STAY UP-TO-DATE:
FREE 30-DAY TEST DRIVE ($47 Value!)

Get Instant Updates, Free Research Requests,
Postage Refunds, Insider Information & More
FREE For 30 Days Using This Activation Link:

www.contactanycelebrity.com/free

You'll get INSTANT ACCESS to the Best Mailing Address,
Agent, Manager, Publicist, Production Company & Charitable Cause
For Over 60,000 Celebrities & Public Figures Worldwide!

You'll Get INSTANT ACCESS To All This & More:

Easy-To-Use, Fully-Searchable Online Database
60,000+ Celebrities & Public Figures Worldwide
Agent, Manager & Publicist Information
Celebrity Causes Database
Daily Real-Time Updates
Free Research Requests
Postage Refund Guarantee
Insider Interviews
Live Customer Service
Plus Much More!

D1289400

Activate Your FREE 30-Day Test Drive ($47 Value!)

www.contactanycelebrity.com/free

Look What People Are Saying:

"The range is amazing – this thing is HUGE!"
- CNN

"The solution to getting your products in celebrities' hands."
- Entrepreneur Magazine

"Recommended for all libraries."
- Library Journal

"The best resource and a great deal."
- Peter Shankman, HARO (Help A Reporter)

"This online directory and its helpful staff will
help you find any celebrity in the world."
- Tim Ferriss, 'The 4-Hour Workweek'

The Celebrity Black Book 2015: Over 50,000 Celebrity Addresses.

Mega Niche Media LLC
8721 Santa Monica Blvd. #431
West Hollywood, CA 90069-4507
310-388-6084 (Phone/Fax)
info@meganiche.com

Printed and bound in the United States of America.

Please visit www.ContactAnyCelebrity.com for updates and new addresses.

ISBN: 978-1-60487-016-9

Edited by Contact Any Celebrity – www.ContactAnyCelebrity.com
Interior Layout by Data Management, Inc. – www.dbman.com

STAY UP-TO-DATE:
FREE 30-DAY TEST DRIVE ($47 Value!)

Get Instant Updates, Free Research Requests,
Postage Refunds, Insider Information & More
FREE For 30 Days Using This Activation Link:

www.contactanycelebrity.com/free

You'll get INSTANT ACCESS to the Best Mailing Address,
Agent, Manager, Publicist, Production Company & Charitable Cause
For Over 60,000 Celebrities & Public Figures Worldwide!

BE KIND – PLEASE REVIEW THIS BOOK ON AMAZON!

BUZZ FOR THE CELEBRITY BLACK BOOK...

"The range is amazing – this thing is huge!"
- CNN

"I can do so much with this!"
- Perez Hilton

"This book is the solution to getting your products or services in celebrities' hands."
- Entrepreneur Magazine

"Of all the resources for celebrity addresses, this book is far and away the most useful."
- Autograph Magazine

"Similar titles do not boast as many entries. Recommended for all libraries."
- Library Journal

"A superb, quick and easy-to-use reference for professionals and fans alike."
- Midwest Book Review

"Priceless information that would otherwise take hours to research."
- Curled Up with a Good Book

"The time saved rather than Googling and cold-calling will pay for this book in the long run."
- Absolute Write

"Some of the best money you'll ever spend. Provides great publicity opportunities."
- Paul Hartunian, Free Publicity Information Center

"The most helpful book I have ever owned – worth every penny."
- Jill Jackson, Syndicated Columnist, Jill Jackson's Hollywood

"If you opt to pursue celebrities on your own, this is the place to get contact information."
- Dan Kennedy, No B.S. Guide to Marketing to the Affluent

STAY UP-TO-DATE:
FREE 30-DAY TEST DRIVE ($47 Value!)

Get Instant Updates, Free Research Requests,
Postage Refunds, Insider Information & More
FREE For 30 Days Using This Activation Link:

www.contactanycelebrity.com/free

You'll get INSTANT ACCESS to the Best Mailing Address,
Agent, Manager, Publicist, Production Company & Charitable Cause
For Over 60,000 Celebrities & Public Figures Worldwide!

ABOUT THE EDITOR

Known as the 'King of Celebrity Contacts,' Jordan McAuley's www.ContactAnyCelebrity.com service helps charities and nonprofits; authors and writers; journalists and the media; and entrepreneurs and small businesses get in touch with celebrities worldwide for promotional and publicity use.

McAuley has been featured by the Associated Press, CNN, USA Today, Investor's Business Daily, Publisher's Weekly, Miami Herald, Village Voice, Writer's Digest, New York Daily News, Fox News, Star Magazine, Sirius/XM Satellite Radio, National Public Radio and more.

Jordan got his start as an intern in the publicity departments of CNN and Turner Entertainment in Atlanta. He also worked at a prominent modeling agency in South Beach, Miami; a film production company in Hollywood, California and a top talent agency in Beverly Hills.

He is featured in several best-selling books including Timothy Ferris' 'The 4-Hour Workweek,' Dan Kennedy's 'Marketing to the Affluent,' Dan Poynter's 'Book Publishing Encyclopedia,' John Kremer's '1001 Ways to Market Your Books' and Robin Blakely's 'PR Therapy.'

McAuley is also the author of 'Secrets to Contacting Celebrities: 101 Ways to Reach the Rich and Famous' 'Celebrity Leverage: Insider Secrets to Getting Celebrity Endorsements, Instant Credibility & Star-Powered Publicity' and 'The Lost Secrets of Fame & Fortune.'

Jordan is a member of the Public Relations Society of America, Association of Fundraising Professionals, GLAAD Media Circle, Independent Book Publishers Association, Information Marketing Association, Society of Professional Journalists and MediaBistro.

Follow him on Facebook and Twitter at:

twitter.com/ContactCelebs
facebook.com/ContactAnyCelebrity

STAY UP-TO-DATE:
FREE 30-DAY TEST DRIVE!

Get Instant Updates, Free Research Requests,
Postage Refunds, Insider Information & More
FREE For 30 Days Using This Activation Link:

www.contactanycelebrity.com/free

**You'll get INSTANT ACCESS to the Best Mailing Address,
Agent, Manager, Publicist, Production Company & Charitable Cause
For Over 60,000 Celebrities & Public Figures Worldwide!**

INTRODUCTION

Welcome to The Celebrity Black Book 2015!

Whether you're a fan, charity, nonprofit, entrepreneur, marketer, author, writer, journalist, publicist, or event planner, you're bound to find this book useful. Inside you'll discover the best mailing addresses for over 50,000 celebrities and public figures worldwide.

Everyone who is anyone is included: actors, musicians, politicians, world leaders, authors, artists, television hosts, even reality TV stars! The list goes on and on as you'll see once you start browsing the following pages.

The Celebrity Black Book 2015 is a staple for fans who want to request autographs, nonprofits who want to hold an autograph auction to raise money for their cause, businesses who want to get their products and services into celebrities' hands, authors who want to get celebrity endorsements for their books, and the media who want to get quotes and interviews.

There are so many uses, the possibilities are endless!

Of course, with over 50,000 celebrities who move and change representation on a daily basis, this book cannot possibly be 100% accurate. That's why you also get a FREE 30-Day Test Drive to our membership Web site and online database, www.ContactAnyCelebrity.com for updates!

Activate your FREE 30 Day Test Drive here: www.contactanycelebrity.com/free

You may be wondering how to write a fan letter, request an autograph, or get your product or service in the hands of celebrities. To find out, check out our other books:

- Secrets to Contacting Celebrities: 101 Ways to Reach the Rich & Famous
- Celebrity Leverage: Insider Secrets to Getting Celebrity Endorsements, Instant Credibility & Star-Powered Publicity
- The Lost Secrets of Fame & Fortune: How to Get – and Keep – Everything You Desire!

Enjoy your new Celebrity Black Book 2015, and let me know your success stories!

Reach for the stars,

Jordan McAuley, Founder
Contact Any Celebrity
8721 Santa Monica Blvd. #431
West Hollywood, CA 90069-4507
310-691-5466 (Phone)
jordan@contactanycelebrity.com
www.ContactAnyCelebrity.com

ALSO BY THE AUTHOR:

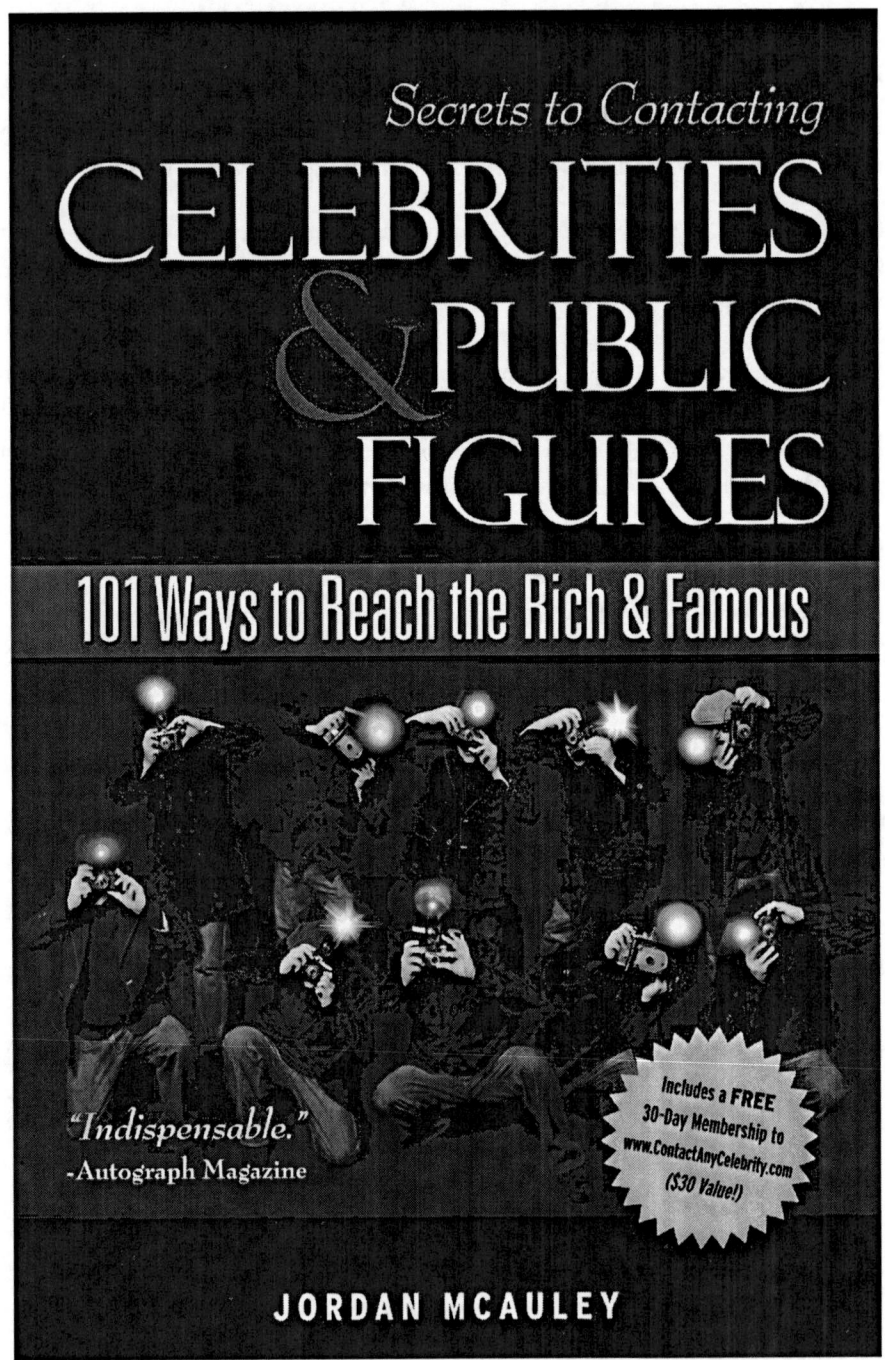

**Secrets to Contacting Celebrities:
101 Ways to Reach the Rich & Famous**

Available on Amazon.com

ALSO BY THE AUTHOR:

Celebrity Leverage:
Insider Secrets to Getting Celebrity Endorsements,
Instant Credibility & Star-Powered Publicity

Available on Amazon.com

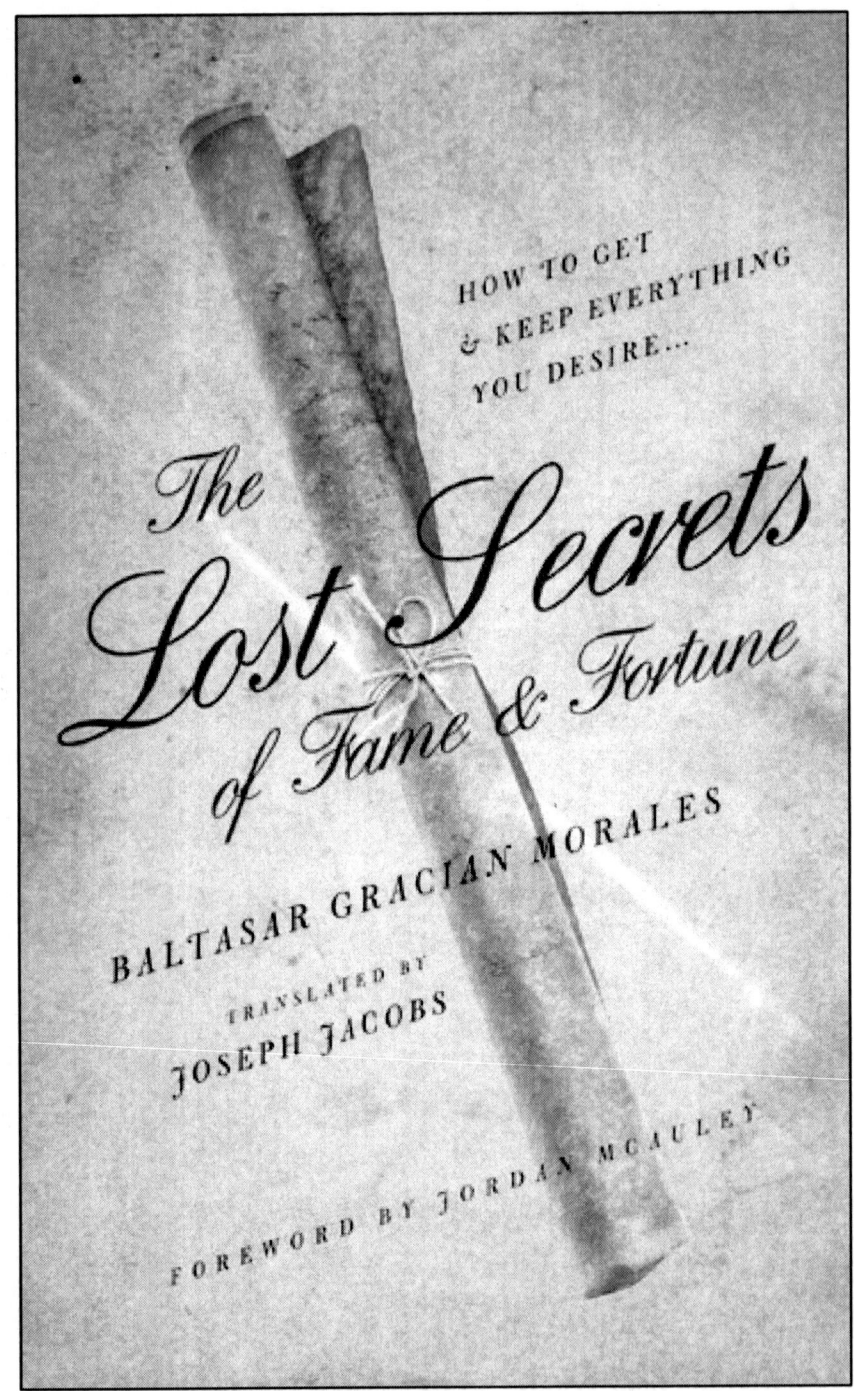

30 Seconds to Mars (Music Group)
c/o Irving Azoff *Azoff Music Management*
1100 Glendon Ave Ste 2000
Los Angeles, CA 90024-3524, USA

311 (Music Group)
c/o Peter Raspler *Raspler Management*
946 N Croft Ave
Los Angeles, CA 90069-4204, USA

3 Doors Down (Music Group)
c/o Staff Member *Marathon Music Management*
310 Greenway Ave
Nashville, TN 37205-2308, USA

98 Degrees (Music Group)
c/o Dvora Vener Englefield *42West (LA)*
1840 Century Park E Ste 700
Los Angeles, CA 90067-2122, USA

A

A3 (Music Group)
c/o Staff Member *Paradigm (Monterey)*
404 W Franklin St
Monterey, CA 93940-2303, USA

Aaker, Lee (Actor)
PO Box 1386
Mammoth Lakes, CA 93546-1386, USA

Aames, Willie (Actor)
c/o Staff Member *Jeff Ballard PR*
4814 Lemona Ave
Sherman Oaks, CA 91403-2010, USA

Aardsma, David (Athlete, Baseball Player)
6009 E Turquoise Ave
Paradise Valley, AZ 85253-1234, USA

Aaron, Caroline (Actor)
Mindel/Donigan
9057-C Nemo St
W Hollywood, CA 90069, USA

Aaron, Hank (Athlete, Baseball Player)
Atlanta Braves
PO Box 4064
Attn: Sr Vice President
Atlanta, GA 30302-4064, USA

Aaron, Paul (Director)
c/o Staff Member *Elsboy Entertainment*
1581 N Crescent Heights Blvd
West Hollywood, CA 90046-2405, USA

Aaron, Quinton (Actor)
Suzelle Enterprises
853 7th Ave Apt 8D
New York, NY 10019-5222, USA

Aaron, Tommy (Athlete, Golfer)
440 E Lake Dr
Gainesville, GA 30506-1740, USA

Aase, Don (Athlete, Baseball Player)
5055 Via Ricardo
Yorba Linda, CA 92886-4526, USA

Abad, Andy (Athlete, Baseball Player)
1092 Chickasaw St
Jupiter, FL 33458-5610, USA

Abagnale, Frank (Business Person)
Abagnale & Associates
PO Box 701290
Tulsa, OK 74170-1290, USA

Abbass, Hiam (Actor)
c/o Michael Lazo *Untitled Entertainment (LA)*
350 S Beverly Dr Ste 200
Beverly Hills, CA 90212-4819, USA

Abbatiello, Carmine (Horse Racer)
7 Whirlaway Rd
Manalapan, NJ 07726-9566, USA

Abbatiello, Tony (Horse Racer)
176 Stone Hill Rd
Colts Neck, NJ 07722-1730, USA

Abbott, Christie (Actor)
c/o Gene Parseghian *Parseghian Planco LLC*
388 2nd Ave
New York, NY 10010-5616, USA

Abbott, Diahnne (Actor)
460 W Avenue 46
Los Angeles, CA 90065-5006, USA

Abbott, D Thomas (Business Person)
Salvin Corp
333 Ludlow St
Stamford, CT 06902-6987, USA

Abbott, Glenn (Athlete, Baseball Player)
4413 Dawson Dr
North Little Rock, AR 72116-7037, USA

Abbott, Gregory (Musician)
PO Box 68
Bergenfield, NJ 07621-0068, USA

Abbott, Jeff (Athlete, Baseball Player)
1095 Stonegate Ct
Roswell, GA 30075-2265, USA

Abbott, Jim (Athlete, Baseball Player, Olympic Athlete)
3449 Quiet Cv
Corona Del Mar, CA 92625-1637, USA

Abbott, Josh (Musician)
c/o Joey Lee *William Morris Endeavor (Nashville)*
1600 Division St Ste 300
Nashville, TN 37203-2755, USA

Abbott, Kurt (Athlete, Baseball Player)
1704 NW Spruce Ridge Dr
Stuart, FL 34994-9528, USA

Abbott, Kyle (Athlete, Baseball Player)
2817 Hamlett Ln
Flower Mound, TX 75028-1545, USA

Abbott, Norman (Director)
1520 San Ysidro Dr
Beverly Hills, CA 90210-2111, USA

Abbott, Paul (Athlete, Baseball Player)
330 E Rosslynn Ave
Fullerton, CA 92832-2525, USA

Abboud, A Robert (Business Person)
A Robert Abboud Co
960 Route 22
#212
Fox River Grove, IL 60021, USA

Abboud, Joseph M (Designer, Fashion Designer)
650 5th Ave Ste 2700
New York, NY 10019-6108, USA

Abbrederis, Jared (Athlete, Football Player)
c/o Michael McCartney *Priority Sports & Entertainment - Chicago*
312 N La Salle
Suite 650
Chicago, IL 60610, USA

Abdelkader, Justin (Athlete, Hockey Player)
1080 Edinborough Dr
Norton Shores, MI 49441-5371, USA

Abdi, Barkhad (Actor)
c/o Staff Member *SMS Talent*
8383 Wilshire Blvd Ste 230
Beverly Hills, CA 90211-2436, USA

Abdoo, Rose (Actor)
c/o Judy Orbach *Judy O Productions*
6136 Glen Holly St
Los Angeles, CA 90068-2338, USA

Abdul, Paula (Dancer, Musician)
c/o Marty Tudor *Tudor Management Group*
300 S Beverly Dr Ste 102
Beverly Hills, CA 90212-4804, USA

Abdul-Aziz, Zaid (Athlete, Basketball Player)
Sunlight Inc
PO Box 75583
Seattle, WA 98175-0583, USA

Abdul-Jabbar, Kareem (Athlete, Basketball Player, Coach)
c/o Staff Member *Iconomy*
970 Knox St Ste D
Torrance, CA 90502-1099, USA

Abdul-Jabbar, Karim (Athlete, Football Player)
17044 Downing St
Gaithersburg, MD 20877-3602, USA

Abdullah, Khalid (Athlete, Football Player)
7634 Wexford Club Dr E
Jacksonville, FL 32256-2330, USA

Abdullah, Rabih (Athlete, Football Player)
12810 Wallingford Dr
Tampa, FL 33624-6354, USA

Abdullah, Rahim (Athlete, Football Player)
7634 Wexford Club Dr E
Jacksonville, FL 32256-2330, USA

Abdul-Saboor, Mikal (Athlete, Football Player)
5465 Derby Chase Ct
Alpharetta, GA 30005-7882, USA

Abdur-Rahim, Shareef (Athlete, Basketball Player)
c/o Staff Member *Atlanta Hawks*
190 Marietta St NW Ste 405
Atlanta, GA 30303-2717, USA

Abdus-Salaam, Sultan (Athlete, Football Player)
12715 Joust St
North Las Vegas, NV 89030, USA

Abel (DJ)
c/o Len Evans *Project Publicity*
312 W 53rd St Ste 202
New York, NY 10019-5743, USA

Abel, Gerry (Athlete, Hockey Player)
23570 Samoset Trl
Southfield, MI 48033-2820, USA

Abel, Jake (Actor)
c/o Cynthia Campos-Greenberg *Anthem Entertainment*
9595 Wilshire Blvd Ste 900
Beverly Hills, CA 90212-2509, USA

Abel, Joy (Bowler)
2440 187th St
Lansing, IL 60438-4102, USA

Abell, Bud (Athlete, Football Player)
919 E 25th Plz
Panama City, FL 32405-5255, USA

Abell, Tim (Actor)
c/o Staff Member *Tactical Media Productions*
578 Washington Blvd # 346
Marina Del Rey, CA 90292-5442, USA

Abelson, Robert P (Doctor)
1155 Whitney Ave
Hamden, CT 06517-3434

Abendschan, Jack (Athlete, Football Player)
25 Wynrush Cir
Abilene, TX 79606-4363, USA

Abercrombie, John L (Musician)
Joel Chriss
300 Mercer St Apt 3J
New York, NY 10003-6732, USA

Abercrombie, Neil (Congressman, Politician)
300 Ala Moana Blvd Rm 4104
Prince Kuhio Federal Building
Honolulu, HI 96850-4104, USA

Abercrombie, Neil (Governor, Politician)
Governor, State of Hawaii
Executive Chambers, State Capitol
Honolulu, HI 96813, USA

Abercrombie, Reggie (Athlete, Baseball Player)
5920 Buxton Dr
Columbus, GA 31907-3635, USA

Abercrombie, Walter (Athlete, Coach, Football Coach, Football Player)
217 Westlane Cir
Woodway, TX 76712-3186, USA

Abernathy, Brent (Athlete, Baseball Player, Olympic Athlete)
1787 Bridgeport Colony Ln
Fort Walton Beach, FL 32547-5711, USA

Abernathy, Robert (Athlete, Baseball Player)
2491 Walker Ln
Nashville, TN 37207-4213, USA

Abernethy, Tom (Athlete, Basketball Player)
5268 Woodfield Dr N
Carmel, IN 46033-8794, USA

Abert, Donald B (Publisher)
Milwaukee Journal
333 W State St
Milwaukee, WI 53203-1309

Abgrall, Dennis (Athlete, Hockey Player)
16607 S 12th Pl
Phoenix, AZ 85048-4703, USA

Abigail (Musician)
c/o Staff Member *T-Best Talent Agency*
508 Honey Lake Ct
Danville, CA 94506-1237, USA

Able, Forest (Athlete, Basketball Player)
11102 Mitchell Hill Rd
Fairdale, KY 40118-9425, USA

Able, Whitney (Actor)
c/o Lisa Gallant *Gallant Management*
1112 Montana Ave # 454
Santa Monica, CA 90403-1652, USA

Ableson, Andrew (Actor)
c/o Stephanie Blume *Imperium 7 Talent Agency*
5455 Wilshire Blvd Ste 1706
Los Angeles, CA 90036-4217, USA

Ablon, Ralph E (Business Person)
Ogden Corp
PO Box 2615
Fairfield, NJ 07004, USA

Ablow, Keith (Doctor)
c/o Greg Lipstone *ICM Partners (LA)*
9601 Wilshire Blvd
Beverly Hills, CA 90210-5213, USA

Abner, Shawn (Athlete, Baseball Player)
1443 Olde Oak Ct
Mechanicsburg, PA 17050-9198, USA

Abney Culberson, John (Congressman, Politician)
2352 Rayburn Hob
Washington, DC 20515-2201, USA

Aboulhosn, Hassan (Athlete, Football Player)
2703 Oaklawn Blvd
Hopewell, VA 23860-4934, USA

Abourezk, James G (Politician)
1509 E Cedar Ln
Sioux Falls, SD 57103-4516, USA

Abraham, Clifton (Athlete, Football Player)
1413 Dutchman Creek Dr
Desoto, TX 75115-3659, USA

Abraham, Donnie (Athlete, Football Player)
3038 Wentworth Way
Tarpon Springs, FL 34688-8445, USA

Abraham, F Murray (Actor)
c/o Johnnie Planco *Parseghian Planco LLC*
388 2nd Ave
New York, NY 10010-5616, USA

Abraham, John (Athlete, Football Player)
c/o Amanda Mitchell *Southern Hospitality Marketing & PR*
122 W 26th St Ground Floor
New York, NY 10001, USA

Abraham, Nate (Athlete, Football Player)
3038 Wentworth Way
Tarpon Springs, FL 34688-8445, USA

Abraham, Robert (Athlete, Football Player)
831 Canal St
Myrtle Beach, SC 29577-3455, USA

Abraham, Spencer E (Politician)
Energy Dept
8016 Greenwich Woods Dr
Mc Lean, VA 22102-1332, USA

Abrahamian, Emil (Cartoonist)
147 Woodleaf Dr
Winter Springs, FL 32708-6159, USA

Abrahams, Jim S (Director)
c/o Staff Member *ICM Partners (LA)*
10250 Constellation Blvd Fl 7
Los Angeles, CA 90067-6207, USA

Abrahams, Jon (Actor)
c/o Christian Donatelli *The Schiff Company*
9220 W Sunset Blvd Ste 106
West Hollywood, CA 90069-3500, USA

Abrahamson, James A (Astronaut)
20112 Marble Quarry Rd
Keedysville, MD 21756-1508, USA

Abram, Norm (Television Host)
PO Box 2284
South Burlington, VT 05407-2284

Abramovich, Roman (Business Person)
303 Aspen Way
Snowmass Village, CO 81615, USA

Abramowicz, Daniel (Danny) (Athlete, Football Player)
479 N Harlem Ave Apt 801
Oak Park, IL 60301-6409, USA

Abrams, Bobby (Athlete, Football Player)
1470 Pampas Dr
Montgomery, AL 36117-2310, USA

Abrams, Dan (Television Host)
150 Waverly Pl Apt C
New York, NY 10014-6836, USA

Abrams, Elliott (Politician)
10607 Dogwood Farm Ln
Great Falls, VA 22066-2937, USA

Abrams, JJ (Actor, Producer, Writer)
c/o Staff Member *Bad Robot*
1221 Olympic Blvd
Santa Monica, CA 90404-3721, USA

Abrams, Kevin (Athlete, Football Player)
1314 E Wilder Ave
Tampa, FL 33603-2433, USA

Abrams, Robert (Politician)
531 Weaver St
Larchmont, NY 10538-1013, USA

Abramson, Leslie (Actor)
122A E Foothill Blvd # 4
Arcadia, CA 91006-2505, USA

Abramson, Neil (Director, Writer)
c/o Staff Member *United Talent Agency (UTA-LA)*
9336 Civic Center Dr
Beverly Hills, CA 90210-3604, USA

Abrego, Johnny (Athlete, Baseball Player)
PO Box 681144
San Antonio, TX 78268-1144, USA

Abreu, Aldo (Musician)
Concert Artists Guild
850 7th Ave # 1205
New York, NY 10019-5230, USA

Abreu, Bobby (Athlete, Baseball Player)
5 Rockledge Ct
Marlton, NJ 08053-9774, USA

Abreu, Winston
8929 163rd St Apt 3H
Jamaica, NY 11432-5024, USA

Abroms, Edward M (Director)
EMA Enterprises
1866 Marlowe St
Thousand Oaks, CA 91360-3331, USA

Abronzino, Umberto (Soccer Player)
1336 Settle Ave
San Jose, CA 95125-2363, USA

Abrue, Bobby (Athlete, Baseball Player)
c/o Staff Member *Los Angeles Dodgers (LA Dodgers)*
1000 Elysian Park Ave
Los Angeles, CA 90012-1112, USA

Abrunhosa, Pedro (Musician)
Polygram Records
825 8th Ave
Worldwide Plaza
New York, NY 10019-7416, USA

Abruzzo, Ray (Actor)
c/o Staff Member *Peter Strain & Associates Inc (LA)*
5455 Wilshire Blvd Ste 1812
Los Angeles, CA 90036-4268, USA

Absher, Dick (Athlete, Football Player)
567 Battersea Dr
Saint Augustine, FL 32095-8406, USA

Acaba, Joseph M (Astronaut)
2620 Loganberry Cir
Seabrook, TX 77586-1525, USA

Accardo, Jeremy (Athlete, Baseball Player)
4287 E Blue Sage Ct
Gilbert, AZ 85297-4908, USA

Accola, Candice (Actor)
c/o Katie Rhodes *Untitled Entertainment (LA)*
350 S Beverly Dr Ste 200
Beverly Hills, CA 90212-4819, USA

AC/DC (Music Group, Musician)
c/o Christopher Dalston *Creative Artists Agency (CAA-LA)*
2000 Avenue of the Stars Ste 100
Los Angeles, CA 90067-4705, USA

Ace, Buddy (Musician)
Rodgers Redding
1048 Tattnall St
Macon, GA 31201-1537

Acevedo, Juan (Athlete, Baseball Player)
143 Madera Cir
Carpentersville, IL 60110-1110, USA

Acevedo, Kirk (Actor)
c/o Stacy Abrams *Abrams Entertainment*
5225 Wilshire Blvd Ste 515
Los Angeles, CA 90036-4349, USA

Ache, Steve (Athlete, Football Player)
22 Lashley Estates Dr
Swansea, IL 62226-2502, USA

Achica, George (Athlete, Football Player)
3165 Lone Bluff Way
San Jose, CA 95111-1264, USA

Acho, Sam (Athlete, Football Player)
c/o Pat Dye Jr *SportsTrust Advisors (GA)*
3340 Peachtree Rd NE Fl 16
Atlanta, GA 30326-1000, USA

Acid Test (Music Group)
83 Riverside Dr
New York, NY 10024-5713, USA

Acker, Amy (Actor)
3721 Blue Canyon Dr
Studio City, CA 91604-3802, USA

Acker, Bill (Athlete, Football Player)
1809 Walker Dr
Alice, TX 78332-4126, USA

Acker, Jim (Athlete, Baseball Player)
PO Box 1288
Poth, TX 78147-1300, USA

Acker, Joseph E (Doctor)
1307 Old Weisgarber Rd
Knoxville, TN 37909

Acker, Tom (Athlete, Baseball Player)
118 Gloucester Rd
Stuarts Draft, VA 24477-3328, USA

Acker-Macosko, Anna (Athlete, Golfer)
304 Earl Dr
Kerrville, TX 78028-7019, USA

Ackerman, Doug (Horse Racer)
530 Lighthorse Cir
Aberdeen, NC 28315-3770, USA

Ackerman, Gary (Congressman, Politician)
2111 Rayburn Hob
Washington, DC 20515-0201, USA

Ackerman, Joshua (Actor)
c/o Joanna (Joanie) Burstein *Burstein Company, The*
15304 W Sunset Blvd Ste 208
Pacific Palisades, CA 90272-3656, USA

Ackerman, Leslie (Actor)
5065 Calvin Ave
Tarzana, CA 91356-4419, USA

Ackerman, Rick (Athlete, Football Player)
125 Zog Ln
Laramie, WY 82072-9546, USA

Ackerman, Roger G (Business Person)
Coming Inc
Houghton Park
Corning, NY 14831-0001, USA

Ackerman, Thomas E (Cinematographer)
280 Halcyon Ave
Winston Salem, NC 27104-3108, USA

Ackerman, Tom (Athlete, Football Player)
c/o Allain Roy *CMG Sports*
16476 Wild Horse Creek Rd Fl 2
Chesterfield, MO 63017-1404, USA

Ackles, Jensen (Actor)
c/o Lainie Sorkin Becky *Management 360*
9111 Wilshire Blvd
Beverly Hills, CA 90210-5508, USA

Ackroyd, David (Actor)
273 N Many Lakes Dr
Kalispell, MT 59901-8344, USA

Acks, Ron (Athlete, Football Player)
563 Licklog Rdg
Hayesville, NC 28904-4879, USA

Acord, Lance (Cinematographer)
7069 Fernhill Dr
Malibu, CA 90265-4240, USA

Acosta, Eduardo (Ed) (Athlete, Baseball Player)
22822 Boltana
Mission Viejo, CA 92691-1717, USA

Acovone, Jay (Actor)
c/o Richard Lewis *Geddes Agency, The*
1203 Greenacre Ave
West Hollywood, CA 90046-5707, USA

Acre, Mark (Athlete, Baseball Player)
4145 S Camellia Dr
Chandler, AZ 85248-6193, USA

Acres, Mark (Athlete, Basketball Player)
5908 Finecrest Dr
Rancho Palos Verdes, CA 90275-2105, USA

Acta, Manny (Athlete, Baseball Player, Coach)
15208 Gulf Blvd Apt 501
Madeira Beach, FL 33708-1861, USA

Acton, Bud (Athlete, Basketball Player)
PO Box 87
Empire, MI 49630-0087, USA

Acton, Loren W Dr (Astronaut)
8490 Overlook Ln
Bozeman, MT 59715-7753, USA

Acuff, Amy (Athlete, Olympic Athlete, Track Athlete)
4102 Bobwhite
Robstown, TX 78380-6060, USA

Acuna, Alicia (Correspondent)
c/o Staff Member *Fox News (NY)*
1211 Avenue of the Americas Lowr C1
New York, NY 10036-8705, USA

Acuna, Jason (Actor)
1523 Manhattan Ave
Hermosa Beach, CA 90254-3637, USA

Adair, Deborah (Actor)
1605 Lindamere Pl
Los Angeles, CA 90077-1905, USA

Adair, Rick
419 Winding Oak Dr
Woodruff, SC 29388-8015, USA

Adair, Tatum (Actor)
Mission Talent Agency
10929 Vanowen St Ste 138
Atten: Goro Hamasaki
North Hollywood, CA 91605-6435, USA

Adam, Ken (Designer)
c/o Staff Member *Mirisch Agency*
8840 Wilshire Blvd Ste 100
Beverly Hills, CA 90211-2606, USA

Adamchik, Ed (Athlete, Football Player)
234 Princeton Ave
Pittsburgh, PA 15229-1516, USA

Adamek, Donna (Bowler)
25834 Webster Pl
Stevenson Ranch, CA 91381-1244, USA

Adamle, Mike (Sportscaster)
83 Holabird Loop
Highwood, IL 60040-2000, USA

Adamowicz, Tony (Race Car Driver)
633 Skyview Ln
Costa Mesa, CA 92626-3134, USA

Adams, Alvan (Athlete, Basketball Player)
5617 N Palo Cristi Rd
Paradise Valley, AZ 85253-7544, USA

Adams, Amy (Actor)
9030 Briarcrest Ln
Beverly Hills, CA 90210-1818, USA

Adams, Beverly Sassoon (Model)
2533 Benedict Canyon Dr
Beverly Hills, CA 90210-1020, USA

Adams, Bob (Athlete, Baseball Player)
31713 157th St E
Llano, CA 93544-1222, USA

Adams, Brent (Athlete, Football Player)
3615 Parkmont Ct
Peachtree Corners, GA 30092-4521, USA

Adams, Brooke (Actor)
248 S Van Ness Ave
Los Angeles, CA 90004-3921, USA

Adams, Bryan (Athlete, Hockey Player)
c/o Staff Member *Sports Personnel Services*
125 Lake St W Ste 200
Wayzata, MN 55391-1573, USA

Adams, Charles (Athlete, Baseball Player)
6058 Puerto Dr
Rancho Murieta, CA 95683-9314, USA

Adams, Charles J (Religious Leader)
Progressive National Baptist Convention
601 50th St NE
Washington, DC 20019-5498

Adams, Corin (Athlete, Basketball Player)
c/o Gigi Rock *Heraea Marketing*
10905 E Pear Tree Dr
Cornville, AZ 86325-5523, USA

Adams, Craig (Athlete, Hockey Player)
8030 Sherwood Dr
Presto, PA 15142-1078, USA

Adams, Curtis (Athlete, Football Player)
258 W Towering Oaks Cir
Muskegon, MI 49442-8442, USA

Adams, Danny (Athlete, Basketball Player)
16461 Racquet Club Rd
Weston, FL 33326-3131, USA

Adams, Davante (Athlete, Football Player)
c/o Frank Bauer *Sun West Sports*
7883 N Pershing Ave
Stockton, CA 95207-1749, USA

Adams, Dave (Athlete, Football Player)
2780 N La Cienega Dr
Tucson, AZ 85715-3504, us

Adams, Dick (Athlete, Baseball Player)
4650 Dulin Rd Spc 136
Fallbrook, CA 92028-9362, USA

Adams, Doug (Athlete, Baseball Player)
1129 Harmony Cir NE
Janesville, WI 53545-2072, USA

Adams, Earnest (Athlete, Football Player)
1061 NW 25th Way
Ft Lauderdale, FL 33311-5710, USA

Adams, Flozell (Athlete, Football Player)
5201 Reflection Ct
Flower Mound, TX 75022-8144, USA

Adams, George (Athlete, Basketball Player)
508 Watergate Cir
Gastonia, NC 28052-7718, USA

Adams, George (Athlete, Football Player)
2410 Damsel Katie Dr
Lewisville, TX 75056-5801, USA

Adams, Gerard (Gerry) (Politician)
Sinn Fein/IRA
51/55 Falls Rd
Belfast, NO BT 12, USA

Adams, Glenn (Athlete, Baseball Player)
29 SE 87th St
Oklahoma City, OK 73149-9100, USA

Adams, Greg (Athlete, Hockey Player)
19864 N 83rd Pl # Pi
Scottsdale, AZ 85255-3915, USA

Adams, Hank (Athlete, Football Player)
53 4th St
California, PA 15419-1109, USA

Adams, Henry
53 4th St
California, PA 15419-1109, USA

Adams, Jane (Actor)
c/o Staff Member *Framework Entertainment (LA)*
9057 Nemo St Ste C
West Hollywood, CA 90069-5511, USA

Adams, Jeb Stuart (Actor)
1163 Calle Vista Dr
Beverly Hills, CA 90210-2507, USA

Adams, Jeff (Athlete, Football Player)
c/o Alan Herman *Sportstars Inc*
1350 Avenue of the Americas Fl 28
New York, NY 10019-4702, USA

Adams, Joey Lauren (Actor)
c/o Staff Member *Caliber Media Company*
5670 Wilshire Blvd Ste 1600
Los Angeles, CA 90036-5659, USA

Adams, John (Athlete, Golfer)
4610 County Road 42200
Paris, TX 75462-1391, USA

Adams, John C (Musician)
c/o Staff Member *Elektra Records*
75 Rockefeller Plz Fl 17
New York, NY 10019-6927, USA

Adams, John H (Religious Leader)
African Methodist Church
1134 11th St NW
Washington, DC 20001-4316

Adams, Julie (Actor)
2446 N Commonwealth Ave
Los Angeles, CA 90027-1206, USA

Adams, Julius (Athlete, Football Player)
2135 Jefferson Davis St
MacOn, GA 31201, USA

Adams, Kev (Actor)
c/o Staff Member *United Talent Agency (UTA-LA)*
9336 Civic Center Dr
Beverly Hills, CA 90210-3604, USA

Adams, Kevyn (Athlete, Hockey Player)
Buffalo Sabres 1 Seymour H Knox III Plz
Ste 1
Buffalo, NY 14203

Adams, Linda
c/o Staff Member *Crews*
828 Clemont Dr NE
Atlanta, GA 30306-3694, USA

Adams, Lindsey (Race Car Driver)
819 W Arapaho Rd # 24B-188
Richardson, TX 75080-5045, USA

Adams, Lorraine (Journalist)
Washington Post - Editorial Dept
1150 15th St
Washington, DC 20071-0002

Adams, Lynn (Athlete, Golfer)
2445 Brant St Unit 207
San Diego, CA 92101-1364, USA

Adams, Mary Kay (Actor)
Roe Enterprises
PO Box 2023
Fairfield, IA 52556-0034, USA

Adams, Maud (Actor)
9420 Eden Dr
Beverly Hills, CA 90210-1309, USA

Adams, Mike (Athlete, Baseball Player)
800 Booty St
Sinton, TX 78387-3210, USA

Adams, Mike (Athlete, Baseball Player)
13205 Jo Ln NE
Albuquerque, NM 87111-7112, USA

Adams, Mike (Athlete, Football Player)
70 Graham Ave # 1
Paterson, NJ 07524-2423, USA

Adams, Mike (Athlete, Football Player)
228 Flinn St
Hutto, TX 78634-3298, USA

Adams, Neal (Producer)
Continuity Studios
15 W 39th St Fl 9
New York, NY 10018-0631, USA

Adams, Neile McQueen (Actor)
10128 Empyrean Way Apt 203
Los Angeles, CA 90067-3801, USA

Adams, Noah (Correspondent)
National Public Radio
1111 N Capitol St NE
Washington, DC 20002-7502, USA

Adams, Oleta (Music Group)
c/o Tom Estey *Tom Estey Publicity*
144 E 22nd St Apt 1B
New York, NY 10010-6333, USA

Adams, Patch (Doctor)
122 Franklin St
Urbana, IL 61801-1714, USA

Adams, Patrick (Actor)
c/o Andy Corren *Andy Corren Management*
Prefers to be contacted via email or telephone
CA, USA

Adams, Pete (Athlete, Football Player)
1443 Hygeia Ave
Encinitas, CA 92024-1624, USA

Adams, Red (Athlete, Baseball Player)
6058 Puerto Dr
Rancho Murieta, CA 95683-9314, USA

Adams, Russ (Athlete, Baseball Player)
443 Sells Rd
Salisbury, NC 28144-9432, USA

Adams, Ryan (Music Group, Songwriter, Writer)
High Road
751 Bridgeway Fl 2
Sausalito, CA 94965-2174, USA

Adams, Sam (Athlete, Football Player)
13245 Holmes Point Dr NE
Kirkland, WA 98034-1602, USA

Adams, Sam E (Athlete, Football Player)
12010 Holly Stone Dr
Houston, TX 77070-5420, USA

Adams, Sandy (Congressman, Politician)
216 Cannon Hob
Washington, DC 20515-4325, USA

Adams, Scott (Cartoonist)
Harper Business Publishers
3647 Whitworth Dr
Dublin, CA 94568-1379, USA

Adams, Scott (Athlete, Football Player)
1171 Middlebrooks Rd
Watkinsville, GA 30677-3820, USA

Adams, Stan (Athlete, Football Player)
502 S Highland Dr
Cedar Hill, TX 75104-2873, USA

Adams, Stefon (Athlete)
1734 Trotters Ln
Stone Mountain, GA 30087-2337, USA

Adams, Stefon (Athlete, Football Player)
937 Bingham Ln
Stone Mountain, GA 30083-2424, us

Adams, Sunrise (Adult Film Star)
c/o Staff Member *Vivid Entertainment*
3599 Cahuenga Blvd W Fl 2
Los Angeles, CA 90068-1397, USA

Adams, Tag (Adult Film Star)
c/o Staff Member *Diva Central Inc*
7510 W Sunset Blvd Ste 1445
Los Angeles, CA 90046-3408, USA

Adams, Terry (Athlete, Baseball Player)
11315 Howells Ferry Rd
Semmes, AL 36575-6655, USA

Adams, Theo (Athlete, Football Player)
9555 Highland Park Dr
Roseville, CA 95678-2911, USA

Adams, Tom (Athlete, Football Player)
20606 Crystal Springs Loop
Grand Rapids, MN 55744-5183, USA

Adams, Tony (Athlete, Football Player)
14012 Juniper St
Overland Park, KS 66224-3578, USA

Adams, Trace (Music Group)
Borman
1222 16th Ave S Ste 23
Nashville, TN 37212-2926, USA

Adams, Valerie (Athlete, Track Athlete)
1155 Union Cir
Denton, TX 76201, USA

Adams, Vashone (Athlete, Football Player)
2940 S Parker Ct
Aurora, CO 80014-3018, USA

Adams, William J (Athlete, Football Player)
12 Willowby Way
Lynnfield, MA 01940-1022, USA

Adams, Willie (Athlete, Baseball Player)
11903 Kibbee Ave
La Mirada, CA 90638-1518, USA

Adams, Willie J (Athlete, Football Player)
2513 Forest Creek Dr
Fort Worth, TX 76123-1145, USA

Adams, Willis (Athlete, Football Player)
7831 Quail Meadow Dr
Houston, TX 77071-2337, USA

Adams, Yolanda (Music Group, Musician)
c/o Lynn Jeter *Lynn Jeter & Associates*
3699 Wilshire Blvd Ste 850
Los Angeles, CA 90010-2737, USA

Adamson, Andrew (Director)
c/o Jeremy Zimmer *United Talent Agency (UTA-LA)*
9336 Civic Center Dr
Beverly Hills, CA 90210-3604, USA

Adamson, James C Colonel (Astronaut)
25 Tradewind Cir
Fishersville, VA 22939-2141, USA

Adamson, Joel (Athlete, Baseball Player)
14832 S 46th Pl
Phoenix, AZ 85044-6872, USA

Adamson, Ken (Athlete, Football Player)
5061 Jardin Ln
Carmichael, CA 95608-6070, USA

Adamson, Mike (Athlete, Baseball Player)
17610 Canterbury Dr
Monument, CO 80132-8310, USA

Adamson IV, Robert (Actor)
c/o Theo Swerissen *Theo Swerissen Management*
Prefers to be contacted via telephone or email
Los Angeles, CA, USA

Addai, Joseph (Athlete, Football Player)
5006 Manzanilla View Ln
Sugar Land, TX 77479-6779, USA

Addams, Abe (Athlete, Football Player)
477 Colesburg Rd
Elizabethtown, KY 42701-6144, USA

Addams, Calpernia (Actor, Reality Star)
c/o Staff Member *Deep Stealth Productions*
5419 Hollywood Blvd # C-142
Los Angeles, CA 90027-3480, USA

Addazio, Steve (Athlete, Football Coach, Football Player)
Boston College
Athletic Dept
Chestnut Hill, MA 02467, USA

Adderley, Herb (Athlete, Football Player)
1058 Tristram Cir
Mantua, NJ 08051-2204, us

Addis, Bob (Athlete, Baseball Player)
7466 Hollycroft Ln
Mentor, OH 44060-5611, USA

Addison, Rafael (Athlete, Basketball Player)
6 Bernadette Ct
East Hanover, NJ 07936-3425, USA

Addonizio, Kim (Writer)
3749 Park Boulevard Way
Oakland, CA 94610-2837, USA

Adduci, Jim (Athlete, Baseball Player)
9529 S Sawyer Ave
Evergreen Park, IL 60805-2343, USA

Addy, Mark (Actor)
c/o Staff Member *ID Public Relations (LA)*
7060 Hollywood Blvd Fl 8th
Los Angeles, CA 90028-6021, USA

Ade, King Sunny (Music Group)
Monterey International
200 W Superior St Ste 202
Chicago, IL 60654-6422, USA

Adelman, Jason (Actor)
21747 Erwin St # 2
Woodland Hills, CA 91367-3608, USA

Adelman, Kenneth L (Government Official)
Int'l Contemporary Studies Institute
1601 Clarendon Blvd Apt 1501
Arlington, VA 22209-2866, USA

Adelman, Rick (Athlete, Basketball Player, Coach)
11919 SW Breyman Ave
Portland, OR 97219-8412, USA

Adelson, Sheldon (Business Person)
Venetian Resort Hotel Casino
3355 Las Vegas Blvd S
Las Vegas, NV 89109-8931, USA

Adelstein, Paul (Actor)
2789 Westshire Dr
Los Angeles, CA 90068-1929, USA

Adem (Music Group)
c/o Staff Member *Paradigm (Monterey)*
404 W Franklin St
Monterey, CA 93940-2303, USA

Aderholt, Robert (Congressman, Politician)
205 4th Ave NE Ste 104
Cullman, AL 35055-1965, USA

Adeyamju, Victor (Athlete, Football Player)
5375 S Maplewood Ave
Chicago, IL 60632-1537, USA

Adeyanju, Victor (Athlete, Football Player)
5218 W Cavedale Dr
Phoenix, AZ 85083-1270, us

Adickes, John M (Athlete, Football Player)
205 W Fair Oaks Pl
San Antonio, TX 78209-3710, USA

Adickes, Mark (Athlete, Football Player)
6146 Bordley Dr
Houston, TX 77057-1124, USA

Adkins, Derrick (Athlete, Olympic Athlete, Track Athlete)
909 Derrick Adkins Ln
W Hempstead, NY 11552-3915, USA

Adkins, James (Athlete, Baseball Player)
185 Cedar Ridge Ct
Coppell, TX 75019-2981, USA

Adkins, Jim (Musician)
21 W Berridge Ln
Phoenix, AZ 85013-1509, USA

Adkins, Jon (Athlete, Baseball Player)
5322 Fisher Bowen Branch Rd
Wayne, WV 25570-5946, USA

Adkins, Kevin (Athlete, Football Player)
209 Redwood Dr
Coppell, TX 75019-5422, USA

Adkins, Margene (Athlete, Football Player)
2312 Donnyville Ct
Fort Worth, TX 76119-3111, USA

Adkins, Sam (Athlete, Football Player)
PO Box 996
Ferndale, WA 98248-0996, USA

Adkins, Seth (Actor)
c/o Alisa Adler *Paradigm (LA)*
360 N Crescent Dr
North Bldg
Beverly Hills, CA 90210-4874, USA

Adkins, Steve
16225 Sierra De Avila
Tampa, FL 33613-5222, USA

Adkins, Trace (Musician)
1607 17th Ave S
Nashville, TN 37212-2812, USA

Adler, Andy (Sportscaster)
c/o Staff Member *William Morris Endeavor (LA)*
9601 Wilshire Blvd
Beverly Hills, CA 90210-5213, USA

Adler, Charles (Actor)
c/o Luanne Salandy-Regis *Innovative Artists (LA)*
1505 10th St
Santa Monica, CA 90401-2805, USA

Adler, Cisco (Musician)
21653 Rambla Vis
Malibu, CA 90265-5125, USA

Adler, Gilbert (Director, Producer)
17547 Ventura Blvd
Encino, CA 91316-3853, USA

Adler, Jerry (Actor)
c/o Alisa Adler *Paradigm (LA)*
360 N Crescent Dr
North Bldg
Beverly Hills, CA 90210-4874, USA

Adler, Jonathan (Designer)
74 Gardiners Bay Dr
Shelter Island, NY 11964, USA

Adler, Lou (Actor, Director, Producer)
21750/21756 Pacific Coast Hwy
Malibu, CA 90265, USA

Adler, Matt
PO Box 1866
Studio City, CA 91614-0866, USA

Adler, Max (Actor)
c/o Rodney Ponder *Justice & Ponder*
PO Box 480033
Los Angeles, CA 90048-1033, USA

Adler, Steven (Music Group)
Adler's Appetite
PO Box 8074
Huntington Beach, CA 92615-8074, USA

Adlesh, Dave (Athlete, Baseball Player)
9770 Avenida Monterey
Cypress, CA 90630-3446, USA

Adoti, Rasaaq (Actor)
c/o Staff Member *Coast to Coast Talent Group*
3350 Barham Blvd
Los Angeles, CA 90068-1404, USA

Adoti, Razaaq (Actor, Producer)
c/o Staff Member *Coast II Coast Entertainment*
204 S Beverly Dr Ste 110
Beverly Hills, CA 90212-3800, USA

Adotta, Kip (Actor, Comedian)
PO Box 5734
Santa Rosa, CA 95402-5734, USA

Adrian, Nathan (Athlete, Swimmer)
University of California
Athletic Dept
Dwinelle Hall
Berkeley, CA 94720-0001, USA

Adsit, Scott (Actor)
c/o Melanie Truhett *Messina Baker Entertainment*
955 Carrillo Dr Ste 100
Los Angeles, CA 90048-5400, USA

Adu, Sade (Musician)
c/o Steven Manzano *RDWM America*
1158 26th St Ste 564
Santa Monica, CA 90403-4698, USA

Aduba, Uzo (Actor)
c/o Lainie Sorkin Becky *Management 360*
9111 Wilshire Blvd
Beverly Hills, CA 90210-5508, USA

Adubato, Richie (Basketball Coach, Coach)
290 Chiswell Pl
Lake Mary, FL 32746-4123, USA

Adway, Dwayne (Actor)
c/o Mark Schumacher *Schumacher Management*
2018 Glendon Ave
Los Angeles, CA 90025-6324, USA

Aebischer, David (Athlete, Hockey Player)
365 Jackson St
Denver, CO 80206-4538, USA

Aerosmith (Music Group)
c/o Irving Azoff *Azoff Music Management*
1100 Glendon Ave Ste 2000
Los Angeles, CA 90024-3524, USA

Afenir, Troy (Athlete, Baseball Player)
459 Old Via Rancho Dr
Escondido, CA 92029-7959, USA

Affeldt, Jeremy (Athlete, Baseball Player)
6211 E Mandalay Ln
Spokane, WA 99217-9339, USA

Affholter, Erik (Athlete, Football Player)
41734 N Maidstone Ct
Anthem, AZ 85086-1187, USA

Afflalo, Arron (Athlete, Basketball Player)
705 W Tichenor St
Compton, CA 90220-4415, USA

Affleck, Ben (Actor, Director, Producer)
1700 San Remo Dr
Pacific Palisades, CA 90272-2743, USA

Affleck, Bruce (Athlete, Hockey Player)
2439 Baxton Way
Chesterfield, MO 63017-7809, USA

Affleck, Bruce (Athlete, Hockey Player)
StLouis Blues 1401
Saint Louis, MO 63103

Affleck, Casey (Actor, Producer, Writer)
c/o Cynthia Pett-Dante *Brillstein Entertainment Partners (LA)*
9150 Wilshire Blvd Ste 350
Beverly Hills, CA 90212-3453, USA

Affleck, James G (Business Person)
American Cyanamid
5 Giralda Farms
Madison, NJ 07940-1027, USA

Afghan Raiders (Music Group)
c/o David Benveniste *Velvet Hammer*
9014 Melrose Ave
West Hollywood, CA 90069-5610, USA

AFI (Music Group)
c/o John Silva *SAM*
722 Seward St
Los Angeles, CA 90038-3504, USA

Afinogenov, Maxim (Athlete, Hockey Player)
3700 S Ocean Blvd Apt 1502
Highland Beach, FL 33487-3376, USA

Afrika, Bambaataa (Artist, Musician)
KLB Productions
70A Greenwich Ave # 441
New York, NY 10011-8300, USA

Afrojack (DJ, Musician)
c/o Joel Zimmerman *William Morris Endeavor (NY)*
1325 Avenue of the Americas
New York, NY 10019-6026, USA

Afroman (Artist, Music Group)
Crescent Moon
20 Music Sq W
Nashville, TN 37203-6225, USA

Aftermath (Music Group)
c/o Tom Workman *Starcrest Entertainment Corp*
4585 N River Rd
Zanesville, OH 43701-7768, USA

Agajanian, Ben (Athlete, Football Player)
27950 Avenida Terrazo
Cathedral City, CA 92234-9401, us

Agajanian, Benjamin (Ben) (Athlete, Football Player)
27950 Avenida Terrazo
Cathedral Cty, CA 92234-9401, USA

Agassi, Andre (Athlete, Olympic Athlete, Tennis Player)
c/o Staff Member *Andre Agassi Charitable Foundation*
1120 N Town Center Dr Ste 160
Las Vegas, NV 89144-6303, USA

Agbayani, Benny (Athlete, Baseball Player)
66-948 Kolu Pl
Waialua, HI 96791-9743, USA

Age, Louis (Athlete, Football Player)
7517 Park Ave
Houma, LA 70364-3631, USA

Agee, Tommie (Athlete, Football Player)
1505 Blackhawk Dr
Opelika, AL 36801-3513, USA

Agena, Keiko (Actor)
c/o Staff Member *Fenton Kritzer Entertainment*
8840 Wilshire Blvd Fl 3
Beverly Hills, CA 90211-2606, USA

Ager, Nikita (Actor)
c/o Kim Byrd *Innovative Artists (LA)*
1505 10th St
Santa Monica, CA 90401-2805, USA

Aghdashloo, Shohreh (Actor)
c/o Tamara Houston *Round Table Entertainment*
15301 Ventura Blvd Ste 400
Sherman Oaks, CA 91403-6629, USA

Agna, Tom (Actor, Producer, Writer)
c/o Lisa Harrison *William Morris Endeavor (LA)*
9601 Wilshire Blvd
Beverly Hills, CA 90210-5213, USA

Agnello Jr, Carmine (Actor)
c/o Staff Member *Britto Agency PR*
90 Franklin St Apt 4N
New York, NY 10013-3489, USA

Agnew, Jim (Athlete, Hockey Player)
2747 Ancabide Ln
Missoula, MT 59803-2904, USA

Agnew, Ray (Athlete, Football Player)
2215 Cline St
Winston Salem, NC 27107-2411, USA

Agoos, Jeff (Athlete, Soccer Player)
235 Pascack Rd
Park Ridge, NJ 07656-1125, USA

Agosto, Ben (Athlete, Figure Skater, Olympic Athlete)
529 Kingsmoor Dr
Simpsonville, SC 29681-3500, USA

Agosto, Juan (Athlete, Baseball Player)
104 79th St
Holmes Beach, FL 34217-1050, USA

Agron, Dianna (Actor, Musician)
3225 Oakshire Dr
Los Angeles, CA 90068-1744, USA

Aguayo, Luis (Athlete, Baseball Player)
501 Calle Julio Andino
San Juan, PR 00924-2106, USA

Aguiar, Louie (Athlete, Football Player)
1411 Palmer Creek Dr
Columbia, IL 62236-2747, USA

Aguila, Chris (Athlete, Baseball Player)
3955 Falling Water Dr
Reno, NV 89519-2143, USA

Aguilar, Pepe (Musician)
c/o Eric Rovner *William Morris Endeavor (Miami)*
119 Washington Ave Ste 400
Miami Beach, FL 33139-7202, USA

Aguilera, Christina (Musician)
14143 Beresford Rd
Beverly Hills, CA 90210-1067, USA

Aguilera, Hellweg Max (Artist, Photographer)
PO Box 289
White Plains, NY 10605-0289, USA

Aguilera, Richard W (Rick) (Athlete, Baseball Player)
PO Box 174
Rancho Santa Fe, CA 92067-0174, USA

Aguirre, Mark (Basketball Player, Olympic Athlete)
10281 Highland Ct
Frisco, TX 75033-2415, USA

Ahanotu, Chidi (Athlete, Football Player)
301 W Platt St
Tampa, FL 33606-2292, USA

Ahdout, Jonathan (Actor)
c/o Leonard Torgan *The Collective*
8383 Wilshire Blvd Ste 1050
Beverly Hills, CA 90211-2415, USA

Aheam, Kevin (Athlete, Hockey Player)
174 Marlborough St
Boston, MA 02116-1822, USA

Ahearn, Kevin (Athlete, Hockey Player, Olympic Athlete)
174 Marlborough St
Boston, MA 02116-1822, USA

Ahearne, Pat (Athlete, Baseball Player)
246 Milam Ln
Bastrop, TX 78602-3108, USA

Ahem, Jim (Golfer)
314 E Wagon Wheel Dr
Phoenix, AZ 85020-4066, USA

Ahern, Fred (Athlete, Hockey Player)
807 E 5th St
Boston, MA 02127-3217, USA

Ahern, Jim (Athlete, Golfer)
130 E Glendale Ave
Phoenix, AZ 85020-4824, USA

Ahern, Neal (Producer)
c/o Staff Member *William Morris Endeavor (LA)*
9601 Wilshire Blvd
Beverly Hills, CA 90210-5213, USA

Ahrens, Chris (Athlete, Hockey Player)
1412 Linstock Dr
Holiday, FL 34690-6634, USA

Ahrens, Dave (Athlete, Football Player)
6451 Woodhaven Ct
Avon, IN 46123-7220, us

Ahrens, David (Dave) (Athlete, Football Player)
5864 Manchester Ct
Pittsboro, IN 46167-9064, USA

Ahrens, Lynn (Musician)
c/o Staff Member *Gersh (LA)*
9465 Wilshire Blvd Ste 600
Beverly Hills, CA 90212-2605, USA

Ah You, Junior (Athlete, Football Player)
55-690 Wahinepee St
Las Vegas, NV 89129, USA

Aiello, Anthony (Athlete, Football Player)
9 Taylor Ave
Norwalk, OH 44857-1645, USA

Aiello, Danny (Actor, Director, Producer)
30 Chestnut Ridge Rd
Saddle River, NJ 07458-3302, USA

Aiken, Blair (Race Car Driver)
4855 Highland Springs Rd
Lakeport, CA 95453-9346, USA

Aiken, Clay (Musician)
c/o Simon Renshaw *Strategic Artist Management*
1100 Glendon Ave Ste 1000
Los Angeles, CA 90024-3514, USA

Aiken, John (Athlete, Hockey Player)
18 Pinetree Rd
Billerica, MA 01821-3446, USA

Aiken, Johnny (Athlete, Hockey Player)
18 Pinetree Rd
Billerica, MA 01821-3446, USA

Aiken, Liam (Actor)
c/o Ellen Gilbert *Paradigm (NY)*
360 Park Ave S Fl 16
New York, NY 10010-1716, USA

Aiken, Sam (Athlete, Football Player)
PO Box 32
Wake Forest, NC 27588-0032, us

Aiken, Sam (Athlete, Football Player)
103 New Bingham Ct
Cary, NC 27513-4093, USA

Aikens, Carl (Athlete, Football Player)
931 W Arquilla Dr Apt 114
Glenwood, IL 60425-1143, USA

Aikens, Curtis (Chef)
68 Baca Vis
Novato, CA 94947-2102, USA

Aikens, Willie (Athlete, Baseball Player)
10206 Locust St
Kansas City, MO 64131-4214, USA

Aikman, Troy (Athlete, Football Player, Sportscaster)
Aikman Enterprises
PO Box 192309
Dallas, TX 75219-8517, USA

Ailes, Roger (Journalist)
218 Truman Dr
Cresskill, NJ 07626-1720, USA

Ailes, Roger E (Business Person)
c/o Staff Member *Fox News (NY)*
1211 Avenue of the Americas Lowr C1
New York, NY 10036-8705, USA

Aimi, Milton (Athlete, Soccer Player)
19927 Stonelodge Dr
Katy, TX 77450-5201, USA

Ainge, Danny (Athlete, Baseball Player)
140 Wellesley Ave
Wellesley Hills, MA 02481-7209, USA

Ainge, Erik (Athlete, Football Player)
634 NE Kathleen Ct
Hillsboro, OR 97124-4029, USA

Ainsleigh, H Gordon (Athlete, Track Athlete)
17119 Placer Hills Rd
Meadow Vista, CA 95722-9508, USA

Ainsworth, Kurt (Athlete, Baseball Player, Olympic Athlete)
15220 Memorial Tower Dr
Baton Rouge, LA 70810-0301, USA

Airborne Toxic Event, The (Music Group)
c/o Staff Member *Paradigm (Monterey)*
404 W Franklin St
Monterey, CA 93940-2303, USA

Airpushers (Music Group)
c/o Staff Member *Paradigm (Monterey)*
404 W Franklin St
Monterey, CA 93940-2303, USA

Air Supply (Music Group, Musician)
c/o Staff Member *Agency for the Performing Arts (APA-LA)*
405 S Beverly Dr Ste 500
Beverly Hills, CA 90212-4425, USA

Aitay, Victor (Musician)
50 S La Salle St
Chicago, IL 60603-1008, USA

Aitch, Matt (Athlete, Basketball Player)
1525 Bentbrook Cir
Lansing, MI 48917-1402, USA

Aitchison, Charlotte (Charli XCX) (Musician)
c/o Marty Diamond *Paradigm (NY)*
360 Park Ave S Fl 16
New York, NY 10010-1716, USA

Aizley, Carrie (Actor)
c/o Staff Member *Much and House Public Relations*
8075 W 3rd St Ste 500
Los Angeles, CA 90048-4325, USA

Aja, Alexandre (Director)
c/o Sara Bottfeld *Industry Entertainment*
955 Carrillo Dr Ste 300
Los Angeles, CA 90048-5400, USA

Ajae, Franklyn (Comedian)
1312 S Orange Dr
Los Angeles, CA 90019-2901, USA

Akaka, Daniel (Politician)
3125 Kaohinani Dr
Honolulu, HI 96817-1040, USA

Akaka, Daniel K. (Senator)
141 Hart Senate Office Building
Washington, DC 20510-0001, USA

Akbar, Hakim (Athlete, Football Player)
300 W Ocean Blvd Apt 6510
Long Beach, CA 90802-7959, us

Akbar, Hakim (Athlete, Football Player)
29869 Vanderbilt St Apt 4
Hayward, CA 94544-6873, USA

Aker, Jack (Athlete, Baseball Player)
5911 E Bloomfield Rd
Scottsdale, AZ 85254-4338, USA

Akerlund, Jonas (Director)
c/o Staff Member *ICM Partners (LA)*
10250 Constellation Blvd Fl 7
Los Angeles, CA 90067-6207, USA

Akerman, Malin (Actor)
2738 Ivan Hill Ter
Los Angeles, CA 90039-2717, USA

Akers, David (Athlete, Football Player)
2509 Belle Brook Dr
Franklin, TN 37067-8154, USA

Akers, Fred (Coach, Football Coach)
Purdue University
Athletic Dept
West Lafayette, IN 47907, USA

Akers, Michelle (Athlete, Olympic
Athlete, Soccer Player)
c/o Staff Member *US Soccer Federation*
1801 S Prairie Ave
Chicago, IL 60616-1356, USA

Akers, Thomas D Colonel (Astronaut)
HC 3 Box 35
Eminence, MO 65466-9504, USA

Akil, Mara Brock (Producer, Writer)
c/o Chris Chambers *The Chamber Group*
75 Broad St Ste 2710
New York, NY 10004-2679, USA

Akil, Salim (Director)
c/o Staff Member *ICM Partners (LA)*
10250 Constellation Blvd Fl 7
Los Angeles, CA 90067-6207, USA

Akili, Samaji (Athlete, Football Player)
10605 Caminito Cascara
San Diego, CA 92108-2601, USA

Akin, Harold (Athlete, Football Player)
12608 Cobblestone Pkwy
Oklahoma City, OK 73142-2217, us

Akin, Harold (Athlete, Football Player)
8216 NW 99th St
Oklahoma City, OK 73162-5002, USA

Akin, Henry (Athlete, Basketball Player)
18924 40th Pi NE
Seattle, WA 98155, USA

Akin, W. Todd (Congressman, Politician)
117 Cannon Hob
Washington, DC 20515-2502, USA

Akinnouye-Agbaje, Adawale (Actor)
c/o Erik Kritzer *LINK Entertainment*
11872 La Grange Ave
Los Angeles, CA 90025-5282, USA

Akinnuoye-Agbaje, Adewale (Actor)
c/o Pamela Kohl *3 Arts Entertainment (LA)*
9460 Wilshire Blvd Fl 7
Beverly Hills, CA 90212-2713, USA

Akinradewo, Foluke (Athlete, Volleyball
Player)
1181 NW 101st Way
Plantation, FL 33322-6556, USA

Akins, Chris (Athlete, Football Player)
4835 Shepherds Creek Dr Apt 2
Conway, AR 72034-9271, USA

Akins, Chris (Athlete, Football Player)
11 McClure Acres Rd Apt 6
Conway, AR 72032-9291, us

Akins, Rhett (Musician, Songwriter)
PO Box 331847
Nashville, TN 37203-7517, USA

Akins, Sid (Athlete, Baseball Player,
Olympic Athlete)
1655 W Sandtown Rd SW
Marietta, GA 30064-3744, USA

Akiu, Mike (Athlete, Football Player)
PO Box 1845
Kailua, HI 96734-8845, USA

Akiu, Mike (Athlete, Football Player)
297 Kakahiaka St
Kailua, HI 96734-3461, us

Akon (Musician)
Konfidence Foundation
PO Box 191188
Atlanta, GA 31119-1188, USA

Akroyd, Dan (Actor, Musician, Producer,
Writer)
c/o Fred Specktor *Creative Artists Agency
(CAA-LA)*
2000 Avenue of the Stars Ste 100
Los Angeles, CA 90067-4705, USA

Aksyonov, Vassily P (Writer)
Random House
1745 Broadway Frnt 3 # B1
New York, NY 10019-4343, USA

Alabama (Music Group)
c/o Coran Capshaw *Red Light
Management (VA)*
321 E Main St Ste 500
Charlottesville, VA 22902-3201, USA

Alagia, John (Producer)
c/o Sandy Robertson *Twenty First
Republic Creative Management*
Prefers to be contact via telephone
CA, USA

Alaimo, Marc (Actor)
1936 Seminole Dr
Agoura Hills, CA 91301-2942, USA

Alaina, Lauren (Musician)
c/o Michelle Young *19 Entertainment (LA)*
9000 W Sunset Blvd Ste 1574
West Hollywood, CA 90069-5817, USA

Alan, Buddy (Musician)
600 E Gilbert Dr
Tempe, AZ 85281-2021, USA

Alan, Reuber (Athlete, Football Player)
1202 Crosswind Dr
Murphy, TX 75094-4110, USA

Al and the Transamericans (Music Group)
c/o Staff Member *Paradigm (Monterey)*
404 W Franklin St
Monterey, CA 93940-2303, USA

Alapa, Clifton (Athlete, Football Player)
3928 Country Lights St
Las Vegas, NV 89129-7657, USA

Alarie, Mark (Athlete, Basketball Player)
8514 Country Club Dr
Bethesda, MD 20817-4581, USA

Alazraqui, Carlos (Actor)
242 N Avon St
Burbank, CA 91505-3501, USA

Alba, Gibson (Athlete, Baseball Player)
87 E 17th St
Paterson, NJ 07524-1516, USA

Alba, Jessica (Actor)
1913 N Beverly Dr
Beverly Hills, CA 90210-1612, USA

Albaladejo, Jonathan (Athlete, Baseball
Player)
12517 River Birch Dr
Riverview, FL 33569-8206, USA

Alban, Carlo (Actor)
c/o Don Buchwald *Don Buchwald &
Associates (NY)*
10 E 44th St Frnt 1
New York, NY 10017-3654, USA

Alban, Richard (Dick) (Athlete, Football
Player)
306 Belpaire Ct
Newtown Square, PA 19073-2128, USA

Albea, Troy (Athlete, Football Player)
1070 L and N Rd
Lincolnton, GA 30817-4724, USA

Albeck, Stan (Basketball Coach, Coach)
130 Tall Oak Dr
San Antonio, TX 78232-1316, USA

Albee, Edward (Writer)
PO Box 697
Montauk, NY 11954-0503, USA

Albee, Edward F (Writer)
14 Harrison St Apt 5
New York, NY 10013-2842, USA

Albelin, Tommy (Athlete, Coach, Hockey
Player)
c/o Staff Member *New Jersey Devils*
165 Mulberry St
Continental Arena
Newark, NJ 07102-3607, USA

Albelin, Tommy (Athlete, Hockey Player)
51 S Pearl St Ste 14
Attn: Coaching Staff
Albany, NY 12207-1500, USA

Alberghetti, Anna Maria (Actor, Musician)
2800 28th St Ste 101
Santa Monica, CA 90405-6212, USA

Alberoni, Sherry (Actor)
PO Box 161936
Altamonte Springs, FL 32716-1936, USA

Alberro, Jose
HC 2 Box 4649
Sabana Hoyos, PR 00688-9405, USA

Albers, Kristi (Athlete, Golfer)
5872 Via Cuesta Dr
El Paso, TX 79912-6608, USA

Albers, Matthew James (Athlete, Baseball
Player)
15 S Swanwick Pl
Tomball, TX 77375-4478, USA

Alberstein, Chara (Musician)
DL Media
PO Box 2728
Bala Cynwyd, PA 19004-6728, USA

Albert, Branden (Athlete, Football Player)
c/o Staff Member *Kansas City Chiefs*
1 Arrowhead Dr
Kansas City, MO 64129-1651, USA

Albert, Lewis (Athlete, Football Player)
3532 Macedonia Rd
Centreville, MS 39631-3634, USA

Albert, Marv (Sportscaster)
150 Columbus Ave PH 2A
New York, NY 10023-5972, USA

Alberti, Micah (Actor)
c/o David Dean Portelli *David Dean
Management*
6338 Wilshire Blvd
Los Angeles, CA 90048-5002, USA

Alberto, Padre (Actor)
c/o Staff Member *Telemundo*
2470 W 8th Ave
Hialeah, FL 33010-2000, USA

Alberts, Andrew (Athlete, Hockey Player)
4265 Cottonwood Ln
Excelsior, MN 55331-9328, USA

Alberts, Francis (Butch) (Athlete, Baseball
Player)
3063 Amberlea Ln
Baldwinsville, NY 13027-1613, USA

Alberts, Francis ""Butch""
3063 Amberlea Ln
Baldwinsville, NY 13027-1613, USA

Alberts, Trev (Athlete, Football Player)
8901 W Cedar Wapsie Rd
Cedar Falls, IA 50613-9448, USA

Albita (Musician)
Estefan Enterprises
6205 Bird Rd
Miami, FL 33155-4823, USA

Albom, Mitch (Writer)
25600 Franklin Park Dr
Franklin, MI 48025-1211, USA

Alborn, Alan (Athlete, Olympic Athlete,
Skier)
PO Box 109
Willow, AK 99688-0109, USA

Albrecht, A Chim (Wrestler)
Physique Promotions
9668 Moss Glen Ave
Fountain Valley, CA 92708-1053, USA

Albrecht, Kate (Actor)
c/o Brad Petrigala *Brillstein Entertainment
Partners (LA)*
9150 Wilshire Blvd Ste 350
Beverly Hills, CA 90212-3453, USA

Albrecht, Ted (Athlete, Football Player)
1314 S West Fork Dr
Lake Forest, IL 60045-3539, us

Albrecht, Ted (Athlete, Football Player)
1205 Cherry St
Winnetka, IL 60093-2116, USA

Albright, Ethan (Athlete, Football Player)
19181 Ferry Field Ter
Leesburg, VA 20176-1276, USA

Albright, Ethan (Athlete, Football Player)
PO Box 38337
Greensboro, NC 27438-8337, us

Albright, Ira (Athlete, Football Player)
PO Box 398143
Dallas, TX 75339-8143, USA

Albright, Lola (Actor)
4610 Coldwater Canyon Ave # 223
Studio City, CA 91604-1031, USA

Albright, Madeleine (Politician)
1318 34th St NW
Washington, DC 20007-2801, USA

Albright, Tenley (Athlete, Figure Skater,
Olympic Athlete)
70 Suffolk Rd
Chestnut Hill, MA 02467-1218, USA

Albright, William (Bill) (Athlete, Football
Player)
N4591 Meadow Wood Rd
Onalaska, WI 54650-8727, USA

Albritton, Vince (Athlete, Football Player)
2801 Denton Tap Rd Apt 1113
Lewisville, TX 75067-8162, us

Albury, Victor (Vic) (Athlete, Baseball
Player)
2109 E Bougainvillea Ave
Tampa, FL 33612-7035, USA

Albus, Jim (Athlete, Golfer)
3972 Somerset Dr Unit 1
Sarasota, FL 34242-1110, USA

Alcantara, Izzy (Athlete, Baseball Player)
4059 240th Pl SE
Issaquah, WA 98029-6304, USA

Alcaraz, Luis (Athlete, Baseball Player)
679 Calle Chihuahua
Urb Venus Gdns Norte
San Juan, PR 00926-4614, USA

Alcivar, Patricia (Athlete, Boxer)
c/o Gigi Rock *Heraea Marketing*
10905 E Pear Tree Dr
Cornville, AZ 86325-5523, USA

Alcorn, Gary (Athlete, Basketball Player)
2059 E Lexington Ave
Fresno, CA 93720-0474, USA

Alcorn, Randy (Motivational Speaker,
Writer)
Eternal Perspective Ministries
39085 Pioneer Blvd Ste 206
Sandy, OR 97055-8062, USA

Alcott, Amy S (Athlete, Golfer)
323 Amalfi Dr
Santa Monica, CA 90402-1127, USA

Alda, Alan (Actor)
c/o Toni Howard *ICM Partners (LA)*
10250 Constellation Blvd Fl 7
Los Angeles, CA 90067-6207, USA

Alda, Rutanya (Actor)
c/o Hazel Shallon *Shallon Star
Management*
14320 Ventura Blvd # 624
Sherman Oaks, CA 91423-2717, USA

Aldean, Jason (Musician)
4637 Reed Rd
Thompsons Station, TN 37179-9240, USA

Alden, Bruce (Producer)
c/o Staff Member *Vision Art Management*
9465 Wilshire Blvd Ste 870
Beverly Hills, CA 90212-2610, USA

Alden, Ginger (Actor, Model, Musician)
25 Rolling Hill Ct W
Sag Harbor, NY 11963-2012, USA

Alden Robinson, Phil (Director, Producer,
Writer)
Writers Co-op
4000 Warner Blvd Bldg 1
Burbank, CA 91522-0001, USA

Alderete, Loretta (Athlete, Golfer)
80194 Delphi Ct
Indio, CA 92201-8430, USA

Alderfer-Benner, Gertrude (Athlete,
Baseball Player)
2191 County Line Rd
East Greenville, PA 18041-2700, USA

Alderman, Darrell (Race Car Driver)
DA Construction Co
8130 Flemingsburg Rd
Morehead, KY 40351, USA

Alderman, Grady (Athlete, Football
Player)
62 Elk Valley Way
Evergreen, CO 80439-4951, us

Alderson, Kristen (Actor)
c/o Staff Member *One Life to Live*
56 W 66th St
New York, NY 10023-6225, USA

Alderson, Richard Sandy (Commentator)
305 E 85th St PH B
New York, NY 10028-4672, USA

Alderton, John (Athlete, Football Player)
12314 Williams Rd SE
Cumberland, MD 21502-7961, USA

Aldred, Scott (Athlete, Baseball Player)
13435 Lakebrook Dr
Fenton, MI 48430-8420, USA

Aldrete, Mike (Athlete, Baseball Player)
22160 Toro Hills Dr
Salinas, CA 93908-1131, USA

Aldrich, Cole (Athlete, Basketball Player)
c/o Jeff Schwartz *Excel Sports
Management (NY)*
1700 Broadway Fl 29
New York, NY 10019-5905, USA

Aldrich, Jay (Athlete, Baseball Player)
6218 S Indiana Ave
Cudahy, WI 53110-2870, USA

Aldrich, John H (Politician, Scientist)
Duke University
Political Science Dept
Durham, NC 27708-0001, USA

Aldridge, Allen (Athlete, Football Player)
PO Box 717
Fresno, TX 77545-0717, us

Aldridge, Cory (Athlete, Baseball Player)
417 Penrose Dr
Abilene, TX 79601-6228, USA

Aldridge, Edward C (pete) Jr
(Government Official)
Aerospace Corp
2350 E El Segundo Blvd
El Segundo, CA 90245-4691, USA

Aldridge, Jerry
307 Park Ln
Jacksonville, TX 75766-5773, us

Aldridge, Jerry (Athlete, Football Player)
297 Ellis
Jacksonville, TX 75766, USA

Aldridge, Keith (Athlete, Hockey Player)
80 Joslyn Rd
Lake Orion, MI 48362-2215, USA

Aldridge, Kevin (Athlete, Football Player)
3130 Brookhaven Club Dr
Dallas, TX 75234-3710, us

Aldridge, Kevin (Athlete, Football Player)
2820 McKinnon St Apt 3009
Dallas, TX 75201-1025, USA

Aldridge, Lamarcus (Athlete, Basketball
Player)
1410 Montgomery Ln
Southlake, TX 76092-9602, USA

Aldridge, Lily (Model)
184 Thompson St Apt 5M
New York, NY 10012-2533, USA

Aldridge, Melvin (Athlete, Football Player)
14618 Braden Dr E
Houston, TX 77047-6752, USA

Aldridge, Sabrina (Actor)
c/o Allee Newhoff *Elite Model
Management (Miami)*
119 Washington Ave Ste 501
Miami Beach, FL 33139-7228, USA

Aldridge Jr, Allen (Athlete, Football
Player)
2111 Hammerwood Dr
Missouri City, TX 77489-4137, USA

Aldridge Sr, Allen (Athlete, Football
Player)
2111 Hammerwood Dr
Missouri City, TX 77489-4137, USA

Aldrin Jr, Edwin (Buzz) (Astronaut)
Buzz Aldrin Enterprises
11901 Santa Monica Blvd Ste 496
Los Angeles, CA 90025-2767, USA

Ale, Arnold (Athlete, Football Player)
308 E Desford St
Carson, CA 90745-2111, USA

Aleaga, Ink (Athlete, Football Player)
14612 22nd Ave SW
Burien, WA 98166-1610, USA

Alejandro, Kevin (Actor)
c/o Stewart Strunk *Main Title
Entertainment*
8383 Wilshire Blvd Ste 408
Beverly Hills, CA 90211-2435, USA

Alejo, Bob
3724A Portofino Way # A
Santa Barbara, CA 93105-4453, USA

Aleksander, Grant (Actor)
66 Crow Hill Rd
Freehold, NJ 07728-8404, USA

Aleksinas, Charles (Chuck) (Athlete,
Basketball Player)
16 Litchfield Rd
Morris, CT 06763-1522, USA

Aleno, Charles (Athlete, Baseball Player)
601 Marion Ct
Deland, FL 32720-3217, USA

Alessi, Raquel (Actor)
c/o Rhonda Price *Gersh (NY)*
41 Madison Ave
New York, NY 10010-2202, USA

Alex (Actor)
2 Rajaji North St
Pushpa Nagar Nungambakkam
Chennai, TN 600 0, USA

Alex, Keith (Athlete, Football Player)
9750 Windwater Dr Apt 128
Houston, TX 77075-2379, us

Alex, Keith (Athlete, Football Player)
6985 Reno Cir
Beaumont, TX 77708-3594, USA

Alexakis, Art (Musician)
Pinnacle Entertainment
30 Glenn St
White Plains, NY 10603-3254, USA

Alexakos, Steve (Athlete, Football Player)
306 W Linden St
Boise, ID 83706-4830, USA

Alexakos, Steve (Athlete, Football Player)
22300 Hathaway Ave Unit A
Hayward, CA 94541-4896, us

Alexander, Andrew (Producer)
1569 Lindacrest Dr
Beverly Hills, CA 90210-2521, USA

Alexander, Brent (Athlete, Football Player)
349 Remington Ave
Gallatin, TN 37066-7536, USA

Alexander, Brooke (Actor)
c/o Staff Member *Abrams Artists Agency
(LA)*
9200 W Sunset Blvd PH 11
West Hollywood, CA 90069-3601, USA

Alexander, Bruce (Athlete, Football
Player)
508 Englewood Dr
Lufkin, TX 75901-5844, USA

Alexander, Charles (Athlete, Football
Player)
3711 Heritage Colony Dr
Missouri City, TX 77459-4055, USA

Alexander, Corey (Athlete, Basketball
Player)
440 Alpha St
Waynesboro, VA 22980-3904, USA

Alexander, Cory (Athlete, Basketball
Player)
1226 Cardwell Rd
Crozier, VA 23039-2402, USA

Alexander, Dan (Athlete, Football Player)
3846 Somers Ln
Thompsons Station, TN 37179-9617, USA

Alexander, Dan (Athlete, Football Player)
58520 Saint Clement Ave
Plaquemine, LA 70764-3532, USA

Alexander, David (Athlete, Football
Player)
11420 S Granite Pl
Tulsa, OK 74137-8113, USA

Alexander, Denise (Actor)
270 N Canon Dr
Beverly Hills, CA 90210-5323, USA

Alexander, Derrick (Athlete, Football
Player)
PO Box 272626
Tampa, FL 33688-2626, USA

Alexander, Doyle (Athlete, Baseball
Player)
6821 Greenlee St
Fort Worth, TX 76112-5633, USA

Alexander, Eric
2213 Dante St
New Orleans, LA 70118-2956, USA

Alexander, Eric (Musician)
Joel Chriss
300 Mercer St Apt 3J
New York, NY 10003-6732, USA

Alexander, Erika (Actor)
c/o Staff Member *Untitled Entertainment (LA)*
350 S Beverly Dr Ste 200
Beverly Hills, CA 90212-4819, USA

Alexander, Flex (Actor)
c/o Joel Zadak *Principato/Young Management (LA)*
9465 Wilshire Blvd Ste 900
Beverly Hills, CA 90212-2608, USA

Alexander, Frank (Athlete, Football Player)
c/o Bus Cook *Bus Cook Sports, Inc*
1 Willow Bend Dr
Hattiesburg, MS 39402-8552, USA

Alexander, Gary (Athlete, Baseball Player)
5420 Senford Ave
Los Angeles, CA 90056-1029, USA

Alexander, Gerald (Athlete, Baseball Player)
307 Woodland Dr
Donaldsonville, LA 70346-9752, USA

Alexander, Gwen Cheeseman (Athlete, Hockey Player, Olympic Athlete)
502 Maury St
Lexington, VA 24450-2626, USA

Alexander, Harold (Athlete, Football Player)
590 J D Dr
Pickens, SC 29671-9035, USA

Alexander, J (Reality Star, Television Host)
c/o Staff Member *Bankable Productions*
226 W 26th St Fl 4
New York, NY 10001-6700, USA

Alexander, Jaimie (Actor)
c/o David (Dave) Fleming *Mosaic Media Group*
9200 W Sunset Blvd Ste 10
West Hollywood, CA 90069-3608, USA

Alexander, Jamie (Actor)
c/o Alicia Gelernt *Noble Media Management*
275 Madison Ave Fl 28
New York, NY 10016-1101, USA

Alexander, Jane (Actor, Government Official)
William Morris Agency
1325 Avenue Of Americans
New York, NY 10019, USA

Alexander, Jason (Actor, Comedian, Producer)
c/o Carol Yumkas *Yumkas Management*
915 12th St Apt 1
Santa Monica, CA 90403-6047, USA

Alexander, Jeff (Athlete, Football Player)
5283 Elkhart St
Denver, CO 80239-6042, USA

Alexander, John (Athlete, Football Player)
312 Lee Pl
Plainfield, NJ 07063-1337, USA

Alexander, Jules (Musician)
Variety Artists
1924 Spring St
Paso Robles, CA 93446-1620, USA

Alexander, Keith (Actor)
c/o Staff Member *Cunningham Escott Slevin & Doherty (CESD-LA)*
10635 Santa Monica Blvd Ste 130
Los Angeles, CA 90025-8306, USA

Alexander, Kenneth (Cartoonist)
1182 Glen Rd
Lafayette, CA 94549-3044, USA

Alexander, Kermit (Athlete, Football Player)
16651 Stallion Pl
Riverside, CA 92504-5872, USA

Alexander, Khandi (Actor)
8262 Woodshill Trl
Los Angeles, CA 90069-1636, USA

Alexander, Lamar (Politician)
565 Pennsylvania Ave NW Apt 702
Washington, DC 20001-4936, USA

Alexander, Manny (Athlete, Baseball Player)
3660 N Lake Dr
Apt 2664
Chicago, IL 60613, USA

Alexander, Matt (Athlete, Baseball Player)
2419 Stonewall St
Shreveport, LA 71103-3451, USA

alexander, maximillian (Actor)
c/o Staff Member *Schumacher Management*
2018 Glendon Ave
Los Angeles, CA 90025-6324, USA

Alexander, Michelle (Writer)
c/o Julie McCarroll *The New Press*
120 Wall St Fl 31
New York, NY 10005-4007, USA

Alexander, Mike
2700 N Hayden Rd Apt 1096
Scottsdale, AZ 85257-1761, USA

Alexander, Millette (Actor)
157 Roseville Rd
Westport, CT 06880-2615, USA

Alexander, Monty (Musician)
Bennett Morgan
1282 RR 376
Wappingers Falls, NY 12590, USA

Alexander, Narond
530 Winnepeg Dr
Colorado Springs, CO 80910-3360, USA

Alexander, Newell (Actor)
5830 Morella Ave
Valley Village, CA 91607-1322, USA

Alexander, Patrise (Athlete, Football Player)
15035 Westpark Dr Apt 514
Houston, TX 77082-3942, USA

Alexander, P J
5045 Mohegan Ln
Frisco, TX 75034-1278, USA

Alexander, Ray (Athlete, Football Player)
1631 Royal Palm Dr
Edgewater, FL 32132-3213, USA

Alexander, Robert (Athlete, Football Player)
10147 Tramore Ave Apt B
Englewood, FL 34224-9303, USA

Alexander, Roc (Athlete, Football Player)
22020 E Belleview Pl
Aurora, CO 80015-6597, USA

Alexander, Rodney (Congressman, Politician)
316 Cannon Hob
Washington, DC 20515-1805, USA

Alexander, Rogers (Athlete, Football Player)
8182 Rainwater Cir
Manassas, VA 20111-5231, USA

Alexander, Sasha (Actor, Producer)
2241 Chelan Dr
Los Angeles, CA 90068-2625, USA

Alexander, Shasha (Actor, Producer)
c/o Steve Dontanville *Circle of Confusion (NY)*
8931 Ellis Ave
Los Angeles, CA 90034-3336, USA

Alexander, Shaun (Athlete, Football Player)
c/o Ben Dogra *CAA (St. Louis)*
222 S Central Ave Ste 1008
Saint Louis, MO 63105-3509, USA

Alexander, Stephen (Athlete, Football Player)
30677 Santa Fe Ave
Norman, OK 73072-8768, USA

Alexander, Victor (Athlete, Basketball Player)
3450 Holly Trail Ln
Alpharetta, GA 30022-5943, USA

Alexander, Vincent (Athlete, Football Player)
622 W 30th Ave
Covington, LA 70433-2012, USA

Alexander, Willie (Athlete, Football Player)
7219 Holder Forest Cir
Houston, TX 77088-7431, USA

Alexander, Willie (Musician)
Tourmaline Music Group
894 Mayville Rd
Bethel, ME 04217-4605, USA

Alexeev, Nikita (Athlete, Hockey Player)
PO Box 3342
Riverview, FL 33568-3342, USA

Alexie, Sherman (Writer)
PO Box 376
Wellpinit, WA 99040-0376, USA

Alexis, Alton (Athlete, Football Player)
7020 Shadow Creek Ct
Fort Worth, TX 76132-4550, USA

Alexis, Kim (Athlete, Hockey Player)
982 Ponte Vedra Blvd
Ponte Vedra Beach, FL 32082-4068, USA

Alfaro, Jason (Athlete, Baseball Player)
5912 Oak Hill Rd
Watauga, TX 76148-1652, USA

Alfieri, Janet (Cartoonist)
15 Bumpus Rd
Plymouth, MA 02360-3511, USA

Alflen, Ted (Athlete, Football Player)
960 NE 27th Ave
Pompano Beach, FL 33062-4214, USA

Alfonseca, Antonio (Athlete, Baseball Player)
3020 SW 189th Ter
Miramar, FL 33029-5861, USA

Alfonsi, Sharyn (Correspondent)
c/o Staff Member *ABC News*
77 W 66th St Fl 3
New York, NY 10023-6201, USA

Alfonso, Carlos (Athlete, Baseball Player, Coach)
1171 Royal Palm Dr
Naples, FL 34103-4849, USA

Alfonso, Kristian (Actor)
7577 Mulholland Dr
Los Angeles, CA 90046-1238, USA

Alfonzo, Edgar (Athlete, Baseball Player)
9019 Cormorant Ct
Tampa, FL 33647-2980, USA

Alfonzo, Edgardo (Athlete, Baseball Player)
9019 Cormorant Ct
Tampa, FL 33647-2980, USA

Alford, Brian (Athlete, Football Player)
21011 Kenosha St
Oak Park, MI 48237-3813, USA

Alford, Bruce
105 County Road 2965
Kopperl, TX 76652-4610, USA

Alford, Darnell (Athlete, Football Player)
3407 NW Duncan Rd Apt 6
Blue Springs, MO 64015-7209, USA

Alford, David (Actor)
651 Good Springs Rd
Brentwood, TN 37027-5192, USA

Alford, Jay
150 Brittany Ct
Clifton, NJ 07013-2672, USA

Alford, Lynwood (Athlete, Football Player)
355 Moon Clinton Rd Apt 2
Coraopolis, PA 15108-2486, USA

Alford, Mike (Athlete, Football Player)
801 Valparaiso Blvd
Niceville, FL 32578-3406, USA

Alford, Robert (Athlete, Football Player)
c/o Alan Herman *Sportstars Inc*
1350 Avenue of the Americas Fl 28
New York, NY 10019-4702, USA

Alford, Steve (Basketball Player, Olympic Athlete)
5425 Collingwood Cir
Calabasas, CA 91302-3141, USA

Alfredsson, Helen (Athlete, Golfer)
6043 Jamestown Park
Orlando, FL 32819-4435, USA

Alger, Brittney (Actor)
c/o Alex Czuleger *Open Entertainment*
1051 Cole Ave Ste B
Los Angeles, CA 90038-2601, USA

Ali, Laila (Athlete, Boxer)
4801 Azucena Rd
Woodland Hills, CA 91364-4039, USA

Ali, Mahershala (Actor)
c/o Carolyn Govers *Anonymous Content (LA)*
3532 Hayden Ave
Culver City, CA 90232-2413, USA

Ali, May May (Actor)
c/o Kristene Wallis *Wallis Agency*
210 N Pass Ave Ste 205
Burbank, CA 91505-3936, USA

Ali, Muhammad (Athlete, Boxer)
c/o Craig Bankey *Craig Bankey Public Relations*
4470 W Sunset Blvd # 315
Los Angeles, CA 90027-6302, USA

Ali, Tariq (Writer)
c/o Anthony Arnove *Roam Agency*
45 Main St Ste 727
Brooklyn, NY 11201-1076

Ali, Tatyana (Actor)
c/o Staff Member *S/W PR Shop*
7083 Hollywood Blvd Ste 650
Los Angeles, CA 90028-7584, USA

Alibar, Lucy (Writer)
c/o David Gersh *Gersh (LA)*
9465 Wilshire Blvd Ste 600
Beverly Hills, CA 90212-2605, USA

Alicea, Luis (Athlete, Baseball Player)
346 Moorings Dr
Lantana, FL 33462-8022, USA

Alicea, Wilmer (Baby Rasta) (Musician)
c/o Staff Member *Universal Music Publishing Group*
2100 Colorado Ave
Santa Monica, CA 90404-3504, USA

Alice In Chains (Music Group)
c/o David Benveniste *Velvet Hammer*
9014 Melrose Ave
West Hollywood, CA 90069-5610, USA

Alicia, Ana (Actor)
3446 Longridge Ave
Sherman Oaks, CA 91423-4914, USA

Alien Ant Farm (Music Group)
c/o David Gibson *New Ocean Media*
270 Doug Baker Blvd Ste 700
Birmingham, AL 35242-8300, USA

Aliens, The (Music Group)
c/o Staff Member *Paradigm (Monterey)*
404 W Franklin St
Monterey, CA 93940-2303, USA

Alipate, Tuineau (Athlete, Football Player)
9029 18th Ave S
Minneapolis, MN 55425-2321, USA

Alisha (Musician)
Famous Artists Agency
250 W 57th St Ste 901
New York, NY 10107-0008, USA

Alison, Jane (Writer)
FarrarStraus Giroux
19 Union Sq W
New York, NY 10003-3304, USA

Alkan, Erol (Musician)
c/o Joel Zimmerman *William Morris Endeavor (NY)*
1325 Avenue of the Americas
New York, NY 10019-6026, USA

All American Rejects (Music Group, Musician)
c/o Staff Member *PMK/BNC Public Relations (PMK-LA)*
8687 Melrose Ave Ste 8
West Hollywood, CA 90069-5746, USA

Allan, Gabrielle (Producer)
c/o Staff Member *United Talent Agency (UTA-LA)*
9336 Civic Center Dr
Beverly Hills, CA 90210-3604, USA

Allan, Gary (Musician)
114 Walnut Dr
Hendersonville, TN 37075-5030, USA

Allan, Jed (Actor)
76470 Minaret Way
Palm Desert, CA 92211, USA

Allan, Stephen D (Steve) (Golfer)
c/o Staff Member *Pro-Sport Management*
8355 E Hartford Dr Ste 105
Scottsdale, AZ 85255-2533, USA

Allanson, Andy (Athlete, Baseball Player)
38713 Tierra Subida Ave # 102
Palmdale, CA 93551-4562, USA

Allard, Beatrice (Athlete, Baseball Player)
1040 Ridgewood Dr
Lillian, AL 36549-5334, USA

Allard, Brian (Athlete, Baseball Player)
22102 N Perry Rd
Colbert, WA 99005-9488, USA

Allard, Wayne (Politician)
5328 Lighthouse Point Ct
Loveland, CO 80537-7915, USA

Allegre, Raul (Athlete, Football Player)
6500 Rain Creek Pkwy
Austin, TX 78759-6147, USA

Allem, Fulton (Athlete, Golfer)
6876 Hidden Glade Pl
Sanford, FL 32771-6429, USA

Allen, Aleisha (Actor)
c/o Jan Jarrett *Jordan Gill & Dornbaum*
150 5th Ave Ste 308
New York, NY 10011-4311, USA

Allen, Andrew (Astronaut)
4151 Tradewinds Trl
Merritt Island, FL 32953-8078, USA

Allen, Andrew M Lt Colonel (Astronaut)
4151 Tradewinds Trl
Merritt Island, FL 32953-8078, USA

Allen, Anthony (Athlete, Football Player)
956 20th Ave
Seattle, WA 98122-4736, USA

Allen, Bernie (Athlete, Baseball Player)
3725 Coventry Way
Carmel, IN 46033-3026, USA

Allen, Beth (Athlete, Golfer)
1602 Peacock Ave
Sunnyvale, CA 94087-4917, USA

Allen, Bob (Athlete, Baseball Player)
PO Box 677
Tatum, TX 75691-0677, USA

Allen, Bob (Athlete, Basketball Player)
117 Quarter Mile Way
Nicholasville, KY 40356-8220, USA

Allen, Bruce (Race Car Driver)
Reher Morrison Motorsports
1120 Enterprise Pl
Arlington, TX 76001-7138, USA

Allen, Buddy (Athlete, Football Player)
3689 Westmoreland Dr
Mays Landing, NJ 08330-3240, USA

Allen, Byron (Comedian)
c/o Staff Member *Entertainment Studios*
1925 Century Park E Ste 1025
Los Angeles, CA 90067-2729, USA

Allen, Carl
1614 Hornsby Ave
Saint Louis, MO 63147-1410, USA

Allen, Chad (Actor)
7326 Brightwater Oaks Dr
Tampa, FL 33625-4070, USA

Allen, Chad (Athlete, Baseball Player, Olympic Athlete)
7152 Blackwood Dr
Dallas, TX 75231-5604, USA

Allen, Chuck
192 Victoria Loop
Port Townsend, WA 98368-9400, USA

Allen, Dalva (Athlete, Football Player)
411 County Road 1925
Mount Pleasant, TX 75455-6912, USA

Allen, Danielle Sherie (Actor)
c/o Staff Member *Privilege Talent Agency*
PO Box 260860
Encino, CA 91426-0860, USA

Allen, Debbie (Actor, Dancer)
c/o Staff Member *Red Bird Productions*
3791 Santa Rosalia Dr
Los Angeles, CA 90008-3603, USA

Allen, Dennis (Football Coach)
c/o Team Member *Oakland Raiders*
1220 Harbor Bay Pkwy
Alameda, CA 94502-6570, USA

Allen, Derek (Athlete, Football Player)
6206 Woodward Ln
Milton, FL 32570-4577, USA

Allen, Dick (Athlete, Baseball Player)
983 Possum Hollow Rd
Wampum, PA 16157-2817, USA

Allen, Dick (Athlete, Baseball Player)
PO Box 254
Wampum, PA 16157-0254, USA

Allen, Don (Athlete, Football Player)
17303 Kermier Rd
Hockley, TX 77447-9100, USA

Allen, Doug (Athlete, Football Player)
291 E McCormick Ave
State College, PA 16801-6122, USA

Allen, Duane (Actor)
216 Spring Valley Rd
Hendersonville, TN 37075-9657, USA

Allen, Dusty (Athlete, Baseball Player)
208 Valiente St
Las Vegas, NV 89144-1518, USA

Allen, Dwayne (Athlete, Football Player)
c/o Michael Perrett *SportsTrust Advisors (GA)*
3340 Peachtree Rd NE Fl 16
Atlanta, GA 30326-1000, USA

Allen, Earl (Athlete, Football Player)
8015 Duffield Ln
Houston, TX 77071-2016, USA

Allen, Eddie (Athlete, Football Player)
3321 W Fisher St
Pensacola, FL 32505-4909, USA

Allen, Egypt (Athlete, Football Player)
2115 Rubens Dr
Dallas, TX 75224-4146, USA

Allen, Eric (Athlete, Football Player)
484 San Elijo St
San Diego, CA 92106-3463, USA

Allen, George (Politician)
4296 Neitzey Pl
Alexandria, VA 22309-3069, USA

Allen, George F (Ex-Governor, Ex-Senator)
Young America's Foundation
110 Elden St Ste A
F.M. Kirby Freedom Center
Herndon, VA 20170-4800, USA

Allen, Grady (Athlete, Football Player)
317 Circleview Dr N
Hurst, TX 76054-3518, USA

Allen, Greg (Athlete, Football Player)
5006 Persimmon Hollow Rd
Milton, FL 32583-2739, USA

Allen, Hank (Athlete, Baseball Player)
PO Box 4612
Upper Marlboro, MD 20775-0612, USA

Allen, Herb (Business Person)
Allen & Co
711 5th Ave Fl 9
New York, NY 10022-3168, USA

Allen, Jackie (Athlete, Football Player)
7152 Blackwood Dr
Dallas, TX 75231-5604, USA

Allen, Jamie (Athlete, Baseball Player)
1920 E Belmont Dr
Tempe, AZ 85284-1719, USA

Allen, Jared (Athlete, Football Player)
c/o Ken Harris *Optimum Sports Management*
3225 S Macdill Ave Ste 330
Tampa, FL 33629-8171, USA

Allen, Jared (Athlete, Football Player)
c/o Denise White *EAG Sports Management*
909 N Sepulveda Blvd Ste 360
El Segundo, CA 90245-3864, USA

Allen, Jason (Athlete, Football Player)
104 Napa Valley Way
Madison, AL 35758-2227, USA

Allen, Jeff (Athlete, Football Player)
902 Warren Dr
Centerville, IN 47330-9533, USA

Allen, Jerry (Athlete, Football Player)
14 Washington Valley Rd
Morristown, NJ 07960-3412, USA

Allen, Jimmy (Athlete, Football Player)
12650 Garden Way
Victorville, CA 92395-9702, USA

Allen, Joan (Actor)
250 W 94th St # 15G
New York, NY 10025-6954, USA

Allen, Johnny (Race Car Driver)
7403 S County Road 825 E
Plainfield, IN 46168-8745, USA

Allen, Jonelle (Actor)
c/o Staff Member *SMS Talent*
8383 Wilshire Blvd Ste 230
Beverly Hills, CA 90211-2436, USA

Allen, Joseph P (Astronaut)
LBJ Space Center
2101 Nasa Pkwy # 1
C/O Astronaut Office
Houston, TX 77058-3607, USA

Allen, Joseph P Dr (Astronaut)
4051 Mansion Dr NW
Washington, DC 20007-2135, USA

Allen, Karen (Actor)
Karen Allen Fiber Arts
8 Railroad St
Great Barrington, MA 01230-1521, USA

Allen, Keegan (Actor)
c/o Konrad Leh *Creative Talent Group*
1900 Avenue of the Stars Ste 2475
Los Angeles, CA 90067-4512, USA

Allen, Keith (Athlete, Hockey Player)
275 Evergreen Rd
Barrington, NJ 08007-1457, USA

Allen, Kenderick (Athlete, Football Player)
5921 Oxford Chase Cir
Peachtree Corners, GA 30092-3514, USA

Allen, Kevin (Athlete, Football Player)
2422 Hazelcrest Ln
Cincinnati, OH 45231-1132, USA

Allen, Kim (Athlete, Baseball Player)
2705 La Praix St
Highland, CA 92346-1928, USA

Allen, Krista (Actor)
c/o Todd Eisner *Innovative Artists (LA)*
405 S Beverly Dr Ste 500
Beverly Hills, CA 90212-4425, USA

Allen, Larry C (Athlete, Football Player)
401 Kingswood Ln
Danville, CA 94506-6066, USA

Allen, Leo (Writer)
c/o Staff Member *Saturday Night Live*
30 Rockefeller Plz Fl 2
New York, NY 10112-0044, USA

Allen, Lily (Musician)
c/o Brad Petrigala *Brillstein Entertainment Partners (LA)*
9150 Wilshire Blvd Ste 350
Beverly Hills, CA 90212-3453, USA

Allen, Lloyd (Athlete, Baseball Player)
2340 Castlewood Dr
Toledo, OH 43613-3923, USA

Allen, Loy Jr (Race Car Driver)
1508 Kildaire Farm Rd
Cary, NC 27511-6552, USA

Allen, Lucius (Athlete, Basketball Player)
1915 Buckingham Rd
Los Angeles, CA 90016-1701, USA

Allen, Luke (Athlete, Baseball Player)
282 Cooper Rd
Social Circle, GA 30025-5119, USA

Allen, Marcus (Athlete, Football Player)
5301 Forecastle Ct
Carlsbad, CA 92008-3826, USA

Allen, Marty (Actor, Comedian)
3847 Tropical Vine St
Las Vegas, NV 89147-8079, USA

Allen, Marvin (Athlete, Football Player)
1806 Las Cruces Ln
Wichita Falls, TX 76306-5205, USA

Allen, Maryon P (Ex-Senator, Politician)
1551 Creekstone Cir
Birmingham, AL 35243-2827, USA

Allen, Michael (Athlete, Football Player)
8839 NE 147th St
Kenmore, WA 98028-4727, USA

Allen, Michael (Athlete, Golfer)
5827 E Anderson Dr
Scottsdale, AZ 85254-5941, USA

Allen, Mike (Athlete, Hockey Player)
PO Box 1416
International Falls, MN 56649-1416, USA

Allen, Nancy (Actor)
weSPARK
13520 Ventura Blvd
Sherman Oaks, CA 91423-3802, USA

Allen, Natalie (Correspondent)
Cable News Network
1050 Techwood Dr NW
News Dept
Atlanta, GA 30318-5695, USA

Allen, Nate (Athlete, Football Player)
8239 Queen Ave N
Minneapolis, MN 55444-1513, USA

Allen, Neil (Athlete, Baseball Player)
3619 Torrey Pines Blvd
Sarasota, FL 34238-2828, USA

Allen, Pam (Athlete, Golfer)
809 Delphinium Dr
Billings, MT 59102-3409, USA

Allen, Patrick (Athlete, Football Player)
427 20th Ave E
Seattle, WA 98112-5313, USA

Allen, Paul (Business Person, Football Executive)
The Paul G Allen Family Foundation
505 5th Ave S Ste 900
Seattle, WA 98104-3821, USA

Allen, Rae (Actor)
c/o Staff Member *Kyle Fritz Management*
6325 Heather Dr
Los Angeles, CA 90068-1633, USA

Allen, Randy (Athlete, Basketball Player)
10185 Nichols Lake Rd
Milton, FL 32583-9267, USA

Allen, Rax Jr (Music Group)
209 10th Ave # 527
Nashville, TN 37203, USA

Allen, Ray (Actor, Athlete, Basketball Player)
7984 Esta Ln
Orlando, FL 32827-7172, USA

Allen, Ricardo (Athlete, Football Player)
c/o Eugene Parker *Maximum Sports Management*
6435 W Jefferson Blvd # 197
Fort Wayne, IN 46804-6203, USA

Allen, Rice (Athlete, Football Player)
4906 Laurel Hill Ct
Sugar Land, TX 77478-5424, USA

Allen, Richard A (Richie) (Athlete, Baseball Player)
RR 2
Possum Hollow Rd
Wampum, PA 16157, USA

Allen, Richard V (Government Official)
905 16th St NW
Washington, DC 20006-1703, USA

Allen, Rick (Musician)
935 Camino Colibri
Calabasas, CA 91302-2106, USA

Allen, Robert (Business Person, Writer)
Multiple Streams of Income
1353 W 760 N
Orem, UT 84057-6102, USA

Allen, Rod (Athlete, Baseball Player)
3150 E Woodland Dr
Phoenix, AZ 85048-7702, USA

Allen, Ron (Athlete, Baseball Player)
917 Winona Dr
Youngstown, OH 44511-1404, USA

Allen, Rosalind (Actor)
c/o John Carrabino *John Carrabino Management*
5900 Wilshire Blvd Ste 406
Los Angeles, CA 90036-5015, USA

Allen, Ryan (Athlete, Football Player)
c/o Ryan Morgan *MAG Sports Agency*
8222 Melrose Ave Fl 2
Los Angeles, CA 90046-6825, USA

Allen, Sam (Athlete, Baseball Player)
2734 Gate House Rd Apt 108
Norfolk, VA 23504-4057, USA

Allen, Sian Barbara (Actor, Writer)
1411 N Alberta St Apt 7
Portland, OR 97217-3761, USA

Allen, Taje (Athlete, Football Player)
1209 Valorie Ct
Cedar Park, TX 78613-4023, USA

Allen, Ted (Chef, Television Host)
c/o Staff Member *Creative Artists Agency (CAA-NY)*
162 5th Ave Fl 6
New York, NY 10010-6047, USA

Allen, Terry (Athlete, Football Player)
2729 Kelly Cove Dr
Buford, GA 30519-3474, USA

Allen, Tessa (Actor)
c/o Staff Member *Bobby Ball Talent Agency*
3500 W Olive Ave Ste 300
Burbank, CA 91505-4647, USA

Allen, Tim (Actor, Comedian, Producer)
8430 Edwin Dr
Los Angeles, CA 90046-1026, USA

Allen, Todd (Actor, Producer)
c/o David (Dave) Fleming *Mosaic Media Group*
9200 W Sunset Blvd Ste 10
West Hollywood, CA 90069-3608, USA

Allen, Tony (Athlete, Basketball Player)
70 Kodiak Way Unit 2628
Waltham, MA 02451-0296, USA

Allen, Tremayne (Athlete, Football Player)
2910 Girvan Dr
Land O Lakes, FL 34638-7877, USA

Allen, Will (Athlete, Football Player)
15 Fox Hill Dr
Wayne, NJ 07470-2539, USA

Allen, Will (Athlete, Football Player)
2325 SW 105th Ter
Davie, FL 33324-7608, USA

Allen, Will (Athlete, Football Player)
12721 Tar Flower Dr
Tampa, FL 33626-2341, USA

Allen, Willard M (Doctor)
211 Key Haighway
Baltimore, MD 21230, USA

Allen, Willie (Race Car Driver)
Modern Management
1625 Broadway Ste 600
Nashville, TN 37203-3141, USA

Allen, Woody (Actor, Comedian, Director, Writer)
118 E 70th St
New York, NY 10021-5007, USA

Allen, Wyatt (Athlete, Olympic Athlete, Rower)
University of California
2227 Piedmont Ave
Attn: Men's Crew Coaching Staff
Berkeley, CA 94720-2325, USA

Allenby, Robert (Athlete, Golfer)
4901 Pacifico Ct
Palm Beach Gardens, FL 33418-8995, USA

Allende, Fernando (Actor)
c/o Staff Member *El Dorado Pictures*
725 Arizona Ave Ste 100
Santa Monica, CA 90401-1734, USA

Allende, Isabel (Writer)
116 Caledonia St
Sausalito, CA 94965-1925, USA

Allende, Isabel (Writer)
92 Fernwood Dr
San Rafael, CA 94901-1533, USA

Allen Jr, Glenn (Race Car Driver)
7280 Jerry Dr
West Chester, OH 45069-4216, USA

Allen Jr, Rex (Musician)
Friends of Rex Allen Jr
PO Box 13436
Wichita, KS 67213-0436, USA

Allen-Mullins, Doreen (Athlete, Baseball Player)
1104 Somonauk St
Sycamore, IL 60178-2521, USA

Allenson, Gary (Athlete, Baseball Player)
711 SE 34th St
Cape Coral, FL 33904-4900, USA

Allensworth, Jermaine (Athlete, Baseball Player)
3410 Crossgate Dr
Bloomington, IL 61704-9662, USA

Allerman, Kurt (Athlete, Football Player)
2511 Blue Heron Dr
Hudson, OH 44236-1866, USA

Allernnan, Kurt (Athlete, Football Player)
2511 Blue Heron Dr
Hudson, OH 44236-1866, USA

Allert, Ty (Athlete, Football Player)
1504 County Road 308
Lexington, TX 78947-4113, USA

Alley, Donald (Athlete, Football Player)
3258 W Parade Cir
Colorado Springs, CO 80917-2931, USA

Alley, Gene (Athlete, Baseball Player)
10236 Steuben Dr
Glen Allen, VA 23060-3072, USA

Alley, Kirstie (Actor, Producer)
2600 Aberdeen Ave
Los Angeles, CA 90027-1222, USA

Alley, Steve (Athlete, Hockey Player)
545 College Rd
Lake Forest, IL 60045-2319, USA

Alley Cats, The (Music Group, Musician)
c/o Staff Member *Harmony Artists*
8455 Beverly Blvd Ste 400
Los Angeles, CA 90048-3437, USA

All For One / All-4-One (Music Group)
c/o Staff Member *Performers of the World*
5657 Wilshire Blvd Ste 280
Los Angeles, CA 90036-3755, USA

Allgaier, Justin (Race Car Driver)
c/o Staff Member *Penske Racing South*
200 Penske Way
Mooresville, NC 28115-8022, USA

Allgood, Lonnie (Athlete, Football Player)
12 Drake Rd
Somerset, NJ 08873-2369, USA

Allie, Gair (Athlete, Baseball Player)
11818 Button Willow Cv
San Antonio, TX 78213-1220, USA

Allietta, Bob
25 Robinson Rd
Falmouth, MA 02540-3840

Allinson, Michael (Actor)
112 Knollwood Dr
Larchmont, NY 10538, USA

Allione, Tsultrim (Religious Leader)
Tara Mandala Retreat Center
PO Box 3040
Pagosa Springs, CO 81147-3040, USA

Allison, Aundrae (Athlete, Football Player)
2024 Summit Ridge Ln
Kannapolis, NC 28083-6284

Allison, Bobby (Race Car Driver)
PO Box 3696
Mooresville, NC 28117-3696, USA

Allison, Dana (Athlete, Baseball Player)
322 Thomas Dr
Middletown, VA 22645-3992, USA

Allison, Dave (Athlete, Coach, Hockey Player)
c/o Staff Member *Iowa Stars*
833 5th Ave
Des Moines, IA 50309-1399, USA

Allison, Donnie (Race Car Driver)
355 Quail Dr
Salisbury, NC 28147-8860, USA

Allison, Glenn (Bowler)
1844 S Haster St Spc 138
Anaheim, CA 92802-3750, USA

Allison, Henry (Hank) (Athlete, Football Player)
458 W Ellis Ave
Inglewood, CA 90302-1109, USA

Allison, Jerry (Musician, Songwriter, Writer)
8455 New Bethel Rd
Lyles, TN 37098-1909, USA

Allison, Jim (Athlete, Football Player)
5706 Laramie Way
San Diego, CA 92120-1426, USA

Allison, Kate (Athlete, Golfer)
349 Canterbury Ln
Wyckoff, NJ 07481-2305, USA

Allison, Mike (Athlete, Hockey Player)
PO Box 1416
International Falls, MN 56649-1416, USA

Allison, Odis (Athlete, Basketball Player)
2945 20th St
San Pablo, CA 94806-2431, USA

Allison, Ray (Athlete, Hockey Player)
106 N Valleybrook Rd
Cherry Hill, NJ 08034-3809, USA

Allison, Robert J Jr
Anadarko Petroleum Corp
1201 Lake Robbins Dr
Spring, TX 77380-1124, USA

Allison, Stacy (Mountaineer)
6633 SE 29th Ave
Portland, OR 97202-8721, USA

Alliss, Peter (Sportscaster)
Int'l Mgmt Group
1 Erieview Plz
1360 E 9th St #1300
Cleveland, OH 44114-1738, USA

Alliston, Vaughn (Buddy) (Athlete, Football Player)
7493 Apple Yard Ln
Cordova, TN 38016-8770, USA

Allman, Gregg (Musician)
706 Buckland Hall Rd
Richmond Hill, GA 31324-5352, USA

Allman, Jamie Anne (Actor)
c/o Jordyn Palos *Persona PR (LA)*
8840 Wilshire Blvd Ste 212
Beverly Hills, CA 90211-2606, USA

Allman, Marshall (Actor)
c/o Nate Steadman *Gersh (LA)*
9465 Wilshire Blvd Ste 600
Beverly Hills, CA 90212-2605, USA

Allmendinger, AJ (Race Car Driver)
Richard Petty Motorsports
1120 Enterprise Pl
Arlington, TX 76001-7138, USA

Allor, Kristin
11940 Willow Ridge Dr
Willow Springs, IL 60480-1187, USA

Allport, Chris M (Actor)
1324 Pine St
Santa Monica, CA 90405-2612, USA

Allport, Christopher (Actor)
c/o Staff Member *Pakula/King & Associates*
9229 W Sunset Blvd Ste 315
West Hollywood, CA 90069-3403, USA

Allred, Beau (Athlete, Baseball Player)
690 S Aspen Ln
Thatcher, AZ 85552-4441, USA

Allred, Brian (Athlete, Football Player)
16470 Ed Warfield Rd
Woodbine, MD 21797-7806, USA

Allred, Gloria (Attorney)
6300 Wilshire Blvd Ste 1500
Los Angeles, CA 90048-5217, USA

Allred, Jason (Athlete, Golfer)
10239 E Salt Bush Dr
Scottsdale, AZ 85255-8637, USA

Allred, John (Athlete, Football Player)
25582 Paseo De La Paz
San Juan Capistrano, CA 92675-4010, USA

Allstar Weekend (Music Group, Musician)
c/o Staff Member *Hollywood Records*
500 S Buena Vista St
Burbank, CA 91521-0002, USA

Allston, Aaron (Writer)
PO Box 564
Round Rock, TX 78680-0564, USA

Allsup, Mike (Music Group, Musician)
Mckenzie Accountancy
5171 Caliente St Unit 134
Las Vegas, NV 89119-2198, USA

Allsup, Tommy (Music Group)
Tophands Talent
PO Box 1547
Arlington, TX 76004-1547, USA

All Time Low (Music Group)
Hopeless Records
PO Box 7495
Van Nuys, CA 91409-7495, USA

Allums, Darrell (Athlete, Basketball Player)
3584 Brenton Ave Apt B
Lynwood, CA 90262-2054, USA

Almanza, Armando (Athlete, Baseball Player)
2024 Paseo Del Prado Dr
El Paso, TX 79936-3737, USA

Almanzar, Carlos (Athlete, Baseball Player)
c/o Staff Member *San Diego Padres*
100 Park Blvd
San Diego, CA 92101-7405, USA

Almen, Lowell G (Religious Leader)
Evangelical Lutheran Church
8765 W Higgins Rd Ste 600
Chicago, IL 60631-4100, USA

Almirola, Aric (Race Car Driver)
Aric Almirola Inc
215 Overhill Dr Ste A
Mooresville, NC 28117-7037, USA

Almon, Bill (Athlete, Baseball Player)
42 Channel Vw Unit 4
Warwick, RI 02889-6544, USA

Almond, David (Writer)
c/o Staff Member *Doubleday/RandomHouse*
1745 Broadway
New York, NY 10019-4640, USA

Almond, Marc (Musician)
105 Shad Row Ste B
Piermont, NY 10968-3001, USA

Almonte, Edwin (Athlete, Baseball Player)
3078 Clairmont Rd NE
NE Act 231
Atlanta, GA 30329-1656, USA

Almonte, Erick (Athlete, Baseball Player)
1105 NW 90th Ter
Hollywood, FL 33024-4642, USA

Almonte, Hector (Athlete, Baseball Player)
16742 SW 12th St
Pembroke Pines, FL 33027-1408, USA

Almy, Brook (Actor)
c/o Nyle Brenner *Brenner Management*
9171 Wilshire Blvd Ste 441
Beverly Hills, CA 90210-5516, USA

Alomar, Roberto (Athlete, Baseball Player)
901 Palacio De Avila
Tampa, FL 33613-5224, USA

Alomar Jr, Sandy (Athlete, Baseball Player)
1906 W Cortland St
Chicago, IL 60622-1037, USA

Alomar Sr, Sandy (Athlete, Baseball Player)
PO Box 367
Salinas, PR 00751-0367, USA

Alonso, Adrian (Actor)
c/o Staff Member *Featured Artists Agency*
1880 Century Park E Ste 1402
Los Angeles, CA 90067-1630, USA

Alonso, Daniella (Actor)
c/o Staff Member *Gersh (LA)*
9465 Wilshire Blvd Ste 600
Beverly Hills, CA 90212-2605, USA

Alonso, Laz (Actor)
c/o Ron West *Thruline Entertainment*
9250 Wilshire Blvd Ste 100
Ground Floor
Beverly Hills, CA 90212-3343, USA

Alonso, Maria Conchita (Actor, Musician)
420 N Palm Dr Apt 103
Beverly Hills, CA 90210-4055, USA

Alonzo, Cristela (Actor)
c/o Stacy Mark *William Morris Endeavor (LA)*
9601 Wilshire Blvd
Beverly Hills, CA 90210-5213, USA

Alosio, Ryan (Actor)
c/o Alexander Shekarchian *AS Management*
9440 Santa Monica Blvd Ste 700
Beverly Hills, CA 90210-4609, USA

Alou, Felipe (Athlete, Baseball Player)
6891 Cobia Cir
Boynton Beach, FL 33437-3639, USA

Alou, Moises (Athlete, Baseball Player)
13095 NW 13th St
Pembroke Pines, FL 33028-2711, USA

Alpay, David (Actor)
c/o Brian Wilkins *Kritzer Levine Wilkins Entertainment (KLWG)*
11872 La Grange Ave Fl 1
Los Angeles, CA 90025-5283, USA

Alpert, Herb (Musician)
216 Notteargenta Rd
Pacific Palisades, CA 90272-3110, USA

Alpert, Joseph S (Doctor)
3440 E Cathedral Rock Cir
Tucson, AZ 85718-1379, USA

Alphin, Big Kenny (Musician)
2325 Golf Club Ln
Nashville, TN 37215-1107, USA

Alphin, Gerald (Athlete, Football Player)
4760 Lorient Ct
Snellville, GA 30039-8721, USA

Alsina, August (Musician)
c/o Staff Member *William Morris Endeavor (LA)*
9601 Wilshire Blvd
Beverly Hills, CA 90210-5213, USA

Alsop, Marin (Musician)
c/o Staff Member *ICM Partners (LA)*
10250 Constellation Blvd Fl 7
Los Angeles, CA 90067-6207, USA

Alston, Barbara (Music Group)
Superstars Unlimited
PO Box 371371
Las Vegas, NV 89137-1371, USA

Alston, Dell (Athlete, Baseball Player)
101 Enchanted Hills Rd Apt 103
Owings Mills, MD 21117-2793, USA

Alston, Garvin (Athlete, Baseball Player)
4705 E Thunderhill Pl
Phoenix, AZ 85044-4905, USA

Alston, Gerald (Musician)
c/o Staff Member *Wenig-LaMonica Associates*
580 White Plains Rd Ste 130
Tarrytown, NY 10591-5106, USA

Alston, Lyneal (Athlete, Football Player)
1318 Morning Sun Cir
Birmingham, AL 35242-2907, USA

Alston, Mack (Athlete, Football Player)
5421 Echols Ave
Alexandria, VA 22311-1344, USA

Alstott, Mike (Athlete, Football Player)
Mike Alstott Family Foundation
PO Box 40055
St Petersburg, FL 33743-0055, USA

Alsup, Bill (Race Car Driver)
93 Rio Grande Dr
Durango, CO 81301-7113, USA

Alt, Carol (Actor)
c/o Scott Hart *Scott Hart Entertainment*
14622 Ventura Blvd # 746
Sherman Oaks, CA 91403-3600, USA

Alt, John M (Athlete, Football Player)
21 Crescent Ln
Saint Paul, MN 55127-6358, USA

Altamirano, Porfi (Athlete, Baseball Player)
3676 SW 24th Ter
Miami, FL 33145-3041, USA

Alther, Lisa (Writer)
1086 Silver St
Hinesburg, VT 05461-9450, USA

Althoff, James (Jim) (Athlete, Football Player)
150 Red Top Dr Apt 302
Libertyville, IL 60048-5237, USA

Altman, Chelsea (Actor)
c/o Matthew Sullivan *Sullivan Talent Group*
305 W 105th St Apt 3B
New York, NY 10025-9116, USA

Altman, George (Athlete, Baseball Player)
915 Midpoint Dr
O Fallon, MO 63366-5906, USA

Altman, Jeff (Actor)
c/o Staff Member *Richard De La Font Agency*
3808 W South Park Blvd
Broken Arrow, OK 74011-1261, USA

Altman, Josh (Business Person, Reality Star)
The Altman Brothers Realty
250 N Canon Dr
Beverly Hills, CA 90210-5322, USA

Altman, Scott D (Astronaut)
1413 36th St NW
Washington, DC 20007-2606, USA

Altman, Scott D Cdr (Astronaut)
1413 36th St NW
Washington, DC 20007-2606, USA

Altmire, Jason (Congressman, Politician)
332 Cannon Hob
Washington, DC 20515-3226, USA

Altobelli, Joe (Athlete, Baseball Player, Coach)
10 Stowell Dr Apt 3
Rochester, NY 14616-1889, USA

Alualu, Tyson (Athlete, Football Player)
c/o Ken Zuckerman *Priority Sports & Entertainment - (LA)*
15233 Ventura Blvd Ste 718
Sherman Oaks, CA 91403-2237, USA

Alusik, George (Athlete, Baseball Player)
581 Garden Ave
Woodbridge, NJ 07095-3850, USA

Alvarado, Allen (Actor)
c/o Scott Appel *Scott Appel Public Relations*
13547 Ventura Blvd # 203
Sherman Oaks, CA 91423-3825, USA

Alvarez, Barry (Coach, Football Coach)
University of Wisconsin
Athletic Dept
Madison, WI 53711, USA

Alvarez, Clemente
18711 NW 46th Ave
Miami Gardens, FL 33055-2655, USA

Alvarez, Frankie J (Actor)
c/o Staff Member *Don Buchwald & Associates (NY)*
10 E 44th St Frnt 1
New York, NY 10017-3654, USA

Alvarez, Gabe (Athlete, Baseball Player)
4401 La Madera Ave
El Monte, CA 91732-2009, USA

Alvarez, Isabel (Athlete, Baseball Player)
2416 Monmouth Ave
Fort Wayne, IN 46809-1732, USA

Alvarez, Jose (Athlete, Baseball Player)
210 Murphy Ln
Greenville, SC 29607-4934, USA

Alvarez, Juan (Athlete, Baseball Player)
10995 SW 107th Ave
Miami, FL 33176-3444, USA

Alvarez, Orlando (Athlete, Baseball Player)
Cummunidad Dolores 37
Rio Grande, PR 00745, USA

Alvarez, Rogelio (Athlete, Baseball Player)
5010 NW 183rd St
Miami Gardens, FL 33055-2929, USA

Alvarez, Victor (Athlete, Baseball Player)
c/o Staff Member *Los Angeles Dodgers (LA Dodgers)*
1000 Elysian Park Ave
Los Angeles, CA 90012-1112, USA

Alvarez, Wilson (Athlete, Baseball Player)
State College Spikes
6927 Westchester Cir
Lakewood Ranch, FL 34202-2584, USA

Alvers, Steve (Athlete, Football Player)
9751 SW 115th Ave
Miami, FL 33176-2553, USA

Alverson, Tommy (Musician)
c/o Staff Member *Ken-Ran Entertainment*
418 S Barton St
Grapevine, TX 76051-5344, USA

Alves, Camila (Model, Television Host)
c/o Jesse Parker Stowell *Full Picture Management (NYC)*
915 Broadway Fl 20
New York, NY 10010-7131, USA

Alves, Joe (Director)
4176 Rosario Rd
Woodland Hills, CA 91364-6025, USA

Alvim, Anna (Actor)
c/o Jean Fox *Fox-Albert Management*
88 Central Park W
New York, NY 10023-5299, USA

Alvin, Dave (Musician, Songwriter, Writer)
Mark Pucci
5000 Oak Bluff Ct
Atlanta, GA 30350-1069, USA

Alvis, Max (Athlete, Baseball Player)
806 Hunterwood Dr
Jasper, TX 75951-2820, USA

Alvord, Steve (Athlete, Football Player)
3624 Westridge Pi
Bellingham, WA 98226, USA

Alward, Tom (Athlete, Football Player)
5051 Bensett Trl
Davison, MI 48423-8781, USA

Alworth, Lance (Athlete, Football Player)
990 Highland Dr Ste 300
Solana Beach, CA 92075-2438, USA

Alyea, Brant (Athlete, Baseball Player)
3323 Manor Rd
Huntingdon Valley, PA 19006-4147, USA

Alyson, Jocelyn E (Musician)
c/o Staff Member *Diva Central Inc*
7510 W Sunset Blvd Ste 1445
Los Angeles, CA 90046-3408, USA

Alzne, Karl (Athlete, Hockey Player)
1301 N Troy St
Arlington, VA 22201-2521

alzner, karl (Athlete, Hockey Player)
1301 N Troy St
Arlington, VA 22201-2521, USA

Amaechi, John (Athlete, Basketball Player)
5747 E Aire Libre Ave
Scottsdale, AZ 85254-1206, USA

Amaker, Tommy (Athlete, Basketball Player, Coach)
University of Michigan
Athletic Dept
Ann Arbor, MI 48109, USA

Amalfitano, J Joseph (Joey) (Athlete, Baseball Player, Coach)
265 Bowstring Dr
Sedona, AZ 86336-6523, USA

amalfitano, joe (Athlete, Baseball Player)
60 Sheath Dr
Sedona, AZ 86336-6510, USA

Amandes, Tom (Actor)
2751 Pelham Pl
Los Angeles, CA 90068-2326, USA

Amano, Eugene (Athlete, Football Player)
495 Jones Pkwy
Brentwood, TN 37027-5045, USA

Amanpour, Christiane (Correspondent, Journalist)
c/o Staff Member *CNN (Atlanta)*
1 Cnn Ctr NW
PO Box 105366
Atlanta, GA 30303-2762, USA

Amante, Tony (Athlete, Hockey Player)
58 Turners Way
Norwell, MA 02061-2339, USA

Amaral, Bob (Actor)
c/o Staff Member *Professional Artists Agency*
321 W 44th St Ste 605
New York, NY 10036-5432, USA

Amaral, Rich (Athlete, Baseball Player)
3122 Country Club Dr
Costa Mesa, CA 92626-2344, USA

Amaro, Melanie (Musician)
6441 NW 24th Pl
Sunrise, FL 33313-2162, USA

Amaro, Ruben (Commentator)
1063 Country Hills Rd
Yardley, PA 19067-6024, USA

Amaro Jr, Ruben (Athlete, Baseball Player)
Philadelphia Phillies
1063 Country Hills Rd
Yardley, PA 19067-6024, USA

Amaro Sr, Ruben (Athlete, Baseball Player)
4098 Cinnamon Way
Weston, FL 33331-3810, USA

Amash, Justin (Congressman, Politician)
114 Cannon Hob
Washington, DC 20515-3601, USA

Amato, Bruno (Actor)
c/o Wendy Peldon *Caviar Entertainment*
2934 N Beverly Glen Cir Ste 115
Los Angeles, CA 90077-1724, USA

Amato, Joe (Race Car Driver)
Amato Racing
44 Tunkhannock Ave
Exeter, PA 18643-1221, USA

Amato, Ken (Athlete, Football Player)
9290 Wardley Park Ln
Brentwood, TN 37027-4465, USA

Amavia, Daniela (Actor, Model)
c/o Tom Greenberg *Del Shaw Moonves Tanaka Finkelstein & Lezcano*
2120 Colorado Ave Ste 200
Santa Monica, CA 90404-3561, USA

Amaya, Rafael (Actor, Model, Musician)
c/o Liza Anderson *Anderson Group Public Relations*
8060 Melrose Ave Fl 4
Los Angeles, CA 90046-7038, USA

Amays, Ashraf (Athlete, Basketball Player)
25030 Round Barn Rd
Plainfield, IL 60585-7490

Amazing Jonathan, The (Actor)
c/o Staff Member *ICM Partners (LA)*
10250 Constellation Blvd Fl 7
Los Angeles, CA 90067-6207, USA

Amazing Rhythm Aces (Music Group)
c/o Staff Member *Fat City Artists*
830 Tannahill Dr SE
Huntsville, AL 35802-1956, USA

Amber (Musician)
Artists & Audience Entertainment
PO Box 35
Pawling, NY 12564-0035, USA

Amber, Britney (Actor, Adult Film Star, Model)
c/o Erika Icon *The Rub PR*
3370 Glendale Blvd
Los Angeles, CA 90039-4836, USA

Ambinder, Marc (Writer)
c/o Staff Member *Cohen & Gardner*
345 N Maple Dr Ste 181
Beverly Hills, CA 90210-5185, USA

Ambres, Chip (Athlete, Baseball Player)
4460 Beale St
Beaumont, TX 77705-4705, USA

Ambrose, Ashley (Athlete, Football Player)
2726 Eudora Trl
Duluth, GA 30097-6284, USA

Ambrose, Lauren (Actor)
c/o Billy Lazarus *United Talent Agency (UTA-LA)*
9336 Civic Center Dr
Beverly Hills, CA 90210-3604, USA

Ambrose, Marcos (Race Car Driver)
Wood Bros Racing
7203 Caldwell Rd
Harrisburg, NC 28075, USA

Ambrose, Richard (Dick) (Athlete, Football Player)
2677 Wrenford Rd
Beachwood, OH 44122-2013, USA

Ambrosio, Alessandra (Model)
2314 La Mesa Dr
Santa Monica, CA 90402-2331, USA

Ambrosius, Marsha (Musician)
c/o Staff Member *ICM Partners (LA)*
10250 Constellation Blvd Fl 7
Los Angeles, CA 90067-6207, USA

Ambroziak, Peter (Athlete, Hockey Player)
6052 Crownpoint Dr NE
Rio Rancho, NM 87144-8714, USA

Ambuehl, Cindy (Actor)
Paul Kohner
9300 Wilshire Blvd Ste 555
Beverly Hills, CA 90212-3211, USA

Ambulance Ltd (Music Group)
c/o Staff Member *Paradigm (Monterey)*
404 W Franklin St
Monterey, CA 93940-2303, USA

Amedori, John Patrick (Actor)
4440 Elmer Ave
North Hollywood, CA 91602-2036, USA

Ameling, Elly (Music Group, Musician)
Hubstein Artist Services
65 W 90th St Apt 13F
New York, NY 10024-1510, USA

Amelio, Gilbert F (Business Person)
InterDigital
781 3rd Ave
King Of Prussia, PA 19406-1409, USA

Amell, Robbie (Actor)
c/o David Eisenberg *Protege Entertainment*
710 E Angeleno Ave
Burbank, CA 91501-2213, USA

Amell, Stephen (Actor)
c/o Michael Garnett *Leverage Management*
3030 Pennsylvania Ave
Santa Monica, CA 90404-4112, USA

Amelung, Ed (Athlete, Baseball Player)
16681 Cedar Cir
Fountain Valley, CA 92708-2310, USA

Amenabar, Alejandro (Director, Musician, Writer)
c/o Sunmin Park *Maxmedia*
1620 Broadway Ste C
Santa Monica, CA 90404-2777, USA

Amend, Bill (Cartoonist)
620 W 51st St
Kansas City, MO 64112-2317, USA

Amendola, Danny (Athlete, Football Player)
c/o Erik Burkhardt *Select Sports Group*
2700 Post Oak Blvd Ste 1450
Houston, TX 77056-5785, USA

Amendola, Tony (Actor)
c/o Staff Member *Beacon Talent Agency*
170 Apple Ridge Rd
Woodcliff Lake, NJ 07677-8149, USA

Ament, Jeff (Musician)
5702 SW Andover St
Seattle, WA 98116-3555, USA

American Gladiators (Reality Star)
MGM Television
10250 Constellation Blvd Ste 1750
Los Angeles, CA 90067-6257, USA

American Young (Music Group, Musician)
c/o Todd Thomas *Caption Management*
47 Music Sq E
Nashville, TN 37203-4324, USA

Amerie (Musician)
c/o Len Nicholson *Feenix Rising Entertainment*
1360 Clifton Ave Ste 318
Clifton, NJ 07012-1453, USA

Amerson, Glenn (Athlete, Football Player)
4857 Mustang Rd
Brenham, TX 77833-8746, USA

Ames, Aldrich (Government Official)
PO Box 3000
Rn# 40087-083, Usp Allenwood
White Deer, PA 17887-3000, USA

Ames, David (Athlete, Football Player)
7909 Alvarado Rd
Henrico, VA 23229-4208, USA

Ames, Denise (Actor)
Studio Talent Group
1328 12th St Apt 1
Santa Monica, CA 90401-2051, USA

Ames, Ed (Actor, Musician)
c/o Staff Member *Paradise Artists*
108 E Matilija St
Ojai, CA 93023-2639, USA

Ames, Frank Anthony (Musician)
1235 Potomac St NW
Washington, DC 20007-3230, USA

Ames, Rachel (Actor)
Atkins Assoc
8040 Ventura Canyon Ave
Panorama City, CA 91402-6313, USA

Ames, Trey (Actor)
TDA Enterprises
2082 Michelson Dr Ste 306
Irvine, CA 92612-1214, USA

Amey, Vince (Athlete, Football Player)
4433 Callecita Ct
Union City, CA 94587-3829, USA

Amezaga, Alfredo
12887 W Virginia Ave
Avondale, AZ 85392-7123, USA

Amick, Madchen (Actor)
c/o Kesha Williams *KW Entertainment*
425 N Robertson Blvd
West Hollywood, CA 90048-1735, USA

Amiel, Jon (Director)
c/o Dave Brown *Echo Lake Management*
9595 Wilshire Blvd Fl 9
Beverly Hills, CA 90212-2512, USA

Amiina (Musician)
c/o Staff Member *Paradigm (Monterey)*
404 W Franklin St
Monterey, CA 93940-2303, USA

Amis, Suzy (Actor, Model)
Amis Construction Co
1647 Exchange Ave
Oklahoma City, OK 73108-3027, USA

Amlong, Joe (Athlete, Olympic Athlete, Rower)
2445 4th Ln SW
Vero Beach, FL 32962-3329, USA

Amlong, Thomas (Athlete)
166 Four Mile River Rd
Old Lyme, CT 06371-1325, USA

Ammaccapane, Danielle (Athlete, Golfer)
13214 N 13th St
Phoenix, AZ 85022, USA

Ammaccapane, Dina (Athlete, Golfer)
4407 E Blanche Dr
Phoenix, AZ 85032-4881, USA

Amman, Dick (Athlete, Football Player)
2907 Lake Joanna Dr
Eustis, FL 32726-7824, USA

Amman, Richard (Athlete, Football Player)
2907 Lake Joanna Dr
Eustis, FL 32726-7824, USA

Among the Oak & Asj (Music Group, Musician)
c/o Staff Member *MCT Management*
104 W 29th St Rm 1101
New York, NY 10001-5310, USA

Amons, Mary Schmidt (Reality Star)
c/o Staff Member *Bravo (NY)*
30 Rockefeller Plz
New York, NY 10112-0015, USA

Amonte, Tony (Athlete, Hockey Player, Olympic Athlete)
58 Turners Way
Norwell, MA 02061-2339, USA

Amor, Vicente (Athlete, Baseball Player)
13871 SW 52nd St
Miramar, FL 33027-5945, USA

Amor, Vincente (Athlete, Baseball Player)
13871 SW 52nd St
Miramar, FL 33027-5945, USA

Amos, John (Actor)
c/o Suzanne Bennett-Harrison *Diverse Talent Group*
9911 W Pico Blvd Ste 340W
Los Angeles, CA 90035-2703, USA

Amos, Tori (Musician)
c/o Carole Kinzel *Creative Artists Agency (CAA-LA)*
2000 Avenue of the Stars Ste 100
Los Angeles, CA 90067-4705, USA

Amos, Wally (Famous) (Business Person)
PO Box 88323
Honolulu, HI 96830-8323, USA

Amplas, John (Actor)
443 Meridian Dr
Pittsburgh, PA 15228-2613, USA

Amsler, Marty (Athlete, Football Player)
4009 Fairfax Rd
Evansville, IN 47710-3718, USA

Amstrong, Otis (Athlete, Football Player)
7183 S Newport Way
Centennial, CO 80112-1613, USA

Amstutz, Joe (Athlete, Football Player)
24840 Arrow Ct Apt 29
Tehachapi, CA 93561-7124, USA

Amukamura, Prince (Football Player)
c/o Todd France *Five Star Athlete Management*
3500 Lenox Rd NE
Atlanta, GA 30326-4228, USA

Amundsen, Norman (Athlete, Football Player)
3901 Hemlock Dr
Valparaiso, IN 46383-1813, USA

Amurri, Eva (Actor)
c/o JJ Harris *One Talent Management*
3680 1/2 Fredonia Dr
Los Angeles, CA 90068-1208, USA

Amy, Susie (Actor, Model)
c/o Marty Berneman *Precision Entertainment*
465 N Croft Ave
Los Angeles, CA 90048-2508, USA

Anae, Tumua (Athlete, Olympic Athlete, Water Polo Player)
Allen F Anae
2311 Santiago St
Santa Ana, CA 92706-2053, USA

Anagarano, Michael (Actor)
c/o Staff Member *Coast to Coast Talent Group*
3350 Barham Blvd
Los Angeles, CA 90068-1404, USA

Anagnostopoulos, Constantine E (Doctor)
3959 Mount Vernon Dr
Bloomfield Hills, MI 48301-3227, USA

Anastacia (Musician)
2501 Bowmont Dr
Beverly Hills, CA 90210-1812, USA

Anastasio, Trey (Musician)
40 Lawrence Ln
Palisades, NY 10964, USA

Anaya, Rudolfo (Writer)
5324 Canada Vista Pl NW
Albuquerque, NM 87120-2412, USA

Anaya, Toney (Ex-Governor)
Anaya Law Firm, P.A.
826 Gonzales Rd
Santa Fe, NM 87501-8741, USA

Anaya, Toney (Politician)
Maldef
634 S Spring St
Los Angeles, CA 90014-3921, USA

Ancheta, Bernie (Director, Writer)
c/o Staff Member *Lenhoff & Lenhoff*
830 Palm Ave
West Hollywood, CA 90069-4009

Anchia, Juan-Ruiz (Cinematographer)
Stanford-Beckett-Skouras
1015 Gayley Ave
Los Angeles, CA 90024-3413, USA

Ancona, Bill (Race Car Driver)
260 Nelson Wyatt Rd
Mansfield, TX 76063-6031, USA

Andabaker, Rudy (Athlete, Football Player)
1050 McNeilly Rd Apt 433
Pittsburgh, PA 15226-2556, USA

Anderegg, Bob (Athlete, Basketball Player)
11708 E Onyx Ave
Scottsdale, AZ 85259-5017, USA

Anders, Andrea (Actor)
3615 Dixie Canyon Ave
Sherman Oaks, CA 91423-4823, USA

Anders, Beth (Athlete, Hockey Player, Olympic Athlete)
9727 Bay Point Dr
Norfolk, VA 23518-2019, USA

Anders, David (Actor)
c/o Kay Liberman *Liberman/Zerman Management*
252 N Larchmont Blvd Ste 200
Los Angeles, CA 90004-3754, USA

Anders, Kimble (Athlete, Football Player)
801 Landing Blvd
League City, TX 77573-3315, USA

Anders, Sean (Director, Producer, Writer)
c/o John Elliott *Mosaic Media Group*
9200 W Sunset Blvd Ste 10
West Hollywood, CA 90069-3608, USA

Anders, William A (Astronaut, General)
c/o Staff Member *NASA-JSC*
2101 Nasa Pkwy # 1
Astronaut Office - Mail Code Cb
Houston, TX 77058-3607, USA

Anders, William A Maj Gen (Astronaut)
1156 Brighton Crest Dr
Bellingham, WA 98229-6905, USA

Andersen, Anthony (Actor)
1619 Broadway # 900
New York, NY 10019-7412, USA

Andersen, Barbara (Actor)
PO Box 10118
Santa Fe, NM 87504, USA

Andersen, Chris (Birdman) (Athlete, Basketball Player)
c/o Staff Member *Miami Heat*
601 Biscayne Blvd
American Airlines Arena
Miami, FL 33132-1801, USA

Andersen, Elmer (Politician)
501 Main St SE Apt 702
Minneapolis, MN 55414-2980, USA

Andersen, Gary (Football Coach)
University of Wisconsin
Athletic Dept
Madison, WI 53706, USA

Andersen, Greta (Athlete, Olympic Athlete, Swimmer)
16222 Monterey Ln Spc 264
Huntington Beach, CA 92649-2248, USA

Andersen, Jason (Athlete, Football Player)
4530 County Road 16 Apt 410
Canandaigua, NY 14424-8316, USA

Andersen, Larry (Athlete, Baseball Player)
120 Dickinson St Rear A
Philadelphia, PA 19147-6100, USA

Andersen, Morten (Athlete, Football Player)
6501 Old Shadburn Ferry Rd
Buford, GA 30518-1137, USA

Andersen, Pip (Actor)
c/o Shani Rosenzweig *United Talent Agency (UTA-LA)*
9336 Civic Center Dr
Beverly Hills, CA 90210-3604, USA

Andersen, Reidar (Skier)
National Ski Hall of Fame
PO Box 191
Ishpeming, MI 49849-0191, USA

Andersen, Watts Teresa (Swimmer)
2582 Marsha Way
San Jose, CA 95125-4029, USA

Andersion, Robert P (Athlete, Football Player)
244 Carmel Dr
Melbourne, FL 32940-7782, USA

Anderson, Alfred (Athlete, Football Player)
2805 Chesterwood Ct
Mansfield, TX 76063-8809, USA

Anderson, Allan (Athlete, Baseball Player)
799 Wagner Dr SW
Lancaster, OH 43130-8219, USA

Anderson, Alyssa (Athlete, Swimmer)
Randy Anderson
9620 Oak Leaf Way
Granite Bay, CA 95746-8919, USA

Anderson, Anthony (Actor, Television Host)
2509 Silver Ridge Ave
Los Angeles, CA 90039-3323, USA

Anderson, Anthony (Athlete, Football Player)
4001 Kennett Pike Ste 134
Wilmington, DE 19807-2000, USA

Anderson, Antonio (Athlete, Football Player)
463 Lexington Ave
Brooklyn, NY 11221-1203, USA

Anderson, Aric (Athlete, Football Player)
528 Halifax Ln
Coppell, TX 75019-2448, USA

Anderson, Aric (Athlete, Football Player)
16306 Rolling View Trl
Cypress, TX 77433-5856, USA

Anderson, Audrey Marie (Actor)
c/o Staff Member *Untitled Entertainment (NY)*
435 Hudson St Fl 9
New York, NY 10014-3995, USA

Anderson, Bennie (Athlete, Football Player)
6450 Virginia Ave
Saint Louis, MO 63111-2705, USA

Anderson, Bill (Athlete, Football Player)
6924 Lark Ln
Knoxville, TN 37919-5928, USA

Anderson, Bill (Whispering) (Musician, Songwriter)
PO Box 888
Hermitage, TN 37076-0888, USA

Anderson, Blake (Actor, Comedian)
3230 N Knoll Dr
Los Angeles, CA 90068-1518, USA

Anderson, Bob (Athlete, Baseball Player)
8417 S 84th East Pl
Tulsa, OK 74133-8028, USA

Anderson, Bob (Athlete, Football Player)
244 Carmel Dr
Melbourne, FL 32940-7782, USA

Anderson, Bobby (Athlete, Football Player)
79125 Big Horn Trl
La Quinta, CA 92253-4523, USA

Anderson, Brad (Athlete, Football Player)
6121 N 34th Pl
Paradise Valley, AZ 85253-3751, USA

Anderson, Brad (Race Car Driver)
1240 S Cucamonga Ave
Ontario, CA 91761-4505, USA

Anderson, Brad
13022 Wood Harbour Dr
Montgomery, TX 77356-8046, USA

Anderson, Brad (Director)
422 Santa Monica Ct
Escondido, CA 92029, USA

Anderson, Bradford (Actor)
c/o Staff Member *General Hospital*
4151 Prospect Ave
Los Angeles, CA 90027-4524, USA

Anderson, Brady (Athlete, Baseball Player)
32800 Pacific Coast Hwy
Malibu, CA 90265, USA

Anderson, Brain (Athlete, Baseball Player)
W275N9303 Lake Five Rd
Hartland, WI 53029-9016, USA

Anderson, Brian (Athlete, Baseball Player)
3750 E Via Palomita Apt 16202
Tucson, AZ 85718-3377, USA

Anderson, Brian (Athlete, Baseball Player)
660 Saxony Blvd
St Petersburg, FL 33716-1284, USA

Anderson, Brian (Commentator)
W275N9303 Lake Five Rd
Hartland, WI 53029-9016, USA

Anderson, Bruce A (Athlete, Football Player)
910 NE Parkview Ct
Roseburg, OR 97470-2136, USA

Anderson, Bud (Athlete, Baseball Player)
240 Twin Ln E
Wantagh, NY 11793-1963, USA

Anderson, Camille (Actor)
c/o Steven Neibert *Imperium 7 Talent Agency*
5455 Wilshire Blvd Ste 1706
Los Angeles, CA 90036-4217, USA

Anderson, Chantelle (Athlete, Basketball Player)
Cleveland Rockers
1 Center Ct
Gund Arena
Cleveland, OH 44115-4001, USA

Anderson, Charlie (Athlete, Football Player)
2323 Melrose Ave
Bossier City, LA 71111-5952, USA

Anderson, Chris (Business Person, Writer)
The Long Tail
1165 Miller Ave
Berkeley, CA 94708-1754, USA

Anderson, C.J. (Athlete, Football Player)
c/o Peter Schaffer *All Pro Sports and Entertainment*
36 Steele St Ste 100
Denver, CO 80206-5709, USA

Anderson, Clayton (Astronaut)
2883 Carrera Ct
League City, TX 77573-2291, USA

Anderson, Clifford (Athlete, Basketball Player)
2096A S John Russell Cir
Elkins Park, PA 19027-1017, USA

Anderson, Courtney (Athlete, Football Player)
340 34th St
Richmond, CA 94805-2168, USA

Anderson, Craig (Athlete, Baseball Player)
19217 SW 96th Loop
Dunnellon, FL 34432-4201, USA

Anderson, Craig (Athlete, Hockey Player)
2828 Carrington Dr
Dundee, IL 60118-1740, USA

Anderson, Curtis (Athlete, Football Player)
967 Kemper Meadow Dr
Cincinnati, OH 45240-1463, USA

Anderson, Damien (Athlete, Football Player)
3563 S Cox Ct
Chandler, AZ 85248-4436, USA

Anderson, Dan (Athlete, Basketball Player)
100 3rd Ave S Unit 2002
Minneapolis, MN 55401-2716, USA

Anderson, Dan (Athlete, Basketball Player)
2230 SW Winchester Ave
Portland, OR 97225-4460, USA

Anderson, Darren (Athlete, Football Player)
7328 Overland Park Ct
West Chester, OH 45069-5560, USA

Anderson, Daryl (Actor)
24136 Friar St
Woodland Hills, CA 91367-1240, USA

Anderson, Dave (Athlete, Baseball Player)
21 Quinn Way
Mission Viejo, CA 92691-5651, USA

Anderson, Dave (Commentator)
8 Inness Rd
Tenafly, NJ 07670-2715, USA

Anderson, David (Athlete, Baseball Player)
207 Athletic Office Bldg
Memphis, TN 38152-3730, USA

Anderson, Dennis (Race Car Driver)
Clear Channel Entertainment
495 N Commons Dr Ste 200
Aurora, IL 60504-8295, USA

Anderson, Derek (Athlete, Football Player)
c/o David Dunn *Athletes First, LLC*
10600 W Charleston Blvd
Las Vegas, NV 89135-1014, USA

Anderson, Derek (Athlete, Basketball Player)
5562 Werburgh St
Charlotte, NC 28209-3693, USA

Anderson, Dick (Athlete, Football Player)
4603 Santa Maria St
Miami, FL 33146-1132, USA

Anderson, Dion (Actor)
S D B Partners
315 S Beverly Dr Ste 411
Beverly Hills, CA 90212-4301, USA

Anderson, Don (Athlete, Football Player)
10090 Beechdale St
Detroit, MI 48204-2567, USA

Anderson, Don
California Institute Of Technology
Geophysics
Pasadena, CA 91125-0001, USA

Anderson, Drew (Athlete, Baseball Player)
209 Golf Ct
Cold Spring, MN 56320-8749, USA

Anderson, Dwain (Athlete, Baseball Player)
1807 Fallbrook Dr
Alamo, CA 94507-2810, USA

Anderson, Earl (Athlete, Hockey Player)
602 3rd Ave NE
Roseau, MN 56751-1809, USA

Anderson, Eddie Lee (Athlete, Football Player)
209 Shenandoah Trl
Warner Robins, GA 31088-6284, USA

Anderson, Erich (Actor)
Paradigm Agency
10100 Santa Monica Blvd Ste 2500
Los Angeles, CA 90067-4116, USA

Anderson, Erick (Athlete, Football Player)
2919 Attleboro Rd
Cleveland, OH 44120-1815, USA

Anderson, Erika (Actor)
c/o Staff Member *Flick Commercials*
9057 Nemo St # A
W Hollywood, CA 90069-5511, USA

Anderson, Erriestine I (Musician)
Thomas Cassidy
11761 E Speedway Blvd
Tucson, AZ 85748-2017, USA

Anderson, Flipper (Athlete, Football Player)
190 Abbey Hill Rd
Suwanee, GA 30024-1976, USA

Anderson, Fred (Athlete, Football Player)
11810 NE 48th Pl
Kirkland, WA 98033-8750, USA

Anderson, Garret (Athlete, Baseball Player)
36 Boulder Vw
Irvine, CA 92603-0410, USA

Anderson, Gary W (Athlete, Football Player)
1 Ridgefield Ct
Little Rock, AR 72223-4608, USA

Anderson, Gayle (Correspondent)
KTLA-TV
5800 W Sunset Blvd
Los Angeles, CA 90028-6607, USA

Anderson, Gillian (Actor)
c/o Justin Grey Stone *Management 360*
9111 Wilshire Blvd
Beverly Hills, CA 90210-5508, USA

Anderson, Glenn (Athlete, Hockey Player)
42 W 69th St Apt 2A
New York, NY 10023-5265, USA

Anderson, Haley (Athlete, Swimmer)
Randy Anderson
9620 Oak Leaf Way
Granite Bay, CA 95746-8919, USA

Anderson, Harry (Actor, Magician)
204 Pearson Dr
Asheville, NC 28801-1614, USA

Anderson, H George (Religious Leader)
Evangelical Lutheran Church
8765 W Higgins Rd Ste 600
Chicago, IL 60631-4100, USA

Anderson, Howard A (Actor)
PO Box 2230
Los Angeles, CA 90028, USA

Anderson, Howard A Jr
(Cinematographer)
c/o Staff Member *Howard Anderson Company*
5161 Lankershim Blvd
North Hollywood, CA 91601-4962, USA

Anderson, Jacob (Actor)
c/o Mike Smith *Principal Entertainment (LA)*
9255 W Sunset Blvd Ste 500
West Hollywood, CA 90069-3301, USA

Anderson, Jamal (Athlete, Football Player)
3733 Golden Ive Dr
Buford, GA 30519-7828, USA

Anderson, James (Athlete, Football Player)
1544 Taylor Point Dr
Chesapeake, VA 23321-0181, USA

Anderson, James F (Religious Leader)
12 Surf Ave
Ocean Grove, NJ 07756-1629, USA

Anderson, James W (Doctor)
University of Kentucky
Medical Center
Endocrinology Dept
Lexington, KY 40506-0001, USA

Anderson, Jamie (Actor)
c/o JoAnn Smolen *Rage Talent Agency (RTA)*
23679 Calabasas Rd Ste 501
Calabasas, CA 91302-1502, USA

Anderson, Janet (Athlete, Golfer)
4311 W Ardmore Rd
Laveen, AZ 85339-2112, USA

Anderson, Jason (Athlete, Baseball Player)
2869 11th St
Cuyahoga Falls, OH 44221-2053, USA

Anderson, J C (Athlete, Golfer)
1418 S 39th St
Quincy, IL 62305-6104, USA

Anderson, Jeff (Actor, Director)
c/o Staff Member *Imperium 7 Talent Agency*
5455 Wilshire Blvd Ste 1706
Los Angeles, CA 90036-4217, USA

Anderson, Jesse (Athlete, Football Player)
4374 Redwood Cir
Jackson, MS 39212-3645, USA

Anderson, Jim (Athlete, Baseball Player)
2111 Bennington Ct
Thousand Oaks, CA 91360-1977, USA

Anderson, Jimmy (Athlete, Baseball Player)
214 Pennington Blvd
Portsmouth, VA 23701-1226, USA

Anderson, Jimmy (Athlete, Hockey Player)
4H Castle Hill Rd
Agawam, MA 01001-2460, USA

Anderson, Jo (Actor)
c/o Staff Member *Innovative Artists (LA)*
1505 10th St
Santa Monica, CA 90401-2805, USA

Anderson, John (Politician)
PO Box 343
Gardner, KS 66030-0343, USA

Anderson, John (Athlete, Football Player)
14730 Crestwood Ct
Elm Grove, WI 53122-1603, USA

Anderson, John (Athlete, Hockey Player)
6751 N Sunset Blvd Ste 200
Glendale, AZ 85305-3162, USA

Anderson, John (Musician)
671/673 Cordell Love Rd
Smithville, TN 37166, USA

Anderson, John B (Politician)
4120 48th St NW
Washington, DC 20016-2336, USA

Anderson, John Jr (Ex-Governor)
PO Box 343
Gardner, KS 66030-0343, USA

Anderson, Josh (Athlete, Baseball Player)
3750 E Highway 452
Eubank, KY 42567-9731, USA

Anderson, Kalen (Athlete, Golfer)
c/o Jim Lehrman *SFX Golf*
36855 W Main St Ste 200
Purcellville, VA 20132-3561, USA

Anderson, Keith (Musician)
c/o Staff Member *Fitzgerald-Hartley Co (Ventura)*
34 N Palm St Ste 100
Ventura, CA 93001-2610, USA

Anderson, Ken (Athlete, Football Player)
41 Sedge Fern Dr
Hilton Head Island, SC 29926-2782, USA

Anderson, Kenny (Athlete, Basketball Player)
18145 SW 5th Ct
Pembroke Pines, FL 33029-4352, USA

Anderson, Kent (Athlete, Baseball Player)
925 E Twin Church Rd
Timmonsville, SC 29161-8528, USA

Anderson, Kevin (Actor)
c/o Staff Member *ICM Partners (LA)*
10250 Constellation Blvd Fl 7
Los Angeles, CA 90067-6207, USA

Anderson, Kevin J (Writer)
Tom Doherty Associates, LLC
175 5th Ave
New York, NY 10010-7703, USA

Anderson, Kim (Athlete, Basketball Player)
1210 Shady Bank Ln
Columbia, MO 65201-2889, USA

Anderson, Kim S (Athlete, Football Player)
3500 W Manchester Blvd Unit 216
Inglewood, CA 90305-4216, USA

Anderson, Larry (Athlete, Baseball Player)
1319 Ronald Pl
Santa Maria, CA 93458-6548, USA

Anderson, Lars (Athlete, Baseball Player)
3948 Bannister Rd
Fair Oaks, CA 95628-6806, USA

Anderson, Laurie (Musician)
195 Chrystie St # 501F
New York, NY 10002-1214, USA

Anderson, Lawrence A (Larry) (Athlete, Football Player)
3170 Blanchard Rd
Shreveport, LA 71103-2142, USA

Anderson, Lloyd L (Astronaut)
1939 Live Oak Cemetery Rd
Killeen, TX 76542-5100, USA

Anderson, Loni (Actor)
14318 Valley Vista Blvd
Sherman Oaks, CA 91423-4028, USA

Anderson, Louie (Actor, Comedian, Producer)
11 Edgewater Dr
Dunedin, FL 34698-7529, USA

Anderson, Loule (Actor, Comedian)
8033 W Sunset Blvd # 605
Los Angeles, CA 90046-2401, USA

Anderson, Lynn (Musician)
c/o Staff Member *Wolfman Jack Entertainment*
105 River Shore Dr
Hertford, NC 27944-8015, USA

Anderson, Marina (Actor)
c/o Nancy Harding *Powerhouse Talent*
PO Box 261939
Encino, CA 91426-1939, USA

Anderson, Mark (Athlete, Football Player)
9725 Woods Dr Unit 1617
Skokie, IL 60077-4456, USA

Anderson, Marlon (Athlete, Baseball Player)
780 Glenleigh Ln
Duluth, GA 30097-8035, USA

Anderson, Marques (Athlete, Football Player)
213 W Gardner St
Long Beach, CA 90805-2034, USA

Anderson, Mary (Actor)
225 Vance St
Pacific Palisades, CA 90272-4413, USA

Anderson, Matt (Athlete, Baseball Player)
4115 Woodmont Park Ln
Louisville, KY 40245-8431, USA

Anderson, Matt (Athlete, Golfer)
c/o Jim Lehrman *SFX Golf*
36855 W Main St Ste 200
Purcellville, VA 20132-3561, USA

Anderson, Melissa Sue (Actor, Producer)
c/o Staff Member *Globe Pequot Press*
246 Goose Ln Ste 200
PO Box 480
Guilford, CT 06437-2186, USA

Anderson, Melody (Actor)
PO Box 24483
Los Angeles, CA 90024-0483, USA

Anderson, Melvin
2747 Sheridan Ave N
Minneapolis, MN 55411-1020, USA

Anderson, Michael (Musician, Songwriter, Writer)
Brock Assoc
7106 Moores Ln # 200
Brentwood, TN 37027-2903, USA

Anderson, Mike (Athlete, Baseball Player)
407 Prairie Grass Ct
Hartland, WI 53029-8562, USA

Anderson, Mike (Athlete, Coach, Football Player)
PO Box 12753
Chandler, AZ 85248-0030, USA

Anderson, Mitchell (Actor)
MetroFresh
931 Monroe Dr NE Ste A106
Atlanta, GA 30308-1795, USA

Anderson, Neal (Athlete, Football Player)
10626 SW 41st Pl
Gainesville, FL 32608-7126, USA

Anderson, Neilson (Athlete, Basketball Player)
163 Harbor Isle Cir N
Memphis, TN 38103-0841, USA

Anderson, Neil T. (Writer)
Freedom in Christ Ministries
9051 Executive Park Dr Ste 503
Knoxville, TN 37923-4632, USA

Anderson, Nick (Athlete, Basketball Player)
6672 Cherry Grove Cir
Orlando, FL 32809-6658, USA

Anderson, Nicole (Actor)
c/o Todd Justice *Justice & Ponder*
PO Box 480033
Los Angeles, CA 90048-1033, USA

Anderson, Ottis (Athlete, Football Player)
47 Duffield Dr
South Orange, NJ 07079-1015, USA

Anderson, Ottis J (O J) (Athlete, Football Player)
PO Box 399
Orange, NJ 07051-0399, USA

Anderson, Pamela (Actor)
c/o Ann Gurrola *Marleah Leslie & Associates PR*
1645 Vine St Apt 712
Los Angeles, CA 90028-8812, USA

Anderson, Paul Thomas (Director, Writer)
4900 Casa Dr
Tarzana, CA 91356-3941, USA

Anderson, Paul W S (Director)
c/o Ken Kamins *Key Creatives*
1800 N Highland Ave Fl 5
Los Angeles, CA 90028-4523, USA

Anderson, Perry (Athlete, Hockey Player)
7724 E Osborn Rd
Scottsdale, AZ 85251-7404, USA

Anderson, Ralph (Athlete, Football Player)
908 Hilltop Dr Apt C
Irving, TX 75060-3925, USA

Anderson, Randy (Race Car Driver)
Anderson Racing
1240 S Cucamonga Ave
Ontario, CA 91761-4505, USA

Anderson, Rashard (Athlete, Football Player)
676 N First Ave
Forest, MS 39074-3637, USA

Anderson, Ray (Musician)
James faith Entertainment
318 Wynn Ln Ste 14
Port Jefferson, NY 11777-1699, USA

Anderson, Renee (Actor)
2818 Laurel Canyon Blvd
Los Angeles, CA 90046, USA

Anderson, Richard (Actor)
10120 Cielo Dr
Beverly Hills, CA 90210-2037, USA

Anderson, Richard Dean (Actor)
28890 Selfridge Dr
Malibu, CA 90265-4264, USA

Anderson, Richard (Dick) J (Athlete, Football Player)
206 Baker St
Lodi, OH 44254-1407, USA

Anderson, Richard P (Dick) (Athlete, Football Player)
4603 Santa Maria St
Miami, FL 33146-1132, USA

Anderson, Richie (Athlete, Football Player)
2570 Carrington Way
Frederick, MD 21702-5973, USA

Anderson, Rick (Athlete, Baseball Player)
3929 Benjamin Dr
Saint Paul, MN 55125-3396, USA

Anderson, Rick (Athlete, Baseball Player)
Minnesota Twins
1 Twins Way
Minneapolis, MN 55403-1418, USA

Anderson, Robert (Writer)
William Morris Agency
1325 Avenue of the Americas Bsmt 2
New York, NY 10019-6047, USA

Anderson, Ross (Journalist)
Seattle Times
1000 Denny Way # 5
Editorial Dept
Seattle, WA 98109-5340, USA

Anderson, Russ (Athlete, Hockey Player)
76 Fern Dr
Plantsville, CT 06479-1810, USA

Anderson, Ryan (Athlete, Basketball Player)
c/o Jeff Austin *Octagon Home Office*
1751 Pinnacle Dr Fl 15
Mc Lean, VA 22102-3833, USA

Anderson, Sam (Actor)
c/o Staff Member *TalentWorks (LA)*
3500 W Olive Ave Ste 1400
Burbank, CA 91505-5512, USA

Anderson, Scot (Writer)
c/o Staff Member *Premiere Speakers Bureau*
109 International Dr Ste 300
Franklin, TN 37067-1764, USA

Anderson, Scott (Athlete, Baseball Player)
13061 Amber Pl
Lake Oswego, OR 97034-1524, United States

Anderson, Scott (Athlete, Football Player)
2836 Queen Bee Ln
Saint Louis, MO 63129-5644, USA

Anderson, Scotty (Athlete, Football Player)
1405 Leon Dr
Jonesboro, LA 71251-2213, USA

Anderson, Shandon (Athlete, Basketball Player)
63 Mangum St SW Unit 5
Atlanta, GA 30313-1355, USA

Anderson, Shelly (Race Car Driver)
1240 S Cucamonga Ave
Ontario, CA 91761-4505, USA

Anderson, Sterling (Writer)
c/o Abram Nalibotsky *Gersh (LA)*
9465 Wilshire Blvd Ste 600
Beverly Hills, CA 90212-2605, USA

Anderson, Stevie (Athlete, Football Player)
1405 Leon Dr
Jonesboro, LA 71251-2213, USA

Anderson, Stuart (Athlete, Football Player)
100 Careys Ln
Cardinal, VA 23025-2006, USA

Anderson, Sunny (Chef)
c/o Jonathan Rosen *William Morris Endeavor (NY)*
1325 Avenue of the Americas
New York, NY 10019-6026, USA

Anderson, Sylvia (Actor)
c/o Staff Member *Hermes Press*
2100 Wilmington Rd
New Castle, PA 16105-1931, USA

Anderson, Taz (Athlete, Football Player)
Taz Anderson Realty
2931 Paces Ferry Rd SE Ste 150
Atlanta, GA 30339-5727, USA

Anderson, Terence (Politician)
668 Oak Tree Rd
Palisades, NY 10964-1532, USA

Anderson, Terence (Terry) (Journalist)
17 Sunlight Hl
Yonkers, NY 10704-2903, USA

Anderson, Tom (Actor, Producer, Writer)
c/o Staff Member *Gersh (LA)*
9465 Wilshire Blvd Ste 600
Beverly Hills, CA 90212-2605, USA

Anderson, Tom (Business Person)
c/o *MySpace, Inc*
6060 Center Dr Ste 300
Los Angeles, CA 90045-8842, USA

Anderson, Tracy (Fitness Expert)
Tracy Anderson Studios
408 Greenwich St Fl 3
New York, NY 10013-2077, USA

Anderson, Vickey Ray (Athlete, Football Player)
9308 S Harvey Ave
Oklahoma City, OK 73139-8636, USA

Anderson, Warren M (Business Person)
270 Park Ave
New York, NY 10017-2014, USA

Anderson, Wayne (Race Car Driver)
Liberty Racing
3086 N US Highway 301
Wildwood, FL 34785-8371, USA

Anderson, Wendell (Athlete, Hockey Player)
108 Chevy Chase Dr
Wayzata, MN 55391-1054, USA

Anderson, Wes (Director, Writer)
c/o Leslee Dart *42West (NYC)*
220 W 42nd St Fl 12
New York, NY 10036-7200, USA

Anderson, Wessell (Musician)
Fat City Artists
830 Tannahill Dr SE
Huntsville, AL 35802-1956, USA

Anderson, Willie (Athlete, Football Player)
1490 Meadowcreek Ct
Atlanta, GA 30338-3803, USA

Anderson, W William (Athlete, Football Player)
6924 Lark Ln
Knoxville, TN 37919-5928, USA

Anderson-Emmons, Aubrey (Actor)
c/o Carlyne Grager *Dramatic Artists Agency*
103 W Alameda Ave Ste 139
Burbank, CA 91502-2253, USA

Anderson III, Shedrack (Actor)
c/o Joy Donnell *720 PR*
9595 Wilshire Blvd Ste 900
Beverly Hills, CA 90212-2509, USA

Anderson-Sheriffs, Vivian (Athlete, Baseball Player)
2654 N 117th St
Milwaukee, WI 53226-1124, USA

Andersson, Henrik (Musician)
MOB Agency
6404 Wilshire Blvd Ste 505
Los Angeles, CA 90048-5507, USA

Andersson, Mikael (Athlete, Hockey Player)
c/o Staff Member *Tampa Bay Lightning*
401 Channelside Dr
Ice Palace
Tampa, FL 33602-5400, USA

Andino, Robert (Athlete, Baseball Player)
645 Santa Clara Trl
Wellington, FL 33414-3921, USA

Andrade, Fernanda (Actor)
c/o Robyn Holt *Genesis Entertainment Partners*
152 S Kilkea Dr
Los Angeles, CA 90048-3526, USA

Andrade, Sergio (Musician)
DreamWorks Records
9268 W 3rd St
Beverly Hills, CA 90210-3713, USA

Andrade, William T (Billy) (Athlete, Golfer)
4439 E Brookhaven Dr NE
Atlanta, GA 30319-1007, USA

Andrascik, Steve (Athlete, Hockey Player)
32 Early Ln
Annville, PA 17003-8623, USA

Andreas, Dwayne O (Business Person)
181 Southmoreland Pl
Decatur, IL 62521-3738, USA

Andreas, G Allen (Business Person)
Archer-Daniels-Midland
4666 E Faries Pkwy Ste 1
Decatur, IL 62526-5632, USA

Andreasen, Nancy C (Doctor)
200 Hawkins Dr
Iowa City, IA 52242-1009, USA

Andreeff, Starr (Actor)
C N A Assoc
1875 Century Park E Ste 2250
Los Angeles, CA 90067-2563, USA

Andreessen, Marc (Business Person)
23910 Malibu Rd
Malibu, CA 90265-4606, USA

Andress, Tuck (Musician)
Windham Hill Records
PO Box 5501
Beverly Hills, CA 90209-5501, USA

Andress, Ursula (Actor)
1740 Clear View Dr
Beverly Hills, CA 90210-2012, USA

Andretti, Jeff (Race Car Driver)
Andretti Racing Group
7615 Zionsville Rd
Indianapolis, IN 46268-2174, USA

Andretti, John (Race Car Driver)
Andretti Autosport
7615 Zionsville Rd
Indianapolis, IN 46268-2174, USA

Andretti, Marco (Race Car Driver)
c/o John Caponigro *Sports Management Network, Inc.*
1301 W Long Lake Rd Ste 250
Troy, MI 48098-6326, USA

Andretti, Mario (Race Car Driver)
457 Rose Inn Ave
Nazareth, PA 18064-9234, USA

Andretti, Michael (Athlete, Race Car Driver)
7615 Zionsville Rd
Indianapolis, IN 46268-2174, USA

Andrew, Kim (Athlete, Baseball Player)
10052 Densmore Ave
North Hills, CA 91343-1454, USA

Andrew, Phillip (Actor)
c/o Bonnie Liedtke *Principato/Young Management (LA)*
9465 Wilshire Blvd Ste 900
Beverly Hills, CA 90212-2608, USA

Andrew, Troy (Athlete, Football Player)
James Crystal Radio Inc
206 Johnstone Ct
Durham, NC 27712-9454, USA

Andrews, Al (Athlete, Boxer)
1119 River St
Rhinelander, WI 54501-2404, USA

Andrews, Al (Athlete, Football Player)
PO Box 82256
Atlanta, GA 30354-0256, USA

Andrews, Amy Leigh (Model)
c/o Staff Member *Playboy Productions*
2300 W Empire Ave
Burbank, CA 91504-3341, USA

Andrews, Andy (Actor, Comedian)
PO Box 17321
Nashville, TN 37217-0321, USA

Andrews, Ariel (Race Car Driver)
PO Box 374
Newburgh, IN 47629-0374, USA

Andrews, Billy (Athlete, Football Player)
PO Box 703
17164 Highway 10 E
Clinton, LA 70722-0703, USA

Andrews, Clayton (Athlete, Baseball Player)
4609 W Bradley St
Tampa, FL 33616-2800, USA

Andrews, Donna (Athlete, Golfer)
2301 Hawthorne Rd
Lynchburg, VA 24503-2903, USA

Andrews, Erin (Journalist, Sportscaster, Television Host)
c/o Staff Member *Fox Sports (LA)*
10201 W Pico Blvd Bldg 101
Los Angeles, CA 90064-2606, USA

Andrews, Fred (Athlete, Baseball Player)
PO Box 898
Wedowee, AL 36278-0898, USA

Andrews, Giuseppe (Actor)
1221 S Congress Ave Apt 612
Austin, TX 78704-2406, USA

Andrews, James (Doctor)
American Sports Medicine Institute
1313 13th St S
Birmingham, AL 35205-5327, USA

Andrews, Jeff (Baseball Player)
2420 NW 177th St
Edmond, OK 73012-7134

Andrews, Jessica (Musician)
6535 Melinda Dr
Nashville, TN 37205-3934, USA

Andrews, John (Athlete, Baseball Player)
6348 Jasper St
Rancho Cucamonga, CA 91701-3226, USA

Andrews, John M (Athlete, Football Player)
7306 Summer Trail Dr
Sugar Land, TX 77479-6233, USA

Andrews, John V (Athlete, Football Player)
7306 Summer Trail Dr
Sugar Land, TX 77479-6233, USA

Andrews, Julie (Actor, Musician)
c/o Gene Schwam *Hanson & Schwam Public Relations*
9350 Wilshire Blvd Ste 315
Beverly Hills, CA 90212-3206

Andrews, Ken (Musician)
c/o Staff Member *Paradigm (Monterey)*
404 W Franklin St
Monterey, CA 93940-2303, USA

Andrews, Lee (Musician)
Mars Talent
27 L Ambiance Ct
Bardonia, NY 10954-1421, USA

Andrews, Mark (Politician)
3354 165th Ave SE
Mapleton, ND 58059-9746, USA

Andrews, Mike (Athlete, Baseball Player)
5 Patriot Ln Unit 10
Georgetown, MA 01833-2246, USA

Andrews, Mitch (Athlete, Football Player)
PO Box 672
Washington, LA 70589-0672, USA

Andrews, Naveen (Actor)
c/o Renee Jennett *Renee Jennett Management*
10028 Farragut Dr
Culver City, CA 90232-3228, USA

Andrews, Patricia (Patti) (Musician)
9823 Aldea Ave
Northridge, CA 91325-1915, USA

Andrews, Rob (Athlete, Baseball Player)
1280 Mountbatten Ct
Concord, CA 94518-3927, USA

Andrews, Robert (Writer)
G P Putnam's Sons
375 Hudson St
New York, NY 10014-3658, USA

Andrews, Robert E (Congressman, Politician)
2265 Rayburn Hob
Washington, DC 20515-0552, USA

Andrews, Shane (Athlete, Baseball Player)
1816 N Guadalupe St
Carlsbad, NM 88220-8813, USA

Andrews, Shawn (Athlete, Football Player)
8 Sezanne Cv
Little Rock, AR 72223-5093, USA

Andrews, Shawn (Athlete, Football Player)
c/o Laura Berwick *Berwick & Kovacik*
9465 Wilshire Blvd Ste 420
Beverly Hills, CA 90212-2603, USA

Andrews, Stacy (Athlete, Football Player)
7 Deauville Cir
Little Rock, AR 72223-5532, USA

Andrews, Theresa (Athlete, Olympic Athlete, Swimmer)
2004 Homewood Rd
Annapolis, MD 21409-5970, USA

Andrews, Thomas (Tom) (Athlete, Football Player)
1918 Wickham Way
Louisville, KY 40223-1059, USA

Andrews, Tina (Actor)
c/o Staff Member *Sharp & Associates Public Relations*
1516 N Fairfax Ave
Los Angeles, CA 90046-2608, USA

Andrews, William D (Athlete, Football Player)
PO Box 703
Clinton, LA 70722-0703, USA

Andrews, William L (Athlete, Football Player)
3916 Toccoa Falls Dr
Duluth, GA 30097-8104, USA

Andrews II, George E (Athlete, Football Player)
10195 Overhill Dr
Santa Ana, CA 92705-1515, USA

Andreychuk, Dave (Athlete, Hockey Player)
401 Channelside Dr
Tampa, FL 33602-5400, USA

Andreychuk, Dave (Athlete, Hockey Player)
107 Sable Park
East Amherst, NY 14051-2209, USA

Andrie, George J (Athlete, Football Player)
26356 E Zeerip Dr
Drummond Island, MI 49726-9597, USA

Androsky, Carol (Actor)
Henderson/Hogan
8285 W Sunset Blvd Ste 1
West Hollywood, CA 90046-2420, USA

Andruff, Ron (Athlete, Hockey Player)
72 1/2 Irving Pl Apt 1F
New York, NY 10003-2223, USA

Andrulis, Greg (Coach, Football Coach)
Columbus Crew
2121 Velma Ave
Columbus, OH 43211-2085, USA

Andrus, Cecil (Politician)
PO Box 852
Boise, ID 83701-0852, USA

Andrus, Lou (Athlete, Football Player)
739 W 550 S
Orem, UT 84058-6070, USA

Andrus, Sheldon (Athlete, Football Player)
210 Belle Meade Blvd
Thibodaux, LA 70301-4908, USA

Andruski, Frank (Athlete, Football Player)
303 W Cody Cir
Payson, AZ 85541-3173, United States

Andrusyshyn, Zenon (Athlete, Football Player)
2823 Lake Saxon Dr
Land O Lakes, FL 34639-6620, USA

Andruzzi, Joe (Athlete, Football Player)
130 Brown Ave
Mansfield, MA 02048-1046, USA

Andy, Dorris (Athlete, Football Player)
12391 Ike White Rd
Conroe, TX 77303-3044, USA

Andy, Ekern (Athlete, Football Player)
2041 W Bradley Pl
Chicago, IL 60618-4907, USA

Ane, Charles T (Charlie) III (Athlete, Football Player)
749 16th Ave
Honolulu, HI 96816-4121, USA

Angarano, Michael (Actor)
23456 Dolorosa St
Woodland Hills, CA 91367-4124, USA

Angel, Ashley Parker (Musician)
c/o Chuck James *ICM Partners (LA)*
10250 Constellation Blvd Fl 7
Los Angeles, CA 90067-6207, USA

Angel, Criss (Magician, Musician)
1 Club Point Ct
Henderson, NV 89052-6641, USA

Angel, Joanna (Actor, Adult Film Star, Model)
c/o Drew Elliot *Artists International Management (NY)*
333 E 43rd St Apt 115
New York, NY 10017-4822, USA

Angel, Joe (Commentator)
4900 Moreau Ct
El Dorado Hills, CA 95762-7625, USA

Angel, Juan Pablo (Athlete, Soccer Player)
c/o Patrick Tully *PR/PR*
1515 Broadway Fl 11
New York, NY 10036-8901, USA

Angel, Ryland (Musician)
c/o Staff Member *Paradigm (Monterey)*
404 W Franklin St
Monterey, CA 93940-2303, USA

Angelil, Rene (Actor, Writer)
c/o Staff Member *United Talent Agency (UTA-LA)*
9336 Civic Center Dr
Beverly Hills, CA 90210-3604, USA

Angelini, Norm (Athlete, Baseball Player)
15063 E Chenango Pl
Aurora, CO 80015-2136, USA

Angello, Steve (DJ, Musician)
c/o Staff Member *Creative Artists Agency (CAA-LA)*
2000 Avenue of the Stars Ste 100
Los Angeles, CA 90067-4705, USA

Angelos, Peter (Commentator)
Baltimore Orioles
100 N Charles St Ste 2200
Baltimore, MD 21201-3804, USA

Angels & Airwaves (Music Group)
c/o Staff Member *Geffen Records*
9126 Sunset Blvd
West Hollywood, CA 90069, USA

Angelycal Musical (Music Group)
c/o Staff Member *Sony Music Miami*
605 Lincoln Rd Ste 700
Miami Beach, FL 33139-2901, USA

Angelyne (Actor, Model)
PO Box 3864
Beverly Hills, CA 90212-0864, USA

Anger, Bryan (Athlete, Football Player)
c/o Frank Bauer *Sun West Sports*
7883 N Pershing Ave
Stockton, CA 95207-1749, USA

Angle, Kurt (Athlete, Olympic Athlete, Wrestler)
c/o Staff Member *Hawk & Company*
PO Box 97007
Pittsburgh, PA 15229-0007, USA

Anglim, Philip (Actor)
2404 Grand Canal
Venice, CA 90291-4508, USA

Anglin, Jennifer (Actor)
651 N Kilkea Dr
Los Angeles, CA 90048-2213, USA

Angotti, Lou (Athlete, Hockey Player)
2850 NE 14th Street Cswy Apt 401B
Pompano Beach, FL 33062-3640, USA

Angullo, Richard (Athlete, Football Player)
4801 W Libby St
Glendale, AZ 85308-1436, USA

Angullq, Richard
4801 W Libby St
Glendale, AZ 85308-1436, USA

Angus & Julia Stone (Music Group, Musician)
c/o Dan Efram *The Muse Box - NY*
205 Lexington Ave Fl 2
New York, NY 10016-6053, USA

Anholt, Christien (Actor)
Covington International
4237 Morro Dr
Woodland Hills, CA 91364-5521, USA

Anikulap-Kuti, Femi (Musician, Songwriter, Writer)
MCA Records
70 Universal City Plz
Universal City, CA 91608-1011, USA

Animal Collective (Music Group)
c/o Tom Windish *The Windish Agency*
1658 N Milwaukee Ave # 211
Chicago, IL 60647-6905, USA

Animals, The (Music Group)
PO Box 1821
Ojai, CA 93024-1821, USA

Anissina, Marina (Figure Skater)
c/o Staff Member *Champions on Ice*
3500 American Blvd W Ste 190
Minneapolis, MN 55431-4431, USA

Aniston, Jennifer (Actor)
901 Airole Way
Los Angeles, CA 90077-2601, USA

Aniston, John (Actor)
PO Box 514
5520 Platt Ave
West Hills, CA 91307, USA

Anka, Paul (Actor, Musician)
2674 Stafford Rd
Thousand Oaks, CA 91361-5039, USA

Ankiel, Rick (Athlete, Baseball Player)
8695 SE Compass Island Way
Jupiter, FL 33458-1102, USA

Ankrom, Scott (Athlete, Football Player)
1206 Harvest Cyn
San Antonio, TX 78258-3836, USA

Anlyan, William G (Doctor)
Duke Medical Center
100 Seeley Mudd Bldg 109
Durham, NC 27710-0001, USA

Annable, Dave (Actor)
1878 Greenfield Ave Apt 106
Los Angeles, CA 90025-6436, USA

Annable, Odette (Actor)
1878 Greenfield Ave Apt 106
Los Angeles, CA 90025-6436, USA

Annenberg, Wallis (Publisher)
10273 Century Woods Dr
Los Angeles, CA 90067-6312, USA

Annett, Chloe (Actor)
c/o Staff Member *Innovative Artists (LA)*
1505 10th St
Santa Monica, CA 90401-2805, USA

Annett, Michael (Race Car Driver)
Germain Racing
218 Raceway Dr
Mooresville, NC 28117-6510, USA

Anno, Sam (Athlete, Football Player)
12934 Ferndale Ave
Los Angeles, CA 90066-3520, USA

Ansah, Ezekiel (Athlete, Football Player)
c/o Frank Bauer *Sun West Sports*
7883 N Pershing Ave
Stockton, CA 95207-1749, USA

Ansara, Edward (Actor)
Jack Scagnetti
5118 Vineland Ave # 102
North Hollywood, CA 91601-3814, USA

Ansari, Anousheh (Astronaut)
6101 W Plano Pkwy # 210
Plano, TX 75093-8201, USA

Ansari, Aziz (Comedian)
5146 Los Franciscos Way
Los Angeles, CA 90027-1022, USA

Anschutz, Jody (Athlete, Golfer)
27307 N Palo Fierro Rd
Rio Verde, AZ 85263-5087, USA

Anschutz, Philip F (Business Person)
c/o Staff Member *Anschutz Film Group*
1888 Century Park E Ste 1400
Los Angeles, CA 90067-1718, USA

Anschutz, Philip F. (Business Person)
Anschutz Company
555 17th St Ste 2400
Denver, CO 80202-3941, USA

Anselmo, Philip (Musician)
Concrete Mgmt
361 W Broadway # 200
New York, NY 10013-2209, USA

Ansley, Michael (Athlete, Basketball Player)
1809 Wood Violet Dr
Orlando, FL 32824-6411, USA

Anspach, Susan (Actor)
PO Box 5605
Santa Monica, CA 90409-5605, USA

Anspaugh, David (Director, Producer)
c/o John Burnham *ICM Partners (LA)*
10250 Constellation Blvd Fl 7
Los Angeles, CA 90067-6207, USA

Ant, Adam (Musician)
c/o Liam Collopy *Levine Communications Office*
9100 Wilshire Blvd Ste 540
Beverly Hills, CA 90212-3470, USA

Antal, Nimrod (Director)
c/o Scott Greenberg *Creative Artists Agency (CAA-LA)*
2000 Avenue of the Stars Ste 100
Los Angeles, CA 90067-4705, USA

Anthony, Carmelo (Athlete, Basketball Player)
c/o Staff Member *New York Knicks*
2 Pennsylvania Plz
New York, NY 10121, USA

Anthony, Charles (Athlete, Football Player)
38709 Farwell Dr
Fremont, CA 94536-7218, USA

Anthony, Denman (Athlete, Football Player)
PO Box 2733
Spring, TX 77383-2733, USA

Anthony, Edward (Athlete, Football Player)
PO Box 605
Pfafftown, NC 27040-0605, USA

Anthony, Eric (Athlete, Baseball Player)
42 Fosters Ct
Sugar Land, TX 77479, USA

Anthony, Greg (Athlete, Basketball Player)
901 Wiggin Rd
Delray Beach, FL 33444-2851, USA

Anthony, Jasmine Jessica (Actor)
c/o Adam Griffin *Kritzer Levine Wilkins Entertainment (KLWG)*
11872 La Grange Ave Fl 1
Los Angeles, CA 90025-5283, USA

Anthony, La La (Actor, Musician)
c/o Christina Gualazzi *Silver Lining Entertainment*
8383 Wilshire Blvd Ste 1050
Beverly Hills, CA 90211-2415, USA

Anthony, Marc (Actor, Musician, Songwriter)
c/o Blanca Lasalle *Creativelink Inc*
PO Box 115
Bronx, NY 10471-0115, USA

Anthony, Michael (Musician)
Van Halen
10100 Santa Monica Blvd Ste 1300
Los Angeles, CA 90067-4114, USA

Anthony, Piers (Writer)
PO Box 2289
Inverness, FL 34451-2289, USA

Anthony, Plers (Writer)
PO Box 2289
Inverness, FL 34451-2289, USA

Anthony, Ray (Musician)
9288 Kinglet Dr
Los Angeles, CA 90069-1114, USA

Anthony, Reidel (Athlete, Football Player)
PO Box 23
South Bay, FL 33493-0023, USA

Anthony, Terry (Athlete, Football Player)
1200 Beville Rd Apt 91
Daytona Beach, FL 32114-5778, USA

Anti, Michael (Athlete, Olympic Athlete, Shooter)
13383 Honey Run Way
Colorado Springs, CO 80921-2072, USA

Antin, Jonathan (Reality Star, Stylist)
Jonathan Salon
901 Westbourne Dr
West Hollywood, CA 90069-4113, USA

Antin, Robin (Actor, Dancer)
8819 Rosewood Ave
West Hollywood, CA 90048-2407, USA

Antin, Steve (Actor, Writer)
c/o Doug MacLaren *ICM Partners (LA)*
10250 Constellation Blvd Fl 7
Los Angeles, CA 90067-6207, USA

Antoine, Lionel (Athlete, Football Player)
1455 Glencliff Dr
Dallas, TX 75217-2686, USA

Antoine, Tamlin (Athlete, Football Player)
5452 New Grange Garth
Columbia, MD 21045-2422, USA

Anton, Craig (Actor)
c/o Staff Member *United Talent Agency (UTA-LA)*
9336 Civic Center Dr
Beverly Hills, CA 90210-3604, USA

Anton, Susan (Actor, Producer)
509 Pinnacle Heights Ln
Las Vegas, NV 89144-0812, USA

Antonelli, Dominic A (Astronaut)
4106 Oak Blossom Ct
Houston, TX 77059-3264, USA

Antonelli, Dominic A Lt Cmdr (Astronaut)
4106 Oak Blossom Ct
Houston, TX 77059-3264, USA

Antonelli, Johnny (Athlete, Baseball Player)
18 Tobey Ct
Pittsford, NY 14534-1854, USA

Antonelli, matt (Baseball Player)
1 Littles Hill Ln
Georgetown, MA 01833-2318, USA

Antonetti, Chris (Commentator)
2994 Riviera Ln
Westlake, OH 44145-6845, USA

Antonio, Banks
6211 Savannah Breeze Ct
Tampa, FL 33625-4078, us

Antonio, Lou (Actor)
530 S Gaylord Dr
Burbank, CA 91505-4714, USA

Antonoff, Jack (Musician)
c/o Matt Galle *Paradigm (NY)*
360 Park Ave S Fl 16
New York, NY 10010-1716, USA

Antonovich, Mike (Athlete, Hockey Player)
PO Box 224
Coleraine, MN 55722-0224, USA

Antoun (Khouri), Bishop (Religious Leader)
Antiochian Orthodox Christian Archdiocese
358 Mountain Rd
Englewood, NJ 07631-3798, USA

Antuofermo, Vito (Boxer)
16452 98th St
Howard Beach, NY 11414-4036, USA

Anwar, Gabrielle (Actor)
c/o Bradley Kramer *Kramer Management*
5699 Kanan Rd # 275
Agoura Hills, CA 91301-3358, USA

Anzulot, Cynthia (Athlete, Golfer)
21 Spring Creek Mnr
Hershey, PA 17033-1327, USA

Aoki, Chieko N (Business Person)
Westin Hotels Co
777 Westchester Ave
Westin Building
West Harrison, NY 10604-3520, USA

Aoki, Devon (Actor)
2828 Benedict Canyon Dr
Beverly Hills, CA 90210-1027, USA

Aoki, Isao (Athlete, Golfer)
I M G
1360 E 9th St Ste 100
Cleveland, OH 44114-1730, USA

Aoki, Rocky (Athlete, Business Person)
Benihana of Tokyo
8750 NW 36th St Ste 300
Doral, FL 33178-2499, USA

Aoki, Steve (DJ, Musician)
c/o Kirk Sommer *William Morris Endeavor (LA)*
9601 Wilshire Blvd
Beverly Hills, CA 90210-5213, USA

Aoloo Sunshine (Music Group)
c/o Staff Member *Paradigm (Monterey)*
404 W Franklin St
Monterey, CA 93940-2303, USA

Apap, Gilles (Musician)
Columbia Artists Mgmt Inc
165 W 57th St
New York, NY 10019-2201, USA

Aparicio, Luis (Athlete, Baseball Player)
Baltimore Orioles
333 W Camden St Attn Alumniassociation
Baltimore, MD 21201-2496, USA

Apatow, Judd (Director, Producer, Writer)
239 N Bristol Ave
Los Angeles, CA 90049-2603, USA

Apice, Robert (Horse Racer)
69 Alissa Ter
Jackson, NJ 08527-3116, USA

Apke, Steve (Athlete, Football Player)
427 Kenmont Ave
Pittsburgh, PA 15228-1405, USA

Apodaca, Bob (Athlete, Baseball Player)
2001 Blake St
Denver, CO 80205-2060, USA

Apodaca, Jerry (Politician)
6223 Utah Ave NW
Washington, DC 20015-2431, USA

Apodaca, Raymond S (Jerry) (Ex-Governor)
1477 Miracerros Loop N
Santa Fe, NM 87505-4021, USA

Appel, Deena (Designer)
c/o Jon Furie *Montana Artists Agency*
16133 Ventura Blvd Ste 620
Encino, CA 91436-2404, USA

Appice, Carmine (Musician)
Long Distance Entertainment
568 E Woolbright Rd # 234
Boynton Beach, FL 33435-6033, USA

Appier, Kevin (Athlete, Baseball Player)
30743 Victory Rd
Paola, KS 66071-9477, USA

Apple, Fiona (Musician)
2212 Meade Pl
Venice, CA 90291-3926, USA

Appleby, Shiri (Actor)
8743 Bonner Dr
West Hollywood, CA 90048-1805, USA

Appleby, Stuart (Athlete, Golfer)
9724 Chestnut Ridge Dr
Windermere, FL 34786-8943, USA

Applegate, Christina (Actor)
11223 Sunshine Ter
Studio City, CA 91604-3123, USA

Applegate, Eddie (Actor)
PO Box 55592
Valencia, CA 91385-0592, USA

Applegate, Fred (Actor)
811 E Olive Ave
Burbank, CA 91501-1425, USA

Applegate, Gideon (Athlete, Baseball Player)
7 Jenness Dr
South Newfane, VT 05351-9753, USA

Applegate, Jodi (Correspondent)
WNYW
205 E 67th St
New York, NY 10065-6089, USA

Applewhite, Major (Athlete, Football Player)
3911 Willow Bay Dr
Baton Rouge, LA 70809-2670, USA

Appolonia (Kotero) (Actor)
c/o Staff Member *TalentWorks (LA)*
3500 W Olive Ave Ste 1400
Burbank, CA 91505-5512, USA

Aprea, John (Actor)
727 N Martel Ave
Los Angeles, CA 90046-7506, USA

April, Johnny (Musician)
c/o Staff Member *Mitch Schneider Organization (MSO)*
14724 Ventura Blvd Ste 410
Sherman Oaks, CA 91403-3537, USA

Apt, Jerome (Jay) (Astronaut)
4 Shadycourt Dr
Pittsburgh, PA 15232-2914, USA

Apted, Michael (Director)
12857 Via Grimaldi
Del Mar, CA 92014-3839, USA

Apuna, Ben (Athlete, Football Player)
94423 Keaoopua St Apt 156
Mililani, HI 96789-2201, USA

Aqualung (Music Group)
c/o Staff Member *Paradigm (Monterey)*
404 W Franklin St
Monterey, CA 93940-2303, USA

Aquarium Rescue Unit (Music Group, Musician)
c/o Staff Member *Skyline Music*
28 Union St
Whitefield, NH 03598-3503, USA

Aquila, Chris
3955 Falling Water Dr
Reno, NV 89519-2143, USA

Aquino, Amy (Actor)
c/o Staff Member *Gersh (LA)*
9465 Wilshire Blvd Ste 600
Beverly Hills, CA 90212-2605, USA

Aquino, Amy (Actor)
c/o August Kammer *TalentWorks (LA)*
3500 W Olive Ave Ste 1400
Burbank, CA 91505-5512, USA

Aquino, Luis (Athlete, Baseball Player)
17201 Collins Ave Apt 606
Apt 606
Sunny Isles Beach, FL 33160-3476, USA

Arad, Avi (Producer)
29 Beverly Park Ter
Beverly Hills, CA 90210-1563, USA

Aragon, Art (Boxer)
19050 Wells Dr
Tarzana, CA 91356-3937, USA

Aragon, Frank (Director)
c/o Reyna Trevino *Trevino Enterprises*
10 Universal City Plz Fl 20
Universal City, CA 91608-1002, USA

Aragones, Sergio (Cartoonist)
PO Box 696
Ojai, CA 93024-0696, USA

Araguz, Leo (Athlete, Football Player)
3201 Leo Araguz St
Harlingen, TX 78552-7835, USA

Araki, Gregg (Director)
c/o Brian Young *Untitled Entertainment (LA)*
350 S Beverly Dr Ste 200
Beverly Hills, CA 90212-4819, USA

Arana, Tomas (Actor)
c/o Kesha Williams *KW Entertainment*
425 N Robertson Blvd
West Hollywood, CA 90048-1735, USA

Arapostathis, Evan (Athlete, Football Player)
4338 Macronald Dr
La Mesa, CA 91941-5608, USA

Arbanas, Frederick V (Fred) (Athlete, Football Player)
3350 SW Hook Rd
Lees Summit, MO 64082-1524, USA

Arbour, Al (Athlete, Hockey Player)
2071 Harbour Links Dr
Longboat Key, FL 34228-4281, USA

Arbour, Louise (Government Official)
UN Human Rights Commision
1 United Nations Plz
New York, NY 10017-3515, USA

Arbour-Parrott, Beatrice (Athlete, Baseball Player)
691 Elm St
Somerset, MA 02726-4034, USA

Arbubakrr, Hasson (Athlete, Football Player)
76 Custer Ave
Newark, NJ 07112-2510, USA

Arbuckle, Charles (Athlete, Football Player)
805 Oak Park Dr
Round Rock, TX 78681-4077, USA

Arbus, Loreen (Producer)
Loreen Arbus Productions
135 Central Park W Apt 9N
New York, NY 10023-5754, USA

Arcelus, Sebastian (Actor)
c/o Tim Sage *Paradigm (LA)*
360 N Crescent Dr
North Bldg
Beverly Hills, CA 90210-4874, USA

Arch, Lisa (Actor)
c/o Staff Member *The Paradise Group*
PO Box 69451
West Hollywood, CA 90069-0451, USA

Archambault, Lee J (Astronaut)
4318 Sweet Cicely Ct
Houston, TX 77059-3126, USA

Archambault, Lee J Lt Colonel (Astronaut)
4318 Sweet Cicely Ct
Houston, TX 77059-3126, USA

Archambeau, Lester (Athlete, Football Player)
10520 Montclair Way
Duluth, GA 30097-1840, USA

Archer, Anne (Actor)
PO Box 57593
Sherman Oaks, CA 91413-2593, USA

Archer, Beverly (Actor)
811 Adelaine Ave
S Pasadena, CA 91030-2403, USA

Archer, Dan (Athlete, Football Player)
65 Sunnyside Ave
Mill Valley, CA 94941-1924, USA

Archer, David (Athlete, Football Player)
3831 Upland Dr
Marietta, GA 30066-3064, USA

Archer, Jim (Athlete, Baseball Player)
1414 Oleander Dr
Tarpon Springs, FL 34689-2308, USA

Archer, John (Writer)
10901 176th Cir NE # 3601
Redmond, WA 98052-7218, USA

Archer, Tommy (Race Car Driver)
Archer Motorsports
4415 Venture Ave
Duluth, MN 55811-5705, USA

Archibaid, Nathaniel (Nate) (Athlete, Basketball Player)
2920 Holland Ave
Bronx, NY 10467-8304, USA

Archibald, Nate (Tiny) (Athlete, Basketball Player)
2920 Holland Ave
Bronx, NY 10467-8304, USA

Archibald, Nolan D (Business Person)
Black & Decker Corp
701 E Joppa Rd
Towson, MD 21286-5502, USA

Archie, Mike (Athlete, Football Player)
1178 Old Hickory Blvd
Brentwood, TN 37027-4221, USA

Archipoeski, Ken (Musician)
PO Box 656507
Fresh Meadows, NY 11365-6507, USA

Architecture in Helsinki (Music Group)
c/o Staff Member *Paradigm (Monterey)*
404 W Franklin St
Monterey, CA 93940-2303, USA

Archuleta, Adam (Athlete, Football Player)
1237 W Galveston St
Chandler, AZ 85224-4335, USA

Archuleta, David (Musician)
c/o Roger Widynowski *19 Entertainment (LA)*
9000 W Sunset Blvd Ste 1574
West Hollywood, CA 90069-5817, USA

Arcia, Jose (Athlete, Baseball Player)
7325 NW 3rd St
Miami, FL 33126-4211, USA

Arcieri, Leila (Actor)
c/o Staff Member *Paradigm (LA)*
360 N Crescent Dr
North Bldg
Beverly Hills, CA 90210-4874, USA

Arctic Monkeys (Music Group)
c/o Staff Member *Paradigm (Monterey)*
404 W Franklin St
Monterey, CA 93940-2303, USA

Arcuri, Mike (Congressman, Politician)
10 Broad St Rm 330
Utica, NY 13501-1233, USA

Ard, Jim (Athlete, Baseball Player)
2325 Wayfarer Dr
Discovery Bay, CA 94505-9225, USA

Ard, Johnny (Athlete, Baseball Player)
3815 Edinburg Cir
Valdosta, GA 31605-7858, USA

Ard, William D (Bill) (Athlete, Football Player)
41 Vail Ln
Watchung, NJ 07069-6149, USA

Ardell, Dan (Athlete, Baseball Player)
554 Hazel Dr
Corona Del Mar, CA 92625-2535, USA

Ardell, Donald B (Doctor)
288 Beach Dr NE Apt 11C
St Petersburg, FL 33701-3481, USA

Arden, Alicia (Actor)
c/o Vance Payton *Advance LA*
7904 Santa Monica Blvd Ste 200
West Hollywood, CA 90046-5170

Arden, Michael (Actor)
3826 Sunset Dr
Los Angeles, CA 90027-4750, USA

Arden, Toni (Musician)
1 N Golfview Rd Apt 300
Lake Worth, FL 33460-3948, USA

Ardito, Doug (Musician)
7820 Caverna Dr
Los Angeles, CA 90068, USA

Ardizoia, Rinaldo (Athlete, Baseball Player)
130 Santa Rosa Ave
San Francisco, CA 94112-1930, USA

Ardizzone, Anthony (Tony) (Athlete, Football Player)
27 S Farview Ave
Paramus, NJ 07652-2629, USA

Ardoin, Danny (Athlete, Baseball Player)
1761 Hollow Cove Ln
Lake Charles, LA 70611-5155, USA

Ardolino, Todd (Director)
c/o Staff Member *Creative Artists Agency (CAA-LA)*
2000 Avenue of the Stars Ste 100
Los Angeles, CA 90067-4705, USA

Aregood, Richards L (Journalist)
Philadelphia Daily News
400 N Broad St
Editorial Dept
Philadelphia, PA 19130-4015, USA

Arellano, Stephanie (Actor)
c/o Ken Jacobson *Ken Jacobson Management*
Preferred to be contacted by phone or email
Woodland Hills, CA 91367, USA

Arenas, Gilbert (Athlete, Basketball Player)
4550 Gable Dr
Encino, CA 91316-4354, USA

Arenas, Javier (Athlete, Football Player)
c/o Hadley Engelhard *Enter-Sports Management*
5 Concourse Pkwy Ste 3000
Atlanta, GA 30328-7106, USA

Arenas, Joe (Athlete, Football Player)
780 W Bay Area Blvd Apt 1215
Webster, TX 77598-4057, USA

Arenberg, Lee (Actor)
c/o Staff Member *Gage Group, The (LA)*
5757 Wilshire Blvd Ste 659
Los Angeles, CA 90036-3682, USA

Arencibia, J P
770 Claughton Island Dr Apt 1104
Miami, FL 33131-2628, USA

Arend, Geoffrey (Actor)
c/o Jason Newman *Untitled Entertainment (LA)*
350 S Beverly Dr Ste 200
Beverly Hills, CA 90212-4819, USA

Arend, Jeff (Race Car Driver)
888 De Anza Heights Dr
La Verne, CA 91750-5702, USA

Aretsky, Ken (Business Person)
21 Club
21 W 52nd St
New York, NY 10019-6181, USA

Arfons, Arthur E (Art) (Race Car Driver)
PO Box 1409
Saint Charles, MO 63302-1409, USA

Argenziano, Carmen (Actor)
824 S Bel Aire Dr
Burbank, CA 91501-1558, USA

Argota, Ashley (Actor)
c/o Monique Moss *Integrated PR*
8060 Melrose Ave Fl 4
Los Angeles, CA 90046-7038, USA

Argott, Don (Director, Producer)
c/o David Gersh *Gersh (LA)*
9465 Wilshire Blvd Ste 600
Beverly Hills, CA 90212-2605, USA

Argov, Sherry (Writer)
PO Box 91298
Los Angeles, CA 90009-1298, USA

Arias, Alex (Athlete, Baseball Player)
37 Edmund Rd
West Park, FL 33023-5231, USA

Arias, George (Athlete, Baseball Player)
4343 W Tellurite Dr
Tucson, AZ 85745-4193, USA

Arias, Moises (Actor)
c/o Matt Fletcher *Greene & Associates*
1901 Avenue of the Stars Ste 130
Los Angeles, CA 90067-6030, USA

Arias, Rudy (Athlete, Baseball Player)
3911 NW 11th St
Miami, FL 33126-3614, USA

Arias, Silvana (Actor)
Diane Perez Entertainment
838 N Fairfax Ave
Los Angeles, CA 90046-7208, USA

Arias, Yancey (Actor)
c/o Chris Henze *Thruline Entertainment*
9250 Wilshire Blvd Ste 100
Ground Floor
Beverly Hills, CA 90212-3343, USA

Arie, India (India.Arie) (Musician, Songwriter)
5666 Stonehaven Dr
Stone Mountain, GA 30087-5766, USA

Aries, Jacqueline Pinol (Actor)
c/o Tracy Quinn *Quinn Management*
17328 Ventura Blvd Ste 416
Encino, CA 91316-3904, USA

Ariey, Mike (Athlete, Football Player)
PO Box 708
Bakersfield, CA 93302-0708, USA

Ariyoshi, George R (Politician)
745 Fort Street Mall Ste 500
Honolulu, HI 96813-3805, USA

Ariza, Trevor (Athlete, Basketball Player)
1111 S Grand Ave PH 2
Los Angeles, CA 90015-2174, USA

Arjona, Ricardo (Musician)
c/o Staff Member *Fenix Entertainment Group*
919 Fourth St
San Francisco, CA 94158, USA

Arkangel R-15 (Music Group)
c/o Staff Member *Sony Music Miami*
605 Lincoln Rd Ste 700
Miami Beach, FL 33139-2901, USA

Arkhipov, Denis (Athlete, Hockey Player)
716 Sweet Cherry Ct
Nashville, TN 37215-6174, USA

Arkin, Adam (Actor)
3531 Coldwater Canyon Ave
Studio City, CA 91604-4060, USA

Arkin, Alan (Actor)
2744 Levante St
Carlsbad, CA 92009-8120, USA

Ark, The (Music Group)
c/o Staff Member *Paradigm (Monterey)*
404 W Franklin St
Monterey, CA 93940-2303, USA

Arlauckas, Joe (Athlete, Basketball Player)
8 Brimley Mnr
Rochester, NY 14612-4414, USA

Arlich, Don (Athlete, Baseball Player)
7877 73rd St S
Cottage Grove, MN 55016-1919, USA

Arlin, Steve (Athlete, Baseball Player)
6819 Claremore Ave
San Diego, CA 92120-3125, USA

Arlovski, Andrei (Athlete, Boxer)
c/o Staff Member *John Lewis Entertainment Group*
3071 S Valley View Blvd
Las Vegas, NV 89102-7889, USA

Arm, Mark (Musician)
Legends of 21st Century
7 Trinity Row
Florence, MA 01062-1931, USA

Armand, Arman
430 Washington St
New York, NY 10013-1721, USA

Armas, Chris (Soccer Player)
Chicago Fire
980 N Michigan Ave Ste 1998
Chicago, IL 60611-7504, USA

Armas, Tony (Athlete, Baseball Player)
c/o Staff Member *Washington Nationals*
1500 S Capitol St SE
Washington, DC 20003-3599, USA

Armato, Ange (Athlete, Baseball Player)
5082 Valley Pines Dr
Rockford, IL 61109-3774, USA

Armdt-Proefrock, Ellen (Athlete, Baseball Player)
905 Alpine St
Brodhead, WI 53520-1052, USA

Armenante, Jillian (Actor)
574 N Irving Blvd
Los Angeles, CA 90004-1407, USA

Armendariz, Ramon
3952 Malaya Ct
Denver, CO 80249-8178, USA

Armisen, Fred (Actor, Comedian)
2445 Riverside Pl
Los Angeles, CA 90039-4010, USA

Armitage, Alison (Actor, Model)
9220 W Sunset Blvd Ste 305
West Hollywood, CA 90069-3503, USA

Armitage, Richard (Actor)
c/o Evelyn O'Neill *Management 360*
9111 Wilshire Blvd
Beverly Hills, CA 90210-5508, USA

Armor, James Majgen (Astronaut)
9120 Maria Ave
Great Falls, VA 22066-4008, USA

Armour, Jojuan (Athlete, Football Player)
1436 Rollins Rd
Toledo, OH 43612-1633, USA

Armour, Justin (Athlete, Football Player)
8 Crystal Park Pl Unit B
Manitou Springs, CO 80829-2654, us

Armour, Justin (Athlete, Football Player)
765 Mays Hollow Ln
Encinitas, CA 92024-2734, USA

Armour, Tommy (Athlete, Golfer)
3006 Woodside St Apt 8017
Dallas, TX 75204-8538, USA

Armstead, Jessie (Athlete, Football Player)
1316 Mill Stream Dr
Dallas, TX 75232-4604, USA

Armstead, Ray (Athlete, Olympic Athlete, Track Athlete)
7953 Bloom Dr
Saint Louis, MO 63133-1109, USA

Armstrong, Adger (Athlete, Football Player)
6403 Paddington St
Houston, TX 77085-3000, USA

Armstrong, Antonio (Athlete, Football Player)
5314 Palmetto St
Houston, TX 77081-4614, USA

Armstrong, Bess (Actor)
1518 N Doheny Dr
Los Angeles, CA 90069-1104, USA

Armstrong, Billie Joe (Musician)
393 Hampton Rd
Piedmont, CA 94611-3525, USA

Armstrong, BJ (Athlete, Basketball Player)
SeS N Lake Shore Dr Apt 64e2
Chicago, IL 6E611, USA

Armstrong, Brad (Adult Film Star)
c/o Staff Member *Vivid Entertainment*
3599 Cahuenga Blvd W Fl 2
Los Angeles, CA 90068-1397, USA

Armstrong, Bruce (Athlete, Football Player)
12543 Brookwood Ct
Davie, FL 33330-1207, USA

Armstrong, Charlotte (Athlete, Baseball Player)
5838 N 81st St
Scottsdale, AZ 85250-6208, USA

Armstrong, Colby (Athlete, Hockey Player)
1597 Washington Pike Ste B14
Bridgeville, PA 15017-2876, USA

Armstrong, Curtis (Actor)
3867 Shannon Rd
Los Angeles, CA 90027-1441, USA

Armstrong, Darrell (Athlete, Basketball Player)
337 Broadmoor Way
McDonough, GA 30253-4290, USA

Armstrong, Debbie (Athlete, Olympic Athlete, Skier)
681 Shekel Ln
Breckenridge, CO 80424-8931, USA

Armstrong, Derek (Athlete, Hockey Player)
9373 S Holland Way
Littleton, CO 80127-5934, USA

Armstrong, Dwight (Actor)
c/o Paul Greenstone *Paul Greenstone Entertainment*
3008 Sorrelwood Dr
San Ramon, CA 94582-5008, USA

Armstrong, Harvey (Athlete, Football Player)
3820 River Mansion Dr
Peachtree Corners, GA 30096-6147, USA

Armstrong, Hilton (Athlete, Basketball Player)
c/o Jeff Schwartz *Excel Sports Management (NY)*
1700 Broadway Fl 29
New York, NY 10019-5905, USA

Armstrong, Jack (Athlete, Baseball Player)
272 E River Park Dr
Jupiter, FL 33477-9381, USA

Armstrong, J D (Athlete, Football Player)
7906 W Meadow Pass Cir
Wichita, KS 67205-1611

Armstrong, Jonas (Actor)
c/o Andrew Kurland *ICM Partners (LA)*
10250 Constellation Blvd Fl 7
Los Angeles, CA 90067-6207, USA

Armstrong, Lance (Athlete, Cycler, Olympic Athlete)
LiveStrong
2201 E 6th St
Austin, TX 78702-3456, USA

Armstrong, Matthew John (Actor)
c/o David Ginsberg *Insight*
PO Box 36359
Los Angeles, CA 90036-0359, USA

Armstrong, Mike (Athlete, Baseball Player)
525 Ashbrook Ct
Athens, GA 30605-3985, USA

Armstrong, Neill (Athlete, Football Player)
312 Lakewood Dr
Roanoke, TX 76262-5292, us

Armstrong, Otis (Athlete, Football Player)
7183 S Newport Way
Centennial, CO 80112-1613, us

Armstrong, Otis (Athlete, Football Player)
9951 E Idaho Cir Apt 202
Aurora, CO 80247-6293, USA

Armstrong, Quincy (Athlete, Football Player)
5801 E FM 4
Grandview, TX 76050-3005, USA

Armstrong, Robb (Cartoonist)
229 E 5th Ave
Conshohocken, PA 19428-1714, USA

Armstrong, Robert (Bob) (Athlete, Basketball Player)
6802 Packer Dr NE
Belmont, MI 49306-9240, USA

Armstrong, Roger (Cartoonist)
21701 Rushford Dr
Lake Forest, CA 92630-6510, USA

Armstrong, Samaire (Actor)
c/o Loch Powell *Leverage Management*
3030 Pennsylvania Ave
Santa Monica, CA 90404-4112, USA

Armstrong, Tate (Athlete, Basketball Player)
14704 Westbury Rd
Rockville, MD 20853-1610, USA

Armstrong, Taylor (Reality Star)
1736 Family Crisis Center
2116 Arlington Ave Ste 200
Los Angeles, CA 90018-1353, USA

Armstrong, Thomas (Race Car Driver)
PacWest Racing Group
PO Box 1717
Bellevue, WA 98009-1717, USA

Armstrong, Trace (Athlete, Football Player)
422 SW 88th Ter
Gainesville, FL 32607-1452, us

Armstrong, Trace (Athlete, Football Player)
10191 Winding Ridge Rd
Saint Louis, MO 63124-1157, USA

Armstrong, Ty (Athlete, Golfer)
11529 Kensington Dr
Eden Prairie, MN 55347-4943, USA

Armstrong, Valorie (Actor)
Contemporary Artists
610 Santa Monica Blvd Ste 202
Santa Monica, CA 90401-1645, USA

Armstrong, Vaughn (Actor)
1903 Apex Ave
Los Angeles, CA 90039-3115, USA

Armstrong, Wally (Athlete, Golfer)
Signature Sports Group
4150 Olson Memorial Hwy Ste 110
Minneapolis, MN 55422-4804, USA

Armstrong, William (Writer)
6 Roland St
Newton Highlands, MA 02461-1920, USA

Armstrong, William L (Ex-Senator, Politician)
23 Sedgwick Dr
Englewood, CO 80113-4109, USA

Armtritraz, Ashok (Producer)
c/o Staff Member *Hyde Park Entertainment*
3500 W Olive Ave Ste 300
Burbank, CA 91505-4647, USA

Arnason, Tyler (Athlete, Hockey Player)
881 N La Salle Dr
Chicago, IL 60610-3259, USA

Arnaz, Lucie (Actor)
3 Big Shop Ln
Ridgefield, CT 06877-4565, USA

Arnaz Jr, Desi (Actor)
516 Avenue M
Boulder City, NV 89005-2831, USA

Arndt, Denis (Actor)
c/o Suzanne DeWalt *Dewalt & Musik Management*
623 N Parish Pl
Burbank, CA 91506-1701, USA

Arndt, Michael (Writer)
c/o Tom Strickler *William Morris Endeavor (LA)*
9601 Wilshire Blvd
Beverly Hills, CA 90210-5213, USA

Arndt, Richard (Athlete, Football Player)
2130 Parkdale Dr
Kingwood, TX 77339-2351, USA

Arnelle, Jesse (Athlete, Basketball Player)
400 Urbano Dr
San Francisco, CA 94127-2827, USA

Arnesen, Liv (Skier)
401 2nd Ave N Ste 406
Minneapolis, MN 55401-2097, USA

Arneson, Jim (Athlete, Football Player)
12649 S 71st St
Tempe, AZ 85284-3105, USA

Arneson, Mark (Athlete, Football Player)
15902 Wetherburn Rd
Chesterfield, MO 63017-7341, USA

Arnett, Jon (Athlete, Football Player)
200 Greenridge Dr Apt 715
Lake Oswego, OR 97035-1475, us

Arnett, Jon D (Athlete, Football Player)
16869 65th Ave Unit 330
Lake Oswego, OR 97035-7865, USA

Arnett, Peter (Journalist)
Cnn News
820 1st St NE Ste 1000
Washington, DC 20002-4363, USA

Arnett, Will (Actor, Comedian)
c/o Peter Principato *Principato/Young Management (LA)*
9465 Wilshire Blvd Ste 900
Beverly Hills, CA 90212-2608, USA

Arnette, Jay (Athlete, Basketball Player, Olympic Athlete)
2 Hillside Ct
Austin, TX 78746-6436, USA

Arnette, Jeanetta (Actor)
466 N Harper Ave
Los Angeles, CA 90048-2221, USA

Arnezeder, Nora (Actor)
c/o Estelle Lasher *Lasher Group*
1133 Avenue Of The Americas Ste 1621
New York, NY 10036-6710, USA

Arnez J (Comedian)
c/o Staff Member *ICM Partners (LA)*
10250 Constellation Blvd Fl 7
Los Angeles, CA 90067-6207, USA

Arngrim, Alison (Actor)
PO Box 98
Tujunga, CA 91043-0098, USA

Arning, Lisa (Actor)
c/o Julie Wolff *Morgan Agency, The*
38 E High St
Ballston Spa, NY 12020-1805, USA

Arno, Ed
11220 72nd Dr
Forest Hills, NY 11375-5631, USA

Arnold, Ben (Musician)
Golden Guru
227 Pine St
Philadelphia, PA 19106-4326, USA

Arnold, Ben (Race Car Driver)
309 Fair Oaks Dr
Fairfield, AL 35064-2418, USA

Arnold, Charles (Athlete, Baseball Player)
19537 Beaverland St
Detroit, MI 48219-5507, USA

Arnold, Chris (Athlete, Baseball Player)
794 E 7th Ave
Denver, CO 80203-3820, USA

Arnold, David (Athlete, Football Player)
1615 Stanley St
New Britain, CT 06053-2439, USA

Arnold, David (Athlete, Football Player)
3079 Solar Dr NW
Warren, OH 44485-1611, us

Arnold, Dr Jennifer (Doctor, Reality Star)
Texas Children's Hospital
6621 Fannin St
Houston, TX 77030-2399, USA

Arnold, Francis (Athlete, Football Player)
3312 W 80th St
Inglewood, CA 90305-1354, USA

Arnold, Jahine (Athlete, Football Player)
4513 W Brookwood Dr
Tampa, FL 33629-4242, USA

Arnold, Jahine (Athlete, Football Player)
8013 Fountain Ave
Tampa, FL 33615-2903, us

Arnold, James E (Athlete, Football Player)
4407 Waterford Cir
Nashville, TN 37221-2153, USA

Arnold, Jamie (Athlete, Baseball Player)
17132 W Tara Ln
Surprise, AZ 85388-1244, USA

Arnold, Jim (Athlete, Football Player)
4407 Waterford Cir
Nashville, TN 37221-2153, us

Arnold, Kristine (Music Group)
Monty Hitchcock Mgmt
5101 Overton Rd
Nashville, TN 37220-1920, USA

Arnold, Lenna (Athlete, Baseball Player)
4312 Dodge Ave
Fort Wayne, IN 46815-6925, USA

Arnold, Lindsay (Dancer)
c/o Rebecca Lambrecht *Chicane Group*
6442 Santa Monica Blvd Ste 200B
Los Angeles, CA 90038-1530, USA

Arnold, Louise (Athlete, Baseball Player)
52806 Brandel Ave
South Bend, IN 46635-1250, USA

Arnold, Monica (Actor, Musician)
c/o Cara Lewis *Creative Artists Agency (CAA-NY)*
162 5th Ave Fl 6
New York, NY 10010-6047, USA

Arnold, Murray (Athlete, Basketball Player, Coach)
Western Kentucky University
Athletic Dept
Bowling Green, KY 42101, USA

Arnold, Richard R (Astronaut)
16302 Heather Bend Ct
Houston, TX 77059-5579, USA

Arnold, Scott (Athlete, Baseball Player)
3282 Gondola Dr
Lexington, KY 40513-1083, USA

Arnold, Stuart (Publisher)
Fortune Magazine
Rockefeller Center
New York, NY 10020, USA

Arnold, Tichina (Actor)
c/o Geoff Cheddy *Brillstein Entertainment Partners (LA)*
9150 Wilshire Blvd Ste 350
Beverly Hills, CA 90212-3453, USA

Arnold, Tom (Actor, Comedian)
9958 Kip Dr
Beverly Hills, CA 90210-2014, USA

Arnold, Tony (Athlete, Baseball Player)
300 S Main St
Akron, OH 44308-1204, USA

Arnold, Walt (Athlete, Football Player)
8503 La Sala Grande NE
Albuquerque, NM 87111-4564, USA

Arnold Jr, Harry L (Doctor, Writer)
250 Laurel St Apt 301
San Francisco, CA 94118-2045, USA

Arnsberg, Brad (Athlete, Baseball Player)
4610 E Thunder Hawk Rd
Cave Creek, AZ 85331-5485, USA

Arnsparger, Bill (Athlete, Football Player)
1574 Pine Needles Ln
Lexington, KY 40513-1503, USA

Arnstein, Rolly (Music Group)
Bad Boy Entertainment
1540 Broadway Ste 3000
New York, NY 10036-4039, USA

Arntz, Jason (Athlete)
95A Finnegan Ln
Kendall Park, NJ 08824-1644, USA

Arnzen, Bob (Athlete, Basketball Player)
8 Grand Lake Dr
Fort Thomas, KY 41075-4100

Arnzen, Robert (Athlete, Basketball Player)
8 Grand Lake Dr
Fort Thomas, KY 41075-4100, USA

Arocha, Rene (Athlete, Baseball Player)
14652 SW 170th St
Miami, FL 33177-2040, USA

Aronofsky, Darren (Director)
200 Diamond Ln
Peconic, NY 11958-3000, USA

Aronsohn, Lee (Writer)
14332 Roblar Pl
Sherman Oaks, CA 91423-4020, USA

Aronson, Doug (Athlete, Football Player)
36 Piermont Ter
Wayne, NJ 07470-3648, us

Aronson, Judie (Actor)
11543 Laurelcrest Dr
Studio City, CA 91604-3875, USA

Arpel, Adrien (Beauty Pageant Winner, Business Person)
Adrien Arpel Cosmetics
400 Hackensack Ave
Hackensack, NJ 07601-6310, USA

Arpey, Gerard (Business Person)
AMR Corp
433 Amon Carter Blvd
Fort Worth, TX 76155, USA

Arquette, Alexis (Actor)
c/o Staff Member Innovative Artists (LA)
1505 10th St
Santa Monica, CA 90401-2805, USA

Arquette, David (Actor, Director, Producer)
27460 Pacific Coast Hwy
Malibu, CA 90265-4336, USA

Arquette, Patricia (Actor)
c/o Molly Madden 3 Arts Entertainment (LA)
9460 Wilshire Blvd Fl 7
Beverly Hills, CA 90212-2713, USA

Arquette, Rosanna (Actor)
c/o Laina Cohn Cohn / Torgan Management
Prefers to be contacted by telephone or email
Los Angeles, CA, USA

Arrants, Rod (Actor)
115 Maitland Dr
Alameda, CA 94502-6725, USA

Arras, Maria Celeste (Actor)
c/o Staff Member Telemundo
2470 W 8th Ave
Hialeah, FL 33010-2000, USA

Arredondo, Rosa (Actor)
c/o Suzanne (Sue) Wohl TalentWorks (LA)
3500 W Olive Ave Ste 1400
Burbank, CA 91505-5512, USA

Arriale, Lynne (Musician)
c/o Suzi Reynolds Suzi Reynolds Associates
2055 Center Ave PH A
Fort Lee, NJ 07024-4947, USA

Arrieta, Jacob '"Jake'"
207 Golden Bear Dr
Austin, TX 78738-1721, USA

Arrigo, Gerry (Athlete, Baseball Player)
3740 Redthorne Dr
Amelia, OH 45102-1263, USA

Arrillaga, John (Business Person, Philanthropist)
John Arrillaga Foundation
2450 Watson Ct
Palo Alto, CA 94303-3216, USA

Arrington, Buddy (Race Car Driver)
2820 Kings Mountain Rd
Martinsville, VA 24112-6751, USA

Arrington, Jill (Sportscaster)
CBS-TV
51 W 52nd St
New York, NY 10019-6119, USA

Arrington, J J (Athlete, Football Player)
1599 E Beretta Pl
Chandler, AZ 85286-1152, USA

Arrington, LaVar (Athlete, Football Player)
1514 Cedar Lane Farm Rd
Annapolis, MD 21409-5625, USA

Arrington, Michael (Business Person, Internet Star)
3800 the Strand Apt 6
Manhattan Beach, CA 90266-3136, USA

Arrington, Richard (Athlete, Football Player)
2585 King Cir SE
Conyers, GA 30013-1981, USA

Arrington, Rick (Athlete, Football Player)
2585 King Cir SE
Conyers, GA 30013-1981, us

Arriola, Dante (Director)
c/o Staff Member MJZ
2201 S Carmelina Ave
Los Angeles, CA 90064-1001, USA

Arriota, Gus (Cartoonist)
PO Box 3275
Carmel By The Sea, CA 93921-3275, USA

Arrobio, Charles (Chuck) (Athlete, Football Player)
35 Essex St Apt 5A
New York, NY 10002-4716, USA

Arrobio, Chuck (Athlete, Football Player)
481 Linda Vista Ave
Pasadena, CA 91105-1119, us

Arrojo, Luis (Athlete, Baseball Player)
5684 36th Ave N
Saint Petersburg, FL 33710-1914, USA

Arrolo, Rolando (Athlete, Baseball Player)
5684 36th Ave N
Saint Petersburg, FL 33710-1914, USA

Arroyo, Bronson (Athlete, Baseball Player)
9256 Scarlette Oak Ave
Fort Myers, FL 33967-5145, USA

Arroyo, Carlos (Athlete, Basketball Player)
1115 NW 126th Ct
Miami, FL 33182-2033, USA

Arroyo, Fernando (Athlete, Baseball Player)
702 Hampton Woods Ln SW
Vero Beach, FL 32962-7052, USA

Arroyo, Jose (Writer)
c/o Staff Member Kaplan-Stahler Agency
8383 Wilshire Blvd Ste 923
Beverly Hills, CA 90211-2443, USA

Arroyo, Luis (Athlete, Baseball Player)
PO Box 1452
Yauco, PR 00698-1452, USA

Arroyo, Rudolph (Athlete, Baseball Player)
28799 Sequoia Ct
Coarsegold, CA 93614-9161, USA

Arroyo, Rudy
28799 Sequoia Ct
Coarsegold, CA 93614-9161, USA

Arsmstrong, Colby (Athlete, Hockey Player)
8030 Sherwood Dr
Presto, PA 15142-1078, USA

Arterburn, Elmer (Athlete, Football Player)
3819 29th St
Lubbock, TX 79410-2508, USA

Arterburn, Stephen (Writer)
New Life Ministries
PO Box 1018
Laguna Beach, CA 92652-1018, USA

Arteta, Miguel (Director)
c/o David Lubliner William Morris Endeavor (LA)
9601 Wilshire Blvd
Beverly Hills, CA 90210-5213, USA

Arthur, Maureen (Actor)
9171 Wilshire Blvd # 530
Beverly Hills, CA 90210-5530, USA

Arthur, Michelle (Actor)
c/o Steven Neibert Imperium 7 Talent Agency
5455 Wilshire Blvd Ste 1706
Los Angeles, CA 90036-4217, USA

Arthur, Mike (Athlete, Football Player)
10445 Sharondale Rd
Cincinnati, OH 45241-3077, USA

Arthur, Mike (Athlete, Football Player)
11271 Terwilligers Valley Ln
Cincinnati, OH 45249-2740, us

Arthur, Perry (Athlete, Golfer)
7513 Zurich Dr
Plano, TX 75025-3118, USA

Arthur, Rebeca (Actor)
Epstein-Wyckoff
280 S Beverly Dr Ste 400
Beverly Hills, CA 90212-3904, USA

Arthurs, John (Athlete, Basketball Player)
1429 Henry Clay Ave
New Orleans, LA 70118-6059, USA

Artist, Jacob (Actor, Musician)
c/o Tej Bhatia Herring Rogers & Cowan PR (LA)
8687 Melrose Ave Ste 7
West Hollywood, CA 90069-5721, USA

Artoe, Mike (Athlete, Football Player)
17 Canterbury Ct
Wilmette, IL 60091-2822, USA

Arturo, Lisa (Actor)
c/o Mitch Clem Shadow Entertainment
655 N Central Ave Fl 17
Glendale, CA 91203-1439, USA

Artz, Mary Gail (Actor)
20501 Ventura Blvd Ste 380
Woodland Hills, CA 91364-6432, USA

Artzt, Alice J (Musician)
51 Hawthorne Ave
Princeton, NJ 08540-3803, USA

Artzt, Edwin L (Business Person)
3849 Hedgewood Dr
Lawrenceburg, IN 47025-8047, USA

Arum, Robert (Bob) (Boxer)
36 Gulf Stream Ct
Las Vegas, NV 89113-1354, USA

Arute, Jack (Commentator, Race Car Driver)
342 Southwick Rd Apt 104
Westfield, MA 01085-4753, USA

Arvesen, Nina (Actor)
20315 Lanark St
Winnetka, CA 91306-1819, USA

Arvie, Herman (Athlete, Football Player)
33844 Canterbury Rd
Solon, OH 44139-5617, USA

Arvizu, Reginald (Musician)
27511 Hidden Trail Rd
Laguna Hills, CA 92653-7841, USA

Asad, Doug (Athlete, Football Player)
1701 Marquette Ct
Lake Forest, IL 60045-5115, us

Asay, Chuck (Cartoonist)
Colorada Springs Gazette
303 S Prospect St
Colorado Springs, CO 80903-3748, USA

Asbury, Kelly (Actor)
c/o Staff Member Creative Artists Agency (CAA-LA)
2000 Avenue of the Stars Ste 100
Los Angeles, CA 90067-4705, USA

Ascencio, Nelson (Actor)
c/o Heidi Rotbart Heidi Rotbart Management
1810 Malcolm Ave Apt 207
Los Angeles, CA 90025-7610, USA

Asch, Peter (Athlete, Olympic Athlete, Water Polo Player)
1946 Green St
San Francisco, CA 94123-4811, USA

Aschbacher, Darrel (Athlete, Football Player)
915 NE Wyoming Dr
Prineville, OR 97754-7905, USA

Aschwege, David (Athlete, Baseball Player)
3027 S 27th St
Lincoln, NE 68502-5010, USA

Asghedom, Ermias (Nipsey Hussle) (Musician)
c/o John Pantle Agency for the Performing Arts (APA-LA)
405 S Beverly Dr Ste 500
Beverly Hills, CA 90212-4425, USA

Ash, Brandon (Race Car Driver)
Racing West
1772 Los Arboles # J-186
Thousand Oaks, CA 91362, USA

Ash, Brian (Producer, Writer)
c/o Simon Millar Rumble Media
1620 Broadway Ste C
Santa Monica, CA 90404-2777, USA

Ashanti (Musician)
23 Saint Andrews Ct
Old Westbury, NY 11568-1711, USA

Ashbery, John L (Writer)
326 Belmont Ave
Buffalo, NY 14223-1550, USA

Ashbrook, Dana (Actor)
Rigberg Roberts Rugolo
1180 S Beverly Dr Ste 601
Los Angeles, CA 90035-1158, USA

Ashbrook, Daphne (Actor)
Innovative Atrists
1505 10th St
Santa Monica, CA 90401-2805, USA

Ashbrook, Stephen (Musician)
Green Room
2280 NW Thurman St
Portland, OR 97210-2519, USA

Ashby, Alan (Athlete, Baseball Player)
12011 Cypress Creek Lakes Dr
Cypress, TX 77433-1872, USA

Ashby, Andy (Athlete, Baseball Player)
5701 NW Parkdale Cir
Kansas City, MO 64151-3281, USA

Ashby, Jeffrey S (Astronaut)
NASA
2101 Nasa Pkwy Spc Ctr
Houston, TX 77058-3696, USA

Ashby, JeffreyS Captain (Astronaut)
2834 W Nasa Rd # 1
Webster, TX 77598-6202, USA

Ashby, Jeffrey S Captain
2834 W Nasa Rd # 1
Webster, TX 77598-6202, USA

Ashby, Linden (Actor)
639 N Larchmont Blvd Ste 207
Los Angeles, CA 90004-1323, USA

Ashcroft, John (Politician)
5603 W Farm Road 54
Willard, MO 65781-8405, USA

Ashcroft, John D (Ex-Governor, Ex-Senator)
The Ashcroft Group, LLC
950 N Glebe Rd Ste 240
Arlington, VA 22203-4181, USA

Ashcroft, Richard (Musician, Songwriter)
c/o Marty Diamond *Paradigm (NY)*
360 Park Ave S Fl 16
New York, NY 10010-1716, USA

Ashe, Chrstopher (Actor)
c/o Paul Greenstone *Paul Greenstone Entertainment*
3008 Sorrelwood Dr
San Ramon, CA 94582-5008, USA

Ashenfelter III, Horace (Athlete, Track Athlete)
100 Hawthome Ave
Glen Ridge, NJ 07028, USA

Asher, Barry (Bowler)
Professional Bowlers Assn
55 E Jackson Blvd Ste 401
Chicago, IL 60604-4307, USA

Asher, Jamie (Athlete, Football Player)
6840 S Arlington Ave
Indianapolis, IN 46237-9722, us

Asher, Peter (Musician, Producer)
23446 Malibu Colony Rd
Malibu, CA 90265-4640, USA

Asher, Robert (Bob) (Athlete, Football Player)
4800 S Chicago Beach Dr Apt 612S
Chicago, IL 60615-3569, USA

Ashford, Mandy (Music Group)
Evolution Talent
1776 Broadway # 1500
New York, NY 10019-2002, USA

Ashford, Matthew (Actor)
c/o Staff Member *Tranquil Bay Entertainment*
330 Island Cove Rd
Norwood, NC 28128-6494, USA

Ashford, Michelle (Producer, Writer)
c/o Staff Member *William Morris Endeavor (LA)*
9601 Wilshire Blvd
Beverly Hills, CA 90210-5213, USA

Ashford, Rob (Actor)
c/o Staff Member *Creative Artists Agency (CAA-LA)*
2000 Avenue of the Stars Ste 100
Los Angeles, CA 90067-4705, USA

Ashford, Roslyn (Music Group)
Thomas Cassidy
11761 E Speedway Blvd
Tucson, AZ 85748-2017, USA

Ashford, Tucker (Athlete, Baseball Player)
122 E Church Ave
Covington, TN 38019-2504, USA

Ashford & Simpson (Music Group)
254 W 72nd St Apt 1A
New York, NY 10023-2851, USA

Ashkenasi, Shmuel (Musician)
3800 N Lake Shore Dr
Chicago, IL 60613-3301, USA

Ashley, Billy (Athlete, Baseball Player)
2787 Autumn Ridge Dr
Thousand Oaks, CA 91362-4934, USA

Ashley, Elizabeth (Actor)
1223 N Ogden Dr
West Hollywood, CA 90046-4706, USA

Ashley, Jennifer (Actor)
129 W Wilson St Ste 202
Costa Mesa, CA 92627-1586, USA

Ashley, Leon (Musician)
PO Box 567
Hendersonville, TN 37077-0567, USA

Ashley, Mike (Race Car Driver)
Gotham City Racing
201 Old Country Rd Ste 101
Melville, NY 11747-2731, USA

Ashley, Walker (Athlete, Football Player)
4A Dwight St
Jersey City, NJ 07305-4139, USA

Ashman, Duane (Athlete, Football Player)
2625 Antler Ct
Silver Spring, MD 20904-7157, USA

Ashmore, Darryl (Athlete, Football Player)
8695 Thornbrook Terrace Pt
Boynton Beach, FL 33473-4882, USA

Ashmore, Frank (Actor)
c/o Staff Member *Howard Talent West*
17000 Ventura Blvd Ste 210
Encino, CA 91316-4153, USA

Ashmore, Shawn (Actor)
4248 Wilkinson Ave
Studio City, CA 91604-1661, USA

Ashton, John (Actor)
PO Box 272489
Fort Collins, CO 80527-2489, USA

Ashton, Susan (Music Group)
Bob Doyle Assoc
713 18th Ave S
Nashville, TN 37203-3214, USA

Ashwell, Rachel (Business Person, Designer)
739 Superba Ave
Venice, CA 90291-3868, USA

Ashworth, Gerald (Gerry) (Athlete, Track Athlete)
PO Box 2
Ogunquit, ME 03907-0002, USA

Ashworth, Jeanne (Athlete, Olympic Athlete, Speed Skater)
92 Esther Vue Way
Wilmington, NY 12997-1918, USA

Ashworth, Landon (Actor)
c/o Staff Member *Snyder Management*
PO Box 5728
Beverly Hills, CA 90209-5728, USA

Ashworth, Thomas (Athlete, Football Player)
7329 S Xanthia Way
Centennial, CO 80112-1962, USA

Asia (Music Group)
%Michael Rosen
7715 W Sunset Blvd Fl 3
Los Angeles, CA 90046-3912, USA

Asian Dub Foundation (Music Group)
c/o Staff Member *Paradigm (Monterey)*
404 W Franklin St
Monterey, CA 93940-2303, USA

As I Lay Dying (Music Group, Musician)
c/o Staff Member *Strong Management*
17625 Union Tpke # 405
Fresh Meadows, NY 11366-1515, USA

Askea, Mike (Athlete, Football Player)
PO Box 2391
Ooltewah, TN 37363-2391, USA

Askea, Mike (Athlete, Football Player)
Front Gate Cir
Ooltewah, TN 37363, us

Askew, B J (Athlete, Football Player)
4216 Lantana Dr
Lebanon, OH 45036-4022, USA

Askew, Desmond (Actor)
c/o Staff Member *Envision Entertainment*
8840 Wilshire Blvd Fl 3
Beverly Hills, CA 90211-2606, USA

Askew, Matthias (Athlete, Football Player)
4100 SW 2nd St
Plantation, FL 33317-3722, us

Askew, Matthias (Athlete, Football Player)
220 Greenup St
Covington, KY 41011-1787, USA

Askey, Tom (Athlete, Hockey Player)
5732 S 6th St
Kalamazoo, MI 49009-9438, USA

Asking Alexandria (Music Group, Musician)
c/o Devin Timmons *The Artery Foundation*
PO Box 160451
Sacramento, CA 95816-0451, USA

Askson, Bert (Athlete, Football Player)
7713 Charlesmont St
Houston, TX 77016-3927, USA

Asleep At The Wheel (Music Group)
PO Box 463
Austin, TX 78767-0463, USA

Aslyn (Musician)
c/o Staff Member *Paradigm (Monterey)*
404 W Franklin St
Monterey, CA 93940-2303, USA

Asmonga, Don (Athlete, Basketball Player)
124 Naylor Dr
Belle Vernon, PA 15012-4729, USA

Asmussen, Cash (Horse Racer)
111 Devonshire Ct
Laredo, TX 78041-2659, USA

Asner, Ed (Actor)
11970 Montana Ave Apt 210
Los Angeles, CA 90049-6601, USA

Asner, Jules (Producer, Television Host)
c/o John Ferriter *Octagon Entertainment*
8687 Melrose Ave Ste 7
West Hollywood, CA 90069-5721, USA

Asomugha, Nnamdi (Athlete, Football Player)
22632 Felbar Ave
Torrance, CA 90505-2825, us

Asomugha, Nnamdi (Athlete, Football Player)
1050 Armitage St
Alameda, CA 94502-7931, USA

Aspen, Jennifer (Actor)
c/o Joel Stevens *Joel Stevens Entertainment*
5627 Allott Ave
Van Nuys, CA 91401-4502, USA

Aspromonte, Bob
Brooklyn Dodgers
1000 Uptown Park Blvd Apt 241
Houston, TX 77056-3243, USA

Aspromonte, Ken (Athlete, Baseball Player, Coach)
2 Derham Parc St
Houston, TX 77024-5200, USA

Assante, Armand (Actor)
c/o Michael Kaliski *Omniquest Entertainment (LA)*
1416 N La Brea Ave
Los Angeles, CA 90028-7506, USA

Assaraf, John (Writer)
PO Box 5020 PMB 1101
Rancho Santa Fe, CA 92067-5020, USA

Asselstine, Brian (Athlete, Baseball Player)
1488 Country Ct
Santa Ynez, CA 93460-9754, USA

Assenmacher, Paul (Athlete, Baseball Player)
500 Covington Cv
Alpharetta, GA 30022-5574, USA

Assuras, Thalia (Television Host)
c/o Staff Member *CBS News (NY)*
524 W 57th St Fl 8
New York, NY 10019-2930, USA

Astacio, Pedro (Athlete, Baseball Player)
123 Blue Heron Dr
Greenwood Village, CO 80121-2162, USA

Astaire, Robyn (Horse Racer)
1155 San Ysidro Dr
Beverly Hills, CA 90210-2102, USA

As Tall as Lions (Music Group)
c/o Staff Member *Paradigm (Monterey)*
404 W Franklin St
Monterey, CA 93940-2303, USA

Astanova, Lola (Musician)
c/o Gail Parenteau *Parenteau Guidance*
132 E 35th St # 3J
New York, NY 10016-3892, USA

Astin, John (Actor, Director)
3801 Canterbury Rd
Baltimore, MD 21218-2370, USA

Astin, Mackenzie (Actor)
c/o Staff Member *William Morris Endeavor (LA)*
9601 Wilshire Blvd
Beverly Hills, CA 90210-5213, USA

Astin, Sean (Actor, Director, Producer)
24935 Normans Way
Calabasas, CA 91302-3090, USA

Astin, Skylar (Actor)
c/o Mike Smith *Snax Memphis*
67 N Cox St
Memphis, TN 38104-6520, USA

Astroth, Joe (Athlete, Baseball Player)
6035 Verde Trl S Apt J310
Boca Raton, FL 33433-4435, USA

Asturaga, Nova (Government Official)
Permanent Mission of Nicaragua
820 2nd Ave Rm 801
New York, NY 10017-4556, USA

Asuma, Linda (Actor)
c/o JR Dibbs *Malaky International*
205 S Beverly Dr Ste 211
Beverly Hills, CA 90212-3893, USA

Atari Teenage Riot (Music Group)
c/o Staff Member *Girlie Action*
243 W 30th St Fl 12
New York, NY 10001-2812, USA

Atchison, Scott (Race Car Driver)
Day Enterprises Racing
1820 Barrington Dr
Keller, TX 76262-9004, USA

Atchley, Justin (Athlete, Baseball Player)
17958 Cove Ln
Mount Vernon, WA 98274-8126, USA

Aterciopelados (Musician)
c/o Staff Member *BMG*
1540 Broadway
New York, NY 10036-4039, USA

Atessis, Bill (Athlete, Football Player)
PO Box 616
Phoenix, AZ 85001-0616, USA

Atha, Dick (Athlete, Basketball Player)
PO Box 256
4E2 N Justus
Oxford, IN 47971-0256, USA

Atha, Richard (Athlete, Basketball Player)
PO Box 256
402 N. Justus
Oxford, IN 47971-0256, USA

Athas, Pete (Athlete, Football Player)
1539 Mayo St
Hollywood, FL 33020-6514, USA

Atherton, Keith (Athlete, Baseball Player)
1014 Cobbs Creek Ln
Cobbs Creek, VA 23035-2137, USA

Atherton, William (Actor)
5102 San Feliciano Dr
Woodland Hills, CA 91364-1624, USA

Athlete (Music Group)
c/o Staff Member *Paradigm (Monterey)*
404 W Franklin St
Monterey, CA 93940-2303, USA

Atias, Moran (Actor)
c/o Carolyn Govers *Anonymous Content (LA)*
3532 Hayden Ave
Culver City, CA 90232-2413, USA

Atkin, Harvey (Actor)
527 S Curson Ave
Los Angeles, CA 90036-3252, USA

Atkins, Bob (Athlete, Football Player)
15871 Misty Loch Ln
Houston, TX 77084-6795, USA

Atkins, Christopher (Actor)
6934 Bevis Ave
Van Nuys, CA 91405-3844, USA

Atkins, Dave (Athlete, Football Player)
737 W Wildwood Dr
Phoenix, AZ 85045-0632, USA

Atkins, Doug (Athlete, Football Player)
PO Box 14007
Knoxville, TN 37914-1007, us

Atkins, Doug (Athlete, Football Player)
5312 Sunset Rd
Knoxville, TN 37914-4304, USA

Atkins, Eileen (Actor, Writer)
c/o Staff Member *ICM Partners (LA)*
10250 Constellation Blvd Fl 7
Los Angeles, CA 90067-6207, USA

Atkins, Essence (Actor)
11030 Sunnybrae Ave
Chatsworth, CA 91311-1651, USA

Atkins, Garrett (Athlete, Baseball Player)
25201 Derbyhill Dr
Laguna Hills, CA 92653-5894, USA

Atkins, Gene (Athlete, Football Player)
3970 NW 84th Way
Pembroke Pines, FL 33024-5059, us

Atkins, Gene (Athlete, Football Player)
3515 Sunnyside Dr
Tallahassee, FL 32305-6964, USA

Atkins, Geno (Athlete, Football Player)
c/o Pat Dye Jr *SportsTrust Advisors (GA)*
3340 Peachtree Rd NE Fl 16
Atlanta, GA 30326-1000, USA

Atkins, George (Athlete, Football Player)
3445 Polo Downs
Hoover, AL 35226-3371, USA

Atkins, Kelvin (Athlete, Football Player)
4978 Timber Ridge Trl
Ocoee, FL 34761-8460, USA

Atkins, Kenneth ""Chucky"" (Athlete, Basketball Player)
7618 Colebrook Dr
Orlando, FL 32818-3317, USA

Atkins, Larry (Athlete, Football Player)
25982 Vista Dr E
Capistrano Beach, CA 92624-1226, USA

Atkins, Rodney (Musician)
751 Valhalla Ln
Brentwood, TN 37027-6414, USA

Atkins, Sharif (Actor)
c/o Christopher Wright *Christopher Wright Management*
3207 Winnie Dr
Los Angeles, CA 90068-1439, USA

Atkins, Tom (Actor)
Paradigm Agency
10100 Santa Monica Blvd Ste 2500
Los Angeles, CA 90067-4116, USA

Atkins, Veronica (Business Person)
100 Park Ave Rm 1600
New York, NY 10017-5538, USA

Atkinson, Al (Athlete, Football Player)
218 Wells Ln
Springfield, PA 19064-3038, USA

Atkinson, Frank (Athlete, Football Player)
PO Box 610
Menlo Park, CA 94026-0610, USA

Atkinson, George (Athlete, Football Player)
3570 Caldeira Dr
Livermore, CA 94550-6563, USA

Atkinson, Jayne (Actor)
Innovative Artists
1505 10th St
Santa Monica, CA 90401-2805, USA

Atkinson, Jess (Athlete, Football Player)
2913 Southaven Dr
Annapolis, MD 21401-7125, USA

Atkinson, Matthew (Actor)
c/o Theo Swerissen *Theo Swerissen Management*
Prefers to be contacted via telephone or email
Los Angeles, CA, USA

Atkinson, Ray N (Business Person)
Guy F Atkinson Co
1001 Bayhill Dr
San Bruno, CA 94066-3062, USA

Atkinson, Rick (Journalist)
Kansas City Times
1729 Grand Blvd
Attn Editorial Dept
Kansas City, MO 64108-1458, USA

Atkisson, Sharyl (Correspondent)
Cable News Network
News Dept 1051 Techwood Dr NW
Atlanta, GA 30318, USA

Atogwe, Oshiomogho (Athlete, Football Player)
43263 Parkers Ridge Dr
Leesburg, VA 20176-5108, us

A Tribe Called Quest (Music Group)
c/o Staff Member *The Agency Group (NYC)*
142 W 57th St Fl 6
New York, NY 10019-3300, USA

Attanasio, Paul (Producer, Writer)
236 Adelaide Dr
Santa Monica, CA 90402-1228, USA

Attardi, Michael (Athlete, Football Player)
11 Walada Ave
Port Monmouth, NJ 07758-1325, USA

Attell, Dave (Actor, Comedian, Producer)
500 W 43rd St Apt 35A
New York, NY 10036-4338, USA

Attlee, Frank III (Business Person)
Monsanto Co
800 N Lindbergh Blvd
Saint Louis, MO 63167-0001, USA

Attles, Al (Athlete, Basketball Player, Coach)
195 Villanova Dr
Oakland, CA 94611-1108, USA

Atwater, Stephen D (Steve) (Athlete, Football Player)
2424 Sapling Ridge Ln
Brookeville, MD 20833-1833, USA

Atwater Rhodes, Amelia (Writer)
c/o Staff Member *Random House Publicity*
1745 Broadway Frnt 3
New York, NY 10019-4343, USA

Atwell, Alfred (Astronaut)
3253 Ennis Ct
Las Vegas, NV 89121-5761, USA

Atwood, Casey (Race Car Driver)
Day Enterprises Racing
107 Flat Ridge Rd
Goodlettsville, TN 37072-8509, USA

Atwood, Margare (Writer)
c/o Ron Bernstein *ICM Partners (LA)*
10250 Constellation Blvd Fl 7
Los Angeles, CA 90067-6207, USA

Atwood, Susie (Sue) (Swimmer)
5624 E 2nd St
Long Beach, CA 90803-3904, USA

Auberjonois, Rene (Actor)
3629 Wonder View Dr
Los Angeles, CA 90068-1539, USA

Aubert, KD (Actor)
c/o Scott Karp *The Syndicate*
10203 Santa Monica Blvd Fl 5
Los Angeles, CA 90067-6416, USA

Aubin, Serge (Athlete, Hockey Player)
PO Box 105366
Atlanta, GA 30348-5366, USA

Aubrey, Emlyn (Athlete, Golfer)
2013 Surrey Ln
Bossier City, LA 71111-5534, USA

Aubrey, Michael (Athlete, Baseball Player)
9622 Gardere Dr
Shreveport, LA 71115-4602, USA

Aubuchon, Remi (Producer)
c/o Staff Member *United Talent Agency (UTA-LA)*
9336 Civic Center Dr
Beverly Hills, CA 90210-3604, USA

Auburn, David (Writer)
97 W Elmwood Ave
Clawson, MI 48017-1228, USA

Aucoin, Adrian (Athlete, Hockey Player)
421 N Grant St
Hinsdale, IL 60521-3339, USA

Aucoin, Derek (Athlete, Baseball Player)
233 W 77th St Apt 5E
New York, NY 10024-6809, USA

Aude, Rich (Athlete, Baseball Player)
4817 Natoma Ave
Woodland Hills, CA 91364-3416, USA

Audick, Daniel (Athlete, Football Player)
13253 Sparren Ave
San Diego, CA 92129-2324, USA

Auel, Jean M (Writer)
PO Box 8278
Portland, OR 97207-8278, USA

Auel, Jean Marie (Writer)
PO Box 8278
Portland, OR 97207-8278, USA

Auer, Joe (Athlete, Football Player)
1138 Washington Ave
Winter Park, FL 32789-5657, USA

Auer, Scott (Athlete, Football Player)
2921 Burge Dr
Crown Point, IN 46307-8172, USA

Auerbach, Dan (Musician)
2013 19th Ave S
Nashville, TN 37212-4305, USA

Auerbach, Rick (Athlete, Baseball Player)
2139 Stunt Rd
Calabasas, CA 91302-2358, USA

Auermann, Nadja (Model)
c/o Staff Member *DNA Model Management*
555 W 25th St Fl 6
New York, NY 10001-5542, USA

AufDerMaur, Melissa (Music Group, Musician)
Artist Group International
9560 Wilshire Blvd Ste 400
Beverly Hills, CA 90212-2442, USA

Auferio, Tony (Athlete, Baseball Player)
493 Indian Rd
Wayne, NJ 07470-4922, USA

Augenstein, Bryan (Athlete, Baseball Player)
179 Cili Rona St
Sebastian, FL 32958, USA

Auger, Brian (Music Group, Musician)
Earthtone
8306 Wilshire Blvd # 981
Beverly Hills, CA 90211-2304, USA

Aughtman, Dowe (Athlete, Football Player)
2 Buckhead Ln
Opelika, AL 36804-7645, USA

The Celebrity Black Book 2015

Augmon, Stacey (Athlete, Basketball Player)
2761 Josephine Dr
Henderson, NV 89044-0307, USA

August, Don (Athlete, Baseball Player, Olympic Athlete)
N88W17812 Christman Rd
Menomonee Falls, WI 53051-2630, USA

August, John (Director, Musician, Producer)
644 S June St
Los Angeles, CA 90005-3821, USA

August, Steve (Athlete, Football Player)
7704 E 86th St
Tulsa, OK 74133-6651, USA

Augusta, Kim (Athlete, Golfer)
16 Rachella Ct
East Providence, RI 02914-3063, USA

Augusta, Patrik (Athlete, Hockey Player)
c/o Staff Member *Phoenix Coyotes*
9400 W Maryland Ave
Glendale, AZ 85305-3114, USA

Augustain, Ira (Actor)
c/o Staff Member *Diamond Artists*
9200 W Sunset Blvd Ste 701
W Hollywood, CA 90069-3602, USA

Augustana (Musician)
c/o Staff Member *Paradigm (Monterey)*
404 W Franklin St
Monterey, CA 93940-2303, USA

Augustine, Dave (Athlete, Baseball Player)
PO Box 1114
Saint Albans, WV 25177-1114, USA

Augustine, Jerry (Athlete, Baseball Player)
S74W13490 Courtland Ln
Muskego, WI 53150-3937, USA

Augustine, Norman R (Business Person)
Review of U.S. Human Space Flight Plans Committee
300 E St SW
Nasa Headquarters
Washington, DC 20024-3210, USA

Augustnyiak, Jerry (Music Group, Musician)
Agency for Performing Arts
9200 W Sunset Blvd Ste 900
West Hollywood, CA 90069-3604, USA

Augustus, Seimone (Athlete, Basketball Player)
Matheny Sears Linkert & Long, LLP
3638 American River Dr
Sacramento, CA 95864-5901, USA

Augustus, Sherman (Actor)
c/o Steven Jensen *Independent Group, The*
6363 Wilshire Blvd Ste 115
Los Angeles, CA 90048-5734, USA

Augustyniak, Jerry (Musician)
c/o Staff Member *Agency for the Performing Arts (APA-LA)*
405 S Beverly Dr Ste 500
Beverly Hills, CA 90212-4425, USA

Augustyniak, Mike (Athlete, Football Player)
10540 Castlebrook Dr
Jacksonville, FL 32257-6478, USA

Augustyniak, Mike (Athlete, Football Player)
244 Sweetbrier Branch Ln
Saint Johns, FL 32259-4407, us

Aukerman, Scott (Actor, Comedian, Television Host)
c/o Christie Smith *Mosaic Media Group*
9200 W Sunset Blvd Ste 10
West Hollywood, CA 90069-3608, USA

Auktyon (Music Group, Musician)
c/o Staff Member *Skyline Music*
28 Union St
Whitefield, NH 03598-3503, USA

Aulby, Mike (Bowler)
1591 Springmill Ponds Cir
Carmel, IN 46032-8552, USA

Ault, Chris (Coach, Football Coach)
University of Nevada
Athletic Dept
Reno, NV 89557-0001, USA

Ault, James M (Religious Leader)
1 Amoskegan Dr
Brunswick, ME 04011-9524, USA

Aunon, Serena Dr (Astronaut)
2536 Goldeneye Ln
League City, TX 77573-6434, USA

Auriemma, Frank (Horse Racer)
21 Jacob Rd
Plainview, NY 11803-6462, USA

Auriemma, Geno (Athlete, Basketball Player, Coach)
180 Garth Rd
Manchester, CT 06040-5644, USA

Aurilia, Rich
4525 E Cheery Lynn Rd
Phoenix, AZ 85018-6448, USA

Aurilla, Rich (Athlete, Baseball Player)
4525 E Cheery Lynn Rd
Phoenix, AZ 85018-6448, USA

Ausanio, Joe (Athlete, Baseball Player)
PO Box 213
Marlboro, NY 12542-0213, USA

Ausbie, Hubert (Athlete, Basketball Player)
902 Arthur Dr
Little Rock, AR 72204-1524, USA

Ausmus, Brad (Athlete, Baseball Player)
1644 Stratford Way
Del Mar, CA 92014-2444, USA

Ausoin, Derek (Athlete, Baseball Player)
233 W 77th St Apt 5E
New York, NY 10024-6809, USA

Aust, Dennis (Athlete, Baseball Player)
16252 Estuary Ct
Bokeelia, FL 33922-1535, USA

Auster, Paul (Director, Writer)
c/o Ron Bernstein *ICM Partners (LA)*
10250 Constellation Blvd Fl 7
Los Angeles, CA 90067-6207, USA

Austin, Alana (Actor)
c/o Lena Roklin *Luber Roklin Management*
5815 W Sunset Blvd Ste 206
Los Angeles, CA 90028-6481, USA

Austin, A Woody (Athlete, Golfer)
10906 W Havenhurst St
Maize, KS 67101-3712, USA

Austin, Billy (Athlete, Football Player)
12723 Timbermeadow Dr
Houston, TX 77070-4754, us

Austin, Charles (Athlete, Olympic Athlete, Track Athlete)
514 Duncan Dr
San Marcos, TX 78666-4900, USA

Austin, Cliff (Athlete, Football Player)
5410 Maltdie Ct
Sugar Hill, GA 30518-5964, us

Austin, Cliff (Athlete, Football Player)
1652 Valencia Rd
Decatur, GA 30032-5263, USA

Austin, Coco (Model, Reality Star)
8125 River Rd Apt 6B
North Bergen, NJ 07047-7202, USA

Austin, Dallas (Musician, Producer, Songwriter)
5335 Northside Dr
Atlanta, GA 30327-4252, USA

Austin, Darlene (Musician, Songwriter)
PO Box 171143
Nashville, TN 37217-8143, USA

Austin, Darrell (Athlete, Football Player)
720A S Duncan Byp
Union, SC 29379-7830, us

Austin, Darrell (Athlete, Football Player)
268 Austin Rd
Union, SC 29379-7658, USA

Austin, Debbie (Athlete, Golfer)
6733 Bittersweet Ln
Orlando, FL 32819-4635, USA

Austin, Denise (Fitness Expert)
PrimeCare Systems, Inc
PO Box 796
Fairfax, VA 22038-0796, USA

Austin, Hise (Athlete, Football Player)
53 N Deerfoot Cir
Spring, TX 77380-1523, USA

Austin, Ike (Athlete, Basketball Player)
1448 S Roberta St
Salt Lake City, UT 84115-1619, USA

Austin, Isaac (Athlete, Basketball Player)
2451 Brickell Ave Apt 15J
Miami, FL 33129-2421, USA

Austin, Jake (Actor)
c/o Ryan Bartlett *Paradigm (LA)*
360 N Crescent Dr
North Bldg
Beverly Hills, CA 90210-4874, USA

Austin, Jeff (Athlete, Baseball Player)
1723 Milton St
Redwood City, CA 94061-3419, USA

Austin, Jeff (Musician)
c/o Staff Member *Paradigm (Monterey)*
404 W Franklin St
Monterey, CA 93940-2303, USA

Austin, Jim (Athlete, Baseball Player)
20974 Rootstown Ter
Ashburn, VA 20147-4839, USA

Austin, John (Athlete, Basketball Player)
1330 Riggs St NW
Washington, DC 20009-4325, USA

Austin, Johnny (Athlete, Basketball Player)
1330 Riggs St NW
Washington, DC 20009-4325, USA

Austin, Kent (Athlete, Football Player)
704 Legends Crest Dr
Franklin, TN 37069-4659, USA

Austin, Marvin (Athlete, Football Player)
c/o Peter Schaffer *All Pro Sports and Entertainment*
36 Steele St Ste 100
Denver, CO 80206-5709, USA

Austin, Miles (Athlete, Football Player)
c/o David Dunn *Athletes First, LLC*
23091 Mill Creek Dr
Laguna Hills, CA 92653-1258, USA

Austin, Ocie (Athlete, Football Player)
750 MacArthur Blvd Apt 301
Oakland, CA 94610-3702, USA

Austin, Pat (Race Car Driver)
14823 47th Ave E
Tacoma, WA 98446-4033, USA

Austin, Patti (Music Group)
3 Loudon Dr Unit 8
Fishkill, NY 12524-1870, USA

Austin, Reggie (Athlete, Football Player)
3339 Deerwood Ln
Rex, GA 30273-2475, USA

Austin, Rick (Athlete, Baseball Player)
8107 Forest Parks Dr
Kansas City, MO 64152-3172, USA

Austin, Scott (Race Car Driver)
Meads Creek Rd
Painted Post, NY 14870, USA

Austin, Sherrie (Musician)
Splash Publications
1520 16th Ave S Unit 2
Nashville, TN 37212-2938, USA

Austin, Steve (Stone Cold) (Athlete, Wrestler)
906 Howard St
Marina Del Rey, CA 90292-5519, USA

Austin, Teri (Actor)
4245 Laurelgrove Ave
Studio City, CA 91604-1624, USA

Austin, Thea (Musician)
c/o Stephen Ford *Diva Central Inc*
7510 W Sunset Blvd Ste 1445
Los Angeles, CA 90046-3408, USA

Austin, Thomas (Athlete, Football Player)
500 Almer Rd Apt 306
Burlingame, CA 94010-3966, USA

Austin, Tracy (Athlete, Tennis Player)
5 Williamsburg Ln
Rolling Hills, CA 90274-4056, USA

Austin, Walt (Race Car Driver)
Pro/Max Performance
5602 S Tacoma Way
Tacoma, WA 98409-4216, USA

Austin-Antelline, Charlotte (Actor)
3053 Valevista Trl
Los Angeles, CA 90068-1724, USA

Austin Jr, M P (Business Person)
BMC Software
2101 Citywest Blvd
Houston, TX 77042-2828, USA

Auston, Jim (Musician)
c/o Staff Member *Curb Records (Nashville)*
48 Music Sq E
Nashville, TN 37203-4639, USA

Austria, Steve (Congressman, Politician)
439 Cannon Hob
Washington, DC 20515-2801, USA

Autrey, Billy (Athlete, Football Player)
303 Ranch Gate
Mc Gregor, TX 76657-3979, USA

Autry, Al
3108 Lennox Dr
El Dorado Hills, CA 95762-5662, USA

Autry, Alan (Actor)
c/o Staff Member *David Shapira & Associates*
193 N Robertson Blvd
Beverly Hills, CA 90211-2103, USA

Autry, Albert (Al) (Athlete, Baseball Player)
3108 Lennox Dr
El Dorado Hills, CA 95762-5662, USA

Autry, Jim (Golfer, Misc)
Professional Golfer's Assn
PO Box 109601
Palm Beach Gardens, FL 33410-9601, USA

Auyeung, Jin (Musician)
c/o Staff Member *Virgin Records (NY)*
150 5th Ave Fl 7
New York, NY 10011-4372, USA

Auzenne, Troy (Athlete, Football Player)
1501 Bluff Ct
Diamond Bar, CA 91765-4301, USA

Auzenne, Troy (Athlete, Football Player)
118 Oak Rd
Orinda, CA 94563-3348, us

Avala, Benny (Athlete, Baseball Player)
PO Box 222
Dorado, PR 00646-0222, USA

Avalon (Music Group)
PO Box 150867
Nashville, TN 37215-0867, USA

Avalon, Frankie (Actor, Musician)
4303 Spring Forest Ln
Westlake Village, CA 91362-5605, USA

Avant, Jason (Athlete, Football Player)
12136 S State St
Chicago, IL 60628-6629, USA

Avant, Jason (Athlete, Football Player)
c/o Doug Hendrickson *Octagon Football*
832 Sansome St Fl 1
San Francisco, CA 94111-1558, USA

Avants, Nick (Athlete, Baseball Player)
2901 Aldersgate Rd Apt 202
Little Rock, AR 72205-7096, USA

Avari, Erick (Actor)
c/o Michael Greene *Greene & Associates*
1901 Avenue of the Stars Ste 130
Los Angeles, CA 90067-6030, USA

Avary, Roger (Director)
c/o Brian Siberell *Creative Artists Agency (CAA-LA)*
2000 Avenue of the Stars Ste 100
Los Angeles, CA 90067-4705, USA

Avdelsayed, Gabriel (Religious Leader)
Coptic Orthodox Curch
427 W Side Ave
Jersey City, NJ 07304-1403, USA

Avedon, Gregg (Model)
c/o Sid Craig *Craig Management*
125 S Sycamore Ave
Los Angeles, CA 90036-2938, USA

Avellan, Elizabeth (Producer)
c/o Staff Member *ICM Partners (LA)*
10250 Constellation Blvd Fl 7
Los Angeles, CA 90067-6207, USA

Avellini, Bob (Athlete, Football Player)
1085 Flamingo Dr
Roselle, IL 60172-4731, USA

Aven, Bruce (Athlete, Baseball Player)
4223 SW 141st Ave
Davie, FL 33330-5724, USA

Avenged Sevenfold (Music Group)
c/o Brian Bumbery *BB Gun Press*
9229 W Sunset Blvd Ste 305
West Hollywood, CA 90069-3403, USA

Avent, Anthony (Athlete, Basketball Player)
1166 Croton Rd
Flemington, NJ 08822-5607, USA

Averell, Tom (Athlete, Football Player)
100 Highland Pines Ct Apt 32
Pittsburgh, PA 15237-2038, USA

Averill Jr., Earl (Athlete, Baseball Player)
1806 19th Sr NE
Auburn, WA 98002, USA

Averitt, William (Athlete, Basketball Player)
PO Box 802
Hopkinsville, KY 42241-0802, USA

Averre, Berton (Music Group, Musician)
17510 Posetano Rd
Pacific Palisades, CA 90272-4175, USA

Avery, Eric (Actor, Musician)
c/o Jeff Frasco *Creative Artists Agency (CAA-LA)*
2000 Avenue of the Stars Ste 100
Los Angeles, CA 90067-4705, USA

Avery, John (Athlete, Football Player)
204 Peacock Ln
Arden, NC 28704-6101, us

Avery, John (Athlete, Football Player)
12 Ballantree Dr
Asheville, NC 28803-2018, USA

Avery, Ken (Athlete, Football Player)
625 Indian Ridge Dr
Nashville, TN 37221-4035, USA

Avery, Margaret (Actor)
2807 Pelham Pl
Los Angeles, CA 90068-2328, USA

Avery, Rick (Actor)
4 Blades Inc
11991 Wood Ranch Rd
Granada Hills, CA 91344-2144, USA

Avery, Shondrella (Actor)
c/o Vincent Cirrincione *Vincent Cirrincione Associates*
1516 N Fairfax Ave
Los Angeles, CA 90046-2608, USA

Avery, Steve (Athlete, Baseball Player)
2 Gleneagles Ct
Dearborn, MI 48120-1165, USA

Avery, Tom (Athlete, Mountaineer)
c/o Staff Member *William Morris Endeavor (LA)*
9601 Wilshire Blvd
Beverly Hills, CA 90210-5213, USA

Avery, Val (Actor)
84 Grove St Apt 19
New York, NY 10014-3567, USA

Avery, William J (Business Person)
Crown Cork & Seal
1 Crown Way
Philadelphia, PA 19154-4599, USA

Aviance, Kevin (Musician)
Kevin Aviance World
115 E 57th St Fl 11
New York, NY 10022-2120, USA

Avicii (DJ, Musician)
1474 Blue Jay Way
Los Angeles, CA 90069-1213, USA

Avila, Alex (Athlete, Baseball Player)
2941 SW 155th Ln
Davie, FL 33331-1527, USA

Avildsen, John (Director)
2423 Briarcrest Rd
Beverly Hills, CA 90210-1819, USA

Aviles, Ramon (Athlete, Baseball Player)
C19 Calle Juan Morell Campos
Jard De Monaco 1
Manati, PR 00674-6618, USA

Avinger, Clarence (Athlete, Football Player)
2021 Chardonnay Way
Birmingham, AL 35216-1650, USA

Avital, Mili (Actor)
c/o Craig Shapiro *ICM Partners (LA)*
10250 Constellation Blvd Fl 7
Los Angeles, CA 90067-6207, USA

Aviva (Actor)
4455 Los Feliz Blvd Apt 604
Los Angeles, CA 90027-2138, USA

Avnet, Jon (Director, Producer)
20911/20929 Colina Dr
Topanga, CA 90290, USA

Avni, Aki
c/o Staff Member *Marshak/Zachary Company, The*
8840 Wilshire Blvd Fl 1
Beverly Hills, CA 90211-2606, USA

Awalt, Rob (Athlete, Football Player)
5011 Highgrove Ct
Granite Bay, CA 95746-7101, USA

Awasom, Adrian (Athlete, Football Player)
12330 Grove Meadow Dr
Stafford, TX 77477-2204, USA

Awasom, Adrian (Athlete, Football Player)
5011 Highgrove Ct
Stafford, TX 77477, us

Awrey, Donald W (Don) (Athlete, Hockey Player)
1015 Alaska Ave
Lehigh Acres, FL 33971-6447, USA

Awtrey, Dennis (Athlete, Basketball Player)
3823E James Rd
Nehalem, OR 97131, USA

Axelrod, Jack (Actor)
c/o Jennifer Lee Garland *Circle Talent Associates*
433 N Camden Dr Ste 400
Beverly Hills, CA 90210-4408, USA

Axelsson, PJ (Athlete, Hockey Player)
121 Mount Vernon St
Boston, MA 02108-1104, USA

Axelsson, P. J. (Athlete, Hockey Player)
50 Fleet St Ste 301
Boston, MA 02109-1129, USA

Axley, Eric (Athlete, Golfer)
4708 Calumet Dr
Knoxville, TN 37919-7617, USA

Axum, Donna (Beauty Pageant Winner)
6312 Indian Creek Dr
Fort Worth, TX 76116-1610, USA

Ayala, Bobby (Athlete, Baseball Player)
11011 W Cottonwood Ln
Avondale, AZ 85392-4324, USA

Ayala, Paul (Boxer)
7524 Creek Meadow Dr
Fort Worth, TX 76123-1980, USA

Ayanbadejo, Brendon (Athlete, Football Player)
1111 E Sunrise Blvd Unit 103
Fort Lauderdale, FL 33304-2857, USA

Ayanbadejo, Obafemi (Athlete, Football Player)
707 President St Apt 438
Baltimore, MD 21202-4477, USA

Ayanna, Charlotte (Actor)
Industry Entertainment
955 Carrillo Dr Ste 300
Los Angeles, CA 90048-5400, USA

Aybar, Erick (Athlete, Baseball Player)
1636 Orchard Dr Apt C
Placentia, CA 92870-5455, USA

Aybar, Manny (Athlete)
401 E Jefferson St
Phoenix, AZ 85004-2438

Aybar, Manuel (Athlete, Baseball Player)
3020 SW 189th Ter
Miramar, FL 33029-5861, USA

Aycock, H David (Business Person)
Nucor Corp
2100 Rexford Rd
Charlotte, NC 28211-3589, USA

Aycox, Nicki (Actor)
c/o Jeb Brandon *Kritzer Levine Wilkins Entertainment (KLWG)*
11872 La Grange Ave Fl 1
Los Angeles, CA 90025-5283, USA

Aydelette, William (Athlete, Football Player)
7988 Wynwood Rd
Trussville, AL 35173-2270, USA

Ayer, David (Producer, Writer)
Crave Films
3312 W Sunset Blvd
Los Angeles, CA 90026-2118, USA

Ayers, Chuck (Cartoonist)
c/o Staff Member *King Features Syndication*
300 W 57th St Fl 15
New York, NY 10019-5238, USA

Ayers, Dick (Cartoonist)
64 Beech St W
White Plains, NY 10604-2230, USA

Ayers, Randy (Athlete, Basketball Player, Coach)
Philadelphia 76ers
1st Union Center 3601 South Broad St
Philadelphia, PA 19148, USA

Ayers, Roy E Jr (Music Group, Musician)
Roy Ayers Ubiquity Inc
209 W 97th St Apt 4D
New York, NY 10025-5602, USA

Ayers, Sam (Actor)
c/o Staff Member *Bobby Ball Talent Agency*
3500 W Olive Ave Ste 300
Burbank, CA 91505-4647, USA

Aykroyd, Dan (Actor, Comedian)
851 Paseo Miramar
Pacific Palisades, CA 90272-3028, USA

Aylesworth, Reiko (Actor)
c/o Staff Member *Innovative Artists (LA)*
1505 10th St
Santa Monica, CA 90401-2805, USA

Aylward, John (Actor)
c/o Staff Member *Mitchell K Stubbs & Assoc (MKS)*
8675 Washington Blvd Ste 203
Culver City, CA 90232-7486, USA

Ayodele, Akin (Athlete, Football Player)
7105 David Ln
Colleyville, TX 76034-6664, USA

Ayotte, Kelly (Senator)
188 Russell Senate Office Building
Washington, DC 20510-0001, USA

Ayrault, Bob (Athlete, Baseball Player)
3012 Green Dr
Carson City, NV 89701-3363, USA

Ayrault, Joe (Athlete, Baseball Player)
PO Box 6756
Attn: Managers Office
Helena, MT 59604-6756, USA

Ayres, Travis (Race Car Driver)
Ayres Motorsports
1186 Buckwheat Rd
Granville Summit, PA 16926-9364, USA

Ayres Kalish, Leah (Actor)
15718 Milbank St
Encino, CA 91436-1637, USA

Aytes, Rochelle (Actor)
c/o Ryan Daly *Zero Gravity Management*
1531 14th St
Santa Monica, CA 90404-3302, USA

Azar, Steve (Music Group)
PO Box 4613
Greenville, MS 38704-4613, USA

Azarenka, Victoria (Athlete, Tennis Player)
725 12th St
Manhattan Beach, CA 90266-4829, USA

Azaria, Hank (Actor)
8950 W Olympic Blvd Ste 402
Beverly Hills, CA 90211-3565, USA

Azcue, Jose (Joe) (Athlete, Baseball Player)
7609 W 115th St
Overland Park, KS 66210-2614, USA

Azelby, Joe (Athlete, Football Player)
14 Pierce Ave
Cresskill, NJ 07626-1126, USA

Azinger, Paul (Athlete, Golfer)
8910 21st Ave NW
Bradenton, FL 34209-9414, USA

Azizi, Anthony (Actor)
c/o Karen Embry *Sky Unlimited Arts*
7510 W Sunset Blvd # 554
Los Angeles, CA 90046-3408, USA

Azlynn, Valerie (Actor)
c/o Devon Jackson *Trademark Talent*
144 S Beverly Dr Ste 404
Beverly Hills, CA 90212-3022, USA

Azoff, Irving (Business Person)
10224 Charing Cross Rd
Los Angeles, CA 90024-1815, USA

Azria, Max (Designer, Fashion Designer)
2761 Fruitland Ave
Vernon, CA 90058-3607, USA

Azul Azul (Music Group)
c/o Staff Member *Sony Music Miami*
605 Lincoln Rd Ste 700
Miami Beach, FL 33139-2901, USA

Azumah, Jerry (Athlete, Football Player)
462 W Superior St
Chicago, IL 60654-3497, USA

Azzaro, Chrissy (Designer, Fashion Designer)
c/o Staff Member *Perception Public Relations LLC*
3940 Laurel Canyon Blvd Ste 169
Studio City, CA 91604-3709, USA

Azzi, Jennifer (Athlete, Basketball Player, Olympic Athlete)
144 S 3rd St Unit 241
San Jose, CA 95112-6503, USA

B

B, Jon (Musician, Songwriter, Writer)
Devour Mgmt
6399 Wilshire Blvd Ste 426
Los Angeles, CA 90048-5714, USA

B, Sandy (Musician)
c/o Stephen Ford *Diva Central Inc*
7510 W Sunset Blvd Ste 1445
Los Angeles, CA 90046-3408, USA

B2K (Music Group)
c/o Staff Member *Pyramid Entertainment Group*
377 Rector Pl Apt 21A
New York, NY 10280-1439, USA

B-52's, The (Music Group)
c/o Staff Member *Astralwerks Records*
150 5th Ave Fl 4
New York, NY 10011-4346, USA

Baab, Mike (Athlete, Football Player)
411 Westover Dr
Euless, TX 76039-2039, us

Baab, Mike (Athlete, Football Player)
1705 Windlea Dr
Euless, TX 76040-4016, USA

Baack, Steve (Athlete, Football Player)
14370 SW Wilson Dr
Beaverton, OR 97008-6139, us

Baack, Steve (Athlete, Football Player)
12322 SW Autumn View St
Portland, OR 97224-2581, USA

Baas, David (Athlete, Football Player)
7004 Lacantera Cir
Lakewood Ranch, FL 34202-5116, us

Babashoff, Jack (Athlete, Olympic Athlete, Swimmer)
17254 Santa Clara St
Fountain Valley, CA 92708-3337, USA

Babashoff, Shirley (Athlete, Olympic Athlete, Swimmer)
17254 Santa Clara St
Fountain Valley, CA 92708-3337, USA

Babatunde, Obba (Actor)
Stone Manners
6500 Wilshire Blvd # 550
Los Angeles, CA 90048-4920, USA

Babb, Charlie (Athlete, Football Player)
371 Heron Ave
Naples, FL 34108-2115, USA

Babb, Eugene (Gene) (Athlete, Football Player)
5110 W 9th Ave
Stillwater, OK 74074-1465, USA

Babbit, Jamie (Director, Producer, Writer)
c/o Staff Member *Innovative Artists (LA)*
1505 10th St
Santa Monica, CA 90401-2805, USA

Babbitt, Bruce E (Politician)
5169 Watson St NW
Washington, DC 20016-5330, USA

Babbs, Durrell (Tank) (Musician)
c/o Amy Malone *GIC Public Relations*
Prefers to be contacted via email or telephone
West Hollywood, CA 90069, USA

Babb-Sprague, Kristen (Swimmer)
4677 Pine Valley Cir
Stockton, CA 95219-1881, USA

Babcock, Barbara (Actor)
PO Box 222271
Carmel, CA 93922-2271, USA

Babcock, Bob (Athlete, Baseball Player)
7123 Fairway Dr
Butler, PA 16001-8597, USA

Babcock, Mike (Athlete, Coach, Hockey Player)
c/o Staff Member *Detroit Red Wings*
600 Civic Center Dr
Joe Luis Arena
Detroit, MI 48226-4419, USA

Babcock, Tim M (Politician)
Ox Bow Ranch
PO Box 877
Helena, MT 59624-0877, USA

Babcock, Todd (Actor)
c/o Staff Member *Gage Group, The (LA)*
5757 Wilshire Blvd Ste 659
Los Angeles, CA 90036-3682, USA

Babenco, Hector E (Director)
c/o Johnnie Planco *Parseghian Planco LLC*
388 2nd Ave
New York, NY 10010-5616, USA

Baber, Billy (Athlete, Football Player)
12001 W 160th Pl
Overland Park, KS 66062-7980, USA

Babers, Roderick (Athlete, Football Player)
11838 Murr Way
Houston, TX 77048-2528, USA

Babic, Milos (Athlete, Basketball Player)
1500 Doris Dr
Cookeville, TN 38501-2026, USA

Babich, Bob (Athlete, Football Player)
4994 Mount Ashmun Dr
San Diego, CA 92111-3930, USA

Babilonia, Tai (Athlete, Figure Skater, Olympic Athlete)
13889 Valley Vista Blvd
Sherman Oaks, CA 91423-4662, USA

Babin, Jason (Athlete, Football Player)
2735 Peninsulas Dr
Missouri City, TX 77459-4317, USA

Babin, Mitch (Athlete, Hockey Player)
519 Pleasant St Apt 306
Leominster, MA 01453-6219, USA

Babineaux, Jonathan (Athlete, Football Player)
2362 Strand Ave
Lawrenceville, GA 30043-8199, USA

Babineaux, Jordan (Athlete, Football Player)
801 Dewalt Ave
Port Arthur, TX 77640-4814, USA

Babinecz, John (Athlete, Football Player)
810 Trout Run Dr
Malvern, PA 19355-3148, USA

Babitt, Shooty (Athlete, Baseball Player)
4912 Plaza Way
Richmond, CA 94804-4346, USA

Baby, Peggy (Actor)
2219 Canyon Brook Ln
Newman, CA 95360-2407, USA

Baca, Jason Aaron (Race Car Driver)
20770 Wildwood Way Apt 4
Saratoga, CA 95070-5898, USA

Baca, Jimmy Santiago (Writer)
c/o Staff Member *Blue Flower Arts*
PO Box 1361
Millbrook, NY 12545-1361, USA

Baca, Joe (Congressman, Politician)
2366 Rayburn Hob
Washington, DC 20515-3509, USA

Bacashihua, Jason (Athlete, Hockey Player)
23411 Annapolis St
Dearborn Heights, MI 48125-2200, USA

Baccaglio, Marty (Athlete, Football Player)
15030 Montebello Rd
Cupertino, CA 95014-5470, USA

Baccarin, Morena (Actor)
c/o Sarah Jackson *Seven Summits Pictures & Management*
8906 W Olympic Blvd
Ground Floor
Beverly Hills, CA 90211-3550, USA

Bach, Barbara (Actor)
918 N Hillcrest Rd
Beverly Hills, CA 90210-2611, USA

Bach, Catherine (Actor)
15930 Woodvale Rd
Encino, CA 91436-3445, USA

Bach, David (Writer)
c/o John Ferriter *Octagon Entertainment*
8687 Melrose Ave Ste 7
West Hollywood, CA 90069-5721, USA

Bach, Jillian (Actor)
c/o Staff Member *Metropolitan (MTA)*
4526 Wilshire Blvd
Los Angeles, CA 90010-3801, USA

Bach, John (Athlete, Basketball Player)
182 W Lake St Apt 21E6
Chicago, IL 60601-1049, USA

Bach, Pamela (Actor)
c/o Nelson Parks *ESI Network*
6310 San Vicente Blvd Ste 340
Los Angeles, CA 90048-5499, United States

Bach, Richard (Writer)
Dell Publishing
1540 Broadway
New York, NY 10036-4039, USA

Bach, Sebastian (Actor, Music Group)
99 Swimming River Rd
Lincroft, NJ 07738-1735, USA

Bachar, Carmit (Musician)
5778 Bucknell Ave
Valley Village, CA 91607-1302, USA

Bacharach, Burt (Musician)
681 Amalfi Dr
Pacific Palisades, CA 90272-4507, USA

Bachardy, Don (Writer)
145 Adelaide Dr
Santa Monica, CA 90402-1223, USA

Bachchan, Aisawarya Rai (Actor)
c/o Rick Genow *Stone, Meyer, Genow, Smelkinson and Binder*
9665 Wilshire Blvd Ste 500
Beverly Hills, CA 90212-2312, USA

Bachelart, Eric (Race Car Driver)
7326 W 88th St
Indianapolis, IN 46278-1106, USA

Bachelor, Andrew (Actor, Internet Star, Musician)
c/o Allan Haldeman *United Talent Agency (UTA-LA)*
9336 Civic Center Dr
Beverly Hills, CA 90210-3604, USA

Bachleda-Curus, Alicja (Actor)
2966 Passmore Dr
Los Angeles, CA 90068-1717, USA

Bachman, Jay (Athlete, Football Player)
4602 Delphene Cir
Louisville, KY 40241-6109, USA

Bachman, Michelle (Congressman, Politician)
103 Cannon Hob
Washington, DC 20515-2303, USA

Bachman, Randy (Music Group, Songwriter, Writer)
Entertainment Services
6400 Pleasant Park Dr
Chanhassen, MN 55317-8804, USA

Bachman, Tal (Music Group, Musician, Songwriter, Writer)
Q Prime
729 7th Ave Ste 1600
New York, NY 10019-6880, USA

Bachman, Ted (Athlete, Football Player)
2890 Huntington Blvd Apt 110
Fresno, CA 93721-2346, USA

Bachmann, Michele (Congressman, Politician)
412 Cannon Hob
Washington, DC 20515-2509, USA

Bachus, Spencer (Congressman, Politician)
2246 Rayburn Hob
Washington, DC 20515-3224, USA

Bacic, Steve (Actor, Producer)
c/o Staff Member *Pipeline Productions*
25715 Haskell St
Taylor, MI 48180-2076, USA

Backe, Brandon (Athlete, Baseball Player)
2116 Eastland Ct
League City, TX 77573-4980, USA

Backe, John D (Business Person)
Backe Group
83 General Warren Blvd Ste 100
Malvern, PA 19355-1252, USA

Backer, Brian (Actor)
400 E 56th St Apt 17E
New York, NY 10022-4339, USA

Backes, David (Athlete, Hockey Player)
323 N Forsyth Blvd
Saint Louis, MO 63105-3617, USA

Backhaus, Robin (Athlete, Olympic Athlete, Swimmer)
PO Box 6271
Ocean View, HI 96737-6271, USA

Backlund, Bob (Athlete, Wrestler)
PO Box 973
Glastonbury, CT 06033-0973

Backman, Mike (Athlete, Hockey Player)
50 Pond Pl
Cos Cob, CT 06807-2220, USA

Backman, Wally (Athlete, Baseball Player)
PO Box 598
Attn: Managers Office
Binghamton, NY 13902-0598, USA

Backman, Walter W (Wally) (Athlete, Baseball Player)
241 SE Mercury Ln
Prineville, OR 97754-2803, USA

Backstreet Boys (Music Group)
c/o Johnny Wright *Wright Entertainment Group*
PO Box 590009
Orlando, FL 32859-0009, USA

Backstrom, Niklas (Athlete, Hockey Player)
4908 E Sunnyslope Rd
Minneapolis, MN 55424-1165, USA

Backstrom, Ralph (Athlete, Hockey Player)
220 Habitat Cir
Windsor, CO 80550-6196, USA

Backus, Billy (Boxer)
308 N Main St
Canastota, NY 13032-1070, USA

Backus, Gus (Musician)
Lustig Talent
PO Box 770850
Orlando, FL 32877-0850, USA

Backus, Jeff (Athlete, Football Player)
48075 Bellagio Ct
Northville, MI 48167-9808, USA

Backus, Sharon (Coach)
University of California
Athletic Dept
Los Angeles, CA 90024, USA

Bacon, Henry (Athlete, Basketball Player)
10103 Grand Ave Apt 218
Louisville, KY 40299-3145, USA

Bacon, Kelvin (Actor)
PO Box 668
Sharon, CT 06069-0668, USA

Bacon, Kevin (Actor)
2800 Glendower Ave
Los Angeles, CA 90027-1119, USA

Bacon, Michael (Actor)
12 Garnet Rd
Roxbury, CT 06783-2033, USA

Bacon, Waine (Athlete, Football Player)
2900 McFarland Blvd E
Apt 516
Tuscaloosa, AL 35405, USA

Bacon Brothers, The (Music Group)
c/o Staff Member *Paradigm (Monterey)*
404 W Franklin St
Monterey, CA 93940-2303, USA

Bacsik, Mike (Athlete, Baseball Player)
709 Haines Ave
Dallas, TX 75208-4032, USA

Bacsik, Mike (Athlete, Baseball Player)
4014 Falcon Lake Dr
Arlington, TX 76016-4126, USA

Badalucco, Michael (Actor)
516 Highland Ave # 1A
Manhattan Beach, CA 90266-5747, USA

Badar, Rich (Athlete, Football Player)
10380 Saint Andrews Ct
Newburgh, IN 47630-1029, USA

Bad Brains (Music Group)
c/o Jeremy Holgersen *The Agency Group (NYC)*
142 W 57th St Fl 6
New York, NY 10019-3300, USA

Bad Company (Music Group)
c/o Kirt Webster *Webster & Associates PR*
3573 Couchville Pike
Hermitage, TN 37076-4012, USA

Baddeley, Aaron (Athlete, Golfer)
8606 E Via Del Sol Dr
Scottsdale, AZ 85255-5253, USA

Bade, Lance (Athlete, Olympic Athlete, Shooter)
9491 Berrey Ln
Colorado Springs, CO 80925-1320, USA

Badelt, Klaus (Musician)
c/o John Tempereau *Soundtrack Music Assoc*
1460 4th St Ste 308
Santa Monica, CA 90401-3483, USA

Badenhop, Burke (Athlete, Baseball Player)
1421 Rivercrest Dr
Perrysburg, OH 43551-1095, USA

Bader, Beth (Athlete, Golfer)
713 S 7th St
Eldridge, IA 52748-1537, USA

Bader, Diedrich (Actor)
131 N June St
Los Angeles, CA 90004-1039, USA

Baderinwa, Sade (Correspondent)
WABC-TV
7 Lincoln Sq
New York, NY 10023-7219, USA

Badger, Brad (Athlete, Football Player)
2552 Milleford Ct
Pleasanton, CA 94588, USA

Badgley, Mark (Fashion Designer)
c/o Staff Member *Badgley Mischka*
550 Fashion Ave Fl 22
New York, NY 10018-3223, USA

Badgley, Penn (Actor)
c/o Doug Wald *Anonymous Content (LA)*
3532 Hayden Ave
Culver City, CA 90232-2413, USA

Badham, John (Director)
Badham Company
344 Clerendon Rd
Beverly Hills, CA 90210, USA

Badham, Mary (Actor)
3720 Whitehall Rd
Sandy Hook, VA 23153-2204, USA

Badie, Mina (Actor)
c/o Staff Member *Rugolo Entertainment*
195 S Beverly Dr Ste 400
Beverly Hills, CA 90212-3044, USA

Badillo, Herman (Politician)
200 E 72nd St Apt 8K
New York, NY 10021-4539, USA

Badly Drawn Boy (Music Group)
c/o Staff Member *Paradigm (Monterey)*
404 W Franklin St
Monterey, CA 93940-2303, USA

Badnarik, Michael (Politician)
Badnarik Campaign Headquarters
6633 E Highway 290
Austin, TX 78723-1172, USA

Badu, Erykah (Musician, Songwriter)
Badu World, Inc.
PO Box 25092
Arlington, VA 22202-8992, USA

Bae, Doona (Actor)
c/o David Wirtschafter *William Morris Endeavor (LA)*
9601 Wilshire Blvd Fl 3
Beverly Hills, CA 90210-5219, USA

Baechtold, James (Jim) (Athlete, Basketball Player)
225 W Irvine St Ste 7
Richmond, KY 40475-2702, USA

Baeling, Becky (Musician)
c/o Staff Member *Diva Central Inc*
7510 W Sunset Blvd Ste 1445
Los Angeles, CA 90046-3408, USA

Baena, Marisa (Athlete, Golfer)
3605 Dandelion Dr
Plano, TX 75093-7230, USA

Baer, Gordy (Bowler)
8577 Tullamore Dr
Tinley Park, IL 60487-4774, USA

Baer, Neal (Actor, Producer, Writer)
Wolf Films
100 Universal City Plz Bldg 2252
Universal City, CA 91608-1002, USA

Baerga, Carlos (Athlete, Baseball Player)
PO Box 1667
Bayamon, PR 00960-1667, USA

Baer Jr, Max (Actor, Director, Producer)
3456 Pueblo Way
Las Vegas, NV 89169-3337, USA

Baetens, Veerle (Actor)
c/o Carter Cohn *ICM Partners (LA)*
10250 Constellation Blvd Fl 7
Los Angeles, CA 90067-6207, USA

Baez, Danys (Athlete, Baseball Player)
8975 SW 63rd Ct
Miami, FL 33156-1857, USA

Baez, Eddie (DJ)
c/o Staff Member *Diva Central Inc*
7510 W Sunset Blvd Ste 1445
Los Angeles, CA 90046-3408, USA

Baez, Joan (Musician, Songwriter)
510 Whiskey Hill Rd
Woodside, CA 94062-1233, USA

Baez, Jose (Athlete, Baseball Player)
1028 E Jersey St Apt 2
Elizabeth, NJ 07201-2532, USA

Baez, Kevin (Athlete, Baseball Player)
72 Hollywood Dr
Oakdale, NY 11769-1941, USA

Baez, Kevin
Long Island Ducks 3 Court House Dr
Attn: Managers Office
Central Islip, NY 11722, USA

Baeza, Braulio (Jockey)
Janice Blake
191 Hunnewell Ave
Elmont, NY 11003-2711, USA

Baeza, Braulio (Horse Racer)
1588 Rosalind Ave
Elmont, NY 11003-1821, USA

Bafaro, Michael (Director, Writer)
c/o Staff Member *Lenhoff & Lenhoff*
830 Palm Ave
West Hollywood, CA 90069-4009

Baffert, Bob (Horse Racer)
4244 Woodleigh Ln
La Canada Flintridge, CA 91011-3537,
USA

Bagdasarian Jr, Ross (Actor, Producer)
c/o Staff Member *Bagdasarian Productions*
1192 E Mountain Dr
Santa Barbara, CA 93108-1119

Baggetta, Vincent (Actor)
4812 Ranchito Ave
Sherman Oaks, CA 91423-1913, USA

Bagian, James P (Astronaut)
21537 Holmbury Rd
Northville, MI 48167-1021, USA

Bagian, James P Dr (Astronaut)
21537 Holmbury Rd
Northville, MI 48167-1021, USA

Bagley, John (Athlete, Basketball Player)
828 Beechwood Ave
Bridgeport, CT 06605-1609, USA

Bagley, Tom (Race Car Driver)
109 Walnut Dr
Shorewood, IL 60404-5302, USA

Baglietto, Tara (Actor)
c/o Staff Member *Innovative Artists (NY)*
235 Park Ave S Fl 7
New York, NY 10003-1405, USA

Bagwell, Jeffrey R (Jeff) (Athlete, Baseball
Player)
601 Lindenwood Dr
Houston, TX 77024-6911, USA

Baham, Curtis (Athlete, Football Player)
5936 Oxford Pl
New Orleans, LA 70131-3908, USA

Bahns, Maxine (Actor)
c/o Steven Jensen *Independent Group,
The*
6363 Wilshire Blvd Ste 115
Los Angeles, CA 90048-5734, USA

Bahnsen, Ken (Athlete, Football Player)
671 N Masch Branch Rd
Denton, TX 76207-3633, USA

Bahnsen, Stan (Athlete, Baseball Player)
3500 Blue Lake Dr Apt 402
Pompano Beach, FL 33064-2026, USA

Bahr, Chris (Athlete, Football Player)
122 Kaywood Dr
Boalsburg, PA 16827-1686, USA

Bahr, Matthew D (Matt) (Athlete, Football
Player)
53 Parkridge Ln
Pittsburgh, PA 15228-1105, USA

Bahr, Walter (Athlete, Olympic Athlete,
Soccer Player)
122 Glory Way
Boalsburg, PA 16827-1263, USA

Bahrke, Shannon (Athlete, Olympic
Athlete, Skier)
3556 S Crestwood Dr
Salt Lake City, UT 84109-3206, USA

Bailes, Margaret (Athlete, Olympic
Athlete, Track Athlete)
11136 Vista Sorrento Pkwy Apt 203
San Diego, CA 92130-7606, USA

Bailes, Scott (Athlete, Baseball Player)
2920 S Ranch Dr
Springfield, MO 65809-2204, USA

Bailey, Allen (Athlete, Football Player)
c/o Drew Rosenhaus *Rosenhaus Sports
Representation*
6400 Allison Rd
Miami Beach, FL 33141-4540, USA

Bailey, Ben (Actor, Television Host)
c/o Amy Brownstein *PRStudio USA*
630 9th Ave Ste 209
New York, NY 10036-4752, USA

Bailey, Bob (Athlete, Hockey Player)
3190 W 140th St
Cleveland, OH 44111-1443, USA

Bailey, Buddy (Athlete)
PO Box 590
Amherst, VA 24521-0590, USA

Bailey, Champ (Athlete, Football Player)
8287 Whisper Wood Ct
Parker, CO 80134-3245, USA

Bailey, Chris (Athlete, Hockey Player,
Olympic Athlete)
13510 High Stone Cir
Pittsford, NY 14534, USA

Bailey, Claron (Athlete, Football Player)
9624 E Navarro Ave
Mesa, AZ 85209-2491, USA

Bailey, Cory (Athlete, Baseball Player)
10877 Paulton Rd
Pittsburg, IL 62974-1705, USA

Bailey, Cynthia (Model, Reality Star)
c/o Marcus Jackson *Caliber Models &
Talent*
PO Box 79065
Atlanta, GA 30357-7065, USA

Bailey, Damon (Athlete, Basketball Player)
723 Diamond Rd
Heltonville, IN 47436-8559, USA

Bailey, Dan (Athlete, Football Player)
c/o Jordan Woy *Willis and Woy
Management*
3030 Olive St Ste 520
Dallas, TX 75219-7629, USA

Bailey, David (Athlete, Football Player)
1916 NE 29th St
Oklahoma City, OK 73111-3346, USA

Bailey, David ""Homer"" (Athlete, Baseball
Player)
4327 O Quinn Branch Rd # 0
La Grange, TX 78945-5695, USA

Bailey, Don (Athlete, Football Player)
14831 NW 7th Ave
Miami, FL 33168-3105, USA

Bailey, Edwin (Athlete, Football Player)
3677 Cypress Point Dr
Augusta, GA 30907-9021, USA

Bailey, Eion (Actor)
5601 Briarcliff Rd
Los Angeles, CA 90068-3630, USA

Bailey, Elmer (Athlete, Football Player)
13390 NE 7th Ave Apt 406
Miami, FL 33161-7562, USA

Bailey, F Lee (Attorney)
6231 Tidewater Island Cir
Fort Myers, FL 33908-4686, USA

Bailey, GW (Actor)
22415 La Rochelle Dr
Santa Clarita, CA 91350-1308, USA

Bailey, Harold (Athlete, Football Player)
22502 Prince George St
Katy, TX 77449-2723, USA

Bailey, HB (Race Car Driver)
PO Box 450288
Houston, TX 77245-0288, USA

Bailey, Howard (Athlete, Baseball Player)
11674 156th Ave
West Olive, MI 49460-9388, USA

Bailey, Jeff (Athlete, Baseball Player)
709 N 18th Ave
Kelso, WA 98626-5036, USA

Bailey, Jerry (Athlete, Horse Racer)
105 Nurmi Dr
Ft Lauderdale, FL 33301-1404, USA

Bailey, Jim (Athlete, Baseball Player)
250 Cade Rd
Ten Mile, TN 37880-2149, USA

Bailey, Jim (Athlete, Football Player)
5219 Stone Creek Ct
Lawrence, KS 66049-4792, USA

Bailey, John (Cinematographer)
United Talent Agency
9336 Civic Center Dr
Beverly Hills, CA 90210-3604, USA

Bailey, Karsten (Athlete, Football Player)
16 Salbide Ave
Newnan, GA 30263-2501, USA

Bailey, Keith E (Business Person)
Williams Companies
1 One Williams Ctr Bsmt 2
Tulsa, OK 74172-0172, USA

Bailey, Leonard L (Doctor)
Loma Linda University
Medical School
Loma Linda, CA 92350-0001, USA

Bailey, Mark (Athlete, Baseball Player)
PO Box 694
Attn: Coaching Staff
Troy, NY 12181-0694, USA

Bailey, Mark (Athlete, Baseball Player)
32703 Waltham Xing
Fulshear, TX 77441-4203, USA

Bailey, Mark (Athlete, Football Player)
3229 Corniche Ln
Roseville, CA 95661-3970, USA

Bailey, Michael (Doctor)
Northwestern University
Psychology Dept
Evanston, IL 60208-0001, USA

Bailey, Otha (Athlete, Baseball Player)
937 6th Pl SW
Birmingham, AL 35211-1743, USA

Bailey, Palmer (Astronaut)
64710 Knob Hill Rd
Anchor Point, AK 99556-9160, USA

Bailey, Philip (Musician)
c/o Staff Member *Richard De La Font
Agency*
3808 W South Park Blvd
Broken Arrow, OK 74011-1261, USA

Bailey, Preston (Actor)
c/o Staff Member *Elements Entertainment*
312 W 5th St Apt 815
Los Angeles, CA 90013-1750, USA

Bailey, Razzy (Musician, Songwriter,
Writer)
Doc Sedelmeier
PO Box 62
Geneva, NE 68361-0062, USA

Bailey, Robert M (Athlete, Football Player)
15325 SW 99th Ave
Miami, FL 33157-1708, USA

Bailey, Roger (Athlete, Baseball Player)
6186 Massive Peak Cir
Castle Rock, CO 80108-9484, USA

Bailey, Scott (Actor)
c/o Staff Member *Stone Manners Salners
Agency (LA)*
6100 Wilshire Blvd Ste 1500
Los Angeles, CA 90048-5110, USA

Bailey, Sean (Producer)
c/o Patrick Whitesell *William Morris
Endeavor (LA)*
9601 Wilshire Blvd
Beverly Hills, CA 90210-5213, USA

Bailey, Stacey (Athlete, Football Player)
770 Hopewell Place Dr
Alpharetta, GA 30004-8100, USA

Bailey, Steve (Athlete, Baseball Player)
4600 Queen Anne Ave
Lorain, OH 44052-5648, USA

Bailey, Steven W (Reality Star)
c/o Scott Fedro *Lone Star Entertainment*
139 S Beverly Dr Ste 314
Beverly Hills, CA 90212-3040, USA

Bailey, Teddy (Athlete, Football Player)
7825 Elbrook Ave
Cincinnati, OH 45237-2207, USA

Bailey, Thurl (Athlete, Basketball Player)
10265 N 6960 W
Highland, UT 84003-9337, USA

Bailey, Victor (Athlete, Football Player)
9700 Palmbrook Dr
Austin, TX 78717-3892, USA

Bailey, Welby (Buddy) (Athlete, Baseball
Player)
PO Box 590
Amherst, VA 24521-0590, USA

Bailey II, Irving W (Business Person)
Providian Corp
4333 Edgewood Rd NE
Cedar Rapids, IA 52499-3830, USA

Bailon, Adrienne (Actor, Musician)
c/o Staff Member *FYI Public Relations*
174 5th Ave Ste 404
New York, NY 10010-5964, USA

Bailor, Bob (Athlete, Baseball Player)
1950 Swan Ln
Palm Harbor, FL 34683-6275, USA

Baily, Kirk (Actor)
c/o Staff Member *Independent Artists (LA)*
9601 Wilshire Blvd Ste 750
Beverly Hills, CA 90210-5228, USA

Bain, Barbara (Actor)
831 S Dunsmuir Ave
Los Angeles, CA 90036-4731, USA

Bain, William E (Bill) (Athlete, Football
Player)
27661 Paseo Barona
San Juan Capistrano, CA 92675-2851,
USA

Baines, Harold (Athlete, Baseball Player)
40 Grove St Ste 430
Wellesley, MA 02482-7774, USA

Baio, Scott (Actor)
20524 Chatsboro Dr
Woodland Hills, CA 91364-5652, USA

Baiocchi, Hugh (Athlete, Golfer)
3656 Half Moon Dr
Orlando, FL 32812-3816, USA

Bair, Doug (Athlete, Baseball Player)
11545 Kemper Woods Dr
Cincinnati, OH 45249-1753, USA

Baird, Allard (Commentator)
1425 Brickell Ave Apt 62C
Miami, FL 33131-3424, USA

Baird, Bill (Athlete, Football Player)
6050 E Heaton Ave
Fresno, CA 93727-5606, USA

Baird, Briny (Athlete, Golfer)
3340 SW Rivers End Way
Palm City, FL 34990-7603, USA

Baird, Butch (Athlete, Golfer)
PO Box 2663
Carefree, AZ 85377-2663, USA

Baird, Diora (Actor)
c/o Lena Roklin *Luber Roklin Management*
5815 W Sunset Blvd Ste 206
Los Angeles, CA 90028-6481, USA

Baird, James M (Religious Leader)
Presbyterian Church
PO Box 1428
Decatur, GA 30031-1428, USA

baird, jenni (Actor)
c/o Michael P Levine *Levine Management*
9028 W Sunset Blvd PH 1
West Hollywood, CA 90069-1830, USA

Baird, Stuart (Director)
c/o Staff Member *Mirisch Agency*
8840 Wilshire Blvd Ste 100
Beverly Hills, CA 90211-2606, USA

Baisden, Michael (Producer, Radio Personality, Writer)
c/o Pamela Yvette Exum *PYE Enterprises Agency*
13901 Midway Rd Ste 102
Dallas, TX 75244-4388, USA

Baisley, Jeff (Athlete, Baseball Player)
16222 Pebblebrook Dr
Tampa, FL 33624-1072, USA

Baitz, Jon Robin (Producer)
c/o Simon Halls *Slate Public Relations*
9000 W Sunset Blvd Ste 915
West Hollywood, CA 90069-5809, USA

Baiul, Oksana (Figure Skater)
c/o Phil Viardo *The Viardo Agency*
8484 Wilshire Blvd Ste 220
Beverly Hills, CA 90211-3223, USA

Bajardi, Lane (Television Host)
c/o Staff Member *Bloomberg Television*
731 Lexington Ave
New York, NY 10022-1331, USA

Bajema, Billy (Athlete, Football Player)
2605 SW 120th St
Oklahoma City, OK 73170-4735, USA

Bajenaru, Jeff (Athlete, Baseball Player)
3717 E Megan St
Gilbert, AZ 85295-4818, USA

Bakalyan, Richard (Actor)
1070 S Bedford St
Los Angeles, CA 90035-2102, USA

Bakanic, Laddie (Athlete, Gymnast, Olympic Athlete)
7 David Ter
White Plains, NY 10603-3516, USA

Bakay, Nick (Actor)
1437 Bluebird Ave
Los Angeles, CA 90069-1714, USA

Bakenhaster, Dave (Athlete, Baseball Player)
3710 Rome Corners Rd
Galena, OH 43021-9490, USA

Baker, Al (Athlete, Football Player)
2784 Trinity Ct
Avon, OH 44011-1951, USA

Baker, Anita (Actor, Musician, Songwriter)
c/o Staff Member *Blue Note Label Group*
150 5th Ave
New York, NY 10011-4311, USA

Baker, Art (Athlete, Football Player)
5300 Washington St Apt L235
Hollywood, FL 33021-7726, us

Baker, Art (Athlete, Football Player)
247 Main St # B
Buzzards Bay, MA 02532-3232, USA

Baker, Becky Ann
484 W 43rd St Apt 31H
New York, NY 10036-6333, USA

Baker, Bill (Athlete, Hockey Player, Olympic Athlete)
5638 Ojibwa Rd
Brainerd, MN 56401-7017, USA

Baker, Blanche (Actor)
4695 Independence Ave
Bronx, NY 10471-3538, USA

Baker, Brad (Race Car Driver)
565 Brick Church Park Dr
Nashville, TN 37207-3219, USA

Baker, Brenda (Actor)
Agency for Performing Arts
9200 W Sunset Blvd Ste 900
West Hollywood, CA 90069-3604, USA

Baker, Buddy (Race Car Driver)
4860 Moonlite Bay Dr
Sherrills Ford, NC 28673-9242, USA

Baker, Carroll (Actor)
Abrams Artists
9200 W Sunset Blvd Ste 1125
West Hollywood, CA 90069-3610, USA

Baker, Charles (Actor)
c/o Anna Kreynes *Persona PR (LA)*
8840 Wilshire Blvd Ste 212
Beverly Hills, CA 90211-2606, USA

Baker, Charles (Charlie) (Athlete, Football Player)
PO Box 112593
Carrollton, TX 75011-2593, USA

Baker, Chuck (Athlete, Baseball Player)
3035 Mescalero Dr
Lake Havasu City, AZ 86404-9605, USA

Baker, Dave (Athlete, Baseball Player)
5334 Cervantes Dr
Ames, IA 50014-6917, USA

Baker, Diane (Actor)
2733 Outpost Dr
Los Angeles, CA 90068-2061, USA

Baker, Donald K (Cinematographer)
11789 Lakeshore N
Auburn, CA 95602-8326, USA

Baker, Doug (Athlete, Baseball Player)
116 Woodthrush Ln
Fallbrook, CA 92028-4149, USA

Baker, Dusty (Athlete, Baseball Player)
100 Joe Nuxhall Way
Attn Managers Office
Cincinnati, OH 45202-4109, USA

Baker, Dylan (Actor)
484 W 43rd St Apt 31H
New York, NY 10036-6333, USA

Baker, Edward (Athlete, Football Player)
45 Smull Ave
Caldwell, NJ 07006-5001, USA

Baker, Edward Dr
45 Smull Ave
Caldwell, NJ 07006-5001, us

Baker, Ellen Dr (Astronaut)
2207 Garden Stream Ct
Houston, TX 77062-3650, USA

Baker, Ellen Shulman (Astronaut)
2207 Garden Stream Ct
Houston, TX 77062-3650, USA

Baker, Frank
PO Box 3066
Meridian, MS 39303-3066, USA

Baker, Ginger (Musician)
Twist Mgmt
4230 Del Rey Ave # 621
Marina Del Rey, CA 90292-5606, USA

Baker, Jack (Athlete, Baseball Player)
5513 Hunters Hill Rd
Irondale, AL 35210-3011, USA

Baker, James A (Bubba) (Athlete, Football Player)
2784 Trinity Ct
Avon, OH 44011-1951, USA

Baker, Jamie (Athlete, Hockey Player)
801 Seabury Dr
San Jose, CA 95136-1850, USA

Baker, Jamie (Athlete, Hockey Player)
San Jose Sharks
525 W Santa Clara St
San Jose, CA 95113-1500

Baker, Jason (Athlete, Football Player)
435 S Tryon St Unit 906
Charlotte, NC 28202-1922, USA

Baker, Jeff Baker (Athlete, Baseball Player)
4747 Timber Ridge Dr
Dumfries, VA 22025-1081, USA

Baker, Jerry (Athlete, Football Player)
7780 W 38th Ave Apt 305
Wheat Ridge, CO 80033-6103, USA

Baker, John (Athlete, Baseball Player)
222 Weber Ln
Danville, CA 94526-1991, USA

Baker, Johnnie B (Dusty) (Athlete, Baseball Player, Coach)
9090 Stockhorse Ln
Granite Bay, CA 95746-7165, USA

Baker, Johnny (Athlete, Football Player)
466 Jan Kelly Ln
Houston, TX 77024-6511, us

Baker, John W (Athlete, Football Player)
72 Oak Village Blvd S
Homosassa, FL 34446-5945, USA

Baker, Kathy (Actor)
c/o Becca Kovacik *Berwick & Kovacik*
9465 Wilshire Blvd Ste 420
Beverly Hills, CA 90212-2603, USA

Baker, Keith (Athlete, Football Player)
3203 S Marsalis Ave
Dallas, TX 75216-5203, USA

Baker, Ken (Journalist)
1155 7th Pl
Hermosa Beach, CA 90254-4912, USA

Baker, Kitana (Actor)
c/o Jason Newman *Untitled Entertainment (LA)*
350 S Beverly Dr Ste 200
Beverly Hills, CA 90212-4819, USA

Baker, Laurie (Athlete, Hockey Player, Olympic Athlete)
85 Monsen Rd
Concord, MA 01742-1924, USA

Baker, Leslie David (Actor)
13952 Hartsook St
Sherman Oaks, CA 91423-1210, USA

Baker, Lewis (Musician)
Joe Terry Mgmt
PO Box 1017
Blackwood, NJ 08012-0837, USA

Baker, Loris (Athlete, Football Player)
1009 Brentwood Pl
Fircrest, WA 98466-5922, USA

Baker, Michael A Captain (Astronaut)
18138 Lakeside Ln
Houston, TX 77058-4331, USA

Baker, Michael A (Mike) (Astronaut)
NASA
2101 Nasa Pkwy Spc Johnsoncenter
Houston, TX 77058-3696, USA

Baker, Michael Andrew (Actor)
c/o David Chandler Secor *Daniel Hoff Agency*
5455 Wilshire Blvd Ste 1100
Los Angeles, CA 90036-4277, USA

Baker, Myron (Athlete, Football Player)
297 Peart Rd
Alexandria, LA 71302-9344, USA

Baker, Ralph (Athlete, Football Player)
36 Sunshine Cir
Lewistown, PA 17044-9264, USA

Baker, Randy (Race Car Driver)
Speed Tech
4333 Motorsports Dr SW
Concord, NC 28027-8977, USA

Baker, Ray (Actor)
11749 Chenault St
Los Angeles, CA 90049-4230, USA

Baker, Robert (Actor)
c/o Amanda Glazer *Kohner Agency, The*
9300 Wilshire Blvd Ste 555
Beverly Hills, CA 90212-3211, USA

Baker, Ron (Athlete, Football Player)
1119 S Main St
Stillwater, OK 74074-4639, USA

Baker, Russell (Journalist)
202 W Market St
Leesburg, VA 20176-2709, USA

Baker, Sam (Athlete, Football Player)
c/o Tom Condon *CAA (St. Louis)*
222 S Central Ave Ste 1008
Saint Louis, MO 63105-3509, USA

Baker, Scott (Athlete, Baseball Player)
904 Shining Arrows St
Henderson, NV 89002-0408, USA

Baker, Scott (Athlete, Baseball Player)
340 Johns Bluff Cir
Shreveport, LA 71106-4733, USA

Baker, Scott Thompson (Actor)
17651 Sidwell St
Granada Hills, CA 91344-1054, USA

Baker, Shaun (Actor)
c/o Staff Member *Brady, Brannon & Rich Talent*
5670 Wilshire Blvd Ste 820
Los Angeles, CA 90036-5613, USA

Baker, Simon (Actor)
425 23rd St
Santa Monica, CA 90402-3125, USA

Baker, Stephen (Athlete, Football Player)
280 Water St
Perth Amboy, NJ 08861-4427, USA

Baker, Steve (Athlete, Hockey Player)
2929 N 70th St Apt 3087
Scottsdale, AZ 85251-6235, USA

Baker, Steve (Athlete, Baseball Player)
27527 Easy Acres Dr
Eugene, OR 97405-4500, USA

Baker, Terry (Athlete, Football Player, Heisman Trophy Winner)
3208 SW Fairmount Blvd
Portland, OR 97239-1443, USA

Baker, Tim
PO Box 483
Wolcott, CO 81655-0483, us

Baker, Tony (Athlete, Football Player)
3847 Eagleston Ct
High Point, NC 27265-7928, us

Baker, Vin (Athlete, Basketball Player)
PO Box 179
Old Saybrook, CT 06475-0179, USA

Baker, Wayne (Athlete, Football Player)
209 Needmore Rd
Waco, KY 40385-9030, USA

Baker, W Thane (Athlete, Track Athlete)
6704 Saint John Ct
Granbury, TX 76049-4520, USA

Baker-Finch, Ian (Athlete, Golfer)
11309 Caladium Ln
Palm Beach Gardens, FL 33418-1506, USA

Baker III, James A (Politician)
Baker And Botts
1299 Pennsylvania Ave NW Ste 1200
NW Ste 1200
Washington, DC 20004-2408, USA

Bakhtair, Rudi (Correspondent)
Cable News Network
1050 Techwood Dr NW
News Dept
Atlanta, GA 30318-5695, USA

Bakhtiar, Jim (Athlete, Football Player)
PO Box 863
Charles Town, WV 25414-0863, USA

Bakke, Brenda (Actor)
c/o Staff Member *House of Representatives, The*
1434 6th St Ste 1
Santa Monica, CA 90401-2527, USA

Bakkedahl, Dan (Actor)
c/o Meg Mortimer *Principal Entertainment (NY)*
1133 Avenue Of The Americas Ste 1621
New York, NY 10036-6710, USA

Bakken, James L (Jim) (Athlete, Football Player)
230 Glen Hollow Rd
Madison, WI 53705-1166, USA

Bakker, James O (Jim) (Religious Leader)
123 E End Rd
Branson, MO 65616-3701, USA

Bako, Brigitte (Actor)
8329 Anthony Cir
Los Angeles, CA 90046-1901, USA

Bako, Paul (Athlete, Baseball Player)
500 Princeton Woods Loop
Lafayette, LA 70508-6672, USA

Bakovic, Pete (Athlete, Hockey Player)
7991 S 47th St
Franklin, WI 53132-8468, USA

Bakshi, Ralph (Cartoonist)
PO Box 2858
Silver City, NM 88062-2858, USA

Bakula, Scott (Actor)
Bakula Pictures
16255 Ventura Blvd Ste 625
Encino, CA 91436-2307, USA

Bala, Chris (Athlete, Hockey Player)
271 Beacon Dr
Phoenixville, PA 19460-2046, USA

Balaban, Bob (Director, Producer)
310 Highland Ter
Bridgehampton, NY 11932, USA

Balas, Mike
1 Heather Rd
Rye, NH 03870-6123, USA

Balaski, Belinda (Actor)
731 N Laurel Ave
Los Angeles, CA 90046-7007, USA

Balaz, John (Athlete, Baseball Player)
3982 Valeta St Unit 278
San Diego, CA 92110-5810, USA

Balazs, Andre (Business Person)
Andre Balazs Properties
295 Lafayette St Fl 7
the Puck Bldg
New York, NY 10012-2701, USA

Balboa, Marcelo (Soccer Player)
13139 Hedda Dr
Cerritos, CA 90703-6146, USA

Balboni, Steve (Athlete, Baseball Player)
PO Box 87
Berkeley Heights, NJ 07922-0087, USA

Balcer, Rene (Producer, Writer)
c/o Missy Malkin *Brillstein Entertainment Partners (LA)*
9150 Wilshire Blvd Ste 350
Beverly Hills, CA 90212-3453, USA

Baldacci, David (Writer)
c/o Aaron Priest *Aaron M. Priest Literary Agency*
708 3rd Ave Rm 2301
New York, NY 10017-4212, USA

Baldacci, John (Politician)
192 State St
Augusta, ME 04330-6406, USA

Baldacci, Lou (Athlete, Football Player)
983 Coral Dr
Pebble Beach, CA 93953-2538, USA

Baldachino, Gerald (Horse Racer)
208 Sweetmans Ln
Millstone Township, NJ 08535-8110, USA

Baldassin, Mike (Athlete, Football Player)
7914 Interlaaken Dr SW
Lakewood, WA 98498-5707, USA

Baldavin, Barbara (Actor)
228 17th St
Manhattan Beach, CA 90266-4634, USA

Baldelli, Rocco (Athlete, Baseball Player)
5301 Gulf Blvd Unit 610
St Pete Beach, FL 33706-2307, USA

Balderson, Dick (Commentator)
607 Wood Valley Dr
Collierville, TN 38017-6101, USA

Balding, Rebecca (Actor)
2001 Winnetka Pl
Woodland Hills, CA 91364, USA

Baldinger, Brian (Athlete, Football Player, Sportscaster)
21 S Elmwood Rd
Marlton, NJ 08053-2562, USA

Baldinger, Gary (Athlete, Football Player)
114 Adam Rd
Massapequa, NY 11758-8102, USA

Baldinger, Rich (Athlete, Football Player)
5401 Phelps Rd
Kansas City, MO 64136-1224, USA

Baldischwiler, Karl (Athlete, Football Player)
3033 N Willow Dr
Newcastle, OK 73065-6456, USA

Baldissin, Mike (Athlete, Football Player)
13834 Bandix Rd SE
Olalla, WA 98359-9467, USA

Baldoni, Justin (Actor)
c/o Adam Griffin *Kritzer Levine Wilkins Entertainment (KLWG)*
11872 La Grange Ave Fl 1
Los Angeles, CA 90025-5283, USA

Baldrige, Leticia (Writer)
Letitia Baldrige Enterprises Inc
2339 Massachusetts Ave NW
Washington, DC 20008-2803, USA

Baldschun, Jack (Athlete, Baseball Player)
311 Erie Rd
Green Bay, WI 54311-7706, USA

Baldschun, Jack E (Athlete, Baseball Player)
311 Erie Rd
Green Bay, WI 54311-7706, USA

Baldwin, Adam (Actor)
c/o Abe Hoch *A Management Company*
9107 Wilshire Blvd Ste 650
Beverly Hills, CA 90210-5544, USA

Baldwin, Alec (Actor)
28 E 10th St PH 12E
New York, NY 10003-6208, USA

Baldwin, Daniel (Actor)
c/o John McGalliard *Chaotik*
732 1/2 N Edinburgh Ave
Los Angeles, CA 90046-7004, USA

Baldwin, Dave (Athlete, Baseball Player)
PO Box 190
Yachats, OR 97498-0190, USA

Baldwin, Don (Athlete, Football Player)
14 Beacon Trail Ct
O Fallon, MO 63366-1495, USA

Baldwin, Hilaria (Television Host)
c/o Mark Mullett *William Morris Endeavor (LA)*
9601 Wilshire Blvd
Beverly Hills, CA 90210-5213, USA

Baldwin, Howard (Producer)
c/o Staff Member *Baldwin Entertainment*
9200 W Sunset Blvd Ste 550
West Hollywood, CA 90069-3611, USA

Baldwin, Jack (Race Car Driver)
4748 Balmoral Way NE
Marietta, GA 30068-1604, USA

Baldwin, James (Athlete, Baseball Player)
18 Monteith Pl
Pinehurst, NC 28374-8542, USA

Baldwin, Jeff (Athlete, Baseball Player)
70 Goodwill Rd
Huntington, WV 25704-8820, USA

Baldwin, Jerry (Business Person)
1400 Park Ave
Emeryville, CA 94608-3520, USA

Baldwin, Jonathan (Football Player)
c/o Ken Zuckerman *Priority Sports & Entertainment - (LA)*
15233 Ventura Blvd Ste 718
Sherman Oaks, CA 91403-2237, USA

Baldwin, Judy (Actor)
c/o Larry Metzger *Grant Savic Kopaloff & Associates*
6399 Wilshire Blvd Ste 414
Los Angeles, CA 90048-5716, USA

Baldwin, Keith M (Athlete, Football Player)
124 Leonardville Rd
Belford, NJ 07718-1131, USA

Baldwin, Margaret (Writer)
PO Box 1106
Williams Bay, WI 53191-1106, USA

Baldwin, Matisha (Actor)
c/o Marianne Golan *Golan & Blumberg*
6528 W 6th St
Los Angeles, CA 90048-4716, USA

Baldwin, Randy (Athlete, Football Player)
862 S 9th St
Griffin, GA 30224-4823, USA

Baldwin, Reggie (Athlete, Baseball Player)
PO Box 970816
Ypsilanti, MI 48197-0116, USA

Baldwin, Rick (Athlete, Baseball Player)
2601 Stoneridge Dr
Modesto, CA 95355-3454, USA

Baldwin, Stephen (Actor)
98 Buckberg Mountain Rd
Tomkins Cove, NY 10986-1013, USA

Baldwin, Tammy (Congressman, Politician)
2446 Rayburn Hob
Washington, DC 20515-3703, USA

Baldwin, William (Billy) (Actor)
c/o Lee Wallman *Wallman Public Relations*
10323 Santa Monica Blvd Ste 109
Los Angeles, CA 90025-5056, USA

Bale, Christian (Actor)
150 Mabery Rd
Santa Monica, CA 90402-1204, USA

Bale, John (Athlete, Baseball Player)
2000 Echo Creek Cv
Niceville, FL 32578-1512, USA

Bales, Lee (Athlete, Baseball Player)
7422 Greatwood Lake Dr
Sugar Land, TX 77479-6302, USA

Balester, Collin (Athlete, Baseball Player)
5614 52nd Ave W
Bradenton, FL 34210-4919, USA

Balfour, Eric (Actor)
c/o Brian Medavoy *Medavoy Management*
10203 Santa Monica Blvd Ste 400
Los Angeles, CA 90067-6405, USA

Balfour, Grant (Athlete, Baseball Player)
2678 N McMullen Booth Rd
Clearwater, FL 33761-4409, USA

Baliles, Gerald L (Politician)
951 E Byrd St
Riverfront Plaza East Tower
Richmond, VA 23219-4040, USA

Balin, Marty (Musician)
12413 Stillwater Terrace Dr
Tampa, FL 33618-8738, USA

Balk, Fairuza (Actor)
Rigberg Roberts Rugolo
1180 S Beverly Dr Ste 601
Los Angeles, CA 90035-1158, USA

Ball, Alan (Athlete, Football Player)
c/o Ryan Morgan *MAG Sports Agency*
8222 Melrose Ave Fl 2
Los Angeles, CA 90046-6825, USA

Ball, Alan (Producer)
7443 Woodrow Wilson Dr
Los Angeles, CA 90046-1322, USA

Ball, Dave (Athlete, Football Player)
9234 Carrisbrook Ln
Brentwood, TN 37027-4883, us

Ball, Dave (Athlete, Football Player)
1020 Hillview Dr
Dixon, CA 95620-3729, USA

Ball, Edward (Writer)
Farrar Straus Giroux
19 Union Sq W
New York, NY 10003-3304, USA

Ball, Eric C (Athlete, Football Player)
10614 Margate Ter
Cincinnati, OH 45241-3000, USA

Ball, Ian (Musician)
c/o Staff Member *Paradigm (Monterey)*
404 W Franklin St
Monterey, CA 93940-2303, USA

Ball, Jason
22 Coe Dr
Durham, NH 03824-2206, us

Ball, Jason (Athlete, Football Player)
325 S Jessie Doe
Durham, NH 03824, USA

Ball, Jeff (Athlete, Baseball Player)
1166 6th Ave Apt 9C
Vero Beach, FL 32960-5960, USA

Ball, Jerry L (Athlete, Football Player)
3311 Meadowside Dr
Sugar Land, TX 77478-4051, USA

Ball, Larry (Athlete, Football Player)
8830 SW 57th St
Cooper City, FL 33328-5100, USA

Ball, Marcia (Musician)
PO Box 2629
Austin, TX 78768-2629, USA

Ball, Montee (Athlete, Football Player)
c/o Neil Cornrich *NC Sports, LLC*
best to contact via email
Columbus, OH 43201, USA

Ball, Robert (Athlete, Football Player)
6412 E Claire Dr
Scottsdale, AZ 85254-2623, USA

Ball, Sam (Actor)
c/o Robert Stein *Robert Stein Management*
PO Box 3797
Beverly Hills, CA 90212-0797, USA

Ball, Sam (Athlete, Football Player)
1220 Glenshiel Dr
Henderson, KY 42420-2530, USA

Ball, Taylor (Actor)
c/o Shannon Barr *Rogers & Cowan PR (LA)*
8687 Melrose Ave Ste 7
West Hollywood, CA 90069-5721, USA

Ball, Terry (Athlete, Hockey Player)
4502 Torrington Ave
Cleveland, OH 44134-2163, USA

Ballantine, Sara (Actor)
Talent Group
5670 Wilshire Blvd Ste 820
Los Angeles, CA 90036-5613, USA

Ballard, Carroll (Director)
PO Box 556
Saint Helena, CA 94574-5056, USA

Ballard, Del Jr (Bowler)
Ebonite International
PO Box 746
Hopkinsville, KY 42241-0746, USA

Ballard, Florence (Musician)
c/o Staff Member *Diva Central Inc*
7510 W Sunset Blvd Ste 1445
Los Angeles, CA 90046-3408, USA

Ballard, Glen (Musician, Songwriter)
16214 Morrison St
Encino, CA 91436-1332, USA

Ballard, Greg (Athlete, Basketball Player)
100 Arborcrest Ct
Tyrone, GA 30290-1555, USA

Ballard, Howard (Athlete, Football Player)
PO Box 584
Ashland, AL 36251-0584, USA

Ballard, Jeff (Athlete, Baseball Player)
4828 Rimrock Rd
Billings, MT 59106-1317, USA

Ballard, J G (Writer)
36 Old Charlton Rd
Shepperton, MI ENGLA, USA

Ballard, Jim (Athlete, Football Player)
1215 Stone Crossing St NE
Canton, OH 44721-2475, us

Ballard, Kaye (Actor)
PO Box 922
Rancho Mirage, CA 92270-0922, USA

Ballard, Keith (Athlete, Hockey Player)
2336 River Pointe Cir
Minneapolis, MN 55411-4414, USA

Ballard, Quinton (Athlete, Football Player)
4005 Saint Patrick Dr
Greensboro, NC 27406-6420, USA

Ballard, Robert
Woods Hole Oceanographic Institute
86 Water St
Woods Hole, MA 02543-1052, USA

Ballard, Vick (Athlete, Football Player)
c/o Bus Cook *Bus Cook Sports, Inc*
1 Willow Bend Dr
Hattiesburg, MS 39402-8552, USA

Ballas, Mark (Dancer, Reality Star)
3161 Dona Maria Dr
Studio City, CA 91604-4258, USA

Ballentine, Lonnie (Athlete, Football Player)
c/o Harold C Lewis *National Sports Agency*
15400 Timpaige Dr
Chesterfield, MO 63017-1762, USA

Baller, Jay (Athlete, Baseball Player)
303 Spring Valley Rd
Reading, PA 19605-2747, USA

Ballerini, Edoardo (Actor)
3350 Atwater Ave
Los Angeles, CA 90039-2204, USA

Ballestros, Anderson (Actor)
c/o J R Heermans *LatinActors*
920 Leavenworth St Apt 302
San Francisco, CA 94109-4907

Balley, Otha (Athlete, Baseball Player)
937 6th Pl SW
Birmingham, AL 35211-1743, USA

Ballhaus, Florian M (Cinematographer)
115 Berkeley Pl
Brooklyn, NY 11217-3603, USA

Ballhaus, Michael (Cinematographer)
11 Elm Pl
Rye, NY 10580-2918, USA

Ballina, Frank (Athlete, Baseball Player)
534 Lori Dr
Leechburg, PA 15656-9414, USA

Ballingall, Chris (Athlete, Baseball Player)
52879 25th St
Mattawan, MI 49071-8803, USA

Ballinger, Mark (Athlete, Baseball Player)
1212 SW 5th Ave
Okeechobee, FL 34974-5014, USA

Ballmer, Steve (Business Person)
Microsoft Corp
1 Microsoft Way
Redmond, WA 98052-8300, USA

Ballon, Adrienne (Actor)
c/o Staff Member *ICM Partners (LA)*
10250 Constellation Blvd Fl 7
Los Angeles, CA 90067-6207, USA

Ballou, Mark (Actor)
c/o Staff Member *Imperium 7 Talent Agency*
5455 Wilshire Blvd Ste 1706
Los Angeles, CA 90036-4217, USA

Ballou, Tyson (Model)
c/o Staff Member *IMG*
304 Park Ave S Fl 12
New York, NY 10010-4314, USA

Balmaseda, Liz (Journalist)
Miami Herald
PO Box 3028
Editorial Dept
Livonia, MI 48151-3028, USA

Balmer, Earl (Race Car Driver)
8115 N Skyline Dr
Floyds Knobs, IN 47119-8925, USA

Balmilero, Kimee (Actor)
c/o Staff Member *Rogers Orion Talent Agency*
13731 Ventura Blvd Ste D
Sherman Oaks, CA 91423-3078, USA

Balsam, Talia (Actor)
c/o Sue Leibman *Barking Dog Entertainment*
609 Greenwich St Fl 6
New York, NY 10014-3610, USA

Balsamo, Tony (Athlete, Baseball Player)
15 Doral Ln
Bay Shore, NY 11706-8840, USA

Balsley, Darren (Athlete, Baseball Player, Coach)
1200 Harper Pl
Knoxville, TN 37922-5560, USA

Balsley, Phil (Musician)
1409 N Augusta St
Staunton, VA 24401-2402, USA

Baltes, Jameson (Actor)
Hervey/Grimes
PO Box 64249
Los Angeles, CA 90064-0249, USA

Baltica, Kremerata (Musician)
c/o Staff Member *ICM Partners (LA)*
10250 Constellation Blvd Fl 7
Los Angeles, CA 90067-6207, USA

Baltron, Donna (Actor)
C N A Assoc
1925 Century Park E Ste 750
Los Angeles, CA 90067-2708, USA

Baluik, Stan (Athlete, Hockey Player)
809 8th Ter
Palm Beach Gardens, FL 33418-3607, USA

Balul, Oksana (Figure Skater)
Bob Young
PO Box 988
Niantic, CT 06357-0988, USA

Bamber, Jamie
c/o Alan Siegel *Alan Siegel Entertainment*
9200 W Sunset Blvd Ste 407
West Hollywood, CA 90069-3511, USA

Bamford, Maria (Actor)
c/o Bob Read *ReBar Management*
10061 Riverside Dr # 722
Toluca Lake, CA 91602-2560

Bamman, Gerry (Actor)
c/o Bill Timms *Lava Entertainment*
1560 Broadway Ste 1001
New York, NY 10036-1537, USA

Banach, Ed (Athlete, Olympic Athlete, Wrestler)
2128 Country Club Blvd
Ames, IA 50014-7061, USA

Banach, Lou (Athlete, Olympic Athlete, Wrestler)
36735 Hollyhock Woods Dr
Oconomowoc, WI 53066-8611, USA

Banachowski, Andy (Athlete, Coach, Volleyball Player)
University of California
PO Box 24044
Athletic Dept - J.D. Morgan Center
Los Angeles, CA 90024-0044, USA

Banaszak, John A (Athlete, Football Player)
420 Robinhood Ln
Canonsburg, PA 15317-2717, USA

Banaszak, Pete (Athlete, Football Player)
1021 Inverness Dr
Saint Augustine, FL 32092-2787, USA

Banaszek, Cas (Athlete, Football Player)
1877 Castle Dr
Petaluma, CA 94954-8506, USA

Banaszynski, Jacqui (Journalist)
Saint Paul Pioneer Press
345 Cedar St
Editorial Dept
Saint Paul, MN 55101-1057, USA

Bancroft, Cameron (Actor)
c/o Staff Member *Gersh (LA)*
9465 Wilshire Blvd Ste 600
Beverly Hills, CA 90212-2605, USA

Banda El Limon, Arrolladora (Music Group)
c/o Staff Member *Sony Music Miami*
605 Lincoln Rd Ste 700
Miami Beach, FL 33139-2901, USA

Banda Imperio (Music Group, Musician)
c/o Staff Member *Morena Music*
5021 Columbus Ave
Sherman Oaks, CA 91403-1251, USA

Banda Pachuco (Music Group)
c/o Staff Member *Sony Music Miami*
605 Lincoln Rd Ste 700
Miami Beach, FL 33139-2901, USA

Banderas, Antonio (Actor, Director, Musician, Producer)
611 S Muirfield Rd
Los Angeles, CA 90005-3832, USA

B. Anderholf, Robert (Congressman, Politician)
2264 Rayburn Hob
Washington, DC 20515-3217, USA

Bandiera, Bob (Bobby) (Musician)
29 Court B Apt C
Brick, NJ 08724-3058, USA

Bando, Chris (Athlete, Baseball Player)
1 Washington Federal Way
Attn:Maeers Office
Washington, PA 15301-5873, USA

Bando, Chris (Athlete, Baseball Player)
5811 S Mack Ave
Gilbert, AZ 85298-8709, USA

Bando, Salvatore L (Sal) (Athlete, Baseball Player)
W308N6225 Shore Acres Rd
Hartland, WI 53029-8723, USA

Band of Bees, A (Music Group)
c/o Staff Member *Paradigm (Monterey)*
404 W Franklin St
Monterey, CA 93940-2303, USA

Band of Horses (Music Group)
c/o Staff Member *Silva Artist Management (SAM)*
722 Seward St
Los Angeles, CA 90038-3504, USA

Band of Skulls (Music Group, Musician)
c/o Staff Member *Vagrant Records*
2118 Wilshire Blvd # 361
Santa Monica, CA 90403-5704, USA

Bandy, Don (Athlete, Football Player)
215 E Calvin St
Taft, CA 93268-2915, USA

Bandy, Moe (Musician, Songwriter)
2577 US 160
Reeds Spring, MO 65737, USA

Bane (Music Group, Musician)
c/o Mike Pike *Kenmore Agency, The*
1032 W 18th St Ste A3
Costa Mesa, CA 92627-4553, USA

Bane, Eddie (Athlete, Baseball Player)
7790 Via Francesco Unit 1
San Diego, CA 92129-5153, USA

Banes, Lisa (Actor)
c/o Tim Angle *Don Buchwald & Associates (LA)*
6500 Wilshire Blvd Ste 2200
Los Angeles, CA 90048-4942, USA

Baney, Dick (Athlete, Baseball Player)
2231 Northup Dr
Tustin, CA 92782-1028, USA

Banfield, Ashleigh (Correspondent)
c/o Staff Member *NBC News (NY)*
30 Rockefeller Plz
New York, NY 10112-0015, USA

Banfield, Tony (Athlete, Football Player)
1102 Myrtlewood Dr
Friendswood, TX 77546-2015, us

Bang, Molly (Writer)
43 Drumlin Rd
Falmouth, MA 02540-2505, USA

Bangerter, Norman (Politician)
9947 S Congressional Way
South Jordan, UT 84095-3304, USA

Bang Lime (Music Group)
c/o Staff Member *Paradigm (Monterey)*
404 W Franklin St
Monterey, CA 93940-2303, USA

Banham, Frank (Athlete, Hockey Player)
139 W Grayling Ln
Suffield, CT 06078-1960, USA

Banhart, Bobby (Reality Star)
c/o Elizabeth Much *Much and House Public Relations*
8075 W 3rd St Ste 500
Los Angeles, CA 90048-4325, USA

Banhart, Devendra (Musician)
c/o Staff Member *Kill Rock Stars (KRS)*
107 SE Washington St Ste 155
Portland, OR 97214-2105, USA

Banister, Jeff (Athlete, Baseball Player)
5228 Hidden Brook Ln
League City, TX 77573-5783, USA

Banister, Jeff
PO Box 7000
Attn Coaching Staff
Pittsburgh, PA 15212-0038, USA

Bank, Melissa (Producer, Writer)
c/o Sylvie Rabineau *Rabineau Wachter and Sanford Literary Agency*
522 Wilshire Blvd Ste L
Santa Monica, CA 90401-1445, USA

Bank, Raymond
254 Embassy Ct
Columbus, OH 43230-2517, USA

Banke, Paul (Boxer)
1926 Bobolink Way
Pomona, CA 91767-2828, USA

Banker, Ted (Athlete, Football Player)
1862 Park Ave
East Meadow, NY 11554-4007, USA

Bankhead, Scott (Athlete, Baseball Player, Olympic Athlete)
1236 Idlewood Dr
Asheboro, NC 27205-4119, USA

Banks, Brian (Athlete, Baseball Player)
3243 E Jacaranda Cir
Mesa, AZ 85213-3242, USA

Banks, Briana (Actor, Adult Film Star, Model)
c/o Mike Esterman *Esterman.Com, LLC*
Prefers to be contacted via email
Baltimore, MD XXXXX, USA

Banks, Brianna (Adult Film Star)
c/o Staff Member *Atlas Multimedia Inc*
9005 Eton Ave Ste C
Canoga Park, CA 91304-6533, USA

Banks, Carl (Athlete, Football Player)
7 Glenview Dr
Warren, NJ 07059-5476, USA

Banks, Chip (Athlete, Football Player)
55 Fair Haven Way SE
Smyrna, GA 30080-8087, USA

Banks, Chuck (Athlete, Football Player)
3705 Valley Hill Dr
Randallstown, MD 21133-4822, USA

Banks, Darren (Athlete, Hockey Player)
11 Millington Rd
Pleasant Ridge, MI 48069-1108, USA

Banks, Elizabeth (Actor)
11635 Canton Pl
Studio City, CA 91604-4164, USA

Banks, Ernie (Athlete, Baseball Player)
1008 Harbor Crossing Ln
Marina Del Rey, CA 90292-5452, USA

Banks, Estes (Athlete, Football Player)
640 Gooseberry Dr Unit 703
Longmont, CO 80503-6432, us

Banks, Fred (Athlete, Football Player)
PO Box 358
Douglasville, GA 30133-0358, USA

Banks, Gene (Athlete, Basketball Player)
Bluefield State College
219 Rock St
Athletic Dept
Bluefield, WV 24701-2198, USA

Banks, Gene (Athlete, Basketball Player)
1210 Sloan St
Greensboro, NC 27401-3442, USA

Banks, Gordon (Athlete, Football Player)
2644 E Trinity Mills Rd
Carrollton, TX 75006-2136, USA

Banks, Jonathan (Actor)
29734 Harvester Rd
Malibu, CA 90265-3727, USA

Banks, Josh (Athlete, Baseball Player)
8605 Wandering Fox Trl Unit 204
Odenton, MD 21113-3746, USA

Banks, Lloyd (Musician)
1 Fox Hunt Ct
Huntington, NY 11743-6542, USA

Banks, Lynne Reid (Writer)
c/o Staff Member *HarperCollins Publishers*
195 Broadway Fl 2
Cellar 1
New York, NY 10007-3132, USA

Banks, Mike (Athlete, Football Player)
1615 1 Ave
Boone, IA 50036, us

Banks, Morwenna (Actor, Writer)
c/o Staff Member *ICM Partners (LA)*
10250 Constellation Blvd Fl 7
Los Angeles, CA 90067-6207, USA

Banks, Robert (Athlete, Football Player)
PO Box 1209
Hampton, VA 23661-0209, USA

Banks, Russell (Writer)
Princeton University
English Debt
Princeton, NJ 08544-0001, USA

Banks, Sandy (Journalist)
Los Angeles Times
202 W 1st St Ste 500
Los Angeles, CA 90012-4401, USA

Banks, Skeeter (Athlete, Baseball Player)
3810 Castlewood Rd
Richmond, VA 23234-2612, USA

Banks, Steven (Actor, Comedian)
c/o Rob Kenneally *Creative Artists Agency (CAA-LA)*
2000 Avenue of the Stars Ste 100
Los Angeles, CA 90067-4705, USA

Banks, Steven Gary (Producer, Writer)
c/o Staff Member *Evolution Entertainment (LA)*
901 N Highland Ave
Los Angeles, CA 90038-2412, USA

Banks, Ted (Coach)
Riverside Community College
Athletic Dept
Riverside, CA 92506, USA

Banks, Tom (Athlete, Football Player)
358 Wisteria St
Fairhope, AL 36532-1729, USA

Banks, Tony (Athlete, Football Player)
735 Laguna
Irving, TX 75039-3218, USA

Banks, Tyra (Actor, Model, Producer)
9308 Readcrest Dr
Beverly Hills, CA 90210-2533, USA

Banks, Walker (Athlete, Basketball Player)
3207 Brentwood Dr
Champaign, IL 61821-3482, USA

Banks, William
709 Albany Ave
Augusta, GA 30901-1807, us

Banks, Willie (Athlete, Baseball Player)
3443 Corte Sonrisa
Carlsbad, CA 92009-9341, USA

Bankston, Michael (Athlete, Football Player)
938 Kingwood Dr Apt 220
Kingwood, TX 77339-4446, USA

Bankston, Michael (Athlete, Football Player)
182 N Burberry Park Cir
Spring, TX 77382-5425, us

Bankston, Warren (Athlete, Football Player)
4201 Bordeaux Dr
Kenner, LA 70065-1739, USA

Bankston, Wes
599 Ewing Way
Wylie, TX 75098-7283, USA

Bannan, Justin (Athlete, Football Player)
561 Mockingbird Dr Belgrade Mt 59714-8139
Belgrade, MT 59714, us

Banner, David (Actor, Musician, Producer)
c/o Peter Schwartz *The Agency Group (NYC)*
142 W 57th St Fl 6
New York, NY 10019-3300, USA

Bannerman, Bill (Director, Producer)
Mirisch Agency
1875 Century Park E Ste 2025
C/O Lawrence Mirisch
Los Angeles, CA 90067-2337, USA

Bannerman, Isabella (Cartoonist)
41 South Dr
Hastings On Hudson, NY 10706-1813, USA

Bannerman, Murray (Athlete, Hockey Player)
826 Raintree Dr
Naperville, IL 60540-6381, USA

Bannister, Alan (Athlete, Baseball Player)
JDH Insurance Brokerage Services
20403 N Lake Pleasant Rd Ste 117
Peoria, AZ 85382-9707, USA

Bannister, Brian (Athlete, Baseball Player)
6701 E Caballo Dr
Paradise Valley, AZ 85253-2706, USA

Bannister, Floyd (Athlete, Baseball Player)
6701 E Caballo Dr
Paradise Valley, AZ 85253-2706, USA

Bannister, Ken (Athlete, Basketball Player)
2322 Broadgreen Dr
Missouri City, TX 77489-5002, USA

Bannister, Reggie (Actor, Musician)
Magic Inc
4450 California Pl # 315
Long Beach, CA 90807-2209, USA

Bannon, Bruce (Athlete, Football Player)
5765 Valley Stream Dr
Doylestown, PA 18902-9417, USA

Bannon, Jack (Actor)
6470 E Sunnyside Rd
Coeur D Alene, ID 83814-9503, USA

Bannon, Shaun (Musician)
Artist Group International
9560 Wilshire Blvd Ste 400
Beverly Hills, CA 90212-2442, USA

Banois, Vincent J (Athlete, Football Player)
24256J Tamarack Trl
Southfield, MI 48075, USA

Banta, Brad (Athlete, Football Player)
2069 Linwood Cir
Soddy Daisy, TN 37379-8139, USA

Banta, Brad (Athlete, Football Player)
1100 Smith Ave Birmingham MI48009-2031
Birmingham, MI 48009-2031, us

Banta-Cain, Tully (Athlete, Football Player)
111 Ruest Rd Attleboro MA2760-6610
North Attleboro, MA 02760-6610, us

Bantom, Michael (Basketball Player, Olympic Athlete)
418 Egret Ln
Secaucus, NJ 07094-2219, USA

Bantom, Mike (Athlete, Basketball Player)
418 Egret Ln
Secaucus, NJ 07094-2219, USA

Banx, Brooke (Model)
8491 W Sunset Blvd # 285
W Hollywood, CA 90069-1911, USA

Bao, Joseph Y (Doctor)
17436 Terry Lyn Ln
Cerritos, CA 90703-8522, USA

Baptist, Travis (Athlete, Baseball Player)
12269 Deersong Dr
Jacksonville, FL 32218-9038, USA

Baptiste, Baron (Athlete)
c/o Staff Member St Martins Press
175 5th Ave Ste 400
Publicity Dept
New York, NY 10010-7848, USA

Baquero, Ivana (Actor)
c/o Tom Drumm The Safran Company
8748 Holloway Dr
West Hollywood, CA 90069-2327, USA

Bar, Sendi (Actor)
c/o Peter Young Sovereign Talent Group
8421 Wilshire Blvd Ste 200
Beverly Hills, CA 90211-3204, USA

Barahona, Ralph (Athlete, Hockey Player)
4608 Bellflower Blvd
Lakewood, CA 90713-2502, USA

Barajas, Rod (Athlete, Baseball Player)
PO Box 7192
Rancho Santa Fe, CA 92067-7192, USA

Baraka, Imiri (Writer)
State University Of New York
Dept of African Studies
Stony Brook, NY 11794-0001, USA

Baranova, Anastasia (Actor)
c/o Staff Member Gersh (LA)
9465 Wilshire Blvd Ste 600
Beverly Hills, CA 90212-2605, USA

Baranski, Christine (Actor)
316 Wood Creek Rd
Bethlehem, CT 06751-1012, USA

Barash, Brandon (Actor)
c/o Marty Berneman Precision Entertainment
465 N Croft Ave
Los Angeles, CA 90048-2508, USA

Baratta, Adam (Actor)
c/o Gary Raskin Raskin Peter Rubin & Simon
1801 Century Park E Ste 2300
Los Angeles, CA 90067-2325, USA

Barbara, Kingsolver E (Writer)
c/o Staff Member HarperCollins Publishers
195 Broadway Fl 2
Cellar 1
New York, NY 10007-3132, USA

Barbaro, Gary W (Athlete, Football Player)
1000 Giuffrias Ave
Metairie, LA 70001-3649, USA

Barbat, Roxanne (Director, Producer, Writer)
c/o Staff Member Fantastic Films
3854 Clayton Ave
Los Angeles, CA 90027-4720, USA

Barbeau, Adrienne (Actor, Musician)
3851 Avenida Del Sol
Studio City, CA 91604-4025, USA

Barber, Aaron (Athlete, Basketball Player)
2830 Fillmore St NE
Minneapolis, MN 55418-2936, USA

Barber, Andrea (Actor)
1391 Beechwood Dr
Brea, CA 92821-2056, USA

Barber, Ava (Musician)
1508 N Courtney Oak Ln
Knoxville, TN 37938-4413, USA

Barber, Bill (Athlete, Hockey Player)
105 Harmon Dr
Blackwood, NJ 08012-5198, USA

Barber, Bob (Athlete, Football Player)
PO Box 552
Shreveport, LA 71162-0552, us

Barber, Brian (Athlete, Baseball Player)
1081 Vinsetta Cir
Winter Garden, FL 34787-9610, USA

Barber, Christopher E (Athlete, Football Player)
2621 Monaco Cove Cir
Orlando, FL 32825-8442, USA

Barber, Don (Athlete, Hockey Player)
1275 Park Ave
Washington, PA 15301-5949, USA

Barber, Gary (Producer)
6114 Camino De La Costa
La Jolla, CA 92037-6520, USA

Barber, John (Athlete, Basketball Player)
1554 Mahan St
Orangeburg, SC 29118-3546, USA

Barber, Kurt (Athlete, Football Player)
6850 Silver Eagle Ave Las Vegas
NV89122-8387
Las Vegas, NV 89122-8387, us

Barber, Kurt (Athlete, Football Player)
400 E Main St
Frankfort, KY 40601-2334, USA

Barber, Marion (Athlete, Football Player)
PO Box 46106
Minneapolis, MN 55446-0106, USA

Barber, Michael (Athlete, Football Player)
3020 Prosperity Church Rd Ste 1
Charlotte, NC 28269-7197, USA

Barber, Mike (Athlete, Football Player)
PO Box 2424
Desoto, TX 75123-2424, USA

Barber, Paul (Actor, Producer, Writer)
c/o Staff Member Paradigm (LA)
360 N Crescent Dr
North Bldg
Beverly Hills, CA 90210-4874, USA

Barber, Ronde (Athlete, Football Player)
17119 Journeys End Dr
Odessa, FL 33556-2442, USA

Barber, Rudy (Athlete, Football Player)
1411 NW 175th St
Miami, FL 33169-4660, USA

Barber, Shawn (Athlete, Football Player)
20035 Canterbury Dr
Stilwell, KS 66085-9394, USA

Barber, Steve (Athlete, Baseball Player)
902 San Eduardo Ave
Henderson, NV 89002-8900, USA

Barber, Stewart C (Stew) (Athlete, Football Player)
1447 Cardinal Hill Dr N
Mount Pleasant, SC 29466-8652, USA

Barber, Tiki (Athlete, Football Player, Sportscaster)
c/o Mark Lepselter Maxx Sports & Entertainment
546 5th Ave Fl 6
New York, NY 10036-5000, USA

Barber, William (Cinematographer)
2509 Whitechapel Pl
Thousand Oaks, CA 91362-5356, USA

Barberie, Bret (Athlete, Baseball Player)
11607 Bos St
Cerritos, CA 90703-6744, USA

Barberie, Jillian (Actor, Television Host)
19413 Bilmoor Pl
Tarzana, CA 91356-4416, USA

Barbieri, Gato (Musician)
Central Entertainment Services
123 Hardvard Ave
Staten Island, NY 10310, USA

Barbieri, Jim (Athlete, Baseball Player)
13619 E 5th Ave
Spokane Valley, WA 99216-0600, USA

Barbosa, Derek Keith (Chino XL) (Musician)
c/o Staff Member Universal Music Publishing Group (Latin)
420 Lincoln Rd Ste 200
Miami Beach, FL 33139-3014, USA

Barbosa, Leandro (Athlete, Basketball Player)
3EE1 NW 4th Ter
Apt 175
Pompano Beach, FL 33064, USA

Barbour, Benny (Athlete, Football Player)
661 Barbour Rd
Smithfield, NC 27577-5579, USA

Barbour, Haley R (Politician)
648 Dogwood Dr
Yazoo City, MS 39194-8205, USA

Barbour, John (Actor, Comedian, Writer)
10309 Denman St
Las Vegas, NV 89178-8031, USA

Barbree, Jay (Journalist)
9320 S Tropical Trl
Merritt Island, FL 32952-6821, USA

Barbutti, Pete (Musician)
Thomas Cassidy
11761 E Speedway Blvd
Tucson, AZ 85748-2017, USA

Barcelo, Lorenzo (Athlete, Baseball Player)
740 W Alameda St
Tucson, AZ 85745-2937, USA

Barcelo, Rich (Athlete, Basketball Player)
6308 Lakecrest Dr
Sachse, TX 75048-5577, USA

Barch, Krys (Athlete, Hockey Player)
2601 Aye Of The Stars
Houston, TX 77034

Barch, Krystofer (Athlete, Hockey Player)
6990 Long Leaf Dr
Parkland, FL 33076-3946, USA

Barclay, Dave (Actor)
c/o Staff Member Coolwaters Productions
10061 Riverside Dr # 531
Toluca Lake, CA 91602-2560, USA

Barclay, Don (Athlete, Football Player)
c/o Joe Linta JL Sports
1204 Main St Ste 179
Branford, CT 06405-3787, USA

Barclay, Paris (Director, Producer)
c/o Steve Lovett Lovett Management
1327 Brinkley Ave
Los Angeles, CA 90049-3619, USA

Bard, Daniel
205 Clermont Dr
Madison, MS 39110-4526, USA

Bard, Josh (Athlete, Baseball Player)
2139 Beechnut Pl
Castle Rock, CO 80108-7827, USA

Bardem, Javier E (Actor, Producer)
c/o Kelly Bush ID Public Relations (LA)
7060 Hollywood Blvd Fl 8th
Los Angeles, CA 90028-6021, USA

Barden, Brian (Athlete, Baseball Player)
10452 E Cannon Dr
Scottsdale, AZ 85258-4929, USA

Bare, Bobby (Musician)
112 Galway Lk S
Hendersonville, TN 37075-4583, USA

Barefoot, Ken (Athlete, Football Player)
1204 Lawrence Grey Dr
Virginia Beach, VA 23455-5605, USA

Bareikis, Arija (Actor)
c/o Rhonda Price *Gersh (NY)*
41 Madison Ave
New York, NY 10010-2202, USA

Bareikis, Arlia (Actor)
360 W 23rd St
New York, NY 10011-2258, USA

Bareilles, Sara (Musician)
c/o Jordan Feldstein *Career Artist Management*
9350 Civic Center Dr Ste 100
Beverly Hills, CA 90210-3629, USA

Baretto, Ray (Musician)
Creative Music Consultants
181 Christle St # 300
New York, NY 10002, USA

Barfield, Amanda (Actor)
Snyder Management
6409 Primrose Ave Ste 7
Los Angeles, CA 90068-2865, USA

Barfield, Jesse L (Athlete, Baseball Player)
5814 Spanish Moss Ct
Spring, TX 77379-6482, USA

Barfield, John (Athlete, Baseball Player)
2107 Hobson Ave
Hot Springs National Park,
AR 71913-3037, USA

Barfield, Josh (Athlete, Baseball Player)
18082 N 93rd Pi
Scottsdale, AZ 85255, USA

Barfield, Ron (Race Car Driver)
PO Box 6495
Florence, SC 29502-6495, USA

Bargar, Greg (Athlete, Baseball Player)
22682 Lupine Dr
Torrance, CA 90505-3332, USA

Barger, Ralph (Sonny) (Actor)
c/o Staff Member *HarperCollins Publishers*
195 Broadway Fl 2
Cellar 1
New York, NY 10007-3132, USA

Bargnani, Andrea (Athlete, Basketball Player)
c/o Leon Rose *Creative Artists Agency (CAA-NY)*
162 5th Ave Fl 6
New York, NY 10010-6047, USA

Barhorst, Barney (Athlete, Basketball Player)
8004 River Bay Dr E
Indianapolis, IN 46240-2994, USA

Barinholtz, Ike (Actor, Comedian)
c/o Peter Principato *Principato/Young Management (LA)*
9465 Wilshire Blvd Ste 900
Beverly Hills, CA 90212-2608, USA

Barisich, Carl J (Athlete, Football Player)
16566 W Lilac St
Goodyear, AZ 85338-4535, USA

Bark, Brian (Athlete, Baseball Player)
3752 Spring Lake Ln
Owings Mills, MD 21117-1432, USA

Barker, Bob (Game Show Host)
The Prappas Company
9201 Wilshire Blvd Ste 204
Beverly Hills, CA 90210-5537, USA

Barker, Bryan (Athlete, Football Player)
1225 Selva Marina Cir
Atlantic Beach, FL 32233-5525, USA

Barker, Clive (Writer)
1875 Century Park E Ste 2060
Los Angeles, CA 90067-2521, USA

Barker, Clyde F (Doctor)
3 Coopertown Rd
Haverford, PA 19041-1012, USA

Barker, Ed (Athlete, Football Player)
12002 Clover Creek Dr SW
Lakewood, WA 98499-5210, USA

Barker, Glen (Athlete, Baseball Player)
363 2nd Ave
Albany, NY 12209-1924, USA

Barker, Jay (Athlete, Football Player, Talk Show Host)
4120 Montevallo Rd S
Mountain Brk, AL 35213-3114, USA

Barker, Jordan (Actor)
c/o Staff Member *Select Artists Ltd (CA-Westside Office)*
1138 12th St Apt 1
Santa Monica, CA 90403-5459, USA

Barker, Kevin (Athlete, Baseball Player)
PO Box 96
Mendota, VA 24270-0096, USA

Barker, Len (Athlete, Baseball Player)
10690 Locust Grove Dr
Chardon, OH 44024-8870, USA

Barker, Leo (Athlete, Football Player)
25 Via Lucena
San Clemente, CA 92673-7045, USA

Barker, Lois (Athlete, Baseball Player)
195 W Main St Apt 6
Chester, NJ 07930-2451, USA

Barker, Ray (Athlete, Baseball Player)
303 Greenbriar Rd
Martinsburg, WV 25401-2827, USA

Barker, Rich (Athlete, Baseball Player)
17 Landers Rd
Stoneham, MA 02180-1409, USA

Barker, Richard A (Religious Leader)
Orthodox Presbyterian Church
PO Box P
Willow Grove, PA 19090, USA

Barker, Roy (Athlete, Football Player)
23 Saint Marks Cir
Islandia, NY 11749-1728, USA

Barker, Sean (Athlete, Baseball Player)
2454 C St
Bakersfield, CA 93301-2716, USA

Barker, Travis (Musician)
2371 Buckingham Ln
Los Angeles, CA 90077-1339, USA

Barker-Lequia, Joan (Athlete, Baseball Player)
3236 34th St SW
Grandville, MI 49418-1905, USA

Barkett, Andy (Athlete, Baseball Player)
503 Yorkshire Dr
Oviedo, FL 32765-8157, USA

Barkin, Ellen (Actor)
c/o Stephen Huvane *Slate Public Relations*
9000 W Sunset Blvd Ste 915
West Hollywood, CA 90069-5809, USA

Barkley, Brian (Athlete, Baseball Player)
10426 Cooks Lake Rd
Lumberton, TX 77657-8864, USA

Barkley, Charles (Athlete, Basketball Player, Olympic Athlete)
7615 E Vaquero Dr
Scottsdale, AZ 85258-2100, USA

Barkley, Dean M (Politician)
1300 W Medicine Lake Dr Apt 101
Minneapolis, MN 55441-4854, USA

Barkley, Iran (Boxer)
2645 3rd Ave
Bronx, NY 10451-6329, USA

Barkley, Jeff (Athlete, Baseball Player)
264 3rd Ave NE
Hickory, NC 28601-5016, USA

Barkley, Matt (Athlete, Football Player)
c/o Jimmy Sexton *CAA (Memphis)*
6060 Poplar Ave Ste 470
Memphis, TN 38119-0910, USA

Barkman, Tyler Jane (Janie) (Swimmer)
Princeton University
Athletic Dept
Princeton, NJ 08544-0001, USA

Barksdale, James (Jim) (Business Person)
Time Warner Inc.
1 Time Warner Ctr Bsmt B
New York, NY 10019-6010, USA

Barksdale, Lance (Athlete, Baseball Player)
4507 Pine Lake Dr
Terry, MS 39170-8741, USA

Barksdale, LaQuanda (Athlete, Basketball Player)
San Antonio Silver Stars
1 at and T Center Pkwy
San Antonio, TX 78219-3604, USA

Barkum, Jerome P (Athlete, Football Player)
2720 Palmer Dr Apt J5
Gulfport, MS 39507-2854, USA

Barletta, Joseph (Publisher)
TV Guide Magazine
100 Matsonford Rd Ste 1
Wayne, PA 19087-4565, USA

Barletta, Lou (Congressman, Politician)
510 Cannon Hob
Washington, DC 20515-1402, USA

Barlow, Corey (Athlete, Football Player)
30 Wisteria Cir
Covington, GA 30016-7260, USA

Barlow, Craig (Athlete, Golfer)
1037 Copper Palm Ct
Henderson, NV 89002-0508, USA

Barlow, Kevan (Athlete)
c/o Doug Hendrickson *Octagon Football*
832 Sansome St Fl 1
San Francisco, CA 94111-1558, USA

Barlow, Mike (Athlete, Baseball Player)
4524 Francis Rd
Cazenovia, NY 13035-8470, USA

Barlow, Perry (Cartoonist)
New Yorker Magazine
4 Times Sq Fl 22
Editorial Dept
New York, NY 10036-6592, USA

Barlow, Reggie (Athlete, Football Player)
8311 Timber Trace Ln
Pike Road, AL 36064-3444, USA

BarlowGirl (Music Group, Musician)
c/o Greg Oliver *Greg Oliver Agency*
1710 General George Patton Dr Ste 104
Brentwood, TN 37027-2904, USA

Barmes, Bruce (Athlete, Baseball Player)
300 Southerby Dr
Garner, NC 27529-4981, USA

Barmes, Clnt (Athlete, Baseball Player)
113 Mallard Ct
Mead, CO 80542-8802, USA

Barmore, Leon (Athlete, Basketball Player)
1100 Brookhaven Ave
Ruston, LA 71270-8505, USA

Barnaby, Matthew (Athlete, Hockey Player)
134 King Anthony Way
Getzville, NY 14068-1414, USA

Barndt, Tom (Athlete, Football Player)
11041 Romola St
Las Vegas, NV 89141-3410, USA

Barner, Kenjon (Athlete, Football Player)
c/o Frank Bauer *Sun West Sports*
7883 N Pershing Ave
Stockton, CA 95207-1749, USA

Barnes, Ben (Actor)
c/o Lena Roklin *Luber Roklin Management*
5815 W Sunset Blvd Ste 206
Los Angeles, CA 90028-6481, USA

Barnes, Benny J (Athlete, Football Player)
5003 Fleming Ave
Richmond, CA 94804-4718, USA

Barnes, Billy Ray (Athlete, Football Player)
501 W Ryder Ave
Landis, NC 28088-1238, USA

Barnes, Brandon (Athlete, Football Player)
912 Westview Dr
Sikeston, MO 63801-4661, USA

Barnes, Brian (Athlete, Baseball Player)
1006 Arrowhead Pt
Anderson, SC 29625-6500, USA

Barnes, Bruce (Athlete, Football Player)
7129 Alexandria Pl
Stockton, CA 95207-1503, USA

Barnes, Christopher Daniel (Actor)
3824 Fairway Ave
Studio City, CA 91604-2303, USA

Barnes, Darian (Athlete, Football Player)
554 Clifton Ave
Toms River, NJ 08753-6791, USA

Barnes, Erich (Athlete, Football Player)
712 Warburton Ave
Yonkers, NY 10701-1501, USA

Barnes, Ernest E (Athlete, Football Player)
8613 Sherwood Dr
West Hollywood, CA 90069-4607, USA

Barnes, Frank (Athlete, Baseball Player)
1508 Brazil St
Greenville, MS 38701-2622, USA

Barnes, Gary (Athlete, Football Player)
172 Falling Springs Rd
Central, SC 29630-9406, USA

Barnes, Jeff (Athlete, Football Player)
10738 Versailles Blvd
Clermont, FL 34711-7342, USA

Barnes, Jhane (Designer, Fashion
Designer)
Jhane Barnes Inc
18 Five Ponds Dr
Waccabuc, NY 10597-1032, USA

Barnes, Joanna (Actor)
PO Box 1103
Gualala, CA 95445-1103, USA

Barnes, Joe (Race Car Driver)
Barnes Racing
200 Neil Thompson Rd
Lackawaxen, PA 18435-9601, USA

Barnes, John (Athlete, Baseball Player)
1455 Godell St
Templeton, CA 93465-9424, USA

Barnes, Johnnie (Athlete, Football Player)
212 Charlemagne Dr
Suffolk, VA 23435-1453, USA

Barnes, Khalif (Athlete, Football Player)
7967 Monterey Bay Dr
Jacksonville, FL 32256-2927, USA

Barnes, Kim (Writer)
c/o Staff Member Knopf
1745 Broadway
New York, NY 10019-4640, USA

Barnes, Larry (Athlete, Baseball Player)
11906 Crockett Ct
Bakersfield, CA 93312-5710, USA

Barnes, Larry (Athlete, Football Player)
410 Navajo Ave
Simla, CO 80835, USA

Barnes, Larry (Athlete, Football Player)
2202 Belle Chase Cir
Tampa, FL 33634, USA

Barnes, Linda (Writer)
56 Seaver St
Brookline, MA 02445-5749, USA

Barnes, Lute (Athlete, Baseball Player)
37329 S Blackfoot Dr
Tucson, AZ 85739-1042, USA

Barnes, Marlon (Athlete, Football Player)
7092 W Autumn Gold Ct
Tucson, AZ 85743-5029, USA

Barnes, Matt (Athlete, Basketball Player)
c/o Aaron Goodwin Goodwin Sports
Management
121 Lakeside Ave Ste 100B
Seattle, WA 98122-6587, USA

Barnes, Mike H (Athlete, Football Player)
205 Cindy St S
Keller, TX 76248-2341, USA

Barnes, Mike J (Athlete, Football Player)
27474 Plank Rd
Guys Mills, PA 16327-5434, USA

Barnes, Norm (Athlete, Hockey Player)
17 Meadow Xing
Simsbury, CT 06070-1006, USA

Barnes, Pat (Athlete, Football Player)
5 Willowglade
Trabuco Canyon, CA 92679-3813, USA

Barnes, Priscilla (Actor)
3109 Buckingham Rd
Glendale, CA 91206-1406, USA

Barnes, Rashidi (Athlete, Football Player)
8748 Kentshire Way
Sacramento, CA 95828-6173, USA

Barnes, Reggie (Athlete, Football Player)
3110 Merrimac Ct
Southlake, TX 76092-8109, USA

Barnes, Rich (Athlete, Baseball Player)
2845 Wilderness Rd
West Palm Beach, FL 33409-2030, USA

Barnes, Rick (Athlete, Basketball Player)
Texas University
Athletic Dept
Austin, TX 78713, USA

Barnes, Rod (Athlete, Basketball Player)
Mississippi State University
Athletic Dept
Mississippi State, MS 39762, USA

Barnes, Rodrigo (Athlete, Football Player)
4310 Gram Ln
Waco, TX 76705-2662, USA

Barnes, Ron (Athlete, Baseball Player)
5304 MacDonald Ave
El Cerrito, CA 94530-1636, USA

Barnes, Skeeter (Athlete, Baseball Player)
11544 Winding Wood Dr
Indianapolis, IN 46235-9731, USA

Barnes, Stu (Athlete, Hockey Player)
5069 Royal Creek Ln
Plano, TX 75093-4069, USA

Barnes, Stu (Athlete, Hockey Player)
Dallas Stars
2601 Avenue of the Stars Ste 100
Attn: Hockey Operations Dept
Frisco, TX 75034-9016, USA

Barnes, Tomur (Athlete, Football Player)
2518 Broad St
Baytown, TX 77521-1265, USA

Barnes, Wallace (Business Person)
Barnes Group
123 Main St
Bristol, CT 06010-6376, USA

Barnes, William (Athlete, Baseball Player)
19792 Ardmore St
Detroit, MI 48235-1503, USA

Barnes Jr, Roosevelt (Athlete, Football
Player)
3128 Covington Manor Rd
Fort Wayne, IN 46814-9126, USA

Barnes-McCoy, Joyce (Athlete, Baseball
Player)
1313 E 19th Ave
Hutchinson, KS 67502-5061, USA

Barnett, Charlie (Actor)
c/o Carl Rumbaugh Simmons & Scott
Entertainment
7942 Mulholland Dr
Los Angeles, CA 90046-1225, USA

Barnett, Dave (Commentator)
Sb24 Lake Cherokee
Tatum, TX 75691-3289, USA

Barnett, Dean (Athlete, Football Player)
8 Cozy Glen Cir
Henderson, NV 89074-1563, USA

Barnett, Dick (Athlete, Basketball Player)
1227 Pine Rdg
Bushkill, PA 18324, USA

Barnett, Douglas (Athlete, Football Player)
651 Park Ln
Billings, MT 59102-1930, USA

Barnett, Doyle (Writer)
c/o Staff Member New World Library
14 Pamaron Way Ste 1
Novato, CA 94949-6215, USA

Barnett, Fred (Athlete, Football Player)
PO Box 604
Bala Cynwyd, PA 19004-0604, USA

Barnett, Gary (Coach, Football Coach)
Colorado University
Athletic Dept
Boulder, CO 80309-0001, USA

Barnett, Jim (Athlete, Basketball Player)
7 Kittiwake Rd
Orinda, CA 94563-1716, USA

Barnett, Larry (Athlete, Baseball Player)
6298 Hughes Rd
Prospect, OH 43342-9602, USA

Barnett, Mandy (Musician)
320 Old Hickory Blvd Apt 1911
Nashville, TN 37221-1312, USA

Barnett, Mike (Athlete, Baseball Player)
PO Box 53625
Knoxville, TN 37950-3625, USA

Barnett, Nate (Athlete, Basketball Player)
1001 N Jefferson St Ste 71E
Wilmington, DE 19801-1447, USA

Barnett, Nick (Athlete, Football Player)
3496 Country Winds Ct
Green Bay, WI 54311-6906, USA

Barnett, Oliver (Athlete, Football Player)
1133 Autumn Ridge Dr
Lexington, KY 40509-2055, USA

Barnett, Pam (Athlete, Golfer)
4908 E Rancho Tierra Dr
Cave Creek, AZ 85331-5912, USA

Barnett, Sloan (Correspondent, Writer)
c/o Staff Member Simon & Schuster
1230 Avenue of the Americas Fl CONC1
New York, NY 10020-1586, USA

Barnett, Steven (Steve) (Athlete, Football
Player)
308 Romae Ct
Danville, CA 94526-1863, USA

Barnette, Curtis H (Business Person)
Bethlehem Steel
1170 8th Ave
Bethlehem, PA 18018-2255, USA

Barney, Darwin (Athlete, Baseball Player)
20467 SW Skiver St
Beaverton, OR 97078-5815, USA

Barney, Edith (Athlete, Baseball Player)
329 Blackburn Blvd
North Port, FL 34287-1507, USA

Barney, Tamra (Reality Star)
c/o Pamela Hicks Hicks and Associates
Prefers to be contacted via email or
telephone
West Hollywood, CA 90069, USA

Barney Jr, Lemuel J (Lem) (Athlete,
Football Player)
775 Kentbrook Dr
Commerce Township, MI 48382-5013,
USA

Barnhardt, Tom (Athlete, Football Player)
503 Park St
China Grove, NC 28023-2154, USA

Barnhart, Vic (Athlete, Baseball Player)
13102 Unger Rd
Hagerstown, MD 21742-1428, USA

Barnhill, Herbert (Athlete, Baseball
Player)
Jacksonville Red Caps
3712 Owen Ave
Jacksonville, FL 32208-2910, USA

Barnhill, John (Athlete, Basketball Player)
28511 Lomo Dr
Rancho Palos Verdes, CA 90275-3137,
USA

Barnhill, Norton (Athlete, Basketball
Player)
3355 Kensington Pl
Winston Salem, NC 27103-6456, USA

Barnhill, Scott (Model)
c/o Staff Member IMG
304 Park Ave S Fl 12
New York, NY 10010-4314, USA

Barnowski, Ed (Athlete, Baseball Player)
2380 Lake Lucy Rd
Chanhassen, MN 55317-7561, USA

Barnwell, Chris (Athlete, Baseball Player)
PO Box 600070
Jacksonville, FL 32260-0070, USA

Barnwell, Malcolm (Athlete, Football
Player)
4 Flood St Apt A
Charleston, SC 29403-5167, USA

Barnwell, Ysaye (Musician)
Sweet Honey Agency
PO Box 600099
Newtonville, MA 02460-0001, USA

Baron, Caroline (Producer)
c/o Paul Hook ICM Partners (LA)
10250 Constellation Blvd Fl 7
Los Angeles, CA 90067-6207, USA

Baron, Jimmy (Athlete, Baseball Player)
7402 Conner Ln
Edwardsville, IL 62025-4668, USA

Baron, Joanne (Actor)
940 N Tigertail Rd
Los Angeles, CA 90049-1419, USA

Baron, Murray (Athlete, Hockey Player)
23723 N Scottsdale Rd
#D-3
Scottsdale, AZ 85255, USA

Baron, Natalia (Actor)
c/o Tiffany Kuzon Evolution Entertainment
(LA)
901 N Highland Ave
Los Angeles, CA 90038-2412, USA

Barone, Anita (Actor)
17628 McCormick St
Encino, CA 91316-2551, USA

Barone, Daniel (Athlete, Baseball Player)
120 Joes Ln
Hollister, CA 95023-6353, USA

Barone, Dick (Athlete, Baseball Player)
1481 McDonald Cir
Hollister, CA 95023-6743, USA

Baron-Reid, Colette Baron-Reid (Writer)
c/o Staff Member Hay House, Inc
PO Box 5100
Carlsbad, CA 92018-5100, USA

Barr, Bob (Business Person, Politician)
Office of Bob Barr
4401 Northside Pkwy NW # 100
Atlanta, GA 30327-3065, USA

Barr, Cynthia (Athlete, Olympic Athlete, Swimmer)
3995 Aiken Rd
Pensacola, FL 32503-3301, USA

Barr, Doug (Actor)
PO Box 63
Rutherford, CA 94573-0063, USA

Barr, Jim (Athlete, Baseball Player)
6335 Oak Hill Dr
Granite Bay, CA 95746-8908, USA

Barr, Julia (Actor)
c/o Robert Attermann *Abrams Artists Agency (NY)*
9200 W Sunset Blvd PH 11
West Hollywood, CA 90069-3601, USA

Barr, Matt (Actor)
c/o Matt Luber *Luber Roklin Management*
5815 W Sunset Blvd Ste 206
Los Angeles, CA 90028-6481, USA

Barr, Mike (Athlete, Basketball Player)
350 38th St NW
Canton, OH 44709-1523, USA

Barr, Nevada (Writer)
G P Putnam's Sons
375 Hudson St
New York, NY 10014-3658, USA

Barr, Roseanne (Actor, Comedian, Producer)
8142 Billowvista Dr
Playa Del Rey, CA 90293-7806, USA

Barr, Steve (Athlete, Baseball Player)
470 Village Cir SW
Winter Haven, FL 33880-1668, USA

Barr, William (Politician)
1 Stamford Forum
Stamford, CT 06901-3516, USA

Barra, Mary (Business Person)
General Motors Company
P.O. Box 3170
Highland Park, MI 48203, USA

Barragan, Cuno (Athlete, Baseball Player)
1824 Saint Ann Ct
Carmichael, CA 95608-5643, USA

Barranca, German (Athlete, Baseball Player)
199 Kreidler Ave
York, PA 17402-4976, USA

Barrasso, John (Senator)
307 Dirksen Senate Office Building
Washington, DC 20510-0001, USA

Barrasso, Tom (Athlete, Hockey Player)
1400 Edwards Mill Rd
Attn Coaching Staff
Raleigh, NC 27607-3624, USA

Barrasso, Tom (Athlete, Hockey Player)
12820 Rosalie St
Raleigh, NC 27614-7970, USA

Barratt, Michael R (Astronaut)
2102 Pleasant Palm Cir
League City, TX 77573-6670, USA

Barratt, Michael R Dr (Astronaut)
2102 Pleasant Palm Cir
League City, TX 77573-6670, USA

Barraza, Adriana (Actor)
c/o Ivan De Paz *DePaz Management*
2011 N Vermont Ave
Los Angeles, CA 90027-1931, USA

Barrese, Sasha (Actor)
c/o Erik Kritzer *LINK Entertainment*
11872 La Grange Ave Fl 1
Los Angeles, CA 90025-5283, USA

Barreto, Alexandra (Actor)
c/o Robert Marsala *Wishlab*
2225A Hyperion Ave
Los Angeles, CA 90027-4709, USA

Barreto, Bruno (Director)
c/o Martin Spencer *Paradigm (LA)*
2000 Avenue of the Stars
Los Angeles, CA 90067-4700, USA

Barrett, Alice (Actor)
Alliance Talent
9171 Wilshire Blvd Ste 441
Beverly Hills, CA 90210-5516, USA

Barrett, Bo (Actor)
c/o Staff Member *Badass Haircut Productions*
4425 Avocado St
Los Angeles, CA 90027-2104, USA

Barrett, Bob (Athlete, Football Player)
610 54th Ave W
Bradenton, FL 34210, USA

Barrett, Brendan Ryan (Actor)
c/o Carol Elsner *AMT Artists*
14724 Ventura Blvd Ste 505
Sherman Oaks, CA 91403-3505, USA

Barrett, Brendon Ryan (Actor)
9255 W Sunset Blvd Ste 1010
West Hollywood, CA 90069-3307, USA

Barrett, Colleen (Business Person)
Southwest Airlines
PO Box 36611
2702 Love Field Dr
Dallas, TX 75235-1611, USA

Barrett, Craig R (Business Person)
Intel Corp
2200 Mission College Blvd
Santa Clara, CA 95054-1549, USA

Barrett, Danny
University At Buffalo
104 Stadium Complex Attn Footballcouchingstaff
Buffalo, NY 14260-5100, USA

Barrett, David (Athlete, Football Player)
1423 E Rose St
Blytheville, AR 72315-3714, USA

Barrett, Ernie (Athlete, Basketball Player)
2105 Grand Ridge Ct
Manhattan, KS 66503-8695, USA

Barrett, Jacinda (Actor)
c/o Joan Green *Joan Green Management*
1836 Courtney Ter
Los Angeles, CA 90046-2106, USA

Barrett, Jean (Athlete, Football Player)
7494 S Sleepy Hollow Dr
Tulsa, OK 74136-5919, USA

Barrett, Kelli (Actor)
c/o Emily Gerson Saines *Brookside Artists Management (NY)*
250 W 57th St Ste 2303
New York, NY 10107-2399, USA

Barrett, Malcolm (Actor)
c/o Craig Dorfman *Frontline Management*
5670 Wilshire Blvd Ste 1370
Los Angeles, CA 90036-5679, USA

Barrett, Mario (Actor, Musician)
c/o Heather Weiss *Much and House Public Relations*
8075 W 3rd St Ste 500
Los Angeles, CA 90048-4325, USA

Barrett, Martin G (Marty) (Athlete, Baseball Player)
3552 Ridge Meadow St
Las Vegas, NV 89135-7811, USA

Barrett, Michael (Athlete, Baseball Player)
600 Galleria Pkwy SE Ste 1900
Atlanta, GA 30339-5990, USA

Barrett, Stanton (Race Car Driver)
Sky Motorsports
1055 Gateway Dr
Mooresville, NC 28115-8341, USA

Barrett, Ted (Athlete, Baseball Player)
4380 E Sundance Ct
Gilbert, AZ 85297-9640, USA

Barrett, Tim (Athlete, Baseball Player)
5588 Jandel Dr
Aurora, IN 47001-3010, USA

Barrett, Tom (Athlete, Baseball Player)
5306 W Jupiter Way
Chandler, AZ 85226-8622, USA

Barrie, Barbara (Actor)
c/o Staff Member *Innovative Artists (LA)*
1505 10th St
Santa Monica, CA 90401-2805, USA

Barrie, Sebastian (Athlete, Football Player)
1369 E Canyon Way
Chandler, AZ 85249-4738, USA

Barrile, Anthony (Actor)
Alliance Talent
9171 Wilshire Blvd Ste 441
Beverly Hills, CA 90210-5516, USA

Barrino, Fantasia (Musician)
7721 Seton House Ln
Charlotte, NC 28277-5563, USA

Barrios, Jose (Athlete, Baseball Player)
6484 SW 25th St
Miami, FL 33155-2958, USA

Barris, Chuck (Television Host)
80 Washington Spring Rd
Palisades, NY 10964-1624, USA

Barris, George (Designer, Misc)
Barris Kustom Industries
10811 Riverside Dr
North Hollywood, CA 91602-2308, USA

Barriw, Barbara (Actor)
15 W 72nd St Apt 2A
New York, NY 10023-3419, USA

Barron, Alex (Athlete, Football Player)
630 Emerson Rd Apt 206
Saint Louis, MO 63141-6751, USA

Barron, Alex (Race Car Driver)
Dan Gurney's Racing
2334 S Broadway
Santa Ana, CA 92707-3250, USA

Barron, Chris (Music Group, Musician)
c/o Staff Member *Skyline Music*
28 Union St
Whitefield, NH 03598-3503, USA

Barron, Dana (Actor)
c/o Kevin Turner *Coast to Coast Talent Group*
3350 Barham Blvd
Los Angeles, CA 90068-1404, USA

Barron, Doug (Athlete, Golfer)
5080 Peg Ln
Memphis, TN 38117-2147, USA

Barron, Mark (Athlete, Baseball Player)
110 N Randolph Ave
Clarksville, IN 47129-2761, USA

Barron, Tony (Athlete, Baseball Player)
16014 123rd Avenue Ct E
Puyallup, WA 98374-9649, USA

Barros, Dana (Athlete, Basketball Player)
10 Arborway
North Easton, MA 02356-1142, USA

Barrow, Barbara (Athlete, Golfer)
11427 Mayapple Way
San Diego, CA 92131-2928, USA

Barrow, John (Athlete, Football Player)
4111 Bay Shore Dr
Missouri City, TX 77459-1829, USA

Barrow, Michael (Athlete, Football Player)
1115 S Alhambra Cir
Coral Gables, FL 33146-3711, USA

Barrowman, Mike (Swimmer)
706 N Wamer St
Bay City, MI 48708, USA

Barrows, Scott (Athlete, Football Player)
3600 Kern Rd
Lake Orion, MI 48360-2351, USA

Barrs, Jay (Athlete, Olympic Athlete, Shooter)
646 E Kings Peak Cv
Draper, UT 84020-7922, USA

Barrueco, Manuel (Musician)
Columbia Artists Mgmt Inc
165 W 57th St
New York, NY 10019-2201, USA

Barry, A L (Religious Leader)
Lutheran Church Missouri Synod
1333 S Kirkwood Rd
Saint Louis, MO 63122-7295, USA

Barry, Allan (Athlete, Football Player)
700 S Myrtle Ave Apt 230
Monrovia, CA 91016-8410, USA

Barry, Brent (Athlete, Basketball Player)
617 Grandview Pl
San Antonio, TX 78209-5417, USA

Barry, Daniel T (Dan) (Astronaut)
46 Ashton Ln
South Hadley, MA 01075-2143, USA

Barry, Daniel T Dr (Astronaut)
46 Ashton Ln
South Hadley, MA 01075-2143, USA

Barry, Dave (Journalist, Writer)
Miami Herald
PO Box 3028
Editorial Dept
Livonia, MI 48151-3028, USA

Barry, Ed (Athlete, Hockey Player)
61 Pleasant St
Needham, MA 02492-2950, USA

Barry, Jeff (Athlete, Baseball Player)
322 N Barneburg Rd
Medford, OR 97504-6683, USA

Barry, Jon (Athlete, Basketball Player)
3325 Piedmont Rd NE
Atlanta, GA 30305-1889, USA

Barry, Kevin (Athlete, Baseball Player)
72 Burlington Path Rd
Cream Ridge, NJ 08514-1601, USA

Barry, Len (Musician)
Cape Entertainment
1161 NW 76th Ave
Plantation, FL 33322-5120, USA

Barry, Lynda (Cartoonist)
PO Box 447
Footville, WI 53537-0447, USA

Barry, Marion S (Politician)
161 Raleigh St SE
Washington, DC 20032-1528, USA

Barry, Odell (Athlete, Football Player)
2561 Ranch Reserve Rdg
Denver, CO 80234-2695, USA

Barry, Patricia (Actor)
12742 Highwood St
Los Angeles, CA 90049-2624, USA

Barry, Paul (Athlete, Football Player)
409 Kingswood Dr
El Paso, TX 79932-2217, USA

Barry, Randy (Reality Star)
c/o Michael Martin *MM Agency*
3937 Nobel Dr
San Diego, CA 92122-6156, USA

Barry, Raymond J (Actor)
c/o Bob McGowan *McGowan Management*
8733 W Sunset Blvd Ste 103
West Hollywood, CA 90069-2241, USA

Barry, Rich (Athlete, Baseball Player)
12020 Hoffman St Apt K
Studio City, CA 91604-4760, USA

Barry, Rick (Athlete, Basketball Player)
5240 Broadmoor Bluffs Dr
Colorado Springs, CO 80906-7912, USA

Barry, Rod (Adult Film Star)
c/o Staff Member *Diva Central Inc*
7510 W Sunset Blvd Ste 1445
Los Angeles, CA 90046-3408, USA

Barry, Scott (Athlete, Baseball Player)
148 Lukesport Dr
Quincy, MI 49082-9595, USA

Barry, Seymour (Sy) (Artist, Cartoonist)
225 Fairfield Dr E
Holbrook, NY 11741-2866, USA

Barry, Todd (Comedian)
c/o David (Dave) Becky *3 Arts Entertainment (LA)*
9460 Wilshire Blvd Fl 7
Beverly Hills, CA 90212-2713, USA

Barry III, Richard F D (Rick) (Athlete, Basketball Player)
KNBR Radio
55 Hawthorne St Ste 1100
San Francisco, CA 94105-3932, USA

Barrymore, Drew (Actor, Producer)
c/o Chris Miller *Flower Films Inc*
7360 Santa Monica Blvd
West Hollywood, CA 90046-6619, USA

Barsh, Gregory S (Doctor)
Stanford University
Medical Center
Pediatrics Dept
Stanford, CA 94305, USA

Bart, Peter (Writer)
c/o Daniel Strone *Trident Media Group LLC*
41 Madison Ave Fl 36
New York, NY 10010-2257, USA

Bart, Roger (Actor)
c/o Michael Baum *Impression Entertainment*
9229 W Sunset Blvd Ste 700
West Hollywood, CA 90069-3407, USA

Bartecko, Lubos (Athlete, Hockey Player)
121 Windy Acres Estates Dr
Ballwin, MO 63021-4232, USA

Bartee, Kimera (Athlete, Baseball Player)
State College Spikes 112 Medlar Field at
Lubrano Park 'Attn Managers Office
University Park, PA 16802, USA

Bartee, William (Athlete, Football Player)
17 Talaquah Blvd
Ormond Beach, FL 32174-3705, USA

Bartek, Steve (Musician)
c/o Staff Member *Kraft-Engel Management*
15233 Ventura Blvd Ste 200
Sherman Oaks, CA 91403-2244, USA

Barth, Robert (Religious Leader)
Churches of Christ in Christian Union
PO Box 30
Circleville, OH 43113-0030, USA

Bartha, Justin (Actor, Producer)
2220 N Berendo St
Los Angeles, CA 90027-1125, USA

Barthmaier, Jimmy (Athlete, Baseball Player)
445 Brook Cir
Roswell, GA 30075-7179, USA

Bartholomay, William C (Commentator)
180 E Pearson St Apt 3307
Chicago, IL 60611-6730, USA

Bartholomew, Brent (Athlete, Football Player)
809 N Lake Pleasant Rd
Apopka, FL 32712-3219, USA

Bartholomew, Jean (Athlete, Golfer)
411 Capistrano Dr
Palm Beach Gardens, FL 33410-4301, USA

Bartholomew, Logan (Actor)
c/o Beverly Strong *Strong Management*
9350 Wilshire Blvd Ste 224
Beverly Hills, CA 90212-3204, USA

Bartilson, Lynsey (Actor)
c/o Staff Member *Karen Renna & Associates*
PO Box 4227
Burbank, CA 91503-4227, USA

Bartirome, Tony (Athlete, Baseball Player)
1104 Palma Sola Blvd
Bradenton, FL 34209-3342, USA

Bartiromo, Maria (Correspondent)
c/o Staff Member *CNBC (DC)*
400 N Capitol St NW Ste 850
Washington, DC 20001-1555, USA

Bartkowski, Steven J (Steve) (Athlete, Football Player)
10745 Bell Rd
Duluth, GA 30097-1801, USA

Bartle, Cheryl (Actor)
8281 Melrose Ave Ste 200
Los Angeles, CA 90046-6890, USA

Bartles, Carl Bartles (Athlete, Football Player)
405 E 4th St
Kannapolis, NC 28083-3606, United States

Bartles, Edward (Athlete, Basketball Player)
105 Hemlock Dr
Killingworth, CT 06419-2225, USA

Bartlett, Bonnie (Actor, Musician)
12805 Hortense St
Studio City, CA 91604-1124, USA

Bartlett, Doug (Athlete, Football Player)
9133 26th St
Brookfield, IL 60513-1006, USA

Bartlett, Erinn (Actor)
c/o Randy James *James/Levy Management Inc*
3500 W Olive Ave Ste 1470
Burbank, CA 91505-5514, USA

Bartlett, Jason (Athlete, Baseball Player)
730 Washington Ave N Unit 326
Minneapolis, MN 55401-2805, USA

Bartlett, Jim (Athlete, Hockey Player)
8718 Chadwick Dr
Tampa, FL 33635-6212, USA

Bartlett, Murray (Actor)
c/o Rosanne Quezada *Paradigm (LA)*
360 N Crescent Dr
North Bldg
Beverly Hills, CA 90210-4874, USA

Bartlett, Robin (Actor)
2202 Pearl St
Santa Monica, CA 90405-2828, USA

Bartletti, Don (Journalist)
Los Angeles Times
202 W 1st St Ste 500
Editorial Dept
Los Angeles, CA 90012-4401, USA

Bartlett O'Reilly, Alison (Actor)
c/o Carolyn Anthony *Anthony & Associates*
PO Box 910
New York, NY 10108-1201, USA

Bartley, Boyd (Athlete, Baseball Player)
7500 Noreast Dr
North Richland Hills, TX 76180-6736, USA

Bartley, Ephesians (Athlete, Football Player)
3552 Kittery Dr
Snellville, GA 30039-6033, USA

Bartmann, Bill (Business Person)
8556 E 101st St Ste 200
Tulsa, OK 74133-7036, USA

Bartoe, John-David F (Astronaut)
2724 Lighthouse Dr
Houston, TX 77058-4318, USA

Bartoletti, Louis (Athlete, Golfer)
1450 Longlea Ter
Wellington, FL 33414-9017, USA

Bartolome, Victor (Athlete, Basketball Player)
130 Sumida Gardens Ln Apt 205
Santa Barbara, CA 93111-3359, USA

Bartolomeo, Marc (Reality Star)
c/o Jessie Blackhall *Cunningham Escott Slevin & Doherty (CESD-LA)*
10635 Santa Monica Blvd Ste 130
Los Angeles, CA 90025-8306, USA

Barton, Bob (Athlete, Baseball Player)
37193 Stardust Way
Murrieta, CA 92563-5076, USA

Barton, Brian (Athlete, Baseball Player)
1217 W 76th St
Los Angeles, CA 90044-2411, USA

Barton, Daric (Athlete, Baseball Player)
958 Naples Dr
Corona, CA 92882-6350, USA

Barton, Dorie (Actor)
c/o Daniel Spilo *Industry Entertainment*
955 Carrillo Dr Ste 300
Los Angeles, CA 90048-5400, USA

Barton, Eric (Athlete, Football Player)
23 Hayes Hill Dr
Northport, NY 11768-1331, USA

Barton, Greg (Athlete, Football Player)
13965 SW Barlow Ct
Beaverton, OR 97008-5525, USA

Barton, Greg (Athlete, Olympic Athlete)
Epic Kayaks Inc
645 Marina Dr
Charleston, SC 29492-7626, USA

Barton, Harris S (Athlete, Football Player)
334 Lincoln Ave
Palo Alto, CA 94301-2730, USA

Barton, Jim (Athlete, Football Player)
2126 Taylor Ln
Newark, OH 43055-6091, USA

Barton, Joe (Congressman, Politician)
2109 Rayburn Hob
Washington, DC 20515-4306, USA

Barton, Lou Ann (Musician)
2004 Courtney St # B
Austin, TX 78745-5299, USA

Barton, Mischa (Actor)
2670 Bowmont Dr
Beverly Hills, CA 90210-1815, USA

Barton, Peter (Actor)
10417 Eastborne Ave Apt 3
Los Angeles, CA 90024-6130, USA

Barton, Rachel (Musician)
I C M Artists
40 W 57th St
New York, NY 10019-4001, USA

Barton, Shawn (Athlete, Baseball Player)
1009 Helm Ln
Reading, PA 19605-3313, USA

Bartosh, Cliff (Athlete, Baseball Player)
939 Fairlawn Dr
Duncanville, TX 75116-3003, USA

Bartosik, Alison (Swimmer)
c/o Staff Member *Premier Management Group (PMG Sports)*
115 Crescent Commons Dr Ste 250
Cary, NC 27518-8134, USA

Bartovic, Milan (Athlete, Hockey Player)
141 Bennington Hills Ct
West Henrietta, NY 14586-9768, USA

Bartrum, Mike (Athlete, Football Player)
43375 Carlton Pl
Pomeroy, OH 45769-9462, USA

Bartulis, Oskars (Athlete, Hockey Player)
86 Euston Rd S
Marlton, NJ 08053-3901, USA

Bartz, Carol A (Business Person)
Autodesk Inc
111 McInnis Pkwy
San Rafael, CA 94903-2700, USA

Bartz, Randall (Athlete, Olympic Athlete, Speed Skater)
3820 Baker Rd
Hopkins, MN 55305-4908, USA

Baruchel, Jay (Actor)
c/o Willie Mercer *Thruline Entertainment*
9250 Wilshire Blvd Ste 100
Ground Floor
Beverly Hills, CA 90212-3343, USA

Baryshnikov, Mikhail (Actor, Dancer)
12 Lawrence Ln
Palisades, NY 10964-1604, USA

Barzilauskas, Carl (Athlete, Football Player)
4444 Lower Schooner Rd
Nashville, IN 47448-9476, USA

Barzilla, Phil (Athlete, Baseball Player)
3310 Crystal Creek Dr
Sugar Land, TX 77478-4045, USA

Basak, Chris (Athlete, Baseball Player)
1371 N Mohawk St
Chicago, IL 60610-1713, USA

Basana, Fred (Athlete, Baseball Player)
222 Diamond Oaks Rd
Roseville, CA 95678-1007, USA

Basch, Harry (Actor)
920 1/2 S Serrano Ave
Los Angeles, CA 90006-1108, USA

Basche, David (Actor)
c/o Mark Rousso *New Wave Entertainment (LA)*
2660 W Olive Ave
Burbank, CA 91505-4525, USA

Basche, David Alan (Actor)
c/o Brad Mendelsohn *New Wave Entertainment (LA)*
2660 W Olive Ave
Burbank, CA 91505-4525, USA

Baschnagel, Brian D (Athlete, Football Player)
1824 Ridgewood Ln W
Glenview, IL 60025-2206, USA

Basco, Dante (Actor)
Don Buchwald
6500 Wilshire Blvd Ste 2200
Los Angeles, CA 90048-4942, USA

Basco, Derek (Actor)
c/o Staff Member *GVA Talent Agency Inc*
8981 W Sunset Blvd Ste 101
West Hollywood, CA 90069-1850, USA

Basco, Dion (Actor)
Schiowitz/Clay/Rose
1680 Vine St Ste 1016
Los Angeles, CA 90028-8800, USA

Bash, Dana (Correspondent, Television Host)
5003 Belt Rd NW
Washington, DC 20016-4234, USA

Bashir, Idrees (Athlete, Football Player)
5579 Mountain View Pass
Stone Mountain, GA 30087-6020, USA

Bashir, Idrees
5579 Mountain View Pass
Stone Mountain, GA 30087-6020, USA

Bashoff, Blake (Actor)
c/o Marni Rosenzweig *Abrams Artists Agency (LA)*
9200 W Sunset Blvd PH 11
West Hollywood, CA 90069-3601, USA

Basia (Music Group)
c/o Staff Member *Creative Artists Agency (CAA-LA)*
2000 Avenue of the Stars Ste 100
Los Angeles, CA 90067-4705, USA

Basil, Toni (Musician)
830 S Ridgeley Dr
Los Angeles, CA 90036-4727, USA

Basinger, Kim (Actor)
4833 Don Juan Pl
Woodland Hills, CA 91364-4705, USA

Basinski, Ed (Athlete, Baseball Player)
8530 SW Curry Dr Unit B
Wilsonville, OR 97070-8448, USA

Basinski, Eddie (Athlete, Baseball Player)
4110 SE Jackson St
Portland, OR 97222-5936, USA

Basis, Austin (Actor)
c/o Sandy Erickson *Vic Ramos Management*
337 E 13th St Apt 6
New York, NY 10003-5852, USA

Baska, Richard (Rick) (Athlete, Football Player)
176 Josephine Ct
Central Point, OR 97502-3709, USA

Bass, Anthony (Athlete, Football Player)
120 Ridgewood Frst
Saint Albans, WV 25177-9502, USA

Bass, Bob (Athlete, Basketball Player, Coach)
2266 Deerfield Dr
Fort Mill, SC 29715-6941, USA

Bass, Brian (Athlete, Baseball Player)
1101 Berrymans Ln
Reisterstown, MD 21136-6014, USA

Bass, David (Athlete, Football Player)
c/o Harold C Lewis *National Sports Agency*
15400 Timpaige Dr
Chesterfield, MO 63017-1762, USA

Bass, Doug (Actor)
c/o Jana Marimpietri *Mosaic Media Group*
9200 W Sunset Blvd Ste 10
West Hollywood, CA 90069-3608, USA

Bass, Glenn (Athlete, Football Player)
4185 Diplomacy Cir
Tallahassee, FL 32308-8720, USA

Bass, Jules (Director, Musician, Producer, Writer)
c/o Staff Member *Rankin/Bass Productions*
24 W 55th St
New York, NY 10019-5456, USA

Bass, Karen (Congressman, Politician)
405 Cannon Hob
Washington, DC 20515-4309, USA

Bass, Kevin (Athlete, Baseball Player)
3630 Maranatha Dr
Sugar Land, TX 77479-9665, USA

Bass, Lance (Musician)
c/o John Ferriter *Octagon Entertainment*
8687 Melrose Ave Ste 7
West Hollywood, CA 90069-5721, USA

Bass, Michael T (Athlete, Football Player)
4703 NW 36th St
Gainesville, FL 32605-1017, USA

Bass, Mike (Athlete, Football Player)
4703 NW 36th St
Gainesville, FL 32605-1017, USA

Bass, Norm (Athlete, Baseball Player)
156 E 70th St
Los Angeles, CA 90003-2102, USA

Bass, Randy (Athlete, Baseball Player)
2709 SW Coombs Rd
Lawton, OK 73505-0809, USA

Bass, Ronald (Writer)
c/o Staff Member *Creative Artists Agency (CAA-LA)*
2000 Avenue of the Stars Ste 100
Los Angeles, CA 90067-4705, USA

Bass, Ronald (Ron) (Actor, Producer, Writer)
c/o Staff Member *Writers Co-Op*
4000 Warner Blvd Bldg 1
Burbank, CA 91522-0001, USA

Bass, Sid (Business Person)
4824 Crestline Rd
Fort Worth, TX 76107-3708, USA

Bassen, Bob (Athlete, Coach, Hockey Player)
12 Chapman Chase
Windsor Locks, CT 06096-1343, USA

Bassett, Angela (Actor)
4710 Hillard Ave
La Canada Flintridge, CA 91011-2006, USA

Bassett, Tim (Athlete, Basketball Player)
1143 Dorsey Pl
Plainfield, NJ 07062-2207, USA

Bassey, Jennifer (Actor)
12 E 86th St Apt 1728
New York, NY 10028-0517, USA

Bassham, Lanny (Athlete, Olympic Athlete, Shooter)
7101 Lake Mead Ct
Frisco, TX 75034-3369, USA

Bassman, Herman (Red) (Athlete, Football Player)
7860 Rolling Woods Ct Apt 305
Springfield, VA 22152-3629, USA

Basso, Gabriel (Actor)
c/o David Eisenberg *Protege Entertainment*
710 E Angeleno Ave
Burbank, CA 91501-2213, USA

Bast, William (Producer)
6691 Whitley Ter
Los Angeles, CA 90068-3220, USA

Bastel, Emily (Athlete, Golfer)
5377 County Highway 330
Upper Sandusky, OH 43351-9772, USA

Baston, Maceo (Athlete, Basketball Player)
PO Box 4846
Troy, MI 48099-4846, USA

Basu, Bipasha (Actor)
c/o Simone Sheffield *Canyon Entertainment*
PO Box 256
Palm Springs, CA 92263-0256, USA

Baswell, Jack (Athlete, Baseball Player)
9629 Bella Dr
Daphne, AL 36526-6271, USA

Batali, Dean (Writer)
c/o Michael Van Dyck *Paradigm (LA)*
360 N Crescent Dr
Beverly Hills, CA 90210-4874, USA

Batali, Mario (Chef, Television Host)
Otto Enoteca Pizzeria
1 5th Ave Frnt 2
New York, NY 10003-4312, USA

Batalla, Rick (Actor)
c/o Staff Member *Halpern Management*
PO Box 5042
Santa Monica, CA 90409-5042, USA

Batch, Baron (Athlete, Football Player)
c/o Jordan Woy *Willis and Woy Management*
3030 Olive St Ste 520
Dallas, TX 75219-7629, USA

Batch, Charlie (Athlete, Football Player)
1844 Willow Oak Dr
Wexford, PA 15090-2506, USA

Batchelder, Joseph (Athlete, Olympic Athlete, Sailor)
2205 Ezra Ct
Cedar Park, TX 78613-7461, USA

Batchelor, Rich (Athlete, Baseball Player)
1004 Pineneedle Rd
Hartsville, SC 29550-8452, USA

Bateman, Brian (Athlete, Golfer)
100 Brunswick Ave
Saint Simons Island, GA 31522-2605, USA

Bateman, Jason (Actor)
3055 Lake Glen Dr
Beverly Hills, CA 90210-1313, USA

Bateman, Justine (Actor)
7445 Woodrow Wilson Dr
Los Angeles, CA 90046-1322, USA

Bateman, Marv (Athlete, Football Player)
1022 W Smithsonian Way
Apple Valley, UT 84737-4830, USA

Bates, Alfred (Athlete, Track Athlete)
4215 Skymont Dr
Belmont, CA 94002-1245, USA

Bates, Bill (Athlete, Football Player)
1252 Neck Rd
Ponte Vedra Beach, FL 32082-4112, USA

Bates, Billy Ray (Athlete, Basketball Player)
340 Eastbrook Rd
Ridgewood, NJ 07450-2108, USA

Bates, Dick (Athlete, Baseball Player)
5859 W Cielo Grande
Glendale, AZ 85310-3631, USA

Bates, Dwayne (Athlete, Football Player)
PO Box 331
Peru, IL 61354-0331, USA

Bates, Emma (Actor)
c/o Marianne Golan *Golan & Blumberg*
6528 W 6th St
Los Angeles, CA 90048-4716, USA

Bates, Jason (Athlete, Baseball Player)
2487 Paint Pony Ct
Castle Rock, CO 80108-8452, USA

Bates, Kathy (Actor)
243 S Muirfield Rd
Los Angeles, CA 90004-3730, USA

Bates, Mario (Athlete, Football Player)
PO Box 5832
Scottsdale, AZ 85261-5832, USA

Bates, Michael (Athlete, Football Player)
1239 W Keuhne Ct
Tucson, AZ 85755-8506, USA

Bates, Pat (Athlete, Golfer)
215 Ward Cir Ste 200
Brentwood, TN 37027-2304, USA

Bates, Patrick J (Athlete, Football Player)
2745 N Collins St Apt 11123
Arlington, TX 76006-7108, USA

Bates, Shawn (Athlete, Hockey Player)
35 Bradshaw St
Medford, MA 02155-4819, USA

Bates, Ted (Athlete, Football Player)
245 E Colorado Blvd Apt 4
Monrovia, CA 91016-6106, USA

Bates, Tyler (Musician)
317 N Van Ness Ave
Los Angeles, CA 90004-1523, USA

Bat for Lashes (Music Group)
c/o Staff Member *Red Light Management
(LA)*
8439 W Sunset Blvd Ste 2
West Hollywood, CA 90069-1925, USA

Bathe, Bill (Athlete, Baseball Player)
5378 N Ridge Spring Pl
Tucson, AZ 85749-7106, USA

Bathe, Frank (Athlete, Hockey Player)
2 Meadowood Dr
Scarborough, ME 04074-9421, USA

Bathe, Ryan Michelle (Actor)
c/o Nick Campbell *Commonwealth Talent
Group*
PO Box 36514
Los Angeles, CA 90036-0514, USA

Batikis, Annastasia (Athlete, Baseball
Player)
1023 Crab Tree Ln
Racine, WI 53406-4109, USA

Batinkoff, Randall (Actor)
1330 4th St
Santa Monica, CA 90401-1302, USA

Batista, Tony (Athlete)
333 W Camden St
Baltimore, MD 21201-2496

Batiste, Kevin (Athlete, Baseball Player)
2501 Westridge St Apt 255
Houston, TX 77054-1519, USA

Batiste, Kim (Athlete, Baseball Player)
16163 Aikens Rd
Prairieville, LA 70769-4903, USA

Batiste, Michael (Athlete, Football Player)
2720 Edmonds St
Beaumont, TX 77705-1437, USA

Batiuk, Thomas M (Tom) (Cartoonist)
c/o Staff Member *King Features
Syndication*
300 W 57th St Fl 15
New York, NY 10019-5238, USA

Batson, Susan (Actor)
Black Nexxus Inc.
300 W 43rd St Ste 300
New York, NY 10036-6404, USA

Batt, Bryan (Actor)
c/o Marc Chancer *Origin Talent Agency*
4705 Laurel Canyon Blvd Ste 303
Valley Village, CA 91607-5943, USA

Battaglia, Bates (Athlete, Hockey Player)
832 Graham St
Raleigh, NC 27605-1125, USA

Battaglia, Marco (Athlete, Football Player)
15832 79th St
Howard Beach, NY 11414-2907, USA

Battaglia, Matt (Actor)
c/o Stewart Strunk *Main Title
Entertainment*
8383 Wilshire Blvd Ste 408
Beverly Hills, CA 90211-2435, USA

Battelle, Ann (Athlete, Olympic Athlete,
Skier)
1355 Walton Creek Rd
Steamboat Springs, CO 80487-1702, USA

Batten, Kim (Athlete, Olympic Athlete,
Track Athlete)
24107 Plantation Dr NE
Atlanta, GA 30324-2942, USA

Batten, Pat (Athlete, Football Player)
9403 E 64th Ter
Raytown, MO 64133-4916, USA

Battie, Demetrius (Tony) (Athlete,
Basketball Player)
11264 Bridge House Rd
Windermere, FL 34786-5405, USA

Battie, Demetrius ""Tony"" (Athlete,
Basketball Player)
11264 Bridge House Rd
Windermere, FL 34786-5405

Battier, Shane (Athlete, Basketball Player)
490 Bruin Lake Rd
Gregory, MI 48137-9648, USA

Battista, Bobbie
c/o Staff Member *Atamira*
3400 Peachtree Rd NE Ste 300
Atlanta, GA 30326-1107, USA

Battle, Allen (Athlete, Baseball Player)
106 Donette Loop
Daphne, AL 36526-7764, USA

Battle, Arnaz (Athlete, Football Player)
1091 Broadmoor Ln
Prosper, TX 75078-8940, USA

Battle, Greg (Athlete, Football Player)
1217 W Saltsage Dr
Phoenix, AZ 85045-0735, USA

Battle, Howard (Athlete, Baseball Player)
238 Romana Ave SE
Albuquerque, NM 87102-5039, USA

Battle, John (Athlete, Basketball Player)
145 Covey Xing
Fayetteville, GA 30215-7629, USA

Battle, Julian (Athlete, Football Player)
196 Monterey Way
West Palm Beach, FL 33411-7817, USA

Battle, Kenny (Athlete, Basketball Player)
Northwest Sports and Entertainment Inc
835 W Warner Rd Ste 101-445
Gilbert, AZ 85233-7296, USA

Battle, Lois (Writer)
Viking Press
375 Hudson St
New York, NY 10014-3658, USA

Battle, Mike (Athlete, Football Player)
712 Rodes Valley Dr
Nellysford, VA 22958-8049, USA

Battle, Ralph (Athlete, Football Player)
184 Timber Oak Rd
Huntsville, AL 35806-4110, USA

Battle, Terry (Athlete, Football Player)
7049 N 7th Ave
Phoenix, AZ 85021-8690, USA

Battle, Texas (Actor)
c/o Ryan Daly *Zero Gravity Management*
1531 14th St
Santa Monica, CA 90404-3302, USA

Battles, Ainslev (Athlete, Football Player)
493 Villa Dr SW
Lilburn, GA 30047-5318, USA

Battles, Ainsley (Athlete, Football Player)
2859 Yellow Pine Dr
Jacksonville, FL 32277-3462, USA

Batton, Chris (Athlete, Baseball Player)
30221 Savoie St
Murrieta, CA 92563-1816, USA

Batton, Dave (Athlete, Basketball Player)
8627 Hufsmith Rd Apt 1221
Tomball, TX 77375-2874, USA

Batts, Lloyd (Athlete, Basketball Player)
500 S Denton Ave
Glenwood, IL 60425, USA

Batts, Matt (Athlete, Baseball Player)
3342 Vintage Ct
Baton Rouge, LA 70809-8529, USA

Batts, Warren L (Business Person)
Premark International
3600 W Lake Ave
Glenview, IL 60026-1215, USA

Baty, Greg (Athlete, Football Player)
4 King St
Redwood City, CA 94062-1938, USA

Bauchau, Patrick (Actor)
1941 Lookout Dr
Agoura Hills, CA 91301-2928, USA

Baucus, Max (Senator)
511 Hart Senate Office Bldg NE
Washington, DC 20510-0001, USA

Baudin, Belinda (Horse Racer, Olympic
Athlete)
15939 NW 162nd Ter
Williston, FL 32696-4356, USA

Bauer, Alice (Athlete, Golfer)
LPGA Pioneer
77165 Avenida Arteaga
La Quinta, CA 92253-2552, USA

Bauer, Chris (Actor)
c/o Peg Donegan *Framework
Entertainment (LA)*
9057 Nemo St Ste C
West Hollywood, CA 90069-5511, USA

Bauer, Donna (Business Person)
The Note Buyer
11006 Reading Rd Ste 201
Cincinnati, OH 45241-1980, USA

Bauer, Hank (Athlete, Football Player)
11150 Alejo Pl
San Diego, CA 92124-1521, USA

Bauer, Jaime Lyn (Actor)
4212 Camellia Ave
Studio City, CA 91604-2936, USA

Bauer, Linda Susan (Actor)
2476 Glendale Cir SE
Smyrna, GA 30080-1830, USA

Bauer, Peter (Publisher)
People Magazine
Time-Life Building
Rockefeller Center
New York, NY 10020, USA

Bauer, Rick (Athlete, Baseball Player)
6643 W Limelight Dr
Boise, ID 83714-6109, USA

Bauer, Steven (Actor)
c/o Liza Anderson *Anderson Group Public
Relations*
8060 Melrose Ave Fl 4
Los Angeles, CA 90046-7038, USA

Bauer van Straten, Kristin (Actor)
c/o Ben Levine *LINK Entertainment*
11872 La Grange Ave Fl 1
Los Angeles, CA 90025-5283, USA

Baugh, Gavin (Athlete, Baseball Player)
3605 Pasadena Dr
San Mateo, CA 94403-2947, USA

Baugh, Laura (Athlete, Golfer)
3024 Cardinal Dr
Augusta, GA 30909-3040, USA

Baugh, Sammy (Athlete, Football Coach,
Football Player)
General Delivery
Rotan, TX 79546-9999, USA

Baugh, Tom (Athlete, Football Player)
14716 S Bynum Rd
Lone Jack, MO 64070-9286, USA

Baughan, Maxie C (Athlete, Coach,
Football Player)
3355 Lawndale Rd
Reisterstown, MD 21136-4026, USA

Baughman, J Ross (Journalist, Misc,
Photographer)
203 S Payne St
Alexandria, VA 22314-3529, USA

Baughman, Justin (Athlete, Baseball
Player)
4052 NE 21st Ave
Portland, OR 97212-1433, USA

Bauhaus (Music Group)
c/o Pete Riedling *Satellite Artist
Management*
5653 1/2 Hollywood Blvd Ste 7
Los Angeles, CA 90028-6813, USA

Baum, Herbert M (Business Person)
Quarker State Corp
700 Milam St
Houston, TX 77002-2806, USA

Baum, John (Athlete, Basketball Player)
8216 Fenton Rd
Glenside, PA 19038-7144, USA

Bauman, Jon (Bowzer) (Musician)
3168 Oakshire Dr
Los Angeles, CA 90068-1743, USA

Bauman, Rashad (Athlete, Football Player)
14724 SE Loren Ln
Portland, OR 97267-1700, USA

Baumann, Charlie
8617 Summerville Pl
Orlando, FL 32819-3850, USA

Baumann, Frank M (Athlete, Baseball
Player)
7712 Sunray Ln
Saint Louis, MO 63123-1938, USA

Baumann, Kenny (Actor)
c/o Michael Valeo *Valeo Entertainment*
8581 Santa Monica Blvd Ste 570
West Hollywood, CA 90069-4120, USA

Baumgardner, Larry (Athlete, Football
Player)
1125 Loma Ave
Coronado, CA 92118-2835, USA

Baumgarten, Ross (Athlete, Baseball
Player)
399 Sunset Ln
Glencoe, IL 60022-1238, USA

Baumgartner, Brian (Actor)
3896 Franklin Ave
Los Angeles, CA 90027-4661, USA

Baumgartner, Bruce (Athlete, Motivational Speaker, Olympic Athlete, Wrestler)
12765 Forrest Dr
Edinboro, PA 16412-1281, USA

Baumgartner, John (Athlete, Baseball Player)
1215 Oxford Ct
Birmingham, AL 35242-4676, USA

Baumgartner, Ken (Athlete, Hockey Player)
39 Court St Apt 1
Newton, MA 02458-1372, USA

Baumgartner, Mary (Athlete, Baseball Player)
60 Lane
440 Jimmerson Lk
Fremont, IN 46737, USA

Baumgartner, Mike (Athlete, Hockey Player)
39998 290th St
Roseau, MN 56751-8321, USA

Baumgartner, Steve (Athlete, Football Player)
144 Brookside Dr
Mandeville, LA 70471-3202, USA

Baumgartner, William (Doctor)
Johns Hopkins Hospital
600 N Wolfe St # 100
Baltimore, MD 21287-0005, USA

Baumhower, Robert G (Bob) (Athlete, Football Player)
21201 Ayrshire Ln
Fairhope, AL 36532-4479, USA

Bauta, Ed (Athlete, Baseball Player)
3792 Long Grove Ln
Port Orange, FL 32129-8617, USA

Baute, Joseph A (Business Person)
Nashua Corp
11 Trafalgar Sq Ste 200
Nashua, NH 03063-1991, USA

Bautin, Sergei (Athlete, Hockey Player)
22140 E Euclid Pl
Aurora, CO 80016-2361, USA

Bautista, Danny (Athlete, Baseball Player)
901 E Van Buren St Apt 1063
Phoenix, AZ 85006-4014, USA

Bautista, Dave (Actor)
c/o Jonathan Meisner *DMBV*
2020 Pennsylvania Ave NW Ste 179
Washington, DC 20006-1811, USA

Bautista, David (Athlete, Wrestler)
c/o Jonathan Meisner *DMBV*
2020 Pennsylvania Ave NW Ste 179
Washington, DC 20006-1811, USA

Bautista, Franciso Javier Jr (Frankie J) (Musician)
c/o Staff Member *BMG*
1540 Broadway
New York, NY 10036-4039, USA

Bautista, Jose (Athlete, Baseball Player)
2 Sandpiper Rd
Tampa, FL 33609-3592, USA

Bavaro, David (Athlete, Football Player)
55 Ash St Unit 14
Danvers, MA 01923-2710, USA

Bavaro, Mark (Athlete, Football Player)
17 Long Hl
Boxford, MA 01921-2453, USA

Bavasi, Peter (Commentator)
1001 Genter St Unit 3G
La Jolla, CA 92037-5531, USA

Bawel, Edward (Athlete, Football Player)
1169 2nd Ave
Jasper, IN 47546-3411, USA

Bax, Kylie (Actor, Model)
8309 Kirkwood Dr
Los Angeles, CA 90046-1925, USA

Baxes, Mike (Athlete, Baseball Player)
303 Wickham Dr
Mill Valley, CA 94941-3443, USA

Baxley, Rob (Athlete, Football Player)
39 Oak Creek Dr
Yorkville, IL 60560-9779, USA

Baxter, Fred (Athlete, Football Player)
PO Box 14
Brundidge, AL 36010-0014, USA

Baxter, Jeff (Skunk) (Music Group, Musician)
Monterey Peninsula Artists
509 Hartnell St
Monterey, CA 93940-2825, USA

Baxter, Lloyd (Athlete, Football Player)
718 Minturn Ln
Austin, TX 78748-6568, USA

Baxter, Meredith (Actor)
14186 Alisal Ln
Santa Monica, CA 90402-1312, USA

Baxter, Paul (Athlete, Hockey Player)
1610 Saint John St
Wichita Falls, TX 76302-3315, USA

Baxter, Stephen (Writer)
Tom Doherty Associates, LLC
175 5th Ave
New York, NY 10010-7703, USA

Baxter-Johnson, Patricia (Athlete, Golfer)
111 Bryn Mawr Dr
Lake Worth, FL 33460-6311, USA

Bay, Jason (Athlete, Baseball Player)
c/o Joe Urbon *Creative Artists Agency (CAA-NY)*
162 5th Ave Fl 6
New York, NY 10010-6047, USA

Bay, Michael (Actor, Director, Producer)
960 Bel Air Rd
Los Angeles, CA 90077-3010, USA

Bay, Susan (Actor)
801 Stone Canyon Rd
Los Angeles, CA 90077-2911, USA

Bay, Willow
1050 Techwood Dr NW
Atlanta, GA 30318-5604

Bay City Rollers (Music Group)
297 Kinderkamack Rd Ste 101
Oradell, NJ 07649-1535, USA

Bayer, Samuel (Director)
c/o Doreen Wilcox Little *Anonymous Content (LA)*
3532 Hayden Ave
Culver City, CA 90232-2413, USA

Bayless, Jerryd (Athlete, Basketball Player)
c/o Jeff Schwartz *Excel Sports Management (NY)*
1700 Broadway Fl 29
New York, NY 10019-5905, USA

Bayless, Martin (Athlete, Football Player)
757 Ernroe Dr
Dayton, OH 45417-3507, USA

Bayless, Rick (Athlete, Football Player)
885 Dawn Ave
Saint Paul, MN 55126-6403, USA

Baylis, Jerald (Athlete, Football Player)
PO Box 33921
Portland, OR 97292-3921, USA

Bayliss, Jonah (Athlete, Baseball Player)
41 Front St
Williamstown, MA 01267-2403, USA

Baylon, Noah (Writer)
c/o James (Jamie) Feldman *Lichter Grossman Nichols Adler & Goodman*
9200 W Sunset Blvd Ste 1200
West Hollywood, CA 90069-3607, USA

Baylor, Don (Athlete, Baseball Player, Coach)
PO Box 2095
Phoenix, AZ 85001-2095, USA

Baylor, Elgin (Athlete, Basketball Player)
2480 Briarcrest Rd
Beverly Hills, CA 90210-1820, USA

Baylor, John (Athlete, Football Player)
7436 Freeport Ln Apt A
Indianapolis, IN 46214-1037, USA

Baylor, Raymond (Athlete, Football Player)
5302 Heathercrest St
Houston, TX 77045-5230, USA

Baylor, Tim (Athlete, Football Player)
1302 Douglas Ave
Minneapolis, MN 55403-2904, USA

Bayne, Howard (Athlete, Basketball Player)
11840 Yarnell Rd
Knoxville, TN 37932-2354, USA

Bayne, Trevor (Race Car Driver)
Wood Bros Racing
7291 Caldwell Rd
Harrisburg, NC 28075, USA

Baynes, Michelle (Race Car Driver)
Bayshore Communications
2839 Ogletown Rd
Newark, DE 19713-1837, USA

Baynham, Craig (Athlete, Football Player)
1 7th St Ste 1102
Augusta, GA 30901-1397, USA

Bayona, Juan Antonio (Director, Producer, Writer)
c/o Robert Newman *William Morris Endeavor (LA)*
9601 Wilshire Blvd
Beverly Hills, CA 90210-5213, USA

Bays, Carter (Producer)
Bays Thomas Productions
10201 W Pico Blvd Bldg 88
Los Angeles, CA 90064-2606, USA

Baze, Winiford (Athlete, Football Player)
5317 New Copeland Rd Apt 119
Tyler, TX 75703-3964, USA

Bazell, Josh (Writer)
c/o Staff Member *Regal Literary Inc.*
236 W 26th St Rm 801
the Capitol Building
New York, NY 10001-6882, USA

Bazell, Robert J (Correspondent)
NBC-TV News Dept
4001 Nebraska Ave NW
Washington, DC 20016-2795, USA

Bazemore, Whit (Race Car Driver)
50 Gasoline Aly Ste H
Indianapolis, IN 46222-5906, USA

BB Mak (Music Group)
c/o Staff Member *Hollywood Records*
500 S Buena Vista St
Burbank, CA 91521-0002, USA

Beach, Adam (Actor)
c/o Daniel Spilo *Industry Entertainment*
955 Carrillo Dr Ste 300
Los Angeles, CA 90048-5400, USA

Beach, Bill (Bowler)
3715 Lee Run Rd
Hermitage, PA 16148-6185, USA

Beach, Ed (Athlete, Football Player)
938 Sedgewick Ave
Scotch Plains, NJ 07076, USA

Beach, Gary (Actor)
122 Andalusia Way
Palm Bch Gdns, FL 33418-1723, USA

Beach, Michael (Actor)
4434 Moorpark Way # 107
Toluca Lake, CA 91602-2474, USA

Beach, Pat (Athlete, Football Player)
2523 W Beach Rd
Oak Harbor, WA 98277-8865, USA

Beach, Roger C (Business Person)
Unocal Corp
2141 Rosecrans Ave
El Segundo, CA 90245-4747, USA

Beach, Sanjay (Athlete, Football Player)
2989 Riviera Ln
Westlake, OH 44145-6844, USA

Beach, Walter
2010 Winthrop Way
Macungie, PA 18062-8043, USA

Beacher, Jeff (Producer, Television Host)
5777 W Century Blvd Ste 1600
Los Angeles, CA 90045-5671, USA

Beach House (Music Group)
c/o Staff Member *We Are Free*
61 Greenpoint Ave Ste 508
Brooklyn, NY 11222-1526, USA

Beachy, Brandon (Athlete, Baseball Player)
339 Caswyck Tree
Alpharetta, GA 30022, USA

Beadles, Zane (Athlete, Football Player)
c/o Bruce Tollner *REP 1 Sports Group*
2 Corporate Park Ste 106
Irvine, CA 92606-5103, USA

Beagle, Ronald G (Ron) (Athlete, Football Player)
3830 San Ysidro Way
Sacramento, CA 95864-5260, USA

Beahan, Kate (Actor)
c/o Suzan Bymel *Management 360*
9111 Wilshire Blvd
Beverly Hills, CA 90210-5508, USA

Beal, Andrew (Business Person)
Beal Bank
6000 Legacy Dr
Plano, TX 75024-3601, USA

Beal, Damien (Athlete, Baseball Player)
5325 Archstone Dr Apt 101
Tampa, FL 33634-4225, USA

Beal, Jeremy (Athlete, Football Player)
3709 Furneaux Ln
Carrollton, TX 75007-2455, USA

Beal, Norm (Athlete, Football Player)
21246 Jade Dr
Rocky Mount, MO 65072-2953, USA

Beale, Betty (Writer)
2926 Garfield St NW
Washington, DC 20008-3536, USA

Beale, Simon Russell (Actor)
c/o Tony Lipp *Anonymous Content (LA)*
3532 Hayden Ave
Culver City, CA 90232-2413, USA

Beall, Bob (Athlete, Baseball Player)
1950 NW 192nd Ave Unit 451
Beaverton, OR 97006-6592, USA

Bealor, Bruce (Athlete, Football Player)
409 Skyforest Dr
San Antonio, TX 78232-2015, USA

Beals, Jennifer (Actor)
c/o Adena Chawke *Greenlight Management and Production*
9713 Santa Monica Blvd Ste 219
Beverly Hills, CA 90210-4215, USA

Beals, Shawn (Athlete, Football Player)
250 Edward Ave
Pittsburg, CA 94565-4107, USA

Beals, Vaughn L Jr (Business Person)
Harley-Davidson Inc
3700 W Juneau Ave
Milwaukee, WI 53208-2865, USA

Beam, T J (Athlete, Baseball Player)
8505 E Pepper Tree Ln
Scottsdale, AZ 85250-4912, USA

Beaman, Lee Anne (Actor)
Cavaleri Assoc
3500 W Olive Ave Ste 300
Burbank, CA 91505-4647, USA

Beamer, Frank (Coach, Football Coach)
Virginia Polytechnic Institute
Athletic Dept
Blacksburg, VA 24061, USA

Beamer, Lisa (Writer)
The Todd M Beamer Foundation
PO Box 32
Cranbury, NJ 08512-0032

Beamon, Autry (Athlete, Football Player)
14345 Parkside Ct NW
Prior Lake, MN 55372-4482, USA

Beamon, Bob (Athlete, Hockey Player, Olympic Athlete)
20533 Biscayne Blvd # 113
Miami, FL 33180-1529, USA

Beamon, Clifford ""Trey"" (Athlete, Baseball Player)
2125 Highwood St
Mesquite, TX 75181-1727, USA

Beamon, Trey (Athlete, Baseball Player)
9730 Whitehurst Dr Apt 51
Dallas, TX 75243-8756, USA

Beamon Jr, Charlie (Athlete, Baseball Player)
2921 Isabelle Ave
San Mateo, CA 94403-2707, USA

Beamon Sr, Charlie (Athlete, Baseball Player)
355 W Grant Line Rd Apt 212
Tracy, CA 95376-2579, USA

Bean, Alan L (Astronaut)
9173 Briar Forest Dr
Houston, TX 77024-7222, USA

Bean, Andy (Athlete, Golfer)
2912 Grasslands Dr
Lakeland, FL 33803-5418, USA

Bean, Bill (Athlete, Baseball Player)
520 Brickell Key Dr Apt A1705
Miami, FL 33131-2616, USA

Bean, Bubba (Athlete, Football Player)
4252 Ashley Ln
College Station, TX 77845-4798, USA

Bean, Colter (Athlete, Baseball Player)
2116 Shades Crest Rd
Vestavia, AL 35216-1534, USA

Bean, Dawn Pawson (Swimmer)
11902 Red Hill Ave
Santa Ana, CA 92705-3106, USA

Bean, Dexter (Race Car Driver)
Black Cat Racing
304 Performance Rd
Mooresville, NC 28115-9592, USA

Bean, Earnest (Athlete, Football Player)
4252 Ashley Ln
College Station, TX 77845-4798, USA

Bean, Ed (Athlete, Baseball Player)
827 3rd Ct SE
Winter Haven, FL 33881, USA

Bean, Henry (Director)
c/o Staff Member *Fuller Films*
625 Santa Clara Ave
Venice, CA 90291-3445, USA

Bean, Noah (Actor)
c/o Nick Campbell *Commonwealth Talent Group*
PO Box 36514
Los Angeles, CA 90036-0514, USA

Bean, Orson (Actor, Comedian)
444 Carroll Canal
Venice, CA 90291-4682, USA

Bean, Robert (Athlete, Football Player)
4197 Summit Crossing Dr
Decatur, GA 30034-3544, USA

Bean, Shoshana (Actor, Musician)
c/o Tim Marshal *Bauman Redanty & Shaul Agency*
5757 Wilshire Blvd
Suite 473
Beverly Hills, CA 90212, USA

Beane, Billy (Commentator)
15 Saddleback Ct
Danville, CA 94506-3109, USA

Beane, Billy (Athlete, Baseball Player)
7000 Coliseum Way Ste 3
Attn: General Manager
Oakland, CA 94621-1917, USA

Bear, Greg
c/o Vince Gerardis *Grok! Studio*
Prefers to be contacted via email or telephone
Los Angeles, CA, USA

Beard, Al (Athlete, Basketball Player)
653 Sprite Way
Glen Burnie, MD 21061-7600, USA

Beard, Alana (Athlete, Basketball Player)
Washington Mystics
601 F St NW
Mci Center
Washington, DC 20004-1605, USA

Beard, Alfred (Butch) (Athlete, Basketball Player, Coach)
3834 Berleigh Hill Ct
Burtonsville, MD 20866-1392, USA

Beard, Alfred ""Butch"" (Athlete, Basketball Player)
gee Palisade Ave Apt 6E
Fort Lee, NJ 07024, USA

Beard, Amanda (Athlete, Olympic Athlete, Swimmer)
212 Fir Dr NW
Gig Harbor, WA 98335-5900, USA

Beard, Dave (Athlete, Baseball Player)
2570 Lakeview Trl
Cumming, GA 30041-8462, USA

Beard, Ed (Athlete, Football Player)
4861 Strand Dr
Virginia Beach, VA 23462-6449, USA

Beard, Frank (Athlete, Golfer)
70 Rocio Ct
Palm Desert, CA 92260-3160, USA

Beard, Frank (Musician)
918 Pitts Rd
Richmond, TX 77406-1304, USA

Beard, Mike (Athlete, Baseball Player)
90 Elcano Dr
Hot Springs Village, AR 71909-7833, USA

Beard, Tom (Athlete, Football Player)
164 Gale Rd
Mason, MI 48854-9735, USA

Beare, Gary (Athlete, Baseball Player)
31167 Old River Rd
Bonsall, CA 92003-5104, USA

Bearse, Amanda (Actor)
629 Elmwood Dr NE
Atlanta, GA 30306-3643, USA

Bearse, Kevin (Athlete, Baseball Player)
656 Saint Andrews Pl
Manalapan, NJ 07726-9551, USA

Beasley, Aaron (Athlete, Football Player)
1635 Braid Hills Dr
Pasadena, MD 21122-3533, USA

Beasley, Allyce (Actor)
SBV
5900 Wilshire Blvd Ste 700
Los Angeles, CA 90036-5009, USA

Beasley, Alyce (Actor)
c/o Staff Member *TalentWorks (LA)*
3500 W Olive Ave Ste 1400
Burbank, CA 91505-5512, USA

Beasley, Charles (Athlete, Basketball Player)
4404 Copper Xing
McKinney, TX 75070-6463, USA

Beasley, Chris (Athlete, Baseball Player)
1013 W Cooley Dr
Gilbert, AZ 85233-2540, USA

Beasley, Derrick (Athlete, Football Player)
141 North St
Andover, MA 01810-1131, USA

Beasley, Fred (Athlete, Football Player)
PO Box 210931
Montgomery, AL 36121-0931, USA

Beasley, John (Athlete, Basketball Player)
113 Oak Acres Dr W
Malakoff, TX 75148-3163, USA

Beasley, John
W3848 Turtle Patch Rd
Pine River, WI 54965-8113, USA

Beasley, John (Actor)
c/o Staff Member *Bauman Redanty & Shaul Agency*
5757 Wilshire Blvd
Suite 473
Beverly Hills, CA 90212, USA

Beasley, Lew (Athlete, Baseball Player)
24653 Newtown Rd
Bowling Green, VA 22427-2725, USA

Beasley, Michael (Athlete, Basketball Player)
c/o Jeff Schwartz *Excel Sports Management (NY)*
1700 Broadway Fl 29
New York, NY 10019-5905, USA

Beasley, Terry (Athlete, Football Player)
4052 Wellington Way
Moody, AL 35004-3507, USA

Beasley, Tom (Athlete, Football Player)
RR 1 Box 185
Hiltons, VA 24258, USA

Beasley, Tony (Athlete, Baseball Player)
4490 Ccc Rd
Ruther Glen, VA 22546, USA

Beastie Boys (Music Group)
c/o John Silva *SAM*
722 Seward St
Los Angeles, CA 90038-3504, USA

Beathard, Pete (Athlete, Football Player)
3770 Drake St
Houston, TX 77005-1118, USA

Beaton, Frank (Athlete, Hockey Player)
3327 Chapel Hills Pkwy
Fultondale, AL 35068-1596, USA

Beatriz, Stephanie (Actor)
c/o Elizabeth Much *Much and House Public Relations*
8075 W 3rd St Ste 500
Los Angeles, CA 90048-4325, USA

Beattie, Jim (Athlete, Baseball Player)
PO Box 231
Quechee, VT 05059-0231, USA

Beattle, Ann (Writer)
janklow & Nesbit
445 Park Ave Fl 13
New York, NY 10022-8628, USA

Beattle, Bob (Skier)
210 Aabc Ste N
Aspen, CO 81611-3537, USA

Beattle, Bruce (Cartoonist)
Daytona Beach News-Journal
901 6th St
Editorial Dept
Daytona Beach, FL 32117-8099, USA

Beatty, Blaine (Athlete, Baseball Player)
867 Kolodzey Rd
Victoria, TX 77905-2520, USA

Beatty, Blaine (Athlete, Baseball Player)
Frederick Keys 21 Stadium Dr
Attn: Coaching Staff
Frederick, MD 21703, USA

Beatty, Charles (Athlete, Football Player)
PO Box 2634
Waxahachie, TX 75168-8634, USA

Beatty, Chuck
300 Oldham St
Waxahachie, TX 75165-3332, USA

Beatty, Jim (Athlete, Olympic Athlete, Track Athlete)
1516 Larochelle Ln
Charlotte, NC 28226-6868, USA

Beatty, Ned (Actor)
923 N Orchard Dr
Burbank, CA 91506-1540, USA

Beatty, Warren (Actor, Director, Producer)
13671 Mulholland Dr
Beverly Hills, CA 90210-1135, USA

Beaty, Zelmo (Athlete, Basketball Player)
6633 E Greenway Pkwy Apt 1100
Scottsdale, AZ 85254-2032, USA

Beau Brummels, The (Music Group, Musician)
PO Box 53664
C/O Jeff Hubbard
Indianapolis, IN 46253-0664, USA

Beauchamp, Al (Athlete, Football Player)
533 Pinegate Rd
Peachtree City, GA 30269-1120, USA

Beauchamp, Joe (Athlete, Football Player)
10525 Vista Sorrento Pkwy
Pkwy Ste 110
San Diego, CA 92121-2745, USA

Beaudin, Norm (Athlete, Hockey Player)
9595 E Thunderbird Rd Apt 1103
Scottsdale, AZ 85260-3746, USA

Beaudoin, Doug (Athlete, Football Player)
15143 Springview St
Tampa, FL 33624-2374, USA

Beaufait, Mark (Athlete, Hockey Player, Olympic Athlete)
5454 Longwood Ct SE
Ada, MI 49301-7755, USA

Beauford, Carter (Musician)
3000 Lonesome Mountain Rd
Charlottesville, VA 22911-6009, USA

Beaumon, Sterling (Actor)
c/o Bernard Kira *Vanguard Management Group*
8060 Melrose Ave Fl 4
Los Angeles, CA 90046-7038, USA

Beaumont, Jimmy (Musician)
2002 Duquesne Ave
McKeesport, PA 15132-5103, USA

Beaumont, Thomas (Actor)
c/o Staff Member *Scott Stander & Associates*
13701 Riverside Dr Ste 201
Sherman Oaks, CA 91423-2447, USA

Beaupre, Don (Athlete, Hockey Player)
5020 Scriver Rd
Minneapolis, MN 55436-1158, USA

Beauregard, DJ Paul (DJ, Musician)
5073 Topeka Dr
Tarzana, CA 91356-3909, USA

Beauregard, Robin (Athlete, Olympic Athlete, Water Polo Player)
467 Midvale Ave
Los Angeles, CA 90024-6707, USA

Beauvais, Garcelle (Actor)
3971 Murietta Ave
Sherman Oaks, CA 91423-4646, USA

Beaver, Jim (Actor)
4213 Gentry Ave
Studio City, CA 91604-2024, USA

Beaver, Joe (Rodeo Rider)
PO Box 1595
Huntsville, TX 77342-1595, USA

Beaver, Terry (Actor)
Paradigm Agency
10100 Santa Monica Blvd Ste 2500
Los Angeles, CA 90067-4116, USA

Beavers, Aubrey (Athlete, Football Player)
7035 Bellfort St Apt 204
Houston, TX 77087-5975, USA

Beavers, Scott (Athlete, Football Player)
4030 Pittman Rd
Atlanta, GA 30349-1439, USA

Beban, Gary (Athlete, Football Player)
70 W Huron St Apt 2308
Chicago, IL 60654-5351, USA

Bebout, Nick (Athlete, Football Player)
549 Downs Cir
Riverton, WY 82501-2211, USA

Becerra, Xavier (Congressman, Politician)
1226 Longworth Hob
Washington, DC 20515-4208, USA

Bech, Brett (Athlete, Football Player)
2701 White Oak Dr
Grapevine, TX 76051-2676, USA

Bech, Debra (Actor)
Minnesota Public Radio
480 Cedar St
Saint Paul, MN 55101-2230, USA

Becht, Anthony (Athlete, Football Player)
4657 Artesian Rd
Land O Lakes, FL 34638-3748, USA

Bechtel, Riley P (Business Person)
Bechtel Group
50 Beale St
San Francisco, CA 94105-1813, USA

Bechtel, Stefan (Writer)
Center for Creative Voices in Media
PO Box 331
Keswick, VA 22947-0331, USA

Bechtel, Stephen D Jr (Business Person)
Bechtel Group
50 Beale St
San Francisco, CA 94105-1813, USA

Beck, Aaron T (Doctor)
3600 Market St Ste 700
Philadelphia, PA 19104-2650, USA

Beck, Braden (Athlete, Football Player)
691 Milverton Rd
Los Altos, CA 94022-3928, USA

Beck, Byron (Athlete, Basketball Player)
1909 S Williams St
Kennewick, WA 99338-1820, USA

Beck, Chip (Athlete, Golfer)
11 Pembroke Dr
Lake Forest, IL 60045-2147, USA

Beck, Corey (Athlete, Basketball Player)
9444 Austin Dr
Olive Branch, MS 38654-7647, USA

Beck, Ernie (Athlete, Basketball Player)
1523 Brierwood Rd
Havertown, PA 19083-2910, USA

Beck, Glenn (Radio Personality, Television Host)
8528 Davis Blvd # 134-357
North Richland Hills, TX 76182-8367, USA

Beck, John (Athlete, Football Player)
17172 Glen Aspen Dr
San Diego, CA 92127-7830, USA

Beck, Jordan (Athlete, Football Player)
1042 Pinyon Ct
Windsor, CO 80550-4983, USA

Beck, Kimberly (Actor)
941 Kagawa St
Pacific Palisades, CA 90272-3834, USA

Beck, Maria (Actor)
c/o Staff Member *Shamon Freitas Talent Agency*
3916 Oregon St
San Diego, CA 92104-2806, USA

Beck, Martha (Writer)
1015 Ditmas Way
Arroyo Grande, CA 93420-6918, USA

Beck, Martin (Actor)
c/o Dale Garrick *Dale Garrick International Agency*
1017 N La Cienega Blvd Ste 109
West Hollywood, CA 90069-4196, USA

Beck, Mat (Cinematographer)
621 Via De La Paz
Pacific Palisades, CA 90272-4365, USA

Beck, Michael (Actor)
c/o Staff Member *Paradigm (LA)*
360 N Crescent Dr
North Bldg
Beverly Hills, CA 90210-4874, USA

Beck, Rich (Athlete, Baseball Player)
8218 N Sumter Ct
Spokane, WA 99208-5749, USA

Beck, Robin (Musician)
Cavaricci & White
156 W 56th St Ste 1803
New York, NY 10019-3899, USA

Beck, Tom (Athlete, Football Player)
806 Saddlewood Dr
Glen Ellyn, IL 60137-3202, USA

Beckel, Heather (Writer)
Milkshake Media
2210 S Congress Ave
Austin, TX 78704-4319, USA

Becker, Arthur (Athlete, Basketball Player)
1879 E Brentrup Dr
Tempe, AZ 85283-4275, USA

Becker, Boris (Athlete, Tennis Player)
c/o Staff Member *IMG (Cleveland)*
1360 E 9th St Ste 100
Cleveland, OH 44114-1730, USA

Becker, Donna (Athlete, Baseball Player)
5316 40th Ave
Kenosha, WI 53144-2707, USA

Becker, Doug (Athlete, Football Player)
6716 Lincoln Ave
Evansville, IN 47715-6920, USA

Becker, Gerry (Actor)
c/o Oliver Mossi *Paradigm (LA)*
360 N Crescent Dr
North Bldg
Beverly Hills, CA 90210-4874, USA

Becker, Gretchen (Actor)
Acme Talent
4727 Wilshire Blvd Ste 333
Los Angeles, CA 90010-3874, USA

Becker, Harold (Director, Producer)
c/o Jack Gilardi *ICM Partners (LA)*
10250 Constellation Blvd Fl 7
Los Angeles, CA 90067-6207, USA

Becker, Kuno (Actor)
c/o Ivan De Paz *DePaz Management*
2011 N Vermont Ave
Los Angeles, CA 90027-1931, USA

Becker, Kurt (Athlete, Football Player)
49W412 Scott Rd
Big Rock, IL 60511-9489, USA

Becker, Margaret (Musician)
Sparrow Communications
101 Winners Cir N
Brentwood, TN 37027-5352, USA

Becker, Quinn H (Doctor, General)
2111 Peninsula Dr
San Antonio, TX 78239-3077, USA

Becker, Rich (Athlete, Baseball Player)
210 Mary Senica Ct
La Salle, IL 61301-9676, USA

Becker, Rob (Actor, Comedian)
c/o Staff Member *William Morris Endeavor (LA)*
9601 Wilshire Blvd
Beverly Hills, CA 90210-5213, USA

Becker, Tony (Actor)
Howard Talent West
17000 Ventura Blvd Ste 210
C/O Bonnie Howard
Encino, CA 91316-4153, USA

Becker, Walt (Director)
c/o Matt Luber *Luber Roklin Management*
5815 W Sunset Blvd Ste 206
Los Angeles, CA 90028-6481, USA

Becker, Walter (Musician)
543 Hana Hwy
Paia, HI 96779-9732, USA

Beckert, Glenn (Athlete, Baseball Player)
1953 Arkansas Ave
Englewood, FL 34224-5505, USA

Beckett, Josh (Athlete, Baseball Player)
635 Sisterdale Rd
Bigfoot, TX 78005, USA

Beckett, Robbie (Athlete, Baseball Player)
15625 Harry Lind Rd
Elgin, TX 78621-3824, USA

Beckett, Rogers (Athlete, Football Player)
635 Gaelic Ct
Apopka, FL 32712-4724, USA

Beckett, Wendy (Sister) (Writer)
BBC-TV
Center Wood Ln
London, EN W12 7

Beckett, William (Musician)
c/o Bob McLynn *Crush Management*
60-62 E 11th St
7th Floor
New York, NY 10003, USA

Beckford, Roxanne (Actor)
9255 W Sunset Blvd Ste 401
West Hollywood, CA 90069-3302, USA

Beckford, Tyson (Actor, Model)
Bethann Entertainment
388 2nd Ave # 223
New York, NY 10010-5616, USA

Beckham, Brice (Actor)
6561 E Espanita St
Long Beach, CA 90815-4635

Beckham, David (Athlete, Soccer Player)
1105 San Ysidro Dr
Beverly Hills, CA 90210-2102, USA

Beckham, Gordon (Athlete, Baseball Player)
8 Habersham Park NW
Atlanta, GA 30305-2856, USA

Beckham, Victoria (Actor, Musician)
1105 San Ysidro Dr
Beverly Hills, CA 90210-2102, USA

Beckinsale, Kate (Actor)
c/o Geyer Kosinski *Media Talent Group*
9200 W Sunset Blvd Ste 550
West Hollywood, CA 90069-3611, USA

Becklean, William (Athlete, Olympic Athlete, Rower)
254 Fairhaven Hill Rd
Concord, MA 01742-4404, USA

Beckless, Ian (Athlete, Football Player)
4915 Andros Dr
Tampa, FL 33629-4801, USA

Beckley, Gerry (Music Group, Musician)
Agency for Performing Arts
9200 W Sunset Blvd Ste 900
West Hollywood, CA 90069-3604, USA

Beckman, Cameron (Athlete, Golfer)
191 Birnamwood Dr
Burnsville, MN 55337-6815, USA

Beckman, Ed (Athlete, Football Player)
4295 18th St NE
Naples, FL 34120-6409, USA

Beckman, Thomas (Athlete, Football Player)
3672 Cedar Shake Dr
Rochester Hills, MI 48309-1013, USA

Beckman, Tom (Athlete, Football Player)
3672 Cedar Shake Dr
Rochester Hills, MI 48309-1013, USA

Beckman, Witt (Athlete, Football Player)
568 Peachtree Pkwy Ste 116
Cumming, GA 30041-7404, United States

Beckum, Travis (Athlete, Football Player)
c/o Roosevelt Barnes *Maximum Sports Management*
6435 W Jefferson Blvd # 197
Fort Wayne, IN 46804-6203, USA

Beckwith, Alan (Actor)
3928 Carpenter Ave
Studio City, CA 91604-3764, USA

Beckwith, Darry (Athlete, Football Player)
c/o Jimmy Sexton *CAA (Memphis)*
6060 Poplar Ave Ste 470
Memphis, TN 38119-0910, USA

Beckwith, Joe (Athlete, Baseball Player)
859 Annabrook Dr
Auburn, AL 36830-7531, USA

Becquer, Julio (Athlete, Baseball Player)
2461 Kyle Ave N
Minneapolis, MN 55422-3626, USA

Becton, C W (Religious Leader)
United Pentecostal Free Will Baptist Church
8855 Dunn Rd
Hazelwood, MO 63042-2212, USA

Bedard, Irene (Actor)
Don Buchwald
6500 Wilshire Blvd Ste 2200
Los Angeles, CA 90048-4942, USA

Bedard, James A (Athlete, Hockey Player)
c/o Staff Member *Detroit Red Wings*
600 Civic Center Dr
Joe Luis Arena
Detroit, MI 48226-4419, USA

Bedard, Jim (Athlete, Hockey Player)
600 Civic Center Dr
Attn Coaching Staff
Detroit, MI 48226-4408, USA

Bedard, Patrick (Race Car Driver)
1462 Indian Pass Rd
Port Saint Joe, FL 32456-7811, USA

Bedelia, Bonnie (Actor)
c/o Nevin Dolcefino *Innovative Artists (LA)*
1505 10th St
Santa Monica, CA 90401-2805, USA

Bedell, Bob (Athlete, Basketball Player)
802 Exmoor Ave
Louisville, KY 40223-2715, USA

Bedell, Brad (Athlete, Football Player)
545 N Altura Rd
Arcadia, CA 91007-6059, USA

Bedell, Howie (Athlete, Baseball Player)
1187 Crestwood Dr
Pottstown, PA 19464-2931, USA

Bedford, Brian (Actor)
Arts Management Group
1133 Broadway Ste 1025
New York, NY 10010-7985, USA

Bedford, Vance (Athlete, Football Player)
3200 Grandview St Apt 9
Austin, TX 78705-2106, USA

Bedingfield, Natasha (Musician)
4130 Warner Blvd # D
Burbank, CA 91505-4130, USA

Bednarik, Charles P (Chuck) (Athlete, Football Player)
6379 Winding Rd
Coopersburg, PA 18036-9410, USA

Bednarski, John (Athlete, Hockey Player)
22917 Forest Edge Ct
Bonita Springs, FL 34135-2026, USA

Bedore, Thomas (Athlete, Football Player)
211 73rd St
Niagara Falls, NY 14304-4028, USA

Bedore, Tom (Athlete, Football Player)
9 Catherine Ave
Latrobe, PA 15650-2602, USA

Bedrosian, Steve (Athlete, Baseball Player)
11 Thomaston St
Newnan, GA 30263-5778, USA

Bedsole, Harold (Hal) (Athlete, Football Player)
78661 Rainswept Way
Palm Desert, CA 92211-3035, USA

Bee, Samantha (Actor, Comedian, Producer, Writer)
c/o Brian Stern *Brillstein Entertainment Partners (NYC)*
375 Greenwich St
New York, NY 10013-2376, USA

Beebe, Dion (Cinematographer)
International Creative Mgmt
10250 Constellation Blvd Fl 1
Los Angeles, CA 90067-6241, USA

Beebe, Don (Athlete, Football Player)
1246 Verona Ridge Dr
Aurora, IL 60506-6510, USA

Beebe, Mike (Governor, Politician)
Office of the Governor
State Capitol
Room 250
Little Rock, AR 72201, USA

Beech, Matt (Athlete, Baseball Player)
516 Sheffield Dr
Richardson, TX 75081-5610, USA

Beecham, Earl (Athlete, Football Player)
11 Terrace Cir Apt 1E
Great Neck, NY 11021-4143, USA

Beechen, Adam (Writer)
c/o Staff Member *Natural Talent Inc*
3331 Ocean Park Blvd Ste 203
Santa Monica, CA 90405-3225, USA

Beechler, Donnie (Race Car Driver)
1605 Arlington Chase
Sherman, IL 62684-8036, USA

Beecroft, David
1231 N Vista St
West Hollywood, CA 90046-6650, USA

Beede, Frank (Athlete, Football Player)
1645 Somerset Pl
Antioch, CA 94509-2183, USA

Bee Gees, The (Music Group)
c/o Staff Member *United Talent Agency (UTA-LA)*
9336 Civic Center Dr
Beverly Hills, CA 90210-3604, USA

Beekley, Bruce (Athlete, Football Player)
1351 Eaton Ave
San Carlos, CA 94070-4940, USA

Beem, Rich (Athlete, Golfer)
104 Bella Cima Dr
Austin, TX 78734-2670, USA

Beene, Andy (Athlete, Baseball Player)
113 Forest Brook St
Red Oak, TX 75154-6028, USA

Beene, Fred (Athlete, Baseball Player)
PO Box 143
Oakhurst, TX 77359-0143, USA

Beer, Tom (Athlete, Football Player)
292 Changebridge Rd Apt 2
Pine Brook, NJ 07058-9543, USA

Beers, Bob (Athlete, Hockey Player)
Boston Bruins
100 Legends Way Ste 250
Attn: Broadcast Dept
Boston, MA 02114-1389, USA

Beers, Bob (Athlete, Hockey Player)
97 Blake Rd
Lexington, MA 02420-3212, USA

Beesley, Max (Actor)
c/o Beth Holden-Garland *Untitled Entertainment (LA)*
350 S Beverly Dr Ste 200
Beverly Hills, CA 90212-4819, USA

Beeson, Paul B (Doctor, Physicist)
7 Riverwoods Dr Apt F125
Exeter, NH 03833-4385, USA

Beeson, Terry (Athlete, Football Player)
1302 Hibbard St
Coffeyville, KS 67337-1412, USA

Bega, Leslie (Actor)
31 1/2 Buccaneer St
Marina Del Rey, CA 90292-5103, USA

Begala, Paul (Commentator, Television Host)
1581 Highland Glen Pl
Mc Lean, VA 22101-4158, USA

Begay, Notah (Athlete, Golfer)
3620 Vista Del Sur St NW
Albuquerque, NM 87120-1583, USA

Beggs, James M (Government Official, Misc)
1177 N Great Southwest Pkwy
Grand Prairie, TX 75050-2629, USA

Beghe, Jason (Actor)
3800 Decker Edison Rd
Malibu, CA 90265-2330, USA

Begich, Mark
111 Russell Senate Office Building
Washington, DC 20510-0001, USA

Begler, Michael (Producer)
c/o Staff Member *William Morris Endeavor (LA)*
9601 Wilshire Blvd
Beverly Hills, CA 90210-5213, USA

Begley Jr, Ed (Actor, Director)
3850 Mound View Ave
Studio City, CA 91604-3630, USA

Beglin, Elizabeth (Athlete, Hockey Player, Olympic Athlete)
2070 Silver Maple Trl
North Liberty, IA 52317-4765, USA

Begovich, Mike (Actor)
c/o Beverly Strong *Strong Management*
9350 Wilshire Blvd Ste 224
Beverly Hills, CA 90212-3204, USA

Behagen, Ron (Athlete, Basketball Player)
1101 Juniper St NE Apt 401
Atlanta, GA 30309-7655, USA

Behar, Joy (Comedian, Talk Show Host, Television Host)
205 W 89th St Apt 9H
New York, NY 10024-1835, USA

Beharie, Nicole (Actor)
c/o Andrew Rogers *ICM Partners (LA)*
10250 Constellation Blvd Fl 7
Los Angeles, CA 90067-6207, USA

Behe, Michael (Writer)
Lehigh University
Biochemistry Dept
Bethlehem, PA 18015, USA

Behm, Donald (Athlete, Olympic Athlete, Wrestler)
PO Box 4401
East Lansing, MI 48826-4401, USA

Behm, Forrest E (Athlete, Football Player)
3 Briarcliff Dr
Corning, NY 14830-3328, USA

Behney, Mel (Athlete, Baseball Player)
2800 Woodshire Dr
Arlington, TX 76016-1553, USA

Behning, Mark (Athlete, Football Player)
2224 Woodbrook St
Denton, TX 76205-8254, USA

Behnke, Elmer (Athlete, Basketball Player)
3412 Ivy Chase Cir
Hoover, AL 35226-2276, USA

Behnken, Robert L (Astronaut)
43708 Dejay St
Lancaster, CA 93536-5781, USA

Behr, Aaron (Actor)
c/o Staff Member *Acme Talent & Literary (LA)*
1400 Atlantic Ave Ste 274
Long Beach, CA 90813-2013, USA

Behr, Ira Steven (Producer, Writer)
c/o Staff Member *Simon & Schuster*
1230 Avenue of the Americas Fl CONC1
New York, NY 10020-1586, USA

Behr, Jason (Actor)
c/o Robert Stein *Robert Stein Management*
PO Box 3797
Beverly Hills, CA 90212-0797, USA

Behrend, Marc (Athlete, Hockey Player, Olympic Athlete)
6805 Cross Country Rd
Verona, WI 53593-8203, USA

Behrendt, Greg (Actor, Writer)
c/o Staff Member *Simon & Schuster*
1230 Avenue of the Americas Fl CONC1
New York, NY 10020-1586, USA

Behrendt, Greg (Comedian, Radio Personality)
The Greg Behrendt Show
9336 Washington Blvd
Culver City, CA 90232-2628, USA

Behrens, Sam (Actor)
530 Bryant Dr
Canoga Park, CA 91304-1019, USA

Behrman, Dave (Athlete, Football Player)
10713 M 60
Three Rivers, MI 49093-9290, USA

Behrs, Beth (Actor)
c/o Chuck Binder *Binder & Associates*
1465 Lindacrest Dr
Beverly Hills, CA 90210-2519, USA

Beier, Thomas (Athlete, Football Player)
5055 Hammock Lake Dr
Coral Gables, FL 33156-2221, USA

Beilina, Nina (Musician)
400 W 43rd St Apt 7D
New York, NY 10036-6304, USA

Beimel, Joe (Athlete, Baseball Player)
4723 Boone Mountain Rd
Kersey, PA 15846-2109, USA

Beinfest, Larry (Commentator)
13700 Mustang Trl
Southwest Ranches, FL 33330-3610, USA

Beirne, Jim (Athlete, Football Player)
11173 Cox Rd
Conroe, TX 77385-7319, USA

Beirne, Kevin (Athlete, Baseball Player)
2 Cedar Chase Pl
Spring, TX 77381-3030, USA

Beisel, Monty (Athlete, Football Player)
2149 Sunset Plaza Dr
Los Angeles, CA 90069-1204, USA

Beisler, Randy (Athlete, Football Player)
306 Ramona St
Palo Alto, CA 94301-1438, USA

Bekar, Derek (Athlete, Hockey Player)
10 Cottage Rd
Meredith, NH 03253-7110, USA

Belafonte, Harry (Actor, Musician)
c/o Kaleigh Thomas *Sunshine Sachs (LA)*
8409 Santa Monica Blvd
West Hollywood, CA 90069-4209, USA

Belafonte, Shari (Actor, Musician)
530 Bryant Dr
Canoga Park, CA 91304-1019, USA

Belanger, Eric (Athlete, Hockey Player)
957 7th St
Hermosa Beach, CA 90254-4824, USA

Belanova (Music Group, Musician)
c/o Staff Member *APA Talent and Literary Agency*
9200 W Sunset Blvd Ste 900
West Hollywood, CA 90069-3604, USA

Belbin, Tanith (Figure Skater)
c/o Staff Member *Champions on Ice*
3500 American Blvd W Ste 190
Minneapolis, MN 55431-4431, USA

Bel Biv Devoe (Music Group, Musician)
8942 Wilshire Blvd
Beverly Hills, CA 90211-1908, USA

Belcher, Kevin (Athlete, Baseball Player)
2957 Silvercrest Ln
Grapevine, TX 76051-2423, USA

Belcher, Tim (Athlete, Baseball Player)
PO Box 153
Sparta, OH 43350-0153, USA

Belden, Bob (Athlete, Football Player)
6701 Militia Hill St NW
Canton, OH 44718-1391, USA

Belew, Adrian (Musician)
Umbrella Artists Mgmt
2595 Perkins Ln
Cincinnati, OH 45208-2722, USA

Belew, Adrian (Musician)
2004 Hidden Ridge Ct
Mount Juliet, TN 37122-2366, USA

Belfi, Jordan (Actor)
c/o Mark Schumacher *Schumacher Management*
2018 Glendon Ave
Los Angeles, CA 90025-6324, USA

Belford, Christine (Actor)
116 Inlet Ct
Hampstead, NC 28443-2558, USA

Belfort, Jordan (Business Person)
Global Motivation Inc
2711 N Sepulveda Blvd Ste 287
Manhattan Beach, CA 90266-2725, USA

Belfour, Ed (Athlete, Hockey Player)
420 Studebaker Rd
Whitewright, TX 75491-7297, USA

Belhumeur, Michel (Athlete, Hockey Player)
58 Little Falls Ln
Rockville, VA 23146-2123, USA

Belichick, Bill (Athlete, Football Coach, Football Player)
5028 Calais Dr
Columbus, OH 43221-5685, USA

Belichik, William S (Bill) (Coach, Football Coach)
New England Patriots
60 Washington St
Gillette Stadium RR1
Foxboro, MA 02035-1388, USA

Belinda, Stan (Athlete, Baseball Player)
4208 Reservoir Cir
Alexandria, PA 16611-2300, USA

Belisle, Danny (Athlete, Hockey Player)
3967 Glen Oaks Manor Dr
Sarasota, FL 34232-1045, USA

Belisle, Matt (Athlete, Baseball Player)
4009 Sierra Dr
Austin, TX 78731-3913, USA

Belitz, Todd (Athlete, Baseball Player)
17901 N Colton Ct
Colbert, WA 99005-9174, USA

Belk, Bill (Athlete, Football Player)
12 Ricemill Fry
Columbia, SC 29229-9034, USA

Belk, Tim (Athlete, Baseball Player)
14714 Carolcrest Dr
Houston, TX 77079-6408, USA

Belknap, Anna (Actor)
c/o Steve Stone *Cornerstone Talent Agency*
37 W 20th St Ste 1007
New York, NY 10011-3714, USA

Bell, Albert (Athlete, Football Player)
PO Box 3802
Lakewood, CA 90711-3802, USA

Bell, Andy (Musician)
c/o Stephen Ford *Diva Central Inc*
7510 W Sunset Blvd Ste 1445
Los Angeles, CA 90046-3408, USA

Bell, Anthony (Athlete, Football Player)
2021 Illinois St
Vallejo, CA 94590-4730, USA

Bell, Art (Business Person)
c/o Staff Member *Court TV*
600 3rd Ave Fl 2
New York, NY 10016-1919, USA

Bell, Art (Radio Personality)
c/o Staff Member *Simon & Schuster*
1230 Avenue of the Americas Fl CONC1
New York, NY 10020-1586, USA

Bell, Ashley (Actor)
c/o David Guillod *Intellectual Artists Management*
10585 Santa Monica Blvd Ste 135
Los Angeles, CA 90025-6392, USA

Bell, Bill (Athlete, Baseball Player)
3401 Urbandale Ave
Des Moines, IA 50310-4006, USA

Bell, Bill (Athlete, Football Player)
1601 Walnut St Apt 611
Kansas City, MO 64108-1350, USA

Bell, Billy Ray (Athlete, Football Player)
4006 Mossy Grove Ct
Humble, TX 77346-2498, USA

Bell, Bob (Athlete, Football Player)
700 Lower State Rd # 128G
North Wales, PA 19454-2167, USA

Bell, Brad (Athlete, Golfer)
2286 Stone Blvd
West Sacramento, CA 95691-4050, USA

Bell, Brian (Musician)
3611 Sapphire Dr
Encino, CA 91436-4233, USA

Bell, Buddy (Athlete, Baseball Player, Coach)
2100 S Sycamore St
Chandler, AZ 85286-5161, USA

Bell, Buddy (Athlete, Baseball Player)
333 W 35th St
Attn Director of Player Development
Chicago, IL 60616-3621

Bell, Byron (Athlete, Basketball Player)
1141 Williams St
Lake Geneva, WI 53147-1260, USA

Bell, Carl (Musician)
10690 Fairfield Ave
Las Vegas, NV 89183-4636, USA

Bell, Carlos (Athlete, Football Player)
14411 Hartshill Dr
Houston, TX 77044-4925, USA

Bell, Catherine (Actor)
c/o Daniel (Danny) Sussman *Brillstein Entertainment Partners (LA)*
9150 Wilshire Blvd Ste 350
Beverly Hills, CA 90212-3453, USA

Bell, Charles (Business Person)
McDonald's Corp
1 Kroc Dr
1 McDonald's Plaza
Oak Brook, IL 60523-2275, USA

Bell, Coby (Actor)
5534 E Oleta St
Long Beach, CA 90815-4433, USA

Bell, Coleman (Athlete, Football Player)
3236 Gianna Way
Land O Lakes, FL 34638-7823, USA

Bell, David (Athlete, Baseball Player)
244 W Goldfinch Way
Chandler, AZ 85286-4547, USA

Bell, Dennis (Athlete, Basketball Player)
111 Springfield Pike
Cincinnati, OH 45215-4263, USA

Bell, Derek (Athlete, Baseball Player)
3404 Pine Top Dr
Valrico, FL 33594-7618, USA

Bell, Drake (Actor)
3356 Ley Dr
Los Angeles, CA 90027-1316, USA

Bell, Drew Tyler (Actor, Dancer)
c/o Brad Diffley *Mavrick Artists Agency*
6100 Wilshire Blvd Ste 550
Los Angeles, CA 90048-5164, USA

Bell, Eddie (Athlete, Football Player)
4529 Tacoma Ter
Fort Worth, TX 76123-4005, USA

Bell, Eddie A (Actor)
4529 Tacoma Ter
Fort Worth, TX 76123-4005, USA

Bell, Emma (Actor)
c/o Scott Wexler *Brillstein Entertainment Partners (LA)*
9150 Wilshire Blvd Ste 350
Beverly Hills, CA 90212-3453, USA

Bell, Eric (Athlete, Baseball Player)
1140 S 124th St
Chandler, AZ 85286-1121, USA

Bell, Gary (Athlete, Baseball Player)
2107 Oak Rnch
San Antonio, TX 78259-1819, USA

Bell, Gerard (Athlete, Football Player)
1347 Deerbourne Dr
Wesley Chapel, FL 33543-6754, USA

Bell, Glen (Business Person)
Bell Charitable Foundation
PO Box 642
Rancho Santa Fe, CA 92067-0642, USA

Bell, Gordon (Athlete, Football Player)
205 Le Moyne Pkwy
Oak Park, IL 60302-1121, USA

Bell, Grantis (Athlete, Football Player)
3049 La Mirage Dr
Lauderhill, FL 33319-4246, USA

Bell, Greg (Athlete, Football Player)
5662 Calle Real
Goleta, CA 93117-2317, USA

Bell, Greg (Athlete, Track Athlete)
831 W Miami Ave
Logansport, IN 46947-2543, USA

Bell, Harry (Athlete, Hockey Player)
7711 N Invergordon Rd
Paradise Valley, AZ 85253-3169, USA

Bell, Heath (Athlete, Baseball Player)
7437 Los Brazos
San Diego, CA 92127-3852, USA

Bell, Hilari (Writer)
PO Box 877
Chestertown, MD 21620-0877, USA

Bell, Jacob (Athlete, Football Player)
2175 W California St
San Diego, CA 92110-2124, USA

Bell, Jaime (Actor)
c/o Staff Member *William Morris Endeavor (LA)*
9601 Wilshire Blvd
Beverly Hills, CA 90210-5213, USA

Bell, Jamie (Actor)
c/o Brian Swardstrom *United Talent Agency (UTA-NYC)*
9601 Wilshire Blvd
Beverly Hills, CA 90210-5213, USA

Bell, Jason (Athlete, Football Player)
3387 N Studebaker Rd
Long Beach, CA 90808-4258, USA

Bell, Jay (Athlete, Baseball Player)
3217 E Piro St
Phoenix, AZ 85044-3618, USA

Bell, Jerry (Athlete, Baseball Player)
631 Audrey Rd
Mount Juliet, TN 37122-3844, USA

Bell, Jerry (Athlete, Football Player)
1347 Deerbourne Dr
Wesley Chapel, FL 33543-6754, USA

Bell, John (Musician)
Brown Cat Inc
400 Foundry St
Athens, GA 30601-2623, USA

Bell, Joshua (Musician)
24 E 22nd St PH 7
New York, NY 10010-6146, USA

Bell, Ken (Athlete, Football Player)
8335 Fairmount Dr Unit 9-106
Denver, CO 80247-1137, us

Bell, Kendrell (Athlete, Football Player)
1270 Caroline St NE Ste D120
Atlanta, GA 30307-2758, us

Bell, Kendrell (Athlete, Football Player)
400 W Peachtree St NW Unit 1211
Atlanta, GA 30308-3547, USA

Bell, Kerwin (Athlete, Football Player)
525 3rd St N Apt 508
Jacksonville Beach, FL 32250-7039, USA

Bell, Kerwin (Athlete, Football Player)
1822 Waterbury Lane Fleming Is Fl
32003-7749
Fleming Island, FL 32003, us

Bell, Kevin (Athlete, Baseball Player)
621 Sue St
Little Chute, WI 54140-2424, USA

Bell, Kevin (Athlete, Football Player)
5780 Phyllis Ln
Beaumont, TX 77713-9539, USA

Bell, Kristen (Actor)
c/o Emily Gerson Saines *Brookside Artists Management (NY)*
250 W 57th St Ste 2303
New York, NY 10107-2399, USA

Bell, Lake (Actor)
c/o Joanna (Joanie) Burstein *Burstein Company, The*
15304 W Sunset Blvd Ste 208
Pacific Palisades, CA 90272-3656, USA

Bell, Lauralee (Actor)
23713 Malibu Colony Rd
Malibu, CA 90265-6629, USA

Bell, Madison Smartt (Writer)
Random House
1745 Broadway Frnt 3 # B1
New York, NY 10019-4343, USA

Bell, Marcus (Athlete, Football Player)
PO Box 263
Eagar, AZ 85925-0263, USA

Bell, Mark E (Athlete, Football Player)
2701 N Wild Rose St
Wichita, KS 67205-1607, USA

Bell, Marshall (Actor)
IFA Talent Agency
2000 Avenue Of The Stars
Los Angeles, CA 90067-4700, USA

Bell, Michael (Actor)
4906 Encino Ave
Encino, CA 91316-3816, USA

Bell, Michelle (Athlete, Golfer)
18895 Pond Cypress Ct
Jupiter, FL 33458-3735, USA

Bell, Mike (Athlete, Baseball Player)
5125 Piney Grove Dr
Cumming, GA 30040-9673, USA

Bell, Mike (Race Car Driver)
American Motorcycle Assn
13515 Yarmouth Dr
Pickerington, OH 43147-8273, USA

Bell, Mike J (Athlete, Football Player)
7405 W Lakewood Cir
Wichita, KS 67205-1608, USA

Bell, Mikw (Athlete)
244 W Goldfinch Way
Chandler, AZ 85286-4547, USA

Bell, Myron (Athlete, Football Player)
3027 Crawford Ave Gastonia NC28052-6076
Gastonia, NC 28052-6076, USA

Bell, Nick (Athlete, Football Player)
1641 Minorca Dr
Costa Mesa, CA 92626-4854, USA

Bell, Peggy (Athlete, Golfer)
400 Grove Rd
Southern Pines, NC 28387-2839, USA

Bell, Raja (Athlete, Basketball Player)
22 E Cactus601 NE 36th St
Apt 1812 Wren Dr
Miami, FL 33137, USA

Bell, Richard T (Athlete, Football Player)
12106 City View Ln SE
Chatfield, MN 55923-1719, USA

Bell, Ricky (Athlete, Football Player)
c/o Staff Member *Sosincere Entertainment*
2054 Nostrand Ave Apt 4F
Brooklyn, NY 11210-2526, USA

Bell, Rini (Actor)
c/o Sherry Marsh *Marsh Entertainment*
12444 Ventura Blvd Ste 203
Studio City, CA 91604-2409, USA

Bell, Rob (Athlete, Baseball Player)
28 Blossom Hill Dr
Marlboro, NY 12542-6000, USA

Bell, Robert (Musician)
c/o Staff Member *J Bird Entertainment Agency*
4905 S Atlantic Ave
Ponce Inlet, FL 32127-7311, USA

Bell, Robert F (Athlete, Football Player)
7415 N 12th St
Elkins Park, PA 19027-3052, USA

Bell, Sam (Coach)
2310 E Woodstock Pl
Bloomington, IN 47401-6179, USA

Bell, Sean (Actor)
c/o Daniel Sladek *Daniel Sladek Entertainment Corporation*
8306 Wilshire Blvd # 510
Beverly Hills, CA 90211-2304, USA

Bell, Tatum (Athlete, Football Player)
18754 E Powers Dr
Aurora, CO 80015-3162, us

Bell, Terry (Athlete, Baseball Player)
8352 Normandy Creek Dr
Dayton, OH 45458-3284, USA

Bell, Tobin (Actor)
c/o Alan Saffron *Saffron Management*
9171 Wilshire Blvd Ste 441
Beverly Hills, CA 90210-5516, USA

Bell, Townsend (Race Car Driver)
524 15th St
Santa Monica, CA 90402-2934, USA

Bell, Wally (Athlete, Baseball Player)
725 Purdue Ave
Youngstown, OH 44515-4220, USA

Bell, W Kamau (Comedian, Television Host)
c/o Keri Smith Esguia *Whitesmith Entertainment*
Prefers to be contact via email or telephone
West Hollywood, CA 90069, USA

Bell, Yeremiah (Athlete, Football Player)
1215 Delong Pl
Lexington, KY 40515-8522, us

Bell, Zoe (Actor)
c/o Todd Diener *Untitled Entertainment (LA)*
350 S Beverly Dr Ste 200
Beverly Hills, CA 90212-4819, USA

Bella, John (Athlete, Baseball Player)
409 N Cypress Dr Apt 7
Jupiter, FL 33469-2656, USA

Bella, Rachael (Actor)
c/o Leonard Torgan *The Collective*
8383 Wilshire Blvd Ste 1050
Beverly Hills, CA 90211-2415, USA

Bellamy, Bill (Actor, Comedian)
17219 Benner Pl
Encino, CA 91316-3908, USA

Bellamy, Ned (Actor)
c/o Laina Cohn *Cohn / Torgan Management*
Prefers to be contacted by telephone or email
Los Angeles, CA, USA

Bellani, Adrian (Actor)
8004 Woodrow Wilson Dr
Los Angeles, CA 90046-1117, USA

Bell Calloway, Vanessa (Actor)
c/o Katie Mason *Luber Roklin Management*
5815 W Sunset Blvd Ste 206
Los Angeles, CA 90028-6481, USA

Belle, Albert (Athlete, Baseball Player)
9299 E Marioosa Grande Dr
Scottsdale, AZ 85255, USA

Belle, Camilla (Actor)
c/o Brad Cafarelli *PMK/BNC Public Relations (PMK-LA)*
8687 Melrose Ave Ste 8
West Hollywood, CA 90069-5746, USA

Belle, David (Actor)
c/o Emanuel Nunez *Paradigm (LA)*
360 N Crescent Dr
North Bldg
Beverly Hills, CA 90210-4874, USA

Belle, Regina (Musician)
Green Light
PO Box 3172
Beverly Hills, CA 90212-0172, USA

Bellefeuille, Blake (Athlete, Hockey Player)
716 Berlin Rd
Marlborough, MA 01752-4592, USA

Beller, Kathleen (Actor)
PO Box 806
Half Moon Bay, CA 94019-0806, USA

Bellflower, Nellie (Actor, Producer)
c/o Staff Member *Keylight Entertainment Group*
10590 Wilshire Blvd Apt 301
Los Angeles, CA 90024-4531, USA

Bellhorn, Mark (Athlete, Baseball Player)
19550 N Grayhawk Dr Unit 1083
Scottsdale, AZ 85255-3993, USA

Bellhorn, Mark (Athlete, Basketball Player)
1447 Palomino Way
Oviedo, FL 32765-9304, USA

Belliard, Rafael (Athlete, Baseball Player)
10846 King Bay Dr
Boca Raton, FL 33498-4548, USA

Belliard, Ronnie (Athlete, Baseball Player)
2999 NW 96th St
Miami, FL 33147-2337, USA

Bellinger, Clay (Athlete, Baseball Player)
1390 E Horseshoe Dr
Chandler, AZ 85249-4761, USA

Bellinger, Rodney (Athlete, Football Player)
6721 SW 48th Ter
Miami, FL 33155-5745, USA

Bellingham, Norman (Athlete, Olympic Athlete)
1825 Cantwell Grv
Colorado Springs, CO 80906-6911, USA

Bellino, Dan (Athlete, Baseball Player)
8820 Belfield Rd
Crystal Lake, IL 60014-8503, USA

Bellino, Joe (Athlete, Football Player)
45 Hayden Ln
Bedford, MA 01730-1140, USA

Bellisario, Donald P (Actor, Director, Producer, Writer)
1565 Las Tunas Rd
Santa Barbara, CA 93108-1334, USA

Bellisario, Troian (Actor)
c/o Matthew Lesher *Insight*
PO Box 36359
Los Angeles, CA 90036-0359, USA

Bellman, Gina (Actor)
c/o Matthew Lesher *Insight*
PO Box 36359
Los Angeles, CA 90036-0359, USA

Bellman-Balchunas, Lois (Athlete, Baseball Player)
1008 Southport Ave
Lisle, IL 60532-1346, USA

Bello, Maria (Actor)
132 Mabery Rd
Santa Monica, CA 90402-1204, USA

Belloir, Rob (Athlete, Baseball Player)
PO Box 2933
Savannah, GA 31402-2933, USA

Bellorin, Edwin
44523 Fenhold St
Lancaster, CA 93535-3420, USA

Bellotti, Mike (Coach, Football Coach)
University of Oregon
Athletic Dept
Eugene, OR 97403, USA

Bellows, Brian (Athlete, Hockey Player)
6824 Valley View Rd
Minneapolis, MN 55439-1646, USA

Bellows, Gil (Actor)
c/o Emily Gerson Saines *Brookside Artists Management (NY)*
250 W 57th St Ste 2303
New York, NY 10107-2399, USA

Bellwood, Pamela (Actor)
1696 San Leandro Ln
Santa Barbara, CA 93108-2638, USA

Bell X1 (Music Group)
c/o Staff Member *Paradigm (Monterey)*
404 W Franklin St
Monterey, CA 93940-2303, USA

Belmares, Roland (DJ)
c/o Staff Member *Diva Central Inc*
7510 W Sunset Blvd Ste 1445
Los Angeles, CA 90046-3408, USA

Belote, Melissa (Athlete, Olympic Athlete, Swimmer)
1504 E Coronado Dr
Tempe, AZ 85282-5763, USA

Below, Duane
4330 Eaglehurst Rd
Sylvania, OH 43560-3411, USA

Belser, Ceaser (Athlete, Football Player)
317 Cooper Dr
Hurst, TX 76053-6130, USA

Belser, Jason (Athlete, Football Player)
20150 Valhalla Sq
Ashburn, VA 20147-4104, USA

Belton, Horace (Athlete, Football Player)
2047 General Lee Ave
Baton Rouge, LA 70810-6325

Beltran, Carlos (Athlete, Baseball Player)
1450 Brickell Ave Ste 1800
Miami, FL 33131-3452, USA

Beltran, Rigo (Athlete, Baseball Player)
3950 Laurelwood Ln
Delray Beach, FL 33445-3503, USA

Beltran, Robert (Actor)
2210 Talmadge St
Los Angeles, CA 90027-2918, USA

Beltre, Adrian (Athlete, Baseball Player)
1204 Suncast Ln Ste 2
El Dorado Hills, CA 95762-9665, USA

Belushi, James (Jim) (Actor)
c/o Marc Gurvitz *Brillstein Entertainment Partners (LA)*
9150 Wilshire Blvd Ste 350
Beverly Hills, CA 90212-3453, USA

Belushi-Pisano, Judith (Writer)
c/o Staff Member *CMG Worldwide*
10500 Crosspoint Blvd
Indianapolis, IN 46256-3331, USA

Belvin, Art (Athlete, Football Player)
6506 Centre Place Cir
Spring, TX 77379-2937, USA

Belzer, Richard (Actor, Comedian)
60 Riverside Dr # 14C/D
New York, NY 10024-6108, USA

Beman, Deane R (Athlete, Golfer)
Golf HOF
255 Deer Haven Dr
Ponte Vedra Beach, FL 32082-2108, USA

Bemiller, Al (Athlete, Football Player)
Buffalo Bills
5002 Armor Duells Rd
Orchard Park, NY 14127-4401, USA

Bemis, Cliff (Actor)
Beartooth Productions
11271 Ventura Blvd PMB 366
Studio City, CA 91604-3136, USA

Bemvenuti, Luciana (Athlete, Golfer)
2208 Craftsman St
Duluth, GA 30097-2516, USA

Benanti, Laura (Actor)
c/o Emily Gerson Saines *Brookside Artists Management (NY)*
250 W 57th St Ste 2303
New York, NY 10107-2399, USA

Benard, Marcus (Athlete, Football Player)
c/o Drew Rosenhaus *Rosenhaus Sports Representation*
6400 Allison Rd
Miami Beach, FL 33141-4540, USA

Benard, Marvin (Athlete, Baseball Player)
30405 S 903 PR SE
Kennewick, WA 99338-7346, USA

Benard, Maurice (Actor)
c/o Staff Member *Benard Management*
15300 Ventura Blvd Ste 315
Sherman Oaks, CA 91403-5870, USA

Benatar, Pat (Musician, Songwriter)
c/o John Malta *Bel Chiasso Entertainment*
7956 Glade Ave
Canoga Park, CA 91304-4718, USA

Benavides, Freddie (Athlete, Baseball Player)
3007 Wincrest Cir
Laredo, TX 78045-8149, USA

Benben, Brian (Actor)
c/o Erwin More *Paradigm (LA)*
360 N Crescent Dr
North Bldg
Beverly Hills, CA 90210-4874, USA

Bench, Johnny (Athlete, Baseball Player)
Johnny Bench Enterprises
3899 Ridgedale Dr
Cincinnati, OH 45247-6946, USA

Bendekovits, Joe (Athlete, Baseball Player)
9410 N Newport Ave
Tampa, FL 33612-7724, USA

Bender, Carey (Athlete, Football Player)
716 Delta Downs Dr
Cary, NC 27519-8750, USA

Bender, Gary N (Sportscaster)
TNT-TV
1050 Techwood Dr NW
Sports Dept
Atlanta, GA 30318-5604, USA

Bender, Jack (Director)
13055 Evanston St
Los Angeles, CA 90049-3642, USA

Bender, Jennie (Athlete, Olympic Athlete, Skier)
c/o Gigi Rock *Heraea Marketing*
10905 E Pear Tree Dr
Cornville, AZ 86325-5523, USA

Bender, Wes (Athlete, Football Player)
114 Skyline Dr
Burbank, CA 91501-1132, USA

Bendross, Jesse (Athlete, Football Player)
5226 SW 22nd St
West Park, FL 33023-3118, USA

Bene, Bill (Athlete, Baseball Player)
1063 Bella Vista Ave
San Gabriel, CA 91775, USA

Benedeti, Paulo (Actor)
1560 NW 13th Ave
Boca Raton, FL 33486-1217, USA

Benedict, Bruce (Athlete, Baseball Player)
335 Quiet Water Ln
Atlanta, GA 30350-3724, USA

Benedict, Dirk (Actor, Director, Writer)
c/o Staff Member *Acme Talent & Literary (LA)*
1400 Atlantic Ave Ste 274
Long Beach, CA 90813-2013, USA

Benedict, Robert Patrick (Actor)
c/o Charles Silver *SMS Talent*
8383 Wilshire Blvd Ste 230
Beverly Hills, CA 90211-2436, USA

Benedicto, Lourdes (Actor)
23325 Collins St
Woodland Hills, CA 91367-4119, USA

Benefield, Daved (Athlete, Football Player)
420 N Rodeo Dr Apt 15281
Beverly Hills, CA 90210-4502, USA

Benepe, Jim (Athlete, Golfer)
1955 1/2 Frackelton St
Sheridan, WY 82801-2526, USA

Benes, Alan (Athlete, Baseball Player)
754 Kraffel Ln
Chesterfield, MO 63017-8057, USA

Benes, Andy (Athlete, Baseball Player, Olympic Athlete)
1127 Highland Pointe Dr
Saint Louis, MO 63131-1420, USA

Benet, Eric (Actor, Musician)
3312 Via Verde Ct
Calabasas, CA 91302-3085, USA

Benfatti, Lou (Athlete, Football Player)
29 Colonial Oaks Dr
Oak Ridge, NJ 07438-9196, USA

Bengis, Fred (Athlete, Baseball Player)
546 Quail Ct
Longs, SC 29568-8638, USA

Bening, Annette (Actor)
13671 Mulholland Dr
Beverly Hills, CA 90210-1135, USA

Benioff, David (Producer)
1228 N Wetherly Dr
Los Angeles, CA 90069-1816, USA

Beniquez, Juan (Athlete, Baseball Player)
87-12 Calle 99A
Carolina, PR 00985-4127, USA

Benirschke, Rolf J (Athlete, Football Player)
4326 Vista De La Tierra
Del Mar, CA 92014-4101, USA

Benish, Dan (Athlete, Football Player)
2885 Cross Creek Dr
Cumming, GA 30040-6344, USA

Benishek, Dan (Congressman, Politician)
514 Cannon Hob
Washington, DC 20515-0103, USA

Benitez, Armando (Athlete, Baseball Player)
2205 Warwick Way Ste 200
Marriottsville, MD 21104-1632, USA

Benitez, Jellybean (Musician)
Jellybean Recordings
235 Park Ave S
New York, NY 10003-1405, USA

Benitez, Wilfred (Athlete, Boxer)
Wilfred Benitez Foundation, NFP
PO Box 2338
Temecula, CA 92593-2338, USA

Benitez, Yamil (Athlete, Baseball Player)
13 Calle Un
918 Caperra Terrace
San Juan, PR 00915-2401, USA

Benitz, Max (Actor)
c/o Michael Baum *Impression Entertainment*
9229 W Sunset Blvd Ste 700
West Hollywood, CA 90069-3407, USA

Benjamin, Andre 3000 (Artist, Musician)
c/o Kaleigh Thomas *Sunshine Sachs (LA)*
8409 Santa Monica Blvd
West Hollywood, CA 90069-4209, USA

Benjamin, Benoit (Athlete, Basketball Player)
28 Morning Grn
San Antonio, TX 78257-2602, USA

Benjamin, Guy (Athlete, Football Player)
91-443 Ewa Beach Rd Apt B
Ewa Beach, HI 96706-2974, USA

Benjamin, Jill (Actor)
c/o Staff Member *Principato/Young Management (LA)*
9465 Wilshire Blvd Ste 900
Beverly Hills, CA 90212-2608, USA

Benjamin, Kelvin (Athlete, Football Player)
c/o Eugene Parker *Maximum Sports Management*
6435 W Jefferson Blvd # 197
Fort Wayne, IN 46804-6203, USA

Benjamin, Mike (Athlete, Baseball Player)
25608 S 182nd Pl
Queen Creek, AZ 85142-8188, USA

Benjamin, Richard (Actor, Director)
c/o Staff Member *Gersh (LA)*
9465 Wilshire Blvd Ste 600
Beverly Hills, CA 90212-2605, USA

Benjamin, Ryan (Athlete, Football Player)
8332 Boyce Ct
New Port Richey, FL 34654-5602, USA

Benjamin, Steve (Athlete, Olympic Athlete, Sailor)
PO Box 399
Norwalk, CT 06856-0399, USA

Benjamin, Tony (Athlete, Football Player)
7448 E Leland Cir
Mesa, AZ 85207-2030, us

Benjamin, Travis (Athlete, Football Player)
c/o Mitchell Frankel *Impact Sports - Boca Raton*
2799 NW 2nd Ave Ste 203
Boca Raton, FL 33431-6709, USA

Benmosche, Robert H (Business Person)
Metropolitan Life Insurance
1 Madison Ave
New York, NY 10010-3603, USA

Benners, Fred (Athlete, Football Player)
5211 Shadywood Ln
Dallas, TX 75209-2207, USA

Bennet, Chloe (Actor)
c/o Alexandra Crotin *42West (LA)*
1840 Century Park E Ste 700
Los Angeles, CA 90067-2122, USA

Bennet, Michael F. (Senator)
458 Russell Senate Office Building
Washington, DC 20510-0001, USA

Bennett, A L (Athlete, Basketball Player)
523 N Willow Pl
Jenks, OK 74037-3489, USA

Bennett, Antoine
5011 SW 173rd Ave
Miramar, FL 33029-5095, USA

Bennett, Barry (Athlete, Football Player)
22047 Ginseng Rd
Long Prairie, MN 56347-4754, USA

Bennett, Bennett (Actor)
c/o Paul Young *Principato/Young Management (LA)*
9465 Wilshire Blvd Ste 900
Beverly Hills, CA 90212-2608, USA

Bennett, Bill (Athlete, Hockey Player)
14 Glen Ave
Cranston, RI 02905-3702, USA

Bennett, Bill (DJ)
c/o Staff Member *Diva Central Inc*
7510 W Sunset Blvd Ste 1445
Los Angeles, CA 90046-3408, USA

Bennett, Bob (Athlete, Olympic Athlete, Swimmer)
70 Rivo Alto Canal
Long Beach, CA 90803-4047, USA

Bennett, Bob (Musician, Songwriter, Writer)
c/o Vicki Jennette *The Benjamin Artist Agency*
PO Box 92348
Nashville, TN 37209-8348, USA

Bennett, Brad (Race Car Driver)
PO Box 16759
Stamford, CT 06905-8759, USA

Bennett, Brandon (Athlete, Football Player)
308 Daybrook Ct
Greenville, SC 29605-5963, us

Bennett, Brooke (Athlete, Olympic Athlete, Swimmer)
2585 Rowe Rd
Milford, MI 48380-2337, USA

Bennett, Carl (Athlete, Basketball Player)
2834 Little River Run
Fort Wayne, IN 46804-2573, USA

Bennett, Charles (Athlete, Football Player)
10240 Red Currant Ct
Riverview, FL 33578-3657, USA

Bennett, Clay (Cartoonist)
Christian Science Monitor
1 Norway Park
Editorial Dept
Hyde Park, MA 02136-4016, USA

Bennett, Cornelius (Athlete, Football Player)
818 S 7th Ave
Hollywood, FL 33019-1100, us

Bennett, Curt (Athlete, Hockey Player)
260 Awapuhi Pl
Wailuku, HI 96793-2117, USA

Bennett, Darren (Athlete, Football Player)
3347 Corte Del Cruce
Carlsbad, CA 92009-9548, USA

Bennett, Dave (Athlete, Baseball Player)
101 S Fairchild St
Yreka, CA 96097-2263, USA

Bennett, Donnell (Athlete, Football Player)
129 NW 16th Ave
Pompano Beach, FL 33069-2803, USA

Bennett, Drew (Athlete, Football Player)
93 Stephanie Ln
Alamo, CA 94507-1225, us

Bennett, Edgar (Athlete, Football Player)
1880 Horseshoe Ln
De Pere, WI 54115-7947, USA

Bennett, Elmer (Athlete, Basketball Player)
2820 Avenue of the Woods
Louisville, KY 40241-6232, USA

Bennett, Erik (Athlete, Baseball Player)
PO Box 4108
Salt Lake City, UT 84110-4108, USA

Bennett, Fran (Actor)
749 N La Fayette Park Pl
Los Angeles, CA 90026-2917, USA

Bennett, Gary (Athlete, Baseball Player)
14905 Creekside Path
Libertyville, IL 60048-1104, USA

Bennett, Haley (Actor)
c/o Mimi DiTrani *The Schiff Company*
9220 W Sunset Blvd Ste 106
West Hollywood, CA 90069-3500, USA

Bennett, Harvey (Athlete, Hockey Player)
1096 Warwick Neck Ave
Warwick, RI 02889-6815, USA

Bennett, Jeff (Athlete, Baseball Player)
408 Five Oaks Blvd
Lebanon, TN 37087-1321, USA

Bennett, Joel (Athlete, Baseball Player)
401 Riley Rd
Windsor, NY 13865-1043, USA

Bennett, John
5151 Collins Ave Apt 426
Miami Beach, FL 33140-2714, USA

Bennett, Jonathan (Actor)
c/o Staff Member *Amplitude Entertainment*
8033 W Sunset Blvd # 823
Los Angeles, CA 90046-2401

Bennett, Leeman (Athlete, Football Coach, Football Player)
PO Box 9269
Fleming Island, FL 32006-0026, USA

Bennett, Manu (Actor)
c/o Ruth Bornhauser *Sanders Armstrong Caserta*
2120 Colorado Ave Ste 120
Santa Monica, CA 90404-3561, USA

Bennett, Martellus (Athlete, Football Player)
c/o Kennard McGuire *MS World LLC*
1270 Crabb River Rd Ste 600-104
Richmond, TX 77469-5636, USA

Bennett, Michael (Athlete, Football Player)
17110 Journeys End Dr
Odessa, FL 33556-2441, USA

Bennett, Monte (Athlete, Football Player)
2075 Avenue U
Sterling, KS 67579-8917, USA

Bennett, Nelson (Skier)
807 S 20th Ave
Yakima, WA 98902-4228, USA

Bennett, Paris (Musician)
c/o Stephen Ford *Diva Central Inc*
7510 W Sunset Blvd Ste 1445
Los Angeles, CA 90046-3408, USA

Bennett, Rick (Athlete, Hockey Player)
4 N Center Ln
Ballston Lake, NY 12019-1403, USA

Bennett, Robert R (Business Person)
Home Shopping Network
2501 118th Ave N
Saint Petersburg, FL 33716-1900, USA

Bennett, Roy (Athlete, Football Player)
6509 Tree Mountain Pkwy
Stone Mountain, GA 30083-6738, USA

Bennett, Sean (Athlete, Football Player)
12163 E State Road 62
Saint Meinrad, IN 47577-9673, USA

Bennett, Tony (Athlete, Basketball Player)
306 Ednam Dr
Charlottesville, VA 22903-4714, USA

Bennett, Tony (Musician)
Benedetto Arts LLC
48 W 10th St Ste B
New York, NY 10011-8702, USA

Bennett, Wendell (Athlete, Hockey Player)
133 Sun Villa Ct
Vista, CA 92084-5851, USA

Bennett, William (Athlete, Hockey Player)
20 Versailles St
Cranston, RI 02920-1420, USA

Bennett, William J. (Politician)
1901 N Moore St Ste 201B
Arlington, VA 22209-1706, USA

Bennett, Winston (Athlete, Basketball Player)
5108 Forest Grove Ct
Prospect, KY 40059-9672, USA

Bennett, Woody (Athlete, Football Player)
5678 Saddle Trail Ln
Lake Worth, FL 33449-5449, us

Bennie, Dan (Musician)
22121 Cleveland St
Dearborn, MI 48124-3462, USA

Benning, Jim (Athlete, Hockey Player)
Boston Bruins
100 Legends Way Ste 250
Attn: Asst General Manager
Boston, MA 02114-1389, USA

Benning, Jim (Athlete, Hockey Player)
PO Box 1264
Sherwood, OR 97140-1264, USA

Benning, Norm (Race Car Driver)
3359 Babcock Blvd
Pittsburgh, PA 15237-2421, USA

Bennington, Chester (Musician)
2959 E Bonanza Rd
Gilbert, AZ 85297-7607, USA

Benny, Joan (Actor)
1131 Coldwater Canyon Dr
Beverly Hills, CA 90210-2402

Benoit, David (Musician)
Fitzgerald-Hartley
34 N Palm St Ste 100
Ventura, CA 93001-2610, USA

Benoit, Morgan (Actor)
c/o Staff Member *Bluestone Entertainment*
9000 W Sunset Blvd Ste 700
West Hollywood, CA 90069-5807, USA

Benrubi, Abraham (Actor)
c/o Erik Kritzer *LINK Entertainment*
11872 La Grange Ave Fl 1
Los Angeles, CA 90025-5283, USA

Bensimon, Kelly Killoren (Model, Reality Star, Writer)
c/o Staff Member *Bravo (NY)*
30 Rockefeller Plz
New York, NY 10112-0015, USA

Benson, Amber (Actor)
c/o Staff Member *United Talent Agency (UTA-LA)*
9336 Civic Center Dr
Beverly Hills, CA 90210-3604, USA

Benson, Anna (Model, Reality Star)
c/o Jon Orlando *WNWN Media*
348 Hauser Blvd # PH414
Los Angeles, CA 90036-3276, USA

Benson, Ashley (Actor)
c/o Thor Bradwell *LBI Entertainment*
2000 Avenue of the Stars
Floor 3, North Tower
Los Angeles, CA 90067-4700, USA

Benson, Brad (Athlete, Football Player)
840 Amwell Rd
Hillsborough, NJ 08844-3900, USA

Benson, Brendan (Musician)
1504 Woodmont Blvd
Nashville, TN 37215-1632, USA

Benson, Cedric (Athlete, Football Player)
15365 W Rockland Ln
Libertyville, IL 60048-9721, USA

Benson, Charles (Athlete, Football Player)
1514 Hanover Ln
Van Alstyne, TX 75495-7086, USA

Benson, Cliff (Athlete, Football Player)
PO Box 821957
Vancouver, WA 98682-0045, USA

Benson, Darren (Athlete, Football Player)
PO Box 742614
Dallas, TX 75374-2614, USA

Benson, Doug (Comedian)
c/o Bruce Smith *OmniPop Talent Group (LA)*
4605 Lankershim Blvd Ste 201
North Hollywood, CA 91602-1874, USA

Benson, George (Actor, Musician)
6132 E Foothill Dr N
Paradise Valley, AZ 85253-3072, USA

Benson, George (Race Car Driver)
16700 State Highway 96 Spc 16
96 Unit 16
Klamath River, CA 96050-9105, USA

Benson, Herbert (Doctor)
Mind/Body Medical Institute
Beth Israel Hospital
Brookline, MA 02146, USA

Benson, Joyce (Athlete, Golfer)
5310 Papaya Cir
Harlingen, TX 78552-8956, USA

Benson, Kent (Athlete, Basketball Player)
3921 W Maybury Mall Apt 12
Bloomington, IN 47403-3738, USA

Benson, Kris (Athlete, Baseball Player, Olympic Athlete)
2862 Howard Dr NE
Marietta, GA 30062-6676, USA

Benson, Robby (Actor)
c/o Staff Member *Creative Artists Agency (CAA-LA)*
2000 Avenue of the Stars Ste 100
Los Angeles, CA 90067-4705, USA

Benson, Steve (Cartoonist)
Arizona Republic
200 E Van Buren St
Editorial Dept
Phoenix, AZ 85004-2238, USA

Benson, Thomas (Athlete, Football Player)
PO Box 701341
Dallas, TX 75370-1341, USA

Benson, Troy (Athlete, Football Player)
1038 Victoria Pl
Gibsonia, PA 15044-9200, USA

Benson-Landes, Wendy (Actor)
1236 N Doheny Dr
Los Angeles, CA 90069-1723, USA

Bent, Lyriq (Actor)
c/o Staff Member *Stone Manners Salners Agency (LA)*
6100 Wilshire Blvd Ste 1500
Los Angeles, CA 90048-5110, USA

Bentham, Lee (Race Car Driver)
Forsythe Racing Inc
1111 Willis Ave
Wheeling, IL 60090-5816, USA

Bentley, Albert (Athlete, Football Player)
13631 Eagle Ridge Dr Apt 223
Fort Myers, FL 33912-1878, USA

Bentley, Dierks (Musician)
4410 Granny White Pike
Nashville, TN 37204-4118, USA

Bentley, Eric (Writer)
194 Riverside Dr Apt 4E
New York, NY 10025-7276, USA

Bentley, Kevin (Athlete, Football Player)
3001 Murworth Dr Unit 904
Houston, TX 77025-4430, us

Bentley, Lecharles (Athlete, Football Player)
1177 Windsor Ave
Broadview Heights, OH 44147, USA

Bentley, Ray (Athlete, Football Player, Sportscaster)
16543 Lake Shore Dr
Gowen, MI 49326-9513, USA

Bentley, Robert (Governor, Politician)
Office of the Governor
600 Dexter Ave
Montgomery, AL 36130-3024, USA

Bentley, Scott (Athlete, Football Player)
7756 S Trenton Ct
Centennial, CO 80112-2636, us

Bentley, Wes (Actor)
c/o Kevin Morris *Morris Yorn Barnes Levine Krintzman Rubenstein Kohner & Gellman*
2000 Avenue of the Stars Ste 300N
3rd Floor, North Tower
Los Angeles, CA 90067-4704, USA

Benton, Barbi (Actor, Model)
840 N Starwood Dr
Aspen, CO 81611-9717, USA

Benton, Brad (Adult Film Star)
c/o Staff Member *Diva Central Inc*
7510 W Sunset Blvd Ste 1445
Los Angeles, CA 90046-3408, USA

Benton, Butch (Athlete, Baseball Player)
12314 SE 60th Ave
Belleview, FL 34420-5200, USA

Benton, Robert (Director, Writer)
c/o Brian Siberell *Creative Artists Agency (CAA-LA)*
2000 Avenue of the Stars Ste 100
Los Angeles, CA 90067-4705, USA

Bentsen, William (Athlete, Sailor)
N1946 Birches Dr
Lake Geneva, WI 53147-4119, USA

Bentz, Chad (Athlete, Baseball Player)
78 Skyline Dr
West Rutland, VT 05777-9808, USA

Benvenuti, Leo (Director, Producer, Writer)
c/o John Elliott *Mosaic Media Group*
9200 W Sunset Blvd Ste 10
West Hollywood, CA 90069-3608, USA

Ben-Victor, Paul (Actor)
c/o Michael Garnett *Leverage Management*
3030 Pennsylvania Ave
Santa Monica, CA 90404-4112, USA

Benymon, Chico (Actor)
c/o Staff Member *Gersh (LA)*
9465 Wilshire Blvd Ste 600
Beverly Hills, CA 90212-2605, USA

Benz, Amy (Athlete, Golfer)
85133 Shinnecock Hills Dr
Fernandina Beach, FL 32034-8177, USA

Benz, Julia (Actor)
Innovative Artists
1505 10th St
Santa Monica, CA 90401-2805, USA

Benz, Julie (Actor)
9031 Ashcroft Ave
West Hollywood, CA 90048-1704, USA

Benz, Larry (Athlete, Football Player)
1526 Brummel St
Evanston, IL 60202-3708, USA

Benz, Nikki (Actor, Adult Film Star, Model)
Nikki Benz, Inc.
15030 Ventura Blvd Ste 19654
Sherman Oaks, CA 91403-5470, USA

Benza, AJ (Actor)
5670 Wilshire Blvd # 400W
Los Angeles, CA 90036-5679, USA

Benzali, Daniel (Actor)
c/o Staff Member *William Morris Endeavor (LA)*
9601 Wilshire Blvd
Beverly Hills, CA 90210-5213, USA

Benzinger, Todd (Athlete, Baseball Player)
1047 Shore Point Ct
Loveland, OH 45140-6970, USA

Beracasa, Fabiola
Circa Inc
415 Madison Ave Fl 19
New York, NY 10017-7948, USA

Berard, Bryan (Athlete, Hockey Player, Olympic Athlete)
17 Summit Cir
Wrentham, MA 02093-1909, USA

Berardino, Dick
37 Emmeline Ave
Waltham, MA 02452-7935, USA

Berblinger, Jeff (Athlete, Baseball Player)
102 Swanee Dr
Goddard, KS 67052-9420, USA

Berce, Gene (Athlete, Basketball Player)
13900 W Burleigh Rd
Brookfield, WI 53005-3019, USA

Bercich, Bob (Athlete, Football Player)
19017 Edward Pkwy
Mokena, IL 60448-8565, USA

Bercich, Pete (Athlete, Football Player)
17448 Honeysuckle Ave
Lakeville, MN 55044-7824, USA

Bercu, Michaela (Actor, Model)
c/o Staff Member *Elite Model Management (NY)*
245 5th Ave Fl 24
New York, NY 10016-8728, USA

Berdy, Sean (Actor)
18685 Main St Ste 101 PMB 331
Huntington Beach, CA 92648-1719, USA

Berdych, Thomas (Athlete, Tennis Player)
c/o Staff Member *ATP Tour*
201 Atp Tour Blvd
Ponte Vedra Beach, FL 32082-3211, USA

Bere, Jason (Athlete, Baseball Player)
40 Berrington Pl
North Andover, MA 01845-2152, USA

Berehowsky, Drake (Athlete, Hockey Player)
20455 N 95th St
Scottsdale, AZ 85255-6629, USA

Berendt, John (Writer)
c/o Suzanne Gluck *William Morris Endeavor (NY)*
1325 Avenue of the Americas
New York, NY 10019-6026, USA

Berenger, Tom (Actor)
65/67/70 Camp Saint Mary Rd
Okatie, SC 29909, USA

Berenguer, Juan (Athlete, Baseball Player)
8616 Alisa Ct
Chanhassen, MN 55317-9373, USA

Berens, Ricky (Athlete, Swimmer)
1 Olympic Plz Bldg 2A
Colorado Springs, CO 80909-5746, USA

Berenson, Ken (Red) (Athlete, Coach, Hockey Player)
3555 Daleview Dr
Ann Arbor, MI 48105-9686, USA

Berenyi, bruce (Baseball Player)
10 Pine Grove Rd
Exeter, NH 03833-4718, USA

Berenyl, Bruce (Athlete, Baseball Player)
PO Box 133
Sherwood, OH 43556-0133, USA

Berenzweig, Andrew (Athlete, Hockey Player)
4603 Brookside Rd
Ottawa Hills, OH 43615-2207, USA

Berezhnaya, Yelena (Figure Skater)
Ice House Skating Rink
111 Midtown Bridge Approac
Hackensack, NJ 07601-7505, USA

Berezin, Sergei (Athlete, Hockey Player)
1645 SW 4th Ave
Boca Raton, FL 33432-7232, USA

Berfield, Justin (Actor, Director, Producer)
24944 Lorena Dr
Calabasas, CA 91302-3048, USA

Berg, Aki (Athlete, Hockey Player)
7400 Metro Blvd Ste 280
Minneapolis, MN 55439-2363, USA

Berg, Aki-Petteri (Athlete, Hockey Player)
1751 Pinnacle Dr Ste 1500
Mc Lean, VA 22102-3833, USA

Berg, Dave (Baseball Player)
1620 Bradford Grove Trl
Keller, TX 76248-9729, USA

Berg, Dave (Athlete, Baseball Player)
PO Box 638
Jamestown, NY 14702-0638, USA

Berg, justin (Baseball Player)
N3628 Heights Dr
Bryant, WI 54418-9563, USA

Berg, Kevin (Business Person)
c/o Staff Member *CBS Paramount Network Television*
4024 Radford Ave
Cbs Studios
Studio City, CA 91604-2190, USA

Berg, Laura (Athlete, Olympic Athlete, Softball Player)
2801 NE 50th St
Usa Softball
Oklahoma City, OK 73111-7203, USA

Berg, Matraca (Musician)
Joe's Garage
4405 Belmont Park Ter
Nashville, TN 37215-3609, USA

Berg, Peter (Actor)
2125 Glencoe Ave
Venice, CA 90291-4008, USA

Berg, Rick (Congressman, Politician)
323 Cannon Hob
Washington, DC 20515-0924, USA

Berg, Steve (Actor)
c/o Ilan Breil *Mosaic Media Group*
9200 W Sunset Blvd Ste 10
West Hollywood, CA 90069-3608, USA

Berg, Yehuda (Religious Leader)
Kabbalah Center International
1066 S La Cienega Blvd
Los Angeles, CA 90035-2508, USA

Berganio, David Jr (Athlete, Golfer)
17811 Lahey St
Granada Hills, CA 91344-4030, USA

Bergen, Candice (Actor)
222 Central Park W
New York, NY 10024, USA

Bergen, Danny (Actor)
c/o Staff Member *Paul Lane Entertainment*
468 N Camden Dr
Beverly Hills, CA 90210-4507, USA

Bergen, Gary (Athlete, Basketball Player)
1386 Graham Cir
Erie, CO 80516-3617, USA

Berger, Brandon (Athlete, Baseball Player)
2276 Dixie Hwy
Ft Mitchell, KY 41017-2949, USA

Berger, Isaac (Athlete, Olympic Athlete, Weightlifter)
206 E 31st St Apt 8A
New York, NY 10016-6357, USA

Berger, Lee (Actor)
57 Fellows Rd
Brentwood, NH 03833-6130, USA

Berger, Mike (Athlete, Hockey Player)
118 SW Santee Dr
Greensburg, IN 47240-7802, USA

Berger, Ronald (Athlete, Football Player)
6000 Lagorce Dr
Miami Beach, FL 33140-2117, USA

Berger, Sy (Commentator)
36 Whitehall Rd
Rockville Centre, NY 11570-3244, USA

Berger-Brown, Barbara (Athlete, Baseball Player)
1321 S Finley Rd Apt 109
Lombard, IL 60148-4355, USA

Berger-Knebl, Joan (Athlete, Baseball Player)
8 Lochmeath Way
Dover, DE 19904-6447, USA

Bergeron, Patrice (Athlete, Hockey Player)
c/o Staff Member *Boston Bruins*
100 Legends Way Ste 250
Td Banknorth Garden
Boston, MA 02114-1389, USA

Bergeron, Peter (Athlete, Baseball Player)
3495 Manatee Dr SE
Saint Petersburg, FL 33705-4144, USA

Bergeron, Tom (Actor, Producer)
24856 Paseo Del Rancho
Calabasas, CA 91302-3083, USA

Berger-Taylor, Norma (Athlete, Baseball Player)
529 N Bierman Ave
Villa Park, IL 60181-1437, USA

Bergeson, Eric (Athlete, Football Player)
2579 E Sherwood Dr
Salt Lake City, UT 84108-2457, USA

Bergeson, James (Athlete, Olympic Athlete, Water Polo Player)
7 Promontory
Trabuco Canyon, CA 92679-3811, USA

Bergeson, Pat (Musician)
3614 Central Ave
Nashville, TN 37205-2344, USA

Bergevin, Marc (Athlete, Hockey Player)
404 Canterbury Ct
Hinsdale, IL 60521-2826, USA

Bergevin, Marc (Athlete, Hockey Player)
Chicago Blackhawks
1901 W Madison St
Attn Assistant G M
Chicago, IL 60612-2459, USA

Bergey, Bruce (Athlete, Football Player)
7700 SW River Rd
Hillsboro, OR 97123-9108, USA

Bergey, William E (Bill) (Athlete, Football Player)
2 Hickory Ln
Chadds Ford, PA 19317-9715, USA

Bergh, Larry (Athlete, Basketball Player)
7020 Peoto Ln
Crossville, TN 38572-4501, USA

Bergi, Emily (Actor)
Innovative Artists
1505 10th St
Santa Monica, CA 90401-2805, USA

Bergin, Michael (Actor, Model)
c/o Tom Chasin *Chasin Agency, The*
8899 Beverly Blvd Ste 716
Los Angeles, CA 90048-2449, USA

Bergin, Patrick (Actor)
Hyler Mgmt
25 Sea Colony Dr
Santa Monica, CA 90405-5495, USA

Bergl, Emily (Actor)
c/o Craig Shapiro *ICM Partners (LA)*
10250 Constellation Blvd Fl 7
Los Angeles, CA 90067-6207, USA

Bergland, Tim (Athlete, Hockey Player)
721 Labree Ave N
Thief River Falls, MN 56701-1632, USA

Berglind (Icey) (Television Host)
c/o Staff Member *E! Entertainment Television (LA)*
5750 Wilshire Blvd Ste 500
Los Angeles, CA 90036-3635, USA

Bergloff, Bob (Athlete, Hockey Player)
10200 Harriet Ave S
Minneapolis, MN 55420-5233, USA

Berglund, Art (Athlete, Hockey Player)
3749 Blue Merion Ct
Colorado Springs, CO 80906-4444, USA

Berglund, Bo (Athlete, Hockey Player)
c/o Staff Member *Buffalo Sabres*
1 Seymour H Knox III Plz Ste 1
Buffalo, NY 14203-3096, USA

Bergman, Alan (Musician)
714 N Maple Dr
Beverly Hills, CA 90210-3411, USA

Bergman, Andrew C (Director, Writer)
c/o Robert (Bob) Bookman *Paradigm (LA)*
2000 Avenue of the Stars
Los Angeles, CA 90067-4700, USA

Bergman, Dave (Athlete, Baseball Player)
PO Box 380135
Clinton Township, MI 48038-0060, USA

Bergman, Dusty (Athlete, Baseball Player)
1549 Koontz Ln
Carson City, NV 89701-6504, USA

Bergman, Jaime
c/o Holly Shelton *Precision Entertainment*
465 N Croft Ave
Los Angeles, CA 90048-2508, USA

Bergman, Jamie (Actor, Model)
c/o Staff Member *Special Artists Agency*
9200 W Sunset Blvd Ste 410
West Hollywood, CA 90069-3506, USA

Bergman, Marilyn K (Musician)
714 N Maple Dr
Beverly Hills, CA 90210-3411, USA

Bergman, Peter (Actor)
4799 White Oak Ave
Encino, CA 91316-3719, USA

Bergman, Sean (Athlete, Baseball Player)
14421 Scott Rd
Bryan, OH 43506-9624, USA

Bergmann, Erma (Athlete, Baseball Player, Commentator)
6613 Morganford Rd
Saint Louis, MO 63116-2835, USA

Bergmann, Jay (Athlete, Baseball Player)
13 Abilene Ln
Manalapan, NJ 07726-4527, USA

Bergmann, S
3620 Gatlin Dr
Rockledge, FL 32955-6049, USA

Bergoust, Eric (Athlete, Olympic Athlete, Skier)
1430 Shadow Ln
Missoula, MT 59803-3405, USA

Bergstein, Eleanor (Director, Producer, Writer)
c/o Staff Member *Creative Artists Agency (CAA-LA)*
2000 Avenue of the Stars Ste 100
Los Angeles, CA 90067-4705, USA

Beristain, Gabriel L (Cinematographer)
United Talent Agency
9336 Civic Center Dr
Beverly Hills, CA 90210-3604, USA

Berkeley, Xander (Actor, Producer)
2946 N Beachwood Dr
Los Angeles, CA 90068-1926, USA

Berken, Jason
1303 Grasswoods Ct
De Pere, WI 54115-7613, USA

Berkhoel, Adam (Athlete, Hockey Player)
1744 Manning Aves
Saint Paul, MN 55129, USA

Berkley, Elizabeth (Actor, Producer)
c/o Adam Griffin *Kritzer Levine Wilkins Entertainment (KLWG)*
11872 La Grange Ave Fl 1
Los Angeles, CA 90025-5283, USA

Berkley, Shelley (Congressman, Politician)
405 Cannon Hob
Washington, DC 20515-4309, USA

Berkman, Lance (Athlete, Baseball Player)
5 Farnham Park Dr
Houston, TX 77024-7501, USA

Berkner, Laurie (Musician)
PO Box 250774
Columbia University Station
New York, NY 10025-1529, USA

Berkoff, David (Swimmer)
Harvard University
Athletic Dept
Cambridge, MA 02138, USA

Berkowitz, Bob (Journalist, Television Host)
c/o Staff Member *CNBC (Main)*
900 Sylvan Ave
Englewood Cliffs, NJ 07632-3312, USA

Berkus, Nate (Designer, Television Host)
406 N Wood St
Chicago, IL 60622-6260, USA

Berlanti, Greg (Producer)
PO Box 5623
Beverly Hills, CA 90209-5623, USA

Berlin, Clay (Publisher)
2935 Franciscan Way
Carmel, CA 93923-9216, USA

Berlin, Eddie (Athlete, Football Player)
1527 W School St # 3
Chicago, IL 60657-2121, USA

Berlin, Mike (Bowler)
12 Coventry Ln
Muscatine, IA 52761-5659, USA

Berlin, Steve (Musician)
c/o Staff Member *Paradigm (Monterey)*
404 W Franklin St
Monterey, CA 93940-2303, USA

Berliner, Alain (Director)
United Talent Agency
9336 Civic Center Dr
Beverly Hills, CA 90210-3604, USA

Berlinger, Warren (Actor)
10642 Arnel Pl
Chatsworth, CA 91311-2501, USA

Berlinsky, Dmitri (Musician)
35 W 64th St Apt 7F
New York, NY 10023-6757, USA

Berman, Andy (Actor)
c/o Staff Member *Gersh (LA)*
9465 Wilshire Blvd Ste 600
Beverly Hills, CA 90212-2605, USA

Berman, Boris (Musician)
Columbia Artists Mgmt Inc
165 W 57th St
New York, NY 10019-2201, USA

Berman, Chris (Commentator, Sportscaster)
31 Peach Tree Ct
Cheshire, CT 06410-2367, USA

Berman, David (Musician)
2326 Hollyridge Dr
Los Angeles, CA 90068-3518, USA

Berman, Jennifer (Doctor)
University of California
Women's Sexual Health Center
Los Angeles, CA 90024, USA

Berman, Josh (Producer)
c/o Staff Member *Creative Artists Agency (CAA-LA)*
2000 Avenue of the Stars Ste 100
Los Angeles, CA 90067-4705, USA

Berman, Julie (Actor)
c/o Nicole Nassar *Nicole Nassar PR*
1111 10th St Unit 104
Santa Monica, CA 90403-5363, USA

Berman, Laura (Doctor, Writer)
Laura A Berman, PhD
625 N Michigan Ave Ste 2500
Chicago, IL 60611-3835, USA

Berman, Lazar N (Musician)
12 Nicola Ln
Nesconset, NY 11767-1550, USA

Berman, Shari Springer (Director)
c/o Staff Member *Creative Artists Agency (CAA-LA)*
2000 Avenue of the Stars Ste 100
Los Angeles, CA 90067-4705, USA

Berman, Shelley (Actor, Comedian)
268 Bell Canyon Rd
Bell Canyon, CA 91307-1112, USA

Bermudez, Carolina (Musician)
c/o Staff Member *Don Buchwald & Associates (LA)*
6500 Wilshire Blvd Ste 2200
Los Angeles, CA 90048-4942, USA

Bermudez, Joe (DJ)
c/o Staff Member *Diva Central Inc*
7510 W Sunset Blvd Ste 1445
Los Angeles, CA 90046-3408, USA

Bernard, Betsy (Business Person)
American Telephone & Telegraph Corp
32 Avenue of the Americas Bldg 1
New York, NY 10013-2473, USA

Bernard, Carlos (Actor)
8901 Wonderland Ave
Los Angeles, CA 90046-1853, USA

Bernard, Crystal (Actor, Musician, Songwriter, Writer)
PO Box 202
Montrose, CA 91021-0202, USA

Bernard, Dwight (Athlete, Baseball Player)
5120 N Norwich Ln
Belle Rive, IL 62810-2703, USA

Bernard, Ed (Actor)
PO Box 7965
Northridge, CA 91327-7965, USA

Bernard, Giovani (Athlete, Football
Player)
c/o Jamie Fritz *Fritz Martin Management*
1801 Avenue of the Stars Ste 250
Los Angeles, CA 90067-5914, USA

Bernard, James (Race Car Driver)
PO Box 758
Mc Henry, MD 21541-0758, USA

Bernard, Robyn (Actor)
The Bernard Bookstore
PO Box 202
Montrose, CA 91021-0202, USA

Bernardi, Barry (Producer)
c/o Staff Member *Gersh (LA)*
9465 Wilshire Blvd Ste 600
Beverly Hills, CA 90212-2605, USA

Bernardi, Frank (Athlete, Football Player)
PO Box 1015
Broomfield, CO 80038-1015, USA

Bernazard, Tony (Athlete, Baseball Player)
D25 Calle Santa Ana
Caguas, PR 00725-3418, USA

Bernero, Adam (Athlete, Baseball Player)
11 Columbus Dr
Savannah, GA 31405-4101, USA

Bernero, Ed (Writer)
c/o Jeff Jacobs *Creative Artists Agency
(CAA-LA)*
2000 Avenue of the Stars Ste 100
Los Angeles, CA 90067-4705, USA

Bernet, Ed (Athlete, Football Player)
7967 Caruth Ct
Dallas, TX 75225-8135, USA

Bernet, Lee (Athlete, Football Player)
4689 Stoddart Ln
Saint Paul, MN 55127-2334, USA

Berney, Bob (President)
c/o Staff Member *Newmarket Films*
597 5th Ave Fl 7
New York, NY 10017-8264, USA

Bernhard, Sandra (Actor, Comedian,
Musician)
6145 Shadyglade Ave
North Hollywood, CA 91606-4635, USA

Bernhardt, Daniel (Actor)
6500 Wilshire Blvd Ste 2200
Los Angeles, CA 90048-4942

Bernhardt, Kevin (Writer)
c/o Luke Rivett *Anonymous Content (LA)*
3532 Hayden Ave
Culver City, CA 90232-2413, USA

Bernhardt, Roger (Athlete, Football
Player)
PO Box 4631
Lawrence, KS 66046-1631, USA

Bernheimer, Martin (Musician)
17350 W Sunset Blvd Apt 702C
Pacific Palisades, CA 90272-4109, USA

Bernice Johnson, Eddie (Congressman,
Politician)
2468 Rayburn Hob
Washington, DC 20515-3306, USA

Bernich, Ken (Athlete, Football Player)
504 Woodland Park Cir
Mary Esther, FL 32569-1577, USA

Berning, Susie (Athlete, Golfer)
80413 Portobello Dr
Indio, CA 92201-1877, USA

Berns, Rick (Athlete, Football Player)
127 Merry Trl
San Antonio, TX 78232-1330, USA

Bernsen, Corbin (Actor)
11955 Addison St
Valley Village, CA 91607-3106, USA

Bernstein, Adam (Director, Producer,
Writer)
c/o Sean Freidin *ICM Partners (LA)*
10250 Constellation Blvd Fl 7
Los Angeles, CA 90067-6207, USA

Bernstein, Al (Actor)
c/o Gisela Shiffer *3G Management*
Prefers to be contacted via telephone or
email
Los Angeles, CA, USA

Bernstein, Assaf (Director)
c/o Brad Kaplan *Evolution Entertainment
(LA)*
901 N Highland Ave
Los Angeles, CA 90038-2412, USA

Bernstein, Bonnie (Television Host)
c/o Staff Member *CBS Television*
51 W 52nd St Fl 29
New York, NY 10019-6116, USA

Bernstein, Carl (Journalist, Writer)
9 Salt Meadow Ln
Sag Harbor, NY 11963-4324, USA

Bernstein, Josh (Television Host)
c/o Mark Schulman *3 Arts Entertainment
(LA)*
9460 Wilshire Blvd Fl 7
Beverly Hills, CA 90212-2713, USA

Bernstein, Kenny (Race Car Driver)
King Racing
26231 Dimension Dr
Lake Forest, CA 92630-7805, USA

Bernstine, Rod (Athlete, Football Player)
6675 S Robertsdale Way
Aurora, CO 80016-7500, USA

Bernthal, Jon (Actor)
3028 Stanford Ave
Marina Del Rey, CA 90292-5527, USA

Berra, Dale (Athlete, Baseball Player)
164 Eagle Rock Way
Montclair, NJ 07042-1623, USA

Berra, Steve (Skateboarder)
3716 Clayton Ave
Los Angeles, CA 90027-4614, USA

Berra, Tim (Athlete, Football Player)
23 Wilson Ter
West Caldwell, NJ 07006-7953, USA

Berra, Yogi (Athlete, Baseball Player,
Coach)
The Yogi Berra Museum
8 Quarry Rd
Little Falls, NJ 07424-2161, USA

Berresford, Josh (Actor)
Auz & Associates PR
PO Box 601
Homewood, IL 60430-8601

Berrian, Bernard (Athlete, Football Player)
7209 Tokay Cir
Winton, CA 95388-9358, USA

Berridge, Elizabeth (Actor)
Judy Schoen
606 N Larchmont Blvd Ste 309
Los Angeles, CA 90004-1309, USA

Berrier, Max (Race Car Driver)
6262 N N C Highway 109
High Point, NC 27265, USA

Berrigan, Daniel (Politician)
220 W 98th St Apt 11L
New York, NY 10025-5677, USA

Berroa, Geronimo (Athlete, Baseball
Player)
3681 Broadway Act 23
New York, NY 10031, USA

Berry, Bert (Athlete, Football Player)
1402 E Coral Cove Dr
Gilbert, AZ 85234-2600, USA

Berry, Bill (Baseball Player)
Negro Baseball Leagues
2231 Dickinson St
Philadelphia, PA 19146-4204, USA

Berry, Bill (Musician)
1661 Old Farmington Rd
Watkinsville, GA 30677-3208, USA

Berry, Bob (Athlete, Football Player)
114 Vista Mar Ct
Aptos, CA 95003-3925, USA

Berry, Brad (Athlete, Hockey Player)
Columbus Blue Jackets
200 W Nationwide Blvd Unit 1
Attn Coaching Staff
Columbus, OH 43215-2564, USA

Berry, Brad (Athlete, Hockey Player)
PO Box 5182
Grand Forks, ND 58206-5182, USA

Berry, Chuck (Musician, Songwriter)
691 Buckner Rd
Berry Park
Wentzville, MO 63385-5442, USA

Berry, David (Actor)
5903 Winton St
Dallas, TX 75206-5536, USA

Berry, Ed (Athlete, Football Player)
4215 Skymont Dr
Belmont, CA 94002-1245, USA

Berry, Eric (Athlete, Football Player)
c/o Chad Speck *Allegiant Athletic Agency*
35 Market Sq Ste 201
Knoxville, TN 37902-1420, USA

Berry, Fred (Athlete, Hockey Player)
1330 Jaclyn Dr
Brookfield, WI 53045-4452, USA

Berry, Halle (Actor, Model)
1164 N Doheny Dr
Los Angeles, CA 90069-1750, USA

Berry, Jadagrace (Actor)
c/o Monique Moss *Integrated PR*
8060 Melrose Ave Fl 4
Los Angeles, CA 90046-7038, USA

Berry, Jim (Artist, Cartoonist)
United Feature Syndicate
PO Box 5610
Cincinnati, OH 45201-5610, USA

Berry, John (Musician)
2162 Elder Mill Rd
Watkinsville, CA 90677, USA

Berry, Joy (Writer)
c/o Staff Member *Trident Media Group
LLC*
41 Madison Ave Fl 36
New York, NY 10010-2257, USA

Berry, Ken (Actor)
13911 Fenton Ave
Sylmar, CA 91342-1653, USA

Berry, Ken (Athlete, Baseball Player)
1131 SW Camden Ln
Topeka, KS 66604-1980, USA

Berry, Latin (Athlete, Football Player)
925 Prater Rd
Sulphur, LA 70663-4243, USA

Berry, Mark (Athlete, Baseball Player)
5201 Keene Dr
Plant City, FL 33566-9798, USA

Berry, Matthew (Commentator)
c/o Jonathan Berry *3 Arts Entertainment
(LA)*
9460 Wilshire Blvd Fl 7
Beverly Hills, CA 90212-2713, USA

Berry, Neil (Athlete, Baseball Player)
407 Inkster Ave
Kalamazoo, MI 49001-4220, USA

Berry, Ray (Athlete, Football Player)
12 Winged Foot Cir W
Abilene, TX 79606-5026, USA

Berry, Raymond E (Athlete, Football
Coach, Football Player)
1110 SE Broad St
Murfreesboro, TN 37130-5027, USA

Berry, Reggie (Athlete, Football Player)
1803 E Ocean Blvd Unit 402
Long Beach, CA 90802-6045, USA

Berry, Robert V (Bob) (Athlete, Coach,
Hockey Player)
640 3rd St
Hermosa Beach, CA 90254-4710, USA

Berry, Royce (Athlete, Football Player)
PO Box 909
Comfort, TX 78013-0909, USA

Berry, Sean (Athlete, Baseball Player)
307 Susannah Ln
Paso Robles, CA 93446-7114, USA

Berry, Walter (Athlete, Basketball Player)
PO Box 81
Union City, GA 30291-0081, USA

Berry, Wendell E (Writer)
Lanes Landing Farm
PO Box 1
Port Royal, KY 40058-0001, USA

Berryhill, Damon (Athlete, Baseball
Player)
11 Springbrook Rd
Laguna Niguel, CA 92677-5719, USA

Berryman, Michael (Actor)
5806 Hannah Pierce Rd W Apt G
University Place, WA 98467-4201, USA

Bersia, John (Journalist)
Orlando Sentinel
633 N Orange Ave Lbby
Editorial Dept
Orlando, FL 32801-1349, USA

Bertelsen, Jim (Athlete, Football Player)
2001 Days End Rd
Wimberley, TX 78676-9153, USA

Berteotti, Missy (Athlete, Golfer)
3065 Annandale Dr
Presto, PA 15142, USA

Berthiaume, Daniel (Athlete, Hockey Player)
PO Box 673
Hardy, VA 24101-0673, USA

Berti, Joel (Actor)
c/o Melissa Hirschenson *Innovative Artists (LA)*
1505 10th St
Santa Monica, CA 90401-2805, USA

Bertinelli, Valerie (Actor)
3496 Berry Dr
Studio City, CA 91604-4152, USA

Bertold, Isabella (Athlete, Olympic Athlete, Sailor)
c/o Gigi Rock *Heraea Marketing*
10905 E Pear Tree Dr
Cornville, AZ 86325-5523, USA

Bertotti, Mike (Athlete, Baseball Player)
14 Jupiter Rd
Highland Mls, NY 10930-2916, USA

Bertsch, Jackie (Athlete, Golfer)
8215 E Bronco Trl
Scottsdale, AZ 85255-2171, USA

Bertuca, Tony (Athlete, Football Player)
2014 N Newcastle Ave
Chicago, IL 60707-3332, USA

Berube, Craig (Athlete, Hockey Player)
1341 Durham Rd
New Hope, PA 18938-9479, USA

Berube, Craig (Athlete, Hockey Player)
Philadelphia Flyers
3601 S Broad St Ste 2
Attn Coaching Staff
Philadelphia, PA 19148-5297, USA

Berumen, Andres (Athlete, Baseball Player)
PO Box 1436
Banning, CA 92220-0010, USA

Besana, Fred (Baseball Player)
Baltimore Orioles
222 Diamond Oaks Rd
Roseville, CA 95678-1007, USA

Beschorner-Baskovich, Mary (Baseball Player)
211 Sandy Ln
Plano, IL 60545-2054, USA

Besedin, Vladimir (Figure Skater)
c/o Staff Member *Champions on Ice*
3500 American Blvd W Ste 190
Minneapolis, MN 55431-4431, USA

Beshear, Steve (Governor, Politician)
Office of the Governor
700 Capital Ave Rm 142
Frankfort, KY 40601-3458, USA

Beshore, Del (Athlete, Basketball Player)
1404 Cobblestone Ln
Pomona, CA 91767-3562, USA

Bess, Daniel (Actor)
c/o Raelle Koota *Anonymous Content (LA)*
3532 Hayden Ave
Culver City, CA 90232-2413, USA

Bess, Rufus (Athlete, Football Player)
8685 Magnolia Trl Apt 214
Eden Prairie, MN 55344-7664, USA

Bessey, Joe
c/o Joe Bessey Motorsport
PO Box 525
Scarborough, ME 04070-0525, USA

Bessillieu, Donald A (Don) (Athlete, Football Player)
4787 Gardiner Dr
Columbus, GA 31907-3441, USA

Besson, Luc (Director, Producer, Writer)
1415 Devlin Dr
Los Angeles, CA 90069-1804, USA

Best, Art (Athlete, Football Player)
420 Lockville Rd
Pickerington, OH 43147-1360, USA

Best, Greg (Athlete, Football Player)
2859 Darlington Rd
Beaver Falls, PA 15010-1054, USA

Best, Jahvid (Athlete, Football Player)
c/o Tony Fleming *Impact Sports - LA*
11331 Ventura Blvd Ste 1A
Studio City, CA 91604-3147, USA

Best, John O (Soccer Player)
1065 Lomita Blvd Spc 348
Harbor City, CA 90710-5045, USA

Best, Karl (Athlete, Baseball Player)
PO Box 12698
Everett, WA 98206-2698, USA

Best, Travis (Athlete, Basketball Player)
703 Bradley Rd
Springfield, MA 01109-1424, USA

Bestar, Maria (Musician)
c/o Staff Member *Sony Music Miami*
605 Lincoln Rd Ste 700
Miami Beach, FL 33139-2901, USA

Bester, Allan (Athlete, Hockey Player)
12527 Crayford Ave
Orlando, FL 32837-8536, USA

Bestwick, Arnie (Race Car Driver)
10643 Court Rd
Morrison, IL 61270-9386, USA

Bestwicke, Martine (Actor)
Goldey Co
1156 S Carmelina Ave # B
Los Angeles, CA 90049-5812, USA

Beswick, Jim (Athlete, Baseball Player)
6911 Buckhorn Dr
Columbus, GA 31904-3212, USA

Beswicke, Martine (Actor)
Goldey Co
1156 S Carmelina Ave # 8
Los Angeles, CA 90049-5812, USA

Betancourt, Jeff (Director)
c/o Staff Member *Broder Webb Chervin Silbermann Agency, The (BWCS)*
10250 Constellation Blvd
Los Angeles, CA 90067-6200, USA

Betancourt, Rafael
6857 Valhalla Way
Windermere, FL 34786-5627, USA

Betancourt, Yuniesky (Athlete, Baseball Player)
1225 SW 78th Ct
Miami, FL 33144-4309, USA

Bethea, Antoine (Athlete, Football Player)
5680 La Seyne Pl
San Jose, CA 95138-2240, us

Bethea, Bill (Athlete, Baseball Player)
166 Penny Ln
Georgetown, TX 78633-2016, USA

Bethea, Ellen (Actor)
Independent Artists
505 8th Ave Ste 2208
New York, NY 10018-6505, USA

Bethea, Elvin L (Athlete, Football Player)
16211 Leslie Ln
Missouri City, TX 77489-1012, USA

Bethel, Wilson (Actor)
c/o Ryan Daly *Zero Gravity Management*
1531 14th St
Santa Monica, CA 90404-3302, USA

Beth Hart Band (Music Group, Musician)
c/o Staff Member *William Morris Endeavor (LA)*
9601 Wilshire Blvd
Beverly Hills, CA 90210-5213, USA

Bethke, Jim (Athlete, Baseball Player)
4305 N Jarboe Ct
Kansas City, MO 64116-4655, USA

Bethune, Bobby (Athlete, Football Player)
PO Box 692
Leeds, AL 35094-0011, USA

Bethune, George (Athlete, Football Player)
2817 Gaslight Ln W
Mobile, AL 36695-3130, USA

Bethune, Patricia (Actor)
c/o Peter Himberger *Impact Artists Group LLC*
42 Hamilton Ter
New York, NY 10031-6403, USA

Bets, Maxim (Athlete, Hockey Player)
5566 Candlelight Dr
La Jolla, CA 92037-7711, USA

Bettany, Paul (Actor)
288 West St # 8E/8W
New York, NY 10013-1367, USA

Bettencourt, Nuno (Musician)
3001 Durand Dr
Los Angeles, CA 90068-1909, USA

Bettendorf, Jeff (Athlete, Baseball Player)
10349 SE Nicole Loop
Happy Valley, OR 97086-6881, USA

Betters, Doug L (Athlete, Football Player)
77 Better Way
Whitefish, MT 59937-3471, USA

Betterson, Doug (Athlete, Football Player)
2442 46th St
Pennsauken, NJ 08110-2018, USA

Betterson, James (Athlete, Football Player)
234 Allens Ln
Mullica Hill, NJ 08062-2005, USA

Bettiga, Mike (Athlete, Football Player)
PO Box 657
Hydesville, CA 95547-0657, USA

Bettis, Angela (Actor)
c/o Ryan Revel *Benderspink*
8447 Wilshire Blvd Ste 250
Studio E
Beverly Hills, CA 90211-3224, USA

Bettis, Jerome (Athlete, Football Player)
1651 Randall Mill Pl NW # Pi
Atlanta, GA 30327-3136, USA

Bettis, Tom (Athlete, Football Coach, Football Player)
3523 N Peach Hollow Cir
Pearland, TX 77584-4007, USA

Bettman, Gary (Athlete, Hockey Player)
23 Baldwin Rd
Saddle River, NJ 07458-3203, USA

Bettridge, Ed (Athlete, Football Player)
505 Aqua Marine Blvd
Avon Lake, OH 44012-2588, USA

Betts, Dickie (Musician)
FreeFalls
PO Box 604
Chagrin Falls, OH 44022-0604, USA

Betts, Erik (Actor)
9068 Hayvenhurst Ave
North Hills, CA 91343-3600, USA

Betts, Jack (Actor)
c/o Jon Simmons *Simmons & Scott Entertainment*
7942 Mulholland Dr
Los Angeles, CA 90046-1225, USA

Betts, Ladell (Athlete, Football Player)
4765 W Leitner Dr
Coral Springs, FL 33067-2030, USA

Betts, Richard (Dickey) (Musician)
325 Palmetto Ave
Osprey, FL 34229-9381, USA

Beuchel, Ted (Musician)
Variety Artists
1924 Spring St
Paso Robles, CA 93446-1620, USA

Beueriein, Stephen T (Steve) (Athlete, Football Player)
15624 McCullers Ct
Charlotte, NC 28277-1478, USA

Beuerlein, Steve (Athlete, Football Player)
8 Capistrano By The Sea
Dana Point, CA 92629-5907, USA

Beutler, Ernest (Doctor)
2707 Costebelle Dr
La Jolla, CA 92037-3518, USA

Beutler, Tom (Athlete, Football Player)
7218 Longwater Dr
Maumee, OH 43537-8663, USA

Bevacqua, Kurt (Athlete, Baseball Player)
7679 Sitio Manana
Carlsbad, CA 92009-8960, USA

Bevan, Tim (Actor, Producer)
c/o Staff Member *Working Title Films*
9720 Wilshire Blvd Fl 4
Beverly Hills, CA 90212-2000, USA

Beverley, Frankie (Musician)
115 Cherokee Rose Ln
Fairburn, GA 30213, USA

Beverley, Nick (Athlete, Coach, Hockey Player)
c/o Staff Member *Nashville Predators*
501 Broadway
Nashville, TN 37203-3980, USA

Beverlin, Jason (Athlete, Baseball Player)
2300 N Atlantic Ave Apt 702
Daytona Beach, FL 32118-3378, USA

Beverly, David (Athlete, Football Player)
301 N 9th St Apt 2
Opelika, AL 36801-4274, USA

Beverly, Don (Race Car Driver)
1801 Coxendale Rd
Chester, VA 23836-2442, USA

Beverly, Ed (Athlete, Football Player)
13051 Golansville Rd
Ruther Glen, VA 22546-4029, USA

Beverly, Eric (Athlete, Football Player)
PO Box 492433
Lawrenceville, GA 30049-0041, USA

Beverly, Randy (Athlete, Football Player)
PO Box 425
Westbury, NY 11590-0130, USA

Bevil, Brian (Athlete, Baseball Player)
210 Maurine Ln
Cleveland, TX 77328-3245, USA

Bevill, Lisa (Musician)
Jeff Roberts
206 Bluebird Dr
Goodlettsville, TN 37072-2302, USA

Bevington, Terry (Athlete, Baseball Player, Coach)
2600 Halle Pkwy # Y
Collierville, TN 38017-8888, USA

Bevis, Muriel (Baseball Player)
538 Idlewood Dr
Mount Juliet, TN 37122-2118, USA

Bey, Andy (Musician)
Megaforce Entertainment
PO Box 779
New Hope, PA 18938-0779, USA

Beyer, Andy (Sportscaster)
4237 Lenore Ln NW
Washington, DC 20008-3835, USA

Beyer, Brad (Actor)
c/o Jeff Hunter *William Morris Endeavor (NY)*
1325 Avenue of the Americas
New York, NY 10019-6026, USA

Beyer, Troy (Actor)
14333 Greenleaf St
Sherman Oaks, CA 91423-4013, USA

Beymer, Richard (Actor)
147 N Ridgewood Pl
Los Angeles, CA 90004-4002, USA

Bezic, Sandra (Figure Skater, Sportscaster)
c/o Staff Member *NBC Sports (NY)*
30 Rockefeller Plz
New York, NY 10112-0015, USA

Bezos, Jeff (Business Person)
Amazon Inc
PO Box 907
Bellevue, WA 98009-0907, USA

Bezucha, Tom (Director)
c/o Simon Halls *Slate Public Relations*
9000 W Sunset Blvd Ste 915
West Hollywood, CA 90069-5809, USA

Bhakta, Raj (Business Person)
238 E 50th St
New York, NY 10022-7704, USA

Bhardwaj, Mohini (Athlete, Gymnast, Olympic Athlete)
53 Juergens Ave
Cincinnati, OH 45220-1227, USA

Bhatt, Brinda (Actor)
c/o Staff Member *Innovative Artists (LA)*
1505 10th St
Santa Monica, CA 90401-2805, USA

Bhavsar, Raj (Athlete, Gymnast)
201 S Capitol Ave
Pan American Plaza, Suite 300
Indianapolis, IN 46225-1000

Biafra, Jello (Musician)
c/o Staff Member *Simon & Schuster*
1230 Avenue of the Americas Fl CONC1
New York, NY 10020-1586, USA

Biakabutuka, Tshimanga (Tim) (Athlete, Football Player)
110 Sonnys Way
Fort Mill, SC 29708-6415, USA

Bialas, Dave (Baseball Player)
14080 N Bayshore Dr
Madeira Beach, FL 33708-2211, USA

Bialik, Mayim (Actor)
c/o Tiffany Kuzon *Evolution Entertainment (LA)*
901 N Highland Ave
Los Angeles, CA 90038-2412, USA

Bialorucki, Larry (Athlete, Baseball Player)
PO Box 1933
Toledo, OH 43603-1933, USA

Bialosuknia, Wesley (Athlete, Basketball Player)
29 Bayberry Dr
Bristol, CT 06010-7604, USA

Bialowas, Dwight (Athlete, Hockey Player)
15616 Park Terrace Dr
Eden Prairie, MN 55346-2429, USA

Bialowas, Frank (Athlete, Hockey Player)
1640 New Brooklyn Rd
Williamstown, NJ 08094-3717, USA

Biancalana, Buddy (Athlete, Baseball Player)
4125 E Prickly Pear Trl
Phoenix, AZ 85050-9005, USA

Bianchi, Al (Athlete, Baseball Player, Basketball Coach, Basketball Player, Coach)
4350 N 40th St
Phoenix, AZ 85018-4105, USA

Bianchl, Alfred (Al) (Athlete, Basketball Player, Coach)
Miami Heat
601 Biscayne Blvd
American Airlines Arena
Miami, FL 33132-1801, USA

Bianco, Tom (Athlete, Baseball Player)
12 Knolltop Dr
Nesconset, NY 11767-2222, USA

Bianco, tommy
12 Knolltop Dr
Nesconset, NY 11767-2222, USA

Biasucci, Dean (Athlete, Football Player)
3484 Sandy Beach Dr
Canandaigua, NY 14424-2348, USA

Bibb, John (Writer)
Nashville Tennessean
1100 Broadway
Editorial Dept
Nashville, TN 37203-3134, USA

Bibb, Laslie (Actor)
9615 Brighton Way Ste 300
Beverly Hills, CA 90210-5118, USA

Bibb, Leslie (Actor)
c/o John Carrabino *John Carrabino Management*
5900 Wilshire Blvd Ste 406
Los Angeles, CA 90036-5015, USA

Bibby, Henry (Athlete, Basketball Player)
Memphis Grizzlies
191 Beale St
Memphis, TN 38103-3715, USA

Bibby, Mike (Athlete, Basketball Player)
c/o David Falk *F.A.M.E*
Prefers to be contacted via telephone
Washington, DC, USA

Bible, Jon (Athlete, Baseball Player)
11254 Pinehurst Dr
Austin, TX 78747-1432, USA

Biccum, Del (Horse Racer)
RR 23 Box 27
Montague, NJ 07827, USA

Bice, Bo (Musician)
469 Parker Rd
Covington, GA 30014-5947, USA

Bichette, Dante (Athlete, Baseball Player)
1830 Gipson Green Ln
Winter Park, FL 32789-1480, USA

Bichir, Demian (Actor)
c/o Sekka Scher *Evolution Entertainment*
175 Varick St
New York, NY 10014-4604, USA

Bickerstaff, Bernard T (Bernie) (Coach)
Charlotte Bobcats
129 W Trade St Ste 700
Charlotte, NC 28202-5301, USA

Bickett, Duane (Athlete, Football Player)
508 Van Dyke Ave
Del Mar, CA 92014-2545, USA

Bickford, Valerie (Actor)
c/o Staff Member *TLC*
10100 Santa Monica Blvd Ste 1500
Los Angeles, CA 90067-4117, USA

Bickle, Dick (Race Car Driver)
9L6-A Bambi Dr
Destin, FL 32541, USA

Bickle, Mike (Religious Leader)
International House of Prayer
3535 E Red Bridge Rd
Kansas City, MO 64137-2135, USA

Bickle, Jr., Rich (Race Car Driver)
2119 W Glenmoor Ln
Janesville, WI 53545-9639, USA

Bicknell, Charlie (Athlete, Baseball Player)
319 W Gold St
Butte, MT 59701-2405, USA

Bicks, Jenny (Producer)
9003 St Ives Dr
Los Angeles, CA 90069-1704, USA

Bidart, Frank (Writer)
Wellesley College
106 Central St
English Dept
Wellesley Hills, MA 02481-8203, USA

Biddle, Dennis (Bose) (Athlete, Baseball Player)
9418 N Green Bay Rd Apt 241
Milwaukee, WI 53209-1070, USA

Biddle, Dennis ""Bose"" (Athlete, Baseball Player)
9418 N Green Bay Rd Apt 241
Milwaukee, WI 53209-1070, USA

Biddle, Rocky (Athlete, Baseball Player)
2031 E Rancho Culebra Dr
Covina, CA 91724-3331, USA

Biden, Joe (Politician)
Office Of The Vice President
1600 Pennsylvania Ave NW
the White House
Washington, DC 20500-0001, USA

Biden, Joseph (Politician)
404 Hillside Rd
Wilmington, DE 19807-2248, USA

Bidwell, Josh (Athlete, Football Player)
1380 W 40th Ave
Eugene, OR 97405-2001, USA

Bieber, Justin (Musician)
25202 Prado Del Grandioso
Calabasas, CA 91302-3654, USA

Bieber, Nita (Actor)
PO Box 1889
Avalon, CA 90704-1889, USA

Biedenbach, Edward (Athlete, Basketball Player)
9 E Fayetteville St
Wrightsville Beach, NC 28480-1886, USA

Biedermann, Leo (Athlete, Football Player)
11527 Noors Ave
Las Vegas, NV 89138-1547, USA

Biegler, David W (Business Person)
Texas Utilities Co
1601 Bryan St
Energy Plaza
Dallas, TX 75201-3431, USA

Biehn, Michael (Actor)
14358 Magnolia Blvd Apt 229
Sherman Oaks, CA 91423-1026, USA

Biekert, Gregory (Athlete, Football Player)
2360 Fish Creek Pl
Danville, CA 94506-2063, USA

Biel, Jessica (Actor)
c/o Rick Yorn *LBI Entertainment*
2000 Avenue of the Stars
Floor 3, North Tower
Los Angeles, CA 90067-4700, USA

Bielecki, Mike (Athlete, Baseball Player)
1505 Habersham Pl
Crownsville, MD 21032-2230, USA

Bielke, Don (Athlete, Basketball Player)
3768 Corte Cancion
Thousand Oaks, CA 91360-7017, USA

Bielski, Dick (Athlete, Football Player)
27 Malibu Ct
Towson, MD 21204-2047, USA

Bienen, Andy (Writer)
c/o Staff Member *United Talent Agency (UTA-LA)*
9336 Civic Center Dr
Beverly Hills, CA 90210-3604, USA

Bieniemy, Eric (Athlete, Football Player)
11478 S Carbondale St
Olathe, KS 66061-4515, USA

Bierbrodt, Nick (Athlete, Baseball Player)
1200 White Hawk Ranch Dr
Boulder, CO 80303-1668, USA

Biercevicz, Greg (Baseball Player)
21 Mead Farm Rd
Seymour, CT 06483-2453, USA

Bierko, Craig (Actor, Musician)
c/o Jill Littman *Impression Entertainment*
9229 W Sunset Blvd Ste 700
West Hollywood, CA 90069-3407, USA

Bies, Don (Athlete, Golfer)
1262 NW Blakely Ct
Seattle, WA 98177-4340, USA

Bieser, Steve (Athlete, Baseball Player)
1243 Timber Creek Dr
Cpe Girardeau, MO 63701-2621, USA

Bies Susan, Schmidt (Government Official)
Federal Reserve Board
20th St & Constitution Ave
Washington, DC 20551-0001, USA

Biffle, Greg (Race Car Driver)
319/323 Doolie Rd
Mooresville, NC 28117, USA

Biffle, Jerome (Athlete, Track Athlete)
3205 Monaco Pkwy
Denver, CO 80207-2203, USA

Big & Rich (Music Group)
c/o Keith Miller *William Morris Endeavor (Nashville)*
1600 Division St Ste 300
Nashville, TN 37203-2755, USA

Big Bad Voodoo Daddy (Music Group, Musician)
c/o Staff Member *Vanguard Records*
11400 W Olympic Blvd Ste 1450
Los Angeles, CA 90064-1649, USA

Bigbie, Larry (Athlete, Baseball Player)
102 Brooke Ln
Centreville, MD 21617-2755, USA

Big Dismal (Music Group)
c/o Staff Member *Wind-up Records*
72 Madison Ave Fl 8
New York, NY 10016-8731, USA

Bigelow, Kathryn (Director, Producer, Writer)
2934 1/2 N Beverly Glen Cir # 390
Los Angeles, CA 90077-1724, USA

Bigelow, Tom (Race Car Driver)
Rt. 1
Box 158A
Winchester, IN 47394, USA

Biggerstaff, Sean (Actor)
c/o Jeff Morrone *Intellectual Artists Management*
9350 Wilshire Blvd Ste 224
Beverly Hills, CA 90212-3204, USA

Biggert, Judy (Congressman, Politician)
2113 Rayburn Hob
Washington, DC 20515-0706, USA

Biggins, Al-Mela (Reality Star)
c/o Staff Member *Trading Spouses*
3151 Cahuenga Blvd W Ste 300
Rocket Science Laboratories
Los Angeles, CA 90068-1768, USA

Biggio, Craig (Athlete, Baseball Player)
6520 Belmont St
Houston, TX 77005-3804, USA

Bigglo, Craig A (Baseball Player)
6520 Belmont St
Houston, TX 77005-3804, USA

Biggs, Don (Athlete, Hockey Player)
10050 Somerset Dr
Loveland, OH 45140-1863, USA

Biggs, Jason (Actor)
2515 Benedict Canyon Dr
Beverly Hills, CA 90210-1020, USA

Biggs, John H (Business Person)
240 E 47th St # 47D
New York, NY 10017-2131, USA

Biggs-Dawson, Roxann (Actor)
Innovative Artists
1505 10th St
Santa Monica, CA 90401-2805, USA

Biggs-Dawson, Rozann
c/o Staff Member *Innovative Artists (LA)*
1505 10th St
Santa Monica, CA 90401-2805, USA

Bignotti, George (Race Car Driver)
1150 W Capitol Dr Unit 25
San Pedro, CA 90732-2268, USA

Big Preach (Musician)
c/o Staff Member *UGF Entertainment Inc*
3105 S Martin Luther King Jr Blvd # 313
Lansing, MI 48910-2939, USA

Big Sean (Musician)
3535 Multiview Dr
Los Angeles, CA 90068-1221, USA

Big Tigger (Television Host)
c/o Staff Member *Britto Agency PR*
90 Franklin St Apt 4N
New York, NY 10013-3489, USA

Big Time Rush (Music Group)
c/o Erica Gerard *PMK/BNC Public Relations (PMK-NY)*
622 3rd Ave Fl 8
New York, NY 10017-6707, USA

Big Tymers (Music Group)
c/o Staff Member *ICM Partners (LA)*
10250 Constellation Blvd Fl 7
Los Angeles, CA 90067-6207, USA

Biil Young, C.W (Congressman, Politician)
2407 Rayburn Hob
Washington, DC 20515-0910, USA

Biittner, Larry (Athlete, Baseball Player)
915 3rd Ave NW
Pocahontas, IA 50574-1413, USA

Bikel, Theodore (Actor)
167 Langley Rd
Newton Center, MA 02459-2328, USA

Bilardello, Dann (Athlete, Baseball Player)
299 Bank St
Batavia, NY 14020-1615, USA

Bilderback, Nicole (Actor)
c/o Jeff Morrone *Intellectual Artists Management*
9350 Wilshire Blvd Ste 224
Beverly Hills, CA 90212-3204, USA

Bileck, Pamela (Athlete, Gymnast, Olympic Athlete)
2475 Redbud Ct
San Jose, CA 95128-4226, USA

Biletnikoff, Frederick (Fred) (Athlete, Football Player)
1736 Avondale Dr
Roseville, CA 95747-8389, USA

Bilheimer, Robert S (Religious Leader)
15256 Knightwood Rd
Cold Spring, MN 56320-9649, USA

Bill, Dunstan (Athlete, Football Player)
PO Box 514
Rancho Mirage, CA 92270-0514, USA

Bill, Tony (Actor, Director, Producer)
Barnstorm Films
3163 Donald Douglas Loop S
Santa Monica, CA 90405-3210, USA

Billick, Brian (Athlete, Football Coach, Football Player)
12500 Ivy Mill Rd
Reisterstown, MD 21136-5135, USA

Billingham, Jack (Athlete, Baseball Player)
625 Faulkner St
New Smyrna Beach, FL 32168-6421, USA

Billings, Dick (Athlete, Baseball Player)
6025 Cedar Bend Dr
Clarkston, MI 48346-2291, USA

Billings, Earl (Actor)
c/o Staff Member *Stone Manners Salners Agency (LA)*
6100 Wilshire Blvd Ste 1500
Los Angeles, CA 90048-5110, USA

Billingslea, Beau (Actor)
6025 Sepulveda Blvd Ste 201
Van Nuys, CA 91411-2513, USA

Billingslea, Shavonda (Reality Star)
c/o Michael Martin *MM Agency*
3937 Nobel Dr
San Diego, CA 92122-6156, USA

Billingsley, Brent (Athlete, Baseball Player)
16112 Medlar Ln
Chino Hills, CA 91709-3625, USA

Billingsley, Chad (Athlete, Baseball Player)
1434 Monarch Dr
Lemoore, CA 93245-1786, USA

Billingsley, John (Actor)
8480 Hillside Ave
Los Angeles, CA 90069-1505, USA

Billingsley, John (Athlete, Baseball Player)
3614 N 24th Pl
Milwaukee, WI 53206-1325, USA

Billingsley, Peter (Director)
6225 Winans Dr
Los Angeles, CA 90068-2250, USA

Billingsley, Ray (Cartoonist)
c/o Staff Member *King Features Syndication*
300 W 57th St Fl 15
New York, NY 10019-5238, USA

Billingsley, Ron (Athlete, Football Player)
PO Box 2455
Gadsden, AL 35903-0455, USA

Billingsley, Sam (Baseball Player)
Memphis Red Sox
1426 W State St
Milwaukee, WI 53233-1249, USA

Billington, Craig (Athlete, Hockey Player)
c/o Staff Member *Colorado Avalanche*
1000 Chopper Cir
Pepsi Center
Denver, CO 80204-5805, USA

Billington, Craig (Athlete, Hockey Player)
3254 Elk View Dr
Evergreen, CO 80439-7972, USA

Billmeyer, mick (Baseball Player)
10921 Sassan Ln
Hagerstown, MD 21742-4070, USA

Billups, Chauncey (Athlete, Basketball Player)
c/o Andy Miller *ASM Sports*
920 Undercliff Ave
Edgewater, NJ 07020-1558, USA

Billups, Terry (Athlete, Football Player)
1801 E 12th St Apt 1721
Cleveland, OH 44114-3528, USA

Bill Wyman's Rhythm Kings (Music Group, Musician)
c/o Staff Member *Concerted Efforts*
PO Box 440326
Somerville, MA 02144-0004, USA

Billy Vera and the Beaters (Music Group)
c/o Troy Blakely *Agency for the Performing Arts (APA-LA)*
405 S Beverly Dr Ste 500
Beverly Hills, CA 90212-4425, USA

Bilodeau, Jean-Luc (Actor)
c/o Allan Grifka *Alchemy Entertainment*
7024 Melrose Ave Ste 420
Los Angeles, CA 90038-3394, USA

Bilson, Bruce (Director)
Downwind Enterprices
12505 Sarah St
Studio City, CA 91604-1113, USA

Bilson, Malcolm (Musician)
132 N Sunset Dr
Ithaca, NY 14850-1460, USA

Bilson, Rachel (Actor)
c/o Alissa Vradenburg *Untitled Entertainment (LA)*
350 S Beverly Dr Ste 200
Beverly Hills, CA 90212-4819, USA

Binder, John (Religious Leader)
North American Baptist Conference
1219 Pleasant Grove Blvd
Roseville, CA 95678-6987, USA

Binder, Mike (Actor, Director, Writer)
c/o Jason Hodes *William Morris Endeavor (NY)*
1325 Avenue of the Americas
New York, NY 10019-6026, USA

Binder, Steve (Director)
c/o Staff Member *Freeman, Heinecke and Sutton*
8961 W Sunset Blvd
West Hollywood, CA 90069-1807, USA

Bindler, Robb (Director, Writer)
c/o Susan Weaving *William Morris Endeavor (NY)*
1325 Avenue of the Americas
New York, NY 10019-6026, USA

Bing, Dave (Athlete, Basketball Player)
29555 Woodhaven Ln
Southfield, MI 48076-5281, USA

Bing, Jonathan
c/o Daniel Strone *Trident Media Group LLC*
41 Madison Ave Fl 36
New York, NY 10010-2257, USA

Bingaman, Jeff (Senator)
703 Hart Senate Office Bldg
Washington, DC 20510-0001, USA

Bingaman, Jeff (Politician)
5028 Overlook Rd NW
Washington, DC 20016-1912, USA

Bingham, Craig (Athlete, Football Player)
179 Black Oak Dr
Pittsburgh, PA 15220-2007, USA

Bingham, Gregory R (Greg) (Athlete, Football Player)
3710 W Valley Dr
Missouri City, TX 77459-4320, USA

Bingham, Guy (Athlete, Football Player)
9214 Keegan Trl
Missoula, MT 59808-9382, USA

Bingham, Ryan (Musician)
c/o Jenna Adler *Creative Artists Agency (CAA-LA)*
2000 Avenue of the Stars Ste 100
Los Angeles, CA 90067-4705, USA

Bingham, Traci (Actor, Model)
c/o Gloria Kisel *Trendy P.R.*
264 S La Cienega Blvd Ste 968
Beverly Hills, CA 90211-3302, USA

Binkley, Gregg (Actor)
c/o Staff Member *Schachter Entertainment*
1157 S Beverly Dr Fl 2
Los Angeles, CA 90035-1119, USA

Binn, Dave (Athlete, Football Player)
2005 Loring St
San Diego, CA 92109-1407, USA

Binnie, William B (Astronaut)
3756 Bottlebrush St
Rosamond, CA 93560-7677, USA

Binoche, Juliette (Actor)
c/o Jason Weinberg *Untitled Entertainment (LA)*
350 S Beverly Dr Ste 200
Beverly Hills, CA 90212-4819, USA

Binotto, John (Athlete, Football Player)
277 E McMurray Rd
Canonsburg, PA 15317-2929, USA

Binyon, Conrad (Actor)
17805 Margate St
Encino, CA 91316-2306, USA

Biodrowski, Denny (Athlete, Football Player)
2305 Grizzly Run Ln
Euless, TX 76039-6073, USA

Biondi, Matt (Athlete, Olympic Athlete, Swimmer)
6223 Tangelo Pl
Simi Valley, CA 93063-7072, USA

Birch, Thora (Actor)
c/o Jack Birch *Keep the Peace Productions*
PO Box 691576
West Hollywood, CA 90069-9576, USA

Birchard, Bruce (Religious Leader)
Friends General Conference
1216 Arch St Ste 2B
Philadelphia, PA 19107-2835, USA

Birck, Michael J (Business Person)
Tellabs Inc
1415 W Diehl Rd
Naperville, IL 60563-9950, USA

Bird, Brad (Director, Writer)
170 San Geronimo Valley Dr
Woodacre, CA 94973, USA

Bird, Cory (Athlete, Football Player)
4618 Harding Hwy
Mays Landing, NJ 08330-2736, USA

Bird, Doug (Athlete, Baseball Player)
11821 Lady Anne Cir
Cape Coral, FL 33991-7548, USA

Bird, Jerry Lee (Athlete, Basketball Player)
1114 Scenic View Hts
Corbin, KY 40701-2156, USA

Bird, Larry (Athlete, Basketball Player, Olympic Athlete)
4715 Ellery Ln
Indianapolis, IN 46250-5677, USA

Bird, Rodger (Athlete, Football Player)
215 S Elm St
Henderson, KY 42420-3510, USA

Bird, Sue (Athlete, Basketball Player)
c/o Dan Levy *Wasserman Media Group (NC)*
4208 Six Forks Rd Ste 1020
Raleigh, NC 27609-5738, USA

Bird-Phillips, Nalda (Baseball Player)
2033 Honeydew Ln NW
Kennesaw, GA 30152-5852, USA

Birdsell, Lilli (Actor)
c/o John Crosby *John Crosby Management*
1357 N Spaulding Ave
Los Angeles, CA 90046-4009, USA

Birdsong, Carl (Athlete, Football Player)
1807 Clubview Dr
Amarillo, TX 79124-1731, USA

Birdsong, Cindy (Musician)
c/o Staff Member *Diva Central Inc*
7510 W Sunset Blvd Ste 1445
Los Angeles, CA 90046-3408, USA

Birdsong, Mary (Actor, Writer)
c/o Stacy Abrams *Abrams Entertainment*
5225 Wilshire Blvd Ste 515
Los Angeles, CA 90036-4349, USA

Birdsong, Otis (Athlete, Basketball Player)
PO Box 316
Little Rock, AR 72203-0316, USA

Bires, Kally (Race Car Driver)
Black Cat Racing
304 Performance Rd
Mooresville, NC 28115-9592, USA

Bires, Kelly (Race Car Driver)
JTG Racing
304 Performance Rd
Mooresville, NC 28115-9592, USA

Birk, Matt (Athlete, Football Player)
26 Cobb Island Dr
Greenwich, CT 06830-7244, USA

Birk, Roger E (Business Person)
Federal National Mortgage Assn
3900 Wisconsin Ave NW
Washington, DC 20016-2806, USA

Birkbeck, Mike (Athlete, Baseball Player)
1705 W Hill Dr
Orrville, OH 44667-1331, USA

Birkell, Lauren (Actor)
c/o Tiffany Kuzon *Evolution Entertainment (LA)*
901 N Highland Ave
Los Angeles, CA 90038-2412, USA

Birkhead, Larry
PO Box 99800
Emeryville, CA 94662-9809, USA

Birkin, David (Actor)
c/o Scott Zimmerman *Evolution Entertainment (LA)*
901 N Highland Ave
Los Angeles, CA 90038-2412, USA

Birkins, Kurt (Athlete, Baseball Player)
24106 Vanowen St
West Hills, CA 91307-2932, USA

Birman, Len (Actor)
Michael Mann talent
617 S Olive St Ste 311
Los Angeles, CA 90014-1624, USA

Birmingham, Stephen (Writer)
Brandt & Brandt
1501 Broadway Ste 2310
New York, NY 10036-5689, USA

Birnes, William J. (Writer)
c/o Staff Member *Simon & Schuster*
1230 Avenue of the Americas Fl CONC1
New York, NY 10020-1586, USA

Birney, David (Actor)
20 Ocean Park Blvd # 118
Santa Monica, CA 90405-3589, USA

Birney, Frank (Actor)
c/o Staff Member *Bauman Redanty & Shaul Agency*
5757 Wilshire Blvd
Suite 473
Beverly Hills, CA 90212, USA

Biron, Martin (Athlete, Hockey Player)
Sport Prospects Inc
488 Willardshire Rd
East Aurora, NY 14052-9442, USA

Biron, Mathieu (Athlete, Hockey Player)
5723 NW 199th Dr
Pompano Beach, FL 33076, USA

Birrer, Babe (Athlete, Baseball Player)
9705 the Maples
Clarence, NY 14031-1594, USA

Birthistle, Eva (Actor)
c/o Staff Member *William Morris Endeavor (LA)*
9601 Wilshire Blvd
Beverly Hills, CA 90210-5213, USA

Birtsas, Tim (Athlete, Baseball Player)
43 Robertson Ct
Clarkston, MI 48346-1547, USA

Biscaha, Joe (Athlete, Football Player)
700 N Delaware Ave
Apt 3
Beach Haven, NJ 08008, USA

Bischoff, Eric (Athlete, Wrestler)
35011 N Sunset Trl
Cave Creek, AZ 85331-9126, USA

Bisciotti, Steve (Business Person, Football Executive)
511 Point Field Dr
Millersville, MD 21108-2052, USA

Bisenius, Joe (Athlete, Baseball Player)
19027 Atlas St
Omaha, NE 68130-4292, USA

Bishe, Kerry (Actor)
c/o Staff Member *Brookside Artists Management (NY)*
250 W 57th St Ste 2303
New York, NY 10107-2399, USA

Bishil, Summer (Actor)
c/o Brian Swardstrom *United Talent Agency (UTA-NYC)*
9601 Wilshire Blvd
Beverly Hills, CA 90210-5213, USA

Bishop, Ben (Athlete, Hockey Player)
11 Huntleigh Trails Ln
Saint Louis, MO 63131-4801, USA

Bishop, Elvin (Musician)
DeLeon Artists
4031 Panama Ct
Oakland, CA 94611-4930, USA

Bishop, Greg (Athlete, Football Player)
PO Box 2263
Lodi, CA 95241-2263, USA

Bishop, Harold (Athlete, Football Player)
4113 Woodland Hills Dr
Tuscaloosa, AL 35405-2777, USA

Bishop, Keith (Athlete, Football Player)
PO Box 133111
Spring, TX 77393-3111, USA

Bishop, Kelly (Actor)
c/o Robert Attermann *Abrams Artists Agency (NY)*
9200 W Sunset Blvd PH 11
West Hollywood, CA 90069-3601, USA

Bishop, Michael (Athlete, Football Player)
113 Philpot St
Willis, TX 77378, USA

Bishop, Rob (Congressman, Politician)
123 Cannon Hob
Washington, DC 20515-3805, USA

Bishop, Sonny (Athlete, Football Player)
22843 Hale Rd
Land O Lakes, FL 34639-4030, USA

Bisset, Jacqueline (Actor)
1815 Benedict Canyon Dr
Beverly Hills, CA 90210-2006, USA

Bissett, Josie (Actor)
1020 91st Ave NE
Bellevue, WA 98004-3901, USA

Bissett, Tom (Athlete, Hockey Player)
285 Saddleback Dr NE
Grand Rapids, MI 49525-3496, United States

Bissinger, Buzz (Writer)
c/o Houghton Mifflin Company Trade Division
222 Berkeley St Fl 8
Boston, MA 02116-3748, USA

Bisutti, Kylie (Model)
c/o Anne Watkins *Primary Wave Music Publishing*
116 E 16th St Fl 9
New York, NY 10003-2123, USA

Bitker, Joe (Athlete, Baseball Player)
39 Blackstone Ct
Chico, CA 95928-9428, USA

Bitonio, Joel (Athlete, Football Player)
c/o Bruce Tollner *REP 1 Sports Group*
2 Corporate Park Ste 106
Irvine, CA 92606-5103, USA

Bitsui, Jeremiah (Actor)
c/o Sarah Baker *Open Entertainment*
1051 Cole Ave Ste B
Los Angeles, CA 90038-2601, USA

Bittan, Roy (Musician)
28929 Boniface Dr
Malibu, CA 90265-4207, USA

Bitterlich, Don (Athlete, Football Player)
101 Medinah Dr
Blue Bell, PA 19422-3213, USA

Bitterman, Shem (Writer)
6616 Colgate Ave
Los Angeles, CA 90048-4205, USA

Bittiger, Jeff (Athlete, Baseball Player)
2163 Valley View Dr S
Saylorsburg, PA 18353-8359, USA

Bittinger, Ned (Designer)
16 Camino De Vecinos
Santa Fe, NM 87507-7901, USA

Bittle, Ryan (Actor)
1345 Paseo Isabella
San Dimas, CA 91773-4076, USA

Bittner, Jayne (Baseball Player)
15536 Northville Forest Dr Apt U250
Plymouth, MI 48170, USA

Bittner, Jaynne (Athlete, Baseball Player, Commentator)
15535 Northville Forest Dr Apt 250
Plymouth, MI 48170-4947, USA

Bittner, Lauren (Actor)
c/o Jill McGrath *The Group Entertainment*
115 W 29th St Rm 1102
New York, NY 10001-5106, USA

Bixler, Brian (Athlete, Baseball Player)
3525 Teakwood Ln
Plano, TX 75075-1783, USA

B. Jones, Walter (Congressman, Politician)
2333 Rayburn Hob
Washington, DC 20515-3223, USA

Bjorge, Jamie (Actor)
10061 Riverside Dr # 113
Toluca Lake, CA 91602-2560

Bjork (Musician)
160 Henry St PH
Brooklyn, NY 11201-2503, USA

Bjorkman, George (Athlete, Baseball Player)
3525 Teakwood Ln
Plano, TX 75075-1783, USA

Bjorkman, Jonas (Tennis Player)
Octagon
7950 Jones Branch Dr
Mc Lean, VA 22102-3302, USA

Bjorkman, Reuben (Athlete, Hockey Player, Olympic Athlete)
504 Lake St NE
Warroad, MN 56763-2308, USA

Bjorlin, Nadia (Actor)
14439 Glorietta Dr
Sherman Oaks, CA 91423-4533, USA

Bjornson, Eric (Athlete, Football Player)
40 Orchard Rd
Orinda, CA 94563-3421, USA

Bjugstad, Scott (Athlete, Hockey Player, Olympic Athlete)
2874 Lisbon Ave N
Lake Elmo, MN 55042-8554, USA

Blab, Uwe (Athlete, Basketball Player)
5993 Mount Gainor
Wimberley, TX 78676-4278, USA

Blacc, Aloe (Musician)
3111 Paddington Rd
Glendale, CA 91206-1336, USA

Black, Avion (Athlete, Football Player)
7140 Park Glen Dr
Fairview, TN 37062-5129, USA

Black, BiBi (Musician)
c/o Staff Member *EMI Music Group (NY)*
150 5th Ave Fl 7
New York, NY 10011-4372, USA

Black, Bibi (Musician)
Columbia Artists Mgmt Inc
165 W 57th St
New York, NY 10019-2201, USA

Black, Bill (Baseball Player)
Detroit Tigers
264 Braeshire Dr
Ballwin, MO 63021-5659, USA

Black, Brantley (Actor)
c/o Taylor Jacobs *Cinema Talent Agency*
468 N Camden Dr # 200
Beverly Hills, CA 90210-4507, USA

Black, Bud (Athlete, Baseball Player)
PO Box 2133
Rancho Santa Fe, CA 92067-2133, USA

Black, Bud (Athlete, Baseball Player)
PO Box 122000
San Diego, CA 92112-2000, USA

Black, Carole (Business Person)
c/o Staff Member *Lifetime Entertainment Services*
309 W 49th St
New York, NY 10019-7316, USA

Black, Cathie (Business Person, Writer)
c/o Staff Member *Hearst Magazines*
959 8th Ave Sutie 100
New York, NY 10019-3737, USA

Black, Claudia (Actor)
c/o Vanessa Pereira *Artists Independent Management (LA)*
1522 2nd St
Santa Monica, CA 90401-2303, USA

Black, Clint (Actor, Musician)
141 Chickering Mdws
Nashville, TN 37215-5507, USA

Black, David (Producer, Writer)
c/o Johnnie Planco *Parseghian Planco LLC*
388 2nd Ave
New York, NY 10010-5616, USA

Black, Debbie (Athlete, Basketball Player)
2319 Tippecanoe Dr
Charleston, IL 61920-6655, USa

Black, Diane (Congressman, Politician)
1531 Longworth Hob
Washington, DC 20515-1310, USA

Black, Dustin Lance (Producer, Writer)
1618 N Fairfax Ave
Los Angeles, CA 90046-2610, USA

Black, Holly (Writer)
10 Pleasant Ct
Amherst, MA 01002-1513, USA

Black, Jack (Actor, Comedian, Musician)
4900 Los Feliz Blvd
Los Angeles, CA 90027-1739, USA

Black, Jay (Musician)
c/o Staff Member *Charles Rapp Enterprises Inc*
88 Pine St Ste 2601
New York, NY 10005-1826, USA

Black, Leonard (Athlete, Football Player)
2112 Winterlochen Rd
Fayetteville, NC 28305-5200, USA

Black, Lewis (Actor, Comedian)
c/o Staff Member *Agency for the Performing Arts (APA-LA)*
405 S Beverly Dr Ste 500
Beverly Hills, CA 90212-4425, USA

Black, Lisa Hartman (Actor)
141 Chickering Mdws
Nashville, TN 37215-5507, USA

Black, Lucas (Actor)
c/o Staff Member *Agency for the Performing Arts (APA-LA)*
405 S Beverly Dr Ste 500
Beverly Hills, CA 90212-4425, USA

Black, Marina (Actor)
c/o Matt Schwartz *Christopher Wright Management*
3207 Winnie Dr
Los Angeles, CA 90068-1439, USA

Black, Mary (Musician)
International Music Network
278 Main St
#400
Gloucester, MA 01930-6022, USA

Black, Michael Ian (Actor, Comedian)
c/o Ted Schachter *Schachter Entertainment*
1157 S Beverly Dr Fl 2
Los Angeles, CA 90035-1119, USA

Black, Mike (Athlete, Football Player)
608 Andalusia St
Los Angeles, CA 90065-2547, USA

Black, Mike D (Athlete, Football Player)
609 Grider Dr
Roseville, CA 95678-1244, USA

Black, Pippa (Actor)
c/o Kimberlin Dalehite *Magnolia Entertainment (LA)*
9595 Wilshire Blvd Ste 601
Beverly Hills, CA 90212-2506, USA

Black, Rebecca (Musician)
c/o Debra Baum *DB Entertainment Group*
8033 W Sunset Blvd # 1062
Los Angeles, CA 90046-2401, USA

Black, Ronnie (Athlete, Golfer)
5118 N Ocean Ave
Tucson, AZ 85704-2545, USA

Black, Shane (Writer)
104 Fremont Pl
Los Angeles, CA 90005-3867, USA

Black, Stan (Athlete, Football Player)
470 Johnstone Dr
Madison, MS 39110-7586, USA

Black, Tim (Athlete, Football Player)
10520 Kilo Rd
Clarendon, TX 79226-5100, USA

Black, Todd (Producer)
c/o Staff Member *ICM Partners (LA)*
10250 Constellation Blvd Fl 7
Los Angeles, CA 90067-6207, USA

Black, Tori (Actor, Adult Film Star, Model)
c/o Staff Member *LA Direct Models*
5535 Balboa Blvd Ste 103
Encino, CA 91316-1575, USA

Black 47 (Music Group, Musician)
c/o Staff Member *Skyline Music*
28 Union St
Whitefield, NH 03598-3503, USA

Blackabv, Ethan (Athlete, Baseball Player)
2308 E Orangewood Ave
Phoenix, AZ 85020-4730, USA

Blackaby, Ethan (Athlete, Baseball Player)
2308 E Orangewood Ave
Phoenix, AZ 85020-4730, USA

Black Box Recorder (Music Group)
c/o Staff Member *Paradigm (Monterey)*
404 W Franklin St
Monterey, CA 93940-2303, USA

Blackburn, Al (Astronaut)
1300 Woodside Dr
Mc Lean, VA 22102-1529, USA

Blackburn, Chase (Athlete, Football Player)
562 Wagonwheel Ln
Marysville, OH 43040-1251, USA

Blackburn, Dan (Athlete, Hockey Player)
12 Carey Dr
Bedford, NY 10506-2025, USA

Blackburn, Don (Athlete, Hockey Player)
637 S Owl Dr
Sarasota, FL 34236-1907, USA

Blackburn, Greta (Actor)
Dade/Schultz
6442 Coldwater Canyon Ave Ste 206
North Hollywood, CA 91606-1174, USA

Blackburn, Marsha (Congressman, Politician)
217 Cannon Hob
Washington, DC 20515-2507, USA

Blackburn, Tyler (Actor)
c/o Jason Carter *Society Entertainment*
15303 Ventura Blvd # C
Sherman Oaks, CA 91403-3110, USA

Blackburn, Woody (Athlete, Golfer)
PO Box 215
Orange Park, FL 32067-0215, USA

Black Crowes (Music Group)
c/o Staff Member *Mitch Schneider Organization (MSO)*
14724 Ventura Blvd Ste 410
Sherman Oaks, CA 91403-3537, USA

Black Eyed Peas, The (Music Group, Musician)
c/o David Sonenberg *DAS Communications*
83 Riverside Dr
New York, NY 10024-5713, USA

Black Flag (Music Group)
c/o Heidi May *Rollins Management*
7510 W Sunset Blvd # 602
Los Angeles, CA 90046-3408, USA

Black Keys, The (Music Group)
c/o John Peets *Q Prime South*
131 S 11th St
Nashville, TN 37206-2954, USA

Blackledge, Todd A (Athlete, Football Player, Sportscaster)
2711 Glenmont Rd NW
Canton, OH 44708-1345, USA

Blacklev, Travis (Athlete, Baseball Player)
8510 E 29th St N Apt 1517
Wichita, KS 67226-2254, USA

Blackman, Don (Athlete, Football Player)
48 Shire Dr S
East Amherst, NY 14051-1814, USA

Blackman, Ken (Athlete, Football Player)
5914 Northcrest Village Way
Spring, TX 77388-6916, USA

Blackman, Robert (Athlete, Football Player)
70 Glenwood N
Van Vleck, TX 77482-6292, USA

Blackman, Rolando (Athlete, Basketball Player, Olympic Athlete)
2649 Peavy Rd
Dallas, TX 75228-4211, USA

Blackmar, Phil (Athlete, Golfer)
4420 Janssen Dr
Corpus Christi, TX 78411-2817, USA

Blackmon, Don (Athlete, Football Player)
4340 Lansfaire Ter
Suwanee, GA 30024-6956, USA

Blackmon, Harold (Athlete, Football Player)
6937 S Crandon Ave Apt 4E
Chicago, IL 60649-2944, USA

Blackmon, Robert (Athlete, Football Player)
70 Glenwood N
Van Vleck, TX 77482-6292, USA

Blackmon, Roosevelt (Athlete, Football Player)
PO Box 1347
Belle Glade, FL 33430-6347, USA

Blackmon, Will (Athlete, Football Player)
7967 Monterey Bay Dr
Jacksonville, FL 32256-2927, USA

Blackmon, Will (Athlete, Football Player)
c/o Eugene Parker *Maximum Sports Management*
6435 W Jefferson Blvd # 197
Fort Wayne, IN 46804-6203, USA

Blackmore, Ritchie (Musician)
Blackmore Productions
PO Box 735
Nesconset, NY 11767-0735, USA

Blackmore, Stephanie (Actor)
1265 Leona Dr
Beverly Hills, CA 90210-2147, USA

Blacknall, Hubert (Athlete, Baseball Player)
46 Avenue A
Freehold, NJ 07728-1738, USA

Black Sabbath (Music Group)
c/o Rob Light *Creative Artists Agency (CAA-LA)*
2000 Avenue of the Stars Ste 100
Los Angeles, CA 90067-4705, USA

Blackshear, Jeff (Athlete, Football Player)
9229 Christo Ct
Owings Mills, MD 21117-3596, USA

Blackthorne, Paul (Actor)
8906 W Olympic Blvd
Beverly Hills, CA 90211-3550, USA

Black Veil Brides (Music Group)
c/o Ash Avildsen *The Pantheon Agency*
10866 Wilshire Blvd Ste 700
Los Angeles, CA 90024-4321, USA

Blackwelder, Myra (Athlete, Golfer)
2009 Hill Gail Way
Versailles, KY 40383-9132, USA

Blackwell, Alois (Athlete, Football Player)
2450 Louisiana St Ste 400
Houston, TX 77006-2318, USA

Blackwell, Nathaniel (Athlete, Basketball Player)
1716 Manor Pl
Clementon, NJ 08021-5811, USA

Blackwell, Tim (Athlete, Baseball Player)
8854 Whiteport Ln
San Diego, CA 92119-2135, USA

Blackwell, Will (Athlete, Football Player)
4801 Grass Valley Rd
Oakland, CA 94605-5600, USA

Blackwell, Willie (Athlete, Football Player)
152 Glenmore Ln
McDonough, GA 30253-8743, USA

Blackwood, Glenn (Athlete, Football Player)
24 Marina Gardens Dr
Palm Beach Gardens, FL 33410-3503, USA

Blackwood, Lyle (Athlete, Football Player)
4930 Stanford Ave
Dallas, TX 75209-3122, USA

Blackwood, Nina (DJ)
c/o Staff Member *Sirius/XM Satellite Radio*
1221 Avenue of the Americas Fl 19
New York, NY 10020-1011, USA

Blackwood, Vas (Actor)
c/o David Ginsberg *Insight*
PO Box 36359
Los Angeles, CA 90036-0359, USA

Blacque, Taurean (Actor)
5049 Rock Springs Rd
Lithonia, GA 30038-2239, USA

Bladd, Stephen Jo (Musician)
Nick Ben-Meir
652 N Doheny Dr
West Hollywood, CA 90069-5526, USA

Blade, Brian (Musician)
Ted Kurland
173 Brighton Ave
Allston, MA 02134-2003, USA

Blade, Willie (Athlete, Football Player)
331 Cobblestone Rd
Auburn, GA 30011-3022, USA

Blades, Bennie (Athlete, Football Player)
3409 NW 14th Ct Ft
Fort Lauderdale, FL 33311, USA

Blades, Brian K (Athlete, Football Player)
5124 NW 30th Ln
Fort Lauderdale, FL 33309-3310, USA

Blades, Jack (Musician)
2000/2200 Warrington Rd
Santa Rosa, CA 95404, USA

Blados, Brian (Athlete, Football Player)
7087 Clawson Ridge Ct
Liberty Twp, OH 45011-9121, USA

Bladt, Rick (Athlete, Baseball Player)
8600 Wilco Hwy NE
Mount Angel, OR 97362-9747, USA

Blagojevich, Rod (Politician)
2934 W Sunnyside Ave
Chicago, IL 60625-3845, USA

Blaha, John E (Astronaut)
346 Whitestone Dr
Spring Branch, TX 78070-6046, USA

Blahak, Joseph (Athlete, Football Player)
4040 N 21st St
Lincoln, NE 68521-1203, USA

Blahoski, Alana (Athlete, Hockey Player, Olympic Athlete)
60 E 9th St Apt 315
New York, NY 10003-6400, USA

Blaine, David (Magician)
354 Broadway Apt 1B
New York, NY 10013-3908, USA

Blaine, Ed (Athlete, Football Player)
4 E Clarkson Rd Apt B
Columbia, MO 65203-3520, USA

Blair, Dennis (Athlete, Baseball Player)
1706 Aurora Dr
Richardson, TX 75081-2115, USA

Blair, George (Athlete, Football Player)
1233 Karen Dr
Laurel, MS 39440-2186, USA

Blair, Jayson (Actor)
c/o Todd Justice *Justice & Ponder*
PO Box 480033
Los Angeles, CA 90048-1033, USA

Blair, Ken (Athlete, Football Player)
1837 NE 51st St
Oklahoma City, OK 73111-7005, USA

Blair, Kimberly (Actor)
c/o John Elliott *Mosaic Media Group*
9200 W Sunset Blvd Ste 10
West Hollywood, CA 90069-3608, USA

Blair, Linda (Actor)
The Linda Blair WorldHeart Foundation
10061 Riverside Dr Ste 1003
Toluca Lake, CA 91602-2560, USA

Blair, Matt (Athlete, Football Player)
16725 43rd Ave N
Minneapolis, MN 55446-2442, USA

Blair, Maybelle (Athlete, Baseball Player, Commentator)
39220 Palm Greens Pkwy
Palm Desert, CA 92260-1362, USA

Blair, Paul (Athlete, Football Player)
5301 Carrington Pl
Oklahoma City, OK 73131-6613, USA

Blair, Selma (Actor)
3224 Oakdell Rd
Studio City, CA 91604-4221, USA

Blair, Stanley (Athlete, Football Player)
901 Deer Run N
Pine Bluff, AR 71603-8158, USA

Blair, William (Athlete, Baseball Player)
1411 E Red Bird Ln
Dallas, TX 75241-2111, USA

Blair, William (Director)
c/o Staff Member *New Star Entertainment*
PO Box 84172
San Diego, CA 92138-4172, USA

Blair, Willie (Athlete, Baseball Player)
Fort Wayne Tincaps 1301
Fort Wayne, IN 46802, USA

Blair-Cruikshank, Bonnie (Athlete, Olympic Athlete, Speed Skater)
1223 Aspen Ct
Delafield, WI 53018-1300, USA

Blais, Madeleine H (Journalist)
Miami Herald
PO Box 3028
Editorial Dept
Livonia, MI 48151-3028, USA

Blais, Richard (Chef, Reality Star)
c/o Staff Member *Creative Artists Agency (CAA-LA)*
2000 Avenue of the Stars Ste 100
Los Angeles, CA 90067-4705, USA

Blaise, Kerlin (Athlete, Football Player)
17786 Parkshore Dr
Northville, MI 48168-8580, USA

Blake, Andre (Actor)
c/o Staff Member *Kerin-Goldberg Associates*
155 E 55th St Ste 5D
New York, NY 10022-4038, USA

Blake, Asha (Correspondent)
NBC-TV
30 Rockefeller Plz Fl 31
News Dept
New York, NY 10112-3199, USA

Blake, Casey (Athlete, Baseball Player)
8224 150th Ave
Indianola, IA 50125-8683, USA

Blake, David (DJ Quik) (Musician)
c/o Linda Jones *The Mass Appeal*
11607 Burbank Blvd Ste A
North Hollywood, CA 91601-2345, USA

Blake, Geoffrey (Writer)
2038 Kelton Ave
Los Angeles, CA 90025-5704, USA

Blake, James (Athlete, Tennis Player)
35 Prospect Rd
Westport, CT 06880-5206, USA

Blake, Jason (Athlete, Olympic Athlete)
11322 S Lake Eunice Rd
Detroit Lakes, MN 56501-7045, USA

Blake, Jay Don (Athlete, Golfer)
2859 Calle Del Sol
Saint George, UT 84790-7968, USA

Blake, Jeff (Athlete, Football Player)
1 Novacare Way
Philadelphia, PA 19145-5900, USA

Blake, Jim (Race Car Driver)
Wild Side Racing
107 Highway 198 E
Norris, MS 29667, USA

Blake, Josh (Actor)
c/o Staff Member *Pakula/King & Associates*
9229 W Sunset Blvd Ste 315
West Hollywood, CA 90069-3403, USA

Blake, Julian W (Bud) (Cartoonist)
PO Box 146
Damariscotta, ME 04543-0146, USA

Blake, Kayla (Actor)
c/o Todd Diener *Untitled Entertainment (LA)*
350 S Beverly Dr Ste 200
Beverly Hills, CA 90212-4819, USA

Blake, Marcia (Writer)
c/o Staff Member *Creative Artists Agency (CAA-LA)*
2000 Avenue of the Stars Ste 100
Los Angeles, CA 90067-4705, USA

Blake, Norman (Musician)
Scott O'Malley Assoc
433 E Cucharras St
Colorado Springs, CO 80903-3609, USA

Blake, Ricky (Athlete, Football Player)
2925 Baby Ruth Ln Apt 413
Antioch, TN 37013-2497, USA

Blake, Rob (Athlete, Hockey Player)
C A A Sports
2000 Avenue of the Stars Fl 3
Los Angeles, CA 90067-4704, USA

Blake, Sherry (Doctor)
Touchstone Psychological Services
1897 Godby Rd
Atlanta, GA 30349-5235, USA

Blake, Stephanie (Actor)
First Artists
1631 N Bristol St # 820
Santa Ana, CA 92706-3342, USA

Blake, Steve (Athlete, Basketball Player)
3479 Cascade Ter
West Linn, OR 97068-9271, USA

Blake, Susan (Correspondent)
News Center 4
1001 Van Ness Ave
San Francisco, CA 94109-6913, USA

Blake, Tchad (Musician)
Monterey International
200 W Superior St Ste 202
Chicago, IL 60654-6422, USA

Blake, Teresa (Actor)
Stone Manners
6500 Wilshire Blvd # 550
Los Angeles, CA 90048-4920, USA

Blake, Theo (Adult Film Star)
c/o Staff Member *Diva Central Inc*
7510 W Sunset Blvd Ste 1445
Los Angeles, CA 90046-3408, USA

Blake, Tom (Athlete, Football Player)
2017 Tullis Dr
Middletown, OH 45042-2962, USA

Blake, Victoria (Actor)
23801 Calabasas Rd Ste 2023
Calabasas, CA 91302-1558, USA

Blakeley, Ronee (Actor, Musician)
8033 W Sunset Blvd # 693
Los Angeles, CA 90046-2401, USA

Blakely, Sara (Business Person)
Spanx Inc.
3344 Peachtree Rd NE Ste 1700
Atlanta, GA 30326-4800, USA

Blakely, Susan (Actor, Model)
c/o Kim Dorr *Defining Artists Agency*
4370 Tujunga Ave Ste 120
Studio City, CA 91604-2763, USA

Blakemore, Sean (Actor)
c/o Steven Jang *SDB Partners Inc*
315 S Beverly Dr Ste 411
Beverly Hills, CA 90212-4301, USA

Blaker, Clay (Musician, Songwriter, Writer)
Texas Sounds Entertainment
2317 Pecan St
Dickinson, TX 77539-4949, USA

Blakey, Marion (Government Official)
Federal Aviation Agency
800 Independence Ave SW
Washington, DC 20591-0004, USA

Blalack, Robert (Cinematographer)
12251 Huston St
Valley Village, CA 91607-3616, USA

Blalock, Hank (Athlete, Baseball Player)
1541 Black Walnut Dr
San Marcos, CA 92078-7985, USA

Blalock, Jane (Athlete, Golfer)
197 8th St Ste 300
Charlestown, MA 02129-4236, USA

Blalock, Jolene (Actor)
7651 Willow Glen Rd
Los Angeles, CA 90046-1656, USA

Blalock, Justin (Athlete, Football Player)
c/o Ben Dogra *CAA (St. Louis)*
222 S Central Ave Ste 1008
Saint Louis, MO 63105-3509, USA

Blamire, Larry (Actor, Director, Writer)
10878 Bloomfield St
North Hollywood, CA 91602-2264, USA

Blanc, Jennifer (Actor)
c/o Melanie Sharp *Sharp Talent*
5538 Willowcrest Ave
North Hollywood, CA 91601-2830, USA

Blancas, Homero (Athlete, Golfer)
6826 Queensclub Dr
Houston, TX 77069-1216, USA

Blanchard, Cary (Athlete, Football Player)
7528 NW 132nd St
Oklahoma City, OK 73142-2405, USA

Blanchard, John A (Business Person)
Delux Corp
3680 Victoria St N
Saint Paul, MN 55126-2906, USA

Blanchard, Ken (Business Person, Writer)
The Ken Blanchard Companies
125 State Pl
Escondido, CA 92029-1398, USA

Blanchard, Rachel (Actor)
c/o Christian Donatelli *The Schiff Company*
9220 W Sunset Blvd Ste 106
West Hollywood, CA 90069-3500, USA

Blanchard, Tammy (Actor)
c/o Carol Bodie *Radius Entertainment*
10250 Constellation Blvd Fl 7
Los Angeles, CA 90067-6207, USA

Blanchard, Tim (Religious Leader)
Conservative Baptist Assn
1501 W Mineral Ave # B
Littleton, CO 80120-5612, USA

Blanchard, Tom (Athlete, Football Player)
217 Independence Dr
Grants Pass, OR 97527-5684, USA

Blanchard, Tully (Athlete, Wrestler)
922 Serenade Dr
San Antonio, TX 78213-1335, USA

Blanco, Gil (Athlete, Baseball Player)
18403 N 16th Pl
Phoenix, AZ 85022, USA

Blanco, Henry (Athlete, Baseball Player)
5510 N 132nd Dr
Litchfield Park, AZ 85340-8328, USA

Blanco, Kathleen (Politician)
506 Beverly Dr
Lafayette, LA 70503-3114, USA

Bland, Anthony (Tony) (Athlete, Football Player)
20429 Walnut Grove Ln
Tampa, FL 33647-3352, USA

Bland, Carl (Athlete, Football Player)
1985 Crossbridge Ct
Saint Charles, MO 63303-4810, USA

Bland, John (Athlete, Golfer)
PO Box 451436
Westlake, OH 44145-0638, USA

Bland, Nate (Athlete, Baseball Player)
1504 Oxmoor Rd
Birmingham, AL 35209-3908, USA

Bland, Tom (Athlete, Football Player)
66 S Winter Park Dr
Casselberry, FL 32707-4409, USA

Blandi, Oscar (Business Person)
Oscar Blandi Salon
746 Madison Ave
New York, NY 10065-7052, USA

Blaney, George (Athlete, Basketball Player)
21 Holland St
Falmouth, MA 02540-3665, USA

Blank, Arthur (Business Person, Football Executive)
1080 W Paces Ferry Rd NW
Atlanta, GA 30327-2600, USA

Blank, Barbie (Actor, Wrestler)
1157 Ovington Rd S
Jacksonville, FL 32216-2631, USA

Blank, Matt (Athlete, Baseball Player)
28610 Hidden Lk W
Magnolia, TX 77354-6548, USA

Blankenship, Greg (Athlete, Football Player)
PO Box 945
Cambria, CA 93428-0945, USA

Blankenship, Kevin (Athlete, Baseball Player)
5014 Regency Dr
Rocklin, CA 95677-4420, USA

Blankenship, Lance (Athlete, Baseball Player)
340 Kimberwicke Ct
Alamo, CA 94507-2703, USA

Blankley, Anthony (Tony) (Correspondent)
Edelman
1875 I St NW Ste 900
International Square
Washington, DC 20006-5422, USA

Blanks, Billy (Actor, Athlete)
c/o Staff Member *William Morris Endeavor (LA)*
9601 Wilshire Blvd
Beverly Hills, CA 90210-5213, USA

Blanks, Larvell (Athlete, Baseball Player)
PO Box 562
Del Rio, TX 78841-0562, USA

Blanks, Sid (Athlete, Football Player)
4402 Warm Springs Rd
Houston, TX 77035-6026, USA

Blanton, Dain (Athlete, Olympic Athlete, Volleyball Player)
1615 Stoner Ave Apt 3
Los Angeles, CA 90025-7340, USA

Blanton, Jerry (Athlete, Football Player)
1942 Calumet Ave
Toledo, OH 43607-1605, USA

Blanton, Joe (Athlete, Baseball Player)
1041 Germano Way
Pleasanton, CA 94566-2240, USA

Blanton, Robert (Athlete, Football Player)
c/o Scott Smith *XAM Sports*
PO Box 1725
Madison, WI 53701-1725, USA

Blaqk Audio (Music Group)
c/o Staff Member *Silva Artist Management (SAM)*
722 Seward St
Los Angeles, CA 90038-3504, USA

Blarikfield, Mark (Actor)
Artists Group
10 100 Santa Monica Blvd
#2490
Los Angeles, CA 90067, USA

B. Larson, John (Congressman, Politician)
1501 Longworth Hob
Washington, DC 20515-4708, USA

Blasberg, Erica (Athlete, Golfer)
2280 Treemont Pl Apt 206
Corona, CA 92879-7868, USA

Blasco, Chuck (Musician)
Media Promotion Enterprises
423 6th Ave
Huntington, WV 25701-1935, USA

Blaser, Cory (Athlete, Baseball Player)
10528 Ross Pi
Broomfield, CO 80021, USA

Blasi, Rosa (Actor)
c/o Cheryl McLean *Creative Public Relations*
3385 Oak Glen Dr
Los Angeles, CA 90068-1311, USA

Blasingame, Wade (Athlete, Baseball Player)
5207 Riverhill Rd NE
Marietta, GA 30068-4865, USA

Blass, (Steve) (Athlete, Baseball Player)
PO Box 7000
Pittsburgh, PA 15212-0038, USA

Blasucci, Dick (Producer)
c/o Staff Member *Kaplan-Stahler Agency*
8383 Wilshire Blvd Ste 923
Beverly Hills, CA 90211-2443, USA

Blatche, Andray (Athlete, Basketball Player)
914 Jennings Mill Dr
Bowie, MD 20721-6223, USA

Blateric, Steve (Athlete, Baseball Player)
2855 S Monaco Pkwy Apt 2-304
Denver, CO 80222-7191, USA

Blatny, Zdenek (Athlete, Hockey Player)
c/o Staff Member *International Sports Advisors*
878 Ridge View Way
Franklin Lakes, NJ 07417-1524, USA

Blatty, William Peter (Writer)
7018 Longwood Dr
Bethesda, MD 20817-2118, USA

Blatz, Kelly (Actor, Musician)
c/o Lena Roklin *Luber Roklin Management*
5815 W Sunset Blvd Ste 206
Los Angeles, CA 90028-6481, USA

Blauser, Jeff (Athlete, Baseball Player)
6080 Carlisle Ln
Alpharetta, GA 30022-6279, USA

Blavatnik, Leonard (Business Person)
128 Porchuck Rd
Greenwich, CT 06831-2926, USA

Blaylock, Anthony (Athlete, Football Player)
604 Glen Iris Dr NE
Atlanta, GA 30308-2717, USA

Blaylock, Bob (Athlete, Baseball Player)
36460 N 4030 Rd
Talala, OK 74080-3509, USA

Blaylock, Caroline (Athlete, Golfer)
232 Hennon Dr NW # B
Rome, GA 30165-9725, USA

Blaylock, Daren ""Mookie"" (Athlete, Basketball Player)
7601 Belmount Rd
Rowlett, TX 75089-7479, USA

Blaylock, Daron (Athlete, Basketball Player)
1017 Gresham Rd
Zebulon, GA 30295-3141, USA

Blaylock, Derrick (Athlete, Football Player)
1471 Edgewater Rd
Crown Point, IN 46307-8255, USA

Blaylock, Gary (Athlete, Baseball Player)
PO Box 241
Malden, MO 63863-0241, USA

Blazejowski, Carol (Athlete, Basketball Player, Olympic Athlete)
126 Walnut St
Nutley, NJ 07110-2851, USA

Blazelowski, Carol A (Athlete, Basketball Player)
New York Liberty
125 W End Ave # 6
Madison Square Garden
New York, NY 10023-6387, USA

Blazer, Phil (Athlete, Football Player)
16 Tranquil Ave
Greenville, SC 29615-1516, USA

Blazier, Ron (Athlete, Baseball Player)
610 N 9th St
Bellwood, PA 16617-1524, USA

Blazitz, Micael (Athlete, Football Player)
27100 Bunert Rd
Warren, MI 48088-6013, USA

Bledel, Alexis (Actor, Model)
c/o Paul Brown *New Wave Entertainment (LA)*
2660 W Olive Ave
Burbank, CA 91505-4525, USA

Bledsoe, Curtis (Athlete, Football Player)
1012 Red Oak Pl
Chula Vista, CA 91910-6750, USA

Bledsoe, Drew (Athlete, Football Player)
845 Delrey Rd
Whitefish, MT 59937-8020, USA

Bledsoe, Tempestt (Actor)
c/o Staff Member *GVA Talent Agency Inc*
8981 W Sunset Blvd Ste 101
West Hollywood, CA 90069-1850, USA

Bleek (Cox), Memphis (Malik) (Artist, Musician)
Green Light Talent Agency
PO Box 3172
Beverly Hills, CA 90212-0172, USA

Bleeth, Yasmine (Actor)
308 N Sycamore Ave Apt 202
Los Angeles, CA 90036-2661, USA

Bleick, Tom (Athlete, Football Player)
PO Box 187
Talladega, AL 35161-0187, USA

Bleier, Robert P (Rocky) (Athlete, Football Player)
929 Osage Rd
Pittsburgh, PA 15243-1011, USA

Bleiler, Gretchen (Athlete, Olympic Athlete, Speed Skater)
USOC Headquarters
PO Box 5774
Snowmass Village, CO 81615-5774, USA

Blessen, Karen A (Journalist)
Karen Blessen Illustration
6327 Vickery Blvd
Dallas, TX 75214-3348, USA

Blessing, Jack (Actor)
c/o Marianne Golan *Golan & Blumberg*
6528 W 6th St
Los Angeles, CA 90048-4716, USA

Blessitt, Ike (Athlete, Baseball Player)
19712 Anglin St
Detroit, MI 48234-1469, USA

Blethen, Frank A (Publisher)
Seatle Times Publisher's Office
1120 John St
Seattle, WA 98109-5321, USA

Bleu, Corbin (Actor)
c/o Randy James *James/Levy Management Inc*
3500 W Olive Ave Ste 1470
Burbank, CA 91505-5514, USA

Blevins, Michael (Actor)
13 W 100th St Apt 2C
New York, NY 10025-4815, USA

Blewett III, John (Race Car Driver)
John Blewett Motorsports
246 Herbertsville Rd
Howell, NJ 07731-8787, USA

Blick, Richard (Dick) (Athlete, Swimmer)
1602 N Nye Ave
Fremont, NE 68025-3328, USA

Blige, Mary J (Musician)
c/o Dvora Vener Englefield *42West (LA)*
1840 Century Park E Ste 700
Los Angeles, CA 90067-2122, USA

Bligen, Dennis (Athlete, Football Player)
PO Box 101
West Hempstead, NY 11552-0101, USA

Blim, Richard D (Doctor)
304 W 172nd St
Belton, MO 64012, USA

Blind Boys of Alabama, The (Music Group, Musician)
192 Warren St SE
C/O Eric (Ricky) McKinnie
Atlanta, GA 30317-2243, USA

Blink 182 (Music Group)
c/o Karen Wiessen *Universal Music Group*
1755 Broadway Fl 6
New York, NY 10019-3768, USA

Blinka, Stan (Athlete, Football Player)
1966 Lincoln Hwy
North Versailles, PA 15137-2734, USA

Blinks, Susan (Athlete, Horse Racer, Olympic Athlete)
42 Thayer St
S Deerfield, MA 01373-1137, USA

Bliss, Boti Anne (Actor)
Chase/Goldberg Management
3400 San Marino St # A
Los Angeles, CA 90006-1106

Bliss, Mike (Race Car Driver)
195 Jones Rd
Spartanburg, SC 29307-5448, USA

Blitt, Ricky (Writer)
c/o Nick Reed *ICM Partners (LA)*
10250 Constellation Blvd Fl 7
Los Angeles, CA 90067-6207, USA

Blittner, Larry (Baseball Player)
Washington Senators
915 3rd Ave NW
Pocahontas, IA 50574-1413, USA

Blitz, Andy (Writer)
c/o Staff Member *3 Arts Entertainment (LA)*
9460 Wilshire Blvd Fl 7
Beverly Hills, CA 90212-2713, USA

Blitzer, Wolf (Correspondent, Television Host)
8929 Holly Leaf Ln
Bethesda, MD 20817-2654, USA

Bloch, Henry W (Business Person)
H & R Block Inc
4410 Main St
Kansas City, MO 64111-1812, USA

Block, Francesca Lia (Writer)
c/o Angela Cheng Caplan *Cheng Caplan Co*
3136 S Bentley Ave
Los Angeles, CA 90034-3008, USA

Block, Hunt (Actor)
PO Box 462
Greens Farms, CT 06838-0462, USA

Block, John (Athlete, Basketball Player)
Point Loma Nazarene College
1069 Santa Barbara St
San Diego, CA 92107-4160, USA

Block, John R (Politician, Secretary)
National Wholesale Grocers Assn
201 Park Washington Ct
Falls Church, VA 22046-4527, USA

Block, Ken (Athlete, Hockey Player)
15762 Bethpage Trl
Carmel, IN 46033-5513, USA

Block, Lawrence (Writer)
299 W 12th St Apt 12D
New York, NY 10014-1829, USA

Block, Ron (Musician)
2065 Carters Creek Pike
Franklin, TN 37064-5914, USA

Blocker, Dirk (Actor)
5063 La Ramada Dr
Santa Barbara, CA 93111-1846, USA

Blocker, Terry (Athlete, Baseball Player)
745 Guide Post Ln
Stone Mountain, GA 30088-1943, USA

Blodgett, Cindy (Athlete, Basketball Player)
25 Liberty St
Wakefield, RI 02879-2906, USA

Bloedorn, Greg (Athlete, Football Player)
816 N Catherine Ave
La Grange Park, IL 60526-1511, USA

Blomberg, Ron (Athlete, Baseball Player)
11660 Mountain Laurel Dr
Roswell, GA 30075-1329, USA

Blomdahl, Ben (Athlete, Baseball Player)
6 Pleasanton Ln
Ladera Ranch, CA 92694-0222, USA

Blomgren, Jim (Race Car Driver)
1206 S 13th Ave
Yakima, WA 98902-5311, USA

Blomgren, Michael (Actor)
c/o Staff Member *Select Artists Ltd (CA-Westside Office)*
1138 12th St Apt 1
Santa Monica, CA 90403-5459, USA

Blonde streak (Music Group)
c/o John Elias *Three Twins Entertainment, Inc*
PO Box 100210
Staten Island, NY 10310-0210, USA

Blondie (Musician)
c/o Staff Member *10th Street Entertainment (NY)*
38 W 21st St Rm 300
New York, NY 10010-6979, USA

Blong, Jenni (Actor)
c/o Susan Smith *Susan Smith Company, The*
2001 Wilshire Blvd Ste 400
Santa Monica, CA 90403-5686, USA

Blonsky, Nikki (Actor)
c/o Teal Cannaday *Rogers & Cowan PR (LA)*
8687 Melrose Ave Ste 7
West Hollywood, CA 90069-5721, USA

Blood, Edward J (Skier)
2 Beech Hill Rd
Durham, NH 03824-1803, USA

Blood, Peter (Horse Racer)
290 SE 5th Ave
Pompano Beach, FL 33060-8024, USA

Bloodgood, Moon (Actor)
1238 S Holt Ave Apt 4
Los Angeles, CA 90035-5100, USA

Bloodworth-Thomason, Linda (Producer, Writer)
c/o Jim Stein *Innovative Artists (LA)*
1505 10th St
Santa Monica, CA 90401-2805, USA

Bloom, Anne (Actor)
Abrams Artists
9200 W Sunset Blvd Ste 1125
West Hollywood, CA 90069-3610, USA

Bloom, Brian (Actor)
16760 Escalon Dr
Encino, CA 91436-3832, USA

Bloom, Jeremy (Athlete, Olympic Athlete, Sportscaster)
c/o Staff Member *Maxx Sports & Entertainment*
546 5th Ave Fl 6
New York, NY 10036-5000, USA

Bloom, Lisa (Attorney, Commentator)
The Bloom Firm
20700 Ventura Blvd Ste 301
Woodland Hills, CA 91364-6272, USA

Bloom, Mike (Athlete, Hockey Player)
3214 Marina Cir
Marina, CA 93933, USA

Bloom, Orlando (Actor)
c/o Robin Baum *Slate Public Relations*
9000 W Sunset Blvd Ste 915
West Hollywood, CA 90069-5809, USA

Bloom, Verna (Actor)
327 E 82nd St
New York, NY 10028-4659, USA

Bloomauist, Willie (Athlete, Baseball Player)
7026 E Blue Sky Dr
Scottsdale, AZ 85266-7518, USA

Bloomberg, Michael (Business Person, Politician)
17 E 79th St
New York, NY 10075-0101

Bloomfield, Jack (Athlete, Baseball Player)
1310 W Iris Ave
McAllen, TX 78501-3995, USA

Bloomfield, Michael J (Mike) (Astronaut)
14302 Autumn Canyon Trce
Houston, TX 77062-2193, USA

Bloomfield, Sara (Director, Misc)
Holocaust Memorial Museum
100 Wallenberg Pl SW
Washington, DC 20024, USA

Bloomfield, Willie (Athlete, Baseball Player)
3145 NE Magnolia St
Issaquah, WA 98029-3603, USA

Bloomquist, Scott (Race Car Driver)
219 Brooks Ln
Mooresburg, TN 37811-2113, USA

Blosser, Greg (Athlete, Baseball Player)
5525 47th Ct E
Bradenton, FL 34203-5655, USA

Blount, Alvin (Athlete, Football Player)
1943 Lakeshore Overlook Cir NW
Cir NW
Kennesaw, GA 30152-6711, USA

Blount, Corie (Athlete, Basketball Player)
5427 Kyles Ln
Liberty Township, OH 45044-9462, USA

Blount, Eric (Athlete, Football Player)
1388 Institute Rd
Kinston, NC 28504-7308, USA

Blount, Jeb (Athlete, Football Player)
1212 Daffodil Ln
Longview, TX 75604-2834, USA

Blount, John E (Athlete, Football Player)
1212 Daffodil Ln
Longview, TX 75604-2834, USA

Blount, Mark (Athlete, Basketball Player)
PO Box 33268
West Palm Beach, FL 33420-3268, USA

Blount, Mel (Athlete, Football Player)
6 Mel Blount Dr
Claysville, PA 15323-1329, USA

Blount, Melvin C (Mel) (Athlete, Football Executive, Football Player)
6 Mel Blount Dr
Claysville, PA 15323-1329, USA

Blount, Winton M III (Business Person)
Blount Inc
4909 SE International Way
Portland, OR 97222-4679, USA

Blow, Kurtis (Music Group)
Entertainment Artists
2409 21st Ave S Ste 100
Nashville, TN 37212-5317, USA

Blowers, Mike (Athlete, Baseball Player)
PO Box 4100
Seattle, WA 98194-0100, USA

Blu, D K (Musician)
c/o Mike Rosen *Working Artists Agency*
13525 Ventura Blvd
Sherman Oaks, CA 91423-3801

Blucas, Marc (Actor)
c/o Sandra Chang *Anonymous Content (LA)*
3532 Hayden Ave
Culver City, CA 90232-2413, USA

Blue, Callum (Actor)
c/o Staff Member *Untitled Entertainment (LA)*
350 S Beverly Dr Ste 200
Beverly Hills, CA 90212-4819, USA

Blue, John (Athlete, Hockey Player)
1724 Tustin Ave
Costa Mesa, CA 92627-3230, USA

Blue, Linda Bell (Producer)
c/o Staff Member *N.S. Bienstock*
250 W 57th St Ste 333
New York, NY 10107-0302, USA

Blue, Luther (Athlete, Football Player)
6952 Ravines Cir
West Bloomfield, MI 48322-2757, USA

Blue, Sam (Race Car Driver)
Blue Racing
1400 W 6th St
Red Wing, MN 55066-2174, USA

Blue, Vida (Athlete, Baseball Player)
PO Box 1449
Pleasanton, CA 94566-0349, USA

Blues Traveler (Music Group)
c/o Keith Sarkisian *William Morris Endeavor (LA)*
9601 Wilshire Blvd
Beverly Hills, CA 90210-5213, USA

Bluford, Guion (Astronaut)
PO Box 549
North Olmsted, OH 44070-0549, USA

Blum, Arlene (Mountaineer)
University of California
Biochemistry Dept
Berkeley, CA 94720-0001, USA

Blum, Geoff (Athlete, Baseball Player)
29 Groveside Dr
Aliso Viejo, CA 92656-7070, USA

Blum, John (Athlete, Coach, Hockey Player)
416 Marlborough St Apt 903
Boston, MA 02115-1508, USA

Blum, Stephanie (Comedian)
c/o Staff Member *Don Buchwald & Associates (LA)*
6500 Wilshire Blvd Ste 2200
Los Angeles, CA 90048-4942, USA

Blum, Steve (Actor)
c/o Staff Member *Arlene Thornton & Associates*
12711 Ventura Blvd Ste 490
Studio City, CA 91604-2477, USA

Blum, Walter (Horse Racer)
5710 NW 65th Way
Tamarac, FL 33321-5778, USA

Bluma, Jaime (Athlete, Baseball Player)
15219 Reeds St
Overland Park, KS 66223-3241, USA

Blume, Bernard (Athlete, Basketball Player)
626 SE 38th Dr
Gresham, OR 97080-8459, USA

Blume, Judy (Writer)
JB Props Inc
C/o Tashmoo Productions 244 Fifth Ave 11th Fl
New York, NY 10023, USA

Blumenauer, Earl (Congressman, Politician)
1502 Longworth Hob
Washington, DC 20515-1101, USA

Blumenthal, Richard (Senator)
702 Hart Senate Office Bldg
Washington, DC 20510-0001, USA

Blundell, Mark (Race Car Driver)
4001 Methanol Ln
Indianapolis, IN 46268-4855, USA

Blundin, Matt (Athlete, Football Player)
731 Milmont Ave
Swarthmore, PA 19081-2519, USA

Blunt, Emily (Actor)
c/o BeBe Lerner *ID Public Relations (LA)*
7060 Hollywood Blvd Fl 8th
Los Angeles, CA 90028-6021, USA

Blunt, Matt (Ex-Governor)
The Ashcroft Group, LLC
950 N Glebe Rd Ste 240
Arlington, VA 22203-4181, USA

Blunt, Roy (Senator)
260 Russell Senate Office Building
Washington, DC 20510-0001, USA

Blur (Music Group)
c/o Greg Janese *Paradigm (Nashville)*
124 12th Ave S Ste 410
Nashville, TN 37203-3170, USA

Blurth, Ray (Bowler)
569 Beauford Dr
Saint Louis, MO 63122-1413, USA

Blush (Music Group, Musician)
c/o Staff Member *Mitch Schneider Organization (MSO)*
14724 Ventura Blvd Ste 410
Sherman Oaks, CA 91403-3537, USA

Bluth, Don (Cartoonist)
10121 E Shangri La Rd
Scottsdale, AZ 85260-6302, USA

Bluth, Ray (Bowler)
569 Beauford Dr
Saint Louis, MO 63122-1413, USA

BLVD (Music Group, Musician)
c/o Staff Member *Skyline Music*
28 Union St
Whitefield, NH 03598-3503, USA

Bly, Dre' (Athlete, Football Player)
4312 Topsail Lndg
Chesapeake, VA 23321-6601, USA

Bly, Dre (Athlete, Football Player)
4312 Topsail Lndg
Chesapeake, VA 23321-6601, USA

Blyleven, Bert (Athlete, Baseball Player)
1 Twins Way
Minneapolis, MN 55403-1418, USA

Blyth, Ann (Actor, Music Group)
PO Box 9754
Rancho Santa Fe, CA 92067-4754, USA

Blythe, Jamie (Reality Star)
c/o Mike Esterman *Esterman.Com, LLC*
Prefers to be contacted via email
Baltimore, MD XXXXX, USA

B. Maloney, Carolyn (Congressman, Politician)
2332 Rayburn Hob
Washington, DC 20515-3513, USA

B. McKinley, David (Congressman, Politician)
313 Cannon Hob
Washington, DC 20515-0925, USA

B. Nugent, Richard (Congressman, Politician)
1517 Longworth Hob
Washington, DC 20515-1004, USA

Boal, Mark (Writer)
c/o Staff Member *Creative Artists Agency (CAA-LA)*
2000 Avenue of the Stars Ste 100
Los Angeles, CA 90067-4705, USA

Board, Dwaine (Athlete, Football Player)
651 Arlington Rd
Redwood City, CA 94062-1842, USA

Boat, Billy (Race Car Driver)
23045 N 15th Ave
Phoenix, AZ 85027-1316, USA

Boatman, Michael (Actor)
1432 Sunnycrest Dr
Fullerton, CA 92835-3751, USA

Boatwright, Bon (Athlete, Football Player)
1801 E Main St
Henderson, TX 75652-3324, USA

Boatwright, Ron (Athlete, Football Player)
1801 E Main St
Henderson, TX 75652-3324, USA

Bob, Tim (Music Group, Musician)
c/o Staff Member *ArtistDirect*
9046 Lindblade St
Culver City, CA 90232-2513, USA

Bobadilla, Daniela (Actor)
c/o Michael Abrams *The Michael Abrams Group*
10250 Constellation Blvd Fl 23
Los Angeles, CA 90067-6237, USA

Bobby Chacon, Bobby Chacon (Boxer)
Main Street III Gym
752 S Main St
Huntington Hotel
Los Angeles, CA 90014-2013, USA

Bobek, Nicole (Figure Skater)
19220 Seaview Rd # 100
Jupiter, FL 33469-2402, USA

Bober, Chris (Athlete, Football Player)
4406 N 195th Cir
Elkhorn, NE 68022-5167, USA

Bobko, Karol J (Astronaut)
32 Mansion Ct
Menlo Park, CA 94025-6658, USA

Bobo, Jonah (Actor)
c/o Ellen Gilbert *Abrams Artists Agency (LA)*
9200 W Sunset Blvd PH 11
West Hollywood, CA 90069-3601, USA

Bocachica, Hiram (Athlete, Baseball Player)
PO Box 364952
San Juan, PR 00936-4952, USA

Bocanegra, Carlos (Athlete, Soccer Player)
c/o Lyle York *Proactive Sports Management USA*
3233 M St NW
Washington, DC 20007-3556, USA

Boccabella, John (Athlete, Baseball Player)
1035 Lea Dr
San Rafael, CA 94903-3747, USA

Bochco, Steven (Producer, Writer)
c/o Staff Member *Steven Bochco Productions*
3000 Olympic Blvd Ste 1310
Santa Monica, CA 90404-5073, USA

Bochenski, Brandon (Athlete, Hockey Player)
10590 Kumquat St NW Apt 3
Minneapolis, MN 55448-1516, USA

Bochner, Hart (Actor)
1746 Correa Way
Los Angeles, CA 90049-2202, USA

Bochte, Bruce (Athlete, Baseball Player)
80 Century Ln
Petaluma, CA 94952-1218, USA

Bochtler, Doug (Athlete, Baseball Player)
PO Box 483
Yakima, WA 98907-0483, USA

Bochy, Bruce (Athlete, Baseball Player, Coach)
24 Willie Mays Plz
San Francisco, CA 94107-2134, USA

Bock, Charles Col
PO Box 4197
Incline Village, NV 89450-4197, USA

Bock, Edward J (Athlete, Business Person, Football Player)
2232 Clifton Forge Dr
Saint Louis, MO 63131-3107, USA

Bock, Joe (Athlete, Football Player)
2896 Kingston Ct
Irwin, PA 15642-9632, USA

Bock, John (Athlete, Football Player)
7394 NW 114th Ter
Parkland, FL 33076-4242, USA

Bock, Joseph (Athlete, Football Player)
2896 Kingston Ct
Irwin, PA 15642-9632, USA

Bockhorn, Arlen (Athlete, Basketball Player)
3540 Big Tree Rd
Bellbrook, OH 45305-1971, USA

Bockus, Randy (Athlete, Baseball Player)
560 Helena Dr
Tallmadge, OH 44278-2667, USA

Bockwoldt, Colby (Athlete, Football Player)
1630 E 2450 S Unit 220
Saint George, UT 84790-6487, USA

Bocock, Brian (Baseball Player)
140 Cantermill Ln
Mount Crawford, VA 22841-2355, USA

Bodden, Alonzo (Actor, Comedian)
c/o Staff Member *Rozon/Mercer Management*
9250 Wilshire Blvd Ste 100
Beverly Hills, CA 90212-3343, USA

Bodden, Leigh (Athlete, Football Player)
14409 Woodmore Oaks Ct
Bowie, MD 20721-3012, USA

Boddicker, Michael J (Mike) (Athlete, Basketball Player)
11324 W 121st Ter
Overland Park, KS 66213-1978, USA

Boddicker, Mike (Athlete, Baseball Player)
11324 W 121st Ter
Overland Park, KS 66213-1978, USA

Boddie, Tony (Athlete, Football Player)
330 Golden Pond St
Port Orchard, WA 98366-3300, USA

Boden, Lynn (Athlete, Football Player)
7103 N 146th St
Bennington, NE 68007-1527, USA

Bodenheimer, George W. (Business Person)
c/o Staff Member *ESPN (Main)*
935 Middle St
Espn Plaza
Bristol, CT 06010-1000, USA

Bodine, Brett (Race Car Driver)
304 Performance Rd
Mooresville, NC 28115-9592, USA

Bodine, Eric (Race Car Driver)
Billy Hill Vineyards
6843 Georgetown Taylor Memori Al Dr
Hammondsport, NY 14840, USA

Bodine, Geoff (Athlete, Race Car Driver)
Geoff Bodine Fan Club
3672 Joslin Way
Melbourne, FL 32904-8498, USA

Bodine, Geoffrey (Race Car Driver)
Gunselman Motorsports
208 Rolling Hill Rd
Mooresville, NC 28117-6845, USA

Bodine, Todd (Race Car Driver)
Team Onion Racing
PO Box 419
Mooresville, NC 28115-0419, USA

Bodine, Vance (Race Car Driver)
11881 Vance Davis Dr
Charlotte, NC 28269-7694, USA

Bodison, Wolfgang (Actor)
c/o Amy Macnow *Envoy Entertainment*
2637 Centinela Ave Apt 8
Santa Monica, CA 90405-3162, USA

Bodrov, Sergei (Director)
c/o Steve Rabineau *United Talent Agency (UTA-LA)*
9336 Civic Center Dr
Beverly Hills, CA 90210-3604, USA

Boe, Eric A Major
16702 Mighty Redwood Ct
Houston, TX 77059-5595, USA

Boeheim, Jim (Athlete, Basketball Player, Coach)
702 Tiffany Cir
Fayetteville, NY 13066, USA

Boehmer, Len (Athlete, Baseball Player)
206 Townview Ct
Wentzville, MO 63385-2925, USA

Boehner, John (Congressman, Politician)
1011 Longworth Hob
Washington, DC 20515-3508, USA

Boehringer, Brian (Athlete, Baseball Player)
10 Sunset Dr
Fenton, MO 63026-4959, USA

Boeke, Jim (Athlete, Football Player)
18914 San Blas St
Fountain Valley, CA 92708-7430, USA

Boen, Earl (Actor)
3015 Kalakaua Ave Apt 902
Honolulu, HI 96815-4750, USA

Boerigter, Marc (Athlete, Football Player)
210 W 2nd St Apt 1412
Kansas City, MO 64105-2171, USA

Boeschenstein, William W (Business Person)
10617 Cardiff Rd
Perrysburg, OH 43551-3404, USA

Boesel, Raul (Athlete, Race Car Driver)
150 SE 25th Rd Apt 4E
Miami, FL 33129-2403, USA

Boesen, Dannis L (Astronaut)
6613 Sandra Ave NE
Albuquerque, NM 87109-3639, USA

Boesen, Dennis (Astronaut)
6613 Sandra Ave NE
Albuquerque, NM 87109-3639, USA

Boever, Joe (Athlete, Baseball Player)
4701 Sawbuck St
Saint Augustine, FL 32092-3690, USA

Boffill, Angela (Music Group)
1385 York Ave Apt 6B
New York, NY 10021-3906, USA

Bogans, Keith (Athlete, Basketball Player)
8345 Lake Burden Cir
Windermere, FL 34786-5322, USA

Bogar, Tim (Athlete, Baseball Player)
4 Yawkey Way
Boston, MA 02215-3409, USA

Bogart, Andrea (Actor)
c/o Staff Member *Kazarian, Measures, Ruskin & Associates (LA)*
11969 Ventura Blvd Fl 3
Studio City, CA 91604-2630, USA

Bogart, Stephen (Producer)
c/o Staff Member *MODA Entertainment*
590 Madison Ave Fl 21
New York, NY 10022-2545, USA

Bogdanovich, Peter (Director)
c/o Oren Segal *Radius Entertainment*
9229 W Sunset Blvd Ste 310
West Hollywood, CA 90069-3403, USA

Bogener, Terry (Athlete, Baseball Player)
311 Virginia Dr
Estes Park, CO 80517-9041, USA

Boggs, Bill (Journalist)
400 Central Park W Apt 18H
New York, NY 10025-5856, USA

Boggs, Brandon (Athlete, Baseball Player)
520 Summerset Ln
Aot 41
Atlanta, GA 30328-1693, USA

Boggs, Haskell (Cinematographer)
3710 Goodland Ave
Studio City, CA 91604-2312, USA

Boggs, Mitchell Boggs (Athlete, Baseball Player)
901 W Walnut Ave
Dalton, GA 30720-3952, USA

Boggs, Taylor (Athlete, Football Player)
c/o Adam Heller *Vantage Management Group*
518 Reamer Dr
Carnegie, PA 15106-1845, USA

Boggs, Tommy (Athlete, Baseball Player)
1450 Long Mdw
Salado, TX 76571-5367, USA

Boggs, Wade (Athlete, Baseball Player)
6006 Windham Pl
Tampa, FL 33647-1149, USA

Bogguss, Suzy (Musician, Songwriter)
707 Sneed Rd W
Franklin, TN 37069-7045, USA

Bogle, Warren (Athlete, Baseball Player)
3400 Gulf Shore Blvd N Apt M8
Naples, FL 34103-3609, USA

Boglioli, Wendy (Athlete, Olympic Athlete, Swimmer)
2014 210th Cir NE
Sammamish, WA 98074-4210, USA

Bogosian, Eric (Actor, Artist)
100 Hudson St Apt 3D
New York, NY 10013-2881, USA

BOGRAKOS, Steve (Athlete, Football Player)
7615 E Jamison Dr
Centennial, CO 80112-2623, USA

Bogues, Muggsy (Athlete, Basketball Player)
527 E 83rd St Apt 2W
New York, NY 10028-7281, USA

Bogues, Tyrone ""Muggsy"" (Athlete, Basketball Player)
2318 Houston Branch Rd
Charlotte, NC 28270-0795, USA

Boguniecki, Eric (Athlete, Hockey Player)
58 Hine St
West Haven, CT 06516-4707, USA

Bogusevic, Brian (Athlete, Baseball Player)
12623 S 69th Ct Apt 3
Palos Heights, IL 60463-1746, USA

Bogush, Elizabeth (Actor)
c/o Craig Shapiro *ICM Partners (LA)*
10250 Constellation Blvd Fl 7
Los Angeles, CA 90067-6207, USA

Bohanon, Brian (Athlete, Baseball Player)
243 W Thorn Way
Houston, TX 77015-2069, USA

Bohay, Heidi (Actor)
5004 Sanlo Pl
Woodland Hills, CA 91364-3528, USA

Bohbot, Daniel (Designer)
Hale Bob
2711 Beverly Blvd
C/O Marc Springer
Los Angeles, CA 90057-1007, USA

Bohem, Les (Producer, Writer)
c/o Staff Member *United Talent Agency (UTA-LA)*
9336 Civic Center Dr
Beverly Hills, CA 90210-3604, USA

Bohling, Dewey (Athlete, Football Player)
5705 Cambria Rd NW
Albuquerque, NM 87120-2317, USA

Bohlinger, Rob (Athlete, Football Player)
12650 69th Ave N
Maple Grove, MN 55369-5438, USA

Bohlke, Sanders (Musician)
c/o Staff Member *Paradigm (Monterey)*
404 W Franklin St
Monterey, CA 93940-2303, USA

Bohlmann, Ralph A (Religious Leader)
Lutheran Church Missouri Synod
1333 S Kirkwood Rd
Saint Louis, MO 63122-7295, USA

Bohm-Vitense, Erika
750 Edmonds Way # 219
Edmonds, WA 98020-5126, USA

Bohn, Jason (Athlete, Golfer)
161 Graves Rd
Acworth, GA 30101-6117, USA

Bohn, Parker III (Bowler)
25 Pitney Ln
Jackson, NJ 08527-2933, USA

Bohn, T J (Athlete, Baseball Player)
PO Box 332
Millerstown, PA 17062-0332, USA

Bohnet, John (Athlete, Baseball Player)
224 Panorama Dr
Benicia, CA 94510-1523, USA

Bohrer, Thomas (Athlete, Olympic Athlete, Rower)
77 Crest St
Concord, MA 01742-3006, USA

Boi, Big (Artist, Music Group, Musician)
180 Parkwood Ln
Fayetteville, GA 30215-5082, USA

Boikov, Alexandre (Athlete, Hockey Player)
2138 Charleys Creek Rd
Culloden, WV 25510, USA

Boiman, Rocky (Athlete, Football Player)
10105 County Line Rd
Brookville, IN 47012-1298, USA

Boiovic, Novo (Athlete, Football Player)
22097 Worcester Dr
Novi, MI 48374-3956, USA

Boireau, Michael (Athlete, Football Player)
1729 SW 101st Way
Miramar, FL 33025-6537, USA

Boisclair, Bruce (Athlete, Baseball Player)
5423 Spanish Oak Ln Unit D
Oak Park, CA 91377-3728, USA

Boisvert, Gilles (Athlete, Hockey Player)
10213 Greenside Dr
Cockeysville, MD 21030-3332, USA

Boitano, Brian (Athlete, Figure Skater, Olympic Athlete)
Brian Boitano Enterprises
1072 Inverness Way
Sunnyvale, CA 94087-4921, USA

Boitano, Danny (Athlete, Baseball Player)
2343 Deauville Cir
Clovis, CA 93619-4292, USA

Bok, Arthur (Athlete, Football Player)
3280 Early Rd
Dayton, OH 45415-2705, USA

Bokamper, Kim (Athlete, Football Player)
301 NW 127th Ave
Plantation, FL 33325-2318, USA

Bokelmann, Dick (Athlete, Baseball Player)
629 N Belmont Ave
Arlington Heights, IL 60004-5601, USA

Bolden, Charles F (Astronaut, General)
Natl Aviation & Space Admin
300 C St NE
Washington, DC 20002-5710, USA

Bolden, Juran (Athlete, Football Player)
1606 Deep Well Ct
Valrico, FL 33594-5156, USA

Bolden, Omar (Athlete, Football Player)
c/o Joel Segal *Lagardere Unlimited (NYC)*
845 United Nations Plz
New York, NY 10017-3540, USA

Bolden, Rickey (Athlete, Football Player)
112 Beeman St
Lagrange, GA 30241-2810, USA

Boldin, Anquan (Athlete, Football Player)
16225 Bridlewood Cir
Delray Beach, FL 33445-6675, USA

Boldirev, Ivan (Athlete, Hockey Player)
2003 Woodmere Dr
Valparaiso, IN 46383-6680, USA

Boldman, Spencer (Actor)
c/o Meredith Fine *Coast to Coast Talent Group*
3350 Barham Blvd
Los Angeles, CA 90068-1404, USA

Bolduc, Dan (Athlete, Hockey Player, Olympic Athlete)
27 Daisy Ln
Sidney, ME 04330-1809, USA

Bolek, Ken (Athlete, Baseball Player)
4816 1st Avenue Dr NW
Bradenton, FL 34209-2861, USA

Boles, Carl (Athlete, Baseball Player)
5618 Pine Bay Dr
Tampa, FL 33625-4025, USA

Boles, John E (Athlete, Baseball Player, Coach)
7901 Timberlake Dr
Melbourne, FL 32904-2151, USA

Boley, Michael (Athlete, Football Player)
2934 Misty Rock Cv
Dacula, GA 30019-3156, USA

Bolger, Bill (Athlete, Basketball Player)
525 Ahlstrand Rd
Glen Ellyn, IL 60137-6926, USA

Bolger, Emma (Actor)
c/o Abby Bluestone *Innovative Artists (LA)*
1505 10th St
Santa Monica, CA 90401-2805, USA

Bolger, Gary (Race Car Driver)
3632 Washington St
Lansing, IL 60438-2425, USA

Bolger, James B (Jim) (Prime Minister)
New Zealand Embassy
37 Observatory Cir NW
Washington, DC 20008-3686, USA

Bolger, Jim (Athlete, Baseball Player)
5524 Sidney Rd
Cincinnati, OH 45238-3215, USA

Bolger, Sarah (Actor)
c/o Hylda Queally *Creative Artists Agency (CAA-LA)*
2000 Avenue of the Stars Ste 100
Los Angeles, CA 90067-4705, USA

Bolick, Frank (Athlete, Baseball Player)
381 Virginia Ln
Kulpmont, PA 17834-2024, USA

Bolin, Bobby D (Athlete, Baseball Player)
100 Medinah Dr
Easley, SC 29642-3126, USA

Bolin, Treva (Athlete, Football Player)
PO Box 281
New Waverly, TX 77358-0281, USA

Boling, Clint (Athlete, Football Player)
c/o Pat Dye Jr *SportsTrust Advisors (GA)*
3340 Peachtree Rd NE Fl 16
Atlanta, GA 30326-1000, USA

Bolkovac, Nick (Athlete, Football Player)
1418 Humbolt Ave
Youngstown, OH 44502-2755, USA

Bollen, Roger (Cartoonist)
Tribune Media Services
435 N Michigan Ave Ste 1500
Chicago, IL 60611-4012, USA

Boller, Kyle (Athlete, Football Player)
2365 Jennifer Ln
Encinitas, CA 92024-6438, USA

Bolles, Richard N (Writer)
10 Stirling Dr
Danville, CA 94526-2921, USA

Bollettieri, Nick (Coach, Tennis Player)
Nick Bollettieri Tennis Academy
5500 34th St W
Bradenton, FL 34210-3596, USA

Bolli, Justin (Athlete, Golfer)
3309 Buckhead Forest Mews NE
Atlanta, GA 30305-1706, USA

Bolling, Eric (Television Host)
c/o Staff Member *Fox News (NY)*
1211 Avenue of the Americas Lowr C1
New York, NY 10036-8705, USA

Bolling, Frank (Athlete, Baseball Player)
171 Fenwick Rd
Mobile, AL 36608-1743, USA

Bolling, Milt (Athlete, Baseball Player)
4009 Old Shell Rd Apt E11
Mobile, AL 36608-1385, USA

Bolling, Tiffany (Actor)
116 S Burris Ave
Compton, CA 90221-3315, USA

Bollinger, Brian (Athlete, Football Player)
1010 Winding Waters Cir
Winter Springs, FL 32708-6324, USA

Bollinger, Brooks (Athlete, Football Player)
3549 Birchpond Rd
Saint Paul, MN 55122-4900, USA

Bollinger, Danielle (Musician)
c/o Len Evans *Project Publicity*
312 W 53rd St Ste 202
New York, NY 10019-5743, USA

Bollman, Ryan (Actor)
c/o Staff Member *Lichtman/Salners Company*
12216 Moorpark St
Studio City, CA 91604-5228, USA

Bollo, Greg (Athlete, Baseball Player)
4105 7th St
Wyandotte, MI 48192-7109, USA

Bologna, Joseph (Actor, Director, Writer)
613 N Arden Dr
Beverly Hills, CA 90210-3509, USA

Bolstorff, Douglas (Athlete, Basketball Player)
1553 Skyline Ct
Saint Paul, MN 55121-1148, USA

Bolt, Jackson (Actor)
c/o Jack Scagnetti *Jack Scagnetti Agency*
5118 Vineland Ave
North Hollywood, CA 91601-3814, USA

Bolt, Jeremy (Producer)
c/o Ken Kamins *Key Creatives*
1800 N Highland Ave Fl 5
Los Angeles, CA 90028-4523, USA

Bolt, Mae (Athlete, Bowler)
1516 Robinhood Ln
La Grange Park, IL 60526-1129, USA

Bolt, Tommy (Athlete, Golfer)
8 Whispering Winds Tc
Cherokee Village, AR 72529, USA

Bolt, Usain (Athlete, Olympic Athlete, Track Athlete)
c/o Jason Hodes *William Morris Endeavor (NY)*
1325 Avenue of the Americas Fl 28
New York, NY 10019-6583, USA

Bolten, Joshua (Government Official)
Office of Management/Budget
Executive Office Building
Washington, DC 20503-0001, USA

Bolton, Michael (Musician, Songwriter)
c/o Erin Culley *Creative Artists Agency (CAA-LA)*
2000 Avenue of the Stars Ste 100
Los Angeles, CA 90067-4705, USA

Bolton, Rodney (Athlete, Baseball Player)
2195 Ooltewah Ringgold Rd
Ooltewah, TN 37363-9392, USA

Bolton, Ron (Athlete, Football Player)
408 Maiden Ln
Chesapeake, VA 23325-4607, USA

Bolton, Ruthie (Athlete, Basketball Player)
PO Box 188463
Sacramento, CA 95818-8463, USA

Bolton, Scott (Athlete, Football Player)
1635 Ashmoor Dr E
Mobile, AL 36695-4345, USA

Bolton, Tom (Athlete, Baseball Player)
2288 Rolling Hills Dr
Nolensville, TN 37135-9483, USA

Boltz, Ray (Musician)
c/o Staff Member *Ray Boltz Music*
1767 NE 16th St
Fort Lauderdale, FL 33304-1357, USA

Bolzan, Scott (Athlete, Football Player)
2074 E Linda Ln
Gilbert, AZ 85234-6210, USA

Bomback, Mark (Athlete, Baseball Player)
2482 Riverside Ave
Somerset, MA 02726-5149, USA

Bombard, Marc (Athlete, Baseball Player)
8612 Barkwood Pi
Tampa, FL 33615, USA

Bombardir, Brad (Athlete, Hockey Player)
Minnesota Wild
317 Washington St
Player Development
Saint Paul, MN 55102-1667, USA

Bomer, Matt (Actor)
444 S Rossmore Ave
Los Angeles, CA 90020-4742, USA

Bonaduce, Danny (Actor, Musician, Producer)
4039 Cromwell Ave
Los Angeles, CA 90027-1351, USA

Bonaly, Surya (Figure Skater)
c/o Staff Member *Champions on Ice*
3500 American Blvd W Ste 190
Minneapolis, MN 55431-4431, USA

Bonamassa, Joe (Musician)
c/o Andrew Lanoie *William Morris Endeavor (LA)*
9601 Wilshire Blvd
Beverly Hills, CA 90210-5213, USA

Bonamy, James (Musician)
Hallmark Direction
15 Music Sq W
Nashville, TN 37203-6200, USA

Bonanno, Louis (Louie) (Actor)
24822 Largo Dr
Laguna Hills, CA 92653-5356, USA

Bond, Christopher S (Kit) (Ex-Governor, Ex-Senator, Politician)
14 Jefferson Rd
Mexico, MO 65265-3732, USA

Bond, Larry (Writer)
c/o Robert Gottlieb *Trident Media Group LLC*
41 Madison Ave Fl 36
New York, NY 10010-2257, USA

Bond, Phillip (Phil) (Athlete, Basketball Player)
208 Northwestern Pkwy
Louisville, KY 40212-2732, USA

Bond, Samatha (Actor)
c/o Staff Member *Innovative Artists (LA)*
1505 10th St
Santa Monica, CA 90401-2805, USA

Bond, Walter (Athlete, Basketball Player)
3610 Gardens Pkwy Unit 303
Palm Beach Gardens, FL 33410-2788, USA

Bonderman, Jeremy (Athlete, Baseball Player)
=
10 Ridgeview Dr
Pasco, WA 99301-8808, USA

Bondra, Peter (Athlete, Hockey Player)
372 Carriage Park Way
Annapolis, MD 21401-7709, USA

Bonds, Barry (Athlete, Baseball Player)
3 Lagoon Dr Ste 400
Redwood City, CA 94065-5157, USA

Bonds, Gary U S (Music Group)
Entity Communications
875 Avenue of the Americas # 1908
New York, NY 10001-3507, USA

Bondurant, Bob (Race Car Driver)
Firebird Racing School
20 0 S Maricopa Rd
Box 5023
Chandler, AZ 85226, USA

Bondy, A.A. (Musician)
c/o Ken Weinstein *Big Hassle Media*
40 Exchange Pl Ste 1900
New York, NY 10005-2714, USA

Bone, Bizzy (Musician)
c/o Mary Bowlin *7th Sign Records*
145 Baker St
Marion, OH 43302-4111, USA

Boneham, Rupert (Reality Star)
c/o Staff Member *Abrams Artists Agency (NY)*
275 7th Ave Fl 26
New York, NY 10001-6708, USA

Bonehman, Rupert (Actor)
c/o Staff Member *Ruth Webb Enterprises*
10580 Des Moines Ave
Porter Ranch, CA 91326-2926, USA

Bonelli, Ernest (Athlete, Football Player)
1200 E Peppertree Ln Apt 602
Sarasota, FL 34242-8712, USA

Bonerz, Peter (Actor, Comedian, Director)
3637 Lowry Rd
Los Angeles, CA 90027-1435, USA

Bones, Ricky (Athlete, Baseball Player)
908 NW Looth Ave
Hollywood, FL 33024, USA

Bonet, Lisa (Actor)
1551 Will Geer Rd
Topanga, CA 90290-4291, USA

Boneta, Diego (Actor)
c/o Lena Roklin *Luber Roklin Management*
5815 W Sunset Blvd Ste 206
Los Angeles, CA 90028-6481, USA

Bone Thugs-N-Harmony (Music Group)
c/o Staff Member *Sony Music Entertainment*
555 Madison Ave
New York, NY 10022-3301, USA

Bong, Jung (Baseball Player)
Atlanta Braves
2917 Asteria Pointe
Duluth, GA 30097-5221, USA

Bongiovi, Tony (Producer)
Bongiovi Acoustics
649 SW Whitmore Dr
Port St Lucie, FL 34984-3567, USA

Bonham, Bill (Athlete, Baseball Player)
2135 Holly Ln
Solvang, CA 93463-2207, USA

Bonham, Jason (Musician)
10324 El Caballo Ct
Delray Beach, FL 33446-2712, USA

Bonham, Ron (Athlete, Basketball Player)
8020 S County Road 700 E
Selma, IN 47383-9621, USA

Bonham, Shane (Athlete, Football Player)
321 Clover Hill Rd
Maryville, TN 37801-9587, USA

Bonham, Tracy (Music Group, Songwriter)
c/o Staff Member *Paradigm (Monterey)*
404 W Franklin St
Monterey, CA 93940-2303, USA

Bonham Carter, Helena (Actor)
c/o Adam Isaacs *The Schiff Company*
9220 W Sunset Blvd Ste 106
West Hollywood, CA 90069-3500, USA

Bonikowski, Joe (Athlete, Baseball Player)
6701 Old Reid Rd
Charlotte, NC 28210-4622, USA

Bonilla, Juan (Athlete, Baseball Player)
2902 Orchidcrest Dr
Crestview, FL 32539-8528, USA

Bonilla, Roberto M A (Bobby) (Athlete, Baseball Player)
1403 Kenilworth St
Sarasota, FL 34231-3521, USA

Bonin, Brian (Athlete, Hockey Player)
2279 8th St
Saint Paul, MN 55110-2869, USA

Bonin, Celeste Beryl (Athlete, Wrestler)
c/o Staff Member *World Wrestling Entertainment (WWE)*
1241 E Main St
Titan Towers
Stamford, CT 06902-3520, USA

Bonin, Greg (Athlete, Baseball Player)
509 Boulder Creek Pkwy
Lafayette, LA 70508-1717, USA

Bonine, Eddie (Athlete, Baseball Player)
5809 W Plum Rd
Phoenix, AZ 85083-9346, USA

Boniol, Chris (Athlete, Football Player)
3413 Monaghan St
Dublin, CA 94568-4569, USA

Bonjour, Daniel (Actor)
c/o Staff Member *Tinoco Management*
8033 W Sunset Blvd Ste 573
Los Angeles, CA 90046-2401, USA

Bon Jovi, Jon (Actor, Musician, Songwriter)
740 Navesink River Rd
Red Bank, NJ 07701, USA

Bonk, Radek (Athlete, Hockey Player)
137 Allenhurst Cir
Franklin, TN 37067-7272, USA

Bonnaire, Sandrine (Actor)
36 Rue De Ponthieu
Paris, FR F-750

Bonnell, Barry (Athlete, Baseball Player)
2102 179th Ct NE
Redmond, WA 98052-6064, USA

Bonner, Alan (Athlete, Football Player)
c/o Bus Cook *Bus Cook Sports, Inc*
1 Willow Bend Dr
Hattiesburg, MS 39402-8552, USA

Bonner, Anthony (Athlete, Basketball Player)
5854 Elmbank Ave
Saint Louis, MO 63120-1116, USA

Bonner, Bobby (Athlete, Baseball Player)
990 Manitou Rd
Hilton, NY 14468-9390, USA

Bonner, Frank (Actor)
Stone Manners
6500 Wilshire Blvd # 550
Los Angeles, CA 90048-4920, USA

Bonner, Jo (Congressman, Politician)
2236 Rayburn Hob
Washington, DC 20515-3312, USA

Bonner, Melvin (Athlete, Football Player)
415 N Beauregard St Apt 16
Alvin, TX 77511-2107, USA

Bonness, Rik (Athlete, Football Player)
18914 Boyle Cir
Elkhorn, NE 68022-3953, USA

Bonneville, Hugh (Actor)
c/o Staff Member *Paradigm (LA)*
360 N Crescent Dr
North Bldg
Beverly Hills, CA 90210-4874, USA

Bono (Musician, Songwriter)
145 Central Park W # 27E/ PMB 28E
New York, NY 10023-6296, USA

Bono, Chaz (Actor, Musician, Writer)
c/o Howard Bragman *Fifteen Minutes (LA)*
8436 W 3rd St Ste 650
Los Angeles, CA 90048-4131, USA

Bono, Steven C (Steve) (Athlete, Football Player)
1100 Hamilton Ave
Palo Alto, CA 94301-2216, USA

Bonoff, Karla (Musician, Songwriter)
2122 E Valley Rd
Santa Barbara, CA 93108-1513, USA

Bono Mack, Mary (Congressman, Politician)
104 Cannon Hob
Washington, DC 20515-0916, USA

Bonsall, Joe (Musician)
100 Surrey Hill Pt
Hendersonville, TN 37075-5212, USA

Bonsalle, George (Athlete, Basketball Player)
11804 Del Rey Ave NE
Albuquerque, NM 87122-2417, USA

Bonser, Boof (Athlete, Baseball Player)
1004 Colonel Ledyard Hwy
Ledyard, CT 06339-1104, USA

Bonsignore, Jason (Athlete, Hockey Player)
2152 Edgemere Dr
Rochester, NY 14612-1102, USA

Bontemps, Ron (Athlete, Basketball Player, Olympic Athlete)
133 S Illinois Ave
Morton, IL 61550-2683, USA

Bonvicini, Joan (Athlete, Basketball Player, Coach)
University of Arizona
McKale Memorial Center
Atheletic Dept
Tucson, AZ 85721-0001, USA

Bonvie, Dennis (Athlete, Hockey Player)
54 Grandville Dr
Kingston, PA 18704-1251, USA

Boo, Jim (Athlete, Hockey Player)
416 4th St S
Stillwater, MN 55082-4912, USA

Boo, Katherine (Journalist, Writer)
c/o Staff Member *Random House Publicity*
1745 Broadway
New York, NY 10019-4640, USA

Booher, Paul (Race Car Driver)
653 Powers Dr
El Dorado Hills, CA 95762-4443, USA

Book, Asher (Actor)
c/o Bryan Leder *Management 101*
11271 Ventura Blvd # 102
Studio City, CA 91604-3136, USA

Booka Shade (Music Group)
c/o Joel Zimmerman *William Morris Endeavor (NY)*
1325 Avenue of the Americas
New York, NY 10019-6026, USA

Booker, Buddy (Athlete, Baseball Player)
PO Box 59
Brookneal, VA 24528-0059, USA

Booker, Butch (Athlete, Basketball Player)
305 Barker Ave
Lansdowne, PA 19050-1215, USA

Booker, Chris (Athlete, Baseball Player)
2052 Perryville Rd
Monroeville, AL 36460-6852, USA

Booker, Chris (Correspondent)
c/o Staff Member *Entertainment Tonight (ET)*
4024 Radford Ave
Studio City, CA 91604-2101, USA

Booker, Greg (Athlete, Baseball Player)
1535 Charleigh Ct
Elon, NC 27244-9770, USA

Booker, Marty (Athlete, Football Player)
15982 SW 11th St
Pembroke Pines, FL 33027-5051, USA

Booker, Rod (Athlete, Baseball Player)
526 W Altadena Dr
Altadena, CA 91001-4204, USA

Booker, Vaughn (Athlete, Football Player)
56 E Mitchell Ave
Cincinnati, OH 45217-1520, USA

Booko, Daniel (Actor)
c/o Glenn Hughes III *Gem Entertainment Group*
10920 Wilshire Blvd Ste 150
Los Angeles, CA 90024-3990, USA

Bookwalter, JR (Director)
PO Box 6573
Akron, OH 44312-0573, USA

Boom, Benn (Actor)
c/o Staff Member *William Morris Endeavor (LA)*
9601 Wilshire Blvd
Beverly Hills, CA 90210-5213, USA

Boomer, Linwood (Producer)
c/o Rick Rosen *William Morris Endeavor (LA)*
9601 Wilshire Blvd
Beverly Hills, CA 90210-5213, USA

Boone, Aaron (Athlete, Baseball Player)
10111 E Phantom Way
Scottsdale, AZ 85255-6696, USA

Boone, Alfonso (Athlete, Football Player)
14290 W Lyle Ct
Libertyville, IL 60048-4835, USA

Boone, Bob (Athlete, Baseball Player)
1432 Misty Sea Way
San Marcos, CA 92078-1010, USA

Boone, Bret (Athlete, Baseball Player)
804 Midori Ct
Solana Beach, CA 92075-1291, USA

Boone, Danny (Athlete, Baseball Player)
320 Minnesota Ave
El Cajon, CA 92020-6118, USA

Boone, Debby (Actor, Musician)
4334 Kester Ave
Sherman Oaks, CA 91403-4135, USA

Boone, Greg (Athlete, Football Player)
604 Talwood Cir Apt B
Brandon, FL 33510-3605

Boone, James (Athlete, Football Player)
2529 Butler Bay Dr N
Windermere, FL 34786-6111, USA

Boone, Jim (Athlete, Football Player)
2529 Butler Bay Dr N
Windermere, FL 34786-6111, USA

Boone, Lesley (Actor)
12523 Landale St
Studio City, CA 91604-1306, USA

Boone, Pat (Actor, Musician)
904 N Beverly Dr
Beverly Hills, CA 90210-2913, USA

Boone, Ron (Athlete, Basketball Player)
2200 S 100 E
Salt Lake City, UT 84106, USA

Boone, Steve (Music Group, Musician)
Pipeline Artists Mgmt
620 16th Ave S
Hopkins, MN 55343-7833, USA

Boone Junior, Mark (Actor)
c/o Michael Greenwald *Don Buchwald &
Associates (LA)*
6500 Wilshire Blvd Ste 2200
Los Angeles, CA 90048-4942, USA

Booras, Steve (Athlete, Football Player)
1441 Parkhill Dr
Billings, MT 59102-3147, USA

Boorem, Mika (Actor)
129 N Lincoln St
Burbank, CA 91506-2304, USA

Booros, James (Athlete, Golfer)
2615 W Pennsylvania St
Allentown, PA 18104-2921, USA

Boortz, Neal (Radio Personality)
1601 W Peachtree St NE
Atlanta, GA 30309-2641, USA

Boose, Dorian (Athlete, Football Player)
1630 NE Valley Rd
Apt K102T Ct
Pullman, WA 99163-4400, USA

Boosler, Elayne (Actor, Comedian)
11061 Wrightwood Ln
Studio City, CA 91604-3959, USA

Bootcheck, Chris (Athlete, Baseball
Player)
6105 Lakeaires Dr
Cumming, GA 30040-1109, USA

Booth, Adrian (Actor)
3922 Glenridge Dr
Sherman Oaks, CA 91423-4645, USA

Booth, Brad (Athlete, Football Player)
2201 W 229th Pi
Torrance, CA 90501, USA

Booth, Calvin (Athlete, Basketball Player)
6001 E Horseshoe Rd
Paradise Valley, AZ 85253-8125, USA

Booth, Clarence (Athlete, Football Player)
33 Cor Dale Ct
Lafayette, IN 47904-1043, USA

Booth, David (Athlete, Hockey Player)
Octagon Sports Management
5110 Crystal Creek Ln
Washington, MI 48094-4238, USA

Booth, George (Cartoonist)
PO Box 1539
Stony Brook, NY 11790-0830, USA

Booth, Kellee (Athlete, Golfer)
4804 Goldeneyes Ln
McKinney, TX 75070-9037, USA

Booth, Kristin (Actor)
c/o Vicki McCarty *Covington International*
4237 Morro Dr
Woodland Hills, CA 91364-5521, USA

Booth, Lindy (Actor)
c/o Christopher Wright *Christopher
Wright Management*
3207 Winnie Dr
Los Angeles, CA 90068-1439, USA

Boothe, Kevin (Athlete, Football Player)
12100 NW 18th St
Plantation, FL 33323-2120, USA

Boothe, Powers (Actor)
23629 Long Valley Rd
Hidden Hills, CA 91302-2406, USA

Boothie, Powers (Actor)
23629 Long Valley Rd
Hidden Hills, CA 91302-2406, USA

Booty, John (Athlete, Football Player)
1408 Flatwood Ct
Crofton, MD 21114-1440, USA

Booty, Josh (Athlete, Baseball Player)
6248 N Windermere Dr
Shreveport, LA 71129-3423, USA

Boozer, Carlos (Athlete, Basketball Player)
c/o Rob Pelinka *Landmark Sports Agency*
881 N Park View Dr
El Segundo, CA 90245-4932, USA

Boozer, Emerson (Athlete, Football Player)
25 Windham Dr
Huntington Station, NY 11746-4541, USA

Boozman, John
320 Hart Senate Office Building
Washington, DC 20510-0001, USA

Borbon, Julio (Athlete, Baseball Player)
522 Vinings Oaks Run
Mableton, GA 30126-7239, USA

Borchard, Joe (Athlete, Baseball Player)
712 Camino Del Sol
Newbury Park, CA 91320-6701, USA

Borchardt, Jon (Athlete, Football Player)
18815 201st Ave NE
Woodinville, WA 98077-5953, USA

Borchelt, Earl (Athlete, Olympic Athlete,
Rower)
7 Blueberry Ln
Sterling, MA 01564-2143, USA

Borcky, Dennis (Athlete, Football Player)
18 Weathervane Rd
Aston, PA 19014-2616, USA

Bordano, Chris (Athlete, Football Player)
2788 Morning Moon
New Braunfels, TX 78132-4785, USA

Bordelon, Ben (Athlete, Football Player)
PO Box 250
Lockport, LA 70374-0250, USA

Bordelon, Kenneth (Athlete, Football
Player)
1224 Octavia St
New Orleans, LA 70115-4223, USA

Borden, Amanda (Gymnast)
Cincinnati Gymnastics Acadamy
3536 Woodridge Blvd
Fairfield, OH 45014, USA

Borden, Lynn (Actor)
Associated Artists
6399 Wilshire Blvd Ste 211
Los Angeles, CA 90048-5705, USA

Borden, Robert (Producer)
c/o Staff Member *United Talent Agency
(UTA-LA)*
9336 Civic Center Dr
Beverly Hills, CA 90210-3604, USA

Borden, Scott (Actor)
c/o Staff Member *Progressive Artists
Agency*
1041 N Formosa Ave
West Hollywood, CA 90046-6703, USA

Borden, Steve (Sting) (Athlete, Wrestler)
c/o Steve Martinez *Stonewood
Entertainment*
Prefers to be contacted by telephone or
email
Los Angeles, CA, USA

Borders, Nate (Athlete, Football Player)
950 Franklin St
Winchester, VA 22601-5810, USA

Borders, Pat (Athlete, Baseball Player,
Olympic Athlete)
2650 Burns Ave
Lake Wales, FL 33898-7947, USA

Bordi, Rich (Athlete, Baseball Player)
1133 Hailey Ct
Rohnert Park, CA 94928-1875, USA

Bordick, Mike (Athlete, Baseball Player)
1724 Circle Rd
Towson, MD 21204-6412, USA

Bordley, Bill (Athlete, Baseball Player)
39 Moccasin Ln
Rolling Hills Estates, CA 90274-2506,
USA

Boreanaz, David (Actor)
5739 Penland Rd
Hidden Hills, CA 91302-2443, USA

Borel, Calvin (Jockey)
16502 Briston Avon Ln
Louisville, KY 40245-4280, USA

Boren, Dan (Congressman, Politician)
2447 Rayburn Hob
Washington, DC 20515-4203, USA

Boren, David L (Ex-Governor, Ex-Senator)
University of Oklahoma
President's Office, Evans Hall, Room 101
660 Parrington Oval
Norman, OK 73019-0001, USA

Boren, Matt (Actor)
c/o Steven Jensen *Independent Group,
The*
6363 Wilshire Blvd Ste 115
Los Angeles, CA 90048-5734, USA

Borg-Aplin, Lorraine (Baseball Player)
5827 Laverne Cir Apt 2
Baxter, MN 56425-8231, USA

Borgeson, Don (Athlete, Hockey Player)
2211 Highway 49 W
Ashland City, TN 37015-5001, USA

Borghi, Frank (Soccer Player)
4123 Poepping St
Saint Louis, MO 63123-7726, USA

Borgmann, Glenn (Athlete, Baseball
Player)
16 Lundy Ter
Butler, NJ 07405-1926, USA

Borgognone, Dirk (Athlete, Football
Player)
29601 NE 173rd St
Duvall, WA 98019-8615, USA

Boris, Angel (Actor)
c/o Staff Member *Acme Talent & Literary
(LA)*
1400 Atlantic Ave Ste 274
Long Beach, CA 90813-2013, USA

Boris, Paul (Athlete, Baseball Player)
28 Sunnyside Ln
Hillsborough, NJ 08844-4738, USA

Bork, Erik (Producer, Writer)
c/o Staff Member *Creative Artists Agency
(CAA-LA)*
2000 Avenue of the Stars Ste 100
Los Angeles, CA 90067-4705, USA

Bork, Frank (Athlete, Baseball Player)
8488 Dunsinane Dr
Dublin, OH 43017-9420, USA

Bork, George (Athlete, Football Player)
7316 Coventry Dr S
Spring Grove, IL 60081-9379, USA

Borkowski, Bob (Athlete, Baseball Player)
1031 Gerhard St
Dayton, OH 45404-2052, USA

Borkowski, David (Dave) (Athlete,
Baseball Player)
2124 McIntosh Dr
Holland, OH 43528-7930, USA

Borland, Toby (Athlete, Baseball Player)
8642 Quitman Hwy
Quitman, LA 71268-1282, USA

Borland, Tom (Athlete, Baseball Player)
624 W Cherokee Ave
Stillwater, OK 74075-1405, USA

Borland, Wes (Musician)
8464 Brier Dr
Los Angeles, CA 90046-1908, USA

Borle, Christian (Actor)
c/o Peter Kiernan *Management 360*
9111 Wilshire Blvd
Beverly Hills, CA 90210-5508, USA

Borlenghi, Matthew (Actor)
16327 Blackhawk St
Granada Hills, CA 91344-6816, USA

Borman, Frank (Astronaut, Business
Person)
PO Box 64
Bighorn, MT 59010-0064, USA

Born, Ruth (Athlete, Baseball Player,
Commentator)
3307 Pines Village Cir Apt 183
Valparaiso, IN 46383-2671, USA

Bornheimer, Kyle (Actor, Comedian)
611 Lorraine Blvd
Los Angeles, CA 90005-3610, USA

Bornstein, Jonathan (Athlete, Soccer
Player)
c/o Lyle York *Proactive Sports
Management USA*
3233 M St NW
Washington, DC 20007-3556, USA

Borntrager, Mary Christner (Writer)
c/o Staff Member *Herald Press*
1251 Virginia Ave
Harrisonburg, VA 22802-2434, USA

Boros, Guy (Athlete, Golfer)
2900 NE 40th St
Ft Lauderdale, FL 33308-5743, USA

Borowski, Joe (Athlete, Baseball Player)
13782 E Gail Rd
Scottsdale, AZ 85259-4642, USA

Borrego, Jesse (Actor)
c/o Kay Liberman *Liberman/Zerman
Management*
252 N Larchmont Blvd Ste 200
Los Angeles, CA 90004-3754, USA

Borresen, Richard (Athlete, Football
Player)
2291 Jefferson St
East Meadow, NY 11554-1907, USA

Borris, Angel (Actor)
c/o Lara Rosenstock *Lara Rosenstock Management*
8371 Blackburn Ave Apt 1
Los Angeles, CA 90048-4245, USA

Borsavage, Ike (Athlete, Basketball Player)
219 Doris Ave
Southampton, PA 18966-2771, USA

Borstein, Alex (Actor)
c/o Brandon Liebman *William Morris Endeavor (LA)*
9601 Wilshire Blvd
Beverly Hills, CA 90210-5213, USA

Borth, Michelle (Actor)
c/o Mark Rousso *New Wave Entertainment (LA)*
2660 W Olive Ave
Burbank, CA 91505-4525, USA

Bortles, Blake (Athlete, Football Player)
c/o Ryan Tollner *REP 1 Sports Group*
2 Corporate Park Ste 106
Irvine, CA 92606-5103, USA

Bortnick, Ethan (Actor, Musician)
c/o Michael Katcher *Creative Artists Agency (CAA-LA)*
2000 Avenue of the Stars Ste 100
Los Angeles, CA 90067-4705, USA

Borton, Della (D B) (Writer)
Ohio Wesleyan University
Dept of English
Delaware, OH 43015, USA

Bortz, Mark (Athlete, Football Player)
PO Box 3504
Quincy, IL 62305-3504, USA

Boryla, Mike (Athlete, Football Player)
1220 Purple Sage Loop
Castle Rock, CO 80104-7845, USA

Boryla, Vince (Athlete, Basketball Player, Olympic Athlete)
5577 S Emporia Cir
Greenwood Village, CO 80111-3543, USA

Borysenko, Joan (Doctor, Writer)
Mind-Body Health Sciences Inc
393 Dixon Rd
Boulder, CO 80302-9769, USA

Bosa, John (Athlete, Football Player)
2101 NE 21st St
Ft Lauderdale, FL 33305-2522, USA

Bosarge, Wade (Athlete, Football Player)
8366 Via Rosa
Orlando, FL 32836-8788, USA

Bosch, Don (Athlete, Baseball Player)
14446 N State Highway 3
Fort Jones, CA 96032-9773, USA

Boschetti, Ryan (Athlete, Football Player)
120 23rd Ave
San Mateo, CA 94403-2204, USA

Boschman, Ed (Religious Leader)
Mennonite Brethren Churches General Conference
PO Box 347
Newton, KS 67114-0347, USA

Bosco, Philip (Actor)
Judy Schoen
606 N Larchmont Blvd Ste 309
Los Angeles, CA 90004-1309, USA

Bose, Eleanora (Model)
I M G Models
304 Park Ave S # 1200
New York, NY 10010-4301, USA

Bose III, Tony (Athlete, Football Player)
6 Glendenning Ln
Houston, TX 77024-6827, USA

Boselli, Tony (Athlete, Football Player)
356 San Juan Dr
Ponte Vedra Beach, FL 32082-2821, USA

Boseman, Chadwick (Actor)
c/o Darin Friedman *Management 360*
9111 Wilshire Blvd
Beverly Hills, CA 90210-5508, USA

Bosetti, Rick (Athlete, Baseball Player)
1471 Arroyo Manor Dr
Redding, CA 96003-9215, USA

Bosh, Chris (Athlete, Basketball Player)
16670 Via La Costa
Pacific Palisades, CA 90272-1950, USA

Bosio, Chris (Athlete, Baseball Player)
Lawrence University
821 Rundquist Way
Attn: Baseball Office
Kimberly, WI 54136-2348, USA

Boskie, Shawn (Athlete, Baseball Player)
10220 N 55th St
Paradise Valley, AZ 85253-1168, USA

Boskin, Michael J (Government Official)
Stanford University
Hoover Instution
Stanford, CA 94305, USA

Bosley, Thad (Athlete, Baseball Player)
20660 Stevens Creek Blvd
Cupertino, CA 95014-2120, USA

Bosman, Dick (Athlete, Baseball Player)
1211 Sid Sites Rd
Irmo, SC 29063-9643, USA

Boso, Casper (Athlete, Football Player)
8811 Calumet Dr
Indianapolis, IN 46236-9031, USA

Bosseler, Don J (Athlete, Football Player)
7782 SW 54th Ave
Miami, FL 33143-5851, USA

Bosson, Barbara (Actor)
742 Milwood Ave
Venice, CA 90291-3829, USA

Bostic, Jeff (Athlete, Football Player)
8250 Royal Saint Georges Ln
Duluth, GA 30097-1649, USA

Bostic, Jim (Athlete, Basketball Player)
111 Valentine Ln Apt 2D
Yonkers, NY 10705-3426, USA

Bostic, Joe (Athlete, Football Player)
3507 Bromley Wood Ln
Greensboro, NC 27410-2182, USA

Bostic, John (Athlete, Football Player)
611 Canaveral Ave
Titusville, FL 32796-7615, USA

Bostic, Jon (Athlete, Football Player)
c/o Tony Paige *Perennial Sports and Entertainment*
1455 Pennsylvania Ave NW Ste 225
Washington, DC 20004-1026, USA

Bostic, Keith (Athlete, Football Player)
2419 Duchess Way
Stafford, TX 77477-6227, USA

Bostick, Brandon (Athlete, Football Player)
c/o Blake Baratz *The Institute for Athletes*
3600 Minnesota Dr Ste 550
Minneapolis, MN 55435-7925, USA

Boston (Music Group, Musician)
c/o Staff Member *Agency for the Performing Arts (APA-LA)*
405 S Beverly Dr Ste 500
Beverly Hills, CA 90212-4425, USA

Boston, Daryl (Athlete, Baseball Player)
3136 Northchester Pl
Lithonia, GA 30038-2292, USA

Boston, David (Athlete, Football Player)
5580 SW 104th Ter
Cooper City, FL 33328-5635, USA

Boston, Lawrence (Athlete, Basketball Player)
93 Greencliff Dr
Bedford, OH 44146-3439, USA

Boston, McKinley (Athlete, Football Player)
1986 Coyote Ridge Dr
Las Cruces, NM 88011-4042, us

Boston, Rachel (Actor)
c/o Vera Mihailovich *Forward Entertainment*
9255 W Sunset Blvd Ste 805
West Hollywood, CA 90069-3305, USA

Boston, Ralph (Athlete, Olympic Athlete)
3301 Woodbine Ave
Knoxville, TN 37914-4448, USA

Boston, Tre (Athlete, Football Player)
c/o Bus Cook *Bus Cook Sports, Inc*
1 Willow Bend Dr
Hattiesburg, MS 39402-8552, USA

Bostridge, Ian (Musician)
c/o Staff Member *ICM Partners (LA)*
10250 Constellation Blvd Fl 7
Los Angeles, CA 90067-6207, USA

Bostrom, Zachary (Actor)
Kazarian/Spencer
11365 Ventura Blvd Ste 100
Box 7403
Studio City, CA 91604-3148

Bostwick, Barry (Actor, Musician)
c/o Staff Member *Vanguard Management Group*
8060 Melrose Ave Fl 4
Los Angeles, CA 90046-7038, USA

Bostwick, Dunbar (Race Car Driver)
1623 Dewey Ave
Pompano Beach, FL 33060, USA

Bostwick, Jackson
Shazam!
PO Box 1452
Mount Juliet, TN 37121-1452, USA

Boswell, Ken (Athlete, Baseball Player)
1103 Live Oak Dr
Marble Falls, TX 78654-7258, USA

Boswell, Thomas M (Writer)
Washington Post
1150 15th St NW
Washington, DC 20071-0002, USA

Boswell, Tom (Athlete, Basketball Player)
341 N Anton Dr
Montgomery, AL 36105-2112, USA

Bosworth, Brian (Actor, Athlete, Football Player)
4400 Arlen Ct
Plano, TX 75093-6701, USA

Bosworth, Kate (Actor)
2633 La Cuesta Dr
Los Angeles, CA 90046-1336, USA

Bosworth, Lauren (Lo) (Reality Star)
c/o Nicole Perez-Krueger *PMK/BNC Public Relations (PMK-LA)*
8687 Melrose Ave Ste 8
West Hollywood, CA 90069-5746, USA

Botchan, Ron (Athlete, Football Player)
55 Toscana Way E
Rancho Mirage, CA 92270-1977, USA

Botelho, Derek (Athlete, Baseball Player)
1819 Orchard St
Burlington, IA 52601-6136, USA

Botha, Francois (Frans) (Boxer)
White Buffalo
PO Box 3982
Clearwater Beach, FL 33767-8982, USA

Botkin, Kirk (Athlete, Football Player)
1414 Pinemont Dr
Columbia, SC 29206-4420, USA

Botsford, Beth (Athlete, Olympic Athlete, Swimmer)
2210 River Bend Ct
White Hall, MD 21161-9214, USA

Botsford, Sara (Actor)
Kordek Agency
8490 W Sunset Blvd # 403
West Hollywood, CA 90069-1912, USA

Bottalico, Ricky (Athlete, Baseball Player)
37 Valley View Dr
Newington, CT 06111-5309, USA

Bottenfield, Kent (Athlete, Baseball Player)
12168 142nd Ct N
West Palm Beach, FL 33418-7901, USA

Botterill, Jason (Athlete, Hockey Player)
5315 Westminster Pl
Pittsburgh, PA 15232-2120, USA

Botti, Chris (Musician)
c/o Bobby Colomby *The Colomby Group*
2110 Main St Ste 302
Santa Monica, CA 90405-2276, USA

Botting, Ralph (Athlete, Baseball Player)
7 Somerset
Trabuco Canyon, CA 92679-3701, USA

Bottom, Joe (Swimmer)
PO Box 3840
Chico, CA 95927-3840, USA

Bottom, Joseph (Athlete, Olympic Athlete, Swimmer)
374 Spanish Garden Dr
Chico, CA 95928-8869, USA

Bottoms, Joseph (Actor)
c/o Belle Zwerdling *B and B Management*
9696 Culver Blvd Ste 110
Culver City, CA 90232-2737, USA

Bottoms, Timothy (Actor)
PO Box 15559
Sn Luis Obisp, CA 93406-5559, USA

Bottrell, David Dean (Actor, Writer)
c/o Alan Gasmer *Alan Gasmer Management Company*
10877 Wilshire Blvd Ste 603
Los Angeles, CA 90024-4348, USA

Botts, Jason (Athlete, Baseball Player)
405 Peachtree Ln
Paso Robles, CA 93446-2869, USA

Botts, Mike (Athlete, Football Player)
PO Box 247
105 S Market St
Elizabethville, PA 17023-0247, USA

Botz, Bob (Athlete, Baseball Player)
2459 N Ranch Estates Blvd
New Braunfels, TX 78130-9124, USA

Boucha, Henry (Athlete, Hockey Player, Olympic Athlete)
7200 Biglerville Cir
Anchorage, AK 99507-2885, USA

Bouchard, Dan (Athlete, Hockey Player)
3111 Hillsdale Ct SE
Marietta, GA 30067-5431, USA

Bouchard, Daniel (Athlete, Hockey Player)
3111 Hillsdale Ct SE
Marietta, GA 30067-5431, USA

Bouchard, Ken (Race Car Driver)
PO Box 60
Thompson, CT 06277-0060, USA

Bouchard, Pierre-Marc (Athlete, Hockey Player)
7950 Jones Branch Dr
Mc Lean, VA 22102-3302, USA

Bouchard, Ron (Race Car Driver)
300 Lunenburg St
Fitchburg, MA 01420-4504, USA

Bouchee, Ed (Athlete, Baseball Player)
1621 E Tremaine Ave
Gilbert, AZ 85234-8140, USA

Boucher, Brian (Athlete, Hockey Player)
416 Overhill Rd
Haddonfield, NJ 08033-3822, USA

Boucher, Guy (Athlete, Hockey Player)
5224 Paylor Ln
Lakewood Ranch, FL 34240-2204, USA

Boucher, Guy (Athlete, Hockey Player)
Tampa Bay Lightning
401 Channelside Dr
Attn Coaching Staff
Tampa, FL 33602-5400, USA

Boucher, Savannah (Actor)
H W A Talent
3500 W Olive Ave Ste 1400
Burbank, CA 91505-5512, USA

Bouchez, Elodie (Actor)
c/o Scott Zimmerman Evolution
Entertainment (LA)
901 N Highland Ave
Los Angeles, CA 90038-2412, USA

Bouck, Brittany Paige (Actor)
c/o Henry Penner Penner PR
8225 Santa Monica Blvd
West Hollywood, CA 90046-5912

Boudia, David (Athlete, Olympic Athlete)
USA Diving Inc
201 S Capitol Ave
Pan American Plaza #430
Indianapolis, IN 46225-1000, USA

Boudreau, Bruce (Athlete, Hockey Player)
PO Box 27280
Anaheim, CA 92809-0108, USA

Boudreau, Bruce (Athlete, Hockey Player)
627 N Glebe Rd Ste 850
Attn: Coaching Staff
Arlington, VA 22203-2144, United States

Bouette, Marc (Athlete, Football Player)
8787 Sienna Springs Blvd Apt 334
Missouri City, TX 77459-6070, USA

Bouggess, Lee (Athlete, Football Player)
121 Christmas Tree Ct
Sicklerville, NJ 08081-9441, USA

Boukadakis, Joey (Director, Producer, Writer)
c/o Michael Lasker Mosaic Media Group
9200 W Sunset Blvd Ste 10
West Hollywood, CA 90069-3608, USA

Boulanger, Pierre (Actor)
c/o Paul Nelson Mosaic Media Group
9200 W Sunset Blvd Ste 10
West Hollywood, CA 90069-3608, USA

Bouldin, Carl (Athlete, Baseball Player)
42 Fairway Dr
Southgate, KY 41071-3024, USA

Boulerice, Jesse (Athlete, Hockey Player)
249 Waterville St
Raleigh, NC 27603-1989, USA

Boulos, Frenchy (Soccer Player)
20 Elvin St
Staten Island, NY 10314-4049, USA

Boulton, Eric (Athlete, Hockey Player)
41 Cove Rd
Huntington, NY 11743-2251, USA

Boulud, Daniel (Chef)
Daniel Restaurant
60 E 65th St
New York, NY 10065-7056, USA

Boulware, Michael (Athlete, Football Player)
c/o Eugene Parker Maximum Sports
Management
6435 W Jefferson Blvd # 197
Fort Wayne, IN 46804-6203, USA

Boulware, Peter (Athlete, Football Player)
305 Leaning Tree Rd
Columbia, SC 29223-3010, USA

Bouman, Todd (Athlete, Football Player)
3070 Dartmouth Dr
Excelsior, MN 55331-7849, USA

Bourbeau, Allen (Athlete, Hockey Player, Olympic Athlete)
2210 Robinswood Rd
Titusville, FL 32780-4513, USA

Bourbonnais, Claude (Race Car Driver)
122 S Southgate Dr
Chandler, AZ 85226-3204, USA

Bourbonnais, Rick (Athlete, Hockey Player)
643 E Parkway Ct
Boise, ID 83706-6526, USA

Bourbonnais, Rick (Athlete, Hockey Player)
643 E Parkway Ct
Boise, ID 83706-6526, USA

Bource, Ludovic (Musician)
c/o Vasi Vangelos First Artists
Management
4764 Park Granada Ste 210
Calabasas, CA 91302-3333, USA

Bourdain, Anthony (Chef, Television Host)
40 E 94th St # 2HJ
New York, NY 10128-0709, USA

Bourdian, Anthony (Chef)
Food Network
1180 Avenue of the Americas Ste 1220 # 1200
New York, NY 10036-8406, USA

Boures, Emil (Athlete, Football Player)
426 W Swissvale Ave
Pittsburgh, PA 15218-1637, USA

Bourgeois, Jason (Athlete, Baseball Player)
16755 Ella Blvd Apt 245
Ant 178
Houston, TX 77090-4217, USA

Bourgeois, Steve (Athlete, Baseball Player)
PO Box 143
Paulina, LA 70763-0143, USA

Bourgoin, Louise (Actor)
c/o Jessica Kovacevic William Morris
Endeavor (LA)
9601 Wilshire Blvd
Beverly Hills, CA 90210-5213, USA

Bourjos, Chris (Athlete, Baseball Player)
10345 E Dreyfus Ave
Scottsdale, AZ 85260-9006, USA

Bourjos, Peter (Athlete, Baseball Player)
3872 E Melinda Dr
Phoenix, AZ 85050-4999, USA

Bourn, Michael (Athlete, Baseball Player)
24604 Belvon Valley Ln
Porter, TX 77365-5743, USA

Bourne, JR (Actor)
c/o John Elliott Mosaic Media Group
9200 W Sunset Blvd Ste 10
West Hollywood, CA 90069-3608, USA

Bourne, Shae-Lynn (Figure Skater)
Connecticut Skating Center
300 Alumni Rd
Newington, CT 06111-1868, USA

Bournigal, Rafael (Athlete, Baseball Player)
230 Canterwood Ln
Mulberry, FL 33860-7637, USA

Bourque, Pat (Athlete, Baseball Player)
PO Box 17593
Munds Park, AZ 86017-7593, USA

Bourque, Phil (Athlete, Hockey Player)
5117 Yale Dr
Aliquippa, PA 15001-4949, USA

Bourque, Phil (Athlete, Hockey Player)
Pittsburgh Penguins
66 Mario Lemieux Pl Ste 2
Attn: Broadcast Dept
Pittsburgh, PA 15219-3504, USA

Bourque, Raymond J (Athlete, Hockey Player)
Tresca Restaurant
233 Hanover St
Boston, MA 02113-2310, USA

Bourret, Caprice (Actor)
c/o Nadja Koglin Richard Schwartz
Management
2934 1/2 N Beverly Glen Cir # 107
Los Angeles, CA 90077-1724, USA

Boushka, Dick (Athlete, Basketball Player, Olympic Athlete)
9844 Cypresswood Dr Apt 209
Houston, TX 77070-3822, USA

Boutiette, K C (Athlete, Olympic Athlete, Speed Skater)
1911 E 72nd St
Tacoma, WA 98404-5408, USA

Bouton, Jim (Athlete, Baseball Player)
PO Box 909
Great Barrington, MA 01230-0909, USA

Boutte, Denise (Actor)
c/o Charles Newman Newman-Thomas
Management
8306 Wilshire Blvd # 996
Beverly Hills, CA 90211-2304, USA

Boutte, Marc (Athlete, Football Player)
906 Derby Ln
Missouri City, TX 77489-3260, us

Boutwell, Thomas (Athlete, Football Player)
32353 Oaken Wood St
Denham Springs, LA 70726-1666, USA

Boutwell, Tommy (Athlete, Football Player)
32353 Oaken Wood St
Denham Springs, LA 70726-1666, us

Bouvia, Gloria (Bowler)
2827 SW Corbeth Ln
Troutdale, OR 97060-3137, USA

Bouyer, Willie (Athlete, Football Player)
6560 Chesterbrook Dr
Elk Grove, CA 95758-6326, USA

Bouza, Matt (Athlete, Football Player)
1042 Via Nueva
Lafayette, CA 94549-2726, USA

Bouzeos, Phil (Athlete, Football Player)
2001 S Meyers Rd Apt 302
Oakbrook Terrace, IL 60181-5271, USA

Bova, Raoul (Actor)
c/o Alan Siegel Alan Siegel Entertainment
9200 W Sunset Blvd Ste 407
West Hollywood, CA 90069-3511, USA

Bovee, Mike (Athlete, Baseball Player)
11405 Affinity Ct Unit 236
San Diego, CA 92131-2718, USA

Boven, Don (Athlete, Basketball Player)
4434 Garth Rd
Charlottesville, VA 22901-5103, USA

Bovey, Terry (Athlete, Baseball Player)
7700 E Speedway Blvd Apt 206
Tucson, AZ 85710-1619, usa

Bowa, Lawrence R (Larry) (Athlete, Baseball Player, Coach)
302 Overlook Ln
Conshohocken, PA 19428-2634, USA

Bowab, John (Actor)
2598 Greenvalley Rd
Los Angeles, CA 90046-1438, USA

Bowdell III, Gordon (Athlete, Football Player)
10929 Stoney Point Dr
South Lyon, MI 48178-9296, USA

Bowden, Craig (Athlete, Golfer)
1101 E Benson Ct
Bloomington, IN 47401-8828, USA

Bowden, James (Commentator)
2333 Indian River Blvd Apt 501
Vero Beach, FL 32960-5295, USA

Bowden, Joe (Athlete, Football Player)
7026 Thistlewood Park Ct
Katy, TX 77494-4252, us

Bowden, Katrina (Actor)
c/o William Choi Management 360
9111 Wilshire Blvd
Beverly Hills, CA 90210-5508, USA

Bowden, Mark (Director, Writer)
c/o Ron Bernstein ICM Partners (LA)
10250 Constellation Blvd Fl 7
Los Angeles, CA 90067-6207, USA

Bowden, Michael (Athlete, Baseball Player)
596 Sudbury Cir
Oswego, IL 60543-7147

Bowden, Robert (Bobby) (Athlete, Coach, Football Coach, Football Player)
2813 Shamrock St
Tallahassee, FL 32309, USA

Bowden, Terry (Coach, Football Coach, Sportscaster)
ABC-TV
77 W 66th St
New York, NY 10023-6201, USA

Bowden, Tommy (Coach, Football Coach)
Clemson University
Athletic Dept
Lockhart, SC 29364, USA

Bowe, David (Actor)
Karg/Weissenbach
329 N Wetherly Dr Ste 101
Beverly Hills, CA 90211-1674, USA

Bowe, Dwayne (Athlete, Football Player)
4509 N Hickory Ln
Kansas City, MO 64116-4660, us

Bowe, Riddick L (Boxer)
714 Amer Dr
Fort Washington, MD 20744-5943, USA

Bowe, Rosemarie (Actor)
321 St Pierre Rd
Los Angeles, CA 90077-3432, USA

Bowen, Andrea (Actor)
790 Riverside Dr Apt 1F
New York, NY 10032-7441, USA

Bowen, Bruce (Athlete, Basketball Player)
18847 Calle Cierra
San Antonio, TX 78258-4032, USA

Bowen, Clare (Actor, Musician)
c/o Anne Woodward *ROAR (LA)*
9701 Wilshire Blvd Fl 8
Beverly Hills, CA 90212-2008, USA

Bowen, Jason (Athlete, Hockey Player)
4900 W 14th Ave
Kennewick, WA 99338-1723, USA

Bowen, Jimmy (Music Group, Musician)
PO Box 454
Lebanon, TN 37088-0454, USA

Bowen, Julie (Actor)
3253 Oakdell Rd
Studio City, CA 91604-4223, USA

Bowen, Michael (Actor)
Diverse Talent Agency
1875 Century Park E Ste 2250
Los Angeles, CA 90067-2563, USA

Bowen, Nanci (Athlete, Golfer)
201 Carolina Point Pkwy Apt 1119
Greenville, SC 29607-6580, USA

Bowen, Pamela (Actor)
c/o Staff Member *Henderson Hogan Agency (LA)*
8929 Wilshire Blvd Ste 312
Beverly Hills, CA 90211-1969, USA

Bowen, Rob (Athlete, Baseball Player)
389 Knight Dr
Ellijay, GA 30540-4381, USA

Bowen, Ryan (Athlete, Baseball Player)
3702 Frankford Rd Apt 18203
Dallas, TX 75287-7811, USA

Bowen, Sam (Athlete, Baseball Player)
8219 Victory Trl
Brentwood, TN 37027-7374, USA

Bowen, Stephen G Cdr (Astronaut)
508 Oak Dr
Friendswood, TX 77546-5531, USA

Bowen, Wade (Musician)
c/o Joey Lee *William Morris Endeavor (Nashville)*
1600 Division St Ste 300
Nashville, TN 37203-2755, USA

Bowens, David (Athlete, Football Player)
12900 SW 33rd Dr
Davie, FL 33330-1246, USA

Bowens, Tim (Athlete, Football Player)
PO Box 93
Okolona, MS 38860-0093, USA

Bowens, Tom (Athlete, Basketball Player)
304 Martin Luther King St
Okolona, MS 38860-1330, USA

Bower, Antoinette (Actor)
1529 N Beverly Glen Blvd
Los Angeles, CA 90077-3129, USA

Bower, Michael (Actor)
c/o Dora Whitaker *Whitaker Agency, The*
4924 Vineland Ave
N Hollywood, CA 91601-3847, USA

Bowers, Brent (Athlete, Baseball Player)
19257 Manchester Dr
Mokena, IL 60448-7747, USA

Bowers, Cedrick
10336 NW 28th Pl # Pi
Gainesville, FL 32606-8666, USA

Bowers, Chris (Actor)
c/o Staff Member *Gersh (LA)*
9465 Wilshire Blvd Ste 600
Beverly Hills, CA 90212-2605, USA

Bowers, John (Football Player, Misc)
International Longshoremen's Assn
198 Woodland Dr
Pulaski, PA 16143-3818, USA

Bowers, John W (Religious Leader)
Foursquare Gospel Int'l Church
1100 Glendale Blvd
Los Angeles, CA 90026-3203, USA

Bowers, RJ (Athlete, Football Player)
109 Waterside Ln
Cross Junction, VA 22625-2469, USA

Bowers, Sam (Athlete, Football Player)
1741 Edgewood Hill Cir Apt 204
Hagerstown, MD 21740-3347, USA

Bowers, Scotty (Writer)
c/o Staff Member *Grove / Atlantic, Inc*
154 W 14th St Fl 12
New York, NY 10011-7300, USA

Bowers, Shane (Athlete, Baseball Player)
535 S Rancho Alegre Dr
Covina, CA 91724-3325, USA

Bowers, William (Athlete, Football Player)
43295 Lacovia Dr
Bermuda Dunes, CA 92203-8016, USA

Bowersox, Kenneth D (Astronaut)
16907 Soaring Forest Dr
Houston, TX 77059-4003, USA

Bowersox, Kenneth D Captain (Astronaut)
16907 Soaring Forest Dr
Houston, TX 77059-4003, USA

Bowes, Margie (Musician)
1502 Brentwood Pt
Brentwood, TN 37027-2801, USA

Bowick, Tony (Athlete, Football Player)
PO Box 234
Slocomb, AL 36375-0234

Bowick, Vantonio (Athlete, Football Player)
PO Box 234
Slocomb, AL 36375-0234, USA

Bowie, David (Actor, Musician)
285 Lafayette St # 7DE
New York, NY 10012-3367, USA

Bowie, Heather (Athlete, Golfer)
3017 Elm River Dr
Fort Worth, TX 76116-0697, USA

Bowie, Jim (Athlete, Baseball Player)
1241 Swan Lake Dr
Fairfield, CA 94533-8137, USA

Bowie, John Ross (Actor, Comedian)
201 N Irving Blvd
Los Angeles, CA 90004-3806, USA

Bowie, Larry D (Athlete, Football Player)
739 Echo Shores Ct
Saint Paul, MN 55115-1473, USA

Bowie, Larry G (Athlete, Football Player)
260 Clarence St
Saint Paul, MN 55106-6572, USA

Bowie, Micah (Athlete, Baseball Player)
2039 Small Town Dr
New Braunfels, TX 78130-9063, USA

Bowie, Michael (Athlete, Football Player)
c/o Peter Schaffer *All Pro Sports and Entertainment*
36 Steele St Ste 100
Denver, CO 80206-5709, USA

Bowie, Sam (Athlete, Basketball Player, Olympic Athlete)
PO Box 306
Lexington, KY 40588-0306, USA

Bowker, John
3912 Cayente Way
Sacramento, CA 95864-2938, USA

Bowlby, April (Actor)
3095 Passmore Dr
Los Angeles, CA 90068-1718, USA

Bowler, Grant (Actor)
c/o Beth Holden-Garland *Untitled Entertainment (LA)*
350 S Beverly Dr Ste 200
Beverly Hills, CA 90212-4819, USA

Bowles, Brian (Athlete, Baseball Player)
1535 Steinhart Ave
Redondo Beach, CA 90278-2745, USA

Bowles, Charlie (Athlete, Golfer)
42009 Cherry Hill Rd
Novi, MI 48375-2518, USA

Bowles, Crandall C (Business Person)
Springs Industries
205 N White St
Fort Mill, SC 29715-1654, USA

Bowles, Erskine B (Politician)
6725 Old Providence Rd
Charlotte, NC 28226-7735, USA

Bowles, Lauren (Actor)
c/o Staff Member *Main Title Entertainment*
8383 Wilshire Blvd Ste 408
Beverly Hills, CA 90211-2435, USA

Bowlin, Weldon (Hoss) (Athlete, Baseball Player)
PO Box 1026
Livingston, AL 35470-1026, USA

Bowling, Andy (Athlete, Football Player)
7421 Straightstone Rd
Long Island, VA 24569-2945, USA

Bowling, Orbie (Athlete, Basketball Player)
10179 Frank Rd
Collierville, TN 38017-3623, USA

Bowling, Steve (Athlete, Baseball Player)
524 E 117th St S
Jenks, OK 74037-3618, USA

Bowman, Bob
8340 Riesling Way
San Jose, CA 95135-1435, USA

Bowman, Elizabeth (Athlete, Golfer)
82 Davidson St
Chula Vista, CA 91910-3002, USA

Bowman, Ernie (Athlete, Baseball Player)
123 Carter Dr Apt 8
Johnson City, TN 37601-2973, USA

Bowman, Harry W (Business Person)
Outboard Marine
PO Box 410
Waukegan, IL 60079-0410, USA

Bowman, Jim (Athlete, Football Player)
12 Stony Field Rd
Norton, MA 02766-1143, USA

Bowman, Joshua (Actor)
c/o Eric Kranzler *Management 360*
9111 Wilshire Blvd
Beverly Hills, CA 90210-5508, USA

Bowman, Ken (Athlete, Football Player)
13664 N Placita Montanas De Oro
Oro Valley, AZ 85755-8687, USA

Bown, Chuck (Race Car Driver)
2503 Wedge Pl
Asheboro, NC 27205-0811, USA

Bown, Jim (Race Car Driver)
5045 Old Nc 49
Asheboro, NC 27203, USA

Bownes, Fabien (Athlete, Football Player)
8127 149th Pl NE Unit B112
Redmond, WA 98052-6582, USA

Bowness, Rick (Athlete, Hockey Player)
10 Shadowstone Ln
Lawrence Township, NJ 08648-1027, USA

Bowser, Charles (Athlete, Football Player)
1188 Dovetail Ct
Virginia Beach, VA 23464-8832, us

Bowsfield, Ted (Athlete, Baseball Player)
980 Briar Rose Ln
Nipomo, CA 93444-8989, USA

Bowyer, Clint (Race Car Driver)
828 Woodward Rd
Mocksville, NC 27028-5860, USA

Bowyer Jr, Walter (Athlete, Football Player)
203 Main St N
Bethlehem, CT 06751-1400, USA

Boxberger, Loa (Politician)
PO Box 708
Russell, KS 67665-0708, USA

Boxer, Barbara (Politician)
136 Yale Dr
Rancho Mirage, CA 92270-3677, USA

Boxerbaum, David (Actor)
c/o Staff Member *Agency for the Performing Arts (APA-Nashville)*
3017 Poston Ave
Nashville, TN 37203-1313

Boxleitner, Bruce (Actor, Writer)
c/o Alan Iezman *Shelter Entertainment*
9255 W Sunset Blvd Ste 320
West Hollywood, CA 90069-3313, USA

Box Tops, The (Music Group)
c/o Staff Member *Rick Levy Management*
Prefers to be contacted by telephone or
email
Jacksonville, FL, USA

Boxx, Gillian (Athlete, Olympic Athlete,
Softball Player)
15111 Chelsea Dr
San Jose, CA 95124-2704, USA

Boxx, Shannon (Athlete, Olympic Athlete,
Soccer Player)
2321 SW Montgomery Dr
Portland, OR 97201-2388, USA

Boy, Soulja (Musician)
c/o Michael Becker *Imprint Entertainment*
100 Universal City Plz
Bungalow #7152
Universal City, CA 91608-1002, USA

Boyar, Lombardo (Actor)
Greene & Associates
526 N Larchmont Blvd # 201
Los Angeles, CA 90004-1300

Boyarsky, Jerry (Athlete, Football Player)
229 Boyarsky Rd
Scott Township, PA 18447-7710, USA

Boyce, Cameron (Actor)
c/o Emily Urbani *Osbrink Talent Agency*
4343 Lankershim Blvd Ste 100
North Hollywood, CA 91602-2705, USA

Boyce, Charles (Cartoonist)
563 Shorely Dr Apt 101
Barrington, IL 60010-3313, USA

Boyce, Kim (Music Group)
200 Nathan Dr
Hollister, MO 65672-6123, USA

Boyd, Billy (Actor)
c/o Sarah Jackson *Seven Summits Pictures
& Management*
8906 W Olympic Blvd
Ground Floor
Beverly Hills, CA 90211-3550, USA

Boyd, Bobby (Athlete, Football Player)
2105 Lansdowne Dr
Garland, TX 75040-3343, us

Boyd, Brandon (Musician)
515 Marguerita Ave
Santa Monica, CA 90402-1917, USA

Boyd, Brent (Athlete, Football Player)
948 N Coast Highway 101 Apt 185
Encinitas, CA 92024-2078, USA

Boyd, Cayden (Actor)
c/o Ellen Drantch-Billet *EDB Management*
1953 Barry Ave
Los Angeles, CA 90025-5381, USA

Boyd, Cletis L (Clete) (Baseball Player)
2034 20th Avenue Pkwy
Indian Rocks Beach, FL 33785-2967, USA

Boyd, Danny (Athlete, Football Player)
619 Spring Lakes Blvd
Bradenton, FL 34210-4558, us

Boyd, Davis (Oil Can) (Athlete, Baseball
Player)
PO Box 8058
Meridian, MS 39303-8058, USA

Boyd, Dennis (Athlete, Baseball Player)
45 Swan St
East Providence, RI 02914-2406, USA

Boyd, Elmo (Athlete, Football Player)
219 S Short St
Troy, OH 45373-3360, USA

Boyd, Fred (Athlete, Basketball Player)
10915 Open Trail Rd
Bakersfield, CA 93311-2892, USA

Boyd, Gary (Athlete, Baseball Player)
15308 Haas Ave
Gardena, CA 90249-4239, USA

Boyd, Greg (Baseball Player)
9 Inez Way
Stafford, VA 22554-5515, USA

Boyd, Greg P (Athlete, Football Player)
4621 N 65th St
Scottsdale, AZ 85251-1037, USA

Boyd, James (Athlete, Football Player)
3355 Sweetwater Rd Apt 10204
Lawrenceville, GA 30044-8544, USA

Boyd, Jason (Athlete, Baseball Player)
7962 State Route 140
Edwardsville, IL 62025-6110, USA

Boyd, Jenna (Actor)
c/o Ellen Drantch-Billet *EDB Management*
1953 Barry Ave
Los Angeles, CA 90025-5381, USA

Boyd, Johnny (Race Car Driver)
7635 N Gearhart Ave
Fresno, CA 93720-2548, USA

Boyd, Lavell (Athlete, Football Player)
4421 Charlotte Ann Dr
Louisville, KY 40216-3403, us

Boyd, Lynda (Actor)
c/o Michael Greene *Greene & Associates*
1901 Avenue of the Stars Ste 130
Los Angeles, CA 90067-6030, USA

Boyd, Malcolm (Religious Leader, Writer)
Saint Augustine-by-Sea Episcpal Church
1227 4th St
Santa Monica, CA 90401-1390, USA

Boyd, Malik (Athlete, Football Player)
2067 E Pickett Ct
Gilbert, AZ 85298-6103, USA

Boyd, Randy (Athlete, Hockey Player)
1769 Blackwillow Dr
Marietta, GA 30066-1954, USA

Boyd, Robert (Athlete, Golfer)
828 Robert E Lee Dr
Wilmington, NC 28412-7138, USA

Boyd, Stephen (Athlete, Football Player)
1268 Marginal Rd
Atlantic Beach, NY 11509-1651, USA

Boyd, Tommie (Athlete, Football Player)
46824 Amberwood Dr
Shelby Township, MI 48317-4100, us

Boyens, Philippa (Writer)
c/o Nick Reed *ICM Partners (LA)*
10250 Constellation Blvd Fl 7
Los Angeles, CA 90067-6207, USA

Boyer, Blaine (Athlete, Baseball Player)
133 Johnson Ferry Rd # 108
Marietta, GA 30068-4923, USA

Boyer, Brant (Athlete, Football Player)
1683 Old Lake Ln
Kaysville, UT 84037-3231, USA

Boyer, Cloyd (Athlete, Baseball Player)
14528 County Road 210
Jasper, MO 64755, USA

Boyer, Mark (Athlete, Football Player)
21942 Kaneohe Ln
Huntington Beach, CA 92646-7828, USA

Boyer, Verdi (Athlete, Football Player)
300 N Lake Ave Ste 930
Pasadena, CA 91101-4106, USA

Boyes, Brad (Athlete, Hockey Player)
11711 Fawnridge Dr
Saint Louis, MO 63131-4235, USA

Boyett, Lon (Athlete, Football Player)
902 W Newgrove St
Lancaster, CA 93534-3012, USA

Boyette, Garland (Athlete, Football
Player)
4003 E Valley Dr
Missouri City, TX 77459-4322, USA

Boy Hits Car (Music Group)
c/o Staff Member *Wind-up Records*
72 Madison Ave Fl 8
New York, NY 10016-8731, USA

Boykin, Deral (Athlete, Football Player)
3972 Lake Run Blvd
Stow, OH 44224-4351, USA

Boykin, Gerda (Athlete, Golfer)
3019 Colonnade Ct NW
Albuquerque, NM 87107-2961, USA

Boykin, Jarrett (Athlete, Football Player)
c/o Kevin Poston *Deal LLC*
28025 S Harwich Dr
Farmington Hills, MI 48334-4259, USA

Boykins, Earl
7572 Sanctuary Cir
Brecksville, OH 44141-3195, USA

Boylan, Barbara (Dancer)
7945 S Eudora Cir
Centennial, CO 80122-3844, USA

Boylan, Dean (Athlete, Hockey Player)
14 Powers Rd
Andover, MA 01810-6070, USA

Boylan, Jeanne
c/o Staff Member *William Morris
Endeavor (LA)*
9601 Wilshire Blvd
Beverly Hills, CA 90210-5213, USA

Boylan, Jim (Athlete, Football Player)
13155 Portofino Dr
Del Mar, CA 92014-3827, USA

Boyland, Dorian (Athlete, Baseball Player)
548 Setting Sun Dr
Winter Garden, FL 34787-5933, USA

Boyle, Brian (Athlete, Hockey Player)
The Orr Hockey Group
PO Box 290836
Charlestown, MA 02129-0215, USA

Boyle, Clune Charlotte (Swimmer)
50 Browns Grv # 31
Scottsville, NY 14546-1302, USA

Boyle, Dan (Athlete, Hockey Player)
348 Sound Beach Ave
Old Greenwich, CT 06870-1930, USA

Boyle, Danny (Director)
c/o Robert Newman *William Morris
Endeavor (LA)*
9601 Wilshire Blvd
Beverly Hills, CA 90210-5213, USA

Boyle, Jim (Athlete, Football Player)
920 Beechmeadow Ln
Cincinnati, OH 45238-4350, USA

Boyle, Lara Flynn (Actor)
c/o Gina Rugolo *Rugolo Entertainment*
195 S Beverly Dr Ste 400
Beverly Hills, CA 90212-3044, USA

Boyle, Lisa (Actor, Model)
7336 Santa Monica Blvd # 776
West Hollywood, CA 90046-6616, USA

Boyle, T Coraghessan (Writer)
University of Southern California
English Dept
Los Angeles, CA 90089-0001, USA

Boyne, Walter (Writer)
10833 Margate Rd
Silver Spring, MD 20901-1615, USA

Boynes, Winford (Athlete, Basketball
Player)
8979 Haflinger Way
Elk Grove, CA 95757-3262, USA

Boynton, George (Athlete, Football
Player)
917 Sartain Dr
Andrews, TX 79714-3817, USA

Boynton, John (Athlete, Football Player)
PO Box 468
Pikeville, TN 37367-0468, USA

Boynton, Nick (Athlete, Hockey Player)
3326 N Valencia Ln
Phoenix, AZ 85018-6611, USA

Boynton, Robert M (Doctor, Misc)
6632 Grulla St
Carlsbad, CA 92009-5315, USA

Boynton, Sandra (Artist, Writer)
c/o Staff Member *Simon & Schuster*
1230 Avenue of the Americas Fl CONC1
New York, NY 10020-1586, USA

Boys, Trevor (Race Car Driver)
Boys Will Be Boys Racing
610 Performance Rd
Mooresville, NC 28115-9595, USA

Boysaw, Gregory (Athlete, Football
Player)
PO Box 501762
Indianapolis, IN 46250-6762, USA

boysetsfire (Music Group)
c/o Staff Member *Wind-up Records*
72 Madison Ave Fl 8
New York, NY 10016-8731, USA

Boyz II Men (Music Group)
c/o Joann Mignano *Krupp
Kommunications*
59 W 19th St Rm 4C
New York, NY 10011-4245, USA

Bozarth, Marci (Athlete, Golfer)
2929 Buffalo Speedway Unit 1612
Houston, TX 77098-1715, USA

Boze, Marshall (Athlete, Baseball Player)
16114 McCormick Pl
Huntersville, NC 28078-9099, USA

Bozek, Steve (Athlete, Hockey Player)
8410 E Whispering Wind Dr
Scottsdale, AZ 85255-2863, USA

Bozilovic, Ivana (Actor)
c/o Jon Orlando *WNWN Media*
348 Hauser Blvd # PH414
Los Angeles, CA 90036-3276, USA

Bozo, Laura (Actor)
c/o Staff Member *Telemundo*
2470 W 8th Ave
Hialeah, FL 33010-2000, USA

Bozza, Anthony (Writer)
c/o Richard Abate *3 Arts Entertainment*
(NY)
16 W 22nd St Ste 201
New York, NY 10010-5842, USA

BR5-49 (Music Group, Musician)
c/o Staff Member *Creative Artists Agency*
(CAA-TN)
401 Commerce St PH
Nashville, TN 37219-2516, USA

Braase, Ordell (Athlete, Football Player)
PO Box 5417
Towson, MD 21285-5417, USA

Bracco, Lorraine (Actor)
460 Butter Ln
Bridgehampton, NY 11932, USA

Bracelin, Greg (Athlete, Football Player)
5465 Calumet Ave
La Jolla, CA 92037-7604, USA

Bracht, Stephanie (Athlete, Golfer)
2004 Delancey Dr
Norman, OK 73071-3872, USA

Brack, Kenny (Race Car Driver)
Team Rahal
4601 Lyman Dr
Hilliard, OH 43026-1249, USA

Brack, Reginald K Jr (Publisher)
12 Huntzinger Dr
Greenwich, CT 06831-4110, USA

Bracken, Don (Athlete, Football Player)
15950 W Diamond St
Goodyear, AZ 85338-2763, USA

Brackenbury, Curt (Athlete, Hockey Player)
W378N5861 Valley Rd
Oconomowoc, WI 53066-2246, USA

Brackens, Tony (Athlete, Football Player)
193 Private Road 407
Fairfield, TX 75840-6022, USA

Brackensick, Deandre (Musician)
c/o Staff Member *19 Entertainment (LA)*
9000 W Sunset Blvd Ste 1574
West Hollywood, CA 90069-5817, USA

Brackett, Gary (Athlete, Football Player)
3591 Hintocks Cir
Carmel, IN 46032-9178, us

Brackett, Griffin (Model)
860 NE 73rd St
Miami, FL 33138-5228

Brackett, M L (Athlete, Football Player)
1216 Monte Vista Dr
Gadsden, AL 35904-3643, USA

Brackins, Charles (Athlete, Football Player)
7227 Haverton Dr
Apt 1907
Houston, TX 77016-2333, USA

Bradberry, Gary (Race Car Driver)
c/o *Tri Star Motorsports*
6006 Ball Park Rd
Thomasville, NC 27360-7942, USA

Bradbery, Danielle (Musician)
c/o Joey Lee *William Morris Endeavor*
(Nashville)
1600 Division St Ste 300
Nashville, TN 37203-2755, USA

Bradbury, Gary (Race Car Driver)
Hoover Motorsports
10705 Bringle Ferry Rd
Salisbury, NC 28146-9576, USA

Bradbury, Janette Lane (Actor)
258 Woodlawn Ave
Jersey City, NJ 07305-2127, USA

Braddock, Paige (Cartoonist)
7596 Bodega Ave
Sebastopol, CA 95472-3654, USA

Braddy, Johanna (Actor)
c/o Julian Rosenberg *Tower 10*
Entertainment
412 S Willaman Dr Apt 507
Los Angeles, CA 90048-3990, USA

Braden, Dallas
1459 W Walnut St
Stockton, CA 95203-1527, USA

Braden, Gregg (Writer)
Wisdom Traditions
PO Box 14668
North Palm Beach, FL 33408-0668, USA

Bradey, Don (Athlete, Baseball Player)
330 Council Bluff Pkwy
Murfreesboro, TN 37127-8317, USA

Bradford, Barbara Taylor (Writer)
Bradford Enterprises
505 Park Ave Ste 403
New York, NY 10022-9339, USA

Bradford, Buddy (Athlete, Baseball Player)
6440 Springpark Ave
Los Angeles, CA 90056-2222, USA

Bradford, Carl (Athlete, Football Player)
c/o David Dunn *Athletes First, LLC*
23091 Mill Creek Dr
Laguna Hills, CA 92653-1258, USA

Bradford, Chad (Athlete, Baseball Player)
4547 Bill Downing Rd
Raymond, MS 39154-8100, USA

Bradford, Corey (Athlete, Football Player)
13002 Highway 955 E
Ethel, LA 70730-3952, us

Bradford, Jesse (Actor)
8020 Briar Summit Dr
Los Angeles, CA 90046-1127, USA

Bradford, Paul (Athlete, Football Player)
2239 Pulgas Ave
East Palo Alto, CA 94303-1755, USA

Bradford, Richard (Actor)
2511 Canyon Dr
Los Angeles, CA 90068-2415, USA

Bradford, Ronnie (Athlete, Football Player)
965 Allen Lake Ln
Suwanee, GA 30024-4179, USA

Bradford, Sam (Athlete, Football Player)
c/o Tom Condon *CAA (St. Louis)*
222 S Central Ave Ste 1008
Saint Louis, MO 63105-3509, USA

Bradford, William (Business Person)
Halliburton Co
Lincoln Plaza 500 N Akard St
Dallas, TX 75201, USA

Bradfute, Byron (Athlete, Football Player)
939 Moonglow Ave
New Braunfels, TX 78130-6081, USA

Bradham, Nigel (Athlete, Football Player)
c/o Mitchell Frankel *Impact Sports - Boca*
Raton
2799 NW 2nd Ave Ste 203
Boca Raton, FL 33431-6709, USA

Bradley, Alonzo (Athlete, Basketball Player)
1713 Briaroaks Dr
Flower Mound, TX 75028-3482, USA

Bradley, Bert (Athlete, Baseball Player)
6039 Old State Rd
Mattoon, IL 61938, USA

Bradley, Bill (Basketball Player, Olympic Athlete, Politician)
Betty Sue Flowers
200 Central Park S Apt 15B
New York, NY 10019-1443, USA

Bradley, Bob (Coach, Soccer Player)
Chicago Fire
980 N Michigan Ave Ste 1998
Chicago, IL 60611-7504, USA

Bradley, Brian (Athlete, Hockey Player)
27116 Winged Elm Dr
Wesley Chapel, FL 33544-7773, USA

Bradley, Bruce (Athlete, Misc)
262 Saint Joseph Ave
Long Beach, CA 90803-1720, USA

Bradley, Carlos (Athlete, Football Player)
1316 E Cliveden St
Philadelphia, PA 19119-3948, USA

Bradley, Charles (Athlete, Basketball Player)
10310 Mountshire Cir
Littleton, CO 80126, USA

Bradley, Christopher (Actor)
c/o Staff Member *Ford/Robert Black*
Agency
4032 N Miller Rd Ste 104
Scottsdale, AZ 85251-4572, USA

Bradley, Dick (Cartoonist, Misc)
10176 Corporate Square Dr Ste 200
Saint Louis, MO 63132-2924, USA

Bradley, Dudley (Athlete, Basketball Player)
9830 Clanford Rd
Randallstown, MD 21133-2508, USA

Bradley, Ed (Athlete, Football Player)
206 Mossy Oak Dr
Winston Salem, NC 27127-9234, us

Bradley, Frank (Baseball Player)
Kansas City Monarchs
PO Box 516
Benton, LA 71006-0516, USA

Bradley, Gordon (Coach, Soccer Player)
14300 Bakerwood Pl
Haymarket, VA 20169-2638, USA

Bradley, Henry (Athlete, Football Player)
42927 Corte Siero
Temecula, CA 92592-3639, us

Bradley, Kathleen (Actor)
Kazarian/Spencer
11365 Ventura Blvd Ste 100
Studio City, CA 91604-3148, USA

Bradley, Keegan (Athlete, Golfer)
c/o Ben Harrison *Lagardere Unlimited*
(AZ)
13845 N Northsight Blvd Ste 200
Scottsdale, AZ 85260-3609, USA

Bradley, Luther (Athlete, Football Player)
19575 Stratford Rd
Detroit, MI 48221-1848, USA

Bradley, Mark (Athlete, Baseball Player)
1605 S Nebraska St
Pine Bluff, AR 71601-6133, USA

Bradley, Michael (Athlete, Basketball Player)
6150 Blackjack Ct N
Punta Gorda, FL 33982-9606, USA

Bradley, Michael (Mike) (Athlete, Golfer)
5501 Branch Oak Pl
Lithia, FL 33547-4801, USA

Bradley, Milton (Athlete, Baseball Player)
5359 Oak Park Ave
Encino, CA 91316-2627, USA

Bradley, Myron (Athlete, Olympic Athlete, Water Polo Player)
262 Saint Joseph Ave
Long Beach, CA 90803-1720, USA

Bradley, Otha (Athlete, Football Player)
PO Box 59071
Los Angeles, CA 90059-0071, USA

Bradley, Phil (Athlete, Baseball Player)
6950 Seminole Ct
Columbia, MO 65203-9669, USA

Bradley, Rebecca (Athlete, Golfer)
14443 W Lee Shore Dr
Willis, TX 77318-7407, USA

Bradley, Ryan (Athlete, Baseball Player)
3454 Alder Pl
Chino Hills, CA 91709-2005, USA

Bradley, Scott (Athlete, Baseball Player)
43 Chicory Ln
Pennington, NJ 08534-1926, USA

Bradley, Shawn (Athlete, Basketball Player)
6E6 Sunny Flowers Ln
Frederiksted, UT 8410000000, USA

Bradley, Tom (Athlete, Baseball Player)
904 Main St
Barboursville, WV 25504-1411, USA

Bradley Baker, Dee (Actor)
13104 Bloomfield St
Sherman Oaks, CA 91423-3206, USA

Bradley Jr, Harold (Athlete, Football Player)
1302 Asbury Ave
Evanston, IL 60201-4108, USA

Bradley Jr, Timothy (Athlete, Boxer)
307 W Bon Air Dr
Palm Springs, CA 92262-1410, USA

Bradshaw (Wrestler)
139 Denny Ln
Athens, TX 75751

Bradshaw, Ahmad (Athlete, Football Player)
c/o Drew Rosenhaus *Rosenhaus Sports*
Representation
6400 Allison Rd
Miami Beach, FL 33141-4540, USA

Bradshaw, Craig (Athlete, Football Player)
9481 Carson Dr
Lantana, TX 76226-7319, us

Bradshaw, James A (Athlete, Football Player)
449 Tresham Rd
Columbus, OH 43230-2224, USA

Bradshaw, Jim (Athlete, Football Player)
5653 Eagle Harbor Dr
Westerville, OH 43081-7085, us

Bradshaw, John (Actor, Director, Writer)
c/o Victoria Wisdom *Wisdom Literary*
287 S Robertson Blvd Ste 258
Beverly Hills, CA 90211-2810, USA

Bradshaw, Morris (Athlete, Football Player)
82 Steuben Bay
Alameda, CA 94502-6406, USA

Bradshaw, Sufe (Actor)
c/o Sarah Baker Grillo *Open Entertainment*
1051 Cole Ave Ste B
Los Angeles, CA 90038-2601, USA

Bradshaw, Terry (Athlete, Football Player, Sportscaster)
5912 Eagle Mountain Dr
Argyle, TX 76226-4266, USA

Brady, Brian (Athlete, Baseball Player)
920 W 23rd St
Odessa, TX 79763-2504, USA

Brady, Charles E (Astronaut)
92 Red Wing Ln
Eastsound, WA 98245-8517, USA

Brady, Doug (Athlete, Baseball Player)
5878 Iron Bridge Rd
Chatham, IL 62629-8014, USA

Brady, Ed (Athlete, Football Player)
5755 White Path Ln
Liberty Twp, OH 45011-1273, USA

Brady, Jeff (Athlete, Football Player)
1506 NW 37th Pi
Cape Coral, FL 33993, USA

Brady, Jim (Athlete, Baseball Player)
1072 Meadow View Ln
Saint Augustine, FL 32092-1055, USA

Brady, Kevin (Congressman, Politician)
301 Cannon Hob
Washington, DC 20515-1701, USA

Brady, Kyle (Athlete, Football Player)
2221 Alicia Ln
Atlantic Beach, FL 32233-5975, USA

Brady, Nicholas F (Politician)
Darby Overseas Investments
PO Box 1410W
Easton, MD 21601, USA

Brady, Orla (Actor)
12440 Yellow Hill Rd
Malibu, CA 90265-2266, USA

Brady, Pat (Cartoonist)
United Feature Syndicate
PO Box 5610
Cincinnati, OH 45201-5610, USA

Brady, Patrick (Athlete, Football Player)
8990 Lombardi Rd
Reno, NV 89511-9537, USA

Brady, Ray (Correspondent)
CBS-TV
524 W 57th St
New York, NY 10019-2924, USA

Brady, Rickey
609 Holly Dr
Edmond, OK 73034-4923, us

Brady, Robert (Congressman, Politician)
102 Cannon Hob
Washington, DC 20515-0516, USA

Brady, Tom (Athlete, Football Player)
400 Heath St
Chestnut Hill, MA 02467-2332, USA

Brady, Wayne (Actor, Comedian, Musician, Producer)
c/o Andy Elkin *Creative Artists Agency (CAA-LA)*
2000 Avenue of the Stars Ste 100
Los Angeles, CA 90067-4705, USA

Braeden, Eric (Actor)
13723 Romany Dr
Pacific Palisades, CA 90272-2733, USA

Braff, Zach (Actor, Writer)
8816 Lookout Mountain Ave
Los Angeles, CA 90046-1820, USA

Braga, Alice (Actor)
c/o Will Ward *ROAR (LA)*
9701 Wilshire Blvd Fl 8
Beverly Hills, CA 90212-2008, USA

Braga, Brannon (Writer)
c/o Staff Member *William Morris Endeavor (LA)*
9601 Wilshire Blvd
Beverly Hills, CA 90210-5213, USA

Braga, Sonia (Actor)
149 Avenue C Apt 2R
New York, NY 10009-5306, USA

Bragg, Darren (Athlete, Baseball Player)
163 Patriot Rd
Southbury, CT 06488-1274, USA

Bragg, Don (Athlete, Olympic Athlete, Track Athlete)
965 Oak St
Clayton, CA 94517-1313, USA

Bragg, Mike (Athlete, Football Player)
807 S 6th St
Saint Charles, MO 63301, USA

Bragg, Rick (Journalist)
229 W 43rd St
New York, NY 10036-3982, USA

Braggs, Byron (Athlete, Football Player)
19469 Mill Dam Pl
Leesburg, VA 20176-8428, USA

Braggs, Glenn (Athlete, Baseball Player)
28369 Falcon Crest Dr
Canyon Country, CA 91351-5016, USA

Braggs, Stephen (Athlete, Football Player)
4110 Pickfair St
Houston, TX 77026-3924, USA

Bragonier, Dennis (Athlete, Football Player)
PO Box 1206
Roseville, CA 95678-8206, USA

Braham, Rich (Athlete, Football Player)
19 Miramichi Trl
Morgantown, WV 26508-2928, USA

Brahaney, Thomas F (Tom) (Athlete, Football Player)
1602 W Cuthbert Ave
Midland, TX 79701-5724, USA

Brainard, Don (Horse Racer)
880 Banks Rd
Coconut Creek, FL 33063-4621, USA

Brakes, The (Music Group)
c/o Staff Member *Paradigm (Monterey)*
404 W Franklin St
Monterey, CA 93940-2303, USA

Braman, Norman (Business Person, Football Executive)
1 Indian Creek Island Rd
Indian Creek Village, FL 33154-2903, USA

Bramhall, Mark (Actor)
c/o Alexandra Karrys *Divine Management*
3822 Latrobe St
Los Angeles, CA 90031-1446

Bramlet, Casey (Athlete, Football Player)
801 15th St
Wheatland, WY 82201-2709, US

Bramlett, John (Athlete, Football Player)
159 Cotton Ridge Cv S
Cordova, TN 38018-7409, USA

Brammell, Abby (Actor)
c/o Robert (Rob) Gomez *Precision Entertainment*
465 N Croft Ave
Los Angeles, CA 90048-2508, USA

Brammer, Mark (Athlete, Football Player)
1680 Amherst St
Buffalo, NY 14214-2002, USA

Branagh, Kenneth (Actor, Director)
c/o Staff Member *Berwick & Kovacik*
6300 Wilshire Blvd Ste 1410
Los Angeles, CA 90048-5216, USA

Branca, Ralph (Athlete, Baseball Player)
99 Biltmore Ave
Rye, NY 10580-1837, USA

Brancaccio, David
2100 Crystal Dr
Arlington, VA 22202-3784, USA

Brancato, George (Athlete, Football Player)
25 Nancy Ave
Nepean, ON K2H 8L3, USA

Brancato, John D (JD) (Producer, Writer)
c/o Staff Member *Broder Webb Chervin Silbermann Agency, The (BWCS)*
10250 Constellation Blvd
Los Angeles, CA 90067-6200, USA

Brancato Jr, Lillo (Actor)
c/o Craig Shapiro *ICM Partners (LA)*
10250 Constellation Blvd Fl 7
Los Angeles, CA 90067-6207, USA

Branch, Adrian (Athlete, Basketball Player)
803 Grand Provincial Ave
Matthews, NC 28105-1833, USA

Branch, Alan (Athlete, Football Player)
c/o Blake Baratz *The Institute for Athletes*
3600 Minnesota Dr Ste 550
Minneapolis, MN 55435-7925, USA

Branch, Andre (Athlete, Football Player)
c/o Hadley Engelhard *Enter-Sports Management*
5 Concourse Pkwy Ste 3000
Atlanta, GA 30328-7106, USA

Branch, Clifford (Cliff) (Athlete, Coach, Football Coach, Football Player)
2071 Stonefield Ln
Santa Rosa, CA 95403-0952, USA

Branch, Colin (Athlete, Football Player)
121 Three Greens Dr
Huntersville, NC 28078-2633, us

Branch, Deion (Athlete, Football Player)
13382 W Sherbern Dr
Carmel, IN 46032-1309, us

Branch, Harvey (Athlete, Baseball Player)
4995 Jolly Dr
Memphis, TN 38109-7123, USA

Branch, Michelle (Musician, Songwriter)
8561 E Old Field Rd
Scottsdale, AZ 85266-1636, USA

Branch, Reggie (Athlete, Football Player)
515 San Lanta Cir
Sanford, FL 32771-5903, USA

Branch, Roy (Athlete, Baseball Player)
5322 Terry Ave
Saint Louis, MO 63120-2021, USA

Branch, Vanessa (Actor)
c/o Staff Member *3 Arts Entertainment (LA)*
9460 Wilshire Blvd Fl 7
Beverly Hills, CA 90212-2713, USA

Branch, William B (Writer)
53 Cortlandt Ave
New Rochelle, NY 10801-2032, USA

Brand, Daniel (Dan) (Wrestler)
4321 Bridgeview Dr
Oakland, CA 94602-1910, USA

Brand, Elton (Athlete, Basketball Player)
942 S Mansfield Ave
Los Angeles, CA 90036-4940, USA

Brand, Glen (Athlete, Olympic Athlete, Wrestler)
PO Box 6069
Omaha, NE 68106-0069, USA

Brand, Jolene (Actor)
G.S. Prod
8321 Beverly Blvd
Los Angeles, CA 90048-2607, USA

Brand, Joshua (Producer)
c/o Staff Member *William Morris Endeavor (LA)*
9601 Wilshire Blvd
Beverly Hills, CA 90210-5213, USA

Brand, Julie (Athlete, Golfer)
7546 Gulf Brook Dr
Remsen, NY 13438-4294, USA

Brand, Neville (Actor)
c/o Staff Member *ICM Partners (LA)*
10250 Constellation Blvd Fl 7
Los Angeles, CA 90067-6207, USA

Brand, Oscar (Musician, Songwriter, Writer)
Gypsy Hill Music
141 Baker Hill Rd
Great Neck, NY 11023-1715, USA

Brand, Robert (Designer)
508 W End Ave
New York, NY 10024-4328, USA

Brand, Ron (Athlete, Baseball Player)
1301 Hudson Ln
Prosper, TX 75078-5013, USA

Brand, Russell (Actor, Comedian)
8856 Appian Way
Los Angeles, CA 90046-7735, USA

Brand, Simon (Director)
5513 Tuxedo Ter
Los Angeles, CA 90068-2453, USA

Brand, Steven (Actor)
c/o Brian Medavoy *Medavoy Management*
10203 Santa Monica Blvd Ste 400
Los Angeles, CA 90067-6405, USA

Brand, Vance D (Astronaut)
NASA Dryden Flight Center
21825 Hidden Canyon Dr
Tehachapi, CA 93561-9528, USA

Brandenburg, Dan''' (Athlete, Football
Player)
PO Box 22533
Fort Lauderdale, FL 33335-2533, us

Brandenburg, Mark (Athlete, Baseball
Player)
152 Cottonwood Dr
Coppell, TX 75019-2511, USA

Brandenstein, Daniel C (Astronaut)
648 N Tailwind
Blanco, TX 78606-5888, USA

Brandenstein, Daniel C Captain
(Astronaut)
648 N Tailwind
Blanco, TX 78606-5888, USA

Brandes, John (Athlete, Football Player)
905 Ashland Ct
Mansfield, TX 76063-3802, USA

Brandi (Model)
Next Model Mgmt
23 Watts St
New York, NY 10013, USA

Brandler, Shellylyn (Actor)
c/o Simon Millar *Rumble Media*
1620 Broadway Ste C
Santa Monica, CA 90404-2777, USA

Brandon, Barbara (Cartoonist)
Universal Press Syndicate
4520 Main St Ste 340
Kansas City, MO 64111-7705, USA

Brandon, Clark (Actor)
Jennings Assoc
28035 Dorothy Dr Ste 210A
Agoura Hills, CA 91301-2685, USA

Brandon, Darrell (Athlete, Baseball
Player)
590 White Cliff Dr
Plymouth, MA 02360-1483, USA

Brandon, David (Athlete, Football Player)
218 Crystal Downs Way
Suwanee, GA 30024-7630, us

Brandon, Jay (Writer)
PO Box 6764
San Antonio, TX 78209-0764, USA

Brandon, Jeb (Actor)
c/o Staff Member *William Morris
Endeavor (LA)*
9601 Wilshire Blvd
Beverly Hills, CA 90210-5213, USA

Brandon, John (Actor)
Coast to Coast Talent
3350 Barham Blvd
Los Angeles, CA 90068-1404, USA

Brandon, Michael (Actor)
c/o Joel Dean *TalentWorks (LA)*
3500 W Olive Ave Ste 1400
Burbank, CA 91505-5512, USA

Brandon, Michael (Athlete, Football
Player)
910 E Green St
Perry, FL 32347-3514, USA

Brandon, Sam (Athlete, Football Player)
5412 Norris Dr
The Colony, TX 75056-3701, us

Brandon, Terrell (Athlete, Basketball
Player)
3310 NE Shaver St
Portland, OR 97212-1860, USA

Brands, Terry (Athlete, Olympic Athlete,
Wrestler)
4595 Hazelwood Ave SW
Iowa City, IA 52240-8548, USA

Brands, Tom (Wrestler)
4494 Taft Ave SE
Iowa City, IA 52240-8166, USA

Brands, X (Actor)
17171 Roscoe Blvd # 104
Northridge, CA 91325-4060, USA

Brandt, Betsy (Actor)
105 W 72nd St Apt 3B
New York, NY 10023-3242, USA

Brandt, David''' (Athlete, Football Player)
2214 Christine Ct SE
Grand Rapids, MI 49546-6468, us

Brandt, Hank (Actor)
Contemporary Artists
610 Santa Monica Blvd Ste 202
Santa Monica, CA 90401-1645, USA

Brandt, Jackie (Athlete, Baseball Player)
103 Sugar Maple Ave
Wildwood, FL 34785-9246, USA

Brandt, Jim (Athlete, Football Player)
714 Zumbro Dr NW
Rochester, MN 55901-2379, USA

Brandt, Jon (Musician)
Monterey Peninsula Artists
509 Hartnell St
Monterey, CA 93940-2825, USA

Brandt, Kyle (Actor, Producer, Reality
Star)
22921 Bergantin
Mission Viejo, CA 92692-1203, USA

Brandt, Paul (Musician)
c/o Staff Member *William Morris
Endeavor (LA)*
9601 Wilshire Blvd
Beverly Hills, CA 90210-5213, USA

Brandt, Victor (Actor)
H David Moss
733 Seward St PH
Los Angeles, CA 90038-3503, USA

Brandy, J C (Actor)
Henderson/Hogan
8285 W Sunset Blvd Ste 1
West Hollywood, CA 90046-2420, USA

Brandywine, Marcia (Correspondent)
743 Huntley Dr
West Hollywood, CA 90069-5008, USA

B. Rangel, Charles (Congressman,
Politician)
2354 Rhob
Washington, DC 20515-0001, USA

Brannagh, Brigid (Actor)
c/o Adam Levine *Levine Okwu Erickson
Management*
2126 N Commonwealth Ave
Los Angeles, CA 90027-2118, USA

Brannan, Solomon (Athlete, Football
Player)
2500 Cascade Rd SW
Atlanta, GA 30311-3228, USA

Brannon, Ronald (Religious Leader)
Wesleyan Church
PO Box 50434
Indianapolis, IN 46250-0434, USA

Branshaw, David (Athlete, Golfer)
1617 Renaissance Way
Tampa, FL 33602-5981, USA

Branson, Brad (Athlete, Basketball Player)
7419 Cortes Dr
Houston, TX 77083-3617, USA

Branson, Jeff (Athlete, Baseball Player)
10749 Spokane Ct
Union, KY 41091-7160, USA

Branson, Jeff (Athlete, Baseball Player)
501 W Maryland St
Attn Coaching Staff
Indianapolis, IN 46225-1041, USA

Branson, Jeff Branson (Actor)
c/o Robert Attermann *Abrams Artists
Agency (NY)*
9200 W Sunset Blvd PH 11
West Hollywood, CA 90069-3601, USA

Branson, Jesse (Athlete, Basketball Player)
100 Sadie Ln
Gibsonville, NC 27249-2673, USA

Branstad, Terry (Governor, Politician)
Governor's Office
1007 E Grand Ave Rm 109
Des Moines, IA 50319-0001, USA

Branstad, Terry (Politician)
E Grand Ave
Des Moines, IA 50319, USA

Brant, Marshall (Athlete, Baseball Player)
604 Scotland Dr
Santa Rosa, CA 95409-4419, USA

Brant, Peter (Business Person)
385 Taconic Rd
Greenwich, CT 06831-2828, USA

Brant, Tim (Sportscaster)
ABC-TV
77 W 66th St
Sports Dept
New York, NY 10023-6201, USA

Brantley, Betsy (Actor)
c/o Staff Member *Mitchell K Stubbs &
Assoc (MKS)*
8675 Washington Blvd Ste 203
Culver City, CA 90232-7486, USA

Brantley, Chris (Athlete, Football Player)
257 Hamilton Rd
Teaneck, NJ 07666-6367, USA

Brantley, Cliff (Athlete, Baseball Player)
90 Grandview Ave
Staten Island, NY 10303-2000, USA

Brantley, Jeff (Athlete, Baseball Player)
104 Cherry Laurel Cv
Ridgeland, MS 39157-8643, USA

Brantley, Jeff (Athlete, Baseball Player)
100 Joe Nuxhall Way
Attn Broadcast Dept
Cincinnati, OH 45202-4109, USA

Brantley, John (Athlete, Football Player)
1021 Manor Ridge Dr
Bishop, GA 30621-1369, USA

Brantley, Michael (Athlete, Baseball
Player)
7640 NW 79th Ave
Apt L8
Tamarac, FL 33321-2868, USA

Brantley, Mickey (Athlete, Baseball
Player)
3095 SW Boxwood Cir
Port Saint Lucie, FL 34953-6971, USA

Brantley, Ollie (Athlete, Baseball Player)
215 S Alabama St
Marianna, AR 72360-2578, USA

Brantley, Rick (Musician)
c/o Staff Member *Paradigm (Monterey)*
404 W Franklin St
Monterey, CA 93940-2303, USA

Brantley, Scot (Athlete, Football Player)
326 SE 32nd Ave
Ocala, FL 34471-2841, USA

Branton, Gene (Athlete, Football Player)
7008 Hazelhurst Ct
Tampa, FL 33615-2945, USA

Branyan, Russell (Athlete, Baseball Player)
8209 Penn Way Ct
Franklin, TN 37064-7630, USA

Brar, Karan (Actor)
c/o Bill Perlman *Perlman Management
Group*
PO Box 2939
Beverly Hills, CA 90213-2939, USA

Brasco, Jim (Athlete, Basketball Player)
225 W Neck Rd
Huntington, NY 11743-2458, USA

Brashares, Ann (Writer)
c/o Jennifer Rudolph Walsh *William
Morris Endeavor (NY)*
1325 Avenue of the Americas
New York, NY 10019-6026, USA

Brassette, Amy (Actor)
c/o Marv Dauer *Marv Dauer Management*
2236 The Terrace
Los Angeles, CA 90049-1171, USA

Brassfield, Darin (Race Car Driver)
541 Division St
Campbell, CA 95008-6934, USA

Bratkowski, Edmund R (Zeke) (Athlete,
Coach, Football Player)
224 Anchors Lake Dr N
Santa Rosa Beach, FL 32459-4106, USA

Bratt, Benjamin (Actor)
c/o Staff Member *5 Stick Films*
7336 Santa Monica Blvd Ste 745
West Hollywood, CA 90046-6616, USA

Bratton, Creed (Musician)
Thomas Cassidy
11761 E Speedway Blvd
Tucson, AZ 85748-2017, USA

Bratton, Jason (Athlete, Football Player)
1104 Regal Oak Dr
Longview, TX 75604-2141, USA

Bratz, Mike (Athlete, Basketball Player)
7503 Tillman Hill Rd
Colleyville, TX 76034-6929, USA

Bratzke, Chad (Athlete, Football Player)
10850 Ruby Ct
Carmel, IN 46032-9303, USA

Braugher, Andre (Actor)
393 Charlton Ave
South Orange, NJ 07079-2405, USA

Braun, Carol Moseley (Politician)
PO Box 8155
Chicago, IL 60680-8155, USA

Braun, Colin (Race Car Driver)
c/o Staff Member *Roush Fenway Racing Team*
4600 Roush Pl NW
Concord, NC 28027-7116, USA

Braun, Nicholas (Actor)
c/o Susan Patricola *Patricola Lust PR*
9171 Wilshire Blvd Ste 441
Beverly Hills, CA 90210-5516, USA

Braun, Rick (Musician)
c/o Staff Member *APA Talent And Literary Agency (NY)*
45 W 45th St Ste 804
New York, NY 10036-4602, USA

Braun, Ryan (Athlete, Baseball Player)
3769 Puerco Canyon Rd
Malibu, CA 90265-4551, USA

Braun, Scooter (Business Person, Producer)
9066 St Ives Dr
Los Angeles, CA 90069-1705, USA

Braun, Steve (Actor)
c/o Tiffany Kuzon *Evolution Entertainment (LA)*
901 N Highland Ave
Los Angeles, CA 90038-2412, USA

Braun, Steve (Athlete, Baseball Player)
108 Gainsboro Rd
Lawrence Township, NJ 08648-3916, USA

Braun, Tamara (Actor)
c/o Brianne Castillo-Huang *The Schiff Company*
9220 W Sunset Blvd Ste 106
West Hollywood, CA 90069-3500, USA

Braun, Wendy (Actor)
c/o Staff Member *House of Representatives, The*
1434 6th St Ste 1
Santa Monica, CA 90401-2527, USA

Braver, Rita (Correspondent)
CBS-TV
2020 M St NW
News Dept
Washington, DC 20036-3368, USA

Braverman, Bart (Actor)
c/o Staff Member *Henriksen Talent Management*
13024 Hesby St
Sherman Oaks, CA 91423-2134, USA

Braverman, Chuck (Director, Producer)
Braverman Productions Inc
3961 Sepulveda Blvd Ste 206
Culver City, CA 90230-4600, USA

Bravo, Alex (Athlete, Football Player)
2316 Pine Ave
Manhattan Beach, CA 90266-2835, USA

Bravo, Duncan (Actor)
3401 Oak Glen Dr
Los Angeles, CA 90068-1313, USA

Braxton, David (Athlete, Football Player)
26898 Primrose Ln
Westlake, OH 44145-5487, USA

Braxton, Tamar (Actor, Musician)
c/o Josh Pyatt *William Morris Endeavor (LA)*
9601 Wilshire Blvd
Beverly Hills, CA 90210-5213, USA

Braxton, Toni (Musician, Songwriter)
16000 Ventura Blvd Ste 600
Encino, CA 91436-2753, USA

Braxton, Trina (Musician, Reality Star)
c/o Staff Member *Primary Wave Music Publishing*
116 E 16th St Fl 9
New York, NY 10003-2123, USA

Braxton, Tyrone S (Athlete, Football Player)
8155 E Fairmount Dr Unit 171
Denver, CO 80230-6827, USA

Braxton III, Hezekiah (Athlete, Football Player)
12715 Norwood Ln
Fort Washington, MD 20744-6312, USA

Bray, Charles (Athlete, Football Player)
1321 Millersport Hwy
Buffalo, NY 14221-2900, USA

Bray, Deanne (Actor)
c/o Sid Craig *Craig Management*
125 S Sycamore Ave
Los Angeles, CA 90036-2938, USA

Bray, Kevin (Actor, Director, Producer)
c/o Simon Millar *Rumble Media*
1620 Broadway Ste C
Santa Monica, CA 90404-2777, USA

Bray, Tyler (Athlete, Football Player)
c/o Don Yee *Yee & Dubin Sports, LLC*
725 S Figueroa St Ste 3085
Los Angeles, CA 90017-5430, USA

Brayton, Tyler (Athlete, Football Player)
91 W Fremont Ave
Littleton, CO 80120-4242, USA

Brazell, Craig (Athlete, Baseball Player)
8512 Rockbridge Cir
Montgomery, AL 36116-8807, USA

Brazelton, Dewon (Athlete, Baseball Player)
107 Scenic Dr
Tullahoma, TN 37388-5422, USA

Brazelton, T Berry (Doctor)
23 Hawthorne St
Cambridge, MA 02138-4829, USA

Brazen, Randi
10138 Main St
Bellevue, WA 98004-6022, USA

Braziel, Larry (Athlete, Football Player)
831 Netherland Dr
Arlington, TX 76017-6019, USA

Brazier, Garry (Race Car Driver)
Stanton Racing
100 Memorial Dr
Nicholasville, KY 40356-1082, USA

Brazil, Jeff (Journalist)
Orlando Sentinel
633 N Orange Ave Lbby
Editorial Dept
Orlando, FL 32801-1349, USA

Brazile Jr, Robert L (Athlete, Football Player)
813 Felder Ave
Mobile, AL 36612-1338, USA

Brazill, Mark (Producer)
10428 Valley Spring Ln
Toluca Lake, CA 91602-2806, USA

Brazoban, Yhency (Athlete, Baseball Player)
13609 N 20th St
Tampa, FL 33613-4324, USA

Brazzell, Chris (Athlete, Football Player)
1205 Las Palmas Cir
Alice, TX 78332-3169, USA

Brea, Leslie (Athlete, Baseball Player)
222 N 153rd Ave
Goodyear, AZ 85338-2966, USA

Bready, Richard L (Business Person)
166 President Ave
Providence, RI 02906-4616, USA

Breaker, Daniel (Actor)
c/o Brian Liebman *Liebman Entertainment*
12 E 46th St Fl 5
New York, NY 10017-2418, USA

Breaking Benjamin (Music Group)
c/o Staff Member *Hollywood Records*
500 S Buena Vista St
Burbank, CA 91521-0002, USA

Breaking Point (Music Group)
c/o Staff Member *Wind-up Records*
72 Madison Ave Fl 8
New York, NY 10016-8731, USA

B-Real (Artist, Musician)
17116 Labrador St
Northridge, CA 91325-1900, USA

Bream, Sid (Athlete, Baseball Player)
115 Sable Run
Zelienople, PA 16063-3141, USA

Breathed, Berkeley (Cartoonist)
Washington Post Writers Group
1150 15th St NW
Washington, DC 20071-0002, USA

Breaux, Don (Athlete, Football Player)
19027 Southport Dr
Cornelius, NC 28031-6478, USA

Breaux, John (Politician)
25860 Royal Oak Rd
Royal Oak, MD 21662, USA

Breaux, Tim (Athlete, Basketball Player)
6410 Del Monte Dr Apt 1
Apt E75
Houston, TX 77057-3329, USA

Breazeale, Jim (Athlete, Baseball Player)
790 County Road 297
Bay City, TX 77414-3644, USA

Breck, Jonathan (Actor)
c/o Eric Stevens *Rainbow High Entertainment*
3500 W Olive Ave Ste 300
Burbank, CA 91505-4647, USA

Breckenridge, Alex (Actor)
c/o Staff Member *Kritzer Levine Wilkins Entertainment (KLWG)*
11872 La Grange Ave Fl 1
Los Angeles, CA 90025-5283, USA

Breckenridge, Laura (Actor)
c/o Glenn Rigberg *Inphenate*
9701 Wilshire Blvd Fl 10
Beverly Hills, CA 90212-2010, USA

Brecker, Randy (Musician)
Tropix International
163 3rd Ave # 206
New York, NY 10003-2523, USA

Bredahl, Charlotte (Athlete, Horse Racer, Olympic Athlete)
PO Box 318
Solvang, CA 93464-0318, USA

Brede, Brent (Athlete, Baseball Player)
1891 J Rock Rd
Trenton, IL 62293-2924, USA

Bredesen, Philip (Politician)
1724 Chickering Rd
Nashville, TN 37215-4908, USA

Breding, Ed (Athlete, Football Player)
126 NW Pritchard St
Harlowton, MT 59036, USA

Breech, Jim (Athlete, Football Player)
3189 Princeton Rd # 266
Hamilton, OH 45011-5338, USA

Breeden, Danny (Athlete, Baseball Player)
5111 B Ave
Loxley, AL 36551-4537, USA

Breeden, Hal (Athlete, Baseball Player)
665 Middle Rd S
Leesburg, GA 31763-3442, USA

Breeden, Joe (Athlete, Baseball Player)
1305 Bonaventure Dr
Melbourne, FL 32940-1904, USA

Breeden, Louis (Athlete, Football Player)
11264 Grooms Rd Ste E
Blue Ash, OH 45242-1418, USA

Breeden, Richard C (Government Official)
Coopers & Lybrand
1800 M St NW
Washington, DC 20036-5802, USA

Breedlove, Craig (Race Car Driver)
200 N Front St
Rio Vista, CA 94571-1420, USA

Breedlove, Leory (Athlete, Baseball Player)
1910 N 16th St
Orange, TX 77630-3311, USA

Breedlove, Rod (Athlete, Football Player)
1664 Carlyle Dr Apt H
Crofton, MD 21114-1430, USA

Breen, Adrian (Athlete, Football Player)
1317 N 138th St
Omaha, NE 68154-5101, USA

Breen, Bobby (Actor)
3701 W McNab Rd Apt 206
Pompano Beach, FL 33069-4933, USA

Breen, Edward D (Business Person)
Tyco International
273 Corporate Dr Ste 100
Portsmouth, NH 03801-6863, USA

Breen, Gene (Athlete, Football Player)
1018 Henley Downs Pl
Lake Mary, FL 32746-1972, USA

Breen, George (Athlete, Olympic Athlete, Swimmer)
425 Pepper Mill Ct
Sewell, NJ 08080-2963, USA

Breen, John G (Business Person)
18800 N Park Blvd
Shaker Heights, OH 44122-1809, USA

Breen, Monica (Producer, Writer)
c/o Ilan Breil *Mosaic Media Group*
9200 W Sunset Blvd Ste 10
West Hollywood, CA 90069-3608, USA

Breen, Patrick (Actor)
Gersh Agency
232 N Canon Dr
Beverly Hills, CA 90210-5302, USA

Breen, Shelley (Musician)
8106 Patrice Dr
Brentwood, TN 37027-7126, USA

Breen, Stephen (Steve) (Cartoonist)
San Diego Union-Telegram
PO Box 120191
San Diego, CA 92112-0191, USA

Breer, Murle (Athlete, Golfer)
7008 Sand Rd
Savannah, GA 31410-2314, USA

Brees, Drew (Athlete, Football Player)
576 Audubon St
New Orleans, LA 70118-4950, USA

Bregel, Jeff (Athlete, Football Player)
15431 Tulsa St Spc 33
Mission Hills, CA 91345-1349, USA

Bregman, Buddy (Actor)
c/o Staff Member *Paul Lane Entertainment*
468 N Camden Dr
Beverly Hills, CA 90210-4507, USA

Bregman, Martin (Producer)
Martin Bregman Productions
240 E 39th St Apt 47B
New York, NY 10016-7213, USA

Bregman, Tracey (Actor)
5957 Cavalleri Rd
Malibu, CA 90265-4011, USA

Brehaut, Jeff (Athlete, Golfer)
1085 Leonello Ave
Los Altos, CA 94024-4914, USA

Breidenbach, Warren (Doctor)
Jewish Hospital
217 E Chestnut St
Surgery Dept
Louisville, KY 40202-1821, USA

Breiman, Valerie (Director)
c/o Staff Member *Industry Entertainment*
955 Carrillo Dr Ste 300
Los Angeles, CA 90048-5400, USA

Breining, Fred (Athlete, Baseball Player)
2120 Ticonderoga Dr
San Mateo, CA 94402-4045, USA

Breitenstein, Robert (Athlete, Football Player)
4215 We 95th St
Tulsa, OK 74137, USA

Breitenstien, Robert (Athlete, Football Player)
8524 S Winston Ave
Tulsa, OK 74137-1914, USA

Breitmayer, Peter (Actor)
2582 Lake View Ave
Los Angeles, CA 90039-3317, USA

Breland, Mark (Athlete, Boxer)
20514 Heritage Hwy
Denmark, SC 29042-8831, USA

Bremer, Dick (Commentator)
15910 56th St NE
Saint Michael, MN 55376-3201, USA

Bremmer, Paul L (Politician, Writer)
c/o Staff Member *Simon & Schuster*
1230 Avenue of the Americas Fl CONC1
New York, NY 10020-1586, USA

Bren, Donald (Business Person, Philanthropist)
Donald Bren School of Environmental Science & Management
2400 Bren Hall
University of California
Santa Barbara, CA 93106-0001, USA

B. Renacci, James (Congressman, Politician)
130 Cannon Hob
Washington, DC 20515-3308, USA

Brendel, Alfred (Musician)
Vanguard/Omega Classics
27 W 72nd St
New York, NY 10023-3498, USA

Brendi, Pavel (Athlete, Hockey Player)
1400 Edwards Mill Rd
Raleigh, NC 27607-3624, USA

Brendon, Nicholas (Actor)
Platform
2666 N Beachwood Dr
Los Angeles, CA 90068-2308, USA

Brenly, Bob (Athlete, Baseball Player, Coach)
9726 E Laurel Ln
Scottsdale, AZ 85260-5959, USA

Brenly, Bob (Athlete, Basketball Player)
1060 W Addison St Ste 1
Attn: Broadcast Dept
Chicago, IL 60613-4383, USA

Brennaman, Marty (Commentator)
Cincinnati Reds
2363 Heather Hill Blvd N
Cincinnati, OH 45244-2666, USA

Brennaman, Thom (Commentator)
738 Park Ave
Terrace Park, OH 45174-1021, USA

Brennan, Brian (Athlete, Football Player)
2961 Edgewood Rd
Cleveland, OH 44124-5101, USA

Brennan, Christine (Writer)
Washington Post
Sports Dept
1150 15th Ave NW
Washington, DC 20071-0001, USA

Brennan, Edward A (Business Person)
AMR Corp
433 Amon Carter Blvd
Fort Worth, TX 76155, USA

Brennan, Ian (Actor, Producer, Writer)
c/o Philip Raskind *William Morris Endeavor (LA)*
9601 Wilshire Blvd
Beverly Hills, CA 90210-5213, USA

Brennan, Joseph E (Politician)
104 Frances St
Portland, ME 04102-2512, USA

Brennan, Kevin (Actor, Comedian)
United Talent Agency
9336 Civic Center Dr
Beverly Hills, CA 90210-3604, USA

Brennan, Melissa (Actor)
6520 Platt Ave # 634
West Hills, CA 91307-3218, USA

Brennan, Mike (Athlete, Football Player)
33660 Fox Rd
Easton, MD 21601-6746, USA

Brennan, Neal (Actor, Comedian)
c/o Gregory McKnight *Creative Artists Agency (CAA-LA)*
2000 Avenue of the Stars Ste 100
Los Angeles, CA 90067-4705, USA

Brennan, Rich (Athlete, Hockey Player)
96 Prospect St
Hingham, MA 02043-3442, USA

Brennan, Terrance P (Terry) (Athlete, Coach, Football Player)
1731 Wildberry Dr Unit C
Glenview, IL 60025-1742, USA

Brennan, Tom (Athlete, Baseball Player)
8204 Millbank Dr
Orland Park, IL 60462-1726, USA

Brennan, William (Athlete, Baseball Player)
802 Cottage Hill Dr
Macon, GA 31210-7628, USA

Brenneman, Amy (Actor, Producer)
17145 Rancho St
Encino, CA 91316-4023, USA

Brenner, Dori (Actor)
210 W 101st St Apt 15C
New York, NY 10025-5040, USA

Brenner, Hoby (Athlete, Football Player)
40 Calle Ameno
San Clemente, CA 92672-2367, USA

Brenner, Lisa (Actor)
7729 Sunset Blvd
Los Angeles, CA 90046, USA

Brenner, Teddy (Boxer)
24 W 55th St Apt 9C
New York, NY 10019-5456, USA

Bresee, Bobbie (Actor)
8282 Hollywood Blvd
Los Angeles, CA 90069-1612, USA

Breslawsky, Marc C (Business Person)
Pitney Bowes Inc
1 Elmcroft Rd # 807
Stamford, CT 06926-0700, USA

Breslin, Abigail (Actor)
c/o Elis Pacheco *Digital Launch*
40 W 37th St Rm 1100
New York, NY 10018-7403, USA

Breslin, Jimmy (Journalist)
Newsday
235 Pinelawn Rd
Editorial Dept
Melville, NY 11747-4250, USA

Breslin, Spencer (Actor)
c/o Beth Cannon *Envision Entertainment*
8840 Wilshire Blvd Fl 3
Beverly Hills, CA 90211-2606, USA

Breslow, Craig (Athlete, Baseball Player)
26 Finchwood Dr
Trumbull, CT 06611-4040, USA

Bresnik, Randolph J Major (Astronaut)
14119 Lake Scene Trl
Houston, TX 77059-4406, USA

Bress, Eric (Director, Producer, Writer)
c/o Tobin Babst *Kaplan/Perrone Entertainment*
9560 Wilshire Blvd Fl 5
Beverly Hills, CA 90212-2401, USA

Bressoud, Eddie (Athlete, Baseball Player)
515 Marble Canyon Ln
San Ramon, CA 94582-4830, USA

Brest, Martin (Director, Producer)
c/o John Burnham *ICM Partners (LA)*
10250 Constellation Blvd Fl 7
Los Angeles, CA 90067-6207, USA

Bretche, Fred
3330 Chimney Rock Ln
Sedona, AZ 86336-3020, USA

Bretherton, Billy (Reality Star)
Vexcon Inc.
1201 Linton Rd
Animal and Pest Control
Benton, LA 71006-8736, USA

Bretos, Max (Athlete, Soccer Player)
c/o Staff Member *Maxx Sports & Entertainment*
546 5th Ave Fl 6
New York, NY 10036-5000, USA

Brett, George (Athlete, Baseball Player)
PO Box 419969
Attn Vice President - Bb Operations
Kansas City, MO 64141-6969, USA

Brett, George (Athlete, Baseball Player)
6528 Seneca Rd
Mission Hills, KS 66208-1718, USA

Brett, Jonathan (Actor)
Agency for Performing Arts
9200 W Sunset Blvd Ste 900
West Hollywood, CA 90069-3604, USA

Brettschneider, Carl (Athlete, Football Player)
4649 Bird View Ct
Las Vegas, NV 89129-5326, USA

Breuer, Jim (Comedian)
5 Erick Ct
Chester, NJ 07930-2826, USA

Breuer, Randy (Athlete, Basketball Player)
10481 Misty Morning Ln
Eden Prairie, MN 55347-5023, USA

Breunig, Robert P (Bob) (Athlete, Football Player)
4307 W Lawther Dr
Dallas, TX 75214-2921, USA

Brevak, Bob (Race Car Driver)
Brevak Racing
206 Performance Rd
Mooresville, NC 28115-9591, USA

Brew, Dorian (Athlete, Football Player)
PO Box 1325
Saint Peters, MO 63376-0023, USA

Brewer, Aaron (Athlete, Football Player)
c/o Frank Bauer *Sun West Sports*
7883 N Pershing Ave
Stockton, CA 95207-1749, USA

Brewer, Albert P (Politician)
800 Lakeshore Dr
Birmingham, AL 35229-0001, USA

Brewer, Billy (Athlete, Baseball Player)
7405 Woodway Dr
Woodway, TX 76712-6153, USA

Brewer, Chris (Athlete, Football Player)
6703 Saint Augustine Rd Apt 116
Jacksonville, FL 32217-2859, USA

Brewer, Craig (Director, Producer)
c/o Brad Gross *Brad Gross Agency, The*
161 S Arden Blvd
Los Angeles, CA 90004-3716, USA

Brewer, Dewell (Athlete, Football Player)
4804 Bloomfield Dr
Memphis, TN 38125-3356, USA

Brewer, Donald (Musician)
Lustig Talent
PO Box 770850
Orlando, FL 32877-0850, USA

Brewer, Eric (Athlete, Hockey Player)
634 Riviera Dr
Tampa, FL 33606-3810, USA

Brewer, Jamie (Actor)
c/o Jenn Fernandez *Mosaic Public Relations*
856 N Hayworth Ave
Los Angeles, CA 90046-7107, USA

Brewer, Jamison (Athlete, Basketball Player)
1322 Wind Castle Trl
Indianapolis, IN 46280-2723, USA

Brewer, Janice (Governor, Politician)
Governor of Arizona
1700 W Washington St Ste H
Phoenix, AZ 85007-2810, USA

Brewer, Jim (Athlete, Basketball Player, Olympic Athlete)
1814 S 23rd Ave
Maywood, IL 60153-2810, USA

Brewer, Madeline (Actor)
c/o Glenn Rigberg *Inphenate*
9701 Wilshire Blvd Fl 10
Beverly Hills, CA 90212-2010, USA

Brewer, Mike (Athlete, Baseball Player)
40 Amherst Ave
Menlo Park, CA 94025-3802, USA

Brewer, Rod (Athlete, Baseball Player)
1063 E Sandpiper St
Apopka, FL 32712-2909, USA

Brewer, Sean (Athlete, Football Player)
9232 Grangehill Dr
Riverside, CA 92508-9329, USA

Brewer, Tom (Athlete, Baseball Player)
409 State Rd
Cheraw, SC 29520-1621, USA

Brewer, Tony (Athlete, Baseball Player)
659 Wildwood Ln
Palo Alto, CA 94303-3117, USA

Brewer, Tony
Los Angeles Dodgers
839 Golden Poppy St
Las Vegas, NV 89110-2858, USA

Brewington, Jamie (Athlete, Baseball Player)
3370 S Roger Ct
Chandler, AZ 85286-2481, USA

Brewster, Darrel '"Pete'" (Athlete, Football Player)
PO Box 183
Peculiar, MO 64078-0183, USA

Brewster, Jordana (Actor)
8383 Wilshire Blvd Ste 1000
Beverly Hills, CA 90211-2439, USA

Brewster, Paget (Actor)
4978 Cromwell Ave
Los Angeles, CA 90027-1060, USA

Brewster, Pete (Athlete, Football Player)
PO Box 183
Peculiar, MO 64078-0183, USA

Brewton, Maia (Actor)
525 W 49th St Apt 5A
New York, NY 10019-7148, USA

Brey, Mike (Coach)
Notre Dame University
Athletic Dept
Notre Dame, IN 46556, USA

Breyer, Stephen G (Attorney)
US Supreme Court
United States Supreme Court 11th St NE
Washington, DC 20543-0001, USA

Brezec, Primoz (Athlete, Basketball Player)
10030 Hazelview Dr
Charlotte, NC 28277-2948, USA

Brezina, Bobby (Athlete, Football Player)
1204 Pine Hollow Dr
Friendswood, TX 77546-4634, USA

Brezina, Greg (Athlete, Football Player)
155 Tillinghast Trce
Newnan, GA 30265-6000, USA

Brezner, Larry (Producer)
c/o Larry Brezner *Morra Brezner Steinberg & Tenenbaum (MBST) Entertainment*
345 N Maple Dr Ste 200
Beverly Hills, CA 90210-5174, USA

Brian, Demarco (Athlete, Football Player)
4364 Tomahawk Ln
Vermilion, OH 44089-3323, USA

Brian, Frank (Athlete, Basketball Player)
23757 Brian Rd
Zachary, LA 70791-6231, USA

Brian duffy, colonel (Astronaut)
2625 Bay Area Blvd Spc V
Houston, TX 77058-1523, USA

Brice, Alan (Athlete, Baseball Player)
6726 71st St E
Bradenton, FL 34203-7173, USA

Brice, Alundis (Athlete, Football Player)
928 N Egypt Cir
Brookhaven, MS 39601-3556, USA

Brice, Lee (Musician)
c/o Jeremy Westby *Webster & Associates PR*
3573 Couchville Pike
Hermitage, TN 37076-4012, USA

Brice, Will (Athlete, Football Player)
1139 Craig Ave
Lancaster, SC 29720-8227, USA

Bricekell, Beth (Director)
PO Box 119
Paron, AR 72122-0119, USA

Brickell, Edie (Musician, Songwriter, Writer)
88 Central Park W
New York, NY 10023-5299, USA

Brickell, Beth (Actor)
3001 N Grant St
Little Rock, AR 72207-2819, USA

Brickell, Edie (Musician)
82 Brookwood Ln
New Canaan, CT 06840-3101, USA

Brickhouse, Smith N (Religious Leader)
Church of Christ
PO Box 472
Independence, MO 64051-0472, USA

Brickley, Andy (Athlete, Hockey Player)
5 Mill River Ln
Hingham, MA 02043-3455, USA

Brickley, Andy (Athlete, Hockey Player)
Boston Bruins
100 Legends Way Ste 250
Attn: Broadcast Dept
Boston, MA 02114-1389, United States

Bricklin, Daniel S (Designer)
Trellix Corp
300 Bahr Ave
Concord, MA 01742, USA

Brickman, Paul (Director)
4116 Holly Knoll Dr
Los Angeles, CA 90027-3222, USA

Brickowski, Frank (Athlete, Basketball Player)
589 7th St
Lake Oswego, OR 97034-2906, USA

Briclges, Roy D Maj Gen (Astronaut)
113 William Barksdale
Williamsburg, VA 23185-8211, USA

Bridgeforth, William (Athlete, Baseball Player)
4766 Drakes Branch Rd
Nashville, TN 37218-1436, USA

Bridgeman, Ulysses (Athlete, Basketball Player)
16E4 Cherokee Rd
Apt 5
Louisville, KY 40205, USA

Bridgers, Sean (Actor)
c/o Darris Hatch *Daris Hatch Management*
10027 Rossbury Pl
Los Angeles, CA 90064-4825, USA

Bridges, Angelica (Actor, Model)
c/o Marv Dauer *Marv Dauer Management*
2236 The Terrace
Los Angeles, CA 90049-1171, USA

Bridges, Beau (Actor)
3129 N Summit Pointe Dr
Topanga, CA 90290-4483, USA

Bridges, Bill (Athlete, Basketball Player)
2322 44th St
Santa Monica, CA 90405, USA

Bridges, Chloe (Actor)
c/o Daniel Spilo *Industry Entertainment*
955 Carrillo Dr Ste 300
Los Angeles, CA 90048-5400, USA

Bridges, Jeff (Actor, Producer)
985 Hot Springs Rd
Santa Barbara, CA 93108-1110, USA

Bridges, Jeremy (Athlete, Football Player)
4502 E Ivanhoe St
Gilbert, AZ 85295-5831, USA

Bridges, Jordan (Actor)
c/o Myrna Jacoby *MJ Management*
130 W 57th St Apt 11A
New York, NY 10019-3311, USA

Bridges, Krista (Actor)
c/o JJ Harris *One Talent Management*
3680 1/2 Fredonia Dr
Los Angeles, CA 90068-1208, USA

Bridges, Rocky (Athlete, Baseball Player)
1128 W Shane Dr
Coeur D Alene, ID 83815-9788, USA

Bridges, Todd (Actor)
16002 Nordhoff St
North Hills, CA 91343-3042, USA

Bridges Jr, Roy D (Astronaut, General)
19035 Merry Men Cir
Monument, CO 80132-8731, USA

Bridgewater, Brad (Athlete, Olympic Athlete, Swimmer)
3843 Echo Brook Ln
Dallas, TX 75229-5222, USA

Bridgewater, Teddy (Athlete, Football Player)
c/o Kennard McGuire *MS World LLC*
1270 Crabb River Rd Ste 600-104
Richmond, TX 77469-5636, USA

Bridgman, Mel (Athlete, Hockey Player)
221 Concord St # 17
El Segundo, CA 90245-3799, USA

Bridgmohan, Shaun (Horse Racer)
4541 NW 5th St
Plantation, FL 33317-2132, USA

Brief Smile, A (Music Group)
c/o Staff Member *Paradigm (Monterey)*
404 W Franklin St
Monterey, CA 93940-2303, USA

Briehl, Tom (Athlete, Football Player)
7501 N Via De Los Libros
Scottsdale, AZ 85258-3235, USA

Briem, Anita (Actor)
c/o Steve Cohen *United Talent Agency (UTA-LA)*
9336 Civic Center Dr
Beverly Hills, CA 90210-3604, USA

Brien, Doug (Athlete, Football Player)
55 Cambrian Ave
Piedmont, CA 94611-3606, USA

Brier, Kathy (Actor, Musician)
c/o Judy Katz *Judy Katz PR*
1745 Broadway Fl 17
New York, NY 10019-4642, USA

Briere, Daniel (Athlete, Hockey Player)
17 S Hinchman Ave
Haddonfield, NJ 08033-3714, USA

Brigance, 0 J (Athlete, Football Player)
14 Woodfield Ct
Reisterstown, MD 21136-4639, USA

Brigati, Eddie (Musician, Songwriter, Writer)
Dassinger Creative
32 Ardsley Rd # 201
Montclair, NJ 07042-5002, USA

Briggs, Dan (Athlete, Baseball Player)
8270 Rookery Way
Westerville, OH 43082-8236, USA

Briggs, Danny (Athlete, Golfer)
115 Pearl St
Franklin, TN 37064-8602, USA

Briggs, Greg (Athlete, Football Player)
11115 Harvest Dale Ave
Houston, TX 77065-3338, USA

Briggs, John (Johnny) (Athlete, Baseball Player)
238 Wall Ave
Paterson, NJ 07504-1016, USA

Briggs, Johnny T (Athlete, Baseball Player)
340 Tom Bell Rd Spc 133
Murphys, CA 95247-9735, USA

Briggs, Lance (Athlete, Football Player)
225 NE Mizner Blvd Ste 685
Boca Raton, FL 33432-4080, USA

Briggs, Wilma (Athlete, Baseball Player, Commentator)
111 Summit Ave
Wakefield, RI 02879-2228, USA

Brigham, Jeremy (Athlete, Football Player)
1141 Catalina Dr
Livermore, CA 94550-5928, USA

Bright, Cameron (Actor)
c/o Stephanie Comer *United Talent Agency (UTA-LA)*
9336 Civic Center Dr
Beverly Hills, CA 90210-3604, USA

Bright, Greg
PO Box 41761
Arlington, VA 22204-8761, USA

Bright, Jason (Race Car Driver)
29103 Arnold Dr
Sonoma, CA 95476-9761, USA

Bright, Kevin (Director, Producer)
12903 Chalon Rd
Los Angeles, CA 90049-1253, USA

Bright, Leon (Athlete, Football Player)
1183 Dutton Ave
Deland, FL 32720-5011, USA

Brightbill, Susan (Actor, Writer)
c/o Michael Lasker *Mosaic Media Group*
9200 W Sunset Blvd Ste 10
West Hollywood, CA 90069-3608, USA

Brightman, Sarah (Musician)
374 E Rustic Rd
Santa Monica, CA 90402-1145, USA

Brigman, D J (Athlete, Golfer)
7136 Calle Alegria NE
Albuquerque, NM 87113-1368, USA

Briley, Greg (Athlete, Baseball Player)
2170 Sunnybrook Rd
Greenville, NC 27834-1164, USA

Briley, John (Writer)
c/o Jack Gilardi *ICM Partners (LA)*
10250 Constellation Blvd Fl 7
Los Angeles, CA 90067-6207, USA

Brill, Charlie (Actor)
3635 Wrightwood Dr
Studio City, CA 91604-3947, USA

Brilley, Greg (Athlete, Baseball Player)
2170 Sunnybrook Rd
Greenville, NC 27834-1164, usa

Brilz, Darrick (Athlete, Football Player)
794 Riverwatch Dr
Crescent Springs, KY 41017-5389, USA

Brim, James (Athlete, Football Player)
4310 Alderny Pl
High Point, NC 27265-9277, USA

Brimanis, Aris (Athlete, Hockey Player)
12909 Badger Ln
Anchorage, AK 99516-3034, USA

Brimley, Wilford (Actor)
2477 Riverfront Dr
Santa Clara, UT 84765-5437, USA

Brin, Sergey (Business Person)
c/o Staff Member *Google Inc*
1600 Amphitheatre Pkwy
Mountain View, CA 94043-1351, USA

Brind'amour, Rod (Athlete, Hockey Player)
Carolina Hurricanes
1400 Edwards Mill Rd Attn Coachingstaff
Raleigh, NC 27607-3624, USA

Brind'amour, Rod (Athlete, Hockey Player)
12304 Birchfalls Dr
Raleigh, NC 27614-7900, USA

Brinegar, Claude (Politician)
2444 Sharon Oaks Dr
Menlo Park, CA 94025-6829, USA

Bring, Murray H (Business Person)
Altria Group
120 Park Ave
New York, NY 10017-5577, USA

Brink, Brad (Athlete, Baseball Player)
2628 Surrey Ave
Modesto, CA 95355-4668, USA

Brink, Larry (Athlete, Football Player)
13310 Tierra Heights Rd13310 Tierra
Heights Rd13310 Tierra Heights Rd
Redding, CA 96003, USA

Brinker, Christopher (Producer)
c/o David Krintzman *Morris Yorn Barnes
Levine Krintzman Rubenstein Kohner &
Gellman*
2000 Avenue of the Stars Ste 300N
3rd Floor, North Tower
Los Angeles, CA 90067-4704, USA

Brinker, Nancy (Business Person)
*The Susan G. Komen Breast Cancer
Foundation, Inc*
5005 Lbj Fwy Ste 250
Dallas, TX 75244-6125

Brinkley, Christie (Model)
1265 Flying Point Rd
Water Mill, NY 11976-3424, USA

Brinkman, Chuck (Athlete, Baseball
Player)
126 Country Club Rd
Bryan, OH 43506-9136, USA

Brinkman, Joe (Athlete, Baseball Player)
10351 NW 70th St
Chiefland, FL 32626-5042, USA

Brinkmann, Robert S (Cinematographer)
Murtha Agency
1025 Colorado Ave # B
C/O Ann Murtha
Santa Monica, CA 90401-2847, USA

Brino, Lorenzo (Actor)
c/o Wendy Wilke *Media Partners*
636 Acanto St Apt 207
Los Angeles, CA 90049-2128, USA

Brino, Nikolas (Actor)
c/o Wendy Wilke *Media Partners*
636 Acanto St Apt 207
Los Angeles, CA 90049-2128, USA

Brino, Zachary (Actor)
c/o Wendy Wilke *Media Partners*
636 Acanto St Apt 207
Los Angeles, CA 90049-2128, USA

Brinson, Dana (Athlete, Football Player)
202 Walnut St
Valdosta, GA 31601-3707, USA

Brinson, Larry (Athlete, Football Player)
4614 Rainbow Run
Sugar Land, TX 77479-2039, USA

Brisbin, David (Actor)
c/o Geneva Bray *GVA Talent Agency Inc*
8981 W Sunset Blvd Ste 101
West Hollywood, CA 90069-1850, USA

Brisby, Vincent (Athlete, Football Player)
PO Box 20131
Houston, TX 77225-0131, USA

Brisco, Jack (Wrestler)
3961 SE 26th Court Rd
Ocala, FL 34480-7280, USA

Brisco, Marlin (Athlete, Football Player)
379 Newport Ave Apt 107
Long Beach, CA 90814-7011, USA

Brisco, Valerie (Athlete, Track Athlete)
USA Track & Field
4341 Starlight Dr
Indianapolis, IN 46239-1473, USA

Briscoe, Brent (Actor)
c/o Robert Enriquez *Red Baron
Management*
1600 Rosecrans Ave
Manhattan Beach, CA 90266-3708, USA

Briscoe, John (Athlete, Baseball Player)
2705 Arbor Ct
Richardson, TX 75082-3802, USA

Briscoe, Marlin (Athlete, Football Player)
675 Coronado Ave
Long Beach, CA 90814-1439, USA

Briscoe, Ryan (Race Car Driver)
108 Hickory Hill Rd
Mooresville, NC 28117-8086, USA

Brisebois, Danielle (Musician, Producer)
1034 Garfield Ave
Venice, CA 90291-4935, USA

Brisebois, Patrice (Athlete, Hockey Player)
4723 Castle Cir
Broomfield, CO 80023-4079, USA

Brisson, Elzear (Horse Racer)
PO Box 228
New Kent, VA 23124-0228, USA

Brisson, Lance (Actor)
4570 Noeline Way
Encino, CA 91436-2108, USA

Brister, Walter A (Bubby) III (Athlete,
Football Player)
139 Fontainbleau Dr
Mandeville, LA 70471-6434, USA

Bristol, Dave (Athlete, Baseball Player,
Coach)
1748 Fairview Rd
Andrews, NC 28901-7426, USA

Bristor, John (Athlete, Football Player)
70 Rinehart Ln
Waynesburg, PA 15370-3412, USA

Bristow, Allan (Athlete, Basketball Player)
510 Sand Hill Ct
Marco Island, FL 34145-5859, USA

Bristow, Allan M (Athlete, Basketball
Player, Coach)
PO Box 635
Gloucester Point, VA 23062-0635, USA

Brito, Jorge (Athlete, Baseball Player)
9348 Snake Rd
Athens, AL 35611-8031, USA

Brito, Tilson (Athlete, Baseball Player)
6809 Fishers Farm Ln Unit F1
Charlotte, NC 28277-0334, USA

Britt, Charley (Athlete, Football Player)
128 Savannah Pointe
North Augusta, SC 29841-3586, USA

Britt, Chris (Cartoonist)
State Journal-Register
1 Copley Plz
Editorial Dept
Springfield, IL 62701-1619, USA

Britt, James (Athlete, Football Player)
PO Box 371202
Decatur, GA 30037-1202, USA

Britt, Jessie (Athlete, Football Player)
4003 Coltrain Rd
Greensboro, NC 27455-2631, USA

Britt, May (Actor)
5059 Enfield Ave
Encino, CA 91316-3502, USA

Britt, Tyrone (Athlete, Basketball Player)
4631 Germantown Ave
Philadelphia, PA 19144-3010, USA

Britt, Wayman (Athlete, Basketball Player)
973 Paradise Lake Dr SE
Grand Rapids, MI 49546-3828, USA

Brittain, Michael (Mike) (Athlete,
Basketball Player)
2101 Sunset Point Rd Apt 602
Clearwater, FL 33765-1277, USA

Brittany, Morgan (Actor, Model)
3434 Cornell Rd
Agoura Hills, CA 91301-2714, USA

Brittenum, John (Athlete, Football Player)
PO Box 3773
Fayetteville, AR 72702-3773, USA

Britton, Bill (Athlete, Golfer)
41 Allen St
Rumson, NJ 07760-1316, USA

Britton, Chris (Athlete, Baseball Player)
7481 NW 11th Ct
Plantation, FL 33313-5913, USA

Britton, Connie (Actor, Musician)
240 Centre St # 4H
New York, NY 10013-3215, USA

Britton, Dave (Athlete, Basketball Player)
6321 Old Ox Rd
Dallas, TX 75241-2733, USA

Britton, Eben (Athlete, Football Player)
c/o Tom Condon *CAA (St. Louis)*
222 S Central Ave Ste 1008
Saint Louis, MO 63105-3509, USA

Britton, Jim (Athlete, Baseball Player)
825 Forestwalk Dr
Suwanee, GA 30024-4243, USA

Britton, Zach (Athlete, Baseball Player)
101 Heritage Ln
Weatherford, TX 76087-4422, USA

Britts, Sam (Athlete, Football Player)
10 Kingsbrook Ln
Saint Louis, MO 63132-3006, USA

Britz, Greg (Athlete, Hockey Player)
245 Ocean Ave
Marblehead, MA 01945-3700, USA

Britz, Jerilyn (Athlete, Golfer)
415 E Lincoln St Apt 7
Luverne, MN 56156-1643, USA

Brizendine, Louann (Writer)
UCSF School of Medicine
401 Parnassus Ave
Langporter
San Francisco, CA 94143-2211, USA

Brizzolara, Tony (Athlete, Baseball Player)
1638 Princess Cir NE
Atlanta, GA 30345-4160, USA

Broad, Eli (Business Person)
Eli and Edythe Broad Foundation
10900 Wilshire Blvd Fl 12
Los Angeles, CA 90024-6548, USA

Broadhead, James L (Business Person)
FPL Group
700 Universe Blvd
North Palm Beach, FL 33408-2657, USA

Broadnax, Jerry (Athlete, Football Player)
429 Weaver St
Cedar Hill, TX 75104-9074, USA

Broadway, Lance (Athlete, Baseball
Player)
4106 Greenwood Way
Mansfield, TX 76063-5562, USA

Broberg, Gus (Athlete, Basketball Player)
208 El Pueblo Way
Palm Beach, FL 33480-3218, USA

Broberg, Pete (Athlete, Baseball Player)
220 Monterey Rd
Palm Beach, FL 33480-3228, USA

Brocail, Doug (Athlete, Baseball Player)
8011 Meadow Vista Dr
Missouri City, TX 77459-5734, USA

Broccoli, Barbara (Producer)
709 N Hillcrest Rd
Beverly Hills, CA 90210-3516, USA

Brochtrup, William (Bill) (Actor)
S D B Partners
315 S Beverly Dr Ste 411
Beverly Hills, CA 90212-4301, USA

Brochu, Stephane (Athlete, Hockey Player)
10178 Hawthorne Cir
Goodrich, MI 48438-9224, USA

Brock, Chris (Athlete, Baseball Player)
7684 Markham Bend Pl
Sanford, FL 32771-8107, USA

Brock, Clyde (Athlete, Football Player)
5592 Yorkshire Pl
Lake Oswego, OR 97035-3382, USA

Brock, Dieter (Athlete, Football Player)
218 Brookhollow Dr
Pelham, AL 35124-1898, USA

Brock, Greg (Athlete, Baseball Player)
3727 Valley Oak Dr
Loveland, CO 80538-8930, USA

Brock, Lou (Athlete, Baseball Player)
9716 Bonhomme Estates Dr
Saint Louis, MO 63132-4102, USA

Brock, Matt (Athlete, Football Player)
3105 SW 98th Ave
Portland, OR 97225-2924, USA

Brock, Pete (Athlete, Football Player)
29 Canterbury Hill Rd
Topsfield, MA 01983-1521, USA

Brock, Raheem (Athlete, Football Player)
1017 Serpentine Ln
Wyncote, PA 19095-1616, USA

Brock, Stanley J (Stan) (Athlete, Football Player)
4820 SW 141st Ave
Beaverton, OR 97005-3747, USA

Brock, Stevie (Actor)
c/o Johnny Wright *Wright Entertainment Group*
PO Box 590009
Orlando, FL 32859-0009, USA

Brock, Tarrik (Athlete, Baseball Player)
8111 Fairchild Ave
Winnetka, CA 91306-2012, USA

Brock, Willie (Athlete, Football Player)
3732 NE 70th Ave
Portland, OR 97213-5141, USA

Brockermeyer, Blake (Athlete, Football Player)
413 Crestwood Dr
Fort Worth, TX 76107-1079, USA

Brock III, William E (Bill) (Politician)
222 Severn Ave Ste 1
Annapolis, MD 21403-2566, USA

Brockington, John (Athlete, Football Player)
The Guardian 311 Camino Del Rio N Ste 1150
Suite1500
San Diego, CA 92108, USA

Brock Jr, Lou (Athlete, Football Player)
1015 Sandstone Dr
Saint Louis, MO 63146-5031, USA

Brocklander, Fred (Athlete, Baseball Player)
7903 Severn Hills Way
Severn, MD 21144-1066, USA

Brockovich, Erin (Activist)
29365 Castlehill Dr
Agoura Hills, CA 91301-4432, USA

Broderick, Beth (Actor)
Innovative Artists
1505 10th St
Santa Monica, CA 90401-2805, USA

Broderick, Len (Athlete, Hockey Player)
216 Inverness Way
Easley, SC 29642-3116, USA

Broderick, Matthew (Actor)
PO Box 10459
Burbank, CA 91510-0459, USA

Brodeur, Martin (Athlete, Hockey Player)
22 Baxter Ln
West Orange, NJ 07052-1429, USA

Brodie, John (Athlete, Football Player, Golfer)
49350 Avenida Fernando
La Quinta, CA 92253-2742, USA

Brodie, Kevin (Actor)
3925 Big Oak Dr Apt 5
Studio City, CA 91604-3800, USA

Brodowski, Dick (Athlete, Baseball Player)
120 Pine St
Manchester, MA 01944-1022, USA

Brodsky, Julian A (Business Person)
Comcast Corp
1500 Market St Fl 11E
Philadelphia, PA 19102-2107, USA

Brody, Adam (Actor)
1539 N Laurel Ave Apt 305
Los Angeles, CA 90046-2591, USA

Brody, Adrien (Actor)
737 Stone Barn Rd
Cleveland, NY 13042-3280, USA

Brody, Jon Lee (Actor)
c/o Terry Cohen *Cohen Entertainment*
964 Hancock Ave Apt 305
West Hollywood, CA 90069-4091, USA

Brody, Lane (Music Group)
Black Stallion Country Productions
PO Box 368
Tujunga, CA 91043-0368, USA

Broelsch, Christopher E (Doctor, Misc)
University of Chicago
Medical Center Surgery Dept Box 259
Chicago, IL 60690, USA

Brogan, James (Athlete, Basketball Player)
6631 Hollycrest Ct
San Diego, CA 92121-4137, USA

Brogdon, Cindy (Athlete, Basketball Player, Olympic Athlete)
4162 Anson Trl
Suwanee, GA 30024-6753, USA

Broglio, Ernie (Athlete, Baseball Player)
2838 Via Carmen
San Jose, CA 95124-1442, USA

Brogna, Rico (Athlete, Baseball Player)
2 Gate Post Ln
Woodbury, CT 06798-2136, USA

Brohamer, Jack (Athlete, Baseball Player)
39017 Narcissus Dr
Palm Desert, CA 92211-1882, USA

Brohawn, Troy (Athlete, Baseball Player)
1619 Taylors Island Rd
Woolford, MD 21677-1328, USA

Brohm, Jeff (Athlete, Football Player)
11016 Perwinkle Ln
Louisville, KY 40291-3999, USA

Brokaw, Gary (Athlete, Basketball Player)
6614 Augustine Way
Charlotte, NC 28270-0891, USA

Brokaw, Tom (Journalist)
66 E 79th St Apt 11S
New York, NY 10075-0274, USA

Broken Lizard (Comedian)
c/o Staff Member *United Talent Agency (UTA-LA)*
9336 Civic Center Dr
Beverly Hills, CA 90210-3604, USA

Brolin, James (Actor)
6838 Zumirez Dr
Malibu, CA 90265-4317, USA

Brolin, Josh (Actor)
8200 Dover Canyon Rd
Paso Robles, CA 93446-6604, USA

Brolly, Shane (Actor)
1416 Havenhurst Dr Apt 3C
West Hollywood, CA 90046-3885, USA

Bromberg, David (Musician)
c/o Staff Member *Agency Group Ltd, The (LA)*
1880 Century Park E Ste 711
Los Angeles, CA 90067-1618, USA

Bromell, Loranzo (Athlete, Football Player)
18 Forest View Rd
Cumberland, VA 23040-2508, USA

Bromstad, David (Designer)
c/o Ken Slotnick *William Morris Endeavor (NY)*
1325 Avenue of the Americas
New York, NY 10019-6026, USA

Bronfman, Charles (Commentator)
501 N Lake Way
Palm Beach, FL 33480-3520, USA

Bronfman, Yefin (Musician)
I C M Artists
40 W 57th St
New York, NY 10019-4001, USA

Bronkey, Jeff (Athlete, Baseball Player)
2101 Cliffgate Dr
Edmond, OK 73003-2666, USA

Bronleewe, Matt (Musician)
Flood Burnstead McCready McCarthy
1700 Hayes St Ste 304
Nashville, TN 37203-3593, USA

Bronson, Ben (Athlete, Football Player)
13333 West Rd Apt 1717
Houston, TX 77041-6153, USA

Bronson, John
4374 N 36th St
Phoenix, AZ 85018-4072, USA

Bronson, Po (Writer)
Random House
1745 Broadway Frnt 3 # B1
New York, NY 10019-4343, USA

Bronson, Zack (Athlete, Football Player)
5735 Jackie Ln
Beaumont, TX 77713-9261, USA

Bronstad, Jim (Athlete, Baseball Player)
63 One Main Pl
Benbrook, TX 76126-2206, USA

Bronstein, Elizabeth (Producer)
c/o Staff Member *Creative Artists Agency (CAA-LA)*
2000 Avenue of the Stars Ste 100
Los Angeles, CA 90067-4705, USA

Brook, Holly (Musician)
c/o Staff Member *Paradigm (Monterey)*
404 W Franklin St
Monterey, CA 93940-2303, USA

Brook, Jayne (Actor)
c/o Leslie Siebert *Gersh (LA)*
9465 Wilshire Blvd Ste 600
Beverly Hills, CA 90212-2605, USA

Brook, Kelly (Actor)
c/o Evan Hainey *Untitled Entertainment (LA)*
350 S Beverly Dr Ste 200
Beverly Hills, CA 90212-4819, USA

Brooke, Allison (Music Group, Songwriter, Writer)
2-K/EMI Records
6920 W Sunset Blvd
Los Angeles, CA 90028-7010, USA

Brooke, Bob (Athlete, Hockey Player, Olympic Athlete)
2994 Hilltop Dr
Chaska, MN 55318-3224, USA

Brooke, Edward (Politician)
NLIHC
808 Brickell Key Dr Apt 3204
Miami, FL 33131-2692, USA

Brooke, Jonatha (Musician, Songwriter, Writer)
Brooke
1255 5th Ave Apt 7J
New York, NY 10029-3848, USA

Brookens, Ike (Athlete, Baseball Player)
1053 Brookens Rd
Fayetteville, PA 17222-9314, USA

Brookens, Tom (Athlete, Baseball Player)
488 Black Gap Rd
Fayetteville, PA 17222-9717, USA

Brooker, Tommy (Athlete, Football Player)
306 Woodridge Dr
Tuscaloosa, AL 35406-1923, USA

Brooking, Keith (Athlete, Football Player)
15400 Emerald Coast Pkwy Unit 1207
Destin, FL 32541-8537, USA

Brookins, Clarence (Athlete, Basketball Player)
8266 Fayette St
Philadelphia, PA 19150-2002, USA

Brookins, Gary (Cartoonist)
Richmond Newspapers
Editorial Dept
PO Box 85333
Richmond, VA 23293-0001, USA

Brookins, Jason (Athlete, Football Player)
523 N Wade St Apt C
Mexico, MO 65265-1880, USA

Brooks, Aaron (Athlete, Football Player)
1005 Middle Quarter Ct
Henrico, VA 23238-5920, USA

Brooks, Adam (Director)
c/o Jeff Gorin *William Morris Endeavor (LA)*
9601 Wilshire Blvd
Beverly Hills, CA 90210-5213, USA

Brooks, Albert (Actor, Director, Writer)
3051 Antelo View Dr
Los Angeles, CA 90077-1607, USA

Brooks, Alex (Athlete, Hockey Player)
423 Glenmeadow Dr
Ballwin, MO 63011-3466, USA

Brooks, Amanda (Actor)
c/o Staff Member *Nine Yards Entertainment*
5815 W Sunset Blvd Ste 206
Los Angeles, CA 90028-6481, USA

Brooks, Angelle (Actor)
c/o Staff Member *Pakula/King & Associates*
9229 W Sunset Blvd Ste 315
West Hollywood, CA 90069-3403, USA

Brooks, Avery (Actor)
c/o Steven Arcieri *Arcieri & Associates Inc*
60 E 42nd St Ste 2315
New York, NY 10165-5015, USA

Brooks, Barrett (Athlete, Football Player)
11 Berkshire Dr
Voorhees, NJ 08043-3448, USA

Brooks, Bill (Athlete, Football Player)
1088 Laurelwood
Carmel, IN 46032-8742, USA

Brooks, Bobby D (Athlete, Football Player)
7416 Red Osier Rd
Dallas, TX 75249-1349, USA

Brooks, Brandon (Athlete, Football Player)
c/o Joe Panos *Athletes First, LLC*
23091 Mill Creek Dr
Laguna Hills, CA 92653-1258, USA

Brooks, Bucky (Athlete, Football Player)
1336 Vanagrif Ct
Wake Forest, NC 27587-4479, USA

Brooks, Chet (Athlete, Football Player)
655 Shadyway Dr
Dallas, TX 75232-4821, USA

Brooks, Conrad (Actor)
PO Box 264
Inwood, WV 25428-0264, USA

Brooks, Danielle (Actor)
c/o Jill McGrath *The Group Entertainment*
115 W 29th St Rm 1102
New York, NY 10001-5106, USA

Brooks, Danny (Musician)
American Promotions
2011 Ferry Ave Apt U19
Camden, NJ 08104-1900, USA

Brooks, David Allen (David A) (Actor)
c/o Staff Member *Candy Entertainment Management*
8981 W Sunset Blvd Ste 310
West Hollywood, CA 90069-1848, USA

Brooks, Derrick (Athlete, Football Player)
Derrick Brooks Charities 10014 N Dale Mabry Hwy Ste 101
Tampa, FL 33618, USA

Brooks, Donnie (Musician)
Al Lampkin Entertainment
1817 W Verdugo Ave
Burbank, CA 91506-2149, USA

Brooks, Ed (Athlete, Golfer)
6604 Augusta Rd
Fort Worth, TX 76132-4564, USA

Brooks, E R (Business Person)
Central & South West Corp
1616 Woodall Rodgers Fwy
Dallas, TX 75202-1234, USA

Brooks, Ethan (Athlete, Football Player)
8 Gatewood
Avon, CT 06001-3949, USA

Brooks, Garth (Actor, Musician, Producer, Songwriter)
c/o Staff Member *Bob Doyle & Associates*
1111 17th Ave S
Nashville, TN 37212-2203, USA

Brooks, Geraldine (Writer)
c/o Staff Member *Viking Press*
375 Hudson St
New York, NY 10014-3658, USA

Brooks, Golden (Actor)
7230 Pacific View Dr
Los Angeles, CA 90068-2042, USA

Brooks, Greg (Athlete, Football Player)
3041 Alex Kornman Blvd
Harvey, LA 70058-2012, USA

Brooks, Hubert (Hubie) (Athlete, Baseball Player)
15001 Olive St
Hesperia, CA 92345-3306, USA

Brooks, Jamal (Athlete, Football Player)
8 Chestnut Bluffs Ct
Greensboro, NC 27407-6376, USA

Brooks, James (Athlete, Football Player)
2876 Sycamore Creek Dr
Independence, KY 41051-8410, USA

Brooks, James L (Actor, Director, Producer)
1716 Westridge Rd
Los Angeles, CA 90049-2516, USA

Brooks, Jason (Actor)
c/o Staff Member *Commonwealth Talent Group*
PO Box 36514
Los Angeles, CA 90036-0514, USA

Brooks, Jerry (Athlete, Baseball Player)
15152 Mountain View Ln
Frisco, TX 75035-6882, USA

Brooks, Jimmie (Athlete, Football Player)
4505 Cherry Forest Cir
Louisville, KY 40245-2124

Brooks, Jon (Athlete, Football Player)
104 Carver St
Saluda, SC 29138-1514, USA

Brooks, Karen (Musician)
5408 Clearview Ln
Waterford, WI 53185-2950, USA

Brooks, Kevin (Athlete, Football Player)
11620 Audelia Rd Apt 614
Dallas, TX 75243-5683, USA

Brooks, Kimberly A (Actor)
c/o Kevin Turner *Coast to Coast Talent Group*
3350 Barham Blvd
Los Angeles, CA 90068-1404, USA

Brooks, Kix (Musician, Songwriter)
Brooks & Dunn
PO Box 120669
Nashville, TN 37212-0669, USA

Brooks, Larry (Athlete, Football Player)
PO Box 9058 Attn Football Coaching Staff
Virginia State University, VA 23806-0001, USA

Brooks, Lee (Athlete, Football Player)
4206 Bamford Dr
Austin, TX 78731-1355, USA

Brooks, Macey (Athlete, Football Player)
693 Manhattan Cir
Oswego, IL 60543-9802, USA

Brooks, Mark (Athlete, Golfer)
1712 S Adams St
Fort Worth, TX 76110-1401, USA

Brooks, Mehcad (Actor)
c/o David (Dave) Fleming *Mosaic Media Group*
9200 W Sunset Blvd Ste 10
West Hollywood, CA 90069-3608, USA

Brooks, Mel (Actor, Director)
c/o Staff Member *BrooksFilms Ltd / Culver Studios*
9336 Washington Blvd
Culver City, CA 90232-2600

Brooks, Meredith (Musician)
2591 Leicester Dr
Los Angeles, CA 90046-1662, USA

Brooks, Michael (Athlete, Football Player)
15004 W Georgia Dr
Surprise, AZ 85379-4249, USA

Brooks, Michael (Athlete, Basketball Player, Olympic Athlete)
495 Bethany St
San Diego, CA 92114-5539, USA

Brooks, Michael (Athlete, Football Player)
30 Pine Tree Dr
Honey Brook, PA 19344-1254, USA

Brooks, Mike (Athlete, Football Player)
716 2nd Ave
Ruston, LA 71270-6066, USA

Brooks, Nate (Athlete, Boxer, Olympic Athlete)
21274 Ellacott Pkwy Apt M208
Cleveland, OH 44128-6600, USA

Brooks, Nathan (Boxer)
3139 Albion Rd
Cleveland, OH 44120-2803, USA

Brooks, Reggie (Athlete, Football Player)
17970 Buckland Dr
Granger, IN 46530-8908, USA

Brooks, Rich (Athlete, Coach, Football Coach, Football Player)
88725 Sky High Dr
Springfield, OR 97478-8211, USA

Brooks, Richard (Actor)
333 Washington Blvd # 102
Marina Del Rey, CA 90292-5152, USA

Brooks, Robert (Athlete, Football Player)
8611 N 17th Pl # Pi
Phoenix, AZ 85020-3320, USA

Brooks, Ron (Athlete, Football Player)
c/o Pat Dye Jr *SportsTrust Advisors (GA)*
3340 Peachtree Rd NE Fl 16
Atlanta, GA 30326-1000, USA

Brooks, Ross (Athlete, Hockey Player)
196 Old River Rd Apt 215
Lincoln, RI 02865-1133, USA

Brooks, Scott (Athlete, Basketball Coach, Basketball Player, Coach)
c/o Warren LeGarie *Warren LeGarie Sports Management*
1108 Masonic Ave
San Francisco, CA 94117-2915, USA

Brooks, Steve (Athlete, Football Player)
3403 36th St
Lubbock, TX 79413-2233, USA

Brooks, Terry (Writer)
Del Rey Books
1540 Broadway
New York, NY 10036-4039, USA

Brooks, Tony (Athlete, Football Player)
19626 Northrop St
Cassopolis, MI 49031-9328, USA

Brooks & Dunn (Music Group, Musician)
c/o Rick Shipp *William Morris Endeavor (Nashville)*
1600 Division St Ste 300
Nashville, TN 37203-2755, USA

Brooks Jr, Cliff (Athlete, Football Player)
12023 Briar Forest Dr
Houston, TX 77077-3027, USA

Brooks Jr., Mo (Congressman, Politician)
1641 Longworth Hob
Washington, DC 20515-3005, USA

Brophy, Jay (Athlete, Football Player)
3623 Oak Rd
Stow, OH 44224-3934, USA

Brophy, John (Athlete, Hockey Player)
141 Carpenter Ln
Harrisonburg, VA 22801-9777, USA

Brophy, Kevin (Actor)
15010 Hamlin St
Van Nuys, CA 91411-1408, USA

Brophy, Nancy (Athlete, Golfer)
141 Carpenter Ln
Harrisonburg, VA 22801-9777, USA

Brophy, Theodore F (Business Person)
60 Arch St
Greenwich, CT 06830-2507, USA

Brosius, Scott D (Athlete, Baseball Player)
Linfield College
900 SE Baker St
Hhpa Complex, Mail Code A440
McMinnville, OR 97128-6894, USA

Brosnahan, Rachel (Actor)
c/o Carole Dibo *Carole Dibo Talent Management*
Prefers to be contacted by telephone or email
Los Angeles, CA, USA

Brosnan, Jim (Athlete, Baseball Player)
7742 Churchill St
Morton Grove, IL 60053-1805, USA

Brosnan, Pierce (Actor, Producer)
31112 Broad Beach Rd
Malibu, CA 90265, USA

Bross, Terry (Athlete, Baseball Player)
7952 E Camino Real
Scottsdale, AZ 85255-6136, USA

Brossart, Willie (Athlete, Hockey Player)
9318 Susquehanna Trl
Ashland, VA 23005-3382, USA

Brosseau, Frank (Athlete, Baseball Player)
41 Island Rd
Saint Paul, MN 55127-2635, USA

Brostek, Bern (Athlete, Football Player)
PO Box 44552
Kamuela, HI 96743-4552, USA

Broten, Aaron (Athlete, Hockey Player)
307 3rd Ave
Roseau, MN 56751, USA

Broten, Neal (Athlete, Hockey Player, Olympic Athlete)
N8216 690th St
River Falls, WI 54022-4535, USA

Broten, Paul (Athlete, Hockey Player)
2971 Jordan Ct
Saint Paul, MN 55125-2821, USA

Brothers, Bellamy, The (Musician)
c/o Staff Member *Agency for the Performing Arts (APA-LA)*
405 S Beverly Dr Ste 500
Beverly Hills, CA 90212-4425, USA

Brotherton, John (Actor)
c/o Gabrielle Krengel *Domain Talent*
9229 W Sunset Blvd Ste 710
West Hollywood, CA 90069-3407, USA

Brotherton, Michael (Race Car Driver)
1317 Summertime Trl
Lewisville, TX 75067-5507, USA

Brotman, Jeffrey (Business Person)
Costco Wholesale Corp
999 Lake Dr
Issaquah, WA 98027-8990, USA

Brough, Randi (Actor)
11684 Ventura Blvd # 476
Studio City, CA 91604-2699, USA

Broughton, Luther (Athlete, Football Player)
PO Box 371
Huger, SC 29450-0371, USA

Broughton, Willie (Athlete, Football Player)
1724 Lacy Ln
Mesquite, TX 75181-1560, USA

Brouhard, Mark (Athlete, Baseball Player)
6289 Jackie Ave
Woodland Hills, CA 91367-1424, USA

Broussard, Ben (Athlete, Baseball Player)
1899 Crockett Gardens Rd
Georgetown, TX 78633-1805, USA

Broussard, Fred (Athlete, Football Player)
2856 Fm 1011 RR
Liberty, TX 77575-7430, USA

Broussard, Marc (Musician)
c/o Staff Member *Paradigm (Monterey)*
404 W Franklin St
Monterey, CA 93940-2303, USA

Broussard, Rebecca (Actor)
413 Howland Canal
Venice, CA 90291-4619, USA

Broussard, Steve (Athlete, Football Player)
113 Waterland Way
Frederick, MD 21702-4094, USA

Brow, Scott (Athlete, Baseball Player)
3749 NW 4th Ave
Hillsboro, OR 97124-1610, USA

Browder, Ben (Actor)
551 Live Oak Circle Dr
Calabasas, CA 91302-2140, USA

Brower, Bob (Athlete, Baseball Player)
2703 N Van Buren St
Hutchinson, KS 67502-2017, USA

Brower, James (Jim) (Athlete, Baseball Player)
34W002 Cherry Ln
Geneva, IL 60134-4104, USA

Brower, Jordan
9100 Wilshire Blvd Ste 503E
Beverly Hills, CA 90212-3419

Brower, Jordan Lloyd (Actor)
c/o Beverly Strong *Strong Management*
9350 Wilshire Blvd Ste 224
Beverly Hills, CA 90212-3204, USA

Brower, Laurie (Athlete, Golfer)
10325 Cypresswood Dr Apt 1024
Houston, TX 77070-3420, USA

Brown, Aaron (Correspondent)
c/o Carole Cooper *N.S. Bienstock*
250 W 57th St Ste 333
New York, NY 10107-0302, USA

Brown, Aaron C (Athlete, Football Player)
3922 W Robson St
Tampa, FL 33614-2636, USA

Brown, A B (Athlete, Football Player)
224 Wesley St
Salem, NJ 08079-1714, USA

Brown, Adrian (Baseball Player)
Pittsburgh Pirates
604 Pike St
McComb, MS 39648-2250, USA

Brown, Alison (Musician, Songwriter, Writer)
SRO Artists
6629 University Ave Ste 206
Middleton, WI 53562-3037, USA

Brown, Allen (Athlete, Football Player)
454 Highway 569
Ferriday, LA 71334-4445, USA

Brown, Alton (Athlete, Baseball Player)
253 Consul Ave
Virginia Beach, VA 23462-3511, USA

Brown, Alton (Chef, Television Host)
441 Church St NE
Marietta, GA 30060-1319, USA

Brown, Amanda (Musician)
c/o Staff Member *ReverbNation (NY)*
15 E 36th St Apt 3A
2D
New York, NY 10016-3308, USA

Brown, Andre (Athlete, Football Player)
11245 S Emerald Ave
Chicago, IL 60628-4706, USA

Brown, Andrew
561 Placid Run Rd
Orange City, FL 32763-6626, USA

Brown, Andy (Athlete, Hockey Player)
6243 S 125 W
Trafalgar, IN 46181-8799, USA

Brown, Anthony (Athlete, Football Player)
42561 Cavalier Ct
Canton, MI 48187-2375, USA

Brown, Antonio (Athlete, Football Player)
c/o Drew Rosenhaus *Rosenhaus Sports Representation*
6400 Allison Rd
Miami Beach, FL 33141-4540, USA

Brown, Antron (Race Car Driver)
45 Waln Rd
Trenton, NJ 08620, USA

Brown, Arnold (Athlete, Football Player)
8763 Stephens Church Rd
Wilmington, NC 28411-7985, USA

Brown, Arthur (Athlete, Football Player)
c/o Doug Hendrickson *Octagon Football*
832 Sansome St Fl 1
San Francisco, CA 94111-1558, USA

Brown, Ashley Nicole (Actor)
Hervey/Grimes
PO Box 64249
Los Angeles, CA 90064-0249, USA

Brown, Bill (Athlete, Football Player)
7501 W 101st St Apt 322
Minneapolis, MN 55438-2530, USA

Brown, Bill (Commentator)
9807 Cat Hollows Ct
Cypress, TX 77433-4014, USA

Brown, Billy Aaron (Actor)
c/o Staff Member *Stone Manners Salners Agency (LA)*
6100 Wilshire Blvd Ste 1500
Los Angeles, CA 90048-5110, USA

Brown, Billy Ray (Athlete, Golfer)
7502 Whitman Ln
Sugar Land, TX 77479-4452, USA

Brown, Blair (Actor)
18 E 53rd St
#140
New York, NY 10022, USA

Brown, Bob (Athlete, Basketball Player)
7 Charleston St S
Sugar Land, TX 77478-3656, USA

Brown, Bob (Athlete, Football Player)
PO Box 211081
Saint Louis, MO 63121-9081, USA

Brown, Bobby (Athlete, Baseball Player)
112 Avonlea Dr
Chesapeake, VA 23322-4270, USA

Brown, Bobby (Actor, Dancer, Musician, Producer, Songwriter)
c/o Staff Member *William Morris Endeavor (LA)*
9601 Wilshire Blvd
Beverly Hills, CA 90210-5213, USA

Brown, Bobby (Athlete, Baseball Player)
4100 Clarke Ave
Fort Worth, TX 76107-2407, USA

Brown, Booker (Athlete, Football Player)
26321 Olanche St
Mojave, CA 93501-7528, USA

Brown, Boyd (Athlete, Football Player)
1610 167th Ave NE
Bellevue, WA 98008-2909, USA

Brown, Brant (Athlete, Baseball Player)
7300 Rough Riders Trl
Frisco, TX 75034-9088, USA

Brown, Brene (Doctor, Writer)
c/o Jennifer Rudolph Walsh *William Morris Endeavor (NY)*
1325 Avenue of the Americas
New York, NY 10019-6026, USA

Brown, Brianna (Actor)
c/o Gladys Gonzalez *John Carrabino Management*
5900 Wilshire Blvd Ste 406
Los Angeles, CA 90036-5015, USA

Brown, Bryan (Actor)
c/o Staff Member *Steve Himber Entertainment*
211 S Beverly Dr # 601
Beverly Hills, CA 90212-3807, USA

Brown, Campbell (Correspondent, Journalist)
Partnership for Educational Justice
5252 11th St S
Arlington, VA 22204-3217, USA

Brown, Candace (Actor)
c/o Judy Orbach *Judy O Productions*
6136 Glen Holly St
Los Angeles, CA 90068-2338, USA

Brown, Carlos (Athlete, Football Player)
10840 N Bunkerhill Dr
Fresno, CA 93730-5901, USA

Brown, Cedric (Athlete, Football Player)
PO Box 23201
Oklahoma City, OK 73123-2201, USA

Brown, Cedrick (Athlete, Football Player)
74 Arbor Meadow Dr
Sicklerville, NJ 08081-1754, USA

Brown, C Edward (Eddie) (Athlete, Football Player)
3465 Commodore Pt
Knoxville, TN 37922-6566, USA

Brown, Chad (Actor)
c/o Staff Member *Sterling/Winters Company, The*
10877 Wilshire Blvd Fl 15
Los Angeles, CA 90024-4341, USA

Brown, Chad (Athlete, Football Player)
10287 Dowling Way
Highlands Ranch, CO 80126-4769, USA

Brown, Charles (Athlete, Football Player)
1215 Brittany Dr Apt F
Florence, SC 29501-6250, USA

Brown, Charles E (Athlete, Football Player)
7317 S Merrill Ave
Chicago, IL 60649-3208, USA

Brown, Charlie (Athlete, Hockey Player, Olympic Athlete)
7676 Ranier Ln N
Osseo, MN 55311-4322, USA

Brown, Charlie (Athlete, Football Player)
7317 S Merrill Ave # 5
Chicago, IL 60649-3208, USA

Brown, Charlie (Athlete, Football Player)
5243 Wabada Ave
Saint Louis, MO 63113-1121, USA

Brown, Charlie (Athlete, Football Player)
3113 Cherry Valley Cir
Fairfield, CA 94534-7510, USA

Brown, Charlie R (Athlete, Football Player)
5226 Washington Pl
Saint Louis, MO 63108-1117, USA

Brown, Chris (Musician)
14975 Patrick Meadows Way
Montpelier, VA 23192-2947, USA

Brown, Chris (Athlete, Football Player)
7161 Cypress Dr
Westerville, OH 43082-8111, USA

Brown, Chris (Athlete, Football Player)
251 Riverbend Dr
Franklin, TN 37064-5518, USA

Brown, Chuck (Race Car Driver)
5082 Old NC Highway 49
Asheboro, NC 27205-0118, USA

Brown, Chucky (Athlete, Basketball Player)
102 Balsamwood Ct
Cary, NC 27513-3456, USA

Brown, Chykie (Athlete, Football Player)
c/o Kevin Poston *Deal LLC*
28025 S Harwich Dr
Farmington Hills, MI 48334-4259, USA

Brown, Cindy (Athlete, Basketball Player)
2 Championship Dr
Auburn Hills, MI 48326-1753, USA

Brown, Clancy (Actor)
3141 Oakdell Ln
Studio City, CA 91604-4218, USA

Brown, Clay (Athlete, Football Player)
PO Box 265
Lakeside, AZ 85929-0265, USA

Brown, Cleophus (Athlete, Baseball Player)
3912 Sharon Church Rd
Pinson, AL 35126-2660, USA

Brown, Clifford (Athlete, Baseball Player)
5104 N 37th St
Tampa, FL 33610-6421, USA

Brown, Cornell (Athlete, Football Player)
1600 Sangloe Pl
Lynchburg, VA 24502-1822, USA

Brown, Corrine (Congressman, Politician)
2336 Rayburn Hob
Washington, DC 20515-2305, USA

Brown, Corwin (Athlete, Football Player)
613 Primrose Ln
Matteson, IL 60443-1762, USA

Brown, Courtney (Athlete, Football Player)
1133 Schurlknight Rd
Saint Stephen, SC 29479-3617, USA

Brown, Curt (Athlete, Baseball Player)
5099 Coronado Rdg
Boca Raton, FL 33486-1416, USA

Brown, Curtis (Athlete, Baseball Player)
3200 Cloudview Dr
Sacramento, CA 95833-2700, USA

Brown, Curtis (Athlete, Football Player)
7370 San Diego Ave Apt 1
Saint Louis, MO 63121-2259, USA

Brown, Curtis (Athlete, Hockey Player)
467 Carroll St
Sunnyvale, CA 94086-6204, USA

Brown, Curtis L Colonel (Astronaut)
19500 E Highway 6
Alvin, TX 77511-7458, USA

Brown, Curtis L Jr (Astronaut)
204 Starrwood
Hudson, WI 54016-7174, USA

Brown, Dale (Writer)
c/o Robert Gottlieb *Trident Media Group LLC*
41 Madison Ave Fl 36
New York, NY 10010-2257, USA

Brown, Dale D (Coach, Sportscaster)
ESPN-TV
935 Middle St
Sports Dept Espn Plaza
Bristol, CT 06010-1000, USA

Brown, Dan (Writer)
c/o Michael Rudell *Franklin Weinrib Rudell & Vassallo*
488 Madison Ave Fl 18
New York, NY 10022-5707, USA

Brown, Dante (Athlete, Football Player)
c/o Liza Anderson *Anderson Group Public Relations*
8060 Melrose Ave Fl 4
Los Angeles, CA 90046-7038, USA

Brown, Daren (Athlete, Baseball Player)
2502 S Tyler St Attn Managersofc
Tacoma, WA 98405-1051, USA

Brown, Darrell (Athlete, Baseball Player)
Detroit Tigers
2808 Northampton Pl
Oklahoma City, OK 73120-3010, USA

Brown, Dave (Athlete, Hockey Player)
c/o Staff Member *Philadelphia Flyers*
3601 S Broad St Ste 2
First Union Spectrum
Philadelphia, PA 19148-5297, USA

Brown, Dave
216 Watchung Frk
Westfield, NJ 07090-3814, USA

Brown, David P (Athlete)
776 W Valley View Rd
Ashland, OR 97520-9479, USA

Brown, Dee (Athlete, Basketball Player)
1 Sports Pkwy
Sacramento, CA 95834-2300, USA

Brown, Dee (Athlete, Baseball Player)
2626 Balmoral Ct
Kissimmee, FL 34744-8442, USA

Brown, Dee (Athlete, Football Player)
3278 Margellina Dr
Charlotte, NC 28210-4086, USA

Brown, Derek (Athlete, Football Player)
13 Four Leaf Mnr
Rexford, NY 12148-1490, USA

Brown, Derek
1283 Carrizo St NW
Los Lunas, NM 87031-6938, USA

Brown, Dermal (Baseball Player)
Kansas City Royals
7118 Grapetree Trl
Cordova, TN 38018-7937, USA

Brown, Don (Athlete, Football Player)
5167 SW 129th Ter
Miramar, FL 33027-5837, USA

Brown, Donald C (Athlete, Football Player)
2797 Union Ave
San Jose, CA 95124-1433, USA

Brown, Dorian (Actor)
c/o Staff Member *McKeon-Myones Management*
3500 W Olive Ave Ste 770
Burbank, CA 91505-5527, USA

Brown, Doug (Athlete, Hockey Player)
11 Chieftans Rd
Greenwich, CT 06831-3260, USA

Brown, Duane (Athlete, Football Player)
c/o Andy Ross *Octagon Football*
832 Sansome St Fl 1
San Francisco, CA 94111-1558, USA

Brown, Dustin (Athlete, Hockey Player)
226 Bundy Rd
Ithaca, NY 14850-9249, USA

Brown, Dwier (Actor)
c/o Michael Slessinger *Michael Slessinger & Associates*
8730 W Sunset Blvd Ste 1125
W Hollywood, CA 90069-2210, USA

Brown, Eddie (Athlete, Football Player)
8400 SW 133rd Avenue Rd Apt 214
Miami, FL 33183-4543, USA

Brown, Elton
1955 W Yosemite Dr
Chandler, AZ 85248-4897, USA

Brown, Emil (Athlete, Baseball Player)
18361 Olde Farm Rd
Lansing, IL 60438-2575, USA

Brown, Eric (Athlete, Football Player)
2226 Drake Falls Dr
Pearland, TX 77584-1760, USA

Brown, Foxy (Musician)
c/o Marvet Britto *Britto Agency PR*
90 Franklin St Apt 4N
New York, NY 10013-3489, USA

Brown, Fred (Athlete, Basketball Player, Coach)
3696 72nd Pl SE
Mercer Island, WA 98040-3353, USA

Brown, Fred (Athlete, Football Player)
1050 Riverbend Club Dr SE
Atlanta, GA 30339-2805, USA

Brown, Fred R (Athlete, Football Player)
4128 Rigel Ave
Lompoc, CA 93436-1248, USA

Brown, Gary (Athlete, Football Player)
1605 Coyote Ct
Keller, TX 76248-5371, USA

Brown, Gary (Athlete, Football Player)
5 Crystal Ln
Brentwood, NY 11717-1114, USA

Brown, Gates (Athlete, Baseball Player)
17206 Santa Barbara Dr
Detroit, MI 48221-2525, USA

Brown, George (Athlete, Basketball Player)
24652 Santa Barbara St
Southfield, MI 48075-2526, USA

Brown, Georg Stanford (Actor)
2565 Greenvalley Rd
Los Angeles, CA 90046-1437, USA

Brown, Gilbert (Athlete, Football Player)
49374 Sherwood Ct
Belleville, MI 48111-8844, USA

Brown, Gordie (Comedian)
c/o Staff Member *William Morris Endeavor (LA)*
9601 Wilshire Blvd
Beverly Hills, CA 90210-5213, USA

Brown, Greg (Athlete, Football Player)
1016 Hartley Ct
Sicklerville, NJ 08081-1109, USA

Brown, Greg (Athlete, Hockey Player)
43 Ladds Way
Scituate, MA 02066-1901, USA

Brown, Guy (Athlete, Football Player)
2233 Forest Hollow Park
Dallas, TX 75228-7826, USA

Brown, Hal (Athlete, Baseball Player)
4216 Henderson Rd
Greensboro, NC 27410-4305, USA

Brown, Harold (Politician)
Strategic/International Studies Center
Strategic Study Center1800 K St NW
Washington, DC 20006, USA

Brown, Henry (Actor)
1101 E Pike St Ste 300
Seattle, WA 98122-3938, USA

Brown, Henry (Athlete, Baseball Player)
4075 N 61st St
Milwaukee, WI 53216-1210, USA

Brown, Heritage Doris (Athlete, Track Athlete)
Seattle Pacific College
Athletic Dept
Seattle, WA 98119, USA

Brown, Hubie (Basketball Coach, Coach)
120 Foxridge Rd
Atlanta, GA 30327-4310, USA

Brown, Ivory Lee (Athlete, Football Player)
9811 Dale Crest Dr Apt 1026
Dallas, TX 75220-3029, USA

Brown, Jackie (Athlete, Baseball Player)
8181 Fannin St Apt 2518
Houston, TX 77054-2991, USA

Brown, James (Musician)
c/o Rob Heller *William Morris Endeavor (LA)*
9601 Wilshire Blvd
Beverly Hills, CA 90210-5213, USA

Brown, James (Sportscaster)
Fox-TV
205 E 67th St
Sports Dept
New York, NY 10065-6089, USA

Brown, James (Athlete, Football Player)
3723 SW 49th Pi
Fort Lauderdale, FL 33312, USA

Brown, Jamie (Actor)
c/o Melisa Spamer *Domain Talent*
9229 W Sunset Blvd Ste 710
West Hollywood, CA 90069-3407, USA

Brown, Jamie (Athlete, Baseball Player)
4050 Bailey Acres Cir
Meridian, MS 39305-9263, USA

Brown, Jamie (Athlete, Football Player)
25023 Riding Center Dr
Chantilly, VA 20152-6039, USA

Brown, Jammal (Athlete, Football Player)
2223 NE 36th St
Lawton, OK 73507, USA

Brown, Jarvis (Athlete, Baseball Player)
1537 Teal Dr
Lawrenceville, GA 30043-3296, USA

Brown, Jason (Athlete, Football Player)
8810 Gilly Way
Randallstown, MD 21133-5300, USA

Brown, J B (Athlete, Football Player)
12520 Woodsong Ln
Bowie, MD 20721-4224, USA

Brown, J Cristopher (Cris) (Baseball Player)
5015 Brighton Ave
Los Angeles, CA 90062-2434, USA

Brown, Jeff (Athlete, Hockey Player)
800 Tara Oaks Dr
Chesterfield, MO 63005, USA

Brown, Jeremy (Athlete, Baseball Player)
704 Cobb St
Birmingham, AL 35209-6515, USA

Brown, J Glen (Horse Racer)
750 Michigan Ave
Columbus, OH 43215-1107, USA

Brown, Jim (Athlete, Football Player)
Amer-I-Can
269 S Beverly Dr # 1048
Beverly Hills, CA 90212-3851, USA

Brown, Jim Ed (Musician)
7000 Cloverland Dr
Brentwood, TN 37027-7660, USA

Brown, John (Athlete, Basketball Player)
1329 N Florissant Rd
Saint Louis, MO 63135-1153, USA

Brown, John (Athlete, Football Player)
101 Gadshill Pl
Pittsburgh, PA 15237-2341, USA

Brown, Johnny (Actor)
2732 Woodhaven Dr
Los Angeles, CA 90068-1934, USA

Brown, Jonathan (Athlete, Football Player)
c/o Chad Wiestling *Integrated Sports Management*
2120 Texas St Apt 2204
Houston, TX 77003-3054, USA

Brown, Jonathan Daniel (Actor)
c/o Staff Member *ICM Partners (LA)*
10250 Constellation Blvd Fl 7
Los Angeles, CA 90067-6207, USA

Brown, Jophrey (Athlete, Baseball Player)
3008 W 81st St
Inglewood, CA 90305-1425, USA

Brown, Julie (Downtown) (DJ)
c/o Steven Jensen *Independent Group, The*
6363 Wilshire Blvd Ste 115
Los Angeles, CA 90048-5734, USA

Brown, Junior (Musician)
c/o Staff Member *Paradigm (Monterey)*
404 W Franklin St
Monterey, CA 93940-2303, USA

Brown, Kaci (Musician)
c/o Staff Member *Interscope Records (LA) - Main*
2220 Colorado Ave
Santa Monica, CA 90404-3506, USA

Brown, Kale (Actor)
c/o Staff Member *Gage Group, The (LA)*
5757 Wilshire Blvd Ste 659
Los Angeles, CA 90036-3682, USA

Brown, Katie (Designer, Television Host)
c/o Staff Member *Style Network*
5750 Wilshire Blvd
Los Angeles, CA 90036-3697, USA

Brown, Kedrick (Athlete, Basketball Player)
151 Merrimac St # 1
Boston, MA 02114-4714, USA

Brown, Keith (Athlete, Hockey Player)
8515 Woodland Brooke Trl
Cumming, GA 30028-5048, USA

Brown, Keith (Athlete, Baseball Player)
820 Harbor View Ter
Old Hickory, TN 37138-1013, USA

Brown, Ken (Athlete, Football Player)
1952 S Magnolia St Apt 3T
Denver, CO 80224-2208, USA

Brown, Ken (Athlete, Football Player)
14811 Valleyheart Dr
Sherman Oaks, CA 91403-1602, USA

Brown, Ken (Athlete, Hockey Player)
2708 Checker Dr
Cedar Park, TX 78613-1640, USA

Brown, Ken J (Athlete, Football Player)
2004 Miramar Blvd
Oklahoma City, OK 73111-1808, USA

Brown, Kevin (Athlete, Baseball Player)
4451 Gateway Park Blvd Apt 565
Sacramento, CA 95834-2409, USA

Brown, Kevin (Athlete, Baseball Player)
10400 Wolfinger Rd
Mount Vernon, IN 47620-8303, USA

Brown, Kevin (Athlete, Baseball Player)
105 Browns Rdg
Macon, GA 31210-8614, USA

Brown, Kevin (Race Car Driver)
Jokers Wild Racing
99 S 1000 W
Clearfield, UT 84015-9234, USA

Brown, Kimberlin Ann (Actor)
c/o Staff Member *Pakula/King & Associates*
9229 W Sunset Blvd Ste 315
West Hollywood, CA 90069-3403, USA

Brown, Kimberly J (Actor)
c/o Diane Brown *Gemstone Talent*
27943 Seco Canyon Rd # 212
Santa Clarita, CA 91350-3872, USA

Brown, Koffee (Musician)
Red Entertainment Group
481 Eight Ave
#1750
New York, NY 10001

Brown, Kris (Athlete, Football Player)
9715 Rockbrook Rd
Omaha, NE 68124-1928, USA

Brown, Kwame
203 Liberty Sq
Brunswick, GA 31525-4774, USA

Brown, Kwarne (Athlete, Basketball Player)
601 F St NW
Washington, DC 20004-1605, USA

Brown, Larry (Basketball Coach, Basketball Player, Coach, Olympic Athlete)
72 Egypt Ln
East Hampton, NY 11937-2693, USA

Brown, Larry (Athlete, Baseball Player)
13158 La Mirada Cir
Wellington, FL 33414-3997, USA

Brown, Larry (Athlete, Football Player)
1377 Glencoe Ave
Pittsburgh, PA 15205-4342, USA

Brown, Larry (Athlete, Football Player)
12004 Piney Glen Ln
Potomac, MD 20854-1417, USA

Brown, Larry (Athlete, Hockey Player)
21 Landing Dr
Dobbs Ferry, NY 10522-1181, USA

Brown, Larry (Athlete, Hockey Player)
5781 Eucalyptus Dr
Garden Valley, CA 95633-9622, USA

Brown, Lee P (Government Official)
Mayor's Office
901 Bagby St # 300
City Hall
Houston, TX 77002-2526, USA

Brown, Leon (Athlete, Baseball Player)
7537 S La Rosa Dr
Tempe, AZ 85283-4627, USA

Brown, Leonard (Baseball Player)
Homestead Grays
4411 19th St NE
Washington, DC 20018-3305, USA

Brown, Les (Motivational Speaker)
PO Box 806217
Chicago, IL 60680-4123, USA

Brown, Levi (Athlete, Football Player)
c/o Joe Linta *JL Sports*
1204 Main St Ste 179
Branford, CT 06405-3787, USA

Brown, Lomas (Athlete, Football Player)
974 Stratton Dr
Waterford, MI 48328-3929, USA

Brown, Louis (Business Person)
Street Smart Systems
4426B Hugh Howell Rd Ste 200
Tucker, GA 30084-4905, USA

Brown, Mack (Coach)
University of Texas
Athletic Dept
Austin, TX 78712, USA

Brown, Marc (Writer)
PO Box 873
West Tisbury, MA 02575-0873, USA

Brown, Mark (Athlete, Baseball Player)
108 NE 1st Street Ter
Blue Springs, MO 64014-2814, USA

Brown, Mark (Athlete, Football Player)
27615W 81st Way
Fort Lauderdale, FL 33328, USA

Brown, Mark N (Astronaut)
80 Earlsgate Rd
Beavercreek, OH 45440-3664, USA

Brown, Mark N Colonel (Astronaut)
4032 Linden Ave Attn Ofc
Dayton, OH 45432-3006, USA

Brown, Marty (Athlete, Baseball Player)
850 Las Vegas Blvd N Attn Managersofc
Las Vegas, NV 89101-2062, USA

Brown, Matt (Director)
c/o James Adams *Schreck Rose Dapello & Adams*
1790 Broadway Fl 20
New York, NY 10019-1412, USA

Brown, Matthew (Athlete, Baseball Player)
11259 N Cutlass St
Hayden, ID 83835-8654, USA

Brown, Max (Actor)
c/o Lena Roklin *Luber Roklin Management*
5815 W Sunset Blvd Ste 206
Los Angeles, CA 90028-6481, USA

Brown, Melanie (Dancer, Musician)
2132 Mount Olympus Dr
Los Angeles, CA 90046-1636, USA

Brown, Mike (Athlete, Baseball Player)
710 95th Ave N
Naples, FL 34108-2457, USA

Brown, Mike (Athlete, Baseball Player)
2904 E Minton St
Mesa, AZ 85213-1697, USA

Brown, Mike (Basketball Coach)
304 Rays Mill Rd
Aberdeen, NC 28315-3323, USA

Brown, Milford (Athlete, Football Player)
6282 Chamar Cir
Kannapolis, NC 28081-7726, USA

Brown, Myron (Athlete, Basketball Player)
3025 Timbercreek Dr
Mc Kees Rocks, PA 15136-1509, USA

Brown, Na (Athlete, Football Player)
PO Box 853
Fletcher, NC 28732-0853, USA

Brown, Norman (Musician)
c/o Staff Member *APA Talent And Literary Agency (NY)*
45 W 45th St Ste 804
New York, NY 10036-4602, USA

Brown, Norman W (Business Person)
Foote Cone Belding
101 E Erie St
Chicago, IL 60611-2812, USA

Brown, Norris (Athlete, Football Player)
320 Pinehaven St Ext
Laurens, SC 29360, USA

Brown, Ollie (Athlete, Baseball Player)
8462 Country Club Dr
Buena Park, CA 90621-1421, USA

Brown, Orlando (Actor)
c/o Sharyn Berg *Sharyn Talent Management*
PO Box 18033
Encino, CA 91416-8033, USA

Brown, Oscar (Athlete, Baseball Player)
19113 Gunlock Ave
Carson, CA 90746-2825, USA

Brown, Owsley II (Business Person)
Brown-Forman Corp
850 Dixie Hwy
Louisville, KY 40210-1038, USA

Brown, Patricia (Athlete, Baseball Player, Commentator)
821 Solar Ln
Glenview, IL 60025-4464, USA

Brown, Paul (Athlete, Baseball Player)
3617 Highway 75
Holdenville, OK 74848-9421, USA

Brown, Paul (Musician)
c/o Staff Member *Verve Music Group*
1755 Broadway Frnt 3
New York, NY 10019-3743, USA

Brown, Peter (Actor)
5328 Alhama Dr
Woodland Hills, CA 91364-2013, USA

Brown, Philip (Actor)
c/o Staff Member *Independent Artists (LA)*
9601 Wilshire Blvd Ste 750
Beverly Hills, CA 90210-5228, USA

Brown, P J (Athlete, Basketball Player)
2142 Hampshire Dr
Slidell, LA 70461-5065, USA

Brown, Preston (Athlete, Football Player)
6804 Jones Valley Dr SE
Huntsville, AL 35802-1920, USA

Brown, Ralph (Athlete, Football Player)
9395 Old Post Dr
Rancho Cucamonga, CA 91730-5765, USA

Brown, Randy (Baseball Player)
California Angels
PO Box 326
Plymouth, FL 32768-0326, USA

Brown, Ray (Athlete, Football Player)
4936 Lake Fjord Pass
Marietta, GA 30068-1639, USA

Brown, Ray (Athlete, Football Player)
1 Bills Dr
Orchard Park, NY 14127-2237, USA

Brown, Ray (Athlete, Football Player)
1225 Stanfield Point Rd
Gautier, MS 39553-3204, USA

Brown, Raymond (Athlete, Football Player)
4936 Lake Fjord Pass
Marietta, GA 30068-1639, USA

Brown, Reb (Actor)
c/o Staff Member *Gyst Management*
9107 Wilshire Blvd Ste 450
Beverly Hills, CA 90210-5535, USA

Brown, Reggie (Athlete, Football Player)
15635 Canterbury Chase
Alpharetta, GA 30004-8027, USA

Brown, Reggie (Athlete, Football Player)
2242 NW 93rd Ter
Miami, FL 33147-3068, USA

Brown, Reggie D (Athlete, Football Player)
4301 Roseneath Dr
Houston, TX 77021-1614, USA

Brown, Reggie V (Athlete, Football Player)
1325 Oxford Ln
Union, NJ 07083-5447, USA

Brown, Richard (Athlete, Football Player)
5652 Alfred Ave
Westminster, CA 92683-2810, USA

Brown, Rita Mae (Actor, Writer)
c/o Staff Member *Random House Publicity*
1745 Broadway Frnt 3
New York, NY 10019-4343, USA

Brown, Rob (Actor)
c/o Gabrielle (Gaby) Morgerman *William Morris Endeavor (LA)*
9601 Wilshire Blvd
Beverly Hills, CA 90210-5213, USA

Brown, Robert (Athlete, Football Player)
PO Box 211081
Saint Louis, MO 63121-9081, USA

Brown, Robert (Athlete, Football Player)
8624 Oak Chase Cir
Fairfax Station, VA 22039-3328, USA

Brown, Robert Curtis (Actor)
2401 Pier Ave
Santa Monica, CA 90405-6053, USA

Brown, Robert D (Business Person)
Milacron Inc
2090 Florence Ave Ste 100
Cincinnati, OH 45206-2489, USA

Brown, Robert S (Bob) (Athlete, Football Player)
1200 Lakeshore Ave Apt 25G
Oakland, CA 94606-1689, USA

Brown, Roger (Athlete, Football Player)
9 N Point Dr
Portsmouth, VA 23703-3644, USA

Brown, Ron (Athlete, Football Player)
22138 Roundup Dr
Walnut, CA 91789-1482, USA

Brown, Ronnie (Athlete, Football Player)
4994 Long Island Dr NW
Atlanta, GA 30327-4904, USA

Brown, Roosevelt (Athlete)
6551 Thea Ln Apt S17
Columbus, GA 31907-0822

Brown, Roosevelt (Athlete, Baseball Player)
308 Newitt Vick Dr
Vicksburg, MS 39183-8741, USA

Brown, Ruben (Athlete, Football Player)
170 Fox Meadow Ln
Orchard Park, NY 14127-2866, USA

Brown, Rush (Athlete, Football Player)
2425 Cartertown Rd
Clinton, NC 28328-7467, USA

Brown, Samantha (Actor)
c/o Erika Martineau *Brooks Group*
10 W 37th St Fl 5
New York, NY 10018-7396, USA

Brown, Samuel M (Athlete, Football Player)
25 Franklin Creek Rd N
Savannah, GA 31411-2826, USA

Brown, Sandra (Writer)
1306 W Abram St
Arlington, TX 76013-1703, USA

Brown, Sara (Actor)
Media Artists Group
6300 Wilshire Blvd Ste 1470
Los Angeles, CA 90048-5200, USA

Brown, Sarah (Actor)
c/o Staff Member *McKeon-Myones Management*
3500 W Olive Ave Ste 770
Burbank, CA 91505-5527, USA

Brown, Scott (Athlete, Baseball Player)
1238 Alton Pierce Rd
Dequincy, LA 70633-4501, USA

Brown, Scott P. (Senator)
359 Dirksen Senate Office Building
Washington, DC 20510-0001, USA

Brown, Selwyn (Athlete, Football Player)
3533 Inverrary Blvd W
Lauderhill, FL 33319-7114, USA

Brown, Shane (Athlete, Basketball Player, Coach)
Ohio Valley University
1 Campus View Dr
Athletic Dept
Vienna, WV 26105-8000, USA

Brown, Shay (Athlete, Misc)
World Skating League
499 Erin Dr
Knoxville, TN 37919, USA

Brown, Sheldon (Athlete, Football Player)
2616 Stonetrace Dr
Rock Hill, SC 29730-6664, USA

Brown, Sherrod (Senator)
713 Hart Senate Office Bldg
Washington, DC 20510-0001, USA

Brown, Sonny (Athlete, Football Player)
825 Shadow Wood Dr
Edmond, OK 73034-7061, USA

Brown, Stan (Athlete, Basketball Player)
2201 Tremont St
Philadelphia, PA 19115-5041, USA

Brown, Stan (Athlete, Football Player)
PO Box 533
Benicia, CA 94510-0533, USA

Brown, Steve (Athlete, Baseball Player)
9626 Cecilwood Dr
Santee, CA 92071-1428, USA

Brown, Steve (Athlete, Football Player)
2207 Osage St
Saint Louis, MO 63118-4725, USA

Brown, Susan (Actor)
11931 Addison St
Valley Village, CA 91607-3106, USA

Brown, Tarrick (Baseball Player)
Chicago Cubs
18631 Collins St Apt 33
Tarzana, CA 91356-2178, USA

Brown, Ted (Athlete, Football Player)
7320 130th St W
Saint Paul, MN 55124-9501, USA

Brown, Terry (Athlete, Football Player)
605 W Apache St
Marlow, OK 73055-1831, USA

Brown, T Graham (Musician)
8437 Rolling Hills Dr
Nashville, TN 37221-5616, USA

Brown, Theotis (Athlete, Football Player)
9604 W 121st Ter
Overland Park, KS 66213-1691, USA

Brown, Thomas M (Athlete, Football Player)
6024 Approach Rd
Sarasota, FL 34238-5721, USA

Brown, Thomas W (Athlete, Football Player)
201 High Point Dr
Waco, TX 76705-1750, USA

Brown, Thomas Wilson (Actor)
c/o Staff Member *SDB Partners Inc*
315 S Beverly Dr Ste 411
Beverly Hills, CA 90212-4301, USA

Brown, Tim (Athlete, Football Player, Heisman Trophy Winner)
1107 W Pleasant Run Rd
Desoto, TX 75115-7402, USA

Brown, Timmy (Athlete, Football Player)
505 S Farrell Dr Unit E28
Palm Springs, CA 92264-8071, USA

Brown, Tina (Talk Show Host, Writer)
c/o Staff Member *Topic A With Tina Brown*
900 Sylvan Ave
Cnbc
Englewood Cliffs, NJ 07632-3312, USA

Brown, Tom (Athlete, Baseball Player)
27981 Nanticoke Rd
Salisbury, MD 21801-1645, USA

Brown, Tom (Athlete, Baseball Player)
600 Valencia Rd
Venice, FL 34285-2538, USA

Brown, Tom (Athlete, Football Player)
10143 Deer Run
Brecksville, OH 44141-3637, USA

Brown, Tommy (Athlete, Baseball Player)
580 S Indigo Rd
Altamonte Springs, FL 32714-3137, USA

Brown, Tom W (Athlete, Football Player)
201 High Point Dr
Waco, TX 76705-1750, USA

Brown, Tony (Athlete, Football Player)
11629 Garrick Ave
Sylmar, CA 91342-6533, USA

Brown, Travis (Athlete, Football Player)
5646 E Ocupado Dr
Cave Creek, AZ 85331-1557, USA

Brown, Troy (Athlete, Football Player)
3 Edgewater Dr
Norton, MA 02766-2120, USA

Brown, Troy (Athlete, Football Player)
124 Pine Hvn
Barnwell, SC 29812-2817, USA

Brown, Tyree (Actor)
c/o Nicole Jolley *Amsel, Eisenstadt & Frazier Talent Agency (AEF)*
5055 Wilshire Blvd Ste 860
Los Angeles, CA 90036-6108, USA

Brown, Vincent (Athlete, Football Player)
PO Box 71268
Henrico, VA 23255-1268, USA

Brown, W Earl (Actor)
c/o Staff Member *William Morris Endeavor (LA)*
9601 Wilshire Blvd
Beverly Hills, CA 90210-5213, USA

Brown, Wes (Actor)
c/o Stacy Abrams *Abrams Entertainment*
5225 Wilshire Blvd Ste 515
Los Angeles, CA 90036-4349, USA

Brown, Wilbert (Athlete, Football Player)
1707 Dominic Ln
Houston, TX 77049-1592, USA

Brown, William D (Bill) (Athlete, Coach, Football Player)
514 Northdale Blvd NW
Minneapolis, MN 55448-3357, USA

Brown, William F (Willie) (Athlete, Coach, Football Player)
27138 Lillegard Ct
Tracy, CA 95304-8866, USA

Brown, William S (Horse Racer)
750 Michigan Ave
Columbus, OH 43215-1107, USA

Brown, Willie (Baseball Player)
3430 John Hancock Dr
Tallahassee, FL 32312-1536, USA

Brown, Winston (Baseball Player)
12144 SW 50th St
Cooper City, FL 33330-4476, USA

Brown, Woody (Actor)
11844 Otsego St
Valley Village, CA 91607-3223, USA

Brown, Wren (Actor)
1861 Wellington Rd
Los Angeles, CA 90019-5945, USA

Brown, Yvette Nicole (Actor)
c/o Jelani Johnson *Generate Management*
8750 Wilshire Blvd Ste 200
Beverly Hills, CA 90211-2707, USA

Brownback, Sam (Governor, Politician)
Office of the Governor
300 SW 10th Ave Ste 222S
Topeka, KS 66612-1514, USA

Brownback, Sam (Politician)
1 SW Cedar Crest Rd
Topeka, KS 66606-2275, USA

Browne, Byron (Athlete, Baseball Player)
2831 S 83rd Dr
Tolleson, AZ 85353-7603, USA

Browne, Chris (Cartoonist)
c/o Staff Member *King Features Syndication*
300 W 57th St Fl 15
New York, NY 10019-5238, USA

Browne, Gordie (Athlete, Football Player)
1001 Lakeridge Ct
Colleyville, TX 76034-2825, USA

Browne, Gordon (Athlete, Football Player)
25 Harbourside Rd
Quincy, MA 02171-1555, USA

Browne, Jackson (Musician, Songwriter)
5075 Porter Gulch Rd
Aptos, CA 95003-2736, USA

Browne, Jerry (Athlete, Baseball Player)
Hagerstown Suns
274 Memorial Blvd E
Attn: Coaching Staff
Hagerstown, MD 21740-6200, USA

Browne, Kale (Actor)
c/o Staff Member *Gage Group, The (LA)*
5757 Wilshire Blvd Ste 659
Los Angeles, CA 90036-3682, USA

Browne, Olin (Athlete, Golfer)
9562 SE Sandpine Ln
Hobe Sound, FL 33455-6356, USA

Browne, Victor (Actor)
c/o Lara Rosenstock *Lara Rosenstock Management*
8371 Blackburn Ave Apt 1
Los Angeles, CA 90048-4245, USA

Browne, Zachary (Actor)
c/o Staff Member *Iris Burton Agency*
10100 Santa Monica Blvd Ste 1300
Los Angeles, CA 90067-4114, USA

Browner, Brandon (Athlete, Football Player)
c/o Peter Schaffer *All Pro Sports and Entertainment*
36 Steele St Ste 100
Denver, CO 80206-5709, USA

Browner, Jim (Athlete, Football Player)
6265 Crest Forest Ct E
Clarkston, MI 48348-4581, USA

Browner, Joey (Athlete, Football Player)
PO Box 22721
Saint Paul, MN 55122-0721, USA

Browner, Joey (Athlete, Football Player)
PO Box 571
Pierz, MN 56364-0571, USA

Browner, Keith (Athlete, Football Player)
14534 Locust St
San Leandro, CA 94579-1047, USA

Browner, Ross (Athlete, Football Player)
7900 Indian Springs Dr
Nashville, TN 37221-1147, USA

Brown-Findlay, Jessica (Actor)
c/o Duncan Millership *William Morris Endeavor (LA)*
9601 Wilshire Blvd
Beverly Hills, CA 90210-5213, USA

Browning, Cal (Athlete, Baseball Player)
111 N Eagle Dr
Ruidoso, NM 88345-6832, USA

Browning, Dave (Athlete, Football Player)
10117 S Lambs Ln
Mica, WA 99023-6031, USA

Browning, Edmond L (Religious Leader)
5164 Imai Rd
Hood River, OR 97031-9442, USA

Browning, Emily (Actor)
c/o Michael D Aglion *Signpost Management*
280 S Beverly Dr Ste 315
Beverly Hills, CA 90212-3903, USA

Browning, Kurt (Figure Skater)
c/o Nicole Cobuzio *Rob Bailey Communications*
310 State Rt 17
Upper Saddle River, NJ 07458-2308, USA

Browning, Logan (Actor)
c/o Ken Jacobson *Ken Jacobson Management*
Preferred to be contacted by phone or email
Woodland Hills, CA 91367, USA

Browning, Ricou (Actor)
5221 SW 196th Ln
Southwest Ranches, FL 33332-1111, USA

Browning, Ryan (Actor)
United Talent Agency
9336 Civic Center Dr
Beverly Hills, CA 90210-3604, USA

Browning, Thomas L (Tom) (Athlete, Baseball Player)
3094 Friars Ln
Edgewood, KY 41017-8126, USA

Brown Jr, Larry (Athlete, Football Player)
5603 Sycamore Dr
Colleyville, TX 76034-5063, USA

Brownlee, Claude (Athlete, Football Player)
2711 Hood St
Columbus, GA 31906-3251, USA

Brownlee, Sophia Grace (Musician)
c/o Jason Egenberg *United Talent Agency (UTA-LA)*
9336 Civic Center Dr
Beverly Hills, CA 90210-3604, USA

Brown-Miller, Lisa (Athlete, Hockey Player, Olympic Athlete)
1 Olympic Plz Bldg 4E
US Olympic Committee
Colorado Springs, CO 80909-5746, USA

Brownschidle, Jack (Athlete, Hockey Player)
35 Hidden Pines Ct
East Amherst, NY 14051-1688, USA

Brownson, Mark (Athlete, Baseball Player)
13992 Aster Ave
Wellington, FL 33414-8509, USA

Brownstein, Carrie (Music Group, Musician)
Legends of 21st Century
7 Trinity Row
Florence, MA 01062-1931, USA

Broxton, Jonathan (Athlete, Baseball Player)
4751 Rocky Creek Church Rd
Waynesboro, GA 30830-4106, USA

Broyles, Frank F (Coach, Football Player, Sportscaster)
517 E Lafayette St
Fayetteville, AR 72701-4312, USA

Brozer, Kim (Athlete, Golfer)
2700 N 16th St
Beaumont, TX 77703-4624, USA

Brubaker, Bruce (Athlete, Baseball Player)
Champion Ford
140 Southtown Blvd
Owensboro, KY 42303-7759, USA

Brubaker, Jeff (Athlete, Hockey Player)
1827 Oak Ridge Rd Unit A
Oak Ridge, NC 27310-9865, USA

Bruce, Aundray (Athlete, Football Player)
1730 Wentworth Dr
Montgomery, AL 36106-2639, USA

Bruce, Bob (Athlete, Baseball Player)
633 Mission Cir
Irving, TX 75063-6617, USA

Bruce, Bruce (Comedian)
c/o Staff Member *Agency for the Performing Arts (APA-LA)*
405 S Beverly Dr Ste 500
Beverly Hills, CA 90212-4425, USA

Bruce, David (Athlete, Hockey Player)
909 Orchid Pl Unit 201
Bellingham, WA 98226-8768, USA

Bruce, Earle (Athlete, Football Player)
2778 Scioto Station Dr
Columbus, OH 43204-3696, USA

Bruce, Ed
1022 16th Ave S
Nashville, TN 37212-2303, USA

Bruce, Elia (Athlete, Football Player)
1110 Hudson St Apt 4N
Hoboken, NJ 07030-5318, USA

Bruce, George (Writer)
c/o Staff Member *Counterpoint*
2117 4th St Ste D
Berkeley, CA 94710-2205, USA

Bruce, Isaac (Athlete, Football Player)
333 Las Olas Way Apt 2606
Fort Lauderdale, FL 33301-2389, USA

Bruce, Jack (Music Group, Songwriter, Writer)
International Creative Mgmt
40 W 57th St Fl 5
New York, NY 10019-4001, USA

Bruce, Thomas (Tom) (Swimmer)
122 Sea Terrace Way
Aptos, CA 95003-4521, USA

Bruce, Tom (Athlete, Swimmer)
USOC Alumni Relations
1750 E Boulder St
Colorado Springs, CO 80909-5724, USA

Bruckheimer, Jerry (Director, Producer)
12822 Highwood St
Los Angeles, CA 90049-2626, USA

Bruckner, Agnes (Actor)
c/o Oren Segal *Radius Entertainment*
9229 W Sunset Blvd Ste 310
West Hollywood, CA 90069-3403, USA

Bruckner, Amy (Actor)
c/o Susan Curtis *Curtis Talent Management*
9607 Arby Dr
Beverly Hills, CA 90210-1202, USA

Bruckner, Greg (Athlete, Golfer)
3906 E Potter Dr
Phoenix, AZ 85050-4837, USA

Bruckner, Les (Athlete, Football Player)
842 E Villa St Apt 310
Pasadena, CA 91101-1283, USA

Brudzinski, Robert L (Bob) (Athlete, Football Player)
1057 Lido Ct
Weston, FL 33326-2903, USA

Brue, Bob (Athlete, Golfer)
4316 N Sheffield Ave
Milwaukee, WI 53211-1432, USA

Brueckman, Charlie (Athlete, Football Player)
7439 Plott Rd
Charlotte, NC 28215-9440, USA

Bruen, John D (Business Person, General)
6104 Greenlawn Ct
Springfield, VA 22152-1314, USA

Bruener, Mark (Athlete, Football Player)
26 Commanders Pl
Missouri City, TX 77459, USA

Bruening, Justin (Actor)
c/o Marnie Sparer *Innovative Artists (LA)*
1505 10th St
Santa Monica, CA 90401-2805, USA

Bruett, J T (Athlete, Baseball Player)
1437 Woods Creek Dr
Delano, MN 55328-9266, USA

Bruhert, Mike (Athlete, Baseball Player)
907 Center Dr
Franklin Square, NY 11010-2005, USA

Bruhin, John (Athlete, Football Player)
6960 Taylors View Ln
Knoxville, TN 37921-2843, USA

Brumback, Charles T (Publisher)
435 N Michigan Ave Fl 7
Chicago, IL 60611-4027, USA

Brumbaugh, Cliff (Athlete, Baseball Player)
216 Moore Ave
New Castle, DE 19720-3559, USA

Brumbly, Charlie (Actor)
c/o Staff Member *DDO Artist Agency (LA)*
4605 Lankershim Blvd Ste 340
North Hollywood, CA 91602-1876, USA

Brumfield, Jackson (Athlete, Football Player)
25644 Highway 25
Franklinton, LA 70438-5126, USA

Brumfield, Jacob D (Athlete, Baseball Player)
7970 Creekstone Way
Riverdale, GA 30274-3929, USA

Brumfield, Scott (Athlete, Football Player)
1150 E 900 S
Spanish Fork, UT 84660-2629, USA

Brumfield-White, Dolly (Athlete, Baseball Player, Commentator)
1604 Millcreek Dr
Arkadelphia, AR 71923-3024, USA

Brumfield-White, Dolores (Baseball Player)
1604 Millcreek Dr
Arkadelphia, AR 71923-3024, USA

Brumley, Duff (Athlete, Baseball Player)
230 Cg Earnest Rd NW
Charleston, TN 37310-6625, USA

Brumley, Mike (Athlete, Baseball Player)
1020 Western Trl
Keller, TX 76248-4924, USA

Brumley, Robert L (Athlete, Football Player)
256 E Sunset Rd
San Antonio, TX 78209-2760, USA

Brumm, Donald D (Don) (Athlete, Football Player)
511 County Road 442
New Franklin, MO 65274-9704, USA

Brummer, Glenn (Athlete, Baseball Player)
1830 Dalton Dr
Belleville, IL 62226-8207, USA

Brummer, Renate (Astronaut)
NOAA/FSL
325 Broadway St
Boulder, CO 80305-3337, USA

Brummett, Greg (Athlete, Baseball Player)
605 W 10th St
Concordia, KS 66901-4011, USA

Brumwell, Murray (Athlete, Hockey Player)
3036 Lloyd Mangrum Ln
Billings, MT 59106-1242, USA

Brunansky, Thomas A (Tom) (Athlete, Baseball Player)
13411 Summit Cir
Poway, CA 92064-2169, USA

Brundage, Dewey (Athlete, Football Player)
220 S 400 W
Orem, UT 84058-5329, USA

Brundage, Howard D (Publisher)
RR 2 Box 332-47
Old Lyme, CT 06371, USA

Brundage, Jennifer (Athlete, Olympic Athlete, Softball Player)
4487 Augusta Ct
Ann Arbor, MI 48108-9789, USA

Brundige, Bill (Athlete, Football Player)
2050 Roanoke St
Christiansburg, VA 24073-2510, USA

Brundy, Stan (Athlete, Basketball Player)
4644 Stephen Girard Ave
New Orleans, LA 70126-4756, USA

Brune, Jesse (Actor)
c/o Cat Josell *Synergy Management*
11271 Ventura Blvd Ste 495
Studio City, CA 91604-3136, USA

Brunell, Mark (Athlete, Football Player)
876 Rock Mesa Pt
Castle Rock, CO 80108-7435, USA

Brunelli, Sam (Athlete, Football Player)
1080 Wisconsin Ave NW Apt 104
Washington, DC 20007-6052, USA

Bruner, Jack (Athlete, Football Player)
701 Lewiston St
Cottonwood, ID 83522, USA

Bruner, Michael L (Mike) (Athlete, Olympic Athlete, Swimmer)
339 Garcia Ave
Half Moon Bay, CA 94019-1886, USA

Brunet, Andree Joly (Figure Skater)
2805 Boyne City Rd
Boyne City, MI 49712, USA

Brunet, Bob (Athlete, Football Player)
25011 La Highway 1032
Denham Springs, LA 70726-5637, USA

Brunette, Andrew (Athlete, Hockey Player)
2392 Morgan Ave N
Stillwater, MN 55082-1967, USA

Brunette, Justin (Athlete, Baseball Player)
11 Atherton
Irvine, CA 92620-2502, USA

Brunettes, The (Music Group)
c/o Staff Member *Paradigm (Monterey)*
404 W Franklin St
Monterey, CA 93940-2303, USA

Brunetti, Wayne H (Business Person)
New Century Energies
1225 17th St Ste 100
Denver, CO 80202-5518, USA

Bruney, Brian (Athlete, Baseball Player)
c/o Staff Member *Gaylord Sports Management*
13845 N Northsight Blvd Ste 200
Scottsdale, AZ 85260-3609, USA

Bruney, Fred (Athlete, Football Coach, Football Player)
800 Mountain Creek Trce
Atlanta, GA 30328-3532, USA

Brungardt, Kurt
c/o Daniel Strone *Trident Media Group LLC*
41 Madison Ave Fl 36
New York, NY 10010-2257, USA

Brunkhorst, Brian (Athlete, Basketball Player)
6182 Brumder Rd
Hartland, WI 53029-9709, USA

Bruno, Chris (Actor)
3678 Alta Mesa Dr
Studio City, CA 91604-4003, USA

Bruno, Dylan (Actor)
1481 W Paseo Del Mar
San Pedro, CA 90731-6055, USA

Bruno, Tom (Athlete, Baseball Player)
316 Ft Sully Trl
Pierre, SD 57501-8309, USA

Bruns, George (Athlete, Basketball Player)
16 E Poplar St
Floral Park, NY 11001-3145, USA

Brunsberg, Ario (Athlete, Baseball Player)
883 104th Ln NW
Minneapolis, MN 55433-6542, USA

Brunson, Larry (Athlete, Football Player)
6104 E Peakview Pl
Centennial, CO 80111-4326, USA

Brunson, Will (Athlete, Baseball Player)
718 Nandina Way
Waxahachie, TX 75165-4643, USA

Brunt, Maureen (Athlete, Olympic Athlete)
430 Silver Lake Dr
Portage, WI 53901-1340, USA

Bruntlett, Eric (Athlete, Baseball Player)
1106 Marconi St Apt A
Houston, TX 77019-4261, USA

Brupbacher, Ross (Athlete, Football Player)
200 Pembroke Ln
Lafayette, LA 70508-5616, USA

Bruschi, Tedy (Athlete, Football Player)
31 Jeffrey Dr
North Attleboro, MA 02760-2761, USA

Bruske, Jim (Athlete, Baseball Player)
5242 N Quail Run Pl
Paradise Valley, AZ 85253-7051, USA

Brusstar, Warren (Athlete, Baseball Player)
3320 Redwood Rd
Napa, CA 94558-9544, USA

Brutcher, Len (Baseball Player)
4510 Hallam Hill Ln
Lakeland, FL 33813-1808, USA

Bruton, David (Athlete, Football Player)
c/o David Dunn *Athletes First, LLC*
23091 Mill Creek Dr
Laguna Hills, CA 92653-1258, USA

Bry, Ellen (Actor)
Media Artists Group
6300 Wilshire Blvd Ste 1470
Los Angeles, CA 90048-5200, USA

Bryan, Ashley (Writer)
General Delivery
Islesford, ME 04646-9999, USA

Bryan, Billy (Athlete, Football Player)
3413 Wren Rd
Vestavia, AL 35243-4326, USA

Bryan, Billy (Athlete, Baseball Player)
3001 Hickory Ln
Opelika, AL 36801-2221, USA

Bryan, Billy (Athlete, Football Player)
3408 Creekwood Dr
Cottondale, AL 35453, USA

Bryan, Bob (Athlete, Tennis Player)
3931 Fawnmist Dr
Wesley Chapel, FL 33544-8190, USA

Bryan, David (Musician)
45 Phalanx Rd
Colts Neck, NJ 07722-1510, USA

Bryan, Jimmy (Race Car Driver)
PO Box 194
Novi, MI 48376-0194, USA

Bryan, Luke (Musician)
373 Childe Harolds Cir
Brentwood, TN 37027-1814, USA

Bryan, Mark (Musician)
816 Stone Pt
Awendaw, SC 29429-6131, USA

Bryan, Mary (Athlete, Golfer)
13001 Reading Rd
Goshen, KY 40026-9796, USA

Bryan, Mike (Athlete, Tennis Player)
3931 Fawnmist Dr
Wesley Chapel, FL 33544-8190, USA

Bryan, Richard (Politician)
269 Russell
Washington, DC 20510-0001, USA

Bryan, Sabrina (Actor, Dancer)
c/o Staff Member *Puravida Enterprises*
2480 Corinth Ave Ste 3
Los Angeles, CA 90064-3012, USA

Bryan, Steve (Athlete, Football Player)
33659 E 147th St S
Coweta, OK 74429-7764, USA

Bryan, Walter (Athlete, Football Player)
757 Kenwood Dr
Abilene, TX 79601-5539, USA

Bryan, Zachery Ty (Actor)
2 Vernal Spg
Irvine, CA 92603-0405, USA

Bryant, Anita (Beauty Pageant Winner, Musician)
2377 NW 206th St
Edmond, OK 73012-9074, USA

Bryant, Anthony (Athlete, Football Player)
1136 County Road 16
Newbern, AL 36765-3712, USA

Bryant, Antonio (Athlete, Football Player)
c/o Staff Member *All Pro Sports and Entertainment*
36 Steele St Ste 100
Denver, CO 80206-5709, USA

Bryant, Bart (Athlete, Golfer)
1318 Sunland Park Dr
Frisco, TX 75033-0206, USA

Bryant, Bill (Athlete, Football Player)
3516 Dewberry Dr
Shreveport, LA 71118-3606, USA

Bryant, Bobby (Athlete, Football Player)
509 Nottingham Rd
Columbia, SC 29210-3719, USA

Bryant, Bonnie (Athlete, Golfer)
2427 Wasabinang St
Hastings, MI 49058-8912, USA

Bryant, Brad (Athlete, Golfer)
3407 Bridgefield Dr
Lakeland, FL 33803-5914, USA

Bryant, Clark Rosalyn (Athlete, Track Athlete)
3901 Somerset Dr
Los Angeles, CA 90008-1704, USA

Bryant, Darrell (Race Car Driver)
171 Brenda Dr
Thomasville, NC 27360-8209, USA

Bryant, Derek (Athlete, Baseball Player)
1047 Redwood Dr
Lexington, KY 40511-1133, USA

Bryant, Desmond (Athlete, Football Player)
c/o Joby Branion *Athletes First, LLC*
23091 Mill Creek Dr
Laguna Hills, CA 92653-1258, USA

Bryant, Dez (Athlete, Football Player)
c/o Eugene Parker *Maximum Sports Management*
6435 W Jefferson Blvd # 197
Fort Wayne, IN 46804-6203, USA

Bryant, Domingo (Athlete, Football Player)
19703 Campfield Dr
Katy, TX 77449-6691, USA

Bryant, Don (Athlete, Baseball Player)
270 Stonewell Dr
Saint Johns, FL 32259-8388, USA

Bryant, Edward (Junior) (Athlete, Football Player)
2906 S 102nd St
Omaha, NE 68124-2639, USA

Bryant, Emmette (Athlete, Basketball Player)
PO Box 6229
Chicago, IL 60680-6229, USA

Bryant, Fernando (Athlete, Football Player)
1740 Hudson Bridge Rd
Stockbridge, GA 30281-6331, USA

Bryant, Hubie (Athlete, Football Player)
4804 Branch Rd
Roanoke, VA 24014-6702, USA

Bryant, Jeff (Athlete, Football Player)
PO Box 362240
Decatur, GA 30036-2240, USA

Bryant, Joe (Athlete, Basketball Player)
1835 N 72nd St
Philadelphia, PA 19151-2311, USA

Bryant, Joshua (Actor)
216 Paseo Del Pueblo Norte Ste M
Taos, NM 87571-5912, USA

Bryant, Joy (Actor)
c/o David Schiff *The Schiff Company*
9220 W Sunset Blvd Ste 106
West Hollywood, CA 90069-3500, USA

Bryant, Kevin (Athlete, Football Player)
701 E Church St
Tarboro, NC 27886-4505, USA

Bryant, Kobe (Athlete, Basketball Player)
1551 N Tustin Ave Ste 1000
Santa Ana, CA 92705-8635, USA

Bryant, Mark (Athlete, Basketball Player)
3300 Everett Dr
Edmond, OK 73013-7443, USA

Bryant, Matt (Athlete, Football Player)
c/o Jordan Woy *Willis and Woy Management*
3030 Olive St Ste 520
Dallas, TX 75219-7629, USA

Bryant, Phil (Governor, Politician)
Office of the Governor
PO Box 139
Jackson, MS 39205-0139, USA

Bryant, Ralph (Athlete, Baseball Player)
367 Spruill Bridge Rd
Temple, GA 30179-4568, USA

Bryant, Red (Athlete, Football Player)
c/o Jimmy Sexton *CAA (Memphis)*
6060 Poplar Ave Ste 470
Memphis, TN 38119-0910, USA

Bryant, Ron (Baseball Player)
San Francisco Giants
90 Oak St # 1
Westerly, RI 02891-1737, USA

Bryant, Ronald Ray (Baby Bash) (Actor,
Musician, Producer)
c/o Staff Member *Sony Music
International*
550 Madison Ave Fl 6
New York, NY 10022-3211, USA

Bryant, Steve (Athlete, Football Player)
12618 Laleu Ln
Houston, TX 77071-3735, USA

Bryant, Taman (Athlete, Football Player)
2742 Bryant St
Vineland, NJ 08361-3021, USA

Bryant, Todd (Actor)
9150 Wilshire Blvd Ste 175
Beverly Hills, CA 90212-3450, USA

Bryant, Tony (Athlete, Football Player)
2351 Sombrero Blvd
Marathon, FL 33050-2468, USA

Bryant, Trent (Athlete, Football Player)
4801 S Tiemey Dr
Independence, MO 64055, USA

Bryant, Walter (Athlete, Football Player)
509 Nottingham Rd
Columbia, SC 29210-3719, USA

Bryant, Waymond (Athlete, Football
Player)
2440 Covington Dr
Flower Mound, TX 75028-4666, USA

Bryant, Wendell (Athlete, Football Player)
PO Box 888
Phoenix, AZ 85001-0888, USA

Bryce, Ian (Producer)
Ian Bryce Productions
5555 Melrose Ave
Wallis Building, 105-106
Los Angeles, CA 90038-3989, USA

Bryden, T R (Athlete, Baseball Player)
1021 9th St
Clarkston, WA 99403-2505, USA

Brye, Steve (Athlete, Baseball Player)
255 S Grand Ave Apt 858
Los Angeles, CA 90012-3038, USA

Brylin, Sergei (Athlete, Hockey Player)
32 Robert Dr
Short Hills, NJ 07078-1507, USA

Bryson, Bill (Writer)
c/o Staff Member *Random House
Publicity*
1745 Broadway Frnt 3
New York, NY 10019-4343, USA

Bryson, David (Musician)
1276 Hudson Ave
Saint Helena, CA 94574-1920, USA

Bryson, Peabo (Music Group, Musician,
Songwriter, Writer)
Agency for the Performing Arts
9200 W Sunset Blvd Ste 900
West Hollywood, CA 90069-3604, USA

Bryson, Peabo (Musician)
c/o Staff Member *Agency for the
Performing Arts (APA-LA)*
405 S Beverly Dr Ste 500
Beverly Hills, CA 90212-4425, USA

Bryson, Shawn (Athlete, Football Player)
418 Heatherstone Dr
Franklin, NC 28734-0274, USA

Bryzgalov, Ilya (Athlete, Hockey Player)
4092 Santa Anita Ln
Yorba Linda, CA 92886-7014, USA

Brzezinski, Mika (Talk Show Host)
MSNBC
30 Rockefeller Plz
New York, NY 10112-0015, USA

Brzezinski, Zbigniew (Politician)
1061 Spring Hill Rd
Mc Lean, VA 22102-2304, USA

B. Schiff, Adam (Congressman, Politician)
2411 Rayburn Hob
Washington, DC 20515-0511, USA

B-Side Players (Music Group, Musician)
c/o Staff Member *Skyline Music*
28 Union St
Whitefield, NH 03598-3503, USA

Buatta, Mario (Designer)
120 E 80th St
New York, NY 10075-0306, USA

Bubas, Vic (Athlete, Basketball Player,
Coach)
12960 Crescent Green Apt 104
Midlothian, VA 23114-5570, USA

Bubela, Jaime (Athlete, Baseball Player)
14927 Royal Birkdale St
Houston, TX 77095-2812, USA

Buble, Michael (Musician)
c/o Liz Rosenberg *Liz Rosenberg Media*
1650 Broadway
505A
New York, NY 10019-6833, USA

Bubna, P F (Religious Leader)
Christian & Missionary Alliance
PO Box 3500
Colorado Springs, CO 80935, USA

Bucatinsky, Dan (Actor, Producer, Writer)
c/o Staff Member *William Morris
Endeavor (LA)*
9601 Wilshire Blvd
Beverly Hills, CA 90210-5213, USA

Bucci, George (Athlete, Basketball Player)
15 Peter Ave
Newburgh, NY 12550-8812, USA

Buchan, William E (Athlete, Olympic
Athlete, Sailor)
4530 Bennett View Dr
Santa Rosa, CA 95404-6204, USA

Buchanan, Bill (Athlete, Baseball Player)
94 Twill Valley Dr
Saint Peters, MO 63376-6566, USA

Buchanan, Bob (Athlete, Baseball Player)
2035 Bever Ave SE
Cedar Rapids, IA 52403-2716, USA

Buchanan, Brian (Athlete, Baseball Player)
136 Steeple Cir
Jupiter, FL 33458-1649, USA

Buchanan, Charles (Athlete, Football
Player)
1715 Windover Dr
Nashville, TN 37218-2410, USA

Buchanan, Edna (Writer)
156 5th Ave Ste 625
New York, NY 10010-7002, USA

Buchanan, Ian (Actor, Model)
Gold Marshak Liedtke
3500 W Olive Ave Ste 1400
Burbank, CA 91505-5512, USA

Buchanan, Jeff (Athlete, Hockey Player)
Wealth Management
1404 E Chocolate Ave
Hershey, PA 17033-1118, USA

Buchanan, Jensen (Actor)
Paradigm Agency
10100 Santa Monica Blvd Ste 2500
Los Angeles, CA 90067-4116, USA

Buchanan, Pat (Politician)
1017 Savile Ln
Mc Lean, VA 22101-1830, USA

Buchanan, Phillip (Athlete, Football
Player)
6185 Meadowview Cir
Fort Myers, FL 33916-4906, USA

Buchanan, Ray (Athlete, Football Player)
2888 Major Ridge Trl
Duluth, GA 30097-4987, USA

Buchanan, Richard (Athlete, Football
Player)
216 Brookwood Ln W
Bolingbrook, IL 60440-5511, USA

Buchanan, Robert S (Astronaut)
3 Lariat Ln
Rolling Hills Estates, CA 90274-4119,
USA

Buchanan, Ron (Athlete, Hockey Player)
200 Telluride Trl
Ruidoso, NM 88345-7123, USA

Buchanan, Tim (Athlete, Football Player)
888 Magnolia Ave Apt 1
Pasadena, CA 91106-3700, USA

Buchanan, Tom (Reality Star)
3130 Valley Rd
Saltville, VA 24370-4373

Buchanan, Vern (Congressman, Politician)
221 Cannon Hob
Washington, DC 20515-3515, USA

Buchanan, Willie J (Athlete, Football
Player)
2742 Mesa Dr
Oceanside, CA 92054-3717, USA

Buchanon, Willie (Athlete, Football
Player)
2742 Mesa Dr
Oceanside, CA 92054-3717, USA

Buchberger, Kelly (Athlete, Hockey
Player)
c/o Staff Member *Springfield Falcons*
45 Falcons Way
Springfield, MA 01103-1742, USA

Buchbinder, Rudolf (Music Group,
Musician)
Columbia Artists Mgmt Inc
165 W 57th St
New York, NY 10019-2201, USA

Buchek, Jerry (Athlete, Baseball Player)
815 NW Flagler Ave Apt 303
Stuart, FL 34994-1158, USA

Buchholz, Clay (Athlete, Baseball Player)
630 King Oaks St
Lumberton, TX 77657-7210, USA

Buchholz, Taylor (Athlete, Baseball
Player)
321 Southcroft Rd
Springfield, PA 19064-1353, USA

Buchli, James F Colonel (Astronaut)
14761A Lnnerarity Point Rd
Pensacola, FL 32507, USA

Buchli, James F (Jim) (Astronaut)
1602 Fairoaks St
El Lago, TX 77586-5921, USA

Buck, Craig (Athlete, Olympic Athlete,
Volleyball Player)
2208 Moline Ave
Pueblo, CO 81003-3810, USA

Buck, Joe (Commentator, Television Host)
40 Overhills Dr
Saint Louis, MO 63124-1532, USA

Buck, Mike E (Athlete, Football Player)
321 Fox Den Ct
Destin, FL 32541-4317, USA

Buck, Peter (Musician)
2033 2nd Ave Apt 2003
Seattle, WA 98121-2255, USA

Buck, Robert T Jr (Director, Misc)
Brooklyn Museum
200 Eastern Pkwy
Brooklyn, NY 11238-6099, USA

Buck, Samantha (Actor)
c/o Elise Konialian *Untitled Entertainment
(NY)*
435 Hudson St Fl 9
New York, NY 10014-3995, USA

Buck, Scott (Producer)
c/o Ann Blanchard *Creative Artists
Agency (CAA-LA)*
2000 Avenue of the Stars Ste 100
Los Angeles, CA 90067-4705, USA

Buckcherry (Music Group, Musician)
c/o Frank Cimler *10th Street
Entertainment (LA)*
700 N San Vicente Blvd Ste G410
West Hollywood, CA 90069-5060, USA

Buckels, Gary (Athlete, Baseball Player)
3510 E Longridge Dr
Orange, CA 92867-2021, USA

Buckey, Don (Athlete, Football Player)
3401 Melbourne Ln
The Villages, FL 32163-6363, USA

Buckey, Jay C Dr (Astronaut)
1 Sargent St
Hanover, NH 03755-1912, USA

Buckey, Jay C Jr (Astronaut)
14 Valley Rd
Hanover, NH 03755-2228, USA

Buckhalter, Joe (Athlete, Basketball
Player)
3131 Bellewood Ave # 1
Cincinnati, OH 45213-1603, USA

Buckingham, Gregory (Greg) (Swimmer)
338 Ridge Rd
San Carlos, CA 94070-4423, USA

Buckingham, Jane (Television Host)
c/o Staff Member *Style Network*
5750 Wilshire Blvd
Los Angeles, CA 90036-3697, USA

Buckingham, Lindsay (Musician)
299 N Saltair Ave
Los Angeles, CA 90049-2912, USA

Buckingham, Lindsey (Musician)
310 N Carmelina Ave
Los Angeles, CA 90049-2702, USA

Buckingham, Marcus (Business Person,
Writer)
Simon & Schuster/Pocket/Summit
1230 Avenue of the Americas
New York, NY 10020-1513, USA

Buckinghams, The (Music Group)
Paradise Artists
PO Box 1821
Ojai, CA 93024-1821, USA

Buckland, Jonny (Musician)
21 Astor Pl Apt 6C
New York, NY 10003-6940, USA

Buckles, Bradley (Government Official, Misc)
Alcohol Tobacco Firearms Agency
650 Massachusetts Ave NW
Washington, DC 20001-3796, USA

Buckley, A J (Actor)
Innovative Artists
1505 10th St
Santa Monica, CA 90401-2805, USA

Buckley, Barry (Athlete, Football Player)
26 Forest Notch
Cohasset, MA 02025-1133, USA

Buckley, Betty (Actor, Director, Musician)
233 Russell Bend Rd
Weatherford, TX 76088-1217, USA

Buckley, Curtis (Athlete, Football Player)
2208 Cantura Dr
Mesquite, TX 75181-4653, USA

Buckley, D Terrell (Athlete, Football Player)
11111 Pine Lodge Trl
Davie, FL 33328-7317, USA

Buckley, James L (Politician)
PO Box 597
Sharon, CT 06069-0597, USA

Buckley, Jean (Athlete, Baseball Player, Commentator)
143 Monarch Dr
Fortuna, CA 95540-3451, USA

Buckley, Kevin (Athlete, Baseball Player)
34 Calvin St
Braintree, MA 02184-3814, USA

Buckley, Marcus W (Athlete, Football Player)
7100 Monterrey Dr
Fort Worth, TX 76112-4234, USA

Buckley, Mike (Race Car Driver)
Buckley Racing
424 Hollister Ct
Ann Arbor, MI 48103-9335, USA

Buckley, Robert (Actor)
c/o Gary Mantoosh *Baker Winokur Ryder Public Relations (BWR-LA)*
9100 Wilshire Blvd Ste 500
West Tower Suite 500
Beverly Hills, CA 90212-3426, USA

Buckley, Roy (Bowler)
6900 Lee Rd
Westerville, OH 43081-9556, USA

Buckley, Travis (Baseball Player)
10020 England Dr
Overland Park, KS 66212-4138, USA

Buckman, James E (Business Person)
Cendant Corp
9 W 57th St
New York, NY 10019-2701, USA

Buckman, Tara (Actor)
561 Fords Rd
Manakin Sabot, VA 23103-2141, USA

Buckman, Tom (Athlete, Football Player)
212 Foxford Dr
Keller, TX 76248-2532, USA

Buckner, Betty (Actor)
10643 Riverside Dr
North Hollywood, CA 91602-2341, USA

Buckner, Bill (Athlete, Baseball Player)
4405 E Wild Horse Ln
Boise, ID 83712-7593, USA

Buckner, Brentson (Athlete, Football Player)
423 Leary Ct
Columbus, GA 31907-5403, USA

Buckner, Cleveland (Athlete, Basketball Player)
19227 S Grandee Ave
Carson, CA 90746-2805, USA

Buckner, Greg (Athlete, Baseball Player)
4129 Catawba Ave
Newburgh, NY 12550, USA

Buckner, Pam (Bowler)
645 Utah St
Reno, NV 89506-8979, USA

Buckner, Quinn (Athlete, Basketball Player, Olympic Athlete)
857 Valencia Blvd
Irving, TX 75039-3057, USA

Buckner, Shelley (Actor)
c/o Staff Member *Cunningham Escott Slevin & Doherty (CESD-LA)*
10635 Santa Monica Blvd Ste 130
Los Angeles, CA 90025-8306, USA

Bucknor, C B (Athlete, Baseball Player)
46 Midwood St
Brooklyn, NY 11225-5004, USA

Bucknum, Jeff (Race Car Driver)
924 Paso Dr
Lake Havasu City, AZ 86406-8216, USA

Buckson, David P (Politician)
2710 Rismen Ct
Kissimmee, FL 34743-5370, USA

Bucshon, Larry (Congressman, Politician)
1123 Longworth Hob
Washington, DC 20515-4601, USA

Bucyk, John (Athlete, Hockey Player)
c/o Staff Member *Boston Bruins*
100 Legends Way Ste 250
Td Banknorth Garden
Boston, MA 02114-1389, USA

Buczkowski, Bob (Athlete, Football Player)
4515 Northern Pike
Monroeville, PA 15146-2915, USA

Budaj, Peter (Athlete, Hockey Player)
10140 Ridgegate Cir
Lone Tree, CO 80124-5538, USA

Budaska, Mark (Athlete, Baseball Player)
15025 W Buttonwood Dr
Sun City West, AZ 85375-5750, USA

Budd, Boyce (Athlete, Olympic Athlete, Rower)
PO Box 203
160 Geiger Rd
Erwinna, PA 18920-0203, USA

Budd, David (Athlete, Basketball Player)
40 N Woodland Ave
Woodbury, NJ 08096-2517, USA

Budd, Julie (Actor, Music Group)
Julie Budd Productions
163 Amsterdam Ave # 224
New York, NY 10023-5001, USA

Budde, Brad E (Athlete, Football Player)
5121 W 159th Ter
Stilwell, KS 66085-8956, USA

Budde, Ed (Athlete, Football Player)
5121 W 159th Ter
Stilwell, KS 66085-8956, USA

Budde, Jordan (Producer, Writer)
c/o Ann Blanchard *Creative Artists Agency (CAA-LA)*
2000 Avenue of the Stars Ste 100
Los Angeles, CA 90067-4705, USA

Budde, Ryan (Athlete, Baseball Player)
3109 N Peebly Dr
Oklahoma City, OK 73110-1509, USA

Budden, Joe (Actor)
c/o Staff Member *ICM Partners (LA)*
10250 Constellation Blvd Fl 7
Los Angeles, CA 90067-6207, USA

Buddie, Mike (Athlete, Baseball Player)
157 Scottsdale Dr
Advance, NC 27006-6933, USA

Buddy, Brandon (Actor)
c/o Jon Simmons *Simmons & Scott Entertainment*
7942 Mulholland Dr
Los Angeles, CA 90046-1225, USA

Budenholzer, Mike (Basketball Coach)
c/o Michael Hawkins *Hawkins Law Firm*
1535 Mount Vernon Rd Ste 200
Atlanta, GA 30338-4149, USA

Budig, Gene (Commentator)
5 Sandwedge Ln
Isle Of Palms, SC 29451-2820, USA

Budig, Rebecca (Actor)
83 Kellogg Hill Rd
Weston, CT 06883-2619, USA

Budka, Frank (Athlete, Football Player)
2637 SW Abel St
Port Saint Lucie, FL 34953-2834, USA

Budko, Walter (Athlete, Basketball Player)
7 Drumlin Dr
Morris Plains, NJ 07950-2718, USA

Budness, Bill (Athlete, Football Player)
401 Huckle Hill Rd
Bernardston, MA 01337-9423, USA

Budrewicz, Tom (Athlete, Football Player)
13 Olde Farms Rd
Boxford, MA 01921-1915, USA

Budzinski, Mark (Athlete, Baseball Player)
4919 Packard Rd
Glen Allen, VA 23060-3536, USA

Bueche, Wendell F (Business Person)
IMC Global
2100 Sanders Rd
Northbrook, IL 60062-6139, USA

Buechele, Steve (Athlete, Baseball Player)
1810 Prince John Dr
Grand Prairie, TX 75050-2159, USA

Buechler, John Carl (Director)
19528 Gilmore St
Reseda, CA 91335-5718, USA

Buechler, Jud (Athlete, Basketball Player)
680 W Circle Dr
Solana Beach, CA 92075-1114, USA

Buechrle, James (Baseball Player)
Chicago White Sox
Comiskey Park 333 W 35th St
Chicago, IL 60616, USA

Buehler, George (Athlete, Football Player)
201 E Grant Line Rd Apt 16
Tracy, CA 95376-2763, USA

Buehler, Jud (Athlete, Basketball Player)
4576 South Ln
Del Mar, CA 92014-4139, USA

Buehrle, Mark (Athlete, Baseball Player)
5653 N Ridge Ave
Chicago, IL 60660-5549, USA

Buell, Bebe (Actor)
c/o Ivan Bart *IMG Models (NY)*
304 Park Ave S Fl 12
New York, NY 10010-4314, USA

Buenning, Dan
E1806 Melody Ln
Waupaca, WI 54981-8318, us

Buer, Aaron (Actor)
c/o Staff Member *RPM Talent Agency*
2600 W Olive Ave Fl 5
Burbank, CA 91505-4572, USA

Buerge, Aaron (Reality Star)
c/o Staff Member *Maximum Talent*
6000 E Evans Ave Ste 1341
Denver, CO 80222-5428, USA

Buerkle, Ann Marie (Congressman, Politician)
1630 Longworth Hob
Washington, DC 20515-2002, USA

Buerkle, Dick (Athlete, Olympic Athlete, Track Athlete)
3086 Dale Dr NE
Atlanta, GA 30305-2776, USA

Buetow, Brad (Athlete, Hockey Player)
1419 Alamo Ave
Colorado Springs, CO 80907-7301, USA

Buffett, Howard Graham (Business Person)
407 Southmoreland Pl
Decatur, IL 62521-3754, USA

Buffett, Jimmy (Musician)
424A Fleming St
Key West, FL 33040-6529, USA

Buffett, Peter (Musician)
c/o Staff Member *Paradigm (Monterey)*
404 W Franklin St
Monterey, CA 93940-2303, USA

Buffett, Warren (Business Person)
Berkshire Hathaway
1440 Kiewit Plz
Omaha, NE 68131, USA

Buffone, Douglas J (Doug) (Athlete, Football Player)
1272 W Lexington St
Chicago, IL 60607-4110, USA

Bufman, Zev (Producer)
520 Brickell Key Dr # 612
Miami, FL 33131-2660, USA

Buford, Damon J (Athlete, Baseball Player)
791 E Birchwood Pl
Chandler, AZ 85249-3311, USA

Buford, Don (Athlete, Baseball Player)
15412 Valley Vista Blvd
Sherman Oaks, CA 91403-3812, USA

Buford, Maury (Athlete, Football Player)
2901 Sweet Briar St
Grapevine, TX 76051-2651, USA

Bugel, Joe (Athlete, Football Coach, Football Player)
15517 E Cactus Dr
Fountain Hills, AZ 85268-4123, USA

Bugenhagen, Gary (Athlete, Football Player)
4337 Henneberry Rd
Manlius, NY 13104-8425, USA

Buggs, Danny
190 Austin Oaks Dr
Ellenwood, GA 30294-3161, us

Buggs, Dany (Athlete, Football Player)
3186 Evans Mill Rd
Lithonia, GA 30038-2420, USA

Buggs, Wamon (Athlete, Football Player)
5700 Sonoma Trce
Antioch, TN 37013-4273, USA

Buggy, Regina (Athlete, Hockey Player)
550 N Limekiln Pike
Chalfont, PA 18914-2739, USA

Bugliosi, Vincent (Writer)
663 Arbor St
Pasadena, CA 91105-1519, USA

Buhl, Robbie (Race Car Driver)
24530 Hilliard Blvd
Westlake, OH 44145-3517, USA

Buhner, Jay (Athlete, Baseball Player)
David and Kay Buhner
7201 Westover Rd
Waco, TX 76710-6106, USA

Buhrmaster, Robert C (Business Person)
Jostens Inc
3601 Minnesota Dr Ste 400
Minneapolis, MN 55435-6008, USA

Buice, Dewayne (Athlete, Baseball Player)
PO Box 5185
Incline Village, NV 89450-5185, USA

Buie, Drew (Athlete, Football Player)
2815 Eland Dr
Winston Salem, NC 27127-7284, USA

Bujnoch, Glenn (Athlete, Football Player)
7598 Fairwayglen Dr
Cincinnati, OH 45248-2800, USA

Bujold, Genevieve (Actor)
1327 Ocean Ave Ste J
Blake Agency
Santa Monica, CA 90401-1033, USA

Bukich, Rudy (Athlete, Football Player)
12370 Carmel Country Rd Unit 109
San Diego, CA 92130-4518, USA

Buktenica, Raymond (Actor)
Special Artists Agency
345 N Maple Dr # 302
Beverly Hills, CA 90210-3869, USA

Bukvich, Ryan (Athlete, Baseball Player)
200 Apple Blossom Cir
Brandon, MS 39047-7691, USA

Bulaga, Bryan (Athlete, Football Player)
c/o Ben Dogra *CAA (St. Louis)*
222 S Central Ave Ste 1008
Saint Louis, MO 63105-3509, USA

Bulaich, Norman B (Norm) (Athlete, Football Player)
421 Lynndale Ct
Hurst, TX 76054-2725, USA

Bulger, Jason (Athlete, Baseball Player)
1898 Harbour Oaks Dr
Snellville, GA 30078-2316, USA

Bulger, Marc (Athlete, Football Player)
c/o Tom Condon *CAA (St. Louis)*
222 S Central Ave Ste 1008
Saint Louis, MO 63105-3509, USA

Bulifant, Joyce (Actor)
James/Levy/Jacobson
3500 W Olive Ave Ste 1470
Burbank, CA 91505-5514, USA

Buljung, Erich (Athlete, Olympic Athlete, Shooter)
7570 Stampede Dr
Colorado Springs, CO 80920-3715, USA

Bull, Ronald D (Ronnie) (Athlete, Football Player)
15 Redspire Ct
Bolingbrook, IL 60490-3175, USA

Bull, Scott (Athlete, Football Player)
11446 Mountain Spring Dr
Fayetteville, AR 72701-0422, USA

Bullard, Courtland (Athlete, Football Player)
22200 SW 113th Ct
Miami, FL 33170-4762, us

Bullard, Kendricke (Athlete, Football Player)
PO Box 2330
North Little Rock, AR 72115-2330, US

Bullard, Matt (Athlete, Basketball Player)
10 Balmoral Pl
Spring, TX 77382-1343, USA

Bullet, Scott (Athlete, Baseball Player)
218 Vicky Bullett St
Martinsburg, WV 25404-4511, USA

Bulling, Terry (Bud) (Athlete, Baseball Player)
203 Laurelhurst Dr
Newport, WA 99156, USA

Bullinger, Jim (Athlete, Baseball Player)
2504 Elise Ave
Metairie, LA 70003-1931, USA

Bullinger, Kirk (Athlete, Baseball Player)
3608 David Dr
Metairie, LA 70003-3413, USA

Bullington, Bryan (Athlete, Baseball Player)
20116 Oakwood Dr
Mokena, IL 60448-1395, USA

Bullins, Ed (Writer)
425 Lafayette St
New York, NY 10003-7021, USA

Bullock, Bruce (Athlete, Hockey Player)
5226 W Redbird Rd
Phoenix, AZ 85083-6317, USA

Bullock, Eric (Athlete, Baseball Player)
17503 Harwick Ct
Carson, CA 90746-1617, USA

Bullock, Jim J (Actor)
c/o Staff Member *Bohemia Group (LA)*
1680 Vine St Ste 505
Los Angeles, CA 90028-8833, USA

Bullock, Jim J (Actor)
612 Lighthouse Ave # 200
Pacific Grove, CA 93950-2615, USA

Bullock, Randy (Athlete, Football Player)
c/o Eric Metz *Lock Metz Milanovic LLC*
6900 E Camelback Rd Ste 600
Scottsdale, AZ 85251-8044, USA

Bullock, Sandra (Actor, Producer)
c/o Staff Member *Fortis Films*
8581 Santa Monica Blvd # 1
West Hollywood, CA 90069-4120, USA

Bullock, Steve (Governor, Politician)
Office of the Governor
PO Box 200801
Helena, MT 59620-0801, USA

Bullock, Vicki (Athlete, Basketball Player)
Charlotte Sting
100 Hive Dr
Charlotte, NC 28217-4524, USA

Bullocks, Amos (Athlete, Football Player)
17209 Dobson Ave
South Holland, IL 60473-3535, USA

Bullough, Hank (Athlete, Football Player)
4439 Copperhill Dr
Okemos, MI 48864-2067, USA

Bulluck, Keith (Athlete, Football Player)
874 Nialta Ln
Brentwood, TN 37027-8232, USA

Bulriss, Mark P (Business Person)
Great Lakes Chemical
9025 River Rd Ste 400
Indianapolis, IN 46240-6443, USA

Bumbry, Alonzo B (Al) (Athlete, Baseball Player)
28 Tremblant Ct
Lutherville Timonium, MD 21093-3748, USA

Bumgarner, Wayne (Actor)
PO Box 208
Claremont, NC 28610-0208, USA

Bump, Nate (Athlete, Baseball Player)
274 Caravelle Dr
Jupiter, FL 33458-8200, USA

Bumpas, Dick (Athlete, Football Player)
22262 Dam Site Rd
Garfield, AR 72732-8515, USA

Bumpers, Dale (Politician)
Arent Fox
12723 Hunters Field Rd
Little Rock, AR 72211-2248, USA

Bunce, Gregory (Athlete, Basketball Player)
1710 Redwood Way
Upland, CA 91784-1767, USA

Bunce, Larry (Attorney, Basketball Player)
1000 Vintage Ln Apt 338
Mount Vernon, WA 98273-5532, USA

Bunch, Ashli (Athlete, Golfer)
1629 Country Club Dr
Morristown, TN 37814-3316, USA

Bunch, Jarrod (Athlete, Football Player)
1580 Hemlock Dr
Ashtabula, OH 44004-9360, USA

Bunch, Melvin (Athlete, Baseball Player)
782 Horseshoe Loop
Texarkana, TX 75501-1322, USA

Bunch, Sidney (Athlete, Baseball Player)
3285 Towne Village Rd
Antioch, TN 37013-1280, USA

Bundchen, Gisele (Model)
c/o Anne Nelson *IMG Models (NY)*
304 Park Ave S Fl 12
New York, NY 10010-4314, USA

Bundren, Jim (Athlete, Football Player)
34 Sovern Dr
Greenville, SC 29607-5498, us

Bundy, Brooke (Actor)
833 N Martel Ave
Los Angeles, CA 90046-7508, USA

Bundy, Laura Bell (Actor, Musician)
c/o CeCe Yorke *True Public Relations*
6725 W Sunset Blvd Ste 470
Los Angeles, CA 90028-7180, USA

Bunker, Wallace E (Wally) (Athlete, Baseball Player)
330 Coosaw Way Unit 38
Ridgeland, SC 29936-4968, USA

Bunkowsky-Scherbak, Barb (Athlete, Golfer)
8725 Marlamoor Ln
West Palm Beach, FL 33412-1614, USA

Bunnell, John (Actor, Television Host)
c/o Greg Horangic *William Morris Endeavor (LA)*
9601 Wilshire Blvd
Beverly Hills, CA 90210-5213, USA

Bunnetta, Bill (Bowler)
1176 E San Bruno Ave
Fresno, CA 93710-7109, USA

Bunning, James P D (Jim) (Politician)
4 Fairway Dr
Southgate, KY 41071-3022, USA

Bunny, Lady (Comedian, DJ, Impersonator)
c/o Stephen Ford *Diva Central Inc*
7510 W Sunset Blvd Ste 1445
Los Angeles, CA 90046-3408, USA

Bunt, Dick (Actor)
11 Irving Pl
Greenlawn, NY 11740-3113, USA

Bunt, Richard (Athlete, Basketball Player)
38 Lawrence Ave
Danbury, CT 06810-5181, USA

Bunting, Eve (Writer)
Harper Collins Publishers
1512 Rose Villa St
Pasadena, CA 91106-3525, USA

Bunting, John (Athlete, Football Player)
134 Soundview Dr
Hampstead, NC 28443-2510, USA

Bunting, William (Athlete, Basketball Player)
11000 Pacer Ct
Raleigh, NC 27614-9604, USA

Bunton, Emma (Music Group, Musician)
c/o Jeff Frasco *Creative Artists Agency (CAA-LA)*
2000 Avenue of the Stars Ste 100
Los Angeles, CA 90067-4705, USA

Bunyan, John (Athlete, Football Player)
132 Ringneck Trl
Mooresville, NC 28117-8124, USA

Bunz, Dan (Athlete, Football Player)
4230 Rocklin Rd Apt 2
Rocklin, CA 95677-2869, USA

Buoniconti, Nicholas A (Nick) (Athlete, Business Person, Football Player)
445 Grand Bay Dr Apt 803
Key Biscayne, FL 33149-1907, USA

Buono, Cara (Actor)
c/o Joanna (Joanie) Burstein *Burstein Company, The*
15304 W Sunset Blvd Ste 208
Pacific Palisades, CA 90272-3656, USA

Buono, Carla (Actor)
25 Sea Colony Dr
Santa Monica, CA 90405-5495, USA

Burba, Dave (Athlete, Baseball Player)
984 E Erie Ct
Gilbert, AZ 85295-5476, USA

Burbach, Bill (Athlete, Baseball Player)
147 Shenandoah Dr
Johnson City, TN 37601-5459, USA

Burbage, Cornell (Athlete, Football Player)
1309 Copper Run Blvd
Lexington, KY 40514-2217, us

Burbank, Daniel C Cdr (Astronaut)
364 Route 6A
Yarmouth Port, MA 02675-1820, USA

Burbank, Daniel C (Dan) (Astronaut)
3210 Water Elm Way
Houston, TX 77059, USA

Burbano, Mindy (Actor)
12 Fairway Pt
Newport Coast, CA 92657-1721, USA

Burch, Elliot (Race Car Driver)
108 Feroe Ct
Rotonda West, FL 33947-3819, USA

Burch, Jerry (Athlete, Football Player)
1501 Plantation Dr
Simpsonville, SC 29681-4658, USA

Burch, Matt (Reality Star)
PO Box 802227
Santa Clarita, CA 91380-2227, USA

Burch, Rick (Musician)
3302 E Mitchell Dr
Phoenix, AZ 85018-5737, USA

Burch, Tory (Business Person, Designer)
Tory Burch
11 W 19th St Fl 7
New York, NY 10011-4277, USA

Burchard, Brendon (Business Person, Motivational Speaker)
The Burchard Group
PO Box 5368
Portland, OR 97228-5368, USA

Burchart, Larry (Athlete, Baseball Player)
5310 E 94th St
Tulsa, OK 74137-4417, USA

Burchfield, Don (Athlete, Football Player)
26450 Summer Greens Dr
Bonita Springs, FL 34135-2328, USA

Burd, Steven A (Business Person)
Safeway Inc
5918 Stoneridge Mall Rd
Pleasanton, CA 94588-3229, USA

Burda, Bob (Athlete, Baseball Player)
5285 S Roanoke
Mesa, AZ 85206, USA

Burden, Ticky (Athlete, Basketball Player)
4332 Grove Ave Apt C
Winston Salem, NC 27105-2837, USA

Burden, Willie (Athlete, Football Player)
112 Olde Towne Dr
Statesboro, GA 30458-1673, USA

Burditt, Joyce (Producer, Writer)
c/o Staff Member *William Morris Endeavor (LA)*
9601 Wilshire Blvd
Beverly Hills, CA 90210-5213, USA

Burdon, Eric (Music Group, Songwriter, Writer)
Lustig Talent
PO Box 770850
Orlando, FL 32877-0850, USA

Bure, Pavel (Athlete, Hockey Player)
7632 Fisher Island Dr
Miami Beach, FL 33109-0780, USA

Bure, Valeri (Athlete, Hockey Player)
10371 Golden Eagle Ct
Plantation, FL 33324-2161, USA

Bureker-Stopper, Geraldine (Baseball Player)
2006 SE 41st Ave
Portland, OR 97214-5966, USA

Buress, Hannibal (Actor, Comedian)
c/o David (Dave) Becky *3 Arts Entertainment (LA)*
9460 Wilshire Blvd Fl 7
Beverly Hills, CA 90212-2713, USA

Burfeindt, Betty (Athlete, Golfer)
70 San Simeon Pl
Rancho Mirage, CA 92270-1951, USA

Burford, Christopher W (Chris) (Athlete, Football Player)
1215 Broken Feather Ct
Reno, NV 89511-5350, USA

Burg, Bob (Writer)
Burg Communications Inc
3607 Fairway Dr N
Jupiter, FL 33477-9525, USA

Burg, Mark (Producer)
14050 Aubrey Rd
Beverly Hills, CA 90210-1064, USA

Burger, Michael (Actor)
c/o Staff Member *Richard De La Font Agency*
3808 W South Park Blvd
Broken Arrow, OK 74011-1261, USA

Burger, Neil (Director)
c/o Staff Member *William Morris Endeavor (LA)*
9601 Wilshire Blvd
Beverly Hills, CA 90210-5213, USA

Burgess, Adrian (Mountaineer)
324 G St
Anderson, SC 29625-4147, USA

Burgess, Annie (Athlete)
601 F St NW
Washington, DC 20004-1605

Burgess, Bobby (Actor)
11684 Ventura Blvd # 691
Studio City, CA 91604-2699, USA

Burgess, Don (Cinematographer)
Gersh Agency
232 N Canon Dr
Beverly Hills, CA 90210-5302, USA

Burgess, Mitchell (Writer)
c/o Staff Member *Broder Webb Chervin Silbermann Agency, The (BWCS)*
10250 Constellation Blvd
Los Angeles, CA 90067-6200, USA

Burgess, Ronnie (Athlete, Football Player)
303 Brandymill Blvd
Myrtle Beach, SC 29588-7227, USA

Burgess, Tom (Athlete, Football Player)
1399 Maryland Rd
Phelps, NY 14532-9508, USA

Burgess, Warren D (Religious Leader)
Reformed Church in America
475 Riverside Dr Ste 1606
New York, NY 10115-0093, USA

Burghoff, Gary (Actor)
1271 Nunneley Rd
Paradise, CA 95969-4843, USA

Burgi, Richard (Actor)
1019 Baja St
Laguna Beach, CA 92651-3546, USA

Burgio, Danielle (Actor)
c/o Carl Scott *Simmons & Scott Entertainment*
7942 Mulholland Dr
Los Angeles, CA 90046-1225, USA

Burgmeier, Ted (Athlete, Football Player)
861 Scenic Hts
East Dubuque, IL 61025-1041, USA

Burgmeler, Tom (Athlete, Baseball Player)
13118 Walmer St
Leawood, KS 66209-3618, USA

Burham, Daniel (Business Person)
Raytheon Co
870 Winter St
Waltham, MA 02451-1449, USA

Burish, Adam (Athlete, Hockey Player)
100 Wisconsin Ave Apt 1001
Madison, WI 53703-4169, USA

Burk, Mack (Athlete, Baseball Player)
5710 Glen Pines Dr
Houston, TX 77069-1852, USA

Burk, Scott (Athlete, Football Player)
2608 SW 121st Ct
Oklahoma City, OK 73170-4757, USA

Burka, Vern (Athlete, Football Player)
580 Riviera Cir
Nipomo, CA 93444-8866, USA

Burkart, Phil (Race Car Driver)
114 Oriskany Blvd
Yorkville, NY 13495-1328, USA

Burke, Alexandra (Musician)
c/o Joseph Carozza *Epic Records Group*
550 Madison Ave Fl 6
New York, NY 10022-3211, USA

Burke, Billy (Actor)
4180 Crisp Canyon Rd
Sherman Oaks, CA 91403-4646, USA

Burke, Brooke (Actor, Model)
2221 Ocean Ave Apt 302
Santa Monica, CA 90405-2238, USA

Burke, Cheryl (Dancer, Reality Star)
3520 Multiview Dr
Los Angeles, CA 90068-1222, USA

Burke, Chris (Actor)
c/o Staff Member *Abrams Artists Agency (LA)*
9200 W Sunset Blvd PH 11
West Hollywood, CA 90069-3601, USA

Burke, Chris (Athlete, Baseball Player)
15415 Crystal Springs Way
Louisville, KY 40245-5298, USA

Burke, Clement (Clem) (Musician)
Shore Fire Media
32 Court St Ste 1600
Brooklyn, NY 11201-4441, USA

Burke, Delta (Actor)
4270 Farmdale Ave
Studio City, CA 91604-2733, USA

Burke, Ed (Actor)
16717 La Mirada Rd
Los Gatos, CA 95030-4118, USA

Burke, Edward (Athlete, Olympic Athlete)
16717 La Mirada Rd
Los Gatos, CA 95030-4118, USA

Burke, Ernest (Athlete, Baseball Player)
9451 Common Brook Rd Apt 302
Owings Mills, MD 21117-7582, USA

Burke, Hederman Lynn (Swimmer)
26 White Oak Tree Rd
Syosset, NY 11791-1210, USA

Burke, James D (Director)
Saint Louis Art Museum
Forest Park
Saint Louis, MO 63110, USA

Burke, James Lee (Writer)
c/o Joel Gotler *Intellectual Property Group (IPG)*
10585 Santa Monica Blvd Ste 140
Los Angeles, CA 90025-4984, USA

Burke, Joe (Athlete, Football Player)
7 Maplewood St
Albany, NY 12208-2413, USA

Burke, John (Athlete, Baseball Player)
3490 Westbrook Ln
Highlands Ranch, CO 80129-1527, USA

Burke, John (Athlete, Football Player)
612 Valley Rd
Brielle, NJ 08730-1229, USA

Burke, Leo (Athlete, Baseball Player)
12916 Woodburn Dr
Hagerstown, MD 21742-2866, USA

Burke, Mark (Athlete, Football Player)
10 Maple Shade Dr
Marietta, OH 45750-1124, US

Burke, Michael Reilly (Actor)
c/o Staff Member *Paradigm (LA)*
360 N Crescent Dr
North Bldg
Beverly Hills, CA 90210-4874, USA

Burke, Mike (Athlete, Football Player)
720 Deodara Pl
Dixon, CA 95620-3639, USA

Burke, Patrick (Athlete, Golfer)
24 Saint Georges Ct
Trabuco Canyon, CA 92679-4926, USA

Burke, Randall (Athlete, Football Player)
3420 Chestnut Hill Ln
Lexington, KY 40509-1916, USA

Burke, Randy (Athlete, Football Player)
3420 Chestnut Hill Ln
Lexington, KY 40509-1916, US

Burke, Sarah (Reality Star)
c/o Mike Esterman *Esterman.Com, LLC*
Prefers to be contacted via email
Baltimore, MD XXXXX, USA

Burke, Sean (Athlete, Hockey Player)
9016 N 60th St
Paradise Valley, AZ 85253-1718, USA

Burke, Sean (Athlete, Hockey Player)
7701 N Calle Caballeros
Paradise Valley, AZ 85253-3116, USA

Burke, Shawn (Athlete, Hockey Player)
7701 N Calle Caballeros
Paradise Valley, AZ 85253-3116, USA

Burke, Steve (Athlete, Baseball Player)
1812 Amber Leaf Way
Lodi, CA 95242-4468, USA

Burke, Steve (Athlete, Football Player)
RR 3 Box 553-F
Austin, TX 78754, USA

Burke, Tim (Athlete, Baseball Player)
12108 W Ida Ln
Littleton, CO 80127-3106, USA

Burke Sr, Jack (Athlete, Golfer)
5602 Glen Pines Dr
Houston, TX 77069-1834, USA

Burkett, Chris (Athlete, Football Player)
296 Dover Ln
Madison, MS 39110-9726, USA

Burkett, Jackie (Athlete, Football Player)
895 Santa Rosa Blvd Apt 709
Fort Walton Beach, FL 32548-1913, USA

Burkett, John D (Athlete, Baseball Player)
1404 Laurel Ln
Southlake, TX 76092-3573, USA

Burkhalter, Correll (Athlete, Football Player)
221 Robert Owens Rd
Mount Olive, MS 39119-4651, USA

Burkhardt, Lisa (Sportscaster)
Madison Square Garden Network
4 Pennsylvania Plz
New York, NY 10001, USA

Burkhart, Morgan (Athlete, Baseball Player)
105 Turtle Rock Ct
Saint Charles, MO 63304-7679, USA

Burkhead, Rex (Athlete, Football Player)
c/o Neil Cornrich *NC Sports, LLC*
best to contact via email
Columbus, OH 43201, USA

Burkholder, Max (Actor)
c/o Emily Urbani *Osbrink Talent Agency*
4343 Lankershim Blvd Ste 100
North Hollywood, CA 91602-2705, USA

Burkholder, Owen E (Religious Leader)
421 S 2nd St Ste 600
Elkhart, IN 46516-3243, USA

Burkle, Ron (Business Person)
2607 Glendower Ave
Los Angeles, CA 90027-1114, USA

Burkman, Roger (Athlete, Basketball Player)
3242 Beals Branch Dr
Dallas, TX 75237, USA

Burkovich, Shirley (Athlete, Baseball Player, Commentator)
67430 Ovante Rd
Cathedral City, CA 92234-8402, USA

Burks, Audra (Athlete, Golfer)
2821 Crown Pt
Springfield, IL 62704-1095, USA

Burks, Ellis R (Athlete, Baseball Player)
115 South Ln
Chagrin Falls, OH 44022-1145, USA

Burks, Randy (Athlete, Football Player)
300 Moyer Dr
Broken Bow, OK 74728-1519, USA

Burks, Shawn (Athlete, Football Player)
5752 Nottaway Dr
Baton Rouge, LA 70820-5415, USA

Burks, Steve (Athlete, Football Player)
2568 Mount Tabor Rd
Cabot, AR 72023-9596, USA

Burleson, Dyrol (Athlete, Olympic Athlete, Track Athlete)
12024 S Shadow Hills Ct SE
Turner, OR 97392-9353, USA

Burleson, Richard P (Rick) (Athlete, Baseball Player)
241 E Country Hills Dr
La Habra, CA 90631-7623, USA

Burleson, Tom (Athlete, Basketball Player, Olympic Athlete)
PO Box 861
Newland, NC 28657-0861, USA

Burley, Gary (Athlete, Football Player)
8228 Castlehill Rd
Birmingham, AL 35242-7233, USA

Burman, George (Athlete, Football Player)
1646 James St
Syracuse, NY 13203-2816, USA

Burn, Scott (Writer)
c/o Staff Member *Creative Artists Agency (CAA-LA)*
2000 Avenue of the Stars Ste 100
Los Angeles, CA 90067-4705, USA

Burner, David L (Business Person)
B F Goodrich Co
2550 W Tyvola Rd
3 Coliseum Centre
Charlotte, NC 28217-4574, USA

Burnes, Karen (Correspondent)
CBS-TV
51 W 52nd St
News Dept
New York, NY 10019-6119, USA

Burnett, A J (Athlete, Baseball Player)
15208 Jarrettsville Pike
Monkton, MD 21111, USA

Burnett, Bobby (Athlete, Football Player)
4521 N Diamond Leaf Dr
Castle Rock, CO 80109-8684, USA

Burnett, Carol (Actor, Comedian)
c/o Angie Horejsi *Mabel Cat*
9663 Santa Monica Blvd Ste 643
Beverly Hills, CA 90210-4303, USA

Burnett, Chester (Athlete, Football Player)
2610 Ivanhoe St
Denver, CO 80207-3409, USA

Burnett, Erin (Correspondent)
c/o Staff Member *CNBC (DC)*
400 N Capitol St NW Ste 850
Washington, DC 20001-1555, USA

Burnett, James E (Government Official)
Transportations Safety Board
800 Independence Ave SW
Washington, DC 20594, USA

Burnett, Mark (Producer)
27540 Pacific Coast Hwy
Malibu, CA 90265-4338, USA

Burnett, Molly (Actor)
c/o Shepard Smith *Luber Roklin Management*
1608 Argyle Ave
Los Angeles, CA 90028-6408, USA

Burnett, Nancy (Director)
Nancy Burnett Productions
32 Watson St
Unadilla, NY 13849, USA

Burnett, Sean (Athlete, Baseball Player)
14016 Aster Ave
Wellington, FL 33414-2145, USA

Burnett, T-Bone (Musician, Producer, Songwriter)
c/o Staff Member *Paradigm (Monterey)*
404 W Franklin St
Monterey, CA 93940-2303, USA

Burnett, Webbie D (Athlete, Football Player)
5305 San Antonio Ave Apt 128
Orlando, FL 32839-2222, USA

Burnette, Dave (Athlete, Football Player)
4201 Senator St
Texarkana, AR 71854-1528, USA

Burnette, Olivia (Actor)
c/o Staff Member *RPM Talent Agency*
2600 W Olive Ave Fl 5
Burbank, CA 91505-4572, USA

Burnette, Reggie (Athlete, Football Player)
7803 Chasewood Dr
Missouri City, TX 77489-1836, USA

Burnette, Rocky (Musician)
1900 Ave of Stars # 2530
Los Angeles, CA 90067-4301, USA

Burnine, Hank (Athlete, Football Player)
709 W Rieck Rd
Tyler, TX 75703-3559, USA

Burning, Spear (Musician)
13034 231st St
Laurelton, NY 11413-1832, USA

Burnitz, Jeromv (Athlete, Baseball Player)
PO Box 676032
Rancho Santa Fe, CA 92067-6032, USA

Burnitz, Jeromy (Athlete, Baseball Player)
PO Box 676032
Rcho Santa Fe, CA 92067-6032, USA

Burnley, James H IV (Politician)
Shaw Pittman Potts Trowbridge
9401 Mount Vernon Cir
Alexandria, VA 22309-3221, USA

Burns, Annie (Musician, Songwriter, Writer)
Drake Assoc
177 Woodland Ave
Westwood, NJ 07675-3218, USA

Burns, Bob (Athlete, Golfer)
12512 Fraser Ave
Granada Hills, CA 91344-1321, USA

Burns, Brent
1460 Newport Ave
San Jose, CA 95125-3329, USA

Burns, Britt (Athlete, Baseball Player)
1550 Katy Gap Rd Apt 903
Katy, TX 77494-5872, USA

Burns, Brooke (Actor, Model)
4320 Mariota Ave
Toluca Lake, CA 91602-2912, USA

Burns, Charlie (Athlete, Hockey Player)
7 Fawn Dr
Wallingford, CT 06492-3307, USA

Burns, Conrad (Politician)
PO Box 51293
Billings, MT 59105-1293, USA

Burns, David (Athlete, Basketball Player)
2623 Bainbridge Dr
Dallas, TX 75237-2801, USA

Burns, Edward (Actor, Director)
c/o JoAnne Colonna *Brillstein Entertainment Partners (LA)*
9150 Wilshire Blvd Ste 350
Beverly Hills, CA 90212-3453, USA

Burns, Eileen (Actor)
4000 W 43rd St
New York, NY 10036, USA

Burns, Evers (Athlete, Basketball Player)
7216 Lost Spring Ct
Lanham, MD 20706-3834, USA

Burns, George (Athlete, Basketball Player)
16 E Poplar St
Floral Park, NY 11001-3145, USA

Burns, George (Athlete, Golfer)
10459 Prestwick Rd
Boynton Beach, FL 33436-4418, USA

Burns, Heather (Actor)
c/o Courtney Kivowitz *The Schiff Company*
9220 W Sunset Blvd Ste 106
West Hollywood, CA 90069-3500, USA

Burns, James (Athlete, Basketball Player)
2706 Lincoln St
Evanston, IL 60201-2043, USA

Burns, Jason (Athlete, Football Player)
8923 S Marshfield Ave
Chicago, IL 60620-4955, USA

Burns, Jeannie (Musician, Songwriter, Writer)
Drake Assoc
177 Woodland Ave
Westwood, NJ 07675-3218, USA

Burns, Jere (Actor)
c/o Staff Member *ICM Partners (LA)*
10250 Constellation Blvd Fl 7
Los Angeles, CA 90067-6207, USA

Burns, Jerry (Athlete, Football Coach, Football Player)
9520 Viking Dr
Eden Prairie, MN 55344-3825

Burns, Jim (Writer)
c/o Staff Member *Da Capo Press*
44 Farnsworth St Fl 3
Boston, MA 02210-1223, USA

Burns, Keith (Athlete, Football Player)
7991 S Kittredge Way
Englewood, CO 80112-4631, USA

Burns, Kenneth L (Ken) (Director)
Florentine Films
Maple Grove Road
Walpole, NH 03608, USA

Burns, Lamont (Athlete, Football Player)
104 Northwood St
Greensboro, NC 27417, USA

Burns, M Anthony (Business Person)
Ryder System Inc
3600 NW 82nd Ave
Doral, FL 33166-6623, USA

Burns, Marie (Musician, Songwriter, Writer)
Drake Assoc
177 Woodland Ave
Westwood, NJ 07675-3218, USA

Burns, Marilyn (Actor)
12951 Briar Forest Dr Apt 926
Houston, TX 77077-2058, USA

Burns, Marilyn (Writer)
150 Gate 5 Rd Ste 101
Sausalito, CA 94965-1486, USA

Burns, Michael (Business Person)
8365 Sunset View Dr
Los Angeles, CA 90069-1517, USA

Burns, Mike (Athlete, Football Player)
540 Stege Ave
Richmond, CA 94804-4133, USA

Burns, Pat (Coach)
New Jersey Devils
Continental Arena
50 RR 120 N
East Rutherford, NJ 07073, USA

Burns, Regan (Actor)
c/o Bruce Smith *OmniPop Talent Group (LA)*
4605 Lankershim Blvd Ste 201
North Hollywood, CA 91602-1874, USA

Burns, Steven (Actor)
c/o Staff Member *Davis Spylios Management*
244 W 54th St Ste 707
New York, NY 10019-5515

Burns, Todd (Athlete, Baseball Player)
PO Box 111
Princeton, AL 35766-0111, USA

Burnside, Pete (Athlete, Baseball Player)
1041 Ridge Rd Unit 210
Wilmette, IL 60091-1569, USA

Burnside, Sheldon (Athlete, Baseball Player)
7519 Wynford Cir
Montgomery, AL 36117-7483, USA

Burns Jr, Jere (Actor)
Binder
1465 Lindacrest Dr
Beverly Hills, CA 90210-2519, USA

Burnstein, Nanette (Director, Producer)
c/o Scott Greenberg *Creative Artists Agency (CAA-LA)*
2000 Avenue of the Stars Ste 100
Los Angeles, CA 90067-4705, USA

Burpo, George (Athlete, Baseball Player)
8981 E Palms Park Dr
Tucson, AZ 85715-5644, USA

Burr, Bill (Actor, Comedian)
c/o Michael O'Brien *Michael OBrien Entertainment*
Prefers to be contacted by telephone or email
New York, NY 10012, USA

Burr, Gary (Musician)
833 Highland Park Ct
Nashville, TN 37205-4003, USA

Burr, Richard (Senator)
217 Russell Senate Office Building
Washington, DC 20510-0001, USA

Burr, Shawn (Athlete, Hockey Player)
1615 River Rd
Saint Clair, MI 48079-3552, USA

Burrell, George R (Athlete, Football Player)
129 W Upsal St
Philadelphia, PA 19119-4003, USA

Burrell, John (Athlete, Football Player)
376 Park Lake Dr
Mead, OK 73449-6352, USA

Burrell, Kenny (Musician)
c/o Staff Member *Concord Music Group, Inc*
900 N Rohlwing Rd
Itasca, IL 60143-1161, USA

Burrell, Leroy (Athlete, Track Athlete)
University of Houston
Athletic Dept
Houston, TX 77023, USA

Burrell, Orville (Shaggy) (Musician)
c/o Staff Member *Big Yard Music Group*
PO Box 1060
Valley Stream, NY 11582-1060, USA

Burrell, Pat (Athlete, Baseball Player)
PO Box 1770
Boulder Creek, CA 95006-1770, USA

Burrell, Scott (Athlete, Basketball Player)
331 Evergreen Ave
Hamden, CT 06518-2745, USA

Burres, Brian (Athlete, Baseball Player)
533 SW Edgefield Meadows Ave
Troutdale, OR 97060-5451, USA

Burress, Hedy (Actor)
c/o David Lillard *Paradigm (LA)*
8730 W Sunset Blvd Ste 490
West Hollywood, CA 90069-2248, USA

Burress, Plaxico (Athlete, Football Player)
47 Huntington Ter
Totowa, NJ 07512-2181, USA

Burridge, Randy (Athlete, Hockey Player)
1911 Nuevo Rd
Henderson, NV 89014-5134, USA

Burright, Larry
1239 E Palm Dr
Glendora, CA 91741-2347, USA

Burright, Larry (Athlete, Baseball Player)
1239 E Palm Dr
Glendora, CA 91741-2347, USA

Burris, Jeffrey L (Jeff) (Athlete, Football Player)
77 Reynolds St
Rock Hill, SC 29730-4368, USA

Burris, Ray (Athlete, Baseball Player)
Erie Sea Wolves 110 E lOth St
Erie, PA 16501, USA

Burris, Ray (Athlete, Baseball Player)
2708 Golden Creek Ln Apt 1208
Arlington, TX 76006-3557, USA

Burriss, Bo (Athlete, Football Player)
818 Pinemont Dr Apt 38
Houston, TX 77018-1529, USA

Burrough, Junior (Athlete, Basketball Player)
625 Harwyn Dr
Charlotte, NC 28215-2029, USA

Burrough, Kenneth O (Ken) (Athlete, Football Player)
7979 Westheimer Rd
Houston, TX 77063-4550, USA

Burroughs, Augusten (Writer)
c/o Christopher Schelling *Ralph Vicinanza, Ltd.*
303 W 18th St
New York, NY 10011-4440, USA

Burroughs, Jeffrey A (Jeff) (Athlete, Baseball Player)
6155 Laguna Ct
Long Beach, CA 90803-4812, USA

Burroughs, Sean (Athlete, Baseball Player, Olympic Athlete)
6155 Laguna Ct
Long Beach, CA 90803-4812, USA

Burroughs, William S (Musician)
PO Box 147
Lawrence, KS 66044-0147, USA

Burrow, Bob (Athlete, Basketball Player)
2228 Oakbranch Cir
Franklin, TN 37064-7407, USA

Burrow, Curtis (Athlete, Football Player)
51 W Cadron Ridge Rd
Greenbrier, AR 72058-9102, USA

Burrow, Jim (Athlete, Football Player)
7961 Floyd Dr
The Plains, OH 45780-1403, USA

Burrow, Ken (Athlete, Football Player)
3206 Greenwood Oak Dr
Peachtree Corners, GA 30092-3510, USA

Burrow, Robert (Athlete, Basketball Player)
2228 Oakbranch Cir
Franklin, TN 37064-7407, USA

Burrows, Darren E (Actor)
c/o Deborah Miller *Shelter Entertainment*
9255 W Sunset Blvd Ste 320
West Hollywood, CA 90069-3313, USA

Burrows, Edwin G (Writer)
Oxford University Press
198 Madison Ave Fl 8
New York, NY 10016-4341, USA

Burrows, Irv
555 Couch Ave Apt 261
Saint Louis, MO 63122-5664, USA

Burrows, James (Director)
10702 Levico Way
Los Angeles, CA 90077-1917, USA

Burrows, Terry (Athlete, Baseball Player)
7019 Burgandy Dr
Lake Charles, LA 70605-0252, USA

Burrows, Terry (Athlete, Baseball Player)
7019 Burgandy Dr
Lake Charles, LA 70605-0252, USA

Burruss, Kandi (Musician, Reality Star)
525 Carondelett Cv SW
Atlanta, GA 30331-8354, USA

Bursch, Daniel W (Astronaut)
1305 Buena Vista Ave
Pacific Grove, CA 93950-5505, USA

Burse, Isaiah (Athlete, Football Player)
c/o Jim Ivler *Sportstars Inc*
1350 Avenue of the Americas Fl 28
New York, NY 10019-4702, USA

Burson, Jim (Athlete, Football Player)
351 Heath Rd
Dawsonville, GA 30534-5603, USA

Burstyn, Ellen (Actor)
c/o Courtney Kivowitz *The Schiff Company*
9220 W Sunset Blvd Ste 106
West Hollywood, CA 90069-3500, USA

Burt, Adam (Athlete, Hockey Player)
34 Smull Ave
Caldwell, NJ 07006-5012, USA

Burt, Jim (Athlete, Football Player)
10 River Farms Ln
Saddle River, NJ 07458-3028, USA

Burtnett, Wellington (Athlete, Hockey Player)
121 Pine Lakes Pkwy N Apt 1102
Palm Coast, FL 32137-3653, USA

Burton, Albert (Athlete, Football Player)
3768 London Dr
Decatur, GA 30032-2359, USA

Burton, Brandie (Athlete, Golfer)
27102 Pleasant Hill Dr
Highland, CA 92346, USA

Burton, Brian (Danger Mouse) (Musician)
960 W Avenue 37
Los Angeles, CA 90065-3240, USA

Burton, Dan (Congressman, Politician)
2308 Raybunn Hob
Washington, DC 20515-0001, USA

Burton, Ed (Actor)
660 W Hile Rd
Norton Shores, MI 49441-5467, USA

Burton, Edward (Athlete, Basketball Player)
660 W Hile Rd
Norton Shores, MI 49441-5467, USA

Burton, Ellis (Athlete, Baseball Player)
15621 Beach Blvd Spc 7
Westminster, CA 92683-7120, USA

Burton, Gary (Musician)
Berklee College of Music
1140 Boylston St
Boston, MA 02215-3693, USA

Burton, Hilarie (Actor)
4176 Farmdale Ave
Studio City, CA 91604-3016, USA

Burton, Jake (Skier)
Burton Snowboards
80 Industrial Pkwy
Burlington, VT 05401-5434, USA

Burton, James (Athlete, Football Player)
458 W Altadena Dr
Altadena, CA 91001-4202, USA

Burton, James (Musician)
James Burton Foundation
714 Elvis Presley Ave
Shreveport, LA 71101-3406, USA

Burton, Jared
PO Box 506
Westminster, SC 29693-0506, USA

Burton, Jeff (Race Car Driver)
15555 Huntersville Concord Rd
Huntersville, NC 28078-6642, USA

Burton, Kate (Actor, Musician)
c/o Larry Taube *Principal Entertainment (LA)*
9255 W Sunset Blvd Ste 500
West Hollywood, CA 90069-3301, USA

Burton, Lance (Magician)
Monte Carlo Hotel
3770 Las Vegas Blvd S
Las Vegas, NV 89109-4323, USA

Burton, Lawrence (Athlete, Football Player)
41 San Gabriel
Rancho Santa Margarita, CA 92688-3127, USA

Burton, Leonard (Athlete, Football Player)
3436 Beech Grove Rd
Memphis, TN 38118-7269, USA

Burton, LeVar (Actor)
13251 Stoneridge Pl
Sherman Oaks, CA 91423-4933, USA

Burton, Mike (Athlete, Olympic Athlete, Swimmer)
1119 N 31st St
Billings, MT 59101-0132, USA

Burton, Nelson (Athlete, Hockey Player)
128 Collington Ct
Arnold, MD 21012-2305, USA

Burton, Nelson Jr (Bowler)
9359 SW Eagles Lndg
Stuart, FL 34997-7969, USA

Burton, Robert G (Publisher)
World Color Press
101 Park Ave Fl 40
New York, NY 10178-4499, USA

Burton, Shane (Athlete, Football Player)
PO Box 522
Hewitt Road
Catawba, NC 28609-0522, USA

Burton, Steve (Actor)
2017 Legends Ridge Dr
Franklin, TN 37069-4549, USA

Burton, Tim (Director, Producer)
Tim Burton Productions
8033 W Sunset Blvd # 7500
Los Angeles, CA 90046-2401, USA

Burton, Tony (Actor)
3500 W Olive Ave Ste 1400
Burbank, CA 91505-5512, USA

Burton, Ward (Race Car Driver)
The Ward Burton Wildlife Foundation
PO Box 519
Halifax, VA 24558-0519, USA

Burton, Warren
c/o Steven Neibert *Imperium 7 Talent Agency*
5455 Wilshire Blvd Ste 1706
Los Angeles, CA 90036-4217, USA

Burton, Willie (Athlete, Basketball Player)
18900 Fleming St
Detroit, MI 48234-1392, USA

Burton Jr, John (Actor)
12711 Ventura Blvd Ste 490
Studio City, CA 91604-2477, USA

Burton-Woody, Patty (Baseball Player)
918 N Walnut St
Steele, MO 63877-1316, USA

Burtt, Dennis (Athlete, Baseball Player)
135 W Stadium Dr
Stockton, CA 95204-3117, USA

Burtt, Steve (Athlete, Basketball Player)
200 W 143rd St Apt 12D
New York, NY 10030-1527, USA

Burwell, Barbara (Actor)
1100 Millston Rd
Wayzata, MN 55391-9411, USA

Burwell, Dick (Athlete, Baseball Player)
7424 N San Manuel Rd
Scottsdale, AZ 85258-3461, USA

Busbv, Mike
20251 N 75th Ave Apt 2006
Glendale, AZ 85308-7911, USA

Busby, Mike (Athlete, Baseball Player)
27399 N 84th Gln
Peoria, AZ 85383-4800, USA

Busby, Steve (Athlete, Baseball Player)
2701 Brittany Ln
Grapevine, TX 76051-4302, USA

Busby, Wayne (Athlete, Baseball Player)
287 S Tampa Ave
Orlando, FL 32805-2157, USA

Buscemi, Steve (Actor, Director)
c/o Lee Stollman *The Gotham Group Inc*
9255 W Sunset Blvd Ste 515
West Hollywood, CA 90069-3308, USA

Busch, Adam (Actor)
c/o Ryan Revel *Benderspink*
8447 Wilshire Blvd Ste 250
Studio E
Beverly Hills, CA 90211-3224, USA

Busch, August A III (Business Person)
Anheuser-Busch Cos
1 Busch Pl
Saint Louis, MO 63118-1852, USA

Busch, Charles (Actor, Writer)
c/o Jeff Melnick *Eighth Square Entertainment*
456 S Ogden Dr
Los Angeles, CA 90036-3121, USA

Busch, Kurt (Race Car Driver)
Kurt Busch Inc
151 Lugnut Ln
Mooresville, NC 28117-9300, USA

Busch, Kyle (Race Car Driver)
351 Mazeppa Rd
Mooresville, NC 28115-7929, USA

Busch, Mike (Athlete, Baseball Player)
103 E 1st Ave
Donahue, IA 52746-9648, USA

Buscher, Brian (Athlete, Baseball Player)
39 Westshire Ct
Columbia, SC 29209-1967, USA

Buschhorn, Don (Athlete, Baseball Player)
17804 E 26th St S
Independence, MO 64057-1350, USA

Buse, Don (Athlete, Basketball Player)
7300 W State Road 64
Huntingburg, IN 47542-9781, USA

Buser, Martin (Race Car Driver)
PO Box 520997
Big Lake, AK 99652-0997, USA

Busey, Gary (Actor)
c/o April Lim *Global Artists Agency*
6253 Hollywood Blvd Apt 508
Los Angeles, CA 90028-8251, USA

Busey, Jake (Actor)
4726 Templeton St
Ventura, CA 93003-0388, USA

Busfield, Timothy (Actor)
435 Locust St Apt 2
San Francisco, CA 94118-5000, USA

Bush, Barbara (Politician)
10000 Memorial Dr Ste 900
Houston, TX 77024-3412, USA

Bush, Barbara Pierce (Business Person)
Global Health Corps
5 Penn Plz Frnt 2
New York, NY 10001-1810, USA

Bush, Billy (Television Host)
4161 High Valley Rd
Encino, CA 91436-3350, USA

Bush, Blair (Athlete, Football Player)
1223 Spring St Apt 601
Seattle, WA 98104-3573, USA

Bush, David (Athlete, Baseball Player)
518 Delancy Cir
Devon, PA 19333-1008, USA

Bush, Frank (Athlete, Football Player)
1126 W Armstrong Way
Chandler, AZ 85286-6306, USA

Bush, George (Ex-President, Politician)
Office Of George W. Bush
PO Box 259000
Dallas, TX 75225-9000, USA

Bush, George HW (Ex-President, President)
The Office of George Bush
10000 Memorial Dr Ste 900
Houston, TX 77024-3412, USA

Bush, Homer (Athlete, Baseball Player)
1402 Exeter Ct
Southlake, TX 76092-4219, USA

Bush, Jarrett (Athlete, Football Player)
c/o Derrick Fox *Derrick Fox Management*
Prefers to be contacted by telephone
CA, USA

Bush, Jeb (Governor) (Politician)
651 Almeria Ave
Coral Gables, FL 33134-5602, USA

Bush, Jenna (Writer)
1345 S Charles St
Baltimore, MD 21230-4226, USA

Bush, Jim (Coach)
5106 Bounty Ln
Culver City, CA 90230-4302, USA

Bush, Kristian (Musician)
917 Stratford Rd
Avondale Estates, GA 30002-1435, USA

Bush, Laura (Politician)
Office Of George W. Bush
PO Box 259000
Dallas, TX 75225-9000, USA

Bush, Lauren (Model)
c/o Staff Member *Elite Model Management (NY)*
245 5th Ave Fl 24
New York, NY 10016-8728, USA

Bush, Randv (Athlete, Baseball Player)
1000 Chestnut Ct
Slidell, LA 70458-5486, USA

Bush, Randy (Athlete, Baseball Player)
37 Kings Canyon Dr
New Orleans, LA 70131-8611, USA

Bush, Rebeccah (Actor)
c/o Staff Member *Cunningham Escott Slevin & Doherty (CESD-LA)*
10635 Santa Monica Blvd Ste 130
Los Angeles, CA 90025-8306, USA

Bush, Reggie (Athlete, Football Player)
1501 Viewsite Ter
Los Angeles, CA 90069-1324, USA

Bush, Sophia (Actor)
c/o Joan Green *Joan Green Management*
1836 Courtney Ter
Los Angeles, CA 90046-2106, USA

Bush, William Green (Actor)
Gold Marshak Liedtke
3500 W Olive Ave Ste 1400
Burbank, CA 91505-5512, USA

Bushbeck, Chuck (Athlete, Football Player)
2806 Angus Rd
Philadelphia, PA 19114-3414, USA

Bushell, Matt (Actor)
c/o Sandra Joseph *SLJ Management*
833 N Edinburgh Ave Unit 203
Los Angeles, CA 90046-6947, USA

Bushing, Chris (Athlete, Baseball Player)
12830 NW 21st St
Pembroke Pines, FL 33028-2534, USA

Bush, Jr., Walter L (Athlete, Hockey Player)
5200 Malibu Dr
Minneapolis, MN 55436-1030, USA

Bushnell, Bill (Director)
2751 Pelham Pl
Los Angeles, CA 90068-2326, USA

Bushnell, Candace (Producer, Writer)
253 Tophet Rd
Roxbury, CT 06783-1523, USA

Bushrod, Jermon (Athlete, Football Player)
c/o Anthony J. Agnone *Eastern Athletic Services*
11350 McCormick Rd
Suite 800 - Executive Plaza
Hunt Valley, MD 21031-1002, USA

Bushy, Ronald (Ron) (Musician)
Entertainment Services Int'l
6400 Pleasant Park Dr
Chanhassen, MN 55317-8804, USA

Busick, Steve (Athlete, Football Player)
6246 W Long Dr
Littleton, CO 80123-5172, USA

Busino, Orlando (Cartoonist)
12 Shadblow Hill Rd
Ridgefield, CT 06877-5221, USA

Buskas, Rod (Athlete, Hockey Player)
182 Wentworth Dr
Henderson, NV 89074-1049, USA

Buskey, Mike (Athlete, Baseball Player)
2509 Highland Park Ct
Colleyville, TX 76034-5352, USA

Buskey., Mike (Athlete, Baseball Player)
2509 Highland Park Ct
Colleyville, TX 76034-5352, USA

Busse, Ray (Athlete, Baseball Player)
4265 Lemon St
Cocoa, FL 32926-2148, USA

Bussell, Gerry (Athlete, Football Player)
2922 Justin Ct
Orange Park, FL 32065-7338, USA

Bussey, Barney (Athlete, Football Player)
5059 Park Ridge Ct
West Chester, OH 45069-5552, USA

Bussey, Dexter (Athlete, Football Player)
2565 Bloomfield Xing
Bloomfield Hills, MI 48304-1707, US

Bustion, Dave (Athlete, Basketball Player)
706 Tarrant Ct
Gadsden, AL 35901-3150, USA

Butala, Tony (Musician)
PO Box 151
Mc Kees Rocks, PA 15136-0151, USA

Butcher, Garth (Athlete, Hockey Player)
1524 Maple Ln
Bellingham, WA 98229-5242, USA

Butcher, Jade (Athlete, Football Player)
9730 N Moon Rd
Gosport, IN 47433-9517

Butcher, Jim (Writer)
c/o *St. Martin's Press*
175 5th Ave
Attn: Publicity Dept
New York, NY 10010-7703, USA

Butcher, John (Athlete, Baseball Player)
820 Woodridge Dr S
Chaska, MN 55318-1266, USA

Butcher, Mike (Athlete, Baseball Player)
324 33rd Ave
East Moline, IL 61244-3124, USA

Butcher, Paul (Athlete, Football Player)
c/o Mitchell Gossett *Cunningham Escott Slevin & Doherty (CESD-LA)*
10635 Santa Monica Blvd Ste 130
Los Angeles, CA 90025-8306, USA

Butcher, Rodney (Athlete, Golfer)
27211 Iron Gate Ln
Wesley Chapel, FL 33544-5629, USA

Butcher-Marsh, Mary (Athlete, Baseball Player, Commentator)
PO Box 563
Lovelock, NV 89419-0563, USA

Butera, Sal (Athlete, Baseball Player)
324 Tersas Ct
Lake Mary, FL 32746-5143, USA

Butkus, Dick (Actor, Athlete, Football Player)
The Butkus Foundation
18920 NE 227th Ave
Brush Prairie, WA 98606-8114, USA

Butler, Adam (Athlete, Baseball Player)
815 Providence Rd
Towson, MD 21286-2964, USA

Butler, Austin (Actor)
c/o Doug Wald *Anonymous Content (LA)*
3532 Hayden Ave
Culver City, CA 90232-2413, USA

Butler, Bill (Athlete, Baseball Player)
c/o Greg Genske *The Legacy Agency*
500 Newport Center Dr Ste 800
Newport Beach, CA 92660-7008, USA

Butler, Bill C (Cinematographer)
1097 Aviation Blvd
Hermosa Beach, CA 90254-4023, USA

Butler, Bob (Athlete, Football Player)
120 Holly Hills Dr
Mount Sterling, KY 40353-9738, USA

Butler, Bobby (Athlete, Hockey Player)
c/o John and Wendy Butler 56 Ethier Cir
Marlborough, MA 01752, USA

Butler, Brent (Athlete, Baseball Player)
10441 Scotland Farm Rd
Laurinburg, NC 28352-7977, USA

Butler, Brett (Actor, Comedian)
c/o Staff Member *TalentWorks (LA)*
3500 W Olive Ave Ste 1400
Burbank, CA 91505-5512, USA

Butler, Brett M (Athlete, Baseball Player)
4488 E Thomas Rd Unit 2012
Phoenix, AZ 85018-7627, USA

Butler, Caron (Athlete, Basketball Player)
3808 Millard Way
Fairfax, VA 22033, USA

Butler, Cecil (Athlete, Baseball Player)
263 Hickory Gap Trl
Dallas, GA 30157-5353, USA

Butler, Charles (Athlete, Basketball Player)
453 Arbor Cir
Youngstown, OH 44505-1915, USA

Butler, Charles W (Athlete, Football Player)
5496 Celestial Dr
Atwater, CA 95301-3165, USA

Butler, Chuck (Athlete, Football Player)
5496N Celestial Dr
Atwater, CA 95301, US

Butler, Conrad (Actor)
Paradigm Agency
10100 Santa Monica Blvd Ste 2500
Los Angeles, CA 90067-4116, USA

Butler, Dan (Actor)
c/o Staff Member *ATA Management*
12 Desbrosses St
New York, NY 10013-1704, USA

Butler, Darius (Athlete, Football Player)
c/o Drew Rosenhaus *Rosenhaus Sports Representation*
6400 Allison Rd
Miami Beach, FL 33141-4540, USA

Butler, Dean (Actor)
1310 Westholme Ave
Los Angeles, CA 90024-5016, USA

Butler, Donald (Athlete, Football Player)
c/o Roosevelt Barnes *Maximum Sports Management*
6435 W Jefferson Blvd # 197
Fort Wayne, IN 46804-6203, USA

Butler, Elbert (Athlete, Basketball Player)
153 Willow Ave
Rochester, NY 14609-1244, USA

Butler, Gary (Athlete, Football Player)
6660 S Piney Creek Cir
Aurora, CO 80016, USA

Butler, Gary C (Athlete, Football Player)
Automatic Data Processing
212 Oak Hollow St
Conroe, TX 77301-1747, USA

Butler, Gerard (Actor)
c/o Alan Siegel *Alan Siegel Entertainment*
9200 W Sunset Blvd Ste 407
West Hollywood, CA 90069-3511, USA

Butler, Greg (Athlete, Basketball Player)
75 Round Hill Rd
Scarsdale, NY 10583-1703, USA

Butler, James (Athlete, Football Player)
3181 Spring St
Atlanta, GA 30349-2345, USA

Butler, Jerametrius
1717 High Valley Ln
Cedar Hill, TX 75104-2405, US

Butler, Jerry (Iceman) (Musician, Songwriter, Writer)
c/o Jeremy Plager *Creative Artists Agency (CAA-LA)*
2000 Avenue of the Stars Ste 100
Los Angeles, CA 90067-4705, USA

Butler, Jerry O (Athlete, Football Player)
17117 Shaker Blvd
Cleveland, OH 44120-1635, USA

Butler, Joe (Musician)
Pipeline Artists Mgmt
620 16th Ave S
Hopkins, MN 55343-7833, USA

Butler, John (Musician)
c/o Staff Member *Paradigm (Monterey)*
404 W Franklin St
Monterey, CA 93940-2303, USA

Butler, Jonathan (Musician)
12740 Landale St
Studio City, CA 91604-1349, USA

Butler, Keith (Athlete, Football Player)
805 Cavan Dr
Cranberry Twp, PA 16066-2333, USA

Butler, Kerry (Actor)
c/o Erica Tuchman *One Entertainment (NY)*
12 W 57th St PH
New York, NY 10019-3900, USA

Butler, Kevin (Athlete, Football Player)
3256 Bagley Psge
Duluth, GA 30097-3788, USA

Butler, LeRoy (Athlete, Football Player)
2812 Eagle Preserve Blvd
Jacksonville, FL 32226-5895, USA

Butler, Lucy (Actor)
c/o Judy Orbach *Judy O Productions*
6136 Glen Holly St
Los Angeles, CA 90068-2338, USA

Butler, Michael (Athlete, Football Player)
3107 Magdalene Forest Ct
Tampa, FL 33618-2509, USA

Butler, Mike (Athlete, Basketball Player)
3107 Magdalene Forest Ct
Tampa, FL 33618-2509, USA

Butler, Mitchell (Athlete, Basketball Player)
3526 Ocean View Ave
Los Angeles, CA 90066-1910, USA

Butler, Rasual
1463 SW 161st Ave
Pembroke Pines, FL 33027-5139, USA

Butler, Ray (Athlete, Football Player)
3935 Teal Run Place Ct
Fresno, TX 77545-7050, USA

Butler, Robert (Athlete, Football Player)
5567 Naylor Ct
Peachtree Corners, GA 30092-2072, USA

Butler, Robert (Director)
650 Club View Dr
Los Angeles, CA 90024-2624, USA

Butler, Robert Olen (Writer)
1009 Concord Rd Apt 230
Tallahassee, FL 32308-6294, USA

Butler, Robert olen (Writer)
3909 Reserve Dr Apt 1611
Tallahassee, FL 32311-1284, USA

Butler, Skip (Athlete, Football Player)
1311 Spyglass Dr
Mansfield, TX 76063-4023, USA

Butler, Steve (Race Car Driver)
1820 S Buckeye St
Kokomo, IN 46902-2143, USA

Butler, Terence (Geezer) (Musician)
2109 San Ysidro Dr
Beverly Hills, CA 90210-1551

Butler, William D (Athlete, Football Player)
200 E Liberty St
Berlin, WI 54923-1223, USA

Butler, William E (Athlete, Football Player)
3030 Cherry Hl
Manhattan, KS 66503-3011, USA

Butler, William E (Business Person)
Eaton Corp
1111 Superior Ave E Ste 1000
Eaton Center
Cleveland, OH 44114-2568, USA

Butler, Yancy (Actor)
c/o Peg Donegan *Framework Entertainment (LA)*
9057 Nemo St Ste C
West Hollywood, CA 90069-5511, USA

Butler Billv, Billv (Athlete, Baseball Player)
2007 Kansas Citv Rovals
7724 E Santa Catalina Dr, SC AZ, USA

Butsayev, Vyacheslav (Athlete, Hockey Player)
17555 Collins Ave Apt 1704
Sunny Isles Beach, FL 33160-2888, USA

Butsko, Harry (Athlete, Football Player)
4 Milo Cir
Duncannon, PA 17020-9647, USA

Butt, Charles (Business Person)
HEB Corp
646 S Main Ave
San Antonio, TX 78204-1227, USA

Butt, Yondani
Gurtman & Murtha
450 Fashion Ave Ste 603
New York, NY 10123-0691, USA

Buttafuoco, Joey (Actor)
10835 De Soto Ave
Chatsworth, CA 91311-1547, USA

Butterfield, Alexander P (Government Official)
3410 Brookwood Dr
Fairfax, VA 22030-2009, USA

Butterfield, Asa (Actor)
c/o Liz Mahoney *ID Public Relations (LA)*
7060 Hollywood Blvd Fl 8th
Los Angeles, CA 90028-6021, USA

Butterfield, Betty (Comedian)
c/o Staff Member *Diva Central Inc*
7510 W Sunset Blvd Ste 1445
Los Angeles, CA 90046-3408, USA

Butterfield, Brian
PO Box 1538
Standish, ME 04084-1538, USA

Butterfield, G. K. (Congressman, Politician)
2305 Rayburn Hob
Washington, DC 20515-2207, USA

Butterfly Boucher (Music Group)
c/o Staff Member *Paradigm (Monterey)*
404 W Franklin St
Monterey, CA 93940-2303, USA

Butters, Bill (Athlete, Hockey Player)
12579 Europa Ave N
Saint Paul, MN 55110-5957, USA

Butters, Tom (Athlete, Baseball Player)
4 Turnberry Ct
Durham, NC 27712-9465, USA

Butters, Torn (Athlete, Baseball Player)
4 Turnberry Ct
Durham, NC 27712-9465, USA

Butterworth, Dean (Musician)
4310 Canoga Dr
Woodland Hills, CA 91364-5327, USA

Buttke, Nathan (Race Car Driver)
Mark III Motorsports
211 Greenwich Rd
Charlotte, NC 28211-2337, USA

Buttle, Gregory E (Greg) (Athlete, Football Player)
5 Hollacher Dr
Northport, NY 11768-1552, USA

Button, Dick (Athlete, Figure Skater, Olympic Athlete)
Candio Productions
765 Park Ave Fl 6B
New York, NY 10021-4271, USA

Butts, Earl (Actor)
2741 N Salisbury St # 2116
West Lafayette, IN 47906-1431, USA

Butts, James (Athlete, Track Athlete)
16950 Belforest Dr
Carson, CA 90746-1113, USA

Butts, Marion (Athlete, Football Player)
4600 Lacosta Dr
Albany, GA 31721-9475, US

Butts, Robert (Athlete, Football Player)
83 Knox Ln
Wheeling, WV 26003-6407, USA

Butz, David E (Dave) (Athlete, Football Player)
2324 Esther Ave
Saint Louis, MO 63139-2813, USA

Buxton, Sarah (Actor)
1416 Havenhurst Dr Apt 3C
West Hollywood, CA 90046-3885, USA

Buynak, Gordie (Athlete, Hockey Player)
11512 Douglas Lake Rd
Pellston, MI 49769-9105, USA

Buzin, Rich (Athlete, Football Player)
23004 Mastick Rd Apt 216
North Olmsted, OH 44070-3770, USA

Buzolic, Nathaniel (Actor)
c/o Jason Weinberg *Untitled Entertainment (LA)*
350 S Beverly Dr Ste 200
Beverly Hills, CA 90212-4819, USA

Buzolin, Mariah (Actor)
c/o Staff Member *Leslie Allan-Rice Management*
1007 Maybrook Dr
Beverly Hills, CA 90210-2715, USA

Buzzi, Ruth (Actor, Comedian)
31159 N State Highway 108
Mingus, TX 76463-6409, USA

B. West, Allen (Congressman, Politician)
1708 Longworth Hob
Washington, DC 20515-0403, USA

Byars, Betsy C (Writer)
401 Rudder Rdg
Seneca, SC 29678-2035, USA

Byars, Keith (Athlete, Football Player)
23307 Boca Trace Dr
Boca Raton, FL 33433-7641, US

Byas, Rick (Athlete, Football Player)
17110 Westland Ave
Southfield, MI 48075-7627, US

Byce, John (Athlete, Hockey Player)
9701 Hill Creek Dr
Verona, WI 53593-7984, USA

Bychkov, Semyon
Buffalo Symphony Orchestra
71 Symphony Cir
Buffalo, NY 14201-1203, USA

Bye, Karyn (Athlete, Hockey Player, Olympic Athlete)
322 Gandy Dancer Cir
Hudson, WI 54016-8186, USA

Byers, Clinton (Athlete, Basketball Player)
4257 Leewood Rd
Stow, OH 44224-2555, USA

Byers, Ken (Athlete, Football Player)
4650 Willow Hills Ln
Cincinnati, OH 45243-4228, USA

Byers, Lyndon (Athlete, Hockey Player)
654 Central St
20 Guest St, Suite 300
Holliston, MA 01746-2411, USA

Byers, Randall (Randy) (Athlete, Baseball Player)
PO Box 1721
Bridgeton, NJ 08302-0470, USA

Byers, Scott (Athlete, Football Player)
6060 Buckingham Pkwy Apt 314
Culver City, CA 90230-6825, USA

Byers, Walter (Athlete, Basketball Player)
25707 Aiken Switch Rd
Emmett, KS 66422-9719, USA

Byfuglien, Dustin (Athlete, Hockey Player)
33626 State Highway 11
Roseau, MN 56751-8107, USA

Bylsma, Dan (Athlete, Hockey Player)
401 Avonworth Heights Dr
Pittsburgh, PA 15237-1260, USA

Bylsma, Dan (Athlete, Hockey Player)
Pittsburgh Penguins 66 Mario Lemieux Pl Ste 2
Pittsburgh, PA 15219, USA

Byman, Bob (Athlete, Golfer)
9325 Eagle Ridge Dr
Las Vegas, NV 89134-6345, USA

Byner, Earnest A (Athlete, Football Player)
1016 Sattui Ct
Franklin, TN 37064-7909, USA

Byner, John (Actor)
American Mgmt
19948 Mayall St
Chatsworth, CA 91311-3522, USA

Bynes, Amanda (Actor, Comedian)
190 Venus St
Thousand Oaks, CA 91360-2956, USA

Bynes, Josh (Athlete, Football Player)
c/o Chad Speck *Allegiant Athletic Agency*
35 Market Sq Ste 201
Knoxville, TN 37902-1420, USA

Bynum, Andrew (Athlete, Basketball Player)
c/o Philip Button *William Morris Endeavor (LA)*
9601 Wilshire Blvd
Beverly Hills, CA 90210-5213, USA

Bynum, Freddie (Athlete, Baseball Player)
2987 Pope Farm Rd
Stantonsburg, NC 27883-8556, USA

Bynum, Juanita (Actor, Motivational Speaker)
c/o Staff Member *Just Borne Mega Entertainment*
PO Box 2669
Cumming, GA 30028-6508, USA

Bynum, Mike (Athlete, Baseball Player)
9550 Meyer Forest Dr Apt 937
Houston, TX 77096-4350, USA

Bynum, Will (Athlete, Basketball Player)
c/o Brad Ames *Priority Sports & Entertainment - (LA)*
15233 Ventura Blvd Ste 718
Sherman Oaks, CA 91403-2237, USA

Byrd, Benjamin F Jr (Doctor)
4220 Harding Pike # 380
Nashville, TN 37205-2005, USA

Byrd, Boris (Athlete, Football Player)
1376 Richpond Rockfield Rd
Bowling Green, KY 42101-7407, USA

Byrd, Dan (Actor)
2450 Rinconia Dr
Los Angeles, CA 90068-2222, USA

Byrd, Darryl (Athlete, Football Player)
138 Mission Dr
East Palo Alto, CA 94303-2752, USA

Byrd, Dennis (Athlete, Football Player)
10757 E 350 Rd
Talala, OK 74080-9689, USA

Byrd, Dominique (Athlete, Football Player)
c/o Eugene Parker *Maximum Sports Management*
6435 W Jefferson Blvd # 197
Fort Wayne, IN 46804-6203, USA

Byrd, Eugene (Actor)
c/o Steve Caserta *Sanders Armstrong Caserta*
2120 Colorado Ave Ste 120
Santa Monica, CA 90404-3561, USA

Byrd, George (Athlete, Football Player)
23 Wayside Rd
Westborough, MA 01581-3620, USA

Byrd, Gill (Athlete, Football Player)
5347 Notting Hill Rd
Gurnee, IL 60031-1008, US

Byrd, Isaac (Athlete, Football Player)
5712 Astra Ave
Saint Louis, MO 63147-1012, USA

Byrd, Israel (Athlete, Football Player)
5712 Astra Ave
Saint Louis, MO 63147-1012, USA

Byrd, Jairus (Athlete, Football Player)
c/o Eugene Parker *Maximum Sports Management*
6435 W Jefferson Blvd # 197
Fort Wayne, IN 46804-6203, USA

Byrd, Jeff (Athlete, Baseball Player)
39376 Opalocka Rd
Boulevard, CA 91905-9682, USA

Byrd, Jim (Athlete, Baseball Player)
511 NW Woodridge Dr
Lawton, OK 73507-2265, USA

Byrd, Jonathan (Athlete, Golfer)
110 Meadow Bark
Saint Simons Island, GA 31522, USA

Byrd, Marion
2002 Philadelphia Phillies
Chicago, IL 60657, USA

Byrd, Marlon (Athlete, Baseball Player)
3620 E Hamilton KY
West Palm Beach, FL 33411-6436, USA

Byrd, McArthur (Athlete, Football Player)
10291 Sheldon Rd
Elk Grove, CA 95624-9341, USA

Byrd, Paul (Athlete, Baseball Player)
29254 Grande Ct
Westlake, OH 44145-6707, USA

Byrd, Richard (Athlete, Football Player)
2230 Haley Rd
Terry, MS 39170-8820, USA

Byrd, Robin (Adult Film Star)
Robin Byrd Show
PO Box 305
Lenox Hill Station
New York, NY 10021-0009, USA

Byrd, Tom (Actor)
United Talent Agency
14011 Ventura Blvd Ste 213
Sherman Oaks, CA 91423-5222, USA

Byrd, Tracy (Musician)
4695 Monticello St
Beaumont, TX 77706-7710, USA

Byrdak, Tim (Athlete, Baseball Player)
16721 W Seneca Dr
Lockport, IL 60441-4269, USA

Byrds, The (Music Group, Musician)
PO Box 1222
Pleasanton, CA 94566-0122, USA

Byrne, Brendan T (Politician)
Carella Byrne
5 Becker Farm Rd Ste 200
Roseland, NJ 07068-1788, USA

Byrne, Chris (Actor)
c/o Staff Member *Kazarian, Measures, Ruskin & Associates (LA)*
11969 Ventura Blvd Fl 3
Studio City, CA 91604-2630, USA

Byrne, David (Musician, Songwriter)
231 10th Ave # PH1
New York, NY 10011-4702, USA

Byrne, Gabriel (Actor)
211 Elizabeth St Apt 2N
New York, NY 10012-4290, USA

Byrne, Garry (Publisher)
Variety Inc
5700 Wilshire Blvd
Los Angeles, CA 90036-3659, USA

Byrne, Josh (Actor)
Hervey/Grimes
PO Box 64249
Los Angeles, CA 90064-0249, USA

Byrne, Martha
c/o Staff Member *Innovative Artists (LA)*
1505 10th St
Santa Monica, CA 90401-2805, USA

Byrne, Rhonda (Writer)
c/o Staff Member *Simon & Schuster*
1230 Avenue of the Americas Fl CONC1
New York, NY 10020-1586, USA

Byrne, Rose (Actor)
c/o Michael Katcher *Creative Artists Agency (CAA-LA)*
2000 Avenue of the Stars Ste 100
Los Angeles, CA 90067-4705, USA

Byrne, Steve (Musician)
c/o Staff Member *Paradigm (Monterey)*
404 W Franklin St
Monterey, CA 93940-2303, USA

Byrne, Thomas J (Tommy) (Athlete, Baseball Player)
1108 Fairway Villas Dr
Wake Forest, NC 27587-5179, USA

Byrnes, Edd (Actor)
PO Box 1623
Beverly Hills, CA 90213-1623, USA

Byrnes, Eric (Athlete, Baseball Player)
c/o Staff Member *William Morris Endeavor (LA)*
9601 Wilshire Blvd
Beverly Hills, CA 90210-5213, USA

Byrnes, Eric (Athlete, Baseball Player)
24404 N 61st Dr
Glendale, AZ 85310-2704, USA

Byrnes, Marty (Athlete, Basketball Player)
8739 3rd Ave
Pleasant Prairie, WI 53158-4709, USA

Byron, Kari
Mythbusters Beyond Productions
1268 Missouri St
San Francisco, CA 94107-3310, USA

Byrorn, Don (Musician)
Hans Wendl Productions
2220 California St
Berkeley, CA 94703-1608, USA

Byrorn, Monty (Musician, Songwriter, Writer)
Gurley Co
1204B Cedar Ln
Nashville, TN 37212-5910, USA

Byrum, Carl (Athlete, Football Player)
209 Castlewood Dr
Buffalo, NY 14227-2652, us

Byrum, Curt (Athlete, Golfer)
12441 N 86th St
Scottsdale, AZ 85260-5343, USA

Byrum, John W (Director)
7435 Woodrow Wilson Dr
Los Angeles, CA 90046-1322, USA

Byrum, Tom (Athlete, Golfer)
734 Sentry Hl
San Antonio, TX 78260-2977, USA

Bystrom, Marty (Athlete, Baseball Player)
PO Box 89
Geigertown, PA 19523-0089, USA

Byung-Hun, Lee
c/o Larry Galper *Creative Artists Agency
(CAA-LA)*
2000 Avenue of the Stars Ste 100
Los Angeles, CA 90067-4705, USA

Bzdelik, Jeff (Coach)
Denver Nuggets
1000 Chopper Cir
Pepsi Center
Denver, CO 80204-5805, USA

Caan, James (Actor, Director)
2791 Hutton Dr
Beverly Hills, CA 90210-1215, USA

Caan, Scott (Actor)
2049 Oakstone Way
Los Angeles, CA 90046-1821, USA

Caballero, Celestino (Athlete, Boxer)
c/o Jody Kohn *Talent Without Borders*
Prefers to be contacted by telephone
Las Vegas, NV 89145, USA

Caballero, Ralph (Putsy) (Athlete,
Baseball Player)
1120 Shirley Dr
Metairie, LA 70001-3379, USA

Cabana, Robert D (Astronaut)
18315 Cape Bahamas Ln
Houston, TX 77058-3406, USA

cabana, Robert d colonel (Astronaut)
1626 Manor Dr
Cocoa, FL 32922-6922, USA

Cabas (Musician)
c/o Staff Member *Creative Artists Agency
(CAA-LA)*
2000 Avenue of the Stars Ste 100
Los Angeles, CA 90067-4705, USA

Cabel, Barney (Athlete, Basketball Player)
1134 S Main St
Hampstead, MD 21074-2255, USA

Cabell, Enos M (Athlete, Baseball Player)
4103 Frost Lake Ct
Missouri City, TX 77459-2304, USA

Cable, Barney (Athlete, Basketball Player)
1134 S Main St
Hampstead, MD 21074-2255, USA

Cable, Candace (Athlete, Olympic
Athlete)
PO Box 8264
Truckee, CA 96162-8264, USA

Cable, Tom (Athlete, Football Player)
1220 Harbor Bay Pkwy
Alameda, CA 94502-6501, us

Cable Guy, The, Larry (Comedian)
c/o J P Williams *Parallel Entertainment*
9420 Wilshire Blvd Ste 250
Beverly Hills, CA 90212-3151, USA

Cabot, Louis W (Business Person)
Brookings Institution
1775 Massachusetts Ave NW
Washington, DC 20036-2103, USA

Cabot, Meg (Writer)
PO Box 4904
Key West, FL 33041-4904, USA

Cabral, Brian (Athlete, Football Player)
5008 Ellsworth Pl
Boulder, CO 80303-1210, USA

Cabrera, John (Actor)
c/o Adam Griffin *Kritzer Levine Wilkins
Entertainment (KLWG)*
11872 La Grange Ave Fl 1
Los Angeles, CA 90025-5283, USA

Cabrera, Jolbert (Baseball Player)
c/o Staff Member *Los Angeles Dodgers
(LA Dodgers)*
1000 Elysian Park Ave
Los Angeles, CA 90012-1112, USA

Cabrera, Melky (Athlete, Baseball Player)
7912 River Rd
North Bergen, NJ 07047-6271, USA

Cabrera, Miguel (Athlete, Baseball Player)
c/o Aaron Spiewak *Relativity Sports (LA)*
9242 Beverly Blvd Ste 300
Beverly Hills, CA 90210-3728, USA

Cabrera, Orlando (Athlete, Baseball
Player)
9248 Scarlette Oak Ave
Fort Myers, FL 33967-5145, USA

Cabrera, Ryan (Musician)
c/o Staff Member *CEG Talent*
251 W 39th St Fl 7
New York, NY 10018-3171, USA

Cabrera, Santiago (Actor)
c/o Suzan Bymel *Management 360*
9111 Wilshire Blvd
Beverly Hills, CA 90210-5508, USA

Caccialanza, Lorenzo (Actor)
Ambrosio/Mortimer
PO Box 16758
Beverly Hills, CA 90209-2758, USA

Cacek, Craig (Athlete, Baseball Player)
909 6th St Apt 3
Santa Monica, CA 90403-2700, USA

Caceres, Edgar (Athlete, Baseball Player)
7501 50th Ter E
Bradenton, FL 34203-7905, USA

Caceres, Kurt (Actor)
Pakula/King Associates
9229 W Sunset Blvd Ste 315
West Hollywood, CA 90069-3403

Cackowski, Liz (Actor, Comedian)
c/o Staff Member *Creative Artists Agency
(CAA-LA)*
2000 Avenue of the Stars Ste 100
Los Angeles, CA 90067-4705, USA

Cadaret, Greg (Athlete, Baseball Player)
22636 Bridlewood Ln
Palo Cedro, CA 96073-9567, USA

Caddell, Patrick (Politician)
p
1048 Dominion Dr
Hanahan, SC 29410-2408, USA

Cade, Eddie (Athlete, Football Player)
501 W 4th St
Eloy, AZ 85131-2206, USA

Cade, Mossy (Athlete, Football Player)
400 W Pasadena Ave Apt 19
Phoenix, AZ 85013-2367, USA

Cadell, Ava (Actor, Model)
c/o Rick Hersh *Celebrity Consultants LLC*
3340 Ocean Park Blvd Ste 1030
Santa Monica, CA 90405-3259, USA

Cadell, Dr. Ava (Adult Film Star)
Loveology University
26500 Agoura Rd
Calabasas, CA 91302-1952, USA

Cadigan, Dave (Athlete, Football Player)
14416 Katie Rd
Phoenix, MD 21131-1755, USA

Cadile, Jim (Athlete, Football Player)
1746 Dove Ln
Medford, OR 97501-7015, USA

Cadogan, William J (Business Person)
ADC Communications
PO Box 1101
Minneapolis, MN 55440-1101, USA

Cadorette, Mary (Actor)
114 W Granby Rd
Granby, CT 06035-2907, USA

Cadrez, Glenn (Athlete, Football Player)
PO Box 130818
Carlsbad, CA 92013-0818, USA

Caesar, Shirley (Music Group)
Shirley Caesar Outreach Ministries
3310 Croasdaile Dr Ste 902
Durham, NC 27705-6806, USA

Caesars, The (Music Group)
c/o Staff Member *Paradigm (Monterey)*
404 W Franklin St
Monterey, CA 93940-2303, USA

Cafagna-Tesoro, Ashley (Actor)
c/o Staff Member *Tesoro Entertainment*
205D N Stephanie St # NO115
Henderson, NV 89074-8060, USA

Cafferty, Jack (Commentator)
41 Vincent Rd
Cedar Grove, NJ 07009-1337, USA

Caffey, Charlotte (Musician)
4827 Glencairn Rd
Los Angeles, CA 90027-1135, USA

Caffey, Jason (Athlete, Basketball Player)
PO Box 131
Roswell, GA 30077-0131, USA

Caffrey, Bob (Athlete, Baseball Player,
Olympic Athlete)
2305 Sunnyside Ave
Burlington, IA 52601-2537, USA

Cage, Byron (Musician)
c/o Staff Member *Verity Gospel Music
Group*
550 Madison Ave Rm 2356
New York, NY 10022-3211, USA

Cage, Michael (Athlete, Basketball Player)
21163 Newport Coast Dr
Dr
Newport Coast, CA 92657-1123, USA

Cage, Nicolas (Actor)
3200 Encinal Canyon Rd
Malibu, CA 90265-2413, USA

Cage, Wayne (Athlete, Baseball Player)
1305 Davis Blvd
Ruston, LA 71270-6405, usa

Cage, Wayne (Athlete, Baseball Player)
1305 Davis Blvd
Ruston, LA 71270-6405, USA

Cagle, Buddy (Race Car Driver)
11713 E 118th St N
Collinsville, OK 74021-1011, USA

Cagle, Chris (Musician)
c/o Scott McGhee *McGhee Entertainment*
8730 W Sunset Blvd Ste 175
West Hollywood, CA 90069-2246, USA

Cagle, J Douglas (Business Person)
Cagle's Inc
1385 Collier Rd NW
Atlanta, GA 30318-7444, USA

Cagle, Jim (Athlete, Football Player)
745 Sharpshooters Rdg NW
Marietta, GA 30064-4731, USA

Cagle, Johnny (Athlete, Football Player)
1645 Citation Dr
Aiken, SC 29803-5223, USA

Cagle, Yvonne D (Astronaut)
c/o Staff Member *NASA-JSC*
2101 Nasa Pkwy # 1
Astronaut Office - Mail Code Cb
Houston, TX 77058-3607, USA

Cahill, Dave (Athlete, Football Player)
11 Kara E
Irvine, CA 92620-1855, us

Cahill, Eddie (Actor)
c/o David Seltzer *Management 360*
9111 Wilshire Blvd
Beverly Hills, CA 90210-5508, USA

Cahill, Erin (Actor)
c/o Cary Anderson *Simmons & Scott
Entertainment*
7942 Mulholland Dr
Los Angeles, CA 90046-1225, USA

Cahill, Jason (Producer)
2316 Nottingham Ave
Los Angeles, CA 90027-1035, USA

Cahill, Laura (Writer)
c/o Staff Member *Broder Webb Chervin
Silbermann Agency, The (BWCS)*
10250 Constellation Blvd
Los Angeles, CA 90067-6200, USA

Cahill, Mike (Director, Writer)
c/o George Heller *Apostle Management*
9465 Wilshire Blvd Ste 430
Beverly Hills, CA 90212-2613, USA

Cahill, Thomas (Writer)
Doubleday Press
1540 Broadway
New York, NY 10036-4039, USA

Cahill, Trevor (Athlete, Baseball Player)
286 Juaneno Ave
Oceanside, CA 92057-4515, usa

Cahill, William (Bill) (Athlete, Football
Player)
24328 Crystal Lake Way
Woodinville, WA 98077-9514, USA

Cahoon, Todd (Actor)
c/o Laura Pallas *Pallas Management*
5301 Bellaire Ave
Valley Village, CA 91607-2329, US

Caifanes (Music Group)
c/o Staff Member *BMG*
1540 Broadway
New York, NY 10036-4039, USA

Caillat, Colbie (Musician)
31803 Saddletree Dr
Westlake Village, CA 91361-4763, USA

Cain, Betty Ann (Actor)
19379 Arkay Ct
Sonoma, CA 95476-6350, USA

Cain, Carl (Athlete, Basketball Player)
3045 Sun Valley Dr
Pickerington, OH 43147-9090, USA

Cain, Dean (Actor)
24630 Blue Dane Ln
Malibu, CA 90265-4709, USA

Cain, Jeremy (Athlete, Football Player)
c/o Kristen Kuliga *K Sports Entertainment*
236 Huntington Ave Ste 209
Boston, MA 02115-4701, USA

Cain, Joe (Athlete, Football Player)
1219 W Piru St
Compton, CA 90222-1712, us

Cain, John Paul (Athlete, Golfer)
1404 Avondale St
Sweetwater, TX 79556-2614, USA

Cain, Jonathan (Musician)
506 E Iris Dr
Nashville, TN 37204-3110, USA

Cain, Les (Athlete, Baseball Player)
3804 Ohio Ave
Richmond, CA 94804-3325, USA

Cain, Lorenzo (Athlete, Baseball Player)
3680 Lindley Cir
Powder Springs, GA 30127-2702, USA

Cain, Lynn (Athlete, Football Player)
PO Box 90881
Los Angeles, CA 90009-0881, USA

Cain, Matt (Athlete, Baseball Player)
2005 San Francisco Giants
Mesa, AZ 85207, USA

Cain, Mick (Actor)
7800 Beverly Blvd # 3371
Los Angeles, CA 90036-2112, USA

Cain, Scott (Race Car Driver)
6059 W Ashlan Ave
Fresno, CA 93723-9201, USA

Cairns, Leah (Actor)
Armada Partners
PO Box 64547
C/O David M Rudy
Los Angeles, CA 90064-0547, USA

Cairo, Miguel (Athlete, Baseball Player)
2262 Steven St
Clearwater, FL 33759-1419, USA

Calabrese, Gerry (Athlete, Basketball Player)
351 Esplanade Pl
Cliffside Park, NJ 07010-2708, USA

Calabro, Thomas (Actor)
4318 Ben Ave
Studio City, CA 91604-1703, USA

Calacurcio-Thomas, Aldine (Athlete, Baseball Player, Commentator)
5438 Nottingham Dr
Loves Park, IL 61111-3605, USA

Calaway, Mark (The Undertaker) (Athlete, Wrestler)
12904 Hacienda Rdg
Austin, TX 78738-7662, USA

Calcagni, Ron (Athlete, Football Player)
340 Savannah Park Cir
Conway, AR 72034-7277, USA

Calcavecchia, Mark (Athlete, Golfer)
354 W Riverside Dr
Jupiter, FL 33469-2950, USA

Calder, Kyle (Athlete, Hockey Player)
23 Orange Blossom Cir
Ladera Ranch, CA 92694-1251, USA

Calderon, Sila Maria (Ex-Governor)
LA Fortaleza
PO Box 9020082
San Juan, PR 00902-0082, USA

Calderon, Wilmer (Actor)
c/o Lena Roklin *Luber Roklin Management*
5815 W Sunset Blvd Ste 206
Los Angeles, CA 90028-6481, USA

Caldwell, Adrian (Athlete, Basketball Player)
10990 West Rd Apt 311
Houston, TX 77064-5496, USA

Caldwell, Alan (Athlete, Football Player)
1370 Kerner Rd
Kernersville, NC 27284-8943, USA

Caldwell, Andre (Athlete, Football Player)
c/o Tony Fleming *Impact Sports - LA*
11331 Ventura Blvd Ste 1A
Studio City, CA 91604-3147, USA

Caldwell, Bobby (Musician, Songwriter, Writer)
Public Relations Partners
12702 Landale St
Studio City, CA 91604-1349, USA

Caldwell, Darryl (Athlete, Football Player)
4604 Malinta Ln
Chattanooga, TN 37416-3728, USA

Caldwell, Gail (Journalist)
c/o Staff Member *Zachary Shuster Harmsworth Talent Agency*
1776 Broadway Ste 1405
New York, NY 10019-2002, USA

Caldwell, Jim (Athlete, Basketball Player)
705 Freedom Ln
Roswell, GA 30075-7911, USA

Caldwell, Joe (Athlete, Basketball Player, Olympic Athlete)
15 E Pebble Beach Dr
Tempe, AZ 85282-5127, USA

Caldwell, John (Cartoonist)
c/o Staff Member *King Features Syndication*
300 W 57th St Fl 15
New York, NY 10019-5238, USA

Caldwell, Kimberly (Musician, Reality Star)
c/o Anthony Cordova *Story Road Entertainment*
809 S Bundy Dr Apt 209
Los Angeles, CA 90049-5253, USA

Caldwell, Matt (Musician)
c/o Staff Member *Paradigm (Monterey)*
404 W Franklin St
Monterey, CA 93940-2303, USA

Caldwell, Mike (Athlete, Baseball Player)
1645 Brook Run Dr
Raleigh, NC 27614-9732, USA

Caldwell, Mike (Athlete, Football Player)
646 Robertsville Rd
Oak Ridge, TN 37830-4724, USA

Caldwell, Mike T (Athlete, Football Player)
41621 N Bent Creek Ct
Phoenix, AZ 85086-1903, USA

Caldwell, Ralph W (Athlete, Football Player)
4054 Charlene Dr
Windsor Hills, CA 90043-1510, USA

Caldwell, Ravin (Athlete, Football Player)
4415 Johnson St
Fort Smith, AR 72904-4531, USA

Caldwell, Scott (Athlete, Football Player)
1037 Tuskegee St
Grand Prairie, TX 75051-2637, USA

Caldwell, Tracy e dr (Astronaut)
827 Timber Cove Dr
Seabrook, TX 77586-4617, USA

Caldwell, Travis (Actor)
c/o Ellen Meyer *Ellen Meyer Management*
8899 Beverly Blvd Ste 612
Los Angeles, CA 90048-2429, USA

Caldwell, Zoe (Actor)
Whitehead-Stevens
1501 Broadway
New York, NY 10036-5601, USA

Cale, Paula (Actor)
2518 Canyon Dr
Los Angeles, CA 90068-2416, USA

Cale, Puala (Actor)
Gersh Agency
232 N Canon Dr
Beverly Hills, CA 90210-5302, USA

Caleb, Jamie (Athlete, Football Player)
8889 Brandywine Rd
Northfield, OH 44067-2503, USA

Calero, Kiko (Athlete, Baseball Player)
18 Danson Dr
Saint Peters, MO 63376-4028, USA

Caley, Don (Athlete, Hockey Player)
7127 E Aloe Vera Dr
Scottsdale, AZ 85266-7176, USA

Calfa, Don (Actor)
Richard Sundel
1910 Holmby Ave Apt 1
Los Angeles, CA 90025-5936, USA

Calhoun, Bill (Athlete, Basketball Player)
3740 El Cerro View Cir
Reno, NV 89509-5610, USA

Calhoun, David (Athlete, Basketball Player)
17912 Lafayette Dr
Olney, MD 20832-2129, USA

Calhoun, Donald C (Don) (Athlete, Football Player)
PO Box 49104
Wichita, KS 67201-9104, USA

Calhoun, Jeff (Athlete, Baseball Player)
10002 Springwood Forest Dr
Houston, TX 77080-6419, USA

Calhoun, Jim (Athlete, Basketball Player, Coach)
PO Box 379
Pomfret Center, CT 06259-0379, USA

Calhoun, Kole (Athlete, Baseball Player)
662 N Davids Cir
Buckeye, AZ 85326, USA

Calhoun, Monica (Actor)
Innovative Artists
1505 10th St
Santa Monica, CA 90401-2805, USA

Cali, Carmen (Athlete, Baseball Player)
5751 Copper Leaf Ln
Naples, FL 34116-6713, USA

Cali, Joseph (Actor)
25630 Edenwild Rd
Calabasas, CA 91302-2265, USA

Calico, Tyrone (Athlete, Football Player)
678 Uptown St
Memphis, TN 38107-1437, USA

Caliendo, Frank (Actor)
12808 Halkirk St
Studio City, CA 91604-2365, USA

Califano, Joseph A Jr (Politician)
Casa at Columbia
42 Morningside Drs
Westport, CT 06880, USA

Califano Jr, Joseph A (Government Official)
Casa At Columbia
633 3rd Ave # 1900
New York, NY 10017-6706, USA

Caligiuri, Fred (Athlete, Baseball Player)
2101 Runnymede Ln
Charlotte, NC 28209-3316, USA

Calip, Brad
5325 E 92nd St
Tulsa, OK 74137-4004, USA

Calip, Demetrius (Athlete, Basketball Player)
7321 Lennox Ave Unit G5
G5
Van Nuys, CA 91405-6262, USA

Calipari, John (Basketball Coach, Coach)
1732 Richmond Rd
Lexington, KY 40502-1622, USA

Calis, Natasha (Actor)
c/o Jill Littman *Impression Entertainment*
9229 W Sunset Blvd Ste 700
West Hollywood, CA 90069-3407, USA

Calkins, Buzz (Race Car Driver)
1630 Chicago Ave Apt 904
Evanston, IL 60201-4589, USA

Call, Anthony (Actor)
Michael Thomas Agency
134 E 10th St
New York, NY 10003, USA

Call, Brandon (Actor)
c/o Staff Member *SDB Partners Inc*
315 S Beverly Dr Ste 411
Beverly Hills, CA 90212-4301, USA

Call, Jack (Athlete, Football Player)
PO Box 361
Churchville, MD 21028-0361, USA

Call, Kevin (Athlete, Football Player)
839 Carey Rd
Carmel, IN 46033-9324, USA

Callahan, Bill (Athlete, Coach, Football Coach, Football Player)
405 Christinas Ct
Cranberry Township, PA 16066-7805, USA

Callahan, John (Actor)
Levin Representatives
2402 4th St Apt 6
Santa Monica, CA 90405-3664, USA

Callan, Cecile (Actor)
SMZ
8730 W Sunset Blvd Ste 480
West Hollywood, CA 90069-2277, USA

Callan, K (Actor)
4957 Matilija Ave
Sherman Oaks, CA 91423-1921, USA

Callan, Michael (Actor)
23388 Mulholland Dr # 112
Woodland Hills, CA 91364-2733, USA

Calland, Lee (Athlete, Football Player)
6624 Windwood Cir
Douglasville, GA 30135-1647, USA

Callander, Jock (Athlete, Hockey Player)
Lake Erie Monsters 1 Center Ice
Cleveland, OH 44115, USA

Callaway, Mickey (Athlete, Baseball
Player)
8061 Stonewyck Rd
Germantown, TN 38138-2351, USA

Calle 13 (Music Group, Musician)
c/o Staff Member *Sony Music Miami*
605 Lincoln Rd Ste 700
Miami Beach, FL 33139-2901, USA

Callen, Bryan (Actor, Musician)
24741 Via Pradera
Calabasas, CA 91302-1470, USA

Callen, Jones Gloria (Swimmer)
1508 Chafton Rd
Charleston, WV 25314-1603, USA

Callender, Jock (Athlete, Hockey Player)
388 Lear Rd
Avon Lake, OH 44012-2079, USA

Callicutt, Ken (Athlete, Football Player)
919 Suchava Dr
White Lake, MI 48386-4558, USA

Callie, Dayton (Actor)
c/o Staff Member *Commercial Talent
Agency*
12711 Ventura Blvd Ste 285
Studio City, CA 91604-2431, USA

Callier, Frances (Comedian)
c/o Staff Member *Gekis Management*
4217 Verdugo View Dr
Los Angeles, CA 90065-4317, USA

Callies, Sarah Wayne (Actor)
c/o Alissa Vradenburg *Untitled
Entertainment (LA)*
350 S Beverly Dr Ste 200
Beverly Hills, CA 90212-4819, USA

Calling, The (Music Group)
c/o Staff Member *William Morris
Endeavor (LA)*
9601 Wilshire Blvd
Beverly Hills, CA 90210-5213, USA

Callis, James (Actor, Director)
c/o Alan Siegel *Alan Siegel Entertainment*
9200 W Sunset Blvd Ste 407
West Hollywood, CA 90069-3511, USA

Callner, Marty (Director, Producer)
c/o David Steinberg *Morra Brezner
Steinberg & Tenenbaum (MBST)
Entertainment*
345 N Maple Dr Ste 200
Beverly Hills, CA 90210-5174, USA

Calloway, AJ (Television Host)
c/o Mike Esterman *Esterman.Com, LLC*
Prefers to be contacted via email
Baltimore, MD XXXXX, USA

Calloway, Chris (Athlete, Football Player)
3213 Southern Green Dr
Pearland, TX 77584-1799, USA

Calloway, Ernie (Athlete, Football Player)
4027 Lenox Blvd
Orlando, FL 32811-4107, USA

Calloway, Ron (Athlete, Baseball Player)
3868 Las Colinas Dr
Las Cruces, NM 88012-0693, USA

Calmus, Dick (Athlete, Baseball Player)
3823 S 28th West Ave
Tulsa, OK 74107-5452, USA

Calmus, Rocky (Athlete, Football Player)
4131 Trinity Rd
Franklin, TN 37067-7714, USA

Caltabiano, Tom (Comedian)
c/o Staff Member *United Talent Agency
(UTA-LA)*
9336 Civic Center Dr
Beverly Hills, CA 90210-3604, USA

Calvert, Ken (Congressman, Politician)
2269 Rayburn Hob
Washington, DC 20515-0005, USA

Calvert, Mark (Athlete, Baseball Player)
908 W Waco St
Broken Arrow, OK 74011-2819, USA

Calvert, Patricia (Writer)
c/o Staff Member *Simon & Schuster*
1230 Avenue of the Americas Fl CONC1
New York, NY 10020-1586, USA

Calvin, John (Actor)
2503 Ware Rd
Austin, TX 78741-5720, USA

Calvin, Mack (Basketball Player)
930 Figueroa Ter Apt 602
Los Angeles, CA 90012-3076, USA

Calvin, Thomas (Athlete, Football Player)
2712 McTavish Ave SW
Decatur, AL 35603-1106, USA

Calvin, Tom (Athlete, Football Player)
2712 McTavish Ave SW
Decatur, AL 35603-1106, USA

Calvo, Paul M (Ex-Governor)
115 Chalen Sando Papa
Hagatna, GU 96910, USA

Camacho, Ernie (Athlete, Baseball Player)
746 Saint Regis Way
Salinas, CA 93905-1642, USA

Camacho, Joe (Athlete, Baseball Player)
48 Massasoit Ave
Act 3-R
Fairhaven, MA 02719-3266, USA

Camarda, Charles J (Astronaut)
2301 Beach Haven Dr Apt 102
Virginia Beach, VA 23451-1255, USA

Camarillo, Greg (Athlete, Football Player)
PO Box 712827
San Diego, CA 92171-2827, USA

Camarillo, Rich (Athlete, Football Player)
301 E Hiddenview Dr
Phoenix, AZ 85048-1977, USA

Camastra, Danielle (Actor)
c/o Staff Member *Henderson Hogan
Agency (LA)*
8929 Wilshire Blvd Ste 312
Beverly Hills, CA 90211-1969, USA

Cambal, Dennis (Athlete, Football Player)
24 Hedge Row
West Yarmouth, MA 02673-5813, USA

Cambre, Ronald C (Business Person)
Newmont Mining
9903 W Laurel Pl
Littleton, CO 80127-3900, USA

Cambria, Fred (Athlete, Baseball Player)
12 Iris Ct
Northport, NY 11768-3207, USA

Camby, Marcus (Athlete, Basketball
Player)
6725 Fite Rd
Pearland, TX 77584-1089, USA

Cameron, Austin (Race Car Driver)
10 Newbridge Pkwy
Asheville, NC 28804-1256, USA

Cameron, Candace (Actor)
Barbara Camaron Assoc
8369 Sausalito Ave # A
Canoga Park, CA 91304-3342, USA

Cameron, Dallas (Athlete, Football Player)
Hialeah-Miami Lakes High School
7977 W 12th Ave
Hialeah, FL 33014-3595, USA

Cameron, Dean (Actor)
Landmark Artists Mgmt
4116 W Magnolia Blvd
Burbank, CA 91505-2782, USA

Cameron, Duncan (Music Group,
Musician)
Sawyer Brown Inc
5200 Old Harding Rd
Franklin, TN 37064-9406, USA

Cameron, Dwayne (Actor)
c/o Scott Karp *The Syndicate*
10203 Santa Monica Blvd Fl 5
Los Angeles, CA 90067-6416, USA

Cameron, Glenn S (Athlete, Football
Player)
8082 Steeplechase Dr
Palm Beach Gardens, FL 33418-7703,
USA

Cameron, James (Director, Producer)
3211 Retreat Ct
Malibu, CA 90265-3448, USA

Cameron, Jordan (Athlete, Football
Player)
c/o Tom Condon *CAA (St. Louis)*
222 S Central Ave Ste 1008
Saint Louis, MO 63105-3509, USA

Cameron, Julia (Writer)
c/o Staff Member *HarperCollins Publishers*
195 Broadway Fl 2
Cellar 1
New York, NY 10007-3132, USA

Cameron, Kenneth d colonel (Astronaut)
11333 Gulf Beach Hwy
Pensacola, FL 32507-9100, USA

Cameron, Kevin (Athlete, Baseball Player)
26435 S Ivy Ln
Channahon, IL 60410-3341, USA

Cameron, Kirk (Actor)
c/o Mark Craig *Mark Craig Productions*
1383 Callens Rd
Ventura, CA 93003-5602, USA

Cameron, Laura (Actor)
8383 Wilshire Blvd # 954
Beverly Hills, CA 90211-2425, USA

Cameron, Mat (Music Group, Musician)
Susan Silver Mgmt
6523 California Ave SW # 348
Seattle, WA 98136-1833, USA

Cameron, Matt (Musician)
10910 Algonquin Rd
Woodway, WA 98020-6108, USA

Cameron, Mike (Athlete, Baseball Player)
615 Champions Dr
McDonough, GA 30253-4284, USA

Cameron, Paul (Athlete, Football Player)
28072 Klamath Ct
Laguna Niguel, CA 92677-7018, USA

Cameron, Scotty (Golfer)
Acushnet Company
333 Bridge St
C/O Gordon Sanborn
Fairhaven, MA 02719-4900, USA

Cameron, Warren (Horse Racer)
PO Box 1306
De Leon Springs, FL 32130-1306

Cameron, W Bruce (Writer)
c/o Scott Miller *Trident Media Group LLC*
41 Madison Ave Fl 36
New York, NY 10010-2257, USA

Cameron-Bure, Candace (Actor)
c/o Jeffery Brooks *Redrock Entertainment
Development*
118 S Cordova St Fl 3
Burbank, CA 91505-4610, USA

Camerota, Brett (Athlete, Olympic
Athlete, Skier)
3118 Elk Run Dr
Park City, UT 84098-5300, USA

Camerota, Eric (Athlete, Olympic Athlete,
Skier)
3118 Elk Run Dr
Park City, UT 84098-5300, USA

Camiletti, Rob (Actor)
643 N La Cienega Blvd
West Hollywood, CA 90069-5201, USA

Camilleri, Louis C (Business Person)
Altria Group
120 Park Ave Fl 6
New York, NY 10017-5579, USA

Camilleri, Terry (Actor)
c/o Christopher Mario Parker *Access LA
Talent Management*
2850 Ocean Park Blvd Ste 215
Santa Monica, CA 90405-6206, USA

Camilli, Doug (Athlete, Baseball Player)
4245 61st Ave
Vero Beach, FL 32967-8807, USA

Camilli, Lou (Athlete, Baseball Player)
1314 Sigma Chi Rd NE
Albuquerque, NM 87106-4544, USA

Camilo, Michael (Musician)
Joel Chriss
300 Mercer St Apt 3J
New York, NY 10003-6732, USA

Camilo, Michel (Music Group, Musician)
Redondo Music
590 W End Ave # 6
New York, NY 10024-1722, USA

Caminito, Jerry (Race Car Driver)
Blue Thunder Racing
PO Box 1486
Jackson, NJ 08527-0486, USA

Cammack, Eric (Athlete, Baseball Player)
605 Remington Dr
Bridge City, TX 77611-2234, USA

Cammuso, Frank (Cartoonist)
PO Box 4915
Syracuse, NY 13221-4915, USA

Camp, Anna (Actor)
c/o Robert Glennon *Authentic Talent and Literary Management*
20 Jay St Ste M17
Brooklyn, NY 11201-8300, USA

Camp, Colleen (Actor)
473 N Tigertail Rd
Los Angeles, CA 90049-2807, USA

Camp, Dave (Congressman, Politician)
341 Cannon Hob
Washington, DC 20515-1806, USA

Camp, Jeremy (Musician)
1712 Championship Blvd
Franklin, TN 37064-8631, USA

Camp, John (Journalist)
Saint Paul Pioneer Press
345 Cedar St
Saint Paul, MN 55101-1057, USA

Camp, Rick (Athlete, Baseball Player)
F P C Montgomery ID # 11973-021
Maxwell Air Force Base
Montgomery, AL 36112, USA

Camp, Steve (Music Group)
Third Coast Artists
2021 21st Ave S Ste 220
Nashville, TN 37212-4348, USA

Campanella, Joseph (Actor)
4196 Colfax Ave
Studio City, CA 91604-2165, USA

Campaneris, Bert (Athlete, Baseball Player)
PO Box 5096
Scottsdale, AZ 85261-5096, USA

Campanis, Jim (Athlete, Baseball Player)
17082 Cascades Ave
Yorba Linda, CA 92886-4867, USA

Campau, Thomas E (Cinematographer)
2000 S Hammond Lake Rd
West Bloomfield, MI 48324-1816, USA

Campbell, A Kim (Prime Minister)
Harvard University
Kennedy School of Government
Cambridge, MA 02138, USA

Campbell, Alan (Actor)
Gersh Agency
41 Madison Ave Ste 3301
New York, NY 10010-2210, USA

Campbell, Bek David (Beck) (Musician)
c/o John Silva *SAM*
722 Seward St
Los Angeles, CA 90038-3504, USA

Campbell, Ben Nighthorse (Politician)
380 Russell
Washington, DC 20510-0001, USA

Campbell, Bill (Athlete, Baseball Player)
133 S Hale St
Palatine, IL 60067-6211, USA

Campbell, Billy (Actor)
c/o Sean Fay *Kritzer Levine Wilkins Entertainment (KLWG)*
11872 La Grange Ave Fl 1
Los Angeles, CA 90025-5283, USA

Campbell, Brian (Athlete, Hockey Player)
4132 Grove Ave
Western Springs, IL 60558-1344, USA

Campbell, Bruce (Actor, Director, Producer)
735 Roca St
Ashland, OR 97520-3315, USA

Campbell, Bryan (Athlete, Hockey Player)
10895 Tamoron Ln
Boca Raton, FL 33498-6397, USA

Campbell, Carter (Athlete, Football Player)
24834 Winterberry Ln
Plainfield, IL 60585-5685, USA

Campbell, Chad (Athlete, Golfer)
200 Glade Rd
Colleyville, TX 76034-3603, USA

Campbell, Christa (Actor)
c/o Staff Member *Origin Talent Agency*
4705 Laurel Canyon Blvd Ste 303
Valley Village, CA 91607-5943, USA

Campbell, Christian (Actor)
12533 Woodgreen St
Los Angeles, CA 90066-2723, USA

Campbell, Dan (Athlete, Football Player)
PO Box 237
Morgan, TX 76671-0237, USA

Campbell, Dave (Athlete, Baseball Player)
878 Amidon St
Deltona, FL 32725-7206, USA

Campbell, Dave (Athlete, Baseball Player)
726 N Dundee Dr
Post Falls, ID 83854-8886, USA

Campbell, Dick (Athlete, Football Player)
382 NE Jade Cir
Jensen Beach, FL 34957-5411, USA

Campbell, Dick (Athlete, Football Player)
2557 Nicolet Dr
Green Bay, WI 54311-7225, USA

Campbell, Earl (Athlete, Football Player)
The Tyler Rose
701 W 11th St
Austin, TX 78701-2067, USA

Campbell, Elden (Athlete, Basketball Player)
17252 Hawthome Blvd
#493
Torrance, CA 90504, USA

Campbell, Gaetana (Actor)
1620 Richmond Cir Unit 105
Joliet, IL 60435-6751, USA

Campbell, Garry (Producer, Writer)
c/o Staff Member *Creative Artists Agency (CAA-LA)*
2000 Avenue of the Stars Ste 100
Los Angeles, CA 90067-4705, USA

Campbell, Gary (Athlete, Football Player)
PO Box 772992
Steamboat Springs, CO 80477-2992, USA

Campbell, Gene (Athlete, Hockey Player)
6149 Sugar Mill Ln
Mound, MN 55364-8624, USA

Campbell, Glen (Musician)
827 Battery Ln
Nashville, TN 37220-1103, USA

Campbell, Isobel (Music Group, Musician)
Legends of 21st Century
7 Trinity Row
Florence, MA 01062-1931, USA

Campbell, Jack (Politician)
PO Box 2208
Santa Fe, NM 87504-2208, USA

Campbell, James (Jim) (Athlete, Baseball Player)
209 W Seven Pines St
Lamar, SC 29069-8964, USA

Campbell, Jason (Athlete, Football Player)
c/o Joel Segal *Lagardere Unlimited (NYC)*
845 United Nations Plz Apt 77B
New York, NY 10017-3538, USA

Campbell, Jeff (Athlete, Football Player)
10205 Birdlip Cir
Austin, TX 78733-3415, USA

Campbell, Jeff (Baseball Player)
Homestead Grays
4194 San Miguel Ave
San Diego, CA 92113-1842, USA

Campbell, Jennifer Lynn (Actor)
11871 Dubarry Dr
Carmel, IN 46033-8259, USA

Campbell, Jesse (Athlete, Football Player)
875 Piney Neck Rd
Vanceboro, NC 28586-8677, USA

Campbell, Jessica (Actor)
Somers Teitelbaum David
8840 Wilshire Blvd # 200
Beverly Hills, CA 90211-2606, USA

Campbell, Jim (Athlete, Baseball Player)
1924 Knollwood Ln
Los Altos, CA 94024-6720, USA

Campbell, Jim (Athlete, Baseball Player)
1671 6th St
Oroville, CA 95965-4057, USA

Campbell, Jim (Athlete, Hockey Player)
32 Lemp Rd
Saint Louis, MO 63122-6947, USA

Campbell, Jim (Horse Racer)
31 Mill Pond Rd
Jackson, NJ 08527-4888, USA

Campbell, Joe (Athlete, Baseball Player)
330 Legends Ct
Bowling Green, KY 42103-2550, USA

Campbell, John (Congressman, Politician)
1507 Longworth Hob
Washington, DC 20515-4328, USA

Campbell, John (Horse Racer)
John D Campbell Stable
823 Allison Dr
Rivervale, NJ 07675-6602, USA

Campbell, John W (Athlete, Football Player)
12908 Welcome Ln
Burnsville, MN 55337-3626, USA

Campbell, Joshua (Actor)
c/o Staff Member *Select Artists Ltd (CA-Westside Office)*
1138 12th St Apt 1
Santa Monica, CA 90403-5459, USA

Campbell, Julia (Actor)
Innovative Artists
1505 10th St
Santa Monica, CA 90401-2805, USA

Campbell, Kevin (Athlete, Baseball Player)
207 Ridout Dr
Des Arc, AR 72040-3335, USA

Campbell, Kim (Politician)
Canadian Consulate
550 S Hope St Ste 900
Los Angeles, CA 90071-2654, USA

Campbell, Lamar (Athlete, Football Player)
2511 W 7th St
Chester, PA 19013-2109, USA

Campbell, Larry Joe (Actor)
30306 Diamonte Ln
Rancho Palos Verdes, CA 90275-6395, USA

Campbell, Lewis B (Business Person)
Textron Inc
40 Westminster St Ste 500
Providence, RI 02903-2503, USA

Campbell, Luther (Musician)
16571 SW 18th St
Miramar, FL 33027-4468, USA

Campbell, Marion (Athlete, Football Coach, Football Player)
351 Marsh Point Cir
Saint Augustine, FL 32080-5864, USA

Campbell, Mark (Athlete, Football Player)
2425 NW 91st Dr
Gainesville, FL 32606-9146, USA

Campbell, Martin (Director)
International Creative Mgmt
10250 Constellation Blvd Fl 1
Los Angeles, CA 90067-6241, USA

Campbell, Matt (Athlete, Football Player)
9 Timberidge Dr
North Augusta, SC 29860-9725, USA

Campbell, Matthew (Matt) (Athlete, Football Player)
6 Old House Cir
Okatie, SC 29909-7002, USA

Campbell, Mike (Athlete, Baseball Player)
4500 36th Ave SW Apt 12
Seattle, WA 98126-2750, USA

Campbell, Mike (Athlete, Football Player)
383 Inverness Dr
Winston Salem, NC 27107-6030, USA

Campbell, Mike (Musician)
19950 Redwing St
Woodland Hills, CA 91364-2621, USA

Campbell, Naomi (Actor, Model)
c/o David Unger *Resolution (LA)*
1801 Century Park E Ste 2300
Los Angeles, CA 90067-2325, USA

Campbell, Nell (Actor)
246 W 14th St
New York, NY 10011-7201, USA

Campbell, Neve (Actor)
c/o Arlene Forster *Forster Entertainment*
12533 Woodgreen St
Los Angeles, CA 90066-2723, USA

Campbell, Nicholas (Actor)
1206 N Orange Grove Ave
West Hollywood, CA 90046-5351, USA

Campbell, Paul (Actor)
c/o Staff Member *ROAR (LA)*
9701 Wilshire Blvd Fl 8
Beverly Hills, CA 90212-2008, USA

Campbell, Rich (Athlete, Football Player)
8 Gregory Ln
Little Rock, AR 72205-5027, USA

Campbell, Robert H (Business Person)
Sunoco Inc
10 Penn Center 1801 Market St
Philadelphia, PA 19103, USA

Campbell, Ron (Athlete, Baseball Player)
119 Overbriar Dr NE
Cleveland, TN 37312-5453, USA

Campbell, Scott (Athlete, Football Player)
123 Oak Ln
Hershey, PA 17033-1748, USA

Campbell, Scott Michael (Actor)
c/o Danielle Allman-Del *D2 Management*
9255 W Sunset Blvd Ste 600
West Hollywood, CA 90069-3306, USA

Campbell, Sonny (Athlete, Football Player)
6250 N Desert Willow Dr
Tucson, AZ 85743-8701, USA

Campbell, Stacy Dean (Musician)
1105-C 16th Avenue Sq
Nashville, TN 37212, USA

Campbell, Tevin (Musician)
c/o Staff Member *M.A.G./Universal Attractions*
15 W 36th St Fl 8
New York, NY 10018-7927, USA

Campbell, Tony (Athlete, Basketball Player)
1445 Teaneck Rd
Teaneck, NJ 07666-3627, USA

Campbell, Vivian (Musician)
2621 N Vermont Ave
Los Angeles, CA 90027-1244, USA

Campbell, Woodrow (Athlete, Football Player)
9122 Weymouth Dr
Houston, TX 77031-3034, USA

Campbell, Woody (Athlete, Football Player)
9122 Weymouth Dr
Houston, TX 77031-3034, USA

Campbell-Martin, Tisha (Actor)
22401 S Summit Ridge Cir
Chatsworth, CA 91311-2682, USA

Campedelli, Dominic (Athlete, Hockey Player)
732 Jerusalem Rd
Cohasset, MA 02025-1032, USA

Campen, James (Athlete, Football Player)
2789 Ichabod Ln
Green Bay, WI 54313-3209, USA

Campfield, Billy (Athlete, Football Player)
930 Glenmore Way Apt K
Westerville, OH 43082-9429, USA

Campfield, William (Billy) (Athlete, Football Player)
930 Glenmore Way Apt K
Westerville, OH 43082-9429, USA

Campisi, Sal (Athlete, Baseball Player)
644 77th Ave
St Pete Beach, FL 33706-1708, USA

Campo, Dave (Coach, Football Coach)
Celveland Browns
76 Lou Groza Blvd
Berea, OH 44017-1269, USA

Campos, Angel (Athlete, Baseball Player)
6305 W Velvet Senna Dr
Tucson, AZ 85757-7518, USA

Campos, Bruno (Actor)
SDB Partners
315 S Beverly Dr Ste 411
Beverly Hills, CA 90212-4301, USA

Cam'ron (Musician)
c/o Staff Member *ICM Partners (LA)*
10250 Constellation Blvd Fl 7
Los Angeles, CA 90067-6207, USA

Canada, Larry (Athlete, Football Player)
PO Box 2312
Country Club Hills, IL 60478-9412, USA

Canada, Ron (Actor)
c/o Christopher Wright *Christopher Wright Management*
3207 Winnie Dr
Los Angeles, CA 90068-1439, USA

Canadas, Esther (Actor, Model)
Wilhelmina Models
300 Park Ave S # 200
New York, NY 10010-5313, USA

Canady, James (Jim) (Athlete, Football Player)
303 Sunset Dr
Burnet, TX 78611-9737, USA

Canagata, Bill (Baseball Player)
Indianapolis Clowns
25 W 132nd St Apt 10R
New York, NY 10037-3205, USA

Canale, George (Athlete, Baseball Player)
7333 Old Mill Rd
Roanoke, VA 24018-6712, USA

Canalis, Elisabetta (Actor, Model)
c/o Staff Member *Corsa Agency, The*
11704 Wilshire Blvd Ste 204
Los Angeles, CA 90025-1510, USA

Canals-Barrera, Maria (Actor)
c/o Jason Newman *Untitled Entertainment (LA)*
350 S Beverly Dr Ste 200
Beverly Hills, CA 90212-4819, USA

Canary, David (Actor)
110 Belden Hill Rd
Wilton, CT 06897-2911, USA

Candaele, Casey (Athlete, Baseball Player)
251 Broad St
San Luis Obispo, CA 93405-2303, USA

Candelari, Richard
3812 Conough Ln
Las Vegas, NV 89129-2707, USA

Candelaria, John (Athlete, Baseball Player)
3122 Elroy Ave
Pittsburgh, PA 15227-2825, USA

Candiotti, Thomas C (Tom) (Athlete, Baseball Player)
6061 E Jenan Dr
Scottsdale, AZ 85254-4972, USA

Candlebox (Music Group)
c/o Staff Member *Maverick Recording Co (LA)*
3300 Warner Blvd
Burbank, CA 91505-4632, USA

Caneira, John (Athlete, Baseball Player)
18 Spruce Dr
Naugatuck, CT 06770-4231, USA

Canela, Jencarlos (Actor, Musician)
c/o Oswaldo Pisfil *NCM Productions*
10770 NW 66th St Apt 512
Doral, FL 33178-3781, USA

Canerday, Natalie (Actor)
c/o Staff Member *The Agency Inc*
802 W 8th St
Little Rock, AR 72201-4016, USA

Canet, Guillaume (Actor, Director, Writer)
c/o Robert Newman *William Morris Endeavor (LA)*
9601 Wilshire Blvd
Beverly Hills, CA 90210-5213, USA

Canete, Ariel (Athlete, Golfer)
Advantage International
1751 Pinnacle Dr Ste 1500
Mc Lean, VA 22102-3833, USA

Canfield, Jack (Business Person, Writer)
The Jack Canfield Companies
PO Box 30880
Santa Barbara, CA 93130-0880, USA

Cangelosi, John (Athlete, Baseball Player)
10914 Caribou Ln
Orland Park, IL 60467-7843, USA

Canidate, Trung (Athlete, Football Player)
1707 W Clarendon Ave
Phoenix, AZ 85015-5502, USA

Canipe, David (Athlete, Golfer)
505 Oakwood Ave
New Smyrna Beach, FL 32169-2715, USA

Canizales, Gaby (Boxer)
2205 Saint Maria Ave
Laredo, TX 78040, USA

Canizaro, Jay (Athlete, Baseball Player)
19523 Piney Lake Dr
Spring, TX 77388-3060, USA

Canley, Sheldon (Athlete, Football Player)
264 Altair Ave
Lompoc, CA 93436-1424, USA

Cannatella, Trishelle (Reality Star)
c/o Staff Member *Bunim/Murray Productions*
6007 Sepulveda Blvd
Van Nuys, CA 91411-2502, USA

Cannava, Anthony (Tony) (Athlete, Football Player)
26 Royall St
Medford, MA 02155-4512, USA

Cannavale, Bobby (Actor)
c/o Peg Donegan *Framework Entertainment (LA)*
9057 Nemo St Ste C
West Hollywood, CA 90069-5511, USA

Cannavino, Joe (Athlete, Football Player)
346 Claymore Blvd
Cleveland, OH 44143-1730, USA

Canned Heat (Music Group, Musician)
PO Box 3773
San Rafael, CA 94912-3773, USA

Cannida, James (Athlete, Football Player)
4504 Harmony Pl
Rohnert Park, CA 94928-1880, USA

Canning, Doug
700 Brookside Rd
Maitland, FL 32751-5170, USA

Canning, Lisa (Actor, Correspondent)
880 Hilldale Ave Apt 12
West Hollywood, CA 90069-4920, USA

Canning, Sara (Actor)
c/o Laura Myones *McKeon-Myones Management*
3500 W Olive Ave Ste 770
Burbank, CA 91505-5527, USA

Cannizaro, Andy (Athlete, Baseball Player)
429 Marina Oaks
Mandeville, LA 70471-1567, USA

Cannizzaro, Chris (Athlete, Baseball Player)
13597 Grain Ln
San Diego, CA 92129-2851, USA

Cannon, Ace (Musician)
American Mgmt
19948 Mayall St
Chatsworth, CA 91311-3522, USA

Cannon, Billy (Athlete, Football Player)
8857 Sage Hill Rd
Saint Francisville, LA 70775-7168, USA

Cannon, Billy (Athlete, Football Player)
8851 Sage Hill Rd
Saint Francisville, LA 70775-7168, USA

Cannon, Danny (Producer)
c/o Staff Member *Creative Artists Agency (CAA-LA)*
2000 Avenue of the Stars Ste 100
Los Angeles, CA 90067-4705, USA

Cannon, Don (Producer)
Cannon Music Enterprise
PO Box 360055
Decatur, GA 30036-0055, USA

Cannon, Dyan (Actor)
1100 Alta Loma Rd Apt 808
West Hollywood, CA 90069-2438, USA

Cannon, Freddy (Musician)
5119 Surfrider Way
Oxnard, CA 93035-1050, USA

Cannon, Glenn (Actor)
University of Hawaii at Manoa
2500 Campus Rd
C/O Cinematic and Digital Arts
Honolulu, HI 96822-2217, USA

Cannon, Harold (Actor)
c/o Staff Member *Select Artists Ltd (CA-Valley Office)*
PO Box 4359
Burbank, CA 91503-4359, USA

Cannon, Joe (Soccer Player)
c/o Staff Member *Colorado Rapids Soccer Club*
1000 Chopper Cir
Pepsi Center
Denver, CO 80204-5805, USA

Cannon, Joe (J J) (Athlete, Baseball Player)
3017 Cedarwood Village Ln
Pensacola, FL 32514-6251, USA

Cannon, John (Athlete, Football Player)
2911 W Bay Vista Ave
Tampa, FL 33611-1609, USA

Cannon, Katherine (Actor)
1310 Westholme Ave
Los Angeles, CA 90024-5016, USA

Cannon, Larry (Athlete, Basketball Player)
6102 Whiskey Creek Dr Apt 105
Fort Myers, FL 33919-8711, USA

Cannon, Marcus (Athlete, Football Player)
c/o Tom Condon *CAA (St. Louis)*
222 S Central Ave Ste 1008
Saint Louis, MO 63105-3509, USA

Cannon, Mark (Athlete, Football Player)
2604 Riveroaks Dr
Arlington, TX 76006-3638, USA

Cannon, Nick (Actor, Producer)
3130 Antelo Rd
Los Angeles, CA 90077-1604, USA

Cano, Christi (Athlete, Golfer)
PO Box 12792
San Antonio, TX 78212-0792, USA

Cano, Robinson (Athlete, Baseball Player)
c/o Brodie van Wagenen *Creative Artists Agency (CAA-NY)*
162 5th Ave Fl 6
New York, NY 10010-6047, USA

Canonero, Milena (Designer)
c/o Paul Hook *ICM Partners (LA)*
10250 Constellation Blvd Fl 7
Los Angeles, CA 90067-6207, USA

Canova, Diana (Actor)
Grand View Management
578 Washington Blvd Ste 688
Marina Del Rey, CA 90292-5442, USA

Canseco, Jose (Athlete, Baseball Player,
Reality Star)
c/o Susan Haber *Haber Entertainment*
434 S Canon Dr Apt 204
Beverly Hills, CA 90212-4501, USA

Canseco, Ozzie (Athlete, Baseball Player)
10833 Wilshire Blvd Apt 525
Los Angeles, CA 90024-4157, USA

Cansino, Athena (Actor)
c/o Victor Kruglov *Victor Kruglov Talent
Management*
6565 W Sunset Blvd Ste 200
Los Angeles, CA 90028-7219, USA

Cantafio, Jim (Actor)
c/o Laura Lichen *Laura Lichen
Management*
PO Box 33051
Granada Hills, CA 91394-3051, USA

Cantaline, Anita (Bowler)
31455 Pinto Dr
Warren, MI 48093-7624, USA

Cantano, Mark (Athlete, Football Player)
9036 Walton St
Indianapolis, IN 46231-1164, USA

Cantey, Charisie (Sportscaster)
ABC-TV
77 W 66th St
New York, NY 10023-6201, USA

Cantillo, Jose Pablo (Actor)
c/o Staff Member *New Wave
Entertainment (LA)*
2660 W Olive Ave
Burbank, CA 91505-4525, USA

Canto, Adan (Actor)
c/o Aida Bernal *Spellbound Entertainment*
Prefers to be contacted by telephone or
email
Los Angeles, CA, USA

Canton, Denio (Baseball Player)
New York Cubans
1330 NW 5th St Apt 5
Miami, FL 33125-4734, USA

Canton, Joanna (Actor)
c/o Staff Member *Liberman/Zerman
Management*
252 N Larchmont Blvd Ste 200
Los Angeles, CA 90004-3754, USA

Cantone, Mario (Actor)
c/o Jim Mannino *Jim Mannino PR*
1 River Pl Apt 726
New York, NY 10036-4365, USA

Cantor, Andres (Sportscaster)
c/o Staff Member *William Morris
Endeavor (LA)*
9601 Wilshire Blvd
Beverly Hills, CA 90210-5213, USA

Cantor, Eric (Congressman, Politician)
303 Cannon Hob
Washington, DC 20515-1501, USA

Cantrell, Barry (Athlete, Football Player)
142 Underwood Dr
Palatka, FL 32177-8166, USA

Cantrell, Bill (Race Car Driver)
PO Box 194
Novi, MI 48376-0194, USA

Cantrell, Blu (Music Group)
c/o Mike Esterman *Esterman.Com, LLC*
Prefers to be contacted via email
Baltimore, MD XXXXX, USA

Cantrell, Jerry (Musician)
11700 Valleycrest Rd
Studio City, CA 91604-4226, USA

Cantrell, Lana (Musician)
300 E 71st St Apt 19A
New York, NY 10021-5238, USA

Cantu, Jorge (Athlete, Baseball Player)
5009 S 24th St
McAllen, TX 78503-8936, USA

Cantwell, Maria (Politician)
904 7th Ave S
Edmonds, WA 98020-4014, USA

Canty, Chris (Athlete, Football Player)
26 Berkery Pl
Alpine, NJ 07620, USA

Canyon, George (Musician)
c/o Staff Member *Paradigm (Monterey)*
404 W Franklin St
Monterey, CA 93940-2303, USA

Cap, Kelly (Athlete, Golfer)
3023 Alcazar Pl Apt 208
Palm Beach Gardens, FL 33410-2878,
USA

Capalbo, Carmen C (Director, Producer)
500 2nd Ave
New York, NY 10016-8606, USA

Caparulo, John (Comedian)
c/o Staff Member *Brillstein Entertainment
Partners (LA)*
9150 Wilshire Blvd Ste 350
Beverly Hills, CA 90212-3453, USA

Capece, Bill (Athlete, Football Player)
867 Hill Roost Rd
Tallahassee, FL 32312-6716, USA

Capel, Mike (Athlete, Baseball Player)
3901 Northshore Dr
Montgomery, TX 77356-5369, USA

Capellas, Michael (Business Person)
MCI
500 Clinton Center Dr Ste 2200
Clinton, MS 39056-5674, USA

Capers, Dom (Athlete, Coach, Football
Coach, Football Player)
669 Ponte Vedra Blvd Unit A
Ponte Vedra Beach, FL 32082-2984, USA

Capers, Wayne (Athlete, Football Player)
28 Greenlawn Dr
Pittsburgh, PA 15220-2503, USA

Caperton, Gaston (Ex-Governor)
The College Board
PO Box 1386
Charleston, WV 25325-1386, USA

Capilla, Doug (Athlete, Baseball Player)
55 Jeffers Way Apt 3
Campbell, CA 95008-2849, USA

Caplan, Lizzy (Actor)
c/o Julie Darmody *Mosaic Media Group*
9200 W Sunset Blvd Ste 10
West Hollywood, CA 90069-3608, USA

Capleton (Musician)
c/o Staff Member *The Agency Group
(NYC)*
142 W 57th St Fl 6
New York, NY 10019-3300, USA

Caplin, Mortimer M (Government
Official)
5610 Wisconsin Ave PH 18E
Chevy Chase, MD 20815-4442, USA

Capon, Edwin G (Religious Leader)
Swedenborgian Church
50 Quincy St
Cambridge, MA 02138-3013, USA

Capone, Warren (Athlete, Football Player)
1076 W Tom Stokes Ct
Baton Rouge, LA 70810-3194, USA

Caponera, John (Actor, Comedian)
Messina Baker Entertainment
955 Carrillo Dr Ste 100
Los Angeles, CA 90048-5400, USA

Caponi, Donna M (Athlete, Golfer)
2731 Silver River Trl
Orlando, FL 32828-7787, USA

Capp, Dick (Athlete, Football Player)
PO Box 2193
Cary, NC 27512-2193, USA

Cappadona, Robert (Bob) (Athlete,
Football Player)
25 Summer St
Watertown, MA 02472-3457, USA

Cappelletti, Gino (Athlete, Football
Player)
19 Louis Dr
Wellesley Hills, MA 02481-1164, USA

Cappelletti, John (Athlete, Football Player,
Heisman Trophy Winner)
23791 Brant Ln
Laguna Niguel, CA 92677-1341, USA

Cappelman, Bill (Athlete, Football Player)
1506 Sydney Ln
Lynn Haven, FL 32444-2928, USA

Cappleman, William (Bill) (Athlete,
Football Player)
1506 Sydney Ln
Lynn Haven, FL 32444-2928, USA

Capps, Lois (Congressman, Politician)
2231 Rayburn Hob
Washington, DC 20515-4321, USA

Capps, Matt (Athlete, Baseball Player)
4928 Pebblebrook Dr
Douglasville, GA 30135-4520, USA

Capps, Ron (Race Car Driver)
Copenhagen Racing
1232 Distribution Way
Vista, CA 92081-8816, USA

Capps, Thomas E (Business Person)
Dominion Resources
120 Tredegar St
Richmond, VA 23219-4306, USA

Cappuzzello, George (Athlete, Baseball
Player)
2024 Stillwood Pl
Windermere, FL 34786-8329, USA

Capra, Buzz (Athlete, Baseball Player)
15039 W Keswick Pl
Lockport, IL 60441-6251, USA

Capra, Nick (Athlete, Baseball Player)
300 Town Park Rd
Norman, OK 73072-4538, USA

Capri, Ahna (Actor)
16547 Vanowen St Apt 209
Van Nuys, CA 91406-4710, USA

Capri, Mark (Actor)
The Blithe Spirit
225 W 44th St
the Shubert Theatre
New York, NY 10036-3964, USA

Capria, Carl (Athlete, Football Player)
9003 Nautical Watch Dr
Indianapolis, IN 46236-9035, USA

Capriati, Jennifer (Athlete, Olympic
Athlete, Tennis Player)
PO Box 7078
Wesley Chapel, FL 33545-0100, USA

Caprice, Frank (Athlete, Hockey Player)
4770 Aston Gardens Way Apt 114
Naples, FL 34109-3589, USA

Capshaw, Jessica (Actor)
c/o Raj Raghavan *Creative Artists Agency
(CAA-LA)*
2000 Avenue of the Stars Ste 100
Los Angeles, CA 90067-4705, USA

Capshaw, Kate (Actor)
c/o Kevin Huvane *Creative Artists Agency
(CAA-LA)*
2000 Avenue of the Stars Ste 100
Los Angeles, CA 90067-4705, USA

Capuano, Chris (Athlete, Baseball Player)
19550 N Grayhawk Dr Unit 1112
Scottsdale, AZ 85255-3986, USA

Capuano, Dave (Athlete, Hockey Player)
145 Capuano Ave
Cranston, RI 02920-8200, USA

Capuano, Jack (Athlete, Coach, Hockey
Player)
c/o Staff Member *Bridgeport Sound Tigers*
600 Main St Ste 1
Bridgeport, CT 06604-5106, USA

Capucill, Terese (Dancer)
Martha Graham dance Center
440 Lafayette St
New York, NY 10003-6919, USA

Caputo, Theresa (Reality Star)
PO Box 490
Hicksville, NY 11802-0490, USA

Capuzzi, Jim (Athlete, Football Player)
10538 Rancho Carmel Dr
San Diego, CA 92128-3627, USA

Cara, Irene (Actor, Musician)
2160 Moon Shadow Rd
New Port Richey, FL 34655-4031, USA

Carafotes, Paul (Actor)
8033 W Sunset Blvd # 3554
Los Angeles, CA 90046-2401, USA

Caraluzzi, Joseph (Horse Racer)
44 Greenwood Dr
Freehold, NJ 07728-4005

Carano, Gina (Crush) (Athlete, Wrestler)
c/o Scott Karp *The Syndicate*
10203 Santa Monica Blvd Fl 5
Los Angeles, CA 90067-6416, USA

Carano, Glenn (Athlete, Football Player)
2551 E Lake Ridge Shrs
Reno, NV 89519-5787, USA

Carapella, Alfred (Al) (Athlete, Football
Player)
10 Woodlot Rd
Eastchester, NY 10709-1204, USA

Carasco, Joe (King) (Music Group)
Texas Sounds
2317 Pecan St
Dickinson, TX 77539-4949, USA

Caravello, Joe (Athlete, Football Player)
633 W Palm Ave
El Segundo, CA 90245-2065, USA

Caray, Chip (Commentator)
1302 Azalea Ln
Maitland, FL 32751-6404, USA

Carbajal, Michael (Athlete, Boxer, Olympic Athlete)
PO Box 510
Phoenix, AZ 85001-0510, USA

Carbo, Bernie (Athlete, Baseball Player)
6352 Woodside Dr S
Theodore, AL 36582-3992, USA

Carbonaro, Michael (Actor)
c/o Staff Member *Grapevine Public Relations*
5237 Cahuenga Blvd # 2
N Hollywood, CA 91601-3419, USA

Carbone, Frank (Horse Racer)
6004 Dickens Ct
Norristown, PA 19403-1373, USA

Carbonell, Nestor (Actor)
128 S Larchmont Blvd
Los Angeles, CA 90004-3709, USA

Carcaterra, Lorenzo (Producer, Writer)
c/o Staff Member *Pitt Group, The*
8750 Wilshire Blvd Ste 301
Beverly Hills, CA 90211-2700, USA

Carcieri, Donald (Politician)
PO Box 701
Saunderstown, RI 02874-0701, USA

Card, Andrew (Politician)
White House
8405 Spring Crk
College Station, TX 77845-4608, USA

Card, Michael (Music Group, Musician)
1143 Dora Whitley Rd
Franklin, TN 37064-4788, USA

Card, Orson Scott (Writer)
401 Willoughby Blvd
Greensboro, NC 27408-3135, USA

Cardellini, Linda (Actor)
180 Santa Clara Ave
Redwood City, CA 94061-3405, USA

Cardenal, Jose D (Athlete, Baseball Player)
118 Bridgewater Ct
Bradenton, FL 34212-9302, USA

Cardenas, Leo (Athlete, Baseball Player)
4305 Grotto Ct
Cincinnati, OH 45211-5341, USA

Carder, Tank (Athlete, Football Player)
c/o Kelli Masters *Kelli Masters Management*
100 N Broadway Ste 1700
Oklahoma City, OK 73102-9211, USA

Cardigans, The (Music Group)
c/o Larry Webman *Paradigm (NY)*
360 Park Ave S Fl 16
New York, NY 10010-1716, USA

Cardille, Lori (Actor)
c/o Tracey Goldblum *Abrams Artists Agency (NY)*
275 7th Ave Fl 26
New York, NY 10001-6708, USA

Cardin, Benjamin L. (Senator)
509 Hart Senate Office Building
Washington, DC 20510-0001, USA

Cardinal, Brian (Athlete, Basketball Player)
1680 Lane 105
Lake James
Angola, IN 46703, USA

Cardinal, Conrad (Athlete, Baseball Player)
162 E Hunter Ln
Central, UT 84722-3221, USA

Cardinal, Randy (Baseball Player)
Houston Colt 45's
3810 W Verde Way
North Las Vegas, NV 89031-4812, USA

Cardona, Manolo (Actor)
c/o Nina Shaw *Del Shaw Moonves Tanaka Finkelstein & Lezcano*
2120 Colorado Ave Ste 200
Santa Monica, CA 90404-3561, USA

Cardone, Vivien (Actor)
c/o Staff Member *Persona Management*
40 E 9th St Apt 11J
Suite 11J
New York, NY 10003-6426, USA

Cardos, John Bud (Director)
PO Box 7430
Burbank, CA 91510-7430, USA

Cardosa, Patricia (Director)
c/o Staff Member *ICM Partners (LA)*
10250 Constellation Blvd Fl 7
Los Angeles, CA 90067-6207, USA

Cardoso, Patricia (Director)
c/o Rosalie Swedlin *Anonymous Content (LA)*
3532 Hayden Ave
Culver City, CA 90232-2413, USA

Cardoza, Dennis (Congressman, Politician)
2437 Rayburn Hob
Washington, DC 20515-1010, USA

Care, Peter (Cinematographer, Director, Writer)
Bob Industries
1313 5th St
Santa Monica, CA 90401-1414, USA

Carell, Steve (Actor)
4310 Arcola Ave
Toluca Lake, CA 91602-2904, USA

Carelli, Rick (Race Car Driver)
Chesrow Auto Group
2009 Market St
Denver, CO 80205-2022, USA

Carenard, Brian (Saigon) (Musician)
Abandoned Nation Ent. Inc.
86-110 Orchard St Ste 2
Hackensack, NJ 07601-4833, USA

Caretto-Brown, Patty (Swimmer)
16079 Mesquite Cir
Fountain Valley, CA 92708-1513, USA

Carew, Drew (Actor, Comedian)
Messina Baker Entertainment
955 Carrillo Dr Ste 100
Los Angeles, CA 90048-5400, USA

Carew, Rod (Athlete, Baseball Player)
4271 Vale St
Irvine, CA 92604-2208, USA

Carey, Clare (Actor)
1025 Nowita Pl
Venice, CA 90291-3518, USA

Carey, Danny (Musician)
2174 Canyon Dr
Los Angeles, CA 90068-3609, USA

Carey, Drew (Actor, Comedian)
c/o Rick Messina *Messina Baker Entertainment*
955 Carrillo Dr Ste 100
Los Angeles, CA 90048-5400, USA

Carey, Duane G (Astronaut)
5938 Instone Cir
Colorado Springs, CO 80922-1716, USA

Carey, Duane G Lt Colonel (Astronaut)
5938 Instone Cir
Colorado Springs, CO 80922-1716, USA

Carey, Ezekiel (Music Group)
509 E Ridgecrest Blvd Apt A
Ridgecrest, CA 93555-3959, USA

Carey, Jim (Athlete, Hockey Player)
5351 Hunt Club Way
Sarasota, FL 34238-4011, USA

Carey, Ka'Deem (Athlete, Football Player)
c/o Ken Zuckerman *Priority Sports & Entertainment - (LA)*
15233 Ventura Blvd Ste 718
Sherman Oaks, CA 91403-2237, USA

Carey, Marey (Adult Film Star)
c/o *Pure Play Media*
19800 Nordhoff Pl
Chatsworth, CA 91311-6607, USA

Carey, Mariah (Musician, Songwriter)
3130 Antelo Rd
Los Angeles, CA 90077-1604, USA

Carey, Matthew Thomas (Actor)
c/o Abby Bluestone *Innovative Artists (LA)*
1505 10th St
Santa Monica, CA 90401-2805, USA

Carey, Michelle (Actor)
H David Moss
733 Seward St PH
Los Angeles, CA 90038-3503, USA

Carey, Paul (Athlete, Baseball Player)
5334 Olive Ave
Sarasota, FL 34231-2510, USA

Carey, Peter (Writer)
International Creative Mgmt
40 W 57th St Fl 5
New York, NY 10019-4001, USA

Carey, Rick (Athlete, Swimmer)
119 Rockland Ave
Larchmont, NY 10538-1430, USA

Carey, Vernon (Athlete, Football Player)
5321 Thoroughbred Ln
Southwest Ranches, FL 33330-2408, USA

Cargo, David F (Politician)
9415 Dove Meadow Dr
Dallas, TX 75243-6328, USA

Carhart, Timothy (Actor)
29228 Circle Dr
Agoura Hills, CA 91301-2902, USA

Carillo, Mary (Sportscaster)
822 Boylston St Ste 203
Chestnut Hill, MA 02467-2504, USA

Carimi, Gabe (Athlete, Football Player)
c/o Gary Uberstine *Premier Sports Management*
16133 Ventura Blvd Ste 500
Encino, CA 91436-2402, USA

Cariou, Len (Actor)
c/o Clifford Stevens *Paradigm (NY)*
360 Park Ave S Fl 16
New York, NY 10010-1716, USA

Carkner, Terry (Athlete, Hockey Player)
4 Remington Ln
Malvern, PA 19355-2896, USA

Carl, Harland (Athlete, Football Player)
1419 N Douglas St
Appleton, WI 54914-2517, USA

Carl, Jann (Television Host)
704 Magnolia Ave
Pasadena, CA 91106-3624, USA

Carlei, Carlo (Director, Writer)
c/o Staff Member *Creative Artists Agency (CAA-LA)*
2000 Avenue of the Stars Ste 100
Los Angeles, CA 90067-4705, USA

Carlesimo, PJ (Basketball Coach, Coach, Sportscaster)
1429 Willard Ave W
Seattle, WA 98119-3250, USA

Carlile, Brandi (Musician)
25647 SE 179th St
Maple Valley, WA 98038-7329, USA

Carlin, John (Politician)
1208 Wyndham Heights Dr
Manhattan, KS 66503-8676, USA

Carlin, Thomas R (Publisher)
Saint Paul Pioneer Press
345 Cedar St
Publisher's Office
Saint Paul, MN 55101-1057, USA

Carlin, Vidal (Athlete, Football Player)
930 Palm Ave Apt 417
West Hollywood, CA 90069-4080, USA

Carlino, Lewis John (Director, Writer)
991 Oakmont St
Los Angeles, CA 90049-2228, USA

Carlisie, Rick (Basketball Player)
Boston Celtics
RR 4
Ogdensburg, NY 13669, USA

Carlisle, Belinda (Musician, Songwriter)
c/o Carlos Keyes *Red Entertainment Agency*
505 8th Ave Rm 1004
New York, NY 10018-6529, USA

Carlisle, Cooper (Athlete, Football Player)
1693 SW 188th St
Newberry, FL 32669-4757, USA

Carlisle, Jodi (Actor, Comedian)
c/o Staff Member *ICM Partners (LA)*
10250 Constellation Blvd Fl 7
Los Angeles, CA 90067-6207, USA

Carlisle, Mary (Actor)
517 N Rodeo Dr
Beverly Hills, CA 90210-3206, USA

Carlisle, Rick (Athlete, Basketball Coach, Basketball Player, Coach)
3925 Greenbrier Dr
Dallas, TX 75225-5405, USA

Carlos, Bun (Musician)
6951 Belvidere Rd
Caledonia, IL 61011-9605, USA

Carlos, Emmons (Athlete, Football Player)
435 Verdi Ln
Atlanta, GA 30350-6619, USA

Carlos, Francisco (Cisco) (Athlete,
Baseball Player)
6027 N 7th St
Phoenix, AZ 85014-1802, USA

Carlos, John (Athlete, Olympic Athlete,
Track Athlete)
160 Palisade Point Dr
Ellenwood, GA 30294-4530, USA

Carlos, Jordan (Comedian)
c/o Scott Metzger *Paradigm (NY)*
360 Park Ave S Fl 16
New York, NY 10010-1716, USA

Carlos, Roberto (Musician)
c/o Jorge Pinos *William Morris Endeavor
(LA)*
9601 Wilshire Blvd
Beverly Hills, CA 90210-5213, USA

Carlson, Amy (Actor)
c/o Darris Hatch *Daris Hatch
Management*
10027 Rossbury Pl
Los Angeles, CA 90064-4825, USA

Carlson, Arne H (Ex-Governor)
145 Holly Ln N
Minneapolis, MN 55447-3547, USA

Carlson, Brendyn "Tyce" (Race Car
Driver)
13436 Lorenzo Blvd
Carmel, IN 46074-8274, USA

Carlson, Cody (Athlete, Football Player)
3417 Foothill Ter
Austin, TX 78731-5826, USA

Carlson, Dale (Race Car Driver)
Mike Johnson Racing
1931 4th Ave E
Olympia, WA 98506-4631, USA

Carlson, Dan (Athlete, Baseball Player)
334 N Wickford Cir
Shreveport, LA 71115-2935, USA

Carlson, Dan (Athlete, Baseball Player)
Mobile Baybears 755 Boiling Brothers
Blvd
Attn: Coaching Staff
Mobile, AL 36606, USA

Carlson, Gretchen (Television Host)
c/o Staff Member *Fox News (NY)*
1211 Avenue of the Americas Lowr C1
New York, NY 10036-8705, USA

Carlson, Jack (Athlete, Hockey Player)
18259 Embers Ave
Farmington, MN 55024-9259, USA

Carlson, Jeff (Athlete, Football Player)
17129 Dillard Ct
Lutz, FL 33559-2008, USA

Carlson, Jeff (Athlete, Hockey Player)
2935 Princeton Ct
Muskegon, MI 49441-3764, USA

Carlson, Jesse (Athlete, Baseball Player)
654 High Rd
Berlin, CT 06037-1938, USA

Carlson, John (Athlete, Football Player)
c/o Joe Flanagan *BTI Sports Advisors*
170 N Scoville Ave
Oak Park, IL 60302-2647, USA

Carlson, John (Athlete, Golfer)
c/o Jim Lehrman *SFX Golf*
36855 W Main St Ste 200
Purcellville, VA 20132-3561, USA

Carlson, Karen (Actor)
3700 Ventura Canyon Ave
Sherman Oaks, CA 91423-4709, USA

Carlson, Katrina (Actor)
c/o Staff Member *Sara Bennett Agency*
6404 Hollywood Blvd Ste 316
Los Angeles, CA 90028-6244, USA

Carlson, K C (Cartoonist)
DC Comics
1700 Broadway Fl 6
New York, NY 10019-5905, USA

Carlson, Kelly (Actor)
c/o Margot Klar *Cunningham Escott Slevin
& Doherty (CESD-LA)*
10635 Santa Monica Blvd Ste 130
Los Angeles, CA 90025-8306, USA

Carlson, Kent (Athlete, Hockey Player)
58 Branch Tpke Unit 74
Concord, NH 03301-5777, USA

Carlson, Mark (Athlete, Baseball Player)
359 Tall Oak Trl
Tarpon Springs, FL 34688, USA

Carlson, Paulette (Music Group)
Mark Sonder Music
250 W 57th St Bldg 1830
New York, NY 10107-0001, USA

Carlson, Richard (Writer)
Pennsylvania State Univ
613 Moore Bldg
University Park, PA 16802-3106

Carlson, Steve (Athlete, Hockey Player)
PO Box 3476
Rancho Cordova, CA 95741-3476, USA

Carlson, Steve (Race Car Driver)
539 Brickl Rd
West Salem, WI 54669-1177, USA

Carlson, Stuart (Cartoonist)
Universal Press Syndicate
4520 Main St Ste 340
Kansas City, MO 64111-7705, USA

Carlson, Tucker (Correspondent,
Journalist, Television Host)
c/o Staff Member *Fox News (DC)*
5151 Wisconsin Ave NW Fl 1
Washington, DC 20016-4132, USA

Carlson, Vanessa (Musician)
c/o Kurt Steffek *Razor & Tie*
PO Box 585
New York, NY 10276-0585, USA

Carlson, Veronica (Actor)
7844 Kavanagh Ct
Sarasota, FL 34240-7906, USA

Carlton, Carl (Musician)
Randolph Enterprises
Oakland
Inkster, MI 48141, USA

Carlton, Larry (Musician)
c/o Staff Member *Paradigm (Monterey)*
404 W Franklin St
Monterey, CA 93940-2303, USA

Carlton, Steve (Athlete, Baseball Player)
Game Winner Sports
835 E 2nd Ave Ste 203
Durango, CO 81301-5488, USA

Carlton, Vanessa (Musician)
182 Lafayette St Fl 5
New York, NY 10013-3276, USA

Carlton, Venessa (Music Group)
Peter Malkin Mgmt
410 Park Ave Ste 420
New York, NY 10022-9459, USA

Carlton, Wray (Athlete, Football Player)
29 Pine Ter
Orchard Park, NY 14127-3929, USA

Carlucci, Dave (Athlete, Baseball Player)
580 Pond St
Franklin, MA 02038-2710, USA

Carlucci, Frank (Politician)
Carlyle Group
1001 Pennsylvania Ave NW Ste 220
Washington, DC 20004-2525, USA

Carlucci, Frank C
1001 Pennsylvania Ave NW
Washington, DC 20004-2505, USA

Carlyle, Buddy (Athlete, Baseball Player)
205 Ashmere Ct
Tyrone, GA 30290-2845, USA

Carlyle, Randy (Athlete, Hockey Player)
2695 E Katella Ave
Attn Coaching Staff
Anaheim, CA 92806-5904, USA

Carlyle, Randy (Athlete, Coach, Hockey
Player)
180 S Lakeview Ave
Anaheim, CA 92807-3606, USA

Carlyle, Robert (Actor)
c/o Jon Rubinstein *Authentic Talent and
Literary Management*
20 Jay St Ste M17
Brooklyn, NY 11201-8300, USA

Carmack, Chris (Actor)
c/o Theodore B Gekis *Gekis Management*
4217 Verdugo View Dr
Los Angeles, CA 90065-4317, USA

Carman, Don (Athlete, Baseball Player)
1560 Bluefin Ct
Naples, FL 34102-1576, USA

Carman, Jon (Athlete, Football Player)
13 Nautilus Dr
Barnegat, NJ 08005-1302, USA

Carman, Patrick (Writer)
1247 Studebaker Dr
Walla Walla, WA 99362-8845, USA

Carmazzi, Giovanni (Athlete, Football
Player)
9401 Cook Riolo Rd
Roseville, CA 95747-9221, USA

Carmel, duke (Athlete, Baseball Player)
116 Spring Lake Blvd
Waretown, NJ 08758-2671, USA

Carmen, Eric (Musician, Songwriter)
27020 Cedar Rd PH 7
Beachwood, OH 44122-1135, USA

Carmichael, Al (Athlete, Football Player)
72525 Desert Flower Dr
Palm Desert, CA 92260-6269, USA

Carmichael, Greg (Musician)
Monterey International
200 W Superior St Ste 202
Chicago, IL 60654-6422, USA

Carmichael, Harold (Athlete, Football
Player)
38 Birch Ln
Glassboro, NJ 08028-2821, USA

Carmichael, Jesse (Musician)
8062 Woodrow Wilson Dr
Los Angeles, CA 90046-1117, USA

Carmichael, Paul (Athlete, Football
Player)
550 Orange Ave Unit 335
Long Beach, CA 90802-7011, USA

Carmine, Michael (Cinematographer)
3615 West Dr
Little Neck, NY 11363-1243, USA

Carmine, Robert (Musician)
c/o Staff Member *Geffen Records*
9126 Sunset Blvd
West Hollywood, CA 90069, USA

Carmody, Steve (Athlete, Football Player)
PO Box 119
Jackson, MS 39205-0119, USA

Carmona, Richard H (Government
Official, Misc, Physicist)
Surgeon General's Office
200 Independence Ave SW
Washington, DC 20201-0004, USA

Carn, Jean (Musician)
PO Box 27641
Philadelphia, PA 19118-0641, USA

Carnahan, Joe (Director)
7715 Southcliff Dr
Fair Oaks, CA 95628-7329, USA

Carnahan, Russ (Congressman, Politician)
1710 Longworth Hob
Washington, DC 20515-3206, USA

Carne, Jean (Music Group)
Walt Reeder Productions
PO Box 27641
Philadelphia, PA 19118-0641, USA

Carne, Judy (Actor, Comedian)
2 Horatio St Apt 10N
New York, NY 10014-1632, USA

Carnegie, Dale (Business Person)
Dale Carnegie & Associates, Inc
290 Motor Pkwy
Hauppauge, NY 11788-5177, USA

Carnelly, Ray (Athlete, Football Player)
107 Lone Star Dr
Georgetown, TX 78633-4525, USA

Carner, Joanne (Athlete, Golfer)
3030 S Ocean Blvd Apt 325
Palm Beach, FL 33480-6610, USA

Carnes, Kim (Musician, Songwriter)
1829 Tyne Blvd
Nashville, TN 37215-4701, USA

Carnes, Ryan (Actor)
c/o Jon Simmons *Simmons & Scott
Entertainment*
7942 Mulholland Dr
Los Angeles, CA 90046-1225, USA

Carnesecca, Lou (Basketball Coach,
Coach)
18247 Midland Pkwy
Jamaica, NY 11432-1535, USA

Carnett, Eddie (Athlete, Baseball Player)
RR 1 Box 20C
Ringling, OK 73456-9701, USA

Carnevale, Mark (Athlete, Golfer)
24 Loggerhead Ln
Ponte Vedra Beach, FL 32082-2581, USA

Carney, John (Athlete, Football Player)
2950 Wishbone Way
Encinitas, CA 92024-7235, USA

Carney, Keith (Athlete, Hockey Player,
Olympic Athlete)
8701 N 55th Pl # Pi
Paradise Valley, AZ 85253-2107, USA

Carney, Lester (Athlete, Olympic Athlete, Track Athlete)
978 Seward Ave
Akron, OH 44320-2626, USA

Carney, Patrick (Musician)
4330 Chickering Ln
Nashville, TN 37215-4916, USA

Carney, Reeve (Musician)
c/o Staff Member *Paradigm (Monterey)*
404 W Franklin St
Monterey, CA 93940-2303, USA

Caro, Niki (Director, Writer)
c/o Sophy Holodnik *ICM Partners (LA)*
10250 Constellation Blvd Fl 7
Los Angeles, CA 90067-6207, USA

Caro, Robert A (Writer)
Robert A Caro Assoc
250 W 57th St Ste 2215
New York, NY 10107-2209, USA

Carolan, Brett (Athlete, Football Player)
3218 43rd Ave W
Seattle, WA 98199-2437, USA

Caroline, James C (J C) (Athlete, Football Player)
2501 Stanford Dr
Champaign, IL 61820-7634, USA

Carolla, Adam (Radio Personality, Talk Show Host)
c/o Staff Member *Jackhole Industries*
6834 Hollywood Blvd
Los Angeles, CA 90028-6116, USA

Carollo, Joe (Athlete, Football Player)
4634 Meyer Way
Carmichael, CA 95608-1144, USA

Caron, Alain (Athlete, Hockey Player)
6426 Moorings Point Cir Unit 201
Lakewood Ranch, FL 34202-1204, USA

Caron, Jacques (Athlete, Hockey Player)
11105 Bullrush Ter
Lakewood Ranch, FL 34202-4149

Caron, Jacques (Athlete, Hockey Player)
165 Mulberry St
Attn Special Assignment Coach
Newark, NJ 07102-3607, USA

Caron, Jason (Athlete, Golfer)
150 Silo Ridge Ln
Vilas, NC 28692-3002, USA

Caron, Roger (Athlete, Football Player)
10 Main St
Cheshire, CT 06410-2403, USA

Carothers, Veronica (Actor)
535 N Heatherstone Dr
Orange, CA 92869-2648, USA

Carpenetr, M scott cdr (Astronaut)
PO Box 3161
Vail, CO 81658-3161, USA

Carpenter, Andrew (Athlete, Baseball Player)
1894 SW Mistybrook Dr
Grants Pass, OR 97527-6441, USA

Carpenter, Bob
205 S Princeton Ave
Arlington Heights, IL 60005-1666, USA

Carpenter, Bobby (Athlete, Football Player)
2396 Andover Rd
Columbus, OH 43221-3744, USA

Carpenter, Bobby (Athlete, Hockey Player)
71 Chestnut St
North Reading, MA 01864-2823, USA

Carpenter, Brian (Athlete, Football Player)
42486 Belmont Glen Pl
Ashburn, VA 20148-4318, USA

Carpenter, Bubba (Athlete, Baseball Player)
4601 Saddlebrook Ave
Springdale, AR 72762-0503, USA

Carpenter, Carleton (Actor)
RR 2
Warwick, NY 10990, USA

Carpenter, Chad (Athlete, Football Player)
21311 S 187th Way
Queen Creek, AZ 85142-3668, USA

Carpenter, Charisma (Actor, Model)
c/o Gladys Gonzalez *John Carrabino Management*
5900 Wilshire Blvd Ste 406
Los Angeles, CA 90036-5015, USA

Carpenter, Chris (Athlete, Baseball Player)
84 Colonel Daniels Dr
Bedford, NH 03110-5010, USA

Carpenter, Cris (Athlete, Baseball Player)
1484 Heritage Pl
Gainesville, GA 30501-1249, USA

Carpenter, Dave (Cartoonist)
PO Box 520
Emmetsburg, IA 50536-0520, USA

Carpenter, Ed (Race Car Driver)
Vision Racing
6803 Coffman Rd
Indianapolis, IN 46268-2561, USA

Carpenter, James (Football Player)
c/o Ken Zuckerman *Priority Sports & Entertainment - (LA)*
15233 Ventura Blvd Ste 718
Sherman Oaks, CA 91403-2237, USA

Carpenter, Jennifer (Actor)
c/o Stephanie Ritz *William Morris Endeavor (LA)*
9601 Wilshire Blvd
Beverly Hills, CA 90210-5213, USA

Carpenter, John (Director)
8532 Hollywood Blvd
Los Angeles, CA 90069-1414, USA

Carpenter, Keion (Athlete, Football Player)
2009 Shin Ct
Buford, GA 30519-6808, USA

Carpenter, Kip (Athlete, Olympic Athlete, Speed Skater)
W375S10897 Prairie Ln
Eagle, WI 53119-1742, USA

Carpenter, Marj C (Religious Leader)
Presbyterian Church USA
100 Witherspoon St
Louisville, KY 40202-6300, USA

Carpenter, Mary Chapin (Musician)
6734 Plank Rd
Charlottesville, VA 22903-7536, USA

Carpenter, Richard (Musician, Songwriter, Writer)
960 Country Valley Rd
Westlake Village, CA 91362-5631, USA

Carpenter, Rob (Athlete, Football Player)
1601 Wheeling Rd NE
Lancaster, OH 43130-8706, USA

Carpenter, Ron (Athlete, Football Player)
1181 Chersonese Round
Mount Pleasant, SC 29464-9544, USA

Carpenter, Ron (Athlete, Football Player)
1500 Wade Haven Ct
McKinney, TX 75071-5985, USA

Carpenter, Russell P (Cinematographer)
Gersh Agency
232 N Canon Dr
Beverly Hills, CA 90210-5302, USA

Carpenter, Sabrina (Actor, Musician)
c/o Bill Perlman *Perlman Management Group*
PO Box 2939
Beverly Hills, CA 90213-2939, USA

Carpenter, Teresa (Journalist)
Village Voice
80 Maiden Ln Rm 2105
Editorial Dept
New York, NY 10038-4893, USA

Carpenter, William S (Bill) Jr (Athlete, Football Player)
PO Box 4067
Whitefish, MT 59937-4067, USA

Carpenter, W M (Business Person)
Bausch & Lomb
36 Knollwood Dr
Rochester, NY 14618-3513, USA

Carpenter-Phinney, Connie (Athlete, Cycler, Olympic Athlete)
470 Juniper Ave
Boulder, CO 80304-1716, USA

Carper, Thomas R. (Politician)
600 W Matson Run Pkwy
Wilmington, DE 19802-1911, USA

Carpin, Frank (Athlete, Baseball Player)
4014 Park Ave
Richmond, VA 23221-1120, USA

Carpinello, James (Actor)
3721 Blue Canyon Dr
Studio City, CA 91604-3802, USA

Carr, Antoine (Athlete, Basketball Player)
5724 Croyden Cir
Wichita, KS 67220-3119, USA

Carr, Austin (Athlete, Basketball Player)
4547 Saint Germain Blvd
Cleveland, OH 44128-6205, USA

Carr, Brandon (Athlete, Football Player)
c/o Tom Condon *CAA (St. Louis)*
222 S Central Ave Ste 1008
Saint Louis, MO 63105-3509, USA

Carr, Catherine (Cathy) (Swimmer)
409 10th St
Davis, CA 95616-1941, USA

Carr, Charmian (Actor)
PO Box 260584
Encino, CA 91426-0584, USA

Carr, Chuck (Athlete, Baseball Player)
5419 E Greenway St
Mesa, AZ 85205-4360, USA

Carr, Darleen (Actor)
Abrams Artists
9200 W Sunset Blvd Ste 1125
West Hollywood, CA 90069-3610, USA

Carr, David (Athlete, Football Player)
c/o Jeff Sperbeck *The Novo Agency*
2121 N California Blvd Ste 1025
Walnut Creek, CA 94596-7101, USA

Carr, Edwin (Athlete, Football Player)
1908 Scott Rd
Oreland, PA 19075-1519, USA

Carr, Fred (Athlete, Football Player)
6274 S 17th Pl
Phoenix, AZ 85042-4568, USA

Carr, Gene (Athlete, Hockey Player)
PO Box 57258
Sherman Oaks, CA 91413-2258, USA

Carr, Gerald (Astronaut)
49 Maple St Apt 123
Manchester Center, VT 05255-4485, USA

Carr, Gerald P Colonel (Astronaut)
49 Maple St Apt 123
Manchester Center, VT 05255-4485, USA

Carr, Gregg (Athlete, Football Player)
3009 Canterbury Ln
Mountain Brk, AL 35223-1241, USA

Carr, Henry (Athlete, Football Player)
1612 Pinebrook Dr
Griffin, GA 30224-3957, USA

Carr, Jane (Actor)
6200 Mount Angelus Dr
Los Angeles, CA 90042-3526, USA

Carr, Kenny (Athlete, Basketball Player, Olympic Athlete)
1210 W Adams Blvd Apt 106
Los Angeles, CA 90007-7700, USA

Carr, Levert (Athlete, Football Player)
169 Brookwood Ln W
Bolingbrook, IL 60440-5508, USA

Carr, Lloyd (Coach)
University of Michigan
Athletic Dept
Ann Arbor, MI 48109, USA

Carr, Lydell (Athlete, Football Player)
8330 Flintrock Dr
Frisco, TX 75034-8879, USA

Carr, Michael L (M L) (Athlete, Basketball Player, Coach)
168 Beaver Rd
Weston, MA 02493-1036, USA

Carr, M L (Athlete, Basketball Player)
168 Beaver Rd
Weston, MA 02493-1036, USA

Carr, Nathaniel (Athlete, Olympic Athlete, Wrestler)
9401 Foxburrow Way
Dayton, OH 45458-9623, USA

Carr, Roger D (Athlete, Football Player)
222 Broken Arrow Trl
Petal, MS 39465-8956, USA

Carr, Steve (Director, Producer)
c/o Nicole Chabot *Re: Group*
815 Broadway St Ste 2
Venice, CA 90291-3407, USA

Carr, Vikki (Actor, Musician)
PO Box 780968
San Antonio, TX 78278-0968, USA

Carra, Alexis (Actor)
c/o JC Robbins *JC Robbins Management*
865 S Sherbourne Dr
Los Angeles, CA 90035-1809, USA

Carrabba, Chris (Musician)
403 Stafford Close
Franklin, TN 37069-4361, USA

Carrack, Paul (Musician, Songwriter, Writer)
Firstars Mgmt
14724 Ventura Blvd PH
Sherman Oaks, CA 91403-3513, USA

Carradine, Ever (Actor)
c/o Lainie Sorkin Becky *Management 360*
9111 Wilshire Blvd
Beverly Hills, CA 90210-5508, USA

Carradine, Keith (Actor, Musician, Songwriter)
355 S Grand Ave Ste 1710
Los Angeles, CA 90071-1532, USA

Carradine, Robert (Actor, Director, Producer)
c/o Staff Member *Marshak/Zachary Company, The*
8840 Wilshire Blvd Fl 1
Beverly Hills, CA 90211-2606, USA

Carrasco, Carlos (Actor)
c/o Sandy Oroumieh *Rothman / Andres Entertainment*
4400 Coldwater Canyon Ave Ste 125
Studio City, CA 91604-5040, USA

Carrasco, D J (Athlete, Baseball Player)
1216 W 18th St
Safford, AZ 85546-3564, USA

Carreker, Alphonso (Athlete, Football Player)
5599 Asheforde Ln
Marietta, GA 30068-1851, USA

Carrell, Duane (Athlete, Football Player)
6525 Willow Springs Rd
Springfield, IL 62712-9501, USA

Carrell, John (Athlete, Football Player)
2303 Cliffs Edge Dr
Austin, TX 78733-6031, USA

Carreon, Mark (Athlete, Baseball Player)
413 Ashland Crk
Victoria, TX 77901-3687, USA

Carrera, Asia (Adult Film Star)
c/o Staff Member *Atlas Multimedia Inc*
9005 Eton Ave Ste C
Canoga Park, CA 91304-6533, USA

Carrera, Barbara (Actor)
434 S Canon Dr Apt 502
Beverly Hills, CA 90212-4544, USA

Carrera, Carlos (Director)
c/o Staff Member *Creative Artists Agency (CAA-LA)*
2000 Avenue of the Stars Ste 100
Los Angeles, CA 90067-4705, USA

Carrere, Tia (Actor, Model, Producer)
c/o Kieran Maguire *The Arlook Group*
205 S Beverly Dr Ste 209
Beverly Hills, CA 90212-3899, USA

Carretto, Joseph A
2110 Lakeview Lndg
Corsicana, TX 75109-9658, USA

Carretto, Joseph A Jr (Astronaut)
4534 E 85th St
Tulsa, OK 74137-1918, USA

Carrey, Jim (Actor, Comedian)
PO Box 57593
Sherman Oaks, CA 91413-2593, USA

Carrier, Darel (Athlete, Basketball Player)
4224 Glasgow Rd
Oakland, KY 42159-6836, USA

Carrier, Mark A (Athlete, Football Player)
4115 Highland Park Cir
Lutz, FL 33558-5314, USA

carriere, Larry (Athlete, Hockey Player)
94 Dawnbrook Ln
Buffalo, NY 14221-4932, USA

Carrigan, Sam (Athlete, Baseball Player)
607 Sunrise Ave
Alamogordo, NM 88310-4144, USA

Carril, Pete (Athlete, Basketball Player, Coach)
372 Carter Rd
Princeton, NJ 08540-7422, USA

Carrillo, Cesar (Athlete, Baseball Player)
7801 Lamon Ave
Burbank, IL 60459-1522, USA

Carrillo, Elpidia (Actor)
Bresler Kelly Assoc
11500 W Olympic Blvd Ste 510
Los Angeles, CA 90064-1527, USA

Carrillo, Erick (Actor)
c/o Staff Member *Three Moons Entertainment Inc*
7040F W Sunset Blvd # 206
Los Angeles, CA 90028-7521, USA

Carrington, Alex (Athlete, Football Player)
c/o Roosevelt Barnes *Maximum Sports Management*
6435 W Jefferson Blvd # 197
Fort Wayne, IN 46804-6203, USA

Carrington, Bob (Athlete, Basketball Player)
PO Box 131301
Carlsbad, CA 92013-1301, USA

Carrington, Chuck (Actor)
c/o Kate Edwards *Grand View Management*
578 Washington Blvd # 688
Marina Del Rey, CA 90292-5442, USA

Carrington, Darren (Athlete, Football Player)
14097 Montfort Ct
San Diego, CA 92128-4283, USA

Carrington, Debbie Lee (Actor)
Jonis
8147 Tunney Ave
Reseda, CA 91335-1042, USA

Carrington, Rodney (Musician)
c/o Damion Greiman *727 Management*
727 Scotsman Ln
Franklin, TN 37064, USA

Carrithers, Don (Athlete, Baseball Player)
9367 Sunny Glade Ct
Elk Grove, CA 95758-4208, USA

Carroll, Ahmad (Athlete, Football Player)
1389 Pollard Dr SW
Atlanta, GA 30311-3451, USA

Carroll, Brett (Athlete, Baseball Player)
2267 NW 199th St
Miami Gardens, FL 33056-2600, USA

Carroll, Brian (Buckethead) (Musician)
915C W Foothill Blvd Ste 545
Claremont, CA 91711-3304, USA

Carroll, Bruce (Musician, Songwriter, Writer)
William Morris Agency
2100 W End Ave Ste 1000
Nashville, TN 37203-5240, USA

Carroll, Clay P (Athlete, Baseball Player)
12407 Burroughs Ln
Soddy Daisy, TN 37379-9119, USA

Carroll, Diahann (Actor, Musician)
9255 Doheny Rd Apt 1705
West Hollywood, CA 90069-3222, USA

Carroll, James (Athlete, Football Player)
13880 Stirling Rd
Southwest Ranches, FL 33330-3019, USA

Carroll, Jamey (Athlete, Baseball Player)
2789 Wyndham Way
Melbourne, FL 32940-5971, USA

Carroll, Jay (Athlete, Football Player)
117 Homedale Rd
Hopkins, MN 55343-8519, USA

Carroll, Jim (Athlete, Football Player)
13880 Stirling Rd
Southwest Ranches, FL 33330-3019, USA

Carroll, Joe (Athlete, Football Player)
4541 Fairfield St
Pittsburgh, PA 15201-2031, USA

Carroll, Joe Barry (Athlete, Basketball Player)
5220 Cascade Rd SW
Atlanta, GA 30331-7358, USA

Carroll, Julian (Politician)
413 Shelby St
Frankfort, KY 40601-2821, USA

Carroll, Leo (Athlete, Football Player)
34448 Agua Dulce Canyon Rd
Santa Clarita, CA 91390-4668, USA

Carroll, Lester (Les) (Cartoonist)
1715 Ivyhill Loop N
Columbus, OH 43229-5223, USA

Carroll, Madeline (Actor)
c/o Susan Curtis *Curtis Talent Management*
9607 Arby Dr
Beverly Hills, CA 90210-1202, USA

Carroll, Matt (Athlete, Basketball Player)
300 W 5th St Apt 604
Charlotte, NC 28202-1647, USA

Carroll, Pat (Actor)
c/o Gabrielle Allabashi *Ellis Talent Group*
4705 Laurel Canyon Blvd Ste 300
Valley Village, CA 91607-5901, USA

Carroll, Pete (Athlete, Football Player)
0 Openbrand Rd
Rolling Hills, CA 90274-5202, USA

Carroll, Rocky (Actor)
c/o Erik Kritzer *LINK Entertainment*
11872 La Grange Ave
Los Angeles, CA 90025-5282, USA

Carroll, Ron (Ronnie) (Athlete, Football Player)
7665 County Road 112
Van Vleck, TX 77482-2011, USA

Carroll, Sonny (Athlete, Baseball Player)
3311 Lawson St
Richmond, VA 23224-1853, USA

Carroll, Tom (Athlete, Baseball Player)
38572 Pheasant Hill Ln
Hamilton, VA 20158-3302, USA

Carroll, Tom (Tommy) (Athlete, Baseball Player)
304 Sonnet Ct
Peachtree City, GA 30269-3357, USA

Carroll, Wesley (Athlete, Football Player)
13435 SW 119th St
Miami, FL 33186-4513, USA

Carroll, Willard (Director, Producer, Writer)
c/o Staff Member *Hyperion Pictures*
111 N Maryland Ave # 300
Glendale, CA 91206-4238, USA

Carruth, Paul (Athlete, Football Player)
373 Brentwood Ave
Trussville, AL 35173-1103, USA

Carruth, Rae (Athlete, Football Player)
12653 Tucker Crossing Ln
Charlotte, NC 28273-4746, USA

Carruthers, Dwight (Athlete, Hockey Player)
9513 W Nelson Dr
Nine Mile Falls, WA 99026-9620, USA

Carruthers, Garrey E (Politician)
1 Mansion Dr
Santa Fe, NM 87501-6904, USA

Carruthers, James H (Red) (Skier)
8 Malone Ave
Garnerville, NY 10923-1812, USA

Carruthers, Peter (Athlete, Figure Skater, Olympic Athlete)
239 Via Monterey
Newbury Park, CA 91320-6824, USA

Carsey, Marcia (Producer)
27834 Pacific Coast Hwy
Malibu, CA 90265-4342, USA

Carsey, Marcy (Producer)
c/o Staff Member *Carsey-Werner-Mandabach*
16027 Ventura Blvd Ste 600
Encino, CA 91436-2798, USA

Carson, Andre (Congressman, Politician)
425 Cannon Hob
Washington, DC 20515-2301, USA

Carson, Benjamin S (Doctor)
Johns Hopkins University
Medical Center
Baltimore, MD 21218, USA

Carson, Carlos A (Athlete, Football Player)
4747 W 150th Ter
Overland Park, KS 66224-3410, USA

Carson, Crystal (Actor)
6725 McLennan Ave
Van Nuys, CA 91406-5542, USA

Carson, David (Director)
c/o Chris Simonian *Creative Artists Agency (CAA-LA)*
2000 Avenue of the Stars Ste 100
Los Angeles, CA 90067-4705, USA

Carson, Harold (Athlete, Football Player)
Harry Carson Inc
PO Box 852
Westwood, NJ 07675-0852, USA

Carson, Hunter (Actor)
c/o Staff Member *Elkins Entertainment*
8306 Wilshire Blvd Ste 438
Beverly Hills, CA 90211-2304, USA

Carson, James (Jimmy) (Athlete, Hockey Player)
1154 Ridgeway Dr
Rochester, MI 48307-1771, USA

Carson, Jeff (Musician)
2008 Clifton Johnston Ct
Nolensville, TN 37135-9606, USA

Carson, Leonardo (Athlete, Football Player)
7373 Valley View Ln Apt 2089
Dallas, TX 75240-5588

Carson, Lisa Nicole (Actor)
c/o Scott Zimmerman *Evolution Entertainment (LA)*
901 N Highland Ave
Los Angeles, CA 90038-2412, USA

Carson, Malcolm (Athlete, Football Player)
PO Box 11847
Birmingham, AL 35202-1847, USA

Carson, Matt (Athlete, Baseball Player)
33352 Madera De Playa
Temecula, CA 92592-9289, USA

Carson, Rachelle (Actor)
c/o Staff Member *JC Robbins Management*
865 S Sherbourne Dr
Los Angeles, CA 90035-1809, USA

Carson, T C
1505 10th St
Santa Monica, CA 90401-2805, USA

Carstens, Jordan (Athlete, Football Player)
2487 140th St
Bagley, IA 50026-8558, USA

Carswell, Dwayne (Athlete, Football Player)
8202 Abbeyfield Dr
Jacksonville, FL 32277-0966, USA

Carswell, Robert (Athlete, Football Player)
5906 Heritage Walk
Lithonia, GA 30058-3896, USA

Cartagena, Victoria (Actor)
c/o Larry Taube *Principal Entertainment (LA)*
9255 W Sunset Blvd Ste 500
West Hollywood, CA 90069-3301, USA

Carter, Aaron (Actor, Musician)
c/o Roger Paul *Headline Talent*
1650 Broadway Ste 304
New York, NY 10019-6952, USA

Carter, Allen (Athlete, Football Player)
13133 Le Parc Unit 609
Chino Hills, CA 91709-4025, USA

Carter, Andy (Athlete, Baseball Player)
106 Montgomery Ave
Glenside, PA 19038-8228, USA

Carter, Anson (Athlete, Hockey Player)
820 Haven Oaks Ct NE
Atlanta, GA 30342-4348, USA

Carter, Anthony (Athlete, Basketball Player)
15250 E Caley Ave
Centennial, CO 80016-1058, USA

Carter, Anthony (Athlete, Football Player)
4314 Danielson Dr
Lake Worth, FL 33467-3628, USA

Carter, Antonio (Athlete, Football Player)
7839 Maple Grove Dr
Lewis Center, OH 43035-9350, USA

Carter, Bernard (Athlete, Football Player)
261 Pinestraw Cir
Altamonte Springs, FL 32714-5416, USA

Carter, Betsy (Musician)
7561 Brush Lake Rd
North Lewisburg, OH 43060-9649

Carter, Bruce (Athlete, Football Player)
c/o Carl Carey *Champion Pro Consulting Group*
3547 Ruth St
Houston, TX 77004-5515, USA

Carter, Carl (Athlete, Football Player)
3256 Centennial Rd
Forest Hill, TX 76119-7103, USA

Carter, Carl (Athlete, Football Player)
7568 Kings Trl
Fort Worth, TX 76133-8346, USA

Carter, Cheryl (Actor)
CunninghamEscottDipene
10635 Santa Monica Blvd Ste 130
Los Angeles, CA 90025-8306, USA

Carter, Chris (Athlete, Football Player)
606 American Falls Dr
Rio Vista, CA 94571-2205, USA

Carter, Chris (Producer)
566 Picacho Ln
Santa Barbara, CA 93108-1223, USA

Carter, Clarence (Athlete, Basketball Player)
300 Love St SW
Atlanta, GA 30315-1048, USA

Carter, Clarence (Musician)
Rodgers Redding
1048 Tattnall St
Macon, GA 31201-1537, USA

Carter, Cris (Athlete, Football Player)
2493 NW 46th St
Boca Raton, FL 33431-8432, USA

Carter, Darren (Comedian)
c/o Staff Member *AKA Talent Agency*
6310 San Vicente Blvd Ste 200
Los Angeles, CA 90048-5488, USA

Carter, David (Athlete, Football Player)
2401 Long Reach Dr
Sugar Land, TX 77478-4127, USA

Carter, Deana (Musician, Songwriter)
12251 Huston St
Valley Vlg, CA 91607-3616, USA

Carter, Deanna (Actor, Musician)
c/o John Huie *Creative Artists Agency (CAA-TN)*
401 Commerce St PH
Nashville, TN 37219-2516, USA

Carter, Dexter A (Athlete, Football Player)
13715 Richmond Park Dr N Unit 1205
Jacksonville, FL 32224-0241, USA

Carter, Dr Jay (Writer)
PO Box 6048
Reading, PA 19610-0048, USA

Carter, Duane (Pancho) (Race Car Driver)
32 Forest
Brownsburg, IN 46112, USA

Carter, Dyshod (Athlete, Football Player)
916 W Carter Rd
Phoenix, AZ 85041-6750, USA

Carter, Finn (Actor)
c/o Craig Dorfman *Frontline Management*
5670 Wilshire Blvd Ste 1370
Los Angeles, CA 90036-5679, USA

Carter, Fred (Athlete, Basketball Player)
2617 Dekalb Pike
Norristown, PA 19401-1845, USA

Carter, Frederick J (Fred) (Baseball Player, Coach)
5070 Parkside Ave # 3500
Philadelphia, PA 19131-4747, USA

Carter, Gerald (Athlete, Football Player)
3917 Cheshire Ct
Bryan, TX 77802-4905, USA

Carter, Graydon (Writer)
Vanity Fair Magazine
4 Times Sq Bsmt C1B
Basement C1B
New York, NY 10036-6562, USA

Carter, Hodding (Journalist)
1643 Brickell Ave Apt 3604
Miami, FL 33129-1297, USA

Carter, Howard (Athlete, Basketball Player)
8026 Jefferson Hwy Apt 112
Baton Rouge, LA 70809-1661, USA

Carter, Jack (Actor, Comedian)
1023 Chevy Chase Dr
Beverly Hills, CA 90210-2707, USA

Carter, Jake (Athlete, Basketball Player)
4632 Country Creek Dr Apt 1220
Dallas, TX 75236-1253, USA

Carter, Jay (Musician)
Brothers Mgmt
141 Dunbar Ave
Fords, NJ 08863-1551, USA

Carter, Jeff (Athlete, Baseball Player)
4625 River Overlook Dr
Valrico, FL 33596-7878, USA

Carter, Jim (Athlete, Football Player)
1500 Morning Glory Ln
Wausau, WI 54401-7686, USA

Carter, Jim (Athlete, Golfer)
12575 N 130th Way
Scottsdale, AZ 85259-3542, USA

Carter, Jimmy (Politician)
The Carter Center
453 Freedom Pkwy NE
Atlanta, GA 30307-1406, USA

Carter, Jodie (Athlete, Football Player)
5921 Timberview Rd
Little Rock, AR 72204-8559, USA

Carter, Joe (Athlete, Baseball Player)
3000 W 117th St
Leawood, KS 66211-2923, USA

Carter, John (Athlete, Hockey Player)
27 Country Ln
Sharon, MA 02067-2339, USA

Carter, John (Musician)
Resort Attractions
2375 E Tropicana Ave # 304
Las Vegas, NV 89119-6564, USA

Carter, Kent (Athlete, Football Player)
18657 Klum Pl
Rowland Heights, CA 91748-4851, USA

Carter, Kevin (Athlete, Football Player)
1070 Vaughn Crest Dr
Franklin, TN 37069-7211, USA

Carter, Kevin (Athlete, Football Player)
17111 Journeys End Dr
Odessa, FL 33556-2442, USA

Carter, Ki-Jana (Athlete, Football Player)
9721 NW 18th Pl
Plantation, FL 33322-5682, USA

Carter, Lance (Athlete, Baseball Player)
213 172nd St E
Bradenton, FL 34212-3072, USA

Carter, Larry (Athlete, Baseball Player)
4305 Wilmette Dr
Denton, TX 76208-4823, USA

Carter, Louis (Athlete, Football Player)
8209 Swamp Rose Pl
Laurel, MD 20724-1963, USA

Carter, Lynda (Actor)
9200 Harrington Dr
Potomac, MD 20854-4507, USA

Carter, Marty (Athlete, Football Player)
1397 Waterford Green Dr
Marietta, GA 30068-2927, USA

Carter, Mel (Musician)
Cape Entertainment
1161 NW 76th Ave
Plantation, FL 33322-5120, USA

Carter, Michael D (Athlete, Football Player)
901 Red Oak Creek Dr
Red Oak, TX 75154-3615, USA

Carter, Mike (Athlete, Football Player)
10705 Celeo St
San Jose, CA 95127-2706, USA

Carter, Mike (Baseball Player)
Atlanta Braves
12215 Magnolia Crescent Dr Apt D
Roswell, GA 30075-5568, USA

Carter, M L (Athlete, Football Player)
PO Box 1971
Seaside, CA 93955-1971, USA

Carter, M L (Athlete, Football Player)
1765 Napa St
Seaside, CA 93955-4018, USA

Carter, Nick (Musician, Songwriter)
1577 Championship Blvd
Franklin, TN 37064-8668, USA

Carter, Pat (Athlete, Football Player)
11321 Cambray Creek Loop
Riverview, FL 33579-3920, USA

Carter, Paula (Bowler)
10331 SW 102nd Ave
Miami, FL 33176-3507, USA

Carter, Perry (Athlete, Football Player)
15719 Sweeney Park Ln
Houston, TX 77084-2281, USA

Carter, Quinton (Athlete, Football Player)
c/o Kelli Masters *Kelli Masters Management*
100 N Broadway Ste 1700
Oklahoma City, OK 73102-9211, USA

Carter, Rodney (Athlete, Football Player)
4490 Jasmine Dr
Bethlehem, PA 18020-8840, USA

Carter, Rosalynn (Politician)
Carter Center
The Carter Center 453 Freedom Pkwy NE
Atlanta, GA 30307, USA

Carter, Rubin (Athlete, Coach, Football Player)
1793 Vineyard Way
Tallahassee, FL 32317-7915, USA

Carter, Rublin (Athlete, Football Player)
1793 Vineyard Way
Tallahassee, FL 32317-7915, USA

Carter, Russell (Athlete, Football Player)
216 Lilac Ln
Douglassville, PA 19518-1121, USA

Carter, Sarah (Actor)
c/o Darren Goldberg *Global Creative*
1051 Cole Ave # B
Los Angeles, CA 90038-2601, USA

Carter, Steve (Athlete, Baseball Player)
13006 Innisbrook Dr
Beltsville, MD 20705-1196, USA

Carter, Terry (Actor)
244 Madison Ave # 332
New York, NY 10016-2817, USA

Carter, Thomas (Director)
140 N Tigertail Rd
Los Angeles, CA 90049-2706, USA

Carter, Tim (Athlete, Football Player)
4860 26th Ct S
Saint Petersburg, FL 33712-4322, USA

Carter, Tom (Athlete, Football Player)
4548 Bristol Ln
Cincinnati, OH 45229-1214, USA

Carter, Tom (Athlete, Golfer)
3787 County Line Rd
Quakertown, PA 18951-2085, USA

Carter, Tony (Athlete, Football Player)
c/o Sean Kiernan *Impact Sports - LA*
11331 Ventura Blvd Ste 1A
Studio City, CA 91604-3147, USA

Carter, Travis (Race Car Driver)
Carter Motorsports
2668 Peachtree Rd
Statesville, NC 28625-8252, USA

Carter, Vince (Athlete, Basketball Player)
PO Box 9596
Daytona Beach, FL 32120-9596, USA

Carter, Virgil (Athlete, Football Player)
PO Box 9
Helendale, CA 92342-0009, USA

Carter III, W Hodding (Government
Official)
214 N Columbus St
Alexandria, VA 22314-2412, USA

Carteris, Gabrielle (Actor)
4019 Longridge Ave
Sherman Oaks, CA 91423-4925, USA

Carter's Chord (Music Group)
c/o Staff Member *Paradigm (Monterey)*
404 W Franklin St
Monterey, CA 93940-2303, USA

Carthen, Jason (Athlete, Football Player)
10310 Townley Ct
Aurora, OH 44202-8147, USA

Carthon, Maurice (Athlete, Football
Player)
4515 Walnut St Apt 414B
Kansas City, MO 64111-7738, USA

Carthy, Eliza (Musician)
c/o Staff Member *The Agency Group
(NYC)*
142 W 57th St Fl 6
New York, NY 10019-3300, USA

Cartwright, Angela (Actor)
4330 Bakman Ave
N Hollywood, CA 91602-2629, USA

Cartwright, Bill (Athlete, Basketball
Player)
1839 Wedgewood Ct
Lake Forest, IL 60045-3705, USA

Cartwright, Catherine (Athlete, Golfer)
28382 Tasca Dr
Bonita Springs, FL 34135-6840, USA

Cartwright, Nancy (Actor)
The Nancy Show
9420 Reseda Blvd # 572
Northridge, CA 91324-2932, USA

Cartwright, Rock (Athlete, Football
Player)
231 Interstate 45 N Apt 21115
Conroe, TX 77304-2326, USA

Cartwright, Ryan (Actor)
c/o Susan Calogerakis *SC Management*
9250 Wilshire Blvd
Ground Fl
Beverly Hills, CA 90212-3352, USA

Cartwright, Veronica (Actor)
c/o Mitch Clem *Shadow Entertainment*
655 N Central Ave Fl 17
Glendale, CA 91203-1439, USA

Carty, Jay (Athlete, Basketball Player)
5425 Lower Honoapiilani Rd
Lahaina, HI 96761-8766, USA

Carty, Johndale (Athlete, Football Player)
PO Box 552076
Opa Locka, FL 33055-0076, USA

Caruso, David (Actor)
4134 Murietta Ave
Sherman Oaks, CA 91423-4223, USA

Caruso, D.J. (Director)
c/o Geyer Kosinski *Media Talent Group*
9200 W Sunset Blvd Ste 550
West Hollywood, CA 90069-3611, USA

Caruso, Mike (Athlete, Baseball Player)
6305 NW 73rd Ave
Tamarac, FL 33321-5508, USA

Carver, Brent (Actor, Musician)
Live Entertainment
1500 Broadway Ste 902
New York, NY 10036-4055, USA

Carver, Dale (Athlete, Football Player)
1745 Golfview Dr
Titusville, FL 32780-3946, USA

Carver, Dana (Actor, Comedian)
775 E Blithedale Ave # 501
Mill Valley, CA 94941-1554, USA

Carver, Jeremy (Producer)
2004 La Brea Ter
Los Angeles, CA 90046-2314, USA

Carver, Johnny (Musician)
House of Talent
9 Lucy Ln
Sherwood, AR 72120-3612, USA

Carver, Melvin (Mel) (Athlete, Football
Player)
10840 Breaking Rocks Dr
Lithia, FL 33547, USA

Carver, Randall (Actor)
Tyler Kjar
5144 Vineland Ave
North Hollywood, CA 91601-3849, USA

Carver, Shante (Athlete, Football Player)
7360 W Ellis St
Laveen, AZ 85339-2623, USA

Carvey, Dana (Actor)
1 Roosevelt Ave
Mill Valley, CA 94941-1127, USA

Carvilie, C James Jr (Politician)
209 Pennsylvania Ave SE # 800
Washington, DC 20003-1107, USA

Carville, James (Journalist)
1711 Palmer Ave
New Orleans, LA 70118-6115, USA

Carville, James (Television Host)
424 S Washington St Ste 2
Alexandria, VA 22314-4153, USA

Cary, Chuck (Athlete, Baseball Player)
11618 SE Masa Ln
Happy Valley, OR 97086-6475, USA

Cary, Diane (Baby Peggy) Serra (Actor)
738 5th Ave
Gustine, CA 95322-1537, USA

Cary, Duane G (Astronaut)
5938 Instone Cir
Colorado Springs, CO 80922-1716, USA

Cary, W Sterling (Religious Leader)
2344 Vardon Ln
Flossmoor, IL 60422-1363, USA

Cary Brothers (Music Group)
c/o Staff Member *Paradigm (Monterey)*
404 W Franklin St
Monterey, CA 93940-2303, USA

casa, Joseh
11134 Speedway Dr
Shelby Township, MI 48317-3546, USA

Casablancas, Julian (Musician, Songwriter)
c/o Staff Member *Wiz Kid Management*
123 E 7th St
New York, NY 10009-5747, USA

Casados, Eloy (Actor)
c/o Michelle Gordon *Michelle Gordon &
Assoc*
260 S Beverly Dr Ste 308
Beverly Hills, CA 90212-3814, USA

Casady, Jack (Musician)
Ron Rainey Mgmt
315 S Beverly Dr Ste 407
Beverly Hills, CA 90212-4301, USA

Casale, Gerald (Musician)
7960 Fareholm Dr
Los Angeles, CA 90046-2113, USA

Casale, Jerry (Athlete, Baseball Player)
600 County Ave Apt 408
Secaucus, NJ 07094-2610, USA

Casali, Kim (Cartoonist)
Times-Mirror Syndicate
Times-Mirror Square
Los Angeles, CA 90053, USA

Casals, Rosemary (Rosie) (Athlete, Tennis
Player)
c/o Staff Member *Women's Tennis
Association (WTA (US))*
1 Progress Plz Ste 1500
St Petersburg, FL 33701-4335, USA

Casanega, Ken (Athlete, Football Player)
480 Donald Dr
Hollister, CA 95023-6364, USA

Casanova, Paul (Athlete, Baseball Player)
5370 NW 183rd St
Miami Gardens, FL 33055-2304, USA

Casanova, Raul (Athlete, Baseball Player)
1441 Ortiz Ave
Fort Myers, FL 33905-4903, USA

Casanova, Thomas H (Tommy) (Athlete,
Football Player)
345 Casanova Rd
Crowley, LA 70526-0504, USA

Casares, Ricardo (Rick) (Athlete, Football
Player)
4107 Starfish Ln
Tampa, FL 33615-5428, USA

Cascadden, Chad (Athlete, Football
Player)
2611 Winsor Dr
Eau Claire, WI 54703-1778, USA

Cascio, Frank (Writer)
c/o Staff Member *HarperCollins Publishers*
195 Broadway Fl 2
Cellar 1
New York, NY 10007-3132, USA

Case, John (Writer)
Random House
1745 Broadway Frnt 3 # B1
New York, NY 10019-4343, USA

Case, J Scott (Athlete, Football Player)
4930 Price Dr
Suwanee, GA 30024-4186, USA

Case, Ronald (Ron) (Athlete, Football
Player)
6960 Driskell Cir
Cumming, GA 30041-4714, USA

Case, Sharon (Actor)
265 S Linden Dr
Beverly Hills, CA 90212-3704, USA

Case, Steve (Business Person)
700 Chain Bridge Rd
Mc Lean, VA 22101-1812, USA

Case, Stoney (Athlete, Football Player)
4824 Travis Oaks Dr
Marble Falls, TX 78654-3347, USA

case, Walter (Horse Racer)
8795 Crow Dr
Macedonia, OH 44056-1647, USA

Case Jr, Walter (Race Car Driver)
142 Summer St
Lisbon Falls, ME 04252-9732, USA

Casel, Nitanju Bolade (Musician)
Sweet Honey Agency
PO Box 600099
Newtonville, MA 02460-0001, USA

Casella, Max (Actor)
c/o Marcia Hurwitz *Innovative Artists (LA)*
1505 10th St
Santa Monica, CA 90401-2805, USA

Casey, Bernie (Athlete, Football Player)
6145 Flight Ave
Los Angeles, CA 90056-1509, USA

Casey, Dillon (Actor)
c/o Tim Taylor *Luber Roklin Management*
5815 W Sunset Blvd Ste 206
Los Angeles, CA 90028-6481, USA

Casey, Dwane (Basketball Coach)
c/o Warren LeGarie *Warren LeGarie
Sports Management*
1108 Masonic Ave
San Francisco, CA 94117-2915, USA

Casey, Harry Wayne (Musician)
7530 Loch Ness Dr
Miami Lakes, FL 33014-6014, USA

Casey, John D (Writer)
University of Virginia
English Dept
Charlottesville, VA 22903, USA

Casey, Jon (Athlete, Hockey Player)
651 Bluffs View Ct
Eureka, MO 63025-3727, USA

Casey, Lawrence P. (Actor)
4139 Vanetta Pl
Studio City, CA 91604-2342, USA

Casey, Lee
Paul Kohner Agency Inc
9300 Wilshire Blvd Ste 555
Beverly Hills, CA 90212-3211

Casey, Paul (Athlete, Golfer)
29167 N 108th St
Scottsdale, AZ 85262-4665, USA

Casey, Peter (Director)
Jim Preminger Agency
450 N Roxbury Dr Ste 1050
Beverly Hills, CA 90210-4235, USA

Casey, Sean (Athlete, Baseball Player)
40 Hartz Way Ste 10
Attn: on Air Personality
Secaucus, NJ 07094-2403, USA

Casey, Sean (Athlete, Baseball Player)
271 Trotwood Dr
Pittsburgh, PA 15241-2244, USA

Casey Donahew Band, The (Music Group, Musician)
c/o Staff Member William Morris Endeavor (Nashville)
1600 Division St Ste 300
Nashville, TN 37203-2755, USA

Casey Jr, Robert P. (Senator)
393 Russell Senate Office Building
Washington, DC 20510-0001, USA

Cash, Antoine (Athlete, Football Player)
5914 Trevors Way
Tampa, FL 33625-3308, USA

Cash, Cornelius (Athlete, Basketball Player)
1661 Miami Chapel Rd
Dayton, OH 45417-4527, USA

Cash, Dave (Athlete, Baseball Player)
16308 Birkdale Dr
Odessa, FL 33556-2802, USA

Cash, Keith (Athlete, Football Player)
1600 NW 54th Ter
Kansas City, MO 64118-3200, USA

Cash, Kerry (Athlete, Football Player)
1414 Gator Creek Dr
Cedar Park, TX 78613-1442, USA

Cash, Kevin (Athlete, Baseball Player)
32256 Woodfield Dr
Avon Lake, OH 44012-2556, USA

Cash, Rick (Athlete, Football Player)
203 E Benton St
Savannah, MO 64485-1720, USA

Cash, Rosanne (Musician, Songwriter)
c/o Mike Leahy Concerted Efforts
PO Box 440326
Somerville, MA 02144-0004, USA

Cash, Roseanne (Musician)
1309 Boscobel St
Nashville, TN 37206-2917, USA

Cash, Sam (Athlete, Basketball Player)
25825 Karisa Cir
Moreno Valley, CA 92551-1968, USA

Cash, Swin (Basketball Player)
Detroit Shock
2 Championship Dr
Palace
Auburn Hills, MI 48326-1753, USA

Cash, Tommy (Musician, Songwriter, Writer)
PO Box 1230
Hendersonville, TN 37077-1230, USA

Cashion, Red (Athlete, Football Player)
PO Box 3889
Bryan, TX 77805-3889, USA

Cashman, Brian (Commentator)
40 Peach Hill Rd
Darien, CT 06820-2821, USA

Cashman, Terry (Musician)
15 Engle St
Englewood, NJ 07631-2936, USA

Cashman, Wayne (Athlete, Hockey Player)
5150 NW 80th Avenue Rd
Ocala, FL 34482-2028, USA

Cashner, Andrew (Athlete, Baseball Player)
104 Lyndsey Dr
Montgomery, TX 77316-6824, USA

Casian, Larry (Athlete, Baseball Player)
817 Limelight Ave NW
Salem, OR 97304-3291, USA

Casillas, Tony (Athlete, Football Player)
6201 Bay Valley Ct
Flower Mound, TX 75022-5573, USA

Caskey, Craig (Athlete, Baseball Player)
17422 Palomino Dr
Bothell, WA 98012-6419, USA

Casnoff, Philip (Actor)
216 S Plymouth Blvd
Los Angeles, CA 90004-3814, USA

Cason, Antoine (Athlete, Football Player)
c/o Drew Rosenhaus Rosenhaus Sports Representation
6400 Allison Rd
Miami Beach, FL 33141-4540, USA

Cason, Aveion (Athlete, Football Player)
4416 Ashbury Ln
Mansfield, TX 76063-6702, USA

Caspary, Tina (Actor)
11350 Ventura Blvd Ste 206
Studio City, CA 91604-3140, USA

Casper, Billy (Athlete, Golfer)
2561 Stonebury Loop Rd
Springville, UT 84663-3937, USA

Casper, Colonel John H (Astronaut)
4414 Village Corner Dr
Houston, TX 77059-4025, USA

Casper, David J (Dave) (Athlete, Football Player)
11390 Kingsborough Trl
Cottage Grove, MN 55016-4664, USA

Casper, John H (Astronaut)
4414 Village Corner Dr
Houston, TX 77059-4025, USA

Casper, Robert (Actor)
CunninghamEscottDipene
10635 Santa Monica Blvd Ste 130
Los Angeles, CA 90025-8306, USA

Cass, Christopher (Actor)
Halpern Assoc
PO Box 5597
Santa Monica, CA 90409-5597, USA

Cassaday, Leann (Athlete, Golfer)
542 Orpheus Ave
Encinitas, CA 92024-2660, USA

Cassady, Craig (Athlete, Football Player)
3840 Lacon Rd Ste 15
Hilliard, OH 43026-1255, USA

Cassady, Howard (Hopalong) (Athlete, Football Player, Heisman Trophy Winner)
PO Box 7828
Talis Sports Management
Columbus, OH 43207-0828, USA

Cassar, Jon (Producer)
c/o Jeff Benson Paradigm (LA)
360 N Crescent Dr
North Bldg
Beverly Hills, CA 90210-4874, USA

Cassara, Frank (Athlete, Football Player)
834 Perla Ct
San Jacinto, CA 92583-6822, USA

Cassata, Rick (Athlete, Football Player)
133 Burch Ave
Buffalo, NY 14210-2638, USA

Cassatt, Chris (Cartoonist)
PO Box 6334
Snowmass Village, CO 81615-6334, USA

Cassaveters, Nick (Actor, Director)
22223 Buena Ventura St
Woodland Hills, CA 91364-5007, USA

Cassavetes, Nick (Actor, Director, Writer)
2067 Hercules Dr
Los Angeles, CA 90046-2014, USA

Cassel, Jack (Athlete, Baseball Player)
723 Palisades Beach Rd Unit 324
Santa Monica, CA 90402-2650, USA

Cassel, Matt (Athlete, Football Player)
150 Street of Dreams
Village Of Loch Lloyd, MO 64012-4179, USA

Cassel, Seymour (Actor)
c/o Harry Abrams Abrams Artists Agency (LA)
9200 W Sunset Blvd PH 11
West Hollywood, CA 90069-3601, USA

Cassel, Vincent (Actor)
c/o Staff Member United Talent Agency (UTA-LA)
9336 Civic Center Dr
Beverly Hills, CA 90210-3604, USA

Cassell, Sam (Athlete, Basketball Player)
5205 N Charles St
Baltimore, MD 21210-2042, USA

Cassels, Andrew (Athlete, Hockey Player)
8614 Tartan Fields Dr
Dublin, OH 43017-8773, USA

Cassese, Tom (Athlete, Football Player)
80 Van Buren St
Port Jefferson Station, NY 11776-3173, USA

Casseus, Gabriel (Actor)
c/o Dan Baron Agency for the Performing Arts (APA-LA)
405 S Beverly Dr Ste 500
Beverly Hills, CA 90212-4425, USA

Cassevah, Bobby (Athlete, Baseball Player)
11095 Chippewa Way
Pensacola, FL 32534-9755, USA

Cassidy (Musician)
c/o Staff Member J Records (Division of BMG Entertainment)
745 5th Ave Fl 6
New York, NY 10151-0099, USA

Cassidy, Bill (Congressman, Politician)
1535 Longworth Hob
Washington, DC 20515-1410, USA

Cassidy, Bruce
174 Irving Ave
Providence, RI 02906-5407, usa

Cassidy, Christopher (Astronaut)
1207 Spring Cress Ln
Seabrook, TX 77586-4721, USA

Cassidy, David (Actor, Musician, Producer)
DBC, INC.
1536 W 25th St PMB 233
San Pedro, CA 90732-4415, USA

Cassidy, Elaine (Actor)
c/o Staff Member ICM Partners (LA)
10250 Constellation Blvd Fl 7
Los Angeles, CA 90067-6207, USA

Cassidy, Joanna (Actor)
c/o Bette Smith Bette Smith Management
499 N Canon Dr
Beverly Hills, CA 90210-4887, USA

Cassidy, Katie (Actor)
c/o Doreen Wilcox Little Anonymous Content (LA)
3532 Hayden Ave
Culver City, CA 90232-2413, USA

Cassidy, Michael (Actor)
c/o Vic Ramos Vic Ramos Management
337 E 13th St Apt 6
New York, NY 10003-5852, USA

Cassidy, Patrick (Actor)
Innovative Artists
1505 10th St
Santa Monica, CA 90401-2805, USA

Cassidy, Ron (Athlete, Football Player)
2214 W 171st St
Torrance, CA 90504-2925, USA

Cassidy, Scott (Athlete, Baseball Player)
1006 4th St
Liverpool, NY 13088-4407, USA

Cassidy, Shaun (Actor, Musician)
Shaun Cassidy Productions
8530 Wilshire Blvd Ste 200
Beverly Hills, CA 90211-3130, USA

Cassivi, Frederic (Athlete, Hockey Player)
7521 Clover Lee Blvd
Harrisburg, PA 17112-8945, USA

Cassolato, Tony (Athlete, Hockey Player)
576 Camino El Dorado
Encinitas, CA 92024-3820, USA

Casson, Mel (Cartoonist)
c/o Staff Member King Features Syndication
300 W 57th St Fl 15
New York, NY 10019-5238, USA

Cast, PC (Writer)
c/o Sean T. Daily Hotchkiss & Associates
15 1st St Apt 9
Stamford, CT 06905-5127, USA

Cast, Tricia (Actor)
1346 Pond Creek Rd
Ashland City, TN 37015-5517, USA

Casta, Laetitia (Actor)
c/o Staff Member IMG Models (NY)
304 Park Ave S Fl 12
New York, NY 10010-4314, USA

Castaneda, Pedro (Actor)
c/o Maggie Woods Online Talent Group
Prefers to be contacted via email or telephone
West Hollywood, CA 90069, USA

Castellaneta, Dan (Actor, Musician)
c/o Arlene Forster Forster Entertainment
12533 Woodgreen St
Los Angeles, CA 90066-2723, USA

Castellini, Clateo (Business Person)
Becton Dickinson Co
1 Becton Dr
Franklin Lakes, NJ 07417-1880, USA

Castellini, Robert (Commentator)
2180 Grandin Rd
Cincinnati, OH 45208-3306, USA

Castelluccio, Frederico (Actor)
c/o Robyn Ziegler *Robyn Ziegler Management*
30 Irving Pl Fl 6
New York, NY 10003-2303, USA

Caster, Rich (Athlete, Football Player)
41 Lincoln Ct
Rockville Centre, NY 11570-5744, USA

Castete, Jesse (Athlete, Football Player)
302 W Lee St
Sulphur, LA 70663-5440, USA

Castiglia, James (Athlete, Football Player)
5301 Westbard Cir Apt 313
Bethesda, MD 20816-1427, USA

Castiglione, Joe (Commentator)
Boston Red Sox
100 King Phillips Pathe
Marshfield, MA 02050-5714, USA

Castilla, Vinny (Athlete, Baseball Player)
7680 Polo Ridge Dr
Littleton, CO 80128-2502, USA

Castilla, Vinny (Athlete, Baseball Player)
2001 Blake St
Attn Coaching Staff
Denver, CO 80205-2060, USA

Castille, Jeremiah (Athlete, Football Player)
2904 Kirkcaldy Ln
Birmingham, AL 35242-4117, USA

Castillio, Susie (Actor, Beauty Pageant Winner)
c/o Gordon Gilbertson *Gilbertson Management*
1334 3rd Street Promenade Ste 201
Santa Monica, CA 90401-1320, USA

Castillo, Alberto (Athlete, Baseball Player)
400 SW Lakota Ave
Port Saint Lucie, FL 34953-3029, USA

Castillo, Alberto (Athlete, Baseball Player)
13600 Coco Palm Ct
Bakersfield, CA 93314-6662, USA

Castillo, Bobby (Athlete, Baseball Player)
JD Legends Promotions
10808 Foothill Blvd # 160-454
Rancho Cucamonga, CA 91730-3889, USA

Castillo, Carmen (Athlete, Baseball Player)
344 Prospect Ave Apt 6A
Hackensack, NJ 07601-2603, USA

Castillo, Frank (Athlete, Baseball Player)
4283 N 81st St
Scottsdale, AZ 85251-2679, USA

Castillo, Joey (Musician)
120 N Harvard Blvd
Los Angeles, CA 90004-4317, USA

Castillo, Luis (Athlete, Baseball Player)
10782 Hawks Vista St
Plantation, FL 33324-8212, USA

Castillo, Luis (Athlete, Baseball Player)
14165 Augusta Ct
Poway, CA 92064-6645

Castillo, Manny (Athlete, Baseball Player)
Bowling Green Hot Rods 300 8th Ave
Attn: Coaching Staff
Bowling Green, KY 42101, USA

Castillo, Marty (Athlete, Baseball Player)
589 Palisade Dr
Brunswick, GA 31523-8208, USA

Castillo, Raul (Actor)
c/o Michael Gasparro *TMT Entertainment Group*
648 Broadway # 1002
New York, NY 10012-2348, USA

Castillo, Tony (Athlete, Baseball Player)
6402 Silverwood Dr
Huntington Beach, CA 92647-3366, USA

Castillo, Vinicio (Athlete, Baseball Player)
c/o Staff Member *Atlanta Braves*
755 Hank Aaron Dr SW
Atlanta, GA 30315-1120, USA

Casting Crowns (Music Group, Musician)
c/o Stacey Jannette *Proper Management*
PO Box 150867
Nashville, TN 37215-0867, USA

Castino, John (Athlete, Baseball Player)
6290 Bluestern Rd S
Hamel, MN 55340, USA

Castle, Don (Athlete, Baseball Player)
560 Country Club Dr
Senatobia, MS 38668-6317, USA

Castle, Eric (Athlete, Football Player)
41984 Cut Off Dr
Lebanon, OR 97355-9120, USA

Castle, Michael (Congressman, Ex-Governor)
300 S New St
Dover, DE 19904-6726, USA

Castle, Nick (Actor, Director, Writer)
PO Box 92136
Pasadena, CA 91109-2136, USA

Castle-Hughes, Keisha (Actor)
c/o Jennifer Rawlings *Principato/Young Management (LA)*
9465 Wilshire Blvd Ste 900
Beverly Hills, CA 90212-2608, USA

Castleman, Foster (Athlete, Baseball Player)
8250 Graves Rd
Cincinnati, OH 45243-3633, USA

Castles, Neil (Race Car Driver)
1525 Stoneyridge Dr
Charlotte, NC 28214-8656, USA

Casto, Kory (Athlete, Baseball Player)
103 Raska Dr
Yoakum, TX 77995-4609, USA

Castonzo, Anthony (Football Player)
c/o Tom Condon *CAA (St. Louis)*
222 S Central Ave Ste 1008
Saint Louis, MO 63105-3509, USA

Castor, Chris (Athlete, Football Player)
206 Connors Cir
Cary, NC 27511-6100, USA

Castor, Kathy (Congressman, Politician)
137 Cannon Hob
Washington, DC 20515-2204, USA

Castro, Bill (Athlete, Baseball Player)
5217 W Harvard Dr
Franklin, WI 53132-8192, USA

Castro, Cristian (Musician)
c/o Staff Member *BMG*
1540 Broadway
New York, NY 10036-4039, USA

Castro, David (Actor)
c/o Staff Member *Persona Management*
40 E 9th St Apt 11J
Suite 11J
New York, NY 10003-6426, USA

Castro, Jason (Musician)
c/o Staff Member *Atlantic Recording Corporation*
1290 Avenue of the Americas
New York, NY 10104-0101, USA

Castro, Juan (Athlete, Baseball Player)
5605 W Andrea Dr
Phoenix, AZ 85083-7341, USA

Castro, Ramon (Athlete, Baseball Player)
1230 Windway Cir
Kissimmee, FL 34744-2552, USA

Castro, Raquel (Actor)
c/o Staff Member *William Morris Endeavor (LA)*
9601 Wilshire Blvd
Beverly Hills, CA 90210-5213, USA

Castroneves, Helio (Race Car Driver)
325 Seven Isles Dr
Ft Lauderdale, FL 33301-1532, USA

Castronuova, Cara (Actor, Reality Star)
c/o Seth Greenky *Green Key Mgmt (NY)*
251 W 89th St Apt 4A
New York, NY 10024-1713, USA

Catalanotto, Frank (Athlete, Baseball Player)
PO Box 236
Frank Catalanotto Foundation
Saint James, NY 11780-0236, USA

Catan, Pete (Athlete, Football Player)
1261 Blakely St
Woodstock, IL 60098-3631, USA

Catanho, Alcides (Athlete, Football Player)
931 Pennington St Apt 1
Elizabeth, NJ 07202-1584, USA

Catanzaro, Tony (Dancer)
8915 SW 207th St
Miami, FL 33189-3608, USA

Catapano, Mike (Athlete, Football Player)
c/o Alan Herman *Sportstars Inc*
1350 Avenue of the Americas Fl 28
New York, NY 10019-4702, USA

Catchings, Harvey (Athlete, Basketball Player)
17406 Edenwalk
Spring, TX 77379-8513, USA

Catchings, Tamika (Athlete)
125 S Pennsylvania St
Indianapolis, IN 46204-3610

Catchings, Toney (Athlete, Football Player)
6213 Zoellners Pl
Hamilton, OH 45011-1001

Cate, Troy (Athlete, Baseball Player)
32499 Via Destello
Temecula, CA 92592-3961, USA

Cater, Danny (Athlete, Baseball Player)
3268 Candlewood Trl
Plano, TX 75023-1320, USA

Cater, Greg (Athlete, Football Player)
19 Warwick Way SE
Rome, GA 30161-4058, USA

Cates, Challen (Actor)
179 S Hudson Ave
Los Angeles, CA 90004-1033, USA

Cates, Dariene (Actor)
13340 FM 740
Forney, TX 75126-6802, USA

Cates, Georgina (Actor)
118 S Kilkea Dr
Los Angeles, CA 90048-3526, USA

Cates, Phoebe (Actor)
Blue Tree
1283 Madison Ave
New York, NY 10128-0575, USA

Cathcard, Patti (Musician)
Windham Hill Records
PO Box 5501
Beverly Hills, CA 90209-5501, USA

Cathcart, Sam (Athlete, Football Player)
370 Las Alturas Rd
Santa Barbara, CA 93103-2179, USA

Cather, Mike (Athlete, Baseball Player)
19507 Star Cir
Cerritos, CA 90703-7751, USA

Catherwood, Mike (Radio Personality, Reality Star)
c/o Staff Member *Core Entertainment*
14742 Ventura Blvd
Penthouse
Sherman Oaks, CA 91403, USA

Cathey, Reg E (Actor)
c/o Sarah Fargo *Paradigm (NY)*
360 Park Ave S Fl 16
New York, NY 10010-1716, USA

Catledge, Terry (Athlete, Basketball Player)
170 Hall St
Houston, MS 38851-1605, USA

Catlett, Mary Jo (Actor)
4375 Farmdale Ave
Studio City, CA 91604-2737, USA

Catlett, Sid (Athlete, Basketball Player)
3110 Scottish Ave
Suitland, MD 20746-3136, USA

Cato, Keefe (Athlete, Baseball Player)
98 Maryton Rd
White Plains, NY 10603-2016, USA

Cato, Kelvin (Athlete, Basketball Player)
PO Box 1400
Missouri City, TX 77459-1400, USA

Caton Jones, Michael (Director)
c/o Staff Member *William Morris Endeavor (LA)*
9601 Wilshire Blvd Ste 220
Beverly Hills, CA 90210-5205, USA

Cattage, Bobby (Athlete, Basketball Player)
4838 US Highway 29 S
Auburn, AL 36830-8184, USA

Cattrall, Kim (Actor)
105 Gerard Dr
East Hampton, NY 11937-4700, USA

Caudill, Bill (Athlete, Baseball Player)
11605 NE 41st St
Kirkland, WA 98033-8742, USA

Cauffiel, Jessica (Actor)
c/o Michael Greene *Greene & Associates*
1901 Avenue of the Stars Ste 130
Los Angeles, CA 90067-6030, USA

Caufield, Jay (Athlete, Hockey Player)
106 Quail Hollow Ln
Wexford, PA 15090-7596, USA

Caulfield, Emma (Actor)
c/o Ellen Drantch-Billet *EDB Management*
1953 Barry Ave
Los Angeles, CA 90025-5381, USA

Caulfield, Lore (Designer, Fashion Designer)
2228 Cotner Ave
Los Angeles, CA 90064-1802, USA

Caulfield, Maxwell (Actor)
5252 Lennox Ave5252 Lennox Ave
Van Nuys, CA 91401, USA

Caulkins, Tracy (Athlete, Olympic Athlete, Swimmer)
511 Oman St
Nashville, TN 37203-1234, USA

Causey, Kevin (Athlete, Baseball Player)
765 Eldorado Blvd
Broomfield, CO 80021-8828, USA

Causey, Wayne (Athlete, Baseball Player)
2905 Paynter Dr
Ruston, LA 71270-5242, USA

Causwell, Duane (Athlete, Baseball Player)
3 Pierce Dr
Stony Point, NY 10980-3701

Cauterize (Music Group)
c/o Staff Member *Wind-up Records*
72 Madison Ave Fl 8
New York, NY 10016-8731, USA

Cauthen, Steve (Athlete, Jockey)
167 N Main St
Walton, KY 41094-1150, USA

Cauthen, Steve (Horse Racer)
15541 Porter Rd
Verona, KY 41092-9205, USA

Cavadini, Catherine (Cathy) (Actor)
c/o Staff Member *ICM Partners (LA)*
10250 Constellation Blvd Fl 7
Los Angeles, CA 90067-6207, USA

Cavalera, Max (Musician)
Variety Artists
1924 Spring St
Paso Robles, CA 93446-1620, USA

Cavaleri, Ray (Producer)
c/o Staff Member *Cavaleri & Associates*
3500 W Olive Ave Ste 300
Burbank, CA 91505-4647, USA

Cavallari, Kristin (Actor, Reality Star)
c/o Susan Calogerakis *SC Management*
9250 Wilshire Blvd
Ground Fl
Beverly Hills, CA 90212-3352, USA

Cavalli, Carmen (Athlete, Football Player)
13111 Anns Choice Way
Warminster, PA 18974-3318, USA

Cavallini, Gino (Athlete, Hockey Player)
6614 Clayton Rd Unit 315
Saint Louis, MO 63117-1602, USA

Cavallini, Paul (Athlete, Hockey Player)
7201 Kingsbury Blvd
Saint Louis, MO 63130-4139, USA

Cavanagh, Megan (Actor)
c/o Staff Member *Framework Entertainment (LA)*
9057 Nemo St Ste C
West Hollywood, CA 90069-5511, USA

Cavanagh, Tom (Actor)
c/o Daniel Pancotto *Circle of Confusion (LA)*
8607 Washington Blvd
Culver City, CA 90232-7441, USA

Cavanaugh, Christine (Actor)
Allman
342 S Cochran Ave # 30
Los Angeles, CA 90036-3320, USA

Cavanaugh, Joe (Athlete, Hockey Player)
25 Nathaniel Green Dr
East Greenwich, RI 02818-2019, USA

Cavanaugh, Matt (Athlete, Football Player)
644 Robinwood Dr Apt C
Pittsburgh, PA 15216-1034, USA

Cavanaugh, Matthew A (Matt) (Athlete, Football Player)
8 Barstad Ct
Lutherville Timonium, MD 21093-3501, USA

Cavanaugh, Michael (Actor)
Ambrosio/Mortimer
165 W 46th St
New York, NY 10036-2501, USA

Cavanaugh, Page (Musician)
9420 Reseda Blvd
Northridge, CA 91324-2932, USA

Cavaretta, Philip J (Phil) (Athlete, Baseball Player, Coach)
4637 Kellogg Dr SW
Lilburn, GA 30047-4407, USA

Cavazos, Andy (Athlete, Baseball Player)
244 E Bernard St
Clute, TX 77531-4609, USA

Cavazos, Lauro (Politician)
173 Annursnac Hill Rd
Concord, MA 01742-5402, USA

Cavazos, Lumi (Actor)
Visionary Entertainment
8265 W Sunset Blvd Ste 203
West Hollywood, CA 90046-2470, USA

Cave, Nick (Musician, Songwriter, Writer)
Billions Corp
833 W Chicago Ave Ste 101
Chicago, IL 60642-8408, USA

Cavenall, Ron (Athlete, Basketball Player)
PO Box 450983
Houston, TX 77245-0983, USA

Caveness, Ronnie (Athlete, Football Player)
17 Brookridge Cv
Little Rock, AR 72205-2224, USA

Caver, James (Athlete, Football Player)
10722 Mersington Ave
Kansas City, MO 64137-1870, USA

Caver, Quinton (Athlete, Football Player)
PO Box 335
China, TX 77613-0335, USA

Caverly, Kristen (Athlete, Olympic Athlete, Swimmer)
9 Puerto Caravaca
San Clemente, CA 92672-6054, USA

Cavett, Dick (Actor)
181 Deforest Rd
Montauk, NY 11954, USA

Cavic, Milorad (Mike) (Swimmer)
Cal Bears Athletics
Swimming
Haas Pavilion #4422
Berkeley, CA 94720-0001, USA

Caviezel, James (Jim) (Actor)
c/o Hildy Gottlieb *ICM Partners (LA)*
10250 Constellation Blvd Fl 7
Los Angeles, CA 90067-6207, USA

Cavil, Kwame (Athlete, Football Player)
2005 Dan Rowe St
Waco, TX 76704-1016, USA

Cavill, Henry (Actor)
c/o Jennifer Allen *Viewpoint Inc (LA)*
8820 Wilshire Blvd Ste 220
Beverly Hills, CA 90211-2622, USA

Cavness, Grady (Athlete, Football Player)
7007 Roberson Rd
Missouri City, TX 77489-2508, USA

Cavuto, Neil (Television Host)
55 Prentice Ln
Mendham, NJ 07945-2723, USA

Cawley, Tucker (Actor)
c/o Adam Berkowitz *Creative Artists Agency (CAA-LA)*
2000 Avenue of the Stars Ste 100
Los Angeles, CA 90067-4705, USA

Cawley, Warren (Rex) (Athlete, Track Athlete)
17741 Miller Dr
Tustin, CA 92780-2657, USA

Caylor, Lowell (Athlete, Football Player)
403 Woodway Dr
Greer, SC 29651-6869, USA

Cayne, Candis (Actor, Model)
c/o Nikki Weiss *Nikki Weiss & Co.*
4646 Saloma Ave
Sherman Oaks, CA 91403-2511, USA

Cazwell (Musician)
c/o Bill Coleman *Peace Bisquit*
963 Kent Ave Apt E3
Brooklyn, NY 11205-4469, USA

Cazzette (Music Group)
c/o Staff Member *D. Baron Media Relations*
1411 Cloverfield Blvd
Santa Monica, CA 90404-2917, USA

C. Burgess, Michael (Congressman, Politician)
2241 Rayburn Hob
Washington, DC 20515-3212, USA

C. Carney Jr., John (Congressman, Politician)
1429 Longworth Hob
Washington, DC 20515-2302, USA

Ceasar, Shirley (Actor, Musician)
c/o Staff Member *M.A.G./Universal Attractions*
15 W 36th St Fl 8
New York, NY 10018-7927, USA

Ceaser, Curtis (Athlete, Football Player)
4805 Corley St
Beaumont, TX 77707-4224, USA

Ceballos, Cedric (Athlete, Basketball Player)
3068 FM 1252 W
Kilgore, TX 75662-4830, USA

Cechmanek, Roman (Athlete, Hockey Player)
1111 S Figueroa St
Los Angeles, CA 90015-1300, USA

Cecil, Brett (Athlete, Baseball Player)
2989 Estancia Pl
Clearwater, FL 33761-2646, USA

Cedano, Roger (Athlete, Baseball Player)
9325 Byron Ave
Surfside, FL 33154-2437, USA

Cedar, Larry (Actor)
12949 Hartsook St
Sherman Oaks, CA 91423-1614, USA

Cedarstrom, Gary (Athlete, Baseball Player)
1610 18th St SE
Minot, ND 58701-6087, USA

Cedeno, Cesar (Athlete, Baseball Player)
9919 Sagedowne Ln
Houston, TX 77089-4309, USA

Cedeno, Matt (Actor)
c/o Ryan Daly *Zero Gravity Management*
1531 14th St
Santa Monica, CA 90404-3302, USA

Cedeno, Roger (Athlete, Baseball Player)
2950 NE 188th St Apt 538
Miami, FL 33180-2737, USA

Cederstrom, Gary (Athlete, Baseball Player)
755 Whidbey St
Melbourne, FL 32904-7484, USA

Cefalo, Jimmy (Athlete, Football Player)
6675 Roxbury Ln
Miami Beach, FL 33141-4532, USA

Ceglarski, Leonard (Len) (Athlete, Hockey Player, Olympic Athlete)
61 Lantern Ln
Duxbury, MA 02332-4915, USA

Ceika, Alex (Athlete, Golfer)
11589 Caldicot Dr
Las Vegas, NV 89138-1541, USA

Cejka, Alex (Athlete, Golfer)
9484 S Eastern Ave
Las Vegas, NV 89123-3987, USA

Cejudo, Henry (Athlete, Olympic Athlete, Wrestler)
Novuss Media
9943 E Bell Rd Ste 120
Scottsdale, AZ 85260-2530, USA

Celeda (Musician)
c/o Staff Member *Diva Central Inc*
7510 W Sunset Blvd Ste 1445
Los Angeles, CA 90046-3408, USA

Celek, Brent (Athlete, Football Player)
3515 S Reserve Dr
Philadelphia, PA 19145-5752, us

Celestand, John (Athlete, Basketball Player, Sportscaster)
c/o Staff Member *Maxx Sports & Entertainment*
546 5th Ave Fl 6
New York, NY 10036-5000, USA

Celeste, Richard
720 Crestfield Grv
Colorado Springs, CO 80906-1228, USA

Celestin, Oliver (Athlete, Football Player)
PO Box 6963
New Orleans, LA 70174-6963, USA

Celi, AJ (Reality Star)
Playhouse Nightclub
6506 Hollywood Blvd
Los Angeles, CA 90028-6210, USA

Celi, Ari (Actor)
c/o Staff Member *SMS Talent*
8383 Wilshire Blvd Ste 230
Beverly Hills, CA 90211-2436, USA

Cellins, Art (Basketball Player)
Atlanta Hawks
4915 NW 15th Ct
Miami, FL 33142-4122, USA

Celotto, Mario (Athlete, Football Player)
47 Evirel Pl
Oakland, CA 94611-1323, USA

Cena, John (Actor, Wrestler)
2326 Camp Indianhead Rd
Land O Lakes, FL 34639-5287, USA

Cenci, John (Athlete, Football Player)
942 Rita Dr
Pittsburgh, PA 15221-3964, USA

Cenker, Robert J (Astronaut)
GORCA Inc
155 Hickory Corner Rd
East Windsor, NJ 08520-2417, USA

Centers, Larry (Athlete, Football Player)
5023 Stagecoach Way
Southlake, TX 76092, USA

Cepeda, Orlando (Athlete, Baseball Player)
2305 Palmer Ct
Fairfield, CA 94534-7550, USA

Cepicky, Matt (Athlete, Baseball Player)
7 Upper Bluffs View Ct
Eureka, MO 63025-3724, USA

Cepicky, Scott (Athlete, Baseball Player, Olympic Athlete)
1606 Harrison Way
Spring Hill, TN 37174-2669, USA

Cera, Michael (Actor)
c/o William Mercer *Thruline Entertainment*
9250 Wilshire Blvd Ste 100
Ground Floor
Beverly Hills, CA 90212-3343, USA

Cerbone, John (Race Car Driver)
168 Fordham St
Bronx, NY 10464-1445, USA

Cerda, Jaime (Athlete, Baseball Player)
2707 Northhill St
Selma, CA 93662-4313, USA

Ceresine, Ray (Athlete, Hockey Player)
13282 Ocean Vista Rd
San Diego, CA 92130-1862, USA

Ceresino, Gordy (Athlete, Football Player)
PO Box 675515
Rancho Santa Fe, CA 92067-5515, USA

Cernan, Eugene (Astronaut)
11310 Innisfree St
Houston, TX 77024-6748, USA

Cernan, Eugene A. (Astronaut)
c/o Staff Member *St Martins Press*
175 5th Ave Ste 400
Publicity Dept
New York, NY 10010-7848, USA

Cerne, Joseph (Joe) (Athlete, Football Player)
536 Valley West Ct
West Des Moines, IA 50265-3900, USA

Ceron, Laura (Actor)
2338 Holly Dr
Los Angeles, CA 90068-2712, USA

Cerone, Rick (Athlete, Baseball Player)
26 Ocean Ter Apt B2
Long Branch, NJ 07740-2503, USA

Cerqua, Marq (Athlete, Football Player)
6431 Main St Apt 303
Hialeah, FL 33014-2259, USA

Cerrone, Rick (Athlete)
100 Old Palisade Rd
Fort Lee, NJ 07024-7064

Cerruda, Ron (Golfer)
c/o Staff Member *Pro Golfers Association (PGA) Tour*
112 Tpc Blvd
Ponte Vedra Beach, FL 32082, USA

Certo, Tish (Athlete, Golfer)
151 Buffalo Ave Apt 211
Niagara Falls, NY 14303-1200, USA

Cerv, Bob (Athlete, Baseball Player)
805 N 22nd St Apt 1A
Blair, NE 68008-1195, USA

Cervantes, Gary (Actor)
2240 Mardel Ave
Whittier, CA 90601-1532, USA

Cervelli, Francisco (Athlete, Baseball Player)
c/o Team Member *New York Yankees*
Yankee Stadium
161st St & River Ave
Bronx, NY 10451, USA

Cervenak, Mike (Athlete, Baseball Player)
27199 Carol Ln
New Boston, MI 48164-9636, USA

Cervenka, Exene (Musician)
Performers of the World
8901 Melrose Ave # 200
West Hollywood, CA 90069-5605, USA

Cervenka, Kathleen (Doctor, Writer)
c/o Staff Member *New Harbinger Publications*
5674 Shattuck Ave
Oakland, CA 94609-1662, USA

Cerveris, Michael (Musician)
c/o Erica Tarin *ID Public Relations (LA)*
7060 Hollywood Blvd Fl 8th
Los Angeles, CA 90028-6021, USA

Cervl, Alfred N (Al) (Basketball Player)
177 Dunrovin Ln
Rochester, NY 14618-4815, USA

Cesaire, Jacques (Athlete, Football Player)
13388 Greenstone Ct
San Diego, CA 92131-4242, USA

Cesare, Billy (Athlete, Football Player)
1655 Hendry Isles Blvd
Clewiston, FL 33440-5825, USA

Cestaro, Alexander (Athlete, Football Player)
289 Devoe Ave
Yonkers, NY 10705-2709, USA

Cester, Chris (Musician)
2010 Holly Hill Ter
Los Angeles, CA 90068-3812, USA

Cetara, Peter (Musician)
c/o Staff Member *MPI Talent Agency*
12100 Wilshire Blvd Ste 1030
Los Angeles, CA 90025-7129, USA

Cetera, Peter (Musician, Songwriter)
691 N Spruce Ave
Ketchum, ID 83340, USA

Cetlinski, Matthew (Matt) (Swimmer)
13121 SE 93rd Terrace Rd
Summerfield, FL 34491-9347, USA

Cey, Ron (Athlete, Baseball Player)
22714 Creole Rd
Woodland Hills, CA 91364-3925, USA

Chabert, Lacey (Actor)
c/o Aaron Ray *The Collective*
8383 Wilshire Blvd Ste 1050
Beverly Hills, CA 90211-2415, USA

Chablis, Lady (Impersonator)
Club One Savannah
1 Jefferson St
Savannah, GA 31401-2511, USA

Chabon, Michael (Writer)
c/o Staff Member *United Talent Agency (UTA-LA)*
9336 Civic Center Dr
Beverly Hills, CA 90210-3604, USA

Chabot, John (Athlete, Coach, Hockey Player)
c/o Staff Member *New York Islanders*
1535 Old Country Rd
Plainview, NY 11803-5042, USA

Chabot, Steve (Congressman, Politician)
2351 Rayburn Hob
Washington, DC 20515-0525, USa

Chabraja, Nicholas D (Business Person)
General Dynamics
3190 Fairview Park Dr
Falls Church, VA 22042-4530, USA

Chabria, Renee (Director)
c/o Staff Member *Management 360*
9111 Wilshire Blvd
Beverly Hills, CA 90210-5508, USA

Chacon, Alex Pineda (Soccer Player)
Los Angeles Galaxy
1010 Rose Bowl Dr
Pasadena, CA 91103, USA

Chacon, Shawn (Athlete, Baseball Player)
7610 W 19th Street Rd
Greeley, CO 80634-8628, USA

Chacurian, Chico (Soccer Player)
96 Stratford Rd
Stratford, CT 06615-7760, USA

Chadha, Gurinder (Director)
c/o Staff Member *ICM Partners (LA)*
10250 Constellation Blvd Fl 7
Los Angeles, CA 90067-6207, USA

Chadwick, Bill (Athlete, Hockey Player)
7 Country Club Dr # 789
Cutchogue, NY 11935-1700, USA

Chadwick, Jeff (Athlete, Football Player)
23062 Village Dr Apt A
Lake Forest, CA 92630-4955, USA

Chadwick, June (Actor)
Contemporary Artists
610 Santa Monica Blvd Ste 202
Santa Monica, CA 90401-1645, USA

Chadwick, Ray (Athlete, Baseball Player)
607 Gattis St
Durham, NC 27701-2831, USA

Chafee, Lincoln (Governor, Politician)
22 Beachwood Dr
East Greenwich, RI 02818-4733, USA

Chaffee, Don (Director)
7020 La Presa Dr
Los Angeles, CA 90068-3105, USA

Chaffee, Susan (Suzy) (Athlete, Olympic Athlete, Skier)
55 Roadrunner Rd
Sedona, AZ 86336-5204, USA

Chaffetz, Jason (Congressman, Politician)
1032 Longworth Hob
Washington, DC 20515-3819, USA

Chaffey, Pat (Athlete, Football Player)
10415 SW Gardner Ct
Tualatin, OR 97062-7208, USA

Chafin, Bryan (Actor)
c/o Heather Collier *Collier Talent Agency*
1001 S Capital Of Texas Hwy Ste L200
West Lake Hills, TX 78746-6473, USA

Chagall, Rachel (Actor)
251 S Van Ness Ave
Los Angeles, CA 90004-3920, USA

Chagnon, Marcel (Musician)
6535 Melinda Dr
Nashville, TN 37205-3934, USA

Chaiken, Ilene (Producer, Writer)
2614 Reppert Ct
Los Angeles, CA 90046-1605, USA

Chaikin, Carly (Actor)
c/o Andrew Rogers *ICM Partners (LA)*
10250 Constellation Blvd Fl 7
Los Angeles, CA 90067-6207, USA

Chainsmokers, The (Music Group, Musician)
c/o Adam Alpert *4AM*
333 E 23rd St Apt 2H
New York, NY 10010-4742, USA

Chairmen of the Board (Musician)
c/o Staff Member *The Willis Blume Agency*
PO Box 509
Orangeburg, SC 29116-0509, USA

Chalenski, Mike (Athlete, Football Player)
225 S Michigan Ave
Kenilworth, NJ 07033-1727, USA

Chalfant, Kathleen (Actor)
c/o Staff Member *Douglas Gorman Rothacker & Wilhelm Inc*
1501 Broadway Ste 703
New York, NY 10036-5501, USA

Chalk, Dave (Athlete, Baseball Player)
137 Cross Timbers Trl
Coppell, TX 75019-3731, USA

Chalke, Sarah (Actor)
3903 Ethel Ave
Studio City, CA 91604-2204, USA

Chalker, Will (Model)
c/o Staff Member *New York Model Management*
596 Broadway # 701
New York, NY 10012-3396, USA

Chamberlain, Byron (Athlete, Football Player)
PO Box 326
Montclair, CA 91763-0326, USA

Chamberlain, Craig (Athlete, Baseball Player)
11292 Los Alamitos Blvd
Los Alamitos, CA 90720-3958, USA

Chamberlain, Dan (Athlete, Football Player)
6356 Puerto Dr
Rancho Murieta, CA 95683-9357, USA

Chamberlain, Jimmy (Actor, Musician)
c/o Staff Member *William Morris Endeavor (LA)*
9601 Wilshire Blvd
Beverly Hills, CA 90210-5213, USA

Chamberlain, Joba (Athlete, Baseball Player)
c/o Team Member *New York Yankees*
Yankee Stadium
161st St & River Ave
Bronx, NY 10451, USA

Chamberlain, Richard (Actor)
c/o Eric Gardner *Panacea Entertainment*
13587 Andalusia Dr
Santa Rosa Valley, CA 93012-9226, USA

Chamberlain, Wes (Athlete, Baseball Player)
PO Box 1358
Homewood, IL 60430-0358, USA

Chambers, Al (Athlete, Baseball Player)
1303 N 14th St
Harrisburg, PA 17103-1206, USA

Chambers, Anne Cox (Business Person)
Cox Enterprises
1440 Lake Hearn Dr NE
Atlanta, GA 30319, USA

Chambers, Christina (Athlete, Football Player)
c/o Lena Roklin *Luber Roklin Management*
5815 W Sunset Blvd Ste 206
Los Angeles, CA 90028-6481, USA

Chambers, Erin (Actor)
c/o Ted Schachter *Schachter Entertainment*
1157 S Beverly Dr Fl 2
Los Angeles, CA 90035-1119, USA

Chambers, Faune (Actor)
c/o Mara Santino *Luber Roklin Management*
5815 W Sunset Blvd Ste 206
Los Angeles, CA 90028-6481, USA

Chambers, Jerry (Athlete, Basketball Player)
4135 Don Diablo Dr
Los Angeles, CA 90008-4305, USA

Chambers, Justin (Actor)
c/o Sandra Chang *Anonymous Content (LA)*
3532 Hayden Ave
Culver City, CA 90232-2413, USA

Chambers, Kasey (Musician)
c/o Staff Member *Paradigm (Monterey)*
404 W Franklin St
Monterey, CA 93940-2303, USA

Chambers, Kirk (Athlete, Football Player)
1294 Lakeview Dr
Provo, UT 84604-2933, USA

Chambers, Lester (Musician)
Lustig Talent
PO Box 770850
Orlando, FL 32877-0850, USA

Chambers, Munro (Actor)
c/o Paul Young *Principato/Young Management (LA)*
9465 Wilshire Blvd Ste 900
Beverly Hills, CA 90212-2608, USA

Chambers, Shawn (Athlete, Hockey Player)
9999 Wood Rdg
Pequot Lakes, MN 56472-3642, USA

Chambers, Tom (Athlete, Basketball Player)
7437 E Via Dona Rd
Scottsdale, AZ 85266-2154, USA

Chambers, Wallace (Wally) (Athlete, Football Player)
18790 E 14 Mile Rd Apt 201
Roseville, MI 48066-1037, USA

Chambers, Willie (Musician)
Noga Mgmt
PO Box 1428
Studio City, CA 91614-0428, USA

Chamblee, Al (Athlete, Football Player)
845 Garrow Rd
Newport News, VA 23608-3387, USA

Chamblee, Brandel (Athlete, Golfer)
14324 E Coyote Rd
Scottsdale, AZ 85259-3789, USA

Chamblee, Jim (Athlete, Baseball Player)
1408 Broadway St
Denton, TX 76201-2714, USA

Chambliss, Chris (Athlete, Baseball Player)
12755 Wyngate Trl
Alpharetta, GA 30005-7514, USA

Chambliss, Saxby (Politician)
27 Cherokee Rd
Moultrie, GA 31768-6541, USA

Chambliss, Saxby (Senator)
416 Russell Senate Office Building
Washington, DC 20510-0001, USA

Chamitoff, Gregory E Dr (Astronaut)
2742 Dunsmere Ct
Pearland, TX 77584-9273, USA

Champagne, Andre (Athlete, Hockey Player)
6936 E 75th St
Tulsa, OK 74133-3037, USA

Champion, Billy (Athlete, Baseball Player)
240 Triple H Farm Rd
Inman, SC 29349, USA

Champion, Mike (Athlete, Baseball Player)
28952 Modjeska Canyon Rd
Silverado, CA 92676-9779, USA

Champion, Sam (Commentator, Television Host)
c/o Staff Member *The Weather Channel*
300 Interstate North Pkwy SE Ste 300
Atlanta, GA 30339-2424, USA

Champnella, Eric (Actor, Director, Writer)
c/o Paul Nelson *Mosaic Media Group*
9200 W Sunset Blvd Ste 10
West Hollywood, CA 90069-3608, USA

Champoux, Bob (Athlete, Hockey Player)
8861 Centaurus Way
San Diego, CA 92126-1916, USA

Chan, Ernie (Cartoonist)
4131 Vale Ave
Oakland, CA 94619-2223, USA

Chan, Gemma (Actor)
c/o Brantley Brown *Schachter Entertainment*
1157 S Beverly Dr Fl 2
Los Angeles, CA 90035-1119, USA

Chan, Jackie (Actor, Producer)
c/o Philip Button *William Morris Endeavor (LA)*
9601 Wilshire Blvd
Beverly Hills, CA 90210-5213, USA

Chan, Michael Paul (Actor)
13888 Valley Vista Blvd
Sherman Oaks, CA 91423-4663, USA

Chance, Bob (Athlete, Baseball Player)
2258 Oakridge Dr
Charleston, WV 25311-1723, USA

Chance, Bobbie Shaw (Actor)
Expressions Unlimited
13317 Ventura Blvd
Studio G
Sherman Oaks, CA 91423-3966, USA

Chance, Dean (Athlete, Baseball Player)
9505 W Smithville Western Rd
Wooster, OH 44691-9209, USA

Chance, Greyson (Musician)
c/o Guy Oseary *Untitled Entertainment (LA)*
350 S Beverly Dr Ste 200
Beverly Hills, CA 90212-4819, USA

Chance, Larry (Musician)
Brothers Mgmt
141 Dunbar Ave
Fords, NJ 08863-1551, USA

Chancellor, Chris (Athlete, Football Player)
c/o Jordan Woy *Willis and Woy Management*
3030 Olive St Ste 520
Dallas, TX 75219-7629, USA

Chancellor, Justin (Musician)
2746 Harrow Rd
Topanga, CA 90290-3366, USA

Chancellor, Van (Coach)
Houston Cornets
2 Greenway Plz Ste 400
Houston, TX 77046-0202, USA

Chancey, Robert (Athlete, Football Player)
PO Box 212
Coosada, AL 36020-0212, USA

Chandler, Al (Athlete, Football Player)
PO Box 21733
Oklahoma City, OK 73156-1733, USA

Chandler, Ben (Congressman, Politician)
1504 Longworth Hob
Washington, DC 20515-4101, USA

Chandler, Christopher M (Chris) (Athlete, Football Player)
1745 Grand Ave
Del Mar, CA 92014-2253, USA

Chandler, Gene (Athlete, Football Player)
550 Southmoor Cir
Stockbridge, GA 30281-4974, USA

Chandler, Jeff (Boxer)
6242 Horner St
Philadelphia, PA 19144, USA

Chandler, Karl (Athlete, Football Player)
5 Plymouth Rd
Newtown Square, PA 19073-1409, USA

Chandler, Kim (Musician)
c/o Jill Fritzo *PMK/BNC Public Relations (PMK-NY)*
622 3rd Ave Fl 8
New York, NY 10017-6707, USA

Chandler, Kyle (Actor)
222068 Topanga School Rd
Topanga, CA 90290, USA

Chandler, Michael ""Mike"" (Race Car Driver)
218 E Yanonali St Unit A
Santa Barbara, CA 93101-1853, USA

Chandler, Scott (Athlete, Football Player)
c/o Ken Zuckerman *Priority Sports & Entertainment - (LA)*
15233 Ventura Blvd Ste 718
Sherman Oaks, CA 91403-2237, USA

Chandler, Thornton (Athlete, Football Player)
8646 Guinevere St
Houston, TX 77029-3357, USA

Chandler, Tom (Athlete, Football Player)
16310 Axis Trl
San Antonio, TX 78232-2804, USA

Chandler, Tyson (Athlete, Basketball Player)
21731 Ventura Blvd Ste 300
Woodland Hills, CA 91364-1851, USA

Chandler, Wesley S (Wes) (Athlete, Football Player)
207 Howard Ave
New Smyrna Beach, FL 32168-8195, USA

Chandler, Wilson (Athlete, Basketball Player)
c/o Chris Luchey *CGL Sports*
885 Woodstock Rd Ste 430-303
Roswell, GA 30075-2277, USA

Chando, Alexandra (Actor)
c/o Elise Koseff *J Mitchell Management*
440 Park Ave S
New York, NY 10016-8012, USA

Chandrasekhar, Jay (Comedian)
c/o Staff Member *United Talent Agency (UTA-LA)*
9336 Civic Center Dr
Beverly Hills, CA 90210-3604, USA

Chaney, Darrel (Athlete, Baseball Player)
10 Fawn Cir
Sautee Nacoochee, GA 30571-5145, USA

Chaney, Don (Athlete, Basketball Player)
20711 Park Pine Dr
Katy, TX 77450-2811, USA

Chaney, John (Athlete, Basketball Player)
1639 Sharp Rd
Baton Rouge, LA 70815-4879, USA

Chaney, John (Coach)
Temple University
Athletic Dept
Philadelphia, PA 19122, USA

Chang, Christina (Actor)
c/o Myrna Jacoby *MJ Management*
130 W 57th St Apt 11A
New York, NY 10019-3311, USA

Chang, David (Chef, Reality Star)
c/o Lisa Shotland *Creative Artists Agency (CAA-LA)*
2000 Avenue of the Stars Ste 100
Los Angeles, CA 90067-4705, USA

Chang, Do Won (Business Person)
Forever 21
3880 N Mission Rd
Los Angeles, CA 90031-3138, USA

Chang, Emily (Actor)
c/o Scott Fish *Velocity Entertainment Partners*
5455 Wilshire Blvd Ste 802
Los Angeles, CA 90036-4271, USA

Chang, Jin Sook (Business Person)
Forever 21
3880 N Mission Rd
Los Angeles, CA 90031-3138, USA

Chang, Michael (Athlete, Tennis Player)
Chang Family Foundation
28562 Oso Pkwy # D343
Rancho Santa Margarita, CA 92688-5595,
USA

Chang, Sarah (Musician)
I C M Artists
40 W 57th St Fl 22
New York, NY 10019-4001, USA

Chang-Diaz, Franklin R (Astronaut)
NASA
2101 Nasa Pkwy Spc Johnsoncenter
Houston, TX 77058-3696, USA

Chang-Diaz, Franklin R (Astronaut)
1110 Pine Cir
Seabrook, TX 77586-4709, USA

Channing, Carol (Actor, Musician)
c/o Harlan Boll *Davidson & Choy
Publicity*
4311 Wilshire Blvd Ste 515
Los Angeles, CA 90010-3708, USA

Channing, Stockard (Actor)
8044 Woodrow Wilson Dr
Los Angeles, CA 90046-1117, USA

Chant, Charlie (Athlete, Baseball Player)
930 Starlight Ct
Banning, CA 92220-1710, USA

Chantels, The (Music Group)
c/o Staff Member *Creative Entertainment
Associates Inc*
6 Esterbrook Ln
Cherry Hill, NJ 08003-4002, USA

Chanticleer (Musician)
c/o Staff Member *ICM Partners (LA)*
10250 Constellation Blvd Fl 7
Los Angeles, CA 90067-6207, USA

Chantres, Carlos (Baseball Player)
67 Amherst St
Nashua, NH 03064-2561

Chao, Elaine (Politician)
2318 Dundee Rd
Louisville, KY 40205-2070, USA

Chao, Mark (Actor)
c/o Jaeson Ma *East West Artists*
5200 W Century Blvd Ste 701
Los Angeles, CA 90045-5928, USA

Chao, Rosalind (Actor)
305 15th St
Santa Monica, CA 90402-2211, USA

Chao, Vic (Actor)
c/o Staff Member *Osbrink Talent Agency*
4343 Lankershim Blvd Ste 100
North Hollywood, CA 91602-2705, USA

Chapas, Shaun (Athlete, Football Player)
c/o Hadley Engelhard *Enter-Sports
Management*
5 Concourse Pkwy Ste 3000
Atlanta, GA 30328-7106, USA

Chapdelaine, Rene (Athlete, Hockey
Player)
662 S Division Rd
Petoskey, MI 49770-8218, USA

Chapin, Darrin (Athlete, Baseball Player)
328 Portage Easterly Rd
Cortland, OH 44410-9510, USA

Chapin, Doug (Actor, Producer)
Doug Chapin Management
1100 Alta Loma Rd Apt 605
West Hollywood, CA 90069-2436, USA

Chapin, Dwight L (Government Official,
Publisher)
San Francisco Examiner
110 5th St
San Francisco, CA 94103-2972, USA

Chapin, Lauren (Actor)
11940 Reedy Creek Dr Apt 207
Orlando, FL 32836-6834, USA

Chapin, Tom (Musician, Songwriter,
Writer)
57 Piermont Pl
Piermont, NY 10968-1128, USA

Chaplin, Alexander (Actor)
c/o Tammy Rosen *Sanders Armstrong
Caserta*
425 N Robertson Blvd
West Hollywood, CA 90048-1735, USA

Chaplin, Ben (Actor)
c/o Simon Halls *Slate Public Relations*
9000 W Sunset Blvd Ste 915
West Hollywood, CA 90069-5809, USA

Chaplin, Geraldine (Actor, Writer)
c/o Staff Member *William Morris
Endeavor (LA)*
9601 Wilshire Blvd
Beverly Hills, CA 90210-5213, USA

Chaplin, Greg (Athlete, Baseball Player)
12426 Glenfield Ave
Tampa, FL 33626-2606, USA

Chaplin, Kiera (Actor, Producer)
c/o Staff Member *Creative Artists Agency
(CAA-LA)*
2000 Avenue of the Stars Ste 100
Los Angeles, CA 90067-4705, USA

Chapman, Al (Race Car Driver)
PO Box 212
Rd #1
Athens, PA 18810-0212, USA

Chapman, Alvah H Jr (Publisher)
Grove Harbour
1690 S Bayshore Ln Apt 10A
Miami, FL 33133-4067, USA

Chapman, Beth Nielsen (Reality Star)
Sussman Assoc
1383 Queen Emma St
Honolulu, HI 96813-2301, USA

Chapman, Blair (Athlete, Hockey Player)
2068 Redcoach Rd
Allison Park, PA 15101-3231, USA

Chapman, Brian (Athlete, Hockey Player)
32 Deer Run Rd
Agawam, MA 01001-3669, USA

Chapman, Bruce K (Government Official)
Discovery Institute
1201 3rd Ave # 4000
Seattle, WA 98101-3029, USA

Chapman, Clarence (Athlete, Football
Player)
14820 Parkside St
Detroit, MI 48238-2155, USA

Chapman, David S (Athlete, Football
Player)
789 N Main St
New Martinsville, WV 26155-1414, USA

Chapman, Doug (Athlete, Football Player)
6215 Chesterfield Meadows Dr
Chesterfield, VA 23832-6597, USA

Chapman, Dr Philip K (Astronaut)
11460 E Helm Dr
Scottsdale, AZ 85255-1885, USA

**Chapman, Duane Lee (Dog the Bounty
Hunter)** (Actor, Reality Star)
c/o Amy Weiss *Brillstein Entertainment
Partners (LA)*
9150 Wilshire Blvd Ste 350
Beverly Hills, CA 90212-3453, USA

Chapman, Gary (Musician)
8382 Collins Rd
Nashville, TN 37221-3903, USA

Chapman, Georgina (Designer)
Marchesa
601 W 26th St Rm 1425
New York, NY 10001-1160, USA

Chapman, Gil (Athlete, Football Player)
771 Cranford Ave
Westfield, NJ 07090-1308, USA

Chapman, Johnny (Race Car Driver)
Douglas & Sons Racing
1025 N Chipley Ford Rd
Statesville, NC 28625-1574, USA

Chapman, Josh (Athlete, Football Player)
c/o Pat Dye Jr *SportsTrust Advisors (GA)*
3340 Peachtree Rd NE Fl 16
Atlanta, GA 30326-1000, USA

Chapman, Judith (Actor)
11670 W Sunset Blvd Apt 312
Los Angeles, CA 90049-2069, USA

Chapman, Kelvin (Athlete, Baseball
Player)
9301 Laughlin Way
Redwood Valley, CA 95470-6425, USA

Chapman, Kevin (Actor)
c/o Ellen Meyer *Ellen Meyer Management*
8899 Beverly Blvd Ste 612
Los Angeles, CA 90048-2429, USA

Chapman, Lamar (Athlete, Football
Player)
18513 N Whitedove Ln
Cleveland, OH 44130-8429, USA

Chapman, Lanei (Actor)
c/o Judy Page *Mitchell K Stubbs & Assoc
(MKS)*
8675 Washington Blvd Ste 203
Culver City, CA 90232-7486, USA

Chapman, Leland (Actor, Reality Star)
c/o Staff Member *Dog the Bounty Hunter*
235 E 45th St
New York, NY 10017-3305, USA

Chapman, Mark Lindsay (Actor)
c/o Michael Zanuck *Michael Zanuck
Agency*
4929 Wilshire Blvd Ste 808
Los Angeles, CA 90010-3859, USA

Chapman, Michael J (Cinematographer,
Director)
501 S Beverly Dr Ste 300
Beverly Hills, CA 90212-4520, USA

Chapman, Mike (Athlete, Football Player)
8731 Avator Cir
Boerne, TX 78015-4424, USA

Chapman, Nathan (Producer)
c/o Haverly Rauen *Adams and Reese LLP*
424 Church St Ste 2800
Nashville, TN 37219-2386, USA

Chapman, Rex (Athlete, Basketball Player)
2172 Savannah Ln
Lexington, KY 40513-1812, USA

Chapman, Steven Curtis (Musician,
Songwriter)
Sparrow Records
PO Box 5010
Brentwood, TN 37024-5010, USA

Chapman, Thomas F (Business Person)
Equifax Inc
1550 Peachtree St NE
Atlanta, GA 30309-2468, USA

Chapman, Tracy (Musician, Songwriter)
c/o Lee Phillips *Manatt Phelps & Phillips
LLP*
11355 W Olympic Blvd Fl 2
Los Angeles, CA 90064-1656, USA

Chapman, Travis (Athlete, Baseball
Player)
5215 Hickson Rd
Jacksonville, FL 32207-5856, USA

Chapman, Wayne (Athlete, Basketball
Player)
3593 Salisbury Dr
Lexington, KY 40510-9742, USA

Chapot, Frank (Athlete, Horse Racer,
Olympic Athlete)
1075 Opie Rd
Branchburg, NJ 08853-4163, USA

Chappas, Harry (Athlete, Baseball Player)
26 SE 1st Ave
Dania, FL 33004-3611, USA

Chappell, Crystal (Actor)
235 Newport Ave
Grover Beach, CA 93433-1512, USA

Chappell, Fred D (Writer)
305 Kensington Rd
Greensboro, NC 27403-1732, USA

Chappell, Len (Athlete, Basketball Player)
7624 Chestnut Ln
Waterford, WI 53185-1707, USA

Chappelle, Dave (Actor, Comedian,
Producer)
3420 Grinnell Rd
Yellow Springs, OH 45387-9721, USA

Chapple, Dave (Athlete, Football Player)
5 Kara E
Irvine, CA 92620-1855, USA

Chapura, Richard (Dick) (Athlete,
Football Player)
7853 Saddle Creek Trl
Sarasota, FL 34241-9550, USA

Chara, Zdeno (Athlete, Hockey Player)
343 Commercial St Unit 211-213
Boston, MA 02109-1212, USA

Charboneau, Joe (Athlete, Baseball Player)
338 Lakeview Ave # B
Sheffield Lk, OH 44054-1718, USA

Charbonneau, Patricia (Actor)
749 1/2 N La Fayette Park Pl
Los Angeles, CA 90026-6559, USA

Charbonneau, Stephane (Athlete, Hockey
Player)
1 Wilderness Dr
Voorhees, NJ 08043-3415, USA

Charbonnier, CArole (Athlete, Golfer)
19 Carolina Ave
West Orange, NJ 07052-1804, USA

Charen, Mona (Writer)
c/o Staff Member *HarperCollins Publishers*
195 Broadway Fl 2
Cellar 1
New York, NY 10007-3132, USA

Charice (Musician)
c/o Liz Rosenberg *Liz Rosenberg Media*
1650 Broadway
505A
New York, NY 10019-6833, USA

Charland, Colin (Baseball Player)
Fleer
5303 Alta Vista Ln
Arlington, TX 76017-1735, USA

Charlap, Bill (Musician)
Abby Hoffer
223 1/2 E 48th St
New York, NY 10017, USA

Charles, Bob (Athlete, Golfer)
5329 Sea Biscuit Rd
Palm Beach Gardens, FL 33418-7818, USA

Charles, Daedra (Athlete, Basketball Player, Olympic Athlete)
Los Angeles Sparks
26730 Joy Rd Apt 3
Redford, MI 48239-1939, USA

Charles, Ed (Athlete, Baseball Player)
57 Park Ter E Apt B58
New York, NY 10034-0786, USA

Charles, Frank (Athlete, Baseball Player)
6146 Bridlewood Dr S
East Amherst, NY 14051-2010, USA

Charles, Gaius (Actor)
c/o Stephen Hirsh *Gersh (LA)*
9465 Wilshire Blvd Ste 600
Beverly Hills, CA 90212-2605, USA

Charles, Jamaal (Athlete, Football Player)
c/o David Dunn *Athletes First, LLC*
23091 Mill Creek Dr
Laguna Hills, CA 92653-1258, USA

Charles, John (Athlete, Football Player)
5644 Westheimer Rd Apt 164
Houston, TX 77056-4002, USA

Charles, Josh (Actor)
c/o Bryna Rifkin *ID Public Relations (LA)*
7060 Hollywood Blvd Fl 8th
Los Angeles, CA 90028-6021, USA

Charles, Ken (Athlete, Basketball Player)
621 Putnam Ave
Brooklyn, NY 11221-1601, USA

Charles, Max (Actor)
c/o Mona Loring *MLC PR*
7080 Hollywood Blvd Ste 903
Los Angeles, CA 90028-6936, USA

Charles M Brig Gen, Duke (Astronaut)
PO Box 310345
New Braunfels, TX 78131-0345, USA

Charleson, Leslie (Actor)
4851 Cromwell Ave
Los Angeles, CA 90027-1141, USA

Charlesworth, Todd (Athlete, Hockey Player)
914 N Brookside Dr
Norton Shores, MI 49441-5365, USA

Charlie, Diamond
7300 SW 69th Ct
Miami, FL 33143-4420, USA

Charlie, Dupre (Athlete, Football Player)
407 Bay St N
Texas City, TX 77590-6427, USA

Charlton, Clifford (Athlete, Football Player)
3708 Carrington Pl
Tallahassee, FL 32303-2041, USA

Charlton, Norm (Athlete, Baseball Player)
312 Estes Dr
Rockport, TX 78382-9758, USA

Charm City Devils (Music Group, Musician)
c/o Frank Cimler *10th Street Entertainment (LA)*
700 N San Vicente Blvd Ste G410
West Hollywood, CA 90069-5060, USA

Charney, Jordan (Actor)
c/o Staff Member *Leading Artists*
145 W 45th St Rm 1000
New York, NY 10036-4032, USA

Charney, Kim (Actor)
4811 Seashore Dr
Newport Beach, CA 92663-2423, USA

Charo (Musician)
1801 Lexington Rd
Beverly Hills, CA 90210-3001, USA

Charron, Paul R (Business Person)
Liz Claiborne Inc
1441 Broadway
New York, NY 10018-1905, USA

Chartoff, Melanie (Actor)
Artists Agency
1180 S Beverly Dr Ste 301
Los Angeles, CA 90035-1154, USA

Chartoff, Robert (Producer)
PO Box 3628
Granada Hills, CA 91394-0628, USA

Charton, Pete (Athlete, Baseball Player)
104 Hickory Knob Hill Rd
Irmo, SC 29063-9782, USA

Chartraw, Rick (Athlete, Hockey Player)
600 Chaparral Rd
Sierra Madre, CA 91024-1115, USA

Charvet, David (Actor)
3551 Cross Creek Rd
Malibu, CA 90265, USA

Charyk, Joseph V (Business Person)
790 Andrews Ave Apt A302
Delray Beach, FL 33483-7257, USA

Chase, Alison (Director)
Pilolobus Dance Theater
PO Box 388
Washington Depot, CT 06794-0388, USA

Chase, Alston (Writer)
c/o Deborah Clarke Grosvenor *The Bohrman Agency*
8899 Beverly Blvd Ste 811
Los Angeles, CA 90048-2452, USA

Chase, Bailey (Actor)
c/o Staff Member *McKeon-Myones Management*
3500 W Olive Ave Ste 770
Burbank, CA 91505-5527, USA

Chase, Barrie (Actor, Dancer)
446 Carroll Canal
Venice, CA 90291-4682, USA

Chase, Chevy (Actor, Comedian, Producer)
PO Box 257
Bedford, NY 10506-0257, USA

Chase, Daveigh (Actor)
c/o Bonnie Liedtke *Principato/Young Management (LA)*
9465 Wilshire Blvd Ste 900
Beverly Hills, CA 90212-2608, USA

Chase, David (Producer)
c/o Staff Member *United Talent Agency (UTA-LA)*
9336 Civic Center Dr
Beverly Hills, CA 90210-3604, USA

Chase, Hayley (Actor)
c/o Staff Member *Bobby Ball Talent Agency*
3500 W Olive Ave Ste 300
Burbank, CA 91505-4647, USA

Chase, John (Athlete, Hockey Player)
170 Broadway Apt 609
New York, NY 10038-4154, USA

Chase, Jonathan (Actor)
c/o Tracy Steinsapir *Main Title Entertainment*
8383 Wilshire Blvd Ste 408
Beverly Hills, CA 90211-2435, USA

Chase, Kelly (Athlete, Hockey Player)
16476 Horseshoe Ridge Rd
Chesterfield, MO 63005-4422, USA

Chase, Kristen (Writer)
c/o Staff Member *Adams Media Corporation*
57 Littlefield St Ste 3
Avon, MA 02322-1934, USA

Chase, Leah (Chef, Writer)
c/o Staff Member *Pelican Publishing Company*
1000 Burmaster St
Gretna, LA 70053-2246, USA

Chase, Sylvia B (Correspondent)
ABC-TV
77 W 66th St
News Dept
New York, NY 10023-6201, USA

Chasez, JC (Musician)
2304 Sunset Plaza Dr
Los Angeles, CA 90069-1209, USA

Chasin, Liza (Business Person)
c/o Staff Member *Working Title Films*
9720 Wilshire Blvd Fl 4
Beverly Hills, CA 90212-2000, USA

Chass, Murray (Commentator)
22-20 Radburn Rd
Fair Lawn, NJ 07410-4524, USA

Chassey, Steve (Race Car Driver)
6063 W Irma Ln
Glendale, AZ 85308-6751, USA

Chast, Roz (Comedian)
New Yorker Magazine
4 Times Sq Fl 22
Editorial Dept
New York, NY 10036-6592, USA

Chastain, Brandi (Athlete, Olympic Athlete, Soccer Player)
1661 University Way
San Jose, CA 95126-1555, USA

Chastain, Jessica (Actor)
c/o Paul Nelson *Mosaic Media Group*
9200 W Sunset Blvd Ste 10
West Hollywood, CA 90069-3608, USA

Chatham, Matt (Athlete, Football Player)
2502 Old Bridge Ln
Bellingham, MA 02019-3124, USA

Chatham, Wes (Actor)
c/o Robert Stein *Robert Stein Management*
PO Box 3797
Beverly Hills, CA 90212-0797, USA

Chatman, Charles (Baseball Player)
Detroit Clowns
2024 Clarksdale Ave
Memphis, TN 38108-1313, USA

Chatman, Jesse (Athlete, Football Player)
c/o Eugene Parker *Maximum Sports Management*
6435 W Jefferson Blvd # 197
Fort Wayne, IN 46804-6203, USA

Chatwin, Justin (Actor)
c/o Theresa Peters *United Talent Agency (UTA-LA)*
9336 Civic Center Dr
Beverly Hills, CA 90210-3604, USA

Chaves, Richard J (Actor)
c/o Staff Member *Media Artists Group (NY)*
722 Mason Ave
Drexel Hill, PA 19026-2416, USA

Chavez, Anthony (Athlete, Baseball Player)
10569 S Varner Dr
Vail, AZ 85641-2582, USA

Chavez, Eric (Athlete, Baseball Player)
6510 E Bar Z Ln
Paradise Valley, AZ 85253-1873, USA

Chavez, Jorge (Horse Racer)
106 John St
Garden City, NY 11530-3006, USA

Chavez, Julio Cesar (Athlete, Boxer)
c/o Staff Member *Boxing Hall of Fame*
1 Hall of Fame Dr
Canastota, NY 13032-1180, USA

Chavez, Linda (Correspondent)
c/o Staff Member *Fox News (NY)*
1211 Avenue of the Americas Lowr C1
New York, NY 10036-8705, USA

Chavez, Marga (Actor)
c/o Staff Member *Select Artists Ltd (CA-Valley Office)*
PO Box 4359
Burbank, CA 91503-4359, USA

Chavira, Ricardo (Actor)
10866 Wilshire Blvd Ste 1600
Los Angeles, CA 90024-4357, USA

Chavous, Barney L (Athlete, Coach, Football Coach, Football Player)
601 Chavous Rd
Aiken, SC 29803-5031, USA

Chavous, Corey (Athlete, Football Player)
1218 S Main St
Saint Charles, MO 63301-3525, USA

Chayanne (Actor, Musician)
1717 N Bayshore Dr
2146
Miami, FL 33132-1180, USA

Cheadle, Don (Actor)
c/o Jennifer Allen *Viewpoint Inc (LA)*
8820 Wilshire Blvd Ste 220
Beverly Hills, CA 90211-2622, USA

Cheaney, Calbert (Athlete, Basketball Player)
4 Upper Dromara Ln
Saint Louis, MO 63124-1894, USA

Cheatham, Ernie (Athlete, Football Player)
400 Ashton St
Pittsburgh, PA 15207-1786, USA

Cheatham, Maree (Actor)
Yvette Schumer
8787 Shoreham Dr
West Hollywood, CA 90069-2231, USA

Checker, Chubby (Musician, Songwriter, Writer)
Twisted Booking
320 Fayette St Fl 2
C/O Mary Parisi
Conshohocken, PA 19428-1960, USA

Cheechoo, Jonathan (Athlete, Hockey Player)
5081 Indigo Bay Blvd Unit 202
Estero, FL 33928-6999, USA

Cheek, Louis (Athlete, Football Player)
545 Woelke Rd
Seguin, TX 78155-9345, USA

Cheek, Molly (Actor)
c/o Staff Member *Pakula/King & Associates*
9229 W Sunset Blvd Ste 315
West Hollywood, CA 90069-3403, USA

Cheeks, Maurica E (Mo) (Athlete, Basketball Player, Coach)
7325 SW Childs Rd
Portland, OR 97224-7713, USA

Cheeks, Maurice (Athlete, Basketball Player)
34400 Woodward Ave # 200
Birmingham, MI 48009-0978, USA

Cheeseborough, Chandra (Athlete, Olympic Athlete, Track Athlete)
104 W Harbor
Hendersonville, TN 37075-3556, USA

Cheesman, Barry (Athlete, Golfer)
2901 Theresa Ln
Sarasota, FL 34239-7008, USA

Cheetwood, Derk (Actor)
2290 Oxford Ave
Claremont, CA 91711-1632, USA

Cheever, Eddie (Race Car Driver)
1842 Cecil St
Carmel, IN 46032-7216, USA

Cheever, Michael (Athlete, Football Player)
2638 Weddington Pl NE
Marietta, GA 30068-3101, USA

Cheevers, Gary (Athlete, Hockey Player)
2 Jakobek Way
Merrimac, MA 01860-1017, USA

Cheevers, Gerry (Athlete, Hockey Player)
106 Appleton St
North Andover, MA 01845-3138, USA

Chelf, Donald(Don) (Athlete, Football Player)
7329 Bottle Brush Dr
Spring Hill, FL 34606-7023, USA

Cheli, Maurizio (Astronaut)
c/o Staff Member *NASA-JSC*
2101 Nasa Pkwy # 1
Astronaut Office - Mail Code Cb
Houston, TX 77058-3607, USA

Chelios, Chris (Athlete, Hockey Player, Olympic Athlete)
28026 Sea Lane Dr
Malibu, CA 90265-4325, USA

Chellgren, Paul W (Business Person)
Ashland Inc
PO Box 15391
Covington, KY 41015-0391, USA

Chelsom, Peter (Actor)
c/o Staff Member *Principato/Young Management (LA)*
9465 Wilshire Blvd Ste 900
Beverly Hills, CA 90212-2608, USA

Chen, Bruce (Athlete, Baseball Player)
114 Dutchfork Creek Trl
Irmo, SC 29063-7834, USA

Chen, Camille (Actor)
c/o Scott Zimmerman *Evolution Entertainment (LA)*
901 N Highland Ave
Los Angeles, CA 90038-2412, USA

Chen, Da (Writer)
c/o Staff Member *Writers and Artists Group Intl (NY)*
360 Park Ave # 16
New York, NY 10022-5909, USA

Chen, Edith (Musician)
Columbia Artists Mgmt Inc
165 W 57th St
New York, NY 10019-2201, USA

Chen, Joan (Actor, Director)
2601 Filbert St
San Francisco, CA 94123-3215, USA

Chen, Joie (Correspondent)
Cable News Network
1050 Techwood Dr NW
News Dept
Atlanta, GA 30318-5695, USA

Chen, Julie (Reality Star, Television Host)
The Talk
4024 Radford Ave
Studio City, CA 91604-2101, USA

Chen, Kaige (Director)
International Creative Mgmt
10250 Constellation Blvd Fl 1
Los Angeles, CA 90067-6241, USA

Chen, Lynn (Actor)
c/o Staff Member *ICM Partners (LA)*
10250 Constellation Blvd Fl 7
Los Angeles, CA 90067-6207, USA

Chen, Robert (Musician)
Columbia Artists Mgmt Inc
165 W 57th St
New York, NY 10019-2201, USA

Chenault, Kenneth (Business Person)
1044 Brick Kiln Rd
Sag Harbor, NY 11963-2942, USA

Cheney, Lynne V (Government Official)
American Enterprise Institute
1150 17th St NW Ste 1000
Washington, DC 20036-4670, USA

Chenier, Phil
10734 Bridlerein Ter
Columbia, MD 21044-3653, USA

Chenier, Phil (Athlete, Basketball Player)
907 Mount Holly St
Baltimore, MD 21229-1929, USA

Chennault, Anna (Business Person)
TAC International
1049 30th St NW
Chennault Building
Washington, DC 20007-3823, USA

Chenoweth, Kristin (Actor, Musician)
462 W 58th St Apt 8A
New York, NY 10019-1168, USA

Cher (Actor, Director, Musician, Producer)
20243 Piedra Chica Rd
Malibu, CA 90265-5327, USA

Cherilus, Gosder (Athlete, Football Player)
c/o Adam Heller *Vantage Management Group*
518 Reamer Dr
Carnegie, PA 15106-1845, USA

Cherington, Ben (Commentator)
338 Commercial St Apt 401
Boston, MA 02109-1128, USA

Chernin, Peter (Business Person)
2327 La Mesa Dr
Santa Monica, CA 90402-2330, USA

Chernow, Ron (Writer)
63 Joralemon St
Brooklyn, NY 11201-4003, USA

Chernus, Michael (Actor)
c/o Jill Kaplan *Authentic Talent and Literary Management*
20 Jay St Ste M17
Brooklyn, NY 11201-8300, USA

Cherrelle (Musician)
c/o Staff Member *Associated Booking Corp*
PO Box 800137
Miami, FL 33280-0137, USA

Cherry, Deron (Athlete, Football Player)
13800 S Pebblebrook Ln
Greenwood, MO 64034-8216, USA

Cherry, Jeirod (Athlete, Football Player)
8708 Quailridge Ct
Macedonia, OH 44056-1772, USA

Cherry, Je'rod (Athlete, Football Player)
8708 Quailridge Ct
Macedonia, OH 44056-1772, USA

Cherry, Marc (Producer, Writer)
4261 Hazeltine Ave
Sherman Oaks, CA 91423-4245, USA

Cherry, Mike (Athlete, Football Player)
4106 Central Pl
Texarkana, AR 71854-1617, USA

Cherry, Nena (Musician)
c/o Staff Member *Paradigm (Monterey)*
404 W Franklin St
Monterey, CA 93940-2303, USA

Cherry, Raphel (Athlete, Football Player)
1102 Church St
Jacksonville, AR 72076-5410, USA

Cherry, Rocky (Athlete, Baseball Player)
5624 Gleneagles Dr
Plano, TX 75093-5973, USA

Cherry Poppin' Daddies (Music Group, Musician)
c/o Jim Lenz *Paradise Artists*
108 E Matilija St
Ojai, CA 93023-2639, USA

Chertok, Jack (Producer)
515 Ocean Ave # 305
Santa Monica, CA 90402-2609, USA

Cherundolo, Charles (Chuck) (Athlete, Football Player)
4230 Simms Rd
Lakeland, FL 33810-0402, USA

Chervyakov, Denis (Athlete, Hockey Player)
PO Box 2832
Ashburn, VA 20146-2832, USA

Chesley, Al (Athlete, Football Player)
2604 32nd St SE
Washington, DC 20020-1448, USA

Chesney, Kenny (Musician)
414 Lake Valley Dr
Franklin, TN 37069-4661, USA

Chesnutt, Mark (Musician)
2454 S Pine Island Rd
Beaumont, TX 77713-3238, USA

Chesson 3rd, Wes (Athlete, Football Player)
1028 Marlowe Rd
Raleigh, NC 27609-6962, USA

Chester, Colby (Actor)
Talent Group
5670 Wilshire Blvd Ste 820
Los Angeles, CA 90036-5613, USA

Chester, Larry (Athlete, Football Player)
6359 Celtic Dr SW
Atlanta, GA 30331-9414, USA

Chester, Raymond (Athlete, Football Player)
4722 Grass Valley Rd
Oakland, CA 94605-5622, USA

Chestnut, Cyrus (Musician)
Avenue Management Group
250 W 57th St # 407
New York, NY 10107-0001, USA

Chestnut, Morris (Actor)
11551 Jerry St
Cerritos, CA 90703-7416, USA

Chetti, Joseph(Joe) (Athlete, Football Player)
7 Baur St
West Babylon, NY 11704-3320, USA

Chetwynd, Lionel (Producer, Writer)
c/o Bruce Vinokour *Creative Artists Agency (CAA-LA)*
2000 Avenue of the Stars Ste 100
Los Angeles, CA 90067-4705, USA

Cheung, Maggie (Actor)
c/o Ted Schachter *Schachter Entertainment*
1157 S Beverly Dr Fl 2
Los Angeles, CA 90035-1119, USA

Chevalier, Tracy (Writer)
EP Dutton
375 Hudson St
New York, NY 10014-3658, USA

Chevelle (Music Group)
c/o Staff Member *Creative Artists Agency (CAA-LA)*
2000 Avenue of the Stars Ste 100
Los Angeles, CA 90067-4705, USA

Chevrier, Alain (Athlete, Hockey Player)
5138 Greenwich Preserve Ct
Boynton Beach, FL 33436-5802, USA

Chevrier, Alain (Athlete, Hockey Player)
6857 Rain Forest Dr
Boca Raton, FL 33434, USA

Chew, Gloria Ann (Actor)
351 N Eldorado St
San Mateo, CA 94401-1733, USA

Chew Jr, Sam
8075 W 3rd St # 303
Los Angeles, CA 90048-4318, USA

Cheylov, Milan (Director)
c/o Bill Douglass *Paradigm (LA)*
360 N Crescent Dr
North Bldg
Beverly Hills, CA 90210-4874, USA

Cheyunski, Jim (Athlete, Football Player)
3116 Stone Gap Ct
Raleigh, NC 27612-4180, USA

Chiacchia, Darren (Athlete, Horse Racer, Olympic Athlete)
5195 Genesee Rd
Springville, NY 14141-9684, USA

Chiadel, Dana (Athlete)
5302 Flanders Ave
Kensington, MD 20895-1139, USA

Chiamparino, Scott (Athlete, Baseball Player)
179 Ortega Ave
Mountain View, CA 94040-1439, USA

Chianese, Dominic (Actor)
c/o Brian Liebman *Liebman Entertainment*
12 E 46th St Fl 5
New York, NY 10017-2418, USA

Chiarello, Michael (Chef)
Napastyle
360 Industrial Ct # A
Benicia, CA 94510-1138, USA

Chiasson, Scott (Athlete, Baseball Player)
3660 N Lake Rd
Erieville, NY 13061-3106, USA

Chiaverini, Darrin (Athlete, Football Player)
3907 106th St
Lubbock, TX 79423-6739, USA

Chicago (Music Group)
c/o Howard Rose *Howard Rose Agency Ltd, The*
9460 Wilshire Blvd Ste 310
Beverly Hills, CA 90212-2710, USA

Chick, Travis (Athlete, Baseball Player)
2201 Villa Dr
Tyler, TX 75703-1949, USA

Chickillo, Anthony (Tony) (Athlete, Football Player)
6920 Spanish Moss Cir
Tampa, FL 33625-6556, USA

Chieftans, The (Music Group)
c/o Staff Member *ICM Partners (LA)*
10250 Constellation Blvd Fl 7
Los Angeles, CA 90067-6207, USA

Chiesa, Fabrizio (Producer)
c/o Matt Leipzig *Original Artists (LA)*
9465 Wilshire Blvd Ste 870
Beverly Hills, CA 90212-2610, USA

Chievous, Derrick (Athlete, Basketball Player)
5607 Thornbrook Pkwy
Columbia, MO 65203-9799, USA

Chiffer, Floyd (Athlete, Baseball Player)
4325 Levelside Ave
Lakewood, CA 90712-3752, USA

Chiffons, The (Music Group, Musician)
c/o Staff Member *Lustig Talent Enterprises Inc*
PO Box 770850
Orlando, FL 32877-0850, USA

Chiklis, Michael (Actor, Director, Producer)
4310 Sutton Pl
Sherman Oaks, CA 91403-4016, USA

Chilcutt, Pete
9054 High Flight Ct
Fair Oaks, CA 95628-4188

Child, Desmond (Musician)
509 Tuckaway Ct
Nashville, TN 37205-3919, USA

Child, Jane (Musician)
2031 Holly Hill Ter
Los Angeles, CA 90068-3811, USA

Childers, Ambyr (Actor)
c/o Staff Member *McKeon-Myones Management*
3500 W Olive Ave Ste 770
Burbank, CA 91505-5527, USA

Childers, Jason (Athlete, Baseball Player)
417 Aumond Rd
Augusta, GA 30909-3562, USA

Childers, Matt (Athlete, Baseball Player)
417 Aumond Rd
Augusta, GA 30909-3562, USA

Childress, Josh (Athlete, Basketball Player)
1433 Cherokee Trl
Lawrenceville, GA 30043-5807, USA

Childress, Kallie Flynn (Actor)
c/o TJ Stein *Stein Entertainment Group*
1351 N Crescent Heights Blvd Apt 312
West Hollywood, CA 90046-4549, USA

Childress, Randolph (Athlete, Basketball Player)
2293 Ashford Dr
Winston Salem, NC 27103-6259

Childress, Raymond C (Ray) Jr (Athlete, Football Player)
639 Shady Hollow St
Houston, TX 77056-1635, USA

Childress, Richard (Race Car Driver)
Childress Racing
9543 Hampton Rd
Lexington, NC 27295, USA

Childress, Rocky (Athlete, Baseball Player)
5 Meadow Glen Ct
Santa Rosa, CA 95404-1845, USA

Childs, Billy (Musician)
Integrity Talent
PO Box 961
Burlington, MA 01803-5961, USA

Childs, Charissa (Athlete, Golfer)
25 Green Springs Cir
Columbia, SC 29223-6940, USA

Childs, Chris (Athlete, Basketball Player)
10830 Willow Meadow Cir Cir
Alpharetta, GA 30022-6516, USA

Childs, Clarence (Athlete, Football Player)
1652 Lawrence Cir
Daytona Beach, FL 32117-3942, USA

Childs, Henry (Athlete, Football Player)
8304 Allman Rd
Lenexa, KS 66219-2705, USA

Chiles, Lois (Actor)
c/o Staff Member *Abrams Artists Agency (LA)*
9200 W Sunset Blvd PH 11
West Hollywood, CA 90069-3601, USA

Chiles, Rich (Athlete, Baseball Player)
18147 Mallard St
Woodland, CA 95695-6038, USA

Chilies, Lois (Actor)
c/o Staff Member *Abrams Artists Agency (LA)*
9200 W Sunset Blvd PH 11
West Hollywood, CA 90069-3601, USA

Chi-Lites, The (Music Group)
c/o Staff Member *M.A.G./Universal Attractions*
15 W 36th St Fl 8
New York, NY 10018-7927, USA

Chillar, Brandon (Athlete, Football Player)
1030 Iris Ct
Carlsbad, CA 92011-4823, USA

Chillemi, Connie (Athlete, Golfer)
2701 NE 10th St Apt 705
Ocala, FL 34470-5689, USA

Chilton, Gene (Athlete, Football Player)
45828 US Highway 69 N
Jacksonville, TX 75766-8749, USA

Chilton, Kevin P (Astronaut)
2555 Talleson Ct
Colorado Springs, CO 80919-4874, USA

Chimera, Jason (Athlete, Hockey Player)
2468 Club Rd
Columbus, OH 43221-4007, USA

Chiminello, Bianca (Actor)
c/o Staff Member *Matt Sherman Management*
7510 W Sunset Blvd Ste 1413
Los Angeles, CA 90046-3408, USA

Chin, Tessanne (Musician)
c/o Staff Member *ICM Partners (LA)*
10250 Constellation Blvd Fl 7
Los Angeles, CA 90067-6207, USA

Chin, Tsai (Actor)
c/o Donald Spradlin *Essential Talent Management*
6399 Wilshire Blvd Ste 401
Los Angeles, CA 90048-5716, USA

Chinlund, Nick (Actor)
c/o Gordon Gilbertson *Gilbertson Management*
1334 3rd Street Promenade Ste 201
Santa Monica, CA 90401-1320, USA

Chino, Chino
440 E 23rd St Apt 1508
Hialeah, FL 33013-3941, usa

Chiodos (Music Group, Musician)
c/o Staff Member *Equal Vision Records*
PO Box 38202
Albany, NY 12203-8202, USA

Chishholm-Carrillo, Linda (Athlete, Volleyball Player)
17213 Vose St
Van Nuys, CA 91406-3633, USA

Chisholm, Art (Athlete, Hockey Player)
9 Jefferson Ct
Woburn, MA 01801-4326, USA

Chism, Tom (Athlete, Baseball Player)
532 W Brookhaven Rd Apt F1
Brookhaven, PA 19015-1824, USA

Chistov, Stanislav (Athlete, Hockey Player)
Puckagency LLC
1 Sunset Dr N
Attn Jay Grossman
Chappaqua, NY 10514-1613, USA

Chistov, Stanislaw (Athlete, Hockey Player)
c/o Jay Grossman *PuckAgency LLC*
555 Pleasantville Rd
North Building, Suite 210
Briarcliff Manor, NY 10510-1955, USA

Chitren, Steve (Athlete, Baseball Player)
259 Dominican Ave
Henderson, NV 89002-3337, USA

Chittum, Nelson (Athlete, Baseball Player)
1008 Morning View Rd
Lawrenceburg, KY 40342-8931, USA

Chitwood Jr, Joey (Race Car Driver)
Chicagoland Speedway
4410 W Alva St
Tampa, FL 33614-7639, USA

Chiu Wai, Tony Leung (Actor)
c/o Staff Member *William Morris Endeavor (LA)*
9601 Wilshire Blvd
Beverly Hills, CA 90210-5213, USA

Chlebek, Ed (Athlete, Football Player)
6160 Waxmyrtle Way
Naples, FL 34109-5940, USA

Chlumsky, Anna (Actor)
c/o Cory Richman *Liebman Entertainment*
12 E 46th St Fl 5
New York, NY 10017-2418, USA

Chlupsa, Bob (Athlete, Baseball Player)
55 Willow St
Garden City, NY 11530-6316, USA

Chmerkovskiy, Maksim (Dancer, Reality Star)
c/o Lizzie Grubman *Lizzie Grubman Public Relations*
424 W 33rd St Rm 110
New York, NY 10001-2619, USA

Chmerkovskiy, Valentin (Dancer)
c/o Lizzie Grubman *Lizzie Grubman Public Relations*
424 W 33rd St Rm 110
New York, NY 10001-2619, USA

Chmura, Mark W (Athlete, Football Player)
S18W28948 Price Ct
Waukesha, WI 53188-9551, USA

Cho, Alina (Correspondent)
c/o John Ferriter *Octagon Entertainment*
8687 Melrose Ave Ste 7
West Hollywood, CA 90069-5721, USA

Cho, Catherine (Musician)
Columbia Artists Mgmt Inc
165 W 57th St
New York, NY 10019-2201, USA

Cho, Frank (Cartoonist)
Creators Syndicate
737 3rd St
Hermosa Beach, CA 90254-4714, USA

Cho, Henry (Actor, Comedian, Writer)
c/o Alex Murray *Brillstein Entertainment Partners (LA)*
9150 Wilshire Blvd Ste 350
Beverly Hills, CA 90212-3453, USA

Cho, John (Actor)
2152 Panorama Ter
Los Angeles, CA 90039-3541, USA

Cho, Margaret (Actor, Comedian)
1875 Oakwood Ave
Glendale, CA 91208-2164, USA

Cho, Smith (Actor)
c/o Amy Guenther *Gateway Management Company Inc*
860 Via De La Paz Ste F10
Pacific Palisades, CA 90272-3631, USA

Choate, Don (Athlete, Baseball Player)
9506 Maryann Dr
Fairview Heights, IL 62208-1625, USA

Choate, Jerry D (Business Person)
Allstate Insurance
2775 Sanders Rd
Allstate Plaza
Northbrook, IL 60062-6127, USA

Choate, Putt (Athlete, Football Player)
9800 Rockbrook Dr
Dallas, TX 75220-2041, USA

Choate, Randy (Athlete, Baseball Player)
316 Leon Pl
Davis, CA 95616, USA

Chobot, Jessica (Correspondent)
IGN Entertainment
625 2nd St Fl 3
San Francisco, CA 94107-4012, USA

Chodor, Allan (Bowler)
9010 Corbin Ave Ste 6
Northridge, CA 91324-3356

Choi, Hee Seop (Athlete, Baseball Player)
14310 SE 29th Cir
Vancouver, WA 98683-7691, USA

Choi, Kathy (Athlete, Golfer)
7912 Beachpoint Cir Apt 18
Huntington Beach, CA 92648-1478, USA

Choi, Kenneth (Actor)
c/o Gail Abbott *Gail Abbott Management*
3019 Hollycrest Dr
Los Angeles, CA 90068-1801, USA

Choi, KJ (Athlete, Golfer)
1360 E 9th St
Cleveland, OH 44114-1737, USA

Choi, Yun (Actor)
c/o Staff Member *Select Artists Ltd (CA-Westside Office)*
1138 12th St Apt 1
Santa Monica, CA 90403-5459, USA

Chokachi, David (Actor)
1036 S Ridgeley Dr
Los Angeles, CA 90019-2509, USA

Cholodenko, Lisa (Director, Producer, Writer)
c/o Bart Walker *ICM Partners (LA)*
10250 Constellation Blvd Fl 7
Los Angeles, CA 90067-6207, USA

Choma, John (Athlete, Football Player)
1544 Carol Ave
Burlingame, CA 94010-5231, USA

Chomet, Sylvain (Director, Writer)
c/o Robert Newman *William Morris Endeavor (LA)*
9601 Wilshire Blvd
Beverly Hills, CA 90210-5213, USA

Chomsky, Marvin J (Director)
15200 W Sunset Blvd Ste 209
Pacific Palisades, CA 90272-3621

Chon, Justin (Actor)
c/o Staff Member *Abrams Artists Agency (LA)*
9200 W Sunset Blvd PH 11
West Hollywood, CA 90069-3601, USA

Chonacas, Katie (Actor, Model)
c/o Jordyn Palos *Persona PR (LA)*
8840 Wilshire Blvd Ste 212
Beverly Hills, CA 90211-2606, USA

Chones, Jim (Athlete, Basketball Player)
26400 George Zeiger Dr Apt 305
Dr Apt 305
Beachwood, OH 44122-7511, USA

Chong, Rae Dawn (Actor)
c/o David Fox *Myman Greenspan Fineman Fox Rosenberg & Light*
11601 Wilshire Blvd Ste 2200
Los Angeles, CA 90025-1758, USA

Chong, Tommy (Actor, Comedian)
1625 Casale Rd
Pacific Palisades, CA 90272-2717, USA

Chopra, Daniel (Athlete, Golfer)
9838 Laurel Valley Dr
Windermere, FL 34786-8911, USA

Chopra, Deepak (Doctor, Writer)
6878 Country Club Dr
La Jolla, CA 92037-5605, USA

Chopra, Priyanka (Actor)
c/o Troy Carter *Atom Factory/Coalition Media Group*
1630 Colorado Ave
Santa Monica, CA 90404, USA

Choquette, Sonia (Writer)
Sonia and Sabrina Consulting
4759 N Maplewood Ave
Chicago, IL 60625-2952, USA

Chorske, Tom (Athlete, Hockey Player)
23 Cooper Cir
Minneapolis, MN 55436-1316, USA

Chorvat, Scarlett (Actor)
1727 N Crescent Heights Blvd
Los Angeles, CA 90069-1604, USA

Chou, Collin (Actor)
c/o Tim Kwok *Convergence Entertainment*
9150 Wilshire Blvd Ste 247
Beverly Hills, CA 90212-3429, USA

Chou, Jay (Musician)
c/o Staff Member *BMG*
1540 Broadway
New York, NY 10036-4039, USA

Choudhury, Sarita (Actor)
c/o Kathy Atkinson *Washington Square Arts (NY)*
1041 N Formosa Ave
the Lot Writers Bldg, Room 305
West Hollywood, CA 90046-6703, USA

Chouinard, Bobby (Athlete, Baseball Player)
6024 S Paris Pl
Englewood, CO 80111-4152, USA

Chow, Amy (Athlete, Gymnast, Olympic Athlete)
285 Tamarind Ln
Danville, CA 94526-4421, USA

Chow, China (Actor)
c/o Andy Stabile *Creative Artists Agency (CAA-LA)*
2000 Avenue of the Stars Ste 100
Los Angeles, CA 90067-4705, USA

Chow, Steven (Actor)
c/o Alan Grodin *Weissman Wolff Bergman Coleman Silverman Holmes*
9665 Wilshire Blvd Fl 9
Beverly Hills, CA 90212-2316, USA

Chrebet, Wayne (Athlete, Football Player)
147 Heulitt Rd
Colts Neck, NJ 07722-1427, USA

Chretien, Jean-Loup Brig Gen (Astronaut)
2092 N Pointe Alexis Dr
Dr Apt 43
Tarpon Springs, FL 34689-2048, USA

Chriqui, Emmanuelle (Actor)
c/o Emily Gerson Saines *Brookside Artists Management (NY)*
250 W 57th St Ste 2303
New York, NY 10107-2399, USA

Chris, Mike (Athlete, Baseball Player)
31257 Corte Alhambra
Temecula, CA 92592-5420, USA

Chrisley, Neil (Athlete, Baseball Player)
280 Myrtle Greens Dr Apt B
Conway, SC 29526-9040, USA

Christ, Chad (Actor)
c/o Brian Liebman *Liebman Entertainment*
12 E 46th St Fl 5
New York, NY 10017-2418, USA

Christ, Dorothy (Athlete, Baseball Player, Commentator)
1700 I St # 18
La Porte, IN 46350-5750, USA

Christ, Fred (Athlete, Basketball Player)
2500 Eagle Dr Apt D
Melbourne, FL 32935-3526, USA

Christensen, Bruce (Athlete, Baseball Player)
PO Box 178
Moroni, UT 84646-0178, USA

Christensen, Erika (Actor)
2505 Laurel Pass
Los Angeles, CA 90046-1403, USA

Christensen, Hayden (Actor)
11210 Briarcliff Ln
Studio City, CA 91604-4277, USA

Christensen, John (Athlete, Baseball Player)
2931 Yuma Dr
Lake Havasu City, AZ 86406-8568, USA

Christensen, Joss (Olympic Athlete, Skier)
US Ski And Snowboard Association
1 Victory Ln # 100
Park City, UT 84060-7463, USA

Christensen, McKay (Athlete, Baseball Player)
2720 W Shady Hollow Ln
Lehi, UT 84043-5713, USA

Christensen Jr, Erik (Athlete, Football Player)
308 Sentinel Ln
Newark, DE 19702-8504, USA

Christenson, Gary (Athlete, Baseball Player)
436 E Tremaine Ave
Gilbert, AZ 85234-4624, USA

Christenson, Larry (Athlete, Baseball Player)
1465 Le Boutillier Rd
Malvern, PA 19355-8741, USA

Christenson, Ryan (Athlete, Baseball Player)
7513 Terry John Ave
Bakersfield, CA 93308-2774, USA

Christenson, Ryan (Athlete, Baseball Player)
4021 Canario St Unit 136
Carlsbad, CA 92008-6102, USA

Christian, Andrew (Designer, Fashion Designer)
Andrew Christian Clothing
1631 Gardena Ave
Glendale, CA 91204-2713, USA

Christian, Ash (Actor, Director, Writer)
c/o Simon Millar *Rumble Media*
1620 Broadway Ste C
Santa Monica, CA 90404-2777, USA

Christian, Bill (Athlete, Hockey Player, Olympic Athlete)
400 Fox Haven Dr Apt 4207
Naples, FL 34104-5134, USA

Christian, Bob (Athlete, Football Player)
9450 Lincolnwood Dr
Evanston, IL 60203-1114, USA

Christian, Christina (Actor, Musician)
c/o Allee Newhoff *Elite Model Management (Miami)*
119 Washington Ave Ste 501
Miami Beach, FL 33139-7228, USA

Christian, Claudia (Actor)
c/o Staff Member *Abrams Artists Agency (LA)*
9200 W Sunset Blvd PH 11
West Hollywood, CA 90069-3601, USA

Christian, David W (Dave) (Athlete, Hockey Player, Olympic Athlete)
Christian Brothers Hockey Company
3134 Bavaria Hills Trl
Chaska, MN 55318-2723, USA

Christian, Eddie (Baseball Player)
1126 NE Lija Loop
Portland, OR 97211-1318, USA

Christian, Gabrielle (Actor)
c/o Robert Haas *Innovative Artists (LA)*
1505 10th St
Santa Monica, CA 90401-2805, USA

Christian, Gordon (Athlete, Hockey Player)
604 Lake St NW
Warroad, MN 56763-2123, USA

Christian, Jeff (Athlete, Hockey Player)
5471 Eaglesnest Dr
Westerville, OH 43081-4423, USA

Christian, Richard (Actor)
c/o Staff Member *Select Artists Ltd (CA-Westside Office)*
1138 12th St Apt 1
Santa Monica, CA 90403-5459, USA

Christian, Shawn (Actor)
543 N Fuller Ave
Los Angeles, CA 90036-1940, USA

Christiansen, Clay (Athlete, Baseball Player)
7227 Eby Ave Apt 202
Overland Park, KS 66204-1643, USA

Christiansen, Jason (Athlete, Baseball Player)
3428 E Jasmine Cir
Mesa, AZ 85213-3245, USA

Christiansen, Keith (Athlete, Hockey Player, Olympic Athlete)
1023 Timberline Ln
Duluth, MN 55811-4451, USA

Christiansen, Robert S (Bob) (Athlete, Football Player)
5228 G St
Sacramento, CA 95819-3217, USA

Christianson, Bob (Musician)
c/o Mike Rosen *Working Artists Agency*
13525 Ventura Blvd
Sherman Oaks, CA 91423-3801

Christie, Chris (Governor, Politician)
Office of the Governor
PO Box 1
Trenton, NJ 08625-0001, USA

Christie, Doug (Athlete, Basketball Player)
14150 NE 20th St
Bellevue, WA 98007-3700, USA

Christie, Julianna (Actor)
252 N Larchmont Blvd Ste 200
Los Angeles, CA 90004-3754, USA

Christie, Julianne (Actor)
252 N Larchmont Blvd Ste 200
Los Angeles, CA 90004-3754, USA

Christie, Julie (Actor, Model)
c/o Renee Missel *Renee Missel Management*
846 S Wooster St
Los Angeles, CA 90035-1710, USA

Christie, Lou (Musician)
c/o Staff Member *Dick Fox Entertainment*
1650 Broadway
New York, NY 10019-6833, USA

Christie, Mike (Athlete, Hockey Player)
6093 S Krameria St
Centennial, CO 80111-4273, USA

Christie, Steve (Athlete, Football Player)
6150 Gulfport Blvd S Apt 102
Gulfport, FL 33707-3101, USA

Christine, Andrew (Andy) (Cartoonist)
c/o Staff Member *King Features Syndication*
300 W 57th St Fl 15
New York, NY 10019-5238, USA

Christlieb, Peter (Pete) (Musician)
Thomas Cassidy
11761 E Speedway Blvd
Tucson, AZ 85748-2017, USA

Christman, Tim (Athlete, Baseball Player)
213 Dunsbach Ferry Rd
Cohoes, NY 12047-4900, USA

Christmas, Steve (Athlete, Baseball Player)
600 Bentley St
Oviedo, FL 32765-8169, USA

Christoff, Steve (Athlete, Hockey Player, Olympic Athlete)
542 Fairview Ave S
Saint Paul, MN 55116-1466, USA

Christofferson, Debra (Actor)
5658 Lemp Ave
N Hollywood, CA 91601-1754, USA

Christon, Shameka (Athlete, Basketball Player)
c/o Staff Member *New York Liberty*
125 W End Ave # 6
New York, NY 10023-6387, USA

Christopher, Dennis (Actor)
BR&S
5757 Wilshire Blvd Ste 473
Los Angeles, CA 90036-3632, USA

Christopher, Gerald (Actor)
11900 Goshen Ave Apt 203
Los Angeles, CA 90049-6380, USA

Christopher, Gerard (Actor)
11900 Goshen Ave Apt 203
Los Angeles, CA 90049-6380

Christopher, Gretchen (Musician)
509 E Ridgecrest Blvd # 1A
Ridgecrest, CA 93555-3959, USA

Christopher, Herb (Athlete, Football Player)
PO Box 554
Redan, GA 30074-0554, USA

Christopher, Joe (Athlete, Baseball Player)
Chris Potter Sports 9722
Owings Mills, MD 71117, USA

Christopher, Matt (Writer)
c/o Dale Christopher
PO Box 2511
Gansevoort, NY 12831-5511, USA

Christopher, Mike (Athlete, Baseball Player)
8707 Courthouse Rd
Church Road, VA 23833-2712, USA

Christopher, Patrick (Athlete, Basketball Player)
c/o Sam Goldfelder *Excel Sports Management (LA)*
9665 Wilshire Blvd Ste 500
Beverly Hills, CA 90212-2312, USA

Christopher, Ted (Race Car Driver)
Marsh Racing
81 Mile Creek Rd
Old Lyme, CT 06371-1710, USA

Christopher, Thom (Actor)
Ambrosio/Mortimer
PO Box 16758
Beverly Hills, CA 90209-2758, USA

Christopher, Tyler (Actor)
11523 Duque Dr
Studio City, CA 91604-4279, USA

Christopher, William (Actor)
c/o Wes Stevens *Vox*
6420 Wilshire Blvd Ste 1080
Los Angeles, CA 90048-5539, USA

Christopherson, James (Jim) (Athlete, Football Player)
526 Queens Ct
Moorhead, MN 56560-6777, USA

Christy, Barrett (Athlete, Olympic Athlete, Snowboarder)
131 Lois Ln
Sequim, WA 98382-3057, USA

Christy, Earl (Athlete, Football Player)
10825 S Prairie Ave
Chicago, IL 60628-3620, USA

Christy, George
170 N Carmelina Ave
Los Angeles, CA 90049-2737

Christy, Greg (Athlete, Football Player)
505 Freeport Rd
Freeport, PA 16229-2904, USA

Christy, Jeff (Athlete, Football Player)
125 N Rebecca St
Saxonburg, PA 16056-9549, USA

Chryplewicz, Pete (Athlete, Football Player)
24627 Brompton Way
South Lyon, MI 48178-8888, USA

Chrysostom, Bishop (Religious Leader)
Serbian Orthodox Church
PO Box 519
St Sava Monastery
Libertyville, IL 60048-0519, USA

Chu, Judy (Congressman, Politician)
1520 Longworth Hob
Washington, DC 20515-4605, USA

Chu, Julie (Athlete, Hockey Player, Olympic Athlete)
145 Primrose Ln
Fairfield, CT 06825-2309, USA

Chubin, Steve (Athlete, Basketball Player)
2324 S Gray Dr
Lakewood, CO 80227-3954, USA

Chuck, Chuck (Athlete, Football Player)
268 Babbitt Rd Apt M5
Bedford Hills, NY 10507-2123, USA

Chuck, D (Musician)
Richard Walters
1800 Argyle Ave # 408
Los Angeles, CA 90028-5253, USA

Chuck, Wendy (Designer)
c/o Heather Parker *Innovative Artists (LA)*
1505 10th St
Santa Monica, CA 90401-2805, USA

Chuck Wagon Gang
4408 Buffalo Ln
Joshua, TX 76058-5521

Chukwurah, Patrick (Athlete, Football Player)
6757 Camino Rio
Irving, TX 75039-3064

Chulack, Christopher (Director, Producer, Writer)
c/o Staff Member *Creative Artists Agency (CAA-LA)*
2000 Avenue of the Stars Ste 100
Los Angeles, CA 90067-4705, USA

Chulk, Vinnie (Athlete, Baseball Player)
14301 SW 78th Ct
Palmetto Bay, FL 33158-1508, USA

Chum, Chuck
733 Trevino Dr
Lady Lake, FL 32159-5575, USA

Chung, Connie (Correspondent, Journalist)
1 W 72nd St Apt 4
New York, NY 10023-3414, USA

Chung, Doo Ri (Designer)
c/o Meghan Wood *KCD Worldwide Inc*
450 W 15th St Ste 604
New York, NY 10011-7082, USA

Chung, Eugene (Athlete, Football Player)
109 Surrey Ln
Ponte Vedra Beach, FL 32082-3942, USA

Chung, Jamie (Actor, Reality Star)
c/o Sarah Shyn *3 Arts Entertainment (LA)*
9460 Wilshire Blvd Fl 7
Beverly Hills, CA 90212-2713, USA

Chung, Mark (Soccer Player)
Columbus Crew
2121 Velma Ave
Columbus, OH 43211-2085, USA

Chupack, Cindy
c/o Daniel Strone *Trident Media Group LLC*
41 Madison Ave Fl 36
New York, NY 10010-2257, USA

Church, Barry (Athlete, Football Player)
c/o Bruce Tollner *REP 1 Sports Group*
2 Corporate Park Ste 106
Irvine, CA 92606-5103, USA

Church, Eric (Musician)
714 Farrell Rd
Nashville, TN 37220-1207, USA

Church, Ryan (Athlete, Baseball Player)
3500 Thurloe Dr
Rockledge, FL 32955-6066, USA

Churches, Brady J (Business Person)
Consolidated Stores
1105 N Market St
Wilmington, DE 19801-1216, USA

Churchman, Ricky (Athlete, Football Player)
445 Cherry Blossom Loop
Richland, WA 99352-7851, USA

Churla, Shane (Athlete, Hockey Player)
31826 Scotch Pine Ln
Bigfork, MT 59911-8275, USA

Churla, Steve (Athlete, Hockey Player)
19299 E Shore Route
Bigfork, MT 59911, USA

Churn, Chuck (Athlete, Baseball Player)
637 Hickory Hl
Lady Lake, FL 32159-3224, USA

Chvatal, Cynthia (Producer)
c/o Staff Member *United Talent Agency (UTA-LA)*
9336 Civic Center Dr
Beverly Hills, CA 90210-3604, USA

Chychrun, Jeff (Athlete, Hockey Player)
6423 NW 32nd Way
Boca Raton, FL 33496-3396, USA

Ciaffa, Chris
627 N Las Palmas Ave
Los Angeles, CA 90004-1019

Cialini, Julie (Artist, Model)
PO Box 55536
Valencia, CA 91385-0536, USA

Ciampi, Joe (Coach)
Auburn University
Athletic Dept
Auburn, AL 36831, USA

Ciampl, Joe (Coach)
Aubuin University
Athletic Dept
Auburn, AL 36831, USA

Cianfrocco, Archi (Athlete, Baseball Player)
12424 Addax Ct
San Diego, CA 92129-4141, USA

Ciara (Musician)
3286 Northside Pkwy NW Apt 1004
Atlanta, GA 30327-2250, USA

Ciaramello, Benny (Actor)
c/o Scott Zimmerman *Evolution Entertainment (LA)*
901 N Highland Ave
Los Angeles, CA 90038-2412, USA

Ciardi, Mark (Athlete, Baseball Player)
21 Mitchell Ave
Piscataway, NJ 08854-5560, USA

Cias, Darryl (Athlete, Baseball Player)
11510 Poema Pl Unit 101
Chatsworth, CA 91311-1113, USA

Ciavaglia, Peter (Athlete, Hockey Player, Olympic Athlete)
1137 Carrie Ct
Rochester Hills, MI 48309-3766, USA

Cibrian, Eddie (Actor)
5565 Bonneville Rd
Hidden Hills, CA 91302-1202, USA

Cibulkova, Dominika (Athlete, Tennis Player)
WTA
100 2nd Ave S
Saint Petersburg, FL 33701-4360, USA

Ciccarelli, Dino (Athlete, Hockey Player)
37934 Lakeshore Dr
Harrison Township, MI 48045-2853, USA

Ciccippio, Joseph
2107 3rd St
Norristown, PA 19401-1930

Ciccolella, Jude (Actor)
705 N Screenland Dr
Burbank, CA 91505-3123, USA

Ciccolella, Mike (Athlete, Football Player)
8145 Station House Rd
Dayton, OH 45458-2931, USA

Ciccone, Christopher (Designer)
Bernhardt Design/Pacific Design Center
8687 Melrose Ave Ste B230
West Hollywood, CA 90069-5786

Cichocki, Chris (Athlete, Hockey Player)
3955 Pine Lake Cir
Stockton, CA 95219-2021, USA

Cichowski, Gene (Chick) (Athlete,
Football Player)
3903 Oak Ave
Northbrook, IL 60062-4922, USA

Cichowski, Tom (Athlete, Football Player)
443 N Hill Rd
Kalispell, MT 59901-8107, USA

Cichy, Joe J (Athlete, Football Player)
3278 48th St SE
Dawson, ND 58428-9615, USA

Cidre, Cynthia (Producer, Writer)
c/o Ann Blanchard Creative Artists
Agency (CAA-LA)
2000 Avenue of the Stars Ste 100
Los Angeles, CA 90067-4705, USA

Cienfuegos, Mauricio (Soccer Player)
Los Angeles Galaxy
1010 Rose Bowl Dr
Pasadena, CA 91103, USA

Cigliuti, Natalia (Actor)
c/o Felicia Sager Sager Management
260 S Beverly Dr Ste 205
Beverly Hills, CA 90212-3812, USA

Cihocki, Al (Athlete, Baseball Player)
43 Cochise Cir
Medford, NJ 08055-9769, USA

Cihocki, Al (Athlete, Baseball Player)
43 Cochise Cir
Medford, NJ 08055-9769, USA

Cimarro, Mario (Actor)
c/o Arlene Forster Forster Entertainment
12533 Woodgreen St
Los Angeles, CA 90066-2723, USA

Cimber, Matt (Director, Producer, Writer)
Cimero Enterprises
3620 Beverly Glen Blvd # 1A
Sherman Oaks, CA 91423-4403, USA

Cimino, Michael (Director)
9015 Alto Cedro Dr
Beverly Hills, CA 90210-1804, USA

Cimino, Pete (Athlete, Baseball Player)
14 Fillmore St
Bristol, PA 19007-5415, USA

Cimmo, Leonardo (Actor)
Michael Hartig Agency
156 5th Ave Ste 820
New York, NY 10010-7767, USA

Cimorelli, Frank (Athlete, Baseball Player)
2448 N 112th St
Milwaukee, WI 53226-1210, USA

Cincotti, Peter (Musician)
c/o Staff Member William Morris
Endeavor (LA)
9601 Wilshire Blvd
Beverly Hills, CA 90210-5213, USA

Cinderella (Music Group, Musician)
Tom Keifer
6129 S Riverbend Dr
Nashville, TN 37221-3937, USA

Cindric, Ann (Baseball Player)
210 Greenside Ave Apt 4
Canonsburg, PA 15317-3862, USA

Cindrich, Joe (Athlete, Football Player)
1310 Trinity Dr
Menlo Park, CA 94025-6680, USA

Cindrich, Ralph (Athlete, Football Player)
151 Fort Pitt Blvd Apt 1501
Pittsburgh, PA 15222-1572, USA

Cinematic Sunrise (Music Group,
Musician)
c/o Staff Member Equal Vision Records
PO Box 38202
Albany, NY 12203-8202, USA

Cineson All-Stars (Music Group)
c/o Staff Member Paradigm (Monterey)
404 W Franklin St
Monterey, CA 93940-2303, USA

Cink, Stewart (Athlete, Golfer)
1303 Brunson Way
The Villages, FL 32162-8727, USA

Cinninger, Jake (Musician)
1341 Wayne St N
South Bend, IN 46615-1047, USA

Cintron, Alex (Athlete, Baseball Player)
HC 2 Box 8575
Yabucoa, PR 00767-9599, USA

Cioffi, Charles (Actor)
Paradigm Agency
10100 Santa Monica Blvd Ste 2500
Los Angeles, CA 90067-4116, USA

Ciokey, Janna (Actor)
J Michael Bloom
9255 W Sunset Blvd Ste 710
West Hollywood, CA 90069-3304, USA

Cipa, Larry (Athlete, Football Player)
250 Torrent Ct
Rochester Hills, MI 48307-3871, USA

Cipriani, Frank (Athlete, Baseball Player)
14 Oakhill Dr
Buffalo, NY 14224-4214, USA

Circa Survive (Music Group)
c/o Brian Schechter Riot Squad
Management
335 Cortlandt St Fl 2
Belleville, NJ 07109-3201, USA

Cirillo, Jeff (Athlete, Baseball Player)
PO Box 233
Medina, WA 98039-0233, USA

Cirrincione, Vincent (Producer)
Vincent Cirrincione Associates
1516 N Fairfax Ave
Los Angeles, CA 90046-2608, USA

Cisco, Galen (Athlete, Baseball Player)
604 Elmwood Ln
Celina, OH 45822-2966, USA

Cishek, Steven (Athlete, Baseball Player)
4 Clearwater Dr
East Falmouth, MA 02536-4768, USA

Cisneros, Henry (Politician)
2002 W Houston St
San Antonio, TX 78207-3419, USA

Cisowski, Steve (Athlete, Football Player)
1090 3rd St
Gilroy, CA 95020-5302, USA

Citarella, Ralph (Athlete, Baseball Player)
29 E Sherman Ave
Colonia, NJ 07067-1412, USA

Citro, Ralph (Boxer)
32 N Black Horse Pike
Blackwood, NJ 08012-3093, USA

Citron, Ralph (Boxer)
32 N Black Horse Pike
Blackwood, NJ 08012-3093, USA

City High (Music Group)
c/o Staff Member William Morris
Endeavor (LA)
9601 Wilshire Blvd
Beverly Hills, CA 90210-5213, USA

Ciufo, Leonard (Athlete, Football Player)
3300 Pagent Ct
Thousand Oaks, CA 91360-2837

Civiletti, Benjamin (Politician)
5900 Old Ocean Blvd Apt B3
Blvd Apt B3
Boynton Beach, FL 33435-6228, USA

C. Johnson Jr., Henry (Congressman,
Politician)
1427 Longworth Hob
Washington, DC 20515-1503, USA

CK, Louis (Actor, Comedian)
c/o David (Dave) Becky 3 Arts
Entertainment (LA)
9460 Wilshire Blvd Fl 7
Beverly Hills, CA 90212-2713, USA

Claar, Brian (Athlete, Golfer)
28923 Pine Hill Dr
Spring, TX 77381-1116, USA

Clabo, Neal (Athlete, Football Player)
1100 Beaverton Rd Apt 1
Knoxville, TN 37919-7089, USA

Clabo, Neil (Athlete, Football Player)
1100 Beaverton Rd Apt 1
Knoxville, TN 37919-7089, USA

Clabo, Tyson (Athlete, Football Player)
c/o Chad Speck Allegiant Athletic Agency
35 Market Sq Ste 201
Knoxville, TN 37902-1420, USA

Clack, Darryl (Athlete, Football Player)
2050 E Runaway Bay Pl
Chandler, AZ 85249-4853, USA

Clackson, Kim (Athlete, Hockey Player)
342 Thomas Rd
Canonsburg, PA 15317-3534, USA

Claggett, Anthony (Athlete, Baseball
Player)
123 Arezzo Ct
Palm Desert, CA 92211-0715, USA

Claiborne, Chris (Athlete, Football Player)
Premier Sports Management
1000 N Green Valley Pkwy Ste 440-128
Henderson, NV 89074-6170, USA

Claiborne, Craig
30 Park Pl
East Hampton, NY 11937-2407

Claiborne, Morris (Athlete, Football
Player)
c/o Bus Cook Bus Cook Sports, Inc
1 Willow Bend Dr
Hattiesburg, MS 39402-8552, USA

Claire, Fred (Commentator)
1458 Rutherford Dr
Pasadena, CA 91103-2773, USA

Clairmont, Patsy (Writer)
Milk n Honey Inc
PO Box 1674
Franklin, TN 37065-1674, USA

Claitt, Rickey (Athlete, Football Player)
5830 Grand Canyon Dr
Orlando, FL 32810-3232, USA

Clampett, Bobby (Athlete, Golfer)
25941 Hickory Blvd Apt 3
Bonita Springs, FL 34134-3777, USA

Clampi, Joe (Coach)
Auburn University
Athletic Dept
Auburn, AL 36831, USA

Clancy, Jim (Athlete, Baseball Player)
2598 Gary Cir Apt 502
Dunedin, FL 34698-1789, USA

Clancy, Sam (Athlete, Football Player)
1308 Crest Ln
Oakdale, PA 15071-1748, USA

Clancy, Sean (Athlete, Football Player)
211 Bal Cross Dr
Bal Harbour, FL 33154-1318, USA

Clanton, Jimmy (Musician)
Jimmy Clanton Enterprises
409 Pencroft Dr S
Holtwood, PA 17532-9711, USA

Clapinski, Chris (Athlete, Baseball Player)
44355 Via Coronado
La Quinta, CA 92253-6844, USA

Clapp, Gordon (Actor)
Paul Kohner
9300 Wilshire Blvd Ste 555
Beverly Hills, CA 90212-3211, USA

Clapp, Nicholas R (Producer)
PO Box 1019
Borrego Springs, CA 92004-1019, USA

Clapp, Stubby (Athlete, Baseball Player)
140 P Haynes Ln
Savannah, TN 38372-3517, USA

Clapp, Thomas (Athlete, Football Player)
804 Live Oak St
Metairie, LA 70005-1216, USA

Clapto, Eric (Musician)
c/o Kristen Foster PMK/BNC Public
Relations (PMK-NY)
622 3rd Ave Fl 8
New York, NY 10017-6707, USA

Clap Your Hands Say Yeah (Music Group)
c/o Staff Member Paradigm (Monterey)
404 W Franklin St
Monterey, CA 93940-2303, USA

Clarence, Ellis (Athlete, Football Player)
5849 Leisure South Dr SE
Grand Rapids, MI 49548-6855, USA

Clarey, Doug (Athlete, Baseball Player)
2116 Hillhurst Ave
Los Angeles, CA 90027-2004, USA

Claridge, Dennis (Athlete, Football Player)
2621 Calvert St
Lincoln, NE 68502-4935, USA

Clarizio, Louis (Athlete, Baseball Player)
133 Lela Ln
Schaumburg, IL 60193-1339, USA

Clark, Al (Athlete, Baseball Player)
1185 SW 5th Ave
Boca Raton, FL 33432-7140, USA

Clark, Annie (St Vincent) (Musician)
c/o Staff Member Lever and Beam
325 W 38th St Rm 1101
New York, NY 10018-9597, USA

Clark, Anthony (Actor, Comedian)
2796 Outpost Dr
Los Angeles, CA 90068-2008, USA

Clark, Archie (Athlete, Basketball Player)
4268 10th St
Ecorse, MI 48229-1219, USA

Clark, Bernard (Athlete, Football Player)
306 York Dale Dr
Ruskin, FL 33570-3225, USA

Clark, Blake (Actor, Writer)
c/o Adrienne McWhorter *Abrams Artists Agency (LA)*
9200 W Sunset Blvd PH 11
West Hollywood, CA 90069-3601, USA

Clark, Bobby (Athlete, Baseball Player)
1030 Perrisito St
Perris, CA 92570-2345, USA

Clark, Brady (Athlete, Baseball Player)
19275 Green Lakes Loop
Bend, OR 97702-1171, USA

Clark, Bret (Athlete, Football Player)
815 Manes Ct
Lincoln, NE 68505-2021, USA

Clark, Brett (Athlete, Hockey Player)
9708 Sunset Hill Dr
Lone Tree, CO 80124-6720, USA

Clark, Brian (Athlete, Football Player)
811 Woodland Forest Dr
Waxhaw, NC 28173-8546, USA

Clark, Bruce (Athlete, Football Player)
538 W Main St
Boalsburg, PA 16827-1331, USA

Clark, Bryan (Athlete, Football Player)
1482 Lochridge Rd
Bloomfield Hills, MI 48302-0733, USA

Clark, Bryan (Baseball Player)
Seattle Mariners
508 E Clark St
Madera, CA 93638-1662, USA

Clark, Candy (Actor)
13935 Hatteras St
Van Nuys, CA 91401-4342, USA

Clark, Carol Hiqgins (Writer)
300 E 56th St
New York, NY 10022-4136, USA

Clark, Chris (Athlete, Hockey Player)
71 Grand View Dr
Dedham, ME 04429-4753, USA

Clark, Corinne (Athlete, Baseball Player)
7224 Hawthorn Ave NE
Albuquerque, NM 87113-2084, USA

Clark, Dallas (Athlete, Football Player)
2995 Belle Maison Dr
Zionsville, IN 46077-8901, USA

Clark, Daniel (Actor)
c/o Staff Member *Schachter Entertainment*
1157 S Beverly Dr Fl 2
Los Angeles, CA 90035-1119, USA

Clark, Danny (Athlete, Football Player)
213 Seneca Trl
Bloomingdale, IL 60108-2432, USA

Clark, Dave (Athlete, Baseball Player)
4842 Mayfield Rd W
Collierville, TN 38017-3309, USA

Clark, Derrick (Athlete, Football Player)
430 Sunset Dr Apt 2
Orlando, FL 32805-3305, USA

Clark, Desmond (Athlete, Football Player)
2190 Shadow Creek Ct
Vernon Hills, IL 60061-4567

Clark, Doran
6399 Wilshire Blvd Ste 414
Los Angeles, CA 90048-5716

Clark, Doug (Athlete, Baseball Player)
106 Piedmont St
Springfield, MA 01104-2042, USA

Clark, Dwight (Athlete, Football Player)
2211 Vernon Dr
Charlotte, NC 28211-1844, USA

Clark, Earl (Swimmer)
1145 NE 126th St Apt 4
North Miami, FL 33161-5027, USA

Clark, Gail (Athlete, Football Player)
PO Box 335
Bellefontaine, OH 43311-0335, USA

Clark, Gene (Musician)
Artists International Mgmt
9850 Sandaltoot Rd
#458
Boca Raton, FL 33428, USA

Clark, Glen (Athlete, Baseball Player)
5605 Marblehead Dr
Dallas, TX 75232-2356, USA

Clark, Gordie
New York Rangers
125 W End Ave # 6
New York, NY 10023-6387, USA

Clark, Gordie (Athlete, Hockey Player)
28 Rockingham St
Portsmouth, NH 03801-3940, USA

Clark, Guy (Musician, Songwriter)
102 Stoneway Close
Nashville, TN 37209-4538, USA

Clark, Harry (Athlete, Football Player)
1121 Patton Dr
Morgantown, WV 26505-3756, USA

Clark, Helen (Government Official)
United Nations Development Programme
1 United Nations Plz
New York, NY 10017-3515, USA

Clark, Howie (Athlete, Baseball Player)
14204 439th Ave SE
North Bend, WA 98045-9209, USA

Clark, Jack (The Ripper) (Athlete, Baseball Player)
7601 Orvale Rd Apt 8416
Plano, TX 75024-5997, USA

Clark, James (Jim) (Business Person)
My CFO.com
111 W Monroe St
P.O. Box 755
Chicago, IL 60603-4096, USA

Clark, Jerald (Athlete, Baseball Player)
12325 Crisscross Ln
San Diego, CA 92129-3766, USA

Clark, Jermaine (Athlete, Baseball Player)
2 Ute Ct
San Ramon, CA 94583, USA

Clark, Jessie (Athlete, Football Player)
411 E Indian School Rd Apt 2089
Phoenix, AZ 85012-1884, USA

Clark, Jim (Athlete, Baseball Player)
659 S Indian Hill Blvd Apt C
Claremont, CA 91711-5486, USA

Clark, Joe
PO Box 96848
Washington, DC 20090-6848

Clark, Kelly (Athlete, Skier)
178 Route 100
West Dover, VT 05356, USA

Clark, Kelvin (Athlete, Football Player)
3812 Evesham Dr
Plano, TX 75025-3818, USA

Clark, Keon (Basketball Player)
Utah Jazz Delta Center
301 W South Temple
Salt Lake City, UT 84101-1219, USA

Clark, Kevin (Athlete, Football Player)
3902 S Chase Way
Denver, CO 80235-3133, USA

Clark, Kevin Alexander (Actor)
c/o Anne Geddes *Geddes Agency, The*
1203 Greenacre Ave
West Hollywood, CA 90046-5707, USA

Clark, Laurel B (Doctor)
4899 Montrose Blvd Apt 912
Houston, TX 77006-6167, USA

Clark, Leroy (Athlete, Football Player)
5458 Osprey Dr
Houston, TX 77048-1109, USA

Clark, L Hill (Business Person)
Crane Co
100 Stamford Pl Ste 300
Stamford, CT 06902-6784, USA

Clark, Louis S (Athlete, Football Player)
401 Covered Bridge Rd
Cherry Hill, NJ 08034-3105, USA

Clark, Marcia (Attorney)
5457 Hobson Ct
Calabasas, CA 91302-3135, USA

Clark, Mario (Athlete, Football Player)
8155 Bangor Ave Apt 695
Hesperia, CA 92345-6856, USA

Clark, Mark (Athlete, Baseball Player)
18262 E CR 520N
Kilbourne, IL 62655-6628, USA

Clark, Mary Ellen (Athlete, Diver, Olympic Athlete)
90 Irving St
Waltham, MA 02451-0724, USA

Clark, Mary Higgins (Writer)
MHC-Clark
15 Werimus Brook Rd
Saddle River, NJ 07458-3118, USA

Clark, Mary Higgins (Writer)
210 Central Park S
New York, NY 10019-1428, USA

Clark, Matt (Actor)
1199 Park Ave Apt 15D
New York, NY 10128-1791, USA

Clark, Mel (Baseball Player)
Philadelphia Phillies
270 Home Run Dr
West Columbia, WV 25287-8692, USA

Clark, Mystro (Actor, Comedian)
c/o Staff Member *ICM Partners (LA)*
10250 Constellation Blvd Fl 7
Los Angeles, CA 90067-6207, USA

Clark, Nate (Comedian)
c/o Lon Haber *Lon Haber & Co (IPPR)*
10355 NE Valley Rd Ste 4501
Bainbridge Island, WA 98110-4347, USA

Clark, Perry (Coach)
Miami University
Athletic Dept
Miami, FL 33124, USA

Clark, Peter B (Publisher)
7675 La Jolla Blvd Unit 203
La Jolla, CA 92037-4747, USA

Clark, Petula (Musician)
5415 Collins Ave # Phf
Miami Beach, FL 33140-2575, USA

Clark, Phil (Athlete, Baseball Player)
112 Hicks Rd
Dawson, GA 39842-4002, USA

Clark, Phil (Athlete, Football Player)
PO Box 3021
Barrington, IL 60011-3021, USA

Clark, Ramsey (Politician)
37 W 12th St Apt 2B
New York, NY 10011-8503, USA

Clark, Richard (Ex-Senator, Politician)
4424 Edmunds St NW # 1070
Washington, DC 20007-1117, USA

Clark, Rickey (Athlete, Baseball Player)
8953 Emerald Waters Ct
Las Vegas, NV 89147-6501, USA

Clark, Ron (Athlete, Baseball Player)
700 Starkey Rd Apt 511
Largo, FL 33771-2344, USA

Clark, Roy (Musician)
Roy Clark Productions
3225 S Norwood Ave Ste 101
Tulsa, OK 74135-5493, USA

Clark, Ryan (Athlete, Football Player)
42953 Ridgeway Dr
Broadlands, VA 20148-4547, USA

Clark, Sedric (Athlete, Football Player)
7819 Chasewood Dr
Missouri City, TX 77489-1836, USA

Clark, Spencer Treat (Actor)
c/o Katie Rhodes *Untitled Entertainment (LA)*
350 S Beverly Dr Ste 200
Beverly Hills, CA 90212-4819, USA

Clark, Stephen E (Steve) (Swimmer)
29 Martling Rd
San Anselmo, CA 94960-1172, USA

Clark, Susan (Actor)
13400 Riverside Dr Ste 308
Sherman Oaks, CA 91423-2541, USA

Clark, Terry (Athlete, Baseball Player)
1607 E Tam O Shanter St
Ontario, CA 91761-6356, USA

Clark, Tim (Athlete, Golfer)
22400 N 97th St
Scottsdale, AZ 85255-4431, USA

Clark, Tony (Athlete, Baseball Player)
377 Ruckman Rd
Closter, NJ 07624-2311, USA

Clark, Vinnie (Athlete, Football Player)
1120 Virescent Ct
Cincinnati, OH 45224-2789, USA

Clark, Wayne (Athlete, Football Player)
14241 Lambeth Way
Tustin, CA 92780-2230, USA

Clark, Will (Adult Film Star)
c/o Staff Member *Diva Central Inc*
7510 W Sunset Blvd Ste 1445
Los Angeles, CA 90046-3408, USA

Clark, Will (Athlete, Baseball Player, Olympic Athlete)
18555 Saint Andrews Ct E
Prairieville, LA 70769-3248, USA

Clark-Cole, Dorinda (Musician)
c/o Keith Douglas *RKD Music Management*
PO Box 11611
Beverly Hills, CA 90213-4611, USA

Clark-Diggs, Joetta (Athlete, Olympic Athlete, Track Athlete)
1856 Clarence Dr
Hellertown, PA 18055-2701, USA

Clarke, Angela (Actor)
3930 Weeping Willow Dr
Moorpark, CA 93021-2842, USA

Clarke, Bob (Cartoonist)
7480 Rivershore Dr
Seaford, DE 19973-4328, USA

Clarke, Bobby (Athlete, Hockey Player)
Philadelphia Flyers
3601 S Broad St Ste 2
Philadelphia, PA 19148-5297, USA

Clarke, Brian Patrick (Actor)
c/o Staff Member *Orange Grove Group, The*
12178 Ventura Blvd Ste 205
Studio City, CA 91604-2540, USA

Clarke, Emily (Actor)
c/o Darren Goldberg *Global Creative*
1051 Cole Ave # B
Los Angeles, CA 90038-2601, USA

Clarke, Emmy (Actor)
c/o Darren Goldberg *Global Creative*
1051 Cole Ave # B
Los Angeles, CA 90038-2601, USA

Clarke, Frank (Athlete, Football Player)
3121 NE 34th Ave
Portland, OR 97212-2769, USA

Clarke, Gary (Actor, Writer)
1113 Heep Run
Buda, TX 78610-5091, USA

Clarke, Gilby (Music Group, Musician)
Sammy Boyd Entertainment
212 Allen Ave
Allenhurst, NJ 07711-1006, USA

Clarke, Hagood (Athlete, Football Player)
2500 NE 37th Dr
Fort Lauderdale, FL 33308-6323, USA

Clarke, Hansen (Congressman, Politician)
1319 Longworth Hob
Washington, DC 20515-1305, USA

Clarke, Horace (Athlete, Baseball Player)
PO Box 891
Frederiksted, VI 00841-0891, USA

Clarke, John (Actor)
Days of Our Lives Show
3000 W Alameda Ave
Burbank, CA 91523-0001, USA

Clarke, Kate (Actor)
1470 Angelus Ave
Los Angeles, CA 90026-2209, USA

Clarke, Ken (Athlete, Football Player)
7610 Willoughby Ct
Alpharetta, GA 30005-3028, USA

Clarke, Lenny (Actor)
c/o Staff Member *Paradigm (LA)*
360 N Crescent Dr
North Bldg
Beverly Hills, CA 90210-4874, USA

Clarke, Melinda (Actor)
32107 Lindero Canyon Rd Ste 235
Westlake Village, CA 91361-4208, USA

Clarke, Michael (Music Group, Musician)
Artists International Mgmt
9850 Sandalfoot Blvd # 458
Boca Raton, FL 33428-6645, USA

Clarke, Noah
PO Box 36
Claremont, CA 91711-0036

Clarke, Robert L (Government Official)
Bracewell & Patterson
711 Louisiana St Ste 2900
Houston, TX 77002-2770, USA

Clarke, Ronald (Ron) (Athlete, Track Athlete)
1 Bay St
Brighton, VI 03186, USA

Clarke, Sarah (Actor)
c/o Staff Member *Levine Management*
9028 W Sunset Blvd PH 1
West Hollywood, CA 90069-1830, USA

Clarke, Stan (Athlete, Baseball Player)
5333 Sanders Dr
Toledo, OH 43615-6860, USA

Clarke, Stanley (Musician)
880 Greenleaf Canyon Rd
Topanga, CA 90290-4111, USA

Clarke, Susanna (Writer)
Tom Doherty Associates, LLC
175 5th Ave
New York, NY 10010-7703, USA

Clarke, Thomas E (Business Person)
Nice Inc
1 SW Bowerman Dr
Beaverton, OR 97005-0979, USA

Clarke, Will (Athlete, Football Player)
c/o Jim Ivler *Sportstars Inc*
1350 Avenue of the Americas Fl 28
New York, NY 10019-4702, USA

Clark II, Michael (Athlete, Golfer)
4007 Pintail Cir
Rocky Face, GA 30740-8919, USA

Clark-Sheard, Karen (Musician)
c/o Staff Member *Elektra Records*
75 Rockefeller Plz Fl 17
New York, NY 10019-6927, USA

Clarkson, Kelly (Musician, Songwriter)
c/o Narvel Blackstock *Starstruck Entertainment*
40 Music Sq W
Nashville, TN 37203-3206, USA

Clarkson, Patricia (Actor)
c/o Tony Lipp *Anonymous Content (LA)*
3532 Hayden Ave
Culver City, CA 90232-2413, USA

Clary, Marty (Athlete, Baseball Player)
205 Yorktown Ct
Easley, SC 29642-9042, USA

Clary, Robert (Actor)
10001 Sundial Ln
Beverly Hills, CA 90210-2719, USA

Clasby, Bob (Athlete, Football Player)
10757 N 74th St Unit 1017
Scottsdale, AZ 85260-6470, USA

C. LaTourette, Steven (Congressman, Politician)
2371 Rayburn Hob
Washington, DC 20515-0508, USA

Claudel, Aurelie (Model)
c/o Staff Member *IMG*
304 Park Ave S Fl 12
New York, NY 10010-4314, USA

Clausen, Jimmy (Athlete, Football Player)
c/o David Dunn *Athletes First, LLC*
23091 Mill Creek Dr
Laguna Hills, CA 92653-1258, USA

Clauss, Jared (Athlete, Football Player)
215 S 82nd St
West Des Moines, IA 50266-8524, USA

Claussen, Brandon (Athlete, Baseball Player)
4114 124th St
Lubbock, TX 79423-8905, USA

Clawhammer
PO Box 1519
New Haven, CT 06506-1519

Clawson, John (Athlete, Basketball Player, Olympic Athlete)
30 Eagle Lake Pl Unit 31
San Ramon, CA 94582-4858, USA

Claxton, Craig (Speedy) (Athlete, Basketball Player)
Golden State Warriors
57 Hitchcock Ln
Old Westbury, NY 11568-1403, USA

Claxton, Paul (Athlete, Golfer)
PO Box 485
Claxton, GA 30417-0485, USA

Clay, Andrew Dice (Comedian)
c/o Jeff Abraham *Jonas Public Relations*
240 26th St Ste 3
Santa Monica, CA 90402-2542, USA

Clay, Bryan (Athlete, Olympic Athlete)
c/o Staff Member *USA Track & Field*
132 E Washington St Ste 800
Indianapolis, IN 46204-3674, USA

Clay, Danny (Athlete, Baseball Player)
151 Illinois Ave
Westerville, OH 43081-2325, USA

Clay, Hayward (Athlete, Football Player)
PO Box 234
Snyder, TX 79550-0234, USA

Clay, John (Athlete, Football Player)
1302 S 9th St
Saint Louis, MO 63104-3515, USA

Clay, Ken (Athlete, Baseball Player)
4523 60th Street Ct W
Bradenton, FL 34210-2729, USA

Clay, Walter (Athlete, Football Player)
2827 Arlington Ave
Pueblo, CO 81003-1315, USA

Clay, Willie (Athlete, Football Player)
PO Box 680785
Marietta, GA 30068-0014, USA

Clayborn, Adrian (Football Player)
c/o Blake Baratz *The Institute for Athletes*
3600 Minnesota Dr Ste 550
Minneapolis, MN 55435-7925, USA

Clayborn, Raymond D (Ray) (Athlete, Football Player)
20610 Aspen Canyon Dr
Katy, TX 77450-7091, USA

Claybrooks, Devon (Athlete, Football Player)
725 Auburn Pl
Martinsville, VA 24112-4502, USA

Claydon, Phil (Director)
c/o Jason Burns *United Talent Agency (UTA-LA)*
9336 Civic Center Dr
Beverly Hills, CA 90210-3604, USA

Clayman, Ralph V (Doctor, Misc)
Bames Hospital
Surgery Dept
416 S Kingshighway Blvd
Saint Louis, MO 63110, USA

Claypool, James (Athlete, Hockey Player)
302 Paine Farm Rd
Duluth, MN 55804-2632, USA

Claypool, Les (Musician)
3909 Heather Ln
Sebastopol, CA 95472-9352, USA

Clayson, Jane (Correspondent)
c/o Staff Member *CBS Television*
51 W 52nd St
New York, NY 10019-6119, USA

Clayton, Amber (Actor)
c/o Steve Glick *Glick Agency*
1321 7th St Ste 203
Santa Monica, CA 90401-1631, USA

Clayton, Harvey (Athlete, Football Player)
15303 SW 143rd St
Miami, FL 33196-2879, USA

Clayton, Keenan (Athlete, Football Player)
c/o Ashley Smith Becker *Relativity Sports (LA)*
9242 Beverly Blvd Ste 300
Beverly Hills, CA 90210-3728, USA

Clayton, Mark (Athlete, Football Player)
9407 Manor Forge Way
Owings Mills, MD 21117-5161, USA

Clayton, Mark (Athlete, Football Player)
16426 Canyon Chase Dr
Houston, TX 77095-6532, USA

Clayton, Michael (Athlete, Football Player)
10406 Oak Canopy Jct
Thonotosassa, FL 33592-3934, USA

Clayton, Ralph (Athlete, Football Player)
6356 Selkirk St
Detroit, MI 48211-1836, USA

Clayton, Royce (Athlete, Baseball Player)
5924 Paseo Canyon Dr
Malibu, CA 90265-3130, USA

Clayton, Thomas David (Music Group, Musician)
Music Avenue Inc
43 Washington St
Groveland, MA 01834-1142, USA

Cleamons, Jim (Athlete, Basketball Player)
29 Sausalito Cir W
Manhattan Beach, CA 90266-7234, USA

Clear, Mark (Athlete, Baseball Player)
15654 S Rene St
Olathe, KS 66062-4676, USA

Clearwater, Keith (Athlete, Golfer)
967 N 900 W
Orem, UT 84057-7707, USA

Clearwater, Ray (Athlete, Hockey Player)
98 George St
East Haven, CT 06512-4726, USA

Cleary, Beverly (Writer)
c/o Staff Member *HarperCollins Publishers*
195 Broadway Fl 2
Cellar 1
New York, NY 10007-3132, USA

Cleary, Robert (Bob) (Athlete, Hockey Player, Olympic Athlete)
680 South Ave Unit 8
Weston, MA 02493-1192, USA

Cleary, Thomas (Writer)
c/o Staff Member *Random House*
1540 Broadway
New York, NY 10036-4039, USA

Cleary, William J (Bill) Jr (Athlete, Hockey Player, Olympic Athlete)
27 Kingswood Rd
Auburndale, MA 02466-1013, USA

Cleave, Dr Mary L (Astronaut)
596 Pinewood Dr
Annapolis, MD 21401-7113, USA

Cleave, Mary L (Astronaut)
NASA
Earth Science Office
Code AS Room 7R86
Washington, DC 20546-0001, USA

Cleaver, Emanuel (Congressman, Politician)
1433 Longworth Hob
Washington, DC 20515-0104, USA

Cleeland, Cam (Athlete, Football Player)
6216 Buena Vista Dr
Vancouver, WA 98661-7610, USA

Cleese, John (Actor, Comedian, Writer)
c/o Tony Lipp *Anonymous Content (LA)*
3532 Hayden Ave
Culver City, CA 90232-2413, USA

Clef (Music Group, Musician)
DAS Communications
83 Riverside Dr
New York, NY 10024-5713, USA

Clegg, Johnny (Music Group, Musician)
c/o Staff Member *Monterey International (Chicago)*
200 W Superior St Ste 202
Chicago, IL 60654-6422, USA

Cleghorne, Ellen (Actor, Comedian)
c/o Frederick Levy *Management 101*
11271 Ventura Blvd # 102
Studio City, CA 91604-3136, USA

Cleland, Max (Ex-Senator, Politician)
2460 Peachtree Rd NW Apt 1406
Atlanta, GA 30305-4158, USA

Clemens, Barry (Athlete, Basketball Player)
3111 Clinton Ave
Cleveland, OH 44113-2973, USA

Clemens, Donella (Religious Leader)
Monnonite Church
718 N Main St
Newton, KS 67114-1703, USA

Clemens, Doug (Athlete, Baseball Player)
4799 Lower Mountain Rd
New Hope, PA 18938-9454, USA

Clemens, Robert (Bob) (Athlete, Football Player)
2007 Poole Dr NW Ste D
Huntsville, AL 35810-4900, USA

Clemens, Roger (Athlete, Baseball Player)
11535 Quail Hollow Ln
Houston, TX 77024-6508, USA

Clemenson, Christian (Actor)
2666 La Cuesta Dr
Los Angeles, CA 90046-1337, USA

Clement, Anthony (Athlete, Football Player)
141 Navajo Ln
Opelousas, LA 70570-0324, USA

Clement, Bill (Athlete, Hockey Player)
Philadelphia Flyers
3601 S Broad St Ste 2
Philadelphia, PA 19148-5297, USA

Clement, Jeff (Athlete, Baseball Player)
1318 NE 29th St
Ankeny, IA 50021-6723, USA

Clement, Jemaine (Actor, Writer)
c/o Jason Heyman *Creative Artists Agency (CAA-LA)*
3500 W Olive Ave Ste 1400
Burbank, CA 91505-5512, USA

Clement, Matt (Athlete, Baseball Player)
143 Milt Miller Rd
Renfrew, PA 16053-9613, USA

Clement, Skip (Athlete, Football Player)
620 Tennis Club Dr Apt 106
Fort Lauderdale, FL 33311-4030, USA

Clements, Dick (Director, Producer, Writer)
c/o Bruce Kaufman *ICM Partners (LA)*
10250 Constellation Blvd Fl 7
Los Angeles, CA 90067-6207, USA

Clements, Kim (Writer)
c/o Staff Member *Creative Artists Agency (CAA-LA)*
2000 Avenue of the Stars Ste 100
Los Angeles, CA 90067-4705, USA

Clements, Lennie (Athlete, Golfer)
PO Box 182197
Coronado, CA 92178-2197, USA

Clements, Nate (Athlete, Football Player)
1 Bills Dr
Orchard Park, NY 14127-2237, USA

Clements, Pat (Athlete, Baseball Player)
14 Barker Ct
Chico, CA 95928-3842, USA

Clements, Ronald (Director, Producer, Writer)
c/o Staff Member *Creative Artists Agency (CAA-LA)*
2000 Avenue of the Stars Ste 100
Los Angeles, CA 90067-4705, USA

Clements, Tom (Athlete, Football Player)
101 Cherry St Unit 216
Green Bay, WI 54301-4247, USA

Clements, Vincent (Vin) (Athlete, Football Player)
62 Chatham Rd
Berlin, CT 06037-1104, USA

Clemmensen, Scott (Athlete, Hockey Player)
Edge Sports Management
26 Autumn Ridge Rd
Pound Ridge, NY 10576-1400, USA

Clemmer, Ronnie (Producer)
c/o Staff Member *Longbow Productions*
4295 N Norway Rd
Lincoln, MI 48742-9645, USA

Clemons, Charlie (Athlete, Football Player)
1973 Bertha Ct
Hampton, GA 30228-4006, USA

Clemons, Chris (Athlete, Baseball Player)
903 S Robinson Dr
Robinson, TX 76706-6141, USA

Clemons, Chris (Athlete, Football Player)
c/o Drew Rosenhaus *Rosenhaus Sports Representation*
6400 Allison Rd
Miami Beach, FL 33141-4540, USA

Clemons, Craig (Athlete, Football Player)
1517 D Ave NE
Cedar Rapids, IA 52402-5148, USA

Clemons, Duane (Athlete, Football Player)
30181 W 231st St
Spring Hill, KS 66083-6019, USA

Clendenen, Mike (Athlete, Football Player)
1987 Denver Broncos
Dana Point, CA 92629, USA

Clendenin, Robert (Bob) (Actor)
2343 N Reese Pl
Burbank, CA 91504-2214, USA

Clennon, David (Actor)
2309 27th St
Santa Monica, CA 90405-1921, USA

Clervoy, Jean-Francois (Astronaut)
NASA
EAC Postfach 90 26 96
Koln, GE D-511, USA

Cleveland, Davis (Actor)
c/o Mara Santino *Luber Roklin Management*
5815 W Sunset Blvd Ste 206
Los Angeles, CA 90028-6481, USA

Cleveland, Reggie (Athlete, Baseball Player)
11708 Beach St
Frisco, TX 75034-6435, USA

Clevenger, Tex (Athlete, Baseball Player)
31727 Country Club Dr
Porterville, CA 93257-9610, USA

Clevlen, Brent (Athlete, Baseball Player)
14100 Avery Ranch Blvd Unit 1703
Austin, TX 78717-4012, USA

Cliburn, Stan (Athlete, Baseball Player)
Sioux City Explorers 3400
Sioux City, IA 51106, USA

Cliburn, Stew (Athlete, Baseball Player)
425 William Dr
Pleasant View, TN 37146-7910, USA

Click, Shannan (Model)
1672 Mountcrest Ave
Los Angeles, CA 90069-1426, USA

Clifford, Linda (Music Group)
c/o Staff Member *Diva Central Inc*
7510 W Sunset Blvd Ste 1445
Los Angeles, CA 90046-3408, USA

Clifford, Michael R (Astronaut)
601 Hillside Dr N Apt 2344
North Myrtle Beach, SC 29582-8918, USA

Clifford, M Richard (Rich) (Astronaut)
3700 Bay Area Blvd
Houston, TX 77058-1160, USA

Clifford, Steve (Basketball Coach)
c/o Steve Kauffman *Kauffman Sports Management Group*
Prefers to be contacted by telephone
Malibu, CA, USA

Clift, Eleanor
1750 Pennsylvania Ave NW Ste 1220
Washington, DC 20006-4504

Clifton, Chad (Athlete, Football Player)
1641 Whispering Hills Dr
Franklin, TN 37069-7242, USA

Clifton, Greg (Athlete, Football Player)
2717 Botany St
Charlotte, NC 28216-4431, USA

Clifton, Kyle (Athlete, Football Player)
777 S Point Ct
Aledo, TX 76008-4134, USA

Clijsters, Kim (Athlete, Tennis Player)
2120 Baileys Corner Rd
Wall Township, NJ 07719-9539, USA

Cliks, The (Music Group)
c/o Staff Member *Paradigm (Monterey)*
404 W Franklin St
Monterey, CA 93940-2303, USA

Cline, Ernest (Writer)
c/o Dan Farah *Farah Films & Management*
11640 Mayfield Ave Apt 208
Los Angeles, CA 90049-5728, USa

Cline, Jackie (Athlete, Football Player)
5935 High Forest Dr
Mc Calla, AL 35111-4205, USA

Cline, Richard (Cartoonist)
New Yorker Magazine
4 Times Sq Fl 22
Editorial Dept
New York, NY 10036-6592, USA

Cline, Ty (Athlete, Baseball Player)
37 Wappoo Creek Pl
Charleston, SC 29412-2121, USA

Clines, Gene (Athlete, Baseball Player)
5303 9th Avenue Dr W
Bradenton, FL 34209-4205, USA

Cline Sr, Tony (Athlete, Football Player)
59 Chestnut Pl
Danville, CA 94506-4542, USA

Clinkscale, F Dextor (Athlete, Football Player)
206 Michaux Dr
Greenville, SC 29605-3156, USA

Clinkscales, Joey (Athlete, Football Player)
9199 Blufftop Cv
Cordova, TN 38018-7684, USA

Clinkscales, Sherard (Baseball Player)
13688 Oliver Ln
Westfield, IN 46074-8465, USA

Clinton, Bill (Politician)
3067 Whitehaven St NW
Washington, DC 20008-3620, USA

Clinton, George (Musician, Songwriter)
c/o Vasi Vangelos *First Artists Management*
4764 Park Granada Ste 210
Calabasas, CA 91302-3333, USA

Clinton, Hillary Rodham (Politician)
15 Old House Ln
Chappaqua, NY 10514, USA

Clinton, Kate (Comedian)
230 W End Ave Apt 10C
New York, NY 10023-3664, USA

Clippard, Tyler (Athlete, Baseball Player)
2160 Chianti Pl Unit 118
Palm Harbor, FL 34683-7736, USA

Clique Girlz (Music Group, Musician)
c/o Staff Member *Clique Entertainment Productions*
11 Forest View Ct
Egg Harbor Township, NJ 08234-7132, USA

Clisters, Kim (Tennis Player)
Assn of Tennis Professionals
200 Tournament Rd
Ponte Vedra Beach, FL 32082, USA

Clohessy, Robert (Actor)
Don Buchwald
6500 Wilshire Blvd Ste 2200
Los Angeles, CA 90048-4942, USA

Cloke, Kristen (Actor)
c/o Staff Member *Mitchell K Stubbs & Assoc (MKS)*
8675 Washington Blvd Ste 203
Culver City, CA 90232-7486, USA

Cloninger, Tony (Athlete, Baseball Player)
PO Box 1500
Denver, NC 28037-1500, USA

Clontz, Brad (Athlete, Baseball Player)
General Delivery
Alpharetta, GA 30009-9999, USA

Clooney, Nick (Writer)
American University
4400 Massachusetts Ave NW
School of Communication, Room 330A
Washington, DC 20016-8200, USA

Close, Bill (Basketball Player)
555 Byron St Apt 409
Palo Alto, CA 94301-2038, USA

Close, Eric (Actor)
4243 Saugus Ave
Sherman Oaks, CA 91403-4407, USA

Close, Glenn (Actor)
c/o Staff Member *Trillium Productions*
PO Box 1560
New Canaan, CT 06840-1560, USA

Closser, J D (Athlete, Baseball Player)
2202 U 32nd Ave
Alexandria, IN .JL06, USA

Closter, Al (Athlete, Baseball Player)
4103 Hickory Rd
Richmond, VA 23235-1437, USA

Closure In Moscow (Music Group, Musician)
c/o Andrew Cook *Run Artist Management*
5753 Cobblestone Dr
Rocklin, CA 95765-4103, USA

Clotworthy, Bob (Athlete, Olympic Athlete, Swimmer)
2301 Moss Rose Ln
Fort Collins, CO 80526-2178, USA

Cloud, Mike (Athlete, Football Player)
1880 Tahoe Dr
Rockwall, TX 75087-6505, USA

Cloude, Ken (Athlete, Baseball Player)
1414 Martin Meadows Dr
Fallston, MD 21047-2221, USA

Clougherty, Pat (Athlete, Baseball Player)
3160 Arden Dr
Saint Paul, MN 55129-7782, USA

Cloutier, Jacques (Athlete, Hockey Player)
12172 Triple Crown Dr
Parker, CO 80134-7747, USA

Clovers, The
Rt. 1 Box 56
Belvidere, NC 27CA9

Clowe, Ryane
356 Santana Row Apt 303
San Jose, CA 95128-2046

Clowes, Daniel (Writer)
Fantagraphics
7563 Lake City Way NE
Seattle, WA 98115-4218, USA

Clowney, Jadeveon (Actor, Football Player)
c/o Bus Cook *Bus Cook Sports, Inc*
109 Cornerstone Rd
Hattiesburg, MS 39402-8232, USA

Clune, Don (Athlete, Football Player)
322 N Orange St
Media, PA 19063-2308, USA

Clunie, Michelle Renee (Actor)
c/o Bernard Kira *Vanguard Management Group*
8060 Melrose Ave Fl 4
Los Angeles, CA 90046-7038, USA

Clutterbuck, Bryan (Athlete, Baseball Player)
7998 Grand St Apt 1
Dexter, MI 48130-1357, USA

Clwson, John (Basketball Player)
Oakland Oaks
33 San Ysidro Ct
Danville, CA 94526-1545, USA

Clyde, Ben (Basketball Player)
Bosten Celtics
8356 A Street Apt #1
Saint Petersburg, FL 33701, USA

Clyde, David (Athlete, Baseball Player)
7806 Pinehurst Shadows Dr
Humble, TX 77346-1511, USA

Clyde, K C (Actor)
c/o Ted Schachter *Schachter Entertainment*
1157 S Beverly Dr Fl 2
Los Angeles, CA 90035-1119, USA

Clymer, Ben (Athlete, Hockey Player)
7040 Mill Creek Ln
Excelsior, MN 55331-5706, USA

Clyne, Nikki (Actor)
c/o David Miner *3 Arts Entertainment (LA)*
9460 Wilshire Blvd Fl 7
Beverly Hills, CA 90212-2713, USA

CM Punk (Athlete, Wrestler)
1456 N Milwaukee Ave
Chicago, IL 60622-9225, USA

Coachman, Bobby (Baseball Player)
California Angels
PO Box 44
Cottonwood, AL 36320-0044, USA

Coachman, Pete (Athlete, Baseball Player)
8795 S County 55 Rd
Cottonwood, AL 36320-3323, USA

Coady, Richard (Rich) (Athlete, Football Player)
17106 Spanky Pl
Dallas, TX 75248-1533, USA

Coakley, Dexter (Athlete, Football Player)
1304 Sunset Ridge Cir
Cedar Hill, TX 75104-4541, USA

Coan, Bert (Athlete, Football Player)
14517 N US Highway 59
Nacogdoches, TX 75965-9004, USA

Coan, Gil (Athlete, Baseball Player)
PO Box 668
Brevard, NC 28712-0668, USA

Coasters, The (Music Group, Musician)
2756 N Green Valley Pkwy # 449
Henderson, NV 89014-2120, USA

Coates, Ben (Athlete, Football Player)
461 Havenbrook Way NW
Concord, NC 28027-4113, USA

Coates, Jim (Athlete, Baseball Player)
1098 Oak Hill Rd
Lancaster, VA 22503-4009, USA

Coates, Kim (Actor)
11050 Strathmore Dr Apt 317
Los Angeles, CA 90024-1609, USA

Coates, Phyllis (Actor)
PO Box 1969
Boyes Hot Springs, CA 95416-1969, USA

Coates, Ray (Athlete, Football Player)
932 Oaklawn Dr
Metairie, LA 70005-1648, USA

Coates, Sherrod (Athlete, Football Player)
12233 Silveroak Ln
Charlotte, NC 28277-1582, USA

Coates, Steve (Athlete, Hockey Player)
102 Stoney Creek Dr
Egg Harbor Township, NJ 08234-7559, USA

Coates, Steve (Athlete, Hockey Player)
Philadelphia Flyers
3601 S Broad St Ste 2
Philadelphia, PA 19148-5297

Coats, Dan (Ex-Senator)
1700 Pennsylvania Ave NW
Washington, DC 20006-4700, USA

Coats, Daniel (Athlete, Football Player)
419 S 380 W
Tooele, UT 84074-2958, USA

Coats, Daniel (Senator)
United States Senate SR-493
Washington, DC 20510-0001, USA

Coats, Kristi (Athlete, Golfer)
185 Wildwood Trl
Petal, MS 39465-2681, USA

Coats, Michael L (Astronaut)
3203 Acorn Wood Way
Houston, TX 77059-3175, USA

Coats, Michael L Captain (Astronaut)
3203 Acorn Wood Way
Houston, TX 77059-3175, USA

Cobb, Charles (Athlete, Football Player)
6075 N Forkner Ave
Fresno, CA 93711-1827, USA

Cobb, David (Politician)
c/o Staff Member *The Green Party of the United States*
PO Box 57065
Washington, DC 20037-0065, USA

Cobb, Garry (Athlete, Football Player)
1258 Chanticleer
Cherry Hill, NJ 08003-4817, USA

Cobb, Julie (Actor)
S D B Partners
315 S Beverly Dr Ste 411
Beverly Hills, CA 90212-4301, USA

Cobb, Keith Hamilton (Actor)
c/o Steven Jensen *Vincent Cirrincione Associates*
8332 Melrose Ave
West Hollywood, CA 90069-5420, USA

Cobb, Marvin (Athlete, Football Player)
655 S Flower St Unit 290
Los Angeles, CA 90017-2805, USA

Cobb, Mike
969 Pacific Ave Apt C
Hoffman Estates, IL 60169-4725, USA

Cobb, Randall (Athlete, Football Player)
c/o Jimmy Sexton *CAA (Memphis)*
6060 Poplar Ave Ste 470
Memphis, TN 38119-0910, USA

Cobb, Reggie (Athlete, Football Player)
13315 Orchard Harvest Dr
Richmond, TX 77407-3219, USA

Cobb, Trevor (Athlete, Football Player)
1721 Cheston Dr
Houston, TX 77029-2909, USA

Cobbin, James (Athlete, Baseball Player)
389 Redondo Rd
Youngstown, OH 44504-1451, USA

Cobbs, Bill (Actor, Producer)
c/o Staff Member *Forster Entertainment*
12533 Woodgreen St
Los Angeles, CA 90066-2723, USA

Cobbs, Cedric (Athlete, Football Player)
4710 Fairlee Dr
Little Rock, AR 72209-5218, USA

Cobbs, Tasha (Musician)
4209 Northeast Expy
Atlanta, GA 30340-3802, USA

Cobham, William C (Billy) (Music Group, Musician)
Joel Chriss
300 Mercer St Apt 3J
New York, NY 10003-6732, USA

Coble, Drew (Athlete, Baseball Player)
205 80th Ave N
Myrtle Beach, SC 29572-4339, USA

Coble, Howard (Congressman, Politician)
2188 Rayburn Hob
Washington, DC 20515-1303, USA

Coblenz, Walter (Director, Producer)
4310 Cahuenga Blvd Unit 401
Toluca Lake, CA 91602-2713, USA

Cobra Starship (Music Group)
c/o Jonathan Daniel *Crush Management*
60-62 E 11th St
7th Floor
New York, NY 10003, USA

Cobum, Cindy C (Bowler)
Ladies Professional Bowling Tour
7200 Harrison Ave # 7171
Rockford, IL 61112-1017, USA

Cobum, Doris (Bowler)
130 Dalton Dr
Buffalo, NY 14223-2221, USA

Coburn, Doris (Bowler)
130 Dalton Dr
Buffalo, NY 14223-2221, USA

Coburn, Tom (Senator)
172 Russell Senate Office Bldg
Washington, DC 20510-0001, USA

Cocanower, James S (Jaime) (Athlete, Baseball Player)
10777 Gram B Cir
Lowell, AR 72745-8446, USA

Coccioletti, Philip (Actor)
c/o Carmen Lavia *Fifi Oscard Agency*
110 W 40th St Rm 1601
New York, NY 10018-8512, USA

Cochran, Antonio (Athlete, Football Player)
PO Box 9644
Columbus, GA 31908-9644, USA

Cochran, Barbara (Athlete, Olympic Athlete, Skier)
213 Brown Hl W
Starksboro, VT 05487-7283, USA

Cochran, John (Athlete, Football Player)
1249 Driftwood Dr
De Pere, WI 54115-1813, USA

Cochran, John (Correspondent)
ABC-TV
5010 Creston St
Hyattsville, MD 20781-1216, USA

Cochran, Robert (Producer, Writer)
c/o Staff Member *Agency for the Performing Arts (APA-LA)*
405 S Beverly Dr Ste 500
Beverly Hills, CA 90212-4425, USA

Cochran, Russ (Athlete, Golfer)
23 Bayview Rd
Jupiter, FL 33469-2012, USA

Cochran, Shannon (Actor)
Stubbs
1450 S Robertson Blvd
Los Angeles, CA 90035-3402, USA

Cochran, Thad (Politician)
218 Maryland Ave NE
Washington, DC 20002-5704, USA

Cochran, Thad (Senator)
113 Dirksen Senate Office Building
Washington, DC 20510-0001, USA

Cochrane, Dave (Athlete, Baseball Player)
11 Muirfield
Trabuco Canyon, CA 92679-3427, USA

Cochrane, Rory (Actor)
c/o Beth Holden-Garland *Untitled Entertainment (LA)*
350 S Beverly Dr Ste 200
Beverly Hills, CA 90212-4819, USA

Cockburn, Bruce (Musician)
c/o Staff Member *The Agency Group (NYC)*
142 W 57th St Fl 6
New York, NY 10019-3300, USA

Cocker, Jarvis (Musician, Songwriter)
c/o Staff Member *Paradigm (Monterey)*
404 W Franklin St
Monterey, CA 93940-2303, USA

Cocker, Joe (Musician)
43401/43405/43409 Cottonwood Creek Rd
Crawford, CO 81415, USA

Cockerill, Kay (Athlete, Golfer)
1345 Arroyo Ave
San Carlos, CA 94070-3912, USA

Cockrell, Alan (Athlete, Baseball Player)
2220 Skyview Ln Apt 253
Colorado Springs, CO 80904-4866, USA

Cockrell, Gene (Athlete, Football Player)
8652 County Road 21
Pampa, TX 79065-1313, USA

Cockrell, Kenneth D (Astronaut)
2300 Richmond Ave Apt 350
Houston, TX 77098-3265, USA

Cock Robin (Music Group, Musician)
Loft Recording Studio
48 Dellwood Pl
Buffalo, NY 14225-2617, USA

Cockroft, Donald L (Don) (Athlete, Football Player)
2418 Dunkeith Dr NW
Canton, OH 44708-1326, USA

Cockroft, Sherman (Athlete, Football Player)
2504 Christopher Ln
Costa Mesa, CA 92626-6750, USA

Cocks, Burling (Race Car Driver)
PO Box 512
Unionville, PA 19375-0512, USA

Cocroft, Sherman
2504 Christopher Ln
Costa Mesa, CA 92626-6750, USA

Code, Merl (Athlete, Football Player)
100 Rearden Dr
Greenville, SC 29605-3261, USA

Coder, Ron (Athlete, Football Player)
25 N Bryant Ave
Pittsburgh, PA 15202-3346, USA

Codey, Lawrence R (Business Person)
Public Service Enterprise
PO Box 1171
80 Park Plaza
Newark, NJ 07101-1171, USA

Codiroli, Chris (Athlete, Baseball Player)
2700 Hillcrest Dr
Cameron Park, CA 95682-9279, USA

Codrescu, Andrei (Writer)
Louisiana State University
English Dept
Baton Rouge, LA 70803-0001, USA

Cody, Bill (Athlete, Football Player)
209 Orleans Dr
Fairhope, AL 36532-4218, USA

Cody, Commander (Musician)
Skyline Music
Old Cherry Mountain Road
Jefferson, NH 03583, USA

Cody, Dan (Athlete, Football Player)
104 W 17th St
Ada, OK 74820-7612, USA

Cody, Diablo (Writer)
12701 Landale St
Studio City, CA 91604-1350, USA

Cody, Terrence (Athlete, Football Player)
c/o Peter Schaffer *All Pro Sports and Entertainment*
36 Steele St Ste 100
Denver, CO 80206-5709, USA

Coe, Barry (Actor)
PO Box 100
Sun Valley, ID 83353

Coe, David Allan (Musician)
129 Caldwell Dr
Hendersonville, TN 37075-2045, USA

Coe, George (Actor)
c/o Martin Gage *Gage Group, The (LA)*
5757 Wilshire Blvd Ste 659
Los Angeles, CA 90036-3682, USA

Coe-Jones, Dawn (Athlete, Golfer)
17319 Emerald Chase Dr
Tampa, FL 33647-3516, USA

Coelho, Susie (Actor)
3565 Meadowview Dr
Riverside, CA 92503-4722, USA

Coen, Ethan (Director, Writer)
c/o Jim Berkus *United Talent Agency (UTA-LA)*
9336 Civic Center Dr
Beverly Hills, CA 90210-3604, USA

Coen, Joel (Director, Writer)
23 Rafael Ave
Bolinas, CA 94924, USA

Coetzer, Amanda (Tennis Player)
Octagon
7950 Jones Branch Dr
Mc Lean, VA 22102-3302, USA

Cofer, J Michael (Mike) (Athlete, Football Player)
2688 Hollowvale Ln
Henderson, NV 89052-2846, USA

Cofer, Mike (Athlete, Football Player)
270 Ridgewood Dr
Fayetteville, GA 30215-8165, USA

Cofer, Mike (Athlete, Football Player)
2688 Hollowvale Ln
Henderson, NV 89052-2846, USA

Cofer, Mike (Race Car Driver)
Racing West
1772 Los Arboles
#J-186
Thousand Oaks, CA 91362, USA

Coffee, Claire (Actor)
c/o Liza Anderson *Anderson Group Public Relations*
8060 Melrose Ave Fl 4
Los Angeles, CA 90046-7038, USA

Coffey, Don (Athlete, Football Player)
231 Redfield Dr
Jackson, TN 38305-8534, USA

Coffey, Junior L (Athlete, Football Player)
17228 32nd Ave S Apt E-12
Seatac, WA 98188-4402, USA

Coffey, Kellie (Musician)
c/o Staff Member *William Morris Endeavor (Nashville)*
1600 Division St Ste 300
Nashville, TN 37203-2755, USA

Coffey, Ken (Athlete, Football Player)
3322 Medinah Ct
Sugar Land, TX 77479-2459, USA

Coffey, Paul
633 Hawthorne St
Birmingham, MI 48009-1650

Coffey, Richard (Athlete, Basketball Player)
7021 McCauley Trl S
Minneapolis, MN 55439-1027, USA

Coffey, Scott
143 Wadsworth Ave
Santa Monica, CA 90405-3509

Coffey, Tabatha (Reality Star, Stylist)
c/o Tanya Taylor *Triple 7 PR (Nashville)*
1920 Adelicia St Ste 300
Nashville, TN 37212-2231, USA

Coffey, Todd (Athlete, Baseball Player)
320 Widd Lawing Ln
Union Mills, NC 28167-8588, USA

Coffield, Kelly (Actor)
c/o Staff Member *Innovative Artists (NY)*
235 Park Ave S Fl 7
New York, NY 10003-1405, USA

Coffield, Randy (Athlete, Football Player)
7110 Lake Basin Rd
Tallahassee, FL 32312-6708, USA

Coffin, Edmund (Tad) (Horse Racer)
General Delivery
Strafford, VT 05072, USA

Coffin, Jeff (Musician)
5201 Elkins Ave
Nashville, TN 37209-3328, USA

Coffman, Kevin (Athlete, Baseball Player)
1246 Wedgewood Dr
Sugar Land, TX 77478-3938, USA

Coffman, Mike (Congressman, Politician)
1222 Longworth Hob
Washington, DC 20515-1307, USA

Coffman, Paul (Athlete, Football Player)
14103 E 195th St
Peculiar, MO 64078-9199, USA

Coffman, Vance D (Business Person)
Lockheed Martin Corp
6801 Rockledge Dr
Bethesda, MD 20817-1877, USA

Cofield, Tim (Athlete, Football Player)
312 NE Warrington Ct
Lees Summit, MO 64064-1603, USA

Cogan, Kevin (Race Car Driver)
205 Rocky Point Rd
Palos Verdes Estates, CA 90274-2621, USA

Cogan, Tony (Athlete, Baseball Player)
151 Pine Point Dr
Highland Park, IL 60035-5332, USA

Cogdill, Gail (Athlete, Football Player)
12922 E 36th Ave
Spokane Valley, WA 99206-8405, USA

Coggin, David (Athlete, Baseball Player)
861 Emerson St
Upland, CA 91784-1227, USA

Coggins, Rich (Athlete, Baseball Player)
4095 Fruit St Spc 219
La Verne, CA 91750-2930, USA

Coghill, George (Athlete, Football Player)
307 Chancellor Pl
Fredericksburg, VA 22401-2104, USA

Coghlan, Eamon (Athlete, Track Athlete)
Int'l Mgmt Group
1 Erieview Plz
1360 E 9th St #1300
Cleveland, OH 44114-1738, USA

Cohan, Chris (Basketball Player, Misc)
Goldan State Warriors
1001 Broadway
Oakland, CA 94607-4019, USA

Cohan, Lauren (Actor)
c/o Staff Member *Liberman/Zerman Management*
252 N Larchmont Blvd Ste 200
Los Angeles, CA 90004-3754, USA

Coheed and Cambria (Music Group)
c/o Blaze James *Black Sheep Fellowship*
6255 W Sunset Blvd Ste 910
Los Angeles, CA 90028-7410, USA

Cohen, Aaron (Astronaut, Misc)
1310 Essex Grn
College Station, TX 77845-9355, USA

Cohen, Adam (Writer)
c/o Staff Member *Penguin Press HC*
375 Hudson St Bsmt 3
New York, NY 10014-7465, USA

Cohen, Andy (Business Person, Television Host)
Watch What Happens Live
325 Hudson St # 101
New York, NY 10013-1045, USA

Cohen, Avishai (Music Group, Musician)
Ron Moss Mgmt
2635 Griffith Park Blvd
Los Angeles, CA 90039-2519, USA

Cohen, Ben (Business Person)
Ben & Jerry's
30 Community Dr Ste 1
South Burlington, VT 05403-6828, USA

Cohen, Bruce (Actor, Producer)
c/o Staff Member *Jinks/Cohen Company*
4000 Warner Blvd Bldg 138
Burbank, CA 91522-0001, USA

Cohen, Etan (Director, Producer, Writer)
c/o Jimmy Miller *Mosaic Media Group*
9200 W Sunset Blvd Ste 10
West Hollywood, CA 90069-3608, USA

Cohen, Gary (Commentator)
136 Haviland Rd
Ridgefield, CT 06877-2822, USA

Cohen, Hy (Athlete, Baseball Player)
35734 Donny Cir
Palm Desert, CA 92211-2695, USA

Cohen, John (Musician, Photographer)
Deborah Bell Photographs
465 W 23rd St Apt 8l
New York, NY 10011-2113, USA

Cohen, Landon (Athlete, Football Player)
c/o Drew Rosenhaus *Rosenhaus Sports Representation*
6400 Allison Rd
Miami Beach, FL 33141-4540, USA

Cohen, Larry (Director)
2111 Coldwater Canyon Dr
Beverly Hills, CA 90210-1734, USA

Cohen, Leonard (Musician)
954 Venango Ave
Los Angeles, CA 90029-3020, USA

Cohen, Linda (Musician)
c/o Staff Member *Greenspan Artist Management*
8760 W Sunset Blvd
West Hollywood, CA 90069-2206, USA

Cohen, Lyor (Producer)
75 Rockefeller Plz
New York, NY 10019-6908, USA

Cohen, Matt (Actor)
c/o Sharon Lane *Lane Management Group*
13017 Woodbridge St
Studio City, CA 91604-1431, USA

Cohen, Michael (Race Car Driver)
Cohen Motorsports
1210 S 56th Ave
Hollywood, FL 33023-1924, USA

Cohen, Rob (Director)
United Talent Agency
9336 Civic Center Dr
Beverly Hills, CA 90210-3604, USA

Cohen, Sacha Baron (Actor, Producer)
2950 Okean Pl
Los Angeles, CA 90046-1141, USA

Cohen, Sarah (Journalist)
Washington Post
1150 15th St NW
Washington, DC 20071-0002, USA

Cohen, Sasha (Athlete, Figure Skater)
c/o Staff Member *Champions on Ice*
3500 American Blvd W Ste 190
Minneapolis, MN 55431-4431, USA

Cohen, Scott (Actor)
c/o Heather Reynolds *One Entertainment (NY)*
12 W 57th St PH
New York, NY 10019-3900, USA

Cohen, Sheldon S (Government Official)
5518 Trent St
Chevy Chase, MD 20815-5512, USA

Cohen, Steve (Actor)
c/o Staff Member *William Morris Endeavor (LA)*
9601 Wilshire Blvd
Beverly Hills, CA 90210-5213, USA

Cohen, Steve (Congressman, Politician)
1005 Longworth Hob
Washington, DC 20515-0701, USA

Cohen, Steve (Business Person)
SAC Capital Advisors
72 Cummings Ave
Stamford, CT 06902, USA

Cohen, Steven A (Business Person)
S.A.C. Capital Advisors
72 Cummings Point Rd
Stamford, CT 06902-7912, USA

Cohen, William (Politician)
The Cohen Group
500 8th St NW # 200
Washington, DC 20004-2131, USA

Cohn, Al (Bowler)
85 Odyssey Dr
Tinley Park, IL 60477-4853, USA

Cohn, Alfred (Al) (Athlete, Bowler)
5641 Sheer Bliss Loop
Land O Lakes, FL 34639-2811, USA

Cohn, Ethan (Actor)
c/o Darren Goldberg *Global Creative*
1051 Cole Ave # B
Los Angeles, CA 90038-2601, USA

Cohn, Gary (Journalist)
Balitmore Sun
501 N Calvert St
Baltimore, MD 21278-1000, USA

Cohn, Mindy (Actor)
c/o David Guc *Vanguard Management Group*
8060 Melrose Ave Fl 4
Los Angeles, CA 90046-7038, USA

Cohoon Friedman, Patti (Actor)
11630 Dona Teresa Dr
Studio City, CA 91604, USA

Coil, Austin (Race Car Driver)
John Force Racing
22722 Old Canal Rd
Yorba Linda, CA 92887-4602, USA

Coiro, Rhys (Actor)
2233 Baxter St
Los Angeles, CA 90039-3601, USA

Coke, Phil (Athlete, Baseball Player)
c/o Team Member *New York Yankees*
Yankee Stadium
161st St & River Ave
Bronx, NY 10451, USA

Coker, Larry (Coach, Football Coach)
Miami University
Athletic Dept
Miami, FL 33124, USA

Cokes, Curtis (Boxer)
3540 Durango Dr
Dallas, TX 75220-3624, USA

Cola, Angelo (Athlete, Football Player)
11 McDermott Pl
Brigantine, NJ 08203-2934, USA

Colangelo, Jerry (Commentator)
70 E Country Club Dr
Phoenix, AZ 85014-5435, USA

Colangelo, Mike (Athlete, Baseball Player)
5751 Fincastle Dr
Manassas, VA 20112-5439, USA

Colantoni, Enrico (Actor)
11931 Hesby St
Valley Village, CA 91607-3113, USA

Colasanti, Robert (Horse Racer)
4 Duke Pass
Colts Neck, NJ 07722-1761, USA

Colavito, Rocky (Athlete, Baseball Player)
656 Scenic Dr
Bernville, PA 19506-8257, USA

Colavito, Steve (Athlete, Football Player)
57 Fairview Ct
Nanuet, NY 10954-3230, USA

Colbern, Mike (Athlete, Baseball Player)
5120 E Tano St
Phoenix, AZ 85044-4121, USA

Colbert, Craig (Athlete, Baseball Player)
6635 SE 42nd Ave
Portland, OR 97206-7703, USA

Colbert, Darrell (Athlete, Football Player)
6514 River Bluff Dr
Houston, TX 77085-1306, USA

Colbert, Jim (Athlete, Golfer)
118 Wanish Pl
Palm Desert, CA 92260-7316, USA

Colbert, Keary (Athlete, Football Player)
580 Lantana St Apt 80
Camarillo, CA 93010-6107, USA

Colbert, Nate (Athlete, Baseball Player)
2756 N Green Valley Pkwy
Henderson, NV 89014-2120, USA

Colbert, Rondy (Athlete, Football Player)
5118 Madden Ln
Houston, TX 77048-2727, USA

Colbert, Stephen (Producer, Television Host, Writer)
The Colbert Report
513 W 54th St
New York, NY 10019-5014, USA

Colbert, Steve (Actor, Talk Show Host, Writer)
The Colbert Report
513 W 54th St
New York, NY 10019-5014, USA

Colbert, Vince (Athlete, Baseball Player)
18071 Blandford Rd
Cleveland, OH 44121-1040, USA

Colborn, James W (Jim) (Athlete, Baseball Player)
2932 Solimar Beach Dr
Ventura, CA 93001-9754, USA

Colborn, Richard (Musician)
Legends of 21st Century
7 Trinity Row
Florence, MA 01062-1931, USA

Colbrunn, Greg (Athlete, Baseball Player)
3196 Pignatelli Cres
Mount Pleasant, SC 29466-8060, USA

Colby Cushman, Danielle (Reality Star)
4 Miles 2 Memphis
2125 N Whipple St
Chicago, IL 60647-3810, USA

Colchico, Dan (Athlete, Football Player)
5160 Paul Scarlet Dr
Concord, CA 94521-3134, USA

Coldplay (Music Group)
c/o Ambrosia Healy *The Fun Star*
8439 W Sunset Blvd Ste 2
West Hollywood, CA 90069-1925, USA

Cold War Kids (Music Group)
c/o Staff Member *Paradigm (Monterey)*
404 W Franklin St
Monterey, CA 93940-2303, USA

Cole, Alex (Athlete, Baseball Player)
656 30th St
Newport News, VA 23607-4040, USA

Cole, Anne (Designer, Fashion Designer)
Cole of California
6040 Bandini Blvd
Commerce, CA 90040-2905, USA

Cole, Artemas (Cartoonist)
15 Regency Mnr Apt 15-8
Rutland, VT 05701-5310, USA

Cole, Bobby (Athlete, Golfer)
204 W 2nd Ave
Windermere, FL 34786-8507, USA

Cole, Cecil (Baseball Player)
Newark Eagles
201 N 12th St
Connellsville, PA 15425-2422, USA

Cole, Cheryl (Musician)
1322 N Detroit St Unit 12
Los Angeles, CA 90046-4487, USA

Cole, Chris (Athlete, Football Player)
6642 Hudnall Rd
Orange, TX 77632-3589, USA

Cole, Christina (Actor)
c/o Lorrie Bartlett *ICM Partners (LA)*
10250 Constellation Blvd Fl 7
Los Angeles, CA 90067-6207, USA

Cole, Danton (Athlete, Hockey Player)
7180 Wapiti Way
Saline, MI 48176-9176, USA

Cole, Dick (Athlete, Baseball Player)
3149 Madeira Ave
Costa Mesa, CA 92626-2323, USA

Cole, Emerson (Athlete, Football Player)
1661 Indiana Ave
Toledo, OH 43607-3966, USA

Cole, Erik (Athlete, Hockey Player, Olympic Athlete)
Sports Consulting Group
65 Monroe Ave Ste D
Pittsford, NY 14534-1318, USA

Cole, Ford (Athlete, Football Player)
PO Box 3218
Olympic Valley, CA 96146-3218, USA

Cole, Fred (Athlete, Football Player)
10 Tuscan Rd
Livingston, NJ 07039-2919, USA

Cole, Freddy (Music Group)
Producers Inc
11806 N 56th St
Temple Terrace, FL 33617-1652, USA

Cole, Gary (Actor)
3855 Berry Dr
Studio City, CA 91604-3887, USA

Cole, J (Musician)
c/o Sarah Cunningham *The Chamber Group*
75 Broad St Ste 2710
New York, NY 10004-2679, USA

Cole, Joanna (Writer)
c/o Staff Member *Scholastic Entertainment*
557 Broadway
New York, NY 10012-3962, USA

Cole, John (Cartoonist)
Durham Herald-Sun
2828 Pickett Rd
Durham, NC 27705-5613, USA

Cole, Kenneth (Designer)
Kenneth Cole Productions Inc
601 W 50th St
New York, NY 10019, USA

Cole, Keyshia (Musician)
3710 Milton Park Dr
Alpharetta, GA 30022-5801, USA

Cole, Kimberly Lynn (Actor)
36 Longview Ct
Montgomery, AL 36108-2018, USA

Cole, Larry R (Athlete, Football Player)
400 Country Pl
Colleyville, TX 76034-7598, USA

Cole, Linzy (Athlete, Football Player)
7700 Creekbend Dr Apt 18
Houston, TX 77071-1728, USA

Cole, Michael (Actor)
5121 Varna Ave
Sherman Oaks, CA 91423-1526, USA

Cole, Natalie (Actor, Musician)
14320 Ventura Blvd # 450
Sherman Oaks, CA 91423-2717, USA

Cole, Nigel (Director, Writer)
c/o Rosalie Swedlin *Anonymous Content (LA)*
3532 Hayden Ave
Culver City, CA 90232-2413, USA

Cole, Olivia (Actor)
Century Artists
PO Box 59747
Santa Barbara, CA 93150, USA

Cole, Paula (Musician)
675 Hale St # D
Beverly, MA 01915-2179, USA

Cole, P K
32522 Bowman Knoll Dr
Westlake Village, CA 91361-5520, USA

Cole, Robin (Athlete, Football Player)
9 Brook Ln
Eighty Four, PA 15330-2603, USA

Cole, Stu (Athlete, Baseball Player)
6527 Willow Gate Ln
Charlotte, NC 28215-4014, USA

Cole, Taylor (Actor)
c/o Joanna (Joanie) Burstein *Burstein Company, The*
15304 W Sunset Blvd Ste 208
Pacific Palisades, CA 90272-3656, USA

Cole, Tina (Actor)
778 University Ave
Junior League of Sacramento
Sacramento, CA 95825-6703, USA

Cole, Tom (Congressman, Politician)
2458 Rayburn Hob
Washington, DC 20515-4323, USA

Cole, Victor (Athlete, Baseball Player)
138 Estonallie Rd
Mercer, TN 38392-7102, USA

Colella, Richard (Rick) (Swimmer)
217 19th Pl
Kirkland, WA 98033-4903, USA

Coleman, Andre (Athlete, Football Player)
1616 Mulligan Pl
Manhattan, KS 66502-1444, USA

Coleman, Ben (Athlete, Basketball Player)
14211 Fisher Ave NE
Prior Lake, MN 55372-1240, USA

Coleman, Casey (Athlete, Football Player)
11901 Northumberland Dr
Tampa, FL 33626-1327

Coleman, Catherine G (Cady) (Astronaut)
30 Frank Williams Rd
Shelburne Falls, MA 01370-9724, USA

Coleman, Catherine G Lt Colonel (Astronaut)
30 Frank Williams Rd
Shelburne Falls, MA 01370-9724, USA

Coleman, Chris (Athlete, Football Player)
2425 Evans St SW
Lenoir, NC 28645-6358, USA

Coleman, Cosey (Athlete, Football Player)
11901 Northumberland Dr
Tampa, FL 33626-1327, USA

Coleman, Dabney (Actor)
1100 Alta Loma Rd Apt 508
W Hollywood, CA 90069-2436, USA

Coleman, Daniel J (Publisher)
Popular Mechanics Magazine
224 W 57th St
New York, NY 10019-3212, USA

Coleman, Derrick D (Basketball Player)
Philadelphia 76ers
3601 S Broad St Ste 4
1st Union Center
Philadelphia, PA 19148-5287, USA

Coleman, Don E (Athlete, Football Player)
424 McPherson Ave
Lansing, MI 48915-1158, USA

Coleman, E C (Basketball Player)
Houston Rockets
370 E Harmon Ave
Las Vegas, NV 89169-7003, USA

Coleman, Eric (Athlete, Football Player)
2933 Elm St
Denver, CO 80207-2658, USA

Coleman, George E (Musician)
63 E 9th St Apt 4G
New York, NY 10003-6331, USA

Coleman, Greg (Athlete, Football Player)
2313 River Pointe Cir
Minneapolis, MN 55411-4279, USA

Coleman, Harry (Athlete, Football Player)
c/o Tony Paige *Perennial Sports and Entertainment*
1455 Pennsylvania Ave NW Ste 225
Washington, DC 20004-1026, USA

Coleman, Jack (Actor)
3816 Goodland Ave
Studio City, CA 91604-2314, USA

Coleman, Jermaine (Maino) (Musician)
c/o Staff Member *Atlantic Records (NY)*
1290 Avenue of the Americas Fl 28
New York, NY 10104-0106, USA

Coleman, Karon (Athlete, Football Player)
22959 E Smoky Hill Rd Apt K105
Aurora, CO 80015-6735, USA

Coleman, Kelly (Athlete, Basketball Player)
PO Box 183
Higgins Lake, MI 48627-0183, USA

Coleman, Kenyon (Athlete, Football Player)
35723 Stock St
Murrieta, CA 92562-4467, USA

Coleman, Kurt (Athlete, Football Player)
c/o Blake Baratz *The Institute for Athletes*
3600 Minnesota Dr Ste 550
Minneapolis, MN 55435-7925, USA

Coleman, Leonard (Athlete, Football Player)
125 NE 13th Ave
Boynton Beach, FL 33435-3124, USA

Coleman, Leonard (Commentator)
519 S Maple Ave
Basking Ridge, NJ 07920-1318, USA

Coleman, Lincoln (Athlete, Football Player)
PO Box 496
Seguin, TX 78156-0496, USA

Coleman, Marco (Athlete, Football Player)
105 Monarch Ct
Saint Augustine, FL 32095-7043, USA

Coleman, Marco D (Athlete, Football Player)
11036 Turnbridge Dr
Jacksonville, FL 32256-2328, USA

Coleman, Marcus (Athlete, Football Player)
1736 Mapleleaf Dr
Wylie, TX 75098-8166, USA

Coleman, Mark (Athlete, Wrestler)
Dream Stage Entertainment
6535 Wilshire Blvd Ste 208
Los Angeles, CA 90048-4963, USA

Coleman, Michael (Mike) (Athlete, Baseball Player)
1053 Mallow Dr
Madison, TN 37115-4219, USA

Coleman, Monique (Actor)
c/o Gina Sorial *Rogers & Cowan PR (LA)*
8687 Melrose Ave Ste 7
West Hollywood, CA 90069-5721, USA

Coleman, Monte (Athlete, Football Player)
4700 S Beech St
Pine Bluff, AR 71603-7327, USA

Coleman, Norm (Politician)
909 Osceola Ave
Saint Paul, MN 55105-3209, USA

Coleman, Norris (Athlete, Basketball Player)
445 Monument Rd Apt 1007
Jacksonville, FL 32225-6456, USA

Coleman, Oliver (Actor)
c/o Troy Zien *3 Arts Entertainment (LA)*
9460 Wilshire Blvd Fl 7
Beverly Hills, CA 90212-2713, USA

Coleman, Paul (Athlete, Baseball Player)
2704 Brentwood Dr
Tyler, TX 75701-5902, USA

Coleman, Roderick (Rod) (Athlete, Football Player)
6735 Great Water Dr
Flowery Branch, GA 30542-6639, USA

Coleman, Ronnie (Athlete, Football Player)
16039 Williwaw Dr
Houston, TX 77083-5375, USA

Coleman, Sidney (Athlete, Football Player)
8034 King Rd
Meridian, MS 39305-9261, USA

Coleman, Signy (Actor)
9200 W Sunset Blvd Ste 625
West Hollywood, CA 90069-3609, USA

Coleman, Steve (Athlete, Football Player)
81 W Johnson St
Philadelphia, PA 19144-1937, USA

Coleman, Vincent M (Vince) (Athlete, Baseball Player)
12936 N 137th St
Scottsdale, AZ 85259-2333, USA

Coleman, Walter (Baseball Player)
New York Yankees
HC 1 Box 236
New Russia, NY 12964, USA

Coleman, William (Politician, Secretary)
O'Melveny & Myers
1625 I St NW
O'Melveny and Myers Llp
Washington, DC 20006-4061, USA

Coleman Jr, Leonard (Baseball Player)
283 3rd St
Beach Haven, NJ 08008, USA

Coles, Bimbo (Athlete, Basketball Player)
203 E Washington St
Lewisburg, WV 24901-1423, USA

Coles, Darnell (Athlete, Baseball Player)
10021 Brompton Dr
Tampa, FL 33626-5408, USA

Coles, Janet (Athlete, Golfer)
6083 Alumni Gym
Hanover, NH 03755-3501, USA

Coles, Kim (Actor, Comedian)
9000 Cynthia St Apt 403
West Hollywood, CA 90069-4871, USA

Coles, Laveranues (Athlete, Football Player)
87 Coles Ct
Saint Johns, FL 32259-8898, USA

Coletta, Chris (Athlete, Baseball Player)
206 SW 45th St
Cape Coral, FL 33914-5906, USA

Coley, Daryl (Musician)
Daryl Coley Ministries
417 E Regent St
Inglewood, CA 90301-1315, USA

Coley, James (Athlete, Football Player)
111 Pebble Park Rd
Starr, SC 29684-9259, USA

Coley, John Ford (Musician, Songwriter, Writer)
Earthtone
8306 Wilshire Blvd # 981
Beverly Hills, CA 90211-2304, USA

Colfer, Chris (Actor, Musician)
2654 Charl Pl
Los Angeles, CA 90046-1023, USA

Colfer, Eoin (Writer)
c/o Staff Member *HarperCollins Publishers*
195 Broadway Fl 2
Cellar 1
New York, NY 10007-3132, USA

Colicchio, Tom (Chef, Reality Star, Television Host)
Colicchio & Sons
85 10th Ave Frnt B
New York, NY 10011-4725, USA

Colier, Jason (Basketball Player)
Houston Rockets
19318 Kristen Pine Dr
Humble, TX 77346-2084, USA

Colin, Charlie (Musician)
Jon Landau
80 Main St
Greenwich, CT 06830, USA

Colin, Margaret (Actor)
366 W 11th St Ph C
New York, NY 10014-6227, USA

Colinet, Stalin (Athlete, Football Player)
3 Mohawk Dr
Framingham, MA 01701-3041, USA

Coll, Stephen W (Journalist)
Washington Post
Editorial Dept
1150 15th St NW
Washington, DC 20071-0001, USA

Collective Soul (Music Group)
c/o Jordan Feldstein *Career Artist Management*
9350 Civic Center Dr Ste 100
Beverly Hills, CA 90210-3629, USA

Colledge, Daryn (Athlete, Football Player)
c/o Jeff Sperbeck *The Novo Agency*
3201 Danville Blvd Ste 295
Alamo, CA 94507-1978, USA

Collee, John (Writer)
c/o Alex Lerner *Kaplan/Perrone Entertainment*
280 S Beverly Dr Ste 513
Beverly Hills, CA 90212-3908, USA

Collen, Phil (Musician)
26971 Highwood Cir
Laguna Hills, CA 92653-7828, USA

Collet, Christopher (Actor)
54 Vermont Ter
Tuckahoe, NY 10707-2314, USA

Collett, Elmer (Athlete, Football Player)
PO Box 522
10 Avenida
Stinson Beach, CA 94970-0522, USA

Collette, Toni (Actor)
848 N Las Palmas Ave
Los Angeles, CA 90038-3516, USA

Colletti, Roseanne (Correspondent)
WNBC-TV
30 Rockefeller Plz Fl 7
New York, NY 10112-0015, USA

Colletti, Stephen (Reality Star)
14635 Hawes St
Whittier, CA 90604-1160, USA

Collett-Serra, Jaume (Director)
1662 Marmont Ave
Los Angeles, CA 90069-1514, USA

Colley, Dana (Musician)
Creative Performance Group
48 Laight St
New York, NY 10013-2156, USA

Colley, Ed (Artist, Cartoonist)
11 Blaisdell Ter
Ipswich, MA 01938-1706, USA

Colley-Lee, Myrna (Designer)
Mississippi State University Libraries
PO Box 5408
395 Hardy Road
Mississippi State, MS 39762-5408

Collie, Bruce (Athlete, Football Player)
9595 Ranch Road 12 Ste 13
Wimberley, TX 78676-5248, USA

Collie, Mark (Actor, Musician, Songwriter, Writer)
2709 Tyne Blvd
Nashville, TN 37215-4531, USA

Collier, Don (Actor)
9024 E 21st St
Tucson, AZ 85710-6213, USA

Collier, James (Athlete, Football Player)
922 Bromley Dr
Baton Rouge, LA 70808-5814, USA

Collier, Jim (Athlete, Football Player)
1670 Terral Island Rd
Farmerville, LA 71241-4013, USA

Collier, Lou (Athlete, Baseball Player)
115 E 42nd St # 2E
Chicago, IL 60653-2103, USA

Collier, Mark (Actor)
c/o John Crosby *John Crosby Management*
1357 N Spaulding Ave
Los Angeles, CA 90046-4009, USA

Collier, Mike (Athlete, Football Player)
528 W Church St Apt B
Hagerstown, MD 21740-4630, USA

Collier, Steve (Athlete, Football Player)
3473 S King Dr
Chicago, IL 60616-4108, USA

Collier, Timothy (Tim) (Athlete, Football Player)
3116 50th St
Dallas, TX 75216-7343, USA

Collingwood, Chris (Musician, Songwriter, Writer)
MOB Agency
6404 Wilshire Blvd Ste 505
Los Angeles, CA 90048-5507, USA

Collins, Alfred (Sonny) (Athlete, Football Player)
2455 Cedar Canyon Ct SE
Marietta, GA 30067-6617, USA

Collins, Art (Athlete, Basketball Player)
1812 NW 55th Ter
Miami, FL 33142-3044, USA

Collins, Arthur D Jr (Business Person)
7000 Central Ave NE
Medtronic Inc
Minneapolis, MN 55432-3568, USA

Collins, Bill (Athlete, Hockey Player)
5000 Town Ctr Ste 505
Southfield, MI 48075-1112, USA

Collins, Billy (Writer)
PO Box 2487
Winter Park, FL 32790-2487, USA

Collins, Bootsy (Musician)
817 Barg Salt Run Rd
Cincinnati, OH 45244-1105, USA

Collins, Brett W (Athlete, Football Player)
21275 NW Rock Creek Blvd
Portland, OR 97229-1041, USA

Collins, Brian (Kid Ink) (Musician)
c/o Staff Member *Sony/RCA Records*
550 Madison Ave Fl 6
New York, NY 10022-3211, USA

Collins, Bud (Sportscaster)
822 Boylston St Ste 203
Chestnut Hill, MA 02467-2504, USA

Collins, C F (Athlete, Football Player)
10065 Garden St
Livonia, MI 48150-3110, USA

Collins, Clarence
3697 Blake Canyon Dr
North Las Vegas, NV 89032-0834, USA

Collins, Clifton (Actor)
12933 Bloomfield St
Studio City, CA 91604-1402, USA

Collins, David S (Dave) (Athlete, Baseball Player)
718 Oakland Dr
Taylor Mill, KY 41015-2116, USA

Collins, Donald E (Don) (Athlete, Baseball Player)
127 Deerwood Trl
Sharpsburg, GA 30277-2002, USA

Collins, Douglas (Doug) (Athlete, Basketball Player, Coach, Sportscaster)
10040 E Happy Valley Rd Unit 617
Scottsdale, AZ 85255-2355, USA

Collins, Duane E (Business Person)
Parker Hannifin Corp
6035 Parkland Blvd
Cleveland, OH 44124-4141, USA

Collins, Dwight (Athlete, Football Player)
821 12th St
Beaver Falls, PA 15010-4416, USA

Collins, Gary J (Athlete, Football Player)
221 Lamp Post Ln
Hershey, PA 17033-1881, USA

Collins, George (Athlete, Football Player)
2043 Northside Rd
Perry, GA 31069-2224, USA

Collins, Glen L (Athlete, Football Player)
17 Autumn Park
Jackson, MS 39206-6241, USA

Collins, Jack (Actor)
Contemporary Artists
610 Santa Monica Blvd Ste 202
Santa Monica, CA 90401-1645, USA

Collins, Jackie (Writer)
1580 Stone Canyon Rd
Los Angeles, CA 90077-1911, USA

Collins, Jamie (Athlete, Football Player)
c/o Bus Cook *Bus Cook Sports, Inc*
1 Willow Bend Dr
Hattiesburg, MS 39402-8552, USA

Collins, Jarron (Athlete, Basketball Player)
11173 Cashmere St
Los Angeles, CA 90049-3233, USA

Collins, Jason (Athlete, Basketball Player)
12639 Promontory Rd
Los Angeles, CA 90049-1186, USA

Collins, Javiar (Athlete, Football Player)
2503 S Pennsylvania St
Denver, CO 80210-5722, USA

Collins, Jed (Athlete, Football Player)
c/o Derrick Fox *Derrick Fox Management*
Prefers to be contacted by telephone
CA, USA

Collins, Jerome (Athlete, Football Player)
25540 Soya Ln
Warrenville, IL 60555, USA

Collins, Jerry (Athlete, Football Player)
405 Monterey Ave
Annapolis, MD 21401-1329, USA

Collins, Jessica
c/o Rick Ax *Gold Coast Management*
438 S Venice Blvd Apt 5
Venice, CA 90291-4695, USA

Collins, Jim (Athlete, Football Player)
2140 E Oceanfront
Newport Beach, CA 92661-1525, USA

Collins, Joan (Actor)
9255 Doheny Rd Apt 2501
West Hollywood, CA 90069-3235, USA

Collins, Joely (Actor)
c/o Staff Member *TalentWorks (LA)*
3500 W Olive Ave Ste 1400
Burbank, CA 91505-5512, USA

Collins, Judy (Musician, Songwriter, Writer)
Rocky Mountains Production
PO Box 1296
New York, NY 10025-1296, USA

Collins, Kate (Actor)
1410 York Ave Apt 4D
New York, NY 10021-3401, USA

Collins, Kerry (Athlete, Football Player)
1090 Stockett Dr
Nashville, TN 37221-4431, USA

Collins, Kevin (Athlete, Baseball Player)
9121 Point Charity Dr
Pigeon, MI 48755-9624, USA

Collins, Lauren (Actor)
c/o Steven Kavovit *Thruline Entertainment*
9250 Wilshire Blvd Ste 100
Ground Floor
Beverly Hills, CA 90212-3343, USA

Collins, Lily (Actor)
c/o Will Ward *ROAR (LA)*
9701 Wilshire Blvd Fl 8
Beverly Hills, CA 90212-2008, USA

Collins, Lynn (Actor)
c/o Christine Tripicchio *Shelter PR*
9350 Wilshire Blvd Ste 450
Beverly Hills, CA 90212-3230, USA

Collins, Mark (Athlete, Football Player)
PO Box 24032
2X Champ Sports
Overland Park, KS 66283-4032, USA

Collins, Michael (Astronaut)
c/o Staff Member *Farrar, Straus and Giroux*
18 W 18th St Fl 7
New York, NY 10011-4675, USA

Collins, Michael Brig Gen (Astronaut)
272 Polynesia Ct
Marco Island, FL 34145-3826, USA

Collins, Michelle (Actor)
c/o Tanya Kleckner *Henderson Represents*
100 Universal City Plz Ste 7152
Universal City, CA 91608-1002, USA

Collins, Misha
c/o Carolyn Govers *Anonymous Content (LA)*
3532 Hayden Ave
Culver City, CA 90232-2413, USA

Collins, Mo (Actor)
c/o Nicole Cataldo *Diverse Talent Group*
9911 W Pico Blvd Ste 340W
Los Angeles, CA 90035-2703, USA

Collins, Paul (Athlete, Football Player)
1441 Bayshore Dr
Kemah, TX 77565-3045, USA

Collins, Paul (Athlete, Football Player)
4370 Chamberlain Dr
Bloomfield Hills, MI 48301-3741, USA

Collins, Roosevelt (Athlete, Football Player)
3600 Holly St
Denison, TX 75020-3714, USA

Collins, Shane (Athlete, Football Player)
PO Box 11090
Bozeman, MT 59719-1090, USA

Collins, Shanna (Actor)
c/o Stephanie Simon *Untitled Entertainment (LA)*
350 S Beverly Dr Ste 200
Beverly Hills, CA 90212-4819, USA

Collins, Shawn (Athlete, Football Player)
PO Box 711933
San Diego, CA 92171-1933, USA

Collins, Stephen (Actor)
5153 Chimineas Ave
Tarzana, CA 91356-4305, USA

Collins, Susan (Senator)
413 Dirksen Senate Office Building
Washington, DC 20510-0001, USA

Collins, Suzanne (Writer)
c/o Rosemary B. Stimola *Stimola Literary Studio*
306 Chase Ct
Edgewater, NJ 07020-1601, USA

Collins, Terry (Athlete, Baseball Player, Coach)
Roosevelt Ave Attn
NEWYORKMETS12301MANAGERSO
Corona, NY 11368-9993, USA

Collins, Todd
1279 Collins Rd
New Market, TN 37820-3837, USA

Collins, Todd F (Athlete, Football Player)
1279 Collins Rd
New Market, TN 37820-3837, USA

Collins, Todd S (Athlete, Football Player)
26 Cambridge Cir
Victor, NY 14564-1503, USA

Collins, Tony (Athlete, Football Player)
10709 N Preserve Way Apt 203
Miramar, FL 33025-6553, USA

Collinsworth, Cris (Athlete, Football Player, Sportscaster)
31 Crow Hill Rd
Fort Thomas, KY 41075-1801, USA

Collison, Darren (Athlete, Basketball Player)
c/o Bill Duffy *BDA Sports Management (BDA-CA)*
700 Ygnacio Valley Rd Ste 330
Walnut Creek, CA 94596-3838, USA

Collison, Nick (Athlete, Basketball Player)
Seattle SuperSonics
3012 N Robinson Ave
Oklahoma City, OK 73103-4125, USA

Collyard, Bob (Athlete, Hockey Player)
5300 Knox Ave N
Minneapolis, MN 55430-3058, USA

Colman, Booth (Actor)
2160 Century Park E Apt 603
Los Angeles, CA 90067-2214, USA

Colman, Olivia (Actor)
c/o Bryna Rifkin *ID Public Relations (LA)*
7060 Hollywood Blvd Fl 8th
Los Angeles, CA 90028-6021, USA

Colman, Wayne (Athlete, Football Player)
604 N Somerset Ave
Ventnor City, NJ 08406-1551, USA

Colmes, Alan (Correspondent)
c/o Staff Member *Hannity & Colmes*
1211 Avenue of the Americas Fl 18
New York, NY 10036-8705, USA

Colo, Don (Athlete, Football Player)
7355 E Claremont St
Scottsdale, AZ 85250-5526, USA

Coloma, Marcus (Actor)
c/o Paul Rosicker *Gersh (LA)*
9465 Wilshire Blvd Ste 600
Beverly Hills, CA 90212-2605, USA

Colombini, Aldo (Director, Producer)
PO Box 829
Newbury Park, CA 91319-0829, USA

Colombo, Marc (Athlete, Football Player)
1250 Biltmore Dr
Southlake, TX 76092-3462, USA

Colomby, Bobby
1423 Holmby Ave
Los Angeles, CA 90024-5104

Colomby, Scott (Actor)
Borinstein Oreck Bogart
3172 Dona Susana Dr
Studio City, CA 91604-4356, USA

Colon, Bartolo (Athlete, Baseball Player)
14 Federal St # 1
Passaic, NJ 07055-3209, USA

Colon, Harry (Athlete, Football Player)
10337 Alvarado Way
Charlotte, NC 28277-3459, USA

Colon, Mercedes (Actor)
c/o Jay Schachter *Prestige Talent Agency*
6100 Wilshire Blvd Ste 550
Los Angeles, CA 90048-5164, USA

Colon, Miriam (Actor)
51 W 52nd St
New York, NY 10019-6119, USA

Colonna, Sarah (Actor, Writer)
c/o Abbey Sibucao-MacDonald *New Wave Entertainment (LA)*
2660 W Olive Ave
Burbank, CA 91505-4525, USA

Colorito, Tony (Athlete, Football Player)
17805 SW Cicero Ct
Beaverton, OR 97007-9036, USA

Color Me Badd (Music Group, Musician)
PO Box 552113
Opa Locka, FL 33055-0113, USA

Colpaert, Dick (Athlete, Baseball Player)
47412 Eldon Dr
Shelby Township, MI 48317-2912, USA

Colquitt, Craig (Athlete, Football Player)
1905 Pitts Field Ln
Knoxville, TN 37922-6197, USA

Colquitt, Dustin (Athlete, Football Player)
1905 Pitts Field Ln
Knoxville, TN 37922-6197, USA

Colquitt, Jimmy (Athlete, Football Player)
11722 Hardin Valley Rd
Knoxville, TN 37932-2319, USA

Colson, Loyd A (Athlete, Baseball Player)
309 E Sycamore St
Hollis, OK 73550-1233, USA

Colston, Marques (Athlete, Football Player)
c/o Joel Segal *Lagardere Unlimited (NYC)*
845 United Nations Plz
New York, NY 10017-3540, USA

Colston, Tim (Athlete, Football Player)
6804 N 47th St
Tampa, FL 33610-1808, USA

Colt, Marshall (Actor)
1150 Anchorage Ln Unit 612
San Diego, CA 92106-3124, USA

Colter, Jessie (Musician)
Shout Factory
2042-A Armacost Ave
Los Angeles, CA 90025, USA

Colter, Steve (Athlete, Basketball Player)
802 E Mountain Sage Dr
Phoenix, AZ 85048-4428, USA

Colton, Graham (Musician)
c/o Staff Member *Red Light Management (LA)*
8439 W Sunset Blvd Ste 2
West Hollywood, CA 90069-1925, USA

Colton, Lawrence R (Larry) (Athlete, Baseball Player)
3027 NE 68th Ave
Portland, OR 97213-5215, USA

Colton, Michael (Writer)
c/o Tony Etz *Creative Artists Agency (CAA-LA)*
2000 Avenue of the Stars Ste 100
Los Angeles, CA 90067-4705, USA

Coltrane, Chi
5955 Tuxedo Ter
Los Angeles, CA 90068-2461

Coluccio, Bob (Athlete, Baseball Player)
369 Flower St
Costa Mesa, CA 92627-2352, USA

Columbus, Chris (Director, Producer)
c/o Simon Halls *Slate Public Relations*
9000 W Sunset Blvd Ste 915
West Hollywood, CA 90069-5809, USA

Columbus, Chris (Writer)
290 W End Ave
New York, NY 10023-8106, USA

Colunga, Fernando (Actor)
c/o Staff Member *Crossover Agency*
801 SW 3rd Ave Ste 302
Miami, FL 33130-3576, USA

Colussy, Dan A (Business Person)
20 Saint Thomas Dr
Palm Beach Gardens, FL 33418-4598, USA

Colvin, James (Jim) (Athlete, Football Player)
4583 S Deer Poppy Cir
Saint George, UT 84790-4722, USA

Colvin, Roosevelt (Athlete, Football Player)
9340 Sargent Rd
Indianapolis, IN 46256-1128, USA

Colvin, Shawn (Musician, Songwriter)
615 Pressler St
Austin, TX 78703-5125, USA

Colvin, Tyler (Athlete, Baseball Player)
4335 E Fox Cir
Mesa, AZ 85205-5104, USA

Colyar, Michael (Actor, Comedian)
c/o Vanzil Burke *Burke Management*
810 S Flower St Apt 1108
Los Angeles, CA 90017-4654, USA

Colyer, Steve (Athlete, Baseball Player)
205 S Saint Jacques St
Florissant, MO 63031-6950, USA

Colzie, Jim (Athlete, Baseball Player)
3140 Day Ave
Miami, FL 33133-5111, USA

Comaneci, Nadia (Gymnast)
Paul Ziert and Associates
3214 Bart Conner Dr
Norman, OK 73072-2406, USA

Combe, Geoff (Athlete, Baseball Player)
743 Tudor Cir
Thousand Oaks, CA 91360-5246, USA

Combes, Willard W (Cartoonist)
1266 Oakridge Dr
Cleveland, OH 44121-1623, USA

Combichrist (Music Group, Musician)
c/o Staff Member *Metropolis Records*
PO Box 974
Media, PA 19063-0974, USA

Combs, Chris (Athlete, Football Player)
3435 Cromwell Rd
Durham, NC 27705-5408, USA

Combs, Glenn (Athlete, Basketball Player)
3627 Dogwood Ln SW
Roanoke, VA 24015-4503, USA

Combs, Holly Marie (Actor, Producer, Writer)
223 Saddlebow Rd
Bell Canyon, CA 91307-1035, USA

Combs, Jeffrey (Actor)
c/o Leland LaBarre *Bleu, An Entertainment Company*
5225 Wilshire Blvd Ste 336
Los Angeles, CA 90036-4380, USA

Combs, Jessi (Reality Star)
PO Box 21859
Long Beach, CA 90801-4859, USA

Combs, Leroy (Athlete, Basketball Player)
1631 Glenn Bo Dr
Norman, OK 73071-2813, USA

Combs, Patrick D (Pat) (Athlete, Baseball Player)
203 Timber Lake Way
Southlake, TX 76092-7217, USA

Combs, Rodney (Race Car Driver)
201 Old Country Rd Ste 101
Melville, NY 11747-2731, USA

Combs, Sean (Musician, Producer)
c/o Staff Member *Bad Boy Worldwide Entertainment*
1440 Broadway Fl 19
New York, NY 10018-2301, USA

Comden, Danny (Director)
c/o Ruthanne Secunda *ICM Partners (LA)*
10250 Constellation Blvd Fl 7
Los Angeles, CA 90067-6207, USA

Comeau, Andy (Actor)
c/o Staff Member *Rugolo Entertainment*
195 S Beverly Dr Ste 400
Beverly Hills, CA 90212-3044, USA

Comeaux, Darren (Athlete, Football Player)
15677 W Glenrosa Ave
Goodyear, AZ 85395-7758, USA

Comeaux, John (Athlete, Basketball Player)
PO Box 327
Carencro, LA 70520-0327, USA

Comegys, Dallas (Athlete, Basketball Player)
4330 Wayne Ave
Philadelphia, PA 19140-1745, USA

Comella, Greg (Athlete, Football Player)
90 Fairbanks Ave
Wellesley Hills, MA 02481-5256, USA

Comer, Anjanette (Actor)
Dade/Schultz
6442 Coldwater Canyon Ave Ste 206
North Hollywood, CA 91606-1174, USA

Comer, Steve (Athlete, Baseball Player)
4131 Dynasty Dr
Minnetonka, MN 55345-1812, USA

Comer, Wayne (Athlete, Baseball Player)
145 Marcus St
Shenandoah, VA 22849-3917, USA

Comess, Aaron (Musician)
DAS Communications
83 Riverside Dr
New York, NY 10024-5713, USA

Comfort, Brad
PO Box 715
Mercer Island, WA 98040-0715

Comi, Paul (Actor)
2395 Ridgeway Rd
San Marino, CA 91108-2116, USA

Comiskey, Chuck (Athlete, Football Player)
2502 Convent Ave
Pascagoula, MS 39567-4517, USA

Command, Jim (Athlete, Baseball Player)
2136 Cranbrook Dr NE
Grand Rapids, MI 49505-5721, USA

Commerford, Tim (Musician)
5908 Zumirez Dr
Malibu, CA 90265-4004, USA

Commiskey, Chuck
2502 Convent Ave
Pascagoula, MS 39567-4517, USA

Commodores, The (Music Group, Musician)
1920 Benson Ave
Saint Paul, MN 55116-3214, USA

Common (Musician)
c/o Derek Dudley *Artistic Control Management Inc*
685 Lambert Dr NE
Atlanta, GA 30324-4125, USA

Compte, Maurice (Actor)
c/o British (Brit) Reece *PMK/BNC Public Relations (PMK-LA)*
8687 Melrose Ave Ste 8
West Hollywood, CA 90069-5746, USA

Compton, Clint (Athlete, Baseball Player)
77 Glen St # AJT1
Augusta, ME 04330-3916, USA

Compton, Dick (Athlete, Football Player)
3408 Briarcliff Ct S
Irving, TX 75062-3206, USA

Compton, Forrest (Actor)
PO Box 335
Shelter Island, NY 11964-0335, USA

Compton, Mike (Athlete, Baseball Player)
8624 Leighton Dr
Tampa, FL 33614-1723, USA

Compton, Ogden (Athlete, Football Player)
13918 Preston Valley Pl # Pb
Dallas, TX 75240-4769, USA

Compton, Stacy (Race Car Driver)
15A High Tech Blvd
Thomasville, NC 27360-5560, USA

Comrie, Mike (Athlete, Hockey Player)
10800 Wilshire Blvd Apt 1703
Los Angeles, CA 90024-4217, USA

Comstock, Keith (Athlete, Baseball Player)
9615 E Desert Trl
Scottsdale, AZ 85260-4624, USA

Conant, Sean (Actor)
c/o Staff Member *Rising Picture*
PO Box 2
North Hampton, NH 03862-0002, USA

Conatser, Clint (Athlete, Baseball Player)
26701 Quail Crk Apt 191
Laguna Hills, CA 92656-3010, USA

Conatsor, Clint (Athlete, Baseball Player)
26701 Quail Crk Apt 191
Laguna Hills, CA 92656-3010, USA

Conaty, William (Bill) (Athlete, Football Player)
203 Country Club Dr
Moorestown, NJ 08057-3977, USA

Conaway, Christi
334 Huntley Dr
West Hollywood, CA 90048-1919

Conaway, Cristi (Actor)
1759 Old Ranch Rd
Los Angeles, CA 90049-2507, USA

Conaway, K. Michael (Congressman, Politician)
2430 Rayburn Hob
Washington, DC 20515-3705, USA

Concepcion, Onix (Athlete, Baseball Player)
1486 Steeplechase Ln
Deltona, FL 32725-4752, USA

Concha, Billy (Actor)
PO Box 1129
Hermosa Beach, CA 90254-1129, USA

Concrete Blonde (Music Group)
Concrete Blonde Touring Company Inc
16830 Ventura Blvd Ste 501
Encino, CA 91436-1717, USA

Concretes, The (Music Group)
c/o Staff Member *Paradigm (Monterey)*
404 W Franklin St
Monterey, CA 93940-2303, USA

Conde, Ramon (Athlete, Baseball Player)
PO Box 57
Juana Diaz, PR 00795-0057, USA

Condit, Philip M (Business Person)
Boeing Co
PO Box 3707
Seattle, WA 98124-2207, USA

Condon, Bill (Director, Writer)
c/o Adam Shulman *Anonymous Content (LA)*
3532 Hayden Ave
Culver City, CA 90232-2413, USA

Condon, Tom (Athlete, Football Player)
c/o Staff Member *CAA Sports (LA)*
2000 Avenue of the Stars Ste 100
Los Angeles, CA 90067-4705, USA

Condra, Julie (Actor)
c/o Staff Member *Gold Coast Management*
438 S Venice Blvd Apt 5
Venice, CA 90291-4695, USA

Condredge, Holloway (Athlete, Football Player)
8137 Faircrest Ln
Knoxville, TN 37919-2038, USA

Condren, Glen (Athlete, Football Player)
8557 N 175th East Ave
Owasso, OK 74055-5638, USA

Condrey, Clay (Athlete, Baseball Player)
412 N 8th St
Navasota, TX 77868-2927, USA

Cone, David B (Athlete, Baseball Player)
303 E 83rd St Apt 6A
New York, NY 10028-4316, USA

Cone, Fred (Athlete, Football Player)
111 Elizabeth Ln
Pickens, SC 29671-9003, USA

Confederate Railroad (Music Group)
The Bobby Roberts Company Inc
PO Box 1547
Goodlettsville, TN 37070-1547, USA

Conforti, Gino (Actor)
Orange Gove Group
12178 Ventura Blvd Ste 205
Studio City, CA 91604-2540, USA

Congdon, Jeff (Athlete, Basketball Player)
13712 S 500 E
Draper, UT 84020-8926, USA

Congemi, John (Athlete, Football Player)
1015 Trailmore Ln
Weston, FL 33326-2820

Conger, Harry M (Business Person)
Homestake Mining Co
650 California St
San Francisco, CA 94108-2702, USA

Coniar, Larry (Athlete, Football Player)
PO Box 5133
Evanston, IL 60204-5133, USA

Conigliaro, Billy (Athlete, Baseball Player)
501 Cabot St Unit 2
Beverly, MA 01915-2580, USA

Conine, Jeff (Athlete, Baseball Player)
3166 Inverness
Weston, FL 33332-1816, USA

Conjar, Larry (Athlete, Football Player)
542 Sheridan Rd Apt 2
Evanston, IL 60202-3124, USA

Conklin, Cary (Athlete, Football Player)
13425 W Waldemar St
Boise, ID 83713-0843, USA

Conklin, Ty (Athlete, Hockey Player)
K 0 Sports
501 S Cherry St Ste 580
Attn Kurt Overhardt
Denver, CO 80246-1327, USA

Conlan, Shane P (Athlete, Football Player)
521 East Dr
Sewickley, PA 15143-1114, USA

Conlee, John (Musician)
John Conlee Enterprises
38 Music Sq E Ste 117
Nashville, TN 37203-4334, USA

Conley, Bob (Athlete, Baseball Player)
16A Canton Dr
Whiting, NJ 08759-1977, USA

Conley, Darby (Cartoonist)
c/o Staff Member *United Press Media*
PO Box 5610
Cincinnati, OH 45201-5610, USA

Conley, D Eugene (Gene) (Athlete, Basketball Player)
2105 Grafton Ave
Clermont, FL 34711-5241, USA

Conley, Earl Thomas (Musician, Songwriter)
657 Baker Rd
Smyrna, TN 37167-4777, USA

Conley, Gene (Athlete, Baseball Player)
400 Foxboro Blvd Apt 3102
Foxboro, MA 02035-3803, USA

Conley, Jack (Actor)
c/o Julia Buchwald *Don Buchwald & Associates (LA)*
6500 Wilshire Blvd Ste 2200
Los Angeles, CA 90048-4942, USA

Conley, Joe (Actor)
2227 Bentoak Holw
San Antonio, TX 78248-2306, USA

Conley, Larry (Athlete, Basketball Player)
5422 Forest Springs Dr
Atlanta, GA 30338-3606, USA

Conley, Michael (Mike) (Athlete, Track Athlete)
University of Arkansas
Athletic Dept
Fayetteville, AR 72701, USA

Conley, Mike (Athlete, Basketball Player)
3496 Windgarden Cv
Memphis, TN 38125-1732, USA

Conley, Steve (Athlete, Football Player)
1745 N Independence Pl
Fayetteville, AR 72704-5789, USA

Conlin, Chris (Athlete, Football Player)
4864 Tropicana Ave
Cooper City, FL 33330-4428, USA

Conlin, Edward (Athlete, Basketball Player)
153 N Mountain Ave
Montclair, NJ 07042-2347, USA

Conlin, Michaela (Actor)
2818 Effie St
Los Angeles, CA 90026-1436, USA

Conlon, James J
Shuman Assoc
120 W 58th St Apt 8D
New York, NY 10019-2156, USA

Conlon, Marty (Athlete, Basketball Player)
180 Woodbine Dr
East Hampton, NY 11937-1747, USA

Conn, Didi (Actor, Musician)
250 Piermont Ave
Piermont, NY 10968-1221, USA

Conn, Richard (Dick) (Athlete, Football Player)
430 Southport Commerce Blvd
Spartanburg, SC 29306-3812, USA

Conn, Terri (Actor)
1268 E 14th St
Brooklyn, NY 11230-5241, USA

Connally, Fritzie (Athlete, Baseball Player)
615 Portofino Dr
Arlington, TX 76012-2700, USA

Connell, Albert (Athlete, Football Player)
3328 Clevemont Way
Ellenwood, GA 30294-1323, USA

Connell, Chad (Actor)
c/o Marc Hamou *Thruline Entertainment*
9250 Wilshire Blvd Ste 100
Ground Floor
Beverly Hills, CA 90212-3343, USA

Connell, Jane
905 W End Ave
New York, NY 10025-3530

Connelly, Jennifer (Actor)
288 West St # 8E/8W
New York, NY 10013-1367, USA

Connelly, Lynn (Athlete, Golfer)
40 W Elm St Apt 3L
Greenwich, CT 06830-6418, USA

Connelly, Michael (Writer)
847 S Newport Ave
Tampa, FL 33606-2934, USA

Connelly, Mike (Athlete, Football Player)
9352 Creel Creek Dr
Dallas, TX 75228-4132, USA

Connelly, Steve (Athlete, Baseball Player)
1863 Litchfield Ave
Long Beach, CA 90815-3037, USA

Conner, Bart (Athlete, Gymnast, Olympic Athlete)
4421 Hidden Hill Rd
Norman, OK 73072-2899, USA

Conner, Chris (Actor)
c/o Staff Member *Nine Yards Entertainment*
5815 W Sunset Blvd Ste 206
Los Angeles, CA 90028-6481, USA

Conner, Darion (Athlete, Football Player)
9444 Prairie Point Rd
Macon, MS 39341-8084, USA

Conner, Dennis (Athlete, Olympic Athlete, Sailor)
2525 Shelter Island Dr Ste E
Dennis Conner Sportsdennis Conner Sports
San Diego, CA 92106-3161, USA

Conner, Frank (Golfer)
c/o Staff Member *Pro Golfers Association (PGA) Tour*
112 Tpc Blvd
Ponte Vedra Beach, FL 32082, USA

Conner, Jimmy Dan (Athlete, Basketball Player)
5009 Old Federal Rd
Louisville, KY 40207-1200, USA

Conner, Lester (Athlete, Basketball Player)
12517 Daniels Gate Dr
Castle Pines, CO 80108-9420, USA

Conners, Dan (Athlete, Football Player)
1895 Partridge Dr
San Luis Obispo, CA 93405-6321, USA

Connery, Jason (Actor)
6235 Holly Mont Dr
Los Angeles, CA 90068-3307, USA

Conney, Terry (Athlete, Baseball Player)
3205 Filbert Ave
Clovis, CA 93611-6050, USA

Connick Jr, Harry (Actor, Musician)
671 West Rd
New Canaan, CT 06840-2514, USA

Conniff, Cal (Skier)
157 Pleasantview Ave
Longmeadow, MA 01106-1021, USA

Connolly, Kevin (Actor)
c/o Troy Zien *3 Arts Entertainment (LA)*
9460 Wilshire Blvd Fl 7
Beverly Hills, CA 90212-2713, USA

Connolly, Kristen (Actor)
525 Rialto Ave
Venice, CA 90291-4247, USA

Connolly, Olga Fikotova (Athlete, Track Athlete)
931 W 19th St Apt 35
Costa Mesa, CA 92627-4144, USA

Connolly, Tim (Athlete, Hockey Player)
1266 Greenfield Ln
Skaneateles, NY 13152-9605, USA

Connor, Chris (Musician)
Maxine Harvard Unlimited
7942 W Bell Rd Ste C5
Glendale, AZ 85308-8710, USA

Connor, Christopher M (Business Person)
Sherwin-Williams Co
101 W Prospect Ave Ste 1020
Cleveland, OH 44115-1075, USA

Connor, Joseph E (Business Person, Government Official)
Under-Secretary General's Office
United Nations
UN Plaza
New York, NY 10021, USA

Connor, Mark (Athlete, Baseball Player)
7312 Wheatfield Pl
Knoxville, TN 37919-7201, USA

Connor, Richard L (Publisher)
Fort Worth Star-Telegram
PO Box 1870
Fort Worth, TX 76101-1870, USA

Connor, Shannon (Model)
4 Rockage Rd
Warren, NJ 07059-5506

Connors, Bill (Billy) (Athlete, Baseball Player)
3329 Enterprise Rd E
Safety Harbor, FL 34695-5307, USA

Connors, Carol (Musician, Songwriter)
1709 Ferrari Dr
Beverly Hills, CA 90210-1603, USA

Connors, Jimmy (Athlete, Tennis Player)
c/o Michael Blakey *Electra Star Management*
9229 W Sunset Blvd Ste 415
West Hollywood, CA 90069-3404, USA

Connors, Mike (Actor, Producer)
4810 Louise Ave
Encino, CA 91316-3927, USA

Connors, Patrick (Athlete, Baseball Player)
1075 Maricopa Dr
Oshkosh, WI 54904-8116, USA

Connot, Scott (Athlete, Football Player)
1726 Torrey Pines Dr
Brookings, SD 57006-5498, USA

Conover, Scott (Athlete, Football Player, Sportscaster)
28 Windsor Ter Apt B
Freehold, NJ 07728-3240, USA

Conoway, Cristi (Actor)
Cristi Conaway Design
11973 San Vicente Blvd
Los Angeles, CA 90049-5098, USA

Conrad, Bobby Joe (Athlete, Football Player)
140 County Road 3270
Clifton, TX 76634-4678, USA

Conrad, Brooks (Athlete, Baseball Player)
3672 E Robin Ln
Gilbert, AZ 85296-1849, USA

Conrad, Chris (Athlete, Football Player)
984 Orangewood Dr
Brea, CA 92821-2514, USA

Conrad, David (Actor)
c/o Staff Member *Gersh (LA)*
9465 Wilshire Blvd Ste 600
Beverly Hills, CA 90212-2605, USA

Conrad, Eve Burch
23388 Mulholland Dr
Woodland Hills, CA 91364-2733

Conrad, Kent (Politician, Senator)
530 Hart Senate Office Building
Washington, DC 20003, USA

Conrad, Kimberly (Actor)
10236 Charing Cross Rd
Los Angeles, CA 90024-1815

Conrad, Lauren (Actor, Reality Star, Writer)
110 S La Senda Dr
Laguna Beach, CA 92651-6736, USA

Conrad, Robert (Actor)
6320 Via Cataldo St
Malibu, CA 90265-4445, USA

Conrad, Shane
9255 W Sunset Blvd Ste 620
West Hollywood, CA 90069-3303

Conradt, Jody (Athlete, Basketball Player, Coach)
9614 Leaning Rock Cir
Austin, TX 78730-2725, USA

Conroy, Christopher (Athlete, Baseball Player)
3910 Cephas Child Rd Unit 12
Doylestown, PA 18902-9089, USA

Conroy, Craig (Athlete, Hockey Player, Olympic Athlete)
PO Box 549
Henderson Harbor, NY 13651-0549, USA

Conroy, Jeff (Producer)
Original Productions
308 W Verdugo Ave
Burbank, CA 91502-2340, USA

Conroy, Kevin (Actor)
c/o Staff Member *Imperium 7 Talent Agency*
5455 Wilshire Blvd Ste 1706
Los Angeles, CA 90036-4217, USA

Conroy, Pat (Writer)
c/o Marly Rusoff *Marly Rusoff & Associates Inc*
PO Box 524
Bronxville, NY 10708-0524, USA

Conroy, Tim (Athlete, Baseball Player)
109 Moonlight Dr
Monroeville, PA 15146-2028, USA

Conroy, Zack (Actor)
c/o Danielle Quinoa *Innovative Artists (NY)*
235 Park Ave S Fl 7
New York, NY 10003-1405, USA

Considine, John (Actor)
16 1/2 Red Coat Ln
Greenwich, CT 06830-3432, USA

Considine, Paddy (Actor, Writer)
c/o Staff Member *Creative Artists Agency (CAA-LA)*
2000 Avenue of the Stars Ste 100
Los Angeles, CA 90067-4705, USA

Considine, Tim (Actor)
3708 Mountain View Ave
Los Angeles, CA 90066-3112, USA

Conspirator (Music Group)
c/o Staff Member *Paradigm (Monterey)*
404 W Franklin St
Monterey, CA 93940-2303, USA

Constantine, Kevin
5928 Jenny Lind Ct
San Jose, CA 95120-1789

Constantine, Michael (Actor)
6861 Colbath Ave
Van Nuys, CA 91405-4102, USA

Consuelos, Mark (Actor)
12 E 76th St Apt 1
New York, NY 10021-2669, USA

Conte, Chris (Athlete, Football Player)
c/o Ryan Tollner *REP 1 Sports Group*
2 Corporate Park Ste 106
Irvine, CA 92606-5103, USA

Conte, Dino
2325 Fox Hills Dr
Los Angeles, CA 90064-2603, USA

Conti, Al
PO Box 701
Portsmouth, RI 02871-0701

Conti, Bill (Musician)
117 Fremont Pl
Los Angeles, CA 90005-3868, USA

Conti, Guy (Athlete, Baseball Player)
448 53rd Sq
Vero Beach, FL 32968-1021, USA

Conti, Jason (Athlete, Baseball Player)
740 N April Dr
Chandler, AZ 85226-1632, USA

Contino, Dick (Music Group, Musician)
3355 Nahatan Way
Las Vegas, NV 89169-3119, USA

Contner, James A (Cinematographer)
3020 Kensington Ave
Richmond, VA 23221-2421, USA

Contoulis, John (Athlete, Football Player)
404 Champion Cir
Throop, PA 18512-1451, USA

Contours, The
1161 NW 76th Ave
Plantation, FL 33322-5120

Contreras, Jose (Athlete, Baseball Player)
8501 Lithia Pinecrest Rd
Lithia, FL 33547-2807, USA

Contreras, Nardi (Athlete, Baseball Player)
5052 Lurgan Rd Land 0
Land O Lakes, FL 34638, USA

Contz, Bill (Athlete, Football Player)
106 Grace Dr
Cranberry Twp, PA 16066-2308, USA

Converse, Frank (Actor)
c/o Phil Sutfin *ICM Partners (LA)*
10250 Constellation Blvd Fl 7
Los Angeles, CA 90067-6207, USA

Converse, Jim (Athlete, Baseball Player)
11865 Cobble Brook Dr
Rancho Cordova, CA 95742-8008, USA

Converse-Roberts, William (Actor)
Innovative Artists
1505 10th St
Santa Monica, CA 90401-2805, USA

Convery, Brandon (Athlete, Hockey Player)
PO Box 2556
Manhattan Beach, CA 90267-2556, USA

Conway, Billy (Music Group, Musician)
Creative Performance Group
48 Laight St
New York, NY 10013-2156, USA

Conway, Brett (Athlete, Football Player)
630 Virginia Ave NE
Atlanta, GA 30306-3629, USA

Conway, Curtis (Athlete, Football Player)
c/o Gary Uberstine *Premier Sports Management*
16133 Ventura Blvd Ste 500
Encino, CA 91436-2402, USA

Conway, Gary (Actor)
2035 Mandeville Canyon Rd
Los Angeles, CA 90049-2226, USA

Conway, James (Race Car Driver)
420 Fair Hill Dr # 1
Elkton, MD 21921-2573, USA

Conway, James L (Director, Producer, Writer)
c/o Andrea Simon *Andrea Simon Entertainment*
4230 Woodman Ave
Sherman Oaks, CA 91423-4334, USA

Conway, John W (Business Person)
Crown Cork & Seal
1 Crown Way
Philadelphia, PA 19154-4599, USA

Conway, Kevin (Actor)
25 Centurypark W
New York, NY 10023, USA

Conway, Tim (Actor, Comedian)
4425 Haskell Ave
Encino, CA 91436-3110, USA

Conwell, Angell (Actor)
c/o Staff Member *Evolution Entertainment (LA)*
901 N Highland Ave
Los Angeles, CA 90038-2412, USA

Conwell, Ernie (Athlete, Football Player)
5301 McGavock Rd
Brentwood, TN 37027-5185, USA

Conwell, Joseph (Joe) (Athlete, Football Player)
1301 Stoney River Dr
Ambler, PA 19002-1159, USA

Conwell, Tommy (Music Group, Musician)
Brothers Mgmt
141 Dunbar Ave
Fords, NJ 08863-1551, USA

Conyers Jr., John (Congressman, Politician)
2426 Rayburn Hob
Washington, DC 20515-2214, USA

Cooder, Ry (Musician)
326 Entrada Dr
Santa Monica, CA 90402-1202, USA

Coody, Charles (Athlete, Golfer)
1555 Oldham Ln
Abilene, TX 79602-4143, USA

Coogan, Dodie
PO Box 413
Palm Springs, CA 92263-0413

Coogan, Keith (Actor)
c/o Drew Elliot *Artists International Management (NY)*
333 E 43rd St Apt 115
New York, NY 10017-4822, USA

Coogler, Ryan (Director)
c/o Craig Kestel *William Morris Endeavor (LA)*
9601 Wilshire Blvd
Beverly Hills, CA 90210-5213, USA

Cook, Aaron (Athlete, Baseball Player)
18716 W 56th Dr
Golden, CO 80403-2351, USA

Cook, AJ (Actor)
643 6th St
Hermosa Beach, CA 90254-4702, USA

Cook, Andrea Joy (A.J.) (Actor)
c/o Jeff Morrone *Intellectual Artists Management*
9350 Wilshire Blvd Ste 224
Beverly Hills, CA 90212-3204, USA

Cook, Andy (Athlete, Baseball Player)
3312 Central Ave
Memphis, TN 38111-4402, USA

Cook, Ann T
5412 Riverhills Dr
Temple Terrace, FL 33617-7136, USA

Cook, Ann Turner (Model, Writer)
12401 N 22nd St Apt E501
Tampa, FL 33612-4625, USA

Cook, Anthony (Athlete, Football Player)
PO Box 961404
Riverdale, GA 30296-6905, USA

Cook, Barbara (Actor, Musician)
c/o Staff Member *Cunningham Escott Slevin & Doherty (CESD-LA)*
10635 Santa Monica Blvd Ste 130
Los Angeles, CA 90025-8306, USA

Cook, Bert (Athlete, Basketball Player)
2571 W 5725 S
Roy, UT 84067-1326, USA

Cook, Bob (Athlete, Football Player)
100 Sioux Ct
Hendersonville, TN 37075-4634, USA

Cook, Carole (Actor, Comedian)
8829 Ashcroft Ave
West Hollywood, CA 90048-2401, USA

Cook, Cliff (Athlete, Baseball Player)
6008 Clipper Ln
Fort Worth, TX 76179-5259, USA

Cook, Daequan (Basketball Player)
c/o Staff Member *Miami Heat*
601 Biscayne Blvd
American Airlines Arena
Miami, FL 33132-1801, USA

Cook, Dane (Actor)
1561 Viewsite Dr
Los Angeles, CA 90069-1322, USA

Cook, Darwin (Athlete, Basketball Player)
43541 11th St E
Lancaster, CA 93535-2904, USA

Cook, David (Musician)
1495 Red Oak Dr
Brentwood, TN 37027-7831, USA

Cook, Dennis (Athlete, Baseball Player)
3413 Serene Hills Ct
Austin, TX 78738-1230, USA

Cook, Doris (Athlete, Baseball Player, Commentator)
1059 Airport Rd
Norton Shores, MI 49441-5101, USA

Cook, Edward J (Athlete, Football Player)
902 Briarwood Ct
Sewell, NJ 08080-3508, USA

Cook, Fielder
180 Central Park S
New York, NY 10019-1562

Cook, Fred (Athlete, Football Player)
4402 Market St
Pascagoula, MS 39567-2224, USA

Cook, Gayle (Business Person)
Cook Group Inc
PO Box 489
Bloomington, IN 47402-0489, USA

Cook, Glen (Athlete, Baseball Player)
424 Scarlet Sage Dr
League City, TX 77573-6426, USA

Cook, Jameel (Athlete, Football Player)
PO Box 131647
Houston, TX 77219-1647, USA

Cook, Jason (Actor)
c/o Katie Mason *Luber Roklin Management*
5815 W Sunset Blvd Ste 206
Los Angeles, CA 90028-6481, USA

Cook, Jeff (Athlete, Basketball Player)
4908 E Doubletree Ranch Rd
Paradise Valley, AZ 85253-1556, USA

Cook, Jeff (Music Group, Musician)
PO Box 35967
Fort Payne, AL 35967, USA

Cook, Jerry (Race Car Driver)
117 Palmetto Dr
Mooresville, NC 28117-9406, USA

Cook, John (Athlete, Golfer)
9742 Green Island Cv
Windermere, FL 34786-8953, USA

Cook, Judy (Bowler)
Ladies Professional Bowling Tour
7200 Harrison Ave # 7171
Rockford, IL 61112-1017, USA

Cook, Katie (Television Host)
3056 Old New Cut Rd
Springfield, TN 37172-5716, USA

Cook, Kristy Lee (Musician)
c/o Marty Rendleman *Rendleman Management Group, Inc.*
PO Box 670366
Dallas, TX 75367-0366, USA

Cook, Kyle (Musician)
626 Calverton Ln
Brentwood, TN 37027-8989, USA

Cook, Leigh
9560 Wilshire Blvd # 516
Beverly Hills, CA 90212-2427

Cook, Marv (Athlete, Football Player)
425 Butternut Ln
Iowa City, IA 52246-2782, USA

Cook, Mike (Athlete, Baseball Player)
216 Harlech Way
Charleston, SC 29414-6876, USA

Cook, Paul M (Business Person)
SRI International
333 Ravenswood Ave
Menlo Park, CA 94025-3493, USA

Cook, Rachael Leigh (Actor)
1270 Sunset Plaza Dr
Los Angeles, CA 90069-1245, USA

Cook, Rachel Leigh (Actor, Producer)
c/o Staff Member *James/Levy Management Inc*
3500 W Olive Ave Ste 1470
Burbank, CA 91505-5514, USA

Cook, Rashard (Athlete, Football Player)
425 Coastal Hills Dr
Chula Vista, CA 91914-4308, USA

Cook, Robert (Athlete, Baseball Player)
179 Royal Farm E
Blacklick, OH 43004-9209, USA

Cook, Robin (Writer)
4601 Gulf Shore Blvd N # P4
Naples, FL 34103-2221, USA

Cook, Robin (Writer)
16 Louisburg Sq
Boston, MA 02108-1203, USA

Cook, Ron (Athlete, Baseball Player)
1918 Franklin Dr
Longview, TX 75601-4111, USA

Cook, Stanton R (Publisher)
224 Raleigh Rd
Kenilworth, IL 60043-1209, USA

Cook, Steve (Bowler)
1209 Devonshire Ct
Roseville, CA 95661-5470, USA

Cook, Terry (Race Car Driver)
177 Knob Hill Rd
Mooresville, NC 28117-6847, USA

Cook, Thomas A (Writer)
Bantam Books
1540 Broadway
New York, NY 10036-4039, USA

Cook, Tim (Business Person)
Apple Computer
1 Infinite Loop
Cupertino, CA 95014-2084, USA

Cook, Toi (Athlete, Football Player)
5064 Llano Dr
Woodland Hills, CA 91364-3029, USA

Cooke, Amelia (Actor)
c/o Darren Goldberg *Global Creative*
1051 Cole Ave # B
Los Angeles, CA 90038-2601, USA

Cooke, Christian (Actor)
c/o Chris Huvane *Management 360*
9111 Wilshire Blvd
Beverly Hills, CA 90210-5508, USA

Cooke, David (Athlete, Basketball Player)
PO Box 270591
San Diego, CA 92198-2591, USA

Cooke, Ed (Athlete, Football Player)
2093 Wake Forest St
Virginia Beach, VA 23451-1421, USA

Cooke, Janis (Journalist)
Washington Post
1150 15th St NW
Washington, DC 20071-0002, USA

Cooke, Joe (Athlete, Football Player)
2550 E River Rd Unit 3101
Tucson, AZ 85718-9504, USA

Cooke, Josh (Actor)
620 N Beachwood Dr
Los Angeles, CA 90004-1419, USA

Cooke, Olivia (Actor)
c/o Lena Roklin *Luber Roklin Management*
5815 W Sunset Blvd Ste 206
Los Angeles, CA 90028-6481, USA

Cooke, Steve (Athlete, Baseball Player)
9510 SW 165th Ave
Beaverton, OR 97007-9418, USA

Cooke, William (Bill) (Athlete, Football Player)
1851 Hillside Rd
Fairfield, CT 06824-2017, USA

Cooks, Brandin (Athlete, Football Player)
c/o Jeff Sperbeck *The Novo Agency*
3201 Danville Blvd Ste 295
Alamo, CA 94507-1978, USA

Cooks, Johnie (Athlete, Football Player)
2170 Sun Creek Rd
Starkville, MS 39759-8436, USA

Cooks, Kerry (Athlete, Football Player)
5358 Lismore Ln
Fitchburg, WI 53711-7680, USA

Cooks, Rayford (Athlete, Football Player)
1839 Nomas St
Dallas, TX 75212-3806, USA

Cooksey, Danny
9300 Wilshire Blvd Ste 410
Beverly Hills, CA 90212-3228

Cooksey, Dave (Religious Leader)
Brethren Church
524 College Ave
Ashland, OH 44805-3703, USA

Cooksey, Patty (Athlete)
c/o Churchill Downs
700 Central Ave
Race Office
Louisville, KY 40208-1200

Cookson, Brent (Athlete, Baseball Player)
1232 Manzanita Dr
Santa Paula, CA 93060-1239, USA

Cookson, Peter
30 Norfolk Rd
Southfield, MA 01259

Coolbaugh, Scott (Athlete, Baseball Player)
6708 Carriage Ln
Colleyville, TX 76034-5771, USA

Cool Breeze
PO Box 470642
San Francisco, CA 94147-0642

Cooley, Chris (Athlete, Football Player)
PO Box 144
Hamilton, VA 20159-0144, USA

Cooley, Denton (Doctor, Misc)
3014 Del Monte Dr
Houston, TX 77019-3214, USA

Cooley, Tonya (Reality Star)
c/o Staff Member *Bunim/Murray Productions*
6007 Sepulveda Blvd
Van Nuys, CA 91411-2502, USA

Cooleyb, Chelsea (Beauty Pageant Winner)
c/o Staff Member *Miss Universe Organization, The*
1370 Avenue of the Americas Fl 16
New York, NY 10019-4602, USA

Coolidge, Jennifer (Actor)
c/o Ali Benmohamed *United Talent Agency (UTA-LA)*
9336 Civic Center Dr
Beverly Hills, CA 90210-3604, USA

Coolidge, Martha (Director)
760 N La Cienega Blvd
West Hollywood, CA 90069-5204, USA

Coolidge, Rita (Musician)
560 Hilbert Dr
Fallbrook, CA 92028-1602, USA

Coolio (Actor, Musician)
c/o Susan Haber *Haber Entertainment*
434 S Canon Dr Apt 204
Beverly Hills, CA 90212-4501, USA

Coombs, Danny (Athlete, Baseball Player)
14130 Cleobrook Dr
Houston, TX 77070-3744, USA

Coombs, Torrance (Actor)
c/o Danielle Allman-Del *D2 Management*
9255 W Sunset Blvd Ste 600
West Hollywood, CA 90069-3306, USA

Coombs-Mueller, Carol (Actor)
5200 Irvine Blvd Spc 364
Irvine, CA 92620-2060, USA

Coomer, Ron (Athlete, Baseball Player)
7021 Howard Ln
Eden Prairie, MN 55346-3053, USA

Coon, Christopher (Senator)
127A Russell Senate Office Building # A
Washington, DC 20510-0001, USA

Coonce, Ricky (Music Group, Musician)
Thomas Cassidy
11761 E Speedway Blvd
Tucson, AZ 85748-2017, USA

Cooney, Gerry (Boxer)
370 North Ave
Fanwood, NJ 07023-1320, USA

Cooney, Mark (Athlete, Football Player)
8005 Flower Ct
Arvada, CO 80005-2445, USA

Coonts, Stephen (Writer)
109 Marland Rd S
Colorado Springs, CO 80906-4350

Coonts, Stephen (Writer)
116 W 14th St Apt 8S
New York, NY 10011-7315, USA

Coooinger, Rocky (Athlete, Baseball Player)
7208 Alto Rey Ave
El Paso, TX 79912-2100

Cooper, Adrian (Athlete, Football Player)
4774 Peoria St Apt 602
Denver, CO 80239-2829, USA

Cooper, Alice (Musician)
4135 E Keim Dr
Paradise Valley, AZ 85253-3926, USA

Cooper, Anderson (Correspondent, Journalist, Television Host)
84 W 3rd St
New York, NY 10012-1008, USA

Cooper, Artis (Athlete, Basketball Player)
5013 Millstone Way
Granite Bay, CA 95746-6126, USA

Cooper, Bert (Athlete, Football Player)
3152 Aldon Ave
Las Vegas, NV 89121-5610, USA

Cooper, Bill (Athlete, Football Player)
16056 Greenwood Rd
Monte Sereno, CA 95030-3018, USA

Cooper, Bonnie (Athlete, Baseball Player, Commentator)
PO Box 26
119 Sampson Street
Tremont, IL 61568-0026, USA

Cooper, Bradley (Actor)
733 Brooktree Rd
Pacific Palisades, CA 90272-3902, USA

Cooper, Brian (Athlete, Baseball Player)
346 W Ada Ave
Glendora, CA 91741-4248, USA

Cooper, Brian (Athlete, Baseball Player)
San Jose Giants
PO Box 21727
San Jose, CA 95151-1727, USA

Cooper, Camille (Basketball Player)
New York Liberty
125 W End Ave # 6
Madison Square Garden
New York, NY 10023-6387, USA

Cooper, Carl (Athlete, Golfer)
18 Poplar Hill Pl
Spring, TX 77381-4031, USA

Cooper, Cecil (Athlete, Baseball Player)
24802 Boulder Lakes Ct
Katy, TX 77494-3900, USA

Cooper, Cecil (Athlete, Baseball Player)
7208 Alto Rey Ave
El Paso, TX 79912-2100, U S A

Cooper, Charles (Actor)
c/o Joel Kleinman *Baier/Kleinman International*
3575 Cahuenga Blvd W Ste 500
Los Angeles, CA 90068-1344, USA

Cooper, Chris (Actor)
19 Jones River Dr
Kingston, MA 02364-1519, USA

Cooper, Christin (Athlete, Olympic Athlete, Skier)
1001 E Hyman Ave Apt B
Aspen, CO 81611-2612, USA

Cooper, Darin (Actor)
c/o Marianne Golan *Golan & Blumberg*
6528 W 6th St
Los Angeles, CA 90048-4716, USA

Cooper, Dominic (Actor)
c/o Joel Lubin *Creative Artists Agency (CAA-LA)*
2000 Avenue of the Stars Ste 100
Los Angeles, CA 90067-4705, USA

Cooper, Don (Athlete, Baseball Player)
2109 Willowmet Dr
Brentwood, TN 37027-1812, USA

Cooper, Don (Athlete, Baseball Player)
2320 Arborfield Ln
Sarasota, FL 34235-1807, USA

Cooper, Duane (Athlete, Basketball Player)
13813 Ocana Ave
Bellflower, CA 90706-2528, USA

Cooper, Earl (Athlete, Football Player)
2224 E Highway 21
Lincoln, TX 78948-6496, USA

Cooper, Eric (Athlete, Baseball Player)
5404 Longview Ct Unit 4
Johnston, IA 50131-2706, USA

Cooper, Gary (Athlete, Baseball Player)
1136 Birch Cir
Alpine, UT 84004-1212, USA

Cooper, Gary (Baseball Player)
Atlanta Braves
402 E Victory Dr
Savannah, GA 31405-2254, USA

Cooper, George (Athlete, Football Player)
1230 Bowstring Rd
Monument, CO 80132-8599, USA

Cooper, Hal (Director)
2651 Hutton Dr
Beverly Hills, CA 90210-1213, USA

Cooper, Jim (Athlete, Football Player)
12910 Low Meadow Ct
Charlotte, NC 28277-4030, USA

Cooper, Jim (Congressman, Politician)
1536 Longworth Hob
Washington, DC 20515-4205, USA

Cooper, Joel D (Doctor)
Washington University
Medical School Surgery Dept
Saint Louis, MO 63110, USA

Cooper, Jonathan (Athlete, Football Player)
c/o Todd France *Five Star Athlete Management*
3500 Lenox Rd NE
Atlanta, GA 30326-4228, USA

Cooper, Lester I (Producer)
45 Morningside Dr S
Westport, CT 06880-5414, USA

Cooper, Louis (Athlete, Football Player)
200 Gregg Ave
Marion, SC 29571-3824, USA

Cooper, Marcus Ramone (Pleasure P) (Musician)
c/o Staff Member *Atlantic Records (NY)*
1290 Avenue of the Americas Fl 28
New York, NY 10104-0106, USA

Cooper, Mark S (Athlete, Football Player)
6598 S Telluride St
Aurora, CO 80016-3158, USA

Cooper, Oliver (Actor)
c/o Matthew DelPiano *Creative Artists Agency (CAA-LA)*
2000 Avenue of the Stars Ste 100
Los Angeles, CA 90067-4705, USA

Cooper, Scott (Actor)
c/o Leland LaBarre *Bleu, An Entertainment Company*
5225 Wilshire Blvd Ste 336
Los Angeles, CA 90036-4380, USA

Cooper, Scott (Athlete, Baseball Player)
7 Fairways Cir Apt F
Saint Charles, MO 63303-3353, USA

Cooper, Stephen (Business Person)
Enron Corp
1400 Smith St Ste 501
Houston, TX 77002-7342, USA

Cooper, Wayne (Athlete, Basketball Player)
5013 Millstone Way
Granite Bay, CA 95746-6126, USA

Cooper, Wima Lee (Musician)
c/o Staff Member *Charles Rapp Enterprises Inc*
88 Pine St Ste 2601
New York, NY 10005-1826, USA

Coors, William K (Business Person)
Adolph Coors Co
1221 Ford St
Golden, CO 80401-1132, USA

Coover, Robert (Writer)
Brown University
Linden Press
49 George St
Providence, RI 02912-0001, USA

Copa, Tom (Athlete, Basketball Player)
10068 Circleview Dr
Austin, TX 78733-6302, USA

Cope, Amber (Race Car Driver)
PO Box 44337
Tacoma, WA 98448-0337, USA

Cope, Derrike (Race Car Driver)
CLR Racing
103 Turnerlair Ct
Mooresville, NC 28117-5535, USA

Cope, Julian (Musician, Songwriter, Writer)
International Talent Group
729 7th Ave Ste 1600
New York, NY 10019-6880, USA

Cope, Mike (Race Car Driver)
60th St N
Clearwater, FL 34620, USA

Copeland, Adam (Edge) (Wrestler)
c/o Kerry Rodgerson *World Wrestling Entertainment (WWE)*
1241 E Main St
Titan Towers
Stamford, CT 06902-3520, USA

Copeland, Al (Business Person, Race Car Driver)
1001 S Harimaw Ct
Metairie, LA 70001-6233, USA

Copeland, Cyrus
c/o Daniel Strone *Trident Media Group LLC*
41 Madison Ave Fl 36
New York, NY 10010-2257, USA

Copeland, Danny (Athlete, Football Player)
106 Ruth Ln
Thomasville, GA 31792-6465, USA

Copeland, Gloria (Religious Leader)
Kenneth Copeland Ministries
14355 Morris Dido Rd
Newark, TX 76071-9501, USA

Copeland, Hollis (Athlete, Basketball Player)
257 Upland Ave
Ewing, NJ 08638-2331, USA

Copeland, Horace (Athlete, Football Player)
4195 Blakemore Pl
Spring Hill, FL 34609-0694, USA

Copeland, Joan (Actor)
88 Central Park W Apt 11W
New York, NY 10023-6045, USA

Copeland, John (Athlete, Football Player)
4226 Maxwell Dr
Mason, OH 45040-6504, USA

Copeland, Kenneth (Religious Leader)
Kenneth Copeland Ministries
14355 Morris Dido Rd
Newark, TX 76071-9501, USA

Copeland, Lanard (Athlete, Basketball Player)
4115 Pierce Rd
Atlanta, GA 30349-3648, USA

Copeland, Miles (Musician)
1830 N Sierra Bonita Ave
Los Angeles, CA 90046-2233, USA

Copeland, Stewart (Musician)
2420 Arbutus Dr
Los Angeles, CA 90049-1209, USA

Copeland Jr., Zane (Lil Zane) (Musician)
c/o Gail Del Corral *Del Corral and Associates*
1010 Common St Ste 2550
New Orleans, LA 70112-2461, USA

Copley, Jeff E
687 State Highway 194
Kimper, KY 41539, USA

Copley, Sharlto (Actor)
c/o Phillip d'Amecourt *William Morris Endeavor (LA)*
9601 Wilshire Blvd
Beverly Hills, CA 90210-5213, USA

Copley, Teri (Actor, Model)
13351 Riverside Dr # D513
Sherman Oaks, CA 91423-2542, USA

Copon, Michael (Actor)
c/o Lena Roklin *Luber Roklin Management*
5815 W Sunset Blvd Ste 206
Los Angeles, CA 90028-6481, USA

Coppenbarger, Ron (Athlete, Football Player)
7890 James Island Trl
Jacksonville, FL 32256-7355, USA

Coppens, Gus (Athlete, Football Player)
2413 Deerpark Dr
Fullerton, CA 92835-3001, USA

Copperfield, David (Magician)
111675 Glowing Sunset Ln
Las Vegas, NV 89135, USA

Coppinger, Rocky (Athlete, Baseball Player)
7208 Alto Rey Ave
El Paso, TX 79912-2100, USA

Coppo, Paul (Athlete, Hockey Player)
PO Box 10484
Green Bay, WI 54307-0484, USA

Coppock, Laurel (Actor)
The Groundlings Theatre
7307 Melrose Ave
Los Angeles, CA 90046-7512, USA

Coppola, Alicia (Actor)
12109 Hillslope St
Studio City, CA 91604-3602, USA

Coppola, Chris (Actor)
c/o Staff Member *IMG (LA)*
2049 Century Park E Ste 2460
Los Angeles, CA 90067-3126, USA

Coppola, Francis Ford (Director)
c/o Staff Member *American Zoetrope*
916 Kearny St
San Francisco, CA 94133-5107, USA

Coppola, Roman (Director)
6740 Milner Rd
Los Angeles, CA 90068-3215, USA

Coppola, Sofia (Actor, Director, Writer)
46 Morton St
New York, NY 10014-4021, USA

Coppolla, Alicia (Actor)
c/o Jeff Witjas *Agency for the Performing Arts (APA-LA)*
405 S Beverly Dr Ste 500
Beverly Hills, CA 90212-4425, USA

CopQO, Paul (Athlete, Hockey Player)
3458 Solitude Rd
De Pere, WI 54115-8617, USA

Coquillette, Trace (Athlete, Baseball Player)
5200 Mississippi Bar Dr
Orangevale, CA 95662-5717, USA

Cora, Alex (Athlete, Baseball Player)
F12 Calle 14
Caguas, PR 00727-6935, USA

Cora, Cat (Chef)
c/o Mark Schulman *3 Arts Entertainment (LA)*
9460 Wilshire Blvd Fl 7
Beverly Hills, CA 90212-2713, USA

Cora, Joey (Athlete, Baseball Player)
Florida Marlins
501 Marlins Way
Miami, FL 33125-1121, USA

Cora, Joey (Athlete, Baseball Player)
17734 SW 47th St
Miramar, FL 33029-5050, USA

Cora, Jose M (Joey) (Athlete, Baseball Player)
F12 Calle 14
Villa Nueva
Caguas, PR 00727-6935, USA

Corabi, John (Musician)
c/o Staff Member *Union Entertainment Group*
1323 Newbury Rd Ste 104
Newbury Park, CA 91320-3679, USA

Coraci, Frank (Director)
9738 Arby Dr
Beverly Hills, CA 90210-1203, USA

Coral, The (Music Group)
c/o Staff Member *Paradigm (Monterey)*
404 W Franklin St
Monterey, CA 93940-2303, USA

Corazzini, Carl (Athlete, Hockey Player)
583 Winter St
Framingham, MA 01702-5634, USA

Corbet, Brady (Actor)
c/o Brian Young *Untitled Entertainment (LA)*
350 S Beverly Dr Ste 200
Beverly Hills, CA 90212-4819, USA

Corbett, Doug (Athlete, Baseball Player)
75083 Edwards Rd
Yulee, FL 32097-2660, USA

Corbett, Gretchen (Actor)
6932 N Vincent Ave
Portland, OR 97217-5133, USA

Corbett, James (Athlete, Football Player)
2723 Marlo Way
Lakeside Park, KY 41017-2121, USA

Corbett, John (Actor, Musician)
5323 Baseline Ave
Santa Ynez, CA 93460-9739, USA

Corbett, Luke R (Business Person)
Kerr-McGee Corp
Kerr-McGee Center
Oklahoma City, OK 73125, USA

Corbett, Michael (Actor)
2665 Charl Pl
Los Angeles, CA 90046-1023, USA

Corbett, Mike (Athlete, Football Player)
41828 Road 600
Ahwahnee, CA 93601-9709, USA

Corbett, Sherman (Athlete, Baseball Player)
7031 Washita Way
San Antonio, TX 78256-2310, USA

Corbett, Steve (Athlete, Football Player)
3 Wake Robin Rd
Sudbury, MA 01776-1726, USA

Corbett, Tom (Governor, Politician)
Governor's Office
508 E-Floor Main Capitol Bldg
Harrisburg, PA 17120-0001, USA

Corbin, Archie (Athlete, Baseball Player)
7525 Tram Rd
Beaumont, TX 77713-8723, USA

Corbin, Barry (Actor)
2113 Greta Ln
Fort Worth, TX 76120-5201, USA

Corbin, Easton (Musician)
c/o Staff Member *William Morris Endeavor (Nashville)*
1600 Division St Ste 300
Nashville, TN 37203-2755, USA

Corbin, Ray (Athlete, Baseball Player)
65 Moore St
Franklin, NC 28734-9307, USA

Corbin, Tyrone (Athlete, Basketball Coach, Basketball Player, Coach)
c/o Steve Kauffman *Kauffman Sports Management Group*
Prefers to be contacted by telephone
Malibu, CA, USA

Corbo, Vincent J (Business Person)
Hercules Inc
Hercules Plaza
1313 N Market St
Wilmington, DE 19894-0001, USA

Corbus, William (Athlete, Football Player)
1100 Union St Apt 1100
San Francisco, CA 94109-2019, USA

Corchiani, Chris (Athlete, Basketball Player)
1106 Harvey St
Raleigh, NC 27608-2205, USA

Corcoran, Barbara (Business Person, Reality Star)
The Corcoran Group
226 W 26th St Fl 28
New York, NY 10001-6700, USA

Corcoran, Donna (Actor)
22408 Kanaina Ct
Chatsworth, CA 91311-1275, USA

Corcoran, Kevin (Actor)
8617 Balcom Ave
Northridge, CA 91325-3101, USA

Corcoran, Roy (Athlete, Baseball Player)
PO Box 173
Slaughter, LA 70777-0173, USA

Corcoran, Tim (Athlete, Baseball Player)
PO Box 173
Slaughter, LA 70777-0173, USA

Corcoran, Tim (Athlete, Baseball Player)
4349 Friar Cir
La Verne, CA 91750-2718, USA

Cord, Alex (Actor)
c/o Staff Member *Coast to Coast Talent Group*
3350 Barham Blvd
Los Angeles, CA 90068-1404, USA

Corday, Barbara (Business Person)
317 N Van Ness Ave
Los Angeles, CA 90004-1523, USA

Corday, Mara (Actor)
25932 Mendoza Dr
Valencia, CA 91355-2159, USA

Corddry, Nate (Actor)
c/o Jill McGrath *The Group Entertainment*
115 W 29th St Rm 1102
New York, NY 10001-5106, USA

Corddry, Rob (Actor)
3813 Evans St
Los Angeles, CA 90027-3309, USA

Cordero, Angel (Horse Racer)
4 Osborne Ln
Greenvale, NY 11548-1141, USA

Cordero, Angelo
PO Box 110090
Cambria Heights, NY 11411-0090

Cordero, Angel T Jr (Jockey)
New York Racing Assn
PO Box 170090
Ozone Park, NY 11417-0090, USA

Cordero, Chad (Athlete, Baseball Player)
2825 Live Oak Ave
Fullerton, CA 92835-2237, USA

Cordero, Francisco (Athlete, Baseball Player)
5811 Falling Brook Dr
Mason, OH 45040-2587, USA

Cordero, Wilfredo N (Wil) (Baseball Player)
Montreal Expos
25844 Kensington Dr
Westlake, OH 44145-1472, USA

Cordes-Elliott, Gloria (Athlete, Baseball Player, Commentator)
86 Malone Ave
Staten Island, NY 10306-4110, USA

Cordes-Elliott, Gloria (Baseball Player)
86 Malone Ave
Staten Island, NY 10306-4110, USA

Cordileone, Lou (Athlete, Football Player)
5312 Mark Ct
Agoura Hills, CA 91301-5200, USA

Cordova, Francisco (Athlete, Baseball Player)
c/o Staff Member *San Diego Padres*
100 Park Blvd
San Diego, CA 92101-7405, USA

Cordova, Jorge (Athlete, Football Player)
3256 Katharine Dr
Escondido, CA 92027-6235, USA

Cordova, Marty (Athlete, Baseball Player)
4395 Cameron St Ste C
Las Vegas, NV 89103-3819, USA

Corea, Chick (Musician)
Chick Corea Productions
10400 Samoa Ave
Tujunga, CA 91042-1921, USA

Corella, Angel
890 Broadway
New York, NY 10003-1211

Corev, Brvan (Athlete, Baseball Player)
7829 E Riverdale Cir
Mesa, AZ 85207-0804, USA

Corey, Bryan (Athlete, Baseball Player)
7829 E Riverdale Cir
Mesa, AZ 85207-0804, USA

Corey, Irwin (Professor) (Actor, Comedian)
c/o Richard Corey *Worlds Foremost Management*
165 W 21st St Apt 2
New York, NY 10011-3218, USA

Corey, Jill (Musician)
64 Division Ave
Levittown, NY 11756-2999, USA

Corey, Mark (Athlete, Baseball Player)
PO Box 113
Austin, PA 16720-0113, USA

Corey, Mark (Athlete, Baseball Player)
9321 Cornell Cir
Highlands Ranch, CO 80130-4143, USA

Corey, Walt (Athlete, Football Player)
507 Bowen Dr
Raymore, MO 64083-9114, USA

Corgan, Billy (Musician, Songwriter)
1249 Sheridan Rd
Highland Park, IL 60035-4107, USA

Cori, Carl T (Business Person)
Sigma-Aldrich Corp
3050 Spruce St
Saint Louis, MO 63103-2530, USA

Cori, Yarckin (Musician)
GreeneHouse Management, Inc
PO Box 151234
Altamonte Springs, FL 32715-1234, USA

Corker, Bob (Senator)
Dirksen Senate Office Building SD-185
Washington, DC 20510-0001, USA

Corker, John (Athlete, Football Player)
825 Martin Luther King Jr Blvd
Baltimore, MD 21201-2306, USA

Corkins, Mike (Athlete, Baseball Player)
451 E I St Spc 4
Oakdale, CA 95361-4080, USA

Corkum, Bob (Athlete, Hockey Player)
165 Scotland Rd
Newbury, MA 01951-1004, USA

Corley, Al (Actor)
Code Entertainment
9229 W Sunset Blvd Ste 615
West Hollywood, CA 90069-3419, USA

Corley, Annie (Actor)
c/o Renee Jennett *Renee Jennett Management*
5757 Wilshire Blvd Ste 473
Los Angeles, CA 90036-3632, USA

Corley, Anthony (Athlete, Football Player)
7465 Rodin Ct
Sun Valley, NV 89433-6691, USA

Corley, Ray (Athlete, Basketball Player)
590 Elwood Rd
East Northport, NY 11731-5629, USA

Cormack, Danielle (Actor)
c/o Jane Negline *Platform Public Relations*
2666 N Beachwood Dr
Los Angeles, CA 90068-2308, USA

Corman, Avery (Writer)
International Creative Mgmt
40 W 57th St Fl 5
New York, NY 10019-4001, USA

Corman, Roger (Actor, Director, Producer)
2501 La Mesa Dr
Santa Monica, CA 90402-2334, USA

Cormier, Joe (Athlete, Football Player)
9110 La Salle Ave
Los Angeles, CA 90047-3608, USA

Cormier, Lance (Athlete, Baseball Player)
3630 Windy Rdg
Tuscaloosa, AL 35406-3671, USA

Cormier, Rheal (Athlete, Baseball Player)
2640 Cody Cir
Park City, UT 84098-6281, USA

Corn, Laura (Writer)
c/o Staff Member *Literary Group International*
14 Penn Plz Ste 925
New York, NY 10122-0049, USA

Corneisen, Rufus (Religious Leader)
415 S Chester Rd
Swarthmore, PA 19081-2303, USA

Cornejo, Mardie (Athlete, Baseball Player)
321 E 3rd St
Wellington, KS 67152-2706, USA

Cornejo, Nate (Athlete, Baseball Player)
1600 N B St
Wellington, KS 67152-4405, USA

Cornelison, Jerry (Athlete, Football Player)
12713 Cedar St
Leawood, KS 66209-1873, USA

Cornelius, Charles (Athlete, Football Player)
8865 Okeechobee Blvd Apt 306
West Palm Beach, FL 33411-5125, USA

Cornelius, Helen (Musician, Songwriter, Writer)
PO Box 121089
Nashville, TN 37212-1089, USA

Cornelius, James (Business Person)
Guidant Corp
111 Monument Cir
Indianapolis, IN 46204-5100, USA

Cornelius, Jemalle (Athlete, Football Player)
c/o Chad Speck *Allegiant Athletic Agency*
35 Market Sq Ste 201
Knoxville, TN 37902-1420, USA

Cornelius, Kathy (Athlete, Golfer)
5744 W Del Rio St
Chandler, AZ 85226-6825, USA

Cornelius, Reid (Athlete, Baseball Player)
10117 Hunt Club Ln
Palm Beach Gardens, FL 33418-4568, USA

Cornell, Chris (Musician)
1880 Century Park E Ste 1600
Los Angeles, CA 90067-1661, USA

Cornell, Harry M Jr (Business Person)
leggett & Platt Inc
1 Leggett Rd
Carthage, MO 64836-9649, USA

Cornell, Jeff (Athlete, Baseball Player)
1644 SW Jeffrey Cir
Lees Summit, MO 64081-4115, USA

Cornell, Lydia (Actor)
269 S Beverly Dr
Beverly Hills, CA 90212-3851, USA

Cornell, Robert (Bo) (Athlete, Football Player)
200 Congress Ave Unit 36H
Austin, TX 78701-4558, USA

Cornett, Betty Jane (Athlete, Baseball Player)
99 Corbett Ct Apt 410
Pittsburgh, PA 15237-3030, USA

Cornett, Brad (Athlete, Baseball Player)
1704 N Avenue I
Lamesa, TX 79331-3140, USA

Cornett, Leanza (Actor)
c/o Staff Member *William Morris Endeavor (LA)*
9601 Wilshire Blvd
Beverly Hills, CA 90210-5213, USA

Cornfeld, Stuart (Producer)
1543 Marmont Ave
Los Angeles, CA 90069-1621, USA

Cornforth, Mark (Athlete, Hockey Player)
11 Indian Spring Rd
Milton, MA 02186-3716, USA

Cornish, Abbie (Actor)
c/o Cara Tripicchio *Shelter PR*
9350 Wilshire Blvd Ste 450
Beverly Hills, CA 90212-3230, USA

Cornish, Frank (Athlete, Football Player)
406 20th St Apt 29
Gretna, LA 70053-5736, USA

Cornish, Nick (Actor)
c/o Robert Stein *Robert Stein Management*
PO Box 3797
Beverly Hills, CA 90212-0797, USA

Cornutt, Terry (Athlete, Baseball Player)
179 W Hazel St
Roseburg, OR 97471-2211, USA

Cornwell, Fred (Athlete, Football Player)
2107 Windward Ln
Newport Beach, CA 92660-3820, USA

Cornwell, Johnny (Musician)
Overland Productions
156 W 56th St # 500
New York, NY 10019-3800, USA

Cornwell, Patricia (Actor, Producer, Writer)
c/o Staff Member *Simon & Schuster*
1230 Avenue of the Americas Fl CONC1
New York, NY 10020-1586, USA

Cornyn, John (Politician)
1348 S Carolina Ave SE
Washington, DC 20003-2371, USA

Cornyn, John (Senator)
517 Hart Senate Office Bldg
Washington, DC 20510-0001, USA

Corolla, Adam (Actor, Producer, Writer)
c/o Staff Member *Dixon Talent Agency*
375 Greenwich St Fl 5
New York, NY 10013-2376, USA

Coronado, Bob (Athlete, Football Player)
1539 Sereno Dr
Vallejo, CA 94589-2726, USA

Corone, Antoni (Actor)
c/o Bonni Allen *Allen - O'leary*
1138 12th St Apt 1
Santa Monica, CA 90403-5459, USA

Coronel, Felipe (Immortal Technique) (Musician)
c/o Staff Member *Viper Records*
230 Mott St
New York, NY 10012-4147, USA

Corr, Andrea (Musician)
c/o Staff Member *Luber Roklin Management*
5815 W Sunset Blvd Ste 206
Los Angeles, CA 90028-6481, USA

Corrado, Fred (Business Person)
Great A & P Tea Co
2 Paragon Dr
Montvale, NJ 07645-1768, USA

Corral, Frank (Athlete, Football Player)
Riverside Municipal Building
3900 Main St
Attn Graffiti Control Coordinator
Riverside, CA 92522-0001, USA

Corrales, Pat (Athlete, Baseball Player, Coach)
2 W Wesley Rd NW Apt 18
Atlanta, GA 30305-3500, USA

Correa, Ed (Athlete, Baseball Player)
A2 Calle Milagros Cabezas
Urb Carolina Alta
Carolina, PR 00987-7101, USA

Correal, Charles (Athlete, Football Player)
110 Springbrooke Dr
Venetia, PA 15367-1054, USA

Correale, Pete (Musician)
c/o Staff Member *Monterey International (Chicago)*
200 W Superior St Ste 202
Chicago, IL 60654-6422, USA

Correia, Kevin (Athlete, Baseball Player)
San Francisco Giants
2081 Gatun St
Del Mar, CA 92014-2261, USA

Correia, Rod (Athlete, Baseball Player)
82 Perrwille Rd
Rehoboth, MA 02769, USA

Correll, Alston D (Pete) (Business Person)
Georgia-Pacific Corp
133 Peachtree St NE Ste 4810
Atlanta, GA 30303-1821, USA

Correll, Vic (Athlete, Baseball Player)
119 Kentucky Downs
Perry, GA 31069-8514, USA

Corrente, Michael (Actor, Director, Producer)
c/o David Greenblatt *Greenlit*
1800 N Highland Ave Ste 500
Los Angeles, CA 90028-4527, USA

Correnti, John D (Business Person)
Nucor Corp
2100 Rexford Rd
Charlotte, NC 28211-3589, USA

Corretja, Alex (Tennis Player)
Assn of Tennis Professionals
200 Tournament Rd
Ponte Vedra Beach, FL 32082, USA

Corridon-Mortell, Marie (Swimmer)
13 Heritage Vlg # A
Southbury, CT 06488-1601, USA

Corrigal, Jim (Athlete, Football Player)
560 Deerwood Dr
Tallmadge, OH 44278-2008, USA

Corrigan, Kevin (Actor)
220 W Broadway # 310
New York, NY 10013, USA

Corrigan, Mike (Athlete, Hockey Player)
1661 King St
Enfield, CT 06082-6036, USA

Corrigan, Wilfred J (Business Person)
LSI Logic
1621 Barber Ln
Milpitas, CA 95035-7455, USA

Corrinet, Chris
25 Overland Rd
Greenfield, MA 01301-1127, USA

Corrington, Kip (Athlete, Football Player)
4101 Whispering Creek Dr
College Station, TX 77845-6385, USA

Corriveau, Yvon (Athlete, Hockey Player)
396 Willard Ave Apt A2
Newington, CT 06111-2345, USA

Corrock-Luby, Susan (Athlete, Olympic Athlete, Skier)
3809 S Geiger Blvd Apt 603
Spokane, WA 99224-5427, USA

Corry, Megan (Actor)
c/o Staff Member *Mary Anne Claro Talent Agency*
8600 W Chester Pike Ste 202
Upper Darby, PA 19082-2629, USA

Corsaro, Frank A (Director)
33 Riverside Dr Apt 6C
New York, NY 10023-8025, USA

Corsi, Jim (Athlete, Baseball Player)
48 Eastview Rd
Hopkinton, MA 01748-1853, USA

Corsi, Richard (Race Car Driver)
Cormac Motorsports
7954 S Castle Bay St
Tucson, AZ 85747-9232, USA

Corso, John A (Cinematographer)
241 W 13th St Apt 21
New York, NY 10011-7738, USA

Corson, Keith D (Business Person)
Coachmen Industries
PO Box 1205
Mechanicsburg, PA 17055-1205, USA

Cort, Barry (Athlete, Baseball Player)
1813 E Okaloosa Ave
Tampa, FL 33604-2031, USA

Cort, Bud (Actor)
5707 W Sandstone Ct
Homosassa, FL 34446-2761, USA

Cortazar, Esteban (Designer, Fashion Designer)
Esteban Cortazar Inc
1 NE 1st St Ste 9
Miami, FL 33132-2460, USA

Cortes, Ron (Journalist)
Philadelphia Inquirer
400 N Broad St
Philadelphia, PA 19130-4099, USA

Cortese, Dan (Actor)
c/o Amy Abell *Glick Agency*
1321 7th St Ste 203
Santa Monica, CA 90401-1631, USA

Cortese, Genevieve (Actor)
c/o Joanna (Joanie) Burstein *Burstein Company, The*
15304 W Sunset Blvd Ste 208
Pacific Palisades, CA 90272-3656, USA

Cortese, Joe (Actor)
100 S Hayworth Ave Apt 201
Los Angeles, CA 90048-3658, USA

Cortez, Alfonso (Actor)
CunninghamEscottDipene
10635 Santa Monica Blvd Ste 130
Los Angeles, CA 90025-8306, USA

Corver, Clayton (Athlete, Football Player)
1401 8th St SE
Orange City, IA 51041-7463

Corvino, Anthony (Athlete, Football Player)
PO Box 57
North Haven, CT 06473-0057, USA

Corvo (Musician)
c/o Staff Member *Sony Music Miami*
605 Lincoln Rd Ste 700
Miami Beach, FL 33139-2901, USA

Corvo, Joe (Athlete, Hockey Player)
943 Wenonah Ave
Oak Park, IL 60304-1810, USA

Corwin, Jeff (Actor)
c/o Staff Member *William Morris Endeavor (LA)*
9601 Wilshire Blvd
Beverly Hills, CA 90210-5213, USA

Corwin, Lola (Reality Star)
c/o Cindy Osbrink *Osbrink Talent Agency*
4343 Lankershim Blvd Ste 100
North Hollywood, CA 91602-2705, USA

Coryatt, Quentin J (Athlete, Football Player)
611 Cannon Ln
Sugar Land, TX 77479-5846, USA

Coryell, Larry (Music Group, Musician)
Tedd Kurland
173 Brighton Ave
Allston, MA 02134-2003, USA

Corzine, Dave (Athlete, Basketball Player)
1161 W Hunting Dr
Palatine, IL 60067-6673, USA

Corzine, Jon (Politician)
PO Box 1276
Hoboken, NJ 07030-1276, USA

Corzine, Lester (Athlete, Football Player)
38423 Nasturtium Way
Palm Desert, CA 92211-5075, USA

Cosbie, Doug (Athlete, Football Player)
199 Ke Ala Ola Rd
Honolulu, HI 96817-1580, USA

Cosby, Bill (Actor, Comedian)
PO Box 4049
Santa Monica, CA 90411-4049, USA

Cosby, Rita (Correspondent, Journalist, Television Host)
c/o Staff Member *Inside Edition*
555 W 57th St Ste 1300
King World Productions
New York, NY 10019-2925, USA

Coscarelli, Don (Director, Producer, Writer)
c/o Staff Member *Starway International*
12021 Wilshire Blvd # 661
Los Angeles, CA 90025-1206, USA

Coscina, Dennis (Athlete, Golfer)
211 Main St
East Windsor, CT 06088-9518, USA

Cosey, Ray (Athlete, Baseball Player)
139 Byxbee St
San Francisco, CA 94132-2602, USA

Cosgrove, Daniel (Actor)
c/o Staff Member *James/Levy Management Inc*
3500 W Olive Ave Ste 1470
Burbank, CA 91505-5514, USA

Cosgrove, Mike (Athlete, Baseball Player)
1815 W Road 4 N
Chino Valley, AZ 86323-5269, USA

Cosgrove, Miranda (Actor)
c/o Michael Sugar *Anonymous Content (LA)*
3532 Hayden Ave
Culver City, CA 90232-2413, USA

Coslet, Bruce N (Athlete, Coach, Football Coach, Football Player)
1778 Ivy Pointe Ct
Naples, FL 34109-3375, USA

Cosman, Jim (Athlete, Baseball Player)
299 Northgate Trce
Roswell, GA 30075-2329, USA

Cosner, Don (Athlete, Football Player)
141 NW Carter Farms Ct
Bremerton, WA 98310-2090, USA

Cosper, Kina (Music Group)
Green Light Talent Agency
PO Box 3172
Beverly Hills, CA 90212-0172, USA

Costa, David J (Dave) (Athlete, Football Player)
1732 Latour Ave
Brentwood, CA 94513-4333, USA

Costa, Don
7920 W Sunset Blvd Ste 300
Los Angeles, CA 90046-3300

Costa, Gal (Music Group)
Bridge Agency
2600 John F Kennedy Blvd Apt 1H
Jersey City, NJ 07306-6068, USA

Costa, Jim (Congressman, Politician)
1314 Longworth Hob
Washington, DC 20515-4908, USA

Costa, Mary (Musician, Opera Singer)
3340 Kingston Pike Unit 1
Knoxville, TN 37919-4674, USA

Costa, Nikka (Musician)
3724 Buena Park Dr
Studio City, CA 91604-3809, USA

Costa, Paul (Athlete, Football Player)
8017 Kristina Ln
North Richland Hills, TX 76182-8747, USA

Costa, Shane (Athlete, Baseball Player)
127 E Arlen Ave
Visalia, CA 93277-7691, USA

Costabile, David (Actor)
c/o Craig Gartner *Gartner/Green Entertainment*
5225 Wilshire Blvd # 1200
Los Angeles, CA 90036-4301, USA

Costanza, John (Race Car Driver)
Demand Flow Racing
6625 S Galena St
Englewood, CO 80112, USA

Costanzo, Paulo (Actor)
United Talent Agency
9336 Civic Center Dr
Beverly Hills, CA 90210-3604, USA

Costanzo, Robert (Actor)
832 Masselin Ave
Los Angeles, CA 90036-4722, USA

Costas, Bob (Commentator)
22 Coral Cay
Newport Coast, CA 92657-1908, USA

Coste, Chris (Athlete, Baseball Player)
3774 Polk St S
Fargo, ND 58104-7595, USA

Costello, Brad (Athlete, Football Player)
9 Stout Rd
Princeton, NJ 08540-7440, USA

Costello, John (Athlete, Baseball Player)
16614 Willow Glen Dr
Grover, MO 63040-1750, USA

Costello, Mariclare (Actor)
Borinstein Oreck Bogart
3172 Dona Susana Dr
Studio City, CA 91604-4356, USA

Costello, Mark (Writer)
Fordham Univesity
Law School
Bronx, NY 10458, USA

Costello, Patty (Bowler)
715 S Crystal Lake Dr
Orlando, FL 32803-6906, USA

Costello, Rich (Athlete, Hockey Player)
3 Bay Dr
Laguna Beach, CA 92651-6780, USA

Costello, Sean (Actor, Producer)
c/o Staff Member *Concerted Efforts*
PO Box 440326
Somerville, MA 02144-0004, USA

Costello, Sue (Actor)
United Talent Agency
9336 Civic Center Dr
Beverly Hills, CA 90210-3604, USA

Costello, Thomas (Tom) (Athlete, Football Player)
PO Box 299
Rocky Point, NY 11778-0299, USA

Costello, Vince (Athlete, Football Player)
9914 W 125th Ter
Overland Park, KS 66213-1858, USA

Coster, Nicolas (Actor)
c/o Staff Member *Momentum Talent and Literary Agency*
9401 Wilshire Blvd Ste 501
Beverly Hills, CA 90212-2944, USA

Coster, Ritchie (Actor)
c/o Glenn Daniels *Glenn Daniels Arts Management*
56 Warren St Apt 5E
New York, NY 10007-1097, USA

Coster Waldau, Nikolaj (Actor)
c/o Jill Littman *Impression Entertainment*
9229 W Sunset Blvd Ste 700
West Hollywood, CA 90069-3407, USA

Costner, Kevin (Actor, Director)
3270 Beach Club Rd
Carpinteria, CA 93013, USA

Costo, Tim (Athlete, Baseball Player)
3107 Pintail Ln
Signal Mountain, TN 37377-1439, USA

Cota, Chad (Athlete, Football Player)
216 Island Pointe Dr
Medford, OR 97504-9453, USA

Cota, Humberto (Baseball Player)
c/o Staff Member *Pittsburgh Pirates*
115 Federal St Ste 115B
Pnc Park
Pittsburgh, PA 15212-5740, USA

Cotchery, Jerricho (Athlete, Football Player)
c/o Brian Levy *Goal Line Football Management*
1025 Kane Concourse Ste 207
Bay Harbor Islands, FL 33154-2118, USA

Cote, David (Business Person)
TRW Inc
1900 Richmond Rd
Cleveland, OH 44124, USA

Cote, Del (Horse Racer)
292 Route 539
Cream Ridge, NJ 08514-1516, USA

Cote, Riley (Athlete, Hockey Player)
1485 Kearsley Rd
Sicklerville, NJ 08081-5215, USA

Cote, Sylvain (Athlete, Hockey Player)
1432 Wild Cranberry Ct
Crownsville, MD 21032-2039, USA

Cotham, Frank (Cartoonist)
7763 Sunny Trail Dr
Memphis, TN 38135-0418, USA

Cothran, Jeff (Athlete, Football Player)
5671 Oakview Ter
Liberty Twp, OH 45011-2494, USA

Cothren, Paige (Athlete, Football Player)
1332 Highway 15 S
Woodland, MS 39776-9741, USA

Cotillard, Marion (Actor)
c/o Mara Buxbaum *ID Public Relations (LA)*
7060 Hollywood Blvd Fl 8th
Los Angeles, CA 90028-6021, USA

Cotler, Kami (Actor)
7425 Arizona Ave
Los Angeles, CA 90045-1324, USA

Cotney, Mark (Athlete, Football Player)
4809 Cheval Blvd
Lutz, FL 33558-5338, USA

Cotroneo, Vince (Commentator)
4455 E Palmdale Ln
Gilbert, AZ 85298-4024, USA

Cottet, Mia (Actor)
c/o David Sweeney *Sweeney Entertainment*
6253 Hollywood Blvd Apt 201
Los Angeles, CA 90028-8248, USA

Cottier, Chuck (Athlete, Baseball Player, Coach)
7129 Lake Ballinger Way
Edmonds, WA 98026-8545, USA

Cottle, Tameka (Tiny) (Musician)
Major P Productions LLC
325 Edgewood Ave SE
Atlanta, GA 30312-4003, USA

Cotto, Delilah (Actor)
c/o Ivan De Paz *DePaz Management*
2011 N Vermont Ave
Los Angeles, CA 90027-1931, USA

Cotto, Henry (Athlete, Baseball Player)
1141 W Thomas Rd
Phoenix, AZ 85013-4206, USA

Cotto, Miguel (Athlete, Boxer)
c/o Staff Member *Top Rank Inc.*
3908 Howard Hughes Pkwy
#580
Las Vegas, NV 89109, USA

Cotton, Barney (Athlete, Football Player)
2402 Sundown Dr
Ames, IA 50014-8220, USA

Cotton, Blaine (Actor)
Jack Scagnetti Talent
5118 Vineland Ave # 102
North Hollywood, CA 91601-3814, USA

Cotton, Craig (Athlete, Football Player)
5020 Trabuco Canyon Dr
Bakersfield, CA 93307-6932, USA

Cotton, James (Musician)
James Cotton Mgmt
235 W Eugenie St # G
Chicago, IL 60614-5774, USA

Cotton, John (Athlete, Basketball Player)
11426 Country Road 4 S
Alamosa, CO 81101, USA

Cotton, Josie (Music Group)
2794 Hume Rd
Malibu, CA 90265-3435, USA

Cotton, Marcus (Athlete, Football Player)
484 Lake Park Ave Apt 280
Oakland, CA 94610-2730, USA

Cotton, Mason Vale (Actor)
c/o Nicki Fioravante *PMK/BNC Public Relations (PMK-LA)*
8687 Melrose Ave Ste 8
West Hollywood, CA 90069-5746, USA

Cotton, Maxwell Perry (Actor)
c/o Matt Fletcher *Greene & Associates*
1901 Avenue of the Stars Ste 130
Los Angeles, CA 90067-6030, USA

Cotton, Robin (Doctor)
20271 Goldenrod Ln # 120
Germantown, MD 20876-4064, USA

Cottrell, Dana (Athlete, Football Player)
1 Driftwood Ln
North Billerica, MA 01862-1222, USA

Cottrell, Erin (Actor)
c/o Abbey Sibucao-MacDonald *New Wave Entertainment (LA)*
2660 W Olive Ave
Burbank, CA 91505-4525, USA

Cottrell, Ted (Athlete, Football Player)
135 Spring Meadow Dr Apt 5
Buffalo, NY 14221-8436, USA

Cottrell, William (Bill) (Athlete, Football Player)
39675 Patterson Ln
Solon, OH 44139-6705, USA

Cotts, Neal (Athlete, Baseball Player)
939 N Winchester Ave Apt 1
Aot 1
Chicago, IL 60622-4167, USA

Couch, Chris (Athlete, Golfer)
307 Johns Creek Pkwy
Saint Augustine, FL 32092-5064, USA

Couch, Tim (Athlete, Football Player)
2110 N Ocean Blvd Apt 28-D
Fort Lauderdale, FL 33305-1947, USA

Couchee, Mike (Athlete, Baseball Player)
3060 N Ridgecrest Unit 155
Mesa, AZ 85207-1080, USA

Coughlan, Marisa (Actor)
11725 Laurelcrest Dr
Studio City, CA 91604-3816, USA

Coughlin, John (Race Car Driver)
Jeg's High Performance Racing
751 E 11th Ave
Columbus, OH 43211-2695, USA

Coughlin, Kevin
1090 N Euclid Ave
Sarasota, FL 34237-3013

Coughlin, Mike (Race Car Driver)
Jeg's High Performance Racing
751 E 11th Ave
Columbus, OH 43211-2695, USA

Coughlin, Natalie (Athlete, Olympic Athlete, Swimmer)
4139 Coralee Ln
Lafayette, CA 94549-3356, USA

Coughlin, Tom (Coach, Football Coach)
New York Giants
Giants Stadium
East Rutherford, NJ 07073, USA

Coughlin, Troy (Race Car Driver)
Jeg's High Performance Racing
751 E 11th Ave
Columbus, OH 43211-2695, USA

Coughlin, Jr., Jeg (Race Car Driver)
Jeg's High Performance Racing
751 E 11th Ave
Columbus, OH 43211-2695, USA

Coughran, John (Athlete, Basketball Player)
5476 Morningside Dr
San Jose, CA 95138-2244, USA

Coughtry, Marlan (Athlete, Baseball Player)
5504 NE 55th St
Vancouver, WA 98661-2168, USA

Coulier, Dave (Actor)
4754 Lindley Ave
Encino, CA 91316-4231, USA

Coulson, Catherine E (Actor)
1115 Terra Ave
Ashland, OR 97520-3565, USA

Coulter, Allen (Director)
c/o Paul Alan Smith *Equitable Stewardship for Artists (ESA)*
10250 Constellation Blvd Fl 7
Los Angeles, CA 90067-6207, USA

Coulter, Ann (Writer)
c/o Suzanne Gluck *William Morris Endeavor (NY)*
1325 Avenue of the Americas
New York, NY 10019-6026, USA

Coulter, Art
500 Spanish Fort Blvd Apt 203
Spanish Fort, AL 36527-5008

Coulter, Brian (Music Group, Musician)
Ashley Talent
2002 Hogback Rd Ste 20
Ann Arbor, MI 48105-9736, USA

Coulter, Catherine (Writer)
PO Box 17
Mill Valley, CA 94942-0017, USA

Coulter, Chip (Athlete, Baseball Player)
718 Trenton St
Toronto, OH 43964-1269, USA

Council, Keith (Athlete, Football Player)
4418 Lenox Blvd
Orlando, FL 32811-4541, USA

Counsell, Craig (Athlete, Baseball Player)
992 E Circle Dr
Milwaukee, WI 53217-5361, USA

Counting Crows (Music Group)
c/o Gary Gersh *The Artists Organization*
1811 Centinela Ave
Santa Monica, CA 90404-4203, USA

Counts, Mel (Athlete, Basketball Player, Olympic Athlete)
1581 Matheny Rd NE
Gervais, OR 97026-8762, USA

Coupe, Eliza (Actor)
c/o Rhett Usry *ID Public Relations (NY)*
150 W 30th St Fl 19
New York, NY 10001-4119, USA

Coupland, Douglas (Writer)
c/o Michael Siegel *Michael Siegel & Assoc*
8330 W 3rd St
Los Angeles, CA 90048-4311, USA

Couples, Fred (Athlete, Golfer)
127 S Carmelina Ave
Los Angeles, CA 90049-3901, USA

Couric, Katie (Journalist, Television Host)
c/o Matthew Hiltzik *Hiltzik Strategies*
381 Park Ave S Ste 1212
New York, NY 10016-8806, USA

Courier, Jim (Athlete, Olympic Athlete, Tennis Player)
9533 Blandford Rd
Orlando, FL 32827-7008, USA

Courtenay, Ed (Athlete, Hockey Player)
1422 Whispering Oaks Trl
Mount Pleasant, SC 29466-8584, USA

Courtin, Steve (Athlete, Basketball Player)
1109 Grinnell Rd
Wilmington, DE 19803-5125, USA

Courtney, Jai (Actor)
c/o Sam Maydew *The Collective*
8383 Wilshire Blvd Ste 1050
Beverly Hills, CA 90211-2415, USA

Courtney, Joe (Congressman, Politician)
215 Cannon Hob
Washington, DC 20515-0702, USA

Courtney, Joel (Actor)
c/o Bonnie Liedtke *Principato/Young Management (LA)*
9465 Wilshire Blvd Ste 900
Beverly Hills, CA 90212-2608, USA

Courtney, Patricia (Baseball Player)
8 Eagle Loop Ln
Freedom, NH 03836-5311, USA

Courtney, Stephanie (Actor)
4606 Goodland Ave
Studio City, CA 91604-1118, USA

Courtney, Thomas W (Tom) (Athlete, Olympic Athlete, Track Athlete)
336 Edgemere Way E
Naples, FL 34105-7151, USA

Courtright, John (Athlete, Baseball Player)
316 S Roosevelt Ave
Columbus, OH 43209-1829, USA

Courville, Larry (Athlete, Hockey Player)
559 Royal Rd
Palmyra, PA 17078-9017, USA

Courville, Vince (Athlete, Football Player)
5123 Avenue R
Galveston, TX 77551-5282, USA

Coury, Dick (Athlete, Football Player)
4553 Campus Ave Apt 6
San Diego, CA 92116-1162, USA

Coury, Steve (Athlete, Football Player)
6003 Newcastle Dr
Lake Oswego, OR 97035-8757, USA

Cousin, Terry (Athlete, Football Player)
6556 N Ponchartrain Blvd
Chicago, IL 60646-2725, USA

Cousineau, Tom (Athlete, Football Player)
645 Ridgecrest Rd
Akron, OH 44303-1342, USA

Cousino, Brad (Athlete, Football Player)
8778 Kenwood Rd
Blue Ash, OH 45242-7952, USA

Cousins, Christopher (Actor)
c/o Deborah Miller *Shelter Entertainment*
9255 W Sunset Blvd Ste 320
West Hollywood, CA 90069-3313, USA

Cousins, Derryl (Athlete, Baseball Player)
78136 Desert Mountain Cir
Bermuda Dunes, CA 92203-8151, USA

Cousins, Jomo (Athlete, Football Player)
13194 US Highway 301 S # 309
Riverview, FL 33578-7410, USA

Cousteau, Jean-Michel (Producer)
Ocean Futures Society
325 Chapala St
Santa Barbara, CA 93101-3407, USA

Cousy, Robert J (Bob) (Athlete, Basketball Player)
427 Salisbury St
Worcester, MA 01609-1266, USA

Coutlangus, Jon (Athlete, Baseball Player)
428 Starbridge Ct
Pleasant Hill, CA 94523-4723, USA

Couture, Randy (Athlete, Wrestler)
c/o Samuel Spira *Xtreme Couture Management*
8265 W Sunset Blvd Ste 205
West Hollywood, CA 90046-2470, USA

Covay, Don (Music Group, Songwriter, Writer)
Rawstock
PO Box 110002
Cambria Heights, NY 11411-0002, USA

Covelli, Coco Crisp (Athlete, Baseball Player)
508 Judy Dr
Redondo Beach, CA 90277-3830, USA

Coverdale, David (Musician)
757 Champagne Rd
Incline Village, NV 89451-8001, USA

Cover Girls
141 Dunbar Ave
Fords, NJ 08863-1551

Covert, Allen (Actor, Comedian)
6963 Los Tilos Rd
Los Angeles, CA 90068-3106, USA

Covert, James (Jimbo) (Athlete, Football Player)
2647 Nelson Ct
Weston, FL 33332-1835, USA

Covey, Richard O Colonel (Astronaut)
1155 High Lake Vw
Colorado Springs, CO 80906-8717, USA

Coville, Bruce
PO Box 6110
Syracuse, NY 13217-6110

Covington, John (Athlete, Football Player)
1745 Morningdale Cir
Duluth, GA 30097-5259, USA

Covington, Scott (Athlete, Football Player)
7444 W 81st St
Los Angeles, CA 90045-2304, USA

Covington, Tony (Athlete, Football Player)
11160 S Lakes Dr # C1
Reston, VA 20191-4327, USA

Covington, Warren (Music Group)
1627 Open Field Loop
Brandon, FL 33510-2096, USA

Cowan, Billy (Athlete, Baseball Player)
PO Box 1087
Palos Verdes Estates, CA 90274-7887, USA

Cowan, Dr. Connell (Writer)
c/o Staff Member *Reece Halsey North*
98 Main St # 704
Belvedere Tiburon, CA 94920-2517, USA

Cowan, Elliot (Actor)
c/o Laura Berwick *Berwick & Kovacik*
9465 Wilshire Blvd Ste 420
Beverly Hills, CA 90212-2603, USA

Cowan, Lawrence (Larry) (Athlete, Football Player)
1456 McCluer Rd
Jackson, MS 39212-6224, USA

Coward, Herbert (Actor)
1399 Worley Cove Rd
Canton, NC 28716-7069, USA

Cowart, Sam (Athlete, Football Player)
11110 Fallgate Point Ct
Jacksonville, FL 32256-4833, USA

Cowboy Junkies
c/o Staff Member *Paradigm (Monterey)*
404 W Franklin St
Monterey, CA 93940-2303, USA

Cowboy Mouth (Music Group, Musician)
c/o Konrad Leh *Creative Talent Group*
1900 Avenue of the Stars Ste 2475
Los Angeles, CA 90067-4512, USA

Cowell, Simon (Business Person, Judge, Reality Star)
717 N Palm Dr
Beverly Hills, CA 90210-3416, USA

Cowens, Dave (Athlete, Basketball Player)
132 Deep Cv
Raymond, ME 04071-6523, USA

Cowher, Bill (Athlete, Football Coach, Football Player)
1225 Briar Patch Ln
Raleigh, NC 27615-6902, USA

Cowie, Colin (Designer)
256 W 36th St Apt 4
New York, NY 10018-7712, USA

Cowie, Rob
7501 E Phantom Way
Scottsdale, AZ 85255-4619, USA

Cowley, Joe (Athlete, Baseball Player)
904 Andover Grn
Lexington, KY 40509-2929, USA

Cowlings, Al (Athlete, Football Player)
PO Box 1064
Pacific Palisades, CA 90272-1064, USA

Cowper, Stephen C (Steve) (Ex-Governor)
2301 McGregor Ct
Vienna, VA 22182-5235, USA

Cowper, Steve (Politician)
PO Box A
Juneau, AK 99811, USA

Cowsill, Susan (Musician)
c/o Valerie Turner Polishook *V Public Relations LLC*
PO Box 341810
Bethesda, MD 20827-1810, USA

Cox, Alex (Actor, Director)
United Talent Agency
9336 Civic Center Dr
Beverly Hills, CA 90210-3604, USA

Cox, Billy (Athlete, Football Player)
4227 64th Dr E
Sarasota, FL 34243-7940, USA

Cox, Bobby (Commentator)
2190 Heathermoor Hill Dr
Marietta, GA 30062-6504, USA

Cox, Bryan (Athlete, Football Player)
3040 Peachtree Rd NW Unit 1206
Atlanta, GA 30305-2290, USA

Cox, Casey (Athlete, Baseball Player)
2840 La Concha Dr
Clearwater, FL 33762-2203, USA

Cox, Charles C (Government Official)
Lexecon Inc
332 S Michigan Ave Ste 1300
Chicago, IL 60604-4431, USA

Cox, Charlie (Actor)
c/o Nick Frenkel *3 Arts Entertainment (LA)*
9460 Wilshire Blvd Fl 7
Beverly Hills, CA 90212-2713, USA

Cox, Chris (Musician)
c/o Staff Member *Diva Central Inc*
7510 W Sunset Blvd Ste 1445
Los Angeles, CA 90046-3408, USA

Cox, Christina (Actor)
Rysher Entertainment
3400 W Riverside Dr # 600
Burbank, CA 91505-4669, USA

Cox, C Jay (Director, Producer, Writer)
c/o Scott Zimmerman *Evolution Entertainment (LA)*
901 N Highland Ave
Los Angeles, CA 90038-2412, USA

Cox, Courteney (Actor, Producer)
9255 Doheny Rd Apt 2505
West Hollywood, CA 90069-3238, USA

Cox, Danny (Athlete, Baseball Player)
306 Feagin Mill Rd
Warner Robins, GA 31088-6208, USA

Cox, Danny (Motivational Speaker, Writer)
17381 Bonner Dr
Tustin, CA 92780-1837, USA

Cox, Darron (Athlete, Baseball Player)
13681 Stuart St
Broomfield, CO 80023-5527, USA

Cox, David R (Doctor, Misc)
Stanford University
Human Genome Center
Stanford, CA 94305, USA

Cox, Deborah (Musician, Songwriter)
8348 NW 62nd Pl
Parkland, FL 33067-5019, USA

Cox, Frederick W (Fred) (Athlete, Football Player)
401 E River St
Monticello, MN 55362-9397, USA

Cox, G David (Religious Leader)
Church of God
PO Box 2420
Anderson, IN 46018-2420, USA

Cox, Jeff (Athlete, Baseball Player)
2727 E Vanderhoof Dr
West Covina, CA 91791-2247, USA

Cox, Jennifer Elise (Actor)
c/o Lisa DiSante-Frank *DiSante Frank & Company*
10061 Riverside Dr # 377
Toluca Lake, CA 91602-2560, USA

Cox, Jim (Athlete, Baseball Player)
8370 E Charter Oak Rd
Scottsdale, AZ 85260-5256, USA

Cox, John (Athlete, Football Player)
4227 64th Dr E
Sarasota, FL 34243-7940, USA

Cox, Johnny (Athlete, Basketball Player, Coach)
849 N Main St
Hazard, KY 41701-1345, USA

Cox, Joshua (Actor)
7185 Pacific View Dr
Los Angeles, CA 90068-2039, USA

Cox, Kris (Athlete, Golfer)
2009 Lunenburg Dr
Allen, TX 75013-4708, USA

Cox, Larry (Athlete, Football Player)
10326 Catlett Ln
La Porte, TX 77571-4218, USA

Cox, Laverne (Actor)
c/o Jami Kandel *Baker Winokur Ryder Public Relations (BWR-NY)*
292 Madison Ave Fl 12
New York, NY 10017-6415, USA

Cox, Lynne (Swimmer)
Advanced Sport Research
4141 Ball Rd # 142
Cypress, CA 90630-3465, USA

Cox, Morgan (Athlete, Football Player)
c/o Jimmy Sexton *CAA (Memphis)*
6060 Poplar Ave Ste 470
Memphis, TN 38119-0910, USA

Cox, Nathalie (Actor)
c/o Chuck James *ICM Partners (LA)*
10250 Constellation Blvd Fl 7
Los Angeles, CA 90067-6207, USA

Cox, Nikki (Actor)
737 El Medio Ave
Pacific Palisades, CA 90272-3452, USA

Cox, Ralph (Athlete, Hockey Player)
1 Harborside Dr Ste 200S
Boston, MA 02128-2905, USA

Cox, Richard
9200 W Sunset Blvd Ste 900
West Hollywood, CA 90069-3604

Cox, Richard Ian
8730 W Sunset Blvd Ste 480
West Hollywood, CA 90069-2277

Cox, Ronny (Actor)
13948 Magnolia Blvd
Sherman Oaks, CA 91423-1230, USA

Cox, Steve (Athlete, Baseball Player)
22678 Avenue 188
Strathmore, CA 93267-9680, USA

Cox, Steve (Athlete, Football Player)
Rainwater & Cox LLC
915 Enterprise Dr
Jonesboro, AR 72401-9201, USA

Cox, Ted (Athlete, Baseball Player)
3660 Sunvalley Dr
Oklahoma City, OK 73110-1224, USA

Cox, Terry (Athlete, Baseball Player)
707 N Broadway St
Aot 302
Pittsburg, KS 66762-3905, USA

Cox, Thomas (Race Car Driver)
2321 Race Track Rd
Sophia, NC 27350-8901, USA

Cox, Tom (Athlete, Football Player)
2121 S Mill Ave Apt 231
Tempe, AZ 85282-2138, USA

Cox, Tony (Actor)
c/o Staff Member *New Wave Entertainment (LA)*
2660 W Olive Ave
Burbank, CA 91505-4525, USA

Cox, Torrie (Athlete, Football Player)
42 NW 92nd St
Miami Shores, FL 33150-2227, USA

Cox, Veanne (Actor)
c/o Nyle Brenner *Brenner Management*
Prefers to be contacted via telephone or email
CA, USA

Cox, Vera
345 N Maple Dr Ste 397
Beverly Hills, CA 90210-5179

Coxe, Craig (Athlete, Hockey Player)
W3059 Oak St
Saint Ignace, MI 49781-9849, USA

Coyle, Eric (Athlete, Football Player)
397 County Road 26
Longmont, CO 80504-9515, USA

Coyle, Nadine (Actor, Musician)
c/o Julie Colbert *William Morris Endeavor (LA)*
9601 Wilshire Blvd
Beverly Hills, CA 90210-5213, USA

Coyle, Ross (Athlete, Football Player)
PO Box 68
Blanchard, OK 73010-0068, USA

Coyne, Colleen (Athlete, Hockey Player, Olympic Athlete)
3 Baldwin Ln
North Reading, MA 01864-2277, USA

Coyne, Dale (Race Car Driver)
13627 Sharp Dr
Plainfield, IL 60544-7952, USA

Coyne, Wayne (Musician)
1715 NW 13th St
Oklahoma City, OK 73106-2005, USA

Coyote, Peter (Actor)
774 Marin Dr
Mill Valley, CA 94941-3919, USA

Cozart, Keith (Chief Keef) (Musician)
c/o Staff Member *Interscope Records (LA) - Main*
2220 Colorado Ave
Santa Monica, CA 90404-3506, USA

Cozler, Jimmy (Musician, Songwriter, Writer)
J Racords
745 5th Ave # 600
New York, NY 10151-0099, USA

C. Peters, Gary (Congressman, Politician)
1609 Longworth Hob
Washington, DC 20515-0538, USA

C. Peterson, Collin (Congressman, Politician)
2211 Rayburn Hob
Washington, DC 20515-1317, USA

Crabb, Claude (Athlete, Football Player)
49851 Wayne St
Indio, CA 92201, USA

Crabb, Joey (Athlete, Hockey Player)
1332 Northbluff Dr
Anchorage, AK 99501-1300, USA

Crabbe, Cullen (Actor)
9437 N 122nd Pl
Scottsdale, AZ 85259-6020, USA

Crable, Bob (Athlete, Football Player)
564 Miami Trace Ct
Loveland, OH 45140-8021, USA

Crabtree, Eric (Athlete, Football Player)
3342 Arapahoe St
Denver, CO 80205-2741, USA

Crabtree, Michael (Athlete, Football Player)
c/o Eugene Parker *Maximum Sports Management*
6435 W Jefferson Blvd # 197
Fort Wayne, IN 46804-6203, USA

Crabtree, Tim (Athlete, Baseball Player)
1503 Kingswood Ln
Colleyville, TX 76034-5580, USA

Craddock, Billy Crash
PO Box 428
Portland, TN 37148-0428

Craddock, Billy (Crash) (Musician, Songwriter, Writer)
3007 Old Martinsville Rd
Greensboro, NC 27455, USA

Cradle, Rickey (Athlete, Baseball Player)
1311 Dry Gap Pike
Knoxville, TN 37918-9785, USA

Craft, Chris
14919 Village Elm St
Houston, TX 77062-2914

Craft, Jason (Athlete, Football Player)
11688 Amistad Ct
Jacksonville, FL 32256-2925, USA

Craft, Sammi (Actor)
c/o Staff Member *Paradigm (LA)*
360 N Crescent Dr
North Bldg
Beverly Hills, CA 90210-4874, USA

Craft, Terry (Athlete, Baseball Player)
16 Sheldon Ave
Castle Rock, CO 80104-8820, USA

Crafter, Jane (Athlete, Golfer)
317 W Almeria Rd
Phoenix, AZ 85003-1140, USA

Crafts, Hannah (Writer)
c/o Staff Member *Creative Artists Agency (CAA-LA)*
2000 Avenue of the Stars Ste 100
Los Angeles, CA 90067-4705, USA

Craggs, George (Soccer Player)
6223 6th Ave NW
Seattle, WA 98107-2131, USA

Craig, Adam Jamal (Actor)
c/o Christopher Rockwell *Keyword Entertainment*
1051 Cole Ave # B
Los Angeles, CA 90038-2601, USA

Craig, Daniel (Actor)
c/o Robin Baum *Slate Public Relations*
9000 W Sunset Blvd Ste 915
West Hollywood, CA 90069-5809, USA

Craig, Demeyune (Athlete, Football Player)
5102 31st Ave
Valley, AL 36854-5214, USA

Craig, Elijah (Actor)
Agency for Performing Arts
9200 W Sunset Blvd Ste 900
West Hollywood, CA 90069-3604, USA

Craig, Jenny (Business Person, Doctor)
5973 Rancho Diegueno
Rancho Santa Fe, CA 92067, USA

Craig, Jim (Athlete, Hockey Player, Olympic Athlete)
29907 County Road 3
Merrifield, MN 56465-4402, USA

Craig, Larry (Politician)
8935 W Cornwall Dr
Boise, ID 83704-4310, USA

Craig, Mike (Athlete, Hockey Player)
29907 County Road 3
Merrifield, MN 56465-4402, USA

Craig, Neal (Athlete, Football Player)
2231 Crane Ave
Cincinnati, OH 45207-1322, USA

Craig, Paco (Athlete, Football Player)
23668 Marguerite Cir
Moreno Valley, CA 92557-2853, USA

Craig, Pete (Athlete, Baseball Player)
5915 Carmel Ln
Raleigh, NC 27609-3953, USA

Craig, Rod (Athlete, Baseball Player)
1200 E Kay St Apt C
Compton, CA 90221-1573, USA

Craig, Roger (Athlete, Baseball Player, Coach)
PO Box 2174
Borrego Springs, CA 92004-2174, USA

Craig, Roger (Athlete, Football Player)
271 Vista Verde Way
Portola Valley, CA 94028-8149, USA

Craig, William (Bill) (Swimmer)
PO Box 629
Newport Beach, CA 92661-0629, USA

Craig, Yvonne (Actor)
YC/MC Ltd
PO Box 827
Pacific Palisades, CA 90272-0827, USA

Crain, Jesse (Athlete, Baseball Player)
20702 Hartford Way
Lakeville, MN 55044-4438, USA

Crain, Keith E (Publisher)
Crain Communications
1400 Woodbridge St
Detroit, MI 48207-3110, USA

Crain, Rance (Publisher)
Crain Communications
150 N Michigan Ave Ste 1700
Chicago, IL 60601-7620, USA

Crain, William (Director)
Contemporary Artists
610 Santa Monica Blvd Ste 202
Santa Monica, CA 90401-1645, USA

Crais, Robert (Writer)
1647 Blue Jay Way
Los Angeles, CA 90069-1216, USA

Cram, Jerry (Athlete, Baseball Player)
20638 Furr Rd
Round Hill, VA 20141-1802, USA

Cram, Jerry (Athlete, Baseball Player)
PO Box 20936
Attn: Coaching Staff
Keizer, OR 97307-0936, USA

Cramer, Douglas
738 Sarbonne Rd
Los Angeles, CA 90077-3302

Cramer, Grant (Actor)
Richard Sindell
1910 Holmby Ave Apt 1
Los Angeles, CA 90025-5936, USA

Cramer, James (Television Host)
c/o Staff Member *CNBC (Main)*
900 Sylvan Ave
Englewood Cliffs, NJ 07632-3312, USA

Cramer, Jim (Business Person, Television Host)
c/o Staff Member *CNBC (Main)*
900 Sylvan Ave
Englewood Cliffs, NJ 07632-3312, USA

Cramer, Peggy (Athlete, Baseball Player, Commentator)
1160 E Old Andrew Johnson Hwy
Talbott, TN 37877-3103, USA

Cramps, The (Music Group)
c/o Stormy Shepherd *Leave Home Booking*
1400 S Foothill Dr Ste 34
Salt Lake City, UT 84108-2392, USA

Crampton, Barbara (Actor)
Stone Manners
6500 Wilshire Blvd # 550
Los Angeles, CA 90048-4920, USA

Crampton, Bruce (Athlete, Golfer)
225 Winter Crest Ln
Severna Park, MD 21146-3104, USA

Cranberries, The (Music Group)
c/o Staff Member *Creative Artists Agency (CAA-LA)*
2000 Avenue of the Stars Ste 100
Los Angeles, CA 90067-4705, USA

Crandall, Del (Athlete, Baseball Player, Coach)
1355 Clear Lake Pl
Brea, CA 92821-2807, USA

Crane, Ben (Athlete, Golfer)
2223 Cedar Elm Ter
Westlake, TX 76262-9028, USA

Crane, Brian (Cartoonist)
PO Box 51771
Sparks, NV 89435-1771, USA

Crane, Caprice (Actor, Writer)
c/o Brad Petrigala *Brillstein Entertainment Partners (LA)*
9150 Wilshire Blvd Ste 350
Beverly Hills, CA 90212-3453, USA

Crane, David (Director, Producer, Writer)
c/o Staff Member *Bright Kauffman Crane Productions*
4000 Warner Blvd Bldg 750
Burbank, CA 91522-0001

Crane, Gary (Athlete, Football Player)
6 Greystone
Bentonville, AR 72712-4098, USA

Crane, John (Writer)
c/o Staff Member *Agency for the Performing Arts (APA-LA)*
405 S Beverly Dr Ste 500
Beverly Hills, CA 90212-4425, USA

Crane, Kenneth G (Director)
6627 Lindenhurst Ave
Los Angeles, CA 90048-4611, USA

Crane, Paul (Athlete, Football Player)
12 N Monterey St
Mobile, AL 36604-1317, USA

Crane, Tony (Actor)
Abrams Artists
9200 W Sunset Blvd Ste 1125
West Hollywood, CA 90069-3610, USA

Cranston, Bryan (Actor)
c/o Jodi Gottlieb *Independent Public Relations*
Prefers to be contacted via telephone or email
Los Angeles, CA, USA

Crapo, Michael (Politician)
3212th St SE
Washington, DC 20003, USA

Crapo, Mike (Senator)
239 Dirksen Senate Bldg
Washington, DC 20510-0001, USA

Cravaack, Chip (Congressman, Politician)
508 Cannon Hob
Washington, DC 20515-2210, USA

Craven, Bill (Athlete, Football Player)
4363 N Buckhead Dr NE
Atlanta, GA 30342-3451, USA

Craven, Matt (Actor)
6108 Dorcas Pl
Los Angeles, CA 90068-1662, USA

Craven, Murray (Athlete, Hockey Player)
2802 Rest Haven Dr
Whitefish, MT 59937, USA

Craven, Ricky (Race Car Driver)
PO Box 472
Concord, NC 28026-0472, USA

Craven, Wes (Director)
2419 Solar Dr
Los Angeles, CA 90046-1740, USA

Cravens, Greg (Cartoonist)
312 N McLean Blvd
Memphis, TN 38112-5341, USA

Craver, Aaron (Athlete, Football Player)
821 W Maple St
Compton, CA 90220-1829, USA

Crawford, Bob (Athlete, Hockey Player)
19 Cliff Dr
Avon, CT 06001-3413, USA

Crawford, Brad (Athlete, Football Player)
RR 2
Winamac, IN 46996, USA

Crawford, Carl (Athlete, Baseball Player)
15618 Bristol Lake Dr
Houston, TX 77070-3865, USA

Crawford, Carlos (Athlete, Baseball Player)
1605 Martin Luther King Ave E
Bradenton, FL 34208-2801, USA

Crawford, Chace (Actor)
c/o Eric Podwall *Podwall Entertainment*
710 N Orlando Ave Apt 203
Loft 203
West Hollywood, CA 90069-5549, USA

Crawford, Cheyne (Actor)
c/o Amy Slomovits *Evolution Entertainment (LA)*
9320 Wilshire Blvd Ste 202
Beverly Hills, CA 90212-3217, USA

Crawford, Christina (Writer)
7 Springs Farm Sanders Rd
Tensed, ID 83870, USA

Crawford, Cindy (Actor, Model)
33246 Pacific Coast Hwy
Malibu, CA 90265-2304, USA

Crawford, Clayne (Actor)
c/o Alex Cole *Elevate Entertainment*
5757 Wilshire Blvd Ste 460
Los Angeles, CA 90036-3658, USA

Crawford, Ed (Athlete, Football Player)
204 Country Club Rd
Oxford, MS 38655-2606, USA

Crawford, Eric (Congressman, Politician)
1408 Longworth Hob
Washington, DC 20515-3102, USA

Crawford, Fred (Athlete, Basketball Player)
24 W Lawn Dr
Teaneck, NJ 07666-5612, USA

Crawford, Hilton (Athlete, Football Player)
262 Hagen St
Buffalo, NY 14215-3959, USA

Crawford, Jack (Athlete, Football Player)
c/o Anthony J. Agnone *Eastern Athletic Services*
11350 McCormick Rd
Suite 800 - Executive Plaza
Hunt Valley, MD 21031-1002, USA

Crawford, Jamal (Basketball Player)
Chicago Bulls United Center
1901 W Madison St
Chicago, IL 60612-2459, USA

Crawford, Jerry (Athlete, Baseball Player)
111 9th St E
Saint Petersburg, FL 33715-2204, USA

Crawford, Jim (Athlete, Baseball Player)
4370 E Gemini Pl
Chandler, AZ 85249-5829, USA

Crawford, Joan (Athlete, Basketball Player)
4728 S Harvard Ave Apt 22
Tulsa, OK 74135-3045, USA

Crawford, Joe (Athlete, Baseball Player)
8395 SW County Road 239a
Lake Butler, FL 32054-8942, USA

Crawford, Johnny (Actor, Musician)
PO Box 1851
Los Angeles, CA 90078-1851, USA

Crawford, Keith (Athlete, Football Player)
RR 5 Box 5008
Palestine, TX 75801, USA

Crawford, Marc (Athlete, Coach, Hockey Player)
c/o Staff Member *Los Angeles Kings*
1111 S Figueroa St Ste 3100
Los Angeles, CA 90015-1333, USA

Crawford, Michael (Actor, Musician)
c/o Steve Levine *ICM Partners (LA)*
10250 Constellation Blvd Fl 7
Los Angeles, CA 90067-6207, USA

Crawford, Paxton (Athlete, Baseball Player)
PO Box 345
Plumerville, AR 72127-0345, USA

Crawford, Rachael (Actor)
c/o Staff Member *Coast to Coast Talent Group*
3350 Barham Blvd
Los Angeles, CA 90068-1404, USA

Crawford, Randy (Musician)
911 Park St SW
Grand Rapids, MI 49504-6241, USA

Crawford, Steve (Athlete, Baseball Player)
6122 E 480
Salina, OK 74365-2496, USA

Crawford, Vernon (Athlete, Football Player)
2001 Gemini St Apt 1305
Houston, TX 77058-2062, USA

Crawley, Pauline (Baseball Player)
68670 Raposa Rd
Cathedral City, CA 92234-8148, USA

Crawley, Sylvia (Athlete, Basketball Player)
125 S Pennsylvania St
Indianapolis, IN 46204-3610, USA

Cray, Robert (Musician)
Rosebud Agency
PO Box 170429
San Francisco, CA 94117-0429, USA

Craybas, Jill (Athlete, Tennis Player)
2603 Delaware St Apt C
Huntington Beach, CA 92648-2583, USA

Craymer, Judy (Producer)
Winter Garden Theater
1634 Broadway Ofc
New York, NY 10019-6894, USA

Crayton, Patrick (Athlete, Football Player)
2831 Merlins Rock Ln
Lewisville, TX 75056-5647, USA

Creamer, Paula (Athlete, Golfer)
4812 Alexandra Garden Ct
Windermere, FL 34786-8838, USA

Creamer, Roger W (Writer)
180 E Hartsdale Ave Apt 2E
Hartsdale, NY 10530-3540, USA

Creamer, Timothy J (Astronaut)
5103 Carefree Dr
League City, TX 77573-3195, USA

Creamer, Timothy J Lt Colonel (Astronaut)
5103 Carefree Dr
League City, TX 77573-3195, USA

Crear, Mark (Athlete, Olympic Athlete, Track Athlete)
Octagon
9420 Reseda Blvd Ste 600
Northridge, CA 91324-2932, USA

Crecion, Gabe (Athlete, Football Player)
4800 Coyote Wells Cir
Westlake Village, CA 91362-4712, USA

Crede, Joe (Athlete, Baseball Player)
PO Box 7
Westphalia, MO 65085-0007, USA

Creech, Bob (Athlete, Football Player)
1905 Windsor Dr
Mesquite, TX 75181-2358, USA

Creech, Sharon (Writer)
10 E 53rd St Frnt
New York, NY 10022-5244, USA

Creed (Music Group)
c/o Ken Fermaglich *The Agency Group (NYC)*
142 W 57th St Fl 6
New York, NY 10019-3300, USA

Creed, Clifford Ann (Athlete, Golfer)
240 N Rosemont Dr
Sulphur, LA 70665-7994, USA

Creek, Doug (Athlete, Baseball Player)
25385 Mount Sterling Ct
Mechanicsville, MD 20659-4922, USA

Creel, Gavin (Actor)
c/o Amy Brownstein *PRStudio USA*
630 9th Ave Ste 209
New York, NY 10036-4752, USA

Creel, Keith (Athlete, Baseball Player)
527 Trail Ridge Dr
Duncanville, TX 75116-2433, USA

Creel, Monica (Actor)
c/o Mike Eisenstadt *Amsel, Eisenstadt &
Frazier Talent Agency (AEF)*
5055 Wilshire Blvd Ste 860
Los Angeles, CA 90036-6108, USA

Cregar, Bill (Athlete, Football Player)
22 Locust Ct
Spring Lake, NJ 07762-2109, USA

Creighton, Adam (Athlete, Hockey Player)
Boston Bruins
100 Legends Way Ste 250
Scouting Dept
Boston, MA 02114-1389, USA

creighton, fred
8151 Stallion Way
Sacramento, CA 95830-9334

Creighton, Jim (Athlete, Basketball Player)
5297 S Geneva St
Englewood, CO 80111-6210, USA

Creighton, John O (Astronaut)
2111 SW 174th St
Burien, WA 98166-3259, USA

Creighton, John O Captain (Astronaut)
2111 SW 174th St
Burien, WA 98166-3259, USA

Creighton Sr, Dave (Athlete, Hockey
Player)
5202 Spectacular Bid Dr
Wesley Chapel, FL 33544-1576, USA

Cremins, Bobby (Coach)
150 Bobby John Rd
Atlanta, GA 30332-0001, USA

Crennel, Carl (Athlete, Football Player)
204 Hawthorne Sq
Oakdale, PA 15071-1060, USA

Crennel, Romeo (Athlete, Football Coach,
Football Player)
80 Cayman Pl
Palm Beach Gardens, FL 33418-8096,
USA

Crenshaw, Ander (Congressman,
Politician)
440 Cannon Hob
Washington, DC 20515-1504, USA

Crenshaw, Ben (Athlete, Golfer)
PO Box 50568
Austin, TX 78763-0568, USA

Crenshaw, Marshall (Musician)
c/o Staff Member *MCT Management*
104 W 29th St Rm 1101
New York, NY 10001-5310, USA

Crenshaw, Willis (Athlete, Football Player)
22 Carly Rd
Woodstock, NY 12498-2524, USA

Creole, Kid (Musician)
Ron Rainey Mgmt
315 S Beverly Dr Ste 407
Beverly Hills, CA 90212-4301, USA

Creskoff, Rebecca (Actor)
c/o Steven Levy *Framework Entertainment
(LA)*
9057 Nemo St Ste C
West Hollywood, CA 90069-5511, USA

Crespino, Robert (Athlete, Football Player)
109 Heatherdown Rd
Decatur, GA 30030-3817, USA

Crespo, Elvis (Musician)
c/o Staff Member *Sony Music Miami*
605 Lincoln Rd Ste 700
Miami Beach, FL 33139-2901, USA

Crespo, Felipe (Athlete, Baseball Player)
C2 Calle 6
Caguas, PR 00725-2019, USA

Cresse, Mark (Athlete, Baseball Player)
3222 Clay St
Newport Beach, CA 92663-4207, USA

Cressend, Jack (Athlete, Baseball Player)
723 Libby Ln
Mandeville, LA 70471-2879, USA

cressman, glen
678 E J St
Chula Vista, CA 91910-6541

Cressy, Jr., Dale (Race Car Driver)
1336 Paralllount Pkwy
Batavia, IL 60510, USA

Creswell, Smiley (Athlete, Football Player)
1 Academy Way
Monroe, WA 98272-2006, USA

Crevalle, Laura
PO Box 557
Old Orchard Beach, ME 04064-0557

Crew-Cuts, The
29 Cedar St
Cresskill, NJ 07626-2508

Crewdson, John M (Journalist)
435 N Michigan Ave Fl 2
Chicago, IL 60611-4067, USA

Crews, Albert (Astronaut)
444 SIlja Terway Dr
Satellite Beach, FL 32937, USA

Crews, Gina (Reality Star)
10211 W State Road 235
Alachua, FL 32615-4947, USA

Crews, Terry (Actor)
2935 Lindaloa Ln
Pasadena, CA 91107-1123, USA

Crha, Jiri (Athlete, Hockey Player)
8023 Laurel Ridge Ct
Delray Beach, FL 33446-9537, USA

Crha, Jiri (Athlete, Hockey Player)
16390 Braeburn Ridge Trl
Delray Beach, FL 33446-9508, USA

Crialese, Emanuele (Director)
c/o Staff Member *William Morris
Endeavor (LA)*
9601 Wilshire Blvd
Beverly Hills, CA 90210-5213, USA

Cribbs, Joe S (Athlete, Football Player)
5333 Creekside Loop
Hoover, AL 35244-3985, USA

Cribbs, Joshua (Athlete, Football Player)
1938 Gault St
Columbus, OH 43205-1648, USA

Crichton, Scott (Athlete, Football Player)
c/o Doug Hendrickson *Octagon Football*
832 Sansome St Fl 1
San Francisco, CA 94111-1558, USA

Crick, Jared (Athlete, Football Player)
c/o David Dunn *Athletes First, LLC*
23091 Mill Creek Dr
Laguna Hills, CA 92653-1258, USA

Cricketts, The
3322 W End Ave # 520
Nashville, TN 37203-1031

Crider, Melissa (Missy) (Actor)
Paradigm Agency
10100 Santa Monica Blvd Ste 2500
Los Angeles, CA 90067-4116, USA

Crier, Catherine (Correspondent,
Television Host)
Catherine Crier Live
2001 Junipero Serra Blvd Ste 550
Courtroom Television Network
Daly City, CA 94014-3889, USA

Crier, Catherine (Journalist)
190 Marietta St NW Ste 280
Atlanta, GA 30303-2766, USA

Crim, Chuck (Athlete, Baseball Player)
Chattanooga Lookouts
PO Box 11002
Attn: Coaching Staff
Chattanooga, TN 37401-2002, USA

Crim, Chuck (Athlete, Baseball Player)
50039 Golden Horse Dr
Oakhurst, CA 93644-9497, USA

Crimian, Jack (Athlete, Baseball Player)
3012 Green St
Claymont, DE 19703-2026, USA

Cripe, Dave (Athlete, Baseball Player)
1835 Montara Way
San Jacinto, CA 92583-5832, USA

Crippen, Robert L (Astronaut)
781 Harbour Isle Pl
West Palm Beach, FL 33410-4408, USA

Crippen, Robert L Captain (Astronaut)
781 Harbour Isle Pi
Palm Beach Gardens, FL 33410, USA

Criqui, Don (Sportscaster)
CBS-TV
51 W 52nd St
Sports Dept
New York, NY 10019-6119, USA

Criscione, Dave (Athlete, Baseball Player)
87 Hamlet St
Fredonia, NY 14063-2143, USA

Crisman, Joel (Athlete, Football Player)
10200 Park Meadows Dr Unit 1416
Lone Tree, CO 80124-5465, USA

Crisostomo, Manny (Journalist,
Photographer)
Pacific Daily News
PO Box Dn
Hagatna, GU 96932-7643, USA

Crisp, Coco (Athlete, Baseball Player)
15 Evening Star Dr
Rancho Mirage, CA 92270-3463, USA

crisp, terry (Athlete, Hockey Player)
Nashville Predators
501 Broadway
Nashville, TN 37203-3980

Crisp, Terry A (Athlete, Coach, Hockey
Player)
805 Cherry Laurel Ct
Nashville, TN 37215-6173, USA

Crispin, Anne C (Writer)
175 5th Ave
Tom Doherty Associates, Llc
New York, NY 10010-7703, USA

Criss, Charles (Athlete, Basketball Player)
4310 Melanie Ln
Atlanta, GA 30349-2849, USA

Criss, Darren (Actor, Musician)
1915 N Normandie Ave
Los Angeles, CA 90027-1732, USA

Criss, Peter (Musician)
277 Lakeside Ave
Colts Neck, NJ 07722-1522, USA

Crist, Charlie (Attorney)
Charlie Crist for Governor
PO Box 311
Tallahassee, FL 32302-0311, USA

Crist, Chuck (Athlete, Football Player)
PO Box 369
Greenhurst, NY 14742-0369, USA

Cristal, Linda (Actor)
9129 Hazen Dr
Beverly Hills, CA 90210-1825, USA

Cristofer, Michael (Director, Writer)
c/o Geyer Kosinski *Media Talent Group*
9200 W Sunset Blvd Ste 550
West Hollywood, CA 90069-3611, USA

Cristofer, Michael (Writer)
9830 Wilshire Blvd
Beverly Hills, CA 90212-1804, USA

Criswell, Jeff (Athlete, Football Player)
1101 Walnut St
Kansas City, MO 64106-2110, USA

Criswell, Ray
2216 Jones Rd
Jacksonville, FL 32220-1210, USA

Critchfield, Russell (Athlete, Basketball
Player)
1927 Oak Cir
Yountville, CA 94599-1362, USA

Crite, Winston (Athlete, Basketball Player)
8812 Heely Ct
Bakersfield, CA 93311-1923, USA

Critelli, Michael (Business Person)
Pitney Bowes Inc
1 Elmcroft Rd # 807
Stamford, CT 06926-0700, USA

Criter, Ken (Athlete, Football Player)
PO Box 441343
Aurora, CO 80044-1343, USA

Crittenden, Ray (Athlete, Football Player)
8915 Garden Gate Dr
Fairfax, VA 22031-1475, USA

Crivello, Anthony (Actor)
c/o Neil Bagg *Don Buchwald &
Associates (LA)*
6500 Wilshire Blvd Ste 2200
Los Angeles, CA 90048-4942, USA

Croce, A J
1027 Meade Ave
San Diego, CA 92116-1038, USA

Croce, Pat (Basketball Player, Business
Person, Sportscaster)
c/o Staff Member *William Morris
Endeavor (LA)*
9601 Wilshire Blvd
Beverly Hills, CA 90210-5213, USA

Crocicchia, James (Athlete, Football
Player)
11 Lanesboro Rd
Ladera Ranch, CA 92694-0712, USA

Crocicchia, Jim (Athlete, Football Player)
22 Daisy St
Ladera Ranch, CA 92694-0709, USA

Crocker, Chris (Actor, Reality Star)
44 Blue Productions
4040 Vineland Ave Ste 105
Studio City, CA 91604-3350, USA

Crocker, Dillard (Athlete, Basketball Player)
5601 Holiday Park Blvd
North Port, FL 34287-2615, USA

Crocker, Erin (Race Car Driver)
Evernham Motors
320 Aviation Dr
Statesville, NC 28677-2509, USA

Crocker, Ian (Athlete, Olympic Athlete, Swimmer)
8901 Ovalla Dr
Austin, TX 78749-5100

Crocker, Mary Lou (Athlete, Golfer)
1403 Sutton Dr
Carrollton, TX 75006-2943, USA

Crockett, Bobby (Athlete, Football Player)
PO Box 26
Harriet, AR 72639-0026, USA

Crockett, Gibson (Cartoonist)
4713 Great Oak Rd
Rockville, MD 20853-1607, USA

Crockett, Ivory (Athlete, Track Athlete)
812 N Elm Ave
Saint Louis, MO 63119-1721, USA

Crockett, Monte (Athlete, Football Player)
2696 Halleck Dr
Columbus, OH 43209-3220, USA

Crockett, Ray (Athlete, Football Player)
361 S White Chapel Blvd
Southlake, TX 76092-7312, USA

Crockett, Willis (Athlete, Football Player)
493 Bojo Ella Dr
Douglas, GA 31533-0607, USA

Crockett, Zack (Athlete, Football Player)
6136 NW 120th Ter
Coral Springs, FL 33076-1913, USA

Croel, Mike (Athlete, Football Player)
8305 Lookout Mountain Ave
Los Angeles, CA 90046-1548, USA

Croft, Don (Athlete, Football Player)
511 Larry Dr
Irving, TX 75060-2847, USA

Croftcheck, Don (Athlete, Football Player)
120 Mine St
Allison, PA 15413, USA

Crofts, Dash (Musician, Songwriter, Writer)
Nationwide Entertainment
2756 N Green Valley Pkwy
Henderson, NV 89014-2120, USA

Cromartie, Antonio (Athlete, Football Player)
c/o Ben Dogra *CAA (St. Louis)*
222 S Central Ave Ste 1008
Saint Louis, MO 63105-3509, USA

Cromartie, Warren (Athlete, Baseball Player)
20450 NW 2nd Ave # Waxy
Attn: Talkin' Hardball
Miami, FL 33169-2505, USA

Crombie, Robert B (Astronaut)
20632 Queens Park Ln
Huntington Beach, CA 92646-6018, USA

Cromer, D T (Athlete, Baseball Player)
134 Ridge Top Rd
Lexington, SC 29072-7130, USA

Cromer, Tripp (Athlete, Baseball Player)
32 W Tombee Ln
Columbia, SC 29209-0844, USA

Cromwell, James (Actor)
40452 Via Amapola
Murrieta, CA 92562-7708, USA

Cromwell, Nolan (Athlete, Coach, Football Coach, Football Player)
2624 140th Ave NE
Bellevue, WA 98005-1824, USA

Cron, Chris (Athlete, Baseball Player)
9705 E Villa Park St
Sun Lakes, AZ 85248-7346, USA

Cron, Chris (Athlete, Baseball Player)
Erie Sea Wolves 110 E l0th St
Attn: Managers Office
Erie, PA 16501, USA

Cronan, Pete (Athlete, Football Player)
125 Riverside St
Watertown, MA 02472-2713, USA

Crone, Ray (Athlete, Baseball Player)
508 Panorama
Waxahachie, TX 75165-5919, USA

Cronenberg, David (Actor)
c/o Renee Tab *Sentient*
881 Alma Real Dr
317
Pacific Palisades, CA 90272-3731, USA

Cronenweth, Regina
5410 Wilshire Blvd # 227
Los Angeles, CA 90036-4216

Cronin, Eugene (Athlete, Football Player)
2445 37th Ave
Sacramento, CA 95822-3613, USA

Cronin, Kevin (Musician)
1547 Pathfinder Ave
Westlake Village, CA 91362-5299, USA

Cronin, Mark (Producer)
1015 Oak Grove Ave
San Marino, CA 91108-1025, USA

Cronin, Shawn (Athlete, Hockey Player)
4163 SE Oakland St
Stuart, FL 34997-5415, USA

Cronkite, Kathy (Actor)
PO Box 5261
Austin, TX 78763-5261, USA

Cronyn, Christopher (Producer)
c/o Staff Member *Lichter Grossman Nichols Adler & Goodman*
9200 W Sunset Blvd Ste 1200
West Hollywood, CA 90069-3607, USA

Cronyn, Susan Cooper (Producer, Writer)
c/o Ron Bernstein *ICM Partners (LA)*
10250 Constellation Blvd Fl 7
Los Angeles, CA 90067-6207, USA

Crook, Edward Jr (Boxer)
4512 Moline Ave
Columbus, GA 31907-6625, USA

Crook, Lorianne (Musician)
1111 Wilson Pike
Brentwood, TN 37027-6736, USA

Crook & Chase
3201 Dickerson Pike
Nashville, TN 37207-2905

Crooke, Edward A (Business Person)
Constellation Energy Group
39 W Lexington St
Baltimore, MD 21201-3910, USA

Croom, Corey (Athlete, Football Player)
1423 Carr St
Sandusky, OH 44870-3108, USA

Croom, Sylvester (Athlete, Coach, Football Player)
3909 12th St NE
Tuscaloosa, AL 35404-2004, USA

Crooms, Chris (Athlete, Football Player)
23 Valera Ridge Dr
Spring, TX 77389-5150, USA

Crooms, Chris (Athlete, Football Player)
1522 Beaumont Rd
Baytown, TX 77520-3104, USA

Cropper, Marshall (Athlete, Football Player)
2932 Fort Baker Dr SE
Washington, DC 20020-7222, USA

Cropper, Steve (Musician)
819 Tyne Blvd
Nashville, TN 37220-1504, USA

Crosby, Bobby (Athlete, Baseball Player)
11463 Anticost Way
Cypress, CA 90630-5429, USA

Crosby, Bubba (Athlete, Baseball Player)
5100 Palmetto St
Bellaire, TX 77401-3332, USA

Crosby, Caitlin (Musician)
c/o Gerry Cagle *Crysis Management*
8424 Santa Monica Blvd
West Hollywood, CA 90069-6233, USA

Crosby, Cathy Lee (Actor)
c/o Michael Mann *Michael Mann Management*
18324 Clark St Unit 110
Tarzana, CA 91356-3512, USA

Crosby, Cleveland (Athlete, Football Player)
2703 Sandal Walk
Pearland, TX 77584-3365, USA

Crosby, David (Musician)
1876 Sky Dr
Santa Ynez, CA 93460-9500, USA

Crosby, Denise (Actor, Model)
935 Embury St
Pacific Palisades, CA 90272-3811, USA

Crosby, Ed (Athlete, Baseball Player)
11463 Anticost Way
Cypress, CA 90630-5429, USA

Crosby, Elaine (Athlete, Golfer)
2580 Meadowbrook Ln
Jackson, MI 49201-7702, USA

Crosby, Kathryn
508 W Third St
Carson City, NV 89703-4242

Crosby, Kathryn Grant (Actor)
508 W Third St
Carson City, NV 89703-4242, USA

Crosby, Ken (Athlete, Baseball Player)
PO Box 680306
Park City, UT 84068-0306, USA

Crosby, Lucinda (Actor)
4942 Vineland Ave Ste 200
North Hollywood, CA 91601-5646, USA

Crosby, Mark
3500 W Olive Ave Ste 1400
Burbank, CA 91505-5512

Crosby, Mary
3500 W Olive Ave Ste 1400
Burbank, CA 91505-5512

Crosby, Mason (Athlete, Football Player)
2911 Moose Creek Trl
Suamico, WI 54313-3251, USA

Crosby, Norm (Actor, Comedian)
c/o Staff Member *William Morris Endeavor (LA)*
9601 Wilshire Blvd
Beverly Hills, CA 90210-5213, USA

Crosby, Phil (Athlete, Football Player)
14614 Waterside Dr
Charlotte, NC 28278-7355, USA

Crosby, Sidney (Athlete, Hockey Player)
c/o Staff Member *Pittsburgh Penguins*
1001 5th Ave
Pittsburgh, PA 15219-6201, USA

Crosby, Steve (Athlete, Coach, Football Coach, Football Player)
Vanderbilt University
2201 W End Ave
Attn: Football Coaching Staff
Nashville, TN 37235-0001, USA

Crosby, Steve (Athlete, Football Player)
PO Box 609609
San Diego, CA 92160-9609, USA

Croshere, Austin (Athlete, Basketball Player)
21766 Azurelee Dr
Malibu, CA 90265-3401, USA

Cross, Ben (Actor)
c/o Jeff Goldberg *Jeff Goldberg Management*
817 Monte Leon Dr
Beverly Hills, CA 90210-2629, USA

Cross, Billy (Athlete, Football Player)
PO Box 103
Canadian, TX 79014-0103, USA

Cross, Burton (Politician)
8 Lonsdale Rd
Farmingdale, ME 04344, USA

Cross, Christopher (Musician, Songwriter)
1708 W 29th St
Austin, TX 78703-1806, USA

Cross, Cory (Athlete, Hockey Player)
2963 W Bayshore Ct
Tampa, FL 33611, USA

Cross, David (Actor, Comedian)
c/o Tim Sarkes *Brillstein Entertainment Partners (LA)*
9150 Wilshire Blvd Ste 350
Beverly Hills, CA 90212-3453, USA

Cross, Howard (Athlete, Football Player)
60 Mulberry Ct
Paramus, NJ 07652-1361, USA

Cross, Irv (Athlete, Football Player, Sportscaster)
2196 Marion Rd
Saint Paul, MN 55113-3824, USA

Cross, Iry
2196 Marion Rd
Saint Paul, MN 55113-3824, USA

Cross, Jeff (Athlete, Basketball Player)
6 Bow Center Rd Apt 2303
Bow, NH 03304-4234, USA

Cross, Jeff (Athlete, Football Player)
2715 Walkers Way
Weston, FL 33331-3021, USA

Cross, Jeff (Athlete, Football Player)
8045 SW 100th St
Miami, FL 33156-2523, USA

Cross, Joseph (Actor)
Innovative Artists
1505 10th St
Santa Monica, CA 90401-2805, USA

Cross, Justin (Athlete, Football Player)
PO Box 1967
New London, NH 03257-1967, USA

Cross, Kendall (Athlete, Olympic Athlete, Wrestler)
2209 Kings Pass
Rockwall, TX 75032-5921

Cross, Marcia (Actor)
870 5th Ave
Los Angeles, CA 90005-3522, USA

Cross, Randall L (Randy) (Athlete, Football Player, Sportscaster)
155 Travertine Trl
Alpharetta, GA 30022-5196, USA

Cross, Roger (Actor)
c/o Staff Member *SMS Talent*
8383 Wilshire Blvd Ste 230
Beverly Hills, CA 90211-2436, USA

Cross, Russell (Basketball Player)
Elmhurst College
190 S Prospect Ave
Athletic Dept
Elmhurst, IL 60126-3296, USA

Crossan, Dave (Athlete, Football Player)
3590 Round Bottom Rd
Cincinnati, OH 45244-3026, USA

Crosse, Liris (Actor, Model)
c/o Staff Member *Cinematic Management*
249 1/2 E 13th St
New York, NY 10003-5602, USA

Crossley, Charlotte (Actor, Musician)
Stone Manners Agency
6500 Wilshire Blvd # 550
Los Angeles, CA 90048-4920, USA

Crossman, Doug (Athlete, Hockey Player)
PO Box 634
Somers Point, NJ 08244-0634, USA

Crosswhite, Leon (Athlete, Football Player)
1955 E 120th St Rear
Cleveland, OH 44106-1907, USA

Croston, Dave (Athlete, Football Player)
400 Homestead Ln
Sergeant Bluff, IA 51054-3512, USA

Croteau, Gary (Athlete, Hockey Player)
8380 E Hinsdale Ave
Centennial, CO 80112-1905, USA

Crotty, Jim (Athlete, Football Player)
215 S 195th St # 5
Des Moines, WA 98148-2137, USA

Crotty, John (Athlete, Basketball Player)
685 Destacada Ave
Miami, FL 33156-8001, USA

Crouch, Andrae (Musician, Songwriter)
c/o Staff Member *M.A.G./Universal Attractions*
15 W 36th St Fl 8
New York, NY 10018-7927, USA

Crouch, Eric (Athlete, Football Player, Heisman Trophy Winner)
19453 Walnut Cir
Omaha, NE 68130-3759, USA

Crouch, Jan (Religious Leader)
2442 Michelle Dr
Tustin, CA 92780-7015, USA

Crouch, Lindsay (Actor)
15115 1/2 W Sunset Blvd Ste A
Pacific Palisades, CA 90272-3751, USA

Crouch, Matthew (Producer)
3131 Tara
Costa Mesa, CA 92626-7302, USA

Crouch, Robbie (Race Car Driver)
106 Pierremount Ave
New Britain, CT 06053-2345, USA

Crouch, Roger K (Astronaut)
120 6th St NE Apt B
Washington, DC 20002-8307, USA

Crouch, Sandra (Musician, Songwriter, Writer)
Sparrow Communications Group
101 Winners Cir N
Brentwood, TN 37027-5352, USA

Crouch, William T (Bill) (Journalist, Photographer)
5660 Valley Oaks Ct
Placerville, CA 95667-9363, USA

Crouch, Zach (Athlete, Baseball Player)
9418 San Paulo Cir
Elk Grove, CA 95624-2126, USA

Croucher, Juan
45 Cayuse Ln
Rancho Palos Verdes, CA 90275-5155

Crouse, Lindsay (Actor)
28 Leonard St
Gloucester, MA 01930-1322, USA

Croushore, Rich (Athlete, Baseball Player)
3110 Bastogne Way
Benton, AR 72019-2943, USA

Croushore, Rick (Athlete, Baseball Player)
4001 Tanglewilde St Apt 101
Houston, TX 77063-5164, USA

Crouthamel, Jake (Athlete, Football Player)
3 Martin Ln
Hanover, NH 03755-3110, USA

Crow, Al (Athlete, Football Player)
6191 Occoquan Forest Dr
Manassas, VA 20112-3034, USA

Crow, Bill (Athlete, Basketball Player)
21300 River Rd # 15
Perris, CA 92570-8390, USA

Crow, Dean (Athlete, Baseball Player)
11507 Wickchester Ln
Houston, TX 77043-4521, USA

Crow, Don (Athlete, Baseball Player)
1023 E Lincoln Ave
Nampa, ID 83686-5321, USA

Crow, F Trammell (Business Person)
Trammell Crow Co
2100 McKinney Ave Ste 900
Trammell Crow Center
Dallas, TX 75201-6907, USA

Crow, Harian R (Business Person)
Trammell Crow Co
2100 McKinney Ave Ste 900
Trammell Crow Center
Dallas, TX 75201-6907, USA

Crow, John David (Athlete, Coach, Football Coach, Football Player, Heisman Trophy Winner)
5004 Augusta Cir
College Station, TX 77845-8983, USA

Crow, Lindon (Athlete, Football Player)
2869 Riachuelo
San Clemente, CA 92673-4050, USA

Crow, Mark (Athlete, Basketball Player)
501 W Bay St
Jacksonville, FL 32202-4428, USA

Crow, Rachel (Actor, Musician)
c/o Christian Carino *Creative Artists Agency (CAA-LA)*
2000 Avenue of the Stars Ste 100
Los Angeles, CA 90067-4705, USA

Crow, Sheryl (Musician, Songwriter)
1900 N Vista St
Los Angeles, CA 90046-2239, USA

Crow, Wayne (Athlete, Football Player)
16561 Fawn St
Truckee, CA 96161-3534, USA

Crowder, Bruce (Athlete, Hockey Player)
7 Kyle Dr
Nashua, NH 03062-4539, USA

Crowder, Channing (Athlete, Football Player)
8921 Southern Orchard Rd N
Davie, FL 33328-6986, USA

Crowder, Corey (Athlete, Basketball Player)
725 Ballard Bridge Rd
Carrollton, GA 30117-9104, USA

Crowder, Randy (Athlete, Football Player)
803 Strawberry Ln
Brandon, FL 33511-7533, USA

Crowe, Cameron (Director)
1016 Amalfi Dr
Pacific Palisades, CA 90272-4028, USA

Crowe, James (J.D.) (Musician)
JD Crowe Festival
201 S Lexington Ave Apt D
Wilmore, KY 40390-1200, USA

Crowe, Mia (Actor, Model)
Mia Crowe Official Fan Club
7336 Santa Monica Blvd # 633
West Hollywood, CA 90046-6616, USA

Crowe, Pat (Horse Racer)
202-100 Millside Dr
Milton, ON L9T 5E2, USA

Crowe, Phil (Athlete, Hockey Player)
1409 Pintail Ct
Windsor, CO 80550-6144, USA

Crowe, Tonya (Actor)
70 Sklar St Apt 1209
Ladera Ranch, CA 92694-0777, USA

Crowell, Angelo (Athlete, Football Player)
5309 Dockery Dr
Charlotte, NC 28209-3668, USA

Crowell, Craven H Jr (Government Official)
Tennessee Valley Authority
400 W Summit Hill Dr
Knoxville, TN 37902-1419, USA

Crowell, Germane (Athlete, Football Player)
195 Everidge Rd
Winston Salem, NC 27103-6326, USA

Crowell, Jim (Athlete, Baseball Player)
4003 Sleighbell Ln
Valparaiso, IN 46383-1943, USA

Crowell, Rodney (Musician)
1238 Saddle Springs Dr
Thompsons Station, TN 37179-5419, USA

Crowley, Ben (Actor)
c/o Staff Member *Kass Management*
501 Santa Monica Blvd Ste 604
Santa Monica, CA 90401-2467, USA

Crowley, Candy (Correspondent)
5709 Ridgefield Rd
Bethesda, MD 20816-1250, USA

Crowley, Joseph (Congressman, Politician)
2404 Rayburn Hob
Washington, DC 20515-3605, USA

Crowley, Kevin (Actor)
c/o Lorraine Berglund *Lorraine Berglund Management*
11537 Hesby St
North Hollywood, CA 91601-3618, USA

Crowley, Monica (Television Host)
c/o Staff Member *Fox News (NY)*
1211 Avenue of the Americas Lowr C1
New York, NY 10036-8705, USA

Crowley, Pat (Actor)
551 Perugia Way
Los Angeles, CA 90077-3708, USA

Crowley, Ted (Athlete, Hockey Player)
248 Seaward Bnd Apt 53-2
Teaticket, MA 02536-5843, USA

Crowley, Terry (Athlete, Baseball Player)
18405 Ensor Farm Ct
Parkton, MD 21120-9685, USA

Crowley, Terry (Athlete, Baseball Player)
333 W Camden St
Attn: Coaching Staff
Baltimore, MD 21201-2496, USA

Crown, Lester (Business Person)
Henry Crown & Co
222 N La Salle St Ste 2000
Chicago, IL 60601-1120

Crowton, Gary (Coach, Football Coach)
Brigham Young University
Athletic Dept
Provo, UT 84602, USA

Croyle, Brodie (Athlete, Football Player)
105 Apple Blossom Dr
Brandon, MS 39047-7443, USA

Croyle, Philip (Athlete, Football Player)
5883 Treetop Ct
San Jose, CA 95123-4346, USA

Crozier, Eric (Athlete, Baseball Player)
3142 Clermont Rd
Columbus, OH 43227-1833, USA

Crozier, Joseph R (Joe) (Athlete, Coach, Hockey Player)
299 Randwood Dr
Buffalo, NY 14221-1444, USA

Crudale, Mike (Athlete, Baseball Player)
2319 Tree Creek Pl
Danville, CA 94506-2065, USA

Crudup, Billy (Actor)
c/o Aleen Keshishian *Brillstein Entertainment Partners (LA)*
9150 Wilshire Blvd Ste 350
Beverly Hills, CA 90212-3453, USA

Cruikshank, Dave (Athlete, Olympic Athlete, Speed Skater)
1223 Aspen Ct
Delafield, WI 53018-1300, USA

Cruikshank, Lucas (Actor)
c/o Evan Weiss *The Collective*
8383 Wilshire Blvd Ste 1050
Beverly Hills, CA 90211-2415, USA

Cruikshank, Thomas H (Business Person)
5949 Sherry Ln Ste 1035
Dallas, TX 75225-6521, USA

Cruise, Earl (Horse Racer)
151 Liberty St Apt 16
Little Ferry, NJ 07643-1790, USA

Cruise, Jimmy (Horse Racer)
133 Golf Club Way
Longwood, FL 32779-4622, USA

Cruise, Tom (Actor, Director, Producer)
c/o Amanda Lundberg *42West (NYC)*
220 W 42nd St Fl 12
New York, NY 10036-7200, USA

Cruisie, Jennifer (Writer)
c/o *Argh Ink LLC*
285 5th Ave # 470
Brooklyn, NY 11215-2578, USA

Crum, E Denzel (Denny) (Athlete, Basketball Player, Coach)
6901 Routt Rd
Louisville, KY 40299-5243, USA

Crumb, Robert (Artist, Cartoonist)
c/o Staff Member *Fantagraphics Books*
7563 Lake City Way NE
Seattle, WA 98115-4218, USA

Crumley Jr, James R (Religious Leader)
108 Castle Church Rd
Chapin, SC 29036-7853, USA

Crump, Diane (Horse Racer)
PO Box 297
Linden, VA 22642-0297, USA

Crump, Dwayne (Athlete, Football Player)
35708 Marciel Ave
Madera, CA 93636-8414, USA

Crump, Harry (Athlete, Football Player)
9601 Collins Ave PH 201
Bal Harbour, FL 33154-2220, USA

Crumpler, Alge (Athlete, Football Player)
787 Blackfoot Trl
Suwanee, GA 30024-1753, USA

Crumpler, Carlester (Athlete, Football Player)
4355 River Gate Ln Unit B
Little River, SC 29566-6833, USA

Crusan, Doug (Athlete, Football Player)
6263 Hanover Ct
Fishers, IN 46038-1799, USA

Crutcher, Chris
3405 E Marion Ct
Spokane, WA 99223-7215

Crutcher, Lawrence M (Publisher)
Book-of-the-Month Club
Rockefeller Center
New York, NY 10020, USA

Crutchfield, Dwayne (Athlete, Football Player)
6936 Rebecca Dr
Niagara Falls, NY 14304-3053, USA

Cruz, Alexis (Actor)
c/o Staff Member *Abrams Artists Agency (LA)*
9200 W Sunset Blvd PH 11
West Hollywood, CA 90069-3601, USA

Cruz, Cirilio (Baseball Player)
St Louis Cardinals
E8 Calle H
Arroyo, PR 00714-2236, USA

Cruz, Deivi (Baseball Player)
Detroit Tigers
611 Woodward Ave
Detroit, MI 48226-3408, USA

Cruz, Hector (Athlete, Baseball Player)
1646 N Monticello Ave
Chicago, IL 60647-4719, USA

Cruz, Henry (Athlete, Baseball Player)
Los Angeles Dodgers
PO Box 70012
Fajardo, PR 00738-7012, USA

Cruz, Ivan (Athlete, Baseball Player)
3874 Bright Leaf Ct
Jacksonville, FL 32246-7660, USA

Cruz, Jacob (Athlete, Baseball Player)
1582 W Commerce Ave
Gilbert, AZ 85233-4103, USA

Cruz, Juan (Athlete, Baseball Player)
c/o Staff Member *Chicago Cubs*
1060 W Addison St
Wrigley Field
Chicago, IL 60613-4397, USA

Cruz, Julio (Athlete, Baseball Player)
12212 164th Ct NE
Redmond, WA 98052-2368, USA

Cruz, Mike (DJ)
c/o Staff Member *Diva Central Inc*
7510 W Sunset Blvd Ste 1445
Los Angeles, CA 90046-3408, USA

Cruz, Nelson (Athlete, Baseball Player)
2021 Stone Canyon Ct
Arlington, TX 76012-5762, USA

Cruz, Nicky (Religious Leader)
Nicky Cruz Outreach
PO Box 62010
Colorado Springs, CO 80962-2010, USA

Cruz, Penelope (Actor, Model)
c/o Leslee Dart *42West (NYC)*
220 W 42nd St Fl 12
New York, NY 10036-7200, USA

Cruz, Raymond (Actor)
8383 Wilshire Blvd # 954
Beverly Hills, CA 90211-2425

Cruz, Smith Martin (Writer)
Random House
1745 Broadway Frnt 3 # B1
New York, NY 10019-4343, USA

Cruz, Taio (Musician)
c/o Staff Member *Energon Entertainment*
276 5th Ave Rm 704
New York, NY 10001-4527, USA

Cruz, Tommy (Athlete, Baseball Player)
E8 Calle H
Arroyo, PR 00714-2236, USA

Cruz, Tommy (Athlete, Baseball Player)
12000 Stadium Rd
Attn Coaching Staff
Adelanto, CA 92301-3400, USA

Cruz, Valerie (Actor)
c/o Staff Member *Innovative Artists (LA)*
1505 10th St
Santa Monica, CA 90401-2805, USA

Cruz, Victor (Athlete, Football Player)
c/o Tom Condon *CAA (St. Louis)*
222 S Central Ave Ste 1008
Saint Louis, MO 63105-3509, USA

Cruz, Wilson
Latin Hollywood Films
153 San Vicente Blvd Apt 2G
Santa Monica, CA 90402-1507, USA

Cruz Jr, Jose (Athlete, Baseball Player)
8475 SW 53rd Ave
Miami, FL 33143-8407, USA

Cruz Sr, Jose D (Athlete, Baseball Player)
2309 Delta Bridge Dr
Pearland, TX 77584-1566, USA

Cryder, Robert (Athlete, Football Player)
17411 NE 129th St
Redmond, WA 98052-1323, USA

Crye, John B (Actor, Producer, Writer)
c/o Staff Member *Fewdio*
13348 Reedley St
Panorama City, CA 91402-4061, USA

Cryer, Gretchen (Actor, Songwriter, Writer)
885 W End Ave Apt 1A
New York, NY 10025-3512, USA

Cryer, Jon (Actor)
885 W End Ave Apt 1A
New York, NY 10025-3512, USA

Cryer, Suzanne (Actor)
c/o Chris Schmidt *Paradigm (LA)*
360 N Crescent Dr
North Bldg
Beverly Hills, CA 90210-4874, USA

Crystal, Billy (Actor, Comedian)
860 Chautauqua Blvd
Pacific Palisades, CA 90272-3801, USA

Crystals (Music Group)
27-L Ambiance Ct
Nanuet, NY 10954, USA

C. Scott, Robert (Congressman, Politician)
1201 Longworth Hob
Washington, DC 20515-0520, USA

Csokas, Martin (Actor)
c/o Sandra Chang *Anonymous Content (LA)*
3532 Hayden Ave
Culver City, CA 90232-2413, USA

Csokas, Marton (Actor)
c/o George Freeman *William Morris Endeavor (LA)*
9601 Wilshire Blvd
Beverly Hills, CA 90210-5213, USA

Csonka, Larry (Athlete, Football Player)
37256 Hunter Camp Rd
Lisbon, OH 44432-9464, USA

Csupo, Gabor (Animator, Director, Producer)
c/o Staff Member *Grand Allure Entertainment*
12835 Mulholland Dr
Beverly Hills, CA 90210-1247, USA

Ctvrtlik, Bob (Athlete, Olympic Athlete, Volleyball Player)
5525 E Seaside Walk Apt B
Long Beach, CA 90803-4427, USA

Cua, Rick (Musician)
1086 Rip Steele Rd
Columbia, TN 38401-7745, USA

Cuaron, Alfonso (Director)
c/o Staff Member *Esperanto Filmoj*
37 W 20th St
New York, NY 10011-3706, USA

Cuban, Mark (Business Person, Reality Star)
c/o Staff Member *Dallas Mavericks*
2909 Taylor St
Dallas, TX 75226-1909, USA

Cubbage, Mike (Athlete, Baseball Player, Coach)
3349 Carroll Creek Rd
Keswick, VA 22947-9156, USA

Cube, Ice (Actor, Director, Musician)
4615 Petit Ave
Encino, CA 91436-3215, USA

Cubillan, Darwin (Athlete, Baseball Player)
11505 Clumbet Ln
Lehigh Acres, FL 33971-3748, USA

Cubitt, David (Actor)
c/o Shelley Browning *Magnolia Entertainment (LA)*
9595 Wilshire Blvd Ste 601
Beverly Hills, CA 90212-2506, USA

Cuddy, Jim (Musician)
c/o Staff Member *The Agency Group (NYC)*
142 W 57th St Fl 6
New York, NY 10019-3300, USA

Cuddyer, Michael (Athlete, Baseball Player)
153 Greengable Way
Chesapeake, VA 23322-4274, USA

Cudi, Kid (Musician)
c/o Stephen (Steve) Levinson *Leverage Management*
3030 Pennsylvania Ave
Santa Monica, CA 90404-4112, USA

Cudlitz, Michael (Actor)
4221 Allott Ave
Sherman Oaks, CA 91423-4303, USA

Cuellar, Bobby (Athlete, Baseball Player)
1 Morrie Silver Way
Attn Coaching Staff
Rochester, NY 14608-1754, USA

Cuellar, Bobby (Athlete, Baseball Player)
705 E 6th St
Alice, TX 78332-4651, USA

Cueller, Henry (Congressman, Politician)
2463 Rayburn Hob
Washington, DC 20515-4315, USA

Cueto, Al (Athlete, Basketball Player)
5714 Riviera Dr
Coral Gables, FL 33146-2751, USA

Culbertson, FrankL Captain (Astronaut)
15500 Meherrin Dr
Centreville, VA 20120-3733, USA

Culbertson Jr, Frank L (Astronaut)
15500 Meherrin Dr
Centreville, VA 20120-3733, USA

Culbreath, Jim (Athlete, Football Player)
212 Elder Ave
Lansdowne, PA 19050-3028, USA

Culbreath, Joshua (Josh) (Athlete, Track Athlete)
Central State University
Athletic Dept
Wilberforce, OH 45384, USA

Culbreth, Feildin (Athlete, Baseball Player)
224 Claiborne Ct
Spartanburg, SC 29301-5345, USA

Culhane, Jim (Athlete, Hockey Player)
Western Michigan University
8547 Hathaway Rd
Kalamazoo, MI 49009-6999, USA

Culkin, Kieran (Actor)
c/o Emily Gerson Saines *Brookside Artists Management (NY)*
250 W 57th St Ste 2303
New York, NY 10107-2399, USA

Culkin, Macaulay (Actor)
704 Broadway Fl 8
New York, NY 10003-9504, USA

Culkin, Rory (Actor)
c/o Emily Gerson Saines *Brookside Artists Management (NY)*
250 W 57th St Ste 2303
New York, NY 10107-2399, USA

Cullars, Willie (Athlete, Football Player)
1034 Garfield Ave
Kansas City, KS 66104, USA

Cullen, Betsy (Athlete, Golfer)
4144 Greystone Way Apt 707
Sugar Land, TX 77479-3014, USA

Cullen, Brett (Actor)
2229 Glyndon Ave
Venice, CA 90291-4042, USA

Cullen, Jack (Athlete, Baseball Player)
164 Alexander Ave
Nutley, NJ 07110-1002, USA

Cullen, John (Athlete, Hockey Player)
1002 Legacy Hills Dr
McDonough, GA 30253-8824, USA

Cullen, Kimberly (Actor)
8916 Ashcroft Ave
West Hollywood, CA 90048-2404, USA

Cullen, Matt (Athlete, Hockey Player)
5109 2nd St E
West Fargo, ND 58078-8211, USA

Cullen, Sean M
10100 Santa Monica Blvd Ste 2500
Los Angeles, CA 90067-4116, USA

Cullen, Tim (Athlete, Baseball Player)
159 W G St
Benicia, CA 94510-3114, USA

Cullens, E Van (Business Person)
Harris Corp
1025 W Nasa Blvd
Melbourne, FL 32919-0001, USA

Culligan, Joe (Writer)
Research Investigative Services
650 NE 126th St
North Miami, FL 33161-4821, USA

Cullimore, Jassen (Athlete, Hockey Player)
8610 Dolce Vita Ln
Odessa, FL 33556-1938, USA

Cullity, Dave (Athlete, Football Player)
3015 Birchwood Ct
Fullerton, CA 92835-4317, USA

Cullocks, Josh (Athlete, Football Player)
5511 Eastover Dr S
New Orleans, LA 70128-3658, USA

Cullum, Jamie (Musician)
c/o Martin Kirkup *Direct Management Group*
8332 Melrose Ave
West Hollywood, CA 90069-5420, USA

Cullum, Kaitlin (Actor)
c/o Norma Robbins *Abrams Artists Agency (LA)*
9200 W Sunset Blvd PH 11
West Hollywood, CA 90069-3601, USA

Cullum, Kimberly (Actor)
8916 Ashcroft Ave
West Hollywood, CA 90048-2404

Culos, Chris (Musician)
900 20th Ave S Apt 815
Nashville, TN 37212-2239, USA

Culp, Curley (Athlete, Football Player)
16811 Gravesend Rd
Pflugerville, TX 78660-1830, USA

Culp, Ray (Athlete, Baseball Player)
7400 Waterline Rd
Austin, TX 78731-2055, USA

Culp, Steven (Actor)
1680 Las Lunas St
Pasadena, CA 91106-1303, USA

Culpepper, Brad (Athlete, Football Player)
60 Bahama Cir
Tampa, FL 33606-3318, USA

Culpepper, Daunte (Athlete, Football Player)
16730 Berkshire Ct
Southwest Ranches, FL 33331-1331, USA

Culpepper, Ed (Athlete, Football Player)
811 Bluewater Dr
Sun City Center, FL 33573-6245, USA

Culpepper, Robert E (Athlete, Football Player)
1535 45th Ave E
Ellenton, FL 34222-2643, USA

Cult, The
c/o Staff Member *Immortal Entertainment*
11965 Venice Blvd Ste 204
Los Angeles, CA 90066-3954, USA

Cult Jam
PO Box 30284
Brooklyn, NY 11203-0284

Culver, George (Athlete, Baseball Player)
5409 Rustic Canyon St
Bakersfield, CA 93306-7315, USA

Culver, John C (Ex-Senator, Politician)
5409 Spangler Ave
Bethesda, MD 20816-1847, USA

Culver, Michael (Actor)
77 Beak St
London, EN W1F 9

Culver, Molly (Actor)
29732 Arroyo Oak Ln
Castaic, CA 91384-3214, USA

Cumberland, John (Athlete, Baseball Player)
1771 Muddy Creek Rd
Dandridge, TN 37725-6674, USA

Cumberland Gap
159 Madison Ave Apt 2G
New York, NY 10016-5434

Cumby, George E (Athlete, Football Player)
12090 Cross Fence Trl
Tyler, TX 75706-4239, USA

Cumming, Alan (Actor, Musician)
c/o Danielle Thomas *Untitled Entertainment (LA)*
350 S Beverly Dr Ste 200
Beverly Hills, CA 90212-4819, USA

Cummings, Burton (Musician, Songwriter)
3758 Woodcliff Rd
Sherman Oaks, CA 91403-5050, USA

Cummings, Dave
4130 La Village Dr # 107
La Jolla, CA 92037

Cummings, Ed (Athlete, Football Player)
237 Schearbrook Ln
Stevensville, MT 59870-6405, USA

Cummings, Erin (Actor)
c/o Nate Bryson *Paradigm (LA)*
360 N Crescent Dr
North Bldg
Beverly Hills, CA 90210-4874, USA

Cummings, Joe (Athlete, Football Player)
4034 Oshaughnessy St
Missoula, MT 59808-5659, USA

Cummings, John (Athlete, Baseball Player)
21 Paseo Park
Laguna Niguel, CA 92677-5317, USA

Cummings, Midre (Athlete, Baseball Player)
17741 Jamestown Way
Lutz, FL 33558-7709, USA

Cummings, Quinn (Actor)
3870 Glenfeliz Blvd
Los Angeles, CA 90039-1742, USA

Cummings, Steve (Athlete, Baseball Player)
11010 Sagecrest Ln
Houston, TX 77089-3904, USA

Cummings, Terry (Athlete, Basketball Player)
12820 W Golden Ln
San Antonio, TX 78249-2231, USA

Cummings, Terry (Athlete, Basketball Player)
2400 Parkland Dr NE Unit 108
Atlanta, GA 30324-3592, USA

Cummings, Whitney (Actor)
3633 Bellfield Way
Studio City, CA 91604-3906, USA

Cummins, Gregory Scott (Actor)
Schiowitz/Clay/Rose
1680 Vine St Ste 1016
Los Angeles, CA 90028-8800, USA

Cummins, Jim (Athlete, Hockey Player)
25640 Kinyon St
Taylor, MI 48180-3281, USA

Cumpsty, Michael (Actor)
c/o Staff Member *Innovative Artists (LA)*
1505 10th St
Santa Monica, CA 90401-2805, USA

Cundey, Dean R (Cinematographer)
250 S De Lacey Ave Unit 207
Pasadena, CA 91105-4136, USA

Cundieff, Rusty (Actor)
c/o Norman Aladjem *Levity Entertainment Group (LEG)*
6701 Center Dr W Fl 11
Los Angeles, CA 90045-1535, USA

Cundiff, Billy (Athlete, Football Player)
3426 E Pyrenees Pass
Phoenix, AZ 85018-1553, USA

Cunnane, Will (Athlete, Baseball Player)
10 Calico Pl
Congers, NY 10920-1841, USA

Cunneyworth, Randy (Athlete, Coach, Hockey Player)
c/o Staff Member *Rochester Americans*
1 War Memorial Sq Ste 228
Rochester, NY 14614-2192, USA

Cunniff, Jill (Musician)
Metropolitan Entertainment
2 Penn Plz # 2600
New York, NY 10121-0101, USA

Cunningham, Bennie L (Athlete, Football Player)
PO Box 1086
Seneca, SC 29679-1086, USA

Cunningham, Bill (Musician)
Horizon Mgmt
PO Box 8770
Endwell, NY 13762-8770, USA

Cunningham, Bill (Radio Personality)
8044 Montgomery Rd Ste 650
Cincinnati, OH 45236-2959, USA

Cunningham, Brian (Race Car Driver)
PTG Racing
441 Victory Rd
Winchester, VA 22602-4567, USA

Cunningham, Carl (Athlete, Football Player)
4471 Saddleworth Cir
Orlando, FL 32826-4123, USA

Cunningham, Colin (Actor)
c/o Jordyn Palos *Persona PR (LA)*
8840 Wilshire Blvd Ste 212
Beverly Hills, CA 90211-2606, USA

Cunningham, Dick (Athlete, Basketball Player)
5349 Desoto Pkwy
Sarasota, FL 34234-3076, USA

Cunningham, Dick (Athlete, Football Player)
100 Rosewood Ct
Peachtree City, GA 30269-2237, USA

Cunningham, Doug (Athlete, Football Player)
5060 Harling Pi
Jackson, MS 39211, USA

Cunningham, Ed (Athlete, Football Player)
7416 Alverstone Ave
Los Angeles, CA 90045-1310, USA

Cunningham, Gunther (Athlete, Coach, Football Coach, Football Player)
2250 E Hammond Lake Dr
Bloomfield Hills, MI 48302-0131, USA

Cunningham, Jay (Athlete, Football Player)
13030 Idle Water Ln
Houston, TX 77044-1208, USA

Cunningham, Jeffrey M (Publisher)
Forbes Magazine
60 5th Ave Frnt 1
New York, NY 10011-8868, USA

Cunningham, Joe (Athlete, Baseball Player)
RR 1 Box 80A
Koshkonong, MO 65692, USA

Cunningham, Katherine (Actor)
c/o Jean-Pierre (JP) Henraux *Henraux Management*
Prefers to be contacted by telephone
CA, USA

Cunningham, Kristan (Actor, Television Host)
c/o Cat Josell *Synergy Management*
11271 Ventura Blvd Ste 495
Studio City, CA 91604-3136, USA

Cunningham, Leon (Athlete, Football Player)
5484 Brookwood Dr SW
Mableton, GA 30126-2028, USA

Cunningham, Liam (Actor)
c/o Chris Huvane *Management 360*
9111 Wilshire Blvd
Beverly Hills, CA 90210-5508, USA

Cunningham, Michael (Writer)
Farrar Straus Giroux
19 Union Sq W
New York, NY 10003-3304, USA

Cunningham, Randall (Athlete, Football Player)
9367 Jeremy Blaine Ct
Las Vegas, NV 89139-8358, USA

Cunningham, Richard (Athlete, Football Player)
100 Rosewood Ct
Peachtree City, GA 30269-2237, USA

Cunningham, Richie (Athlete, Football Player)
610 Cheyenne Dr
Houma, LA 70360-6060, USA

Cunningham, Sam (Athlete, Football Player)
9316 S 4th Ave # 5
Inglewood, CA 90305-3002, USA

Cunningham, Sean (Director, Producer)
4420 Hayvenhurst Ave
Encino, CA 91436-3248, USA

Cunningham, T J (Athlete, Football Player)
11640 E Walsh Pl
Aurora, CO 80012-3264, USA

Cunningham, Walter (Astronaut)
AVD
PO Box 604
Glenn Dale, MD 20769-0604, USA

Cunningham, Walter Colonel (Astronaut)
1707 Post Oak Blvd Ste 263
Houston, 77 TX, USA

Cunningham, William J (Billy) (Athlete, Basketball Player, Coach)
Cunningham's Court Restaurant
31 Front St # 33
Conshohocken, PA 19428-2867, USA

Cuoco, Kaley (Actor)
19011 Ashurst Ln
Tarzana, CA 91356-5825, USA

Cuomo, Andrew (Politician)
717 5th Ave
New York, NY 10022-8101, USA

Cuomo, Andrew M (Governor, Politician)
Office of the Governor
NYS State Capitol Building
Albany, NY 12224, USA

Cuomo, Christopher (Chris) (Correspondent)
c/o Staff Member *Primetime*
147 Columbus Ave
New York, NY 10023-6503, USA

Cuomo, Mario (Ex-Governor)
Willkie, Farr & Gallagher LLP
787 7th Ave Fl 2
New York, NY 10019-6099, USA

Cuomo, Mario (Politician)
50 Sutton Pl S Apt 11G
New York, NY 10022-4130, USA

Cuomo, Rivers (Musician)
1027 Chelsea Ave
Santa Monica, CA 90403-4611, USA

Cuozzo, Gary S (Athlete, Football Player)
2201 River Rd Apt 2401
Point Pleasant Boro, NJ 08742-2283, USA

Curatola, Vincent (Actor)
26 Possum Trl
Upper Saddle River, NJ 07458-1825, USA

Curb, Mike
3907 W Alameda Ave Ste 200
Burbank, CA 91505-4359

Curbeam, Robert L Cdr (Astronaut)
13727 Briaridge Ct
Highland, MD 20777-9539, USA

Curbeam, Robert L Jr (Astronaut)
13727 Briaridge Ct
Highland, MD 20777-9539, USA

Curci, Francis (Athlete, Football Player)
14707 Croydon Pl
Tampa, FL 33618-2160, USA

Curcillo, Anthony (Athlete, Football Player)
23887 Corte Emerado
Murrieta, CA 92562-3539, USA

Curcio, Michael (Athlete, Football Player)
165 Lincoln Ave
Hightstown, NJ 08520-4117, USA

Curd, Francis (Athlete, Football Player)
14707 Croydon Pl
Tampa, FL 33618-2160, USA

Cure, Robert (Athlete, Football Player)
145 Main St
Los Altos, CA 94022-2912, USA

Cure, The (Music Group)
c/o Rick Roskin *Creative Artists Agency (CAA-LA)*
2000 Avenue of the Stars Ste 100
Los Angeles, CA 90067-4705, USA

Cureton, Earl (Athlete, Basketball Player)
31190 Country Way
Farmington Hills, MI 48331-1036, USA

Cureton, Will (Athlete, Football Player)
1999 McKinney Ave Apt 1408
Dallas, TX 75201-1713, USA

Curfman, Shannon (Musician)
Monterey International
200 W Superior St Ste 202
Chicago, IL 60654-6422, USA

Curie-Good, Louise
1317 Delresto Dr
Beverly Hills, CA 90210-2100

Curl, Carolyn (Skier)
Robert U Curt
405 N Westridge Dr
Idaho Falls, ID 83402-5447, USA

Curlander, Paul J (Business Person)
Lexmark International
740 W New Circle Rd
Lexington, KY 40511-1876, USA

Curler, James (Business Person)
Bernis Co
222 S 9th St
Minneapolis, MN 55402-3389, USA

Curley, Bill (Athlete, Basketball Player)
377 Autumn Ave
Duxbury, MA 02332-4614, USA

Curley, John J (Publisher)
Gannett Co
1100 Wilson Blvd
Arlington, VA 22209-2249, USA

Curnen, Monique (Actor)
c/o Sheree Cohen *Don Buchwald & Associates (LA)*
6500 Wilshire Blvd Ste 2200
Los Angeles, CA 90048-4942, USA

Curran, Brian (Athlete, Coach, Hockey Player)
c/o Staff Member *Quad City Mallards*
1509 3rd Avenue A
Moline, IL 61265-1363, USA

Curran, Brian (Athlete, Hockey Player)
3600 Vanrick Dr
Attn: Director of Hockey Operations
Kalamazoo, MI 49001-0805, USA

Curran, Kevin (Tennis Player)
5808 Back Ct
Austin, TX 78731-3301, USA

Curran, Mike (Athlete, Hockey Player, Olympic Athlete)
7615 Lanewood Ln N
Osseo, MN 55311-2608, USA

Curran, Pat (Athlete, Football Player)
1525 Glenwood Dr
San Diego, CA 92103-4732, USA

Curran, Tony (Actor)
c/o Tammy Rosen *Sanders Armstrong Caserta*
425 N Robertson Blvd
West Hollywood, CA 90048-1735, USA

Currence, Lafayette (Athlete, Baseball Player)
113 Rock Springs Way
Rock Hill, SC 29730-6149, USA

Currie, Bill (Athlete, Baseball Player)
242 Lakeside Dr SW
Arlington, GA 39813-2345, USA

Currie, Brian (Writer)
c/o David Krintzman *Morris Yorn Barnes Levine Krintzman Rubenstein Kohner & Gellman*
2000 Avenue of the Stars Ste 300N
3rd Floor, North Tower
Los Angeles, CA 90067-4704, USA

Currie, Cherie (Musician)
Cherie Currie's Chainsaw Art Gallery
8511 Hanna Ave
Canoga Park, CA 91304-2322, USA

Currie, Daniel (Dan) (Athlete, Football Player)
6650 W Flamingo Rd Apt 152
Las Vegas, NV 89103-2144, USA

Currie, Louise (Actor)
1317 Delresto Dr
Beverly Hills, CA 90210-2100, USA

Currie, Malcolm R (Business Person)
Hughes Aircraft Co
PO Box 956
El Segundo, CA 90245-0956, USA

Currie, Nancy J (Astronaut)
403 Cranbrook Ln
League City, TX 77573-1850, USA

Currie, Nancy Jane Colonel (Astronaut)
1023 Knoll Bridge Ln
Friendswood, TX 77546-3299, USA

Currie, Sondra (Actor)
3951 Longridge Ave
Sherman Oaks, CA 91423-4923, USA

Currier, William(Bill) (Athlete, Football Player)
8661 Monticello Rd
Columbia, SC 29203-9706, USA

Currin, James A (Athlete, Football Player)
11770 Thayer Ln
Cincinnati, OH 45249-1566, USA

Currington, Billy (Musician)
159 San Marco Dr
Tybee Island, GA 31328, USA

Curry, Adrianne (Model, Reality Star)
425 N Sycamore Ave Apt 8
Los Angeles, CA 90036-2659, USA

Curry, Alana (Actor)
c/o JD Sobol *Almond Talent Agency*
8217 Beverly Blvd Ste 8
Los Angeles, CA 90048-4534, USA

Curry, Ann (Television Host)
181 Ferris Hill Rd
New Canaan, CT 06840-3826, USA

Curry, Bill (Athlete, Coach, Football Coach, Football Player)
2660 Peachtree Rd NW Apt 27H
Atlanta, GA 30305-3680, USA

Curry, Buddy (Athlete, Football Player)
4407 Trestle Way
Buford, GA 30518-6055, USA

Curry, Craig (Athlete, Football Player)
3210 Amber Forest Dr
Houston, TX 77068-2005, USA

Curry, Dell (Athlete, Basketball Player)
1615 Rutledge Ave
Charlotte, NC 28211-2752, USA

Curry, Demarcus (Athlete, Football Player)
765 Forest Crossing Dr SW
Atlanta, GA 30331-7387, USA

Curry, Denise (Athlete, Basketball Player, Coach)
21 Maple Dr
Aliso Viejo, CA 92656-4273, USA

Curry, Don (Athlete, Boxer, Olympic Athlete)
2509 McKenzie St
Fort Worth, TX 76105-3940, USA

Curry, Don (DC) (Actor, Comedian)
c/o Tony Spires *Full Circle Entertainment*
6320 Canoga Ave Ste 1550
Woodland Hills, CA 91367-2563, USA

Curry, Eddy (Athlete, Basketball Player)
17 Magnolia Dr
Purchase, NY 10577-1137, USA

Curry, Eric F (Athlete, Football Player)
PO Box 17321
Jacksonville, FL 32245-7321, USA

Curry, Mark (Actor)
12540 Kling St
Studio City, CA 91604-1108, USA

Curry, Mike (Athlete, Basketball Player)
1086 Hampstead Pl
Augusta, GA 30907-6200, USA

Curry, Ronald (Athlete, Football Player)
PO Box 1072
Salisbury, NC 28145-1072, USA

Curry, Roy (Athlete, Football Player)
9045 S Paxton Ave
Chicago, IL 60617-3814, USA

Curry, Steve (Athlete, Baseball Player)
10725 Obee Rd
Whitehouse, OH 43571-9250, USA

Curry, Tim (Actor, Musician)
4756 Placidia Ave
Toluca Lake, CA 91602-1544, USA

Curry, Valorie (Actor)
c/o Ron West *Thruline Entertainment*
9250 Wilshire Blvd Ste 100
Ground Floor
Beverly Hills, CA 90212-3343, USA

Curtale, Tony (Athlete, Hockey Player)
9601 Presthope Dr
Frisco, TX 75035-5770, USA

Curtin, David S (Journalist)
Colorado Springs Gazette Telegraph
30 E Pikes Peak Ave Ste 100
Colorado Springs, CO 80903-1580, USA

Curtin, Jane (Actor)
181 Mudge Pond Rd
Sharon, CT 06069, USA

Curtin, Valerie
15622 Meadowgate Rd
Encino, CA 91436-3431

Curtis, Ben (Actor)
c/o Staff Member *Abrams Artists Agency (NY)*
275 7th Ave Fl 26
New York, NY 10001-6708, USA

Curtis, Ben (Athlete, Golfer)
8959 Bevington Ln
Orlando, FL 32827-7058, USA

Curtis, Bonnie (Producer)
c/o Staff Member *Mockingbird Pictures, LLC*
2312 Lorenzo Dr
Los Angeles, CA 90068-2726, USA

Curtis, Chad (Athlete, Baseball Player)
1400 Buttrick Ave SE
Ada, MI 49301-9614, USA

Curtis, Cliff (Actor)
c/o Joseph (Joe) Rice *Abrams Artists Agency (LA)*
9200 W Sunset Blvd PH 11
West Hollywood, CA 90069-3601, USA

Curtis, Don (Wrestler)
920 Middleton Rd
Jacksonville, FL 32211-6273, USA

Curtis, Isaac F (Athlete, Football Player)
711 Clinton Springs Ave
Cincinnati, OH 45229-1300, USA

Curtis, Jack (Athlete, Baseball Player)
4949 Ike Starnes Rd
Granite Falls, NC 28630-8631, USA

Curtis, Jamie Lee (Actor)
c/o Heidi Schaeffer *PMK/BNC Public Relations (PMK-LA)*
8687 Melrose Ave Ste 8
West Hollywood, CA 90069-5746, USA

Curtis, John (Athlete, Baseball Player)
1800 Roundhill Rd Apt 1207
Charleston, WV 25314-1559, USA

Curtis, John (Athlete, Baseball Player)
3125 Leeman Ferry Rd SW
Attn Coaching Staff
Huntsville, AL 35801-5331, USA

Curtis, Kelly (Actor)
651 N Kilkea Dr
Los Angeles, CA 90048-2213, USA

Curtis, Kenneth (Politician)
1211 Southport Dr
Sarasota, FL 34242-1716, USA

Curtis, Kenneth M (Ex-Governor)
Curtis Thaxter
1 Canal Plz Ste 1000
Portland, ME 04101-6404, USA

Curtis, King (Baseball Player)
St Louis Cardinals
2538 Beechwood Dr
Vineland, NJ 08361-2932, USA

Curtis, Liane (Actor)
12556 Everglade St
Los Angeles, CA 90066-1818, USA

Curtis, Mike (Athlete, Football Player)
940 Water Lily Ct NE
Saint Petersburg, FL 33703-3136, USA

Curtis, Nicole (Reality Star)
Keller Williams Realty
1350 Lagoon Ave Ste 900
Minneapolis, MN 55408-2692, USA

Curtis, Paul (Athlete, Hockey Player)
PO Box 6325
Abilene, TX 79608-6325, USA

Curtis, Robin (Actor)
1147 Beverly Hill Dr
Cincinnati, OH 45208-4323, USA

Curtis, Scott (Athlete, Football Player)
31661 Prairie Dunes Ct
Evergreen, CO 80439-5902, USA

Curtis, Todd (Actor)
2046 14th St Apt 10
Santa Monica, CA 90405-1641, USA

Curtis, Tom (Athlete, Football Player)
1229 Westward Dr
Miami, FL 33166-5171, USA

Curtis, Travis (Athlete, Football Player)
9905 Sorrel Ave
Potomac, MD 20854-4703, USA

Cusack, Ann (Actor)
Innovative Artists
1505 10th St
Santa Monica, CA 90401-2805, USA

Cusack, Joan (Actor, Comedian)
60 E Cedar St
Chicago, IL 60611-1179, USA

Cusack, John (Actor)
24460 Malibu Rd
Malibu, CA 90265-4613, USA

Cuschieri, Paul (Writer)
c/o Naren Desai *Brillstein Entertainment Partners (LA)*
9150 Wilshire Blvd Ste 350
Beverly Hills, CA 90212-3453, USA

Cuse, Carlton (Producer)
c/o Staff Member *William Morris Endeavor (LA)*
9601 Wilshire Blvd
Beverly Hills, CA 90210-5213, USA

Cushenan, Ian (Athlete, Hockey Player)
4014 Dryden Dr
North Olmsted, OH 44070-1928, USA

Cushing, Brian (Athlete, Football Player)
c/o Drew Rosenhaus *Rosenhaus Sports Representation*
6400 Allison Rd
Miami Beach, FL 33141-4540, USA

Cushing, Matt (Athlete, Football Player)
5752 Lyman Ave
Downers Grove, IL 60516-1401, USA

Cushman, Karen (Writer)
17804 Thorsen Rd SW
Vashon, WA 98070-4502, USA

Cusick, Pete (Athlete, Football Player)
623600 Amaui Pl Apt 302
Kamuela, HI 96743-7733, USA

Cussler, Clive (Writer)
7731 W 72nd Pl
Arvada, CO 80005-4230, USA

Cust, Jack (Athlete, Baseball Player)
9 Club House Dr
Whitehouse Station, NJ 08889-3366, USA

Cutcliffe, David (Coach, Football Coach)
University of Mississippi
Athletic Dept
University, MS 38677, USA

Cute Is What We Aim For (Music Group)
Fueled By Ramen
PO Box 1803
Tampa, FL 33601-1803, USA

Cuthbert, Elisha (Actor)
1531 Marmont Ave
Los Angeles, CA 90069-1621, USA

Cuthbert, Randy (Athlete, Football Player)
6440 Eichler Cir
Coopersburg, PA 18036-1382, USA

Cutler, Alexander M (Business Person)
Eaton Corp
1000 Eaton Blvd
Eaton Center
Beachwood, OH 44122-6058, USA

Cutler, Jay (Athlete)
c/o Brad Marks *Blue Five Media*
1550 17th St
Santa Monica, CA 90404-3402, USA

Cutler, Jay (Athlete, Football Player)
c/o Bus Cook *Bus Cook Sports, Inc*
1 Willow Bend Dr
Hattiesburg, MS 39402-8552, USA

Cutler, RJ (Director, Producer)
c/o Rowena Arguelles *Creative Artists Agency (CAA-LA)*
2000 Avenue of the Stars Ste 100
Los Angeles, CA 90067-4705, USA

Cutliffe, Molly (Actor)
Herney/Grimes
PO Box 64249
Los Angeles, CA 90064-0249, USA

Cutrone, Kelly (Business Person, Reality Star)
People's Revolution Inc
62 Grand St Apt 3
New York, NY 10013-2245, USA

Cutrufello, Mary (Musician, Songwriter, Writer)
Joe's Garage
4405 Belmont Park Ter
Nashville, TN 37215-3609, USA

Cutsinger, Gary (Athlete, Football Player)
5004 W Fm 2147
Horseshoe Bay, TX 78657-9394, USA

Cutter, Kiki (Skier)
PO Box 1317
Carbondale, CO 81623-1317, USA

Cutter, Lise (Actor)
36 Poplar St
Sag Harbor, NY 11963-1718, USA

Cutter, Slade D (Athlete, Football Player)
4000 River Crescent Dr
Annapolis, MD 21401-7721, USA

Cuwinski, Kevin (Race Car Driver)
Brevak Racing
206 Performance Rd
Mooresville, NC 28115-9591, USA

Cuyler, Milt (Athlete, Baseball Player)
962 Lamar Rd
Macon, GA 31210-7109, USA

Cuzzi, Phil (Athlete, Baseball Player)
32 Mapes Ave
Nutley, NJ 07110-1410, USA

Cwiklinski, Stanley (Athlete, Olympic Athlete)
728 W Washington St
San Diego, CA 92103-1938, USA

C. Woolsey, Lynn (Congressman, Politician)
2263 Rayburn Hob
Washington, DC 20515-0506, USA

Cymphonique (Dancer, Musician)
c/o Ben Press *Evolution Entertainment (LA)*
6500 Wilshire Blvd Ste 2200
Los Angeles, CA 90048-4942, USA

C. Young, Todd (Congressman, Politician)
1721 Longworth Hob
Washington, DC 20515-4326, USA

Cypher, John
9229 W Sunset Blvd Ste 315
West Hollywood, CA 90069-3403

Cypher, Jon (Actor)
498 Manzanita Ave
Ventura, CA 93001-2227, USA

Cyphers, Charles (Actor)
8567 E American Dream Way
Sierra Vista, AZ 85650-8413, USA

Cypress, Tawny
c/o Staff Member *Abrams Artists Agency (NY)*
275 7th Ave Fl 26
New York, NY 10001-6708, USA

Cypress Hill (Music Group)
c/o David Benveniste *Velvet Hammer*
9014 Melrose Ave
West Hollywood, CA 90069-5610, USA

Cyprien, Jonathan (Athlete, Football Player)
c/o Drew Rosenhaus *Rosenhaus Sports Representation*
6400 Allison Rd
Miami Beach, FL 33141-4540, USA

Cyr, Denis (Athlete, Hockey Player)
9816 N Townsend Dr
Peoria, IL 61615-1388, USA

Cyrus, Billy Ray (Musician, Songwriter)
c/o Stuart Dill *Sanctuary Artist Management (TN)*
209 10th Ave S Ste 342
Nashville, TN 37203-0758, USA

Cyrus, Brandi (Actor)
c/o Staff Member *United Talent Agency (UTA-LA)*
9336 Civic Center Dr
Beverly Hills, CA 90210-3604, USA

Cyrus, Miley (Actor, Musician)
c/o Larry Rudolph *ReignDeer Entertainment*
100 Glendon Ave
Suite 1100
Los Angeles, CA 90024, USA

Cywinski, Kevin (Race Car Driver)
709 Performance Rd
Mooresville, NC 28115-9596, USA

Czajkowski, Jim (Athlete, Baseball Player)
1648 Rivergate Dr
Sevierville, TN 37862-9321, USA

Czapsky, Stefan (Cinematographer)
RR 3 Box 278
Unadilla, NY 13849, USA

Czuchry, Matt (Actor)
c/o Jeff Golenberg *Silver Lining Entertainment*
421 S Beverly Dr Fl 7
Beverly Hills, CA 90212-4408, USA

Czyz, Bobby (Boxer)
110 Pennsylvania Ave
Flemington, NJ 08822-1202, USA

D, Deezer (Actor)
c/o Staff Member *Acme Talent & Literary (LA)*
1400 Atlantic Ave Ste 274
Long Beach, CA 90813-2013, USA

D, Mike (Musician)
7126 Fernhill Dr
Malibu, CA 90265-4243, USA

D12 (Music Group)
c/o Staff Member *William Morris Endeavor (NY)*
1325 Avenue of the Americas
New York, NY 10019-6026, USA

D-12 (Musician)
Evolution Talent Agency
1776 Broadway Fl 15
New York, NY 10019-2002

Daal, Omar (Athlete, Baseball Player)
3859 E Bellerive Dr
Queen Creek, AZ 85142-3233, USA

Daanen, Jerome (Athlete, Football Player)
1011 S Erie St
De Pere, WI 54115-3109, USA

Da Band (Music Group)
c/o Staff Member *Bad Boy Worldwide Entertainment*
1440 Broadway Fl 19
New York, NY 10018-2301, USA

Dabich, Mike (Athlete, Basketball Player)
PO Box 236
Hudson, WY 82515-0236, USA

Dabney, Carlton (Athlete, Football Player)
2522 Northumberland Ave
Richmond, VA 23220-1504, USA

D'Abo, Olivia (Actor)
3480 Berry Dr
Studio City, CA 91604-4152, USA

Da Brat (Musician)
c/o Staff Member *William Morris Endeavor (LA)*
9601 Wilshire Blvd
Beverly Hills, CA 90210-5213, USA

Dacascos, Mark (Actor)
1479 Aldercreek Pl
Westlake Village, CA 91362-4200, USA

Da Costa, Rebecca (Actor)
c/o Liza Anderson *Anderson Group Public Relations*
8060 Melrose Ave Fl 4
Los Angeles, CA 90046-7038, USA

Dacquisto, John (Athlete, Baseball Player)
32010 N 20th Ln
Phoenix, AZ 85085-7081, USA

D'Acquisto, John F (Athlete, Baseball Player)
1441 Santa Lucia Rd Unit 615
Chula Vista, CA 91913-3600, USA

Dacus, Don (Actor)
8455 Fountain Ave Unit 512
West Hollywood, CA 90069-2543, USA

Daddario, Alex (Actor)
c/o Jerry Shandrew *Shandrew Public Relations*
1050 S Stanley Ave
Los Angeles, CA 90019-6634, USA

Daddario, Alexandra (Actor)
c/o Donnalyn Carfi *Harvest Talent Management*
124 W 80th St Apt 1
New York, NY 10024-6320, USA

Dade, Paul (Athlete, Baseball Player)
5212 66th Street Ct W
University Place, WA 98467-3337, USA

Daetweiler, Louella (Baseball Player)
415 S Poplar Ave
Brea, CA 92821-6650, USA

Dafoe, Willem (Actor)
68 Jane St Apt 7E
New York, NY 10014-0715, USA

Daft, Douglas (Business Person)
Coca Cola Co
1 Coca Cola Plz NW
310 North Ave NW
Atlanta, GA 30313-2499, USA

Daft, Kevin (Athlete, Football Player)
6033 Old Quarry Loop
Oakland, CA 94605-3375, USA

Daggett, Jensen (Actor)
28025 Balkins Dr
Agoura Hills, CA 91301-1801, USA

Daggett, Timothy (Tim) (Gymnast)
134 Country Club Dr
East Longmeadow, MA 01028-5807, USA

Daghe, Noelle (Athlete, Golfer)
1300 Tamarac St
Denver, CO 80220-3325, USA

D'Agosto, Nicholas (Nick) (Actor)
c/o Faras Rabadi *Emerald Talent Group*
10 Universal City Plz Fl 20
Universal City, CA 91608-1002, USA

Dagres, Angie (Athlete, Baseball Player)
PO Box 27
Rowley, MA 01969-0027, USA

Dahl, Ariene (Actor)
Dahlmark Productions
PO Box 116
Sparkill, NY 10976-0116, USA

Dahl, Arlene (Actor)
PO Box 116
Sparkill, NY 10976-0116, USA

Dahl, Bob (Athlete, Football Player)
363 Elliots Hill Ln
Lexington, VA 24450-7202, USA

Dahl, Craig (Athlete, Football Player)
62503 Shorewood Ln
Madison Lake, MN 56063-4434, USA

Dahl, Dave (Correspondent)
KSTP
3415 University Ave SE
Minneapolis, MN 55414-3365, USA

Dahl, John (Director, Writer)
c/o Jason Spitz *William Morris Endeavor (LA)*
9601 Wilshire Blvd
Beverly Hills, CA 90210-5213, USA

Dahl, Kevin (Athlete, Hockey Player)
4000 Astoria Way
Avon, OH 44011-3426, USA

Dahlen, Ulf (Athlete, Hockey Player)
2500 Victory Ave
Dallas, TX 75219-7601, USA

Dahler, Ed (Athlete, Basketball Player)
511 E Tremont St
Hillsboro, IL 62049-1801, USA

Dahllof, Eva (Athlete, Golfer)
419 Glen Crest Dr
Moore, SC 29369-9287, USA

Dahlquist, Chris (Athlete, Hockey Player)
10859 Purdey Rd
Eden Prairie, MN 55347-5236, USA

Dahm, Jaclyn (Actor)
c/o Amy Godsick *Candy Entertainment Management*
8981 W Sunset Blvd Ste 310
West Hollywood, CA 90069-1848, USA

Dai, Sijie (Writer)
c/o Staff Member *Knopf*
1745 Broadway
New York, NY 10019-4640, USA

Daigle, Casey (Athlete, Baseball Player)
2607 Wpa Rd
Sulphur, LA 70663-9408, USA

Daigneau, Maurice (Athlete, Football Player)
32 Redmond Ave
Buffalo, NY 14216-1511, USA

Daigneault, J J (Athlete, Coach, Hockey Player)
c/o Staff Member *Hartford Wolf Pack*
196 Trumbull St Fl 3
Hartford, CT 06103-2200, USA

Daigneault, Rejean (Horse Racer)
95 Hildreth Pl
Yonkers, NY 10704-2220, USA

Dailey, Bill (Athlete, Baseball Player)
5019 Meadow Way
Dublin, VA 24084-5721, USA

Dailey, Bob (Athlete, Hockey Player)
249 Harrison Ave
Elkins Park, PA 19027-2731

Dailey, Dianne (Athlete, Golfer)
4220 Stonehenge Ln
Lakeland, FL 33813, USA

Daily, Bill (Actor)
1331 Park Ave SW Unit 802
Albuquerque, NM 87102-2855, USA

Daily, EG (Actor, Musician)
2324 Jupiter Dr
Los Angeles, CA 90046-2026, USA

Daily, Parker (Religious Leader)
Baptist Bible Fellowship International
PO Box 191
Springfield, MO 65801-0191, USA

Daisey, Gene (Horse Racer)
5335 Havasu Ct
Lake Worth, FL 33467-5533, USA

Dajani, Nadia (Actor)
22 Perry St # 3C/D
New York, NY 10014-2775, USA

Dale, Alan (Actor)
c/o Dan Baron *Agency for the Performing Arts (APA-LA)*
405 S Beverly Dr Ste 500
Beverly Hills, CA 90212-4425, USA

Dale, Carl (Athlete, Baseball Player)
3358 Oak Trl
Cookeville, TN 38506-6144, USA

Dale, Carroll (Athlete, Football Player)
9533 Coeburn Mountain Rd
Wise, VA 24293, USA

Dale, Dick (Actor)
PO Box 1713
Twentynine Palms, CA 92277-1000, USA

Dale, James Badge (Actor)
255 E 7th St Apt 3F
New York, NY 10009-6077, USA

Dale, Jerry (Athlete, Baseball Player)
2112 Middlewood Dr
Maryville, TN 37803-6374, USA

Dale, Jim (Actor)
Mark Sendroff
230 W 56th St Apt 63B
New York, NY 10019-0077, USA

Dale & Grace (Music Group)
Sea Cruise Productions
PO Box 1875
Gretna, LA 70054-1875, USA

Dalembert, Samuel (Athlete, Basketball Player)
899 NE Orchid Bay Dr
Boca Raton, FL 33487-1751, USA

Dalena, Pete (Athlete, Baseball Player)
4951 N Thorne Ave
Fresno, CA 93704-2935, USA

D'Aleo, Angelo (Musician)
Paramount Entertainment
PO Box 12
Far Hills, NJ 07931-0012, USA

Dalesandro, Mark (Athlete, Baseball Player)
1908 Arbor Fields Dr
Plainfield, IL 60586-5729, USA

Dale Scott, Cynthia (Actor)
c/o Derek Maki *Coolwaters Productions*
10061 Riverside Dr # 531
Toluca Lake, CA 91602-2560, USA

Dales-Schuman, Stacey (Basketball Player)
Washington Mystics
601 F St NW
Mci Center
Washington, DC 20004-1605, USA

D'Alessio, Diana (Athlete, Golfer)
6955 Nunn Rd
Lakeland, FL 33813-3821, USA

Daley, Bill (Athlete, Baseball Player)
SBC Communications
5824 Hansen Rd
Minneapolis, MN 55436-2402, USA

Daley, Bud (Athlete, Baseball Player)
922 Moose Dr
Riverton, WY 82501-2537, USA

Daley, John (Golfer)
10015 E Mountain View Rd Apt 2126
Scottsdale, AZ 85258-5221, USA

Daley, John (Golfer)
c/o Staff Member *Pro Golfers Assoc of America (PGA)*
112 Tpc Blvd
Ponte Vedra Beach, FL 32082, USA

Daley, John Francis (Actor)
2400 Crest View Dr
Los Angeles, CA 90046-1407, USA

Daley, Matt (Athlete, Baseball Player)
173 Kildare Rd
Garden City, NY 11530-1120, USA

Daley, Pete (Athlete, Baseball Player)
4019 Calle Mira Monte
Newbury Park, CA 91320-1932, USA

Daley, Richard M (Politician)
Mayor's Office
121 N La Salle St Rm 507
City Hall
Chicago, IL 60602-1281, USA

Dalheimer, Patrick (Musician)
Freedman & Smith
350 W End Ave Apt 1
New York, NY 10024-6818, USA

Dali, Tracy (Actor, Model)
JAS Entertainment Squad
7119 W Sunset Blvd # 261
P.O. Box 261
Los Angeles, CA 90046-4411, USA

Dalian, Susan (Actor)
c/o Staff Member *GVA Talent Agency Inc*
8981 W Sunset Blvd Ste 101
West Hollywood, CA 90069-1850, USA

Dalio, Raymond
40 Glenwood Dr
Greenwich, CT 06830-7015, USA

Dalkas, Nicole (Athlete, Golfer)
288 Green Mountain Dr
Palm Desert, CA 92211-3246, USA

Dalkowski, Steve (Baseball Player)
Walnut Hill Care Center 55 Grand St
New Britain, CT 06052, USA

Dall, Bobby (Musician)
160 Ocean Oaks Dr
Indialantic, FL 32903-2732, USA

Dallafior, Ken (Athlete, Football Player)
4529 Oak Pointe Rd
Brighton, MI 48116-9780, USA

Dallas, Joshua (Actor)
c/o John Carrabino *John Carrabino Management*
5900 Wilshire Blvd Ste 406
Los Angeles, CA 90036-5015, USA

Dallas, Matt (Actor)
c/o Katie Rhodes *Untitled Entertainment (LA)*
350 S Beverly Dr Ste 200
Beverly Hills, CA 90212-4819, USA

Dallas Cowboys Cheerleaders
1 Cowboys Pkwy
Irving, TX 75063-4924

Dallenbach Jr., Wally (Race Car Driver)
2561 Frying Pan Rd
Basalt, CO 81621-9715, USA

Dallimore, Brian (Athlete, Baseball Player)
10531 Haywood Dr
Las Vegas, NV 89135-2850, USA

Dalrymple, Clay (Athlete, Baseball Player)
28248 Mateer Rd
Gold Beach, OR 97444-9618, USA

Dalrymple, Jack (Governor, Politician)
Office of Governor
600 E Boulevard Ave Dept 112
Bismarck, ND 58505-0602, USA

Dalton, Andy (Athlete, Football Player)
c/o W Vann McElroy *Select Sports Group*
2700 Post Oak Blvd Ste 1450
Houston, TX 77056-5785, USA

Dalton, Audrey (Actor)
22461 Labrusca
Mission Viejo, CA 92692-1325, USA

Dalton, Brett (Actor)
c/o Emily Gerson Saines *Brookside Artists Management (NY)*
250 W 57th St Ste 2303
New York, NY 10107-2399, USA

Dalton, Kristin (Actor)
c/o Bob McGowan *McGowan Management*
8733 W Sunset Blvd Ste 103
West Hollywood, CA 90069-2241, USA

Dalton, Lacy J (Musician)
820 Cartwright Rd
Reno, NV 89521-7134, USA

Dalton, Lional (Athlete, Football Player)
9858 Clint Moore Rd Ste 128
Boca Raton, FL 33496-1033, USA

Dalton, Mike (Athlete, Baseball Player)
42410 Palm Ave
Fremont, CA 94539-4729, USA

Dalton, Nic (Musician)
c/o Staff Member *The Agency Group (NYC)*
142 W 57th St Fl 6
New York, NY 10019-3300, USA

Dalton, Nicole (Actor)
c/o Staff Member *Commonwealth Talent Group*
PO Box 36514
Los Angeles, CA 90036-0514, USA

Dalton, Oakley (Athlete, Football Player)
3647 Highway 131
Washburn, TN 37888-4015, USA

Dalton, Timothy (Actor)
8322 Marmont Ln
Los Angeles, CA 90069-1637, USA

Daluiso, Brad (Athlete, Football Player)
13258 Glencliff Way
San Diego, CA 92130-1309, USA

Daly, Carson (Television Host)
133 Elderfields Rd
Manhasset, NY 11030-1648, USA

Daly, Derek (Race Car Driver)
733 E State Road 32
Westfield, IN 46074-8764, USA

Daly, John (Athlete, Golfer)
10093 Par St
Dardanelle, AR 72834-8793, USA

Daly, Robert (Baseball Player)
Los Angeles Dodgers
10779 Bellagio Rd
Los Angeles, CA 90077-3731, USA

Daly, Tim (Actor, Producer)
212 Marine St Unit 203
Santa Monica, CA 90405-6511, USA

Daly, Tyne (Actor)
1617 N Sierra Bonita Ave
Los Angeles, CA 90046-2815, USA

Daly-Donofrio, Heather (Athlete, Golfer)
414 Long Cove Ct Apt 212
Ormond Beach, FL 32174-9290, USA

Damageplan (Music Group)
2706 Monterrey St
Arlington, TX 76015-1323, USA

Damas, Bertila (Actor)
PO Box 17193
Beverly Hills, CA 90209-3193, USA

Damasio, Antonio R (Doctor)
University of Iowa Hospital
Neurology Dept
Iowa City, IA 52242, USA

Damaska, Jack (Athlete, Baseball Player)
252 Blackhawk Rd
Beaver Falls, PA 15010-1404, USA

D'Amato, Lisa (Musician)
c/o Staff Member *Brendan Vaughn*
Prefers to be contact via telephone or email
West Hollywood, CA 90069, USA

D'Amato, Mike (Athlete, Football Player)
7 Lansing Ln
East Northport, NY 11731-5325, USA

DaMatta, Cristiano (Race Car Driver)
Newman-Haas Racing
500 Tower Pkwy
Lincolnshire, IL 60069-3642, USA

Dames, Romi (Actor)
c/o Nicole Walter *Metro Public Relations*
8383 Wilshire Blvd Ste 208
Beverly Hills, CA 90211-2432, USA

Dameshek, David (Actor, Writer)
c/o Staff Member *Creative Artists Agency (CAA-LA)*
2000 Avenue of the Stars Ste 100
Los Angeles, CA 90067-4705, USA

Damian, Michael (Actor, Musician)
Gold Marshak Liedtke
3500 W Olive Ave Ste 1400
Burbank, CA 91505-5512, USA

Damico, Jeff (Athlete, Baseball Player)
757 Santa Clara Ln NE
Bainbridge Island, WA 98110-3928, USA

Damico, Jeff (Athlete, Baseball Player)
2223 Muirfield Way
Oldsmar, FL 34677-1942, USA

D'Amico, Jeff (Athlete, Baseball Player)
400 Carriage House Ln
Tarpon Springs, FL 34688-7250, USA

D'Amico, William D (Athlete)
30 Greenwood St
Lake Placid, NY 12946-1214, USA

Damkroger, Maury (Athlete, Football Player)
6224 Oak Hills Plz
Omaha, NE 68137-4419, USA

Dammerman, Dennis D (Business Person)
General Electric Co
3135 Easton Tumpike
Fairfield, CT 06828-0001, USA

Damon, Grey (Actor)
c/o Toni Benson *Thirdhill Entertainment*
195 S Beverly Dr Ste 400
Beverly Hills, CA 90212-3044, USA

Damon, Johnny (Athlete, Baseball Player)
PO Box 8540
Stockton, CA 95208-0540, USA

Damon, Mark (Actor)
2781 Benedict Canyon Dr
Beverly Hills, CA 90210-1024, USA

Damon, Matt (Actor)
1401 San Remo Dr
Pacific Palisades, CA 90272-2738, USA

Damon, Stuart (Actor)
387 N Van Ness Ave
Los Angeles, CA 90004, USA

Damon, Una (Actor)
c/o Suzanne DeWalt *Dewalt & Musik Management*
623 N Parish Pl
Burbank, CA 91506-1701, USA

Damone, Vic (Actor, Musician)
200 Via Bellaria
Palm Beach, FL 33480-4901

Damore, John (Athlete, Football Player)
627 Citadel Dr
Westmont, IL 60559-1297, USA

D'Amour, Marc
70 Jacobs Creek Dr
Hershey, PA 17033-8918

Dampier, Erick (Athlete, Basketball Player)
18724 Wainsborough Ln
Dallas, TX 75287-5525, USA

Dampier, Louie (Athlete, Basketball Player)
2808 New Moody Ln
La Grange, KY 40031-9453, USA

Dampler, Erick (Basketball Player)
2635 Sea View Pkwy
Alameda, CA 94502, USA

Dampler, Louie (Basketball Player)
Dampler Ditributing
2808 New Moody Ln
La Grange, KY 40031-9453, USA

Damron, Robert (Athlete, Golfer)
6001 Masters Blvd
Orlando, FL 32819-4303, USA

Damus, Mike (Actor)
c/o Staff Member *United Talent Agency (UTA-LA)*
9336 Civic Center Dr
Beverly Hills, CA 90210-3604, USA

Dan, Dercher (Athlete, Football Player)
3448 W 131st St
Leawood, KS 66209-4112, USA

Dan, Reeder (Athlete, Football Player)
703 Southwood Rd
Hockessin, DE 19707-1040, USA

Dan, Rice (Athlete, Football Player)
247 Bramblebush Rd
Stoughton, MA 02072-3096, USA

Dana, Bill (Actor, Comedian)
c/o Staff Member *Amsel, Eisenstadt & Frazier Talent Agency (AEF)*
5055 Wilshire Blvd Ste 860
Los Angeles, CA 90036-6108, USA

Dana, Justin (Actor)
13111 Ventura Blvd Ste 102
Studio City, CA 91604-2218, USA

Danare, Malcolm (Actor)
c/o Monique Moss *Integrated PR*
8060 Melrose Ave Fl 4
Los Angeles, CA 90046-7038, USA

Danby, John (Athlete, Hockey Player)
20 Jb Dr
Marstons Mills, MA 02648-1521, USA

Dance, Charies (Actor)
7812 Forsythe St
Sunland, CA 91040-2502, USA

Dance, Charles (Actor)
c/o Susan Smith *Susan Smith Company, The*
2001 Wilshire Blvd Ste 400
Santa Monica, CA 90403-5686, USA

Dancer, Donald (Horse Racer)
30 Amherst Rd
Marlboro, NJ 07746-1557, USA

Dancer, James (Horse Racer)
102 Ricemill Cir Apt 1
Sunset Beach, NC 28468-4479, USA

Dancer, Rachel (Horse Racer)
649 W Oakland Park Blvd Apt 219A
Wilton Manors, FL 33311-0906, USA

Dancer, Ronald (Horse Racer)
PO Box 235
New Egypt, NJ 08533-0235, USA

Dancer, Stanley F (Race Car Driver)
1300 S Ocean Blvd Apt 101
Pompano Beach, FL 33062-6916, USA

Dancy, Bill (Athlete, Baseball Player)
2225 Hemerick Pl
Clearwater, FL 33765-2228, USA

Dancy, Hugh (Actor)
19 Downing St
New York, NY 10014-4748, USA

Dancy, John (Correspondent)
Harvard University
Kennedy Government School
Cambridge, MA 02138, USA

Dandenault, Mathieu (Athlete, Hockey Player)
2615 Dorchester Rd
Birmingham, MI 48009-5990, USA

Dando, Evan (Musician)
c/o Staff Member *Good Cop Public Relations*
425 W 13th St # 502
New York, NY 10014-1123, USA

Dandridge, Bob (Athlete, Basketball Player)
1708 Saint Denis Ave
Norfolk, VA 23509-1004, USA

Dandy Warholds, The (Music Group)
c/o Staff Member *Tsunami Entertainment*
2525 Hyperion Ave
Los Angeles, CA 90027-3316, USA

Dandy Warhols (Music Group)
c/o Staff Member *Tsunami Entertainment*
2525 Hyperion Ave
Los Angeles, CA 90027-3316, USA

Dane, Eric (Actor)
c/o David Seltzer *Management 360*
9111 Wilshire Blvd
Beverly Hills, CA 90210-5508, USA

Dane, Lloyd (Race Car Driver)
4165 Amarillo Dr SW
Concord, NC 28027-0404, USA

Danehe, Dick (Athlete, Football Player)
612 Berkshire Ave
La Canada Flintridge, CA 91011-3425, USA

Daneker, Pat (Athlete, Baseball Player)
107 Van Buren Rd Apt 5
Voorhees, NJ 08043-2409, USA

Danelli, Dino (Musician)
Rascals Cassidy
11761 E Speedway Blvd
Tucson, AZ 85748-2017, USA

Danelo, Joe (Athlete, Football Player)
3601 Roxbury St
San Pedro, CA 90731-6440, USA

Danenhauer, Bill (Athlete, Football Player)
10 Kirkby Cir
Bella Vista, AR 72715-2349, USA

Danenhauer, Eldon (Athlete, Football Player)
1030 SW Exmoor Ln
Topeka, KS 66604-1977, USA

Danes, Claire (Actor)
19 Downing St
New York, NY 10014-4748, USA

Daney_ko, Ken (Athlete, Hockey Player)
13 Blue Bird Ct
Randolph, NJ 07869-2127

Daneyko, Ken (Athlete, Hockey Player)
11 Combs Hollow Rd
Mendham, NJ 07945-2204, USA

Danforth, Douglas D (Athlete, Baseball Player, Business Person)
8787 Bay Colony Dr Apt 1002
Naples, FL 34108-0784, USA

Danforth, John (Politician)
HC 1 Box 91
Newburg, MO 65550, USA

Danforth, John C (Jack) (Ex-Senator)
US Permanent Mission
799 United Nations Plz
New York, NY 10017-3505, USA

D'Angelo (Musician, Songwriter)
c/o Kevin Liles *KWL Management*
304 Park Ave S Fl 11
New York, NY 10010-4305, USA

D'Angelo, Beverly (Actor)
7708 Woodrow Wilson Dr
Los Angeles, CA 90046-1212, USA

D'Angelo, Josephine (Athlete, Baseball Player, Commentator)
6141 W Higgins Ave Apt 5A
Chicago, IL 60630-1853, USA

Daniel, Brittany (Actor)
c/o Glenn Rigberg *Inphenate*
9701 Wilshire Blvd Fl 10
Beverly Hills, CA 90212-2010, USA

Daniel, Chase (Athlete, Football Player)
10Star Apparel
912 113th St
Arlington, TX 76011-5407, USA

Daniel, Elizabeth A (Beth) (Athlete, Golfer)
219 Palm Trl
Delray Beach, FL 33483-5526, USA

Daniel, Eugene (Athlete, Football Player)
PO Box 80345
Baton Rouge, LA 70898-0345, USA

Daniel, Kenny (Athlete, Football Player)
2911 Center Ave
Richmond, CA 94804-3022, USA

Daniel, Robert (Athlete, Football Player)
9860 Scyene Rd Apt 518
Dallas, TX 75227-1951, USA

Daniel, Willie (Athlete, Football Player)
8323 Oktoc Rd
Starkville, MS 39759-6461, USA

Daniel, Willie (Athlete, Football Player)
508 S Jackson St
Starkville, MS 39759-3352, USA

Danielle, Juliette (Actor)
PO Box 16373
Encino, CA 91416-6373, USA

Daniels, Anthony (Actor)
c/o Fifi Oscard *Fifi Oscard Agency*
110 W 40th St Rm 1601
New York, NY 10018-8512, USA

Daniels, Antonio (Basketball Player)
Seatle SuperSonics
351 Elliott Ave W Ste 500
Seattle, WA 98119-4153, USA

Daniels, Bennie (Athlete, Baseball Player)
938 W 156th St
Compton, CA 90220-3504, USA

Daniels, Charlie (Musician, Songwriter, Writer)
16225/16832/16836/16850/17060 Central Pike
Lebanon, TN 37090, USA

Daniels, Cheryl (Bowler)
6574 Crest Top Dr
West Bloomfield, MI 48322-2656, USA

Daniels, Clem (Athlete, Football Player)
PO Box 18673
Oakland, CA 94619-0673, USA

Daniels, Dexter (Athlete, Football Player)
518 E Magnolia St
Valdosta, GA 31601-5860, USA

Daniels, Erin (Actor)
10171 Valley Spring Ln
Toluca Lake, CA 91602-2901, USA

Daniels, Fred (Athlete, Baseball Player)
PO Box 6208
Statesville, NC 28687-6208, USA

Daniels, Greg (Actor)
c/o Howard Klein *3 Arts Entertainment (LA)*
9460 Wilshire Blvd Fl 7
Beverly Hills, CA 90212-2713, USA

Daniels, Jack (Athlete, Baseball Player)
811 S Lombard Ave
Evansville, IN 47714-0428, USA

Daniels, Jeff (Actor)
701 Glazier Rd
Chelsea, MI 48118-9781, USA

Daniels, Jeff (Athlete, Hockey Player)
108 Delaplane Ct
Morrisville, NC 27560-6987, USA

Daniels, Jenna (Athlete, Golfer)
85140 Amagansett Dr
Fernandina Beach, FL 32034-8711, USA

Daniels, Jerome (Athlete, Football Player)
311 Park Ave
Bloomfield, CT 06002-3103, USA

Daniels, Jon (Athlete, Baseball Player)
425 Pine Dr
Southlake, TX 76092-7407, USA

Daniels, Kal (Athlete, Baseball Player)
100 Echo Ln
Warner Robins, GA 31088-7458, USA

Daniels, Kevin (Actor)
c/o Staff Member *Insight*
PO Box 36359
Los Angeles, CA 90036-0359, USA

Daniels, Kimbi
9159 Cranberry St
Anchorage, AK 99502-5575

Daniels, Lee (Director, Producer)
c/o Staff Member *Lee Daniels Entertainment*
315 W 36th St Rm 1002
New York, NY 10018-6526, USA

Daniels, Leshun (Athlete, Football Player)
865 Landsdowne Ave NW
Warren, OH 44485-2227, USA

Daniels, Marquis (Athlete, Basketball Player)
2501 Sutton Place Dr S
Carmel, IN 46032-8694, USA

Daniels, Marquis
c/o Staff Member *Dallas Mavericks*
2909 Taylor St
Dallas, TX 75226-1909, USA

Daniels, Melvin (Mel) (Athlete, Basketball Player)
19789 Centennial Rd
Sheridan, IN 46069-9789, USA

Daniels, Mike (Athlete, Football Player)
c/o Mark Gordon *ICM Partners (LA)*
10250 Constellation Blvd Fl 7
Los Angeles, CA 90067-6207, USA

Daniels, Owen (Athlete, Football Player)
5425 Inwood Dr
Houston, TX 77056-4215, USA

Daniels, Phillip (Athlete, Football Player)
1703 Pebble Beach Way
Vernon Hills, IL 60061-4520, USA

Daniels, Scott (Athlete, Hockey Player)
36 Deer Run
Southwick, MA 01077-9523, USA

Daniels, Spencer (Actor)
c/o Staff Member *Stone Manners Salners Agency (LA)*
6100 Wilshire Blvd Ste 1500
Los Angeles, CA 90048-5110, USA

Daniels, Stormy (Actor, Adult Film Star, Model)
c/o Gina Rodriguez *GR Media*
Prefers to be contacted via telephone or email
Reseda, CA 91335, USA

Daniels, Susan (Athlete, Golfer)
251 N Lake Blvd
Tahoe City, CA 96145, USA

Daniels, Travis (Athlete, Football Player)
3185 Wilson St
Hollywood, FL 33021-4446, USA

Daniels, William (Actor)
12805 Hortense St
Studio City, CA 91604-1124, USA

Danielson, Gary D (Athlete, Football Player)
10112 Magnolia Bnd
Bonita Springs, FL 34135-8109, USA

Daniloff, Nicholas (Journalist)
PO Box 892
Chester, VT 05143-0892, USA

Danity Kane (Music Group)
c/o Tammy Brook *FYI Public Relations*
174 5th Ave Ste 404
New York, NY 10010-5964, USA

Danks, John (Athlete, Baseball Player)
702 Oaklands Dr
Round Rock, TX 78681-4029, USA

Danley, Kerwin (Athlete, Baseball Player)
2455 E Desert Broom Pl
Chandler, AZ 85286-2336, USA

Danmeier, Rick (Athlete, Football Player)
7475 Flying Cloud Dr Apt 586
Eden Prairie, MN 55344-3842, USA

Danna, Mychael (Musician)
c/o Robert Messinger *First Artists Management*
4764 Park Granada Ste 210
Calabasas, CA 91302-3333, USA

Danner, Blythe (Actor)
101 Ocean Ave Unit E601
Santa Monica, CA 90402-1496, USA

Danning, Sybil (Actor, Model)
8578 Walnut Dr
Los Angeles, CA 90046-1950, USA

Danny & The Juniors (Music Group)
PO Box 279
Williamstown, NJ 08094-0279

Dano, Paul Franklin (Actor)
c/o Sandra Chang *Anonymous Content (LA)*
3532 Hayden Ave
Culver City, CA 90232-2413, USA

Dansby, Karlos (Athlete, Football Player)
2844 E Honeysuckle Pl
Chandler, AZ 85286-2451, USA

Danson, Ted (Actor)
11 Latimer Rd
Santa Monica, CA 90402-1011, USA

Dante, Joe (Director)
c/o Staff Member *Gersh (LA)*
9465 Wilshire Blvd Ste 600
Beverly Hills, CA 90212-2605, USA

Dante, Michael (Actor)
71372 Biskra Rd
Rancho Mirage, CA 92270-4200, USA

Dante, Peter (Actor)
5815 Ramirez Canyon Rd
Malibu, CA 90265-4420, USA

Dante Bichette, Alphonse (Baseball Player)
119 1st St W
Saint Petersburg, FL 33715-1702, USA

Dantine, Nikki (Actor)
707 N Palm Dr
Beverly Hills, CA 90210-3416, USA

Dantley, Adrian (Athlete, Basketball Player, Olympic Athlete)
9 Barn Ridge Ct
Silver Spring, MD 20906-1105, USA

Danton, Mike (Athlete, Hockey Player)
PO Box 1000
Fort Dix F C I
Fort Dix, NJ 08640-0902, USA

Dantoni, Mike (Athlete, Basketball Player)
116 25th St
Manhattan Beach, CA 90266-4332, USA

D'Antoni, Mike (Basketball Coach)
116 25th St
Manhattan Beach, CA 90266-4332, USA

Danz, Shirley (Athlete, Baseball Player, Commentator)
19 Eastbury Dr Apt B
Hendersonville, NC 28792-2691, USA

Danza, Tony (Actor)
11911 Ashdale Ln
Studio City, CA 91604-4202, USA

Danzig
PO Box 884563
San Francisco, CA 94188-4563

Danziger, Cory (Actor)
c/o Staff Member *Iris Burton Agency*
10100 Santa Monica Blvd Ste 1300
Los Angeles, CA 90067-4114, USA

Dao, Chloe (Fashion Designer)
Lot 8 Boutique
6127 Kirby Dr
Houston, TX 77005-3148, USA

Dapkus-Wolf, Eleanor (Baseball Player)
9150 Mallard Cv
Saint John, IN 46373-9019, USA

Dara, Olu (Actor)
c/o Staff Member *Monterey International (Chicago)*
200 W Superior St Ste 202
Chicago, IL 60654-6422, USA

D'Arabian, Melissa (Chef)
c/o Josh Bider *William Morris Endeavor (NY)*
1325 Avenue of the Americas
New York, NY 10019-6026, USA

Darabont, Frank (Director)
4474 Dundee Dr
Los Angeles, CA 90027-1212, USA

D'Arbanville, Patti (Actor)
c/o Staff Member *Moskowit Agency*
10440 Queens Blvd Apt 15V
Forest Hills, NY 11375-8145, USA

Darbo, Patrka (Musician)
346 N Avon St
Burbank, CA 91505-3503, USA

Darby, Chartric (Athlete, Football Player)
14335 Simonds Rd NE Apt A302
Kirkland, WA 98034-9277, USA

Darby, Craig (Athlete, Hockey Player)
40 Vista Dr
Saratoga Springs, NY 12866-8772

Darby, Kim (Actor)
4255 Laurelgrove Ave
Studio City, CA 91604-1624, USA

Darby, Matt (Athlete, Football Player)
501 Sagecreek Ct
Winter Springs, FL 32708-2731, USA

D'Arby, Terence Trent (Musician)
c/o Staff Member *Creative Artists Agency (CAA-LA)*
2000 Avenue of the Stars Ste 100
Los Angeles, CA 90067-4705, USA

Darcey, Pete (Athlete, Basketball Player)
17600 N Anderson Rd
Arcadia, OK 73007-7113, USA

Darche, Jean-Philippe (Athlete, Football Player)
9507 W 160th Ter
Stilwell, KS 66085-8127, USA

Darcum, Max (Skier)
PO Box 189
Dillon, CO 80435-0189, USA

D'Arcy (Musician)
Cohen Brothers Mgmt
500 Molino St Ste 104
Los Angeles, CA 90013-2264, USA

D'Arcy, James (Actor)
c/o Joel Lubin *Creative Artists Agency (CAA-LA)*
2000 Avenue of the Stars Ste 100
Los Angeles, CA 90067-4705, USA

Darcy, Pat (Athlete, Baseball Player)
515 S Columbus Blvd
Tucson, AZ 85711-4753, USA

D'Arcy James, Brian (Actor)
c/o JB Roberts *Thruline Entertainment*
9250 Wilshire Blvd Ste 100
Ground Floor
Beverly Hills, CA 90212-3343, USA

Dar Dar, Kirby (Athlete, Football Player)
PO Box 2872
Syracuse, NY 13220-2872, USA

Darden, Christopher (Attorney)
9551 Baden Ave
Chatsworth, CA 91311-2620, USA

Darden, Ollie
2219 Clipper Pl
Fort Lauderdale, FL 33312-5243, USA

Darden, Thom (Athlete, Football Player)
637 20th Ave SW
Cedar Rapids, IA 52404-5520, USA

Daredevil (Music Group)
c/o Staff Member *Wind-up Records*
72 Madison Ave Fl 8
New York, NY 10016-8731, USA

Darehshori, Nader F (Publisher)
Houghton Mifflin Co
222 Berkeley St
Boston, MA 02116-3760, USA

Darensbourg, Vic (Athlete, Baseball Player)
5884 Alington Bend Dr
Las Vegas, NV 89139-7463, USA

Darensbourg., Vic
4151 Abernethy Forest Pl # Pi
Las Vegas, NV 89141-4336, USA

Dareus, Marcell (Football Player)
c/o Todd France *Five Star Athlete Management*
3500 Lenox Rd NE
Atlanta, GA 30326-4228, USA

Darish, Frank (Horse Racer)
11 March Ln
Westbury, NY 11590-6301, USA

Darius, Donovin (Athlete, Football Player)
1357 Lawrence Rd
Danville, CA 94506-4735, USA

Dark, Al (Athlete, Baseball Player, Coach)
103 Cranberry Way
Easley, SC 29642-3200, USA

Darkins, Chris (Athlete, Football Player)
10903 Shawnbrook Dr
Houston, TX 77071-1515, USA

Dark Star Orchestra (Music Group)
PO Box 1282
Evanston, IL 60204-1282, USA

Darling, Chuck (Athlete, Basketball Player, Olympic Athlete)
8066 S Krameria Way
Centennial, CO 80112-3040, USA

Darling, Devard (Athlete, Football Player)
4504 Canterwood Dr NW
Gig Harbor, WA 98332-8832, USA

Darling, Gary (Athlete, Baseball Player)
16609 S 32nd Ln
Phoenix, AZ 85045-1223, USA

Darling, Jennifer (Actor)
13351 Riverside Dr # 427
Sherman Oaks, CA 91423-2542, USA

Darling, Joan (Actor)
PO Box 6700
Tesuque, NM 87574-6700, USA

Darling, Ron (Athlete, Baseball Player)
c/o Staff Member *SportsNet New York*
1271 Avenue Of The Americas Bsmt S7
New York, NY 10020-1302, USA

Darnell, Erik (Race Car Driver)
Darmer Motorsports Ltd
3627 Washington St Bldg 5
Waukegan, IL 60085-4767, USA

Darnell, Mike (Producer)
24962 Lorenzo Ct
Calabasas, CA 91302-3088, USA

Darr, Mike
1461 Maplebrook Ln
Corona, CA 92881-0704, USA

Darragh, Dan (Athlete, Football Player)
201 Sewickley Ridge Ct
Sewickley, PA 15143-8973, USA

Darren, James (Actor, Musician)
PO Box 1088
Beverly Hills, CA 90213-1088, USA

Darrian, Raquel (Adult Film Star)
49 Eaton Ct
Manhasset, NY 11030-4052

Darrow, Barry (Athlete, Football Player)
2406 Chief Victor Camp Rd
Victor, MT 59875-9410, USA

Darrow, Nathan (Actor)
c/o James Suskin *James Suskin Management*
2 Charlton St Apt 5K
New York, NY 10014-4970, USA

Dart, Iris Rainer (Writer)
938 Coral Dr
Pebble Beach, CA 93953-2503, USA

Darvill, Arthur (Actor)
c/o Jeff Golenberg *Silver Lining Entertainment*
421 S Beverly Dr Fl 7
Beverly Hills, CA 90212-4408, USA

Darwin, Bobby (Athlete, Baseball Player)
6516 Pleasant Hill Cir
Corona, CA 92880-3015, USA

Darwin, Danny (Athlete, Baseball Player)
7520 Bright Pl
Pilot Point, TX 76258-3646, USA

Darwin, Jeff (Athlete, Baseball Player)
1010 W Russell Ave
Bonham, TX 75418-2332, USA

Darwin, Matt (Athlete, Football Player)
414 Love Bird Ln
Murphy, TX 75094-3263, USA

Darwitz, Natalie (Athlete, Hockey Player, Olympic Athlete)
c/o Staff Member *US Olympic Committee*
1750 E Boulder St
Alumni Relations
Colorado Springs, CO 80909-5793, USA

Das, Alisha (Actor)
19583 Bowers Dr
Topanga, CA 90290-3102, USA

Dascascos, Marc (Actor)
PO Box 1549
Studio City, CA 91614-0549, USA

Dascenzo, Doug (Athlete, Baseball Player)
111 Eastgate Rd
Uniontown, PA 15401-5615, USA

Daschle, Thomas (Politician)
1020 N Jay St Apt 212
Aberdeen, SD 57401-2478, USA

Dash, Damon (Actor, Director, Producer, Writer)
c/o Staff Member *Fortitude*
6500 Wilshire Blvd Ste 2200
Los Angeles, CA 90048-4942, USA

Dash, Julie (Actor, Director, Producer, Writer)
c/o Kimber Wheeler *TalentWorks (LA)*
3500 W Olive Ave Ste 1400
Burbank, CA 91505-5512, USA

Dash, Leon O Jr (Journalist)
Washington Post
Editorial Dept
1150 15th Ave NW
Washington, DC 20071-0001, USA

Dash, Sam
110 Newlands
Washington, DC 20015

Dash, Stacey (Actor)
c/o Jay Schachter *Prestige Talent Agency*
9250 Wilshire Blvd Ste 208
Beverly Hills, CA 90212-3344, USA

Dashboard Confessional (Music Group)
c/o Richard Egan *Hard 8 Management*
1709 19th Ave S
Nashville, TN 37212-3701, USA

Daskalakis, Cleon (Athlete, Hockey Player)
752 Main St
Boxford, MA 01921-1127, USA

Datsyuk, Pavel (Athlete, Hockey Player)
3166 Rosedale St
Ann Arbor, MI 48108-1884, USA

Dattilo, Bryan (Actor)
7039 Shoshone Ave
Van Nuys, CA 91406-3529, USA

Datz, Jeff (Athlete, Baseball Player)
4775 Elen Ct
Shingle Springs, CA 95682-9519, USA

Daubach, Brian (Athlete, Baseball Player)
2709 Timberline Dr
Belleville, IL 62226-4933, USA

Dauer, Rich (Athlete, Baseball Player)
4435 Manor Creek Dr
Cumming, GA 30040-6817, USA

Daugaard, Dennis (Governor, Politician)
500 E Capitol Ave Ofc of
Pierre, SD 57501-5007, USA

Daugherty, Brad (Athlete, Basketball Player)
1613 Cimarron Crest St
Las Vegas, NV 89144-1101, USA

Daugherty, Brant (Actor)
c/o David Sweeney *Sweeney Entertainment*
6253 Hollywood Blvd Apt 201
Los Angeles, CA 90028-8248, USA

Daugherty, Doc (Athlete, Baseball Player)
2304 Higgins Cir
Downingtown, PA 19335-5010, USA

Daugherty, Jack (Athlete, Baseball Player)
20360 N 95th Pl
Scottsdale, AZ 85255-6646, USA

Dauline, Marie (Musician)
Todo Mundo
PO Box 652
Cooper Station
New York, NY 10276-0652, USA

Daulton, Darren (Athlete, Baseball Player)
211 N 3rd St
Arkansas City, KS 67005-2452, USA

Dauplaise, Norman (Jockey)
29 W 36th St # 1000
New York, NY 10018-7907, USA

Davalos, Alexa (Actor)
c/o Staff Member *Anonymous Content (LA)*
3532 Hayden Ave
Culver City, CA 90232-2413, USA

Davalos, Elyssa
2934 1/2 N Beverly Glen Cir # 53
Los Angeles, CA 90077-1724

Davalos, Richard (Actor)
23388 Mulholland Dr # 28
Woodland Hills, CA 91364-2733, USA

Davanon, Jeff (Athlete, Baseball Player)
2811 Piedmont Ave
Los Alamitos, CA 90720-4244, USA

Davanon, Jerry (Athlete, Baseball Player)
350 Greypine W
Montgomery, TX 77356-8192, USA

Dave, Al (Athlete, Football Player)
5173 Waring Rd Apt 441
San Diego, CA 92120-2705, USA

Dave, Al
5173 Waring Rd # 441
San Diego, CA 92120-2705, USA

Dave Matthews Band (Music Group)
c/o Coran Capshaw *Red Light Management (VA)*
321 E Main St Ste 500
Charlottesville, VA 22902-3201, USA

Davenport, Adell (Baseball Player)
Topps
PO Box 462490
Garland, TX 75046-2490, USA

Davenport, Charles (Athlete, Football Player)
206 Wapiti Dr
Spring Lake, NC 28390-1530, USA

Davenport, Jim (Athlete, Baseball Player, Coach)
1016 Hewitt Dr
San Carlos, CA 94070-3601, USA

Davenport, Joe (Athlete, Baseball Player)
10102 Wycliffe St
Santee, CA 92071-1176, USA

Davenport, Ken (Producer)
Davenport Theatrical Enterprises
254 W 54th St Fl 14
New York, NY 10019-5516, USA

Davenport, Lindsay (Athlete, Olympic Athlete, Tennis Player)
704 Emerald Bay
Laguna Beach, CA 92651-1272, USA

Davenport, Lindsey (Tennis Player)
PO Box 10179
Newport Beach, CA 92658-0179, USA

Davenport, Madison (Actor)
c/o Erik Kritzer *LINK Entertainment*
11872 La Grange Ave Fl 1
Los Angeles, CA 90025-5283, USA

Davenport, Naieh
792 SW 106th Ave
Pembroke Pines, FL 33025-6911, USA

Davenport, Najeh (Athlete, Football Player)
c/o Brian Lammi *Lammi Sports Management*
310 E Buffalo St
Milwaukee, WI 53202-5808, USA

Davenport Cabinet (Musician)
c/o Blaze James *Black Sheep Fellowship*
6255 W Sunset Blvd Ste 910
Los Angeles, CA 90028-7410, USA

Davenport Jr, Guy M (Writer)
621 Sayre Ave
Lexington, KY 40508-2317, USA

Davey, Don (Athlete, Football Player)
1525 Beach Ave
Atlantic Beach, FL 32233-5735, USA

Davey, Mike (Athlete, Baseball Player)
902 W Melinda Ln
Spokane, WA 99203-1363, USA

Davey, Rohan (Athlete, Football Player)
24696 Plank Rd
Slaughter, LA 70777-9703, USA

Davey, Tom (Athlete, Baseball Player)
13125 Andover Dr
Plymouth, MI 48170-8208, USA

Davi, Robert (Actor)
10044 Calvin Ave
Northridge, CA 91324-1111, USA

Daviau, Allen (Cinematographer)
2249 Bronson Hill Dr
Los Angeles, CA 90068-2407, USA

Davich, Jacob (Actor)
c/o Brad Schenck *Paradigm (LA)*
360 N Crescent Dr
North Bldg
Beverly Hills, CA 90210-4874, USA

David, Andre (Athlete, Baseball Player)
17341 W Banff Ln
Surprise, AZ 85388-7712, USA

David, Craig (Musician)
c/o Peter Nash *William Morris Endeavor (LA)*
9601 Wilshire Blvd
Beverly Hills, CA 90210-5213, USA

David, Duke (Politician)
240 Garden Ave
Mandeville, LA 70471-2910, USA

David, George A L (Business Person)
United Technologies Corp
United Technologies Building
Hartford, CT 06101, USA

David, Keith (Actor)
c/o Josh Silver *Silver Mine Entertainment*
6705 W Sunset Blvd
Los Angeles, CA 90028-7107, USA

David, Larry (Actor, Producer, Writer)
3000 Olympic Blvd
Santa Monica, CA 90404-5073, USA

David, Mack
1575 Toledo Cir
Palm Springs, CA 92264-9535

David, Peter (Writer)
PO Box 239
Bayport, NY 11705-0239, USA

David, Richie (Athlete, Football Player)
3712 NE 110th St
Vancouver, WA 98686-3991, USA

David, Stacey (Reality Star)
c/o Staff Member *Elite Talent Agency*
1200 Clinton St Ste 212
Nashville, TN 37203-2894, USA

David, Stan (Athlete, Football Player)
502 Baja Cir
Denver City, TX 79323-3747, USA

David, Yuval (Actor, Musician)
c/o Stanzi Stokes *Trio Entertainment Group*
16060 Ventura Blvd # 105-349
Encino, CA 91436-2761, USA

David Bossert, David Bossert (Director, Producer)
c/o Staff Member *Disney Animation (LA)*
500 S Buena Vista St
Burbank, CA 91521-9500, USA

David Crowder Band (Musician)
c/o Staff Member *Third Coast Artists Agency*
2021 21st Ave S Ste 220
Nashville, TN 37212-4348, USA

Davidoff, Dov (Actor)
c/o Stephanie Davis *Wet Dog Entertainment*
9460 Wilshire Blvd Fl 7
Beverly Hills, CA 90212-2713, USA

Davidovich, Bella (Musician)
c/o Staff Member *Columbia Artists Mgmt Inc*
1790 Broadway Fl 6
New York, NY 10019-1537, USA

Davidovich, Lolita (Actor)
15200 Friends St
Pacific Palisades, CA 90272-4605, USA

Davids, Hollace (Producer)
c/o Staff Member *Universal Pictures*
100 Universal City Plz
Universal City, CA 91608-1085, USA

Davidson, Adam (Actor)
c/o Andrea Simon *Andrea Simon Entertainment*
4230 Woodman Ave
Sherman Oaks, CA 91423-4334, USA

Davidson, Amy (Actor)
4435 Colfax Ave Unit 112
N Hollywood, CA 91602-4207, USA

Davidson, Bob (Athlete, Baseball Player)
91 Deerwood Dr
Littleton, CO 80127-2626, USA

Davidson, Bob (Athlete, Baseball Player)
1420 Bruton Parish Way
Fairfield, OH 45014-4536, USA

Davidson, Cleatus (Athlete, Baseball Player)
705 E Frederick Ave
Dundee, FL 33838-4240, USA

Davidson, Cotton (Athlete, Football Player)
435 Old Osage Rd
Gatesville, TX 76528-3362, USA

Davidson, Dallas (Musician)
4320 Wallace Ln
Nashville, TN 37215-3234, USA

Davidson, Diane Mott (Writer)
c/o Author Mail *Bantam-Dell Publishing (NY)*
1745 Broadway
New York, NY 10019-4640, USA

Davidson, Doug (Actor)
295 Toro Canyon Rd
Carpinteria, CA 93013-3040, USA

Davidson, Eileen (Actor)
11300 W Olympic Blvd Ste 610
Los Angeles, CA 90064-1643, USA

Davidson, Gary L (Athlete, Hockey Player)
245 Fischer Ave Ste D1
Costa Mesa, CA 92626-4539, USA

Davidson, George A Jr (Business Person)
Consolidated Natural Gas
625 Liberty Ave
Pittsburgh, PA 15222-3110, USA

Davidson, Gordon (Director, Producer)
Center Theatre Group
135 N Grand Ave
Mark Taper Forum
Los Angeles, CA 90012-3013, USA

Davidson, Jeff (Athlete, Football Player)
8971 SW Village Loop
Chanhassen, MN 55317-8589, USA

Davidson, Jeff (Motivational Speaker)
Breathing Space Institute
2417 Honeysuckle Rd
Chapel Hill, NC 27514-6819, USA

Davidson, Jeremy (Actor)
c/o Matthew Lesher *Insight*
PO Box 36359
Los Angeles, CA 90036-0359, USA

Davidson, John (Athlete, Hockey Player)
c/o Josh Pultz *Douglas Gorman Rothacker & Wilhelm Inc*
1501 Broadway Ste 703
New York, NY 10036-5501, USA

Davidson, John (Athlete, Hockey Player)
6 Briarbrook Trl
Saint Louis, MO 63131-3947, USA

Davidson, Ken (Athlete, Football Player)
1922 Thompson Crossing Dr
Richmond, TX 77406-6707, USA

Davidson, Mark (Athlete, Baseball Player)
996 Old Mountain Rd
Statesville, NC 28677-2082, USA

Davidson, Matthew (Athlete, Golfer)
3 Westminster Pl
Cranbury, NJ 08512-3217, USA

Davidson, Owen (Athlete, Tennis Player)
39 N Lakemist Harbour Pl
Spring, TX 77381-3344, USA

Davidson, Ralph P (Publisher)
494 Harbor Rd
Southport, CT 06890-1319, USA

Davidson, Satch (Athlete, Baseball Player)
2400 Westheimer Rd Apt 209W
Houston, TX 77098-1305, USA

Davidson, Tommy (Actor, Comedian)
3800 Weslin Ave
Sherman Oaks, CA 91423-4735, USA

Davidtz, Embeth (Actor)
345 S Chadbourne Ave
Los Angeles, CA 90049-3708, USA

Davie, Jerry (Athlete, Baseball Player)
2800 US Highway 17 92 W Ofc
Haines City, FL 33844, USA

Davies, Gail (Musician)
246 Cherokee Rd
Nashville, TN 37205-1818, USA

Davies, Jeremy (Actor)
United Talent Agency
9336 Civic Center Dr
Beverly Hills, CA 90210-3604, USA

Davies, Kyle (Athlete, Baseball Player)
1495 E Lake Rd
McDonough, GA 30252-2615, USA

Davies, Lane (Actor)
PO Box 20531
Thousand Oaks, CA 91358, USA

Davies, Laura (Athlete, Golfer)
I M G
1360 E 9th St Ste 100
Cleveland, OH 44114-1730, USA

Davies, Russel T (Writer)
c/o Lisa Harrison *William Morris Endeavor (LA)*
9601 Wilshire Blvd
Beverly Hills, CA 90210-5213, USA

Davies, Tamara (Actor)
c/o Staff Member *Bauman Redanty & Shaul Agency*
5757 Wilshire Blvd
Suite 473
Beverly Hills, CA 90212, USA

Davies, Wyn (Actor)
c/o Staff Member *Screen Actors Guild (SAG-LA)*
5757 Wilshire Blvd Ste 124
Los Angeles, CA 90036-3792, USA

Davis, A Dano (Business Person)
Winn-Dixie Stores
5050 Edgewood Ct
Jacksonville, FL 32254-3699, USA

Davis, Alecia (Actor)
c/o Jonathan Clements *Nashville Agency*
501 Metroplex Dr Ste 116
Nashville, TN 37211-3131, USA

Davis, Alvin (Athlete, Baseball Player)
7983 Arma101OSA Dr
Riverside, CA 92S08, USA

Davis, Andra (Athlete, Football Player)
6009 S Olathe St
Centennial, CO 80016-1071, USA

Davis, Andra (Athlete, Football Player)
21230 Greenfield Pl
Strongsville, OH 44149-9218, USA

Davis, Andre (Athlete, Football Player)
11407 Jutland Rd
Houston, TX 77048-2631, USA

Davis, Andrew (Director)
c/o Laurence Becsey *Intellectual Property Group (IPG)*
10585 Santa Monica Blvd Ste 140
Los Angeles, CA 90025-4984, USA

Davis, Andy (Athlete, Football Player)
14500 Fiske Dr
Silver Spring, MD 20906-1737, USA

Davis, Angela (Politician)
10463 Royal Oak Rd
Oakland, CA 94605-5041, USA

Davis, Anthony (Athlete, Football Player)
8500 W 131st Ter Apt 1834
Overland Park, KS 66213-5157, USA

Davis, Anthony (Athlete, Football Player)
A D 28 Development Inc 29 Firwood
Irvine, CA 92604, USA

Davis, Antone (Athlete, Football Player)
2252 Red Bud Rd
Sevierville, TN 37876, USA

Davis, Antonio (Athlete, Basketball Player)
1883 Cedar Glenn Way
Atlanta, GA 30339-8563, USA

Davis, Ardie A (Writer)
c/o Staff Member *Harvard Common Press, The*
535 Albany St Ste 47
Boston, MA 02118-2559, USA

Davis, Aree (Actor)
c/o Myrna Lieberman *Myrna Lieberman Management*
3001 Hollyridge Dr
Los Angeles, CA 90068-1951, USA

Davis, Arthur (Athlete, Football Player)
8260 SW Woodbridge Ct
Wilsonville, OR 97070-7458, USA

Davis, Bard (Basketball Player)
Los Angeles Lakers
2703 Ridge Top Ln
Arlington, TX 76006-2729, USA

Davis, Baron (Athlete, Basketball Player)
c/o Staff Member *BDA Sports Management (BDA-CA)*
700 Ygnacio Valley Rd Ste 330
Walnut Creek, CA 94596-3838, USA

Davis, Barry (Athlete, Olympic Athlete, Wrestler)
417 N High Point Rd
Madison, WI 53717-1849, USA

Davis, Ben (Athlete, Baseball Player)
416 Homestead Dr
West Chester, PA 19382-8242, USA

Davis, Ben (Athlete, Football Player)
1144 Brandon Rd
Cleveland, OH 44112-3632, USA

Davis, Bill (Race Car Driver)
11 N Robbins St
Thomasville, NC 27360-8970, USA

Davis, Bill (Athlete, Baseball Player)
6638 Knox Aves
Minneapolis, MN 55423, USA

Davis, Billy (Athlete, Football Player)
5813 Tautoga Dr
El Paso, TX 79924-5620, USA

Davis, Bob (Athlete, Baseball Player)
PO Box 198
Locust Grove, OK 74352-0198, USA

Davis, Brad (Athlete, Basketball Player)
2703 Ridge Top Ln
Arlington, TX 76006-2729, USA

Davis, Brian (Athlete, Football Player)
9874 Red Sumac Pl
Parker, CO 80138-7868, USA

Davis, Brian (Athlete, Golfer)
10545 Down Lakeview Cir
Windermere, FL 34786-7911, USA

Davis, Brianne (Actor)
c/o Staff Member *Art Work Entertainment*
5900 Wilshire Blvd Ste 2150
Los Angeles, CA 90036-5021, USA

Davis, Brock (Athlete, Baseball Player)
13801 Paramount Blvd Apt 4110
Paramount, CA 90723-6136, USA

Davis, Buddy (Athlete, Basketball Player, Olympic Athlete)
6582 FM 841
Lufkin, TX 75901-4633, USA

Davis, Butch (Athlete, Baseball Player)
1108 Brucemont Dr
Garner, NC 27529-4505, USA

Davis, Carole (Actor)
c/o Judy Orbach *Judy O Productions*
6136 Glen Holly St
Los Angeles, CA 90068-2338, USA

Davis, Charles (Actor)
c/o Anthony Embry *AE Entertainment Public Relations*
124 Evening Shade Dr
Charleston, SC 29414-9144, USA

Davis, Charles (Athlete, Basketball Player)
615 Main St
Nashville, TN 37206-3603, USA

Davis, Charles ""Chili (Athlete, Baseball Player)
2348 E Cinnabar Ave
Phoenix, AZ 85028-3600, USA

Davis, Charles (Chili) (Athlete, Baseball Player)
c/o Team Member *San Francisco Giants*
24 Willie Mays Plz
Sbc Park
San Francisco, CA 94107-2199, USA

Davis, Charles D (Athlete, Football Player)
8935 Aspen Meadow Dr
Houston, TX 77071-3256, USA

Davis, Charles M (Athlete, Football Player)
2391 Crescent Park Dr
Houston, TX 77077-6756, USA

Davis, Charles Michael (Actor)
c/o Mary Erickson *Mary Erickson Management*
2126 N Commonwealth Ave
Los Angeles, CA 90027-2118, USA

Davis, Charlie (Athlete, Basketball Player)
302 Heather Ridge Ct
Greensboro, NC 27455-8360, USA

Davis, Chip (Musician)
c/o Staff Member *Brokaw Company, The*
9255 W Sunset Blvd Ste 804
West Hollywood, CA 90069-3305, USA

Davis, Chris (Athlete, Baseball Player)
c/o Scott Boras *Boras Corporation*
3 San Joaquin Plz Ste 100
Newport Beach, CA 92660-5944, USA

Davis, Christine (Writer)
Lighthearted Press Inc
PO Box 90125
Portland, OR 97290-0125, USA

Davis, Christopher (Chris) W (Athlete, Football Player)
1509 Chateau Run Ct
Virginia Beach, VA 23456-1480, USA

Davis, Clarence (Athlete, Football Player)
171 Longleaf St
Pickerington, OH 43147-7940, USA

Davis, Clifton (Actor)
c/o Staff Member *Agency for the Performing Arts (APA-LA)*
405 S Beverly Dr Ste 500
Beverly Hills, CA 90212-4425, USA

Davis, Clive (Business Person, Producer)
29 Col Sheldon Ln
Pound Ridge, NY 10576-1409, USA

Davis, Dana (Actor)
c/o Darryl Marshak *Marshak/Zachary Company, The*
8840 Wilshire Blvd Fl 1
Beverly Hills, CA 90211-2606, USA

Davis, Daniel (Actor)
c/o Gary Gersh *Innovative Artists (NY)*
235 Park Ave S Fl 7
New York, NY 10003-1405, USA

Davis, David (Dave) (Bowler)
DeStasio
710 Shore Rd
Spring Lake, NJ 07762-1855, USA

Davis, DeRay (Actor)
c/o April Lim *Global Artists Agency*
6253 Hollywood Blvd Apt 508
Los Angeles, CA 90028-8251, USA

Davis, Dexter (Athlete, Football Player)
5078 Old Mountain Trl
Powder Springs, GA 30127-4317, USA

Davis, Dick (Athlete, Football Player)
3425 N 267th Plz
Waterloo, NE 68069-5829, USA

Davis, Dick (Athlete, Baseball Player)
11091 Sultan St
Moreno Valley, CA 92557-4917, USA

Davis, Domanick (Athlete, Football Player)
1223 Nursery Hwy
Breaux Bridge, LA 70517-8217, USA

Davis, Dominique (Athlete, Football Player)
c/o Adisa P. Bakari *Dow Lohnes PLLC*
1299 Pennsylvania Ave NW Ste 700
Washington, DC 20004-2431, USA

Davis, Donald (Athlete, Football Player)
739 E 48th St
Los Angeles, CA 90011-4008, USA

Davis, Don H Jr (Business Person)
Rockwell International
777 E Wisconsin Ave Ste 1400
Milwaukee, WI 53202-5317, USA

Davis, Dorsett (Athlete, Football Player)
605 Rosemary Rd
Cleveland, MS 38732-2048, USA

Davis, Doug (Athlete, Baseball Player)
279 Whites Church Rd
Bloomsburg, PA 17815-7156, USA

Davis, Doug (Athlete, Baseball Player)
26125 N 116th St Unit 7
Scottsdale, AZ 85255-8721, USA

Davis, Drew (Athlete, Football Player)
c/o Derrick Fox *Derrick Fox Management*
Prefers to be contacted by telephone
CA, USA

Davis, Dwight (Athlete, Basketball Player)
PO Box 324
Newfields, NH 03856-0324, USA

Davis, Ed (Athlete, Basketball Player)
36750 US Highway 19 N # 26-3437
Palm Harbor, FL 34684-1239, USA

Davis, Elizabeth (Musician)
Rave Booking
PO Box 310780
Jamaica, NY 11431-0780, USA

Davis, Elliot M (Cinematographer)
1328 Arch St
Berkeley, CA 94708-1825, USA

Davis, Eric K (Athlete, Baseball Player)
6203 Variel Ave Unit 118
Woodland Hills, CA 91367-2472, USA

Davis, Eric W (Athlete, Football Player)
236 S Oakhurst Dr
Beverly Hills, CA 90212-3504, USA

Davis, Frenchie (Musician)
c/o Stephen Ford *Diva Central Inc*
7510 W Sunset Blvd Ste 1445
Los Angeles, CA 90046-3408, USA

Davis, Gary (Athlete, Football Player)
10750 San Marcos Rd
Atascadero, CA 93422-2126, USA

Davis, Geena (Actor)
c/o Jack Whigham *Creative Artists Agency (CAA-LA)*
2000 Avenue of the Stars Ste 100
Los Angeles, CA 90067-4705, USA

Davis, Geoff (Congressman, Politician)
1119 Longworth Hob
Washington, DC 20515-0531, USA

Davis, George (Athlete, Baseball Player)
3334 Sharpe Ave
Memphis, TN 38111-3758, USA

Davis, Gerry (Athlete, Baseball Player)
19856 Saltwater Cir
Huntington Beach, CA 92648-3027, USA

Davis, Gray (Politician)
10430 Wilshire Blvd Apt 605
Los Angeles, CA 90024-4653, USA

Davis, Gray (Ex-Governor)
State Capitol Building
Sacramento, CA 95814, USA

Davis, Greg (Athlete, Football Player)
1550 Dunwoody Club Dr
Atlanta, GA 30350-4436, USA

Davis, Harper (Athlete, Football Player)
1224 Springdale Dr
Jackson, MS 39211-3130, USA

Davis, Harrison (Athlete, Football Player)
6806 W 3rd St Unit 26
Greeley, CO 80634-9030, USA

Davis, Harry (Athlete, Basketball Player)
1966 E 75th St
Cleveland, OH 44103-4125, USA

Davis, Hope (Actor)
152 Jermain Ave
Sag Harbor, NY 11963-3413, USA

Davis, Hubert (Athlete, Basketball Player)
4320 Trenton Rd
Chapel Hill, NC 27517-7833, USA

Davis, Jack (Athlete, Football Player)
305 Crest Ct
Poteau, OK 74953-2128, USA

Davis, Jacke (Athlete, Baseball Player)
6806 Castle Pines Ct
Tyler, TX 75703-5890, USA

Davis, James (Basketball Player)
Rochester Royals
44 Van Ter
Sparkill, NY 10976-1406, USA

Davis, James (Athlete, Football Player)
5701 S St Andrews Pl
Los Angeles, CA 90062, USA

Davis, James (Cartoonist)
5440 E Country Rd 450 N
Albany, IN 47320, USA

Davis, James O (Doctor)
546 Warren Ave
Saint Louis, MO 63130-4154, USA

Davis, Jason (Athlete, Baseball Player)
474 Leatha Ln NW
Cleveland, TN 37312-6522, USA

Davis, Jay (Athlete, Golfer)
2152 S State St
Springfield, IL 62704-4526, USA

Davis, Jeff (Actor)
c/o Staff Member *United Talent Agency (UTA-LA)*
9336 Civic Center Dr
Beverly Hills, CA 90210-3604, USA

Davis, Jeff (Athlete, Football Player)
106 Sycamore Dr
Clemson, SC 29631-2071, USA

Davis, Jeremy (Musician)
245 3rd Ave N
Franklin, TN 37064-2504, USA

Davis, Jerome (Athlete, Football Player)
515 N 4th St
Palatka, FL 32177-3523, USA

Davis, Jerry (Baseball Player)
San Diego Padres
72 Theresa St
Ewing, NJ 08618-1531, USA

Davis, Jesse (Musician)
Concord Records
100 N Crescent Dr Ste 275
Beverly Hills, CA 90210-5412, USA

Davis, Jill A (Writer)
Random House
1745 Broadway Frnt 3 # B1
New York, NY 10019-4343, USA

Davis, Jimmy (Athlete, Football Player)
616 Briar Patch Ter
Waxhaw, NC 28173-6822, USA

Davis, J J (Athlete, Baseball Player)
7302 Forrest Rader Dr
Mint Hill, NC 28227-9830, USA

Davis, Jody (Athlete, Baseball Player)
PO Box 93157
Phoenix, AZ 85070-3157, USA

Davis, Joel (Athlete, Baseball Player)
10075 Gate Pkwy N Apt 2912
Jacksonville, FL 32246-4431, USA

Davis, John (Athlete, Baseball Player)
329 Summit Ave
Redlands, CA 92373-6853, USA

Davis, John (Actor, Director, Producer)
c/o Staff Member *Davis Entertainment*
150 S Barrington Pl
Los Angeles, CA 90049-3306, USA

Davis, John (Athlete, Football Player)
901 Forest Pond Dr
Marietta, GA 30068-4420, USA

Davis, Johnny (Athlete, Basketball Player, Coach)
28 S Kaufman Stone Way
Biltmore Lake, NC 28715-7722, USA

Davis, Johnny (Athlete, Football Player)
PO Box 550
Edgewater, NJ 07020-0550, USA

Davis, Jonathan (Musician)
5253 Horizon Dr
Malibu, CA 90265, USA

Davis, Josie (Actor)
CunninghamEscottDipene
10635 Santa Monica Blvd Ste 130
Los Angeles, CA 90025-8306, USA

Davis, Kane (Athlete, Baseball Player)
1558 Noble Rdg
Reedy, WV 25270-9540, USA

Davis, Kara (Adult Film Star)
PO Box 9465
Newport Beach, CA 92658-9465, USA

Davis, Keith B (Athlete, Football Player)
1004 Peach Ln
Desoto, TX 75115-4122, USA

Davis, Kenneth E (Athlete, Football Player)
1224 Brooklawn Dr
Arlington, TX 76018-2952, USA

Davis, Kristin (Actor)
c/o David (Dave) Fleming *Mosaic Media Group*
9200 W Sunset Blvd Ste 10
West Hollywood, CA 90069-3608, USA

Davis, Kyle (Athlete, Football Player)
104 Futurity Ln
Weatherford, TX 76087-4606, USA

Davis, Lance (Athlete, Baseball Player)
5845 Old Berkley Rd
Auburndale, FL 33823-8361, USA

Davis, L Edward (Religious Leader)
Evangelical Presbyterian Church
26049 5 Mile Rd
Redford, MI 48239-3235, USA

Davis, Lee (Athlete, Basketball Player)
5024 Fieldgreen Xing Apt B2
Stone Mountain, GA 30088-3103, USA

Davis, Lee (Director)
Gersh Agency
232 N Canon Dr
Beverly Hills, CA 90210-5302, USA

Davis, Leonard (Athlete, Football Player)
24012 S 150th St
Chandler, AZ 85249-9600, USA

Davis, Linda (Musician)
PO Box 767
Hermitage, TN 37076-0767, USA

Davis, Lorenzo (Athlete, Football Player)
149 Vista Luna Dr
Davie, FL 33325-6929, USA

Davis, Lucy (Actor, Director)
512 N Gower St
Los Angeles, CA 90004-1302, USA

Davis, Mac (Actor, Musician, Songwriter)
346 N Tigertail Rd
Los Angeles, CA 90049-2806, USA

Davis, Mark (Athlete, Baseball Player)
8867 E Sierra Pinta Dr
Scottsdale, AZ 85255-9174, USA

Davis, Mark A (Athlete, Basketball Player)
108 Government Cir # A
Thibodaux, LA 70301-6615, USA

Davis, Mark G (Basketball Player)
Milwaukee Bucks
3120 Aaron Dr
Chesapeake, VA 23323-2600, USA

Davis, Mark W (Athlete, Baseball Player)
8867 E Sierra Pinta Dr
Scottsdale, AZ 85255-9174, USA

Davis, Martha (Musician)
c/o Trip Brown *Paradise Artists*
108 E Matilija St
Ojai, CA 93023-2639, USA

Davis, Marv (Butch) (Athlete, Football Player)
700 Ponce De Leon Ave
Clewiston, FL 33440-2413, USA

Davis, Mary (Athlete, Football Player)
700 Ponce De Leon Ave
Clewiston, FL 33440-2413, USA

Davis, Matthew (Actor)
1958 Glencoe Way
Los Angeles, CA 90068-3113, USA

Davis, Melvyn (Athlete, Basketball Player)
PO Box 29
Suffern, NY 10901-0029, USA

Davis, Meryl (Athlete, Figure Skater,
Olympic Athlete)
c/o Hailey Ohnuki *IMG World (NY)*
200 5th Ave Bsmt 7
New York, NY 10010-3312, USA

Davis, Michael (Athlete, Basketball Player)
110 W Clay St
Richmond, VA 23220-3913, USA

Davis, Michael A (Athlete, Football
Player)
2229 Durango Dr
Loveland, CO 80538-2947, USA

Davis, Michael L (Athlete, Football Player)
PO Box 614
Beaver Falls, PA 15010-0614, USA

Davis, Mike (Athlete, Baseball Player)
c/o Staff Member *Oakland Athletics*
7000 Coliseum Way Ste 3
Oakland, CA 94621-1992, USA

Davis, Mike (Athlete, Basketball Player)
100 W 92nd St Apt 29E
New York, NY 10025-7546, USA

Davis, Mike (Athlete, Football Player)
37039 N 109th St
Scottsdale, AZ 85262-3582, USA

Davis, Monti (Athlete, Basketball Player)
328 Tod Ln
Youngstown, OH 44504-1403, USA

Davis, Musiello
Janette200 Windemere Way
Naples, FL 33999

Davis, N Jan (Astronaut)
4105 Cumberland Pass Apt 814
Fort Worth, TX 76116-0753, USA

Davis, Odie (Athlete, Baseball Player)
7314 Hidden His N
San Antonio, TX 78244, USA

Davis, Oliver (Athlete, Football Player)
3791 Paces Ferry West SE
Atlanta, GA 30339-4138, USA

Davis, Paige (Television Host)
c/o Staff Member *William Morris
Endeavor (LA)*
9601 Wilshire Blvd
Beverly Hills, CA 90210-5213, USA

Davis, Paschall (Athlete, Football Player)
937 Plumeria Dr
Arlington, TX 76002-2402, USA

Davis, Patti (Writer)
c/o Staff Member *Hay House, Inc*
PO Box 5100
Carlsbad, CA 92018-5100, USA

Davis, Paul (Athlete, Football Player)
227 Oval Park Pl # Pi
Chapel Hill, NC 27517-8116, USA

Davis, Phyllis (Actor)
29330 SE Hillyard Dr # D14
Boring, OR 97009-8502, USA

Davis, Preston (Athlete, Football Player)
1282 W 100th Pi
Denver, CO 80260, USA

Davis, Radric (Gucci Mane) (Musician)
c/o Staff Member *Warner Bros Records
(NY)*
75 Rockefeller Plz
New York, NY 10019-6908, USA

Davis, Raiai (Athlete, Baseball Player)
9 Pear Grv
East Lyme, CT 06333-1177, USA

Davis, Ralph (Athlete, Basketball Player)
2624 S Kathwood Cir
Cincinnati, OH 45236-1026, USA

Davis, Rennie (Politician)
Birth of a New Nation
905 S Gilpin St
Denver, CO 80209-4520, USA

Davis, Reuben (Athlete, Football Player)
515 Ireland St
Greensboro, NC 27406-1236, USA

Davis, Richard (Musician)
SRO Artists
6629 University Ave Ste 206
Middleton, WI 53562-3037, USA

Davis, Ricky (Athlete, Football Player)
2715 Altadena Rd
Vestavia, AL 35243-4506, USA

Davis, Ricky (Athlete, Basketball Player)
c/o Jeff Schwartz *Excel Sports
Management (NY)*
1700 Broadway Fl 29
New York, NY 10019-5905, USA

Davis, Robbie (Horse Racer)
756 Stone Church Rd
Middle Grove, NY 12850-1131, USA

Davis, Roger (Athlete, Football Player)
12501 Mount Overlook Ave
Cleveland, OH 44120-1039, USA

Davis, Roger (Actor)
Janette Anderson Talent Agency
9682 Via Torino
Burbank, CA 91504-1410, USA

Davis, Ron (Athlete, Basketball Player)
11748 N 90th Pl # Pi
Scottsdale, AZ 85260-6841, USA

Davis, Ronald (Ron) (Athlete, Football
Player)
4717 Pompton Ln
Chester, VA 23831-4335, USA

Davis, Ross (Athlete, Baseball Player)
8042 Highway 71
Garwood, TX 77442-4158, USA

Davis, Russ (Athlete, Baseball Player)
3351 Crescent Dr
Bessemer, AL 35023-2919, USA

Davis, Russell (Athlete, Football Player)
1208 Tanbark Ln E
Jackson, MI 49203-1275, USA

Davis, Russell (Athlete, Football Player)
605 Jones Ferry Rd
Carrboro, NC 27510-2106, USA

Davis, Russell A (Athlete, Football Player)
4236 Crosswood Dr
Burtonsville, MD 20866-1350, USA

Davis, Russell S (Russ) (Baseball Player)
3351 Crescent Dr
Bessemer, AL 35023-2919, USA

Davis, Ruth (Athlete, Baseball Player,
Commentator)
1917 Park Ave
Cheyenne, WY 82007-3395, USA

Davis, Sam (Athlete, Football Player)
423 Edgemont St
Mt Washington, PA 15211-2405, USA

Davis, Sammy (Athlete, Football Player)
4020 Murphy Canyon Rd
San Diego, CA 92123-4407, USA

Davis, Spencer
PO Box 1821
Ojai, CA 93024-1821

Davis, Stephen (Athlete, Football Player)
16 Dunleith Ct
Irmo, SC 29063-8042, USA

Davis, Steve (Athlete, Baseball Player)
6011 86th St
Lubbock, TX 79424-6708, USA

Davis, Steve (Athlete, Football Player)
356 E 29th St
Buena Vista, VA 24416-1204, USA

Davis, Steve (Athlete, Baseball Player)
601186th St
Lubbock, TX 79424, USA

Davis, Storm (Athlete, Baseball Player)
8469 Mizner Cir E
Jacksonville, FL 32217-4326, USA

Davis, Storm George (Baseball Player)
7931 Dawsons Creek Dr
Jacksonville, FL 32222-4905, USA

Davis, Susan (Congressman, Politician)
1526 Longworth Hob
Washington, DC 20515-3305, USA

Davis, Tamra (Director)
7126 Fernhill Dr
Malibu, CA 90265-4243, USA

Davis, Ted (Athlete, Football Player)
5401 Riverbend Dr
Knoxville, TN 37919-8953, USA

Davis, Terrell (Athlete, Football Player)
19750 E Geddes Pl
Centennial, CO 80016-2143, USA

Davis, Terry (Athlete, Basketball Player)
2933 Kenmore Rd
Richmond, VA 23225-1429, USA

Davis, Thomas (Athlete, Football Player)
c/o Todd France *Five Star Athlete
Management*
3500 Lenox Rd NE
Atlanta, GA 30326-4228, USA

Davis, Tim (Athlete, Baseball Player)
16161 NW Lakeside Ln
Bristol, FL 32321-3932, USA

Davis, Todd (Actor)
245 S Keystone St
Burbank, CA 91506-2727, USA

Davis, Tommy (Athlete, Baseball Player)
JD Legends Promotions
Chris Potter Sports 9722
Owings Mills, MD 21117, USA

Davis, Travis (Athlete, Football Player)
PO Box 44643
Indianapolis, IN 46244-0643, USA

Davis, Trench (Athlete, Baseball Player)
306 40th Street Cir W
Palmetto, FL 34221-9516, USA

Davis, Troy (Athlete, Football Player)
11861 SW 190th St
Miami, FL 33177-3940, USA

Davis, Vernon (Athlete, Football Player)
c/o Todd France *Five Star Athlete
Management*
3500 Lenox Rd NE
Atlanta, GA 30326-4228, USA

Davis, Vicki (Actor)
c/o Staff Member *Innovative Artists (LA)*
1505 10th St
Santa Monica, CA 90401-2805, USA

Davis, Viola (Actor)
17755 Arvida Dr
Granada Hills, CA 91344-1306, USA

Davis, Vontae (Athlete, Football Player)
c/o Todd France *Five Star Athlete
Management*
3500 Lenox Rd NE
Atlanta, GA 30326-4228, USA

Davis, Wade (Athlete, Baseball Player)
PO Box 46
Marlboro, NY 12542-0046, USA

Davis, Wade (Writer)
c/o Staff Member *Simon & Schuster*
1230 Avenue of the Americas Fl CONC1
New York, NY 10020-1586, USA

Davis, Walter (Athlete, Basketball Player,
Olympic Athlete)
5200 E Donald Ave Apt A
Denver, CO 80222-5539, USA

Davis, Warren (Athlete, Basketball Player)
44429 Oriole Dr Unit 1E1
Fort Mill, SC 29707-5947, USA

Davis, Wendell (Athlete, Football Player)
4020 S Ellis Ave Apt 2
Chicago, IL 60653-2455, USA

Davis, Wendell (Athlete, Football Player)
10850 Green Mountain Cir Unit 117
Columbia, MD 21044-2300, USA

Davis, Will (Athlete, Football Player)
c/o Doug Hendrickson *Octagon Football*
832 Sansome St Fl 1
San Francisco, CA 94111-1558, USA

Davis, William E (Business Person)
Niagara Mohawk Holdings
300 Erie Blvd W
Syracuse, NY 13202-4250, USA

Davis, William L (Business Person)
R R Donnelley & Sons
77 W Wacker Dr Ste 500
Chicago, IL 60601-1671, USA

Davis, Willie (Athlete, Football Player)
7352 Vista Del Mar Ln
Playa Del Rey, CA 90293-7650, USA

Davis Jr, Greg (Actor, Comedian, Internet
Star)
c/o Colleen Schlegel *Artist Management*
1118 15th St Apt 1
Santa Monica, CA 90403-5580, USA

Davison, Beverly C (Religious Leader)
American Baptist Churches
PO Box 851
Valley Forge, PA 19482-0851, USA

Davison, Bruce (Actor)
5144 Boda Pl
Woodland Hills, CA 91367-5814, USA

Davison, Mike (Athlete, Baseball Player)
927 Lewis Ave SW
Hutchinson, MN 55350-2350, USA

Davison, Sam (Religious Leader)
International Baptist Bible Fellowship
720 E Kearney St
Springfield, MO 65803-3428, USA

Davison, Scott (Athlete, Baseball Player)
4507 Sharynne Ln
Torrance, CA 90505-3454, USA

Davis-Wrightsil, Clarissa (Basketball Player)
Phoenix Mercury
201 E Jefferson St
American West Arena
Phoenix, AZ 85004-2412, USA

Davitian, Ken (Actor)
c/o Tess Finkle *Metro Public Relations*
8383 Wilshire Blvd Ste 208
Beverly Hills, CA 90211-2432, USA

Davkin, Tony (Athlete, Football Player)
5204 Cross Ridge Cir
Woodstock, GA 30188-4381, USA

Davoli, Andrew (Actor)
c/o Greg Clark *Untitled Entertainment (LA)*
350 S Beverly Dr Ste 200
Beverly Hills, CA 90212-4819, USA

Daw, Jeff (Athlete, Hockey Player)
100 Fountain St Unit 4B
Providence, RI 02903-1845, USA

Dawber, Pam (Actor)
c/o Staff Member *TalentWorks (LA)*
3500 W Olive Ave Ste 1400
Burbank, CA 91505-5512, USA

Dawe, Jason (Athlete, Hockey Player)
9077 Drayton Ln
Fort Mill, SC 29707-6484, USA

Dawes, Dominique (Athlete, Gymnast, Olympic Athlete)
1611 Hugo Cir
Silver Spring, MD 20906-5921, USA

Dawes, Joseph (Cartoonist)
20 Church Ct
Closter, NJ 07624-2803, USA

Dawkins, Brian (Athlete, Football Player)
10010 Tavistock Rd
Orlando, FL 32827-7053, USA

Dawkins, Dale (Athlete, Football Player)
390 Concord Dr
Bozeman, MT 59715-7100, USA

Dawkins, Darryl (Athlete, Basketball Player)
1708 Glacier Ct
Allentown, PA 18104-1710, USA

Dawkins, Joe (Athlete, Football Player)
9200 S Harvard Blvd
Los Angeles, CA 90047-3801, USA

Dawkins, Joe (Athlete, Football Player)
4235 Ensenada Dr
Woodland Hills, CA 91364-5403, USA

Dawkins, Johnny (Athlete, Basketball Player)
601A Olmsted Rd # A
Stanford, CA 94305-7498, USA

Dawkins, Johnny (Basketball Player)
San Antonio Spurs
2604 Vintage Hill Ct
Durham, NC 27712-9492, USA

Dawkins, Paul (Athlete, Basketball Player)
2728 N Hampton Dr
Grand Prairie, TX 75052-4201, USA

Dawkins, Pete (Business Person, Football Player, General, Heisman Trophy Winner, Politician)
31 Highland Ave
Rumson, NJ 07760-1751, USA

Dawkins, Sean (Athlete, Football Player)
826 Weichert Dr
Morgan Hill, CA 95037-3785, USA

Dawkins, Travis (Athlete, Baseball Player, Olympic Athlete)
1290 Calhoun Rd
Greenwood, SC 29649-1244, USA

Dawley, Bill (Athlete, Baseball Player)
111 N Silver Manor Cir
Montgomery, TX 77316-1455, USA

Dawley, Joey (Athlete, Baseball Player)
27951 Cactus Ave Unit A
Moreno Valley, CA 92555-3609, USA

Dawsey, Lawrence (Athlete, Football Player)
4341 Cheval Blvd
Lutz, FL 33558-5328, USA

Dawson, Andre (Athlete, Baseball Player)
Andre Dawson Foundation
PO Box 431339
Miami, FL 33243-1339, USA

Dawson, Buck (Swimmer)
Swimming Hall of Fame
1 Hall of Fame Dr
Fort Lauderdale, FL 33316-1694, USA

Dawson, Dale (Athlete, Football Player)
1710 E Oak Knoll Cir
Davie, FL 33324-6424, USA

Dawson, Dermontti (Athlete, Football Player)
PO Box 712481
San Diego, CA 92171-2481, USA

Dawson, Douglas A (Doug) (Athlete, Football Player)
Dawson Financial Services
1 Riverway Ste 900
Houston, TX 77056-1906, USA

Dawson, Jajuan (Athlete, Football Player)
610 Harvest Hill Dr
Murphy, TX 75094-4196, USA

Dawson, Jim (Athlete, Basketball Player)
7 Prestbury Ln
Savannah, GA 31411-2559, USA

Dawson, Keyunta (Athlete, Football Player)
2311 Darks Mill Rd
Columbia, TN 38401-7265, USA

Dawson, Kim (Actor, Producer, Writer)
c/o Staff Member *Skydog Productions*
1000 Universal Studios Plz Bldg 22A
Orlando, FL 32819-7601, USA

Dawson, Lake (Athlete, Football Player)
33228 37th Pl SW
Federal Way, WA 98023-2959, USA

Dawson, Lake (Athlete, Football Player)
33228 37th Pi SW
Federal Way, WA 98023, USA

Dawson, Len (Athlete, Football Player)
1025 W 59th Ter
Kansas City, MO 64113-1335, USA

Dawson, Leonard R (Lenny) (Athlete, Football Player, Sportscaster)
4950 Central St Apt 606
Kansas City, MO 64112-2588, USA

Dawson, Marco (Athlete, Golfer)
4360 Stillwater Dr
Merritt Island, FL 32952-6320, USA

Dawson, Phil (Athlete, Football Player)
4000 Dunning Ln
Austin, TX 78746-1927, USA

Dawson, Phil (Athlete, Football Player)
1770 Arlington Row
Westlake, OH 44145-3561, USA

Dawson, Rhett (Athlete, Football Player)
1717 W 6th St Ste 260
Austin, TX 78703-4777, USA

Dawson, Rosario (Actor)
544 E 13th St Apt 1B
New York, NY 10009-3583, USA

Dawson, Roxann (Actor)
227 Bell Canyon Rd
Bell Canyon, CA 91307-1111, USA

Dawson, Shane (Actor)
c/o Staff Member *3 Arts Entertainment (LA)*
9460 Wilshire Blvd Fl 7
Beverly Hills, CA 90212-2713, USA

Day, Bill (Cartoonist)
Memphis Commercial-Appeal
495 Union Ave
Editorial Dept
Memphis, TN 38103-3221, USA

Day, Boots (Athlete, Baseball Player)
1154 Vespasian Way
Chesterfield, MO 63017-3016, USA

Day, Charlie (Actor)
2175 W Live Oak Dr
Los Angeles, CA 90068-3640, USA

Day, Chon (Cartoonist)
127 Main St
Ashaway, RI 02804-2239, USA

Day, Dewon (Athlete, Baseball Player)
1935 Marshall Pl
Jackson, MS 39213-4450, USA

Day, Doris (Actor)
c/o Staff Member *Sugaroo! LLC*
3650 Helms Ave
Culver City, CA 90232-2417, USA

Day, Felicia (Actor)
c/o Ari Greenburg *William Morris Endeavor (LA)*
9601 Wilshire Blvd
Beverly Hills, CA 90210-5213, USA

Day, Gail (Publisher)
Plaboy Magazine
680 N Lake Shore Dr
Chicago, IL 60611-4546, USA

Day, Glen (Athlete, Golfer)
25 Valley Estates Ct
Little Rock, AR 72212, USA

Day, Howie (Musician)
c/o Staff Member *Paradigm (Monterey)*
404 W Franklin St
Monterey, CA 93940-2303, USA

Day, Inaya (Musician)
c/o Staff Member *Diva Central Inc*
7510 W Sunset Blvd Ste 1445
Los Angeles, CA 90046-3408, USA

Day, Jason (Actor)
c/o Julio Caro *Caro Entertainment*
3221 Hutchison Ave Ste H
Los Angeles, CA 90034-3298, USA

Day, Joe (Athlete, Hockey Player)
805 Shoreline Rd
Lake Barrington, IL 60010-3878, USA

Day, Julian (Business Person)
KMART
PO Box 8073
Royal Oak, MI 48068-8073, USA

Day, Mark
Day Enterprises Racing
107 Flat Ridge Rd
Goodlettsville, TN 37072-8509, USA

Day, Morris (Musician)
805 Hampton Bluff Dr
Alpharetta, GA 30004-3074, USA

Day, Pat (Horse Racer)
14703 Isleworth Ct
Louisville, KY 40245-5256, USA

Day, Robert (Actor, Director)
8832 Ferncliff Ave NE
Bainbridge Island, WA 98110-2907, USA

Day, Terry (Athlete, Football Player)
PO Box 85
Pickens, MS 39146-0085, USA

Day, Zach (Athlete, Baseball Player)
9663 Lupine Dr
West Chester, OH 45241-3693, USA

Dayal, Manish (Actor)
c/o Annick Oppenheim *Sunshine Sachs (LA)*
8409 Santa Monica Blvd
West Hollywood, CA 90069-4209, USA

Daye, Darren (Athlete, Basketball Player)
21 Elderberry
Irvine, CA 92603-3703, USA

Dayett, Brian (Athlete, Baseball Player)
276 Phillips Dr
Winchester, TN 37398-4268, USA

Day-George, Lynda (Actor)
10310 Riverside Dr Unit 104
Toluca Lake, CA 91602-2457, USA

Daykin, Anthony (Athlete, Football Player)
5204 Cross Ridge Cir
Woodstock, GA 30188-4381, USA

Day-Lewis, Daniel (Actor)
232 Tophet Rd
Roxbury, CT 06783-1517, USA

Dayley, Ken (Athlete, Baseball Player)
1300 Windgate Way Ct
Chesterfield, MO 63005-4497, USA

Dayne, Ron (Athlete, Football Player, Heisman Trophy Winner)
2135 Regent St
Madison, WI 53726-3941, USA

Dayne, Taylor (Actor, Musician)
5324 Beeman Ave
Valley Village, CA 91607-2310, USA

Dayton, Jonathan (Director)
505 Radcliffe Ave
Pacific Palisades, CA 90272-4330, USA

Dayton, June (Actor)
Abrams Artists
9200 W Sunset Blvd Ste 1125
West Hollywood, CA 90069-3610, USA

Dayton, Mark (Governor, Politician)
Office of the Governor
130 State Capitol
75 Rev Dr Martin Luther King Jr Blvd
Saint Paul, MN 55155-0001, USA

Dayton, Mark (Politician)
330 Maryland Ave NE
Washington, DC 20002-5712, USA

Daze, Eric (Athlete, Hockey Player)
606 S Washington St
Hinsdale, IL 60521-4439, USA

Daze, Skylar (Adult Film Star)
PO Box 89222
Tampa, FL 33689-0403, USA

D. Clarke, Yvette (Congressman,
Politician)
1029 Longworth Hob
Washington, DC 20515-2304, USA

dc Talk (Music Group, Musician)
c/o Staff Member *True Artist Management*
227 3rd Ave N
Franklin, TN 37064-2504, USa

D (DelVecchio), Pauly (DJ, Reality Star)
c/o Michael Schweiger *CEG Management*
520 8th Ave Rm 2001
New York, NY 10018-4166, USA

D. Dicks, Norman (Congressman,
Politician)
2467 Rayburn Hob
Washington, DC 20515-4706, USA

D. Dingell Jr., John (Congressman,
Politician)
2328 Rayburn Hob
Washington, DC 20515-2215, USA

Dea, Bill (Athlete, Hockey Player)
2636 W Bartlett Way
Queen Creek, AZ 85142-6611, USA

Deacon, John (Musician)
The Mill Mill Lane
367 Windsor Hwy
New Windsor, NY 12553-7900, USA

Dead Can Dance (Music Group)
c/o Staff Member *William Morris
Endeavor (LA)*
9601 Wilshire Blvd
Beverly Hills, CA 90210-5213, USA

Dead marsh, Adam (Athlete, Hockey
Player)
Colorado Avalanche
1000 Chopper Cir
Denver, CO 80204-5805

Deadmarsh, Adam (Athlete, Hockey
Player, Olympic Athlete)
PO Box 3346
Coeur D Alene, ID 83816-2509, USA

deadmau5 (Music Group)
c/o Todd Jacobs *William Morris Endeavor
(LA)*
9601 Wilshire Blvd
Beverly Hills, CA 90210-5213, USA

Dead, The (Music Group)
c/o Staff Member *Paradigm (Monterey)*
404 W Franklin St
Monterey, CA 93940-2303, USA

Deakin, Paul (Musician)
AristoMedia
1620 16th Ave S
Nashville, TN 37212-2908, USA

Deakins, Roger (Cinematographer)
International Creative Mgmt
10250 Constellation Blvd Fl 1
Los Angeles, CA 90067-6241, USA

Deal, Cot (Athlete, Baseball Player)
9009 N May Ave Apt 164
Oklahoma City, OK 73120-4464, USA

Deal, Ellis (Athlete, Baseball Player)
9009 N May Ave Apt 164
Oklahoma City, OK 73120-4464, USA

Deal, Kelley (Musician)
Wire & Twine
PO Box 520
Oxford, OH 45056-0520, USA

Deal, Kim (Musician)
348 Hadley Ave
Oakwood, OH 45419-2610, USA

Deal, Lance (Athlete, Olympic Athlete)
4715 Fox Hollow Rd
Eugene, OR 97405-5302, USA

Deal, Nathan (Governor, Politician)
The Office of the Governor
203 State Capitol SW
State of Georgia
Atlanta, GA 30334-1600, USA

de Almeida, Joaquim (Actor)
c/o Estelle Lasher *Lasher Group*
1133 Avenue Of The Americas Ste 1621
New York, NY 10036-6710, USA

DeAlmeida, Joaquin
2372 Veteran Ave # 102
Los Angeles, CA 90064-2108

Dean, Billy (Musician)
c/o Staff Member *Billy Dean Music Group*
PO Box 150889
Nashville, TN 37215-0889, USA

Dean, Eddie (Actor, Musician)
32161 Sailview Ln
Westlake Village, CA 91361-3620, USA

Dean, Fred (Athlete, Football Player)
2411 Highway 3061
Ruston, LA 71270-9626, USA

Dean, Fred (Athlete, Football Player)
3911 Whitchurch Dr
Houston, TX 77066-4535, USA

Dean, Howard (Politician)
325 S Cove Rd
Burlington, VT 05401-5447, USA

Dean, Ira (Musician)
Graham Agency
6999 E Business 20
Odessa, TX 79762-5483, USA

Dean, John (Politician)
9496 Rembert Ln
Beverly Hills, CA 90210-1720, USA

Dean, Kaseem (Swizz Beatz) (Musician,
Producer)
c/o Staff Member *5W Public Relations
(NY)*
1166 6th Ave Frnt 4
New York, NY 10036-2729, USA

Dean, Kevin (Athlete, Hockey Player)
c/o Staff Member *Lowell Devils*
300 Martin Luther King Jr Way
Lowell, MA 01852-1050, USA

Dean, Kiley (Musician)
c/o Staff Member *Interscope Records (LA)
- Main*
2220 Colorado Ave
Santa Monica, CA 90404-3506, USA

Dean, Loren (Actor)
c/o Amy Guenther *Gateway Management
Company Inc*
860 Via De La Paz Ste F10
Pacific Palisades, CA 90272-3631, USA

Dean, Randy (Athlete, Football Player)
11850 N Sandhill Cir
Mequon, WI 53092-2995, USA

Dean, Ted (Athlete, Football Player)
16474 W Lava Dr
Surprise, AZ 85374-6250, USA

Dean, Tommy (Athlete, Baseball Player)
PO Box 1014
Iuka, MS 38852-6014, USA

Dean, Vernon (Athlete, Football Player)
2223 Fall Meadow Dr
Missouri City, TX 77459-3337, USA

DeAngelis, Barbara (Writer)
c/o Staff Member *St Martins Press*
175 5th Ave Ste 400
Publicity Dept
New York, NY 10010-7848, USA

Deangelis, Billy (Athlete, Basketball
Player)
14 Pickering Dr
Trenton, NJ 08691-2332, USA

De Angelis, Rosemary
817 W End Ave Apt 3A
New York, NY 10025-5318

De Aragon, Maria (Actor)
c/o Staff Member *Coolwaters Productions*
10061 Riverside Dr # 531
Toluca Lake, CA 91602-2560, USA

de Aragow, Maria
1159 Tenth Ave
San Diego, CA 92101

Dearden, James (Director)
International Creative Mgmt
10250 Constellation Blvd Fl 1
Los Angeles, CA 90067-6241, USA

Deardorff, Jeff (Athlete, Baseball Player)
1026 Jayhil Dr
Minneola, FL 34715-4701, USA

Deardurff-Schmidt, Deena (Swimmer)
742 Murray Dr
El Cajon, CA 92020-5640, USA

De Armas, Ana (Actor)
c/o Liz Dalling *Special Artists Agency*
9200 W Sunset Blvd Ste 410
West Hollywood, CA 90069-3506, USA

de Armas, Roly (Baseball Player)
2650 Countryside Blvd Apt B102
Clearwater, FL 33761-3604, USA

DeArmond, Frank (Astronaut)
3086 Ravencrest Cir
Prescott, AZ 86303-5790, USA

Deas, Justin (Actor)
366 W 11th St Ph C
New York, NY 10014-6227, USA

D'Eath, Tom (Athlete, Misc)
PO Box 350437
Grand Island, FL 32735-0437, USA

Deavenport, Earnest Jr (Business Person)
Eastman Chemical Co
100 N Eastman Rd
Kingsport, TN 37660-5299, USA

Deaver, Jeffrey (Writer)
Pocket Star Books
1230 Avenue of the Americas
New York, NY 10020-1513, USA

Deaver, Michael K (Government Official)
Deaver Assoc
1025 Thomas Jefferson St NW
Washington, DC 20007-5201, USA

Deb, Debbie (Musician)
c/o Staff Member *Green Light Talent
Agency*
PO Box 3172
Beverly Hills, CA 90212-0172, USA

DeBarge, Eldra (El) (Musician)
c/o Staff Member *Geffen Records*
9126 Sunset Blvd
West Hollywood, CA 90069, USA

DeBarge, Kristinia (Musician)
c/o Staff Member *Edmonds Entertainment*
312 W 5th Apt 815
Los Angeles, CA 90013-1750, USA

Debarr, Denny (Athlete, Baseball Player)
33843 Juliet Cir
Fremont, CA 94555-3452, USA

De Becker, Gain (Commentator)
5064 Lemona Ave
Sherman Oaks, CA 91403-1341, USA

DeBell, Kristine (Actor)
c/o Ted Elston *Karma Talent Management*
453 S Rexford Dr
Beverly Hills, CA 90212-4711, USA

De Bello, James (Actor, Musician)
c/o Craig Shapiro *ICM Partners (LA)*
10250 Constellation Blvd Fl 7
Los Angeles, CA 90067-6207, USA

DeBello, James (Actor)
c/o Craig Shapiro *ICM Partners (LA)*
10250 Constellation Blvd Fl 7
Los Angeles, CA 90067-6207, USA

Debenedet, Nelson (Athlete, Hockey
Player)
38142 N Vista Dr
Livonia, MI 48152-1066, USA

De Benning, Burr (Actor)
4235 Kingfisher Rd
Calabasas, CA 91302-1842, USA

DeBenning, Burr (Actor)
4235 Kingfisher Rd
Calabasas, CA 91302-1842, USA

DeBerg, Steve (Athlete, Coach, Football
Player)
17920 Simms Rd
Odessa, FL 33556-4751, USA

Debney, John (Musician)
2906 Olney Pl
Burbank, CA 91504-1840, USA

DeBoer, Harm E (Business Person)
Russell Corp
1357 Lee St
Alexander City, AL 35010-2613, USA

DeBoer, Nicole (Actor)
c/o Jeff Witjas *Agency for the Performing
Arts (APA-LA)*
405 S Beverly Dr Ste 500
Beverly Hills, CA 90212-4425, USA

Deboer, Peter (Athlete, Hockey Player)
New Jersey Devils
165 Mulberry St
Newark, NJ 07102-3607

Debol, Dave (Athlete, Hockey Player)
207 N Maple Rd
Saline, MI 48176-1219, USA

De Bont, Jan (Director, Producer)
c/o Martin Bauer *Bauer Company, The*
864 S Gretna Green Way
Los Angeles, CA 90049-5223, USA

DeBorda, Dorothy (Actor)
PO Box 2723
Livermore, CA 94551-2723, USA

DeBrunhoff, Laurent (Writer)
527 W 26th St
New York, NY 10001-5503, USA

Debus, Jon (Baseball Player, Basketball Coach)
4875 26th St
Vero Beach, FL 32966-2017, USA

De Caestecker, Iain (Actor)
c/o Sandra Chang *Anonymous Content (LA)*
3532 Hayden Ave
Culver City, CA 90232-2413, USA

Decambra-Kelley, Lillian (Athlete, Baseball Player, Commentator)
250 South St
Somerset, MA 02726-5616, USA

DeCarl, Nancy
4615 Winnetka
Woodland Hills, CA 91364

DeCarlo, Mark (Actor, Television Host)
3292 Carse Dr
Los Angeles, CA 90068-1707, USA

DeCesare, Carmella (Actor, Model)
c/o Staff Member *Alpha Talent Group*
1201 24th St
Santa Monica, CA 90404-1321, USA

Decinces, Doug (Athlete, Baseball Player)
124 Riviera Way
Laguna Beach, CA 92651-1012, USA

Deck, Inspectah (Musician)
A&E Entertainment
13280 NE Fwy # F328
Houston, TX 77015, USA

Decker, Brooklyn (Actor)
c/o Chris Kiely *Marilyn Model Management*
32 Union Sq E PH
New York, NY 10003-3209, USA

Decker, Eric (Athlete, Football Player)
c/o Todd France *Five Star Athlete Management*
3500 Lenox Rd NE
Atlanta, GA 30326-4228, USA

Decker, Marty (Athlete, Baseball Player)
1638 Lancaster Ct
Yuba City, CA 95993-7692, USA

Decker, Steve (Athlete, Baseball Player)
1024 Laurelridge St NE
Keizer, OR 97303-7208, USA

Decker, Susan (Business Person)
33 Old Coach Rd
Napa, CA 94558-3858, USA

DeConcini, Dennis (Politician)
6014 Chesterbrook Rd
Mc Lean, VA 22101-3210, USA

de Cordova, Fred (Actor, Director, Producer)
1875 Carla Rdg
Beverly Hills, CA 90210-1936

DeCosta, Roger (Race Car Driver)
MC Sports
1919 Torrance Blvd
Torrance, CA 90501-2722, USA

DeCosta, Sara (Athlete, Hockey Player, Olympic Athlete)
200 Cowesett Green Dr
Warwick, RI 02886-8570, USA

DeCoster, Roger (Race Car Driver)
MC Sports
1919 Torrance Blvd
Torrance, CA 90501-2722, USA

Decter, Midge (Writer)
120 E 81st St
New York, NY 10028-1428, USA

De De, Dorsey (Athlete, Football Player)
6522 Southern Trace Dr
Leeds, AL 35094-6605, USA

Dedmon, Jeff (Athlete, Baseball Player)
21102 Broadwell Ave
Torrance, CA 90502-1636, USA

Dedrick, Jim (Athlete, Baseball Player)
2929 NW Kennedy Ct
Portland, OR 97229-8099, USA

Dee, Donald (Athlete, Basketball Player, Olympic Athlete)
7924 N Pennsylvania Ave
Kansas City, MO 64118-1416, USA

Dee, Donnie (Athlete, Football Player)
633 Rolling Hills Rd
Vista, CA 92081-7513, USA

Dee, Francine (Adult Film Star)
Extreme Models
PO Box 472170
Reseda, CA 91337, USA

Dee, Joey (Musician)
Horizon Mgmt
PO Box 8770
Endwell, NY 13762-8770, USA

Dee, Sally (Athlete, Golfer)
3508 W Barcelona St
Tampa, FL 33629-7010, USA

Dee, Toni (Fitness Expert)
Toni Dee Fitness
PO Box 834
Corte Madera, CA 94976-0834, USA

Deedle, Nelson
PO Box 5358
Scottsdale, AZ 85261-5358

Deegan, Bill (Athlete, Baseball Player)
8392 77th Ave
Seminole, FL 33777-4413, USA

Deeley, Cat (Actor)
1619 Tower Grove Dr
Beverly Hills, CA 90210-2143, USA

Dee-Lite (Musician)
428 Cedar St NW
Washington, DC 20012, USA

Deemer, Audrey (Athlete, Baseball Player, Commentator)
4401 Country Club Dr Apt 30
Steubenville, OH 43953-3362, USA

Deen, James (Actor, Adult Film Star)
5009 Cerrillos Dr
Woodland Hills, CA 91364-3013, USA

Deen, Paula (Chef, Television Host)
818 Wilmington Island Rd
Savannah, GA 31410-4503, USA

Deer, Ada E (Government Official)
2537 Mutchler Rd
Fitchburg, WI 53711-7011, USA

Deer, Rob (Athlete, Baseball Player)
27030 N 70th Pl
Scottsdale, AZ 85266-8826, USA

Deering, John (Cartoonist)
6701 Westover Dr
Little Rock, AR 72207-3447, USA

Deery, Tom
49 Yale Sq
Morton, PA 19070-1923, USA

Dees, Archie (Athlete, Basketball Player)
4405 N Hillview Dr
Bloomington, IN 47408-9770, USA

Dees, Charlie (Athlete, Baseball Player)
1064 Allison Woods Ct
Lawrenceville, GA 30043-5383, USA

Dees, Rick (DJ)
Dees Entertainment
3601 W Olive Ave Ste 675
Burbank, CA 91505-4622, USA

Deese, Derrick (Athlete, Football Player)
PO Box 3356
Cerritos, CA 90703-3356, USA

De Eugenia, Coco (Actor)
c/o Nancy Harding *Powerhouse Talent*
PO Box 261939
Encino, CA 91426-1939, USA

Deezen, Eddie (Actor)
c/o Staff Member *Coolwaters Productions*
10061 Riverside Dr # 531
Toluca Lake, CA 91602-2560, USA

Default (Music Group)
c/o Staff Member *The Agency Group (NYC)*
142 W 57th St Fl 6
New York, NY 10019-3300, USA

Defauw, Brad (Athlete, Hockey Player)
Jane And Russell Defauw
13030 Florida Ct
Saint Paul, MN 55124-7943, USA

DeFazio, Peter (Congressman, Politician)
2134 Rayburn Hob
Washington, DC 20515-3704, USA

Defebo, Brian (Race Car Driver)
Magic Motorsports
122 E Front St
Berwick, PA 18603-4818, USA

Defee, Lois (Dancer, Model)
223 Wink Rd
Oak Grove, LA 71263-6973, USA

DeFelitta, Raymond (Director, Writer)
c/o Gary Ungar *Exile Entertainment*
732 El Medio Ave
Pacific Palisades, CA 90272-3451, USA

DeFer, Kaylee (Actor)
c/o Staff Member *Abrams Artists Agency (LA)*
9200 W Sunset Blvd PH 11
West Hollywood, CA 90069-3601, USA

de Ferran, Gil (Race Car Driver)
Penske Racing
13400 W Outer Dr
Redford, MI 48239-1309, USA

DeFina, Barbara (Producer)
*Columbia University
School of Arts*
513 Dodge Hall, Mail Code 1808, 2960 Broadway
New York, NY 10027, USA

Deford, Frank (Sportscaster)
23 W 73rd St # 4
New York, NY 10023-3104, USA

DeForrest, Jeff (Sportscaster)
2249 SE 8th Ct
Pompano Beach, FL 33062-6727, USA

DeFrancesco, Tony (Basketball Coach)
7159 E Quince St
Mesa, AZ 85207-1841, USA

DeFranco, Buddy (Musician)
22525 Coral Ave
Panama City Beach, FL 32413-3047, USA

DeFranco, Philip (Actor, Writer)
c/o Staff Member *Creative Artists Agency (CAA-LA)*
2000 Avenue of the Stars Ste 100
Los Angeles, CA 90067-4705, USA

DeFrank, Joe (Horse Racer)
PO Box 655
Lake Pleasant, NY 12108-0655, USA

DeFreitas, Eric (Bowler)
175 W 12th St
New York, NY 10011-8275, USA

Deftones (Music Group)
c/o David Benveniste *Velvet Hammer*
9014 Melrose Ave
West Hollywood, CA 90069-5610, USA

DeGarmo, Diana (Musician)
c/o Drew Elliot *Artists International Management (NY)*
333 E 43rd St Apt 115
New York, NY 10017-4822, USA

Degen, Bruce (Writer)
62 Castle Meadow Rd
Newtown, CT 06470-2502, USA

DeGeneres, Ellen (Actor, Comedian, Talk Show Host)
360 S Mapleton Dr
Los Angeles, CA 90024-1807, USA

Degerick, Mike (Athlete, Baseball Player)
2702 Lake Osborne Dr
Lake Worth, FL 33461-5665, USA

DeGette, Diana (Congressman, Politician)
2335 Rayburn Hob
Washington, DC 20515-4329, USA

Degnan, John J (Business Person)
Chubb Corp
15 Mountainview Rd
Warren, NJ 07059-6795, USA

Degraffenreid, Allen (Athlete, Football Player)
7830 Rodebaugh Rd
Reynoldsburg, OH 43068-9309, USA

DeGrate, Tony (Athlete, Football Player)
203 Newport Landing Pl
Round Rock, TX 78665-2856, USA

DeGrate Jr, Donald Earle (**DeVante Swing**) (Musician)
c/o Staff Member *De Swing Mob Inc / EMI April Music Inc*
810 7th Ave
C/O Emi Music Publishing
New York, NY 10019-5818, USA

DeGraw, Gavin (Musician)
330 N 13th Ave
Hollywood, FL 33019-1012, USA

Degruttola, Raffaello
c/o Lorraine Berglund *Lorraine Berglund Management*
11537 Hesby St
North Hollywood, CA 91601-3618, USA

Dehaan, Dane (Actor)
c/o Christian Donatelli *The Schiff Company*
9220 W Sunset Blvd Ste 106
West Hollywood, CA 90069-3500, USA

Dehaan, Kory (Athlete, Baseball Player)
19040 E Superstition Dr
Queen Creek, AZ 85142-6884, USA

DeHaan, Richard W (Religious Leader)
3000 Kraft Ave SE
Grand Rapids, MI 49512-2024, USA

Dehart, Rick (Athlete, Baseball Player)
811 NE Wabash Ave
Topeka, KS 66616-1443, USA

DeHaven, Gloria (Actor)
9232 Sunnyfield Dr
Las Vegas, NV 89134-6348, USA

DeHaven, Penny
PO Box 83
Brentwood, TN 37024-0083

Dehere, Terry (Athlete, Basketball Player)
120 Wayne St
Jersey City, NJ 07302-3406, USA

Deidel, Jim (Athlete, Baseball Player)
14312 Wright Way
Broomfield, CO 80023-4045, USA

Deidrick, Casey (Actor)
c/o Jon Simmons *Simmons & Scott Entertainment*
7942 Mulholland Dr
Los Angeles, CA 90046-1225, USA

Deitch, Donna (Director)
International Creative Mgmt
10250 Constellation Blvd Fl 1
Los Angeles, CA 90067-6241, USA

Deja (Musician)
c/o Anthony Embry *AE Entertainment Public Relations*
124 Evening Shade Dr
Charleston, SC 29414-9144, USA

Deja, Andreas (Animator)
3494 Berry Dr
Studio City, CA 91604-4152, USA

Dejdel, Jim (Baseball Player)
New York Yankees
14312 Wright Way
Broomfield, CO 80023-4045, USA

DeJean, Mike (Athlete, Baseball Player)
144 Delouche Rd
West Monroe, LA 71291-8717, USA

Dejesus, David (Athlete, Baseball Player)
28 Muirfield Cir
Wheaton, IL 60189-2737, USA

Dejesus, Ivan (Athlete, Baseball Player)
14608 Velleux Dr
Orlando, FL 32837-5467, USA

Dejesus, Jose (Athlete, Baseball Player)
Kansas City Royals
PO Box 9960
Cidra, PR 00739-8960, USA

De Jesus, Wanda (Actor)
c/o Bob McGowan *McGowan Management*
8733 W Sunset Blvd Ste 103
West Hollywood, CA 90069-2241, USA

Dejohn, Mark (Athlete, Baseball Player)
24 New Hampshire Dr Apt 1C
New Britain, CT 06052-1166, USA

DeJong, jordan (Baseball Player)
5305 Via Cartagena
Yorba Linda, CA 92886-4561, USA

De Jong, Michael
c/o Staff Member *Mark Edward Inc*
325 E 8th St
#1011
New York, NY 10009-5280, USA

DeJoria, John Paul (Business Person)
Paul Mitchell Systems
26455 Golden Valley Rd
Santa Clarita, CA 91350-2973, USA

Dejurnett, Charles (Athlete, Football Player)
1355 Heritage Ct
Escondido, CA 92027-3972, USA

DeKay, Tim (Actor)
4027 Farmdale Ave
Studio City, CA 91604-3070, USA

Dekker, Fred (Director)
832 S Wooster St
Los Angeles, CA 90035-1710, USA

Dekker, Thomas (Actor, Director)
c/o Mimi DiTrani *The Schiff Company*
9220 W Sunset Blvd Ste 106
West Hollywood, CA 90069-3500, USA

de la Cruz, Melissa (Writer)
c/o Richard Abate *3 Arts Entertainment (NY)*
16 W 22nd St Ste 201
New York, NY 10010-5842, USA

DeLaCruz, Rosie (Model)
Willhelmina Models
300 Park Ave S # 200
New York, NY 10010-5313, USA

De La Cruz, Veronica (Television Host)
c/o Staff Member *CNN (Atlanta)*
1 Cnn Ctr NW
PO Box 105366
Atlanta, GA 30303-2762, USA

DeLaFuente, Joel (Actor)
LMRK
130 W 42nd St Ste 1906
New York, NY 10036-7902, USA

de la Fuente, Marian (Actor)
c/o Staff Member *Telemundo*
2470 W 8th Ave
Hialeah, FL 33010-2000, USA

De La Garza, Alana (Actor)
10570 Valley Spring Ln
Toluca Lake, CA 91602-2827, USA

Delahoussaye, Eddie (Horse Racer)
317 Turtledove Trl
Lafayette, LA 70508-8077, USA

Delahoussaye, Ryan (Musician)
Ashley Talent
2002 Hogback Rd Ste 20
Ann Arbor, MI 48105-9736, USA

De La Hoya, Oscar (Athlete, Boxer)
c/o Richard Schaefer *Golden Boy Promotions*
626 Wilshire Blvd Ste 350
Los Angeles, CA 90017-3581, USA

De La Hoz, Mike (Athlete, Baseball Player)
PO Box 441233
Miami, FL 33144-1233, USA

de la Huerta, Paz (Actor)
c/o Christina Papadopoulos *Baker Winokur Ryder Public Relations (BWR-NY)*
292 Madison Ave Fl 12
New York, NY 10017-6415, USA

De La Maza, Roland (Athlete, Baseball Player)
28533 Silverking Trl
Santa Clarita, CA 91390-5248, USA

DeLamielleure, Joseph M (Joe) (Athlete, Football Player)
7818 Ridgeloch Pl
Charlotte, NC 28226-3008, USA

Del Amitri (Music Group, Songwriter, Writer)
c/o Scott Clayton *Creative Artists Agency (CAA-TN)*
401 Commerce St PH
Nashville, TN 37219-2516, USA

DeLancie, John (Actor)
1313 Brunswick Ave
South Pasadena, CA 91030-3509, USA

Delaney, Don (Basketball Coach, Coach)
25 High Point Ln
Willoughby, OH 44094-6968, USA

Delaney, Jeff (Athlete, Football Player)
215 Village Green Dr
Canonsburg, PA 15317-5423, USA

Delaney, Kim (Actor, Model)
711 Walden Dr
Beverly Hills, CA 90210-3110, USA

Delaney, Pat
PO Box 273
Tamworth, NH 03886-0273

Delano, Diane (Actor)
Gold Marshak Liedtke
3500 W Olive Ave Ste 1400
Burbank, CA 91505-5512, USA

Delano, Michael (Actor)
c/o Cody Garden *McCarty Agency*
2600 W Olive Ave Fl 5
Burbank, CA 91505-4572, USA

Delany, Dana (Actor)
2522 Beverley Ave
Santa Monica, CA 90405-3719, USA

De La Puente, Brian (Athlete, Football Player)
c/o Bruce Tollner *REP 1 Sports Group*
2 Corporate Park Ste 106
Irvine, CA 92606-5103, USA

Del Arco, Jonathan (Actor)
c/o Kyle Fritz *Kyle Fritz Management*
6325 Heather Dr
Los Angeles, CA 90068-1633, USA

DelArco, Jonathan (Actor)
Michael Slessinger
8730 W Sunset Blvd Ste 220W
West Hollywood, CA 90069-2275, USA

de la Reguera, Ana (Actor)
c/o Will Ward *ROAR (LA)*
9701 Wilshire Blvd Fl 8
Beverly Hills, CA 90212-2008, USA

DeLaRocha, Zack (Musician)
GAS Entertainment
8935 Lindblade St
Culver City, CA 90232-2438, USA

De La Rosa, Jo (Actor)
c/o Jack Ketsoyan *EMC / Bowery*
5971 W 3rd St
Los Angeles, CA 90036-2832, USA

DeLaRosa, Yvonne (Actor)
c/o Staff Member *Heidi Rotbart Management*
1810 Malcolm Ave Apt 207
Los Angeles, CA 90025-7610, USA

Delasin, Dorothy (Athlete, Golfer)
20 Longview Dr
Daly City, CA 94015-4714, USA

De La Soul (Music Group)
2697 Heath Ave
Bronx, NY 10463-7546, USA

De La Tour, Frances (Actor)
c/o Carl Scott *Simmons & Scott Entertainment*
7942 Mulholland Dr
Los Angeles, CA 90046-1225, USA

De Laurentiis, Giada (Chef)
418 Mount Holyoke Ave
Pacific Palisades, CA 90272-4603, USA

De Laurentiis, Raffaella (Actor, Producer)
Rafaella Productions
100 Universal City Plz
Bungalow 5162
Universal City, CA 91608-1002, USA

Delavan, Burt (Athlete, Football Player)
1161 Jacob Ln
Carmichael, CA 95608-6202, USA

DeLay, Tom (Politician)
242 Cannon Hob
Washington, DC 20515-4322, USA

Delays Delirium (Music Group)
c/o Staff Member *Paradigm (Monterey)*
404 W Franklin St
Monterey, CA 93940-2303, USA

Del Bello, Jack (Athlete, Football Player)
391 Belfast Ter
Sebastian, FL 32958-5509, USA

Delcarmen, Manny (Athlete, Baseball Player)
68 Surrey Ln
East Bridgewater, MA 02333-3110, USA

Del Castillo, Kate (Actor)
c/o Jack Ketsoyan *EMC / Bowery*
5971 W 3rd St
Los Angeles, CA 90036-2832, USA

Del Castillo-Kinney, Ysora (Athlete, Baseball Player, Commentator)
1555 W 44th Pl Apt 216C
Hialeah, FL 33012-7837, USA

deLeeuw, Rob (Actor)
5075 Trail Canyon Dr
Mira Loma, CA 91752-1685, USA

DeLeo, Dean (Musician)
Q Prime
729 7th Ave Ste 1600
New York, NY 10019-6880, USA

DeLeo, Robert (Musician)
2225 Via Cerritos
Palos Verdes Estates, CA 90274-2141, USA

Deleon, Jose (Athlete, Baseball Player)
Pittsburgh Pirates
348 Herbert St # 1
Perth Amboy, NJ 08861-3708, USA

Deleone, Tom (Athlete, Football Player)
PO Box 681472
Park City, UT 84068-1472, USA

de Lesseps, LuAnn (Reality Star)
c/o Staff Member *Bravo (NY)*
30 Rockefeller Plz
New York, NY 10112-0015, USA

Delfino, Carlos Francisco (Basketball Player)
Detroit Pistons
2 Championship Dr
Palace
Auburn Hills, MI 48326-1753, USA

Delfino, Majandra (Actor)
c/o Bradley Frank *Platform Public Relations*
2666 N Beachwood Dr
Los Angeles, CA 90068-2308, USA

Delfino, Marieh (Actor)
c/o Amanda Glazer *Kohner Agency, The*
9300 Wilshire Blvd Ste 555
Beverly Hills, CA 90212-3211, USA

Delgado, Carlos (Athlete, Baseball Player)
9 Repto Ramos
Aguadilla, PR 00603-5944, USA

Delgado, Frankie (Actor)
c/o Eric Podwall *Podwall Entertainment*
710 N Orlando Ave Apt 203
Loft 203
West Hollywood, CA 90069-5549, USA

Delgado, Issac (Musician)
Ralph Mercado Mgmt
568 Broadway Rm 806
New York, NY 10012-3253, USA

Del Gaizo, Jim (Athlete, Football Player)
9581 NW 13th St
Plantation, FL 33322-4809, USA

Del Greco, Al (Athlete, Football Player)
1012 Little Turtle Cir
Birmingham, AL 35242-3282, USA

Del Greco, Bobby (Athlete, Baseball Player)
625 Southview Dr
Pittsburgh, PA 15226-2540, USA

Delguidice, Matt (Athlete, Hockey Player)
25 Church St
North Branford, CT 06471-1418, USA

Delhomme, Jake (Athlete, Football Player)
1459 Mills Hwy
Breaux Bridge, LA 70517-7305, USA

Delhoyo, George (Actor)
c/o Staff Member *TalentWorks (LA)*
3500 W Olive Ave Ste 1400
Burbank, CA 91505-5512, USA

D'Elia, Chris (Actor, Comedian, Writer)
6248 Winans Dr
Los Angeles, CA 90068-2251, USA

Delia, Joseph (Athlete, Football Player)
PO Box 19654
Irvine, CA 92623-9654, USA

Delilah (Radio Personality)
Radio Delilah Media Group
15260 Ventura Blvd Ste 400
Sherman Oaks, CA 91403-5300, USA

DeLillo, Don (Writer)
57 Rossmore Ave
Bronxville, NY 10708-5615, USA

DeLine, Donald (Producer)
120 N Hudson Ave
Los Angeles, CA 90004-1032, USA

Delinsky, Barbara (Writer)
c/o Staff Member *Simon & Schuster*
1230 Avenue of the Americas Fl CONC1
New York, NY 10020-1586, USA

Delisle, Jim (Athlete, Football Player)
26301 W Cedar Niles Cir
Olathe, KS 66061-7478, USA

Delizia, Cara (Actor)
6238 De Longpre Ave
Los Angeles, CA 90028-8265

Delk, Joan (Athlete, Golfer)
830 Forest Path Ln
Alpharetta, GA 30022-6468, USA

Delk, Tony (Athlete, Basketball Player)
1843 Glenhill Dr
Lexington, KY 40502-2817, USA

Dell, Donald (Athlete, Tennis Player)
Lagardere Unlimited
5335 Wisconsin Ave NW Ste 850
Washington, DC 20015-2052, USA

Dell, Michael (Business Person)
Dell Inc
1 Dell Way
Round Rock, TX 78682-7000, USA

Dell'Abate, Gary (Producer)
2 Old Farm Ln
Old Greenwich, CT 06870-1021, USA

Dellaero, Jason (Athlete, Baseball Player)
336 Providence Walk Way
Canton, GA 30114-8623, USA

Del La Hoya, Daisy (Actor, Model, Reality Star)
c/o Mike Esterman *Esterman.Com, LLC*
Prefers to be contacted via email
Baltimore, MD XXXXX, USA

Dellanos, Myrka (Actor)
c/o Staff Member *Univision*
605 3rd Ave Fl 12
New York, NY 10158-0034, USA

Dellenbach, Jeff (Athlete, Football Player)
1002 Pine Branch Dr
Weston, FL 33326-2840, USA

Dellinger, Bill (Athlete, Olympic Athlete, Track Athlete)
1993 Fircrest Dr
Eugene, OR 97403-3112, USA

Dellinger, Dustin (Dusty) (Athlete, Baseball Player)
5203 Grindstone Ln
Granite Falls, NC 28630, USA

Dellucci, David (Athlete, Baseball Player)
5512 Summer Lake Dr
Baton Rouge, LA 70817-4313, USA

Delmas, Louis (Athlete, Football Player)
c/o Drew Rosenhaus *Rosenhaus Sports Representation*
6400 Allison Rd
Miami Beach, FL 33141-4540, USA

Del Negro, Matthew (Actor)
c/o Becca Kovacic *Berwick & Kovacik*
6300 Wilshire Blvd Ste 1410
Los Angeles, CA 90048-5216, USA

Del Negro, Vinny (Athlete, Basketball Player)
7320 N 71st St
Paradise Valley, AZ 85253-3616, USA

Delo, Ken (Actor)
161 Avondale Dr # 93-8
Branson, MO 65616-3646, USA

DeLoach, Nikki (Actor)
c/o Carrie Wick *Carrie Wick Public Relations*
1455 4th St Apt 415
Santa Monica, CA 90401-2324, USA

Delock, Ike (Athlete, Baseball Player)
433 Cypress Way E
Naples, FL 34110-1107, USA

Delon, Nathalie
3 Quai Malaquais
Carrollton, TX 75006

Delong, Greg (Athlete, Football Player)
4960 Shady Maple Ln
Winston Salem, NC 27106-8704, USA

DeLong, Keith A (Athlete, Football Player)
6531 S Northshore Dr
Knoxville, TN 37919-8651, USA

Delong, Nate (Athlete, Basketball Player)
PO Box 485
Hayward, WI 54843-0485, USA

DeLonge, Thomas Matthew (Music Group, Musician)
c/o Staff Member *Geffen Records*
9126 Sunset Blvd
West Hollywood, CA 90069, USA

DeLonge, Tom (Actor, Musician)
18433 Via Candela Rancho
Rancho Santa Fe, CA 92091, USA

De Longis, Anthony
PO Box 323
Burbank, CA 91503-0323

DeLongis, Anthony (Actor)
PO Box 2445
Canyon Country, CA 91386-2445, USA

Deloplaine, Jack (Athlete, Football Player)
215 Montana St
Pittsburgh, PA 15214-1630, USA

Delora, Jennifer (Actor)
Gilla Roos
9744 Wilshire Blvd Ste 203
Beverly Hills, CA 90212-1812, USA

Delorenzi, Ray (Athlete, Hockey Player)
184 Lanternback Island Dr
Satellite Beach, FL 32937-4703, USA

DeLorenzo, Michael (Actor)
c/o Staff Member *Shelter Entertainment*
9255 W Sunset Blvd Ste 320
West Hollywood, CA 90069-3313, USA

De Los Santos, Valerio (Athlete, Baseball Player)
9838 N 119th Pl # Pi
Scottsdale, AZ 85259-5069, USA

Delparte, Guy (Athlete, Hockey Player)
74 Harrison Ave
Saco, ME 04072-3250, USA

Delpino, Robert L (Athlete, Football Player)
9569 Calle Del Casa
Riverside, CA 92503, USA

Delpy, Julie (Actor)
534 Westmount Dr
West Hollywood, CA 90048-2006, USA

Del Regil, Estrellita
PO Box 2004
Beverly Hills, CA 90213-2004

del Rincon, Fernando (Actor)
c/o Staff Member *Univision*
605 3rd Ave Fl 12
New York, NY 10158-0034, USA

Del Rio, Jack (Athlete, Football Coach, Football Player)
285 Twisted Pine Trl
Santa Rosa Beach, FL 32459-3223, USA

Del Rio, Rebekah (Musician)
2280 Grass Valley Hwy # 138
Auburn, CA 95603-2536, USA

Del Rubio, Millie
PO Box 6923
San Pedro, CA 90734-6923

Delsing, Jay (Athlete, Golfer)
14020 Woods Mill Cove Dr
Chesterfield, MO 63017-3434, USA

Delson, Brad (Musician)
12097 Summit Cir
Beverly Hills, CA 90210-1376, USA

Delta Spirit (Music Group)
c/o Staff Member *Paradigm (Monterey)*
404 W Franklin St
Monterey, CA 93940-2303, USA

Del Toro, Benicio (Actor)
1511 Malcolm Ave
Los Angeles, CA 90024-5722, USA

Del Toro, Guillermo (Director, Writer)
5970 Kingham Ct
Agoura Hills, CA 91301-4436, USA

Deluca, Annette (Athlete, Golfer)
7 Turtle Creek Dr Apt D
Jupiter, FL 33469-1530, USA

DeLuca, Mike (Producer)
Michael De Luca Productions
10202 Washington Blvd
Astaire Bldg Ste 3028
Culver City, CA 90232-3119, USA

DeLucas, Lawrence J (Astronaut)
909 19th St S
Birmingham, AL 35205, USA

Delucas, Lawrence J Dr (Astronaut)
90819th St S
Birmingham, AL 35205, USA

Deluca-Verley, Ava (Actor)
c/o Pearl Servat *PMK/BNC Public Relations (PMK-LA)*
8687 Melrose Ave Ste 8
West Hollywood, CA 90069-5746, USA

Delucca, Jerry (Athlete, Football Player)
27 Pulaski St
Peabody, MA 01960-1831, USA

Delucia, Rich (Athlete, Baseball Player)
4 Rick Rd
Reading, PA 19607-9704, USA

Delugg, Milton (Musician)
2740 Claray Dr
Los Angeles, CA 90077-2018, USA

DeLuise, David (Actor)
1144 Yale St Apt 6
Santa Monica, CA 90403-4758, USA

Deluise, Michael (Actor)
1186 Corsica Dr
Pacific Palisades, CA 90272-4014, USA

Deluise, Peter (Actor, Director, Producer)
c/o Lee Dinstman *Agency for the Performing Arts (APA-LA)*
405 S Beverly Dr Ste 500
Beverly Hills, CA 90212-4425, USA

Delvecchio, Alexander P (Alex) (Athlete, Hockey Player)
Pen Pro
2602 Stoodleigh Dr
Rochester Hills, MI 48309-2836, USA

Del-Vikings, The (Music Group)
PO Box 770850
Orlando, FL 32877-0850, USA

Demaestri, Joe (Athlete, Baseball Player)
50 Fairway Dr
Novato, CA 94949-5904, USA

Demao, Al (Athlete, Football Player)
16206 Atlantis Dr
Bowie, MD 20716-3839, USA

Demar, Enoch (Athlete, Football Player)
1579 Olympian Cir SW
Atlanta, GA 30310-2440, USA

Demarco, Bob (Athlete, Football Player)
13055 Midfield Ter
Saint Louis, MO 63146-6053, USA

Demarco, Robert (Bob) (Athlete, Football Player)
13055 Midfield Ter
Saint Louis, MO 63146-6053, USA

DeMarco, Tony (Boxer)
PO Box 53664
Indianapolis, IN 46253-0664, USA

DeMarcus, Jay (Musician)
24 Inveraray
Nashville, TN 37215-4129, USA

Demarie, John (Athlete, Football Player)
736 Magazine St
Lake Charles, LA 70607-6322, USA

Demars, Billy (Athlete, Baseball Player)
770 Island Way Apt 305
Clearwater Beach, FL 33767-1824, USA

de Matteo, Drea (Actor)
8803 Appian Way
Los Angeles, CA 90046-7734, USA

Dembo, Fennis (Athlete, Basketball Player)
430 N Pine St
San Antonio, TX 78202-2850, USA

Demel, Sam (Athlete, Baseball Player)
18650 N 120th Pl
Scottsdale, AZ 85259, USA

Demens, Kenny (Athlete, Football Player)
c/o Blake Baratz *The Institute for Athletes*
3600 Minnesota Dr Ste 550
Minneapolis, MN 55435-7925, USA

DeMent, Iris (Songwriter, Writer)
c/o Staff Member *Paradigm (Monterey)*
404 W Franklin St
Monterey, CA 93940-2303, USA

Dement, Kenneth (Athlete, Football Player)
8 Bel Air Dr
Sikeston, MO 63801-1916, USA

Dementieva, Elena (Tennis Player)
c/o Staff Member *Octagon (VA)*
7950 Jones Branch Dr
Mc Lean, VA 22102-3302, USA

DeMerchant, Paul (Religious Leader)
Missionary Church
PO Box 9127
Fort Wayne, IN 46899-9127, USA

Demerit, John (Athlete, Baseball Player)
550 W Walters St
Port Washington, WI 53074-1430, USA

DeMerritt, Marty (Athlete, Baseball Player)
6201 Weatherglass Ct
Orangevale, CA 95662-3915, USA

Demery, Larry (Athlete, Baseball Player)
10627 Kurt St
Sylmar, CA 91342-6838, USA

Demeter, Don (Athlete, Baseball Player)
6240 S Country Club Dr
Oklahoma City, OK 73159-1844, USA

Demeter, Steve (Athlete, Baseball Player)
4173 Bentley Dr
North Olmsted, OH 44070-2802, USA

Demetral, Chris (Actor)
c/o Jamie Gold *JMG Management*
18000 Coastline Dr Apt 8
Malibu, CA 90265-5727, USA

Demetrios (Religious Leader)
Greek Orthodox Church
89 E 79th St
#19
New York, NY 10075, USA

Demic, Larry (Athlete, Basketball Player)
680 S Lassen Ct
Anaheim, CA 92804-3123, USA

DeMille, Nelson (Writer)
61 Hilton Ave Ste 23
Garden City, NY 11530-2813, USA

Deming, Peter (Cinematographer)
Sandra Marsh Mgmt
6420 Wilshire Blvd Ste 880
Los Angeles, CA 90048-5538, USA

Demme, Jonathan (Director, Producer, Writer)
15 Castle Heights Ave
Nyack, NY 10960-1528, USA

Demmings, Pancho (Actor)
c/o Judy Orbach *Judy O Productions*
6136 Glen Holly St
Los Angeles, CA 90068-2338, USA

Demola, Don (Athlete, Baseball Player)
29 Sequoia Dr
Hauppauge, NY 11788-2625, USA

de Molina, Raul (Actor)
c/o Staff Member *Univision*
605 3rd Ave Fl 12
New York, NY 10158-0034, USA

Demong, Bill (Athlete, Olympic Athlete, Skier)
1546 Mallard Cir
Park City, UT 84098-5410, USA

Demon Hunter (Music Group)
c/o Staff Member *The Agency Group (NYC)*
142 W 57th St Fl 6
New York, NY 10019-3300, USA

DeMont, Rick (Athlete, Swimmer)
PO Box 1453
Waianae, HI 96792-6453, USA

DeMornay, Rebecca (Actor)
2179 Castilian Dr
Los Angeles, CA 90068-2610, USA

Demoss, Bob (Athlete, Football Player)
117 Knox Dr
West Lafayette, IN 47906-2147, USA

Demoss, Darcy (Actor)
7732 Chandelle Pl
Los Angeles, CA 90046-1231, USA

Demps, Will (Athlete)
c/o Staff Member *EAG Sports Management*
909 N Sepulveda Blvd Ste 360
El Segundo, CA 90245-3864, USA

Dempsey, Clint (Athlete, Soccer Player)
c/o Lyle Yorks *James Grant Sports Ltd (USA)*
3233 M St NW
Washington, DC 20007-3556, USA

Dempsey, George (Athlete, Basketball Player)
6945 Cedar Ave
Pennsauken, NJ 08109-2713, USA

Dempsey, Mark (Athlete, Baseball Player)
673 W Martindale Rd
Englewood, OH 45322-3043, USA

Dempsey, Michael (Actor)
c/o Vincent Cirrincione *Vincent Cirrincione Associates*
1516 N Fairfax Ave
Los Angeles, CA 90046-2608, USA

Dempsey, Pat (Baseball Player)
10651 Johanna Ave
Sunland, CA 91040-1603, USA

Dempsey, Patrick (Actor)
29715 Cuthbert Rd
Malibu, CA 90265-3707, USA

Dempsey, Rick (Athlete, Baseball Player)
1673 Crown Ridge Ct
Westlake Village, CA 91362-4731, USA

Dempsey, Tanya (Actor)
c/o Dino May *Dino May Management*
6362 Hollywood Blvd # 422
Los Angeles, CA 90028-6323, USA

Dempsey, Thomas (Tom) (Athlete, Football Player)
541 Julius Ave
New Orleans, LA 70121-1613, USA

Dempster, Ryan (Athlete, Baseball Player)
3537 N Greenview Ave
Chicago, IL 60657-1317, USA

Demsey, Todd (Athlete, Golfer)
145 Willow Pond Ln
Ponte Vedra Beach, FL 32082-3570, USA

DeMunn, Jeffrey (Actor)
PO Box 373
Round Top, NY 12473-0373, USA

De Munn, Jeffrey (Jeff) (Actor)
c/o Larry Taube *Principal Entertainment (LA)*
9255 W Sunset Blvd Ste 500
West Hollywood, CA 90069-3301, USA

Demus, Lashinda (Athlete, Track Athlete)
c/o Staff Member *Pure Perception PR*
10535 Rose Ave Apt 2
Los Angeles, CA 90034-4648, USA

Demuth, Dana (Athlete, Baseball Player)
1156 W Wagner Dr
Gilbert, AZ 85233-7980, USA

Denberg, Lori Beth (Actor)
c/o Staff Member *Acme Talent & Literary (LA)*
1400 Atlantic Ave Ste 274
Long Beach, CA 90813-2013, USA

Denbo, Gary (Athlete, Baseball Player)
27740 Water Ash Dr
Wesley Chapel, FL 33544-8752, USA

Dench, Judi (Actor)
c/o Steven Arcieri *Arcieri & Associates Inc*
60 E 42nd St Ste 2315
New York, NY 10165-5015, USA

Dencik, David (Actor)
c/o Alissa Feldman *Magnolia Entertainment (LA)*
9595 Wilshire Blvd Ste 601
Beverly Hills, CA 90212-2506, USA

Denehy, Bill (Athlete, Baseball Player)
5008 Eastwinds Dr
Orlando, FL 32819-3518, USA

Deng, Luol (Athlete, Basketball Player)
5925 N Bayshore Dr
Miami, FL 33137-2305, USA

Denham, Jeff (Congressman, Politician)
1605 Longworth Hob
Washington, DC 20515-1406, USA

Den Herder, Vern W (Athlete, Football Player)
2342 Riviera Rd
Sioux Center, IA 51250-2943, USA

De Niro, Robert (Actor)
242 Old Montauk Hwy
Montauk, NY 11954, USA

Denisof, Alexis (Actor)
c/o Nancy Gates *United Talent Agency (UTA-LA)*
9336 Civic Center Dr
Beverly Hills, CA 90210-3604, USA

Denison, Anthony (Actor)
10100 Santa Monica Blvd Ste 1060
Los Angeles, CA 90067-4151, USA

Denker, Travis (Athlete, Baseball Player)
845 Palmetto Pl
Brea, CA 92821-4127, USA

Denkinger, Don (Athlete, Baseball Player)
1980 Kamille Ct
Waterloo, IA 50701-4537, USA

Denman, Brian (Athlete, Baseball Player)
16 Cindy Dr
Buffalo, NY 14221-3002, USA

Denman, David (Actor)
c/o Becca Kovacik *Berwick & Kovacik*
9465 Wilshire Blvd Ste 420
Beverly Hills, CA 90212-2603, USA

Denman, Tony (Actor)
c/o Beverly Strong *Strong Management*
9350 Wilshire Blvd Ste 224
Beverly Hills, CA 90212-3204, USA

Dennard, Alfonzo (Athlete, Football Player)
c/o David Dunn *Athletes First, LLC*
23091 Mill Creek Dr
Laguna Hills, CA 92653-1258, USA

Dennard, Darqueze (Athlete, Football Player)
c/o Chafie Fields *Lagardere Unlimited (NYC)*
845 United Nations Plz
New York, NY 10017-3540, USA

Dennard, Kenny (Athlete, Basketball Player)
6641 Westchester Ave
Houston, TX 77005-3755, USA

Dennard, Mark (Athlete, Football Player)
4990 Afton Oaks Dr
College Station, TX 77845-7666, USA

Dennard, Preston (Athlete, Football Player)
4545 Greene Ave NW
Albuquerque, NM 87114-4296, USA

Dennehy, Brian (Actor)
141 Joy Rd
Woodstock, CT 06281-2206, USA

Dennehy, Kathleen (Actor)
Susan Nathe
8281 Melrose Ave Ste 200
Los Angeles, CA 90046-6823, USA

Dennen, Barry (Actor, Musician)
6923 Camrose Dr
Los Angeles, CA 90068-3110, USA

Dennen, Brett (Musician)
c/o Michael McDonald *Mick Management*
35 Washington St
Brooklyn, NY 11201-1028, USA

Dennert-Hill, Pauline (Athlete, Baseball Player, Commentator)
415 Clinton St
Owosso, MI 48867-2718, USA

Denney, Kyle (Athlete, Baseball Player)
PO Box 300
Prague, OK 74864-0300, USA

Denney, Mike (Athlete, Football Player)
6419 Oakley St
Philadelphia, PA 19111-5218, USA

Denney, Ryan (Athlete, Football Player)
646 N Country Manor Ln
Alpine, UT 84004-1940, USA

Denning, Blaine (Athlete, Basketball Player)
1283 NW Bentley Cir
Port Saint Lucie, FL 34986-1834, USA

Denning, Hazel M (Writer)
Llewellyn Worldwide
PO Box 64383
Saint Paul, MN 55164-0383

Denning, Jon (Race Car Driver)
Dobbs Motorsports
23 Springfield Ave
Springfield, NJ 07081-1312, USA

Dennings, Kat (Actor)
c/o Nicole King *Management 360*
9111 Wilshire Blvd
Beverly Hills, CA 90210-5508, USA

Dennis, Clark (Athlete, Golfer)
4117 Sarita Dr
Fort Worth, TX 76109-4743, USA

Dennis, Gabrielle (Actor)
c/o Staff Member *JC Robbins Management*
865 S Sherbourne Dr
Los Angeles, CA 90035-1809, USA

Dennis, Guy (Athlete, Football Player)
PO Box 2500
Hawthorne, FL 32640-2500, USA

Dennis, Jim (Race Car Driver)
1810 Little Mastens Corner Rd
Harrington, DE 19952-3219, USA

Dennis, Marc (Athlete, Hockey Player)
16336 Bumiston Dr
Tampa, FL 33647, USA

Dennis, Mark (Athlete, Football Player)
7533 Bittersweet Dr
Gurnee, IL 60031-5106, USA

Dennis, Mike (Athlete, Football Player)
11004 Covington Way
Oxford, MS 38655-7348, USA

Dennis, Mike (Musician)
American Promotions
2011 Ferry Ave Apt U19
Camden, NJ 08104-1900, USA

Dennis, Pamela (Designer, Fashion Designer)
c/o Jerry Shandrew *Shandrew Public Relations*
1050 S Stanley Ave
Los Angeles, CA 90019-6634, USA

Dennis, Pat (Athlete, Football Player)
600 S MacArthur Blvd Apt 2821
Coppell, TX 75019-6733, USA

Dennison, Doug (Athlete, Football Player)
2309 Daybreak Trl
Plano, TX 75093-3808, USA

Dennison, Glenn (Athlete, Football Player)
1104 Tucker Ln
Ashton, MD 20861-9766, USA

Dennison, Rick (Athlete, Football Player)
1 Winning Dr
Owings Mills, MD 21117-4776, USA

Denny, Christopher (Musician)
c/o Staff Member *Paradigm (Monterey)*
404 W Franklin St
Monterey, CA 93940-2303, USA

Denny, Dorothy (Actor)
15707 La Verida Dr
Victorville, CA 92395-3413, USA

Denny, John (Athlete, Baseball Player)
9403 Tower Pine Dr
Winter Garden, FL 34787-9613, USA

Denny, Simone (Musician)
c/o Stephen Ford *Diva Central Inc*
7510 W Sunset Blvd Ste 1445
Los Angeles, CA 90046-3408, USA

Denorfia, Chris (Athlete, Baseball Player)
8 Hawks Nest Dr
Southington, CT 06489-1372, USA

Densham, Gary (Race Car Driver)
Densham Racing
16661 Grand Ave
Bellflower, CA 90706-5037, USA

Densham, Pen (Director)
International Creative Mgmt
10250 Constellation Blvd Fl 1
Los Angeles, CA 90067-6241, USA

Densmore, Elizabeth (Actor)
c/o Sharon Lane *Lane Management Group*
13017 Woodbridge St
Studio City, CA 91604-1431, USA

Densmore, John (Musician)
49 Haldeman Rd
Santa Monica, CA 90402-1003, USA

Denson, Al (Athlete, Football Player)
6019 Bart Rd
Jacksonville, FL 32209-1809, USA

Denson, Autry (Athlete, Football Player)
5386 Hester Rd
Oxford, OH 45056-1023, USA

Denson, Drew (Athlete, Baseball Player)
1718 Avonlea Ave
Cincinnati, OH 45237-6110, USA

Denson, Keith (Athlete, Football Player)
28024 Eagle Peak Ave
Canyon Country, CA 91387-3105, USA

Denson, Moses (Athlete, Football Player)
14005 Drake Dr
Rockville, MD 20853-2641, USA

Dent, Akeem (Athlete, Football Player)
c/o Hadley Engelhard *Enter-Sports Management*
5 Concourse Pkwy Ste 3000
Atlanta, GA 30328-7106, USA

Dent, Bucky (Athlete, Baseball Player, Coach)
8895 Indian River Run
Boynton Beach, FL 33472-2445, USA

Dent, Burnell (Athlete, Football Player)
2904 Essex Ave
La Place, LA 70068-2241, USA

Dent, Catherine (Actor)
3330 Appleton St
Los Angeles, CA 90039-1702, USA

Dent, Frederick (Politician)
221 Montgomery St
Spartanburg, SC 29302, USA

Dent, Jim (Athlete, Golfer)
PO Box 290656
Tampa, FL 33687-0656, USA

Dent, Richard L (Athlete, Coach, Football Coach, Football Player)
4453 RR
Lake Zurich, IL 60047-6900, USA

Dent, Robert (Bob) (Athlete, Football Player)
6669 Embarcadero Dr Apt 7
Stockton, CA 95219-3378, USA

Dent, Russell E (Bucky) (Athlete, Baseball Player)
Bucky Dent Baseball School
490 Dotterel Rd
Delray Beach, FL 33444-3201, USA

Dent, Taylor (Athlete, Tennis Player)
17582 Lebanon Cir
Irvine, CA 92614-6641, USA

Denton, James (Actor)
2101 Timberwood Dr
Chanhassen, MN 55317-9670, USA

Denton, Jeremiah (Politician)
4509 Wishart Rd
Virginia Beach, VA 23455-5526, USA

Denton, Judy (Writer)
400 Main St S
Atwater, MN 56209, USA

Denton, Kelly (Race Car Driver)
Henderson Motosports
532 E Main St
Abingdon, VA 24210-3410, USA

Denton, Mona (Baseball Player)
1880 S Newton St
Denver, CO 80219-4503, USA

Denton, Randy (Athlete, Basketball Player)
515 Sunnybrook Rd
Raleigh, NC 27610-2850, USA

Denton, Sandi (Pepa) (Musician)
Famous Artists Agency
250 W 57th St
New York, NY 10107-0001, USA

Denton, Sandra (Pepa) (Musician)
570/580 Johnson Ave
Aspen, CO 81611, USA

Denvir, John (Athlete, Football Player)
23250 Walker Basin Rd
Caliente, CA 93518-2103, USA

DeOre, Bill (Cartoonist)
Dallas News
Editorial Dept
Communications Center
Dallas, TX 75265, USA

Deossie, Steve (Athlete, Football Player)
835 Chestnut St
North Andover, MA 01845-6010, USA

de Pablo, Cote (Actor)
c/o Catherine Olim *PMK/BNC Public Relations (PMK-LA)*
8687 Melrose Ave Ste 8
West Hollywood, CA 90069-5746, USA

De Palma, Brian (Director)
82 Pantigo Rd
East Hampton, NY 11937-2642, USA

Depalo, Jim (Baseball Player)
TCMA
4727 7th Ave SW
Naples, FL 34119-4039, USA

DePalva, James (Actor)
PO Box 11152
Greenwich, CT 06831-1152, USA

DePaola, Tomie (Actor, Writer)
c/o Staff Member *Penguin Putnam Books for Young Readers*
345 Hudson St Fl 14
New York, NY 10014-4592

Depaolo, Terri (Producer)
184 Thompson St Apt 6N
New York, NY 10012-2534, USA

Departure, Themm (Music Group)
c/o Staff Member *Paradigm (Monterey)*
404 W Franklin St
Monterey, CA 93940-2303, USA

Depaso, Tom (Athlete, Football Player)
2108 Polo Pointe Dr
Vienna, VA 22181-2804, USA

de Passe, Suzanne (Producer)
9701 Oak Pass Rd
Beverly Hills, CA 90210-1222, USA

Depastino, Joe (Athlete, Baseball Player)
12853 Sheringham Way
Sarasota, FL 34240-8762, USA

Depaula, Sean (Athlete, Baseball Player)
2 Thomas St
Derry, NH 03038-2988, USA

DePavia, James
PO Box 11152
Greenwich, CT 06831-1152

Depeche Mode (Music Group)
c/o Jonathan Kessler *Baron, Inc*
235 S Westgate Ave
Los Angeles, CA 90049-4205, USA

DePeyer, Gervase
1250 S Washington St
Porto Vecchio 109
Alexandria, VA 22314-4411, USA

Deply, Julie (Actor)
c/o Glenn Rigberg *Inphenate*
9701 Wilshire Blvd Fl 10
Beverly Hills, CA 90212-2010, USA

Depodesta, Paul (Commentator)
2775 Costebelle Dr
La Jolla, CA 92037-3518, USA

DePoyster, Jerry D (Athlete, Football Player)
PO Box 3029
Rock Springs, WY 82902-3029, USA

Depp, Johnny (Actor, Director)
c/o Robin Baum *Slate Public Relations*
9000 W Sunset Blvd Ste 915
West Hollywood, CA 90069-5809, USA

Depre, Joe (Athlete, Basketball Player)
59 Oneida St
Rochester, NY 14621-4027, USA

DePree, Hopwood (Actor)
c/o Staff Member *ROAR (LA)*
9701 Wilshire Blvd Fl 8
Beverly Hills, CA 90212-2008, USA

DePrume, Cathryn (Actor)
c/o Staff Member *Flick Commercials*
9057 Nemo St # A
W Hollywood, CA 90069-5511, USA

Dequenne, Emilie (Cartoonist)
Houston Post
4888 Loop Central Dr # 390
Editorial Dept
Houston, TX 77081-2227, USA

de Ravin, Emilie (Actor)
c/o Alexandra Crotin *42West (LA)*
1840 Century Park E Ste 700
Los Angeles, CA 90067-2122, USA

Derby, Dean (Athlete, Football Player)
1682 Corkrum Rd
Walla Walla, WA 99362-8628, USA

Derek, Bo (Actor, Model)
PO Box 1940
Santa Ynez, CA 93460-1940, USA

Dereuck, Colleen (Athlete)
4172 Saint Croix St
Boulder, CO 80301, USA

Dergan, Lisa (Actor, Model, Television Host)
c/o Jon Orlando *WNWN Media*
348 Hauser Blvd # PH414
Los Angeles, CA 90036-3276, USA

Derhak, Rob (Musician)
45 Hadlock Rd
Falmouth, ME 04105-2559, USA

Derline, Rodney (Athlete, Basketball Player)
12612 SE 215th St
Kent, WA 98031-2287, USA

Dern, Bruce (Actor)
PO Box 1581
Santa Monica, CA 90406-1581, USA

Dern, Laura (Actor)
c/o Annett Wolf *WKT Public Relations (LA)*
9350 Wilshire Blvd Ste 450
Beverly Hills, CA 90212-3230, USA

Dernier, Bob (Athlete, Baseball Player)
1242 SW Arbormill Ter
Lees Summit, MO 64082-4165, USA

Deroo, Brian (Athlete, Football Player)
49224 Escalante St
Indio, CA 92201-8850, USA

Derosa, Mark (Athlete, Baseball Player)
878 Crescent River Pass
Suwanee, GA 30024-1761, USA

Derosier, Michael (Musician)
Borman Entertainment
1250 6th St Ste 401
Santa Monica, CA 90401-1638, USA

De Rossi, Portia (Actor)
360 S Mapleton Dr
Los Angeles, CA 90024-1807, USA

Derow, Peter A (Publisher)
PO Box 534
Bedford, NY 10506-0534, USA

Derr, Kenneth T (Business Person)
Chevron Corp
6001 Bollinger Canyon Rd
San Ramon, CA 94583-2324, USA

Derrick, Edward (Athlete, Baseball Player)
PO Box 158473
Nashville, TN 37215-8473, USA

Derricks, Cleavant (Actor)
480 Burano Ct
Oak Park, CA 91377, USA

Derrickson, Scott (Director)
2026 W Mountain St
Glendale, CA 91201-1260, USA

D'Errico, Donna (Actor, Model)
4356 Hillview Dr
Malibu, CA 90265-2832, USA

Derringer, Rick (Musician)
c/o Steve Peck *Fantasma Productions Inc*
854 Conniston Rd
West Palm Beach, FL 33405-2131, USA

Derrington, Bob (Race Car Driver)
4614 Connorvale Rd
Houston, TX 77039-3515, USA

Derrington, Jim (Athlete, Baseball Player)
711 Sandlewood Ave
La Habra, CA 90631-7248, USA

Derryberry, Debi (Actor)
PO Box 2726
Toluca Lake, CA 91610-0726, USA

Dersch, Hans (Swimmer)
7217 E 55th Pl
Tulsa, OK 74145-7704, USA

Dershowitz, Alan (Attorney)
1563 Massachusetts Ave
Cambridge, MA 02138-2903, USA

DeRulo, Jason (Musician)
7555 NW 39th Ave
Pompano Beach, FL 33073-3102, USA

Derwin, Mark (Actor)
4034 Lamarr Ave
Culver City, CA 90232-3712, USA

Desalvo, Matt (Athlete, Baseball Player)
9191 N Lima Rd Unit 53B
Youngstown, OH 44514-5285, USA

deSando, Anthony
PO Box 5617
Beverly Hills, CA 90209-5617

DeSantis, Jaclyn (Actor)
c/o Sarah Fargo *Paradigm (NY)*
360 Park Ave S Fl 16
New York, NY 10010-1716, USA

Desanto, Tom (Producer)
c/o Renee Kurtz *Creative Artists Agency (CAA-LA)*
2000 Avenue of the Stars Ste 100
Los Angeles, CA 90067-4705, USA

Des Barres, Michael (Actor)
c/o Pam Ellis *Ellis Talent Group*
4705 Laurel Canyon Blvd Ste 300
Valley Village, CA 91607-5901, USA

Descalso, Daniel (Athlete, Baseball Player)
1937 Eaton Ave
San Carlos, CA 94070-4740, USA

Descendants, The
4230 Del Rey Ave # 621
Marina Del Rey, CA 90292-5606, USA

Deschaine, Dick (Athlete, Football Player)
205 Cavil Way
De Pere, WI 54115-3775, USA

Deschanel, Caleb (Cinematographer)
Dark Light Pictures
844 Chautauqua Blvd
Pacific Palisades, CA 90272-3801, USA

Deschanel, Emily (Actor)
c/o Lainie Sorkin Becky *Management 360*
9111 Wilshire Blvd
Beverly Hills, CA 90210-5508, USA

Deschanel, Mary Jo (Actor)
844 Chautauqua Blvd
Pacific Palisades, CA 90272-3801, USA

Deschanel, Zooey (Actor)
c/o Carly Morgan *PMK/BNC Public Relations (PMK-LA)*
8687 Melrose Ave Ste 8
West Hollywood, CA 90069-5746, USA

Descher, Sandra (Actor)
4544 Arcola Ave
Toluca Lake, CA 91602-1517, USA

Descombes-Dinehart, Nancy (Baseball Player)
59607 County Road 11
Elkhart, IN 46517-9178, USA

DesCombes Lesko, Jeneane (Baseball Player)
4401 145th Ave NE Apt J5
Bellevue, WA 98007-3160, USA

Descombes-Lesko, Jeneane (Athlete, Baseball Player, Commentator)
11227 NE 109th Ln Apt L108
Kirkland, WA 98033-5029, USA

Desert, Alex (Actor)
2572 Verbena Dr
Los Angeles, CA 90068-3017, USA

Deshaies, Jim (Baseball Player)
151 N Tid lor Point Dr
Spring, TX 77382, USA

Deshales, Jim (Athlete, Baseball Player)
151 N Taylor Point Dr
Spring, TX 77382-1240, USA

DeShannon, Jackie (Musician)
606 N Arden Dr
Beverly Hills, CA 90210-3510, USA

DeShields, Delino L (Athlete, Baseball Player)
1051 Heathchase Dr
Suwanee, GA 30024-4633, USA

Desiderio, Robert (Actor)
2934 N Beverly Glen Cir
Los Angeles, CA 90077-1724, USA

Desilva, John (Athlete, Baseball Player)
32750 Airport Rd
Fort Bragg, CA 95437-9514, USA

DeSimone, Livio D (Desi) (Business Person)
Minnesota Mining & Manufacturing
3M Center
Saint Paul, MN 55144-0002, USA

Desjardins, Eric (Athlete, Hockey Player)
9 Woodglen Ln
Voorhees, NJ 08043-9559, USA

DesJarlais, Scott (Congressman, Politician)
413 Cannon Hob
Washington, DC 20515-3301, USA

Deskins, Donald (Athlete, Football Player)
3240 Pittsview Dr
Ann Arbor, MI 48108-1946, USA

Desman, Shawn (Musician)
c/o Staff Member *BMG*
1540 Broadway
New York, NY 10036-4039, USA

Desmond, Ian
8023 36th Street Cir E
Sarasota, FL 34243-6309

Desmormeaux, Kent (Jockey)
Desmormeaux Racing Stable
385 W Huntington Dr
Arcadia, CA 91007, USA

Desormeaux, Kent (Horse Racer)
c/o Staff Member *Jockeys Guild*
448 Lewis Hargett Cir Ste 220
Lexington, KY 40503-3596, USA

De Souza, Steven (Producer, Writer)
c/o Alan Gasmer *Alan Gasmer Management Company*
10877 Wilshire Blvd Ste 603
Los Angeles, CA 90024-4348, USA

Despadovich, Nada
6500 Wilshire Blvd Ste 2200
Los Angeles, CA 90048-4942

Dess, Darrell (Athlete, Football Player)
224 Sumner Ave
New Castle, PA 16105-2579, USA

Dessens, Elmer (Athlete, Baseball Player)
5542 E Estrid Ave
Scottsdale, AZ 85254-2973, USA

DeStefano, Pete (Producer)
c/o Babette Perry *IMG (LA)*
2049 Century Park E Ste 2460
Los Angeles, CA 90067-3126, USA

Destrade, Orestes (Athlete, Baseball Player)
22447 Oakville Dr
Land O Lakes, FL 34639-3938, USA

Desutter, Wayne (Athlete, Football Player)
4450 Antietam Creek Trl
Leesburg, FL 34748-1203, USA

Deters, Harold (Athlete, Football Player)
1602 Woods Creek Dr
Garner, NC 27529-4761, USA

Detherage, Bob (Athlete, Baseball Player)
322 Turf Ln
Carl Junction, MO 64834-9575, USA

Detmer, Amanda (Actor)
c/o John Carrabino *John Carrabino Management*
5900 Wilshire Blvd Ste 406
Los Angeles, CA 90036-5015, USA

Detmer, Koy (Athlete, Football Player)
2906 Spring Bend St
San Antonio, TX 78209-4282, USA

Detmer, Ty (Athlete, Football Player, Heisman Trophy Winner)
18449 Flagler Dr
Austin, TX 78738-7656, USA

Detorie, Rick (Cartoonist)
Creators Syndicate
737 3rd St
Hermosa Beach, CA 90254-4714, USA

Dettlaff, Bill (Athlete, Golfer)
1 Nicklaus Dr
Dearborn, MI 48120-1126, USA

Dettmer, John (Athlete, Baseball Player)
16811 Babler View Dr
Ballwin, MO 63011-1811, USA

Dettore, Tom (Athlete, Baseball Player)
1120 McEwen Ave
Canonsburg, PA 15317-1928, USA

Detweiler, Ducky (Athlete, Baseball Player)
312 Holt St
Federalsburg, MD 21632-1403, USA

Detwiler, Chuck (Athlete, Football Player)
2921 29th Ter
Emporia, KS 66801-8201, USA

Detwiler, Ross (Baseball Player)
359 Brown Swiss Cir
Duncansville, PA 16635-8061, USA

Deukmejian, C George (Ex-Governor)
5366 E Broadway
Long Beach, CA 90803-3549, USA

Deukmejian, George (Politician)
5366 E Broadway
Long Beach, CA 90803-3549, USA

Deutch, Howard (Director)
International Creative Mgmt
10250 Constellation Blvd Fl 1
Los Angeles, CA 90067-6241, USA

Deutch, Howie (Actor, Director, Producer, Writer)
c/o Daniel J Talbot ICM Partners (LA)
10250 Constellation Blvd Fl 7
Los Angeles, CA 90067-6207, USA

Deutch, John (Politician)
51 Clifton St
Belmont, MA 02478-3353, USA

Deutsch, Dave (Athlete, Basketball Player)
315 Fairmount Rd
Long Valley, NJ 07853-3012, USA

Deutsch, Donny (Television Host)
Deutsch
111 8th Ave Fl 14
New York, NY 10011-5295, USA

Deutsch, Patti (Actor)
1811 San Ysidro Dr
Beverly Hills, CA 90210-1518, USA

DeValeria, Dennis (Sportscaster)
213 Hillendale Rd
Pittsburgh, PA 15237-1803, USA

Devane, William (Actor)
c/o Deborah Miller Shelter Entertainment
9255 W Sunset Blvd Ste 320
West Hollywood, CA 90069-3313, USA

Devarez, Cesar (Athlete, Baseball Player)
35 Arden St Apt B
New York, NY 10040-1318, USA

DeVarona, Donna (Athlete, Olympic Athlete, Swimmer)
TWI
3 Avon Ln
Greenwich, CT 06830-3926, USA

DeVasquez, Devin (Model)
9903 Santa Monica Blvd Ste 169
Beverly Hills, CA 90212-1671, USA

Devaughn, Dennis (Athlete, Football Player)
2416 Clear Field Dr
Plano, TX 75025-5184, USA

DeVaughn, Raheem (Actor, Musician)
c/o Eva Arthur M.A.G./Universal Attractions
15 W 36th St Fl 8
New York, NY 10018-7927, USA

Devault, Calvin (Actor)
c/o John Frazier Amsel, Eisenstadt & Frazier Talent Agency (AEF)
5055 Wilshire Blvd Ste 860
Los Angeles, CA 90036-6108, USA

Devellano, Jim (Athlete, Hockey Player)
300 Riverfront Dr Unit 23G
Detroit, MI 48226-4584

Devenzio, Dick (Athlete, Basketball Player)
1116 Home Pl
Matthews, NC 28105-6891, USA

Dever, Kaitlyn (Actor)
c/o Matt Sherman Medavoy Management
7510 W Sunset Blvd Ste 1413
Los Angeles, CA 90046-3408, USA

Dever, Seamus (Actor)
622 N Crescent Heights Blvd
Los Angeles, CA 90048-2210, USA

Deveraux, Jude (Writer)
Pocket Books
1230 Avenue of the Americas Fl CONC1
New York, NY 10020-1586, USA

Devereaux, Boyd (Athlete, Hockey Player)
10766 E Palm Ridge Dr
Scottsdale, AZ 85255-1719, USA

Devereaux, Mike (Athlete, Baseball Player)
2236 W Doublegrove St
West Covina, CA 91790-5607, USA

Devers, Gail (Athlete, Olympic Athlete, Track Athlete)
2825 Victoria Park Dr
Buford, GA 30519-4171, USA

DeVicenzo, Roberto (Golfer)
Nonl Lann
5025 Veloz Ave
Tarzana, CA 91356-4514, USA

Devicq, Paula (Actor, Model)
c/o Joanne Horowitz Joanne Horowitz Management
9350 Wilshire Blvd Ste 224
Beverly Hills, CA 90212-3204, USA

Deville, CC (Musician)
c/o Mike Esterman Esterman.Com, LLC
Prefers to be contacted via email
Baltimore, MD XXXXX, USA

Devine, Adam (Actor)
c/o Isaac Horne Avalon Management
9171 Wilshire Blvd Ste 320
Beverly Hills, CA 90210-5516, USA

Devine, Adrian (Athlete, Baseball Player)
271 Timber Laurel Ln
Lawrenceville, GA 30043-6504, USA

Devine, Harold (Boxer)
595 Wyckoff Ave
Wyckoff, NJ 07481-1337, USA

Devine, Joey (Athlete, Baseball Player)
932 Chattooga Tree
Suwanee, GA 30024, USA

Devine, Loretta (Actor)
3829 Crestway Pl
View Park, CA 90043-1754, USA

DeVink, Lodewijk J R (Business Person)
Warner-Lambert Co
201 Tabor Rd
Morris Plains, NJ 07950-2614, USA

DeVito, Danny (Actor, Comedian, Director)
1028 Ridgedale Dr
Beverly Hills, CA 90210-2731, USA

Devito, Louie (Athlete, Snowboarder)
c/o Len Evans Project Publicity
312 W 53rd St Ste 202
New York, NY 10019-5743, USA

DeVitto, Torrey (Actor)
4037 Via Marina Apt 112
Marina Del Rey, CA 90292-6250, USA

Devliegher, Charles (Chuck) (Athlete, Football Player)
27307 N 89th Ave
Peoria, AZ 85383-4854, USA

Devlin, Bruce (Athlete, Golfer)
3601 Foot Hills Dr
Weatherford, TX 76087-2239, USA

Devlin, Chris (Athlete, Football Player)
100 Meadow Lark Ln
Boalsburg, PA 16827-1800, USA

Devlin, Dean (Actor, Director, Producer)
Electric Entertainment
1438 N Gower St Ste 24
Los Angeles, CA 90028-8306, USA

Devlin, Joseph (Athlete, Football Player)
3715 Schintzius Rd
Eden, NY 14057-9790, USA

Devlin, Mike (Athlete, Football Player)
48 Shore Rd
Mount Sinai, NY 11766-1420, USA

Devlin, Robert M (Business Person)
American General Corp
2929 Allen Pkwy Ste 3800
Houston, TX 77019-2155, USA

Devlins, The (Music Group)
c/o Staff Member Paradigm (Monterey)
404 W Franklin St
Monterey, CA 93940-2303, USA

Devo (Music Group, Musician)
c/o Ian Fintak Agency Group Ltd, The (LA)
1880 Century Park E Ste 711
Los Angeles, CA 90067-1618, USA

De Voe, Ronald (Musician)
c/o Mike Esterman Esterman.Com, LLC
Prefers to be contacted via email
Baltimore, MD XXXXX, USA

DeVoe, Ronnie (Musician)
6440 Queens Court Trce
Mableton, GA 30126-7227, USA

Devon, Dayna (Actor, Television Host)
545 S Plymouth Blvd
Los Angeles, CA 90020-4709, USA

Devore, Doug (Athlete, Baseball Player)
5247 Willow Grove Pl S
Dublin, OH 43017-2116, USA

Devorski, Paul (Athlete, Hockey Player)
6292 Farmers Ln
Harrisburg, PA 17111-7066

DeVos, Richard (Business Person)
7154 Windy Hill Dr SE
Ada, MI 49301-7545, USA

Devries, Greg (Athlete, Hockey Player)
25 Colonel Winstead Dr
Brentwood, TN 37027-8937, USA

Devries, Jared (Athlete, Football Player)
15342 Lambert Dr
Clear Lake, IA 50428-8637, USA

Devries, Jed (Athlete, Football Player)
2433 W 1425 S
Syracuse, UT 84075-6996, USA

De Vries, Peter
170 Cross Hwy
Westport, CT 06880-2841

deVry, William (Actor)
3268 Bennett Dr
Los Angeles, CA 90068-1702, USA

Dewan, Jenna (Actor)
c/o Courtney Knittel Patricola Lust PR
9171 Wilshire Blvd Ste 441
Beverly Hills, CA 90210-5516, USA

Dewar, Faber (Designer)
c/o Staff Member Trading Spaces
7700 Wisconsin Ave
the Learning Channel
Bethesda, MD 20814-3578, USA

Dewar, Susan (Cartoonist)
Universal Press Syndicate
4520 Main St Ste 340
Kansas City, MO 64111-7705, USA

Deward, Scott (Race Car Driver)
479 Bay Rd
South Easton, MA 02375-1424, USA

Dewese, Mohandas (Kool mo Dee) (Actor)
c/o Staff Member Identity Talent Agency (ID)
9107 Wilshire Blvd Ste 500
Beverly Hills, CA 90210-5526, USA

DeWet, Shaun (Model)
c/o Staff Member Elite Model Management (NY)
245 5th Ave Fl 24
New York, NY 10016-8728, USA

Dewey, Mark (Athlete, Baseball Player)
28150 Rivermont Dr
Meadowview, VA 24361-2822, USA

Dewey, Tommy (Actor)
c/o Paul Brown New Wave Entertainment (LA)
2660 W Olive Ave
Burbank, CA 91505-4525, USA

Dewillis, Jeff (Athlete, Baseball Player)
1311 Market St
Galveston, TX 77550-2624, USA

Dewine, Mike (Politician)
336 Phillips St
Yellow Springs, OH 45387-1724, USA

Dewitt, Blake (Athlete, Baseball Player)
212 Holmes Dr
Sikeston, MO 63801-4907, USA

DeWitt, Doug (Boxer)
2035 Central Ave
Yonkers, NY 10710, USA

DeWitt, Joyce (Actor)
c/o Staff Member JG Business Management Inc
PO Box 7309
Santa Monica, CA 90406-7309, USA

Dewitt, Matt (Athlete, Baseball Player)
7704 Bird of Paradise Ct
Las Vegas, NV 89123-0450, USA

DeWitt, Rosemarie (Actor)
c/o Troy Nankin Wishlab
2225A Hyperion Ave
Los Angeles, CA 90027-4709, USA

Dewitt, William 0 (Commentator)
5695 Drake Rd
Cincinnati, OH 45243-3616, USA

Dewitt, William O (Baseball Player)
St Louis Cardinals
5695 Drake Rd
Cincinnati, OH 45243-3616, USA

DeWitt, Willie (Boxer)
605 N Water St
Burnet, TX 78611-1728, USA

Dews, Bobby (Athlete, Baseball Player)
423 S Audubon Dr
Albany, GA 31707-3005, USA

DeWulf, Noureen (Actor)
c/o Tiffany Kuzon *Evolution Entertainment (LA)*
901 N Highland Ave
Los Angeles, CA 90038-2412, USA

Dexter, Mary (Director)
Hank Tani
14542 Delaware Dr
Moorpark, CA 93021-3560, USA

Dexter, Pete (Writer)
c/o Author Mail *Doubleday*
1745 Broadway
New York, NY 10019-4640, USA

Dexter, Peter W (Writer)
Sacramento Bee
Editorial Dept
21st & Q Sts
Sacramento, CA 95852, USA

Dey, Susan (Actor)
210 E 73rd St # 4D
New York, NY 10021-4395, USA

Deyn, Agyness (Actor)
c/o Danie Streisand *United Talent Agency (UTA-NYC)*
1325 Avenue of the Americas
New York, NY 10019-6026, USA

DeYoung, Cliff (Actor)
481 Savona Way
Oak Park, CA 91377-4842, USA

DeYoung, Dennis (Musician)
12/13 Ambriance Dr
Willowbrook, IL 60527, USA

Dezelan, Frank (Athlete, Baseball Player)
7423 Lighthouse Pt
Pittsburgh, PA 15221-2553, USA

Dhavernas, Caroline (Actor)
c/o Marla Farrell *Shelter PR*
584 Broadway Rm 310
New York, NY 10012-5246, USA

D. Hinchey, Maurice (Congressman, Politician)
2431 Rayburn Hob
Washington, DC 20515-3222, USA

Dhonden, Lama Tenzin (Religious Leader)
Seeds of Compassion
2607 2nd Ave Ste 300
Seattle, WA 98121-1289, USA

Diallo, Mmadou (Soccer Player)
New England Revolution
1 Patriot Pl
Cmgi Field
Foxboro, MA 02035-1388, USA

Diamantopoulos, Chris (Actor)
c/o Van Johnson *Van Johnson Company*
350 S Beverly Dr Ste 200
Beverly Hills, CA 90212-4819, USA

Diamond, Bobby
5309 Comercio Way
Woodland Hills, CA 91364-2030

Diamond, Charles (Athlete, Football Player)
7300 SW 69th Ct
Miami, FL 33143-4420, USA

Diamond, Chris (Race Car Driver)
J&L Racing
5171 Icard Ridge Rd
Hickory, NC 28601-8968, USA

Diamond, Diane (Television Host)
c/o Staff Member *Court TV*
600 3rd Ave Fl 2
New York, NY 10016-1919, USA

Diamond, Dustin (Actor)
124 Grandview Dr
Port Washington, WI 53074-2080, USA

Diamond, Joel (Producer)
Joel Diamond Entertainment
3940 Laurel Canyon Blvd Ste 441
Studio City, CA 91604-3709, USA

Diamond, Michael (Mike D) (Musician)
GAS Entertainment
8935 Lindblade St
Culver City, CA 90232-2438, USA

Diamond, Michael T (DJ)
c/o Staff Member *Diva Central Inc*
7510 W Sunset Blvd Ste 1445
Los Angeles, CA 90046-3408, USA

Diamond, Neil (Musician)
PO Box 3357
Los Angeles, CA 90078-3357, USA

Diamond, Reed (Actor)
c/o David Weise *David Weise and Associates*
209 E 31st St
New York, NY 10016-6302, USA

Diamond, Seymour (Doctor)
Diamond Headache Clinic
467 W Deming Pl Ste 500
Chicago, IL 60614-2970, USA

Diamond, Thomas (Athlete, Baseball Player)
310 Edgewood Ln
La Place, LA 70068-8964, USA

Diamond Rio (Music Group)
c/o Staff Member *William Morris Endeavor (Nashville)*
1600 Division St Ste 300
Nashville, TN 37203-2755, USA

Diamonds, The (Music Group)
561 Keystone Ave # 224
Reno, NV 89503-4304, USA

Diamont, Don (Actor)
Craig Mgmt
125 S Sycamore Ave
Los Angeles, CA 90036-2938, USA

Diana, Rich (Athlete, Football Player)
2 Munson Dr Unit 7
Wallingford, CT 06492-5366, USA

Diaw, Boris (Athlete, Basketball Player)
410 Bentley Mnr
Shavano Park, TX 78249-2062, USA

Diaz, Arnold (Correspondent)
c/o Staff Member *Shame on You !*
524 W 57th St
Wcbs-Tv
New York, NY 10019-2930, USA

Diaz, Cameron (Actor)
212 W 18th St Apt 12A
New York, NY 10011-4562, USA

Diaz, Carlos (Athlete, Baseball Player)
3037 Homestead Oaks Dr
Clearwater, FL 33759-1626, USA

Diaz, Carlos (Athlete, Baseball Player)
45-236 Ka Hanahou Cir
Kaneohe, HI 96744-3009, USA

Diaz, David (Athlete, Boxer)
c/o Staff Member *Top Rank Inc.*
3908 Howard Hughes Pkwy
#580
Las Vegas, NV 89109, USA

Diaz, Einar (Athlete, Baseball Player)
4315 70th Ave E
Ellenton, FL 34222-7329, USA

Diaz, Guillermo (Actor)
c/o Meghan Schumacher *Meghan Schumacher Management*
13351D Riverside Dr # 387
Sherman Oaks, CA 91423-2508, USA

Diaz, Izzy (Actor)
c/o Scott Zimmerman *Evolution Entertainment (LA)*
901 N Highland Ave
Los Angeles, CA 90038-2412, USA

Diaz, Joey (Actor)
c/o Justin Edbrooke *Super Artists*
2910 Main St Fl 2
Santa Monica, CA 90405-5316, USa

Diaz, Jorge (Athlete, Football Player)
9395 126th Ave
Largo, FL 33773-1232, USA

Diaz, Laura (Golfer)
c/o Staff Member *Ladies Pro Golf Association (LPGA)*
100 International Golf Dr
Daytona Beach, FL 32124-1092, USA

Diaz, Lazaro (Athlete, Baseball Player)
13557 Meadow Bay Loop
Orlando, FL 32824-5082, USA

Diaz, Manny (Politician)
Mayor's Office
3500 Pan American Dr
Miami, FL 33133-5504, USA

Diaz, Mario (Athlete, Baseball Player)
90 Calle Menta
Gurabo, PR 00778-9655, USA

Diaz, Matt (Athlete, Baseball Player)
1147 Interlochen Blvd
Winter Haven, FL 33884-3707, USA

Diaz, Melonie (Actor)
c/o Ashley Franklin *Thruline Entertainment*
9250 Wilshire Blvd Ste 100
Ground Floor
Beverly Hills, CA 90212-3343, USA

Diaz, Mike (Athlete, Baseball Player)
11626 Sayward Cir
Riverside, CA 92503-5069, USA

Diaz, Rocsi (Actor)
c/o Daniel Ryan Kinney *Artist and Brand Management - NY*
250 Hudson St Fl 2
New York, NY 10013-1413, USA

Diaz Balart, Jose (Actor)
c/o Staff Member *Telemundo*
2470 W 8th Ave
Hialeah, FL 33010-2000, USA

Diaz-Balart, Jose (Correspondent)
CBS-TV
51 W 52nd St
News Dept
New York, NY 10019-6119, USA

Diaz-Balart, Mario (Congressman, Politician)
436 Cannon Hob
Washington, DC 20515-3203, USA

Diaz-Infante, David (Athlete, Football Player)
24723 E Park Crescent Dr
Aurora, CO 80016-3190, USA

Diaz-Rahi, Yamila (Model)
Next Model Mgmt
23 Watts St
New York, NY 10013, USA

Dibaba, Tirunesh (Athlete, Olympic Athlete, Track Athlete)
c/o Staff Member *Global Athletics & Marketing, Inc.*
437 Boylston St Ste 400
Boston, MA 02116-3374, USA

Dibble, Dorne (Athlete, Football Player)
18601 Jamestown Cir
Northville, MI 48168-1834, USA

Dibble, Rob (Athlete, Baseball Player)
PO Box 890
Middlebury, CT 06762-0890, USA

Dibel, John C (Business Person)
Meade Instruments Corp
6001 Oak Cyn
Irvine, CA 92618-5200, USA

Dibernardo, Rick (Athlete, Football Player)
31942 Via Oso
Trabuco Canyon, CA 92679-3900, USA

DiBlasio, Raul (Musician)
Esterfan Enterprises
420 Jefferson Ave
Miami Beach, FL 33139-6503, USA

Diblassio, Raul (Musician)
c/o Staff Member *BMG*
1540 Broadway
New York, NY 10036-4039, USA

DiBona, Craig (Cinematographer)
333 E 66th St Apt 7O
New York, NY 10065-6274, USA

di Bonaventura, Lorenzo (Producer)
332 N Tigertail Rd
Los Angeles, CA 90049-2806, USA

Dibos, Alicia (Athlete, Golfer)
1465 E Putnam Ave Apt 112E
Old Greenwich, CT 06870-1330, USA

Dibra, Bash
c/o Daniel Strone *Trident Media Group LLC*
41 Madison Ave Fl 36
New York, NY 10010-2257, USA

DiCamillo, Brandon (Actor)
c/o Staff Member *Stoic Management*
947 Trinity Ln
King Of Prussia, PA 19406-3603, USA

Dicamillo, Gary T (Business Person)
1001 Saint Georges Rd
Baltimore, MD 21210-1412, USA

DiCaprio, Leonardo (Actor, Producer)
66 E 11th St Apt 1
New York, NY 10003-6013, USA

Dichter, Misha (Musician)
Columbia Artists Mgmt Inc
165 W 57th St
New York, NY 10019-2201, USA

Dicillo, Tom (Cinematographer, Director, Writer)
c/o Jennifer Levine *Untitled Entertainment (LA)*
350 S Beverly Dr Ste 200
Beverly Hills, CA 90212-4819, USA

Di Cione, Sevy (Actor)
c/o Cindy Sheffield *The Sheffield Agency*
14020 NW Passage
Suite 104
Marina Del Rey, CA 90292-7495, USA

Dick, Andy (Actor, Comedian)
c/o Max Burgos *Agency for the Performing Arts (APA-LA)*
405 S Beverly Dr Ste 500
Beverly Hills, CA 90212-4425, USA

Dick, Degen (Athlete, Football Player)
15871 Springdale St
Huntington Beach, CA 92649-1727

Dick, Douglas (Actor)
604 S Gretna Green Way
Los Angeles, CA 90049-4035, USA

Dick, Ed (Baseball Player)
TCMA
501 Washington Ave
Ocean Springs, MS 39564-4631, USA

Dickau, Dan (Athlete, Basketball Player)
c/o Mark Bartelstein *Priority Sports & Entertainment - Chicago*
312 N La Salle
Suite 650
Chicago, IL 60610, USA

Dickel, Dan (Athlete, Football Player)
832 Normandy Dr
Iowa City, IA 52246-2931, USA

Dicken, Paul (Athlete, Baseball Player)
2775 NW 49th Ave Unit 205
Ocala, FL 34482-6213, USA

Dickens, Jimmy (Musician)
5010 W Concord Rd
Brentwood, TN 37027-6520, USA

Dickens, Kim (Actor)
c/o Stephen Hirsh *Gersh (LA)*
9465 Wilshire Blvd Ste 600
Beverly Hills, CA 90212-2605, USA

Dickerson, Dan (Baseball Player)
7950 Brookwood Dr
Clarkston, MI 48348-4471, USA

Dickerson, Eric (Athlete, Football Player, Sportscaster)
26815 Mulholland Hwy
Calabasas, CA 91302-1947, USA

Dickerson, Ernest R (Director)
c/o Staff Member *Chasen & Company*
8899 Beverly Blvd Ste 405
Los Angeles, CA 90048-2431, USA

Dickerson, Henry (Athlete, Basketball Player)
3022 Skybrook Ln
Durham, NC 27703-5979, USA

Dickerson, John (Athlete, Baseball Player)
1702 26th St N
Columbus, MS 39701-2606, USA

Dickerson, Kenneth (Athlete, Football Player)
2406 Alabama Ave
Tuskegee Institute, AL 36088-2410, USA

Dickerson, Marty (Athlete, Golfer)
4225 Luzon Way
Sarasota, FL 34241-5728, USA

Dickerson, Sam (Athlete, Football Player)
551 Waddell Way
Modesto, CA 95357, USA

Dickey, Boh A (Business Person)
SAFECO Corp
Safeco Plaza
Seattle, WA 98185-0001, USA

Dickey, Charlie (Athlete, Football Player)
1992 E Farm Cir
Sandy, UT 84093-6296, USA

Dickey, Curtis (Athlete, Football Player)
702 Glenview Dr
Mansfield, TX 76063-6743, USA

Dickey, Lynn (Athlete, Football Player)
9220 Pawnee Ln
Leawood, KS 66206-1758, USA

Dickey, R A (Athlete, Baseball Player)
c/o Jordan Bazant *The Legacy Agency*
1500 Broadway Ste 2501
New York, NY 10036-4082, USA

Dickey, Richard (Athlete, Basketball Player)
1109 Red Maple Dr
Plymouth, IN 46563-3697, USA

Dickey, Wallace (Athlete, Football Player)
1226 Safari St
San Antonio, TX 78216-2856, USA

Dickinson, Angie (Actor)
1715 Carla Rdg
Beverly Hills, CA 90210-1911, USA

Dickinson, Gary (Bowler)
501 Wade Martin Rd
Edmond, OK 73034-6716, USA

Dickinson, Janice (Model, Reality Star)
c/o Staff Member *William Morris Endeavor (LA)*
9601 Wilshire Blvd
Beverly Hills, CA 90210-5213, USA

Dickinson, Judy (Athlete, Golfer)
18277 SE Heritage Dr
Jupiter, FL 33469-1439, USA

Dickinson, Parnell (Athlete, Football Player)
1646 Wallace Rd
Lutz, FL 33549-3933, USA

Dickinson, Richard (Athlete, Football Player)
2699 Old Richton Rd
Petal, MS 39465-9871, USA

Dickinson, Steve (Cartoonist)
c/o Staff Member *King Features Syndication*
300 W 57th St Fl 15
New York, NY 10019-5238, USA

Dickman, James B (Journalist)
1471 Peach Creek Dr
Splendora, TX 77372, USA

Dickson, Bob (Athlete, Golfer)
140 Woodlands Creek Dr
Ponte Vedra Beach, FL 32082-3217, USA

Dickson, Bruce (Bad) (Race Car Driver)
1370 Bridge Rd
West Chester, PA 19382-2033, USA

Dickson, Jim (Athlete, Baseball Player)
685 Franklin Ave
Astoria, OR 97103-4615, USA

Dickson, John (Athlete, Basketball Player)
4646 Wynmeade Park NE
Marietta, GA 30067-4098, USA

Dickson, Lance (Athlete, Baseball Player)
4615 N Placita Roca Blanca
Tucson, AZ 85718-7476, USA

Dickson, Neil (Actor)
c/o Lorraine Berglund *Lorraine Berglund Management*
11537 Hesby St
North Hollywood, CA 91601-3618, USA

Dickson, Ngila (Designer)
c/o Staff Member *Sandra Marsh Management*
6420 Wilshire Blvd Ste 880
Los Angeles, CA 90048-5538, USA

Dicus, Charles (Chuck) (Athlete, Football Player)
7 Valley Club Cir
Little Rock, AR 72212-3436, USA

Didier, Bob (Athlete, Baseball Player)
1819 N Lynch
Mesa, AZ 85207-3179, USA

Didier, Clint (Athlete, Football Player)
5015 S Regal St Apt L3089
Spokane, WA 99223-7975, USA

Didion, Joan (Writer)
8955 Beverly Blvd
West Hollywood, CA 90048-2423, USA

Dido (Musician, Songwriter)
c/o Staff Member *Paradigm (NY)*
360 Park Ave S Fl 16
New York, NY 10010-1716, USA

Diduck, Gerald (Athlete, Hockey Player)
4555 Elsby Ave
Dallas, TX 75209-3113

Die Antwoord (Music Group)
c/o Joel Zimmerman *William Morris Endeavor (NY)*
1325 Avenue of the Americas
New York, NY 10019-6026, USA

Diebel, Nelson (Athlete, Olympic Athlete, Swimmer)
401 Webb Rd
Newark, DE 19711-2652, USA

Diebold, John (Business Person)
Diebold Group
PO Box 515
Bedford Hills, NY 10507-0515, USA

Diehl, David (Athlete, Football Player)
116 Liberty Ridge Trl
Totowa, NJ 07512-1600, USA

Diehl, Digby (Journalist)
788 S Lake Ave
Pasadena, CA 91106-3948, USA

Diehl, Digby R (Journalist)
788 S Lake Ave
Pasadena, CA 91106-3948, USA

Diehl, John (Actor)
c/o Sandi Dudek *Paradigm (LA)*
360 N Crescent Dr
North Bldg
Beverly Hills, CA 90210-4874, USA

Diehl, John A (Athlete, Football Player)
900 S Henry St
Williamsburg, VA 23185-3989, USA

Dieken, Doug H (Athlete, Football Player)
29876 Lake Rd
Bay Village, OH 44140-1276, USA

Diem, Ryan (Athlete, Football Player)
11522 Willow Ridge Dr
Zionsville, IN 46077-7823, USA

Diener, Robert (Business Person)
9 Indian Creek Island Rd
Indian Creek Village, FL 33154-2903, USA

Diener, Travis (Athlete, Basketball Player)
3808 W Stonefield Rd
Mequon, WI 53092-2788, USA

Dienhart, Mark (Athlete, Football Player)
1944 Bayard Ave
Saint Paul, MN 55116-1216, USA

Dierassi, Issac (Doctor)
2034 Delancey St
Philadelphia, PA 19103-6510, USA

Diercks, Justin (Race Car Driver)
c/o Steve Diercks
1030 E 4th St
Davenport, IA 52807, USA

Dierdof, Daniel L (Dan) (Athlete, Football Player, Sportscaster)
13302 Buckland Hall Rd
Saint Louis, MO 63131-1214, USA

Dierdorf, Dan (Athlete, Football Player)
1316 Litzsinger Woods Ln
Saint Louis, MO 63124-1495, USA

Diering, Chuck (Athlete, Baseball Player)
3161 Blaiser Ln
Maryland Heights, MO 63043-1386, USA

Dierker, Larry (Athlete, Baseball Player, Coach)
8318 N Tahoe Dr
Jersey Village, TX 77040-1258, USA

Dierking, Scott (Athlete, Football Player)
1862 Wingate Ln
Wheaton, IL 60189-7881, USA

Dierkop, Charles (Actor)
c/o Staff Member *The Actors Studio*
432 W 44th St
New York, NY 10036-5205, USA

Diesel, Vin (Actor, Director, Producer)
c/o Stacy O'Neil *Brillstein Entertainment Partners (LA)*
9150 Wilshire Blvd Ste 350
Beverly Hills, CA 90212-3453, USA

Dieselboy (DJ, Musician)
c/o Joel Zimmerman *William Morris Endeavor (NY)*
1325 Avenue of the Americas
New York, NY 10019-6026, USA

Dieterich, Chris (Athlete, Football Player)
804 Edisto River Rd
Myrtle Beach, SC 29588-7439, USA

Dietrich, Dena (Actor)
c/o Staff Member *Bauman Redanty & Shaul Agency*
5757 Wilshire Blvd
Suite 473
Beverly Hills, CA 90212, USA

Dietrich, William A (Bill) (Journalist)
Seattle Times Fairview Avenue NAnd John Street
Attn: Editorial Dept
Seattle, WA 98111, USA

Dietrick, Coby (Athlete, Basketball Player)
644 Patterson Ave
San Antonio, TX 78209-5655, USA

Dietzel, Roy (Athlete, Baseball Player)
8421 Coulwood Oak Ln
Charlotte, NC 28214-1165, USA

Dietzen, Brian (Actor)
c/o Staff Member *Sweeney Entertainment*
6253 Hollywood Blvd Apt 201
Los Angeles, CA 90028-8248, USA

DiEugenio, James (Writer)
17735 Regency Cir
Bellflower, CA 90706-7004, USA

Difelice, Mark (Athlete, Baseball Player)
1215 Belfield Ave
Drexel Hill, PA 19026-4110, USA

Difelice, Mike (Athlete, Baseball Player)
3980 Mimosa Pl
Palm Harbor, FL 34685-3674, USA

Diffie, Joe (Musician)
9435 Weatherly Dr
Brentwood, TN 37027-2612, USA

Diffrient, Niels (Designer)
General Delivery
Ridgefield, CT 06877, USA

DiFranco, Ani (Musician, Songwriter)
PO Box 597
Buffalo, NY 14205-0597, USA

Digby, Marie (Musician)
c/o Staff Member *Nettwerk Management
(LA)*
1545 Wilcox Ace
Suite 200
Los Angeles, CA 90028, USA

Diggins, Ben (Athlete, Baseball Player)
4804 E Merrell St
Phoenix, AZ 85018-7876, USA

Diggs, Nail (Athlete, Football Player)
2006 Connonade Dr
Waxhaw, NC 28173-0109, USA

Diggs, Shelton (Athlete, Football Player)
261 Washington Ave Apt 3R
New Rochelle, NY 10801-5967, USA

Diggs, Taye (Actor)
3121 Oakdell Ln
Studio City, CA 91604-4218, USA

Digiacomo, Curt (Athlete, Football Player)
830 Ida Ave
Solana Beach, CA 92075-2439, USA

Digible Planets (Music Group)
345 N Maple Dr Ste 123
Beverly Hills, CA 90210-5185, USA

Digitalism (Music Group)
c/o Staff Member *Girlie Action*
243 W 30th St Fl 12
New York, NY 10001-2812, USA

DiGregorio, Ernie (Athlete, Basketball
Player)
60 Chestnut Ave
Narragansett, RI 02882-6113, USA

Dilauro, Jack (Athlete, Baseball Player)
85 Oneida Trl
Malvern, OH 44644-9547, USA

Dildarian, Steve (Actor)
2481 N Edgemont St
Los Angeles, CA 90027-1054, USA

Dilfer, Trent F (Athlete, Football Player)
15288 Quito Rd
Saratoga, CA 95070-6227, USA

Dilger, Ken (Athlete, Football Player)
10403 Windemere
Carmel, IN 46032-8594, USA

Dill, Craig (Athlete, Basketball Player)
10200 Thomas Woods Rd
Saginaw, MI 48609-9512, USA

Dill, Terry (Athlete, Golfer)
1420 Successor Rd
Spicewood, TX 78669-2567, USA

Dillahunt, Garret (Actor)
1077 E Santa Anita Ave
Burbank, CA 91501-1509, USA

Dillam, Bradford (Actor)
770 Hot Springs Rd
Santa Barbara, CA 93108-1107, USA

Dillard, Alex (Business Person)
Dillard's Inc
1600 Cantrell Rd
Little Rock, AR 72201-1145, USA

Dillard, Annie (Writer)
Russell Volkering
50 W 29th St
New York, NY 10001-4227, USA

Dillard, Don (Athlete, Baseball Player)
160 Orchard Park Dr
Greenwood, SC 29649-1679, USA

Dillard, Gordon (Athlete, Baseball Player)
840 Via Manzana
Aromas, CA 95004-9026, USA

Dillard, Harrison (Athlete, Olympic
Athlete, Track Athlete)
306 Knollwood Trl
Cleveland, OH 44143-1482, USA

Dillard, Harrison H. (Athlete, Olympic
Athlete, Track Athlete)
3842 E 147th St
Cleveland, OH 44128-1027, USA

Dillard, Mickey (Athlete, Basketball
Player)
224 SW 11th Ave
Dania, FL 33004-3515, USA

Dillard, Phillip (Athlete, Football Player)
c/o Roosevelt Barnes *Maximum Sports
Management*
6435 W Jefferson Blvd # 197
Fort Wayne, IN 46804-6203, USA

Dillard, Rodney (Actor, Musician)
Superior Communications Co. Talent
340 S Columbus Blvd
C/O Randy Campbell
Tucson, AZ 85711-4138, USA

Dillard, Stacey (Athlete, Football Player)
3188 County Road 4220
Annona, TX 75550-4037, USA

Dillard, Steve (Athlete, Baseball Player)
154 Drive 841
Saltillo, MS 38866-9362, USA

Dillard, Tim (Athlete, Baseball Player)
139 Grigsby Rd
Franklin, TN 37064-8334, USA

Dillard, Victoria (Actor)
25 Chittenden Ave Apt 3C
New York, NY 10033-1142, USA

Dillard, William T Jr (Business Person)
Dillard's Inc
1600 Cantrell Rd
Little Rock, AR 72201-1145, USA

Dille, Bob (Athlete, Basketball Player)
138 Quails Nest Rd Apt 1
Naples, FL 34112-5194, USA

Diller, Barry (Business Person)
IAC/InterActive Corp
555 W 18th St
New York, NY 10011-2822, USA

Dillman, Bill (Athlete, Baseball Player)
PO Box 5167
Winter Park, FL 32793-5167, USA

Dillman, Bradford (Actor)
770 Hot Springs Rd
Santa Barbara, CA 93108-1107, USA

Dillman, Brooke (Actor)
1632 S Point View St
Los Angeles, CA 90035-4508, USA

Dillon, Austin (Race Car Driver)
Childress Racing
236 Industrial Dr
Welcome, NC 27374, USA

Dillon, Bobby (Athlete, Football Player)
1289 Morgan Dr
Temple, TX 76502-4245, USA

Dillon, Corey (Athlete, Football Player)
26535 Alsace Dr
Calabasas, CA 91302-3454, USA

Dillon, David B (Business Person)
Kroger Co
1014 Vine St Ste 1000
Cincinnati, OH 45202-1119, USA

Dillon, Denny (Actor, Comedian)
International Creative Mgmt
10250 Constellation Blvd Fl 1
Los Angeles, CA 90067-6241, USA

Dillon, Joe (Athlete, Baseball Player)
2360 Water Way
Rockwall, TX 75087-2892, USA

Dillon, Kevin (Actor)
1259 S Stanley Ave
Los Angeles, CA 90019-6616, USA

Dillon, Matt (Actor, Director)
35 W 81st St # 88BCD
New York, NY 10024-6045, USA

Dillon, Melinda (Actor)
4065 Michael Ave
Los Angeles, CA 90066-5115, USA

Dillon, Mike (Race Car Driver)
PO Box 30414
Winston Salem, NC 27130-0414, USA

Dillon, Steve (Athlete, Baseball Player)
511 Wateredge Ave
Baldwin, NY 11510-3728, USA

Dilmancheff, Babe (Athlete, Football
Player)
3917 Edgehill Dr
Los Angeles, CA 90008-2617, USA

Dils, Steve (Athlete, Football Player)
525 Cameron Manor Way
Atlanta, GA 30328-6202, USA

Dilts, Bucky (Athlete, Football Player)
240 McCaslin Blvd # 101
Louisville, CO 80027-2911, USA

Dilts, Douglas (Athlete, Football Player)
1231 Defoor Ct NW
Atlanta, GA 30318-2973, USA

Dilweg, Anthony (Athlete, Football Player)
5310 S Alston Ave Ste 210
Durham, NC 27713-4381, USA

Dilworth, John (Animator, Director)
Stretch Films
561 Hudson St # 21
New York, NY 10014-2463, USA

DiMaggio, John (Actor)
c/o Paul Rosicker *Gersh (LA)*
9465 Wilshire Blvd Ste 600
Beverly Hills, CA 90212-2605, USA

Dimaio, Rob (Athlete, Hockey Player)
c/o Staff Member *Dallas Stars*
2601 Avenue of the Stars Ste 100
Frisco, TX 75034-9016, USA

DiManche, Jayson (Athlete, Football
Player)
c/o Joe Linta *JL Sports*
1204 Main St Ste 179
Branford, CT 06405-3787, USA

DiMarco, Chris (Athlete, Golfer)
3545 Rice Lake Loop
Longwood, FL 32779-3081, USA

Dimas, Trent (Gymnast)
Gold Cup Gymnastics School
6009 Carmel Ave NE
Albuquerque, NM 87113-1741, USA

DiMeo, Paul (Actor, Reality Star)
c/o Staff Member *Extreme Makeover:
Home Edition*
9225 W Sunset Blvd # 1100
Endemol Entertainment Usa
West Hollywood, CA 90069-3111, USA

Di Meola, Al (Musician)
c/o Staff Member *Entourage Talent
Associates*
133 W 25th St
New York, NY 10001-7206, USA

Dimichele, Frank (Athlete, Baseball
Player)
119 Clemens Cir
Norristown, PA 19403-3087, USA

Dimitrakos, Niko (Athlete, Hockey Player)
149 Timber Ct
Wood Dale, IL 60191-1356

Dimmel, Mike (Athlete, Baseball Player)
526 Country Ln
Coppell, TX 75019-5129, USA

Dimmick, Thomas (Athlete, Football
Player)
110 Marina Ave
Key Largo, FL 33037-4311, USA

Dimon, James (Jamie) (Business Person)
J P Morgan Chase
270 Park Ave Fl 12
New York, NY 10017-2089, USA

Dimry, Charles (Athlete, Football Player)
7522 Circulo Sequoia
Carlsbad, CA 92009-8468, USA

DiMucci, Dion (Actor, Musician)
3099 NW 63rd St
Boca Raton, FL 33496-3309, USA

Dimuro, Mike (Athlete, Baseball Player)
22594 E Peakview Pl
Aurora, CO 80016-3148, USA

Dimuro, Ray (Athlete, Baseball Player)
9625 N 33rd St
Phoenix, AZ 85028-4919, USA

Dinapoli, Gennaro (Athlete, Football
Player)
10 White Oak Farm Rd
Newtown, CT 06470-2501, USA

DiNardo, Gerry (Coach, Football Coach)
Indiana University
Athletic Dept
Bloomington, IN 47405, USA

Dinardo, Lenny (Athlete, Baseball Player)
23015 NW 227th Dr
High Springs, FL 32643-9031, USA

Dindal, Mark (Director)
c/o Peter Nichols *Lichter Grossman Nichols Adler & Goodman*
9200 W Sunset Blvd Ste 1200
West Hollywood, CA 90069-3607, USA

Dineen, Bill (Athlete, Hockey Player)
18 Fairwood Dr
Queensbury, NY 12804-2175

Dineen, Gord (Athlete, Hockey Player)
51 Fitzgerald Rd
Queensbury, NY 12804-1344

Dineen, Kenny (Athlete, Baseball Player)
112 S Ranch St
Santa Maria, CA 93454-5319, USA

Dineen, Kerry
2155 Arrowhead Dr
Santa Maria, CA 93455-5762, USA

Dineen, Kevin (Athlete, Hockey Player)
360 N Oak St
Hinsdale, IL 60521-3848

Dineen, Kevin (Athlete, Hockey Player)
Florida Panthers
1 Panther Pkwy
Sunrise, FL 33323-5315

Dineen, Peter (Athlete, Hockey Player)
65 Birch Rd
Lake George, NY 12845-4323

Dineen, William P (Bill) (Coach)
Saint Louis Blues
1401 Clark Ave
Sawis Center
Saint Louis, MO 63103-2700, USA

Dingle, Adrian (Athlete, Football Player)
3228 W Canyon Ave
San Diego, CA 92123-5429, USA

Dingle, Mike (Athlete, Football Player)
512 Menlo Dr
Columbia, SC 29210-6537, USA

Dingman, Chris (Athlete, Hockey Player)
9220 Pine Island Ct
Tampa, FL 33647-2301

Dingman, Craig (Athlete, Baseball Player)
3573 W Del Sienno St
Wichita, KS 67203-4349, USA

Dini, Paul (Actor, Producer, Writer)
c/o Staff Member *United Talent Agency (UTA-LA)*
9336 Civic Center Dr
Beverly Hills, CA 90210-3604, USA

Dinkel, Tom (Athlete, Football Player)
4883 Dartmouth Dr
Burlington, KY 41005-9186, USA

Dinkelman, Brian (Athlete, Baseball Player)
2621 S Pine St
Centralia, IL 62801-6149, USA

Dinkins, Byron (Athlete, Basketball Player)
10326 Tallent Ln
Huntersville, NC 28078-5903, USA

Dinkins, Darnell (Athlete, Football Player)
9006 Pembroke Ct
Pittsburgh, PA 15237-6366, USA

Dinkins, Howard (Athlete, Football Player)
5980 Covered Creek Ln
Jacksonville, FL 32277-1447, USA

Dinklage, Peter (Actor)
c/o David Ginsberg *Insight*
PO Box 36359
Los Angeles, CA 90036-0359, USA

Dinnel, Harry (Athlete, Basketball Player)
1427 El Nido Dr
Fallbrook, CA 92028-8697, USA

Dinner, Michael (Director)
c/o Staff Member *Creative Artists Agency (CAA-LA)*
2000 Avenue of the Stars Ste 100
Los Angeles, CA 90067-4705, USA

Dinwiddle, Ryan (Athlete, Football Player)
2931 S Zach Pl
Boise, ID 83706-6807

Diogu, Ike
2052 W Lagoon Rd
Pleasanton, CA 94566-3576, USA

DioGuardi, Kara (Musician, Reality Star, Songwriter)
6 Starboard Ln
York, ME 03909-1563, USA

Dion (Musician)
3099 NW 63rd St
Boca Raton, FL 33496-3309, USA

Dion, Celine (Actor, Musician)
Caesars Palace - The Colosseum
3570 Las Vegas Blvd S
Las Vegas, NV 89109-8933, USA

Dion, Colleen (Actor)
Abrams Artists
9200 W Sunset Blvd Ste 1125
West Hollywood, CA 90069-3610, USA

Dion, Michel (Athlete, Hockey Player)
33 Mulrain Way
Bluffton, SC 29910-6530, USA

Dion, Terry (Athlete, Football Player)
106 E Libby Rd
Shelton, WA 98584-8132, USA

Dionne, Joseph L (Business Person, Publisher)
McGraw-Hill Inc
2 Penn Plz Fl 5
New York, NY 10121-0600, USA

Dionne, Marcel E (Athlete, Hockey Player)
Marcel Dionne Inc
PO Box 2596
Niagara Falls, NY 14302-2596

Diop, DeSagana (Athlete, Basketball Player)
308 Harper Dr Ste 210
Moorestown, NJ 08057-3245, USA

Diorio, Nick (Soccer Player)
273 Clark St
Lemoyne, PA 17043-2010, USA

Diorio, Ron (Athlete, Baseball Player)
234 Peach Orchard Rd
Waterbury, CT 06706-2833, USA

Dipierro, Ramon (Athlete, Football Player)
1750 Brownstone Blvd Apt H
Toledo, OH 43614-1362, USA

Dipino, Frank (Athlete, Baseball Player)
5479 Pebble Beach Dr
Camillus, NY 13031-8651, USA

Diplo (DJ, Musician)
c/o Tom Windish *The Windish Agency*
1658 N Milwaukee Ave # 211
Chicago, IL 60647-6905, USA

Dipoto, Jerry (Commentator)
2681 Crestview Dr
Newport Beach, CA 92663-5626, USA

DiPreta, Tony (Cartoonist)
North American Syndicate
235 E 45th St
New York, NY 10017-3305, USA

DiPrete, Edward D (Politician)
555 Wilbur Ave
Cranston, RI 02921-1435, USA

Dirda, Michael (Journalist)
Washington Post
Editorial Dept
1150 15th St NW
Washington, DC 20071-0001, USA

Dirden, Johnnie (Athlete, Football Player)
1403 S Ulster St
Denver, CO 80231-2744, USA

Director, Kim (Actor)
c/o Rachel Sheedy *Resolution (LA)*
10 E 44th St
New York, NY 10017-3601, USA

Direnzo, Daniel (Dan) (Athlete, Football Player)
PO Box 958
Albrightsville, PA 18210-0958, USA

Direnzo, Fred (Athlete, Football Player)
5 Togno St
Netcong, NJ 07857-1608, USA

Diresta, John (Actor, Comedian)
c/o Ruthanne Secunda *ICM Partners (LA)*
10250 Constellation Blvd Fl 7
Los Angeles, CA 90067-6207, USA

Dirks, Andy
11516 E Trail West Rd
Burrton, KS 67020-8810, USA

Dirnt, Mike (Musician)
3457 Bonnie Hill Dr
Los Angeles, CA 90068-1325, USA

Dirt Band, The
PO Box 1915
Aspen, CO 81612-1915

Dirty Pretty Things (Music Group)
c/o Staff Member *Paradigm (Monterey)*
404 W Franklin St
Monterey, CA 93940-2303, USA

DiSalvatore, Jon
16 Saddle Hill Rd
Manchester, CT 06040-6958

Disarcina, Gary (Athlete, Baseball Player)
141 Martingale Ln
Plymouth, MA 02360-3275, USA

Dischinger, Terry (Athlete, Basketball Player, Olympic Athlete)
1730 Oak Ave
Northbrook, IL 60062-5428, USA

Disco Biscuits, The (Music Group)
c/o Staff Member *Red Light Management (LA)*
8439 W Sunset Blvd Ste 2
West Hollywood, CA 90069-1925, USA

Disel, Vin (Actor, Director)
c/o Stacy Boniello *Firm, The*
2049 Century Park E # 2550
Los Angeles, CA 90067-3101, USA

Dishman, Chris E (Athlete, Football Player)
1561 Raymond Rd
Garland, NE 68360-9347, USA

Dishman, Cris (Athlete, Football Player)
5019 Mariposa Cir
Fresno, TX 77545-9219, USA

Dishman, Glenn (Athlete, Baseball Player)
5400 Fairway Dr
San Jose, CA 95127-1609, USA

Dishy, Bob (Actor)
20 E 9th St
New York, NY 10003-5944, USA

Disick, Scott (Reality Star)
25344 Prado De La Felicidad
Calabasas, CA 91302-3649, USA

Disney, Bill (Athlete, Olympic Athlete, Speed Skater)
1610 Kirk Dr
Lake Havasu City, AZ 86404-2449

Disney, William (Speed Skater)
1610 Kirk Dr
Lake Havasu City, AZ 86404-2449, USA

DiSpirito, Rocco (Chef, Reality Star)
60 E Randolph St # 3203
Chicago, IL 60601-7504, USA

Distefano, Benny (Athlete, Baseball Player)
9911 Murray Lndg
Missouri City, TX 77459-6417, USA

Distler, Natalie (Actor)
c/o Cynthia Booth *Resolution (LA)*
6253 Hollywood Blvd Apt 508
Los Angeles, CA 90028-8251, USA

Disturbed (Music Group, Musician)
c/o Silda Palerm *Warner Bros Records (NY)*
75 Rockefeller Plz
New York, NY 10019-6908, USA

Ditka, Mike (Athlete, Coach, Football Coach, Football Player)
161 E Chicago Ave Apt 39F
Chicago, IL 60611-2623, USA

Ditmar, Arthur J (Art) (Athlete, Baseball Player)
6687 Wisteria Dr
Myrtle Beach, SC 29588-6481, USA

Dittmer, Jack (Athlete, Baseball Player)
PO Box 98
Elkader, IA 52043-0098, USA

Ditto, Beth (Musician)
c/o Marc Gerald *Agency Group Ltd, The (LA)*
1880 Century Park E Ste 711
Los Angeles, CA 90067-1618, USA

Ditz, Nancy (Athlete, Track Athlete)
524 Moore Rd
Woodside, CA 94062-1109, USA

Diva, Amanda (Television Host)
c/o Mike Esterman *Esterman.Com, LLC*
Prefers to be contacted via email
Baltimore, MD XXXXX, USA

Divac, Vlade (Athlete, Basketball Player)
c/o Marc Fleisher *Entersport-World HQ*
128 Heather Dr
New Canaan, CT 06840-5224, USA

DiVello, Adam (Producer)
1235 N Kenter Ave
Los Angeles, CA 90049-1317, USA

Divina, Luz (DJ)
c/o Len Evans *Project Publicity*
312 W 53rd St Ste 202
New York, NY 10019-5743, USA

Divine Comedy, The (Music Group)
c/o Staff Member *Paradigm (Monterey)*
404 W Franklin St
Monterey, CA 93940-2303, USA

Divoff, Andrew (Actor)
c/o Staff Member *Marshak/Zachary Company, The*
8840 Wilshire Blvd Fl 1
Beverly Hills, CA 90211-2606, USA

Dixie Chicks (Music Group)
c/o Simon Renshaw *Strategic Artist Management*
1100 Glendon Ave Ste 1000
Los Angeles, CA 90024-3514, USA

Dixie Cups, The (Music Group)
2535 Noble St
North Las Vegas, NV 89030-3819, USA

Dixieland Rhythm Kings, The
PO Box 12403
Atlanta, GA 30355-2403

Dixon, Al (Athlete, Football Player)
386 Somerset St Apt 1
North Plainfield, NJ 07060-4758, USA

Dixon, Alan J (Politician)
7606 Foley Dr
Belleville, IL 62223-2322, USA

Dixon, Becky (Sportscaster)
ABC-TV
77 W 66th St
Sports Dept
New York, NY 10023-6201, USA

Dixon, Cal (Athlete, Football Player)
179 Las Palmas
Merritt Island, FL 32953-2902, USA

Dixon, Craig (Athlete, Olympic Athlete, Track Athlete)
10630 Wellworth Ave
Los Angeles, CA 90024-5012, USA

Dixon, David (Athlete, Football Player)
4795 W 131 1/2 St
Savage, MN 55378-2505, USA

Dixon, Dennis (Athlete, Football Player)
c/o Jeff Sperbeck *The Novo Agency*
3201 Danville Blvd Ste 295
Alamo, CA 94507-1978, USA

Dixon, Donna (Actor)
7708 Woodrow Wilson Dr
Los Angeles, CA 90046-1212, USA

Dixon, Dwayne (Athlete, Football Player)
78 Westfield Pl
Athens, OH 45701-3857, USA

Dixon, Floyd (Musician)
Folklore Prod
PO Box 7003
Santa Monica, CA 90406-7003, USA

Dixon, Gerald (Athlete, Football Player)
1315 Big Rock Ct
Fort Mill, SC 29708-6950, USA

Dixon, Juan (Basketball Player)
Washington Wizards
601 F St NW
Mci Centre
Washington, DC 20004-1605, USA

Dixon, Ken (Athlete, Baseball Player)
3 Croydon Ct
Gwynn Oak, MD 21207-4542, USA

Dixon, Larry (Race Car Driver)
Don Prudhomme Racing
1232 Distribution Way
Vista, CA 92081-8816, USA

Dixon, Leslie (Director, Producer, Writer)
c/o Todd Feldman *Creative Artists Agency (CAA-LA)*
2000 Avenue of the Stars Ste 100
Los Angeles, CA 90067-4705, USA

Dixon, Mark (Athlete, Football Player)
4016 Ivy Ln
Kitty Hawk, NC 27949-4347, USA

Dixon, Randolph C (Randy) (Athlete, Football Player)
9910 Summerlakes Dr
Carmel, IN 46032-9307, USA

Dixon, Ronnie (Athlete, Football Player)
11755 Norbourne Dr Apt 707
Cincinnati, OH 45240-4444, USA

Dixon, Scott (Race Car Driver)
Target Chip Ganassi Racing
7161 Zionville Rd
Indianapolis, IN 46268, USA

Dixon, Steve (Athlete, Baseball Player)
6510 Hollow Tree Rd
Louisville, KY 40228-1336, USA

Dixon, Tamecka (Basketball Player)
Los Angeles Sparks
1111 S Figueroa St
Staples Center
Los Angeles, CA 90015-1300, USA

Dixon, Tom (Athlete, Baseball Player)
540 W Graves Ave
Orange City, FL 32763-5170, USA

Dixon, Tony (Athlete, Football Player)
4588 Gibson Dr
Bessemer, AL 35022-7045, USA

Dixon, Zachary (Athlete, Football Player)
19365 Hottinger Cir
Germantown, MD 20874-1504, USA

Dizon, Jesse
PO Box 572105
Tarzana, CA 91357-2105, USA

Djalili, Omid (Actor)
c/o Brian Stern *Brillstein Entertainment Partners (NYC)*
375 Greenwich St
New York, NY 10013-2376, USA

DJ Ashba (Musician)
c/o Jill Siegel *10th Street Entertainment (LA)*
700 N San Vicente Blvd Ste G410
West Hollywood, CA 90069-5060, USA

DJ Jazzy Jeff (Actor, Musician)
c/o Ron Rivlin *Coast II Coast Entertainment*
204 S Beverly Dr Ste 110
Beverly Hills, CA 90212-3800, USA

Dlouhy, Lukas (Athlete, Tennis Player)
c/o Staff Member *ATP Tour*
201 Atp Tour Blvd
Ponte Vedra Beach, FL 32082-3211, USA

D. Lucas, Frank (Congressman, Politician)
2311 Rayburn Hob
Washington, DC 20515-2404, USA

Dlugach, Brent
9847 Laurel Hollow Cir
Germantown, TN 38139-6967, USA

D'Lyn, Shae (Actor)
c/o Miles Levy *James/Levy Management Inc*
3500 W Olive Ave Ste 1470
Burbank, CA 91505-5514, USA

Doak, Gary (Athlete, Hockey Player)
47 Highland Ave
Lynnfield, MA 01940-1905, USA

Doan, Charles A (Doctor)
4935 Olentangy Blvd
Columbus, OH 43214-2049, USA

Dobbek, Dan (Athlete, Baseball Player)
4042 SE Yamhill St
Portland, OR 97214-4445, USA

Dobbins, Oliver (Athlete, Football Player)
11126 Piscataway Rd
Clinton, MD 20735-9519, USA

Dobbins, Tim (Athlete, Football Player)
c/o Harold C Lewis *National Sports Agency*
15400 Timpaige Dr
Chesterfield, MO 63017-1762, USA

Dobbs, Greg (Athlete, Baseball Player)
2255 Richey Dr
La Canada Flintridge, CA 91011-1350, USA

Dobbs, Lou (Television Host)
74 Quarry Rd
Sussex, NJ 07461-3820, USA

Dobek, Bob (Athlete, Hockey Player, Olympic Athlete)
3813 Observation Pl
Escondido, CA 92025-7933, USA

Dobek, Michelle (Athlete, Golfer)
292 Chicopee St
Chicopee, MA 01013-1744, USA

Dobkin, Alix (Musician)
PO Box 761
Woodstock, NY 12498-0761, USA

Dobkin, David (Director)
H S I Productions
3630 Eastham Dr
Culver City, CA 90232-2411, USA

Dobkin, Lawrence
1787 Old Ranch Rd
Los Angeles, CA 90049-2507

Dobkins, Carl Jr (Musician)
7640 Cheviot Rd Apt 212
Cincinnati, OH 45247-4011, USA

Dobler, Conrad F (Athlete, Football Player)
12600 Fairway Rd
Leawood, KS 66209-2453, USA

Dobler, David (Religious Leader)
Presbyterian Church USA
100 Witherspoon St
Louisville, KY 40202-6300, USA

Dobo, Kata (Actor)
c/o Sara Ramaker *Paradigm (LA)*
360 N Crescent Dr
North Bldg
Beverly Hills, CA 90210-4874, USA

Dobrev, Nina (Actor)
c/o Aleen Keshishian *Brillstein Entertainment Partners (LA)*
9150 Wilshire Blvd Ste 350
Beverly Hills, CA 90212-3453, USA

Dobslow, Bill (Musician)
945 Handlebar Rd
Mishawaka, IN 46544-6647, USA

Dobson, Aaron (Athlete, Football Player)
c/o Chad Speck *Allegiant Athletic Agency*
35 Market Sq Ste 201
Knoxville, TN 37902-1420, USA

Dobson, Chuck (Athlete, Baseball Player)
4208 Locust St
Kansas City, MO 64110-1017, USA

Dobson, Dominic (Race Car Driver)
2719 63rd Ave SE
Mercer Island, WA 98040-2433, USA

Dobson, Fefe (Musician)
c/o Staff Member *Island Records*
825 8th Ave Rm C2
New York, NY 10019-7472, USA

Dobson, Helen (Athlete, Golfer)
7638 Eagle Creek Dr
Sarasota, FL 34243-4613, USA

Dobson, James C (Religious Leader)
Focus on the Family
8605 Explorer Dr
Colorado Springs, CO 80920-1051, USA

Dobson, Kevin (Actor)
12527 Sarah St
Studio City, CA 91604-1113, USA

Dobson, Peter (Actor)
1351 N Crescent Heights Blvd Apt 318
West Hollywood, CA 90046-4579, USA

Dockery, Derrick (Athlete, Football Player)
7102 Jack Franzen Dr
Garland, TX 75043-6600, USA

Dockery, John (Athlete, Football Player)
17 Garden Pl
Brooklyn, NY 11201-4501, USA

Dockery, Michelle (Actor)
c/o Sandra Chang *Anonymous Content (LA)*
3532 Hayden Ave
Culver City, CA 90232-2413, USA

Dockett, Darnell (Athlete, Football Player)
6815 Sand Cherry Way
Clinton, MD 20735-4246, USA

Docter, Mary (Athlete, Olympic Athlete, Speed Skater)
3400 S Russel Rd
New Berlin, WI 53151-4637, USA

Docter, Pete (Actor, Director)
c/o Staff Member *Pixar Animation Studios*
1200 Park Ave
Emeryville, CA 94608-3677, USA

Doctorow, E L (Writer)
c/o Ron Bernstein *ICM Partners (LA)*
10250 Constellation Blvd Fl 7
Los Angeles, CA 90067-6207, USA

Doda, Carol (Actor, Dancer)
PO Box 387
Fremont, CA 94537-0387, USA

Dodd, Alice (Model)
574 N Irving Blvd
Los Angeles, CA 90004-1407, USA

Dodd, Christopher (Politician)
87th St NE
Washington, DC 20002, USA

Dodd, Deryl (Musician, Songwriter, Writer)
823 Mgmt
PO Box 186
Waring, TX 78074-0186, USA

Dodd, Michael T (Mike) (Athlete, Volleyball Player)
AVP Pro Beach Volleyball Tour
960 Knox St Bldg A
Torrance, CA 90502-1086, USA

Dodd, Patty D (Athlete, Volleyball Player)
Fonz
1017 Manhattan Ave
Manhattan Beach, CA 90266-5452, USA

Dodd, Robert (Athlete, Baseball Player)
3467 Overhill Dr
Frisco, TX 75033-1112, USA

Dodd, Tom (Athlete, Baseball Player)
3735 NE Shaver St
Portland, OR 97212-1871, USA

Dodds, Megan (Actor)
c/o Ron West *Thruline Entertainment*
9250 Wilshire Blvd Ste 100
Ground Floor
Beverly Hills, CA 90212-3343, USA

Dodds, Trevor (Athlete, Golfer)
9730 Plummer St
Houston, TX 77029-4230, USA

Dodge, Brooks (Skier)
PO Box C
Jackson, NH 03846-0802, USA

Dodge, Dedrick (Athlete, Football Player)
1109 Bowlin Dr
Locust Grove, GA 30248-7079, USA

Dodge, GeaHrey (Publisher)
Money Magazine
Time-Life Building
New York, NY 10020, USA

Dodge, Geoffrey (Publisher)
Money Magazine
Time-Life Building
New York, NY 10020, USA

Dodge, Kirk (Athlete, Football Player)
110 Roadrunner Ln
Aliso Viejo, CA 92656-1885, USA

Dodrill, Dale (Athlete, Football Player)
2579 S Independence St
Lakewood, CO 80227-2847, USA

Dodson, Pat (Athlete, Baseball Player)
1034 Hillside Rd
Grove, OK 74344-3514, USA

Dodson, Quintin (Reality Star)
4571 Haskell Ave
Encino, CA 91436-3131, USA

Dodson, Richard (Athlete, Football Player)
PO Box 81302
Phoenix, AZ 85069-1302, USA

Doelling, Fred (Athlete, Football Player)
60 South St
Valparaiso, IN 46383-6445, USA

Doerger, Jerome (Athlete, Football Player)
8309 Ridgevalley Ct
Cincinnati, OH 45247-3597, USA

Doering, Chris (Athlete, Football Player)
3843 SW 92nd Ter
Gainesville, FL 32608, USA

Doering, Jason (Athlete, Football Player)
24 Milford St Apt 1
Boston, MA 02118-3612, USA

Doerr, Robert P (Bobby) (Athlete, Baseball Player)
PO Box 430
Junction City, OR 97448-0430, USA

Dogg, Snoop (Actor, Musician)
c/o Staff Member *Stampede Management*
200 Corporate Pointe Ste 480
Culver City, CA 90230-8734, USA

Doggett, Lloyd (Congressman, Politician)
201 Cannon Hob
Washington, DC 20515-4310, USA

Dogins, Kevin (Athlete, Football Player)
8861 Cameron Crest Dr
Tampa, FL 33626-4732, USA

Dog Star (Music Group)
1900 Avenue of the Stars # 1040
Los Angeles, CA 90067-4301, USA

Dohan, Meital (Actor, Musician)
c/o Cory Richman *Liebman Entertainment*
12 E 46th St Fl 5
New York, NY 10017-2418, USA

Doherty, James (Horse Racer)
9 Jane St
East Rutherford, NJ 07073-1420, USA

Doherty, John (Athlete, Baseball Player)
109 Wakefield St
Reading, MA 01867-1854, USA

Doherty, Robert (Producer)
c/o Staff Member *United Talent Agency (UTA-LA)*
9336 Civic Center Dr
Beverly Hills, CA 90210-3604, USA

Doherty, Shannen (Actor)
6910 Solano Verde Dr
Somis, CA 93066-9756, USA

Dohmann, Scott (Athlete, Baseball Player)
3222 W Paxton Ave
Tampa, FL 33611-3920, USA

Dohring, Jason (Actor)
c/o Joel Stevens *Joel Stevens Entertainment*
5627 Allott Ave
Van Nuys, CA 91401-4502, USA

Dohrmann, Angela (Actor)
Innovative Artists
1505 10th St
Santa Monica, CA 90401-2805, USA

Dohrmann, George (Journalist)
Saint Paul Pioneer Press
345 Cedar St
Editorial Dept
Saint Paul, MN 55101-1057, USA

Doig, Jason (Athlete, Hockey Player)
2153 Broderick Ave
Duarte, CA 91010-3508, USA

Doig, Lex (Actor)
Andromeda Productions
8651 Eastlake Dr
Burnaby, BC V5A 4T7

Doig, Steve (Athlete, Football Player)
PO Box 206
North Reading, MA 01864-0206, USA

Dokey, Merritt (Horse Racer)
14109 B Dr
Plymouth, MI 48170-2303, USA

Dokish, Wanita (Athlete, Baseball Player, Commentator)
2480 S Grande Blvd
Greensburg, PA 15601-8902, USA

Dokken, Don (Musician)
Agency for Performing Arts
9200 W Sunset Blvd Ste 900
West Hollywood, CA 90069-3604, USA

Dolan, Chuck (Business Person)
330 Cove Neck Rd
Oyster Bay, NY 11771, USA

Dolan, Don (Actor)
14228 Emelita St
Van Nuys, CA 91401-4208, USA

Dolan, Ellen (Actor)
Don Buchwald
10 E 44th St Frnt 1
New York, NY 10017-3654, USA

Dolan, Lawrence J (Commentator)
16 Windward Way
Chagrin Falls, OH 44023-6705, USA

Dolan, Michael P (Government Official)
Internal Revenue Service
1111 Constitution Ave NW
Washington, DC 20224-0002, USA

Dolan, Tom (Athlete, Olympic Athlete, Swimmer)
610 Poplar Dr
Falls Church, VA 22046-2838

Dolan, Xavier (Actor, Director)
c/o Thor Bradwell *LBI Entertainment*
2000 Avenue of the Stars
Floor 3, North Tower
Los Angeles, CA 90067-4700, USA

Dolbin, Jack (Athlete, Football Player)
4304 Brookside Ct
Orwigsburg, PA 17961-9345, USA

Dolby, Thomas (Musician, Songwriter, Writer)
Inteinational Talent Group
729 7th Ave Ste 1600
New York, NY 10019-6880, USA

Dolce (Musician)
c/o Staff Member *Diva Central Inc*
7510 W Sunset Blvd Ste 1445
Los Angeles, CA 90046-3408, USA

Dold, R Bruce (Journalist)
501 N Park Rd # Hse
La Grange Park, IL 60526-5516, USA

Dole, Bob (Politician)
The Atlantic Building
950 F St NW Fl 10
Washington, DC 20004-1439, USA

Dole, Elizabeth H (Politician)
c/o Staff Member *William Morris Endeavor (LA)*
9601 Wilshire Blvd
Beverly Hills, CA 90210-5213, USA

Doleac, Michael (Athlete, Basketball Player)
1155 Old Rail Ln
Park City, UT 84098-6640, USA

Doleman, Chris (Athlete, Football Player)
7020 Sentara Pl
Alpharetta, GA 30005-3017, USA

Dolenz, Ami (Actor)
1860 Bel Air Rd
Los Angeles, CA 90077-2729, USA

Dolenz, Micky (Actor, Musician)
22 Baymare Rd
Bell Canyon, CA 91307-1101, USA

D'Oliveira, Luisa (Actor)
c/o Staff Member *Levine Okwu Erickson Management*
2126 N Commonwealth Ave
Los Angeles, CA 90027-2118, USA

Dollansky, Craig (Race Car Driver)
Craig Dollansky Racing
28223 Lake Diann Rd
Zimmerman, MN 55398-9228, USA

Dollar, Aubrey (Actor)
c/o Rhonda Price *Gersh (NY)*
41 Madison Ave
New York, NY 10010-2202, USA

Dollar, Creflo (Religious Leader)
Creflo Dollar Ministries
PO Box 490124
Atlanta, GA 30349-0124, USA

Dollar, Linda (Coach)
Southwest Missouri State University
Athletic Dept
Springfield, MO 65804, USA

Dollar, Taffi (Religious Leader)
Creflo Dollar Ministries
PO Box 490124
Atlanta, GA 30349-0124, USA

Dollard, Christopher Edward (Actor)
Gold Marshak Liedtke
3500 W Olive Ave Ste 1400
Burbank, CA 91505-5512, USA

Dollaz, Rich (Producer)
Dollaz Unlimited
171 Hasbrouck Ave
Hasbrouck Heights, NJ 07604-2703, USA

Dollens, Ronald (Business Person)
Guidant Corp
111 Monument Cir
Indianapolis, IN 46204-5100, USA

Dolley, Jason (Actor)
c/o Nils Larsen *Principato/Young Management (LA)*
9465 Wilshire Blvd Ste 900
Beverly Hills, CA 90212-2608, USA

Dolmayan, John (Musician)
Velvet Hammer
9911 W Pico Blvd Ste 350
Los Angeles, CA 90035-2730, USA

Doman, Brandon (Athlete, Football Player)
4616 Pheasant Ridge Trl
Lehi, UT 84043-5288, USA

Doman, John (Actor)
c/o Staff Member *Peter Strain & Associates Inc (LA)*
5455 Wilshire Blvd Ste 1812
Los Angeles, CA 90036-4268, USA

Dombroski, Paul (Athlete, Football Player)
19122 Beckett Dr
Odessa, FL 33556-2274, USA

Dombrowski, Dave (Commentator)
Detroit Tigers
345 Woodridge Rd
Bloomfield Hills, MI 48304-3468, USA

Dombrowski, James M (Jim) (Athlete, Football Player)
220 Evangeline Dr
Mandeville, LA 70471-1874, USA

Domenichelli, Hnat (Athlete, Hockey Player)
1500 Mansell Rd
Alpharetta, GA 30009-4709, USA

Domenici, Pete (Politician)
225 I St NE Apt 901
Washington, DC 20002-4510, USA

Dominczyk, Marika (Actor)
c/o Sally Ware *Gersh (NY)*
41 Madison Ave
New York, NY 10010-2202, USA

Dominguez, Mario (Race Car Driver)
Herdez Racing
57 Gasoline Aly Ste A
Indianapolis, IN 46222-5932, USA

Dominguez, Matt (Athlete, Football Player)
4804 Counts Cv
Austin, TX 78749-3755, USA

Dominic, Rhodes (Athlete, Football Player)
6411 Canyon Lake Dr
Dallas, TX 75249-3021, USA

Dominik, Andrew (Director, Writer)
c/o Spencer Baumgarten *Creative Artists Agency (CAA-LA)*
2000 Avenue of the Stars Ste 100
Los Angeles, CA 90067-4705, USA

Dominique, Andy (Athlete, Baseball Player)
3899 Arrowhead Dr
El Dorado Hills, CA 95762-4547, USA

Domino, Fats (Musician)
9 Wedgwood Ct
Harvey, LA 70058-7473, USA

Domres, Martin F (Marty) (Athlete, Football Player)
Deutsche Bank
1 South St Ste 2400
Baltimore, MD 21202-3348, USA

Donahue, Elinor (Actor)
78533 Sunrise Mountain Vw
Palm Desert, CA 92211-2403, USA

Donahue, Heather (Actor)
Rigberg Roberts Rugolo
118D S Bevedy Dr
#601
Los Angeles, CA 90035, USA

Donahue, Mitch (Athlete, Football Player)
2220 Beloit Dr
Billings, MT 59102-5706, USA

Donahue, Phil (Talk Show Host)
120/122 Beachside Ave
Westport, CT 06880, USA

Donahue, Terry (Athlete, Baseball Player, Commentator)
215 N 3rd Ave
Saint Charles, IL 60174-2005, USA

Donald, Luke (Athlete, Golfer)
8 Bristol Rd
Northfield, IL 60093-3200, USA

Donald, Mike (Athlete, Golfer)
2400 NW 65th Way
Hollywood, FL 33024-4046, USA

Donaldson, James (Athlete, Basketball Player)
5601 Natomas Blvd Apt 6104
Sacramento, CA 95835-2261, USA

Donaldson, Jeff (Athlete, Football Player)
4529 Stover St
Fort Collins, CO 80525-3261, USA

Donaldson, John (Athlete, Baseball Player)
3913 Yates Ct
Charlotte, NC 28215-3955, USA

Donaldson, Ray (Athlete, Football Player)
3128 Crestwell Dr
Indianapolis, IN 46268-8655, USA

Donaldson, Roger (Director, Producer, Writer)
c/o Martin Spencer *Paradigm (LA)*
2000 Avenue of the Stars
Los Angeles, CA 90067-4700, USA

Donaldson, Sam (Journalist)
1211 Crest Ln
Mc Lean, VA 22101-1837, USA

Donaldson, Samuel (Sam) (Correspondent)
1125 Crest Ln
Mc Lean, VA 22101-1805, USA

Donan, Holland R (Athlete, Football Player)
212 Valley Vw
Pompton Plains, NJ 07444-2166, USA

Donatelli, Clark (Athlete, Hockey Player)
1101 Curtis Corner Rd
Wakefield, RI 02879-1470

Donatelli, Don (Athlete, Football Player)
54846 Seneca Lake Rd
Quaker City, OH 43773-9659, USA

Donato, Ted (Athlete, Hockey Player, Olympic Athlete)
34 Whitcomb Rd
Scituate, MA 02066-1123

Donchez, Tom (Athlete, Football Player)
3369 Green Meadow Dr
Bethlehem, PA 18017-1942, USA

Donckers, William (Athlete, Football Player)
13708 SE 141st St
Renton, WA 98059-5416, USA

Donegan, Dan (Musician)
c/o Staff Member *Mitch Schneider Organization (MSO)*
14724 Ventura Blvd Ste 410
Sherman Oaks, CA 91403-3537, USA

Donella, Chad E (Actor)
c/o Staff Member *TalentWorks (LA)*
3500 W Olive Ave Ste 1400
Burbank, CA 91505-5512, USA

Donen, Stanley (Director)
c/o Staff Member *La Grange Group, The*
11828 La Grange Ave
Los Angeles, CA 90025-5212, USA

Donlavey, Junie (Race Car Driver)
5011 Old Midlothian Tpke
Richmond, VA 23224-1119, USA

Donley, Doug (Athlete, Football Player)
8005 Pullam Cir
Plano, TX 75024-6849, USA

Donnahoo, Roger (Athlete, Football Player)
20 Rock Brook Cv
Rossville, GA 30741-5355, USA

Donnalley, Kevin (Athlete, Football Player)
8910 Dove Stand Ln
Charlotte, NC 28226-2671, USA

Donnalley, Rick (Athlete, Football Player)
485 Gramercy Dr NE
Marietta, GA 30068-4876, USA

Donnan, Jim (Coach, Football Coach)
University of Georgia
Athletic Dept
Athens, GA 30602-0001, USA

Donnelley, James R (Business Person)
R R Donnelley & Sons
77 W Wacker Dr Ste 5000
Chicago, IL 60601-1673, USA

Donnelly, Andrew (Actor)
c/o Ruthanne Secunda *ICM Partners (LA)*
10250 Constellation Blvd Fl 7
Los Angeles, CA 90067-6207, USA

Donnelly, Brendan (Athlete, Baseball Player)
2815 E Arrowhead Trl
Gilbert, AZ 85297-5270, USA

Donnelly, George (Athlete, Football Player)
2S530 Beechwood Rd
Glen Ellyn, IL 60137-6955, USA

Donnelly, Jennifer (Writer)
c/o Staff Member *Simon & Schuster*
1230 Avenue of the Americas Fl CONC1
New York, NY 10020-1586, USA

Donnelly, Joe
1530 Longworth Hob
Washington, DC 20515-0601, USA

Donnelly, Mike (Athlete, Hockey Player)
18429 Stoneridge Ct
Northville, MI 48168-8571, USA

Donnelly, Rich (Athlete, Baseball Player)
165 Stardust Dr
Steubenville, OH 43953-3773, USA

Donnelly, Rick (Athlete, Football Player)
PO Box 20441
Cheyenne, WY 82003-7011, USA

Donnels, Chris (Athlete, Baseball Player)
5 Stone Pne
Aliso Viejo, CA 92656-2131, USA

Donner, Richard (Director)
c/o Staff Member *Donners' Company*
9465 Wilshire Blvd Ste 420
Beverly Hills, CA 90212-2603, USA

Donnie, Elder (Athlete, Football Player)
16613 Norwood Dr
Tampa, FL 33624-1168, USA

Donnovan, Elisa (Actor)
SMS Talent
8383 Wilshire Blvd Ste 230
Beverly Hills, CA 90211-2436, USA

Donoahoe, John (Business Person)
10 Palmer Ln
Portola Valley, CA 94028-7918, USA

D'Onofrio, Mark (Athlete, Football Player)
295 Harmon Ave
Fort Lee, NJ 07024-4446, USA

D'Onofrio, Vincent (Actor, Producer)
c/o Sam Maydew *The Collective*
8383 Wilshire Blvd Ste 1050
Beverly Hills, CA 90211-2415, USA

Donohoe, Michael (Athlete, Football Player)
505 Juneberry Rd
Riverwoods, IL 60015-3715, USA

Donohue, Jim (Athlete, Baseball Player)
16 Huntleigh Downs
Saint Louis, MO 63131-3416, USA

Donohue, Leon (Athlete, Football Player)
1904 Bechelli Ln
Redding, CA 96002-0132, USA

Donohue, Terry
11918 Laurelwood Dr
Studio City, CA 91604-3749

Donohue, Timothy (Business Person)
Nextel Communications
2001 Edmund Halley Dr
Reston, VA 20191-3436, USA

Donohue, Tom (Athlete, Baseball Player)
249 Liberty Ave
Westbury, NY 11590-2135, USA

Donovan, Anne (Athlete, Basketball Player, Olympic Athlete)
123 Ledgewood Rd Apt 310
Groton, CT 06340-6626, USA

Donovan, Billy (Athlete, Basketball Player)
8515 SW 31st Ave
Gainesville, FL 32608-2725, USA

Donovan, Brian (Journalist)
Newsday
235 Pinelawn Rd
Melville, NY 11747-4250, USA

Donovan, Elisa (Actor)
c/o Staff Member *Seven Summits Pictures & Management*
8906 W Olympic Blvd
Ground Floor
Beverly Hills, CA 90211-3550, USA

Donovan, Harry (Athlete, Basketball Player)
8303 Bayonet Point Ct Apt C
Fredericksburg, VA 22407-2125, USA

Donovan, Jeffrey (Actor)
PO Box 549
Evergreen, CO 80437-0549, USA

Donovan, Landon (Athlete, Soccer Player)
c/o Staff Member *Los Angeles Galaxy*
18400 Avalon Blvd Ste 200
Carson, CA 90746-2181, USA

Donovan, Martin (Actor)
c/o Gene Parseghian *Parseghian Planco LLC*
388 2nd Ave
New York, NY 10010-5616, USA

Donovan, Pat (Athlete, Football Player)
PO Box 5
Whitefish, MT 59937-0005, USA

Donovan, Raymond J (Politician)
1600 Paterson Park Rd
Secaucus, NJ 07094, USA

Donovan, Shean (Athlete, Hockey Player)
11 Mountain Rd
Lexington, MA 02420-1308, USA

Donovan, Tate (Actor)
654 Ashland Ave
Santa Monica, CA 90405-4558, USA

Donowho, Ryan (Actor)
c/o Staff Member *Brookside Artists Management (NY)*
250 W 57th St Ste 2303
New York, NY 10107-2399, USA

Doobie Brothers (Music Group)
c/o Staff Member *D. Baron Media Relations*
1411 Cloverfield Blvd
Santa Monica, CA 90404-2917, USA

Doocy, Steve (Television Host)
c/o Staff Member *Fox News (NY)*
1211 Avenue of the Americas Lowr C1
New York, NY 10036-8705, USA

Doolan, Wendy (Athlete, Golfer)
3130 Legends Cir
Lakeland, FL 33803-5432, USA

Dooley, Paul (Actor)
4420 N Clybourn Ave
Burbank, CA 91505-4005, USA

Dooley, Taylor (Actor)
c/o Heather Reynolds *One Entertainment*
(NY)
12 W 57th St PH
New York, NY 10019-3900, USA

Dooley, Thomas (Athlete, Soccer Player)
South Coast Bayern Futbol Club
18141 Beach Blvd Ste 110
Huntington Beach, CA 92648-1354, USA

Dooley, Vince
PO Box 1472
Athens, GA 30603-1472

Dooley, Vincent J (Vince) (Athlete,
Coach, Football Coach, Football Player)
University of Georgia
PO Box 1472
Athletic Dept
Athens, GA 30603-1472, USA

Dooling, Brendan (Actor)
c/o Elise Koseff *J Mitchell Management*
440 Park Ave S
New York, NY 10016-8012, USA

Dooling, Keyon (Athlete, Basketball
Player)
Los Angeles Clippers
2016 NW 3rd Ct
Fort Lauderdale, FL 33311-8708, USA

Doolittle, Melinda (Musician, Reality Star)
1524 Braden Cir
Franklin, TN 37067-8595, USA

Doom, Ryan (Actor)
c/o Katie Rhodes *Untitled Entertainment*
(LA)
350 S Beverly Dr Ste 200
Beverly Hills, CA 90212-4819, USA

Doornink, Dan (Athlete, Football Player)
402 S 12th Ave
Yakima, WA 98902-3115, USA

Dope, Edsel (Musician)
c/o Bob Ringe *Survival Management*
30765 Pacific Coast Hwy Ste 325
Malibu, CA 90265-3643, USA

Dopson, John (Athlete, Baseball Player)
3337 Old Gamber Rd
Finksburg, MD 21048-2223, USA

Dora Brown, Kathryne (Actor)
1617 N Sierra Bonita Ave
Los Angeles, CA 90046-2815, USA

Doran, Bill (Athlete, Baseball Player)
1197 Feather Trl
Maineville, OH 45039-5045, USA

Dore, Andre (Athlete, Hockey Player)
73 Betsys Ln
New Canaan, CT 06840-5202, USA

Dore, Daniel (Athlete, Hockey Player)
c/o Staff Member *Boston Bruins*
100 Legends Way Ste 250
Td Banknorth Garden
Boston, MA 02114-1389, USA

Dore, Jimmy (Comedian)
c/o Alex Murray *Brillstein Entertainment
Partners (LA)*
9150 Wilshire Blvd Ste 350
Beverly Hills, CA 90212-3453, USA

Doremus, David (Actor)
6770 San Onofre Dr
Camarillo, CA 93012-8264, USA

Dorff, Stephen (Actor)
21640 Pacific Coast Hwy
Malibu, CA 90265-5209, USA

Dorfman, Ariel (Writer)
Duke University
2122 Campus Dr
International Studies Center
Durham, NC 27708-9963, USA

Dorfman, David (Actor)
c/o Wendi Green *Paradigm (LA)*
360 N Crescent Dr
North Bldg
Beverly Hills, CA 90210-4874, USA

Dorgan, Byron (Politician)
1702 Esquire Ln
Mc Lean, VA 22101-4754, USA

Dorion, Dan (Athlete, Hockey Player)
10910 Queens Blvd Apt 12H
Forest Hills, NY 11375-5319, USA

Dormann, Dana (Athlete, Golfer)
4887 Arlene Pl
Pleasanton, CA 94566-7824, USA

Dormeker, Jerry (Race Car Driver)
Bad Moon Rising
2243 Ravenna St
Hudson, OH 44236-3453, USA

Dormer, Natalie (Actor)
c/o Jason Weinberg *Untitled
Entertainment (LA)*
350 S Beverly Dr Ste 200
Beverly Hills, CA 90212-4819, USA

Dorn, Michael (Actor)
c/o Nicolas Bernheim *NB Management*
8906 W Olympic Blvd
Ground Floor
Beverly Hills, CA 90211-3550, USA

Dornan, Robert (Politician)
8623 Beaver Pond Ln
Fairfax Station, VA 22039-2725, USA

Dornbrook, Thom (Athlete, Football
Player)
5918 Emerald Lakes Dr
Medina, OH 44256-7464, USA

Dorney, Keith R (Athlete, Football Player)
2450 Blucher Valley Rd
Sebastopol, CA 95472-5355, USA

Dornhoefer, Gary (Athlete, Hockey
Player)
267 Chestnut Neck Rd
Port Republic, NJ 08241-9701

Dornseif, Dave (Athlete, Hockey Player)
3989 E Phillips Cir
Centennial, CO 80122-3647, USA

Dorough, Howie (Musician)
PO Box 110697
Palm Bay, FL 32911-0697, USA

Dorrell, Karl (Coach, Football Coach)
University of California
Athletic Dept
Los Angeles, CA 90024, USA

Dorris, Andrew (Athlete, Football Player)
RR 22 Box 549
Conroe, TX 77303, USA

Dorris, Derek (Athlete, Football Player)
4504 Adobe Dr
Fort Worth, TX 76123-1825, USA

Dorsch, Travis (Athlete, Football Player)
PO Box 2086
West Lafayette, IN 47996-2086, USA

Dorsett, Brian (Athlete, Baseball Player)
749 N Forest Dr
Terre Haute, IN 47803-4216, USA

Dorsett, Tony (Athlete, Football Player,
Heisman Trophy Winner)
5990 Haley Way
Frisco, TX 75034-4878, USA

Dorsett Jr, Anthony (Athlete, Football
Player)
3817 Bowser Ave Apt C
Dallas, TX 75219-4385, USA

Dorsey, Christopher (BG) (Musician)
c/o Staff Member *Sosincere Entertainment*
2054 Nostrand Ave Apt 4F
Brooklyn, NY 11210-2526, USA

Dorsey, Eric (Athlete, Football Player)
5 London Ct
Teaneck, NJ 07666-6461, USA

Dorsey, Jack (Business Person)
Twitter Inc
795 Folsom St Fl 6
San Francisco, CA 94107-4226, USA

Dorsey, Jacky (Athlete, Basketball Player)
1231 S Teal Estates Cir
Fresno, TX 77545-8652, USA

Dorsey, Jim (Athlete, Baseball Player)
335 Elm St
Seekonk, MA 02771-1724, USA

Dorsey, John (Athlete, Football Player)
3100 W 68th St
Mission Hills, KS 66208-2133, USA

Dorsey, Ken (Athlete, Football Player)
7108 Presidio Gln
Lakewood Ranch, FL 34202-5038, USA

Dorsey, Kerris (Actor)
c/o DebraLynn Findon *Discover Inc
Management*
11425 Moorpark St
North Hollywood, CA 91602-2009, USA

Dorsey, Nate (Athlete, Football Player)
5023 S 87th St
Tampa, FL 33619-7209, USA

Dorsey, Ron (Athlete, Basketball Player)
3925 Mallard Way
Cumming, GA 30028-4862, USA

Dorsey Brothers Orchestra (Music Group,
Musician)
PO Box 643176
Vero Beach, FL 32964-3176, USA

Dorta, Melvin (Athlete, Baseball Player)
1351 Cambridge Ct
Palmyra, PA 17078-9351, USA

Dossey, M.D., Larry (Doctor, Writer)
c/o Author Mail *Bantam-Dell Publishing
(NY)*
1745 Broadway
New York, NY 10019-4640, USA

Doster, David (Athlete, Baseball Player)
4123 Sugarhill Run
New Haven, IN 46774-2736, USA

Dotel, Octavio (Athlete, Baseball Player)
382 Oakland Rd
Lawrenceville, GA 30044-3726, USA

Dotson, Dewayne (Athlete, Football
Player)
114 Chapman Dr
White House, TN 37188-9335, USA

Dotson, Earl (Athlete, Football Player)
1112 Azalea Dr
Longview, TX 75601-3214, USA

Dotson, Richard E (Rich) (Athlete,
Baseball Player)
7 Colonel Watson Dr
New Richmond, OH 45157-9002, USA

Dotson, Santana (Athlete, Football Player)
PO Box 79134
Houston, TX 77279-9134, USA

Dotter, Bobby (Race Car Driver)
MPH Racing
118 Stutt Rd
Mooresville, NC 28117, USA

Dotter, Gary (Athlete, Baseball Player)
7413 Ravenswood Rd
Granbury, TX 76049-4742, USA

Dotter, Robert (Race Car Driver)
3632 N Pacific Ave
Chicago, IL 60634-2012, USA

Dottley, John (Athlete, Football Player)
PO Box 88
Vicksburg, MS 39181-0088, USA

Doubleday, Nelson (Commentator)
New York Mets
84 Gomez Rd
Hobe Sound, FL 33455-2330, USA

Doucet, Michael (Music Group, Musician)
Rosebud Agency
PO Box 170429
San Francisco, CA 94117-0429, USA

Doucett, Linda (Actor, Model)
c/o Michael Slessinger *Michael Slessinger
& Associates*
8730 W Sunset Blvd Ste 1125
W Hollywood, CA 90069-2210, USA

Doucette, Paul (Musician)
8071 Woodrow Wilson Dr
Los Angeles, CA 90046-1116, USA

Doug, Doug E (Musician)
4024 Radford Ave # 3
Studio City, CA 91604-2101, USA

Dougherty, Ed (Athlete, Golfer)
448 SW Fairway Vis
Port Saint Lucie, FL 34986-2131, USA

Dougherty, Jim (Athlete, Baseball Player)
102 Pinnacle Ct
Kitty Hawk, NC 27949-5911, USA

Dougherty, Joseph (Joe) (Director,
Producer, Writer)
c/o Ken Freimann *Circle of Confusion
(LA)*
1 William Morris Pl
Beverly Hills, CA 90212-4261, USA

Dougherty, Richard (Athlete, Hockey
Player, Olympic Athlete)
1501 W Paulson Rd
Green Bay, WI 54313-6025, USA

Doughty, Glenn (Athlete, Football Player)
1825 Seven Pines Dr
Saint Louis, MO 63146-3715, USA

Doughty, Kenny (Actor)
c/o Alan Siegel *Alan Siegel Entertainment*
9200 W Sunset Blvd Ste 407
West Hollywood, CA 90069-3511, USA

Douglas, Barry (Music Group, Musician)
I C M Artists
40 W 57th St
New York, NY 10019-4001, USA

Douglas, Bobby (Coach, Wrestler)
Iowa State University
Athletic Dept
Ames, IA 50011-0001, USA

Douglas, Carl (Attorney)
6611 Shenandoah Ave
Los Angeles, CA 90056-2115, USA

Douglas, Carol (Music Group)
Famous Artists Agency
250 W 57th St
New York, NY 10107-0001, USA

Douglas, Charles (Whammy) (Athlete, Baseball Player)
1711 Catherines Lake Rd
Jacksonville, NC 28540-8755, USA

Douglas, David (Athlete, Football Player)
610 Tennessee St
Spring City, TN 37381-5412, USA

Douglas, Diana (Actor)
c/o Staff Member Bauman Redanty & Shaul Agency
5757 Wilshire Blvd
Suite 473
Beverly Hills, CA 90212, USA

Douglas, Donna (Actor)
c/o Staff Member Scott Stander & Associates
13701 Riverside Dr Ste 201
Sherman Oaks, CA 91423-2447, USA

Douglas, Gabby (Athlete, Gymnast, Olympic Athlete)
Chow's Gymnastics
2210 Chows Olympic Ave
West Des Moines, IA 50265-5809, USA

Douglas, Harry (Athlete, Football Player)
c/o Todd France Five Star Athlete Management
3500 Lenox Rd NE
Atlanta, GA 30326-4228, USA

Douglas, Hugh (Athlete, Football Player)
5 Pennbrook Ln
Glen Mills, PA 19342-1663, USA

Douglas, Ileana (Actor)
c/o Staff Member Baumgarten Management
1447 Cloverfield Blvd Ste 101
Santa Monica, CA 90404-2979, USA

Douglas, Illeana (Actor, Director, Producer)
1419 N Ogden Dr
Los Angeles, CA 90046-3906, USA

Douglas, James (Buster) (Athlete, Boxer)
PO Box 342
Johnstown, OH 43031-0342, USA

Douglas, Jay (Athlete, Football Player)
715 Loire Ln
Houston, TX 77090-1925, USA

Douglas, Jerry (Actor)
739 Rodney Dr
Nashville, TN 37205-3015, USA

Douglas, Katie (Basketball Player)
Connecticut Sun
Mohegan Sun Arena
Uncasville, CT 06382, USA

Douglas, Kirk (Actor, Producer)
805 N Rexford Dr
Beverly Hills, CA 90210-2908, USA

Douglas, Leon (Athlete, Basketball Player)
PO Box 58
Leighton, AL 35646-0058, USA

Douglas, Merrill (Athlete, Football Player)
2185 E 3970 S
Salt Lake City, UT 84124-1754, USA

Douglas, Michael (Actor, Director, Producer)
151 Central Park W Apt 9C
New York, NY 10023-1577, USA

Douglas, Nik (Writer)
c/o Staff Member Simon & Schuster
1230 Avenue of the Americas Fl CONC1
New York, NY 10020-1586, USA

Douglas, Santiago (Actor)
c/o Charlton Blackburne A Management Company
9107 Wilshire Blvd Ste 650
Beverly Hills, CA 90210-5544, USA

Douglas, Sherman (Athlete, Basketball Player)
10853 Symphony Park Dr
Rockville, MD 20852-3486, USA

Douglass, Bobby (Athlete, Football Player)
151 E Laurel Ave Apt 203
Lake Forest, IL 60045-1296, USA

Douglass, Dale (Athlete, Golfer)
6601 E San Miguel Ave
Paradise Valley, AZ 85253-5983, USA

Douglass, Maurice (Athlete, Football Player)
1021 Sunset Dr
Englewood, OH 45322-2252, USA

Douglass, Mike (Athlete, Football Player)
1725 Porterfield Pl
El Cajon, CA 92019-4122, USA

Douglass, Robyn (Actor)
407 S Dearborn St Ste 1675
Chicago, IL 60605-1144, USA

Douglass, Sean (Athlete, Baseball Player)
43956 Johns Ct
Lancaster, CA 93536-8213, USA

Doumit, Ryan (Athlete, Baseball Player)
4653 Road 6.5 NE
Moses Lake, WA 98837-8932, USA

Doumit, Sam (Actor)
c/o Staff Member Baker Winokur Ryder Public Relations (BWR-LA)
9100 Wilshire Blvd Ste 500
West Tower Suite 500
Beverly Hills, CA 90212-3426, USA

Dourdan, Gary (Actor)
4151 Moore St
Los Angeles, CA 90066-5723, USA

Dourif, Brad (Actor)
173 Macdaniel Rd
Bearsville, NY 12409-5013, USA

Douris, Peter (Athlete, Hockey Player)
PO Box 113
Cape Neddick, ME 03902-0113, USA

Douse, Joseph (Athlete, Baseball Player)
14075 Riverview St Apt 108
Detroit, MI 48223-2421, USA

Douthitt, Earl (Athlete, Football Player)
8100 Central Ave Apt 211
Cleveland, OH 44104-2173, USA

Dove, Dennis (Athlete, Baseball Player)
144 Kirk Ln
Ocilla, GA 31774-3725, USA

Dove, Eddie (Athlete, Football Player)
1750 Poppy Ave
Menlo Park, CA 94025-5738, USA

Dove, Rita F (Writer)
1757 Lambs Rd
Charlottesville, VA 22901-8911, USA

Dove, Ronnie (Music Group)
c/o Staff Member Time Machine
2109 S Wilbur Ave
Walla Walla, WA 99362-9048, USA

Doves (Music Group)
c/o Staff Member Paradigm (Monterey)
404 W Franklin St
Monterey, CA 93940-2303, USA

Dovolani, Tony (Dancer)
c/o Tej Bhatia Herring Rogers & Cowan PR (LA)
8687 Melrose Ave Ste 7
West Hollywood, CA 90069-5721, USA

Dow, Ellen (Actor)
20327 Oxnard St
Woodland Hills, CA 91367-5427, USA

Dow, Peggy (Actor)
2121 S Yorktown Ave
Tulsa, OK 74114-1426, USA

Dow, Tony (Actor)
c/o David Moss David Moss Company, The
733 Seward St PH
Los Angeles, CA 90038-3503, USA

Dowd, Jim (Athlete, Hockey Player)
708 New Jersey Ave
Point Pleasant Beach, NJ 08742-2970, USA

Dowd, Maureen (Writer)
c/o Staff Member 21st Century Speakers
1352 Lake Ave
Gouldsboro, PA 18424, USA

Dowdell, Marcus (Athlete, Football Player)
16 Charleston Park Dr
Houston, TX 77025-5647, USA

Dowdy, Adam (Athlete, Baseball Player)
956 W Desert Broom Ct
Chandler, AZ 85248-3800, USA

Dowell, Jake
2014 Rice Ct
Eau Claire, WI 54701-7977

Dowell, Ken (Athlete, Baseball Player)
5221 Helen Way
Sacramento, CA 95822-2868, USA

Dower, John W (Writer)
Massachusetts Institute of Technology
History Dept
Cambridge, MA 02139, USA

Dowhower, Rod (Athlete, Football Coach, Football Player)
PO Box 1986
Dahlonega, GA 30533-0034, USA

Dowler, Boyd H (Athlete, Football Player)
5309 Creek Heights Dr
Midlothian, VA 23112-6224, USA

Dowling, Brian (Athlete, Football Player)
PO Box 329
Burlington, MA 01803-0529, USA

Dowling, Dave (Athlete, Baseball Player)
2749 Greencliff Dr
Southaven, MS 38672-7813, USA

Dowling, Peter (Director)
3608 Avenida Del Sol
Studio City, CA 91604-4020, USA

Dowling, Timothy (Actor)
c/o Staff Member William Morris Endeavor (LA)
9601 Wilshire Blvd
Beverly Hills, CA 90210-5213, USA

Dowling, Vincent (Director, Writer)
322 E River Rd
Huntington, MA 01050-9645, USA

Down, Lesley-Anne (Actor)
6525 Paseo Canyon Dr
Studio City, CA 91604, USA

Down, Leslie-Anne (Actor)
6252 Paseo Canyon Dr
Malibu, CA 90265-3135, USA

Down, Rick (Athlete, Baseball Player)
10908 Salford Dr
Las Vegas, NV 89144-4498, USA

Down, Sarah (Cartoonist)
Playboy Magazine
680 N Lake Shore Dr Ste 1500
Chicago, IL 60611-4455, USA

Downes, Robin Atkin (Actor)
c/o Staff Member Gordon Agency
260 S Beverly Dr Ste 308
Beverly Hills, CA 90212-3814, USA

Downey, Bill (Athlete, Basketball Player)
1035 S Moorings Dr
Arlington Heights, IL 60005-3217, USA

Downey, James (Writer)
c/o Staff Member 3 Arts Entertainment (LA)
9460 Wilshire Blvd Fl 7
Beverly Hills, CA 90212-2713, USA

Downey, Jim (Writer)
c/o Staff Member 3 Arts Entertainment (LA)
9460 Wilshire Blvd Fl 7
Beverly Hills, CA 90212-2713, USA

Downey, Roma (Actor)
c/o Laurie Pozmantier William Morris Endeavor (LA)
9601 Wilshire Blvd
Beverly Hills, CA 90210-5213, USA

Downey Jr, Robert (Actor)
30228 Morning View Dr
Malibu, CA 90265-3617, USA

Downing, Al (Athlete, Baseball Player)
25343 Silver Aspen Way Apt 735
Wav Ant 735
Valencia, CA 91381-0698, USA

Downing, Alphonso E (Al) (Athlete, Baseball Player)
25343 Silver Aspen Way Apt 735
Valencia, CA 91381-0698, USA

Downing, Brian J (Athlete, Baseball Player)
8095 County Road 135
Celina, TX 75009-2539, USA

Downing, Jim (Race Car Driver)
3918 Chaucer Wood NE
Atlanta, GA 30319-1673, USA

Downing, Kathryn (Publisher)
Mypotential.com
2821 Main St
Santa Monica, CA 90405, USA

Downing, Sara (Actor)
c/o Steven Siebert Lighthouse Entertainment
9220 W Sunset Blvd Ste 200
West Hollywood, CA 90069-3501, USA

Downing, Steve (Athlete, Basketball Player)
6433 Lakeside Woods Cir
Indianapolis, IN 46278-1663, USA

Downing, Vern (Bowler)
523 Napa St
Rodeo, CA 94572-1512, USA

Downing, Walt (Athlete, Football Player)
1141 Durham Cir NW
Massillon, OH 44646-2121, USA

Downs, Dave (Athlete, Baseball Player)
925 E 1050 N
Bountiful, UT 84010-2620, USA

Downs, Gary (Athlete, Football Player)
3953 Balleycastle Ct
Duluth, GA 30097-7368, USA

Downs, Hugh (Correspondent, Journalist)
c/o Rick Hersh *Celebrity Consultants LLC*
3340 Ocean Park Blvd Ste 1030
Santa Monica, CA 90405-3259, USA

Downs, Kelly (Athlete, Baseball Player)
6459 Willow Creek Rd
Morgan, UT 84050-6746, USA

Downs, Lila (Musician)
c/o Bill Traut *Open Door Management*
865 Via De La Paz Ste 365
Pacific Palisades, CA 90272-3618, USA

Downs, Matt (Athlete, Baseball Player)
448 Cruise Ave
Centreville, AL 35042-6653, USA

Downs, Michael (Athlete, Football Player)
1405 Knob Hill Dr
Desoto, TX 75115-5335, USA

Downs, Nicholas (Actor)
c/o Andrew Stawiarski *ADS Management*
269 S Beverly Dr # 441
Beverly Hills, CA 90212-3851, USA

Downs, Robert (Athlete, Football Player)
28024 High Vista Dr
Escondido, CA 92026-7215, USA

Downs, Scott (Athlete, Baseball Player)
6814 Barbrook Rd
Louisville, KY 40258-2668, USA

Doyle, Allen (Athlete, Golfer)
512 Riverside Dr
Lagrange, GA 30240-9633, USA

Doyle, Brian (Athlete, Baseball Player)
PO Box 9156
Winter Haven, FL 33883-9156, USA

Doyle, Christopher (Cinematographer)
c/o Staff Member *ICM Partners (LA)*
10250 Constellation Blvd Fl 7
Los Angeles, CA 90067-6207, USA

Doyle, Dennis (Race Car Driver)
DRG Motorsports
37 Meghan Blvd
Plymouth, CT 06782-2019, USA

Doyle, Denny (Athlete, Baseball Player)
PO Box 9156
Winter Haven, FL 33883-9156, USA

Doyle, James (Politician)
2001 Hawks Ridge Dr
Verona, WI 53593-9195, USA

Doyle, Jeff (Athlete, Baseball Player)
24655 Judy Ln
Monroe, OR 97456-9762, USA

Doyle, Paul (Athlete, Baseball Player)
19361 Brookhurst St Spc 15
Snc 15
Huntington Beach, CA 92646-2949, USA

Doyle, Shawn (Actor)
3744 San Rafael Ave
Los Angeles, CA 90065-3217, USA

Doyle & Debbie Show, The (Music Group)
c/o Staff Member *Paradigm (Monterey)*
404 W Franklin St
Monterey, CA 93940-2303, USA

Doyle-Childress, Cartha (Athlete, Baseball Player, Commentator)
1516 Carowinds Cir
Maryville, TN 37803-7704, USA

Doyle-Murray, Brian (Actor, Comedian)
3611 Grand View Blvd
Los Angeles, CA 90066-3107, USA

Doyne, Cory (Athlete, Baseball Player)
20228 County Line Rd
Lutz, FL 33558-5074, USA

Doyon, Mario (Athlete, Hockey Player)
33 Lexington Blvd
Carmel, IN 46032-2243

Dozier, D J (Athlete, Baseball Player)
5821 N Cherokee Cluster
Virginia Beach, VA 23462-3214, USA

Dozier, Jan Davis Dr (Astronaut)
4105 Cumberland Pass Apt 814
Fort Worth, TX 76116-0753, USA

Dozier, Terry (Athlete, Basketball Player)
521 Sparkleberry Ln
Columbia, SC 29229-8609, USA

Dozier, Tom (Athlete, Baseball Player)
1231 Willow Ave Apt D7
Hercules, CA 94547-1200, USA

Drabek, Doug (Athlete, Baseball Player)
15 Ivy Pond Pl
Spring, TX 77381-6326, USA

Drabek, Kyle (Athlete, Baseball Player)
32826 Couples Ct
Magnolia, TX 77354-6884, USA

Draffen, Willis (Music Group)
16103 Vista Del Mar Dr
Houston, TX 77083-2309, USA

Draft, Chris (Athlete, Football Player)
970 E Oak St
Anaheim, CA 92805-4138, USA

Dragila, Stacy (Athlete, Olympic Athlete, Track Athlete)
730 W Kingsley St
Meridian, ID 83646-6222, USA

Draglia, Stacy (Athlete, Track Athlete)
1436 E Lander St
Pocatello, ID 83201-4160, USA

Drago, Billy (Actor)
3800 Barham Blvd Ste 303
Los Angeles, CA 90068-1095, USA

Drago, Richard A (Dick) (Athlete, Baseball Player)
4703 Belle Chase Cir
Tampa, FL 33634-4256, USA

Dragon, Daryl (Musician)
4225 W Latham Cir
Prescott, AZ 86305-9044, USA

Drahman, Brian (Athlete, Baseball Player)
11002 W Pierson St
Phoenix, AZ 85037-1087, USA

Drahos, Nick (Athlete, Football Player)
3158 State Route 90
Aurora, NY 13026-9741, USA

Drai, Victor (Producer)
10527 Bellagio Rd
Beverly Hills, CA 90210, USA

Draiman, Dave (Musician)
c/o Staff Member *Mitch Schneider Organization (MSO)*
14724 Ventura Blvd Ste 410
Sherman Oaks, CA 91403-3537, USA

Drake, Bebe (Actor)
c/o Staff Member *Baron Entertainment*
13848 Ventura Blvd Ste A
Sherman Oaks, CA 91423-3654

Drake, Betsy (Actor)
10850 Wilshire Blvd Ste 575
Los Angeles, CA 90024-4336, USA

Drake, Dallas (Athlete, Hockey Player)
11472 E Cedar Bay Trl
Traverse City, MI 49684-6841

Drake, Jerry (Athlete, Football Player)
2857 Regal Cir Apt E
Birmingham, AL 35216-4632, USA

Drake, Jerry (Athlete, Football Player)
1893 Colonnade Rd
Cleveland, OH 44112-1567, USA

Drake, Jessica (Actor, Adult Film Star, Model)
c/o Gina Rodriguez *GR Media*
Prefers to be contacted via telephone or email
Reseda, CA 91335, USA

Drake, Judith (Actor)
20th Century Artists
4605 Lankershim Blvd Ste 305
North Hollywood, CA 91602-1875, USA

Drake, Larry (Actor)
15260 Ventura Blvd Ste 2100
Sherman Oaks, CA 91403-5360, USA

Drake, Robert (Athlete, Baseball Player)
2833 N Ricardo
Mesa, AZ 85215-1057, USA

Drake, Solly (Athlete, Baseball Player)
1732 S Corning St
Los Angeles, CA 90035-4302, USA

Drakeford, Tyronne (Athlete, Football Player)
7786 Cedar Branch Dr
Gainesville, VA 20155-1994, USA

Drane, Dwight (Athlete, Football Player)
200 NW 107th Ave
Plantation, FL 33324-1700, USA

Dransfeldt, Kelly (Athlete, Baseball Player)
2011 Prairie Rose Dr
Morris, IL 60450-6851, USA

Draper, Courtnee
c/o Steve Simon *Landis-Simon Productions Talent Management*
625 E Thousand Oaks Blvd # 279
Thousand Oaks, CA 91360, USA

Draper, Denny (Athlete, Football Player)
11105 Baker Creek Rd
McMinnville, OR 97128-8000, USA

Draper, E Lynn Jr (Business Person)
American Electric Power
1 Riverside Plz Fl 1
Columbus, OH 43215-2373, USA

Draper, Kris (Athlete, Hockey Player)
3418 Westchester Rd
Bloomfield Hills, MI 48304-2573

Draper, Mike (Athlete, Baseball Player)
7608 NW 18th St Apt 105
Act 105
Margate, FL 33063-3143, USA

Draper, Polly (Actor)
3856 Berry Dr
Studio City, CA 91604-3859, USA

Draper, Tim (Athlete, Hockey Player)
76 Blackstone Ave
Binghamton, NY 13903-1328, USA

Draper, Tom
76 Blackstone Ave
Binghamton, NY 13903-1328

Dratch, Rachel (Actor, Comedian)
c/o Scott Metzger *Paradigm (NY)*
360 Park Ave S Fl 16
New York, NY 10010-1716, USA

Dravecky, David F (Dave) (Athlete, Baseball Player)
9154 Viaeeio Way
Littleton, CO 80126, USA

Draves, Victoria (Vickie) (Athlete, Swimmer)
23842 Shady Tree Cir
Laguna Niguel, CA 92677-1704, USA

Drayton, Charlie (Music Group, Musician)
Direct Mangement Group
8332 Melrose Ave # 2
West Hollywood, CA 90069-5420, USA

Drayton, Troy (Athlete, Football Player)
601 NW 82nd Ave Apt 208
Plantation, FL 33324-1362, USA

Drdek, John (Writer)
c/o Will Ward *ROAR (LA)*
9701 Wilshire Blvd Fl 8
Beverly Hills, CA 90212-2008, USA

Dr Dog (Musician)
c/o Staff Member *Paradigm (Monterey)*
404 W Franklin St
Monterey, CA 93940-2303, USA

Dr Dre (Actor, Musician)
9161 Oriole Way
Los Angeles, CA 90069-1125, USA

Dre, Dr. (Actor, Musician, Producer)
c/o Staff Member *Crucial Films*
2220 Colorado Ave Fl 5
Santa Monica, CA 90404-3506, USA

Dreamstreet (Music Group)
c/o Staff Member *Adonis Productions*
175 Skillman St
Brooklyn, NY 11205-3901, USA

Drechsler, Dave (Athlete, Football Player)
1135 Arabian Farms Rd
Clover, SC 29710-8562, USA

Dreckman, Bruce (Athlete, Baseball Player)
110 N Maple St
Marcus, IA 51035, USA

Drees, Tom (Athlete, Baseball Player)
18638 Bearpath Trl
Eden Prairie, MN 55347-3459, USA

Dreesen, Tom (Actor, Comedian)
14538 Benefit St Unit 301
Sherman Oaks, CA 91403-5507, USA

Dreifort, Darren (Athlete, Baseball Player, Olympic Athlete)
463 Wynola St
Pacific Palisades, CA 90272-4243, USA

Dreiling, Greg (Athlete, Basketball Player)
5952 Willowross Way
Plano, TX 75093-4776, USA

Dreilling, Greg (Athlete, Basketball Player)
5952 Willowross Way
Plano, TX 75093-4776, USA

Drescher, Aviva (Reality Star)
c/o Michael Schweiger *CEG Management*
520 8th Ave Rm 2001
New York, NY 10018-4166, USA

Drescher, Fran (Actor)
19734 Pacific Coast Hwy
Malibu, CA 90265-5425, USA

Drese, Ryan (Athlete, Baseball Player)
2201 Bear Lake Dr
Euless, TX 76039-6058, USA

Dressel, Chris (Athlete, Football Player)
410 Whiskey Hill Rd
Woodside, CA 94062-2571, USA

Dressendorfer, Kirk (Athlete, Baseball Player)
1004 Oaklands Dr
Round Rock, TX 78681-4033, USA

Dressler, Doug (Athlete, Football Player)
118 Frostwood Dr
Westwood, CA 96137-9647, USA

Dressler, Rob (Athlete, Baseball Player)
2037 17th Ave
Forest Grove, OR 97116-2709, USA

Drew, Alvin (Astronaut)
2814 Lighthouse Dr
Houston, TX 77058-4320, USA

Drew, Cameron (Athlete, Baseball Player)
31 Highbridge Rd
Trenton, NJ 08620-9632, USA

Drew, David Jonathan (J D) (Athlete, Baseball Player)
5006 Old US 41 N
Hahira, GA 31632-4405, USA

Drew, Elizabeth H (Publisher)
Avon/William Morrow
1350 Avenue of the Americas Fl 17
New York, NY 10019-4702, USA

Drew, Heather (Athlete, Golfer)
78160 Desert Mountain Cir
Bermuda Dunes, CA 92203-8151, USA

Drew, JD (Athlete, Baseball Player)
c/o Scott Boras *Boras Corporation*
3 San Joaquin Plz Ste 100
Newport Beach, CA 92660-5944, USA

Drew, John (Athlete, Basketball Player)
2303 W Tidwell Rd Apt 3404
Houston, TX 77091-4766, USA

Drew, Larry (Athlete, Basketball Player)
4942 Densmore Ave
Encino, CA 91436-1538, USA

Drew, Sarah (Actor)
233 Spencer St
Glendale, CA 91202-1813, USA

Drew, Stephen (Athlete, Baseball Player)
4254 Oak Forest Dr
Valdosta, GA 31602-0838, USA

Drew, Tim (Athlete, Baseball Player)
5006 Old US 41 N
Hahira, GA 31632-4405, USA

Drewiske, Davis (Athlete, Hockey Player)
3327 Humboldt Aves # B
Minneapolis, MN 55408

Drewrey, Willie (Athlete, Football Player)
2714 Cheryl Ct
Missouri City, TX 77459-2930, USA

Drexler, Clyde (Athlete, Basketball Player, Olympic Athlete)
4045 Piping Rock Ln
Houston, TX 77027-3916, USA

Drexler, Clyde (Basketball Player, Coach)
Dade/Schultz
6442 Coldwater Canyon Ave Ste 206
North Hollywood, CA 91606-1174, USA

Drexler, Millard (Business Person)
J. Crew
1 Ivy Cres
Lynchburg, VA 24513-1002, USA

Dreyer, Pamela (Athlete, Hockey Player, Olympic Athlete)
111 E 88th St Apt 4A
New York, NY 10128-1158, USA

Dreyer, Steve (Athlete, Baseball Player)
6018 Greywood Cir
Johnston, IA 50131-1687, USA

Dreyfuss, Richard (Actor, Producer)
PO Box 10459
Burbank, CA 91510-0459, USA

Drier, David (Congressman, Politician)
233 Cannon Hob
Washington, DC 20515-1308, USA

Drier, Moosey (Actor)
3501 Camino De La Cumbre
Sherman Oaks, CA 91423-4516, USA

Drier, Moosie (Actor, Director)
3501 Camino De La Cumbre
Sherman Oaks, CA 91423-4516, USA

Driessen, Dan (Athlete, Baseball Player)
208 Mitchellville Rd
Hilton Head Island, SC 29926-2820, USA

Drills, David (Athlete, Cycler, Olympic Athlete)
3736 Brookside Rd
Ottawa Hills, OH 43606-2614

Drinkard, Bobby Jon (Reality Star)
c/o Staff Member *Mark Burnett Productions*
640 N Sepulveda Blvd
Los Angeles, CA 90049-2108, USA

Drinkwater-Simmons, Maxine (Athlete, Baseball Player, Commentator)
18 Belmont Ave
Camden, ME 04843-2028, USA

Driscoll, Edward (Terry) (Athlete, Basketball Player)
William & Mary University
PO Box 399
Athletics Department
Williamsburg, VA 23187-0399, USA

Driscoll, Edward ""Terry"" (Athlete, Basketball Player)
101 Tayloe Cir
Williamsburg, VA 23185-8248, USA

Driscoll, Jean (Athlete, Motivational Speaker, Olympic Athlete)
Pat Fettig
9161 Elizabeth Ln
Mason, OH 45040-7378, USA

Driscoll, Jim (Athlete, Baseball Player)
8050 E Indian School Rd
Scottsdale, AZ 85251-2612, USA

Driscoll, Peter (Athlete, Hockey Player)
2540 S Annapolis Rd
Rockville, IN 47872-7909, USA

Driscoll, Peter (Athlete, Hockey Player)
422 N Cypress Dr Apt B
Jupiter, FL 33469-3712, USA

Driskill, Travis (Athlete, Baseball Player)
800 Blue Spring Cir
Round Rock, TX 78681-4047, USA

Driver, Adam (Actor)
c/o Jodi Gottlieb *Independent Public Relations*
Prefers to be contacted via telephone or email
Los Angeles, CA, USA

Driver, Bruce (Athlete, Hockey Player)
21A Crest Ter
Montville, NJ 07045-9370

Driver, Donald (Athlete, Football Player)
1501 Noble Way
Flower Mound, TX 75022-8117, USA

Driver, Minnie (Actor)
7666 Woodrow Wilson Dr
Los Angeles, CA 90046-1252, USA

Driver, William J (Government Official)
215 W Columbia St
Falls Church, VA 22046-3412, USA

D'Rivera, Paquito
Charismic Productions
2704 Mozart Pl NW
Washington, DC 20009, USA

Dr John (Musician)
53 Millstone Brook Rd
Southampton, NY 11968-2220, USA

Drolet, Claude (Horse Racer)
156 Greeley Lake Rd
Greeley, PA 18425-9765, USA

Drolet, Jean (Horse Racer)
1 White Rd
Airmont, NY 10901-7108, USA

Drollinger, Ralph (Athlete, Basketball Player)
22831 Market St
Newhall, CA 91321-3605, USA

Drosdick, John G (Business Person)
Sunoco Inc
10 Penn Center 1801 Market St
Philadelphia, PA 19103, USA

Drougas, Tom (Athlete, Football Player)
PO Box 1596
Sun Valley, ID 83353-1596, USA

Droughns, Reuben (Athlete, Football Player)
1405 Huntington St Apt C
Huntingtn Bch, CA 92648-3624, USA

Drouin, Jude (Athlete, Hockey Player)
44479 Maltese Falcon Sq
Ashburn, VA 20147-3886

Drowning Pool (Music Group)
c/o Frank Cimler *10th Street Entertainment (LA)*
700 N San Vicente Blvd Ste G410
West Hollywood, CA 90069-5060, USA

Druckenmiller, Jim (Athlete, Football Player)
2351 E Aragon Blvd Unit 6
Sunrise, FL 33313-8045, USA

Drucker, Mort (Cartoonist)
Famous Artists Agency
250 W 57th St
New York, NY 10107-0001, USA

Drudge, Matt (Internet Star, Journalist)
22661 SW 157th Ave
Miami, FL 33170-5906, USA

Drugg, Herb (Race Car Driver)
PO Box 916
Troy, NH 03465-0916, USA

Dru Hill (Music Group)
c/o Staff Member *William Morris Endeavor (LA)*
9601 Wilshire Blvd
Beverly Hills, CA 90210-5213, USA

Druken, Harold (Athlete, Hockey Player)
16 Shaw Dr
Wayland, MA 01778-3214, USA

Drulia, Stan (Athlete, Hockey Player)
11230 W Heritage Dr
Milwaukee, WI 53224-5034, USA

Drummond, Alice (Actor)
351 E 50th St Apt 1
New York, NY 10022-7975, USA

Drummond, Ann Marie (Ree) (Chef, Writer)
100 W Main St
Pawhuska, OK 74056-4149, USA

Drummond, Jonathan (Jon) (Athlete, Track Athlete)
c/o Staff Member *HS International Sports Management, Inc.*
9871 Irvine Center Dr
Irvine, CA 92618-4361, USA

Drummond, Roscoe (Writer)
6637 MacLean Dr Olde Dominion Sq
Mc Lean, VA 22101, USA

Drummond, Ryan (Actor)
c/o Staff Member *Bobby Ball Talent Agency*
3500 W Olive Ave Ste 300
Burbank, CA 91505-4647, USA

Drummond, Tim (Athlete, Baseball Player)
102 Haldane Ct
La Plata, MD 20646-4308, USA

Drungo, Elbert (Athlete, Football Player)
216 Lake Chateau Dr
Hermitage, TN 37076-3072, USA

Drury, Chris (Athlete, Hockey Player, Olympic Athlete)
145 Parsonage Rd
Greenwich, CT 06830-3937, USA

Drury, James (Actor)
12126 Osage Park Dr
Houston, TX 77065-3812, USA

Drury, Ted (Athlete, Hockey Player)
14 Woodley Rd
Winnetka, IL 60093-3735, USA

Drury, Ted (Athlete, Hockey Player)
28 Cottage Pl
Trumbull, CT 06611-5227, USA

Druschel, Rick (Athlete, Football Player)
724 Cochran Dr
Greensburg, PA 15601-4610, USA

Dry, Tim (Actor)
c/o Staff Member *Coolwaters Productions*
10061 Riverside Dr # 531
Toluca Lake, CA 91602-2560, USA

Dryburgh, Stuart (Cinematographer)
Sandra Marsh Mgmt
6420 Wilshire Blvd Ste 880
Los Angeles, CA 90048-5538, USA

Dryer, Fred (Actor, Athlete, Football Player)
10421 Windtree Dr
Los Angeles, CA 90077-2031, USA

Dryke, Matthew (Athlete, Olympic Athlete, Shooter)
292 Dryke Rd
Sequim, WA 98382-7221, USA

Drynan, Jeanie (Actor)
c/o Staff Member *Essential Talent Management*
6399 Wilshire Blvd Ste 401
Los Angeles, CA 90048-5716, USA

Drysdale, Cliff (Sportscaster, Tennis Player)
Landfall
1801 Eastwood Rd # F
Wilmington, NC 28403, USA

Drzewiecki, Ron (Athlete, Football Player)
5977 S 34th St
Milwaukee, WI 53221-4725, USA

D. Schakowsky, Janice (Congressman, Politician)
2367 Rayburn Hob
Washington, DC 20515-1304, USA

DSquared2 (Fashion Designer)
DSquared2
220 W 19th St Fl 11
New York, NY 10011-4035, USA

DuArt, Louise (Religious Leader, Television Host)
c/o Staff Member *Living the Life*
Christian Broadcasting Network
977 Centerville Tpke
Virginia Beach, VA 23463-0001, USA

Dubble, Curtis (Religious Leader)
Church of Brethren
1451 Dundee Ave
Elgin, IL 60120-1694, USA

Dube, Joseph (Joe) (Athlete, Wrestler)
8821 Eaton Ave
Jacksonville, FL 32211-0306, USA

Dubee, Rich (Athlete, Baseball Player)
8517 Eagle Preserve Way
Sarasota, FL 34241-8505, USA

Dubenion, Elbert (Athlete, Football Player)
610 E Walnut St
Westerville, OH 43081-2423, USA

Duberman, Justin (Athlete, Hockey Player)
4 E 4th St
Hinsdale, IL 60521-4460

Dubielewicz, Wade (Athlete, Hockey Player)
41 Benham Hill Pl
Hamden, CT 06514-1935

Dubinsky, Brandon (Athlete, Hockey Player)
10110 Salix Cir
Anchorage, AK 99507-4138, USA

Dubinsky, Steve (Athlete, Hockey Player)
1367 Cavell Ave
Highland Park, IL 60035-2805, USA

Dublinski, James L (Athlete, Football Player)
723 S 900 E
Salt Lake City, UT 84102-3605, USA

Dublinski, Tom (Athlete, Football Player)
15918 E El Lago Blvd
Fountain Hills, AZ 85268-3935, USA

Dubois, Allison
PO Box 7497
Phoenix, AZ 85011-7497, USA

Dubois, Brian (Athlete, Baseball Player)
3 Soartan Pi
Springfield, IL 62703, USA

Dubois, Janet (Actor)
c/o Staff Member *Cunningham Escott Slevin & Doherty (CESD-LA)*
10635 Santa Monica Blvd Ste 130
Los Angeles, CA 90025-8306, USA

Dubois, Jason (Athlete, Baseball Player)
2204 Lord Seaton Cir
Virginia Beach, VA 23454-2923, USA

DuBois, Marta (Actor)
Three Moons Entertainment
5441 E Beverly Blvd Ste G
Los Angeles, CA 90022-2243, USA

Dubois, Phil (Athlete, Football Player)
405 Speedway Ave
Missoula, MT 59802-5475, USA

Dubose, Brian (Baseball Player)
Ted Williams
15336 Oakfield St
Detroit, MI 48227-1532, USA

Dubose, Eric (Athlete, Baseball Player)
326 County Road 8
Gilbertown, AL 36908-2211, USA

DuBose, James (Director, Producer)
c/o Toni Thompson *Toni Thompson PR*
Accepts Calls Only
Los Angeles, CA 90001, USA

Dubose, Jimmy (Athlete, Football Player)
11420 Walker Rd
Thonotosassa, FL 33592-3616, USA

Dubovsky, Dana (Producer)
American World Pictures
21700 Oxnard St Ste 1770
Woodland Hills, CA 91367-7594, USA

Dubrow, Heather (Actor, Reality Star)
c/o Staff Member *Paradigm (LA)*
360 N Crescent Dr
North Bldg
Beverly Hills, CA 90210-4874, USA

Dubzinski, Walt (Athlete, Football Player)
24 Olde Tavern Rd
Leominster, MA 01453-2067, USA

Ducasse, Vladimir (Athlete, Football Player)
c/o Joe Linta *JL Sports*
1204 Main St Ste 179
Branford, CT 06405-3787, USA

Ducey, Rob (Athlete, Baseball Player)
699 Richmond Close
Tarpon Springs, FL 34688-8423, USA

Duchesne, Steve (Athlete, Hockey Player)
2104 Cedar Elm Ter
Westlake, TX 76262-9025, USA

Duchovny, David (Actor, Producer)
320 Central Park W # 19A
New York, NY 10025-7659, USA

Duchscherer, Justin (Athlete, Baseball Player)
18634 E Canary Way
Queen Creek, AZ 85142-5549, USA

DuCille, Michel (Journalist, Photographer)
9571 Pine Meadows Ln
Burke, VA 22015-1550, USA

Duck Dynasty (Reality Star)
Duck Commander
117 Kings Ln
West Monroe, LA 71292-9430, USA

Duckett, Forey (Athlete, Football Player)
7518 Winona Ave N
Seattle, WA 98103-4838, USA

Duckett, Mahlon (Athlete, Baseball Player)
285 Kentucky Ave
Conshohocken, PA 19428-2650, USA

Duckett, Richard (Athlete, Basketball Player)
440 Fox Haven Dr Apt 2206
Naples, FL 34104-5126, USA

Duckett, TJ (Athlete, Football Player)
c/o Joel Segal *Lagardere Unlimited (NYC)*
845 United Nations Plz
New York, NY 10017-3540, USA

Ducksworth, Sheila (Producer)
c/o Staff Member *Creative Artists Agency (CAA-LA)*
2000 Avenue of the Stars Ste 100
Los Angeles, CA 90067-4705, USA

Duckworth, Brandon (Athlete, Baseball Player)
4460 W 6095 S
Salt Lake City, UT 84118-5289, USA

Duckworth, Jim (Athlete, Baseball Player)
3736 Ferrero Way
Redding, CA 96001-0180, USA

Duckworth, Tyler (Reality Star)
c/o Len Evans *Project Publicity*
312 W 53rd St Ste 202
New York, NY 10019-5743, USA

Duda, Mark (Athlete, Football Player)
1707 Cherry St
Scranton, PA 18505-3972, USA

Dudek, Anne (Actor)
2422 21st St
Santa Monica, CA 90405-2712, USA

Dudek, Joseph A (Joe) (Athlete, Football Player)
31 Ryan Rd
Auburn, NH 03032-3341, USA

Dudek, Mitch (Athlete, Football Player)
1241 Forest Ave
Wilmette, IL 60091-1656, USA

Duden, H Richard (Dick) Jr (Athlete, Football Player)
11 Old Station Rd
Severna Park, MD 21146-4618, USA

Dudikoff, Michael (Actor)
11 Santa Bella Rd
Rolling Hills Estates, CA 90274-2435, USA

Dudley, Brian (Athlete, Football Player)
6319 London Ave
Rancho Cucamonga, CA 91737-3646, USA

Dudley, Charles (Athlete, Basketball Player)
4032 42nd Ave S
Seattle, WA 98118-1121, USA

Dudley, Chris (Athlete, Basketball Player)
PO Box 703
Rancho Santa Fe, CA 92067-0703, USA

Dudley, Debra
PO Box 40
Bonnieville, KY 42713-0040

Dudley, James (Baseball Player)
Baltimore Elite Giants
607 Delafield Pl NW
Washington, DC 20011-4054, USA

Dudley, Olivia Taylor (Actor)
c/o Dan McManus *Mosaic Media Group*
9200 W Sunset Blvd Ste 10
West Hollywood, CA 90069-3608, USA

Dudley, Rick (Athlete, Coach, Hockey Player, Misc)
5150 Oakhill Dr
Lewiston, NY 14092-1857, USA

Dudley, Rickey (Athlete, Football Player)
4529 Mahogany Ln
Lewisville, TX 75077-8546, USA

Duell, Chad (Actor)
c/o Joseph Le *Amatruda Benson & Associates (ABA)*
433 N Camden Dr Ste 400
Beverly Hills, CA 90210-4408, USA

Duenkel, Ginny (Athlete, Olympic Athlete, Swimmer)
2132 NE 17th Ter Fl 5
Wilton Manors, FL 33305-2414, USA

Duenkel Fuldner, Virginia (Swimmer)
2132 NE 17th Ter # 508
Wilton Manors, FL 33305-2414, USA

Duensing, Brian Duensing (Athlete, Baseball Player)
524 S 198th St
Elkhorn, NE 68022-6457, USA

Duerod, Terry (Athlete, Basketball Player)
6S42 Chirrewa St
Westland, MI 48185, USA

Dues, Hal (Athlete, Baseball Player)
3932 Amanda Dr
Dickinson, TX 77539-6405, USA

Dueto Voces del Rancho (Musician)
c/o Staff Member *Sony Music Miami*
605 Lincoln Rd Ste 700
Miami Beach, FL 33139-2901, USA

Dufek, Don (Athlete, Football Player)
570 S Maple Rd
Ann Arbor, MI 48103-3837, USA

Dufek, Joe (Athlete, Football Player)
5425 E Bell Rd Ste 108
Scottsdale, AZ 85254-6008, USA

Duff, Haylie (Actor, Musician)
1674 Sunset Plaza Dr
Los Angeles, CA 90069-1354, USA

Duff, Hilary (Actor, Musician)
12092 Summit Cir
Beverly Hills, CA 90210-1371, USA

Duff, Jamal (Athlete, Football Player)
PO Box 20058
Long Beach, CA 90801-3058, USA

Duff, John (Athlete, Football Player)
PO Box 20058
Long Beach, CA 90801-3058, USA

Duff, Matt (Athlete, Baseball Player)
Major League Bowhunter
1805 E 8th St
Chandler, OK 74834-4819, USA

Duffalo, Jim (Athlete, Baseball Player)
1505 Savannah St
Mesquite, TX 75149-8715, USA

Duffie, John (Athlete, Baseball Player)
177 Lakeside Cir
Douglas, GA 31535-6627, USA

Duffield, David (Business Person)
PeopleSoft Inc
4460 Hacienda Dr
Pleasanton, CA 94588-2761, USA

Duffner, Mark (Coach, Football Coach)
University of Maryland
Athletic Dept
College Park, MD 20740, USA

Duffus, Parris (Athlete, Hockey Player)
8609 Timbermill Pl
Fort Wayne, IN 46804-3411, USA

Duffy, Aimee Anne (DUFFY) (Musician)
c/o Staff Member *Island Records*
825 8th Ave Rm C2
New York, NY 10019-7472, USA

Duffy, Brian (Astronaut)
16410 Heather Bend Ct
Houston, TX 77059-5569, USA

Duffy, Chris (Athlete, Baseball Player)
23212 N 70th Ln
Glendale, AZ 85310-5864, USA

Duffy, Frank (Athlete, Baseball Player)
3750 N Country Club Rd Apt 27
Tucson, AZ 85716-1262, USA

Duffy, James (Business Person)
Saint Paul Companies
385 Washington St
Saint Paul, MN 55102-1396, USA

Duffy, JC (Cartoonist)
Universal Press Syndicate
4520 Main St Ste 340
Kansas City, MO 64111-7705, USA

Duffy, Julia (Actor)
540 Live Oak Circle Dr
Calabasas, CA 91302-2139, USA

Duffy, Karen (Actor, Model)
c/o Staff Member *Rebel Entertainment Partners*
5700 Wilshire Blvd Ste 456
Los Angeles, CA 90036-3648, USA

Duffy, Matthew (DJ)
c/o Len Evans *Project Publicity*
312 W 53rd St Ste 202
New York, NY 10019-5743, USA

Duffy, Patrick (Actor, Director, Producer)
1914 Palisades Dr
Pacific Palisades, CA 90272-1916, USA

Duffy, Roger (Athlete, Football Player)
6509 Lutz Ave NW
Massillon, OH 44646-9512, USA

Duffy, Troy (Actor, Director, Writer)
c/o David Krintzman *Morris Yorn Barnes Levine Krintzman Rubenstein Kohner & Gellman*
2000 Avenue of the Stars Ste 300N
3rd Floor, North Tower
Los Angeles, CA 90067-4704, USA

Dufner, Jason (Athlete, Golfer)
c/o Clarke Jones *IMG (Cleveland)*
1360 E 9th St Ste 100
Cleveland, OH 44114-1730, USA

Dugan, Dennis (Actor, Director)
4505 Woodley Ave
Encino, CA 91436-2721, USA

Dugan, Fred (Athlete, Football Player)
1827 Tamiami Trl N
Nokomis, FL 34275, USA

Dugan, Jeff (Athlete, Football Player)
5 Deepwater Ct
Edgewater, MD 21037-1216, USA

Dugans, Ron (Athlete, Football Player)
1549 Coleman St
Tallahassee, FL 32310-6016, USA

Duggan, Catherine (Athlete, Golfer)
5923 Marilyn Dr
Knoxville, TN 37914-5149, USA

Duggan, Jim (Athlete, Football Player)
1328 Hornsby Cir
Lugoff, SC 29078-9722, USA

Duggar, Michelle (Reality Star)
548 Arbor Acres Ave
Springdale, AR 72762-6256, USA

Duguary, Ron (Actor, Athlete, Hockey Player)
982 Ponte Vedra Blvd
Ponte Vedra Beach, FL 32082-4068, USA

Duguay, Ron (Athlete, Hockey Player)
14 Sea Winds Ln N
Ponte Vedra Beach, FL 32082-2731, USA

Duhamel, Josh (Actor)
1310 N Kenter Ave
Los Angeles, CA 90049-1320, USA

Duhe, Adam J (A J) Jr (Athlete, Football Player)
379 Coconut Cir
Weston, FL 33326-3320, USA

Duhon, Chris (Athlete, Basketball Player)
c/o Bill Duffy *BDA Sports Management (BDA-CA)*
700 Ygnacio Valley Rd Ste 330
Walnut Creek, CA 94596-3838, USA

Duhon, Josh (Actor)
c/o Abby Bluestone *Innovative Artists (LA)*
1505 10th St
Santa Monica, CA 90401-2805, USA

Duhon, Robert (Bobby) (Athlete, Football Player)
1060 Fuzzys Way
Greensboro, GA 30642-3929, USA

Duich, Steve (Athlete, Football Player)
PO Box 2
Descanso, CA 91916-0002, USA

Dujardin, Jean (Actor)
c/o Bryna Rifkin *ID Public Relations (LA)*
7060 Hollywood Blvd Fl 8th
Los Angeles, CA 90028-6021, USA

Dukakis, Kitty
85 Perry St
Brookline, MA 02446-6935

Dukakis, Michael (Ex-Governor)
Northeastern University
85 Perry St
Brookline, MA 02446-6935, USA

Dukakis, Olympia (Actor)
684 Broadway Apt 6E
New York, NY 10012-1123, USA

Duke, Bill (Director)
Duke Media
7510 W Sunset Blvd # 523
Los Angeles, CA 90046-3408, USA

Duke, Charles
PO Box 310345
New Braunfels, TX 78131-0345

Duke, Charles M Jr (Astronaut, General)
280 Lakeview Blvd
New Braunfels, TX 78130-5200, USA

Duke, Clark (Actor)
c/o Andy Corren *Andy Corren Management*
1545 26th St Ste 200
Santa Monica, CA 90404-3554, USA

Duke, Ken (Athlete, Golfer)
3612 SW Rivers End Way
Palm City, FL 34990-7606, USA

Duke, Norm (Bowler)
10836 Country Rd 561A
Clermont, FL 34711, USA

Duke, Patty (Actor)
2865 N Sugar Pines Dr
Coeur D Alene, ID 83815-6247, USA

Duke, Randolph (Fashion Designer)
c/o Diana Bianchini *Di Moda Public Relations*
124 S Lasky Dr # 2
Beverly Hills, CA 90212-1718, USA

Duke, Zach (Athlete, Baseball Player)
1644 Jacobs Dr
Gallatin, TN 37066-7461, USA

Dukes, Elijah (Athlete, Baseball Player)
2430 Cedar Trace Cir # B
Tampa, FL 33613-5628, USA

Dukes, Jamie (Athlete, Football Player)
2452 Stone Manor Dr
Buford, GA 30519-7686, USA

Dukes, Jan (Athlete, Baseball Player)
959 Helena Dr
Sunnyvale, CA 94087-4126, USA

Dukes, Michael (Athlete, Football Player)
115 N 23rd St
Nederland, TX 77627-5909, USA

Dukes, Tom (Athlete, Baseball Player)
325 Monte Vista Rd
Arcadia, CA 91007-6147, USA

Dukes of Dixieland, The
PO Box 56757
New Orleans, LA 70156-6757

Duke Special
c/o Staff Member *Paradigm (Monterey)*
404 W Franklin St
Monterey, CA 93940-2303, USA

Duke Spirit, The (Music Group)
c/o Staff Member *Paradigm (Monterey)*
404 W Franklin St
Monterey, CA 93940-2303, USA

Dukochitz, Jonathan (Actor, Musician)
c/o Staff Member *Innovative Artists (LA)*
1505 10th St
Santa Monica, CA 90401-2805, USA

Dulany, Caitlin (Actor)
Gersh Agency
232 N Canon Dr
Beverly Hills, CA 90210-5302, USA

Duley, Ed (Athlete, Football Player)
5219 N Casa Blanca Dr
Paradise Valley, AZ 85253-6201, USA

Duliba, Bob (Athlete, Baseball Player)
327 Philadelphia Ave
West Pittston, PA 18643-2146, USA

Dullea, Keir (Actor)
c/o Staff Member *Bret Adams Agency*
448 W 44th St
New York, NY 10036-5220, USA

Dulli, Greg (Musician)
3211 Hamilton Way
Los Angeles, CA 90026-2147, USA

Dumais, Justin (Athlete, Diver, Olympic Athlete)
2301 N Millbend Dr
Spring, TX 77380-1360, USA

Dumais, Troy (Athlete, Diver, Olympic Athlete)
2301 N Millbend Dr
Spring, TX 77380-1360, USA

Dumars III, Joe (Athlete, Basketball Player)
3499 Franklin Rd
Bloomfield Hills, MI 48302-0960, USA

Dumas, Michel (Athlete, Hockey Player)
c/o Staff Member *Chicago Blackhawks*
1901 W Madison St
Chicago, IL 60612-2459, USA

Dumas, Mike (Athlete, Football Player)
6735 Alden Nash Ave SE
Alto, MI 49302-8969, USA

Dumas, Tony (Athlete, Basketball Player)
674 Jay Ct
San Marcos, CA 92069-7393, USA

Dumatrait, Phil (Athlete, Baseball Player)
1412 Stub Oak Ave
Bakersfield, CA 93307-6917, USA

Dumbauld, Jonathan (Athlete, Football Player)
PO Box 728
Canadian, TX 79014-0728, USA

Dumervil, Elvis (Athlete, Football Player)
1717 N Bayshore Dr Apt A-2641
Miami, FL 33132-1180, USA

Dumler, Doug (Athlete, Football Player)
1526 Peterson St
Fort Collins, CO 80524-4130, USA

Dummar, Melvin
Dummar's Restaurant
Gabbs, NV 89409

Dummit, Dennis (Athlete, Football Player)
111 Via Di Roma Walk
Long Beach, CA 90803-4156, USA

Dumont, J P (Athlete, Hockey Player)
1512 Kimberleigh Ct
Franklin, TN 37069-7226, USA

Dumont, Tom (Musician)
326 Glendora Ave
Long Beach, CA 90803-1924, USA

Dumoulin, Dan (Athlete, Baseball Player)
202 Nancy Dr
Kokomo, IN 46901-5907, USA

Dumpson, William ""Showboat"" (Athlete, Baseball Player)
555 Ellis Ave
Orangeburg, SC 29115-5021, USA

Dunagan, Donnie (Actor)
422 S Bishop St
San Angelo, TX 76901-4126, USA

Dunagin, Ralph (Cartoonist)
North American Syndicate
235 E 45th St
New York, NY 10017-3305, USA

Dunaway, Craig (Athlete, Football Player)
1000 Westchester Way
Birmingham, MI 48009-2954, USA

Dunaway, Faye (Actor)
901 N Spaulding Ave
West Hollywood, CA 90046-6304, USA

Dunaway, James E (Athlete, Football Player)
170 Mount Carmel Church Rd
Sandy Hook, MS 39478-9793, USA

Dunbar, Bonnie J (Astronaut)
2200 Todville Rd
Seabrook, TX 77586-3005, USA

Dunbar, Dale (Athlete, Hockey Player)
41 Nahant Ave
Winthrop, MA 02152-1514, USA

Dunbar, Dr. bonnie j (Astronaut)
2200 Todville Rd
Seabrook, TX 77586-3005, USA

Dunbar, Huey (Musician)
c/o Staff Member *Sony Music Miami*
605 Lincoln Rd Ste 700
Miami Beach, FL 33139-2901, USA

Dunbar, Lance (Athlete, Football Player)
c/o Brian E. Overstreet *E.O. Sports Management*
2211 Norfolk St Ste 210
Houston, TX 77098-4055, USA

Dunbar, Matt (Athlete, Baseball Player)
6328 County Donegal Ct
Charlotte, NC 28277-9652, USA

Dunbar, Rockmond (Actor)
5260 Medina Rd
Woodland Hills, CA 91364-1913, USA

Dunbar, Vaughn (Athlete, Football Player)
1085 Greatwood Mnr
Alpharetta, GA 30005-7459, USA

Duncan, Allison (Race Car Driver)
McNally Racing
8636 Antelope North Rd
Antelope, CA 95843-3930, USA

Duncan, Andy (Basketball Player)
Rochester Royals
608 Berry Pi
Marion, VA 24354, USA

Duncan, Angus (Actor)
Thomas Jennings
28035 Dorothy Dr Ste 210A
Agoura Hills, CA 91301-2685, USA

Duncan, Brian (Athlete, Football Player)
739 Elm St
Graham, TX 76450-3018, USA

Duncan, Charles W Jr (Politician, Secretary)
2 Briarwood Ct
Houston, TX 77019-5802, USA

Duncan, Chris (Athlete, Baseball Player)
11 Doheny
Laguna Niguel, CA 92677-5635, USA

Duncan, Courtney (Athlete, Baseball Player)
121 Adalene Ln
Madison, AL 35757-8423, USA

Duncan, Curtis (Athlete, Football Player)
4915 Glen Hollow St
Sugar Land, TX 77479-3804, USA

Duncan, Dan (Business Person)
Enterprise Products Partners L.P
1100 Louisiana St
Houston, TX 77002-5227, USA

Duncan, Dave (Athlete, Baseball Player)
2941 N Calle Ladera
Ln
Tucson, AZ 85715-3206, USA

Duncan, Dennis (Athlete, Baseball Player)
7650 N Zack Rd
Columbia, MO 65202-9240, USA

Duncan, Donna (Race Car Driver)
Mike Murphy Racing
PO Box 3936
Portsmouth, VA 23701-0936, USA

Duncan, Iain (Athlete, Hockey Player)
453 Cedarwood Rd
Avon Lake, OH 44012-3141, USA

Duncan, Jamie (Athlete, Football Player)
217 Remi Dr
New Castle, DE 19720-5624, USA

Duncan, Jeff (Athlete, Baseball Player)
825 Lincoln Ln
Frankfort, IL 60423-1087, USA

Duncan, Jeff (Congressman, Politician)
116 Cannon Hob
Washington, DC 20515-0913, USA

Duncan, Ken (Athlete, Football Player)
4 Christina Ave
Camarillo, CA 93012-8102, USA

Duncan, Iain (Athlete, Hockey Player)
453 Cedarwood Rd
Avon Lake, OH 44012-3141, USA

Duncan, Leslie (Speedy) (Athlete, Football Player)
1607 Porter Way
Stockton, CA 95207-4126, USA

Duncan, Mariano (Athlete, Baseball Player)
11142 NW 71st Ter
Doral, FL 33178-3789, USA

Duncan, Melvin (Athlete, Baseball Player)
PO Box 980407
470 Bedford Dr
Ypsilanti, MI 48198-0407, USA

Duncan, Meredith (Athlete, Golfer)
244 Arthur Ave
Shreveport, LA 71105-3626, USA

Duncan, Mike (Race Car Driver)
PO Box 21235
Bakersfield, CA 93390-1235, USA

Duncan, Patrick S (Director, Producer, Writer)
c/o David Kanter *Anonymous Content (LA)*
3532 Hayden Ave
Culver City, CA 90232-2413, USA

Duncan, Sandy (Actor)
c/o Andrew Lawler *Douglas Gorman Rothacker & Wilhelm Inc*
1501 Broadway Ste 703
New York, NY 10036-5501, USA

duncan, Shelley (Athlete, Baseball Player)
2941 N Calle Ladera
Tucson, AZ 85715-3206, USA

Duncan, Speedy (Athlete, Football Player)
1607 Porter Way
Stockton, CA 95207-4126, USA

Duncan, Tim (Athlete, Basketball Player)
21321 Babcock Rd Lot 3
San Antonio, TX 78255-2231, USA

Duncan, Todd (Motivational Speaker, Writer)
The Duncan Group
3760 Peachtree Crest Dr Ste A
Duluth, GA 30097-8624, USa

Dunegan, Jim (Athlete, Baseball Player)
20246 180th St
New London, IA 52645-8555, USA

Dungey, Merrin (Actor)
2906 Nichols Canyon Rd
Los Angeles, CA 90046-1241, USA

Dungy, Tony (Athlete, Coach, Football Coach, Football Player)
16604 Villalenda De Avila
Tampa, FL 33613-5200, USA

Dunham, Archie W (Business Person)
ConocoPhilips Inc
600 N Dairy Ashford Rd
Houston, TX 77079-1100, USA

Dunham, Chip (Cartoonist)
Universal Press Syndicate
4520 Main St Ste 340
Kansas City, MO 64111-7705, USA

Dunham, Duane R (Business Person)
Bethlehem Steel Corp
1170 8th Ave
Bethlehem, PA 18018-2255, USA

Dunham, Jeff (Comedian)
4517 Woodley Ave
Encino, CA 91436-2721, USA

Dunham, John L (Business Person)
May Department Stores
611 Olive St Ste 2076
Saint Louis, MO 63101-1721, USA

Dunham, Lena (Actor, Writer)
c/o Jo Yao *United Talent Agency (UTA-LA)*
9336 Civic Center Dr
Beverly Hills, CA 90210-3604, USA

Dunham, Michael (Mike) (Athlete, Hockey Player, Olympic Athlete)
39 Garfield Rd
Concord, MA 01742-4930, USA

Dunham, Mike
New York Islanders
1255 Hempstead Tpke
Attn Coaching Staff
Uniondale, NY 11553-1200, USA

Dunkie, Nancy (Basketball Player)
University of California
Campus Police
Berkeley, CA 94720-0001, USA

Dunkle, Nancy (Athlete, Basketball Player, Olympic Athlete)
1350 Lorawood St
La Habra, CA 90631-7405, USA

Dunlap, Alexander W (Astronaut)
721 Parkside Dr
Woodstock, GA 30188-6057, USA

Dunlap, Carla (Gymnast, Misc)
Diamond
732 Irvington Ave
Maplewood, NJ 07040-1610, USA

Dunlap, Carlos (Athlete, Football Player)
c/o Drew Rosenhaus *Rosenhaus Sports Representation*
6400 Allison Rd
Miami Beach, FL 33141-4540, USA

Dunlap, Grant (Athlete, Baseball Player)
1431 Alga Ct
Vista, CA 92081-5016, USA

Dunlap, Page (Athlete, Golfer)
8728 Misty Creek Dr
Sarasota, FL 34241-9561, USA

Dunlap, Scott (Athlete, Golfer)
104 Summerour Vale
Duluth, GA 30097-2464, USA

Dunleavy, Michael J (Mike) (Athlete, Basketball Player, Coach)
1 W Century Dr OFC
Los Angeles, CA 90067-3417, USA

Dunleavy, Mike (Athlete, Basketball Player)
Golden State Warriors
1 W Century Dr OFC
Los Angeles, CA 90067-3417, USA

Dunleavy Jr, Mike (Athlete, Basketball Player)
127 S Carmelina Ave
Los Angeles, CA 90049-3901, USA

Dunleavy Sr, Mike (Athlete, Basketball Player, Coach)
c/o Warren LeGarie *Warren LeGarie Sports Management*
1108 Masonic Ave
San Francisco, CA 94117-2915, USA

Dunlop, Blake (Athlete, Hockey Player)
8112 Maryland Ave Ste 500
Saint Louis, MO 63105-3920, USA

dunlop, Harry
5605 Laguna Quail Way
Elk Grove, CA 95758-5710, USA

Dunn, Adam (Athlete, Baseball Player)
11 Netherfield Way
Spring, TX 77382-1730, USA

Dunn, Alan (Athlete, Baseball Player)
8536 Glenfield Dr
Baton Rouge, LA 70809-5214, USA

Dunn, Andrew W (Cinematographer)
525 Broadway Ste 250
Santa Monica, CA 90401-2419, USA

Dunn, Colton (Actor)
c/o Joel Zadak *Principato/Young Management (LA)*
9465 Wilshire Blvd Ste 900
Beverly Hills, CA 90212-2608, USA

Dunn, Gary (Athlete, Football Player)
243 Navajo St
Tavernier, FL 33070-2119, USA

Dunn, Gertie (Baseball Player)
PO Box 88
Chadds Ford, PA 19317-0088, USA

Dunn, Gregory (Publisher)
Redbook Magazine
224 W 57th St
New York, NY 10019-3212, USA

Dunn, Holly (Actor, Musician)
Holly Dunn Enterprises
PO Box 2525
Hendersonville, TN 37077-2525, USA

Dunn, Jim (Race Car Driver)
840 Kallin Ave
Long Beach, CA 90815-5004, USA

Dunn, Keldrick (K.D.) (Athlete, Football Player)
1640 Township Ter
McDonough, GA 30252-6813, USA

Dunn, Kevin (Actor)
11651 Picturesque Dr
Studio City, CA 91604-3826, USA

Dunn, Mike (Race Car Driver)
Team Mopar
PO Box 128
Wrightsville, PA 17368-0128, USA

Dunn, Moira (Athlete, Golfer)
15803 Bridgewater Ln
Tampa, FL 33624-1044, USA

Dunn, Nora (Actor, Comedian)
c/o Steven Siebert *Lighthouse Entertainment*
9220 W Sunset Blvd Ste 200
West Hollywood, CA 90069-3501, USA

Dunn, Patricia (Tricia) (Athlete, Hockey Player, Olympic Athlete)
4 Huson Ave
Derry, NH 03038-4217, USA

Dunn, Perry Lee (Athlete, Football Player)
64 Glenway Pl
Brandon, MS 39042-2545, USA

Dunn, Richie (Athlete, Hockey Player)
12229 Clarence Center Rd
Akron, NY 14001-9334, USA

Dunn, Ron (Athlete, Baseball Player)
1161 Husted Ave
San Jose, CA 95125-3633, USA

Dunn, Ronnie (Musician, Songwriter)
PO Box 120669
Nashville, TN 37212-0669, USA

Dunn, Scott (Athlete, Baseball Player)
1331 Arizona Ash St
San Antonio, TX 78232-3409, USA

Dunn, Steve (Athlete, Baseball Player)
484 Broadmoor Dr
Maryville, TN 37803-6575, USA

Dunn, Todd (Athlete, Baseball Player)
12030 London Lake Dr W
Jacksonville, FL 32258-3317, USA

Dunn, T R (Athlete, Basketball Player)
1014 19th St SW
Birmingham, AL 35211-3623, USA

Dunn, Warrick (Athlete, Football Player)
6016 Beacon Shores St
Tampa, FL 33616-1317, USA

Dunn, Winfield (Governor, Politician)
3100 W End Ave Ste 710
Nashville, TN 37203-5801, USA

Dunne, Griffin (Actor, Director)
26 E 10th St # 1011F
New York, NY 10003-5977, USA

Dunne, Mike (Athlete, Baseball Player, Olympic Athlete)
5115 W Ancient Oak Dr
Peoria, IL 61615-2247, USA

Dunne, Robin (Actor)
c/o Chris Fenton *DMG Entertainment*
3431 Wesley St Ste E
Culver City, CA 90232-2365, USA

Dunne, Roisin (Music Group, Musician)
Rave Booking
PO Box 310780
Jamaica, NY 11431-0780, USA

Dunnigan, Frank J (Publisher)
1500 Palisade Ave
Fort Lee, NJ 07024-5337, USA

Dunnigan, T Kevin (Business Person)
Thomas & Betts Corp
8155 Thomas & Betts Blvd
Memphis, TN 38125, USA

Dunning, Debbe (Actor, Model)
2070 Caleta Ct
Carlsbad, CA 92009-6117, USA

Dunning, Steve (Athlete, Baseball Player)
35 Prairie
Irvine, CA 92618-8840, USA

Dunphry, Jessica (Actor)
c/o Staff Member *Station3 (LA)*
1051 Cole Ave Ste B
Los Angeles, CA 90038-2601, USA

Dunphy, Marv (Athlete, Coach, Volleyball Player)
33370 Decker School Rd
Malibu, CA 90265-2344, USA

Dunphy, T J Dermot (Business Person)
Sealed Air Corp
Park 80 Plaza E
Saddle Brook, NJ 07663, USA

Dunsmore, Barrie (Correspondent)
ABC-TV
5010 Creston St
News Dept
Hyattsville, MD 20781-1216, USA

Dunst, Kirsten (Actor)
10056 Toluca Lake Ave
Toluca Lake, CA 91602-2924, USA

Dunst, Kristen (Actor)
8916 Ashcroft Ave
West Hollywood, CA 90048-2404, USA

Dunstan, William (Athlete, Football Player)
PO Box 514
Rancho Mirage, CA 92270-0514, USA

Dunston, Shawon D (Athlete, Baseball Player)
957 Corte Del Sol
Fremont, CA 94539-4925, USA

Dunwoody, Todd (Athlete, Baseball Player)
2172 Ironbridge Ct
Lafayette, IN 47905-8640, USA

Dunye, Cheryl (Actor, Director, Producer, Writer)
c/o Staff Member *Broder Webb Chervin Silbermann Agency, The (BWCS)*
10250 Constellation Blvd
Los Angeles, CA 90067-6200, USA

Duos, Deena (Adult Film Star)
3661 S Maryland Pkwy # 31
Pmb 285
Las Vegas, NV 89169-3003, USA

Dupard, Reggie (Athlete, Football Player)
1316 Green Hills Ct
Duncanville, TX 75137-2842, USA

Duper, Mark (Athlete, Football Player)
1905 Banks Rd
Margate, FL 33063-7713, USA

Duplass, Mark (Director, Producer)
3636 Amesbury Rd
Los Angeles, CA 90027-1304, USA

DuPont, Pierre (Ex-Governor, Politician)
National Center For Policy Analysis
Richards, Layton And Finger Pa PO Box 551 920 N King St Wilmington
Wilmington, DE 19899, USA

DuPont, Pierre S IV (Ex-Governor)
National Center For Policy Analysis
601 Pennsylvania Ave NW Ste 900
Washington, DC 20004-3647, USA

Dupont, Tiffany (Actor)
c/o Leonard Torgan *The Collective*
8383 Wilshire Blvd Ste 1050
Beverly Hills, CA 90211-2415, USA

Dupre, Ashley (Designer, Fashion Designer, Model)
Femme by Ashley Dupre
15 Broad St
Red Bank, NJ 07701-1901, USA

Dupree, Billy Joe (Athlete, Football Player)
2512 Springhill Dr
McKinney, TX 75070, USA

Dupree, Donald (Don) (Athlete)
3 Center St
Saranac Lake, NY 12983, USA

Dupree, Marcus (Athlete, Football Player)
274 Davis St
Philadelphia, MS 39350-3431, USA

Dupree, Mike (Athlete, Baseball Player)
2358 E Richmond Ave
Fresno, CA 93720-0438, USA

Dupree, Myron (Athlete, Football Player)
1553 Tadlock Ave
Rocky Mount, NC 27801-3035, USA

Dupri, Jermaine (Musician)
1240 Mount Paran Rd NW
Atlanta, GA 30327-3704, USA

Dupuis, Roy (Actor)
c/o Robert Stein *Robert Stein Management*
PO Box 3797
Beverly Hills, CA 90212-0797, USA

Duque, Ximena (Actor, Reality Star)
c/o Staff Member *Univision*
605 3rd Ave Fl 12
New York, NY 10158-0034, USA

Duquette, Dan (Commentator)
1632 Carnoustie Dr
Pasadena, MD 21122-6674, USA

Duran, Clarence (Athlete, Football Player)
201 W 54th St
Los Angeles, CA 90037-3803, USA

Duran, Dan (Athlete, Baseball Player)
2438 Pinehurst Ct
Discovery Bay, CA 94505-9219, USA

Duran, German
608 W Bend Blvd
Burleson, TX 76028-8169, USA

Duran, Micki (Actor)
c/o Staff Member *DDO Artist Agency (LA)*
4605 Lankershim Blvd Ste 340
North Hollywood, CA 91602-1876, USA

Durance, Erica (Actor)
c/o Staff Member *Gersh (LA)*
9465 Wilshire Blvd Ste 600
Beverly Hills, CA 90212-2605, USA

Durand, Kevin (Actor)
2608 Hargrave Dr
Los Angeles, CA 90068-2267, USA

Durant, Joe (Athlete, Golfer)
PO Box 910
Gulf Breeze, FL 32562-0910, USA

Durant, Justin (Athlete, Football Player)
7818 Mount Ranier Dr
Jacksonville, FL 32256-2998, USA

Durant, Kevin (Athlete, Basketball Player)
c/o Jay-Z *Roc Nation*
9348 Civic Center Dr Fl 3
Beverly Hills, CA 90210-3600, USA

Durant, Mike (Athlete, Baseball Player)
9437 Cape Wrath Dr
Dublin, OH 43017-7624, USA

Durazo, Erubiel (Athlete, Baseball Player)
3800 S Cantabria Cir Unit 1079
Chandler, AZ 85248-4250, USA

Durbin, Chad (Athlete, Baseball Player)
18652 Montclair Ct
Baton Rouge, LA 70809-6709, USA

Durbin, J D (Athlete, Baseball Player)
1913 E Pinto Dr
Gilbert, AZ 85296-3214, USA

Durbin, Mike (Bowler)
Professional Bowlers Assn
11008 Candlelight Ln
Dallas, TX 75229-3953, USA

Durbin, Richard (Politician, Senator)
1525 S Bates Ave
Springfield, IL 62704-3347, USA

Durcal, Rocio (Musician)
c/o Staff Member *BMG*
1540 Broadway
New York, NY 10036-4039, USA

Duren, Clarence (Athlete, Football Player)
201 W 54th St
Los Angeles, CA 90037-3803, USA

Duren, John (Athlete, Basketball Player)
1107 1st St NW
Washington, DC 20001-1304, USA

Duren, Steven (Musician)
298 W Carlisle Rd
Thousand Oaks, CA 91361-5310, USA

Durenberger, David (Politician, Senator)
1000 Lasalle Ave
Minneapolis, MN 55403-2025, USA

Durfee, Peter (Athlete, Baseball Player)
4216 Magness Ct
Chico, CA 95973-8507, USA

Durham, Don (Athlete, Baseball Player)
2627 Pennington Bend Rd
Nashville, TN 37214-1107, USA

Durham, Hugh (Basketball Player, Coach)
Jacksonville University
Athletic Dept
Jacksonville, FL 32211, USA

Durham, Jarrett (Athlete, Basketball Player)
18 McKelvey Ave
Pittsburgh, PA 15218-1454, USA

Durham, Joe (Athlete, Baseball Player)
9715 Mendoza Rd
Randallstown, MD 21133-2530, USA

Durham, Leon (Athlete, Baseball Player)
1553 Williamson Dr
Cincinnati, OH 45240-1549, USA

Durham, Ray (Sugar Ray) (Athlete, Baseball Player)
199 Lake Rd
Stanley, NC 28164-2312, USA

Duritz, Adam (Musician, Songwriter)
52 Cooper Sq # 5B
New York, NY 10003, USA

Durkee, Charlie (Athlete, Football Player)
1210 Danbury Dr
Mansfield, TX 76063-3809, USA

Durkin, John A (Ex-Senator)
PO Box 437
Rollinsford, NH 03869-0437, USA

Durko, Sandy (Athlete, Football Player)
2020 Paseo Del Mar
Palos Verdes Estates, CA 90274-2659, USA

Durkota, Jeff (Athlete, Football Player)
1020 Lititz Ave
Lancaster, PA 17602-1921, USA

Durnbaugh, Bobby (Athlete, Baseball Player)
1638 N Central Dr
Beavercreek, OH 45432-2118, USA

Durocher, Jayson (Athlete, Baseball Player)
3997 E Robin Ln
Phoenix, AZ 85050-5416, USA

Durr, Jason (Actor)
536 N Gower St
Los Angeles, CA 90004-1302, USA

Durrance, Samuel T Dr (Astronaut, Scientist)
770 Kerry Downs Cir
Melbourne, FL 32940-1774, USA

Durrant, Devin (Athlete, Basketball Player)
1846 N 1350 W
Provo, UT 84604-1151, USA

Durrington, Trent (Athlete, Baseball Player)
499 N Canon Dr Apt 400
Beverly Hills, CA 90210-4887, USA

Durslag, Melvin
PO Box 559
Salisbury, NC 28145-0559

Durst, Fred (Musician)
c/o Joanne Wiles *ICM Partners (LA)*
10250 Constellation Blvd Fl 7
Los Angeles, CA 90067-6207, USA

Durst, Will (Actor, Comedian)
c/o Staff Member *Entertainment Alliance*
PO Box 1544
Mendocino, CA 95460-1544, USA

Dusan, Gene (Athlete, Baseball Player)
2241 SE Pilatus Ln
Bend, OR 97702-2498, USA

Dusay, Debra (Actor)
Susan Nathe
8281 Melrose Ave Ste 200
Los Angeles, CA 90046-6823, USA

Dusay, Mari (Actor)
320 W 66th St
New York, NY 10023-6304, USA

Dusay, Marj (Actor)
Susan Nathe
8281 Melrose Ave Ste 200
Los Angeles, CA 90046-6823, USA

Dusbabek, Mark (Athlete, Football Player)
11452 Dona Dorotea Dr
Studio City, CA 91604-4246, USA

Dusek, Brad (Athlete, Football Player)
The 4th Quarter Ranch 8311 Fm 2086
Temple, TX 76501, USA

Dusenberry, Ann (Actor)
1615 San Leandro Ln
Santa Barbara, CA 93108, USA

Dusendang, Christina (Athlete, Rodeo Rider)
c/o Gigi Rock *Heraea Marketing*
10905 E Pear Tree Dr
Cornville, AZ 86325-5523, USA

Duser, Carl (Athlete, Baseball Player)
3021 Cornwall Rd
Bethlehem, PA 18017-3313, USA

Dushku, Eliza (Actor, Producer)
2548 Laurel Pass
Los Angeles, CA 90046-1404, USA

Dushku, Nate (Actor)
c/o Matt Schwartz *Christopher Wright Management*
6100 Wilshire Blvd Ste 1170
Los Angeles, CA 90048-5116, USA

Dusick, Ryan (Musician)
4905 Calvin Ave
Tarzana, CA 91356-4417, USA

Dusk, Matt (Musician)
c/o Garry Kief *Stiletto Entertainment*
8295 S La Cienega Blvd
Inglewood, CA 90301-1521, USA

Dussault, Nancy (Actor)
c/o Staff Member *The Artists Group Ltd (LA)*
3345 Wilshire Blvd Ste 915
Los Angeles, CA 90010-1820, USA

Dussault, Rebecca (Athlete, Olympic Athlete, Skier)
PO Box 665
Gunnison, CO 81230-0665

Dustal, Bob (Athlete, Baseball Player)
625 Marian Ln
Lakeland, FL 33813-1412, USA

Dustrude-Roberson, Beverly (Baseball Player)
2422 Lobelia Dr
Oxnard, CA 93036-6260, USA

Dutch, Deborah (Actor)
850 N Kings Rd # 100
West Hollywood, CA 90069-5442, USA

du Tertre, Celine (Actor)
c/o Staff Member *Harvest Talent Management*
124 W 80th St Apt 1
New York, NY 10024-6320, USA

Dutt, Hank (Music Group, Musician)
Kronos Quartet
1235 9th Ave # A
San Francisco, CA 94122-2306, USA

Dutton, Charles S (Actor)
2790 Marriottsville Rd
Marriottsville, MD 21104-1626, USA

Dutton, James P Major (Astronaut)
13285 Cedarville Way
Colorado Springs, CO 80921-7637, USA

Dutton, John O (Athlete, Football Player)
5706 Moss Creek Trl
Dallas, TX 75252-2380, USA

Duva, Lou (Boxer, Misc)
Main Events
811 Totowa Rd # 100
Totowa, NJ 07512-1207, USA

Duval, David (Athlete, Golfer)
11 Parkway Dr
Englewood, CO 80113-4227, USA

Duval, Dennis (Athlete, Basketball Player)
8105 Verbeck Dr
Manlius, NY 13104-9306, USA

Duval, Helen (Bowler)
PO Box 2071
Oakland, CA 94604-2071, USA

Duval, James (Actor)
c/o Ryan Revel *Benderspink*
8447 Wilshire Blvd Ste 250
Studio E
Beverly Hills, CA 90211-3224, USA

Duval, Mike (Athlete, Baseball Player)
2743 Nature Pointe Loop
Fort Myers, FL 33905-2468, USA

Duvall, Brad (Baseball Player)
Bowman
438 Sycamore Trl
Woodstock, GA 30189-7423, USA

Duvall, Carol (Television Host)
c/o Staff Member *HGTV*
9721 Sherrill Blvd
Knoxville, TN 37932-3330, USA

DuVall, Clea (Actor)
11283 Canton Dr
Studio City, CA 91604-4155, USA

Duvall, Jed (Correspondent)
ABC-TV
5010 Creston St
Hyattsville, MD 20781-1216, USA

Duvall, Robert (Actor)
PO Box 520
The Plains, VA 20198-0520, USA

Duvall, Sammy (Skier)
PO Box 871
Windermere, FL 34786-0871, USA

Duvall, Shelley (Actor)
c/o Staff Member *Gersh (LA)*
9465 Wilshire Blvd Ste 600
Beverly Hills, CA 90212-2605, USA

Duvall-Hero, Camille (Skier)
PO Box 871
Windermere, FL 34786-0871, USA

Duvernay-Tardif, Laurent (Athlete, Football Player)
c/o Chad Speck *Allegiant Athletic Agency*
35 Market Sq Ste 201
Knoxville, TN 37902-1420, USA

Duwelius, Richard L (Rich) (Athlete, Olympic Athlete, Volleyball Player)
266 Stoddards Wharf Rd
Gales Ferry, CT 06335-1130, USA

Dvorak, Radek (Athlete, Hockey Player)
10342 Lexington Estates Blvd
Boca Raton, FL 33428-4290, USA

Dvorak, Richard (Rick) (Athlete, Football Player)
13587 SE 230 Rd
Spearville, KS 67876-7506, USA

Dwight, Edward Captain (Astronaut)
3824 Dahlia St Studio Gallery
Denver, CO 80207-1020, USA

Dwight, Edward Jr (Astronaut)
4022 Montview Blvd
Denver, CO 80207-3713, USA

Dwight, Tim (Athlete, Football Player)
26164 Indigo Dr
Park Rapids, MN 56470-5189, USA

Dworaczyk, Hope (Model)
c/o Liza Anderson *Anderson Group Public Relations*
8060 Melrose Ave Fl 4
Los Angeles, CA 90046-7038, USA

Dwork, Melvin (Designer)
Melvin Dwork Inc
196 Avenue of the Americas
New York, NY 10013-1234, USA

Dwyer, Bil (Comedian, Game Show Host, Television Host)
c/o Bruce Smith *OmniPop Talent Group (LA)*
4605 Lankershim Blvd Ste 201
North Hollywood, CA 91602-1874, USA

Dwyer, Clark (Race Car Driver)
4610 Spring Canyon Hts Apt 303
Colorado Springs, CO 80907-3459, USA

Dwyer, Jim (Athlete, Baseball Player)
825 Hancock Bridge Pkwy
Cape Coral, FL 33990-1236, USA

Dwyer, Jonathan (Athlete, Football Player)
c/o Adisa P. Bakari *Dow Lohnes PLLC*
1299 Pennsylvania Ave NW Ste 700
Washington, DC 20004-2431, USA

Dwyer, Mary (Athlete, Golfer)
460 Sunningdale Dr
Rancho Mirage, CA 92270-1443, USA

Dyal, Mike (Athlete, Football Player)
609 Rock Creek Loop
Kerrville, TX 78028-6506, USA

Dybdahl, Thomas (Musician)
c/o Staff Member *Paradigm (Monterey)*
404 W Franklin St
Monterey, CA 93940-2303, USA

Dybzinski, Jerry (Athlete, Baseball Player)
2938 Des Moines Dr
Fort Collins, CO 80525-6686, USA

Dychtwald, Ken (Doctor, Misc)
Age Wave Inc
1900 Powell St
Emeryville, CA 94608-1811, USA

Dye, Cameron (Actor)
13035 Woodbridge St
Studio City, CA 91604-1431, USA

Dye, Dale (Actor)
16129 Tupper St
North Hills, CA 91343-3047, USA

Dye, Jermaine (Athlete, Baseball Player)
18776 Heritage Dr
Poway, CA 92064-6643, USA

Dyer, Danny (Actor)
c/o Staff Member *ICM Partners (LA)*
10250 Constellation Blvd Fl 7
Los Angeles, CA 90067-6207, USA

Dyer, Duffy (Athlete, Baseball Player)
742 W Las Palmaritas Dr
Phoenix, AZ 85021-5545, USA

Dyer, Hector (Athlete, Track Athlete)
1620 E Chapman Ave # 214
Fullerton, CA 92831-4016, USA

Dyer, Henry (Athlete, Football Player)
23464 Reames Rd
Zachary, LA 70791-6603, USA

Dyer, Joseph W Jr (Athlete, Football Player)
46 Windy Way
Alexander City, AL 35010-9407, USA

Dyer, Mike (Athlete, Baseball Player)
22392 Manacor
Mission Viejo, CA 92692-1188, USA

Dyer, Wayne (Writer)
1905 N Ocean Blvd
Shore Club Tower House C
Fort Lauderdale, FL 33305-3747, USA

Dykema, Craig (Athlete, Basketball Player)
10525 Destino St
Bellflower, CA 90706-7125, USA

Dykes, Donald
47408 N Cherry St
Hammond, LA 70401-7233, USA

Dykes, Hart Lee (Athlete, Football Player)
30 Dorothea Ln
Sugar Land, TX 77479-2446, USA

Dykes, Keilen (Athlete, Football Player)
2329 W Melody Dr
Phoenix, AZ 85041-7634, USA

Dykes, Sean (Athlete, Football Player)
7186 Copperfield Cir
Lake Worth, FL 33467-7129, USA

Dykhoff, Radhames (Baseball Player)
Baltimore Orioles
105 Angelfish Ln
Jupiter, FL 33477-7227, USA

Dykinga, Jack (Journalist, Photographer)
1519 E Tascal Loop
Tucson, AZ 85737-8570, USA

Dykstra, John (Animator, Artist, Cinematographer)
15060 Encanto Dr
Sherman Oaks, CA 91403-4408, USA

Dykstra, Lenny (Athlete, Baseball Player)
1072 Newbern Ct
Thousand Oaks, CA 91361-5346, USA

Dylan, Bob (Musician, Songwriter)
c/o Elliott Mintz *Elliot Mintz Public Relations*
2934 1/2 N Beverly Glen Cir
Los Angeles, CA 90077-1724, USA

Dylan, Jakob (Musician)
c/o Marty Diamond *Paradigm (NY)*
360 Park Ave S Fl 16
New York, NY 10010-1716, USA

Dylan, Jesse (Director)
2741 Woodstock Rd
Los Angeles, CA 90046-1118, USA

Dynamo (Magician)
c/o Darin Friedman *Management 360*
9111 Wilshire Blvd
Beverly Hills, CA 90210-5508, USA

Dyrdek, Rob (Actor, Athlete, Skateboarder)
8283 Skyline Dr
Los Angeles, CA 90046-1036, USA

Dyroen-Lancer, Rebekah (Athlete, Olympic Athlete, Swimmer)
31101 Via Madera
San Juan Capistrano, CA 92675-2830, USA

Dysart, Richard (Actor)
654 Copeland Ct
Santa Monica, CA 90405-4416, USA

Dyson, Andre (Athlete, Football Player)
3367 N Shoreline Cir
Layton, UT 84040-7128, USA

Dyson, Kevin (Athlete, Football Player)
3109 Chase Point Dr
Franklin, TN 37067-8156, USA

Dyson, Michael Eric (Writer)
DePaul University
English Dept
Chicago, IL 60604, USA

Dziedzic, Joe (Athlete, Hockey Player)
2195 Marion Rd Apt 102
Saint Paul, MN 55113-3805, USA

Dziedzic, Stanley (Athlete, Olympic Athlete, Wrestler)
835 Hedgegate Ct
Roswell, GA 30075-2281, USA

Dziena, Alexis (Actor)
c/o Adam Schweitzer *ICM Partners (NY)*
730 5th Ave
New York, NY 10019-4105, USA

Dzienny, Gracie (Actor)
c/o Cameron Curtis *Curtis Talent Management*
9607 Arby Dr
Beverly Hills, CA 90210-1202, USA

Dziura, Jennifer (Comedian)
334 15th St # 1
Brooklyn, NY 11215-5006, USA

Dzundza, George (Actor)
c/o Glenn Robbins *Raw Talent Management*
2355 Westwood Blvd Ste 418
Los Angeles, CA 90064-2109, USA

E 40 (Music Group)
BME Recordings
2144 Hills Ave NW Ste D2
Atlanta, GA 30318-2805, USA

Eaben, Bill (Athlete, Basketball Player)
12254 Colliers Reserve Dr
Naples, FL 34110-0910, USA

Eackles, Ledell (Athlete, Basketball Player)
9134 Elmgrove Garden Dr
Baton Rouge, LA 70807-4307, USA

Eadie, Betty J. (Writer)
c/o Staff Member *Random House Publicity*
1745 Broadway Frnt 3
New York, NY 10019-4343, USA

Eads, George (Actor)
3060 Nichols Canyon Rd
Los Angeles, CA 90046-1253, USA

Eads, Ora W (Religious Leader)
Christian Congregation
804 E Hemlock St
La Follette, TN 37766-3758, USA

Eagan, James (Writer)
c/o Greg Cavic *Creative Artists Agency (CAA-LA)*
2000 Avenue of the Stars Ste 100
Los Angeles, CA 90067-4705, USA

Eagle, Ian (Sportscaster)
CBS-TV
51 W 52nd St
Sports Dept
New York, NY 10019-6119, USA

Eaglen, Jane (Musician, Opera Singer)
c/o Staff Member *Columbia Artists Mgmt Inc*
1790 Broadway Fl 6
New York, NY 10019-1537, USA

Eagles, The (Music Group)
c/o Irving Azoff *Azoff Music Management*
1100 Glendon Ave Ste 2000
Los Angeles, CA 90024-3524, USA

Eakes, Bobbie (Actor)
c/o Staff Member *William Morris Endeavor (LA)*
9601 Wilshire Blvd
Beverly Hills, CA 90210-5213, USA

Eakin, Bruce
25915 W Perdido Ave
Orange Beach, AL 36561-5808, USA

Eakin, Thomas C (Business Person)
245 Sandover Dr
Aurora, OH 44202-8774, USA

Eakins, Dallas (Athlete, Hockey Player)
21579 N 81st St
Scottsdale, AZ 85255-6477, USA

Eakins, Gretchen (Actor)
Mattie Management
1438 N Gower St Ste 34
C/O Mattie Semradek
Los Angeles, CA 90028-8362, USA

Eakins, Jim (Athlete, Basketball Player)
2575 E Little Cottonwood Rd
Sandy, UT 84092-3469, USA

Eaks, RW (Athlete, Golfer)
14617 E Shadow Canyon Dr
Fountain Hills, AZ 85268-1900, USA

Ealy, Kony (Athlete, Football Player)
c/o Andy Ross *Octagon Football*
832 Sansome St Fl 1
San Francisco, CA 94111-1558, USA

Ealy, Michael (Actor)
c/o Jessica Cohen *JCPR*
9903 Santa Monica Blvd Ste 983
Beverly Hills, CA 90212-1671, USA

Earl, Acie (Athlete, Basketball Player)
301 S Iowa St
Solon, IA 52333-9428, USA

Earl, Anthony (Politician)
2810 Arbor Dr Unit B
Madison, WI 53711-1809, USA

Earl, Denny (Athlete, Football Player)
3600 Ozark Acres Dr
Bentonville, AR 72712-7111, USA

Earl, Glenn (Athlete, Football Player)
838 N Doheny Dr Apt 1207
West Hollywood, CA 90069-4851, USA

Earl, Robbie
8314 Holy Cross Pl
Los Angeles, CA 90045-2633, USA

Earl, Robin D (Athlete, Football Player)
395 Oak Creek Dr Apt 415
Wheeling, IL 60090-6740, USA

Earl, Roger (Musician)
Lustig Talent
PO Box 770850
Orlando, FL 32877-0850, USA

Earl, Scott (Athlete, Baseball Player)
8102 Salt Fork Way
Indianapolis, IN 46256-1679, USA

Earle, Ed (Athlete, Basketball Player)
1940 Burton Ln
Park Ridge, IL 60068-1572, USA

Earle, Steve (Actor, Musician)
c/o Danny Goldberg *Gold Village Entertainment*
37 W 17th St Ste 7W
New York, NY 10011-5525, USA

Earle, Sylvia (Writer)
12812 Skyline Blvd
Oakland, CA 94619-3125, USA

Earley, Anthony F Jr (Business Person)
Detroit Edison
2000 2nd Ave
Detroit, MI 48226-1203, USA

Earley, Bill (Athlete, Baseball Player)
219 Woodland Dr Apt 7
Beaver Dam, WI 53916-9167, USA

Earley, Liz (Athlete, Golfer)
24 Morton Dr
Buffalo, NY 14226-3338, USA

Earley, Michael M (Business Person)
Triton Group
550 W C St Ste 1155
San Diego, CA 92101-8582, USA

Earley, Quinn (Athlete, Football Player)
PO Box 675752
Rancho Santa Fe, CA 92067-5752, USA

Early, David (Actor)
PO Box 154
Homestead, PA 15120-0154, USA

Early, Gerald L (Writer)
Washington University
English Dept
Saint Louis, MO 63130, USA

Early, Quinn (Athlete, Football Player)
10362 Craftsman Way Apt 106
San Diego, CA 92127-3554, USA

Earnhardt, Jeffrey (Race Car Driver)
c/o Staff Member *Rick Ware Racing*
111 Sunrise Center Dr
Thomasville, NC 27360-4928, USA

Earnhardt, Kelley (Race Car Driver)
Dale Earnhardt Inc
1675 Coddle Creek Hwy
Mooresville, NC 28115-8245, USA

Earnhardt, Kerry (Race Car Driver)
Kerry Earnhardt Fan Club
1675 Coddle Creek Hwy
Mooresville, NC 28115-8245, USA

Earnhardt Jr, Dale (Race Car Driver)
1675 Coddle Creek Hwy
Mooresville, NC 28115-8245, USA

Earnie, Rhone (Athlete, Football Player)
3603 Potomac Ave
Texarkana, TX 75503-3519, USA

Earon, Blaine (Athlete, Football Player)
6640 Lake Run Dr
Flowery Branch, GA 30542-3895, USA

Earp, Mildred (Athlete, Baseball Player, Commentator)
PO Box 333
West Fork, AR 72774-0333, USA

Earth Wind & Fire (Music Group)
c/o Damien Smith *Azoff Music Management*
1100 Glendon Ave Ste 2000
Los Angeles, CA 90024-3524, USA

Easler, Mike (Athlete, Baseball Player)
3709 White Lion Ln
North Las Vegas, NV 89084-2334, USA

Easley, Bill (Musician)
Hot Jazz Mgmt
328 W 43rd St
#4FW
New York, NY 10036, USA

Easley, Damion (Athlete, Baseball Player)
6420 W Line Dr
Glendale, AZ 85310-5751, USA

Easley, Kenny (Athlete, Football Player)
2327 Old Greenbrier Rd
Chesapeake, VA 23325-4929, USA

Easley, Logan (Athlete, Baseball Player)
753 W Cagney Dr
Meridian, ID 83646-5299, USA

Easley, Marcus (Athlete, Football Player)
c/o Ed Wasielewski *EMG Sports - PA*
PO Box 22371
Philadelphia, PA 19110-2371, USA

Easley, Michael (Politician)
216 River Dr
Southport, NC 28461-4108, USA

Easmon, Ricky (Athlete, Football Player)
6605 N Riviera Manor Dr Apt A4
Tampa, FL 33604-6444, USA

Eason, Eric (Actor, Director, Writer)
c/o Simon Millar *Rumble Media*
1620 Broadway Ste C
Santa Monica, CA 90404-2777, USA

Eason, Tony (Athlete, Football Player)
PO Box 340
Walnut Grove, CA 95690-0340, USA

East, Jeff (Actor)
c/o Vaughn Hart *Vaughn Hart & Associates*
12304 Santa Monica Blvd Ste 111
Los Angeles, CA 90025-2586, USA

East, Ron (Athlete, Football Player)
PO Box 2228
Anacortes, WA 98221-8106, USA

Easterbrook, Leslie (Actor)
c/o Staff Member *AKA Talent Agency*
6310 San Vicente Blvd Ste 200
Los Angeles, CA 90048-5488, USA

Easterly, David E (Business Person)
Cox Enterprises
1400 Lake Heam Dr NE
Atlanta, GA 30319, USA

Easterly, Dick (Athlete, Football Player)
206 S Gardenia Ave
Tampa, FL 33609-2506, USA

Easterly, Jamie (Athlete, Baseball Player)
1306 Plantation Dr
Crockett, TX 75835-2314, USA

Easterly, Richard (Athlete, Football Player)
206 S Gardenia Ave
Tampa, FL 33609-2506, USA

Eastern Conference Champions (Music Group)
c/o Staff Member *Paradigm (Monterey)*
404 W Franklin St
Monterey, CA 93940-2303, USA

Eastgate, Peter
c/o Staff Member *Poker Royalty, LLC*
10789 W Twain Ave Ste 200
Las Vegas, NV 89135-3030, USA

Eastin, Steve (Actor)
c/o Staff Member *Agency for the Performing Arts (APA-LA)*
405 S Beverly Dr Ste 500
Beverly Hills, CA 90212-4425, USA

Eastman, Kevin (Cartoonist)
1932 Coldwater Canyon Dr
Beverly Hills, CA 90210-1731, USA

Eastman, Madeline (Musician)
Prince/SF Productions
1450 Southgate Ave Apt 206
Daly City, CA 94015-4021, USA

Eastman, Marilyn (Actor)
Hardman-Eastman Studios
138 Hawthome St
Pittsburgh, PA 15218, USA

Eastman, Rodney (Actor)
c/o Justin Evans *The Independent Group*
6363 Wilshire Blvd Ste 115
Los Angeles, CA 90048-5734, USA

Easton, Michael (Actor)
c/o Danielle Allman-Del *D2 Management*
9255 W Sunset Blvd Ste 600
West Hollywood, CA 90069-3306, USA

Easton, Micheal (Actor)
c/o Danielle Allman-Del *D2 Management*
9255 W Sunset Blvd Ste 600
West Hollywood, CA 90069-3306, USA

Easton, Millard E (Bill) (Coach)
1704 NW Weatherstone Dr
Blue Springs, MO 64015-6317, USA

Easton, Robert
Paul Kohner
9300 Wilshire Blvd Ste 555
Beverly Hills, CA 90212-3211, USA

Easton, Sheena (Musician)
Emmis Mgmt
18136 Califa St
Tarzana, CA 91356-1718, USA

Eastwick, Rawly (Athlete, Baseball Player)
10 River Meadow Dr
West Newbury, MA 01985-1400, USA

Eastwood, Alison (Actor, Model)
c/o Bob McGowan *McGowan Management*
8733 W Sunset Blvd Ste 103
West Hollywood, CA 90069-2241, USA

Eastwood, Bob (Athlete, Golfer)
PO Box 14769
Haltom City, TX 76117-0769, USA

Eastwood, Clint (Actor, Producer)
Malpaso Productions
4000 Warner Blvd Bldg 81
Burbank, CA 91522-0001, USA

Eastwood, Dina (Correspondent, Reality Star)
California Museum
1020 O St
Sacramento, CA 95814-5704, USA

Eastwood, Francesca (Actor)
c/o David Sweeney *Sweeney Entertainment*
6253 Hollywood Blvd Apt 201
Los Angeles, CA 90028-8248, USA

Eastwood, Scott (Actor, Producer)
c/o Joanne Horowitz *Joanne Horowitz Management*
9350 Wilshire Blvd Ste 224
Beverly Hills, CA 90212-3204, USA

Easy, Omar (Athlete, Football Player)
8 Edith Ave # 3
Everett, MA 02149-3011, USA

Eathorne, A J (Athlete, Golfer)
23023 N 25th Pl
Phoenix, AZ 85024-7567, USA

Eaton, Adam (Athlete, Baseball Player)
17404 NE 126th Pl # Pi
Redmond, WA 98052-2296, USA

Eaton, Brando (Actor)
c/o Staff Member *Art Work Entertainment*
5900 Wilshire Blvd Ste 2150
Los Angeles, CA 90036-5021, USA

Eaton, Chad (Athlete, Football Player)
1285 SE Sunnymead Way
Pullman, WA 99163-5475, USA

Eaton, Courtney (Actor)
c/o Staff Member *Principato/Young Management (NY)*
54 W 40th St
New York, NY 10018-2602, USA

Eaton, Craig (Athlete, Baseball Player)
3307 Baltusrol Ln
Lake Worth, FL 33467-1301, USA

Eaton, Dan L (Doctor)
Genentech Inc
1 Dna Way
South San Francisco, CA 94080-4990, USA

Eaton, Mark (Athlete, Basketball Player)
484 Shepherd Way
Park City, UT 84098-5704, USA

Eaton, Mark (Athlete, Hockey Player)
3 Fieldstone Cir
Greenville, RI 02828-1033, USA

Eaton, Mark (Basketball Player)
Utah Jazz
2104 Dayton Ave NE
Renton, WA 98056-2719, USA

Eaton, Meredith (Actor)
c/o Staff Member *Bresler Kelly & Associates*
11500 W Olympic Blvd Ste 510
Los Angeles, CA 90064-1527, USA

Eaton, Scott (Athlete, Football Player)
3950 W Lake Sammamish Pkwy SE
Bellevue, WA 98008-5836, USA

Eaton, Tracey (Athlete, Football Player)
208 Mt Park Blvd SW Apt E303
Issaquah, WA 98027-3691, USA

Eaton, Vic (Athlete, Football Player)
100 Promenade Ave Apt 515
Wayzata, MN 55391-4556, USA

Eave, Gary (Athlete, Baseball Player)
1601 King Ave
Bastrop, LA 71220-4957, USA

Eaves, Jerry (Athlete, Basketball Player)
10 Perch Pl
Greensboro, NC 27455-3437, USA

Eaves, Mike (Athlete, Hockey Player)
27 Quail Ridge Dr
Madison, WI 53717-1081, USA

Eaves, Murray (Athlete, Hockey Player)
Shattuck-St Mary's School
3610 Archer Ln N
Minneapolis, MN 55446-2685, USA

Eaves, Patrick (Athlete, Hockey Player)
3615 Culver Trl
Faribault, MN 55021-7366, USA

Ebanks, Devin (Athlete, Basketball Player)
c/o David Bauman *F.A.M.E*
Prefers to be contacted via telephone
Washington, DC, USA

Ebanks, Selita (Actor, Model)
c/o Staff Member *Full Picture Management (NYC)*
915 Broadway Fl 20
New York, NY 10010-7131, USA

Ebben, Bill (Basketball Player)
Detroit Pistons
12254 Colliers Reserve Dr
Naples, FL 34110-0910, USA

Ebebole, Christine (Actor)
c/o Barry McPherson *Agency for the Performing Arts (APA-NY)*
135 W 50th St Fl 17
New York, NY 10020-1201, USA

Ebel, Dino (Athlete, Baseball Player)
c/o Staff Member *Los Angeles Dodgers (LA Dodgers)*
1000 Elysian Park Ave
Los Angeles, CA 90012-1112, USA

Eber, Richard (Athlete, Football Player)
13 Stoney Pt
Laguna Niguel, CA 92677-1000, USA

Eber, Rick (Athlete, Football Player)
13 Stoney Pt
Laguna Niguel, CA 92677-1000, USA

Eberhard, Al (Athlete, Basketball Player)
203 W Parkway Dr
Columbia, MO 65203-3450, USA

Eberle, William D (Business Person)
13 Garland Rd
Concord, MA 01742-2214, USA

Ebersole, Christine (Actor)
c/o Barry McPherson *Agency for the Performing Arts (APA-NY)*
135 W 50th St Fl 17
New York, NY 10020-1201, USA

Ebersole, Dick (Business Person)
174 West St # 54
Litchfield, CT 06759-3434, USA

Ebersole, Drew (Actor)
c/o Staff Member *House of Representatives, The*
1434 6th St Ste 1
Santa Monica, CA 90401-2527, USA

Ebersole, John (Athlete, Football Player)
1470 Village Sq
Mount Pleasant, SC 29464-4626, USA

Ebert, Derrin (Athlete, Baseball Player)
13785 W Acapulco Ln
Surprise, AZ 85379-8303, USA

Ebert, Jeremy (Athlete, Football Player)
c/o Michael McCartney *Priority Sports & Entertainment - Chicago*
312 N La Salle
Suite 650
Chicago, IL 60610, USA

Ebi, Ndudi (Basketball Player)
Minnesota Timberwolves
600 1st Ave N
Target Center
Minneapolis, MN 55403-1400, USA

Ebner, Nate (Athlete, Football Player)
c/o Neil Cornrich *NC Sports, LLC*
best to contact via email
Columbus, OH 43201, USA

Ebron, Eric (Athlete, Football Player)
c/o Bus Cook *Bus Cook Sports, Inc*
1 Willow Bend Dr
Hattiesburg, MS 39402-8552, USA

Ebron, Roy (Athlete, Basketball Player)
7100 Virgilian St
New Orleans, LA 70126-2633, USA

Ebsen, Bonnie (Actor)
PO Box 356
Agoura Hills, CA 91376-0356, USA

E. Capuano, Michael (Congressman, Politician)
1414 Longworth Hob
Washington, DC 20515-3103, USA

Eccleston, Christopher (Actor)
c/o Larry Taube *Principal Entertainment (LA)*
9255 W Sunset Blvd Ste 500
West Hollywood, CA 90069-3301, USA

Ecclestone, Timothy J (Tim) (Athlete, Hockey Player)
10095 Fairway Village Dr
Roswell, GA 30076-3718, USA

Ecclestone Stunt, Petra (Model)
594 S Mapleton Dr
Los Angeles, CA 90024-1811, USA

Echevarria, Angel (Athlete, Baseball Player)
23830 231st Pl SE
Maple Valley, WA 98038-5257, USA

Echeverria, Sandra (Actor)
c/o Sekka Scher *Evolution Entertainment*
175 Varick St
New York, NY 10014-4604, USA

Echikunwoke, Megalyn (Actor)
c/o Ira Belgrade *Ira Belgrade Management*
5850 W 3rd St Ste E
Los Angeles, CA 90036-2836, USA

Echols, Terry (Athlete, Football Player)
6123 Sissonville Dr
Charleston, WV 25312, USA

Eck, Keith (Athlete, Football Player)
7426 Solano St
Carlsbad, CA 92009-7527, USA

Eckenstahler, Eric (Athlete, Baseball Player)
24250 W Alpine Ct
Lake Villa, IL 60046-8637, USA

Ecker, Guy (Actor)
Bossa Sales Inc.
PO Box 490001
Los Angeles, CA 90049-0001, USA

Eckersley, Dennis (Athlete, Baseball Player)
6 Macy Ln
Ipswich, MA 01938-1185, USA

Eckert, Robert (Business Person)
Mattel Inc
333 Continental Blvd
El Segundo, CA 90245-5032, USA

Eckert, Shari (Actor)
PO Box 5761
Sherman Oaks, CA 91413-5761, USA

Eckhart, Aaron (Actor, Producer)
c/o Staci Wolfe *Polaris PR*
8135 W 4th St Fl 2
Los Angeles, CA 90048-4415, USA

Eckholdt, Steven (Actor)
137 N Larchmont Blvd # 138
Los Angeles, CA 90004-3704, USA

Eckhouse, James (Actor, Director)
c/o Tracy Steinsapir *Main Title Entertainment*
8383 Wilshire Blvd Ste 408
Beverly Hills, CA 90211-2435, USA

Ecko, Marc (Fashion Designer, Producer)
c/o Staff Member *5W Public Relations*
11111 Santa Monica Blvd Fl 16
Los Angeles, CA 90025-3333, USA

Eckstein, Ashley (Drane)
c/o Kathy Carter *Carter Management*
10701 Wilshire Blvd Apt 1202
Los Angeles, CA 90024-4437, USA

Eckstein, David (Athlete, Baseball Player)
1917 Lake Markham Preserve Trl
Sanford, FL 32771-8103, USA

Eckstein, Rick
103 Aldean Dr
Sanford, FL 32771-3612, USA

Eckwood, Jerry (Athlete, Football Player)
496 Pickett Rd
Memphis, TN 38109-7365, USA

E. Clyburn, James (Congressman, Politician)
2135 Rayburn Hob
Washington, DC 20515-0005, USA

E. Connolly, Gerald (Congressman, Politician)
424 Cannon Hob
Washington, DC 20515-0306, USA

E. Cummings, Elijah (Congressman, Politician)
2235 Rayburn Hob # B
Washington, DC 20515-0923, USA

Ed, Reynolds (Athlete, Football Player)
173 Moyer Rd
Stoneville, NC 27048-8462, USA

Edberg, Stefan (Athlete, Tennis Player)
International Tennis Hall Of Fame
194 Bellevue Ave
Newport, RI 02840-3586, USA

Eddie, Patrick (Basketball Player)
New York Knicks
4424 N 76th St Apt 3
Milwaukee, WI 53218-5336, USA

Eddie X (DJ)
c/o Staff Member *Diva Central Inc*
7510 W Sunset Blvd Ste 1445
Los Angeles, CA 90046-3408, USA

Eddings, Doug (Athlete, Baseball Player)
1405 5th St
Las Cruces, NM 88005-1942, USA

Eddings, Floyd (Athlete, Football Player)
988 S Brampton Ave # 5
Rialto, CA 92376-7833, USA

Eddy, Chris (Athlete, Baseball Player)
47 Winterbury Cir
Wilmington, DE 19808-1429, USA

Eddy, Don (Athlete, Baseball Player)
421 1st St N
Rockwell, IA 50469-1002, USA

Eddy, Duane (Musician)
1083 Cedarview Ln
Franklin, TN 37067-4074, USA

Eddy, Nicholas M (Nick) (Athlete, Football Player)
2225 London Cir
Modesto, CA 95356-0731, USA

Eddy, Sonya (Actor)
c/o Staff Member *Marshak/Zachary Company, The*
8840 Wilshire Blvd Fl 1
Beverly Hills, CA 90211-2606, USA

Eddy, Steve (Athlete, Baseball Player)
4491 W Folley Pl
Chandler, AZ 85226-4746, USA

Edelen, Joe (Athlete, Baseball Player)
PO Box 38
Washington, OK 73093-0038, USA

Edelin, Kent (Athlete, Basketball Player)
10950 Clara Barton Dr
Fairfax Station, VA 22039-1431, USA

Edelman, Brad M (Athlete, Football Player)
537 Bienville St
New Orleans, LA 70130-2206, USA

Edelman, John (Athlete, Baseball Player)
125 Fernwood Rd
Cochranville, PA 19330-1116, USA

Edelman, Marian Wright (Business Person)
Children's Defense Fund
25 E St NW
Washington, DC 20001-1591, USA

Edelman, Marian Wright (Politician)
Children's Defense Fund 122 C St NW
Washington, DC 20001, USA

Edelman, Pawel (Cinematographer)
c/o Staff Member *ICM Partners (LA)*
10250 Constellation Blvd Fl 7
Los Angeles, CA 90067-6207, USA

Edelstein, Lisa (Actor)
c/o Cynthia Campos-Greenberg *Anthem Entertainment*
9595 Wilshire Blvd Ste 900
Beverly Hills, CA 90212-2509, USA

Edelstein, Michael (Producer)
c/o Staff Member *Industry Entertainment*
955 Carrillo Dr Ste 300
Los Angeles, CA 90048-5400, USA

Eden, Barbara (Actor)
PO Box 6061-617
Sherman Oaks, CA 91413, USA

Eden, Harry (Actor)
c/o Peter McGrath *Station3 (LA)*
1051 Cole Ave Ste B
Los Angeles, CA 90038-2601, USA

Eden, Mike (Athlete, Baseball Player)
11531 Forest Hills Dr
Tampa, FL 33612-5121, USA

Eden, Richard (Actor)
The Agency
1800 Avenue of the Stars Ste 400
Los Angeles, CA 90067-4206, USA

Eden, Sondi (Echo) (Race Car Driver)
Eden Racing
1962 W Crescent Dr
Crawfordsville, IN 47933-8938, USA

Edenfield, Ken (Athlete, Baseball Player)
4627 Aylesbury Dr
Knoxville, TN 37918-7049, USA

Edens, Tom (Athlete, Baseball Player)
2033 Quailridge Ct
Clarkston, WA 99403-1787, USA

Eder, Linda (Actor)
c/o Staff Member *Agency Group Ltd, The (LA)*
1880 Century Park E Ste 711
Los Angeles, CA 90067-1618, USA

Eder, Richard G (Journalist)
Los Angeles Times
202 W 1st St Ste 500
Editorial Dept
Los Angeles, CA 90012-4401, USA

E. Deutch, Theodore (Congressman, Politician)
1024 Longworth Hob
Washington, DC 20515-1409, USA

Edgar, David
917 NE 16th Ave Apt 13
Fort Lauderdale, FL 33304-4497

Edgar, David (Dave) (Swimmer)
2633 Middle River Dr Apt 3
Fort Lauderdale, FL 33306-1437, USA

Edgar, James (Politician)
1007 W Nevada St Attn
Instituteofgovernment
Urbana, IL 61801-3812, USA

Edgar, Jim (Ex-Governor)
1007 W Nevada St
Mc 037
Urbana, IL 61801-3812, USA

Edgar, Robert W (Religious Leader)
National Council of Churches
475 Riverside Dr # 1880
New York, NY 10115-0002, USA

Edge, Butch (Athlete, Baseball Player)
63553 Gold Spur Way
Bend, OR 97701-9182, USA

Edge, Claude (Butch) Edge (Athlete, Baseball Player)
63553 Gold Spur Way
Bend, OR 97701-9182, USA

Edge, Mitzi (Athlete, Golfer)
118 Kings Chapel Rd
Augusta, GA 30907-4002, USA

Edge, Shayne (Athlete, Football Player)
350 SW Legacy Gin
Lake City, FL 32025, USA

Edgerson, Booker (Athlete, Football Player)
68 Union Cmn
Buffalo, NY 14221-7744, USA

Edgerton, Bill (Athlete, Baseball Player)
9700 Fairway Dr
Foley, AL 36535-9334, USA

Edgley, Gigi (Actor)
Forster - Delaney Management
12533 Woodgreen St
Los Angeles, CA 90066-2723, USA

Edinger, Paul (Athlete, Football Player)
2313 York Pl
Lakeland, FL 33810-4883, USA

Edler, Dave (Athlete, Baseball Player)
1504 S 34th Ave
Yakima, WA 98902-4808, USA

Edler, Lee
1725 K St NW # 1202
Washington, DC 20006-1401

Edlund, Richard P (Cinematographer)
2710 Wilshire Blvd
Santa Monica, CA 90403-4706, USA

Edmonds, James P (Jim) (Athlete, Baseball Player)
25 Boulder Vw
Irvine, CA 92603-0409, USA

Edmonds, Kenneth (Babyface) (Musician, Producer)
c/o Staff Member *Edmonds Management*
1635 N Cahuenga Blvd Fl 5
Los Angeles, CA 90028-6201, USA

Edmonds, Louis
250 W 57th St Ste 2317
New York, NY 10107-2306

Edmonds, Tracey E (Producer)
c/o Staff Member *Edmonds Entertainment*
312 W 5th St Apt 815
Los Angeles, CA 90013-1750, USA

Edmondson, Brian (Athlete, Baseball Player)
304 Ridgeview Trce
Canton, GA 30114-7000, USA

Edmunds, Dave (Musician, Songwriter, Writer)
Entertainment Services
1000 Main St Ste 303
Voorhees, NJ 08043-4633, USA

Edmunds, Ferrell (Athlete, Football Player)
PO Box 414
Blairs, VA 24527-0414, USA

Edmunds, Randall (Athlete, Football Player)
2307 Amity Woodlawn Rd
Lincolnton, GA 30817-1910, USA

Edmunds, Randy (Athlete, Football Player)
2307 Amity Woodlawn Rd
Lincolnton, GA 30817-1910, USA

Edmundson, Gary (Athlete, Hockey Player)
Silvercrest Western Homes Corp
299 N Smith Ave
Corona, CA 92880-1741, USA

Edner, Ashley (Actor)
c/o Nicole Cataldo *Diverse Talent Group*
9911 W Pico Blvd Ste 340W
Los Angeles, CA 90035-2703, USA

Edner, Bobby (Actor)
c/o Kendall Park *JLA Talent Agency*
9151 W Sunset Blvd
West Hollywood, CA 90069-3106, USA

Edney, Tyus (Athlete, Basketball Player)
1800 S Floyd Ct
La Habra, CA 90631-2058, USA

Edson, Hilary (Actor)
400 S Beverly Dr Ste 216
Beverly Hills, CA 90212-4404, USA

Edson, James (Actor)
c/o Staff Member *Synergy Talent*
13251 Ventura Blvd Ste 2
Studio City, CA 91604-1838, USA

Edward, John (Television Host)
c/o Jill Fritzo *PMK/BNC Public Relations (PMK-NY)*
622 3rd Ave Fl 8
New York, NY 10017-6707, USA

Edwards, Al (Athlete, Football Player)
3225 Arkansas Ave
Kenner, LA 70065-3612, USA

Edwards, Anthony (Actor, Producer)
955 Park Ave # 11HAL
New York, NY 10028-0321, USA

Edwards, Antonio (Athlete, Football Player)
717 1st St SW
Moultrie, GA 31768-5401, USA

Edwards, Antuan (Athlete, Football Player)
8108 Connestee Dr
McKinney, TX 75070-4820, USA

Edwards, Barbara (Actor, Model)
Hansen
7767 Hollywood Blvd Apt 202
Los Angeles, CA 90046-2643, USA

Edwards, Bill (Athlete, Basketball Player)
6670 Linzie Ct
Franklin, OH 45005-5373, USA

Edwards, Brad (Athlete, Football Player)
4211 Upper Park Dr
Fairfax, VA 22030-8548, USA

Edwards, Braylon (Athlete, Football Player)
2266 Attard
Birmingham, MI 48009-6814, USA

Edwards, Carl (Race Car Driver)
Roush/Fenway Racing
4600 Roush Pl NW
Concord, NC 28027-7116, USA

Edwards, Cid (Athlete, Football Player)
5343 Adobe Falls Rd
San Diego, CA 92120-4403, USA

Edwards, Danny (Athlete, Golfer)
8361 E Evans Rd Ste 106
Scottsdale, AZ 85260-3617, USA

Edwards, Dave (Athlete, Baseball Player)
7356 Walling Cir
Dallas, TX 75231-7332, USA

Edwards, David (Athlete, Golfer)
5 Champion Pl
Stillwater, OK 74074-1065, USA

Edwards, Dennis (Musician, Opera Singer, Songwriter, Writer)
Green Light Talent Agency
PO Box 3172
Beverly Hills, CA 90212-0172, USA

Edwards, Doc (Athlete, Baseball Player, Coach)
3706 Driftwood Dr
San Angelo, TX 76904-5972, USA

Edwards, Don (Athlete, Hockey Player)
c/o Staff Member *Saginaw Spirit*
PO Box 6157
Saginaw, MI 48608-6157, USA

Edwards, Don (Music Group, Musician, Songwriter, Writer)
Scott O'Malley Assoc
433 S Cuchamas St
Colorado Springs, CO 80903, USA

Edwards, Doug (Athlete, Basketball Player)
1100 Bluff Rd Unit P2
Columbia, SC 29201-5422, USA

Edwards, Dwan (Athlete, Football Player)
c/o Frank Bauer *Sun West Sports*
7883 N Pershing Ave
Stockton, CA 95207-1749, USA

Edwards, Earl (Athlete, Football Player)
1534 W Saint Thomas Dr
Gilbert, AZ 85233-6534, USA

Edwards, Eddie (Athlete, Football Player)
2701 NW 1st St Apt 2
Pompano Beach, FL 33069-2550, USA

Edwards, Edwin (Politician)
2225 Edinburgh Ave
Baton Rouge, LA 70808-3920, USA

Edwards, Eric (Cinematographer)
2865 Highway 139
Monroe, LA 71203-8558, USA

Edwards, Gail
651 N Kilkea Dr
Los Angeles, CA 90048-2213

Edwards, Gareth (Soccer Player)
211 West Rd
Nottage
Porthcawl, MI CF363, WALES

Edwards, Gary (Athlete, Hockey Player)
6818 Pecan Ave
Moorpark, CA 93021-1661, USA

Edwards, Glen (Athlete, Football Player)
4115 31st St S
St Petersburg, FL 33712-4049, USA

Edwards, Herm (Athlete, Football Coach, Football Player)
1627 Highland St
Seaside, CA 93955-4511, USA

Edwards, James (Athlete, Basketball Player)
22750 Civic Center Dr Apt B4
Southfield, MI 48033, USA

Edwards, James B (Ex-Governor, Politician)
100 Venning St
Mount Pleasant, SC 29464-5323, USA

Edwards, Jay (Athlete, Basketball Player)
121 N Washington St Apt 506
Marion, IN 46952-2865, USA

Edwards, Jennifer (Actor)
4123 Saint Clair Ave
Studio City, CA 91604-1608, USA

Edwards, Jesse E (Doctor)
211 2nd St NW Apt 1911
Rochester, MN 55901-3101, USA

Edwards, Joe F Cdr (Astronaut)
24051 Hunters Trail Ln
Aldie, VA 20105-2760, USA

Edwards, Joe F Jr (Astronaut)
Enron Broadband Services
PO Box 1188
Houston, TX 77251-1188, USA

Edwards, Joel (Athlete, Golfer)
280 Benson Ln
Coppell, TX 75019-4548, USA

Edwards, John (Musician)
Buddy Allen Mgmt
3750 Hudson Manor Ter Apt 3AE
Bronx, NY 10463-1167, USA

Edwards, John (Politician)
1201 Old Greensboro Rd
Chapel Hill, NC 27516-5224, USA

Edwards, Johnny (Athlete, Baseball Player)
2511 E Blue Lake Dr
Magnolia, TX 77354-4827, USA

Edwards, Jonathan (Music Group, Songwriter, Writer)
Northern Lights
437 Live Oak Loop NE
Albuquerque, NM 87122-1406, USA

Edwards, Kalimba (Athlete)
c/o Staff Member *Detroit Lions*
222 Republic Dr
Allen Park, MI 48101-3650, USA

Edwards, Kalimba (Athlete, Football Player)
6140 Sibling Pine Dr
Durham, NC 27705-7802, USA

Edwards, Kelvin (Athlete, Football Player)
1716 Brookarbor Ct
Arlington, TX 76018-2420, USA

Edwards, Kevin (Athlete, Basketball Player)
821 Reilly Ln
Lake Forest, IL 60045-4915, USA

Edwards, Luke (Actor)
Ensemble Entertainment
10474 Santa Monica Blvd Ste 380
Los Angeles, CA 90025-6943, USA

Edwards, Marc (Athlete, Football Player)
6426 Autumn Crest Ct
Westerville, OH 43082-8963, USA

Edwards, Mario (Athlete, Football Player)
PO Box 216
Prosper, TX 75078-0216, USA

Edwards, Marshall (Baseball Player)
5059 Quail Run Rd Apt 75
Riverside, CA 92507-6485, USA

Edwards, Marv (Athlete, Hockey Player)
3277 1st Ave Lot 40
Mims, FL 32754-3136, USA

Edwards, Michelle (Athlete, Basketball Player)
1602 Barrons Gate Ave
Woodbridge, NJ 07095-3852, USA

Edwards, Mike (Athlete, Baseball Player)
502 Sharon Ave
Mechanicsburg, PA 17055-6630, USA

Edwards, Mike (Athlete, Baseball Player)
11370 Moreno Beach Dr
Moreno Valley, CA 92555-5240, USA

Edwards, Paul A. (Producer)
c/o Geoffrey Brandt *Course Management*
15159 Greenleaf St
Sherman Oaks, CA 91403-4008, USA

Edwards, Randy (Athlete, Football Player)
1369 Mountain Park Dr NW
Kennesaw, GA 30152-4780, USA

Edwards, R Lavell (Coach, Football Coach, Football Player)
Brighan Young University
2161 N 1400 E
Provo, UT 84604-2104, USA

Edwards, Robert (Athlete, Football Player)
931 Knight Rd
Tennille, GA 31089-4210, USA

Edwards, Stacy (Actor)
Paradigm Agency
10 100 Santa Monica Blvd
#2500
Los Angeles, CA 90067, USA

Edwards, Stephanie (Actor)
c/o Staff Member *Tisherman Gilbert Motley Drozdoski Talent Agency (TGMD)*
6767 Forest Lawn Dr Ste 101
Los Angeles, CA 90068-1027, USA

Edwards, Teresa (Athlete, Basketball Player, Olympic Athlete)
2501 Oak Quarters SE
Smyrna, GA 30080-8292, USA

Edwards, Theodore (Blue) (Athlete, Basketball Player)
10914 Lee Manor Ln
Charlotte, NC 28277-2751, USA

Edwards, Tommy Lee (Cartoonist)
DC Comics
1700 Broadway Fl 6
New York, NY 10019-5905, USA

Edwards, Tonya (Basketball Player)
Phoenix Mercury
201 E Jefferson St
American West Arena
Phoenix, AZ 85004-2412, USA

Edwards, Troy (Athlete, Football Player)
6835 Foghorn Ln
Grand Prairie, TX 75054-7276, USA

Edwards, Wayne (Athlete, Baseball Player)
9738 Aqueduct Ave
North Hills, CA 91343-2035, USA

Edwards, Williams (Monk) (Athlete, Football Player)
3518 Teakwood Dr
Pearland, TX 77584-2530, USA

Edwards III, Dixon (Athlete, Football Player)
8959 Zodiac Dr
Cincinnati, OH 45231-4168, USA

Edwards Jr, Charles C (Publisher)
Des Moines Register & Tribune
715 Locust St
Des Moines, IA 50309-3703, USA

Efron, Zac (Actor)
2173 W Live Oak Dr
Los Angeles, CA 90068-3640, USA

Egan, Christopher (Actor)
c/o Sandra Chang *Anonymous Content (LA)*
3532 Hayden Ave
Culver City, CA 90232-2413, USA

Egan, Dick (Athlete, Baseball Player)
709 Carnoustie Ct
Garland, TX 75044-5054, USA

Egan, Edward M Cardinal (Religious Leader)
Archdiocese of New York
1011 1st Ave Fl 6
New York, NY 10022-4112, USA

Egan, Jennifer (Writer)
Doubleday Press
1540 Broadway
New York, NY 10036-4039, USA

Egan, John (Johnny) (Athlete, Basketball Player)
2124 Nantucket Dr Apt B
Houston, TX 77057-2906, USA

Egan, Richard J (Business Person)
ECM Corp
35 Parkwood Dr
Hopkinton, MA 01748-1659, USA

Egan, Susan (Actor)
13801 Ventura Blvd
Sherman Oaks, CA 91423-3603, USA

Egan, Tom (Athlete, Baseball Player)
184 E Myrna Ln
Tempe, AZ 85284-3118, USA

Egbert, Dave (Television Host)
16009 Digger Pine Rd
Cottonwood, CA 96022-8657, USA

Egdahl, Richard H (Doctor)
505 Tremont St Unit 704
Boston, MA 02116-6353, USA

Egender, Joe (Actor)
c/o Howard Green *Gartner/Green Entertainment*
5225 Wilshire Blvd # 1200
Los Angeles, CA 90036-4301, USA

Eger, David (Athlete, Golfer)
3508 Winslow Green Dr
Charlotte, NC 28210-3488, USA

Egerton, Tamsin (Actor)
c/o Sandra Chang *Anonymous Content (LA)*
3532 Hayden Ave
Culver City, CA 90232-2413, USA

Eggar, Robin (Writer)
c/o Staff Member *Simon & Schuster*
1230 Avenue of the Americas Fl CONC1
New York, NY 10020-1586, USA

Eggar, Samantha (Actor)
5005 Varna Ave
Sherman Oaks, CA 91423-1524, USA

Eggby, David (Cinematographer)
c/o Ann Murtha *Murtha Agency*
1025 Colorado Ave Ste B
Santa Monica, CA 90401-2847, USA

Eggeling, Dale (Athlete, Golfer)
8918 Magnolia Chase Cir
Tampa, FL 33647-2219, USA

Eggers, Dave (Writer)
Simon & Schuster
1230 Avenue of the Americas Fl CONC1
New York, NY 10020-1586, USA

Eggers, Doug (Athlete, Football Player)
12803 Cedarbrook Ln
Laurel, MD 20708-2449, USA

Eggert, Nicole (Actor)
c/o David Weintraub *DWE Talent*
Prefers to be contacted via telephone
CA, USA

Egglesfield, Colin (Actor)
c/o Colton Gramm *Brillstein Entertainment Partners (LA)*
9150 Wilshire Blvd Ste 350
Beverly Hills, CA 90212-3453, USA

Eggleston, Rachel (Actor)
c/o Meredith Fine *Coast to Coast Talent Group*
3350 Barham Blvd
Los Angeles, CA 90068-1404, USA

Eggold, Ryan (Actor)
c/o Andy Corren *Andy Corren Management*
1545 26th St Ste 200
Santa Monica, CA 90404-3554, USA

Egielski, Richard
525 B St Ste 1900
San Diego, CA 92101-4495

Egloff, Bruce (Athlete, Baseball Player)
3136 S Emporia Ct
Denver, CO 80231-4739, USA

Egloff, Ron (Athlete, Football Player)
975 Lincoln St # 5G-NT
Denver, CO 80203-2725, USA

Egnew, Danielle (Musician)
Danielle Egnew Spiritual Advisory
15030 Ventura Blvd Ste 843
Sherman Oaks, CA 91403-5470, USA

Ehle, Jennifer (Actor)
c/o Staff Member *ICM Partners (LA)*
10250 Constellation Blvd Fl 7
Los Angeles, CA 90067-6207, USA

Ehlers, Beth (Actor)
c/o Staff Member *Stone Manners Salners Agency (LA)*
6100 Wilshire Blvd Ste 1500
Los Angeles, CA 90048-5110, USA

Ehlers, Edwin (Athlete, Basketball Player)
PO Box 303
Notre Dame, IN 46556-0303, USA

Ehlers, Tom (Athlete, Football Player)
13898 Layton Rd
Mishawaka, IN 46544-9498, USA

Ehlo, Craig (Athlete, Basketball Player)
3323 E 77th Ave
Spokane, WA 99223-1943, USA

Ehrenreich, Alden (Actor)
c/o JoAnne Colonna *Brillstein Entertainment Partners (LA)*
9150 Wilshire Blvd Ste 350
Beverly Hills, CA 90212-3453, USA

Ehret, Gloria (Athlete, Golfer)
3335 Royal Ln
Dallas, TX 75229-5062, USA

Ehrhoff, Christian (Athlete, Hockey Player)
4517 Carlyle Ct
Santa Clara, CA 95054-3917, USA

Ehrlich, Robert (Politician)
110 State Cir
Annapolis, MD 21401-1924, USA

Ehrman, Bart D (Writer)
The Department of Religious Studies
125 Saunders Hall Cb # 3225
University of North Carolina at Chapel Hill
Chapel Hill, NC 27599-0001, USA

Ehrmann, Joe (Athlete, Football Player)
5 Elmhurst Rd
Baltimore, MD 21210-2216, USA

Eiber, Janet
9300 Wilshire Blvd Ste 410
Beverly Hills, CA 90212-3228

Eichelberger, Dave (Athlete, Golfer)
1947 Judd Hillside Rd
Honolulu, HI 96822-2007, USA

Eichelberger, Juan (Athlete, Baseball Player)
14674 Silverset St
Poway, CA 92064-6408, USA

Eichhorn, Mark (Athlete, Baseball Player)
147 Norma Ct
Aptos, CA 95003-9789, USA

Eichhorst, Richard (Athlete, Basketball Player)
2701 Sheridan Rd
Saint Louis, MO 63125-4168, USA

Eichorn, Lisa
1501 Broadway Ste 2600
New York, NY 10036-5600

Eick, Dick (Producer, Writer)
Dick Eick Productions
100 Universal City Plz Bldg E
Universal City, CA 91608-1002, USA

Eidem, Erik (Actor, Producer)
c/o Scott Zimmerman *Evolution Entertainment (LA)*
901 N Highland Ave
Los Angeles, CA 90038-2412, USA

Eidson, Jim (Athlete, Football Player)
2415 Clark St Apt 420
Dallas, TX 75204-2467, USA

Eifert, Tyler (Athlete, Football Player)
c/o Tom Condon *CAA (St. Louis)*
222 S Central Ave Ste 1008
Saint Louis, MO 63105-3509, USA

Eifrid, Jim (Athlete, Football Player)
2710 Tyler Ave
Fort Wayne, IN 46808-1944, USA

Eigeman, Chris (Actor)
c/o Thomas Cushing *Innovative Artists (LA)*
1505 10th St
Santa Monica, CA 90401-2805, USA

Eigenberg, David (Actor)
c/o Sheree Cohen *Don Buchwald & Associates (LA)*
6500 Wilshire Blvd Ste 2200
Los Angeles, CA 90048-4942, USA

Eigsti, Roger H (Business Person)
SAFECO Corp
Safeco Plaza
Seattle, WA 98185-0001, USA

Eikenberry, Jill (Actor)
c/o Wes Stevens *Vox*
6420 Wilshire Blvd Ste 1080
Los Angeles, CA 90048-5539, USA

Eiland, Dave (Athlete, Baseball Player)
2824 Blue Springs Pl
Wesley Chapel, FL 33544-8746, USA

Eilbacher, Cynthia
PO Box 8920
Universal City, CA 91608

Eilbacher, Lisa (Actor)
4600 Petit Ave
Encino, CA 91436-3216, USA

Eilber, Janet (Actor, Dancer)
Martha Graham Dance Center Of Contemporary Dance
344 E 59th St
New York, NY 10022-1593, USA

Eilers, Dave (Athlete, Baseball Player)
602 Perkins Ln
Brenham, TX 77833-4394, USA

Eilers, Pat (Athlete, Football Player)
177 De Windt Rd
Winnetka, IL 60093-3708, USA

Einertson, Darrell (Athlete, Baseball Player)
111 Loomis Ave
Des Moines, IA 50315-2358, USA

Einziger, Mike (Musician)
c/o Staff Member *ArtistDirect*
9046 Lindblade St
Culver City, CA 90232-2513, USA

Eischeid, Mike (Athlete, Football Player)
306 Auburn St
West Union, IA 52175-1067, USA

Eischen, Joey (Athlete, Baseball Player)
10408 Bryant Rd
Lithia, FL 33547-2510, USA

Eischen, Joey (Athlete, Baseball Player)
Asheville Tourists
30 Buchanan Pl
Asheville, NC 28801-4243, USA

Eisen, Erez (Musician)
4373 Irvine Ave
Studio City, CA 91604-2705, USA

Eisen, Herman N (Doctor)
9 Homestead St
Waban, MA 02468-2008, USA

Eisen, Thelma (Athlete, Baseball Player, Commentator)
PO Box 1314
Moriarty, NM 87035-1314, USA

Eisen, Tripp (Music Group)
Andy Gould Mgmt
9100 Wilshire Blvd Ste 400W
Beverly Hills, CA 90212-3464, USA

Eisenberg, Jesse (Actor)
c/o Jennifer Allen *Viewpoint Inc (LA)*
8820 Wilshire Blvd Ste 220
Beverly Hills, CA 90211-2622, USA

Eisenberg, Warren (Business Person)
Bed Bath & Beyond
650 Liberty Ave
Union, NJ 07083-8107, USA

Eisenhauer, Lawrence (Larry) (Athlete, Football Player)
Pro Action
2 Winter St Ste 402B
Waltham, MA 02451-0961, USA

Eisenhauer, Stephen S (Steve) (Athlete, Football Player)
105 Abbey Rd
Winchester, VA 22602-7402, USA

Eisenhooth, John (Athlete, Football Player)
25602 Conde Ln
Watertown, NY 13601-5737, USA

Eisenhower, David (Politician)
255 Foxall Ln
Berwyn, PA 19312-1843, USA

Eisenhower, Julie Nixon
Foxall Lane
Berwyn, PA 19312

Eisenhower, Susan
1050 17th St NW Ste 600
Washington, DC 20036-5517

Eisenreich, Jim (Athlete, Baseball Player)
8320 Kessler St
Overland Park, KS 66212-3568, USA

Eisenstein, Michael (Music Group)
Little Big Man
155 Avenue of the Americas Rm 700
New York, NY 10013-1507, USA

Eisley, Howard (Athlete, Basketball Player)
20250 Rodeo Ct
Southfield, MI 48075-1285, USA

Eisley, India (Actor)
c/o Todd Justice *Justice & Ponder*
PO Box 480033
Los Angeles, CA 90048-1033, USA

Eisman, Hy (Cartoonist)
99 Boulevard
Glen Rock, NJ 07452-2003, USA

Eisner, Breck (Director)
c/o Gregory McKnight *Creative Artists Agency (CAA-LA)*
2000 Avenue of the Stars Ste 100
Los Angeles, CA 90067-4705, USA

Eisner, Michael (Business Person)
Vuguru
315 S Beverly Dr Ste 315
Beverly Hills, CA 90212-4309, USA

E. Issa, Darrell (Congressman, Politician)
2347 Rayburn Hob
Washington, DC 20515-0915, USA

Eitzel, Mark (Music Group, Songwriter, Writer)
Legends of 21st Century
7 Trinity Row
Florence, MA 01062-1931, USA

Ejogo, Carmen (Actor)
c/o Erica Tarin *ID Public Relations (LA)*
7060 Hollywood Blvd Fl 8th
Los Angeles, CA 90028-6021, USA

Ejogo, Carmen (Actor)
c/o Ilene Feldman *LBI Entertainment*
2000 Avenue of the Stars
Floor 3, North Tower
Los Angeles, CA 90067-4700, USA

Ek, Daniel
Spotify
45 W 18th St Fl 7
New York, NY 10011-4655, USA

Eker, T Harv (Business Person)
True Power International Limited
300 N Commercial St
Bellingham, WA 98225-4002

E. Kildee, Dale (Congressman, Politician)
2107 Rayburn Hob
Washington, DC 20515-2205, USA

Ekland, Britt (Actor)
1888 N Crescent Heights Blvd
Los Angeles, CA 90069-1647, USA

Eklund, Brian
66 Blossom Rd
Braintree, MA 02184-3806, USA

Eklund, Greg (Music Group)
Pinnacle Entertainment
30 Glenn St
White Plains, NY 10603-3254, USA

Eklund, Pelle (Athlete, Hockey Player)
c/o Staff Member *San Jose Sharks*
525 W Santa Clara St
San Jose, CA 95113-1500, USA

Ekstran, Garner (Athlete, Football Player)
10867 Samish Beach Ln
Bow, WA 98232-9405

Ekstrom, Mike (Athlete, Baseball Player)
10065 SE Bristol Loop
Happy Valley, OR 97086-3239, USA

Ekuban, Ebenezer (Athlete, Football Player)
5391 Moonlight Way
Parker, CO 80134-4535, USA

El, Antwaan Randle (Athlete, Football Player)
c/o Fletcher Smith *Blueprint Sports Group*
221 W Jefferson Ave Ste 1
Naperville, IL 60540-4546, USA

Elam, Jason (Athlete, Football Player)
PO Box 1425
Soldotna, AK 99669-1425, USA

Elarton, Scott (Athlete, Baseball Player)
13501 County Road 33
Karval, CO 80823-9305, USA

E. Latta, Robert (Congressman, Politician)
1323 Longworth Hob
Washington, DC 20515-4704, USA

Elba, Idris (Actor)
c/o Oronde Garrett *Headshell Management*
1212 Avenue of the Americas Fl 3
New York, NY 10036-1602, USA

El Bambino, Tito (Musician)
c/o Staff Member *EMI Music Publishing (Latin America)*
1688 Meridian Ave Ste 900
Miami Beach, FL 33139-2712, USA

Eldard, Ron (Actor)
c/o William Choi *Management 360*
9111 Wilshire Blvd
Beverly Hills, CA 90210-5508, USA

Elder, Christian (Race Car Driver)
Atkins Motorsports
222 Raceway Dr
Mooresville, NC 28117-6510, USA

Elder, Dave (Athlete, Baseball Player)
2642 High St SW
Conyers, GA 30094-6843, USA

Elder, George (Athlete, Baseball Player)
423 Amethyst Dr
Fruita, CO 81521-8813, USA

Elder, Larry (Actor)
c/o Ari Emanuel *William Morris Endeavor (LA)*
9601 Wilshire Blvd
Beverly Hills, CA 90210-5213, USA

Elder, Lee E (Athlete, Golfer)
PO Box 667200
Pompano Beach, FL 33066-7200, USA

Elder, Ray (Race Car Driver)
15252 S Cherry Ave
Caruthers, CA 93609-9754, USA

Elders, M Jocelyn (Doctor, Government Official)
University of Arkansas Medical School
Pediatrics Dept
Little Rock, AR 72205, USA

Eldred, Brad (Athlete, Baseball Player)
4182 SW Saint Lucie Ln
Palm City, FL 34990-3830, USA

Eldred, Cal (Athlete, Baseball Player)
1893 Horn Rd
Mount Vernon, IA 52314-9517, USA

Eldredge, Allison (Music Group)
C M Artists
40 W 25th St
New York, NY 10010-2707, USA

Eldredge, Todd (Athlete, Olympic Athlete, Speed Skater)
991 Crystal Falls Dr
Prosper, TX 75078-9209, USA

Electra, Carmen (Actor, Model)
c/o Jack Ketsoyan *EMC / Bowery*
5971 W 3rd St
Los Angeles, CA 90036-2832, USA

Electrik Red (Music Group, Musician)
c/o Staff Member *Island Def Jam Group*
825 8th Ave Fl 28
New York, NY 10019-7416, USA

El Fadil, Siddig (Actor)
Paramount
5555 Melrose Ave
Los Angeles, CA 90038-3197, USA

Elfman, Bodhi (Actor)
c/o Staff Member *Stone Manners Salners Agency (LA)*
6100 Wilshire Blvd Ste 1500
Los Angeles, CA 90048-5110, USA

Elfman, Danny (Musician)
Musica de la Muerte
1901 Avenue of the Stars Ste 1450
Los Angeles, CA 90067-6087, USA

Elfman, Jenna (Actor, Model, Producer)
c/o David McIlvain *Brillstein Entertainment Partners (LA)*
9150 Wilshire Blvd Ste 350
Beverly Hills, CA 90212-3453, USA

Elfont, Harry (Director, Writer)
c/o Staff Member *William Morris Endeavor (LA)*
9601 Wilshire Blvd
Beverly Hills, CA 90210-5213, USA

Elgaard, Ray (Athlete, Football Player)
9529 Cloudcroft Ave
Las Vegas, NV 89134-6231, United States

Elgart, Larry
2065 Gulf of Mexico Dr
Longboat Key, FL 34228-3202

Elgart, Larry J (Music Group)
2065 Gulf of Mexico Dr
Longboat Key, FL 34228-3202, USA

Elgort, Ansel (Actor)
c/o Emily Gerson Saines *Brookside Artists Management (NY)*
250 W 57th St Ste 2303
New York, NY 10107-2399, USA

Elia, Bruce (Athlete, Football Player)
7 Grant Ave
Grant, MI 49327, USA

Elia, Lee (Athlete, Baseball Player)
11613 Innfields Dr
Odessa, FL 33556-5407, USA

Elias, Eliane (Musician)
c/o Anders-Chan Tidemann *Word of Mouth Music*
235 E 22nd St Apt 9F
New York, NY 10010-4636, USA

Elias, Keith (Athlete, Football Player)
4507 Norma Pl
Toms River, NJ 08755-1097, USA

Elias, Patrik (Athlete, Hockey Player)
1005 Smith Manor Blvd
West Orange, NJ 07052-4227, USA

Elich, Matt (Athlete, Hockey Player)
276 McKinley Ave
Grosse Pointe Farms, MI 48236-3460, USA

Elie, Mario (Athlete, Basketball Player)
1 Mott Ln
Houston, TX 77024-7315, USA

Eliff, Tom (Religious Leader)
Southern Baptist Convention
901 Commerce St Ste 750
Nashville, TN 37203-3600, USA

Eliopulos, Jim (Athlete, Football Player)
2500 Macero St
Roseville, CA 95747-5000, USA

Eliot, Alison
2 Ironsides # 18
Marina Del Rey, CA 90292

Eliot, Darren (Athlete, Hockey Player)
1100 Grayton St
Grosse Pointe Park, MI 48230-1427, USA

Eliot, Jan (Cartoonist)
PO Box 50032
Eugene, OR 97405-0967, USA

Elise, Christine (Actor, Writer)
c/o Mara Santino *Luber Roklin Management*
5815 W Sunset Blvd Ste 206
Los Angeles, CA 90028-6481, USA

Elise, Kimberly (Actor)
c/o Evan Hainey *Untitled Entertainment (LA)*
350 S Beverly Dr Ste 200
Beverly Hills, CA 90212-4819, USA

Elisha, Walter Y (Business Person)
Springs Industries
205 N White St
Fort Mill, SC 29715-1654, USA

Eli Young Band (Music Group)
c/o George Couri *Triple 8 Management*
5524 W Highway 290 Ste 101
Austin, TX 78735-8837, USA

Elizabeth, Princess
1526 N Beverly Dr
Beverly Hills, CA 90210-2314

Elizabeth, Shannon (Actor, Producer)
c/o Staff Member *Ganesh Productions*
7336 Santa Monica Blvd Ste 690
West Hollywood, CA 90046-6616, USA

Elizondo, Hector (Actor)
c/o Mark Teitelbaum *Teitelbaum Artists Group*
8840 Wilshire Blvd Fl 3
Beverly Hills, CA 90211-2606, USA

Elk, Jim (Actor)
Dade/Schultz
6442 Coldwater Canyon Ave Ste 206
North Hollywood, CA 91606-1174, USA

Elkington, Steve (Athlete, Golfer)
7010 Kelsey Rae Ct
Houston, TX 77069-1102, USA

Elkins, Corey (Athlete, Hockey Player)
2668 Silverside Rd
Waterford, MI 48328-1762, USA

Elkins, Larry (Athlete, Football Player)
4407 McArthur Cir
Brownwood, TX 76801-7334, USA

Elkins, Larry
111 S Saint Joseph St
South Bend, IN 46601-1901

Elkins, Mike (Athlete, Football Player)
743 Drifting Wind Run
Dripping Springs, TX 78620-4487, USA

Ellard, Henry A (Athlete, Football Player)
5800 Airline Dr
Metairie, LA 70003-3876, USA

Ellenbogen, Bill (Athlete, Football Player)
777 Pelham Rd Apt 2G
New Rochelle, NY 10805-1137, USA

Ellenstein, Robert (Actor)
5212 Sepulveda Blvd # 23F
Culver City, CA 90230-5214, USA

Eller, Carl (Athlete, Football Player)
1035 Washburn Ave N
Minneapolis, MN 55411-3557, USA

Ellerbe, Dannell (Athlete, Football Player)
c/o Hadley Engelhard *Enter-Sports Management*
5 Concourse Pkwy Ste 3000
Atlanta, GA 30328-7106, USA

Ellerbee, Linda (Journalist)
LRB Services Inc
96 Morton St Fl 4
C/O Lori Seidner
New York, NY 10014-3326, USA

Ellerson, Gary (Athlete, Football Player)
S86W18643 Sue Marie Ln
Muskego, WI 53150-8718, USA

Ellett, Dave (Athlete, Hockey Player)
36611 N 51st St
Cave Creek, AZ 85331-8820, USA

Elliman, Donald M Jr (Publisher)
Sports Illustrated Magazine
Rockefeller Center
New York, NY 10020, USA

Ellin, Doug (Actor, Director, Producer, Writer)
c/o Stephen (Steve) Levinson *Leverage Management*
3030 Pennsylvania Ave
Santa Monica, CA 90404-4112, USA

Elling, Kurt (Music Group, Musician)
c/o Ted Kurland *Ted Kurland Associates*
173 Brighton Ave
Allston, MA 02134-2003, USA

Ellingsen, Bruce (Athlete, Baseball Player)
25041 De Salle St
Laguna Hills, CA 92653-5042, USA

Ellingson, Evan (Actor)
c/o Staff Member *Reel Talent Management*
PO Box 491035
Los Angeles, CA 90049-9035, USA

Elliot, Ernie (Race Car Driver)
PO Box 476
Dawsonville, GA 30534-0009, USA

Elliot, Larry (Athlete, Baseball Player)
13010 Caminito Bracho
San Diego, CA 92128-1808, USA

Elliot, Lin (Athlete, Football Player)
42 Independence Trl
Waco, TX 76708-9603, USA

Elliot, Ross
5702 Graves Ave
Encino, CA 91316-1441

Elliot, Tony (Athlete, Football Player)
45907 Riverwoods Dr
Macomb, MI 48044-5788, USA

Elliott, Abby (Actor, Comedian)
c/o Diane McGunigle *The Schiff Company*
9220 W Sunset Blvd Ste 106
West Hollywood, CA 90069-3500, USA

Elliott, Alecia (Actor, Music Group)
PO Box 3075
Muscle Shoals, AL 35662-3075, USA

Elliott, Alison (Actor)
2 Ironsides # 18
Marina Del Rey, CA 90292, USA

Elliott, Allison
1505 10th St
Santa Monica, CA 90401-2805

Elliott, Bill (Race Car Driver)
Bill Elliott Racing
200 Woodhaven Ln
Ball Ground, GA 30107-3109, USA

Elliott, Brennan (Actor)
c/o Christopher Wright *Christopher Wright Management*
3207 Winnie Dr
Los Angeles, CA 90068-1439, USA

Elliott, Brook (Actor)
c/o Nancy Curtis *Harden-Curtis Associates*
214 W 29th St Rm 1203
New York, NY 10001-5754, USA

Elliott, Brooke (Actor)
c/o Jonathan Howard *Innovative Artists (LA)*
1505 10th St
Santa Monica, CA 90401-2805, USA

Elliott, Chalmers (Bump) (Coach, Football Coach, Football Player)
University of Iowa
Athletic Dept
Iowa City, IA 52242, USA

Elliott, Chris (Actor, Comedian)
c/o Ben Feigin *Anonymous Content (LA)*
3532 Hayden Ave
Culver City, CA 90232-2413, USA

Elliott, David James (Actor)
c/o Bob McGowan *McGowan Management*
8733 W Sunset Blvd Ste 103
West Hollywood, CA 90069-2241, USA

Elliott, Dennis (Music Group)
Hard to Handle Mgmt
16501 Ventura Blvd Ste 602
Encino, CA 91436-2072, USA

Elliott, DJ (Actor)
c/o Evan Silverberg *Silverberg Management Group (SMG)*
3030 Nebraska Ave Ste 201
Santa Monica, CA 90404-4140, USA

Elliott, Donnie (Athlete, Baseball Player)
1206 Bayou Vista Dr
Deer Park, TX 77536-6902, USA

Elliott, Gordon (Chef, Producer)
c/o Staff Member *Follow Productions*
125 W End Ave # 7
New York, NY 10023-6387, USA

Elliott, Harry (Athlete, Baseball Player)
9608 Los Coches Rd
Lakeside, CA 92040-4240, USA

Elliott, John (Athlete, Golfer)
235 Lexington Rd
Glastonbury, CT 06033-1289, USA

Elliott, John (Jumbo) (Athlete, Football Player)
17 Fieldstone Ln
Oyster Bay, NY 11771-3122, USA

Elliott, Matt (Athlete, Football Player)
42 Independence Trl
Waco, TX 76708-9603, USA

Elliott, Missy (Actor, Musician, Producer)
8 S Glen Rd
Kinnelon, NJ 07405-2700, USA

Elliott, Paul H (Cinematographer)
Sandra Marsh Mgmt
6420 Wilshire Blvd Ste 880
Los Angeles, CA 90048-5538, USA

Elliott, Randy (Athlete, Baseball Player)
1002 Steuben St
Wausau, WI 54403-5157, USA

Elliott, R Keith (Business Person)
Hercules Inc
Hercules Plaza 1313 N Market St
Wilmington, DE 19894-0001, USA

Elliott, Robert (Athlete, Basketball Player)
6760 E Fieldstone Ln
Tucson, AZ 85750-2075, USA

Elliott, Sam (Actor)
c/o Iris Grossman *Paradigm (LA)*
10250 Constellation Blvd Fl 7
Los Angeles, CA 90067-6207, USA

Elliott, Sean (Athlete, Basketball Player)
1726 Greystone Rdg
San Antonio, TX 78258-4506, USA

Elliott, Stephen (Writer)
The Rumpus
490 2nd St Ste 200
San Francisco, CA 94107-1419, USA

Elliott, Steve (Horse Racer)
1070 Club House Blvd
New Smyrna, FL 32168-7964, USA

Elliott, Ted (Writer)
c/o Brian Siberell *Creative Artists Agency (CAA-LA)*
2000 Avenue of the Stars Ste 100
Los Angeles, CA 90067-4705, USA

Ellis, A J (Athlete, Baseball Player)
3252 Mannington Ct
Lexington, KY 40503-1330, USA

Ellis, Alex (Athlete, Basketball Player)
914 S Front St
Hamilton, OH 45011-3016, USA

Ellis, Allan (Athlete, Football Player)
7352 S Dante Ave
Chicago, IL 60619-2117, USA

Ellis, Anita
130 E End Ave
New York, NY 10028-7553

Ellis, Aunjanue (Actor)
c/o Howard Axel *TMT Entertainment Group*
648 Broadway # 1002
New York, NY 10012-2348, USA

Ellis, Bo (Athlete, Basketball Player)
516 N 14th St
Milwaukee, WI 53233, USA

Ellis, Bret Easton (Writer)
International Creative Mgmt
40 W 57th St Fl 5
New York, NY 10019-4001, USA

Ellis, Caroline (Actor)
8060 Saint Clair Ave
North Hollywood, CA 91605-1321, USA

Ellis, Chris (Athlete, Football Player)
c/o Adam Heller *Vantage Management Group*
518 Reamer Dr
Carnegie, PA 15106-1845, USA

Ellis, Cliff (Basketball Player, Coach)
Auburn University
Athletic Dept
Auburn, AL 36831, USA

Ellis, Dale (Athlete, Basketball Player)
3564 W Hampton Dr NW
Marietta, GA 30064-1775, USA

Ellis, Dan (Athlete, Hockey Player)
1490 Overlook Dr
Frisco, TX 75033-8342, USA

Ellis, Danny (Athlete, Golfer)
1543 Cherry Lake Way
Lake Mary, FL 32746-1906, USA

Ellis, Don (Bowler)
34 Crestwood Cir
Sugar Land, TX 77478-3914, USA

Ellis, Gerry (Athlete, Football Player)
250 Cavil Way
De Pere, WI 54115-3772, USA

Ellis, Gregory (Athlete, Football Player)
PO Box 96075
Southlake, TX 76092-0111, USA

Ellis, Harold (Athlete, Basketball Player)
9420 Parkwood Ave
Douglasville, GA 30135-7504, USA

Ellis, Hunter (Actor, Reality Star)
c/o Lauren Feeney *Ideal Management*
172 81st St
Brooklyn, NY 11209-3502, United States

Ellis, Jim (Athlete, Baseball Player)
13608 Avenue 224
Tulare, CA 93274-9304, USA

Ellis, Joe (Athlete, Basketball Player)
Perfect Shot Skills
PO Box 8055
San Mateo, CA 94404-8055, USA

Ellis, John (Athlete, Baseball Player)
Connecticut Sports Foundation
455 Boston Post Rd Ste 203B
Old Saybrook, CT 06475-1554, USA

Ellis, Joseph J (Writer)
Mount Holyoke College
History Dept
South Hadley, MA 01075, USA

Ellis, Kathleen (Kathy) (Swimmer)
3024 Woodshore Ct
Carmel, IN 46033-3643, USA

Ellis, Kenneth (Athlete, Football Player)
13826 Brantley Dr
Baker, LA 70714-4634, USA

Ellis, LaPhonso (Athlete, Basketball Player)
51215 Shannon Brook Ct
Granger, IN 46530-7905, USA

Ellis, Luther (Athlete, Football Player)
527 Riverside Ave
Mancos, CO 81328, USA

Ellis, Mark (Athlete, Baseball Player)
19301 N 100th Way
Scottsdale, AZ 85255-2606, USA

Ellis, Mary Elizabeth (Actor)
2175 W Live Oak Dr
Los Angeles, CA 90068-3640, USA

Ellis, Maurice (Bo) (Athlete, Basketball Player)
1229 E 158th St
South Holland, IL 60473-1804, USA

Ellis, Michelle (Athlete, Golfer)
30842 Temple Stand Ave
Wesley Chapel, FL 33543-7105, USA

Ellis, Nelsan (Actor)
c/o Emily Gerson Saines *Brookside Artists Management (NY)*
250 W 57th St Ste 2303
New York, NY 10107-2399, USA

Ellis, Ray (Athlete, Football Player)
4666 E Olney Ave
Gilbert, AZ 85234-7836, USA

Ellis, Rob (Athlete, Baseball Player)
2020 Krislin Dr NE
Grand Rapids, MI 49505-7160, USA

Ellis, Robert (Athlete, Baseball Player)
2066 75th Ave
Baton Rouge, LA 70807-5836, USA

Ellis, Romallis (Athlete, Boxer, Olympic Athlete)
2062 San Marco Dr
Ellenwood, GA 30294-1009, USA

Ellis, Sammy (Athlete, Baseball Player)
12511 Forest Highlands Dr
Dade City, FL 33525-8273, USA

Ellis, Samuel J (Sam) (Baseball Player)
12511 Forest Highlands Dr
Dade City, FL 33525-8273, USA

Ellis, Scott (Director)
420 Central Park W Apt 5B
New York, NY 10025-4315, USA

Ellis, Sedrick (Athlete, Football Player)
c/o Eugene Parker *Maximum Sports Management*
6435 W Jefferson Blvd # 197
Fort Wayne, IN 46804-6203, USA

Ellis, Shuan (Athlete, Football Player)
1000 Fulton Ave
Hempstead, NY 11550-1030, USA

Ellis, Terry (Music Group)
East West Records
75 Rockefeller Plz # 1200
New York, NY 10019-6908, USA

Ellis Brothers (Music Group, Musician)
PO Box 50221
Nashville, TN 37205-0221, USA

Ellis Jr, Clarence J (Athlete, Football Player)
120 Hights Holw
Fayetteville, GA 30215-5139, USA

Ellison, Chase (Actor)
c/o Staff Member *Artistry Management*
340 N Camden Dr Ste 302
Beverly Hills, CA 90210-5116, USA

Ellison, David (Actor)
c/o Eddie Michaels *Insignia Public Relations*
1507 20th St Ste B
Santa Monica, CA 90404-3474, USA

Ellison, Harlan
PO Box 55548
Sherman Oaks, CA 91413-0548

Ellison, Harlan j (Writer)
Kilimajaro Group
PO Box 55548
Sherman Oaks, CA 91413-0548, USA

Ellison, Jason (Athlete, Baseball Player)
3745 248th Ave SE
Issaquah, WA 98029-7717, USA

Ellison, Keith (Congressman, Politician)
1027 Longworth Hob
Washington, DC 20515-2101, USA

Ellison, Larry (Business Person)
Oracle Systems
500 Oracle Pkwy
Redwood City, CA 94065-1677, USA

Ellison, Lawrence J (Business Person)
Oracle Systems
500 Oracle Pkwy
Redwood City, CA 94065-1677, USA

Ellison, Megan (Producer)
1 Electra Ct
Los Angeles, CA 90046-2061, USA

Ellison, Pervis (Athlete, Basketball Player)
4602 Kettering Dr NE
Roswell, GA 30075-3190, USA

Ellison, Rhett (Athlete, Football Player)
c/o Tony Paige *Perennial Sports and Entertainment*
1455 Pennsylvania Ave NW Ste 225
Washington, DC 20004-1026, USA

Ellison, Riki (Athlete, Football Player)
434 N Saint Asaph St
Alexandria, VA 22314-2318, USA

Ellison, William H (Willie) (Athlete, Football Player)
3503 Mosley Ct
Houston, TX 77004-4114, USA

Elliss, Luther (Athlete, Football Player)
3760 E Evelyn Dr
Salt Lake City, UT 84124-2306, USA

Ellroy, James (Writer)
Sobel Weber Assoc
146 E 19th St
New York, NY 10003-2404, USA

Ellsberg, Daniel (Politician)
90 Norwood Ave
Kensington, CA 94707-1150, USA

Ellsbury, Jacoby (Athlete, Baseball Player)
c/o Scott Boras *Boras Corporation*
3 San Joaquin Plz Ste 100
Newport Beach, CA 92660-5944, USA

Ellsworth, Kiko (Actor)
c/o Staff Member *Psycho Rock Productions*
PO Box 55305
Sherman Oaks, CA 91413-0305, USA

Ellsworth, Percy (Athlete, Football Player)
11261 Fortsville Rd
Drewryville, VA 23844, USA

Ellsworth, Steve (Athlete, Baseball Player)
546 W Enterprise Ave
Clovis, CA 93619-8356, USA

Ellzey, Charley (Athlete, Football Player)
116 Roosevelt St
Quitman, MS 39355-2018, USA

Elman, Jamie (Actor)
c/o Staff Member *Kohner Agency, The*
9300 Wilshire Blvd Ste 555
Beverly Hills, CA 90212-3211, USA

Elmendorf, Dave (Athlete, Football Player)
17990 FM 1452 W
Normangee, TX 77871-4174, USA

Elmore, Henry (Athlete, Baseball Player)
4311 43rd Pl N
Birmingham, AL 35217-3925, USA

Elmore, Len (Athlete, Basketball Player)
PO Box 22
Highland, MD 20777-0022, USA

Eloani, Sandra (Actor)
c/o Marco Rea *Heretic Entertainment*
7711 Santa Monica Blvd
West Hollywood, CA 90046-6207, USA

Elrod, Jack (Cartoonist)
770 Old Loganville Rd
Loganville, GA 30052-2578, USA

Elrod, James (Athlete, Football Player)
10124 S Maplewood Ave
Tulsa, OK 74137-7085, USA

Elrod, Scott (Actor)
c/o Steven Jensen *Vincent Cirrincione Associates*
8332 Melrose Ave
West Hollywood, CA 90069-5420, USA

Elshire, Neil (Athlete, Football Player)
2441 NW Torsway St
Bend, OR 97701-8647, USA

Elsner, Hannelore (Actor)
ZBF Leopoldstr. 19
Munich, GE D-808

Elson, Francisco (Athlete, Basketball Player)
92 Foxton Dr
San Antonio, TX 78260, USA

Elster, Kevin (Athlete, Baseball Player)
5801 Marshall Dr
Huntington Beach, CA 92649-2727, USA

Elston, Darrell (Athlete, Basketball Player)
2596 W State Road 28
Tipton, IN 46072-9787, USA

Elston, Gene (Commentator)
6304 Deerwood Rd
Houston, TX 77057-1072, USA

Elswrit, Richard (Rik) (Music Group)
Artists Int'l Mgmt
9850 Sandalwood Blvd # 458
Boca Raton, FL 33428, USA

E. Lungren, Daniel (Congressman, Politician)
2313 Rayburn Hob
Washington, DC 20515-1401, USA

Elvira (Actor, Television Host)
Queen B Productions
16830 Ventura Blvd Ste 501
Encino, CA 91436-1717, USA

Elway, John A (Athlete, Football Player)
Elway's
4763 S Elizabeth Ct
Englewood, CO 80113-7105, USA

Elwes, Cary (Actor)
c/o Ben Levine *LINK Entertainment*
11872 La Grange Ave
Los Angeles, CA 90025-5282, USA

Ely, Alexandre (Soccer Player)
5526 N 2nd St
Philadelphia, PA 19120-2904, USA

Ely, Jack (Music Group)
Jeff Hubbard Productions
PO Box 53664
Indianapolis, IN 46253-0664, USA

Ely, Joe (Musician, Songwriter)
8949 Appaloosa Run
Austin, TX 78737-4016, USA

Ely, Larry (Athlete, Football Player)
12190 Waters Edge Ct
Loveland, OH 45140-4828, USA

Ely, Melvin (Basketball Player)
Los Angeles Clippers
Staples Center 1111 S Figueroa St
Los Angeles, CA 90015, USA

Emanuel, Bert (Athlete, Football Player)
15 Bees Creek Ct
Missouri City, TX 77459-6734, USA

Emanuel, Frank (Athlete, Football Player)
10211 Deercliff Dr
Tampa, FL 33647-2941, USA

Emberg, Kelly (Actor, Model)
PO Box 675401
Rancho Santa Fe, CA 92067-5401, USA

Embery, Joan
. San Diego Zoo
San Diego, CA 92104

Emblem3 (Music Group)
18685 Main St Ste 101
Huntington Beach, CA 92648-1719, USA

Embrace (Music Group)
c/o Staff Member *Paradigm (Monterey)*
404 W Franklin St
Monterey, CA 93940-2303, USA

Embree, Alan (Athlete, Baseball Player)
238 NW Outlook Vista Dr
Bend, OR 97701-5473, USA

Embree, Jon (Athlete, Football Player)
9450 Owl Ln
Boulder, CO 80301-5503, USA

Embry, Ethan (Actor)
c/o Brad Schenck *Paradigm (LA)*
360 N Crescent Dr
North Bldg
Beverly Hills, CA 90210-4874, USA

Emerson, Chris (Actor)
c/o Lorraine Berglund *Lorraine Berglund Management*
11537 Hesby St
North Hollywood, CA 91601-3618, USA

Emerson, Douglas (Actor)
1450 Belfast Dr
Los Angeles, CA 90069-1327, USA

Emerson, Jo Ann (Congressman, Politician)
2230 Rayburn Hob
Washington, DC 20515-1404, USA

Emerson, Keith (Musician)
c/o Staff Member *Carlini Group*
445 Park Ave Fl 9
New York, NY 10022-8606, USA

Emerson, Michael (Actor)
c/o Staff Member *Vanguard Management Group*
8060 Melrose Ave Fl 4
Los Angeles, CA 90046-7038, USA

Emerson, Nelson (Athlete, Hockey Player)
717 33rd St
Manhattan Beach, CA 90266-3425, USA

Emerson, Roy (Athlete, Tennis Player)
2221 Alta Vista Dr
Newport Beach, CA 92660-4128, USA

Emerson Drive (Music Group)
c/o Staff Member *Creative Artists Agency (CAA-TN)*
401 Commerce St PH
Nashville, TN 37219-2516, USA

Emery, Brent (Athlete, Cycler, Olympic Athlete)
N62W15 Teepee Court
Menomonee Falls, WI 53051

Emery, Gareth (DJ, Musician)
c/o David Lewis *Don Buchwald & Associates (NY)*
10 E 44th St Frnt 1
New York, NY 10017-3654, USA

Emery, John (Athlete)
2001 Union St
San Francisco, CA 94123-4114, USA

Emery, Julie Ann (Actor)
c/o Stacey Bock-McLaughlin *Principal Entertainment (LA)*
9255 W Sunset Blvd Ste 500
West Hollywood, CA 90069-3301, USA

Emery, Oren D (Religious Leader)
Wesleyan International
6060 Castleway West Dr
Indianapolis, IN 46250-1906, USA

Emery, Ralph (DJ)
PO Box 23470
Nashville, TN 37202-3470, USA

Emick, Jarrod (Actor)
Gersh Agency
232 N Canon Dr
Beverly Hills, CA 90210-5302, USA

Emilio (Music Group)
Refugee Mgmt
209 10th Ave South Cummins Sta # 347
Nashville, TN 37203, USA

Emir of Bahrain
721 5th Ave Fl 60
New York, NY 10022-2523

Emma, David (Athlete, Hockey Player, Olympic Athlete)
193 Eugenia Dr
Naples, FL 34108-2929, USA

Emmanuel (Musician)
Sendyk Leonard
532 Colorado Ave
Santa Monica, CA 90401-2408, USA

Emmanuel, Tommy (Musician)
2153 Grand St
Nolensville, TN 37135-5003, USA

Emmanuel, Tommy (Musician)
c/o Staff Member *Paradigm (Monterey)*
404 W Franklin St
Monterey, CA 93940-2303, USA

Emme (Model)
c/o Daniel Strone *Trident Media Group LLC*
41 Madison Ave Fl 36
New York, NY 10010-2257, USA

Emmel, Paul (Athlete, Baseball Player)
2989 N Lakeview Dr
Sanford, MI 48657-9105, USA

Emmerich, Noah (Actor, Producer)
c/o Jason Gutman *Gersh (NY)*
41 Madison Ave
New York, NY 10010-2202, USA

Emmerich, Roland (Director, Producer)
c/o Staff Member *Centropolis Entertainment*
1445 N Stanley Ave Fl 3
Los Angeles, CA 90046-4015, USA

Emmerson, Michael (Actor)
c/o Staff Member *Vanguard Management Group*
8060 Melrose Ave Fl 4
Los Angeles, CA 90046-7038, USA

Emmerton, Bill (Athlete, Track Athlete)
615 Ocean Ave
Santa Monica, CA 90402-2611, USA

Emmons, John (Athlete, Hockey Player)
67589 Rachael Ln
Washington, MI 48095-1844, USA

Emory, Sonny (Musician)
Great Scott Productions
137 N Wetherly Dr Apt 403
Los Angeles, CA 90048-2866, USA

Emotions (Music Group)
c/o Staff Member *Diva Central Inc*
7510 W Sunset Blvd Ste 1445
Los Angeles, CA 90046-3408, USA

Emrick, Mike ""Doc"" (Athlete, Hockey Player)
PO Box 246
Marysville, MI 48040-0246, USA

Emtman, Steven C (Steve) (Athlete, Football Player)
111 Terra Vis
Cheney, WA 99004-2800, USA

Ena, Justin (Athlete, Football Player)
1252 W 2050 S
Syracuse, UT 84075-9566, USA

Enan, Susan (Musician)
c/o Staff Member *Paradigm (Monterey)*
404 W Franklin St
Monterey, CA 93940-2303, USA

Enau, Ron (Race Car Driver)
Bunch Racing
9009 Topsail Cove Dr Unit B
Huntersville, NC 28078-4904, USA

Enberg, Alexander (Actor)
c/o Staff Member *TalentWorks (LA)*
3500 W Olive Ave Ste 1400
Burbank, CA 91505-5512, USA

Enberg, Dick (Commentator)
1275 Virginia Way
La Jolla, CA 92037-5231, USA

En Blanco Y Negro (Music Group)
c/o Staff Member *Sony Music Miami*
605 Lincoln Rd Ste 700
Miami Beach, FL 33139-2901, USA

Enbom, John (Writer)
c/o Staff Member *Creative Artists Agency (CAA-LA)*
2000 Avenue of the Stars Ste 100
Los Angeles, CA 90067-4705, USA

Endelman, Stephen (Musician)
c/o Staff Member *Robert Urband & Associates*
8981 W Sunset Blvd Ste 311
W Hollywood, CA 90069-1881, USA

Enders, Erica (Race Car Driver)
c/o Staff Member *Big Machine Media*
780 3rd Ave Rm 1500
New York, NY 10017-2172, USA

Enders, Trevor (Athlete, Baseball Player)
25906 Silver Timbers Ln
Katy, TX 77494-0726, USA

Endicott, Bill (Athlete, Baseball Player)
14219 Oak Knoll Rd
Sonora, CA 95370-8822, USA

Endicott, Lori (Athlete, Olympic Athlete, Volleyball Player)
351 Dogwood Rdg
Rogersville, MO 65742-8183, USA

End of Fashion (Music Group)
c/o Staff Member *Paradigm (Monterey)*
404 W Franklin St
Monterey, CA 93940-2303, USA

Endress, Albert (al) (Athlete, Football Player)
201 Oregon Ave
Louisville, OH 44641-2332, USA

Endress, Belinda (Race Car Driver)
God Speed on Wheels
PO Box 501
Newbury Park, CA 91319-0501, USA

Endress, Ned (Athlete, Basketball Player)
1632 Highbridge Rd
Cuyahoga Falls, OH 44223-2363, USA

E. Neal, Richard (Congressman, Politician)
2208 Rayburn Hob
Washington, DC 20515-0522, USA

Engblom, Brian (Athlete, Hockey Player)
601 W Burgundy St Unit B
Highlands Ranch, CO 80129-2535, USA

Engel, Bob (Athlete, Baseball Player)
3500 Harmony Dr
Bakersfield, CA 93306-1219, USA

Engel, Georgia (Actor)
c/o Staff Member *Peter Strain & Associates Inc (LA)*
5455 Wilshire Blvd Ste 1812
Los Angeles, CA 90036-4268, USA

Engel, Steve (Athlete, Baseball Player)
7973 Kirkland Dr
Cincinnati, OH 45224-1248, USA

Engelberger, John (Athlete, Football Player)
18229 Glen Abbey Ct
Leesburg, VA 20176-7462, USA

Engelhard, David H (Religious Leader)
Cristian Reformed Church
1700 28th St SE
Grand Rapids, MI 49508-1414, USA

Engen, D Travis (Business Person)
ITT Industries
4 W Red Oak Ln
West Harrison, NY 10604-3603, USA

Enger, John (Athlete, Golfer)
c/o Jim Lehrman *SFX Golf*
36855 W Main St Ste 200
Purcellville, VA 20132-3561, USA

Engibous, Thomas J (Business Person)
Texas Instruments
PO Box 660199
Dallas, TX 75266-0199, USA

England, Anthony W Dr (Astronaut)
7949 Ridgeway Ct
Dexter, MI 48130-9700, USA

England, Audie
6100 Wilshire Blvd Ste 1170
Los Angeles, CA 90048-5116

England, Dan
PO Box 220082
Great Neck, NY 11022-0082

England, Tyler (Music Group)
Buddy Lee
38 Music Sq E Ste 300
Nashville, TN 37203-4304, USA

Englander, Herold R (Doctor, Scientist)
11502 Whisper Bluff St
San Antonio, TX 78230-3704, USA

Engle, Dave (Athlete, Baseball Player)
5343 Castle Hills Dr
San Diego, CA 92109-1926, USA

Engle, Doug (Baseball Player)
Montreal Expos
17282 Heiser Rd
Berlin Center, OH 44401-9784, USA

Engle, Eleanor (Commentator)
Archives
725 Heiden Dr
Hummelstown, PA 17036-8504, USA

Engle, Joe (Astronaut, General)
PO Box 58386
Houston, TX 77258-8386, USA

Engle, Jon (Race Car Driver)
Engle Motorsports
960 Saint Andrews Ln
Louisville, CO 80027-9589, USA

Engle, Joseph H Majgen (Astronaut)
1906 Back Bay Ct
Houston, TX 77058-4202, USA

Engle, Rick (Athlete, Baseball Player)
6413 Seneca Trl
Mentor, OH 44060-3416, USA

Engleberg, Mort (Producer)
Mort Engelberg Productions, Inc.
1504 Rising Glen Rd
Los Angeles, CA 90069-1226, USA

Englehorn, Shirley (Athlete, Golfer)
849 Shrine Vw
Colorado Springs, CO 80906-8500, USA

Engler, James (Politician)
PO Box 3037
Mount Pleasant, MI 48804, USA

Engler, John M (Ex-Governor)
The Hill
1625 K St NW Ste 900
Washington, DC 20006-1606, USA

Engler, Michael (Director, Producer)
c/o Staff Member *United Talent Agency (UTA-LA)*
9336 Civic Center Dr
Beverly Hills, CA 90210-3604, USA

Engles, Rick (Athlete, Football Player)
5621 W Austin St
Broken Arrow, OK 74011-1577, USA

English, A J (Athlete, Basketball Player)
8 Morning Dew Dr
Middletown, DE 19709-2416, USA

English, Alex (Athlete, Basketball Player)
596 Rimer Pond Rd
Blythewood, SC 29016-9448, USA

English, Claude (Athlete, Basketball Player)
14041 Switzer Rd
Overland Park, KS 66221-9735, USA

English, Corri (Actor)
c/o Staff Member *SMS Talent*
8383 Wilshire Blvd Ste 230
Beverly Hills, CA 90211-2436, USA

English, Diane (Writer)
c/o Staff Member *Shukovsky/English Entertainment*
15456 Ventura Blvd Ste 200
Sherman Oaks, CA 91403-3020

English, Edmond J (Business Person)
TJX Companies
770 Cochituate Rd
Framingham, MA 01701-4698, USA

English, Floyd L (Business Person)
Andrew Corp
10500 W 153rd St
Orland Park, IL 60462-3071, USA

English, JoJo (Athlete, Basketball Player)
133 Ramblewood Dr
Columbia, SC 29209-4439, USA

English, Joseph T (Doctor)
Saint Vincent's Hospital
203 W 12th St
New York, NY 10011-7762, USA

English, Kim (Musician)
c/o Staff Member *Diva Central Inc*
7510 W Sunset Blvd Ste 1445
Los Angeles, CA 90046-3408, USA

English, L Douglas (Doug) (Athlete, Football Player)
4306 Bennedict Ln
Austin, TX 78746-1940, USA

English, Madeline (Athlete, Baseball Player)
55 Clinton St
Everett, MA 02149-4640, USA

English, Michael (Music Group)
Trifecta Entertainment
209 10th Ave S Ste 302
Nashville, TN 37203-0730, USA

English, Paul (Actor)
Wurzel Talent Mgmt
19528 Ventura Blvd # 501
Tarzana, CA 91356-2917, USA

English, Ralna (Musician)
PO Box 14522
Scottsdale, AZ 85267-4522, USA

English, Scott (Athlete, Basketball Player)
10740 E Placita Metate
Tucson, AZ 85749-8808, USA

English, Todd (Chef)
c/o Staff Member *Grand Productions*
2811 Champion Rd
Naperville, IL 60564-4958, USA

Engluand, Robert (Actor)
1616 Santa Cruz St
Laguna Beach, CA 92651-3350, USA

Englund, Robert (Actor)
1278 Glenneyre St PMB 73
Laguna Beach, CA 92651-3103, USA

Engram, Simon (Bobby) (Athlete, Football Player)
1104 Black River Rd
Camden, SC 29020-9720, USA

Engstrom, Molly (Athlete, Hockey Player, Olympic Athlete)
7560 Southshore Dr
Siren, WI 54872

Engvall, Bill (Actor, Comedian, Producer)
c/o J P Williams *Parallel Entertainment*
9420 Wilshire Blvd Ste 250
Beverly Hills, CA 90212-3151, USA

Enigma (Music Group)
c/o Staff Member *Virgin Records (NY)*
150 5th Ave Fl 7
New York, NY 10011-4372, USA

Enis, Curtis (Athlete, Football Player)
10972 Comanche Dr
Sidney, OH 45365-9586, USA

Enis, Hunter (Athlete, Football Player)
2521 Marley Rd
Jacksboro, TX 76458-3808, USA

Enke, Fred (Athlete, Football Player)
206 E McMurray Blvd
Casa Grande, AZ 85122-3415, USA

Enlow, Johnny (Religious Leader, Writer)
DAYSTAR
3434 Pleasantdale Rd
Atlanta, GA 30340-4204, USA

Ennis, John (Athlete, Baseball Player)
2231 Agate Ct
Simi Valley, CA 93065-1841, USA

Ennis Sisters, The (Music Group)
c/o Staff Member *Paradigm (Monterey)*
404 W Franklin St
Monterey, CA 93940-2303, USA

Eno, Brian (Musician)
c/o Bryan Loucks *Creative Artists Agency (CAA-LA)*
2000 Avenue of the Stars Ste 100
Los Angeles, CA 90067-4705, USA

Enos, John (Actor)
c/o Lara Rosenstock *Lara Rosenstock Management*
8371 Blackburn Ave Apt 1
Los Angeles, CA 90048-4245, USA

Enos, Lisa (Actor, Producer)
c/o Staff Member *ICM Partners (LA)*
10250 Constellation Blvd Fl 7
Los Angeles, CA 90067-6207, USA

Enos, Mireille (Actor)
c/o Howard Green *Framework Entertainment (LA)*
9057 Nemo St Ste C
West Hollywood, CA 90069-5511, USA

Enos, Randal (Cartoonist)
402 N Park Ave
Easton, CT 06612-1248, USA

Enright, Barry (Athlete, Baseball Player)
17641 N 77th Way
Scottsdale, AZ 85255-0411, USA

Enright, George (Athlete, Baseball Player)
3075 Strawflower Way
Lake Worth, FL 33467-1465, USA

Enrique, Luis
c/o Staff Member *Verve Music Group*
1755 Broadway Frnt 3
New York, NY 10019-3743, USA

Enriquez, Jocelyn
1135 Francisco St Apt 7
San Francisco, CA 94109-1075

Ensberg, Morgan (Athlete, Baseball Player)
5535 Memorial Dr Unit F-114
Houston, TX 77007-8021, USA

Ensign, John
9808 Moon Valley Pl # Pi
Las Vegas, NV 89134-6738, USA

Ensign, Michael (Actor)
Abrams Artists
9200 W Sunset Blvd Ste 1125
West Hollywood, CA 90069-3610, USA

Ensley, Frank (Athlete, Baseball Player)
241 Webster Ave
Grambling, LA 71245-3117, USA

Entner, Warren (Music Group)
Thomas Cassidy
11761 E Speedway Blvd
Tucson, AZ 85748-2017, USA

Entwhistle, John
PO Box 241
Lake Peekskill, NY 10537-0241

Enzi, Michael (Politician)
431 Circle Dr
Gillette, WY 82716-4903, USA

E. Petri, Thomas (Congressman, Politician)
2462 Rayburn Hob
Washington, DC 20515-4906, USA

Ephraim, Alonzo (Athlete, Football Player)
1713 Five Acre Rd
Dolomite, AL 35061-1038, USA

Ephraim, Molly (Actor)
c/o Josh Katz *United Talent Agency (UTA-LA)*
9336 Civic Center Dr
Beverly Hills, CA 90210-3604, USA

Epler, Jim (Race Car Driver)
1600 W Struck Ave # 11
Orange, CA 92867-3427, USA

Eppard, Jim (Athlete, Baseball Player)
23115 153rd Ave
Rapid City, SD 57703-9041, USA

Epperson-Doumani, Brenda (Actor)
kazarian/Spencer
11365 Ventura Blvd Ste 100
Studio City, CA 91604-3148, USA

Epps, Bobby (Athlete, Football Player)
934 Illinois Ave
Pittsburgh, PA 15221-4718, USA

Epps, Jeanette J (Astronaut)
4727 Five Knolls Dr
Friendswood, TX 77546-3160, USA

Epps, Mike (Actor, Comedian)
c/o Samantha Hill *WKT Public Relations (LA)*
9350 Wilshire Blvd Ste 450
Beverly Hills, CA 90212-3230, USA

Epps, Omar (Actor, Producer)
c/o Eli Selden *Anonymous Content (LA)*
3532 Hayden Ave
Culver City, CA 90232-2413, USA

Epps, Raymond (Athlete, Basketball Player)
4030 Old Warwick Rd
Richmond, VA 23234-1975, USA

Epps, Tauheed (2 Chainz) (Musician)
c/o Rupert Lincoln *William Morris Endeavor (LA)*
9601 Wilshire Blvd
Beverly Hills, CA 90210-5213, USA

E. Price, David (Congressman, Politician)
2162 Rayburn Hob
Washington, DC 20515-3304, USA

Epstein, Daniel M (Writer)
843 W University Pkwy
Baltimore, MD 21210-2911, USA

Epstein, Mike (Athlete, Baseball Player)
1265 Nightfire Cir
Castle Rock, CO 80104-7707, USA

Epstein, Theo (Commentator)
75 Peterborough St Apt 703
Boston, MA 02215-4315, USA

Erardi, Greg (Athlete, Baseball Player)
42 Westgate Rd
Massapequa Park, NY 11762-1953, USA

Erasure (Music Group)
c/o Jonny (Jon) Podell *Podell Talent Agency LLC*
22 W 21st St Fl 9
New York, NY 10010-7095, USA

Erat, Martin (Athlete, Hockey Player)
4 Crooked Stick Ln
Brentwood, TN 37027-8938, USA

Erautt, Eddie (Athlete, Baseball Player)
7252 Waite Dr
La Mesa, CA 91941-7631, USA

Erb, Christy (Athlete, Golfer)
4043 Country Trl
Bonita, CA 91902-3025, USA

Erbe, Kathryn (Actor)
101 Warren St Apt 3A
Brooklyn, NY 11201-6084, USA

Erburu, Robert F (Business Person, Publisher)
1518 Blue Jay Way
Los Angeles, CA 90069-1215, USA

Erdman, Dennis (Actor, Director, Producer)
c/o Staff Member *ICM Partners (LA)*
10250 Constellation Blvd Fl 7
Los Angeles, CA 90067-6207, USA

Erdman, Paul E (Writer)
1817 Lytton Springs Rd
Healdsburg, CA 95448-9145, USA

Erdman, Richard (Actor)
5655 Greenbush Ave
Van Nuys, CA 91401-4513, USA

Erdos, Todd (Athlete, Baseball Player)
118 Windsor Ct
Cranberry Twp, PA 16066-3216, USA

Erenberg, Richard (Athlete, Football Player)
318 Snowberry Cir
Venetia, PA 15367-1043, USA

Erhardt, Warren R (Publisher)
455 Wakefield Dr
Metuchen, NJ 08840-1626, USA

Erhuero, Oris (Actor)
c/o Staff Member *Midwest Talent Management Inc*
4821 Lankershim Blvd Ste F
Pmb 149
N Hollywood, CA 91601-4572, USA

Eric, B (Music Group, Musician)
Rush Artists
1600 Varick St
New York, NY 10013, USA

Eric Kaplan, Bruce (Producer)
c/o Staff Member *William Morris Endeavor (LA)*
9601 Wilshire Blvd
Beverly Hills, CA 90210-5213, USA

Ericks, John (Athlete, Baseball Player)
17000 Oketo Ave
Tinley Park, IL 60477-2630, USA

Erickson, Bryan (Athlete, Hockey Player)
40207 County Road 2 Ste A
Roseau, MN 56751-8604, USA

Erickson, Bud (Athlete, Football Player)
14523 165th Pl NE
Woodinville, WA 98072-9037, USA

Erickson, Chad (Athlete, Hockey Player)
219 Birch Dr N
Warroad, MN 56763-3012, USA

Erickson, Craig (Athlete, Football Player)
420 N Country Club Dr
Lake Worth, FL 33462-1004, USA

Erickson, Dennis (Athlete, Coach, Football Coach, Football Player)
4949 Centennial Blvd
Santa Clara, CA 95054-1229, USA

Erickson, Ethan (Actor)
c/o Staff Member *Diverse Talent Group*
9911 W Pico Blvd Ste 340W
Los Angeles, CA 90035-2703, USA

Erickson, Keith (Athlete, Basketball Player, Volleyball Player)
333 23rd St
Santa Monica, CA 90402-2513, USA

Erickson, Matt (Athlete, Baseball Player)
1408 S Fidelis St
Appleton, WI 54915-4069, USA

Erickson, Millard J. (Writer)
c/o Staff Member *Crossway Books*
1300 Crescent St
Wheaton, IL 60187-5815, USA

Erickson, Roger (Athlete, Baseball Player)
PO Box 235
Sautee Nacoochee, GA 30571-0235, USA

Erickson, Scott (Actor)
501 Chicago Ave
Minneapolis, MN 55415-1517, USA

Erickson, Scott G (Athlete, Baseball Player)
1183 Corral Ave
Sunnyvale, CA 94086-7010, USA

Erickson, Steve (Writer)
Poseidon Press
1230 Avenue of the Americas
New York, NY 10020-1513, USA

Erickson-Sauer, Louise (Athlete, Baseball Player, Commentator)
917 Pleasant Ave
Arcadia, WI 54612-1859, USA

Ericson, John (Actor)
7 Avenida Vista Grande # 310
Santa Fe, NM 87508-9198, USA

E. Rigell, Scott (Congressman, Politician)
327 Cannon Hob
Washington, DC 20515-4320, USA

Erik, Erik (Athlete, Olympic Athlete, Skier)
731 Martingale Ln
Park City, UT 84098-7559, USA

Eriksen, Stein (Skier)
7700 Stein Way
Park City, UT 84060-5132, USA

Erikson, Raymond L (Doctor)
Harvard University
25 Shattuck St
Medical School
Boston, MA 02115-6027, USA

Eriksson, Loui
6323 Meadow Rd
Dallas, TX 75230-5140, USA

Erkiletian, Lynda (Reality Star)
c/o Staff Member *Bravo (NY)*
30 Rockefeller Plz
New York, NY 10112-0015, USA

Erlandson, Eric (Songwriter, Writer)
Artist Group International
9560 Wilshire Blvd Ste 400
Beverly Hills, CA 90212-2442, USA

Erlandson, Tom Sr (Athlete, Football Player)
5950 S Ogden Ct
Littleton, CO 80121-2484, USA

Erman, John (Director)
c/o Johnnie Planco *Parseghian Planco LLC*
388 2nd Ave
New York, NY 10010-5616, USA

Ermey, R Lee (Actor)
4348 W Avenue N3
Palmdale, CA 93551-1823, USA

Ermy, R Lee (Actor)
4348 W Avenue N3
Palmdale, CA 93551-1823, USA

Erna, Sully (Actor, Music Group)
c/o Staff Member *William Morris Endeavor (LA)*
9601 Wilshire Blvd
Beverly Hills, CA 90210-5213, USA

Ernaga, Frank (Athlete, Baseball Player)
50 N Roop St
Susanville, CA 96130-3926, USA

Ernest, Dixon (Athlete, Football Player)
324 Viceroy Curv
Stockbridge, GA 30281-9140, USA

Ernie, Nimmons (Athlete, Baseball Player)
500 Pine Hollow Blvd Apt 103D
Lorain, OH 44055-3003, USA

Ernst, Bret (Actor, Comedian)
c/o Joan Green *Joan Green Management*
1836 Courtney Ter
Los Angeles, CA 90046-2106, USA

Ernst, Mark A (Business Person)
H & R Block Inc
4400 Main St
Kansas City, MO 64111-1812, USA

Ernster, Paul (Athlete, Football Player)
6954 S Fultondale Cir
Aurora, CO 80016-4142, USA

Errey, Bob (Athlete, Hockey Player)
213 Fuji Dr
Canonsburg, PA 15317-5245, USA

Errico, Melissa (Actor)
c/o Richard Schmenner *Paradigm (LA)*
360 N Crescent Dr
North Bldg
Beverly Hills, CA 90210-4874, USA

Erskine, Carl D (Athlete, Baseball Player)
4031 Fallbrook Ln
Anderson, IN 46011-1609, USA

Erskine, Peter (Musician)
1727 Hill St
Santa Monica, CA 90405-4843, USA

Erstad, Darin C (Athlete, Baseball Player)
12 Secret Cv
Newport Coast, CA 92657-2107, USA

Ertel, Mark (Athlete, Basketball Player)
855 Cedarwood Pl
Carmel, IN 46032-9663, USA

Ertl, Sue (Athlete, Golfer)
4707 Sabal Key Dr
Bradenton, FL 34203-3126, USA

Eruzione, Mike (Athlete, Hockey Player, Olympic Athlete)
1 Silber Way Fl 7
Boston, MA 02215-1703, USA

Erving, Julius (Athlete, Basketball Player)
5625 Claire Rose Ln
Atlanta, GA 30327-4858, USA

Ervins, Ricky (Athlete, Football Player)
20984 Nightshade Pl
Ashburn, VA 20147-4703, USA

Ervolino, Frank (Politician)
Laundry & Dry Cleaning Union
107 Delaware Ave
Buffalo, NY 14202-2810, USA

Erwin, Hank
4213th St NE
Leeds, AL 35094

Erwin, Mike (Actor)
c/o Loch Powell *Leverage Management*
3030 Pennsylvania Ave
Santa Monica, CA 90404-4112, USA

Erwin, Terry (Athlete, Football Player)
5596 S Lansing Way
Englewood, CO 80111-4104, USA

Erxleban, Russell (Athlete, Football Player)
2031 Beth Ln
Shreveport, LA 71118-2707, USA

Erxleben, Russell A (Athlete, Football Player)
2031 Beth Ln
Shreveport, LA 71118-2707, USA

Esasky, Nick (Athlete, Baseball Player)
1779 Starlight Dr
Marietta, GA 30062-1942, USA

Esbjornson, David (Director)
Mason Gross Performing Arts Center
85 George St
New Brunswick, NJ 08901-1452, USA

Escalera, Nino (Athlete, Baseball Player)
DK20 Calle 201
Carolina, PR 00983-3715, USA

Escape (DJ)
c/o Len Evans *Project Publicity*
312 W 53rd St Ste 202
New York, NY 10019-5743, USA

Escarpeta, Arlen (Actor)
c/o Jerry Shandrew *Shandrew Public Relations*
1050 S Stanley Ave
Los Angeles, CA 90019-6634, USA

Esch, Eric (Butterbean) (Boxer)
Rt 13 Box 254
Jasper, AL 35501, USA

Esche, Robert (Athlete, Hockey Player, Olympic Athlete)
6750 W Carter Rd
Rome, NY 13440-1326, USA

Eschelman, Vaughn (Baseball Player)
Boston Red Sox
30106 Falher Dr
Spring, TX 77386-1683, USA

Eschen, larrv (Athlete, Baseball Player)
3649 Garden Blvd
Gainesville, GA 30506-1552, USA

Eschen, Larry (Athlete, Baseball Player)
3649 Garden Blvd
Gainesville, GA 30506-1552, USA

Esco, Lina (Actor)
c/o Lena Roklin *Luber Roklin Management*
5815 W Sunset Blvd Ste 206
Los Angeles, CA 90028-6481, USA

Escobar, Gavin (Athlete, Football Player)
c/o Alan Herman *Sportstars Inc*
1350 Avenue of the Americas Fl 28
New York, NY 10019-4702, USA

Escobar, Kelvim (Athlete, Baseball Player)
1292 Biscaya Dr
Surfside, FL 33154-3316, USA

Escobar, Yunel (Athlete, Baseball Player)
15763 SW 43rd St
Miami, FL 33185-3815, USA

Escovedo, Pete (Musician)
PO Box 1741
C/O Victor Pamiroyan
Alameda, CA 94501-0199, USA

E. Serrano, Jose (Congressman, Politician)
2227 Rayburn Hob
Washington, DC 20515-3216, USA

Eshelman, Vaughn (Athlete, Baseball Player)
30106 Falher Dr
Spring, TX 77386-1683, USA

Esiason, Norman J (Boomer) (Athlete, Football Player)
25 Heights Rd
Manhasset, NY 11030-1412, USA

Eskridge, Jack (Athlete, Basketball Player)
619 Lakeview Ave
Independence, MO 64050-3154, USA

Espada, Joey (Athlete, Baseball Player)
1409 Islamorada Dr
Jupiter, FL 33458-8765, USA

Esparaza, Michael (Actor)
c/o Carl Scott *Simmons & Scott Entertainment*
7942 Mulholland Dr
Los Angeles, CA 90046-1225, USA

Esparza, Marlen (Athlete, Boxer)
c/o Staff Member *United Talent Agency (UTA-LA)*
9336 Civic Center Dr
Beverly Hills, CA 90210-3604, USA

Esparza, Moctesuma (Producer)
c/o Staff Member *ICM Partners (LA)*
10250 Constellation Blvd Fl 7
Los Angeles, CA 90067-6207, USA

Esparza, Raul (Actor)
c/o Elin McManus-Flack *Elin Flack Management*
435 W 57th St Apt 3M
New York, NY 10019-1724, USA

Espenson, Jane (Producer)
c/o Melanie Marquez *M4 Publicity*
11684 Ventura Blvd # 213
Studio City, CA 91604-2699, USA

Espineli, Geno (Athlete, Baseball Player)
1222 Park Ln
Katy, TX 77450-4613

Espinosa, Danny (Athlete, Baseball Player)
2326 N Towner St
Santa Ana, CA 92706-1942, USA

Espinoza, Alvaro (Athlete, Baseball Player)
124 SW Peacock Blvd # 13
Port Saint Lucie, FL 34986-3484, USA

Espinoza, Mark (Actor)
c/o Staff Member *Howard Entertainment*
16530 Ventura Blvd Ste 305
Encino, CA 91436-4594, USA

Esposito, Brian (Athlete, Baseball Player)
364 Twinbark Ave
Holbrook, NY 11741-5722, USA

Esposito, Frank (Bowler)
200 N State Rt 17
Paramus, NJ 07652-2902, USA

Esposito, Giancarlo (Actor)
1505 10th St
Santa Monica, CA 90401-2805, USA

Esposito, Jennifer (Actor)
c/o Katherine Atkinson *Washington Square Arts (LA)*
1041 N Formosa Ave
the Lot Writers Bldg, Room 305
West Hollywood, CA 90046-6703, USA

Esposito, Laura (Actor)
Gersh Agency
232 N Canon Dr
Beverly Hills, CA 90210-5302, USA

Esposito, Mike (Athlete, Football Player)
35 Hampton Towne Est
Hampton, NH 03842-1941, USA

Esposito, Philip A (Phil) (Athlete, Hockey Player)
4003 W Tacon St
Tampa, FL 33629-8544, USA

Esposito, Sammy (Athlete, Baseball Player)
8303 Amber Leaf Ct
Raleigh, NC 27612-7388, USA

Esposito, Tony (Athlete, Hockey Player)
418 55th Ave
St Pete Beach, FL 33706-2311, USA

EsPv., Duane
9032 E Hannibal St
Mesa, AZ 85207-4234, USA

Espy, Cecil (Athlete, Baseball Player)
5480 Encina Dr
San Diego, CA 92114-6307, USA

Espy, Mike (Politician)
819 7th St NW Ste 205
Washington, DC 20001-3762, USA

Esquivel, Laura (Actor, Producer, Writer)
c/o Staff Member *Doubleday/ RandomHouse*
1745 Broadway
New York, NY 10019-4640, USA

Essany, Michael (Actor, Talk Show Host)
Michael Essany Show
139 Concord Cir
C/O Mike Randazzo
Valparaiso, IN 46385-8070, USA

Essegian, Chuck (Athlete, Baseball Player)
15639 Bronco Dr
Canyon Country, CA 91387-4717, USA

Essensa, Bob (Athlete, Hockey Player)
1130 Iroquois Trl
Oxford, MI 48371-6621, USA

Esser, Mark (Athlete, Baseball Player)
1605 S US Highway 1 Apt E103
Jupiter, FL 33477-8410, USA

Essex, Trai (Athlete, Football Player)
c/o Eugene Parker *Maximum Sports Management*
6435 W Jefferson Blvd # 197
Fort Wayne, IN 46804-6203, USA

Essian, James (Jim) (Athlete, Baseball Player, Coach)
200 Arbutus Ln
Roscommon, MI 48653-8131, USA

Essink, Ron (Athlete, Football Player)
PO Box 265
Hamilton, MI 49419-0265, USA

Esslinger, Hartmut (Designer)
FrogDesign
1327 Chesapeake Ter
Sunnyvale, CA 94089-1104, USA

Essman, Susie (Comedian)
c/o Lee Kernis *Brillstein Entertainment Partners (LA)*
9150 Wilshire Blvd Ste 350
Beverly Hills, CA 90212-3453, USA

Estabrook, Mike (Athlete, Baseball Player)
110 Grove Way
Delray Beach, FL 33444-2918, USA

Estabrook, Wayne (Athlete, Football Player)
6219 S Los Lagos Cv
Fort Mohave, AZ 86426-7046, USA

Estacea, Elizabeth (Musician)
PO Box 691481
Charlotte, NC 28227-7025

Estalella, Bobby (Athlete, Baseball Player)
2550 Pebble Creek Pl
Port Charlotte, FL 33948-1647, USA

Estefan, Emilio (Business Person, Musician)
Estefan Enterprises
420 Jefferson Ave
Miami Beach, FL 33139-6503, USA

Estefan, Gloria (Musician)
39 Star Island Dr
Miami Beach, FL 33139-5146, USA

Estefan, Lili (Actor)
c/o Staff Member *Univision*
605 3rd Ave Fl 12
New York, NY 10158-0034, USA

Estelle (DJ, Musician)
c/o Tracy Nguyen *Industry Public Relations*
1515 Broadway Fl 40
New York, NY 10036-8901, USA

Estelle, Dick (Athlete, Baseball Player)
2221 Taylor St
Point Pleasant Boro, NJ 08742-3839, USA

Esten, Charles (Chip) (Actor)
519 Arden Wood Pl
Brentwood, TN 37027-5659, USA

Estes, A Shawn (Athlete, Baseball Player)
9694 E Legacy Ln
Scottsdale, AZ 85255-6331, USA

Estes, Bob (Athlete, Golfer)
4408 Long Champ Dr Apt 21
Austin, TX 78746-1186, USA

Estes, Clarissa Pinkola (Writer)
c/o Staff Member *Random House Publicity*
1745 Broadway Frnt 3
New York, NY 10019-4343, USA

Estes, Howell M Jr (Business Person, General)
7603 Shadywood Rd
Bethesda, MD 20817-2066, USA

Estes, James (Cartoonist)
1103 Callahan St
Amarillo, TX 79106-4201, USA

Estes, Larry (Athlete, Football Player)
115 Alida St
Hammond, LA 70403-9419, USA

Estes, Rob (Actor)
1020 91st Ave NE
Bellevue, WA 98004-3901, USA

Estes, Will (Actor)
c/o Jason Barrett *Alchemy Entertainment*
7024 Melrose Ave Ste 420
Los Angeles, CA 90038-3394, USA

Estevez, Emilio (Actor, Director)
c/o Scott Melrose *Paradigm (LA)*
Prefers to be contacted via email or telephone
CA, USA

Estevez, Ramon (Actor)
837 Ocean Ave
#101
Santa Monica, CA 90403, USA

Estevez, Renee (Actor)
Michael Mann Talent
617 S Olive St Ste 311
Los Angeles, CA 90014-1624, USA

Esthero (Musician)
c/o Staff Member *ArtistDirect*
9046 Lindblade St
Culver City, CA 90232-2513, USA

Estill, Michelle (Athlete, Golfer)
642 Yacavona St
Kent, OH 44240-3318, USA

Estleman, Loren Daniel (Writer)
5552 Walsh Rd
Whitmore Lake, MI 48189-9673, USA

Estrada, Charle L (Chuck) (Athlete, Baseball Player)
1289 Manzanita Way
San Luis Obispo, CA 93401-7838, USA

Estrada, Erik (Actor, Producer)
3768 Eureka Dr
Studio City, CA 91604-3104, USA

Estrada, Erik-Michael (Musician)
c/o PJ Shapiro *Ziffren, Brittenham, Branca, Fischer, Gilbert-Lurie, Stiffelman & Cook*
1801 Century Park W Fl 7
Los Angeles, CA 90067-6406, USA

estrada, Johnny (Athlete, Baseball Player)
20 Winged Foot Rdg
Newnan, GA 30265-2083, USA

Estrella, Leo (Athlete, Baseball Player)
5462 NW Boydga Ave
Port Saint Lucie, FL 34986-4038, USA

Estrin, Dan (Musician)
24616 Stagg St
Canoga Park, CA 91304-6143, USA

Estrin, Zack (Writer)
c/o Staff Member *William Morris Endeavor (LA)*
9601 Wilshire Blvd
Beverly Hills, CA 90210-5213, USA

Eszterhas, Joe (Writer)
c/o Craig Baumgarten *Baumgarten Management*
1447 Cloverfield Blvd Ste 101
Santa Monica, CA 90404-2979, USA

Eszterhas, Joseph A (Writer)
c/o Craig Baumgarten *Baumgarten Management*
1447 Cloverfield Blvd Ste 101
Santa Monica, CA 90404-2979, USA

Etchebarren, Andy (Athlete, Baseball Player)
439 Santee Dr
Santee, SC 29142-9304, USA

Etcheverry, Marco (Soccer Player)
DC United
14120 Newbrook Dr
Chantilly, VA 20151-2273, USA

Etebari, Eric (Actor)
c/o Staff Member *Agency for the Performing Arts (APA-LA)*
405 S Beverly Dr Ste 500
Beverly Hills, CA 90212-4425, USA

Etel, Alex (Actor)
c/o Staff Member *ICM Partners (LA)*
10250 Constellation Blvd Fl 7
Los Angeles, CA 90067-6207, USA

Etharton, Seth (Baseball Player)
Anaheim Angels
16 Saint John
Dana Point, CA 92629-4127, USA

Ethelle, Chuck (Race Car Driver)
124-126 Pomfret St
Putnam, CT 06260, USA

Etheredge, Carlos (Athlete, Football Player)
7852 Quail Creek Rd
Maumee, OH 43537-8922, USA

Etheridge, Bobby (Athlete, Baseball Player)
118 Portland Rd
Eudora, AR 71640-2174, USA

Etheridge, Joe (Athlete, Football Player)
900 E Bryan St
Kermit, TX 79745-3623, USA

Etheridge, Melissa (Musician, Songwriter)
c/o Bill Leopold *W.F. Leopold Management*
4425 W Riverside Dr Ste 102
Burbank, CA 91505-4057, USA

Etherton, Seth (Athlete, Baseball Player)
1050 Court St Apt 315
San Rafael, CA 94901-2973, USA

Ethier, Andre (Athlete, Baseball Player)
c/o Nez Balelo *CAA Sports (LA)*
2000 Avenue of the Stars Ste 100
Los Angeles, CA 90067-4705, USA

Etienne, Treva (Actor)
c/o Staff Member *London Flair PR*
7119 W Sunset Blvd # 170
Los Angeles, CA 90046-4411, USA

Etter, Bob (Athlete, Football Player)
8609 La Riviera Dr Apt F
Sacramento, CA 95826-1775, USA

Ettinger, Cynthia (Actor)
c/o Dan Barnhardt *Thruline Entertainment*
9250 Wilshire Blvd Ste 100
Ground Floor
Beverly Hills, CA 90212-3343, USA

Etzel, Edward (Athlete, Olympic Athlete, Shooter)
4507 Laurel Ridge Dr
Morgantown, WV 26508-8687

Etzwiler, Donnell D (Doctor)
2323 Northridge Avenue Cir
Stillwater, MN 55082-2511, USA

Eubank, Shari (Actor)
2965 N 625 East Rd
Farmer City, IL 61842-7000, USA

Eubanks, Bob (Motivational Speaker, Television Host)
74 Queens Garden Dr
Westlake Village, CA 91361-5355, USA

Eubanks, Dwight (Reality Star, Stylist)
Purple Door Salon
321 Edgewood Ave SE
Atlanta, GA 30312-4003, USA

Eubanks, Kevin (Musician)
c/o Staff Member *NBC News (NY)*
30 Rockefeller Plz
New York, NY 10112-0015, USA

Eufemia, Frank (Athlete, Baseball Player)
433 6th Ave
Seaside Heights, NJ 08751-1304, USA

Euhus, Tim (Athlete, Football Player)
3520 SE Shoreline Dr
Corvallis, OR 97333-3208, USA

Eunice, Cecil (Race Car Driver)
Rt. 3
Box 77
Blackshear, GA 31516, USA

Eure, Wesley (Actor)
Irv Schechter
9300 Wilshire Blvd Ste 410
Beverly Hills, CA 90212-3228, USA

Eusebio, Tony (Athlete, Baseball Player)
2078 Shannon Lakes Blvd
Kissimmee, FL 34743-3648, USA

Evan & Jaron (Music Group)
c/o Billy Lazarus *United Talent Agency (UTA-LA)*
9336 Civic Center Dr
Beverly Hills, CA 90210-3604, USA

Evancho, Jackie (Musician)
PO Box 11184
Pittsburgh, PA 15237-0484, USA

Evanescence (Music Group)
c/o Dvora Vener Englefield *42West (LA)*
1840 Century Park E Ste 700
Los Angeles, CA 90067-2122, USA

Evangelista, Christine (Actor)
c/o Myrna Jacoby *MJ Management*
130 W 57th St Apt 11A
New York, NY 10019-3311, USA

Evangelista, Daniella (Actor)
c/o Steve Chasman *Current Entertainment*
9200 W Sunset Blvd Ste 600
West Hollywood, CA 90069-3196, USA

Evangelista, Linda (Actor, Model)
c/o Didier Fernandez *DNA Model Management*
555 W 25th St Fl 6
New York, NY 10001-5542, USA

Evanovich, Janet (Writer)
c/o Robert Gottlieb *Trident Media Group LLC*
41 Madison Ave Fl 36
New York, NY 10010-2257, USA

Evans, Aja (Actor)
c/o Staff Member *Precision Entertainment*
465 N Croft Ave
Los Angeles, CA 90048-2508, USA

Evans, Alice (Actor)
c/o Mary Ellen Mulcahy *Framework Entertainment (LA)*
9057 Nemo St Ste C
West Hollywood, CA 90069-5511, USA

Evans, Barry (Athlete, Baseball Player)
128 Russell Dr
McDonough, GA 30252-4531, USA

Evans, Bart (Athlete, Baseball Player)
8323 Rolling Hills Dr
Nixa, MO 65714-7392, USA

Evans, Bentley Kyle (Director, Producer)
c/o Richard Lovett *Creative Artists Agency (CAA-LA)*
2000 Avenue of the Stars Ste 100
Los Angeles, CA 90067-4705, USA

Evans, Bill (Athlete, Basketball Player, Olympic Athlete)
3110 Springstead Cir
Louisville, KY 40241-4416, USA

Evans, Byron (Athlete, Football Player)
1763 E Carter Rd
Phoenix, AZ 85042-5754, USA

Evans, Caryl (Athlete, Hockey Player)
22403 Marjorie Ave
Torrance, CA 90505-2241, USA

Evans, Charlie (Athlete, Football Player)
406 Ozzie St NW
Orting, WA 98360-7405, USA

Evans, Chris (Actor)
13801 Ventura Blvd
Sherman Oaks, CA 91423-3603, USA

Evans, Chris (Athlete, Hockey Player)
c/o Erwin Stoff *3 Arts Entertainment (LA)*
9460 Wilshire Blvd Fl 7
Beverly Hills, CA 90212-2713, USA

Evans, Dale (Athlete, Football Player)
8878 N State Highway 5 Unit 3
Camdenton, MO 65020-4599, USA

Evans, Dan (Commentator)
113 Mineola Ct
Boulder, CO 80303-4417, USA

Evans, Daniel J (Politician)
4000-D NE 41st St
Seattle, WA 98105, USA

Evans, Darrell (Athlete, Baseball Player)
5207 Virtuoso
Irvine, CA 92620-0355, USA

Evans, Daryl (Athlete, Hockey Player)
22403 Marjorie Ave
Torrance, CA 90505-2241, USA

Evans, David (Edge) (Musician)
c/o Allen Grubman *Grubman Indursky Shire & Meiselas*
152 W 57th St Fl 31
New York, NY 10019-3310, USA

Evans, David Mickey (Director)
c/o Staff Member *Bill Thompson Management*
5956 Kanan Dume Rd
Malibu, CA 90265-4027, USA

Evans, Demetric (Athlete, Football Player)
PO Box 2256
Allen, TX 75013-0040, USA

Evans, Dick (Writer)
121 Morning Dove Ct
Daytona Beach, FL 32119-8739, USA

Evans, Donald (Athlete, Football Player)
12407 Beauvoir St
Raleigh, NC 27614-7037, USA

Evans, Donna (Actor)
c/o Staff Member *United Stuntwomen's Association*
3518 Cahuenga Blvd W # 206B
Los Angeles, CA 90068-1304, USA

Evans, Dwayne (Athlete)
PO Box 91219
Phoenix, AZ 85066-1219, USA

Evans, Dwight (Athlete, Baseball Player)
c/o Staff Member *Boston Red Sox*
4 Yawkey Way
Boston, MA 02215-3496, USA

Evans, Evans (Actor)
3114 Abington Dr
Beverly Hills, CA 90210-1101, USA

Evans, Faith (Musician)
7518 Agnew Ave
Los Angeles, CA 90045-1006, USA

Evans, Frank (Athlete, Baseball Player)
c/o Jeanette Kimble 6617 S Monroe St
Tacoma, WA 98409, USA

Evans, George (Cartoonist)
c/o Staff Member *King Features Syndication*
300 W 57th St Fl 15
New York, NY 10019-5238, USA

Evans, Greg (Cartoonist)
216 Country Garden Ln
San Marcos, CA 92069-9759, USA

Evans, Heath (Athlete, Football Player)
16633 Bienveneda Pl
Pacific Palisades, CA 90272-2322, USA

Evans, James B (Jim) (Baseball Player)
1801 Rogge Ln
Austin, TX 78723-3416, USA

Evans, Janet (Athlete, Olympic Athlete, Swimmer)
c/o Staff Member *Premier Management Group (PMG Sports)*
115 Crescent Commons Dr Ste 250
Cary, NC 27518-8134, USA

Evans, Jay (Athlete, Football Player)
328 W Wind Ln
Camdenton, MO 65020-5436, USA

Evans, Jerry (Athlete, Football Player)
4139 Ivanhoe Dr
Lorain, OH 44053-1560, USA

Evans, Joan (Actor)
2289 Merrimack Ave
Henderson, NV 89044, USA

Evans, John A (Athlete, Football Player)
North Carolina State University
P O Box 8501
Attn: Alumni Association
Raleigh, NC 27695-0001, USA

Evans, John E (Business Person)
Allied Group
701 5th Ave
Des Moines, IA 50391-9997, USA

Evans, John V
397 N Overland Ave
Burley, ID 83318-3432, USA

Evans, Josh (Athlete, Football Player)
PO Box 273309
Boca Raton, FL 33427-3309, USA

Evans, J Thomas (Wrestler)
607 S Fir Ct
Broken Arrow, OK 74012-3435, USA

Evans, Larry (Athlete, Football Player)
5316 S Broadway Cir Apt 8-208
Englewood, CO 80113-6735, USA

Evans, Linda (Actor)
PO Box 29
Rainier, WA 98576-0029, USA

Evans, Luke (Actor)
c/o Lena Roklin *Luber Roklin Management*
5815 W Sunset Blvd Ste 206
Los Angeles, CA 90028-6481, USA

Evans, Lynn (Musician)
Richard Paul Assoc
16207 Mott Dr
Macomb, MI 48044-5650, USA

Evans, Mary Beth (Actor, Director)
c/o Michael Bruno *The Michael Bruno Group*
13576 Cheltenham Dr
Sherman Oaks, CA 91423-4818, USA

Evans, Mike (Athlete, Basketball Player)
9931 Cottoncreek Dr
Highlands Ranch, CO 80130-3825, USA

Evans, Mike (Athlete, Football Player)
1 Hunters Run
Greenville, SC 29615-6050, USA

Evans, Murray (Journalist)
19 W Bar Le Doc Dr
Corpus Christi, TX 78414-6157, USA

Evans, Nicholas (Nick) (Writer)
Delacorte Press
1540 Broadway
New York, NY 10036-4039, USA

Evans, Norm (Athlete, Football Player)
360 NW Boulder Pl
Issaquah, WA 98027-5645, USA

Evans, Norm E (Athlete, Football Player)
4143 Via Marina
Marina Del Rey, CA 90292-5303, USA

Evans, Reggie (Athlete, Football Player)
2813 Juniper St
Merrifield, VA 22116, USA

Evans, Richard (Sportscaster)
Madison Square Garden
4 Pennsylvania Plz
New York, NY 10001, USA

Evans, Richard Paul (Writer)
Richard Paul Evans Inc.
PO Box 712137
Salt Lake City, UT 84171-2137, USA

Evans, Rob (Coach)
Arizona State University
Athletic Dept
Tempe, AZ 85287-0001, USA

Evans, Robert (Producer)
Robert Evans Productions
5555 Melrose Ave
Paramount Pictures
Los Angeles, CA 90038-3989, USA

Evans, Robert S (Business Person)
Crane Co
100 Stamford Plz
Stamford, CT 06902, USA

Evans, Ronald E
6134 E Mescal St
Scottsdale, AZ 85254-5419, USA

Evans, Ronald M (Doctor)
Salk Institute
10100 N Torrey Pines Rd
La Jolla, CA 92037, USA

Evans, Sara (Musician)
4120 Montevallo Rd S
Mountain Brk, AL 35213-3114, USA

Evans, Thomas (Business Person)
Collins & Aikman Corporation
PO Box 7054
Troy, MI 48007-7054

Evans, Tom (Athlete, Baseball Player)
32533 SE 68th St
Issaquah, WA 98027-8729, USA

Evans, Tracy (Athlete, Olympic Athlete, Skier)
1406 Meadow Loop Rd
Park City, UT 84098-5941, USA

Evans, Troy (Actor)
PO Box 834
Lakeside, MT 59922-0834, USA

Evans, Vince (Athlete, Football Player)
14084 Bronte Dr
Whittier, CA 90602-2608, USA

Evans, Walker (Race Car Driver)
Walker Evans Racing
PO Box 2469
Riverside, CA 92516-2469, USA

Evans, William (Basketball Player, Olympic Athlete)
3110 Springstead Cir
Louisville, KY 40241-4416, USA

Evashevski, Forest (Coach, Football Coach)
5820 Clubhouse Dr
Vero Beach, FL 32967-7552, USA

Evason, Dean (Athlete, Hockey Player)
c/o Staff Member *Washington Capitals*
627 N Glebe Rd Ste 850
Arlington, VA 22203-2144, USA

Eve (Actor)
c/o Amanda Silverman *42West (NYC)*
220 W 42nd St Fl 12
New York, NY 10036-7200, USA

Eve, Alice (Actor)
c/o Jason Weinberg *Untitled Entertainment (LA)*
350 S Beverly Dr Ste 200
Beverly Hills, CA 90212-4819, USA

Eve, Diva (Athlete, Wrestler)
c/o Staff Member *World Wrestling Entertainment (WWE)*
1241 E Main St
Titan Towers
Stamford, CT 06902-3520, USA

Eve, Trevor J (Actor)
c/o Matthew Lesher *Insight*
PO Box 36359
Los Angeles, CA 90036-0359, USA

Eveland, Dana (Athlete, Baseball Player)
17530 Ventura Blvd Ste 201
Encino, CA 91316-3889, USA

Evelyn, Lionel (Athlete, Baseball Player)
2508 Edgemere Ave
Far Rockaway, NY 11691-2716, USA

Everclear (Music Group)
c/o Staff Member *Tenth Street Entertainment*
270 Lafayette St Ste 706
New York, NY 10012-3397, USA

Everett, Adam (Athlete, Baseball Player, Olympic Athlete)
4374 Oglethorpe Loop NW
Acworth, GA 30101-9533, USA

Everett, Carl E (Athlete, Baseball Player)
19108 Harborbridge Ln
Lutz, FL 33558-9717, USA

Everett, Chad (Actor)
6 Meridian Ln
San Rafael, CA 94901-1384, USA

Everett, Danny (Athlete)
Santa Monica Track Club
1801 Ocean Park Blvd Apt 112
Santa Monica, CA 90405-4925, USA

Everett, Jim (Athlete, Football Player)
555 N El Camino Real Ste A445
San Clemente, CA 92672-6740, USA

Everett, Major (Athlete, Football Player)
PO Box 1441
Pine Lake, GA 30072-1441, USA

Everett, Mark Oliver (Musician)
4046 Cromwell Ave
Los Angeles, CA 90027-1352, USA

Everett, Rupert (Actor)
c/o Annett Wolf *WKT Public Relations (LA)*
9350 Wilshire Blvd Ste 450
Beverly Hills, CA 90212-3230, USA

Everett, Thomas G (Athlete, Football Player)
PO Box 795337
Dallas, TX 75379-5337, USA

Everham, Ray (Race Car Driver)
18917 Peninsula Point Dr
Cornelius, NC 28031-7599, USA

Everhard, Nancy (Actor)
Kazarian /Spencer
11365 Ventura Blvd Ste 100
Studio City, CA 91604-3148, USA

Everhart, Angie (Actor, Producer)
7251 Pacific View Dr
Los Angeles, CA 90068-2041, USA

Everitt, Leon (Athlete, Baseball Player)
367 Henry Everitt Rd
Marshall, TX 75672-3919, USA

Everitt, Mike (Athlete, Baseball Player)
4215 162nd St
Urbandale, IA 50323-2509, USA

Everitt, Mike (Baseball Player)
12381 Walnut Ridge Ct
Clive, IA 50325-8127, USA

Everitt, Steve (Athlete, Football Player)
17252 Snapper Ln
Summerland Key, FL 33042-3669, USA

Everlast (Actor, Musician)
3455 Rubio Crest Dr
Altadena, CA 91001-1529, USA

Evermore (Music Group)
c/o Staff Member *Paradigm (Monterey)*
404 W Franklin St
Monterey, CA 93940-2303, USA

Evernham, Ray (Race Car Driver)
18917 Peninsula Point Dr
Cornelius, NC 28031-7599, USA

Evers, Bill (Athlete, Baseball Player)
PO Box 507
Durham, NC 27702-0507, USA

Evers, Charles (Politician)
1072 J R Lynch St
Jackson, MS 39203-3344, USA

Evers, Jackson (Actor)
232 N Crescent Dr Apt 101
Beverly Hills, CA 90210-4827, USA

Evers, John (Comedian)
PO Box 169
Mount Airy, NC 27030-0169, USA

Eversgerd, Bryan (Baseball Player, Coach)
Swing of the Quad Cities
PO Box 3496
Attn: Coaching Staff
Davenport, IA 52808-3496, USA

Eversman, Nick (Actor)
c/o Brian Medavoy *Medavoy Management*
10203 Santa Monica Blvd Ste 400
Los Angeles, CA 90067-6405, USA

Everson, Cory (Actor, Athlete)
39 Hackamore Ln
Bell Canyon, CA 91307-1019, USA

Everson, Mark (Government Official)
Internal Revenue Service
111 Constitution Ave NW
Washington, DC 20224-0001, USA

Evert, Chris (Athlete, Olympic Athlete, Tennis Player)
8563 Horseshoe Ln
Boca Raton, FL 33496-1231, USA

Every Move A Picture (Music Group)
c/o Staff Member *Paradigm (Monterey)*
404 W Franklin St
Monterey, CA 93940-2303, USA

Everything But The Girl (Music Group, Musician)
c/o Staff Member *High Road Touring*
751 Bridgeway Fl 2
Sausalito, CA 94965-2174, USA

Evigan, Briana (Actor)
c/o Matt Luber *Luber Roklin Management*
5815 W Sunset Blvd Ste 206
Los Angeles, CA 90028-6481, USA

Evigan, Greg (Actor)
5070 Arundel Dr
Woodland Hills, CA 91364-3602, USA

Evo, Bill (Athlete, Hockey Player)
PO Box 430
Fenton, MI 48430-0430, USA

Evre, Willie (Athlete, Baseball Player)
364 S 100 E Apt 211
Cedar City, UT 84720-3810, USA

Ewald, Esther (Athlete, Baseball Player, Commentator)
8455 N Ozanam Ave
Niles, IL 60714-1935, USA

Ewell, Kayla (Actor)
7225 Crescent Park W Apt 224
Playa Vista, CA 90094-2749, USA

Ewen, Todd (Athlete, Hockey Player)
420 Thunderhead Canyon Dr
Ballwin, MO 63011-1732, USA

Ewing, Blake
c/o Jeff Morrone *Intellectual Artists Management*
9350 Wilshire Blvd Ste 224
Beverly Hills, CA 90212-3204, USA

Ewing, Bradie (Athlete, Football Player)
c/o Scott Smith *XAM Sports*
PO Box 1725
Madison, WI 53701-1725, USA

Ewing, Patrick (Athlete, Basketball Player, Coach, Olympic Athlete)
174 Vaccaro Dr
Cresskill, NJ 07626-1740, USA

Ewing, Reid (Actor)
c/o Justin Grey Stone *Management 360*
350 S Beverly Dr Ste 200
Beverly Hills, CA 90212-4819, USA

Ewing, Sam (Athlete, Baseball Player)
1048 Cedarview Ln
Franklin, TN 37067-4068, USA

Exelby, Garnet (Athlete, Hockey Player)
1182 Saint Louis Pl NE
Atlanta, GA 30306-4834, USA

Exelby, Randy (Athlete, Hockey Player)
10040 E Happy Valley Rd Unit 210
Scottsdale, AZ 85255-2368, USA

Exies, The (Music Group)
c/o Frank Cimler *10th Street Entertainment (LA)*
700 N San Vicente Blvd Ste G410
West Hollywood, CA 90069-5060, USA

Exile
PO Box 1547
Goodlettsville, TN 37070-1547

Expose (Music Group)
c/o Stephen Ford *Diva Central Inc*
7510 W Sunset Blvd Ste 1445
Los Angeles, CA 90046-3408, USA

Eyes, Raymond (Publisher)
McCall's Magazine
375 Lexington Ave
New York, NY 10017-5644, USA

Eyharts, Leopold Colonel (Astronaut)
2371 Calypso Ln
League City, TX 77573-0758, USA

Eyre, Richard (Director)
c/o Staff Member *Creative Artists Agency (CAA-LA)*
2000 Avenue of the Stars Ste 100
Los Angeles, CA 90067-4705, USA

Eyre, Scott (Athlete, Baseball Player)
7010 190th St E
Bradenton, FL 34211-7242, USA

Eyre, Willie (Athlete, Baseball Player)
21237 Waymouth Run
Estero, FL 33928-3244, USA

Ezarik, Justine (Internet Star)
c/o Dan Weinstein *The Collective*
8383 Wilshire Blvd Ste 1050
Beverly Hills, CA 90211-2415, USA

Ezell, Glenn (Athlete, Baseball Player)
4790 Brittany Dr S Unit B-7
Saint Petersburg, FL 33715-2606, USA

Ezersky, John (Athlete, Basketball Player)
2564 Walnut Blvd Apt 103
Walnut Creek, CA 94596-4251, USA

Ezor, Blake (Athlete, Football Player)
10622 Salmon Leap St
Las Vegas, NV 89183-4917, USA

Fa, Sione (Reality Star)
43258 W Chisholm Dr
Maricopa, AZ 85138-1500, USA

Fabac-Bretting, Elizabeth (Baseball Player)
1455 Mesa St
Redding, CA 96001-2310, USA

Fabares, Shelley (Actor)
c/o Staff Member *Innovative Artists (LA)*
1505 10th St
Santa Monica, CA 90401-2805, USA

Fabel, Brad (Athlete, Golfer)
247 Windsor Terrace Dr
Nashville, TN 37221-2279, USA

Faber, David (Actor, Writer)
c/o Staff Member *CNBC (Main)*
900 Sylvan Ave
Englewood Cliffs, NJ 07632-3312, USA

Fabi, Ted
9350 Castlegate Dr
Indianapolis, IN 46256-1001

Fabian, John M (Astronaut)
100 Shine Rd
Port Ludlow, WA 98365-9274, USA

Fabian, John M Dr (Astronaut)
100 Shine Rd
Port Ludlow, WA 98365-9274, USA

Fabian, Patrick (Actor)
c/o Donald Spradlin *Essential Talent
Management*
6399 Wilshire Blvd Ste 401
Los Angeles, CA 90048-5716, USA

Fabini, Jason (Athlete, Football Player)
17 Tappanwood Dr
Locust Valley, NY 11560-1321, USA

Fabio (Actor, Model)
19620 Wells Dr
Tarzana, CA 91356-3829, USA

Fabray, Nanette (Actor, Musician)
14350 W Sunset Blvd
Pacific Palisades, CA 90272-3935, USA

Fabregas, Jorge (Athlete, Baseball Player)
4936 SW 6th St
Coral Gables, FL 33134-1346, USA

Fabulous, Moolah (Wrestler)
101 Moolah Dr
Columbia, SC 29223-3931, USA

Face, Elroy L (Roy) (Athlete, Baseball
Player)
608 Della Dr Apt 5F
North Versailles, PA 15137-1518, USA

Facinelli, Peter (Actor)
4355 Clybourn Ave
Toluca Lake, CA 91602-2906, USA

Faedo, Len (Lenny) (Athlete, Baseball
Player)
2920 W Collins St
Tampa, FL 33607-6702, USA

Faedo, Lennv
2920 W Collins St
Tampa, FL 33607-6702, USA

Faerch, Daeg (Actor)
c/o Kieran Maguire *The Arlook Group*
205 S Beverly Dr Ste 209
Beverly Hills, CA 90212-3899, USA

Fagan, Julian (Athlete, Football Player)
PO Box 920
Madison, MS 39130-0920, USA

Fagan, Kevin (Athlete, Football Player)
21555 SW 106th Lane Rd
Dunnellon, FL 34431-6457, USA

Fagan, kevin (Cartoonist)
26771 Ashford
Mission Viejo, CA 92692-4106, USA

Fagen, Clifford B (Basketball Player)
1021 Royal Saint George Dr
Naperville, IL 60563-2322, USA

Fagerbakke, Bill (Actor)
1500 Will Geer Rd
Topanga, CA 90290-4238, USA

Faggins, Demarcus (Athlete, Football
Player)
3002 Southworth Ln
Manvel, TX 77578-4323, USA

Faggs, Starr H Mae (Athlete, Track
Athlete)
10152 Shady Ln
Cincinnati, OH 45215-1322, USA

Fahey, Bill (Athlete, Baseball Player)
5740 Mona Ln
Dallas, TX 75236-1722, USA

Fahey, Brandon (Athlete, Baseball Player)
5740 Mona Ln
Dallas, TX 75236-1722, USA

Fahey, Damien (Television Host)
c/o Mike Esterman *Esterman.Com, LLC*
Prefers to be contacted via email
Baltimore, MD XXXXX, USA

Fahey, Jeff (Actor)
c/o Jeff Goldberg *Jeff Goldberg
Management*
817 Monte Leon Dr
Beverly Hills, CA 90210-2629, USA

Fahey, Jim (Athlete, Hockey Player)
PO Box 1518
East Dennis, MA 02641-1518, USA

Fahey, Siobhan (Musician)
1208 Poinsettia Dr
West Hollywood, CA 90046-5714, USA

Fahey, Trevor (Athlete, Hockey Player)
7629 Bayhill Ct
New Port Richey, FL 34654-6100, USA

Fahnhorst, James (Jim) (Athlete, Football
Player)
4330 Kings Dr
Minnetonka, MN 55345-3010, USA

Fahnhorst, Keith (Athlete, Football Player)
12216 Chadwick Ln
Eden Prairie, MN 55344-3292, USA

Fahy, Bill (Horse Racer)
465 Hewitt Ave
Washington, PA 15301-1538, USA

Faia, Renee (Actor)
c/o Marni Anhalt *Imperium 7 Talent
Agency*
5455 Wilshire Blvd Ste 1706
Los Angeles, CA 90036-4217, USA

Fain, Farris
PO Box 1357
Georgetown, CA 95634

Fain, Richard (Athlete, Football Player)
2705 62nd St W
Lehigh Acres, FL 33971-5849, USA

Faine, Jeff K (Athlete, Football Player)
Forty VII
108 Estates Cir Unit A
Lake Mary, FL 32746-3023, USA

Fair, Lorrie (Athlete, Olympic Athlete,
Soccer Player)
300 3rd St Apt 1515
San Francisco, CA 94107-1259

Fair, Terry (Athlete, Football Player)
1936 Mahogany Wood Trl
Knoxville, TN 37920-6298, USA

Fairbairn, Bruce (Actor)
Century Artists
PO Box 59747
Santa Barbara, CA 93150, USA

Fairband, Bill
13607 E Garigans Gulch
Vail, AZ 85641-6030, USA

Fairchild, Chad (Athlete, Baseball Player)
2700 Coconut Bay Ln Unit 1D
Sarasota, FL 34237-3033, USA

Fairchild, Greg (Athlete, Football Player)
6604 Heege Rd
Saint Louis, MO 63123-2608, USA

Fairchild, John (Athlete, Basketball Player)
9801 Chantilly Rd NW
Albuquerque, NM 87114-4402, USA

Fairchild, Karen (Musician)
56 Annandale
Nashville, TN 37215-5819, USA

Fairchild, Kelly (Athlete, Hockey Player)
14900 43rd Ave N
Minneapolis, MN 55446-2789, USA

Fairchild, Morgan (Actor)
PO Box 57593
Sherman Oaks, CA 91413-2593, USA

Fairchild, Paul (Athlete, Football Player)
22249 W 183rd St
Olathe, KS 66062-9284, USA

Faircloth, Arthur (Athlete, Football Player)
10010 Sandwedge Ct
Fredericksburg, VA 22408-9546, USA

Faircloth, D McLauchlin (Lauch)
(Politician)
803 Beaman St
Clinton, NC 28328-2607, USA

Fairey, Jim (Athlete, Baseball Player)
218 Strawberry Ln
Clemson, SC 29631-1363, USA

Fairey, Shepard
c/o Bradley Frank *Platform Public
Relations*
2666 N Beachwood Dr
Los Angeles, CA 90068-2308, USA

Fairley, Nick (Football Player)
c/o Brian E. Overstreet *E.O. Sports
Management*
2211 Norfolk St Ste 210
Houston, TX 77098-4055, USA

Fairly, Ronald R (Ron) (Athlete, Baseball
Player)
75369 Spyglass Dr
Indian Wells, CA 92210-7650, USA

Fairs, Eric (Athlete, Football Player)
32707 Wales Cir
Fulshear, TX 77441-4250, USA

Faison, Donald (Actor)
c/o Glenn Rigberg *Inphenate*
9701 Wilshire Blvd Fl 10
Beverly Hills, CA 90212-2010, USA

Faison, Matthew (Actor)
13701 E Kagel Canyon Rd
Sylmar, CA 91342, USA

Faison, Tiffani (Chef, Reality Star)
Sweet Cheeks Q
1381 Boylston St
Boston, MA 02215-3936, USA

Faison, William (Earl) (Athlete, Football
Player)
2279 Sequoia Dr
Prescott, AZ 86301-4326, USA

Faithless (Music Group)
c/o Staff Member *Paradigm (Monterey)*
404 W Franklin St
Monterey, CA 93940-2303, USA

Fakih, Rima (Beauty Pageant Winner)
The Miss Universe Organization
1370 Avenue of the Americas Fl 16
New York, NY 10019-4602, USA

Fakir, Abdul (Duke) (Music Group)
c/o Staff Member *ICM Partners (NY)*
730 5th Ave
New York, NY 10019-4105, USA

Falana, Lola (Dancer, Music Group)
Capital Entertainment
217 Seaton Pl NE
Washington, DC 20002-1528, USA

Falchuk, Brad (Producer)
c/o Marc Korman *William Morris
Endeavor (LA)*
9601 Wilshire Blvd
Beverly Hills, CA 90210-5213, USA

Falco, Edie (Actor)
687 Greenwich St Apt 3
New York, NY 10014-6300, USA

Falcone, Ben (Actor, Comedian)
c/o Courtney Kivowitz *The Schiff
Company*
9220 W Sunset Blvd Ste 106
West Hollywood, CA 90069-3500, USA

Falcone, Lisa Maria (Producer)
c/o Staff Member *Everest Entertainment*
450 Park Ave Fl 31
New York, NY 10022-2637, USA

Falcone, Pete (Athlete, Baseball Player)
2232 Thornton Ct
Alexandria, LA 71301-5147, USA

Falconi, Irina (Athlete, Tennis Player)
c/o Dan Nagler *South Beach Sports
Agency*
770 Claughton Island Dr Apt 1510
Miami, FL 33131-2630, USA

Falk, Randall M (Religious Leader)
Temple
5015 Harding Pike
Nashville, TN 37205-2890, USA

Falkenborg, Brian (Athlete, Baseball
Player)
30233 N 125th Dr
Peoria, AZ 85383-3429, USA

Falkman, Craig (Athlete, Hockey Player)
PO Box 1957
Gillette, WY 82717-1957, USA

Fall, Jim (Actor)
c/o Staff Member *United Talent Agency
(UTA-LA)*
9336 Civic Center Dr
Beverly Hills, CA 90210-3604, USA

Fall, Timothy (Actor)
Gersh Agency
232 N Canon Dr
Beverly Hills, CA 90210-5302, USA

Fallin, Mary (Governor, Politician)
Oklahoma State Capitol
2300 N Lincoln Blvd Rm 212
Oklahoma City, OK 73105-4801, USA

Fallon, Bob (Athlete, Baseball Player)
1830 SW 81st Ave Apt 4416
North Lauderdale, FL 33068-4253, USA

Fallon, Jimmy (Actor, Comedian, Talk
Show Host)
Tonight Show with Jimmy Fallon
30 Rockefeller Plz
New York, NY 10112-0015, USA

Fallon, Tiffany (Model, Reality Star)
c/o Cheryl McLean *Creative Public
Relations*
3385 Oak Glen Dr
Los Angeles, CA 90068-1311, USA

Fall Out Boy (Music Group)
c/o Bob McLynn *Crush Management*
60-62 E 11th St
7th Floor
New York, NY 10003, USA

Falls, Mike (Athlete, Football Player)
5831 Secrest Dr
Austin, TX 78759-2416, USA

Faloona, Christopher J (Cinematographer)
138 Via La Soledad
Redondo Beach, CA 90277-6624, USA

Falteisek, Steve (Athlete, Baseball Player)
12 Verbena Ave
Floral Park, NY 11001-2712, USA

Faludi, Susan C (Journalist)
1032 Irving St # 204
San Francisco, CA 94122-2216, USA

Falvey, Justin (Producer)
c/o Staff Member *Dreamworks Television*
100 Universal Plz Bldg 5125
Universal City, CA 91608, USA

Fambrough, Charles (Musician)
Zane Mgmt
Bellvue
Broad & Walnut Sts
Philadelphia, PA 19102, USA

Fambrough, Henry (Music Group)
Buddy Allen Management
3750 Hudson Manor Ter # 3AG
Bronx, NY 10463-1126, USA

Famiglietti, Mark (Actor)
c/o Robert Stein *Robert Stein Management*
PO Box 3797
Beverly Hills, CA 90212-0797, USA

Famuyiwa, Rick (Director, Writer)
c/o Philip Raskind *William Morris
Endeavor (LA)*
9601 Wilshire Blvd
Beverly Hills, CA 90210-5213, USA

Fancher, Hampton (Director)
262 Old Topanga Canyon Rd
Topanga, CA 90290-3810, USA

Fancy, Richard (Actor)
c/o Paul Kohner *Kohner Agency, The*
9300 Wilshire Blvd Ste 555
Beverly Hills, CA 90212-3211, USA

Faneca, Alan (Athlete, Football Player)
8112 Spring Hill Farm Dr
Mc Lean, VA 22102-2330, USA

Faneyte, Rikkert (Baseball Player)
San Francisco Giants
7408 E Osborn Rd
Scottsdale, AZ 85251-6424, USA

Fangio II, Juan Manuel (Race Car Driver)
All-American Racers
2334 S Broadway
Santa Ana, CA 92707-3250, USA

Fankhouser, Scott (Athlete, Hockey
Player)
2043 Crippled Oak Trl
Jasper, GA 30143-7542, USA

Fann, Al (Actor)
6051 Hollywood Blvd Ste 207
Los Angeles, CA 90028-5496, USA

Fanning, Brent (Race Car Driver)
Udder Nonsense Racing
Rt. 4
Box 80
Stephenville, TX 76401, USA

Fanning, Dakota (Actor)
10900 Terryview Dr
Studio City, CA 91604-3908, USA

Fanning, Elle (Actor)
c/o Brittany Kahan *Echo Lake
Management*
421 S Beverly Dr Fl 8
Beverly Hills, CA 90212-4408, USA

Fanning, Jim (Commentator)
8-800 Commissioners Rd W
London, ON N6K 1C2, USA

Fanning, Michael L (Mike) (Athlete,
Football Player)
7107 S Yale Ave # 330
Tulsa, OK 74136-6308, USA

Fanning, Shawn (Business Person)
c/o Staff Member *Roxio Inc*
2830 De La Cruz Blvd
Santa Clara, CA 95050-2619, USA

Fannypack (Music Group)
Famous Celebrity Sound
29 John St Ste 230
New York, NY 10038-4005, USA

Fanok, Harry (Athlete, Baseball Player)
12373 Old State Rd
Chardon, OH 44024-9560, USA

Fansler, Stan (Athlete, Baseball Player)
32 Bunting Ln
Beckley, WV 25801-3656, USA

Fante, Ricky (Musician)
c/o Staff Member *Virgin Records (NY)*
150 5th Ave Fl 7
New York, NY 10011-4372, USA

Fantetti, Ken (Athlete, Football Player)
4652 Sunvalley Dr
Loveland, CO 80538-1981, USA

Fanucchi, Ledio (Athlete, Football Player)
5650 W Dakota Ave
Fresno, CA 93722-9749, USA

Fanucci, Mike (Athlete, Football Player)
1357 N Tercera Ave
Chandler, AZ 85226-1339, USA

Fanzone, Carmen (Athlete, Baseball
Player)
5114 Ranchito Ave
Sherman Oaks, CA 91423-1235, USA

Faracy, Stephanie (Actor)
8765 Lookout Mountain Ave
Los Angeles, CA 90046-1861, USA

Faraldo, Joe (Horse Racer)
12510 Queens Blvd Apt 1206
Kew Gardens, NY 11415-1528, USA

Faralla, Lillian (Athlete, Baseball Player,
Commentator)
102 Antigua Ct
Coronado, CA 92118-3315, USA

Farasopoulos, Chris (Athlete, Football
Player)
151 Water View Way
Folsom, CA 95630-5039, USA

Farber, Barry (Journalist)
2211 Broadway Apt 3A
New York, NY 10024-6264, USA

Farber, Hap (Athlete, Football Player)
200 Dominican Dr
Madison, MS 39110-8630, USA

Far East Movement (Music Group,
Musician)
c/o Staff Member *Stampede Management*
12530 Beatrice St
Los Angeles, CA 90066-7002, USA

Faregalli, Lindy (Bowler)
113 N 5th Ave
Manville, NJ 08835-1201, USA

Farenthold, Blake (Congressman,
Politician)
2110 Rayburn Hob
Washington, DC 20515-1306, USA

Fargas, Antonio (Actor)
H David Moss
733 Seward St PH
Los Angeles, CA 90038-3503, USA

Fargas, Justin (Athlete, Football Player)
9839 Kessler Ave
Chatsworth, CA 91311-5506, USA

Fargis, Joe (Athlete, Horse Racer,
Olympic Athlete)
11744 Marblestone Ct
Wellington, FL 33414-6041, USA

Fargo, Donna (Musician)
PO Box 210877
Nashville, TN 37221-0877, USA

Farhadi, Asghar (Director)
c/o Keya Khayatian *United Talent Agency
(UTA-LA)*
9336 Civic Center Dr
Beverly Hills, CA 90210-3604, USA

Faries, Paul (Athlete, Baseball Player)
3299 Beechwood Dr
Lafayette, CA 94549-4661, USA

Farina, David (Religious Leader)
Chrishtian Church of North America
41 Sherbrooke Rd
Ewing, NJ 08638-2416, USA

Farina, Johnny (Music Group)
Bellrose Music
308 E 6th St Apt 13
New York, NY 10003-8760, USA

Faris, Anna (Actor)
7651 Willow Glen Rd
Los Angeles, CA 90046-1656, USA

Faris, Sean (Actor)
c/o Dino May *Dino May Management*
6362 Hollywood Blvd # 422
Los Angeles, CA 90028-6323, USA

Faris, Valerie (Director, Producer)
Bob Industries
1313 5th St
Santa Monica, CA 90401-1414, USA

Fariss, Monty (Athlete, Baseball Player)
PO Box 1854
Weatherford, OK 73096-1854, USA

Fariss Montv, Montv
PO Box 249
Leedey, OK 73654-0249, USA

Farkas, Jeff (Athlete, Hockey Player)
284 Patrice Ter
Buffalo, NY 14221-3922, USA

Farley, Bob (Athlete, Baseball Player)
1325 Sycamore Rd
Montoursville, PA 17754-9511, USA

Farley, Dale (Athlete, Football Player)
1048 Mount Carmel Church Rd
Sparta, TN 38583-5203, USA

Farley, Dick (Athlete, Football Player)
117 Candlewood Dr
Williamstown, MA 01267-2973, USA

Farley, Jenni (JWoww) (Reality Star)
2284 Clover Hill Ln
Toms River, NJ 08755-1393, USA

Farm, Ali (Athlete)
PO Box 160
Berrien Springs, MI 49103-0160

Farman, Melissa (Actor)
c/o Staff Member *Prodigy Talent Group*
Prefers to be contacted by telephone or
email
Beverly Hills, CA, USA

Farmar, Jordan (Athlete, Basketball
Player)
172 Middlesex Ave
Englewood Cliffs, NJ 07632-1532, USA

Farmer, Billy (Baseball Player)
18987 E Wilshire Blvd
Jones, OK 73049-5917, USA

Farmer, Charles (Red) (Race Car Driver)
143 Foust Ave
Bessemer, AL 35023-2068, USA

Farmer, Danny (Athlete, Football Player)
332 Lorraine Blvd
Los Angeles, CA 90020-4728, USA

Farmer, Dave (Athlete, Football Player)
141 Via Medici
Aptos, CA 95003-5838, USA

Farmer, Ed (Athlete)
333 W 35th St
Chicago, IL 60616-3621

Farmer, Ed (Athlete, Baseball Player)
4581 Camino Del Sol
Calabasas, CA 91302-3836, USA

Farmer, Evan (Actor, Television Host)
c/o Robert Attermann *Abrams Artists
Agency (NY)*
9200 W Sunset Blvd PH 11
West Hollywood, CA 90069-3601, USA

Farmer, Gary (Actor)
c/o Staff Member *Gonzo Dr. Records*
PO Box 31096
Santa Fe, NM 87594-1096, USA

Farmer, George (Athlete, Football Player)
332 Lorraine Blvd
Los Angeles, CA 90020-4728, USA

Farmer, George III (Athlete, Football
Player)
PO Box 1544
Gardena, CA 90249-0544, USA

Farmer, Howard (Athlete, Baseball Player)
1675 W 10th Pl
Gary, IN 46404-1501, USA

Farmer, James (Athlete, Basketball Player)
214 Ashborough Cir
Dothan, AL 36301-1267, USA

Farmer, John Jr (Ex-Governor)
Rutgers School Of Law-Newark
123 Washington St
Newark, NJ 07102-3026, USA

Farmer, Mike (Athlete, Basketball Player, Coach)
2520 Lakeview Dr
Santa Rosa, CA 95405-8657, USA

Farmer, Richard G (Doctor)
9126 Town Gate Ln
Bethesda, MD 20817-4111, USA

Farmer, Robert (Athlete, Football Player)
481 Bergen Ave
Jersey City, NJ 07304-2416, USA

Farmiga, Vera (Actor)
c/o Jon Rubinstein Authentic Talent and Literary Management
20 Jay St Ste M17
Brooklyn, NY 11201-8300, USA

Farm, The (Music Group, Musician)
900 Division St
Nashville, TN 37203-4111, USA

Farner, Mark (Music Group, Musician)
Bobby Roberts
PO Box 1547
Goodlettsville, TN 37070-1547, USA

Farnon, Shannon
12743 Milbank St
Studio City, CA 91604-1310

Farnsworth, Jeff (Athlete, Baseball Player)
704 50th Ave W
Bradenton, FL 34207-2683, USA

Farnsworth, Kyle (Athlete, Baseball Player)
1400 Stickley Ave
Kissimmee, FL 34747-4024, USA

Farquhar, John W (Doctor)
Stanford University
Med School
Disease Prevention Center
Stanford, CA 94305, USA

Farr, Diane (Actor)
c/o Josh Katz United Talent Agency (UTA-LA)
9336 Civic Center Dr
Beverly Hills, CA 90210-3604, USA

Farr, Dmarco (Athlete, Football Player)
2175 Del Monte Dr
San Pablo, CA 94806-1016, USA

Farr, Felicia (Actor)
1143 Tower Rd
Beverly Hills, CA 90210-2130, USA

Farr, Jaime (Actor)
2316 Delaware Ave Ste 266
Buffalo, NY 14216-2638, USA

Farr, Jamie (Actor)
53 Ranchero Rd
Bell Canyon, CA 91307-1032, USA

Farr, Jim (Athlete, Baseball Player)
3 Tyndal Ct
Williamsburg, VA 23188-1552, USA

Farr, Kimberly (Actor)
Tisherman Agency
6767 Forest Lawn Dr # 101
Los Angeles, CA 90068-1027, USA

Farr, Mel Jr (Athlete, Football Player)
4525 Lakeview Ct
Bloomfield Hills, MI 48301-1412, USA

Farr, Melvin (Mel) Sr (Athlete, Football Player)
10550 W 8 Mile Rd
Ferndale, MI 48220-2152, USA

Farr, Michael (Athlete, Football Player)
PO Box 1225
Marietta, GA 30061-1225, USA

Farr, Miller (Athlete, Football Player)
10203 Cascade Hills Dr
Houston, TX 77064-5534, USA

Farr, Norman (Rocky) (Athlete, Hockey Player)
3850 Overton Park Dr W
Fort Worth, TX 76109-3405, USA

Farr, Sam (Congressman, Politician)
1124 Longworth Hob
Washington, DC 20515-4001, USA

Farrakhan, Louis (Religious Leader)
Nation of Islam
734 W 79th St
Chicago, IL 60620-2424, USA

Farrar, Frank L (Politician)
203 Ninth Ave
Britton, SD 57430, USA

Farrel, Franklin (Athlete, Hockey Player)
89 Notch Hill Rd
Apt 223
North Branford, CT 06471, USA

Farrell, Christopher (Musician)
c/o Mike Rosen Working Artists Agency
13525 Ventura Blvd
Sherman Oaks, CA 91423-3801

Farrell, Colin (Actor)
2618 Nottingham Ave
Los Angeles, CA 90027-1041, USA

Farrell, Dave (Musician)
7 Sawgrass
Trabuco Canyon, CA 92679-4906, USA

Farrell, John (Athlete, Baseball Player)
PO Box 3519
Clearwater Beach, FL 33767-8519, USA

Farrell, Margaux (Athlete, Olympic Athlete, Swimmer)
Bob Farrell
55 Wepawaug Rd
Woodbridge, CT 06525-2424, USA

Farrell, Mike (Actor)
11333 Moorpark St # 509
North Hollywood, CA 91602-2618, USA

Farrell, Paul (Athlete, Football Player)
PO Box 804
Dennis Port, MA 02639-0804, USA

Farrell, Sean (Athlete, Football Player)
17754 Esprit Dr
Tampa, FL 33647-2508, USA

Farrell, Sharon (Actor)
c/o Staff Member Sherri Lynn Talent Management
6680 Medford Ct
Chino, CA 91710-3887, USA

Farrell, Shea (Actor)
Artists Agency
1180 S Beverly Dr Ste 301
Los Angeles, CA 90035-1154, USA

Farrell, Terry (Actor)
Don Buchwald
6500 Wilshire Blvd Ste 2200
Los Angeles, CA 90048-4942, USA

Farrelly, Bobby (Director, Producer, Writer)
c/o David O'Connor Creative Artists Agency (CAA-LA)
2000 Avenue of the Stars Ste 100
Los Angeles, CA 90067-4705, USA

Farrelly, Peter (Director, Producer, Writer)
c/o BeBe Lerner ID Public Relations (LA)
7060 Hollywood Blvd Fl 8th
Los Angeles, CA 90028-6021, USA

Farrelly, Stephen (Athlete, Wrestler)
c/o Staff Member World Wrestling Entertainment (WWE)
1241 E Main St
Titan Towers
Stamford, CT 06902-3520, USA

Farren, Paul (Athlete, Football Player)
21 Gammons Rd
Cohasset, MA 02025-1405, USA

Farrer, Kathy (Athlete, Golfer)
4500 Sojourn Dr Apt 2503
Addison, TX 75001-5069, USA

Farrington, Amy
c/o Staff Member Meghan Schumacher Management
13351D Riverside Dr # 387
Sherman Oaks, CA 91423-2508, USA

Farrington, Richard (Horse Racer)
32 Spring St
Wallington, NJ 07057-2045, USA

Farrington, Robert (Horse Racer)
105 Country Pl
Sanford, FL 32771-6502, USA

Farrington, Robert G (Bob) (Race Car Driver)
201 Lake Hinsdale Dr Apt 211
Willowbrook, IL 60527-2688, USA

Farrior, James (Athlete, Football Player)
1004 Summerset Dr
Pittsburgh, PA 15217-2535, USA

Farris, Dionne (Music Group)
c/o Staff Member Creative Artists Agency (CAA-LA)
2000 Avenue of the Stars Ste 100
Los Angeles, CA 90067-4705, USA

Farris, Jerome
US Court of Appeals
1010 5th Ave
Seattle, WA 98104-1195, USA

Farris, Joseph (Cartoonist)
16 Long Meadow Ln
Bethel, CT 06801-2612, USA

Farris, Kris (Athlete, Football Player)
24 Allbrook Ct
Ladera Ranch, CA 92694-0246, USA

Farris, Rachel (Musician)
c/o Staff Member Logic House Media
3123 Traviston Dr
Franklin, TN 37064-6218, USA

Farrish, Dave (Athlete, Hockey Player)
2695 E Katella Ave
Attn Coaching Staff
Anaheim, CA 92806-5904, USA

Farro, Zac (Musician)
210 Countryside Dr
Franklin, TN 37069-4149, USA

Farrow, Mallory (Actor)
Hervey/Grimes
PO Box 64249
Los Angeles, CA 90064-0249, USA

Farrow, Mia (Actor)
c/o Judy Hofflund Hofflund/Polone
6300 Wilshire Blvd Ste 1410
Los Angeles, CA 90048-5216, USA

Farrow, Ronan (Journalist)
225 W 60th St Apt 15E
New York, NY 10023-7430, USA

Farrow, Yvonne (Actor)
Geddes Agency
1203 Greenacre Ave
West Hollywood, CA 90046-5707, USA

Farrow-Rapp, Elizabeth (Baseball Player)
401 Quail Run
Metamora, IL 61548-8360, USA

Farwig, Stephanie (Athlete, Golfer)
5922 Crystal View Dr
Orlando, FL 32819-4207, USA

Faryniarz, Brett (Athlete, Football Player)
1021 S Patrick Way
Anaheim, CA 92808-1471, USA

Fasano, Anthony (Athlete, Football Player)
1016 S Rio Vista Blvd
Ft Lauderdale, FL 33316-1371, USA

Fasano, John (Actor, Director, Producer, Writer)
c/o Craig Baumgarten Baumgarten Management
1447 Cloverfield Blvd Ste 101
Santa Monica, CA 90404-2979, USA

Fasano, Sal (Athlete, Baseball Player)
905 Catherine Gln
Minooka, IL 60447-4528, USA

Fashoway, Gord (Athlete, Hockey Player)
3131 SE 167th Ave
Portland, OR 97236-1525, USA

Fassel, Jim (Athlete, Coach, Football Coach, Football Player)
345 N Quentin Rd Ste 100
Palatine, IL 60067-4896, USA

Fassero, Jeff (Athlete, Baseball Player)
9841 N 56th St
Paradise Valley, AZ 85253-1108, USA

Fast, Darcy (Athlete, Baseball Player)
2981 Harrison Ave
Centralia, WA 98531-9356, USA

Fast, Darrell (Religious Leader)
Mennonite Church General Conference
PO Box 347
Newton, KS 67114-0347, USA

Faszholz, Jack (Athlete, Baseball Player)
18338 Maries Road 308
Belle, MO 65013-2125, USA

Faszhotz, Jack (Athlete, Baseball Player)
18338 Maries Road 308
Belle, MO 65013-2125, USA

Fatafehi, Mario (Athlete, Football Player)
279 W 1360 N
American Fork, UT 84003-2739

Fatefehi, Mario (Athlete, Football Player)
279 W 1360 N
American Fork, UT 84003-2739, USA

Fatel, Mitch (Musician)
c/o Staff Member *Paradigm (Monterey)*
404 W Franklin St
Monterey, CA 93940-2303, USA

Fath, Farah (Actor)
c/o Kurt Patino *Patino Management Company*
4370 Tujunga Ave Ste 120
Studio City, CA 91604-2763, USA

Fat Joe (Actor, Musician)
c/o Staff Member *Jim Havey Public Relations*
2817 W End Ave # 126-203
Nashville, TN 37203-1453, USA

Fatone, Joey (Dancer, Musician)
c/o Joe Mulvihill *LiveWire Entertainment*
100 Universal Studios Plz
Bldg 22 A, Suite 255
Orlando, FL 32819, USA

Fattah, Chaka (Congressman, Politician)
2301 Rayburn Hob
Washington, DC 20515-3802, USA

Faucette, Chuck (Athlete, Football Player)
4117 Hobnail Dr
Saint Charles, MO 63304-2317, USA

Faucette, Mark (Athlete, Hockey Player)
1100 Haley Ln
Dunedin, FL 34698-6120, USA

Faucher, William (Horse Racer)
42 Old Stage Rd
Hinsdale, NH 03451-2308, USA

Fauci, Anthony S (Doctor)
3012 43rd St NW
Washington, DC 20016-3547, USA

Faulconer, Martha (Athlete, Golfer)
374 Stratford Dr
Lexington, KY 40503-1813, USA

Faulk, Amy (Race Car Driver)
Hypertech Inc
1215 Appling Rd
Memphis, TN 38135, USA

Faulk, Kevin (Athlete, Football Player)
249 Magellan Rd
Carencro, LA 70520-5331, USA

Faulk, Marshall (Athlete, Football Player)
c/o Peter Raskin *The Legacy Agency*
1500 Broadway Ste 2501
New York, NY 10036-4082, USA

Faulk, Trev (Athlete, Football Player)
307 Martin Oaks Dr
Lafayette, LA 70501-2507, USA

Faulkner, Chris (Athlete, Football Player)
1596 E 400 S
Tipton, IN 46072-8440, USA

Faulkner, Jeff (Athlete, Football Player)
14150 Carlton Dr
Davie, FL 33330-4659, USA

Faumui, Taase (Athlete, Football Player)
1574 Linapuni St
Honolulu, HI 96819-3507, USA

Fauria, Christian (Athlete, Football Player)
1908 SE Abbey St
Blue Springs, MO 64014-4015, USA

Fauria, Joseph (Athlete, Football Player)
c/o David Dunn *Athletes First, LLC*
23091 Mill Creek Dr
Laguna Hills, CA 92653-1258, USA

Fauser, Mark (Actor)
c/o Staff Member *United Talent Agency (UTA-LA)*
9336 Civic Center Dr
Beverly Hills, CA 90210-3604, USA

Fauss, Ted (Athlete, Hockey Player)
6861 Lowell Rd
Rome, NY 13440-1228, USA

Faust, Andre (Athlete, Hockey Player)
250 Heritage Rd
Cherry Hill, NJ 08034-3150, USA

Faust, August (Athlete, Hockey Player)
250 Heritage Rd
Cherry Hill, NJ 08034-3150, USA

Faust, Chad (Actor)
c/o Evan Hainey *Untitled Entertainment (LA)*
350 S Beverly Dr Ste 200
Beverly Hills, CA 90212-4819, USA

Faust, Paul (Athlete, Football Player)
5522 Highwood Dr W
Minneapolis, MN 55436-1227, USA

Faustino, David (Actor)
17201 Parthenia St
Sherwood Forest, CA 91325-3219, USA

Faut-Eastman, Jean (Athlete, Baseball Player, Commentator)
406 Warrington Pl
Rock Hill, SC 29732-7408, USA

Fauts, Dan (Actor)
4020 Murphy Canyon Rd
San Diego, CA 92123-4407

Fauza, Dario (Doctor, Misc)
Harvard Medical School
25 Shattuck St
Boston, MA 02115-6092, USA

Favela, Marlene (Actor)
Broadcast Music Inc
320 W 57th St
New York, NY 10019-3705, USA

Favino, Pierfrancesco (Actor)
c/o Tammy Rosen *Sanders Armstrong Caserta*
425 N Robertson Blvd
West Hollywood, CA 90048-1735, USA

Favor, Mike (Athlete, Football Player)
8409 Shadow Creek Dr
Osseo, MN 55311-1570, USA

Favor-Hamilton, Suzy (Athlete, Olympic Athlete, Track Athlete)
1014 Beloit Ct
Madison, WI 53705-2233

Favors, Gregory (Athlete, Football Player)
230 Merritt Dr
Roswell, GA 30076-3936, USA

Favre, Brett (Athlete, Football Player)
1 Willow Bend Dr
Hattiesburg, MS 39402-8552, USA

Favreau, Jon (Actor)
509 14th St
Santa Monica, CA 90402-2927, USA

Fawcett, Don W (Doctor, Misc)
3710 American Way Apt 325
Missoula, MT 59808-1927, USA

Fawcett, John (Director)
c/o Scott Yoselow *Gersh (NY)*
41 Madison Ave
New York, NY 10010-2202, USA

Fawcett, Joy (Athlete, Olympic Athlete, Soccer Player)
11 Calle Marta Rancho
Rancho Santa Margarita, CA 92688, USA

Faxon, Nat (Actor)
c/o Paul Young *Principato/Young Management (LA)*
9465 Wilshire Blvd Ste 900
Beverly Hills, CA 90212-2608, USA

Faxon Jr, Brad (Athlete, Golfer)
c/o Staff Member *Pro Golfers Association (PGA) Tour*
112 Tpc Blvd
Ponte Vedra Beach, FL 32082, USA

Fay, David B (Golfer)
US Golf Assn
Golf House
Liberty Corner Road
Far Hills, NJ 07931, USA

Fay, Meagan (Actor)
c/o Staff Member *Paradigm (LA)*
360 N Crescent Dr
North Bldg
Beverly Hills, CA 90210-4874, USA

Fay, Meagen (Actor)
c/o Staff Member *Main Title Entertainment*
8383 Wilshire Blvd Ste 408
Beverly Hills, CA 90211-2435, USA

Faydoedeelay (Music Group, Musician)
Q Prime
729 7th Ave Ste 1600
New York, NY 10019-6880, USA

Fazande, Jermaine (Athlete, Football Player)
3834 Charleston St
Houston, TX 77021-1408, USA

Fazio, Ernie (Athlete, Baseball Player)
776 El Cerro Blvd
Danville, CA 94526-2605, USA

Fazzini, Enrico (Doctor)
New York University
550 1st Ave
Medical Center
New York, NY 10016-6402, USA

F. Bass, Charles (Congressman, Politician)
2350 Rayburn Hob
Washington, DC 20515-0550, USA

F. Costello, Jerry (Congressman, Politician)
2408 Rayburn Hob
Washington, DC 20515-0922, USA

F. Doyle, Michael (Congressman, Politician)
401 Cannon Hob
Washington, DC 20515-3814, USA

Feacher, Ricky (Athlete, Football Player)
684 NE 2nd St
Crystal River, FL 34429-4310, USA

Feagles, Jeff (Athlete, Football Player)
219 Sunset Ave
Ridgewood, NJ 07450-2420, USA

Feamster, Dave (Athlete, Hockey Player)
1058 S May Valley Dr
Pueblo, CO 81007-5033, USA

Feamster, Tom (Athlete, Football Player)
309 Kentucky Blvd
Hazard, KY 41701-2007, USA

Fear Before (Music Group, Musician)
c/o Staff Member *Equal Vision Records*
PO Box 38202
Albany, NY 12203-8202, USA

Fears, Willie (Athlete, Football Player)
1414 S Summit St
Little Rock, AR 72202-5821, USA

Feaster, Allison (Athlete, Basketball Player)
507 Dawley Dr
Fuquay Varina, NC 27526-4825, USA

Featherston, Katie (Actor)
c/o Jillian Roscoe *ID Public Relations (LA)*
7060 Hollywood Blvd Fl 8th
Los Angeles, CA 90028-6021, USA

Featherstone, Glen (Athlete, Hockey Player)
8 Larrabee Ave
Danvers, MA 01923-1828, USA

Febles, Carlos (Athlete, Baseball Player, Coach)
Lancaster Jethawks
45116 Valley Central Way
Attn: Coaching Staff
Lancaster, CA 93536-1508, USA

Fedderly, Bernie (Race Car Driver)
John Force Racing
22722 Old Canal Rd
Yorba Linda, CA 92887-4602, USA

Fede, Terrence (Athlete, Football Player)
c/o Joe Linta *JL Sports*
1204 Main St Ste 179
Branford, CT 06405-3787, USA

Federer, Mike (Race Car Driver)
Mike Federer Racing
23210 54th St E
Buckley, WA 98321-9759, USA

Federico, Anthony (Athlete, Football Player)
12306 Van Nuys Blvd
Sylmar, CA 91342-6049, USA

Federico, Creig (Athlete, Football Player)
303 Ridgewood Dr
Bloomingdale, IL 60108-2533, USA

Federko, Bernie (Athlete, Hockey Player)
2219 Devonsbrook Dr
Chesterfield, MO 63005-4519, USA

Federko, Bernie (Athlete, Hockey Player)
St Louis Blues 1401 Clark Ave
Attn Broadcast Dept
Saint Louis, MO 63103, USA

Federline, Kevin (Actor, Dancer, Musician)
5090 Shady Trail St
Simi Valley, CA 93063-0219, USA

Federov, Sergei (Athlete, Hockey Player)
1865 Huntingwood Ln
Bloomfield Hills, MI 48304-2313, USA

Federspiel, Joe (Athlete, Football Player)
2016 Lakeside Dr
Lexington, KY 40502-3017, USA

Fedewa, Tim (Race Car Driver)
4403 Stough Rd SW
Concord, NC 28027-8964, USA

Fedor, Dave (Athlete, Basketball Player)
4510 Audubon Ave
De Leon Springs, FL 32130-3033

Fedorov, Sergei (Athlete, Hockey Player)
1975 Tiverton Rd
Bloomfield Hills, MI 48304-2348, USA

Fedoruk, Paul (Athlete, Hockey Player)
4578 Liam Dr
Frisco, TX 75034-2139, USA

Fedoruk, Todd (Athlete, Hockey Player)
25 Mallard Dr
Mount Laurel, NJ 08054-3084, USA

Fedotenko, Ruslan (Athlete, Hockey Player)
230 W 56th St Apt 54E
New York, NY 10019-0077, USA

Fedotowsky, Ali (Actor, Reality Star)
c/o Molly Shoneveld *SW PR Shop*
7083 Hollywood Blvd
Los Angeles, CA 90028-8901, USA

F. Edwards, Donna (Congressman, Politician)
318 Cannon Hob
Washington, DC 20515-3101, USA

Fedyk, Brent (Athlete, Hockey Player)
1741 Holland St
Birmingham, MI 48009-7804, USA

Fee, Melinda (Actor)
145 S Fairfax Ave Ste 310
Los Angeles, CA 90036-2176, USA

Feehery, Gerry (Athlete, Football Player)
5 Sharpless Ln
Media, PA 19063-3931, USA

Feeley, A J (Athlete, Football Player)
477 Zuni Or
Del Mar, CA 92014, USA

Feely, Jay (Athlete, Football Player)
7808 River Ridge Dr
Temple Terrace, FL 33637-4933, USA

Feeney, Joe
32630 Concord Dr
Madison Heights, MI 48071-1110

Fegan, Roshon (Actor, Musician)
c/o Bonnie Liedtke *Principato/Young Management (LA)*
9465 Wilshire Blvd Ste 900
Beverly Hills, CA 90212-2608, USA

Fegley, Jr., Don (Race Car Driver)
RD 1
Box 148-J
New Ringgold, PA 17960, USA

Feher, Raymond (Athlete, Basketball Player)
62 Cool Springs Rd
Signal Mountain, TN 37377-2075, USA

Feherty, David (Athlete, Golfer)
6422 Prestonshire Ln
Dallas, TX 75225-2309, USA

Fehr, Brendan (Actor)
c/o Staff Member *ROAR (LA)*
9701 Wilshire Blvd Fl 8
Beverly Hills, CA 90212-2008, USA

Fehr, Donald (Commentator)
34 Rockinghorse Trl
Rye Brook, NY 10573-1038, USA

Fehr, Oded (Actor)
815 Canada St
Ojai, CA 93023-1803, USA

Fehr, Rick (Athlete, Golfer)
3571 W Summit Walk Dr
Anthem, AZ 85086-2767, USA

Fehr, Steve (Bowler)
1329 Castlebridge Ct
Cincinnati, OH 45233-5214, USA

Feick, Jamie (Athlete, Basketball Player)
3 Township Road 200
Centerburg, OH 43011-9674, USA

Feierabend, Ryan (Athlete, Baseball Player)
366 Windsor Dr
Elyria, OH 44035-1732, USA

Feiffer, Jules (Cartoonist, Writer)
35 Cosdrew Ln
East Hampton, NY 11937-2541, USA

Feig, Paul (Actor, Director)
4211 W Hood Ave
Burbank, CA 91505-4015, USA

Feige, Kevin (Producer)
Marvel Studios
500 S Buena Vista St
Burbank, CA 91521-0001, USA

Feinberg, Alan (Musician)
Cramer/Marder Artists
3436 Springhill Rd
Lafayette, CA 94549-2535, USA

Feingold, Russell (Politician)
7114 Donna Dr
Middleton, WI 53562-1709, USA

Feinstein, A Richard (Doctor, Physicist)
1760 2nd Ave Apt 32C
New York, NY 10128-5397, USA

Feinstein, Dianne (Politician)
c/o Staff Member *United States Senate (Hart Office)*
316 Hart Senate Office Building
Washington, DC 20510-0001, USA

Feinstein, Michael (Music Group, Musician)
4647 Kingswell Ave # 110
Los Angeles, CA 90027-4301, USA

Feitle, Dave (Athlete, Basketball Player)
4008 Holly Ln
Flower Mound, TX 75022-5332, USA

Felashia
PO Box 31734
Tucson, AZ 85751-1734

Felber, Dean (Music Group, Musician)
FishCo Mgmt
P O Box 5456
Columbia, SC 29250, USA

Felch, William C (Doctor, Physicist)
8545 Carmel Valley Rd
Carmel, CA 93923-9556, USA

Felder, Benny (Athlete, Baseball Player)
5012 N 39th St
Tampa, FL 33610-6628, USA

Felder, Bobby (Athlete, Football Player)
c/o Ashanti Webb *EMG Sports - OH*
8055 Reynoldswood Dr
Reynoldsburg, OH 43068-9348, USA

Felder, Don (Musician)
PO Box 6051
Malibu, CA 90264-6051, USA

Felder, Kenny (Athlete, Baseball Player)
2902 W Amberwood Dr
Phoenix, AZ 85045-2289, USA

Felder, Mike (Athlete, Baseball Player)
322 S 17th St
Richmond, CA 94804-2606, USA

Felder, Raoul Lionel (Attorney)
437 Madison Ave Ste 30A
New York, NY 10022-7030, USA

Feldhausen, Paul (Athlete, Football Player)
W137S6949 Clarendon Pl
Muskego, WI 53150-3207, USA

Feldman, Ben (Actor)
c/o Michael Baum *Impression Entertainment*
9229 W Sunset Blvd Ste 700
West Hollywood, CA 90069-3407, USA

Feldman, Corey (Actor)
c/o Staff Member *Scott Carlson Entertainment*
5739 Bucknell Ave
Valley Village, CA 91607-1301, USA

Feldman, Donna (Actor)
c/o Allee Newhoff *Elite Model Management (Miami)*
119 Washington Ave Ste 501
Miami Beach, FL 33139-7228, USA

Feldman, Ed
7700 Wisconsin Ave
Bethesda, MD 20814-3578

Feldman, Jerome M (Doctor, Physicist)
2744 Sevier St
Durham, NC 27705-5745, USA

Feldman, Marty (Athlete, Football Player)
100 Louise Ct
Los Gatos, CA 95032-1608, USA

Feldman, Michelle (Bowler)
Gary Feldman
PO Box 713
Skaneateles, NY 13152-0713, USA

Feldman, Myer (Government Official)
Ginsberg Feldman Bress
1250 Connecticut Ave NW
Washington, DC 20036-2603, USA

Feldman, Scott (Athlete, Baseball Player)
1021 Balboa Ave
Burlingame, CA 94010-4928, USA

Feldman, Tamara (Actor)
c/o John Pierce *The Group*
800 S Robertson Blvd Ste 5
Los Angeles, CA 90035-1634, USA

Feldon, Barbara (Actor, Model)
14 E 74th St Apt 1
New York, NY 10021-2628, USA

Feldott, Jennifer (Athlete, Golfer)
PO Box 359
Glenn, MI 49416-0359, USA

Feldshuh, Tovah S (Actor)
c/o Staff Member *Brookside Artists Management (NY)*
250 W 57th St Ste 2303
New York, NY 10107-2399, USA

Feliciano, Jose (Musician)
c/o John Reilly *Rogers & Cowan PR (LA)*
8687 Melrose Ave Ste 7
West Hollywood, CA 90069-5721, USA

Felix, Allyson (Athlete, Olympic Athlete)
c/o Wesley Felix *Evolve Talent Agency*
26519 Sheldon Ave
Canyon Country, CA 91351-6938, USA

Felix, Junior (Athlete, Baseball Player)
7545 Treadway Rd
Gresham, SC 29546-4210, USA

Felix the Cat
12020 Chandler Blvd Ste 200
Valley Village, CA 91607-4617

Felker, Gene (Athlete, Football Player)
945 N Pasadena Unit 160
Mesa, AZ 85201-4319, USA

Fell, Sam (Animator, Director)
c/o Staff Member *United Talent Agency (UTA-LA)*
9336 Civic Center Dr
Beverly Hills, CA 90210-3604, USA

Feller, Happy (Athlete, Football Player)
4225 Camacho St
Austin, TX 78723-5389, USA

Feller, Jack (Athlete, Baseball Player)
145 Oakwood Dr
Coldwater, MI 49036-8606, USA

Fellner, Eric (Producer)
c/o Simon Halls *Slate Public Relations*
9000 W Sunset Blvd Ste 915
West Hollywood, CA 90069-5809, USA

Fellowes, Julian (Actor)
c/o Jeff Sanderson *Chasen & Company*
8899 Beverly Blvd Ste 405
Los Angeles, CA 90048-2431, USA

Fellows, Mark (Athlete, Football Player)
PO Box 517
Choteau, MT 59422-0517, USA

Fellows, Ron (Athlete, Football Player)
202 Creekview Dr
Wylie, TX 75098-7481, USA

Felske, John (Athlete, Baseball Player, Coach)
3804 Ridge Rd
Spring Grove, IL 60081-9390, USA

Felsner, Brian (Athlete, Hockey Player)
28376 Lange Rd
Chesterfield, MI 48047-4855, USA

Felsner, Denny (Athlete, Hockey Player)
16094 Haverhill Dr
Macomb, MI 48044-1946, USA

Felt, Dick
8125 S 1060 E
Sandy, UT 84094-7281, USA

Felt, Richard (Athlete, Football Player)
8125 S 1060 E
Sandy, UT 84094-7281, USA

Felton, Dennis (Basketball Player)
University of Georgia
Athletic Dept
Athens, GA 30602-0001, USA

Felton, Eric (Athlete, Football Player)
PO Box 1355
Coppell, TX 75019-1355, USA

Felton, Jerome (Athlete, Football Player)
c/o Sean Howard *Octagon Football*
832 Sansome St Fl 1
San Francisco, CA 94111-1558, USA

Felton, John (Musician)
GMS
PO Box 1031
Montrose, CA 91021-1031, USA

Felton, Raymond (Athlete, Basketball Player)
15109 Redwood Valley Ln
Charlotte, NC 28277-3282, USA

Felton, Terry (Athlete, Baseball Player)
1253 Cordoba Dr
Zachary, LA 70791-6212, USA

Felton, Tom (Actor)
c/o Clifford Murray *Management 360*
9111 Wilshire Blvd
Beverly Hills, CA 90210-5508, USA

Felts, Narvel (Musician, Songwriter, Writer)
2005 Narvel Felts Dr
Malden, MO 63863-1243, USA

Feltsman, Vladimir (Musician)
Columbia Artists Mgmt Inc
165 W 57th St
New York, NY 10019-2201, USA

Fem 2 Fem
1122 B St Ste 308
Hayward, CA 94541-4274

Femia, John
1650 Broadway Ste 714
New York, NY 10019-6944

Fencik, J Gary (Athlete, Football Player)
1134 W Schubert Ave
Chicago, IL 60614-1309, USA

Fenenbock, Charles (Athlete, Football Player)
2785 Clipper Ct
Cool, CA 95614-2039, USA

Fenerty, Gill (Athlete, Football Player)
2452 Brookhaven Ct NE
Atlanta, GA 30319, USA

Fenn, Sherilyn (Actor)
c/o Cynthia Campos-Greenberg *Anthem Entertainment*
9595 Wilshire Blvd Ste 900
Beverly Hills, CA 90212-2509, USA

Fennema, Carl (Athlete, Football Player)
2470 Dexter Ave N Apt 402
Seattle, WA 98109-2248, USA

Fenner, Derrick (Athlete, Football Player)
7533 33rd Ave NW
Seattle, WA 98117-4712, USA

Fenner, Lane (Athlete, Football Player)
440 Cullen Copse
Alpharetta, GA 30022-7616, USA

Fenney, Rick (Athlete, Football Player)
41594 Margarita Rd
Temecula, CA 92591-2922, USA

Fenoli, Randy (Designer, Reality Star)
c/o Staff Member *Creative Artists Agency (CAA-LA)*
2000 Avenue of the Stars Ste 100
Los Angeles, CA 90067-4705, USA

Fenske, Chuck
3 Tattnall Pl
Hilton Head, SC 29928-3908

Fenson, Pete (Athlete, Olympic Athlete)
3769 Crest Ct NE
Bemidji, MN 56601-6083, USA

Fenton, Paul (Athlete, Hockey Player)
16 Bridle Path Rd
Brewster, MA 02631-1611, USA

Fenton, Paul (Athlete, Hockey Player)
501 Broadway
Attn: Asst General Manager
Nashville, TN 37203-3980, USA

Fenton, Peggy (Athlete, Baseball Player, Commentator)
11131 Cottonwood Dr Unit A
Palos Hills, IL 60465-2528, USA

Fenwick, Bobby (Athlete, Baseball Player)
51201 Hutchinson Rd
Three Rivers, MI 49093-9029, USA

Fenyves, Dave (Athlete, Hockey Player)
940 Parish Pl
Hummelstown, PA 17036-8986, USA

Ferarone, Jessica (Actor)
c/o Tiffany Kuzon *Evolution Entertainment (LA)*
901 N Highland Ave
Los Angeles, CA 90038-2412, USA

Ferdinand, Franz (Musician)
c/o Staff Member *Paradigm (Monterey)*
404 W Franklin St
Monterey, CA 93940-2303, USA

Ferdinand, Marie (Athlete, Basketball Player)
San Antonio Silver Stars
1 at and T Center Pkwy
San Antonio, TX 78219-3604, USA

Ferdinand, Ron (Cartoonist)
PO Box 1997
Monterey, CA 93942-1997

Ference, Andrew (Athlete, Hockey Player)
220 Commercial St Unit 2F
Boston, MA 02109-6304, USA

Ference, Brad (Athlete, Hockey Player)
2424 Gold Canyon Dr
San Antonio, TX 78259-3568, USA

Ferentz, Kirk (Coach, Football Coach)
University of Iowa
Athletic Dept
Iowa City
Iowa City, IA 52242, USA

Fergie (Actor, Musician)
1310 N Kenter Ave
Los Angeles, CA 90049-1320, USA

Fergon, Vicki (Athlete, Golfer)
44 Partridge Ln
Aliso Viejo, CA 92656-1701, USA

Fergus, Keith (Athlete, Golfer)
3807 Louvre Ln
Houston, TX 77082-6695, USA

Ferguson, Charley (Athlete, Football Player)
81 Stonecroft Ln
Buffalo, NY 14226-4129, USA

Ferguson, Christopher (Astronaut)
2405 Airline Dr
Friendswood, TX 77546-5509, USA

Ferguson, Craig (Actor, Comedian, Television Host)
Late Late Show with Craig Ferguson
7800 Beverly Blvd # 244
Los Angeles, CA 90036-2112, USA

Ferguson, Cullum Cathy (Athlete, Olympic Athlete, Swimmer)
3107 San Gabriel Ave
Clovis, CA 93619-9272, USA

Ferguson, George (Athlete, Hockey Player)
5765 Montville Dr
Mc Donald, PA 15057-3548, USA

Ferguson, Jason (Athlete, Football Player)
15139 SW 34th St
Davie, FL 33331-2714, USA

Ferguson, Jay R (Actor)
4460 Stern Ave
Sherman Oaks, CA 91423-3521, USA

Ferguson, Jesse Tyler (Actor)
2566 Aberdeen Ave
Los Angeles, CA 90027-1220, USA

Ferguson, Joe (Athlete, Baseball Player)
11322 River Run Ln
Berlin, MD 21811-3288, USA

Ferguson, Joe (Athlete, Football Player)
12 Mason Ln
Bella Vista, AR 72715-5548, USA

Ferguson, Keith (Athlete, Football Player)
PO Box 19006
Sugar Land, TX 77496-9006, USA

Ferguson, Kent (Athlete, Diver, Olympic Athlete)
809 Olive Way Apt 954
Seattle, WA 98101-1898, USA

Ferguson, Lynda (Actor)
606 N Larchmont Blvd Ste 309
Los Angeles, CA 90004-1309, USA

Ferguson, Nick (Athlete, Football Player)
1114 Arlington Ave SW
Atlanta, GA 30310-3832, USA

Ferguson, Robert (Athlete, Football Player)
15102 Oldtown Bridge Ct
Sugar Land, TX 77498-1298, USA

Ferguson, Sarah (Royalty)
c/o Karen Sellars *ICM Partners (LA)*
10250 Constellation Blvd Fl 7
Los Angeles, CA 90067-6207, USA

Ferguson, Thomas A Jr (Business Person)
Newell Rubbermaid Inc
29 E Stephenson St
Newell Center
Freeport, IL 61032-0943, USA

Ferguson, Vasquero D (Vagas) (Athlete, Football Player)
Richmond High School
380 Hub Etchison Pkwy
Richmond, IN 47374-5398, USA

Ferguson, William (Athlete, Football Player)
9433 N Newport Hwy
Spokane, WA 99218-1244, USA

Ferguson-Winn, Mabel (Athlete, Track Athlete)
2575 Steele Rd Apt 206
San Bernardino, CA 92408-3979, USA

Ferigno, Lou (Actor)
Lou Ferrigno Enterprises Inc
PO Box 1671
Santa Monica, CA 90406-1671, USA

Ferland, E James (Business Person)
Public Service Enterprise
80 Park Plz
PO Box 1171
Newark, NJ 07102-4194, USA

Ferlinghetti, Lawrence (Writer)
City Lights Booksellers
261 Columbus Ave
San Francisco, CA 94133-4586, USA

Fermin, Felix (Athlete, Baseball Player)
Akron Aeros
300 S Main St
Attn: Coaching Staff
Akron, OH 44308-1204, USA

Fernandes, Ron (Athlete, Football Player)
6630 Campbell St
Taylor, MI 48180-1802, USA

Fernandez, Adrian (Race Car Driver)
Fernandez Racing
PO Box 68828
Indianapolis, IN 46268-0828, USA

Fernandez, Alejandro (Musician)
Hauser Entertainment
11003 Rooks Rd
Whittier, CA 90601-1624, USA

Fernandez, Alex (Athlete, Baseball Player)
12323 SW 55th St Ste 107
Cooper City, FL 33330-3312, USA

Fernandez, Bernardo (Athlete, Baseball Player)
6701 Dorita Ave Unit 202
Las Vegas, NV 89108-0355, USA

Fernandez, Chico (Athlete, Baseball Player)
8401 NW 40th Ct
Sunrise, FL 33351-6181, USA

Fernandez, Chico (Athlete, Baseball Player)
1310 SW 97th Ave
Miami, FL 33174-1384, USA

Fernandez, Chico
3322 24th St
Detroit, MI 48208-2412

Fernandez, Craig (Director, Writer)
c/o Staff Member *The Gotham Group Inc*
9255 W Sunset Blvd Ste 515
West Hollywood, CA 90069-3308, USA

Fernandez, C Sidney (Sid) (Athlete, Baseball Player)
25 Aulike St Apt 218
Kailua, HI 96734-2747, USA

Fernandez, Evalina
5911 Allison St
Los Angeles, CA 90022

Fernandez, Frank (Athlete, Baseball Player)
37 Coughlan Ave
Staten Island, NY 10310-3149, USA

Fernandez, Gigi (Tennis Player)
Gigi Tennis Camp
4202 E Fowler Ave # 214
Tampa, FL 33620-9951, USA

Fernandez, Giselle (Television Host)
NHD International Service
PO Box 498
Quakertown, PA 18951-0498, USA

Fernandez, Jared (Athlete, Baseball Player)
4298 S 4625 W
West Valley City, UT 84120-4964, USA

Fernandez, Juan (Actor)
Don Buchwald
6500 Wilshire Blvd Ste 2200
Los Angeles, CA 90048-4942, USA

Fernandez, Lisa (Athlete, Olympic Athlete, Softball Player)
1460 Homewood Rd Apt 95B
Seal Beach, CA 90740-4627, USA

Fernandez, Manny (Athlete, Football Player)
1709 Poplar Ridge Rd
Ellaville, GA 31806-5935, USA

Fernandez, Mary Jo
133 1st St NE
Saint Petersburg, FL 33701-3307

Fernandez, Mary Joe (Athlete, Olympic Athlete, Tennis Player)
3215 Roundwood Rd
Chagrin Falls, OH 44022-6635, USA

Fernandez, Mervyn (Athlete, Football Player)
1454 Hicks Ave
San Jose, CA 95125-3821, USA

Fernandez, O Antonio (Tony) (Athlete, Baseball Player)
19232 N Gardenia Ave
Weston, FL 33332-4409, USA

Fernández, Pedro (Musician)
c/o Staff Member *Machete Music*
2220 Colorado Ave
Santa Monica, CA 90404-3506, USA

Fernandez, Pedro (Musician, Songwriter)
Exclusive Artists Productions
PO Box 65948
Los Angeles, CA 90065-0948, USA

Fernandez, Shiloh (Actor)
c/o Justin Grey Stone *Management 360*
350 S Beverly Dr Ste 200
Beverly Hills, CA 90212-4819, USA

Fernandez, Vicente (Musician)
Hauser Entertainment
11003 Rooks Rd
Whittier, CA 90601-1624, USA

Fernsten, Eric (Athlete, Basketball Player)
5634 Linden St
Dublin, CA 94568-7704

Ferragamo, Vince (Athlete, Football Player)
Touchdown Real Estate
6200 E Canyon Rim Rd Ste 204
Anaheim, CA 92807-4315, USA

Ferrante, Orlando (Athlete, Football Player)
1223 Adair St
San Marino, CA 91108-1806, USA

Ferrara, Abel (Director)
International Creative Mgmt
10250 Constellation Blvd Fl 1
Los Angeles, CA 90067-6241, USA

Ferrara, Adam (Actor)
Conversation Co
697 Middle Neck Rd
Great Neck, NY 11023-1216, USA

Ferrara, Al (Athlete, Baseball Player)
4901 Whitsett Ave Apt 207
Valley Village, CA 91607-3550, USA

Ferrara, Al (Athlete, Baseball Player)
4901 Whitsett Ave Apt 207
Valley Village, CA 91607-3550, USA

Ferrara, Jerry (Actor)
c/o Stephen (Steve) Levinson *Leverage Management*
3030 Pennsylvania Ave
Santa Monica, CA 90404-4112, USA

Ferrare, Cristina (Actor, Model, Television Host)
c/o Lori Jonas *Jonas Public Relations*
240 26th St Ste 3
Santa Monica, CA 90402-2542, USA

Ferrarese, Don (Athlete, Baseball Player)
15290 Myalon Rd
Apple Valley, CA 92307-4938, USA

Ferrari, Al (Athlete, Basketball Player)
5911 Bristlecone Ct
Saint Louis, MO 63129-2917, USA

Ferrari, Anthony (Athlete, Baseball Player)
17 Bretano Way
Greenbrae, CA 94904-1180, USA

Ferrari, Tina (Dancer, Wrestler)
2901 Las Vegas Blvd S
Las Vegas, NV 89109-1933, USA

Ferrario, Bill (Athlete, Football Player)
116 Hensy Ct
Scranton, PA 18504, USA

Ferraris, Jan (Athlete, Golfer)
7108 N 13th Pl
Phoenix, AZ 85020-5408, USA

Ferraro, Chris (Athlete, Hockey Player)
PO Box 155
Sound Beach, NY 11789-0155, USA

Ferraro, Christina (Actor)
c/o Steve Rodriguez *McGowan Management*
8733 W Sunset Blvd Ste 103
West Hollywood, CA 90069-2241, USA

Ferraro, Dave (Bowler)
672 E Chester St
Kingston, NY 12401-1742, USA

Ferraro, Mike (Athlete, Baseball Player, Coach)
5201 Rim View Ln
Las Vegas, NV 89130-3658, USA

Ferraro, Peter (Athlete, Hockey Player)
PO Box 155
Sound Beach, NY 11789-0155, USA

Ferras (Musician)
c/o Staff Member *Monterey International (Chicago)*
200 W Superior St Ste 202
Chicago, IL 60654-6422, USA

Ferratti, Rebecca (Actor, Model)
10061 Riverside Dr # 721
Toluca Lake, CA 91602-2560, USA

Ferree, Jim (Athlete, Golfer)
12 Kings Tree Rd
Hilton Head Island, SC 29928-6101, USA

Ferreira, Sky (Musician)
c/o Ron Laffitte *Red Light Management (LA)*
8439 W Sunset Blvd Ste 2
West Hollywood, CA 90069-1925, USA

Ferreira, Tony (Athlete, Baseball Player)
1661 Oak Spring Dr
Tarpon Springs, FL 34689-1724, USA

Ferreira, Wayne (Tennis Player)
Int'l Mgmt Group
1 Erieview Plz
1360 E 9th St #1300
Cleveland, OH 44114-1738, USA

Ferrell, Bob (Athlete, Football Player)
3800 W Wilson St Spc 262
Banning, CA 92220-3444, USA

Ferrell, Bobby
3800 W Wilson St Spc 262
Banning, CA 92220-3444, USA

Ferrell, Conchata (Actor)
1335 Seward St
Los Angeles, CA 90028-7816, USA

Ferrell, Earl (Athlete, Football Player)
107 E Forest Trl
South Boston, VA 24592-4366, USA

Ferrell, Rachel (Musician)
Vida Music Group
19800 Cornerstone Sq Apt 415
Ashburn, VA 20147-4250, USA

Ferrell, Rachelle (Musician)
Vida Music Group
19800 Cornerstone Sq Apt 415
Ashburn, VA 20147-4250, USA

Ferrell, Tyra (Actor)
c/o Staff Member *Gersh (LA)*
9465 Wilshire Blvd Ste 600
Beverly Hills, CA 90212-2605, USA

Ferrell, Will (Actor, Comedian, Producer)
c/o Jimmy Miller *Mosaic Media Group*
9200 W Sunset Blvd Ste 10
West Hollywood, CA 90069-3608, USA

Ferrell Edmonson, Barbara A (Athlete, Olympic Athlete, Track Athlete)
University of Newada
239 N Hillcrest Blvd
Inglewood, CA 90301-1310, USA

Ferrer, Alex (Judge, Television Host)
c/o Eric Rovner *William Morris Endeavor (Miami)*
119 Washington Ave Ste 400
Miami Beach, FL 33139-7202, USA

Ferrer, Danay (Musician)
Evolution Talent
1776 Broadway # 1500
New York, NY 10019-2002, USA

Ferrer, Lupita
861 Stone Canyon Rd
Los Angeles, CA 90077-2911

Ferrer, Miguel (Actor)
c/o Leslie Allan-Rice *Leslie Allan-Rice Management*
1007 Maybrook Dr
Beverly Hills, CA 90210-2715, USA

Ferrer, Sergio (Athlete, Baseball Player)
37 Coughlan Ave
Staten Island, NY 10310-3149, USA

Ferrer, Tessa (Actor)
c/o Estelle Lasher *Lasher Group*
1133 Avenue Of The Americas Ste 1621
New York, NY 10036-6710, USA

Ferrera, America (Actor)
175 E Broadway Apt 10B
New York, NY 10002-5555, USA

Ferrero, Louis P (Business Person)
PO Box 675744
Rancho Santa Fe, CA 92067-5744, USA

Ferrigno, Lou (Actor)
Lou Ferrigno Enterprises Inc
PO Box 1671
Santa Monica, CA 90406-1671, USA

Ferrin, Arnie (Athlete, Basketball Player)
91E Donner Way
Apt 301
Salt Lake City, UT 84158, USA

Ferrin, Jennifer (Actor)
c/o Staff Member *As The World Turns*
1268 E 14th St
Jc Studios
Brooklyn, NY 11230-5241, USA

Ferris, Bob (Athlete, Baseball Player)
18259 Glen Oak Way
Leesburg, VA 20176-3992, USA

Ferris, John (Swimmer)
1961 Klamath River Dr
Rancho Cordova, CA 95670-2910, USA

Ferris, Michael (Mike) (Producer, Writer)
c/o Staff Member *Broder Webb Chervin Silbermann Agency, The (BWCS)*
10250 Constellation Blvd
Los Angeles, CA 90067-6200, USA

Ferris, Pamela (Actor)
16601 Marquez Ave Unit 405
Pacific Palisades, CA 90272-3263

Ferriss, Dave (Athlete, Baseball Player)
510 Robinson Dr
Cleveland, MS 38732-2214, USA

Ferriss, David M (Boo) (Athlete, Baseball Player)
510 Robinson Dr
Cleveland, MS 38732-2214, USA

Ferriss, Timothy (Writer)
c/o Staff Member *Random House Publicity*
1745 Broadway Frnt 3
New York, NY 10019-4343, USA

Ferro, Cindy (Athlete, Golfer)
1901 Brookside Dr
Scotch Plains, NJ 07076-2601, USA

Ferron (Musician, Songwriter)
c/o Portia Sabin *Shotclock Management*
PO Box 45
Shotclock Management
Olympia, WA 98507-0045, USA

Ferry, Daniel J W (Danny) (Athlete, Basketball Player)
19300 S Park Blvd
Shaker Heights, OH 44122-1859, USA

Ferry, Danny
604 Castano Ave
San Antonio, TX 78209-3617, USA

Ferry, David R (Writer)
Wellesley College
English Dept
Wellesley, MA 02181, USA

Ferry, Robert (Bob) (Athlete, Basketball Player)
2129 Beach Haven Rd
Annapolis, MD 21409-5744, USA

Fersen, Paul (Athlete, Football Player)
PO Box 4
Dorset, VT 05251-0004, USA

Fest, Howard (Athlete, Football Player)
133 Forest Cir
Bandera, TX 78003-4015, USA

Festinger, Robert (Writer)
c/o Bryan Besser *Verve Talent & Literary Agency, LLC*
6310 San Vicente Blvd Ste 100
Los Angeles, CA 90048-5498, USA

Fetisov, Viachesiav (Slava) (Athlete, Hockey Player)
65 Avon Dr
Essex Fells, NJ 07021-1717, USA

Fetisov, Viacheslav (Athlete, Hockey Player)
65 Avon Dr
Essex Fells, NJ 07021-1717, USA

Fetter, Trevor (Business Person)
13737 Noel Rd Ste 100
Dallas, TX 75240-2017, USA

Fetterhoff, Robert (Religious Leader)
Fellowship of Grace Brethem
PO Box 386
Winona Lake, IN 46590-0386, USA

Fetters, Mike (Athlete, Baseball Player)
1816 E Glacier Pl
Chandler, AZ 85249-2884, USA

Fettig, Jeff M (Business Person)
Whirlpool Corp
2000 N State St
RR 63
Benton Harbor, MI 49022, USA

Fetting, Katie (Actor)
c/o Ramses Ishak *United Talent Agency (UTA-LA)*
9336 Civic Center Dr
Beverly Hills, CA 90210-3604, USA

Fettman, Martin (Astronaut)
1572 N Saguaro Cliffs Ct
Tucson, AZ 85745-8839, USA

Fettman, Martin J (Astronaut)
1572 N Saguaro Cliffs Ct
Tucson, AZ 85745-8839, USA

Feuer, Debra
9560 Wilshire Blvd Ste 500
Beverly Hills, CA 90212-2401

Feuerstein, Mark (Actor)
1714 N Orange Grove Ave
Los Angeles, CA 90046-2132, USA

Feustel, Andrew J (Astronaut)
4003 Elm Crest Trl
Houston, TX 77059-3281, USA

Fey, Michael (Cartoonist)
United Feature Syndicate
PO Box 5610
Cincinnati, OH 45201-5610, USA

Fey, Tina (Actor, Comedian)
c/o David Miner *3 Arts Entertainment (LA)*
9460 Wilshire Blvd Fl 7
Beverly Hills, CA 90212-2713, USA

Fezler, Forrest (Athlete, Golfer)
1523 Pine St
Tallahassee, FL 32303-5733, USA

F. H. Faleomavaega Jr., Eni
(Congressman, Politician)
2422 Rayburn Hob
Washington, DC 20515-5201, USA

Fiala, John (Athlete, Football Player)
12113 268th Dr NE
Duvall, WA 98019-9610, USA

Fiala, Neil (Athlete, Baseball Player)
4709 Woody Terrace Ct
Saint Louis, MO 63129-1683, USA

Fiasco, Lupe (Musician)
c/o Cara Lewis *Creative Artists Agency (CAA-NY)*
162 5th Ave Fl 6
New York, NY 10010-6047, USA

Ficca, Dan (Athlete, Football Player)
151 Kansas Ln
Kulpmont, PA 17834-2005, USA

Fichter, Mike (Athlete, Baseball Player)
8821 Jackson Ct
Munster, IN 46321-2410, USA

Fichter, Rick T (Cinematographer)
318 1st Ave S Apt 406
Seattle, WA 98104-2541, USA

Fichtner, Ross (Athlete, Football Player)
46833 Danbridge St
Plymouth, MI 48170-3079, USA

Fichtner, William (Actor)
1556 Puebla Dr
Glendale, CA 91207-1230, USA

Fick, Robert (Athlete, Baseball Player)
832 Dolores Dr
Santa Barbara, CA 93109-1612, USA

Fiddler, Vern (Athlete, Hockey Player)
2601 Avenue Of The Stars
Frisco, TX 75034-9015, USA

Fidler, Mike (Athlete, Hockey Player)
7723 Gleason Rd
Minneapolis, MN 55439-2563, USA

Fiedler, Jay (Athlete, Football Player)
25 Russell Rd
Garden City, NY 11530-1947, USA

Field, Arabella (Actor)
S M S Talent
8383 Wilshire Blvd Ste 230
Beverly Hills, CA 90211-2436, USA

Field, Ayda (Actor)
c/o Staff Member *Brillstein Entertainment Partners (LA)*
9150 Wilshire Blvd Ste 350
Beverly Hills, CA 90212-3453, USA

Field, Chelsea (Actor)
c/o Jay Schwartz *Jay D Schwartz & Associates*
6767 Forest Lawn Dr Ste 211
Los Angeles, CA 90068-1051, USA

Field, Nate (Athlete, Baseball Player)
10199 Lodestone Way
Parker, CO 80134-3740, USA

Field, Sally (Actor)
c/o Heidi Schaeffer *PMK/BNC Public Relations (PMK-LA)*
8687 Melrose Ave Ste 8
West Hollywood, CA 90069-5746, USA

Field, Todd (Actor, Director)
c/o Ari Emanuel *William Morris Endeavor (LA)*
9601 Wilshire Blvd
Beverly Hills, CA 90210-5213, USA

Fielder, Cecil (Athlete, Baseball Player)
Charlotte County Redfish
6907 Smokey Brook Ln
Katy, TX 77494-1607, USA

Fielder, Guyle (Athlete, Hockey Player)
2253 Leisure World
Mesa, AZ 85206-5384, USA

Fielder, Prince (Athlete, Baseball Player)
11171 Sun Center Dr Ste 290
Rancho Cordova, CA 95670-6190, USA

Fielding, Helen (Writer)
c/o Beth Swofford *Creative Artists Agency (CAA-LA)*
2000 Avenue of the Stars Ste 100
Los Angeles, CA 90067-4705, USA

Fielding, Joy (Writer)
Atria Books
1230 Avenue of the Americas
New York, NY 10020-1513, USA

Fielding, Susannah (Actor)
c/o Kim Callahan *Industry Entertainment*
955 Carrillo Dr Ste 300
Los Angeles, CA 90048-5400, USA

Fields, Brandon (Athlete, Football Player)
4509 Holt Rd
Sylvania, OH 43560-9795, USA

Fields, Bruce (Athlete, Baseball Player)
2401 Ontario St
Cleveland, OH 44115-4003, USA

Fields, Debbi (Business Person)
Mrs. Fields Training R&D Ctr
1290 W 2320 S Ste A
West Valley City, UT 84119-1483, USA

Fields, Edgar (Athlete, Football Player)
435 Musket Entry
Roswell, GA 30076-3411, USA

Fields, Freddie
8899 Beverly Blvd Ste 918
Los Angeles, CA 90048-2427

Fields, Holly (Actor)
Don Buchwald
6500 Wilshire Blvd Ste 2200
Los Angeles, CA 90048-4942, USA

Fields, Jitter (Athlete, Football Player)
6008 Kensington Ave
Detroit, MI 48224-2073, USA

Fields, Joseph C (Joe) Jr (Athlete, Football Player)
1 University Pl
Chester, PA 19013-5700, USA

Fields, Josh (Athlete, Baseball Player)
18421 Carillo Rd
Edmond, OK 73012-7655, USA

Fields, Kenny (Athlete, Basketball Player)
Iese E Ramon Rd Unit 81
Palm Springs, CA 92264, USA

Fields, Kim (Actor)
c/o Art Rutter *Critical Mass Management*
1158 26th St Ste 414
Santa Monica, CA 90403-4698, USA

Fields, Landry (Athlete, Basketball Player)
c/o Chris Emens *Octagon Home Office*
1751 Pinnacle Dr Fl 15
Mc Lean, VA 22102-3833, USA

Fields, Mark (Athlete, Football Player)
887 W Palo Brea Dr
Litchfield Park, AZ 85340-6009, USA

Fields, Scott (Athlete, Football Player)
7513 Santa Lucia St
Fontana, CA 92336-3603, USA

Fields, Stephen (Athlete, Baseball Player)
8306 Wickham Rd
Springfield, VA 22152-1708, USA

Fields, Valerie
PO Box 4025
Niagara Falls, NY 14304-8025

Fien, Casey (Athlete, Baseball Player)
7200 Santa Clara St
Buena Park, CA 90620-3116, USA

Fiennes, Joseph (Actor)
c/o Sandra Chang *Anonymous Content (LA)*
3532 Hayden Ave
Culver City, CA 90232-2413, USA

Fiennes, Ralph (Actor)
c/o Nicole Caruso *Relevant*
584 Broadway Rm 310
New York, NY 10012-5246, USA

Fieri, Guy (Chef, Television Host)
2039 Marsh Rd
Santa Rosa, CA 95403-2429, USA

Fierstein, Harvey (Actor, Musician, Writer)
c/o Ron Fierstein *RF Entertainment Inc.*
29 Haines Rd Ste 200
Bedford Hills, NY 10507-1237, USA

Fife, Dan (Danny) (Athlete, Baseball Player)
5854 Misty Hill Dr
Clarkston, MI 48346-3033, USA

Figaro, Cedric (Athlete, Football Player)
205 Staten St
Lafayette, LA 70501-1745, USA

Figga, Mike (Athlete, Baseball Player)
16434 Turnbury Oak Dr
Odessa, FL 33556-2896, USA

Figg-Currier, Cindy (Athlete, Golfer)
109 Blue Jay Dr
Lakeway, TX 78734-5101, USA

Figgins, Chone (Athlete, Baseball Player)
16 San Sovino
Newport Coast, CA 92657-1313, USA

Figgins, Desmond "Chone" (Athlete, Baseball Player)
6SO Bellevue Wav NE
Bellevue, WA 98004, USA

Figgis, Michael (Mike) (Director)
c/o Robert Newman *William Morris Endeavor (LA)*
9601 Wilshire Blvd
Beverly Hills, CA 90210-5213, USA

Figlo-Gill, Josephine (Athlete, Baseball Player, Commentator)
437 N Fork Dr
Lakeland, FL 33809-1426, USA

Figner, George (Athlete, Football Player)
2329 N Recker Rd Unit 116
Mesa, AZ 85215-2766, USA

Figueras, Nacho (Athlete)
c/o Tony Godsick *Team 8 Global*
30650 Pinetree Rd Ste 1
Cleveland, OH 44124-5920, USA

Figueras-Dotti, Marta (Athlete, Golfer)
6174 Palomino Cir
Bradenton, FL 34201-2384, USA

Figueroa, Bien (Athlete, Baseball Player)
3272 Addison Ln
Tallahassee, FL 32317-9045, USA

Figueroa, Ed (Athlete, Baseball Player)
A-N15 Calle 41
Santa Juanita, PR 00619, USA

Figueroa, Efrain (Actor)
c/o Staff Member *Mitchell K Stubbs & Assoc (MKS)*
8675 Washington Blvd Ste 203
Culver City, CA 90232-7486, USA

Figueroa, Nelson (Athlete, Baseball Player)
1950 E Woodsman Pl
Chandler, AZ 85286-2007, USA

Figura, Maria Louisa (Actor)
The Figura Studio
5716 Cahuenga Blvd
North Hollywood, CA 91601-2105, USA

Figures, Deon (Athlete, Football Player)
1520 S Visalia Ave
Compton, CA 90220-3947, USA

Fikac, Jeremy (Athlete, Baseball Player)
PO Box 2187
Wimberley, TX 78676-7087, USA

Fike, Dan (Athlete, Football Player)
23479 Wingedfoot Dr
Westlake, OH 44145-4371, USA

Fikrig, Erol (Doctor)
Yale University
Medical Center
Infectious Disease Dept
New Haven, CT 06510, USA

Fila, Ivan (Writer)
c/o David Krintzman *Morris Yorn Barnes Levine Krintzman Rubenstein Kohner & Gellman*
2000 Avenue of the Stars Ste 300N
3rd Floor, North Tower
Los Angeles, CA 90067-4704, USA

Filardi, Peter (Director, Producer, Writer)
c/o Robert Marsala *Wishlab*
2225A Hyperion Ave
Los Angeles, CA 90027-4709, USA

Filarski-Steffes, Helen (Athlete, Baseball Player, Commentator)
19623 Damman St
Harper Woods, MI 48225-1753, USA

File, Bob (Athlete, Baseball Player)
6412 Riverfront Dr
Palmyra, NJ 08065-2149, USA

Filer, Tom (Athlete, Baseball Player)
501 W Maryland St Attn Coachingstaff
Indianapolis, IN 46225-1041, USA

Files, Jim (Athlete, Football Player)
6303 Fallstone Rd
Fort Smith, AR 72916-8939, USA

Files, Jimmy (Athlete, Football Player)
6303 Fallstone Rd
Fort Smith, AR 72916-8939, USA

Filicia, Thom (Designer, Television Host)
c/o Staff Member *William Morris Endeavor (LA)*
9601 Wilshire Blvd
Beverly Hills, CA 90210-5213, USA

Filiol, Jalme (Tennis Player)
Advantage International
1025 Thomas Jefferson St NW # 430
Washington, DC 20007-5201, USA

Filion, Rheo (Horse Racer)
187 S Franklin St # 251
Wilkes Barre, PA 18766-0998, USA

Filipek, Ron (Athlete, Basketball Player)
933 Hillside Dr
Cookeville, TN 38501-2890, USA

Filipelli, John (Horse Racer)
1949 NE 1st St
Deerfield Beach, FL 33441-4504, USA

Filippo, Lou
7826 Botany St
Downey, CA 90240-2624

Filippo (Fillipo/Filippo), Fabrizio (Fab) (Actor)
c/o David Lillard *Paradigm (LA)*
8730 W Sunset Blvd Ste 490
West Hollywood, CA 90069-2248, USA

Fill, Shannon (Actor)
260 S Beverly Dr Ste 200
Beverly Hills, CA 90212-3812, USA

Fillion, Nathan (Actor)
12196 Iredell St
Studio City, CA 91604-4172, USA

Fillip, Chet (Race Car Driver)
PO Box 220
Ozona, TX 76943-0220, USA

Fillmore, Greg (Athlete, Basketball Player)
7748 Las Palmas Way
Jacksonville, FL 32256-0203

Filner, Bob (Congressman, Politician)
2428 Rayburn Hob
Washington, DC 20515-0551, USA

Filppula, Valttieri (Athlete, Hockey Player)
4927 Lyford Cay Rd
Tampa, FL 33629-4828, USA

Filson, Pete (Athlete, Baseball Player)
1725 Packer Ave
Philadelphia, PA 19145-4119, USA

Filter (Music Group)
c/o Staff Member *Warner Bros Records (NY)*
75 Rockefeller Plz
New York, NY 10019-6908, USA

Fimmel, Travis (Actor, Model)
c/o David Seltzer *Management 360*
9111 Wilshire Blvd
Beverly Hills, CA 90210-5508, USA

Fimple, Dennis
3518 Cahuenga Blvd W # 306
Los Angeles, CA 90068-1304

Fimple, Jack (Athlete, Baseball Player)
8012 Cliffrose St
Windsor, CA 95492-9537, USA

Fina, John (Athlete, Football Player)
5180 E Fort Lowell Rd
Tucson, AZ 85712-1309, USA

Finch, James (Race Car Driver)
Phoenix Racing
1718 Tennessee Ave
Lynn Haven, FL 32444, USA

Finch, Jennie (Athlete, Olympic Athlete, Softball Player)
Finch Windmill
PO Box 97
La Mirada, CA 90637-0097, USA

Finch, Joel (Athlete, Baseball Player)
68571 Oak Springs Rd
Edwardsburg, MI 49112-9502, USA

Finch, Karl (Athlete, Football Player)
4408 Copper Crest Ln
Modesto, CA 95355-8970, USA

Finch, Tyrone (Comedian)
c/o Staff Member *United Talent Agency (UTA-LA)*
9336 Civic Center Dr
Beverly Hills, CA 90210-3604, USA

Finchem, Timothy W (Athlete, Golfer)
c/o Staff Member *Pro Golfers Association (PGA) Tour*
112 Tpc Blvd
Ponte Vedra Beach, FL 32082, USA

Fincher, Alfred (Athlete, Football Player)
1267 Avenue Du Chateau
Covington, LA 70433-6424, USA

Fincher, David (Director)
c/o Bryan Lourd *Creative Artists Agency (CAA-LA)*
2000 Avenue of the Stars Ste 100
Los Angeles, CA 90067-4705, USA

Fincke, Edward
15819 El Dorado Oaks Dr
Houston, TX 77059-4045, USA

Fincke, Edward M (Astronaut)
15819 El Dorado Oaks Dr
Houston, TX 77059-4045, USA

Fincke, E Michael (Mike) (Astronaut)
15819 El Dorado Oaks Dr
Houston, TX 77059-4045, USA

Findlay, Katie (Actor)
c/o Chris Henze *Thruline Entertainment*
9250 Wilshire Blvd Ste 100
Ground Floor
Beverly Hills, CA 90212-3343, USA

Fine, David (Director, Writer)
c/o Melissa Myers *William Morris Endeavor (LA)*
9601 Wilshire Blvd
Beverly Hills, CA 90210-5213, USA

Fine, Jeanna
19 Hanover Pl Pmb 313
Hicksville, NY 11801

Fine, Travis (Actor)
Vaughn D Hart
200 N Robertson Blvd # 219
Beverly Hills, CA 90211-1769, USA

Finfera, Joe (Actor)
c/o Staff Member *Select Artists Ltd (CA-Westside Office)*
1138 12th St Apt 1
Santa Monica, CA 90403-5459, USA

Fingaz, Sticky (Artist, Musician)
c/o David Guc *Vanguard Management Group*
8060 Melrose Ave Fl 4
Los Angeles, CA 90046-7038, USA

Finger Eleven (Music Group)
c/o Staff Member *Wind-up Records*
72 Madison Ave Fl 8
New York, NY 10016-8731, USA

Fingers, Rollie (Athlete, Baseball Player)
PO Box 230729
Las Vegas, NV 89105-0729, USA

Fink, Jason (Athlete, Football Player)
2619 Regatta Ln
Davis, CA 95618-6409, USA

Fink, John
1680 Vine St Ste 614
Los Angeles, CA 90028-8833

Fink, Mitchell
1835 E Michelle St
West Covina, CA 91791-3942

Finkel, Fyvush (Actor)
c/o Dianne Busch *Leading Artists*
145 W 45th St Rm 1000
New York, NY 10036-4032, USA

Finkel, Henry (Hank) (Athlete, Basketball Player)
2 Pocahontas Way
Lynnfield, MA 01940-1042, USA

Finkel, Shelly
310 Madison Ave
#804
New York, NY 10017, USA

Finkelstein, Norman G (Writer)
2245 Ocean Pkwy Apt 3A
Brooklyn, NY 11223-4859, USA

Finkes, Matt (Athlete, Football Player)
5442 Cedar Spgs
Columbus, OH 43228-7200, USA

Finley, Charles E (Chuck) (Athlete, Baseball Player)
500 McCormick Rd
West Monroe, LA 71291-1921, USA

Finley, Jeff (Race Car Driver)
Team Rensi Motorsports
4011 Hands Mill Hwy
York, SC 29745-9647, USA

Finley, John L (Astronaut)
700 Colonial Rd Ste 120
Memphis, TN 38117-5191, USA

Finley, Michael (Athlete, Basketball Player)
6600 Sudbury Rd
Plano, TX 75024-7414, USA

Finley, Steven (Steve) (Athlete, Baseball Player)
c/o Lew Weitzman *Preferred Artists*
16633 Ventura Blvd Ste 1421
Encino, CA 91436-1885, USA

Finn, Jim (Athlete, Football Player)
12-14 Western Dr
Fair Lawn, NJ 07410-2213, USA

Finn, John (Actor)
c/o Gabrielle Krengel *Domain Talent*
9229 W Sunset Blvd Ste 710
West Hollywood, CA 90069-3407, USA

Finn, Neil (Musician, Songwriter, Writer)
c/o Staff Member *William Morris Endeavor (LA)*
9601 Wilshire Blvd
Beverly Hills, CA 90210-5213, USA

Finn, Patrick (Actor)
c/o Staff Member *Brillstein Entertainment Partners (LA)*
9150 Wilshire Blvd Ste 350
Beverly Hills, CA 90212-3453, USA

Finn, Veronica (Musician)
Evolution Talent
1776 Broadway # 1500
New York, NY 10019-2002, USA

Finnegan, Christian (Comedian)
c/o Kara Welker *Generate Management*
8750 Wilshire Blvd Ste 200
Beverly Hills, CA 90211-2707, USA

Finnegan, Cortland (Athlete, Football Player)
PO Box 158187
Nashville, TN 37215-8187, USA

Finneran, Brian (Athlete, Football Player)
1905 Sugarloaf Club Dr
Duluth, GA 30097-7448, USA

Finneran, Garry (Athlete, Football Player)
711 Oak Point Dr
Oak Park, CA 91377-3836, USA

Finneran, Gary (Athlete, Football Player)
711 Oak Point Dr
Oak Park, CA 91377-3836, USA

Finneran, Katie (Actor)
c/o Adena Chawke *Greenlight Management and Production*
9713 Santa Monica Blvd Ste 219
Beverly Hills, CA 90210-4215, USA

Finneran, Rittenhouse Sharon (Swimmer)
212 Harbor Dr
Santa Cruz, CA 95062-3442, USA

Finnessey, Shandi (Beauty Pageant Winner)
c/o Staff Member *Miss Universe Organization, The*
1370 Avenue of the Americas Fl 16
New York, NY 10019-4602, USA

Finney, Allison (Athlete, Golfer)
78160 Desert Mountain Cir
Bermuda Dunes, CA 92203-8151, USA

Finnie, Roger (Athlete, Football Player)
937 NW 58th St
Miami, FL 33127-1321, USA

Finnigan, Jennifer (Actor)
c/o John Carrabino *John Carrabino Management*
5900 Wilshire Blvd Ste 406
Los Angeles, CA 90036-5015, USA

Finnvold, Gar (Athlete, Baseball Player)
1204 NE 4th Ave
Boca Raton, FL 33432-2808, USA

Finsterwald, Dow (Athlete, Golfer)
6330 Masters Blvd
Orlando, FL 32819-4869, USA

Finzer, Dave (Athlete, Football Player)
1435 Kaywood Ln
Glenview, IL 60025-2341, USA

Fiona, Melanie (Musician)
c/o Dennis Ashley *ICM Partners (LA)*
10250 Constellation Blvd Fl 7
Los Angeles, CA 90067-6207, USA

Fiore, Dave (Athlete, Football Player)
668 Willowgate St Apt F
Mountain View, CA 94043-4898, USA

Fiore, Kathryn (Actor)
c/o Michael P Levine *Levine Management*
9028 W Sunset Blvd PH 1
West Hollywood, CA 90069-1830, USA

Fiore, Mike (Athlete, Baseball Player)
17 Silver St
Malverne, NY 11565-1116, USA

Fiore, Tony (Athlete, Baseball Player)
19021 Fishermans Bend Dr
Lutz, FL 33558-9754, USA

Fiorentini, Jeff (Athlete, Baseball Player)
4200 Chardonnay Dr
Rockledge, FL 32955-5133, USA

Fiori, Ed (Athlete, Golfer)
4411 Winding River Dr
Richmond, TX 77406-9218, USA

Fiori, Fernando (Actor)
c/o Staff Member *Latin World Entertainment Agency (LWE)*
3470 NW 82nd Ave
Doral, FL 33122-1024, USA

Fiorito, Jaelle (Actor, Television Host)
c/o Staff Member *Rebel Entertainment Partners*
5700 Wilshire Blvd Ste 456
Los Angeles, CA 90036-3648, USA

Firefall
6400 Pleasant Park Dr
Chanhassen, MN 55317-8804

Fireman, Paul B (Business Person, Misc)
Reebok International
1895 J W Foster Blvd
Canton, MA 02021-1099, USA

Fireovid, Steve (Athlete, Baseball Player)
1408 Woodstream Dr
Bryan, OH 43506-9049, USA

Fires, Earlie S (Horse Racer)
16337 Rivervale Ln
Chicago, AR 60640, USA

Firestone, Andrew (Actor, Reality Star)
c/o Staff Member *Paradigm (LA)*
360 N Crescent Dr
North Bldg
Beverly Hills, CA 90210-4874, USA

Firestone, Dennis (Race Car Driver)
5380 Via Morena
Yorba Linda, CA 92886-5008, USA

Firestone, Eddie
303 S Crescent Heights Blvd
Los Angeles, CA 90048-4403

Firestone, Roy (Sportscaster)
Seizen/Wallach Productions
257 S Rodeo Dr
Beverly Hills, CA 90212-3803, USA

Firova, Dan (Athlete, Baseball Player)
208 Saint John St
Refugio, TX 78377-3436, USA

Firth, Colin (Actor)
c/o Jessica Kolstad *Relevant*
9350 Wilshire Blvd Ste 450
Beverly Hills, CA 90212-3230, USA

Fiscella, Nicole (Model)
c/o Staff Member *New York Model Management*
596 Broadway # 701
New York, NY 10012-3396, USA

Fischer, Bernard
208 King Rd
Kuna, ID 83634

Fischer, Bill (Athlete, Football Player)
509 NW 23rd Ter
Cape Coral, FL 33993-4102, USA

Fischer, Bill (Athlete, Baseball Player)
139 Upland Dr
Council Bluffs, IA 51503-4823, USA

Fischer, Brad (Athlete, Baseball Player)
6110 Forest Ridge Ct
Mc Farland, WI 53558-9020, USA

Fischer, Erich (Athlete, Olympic Athlete, Water Polo Player)
542 Cress St
Laguna Beach, CA 92651-3128, USA

Fischer, Hank (Athlete, Baseball Player)
7024 Summit Dr
Navarre, FL 32566-8745, USA

Fischer, Jack D
PO Box 1407
Friendswood, TX 77549-1407, USA

Fischer, Jeff (Athlete, Baseball Player)
215 Worth Ct N
West Palm Beach, FL 33405-2751, USA

Fischer, Jenna (Actor)
c/o Naomi Odenkirk *Odenkirk Provissiero Entertainment*
1936 N Bronson Ave
Raleigh Studios
Los Angeles, CA 90068-5602, USA

Fischer, Jiri (Athlete, Hockey Player)
20101 Westview Dr
Northville, MI 48167-9206, USA

Fischer, Lisa (Musician)
Alive Enterprices
3264 S Kihei Rd
Kihei, HI 96753-9605, USA

Fischer, Patrick (Pat) (Athlete, Football Player)
45800 Jona Dr Apt 314
Sterling, VA 20165-5690, USA

Fischer, Todd (Athlete, Baseball Player)
12734 Newtown Rd
Unionville, TN 37180-5004, USA

Fischer, Todd (Athlete, Golfer)
7347 Linwood Ct
Pleasanton, CA 94588-4877, USA

Fischer, Van (Director)
Gersh Agency
232 N Canon Dr
Beverly Hills, CA 90210-5302, USA

Fischer, William A (Moose) (Athlete, Football Player)
1790 Pinnacle Ridge Ln
Colorado Springs, CO 80919-3450, USA

Fischerspooner (Music Group)
c/o Staff Member *Paradigm (Monterey)*
404 W Franklin St
Monterey, CA 93940-2303, USA

Fischetti, Brad (Musician)
Evolution Talent Agency
1776 Broadway Fl 15
New York, NY 10019-2002

Fischler, Patrick (Actor)
c/o Stewart Strunk *Main Title Entertainment*
8383 Wilshire Blvd Ste 408
Beverly Hills, CA 90211-2435, USA

Fischlin, Mike (Athlete, Baseball Player)
1010 Curtright Pl
Greensboro, GA 30642-7432, USA

Fish, Ginger (Musician)
c/o Staff Member *Interscope Records (LA) - Main*
2220 Colorado Ave
Santa Monica, CA 90404-3506, USA

Fish, Matt (Athlete, Basketball Player)
4138 E Waterman Ct
Gilbert, AZ 85297-3574, USA

Fishbacher, Siegfried (Magician)
Mirage Hotel & Casino
3400 Las Vegas Blvd S
Las Vegas, NV 89109-8907, USA

Fishback, Joe (Athlete, Football Player)
1402 Battlecreek Village Dr
Jonesboro, GA 30236-8532, USA

Fishbone
PO Box 4450
New York, NY 10163-4450

Fishburne, Laurence (Actor)
c/o Helen Sugland *Landmark Artists*
4116 W Magnolia Blvd Ste 101
Burbank, CA 91505-2700, USA

Fishel, Danielle (Actor)
c/o Ray Moheet *Levity Entertainment Group (LEG)*
6701 Center Dr W Ste 1111
Los Angeles, CA 90045-1552, USA

Fishel, John (Athlete, Baseball Player)
329 Marjoram Dr
Columbus, OH 43230-7027, USA

Fisher, Anna L (Astronaut)
1912 Elmen St
Houston, TX 77019-6144, USA

Fisher, Brian (Athlete, Baseball Player)
3660 S Uravan St
Aurora, CO 80013-3458, USA

Fisher, Bryan (Actor)
c/o Jamie Freed *Paris Hilton Entertainment*
2934 1/2 N Beverly Glen Cir # 383
Los Angeles, CA 90077-1724, USA

Fisher, Carrie (Actor, Writer)
c/o Carol Marshall *Carol Marshall PR*
4730 Woodman Ave Ste 304
Sherman Oaks, CA 91423-2443, USA

Fisher, Charles (Athlete, Football Player)
PO Box 133
Aliquippa, PA 15001-0133, USA

Fisher, Derek (Athlete, Basketball Player)
c/o Staff Member *New York Knicks*
2 Pennsylvania Plz
New York, NY 10121, USA

Fisher, Doug (Athlete, Football Player)
4040 Hancock St Apt 204
San Diego, CA 92110-5154, USA

Fisher, Ed (Athlete, Football Player)
3602 John Simpson Trl
Austin, TX 78732-2239, USA

Fisher, Eddie G (Athlete, Baseball Player)
408 Cardinal Cir S
Altus, OK 73521-1714, USA

Fisher, Elder A (Bud) (Bowler)
7551 Brackenwood Cir N
Indianapolis, IN 46260-5439, USA

Fisher, Eric (Athlete, Football Player)
c/o Joel Segal *Lagardere Unlimited (NYC)*
845 United Nations Plz
New York, NY 10017-3540, USA

Fisher, Evan (Musician)
GEMS
PO Box 1031
Montrose, CA 91021-1031, USA

Fisher, Frances (Actor)
c/o Michael Greene *Greene & Associates*
1901 Avenue of the Stars Ste 130
Los Angeles, CA 90067-6030, USA

Fisher, Fritz (Athlete, Baseball Player)
3703 Barcelona Dr
Toledo, OH 43615-1203, USA

Fisher, Isla (Actor)
c/o Julie Darmody *Mosaic Media Group*
9200 W Sunset Blvd Ste 10
West Hollywood, CA 90069-3608, USA

Fisher, Jack (Athlete, Baseball Player)
95 Moor Dr
Easton, PA 18045-2183, USA

Fisher, Jeff (Athlete, Football Coach, Football Player)
385 Lake Valley Dr
Franklin, TN 37069-4652, USA

Fisher, Jeff (Coach, Football Coach)
460 Great Circle Rd
Nashville, TN 37228-1404, USA

Fisher, Joely (Actor)
c/o John Carrabino *John Carrabino Management*
5900 Wilshire Blvd Ste 406
Los Angeles, CA 90036-5015, USA

Fisher, Jules E (Designer)
Jules Fisher Enterprises
126 5th Ave
New York, NY 10011-5606, USA

Fisher, Kimberly (Model)
c/o Staff Member *ISA Talent Management*
PO Box 5467
North Hollywood, CA 91616-5467, USA

Fisher, Maurice (Maury) (Athlete, Baseball Player)
15920 Lucerne Rd
Fredericktown, OH 43019-9531, USA

Fisher, Ray (Athlete, Football Player)
1066 County Highway 21
Fairfield, IL 62837-3057, USA

Fisher, Robert (Business Person)
Gap Inc
2 Folsom St
San Francisco, CA 94105-1205, USA

Fisher, Roger (Musician)
Borman Entertainment
1250 6th St Ste 401
Santa Monica, CA 90401-1638, USA

Fisher, Sarah (Race Car Driver)
c/o Staff Member *NASCAR*
1801 W Speedway Blvd
Daytona Beach, FL 32114-1243, USA

Fisher, Steve (Coach)
San Diego State University
Athletic Dept
San Diego, CA 92182-0001, USA

Fisher, Terry Louise
5314 Pacific Ave
Marina Del Rey, CA 90292-7118

Fisher, Thomas L
Nicor Inc
1844 W Ferry Rd
Naperville, IL 60563-9600, USA

Fisher, Tom (Athlete, Baseball Player)
7104 Vega Way Apt 222
Indianapolis, IN 46241-7501, USA

Fisher, Trisha Leigh
243 Delfern Dr
Los Angeles, CA 90077-3544

Fisher, William F (Astronaut)
1119 Woodland Dr
El Lago, TX 77586-6044, USA

Fisher-Stevens, Lorraine (Baseball Player)
120 Birdsell St
Jackson, MI 49203-4670, USA

Fishman, Jerald G (Business Person)
Analog Devices Inc
1 Technology Way
Norwood, MA 02062-2666, USA

Fishman, Jon (Musician)
2353 Prindle Rd
Charlotte, VT 05445-4423, USA

Fishman, Michael (Actor)
c/o Ryan Glasgow *Bohemia Group (LA)*
1680 Vine St Ste 412
Los Angeles, CA 90028-8800, USA

Fisk, Carlton (Athlete, Baseball Player)
18705 63rd Ave E
Bradenton, FL 34211-7025, USA

Fisk, Schuyler (Actor)
c/o Staff Member *Fat Dot*
87 Bedford St Apt 1
New York, NY 10014-3769, USA

Fister, Doug (Athlete, Baseball Player)
3279 Leaf Dr
Merced, CA 95340-8304, USA

Fitch, Bill (Basketball Coach, Coach)
3714 Walden Estates Dr
Montgomery, TX 77356-8043, USA

Fitch, Leigh (Horse Racer)
RR 114
Sebago, ME 04029, USA

Fites, Donald V (Business Person)
Caterpillar Inc
100 NE Adams St
Peoria, IL 61629-0002, USA

Fittipaldi, Emerson (Race Car Driver)
735 Crandon Blvd Apt 503
Key Biscayne, FL 33149-2526, USA

Fitts, Rick
1903 Dracena Dr
Los Angeles, CA 90027-3106

Fitzgerald, Brian (Athlete, Baseball Player)
94 Wood Landing Rd
Fredericksburg, VA 22405-3531, USA

Fitzgerald, Caitlin (Actor)
c/o Adam Schweitzer *ICM Partners (NY)*
730 5th Ave
New York, NY 10019-4105, USA

Fitzgerald, Ed (Athlete, Baseball Player)
431 Christopher St
Folsom, CA 95630-1706, USA

Fitzgerald, Fern (Actor)
Boutique
10 Universal City Plz Ste 2000
Universal City, CA 91608-1002, USA

FitzGerald, Frances (Writer)
Simon & Schuster
1230 Avenue of the Americas Fl CONC1
New York, NY 10020-1586, USA

Fitzgerald, Glenn (Actor)
c/o Sue Leibman *Barking Dog Entertainment*
609 Greenwich St Fl 6
New York, NY 10014-3610, USA

FitzGerald, Helen (Actor)
Paul Lohner
9300 Wilshire Blvd Ste 555
Beverly Hills, CA 90212-3211, USA

Fitzgerald, Jack (Actor)
William Kerwin Agency
1605 N Cahuenga Blvd # 202
Los Angeles, CA 90028-6201, USA

Fitzgerald, John (Athlete, Baseball Player)
1913 Greve Ave Apt 1
Spring Lake, NJ 07762-2354, USA

Fitzgerald, John (Athlete, Football Player)
408 Arborcrest Dr
Richardson, TX 75080-2606, USA

Fitzgerald, Larry (Athlete, Football Player)
c/o Ashley Smith Becker *Relativity Sports (LA)*
9242 Beverly Blvd Ste 300
Beverly Hills, CA 90210-3728, USA

Fitzgerald, Marcus (Athlete, Football Player)
c/o Roosevelt Barnes *Maximum Sports Management*
6435 W Jefferson Blvd # 197
Fort Wayne, IN 46804-6203, USA

Fitzgerald, Melissa (Actor)
c/o Staff Member *Geddes Agency, The*
1203 Greenacre Ave
West Hollywood, CA 90046-5707, USA

Fitzgerald, Mickey (Athlete, Football Player)
4579 Somerset Rd SW
Smyrna, GA 30082-4538, USA

Fitzgerald, Mike (Athlete, Baseball Player)
415 Parkview Dr
Rochester, IL 62563-9543, USA

Fitzgerald, Mike (Athlete, Baseball Player)
502 Flint Ave
Long Beach, CA 90814-2039, USA

Fitzgerald, Mosley Benita (Athlete)
Women in Cable/Telecommunications
2000 K St NW Ste 350
Washington, DC 20006-1889, USA

Fitzgerald, Pat (Athlete, Football Player)
2271 Bracken Ln
Northfield, IL 60093-2902

Fitzgerald, Peter
1133 Crest Ln
Mc Lean, VA 22101-1805

Fitzgerald, Rusty (Athlete, Hockey Player)
2224 Catskill St
Duluth, MN 55811-3126, USA

Fitzgerald, Tac (Actor)
c/o Staff Member *Iris Burton Agency*
10100 Santa Monica Blvd Ste 1300
Los Angeles, CA 90067-4114, USA

Fitzgerald, Thom (Director)
c/o Gloria Bonelli *Gloria Bonelli & Associates*
Prefers to be contacted via email or telephone
Pine Bush, NY 12566, USA

Fitzgerald, Tom (Athlete, Hockey Player)
3 Samuel Phelps Way
North Reading, MA 01864-2990, USA

Fitzgerald, Tom (Athlete, Hockey Player)
Pittsburgh Penguins 66 Mario Lemieux Pl Ste 2
Attn: Asst To General Manager
Pittsburgh, PA 15219, USA

Fitzgerald-Leclair, Meryle (Baseball Player)
909 E Hanson Ave
Mitchell, SD 57301-3635, USA

Fitzhugh, Steve (Athlete, Football Player)
1037 James Ave N
Minneapolis, MN 55411-3936, USA

Fitzkee, Scott (Athlete, Football Player)
1611 Grafton Shop Rd
Forest Hill, MD 21050-2535, USA

Fitzmaurice, Shaun (Athlete, Baseball Player)
1911 Normandstone Dr
Midlothian, VA 23113-9669, USA

Fitzmorris, Al (Athlete, Baseball Player)
17512 W 159th Ter
Olathe, KS 66062-4017, USA

Fitzpatrick, Hugh (Producer)
c/o Staff Member *Teakwood Lane Productions*
11845 W Olympic Blvd Ste 1125
Los Angeles, CA 90064-5096, USA

Fitzpatrick, Mark (Athlete, Hockey Player)
10571 SW Kelsey Way
Port Saint Lucie, FL 34987-1989, USA

Fitzpatrick, Michael (Baseball Player)
262 Lodge Ln
Kalamazoo, MI 49009-9161, USA

Fitzpatrick, Mike (Athlete, Baseball Player)
262 Lodge Ln
Kalamazoo, MI 49009-9161, USA

Fitzpatrick, Rory (Athlete, Hockey Player)
580 Colebrook Dr
Rochester, NY 14617-2009, USA

Fitzpatrick, Ross (Athlete, Hockey Player)
PO Box 459
Hershey, PA 17033-0459, USA

Fitzpatrick, Ryan (Athlete, Football Player)
c/o Jimmy Sexton *CAA (Memphis)*
6060 Poplar Ave Ste 470
Memphis, TN 38119-0910, USA

Fitzpatrick, Sandy (Athlete, Hockey Player)
11250 Lakerim Rd
San Diego, CA 92131-2311, USA

Fitzsimmons, Greg (Actor)
c/o Kara Welker *Generate Management*
8750 Wilshire Blvd Ste 200
Beverly Hills, CA 90211-2707, USA

Fitzwater, Marlin (Government Official)
851 Cedar Dr
Deale, MD 20751-9613, USA

Five Finger Death Punch (Music Group, Musician)
c/o Ron Opaleski *William Morris Endeavor (LA)*
9601 Wilshire Blvd
Beverly Hills, CA 90210-5213, USA

Five for Fighting (Music Group)
c/o Staff Member *Paradigm (NY)*
360 Park Ave S Fl 16
New York, NY 10010-1716, USA

Fizer, Marcus (Basketball Player)
Charlotte Bobcats
129 W Trade St Ste 700
Charlotte, NC 28202-5301, USA

Flacco, Joe (Athlete, Football Player)
222 S Haviland Ave
Audubon, NJ 08106-1126, USA

Flach, Ken (Coach, Tennis Player)
Vanderbilt University
Athletic Dept
Nashville, TN 37240-0001, USA

Flack, Enya (Actor)
c/o Paul Barrutia *The Paradise Group*
PO Box 69451
West Hollywood, CA 90069-0451, USA

Flack, Roberta (Musician)
1 W 72nd St Apt 78
New York, NY 10023-3425

Flagg, Fannie (Actor, Comedian)
c/o Sally Willcox *Creative Artists Agency (CAA-LA)*
2000 Avenue of the Stars Ste 100
Los Angeles, CA 90067-4705, USA

Flagg, Josh (Business Person, Reality Star)
1133 Cory Ave
West Hollywood, CA 90069-1701, USA

Flaherty, Harry (Athlete, Football Player)
23 Elizabeth Dr
Oceanport, NJ 07757-1050, USA

Flaherty, Joe
c/o Staff Member *Silver Massetti & Szatmary (SMS-NY)*
145 W 45th St # 1204
New York, NY 10036-4008, USA

Flaherty, John (Athlete, Baseball Player)
17 Joseph Bow Ct
Pearl River, NY 10965-2868, USA

Flaherty, Maureen
PO Box 15967
Long Beach, CA 90815-0967, USA

Flair, Ric (Athlete, Wrestler)
c/o Elaine Gillespie *Gillespie Agency, The*
3007 Millwood Ave
Columbia, SC 29205-1855, USA

Flake, Jeff (Congressman, Politician)
240 Cannon Hob
Washington, DC 20515-1802, USa

Flame, Penny (Adult Film Star)
19422 Archwood St
Reseda, CA 91335-4903, USA

Flame, Waka Flocka (Musician)
103 Bayberry Hls
McDonough, GA 30253-4293, USA

Flaming Lips, The (Music Group, Musician)
c/o Robby Fraser *William Morris Endeavor (LA)*
9601 Wilshire Blvd
Beverly Hills, CA 90210-5213, USA

Flanagan, Crista (Actor)
c/o Kay Liberman *Liberman/Zerman Management*
252 N Larchmont Blvd Ste 200
Los Angeles, CA 90004-3754, USA

Flanagan, Ed (Athlete, Football Player)
10981 Clayton St
Northglenn, CO 80233-4671, USA

Flanagan, Fionnula (Actor)
c/o Dick Guttman *Guttman Associates*
118 S Beverly Dr Ste 201
Beverly Hills, CA 90212-3016, USA

Flanagan, Flonnula (Actor)
Guttman
118 S Beverly Dr Ste 201
Beverly Hills, CA 90212-3016, USA

Flanagan, Mike (Athlete, Football Player)
4631 Waring St
Houston, TX 77027-6217, USA

Flanagan, Shalane (Athlete, Track Athlete)
c/o Staff Member *US Olympic Committee*
1750 E Boulder St
Alumni Relations
Colorado Springs, CO 80909-5793, USA

Flanagan, Tommy (Actor)
c/o Beth Holden-Garland *Untitled Entertainment (LA)*
350 S Beverly Dr Ste 200
Beverly Hills, CA 90212-4819, USA

Flanery, Bridget
8428 Melrose Pl Ste C
West Hollywood, CA 90069-5300

Flanery, Sean Patrick (Actor)
c/o Jeff Golenberg *Silver Lining Entertainment*
421 S Beverly Dr Fl 7
Beverly Hills, CA 90212-4408, USA

Flanigan, Jim (Athlete, Football Player)
3820 Sand Bay Point Rd
Sturgeon Bay, WI 54235-8418, USA

Flanigan, Jim (Athlete, Football Player)
4511 Wyandot Trl
Green Bay, WI 54313-6789, USA

Flanigan, Joe (Actor)
c/o John Carrabino *John Carrabino Management*
5900 Wilshire Blvd Ste 406
Los Angeles, CA 90036-5015, USA

Flanigan, Tom (Athlete, Baseball Player)
114 E 40th St # 1
Covington, KY 41015-1802, USA

Flannery, John (Athlete, Baseball Player)
9002 Scottish Pastures Dr
Austin, TX 78750-3582, USA

Flannery, John (Athlete, Football Player)
7514 Dawn Mist Ct
Sugar Land, TX 77479-6323, USA

Flannery, Kate (Actor)
c/o Kristopher Koller *Seven Summits Pictures & Management*
8906 W Olympic Blvd
Ground Floor
Beverly Hills, CA 90211-3550, USA

Flannery, Susan (Actor)
Flannery-Daedy-Leona
6977 Shepard Mesa Rd
Carpinteria, CA 93013-3134, USA

Flannery, Tim (Athlete, Baseball Player)
715 Hymettus Ave
Encinitas, CA 92024-2148, USA

Flannigan, Maureen (Actor)
Gold Marshak Liedtke
3500 W Olive Ave Ste 1400
Burbank, CA 91505-5512, USA

Flash, Grandmaster (DJ, Musician)
Grandmaster Flash Enterprises
600 Johnson Ave Ste E7
Bohemia, NY 11716-2664, USA

Flaska, Carrie (Actor)
3440 29th St
Astoria, NY 11106-3504, USA

Flatley, Michael (Actor, Dancer)
c/o Staff Member *Creative Artists Agency (CAA-LA)*
2000 Avenue of the Stars Ste 100
Los Angeles, CA 90067-4705, USA

Flatley, Paul R (Athlete, Football Player)
795 Woods Rd
Richmond, IN 47374-9409, USA

Flatt, Lester
PO Box 647
Hendersonville, TN 37077-0647

Flav, Flavor (Actor, Comedian, Reality Star)
7896 Via Ventura Ct
Las Vegas, NV 89123-1828, USA

Flavin, Jennifer (Model)
30 Beverly Park
Beverly Hills, CA 90210-1546, USA

Flavin, John (Athlete, Baseball Player)
23060 16th St
Newhall, CA 91321-1054, USA

Flavio, Alfaro (Athlete, Baseball Player, Olympic Athlete)
3240 N Bass Island Rd
West Sacramento, CA 95691-5848, USA

Flay, Bobby (Chef, Television Host)
c/o Jonathan Rosen *William Morris Endeavor (NY)*
1325 Avenue of the Americas
New York, NY 10019-6026, USA

Flchter, Michael (Baseball Player)
8821 Jackson Ct
Munster, IN 46321-2410, USA

Flea (Actor, Musician)
c/o Peter Mensch *Q Prime*
729 7th Ave Ste 1600
New York, NY 10019-6880, USA

Flebotte, Dave (Producer)
c/o Ann Blanchard *Creative Artists Agency (CAA-LA)*
2000 Avenue of the Stars Ste 100
Los Angeles, CA 90067-4705, USA

Fleck, Bela (Musician)
c/o Ted Kurland *Ted Kurland Associates*
173 Brighton Ave
Allston, MA 02134-2003, USA

Fleckman, Marty (Athlete, Golfer)
26411 Ridgestone Park Ln
Cypress, TX 77433-1279, USA

Fleder, Gary R (Director)
ACTW Filmworks
624 Sunset Ave
Venice, CA 90291-2733, USA

Fleener, Coby (Athlete, Football Player)
c/o Frank Bauer *Sun West Sports*
7883 N Pershing Ave
Stockton, CA 95207-1749, USA

Fleetwood, Mick (Musician)
Fleetwood Marketing
5737 Kanan Rd # 237
Agoura Hills, CA 91301-1601, USA

Fleigel, Bernie (Athlete, Basketball Player)
21 Granville Rd # 3
Cambridge, MA 02138-6806, USA

Fleischer, Charles
749 N Crescent Heights Blvd
Los Angeles, CA 90046-7001

Fleischer, Daniel (Religious Leader)
6486 Lower 35th St N
Saint Paul, MN 55128-3944, USA

Fleischman, Paul (Writer)
PO Box 646
Aromas, CA 95004-0646, USA

Fleisher, Brett (Actor)
c/o Alan Somers *Somers Mauldin The Rose Group*
1925 Century Park E Ste 2320
Los Angeles, CA 90067-2724, USA

Fleisher, Bruce (Athlete, Golfer)
11722 Cardena Ct
Palm Beach Gardens, FL 33418-1564, USA

Fleisher, Leon (Musician)
20 Merrymount Rd
Baltimore, MD 21210-1909, USA

Fleiss, Michael (Mike) (Director, Producer)
c/o Staff Member *Next Entertainment*
10200 Riverside Dr Ste 200
Toluca Lake, CA 91602-2539, USA

Fleiss, Noah (Actor)
c/o Ellen Gilbert *Paradigm (NY)*
360 Park Ave S Fl 16
New York, NY 10010-1716, USA

Fleming, Cory (Athlete, Football Player)
2500 Whitney Pl Apt 8108
Metairie, LA 70002-6257, USA

Fleming, David (Dave) (Athlete, Baseball Player)
37 Laurelwood Ln
Southbury, CT 06488-4657, USA

Fleming, Ed
RR Box 3BOX 261K
Greensburg, PA 15601

Fleming, Eric (Director)
c/o David Krintzman *Morris Yorn Barnes Levine Krintzman Rubenstein Kohner & Gellman*
2000 Avenue of the Stars Ste 300N
3rd Floor, North Tower
Los Angeles, CA 90067-4704, USA

Fleming, George (Athlete, Football Player)
1100 Lake Washington Blvd S
Seattle, WA 98144-3316, USA

Fleming, Gerry (Athlete, Hockey Player)
c/o Staff Member *Florida Everblades*
11000 Everblades Pkwy
Estero, FL 33928-9412, USA

Fleming, Jamell (Athlete, Football Player)
c/o Ken Landphere *Octagon Football*
832 Sansome St Fl 1
San Francisco, CA 94111-1558, USA

Fleming, John (Congressman, Politician)
416 Cannon Hob
Washington, DC 20515-3220, USA

Fleming, Marv (Athlete, Football Player)
909 Howard St
Marina Del Rey, CA 90292-5518, USA

Fleming, Peggy (Athlete, Figure Skater, Olympic Athlete)
16387 Aztec Ridge Dr
Los Gatos, CA 95030-7503, USA

Fleming, Rhonda (Actor)
10281 Century Woods Dr
Los Angeles, CA 90067-6312, USA

Fleming, Scott (Government Official)
2425 Elendil Ln
Davis, CA 95616-3045, USA

Fleming, Troy (Athlete, Football Player)
510 New Highway 96 W Apt A2
Franklin, TN 37064-2471, USA

Fleming, Troy (Athlete, Football Player)
PO Box 789
Knoxville, TN 37901-0789, USA

Fleming, Vern (Athlete, Basketball Player, Olympic Athlete)
10713 Brixton Ln
Fishers, IN 46037-8707, USA

Fleming, Willie (Athlete, Football Player)
195 Gould Ave
Bedford, OH 44146-2611, USA

Flemister, Zeron (Athlete, Football Player)
7345 S Jackson St
Centennial, CO 80122-2215, USA

Flemming, William N (Bill) (Sportscaster)
ABC-TV Sports Dept
77 W 66th St
New York, NY 10023-6201, USA

Flener, Huck (Athlete, Baseball Player)
2186 North Ave
Chico, CA 95926-1430, USA

Flerstein, Harvey F (Actor, Musician, Writer)
1479 Carla Ridge Dr
Beverly Hills, CA 90210, USA

Flesch, John (Athlete, Hockey Player)
74101 8th Ave
South Haven, MI 49090-9750, USA

Flesch, Steve (Athlete, Golfer)
868 Keeneland Green Dr
Union, KY 41091-8016, USA

Flessel, Craig (Cartoonist)
40 Camino Alto Apt 2306
Mill Valley, CA 94941-2976, USA

Fletcher, Andrew (Baseball Player)
3282 Kinderhill Ln
Germantown, TN 38138-8210, USA

Fletcher, Andy (Athlete, Baseball Player)
8696 Belmor Crossing Cv
Olive Branch, MS 38654-6362, USA

Fletcher, Andy (Musician)
Reach Media
295 Greenwich St # 109
New York, NY 10007-1049, USA

Fletcher, Billy (Athlete, Football Player)
3216 Winners Cir
Germantown, TN 38138-8220, USA

Fletcher, Brendan (Actor)
Seven Summits Mgmt
8447 Wilshire Blvd Ste 200
Beverly Hills, CA 90211-3207, USA

Fletcher, Chris (Athlete, Football Player)
4818 La Cruz Dr
La Mesa, CA 91941-4489, USA

Fletcher, Cliff (Athlete, Hockey Player)
3030 Grand Bay Blvd Unit 314
Longboat Key, FL 34228-4407, USA

Fletcher, Darrin (Athlete, Baseball Player)
9146 E 2100 North Rd
Oakwood, IL 61858-6285, USA

Fletcher, Derrick (Athlete, Football Player)
79 Terra Bella Dr
Manvel, TX 77578-3339, USA

Fletcher, Ernest L (Politician)
118 Golf Terrace Dr
Stockbridge, GA 30281-6362, USA

Fletcher, Jamar (Athlete, Football Player)
11063 Worchester Dr
Saint Louis, MO 63136-5828, USA

Fletcher, London (Athlete, Football Player)
300 Oakmont Ln
Waxhaw, NC 28173-6825, USA

Fletcher, Louis (Athlete, Football Player)
18278 Buccaneer Ter
Leesburg, VA 20176-8479, USA

Fletcher, Louise (Actor)
1520 Camden Ave Apt 105
Los Angeles, CA 90025-3443, USA

Fletcher, Maria (Beauty Pageant Winner)
117 Regency Dr
Conway, SC 29526-9018, USA

Fletcher, Martin (Correspondent)
NBC-TV
4001 Nebraska Ave NW
News Dept
Washington, DC 20016-2795, USA

Fletcher, Paul (Athlete, Baseball Player)
431 Harpold Ave
Ravenswood, WV 26164-1333, USA

Fletcher, Scott B (Athlete, Baseball Player)
300 Birkdale Dr
Fayetteville, GA 30215-2720, USA

Fletcher, Simon (Athlete, Football Player)
2225 S Ensenada St
Aurora, CO 80013-6230, USA

Fletcher, Terrell (Athlete, Football Player)
22457 N Summit Ridge Cir
Chatsworth, CA 91311-2691, USA

Fletcher, Tom (Athlete, Baseball Player)
9287 E 2085 North Rd
Oakwood, IL 61858-6252, USA

Fleury, Marc-Andre (Athlete, Hockey Player)
Octagon Sports Management
7950 Jones Branch Dr
Mc Lean, VA 22102-3302, USA

Flichel, Todd (Athlete, Hockey Player)
Bowling Green State University Athletic
9564 Taberna Ln
Olmsted Twp, OH 44138-4257, USA

Flick, Bob (Musician)
Bob Flick Productions
300 Vine St Ste 14
Seattle, WA 98121-1465, USA

Flick, Mick
Sherry Netherlands 5th & 59th
New York, NY 10003

Flick, Tom (Athlete, Football Player)
9718 208th Ave NE
Redmond, WA 98053-5216, USA

Flinn, John (Athlete, Baseball Player)
6221 Lake Providence Ln
Charlotte, NC 28277-0565, USA

Flinn, Ryan (Athlete, Hockey Player)
21611 N 37th St
Phoenix, AZ 85050-4945, USA

Flint, George (Athlete, Football Player)
PO Box 2486
Prescott, AZ 86302-2486, USA

Flint, Judson (Athlete, Football Player)
306 Federal St
Farrell, PA 16121-1925, USA

Flint, Keith (Dancer, Musician)
c/o Staff Member *Maverick Recording Co (LA)*
3300 Warner Blvd
Burbank, CA 91505-4632, USA

Flippin, Lucy Lee (Actor)
50785 Grand Traverse Ave
La Quinta, CA 92253-5845, USA

Flitter, Josh (Actor)
c/o Mara Santino *Luber Roklin Management*
5815 W Sunset Blvd Ste 206
Los Angeles, CA 90028-6481, USA

Flitter, Josh (Actor)
c/o Ellen Gilbert *Paradigm (NY)*
360 Park Ave S Fl 16
New York, NY 10010-1716, USA

Float, Jeffrey (Athlete, Olympic Athlete, Swimmer)
1906 University Park Dr
Sacramento, CA 95825-8210, USA

Flobots (Music Group)
c/o Corrie Christopher *Paradigm (LA)*
405 S Beverly Dr Ste 500
Beverly Hills, CA 90212-4425, USA

Flockhart, Calista (Actor)
c/o Melissa Kates *Viewpoint Inc (LA)*
8820 Wilshire Blvd Ste 220
Beverly Hills, CA 90211-2622, USA

Flock of Seagulls (Music Group, Musician)
c/o Carlos Keyes *Red Entertainment Agency*
505 8th Ave Rm 1004
New York, NY 10018-6529, USA

Floethe, Chris (Baseball Player)
5634 Mount Hood Ct
Martinez, CA 94553-5837, USA

Floetry (Music Group)
c/o Cara Lewis *Creative Artists Agency (CAA-NY)*
162 5th Ave Fl 6
New York, NY 10010-6047, USA

Flogging Molly (Music Group, Musician)
c/o Gary Schwindt *Villam Artist Management*
820 Hyperion Ave
Los Angeles, CA 90029-3106, USA

Flood, Ann (Actor)
15 E 91st St
New York, NY 10128-0648, USA

Flood, Staci (Model, Musician)
Clear Talent Group
10950 Ventura Blvd
Studio City, CA 91604-3340, USA

Flora, Kevin (Athlete, Baseball Player)
25035 Portsmouth
Mission Viejo, CA 92692-2812, USA

Flora, Lars (Athlete, Olympic Athlete, Track Athlete)
6500 Michigan Blvd
Anchorage, AK 99516-1818, USA

Florek, Dann (Actor)
c/o Staff Member *Access Talent Management*
171 Madison Ave Rm 1005
New York, NY 10016-5110, USA

Florence, Don (Athlete, Baseball Player)
144 Bedford Rd
New Boston, NH 03070-4301, USA

Florence, Tyler (Chef, Television Host)
Tyler Florence Shop
59 Throckmorton Ave
Mill Valley, CA 94941-1915, USA

Flores, Bill (Congressman, Politician)
1505 Longworth Hob
Washington, DC 20515-3313, USA

Flores, Jose (Athlete, Baseball Player)
PO Box 81533
Corpus Christi, TX 78468-1533, USA

Flores, Nikki (Musician)
c/o Staff Member *Sony Music International*
550 Madison Ave Fl 6
New York, NY 10022-3211, USA

Flores, Patrick F (Religious Leader)
Archbishop's Residence
2600 W Woodlawn Ave
San Antonio, TX 78228-5122, USA

Flores, Randy (Athlete, Baseball Player)
23 Keepsake
Irvine, CA 92618-8820, USA

Flores, Ron (Athlete, Baseball Player)
12026 Reichling Ln
Whittier, CA 90606-2561, USA

Flores, Thomas R (Tom) (Athlete, Coach, Football Coach, Football Executive, Football Player)
77741 Cove Pointe Cir
Indian Wells, CA 92210-6101, USA

Flores, Tom
11220 NE 53rd St
Kirkland, WA 98033-7505

Florida Georgia Line (Music Group)
c/o Kevin 'Chief' Zaruk *Big Loud Mountain*
1111 16th Ave S Ste 201
Nashville, TN 37212-2336, USA

Florie, Bryce (Athlete, Baseball Player)
1118 Lands End Dr
Hanahan, SC 29410-4752, USA

Florin, Susan (Athlete, Golfer)
1883 Lexington Pl
Tarpon Springs, FL 34688-4965, USA

Florio, James (Politician)
76 Linden Ave
Metuchen, NJ 08840-1449, USA

Florio, Steven T (Publisher)
Conde Nast Publications
4 Times Sq Fl 22
Publisher's Office
New York, NY 10036-6561, USA

Florio, Thomas A (Actor)
New Yorker Magazine
4 Times Sq Fl 22
Publisher's Office
New York, NY 10036-6592, USA

Flory, Med (Actor)
6044 Ensign Ave
North Hollywood, CA 91606-4905, USA

Flournoy, Craig (Journalist)
Dallas News
Editorial Dept
Communications Center
Dallas, TX 75265, USA

Flower, Joseph R (Religious Leader)
Assemblies of God
1445 N Boonville Ave
Springfield, MO 65802-1894, USA

flower, tyler (Athlete, Baseball Player)
109 Newcastle Walk
Woodstock, GA 30188-6088, USA

Flowers, Bernard (Athlete, Football Player)
3819 Old Farm Rd
Lafayette, IN 47909-3521, USA

Flowers, Brandon (Musician)
c/o Staff Member *William Morris Endeavor (LA)*
9601 Wilshire Blvd Ste M300
Beverly Hills, CA 90210-5212, USA

Flowers, Bruce (Athlete, Basketball Player)
276 W Grantley Ave
Elmhurst, IL 60126-2238, USA

Flowers, Charles (Charlie) (Athlete, Football Player)
6170 Mount Brook Way NW
Atlanta, GA 30328, USA

Flowers ', Erik (Athlete, Football Player)
712 Mandalay Pkwy
McDonough, GA 30253-6109, USA

Flowers, Frank E (Director, Writer)
c/o Aleen Keshishian *Brillstein Entertainment Partners (LA)*
9150 Wilshire Blvd Ste 350
Beverly Hills, CA 90212-3453, USA

Flowers, Gennifer
4859 Cedar Springs Rd Apt 241
Dallas, TX 75219-1215

Flowers, Richmond (Athlete, Football Player)
3434 Indian Lake Dr
Pelham, AL 35124-2713, USA

Floyd, Bobby (Athlete, Baseball Player)
1757 SE Dominic Ave
Port Saint Lucie, FL 34952-5815, USA

Floyd, Bobby Jack (Athlete, Football Player)
4133 Tahoe Vista Dr
Rocklin, CA 95765-5089, USA

Floyd, C Clifford (Cliff) (Athlete, Baseball Player)
3283 Birch Ter
Davie, FL 33330-1337, USA

Floyd, Dixon (Athlete, Football Player)
4285 Pierre Dr
Beaumont, TX 77705-1018, USA

Floyd, Eric (Athlete, Football Player)
18047 Sailfish Dr
Lutz, FL 33558-7771, USA

Floyd, Eric (Sleepy) (Athlete, Basketball Player)
3101 Ivy Creek Rd
Gastonia, NC 28056-0301, USA

Floyd, Eric '"Sleepy'" (Athlete, Basketball Player)
5644 Westheimer Rd
Houston, TX 77056-4002, USA

Floyd, Gavin (Athlete, Baseball Player)
9809 Milano Dr
Trinity, FL 34655-4668, USA

Floyd, George (Athlete, Football Player)
7056 Burlington Pike
Attn: Faculty Staff
Florence, KY 41042-1681, USA

Floyd, Larry (Athlete, Hockey Player)
3780 Hancock St
San Diego, CA 92110-4340, USA

Floyd, Leslie (Baseball Player)
Detroit Tigers
PO Box 7619
Texarkana, TX 75505-7619, USA

Floyd, Marlene (Athlete, Golfer)
5370 Clubhouse Ln
Hope Mills, NC 28348-9794, USA

Floyd, Michael (Athlete, Football Player)
c/o David Dunn *Athletes First, LLC*
23091 Mill Creek Dr
Laguna Hills, CA 92653-1258, USA

Floyd, Ray
PO Box 545957
Miami Beach, FL 33154-5957

Floyd, Raymond (Athlete, Golfer)
505 S Flagler Dr Ste 910
West Palm Beach, FL 33401-5948, USA

Floyd, Susan
PO Box 5617
Beverly Hills, CA 90209-5617

Floyd, Tim (Coach)
New Orleans Hornets
1501 Girod St
New Orleans Arena
New Orleans, LA 70113-3124, USA

Floyd, William (Athlete, Football Player)
PO Box 784767
Winter Garden, FL 34778-4767, USA

Fluegel, Darlanne (Actor)
Shelter Entertainment
9255 W Sunset Blvd Ste 1010
West Hollywood, CA 90069-3307, USA

Flueger, Patrick (Actor)
c/o Nancy Kremer *Nancy Kremer Management*
4545 Morse Ave
Studio City, CA 91604-1008, USA

Flueger, Patrick John (Actor)
c/o Nancy Kremer *Nancy Kremer Management*
4545 Morse Ave
Studio City, CA 91604-1008, USA

Fluno, Jere D (Business Person)
W W Grainger Inc
5500 Howard St
Skokie, IL 60077-2620, USA

Flutie, Darren (Athlete, Football Player)
29 Pine St
Natick, MA 01760-1203, USA

Flutie, Doug (Athlete, Football Player, Heisman Trophy Winner)
PO Box 767
Framingham, MA 01701-0767, USA

F. Lynch, Stephen (Congressman, Politician)
2348 Rayburn Hob
Washington, DC 20515-4611, USA

Flynn, Colleen (Actor)
LGM
10390 Santa Monica Blvd Ste 300
Los Angeles, CA 90025-5091, USA

Flynn, Doug (Athlete, Baseball Player)
2465 Vale Dr
Lexington, KY 40514-1421, USA

Flynn, Gillian (Writer)
c/o Stephanie Kip Rostan *Levine Greenberg Literary Agency*
307 7th Ave Rm 2407
New York, NY 10001-6062, USA

Flynn, Jackie (Comedian)
c/o Staff Member *Don Buchwald & Associates (LA)*
6500 Wilshire Blvd Ste 2200
Los Angeles, CA 90048-4942, USA

Flynn, Matt (Athlete, Football Player)
c/o Pat Dye Jr *SportsTrust Advisors (GA)*
3340 Peachtree Rd NE Fl 16
Atlanta, GA 30326-1000, USA

Flynn, Mike (Athlete, Basketball Player)
2138 Woodbourne Ave
Louisville, KY 40205-1912, USA

Flynn, Mike (Athlete, Football Player)
301 Newbury St Ste 13
Danvers, MA 01923-1029, USA

Flynn, Neil (Actor)
c/o Staff Member *Christopher Wright Management*
3207 Winnie Dr
Los Angeles, CA 90068-1439, USA

Flynn, Sean (Actor)
c/o Danielle Lenniger *Luber Roklin Management*
5815 W Sunset Blvd Ste 206
Los Angeles, CA 90028-6481, USA

Flynn, Tom (Athlete, Football Player)
4008 Holiday Park Dr
Murrysville, PA 15668-8529, USA

Flynt, Larry (Publisher)
9211 Robin Dr
Los Angeles, CA 90069-1146, USA

Flynville Train (Music Group)
c/o Staff Member *Paradigm (Monterey)*
404 W Franklin St
Monterey, CA 93940-2303, USA

Flythe, Mark (Athlete, Football Player)
505 Pheasant Run
Monmouth Junction, NJ 08852-1929, USA

F. Napolitano, Grace (Congressman, Politician)
1610 Longworth Hob
Washington, DC 20515-2213, USA

Foa, Barrett (Actor)
c/o Ethan Salter *Greene & Associates*
1901 Avenue of the Stars Ste 130
Los Angeles, CA 90067-6030, USA

Foale, C Michael (Doctor)
2101 Todville Rd # 11
Seabrook, TX 77586-3723, USA

Foale, C Michael Dr
2102 Todville Rd Unit 11
Seabrook, TX 77586-3732, USA

Foale, C Michael (Mike) (Astronaut)
2101 Todville Rd # 11
Seabrook, TX 77586-3723, USA

Fobbs, Brandon
c/o Todd Justice *Justice & Ponder*
PO Box 480033
Los Angeles, CA 90048-1033, USA

Foeger, Luggi (Skier)
Christopher Foeger
110 Oak Knoll Dr
San Anselmo, CA 94960-1121, USA

Foerster, Paul (Athlete, Olympic Athlete, Sailor)
126 Dunford Dr
Rockwall, TX 75032-6625, USA

Fogelnest, Jake (Actor)
c/o Kara Welker *Generate Management*
8750 Wilshire Blvd Ste 200
Beverly Hills, CA 90211-2707, USA

Fogerty, John (Musician, Songwriter)
2700 White Stallion Rd
Thousand Oaks, CA 91361-5012, USA

Fogg, Josh (Athlete, Baseball Player)
4910 S Quincy St
Tampa, FL 33611-3820, USA

Foggie, Fred (Athlete, Football Player)
360 Jackson Rd
Inman, SC 29349-9533, USA

Foggs, Edward L (Religious Leader)
Church of God
PO Box 2420
Anderson, IN 46018-2420, USA

Fogle, Larry (Athlete, Basketball Player)
72 Beechwood St
Rochester, NY 14609, USA

Fogler, Dan (Actor, Producer)
c/o Suzan Bymel *Management 360*
9111 Wilshire Blvd
Beverly Hills, CA 90210-5508, USA

Fogler, Eddie (Basketball Player)
University of South Carolina
Athletic Dept
Milwaukee, SC 53233, USA

Foiles, Hank (Athlete, Baseball Player)
4333 Silverleaf Ct
Virginia Beach, VA 23462-5738, USA

Foiles, Lisa (Actor)
Boutique Talent Agency
9701 Wilshire Blvd Ste 1000
C/O Nancy Schmidt Sanford
Beverly Hills, CA 90212-2010, USA

Folau, Spencer (Athlete, Football Player)
14003 Woodens Ln
Reisterstown, MD 21136-4536, USA

Folder-Powell, Rose (Athlete, Baseball Player, Commentator)
4651 Spilman Ave
Carnation, WA 98014-6326, USA

Folds, Ben (Musician, Songwriter)
c/o Staff Member *ICM Partners (LA)*
10250 Constellation Blvd Fl 7
Los Angeles, CA 90067-6207, USA

Foley, Christopher (Actor)
c/o Scott Zimmerman *Evolution Entertainment (LA)*
901 N Highland Ave
Los Angeles, CA 90038-2412, USA

Foley, Dave (Athlete, Football Player)
4500 Redmond Rd
Springfield, OH 45505-1722, USA

Foley, Dave (Comedian)
c/o Matthew Labov *Forefront Media*
8500 Melrose Ave Ste 205
West Hollywood, CA 90069-5169, USA

Foley, ex-Speaker Tom
601 W 1st Ave # 2W
Spokane, WA 99201-3825

Foley, Glenn (Athlete, Football Player)
3204 Buxmont Rd
Marlton, NJ 08053-8506, USA

Foley, Jeremy (Actor)
Academy Kids Mgmt
4942 Vineland Ave Ste 103
North Hollywood, CA 91601-5639, USA

Foley, John (Athlete, Basketball Player)
PO Box 143
Barre, MA 01005-0143, USA

Foley, Marv (Athlete, Baseball Player)
10166 Glenmore Ave
Bradenton, FL 34202-4049, USA

Foley, Mick (Actor, Wrestler)
c/o Elaine Gillespie *Gillespie Agency, The*
3007 Millwood Ave
Columbia, SC 29205-1855, USA

Foley, Scott (Actor)
24878 Long Valley Rd
Hidden Hills, CA 91302-1262, USA

Foley, Steve (Athlete, Football Player)
9754 Sunset Hill Dr
Lone Tree, CO 80124-6720, USA

Foley, Tim (Athlete, Football Player)
9816 Fairway Cir
Leesburg, FL 34788-3623, USA

Foley, Tim J (Athlete, Football Player)
2851 Old Clifton Rd
Springfield, OH 45502-9455, USA

Foley, Tom (Athlete, Baseball Player)
5237 Karlsburg Pl
Palm Harbor, FL 34685-3696, USA

Folger, Franklin (Cartoonist)
c/o Staff Member *King Features Syndication*
300 W 57th St Fl 15
New York, NY 10019-5238, USA

Foli, Tim (Athlete, Baseball Player)
74 Apian Way
Ormond Beach, FL 32174-1872, USA

Folkenberg, Robert S (Religious Leader)
Seventh-Day Adventists
12501 Old Columbia Pike
Silver Spring, MD 20904-6600, USA

Folkers, Rich (Athlete, Baseball Player)
1121 Cane Mill Ln
Bradenton, FL 34212-2638, USA

Folkins, Lee (Athlete, Football Player)
14439 Fawnhaven Ct
Orlando, FL 32828-7843, USA

Folkl, Kristin (Athlete, Olympic Athlete, Volleyball Player)
4847 Langtree Dr
Saint Louis, MO 63128-2728, USA

Foll, Tim (Baseball Player)
New York Mets
1003 Hilltop Ln
Kodak, TN 37764-1838, USA

Follese, Ryan (Musician)
PO Box 340020
Nashville, TN 37203-0020, USA

Follet, George (Athlete, Football Player)
6254 Parima St
Long Beach, CA 90803-2108, USA

Follmer, George (Race Car Driver)
3529 E Mountain View Dr
Post Falls, ID 83854-7470, USA

Followill, Caleb (Musician)
184 Thompson St Apt 5M
New York, NY 10012-2533, USA

Followill, Matthew (Musician)
874 S Curtiswood Ln
Nashville, TN 37204-4317, USA

Folman, Ari (Director)
c/o Maha Dakhil *Creative Artists Agency
(CAA-LA)*
2000 Avenue of the Stars Ste 100
Los Angeles, CA 90067-4705, USA

Folse, John (Chef)
Chef John Folse and Company
2517 S Philippe Ave
Gonzales, LA 70737-3750, USA

Folsom, James (Politician)
1482 Orchard Dr NE
Cullman, AL 35055-2145, USA

Folsom, Steve (Athlete, Football Player)
6 Woodhollow Trl
Round Rock, TX 78665-9739, USA

Folston, James (Athlete, Football Player)
1450 Victoria Blvd
Rockledge, FL 32955-4312, USA

Fonda, Bridget (Actor)
c/o Staff Member *IFA Talent Agency*
2000 Avenue Of The Stars
Los Angeles, CA 90067-4700, USA

Fonda, Jane (Actor)
Fonda, Inc
PO Box 5840
Atlanta, GA 31107-0840, USA

Fonda, Peter (Actor)
Peter Fonda Collection LLC
9454 Wilshire Blvd Fl 4
Beverly Hills, CA 90212-2907, USA

Fong, Darryl
247 S Beverly Dr # 102
Beverly Hills, CA 90212-3830

Fonoti, Toniu (Athlete, Football Player)
91781 Oama Pl
Ewa Beach, HI 96706-2417, USA

Fonseca (Musician)
c/o Staff Member *William Morris
Endeavor (Miami)*
119 Washington Ave Ste 400
Miami Beach, FL 33139-7202, USA

Fonseca, Chris (Actor)
Strauss-McGarr Entertainment
1199 Boise Way
Costa Mesa, CA 92626-2704, USA

Fonseca, David (Musician)
c/o Staff Member *Universal Music
Publishing Group (Latin)*
420 Lincoln Rd Ste 200
Miami Beach, FL 33139-3014, USA

Fonseca, Lyndsy (Actor)
c/o Felicia Sager *Sager Management*
260 S Beverly Dr Ste 205
Beverly Hills, CA 90212-3812, USA

Fonsi, Luis (Musician)
Tony Mojena Entertainment Inc
463 Sergio Cuevas Bustamante
San Juan, PR 00918, USA

Fontaine, Levi (Athlete, Basketball Player)
805 Rollins Rd Apt 2
Burlingame, CA 94010-2664, USA

Fontana, Santino (Actor)
c/o Christopher Highland *United Talent
Agency (UTA-NYC)*
41 Madison Ave
New York, NY 10010-2202, USA

Fontana, Tom (Producer, Writer)
c/o Peter Benedek *United Talent Agency
(UTA-LA)*
9336 Civic Center Dr
Beverly Hills, CA 90210-3604, USA

Fontas, Jon (Athlete, Hockey Player)
9 Boggs Cir
Nashua, NH 03060-4861, USA

Fontenot, Albert (Athlete, Football Player)
4919 Gammage St
Houston, TX 77021-3205, USA

Fontenot, Jerry (Athlete, Football Player)
938 Bristol Dr
Deerfield, IL 60015-4843, USA

Fontenot, Joe (Athlete, Baseball Player)
1165 Locust Dr
Bethlehem, GA 30620-2593, USA

Fontenot, Ray (Athlete, Baseball Player)
1674 S Crestview Dr
Lake Charles, LA 70605, USA

Fontes, Wayne H (Athlete, Coach,
Football Coach, Football Player)
2043 Harbour Watch Cir
Tarpon Springs, FL 34689-2055, USA

Fonville, Chad (Athlete, Baseball Player)
2338 Piney Green Rd
Midway Park, NC 28544-1112, USA

Fonville, Charles (Athlete, Track Athlete)
1845 Wintergreen Ct
Ann Arbor, MI 48103-9727, USA

Foo, Jon (Actor)
c/o Steve Chasman *Current Entertainment*
9200 W Sunset Blvd Ste 600
West Hollywood, CA 90069-3196, USA

Foo Fighters (Music Group)
c/o Steve Martin *Nasty Little Man*
110 Greene St Ste 605
New York, NY 10012-3838, USA

Foor, Jim (Athlete, Baseball Player)
2018 Bolsover St
Houston, TX 77005-1616, USA

Foose, Chip (Actor)
Foose Design Inc
17811 Sampson Ln Ste A
Huntington Beach, CA 92647-7199, USA

Foote, Adam (Athlete, Hockey Player)
4656 S Ogden St
Englewood, CO 80113-5975, USA

Foote, Barry (Athlete, Baseball Player)
92 Lassiter Pond Rd
Smithfield, NC 27577-7956, USA

Foote, Chris (Athlete, Football Player)
1431 Springpointe Way
Knoxville, TN 37931-4471, USA

Foote, Larry (Athlete, Football Player)
c/o Brian Levy *Goal Line Football
Management*
1025 Kane Concourse Ste 207
Bay Harbor Islands, FL 33154-2118, USA

Footman, Dan (Athlete, Football Player)
7189 Nottinghamshire Dr
Jacksonville, FL 32219-4338, USA

Foppert, Jesse (Athlete, Baseball Player)
PO Box 150682
San Rafael, CA 94915-0682, USA

Foray, June (Actor)
22745 Erwin St
Woodland Hills, CA 91367-3212, USA

Forbert, Steve (Musician, Songwriter,
Writer)
Mongrel Music
743 Center Blvd
Fairfax, CA 94930-1764, USA

Forbes, Dave (Athlete, Hockey Player)
4020 Reserve Pt
Colorado Springs, CO 80904-1043, USA

Forbes, Michelle (Actor)
c/o Laura Berwick *Berwick & Kovacik*
6300 Wilshire Blvd Ste 1410
Los Angeles, CA 90048-5216, USA

Forbes, Mike (Athlete, Hockey Player)
547 Waverly Ave
Grand Haven, MI 49417-2127, USA

Forbes, P J (Athlete, Baseball Player)
10236 W Westlakes Ct
Wichita, KS 67205-5219, USA

Forbes, Steve (Business Person, Publisher)
Forbes Magazine
60 5th Ave Frnt 1
New York, NY 10011-8868, USA

Forbes, West (Musician)
Paramount Entertainment
PO Box 12
Far Hills, NJ 07931-0012, USA

Force, John (Race Car Driver)
John Force Racing
22722 Old Canal Rd
Yorba Linda, CA 92887-4602, USA

Ford, Ben (Athlete, Baseball Player)
1717 Applewood Pl NE
Cedar Rapids, IA 52402-3321, USA

Ford, Bette
1801 Avenue of the Stars Ste 902
Los Angeles, CA 90067-5981

Ford, Charlie (Athlete, Football Player)
2995 South St
Beaumont, TX 77702-2108, USA

Ford, Charlotte
25 Sutton Pl S Apt 14N
New York, NY 10022-2456

Ford, Cheryl (Basketball Player)
Detroit Shock Palace
2 Championship Dr
Auburn Hills, MI 48326-1753, USA

Ford, Chris (Athlete, Basketball Player,
Coach)
424 N Vendome Ave
Margate City, NJ 08402-1265, USA

Ford, Clementine (Actor)
c/o Staff Member *Schumacher
Management*
2018 Glendon Ave
Los Angeles, CA 90025-6324, USA

Ford, Colton (Musician)
c/o Bill Coleman *Peace Bisquit*
963 Kent Ave Apt E3
Brooklyn, NY 11205-4469, USA

Ford, Curt (Athlete, Baseball Player)
6306 Sprig Oak Ct Apt B
Saint Louis, MO 63128-4336, USA

Ford, Dale (Athlete, Baseball Player)
678 Brethern Church Rd
Jonesborough, TN 37659-3923, USA

Ford, Dan (Athlete, Baseball Player)
1271 Linton Rd
Benton, LA 71006-8736, USA

Ford, Darren (Baseball Player)
7640 NW 79th Ave Apt L8
Tamarac, FL 33321-2868, USA

Ford, Dave (Athlete, Baseball Player)
19523 N Sagamore Rd
Cleveland, OH 44126-1662, USA

Ford, David (Musician)
c/o Staff Member *Paradigm (Monterey)*
404 W Franklin St
Monterey, CA 93940-2303, USA

Ford, Dee (Athlete, Football Player)
c/o Adisa P. Bakari *Dow Lohnes PLLC*
1299 Pennsylvania Ave NW Ste 700
Washington, DC 20004-2431, USA

Ford, Diane
201 San Vicente Blvd Apt 6
Santa Monica, CA 90402-1579

Ford, Don (Athlete, Basketball Player)
519 W Quinto St Apt B
Santa Barbara, CA 93105-4800, USA

Ford, Doug (Athlete, Golfer)
3737 Gulfstream Rd
Delray Beach, FL 33483-7411, USA

Ford, Eileen (Business Person)
c/o Staff Member *Ford Models (NY)*
238 E 4th St
New York, NY 10009-7425, USA

Ford, Eileen
344 E 59th St Fl 2
New York, NY 10022-1593

Ford, Ervin (Baseball Player)
Indianapolis Clowns
429 Banks St
Greensboro, NC 27401-3105, USA

Ford, Faith (Actor)
c/o Becca Kovacik *Berwick & Kovacik*
9465 Wilshire Blvd Ste 420
Beverly Hills, CA 90212-2603, USA

Ford, Frankie (Musician, Songwriter,
Writer)
Ken Keane Artists
PO Box 1875
Gretna, LA 70054-1875, USA

Ford, Frederick (Adult Film Star)
c/o Staff Member *Diva Central Inc*
7510 W Sunset Blvd Ste 1445
Los Angeles, CA 90046-3408, USA

Ford, Garrett (Athlete, Football Player)
866 Bancroft Pl
The Villages, FL 32162-3700, USA

Ford, Gib (Athlete, Basketball Player,
Olympic Athlete)
264 Edgemere Way E
Naples, FL 34105-7150, USA

Ford, Harrison (Actor)
655 Macculloch Dr
Los Angeles, CA 90049-2024, USA

Ford, Henry (Athlete, Football Player)
7222 Shannon Rd
Verona, PA 15147-2036, USA

Ford, Henry (Athlete, Football Player)
809 Glendevon Dr
McKinney, TX 75071-6543, USA

Ford, Jack (Correspondent)
CBS-TV
51 W 52nd St
News Dept
New York, NY 10019-6119, USA

Ford, James L (Athlete, Football Player)
2168 College Cir N
Jacksonville, FL 32209-5980, USA

Ford, Kevin A (Astronaut)
1002 Oak Park Ln
Friendswood, TX 77546-3584, USA

Ford, Lew (Athlete, Baseball Player)
2705 Hundred Knights Dr
Lewisville, TX 75056-5421, USA

Ford, Lita (Actor, Musician)
c/o Garry Buck *Monterey International*
PO Box 297
Carmel By The Sea, CA 93921-0297, USA

Ford, Matt (Athlete, Baseball Player)
4933 NW 104th Ave
Coral Springs, FL 33076-1751, USA

Ford, Melissa (Model)
c/o Mike Esterman *Esterman.Com, LLC*
Prefers to be contacted via email
Baltimore, MD XXXXX, USA

Ford, Melyssa (Model)
c/o Mike Esterman *Esterman.Com, LLC*
Prefers to be contacted via email
Baltimore, MD XXXXX, USA

Ford, Mike (Athlete, Football Player)
9798 FM 1565
Terrell, TX 75160-8516, USA

Ford, Phil (Athlete, Basketball Player,
Olympic Athlete)
PO Box 90623
Raleigh, NC 27675-0623, USA

Ford, Richard (Writer)
c/o Staff Member *HarperCollins Publishers*
195 Broadway Fl 2
Cellar 1
New York, NY 10007-3132, USA

Ford, Robert (Athlete, Basketball Player)
202 Pathway Ln
West Lafayette, IN 47906-2162, USA

Ford, Ruth (Actor)
Dakota Hotel
1 W 72nd St
New York, NY 10023-3486, USA

Ford, Scott (Business Person)
Alltel Corp
PO Box 96019
Charlotte, NC 28296-0019, USA

Ford, Sherell (Athlete, Basketball Player)
1509 S 6th Ave
Maywood, IL 60153-2014, USA

Ford, Ted (Athlete, Baseball Player)
712 Nightingale Ave Apt D
McAllen, TX 78504-1768, USA

Ford, Thomas Mikal (Actor)
c/o Staff Member *TalentWorks (LA)*
3500 W Olive Ave Ste 1400
Burbank, CA 91505-5512, USA

Ford, T J (Basketball Player)
Milwaukee Bucks
1001 N 4th St Ste 1
Bradley Center
Milwaukee, WI 53203-1312, USA

Ford, Tom (Designer, Fashion Designer)
Gucci
845 Madison Ave
New York, NY 10021-4908, USA

Ford, Trent (Actor)
c/o Staff Member *Paradigm (LA)*
360 N Crescent Dr
North Bldg
Beverly Hills, CA 90210-4874, USA

Ford, Wendell H (Ex-Governor, Ex-
Senator)
220 Daviess St
Owensboro, KY 42303, USA

Ford, Whitey (Athlete, Baseball Player)
WhiteyFord.com
3750 Galt Ocean Dr Apt 1411
Fort Lauderdale, FL 33308-7623, USA

Ford, Willa (Musician)
c/o Brad Marks *Blue Five Media*
1550 17th St
Santa Monica, CA 90404-3402, USA

Ford, William C Jr (Business Person)
Ford Motor Co
American Road
Dearborn, MI 48121, USA

Ford Bales, Susan (Writer)
6628 S Atlanta Ave
Tulsa, OK 74136-4303, USA

Forde, Brian (Athlete, Football Player)
20225 Bothell Everett Hwy Apt 1131
Bothell, WA 98012-8186, USA

Fordham, Julia (Musician, Songwriter,
Writer)
Vanguard Records
11400 W Olympic Blvd Ste 1450
Los Angeles, CA 90064-1649, USA

Fordham, Tom (Athlete, Baseball Player)
14559 Miguel Ln
El Cajon, CA 92021-2843, USA

Fordham, Willie (Baseball Player)
Negro Baseball Leagues
3608 Tudor Dr
Harrisburg, PA 17109-1235, USA

Fordyce, Brook (Athlete, Baseball Player)
5 River Crest Ct
Stuart, FL 34996-6515, USA

Foreigner (Music Group, Musician)
c/o Dan Weiner *Paradigm (Monterey)*
404 W Franklin St
Monterey, CA 93940-2303, USA

Foreman, Carol L T (Government Official)
5600 Wisconsin Ave Apt 502
Chevy Chase, MD 20815-4410, USA

Foreman, Chuck (Athlete, Football Player)
9716 Mill Creek Dr
Eden Prairie, MN 55347-4307, USA

Foreman, Deborah (Actor)
PO Box 2305
Big Bear City, CA 92314-2305, USA

Foreman, George (Athlete, Boxer,
Olympic Athlete)
George Foreman Enterprises
PO Box 1405
Huffman, TX 77336-1405, USA

Foreman, Walter E (Chuck) (Athlete,
Football Player)
9716 Mill Creek Dr
Eden Prairie, MN 55347-4307, USA

Foremsky, Skee (Bowler)
914 Manchester Dr
Conroe, TX 77304-2713, USA

Forest, Michael (Actor)
1327 N Vista St Apt 203
Los Angeles, CA 90046-4832, USA

Forester, Herschel (Athlete, Football
Player)
8502 Edgemere Rd Apt 227
Dallas, TX 75225-3553, USA

Forester, Nicole (Actor)
c/o Doug Kesten *Paradigm (NY)*
360 Park Ave S Fl 16
New York, NY 10010-1716, USA

Forlani, Claire (Actor)
c/o Marsha McManus *Principal
Entertainment (LA)*
9255 W Sunset Blvd Ste 500
West Hollywood, CA 90069-3301, USA

Forman, Don (Athlete, Basketball Player)
1532 Gormican Ln
Naples, FL 34110-0920, USA

Forman, Milos (Director)
29 Carter Rd
Warren, CT 06754-1612, USA

Forman, Stanley (Journalist, Photographer)
17 Cherry Rd
Beverly, MA 01915-1511, USA

Forman, Tom (Cartoonist)
10544 James Rd
Celina, TX 75009-3744, USA

Formia, Osvaldo (Horse Racer)
6501 Winfield Blvd # A10
Margate, FL 33063-7168, USA

Forney, Carl (Athlete, Baseball Player)
169 Ridley St
Marion, NC 28752-4629, USA

Forney, Kynan (Athlete, Football Player)
2046 Skybrooke Ln
Hoschton, GA 30548-6295, USA

Foronjy, Richard (Actor)
c/o Staff Member *House of
Representatives, The*
1434 6th St Ste 1
Santa Monica, CA 90401-2527, USA

Forrest, Bayard (Athlete, Basketball
Player)
300A Squaw Valley Pl # A
Pagosa Springs, CO 81147-9773, USA

Forrest, Frederic (Actor)
11300 W Olympic Blvd Ste 610
Los Angeles, CA 90064-1643, USA

Forrest, Katherine Virginia (Writer)
PO Box 31613
San Francisco, CA 94131-0613, USA

Forrest, Lili (Designer)
600 Moulton Ave Apt 205
Los Angeles, CA 90031-3485, USA

Forrest, Sally (Actor)
1125 Angelo Dr
Beverly Hills, CA 90210-2703, USA

Forrester, Patrick G (Astronaut)
3923 Park Circle Way
Houston, TX 77059-3019, USA

Forrester Sisters (Music Group)
c/o Staff Member *Warner Bros Music*
301 Arizona Ave Ste 250A
Santa Monica, CA 90401-1345

Forsberg, Fred (Athlete, Football Player)
1727 223rd Ave SE
Sammamish, WA 98075-9570, USA

Forsch, Ken (Athlete, Baseball Player)
881 S Country Glen Way
Anaheim, CA 92808-2635, USA

Forsey, Brock (Athlete, Football Player)
8346 W Sundisk St
Boise, ID 83714-2509, USA

Forslund, Constance (Actor)
165 W 46th St Ste 1109
New York, NY 10036-2516, USA

Forsman, Dan (Athlete, Golfer)
PO Box 1715
Provo, UT 84603-1715, USA

Forst, Bill (Cartoonist)
2320 Byer Rd
Santa Cruz, CA 95062-1949, USA

Forstchen, William (Writer)
c/o Staff Member *Spectrum Literary
Agency*
320 Central Park W Ste 1-D
New York, NY 10025-7659, USA

Forster, Brian
16172 Flamstead Dr
Hacienda Heights, CA 91745-3644

Forster, Marc (Director, Producer)
c/o Guymon Casady *Management 360*
9111 Wilshire Blvd
Beverly Hills, CA 90210-5508, USA

Forster, Robert (Actor)
c/o Eli Selden *Anonymous Content (LA)*
3532 Hayden Ave
Culver City, CA 90232-2413, USA

Forster, Scott (Athlete, Baseball Player)
901 Sturgis Ln
Ambler, PA 19002-2022, USA

Forster, Terry (Baseball Player)
Chicago White Sox
PO Box 711658
Santee, CA 92072-1658, USA

Forsythe, Gerry
9350 Castlegate Dr
Indianapolis, IN 46256-1001

Forsythe, Rosemary (Actor)
1591 Benedict Canyon Dr
Beverly Hills, CA 90210-2023, USA

Forsythe, William (Actor)
c/o Kieran Maguire *The Arlook Group*
205 S Beverly Dr Ste 209
Beverly Hills, CA 90212-3899, USA

Forte, Deborah (Producer)
c/o Staff Member *Scholastic Entertainment*
557 Broadway
New York, NY 10012-3962, USA

Forte, Fabian (Actor)
PO Box 951
Connellsville, PA 15425-0951, USA

Forte, Ike (Athlete, Football Player)
5811 Winchester Dr
Texarkana, TX 75503-4602, USA

Forte, Joseph (Basketball Player)
355 Elmcroft Blvd # 621
Rockville, MD 20850-5662, USA

Forte, Matt (Athlete, Football Player)
601 Riverwoods Rd
Mettawa, IL 60045-2550, USA

Forte, Will (Actor, Writer)
c/o Julie Darmody *Mosaic Media Group*
9200 W Sunset Blvd Ste 10
West Hollywood, CA 90069-3608, USA

Fortenberry, Jeff (Congressman, Politician)
1514 Longworth Hob
Washington, DC 20515-0537, USA

Fortier, Laurie (Actor)
c/o Steven Jensen *Vincent Cirrincione Associates*
8332 Melrose Ave
West Hollywood, CA 90069-5420, USA

Fortin, Roman (Athlete, Football Player)
10741 Bell Rd
Duluth, GA 30097-1801, USA

Fortner, Nell (Coach)
Auburn University
Athletic Dept
Auburn University, AL 36849-0001, USA

For Today (Music Group, Musician)
c/o Shannon Quiggle *Facedown Records*
PO Box 477
Sun City, CA 92586-0477, USA

Fortson, Danny (Athlete, Basketball Player)
341 E Willow Ave
Cincinnati, OH 45246-4621, USA

Fortugno, Tim (Athlete, Baseball Player)
3604 Babson Dr
Elk Grove, CA 95758-4576, USA

Fortunato, Don (Athlete, Football Player)
222 Regent Wood Rd
Northfield, IL 60093-2767, USA

Fortunato, Joseph F (Joe) (Athlete, Football Player)
PO Box 934
Natchez, MS 39121-0934, USA

Fortune, Jimmy (Musician)
American Major Talent
8747 Highway 304
Hernando, MS 38632-8445, USA

Fortuno, Luis (Governor, Politician)
La Fortaleza
San Juan, PR 00901, USA

Foruria, John (Athlete, Football Player)
5603 W Edson St
Boise, ID 83705-1852, USA

Forward, Susan (Writer)
c/o Staff Member *HarperCollins Publishers*
195 Broadway Fl 2
Cellar 1
New York, NY 10007-3132, USA

Forzano, Rick (Athlete, Football Coach, Football Player)
3216 Interlaken St
West Bloomfield, MI 48323-1824, USA

Fosbury, Dick (Athlete, Olympic Athlete, Track Athlete)
PO Box 1791
Ketchum, ID 83340-1791

Fosnow, Jerry (Athlete, Baseball Player)
7028 W Waters Ave
Tampa, FL 33634-2292, USA

Foss, Anita (Athlete, Baseball Player, Commentator)
452 S Highland Ave
Los Angeles, CA 90036-3531, USA

Foss, Larry (Athlete, Baseball Player)
4303 E English St
Wichita, KS 67218-1320, USA

Fossas, Tony (Athlete, Baseball Player)
11302 NW 9th St
Plantation, FL 33325-1501, USA

Fosse, Ray (Athlete, Baseball Player)
PO Box 567
Diablo, CA 94528-0567, USA

Fossum, Casey (Athlete, Baseball Player)
667 Park Ln
Santa Barbara, CA 93108-1415, USA

Fossum, Michael E (Astronaut)
822 Rolling Run Ct
Houston, TX 77062-2100, USA

Foster, Alan (Athlete, Baseball Player)
10330 Grandview Dr
La Mesa, CA 91941-6844, USA

Foster, Alex (Athlete, Hockey Player)
721 S Livernois Rd
Rochester Hills, MI 48307-2770, USA

Foster, Arian (Athlete, Football Player)
5034 Jackwood St
Houston, TX 77096-1507, USA

Foster, Barry (Athlete, Football Player)
PO Box 750
Colleyville, TX 76034-0750, USA

Foster, Ben (Actor)
c/o Ken Jacobson *Ken Jacobson Management*
Preferred to be contacted by phone or email
Woodland Hills, CA 91367, USA

Foster, Bill (Basketball Player)
Virginia Polytechnic Institute
Athletic Dept
Blacksburg, VA 24061, USA

Foster, David (Musician, Songwriter)
3905 Carbon Canyon Rd
Malibu, CA 90265, USA

Foster, Deshaun (Athlete, Football Player)
2391 Apple Tree Dr
Tustin, CA 92780-7134, USA

Foster, Dwight (Athlete, Hockey Player)
721 S Livernois Rd
Rochester Hills, MI 48307-2770, USA

Foster, George (Athlete, Baseball Player)
15 E Putnam Ave Apt 320
Greenwich, CT 06830-5424, USA

Foster, George (Athlete, Football Player)
4057 Meadowbrook Dr
Macon, GA 31204-4752, USA

Foster, Jeff (Athlete, Basketball Player)
12200 Iron Bluff Pl
Austin, TX 78738-6041, USA

Foster, Jerome (Athlete, Football Player)
18900 Goldwin St
Southfield, MI 48075-7218, USA

Foster, Jodie (Actor, Director)
c/o Jennifer Allen *Viewpoint Inc (LA)*
8820 Wilshire Blvd Ste 220
Beverly Hills, CA 90211-2622, USA

Foster, John (Actor)
c/o Staff Member *Windfall*
3000 W Alameda Ave
Burbank, CA 91523-0001, USA

Foster, John (Athlete, Baseball Player)
519 Airway Ave
Lewiston, ID 83501-4503, USA

Foster, Jon (Actor)
c/o Ken Jacobson *Ken Jacobson Management*
Preferred to be contacted by phone or email
Woodland Hills, CA 91367, USA

Foster, Kris (Athlete, Baseball Player)
116 Johns Ave
Lehigh Acres, FL 33936-2135, USA

Foster, Larry (Athlete, Baseball Player)
205 W Obell St
Whitehall, MI 49461-1742, USA

Foster, Leo (Athlete, Baseball Player)
699 Glensprings Dr
Cincinnati, OH 45246-2129, USA

Foster, Mark (Musician)
3549 N Knoll Dr
Los Angeles, CA 90068-1523, USA

Foster, Marty (Athlete, Baseball Player)
1718 Arrowhead Dr
Beloit, WI 53511-3808, USA

Foster, Marty (Baseball Player)
319 W 5th Ave
Denver, CO 80204-5118, USA

Foster, Meg (Actor)
c/o Chris Roe *CR Management*
23852 Pacific Coast Hwy Ste 627
Malibu, CA 90265-4876, USA

Foster, Norm (Athlete, Hockey Player)
632 Rewold Dr
Rochester, MI 48307-2233, USA

Foster, Radney (Musician, Songwriter, Writer)
c/o Staff Member *William Morris Endeavor (LA)*
9601 Wilshire Blvd
Beverly Hills, CA 90210-5213, USA

Foster, Robert W (Bob) (Boxer)
913 Valencia Dr NE
Albuquerque, NM 87108-1753, USA

Foster, Rod (Athlete, Basketball Player)
1246 Armacost Ave Apt 105
Los Angeles, CA 90025-6432, USA

Foster, Ron (Athlete, Football Player)
17819 Merridy St Apt 117
Northridge, CA 91325-4604, USA

Foster, Roy
650 E 27th Pl N
Tulsa, OK 74106-2409, USA

Foster, Roy A (Athlete, Football Player)
5824 Shenandoah Ave
Los Angeles, CA 90056-1424, USA

Foster, Sara (Actor)
c/o Brad Marks *Blue Five Media*
1550 17th St
Santa Monica, CA 90404-3402, USA

Foster, Scott M (Actor)
c/o John Tae Lee *Shapiro/West & Associates*
141 El Camino Dr Ste 205
Beverly Hills, CA 90212-2786, USA

Foster, Scott Michael (Actor)
c/o John Tae Lee *Shapiro/West & Associates*
141 El Camino Dr Ste 205
Beverly Hills, CA 90212-2786, USA

Foster, Steve (Athlete, Baseball Player)
1020 Heathrow Dr
Frisco, TX 75034-7806, USA

Foster, Sutton (Actor)
c/o Joe Machota *Creative Artists Agency (CAA-NY)*
162 5th Ave Fl 6
New York, NY 10010-6047, USA

Foster, Todd (Boxer)
303 13th St NW
Great Falls, MT 59404-2213, USA

Foster, William E (Bill) (Coach)
152 Hollywood Dr
Coppell, TX 75019-7302, USA

Foster, Yolanda (Reality Star)
3905 Carbon Canyon Rd
Malibu, CA 90265, USA

Foster the People (Music Group)
c/o Ian Montone *Monotone Inc.*
820 Seward St
Los Angeles, CA 90038-3602, USA

Foth, Robert (Athlete, Olympic Athlete, Shooter)
2221 Tesla Dr
Colorado Springs, CO 80909-1446, USA

Foti, Tony (Race Car Driver)
LAPD Racing Team
10250 Etiwanda Ave
Northridge, CA 91325-1015, USA

Fotiu, Nick (Athlete, Hockey Player)
16 Backus River Rd
East Falmouth, MA 02536-5205, USA

Foucault, Steve (Athlete, Baseball Player)
24353 Rolling View Ct
Lutz, FL 33559-8642, USA

Fouch, Allison (Athlete, Golfer)
2949 Oakwood Dr SE
Grand Rapids, MI 49506-4235, USA

Foudy, Judy (Julie) (Model, Soccer Player)
US Soccer Federation
1801 S Prairie Ave
Chicago, IL 60616-1356, USA

Foudy, Julie
1801 S Prairie Ave
Chicago, IL 60616-1319

Fought, John (Athlete, Golfer)
5747 E Via Los Ranchos
Paradise Valley, AZ 85253, USA

Foules, Elbert (Athlete, Football Player)
633 E Ohea St
Greenville, MS 38701-3861, USA

Foulke, Keith (Athlete, Baseball Player)
4844 W Electra Ln
Glendale, AZ 85310-3833, USA

Fountain, Peter D (Pete) Jr (Musician)
Paradise Artists
108 E Matilija St
Ojai, CA 93023-2639, USA

Fountain, Rex
10475 Bellagio Rd
Los Angeles, CA 90077-3818

Fountaine, Jamal (Athlete, Football Player)
245 SW Lincoln St Apt 122
Portland, OR 97201-5083, USA

Fountains of Wayne (Music Group)
c/o Staff Member *Big Hassle Media*
40 Exchange Pl Ste 1900
New York, NY 10005-2714, USA

Four Aces, The
11761 E Speedway Blvd
Tucson, AZ 85748-2017

Fourcade, John (Athlete, Football Player)
2749 Long Branch Dr
Marrero, LA 70072-5856, USA

Four Freshman, The
PO Box 93534
Las Vegas, NV 89193-3534

Four Freshmen, The (Music Group)
c/o Staff Member *International Ventures*
25115 Avenue Stanford Ste 102
Valencia, CA 91355-4777, USA

Four Lads, The
11761 E Speedway Blvd
Tucson, AZ 85748-2017

Fournier, Francine
PO Box 935
Bear, DE 19701-0935, USA

Four Non Blondes
PO Box 170545
San Francisco, CA 94117-0545

Foust, Nina (Athlete, Golfer)
901 East Dr
Morehead City, NC 28557-3009, USA

Fouts, Dan (Athlete, Football Player)
16820 Varco Rd
Bend, OR 97701-9135, USA

Fowler, Bobby (Athlete, Football Player)
3702 Alamo Cv
Lago Vista, TX 78645-6601, USA

Fowler, Chris (Sportscaster)
c/o Staff Member *ESPN (Main)*
935 Middle St
Espn Plaza
Bristol, CT 06010-1000, USA

Fowler, Dan (Athlete, Football Player)
18574 Merlon Ct
Leesburg, VA 20176-3912, USA

Fowler, David (Athlete, Football Player)
511 Cove Rd
Shelbyville, KY 40065-7941, USA

Fowler, Jim (Actor)
Wild Kingdom
Mutual of Omaha
Mutual of Omaha Plaza
Omaha, NE 68175-0001, USA

Fowler, Kevin (Musician)
c/o Staff Member *Paradigm (Monterey)*
404 W Franklin St
Monterey, CA 93940-2303, USA

Fowler, Melvin (Athlete, Football Player)
2850 Amsdell Rd Apt 27
Hamburg, NY 14075-7800, USA

Fowler, Peggy Y (Business Person)
Portland General Electric
121 SW Salmon St
Portland, OR 97204-2977, USA

Fowler, Ryan (Athlete, Football Player)
1713 Montclair Blvd
Brentwood, TN 37027-8073, USA

Fowler, Todd (Athlete, Football Player)
10024 FM 3053 N
Kilgore, TX 75662-4721, USA

Fowler, Willmer (Athlete, Football Player)
471 Linwood Ave
Buffalo, NY 14209-1630, USA

Fowlkes, Alan (Athlete, Baseball Player)
405 Emerald Lake Dr
Lumberton, NC 28358-8022, USA

Fox, Allen (Coach, Tennis Player)
Pepperdine University
Athletic Dept
Malibu, CA 90265, USA

Fox, Andy (Athlete, Baseball Player)
9087 Tarmac Ct
Fair Oaks, CA 95628-8142, USA

Fox, Bernard (Actor)
6601 Burnet Ave
Van Nuys, CA 91405-4515, USA

Fox, Billy (Producer)
c/o Gil Harari *Agency for the Performing
Arts (APA-LA)*
405 S Beverly Dr Ste 500
Beverly Hills, CA 90212-4425, USA

Fox, Chad (Athlete, Baseball Player)
15 Tannery Hill Rd
Tomball, TX 77375-4980, USA

Fox, Eric (Athlete, Baseball Player)
2832 S Glacier Bay Way
Meridian, ID 83642-7829, USA

Fox, Greg (Athlete, Hockey Player)
323 Resource Pkwy # 6A
Winder, GA 30680-8364, USA

Fox, Harold (Athlete, Basketball Player)
6511 Wilburn Dr
Capitol Heights, MD 20743-3351, USA

Fox, Jackie
23368 Ostronic Dr
Woodland Hills, CA 91367-6045

Fox, Jake (Athlete, Baseball Player)
7028 Bellona Ave
Baltimore, MD 21212-1111, USA

Fox, Jason (Athlete, Football Player)
c/o Drew Rosenhaus *Rosenhaus Sports
Representation*
6400 Allison Rd
Miami Beach, FL 33141-4540, USA

Fox, Jim (Athlete, Basketball Player)
4136 N 52nd St
Phoenix, AZ 85018-4402, USA

Fox, Jim (Athlete, Hockey Player)
224 S Juanita Ave # A
Redondo Beach, CA 90277-3438, USA

Fox, Jim
1111 S Figueroa St Ste 3100
Los Angeles, CA 90015-1333, USA

Fox, John (Athlete, Coach, Football
Coach, Football Player)
11137 McClure Manor Dr
Charlotte, NC 28277-3027, USA

Fox, Jorja (Actor)
c/o Peg Donegan *Framework
Entertainment (LA)*
9057 Nemo St Ste C
West Hollywood, CA 90069-5511, USA

Fox, Matthew (Actor)
18625 MacAlpine Loop
Bend, OR 97702-9366, USA

Fox, Matthew (Athlete, Baseball Player)
3379 Caruso Pl
Oviedo, FL 32765-8749, USA

Fox, Matthew (Religious Leader)
Grace Episcopal Cathedral
1 Nob Hill Cir
San Francisco, CA 94108-2232, USA

Fox, Megan (Actor)
c/o Dominique Appel *Baker Winokur
Ryder Public Relations (BWR-LA)*
9100 Wilshire Blvd Ste 500
West Tower Suite 500
Beverly Hills, CA 90212-3426, USA

Fox, Michael J (Actor)
*The Michael J. Fox Foundation For
Parkinson's Research*
PO Box 4777
Grand Central Station
New York, NY 10163-4777, USA

Fox, Rick (Actor, Athlete, Basketball
Player)
10727 Wilshire Blvd Apt 302
Los Angeles, CA 90024-4400, USA

Fox, Shayna
6212 Banner Ave
Los Angeles, CA 90038-2802

Fox, Spencer (Actor)
c/o Maggie Schuster *J Mitchell
Management*
440 Park Ave S
New York, NY 10016-8012, USA

Fox, Terry (Athlete, Baseball Player)
2312 Sugar Mill Rd
New Iberia, LA 70563-8648, USA

Fox, Tim (Athlete, Football Player)
11 Glover Ave
Hull, MA 02045-1464, USA

Fox, Tim (Athlete, Football Player)
10 Longmeadow Dr
Westwood, MA 02090-1079, USA

Fox, Vernon (Athlete, Football Player)
6704 Willow River Ct
Las Vegas, NV 89108-5033, USA

Fox, Vivica A (Actor)
c/o BJ Coleman *Coleman Entertainment
Group*
11 Park Pl Fl 19
New York, NY 10007-2801, USA

Fox Brothers
Rt. 6 Bending Chestnut
Franklin, TN 37064

Foxworth, Domonique (Athlete, Football
Player)
3533 S Sherwood Rd SE # 5
Smyrna, GA 30082-2833, USA

Foxworth, Robert (Actor)
c/o Chris Schmidt *Paradigm (LA)*
360 N Crescent Dr
North Bldg
Beverly Hills, CA 90210-4874, USA

Foxworthy, Jeff (Actor, Comedian)
365 High Bridge Chase
Alpharetta, GA 30022-5512, USA

Foxx, Dion (Athlete, Football Player)
6457 Springcrest Ln
Henrico, VA 23231-5325, USA

Foxx, Jamie (Actor, Comedian)
1355 W Potrero Rd
Thousand Oaks, CA 91361-5037, USA

Foxx, Shyla (Adult Film Star)
c/o Staff Member *Atlas Multimedia Inc*
9005 Eton Ave Ste C
Canoga Park, CA 91304-6533, USA

Foxx, Tanya
901 W Victoria St Ste G
Compton, CA 90220-5819

Foxx, Virginia (Congressman, Politician)
1230 Longworth Hob
Washington, DC 20515-0547, USA

Foy, Eddie III (Actor)
3003 W Olive Ave
Burbank, CA 91505-4538, USA

Foy, Mackenzie (Actor)
c/o Christopher Rockwell *Keyword
Entertainment*
1015 Gayley Ave Ste 601
Los Angeles, CA 90024-3413, USA

Foyle, Adonal (Athlete, Basketball Player)
174 Crestview Dr
Orinda, CA 94563-3922, USA

Foyt, Larry (Race Car Driver)
AJ Foyt Racing
128 Commercial Dr
Mooresville, TN 28116, USA

Foytack, Paul (Athlete, Baseball Player)
1910 Portview Dr
Spring Hill, TN 37174-8249, USA

Foyt IV, A.J. (Race Car Driver)
Vision Racing
19480 Stokes Rd
Waller, TX 77484-8785, USA

Foyt, Jr., A.J. (Race Car Driver)
19480 Stokes Rd
Waller, TX 77484-8785, USA

Frabotta, Don (Actor)
PO Box 962
Douglas, MA 01516-0962, USA

Fradon, Dana (Cartoonist)
2 Brushy Hill Rd
Newtown, CT 06470, USA

Fradon, Ramona (Cartoonist)
Tribune Media Services
435 N Michigan Ave Ste 1500
Chicago, IL 60611-4012, USA

Frailing, Ken (Athlete, Baseball Player)
2150 Shadow Oaks Rd
Sarasota, FL 34240-9324, USA

Frain, James (Actor)
c/o Melanie Greene *Affirmative
Entertainment*
425 N Robertson Blvd
West Hollywood, CA 90048-1735, USA

Fraiture, Nikolai (Musician)
3 Sheridan Sq Apt 9C PMB 9C
New York, NY 10014-6832, USA

Frakes, Jonathan (Actor, Director)
5315 Oakdale Ave
Woodland Hills, CA 91364-3635, USA

Fralic, William (Bill) (Athlete, Football
Player)
280 Galsworthy Ct
Roswell, GA 30075-6354, USA

Frampton, Peter (Musician, Songwriter)
c/o Nicki Loranger *Vector Management
(LA)*
1100 Glendon Ave Ste 2000
Los Angeles, CA 90024-3524, USA

France, Brian (Race Car Driver)
1151 N Halifax Ave
Daytona Beach, FL 32118-3654, USA

France, Doug (Athlete, Football Player)
6056 Great Falls Ave
Las Vegas, NV 89110-2709, USA

France, Jim (Business Person)
Nascar
PO Box 2875
Daytona Beach, FL 32120-2875, USA

Francella, Meaghan (Athlete, Golfer)
36000 Portofino Cir Apt 110
Palm Beach Gardens, FL 33418-1284,
USA

Franchione, Dennis (Coach, Football
Coach)
Texas A&M University
Athletic Dept
College Station, TX 77843-0001, USA

Franchitti, Dario (Race Car Driver)
Team Green
7615 Zionsville Rd
Indianapolis, IN 46268-2174, USA

Franci, Jason (Athlete, Football Player)
336 Vintage Glen Ct
Santa Rosa, CA 95403-7567, USA

Francis, Betty (Baseball Player)
11750 S Homan Ave Trlr 19A
Merrionette Park, IL 60803-4513, USA

Francis, Black (Musician)
3970 N Shasta Loop
Eugene, OR 97405-4436, USA

Francis, Bob (Athlete, Coach, Hockey
Player)
23725 N 75th Pi
Scottsdale, AZ 85258, USA

Francis, Clarence (Bevo) (Basketball
Player)
18340 Steubenyille Pike Rd
Salineville, OH 43945, USA

Francis, Connie (Actor, Musician)
6413 NW 102nd Ter
Parkland, FL 33076-2357, USA

Francis, Dillon (Musician)
c/o Staff Member *The Windish Agency*
1658 N Milwaukee Ave # 211
Chicago, IL 60647-6905, USA

Francis, Emile (Athlete, Hockey Player)
7220 Crystal Lake Dr
West Palm Beach, FL 33411-5713, USA

Francis, Emile P (Coach)
7220 Crystal Lake Dr
West Palm Beach, FL 33411-5713, USA

Francis, Fred (Correspondent)
NBC-TV
4001 Nebraska Ave NW
News Dept
Washington, DC 20016-2795, USA

Francis, Genie (Actor)
5315 Oakdale Ave
Woodland Hills, CA 91364-3635, USA

Francis, Harrison (Athlete, Football
Player)
207 S Susan Ave
Wagoner, OK 74467-4843, USA

Francis, James (Athlete, Football Player)
1201 E Old Settlers Blvd Apt 1201
Round Rock, TX 78664-2413, USA

Francis, Jeff (Athlete, Baseball Player)
3191 Quitman St
Denver, CO 80212-1457, USA

Francis, Joe (Producer)
c/o Staff Member *Mantra Films*
1111 Bel Air Pl
Los Angeles, CA 90077-3002, USA

Francis, Joe (Athlete, Football Player)
45-570 Kaaluna Pl
Kaneohe, HI 96744-3410, USA

Francis, Paul (Actor)
c/o Staff Member *Gilbertson Management*
1334 3rd Street Promenade Ste 201
Santa Monica, CA 90401-1320, USA

Francis, Ron (Athlete, Football Player)
3315 Ashton Park Dr
Houston, TX 77082-5307, USA

Francis, Ron (Athlete, Hockey Player)
12312 Birchfalls Dr
Raleigh, NC 27614-7900, USA

Francis, Russ (Athlete, Football Player)
800 Putney Rd
Brattleboro, VT 05301-9058, USA

Francis, Steve (Athlete, Basketball Player)
632 Pifer Rd
Houston, TX 77024-5434, USA

Francis, Wallace (Athlete, Football Player)
2452 Wilshire Way
Douglasville, GA 30135-8129, USA

Francis, Wally (Athlete, Football Player)
1307 Walton Ln SE
Smyrna, GA 30082-3875, USA

Francis, William (Bill) (Musician)
Artists International
9850 Sandalwood Blvd
#458
Boca Raton, FL 33428, USA

Francisco, Aaron (Athlete, Football Player)
7081 S St Ruben Ave
Gilbert, AZ 85298-4147, USA

Francisco, Ben (Athlete, Baseball Player)
689 S Scout Trl
Anaheim, CA 92807-4757, us

Francisco, Don (Television Host)
c/o Staff Member *Univision*
605 3rd Ave Fl 12
New York, NY 10158-0034, USA

Francisco, Pablo (Comedian)
c/o Derek Van Pelt *Levity Entertainment
Group (LEG)*
6701 Center Dr W Ste 1111
Los Angeles, CA 90045-1552, USA

Franckowiak, Mike (Athlete, Football
Player)
730 Lake Dornoch Dr
Pinehurst, NC 28374-7124, USA

Francks, Rainbow Sun (Actor)
c/o Staff Member *Sci-FI Channel, The*
100 Universal Plz
Bldg 1280/12
Universal City, CA 91608, USA

Franco, Brian (Athlete, Football Player)
155 Oceanwalk Dr S
Atlantic Beach, FL 32233-4679

Franco, Carlos (Athlete, Golfer)
10561 NW 51st St
Doral, FL 33178-3209, USA

Franco, Dave (Actor)
c/o Miles Levy *James/Levy Management
Inc*
3500 W Olive Ave Ste 1470
Burbank, CA 91505-5514, USA

Franco, James (Actor)
2430 Hidalgo Ave
Los Angeles, CA 90039-3306, USA

Franco, John (Athlete, Baseball Player)
111 Cliffwood Ave
Staten Island, NY 10304, USA

Franco, Julio (Athlete, Baseball Player)
651 NE 23rd Ct
Pompano Beach, FL 33064-5504, USA

Franco, Liliana (Actor)
c/o Staff Member *Eileen O'farrell Personal
Management*
11653 Blix St Apt 2
North Hollywood, CA 91602-1051,
United States

Franco, Matt (Athlete, Baseball Player)
1008 Clear Sky Pl
Simi Valley, CA 93065-8331, USA

Francoeur, Jeff (Athlete, Baseball Player)
4834 Kettle River Pt
Suwanee, GA 30024-8804, USA

Francona, Terry (Athlete, Baseball Player,
Coach)
750 Newton St
Chestnut Hill, MA 02467-2606, USA

Francona, Tito (Athlete, Baseball Player)
1109 Penn Ave
New Brighton, PA 15066-1632, USA

Frandsen, Kevin (Athlete, Baseball Player)
1044 Camino Ricardo
San Jose, CA 95125-4305, USA

Frangoulis, Mario (Musician)
c/o Staff Member *Sony Music
International*
550 Madison Ave Fl 6
New York, NY 10022-3211, USA

Frank, Barney (Politician)
Congressman Barney Frank
2252 Rayburn Hob
Washington, DC 20515-2104, USA

Frank, Charles (Actor)
S D B Partners
315 S Beverly Dr Ste 411
Beverly Hills, CA 90212-4301, USA

Frank, Claude (Musician)
Columbia Artists Mgmt Inc
165 W 57th St
New York, NY 10019-2201, USA

Frank, Darryl (Producer)
c/o Staff Member *Dreamworks Television*
100 Universal Plz Bldg 5125
Universal City, CA 91608, USA

Frank, Diana (Actor)
The Agency
1800 Avenue of the Stars Ste 400
Los Angeles, CA 90067-4206, USA

Frank, Donald (Athlete, Football Player)
2039 Weston Green Loop
Cary, NC 27513-2268, USA

Frank, Gary (Actor)
861 S Bundy Dr
Los Angeles, CA 90049-5216, USA

Frank, Howard (Business Person)
Carnival Corp
3655 NW 87th Ave
Doral, FL 33178-2428, USA

Frank, Joanna (Actor)
1274 Capri Dr
Pacific Palisades, CA 90272-4001, USA

Frank, John (Athlete, Football Player)
Medical Hair Restoration
227 W 77th St Apt 4H
New York, NY 10024-6695, USA

Frank, Larry (Race Car Driver)
Larry Frank Auto Body Works
832 Fork Shoals Rd
Greenville, SC 29605-5832, USA

Frank, Lawrence
51 Edward St
Demarest, NJ 07627-2205

Frank, Mike (Athlete, Baseball Player)
1343 W 19th St
Upland, CA 91784-7433, USA

Frank, Phil (Cartoonist)
500 Turney St
Sausalito, CA 94965-1840, USA

Frank, Scott (Actor, Director, Writer)
c/o Staff Member *Arroyo Films*
50 W Dayton St Apt 308
Pasadena, CA 91105-2094, USA

Frank, Tellis (Athlete, Basketball Player)
4936 Van Noord Ave
Sherman Oaks, CA 91423-2214, USA

Frank-Dummerth, Edna (Baseball Player)
5044 Tealby Ln
Saint Louis, MO 63128-2952, USA

Franke, Robert (Writer)
c/o Allen Fischer *Principato/Young
Management (LA)*
9465 Wilshire Blvd Ste 900
Beverly Hills, CA 90212-2608, USA

Frankel, Bethenny (Business Person,
Reality Star, Talk Show Host)
195 Hudson St Apt 5B
New York, NY 10013-1894, USA

Frankel, David (Director)
c/o Rosalie Swedlin *Anonymous Content
(LA)*
3532 Hayden Ave
Culver City, CA 90232-2413, USA

Frankel, Felice (Artist, Photographer)
Massachusetts Institute of Technology
Edgerton Center
Cambridge, MA 02139, USA

Frankel, Max (Journalist)
229 W 43rd St Attn Dept
New York, NY 10036-3982, USA

Franken, Al (Actor, Comedian, Writer)
c/o Staff Member *Creative Artists Agency
(CAA-LA)*
2000 Avenue of the Stars Ste 100
Los Angeles, CA 90067-4705, USA

Franklin, Anthony R (Tony) (Athlete,
Football Player)
117 Shady Trail St
San Antonio, TX 78232-1313, USA

Franklin, Aretha (Musician)
8450 Linwood St
Detroit, MI 48206-2379, USA

Franklin, Arnold (Athlete, Football Player)
PO Box 18113
Cincinnati, OH 45218-0113, USA

Franklin, Aubrayo (Athlete, Football
Player)
1 Castleton Ct
Johnson City, TN 37615-4949, USA

Franklin, Bobby (Athlete, Football Player)
384 Country Club Dr
Senatobia, MS 38668-6308, USA

Franklin, Byron (Athlete, Football Player)
1917 Eagle Circle Rd
Demopolis, AL 36732-0016, USA

Franklin, Carl (Actor, Director, Writer)
c/o Alex Goldstone *Anonymous Content* *(LA)*
3532 Hayden Ave
Culver City, CA 90232-2413, USA

Franklin, Cleveland (Athlete, Football Player)
60 Hillary Cir
New Castle, DE 19720-8620, USA

Franklin, Dennis (Athlete, Football Player)
15474 Edmore Dr
Detroit, MI 48205-1351, USA

Franklin, DeVon (Producer)
16030 Ventura Blvd
Encino, CA 91436-2731, USA

Franklin, Diane (Actor)
Third Hill Entertainment
195 S Beverly Dr Ste 400
Beverly Hills, CA 90212-3044, USA

Franklin, Don (Actor)
Paradigm Agency
10100 Santa Monica Blvd Ste 2500
Los Angeles, CA 90067-4116, USA

Franklin, Don (Actor)
10101 Santa Monica Blvd # 2500
Los Angeles, CA 90067

Franklin, Farrah (Musician)
8391 Beverly Blvd
Los Angeles, CA 90048-2633, USA

Franklin, George (Athlete, Football Player)
6727 Feather Creek Dr
Houston, TX 77086-2005, USA

Franklin, Howard (Director, Writer)
c/o Staff Member *Agency for the Performing Arts (APA-LA)*
405 S Beverly Dr Ste 500
Beverly Hills, CA 90212-4425, USA

Franklin, Jay (Baseball Player)
San Diego Padres
2450 Massanutten Ter
Winchester, VA 22601-2774, USA

Franklin, Jerrell (Athlete, Football Player)
2512 Nettleton St
Houston, TX 77004-2042, USA

Franklin, Jethro (Athlete, Football Player)
4806 Keneshaw St
Sugar Land, TX 77479-3984, USA

Franklin, Joe
PO Box 1
Lynbrook, NY 11563-0001

Franklin, John (Actor)
Gilla Roos
9744 Wilshire Blvd Ste 203
Beverly Hills, CA 90212-1812, USA

Franklin, Jon D (Journalist)
9650 Strickland Rd
Raleigh, NC 27615-1902, USA

Franklin, Kirk (Musician)
c/o Michael Van Dyck *Paradigm (LA)*
360 N Crescent Dr
North Bldg
Beverly Hills, CA 90210-4874, USA

Franklin, Larry (Athlete, Football Player)
9390 Afton Grove Rd
Cordova, TN 38018-7519, USA

Franklin, Micah (Athlete, Baseball Player)
3948 E Lafayette Ave
Gilbert, AZ 85298-9139, USA

Franklin, Missy (Athlete, Olympic Athlete, Swimmer)
c/o Staff Member *USA Swimming Association*
1 Olympic Plz Bldg 2A
Colorado Springs, CO 80909-5770, USA

Franklin, Orlando (Athlete, Football Player)
c/o Drew Rosenhaus *Rosenhaus Sports Representation*
6400 Allison Rd
Miami Beach, FL 33141-4540, USA

Franklin, P J (Athlete, Football Player)
903 S Laurel St
Amite, LA 70422-3525, USA

Franklin, Roshawn (Actor)
c/o Staff Member *Freeze Frame Entertainment*
5225 Wilshire Blvd Ste 303
Los Angeles, CA 90036-4347, USA

Franklin, Ryan (Athlete, Baseball Player, Olympic Athlete)
PO Box 723
Shawnee, OK 74802-0723, USA

Franklin, Shirley (Politician)
Mayor's Office
55 Trinity Ave SW Ste 1600
City Hall
Atlanta, GA 30303-3534, USA

Franklin, Wayne (Athlete, Baseball Player)
925 McManness Ave
Findlay, OH 45840-5671, USA

Franklin, William (Boxer, Misc)
920 La Sombra Dr
San Marcos, CA 92078-1320, USA

Franklin, Willie (Athlete, Football Player)
PO Box 62
Lake Dallas, TX 75065-0062, USA

Frankman, Betty Skelton (Astronaut)
651 Allenwood Loop
The Villages, FL 32162-1004, USA

Franks, Daniel (Bubba) (Athlete, Football Player)
1 Cavil Way
De Pere, WI 54115, USA

Franks, Dennis (Athlete, Football Player)
4 Westmount Ct
Greensboro, NC 27410-2183, USA

Franks, Elvis (Athlete, Football Player)
2147 Rusk St
Beaumont, TX 77701-2525, USA

Franks, Gerold
1745 Camino Palmero St Apt 401
Los Angeles, CA 90046-2936

Franks, Hermine (Baseball Player)
422 Pecor St
Oconto, WI 54153-1800, USA

Franks, Michael (Musician, Songwriter, Writer)
c/o Staff Member *Agency for the Performing Arts (APA-LA)*
405 S Beverly Dr Ste 500
Beverly Hills, CA 90212-4425, USA

Franks, Ray (Race Car Driver)
PO Box 151
New Carlisle, OH 45344-0151, USA

Franks, Trent (Congressman, Politician)
2435 Rayburn Hob
Washington, DC 20515-4318, USA

Frankston, Robert M (Bob) (Designer)
State Corp
15035 N 73rd St
Scottsdale, AZ 85260-2468, USA

Franti, Michael (Actor, Musician)
c/o Jamie Simon *PFA Media NYC*
285 W Broadway Rm 630
New York, NY 10013-0465, USA

Frantz, Adrienne (Actor)
c/o Marnie Sparer *Innovative Artists (LA)*
1505 10th St
Santa Monica, CA 90401-2805, USA

Frantz, Chris (Musician)
Premier Talent
3 E 54th St # 1100
New York, NY 10022-3108, USA

Franz, Arthur (Art) (Athlete, Baseball Player)
PO Box 974
El Prado, NM 87529-0974, USA

Franz, Dennis (Actor)
c/o Alisa Adler *Paradigm (LA)*
360 N Crescent Dr
North Bldg
Beverly Hills, CA 90210-4874, USA

Franz, Frederick W (Religious Leader)
Jehovah's Witnesses
25 Columbia Hts
Brooklyn, NY 11201-1300, USA

Franz, Nolan (Athlete, Football Player)
327 31st St
Gulfport, MS 39507-2341, USA

Franz, Rodney T (Rod) (Athlete, Football Player)
1448 Engberg Ct
Carmichael, CA 95608-5812, USA

Franz, Ron (Athlete, Basketball Player)
8590 Beaverwood Dr
Germantown, TN 38138-7715, USA

Franz, Todd (Athlete, Football Player)
5629 N Classen Blvd
Oklahoma City, OK 73118-4015, USA

Franzen, Johan (Athlete, Hockey Player)
1043 Fairfax St
Birmingham, MI 48009-1286, USA

Franzen, Jonathan (Writer)
c/o Richard Green *Resolution (LA)*
1801 Century Park E Ste 2300
Los Angeles, CA 90067-2325, USA

Frascatore, John (Athlete, Baseball Player)
3121 Saturn Rd
Brooksville, FL 34604-7032, USA

Frase, Paul (Athlete, Football Player)
124 Crossroad Lakes Dr
Ponte Vedra Beach, FL 32082-4031, USA

Fraser, Brendan (Actor)
c/o JoAnne Colonna *Brillstein Entertainment Partners (LA)*
9150 Wilshire Blvd Ste 350
Beverly Hills, CA 90212-3453, USA

Fraser, Brooke (Musician)
c/o Jonathan Adelman *Paradigm (NY)*
360 Park Ave S Fl 16
New York, NY 10010-1716, USA

Fraser, Curt (Athlete, Hockey Player)
Grand Rapids Griffins 130 Fulton St W Ste 111
Grand Rapids, MI 49503, USA

Fraser, Gretchen
5023 236th Pl SE
Woodinville, WA 98072-8610

Fraser, Iain
2938 Grinstead Dr
Louisville, KY 40206-2645, USA

Fraser, Laura (Actor)
c/o Tammy Rosen *Sanders Armstrong Caserta*
2120 Colorado Ave Ste 120
Santa Monica, CA 90404-3561, USA

Fraser, Willie (Athlete, Baseball Player)
129 Shagbark Ln
Hopewell Junction, NY 12533-5281, USA

Frashilla, Fran (Coach)
New Mexico University
Athletic Dept
Albuquerque, NM 87131-0001, USA

Frasor, Jason (Athlete, Baseball Player)
12611 SE Old Cypress Dr
Hobe Sound, FL 33455-7923, USA

Fratello, Michael R (Mike) (Athlete, Basketball Player, Coach, Sportscaster)
7952 Fisher Island Dr
Miami Beach, FL 33109-1029, USA

Fratianne, Linda S (Athlete, Figure Skater, Olympic Athlete)
3352 Whispering Glen Ct
Simi Valley, CA 93065-0596, USA

Frattare, Lanny (Commentator)
Pittsburgh Pirates
2032 Croghan Dr
Carnegie, PA 15106-1593, USA

Frauenfelder, Mark (Internet Star)
Boing Boing
13547 Ventura Blvd # 91
Sherman Oaks, CA 91423-3825, USA

Frazar, Harrison (Athlete, Golfer)
3317 Villanova St
Dallas, TX 75225-4842, USA

Frazier, Al (Athlete, Football Player)
17240 133rd Ave Apt 12A
Jamaica, NY 11434-3965, USA

Frazier, Albert (Baseball Player)
Jacksonville Red Caps
5749 Copper Hill Ln E
Jacksonville, FL 32218-7311, USA

Frazier, Andre (Athlete, Football Player)
4295 Cross Creek Ct
Liberty Twp, OH 45011-6618, USA

Frazier, Charley (Athlete, Football Player)
4018 Brookston St
Houston, TX 77045-3412, USA

Frazier, Dallas (Musician, Songwriter, Writer)
RR 5 Box 133
Longhollow Pike
Gallatin, TN 37066, USA

Frazier, George (Athlete, Baseball Player)
6886 S Evanston Ave
Tulsa, OK 74136-4554, USA

Frazier, Guy (Athlete, Football Player)
3944 Dickson Ave
Cincinnati, OH 45229-1306, USA

Frazier, Herman (Athlete, Olympic Athlete, Track Athlete)
1777 Ala Moana Blvd
Honolulu, HI 96815-1603, USA

Frazier, Ian (Writer)
Farrar Straus Giroux
19 Union Sq W
New York, NY 10003-3304, USA

Frazier, Kevin (Actor, Television Host)
c/o Staff Member *Entertainment Tonight (ET)*
4024 Radford Ave
Studio City, CA 91604-2101, USA

Frazier, Leslie (Athlete, Football Player)
867 Normandy Trace Rd
Tampa, FL 33602-5763, USA

Frazier, Lisa (Musician)
c/o Staff Member *Diva Central Inc*
7510 W Sunset Blvd Ste 1445
Los Angeles, CA 90046-3408, USA

Frazier, Lou (Athlete, Baseball Player)
557 N Mondel Dr
Gilbert, AZ 85233-4113, USA

Frazier, Mavis (Boxer)
2917 N Broad St
Philadelphia, PA 19132-2402, USA

Frazier, Owsley B (Business Person)
Brown-Forman Corp
850 Dixie Hwy
Louisville, KY 40210-1038, USA

Frazier, Sheila (Actor)
c/o Daniel Hoff *Daniel Hoff Agency*
5455 Wilshire Blvd Ste 1100
Los Angeles, CA 90036-4277, USA

Frazier, Walt (Athlete, Basketball Player)
381 Malcolm X Blvd PH A
New York, NY 10027-2173, USA

Frazier, Will (Athlete, Basketball Player)
512 E Parkerville Rd
Desoto, TX 75115-7167, USA

Frazier, Willie (Athlete, Football Player)
6203 Bankside Dr
Houston, TX 77096-5608, USA

Freberg, Stanley V (Stan) (Actor, Comedian)
Radio Spirits
PO Box 3107
Wallingford, CT 06494-3107, USA

Frechette, Peter (Actor)
c/o Staff Member *Don Buchwald & Associates (LA)*
6500 Wilshire Blvd Ste 2200
Los Angeles, CA 90048-4942, USA

Frecheville, James (Actor)
c/o Kenny Goodman *The Schiff Company*
9220 W Sunset Blvd Ste 106
West Hollywood, CA 90069-3500, USA

Freddie, Douglas (Athlete, Football Player)
24 Pheasant Run Dr
Cabot, AR 72023-3608, USA

Frederic, Dreux (Lil Fizz) (Musician)
c/o Douglas Mark *Mark Music and Media Law*
Prefers to be contacted via telephone
West Hollywood, CA 90069, USA

Frederick, Andrew B (Athlete, Football Player)
7247 Alexander Dr
Dallas, TX 75214-3216, USA

Frederick, Andy
7247 Alexander Dr
Dallas, TX 75214-3216, USA

Frederick, Kevin (Athlete, Baseball Player)
20512 N Clarice Ave
Lincolnshire, IL 60069-9618, USA

Frederick, Mike (Athlete, Football Player)
425 Fairmont Dr
Chester Springs, PA 19425-3657, USA

Fredericks, Frank (Frankie) (Athlete, Track Athlete)
4497 Wimbledon Dr
Provo, UT 84604-5394, USA

Fredericks, Fred (Cartoonist)
PO Box 475
Eastham, MA 02642-0475, USA

Frederickson, Ivan C (Tucker) (Athlete, Football Player)
12414 Indian Rd
North Palm Beach, FL 33408-2539, USA

Frederickson, Rob (Athlete, Football Player)
11033 N 74th St
Scottsdale, AZ 85260-6403, USA

Frederickson, Scott (Athlete, Baseball Player)
20703 Turning Leaf Lake Ct
Cypress, TX 77433-4612, USA

Fredette, Jimmer (Athlete, Basketball Player)
c/o Chris Emens *Octagon Home Office*
1751 Pinnacle Dr Fl 15
Mc Lean, VA 22102-3833, USA

Fredrickson, Rob (Athlete, Football Player)
7314 E Claremont St
Scottsdale, AZ 85250-5527, USA

Fredrickson, Scott (Athlete, Baseball Player)
20703 Turning Leaf Lake Ct
Cypress, TX 77433-4612, USA

Free (Actor, Musician)
c/o Damu Bobb *Identity Talent Agency (ID)*
9107 Wilshire Blvd Ste 500
Beverly Hills, CA 90210-5526, USA

Free, Doug (Athlete, Football Player)
c/o Jimmy Sexton *CAA (Memphis)*
6060 Poplar Ave Ste 470
Memphis, TN 38119-0910, USA

Free, World B (Athlete, Basketball Player, Coach)
1 Twin Hollow Ct
Sicklerville, NJ 08081-4057, USA

Freebo
740 N Hayworth Ave
Los Angeles, CA 90046-7142

Freed, Andy (Commentator)
4611 Noble Pl
Parrish, FL 34219-7599, USA

Freedman, Alix M (Journalist)
Wall Street Journal
1 World Financial Ctr Fl 8
Editorial Dept
New York, NY 10281-0006, USA

Freedman, Gerald A (Director, Opera Singer)
Theatre Julliard School
Lincoln Center Plaza
New York, NY 10023, USA

Freedman, Russell (Writer)
280 Riverside Dr Apt 10K
New York, NY 10025-9010, USA

Freeh, LouisFBI
9th & Pennsylvania Ave NW
Washington, DC 20035

Freehan, Bill (Athlete, Baseball Player)
6999 Indian Garden Rd
Petoskey, MI 49770-8708, USA

Freelon, Nnenna (Musician)
Ted Kurland
173 Brighton Ave
Allston, MA 02134-2003, USA

Freelon, Solomon (Athlete, Football Player)
2021 Burg Jones Ln
Monroe, LA 71202-4406, USA

Freeman, Antonio (Athlete, Football Player)
11201 NW 18th St
Plantation, FL 33323-2226, USA

Freeman, Arturo (Athlete, Football Player)
14420 Stirling Rd
Southwest Ranches, FL 33330-2908, USA

Freeman, Bernard (Bun B) (Musician)
c/o Marty Diamond *Paradigm (NY)*
360 Park Ave S Fl 16
New York, NY 10010-1716, USA

Freeman, Bobby (Musician)
Lustig Talent
PO Box 770850
Orlando, FL 32877-0850, USA

Freeman, Cassidy (Actor)
c/o Janice Lee *Entertainment Fusion Group*
7080 Hollywood Blvd Ste 903
Los Angeles, CA 90028-6936, USA

Freeman, Crispin (Actor, Writer)
c/o Staff Member *Arlene Thornton & Associates*
12711 Ventura Blvd Ste 490
Studio City, CA 91604-2477, USA

Freeman, Devonta (Athlete, Football Player)
c/o Tony Fleming *Impact Sports - LA*
11331 Ventura Blvd Ste 1A
Studio City, CA 91604-3147, USA

Freeman, Freddie (Athlete, Baseball Player)
c/o Casey Close *Excel Sports Management (LA)*
9665 Wilshire Blvd Ste 500
Beverly Hills, CA 90212-2312, USA

Freeman, Gary (Athlete, Basketball Player)
PO Box 1399
Albany, OR 97321-0548, USA

Freeman, Gregory A (Writer)
4880 Lower Roswell Rd Ste 165210
Marietta, GA 30068-4375, USA

Freeman, Isaac (Musician)
Keith Case Assoc
1025 17th Ave S Fl 2
Nashville, TN 37212-2211, USA

Freeman, Issac (Fatman Scoop) (Musician)
c/o Staff Member *PhreQuency Entertainment*
1830 South Rd Ste 24 PMB 178
Wappingers Falls, NY 12590-1372, USA

Freeman, J E (Actor)
Gersh Agency
232 N Canon Dr
Beverly Hills, CA 90210-5302, USA

Freeman, Jennifer Nicole (Actor)
c/o Nils Larsen *Principato/Young Management (LA)*
9465 Wilshire Blvd Ste 900
Beverly Hills, CA 90212-2608, USA

Freeman, Jimmy (Athlete, Baseball Player)
4716 E 106th St
Tulsa, OK 74137-6805, USA

Freeman, La Vel (Athlete, Baseball Player)
8941 Laguna Place Way
Elk Grove, CA 95758-5351, USA

Freeman, Marvin (Athlete, Baseball Player)
20135 Mohawk Trl
Olympia Fields, IL 60461-1135, USA

Freeman, Michael William (Actor)
c/o Scott Zimmerman *Evolution Entertainment (LA)*
901 N Highland Ave
Los Angeles, CA 90038-2412, USA

Freeman, Mike (Athlete, Football Player)
222 Clubhill Dr
San Antonio, TX 78228-1903, USA

Freeman, Morgan (Actor)
c/o Stan Rosenfield *Stan Rosenfield & Associates*
2029 Century Park E Ste 1190
Los Angeles, CA 90067-2931, USA

Freeman, Phil (Athlete, Football Player)
1222 S Stanley Ave
Los Angeles, CA 90019-6617, USA

Freeman, Reggie (Athlete, Football Player)
3131 Hartridge Ter
Wellington, FL 33414-3431, USA

Freeman, Robin (Athlete, Golfer)
115 Chelsea Cir
Palm Desert, CA 92260-4688, USA

Freeman, Rod (Athlete, Basketball Player)
6308 Murray Ln
Brentwood, TN 37027-6210, USA

Freeman, Russ (Athlete, Football Player)
4090 Summit Crossing Dr
Decatur, GA 30034-3542, USA

Freeman, Russell (Football Coach, Football Player)
4090 Summit Crossing Dr
Decatur, GA 30034-3542, USA

Freeman, Sandi (Correspondent)
Cable News Network
820 1st St NE Ste 1000
News Dept
Washington, DC 20002-4363, USA

Freeman, Steve (Athlete, Football Player)
Mississippi State University
PO Box 5308
Attn: Alumni Association
Mississippi State, MS 39762-5308, USA

Freeman, Yvette (Actor, Musician)
Stone Manners
6500 Wilshire Blvd # 550
Los Angeles, CA 90048-4920, USA

Freeney, Dwight (Athlete, Football Player)
23001 Hawthorne Blvd Ste 202
Torrance, CA 90505-3754, USA

Freer, Mark (Athlete, Hockey Player)
823 Linden Rd
Hershey, PA 17033-1735, USA

Freese, David (Athlete, Baseball Player)
16559 Thunderhead Canyon Ct
Ballwin, MO 63011-1853, USA

Freese, Gene (Athlete, Baseball Player)
6114 Bellaire Dr
New Orleans, LA 70124-1244, USA

Freese, George (Athlete, Baseball Player)
3341 SW Marigold St
Portland, OR 97219-5309, USA

Freese, Louis (Musician)
c/o Jack Iannaci *Brass Artists & Associates*
4749 Bandini Ave
Riverside, CA 92506-1004, USA

Frehley, Ace (Musician)
1347/1357/1363 Spring Valley Rd
Ossining, NY 10562, USA

Freidheim, Cyrus (Business Person)
Chiquita Brands International
550 S Caldwell St Ste 1010
Charlotte, NC 28202-2681, USA

Freire, Nelson (Musician)
Columbia Artists Mgmt Inc
165 W 57th St
New York, NY 10019-2201, USA

Freis, Edward DJ (Doctor)
4515 Willard Ave
Chevy Chase, MD 20815-3622, USA

Freisleben, Dave (Athlete, Baseball Player)
1326 Diamante Dr
Pasadena, TX 77504-1479, USA

Freitas, Jesse (Athlete, Football Player)
8405 Florissant Ct
San Diego, CA 92129-4408, USA

Freitas, Rocky (Athlete, Football Player)
2667 E Manoa Rd
Honolulu, HI 96822-1817, USA

French, Ernest (Athlete, Football Player)
1004 Moran St
Bay Minette, AL 36507-2443, USA

French, Heather (Beauty Pageant Winner)
1361 Tyler Park Dr
Louisville, KY 40204-1539, USA

French, Jane (Musician)
c/o Staff Member *Pixie Publishing*
9611 Ross Ave
Montgomery, OH 45242-7123

French, Jim (Athlete, Baseball Player)
PO Box 39
49594 Ke Rd
Mesa, CO 81643-0039, USA

French, Kate (Actor)
c/o Brooklyn Weaver *Energy Entertainment*
999 N Doheny Dr Apt 711
West Hollywood, CA 90069-3151, USA

French, Leigh (Actor)
1850 N Vista St
Los Angeles, CA 90046-2237, USA

French, Luke (Athlete, Baseball Player)
10090 Severn Ln
Parker, CO 80134-3617, USA

French, Marilyn (Writer)
Charlotte Sheedy Agency
928 Broadway Ste 901
New York, NY 10010-8139, USA

French, Paige (Actor)
Gersh Agency
232 N Canon Dr
Beverly Hills, CA 90210-5302, USA

French, Rufus (Athlete, Football Player)
PO Box 10628
Green Bay, WI 54307-0628, USA

French, Sarah (Model, Television Host)
1 Devonshire Pl Apt 2102
Boston, MA 02109-3541, USA

French, Susan
110 E 9th St Ste C1005
Los Angeles, CA 90079-6112

Freon, Franck (Race Car Driver)
434 E Ma I N St
Brownsburg, IN 46112, USA

Freotte, Gus (Athlete, Football Player)
10040 Litzsinger Rd
Saint Louis, MO 63124-1132, USA

Freotte, Mitch (Athlete, Football Player)
445 Reynolds Ave
Kittanning, PA 16201-2713, USA

Frerotte, Gus (Athlete, Football Player)
1007 Hulton Rd
Oakmont, PA 15139-1131, USA

Fresh, Doug E (Musician)
c/o Reg Reg Askew *Fly Guy Management*
1 W 34th St Rm 201
New York, NY 10001-3011, USA

Fresh, Mannie (Musician, Producer)
c/o Staff Member *Universal Music Group (UMG - LA)*
2220 Colorado Ave
Santa Monica, CA 90404-3506, USA

Freston, Kathy (Writer)
c/o Staff Member *St Martins Press*
175 5th Ave Ste 400
Publicity Dept
New York, NY 10010-7848, USA

Freudenthal, David (Politician)
10020 Yellowstone Rd
Cheyenne, WY 82009-8943, USA

Freudenthal, Thor (Director)
c/o Peter McHugh *The Gotham Group Inc*
9255 W Sunset Blvd Ste 515
West Hollywood, CA 90069-3308, USA

Freundlich, Bart (Director, Producer, Writer)
c/o Bart Walker *ICM Partners (LA)*
10250 Constellation Blvd Fl 7
Los Angeles, CA 90067-6207, USA

Frewer, Matt (Actor)
c/o Gordon Gilbertson *Gilbertson Management*
1334 3rd Street Promenade Ste 201
Santa Monica, CA 90401-1320, USA

Frey, Bob (Race Car Driver)
605 Harvest Ln
Waterford Works, NJ 08089-2117, USA

Frey, Dick
23618 Powder Mill Dr
Tomball, TX 77377-3920, USA

Frey, Glenn (Actor, Musician, Songwriter, Writer)
5020 Brent Knoll Ln
Suwanee, GA 30024-1376, USA

Frey, James (Writer)
c/o Richard Green *Resolution (LA)*
1801 Century Park E Ste 2300
Los Angeles, CA 90067-2325, USA

Frey, Jim (Commentator)
12101 Tullamore Ct Unit 406
Lutherville Timonium, MD 21093-8148, USA

Frey, Richard (Athlete, Football Player)
PO Box 1967
Tomball, TX 77377-1967, USA

Frey, Steve (Athlete, Baseball Player)
1414 2nd Street Pike
Southampton, PA 18966-3931, USA

Frick, Stephen N (Astronaut)
27998 Mercurio Rd
Carmel, CA 93923-8429, USA

Fricke, Janie (Musician)
Janie Fricke Concerts
PO Box 798
Lancaster, TX 75146-0798, USA

Fricker, Brenda (Actor)
c/o Staff Member *IFA Talent Agency*
2000 Avenue Of The Stars
Los Angeles, CA 90067-4700, USA

Frickman, Andy (Director)
c/o Staff Member *William Morris Endeavor (LA)*
9601 Wilshire Blvd
Beverly Hills, CA 90210-5213, USA

Friday, Tim (Athlete, Hockey Player)
14 Parker St
Southborough, MA 01772-1949, USA

Friday Jr, Elbert W (Government Official)
US National Weather Service
1125 East-West Hwy
Silver Spring, MD 20910, USA

Fridell, Squire
15250 Ventura Blvd Ste 200
Sherman Oaks, CA 91403-3215

Fridgen, Dan (Athlete, Hockey Player)
1524 Bouton Rd
Troy, NY 12180-3630, USA

Friebe, Anika
111 E 22nd St # 200
New York, NY 10010-5400

Friede, Mike (Athlete, Football Player)
6943 County Road 56
Johnstown, CO 80534-8237, USA

Friedericy, Bonita (Actor)
8480 Hillside Ave
Los Angeles, CA 90069-1505, USA

Friedgen, Ralph (Coach, Football Coach)
University of Maryland
Athletic Dept
College Park, MD 20742-0001, USA

Friedkin, William (Director)
c/o Renee Tab *Sentient*
1617 Broadway Mezzanine Suite
Santa Monica, CA 90404, USA

Friedlander, Judah (Comedian, Writer)
c/o Kenneth Lee *Innovative Artists (NY)*
235 Park Ave S Fl 7
New York, NY 10003-1405, USA

Friedlander, Lee (Artist, Photographer)
44 S Mountain Rd
New City, NY 10956-2315, USA

Friedle, Will (Actor)
c/o Steven Muller *Innovative Artists (LA)*
1505 10th St
Santa Monica, CA 90401-2805, USA

Friedman, Andrew (Commentator)
1265 Snell Isle Blvd NE
Saint Petersburg, FL 33704-3035, USA

Friedman, Doug (Athlete, Hockey Player)
PO Box 33
Kents Hill, ME 04349-0033, USA

Friedman, Kinky (Writer)
906 1/2 Congress Ave
Austin, TX 78701-2422, USA

Friedman, Lennie (Athlete, Football Player)
1300 Adams Mountain Rd
Raleigh, NC 27614-8191, USA

Friedman, Peter (Actor, Musician)
J Michael Bloom
233 Park Ave S # 1000
New York, NY 10003-1606, USA

Friedman, Philip (Writer)
Ivy Books/Random House Inc
1745 Broadway # B1
New York, NY 10019-4640, USA

Friedman, Sonya
208 Harristown Rd
Glen Rock, NJ 07452-3308

Friedman, Thomas (Journalist)
7117 Bradley Blvd
Bethesda, MD 20817-2125, USA

Friedmann, Phil (Musician)
Overland Productions
156 W 56th St # 500
New York, NY 10019-3800, USA

Friend, Bob (Athlete, Baseball Player)
4 Salem Cir
Pittsburgh, PA 15238-2525, USA

Friend, Rupert (Actor)
c/o Boomer Malkin *William Morris Endeavor (LA)*
9601 Wilshire Blvd
Beverly Hills, CA 90210-5213, USA

Frier, Mike (Athlete, Football Player)
180 Jackson St NE Apt 1615
Atlanta, GA 30312-1358, USA

Fries, Chuck
6922 Hollywood Blvd
Los Angeles, CA 90028-6117

Fries, Donald B (Publisher)
Life Magazine
Time-Life Building
New York, NY 10020, USA

Friesen, David (Musician)
Thomas Cassidy
11761 E Speedway Blvd
Tucson, AZ 85748-2017, USA

Friesen, Don (Musician)
c/o Staff Member *Paradigm (Monterey)*
404 W Franklin St
Monterey, CA 93940-2303, USA

Friesen, Jeff (Athlete, Hockey Player)
96 Dornoch Way
Trabuco Canyon, CA 92679-4920, USA

Friesz, John (Athlete, Football Player)
1454 E West Pebblestone Ct
Hayden, ID 83835-7999, USA

Frig, Len (Athlete, Hockey Player)
7556 S Wynford St
Salt Lake City, UT 84121-5449, USA

Frigid Pink
32885 Northampton Dr
Warren, MI 48093-6164

Frimout, Dirk D (Astronaut)
c/o Staff Member *NASA-JSC*
2101 Nasa Pkwy # 1
Astronaut Office - Mail Code Cb
Houston, TX 77058-3607, USA

Frisbee, Rob (Athlete)
c/o Jerry Shandrew *Shandrew Public Relations*
1050 S Stanley Ave
Los Angeles, CA 90019-6634, USA

Frisch, Byron (Athlete, Football Coach, Football Player)
3492 Corte Curva
Carlsbad, CA 92009-9501, USA

Frisch, David (Athlete, Football Player)
3 Pebble Acres Ct
High Ridge, MO 63049-1665, USA

Frischman, Daniel
145 S Fairfax Ave Ste 310
Los Angeles, CA 90036-2176

Frisell, William R (Bill) (Musician)
Nonesuch Records
75 Rockefeller Plz
New York, NY 10019-6908, USA

Frist, William (Politician)
900 20th Ave S Apt 1705
Nashville, TN 37212-2251, USA

Frist Jr, Thomas (Business Person)
HCA
1 Park Plz
Nashville, TN 37203-6527, USA

Fritsch, Jamie
17 Littlehale Rd
Durham, NH 03824-2106, USA

Fritsche, Dan (Athlete, Hockey Player)
6414 Fordham Dr
Cleveland, OH 44129-5242, USA

Fritsche, Jim (Athlete, Basketball Player)
470 Emerson Ave W
Saint Paul, MN 55118-2034, USA

Fritsch Jr, Ted (Athlete, Football Player)
5014 Odins Way
Marietta, GA 30068-1660, USA

Fritz, Frank (Reality Star)
Antique Archaeology
1300 Clinton St Ste 130
Nashville, TN 37203-7007, USA

Fritz, Nikki (Actor)
PO Box 57764
Sherman Oaks, CA 91413-2764, USA

Frizzell, David (Musician)
4694 E Robertson Rd
Cross Plains, TN 37049-4827, USA

Frizzelle, William J (Athlete, Football Player)
8001 Tylerton Dr
Raleigh, NC 27613-1557, USA

Froboess, Cornelia (Musician)
Rinklhof
Kleinholzhausen
Raubling, GE D-830

Froemming, Bruce (Athlete, Baseball Player)
702 W Haddonstone Pl
Mequon, WI 53092-5966, USA

Froese, Bob (Athlete, Hockey Player)
11701 Clarence Center Rd
Akron, NY 14001-9747, USA

Froggatt, Joanne (Actor)
c/o Mike Smith *Principal Entertainment (LA)*
9255 W Sunset Blvd Ste 500
West Hollywood, CA 90069-3301, USA

Frohnmayer, John E (Government Official)
1335 SW Timian St
Corvallis, OR 97333-3932, USA

Frohwirth, Todd (Athlete, Baseball Player)
S66W24360 Skyline Ave
Waukesha, WI 53189-9254, USA

Frolov, Alexander (Athlete, Hockey Player)
1467 3rd St
Manhattan Beach, CA 90266-6335, USA

Frolov, Diane (Actor)
c/o Richard Weitz *William Morris Endeavor (LA)*
9601 Wilshire Blvd
Beverly Hills, CA 90210-5213, USA

Fron, Kenneth (Designer)
Kenneth Fron Designs
333 W North Ave # 133
Chicago, IL 60610-1293, USA

Frongillo, John (Athlete, Football Player)
10230 Elmhurst Dr NW
Albuquerque, NM 87114-4617, USA

Froning-O'Meara, Mary (Athlete, Baseball Player, Commentator)
417 Bay Hill Dr
Madison, WI 53717-2650, USA

Frontiere, Dominic
280 S Beverly Dr Ste 411
Beverly Hills, CA 90212-3904

Frost, Dave (Athlete, Baseball Player)
2206 Ocana Ave
Long Beach, CA 90815-2125, USA

Frost, Jo (Actor, Reality Star)
c/o Juliette Harris *It Girl Public Relations*
5301 Beethoven St Ste 220
Los Angeles, CA 90066-7052, USA

Frost, Ken (Athlete, Football Player)
22842 Stinnett Hollow Rd
Athens, AL 35614-3516, USA

Frost, Lindsay (Actor)
c/o Staff Member *Allman/Rea Management*
9255 W Sunset Blvd Ste 600
West Hollywood, CA 90069-3306, USA

Frost, Mark (Writer)
Mark Frost Productions
PO Box 1723
Studio City, CA 91614-0723, USA

Frost, Nick (Actor)
c/o Tom Drumm *The Safran Company*
8748 Holloway Dr
West Hollywood, CA 90069-2327, USA

Frost, Scott (Athlete, Football Player)
99 Thomas Lk
Ashland, NE 68003-9400, USA

Fruhwirth, Amy (Athlete, Golfer)
26431 N 44th Way
Phoenix, AZ 85050-8579, USA

Frusciante, John (Musician)
Boeing
8942 Wilshire Blvd
Everett, WA 98208, USA

Fry, Bob (Athlete, Football Player)
1604 Bexley Dr
Wilmington, NC 28412-2049, USA

Fry, Hayden (Athlete, Football Player)
1069 Calais Cir
Mesquite, NV 89027-8803, USA

Fry, Jay (Athlete, Football Player)
PO Box 53
College Corner, OH 45003-0053, USA

Fry, Jerry (Athlete, Baseball Player)
3300 Stanton St
Springfield, IL 62703-4830, USA

Fry, Jordan (Actor)
c/o Carlyne Grager *Dramatic Artists Agency*
103 W Alameda Ave Ste 139
Burbank, CA 91502-2253, USA

Fry, Michael (Cartoonist)
United Feature Syndicate
PO Box 5610
Cincinnati, OH 45201-5610, USA

Fry, Robert (Athlete, Football Player)
1604 Bexley Dr
Wilmington, NC 28412-2049, USA

Fryar, Irving D (Athlete, Football Player, Sportscaster)
51 Applegate Rd
Jobstown, NJ 08041-2202, USA

Fryberger, Dates (Athlete, Hockey Player, Olympic Athlete)
PO Box 564
114 Gin Ridge Rd
Sun Valley, ID 83353-0564, USA

Fryce, Trevor (Athlete, Football Player)
20293 E Lake Cir
Centennial, CO 80016-1282, USA

Frye, Jeff (Athlete, Baseball Player)
1701 Rogers Rd Apt 611
Fort Worth, TX 76107-6591, USA

Frye, Kelly (Actor)
c/o Katie Mason *Luber Roklin Management*
5815 W Sunset Blvd Ste 206
Los Angeles, CA 90028-6481, USA

Frye, Meno
2713 N Keystone St
Burbank, CA 91504-1602

Frye, Shawn (Actor)
2713 N Keystone St
Burbank, CA 91504-1602

Frye, Soleil Moon (Actor)
The Little Seed
219 N Larchmont Blvd
Los Angeles, CA 90004-3706, USA

Fryer, Bernie (Athlete, Basketball Player)
471 E Glacier View Dr
Sequim, WA 98382-3127, USA

Fry-Irvin, Shirley (Tennis Player)
1970 Asylum Ave
West Hartford, CT 06117-3007, USA

Fryling, Victor J (Business Person)
CMS Energy Fairlane Plaza South
330 Town Center Dr
Dearborn, MI 48126-2738, USA

Fryman, Travis (Athlete, Baseball Player)
2600 Highway 196
Molino, FL 32577-9502, USA

F. Sensenbrenner Jr., James (Congressman, Politician)
2449 Rayburn Hob
Washington, DC 20515-4905, USA

Ftorek, Robert B (Robbie) (Athlete, Hockey Player, Olympic Athlete)
79 Sunset Point Rd
Wolfeboro, NH 03894-4907, USA

Fucarino, Frank (Athlete, Basketball Player)
21 Heathcote Ct
Shirley, NY 11967-4423, USA

Fuchs, Joseph L (Publisher)
Mademoiselle Magazine
350 Madison Ave
New York, NY 10017-3700, USA

Fuchs, Leo
609 N Kilkea Dr
Los Angeles, CA 90048-2213

Fuchs, Michael J (Television Host)
Home Box Office
1100 Avenue Of Americans
New York, NY 10036, USA

Fuente, David I (Business Person)
Office Depot Inc
2200 Germantown Rd
Delray Beach, FL 33445-8223, USA

Fuentes, Brian (Athlete, Baseball Player)
1342 El Portal Dr
Merced, CA 95340-0774, USA

Fuentes, Daisy (DJ, Model, Television Host)
20758 Pacific Coast Hwy
Malibu, CA 90265-5405, USA

Fuentes, Mike (Athlete, Baseball Player)
9626 Sycamore Ct
Davie, FL 33328-6768, USA

Fuentes, Rigoberto (Tito) (Athlete, Baseball Player)
61 S Maddux Dr
Reno, NV 89512-1832, USA

Fuentes, Tito (Athlete, Baseball Player)
61 S Maddux Dr
Reno, NV 89512-1832, USA

Fugate, Katherine (Writer)
c/o Bayard Maybank *Hohman Maybank Lieb*
9465 Wilshire Blvd Fl 6
Beverly Hills, CA 90212-2605, USA

Fugees, The
83 Riverside Dr
New York, NY 10024-5713

Fugelsang, John (Actor, Comedian)
c/o Monique Moss *Integrated PR*
9025 Wilshire Blvd Ste 400
Beverly Hills, CA 90211-1828, USA

Fugere, Joe (Athlete, Baseball Player)
415 Cinnamon Rdg
Rutherfordton, NC 28139-6876, USA

Fugett, Jean (Athlete, Football Player)
4801 Westparkway
Baltimore, MD 21229-1336, USA

Fugit, Patrick (Actor)
c/o Brett Norensberg *Gersh (LA)*
9465 Wilshire Blvd Ste 600
Beverly Hills, CA 90212-2605, USA

Fuglesang, Christer (Astronaut)
PO Box 555
Bellaire, TX 77402-0555, USA

Fuglesang, Christer Dr (Astronaut)
PO Box 555
Bellaire, TX 77402-0555, USA

Fuhr, Grant (Athlete, Hockey Player)
c/o Staff Member *Phoenix Coyotes*
9400 W Maryland Ave
Glendale, AZ 85305-3114, USA

Fuhrman, Isabelle (Actor)
c/o Susie Mains *Trilogy Talent*
13425 Ventura Blvd Fl 2
Sherman Oaks, CA 91423-3974, USA

Fuhrman, Mark (Attorney)
PO Box 333
Sagle, ID 83860-0333, USA

Fujisaki, Judge Hiroshi
1705 Main St # Q
Santa Monica, CA 90401

Fujita, Scott (Athlete, Football Player)
27350 Upper Forty Dr
Carmel Valley, CA 93924-9250, USA

Fukunaga, Cary (Actor)
c/o Michael Sugar *Anonymous Content (LA)*
3532 Hayden Ave
Culver City, CA 90232-2413, USA

Fukuto, Maru (Director)
Jim Preminger Agency
450 N Roxbury Dr Ste 1050
Beverly Hills, CA 90210-4235, USA

Fulcher, Bill (Athlete, Football Player)
18 Eagle Pointe Dr
Augusta, GA 30909-6056, USA

Fulcher, David (Athlete, Football Player)
4140 Fieldsedge Dr
Mason, OH 45040-8538, USA

Fulcher, Modriel (Athlete, Football Player)
6010 S Westmoreland Rd Apt 1012
Dallas, TX 75237-2061, USA

Fulchino, Jeff (Athlete, Baseball Player)
11 Laurel Dr
Monroe, CT 06468-1649, USA

Fuld, Sam (Athlete, Baseball Player)
284 Marlberry Cir
Jupiter, FL 33458-2848, USA

Fulgham, John (Athlete, Baseball Player)
769 Cricklewood Ter
Lake Mary, FL 32746-5310, USA

Fulghum, Robert (Writer)
c/o Staff Member *HarperCollins Publishers*
195 Broadway Fl 2
Cellar 1
New York, NY 10007-3132, USA

Fulghum, Robert (Writer)
Random House
1015 Violeta Dr
Alhambra, CA 91801-5332, USA

Fulhage, Scott (Athlete, Football Player)
2340 N Rd
Beloit, KS 67420, USA

Fulks, Robbie (Musician, Songwriter, Writer)
Mongrel Music
743 Center Blvd
Fairfax, CA 94930-1764, USA

Fuller, Amanda (Actor)
c/o JB Roberts *Thruline Entertainment*
9250 Wilshire Blvd Ste 100
Ground Floor
Beverly Hills, CA 90212-3343, USA

Fuller, Bryan (Writer)
c/o Ari Greenburg *William Morris Endeavor (LA)*
9601 Wilshire Blvd
Beverly Hills, CA 90210-5213, USA

Fuller, Carl (Athlete, Basketball Player)
8302 Kirkville Dr
Houston, TX 77089-2194, USA

Fuller, Corey (Athlete, Football Player)
4161 Ballard Rd
Tallahassee, FL 32305-6308, USA

Fuller, Curtis D (Athlete, Football Player)
Denon Records
15635 Sullivan Ridge Dr
Charlotte, NC 28277-2468, USA

Fuller, Deiores (Actor, Songwriter, Writer)
3628 Ottawa Cir
Las Vegas, NV 89169-3301, USA

Fuller, Drew (Actor)
c/o Stephanie Simon *Untitled Entertainment (LA)*
350 S Beverly Dr Ste 200
Beverly Hills, CA 90212-4819, USA

Fuller, Eddie (Athlete, Football Player)
36422 the Bluffs Ave
Prairieville, LA 70769-3197, USA

Fuller, Jeff (Race Car Driver)
Jeff Fuller Motorsports
PO Box 3336
Mooresville, NC 28117-3336, USA

Fuller, Jim (Athlete, Baseball Player)
5107 Bur Oak Dr
Pasadena, TX 77505-3028, USA

Fuller, Joe (Athlete, Football Player)
8906 Farnsworth Ave N
Minneapolis, MN 55443-1752, USA

Fuller, John (Athlete, Baseball Player)
31912 Paseo Terraza
San Juan Capistrano, CA 92675-3060, USA

Fuller, Johnny (Athlete, Football Player)
2013 Chisholm Trl
Salado, TX 76571-5449, USA

Fuller, Kurt (Actor)
c/o Rick Ax *Gold Coast Management*
438 S Venice Blvd Apt 5
Venice, CA 90291-4695, USA

Fuller, Kyle (Athlete, Football Player)
c/o Greg Barnett *Lagardere Unlimited - Miami*
235 Park Ave S Fl 6
New York, NY 10003-1405, USA

Fuller, Lance
1900 S Longwood Ave
Los Angeles, CA 90016-1408

Fuller, Mike (Athlete, Football Player)
4241 Abingdon Trl
Mountain Brk, AL 35243-1737, USA

Fuller, Penny (Actor)
12428 Hesby St
Valley Village, CA 91607-3020, USA

Fuller, Randy (Athlete, Football Player)
2257 Patsy Ln
Columbus, GA 31903-3436, USA

Fuller, Robert (Actor)
PO Box 272
Era, TX 76238-0272, USA

Fuller, Rod (Race Car Driver)
David Powers Motorsports
10205 Westheimer Rd Ste 100
Houston, TX 77042-3164, USA

Fuller, Simon (Producer)
c/o Jeff Frasco *Creative Artists Agency (CAA-LA)*
2000 Avenue of the Stars Ste 100
Los Angeles, CA 90067-4705, USA

Fuller, Steve (Athlete, Football Player)
81 Oak Tree Rd
Bluffton, SC 29910-4960, USA

Fuller, Tony (Athlete, Basketball Player)
4222 Lost Springs Dr
Agoura Hills, CA 91301-5326, USA

Fuller, Vem (Athlete, Baseball Player)
155 Ironwood Cir
Aurora, OH 44202-9156, USA

Fuller, Vern (Athlete, Baseball Player)
155 Ironwood Cir
Aurora, OH 44202-9156, USA

Fuller, Vincent (Athlete, Football Player)
229 W 60th St Apt 24T
New York, NY 10023-7515, USA

Fuller, William H Jr (Athlete, Football Player)
1014 Fairway Dr
Chesapeake, VA 23320-8200, USA

Fullerton, Ed (Athlete, Football Player)
5850 Meridian Rd Apt 315A
Gibsonia, PA 15044-4801, USA

Fullington, Darrell (Athlete, Football Player)
1023 W Patrick Cir
Daytona Beach, FL 32117-4565, USA

Fullmer, Brad (Athlete, Baseball Player)
400 S Barrington Ave Apt 202
Los Angeles, CA 90049-6413, USA

Fullmer, Gene (Boxer)
9217 S Covered Wagon Cir Unit B
West Jordan, UT 84088-5688, USA

Fullone, Sam (Race Car Driver)
Fullone Motorsports
10743 Mileback Rd
North Collins, NY 14111, USA

Fullwood, Brent (Athlete, Football Player)
4002 Maybreeze Rd
Marietta, GA 30066-2734, USA

Fullwood, Troy (Athlete, Baseball Player)
317 Manning Ln
Hampton, VA 23666-5023, USA

Fulmer, Phillip (Coach, Football Coach)
University of Tennessee
Athletic Dept
Knoxville, TN 37996-0001, USA

Fulton, Bill (Athlete, Baseball Player)
3001 Lexington Ct
Export, PA 15632-9061, USA

Fulton, Eileen (Actor, Musician)
As the World Turns Show"" CBS-TV
524 W 57th St
New York, NY 10019-2924, USA

Fulton, Fitz
1023 E Avenue J5
Lancaster, CA 93535-4239, USA

Fulton, Robert (Politician)
PO Box 2634
Waterloo, IA 50704-2634, USA

Fulton, Soren (Actor)
c/o Staff Member *Savage Agency*
6212 Banner Ave
Los Angeles, CA 90038-2802, USA

Fultz, Aaron (Athlete, Baseball Player)
2575 Beaver Rd
Munford, TN 38058-4215, USA

Fultz, Frank (Athlete, Baseball Player)
310 Willow Glade Pt
Alpharetta, GA 30022-1025, USA

Fultz, Jeff (Race Car Driver)
JCR3 Racing
3401 Rotary Dr
Charlotte, NC 28269-4495, USA

Fultz, Mike (Athlete, Football Player)
1900 W Foothills Rd
Lincoln, NE 68523-9389, USA

Fu Manchu (Music Group, Musician)
c/o Staff Member *Agency for the Performing Arts (APA-LA)*
405 S Beverly Dr Ste 500
Beverly Hills, CA 90212-4425, USA

Fumero, David (Actor)
c/o Jerome Martin *Jerome Martin Management*
1655 N Cherokee Ave
2nd Floor
Los Angeles, CA 90028, USA

Fumero, Melissa (Actor)
200 W 60th St
New York, NY 10023-8502, USA

Fumusa, Dominic (Actor)
c/o Robert Stein *Robert Stein Management*
PO Box 3797
Beverly Hills, CA 90212-0797, USA

Fun. (Music Group, Musician)
c/o Dalton Sim *Nettwerk - Boston*
1955 Massachusetts Ave
Cambridge, MA 02140-1405, USA

Funchess, Tom (Athlete, Football Player)
1015 Funchess St
Crystal Springs, MS 39059-3017, USA

Fund, John (Writer)
c/o Staff Member *The American Spectator*
1611 N Kent St Ste 901
Arlington, VA 22209-2111, USA

Funderburk, Mark (Athlete, Baseball Player)
6924 Old Providence Rd
Charlotte, NC 28226-7740, USA

Funderburke, Lawrence (Athlete, Basketball Player)
1688 Meadoway Ct
Blacklick, OH 43004-9759, USA

Funk, Caribbean (Music Group)
c/o Staff Member *Sony Music Miami*
605 Lincoln Rd Ste 700
Miami Beach, FL 33139-2901, USA

Funk, Frank (Athlete, Baseball Player)
4022 S Alamandas Way
Gold Canyon, AZ 85118-1899, USA

Funk, Fred (Athlete, Golfer)
24729 Harbour View Dr
Ponte Vedra Beach, FL 32082-1509, USA

Funk, Nolan Gerard (Actor)
c/o Kim Callahan *Industry Entertainment*
955 Carrillo Dr Ste 300
Los Angeles, CA 90048-5400, USA

Funk, Tom (Athlete, Baseball Player)
6952 N Olive St
Kansas City, MO 64118-2876, USA

Funke, Alex (Cinematographer)
1176 Fiske St
Pacific Palisades, CA 90272-3845, USA

Funkmaster Flex (DJ, Musician)
c/o Ron Rivlin *Coast II Coast Entertainment*
204 S Beverly Dr Ste 110
Beverly Hills, CA 90212-3800, USA

Funt, Peter
PO Box 827
Monterey, CA 93942-0827

Fuqua, Antoine (Director)
c/o Katherine Rowe *Slate Public Relations*
9000 W Sunset Blvd Ste 915
West Hollywood, CA 90069-5809, USA

Fuqua, John (Athlete, Football Player)
13983 Glastonbury Ave
Detroit, MI 48223-2921, USA

Fuqua, John Frenchy
13983 Glastonbury Ave
Detroit, MI 48223-2921, USA

Furay, Richie (Musician)
c/o Staff Member *The Agency Group*
(NYC)
142 W 57th St Fl 6
New York, NY 10019-3300, USA

Furcal, Rafael (Athlete, Baseball Player)
2489 Provence Cir
Weston, FL 33327-1303, USA

Furey, John (Actor)
c/o Staff Member *Hartig Hilepo Agency
Ltd*
54 W 21st St Rm 610
New York, NY 10010-7344, USA

Furian, Mira (Actor)
6410 Blarney Stone Ct
Springfield, VA 22152-2129, USA

Furie, Sidney (Director, Producer, Writer)
c/o Jack Gilardi *ICM Partners (LA)*
10250 Constellation Blvd Fl 7
Los Angeles, CA 90067-6207, USA

Furjanic, Anthony (Athlete, Football
Player)
15220 Cottonwood Ct
Orland Park, IL 60467-7346, USA

Furjanic, Tony
15220 Cottonwood Ct
Orland Park, IL 60467-7346, USA

Furlan, Mira (Actor)
c/o Chris Roe *CR Management*
23852 Pacific Coast Hwy Ste 627
Malibu, CA 90265-4876, USA

Furlong, Edward (Actor)
c/o Mark Rousso *New Wave
Entertainment (LA)*
2660 W Olive Ave
Burbank, CA 91505-4525, USA

Furlong, Shirley (Athlete, Golfer)
16412 S 18th Dr
Phoenix, AZ 85045-1628, USA

Furman, Andrew (Race Car Driver)
Latonio Racing
PO Box 75007
Cincinnati, OH 45275-0007, USA

Furmaniak, J J (Athlete, Baseball Player)
12502 Larkspur Ln
Plainfield, IL 60585-5545, USA

Furness, Deborra-Lee (Actor, Director,
Producer)
c/o Staff Member *Seed Productions*
10201 W Pico Blvd Bldg 52
Los Angeles, CA 90064-2606, USA

Furniss, Bruce (Athlete, Olympic Athlete,
Swimmer)
18452 Old Lamplighter Cir
Villa Park, CA 92861-4528, USA

Furniss, Steve (Athlete, Olympic Athlete,
Swimmer)
6478 Frampton Cir
Huntington Beach, CA 92648-6620, USA

Furr, Brad (Race Car Driver)
8242 Creekside Dr
Dublin, CA 94568-3512, USA

Furrer, Will (Athlete, Football Player)
420 Logan Ranch Rd
Georgetown, TX 78628-1211, USA

Furrey, Mike (Athlete, Football Player)
8579 Newbury Ct N
Canton, MI 48187-4444, USA

Furst, Anthony (Athlete, Football Player)
4315 Promenade Ave
Grove City, OH 43123-8267, USA

Furst, Nathan (Musician)
c/o Mike Rosen *Working Artists Agency*
13525 Ventura Blvd
Sherman Oaks, CA 91423-3801

Furst, Stephen (Actor, Comedian)
Gold Marshak Liedtke
3500 W Olive Ave Ste 1400
Burbank, CA 91505-5512, USA

Furstenfeld, Jeremy (Musician)
Ashley Talent
2002 Hogback Rd Ste 20
Ann Arbor, MI 48105-9736, USA

Furstenfeld, Justin (Musician)
827 W Hopkins St
San Marcos, TX 78666-4200, USA

Furtick, Steven (Writer)
Elevation Church
11416 E Independence Blvd Ste N
Matthews, NC 28105-4947, USA

Fury, Ed (Actor)
6729 Babcock Ave
N Hollywood, CA 91606-1310

Furyk, Jim (Athlete, Golfer)
241 N Roscoe Blvd
Ponte Vedra Beach, FL 32082-3106, USA

Fusco, John (Writer)
c/o Michael Sugar *Anonymous Content
(LA)*
3532 Hayden Ave
Culver City, CA 90232-2413, USA

Fusco, Mark (Athlete, Hockey Player,
Olympic Athlete)
155 Grove St
Westwood, MA 02090-1027, USA

Fusco, Scott (Athlete, Hockey Player,
Olympic Athlete)
41 Wedgemere Ave
Winchester, MA 01890-2439, USA

Fusina, Chuck A (Athlete, Football Player)
1548 King James Dr
Pittsburgh, PA 15237-1588, USA

Fussell, Chris (Athlete, Baseball Player)
3238 N Eastmoreland Dr
Oregon, OH 43616-2933, USA

Futterman, Dan (Actor)
Gersh Agency
232 N Canon Dr
Beverly Hills, CA 90210-5302, USA

Future (Musician)
c/o Michael Forman *Michael Forman
Management*
409 N Camden Dr Ste 205
Beverly Hills, CA 90210-4423, USA

Futureheads, The (Music Group)
c/o Staff Member *Paradigm (Monterey)*
404 W Franklin St
Monterey, CA 93940-2303, USA

Fyhrie, Mike (Athlete, Baseball Player)
54 Panorama
Trabuco Canyon, CA 92679-5362, USA

G, Franky (Actor)
c/o Jimmy Darmody *Creative Artists
Agency (CAA-LA)*
2000 Avenue of the Stars Ste 100
Los Angeles, CA 90067-4705, USA

G, Kenny (Musician)
c/o Irving Azoff *Azoff Music Management*
1100 Glendon Ave Ste 2000
Los Angeles, CA 90024-3524, USA

Gabaldon, Diana (Writer)
10810 N Tatum Blvd # 102-321
Phoenix, AZ 85028-6055, USA

Gabarra, Carin (Athlete, Olympic Athlete,
Soccer Player)
305 Rosslare Dr
Arnold, MD 21012-3007, USA

Gabbard, Kason (Athlete, Baseball Player)
855 D011TOWN Dr
Savannah, TN 38372, USA

Gabbard, Steve (Athlete, Football Player)
7038 Bradfordville Rd
Tallahassee, FL 32309-1806, USA

Gabbert, Blaine (Football Player)
c/o Tom Condon *CAA (St. Louis)*
222 S Central Ave Ste 1008
Saint Louis, MO 63105-3509, USA

Gabel, Seth (Actor)
c/o Peter Kiernan *Management 360*
9111 Wilshire Blvd
Beverly Hills, CA 90210-5508, USA

Gaberino, Geoffrey (Athlete, Olympic
Athlete, Swimmer)
747 Bear Creek Cv
Gulf Shores, AL 36542-3040, USA

Gable, Brian (Cartoonist)
67 Riverside Dr Apt 1D
New York, NY 10024-6155, USA

Gable, Daniel M (Danny) (Athlete,
Olympic Athlete, Wrestler)
4343 Treefarm Ln NE
Iowa City, IA 52240-7829, USA

Gable, John Clark
Jack Scagnetti Talent Agency
5118 Vineland Ave Ste 102
North Hollywood, CA 91601-3814

Gabler, Bill (Baseball Player)
Chicago Cubs
4443 Mattis Rd
Saint Louis, MO 63128-3136, USA

Gabor, William (Athlete, Basketball
Player)
101 Ocean Bluffs Blvd Apt 503
Jupiter, FL 33477-7362, USA

Gabor, Zsa Zsa (Actor)
1001 Bel Air Rd
Los Angeles, CA 90077-3011, USA

Gaborik, Marian (Athlete, Hockey Player)
Icy Luck Inc
108 Avenue F
Redondo Beach, CA 90277-5013, USA

Gabriel, Juan (Musician)
c/o Staff Member *Universal Music
Publishing Group (Latin)*
420 Lincoln Rd Ste 200
Miami Beach, FL 33139-3014, USA

Gabriel, Roman
16817 McKee Rd
Charlotte, NC 28278-8406

Gabriel, Seychelle (Actor)
c/o TJ Stein *Stein Entertainment Group*
1351 N Crescent Heights Blvd Apt 312
West Hollywood, CA 90046-4549, USA

Gabriel Jr, Roman I (Athlete, Football
Player)
PO Box 4173
Calabash, NC 28467-0373, USA

Gabrielle, Josefina (Actor)
c/o Staff Member *Stone Manners Salners
Agency (LA)*
6100 Wilshire Blvd Ste 1500
Los Angeles, CA 90048-5110, USA

Gabrielle, Monique (Actor, Model)
Purrfect Productions
1231 NE 28th Ave
Pompano Beach, FL 33062-3822, USA

Gabrielson, Len (Athlete, Baseball Player)
24230 Hillview Rd
Los Altos, CA 94024-5221, USA

Gad, Josh (Actor)
10556 Clarkson Rd
Los Angeles, CA 90064-4316, USA

Gaddis, Robert (Athlete, Football Player)
1022 Gaddis Rd
Edwards, MS 39066-8007, USA

Gade, Ariel (Actor)
c/o Jennifer Millar *Paradigm (LA)*
9200 W Sunset Blvd PH 11
West Hollywood, CA 90069-3601, USA

Gadinsky, Brian (Producer)
c/o Staff Member *William Morris
Endeavor (LA)*
9601 Wilshire Blvd
Beverly Hills, CA 90210-5213, USA

Gadot, Gal (Actor)
c/o Darren Goldberg *Global Creative*
1051 Cole Ave # B
Los Angeles, CA 90038-2601, USA

Gadsby, William A (Bill) (Athlete, Hockey
Player)
28765 E Kalong Cir
Southfield, MI 48034-5650, USA

Gadsden, Oronde (Athlete, Football
Player)
11241 NW 15th St
Plantation, FL 33323-2433, USA

Gadzuric, Dan (Athlete, Basketball Player)
1312 Villa Barolo Ave
Henderson, NV 89052-4175, USA

Gaechter, Mike (Athlete, Football Player)
13 Horizon Pt
Frisco, TX 75034-6840, USA

Gaerte, Joe (Race Car Driver)
Gaerte Engines
601 Monroe St
Rochester, IN 46975-1426, USA

Gaetti, Gary (Athlete, Baseball Player)
7819 Silent Forest Dr
Sugar Land, TX 77479-6501, USA

Gaff, Brent (Athlete, Baseball Player)
5925 S State Road 9
Albion, IN 46701-9623, USA

Gaffigan, Jim (Actor, Comedian)
c/o Estelle Lasher *Lasher Group*
1133 Avenue Of The Americas Ste 1621
New York, NY 10036-6710, USA

Gaffney, Derrick T (Athlete, Football
Player)
11750 Cherry Bark Dr E
Jacksonville, FL 32218-7674, USA

Gaffney, Drew Dr (Astronaut)
6613 Chatsworth Pl
Nashville, TN 37205-3955, USA

Gaffney, Jabar (Athlete, Football Player)
PO Box 7125
Gaithersburg, MD 20898-7125, USA

Gaffney, Janice (Athlete, Skier)
8118 Vantage Ave
North Hollywood, CA 91605-1437, USA

Gaffney, Mo (Actor)
c/o Staff Member *Stone Manners Salners
Agency (LA)*
6100 Wilshire Blvd Ste 1500
Los Angeles, CA 90048-5110, USA

Gaffney, Tyler (Athlete, Football Player)
c/o Ryan Tollner *REP 1 Sports Group*
2 Corporate Park Ste 106
Irvine, CA 92606-5103, USA

Gaga, Lady (Dancer, Musician)
40 Central Park S # Ph-D
New York, NY 10019-1633, USA

Gage, Jody (Athlete, Hockey Player)
91 W Forest Dr
Rochester, NY 14624-3755, USA

Gage, Nicholas (Journalist, Writer)
37 Nelson St
North Grafton, MA 01536-1424, USA

Gagliano, Phil (Athlete, Baseball Player)
1095 Crescent Dr
Hollister, MO 65672-4884, USA

Gagliano, Ralph (Athlete, Baseball Player)
1756 Overton Park Ave
Memphis, TN 38112-5344, USA

Gagliano, Robert F (Bob) (Athlete,
Football Player)
822 Fitzgerald Ave
Ventura, CA 93003-0228, USA

Gagliardi, John (Coach, Football Coach)
Saint John's University
16446 Jasmine Ct
Cold Spring, MN 56320-9655, USA

Gagne, Eric S (Athlete, Baseball Player)
c/o Scott Boras *Boras Corporation*
3 San Joaquin Plz Ste 100
Newport Beach, CA 92660-5944, USA

Gagne, Greg (Athlete, Baseball Player)
746 Whetstone Hill Rd
Somerset, MA 02726-3702, USA

Gagne, Simone (Athlete, Hockey Player)
116710th St
Manhattan Beach, CA 90266, USA

Gagner, Larry (Athlete, Football Player)
205 W Curtis St
Tampa, FL 33603-3649, USA

Gagnier, Holly (Actor)
Stone Manners
6500 Wilshire Blvd # 550
Los Angeles, CA 90048-4920, USA

Gagnon, Dave (Athlete, Hockey Player)
50495 Corporate Dr Ste 112
Shelby Township, MI 48315-3132, USA

Gago, Jenny (Actor)
c/o Bill Rogin *Bill Rogin Management*
427 N Canon Dr Ste 215
Beverly Hills, CA 90210-4840, USA

Gagosian, Larry (Business Person)
Gagosian Gallery
980 Madison Ave PH
New York, NY 10075-1848, USA

Gahan, Dave (Musician)
27 S Davis Ave
Montauk, NY 11954, USA

Gaikowski, Steve (Athlete, Baseball
Player)
416 Turner St NE
Olympia, WA 98506-4663, USA

Gail, David
c/o Staff Member *Henze Management*
1925 Century Park E Ste 2320
Los Angeles, CA 90067-2724, USA

Gail, Max (Actor)
c/o Laura Pallas *Pallas Management*
5301 Bellaire Ave
Valley Village, CA 91607-2329, US

Gaile, Jeri
880 Hilldale Ave Apt 3
West Hollywood, CA 90069-4921

Gailes, Jason (Athlete, Olympic Athlete,
Rower)
17 Mark Vincent Dr
Westford, MA 01886-4505, USA

Gailey, T Chandler (Chan) (Athlete,
Coach, Football Coach, Football Player)
191 Sterling Hills Dr
Clarkesville, GA 30523-6817, USA

Gaillard, Bob (Coach)
50 Bonnie Brae Dr
Novato, CA 94949-5851, USA

Gaillard, Eddie (Athlete, Baseball Player)
6063 Woodlake Rd
Jupiter, FL 33458-2456, USA

Gaiman, Neil (Writer)
Cat Mihos
4470 W Sunset Blvd # 339
Los Angeles, CA 90027-6302, USA

Gain, Robert (Bob) (Athlete, Football
Player)
11 Nokomis Dr
Eastlake, OH 44095-1943, USA

Gainer, Derrick (Athlete, Football Player)
733 E McDonald Rd
Plant City, FL 33567-3529, USA

Gainer, Jay (Athlete, Baseball Player)
1035 E 8th St
Panama City, FL 32401-3594, USA

Gaines, Bill (Athlete, Basketball Player)
921 Beverly Cir
Cedar Hill, TX 75104-1236, USA

Gaines, Boyd (Actor, Musician)
c/o Elin McManus-Flack *Elin Flack
Management*
435 W 57th St Apt 3M
New York, NY 10019-1724, USA

Gaines, Clark (Athlete, Football Player)
21364 Scara Pl
Broadlands, VA 20148-3602, USA

Gaines, Corey (Athlete, Basketball Player)
3968 Windansea St
Las Vegas, NV 89147-6544, USA

Gaines, Davis
315 W 57th St Frnt 4H
New York, NY 10019-3158

Gaines, Ernest J (Writer)
PO Box 81
Oscar, LA 70762-0081, USA

Gaines, Joe (Athlete, Baseball Player)
77 Anair Way
Oakland, CA 94605-4874, USA

Gaines, Lawrence (Athlete, Football
Player)
4963 Cherry Blossom Cir
West Bloomfield, MI 48324-1297, USA

Gaines, Reese (Baseball Player)
Houston Rockets
2 Greenway Plz
Toyota Center
Houston, TX 77046-0297, USA

Gaines, Rowdy (Athlete, Olympic Athlete,
Swimmer)
6800 Hawaii Kai Dr
Honolulu, HI 96825-1505, USA

Gaines, Wentford (Athlete, Football
Player)
97 Bayview Ave
Jersey City, NJ 07305-3306, USA

Gaines, William C (Journalist)
Chicago Tribune
1326 Marks Ave
Jackson, MS 39213-7113, USA

Gainey, Steve (Athlete, Hockey Player)
900 McGill Rd Box 3010
Attn Hockey Coaching Staff
Kamloops, BC V2C 0C8, USA

Gainey, Telmanch "Ty" (Athlete,
Baseball Player)
123 Presidential Dr Aot D
19807-3213, DE WILMI, USA

Gainey, Ty (Athlete, Baseball Player)
3040 W Market Street Ext
Cheraw, SC 29520-5587, USA

Gaiser, George (Athlete, Football Player)
28752 Kalkallo Dr
Boerne, TX 78015-4614, USA

Gaison, Blane (Athlete, Football Player)
45-444 Koa Kahiko St
Kaneohe, HI 96744-2008, USA

Gaitan, Paulina (Actor)
c/o Dar Rollins *ICM Partners (LA)*
10250 Constellation Blvd Fl 7
Los Angeles, CA 90067-6207, USA

Gaiter, Tony (Athlete, Football Player)
9235 NW 35th Ct
Miami, FL 33147-2829, USA

Gaiters, Bob (Athlete, Football Player)
6909 Knowlton Pl Apt 206
Los Angeles, CA 90045-2036, USA

Gaither, Bill (Musician, Songwriter)
Gaither Music Co
PO Box 737
Alexandria, VA 22313, USA

Gajan, Hokie (Athlete, Football Player)
213 Cottonwood Ln
Mandeville, LA 70471-2552, USA

Gajdusek, Karl (Writer)
c/o Jill McElroy *Management 360*
110 S Fairfax Ave Ste 350
Los Angeles, CA 90036-2165, USA

Gajkowski, Steve (Athlete, Baseball
Player)
416 Turner St NE
Olympia, WA 98506-4663, USA

Gakeler, Dan (Athlete, Baseball Player)
3714 Sawgrass Rd
Greensboro, NC 27410-9068, USA

Gal, Sandra (Athlete, Golfer)
Callaway Golf Company
2180 Rutherford Rd
Carlsbad, CA 92008-7328, USA

Galanos, James (Designer, Fashion
Designer)
1316 Sunset Plaza Dr
Los Angeles, CA 90069-1235, USA

Galanos, Mike (Television Host)
Prime News Tonight
1 Time Warner Ctr
Cnn
New York, NY 10019-6038, USA

Galante, Matt (Baseball Player, Coach)
Houston Astros
85 Hei11HTS Ter
Middletown, NJ 07748, USA

Galarraga, Andres (Athlete, Baseball
Player)
1639 Enclave Cir
West Palm Beach, FL 33411-1862, USA

Galasso, Bob (Athlete, Baseball Player)
267 Adelaide Rd
Connellsville, PA 15425-6215, USA

Galati, Frank J (Director)
990 Blvd of the Arts Apt 1003
Sarasota, FL 34236-4877, USA

Galavis, Juan Pablo (Athlete, Reality Star,
Soccer Player)
c/o Staff Member *DMT Event*
21 Alessio Ter
Trenton, NJ 08620-9772, USA

Galbraith, Clint (Horse Racer)
PO Box 902
Scottsville, NY 14546-0902, USA

Galbraith, Scott (Athlete, Football Player)
3700 Plymouth Dr
North Highlands, CA 95660-3312, USA

Galbreath, Scott (Athlete, Football Player)
3649 Plymouth Dr
North Highlands, CA 95660-3309, USA

Galbreath, Tony (Athlete, Football Player)
411 W 9th St
Fulton, MO 65251-1178, USA

Gale, Ed (Actor)
c/o Cindy Osbrink *Osbrink Talent Agency*
4343 Lankershim Blvd Ste 100
North Hollywood, CA 91602-2705, USA

Gale, Mike (Athlete, Basketball Player)
18003 4th Ave S
Burien, WA 98148-1803, USA

Gale, Rich (Athlete, Baseball Player)
869 Center Park St
Daniel Island, SC 29492-7569, USA

Gale, Tommy (Race Car Driver)
PO Box 375
Elizabeth, PA 15037-0375, USA

Galecki, Johnny (Actor)
c/o Justin Grey Stone *Management 360*
9111 Wilshire Blvd
Beverly Hills, CA 90210-5508, USA

Galeotti, Bethany Joy (Actor)
c/o Jill Fritzo *PMK/BNC Public Relations (PMK-NY)*
622 3rd Ave Fl 8
New York, NY 10017-6707, USA

Galifianakis, Zach (Actor, Producer, Writer)
c/o Marc Gurvitz *Brillstein Entertainment Partners (LA)*
9150 Wilshire Blvd Ste 350
Beverly Hills, CA 90212-3453, USA

Galigher, Ed (Athlete, Football Player)
1025 Prospect St Ste 150
La Jolla, CA 92037-4163, USA

Galik, Denise (Actor)
Badgley Connor Talent
9229 W Sunset Blvd Ste 311
West Hollywood, CA 90069-3403, USA

Galina, Stacy (Actor)
c/o Mark Scroggs *David Shapira & Associates*
193 N Robertson Blvd
Beverly Hills, CA 90211-2103, USA

Galindo, Rudy (Figure Skater)
c/o Staff Member *Champions on Ice*
3500 American Blvd W Ste 190
Minneapolis, MN 55431-4431, USA

Gall, John (Athlete, Baseball Player)
20 Corte Del Sol
Millbrae, CA 94030-2111, USA

Gallagher, Al (Athlete, Baseball Player)
1810 N Parkwood Dr
Harlingen, TX 78550-8027, USA

Gallagher, Bob (Athlete, Baseball Player)
315 Fair Ave
Santa Cruz, CA 95060-6343, USA

Gallagher, Chad (Athlete, Basketball Player)
482 Wynstone Way
Rockton, IL 61072-3434, USA

Gallagher, Dave (Athlete, Baseball Player)
29 Carrs Tavern Rd
Millstone Township, NJ 08510-1505, USA

Gallagher, Dave (Athlete, Football Player)
2740 California Ct
Columbus, IN 47201-2924, USA

Gallagher, David (Actor)
30430 Byfield Rd
Castaic, CA 91384-3406, USA

Gallagher, Doug (Athlete, Baseball Player)
11 Cherokee Dr
Hamilton, OH 45013-4909, USA

Gallagher, Frank (Athlete, Football Player)
6572 Enclave Dr
Clarkston, MI 48348-4859, USA

Gallagher, Helen (Actor, Musician)
260 W End Ave Apt 4A
New York, NY 10023-3658, USA

Gallagher, John (Religious Leader)
Advent Christian Church
PO Box 551
Presque Isle, ME 04769-0551, USA

Gallagher, Liam (Musician)
160 Central Park S # 1709
New York, NY 10019-1502, USA

Gallagher, Mary (Actor)
c/o Michael Greenwald *Don Buchwald & Associates (LA)*
6500 Wilshire Blvd Ste 2200
Los Angeles, CA 90048-4942, USA

Gallagher, Megan (Actor)
Don Buchwald
6500 Wilshire Blvd Ste 2200
Los Angeles, CA 90048-4942, USA

Gallagher, Mike (Radio Personality)
Gallagher Networks
350 5th Ave Ste 1818
New York, NY 10118-1818, USA

Gallagher, Patrick (Actor)
c/o Harold Augenstein *Abrams Artists Agency (LA)*
9200 W Sunset Blvd PH 11
West Hollywood, CA 90069-3601, USA

Gallagher, Peter (Actor)
c/o John Carrabino *John Carrabino Management*
5900 Wilshire Blvd Ste 406
Los Angeles, CA 90036-5015, USA

Gallagher, Sean (Athlete, Baseball Player)
4434 NW 99th Ter
Sunrise, FL 33351-4747, USA

Gallagher Jr, Jim (Athlete, Golfer)
PO Box 507
Greenwood, MS 38935-0507, USA

Gallagher-Smith, Jackie (Athlete, Golfer)
193 Paradise Cir
Jupiter, FL 33458-2853, USA

Gallant, Gerard (Athlete, Coach, Hockey Player)
c/o Staff Member *New York Islanders*
1535 Old Country Rd
Plainview, NY 11803-5042, USA

Gallant, Matt (Actor, Television Host)
608 Idaho Ave Unit 8
Santa Monica, CA 90403-2712, USA

Gallardo, Camillio (Actor)
Innovative Artists
1505 10th St
Santa Monica, CA 90401-2805, USA

Gallardo, Carlos (Actor)
c/o Michael Henderson *Heresun Management*
4119 W Burbank Blvd
Burbank, CA 91505-2122, USA

Gallardo, Silvana
10637 Burbank Blvd
North Hollywood, CA 91601-2512

Gallardo, Yovani (Athlete, Baseball Player)
8556 Waterfront Ct
Fort Worth, TX 76179-2504, USA

Gallatin, Harry (Athlete, Basketball Player, Coach)
2010 Madison Ave
Edwardsville, IL 62025-2623, USA

Gallegly, Elton (Congressman, Politician)
2309 Rayburn Hob
Washington, DC 20515-3211, USA

Gallego, Gina (Actor)
The Agency
1800 Avenue of the Stars Ste 400
Los Angeles, CA 90067-4206, USA

Gallego, Mike (Athlete, Baseball Player)
11 Sunnin11DALE
Trabuco Canyon, CA 92679, USA

Gallery, Robert (Athlete, Football Player)
3163 20th St
Masonville, IA 50654, USA

Galles, Jamie (Race Car Driver)
109 Gasoline Aly Ste C
Indianapolis, IN 46222-5934, USA

Galletti, Carl (Business Person)
PO Box 3934
Sedona, AZ 86340-3934, USA

Galligan, Zach (Actor, Comedian)
c/o Aine Leicht *Horror & Hilarity*
Prefers to be contacted via telephone
Los Angeles, CA 90067, USA

Gallison, Joe (Actor)
PO Box 10187
Wilmington, NC 28404-0187, USA

Gallner, Kyle (Actor)
c/o Sarah Shyn *3 Arts Entertainment (LA)*
9460 Wilshire Blvd Fl 7
Beverly Hills, CA 90212-2713, USA

Gallo, Carla (Actor)
c/o Stacy Abrams *Abrams Entertainment*
5225 Wilshire Blvd Ste 515
Los Angeles, CA 90036-4349, USA

Gallo, George (Director)
c/o Todd Hoffman *ICM Partners (LA)*
10250 Constellation Blvd Fl 7
Los Angeles, CA 90067-6207, USA

Gallo, Mike (Athlete, Baseball Player)
1415 Christine St
Houston, TX 77017-4003, USA

Gallo, Vincent (Actor, Director)
c/o Danny Goldberg *Gold Village Entertainment*
37 W 17th St Ste 7W
New York, NY 10011-5525, USA

Gallop, Tom (Actor)
c/o Dan Baron *Agency for the Performing Arts (APA-LA)*
405 S Beverly Dr Ste 500
Beverly Hills, CA 90212-4425, USA

Galloway, David (Athlete, Football Player)
19331 NW 19th Ave
Miami Gardens, FL 33056-2817, USA

Galloway, Jean (Religious Leader)
Volunteers of America
1660 Duke St Ste 100
Alexandria, VA 22314-3427, USA

Galloway, Joey (Athlete, Football Player)
4340 Hanna Hills Dr
Dublin, OH 43016-9518, USA

Galotti, Ronald A (Publisher)
Conde Nast Publications
4 Times Sq Fl 22
Publisher's Office
New York, NY 10036-6561, USA

Galvez, Balvino (Athlete, Baseball Player)
3986 SW 190th Ave
Miramar, FL 33029-2726, USA

Galvin, James (Writer)
University of Iowa
Writer's Workshop
Iowa City, IA 52242, USA

Galvin, John R (Athlete, Football Player)
136 Parkview Ave
Lowell, MA 01852-3811, USA

Galyon, Gregory (Athlete, Football Player)
2352 Monticello Dr
Maryville, TN 37803-7528, USA

Galyon, Scott (Athlete, Football Player)
758 Deep Woods Ln
Seymour, TN 37865-9100, USA

Gam, Rita (Actor)
180 W 58th St # 8B
New York, NY 10019-2145, USA

Gamar, Charles D
7660 N 159th Street Ct E
Benton, KS 67017-8926, USA

Gambee, Dave (Athlete, Basketball Player)
6175 SW Arrow Wood Ln
Portland, OR 97223-7261, USA

Gamble, Chris (Athlete, Football Player)
111 Harbor Shore Ct
Mooresville, NC 28117-8911, USA

Gamble, David (Athlete, Football Player)
16804 Royal Poinciana Dr
Weston, FL 33326-1582, USA

Gamble, Dick (Athlete, Hockey Player)
1 Vantage Dr
Pittsford, NY 14534-3205, USA

Gamble, Ed (Cartoonist)
Florida Times-Union
1 Riverside Ave
Editorial Dept
Jacksonville, FL 32202-4904, USA

Gamble, Fred (Race Car Driver)
PO Box 5274
Snowmass Village, CO 81615-5274, USA

Gamble, John (Athlete, Baseball Player)
369 Caliente St
Reno, NV 89509-2729, USA

Gamble, Kenny (Ken) (Athlete, Football Player)
4 Algonquin Dr
Wilbraham, MA 01095-2373, USA

Gamble, Kevin (Athlete, Basketball Player)
2366 Sandstone Dr
Mount Pleasant, MI 48858-1539, USA

Gamble, Mason (Actor)
United Talent Agency
9336 Civic Center Dr
Beverly Hills, CA 90210-3604, USA

Gamble, Oscar (Athlete, Baseball Player)
9705 Bent Brook Dr
Montgomery, AL 36117-7445, USA

Gamble, Trent
4481 NW 42nd Ter
Coconut Creek, FL 33073-4721, USA

Gamble, Troy (Athlete, Hockey Player)
12038 Terraza Cove Ln
Houston, TX 77041-6230, USA

Gamboa, Tom (Athlete, Baseball Player)
318 Loch Lomond Rd
Rancho Mirage, CA 92270-5606, USA

Gambol, Chris (Athlete, Football Player)
451 Longfellow Ave
Glen Ellyn, IL 60137-4712, USA

Gambon, Michael J (Actor)
International Creative Mgmt
40 W 57th St Fl 5
New York, NY 10019-4001, USA

Gambon, Sir Michael (Actor)
c/o Staff Member *ICM Partners (LA)*
10250 Constellation Blvd Fl 7
Los Angeles, CA 90067-6207, USA

Gambrell, Bill (Athlete, Football Player)
341 Osceola Ave
Bogart, GA 30622-1511, USA

Gambrell, David (Politician)
3205 Arden Rd NW
Atlanta, GA 30305-1918, USA

Gambril, Don (Coach)
4409 Spring Row
Northport, AL 35473-5231, USA

Gambucci, Andre (Athlete, Hockey
Player, Olympic Athlete)
4365 Carriage View Rd
Colorado Springs, CO 80906, USA

Gambucci, Gary (Athlete, Hockey Player)
9241 Yukon Ave S
Minneapolis, MN 55438-1446, USA

Gamester, Russ (Race Car Driver)
150 W Warren St
Peru, IN 46970-2754, USA

Gamez, Robert (Athlete, Golfer)
1128 Wilde Dr
Kissimmee, FL 34747-4046, USA

Gammino, Thomas (Race Car Driver)
875 Phenix Ave
Cranston, RI 02921-1107, USA

Gammon, John (Actor)
c/o Liza Anderson *Anderson Group Public
Relations*
8060 Melrose Ave Fl 4
Los Angeles, CA 90046-7038, USA

Gammon, Kendall (Athlete, Football
Player)
14429 Maple St
Overland Park, KS 66223-1256, USA

Gammons, Peter (Commentator)
Boston Globe
36 Glen Rd
Brookline, MA 02445-7721, USA

Ganassi, Floyd (Chip) (Race Car Driver)
7777 Woodland Dr
Indianapolis, IN 46278-1794, USA

Ganchar, Perry (Athlete, Hockey Player)
8043 Summerhouse Dr W
Dublin, OH 43016-7062, USA

Gand, Gale (Chef, Television Host)
c/o Staff Member *Food Network, The*
1180 Avenue of the Americas Fl 11
New York, NY 10036-8401, USA

Gandarillas, Gus (Athlete, Baseball Player)
6320 NW 114th St
Hialeah, FL 33012-2334, USA

Gandee, Sherman (Sonny) (Athlete,
Football Player)
148 Viking Way
Naples, FL 34110-1136, USA

Gandolfo, Joseph (Horse Racer)
4 Cameron Rd
Saddle River, NJ 07458-2934, USA

Gandy, David (Model)
c/o Staff Member *Heffner Management*
80 Vine St Apt 203
Seattle, WA 98121-1369, USA

Gandy, Dylan (Athlete, Football Player)
13161 Haskell Pl
Carmel, IN 46074-8332, USA

Gandy, Mike (Athlete, Football Player)
8508 E Sweetwater Ave
Scottsdale, AZ 85260-4110, USA

Gandy, Wayne L (Athlete, Football Player)
406 Pinecrest Rd NE
Atlanta, GA 30342-3827, USA

Ganev, Tzetzi
1751 N Berendo St # 21
Los Angeles, CA 90027

Gangel, Jamie (Correspondent)
NBC-TV News Dept
30 Rockefeller Plz
New York, NY 10112-0015, USA

Gangloff, Mark (Athlete, Olympic Athlete,
Swimmer)
5318 Camden Dr
Stow, OH 44224-5526, USA

Gang of Four (Music Group)
c/o Staff Member *Paradigm (Monterey)*
404 W Franklin St
Monterey, CA 93940-2303, USA

Gann, Mike (Athlete, Football Player)
1479 Ashford Pl NE
Atlanta, GA 30319-1888, USA

Gannascoli, Joseph (Joe) (Actor)
c/o Greg Meyer *Meyer Management
Group (MMG)*
1400 Atlantic Ave Ste 274
Long Beach, CA 90813-2013, USA

Gannon, Richard J (Rich) (Athlete,
Football Player, Sportscaster)
6472 Smithtown Rd
Excelsior, MN 55331-8211, USA

Gano, Graham (Athlete, Football Player)
c/o Dave Butz *Sportstars Inc*
1350 Avenue of the Americas Fl 28
New York, NY 10019-4702, USA

Gansa, Alex (Producer)
c/o BeBe Lerner *ID Public Relations (LA)*
7060 Hollywood Blvd Fl 8th
Los Angeles, CA 90028-6021, USA

Gansler, Bob (Coach, Soccer Player)
Kansas City Wizards
2 Arrowhead Dr
Kansas City, MO 64129, USA

Gant, Harry (Race Car Driver)
7531 Millersville Rd
Taylorsville, NC 28681-8946, USA

Gant, Kenneth (Athlete, Football Player)
1820 W 10th St
Lakeland, FL 33805-3308, USA

Gant, Kenneth (Kenny) (Athlete, Football
Player)
3906 Carrollwood Place Cir Apt 243
Tampa, FL 33624-3064, USA

Gant, Mtume (Actor)
c/o Maggie Woods *Online Talent Group*
Prefers to be contacted via email or
telephone
West Hollywood, CA 90069, USA

Gant, Reuben (Athlete, Football Player)
PO Box 3051
Tulsa, OK 74101-3051, USA

Gant, Robert (Actor)
c/o British (Brit) Reece *PMK/BNC Public
Relations (PMK-LA)*
8687 Melrose Ave Ste 8
West Hollywood, CA 90069-5746, USA

Gant, Ron (Athlete, Baseball Player)
40 Hartz Way Ste 10
Secaucus, NJ 07094-2403, USA

Gantner, Jim (Athlete, Baseball Player)
PO Box 156
Eden, WI 53019-0156, USA

Gantos, Jack (Writer)
Farrar Straus Giroux
19 Union Sq W
New York, NY 10003-3304, USA

Gantt, Harvey
Rt. #1 Box 587
Taylorsville, NC 28681

Gantt, Jerome (Athlete, Football Player)
2035 Long Point Trl
Sanford, NC 27332-7449, USA

Gantt, Jerry (Athlete, Football Player)
1511 Atwick Dr
Fayetteville, NC 28304-3901, USA

Ganzel, Teresa (Actor)
Irv Schechter
9300 Wilshire Blvd Ste 410
Beverly Hills, CA 90212-3228, USA

Gao, Xiang (Musician)
Columbia Artists Mgmt Inc
165 W 57th St
New York, NY 10019-2201, USA

Gaona, Jessica (Actor)
c/o Staff Member *Abrams Artists Agency
(LA)*
9200 W Sunset Blvd PH 11
West Hollywood, CA 90069-3601, USA

Gap Band, The
89 5th Ave Ste 700
New York, NY 10003-3056

Garabaldi, Bob
2143 Oregon Ave
Stockton, CA 95204-4617

Garagiola, Joe (Commentator)
7433 E Tuckey Ln
Scottsdale, AZ 85250-4640, USA

Garagiola, Joe (Commentator)
2701 Calvert St NW Apt 313
Washington, DC 20008-2618, USA

Garagozzo, Keith (Athlete, Baseball
Player)
16 Foxcroft Way
Mount Laurel, NJ 08054-5732, USA

Garai, Romola (Actor)
c/o Billy Lazarus *United Talent Agency
(UTA-LA)*
9336 Civic Center Dr
Beverly Hills, CA 90210-3604, USA

Garalczyk, Mark (Athlete, Football Player)
PO Box 27304
Scottsdale, AZ 85255-0138, USA

Garamendi, John (Congressman,
Politician)
228 Cannon Hob
Washington, DC 20515-3307, USA

Garan, Ronald J Jr (Astronaut)
2002 Sea Cove Ct
Houston, TX 77058-4228, USA

Garan, Ronald J Lt Colonel (Astronaut)
2002 Sea Cove Ct
Houston, TX 77058-4228, USA

Garas, Kaz (Actor)
10145 N Buchanan Ave
Portland, OR 97203, USA

Garbacz, Lori (Athlete, Golfer)
777 Albany Post Rd
Briarcliff Manor, NY 10510-2400, USA

Garbage (Music Group)
c/o Jenna Adler *Creative Artists Agency
(CAA-LA)*
2000 Avenue of the Stars Ste 100
Los Angeles, CA 90067-4705, USA

Garber, Gene (Athlete, Baseball Player)
771 Stonemill Dr
Elizabethtown, PA 17022-9717, USA

Garber, Terri (Actor)
c/o Maggie Smith *Maggie Smith
Management*
3365 Paseo Del Sol
Calabasas, CA 91302-3013, USA

Garber, Victor (Actor)
c/o Bill Butler *Industry Entertainment*
955 Carrillo Dr Ste 300
Los Angeles, CA 90048-5400, USA

Garbey, Barbaro (Athlete, Baseball Player)
14094 Woodside St
Livonia, MI 48154-5206, USA

Garces, Paula (Actor)
c/o Staff Member *Untitled Entertainment
(NY)*
435 Hudson St Fl 9
New York, NY 10014-3995, USA

Garces, Rich (Athlete, Baseball Player)
605 Swigert St
Kerrville, TX 78028-3140, USA

Garcetti, Gil
139 N Cliffwood Ave
Los Angeles, CA 90049-2613, USA

Garcia, Adam (Actor)
c/o Peter Safran *The Safran Company*
8748 Holloway Dr
West Hollywood, CA 90069-2327, USA

Garcia, Aimee (Actor)
c/o William Mercer *Thruline
Entertainment*
9250 Wilshire Blvd Ste 100
Ground Floor
Beverly Hills, CA 90212-3343, USA

Garcia, Andy (Actor, Musician)
4323 Forman Ave
Toluca Lake, CA 91602-2909, USA

Garcia, Carlos (Athlete, Baseball Player)
5208 William St
Lancaster, NY 14086-9448, USA

Garcia, Danay (Actor)
CW Talent Management
PO Box 532
C/O L Travis Clark
Los Angeles, CA 90078-0532, USA

Garcia, Danna (Actor)
c/o Staff Member *Telemundo*
2470 W 8th Ave
Hialeah, FL 33010-2000, USA

Garcia, Danny (Athlete, Baseball Player)
27 Chapel Ln
Levittown, NY 11756-2635, USA

Garcia, Dave (Athlete, Baseball Player,
Coach)
17842 Avenida Cordillera Unit 28
San Diego, CA 92128-1514, USA

Garcia, Eddie (Athlete, Football Player)
4912 Oreilly Rd
Omro, WI 54963-9643, USA

Garcia, Guillermo (Athlete, Baseball
Player)
3806 Shoma Dr
Royal Palm Beach, FL 33414-4374, USA

Garcia, James (Athlete, Football Player)
999 E Basse Rd Ste 180
San Antonio, TX 78209-1807, USA

Garcia, Jeff (Athlete, Football Player)
PO Box 1026
Campbell, CA 95009-1026, USA

Garcia, Jesus (Actor)
c/o Staff Member *Columbia Artists Mgmt Inc*
1790 Broadway Fl 6
New York, NY 10019-1537, USA

Garcia, Jim (Athlete, Football Player)
999 E Basse Rd Ste 180
San Antonio, TX 78209-1807, USA

Garcia, Joanna (Actor)
c/o Pamela Kohl *3 Arts Entertainment (LA)*
9460 Wilshire Blvd Fl 7
Beverly Hills, CA 90212-2713, USA

Garcia, Jorge (Actor)
c/o Erik Kritzer *LINK Entertainment*
11872 La Grange Ave Fl 1
Los Angeles, CA 90025-5283, USA

Garcia, Jsu (Actor)
c/o Phyllis Carlyle *Carlyle Productions & Management*
2050 Laurel Canyon Blvd
Los Angeles, CA 90046-2065, USA

Garcia, Karim (Athlete, Baseball Player)
38 Agnew Farm Rd
Armonk, NY 10504-1371, USA

Garcia, Kiko (Athlete, Baseball Player)
526 Trailview Cir
Martinez, CA 94553-3563, USA

Garcia, Leo (Athlete, Baseball Player)
11264 W Buchanan St
Avondale, AZ 85323-6824, USA

Garcia, Lilian
1100 Valley Brook Ave
Lyndhurst, NJ 07071-3620, USA

Garcia, Mike (Athlete, Baseball Player)
15892 Lasselle St Unit B
Moreno Valley, CA 92551-4775, USA

Garcia, Nina (Reality Star, Writer)
Elle Magazine
1633 Broadway Fl 44
New York, NY 10019-6708, USA

Garcia, Odalys (Actor)
c/o Staff Member *Univision*
605 3rd Ave Fl 12
New York, NY 10158-0034, USA

Garcia, Pedro (Athlete, Baseball Player)
L4 Parq Del Condado
Caguas, PR 00727-1224, USA

Garcia, Ralph (Athlete, Baseball Player)
7441 Brian Ln
La Palma, CA 90623-1312, USA

Garcia, Rich (Athlete, Baseball Player)
PO Box 3276
Clearwater Beach, FL 33767-8276, USA

Garcia, Rodrigo (Director)
c/o Adriana Alberghetti *William Morris Endeavor (LA)*
9601 Wilshire Blvd Ste GL25
Beverly Hills, CA 90210-5217, USA

Garcia, Teddy (Athlete, Football Player)
2203 Cook Rd
Oak Grove, LA 71263-3705, USA

Garciaparra, Nomar (Athlete, Baseball Player, Olympic Athlete)
613 15th St
Manhattan Beach, CA 90266-4804, USA

Garcon, Pierre (Athlete, Football Player)
c/o Staff Member *Terra Firma Sports Management*
330 W Spring St Ste 460
Columbus, OH 43215-2390, USA

Gardell, Billy (Actor)
c/o Nick Nuciforo *Creative Artists Agency (CAA-LA)*
2000 Avenue of the Stars Ste 100
Los Angeles, CA 90067-4705, USA

Gardener, Daryl (Athlete, Football Player)
8925 Legacy Ct Apt 106
Kissimmee, FL 34747-3018, USA

Gardenhire, Ron (Athlete, Baseball Player, Coach)
585 Country Road B2 E
Saint Paul, MN 55117, USA

Gardin, Ron (Athlete, Football Player)
PO Box 66051
Tucson, AZ 85728-6051, USA

Gardiner, Mike (Athlete, Baseball Player)
26 Read Dr
Hanover, MA 02339-2632, USA

Gardner, Art (Athlete, Baseball Player)
1953 Highway 35 S
Walnut Grove, MS 39189-5025, USA

Gardner, Ashley (Actor)
c/o Staff Member *Forster Entertainment*
12533 Woodgreen St
Los Angeles, CA 90066-2723, USA

Gardner, Barry (Athlete, Football Player)
PO Box 175
Crete, IL 60417-0175, USA

Gardner, Bill (Athlete, Hockey Player)
c/o Staff Member *Chicago Wolves*
2301 Ravine Way
Glenview, IL 60025-7627, USA

Gardner, Billy (Athlete, Baseball Player, Coach)
35 Dayton Rd
Waterford, CT 06385-4205, USA

Gardner, Brett (Athlete, Baseball Player)
100 Halcyon Rd
Summerville, SC 29483-4041, USA

Gardner, Carwell (Athlete, Football Player)
9603 Galene Dr
Louisville, KY 40299-3231, USA

Gardner, Chris (Athlete, Baseball Player)
2304 SW Abalon Cir
Port Saint Lucie, FL 34953-5718, USA

Gardner, Christopher (Business Person, Writer)
Rubenstein Communications
1345 Avenue of the Americas Fl 30
C/O Rachel Nagler
New York, NY 10105-0109, USA

Gardner, Cory (Congressman, Politician)
213 Cannon Hob
Washington, DC 20515-0919, USA

Gardner, Dede (Producer)
c/o Staff Member *Plan B Entertainment*
9150 Wilshire Blvd Ste 350
Beverly Hills, CA 90212-3453, USA

Gardner, Guy S (Astronaut)
PO Box 2730
Gainesville, GA 30503-2730, USA

Gardner, Guy S Colonel (Astronaut)
PO Box 4109
Media, PA 19063-7109, USA

Gardner, James H (Basketball Player, Coach)
5465 Bromely Dr
Oak Park, CA 91377-4750, USA

Gardner, Jeff (Athlete, Baseball Player)
1850 Boa Vista Cir
Costa Mesa, CA 92626-4701, USA

Gardner, John (Dancer)
American Ballet Theatre
890 Broadway Fl 3
New York, NY 10003-1278, USA

Gardner, Ken (Athlete, Basketball Player)
3795 S Hawkeye St
West Valley City, UT 84120-3390, USA

Gardner, Lee (Athlete, Baseball Player)
1354 Blue Heron Dr
Highland, MI 48357-3910, USA

Gardner, Mark (Athlete, Baseball Player)
15216 Mesa View Ave
Friant, CA 93626-9780, USA

Gardner, Martin (Writer)
c/o *St. Martin's Press*
175 5th Ave
Attn: Publicity Dept
New York, NY 10010-7703, USA

Gardner, Moe (Athlete, Football Player)
11017 Lorin Way
Duluth, GA 30097-8482, USA

Gardner, Paul (Athlete, Hockey Player)
3687 May Pointe Cv
Southaven, MS 38672-6513, USA

Gardner, Racine (Race Car Driver)
PO Box 934
Buellton, CA 93427-0934, USA

Gardner, Randy (Athlete, Figure Skater, Olympic Athlete)
4640 Glencoe Ave Unit 6
Marina Del Rey, CA 90292-6388, USA

Gardner, Rob (Athlete, Baseball Player)
2001 Gasrilla Rd Lot D21
Placida, FL 33946, USA

Gardner, Rod (Athlete, Football Player)
1883 Executive Dr
Duluth, GA 30096-8922, USA

Gardner, Rulon (Actor)
6791 Brook Forest Dr
Evergreen, CO 80439-6827, USA

Gardner, Rulon (Athlete, Olympic Athlete, Wrestler)
121 Eugene St
North Salt Lake, UT 84054-1764

Gardner, Slick (Race Car Driver)
PO Box 277
Buellton, CA 93427-0277, USA

Gardner, Wee Willie (Athlete, Basketball Player)
Harlem Globetrotters
400 E Van Buren St Ste 300
Phoenix, AZ 85004-0672, USA

Gardner, Wes (Athlete, Baseball Player)
305 Ruth
Benton, AR 72019-2226, USA

Gardocki, Christopher A (Chris) (Athlete, Football Player)
63 Yorkshire Dr
Hilton Head Island, SC 29928-3368, USA

Gardos, Eva (Director)
c/o Staff Member *ICM Partners (LA)*
10250 Constellation Blvd Fl 7
Los Angeles, CA 90067-6207, USA

Gare, Danny (Athlete, Hockey Player)
Buffalo Sabres 1 Seymour H Knox III Plz Ste 1
Attn: Broadcast Dept
Buffalo, NY 14203, USA

Garelick, Jeremy (Producer)
c/o Staff Member *Principato/Young Management (LA)*
9465 Wilshire Blvd Ste 900
Beverly Hills, CA 90212-2608, USA

Garfat, Jance (Musician)
Artists Int'l Mgmt
9850 Sandalwood Blvd
#458
Boca Raton, FL 33428, USA

Garfield, Allen (Actor)
c/o Brian McCabe *Venture IAB*
3211 Cahuenga Blvd W Ste 104
Los Angeles, CA 90068-1372, USA

Garfield, Andrew (Actor)
c/o Jack Whigham *Creative Artists Agency (CAA-LA)*
2000 Avenue of the Stars Ste 100
Los Angeles, CA 90067-4705, USA

Garfinkel, Jack (Athlete, Basketball Player)
19 Dogwood Ln
Glen Head, NY 11545-1006, USA

Garfinkle, David (Producer)
c/o Staff Member *Renegade 83 Entertainment*
5700 Wilshire Blvd Fl 6
Los Angeles, CA 90036-3659, USA

Garfunkel, Art (Musician)
c/o Ken DiCamillo *William Morris Endeavor (NY)*
1325 Avenue of the Americas
New York, NY 10019-6026, USA

Garibaldi, Bob (Athlete, Baseball Player)
2143 Oregon Ave
Stockton, CA 95204-4617, USA

Garity, Troy (Actor)
c/o Jason Weinberg *Untitled Entertainment (LA)*
350 S Beverly Dr Ste 200
Beverly Hills, CA 90212-4819, USA

Garko, Ryan (Athlete, Baseball Player)
9341 E Canyon View Rd
Scottsdale, AZ 85255-6185, USA

Garland, Beverly (Actor)
4222 Vineland Ave
N Hollywood, CA 91602-3318, USA

Garland, Carrington
8014 Briar Summit Dr
Los Angeles, CA 90046-1127

Garland, Jon (Athlete, Baseball Player)
16833 Armstead St
Granada Hills, CA 91344-2704, USA

Garland, Wayne (Athlete, Baseball Player)
7556 Mossback St
Las Vegas, NV 89123-1581, USA

Garland, Winston (Athlete, Basketball Player)
234 Highland Villa Cir
Nashville, TN 37211-7320, USA

Garlick, Scott (Soccer Player)
Colorado Rapids
555 17th St Ste 3350
Denver, CO 80202-3909, USA

Garlin, Jeff (Actor, Comedian)
14312 Millbrook Dr
Sherman Oaks, CA 91423-4427, USA

Garlits, Donald G (Big Daddy) (Race Car Driver)
Garlits Racing Museum
13700 SW 16th Ave
Ocala, FL 34473-3918, USA

Garlitz, Don (Big Daddy) (Race Car Driver)
13700 SW 16th Ave
Ocala, FL 34473-3970, USA

Garmaker, Dick (Athlete, Basketball Player)
5824 E 111th St
Tulsa, OK 74137-7703, USA

Garman, Mike (Athlete, Baseball Player)
15144 Kings Row Rd
Caldwell, ID 83607-8371, USA

Garman-Hosted, Ann (Athlete, Baseball Player, Commentator)
6582 N 100 E
Wawaka, IN 46794-9724, USA

Garmon, Kelvin (Athlete, Football Player)
1424 Creekview Dr
Lewisville, TX 75067-4994, USA

Garn, Jake Brig Gen (Astronaut)
1267 E Chandler Cir
Salt Lake City, UT 84103-4237, USA

Garner, Charlie (Athlete, Football Player)
728 E 5th St
Hobart, OK 73651-4216, USA

Garner, Hal (Athlete, Football Player)
698 S 180 E
Smithfield, UT 84335-1669, USA

Garner, Jennifer (Actor)
c/o Staff Member *Vandalia Films*
4000 Warner Blvd
Burbank, CA 91522-0001, USA

Garner, Kelli (Actor)
c/o John Carrabino *John Carrabino Management*
5900 Wilshire Blvd Ste 406
Los Angeles, CA 90036-5015, USA

Garner, Phil (Athlete, Baseball Player, Coach)
43 Maymont Way
Spring, TX 77382-1328, USA

Garner, William S (Cartoonist)
Memphis Commercial Appeal
495 Union Ave
Editorial Dept
Memphis, TN 38103-3221, USA

Garnes, Sam (Athlete, Football Player)
101 Hearthstone Dr
West Milford, NJ 07480-3751, USA

Garnett, Dave (Athlete, Football Player)
4527 Tyrone Ave
Sherman Oaks, CA 91423-2628, USA

Garnett, Kevin (Athlete, Basketball Player)
c/o Andy Miller *ASM Sports*
920 Undercliff Ave
Edgewater, NJ 07020-1558, USA

Garnett, Scott (Athlete, Football Player)
1637 28th St SE
Puyallup, WA 98372-5188, USA

Garnett, Winfield (Athlete, Football Player)
2029 S 16th Ave
Broadview, IL 60155-3015, USA

Garofalo, Janeane (Actor)
c/o Kara Welker *Generate Management*
8750 Wilshire Blvd Ste 200
Beverly Hills, CA 90211-2707, USA

Garoppolo, Jimmy (Athlete, Football Player)
c/o Don Yee *Yee & Dubin Sports, LLC*
725 S Figueroa St Ste 3085
Los Angeles, CA 90017-5430, USA

Garr, Ralph (Athlete, Baseball Player)
22314 Auburn Canyon Ln
Richmond, TX 77469-5639, USA

Garr, Teri (Terri/Terry) (Actor)
9150 Wilshire Blvd Ste 350
Beverly Hills, CA 90212-3453, USA

Garrard, David (Athlete, Football Player)
4372 Hunterston Ln
Jacksonville, FL 32224-3616, USA

Garrells, Josh (Musician)
Small Voice Records
PO Box 11500
Portland, OR 97211-0500, USA

Garrelts, Scott (Athlete, Baseball Player)
11070 Ashland Way
Shreveport, LA 71106-9348, USA

Garret, Dean
6226 Stevens Ave
Minneapolis, MN 55423-1606, USA

Garrett, Adrian (Athlete, Baseball Player)
401 E Main St
Louisville, KY 40202-1110, USA

Garrett, Alvin (Athlete, Football Player)
2600 Napoleon Ct
Vestavia, AL 35243-5452, USA

Garrett, Beau (Actor)
c/o Sean Fay *Kritzer Levine Wilkins Entertainment (KLWG)*
11872 La Grange Ave Fl 1
Los Angeles, CA 90025-5283, USA

Garrett, Brad (Actor, Comedian)
c/o Eryn Brown *Management 360*
9111 Wilshire Blvd
Beverly Hills, CA 90210-5508, USA

Garrett, Carl (Athlete, Football Player)
203 S Crawford St
Denton, TX 76205-6215, USA

Garrett, Clifton (Athlete, Baseball Player)
7504 Kenicott Ln
Plainfield, IL 60586-4173, USA

Garrett, Dick (Athlete, Basketball Player)
7100 N Park Manor Dr
Milwaukee, WI 53224-4642, USA

Garrett, Drake (Athlete, Football Player)
5040 Fairlawn Rd
Cleveland, OH 44124-1125, USA

Garrett, Jason (Athlete, Football Player)
3656 Maplewood Ave
Dallas, TX 75205-2835, USA

Garrett, Jeremy (Actor)
c/o Staff Member *Paradigm (LA)*
360 N Crescent Dr
North Bldg
Beverly Hills, CA 90210-4874, USA

Garrett, John (Athlete, Football Player)
4948 W Bay Way Dr
Tampa, FL 33629-4804, USA

Garrett, Judd (Athlete, Football Player)
900 Meadow Ln
Southlake, TX 76092-8335, USA

Garrett, Kathleen (Actor)
The Agency
1800 Avenue of the Stars Ste 400
Los Angeles, CA 90067-4206, USA

Garrett, Kenny (Musician)
Von Productions
1915 Cullen Ave
Austin, TX 78757-2435, USA

Garrett, Leif (Actor, Musician)
c/o Barbara Papageorge *Barbara Papageorge Publicity*
790 Amsterdam Ave
New York, NY 10025-5738, USA

Garrett, Len (Athlete, Football Player)
1240 Frenchmans Dr
Desoto, TX 75115-7763, USA

Garrett, Lila (Director)
1245 Laurel Way
Beverly Hills, CA 90210, USA

Garrett, Mike (Athlete, Football Player, Heisman Trophy Winner)
18009 San Mateo Ct
Edmond, OK 73012-4246, USA

Garrett, MJ (Reality Star)
c/o Mike Esterman *Esterman.Com, LLC*
Prefers to be contacted via email
Baltimore, MD XXXXX, USA

Garrett, Pat (Musician, Songwriter, Writer)
Patrick Sickafus
PO Box 84
Strausstown, PA 19559-0084, USA

Garrett, Reggie (Athlete, Football Player)
3 Martino Way
Somerset, NJ 08873-4952, USA

Garrett, Rowland (Athlete, Basketball Player)
219 Western Hills Dr
Jackson, MS 39212-3216, USA

Garrett, Scott (Congressman, Politician)
2244 Rayburn Hob
Washington, DC 20515-0921, USA

Garrett, Spencer (Actor)
c/o Erik Kritzer *LINK Entertainment*
11872 La Grange Ave Fl 1
Los Angeles, CA 90025-5283, USA

Garrett, Wayne (Athlete, Baseball Player)
4331 Linwood St
Sarasota, FL 34232-3905, USA

Garrett III, H Lawrence (Government Official)
RR 1 Box 136-18
Boyce, VA 22620, USA

Garrick, Tom (Athlete, Basketball Player)
235 Providence St
West Warwick, RI 02893-2552, USA

Garrido, Gil (Athlete, Baseball Player)
11311 SW 200th St Apt 110D
Miami, FL 33157-8281, USA

Garrido, Norberto (Athlete, Football Player)
15633 Briarbank St
La Puente, CA 91744-1106, USA

Garrigus, Thomas (Athlete, Olympic Athlete, Shooter)
PO Box 681
Plains, MT 59859-0681, USA

Garriott, Owen E (Doctor)
111 Lost Tree Dr SW
Huntsville, AL 35824-1313, USA

Garriott, Owen K (Astronaut)
111 Lost Tree Dr SW
Huntsville, AL 35824-1313, USA

Garris, John (Athlete, Basketball Player)
308 Carroll St
New Bedford, MA 02740-1415, USA

Garris, Kiwane (Athlete, Basketball Player)
314 W 34th St Apt 107
Steger, IL 60475-1424, USA

Garrison, David (Actor)
630 Estrada Redonda
Santa Fe, NM 87506-7942, USA

Garrison, Gary (Athlete, Football Player)
993 N Vulcan Ave Apt 7
Encinitas, CA 92024-1794, USA

Garrison, John (Athlete, Hockey Player)
Old Concord Rd
Lincoln, MA 01773, USA

Garrison, Lane (Actor)
c/o Dannielle Thomas *Untitled Entertainment (LA)*
350 S Beverly Dr Ste 200
Beverly Hills, CA 90212-4819, USA

Garrison, Walt (Athlete, Football Player)
3475 E Hickory Hill Rd
Argyle, TX 76226-3133, USA

Garrison, Webster (Athlete, Baseball Player)
2038 Rue Racine
Marrero, LA 70072-4729, USA

Garrison-Jackson, Zina (Athlete, Olympic Athlete, Tennis Player)
PO Box 2077
Bowie, MD 20718-2077, USA

Garrity, Gregg (Athlete, Football Player)
86 Seldom Seen Rd
Bradfordwoods, PA 15015-1320, USA

Garrity, Jack (Athlete, Hockey Player, Olympic Athlete)
100 Gas Light Dr Apt 9
South Weymouth, MA 02190-2149, USA

Garrity, Pat (Athlete, Basketball Player)
107 Dunning Rd
New Canaan, CT 06840-4011, USA

Garron, Larry (Athlete, Football Player)
987 Pleasant St
Framingham, MA 01701-8853, USA

Garror, Leon (Athlete, Football Player)
259 Stocking St
Mobile, AL 36604-1948, USA

Garrum, Larry (Athlete, Hockey Player)
987 Pleasant St
Framingham, MA 01701-8853, USA

Garson, Willie (Actor)
c/o Gladys Gonzalez *John Carrabino Management*
5900 Wilshire Blvd Ste 406
Los Angeles, CA 90036-5015, USA

Garten, Ina (Writer)
Clarkson Potter
1745 Broadway
Author Mail
New York, NY 10019-4640, USA

Garth, Jennie (Actor)
c/o Randy James *James/Levy Management Inc*
3500 W Olive Ave Ste 1470
Burbank, CA 91505-5514, USA

Garver, Cathy (Actor)
550 Mountain Home Rd
Woodside, CA 94062-2515, USA

Garver, Kathy (Actor)
170 Woodridge Rd
Hillsborough, CA 94010-7263, USA

Garver, Ned (Athlete, Baseball Player)
1121 Town Line Rd Unit 164
Bryan, OH 43506-8732, USA

Garvey, Mike (Race Car Driver)
Competitive Edge
1033 Louisiana Ave
#1101
Winter Park, FL 32789, USA

Garvey, Steve (Athlete, Baseball Player)
74720 Old Prospector Trl
Palm Desert, CA 92260-5635, USA

Garvey-Truhan, Cyndy
13924 Panay Way Apt 309
Marina Del Rey, CA 90292-4124

Garvin, Jerry (Athlete, Baseball Player)
1952 E 725 S
Springville, UT 84663-3214, USA

Gary, Cleveland (Athlete, Football Player)
720 SE Martin Luther King Jr Blvd
Stuart, FL 34994-2368, USA

Gary, Cleveland E (Athlete, Football Player)
1446 SW 169th Ave
Indiantown, FL 37956, USA

Gary, Dunn (Athlete, Football Player)
243 Navajo St
Tavernier, FL 33070-2119, USA

Gary, Keith (Athlete, Football Player)
1401 N Taft St Apt 821
Arlington, VA 22201-2650, USA

Gary, Leonard (Athlete, Basketball Player)
3318 N Decatur Blvd Unit 2086
Las Vegas, NV 89130-3253, USA

Gary, Lorraine (Actor)
1158 Tower Rd
Beverly Hills, CA 90210-2131, USA

Garza, David (Musician)
Partisan Arts
1505 Bridgeway Ste 205
Sausalito, CA 94965-1968, USA

Garza, Joselle (Race Car Driver)
865 Comstock Ave Apt 11A
Los Angeles, CA 90024-2585, USA

Garza, Nicole (Actor)
c/o David Rudy *Armada Partners*
PO Box 64547
Los Angeles, CA 90064-0547, USA

Gascon, Eileen (Athlete, Baseball Player, Commentator)
249 Trowbridge Rd
Elk Grove Village, IL 60007-3820, USA

Gascon, Elleen (Baseball Player)
249 Trowbridge Rd
Elk Grove Village, IL 60007-3820, USA

Gash, Samuel L (Sam) (Athlete, Football Player)
46544 Galway Dr
Novi, MI 48374-3871, USA

Gash, Thane (Athlete, Football Player)
201 Whispering Hills Dr
Hendersonville, NC 28792-1213, USA

Gaskill, Brian (Actor)
c/o Marie Mathews *Marie Mathews Management*
8730 W Sunset Blvd Ste 200
West Hollywood, CA 90069-2275, USA

Gasol, Pau (Athlete, Basketball Player)
c/o Arn Tellem *Wasserman Media Group (LA)*
12100 W Olympic Blvd Ste 200
Los Angeles, CA 90064-1075, USA

Gaspar, Rod (Athlete, Baseball Player)
28771 Peach Blossom
Mission Viejo, CA 92692-1072, USA

Gass, William H (Writer)
6304 Westminster Pl
Saint Louis, MO 63130-4727, USA

Gassert, Ron (Athlete, Football Player)
11 Sheffield Pl
Southampton, NJ 08088-1306, USA

Gassner, Dave (Athlete, Baseball Player)
N1376 Woodland Dr
Greenville, WI 54942-8035, USA

Gast, Paul (Race Car Driver)
120 Industrial Dr
Grand Island, NY 14072-1219, USA

Gasteyer, Ana (Actor, Comedian)
c/o Frank Frattaroli *Circle of Confusion (LA)*
8931 Ellis Ave
Los Angeles, CA 90034-3336, USA

Gastineau, Brittny (Actor, Reality Star)
c/o Dana-Lee Schuman *ICM Partners (LA)*
10250 Constellation Blvd Fl 7
Los Angeles, CA 90067-6207, USA

Gastineau, Marcus D (Mark) (Athlete, Football Player)
22202 N 48th St
Phoenix, AZ 85054-6171, USA

Gastineau, Mark (Athlete, Football Player)
53 Honey Flower Dr
Trenton, NJ 08620-9687, USA

Gaston, Cito (Athlete, Baseball Player, Coach)
1454 Woodstream Dr
Oldsmar, FL 34677-4832, USA

Gaston, Michael (Actor)
c/o Lisa Lieberman *Innovative Artists (NY)*
235 Park Ave S Fl 7
New York, NY 10003-1405, USA

Gates, Antonio (Athlete, Football Player)
c/o Staff Member *EAG Sports Management*
909 N Sepulveda Blvd Ste 360
El Segundo, CA 90245-3864, USA

Gates, Bill (Business Person, Philanthropist)
Bill & Melinda Gates Foundation
500 5th Ave N
Seattle, WA 98109-4636, USA

Gates, Brent (Athlete, Baseball Player)
2125 Shawnee Dr SE
Grand Rapids, MI 49506-5332, USA

Gates, Daryl (Actor)
24876 Sunstar Ln
Dana Point, CA 92629-1930, USA

Gates, David (Musician, Songwriter, Writer)
Paradise Artists
108 E Matilija St
Ojai, CA 93023-2639, USA

Gates, Josh (Actor)
c/o Noreen Savides *323 Talent Management*
PO Box 1005
Lake Hughes, CA 93532-2005, USA

Gates, Joshua (Actor)
c/o Feroz Taj *United Talent Agency (UTA-LA)*
9336 Civic Center Dr
Beverly Hills, CA 90210-3604, USA

Gates, Mike (Athlete, Baseball Player)
131 Edgewater Rd
Kooskia, ID 83539-5024, USA

Gatewood, Aubrey (Athlete, Baseball Player)
5 Pine Tree Loop
North Little Rock, AR 72116-8313, USA

Gatewood, Les (Athlete, Football Player)
PO Box 414
Kirbyville, TX 75956-0414, USA

Gatewood, Tom (Athlete, Football Player)
101 Cambridge Dr
Nutley, NJ 07110-3913, USA

Gathegi, Edi (Actor)
c/o Mary Ellen Mulcahy *Framework Entertainment (LA)*
9057 Nemo St Ste C
West Hollywood, CA 90069-5511, USA

Gathright, Joey (Athlete, Baseball Player)
20100 Park Row Dr Apt 1307
Katy, TX 77449-4985, USA

Gatlin, Justin (Athlete, Track Athlete)
c/o Staff Member *USA Track & Field*
132 E Washington St Ste 800
Indianapolis, IN 46204-3674, USA

Gatlin, Larry (Musician)
5100 Harris Ave
Kansas City, MO 64133-2331, USA

Gatlin, Steve (Musician)
5103 Fountainhead Dr
Brentwood, TN 37027-5809, USA

Gatling, Chris (Athlete, Basketball Player)
175 Canon Dr
Orinda, CA 94563-2218, USA

Gatti, Bill (Athlete, Football Player)
1400 Regal Springs Ct
Louisville, KY 40205-3334

Gatti, Jennifer (Actor)
S D B Partners
315 S Beverly Dr Ste 411
Beverly Hills, CA 90212-4301, USA

Gattison, Kenny (Athlete, Basketball Player)
1204 Northern Lights Dr
Upper Marlboro, MD 20774-6049, USA

Gaubatz, Dennis (Athlete, Football Player)
1250 County Road 943
West Columbia, TX 77486-9454, USA

Gaudet, Jim (Athlete, Baseball Player)
3336 Vineville Ave
Macon, GA 31204-2328, USA

Gaudin, Chad (Athlete, Baseball Player)
511 Vecino St
Benicia, CA 94510-2333, USA

Gaudreau, Rob (Athlete, Hockey Player)
22 Briarbrooke Ln
Cranston, RI 02921-2111, USA

Gaughan, Brendan (Race Car Driver)
Rusty Wallace Racing
1459 Knob Hill Rd
Mooresville, NC 28117, USA

Gaul, Frank (Athlete, Football Player)
3420 Balsam Dr
Westlake, OH 44145-4407, USA

Gaul, Gilbert M (Journalist)
Philadelphia Inquirer
400 N Broad St
Editorial Dept
Philadelphia, PA 19130-4099, USA

Gault, Bill (Athlete, Football Player)
1197 Balcones Dr
Fredericksbrg, TX 78624-7500, USA

Gault, William Campbell (Writer)
481 Mountain Dr
Santa Barbara, CA 93103-1700, USA

Gault, Willie (Athlete, Football Player)
15460 La Maida St
Sherman Oaks, CA 91403-1043, USA

Gaustad, Paul (Athlete, Hockey Player)
508 Huckleberry Rd
Nashville, TN 37205-2635, USA

Gauthier, Luc (Athlete, Hockey Player)
c/o Staff Member *Colorado Avalanche*
1000 Chopper Cir
Pepsi Center
Denver, CO 80204-5805, USA

Gauthier, Jr., Denis (Athlete, Hockey Player)
1658 9th St
Manhattan Beach, CA 90266-6129, USA

Gauthreaux, Joe (DJ)
c/o Staff Member *Diva Central Inc*
7510 W Sunset Blvd Ste 1445
Los Angeles, CA 90046-3408, USA

Gautier, Dick (Actor)
c/o Staff Member *Beacon Talent Agency*
170 Apple Ridge Rd
Woodcliff Lake, NJ 07677-8149, USA

Gava, Cassandra (Actor)
1745 Camino Palmero St Apt 210
Los Angeles, CA 90046-2918, USA

Gavankar, Janina (Actor)
c/o Arlene Forster *Forster Entertainment*
12533 Woodgreen St
Los Angeles, CA 90066-2723, USA

Gavaris, Jordan (Actor)
c/o Staff Member *Echo Lake Management*
421 S Beverly Dr Fl 8
Beverly Hills, CA 90212-4408, USA

Gavin, Charles E (Chuck) (Athlete, Football Player)
2800 Grape St
Denver, CO 80207-2730, USA

Gavin, Erica
c/o Siouxzan Perry *Girlwerks Management*
3395 E Camino Rojos
Palm Springs, CA 92262-5417, USA

Gavin, John (Actor)
4 Watchet Ln
Fairport, NY 14450-4122, USA

Gaviria, Trujillo Cesar (President)
Organization of American States
& 17th Constitution NW
Washington, DC 20006, USA

Gavitt, Dave (Basketball Player, Misc)
Boston Celtics
151 Merrimac St # 1
Boston, MA 02114-4714, USA

Gavron, Rafi (Actor)
c/o Melanie Greene *Affirmative*
Entertainment
425 N Robertson Blvd
West Hollywood, CA 90048-1735, USA

Gay, Billy (Athlete, Football Player)
824 Lisdowney Dr
Lockport, IL 60441-2794, USA

Gay, Brian (Athlete, Golfer)
6809 Valhalla Way
Windermere, FL 34786-5627, USA

Gay, Don
1818 Rodeo Dr
Mesquite, TX 75149-3800

Gay, Everett (Athlete, Football Player)
700 E Johnson St
Waco, TX 76705-3816, USA

Gay, George
588 Charlton Ct NW
Marietta, GA 30064-1451

Gay, Randall (Athlete, Football Player)
116 Cocasset St Apt 14
Foxboro, MA 02035-2067, USA

Gay, Rudy (Athlete, Basketball Player)
91 W Galloway Dr
Memphis, TN 38111-6839, USA

Gay, William (Athlete, Football Player)
8200 E Jefferson Ave Apt 804
Detroit, MI 48214-2681, USA

Gaydos, Joey (Actor)
c/o Staff Member *Cunningham Escott*
Slevin & Doherty (CESD-LA)
10635 Santa Monica Blvd Ste 130
Los Angeles, CA 90025-8306, USA

Gaydos, Kent (Athlete, Football Player)
1107 Mallard Ct
Granbury, TX 76048-2676, USA

Gaydos Jr, Joey (Actor)
4021 Ice Castle Way Apt 6
Naples, FL 34112-1013, USA

Gaye, Nona (Actor)
c/o Steven Muller *Innovative Artists (LA)*
1505 10th St
Santa Monica, CA 90401-2805, USA

Gayheart, Rebecca (Actor, Model)
c/o Stephanie Simon *Untitled*
Entertainment (LA)
350 S Beverly Dr Ste 200
Beverly Hills, CA 90212-4819, USA

Gayle, Crystal (Actor, Musician)
c/o Staff Member *Webster & Associates*
PR
3573 Couchville Pike
Hermitage, TN 37076-4012, USA

Gayle, Sami (Actor)
c/o David Guillod *Intellectual Artists*
Management
10585 Santa Monica Blvd Ste 135
Los Angeles, CA 90025-6392, USA

Gayle, Shaun (Athlete, Football Player)
PO Box 803887
Chicago, IL 60680-3887, USA

Gaylor, Trevor (Athlete, Football Player)
5855 Hammond Dr
Norcross, GA 30071-3412, USA

Gaylord, Mitch (Athlete, Gymnast,
Olympic Athlete)
9601 Bowman Dr
Fort Worth, TX 76244-9180, USA

Gaylord, Scott (Race Car Driver)
Scott Gaylord Racing
1451 Depew St
Lakewood, CO 80214-2236, USA

Gaylords, The
32630 Concord Dr
Madison Heights, MI 48071-1110

Gaynes, George (Actor)
5500 Calle Real Bldg A
Santa Barbara, CA 93111-3606, USA

Gaynor, Gloria (Music Group, Musician)
c/o Staff Member *Richard De La Font*
Agency
3808 W South Park Blvd
Broken Arrow, OK 74011-1261, USA

Gaynor, Mitzi (Actor, Dancer, Musician)
517 N Bedford Dr
Beverly Hills, CA 90210-3213, USA

Gayton, Joe (Writer)
c/o David Saunders *Agency for the*
Performing Arts (APA-LA)
405 S Beverly Dr Ste 500
Beverly Hills, CA 90212-4425, USA

Gayton, Tony (Writer)
c/o Matt Ochacher *Agency for the*
Performing Arts (APA-LA)
405 S Beverly Dr Ste 500
Beverly Hills, CA 90212-4425, USA

Gbaja-Biamila, Akbar (Athlete, Football
Player)
1050 Armitage St
Alameda, CA 94502-7931, USA

Gbaja-Biamila, Kabeer (Athlete, Football
Player)
1071 Hill Dr
Oneida, WI 54155-9114, USA

Geale, Rob (Athlete, Hockey Player)
4167 NW 178th Pl
Portland, OR 97229-7703, USA

Geary, Anthony (Actor)
7010 Pacific View Dr
Los Angeles, CA 90068-2038, USA

Geary, Cynthia (Actor)
Baumgarten/Prophet
1041 N Formosa Ave # 200
West Hollywood, CA 90046-6703, USA

Geary, Geoff (Athlete, Baseball Player)
2735 Callaway Ln
Kissimmee, FL 34744-8533, USA

Geary, Tony
7010 Pacific View Dr
Los Angeles, CA 90068-2038

Geater, Ron (Athlete, Football Player)
1134 Bull Valley Dr
Woodstock, IL 60098-8001, USA

Geathers, James (Athlete, Football Player)
200 Tony Dr
Georgetown, SC 29440-2059, USA

Geathers, Robert (Athlete, Football
Player)
1 Dab Dr
Georgetown, SC 29440-6059, USA

Gebert, Gordon (Actor)
8 Dwight St
Poughkeepsie, NY 12601-4408, USA

Gebhard, Bob (Commentator)
5242 E Otero Pl
Centennial, CO 80122-3889, USA

Geddes, Bob (Athlete, Football Player)
79251 Tom Fazio Ln S
La Quinta, CA 92253-8031, USA

Geddes, Jane (Athlete, Golfer)
72 Shady Knoll Ln
New Canaan, CT 06840-6516, USA

Geddes, Jim (Athlete, Baseball Player)
6738 Harrisburg London Rd
Orient, OH 43146-9454, USA

Geddes, Ken (Athlete, Football Player)
7702 147th Ave NE
Redmond, WA 98052-4168, USA

Gedman, Rich (Athlete, Baseball Player)
10 Parmenter Rd
Framingham, MA 01701-3019, USA

Gedney, Chris (Athlete, Football Player)
125 Robineau Rd
Syracuse, NY 13207-1645, USA

Gedrick, Jason (Actor)
c/o Staff Member *IFA Talent Agency*
2000 Avenue Of The Stars
Los Angeles, CA 90067-4700, USA

Gee, Dillon (Athlete, Baseball Player)
4612 Pershing Ave
Fort Worth, TX 76107-4926, USA

Gee, James D (Religious Leader)
Penecostal Church of God
PO Box 211866
Bedford, TX 76095-8866, USA

Geer, Charlotte (Athlete, Olympic
Athlete, Rower)
PO Box 324
Hinesburg, VT 05461-0324, USA

Geer, Ellen (Actor)
21418 Entrada Rd
Topanga, CA 90290-3539, USA

Geer, Josh (Athlete, Baseball Player)
10836 Peach Cir
Forney, TX 75126-6666, USA

Geer, Julia (Athlete, Olympic Athlete,
Rower)
243 Lyle McKee Rd
Morrisville, VT 05661-8902, USA

Geeson, Judy (Actor)
Media Artists Group
6300 Wilshire Blvd Ste 1470
Los Angeles, CA 90048-5200, USA

Geffen, David (Business Person, Producer)
1801 Angelo Dr
Beverly Hills, CA 90210-2723, USA

Geffner, Glenn (Commentator)
4058 Palm Pi
Fort Lauderdale, FL 33331, USA

Gegenhuber, John
9171 Wilshire Blvd Ste 441
Beverly Hills, CA 90210-5516

Gehlhausen, Spike (Race Car Driver)
5456 Meadowood Dr
Indianapolis, IN 46224-3338, USA

Gehman, Martha
2488 Cheremoya Ave
Los Angeles, CA 90068-3070

Gehringer, Rick (Musician)
c/o Staff Member *Brothers Management*
Associates Inc
141 Dunbar Ave
Fords, NJ 08863-1551

Gehrke, Jack (Athlete, Football Player)
5402 Nassau Cir E
Englewood, CO 80113-5134, USA

Gehry, Frank (Designer)
Gehry Partners
12541 Beatrice St
Los Angeles, CA 90066-7001, USA

Geiberger, Al (Athlete, Golfer)
73091 Country Club Dr Ste A4
Palm Desert, CA 92260-2338, USA

Geiberger, Brent (Athlete, Golfer)
113 Chelsea Cir
Palm Desert, CA 92260-4688, USA

Geier, Philip H Jr (Business Person)
Interpublic Group
1271 Avenue of the Americas Fl 43
New York, NY 10020-1309, USA

Geiger, Ken (Journalist, Photographer)
Dallas Mornig News
Communications Center
Dallas, TX 75265, USA

Geiger, Matt (Athlete, Basketball Player)
11476 Trotting Down Dr
Odessa, FL 33556-5900, USA

Geiger, Teddy (Musician)
c/o John Geiger
11 Tamarron Way
Pittsford, NY 14534-3347, USA

Geimer, Samantha
4245 Waipua St
Kilauea, HI 96754-5336

Geisel, Dave (Athlete, Baseball Player)
4 Blacksmith Ln
Media, PA 19063-4411, USA

Geishert, Vern (Athlete, Baseball Player)
1440 W Seminary St
Richland Center, WI 53581-2036, USA

Geisinger, Justin (Athlete, Football Player)
433 Buffalo Run
Goodlettsville, TN 37072-3313, USA

Geissinger-Harding, Jean (Athlete,
Baseball Player, Commentator)
539 Hodunk Rd
Coldwater, MI 49036-9273, USA

Geist, William (Bill) (Commentator,
Writer)
c/o Staff Member *CBS News (NY)*
524 W 57th St Fl 8
New York, NY 10019-2930, USA

Gelbaugh, Stan (Athlete, Football Player)
10389 Derby Dr
Laurel, MD 20723-5743, USA

Geldart, Gary (Athlete, Hockey Player)
1701 Kemah Village Dr
Kemah, TX 77565-1709, USA

Geldof, Bob (Actor, Musician)
c/o Rick Shoor *Red Entertainment Agency*
505 8th Ave Rm 1004
New York, NY 10018-6529, USA

Gelfant, Alan (Actor)
Peter Strain
5724 W 3rd St Ste 302
Los Angeles, CA 90036-3085, USA

Gellar, Sarah Michelle (Actor)
2435 Mandeville Canyon Rd
Los Angeles, CA 90049-1235, USA

Geller, Glenn (Business Person)
c/o Staff Member *CBS Paramount Network Television*
4024 Radford Ave
Cbs Studios
Studio City, CA 91604-2190, USA

Gelman, Larry (Actor)
5121 Greenbush Ave
Sherman Oaks, CA 91423-1507, USA

Gelman, Michael (Producer)
7 Lincoln Sq
New York, NY 10023-7219

Gelnar, John (Athlete, Baseball Player)
1811 Suzanne Dr Apt 2
Weatherford, OK 73096-2383, USA

Gemar, Charles D (Astronaut)
7660 N 159th Street Ct E
Benton, KS 67017-8926, USA

Gemar, Charles D Lt Colonel (Astronaut)
7660 N 159th Street Ct E
Benton, KS 67017-8926, USA

Genet, Sabryn
7800 Beverly Blvd # 3305
Los Angeles, CA 90036-2112

Genilas, Eric (Athlete, Hockey Player)
165 Mulberry St
Newark, NJ 07102-3607, USA

Genitallica (Music Group)
c/o Staff Member *Sony Music Miami*
605 Lincoln Rd Ste 700
Miami Beach, FL 33139-2901, USA

Genovese, George (Athlete, Baseball Player)
11474 Erwin St
North Hollywood, CA 91606-4126, USA

Gentile, Jim (Athlete, Baseball Player)
1016 S Neptune Rd
Edmond, OK 73003-6071, USA

Gentile, Troy (Actor)
c/o Leonard Torgan *The Collective*
8383 Wilshire Blvd Ste 1050
Beverly Hills, CA 90211-2415, USA

Gentilozzi, Paul (Race Car Driver)
201 N Washington Sq Ste 900
Lansing, MI 48933-1323, USA

Gentry, Alvin (Basketball Player, Coach, Misc)
New Orleans Homets
1501 Girod St
New Orleans, LA 70113-3124, USA

Gentry, Craig (Athlete, Baseball Player)
1209 Cartwright St
Van Buren, AR 72956-2809, USA

Gentry, Curtis (Athlete, Football Player)
387 Meadow Green Ln
Round Lake Beach, IL 60073-1326, USA

Gentry, Dennis (Athlete, Football Player)
916 Queen Elizabeth Dr
Mc Gregor, TX 76657-4000, USA

Gentry, Harvey (Athlete, Baseball Player)
9030 Carriage Ct
Pickerington, OH 43147-9731, USA

Gentry, Montgomery (Music Group)
c/o John Dorris Sr *Hallmark Direction Company*
713 18th Ave S
Nashville, TN 37203-3214, USA

Gentry, Teddy W (Music Group, Musician)
P O Box 529
Fort Payne, AL 35968, USA

Gentry, Troy (Musician)
c/o Staff Member *Hallmark Direction Company*
713 18th Ave S
Nashville, TN 37203-3214, USA

Genzel, Carrie (Actor)
Pakula/King
9229 W Sunset Blvd Ste 315
West Hollywood, CA 90069-3403, USA

Genzman, Andy (Race Car Driver)
Genzman Racing
2145 Napoleon Rd
Fremont, OH 43420-1502, USA

Geoffrion, Dan (Athlete, Hockey Player)
413 Overall Dr
Brentwood, TN 37027-7649, USA

Geoffrion, Daniel (Athlete, Hockey Player)
413 Overall Dr
Brentwood, TN 37027-7649, USA

Geoffrion, Scott (Race Car Driver)
Team Mopar
27608 La Paz
#506
Laguna Niguel, CA 92677, USA

George, Alex (Athlete, Baseball Player)
8432 Linden Ln
Prairie Village, KS 66207-1834, USA

George, Boy (Musician)
c/o Ian Fintak *Agency Group Ltd, The (LA)*
1880 Century Park E Ste 711
Los Angeles, CA 90067-1618, USA

George, Chris (Athlete, Baseball Player, Olympic Athlete)
121 E Maranta Rd
Mooresville, NC 28117-6335, USA

George, Christopher S (Chris) (Baseball Player)
121 E Maranta Rd
Mooresville, NC 28117-6335, USA

George, Devean (Athlete, Basketball Player)
14001 53rd Ave N
Minneapolis, MN 55446-1834, USA

George, Ed (Athlete, Football Player)
1220 S Orange Ave
Sarasota, FL 34239-2028, USA

George, Eddie (Athlete, Football Player, Heisman Trophy Winner, Television Host)
9538 Sanctuary Pl
Brentwood, TN 37027-8498, USA

George, Elizabeth (Writer)
c/o Robert Gottlieb *Trident Media Group LLC*
41 Madison Ave Fl 36
New York, NY 10010-2257, USA

George, Eric (Actor)
Lasher McManus Robinson
1964 Westwood Blvd Ste 400
Los Angeles, CA 90025-4695, USA

George, Francis E Cardinal (Religious Leader)
Chicago Archidiocese
1555 N State Pkwy
Chicago, IL 60610-1613, USA

George, Jason Winston (Actor)
c/o Barry McPherson *Agency for the Performing Arts (APA-NY)*
135 W 50th St Fl 17
New York, NY 10020-1201, USA

George, Jeffrey S (Jeff) (Athlete, Football Player)
1908 Schwier Ct
Indianapolis, IN 46229-2154, USA

George, Lynda Day (Actor)
10310 Riverside Dr Unit 104
Toluca Lake, CA 91602-2457

George, Matt (Athlete, Football Player)
24403 Newhall Ave Apt 3
Newhall, CA 91321-2771, USA

George, Melissa (Actor)
c/o Pamela Kohl *3 Arts Entertainment (LA)*
9460 Wilshire Blvd Fl 7
Beverly Hills, CA 90212-2713, USA

George, Paul (Athlete, Basketball Player)
9238 Diamond Pointe Dr
Indianapolis, IN 46236-9055, USA

George, Peter (Athlete, Olympic Athlete, Weightlifter)
1649 Kalakaua Ave Ste 204
Honolulu, HI 96826-2494, USA

George, Phyllis (Beauty Pageant Winner, Television Host)
c/o Staff Member *The Miss America Organization*
222 New Rd Ste 700
Linwood, NJ 08221-1286, USA

George, Ron (Athlete, Football Player)
10136 Middlebrooks Ter
Nokesville, VA 20181-3669, USA

George, Steve (Athlete, Football Player)
5922 W Airport Blvd
Houston, TX 77035-5302, USA

George, Tate (Athlete, Basketball Player)
55 Georgetown Rd
Bristol, CT 06010-5510, USA

George, Terry (Writer)
c/o Ari Emanuel *William Morris Endeavor (LA)*
9601 Wilshire Blvd
Beverly Hills, CA 90210-5213, USA

George, Tim (Athlete, Football Player)
77 Saddle Ln
Easton, PA 18045-3115, USA

George, Tony (Race Car Driver)
Vison Racing
6803 Coffman Rd
Indianapolis, IN 46268-2561, USA

George, William W (Business Person)
Medtronic Inc
7000 Central Ave NE
Minneapolis, MN 55432-3576, USA

Georges, Anne (Baseball Player)
407 Oak St
Des Plaines, IL 60016-4429, USA

Georgian, Theodore J (Religious Leader)
Orthodox Presbyterian Church
PO Box P
Willow Grove, PA 19090, USA

Georgije, Bishop (Religious Leader)
Serbian Orthodox Church
PO Box 519
Libertyville, IL 60048-0519, USA

Georgoulis, Alexis (Actor)
c/o Ali Sages *Sages Entertainment Group*
5213 Meridian St Apt 7
Los Angeles, CA 90042-1745, USA

Gephardt, Richard (Politician)
DLA Piper
PO Box 9945
Mc Lean, VA 22102-0945, USA

Geraci, Sonny (Music Group)
Mars Talent
27 L Ambiance Ct
Bardonia, NY 10954-1421, USA

Geraghty, Brian (Actor)
c/o Lena Roklin *Luber Roklin Management*
5815 W Sunset Blvd Ste 206
Los Angeles, CA 90028-6481, USA

Gerard, Caitlin (Actor)
c/o Mara Buxbaum *ID Public Relations (LA)*
7060 Hollywood Blvd Fl 8th
Los Angeles, CA 90028-6021, USA

Gerard, Gil (Actor)
c/o Michael Einfeld *Michael Einfeld Management*
10630 Moorpark St Unit 101
North Hollywood, CA 91602-2797, USA

Gerard, Gus (Athlete, Basketball Player)
614 Cypresswood Dr
Spring, TX 77388-5913, USA

Gerard, Tara (Reality Star)
c/o Mike Esterman *Esterman.Com, LLC*
Prefers to be contacted via email
Baltimore, MD XXXXX, USA

Gerber, Craig (Athlete, Baseball Player)
4297 N Pershing Ave
San Bernardino, CA 92407-3737, USA

Gerber, H Joseph (Business Person)
Gerber Scientific Inc
83 Gerber Rd W
South Windsor, CT 06074-3230, USA

Gerber, Michael (Business Person, Writer)
E-Myth Worldwide
139 E Main St
Ashland, OR 97520-1830, USA

Gerber, Rande (Business Person)
33246 Pacific Coast Hwy
Malibu, CA 90265-2304, USA

Gerberding, Julie (Doctor, Government Official, Physicist)
Centers for Disease Control
1600 Clifton Rd NE
Atlanta, GA 30329-4018, USA

Gerberman, George (Athlete, Baseball Player)
1501 Michael St
El Campo, TX 77437-9345, USA

Gere, Richard (Actor)
c/o Alan Nierob *Rogers & Cowan PR (LA)*
8687 Melrose Ave Ste 7
West Hollywood, CA 90069-5721, USA

Geredine, Tom (Athlete, Football Player)
1155 Woodlands Dr
Kyle, TX 78640-5530, USA

Gerela, Roy (Athlete, Football Player)
3933 Ramrod Frg
Las Cruces, NM 88012-6008, USA

Geren, Bob (Athlete, Baseball Player, Coach)
32 Bottlebrush Ct
Danville, CA 94506-4743, USA

Gerena, Samuel (Gringo) (Musician)
c/o Staff Member *Universal Music Publishing Group (Latin)*
420 Lincoln Rd Ste 200
Miami Beach, FL 33139-3014, USA

Gergen, David R (Politician)
31 Ash St
Cambridge, MA 02138-4840, USA

Gerhardt, Alben (Musician)
Columbia Artists Mgmt Inc
165 W 57th St
New York, NY 10019-2201, USA

Gerhardt, Don (Athlete, Football Player)
1465 Waterford Dr
Minneapolis, MN 55422-4274, USA

Gerhardt, Jason (Actor)
Hollywood Entertainment
9255 W Sunset Blvd Ste 803
C/O Ron Scott
West Hollywood, CA 90069-3305, USA

Gerhardt, Rusty (Athlete, Baseball Player)
PO Box 426
New London, TX 75682-0426, USA

Gerhart, Bobby (Race Car Driver)
305 Lights St
Lebanon, PA 17042, USA

Gerhart, Garth (Athlete, Football Player)
c/o David Dunn *Athletes First, LLC*
23091 Mill Creek Dr
Laguna Hills, CA 92653-1258, USA

Gerhart, Ken (Athlete, Baseball Player)
1603 Ashford Ct
Murfreesboro, TN 37129-5888, USA

Gering, Galen (Actor)
c/o Staff Member *Schumacher Management*
2018 Glendon Ave
Los Angeles, CA 90025-6324, USA

Gering, Jenna (Actor)
c/o Jonathan Bluman *William Morris Endeavor (LA)*
9601 Wilshire Blvd
Beverly Hills, CA 90210-5213, USA

Gerlach, Gary (Publisher)
Des Moines Register & Tribune
715 Locust St
Des Moines, IA 50309-3703, USA

Gerlach, Jim (Congressman, Politician)
2442 Rayburn Hob
Washington, DC 20515-3011, USA

Germain, Dorothy (Athlete, Golfer)
202 NC Highway 62 W
Randleman, NC 27317-9774, USA

Germain, Eric (Athlete, Hockey Player)
46 Dawes Ave
Hamden, CT 06517-2331, USA

Germain, Stephanie (Producer)
c/o Staff Member *Creative Artists Agency (CAA-LA)*
2000 Avenue of the Stars Ste 100
Los Angeles, CA 90067-4705, USA

German, Jammi (Athlete, Football Player)
3702 Highland Ave
Fort Myers, FL 33916-6529, USA

German, Lauren (Actor)
c/o Doug Wald *Anonymous Content (LA)*
3532 Hayden Ave
Culver City, CA 90232-2413, USA

Germann, Greg (Actor, Director)
c/o Jeff Golenberg *Silver Lining Entertainment*
421 S Beverly Dr Fl 7
Beverly Hills, CA 90212-4408, USA

Germano, Justin (Athlete, Baseball Player)
1156 Festival Rd
San Marcos, CA 92078-2806, USA

Germano, Lisa (Music Group, Musician)
Artists & Audience Entertainment
PO Box 35
Pawling, NY 12564-0035, USA

Germany, Reggie (Athlete, Football Player)
246 Haystack Ave
Pataskala, OH 43062-7359, USA

Germany, Willie (Athlete, Football Player)
4401 Pratt St
Omaha, NE 68111-2533, USA

Gernander, Ken (Athlete, Hockey Player)
93 Jeffrey Ln
Newington, CT 06111-1617, USA

Gerner, Robert (Doctor, Misc)
University of California Neuropsychiatric Institute
Los Angeles, CA 90024, USA

Gernert, David (Publisher)
The Gernet Co
136 E 57th St Fl 18
New York, NY 10022-2923, USA

Gernert, Dick (Athlete, Baseball Player)
1801 Cambridge Ave Apt C12
Reading, PA 19610-2669, USA

Gernhardt, Michael L (Astronaut)
2022 Lakeside Lndg
Seabrook, TX 77586-8301, USA

Gernon, Bruce (Writer)
c/o Staff Member *Llewellyn Worldwide, LTD*
2143 Wooddale Dr
Saint Paul, MN 55125-2989, USA

Gero, Gary D (Cinematographer)
2 McLaren Ste A
Irvine, CA 92618-2815, USA

Gerrard, Steven (Athlete, Soccer Player)
c/o Dan Levy *Wasserman Media Group (NC)*
4208 Six Forks Rd Ste 1020
Raleigh, NC 27609-5738, USA

Gerring, Cathy (Athlete, Golfer)
3328 Tarrant Springs Trl
Fort Wayne, IN 46804-6161, USA

Gersbach, Carl (Athlete, Football Player)
PO Box 433
Devon, PA 19333-0433, USA

Gershman, Benj (Musician)
275 Greenwich St # 9JS
New York, NY 10007-2150, USA

Gershon, Gina (Actor)
6 Varick St Apt 7C
New York, NY 10013-2452, USA

Gerstell, A Frederick (Business Person)
CalMat Co
500 N Brand Blvd Ste 500
Glendale, CA 91203-3319, USA

Gerstner, Lou (Business Person)
IBM Corp
1 N Castle Dr Ste 2
Armonk, NY 10504-1784, USA

Gertz, Jami (Actor)
c/o Jason Barrett *Alchemy Entertainment*
7024 Melrose Ave Ste 420
Los Angeles, CA 90038-3394, USA

Gerut, Jody (Athlete, Baseball Player)
623 Rochdale Cir
Lombard, IL 60148-4730, USA

Gerut, Joseph ""Jody"" (Athlete, Baseball Player)
746 N Cuyler Ave
Oak Park, IL 60302-1775, USA

Gervin, Derrick (Athlete, Basketball Player)
8147 Babe Ruth St
San Antonio, TX 78240-2902, USA

Gervin, George (Athlete, Basketball Player, Coach)
44 Gervin Pass
Spring Branch, TX 78070-6370, USA

Geschke, Charles (Business Person)
Adobe Systems
345 Park Ave
San Jose, CA 95110-2704, USA

Gesek, John (Athlete, Football Player)
105 Sand Point Ct
Coppell, TX 75019-5359, USA

G. Eshoo, Anna (Congressman, Politician)
205 Cannon Hob
Washington, DC 20515-0514, USA

Gessford, Jim (Athlete, Football Player)
6515 Teton Dr
Lincoln, NE 68510-4123

Getherall, Joey (Athlete, Football Player)
3105 Las Marias Ave
Hacienda Heights, CA 91745-6219, USA

Gethers, Peter (Writer)
c/o Catherine Brackey *ICM Partners (LA)*
10250 Constellation Blvd Fl 7
Los Angeles, CA 90067-6207, USA

Gets, Malcolm (Actor)
c/o Lisa Loosemore *Viking Entertainment*
445 W 23rd St Ste 1A
New York, NY 10011-1445, USA

Gettis, Byron (Athlete, Baseball Player)
6313 Whalen Ave
East Saint Louis, IL 62207-1051, USA

Getty, Andrew
2936 Montcalm Ave
Los Angeles, CA 90046-1304

Getty, Balthazar (Actor)
c/o Jeff Golenberg *Silver Lining Entertainment*
421 S Beverly Dr Fl 7
Beverly Hills, CA 90212-4408, USA

Getty, Charlie (Athlete, Football Player)
3736 W Morningside St
Springfield, MO 65807-5581, USA

Getty, Gordon
2880 Broadway St
San Francisco, CA 94115-1061

Get Up Kids (Music Group)
c/o Staff Member *Creative Artists Agency (CAA-LA)*
2000 Avenue of the Stars Ste 100
Los Angeles, CA 90067-4705, USA

Getz, John (Actor)
3613 Greenwood Ave
Los Angeles, CA 90066-3017, USA

Getzlaff, James (Actor)
c/o Staff Member *Douglas Gorman Rothacker & Wilhelm Inc*
1501 Broadway Ste 703
New York, NY 10036-5501, USA

Geyer, Dean (Actor)
c/o David Seltzer *Management 360*
9111 Wilshire Blvd
Beverly Hills, CA 90210-5508, USA

Geyer, Georgie Anne (Journalist)
The Plaza Suite 800 25th St NW
Washington, DC 20037, USA

Geyer, Hugh (Music Group)
2218 Ridge Rd
McKeesport, PA 15135-3037, USA

G. Fitzpatrick, Michael (Congressman, Politician)
1224 Longworth Hob
Washington, DC 20515-0553, USA

G. Grimm, Michael (Congressman, Politician)
512 Cannon Hob
Washington, DC 20515-1012, USA

Ghaffari, Matt (Athlete, Olympic Athlete, Wrestler)
32834 Fox Chappel Ln
Avon Lake, OH 44012-2331, USA

Ghauri, Yasmeen (Model)
c/o Staff Member *Next Model Management (NY)*
15 Watts St Fl 6
New York, NY 10013-1677, USA

Ghelfi, Tony (Athlete, Baseball Player)
3414 Geneva Ln
La Crosse, WI 54601-8302, USA

Ghigliotti, Marilyn (Actor)
Redrock Entertainment Development
118 S Cordova St Fl 3
Burbank, CA 91505-4610, USA

Ghost, Amanda (Musician)
c/o Staff Member *Basina Recording Company*
PO Box 8121
Pittsburgh, PA 15217-0121, USA

Ghostface, Killa (Music Group, Musician)
Famous Artists Agency
250 W 57th St
New York, NY 10107-0001, USA

Ghostland Observatory (Music Group)
c/o Staff Member *Paradigm (Monterey)*
404 W Franklin St
Monterey, CA 93940-2303, USA

Ghuman Jr, JB (Actor)
c/o Harry Gold *TalentWorks (LA)*
3500 W Olive Ave Ste 1400
Burbank, CA 91505-5512, USA

Giacchino, Michael (Musician)
4740 Viviana Dr
Tarzana, CA 91356-5039, USA

Giacomarro, Ralph (Athlete, Football Player)
307 Canterbury Rd
Gainesville, GA 30504-2666, USA

Giacomin, Edward (Eddie) (Athlete, Hockey Player)
6575 Red Maple Ln
Bloomfield Hills, MI 48301-3225, USA

Giaffone, Felipe (Race Car Driver)
Conquest Racing
5062 W 79th St
Indianapolis, IN 46268-1645, USA

Giallombardo, Bob (Athlete, Baseball Player)
7903 Antique Cir
Waxhaw, NC 28173-7858, USA

Giamatti, Marcus
c/o Mitchell Stubbs *Mitchell K Stubbs & Assoc (MKS)*
8675 Washington Blvd Ste 203
Culver City, CA 90232-7486, USA

Giamatti, Paul (Actor)
187 Hicks St Apt 4D
Brooklyn, NY 11201-2380, USA

Giambalvo, Louis (Actor)
c/o Staff Member *Judy Schoen & Associates*
606 N Larchmont Blvd Ste 309
Los Angeles, CA 90004-1309, USA

Giambi, Jason (Athlete, Baseball Player)
34 Isleworth Dr
Henderson, NV 89052-6465, USA

Giambi, Jeremy (Athlete, Baseball Player)
23360 S Power Rd
Gilbert, AZ 85298-8904, USA

Giambra, Joey (Boxer)
4673 Ashington St
Las Vegas, NV 89147-6068, USA

Giambrone, Art (Horse Racer)
398 Brickyard Rd
Freehold, NJ 07728-8414, USA

Giammona, Louie (Athlete, Football Player)
116 Manton St
Philadelphia, PA 19147-5423, USA

Gian, Joey (Musician)
Joey Gian Entertainment
13351D Riverside Dr # 294
Sherman Oaks, CA 91423-2508, USA

Gian, Joseph
8271 Melrose Ave Ste 110
Los Angeles, CA 90046-6800

Giancanelli, Hal (Athlete, Football Player)
2227 Portola Ln
Westlake Village, CA 91361-1748, USA

Giancola, Sammi (Reality Star)
c/o Sal Bonaventura *CEG Talent*
251 W 39th St Fl 7
New York, NY 10018-3171, USA

Gianelli, John (Athlete, Basketball Player)
PO Box 1097
Pinecrest, CA 95364-0097, USA

Giannelli, Ray (Athlete, Baseball Player)
56 E Saltaire Rd
Lindenhurst, NY 11757-6829, USA

Giannoulas, Ted (Commentator)
6549 Mission Gorge Rd Ste 247
San Diego, CA 92120-2306, USA

Gianopoulos, David (Actor)
c/o Staff Member *GVA Talent Agency Inc*
8981 W Sunset Blvd Ste 101
West Hollywood, CA 90069-1850, USA

Gianulias, Nicole (Nikki) (Bowler)
Ladies Professional Bowling Tour
7200 Harrison Ave # 7171
Rockford, IL 61112-1017, USA

Giaquinto, Nick (Athlete, Football Player)
316 3rd Ave
Stratford, CT 06615-7736, USA

Giarraputo, Jack (Producer, Writer)
c/o Staff Member *Happy Madison Productions*
10202 Washington Blvd
Judy Garland Bldg
Culver City, CA 90232-3119, USA

Giarratano, Tony (Athlete, Baseball Player)
17 Winnetka Ln
Saint Louis, MO 63122-3220, USA

Gibara, Samir (Business Person)
Goodyear Tire & Rubber
1144 W Market St
Akron, OH 44316-0001, USA

Gibb, Barry (Musician, Songwriter)
c/o Paul Bloch *Rogers & Cowan PR (LA)*
8687 Melrose Ave Ste 7
West Hollywood, CA 90069-5721, USA

Gibb, Cynthia (Actor)
c/o Scott Hart *Scott Hart Entertainment*
14622 Ventura Blvd # 746
Sherman Oaks, CA 91403-3600, USA

Gibb, Donald (Actor)
Ashby/Rojo Entertainment
1485 S Beverly Dr
Los Angeles, CA 90035-3021, USA

Gibbard, Ben (Musician)
c/o Staff Member *Zeitgeist Artist Management*
600 York St # 216
San Francisco, CA 94110-2119, USA

Gibbon, Joe (Athlete, Baseball Player)
26 County Road 24142
Newton, MS 39345-8946, USA

Gibbons, Billy (Music Group, Musician)
c/o Rick Canny *Sanctuary Artist Management*
8750 Wilshire Blvd Ste 200
Beverly Hills, CA 90211-2707, USA

Gibbons, Brian (Athlete, Baseball Player)
51788 Whitestable Ln
South Bend, IN 46637-1370, USA

Gibbons, Gail (Writer)
c/o Staff Member *Simon & Schuster*
1230 Avenue of the Americas Fl CONC1
New York, NY 10020-1586, USA

Gibbons, Jay (Athlete, Baseball Player)
1659 Ryder Cup Dr
Westlake Village, CA 91362-4325, USA

Gibbons, Jim (Athlete, Football Player)
891 Valley Rd
Carbondale, CO 81623-9712, USA

Gibbons, John (Athlete, Baseball Player, Coach)
3602 Hunters Quail
San Antonio, TX 78230-2052, USA

Gibbons, Kaye (Writer)
c/o Lynn Pleshette *Lynn Pleshette Literary Agency*
2700 N Beachwood Dr
Los Angeles, CA 90068-1922, USA

Gibbons, Leeza (Producer, Television Host)
c/o Rick Bradley *Celebrity Consultants LLC*
3340 Ocean Park Blvd Ste 1030
Santa Monica, CA 90405-3259, USA

Gibbons, Tim (Producer)
c/o Staff Member *ICM Partners (LA)*
10250 Constellation Blvd Fl 7
Los Angeles, CA 90067-6207, USA

Gibbons, Walter (Athlete, Baseball Player)
103 E North St
Tampa, FL 33604-6156, USA

Gibbs, Bob (Congressman, Politician)
329 Cannon Hob
Washington, DC 20515-4607, USA

Gibbs, Connor (Actor)
c/o Geoff Cheddy *Brillstein Entertainment Partners (LA)*
9150 Wilshire Blvd Ste 350
Beverly Hills, CA 90212-3453, USA

Gibbs, Coy (Race Car Driver)
c/o Staff Member *NASCAR*
1801 W Speedway Blvd
Daytona Beach, FL 32114-1243, USA

Gibbs, H Jarrell (Business Person)
Texas Utilities Co
Energy Plaza 1601 Bryan St
Dallas, TX 75201, USA

Gibbs, Jake (Athlete, Baseball Player)
223 Saint Andrews Cir
Oxford, MS 38655-2518, USA

Gibbs, Joe (Athlete, Football Player)
19133 Peninsula Point Dr
Cornelius, NC 28031-7603, USA

Gibbs, Joe (Athlete, Football Coach, Football Player, Race Car Driver)
Joe Gibbs Racing
19122 Peninsula Point Dr
Cornelius, NC 28031, USA

Gibbs, Lawrence B (Government Official)
Miller & Chevaliar
655 15th St NW Ste 900
Washington, DC 20005-5799, USA

Gibbs, Marla (Actor, Music Group)
3500 W Manchester Blvd Unit 267
Inglewood, CA 90305-4267, USA

Gibbs, Mickey (Race Car Driver)
3 Grandview Cir
Gadsden, AL 35905-8837, USA

Gibbs, Pat (Athlete, Football Player)
4835 Corley St
Beaumont, TX 77707-4224, USA

Gibbs, Sonny (Athlete, Football Player)
2708 Halbert St
Fort Worth, TX 76112-5531, USA

Gibbs, Terri (Musician, Songwriter)
1439 Clary Cut Rd
Harlem, GA 30814-3109, USA

Gibbs, Terry (Music Group, Musician)
Thomas Cassidy
11761 E Speedway Blvd
Tucson, AZ 85748-2017, USA

Gibbs, Timothy (Actor)
c/o Julia Buchwald *Don Buchwald & Associates (LA)*
6500 Wilshire Blvd Ste 2200
Los Angeles, CA 90048-4942, USA

Gibgot, Adam (Writer)
c/o Adriana Alberghetti *William Morris Endeavor (LA)*
9601 Wilshire Blvd
Beverly Hills, CA 90210-5213, USA

Giblett, Eloise R (Doctor, Misc)
2518 3rd Ave W
Seattle, WA 98119-2306, USA

Giblin, Robert (Athlete, Football Player)
2818 Reynolds Ln
Port Neches, TX 77651-5410, USA

Gibney, Susan (Actor)
c/o Matthew Lesher *Insight*
PO Box 36359
Los Angeles, CA 90036-0359, USA

Gibralter, Steve (Athlete, Baseball Player)
3012 Barton Springs Ln
Rockwall, TX 75087-6427, USA

Gibraltor, Steve (Athlete, Baseball Player)
3651 Asbury St
Dallas, TX 75205-1848, USA

Gibson, Aaron (Athlete, Football Player)
1777 Timber Creek Rd Apt 2122
Flower Mound, TX 75028-7342, USA

Gibson, Andy (Musician)
c/o Staff Member *Curb Records (Nashville)*
48 Music Sq E
Nashville, TN 37203-4639, USA

Gibson, Antonio (Athlete, Football Player)
2320 Jaguar Dr Apt 502
Bryan, TX 77807-2346, USA

Gibson, Bob (Athlete, Basketball Player)
1409 N 113th Ct Apt 5823
Omaha, NE 68154-5842, USA

Gibson, Bob (Athlete, Baseball Player)
215 Bellevue Blvd S
Bellevue, NE 68005-2442, USA

Gibson, Charles (Television Host)
c/o Staff Member *ABC News*
77 W 66th St Fl 3
New York, NY 10023-6201, USA

Gibson, Claude (Athlete, Football Player)
47 Gladstone Rd
Asheville, NC 28805-2454, USA

Gibson, Damon (Athlete, Football Player)
4332 Dell Rd Apt J
Lansing, MI 48911-8126, USA

Gibson, Deborah (Debbie) (Actor, Musician)
156 W 56th St Ste 1803
New York, NY 10019-3899, USA

Gibson, Dennis (Athlete, Football Player)
6900 NE 11th Ct
Ankeny, IA 50023-9300, USA

Gibson, Derrick (Athlete, Baseball Player)
138 Buckeye Loop Rd
Winter Haven, FL 33881-2703, USA

Gibson, Derrick (Athlete, Football Player)
303 Avenue O NW
Winter Haven, FL 33881, USA

Gibson, Edward G (Astronaut)
Aviation Management Services
1658 S Litchfield Rd
Goodyear, AZ 85338-1509, USA

Gibson, Edward G Dr (Astronaut)
34022 N 85th St
Scottsdale, AZ 85266-1345, USA

Gibson, Ellie (Athlete, Golfer)
35705 N 29th Ln
Phoenix, AZ 85086-4219, USA

Gibson, Ernest (Athlete, Football Player)
1749 Kinsmon Cv
Marietta, GA 30062-8173, USA

Gibson, Fred (Athlete, Golfer)
2006 Avenel St
Orlando, FL 32828-7813, USA

Gibson, Greg (Athlete, Baseball Player)
5222 Dog Fork Laurel Rd
Catlettsburg, KY 41129-9019, USA

Gibson, Greg (Baseball Player)
3628 Briarwood Dr
Catlettsburg, KY 41129-9298, USA

Gibson, Janice (Athlete, Golfer)
9747 S Granite Ave
Tulsa, OK 74137-4931, USA

Gibson, John (Correspondent)
c/o Staff Member *Fox News (NY)*
1211 Avenue of the Americas Lowr C1
New York, NY 10036-8705, USA

Gibson, Kelly (Athlete, Golfer)
PO Box 57478
New Orleans, LA 70157-7478, USA

Gibson, Kirk (Athlete, Baseball Player)
15135 Charlevoix St
Grosse Pointe Park, MI 48230-1007, USA

Gibson, Laurieann (Dancer)
c/o Stephanie Molina *Rogers & Cowan PR (LA)*
8687 Melrose Ave Ste 7
West Hollywood, CA 90069-5721, USA

Gibson, Leah (Actor)
c/o Kim Matuka *Online Talent Group*
Prefers to be contacted via email or
telephone
West Hollywood, CA 90069, USA

Gibson, Mark (Race Car Driver)
Mark Gibson Racing
308 Wages Rd
Auburn, GA 30011-2856, USA

Gibson, Mel (Actor, Director, Producer)
22313 Carbon Mesa Rd
Malibu, CA 90265-5014, USA

Gibson, Oliver (Athlete, Football Player)
1448 E 52nd St # 406
Chicago, IL 60615-4122, USA

Gibson, Paul (Athlete, Baseball Player)
23421 Water Cir
Boca Raton, FL 33486-8547, USA

Gibson, Robert L
1709 Shagbark Trl
Murfreesboro, TN 37130-1136, USA

Gibson, Robert L Captain (Astronaut)
1709 Shagbark Trl
Murfreesboro, TN 37130-1136, USA

Gibson, Robert L (Hoot) (Astronaut)
1709 Shagbark Trl
Murfreesboro, TN 37130-1136, USA

Gibson, Russ (Athlete)
495 Gardners Neck Rd
Swansea, MA 02777-3131, USA

Gibson, Thomas (Actor, Director)
c/o Craig Dorfman *Frontline Management*
5670 Wilshire Blvd Ste 1370
Los Angeles, CA 90036-5679, USA

Gibson, Tyrese (Actor, Musician,
Producer)
c/o Craig Shapiro *ICM Partners (LA)*
10250 Constellation Blvd Fl 7
Los Angeles, CA 90067-6207, USA

Gibson, William (Writer)
General Delivery
Stockbridge, MA 01262-9999, USA

Gick, George (Athlete, Baseball Player)
875 Elston Rd
Lafayette, IN 47909-6322, USA

Giddish, Kelli (Actor)
c/o Jean-Louis Diamonika *One
Entertainment (NY)*
12 W 57th St PH
New York, NY 10019-3900, USA

Gideon, Brett (Athlete, Baseball Player)
PO Box 822
Georgetown, TX 78627-0822, USA

Gideon, Jim (Athlete, Baseball Player)
2509 McCallum Dr
Austin, TX 78703-2520, USA

Gideon, Raynold (Actor, Writer)
3524 Multiview Dr
Los Angeles, CA 90068-1222, USA

Gidley, Pamela (Actor)
c/o Tom Harrison *Diverse Talent Group*
9911 W Pico Blvd Ste 340W
Los Angeles, CA 90035-2703, USA

Giella, Joseph (Cartoonist)
191 Morris St
East Meadow, NY 11554-1317, USA

Gien, Pamela (Actor, Writer)
c/o Heather Schroder *ICM Partners (NY)*
730 5th Ave
New York, NY 10019-4105, USA

Gierasch, Stefan (Actor)
c/o Staff Member *Brandon's Commercials
Unlimited*
8383 Wilshire Blvd Ste 850
Beverly Hills, CA 90211-2443, USA

Gierer, Vincent A Jr (Business Person)
UST Inc
100 W Putnam Ave
Greenwich, CT 06830-5361, USA

Giesler, Jon (Athlete, Football Player)
129 Umbrella Pl
Jupiter, FL 33458-1622, USA

Giessinger, Andrew (Athlete, Football
Player)
1667 Union Ave
Barberton, OH 44203-7644, USA

Gietzen, Pam (Athlete, Golfer)
1029 Windstone Dr
Woodway, TX 76712-7500, USA

Gifford, Frank (Athlete, Football Player,
Sportscaster)
Lambchop Productions
PO Box 275
Cos Cob, CT 06807-0275, USA

Gifford, Gloria (Actor)
Schiowitz/Clay/Rose
1680 Vine St Ste 1016
Los Angeles, CA 90028-8800, USA

Gifford, Kathie Lee (Television Host)
c/o Staff Member *The Today Show*
30 Rockefeller Plz
New York, NY 10112-0015, USA

Giffords, Gabrielle (Congressman,
Politician)
Americans For Responsible Solutions PAC
PO Box 15642
Washington, DC 20003-0642, USA

Gigandet, Cam (Actor)
3329 Cabrillo Blvd
Los Angeles, CA 90066-1501, USA

Giggie, Bob (Athlete, Baseball Player)
8 Royal Lake Dr Apt 3
Braintree, MA 02184-5457, USA

Gigli, Romeo (Designer, Fashion
Designer)
37 W 57th St Ste 900
New York, NY 10019-3411, USA

Gigliotti, Lou (Race Car Driver)
LG Motorsports
4314 Action St
Garland, TX 75042-6805, USA

Gigon, Norm (Athlete, Baseball Player)
201 Paxinosa Rd E
Easton, PA 18040-1334, USA

Gigot, Paul (Journalist)
Wall Street Journal
200 Liberty St
New York, NY 10281-1003, USA

Giguere, Jean-Sebastien (Athlete, Hockey
Player)
2066 Port Bristol Cir
Newport Beach, CA 92660-5413, USA

Giguere, Russ (Music Group, Musician)
Variety Artists
1924 Spring St
Paso Robles, CA 93446-1620, USA

Gil, Benii (Athlete, Baseball Player)
11712 Wild Pear Ln
Fort Worth, TX 76244-8815, USA

Gil, Geronimo (Athlete, Baseball Player)
c/o Staff Member *Baltimore Orioles*
333 W Camden St
Baltimore, MD 21201-2496, USA

Gil, Gus (Athlete, Baseball Player)
2240 SW 42nd Ter
Fort Lauderdale, FL 33317-6618, USA

Gil, R Benjamin (Benji) (Athlete, Baseball
Player)
504 Unbridled Ln
Keller, TX 76248-8724, USA

Gilberry, Wallace (Athlete, Football
Player)
c/o Jimmy Sexton *CAA (Memphis)*
6060 Poplar Ave Ste 470
Memphis, TN 38119-0910, USA

Gilbert, Brad
888 17th St NW Ste 1200
Washington, DC 20006-3320

Gilbert, Brad (Athlete, Tennis Player)
ProServe
1101 Woodrow Wilson Blvd # 1800
Arlington, VA 22209, USA

Gilbert, Brantley (Musician)
152 Courtland Dr
Jefferson, GA 30549-6732, USA

Gilbert, Buddy (Athlete, Baseball Player)
1913 Belcaro Dr
Knoxville, TN 37918-3709, USA

Gilbert, Chris (Athlete, Football Player)
6619 Blue Hills Rd
Houston, TX 77069-2412, USA

Gilbert, Daren (Athlete, Football Player)
6945 Edinboro St
Chino, CA 91710-1339, USA

Gilbert, David (Cartoonist)
c/o Staff Member *King Features
Syndication*
300 W 57th St Fl 15
New York, NY 10019-5238, USA

Gilbert, Ed (Athlete, Hockey Player)
657 Jacksonville Rd
Warminster, PA 18974-1508, USA

Gilbert, Elizabeth (Writer)
c/o Sarah Chalfant *The Andrew Wylie
Agency*
250 W 57th St Ste 2114
New York, NY 10107-2114, USA

Gilbert, Elsie
1016 N Orange Grove Ave Apt 4
West Hollywood, CA 90046-6127

Gilbert, Freddie (Athlete, Football Player)
110 Camden Rd
Griffin, GA 30223-1677, USA

Gilbert, Gary (Producer)
c/o Staff Member *Gilbert Films*
8409 Santa Monica Blvd
West Hollywood, CA 90069-4209, USA

Gilbert, Gibby (Athlete, Golfer)
7070 Sunset Mountain Dr
Chattanooga, TN 37421, USA

Gilbert, Joe (Athlete, Baseball Player)
512 W Martin Luther King Blvd
Jasper, TX 75951-2527, USA

Gilbert, Justin (Athlete, Football Player)
c/o Jimmy Sexton *CAA (Memphis)*
6060 Poplar Ave Ste 470
Memphis, TN 38119-0910, USA

Gilbert, Lewis (Athlete, Football Player)
6331 SW 1st St
Plantation, FL 33317-3407, USA

Gilbert, Mark (Athlete, Baseball Player)
PO Box 3326
Palm Beach, FL 33480-1526, USA

Gilbert, Melissa (Actor)
c/o Marc Schwartz *Fusion Management*
2314 San Ysidro Dr
Beverly Hills, CA 90210-1556, USA

Gilbert, O'Neill (Athlete, Coach, Football
Coach, Football Player)
460 Great Circle Rd
Nashville, TN 37228-1404, USA

Gilbert, Peter (Director)
Innovative Artists
1505 10th St
Santa Monica, CA 90401-2805, USA

Gilbert, Richard W (Publisher)
Des Moines Register & Tribune
715 Locust St
Des Moines, IA 50309-3703, USA

Gilbert, Rod
2 Penn Plz Fl 22
Attn: Director, Special Projects
New York, NY 10121-2299, USA

Gilbert, Rodrique G (Rod) (Athlete,
Hockey Player)
52 E End Ave Apt 33A
New York, NY 10028-8116, USA

Gilbert, Ronnie (Music Group)
Donna Korones Mgmt
PO Box 8388
Berkeley, CA 94707-8388, USA

Gilbert, Sara (Actor, Talk Show Host)
1355 Devlin Dr
Los Angeles, CA 90069-1801, USA

Gilbert, Sean (Athlete, Football Player)
7912 Baltusrol Ln
Charlotte, NC 28210-4933, USA

Gilbert, Shawn (Athlete, Baseball Player)
9656 Kathleen Dr
Cypress, CA 90630-4023, USA

Gilbert, S J Sr (Religious Leader)
Baptist Convention of America
6717 Centennial Blvd
Nashville, TN 37209-1017, USA

Gilberto, Astrud (Music Group)
Absolute Artists
530 Howard St Ste 200
San Francisco, CA 94105-3018, USA

Gilbertson, Bob (Race Car Driver)
2250 Toomey Ave
Charlotte, NC 28203-4635, USA

Gilbertson, Harrison (Actor)
c/o Laina Cohn *Cohn / Torgan Management*
Prefers to be contacted by telephone or email
Los Angeles, CA, USA

Gilbertson, Keith (Coach, Football Coach)
University of Washington
Athletic Dept
Seattle, WA 98195-0001, USA

Gilbertson, Stan (Athlete, Hockey Player)
2924 Mosswood Dr
Lodi, CA 95242-2051, USA

Gilbreath, Rod (Athlete, Baseball Player)
1438 Ridgeland Way SW
Lilburn, GA 30047-4352, USA

Gilbreth, Bill (Athlete, Baseball Player)
709 Gary Ln
Abilene, TX 79601-5537, USA

Gilbride, Kevin (Athlete, Coach, Football Player)
3400 S Water St
Pittsburgh, PA 15203-2349, USA

Gilburg, Tom (Athlete, Football Player)
35 Hess Blvd
Lancaster, PA 17601-4043, USA

Gilchrist, Guy (Cartoonist)
20 Bristol Dr
Canton, CT 06019-2214, USA

Gilchrist, Keir (Actor)
c/o Willie Mercer *Thruline Entertainment*
9250 Wilshire Blvd Ste 100
Ground Floor
Beverly Hills, CA 90212-3343, USA

Gilchrist, Pual R (Religious Leader)
Presbyterian Church in America
1862 Century Pl
Atlanta, GA 30345, USA

Gilder, Bob (Athlete, Golfer)
1977 NW Bonney Dr
Corvallis, OR 97330-9161, USA

Gildon, Jason (Athlete, Football Player)
1562 Barrington Dr
Wexford, PA 15090-9377, USA

Gile, Don (Athlete, Baseball Player)
624 W Cherokee Ave
Stillwater, OK 74075-1405, USA

Giles, Bill (Commentator)
Philadelphia Phillies
1400 Waverly Rd Apt B317
Gladwyne, PA 19035-1269, USA

Giles, Brian (Athlete, Baseball Player)
8020 Las Vegas Blvd S # 81
Las Vegas, NV 89123-1014, USA

Giles, Curt (Athlete, Hockey Player)
5225 Grandview Sq Apt 402
Minneapolis, MN 55436-1691, USA

Giles, Jimmie (Athlete, Football Player)
3959 Van Dyke Rd # 298
Lutz, FL 33558-8025, USA

Giles, Marcus (Athlete, Baseball Player)
26132 Old Highway 80
Descanso, CA 91916-9797, USA

Giles, Nancy (Actor)
12047 178th St
Jamaica, NY 11434-2719, USA

Giles, Sandra
350 N Crescent Dr Apt 108
Beverly Hills, CA 90210-4875

Gilfillan, Jason (Athlete, Baseball Player)
153 Gilfillan Rd
Blacksburg, SC 29702-8521, USA

Gilford, Zach (Actor)
c/o Charles Mastropietro *Circle of Confusion (LA)*
8931 Ellis Ave
Los Angeles, CA 90034-3336, USA

Gilk, Shelley (Athlete, Golfer)
10537 Toledo Dr N
Minneapolis, MN 55443-5424, USA

Gilkey, Bernard (Athlete, Baseball Player)
2200 Dunhill Way Ct
Chesterfield, MO 63005-4511, USA

Gill, George N (Publisher)
Louisville Courier-Journal & Times
525 W Broadway
Louisville, KY 40202-2137, USA

Gill, Hal (Athlete, Hockey Player)
11 Reiling Pond Rd
Lincoln, MA 01773-2311, USA

Gill, Janis (Music Group)
Monty Hitchcock Mgmt
5101 Overton Rd
Nashville, TN 37220-1920, USA

Gill, Johnny (Music Group, Musician, Songwriter, Writer)
4924 Balboa Blvd # 366
Encino, CA 91316-3402, USA

Gill, Johnny Ray (Actor)
c/o Jordyn Palos *Persona PR (LA)*
8840 Wilshire Blvd Ste 212
Beverly Hills, CA 90211-2606, USA

Gill, Kendall (Athlete, Basketball Player)
c/o Staff Member *Milwaukee Bucks*
1001 N 4th St Ste 1
Milwaukee, WI 53203-1312, USA

Gill, Michael (Actor)
c/o David Williams *David Williams Management*
9614 W Olympic Blvd Apt F
Beverly Hills, CA 90212-3761, USA

Gill, Thea (Actor)
c/o Cynthia Campos-Greenberg *Anthem Entertainment*
9595 Wilshire Blvd Ste 900
Beverly Hills, CA 90212-2509, USA

Gill, Tonya (Athlete, Golfer)
3655 Habersham Rd NE Apt B2229
Atlanta, GA 30305-1142, USA

Gill, Vince (Musician, Songwriter)
515 Park Center Ave
Nashville, TN 37205-3429, USA

Gill, William A Jr (Government Official, Misc)
15975 Cove Ln
Dumfries, VA 22025-1412, USA

Gillanders, David (Athlete, Olympic Athlete, Swimmer)
1617 Briarwood Dr
Jonesboro, AR 72401-4632, USA

Gillaspie, Conor (Athlete, Baseball Player)
5601 Pacific St
Omaha, NE 68106-1640, USA

Gillbreath, Rod (Baseball Player)
Atlanta Braves
1438 Ridgeland Way SW
Lilburn, GA 30047-4352, USA

Gillen, Aidan (Actor)
c/o Leanne Coronel *Coronel Group*
1100 Glendon Ave Fl 17
Los Angeles, CA 90024-3588, USA

Gilles, Tom (Athlete, Baseball Player)
14615 W Southern St
Princeville, IL 61559-9375, USA

Gillespie, Ann (Actor)
Greene Assoc
7080 Hollywood Blvd Ste 1017
Los Angeles, CA 90028-6937, USA

Gillespie, Cole (Athlete, Baseball Player)
5455 Summit St
West Linn, OR 97068-2822, USA

Gillespie, Craig (Director)
c/o Simon Millar *Rumble Media*
1620 Broadway Ste C
Santa Monica, CA 90404-2777, USA

Gillespie, Darlene (Actor)
2117 Bermuda Dunes Pl
Oxnard, CA 93036-2787, USA

Gillespie, Jack (Athlete, Basketball Player)
1104 37th Ave NE
Great Falls, MT 59404-4722, USA

Gillespie, Willie (Athlete, Football Player)
102 Aztec Dr
Starkville, MS 39759-2006, USA

Gillette (Musician)
c/o Staff Member *Diva Central Inc*
7510 W Sunset Blvd Ste 1445
Los Angeles, CA 90046-3408, USA

Gillette, Anita (Actor)
501 S Beverly Dr Fl 3
Beverly Hills, CA 90212-4520, USA

Gillette, Walker (Athlete, Football Player)
401 N College Dr
Franklin, VA 23851-2401, USA

Gilley, Mickey (Music Group, Songwriter, Writer)
Gilley's Interests
PO Box 1242
Pasadena, TX 77501-1242, USA

Gilliam, Burton
1427 Tascosa Ct
Allen, TX 75013-1111

Gilliam, Dondre (Athlete, Football Player)
6858 Sturbridge Dr Apt D
Parkville, MD 21234-7426, USA

Gilliam, Elijah (Baseball Player)
Birmingham Black Barons
1617 5th Ave N
Birmingham, AL 35203-1953, USA

Gilliam, John (Athlete, Football Player)
4045 Moheb St SW
Atlanta, GA 30331-6418, USA

Gilliam, Jon (Athlete, Football Player)
440 S Walnut Grove Rd
Midlothian, TX 76065-6206, USA

Gilliam, Seth (Actor)
c/o Jason Gutman *Gersh (NY)*
41 Madison Ave
New York, NY 10010-2202, USA

Gilliand, David (Race Car Driver)
7777 Woodland Dr
Indianapolis, IN 46278-1794, USA

Gilliand, Herman (Baseball Player)
Chicago Cubs
1833 Kern Mountain Way
Antioch, CA 94531-7497, USA

Gilliard, Cory (Athlete, Football Player)
3951 Zinsle Ave
Cincinnati, OH 45213-2348, USA

Gillick, Pat (Commentator)
PO Box 99405
Seattle, WA 98139-0405, USA

Gillie, Nick (Producer)
c/o Staff Member *Metropolitan (MTA)*
4526 Wilshire Blvd
Los Angeles, CA 90010-3801, USA

Gillies, Clark (Athlete, Hockey Player)
17 Pinta Ct
Greenlawn, NY 11740-2314, USA

Gillies, Daniel (Actor, Director, Writer)
c/o Ben Levine *LINK Entertainment*
11872 La Grange Ave Fl 1
Los Angeles, CA 90025-5283, USA

Gillies, Elizabeth (Actor)
c/o Amy Zvi *Thruline Entertainment*
9250 Wilshire Blvd Ste 100
Ground Floor
Beverly Hills, CA 90212-3343, USA

Gillies, Isabel (Actor, Writer)
315 W 106th St Apt 8A
New York, NY 10025-3475, USA

Gilliford, Paul (Athlete, Baseball Player)
7 Woodland Dr
Malvern, PA 19355-3308, USA

Gillig, Tony (Race Car Driver)
Gillig Motorsports
PO Box 823
Lake Zurich, IL 60047-0823, USA

Gilligan, Vince (Producer, Writer)
c/o Mark Gordon *ICM Partners (LA)*
10250 Constellation Blvd Fl 7
Los Angeles, CA 90067-6207, USA

Gillilan, William J III (Business Person)
Centex Corp
PO Box 199000
Dallas, TX 75219-9000, USA

Gilliland, Butch (Race Car Driver)
Gilliland Racing
912 N Anaheim Blvd
Anaheim, CA 92805-1903, USA

Gilliland, David (Race Car Driver)
The Racers Group
292 Rolling Hill Rd
Mooresville, NC 28117-6845, USA

Gilliland, Richard (Actor)
c/o Anthony DeMichele *Beacon Talent Agency*
170 Apple Ridge Rd
Woodcliff Lake, NJ 07677-8149, USA

Gillingwater, Leah (Reality Star)
c/o Staff Member *Real World, The*
6007 Sepulveda Blvd
Van Nuys, CA 91411-2502, USA

Gillis, Don (Athlete, Football Player)
4658 Oso Pkwy
Corpus Christi, TX 78413-5269, USA

Gillis, Louis (Baseball Player)
Birmingham Black Barons
2920 33rd Way N
Birmingham, AL 35207-3720, USA

Gillis, Paul
2210 Medford Ct
Odessa, TX 79762-4504, USA

Gillis, Tom (Athlete, Golfer)
527 Tanview Dr
Oxford, MI 48371-4769, USA

Gillom, Jennifer (Basketball Player)
c/o Staff Member *LA Sparks*
555 N Nash St
El Segundo, CA 90245-2818, USA

Gillooly (Stone), Jeff
10408 SE 82nd Ave
Portland, OR 97266

Gillow, Russ (Athlete, Hockey Player)
1517 W Songbird Dr
Saint George, UT 84790-7261, USA

Gilman, Billy (Music Group)
c/o Rodney Essig *Creative Artists Agency (CAA-TN)*
401 Commerce St PH
Nashville, TN 37219-2516, USA

Gilman, Kenneth B (Business Person)
Limited Inc
3 Limited Pkwy
P O Box 1600
Columbus, OH 43230-1467, USA

Gilman, Richard H (Publisher)
Boston Globe
135 William T Morrissey Blvd # T
Publisher's Office
Dorchester, MA 02125-3310, USA

Gilman, Sid (Doctor, Misc)
3441 Geddes Rd
Ann Arbor, MI 48105, USA

Gilmartin, Paul (Comedian)
c/o Staff Member *Agency for the Performing Arts (APA-LA)*
405 S Beverly Dr Ste 500
Beverly Hills, CA 90212-4425, USA

Gilmartin, Raymond V (Business Person)
Merck Co
PO Box 100
Whitehouse Station, NJ 08889-0100, USA

Gilmer, Harry V (Athlete, Football Player)
7467 Highway N
O Fallon, MO 63368-7003, USA

Gilmore, Artis (Athlete, Basketball Player)
11043 Turnbridge Dr
Jacksonville, FL 32256-2329, USA

Gilmore, Bryan (Athlete, Football Player)
123 Houston St
Lufkin, TX 75904, USA

Gilmore, Jared (Actor)
c/o David Dean Portelli *David Dean Management*
Prefers to be contacted via telephone or email
Los Angeles, CA, USA

Gilmore, Jimmie Dale (Music Group, Songwriter, Writer)
c/o Staff Member *Concerted Efforts*
PO Box 440326
Somerville, MA 02144-0004, USA

Gilmore, Stephon (Athlete, Football Player)
c/o Alan Herman *Sportstars Inc*
1350 Avenue of the Americas Fl 28
New York, NY 10019-4702, USA

Gilmore, Walt (Athlete, Basketball Player)
257 Benjamin Blvd
Bear, DE 19701-1693, USA

Gilmour, Buddy (Horse Racer)
50 Merrick Ave Unit 410
East Meadow, NY 11554-1593, USA

Gilmour, David (Music Group, Musician)
c/o Steve Martin *The Agency Group (NYC)*
142 W 57th St Fl 6
New York, NY 10019-3300, USA

Gilmour, George (Horse Racer)
1445 NW 69th Ave
Margate, FL 33063-2552, USA

Gilmur, Chuck (Athlete, Basketball Player)
PO Box 64290
Tacoma, WA 98464-0290, USA

Gilpin, Peri (Actor)
c/o Joanna (Joanie) Burstein *Burstein Company, The*
15304 W Sunset Blvd Ste 208
Pacific Palisades, CA 90272-3656, USA

Gilroy, Frank D (Writer)
8 Mangin Rd
Monroe, NY 10950-2203, USA

Gilroy, Tom (Actor, Director, Producer, Writer)
c/o Staff Member *William Morris Endeavor (LA)*
9601 Wilshire Blvd
Beverly Hills, CA 90210-5213, USA

Gilroy, Tony (Director, Writer)
c/o Risa Gertner *Creative Artists Agency (CAA-LA)*
2000 Avenue of the Stars Ste 100
Los Angeles, CA 90067-4705, USA

Gilsig, Jessalyn (Actor)
c/o Steven Levy *Framework Entertainment (LA)*
9057 Nemo St Ste C
West Hollywood, CA 90069-5511, USA

Gilson, Hal (Athlete, Baseball Player)
15247 E Sage Dr
Fountain Hills, AZ 85268-4373, USA

Gimbel, Norman (Songwriter, Writer)
PO Box 50013
Santa Barbara, CA 93150-0013, USA

Gimbrone, Michael A Jr (Doctor, Misc)
Brigham & Women's Hospital
Vascular Pathlogy Dept
Boston, MA 02115, USA

Gimenez, Chris (Athlete, Baseball Player)
781 Eschenburg Dr
Gilroy, CA 95020-5610, USA

Gimpel, Erica
c/o Staff Member *Innovative Artists (LA)*
1505 10th St
Santa Monica, CA 90401-2805, USA

Gina G (Music Group)
What Mgmt
PO Box 1463
Culver City, CA 90232-1463, USA

Gin Blossoms (Music Group)
PO Box 429094
San Francisco, CA 94142, USA

Ging, Jack (Actor)
48701 San Pedro St
La Quinta, CA 92253-6229, USA

Gingrey, Phil (Congressman, Politician)
442 Cannon Hob
Washington, DC 20515-0106, USA

Gingrich, Callista (Cally) (Business Person, Writer)
Gingrich Productions
4501 Fairfax Dr Ste 900
Arlington, VA 22203-1660, USA

Gingrich, Newt (Politician)
Gingrich Productions
4501 Fairfax Dr Ste 900
Arlington, VA 22203-1660, USA

Ginn, Chad (Athlete, Golfer)
c/o Staff Member *Signature Sports Group*
4150 Olson Memorial Hey
Suite 110
Minneapolis, MN 55422, USA

Ginn, Hubert (Athlete, Football Player)
16 Egrets Nest Dr
Savannah, GA 31406-4258, USA

Ginn Jr, Ted (Athlete, Football Player)
c/o Randy Mims *LRMR Marketing*
3800 Embassy Pkwy Ste 360
Akron, OH 44333-8389, USA

Ginobili, Emanuel (Manu) (Athlete, Basketball Player)
10 Queens Hi
San Antonio, TX 78257, USA

Ginsberg, Joe (Athlete, Baseball Player)
12635 SW Kingsway Cir # D1
Lake Suzy, FL 34269-4585, USA

Ginsberg, Justice Ruth Bader
700 New Hampshire Ave NW
Washington, DC 20037-2407

Ginter, Keith (Athlete, Baseball Player)
2907 Maple Ave
Fullerton, CA 92835-2126, USA

Ginter, Matt (Athlete, Baseball Player)
3320 Boonesboro Rd
Winchester, KY 40391-9292, USA

Ginter-Brooker, Susan (Athlete, Golfer)
314 Yorkshire Dr
Greenville, SC 29615-1133, USA

Ginzburg, Esti (Actor)
c/o Michael Williams *Frankfurt Kurnit Klein & Selz*
488 Madison Ave Fl 10
New York, NY 10022-5754, USA

Giofriddo, Al
64 Bristol Pl
Goleta, CA 93117-1949

Gioia (Musician)
c/o Staff Member *Diva Central Inc*
7510 W Sunset Blvd Ste 1445
Los Angeles, CA 90046-3408, USA

Giola, Dana (Government Official, Writer)
National Endowment for Arts
1100 Pennsylvania Ave NW
Washington, DC 20004-2501, USA

Gionta, Brian (Athlete, Hockey Player, Olympic Athlete)
Sports Consulting Group
65 Monroe Ave Ste D
Pittsford, NY 14534-1318, USA

Giordano, Tommy (Athlete, Baseball Player)
176 Riverside Ave
Amityville, NY 11701-3738, USA

Giosia, Nadia (Nadia G) (Chef)
c/o Jason Pinyan *Artist & Brand Management (LA)*
132 N Laurel Ave
Los Angeles, CA 90048-3512, USA

Giovanelli, Gordon (Athlete, Olympic Athlete, Rower)
332 Pico De La Loma
Escondido, CA 92029-7912, USA

Giovanni, Nikki E (Writer)
Virginia Polytechnic Institute
English Dept
Blacksburg, VA 24061, USA

Giovanola, Ed (Athlete, Baseball Player)
1741 Nomark Ct
San Jose, CA 95125-3948, USA

Giovinazzo, Carmine (Actor)
6626 Cahuenga Ter
Los Angeles, CA 90068-2747, USA

Gipson, Charles (Athlete, Baseball Player)
632 S Earlham St
Orange, CA 92869-5406, USA

Gipsy Kings (Music Group)
c/o Staff Member *Podell Talent Agency LLC*
22 W 21st St Fl 9
New York, NY 10010-7095, USA

Giraldo, Neil (Musician, Producer)
0 Hana Hwy
Hana, HI 96713, USA

Girardi, Joseph E (Joe) (Athlete, Baseball Player)
5 Laurel Way
Purchase, NY 10577-1101, USA

Giraud, Joyce (Beauty Pageant Winner, Model, Reality Star)
c/o Danny Duran *DDPR*
8840 Wilshire Blvd
Beverly Hills, CA 90211-2606, USA

Giroux, Larry (Athlete, Hockey Player)
10 Colleen Dr
Edwardsville, IL 62025-4242, USA

Gish, Annabeth (Actor)
c/o Joan Hyler *Hyler Management*
20 Ocean Park Blvd Unit 25
Santa Monica, CA 90405-3590, USA

Gisler, Mike (Athlete, Football Player)
407 Tampa Dr
Victoria, TX 77904-1649, USA

Gismonti, Egberto (Music Group, Musician)
International Music Network
278 S Main St # 400
Gloucester, MA 01930, USA

Gissell, Chris (Athlete, Baseball Player)
4310 NW 121st Cir
Vancouver, WA 98685-2052, USA

Gissinger, Andy (Athlete, Football Player)
1667 Union Ave
Barberton, OH 44203-7644, USA

Gitomer, Jeffrey (Business Person)
BuyGitomer Inc
310 Arlington Ave Unit 329
Charlotte, NC 28203-4296, USA

Giudice, Teresa (Reality Star)
6 Indian Ln
Towaco, NJ 07082-1005, USA

Giuffre, James P (Jimmy) (Music Group, Musician)
Legacy Records
550 Madison Ave Fl 6
New York, NY 10022-3211, USA

Giuliani, Rudy (Politician)
Giuliani Partners
1251 Avenue of the Americas Fl 48
New York, NY 10020-1100, USA

Giuliano, Jeff (Athlete, Hockey Player)
46 Lutheran Dr
Nashua, NH 03063-2914, USA

Giuliano, Louis J (Business Person)
ITT Industries
4 W Red Oak Ln
West Harrison, NY 10604-3603, USA

Giuliano, Tom (Music Group)
6929 N Hayden Rd
Scottsdale, AZ 85250-7978, USA

Giuntoli, David (Actor)
c/o Judy Hofflund *Hofflund/Polone*
6300 Wilshire Blvd Ste 1410
Los Angeles, CA 90048-5216, USA

Giusti, David J (Dave) (Athlete, Baseball Player)
524 Clair Dr
Pittsburgh, PA 15241-2013, USA

Givaty, Sarai (Actor)
c/o Siri Garber *Platform Public Relations*
2666 N Beachwood Dr
Los Angeles, CA 90068-2308, USA

Givens, Adele (Actor, Comedian)
c/o Ricky Anderson *Anderson & Smith P.C.*
7322 Southwest Fwy Ste 2010
One Arena Place
Houston, TX 77074-2077, USA

Givens, Brian (Athlete, Baseball Player)
945 E Virginia Ave
Denver, CO 80209-2311, USA

Givens, Jack (Athlete, Basketball Player, Misc)
929 Dustwhirl Dr
Union, KY 41091-7918, USA

Givens, Robin (Actor)
c/o Darryl Marshak *Marshak/Zachary Company, The*
8840 Wilshire Blvd Fl 1
Beverly Hills, CA 90211-2606, USA

Givins, Brian (Athlete, Baseball Player)
945 E Virginia Ave
Denver, CO 80209-2311, USA

Givins, Ernest (Athlete, Football Player)
924 58th St S
Gulfport, FL 33707-2548, USA

Gjertsen, Douglas (Athlete, Olympic Athlete, Swimmer)
7130 Havenridge Way
McDonough, GA 30253-8511, USA

Gladden, Danny (Dan) (Athlete, Baseball Player)
6543 Pinnacle Dr
Eden Prairie, MN 55346-1906, USA

Gladding, Fred (Athlete, Baseball Player)
436 Marsh Pointe Dr
Columbia, SC 29229-7025, USA

Gladieux, Robert (Athlete, Football Player)
802 Arch Ave
South Bend, IN 46601-3204, USA

Gladis, Michael (Actor)
c/o Lisa Gallant *Gallant Management*
1112 Montana Ave # 454
Santa Monica, CA 90403-1652, USA

Gladwell, Malcolm (Writer)
c/o Staff Member *Black Bay / Little Brown*
3 Center Plz
Boston, MA 02108-2003, USA

Glance, Harvey (Athlete, Track Athlete)
2408 Old Creek Rd
Montgomery, AL 36117-2420, USA

Glanville, Brandi (Model, Reality Star)
c/o Staff Member *Persona PR (LA)*
8840 Wilshire Blvd Ste 212
Beverly Hills, CA 90211-2606, USA

Glanville, Doug (Athlete, Baseball Player)
153 N Beacon St
Hartford, CT 06105-2246, USA

Glanville, Jerry (Athlete, Coach, Football Coach, Football Player, Sportscaster)
1215 Cherokee Blvd
Knoxville, TN 37919-7854, USA

Glasbergen, Randy (Cartoonist)
c/o Staff Member *King Features Syndication*
300 W 57th St Fl 15
New York, NY 10019-5238, USA

Glaser, Jim (Music Group)
Joe Taylor Artist Agency
2802 Columbine Pl
Nashville, TN 37204-3104, USA

Glaser, Jon (Actor, Writer)
c/o Staff Member *3 Arts Entertainment (LA)*
9460 Wilshire Blvd Fl 7
Beverly Hills, CA 90212-2713, USA

Glaser, Paul Michael (Actor, Director)
c/o Mark Teitelbaum *Teitelbaum Artists Group*
8840 Wilshire Blvd Fl 3
Beverly Hills, CA 90211-2606, USA

Glaser, Rose Mary (Athlete, Baseball Player, Commentator)
8929 Long Ln
Cincinnati, OH 45231-5024, USA

Glasgow, Brian (Athlete, Football Player)
5 Sage Ct
Bolingbrook, IL 60490-3220, USA

Glasgow, Nesby (Athlete, Football Player)
18125 96th Ave NE Apt 8
Bothell, WA 98011-3331, USA

Glasgow, Walter (Athlete, Olympic Athlete, Sailor)
781 Silver Spur Dr
Weatherford, TX 76087-6417, USA

Glass, Chip (Athlete, Football Player)
7704 NE 140th St
Bothell, WA 98011, USA

Glass, David (Commentator)
Kansas City Royals
17 Glenbrook
Bentonville, AR 72712-3840, USA

Glass, Gerald (Athlete, Basketball Player)
1123 Tillman Rd
Port Gibson, MS 39150-2890, USA

Glass, Glenn (Athlete, Football Player)
301 Portsmouth Rd
Knoxville, TN 37909-3020, USA

Glass, Ira (Writer)
c/o Steven Barclay *Steven Barclay Agency*
12 Western Ave
Petaluma, CA 94952-2907, USA

Glass, Leland (Athlete, Football Player)
9 Bayou Ct
Sacramento, CA 95831-2403, USA

Glass, Nancy (Journalist)
Glass DiFede Productions
345 Montgomery Ave
Bala Cynwyd, PA 19004-2801

Glass, Philip (Musician)
48 E 3rd St # 2
New York, NY 10003-9271, USA

Glass, Ron (Actor)
c/o Mitchell Stubbs *Mitchell K Stubbs & Assoc (MKS)*
8675 Washington Blvd Ste 203
Culver City, CA 90232-7486, USA

Glass, Todd (Actor)
c/o Alex Murray *Brillstein Entertainment Partners (LA)*
9150 Wilshire Blvd Ste 350
Beverly Hills, CA 90212-3453, USA

Glass, William S (Bill) (Athlete, Football Player)
Bill Glass Ministries
1101 S Cedar Ridge Dr
Duncanville, TX 75137-3070, USA

Glassford, Bill (Athlete, Football Player)
3212 N Miller Rd Apt 138
Scottsdale, AZ 85251-6984, USA

Glassic, Tom (Athlete, Football Player)
1030 S Pine Dr
Bailey, CO 80421-2333, USA

Glasson, Bill (Athlete, Golfer)
4920 W Woodland Ct
Stillwater, OK 74074-1327, USA

Glatter, Lesli L (Director)
United Talent Agency
9336 Civic Center Dr
Beverly Hills, CA 90210-3604, USA

Glatz, Fred (Athlete, Football Player)
224 Perkins Row
Topsfield, MA 01983-1532, USA

Glau, Summer (Actor)
c/o Christine Tripicchio *Shelter PR*
9350 Wilshire Blvd Ste 450
Beverly Hills, CA 90212-3230, USA

Glauber, Keith (Athlete, Baseball Player)
20 Highland Ct
Freehold, NJ 07728-9041, USA

Glaudini, Lola (Actor, Producer)
c/o Staff Member *Mosaic Media Group*
9200 W Sunset Blvd Ste 10
West Hollywood, CA 90069-3608, USA

Glaus, Troy (Athlete, Baseball Player)
5865 Neal Ave N
Stillwater, MN 55082-2177, USA

Glave, Matthew (Actor)
17628 McCormick St
Encino, CA 91316-2551, USA

Glavine, Mike (Athlete, Baseball Player)
89 Treble Cove Rd
North Billerica, MA 01862-2215, USA

Glavine, Tom (Athlete, Baseball Player)
8925 Old Southwick Pass
Alpharetta, GA 30022-7140, USA

Glazer, Jay (Sportscaster)
CBS-TV
51 W 52nd St
New York, NY 10019-6119, USA

Glazer, Jonathan (Director, Writer)
c/o David Naylor *David Naylor & Associates*
6535 Santa Monica Blvd
Los Angeles, CA 90038-1407, USA

Glazer, Mitch (Producer)
c/o Staff Member *Creative Artists Agency (CAA-LA)*
2000 Avenue of the Stars Ste 100
Los Angeles, CA 90067-4705, USA

Gleason, Joanna (Actor)
c/o Vera Mihailovich *Forward Entertainment*
9255 W Sunset Blvd Ste 805
West Hollywood, CA 90069-3305, USA

Gleason, Mary Pat (Actor, Writer)
c/o Tim Stone *Stone Manners Salners Agency (LA)*
6100 Wilshire Blvd Ste 1500
Los Angeles, CA 90048-5110, USA

Gleason, Roy (Athlete, Baseball Player)
35218 Fir Ave Spc 93
Yucaipa, CA 92399-3078, USA

Gleason, Tim (Athlete, Hockey Player)
1196 Stone Kirk Dr
Raleigh, NC 27614-7289, USA

Gleaton, Jerry Don (Athlete, Baseball Player)
3008 Avenue K
Brownwood, TX 76801-6016, USA

Gleeson, Brendan (Actor)
c/o Larry Taube *Principal Entertainment (LA)*
9255 W Sunset Blvd Ste 500
West Hollywood, CA 90069-3301, USA

Glen, John (Director)
Spyros Skouras
1015 Gayley Ave Ste 300
Los Angeles, CA 90024-3440, USA

Glenesk, Dean (Athlete, Olympic Athlete, Pentathlete)
1705 Ben Crenshaw Way
Austin, TX 78746-6120, USA

Glenn, Aaron (Athlete, Football Player)
30 Commanders Cv
Missouri City, TX 77459-6518, USA

Glenn, Cordy (Athlete, Football Player)
c/o Pat Dye Jr *SportsTrust Advisors (GA)*
3340 Peachtree Rd NE Fl 16
Atlanta, GA 30326-1000, USA

Glenn, Dorsey (Athlete, Football Player)
4242 NE Edmonson Ct
Lees Summit, MO 64064-1681, USA

Glenn, Jason (Athlete, Football Player)
15530 Ella Blvd Apt 501
Houston, TX 77090-5309, USA

Glenn, Mike (Athlete, Basketball Player)
3571 Kilpatrick Ln
Snellville, GA 30039-8643, USA

Glenn, Scott (Actor)
491 E 10th St Ste A12
Ketchum, ID 83340, USA

Glenn, Stanley (Athlete, Baseball Player)
PO Box 30531
West Palm Beach, FL 33420-0531, USA

Glenn, Tarik (Athlete, Football Player)
2224 Ward St
Berkeley, CA 94705-1065, USA

Glenn, Terry
1619 Fair Oaks Ct
Westlake, TX 76262-8224, USA

Glenn, Vencie (Athlete, Football Player)
718 Casita Ln
San Marcos, CA 92069-7397, USA

Glenn Jr, John H (Astronaut, Ex-Senator)
Ohio State University
1947 N College Rd
Columbus, OH 43210-1181, USA

Glennon, Matt (Athlete, Hockey Player)
6 Gardner St
Hingham, MA 02043, USA

Gless, Sharon (Actor)
Rosenzweig Productions
PO Box 48005
Los Angeles, CA 90048-0005, USA

Glick, Alexis (Correspondent)
c/o Staff Member *Fox News (NY)*
1211 Avenue of the Americas Lowr C1
New York, NY 10036-8705, USA

Glick, Frederick (Freddie) (Athlete,
Football Player)
4226 Antlers Ct
Fort Collins, CO 80526-6411, USA

Glick, Gary (Athlete, Football Player)
2801 Middlesborough Ct
Fort Collins, CO 80525-2331, USA

Glidden, Bob (Race Car Driver)
PO Box 236
Rt. 1
Whiteland, IN 46184-0236, USA

Glinatsis, George (Athlete, Baseball
Player)
13742 W 59th Ave
Arvada, CO 80004-3740, USA

Gload, Ross (Athlete, Baseball Player)
23 Harrison Ave
East Hampton, NY 11937-2051, USA

Globensky, Alan (Athlete, Hockey Player)
20 Myrtle St Apt 2
Augusta, ME 04330-4736

Globke, Rob (Athlete, Hockey Player)
149 Pine Creek Dr
Hampton, VA 23669-1245, USA

Gloden, Fred (Athlete, Football Player)
3821 Andrea Rd
Philadelphia, PA 19154-4211, USA

Gloriana (Music Group)
c/o Haley Melikian *Matchbook Company*
221 E 31st St
New York, NY 10016-6302, USA

Glory, New Found (Music Group)
c/o Staff Member *Ellis Industries Inc*
234 Shoreward Dr
Great Neck, NY 11021-2734, USA

Glosson, Clyde (Athlete, Football Player)
5803 Lake Falls Dr
San Antonio, TX 78222-2405, USA

Glotzbach, Charlie (Race Car Driver)
2513 Coopers Ln
Sellersburg, IN 47172-9564, USA

Glotzbatch, Charles (Race Car Driver)
2513 Coopers Ln
Sellersburg, IN 47172-9564, USA

Glouberman, Michael (Producer)
c/o Staff Member *United Talent Agency
(UTA-LA)*
9336 Civic Center Dr
Beverly Hills, CA 90210-3604, USA

G Love & Special Sauce (Music Group)
c/o Staff Member *Paradigm (Monterey)*
404 W Franklin St
Monterey, CA 93940-2303, USA

Glover, Andrew (Athlete, Football Player)
33226 Magnolia Cir
Magnolia, TX 77354-1523, USA

Glover, Bruce (Actor)
11449 Woodbine St
Los Angeles, CA 90066-1229, USA

Glover, Chris (Musician)
c/o Staff Member *Paradigm (Monterey)*
404 W Franklin St
Monterey, CA 93940-2303, USA

Glover, Clarence (Athlete, Basketball
Player)
811 Lake Forest Pkwy
Louisville, KY 40245-5138, USA

Glover, Crispin (Actor, Director,
Producer)
3573 Carnation Ave
Los Angeles, CA 90026-1103, USA

Glover, Danny (Actor)
8290 Shrader St
San Francisco, CA 94117, USA

Glover, Dion (Athlete, Basketball Player)
3691 Seton Hall Way
Decatur, GA 30034-5509, USA

Glover, Donald (Actor, Writer)
c/o Diane McGunigle *The Schiff
Company*
9220 W Sunset Blvd Ste 106
West Hollywood, CA 90069-3500, USA

Glover, Gary (Athlete, Baseball Player)
19704 Kell Estates Ln
Lutz, FL 33549-4092, USA

Glover, Jane A
Kaylor Mgmt
130 W 57th St Apt 8G
New York, NY 10019-3311, USA

Glover, John (Actor)
c/o Nevin Dolcefino *Innovative Artists
(LA)*
1505 10th St
Santa Monica, CA 90401-2805, USA

Glover, Kevin B (Athlete, Football Player)
11553 Manorstone Ln
Columbia, MD 21044-5413, USA

Glover, La'Roi (Athlete, Football Player)
PO Box 410589
Saint Louis, MO 63141-0589, USA

Glover, Lucas (Athlete, Golfer)
105 Annas Pl
Simpsonville, SC 29681-4813, USA

Glover, Richard E (Rich) (Athlete,
Football Player)
3 Smit Ct
Jersey City, NJ 07305-5509, USA

Glover, Stephen (Steve-O) (Actor, Writer)
c/o Mike Liotta *True Public Relations*
6725 W Sunset Blvd Ste 470
Los Angeles, CA 90028-7180, USA

Glowacki, Janusz (Writer)
845 W End Ave Apt 4B
New York, NY 10025-8436, USA

Gloy, Tom (Race Car Driver)
Rahal/Gloy Racing
804A Performance Rd
Mooresville, NC 28115-9597, USA

Gluck, Griffin (Actor)
c/o Leslie Allan-Rice *Leslie Allan-Rice
Management*
1007 Maybrook Dr
Beverly Hills, CA 90210-2715, USA

Gluck, Louise E (Writer)
14 Ellsworth Park
Cambridge, MA 02139-1011, USA

Glueck, Larry (Athlete, Football Player)
10 Cooper Rd
East Falmouth, MA 02536-7413, USA

Glymph, Junior (Athlete, Football Player)
7300 Fontana Dr
Columbia, SC 29209-3248, USA

Glynn, Bill (Athlete, Baseball Player)
6916 51st St
San Diego, CA 92120-1212, USA

Glynn, Carlin (Actor)
1165 5th Ave
New York, NY 10029-6931, USA

Glynn, Ed (Athlete, Baseball Player)
5212 Stratford Chase Dr
Virginia Beach, VA 23464-5621, USA

Glynn, Gene (Athlete, Baseball Player)
15329 Snake Trl
Waseca, MN 56093-4733, USA

Glynn, Robert D Jr (Business Person)
PG&E Corp
1 Market St
San Francisco, CA 94105-1420, USA

Glynn, Ryan (Athlete, Baseball Player)
14010 W Hyde Park Dr Apt 201
Fort Myers, FL 33912-0207, USA

G. McCotter, Thaddeus (Congressman,
Politician)
1632 Longworth Hob
Washington, DC 20515-2007, USA

G. Miller, Gary (Congressman, Politician)
2349 Rayburn Hob
Washington, DC 20515-2209, USA

Gminski, Mike (Athlete, Basketball Player,
Sportscaster)
3635 Eastover Ridge Dr Apt 1518
Charlotte, NC 28211-1587, USA

Gnarls Barkley (Music Group)
Downtown Records
73 Spring St Rm 504
New York, NY 10012-5802, USA

Goad, Tim (Athlete, Football Player)
138 Birchwood Dr
Pittsboro, NC 27312-8737, USA

Goalby, Bob (Athlete, Golfer)
904 Briar Hill Rd
Belleville, IL 62223-1133, USA

Gob, Art (Athlete, Football Player)
123 Hiscott Dr
Pittsburgh, PA 15241-1105, USA

Gobble, Jimmy (Athlete, Baseball Player)
150 Lake View Estates Dr
Bristol, TN 37620-1307, USA

Goble, Les (Athlete, Football Player)
21 Dodge Ave Apt 1
Waverly, NY 14892-9651, USA

Goc, Marcel (Athlete, Hockey Player)
8061 Sherwood Dr
Presto, PA 15142-1079, USA

Gocke, Justin
6763 Pistachio Pl
Palmdale, CA 93551-1930

Gocong, Chris (Athlete, Football Player)
4664 4th St # B
Carpinteria, CA 93013-2208, USA

Godard, Eric (Athlete, Hockey Player)
201 Lavaca St Apt 208
Austin, TX 78701-3962, USA

Godboldo, Dale (Actor)
c/o Joanna (Joanie) Burstein *Burstein
Company, The*
15304 W Sunset Blvd Ste 208
Pacific Palisades, CA 90272-3656, USA

Godby, Danny (Athlete, Baseball Player)
RR 2 Box 17A
Chapmanville, WV 25508-9773, USA

Godchaux, Stephen (Producer)
c/o Staff Member *William Morris
Endeavor (LA)*
9601 Wilshire Blvd
Beverly Hills, CA 90210-5213, USA

Goddard, Daniel (Actor)
c/o Staff Member *Luber Roklin
Management*
5815 W Sunset Blvd Ste 206
Los Angeles, CA 90028-6481, USA

Goddard, Joe (Athlete, Baseball Player)
304 Ridgepark Dr
Beckley, WV 25801-9593, USA

Goddard, Mark (Actor)
PO Box 778
Middleboro, MA 02346-0778, USA

Godecki, Marzena (Actor)
Jonathan M. Shiff Productions
373 Bay St
Port Melbourne
Victoria, AU 03207

Godfread, Dan (Athlete, Basketball
Player)
622 Michigan St
Eagle River, WI 54521-8929, USA

Godfrey (Actor, Comedian)
c/o Matt Luber *Luber Roklin Management*
5815 W Sunset Blvd Ste 206
Los Angeles, CA 90028-6481, USA

Godfrey, Charles (Athlete, Football
Player)
c/o Doug Hendrickson *Octagon Football*
832 Sansome St Fl 1
San Francisco, CA 94111-1558, USA

Godfrey, Chris (Athlete, Football Player)
52383 Swanson Dr
South Bend, IN 46635-1067, USA

Godfrey, Randall (Athlete, Football
Player)
4102 Mount Zion Church Rd
Valdosta, GA 31605-6506, USA

Godin, Seth (Business Person, Writer)
Do You Zoom Inc
PO Box 305
Irvington, NY 10533-0305, USA

Godina, John
PO Box 120
Indianapolis, IN 46204

Godsmack (Music Group)
c/o John Branigan *William Morris Endeavor (LA)*
9601 Wilshire Blvd
Beverly Hills, CA 90210-5213, USA

Godwin, Gail K (Writer)
PO Box 946
Woodstock, NY 12498-0946, USA

Godwin, John (Reality Star)
c/o Theresa Brown *William Morris Endeavor (LA)*
9601 Wilshire Blvd
Beverly Hills, CA 90210-5213, USA

Godwin, Linda M (Astronaut, Physicist)
3801 Eagle View Ct
Columbia, MO 65203-1064, USA

Godynyuk, Alexander (Athlete, Hockey Player)
217 Follen Rd
Lexington, MA 02421-5802, USA

Goeas, Leo (Athlete, Football Player)
113 Shady Ln
Longwood, FL 32750-2867, USA

Goebel, Brad (Athlete, Football Player)
PO Box 4006
Horseshoe Bay, TX 78657-4006, USA

Goebel, Timothy (Athlete, Figure Skater, Olympic Athlete)
c/o Staff Member *Champions on Ice*
3500 American Blvd W Ste 190
Minneapolis, MN 55431-4431, USA

Goeddeke, George (Athlete, Football Player)
45575 N Stonewood Rd
Canton, MI 48187-6645, USA

Goen, Bob (Game Show Host, Television Host)
c/o Staff Member *Rebel Entertainment Partners*
5700 Wilshire Blvd Ste 456
Los Angeles, CA 90036-3648, USA

Goepper, Nick (Olympic Athlete, Skier)
US Ski And Snowboard Association
1 Victory Ln # 100
Park City, UT 84060-7463, USA

Goestenkors, Gail (Basketball Player, Coach)
Duke University
Athletic Dept
Durham, NC 27708-0001, USA

Goettmann, Georgia
344 E 59th St
New York, NY 10022-1593

Goetz, Bernhard
55 W 14th St Apt 7D
New York, NY 10011-7410

Goetz, Dick (Athlete, Golfer)
4301 Fillbrook Ln
Tyler, TX 75707-5465, USA

Goetz, Peter Michael (Actor)
c/o Staff Member *SMS Talent*
8383 Wilshire Blvd Ste 230
Beverly Hills, CA 90211-2436, USA

Goetz, Russ (Athlete, Baseball Player)
937 Fawcett Ave
McKeesport, PA 15132-1409, USA

Goetze-Ackerman, Vicki (Athlete, Golfer)
3621 Sally Parrish Trl
Valrico, FL 33596-8433, USA

Goetzman, Gary (Producer)
c/o Staff Member *Creative Artists Agency (CAA-LA)*
2000 Avenue of the Stars Ste 100
Los Angeles, CA 90067-4705, USA

Goff, Jerry (Athlete, Baseball Player)
3 Oak Valley Dr
Novato, CA 94947-1964, USA

Goff, Mike (Athlete, Baseball Player)
153 Norton Pl Apt D
Mobile, AL 36607-2235, USA

Goff, Mike (Athlete, Football Player)
2225 5th St
Peru, IL 61354-2506, USA

Goff, Willard (Athlete, Football Player)
441 E 10th Ave
Springfield, CO 81073, USA

Goffin, David (Producer)
c/o Staff Member *Creative Artists Agency (CAA-LA)*
2000 Avenue of the Stars Ste 100
Los Angeles, CA 90067-4705, USA

Goffin, Louise (Musician)
c/o Staff Member *Evolution Music Partners*
1680 Vine St Ste 500
Los Angeles, CA 90028-8800, USA

Goforth, Bart (Athlete, Football Player)
7000 Greenbriar St Apt 20
Houston, TX 77030-3244, USA

Gofourth, Derrel (Athlete, Football Player)
1119 S Woodcrest Dr
Stillwater, OK 74074-1433, USA

Gogan, Kevin (Athlete, Football Player)
4643 286th Ave SE
Fall City, WA 98024-6907, USA

Goganious, Keith (Athlete, Football Player)
4173 Cheswick Ln
Virginia Beach, VA 23455-6560, USA

Gogel, Matt (Athlete, Golfer)
3509 W 68th St
Mission Hills, KS 66208-2142, USA

Goggin, Chuck (Athlete, Baseball Player)
1224 Roundhouse Ln
Alexandria, VA 22314-5908, USA

Goggins, Walton (Actor, Producer)
c/o Darris Hatch *Daris Hatch Management*
10027 Rossbury Pl
Los Angeles, CA 90064-4825, USA

Gogolak, Charlie (Athlete, Football Player)
PO Box 361
Northeast Harbor, ME 04662-0361, USA

Gogolak, Peter (Pete) (Athlete, Football Player)
394 Mansfield Ave
Darien, CT 06820-2112, USA

Gogolewski, Bill (Athlete, Baseball Player)
1522 Graham Ave
Oshkosh, WI 54902-2623, USA

Go-Go's, The (Music Group)
c/o Martin Kirkup *Direct Management Group*
8332 Melrose Ave
West Hollywood, CA 90069-5420, USA

Goh, Rex (Music Group, Musician)
Agency for Performing Arts
9200 W Sunset Blvd Ste 900
West Hollywood, CA 90069-3604, USA

Gohmert, Louie (Congressman, Politician)
2440 Rayburn Hob
Washington, DC 20515-2508, USA

Gohr, Greg (Athlete, Baseball Player)
77 Scotland Rd
Reading, MA 01867-3323, USA

Goich, Dan (Athlete, Football Player)
PO Box 19068
Las Vegas, NV 89132-0068, USA

Going, Joanna (Actor)
c/o Nevin Dolcefino *Innovative Artists (LA)*
1505 10th St
Santa Monica, CA 90401-2805, USA

Goings, E V (Business Person)
Tupperware Corp
PO Box 2353
Orlando, FL 32802-2353, USA

Goings, Nick (Athlete, Football Player)
660 Caicos Ct
Wilmington, NC 28405-8369, USA

Goings, Nick (Athlete)
c/o Staff Member *Carolina Panthers*
800 S Mint St
Ericsson Stadium
Charlotte, NC 28202-1640, USA

Gokey, Danny (Musician)
802 Huntington Cir
Nashville, TN 37215-6112, USA

Golay, Jeanne (Athlete, Cycler, Olympic Athlete)
1125 Red Mountain Dr
Glenwood Springs, CO 81601-3257, USA

Gold, Ari (Musician)
c/o Staff Member *Grapevine Public Relations*
5237 Cahuenga Blvd # 2
N Hollywood, CA 91601-3419, USA

Gold, Brandy (Actor)
Gold Marshak Liedtke
3500 W Olive Ave Ste 1400
Burbank, CA 91505-5512, USA

Gold, Elon (Actor, Comedian)
c/o Ruthanne Secunda *ICM Partners (LA)*
10250 Constellation Blvd Fl 7
Los Angeles, CA 90067-6207, USA

Gold, Herbert (Writer)
1051 Broadway # A
San Francisco, CA 94133-4205, USA

Gold, Ian (Athlete, Football Player)
10275 Tradition Pl
Lone Tree, CO 80124-8505, USA

Gold, Jimmy
11990 San Vicente Blvd Ste 340
Los Angeles, CA 90049-6608

Gold, Judy (Comedian)
c/o Jodi Schoenbrun Carter *1022m*
407 W 43rd St Fl 3
New York, NY 10036-5330, USA

Gold, Missy
3500 W Olive Ave Ste 1400
Burbank, CA 91505-5512

Gold, Seth (DJ)
c/o Len Evans *Project Publicity*
312 W 53rd St Ste 202
New York, NY 10019-5743, USA

Gold, Todd
c/o Daniel Strone *Trident Media Group LLC*
41 Madison Ave Fl 36
New York, NY 10010-2257, USA

Gold, Tracey (Actor)
c/o Harry Gold *TalentWorks (LA)*
3500 W Olive Ave Ste 1400
Burbank, CA 91505-5512, USA

Goldberg, Adam (Actor, Comedian)
2055 N Gramercy Pl
Los Angeles, CA 90068-3616, USA

Goldberg, Bernard (Writer)
c/o Staff Member *HarperCollins Publishers*
195 Broadway Fl 2
Cellar 1
New York, NY 10007-3132, USA

Goldberg, Bill (Athlete, Football Player, Wrestler)
7082 Eagle Mountain Rd
Bonsall, CA 92003-7001, USA

Goldberg, Eric (Animator)
c/o Ellen Goldsmith-Vein *The Gotham Group Inc*
9255 W Sunset Blvd Ste 515
West Hollywood, CA 90069-3308, USA

Goldberg, Hank (Sportscaster)
3300 NE 192nd St Apt 418
Miami, FL 33180-2429, USA

Goldberg, Leonard (Producer)
Spectradyne Inc
1198 Commerce Dr
Richardson, TX 75081-2307, USA

Goldberg, Lucianne
4 Oak St
Weehawken, NJ 07086-5608

Goldberg, Whoopi (Actor, Comedian, Talk Show Host)
c/o Staff Member *Whoop Inc*
1650 Broadway Ste 1400
New York, NY 10019-6985, USA

Goldblum, Jeff (Actor)
8225 Hollywood Blvd
Los Angeles, CA 90069-1611, USA

Golden, Arthur (Writer)
c/o Lynn Pleshette *Lynn Pleshette Literary Agency*
2700 N Beachwood Dr
Los Angeles, CA 90068-1922, USA

Golden, Clyde (Athlete, Baseball Player)
26 E 59th St Apt 503
Jacksonville, FL 32208-4725, USA

Golden, Harry (Bowler, Misc)
Professional Bowlers Assn
55 E Jackson Blvd Ste 401
Chicago, IL 60604-4307, USA

Golden, Jim (Athlete, Baseball Player)
8630 SW 10th Ave
Topeka, KS 66615-9688, USA

Golden, Kate (Athlete, Golfer)
969 Hunterwood Dr
Jasper, TX 75951-2821, USA

Golden, Kit (Producer)
c/o Staff Member *Manhattan Project*
1775 Broadway Ste 410
New York, NY 10019-1903, USA

Golden, Tim (Athlete, Football Player)
11060 NW 20th Ct
Sunrise, FL 33322-3432, USA

Golden, William Lee (Musician, Songwriter)
49 Music Sq W Ste 503
Nashville, TN 37203-3289, USA

Goldens, The
PO Box 1795
Hendersonville, TN 37077-1795

Goldenthal, Elliot (Musician)
c/o Sam Schwartz *Gorfaine/Schwartz Agency Inc*
4111 W Alameda Ave Ste 509
Burbank, CA 91505-4171, USA

Goldfaden, Ben (Athlete, Basketball Player)
5819 Bounty Cir
Tavares, FL 32778-9293, USA

Goldin, Ricky Paull (Actor)
c/o Staff Member *Stone Manners Salners Agency (LA)*
6100 Wilshire Blvd Ste 1500
Los Angeles, CA 90048-5110, USA

Golding, Meta (Actor)
c/o Charlton Blackburne *A Management Company*
9107 Wilshire Blvd Ste 650
Beverly Hills, CA 90210-5544, USA

Goldman, Bo (Producer, Writer)
c/o David O'Connor *Creative Artists Agency (CAA-LA)*
2000 Avenue of the Stars Ste 100
Los Angeles, CA 90067-4705, USA

Goldman, Duff (Chef)
Charm City Cakes
2936 Remington Ave
Baltimore, MD 21211-2830, USA

Goldman, Hersh
62 Essex St
Swampscott, MA 01907-1713, USA

Goldman, Julie (Actor, Comedian)
c/o Staff Member *Ellis Talent Group*
4705 Laurel Canyon Blvd Ste 300
Valley Village, CA 91607-5901, USA

Goldman, Les (Athlete, Football Player)
800 E Cypress Creek Rd Ste 203
Fort Lauderdale, FL 33334-3522, USA

Goldman, Matt (Musician)
Blue Man Group
3900 Las Vegas Blvd S
Luxor Hotel
Las Vegas, NV 89119-1004, USA

Goldman, William (Writer)
Janklow & Nesbit
50 E 77th St Apt 30
New York, NY 10075-1842, USA

Goldoni, Lelia
15459 Wyandotte St
Van Nuys, CA 91406-3334

Goldrup, Ray
2383 Broderick
West Jordan, UT 84084

Goldsboro, Bobby (Musician, Songwriter)
La Rana Productions
PO Box 5250
Ocala, FL 34478-5250, USA

Goldschmidt, Neil (Politician)
1150 SW King Ave
Portland, OR 97205-1116, USA

Goldsman, Akiva (Director, Producer)
c/o Staff Member *Weed Road Pictures*
9100 Wilshire Blvd Ste 1000W
Beverly Hills, CA 90212-3463, USA

Goldsmith, Bethany (Baseball Player)
1000 E Michigan St Apt A
Orlando, FL 32806-4736, USA

Goldsmith, Jonathan (Actor)
c/o Stephanie Gabriel *James/Levy Management Inc*
3500 W Olive Ave Ste 1470
Burbank, CA 91505-5514, USA

Goldsmith, Kelly (Actor)
c/o Dede Binder-Goldsmith *Defining Artists Agency*
4370 Tujunga Ave Ste 120
Studio City, CA 91604-2763, USA

Goldsmith, Paul (Race Car Driver)
1705 E Main St
Griffith, IN 46319-2941, USA

Goldsmith, Stephen (Politician)
Governor's Office
State House
Indianapolis, IN 46204, USA

Goldspink, Calvin (Actor)
c/o Staff Member *Reel Talent Management*
PO Box 491035
Los Angeles, CA 90049-9035, USA

Goldstein, Jenette
3932 Marathon St
Los Angeles, CA 90029-3602

Goldstein, Lonnie (Athlete, Baseball Player)
3401 Premier Dr Apt 213
Plano, TX 75023-7093, USA

Goldthwait, Bob (Bobcat) (Actor, Comedian)
c/o Rick Greenstein *Gersh (LA)*
9465 Wilshire Blvd Ste 600
Beverly Hills, CA 90212-2605, USA

Goldwater Jr, Barry
4401 Connecticut Ave NW PMB 850
Washington, DC 20008-2322, USA

Goldwire, Anthony
2007 Birnam Glen Dr
Sugar Land, TX 77479-6421

Goldwyn, Tony (Actor, Director)
c/o Jason Weinberg *Untitled Entertainment (LA)*
350 S Beverly Dr Ste 200
Beverly Hills, CA 90212-4819, USA

Goldwyn Jr, Samuel (Producer)
c/o Staff Member *Samuel Goldwyn Company*
9570 W Pico Blvd Ste 400
Los Angeles, CA 90035-1216, USA

Golembiewski, Billy (Bowler)
4966 N Wise Rd
Coleman, MI 48618-9658, USA

Golembrosky, Frank (Athlete, Hockey Player)
4 Francis Cir
Newark, DE 19711-2625

Golenbock, Peter (Sportscaster)
849 Jennings Ave N
Saint Petersburg, FL 33704-1142, USA

Golic, Bob (Athlete, Football Player, Sportscaster)
6130 Loch Lomond Ct
Solon, OH 44139-5945, USA

Golic, Mike (Athlete, Football Player)
12110 E Gold Dust Ave
Scottsdale, AZ 85259-5117, USA

Goligoski, Alex
916 Golf Course Rd
Grand Rapids, MN 55744-3440, USA

Golina, Stacy
325 S Swall Dr Apt 502
Los Angeles, CA 90048-3078

Golino, Valeria (Actor, Producer)
c/o Michael (Mike) Jelline *United Talent Agency (UTA-LA)*
9336 Civic Center Dr
Beverly Hills, CA 90210-3604, USA

Golisano, B Thomas (Business Person)
Paychex Inc
911 Panorama Trl S
Rochester, NY 14625-2396, USA

Golisano, Tom (Business Person)
911 Panorama Trl S
Rochester, NY 14625-2311, USA

Gollat, Mike (Baseball Player)
Philadelphia Phillies
2650 Greenlawn Dr
Seven Hills, OH 44131-3623, USA

Golodryga, Bianna (Television Host)
c/o Staff Member *Good Morning America (NY)*
147 Columbus Ave Fl 6
Abc
New York, NY 10023-6503, USA

Golonka, Arlene (Actor)
Silver/Kass/Massetti
8730 W Sunset Blvd Ste 480
West Hollywood, CA 90069-2277, USA

Golson, Greg (Athlete, Baseball Player)
1535 Tamar Ln
Austin, TX 78727-3329, USA

Golsteyn, Jerry (Athlete, Football Player)
2620 Lockwood Rd Unit 202
Fayetteville, NC 28303-5048, USA

Goltz, Dave (Athlete, Baseball Player)
1009 Stony Brook Mnr
Fergus Falls, MN 56537-4413, USA

Gomes, Jessica (Model)
c/o Emily Yomtobian *PMK/BNC Public Relations (PMK-LA)*
8687 Melrose Ave Ste 8
West Hollywood, CA 90069-5746, USA

Gomes, Jonny (Athlete, Baseball Player)
22441 N Church Rd
Scottsdale, AZ 85255-4444, USA

Gomes, Wayne (Athlete, Baseball Player)
5104 W Creek Ct
Suffolk, VA 23435-3523, USA

Gomez (Music Group)
c/o Jason Colton *Red Light Management (VA)*
321 E Main St Ste 500
Charlottesville, VA 22902-3201, USA

Gomez, Andres (Tennis Player)
ProServe
1101 Woodrow Wilson Blvd # 1800
Arlington, VA 22209, USA

Gomez, Carlos (Actor)
c/o Billy Miller *Billy Miller Management*
8322 Ridpath Dr
Los Angeles, CA 90046-7710, USA

Gomez, Carlos
15520 Flyboat Ln
Saint Paul, MN 55124-6021, USA

Gomez, Chris (Athlete, Baseball Player)
2618 San Miguel Dr # 183
Newport Beach, CA 92660-5437, USA

Gomez, Edgar (Eddie) (Music Group, Musician)
Integrity Talent
PO Box 961
Burlington, MA 01803-5961, USA

Gomez, Ian (Actor)
c/o Staff Member *Handprint Entertainment*
1100 Glendon Ave Ste 100
Los Angeles, CA 90024-3593, USA

Gomez, Jeff (Cartoonist)
5 Union Sq W Attn of
New York, NY 10003-3306, USA

Gomez, Juan ""A Orlando"" (Athlete, Baseball Player)
Frederick Keys
21 Stadium Dr
Attn: Manager's Office
Frederick, MD 21703-6553, USA

Gomez, Leo (Athlete, Baseball Player)
273 Portofino Dr
North Venice, FL 34275-6654, USA

Gomez, Luis (Athlete, Baseball Player)
676 Chesterfield Dr
Lawrenceville, GA 30044-5624, USA

Gomez, Marga (Comedian)
PO Box 460368
San Francisco, CA 94146-0368, USA

Gomez, Natalie (Actor)
c/o Staff Member *Advance LA*
7904 Santa Monica Blvd Ste 200
West Hollywood, CA 90046-5170

Gomez, Nick (Director)
c/o Staff Member *Evolution Entertainment (LA)*
901 N Highland Ave
Los Angeles, CA 90038-2412, USA

Gomez, Panchito (Actor)
240 N Hollywood Way
Burbank, CA 91505-3431, USA

Gomez, Pat (Athlete, Baseball Player)
2257 Quarry Way
Rocklin, CA 95765-4292, USA

Gomez, Randy (Athlete, Baseball Player)
50 Oak St
San Martin, CA 95046-9592, USA

Gomez, Rick (Actor)
c/o Sam Maydew *The Collective*
8383 Wilshire Blvd Ste 1050
Beverly Hills, CA 90211-2415, USA

Gomez, Selena (Actor)
5150 Garrett Ct
Hidden Hills, CA 91302-1143, USA

Gomez, Wilfredo (Athlete, Boxer)
Boxing Hall of Fame
1 Hall of Fame Dr
Canastota, NY 13032-1180, USA

Gomez-Preston, Reagen (Actor)
c/o Staff Member *Jeff Morrone Entertainment*
9350 Wilshire Blvd Ste 224
Beverly Hills, CA 90212-3204, USA

Gomez-Rejon, Alfonso (Director, Producer)
c/o Chris Donnelly *William Morris Endeavor (LA)*
9601 Wilshire Blvd
Beverly Hills, CA 90210-5213, USA

Gompers, Bill (Athlete, Football Player)
1060 Montego Bay Dr N
Merritt Island, FL 32953-3152, USA

Gompf, Thomas (Tom) (Athlete, Diver, Olympic Athlete)
2716 Barret Ave
Plant City, FL 33566-9550, USA

Gonchar, Sergei (Athlete, Hockey Player)
3401 Cornell Ave
Dallas, TX 75205-2901, USA

Gondrezick, Grant (Athlete, Basketball Player)
5906 Etiwanda Ave Unit 19
Tarzana, CA 91356-1649, USA

Gondry, Michel (Director, Writer)
c/o Dan Aloni *William Morris Endeavor (LA)*
9601 Wilshire Blvd
Beverly Hills, CA 90210-5213, USA

Gonick, Larry (Cartoonist)
247 Missouri St
San Francisco, CA 94107-2404, USA

Gonsoulin, Austin (Goose) (Athlete, Football Player)
7720 Summer Wind Dr
Beaumont, TX 77713-8492, USA

Gonzales, Carlos (Cinematographer)
3850 Tracy St
Los Angeles, CA 90027-4610, USA

Gonzales, Dan (Athlete, Baseball Player)
429 W Silvertip Rd
Tucson, AZ 85737-3704, USA

Gonzales, Jaslene (Model)
c/o Lizzie Grubman *Lizzie Grubman Public Relations*
424 W 33rd St Rm 110
New York, NY 10001-2619, USA

Gonzales, Larry (Athlete, Baseball Player)
3800 Bradford St Spc 248
La Verne, CA 91750-3151, USA

Gonzales, Rene (Athlete, Baseball Player)
755 E Orangewood Dr
Covina, CA 91723-3620, USA

Gonzalez, Alex (Athlete, Baseball Player)
192 Acorn Trl
Fleetwood, NC 28626-6000, USA

Gonzalez, Anthony (Athlete, Football Player)
314 Brunswick Dr
Avon Lake, OH 44012-2918, USA

Gonzalez, Charles (Congressman, Politician)
1434 Longworth Hob
Washington, DC 20515-0004, USA

Gonzalez, edgar (Athlete, Baseball Player)
2829 Echo Ridge Pl
Chula Vista, CA 91915-1617, USA

Gonzalez, Fredi (Athlete, Baseball Player, Coach)
2768 Pete Shaw Rd
Marietta, GA 30066-2206, USA

Gonzalez, Gabe (Athlete, Baseball Player)
920 Cerritos Ave
Long Beach, CA 90813-4812, USA

Gonzalez, gio
920 Cerritos Ave
Long Beach, CA 90813-4812, United States

Gonzalez, Hector (Religious Leader)
Baptist Churches USA
718 Arch St Ste 500N
Philadelphia, PA 19106-1529, USA

Gonzalez, Jeremi (Athlete, Baseball Player)
1120 N La Salle Dr Apt 14N
Chicago, IL 60610-7609, USA

Gonzalez, Juan (Athlete, Baseball Player)
c/o Staff Member *Texas Rangers*
1000 Ballpark Way Ste 400
Arlington, TX 76011-5170, USA

Gonzalez, Juan A (Baseball Player)
Ext Catoni A9
Vega Baja, PR 00693, USA

Gonzalez, Lazaro Naranjo (Cholly) (Athlete, Baseball Player)
8306 NW 7th St Apt 32
Miami, FL 33126-3924, USA

Gonzalez, Leon (Athlete, Football Player)
4025 Leonnie Rd
Jacksonville, FL 32208-2947, USA

Gonzalez, Luis (Athlete, Baseball Player)
8902 Ilona Ln Apt 8
Houston, TX 77025-3636, USA

Gonzalez, Mike (Athlete, Baseball Player)
2414 Pine Brook Ct
Deer Park, TX 77536-1518, USA

Gonzalez, Nicholas (Actor)
c/o Chuck James *ICM Partners (LA)*
10250 Constellation Blvd Fl 7
Los Angeles, CA 90067-6207, USA

Gonzalez, Orlando (Athlete, Baseball Player)
4309 SW 164th Ct
Miami, FL 33185-5294, USA

Gonzalez, Phoenix (Actor)
c/o Staff Member *Select Artists Ltd (CA-Westside Office)*
1138 12th St Apt 1
Santa Monica, CA 90403-5459, USA

Gonzalez, Rick (Actor)
c/o Stephanie Nese *Framework Entertainment (LA)*
9057 Nemo St Ste C
West Hollywood, CA 90069-5511, USA

Gonzalez, Tony (Athlete, Baseball Player)
8011 SW 196th Ter
Cutler Bay, FL 33189-2103, USA

Gonzalez, Tony (Athlete, Football Player)
c/o Denise White *EAG Sports Management*
909 N Sepulveda Blvd Ste 360
El Segundo, CA 90245-3864, USA

Gonzalo, Julie (Actor)
c/o Ben Levine *LINK Entertainment*
11872 La Grange Ave Fl 1
Los Angeles, CA 90025-5283, USA

Gooch, Jeff (Athlete, Football Player)
12709 Seronera Valley Ct
Spring Hill, FL 34610-7658, USA

Good, Andrew (Athlete, Baseball Player)
1433 S Belcher Rd Apt G4
Clearwater, FL 33764-2863, USA

Good, Hugh W (Religious Leader)
Primitive Advent Christian Church
6403 Frame Rd
Elkview, WV 25071-7040, USA

Good, Jonathan (Dean Ambrose) (Wrestler)
c/o Staff Member *World Wrestling Entertainment (WWE)*
1241 E Main St
Titan Towers
Stamford, CT 06902-3520, USA

Good, Meagan (Actor)
c/o Evan Hainey *Untitled Entertainment (LA)*
350 S Beverly Dr Ste 200
Beverly Hills, CA 90212-4819, USA

Good, Melanie (Actor)
c/o Staff Member *Bobby Ball Talent Agency*
3500 W Olive Ave Ste 300
Burbank, CA 91505-4647, USA

Good, Michael T (Astronaut)
3874 Cherry Plum Dr
Colorado Spgs, CO 80920-2802, USA

Good, Michael T Lt Colonel (Astronaut)
2617 Broussard Ct
Seabrook, TX 77586-3361

Goodacre, Connick Jill (Model)
Harry Connick
323 Broadway
Cambridge, MA 02139-1801, USA

Goodall, Jane (Writer)
The Jane Goodall Institute
1595 Spring Hill Rd Ste 550
Vienna, VA 22182-4100, USA

Goodburn, Kelly (Athlete, Football Player)
3710 W 52nd Pl
Roeland Park, KS 66205-2766, USA

Good Charlotte (Music Group)
81 Pondfield Rd # 358
Bronxville, NY 10708-3818, USA

Goode, Chris (Athlete, Football Player)
1428 Egret Ln
Birmingham, AL 35214-3410, USA

Goode, David R (Business Person)
Norfolk Southern Corp
3 Commercial Pl Ste 1A
Norfolk, VA 23510-2108, USA

Goode, Irvin (Irv) (Athlete, Football Player)
1030 Schnucks Woodsmill Plz
Chesterfield, MO 63017-0606, USA

Goode, Kerry (Athlete, Football Player)
639 Herron Ct
Fairburn, GA 30213-2398, USA

Goode, Matthew (Actor)
c/o Craig Bankey *Craig Bankey Public Relations*
4470 W Sunset Blvd # 315
Los Angeles, CA 90027-6302, USA

Goode, Rob (Athlete, Football Player)
1902 Oakridge Trl
Bridgeport, TX 76426-2620, USA

Goode, Tom (Athlete, Football Player)
9190 Tom Goode Rd
West Point, MS 39773-4487, USA

Goodell, Brian S (Athlete, Olympic Athlete, Swimmer)
27040 S Ridge Dr
Mission Viejo, CA 92692-5015, USA

Goodell, Roger (Business Person, Football Executive)
National Football League
280 Park Ave Fl 12W
Commissioner's Office
New York, NY 10017-1298, USA

Gooden, Drew (Basketball Player)
Orlando Magic
8701 Maitland Summit Blvd
Waterhouse Center
Orlando, FL 32810-5915, USA

Gooden, Dwight (Athlete, Baseball Player)
55 North Dr
Westbury, NY 11590-1011, USA

Gooden, Harry (Athlete, Football Player)
5001 Rime Vlg
Birmingham, AL 35216-6456, USA

Goodenough, Larry (Athlete, Hockey Player)
3677 Spruce Hill Rd
Ottsville, PA 18942-9508, USA

Goodeve, Charles P (Athlete, Football Player)
30177 Tattersail Way
Menifee, CA 92584-7366, USA

Goodeve, Grant (Actor)
2407 Loxford Ln
Alpharetta, GA 30009-8751, USA

Goodfriend, Lynda (Actor)
c/o Lynda Goodfriend *Lynda Goodfriend Management*
338 S Beachwood Dr
Burbank, CA 91506-2713, USA

Gooding, Cuba Jr (Actor)
14230 W Sunset Blvd
Pacific Palisades, CA 90272-3933, USA

Gooding, Omar (Actor)
c/o Ericalane Brown *The Kartel Company*
1304 W 2nd St Apt 310
Los Angeles, CA 90026-7011, USA

Goodlatte, Bob (Congressman, Politician)
2240 Rayburn Hob
Washington, DC 20515-4606, USA

Goodman, Allegra (Writer)
Dial Press
375 Hudson St
New York, NY 10014-3658, USA

Goodman, Amy (Journalist)
Democracy Now!
207 W 25th St Fl 11
New York, NY 10001-7161, USA

Goodman, Andre (Athlete, Football Player)
125 Island View Cir
Elgin, SC 29045-9182, USA

Goodman, Brian (Actor)
c/o Paul Santana *Agency for the Performing Arts (APA-LA)*
405 S Beverly Dr Ste 500
Beverly Hills, CA 90212-4425, USA

Goodman, Brian (Athlete, Football Player)
15009 S 14th Pl
Phoenix, AZ 85048-6242, USA

Goodman, David A. (Writer)
c/o Jon Huddle *United Talent Agency (UTA-LA)*
9336 Civic Center Dr
Beverly Hills, CA 90210-3604, USA

Goodman, Drew (Commentator)
5721 Green Oaks Dr
Greenwood Village, CO 80121-1336,
USA

Goodman, Harvey (Athlete, Football
Player)
2689 County Road 318
Westcliffe, CO 81252-8704, USA

Goodman, Henry
2015 Broad St Apt 108
Cranston, RI 02905-3346, USA

Goodman, John (Actor, Musician,
Producer)
c/o Bob Gersh *Gersh (LA)*
9465 Wilshire Blvd Ste 600
Beverly Hills, CA 90212-2605, USA

Goodman, John (Athlete, Football Player)
800 E 9th St
Edmond, OK 73034-5407, USA

Goodman, Malliciah (Athlete, Football
Player)
c/o Chad Speck *Allegiant Athletic Agency*
35 Market Sq Ste 201
Knoxville, TN 37902-1420, USA

Goodman, Richard (Producer)
c/o Staff Member *William Morris
Endeavor (LA)*
9601 Wilshire Blvd
Beverly Hills, CA 90210-5213, USA

Goodnight, James (Jim) (Business Person)
SAS Institute Inc
100 Sas Campus Dr
Cary, NC 27513-8617, USA

Goodnoff, Irvin (Cinematographer)
29997 Mulholland Hwy
Agoura Hills, CA 91301-3009, USA

Goodrem, Delta (Actor, Musician)
c/o Staff Member *Rebel One*
142 W 57th St Fl 5
New York, NY 10019-3300, USA

Goodrich, Dwayne (Athlete, Football
Player)
533 Oakcrest Dr
Coppell, TX 75019-4082, USA

Goodrich, Gail (Actor, Athlete, Basketball
Player, Sportscaster)
PO Box 6999
Ketchum, ID 83340-6999, USA

Goodrich, Jon (Baseball Player)
123 W Agua Caliente Rd
Sonoma, CA 95476-3340, USA

Goodrich Jr, Gail C (Athlete, Basketball
Player)
270 Oceano Dr
Los Angeles, CA 90049-4124, USA

Goodrum, Charles (Athlete, Football
Player)
117 Pico Rd
East Palatka, FL 32131, USA

Goodson, Ed (Athlete, Baseball Player)
2330 Cold Springs Ln
Galax, VA 24333-3763, USA

Goodwill, Oliver (Actor)
Asylum Entertainment
15503 Ventura Blvd Ste 240
C/O Marcello Robinson
Encino, CA 91436-3162, USA

Goodwin, Curtis (Athlete, Baseball Player)
14939 Western Ave
San Leandro, CA 94578-3627, USA

Goodwin, Danny (Athlete, Baseball
Player)
1555 Linksview Close
Stone Mountain, GA 30088-3768, USA

Goodwin, Doug (Athlete, Football Player)
400 Waverly Place Cir Apt B1
North Charleston, SC 29418-2010, USA

Goodwin, Ginnifer (Actor)
c/o John Carrabino *John Carrabino
Management*
5900 Wilshire Blvd Ste 406
Los Angeles, CA 90036-5015, USA

Goodwin, Hunter (Athlete, Football
Player)
1011 Lyceum Ct
College Station, TX 77840-2342, USA

Goodwin, Marquise (Athlete, Football
Player)
c/o Joby Branion *Athletes First, LLC*
23091 Mill Creek Dr
Laguna Hills, CA 92653-1258, USA

Goodwin, Michael (Actor)
8271 Melrose Ave Ste 110
Los Angeles, CA 90046-6800, USA

Goodwin, Randy (Race Car Driver)
Randy Goodwin Racing
2009 Somerset Ln
Fullerton, CA 92833, USA

Goodwin, Tom (Athlete, Baseball Player,
Olympic Athlete)
8 Maple St
Massapequa, NY 11758-5717, USA

Goodyear, Scott (Race Car Driver)
Scott Goodyear Racing
PO Box 589
Carmel, IN 46082-0589, USA

Goo Goo Dolls (Music Group)
c/o David Levine *William Morris
Endeavor (LA)*
9601 Wilshire Blvd
Beverly Hills, CA 90210-5213, USA

Goorjian, Michael (Actor)
Evolution Entertainment
901 N Highland Ave
Los Angeles, CA 90038-2412, USA

Goosen, Don (Boxer, Misc)
6320 Van Nuys Blvd
Van Nuys, CA 91401-2617, USA

Gorani, Hala (Correspondent)
c/o Staff Member *CNN (Atlanta)*
1 Cnn Ctr NW
PO Box 105366
Atlanta, GA 30303-2762, USA

Goranson, Alicia (Actor)
c/o Staff Member *Paradigm (LA)*
360 N Crescent Dr
North Bldg
Beverly Hills, CA 90210-4874, USA

Gordeeva, Ekaterina (Athlete, Figure
Skater)
c/o Staff Member *IMG (LA)*
2049 Century Park E Ste 2460
Los Angeles, CA 90067-3126, USA

Gorder, Genevieve (Designer, Television
Host)
c/o Ken Slotnick *William Morris Endeavor
(NY)*
1325 Avenue of the Americas
New York, NY 10019-6026, USA

Gordin, Charles (Actor)
187 Chestnut Hill Rd
Wilton, CT 06897-4108, USA

Gordon, Barry (Actor, Music Group)
1912 Kaweah Dr
Pasadena, CA 91105-3604, USA

Gordon, Ben (Athlete, Basketball Player)
c/o Raymond Brothers *International
Athlete Management, Inc*
433 N Camden Dr Ste 600
Beverly Hills, CA 90210-4416, USA

Gordon, Bert I (Director)
9640 Arby Dr
Beverly Hills, CA 90210-1202, USA

Gordon, Bing
Kleiner, Perkins, Caufield, Byers
2750 Sand Hill Rd
Menlo Park, CA 94025-7020, USA

Gordon, Bobby (Race Car Driver)
6300 Valley View St
Buena Park, CA 90620-1032, USA

Gordon, Bridgette (Athlete, Basketball
Player, Olympic Athlete)
3400 Sweetwater Rd Apt 1309
Lawrenceville, GA 30044-2495, USA

Gordon, Carl
8661 Pine Tree Pl
Los Angeles, CA 90069-1201

Gordon, Cornell (Athlete, Football Player)
4029 Spring Meadow Cres
Chesapeake, VA 23321-3117, USA

Gordon, Danso (Actor)
c/o Paul Nicholls *Industry Entertainment*
955 Carrillo Dr Ste 300
Los Angeles, CA 90048-5400, USA

Gordon, Darrien (Athlete, Football Player)
1500 Pecos Dr
Southlake, TX 76092-5933, USA

Gordon, Dick (Athlete, Football Player)
5017 Anderson Pl
Cincinnati, OH 45227-1601, USA

Gordon, Don (Actor)
Acme Talent
4727 Wilshire Blvd Ste 333
Los Angeles, CA 90010-3874, USA

Gordon, Don (Athlete, Baseball Player)
711 Sunset Mountain Dr
Dr
Chattanooga, TN 37421-2076, USA

Gordon, Don
6853 Pacific View Dr
Los Angeles, CA 90068-1831

Gordon, Ed (Correspondent)
NBC-TV
30 Rockefeller Plz Ste 4340
New York, NY 10112-4301, USA

Gordon, Eve (Actor)
10100 Santa Monica Blvd Ste 2500
Los Angeles, CA 90067-4116

Gordon, Harold P (Business Person)
Hasbro Inc
1027 Newport Ave
Pawtucket, RI 02861-2500, USA

Gordon, Herold (Athlete, Baseball Player)
8798 Traverse St
Detroit, MI 48213-1158, USA

Gordon, Howard (Producer, Writer)
c/o Rick Rosen *William Morris Endeavor
(LA)*
9601 Wilshire Blvd
Beverly Hills, CA 90210-5213, USA

Gordon, Ira (Athlete, Football Player)
PO Box 24526
Federal Way, WA 98093-1526, USA

Gordon, Jeff (Race Car Driver)
c/o Zak Brown *Just Marketing
International*
10960 Bennett Pkwy
Zionsville, IN 46077-8195, USA

Gordon, John (Commentator)
13011 Milford Pl
Fort Myers, FL 33913-8454, USA

Gordon, Josh (Athlete, Football Player)
c/o Drew Rosenhaus *Rosenhaus Sports
Representation*
6400 Allison Rd
Miami Beach, FL 33141-4540, USA

Gordon, Keith (Actor, Director, Writer)
c/o Dan Aloni *William Morris Endeavor
(LA)*
9601 Wilshire Blvd
Beverly Hills, CA 90210-5213, USA

Gordon, Keith (Athlete, Baseball Player)
4601 Thornhurst Dr
Olney, MD 20832-1826, USA

Gordon, Kiowa (Actor)
c/o Ryan Martin *Agency for the
Performing Arts (APA-LA)*
405 S Beverly Dr Ste 500
Beverly Hills, CA 90212-4425, USA

Gordon, Lamar (Athlete, Football Player)
4331 N 16th St
Milwaukee, WI 53209-6924, USA

Gordon, Lancaster (Athlete, Basketball
Player)
550 Robinhood Rd
Jackson, MS 39206-5403, USA

Gordon, Lawrence (Business Person)
Largo Entertainment
10201 W Pico Blvd
Los Angeles, CA 90064-2606, USA

Gordon, Leo
9977 Wornom Ave
Sunland, CA 91040-1549

Gordon, Mark (Producer)
Mark Gordon Productions
12200 W Olympic Blvd Ste 250
Los Angeles, CA 90064-1038, USA

Gordon, Mikalah (Musician)
c/o Stephen Ford *Diva Central Inc*
7510 W Sunset Blvd Ste 1445
Los Angeles, CA 90046-3408, USA

Gordon, Mike (Athlete, Baseball Player)
35 Longview Rd
Brockton, MA 02301-5637, USA

Gordon, Mike (Musician)
c/o Jason Colton *Red Light Management
(VA)*
321 E Main St Ste 500
Charlottesville, VA 22902-3201, USA

Gordon, Nina (Musician)
c/o Staff Member *Paradigm (Monterey)*
404 W Franklin St
Monterey, CA 93940-2303, USA

Gordon, Richard (Astronaut)
65 Woodside Dr
Prescott, AZ 86305-5092, USA

Gordon, Richard F Jr (Astronaut)
65 Woodside Dr
Prescott, AZ 86305-5092, USA

Gordon, Robby (Race Car Driver)
Robby Gordon Motorsports
10615 Twin Lakes Pkwy
Charlotte, NC 28269-7659, USA

Gordon, Scott (Athlete, Coach, Hockey Player)
c/o Staff Member *Providence Bruins*
1 La Salle Sq
Providence, RI 02903-1888, USA

Gordon, Sean (Model)
c/o Staff Member *IMG*
304 Park Ave S Fl 12
New York, NY 10010-4314, USA

Gordon, Seth (Director)
5507 Ridge Oak Dr
Los Angeles, CA 90068-2553, USA

Gordon, Stuart (Director, Producer)
c/o Staff Member *Red Hen Productions*
13500 Crewe St
Van Nuys, CA 91405-4233, USA

Gordon, Tom (Athlete, Baseball Player)
2006 Lake Lotela Dr
Avon Park, FL 33825-8030, USA

Gordon, Tracy (Race Car Driver)
Beal's General Store
Main St.
Strong, ME 02983, USA

Gordon, Zachary (Actor)
c/o Daniel Spilo *Industry Entertainment*
955 Carrillo Dr Ste 300
Los Angeles, CA 90048-5400, USA

Gordon-Levitt, Joseph (Actor)
2554 Micheltorena St
Los Angeles, CA 90039-2534, USA

Gordy, Berry (Musician, Producer)
801 Sarbonne Rd
Los Angeles, CA 90077-3303, USA

Gore, Al (Politician)
The Office of Al & Tipper Gore
3810 Bedford Ave Ste 250
Nashville, TN 37215-2563, USA

Gore, Frank (Athlete, Football Player)
16820 NE 8th Pl
North Miami Beach, FL 33162-2511, USA

Gore, Lesley (Musician, Songwriter, Writer)
World Entertainment Assoc
297101 Kinderkamack Rd
#128
Oradell, NJ 07649, USA

Gore, Michael
15622 Royal Oak Rd
Encino, CA 91436-3906

Gore, Tipper (Politician)
The Office of Al & Tipper Gore
3810 Bedford Ave Ste 250
Nashville, TN 37215-2563, USA

Gorecki, Reid (Athlete, Baseball Player)
1017 Crestdale
Crossing Dr
Avon Park, FL 33825, USA

Gorecki, Rick (Athlete, Baseball Player)
8703 Powers Ct
Orland Park, IL 60462-5695, USA

Gore Jr, Albert A (President, Vice President)
312 Lynnwood Blvd
Nashville, TN 37205-2927, USA

Gorence, Tom (Athlete, Hockey Player)
36666 Tallowood Dr
Palm Desert, CA 92211-2394, USA

Gores, Tom (Business Person)
78 Beverly Park Ln
Beverly Hills, CA 90210-1573, USA

Gorga, Melissa (Musician, Reality Star)
c/o Jaime Cassavechia *EJ Media Group*
349 5th Ave Fl 3
New York, NY 10016-5019, USA

Gorgal, Ken (Athlete, Football Player)
4 the Court of Harborside
Northbrook, IL 60062-3207, USA

Gorham, Christopher (Actor)
c/o Glenn Rigberg *Inphenate*
9701 Wilshire Blvd Fl 10
Beverly Hills, CA 90212-2010, USA

Gorie, Docominic L
13656 Hidden Valley Ln
Salida, CO 81201-9760, USA

Gorie, Dominic L Pudwill (Astronaut)
13656 Hidden Valley Ln
Salida, CO 81201-9760, USA

Gorin, Brandon (Athlete, Football Player)
5277 N College Ave
Indianapolis, IN 46220-3139, USA

Goring, Robert T (Butch) (Athlete, Hockey Player)
1255 Hempstead Tpke
Attn: Broadcast Dept
Uniondale, NY 11553-1260, USA

Gorinski, Bob (Athlete, Baseball Player)
758 Claypike Rd
Acme, PA 15610-2177, USA

Goris, Eva (Actor)
International Creative Mgmt
10250 Constellation Blvd Fl 1
Los Angeles, CA 90067-6241, USA

Gorman, Brian (Athlete, Baseball Player)
1381 Via Latina Dr
Camarillo, CA 93012-9294, USA

Gorman, Brian (Baseball Player)
PO Box 1208
Somis, CA 93066-1208, USA

Gorman, Bryan (Athlete, Golfer)
525 Hunte Pkwy
the Auld Course
Chula Vista, CA 91914-4137, USA

Gorman, Burn (Actor)
c/o Chris Huvane *Management 360*
9111 Wilshire Blvd
Beverly Hills, CA 90210-5508, USA

Gorman, Cliff
333 W 57th St Apt 708
New York, NY 10019-3108

Gorman, E J (Writer)
PO Box 669
Cedar Rapids, IA 52406-0669, USA

Gorman, Joseph T (Business Person)
TRW Inc
1900 Richmond Rd
Cleveland, OH 44124, USA

Gorman, Steve (Musician)
c/o Staff Member *Mitch Schneider Organization (MSO)*
14724 Ventura Blvd Ste 410
Sherman Oaks, CA 91403-3537, USA

Gorman, Tom (Athlete, Baseball Player)
1615 SW 5th Ave
Portland, OR 97201-5403, USA

Gorman, Tom (Tennis Player)
ProServe
1101 Woodrow Wilson Blvd
#1800
Arlington, VA 22209, USA

Gorman-Cahill, Margaret
4216 38th St NW
Washington, DC 20016-2258

Gorneault, Nick (Athlete, Baseball Player)
94 Seymour Ave
Springfield, MA 01109-1330, USA

Gorney, Karen Lynn (Actor)
Karen Company
PO Box 23-1060
New York, NY 10023, USA

Gorrell, Bob (Cartoonist)
Creators Syndicate
737 3rd St
Hermosa Beach, CA 90254-4714, USA

Gorrer, Danny (Athlete, Football Player)
c/o David Dunn *Athletes First, LLC*
23091 Mill Creek Dr
Laguna Hills, CA 92653-1258, USA

Gorski, Mark (Athlete, Cycler, Olympic Athlete)
17 Colonial Hills Pkwy
Saint Louis, MO 63141-7765, USA

Gortman, Shaunzinski (Basketball Player)
Charlotte Sting
100 Hive Dr
Charlotte, NC 28217-4524, USA

Gortner, Marjoe (Actor)
PO Box 356
Sun Valley, ID 83353-0356, USA

Gorvl, John (Athlete, Baseball Player)
1888 Cranberry Isle
Way
Apopka, FL 32712, USA

Goryl, John (Athlete, Baseball Player, Coach)
528 Dry Run Rd
Monongahela, PA 15063-1223, USA

Gorzelanny, Tom (Athlete, Baseball Player)
10522 Louetta Ln
Orland Park, IL 60467-1350, USA

Gosar, Paul (Congressman, Politician)
504 Cannon Hob
Washington, DC 20515-4204, USA

Gosger, Jim (Athlete, Baseball Player)
1823 7th St
Port Huron, MI 48060-6301, USA

Gosling, Mike (Athlete, Baseball Player)
2016 Crest Dr
Encinitas, CA 92024-5218, USA

Gosling, Ryan (Actor)
3815 Berry Dr
Studio City, CA 91604-3858, USA

Gosnell, Raja (Director)
c/o Staff Member *Creative Artists Agency (CAA-LA)*
2000 Avenue of the Stars Ste 100
Los Angeles, CA 90067-4705, USA

Goss, Luke (Actor)
Insomnia Media Group
100 Universal Dr Bungalow 7151
Universal City, CA 91608, USA

Goss, Matt (Actor)
c/o Staff Member *Andrew Freedman Public Relations*
9127 Thrasher Ave
Los Angeles, CA 90069-1144, USA

Gossage, Goose (Athlete, Baseball Player)
Wish You Were Here Productions
303 E 83rd St Apt 6A
New York, NY 10028-4316, USA

Gossage, Rich (Athlete, Baseball Player)
35 Marland Rd
Colorado Springs, CO 80906-4328, USA

Gosselaar, Mark-Paul (Actor)
c/o Staff Member *James/Levy Management Inc*
3500 W Olive Ave Ste 1470
Burbank, CA 91505-5514, USA

Gosselin, Guy (Athlete, Hockey Player, Olympic Athlete)
Mlkern sports
131 Bissen St
Caledonia, MN 55921-1811, USA

Gosselin, Jonathan (Reality Star)
c/o Mike Heller *Talent Resources*
124 E 36th St Ste A
New York, NY 10016-3402, USA

Gosselin, Kate (Reality Star)
c/o Julie May *Media Motion International (MMI)*
15332 Antioch St # 726
Pacific Palisades, CA 90272-3628, USA

Gosselin, Mario (Race Car Driver)
Wing's Racing
270 Parkside Ln
Rocky Mount, VA 24151-2671, USA

Gossett, David (Athlete, Golfer)
3405 Normandy Ridge Ln
Austin, TX 78738-5446, USA

Gossett, D Bruce (Athlete, Football Player)
6109 Puerto Dr
Rancho Murieta, CA 95683-9320, USA

Gossett, Jeff (Athlete, Football Player)
6 Lake Forest Ct
Roanoke, TX 76262-5504, USA

Gossett, Robert (Actor)
c/o Staff Member *Leavitt Talent Group*
8222 Melrose Ave Ste 203
Los Angeles, CA 90046-6838, USA

Gossett Jr, Louis (Actor)
c/o Hillard Elkins *Elkins Entertainment*
8306 Wilshire Blvd Ste 438
Beverly Hills, CA 90211-2304, USA

Gossick, Sue (Athlete, Diver, Olympic Athlete)
11738 Villageview Ct
Moorpark, CA 93021-3759, USA

Gossick Crockatt, Sue (Swimmer)
13768 Christian Barrett Dr
Moorpark, CA 93021-2802, USA

Gossin, Tom (Musician)
1701 Russell St
Nashville, TN 37206-2047, USA

Gossip (Music Group)
c/o Sara Newkirk Simon *William Morris Endeavor (LA)*
9601 Wilshire Blvd
Beverly Hills, CA 90210-5213, USA

Gossom, Thom (Athlete, Football Player)
25 Bay Dr SE
Fort Walton Beach, FL 32548-5701, USA

Gostkowski, Stephen (Athlete, Football Player)
2104 Old Bridge Ln
Bellingham, MA 02019-3137, USA

Gotch, Karl
18530 Wayne Rd
Odessa, FL 33556-4739

Gothard, Preston (Athlete, Football Player)
448 Merry Way
Pike Road, AL 36064-2282, USA

Gotshalk, Len (Athlete, Football Player)
1200 Butler Creek Rd
Ashland, OR 97520-9370, USA

Gotshalk, Leonard (Athlete, Football Player)
1200 Butler Creek Rd
Ashland, OR 97520-9370, USA

Gott, Jim (Athlete, Baseball Player)
2275 Huntil Lgton
Dr Unit 177
San Marino, CA 91108, USA

Gottfried, Brian (Tennis Player)
PO Box 417
Ponte Vedra Beach, FL 32004-0417, USA

Gottfried, Gilbert (Actor, Comedian)
c/o Steve Honig *Honig Company, The*
4804 Laurel Canyon Blvd Ste 828
Valley Village, CA 91607-3717, USA

Gotti, Carmine (Reality Star)
c/o Staff Member *Growing Up Gotti*
13400 Riverside Dr Ste 300
Sherman Oaks, CA 91423-2546, USA

Gotti, John, Jr (Reality Star)
c/o Staff Member *Growing Up Gotti*
13400 Riverside Dr Ste 300
Sherman Oaks, CA 91423-2546, USA

Gotti, Victoria (Actor, Producer, Reality Star)
6 Birch Hill Ct
Old Westbury, NY 11568-1218, USA

Gottlieb, Bill (Writer)
c/o Staff Member *Simon & Schuster*
1230 Avenue of the Americas Fl CONC1
New York, NY 10020-1586, USA

Gottlieb, Bill J (Producer)
c/o Staff Member *Gorilla Pictures*
2000 W Olive Ave
Burbank, CA 91506-2642, USA

Gottman, John (Writer)
The Gottman Institute, Inc
1401 E Jefferson St Ste 501
Seattle, WA 98122-5570, USA

Gottwald, Lukasz (Dr. Luke) (Producer)
Kemosabe Entertainment, LLC
9111 W Sunset Blvd
West Hollywood, CA 90069-3106, USA

Goude, Ingrid (Model)
511 Las Fuentes Dr
Santa Barbara, CA 93108-2250, USA

Gough, Alfred (Writer)
c/o Renee Kurtz *Creative Artists Agency (CAA-LA)*
2000 Avenue of the Stars Ste 100
Los Angeles, CA 90067-4705, USA

Gough, Tommy (Musician)
Brothers Mgmt
141 Dunbar Ave
Fords, NJ 08863-1551, USA

Goulart, Izabel (Actor, Model)
c/o Staff Member *Women Model Management*
199 Lafayette St Fl 7
New York, NY 10012-4281, USA

Gould, Alexander (Actor)
c/o TJ Stein *Stein Entertainment Group*
1351 N Crescent Heights Blvd Apt 312
West Hollywood, CA 90046-4549, USA

Gould, Elizabeth (Doctor)
Princeton University
Medical Center
Neurosciences Dept
Princeton, NJ 08544-0001, USA

Gould, Elliott (Actor)
c/o Jeff Witjas *Agency for the Performing Arts (APA-LA)*
405 S Beverly Dr Ste 500
Beverly Hills, CA 90212-4425, USA

Gould, Hal (Athlete, Baseball Player)
126 Rogers Ave
Millville, NJ 08332-9723, USA

Gould, Kelly (Actor)
c/o TJ Stein *Stein Entertainment Group*
1351 N Crescent Heights Blvd Apt 312
West Hollywood, CA 90046-4549, USA

Gould, Larry
2918 Wright St
Port Huron, MI 48060-8529

Gould, Matt Kennedy (Reality Star)
c/o Staff Member *William Morris Endeavor (LA)*
9601 Wilshire Blvd
Beverly Hills, CA 90210-5213, USA

Gould, Nolan (Actor)
c/o Jamie Malone *MC Talent Management*
4821 Lankershim Blvd # F329
N Hollywood, CA 91601-4538, USA

Gould, Robbie
22394 N Prairie Ln
Kildeer, IL 60047-9771, USA

Gould, Terry (Producer)
c/o Staff Member *Lenhoff & Lenhoff*
830 Palm Ave
West Hollywood, CA 90069-4009

Goulding, Ellie (Musician)
c/o Staff Member *Next Model Management (LA)*
8447 Wilshire Blvd PH
Beverly Hills, CA 90211-1683, USA

Goulet, Michael (Athlete, Hockey Player)
PO Box 656
Sedalia, CO 80135-0656, USA

Goulet, Michel (Athlete, Hockey Player)
17 Viking Dr
Englewood, CO 80113-7054, USA

Gourdine, Jerome (Musician)
188 Tamarron Cliffs St
Las Vegas, NV 89148-2794, USA

Gouveia, Kurt (Athlete, Football Player)
138 Seagrove Ln
Mooresville, NC 28117-8976, USA

Govan, Gerald (Athlete, Basketball Player)
30 Newport Pkwy Apt 2112
Jersey City, NJ 07310-1512, USA

Gove, David
59 Blackthorn Rd
Marstons Mills, MA 02648-1026

Gove, Jeff (Athlete, Golfer)
6500 NE 171st Pl
Kenmore, WA 98028-3932, USA

Govedaris, Chris (Athlete, Hockey Player)
123 Farmington Ave Ste 3
Bristol, CT 06010-4200, USA

Govedaris, David (Athlete, Hockey Player)
3838B Lower Union Rd
Orlando, FL 32814-6508, USA

Goverde, David (Athlete, Hockey Player)
3838B Lower Union Rd
Orlando, FL 32814-6508

Govich, Milena (Actor)
c/o Rhonda Price *Gersh (NY)*
41 Madison Ave
New York, NY 10010-2202, USA

Gov't Mule (Music Group)
c/o Staff Member *Paradigm (Monterey)*
404 W Franklin St
Monterey, CA 93940-2303, USA

Gowan, Caroline (Athlete, Golfer)
209 Crescent Ave
Greenville, SC 29605-2814, USA

Gowan, Lawrence (Musician)
c/o Sterling Bacon *TBA Artist Management (Atlanta)*
1111 Alderman Dr Ste 285
Alpharetta, GA 30005-5433, USA

Gowdy, Cornell (Athlete, Football Player)
4611 John St
Suitland, MD 20746-3772, USA

Gowdy, Trey (Congressman, Politician)
1237 Longworth Hob
Washington, DC 20515-0302, USA

Gowell, Larry (Athlete, Baseball Player)
45 Seventh St Apt 2
Auburn, ME 04210-5692, USA

Gower, Jessica (Actor)
c/o Jason Newman *Untitled Entertainment (LA)*
350 S Beverly Dr Ste 200
Beverly Hills, CA 90212-4819, USA

Gowin, Toby (Athlete, Football Player)
847 Fort Worth St
Jacksonville, TX 75766-2709, USA

Goydos, Paul (Athlete, Golfer)
1864 Stearnlee Ave
Long Beach, CA 90815-3040, USA

Goyer, David (Director, Producer, Writer)
c/o Dan Aloni *William Morris Endeavor (LA)*
9601 Wilshire Blvd
Beverly Hills, CA 90210-5213, USA

Goyo, Dakota (Actor)
c/o Steven Kavovit *Thruline Entertainment*
9250 Wilshire Blvd Ste 100
Ground Floor
Beverly Hills, CA 90212-3343, USA

Gozzo, Mauro (Athlete, Baseball Player)
156 Newton St
Berlin, CT 06037-1254, USA

Grabarkewitz, Billy (Athlete, Baseball Player)
2162 Estes Park Rd
Southlake, TX 76092-3835, USA

Grabe, Ronald J (Astronaut)
2652 E Scorpio Pl
Chandler, AZ 85249-5253, USA

Grabe, Ronald J Colonel (Astronaut)
2653 E Scorpio Pl
Chandler, AZ 85249-5257, USA

Grabeel, Lucas (Actor)
c/o Robert C. Thompson *Group III Management*
13914 Addison St
Sherman Oaks, CA 91423-1214, USA

Graber, Bill (Athlete, Track Athlete)
PO Box 5019
Upland, CA 91785-5019, USA

Graber, Rod (Athlete, Baseball Player)
1750 Arnold Way Apt 112
Alpine, CA 91901-3759, USA

Grabow, John (Athlete, Baseball Player)
19415 E Via Del Palo
Queen Creek, AZ 85142-8276, USA

Grabowski, James S (Jim) (Athlete, Football Player)
1523 Withorn Ln
Inverness, IL 60067-4367, USA

Grabowski, Jason (Athlete, Baseball Player)
3328 E Franklin Ave
Gilbert, AZ 85295-3401, USA

Grace, April (Actor)
c/o Lenore Zerman *Liberman/Zerman Management*
252 N Larchmont Blvd Ste 200
Los Angeles, CA 90004-3754, USA

Grace, Bud (Cartoonist)
PO Box 66
Oakton, VA 22124-0066, USA

Grace, Maggie (Actor)
c/o Darren Goldberg *Global Creative*
1051 Cole Ave # B
Los Angeles, CA 90038-2601, USA

Grace, Mark (Athlete, Baseball Player)
5624 E Via Buena Vis
Paradise Valley, AZ 85253-8129, USA

Grace, Mike (Athlete, Baseball Player)
12791 Big Lake Rd
Davisburg, MI 48350-3419, USA

Grace, Nancy (Attorney, Television Host)
1 Cnn Ctr SE 310E
Atlanta, GA 30303, USA

Grace, Robert Bud (Cartoonist)
1401 Park Garden Ln
Reston, VA 20194-1994, USA

Grace, Topher (Actor)
8707 Sunset Plaza Pl
Los Angeles, CA 90069-1345, USA

Graceffa, Joey (Actor)
PO Box 5344
Culver City, CA 90231-5344, USA

Graceland
3765 Elvis Presley Blvd
Memphis, TN 38116-4105

Gracie, Charlie (Musician)
Jeff Hubbard Productions
PO Box 53664
Indianapolis, IN 46253-0664, USA

Gracie, Royce (Athlete, Wrestler)
KhonKhor Enterprises Inc
9806 Zackery Ave
Charlotte, NC 28277-2124, USA

Gracin, Joshua (Musician)
c/o Rob Beckham *William Morris Endeavor (Nashville)*
1600 Division St Ste 300
Nashville, TN 37203-2755, USA

Graddy, Sam (Athlete, Football Player)
4792 Brasac Dr
Stone Mountain, GA 30083-5100, USA

Gradishar, Randy C (Athlete, Football Player)
7628 Pineridge Ter
Castle Pines, CO 80108-8260, USA

Gradison, Ronnie (Athlete, Basketball Player)
6151 Chappellfield Dr
West Chester, OH 45069-6648, USA

Gradkowski, Bruce (Athlete, Football Player)
1120 Peermont Ave
Pittsburgh, PA 15216-2214, USA

Gradkowski, Gino (Athlete, Football Player)
c/o Joe Linta *JL Sports*
1204 Main St Ste 179
Branford, CT 06405-3787, USA

Grady, Ellen
150 E Olive Ave Ste 111
Burbank, CA 91502-1849

Grady, James T (Politician)
International Teamsters Brotherhood
25 Louisiana Ave NW
Washington, DC 20001-2198, USA

Graeber, Clark (Tennis Player)
411 Harbor Rd
Fairfield, CT 06431, USA

Graef, Jed (Athlete, Olympic Athlete, Swimmer)
PO Box 880
Shelburne, VT 05482-0880, USA

Graf, Dave (Athlete, Football Player)
1825 Bel Air Ave
Pompano Beach, FL 33062-7672, USA

Graf, Richard (Athlete, Football Player)
11108 Bluestem Ln
Eden Prairie, MN 55347-4731, USA

Graf, Rick (Athlete, Football Player)
6609 Biscayne Blvd
Minneapolis, MN 55436-1703, USA

Graf, Stefanie (Steffi) (Athlete, Tennis Player)
8921 Andre Dr
Las Vegas, NV 89148-1405, USA

Graff, Ilena (Actor)
11455 Sunshine Ter
Studio City, CA 91604-3129, USA

Graff, Neil (Athlete, Football Player)
Graff Capital Management
PO Box 2696
Sioux Falls, SD 57101-2696, USA

Graff, Randy (Actor)
Peter Strawn Assoc
1501 Broadway Ste 2900
New York, NY 10036-5600, USA

Graff, Todd (Actor)
547 Hudson St
New York, NY 10014-3290

Graffanino, Tony (Athlete, Baseball Player)
6744 W Lucia Dr
Peoria, AZ 85383-6612, USA

Graffman, Gary (Musician)
Curtis Institute of Music
1726 Locust St
Philadelphia, PA 19103-6187, USA

Grafton, Sue (Writer)
PO Box 41446
Santa Barbara, CA 93140-1446, USA

Gragg, Chris (Athlete, Football Player)
c/o Joel Segal *Lagardere Unlimited (NYC)*
845 United Nations Plz
New York, NY 10017-3540, USA

Gragg, Scott (Athlete, Football Player)
583 Cash Nichols Rd
Stevensville, MT 59870-6625, USA

Graham, Art (Athlete, Football Player)
PO Box 785
South Orleans, MA 02662-0785, USA

Graham, Aubrey (Drake) (Actor, Musician)
c/o Cortez Bryant *Blueprint Group*
659 Auburn Ave NE Apt 114
Atlanta, GA 30312-1954, USA

Graham, Bill (Athlete, Football Player)
11013 Sierra Verde Trl
Austin, TX 78759-5129, USA

Graham, Bob (Politician)
14814 Breckness Pl
Miami Lakes, FL 33016-1458, USA

Graham, Brendan (Musician, Writer)
c/o Staff Member *PeerMusic USA*
3260 Blume Dr Ste 405
San Pablo, CA 94806-5277, USA

Graham, Brian (Athlete, Baseball Player)
11995 El Camino Real Ste 305
San Diego, CA 92130-2567, USA

Graham, Chris (Director)
c/o Simon Millar *Rumble Media*
1620 Broadway Ste C
Santa Monica, CA 90404-2777, USA

Graham, Currie
c/o Vera Mihailovich *Forward Entertainment*
9255 W Sunset Blvd Ste 805
West Hollywood, CA 90069-3305, USA

Graham, Dan (Athlete, Baseball Player)
6444 Little Pine Way
Las Vegas, NV 89108-3420, USA

Graham, David (Athlete, Golfer)
4201 Lomo Alto Dr Apt 305
Dallas, TX 75219-1515, USA

Graham, Demingo (Athlete, Football Player)
179 Hillside Ter
Irvington, NJ 07111-1506

Graham, Derrick (Athlete, Football Player)
203 Pine Hill Rd
West End, NC 27376-8848, USA

Graham, Dick (Athlete, Hockey Player)
13580 Technology Dr Apt 3314
Eden Prairie, MN 55344-2317, USA

Graham, Dirk (Athlete, Coach, Hockey Player)
17001 S Blackfoot Dr
Lockport, IL 60441-4367

Graham, Donald E (Publisher)
Washington Post Co
1150 15th St NW
Washington, DC 20071-0002, USA

Graham, Franklin (Religious Leader)
Samantan's Purse
PO Box 3000
Boone, NC 28607-3000, USA

Graham, Garrett (Athlete, Football Player)
c/o David Dunn *Athletes First, LLC*
23091 Mill Creek Dr
Laguna Hills, CA 92653-1258, USA

Graham, Gerrit (Actor)
S M S Talent
8383 Wilshire Blvd Ste 230
Beverly Hills, CA 90211-2436, USA

Graham, Glen (Musician)
Shapiro Co
9229 W Sunset Blvd Ste 607
West Hollywood, CA 90069-3406, USA

Graham, Greg (Athlete, Basketball Player)
12636 Wolf Run Rd
Noblesville, IN 46060-8001, USA

Graham, Hason (Athlete, Football Player)
PO Box 422281
Atlanta, GA 30342-9281, USA

Graham, Heather (Actor, Producer)
c/o Risa Shapiro *The Schiff Company*
9220 W Sunset Blvd Ste 106
West Hollywood, CA 90069-3500, USA

Graham, Jeff (Athlete, Football Player)
1840 Infirmary Rd
Dayton, OH 45417-5730, USA

Graham, Jimmy (Athlete, Football Player)
c/o Jimmy Sexton *CAA (Memphis)*
6060 Poplar Ave Ste 470
Memphis, TN 38119-0910, USA

Graham, John R (Writer)
University of California
Astronomy Dept
Berkeley, CA 94720-0001, USA

Graham, Jorie (Writer)
General Delivery
12 Quincy St
Cambridge, MA 02138-3804, USA

Graham, Kat (Katerina) (Actor, Musician)
c/o Jon Simmons *Simmons & Scott Entertainment*
7942 Mulholland Dr
Los Angeles, CA 90046-1225, USA

Graham, Kenny (Athlete, Football Player)
PO Box 7402
Santa Monica, CA 90406-7402, USA

Graham, Kent (Athlete, Football Player)
1001 N Washington St
Wheaton, IL 60187-3857, USA

Graham, Larry (Musician)
c/o Staff Member *Variety Artists International Inc*
1924 Spring St
Paso Robles, CA 93446-1620, USA

Graham, Lauren (Actor)
c/o Staff Member *Good Game Entertainment*
4000 Warner Blvd Bldg 101
Burbank, CA 91522-0001, USA

Graham, Lee (Athlete, Baseball Player)
481 Richmond Rd
Cleveland, OH 44143-2745, USA

Graham, Linda (Bowler)
4147 E Seneca Ave
Des Moines, IA 50317-8123, USA

Graham, Lindsey (Politician)
PO Box 486
Seneca, SC 29679-0486, USA

Graham, Lou (Athlete, Golfer)
85 Concord Park W
Nashville, TN 37205-4707, USA

Graham, Mal (Athlete, Basketball Player)
122 Christina St
Newton Highlands, MA 02461-1916, USA

Graham, Milt (Athlete, Football Player)
21 Wildflower Ln
Yarmouth Port, MA 02675-1474, USA

Graham, Parker (Musician)
Performers of the World
8901 Melrose Ave # 200
West Hollywood, CA 90069-5605, USA

Graham, Paul (Athlete, Basketball Player)
5255 N Marshall St
Philadelphia, PA 19120-3134, USA

Graham, Roger (Athlete, Football Player)
1996 Jacksonville Jaguars
Monroe, NY 10950, USA

Graham, Samaria
c/o Steven Jensen *Vincent Cirrincione Associates*
8332 Melrose Ave
West Hollywood, CA 90069-5420, USA

Graham, Stedman (Business Person)
737 N Michigan Ave Ste 1050
Chicago, IL 60611-7019, USA

Graham, Stephen (Actor)
c/o Ben Levine *LINK Entertainment*
425 N Robertson Blvd
West Hollywood, CA 90048-1735, USA

Graham, T J (Athlete, Football Player)
c/o Alan Herman *Sportstars Inc*
1350 Avenue of the Americas Fl 28
New York, NY 10019-4702, USA

Graham, Tommy (Athlete, Football Player)
4084 S Wisteria Way
Denver, CO 80237-1714, USA

Graham, Wayne (Athlete, Baseball Player)
2017 Dryden Rd
Houston, TX 77030-1205, USA

Graham, William B (Business Person)
40 Devonshire Ln
Kenilworth, IL 60043-1205, USA

Graham, William F (Billy) (Religious Leader, Writer)
Billy Graham Evangelistic Assoc
1 Billy Graham Pkwy
Charlotte, NC 28201-0001, USA

Graham, William R (Government Official)
Xsirius Inc
1110 N Glebe Rd # 620
Arlington, VA 22201-4795, USA

Graham-Douglas, Mary Lou (Baseball Player)
9990 N Hillview Dr
Tucson, AZ 85737-7940, USA

Grahame, John (Athlete, Hockey Player, Olympic Athlete)
9000 E Jewell Cir
Denver, CO 80231-3450

Grahame, Ron (Athlete, Hockey Player)
9000 E Jewell Cir
Denver, CO 80231-3450

Grahame-Smith, Seth (Writer)
c/o Melissa Kates *Viewpoint Inc (LA)*
8820 Wilshire Blvd Ste 220
Beverly Hills, CA 90211-2622, USA

Grahe, Joe (Athlete, Baseball Player)
2317 N Wallen Dr
West Palm Beach, FL 33410-2558, USA

Grahn, Nancy
4910 Agnes Ave
Valley Village, CA 91607-3705

Grahn, Nancy Lee (Actor)
4910 Agnes Ave
Valley Village, CA 91607-3705, USA

Grainger, David W (Business Person)
WW Grainger Inc
100 Grainger Pkwy
Lake Forest, IL 60045-5202, USA

Gralish, Tom (Journalist, Photographer)
203 E Cottage Ave
Haddonfield, NJ 08033-1824, USA

Gralla, Milton (Publisher)
Gralla Publications
1515 Broadway
New York, NY 10036-8901, USA

Graman, Alex (Athlete, Baseball Player)
450 E Sunset Dr
Huntingburg, IN 47542-9316, USA

Gramanis, Paul (Athlete, Football Player)
989 Parkview Dr
Tallahassee, FL 32311-1245, USA

Gramatica, Guillermo (Bill) (Athlete, Football Player)
3912 Northampton Way
Tampa, FL 33618-8443, USA

Gramatica, Martin (Athlete, Football Player)
3912 Northampton Way
Tampa, FL 33618-8443, USA

Gramly, Tommy (Athlete, Baseball Player)
16485 Red Wood Cir W
McKinney, TX 75071-6198, USA

Gramm, Lou (Musician)
c/o Staff Member *Creative Artists Agency (CAA-LA)*
2000 Avenue of the Stars Ste 100
Los Angeles, CA 90067-4705, USA

Gramm, Wendy L (Government Official)
Commodity Futures Trading Commission
2033 K St NW
Washington, DC 20006-1002, USA

Gramm, W Philip (Phil) (Politician)
UBS Warburg
PO Box 1559
Helotes, TX 78023-1559, USA

Grammas, Alex (Athlete, Baseball Player, Coach)
4030 Vestview Dr
Vestavia, AL 35242-2554, USA

Grammer, Andy (Musician)
c/o Ben Singer *Silverberg Management Group (SMG)*
3030 Nebraska Ave Ste 201
Santa Monica, CA 90404-4140, USA

Grammer, Camille (Actor, Reality Star)
c/o Jill Fritzo *PMK/BNC Public Relations (PMK-NY)*
622 3rd Ave Fl 8
New York, NY 10017-6707, USA

Grammer, Kathy (Actor)
Artists Agency
1180 S Beverly Dr Ste 301
Los Angeles, CA 90035-1154, USA

Grammer, Kelsey (Actor)
261 Baroda Dr
Los Angeles, CA 90077-3532, USA

Grammer, Spencer (Actor)
c/o Evan Hainey *Untitled Entertainment (LA)*
350 S Beverly Dr Ste 200
Beverly Hills, CA 90212-4819, USA

Gran, Phyllis
Penguin/Pitnam Publishing
200 Madison Ave
New York, NY 10016-3903

Granat, Cary (Producer)
c/o Staff Member *Bedrock Studios*
2115 Colorado Ave
Santa Monica, CA 90404-3503, USA

Granato, Tony (Athlete, Hockey Player, Olympic Athlete)
44537 Spring Hill Rd
Northville, MI 48168-4365

Granato, Tony (Athlete, Hockey Player)
Pittsburgh Penguins
66 Mario Lemieux Pl Ste 2
Pittsburgh, PA 15219-3504

Granby, John (Athlete, Football Player)
2870 Addison Cir S
Rochester, MI 48306-4923, USA

Grandberry, Ken (Athlete, Football Player)
108 E Mark Rd
Harker Heights, TX 76548-1224, USA

Grandberry, Omarion (Actor)
c/o Staff Member *Ultimate Group, The*
6320 Canoga Ave # 420
Woodland Hills, CA 91367-2526, USA

Grande, Ariana (Actor)
265 S Federal Hwy Ste 331
Deerfield Beach, FL 33441-4146, USA

Grande, George (Commentator)
70 Four Rod Rd
Hamden, CT 06514-1615, USA

Grandelius, Everett (Sonny) (Athlete, Football Player)
31531 Robinhood Dr
Beverly Hills, MI 48025-3532, USA

Granderson, Curtis (Athlete, Baseball Player)
1450 S Emerald St
Chicago, IL 60607-4440, USA

Granderson, Rufus (Athlete, Football Player)
1717 Paris Ave SE
Grand Rapids, MI 49507-2633, USA

Grand Funk Railroad (Musician)
c/o Staff Member *Paradigm (Monterey)*
404 W Franklin St
Monterey, CA 93940-2303, USA

Grandholm, Jim (Athlete, Basketball Player)
211 Spring Park Ave
Sawyer, MI 49125-8353, USA

Grandison, Ronnie (Athlete, Basketball Player)
6151 Chappellfield Dr
West Chester, OH 45069-6648, USA

Grand Ole Opry
2804 Opryland Dr
Nashville, TN 37214-1209

Grand-Pierre, Jean-Luc (Athlete, Hockey Player)
8432 Galdino Dr
New Albany, OH 43054-7149

Grandpre, Mary (Designer)
Scholastic Press
555 Broadway
New York, NY 10012-3919, USA

Grandy, Fred (Politician)
10806 Waring Pl
Charlotte, NC 28277-2765, USA

Granger, Charley (Athlete, Football Player)
621 Burbridge St
Port Allen, LA 70767-2128, USA

Granger, Danny (Athlete, Basketball Player)
141 S Meridian St Ste 602
Indianapolis, IN 46225-1033, USA

Granger, David (Athlete)
Ingalls & Snyder
1325 Avenue Of The Americas Fl 18
New York, NY 10019-6066, USA

Granger, Hoyle (Athlete, Football Player)
13427 Paradise Valley Dr
Houston, TX 77069-2532, USA

Granger, Jeff (Athlete, Baseball Player)
2905 Glasgow Dr
Arlington, TX 76015-2226, USA

Granger, Kay (Congressman, Politician)
320 CAJ1LLLON Hob
Washington, DC 20515-0001, USA

Granger, Stewart (Athlete, Basketball Player)
552 E 53rd St
Brooklyn, NY 11203-5323, USA

Granger, Wayne (Athlete, Baseball Player)
133 Redtail Pl
Winter Springs, FL 32708-5626, USA

Granholm, Jennifer (Politician)
21 Chelsea Ct
Oakland, CA 94611-2416, USA

Granik, Debra (Director, Writer)
c/o Frank Wuliger *Gersh (LA)*
9465 Wilshire Blvd Ste 600
Beverly Hills, CA 90212-2605, USA

Grant, Alan (Athlete, Football Player)
2474 40th Ave
San Francisco, CA 94116-2115, USA

Grant, Alexander (Alex da Kid) (Musician)
9126 Cordell Dr
Los Angeles, CA 90069-1718, USA

Grant, Amy (Musician, Songwriter)
515 Park Center Ave
Nashville, TN 37205-3429, USA

Grant, Beth (Actor)
c/o Staff Member *Big Leap Productions*
12439 Magnolia Blvd Ste 282
Valley Village, CA 91607-2450, USA

Grant, Bob (Athlete, Football Player)
10153 Riverside Dr
Toluca Lake, CA 91602-2562, USA

Grant, Boyd (Coach)
Colorado State University
Athletic Dept
Fort Collins, CO 80523-0001, USA

Grant, Brea (Actor)
c/o Nicole Perna *Baker Winokur Ryder Public Relations (BWR-LA)*
9100 Wilshire Blvd Ste 500
West Tower Suite 500
Beverly Hills, CA 90212-3426, USA

Grant, Brian (Athlete, Basketball Player)
5405 Childs Rd
Lake Oswego, OR 97035-8033, USA

Grant, Bud (Athlete, Football Coach, Football Player)
8134 Oakmere Rd
Minneapolis, MN 55438-1333, USA

Grant, Charles (Actor)
Media Artists Group
6300 Wilshire Blvd Ste 1470
Los Angeles, CA 90048-5200, USA

Grant, Darryl (Athlete, Football Player)
6931 Compton Ln
Centreville, VA 20121-5009, USA

Grant, David (Athlete, Football Player)
c/o Michael Katcher *Creative Artists Agency (CAA-LA)*
2000 Avenue of the Stars Ste 100
Los Angeles, CA 90067-4705, USA

Grant, Deon (Athlete, Football Player)
2001 Carolina Panthers
Evans, GA 30809, USA

Grant, Faye (Actor)
13000 Brentwood Ter
Los Angeles, CA 90049-4807, USA

Grant, Frank (Athlete, Football Player)
PO Box 14536
Myrtle Beach, SC 29587-4536, USA

Grant, Gil (Producer)
c/o Staff Member *Principal Entertainment (LA)*
9255 W Sunset Blvd Ste 500
West Hollywood, CA 90069-3301, USA

Grant, Gogi (Musician)
10323 Alamo Ave
#202
Los Angeles, CA 90064, USA

Grant, Harry (Race Car Driver)
7531 Millersville Rd
Taylorsville, NC 28681-8946, USA

Grant, Harvey (Athlete, Basketball Player)
15604 Marathon Cir Apt 401
Gaithersburg, MD 20878-5363, USA

Grant, Horace (Athlete, Basketball Player)
195 Michael Ln
Arroyo Grande, CA 93420-5323, USA

Grant, Hugh (Actor)
c/o Leslee Dart *42West (NYC)*
220 W 42nd St Fl 12
New York, NY 10036-7200, USA

Grant, HUgh (Horse Racer)
35 E 84th St Apt 8B
New York, NY 10028-0871, USA

Grant, James T (Mudcat) (Athlete, Baseball Player)
1020 S Dunsmuir Ave
Los Angeles, CA 90019-6754, USA

Grant, Jennifer (Actor)
c/o Mark Teitelbaum *Teitelbaum Artists Group*
8840 Wilshire Blvd Fl 3
Beverly Hills, CA 90211-2606, USA

Grant, Jim ""Mudcat"" (Athlete, Baseball Player)
1020 S Dunsmuir Ave
Los Angeles, CA 90019-6754, USA

Grant, John (Athlete, Football Player)
623 Clayton St
Denver, CO 80206-3812, USA

Grant, Josh (Athlete, Basketball Player)
3191 S Davis Blvd
Bountiful, UT 84010-5764, USA

Grant, Kate Jennings (Actor)
c/o Tammy Rosen *Sanders Armstrong Caserta*
2120 Colorado Ave Ste 120
Santa Monica, CA 90404-3561, USA

Grant, Lee (Actor, Director)
Feury/Grant Entertainment
610 W End Ave Apt 7B
New York, NY 10024-1644, USA

Grant, Leonard (Uncle Murda) (Musician)
c/o Staff Member *Violator Management*
36 W 25th St Fl 2
New York, NY 10010-2768, USA

Grant, Mark (Commentator)
2837 Via Dieguenos
Alpine, CA 91901-3638, USA

Grant, Mickie (Actor)
250 W 94th St # 6G
New York, NY 10025-6954, USA

Grant, Orantes (Athlete, Football Player)
5103 Ashford Gables Dr
Atlanta, GA 30338-6780, USA

Grant, Paul (Basketball Player)
Milwaukee Bucks
1001 N 4th St Ste 1
Bradley Center
Milwaukee, WI 53203-1312, USA

Grant, Reggie
PO Box 15602
Los Angeles, CA 90015-0602, USA

Grant, Reginald (Athlete, Football Player)
PO Box 15602
Los Angeles, CA 90015-0602, USA

Grant, Steve (Athlete, Football Player)
20134 SW 123rd Dr
Miami, FL 33177-5201, USA

Grant, Susannah (Director, Writer)
c/o Risa Gertner *Creative Artists Agency (CAA-LA)*
2000 Avenue of the Stars Ste 100
Los Angeles, CA 90067-4705, USA

Grant, Tom (Athlete, Baseball Player)
36 Millville Rd
Mendon, MA 01756-1231, USA

Grant, Travis (Athlete, Basketball Player)
3314 Pointe Bleue Ct
Decatur, GA 30034-5118, USA

Grant, Wally (Athlete, Hockey Player)
4853 Lone Oak Ct
Ann Arbor, MI 48108-8575

Grant, Wes (Athlete, Football Player)
3014 North St # B
Atlanta, GA 30344-4355, USA

Grant, Wesley (Athlete, Football Player)
3870 Crenshaw Blvd Apt 926
Los Angeles, CA 90008-1837, USA

Grantham, Larry (Athlete, Football Player)
1971 Tissington Dr
Horn Lake, MS 38637-3752, USA

Granville, Billy (Athlete, Football Player)
7 Oakmere Pl
Sugar Land, TX 77479-5611, USA

Grapenthin, Dick (Athlete, Baseball Player)
5040 170th Ave
Linn Grove, IA 51033-8023, USA

Grapenthin, Rick (Athlete, Baseball Player)
500 Argylls Crst
Alpharetta, GA 30022-6118, USA

Grasmanis, Paul (Athlete, Football Player)
7734 Cricklewood Dr
Tallahassee, FL 32312-6785, USA

Grasmick, Lou (Athlete, Baseball Player)
6715 Quad Ave
Rosedale, MD 21237-2406, USA

Grass, Darren (Athlete, Baseball Player, Olympic Athlete)
1086 174th St
Hammond, WI 54015-4831, USA

Grassie, Karen (Actor)
PO Box 913
Pacific Palisades, CA 90272-0913, USA

Grassle, Karen (Actor)
2646 Francisco Way
El Cerrito, CA 94530-1531, USA

Grassley, charles (Politician)
2342 S Rolfe St
Arlington, VA 22202-1545, USA

Grassroots, The
108 E Matilija St
Ojai, CA 93023-2639

Grata, Enrique (Actor)
c/o Staff Member *Univision*
605 3rd Ave Fl 12
New York, NY 10158-0034, USA

Grate, Carl (Athlete, Football Player)
205 Wind Ship Ln
Woodstock, GA 30189-5286, USA

Grate, Don (Athlete, Baseball Player)
1245 NW 203rd St
Miami, FL 33169-2312, USA

Grater, Mark (Athlete, Baseball Player)
1136 Indiana Ave
Monaca, PA 15061-2025, USA

Graterol, Belker (Athlete, Baseball Player)
2301 Lakeland Hills Blvd
Lakeland, FL 33805-2909, USA

Gratham, Larry (Athlete, Football Player)
1971 Tissington Dr
Horn Lake, MS 38637-3752, USA

Gratton, Chris (Athlete, Hockey Player)
8801 Fazio Ct
Tampa, FL 33647-2292

Grau, Shirley Ann (Writer)
12 Nassau Dr
Metairie, LA 70005-4434, USA

Gravel, Gerry (Ge Ge) (Race Car Driver)
52 Mount Auburn St
Somersworth, NH 03878-2417, USA

Gravel, Maurice R (Mike) (Politician)
3133 Frontera Way Apt 341
Burlingame, CA 94010-5767, USA

Graveline, Duane (Astronaut)
4414 Cormorant Ln
Merritt Island, FL 32953-8504, USA

Graveline, Duane E (Astronaut)
494 Pleasant St
Island Pond, VT 05846-9738, USA

Gravelle, Gordon (Athlete, Football Player)
186 Kuss Rd
Danville, CA 94526-2230, USA

Graves, Adam (Athlete, Hockey Player)
c/o Staff Member *New York Rangers*
2 Pennsylvania Plz
Rm 2200
New York, NY 10121, USA

Graves, Alex (Producer)
c/o Staff Member *ICM Partners (LA)*
10250 Constellation Blvd Fl 7
Los Angeles, CA 90067-6207, USA

Graves, Danny (Athlete, Baseball Player)
1241 Seburn Rd
Apopka, FL 32703-8466, USA

Graves, Earl (Athlete, Basketball Player)
123 Random Farms Dr
Chappaqua, NY 10514-1018, USA

Graves, Earl G (Writer)
130 5th Ave
New York, NY 10011-4306, USA

Graves, Harold N Jr (Government Official, Journalist)
4816 Grantham Ave
Chevy Chase, MD 20815-5538, USA

Graves, Marsharne (Athlete, Football Player)
2233 W Pima Ave
Coolidge, AZ 85128-3288, USA

Graves, Michael (Designer)
341 Nassau St
Princeton, NJ 08540-4602, USA

Graves, Ray (Athlete, Coach, Football Coach, Football Player)
420 Bay Ave Apt 821
Clearwater, FL 33756-5249, USA

Graves, Rory (Athlete, Football Player)
7585 Shadow Wood Dr
Jonesboro, GA 30236-7302, USA

Graves, Rupert (Actor)
c/o Barry McPherson *Agency for the Performing Arts (APA-NY)*
135 W 50th St Fl 17
New York, NY 10020-1201, USA

Graves, Sam (Congressman, Politician)
1415 Longworth Hob
Washington, DC 20515-2306, USA

Graves, Tom (Athlete, Football Player)
1902 Montclair Ave
Norfolk, VA 23523-2322, USA

Graves, Tom (Congressman, Politician)
1113 Longworth Hob
Washington, DC 20515-0401, USA

Graves, White (Athlete, Football Player)
2610 Birchwood Dr
Monroe, LA 71201-2337, USA

Gravitte, Beau (Actor)
Paradigm Agency
10100 Santa Monica Blvd Ste 2500
Los Angeles, CA 90067-4116, USA

Gray, Alec (Actor)
c/o Delaney Andrews *Strategic Talent Group*
4804 Laurel Canyon Blvd # 149
Valley Village, CA 91607-3717, USA

Gray, Billy (Actor)
19612 Grand View Dr
Topanga, CA 90290-3353, USA

Gray, Carlton (Athlete, Football Player)
11981 Kenn Rd
Cincinnati, OH 45240-1313, USA

Gray, C Boyden (Government Official)
Wilmer Cutler Pickering
1875 Pennsylvania Ave NW
Washington, DC 20006-3642, USA

Gray, Coleen (Actor)
2337 Roscomare Rd # 2-112
Los Angeles, CA 90077-1854, USA

Gray, Cyrus (Athlete, Football Player)
c/o David Dunn *Athletes First, LLC*
23091 Mill Creek Dr
Laguna Hills, CA 92653-1258, USA

Gray, Dave (Athlete, Baseball Player)
1823 E 5650 S
Ogden, UT 84403-5909, USA

Gray, Dick (Athlete, Baseball Player)
5405 Granby Dr
Yorba Linda, CA 92887-3714, USA

Gray, Doug (Musician)
Ron Rainey Mgmt
315 S Beverly Dr Ste 407
Beverly Hills, CA 90212-4301, USA

Gray, Earnest (Athlete, Football Player)
6746 Kirby Oaks Ln
Memphis, TN 38119-8328, USA

Gray, Ed (Basketball Player)
Houston Rockets
2 Greenway Plz
Toyota Center
Houston, TX 77046-0297, USA

Gray, Erin (Actor)
c/o Geneva Bray *GVA Talent Agency Inc*
8981 W Sunset Blvd Ste 101
West Hollywood, CA 90069-1850, USA

Gray, Erin (Actor, Model)
10921 Alta View Dr
Studio City, CA 91604-3904, USA

Gray, F Gary (Director)
c/o Staff Member *Management 360*
9111 Wilshire Blvd
Beverly Hills, CA 90210-5508, USA

Gray, Gary (Athlete, Basketball Player)
541 Janice Ln
La Place, LA 70068-5680, USA

Gray, Gary G. (Athlete, Baseball Player)
PO Box 98
La Place, LA 70069-0098, USA

Gray, Hector (Athlete, Football Player)
Miami Springs High School
751 Dove Ave
Miami Springs, FL 33166-3299, USA

Gray, James (Director, Writer)
c/o Todd Feldman *Creative Artists Agency (CAA-LA)*
2000 Avenue of the Stars Ste 100
Los Angeles, CA 90067-4705, USA

Gray, Jeff (Athlete, Baseball Player)
3229 Stonebridge Trl
Valrico, FL 33596-9252, USA

Gray, Jerry (Athlete, Football Player)
1403 Willowbrooke Cir
Franklin, TN 37069-7218, USA

Gray, Jim (Actor)
3325 Blair Dr
Los Angeles, CA 90068-1409, USA

Gray, John (Athlete, Hockey Player)
23 Bear Path
Hampton, NH 03842-1300

Gray, John (Director, Writer)
c/o Steve Rabineau *United Talent Agency (UTA-LA)*
9336 Civic Center Dr
Beverly Hills, CA 90210-3604, USA

Gray, John (Writer)
John Gray's Mars Venus
20 Sunnyside Ave # A130
Mill Valley, CA 94941-1933, USA

Gray, John (Johnny) (Athlete, Baseball Player)
721 NE Orchid Bay Dr
Boca Raton, FL 33487-1734, USA

Gray, Johnnie (Athlete, Football Player)
535 Brule Rd Unit 13
De Pere, WI 54115-3720, USA

Gray, Ken (Athlete, Football Player)
1102 Castleford Rd
Midland, TX 79705-2807, USA

Gray, Linda (Actor)
PO Box 5064
Sherman Oaks, CA 91413-5064, USA

Gray, Lorenzo (Athlete, Baseball Player)
2680 E 19th St Apt 1
Signal Hill, CA 90755-1106, USA

Gray, Macy (Musician, Songwriter)
c/o Bobby Collin *Morey Management Group*
4640 White Oak Ave
Encino, CA 91316-3831, USA

Gray, MarQueis (Athlete, Football Player)
c/o Eugene Parker *Maximum Sports Management*
6435 W Jefferson Blvd # 197
Fort Wayne, IN 46804-6203, USA

Gray, Mel (Athlete, Football Player)
PO Box 1986
Sugar Land, TX 77487-1986, USA

Gray, Mel (Athlete, Football Player)
3504 Rural St
Rockford, IL 61107-3502, USA

Gray, Michael
9294 Civic Center Dr
Beverly Hills, CA 90210-3714

Gray, Moses (Athlete, Football Player)
1331 Aggie Ln
Indianapolis, IN 46260-4096, USA

Gray, Nel (Athlete, Football Player)
6549 Samantha Ln
Rockford, IL 61107-6307, USA

Gray, Scott (Cartoonist)
c/o Staff Member *Marvel Entertainment, Inc.*
135 W 50th St Fl 7
New York, NY 10020-1201, USA

Gray, Spaiding (Artist, Writer)
22 Wooster St
New York, NY 10013-2300, USA

Gray, Stuart (Athlete, Basketball Player)
909 Andover Grn
Lexington, KY 40509-2930, USA

Gray, Sylvester (Athlete, Basketball Player)
4929 Bilrae Cir S
Millington, TN 38053-1612, USA

Gray, Tamyra (Musician)
c/o Jeff Frasco *Creative Artists Agency (CAA-LA)*
2000 Avenue of the Stars Ste 100
Los Angeles, CA 90067-4705, USA

Gray, Tim (Athlete, Football Player)
6109 Crane St
Houston, TX 77026-4234, USA

Gray, Torrian (Athlete, Football Player)
370 Oaktree Blvd
Christiansburg, VA 24073-4740, USA

Gray, Vincent (Governor, Politician)
Executive Office of the Mayor
1350 Pennsylvania Ave NW Ste 316
Washington, DC 20004-3003, USA

Gray Cabey, Noah (Actor)
c/o Blake Bandy *Kritzer Levine Wilkins Entertainment (KLWG)*
11872 La Grange Ave Fl 1
Los Angeles, CA 90025-5283, USA

Grayden, Sprague (Actor)
c/o Katie Rhodes *Untitled Entertainment (LA)*
350 S Beverly Dr Ste 200
Beverly Hills, CA 90212-4819, USA

Graye, Devon (Actor)
c/o Adam Griffin *Kritzer Levine Wilkins Entertainment (KLWG)*
11872 La Grange Ave Fl 1
Los Angeles, CA 90025-5283, USA

Grayer, Jeff (Athlete, Basketball Player)
1617 Barbara Dr
Flint, MI 48504-1637, USA

Grayhm, Steven (Actor, Director, Writer)
c/o Adam Griffin *Kritzer Levine Wilkins Entertainment (KLWG)*
425 N Robertson Blvd
West Hollywood, CA 90048-1735, USA

Graynor, Ari (Actor)
c/o Jill Kaplan *Authentic Talent and Literary Management*
20 Jay St Ste M17
Brooklyn, NY 11201-8300, USA

Grayson, David Lee (Athlete, Football Player)
5962 Rancho Mission Rd Unit 218
San Diego, CA 92108-2552, USA

Grayson Sr, Dave (Athlete, Football Player)
7116 Los Soneto Ct
San Diego, CA 92114-5918, USA

Gray-Stanford, Jason (Actor)
c/o Scott Zimmerman *Evolution Entertainment (LA)*
901 N Highland Ave
Los Angeles, CA 90038-2412, USA

Grazer, Brian (Producer)
1605 San Vicente Blvd
Santa Monica, CA 90402-2207, USA

Grazia, Eugene (Athlete, Hockey Player)
2421 NE 49th St
Fort Lauderdale, FL 33308-4788, USA

Graziadei, Michael (Actor)
c/o Amy Abell *Glick Agency*
1505 10th St
Santa Monica, CA 90401-2805, USA

Graziani, Ariel (Soccer Player)
San Jose Earthquakes
3550 Stevens Creek Blvd Ste 200
San Jose, CA 95117-1031, USA

Graziano, Renee (Reality Star)
c/o Staff Member *CEG Talent*
251 W 39th St Fl 7
New York, NY 10018-3171, USA

Grazioso, Claudia (Producer, Writer)
c/o Nicole Clemens *ICM Partners (LA)*
10250 Constellation Blvd Fl 7
Los Angeles, CA 90067-6207, USA

Grazzola, Kenneth E (Publisher)
Aviation Week Magazine
1221 Avenue of the Americas
New York, NY 10020-1001, USA

Grba, Eli (Athlete, Baseball Player)
106 Fox Run
Florence, AL 35633-1465, USA

Grbac, Elvis (Athlete, Football Player)
17361 Coldwater Trl
Chagrin Falls, OH 44023-1413, USA

Greacen, Bob (Athlete, Basketball Player)
333 Reeder St
Easton, PA 18042-7663, USA

Greason, Bill (Athlete, Baseball Player)
4536 Hillman Dr SW
Birmingham, AL 35221-1816, USA

Greason, Staci
8831 Sunset Blvd # 304
West Hollywood, CA 90069

Greason, William (Baseball Player)
Birmingham Black Barons
4536 Hillman Dr SW
Birmingham, AL 35221-1816, USA

Great Big Sea (Musician)
Fleming & Associates
733-735 N Main
Ann Arbor, MI 48104

Greaves, Gary (Athlete, Football Player)
8221 SW 176th St
Palmetto Bay, FL 33157-6147, USA

Grebeck, Craig (Athlete, Baseball Player)
24202 Juanita Dr
Laguna Niguel, CA 92677-4064, USA

Greco, Buddy (Musician)
Zane Mgmt
5 Monte Verde Way
Palm Desert, CA 92260, USA

Greco, John (Athlete, Football Player)
c/o Adam Heller *Vantage Management Group*
518 Reamer Dr
Carnegie, PA 15106-1845, USA

Greco, Marco (Race Car Driver)
11717 W Rockville Rd
Indianapolis, IN 46232, USA

Greczyn, Alice (Actor)
c/o Adam Griffin *Kritzer Levine Wilkins Entertainment (KLWG)*
11872 La Grange Ave Fl 1
Los Angeles, CA 90025-5283, USA

Greeley, Andrew
6030 S Ellis Ave
Chicago, IL 60637-2608

Greeley, Andrew M (Andy) (Writer)
6030 S Ellis Ave
Chicago, IL 60637-2608, USA

Green, AC (Athlete, Basketball Player)
904 Silver Spur Rd # 416
Rolling Hills Estates, CA 90274-3800, USA

Green, A C (Athlete, Basketball Player)
904 Silver Spur Rd
Rolling Hills Estates, CA 90274-3800, USA

Green, Adolph
211 Central Park W # 19E
New York, NY 10024-6020

Green, Ahman (Athlete, Football Player)
1750 Limestone Trl
De Pere, WI 54115-7973, USA

Green, A.J. (Football Player)
c/o Tom Condon *CAA (St. Louis)*
222 S Central Ave Ste 1008
Saint Louis, MO 63105-3509, USA

Green, Al (Congressman, Politician)
220.1 Rayburn Hob
Washington, DC 20515-0001, USA

Green, Al (Musician)
Al Green Music
PO Box 456
Millington, TN 38083-0456, USA

Green, Andy (Athlete, Baseball Player)
1025 Lakefront Dr
Lexington, KY 40517-2658, USA

Green, Anthony (Athlete, Football Player)
9611 Wesland Cir
Randallstown, MD 21133-2043, USA

Green, Barrett (Athlete, Football Player)
2650 Lake Shore Dr Unit 755
Riviera Beach, FL 33404-4608, USA

Green, Benny (Musician)
Jazz Tree
211 Thompson St Apt 1D
New York, NY 10012-1335, USA

Green, B Eric (Athlete, Football Player)
13131 Luntz Point Ln
Windermere, FL 34786-5802, USA

Green, Boyce (Athlete, Football Player)
4156 1st Street Pl NW
Hickory, NC 28601-8075, USA

Green, Brian Austin (Actor, Director, Producer)
1605 San Vicente Blvd
Santa Monica, CA 90402-2207, USA

Green, Cee Lo (Musician)
165 Pointer Ridge Trl
Fayetteville, GA 30214-7405, USA

Green, Charlie (Athlete, Football Player)
c/o Staff Member *Bryan Bantry*
900 Broadway Ste 400
New York, NY 10003-1239, USA

Green, Charlie (Athlete, Football Player)
255 S Kyrene Rd Unit 214
Chandler, AZ 85226-4460, USA

Green, Chris (Athlete, Baseball Player)
4054 Uppergate Ln
Charlotte, NC 28215-3831, USA

Green, Chris (Athlete, Football Player)
331 Village Ter Patio
Fort Lauderdale, FL 33326-1622, USA

Green, Cleveland (Athlete, Football Player)
5537 Robinson Road Ext
Jackson, MS 39204-4142, USA

Green, Cornell (Athlete, Football Player)
2106 Trinidad Dr
Dallas, TX 75232-2750, USA

Green, Dallas (Athlete, Baseball Player, Coach)
846 Conowingo Rd
Conowingo, MD 21918-1307, USA

Green, Darrell (Athlete, Football Player)
20998 Rostormel Ct
Ashburn, VA 20147-4780, USA

Green, Dave (Athlete, Football Player)
8311 Pat Blvd
Tampa, FL 33615-1810, USA

Green, David (Race Car Driver)
118 Reel Brook Ln
Mooresville, NC 28117, USA

Green, David E (Athlete, Football Player)
8311 Pat Blvd
Tampa, FL 33615-1810, USA

Green, David Gordon (Director, Producer, Writer)
c/o Staff Member *The Gotham Group Inc*
9255 W Sunset Blvd Ste 515
West Hollywood, CA 90069-3308, USA

Green, Debbie (Athlete, Olympic Athlete, Volleyball Player)
239 5th St
Seal Beach, CA 90740-6116, USA

Green, Dennis (Athlete, Coach, Football Coach, Football Player)
3930 Torrey Hill Ln
San Diego, CA 92130-1289, USA

Green, Dick (Athlete, Baseball Player)
3924 Ridgemoor Dr
Rapid City, SD 57702-5328, USA

Green, Donnie (Athlete, Football Player)
11 S Walnut St Apt 316
Hagerstown, MD 21740-5499, USA

Green, EG (Athlete, Football Player)
242 Echo Cir
Fort Walton Beach, FL 32548-6315, USA

Green, E.G. (Athlete, Football Player)
26620 Castleview Way
Wesley Chapel, FL 33544-4739, USA

Green, E G (Athlete, Football Player)
3505 45th Ter W Unit 105
Bradenton, FL 34210-3177, USA

Green, Eric (Athlete, Football Player)
PO Box 204
Clewiston, FL 33440-0204, USA

Green, Ernie (Athlete, Football Player)
424 Rue Marseille
Dayton, OH 45429-1878, USA

Green, Gary (Athlete, Baseball Player)
939 Kennebec St
Pittsburgh, PA 15217-2604, USA

Green, Gary F (Athlete, Football Player)
16330 Walnut Creek Dr
San Antonio, TX 78247-5636, USA

Green, Gaston (Athlete, Football Player)
13524 Stanford Ave
Los Angeles, CA 90059-3538, USA

Green, Gene (Congressman, Politician)
2470 Rayburn Hob
Washington, DC 20515-4327, USA

Green, George (Athlete, Baseball Player)
3185 Wilshire Blvd Unit 764
Los Angeles, CA 90010-1253, USA

Green, Gerald (Writer)
88 Arrowhead Trl
New Canaan, CT 06840-3441, USA

Green, Harold (Athlete, Football Player)
145 Folk Rd
Blythewood, SC 29016-9031, USA

Green, Hubert (Athlete, Golfer)
5141 Gulf Dr
Panama City, FL 32408-6903, USA

Green, Hugh (Athlete, Football Player)
4758 Highway 61
Fayette, MS 39069-5422, USA

Green, Jacob (Athlete, Football Player)
4921 Whistling Straits Loop
College Station, TX 77845-3866, USA

Green, Jacquez (Athlete, Football Player)
5102 Madison Lakes Cir W
Davie, FL 33328-4519, USA

Green, Janine (Actor)
c/o David Sweeney *Sweeney Entertainment*
6253 Hollywood Blvd Apt 201
Los Angeles, CA 90028-8248, USA

Green, Jarvis (Athlete, Football Player)
21717 Turkey Creek Dr
Baton Rouge, LA 70817-8157, USA

Green, Jeff (Athlete, Basketball Player)
c/o Staff Member *Oklahoma City Thunder*
208 Thunder Dr
Two Leadership Square
Oklahoma City, OK 73102-2002, USA

Green, Jeff (Race Car Driver)
Haas CNC Racing
6001 Haas Way
Kannapolis Gateway Business Park
Kannapolis, NC 28081-7730, USA

Green, Jenna Leigh (Actor)
c/o Aaron Kogan *Sovereign Talent Group*
8421 Wilshire Blvd Ste 200
Beverly Hills, CA 90211-3204, USA

Green, Jessie (Athlete, Football Player)
638 County Road 2470
Mount Pleasant, TX 75455-9255, USA

Green, Jimmy (Athlete, Golfer)
2130 Keystone Dr
Auburn, AL 36830-2593, USA

Green, John (Athlete, Football Player)
7417 Jester Ct
Ooltewah, TN 37363-7150, USA

Green, John (Writer)
PO Box 8147
Missoula, MT 59807-8147, USA

Green, John M (Johnny) (Athlete, Basketball Player)
9 Susan Ln
Dix Hills, NY 11746-5140, USA

Green, John N (Jack) Jr
(Cinematographer)
516 Esplanade Apt E
Redondo Beach, CA 90277-4077, USA

Green, Jordan-Claire (Actor)
c/o Staff Member *Cunningham Escott Slevin & Doherty (CESD-LA)*
10635 Santa Monica Blvd Ste 130
Los Angeles, CA 90025-8306, USA

Green, Kate (Writer)
Bantam/Delacorte/Dell/Doubleday Press
1540 Broadway
New York, NY 10036-4039, USA

Green, Ken (Athlete, Golfer)
4520 Feivel Rd Apt 56
West Palm Beach, FL 33417-8078, USA

Green, Lamar (Athlete, Basketball Player)
PO Box 490208
Chicago, IL 60649-0019, USA

Green, Lenny (Athlete, Baseball Player)
18693 Sunset St
Detroit, MI 48234-2043, USA

Green, Leonard I (Business Person)
Rite Aid Corp
30 Hunter Ln
Camp Hill, PA 17011-2400, USA

Green, Litterial (Athlete, Basketball Player)
160 McIntosh Place Dr
Fayetteville, GA 30214-7318, USA

Green, Marilyn (Race Car Driver)
601 Norwalk St
Greensboro, NC 27407-1409, USA

Green, Mark (Race Car Driver)
Hensley Racing
1542 Js Holland Rd
Ridgeway, VA 24148-3726, USA

Green, Mark (Race Car Driver)
Trackside Marketing Group
345 Marblerock Way
Lexington, KY 40503-6321, USA

Green, Mark A (Athlete, Football Player)
60 Seneca Ave E
Lake Zurich, IL 60047-1915, USA

Green, Michael (Cinematographer)
11 Stevenson Ln
Upper Saddle River, NJ 07458-2136, USA

Green, Mike
1919 Valleywood Rd
Mc Lean, VA 22101-4931

Green, Mike (Athlete, Football Player)
14709 Marist Ln
Chino, CA 91710-7604, USA

Green, Nick (Athlete, Baseball Player)
1380 Lake Washington Cir
Cir
Lawrenceville, GA 30043-6664, USA

Green, Pat (Musician)
c/o Staff Member *William Morris Endeavor (Nashville)*
1600 Division St Ste 300
Nashville, TN 37203-2755, USA

Green, Patricia (Producer, Writer)
c/o David Greenblatt *Greenlit*
1800 N Highland Ave Ste 500
Los Angeles, CA 90028-4527, USA

Green, Paul (Athlete, Football Player)
1635 N Formosa Ave Apt 208
Los Angeles, CA 90046-3993, USA

Green, Pumpsie (Athlete, Baseball Player)
2105 Harper St
El Cerrito, CA 94530-1724, USA

Green, Ray (Athlete, Football Player)
2738 S University Dr Apt 15A
Davie, FL 33328-1428, USA

Green, Rickey (Athlete, Basketball Player)
20584 Tyler Dr
Lynwood, IL 60411-8571, USA

Green, Robin (Writer)
c/o Staff Member *Broder Webb Chervin Silbermann Agency, The (BWCS)*
10250 Constellation Blvd
Los Angeles, CA 90067-6200, USA

Green, Sarah (Producer)
c/o Staff Member *ICM Partners (LA)*
10250 Constellation Blvd Fl 7
Los Angeles, CA 90067-6207, USA

Green, Scarborough (Athlete, Baseball Player)
2020 Crimson Meadows Dr
O Fallon, MO 63366-4186, USA

Green, sean
3823 Fieldside Cir
Louisville, KY 40299-6545, USA

Green, Seth (Actor, Comedian, Producer)
c/o Trice Koopman *Koopman Management*
PO Box 1317
Pacific Palisades, CA 90272-1317, USA

Green, Shawn (Athlete, Baseball Player)
c/o Chris Stuart *Encore Sports and Entertainment*
703 Palomar Airport Rd Ste 200
Carlsbad, CA 92011-1042, USA

Green, Sidney (Basketball Player, Coach)
Florida Atlantic University
Athletic Dept
Boca Raton, FL 33431, USA

Green, Skylar (Athlete, Football Player)
3121 Thomas Ave Apt D
Dallas, TX 75204-2605, USA

Green, Steve (Athlete, Basketball Player)
942 Round Table Ct
Indianapolis, IN 46260-4923, USA

Green, Suzy (Athlete, Golfer)
26006 Carol Ave
Franklin, MI 48025-1107, USA

Green, Tammie (Athlete, Golfer)
4990 Township Road 147 NE
Somerset, OH 43783-9753, USA

Green, Taylor (Athlete, Baseball Player)
7640 NW 79th Ave
Apt L8
Tamarac, FL 33321-2868, USA

Green, Timothy J (Tim) (Athlete, Football Player, Sportscaster)
1194 Greenfield Ln
Skaneateles, NY 13152-9666, USA

Green, Tom (Actor, Comedian)
c/o Howard Lapides *Core/Lapides Lear Entertainment*
14724 Ventura Blvd PH
Sherman Oaks, CA 91403-3513, USA

Green, Travis (Athlete, Hockey Player)
2 Riverside
Irvine, CA 92602-0903, USA

Green, Trent (Athlete, Football Player)
570 Chestnut Forest Cv
Fort Wayne, IN 46814, USA

Green, Tyler (Athlete, Baseball Player)
3236 E Chandler Blvd Unit 1040
Phoenix, AZ 85048-7281, USA

Green, Van (Athlete, Football Player)
549 Pintail Cir
Auburndale, FL 33823-8368, USA

Green, Victor (Athlete, Football Player)
802 Jamont Cir
Alpharetta, GA 30022-7681, USA

Green, Virgil (Athlete, Football Player)
c/o Scott Smith *XAM Sports*
PO Box 1725
Madison, WI 53701-1725, USA

Green, Vivian (Actor)
c/o Staff Member *William Morris Endeavor (LA)*
9601 Wilshire Blvd
Beverly Hills, CA 90210-5213, USA

Green, Willie (Athlete, Football Player)
152 Farmington Rd
Shelby, NC 28150-8698, USA

Green, Woody (Athlete, Football Player)
702 SE Palmblad Pl
Gresham, OR 97080-1496, USA

Green, Yatil (Athlete, Football Player)
2000 Island Blvd Apt 3002
Aventura, FL 33160-4966, USA

Greenberg, Adam (Athlete, Baseball Player)
79 Fernwood Dr
Guilford, CT 06437-2367, USA

Greenberg, Adam (Cinematographer)
Gersh Agency
232 N Canon Dr
Beverly Hills, CA 90210-5302, USA

Greenberg, Bryan (Actor)
c/o Ellen Meyer *Ellen Meyer Management*
8899 Beverly Blvd Ste 612
Los Angeles, CA 90048-2429, USA

Greenberg, Carl (Journalist)
6001 Canterbury Dr
Culver City, CA 90230-6876, USA

Greenberg, Maurice R (Business Person)
American International Group
70 Pine St
New York, NY 10270-0001, USA

Greenberg, Mike (Sportscaster, Television Host)
c/o Lou Oppenheim *Headline Media Management*
888 7th Ave Ste 503
New York, NY 10106-0501, USA

Greenberg, Peter (Television Host)
c/o Staff Member *The Today Show*
30 Rockefeller Plz
New York, NY 10112-0015, USA

Greenberg, Robbie S (Cinematographer)
11 Reef St
Marina Del Rey, CA 90292-6725, USA

Greenberg, Ross (Producer, Writer)
c/o Staff Member *Shed Media US*
3800 Barham Blvd Ste 410
Los Angeles, CA 90068-1042, USA

Greenblatt, Stephen J (Writer)
Harvard University
English Dept
Cambridge, MA 02138, USA

Greenblatt, William
30710 Monte Lado Dr
Malibu, CA 90265-3128

Greenburg, Dan (Writer)
323 E 50th St
New York, NY 10022-7901, USA

Greenburg, Paul (Journalist)
5900 Scenic Dr
Little Rock, AR 72207-2833, USA

Greenbush, Rachel Lindsay (Actor)
Gold Marshak Liedtke
3500 W Olive Ave Ste 1400
Burbank, CA 91505-5512, USA

Greenbush, Sidney Robin (Actor)
Gold Marshak Liedtke
3500 W Olive Ave Ste 1400
Burbank, CA 91505-5512, USA

Green Day (Music Group)
c/o Brian Bumbery *BB Gun Press*
9229 W Sunset Blvd Ste 305
West Hollywood, CA 90069-3403, USA

Greene, A J (Athlete, Football Player)
3900 Braxton Dr
Charlotte, NC 28226-7003, USA

Greene, Al (Athlete, Baseball Player)
18294 Marlowe St
Detroit, MI 48235-2762, USA

Greene, Andrew
330 Richmond Ave
South Orange, NJ 07079-2134

Greene, Ashley (Actor)
9559 Sherwood Forest Ln
Beverly Hills, CA 90210-1721, USA

Greene, Biloah (Actor)
c/o Vincent Cirrincione *Vincent Cirrincione Associates*
1516 N Fairfax Ave
Los Angeles, CA 90046-2608, USA

Greene, Bob (Fitness Expert)
c/o Bill Stankey *Westport Entertainment Associates*
1120 W State Route 89a
Sedona, AZ 86336-5759, USA

Greene, Charles E (Charlie) (Athlete, Olympic Athlete, Track Athlete)
PO Box 6938
Lincoln, NE 68506-0938, USA

Greene, Charlie (Athlete, Baseball Player)
10760 S Kendale Blvd
Miami, FL 33176-3459, USA

Greene, David (Football Coach, Football Player)
c/o Lenore Zerman *Liberman/Zerman Management*
252 N Larchmont Blvd Ste 200
Los Angeles, CA 90004-3754, USA

Greene, Ellen (Musician)
Innovative Artists
1505 10th St
Santa Monica, CA 90401-2805, USA

Greene, Graham (Actor)
c/o Susan Smith *Susan Smith Company, The*
2001 Wilshire Blvd Ste 400
Santa Monica, CA 90403-5686, USA

Greene, Jay
16502 Craighurst Dr
Houston, TX 77059-6518, USA

Greene, Joe (Athlete, Football Player)
PO Box 270953
Flower Mound, TX 75027-0953, USA

Greene, Ken (Athlete, Football Player)
6002 Yeats Manor Dr Unit 101
Tampa, FL 33616-1439, USA

Greene, Kevin (Athlete, Football Player)
c/o David Dunn *Athletes First, LLC*
23091 Mill Creek Dr
Laguna Hills, CA 92653-1258, USA

Greene, Khalil (Athlete, Baseball Player)
10 Green Hill Dr
Simpsonville, SC 29681-4148, USA

Greene, Maurice (Athlete, Track Athlete)
c/o Staff Member *Exposure Marketing Group*
348 Hauser Blvd # PH414
Los Angeles, CA 90036-3276, USA

Greene, Michele (Actor, Musician)
PO Box 382
Skyforest, CA 92385-0382, USA

Greene, Michelle
PO Box 382
Skyforest, CA 92385-0382

Greene, Pat (Writer)
c/o Staff Member *Playscripts, Inc.*
450 7th Ave Ste 1502
New York, NY 10123-0083, USA

Greene, Paul (Actor)
c/o Jessica Cohen *JCPR*
9903 Santa Monica Blvd Ste 983
Beverly Hills, CA 90212-1671, USA

Greene, Shecky (Actor, Comedian)
1642 S La Verne Way
Palm Springs, CA 92264-9296, USA

Greene, Todd (Athlete, Baseball Player)
725 Pine Leaf Ct
Alpharetta, GA 30022-1026, USA

Greene, Tommy (Athlete, Baseball Player)
PO Box 10
Warrington, PA 18976-0010, USA

Greene, Tony (Athlete, Football Player)
9001 Brookville Rd
Silver Spring, MD 20910-1819, USA

Greene, Tony (Athlete, Football Player)
1890 Briarcliff Cir NE Apt D
Atlanta, GA 30329-2574, USA

Greene, Willie (Athlete, Baseball Player)
1044 GA Highway 22 E
Haddock, GA 31033-2360, USA

Greenfield, James L (Journalist)
470 Park Ave Apt 9A
New York, NY 10022-1946, USA

Greenfield, Jeff (Correspondent)
Cable News Network
820 1st St NE Ste 1000
News Dept
Washington, DC 20002-4363, USA

Greenfield, Lauren (Director, Photographer, Producer)
Lauren Greenfield Photography
1221 Preston Way
Venice, CA 90291-2943, USA

Greenfield-Sanders, Timothy (Artist, Photographer)
821 Broadway Fl 4
New York, NY 10003-4702, USA

Greengrass, Jim (Athlete, Baseball Player)
232 Talking Rock Creek Pro Rd
Chatsworth, GA 30705-6895, USA

Greengrass, Paul (Director)
c/o Beth Swofford *Creative Artists Agency (CAA-LA)*
2000 Avenue of the Stars Ste 100
Los Angeles, CA 90067-4705, USA

Greenlaw, Jeff (Athlete, Hockey Player)
9213 Colberg Dr
Austin, TX 78749-4151, USA

Greenlay, Mike (Athlete, Hockey Player)
c/o Staff Member *Minnesota Wild*
317 Washington St
Saint Paul, MN 55102-1667, USA

Greenlay, Mike (Athlete, Hockey Player)
3338 Richmond Bay
Saint Paul, MN 55129-4925

Greenlee, David (Actor)
1811 Whitley Ave Apt 800
Los Angeles, CA 90028-4960, USA

Greenspan, Alan (Politician)
Greenspan Associates LLC
2710 Chain Bridge Rd NW
Washington, DC 20016-3404, USA

Greenspan, Jerry (Athlete, Basketball Player)
156 E Cedar St Apt 3314
Livingston, NJ 07039-4154, USA

Greenspan, Melissa (Actor)
c/o Jeff Danis *Danis, Panaro, Nist (DPN)*
9201 W Olympic Blvd
Beverly Hills, CA 90212-4605, USA

Greenstein, Jeff (Producer)
c/o Staff Member *ICM Partners (LA)*
10250 Constellation Blvd Fl 7
Los Angeles, CA 90067-6207, USA

Greenway, Chad (Athlete, Football Player)
39448 250th St
Mount Vernon, SD 57363-5005, USA

Greenwell, Mike (Athlete, Baseball Player)
18500 State Road 31
Alva, FL 33920-3016, USA

Greenwood, Bruce (Actor)
c/o Chuck Binder *Binder & Associates*
1465 Lindacrest Dr
Beverly Hills, CA 90210-2519, USA

Greenwood, Colin (Musician)
Nasty Little Man
72 Spring St # 1100
New York, NY 10012-4019, USA

Greenwood, David (Athlete, Basketball Player)
18857 Whitney Pl
Rowland Heights, CA 91748-4873, USA

Greenwood, Jonny (Musician)
Nasty Little Man
72 Spring St # 1100
New York, NY 10012-4019, USA

Greenwood, L C (Athlete, Football Player)
PO Box 3528
Parkersburg, WV 26103-3528, USA

Greenwood, Lee (Musician, Songwriter)
Lee Greenwood Inc
142 Harbin Rd
Madison, AL 35757-7500, USA

Greenwood, Morlon (Athlete, Football Player)
2 Waters Lake Blvd
Missouri City, TX 77459, USA

Greer, Brian (Athlete, Baseball Player)
21810 Clearwater Dr
Yorba Linda, CA 92887-3756, USA

Greer, Brodie
300 S Raymond Ave # 11
Pasadena, CA 91105-2620

Greer, Donovan (Athlete, Football Player)
3423 Shadowside Ct
Houston, TX 77082-8303, USA

Greer, Hal (Athlete, Basketball Player)
c/o Staff Member *Naismith Memorial Basketball Hall of Fame*
1000 W Columbus Ave
Springfield, MA 01105-2518, USA

Greer, Judy (Actor)
c/o Staff Member *Principato/Young Management (LA)*
9465 Wilshire Blvd Ste 900
Beverly Hills, CA 90212-2608, USA

Greer, Kenny (Athlete, Baseball Player)
17 Hill St
Cohasset, MA 02025-2218, USA

Greer, Raeden (Actor)
c/o Mona Loring *MLC PR*
7080 Hollywood Blvd Ste 903
Los Angeles, CA 90028-6936, USA

Greer, Rusty (Athlete, Baseball Player)
4703 Patterson Ln
Colleyville, TX 76034-4507, USA

Greezyn, Alice (Actor)
c/o Staff Member *Windfall*
3000 W Alameda Ave
Burbank, CA 91523-0001, USA

Gregerson, Luke (Athlete, Baseball Player)
109 N Aldine Ave
Park Ridge, IL 60068-3007, USA

Gregg, Clark (Actor)
c/o Paulette Bartlett *Paulette Bartlett Management*
3000 Olympic Blvd Ste 1364
Santa Monica, CA 90404-5073, USA

Gregg, Forrest (Athlete, Coach, Football Coach, Football Executive, Football Player)
2985 Plaza Azul
Santa Fe, NM 87507-5337, USA

Gregg, Judd A (Politician)
1234 Ocean Blvd
Rye, NH 03870-2209, USA

Gregg, Kelly (Athlete, Football Player)
13800 Hollow Glen Rd
Edmond, OK 73013-7278, USA

Gregg, Kevin (Athlete, Baseball Player)
1907 SW Brooklane Dr
Corvallis, OR 97333-1627, USA

Gregg, Stephen (Writer)
c/o Staff Member *Creative Artists Agency (CAA-LA)*
2000 Avenue of the Stars Ste 100
Los Angeles, CA 90067-4705, USA

Gregg, Tommy (Athlete, Baseball Player)
531 Timbercreek Estates Dr
Sharpsburg, GA 30277-3598, USA

Gregg, Tommy (Athlete, Baseball Player)
12356 Ballpark Way
Attn: Coaching Staff
Papillion, NE 68046-4817, USA

Gregoire, Chris (Governor, Politician)
Legislative Bldg
P.O. Box 40002
Olympia, WA 98504-0001, USA

Gregoire, Stephan (Race Car Driver)
Dick Simon Racing
25801 Victoria Blvd
Capistrano Beach, CA 92624-1124, USA

Gregor, Bob (Athlete, Football Player)
14128 180th Ave NE
Redmond, WA 98052-1220, USA

Gregor, Gary (Athlete, Basketball Player)
444 Dove Ridge Rd
Columbia, SC 29223-5589, USA

Gregorio, Rose (Actor)
29 W 10th St Apt 3
New York, NY 10011-8739, USA

Gregorio, Tom (Athlete, Baseball Player)
30 Trina Ln
Staten Island, NY 10309-1532, USA

Gregory, Adam (Actor)
c/o Beverly Strong *Strong Management*
9350 Wilshire Blvd Ste 224
Beverly Hills, CA 90212-3204, USA

Gregory, Andre (Actor)
c/o Jeff Hunter *William Morris Endeavor (NY)*
1325 Avenue of the Americas
New York, NY 10019-6026, USA

Gregory, Bettina L (Correspondent)
ABC-TV
5010 Creston St
News Dept
Hyattsville, MD 20781-1216, USA

Gregory, Bill (Athlete, Football Player)
4317 Cityview Dr
Plano, TX 75093-3236, USA

Gregory, Claude (Athlete, Basketball Player)
14621 Blackburn Rd
Burtonsville, MD 20866-1303, USA

Gregory, Damian (Athlete, Football Player)
7 Surry Ct
Jersey City, NJ 07305-5504, USA

Gregory, David A (Actor)
c/o Staff Member *Leading Artists*
145 W 45th St Rm 1000
New York, NY 10036-4032, USA

Gregory, Dorian (Actor, Television Host)
c/o Staff Member *Creative Management Entertainment Group (CMEG)*
2050 S Bundy Dr Ste 280
Los Angeles, CA 90025-6128, USA

Gregory, Frederick D (Astronaut)
506 Tulip Rd
Annapolis, MD 21403-1326, USA

Gregory, Frederick D Colonel (Astronaut)
506 Tulip Rd
Annapolis, MD 21403-1326, USA

Gregory, Glynn (Athlete, Football Player)
7007 Joyce Way
Dallas, TX 75225-1728, USA

Gregory, Kathy (Cartoonist)
Playboy Magazine
680 N Lake Shore Dr Ste 1500
Reader Services
Chicago, IL 60611-4455, USA

Gregory, Lee (Athlete, Baseball Player)
6456 N Teilman Ave
Fresno, CA 93711-1315, USA

Gregory, Nick (Actor)
c/o Staff Member *Kerin-Goldberg Associates*
155 E 55th St Ste 5D
New York, NY 10022-4038, USA

Gregory, Paul (Actor)
PO Box 415
Desert Hot Springs, CA 92240-0415, USA

Gregory, William G (Astronaut)
2027 E Freeport Ln
Gilbert, AZ 85234-2829, USA

Gregory, William G Lt Colonel (Astronaut)
2027 E Freeport Ln
Gilbert, AZ 85234-2829, USA

Gregory, William Jr (Athlete, Football Player)
4317 Cityview Dr
Plano, TX 75093-3236, USA

Gregory, Wilton D (Religious Leader)
Illinois Diocese
222 S 3rd St
Chancery Office
Belleville, IL 62220-1916, USA

Gregson, Glenn (Athlete, Baseball Player)
719 Touchstone Dr
Helena, MT 59601-5488, USA

Gregson-Williams, Harry (Musician)
c/o Staff Member *Chasen & Company*
8899 Beverly Blvd Ste 405
Los Angeles, CA 90048-2431, USA

Greif, Bill (Athlete, Baseball Player)
807 E 31st St
Austin, TX 78705-3205, USA

Greig, John (Athlete, Basketball Player)
2031 218th Pl NE
Sammamish, WA 98074-4049, USA

Greiner, Lori (Business Person, Reality Star, Television Host)
400 N Saint Paul St Ste 1040
Dallas, TX 75201-6845, USA

Greinke, Zack (Athlete, Baseball Player)
8629 Vista Pine Ct
Orlando, FL 32836-6307, USA

Greise, Bob (Athlete)
12044 SE Birkdale Run
Jupiter, FL 33469-1740

Greisen, Chris (Athlete, Football Player)
1710 Arabian Dr
Green Bay, WI 54313-4388, USA

Greisen, Nick (Athlete, Football Player)
c/o Brad Leshnock *BTI Sports Advisors*
170 N Scoville Ave
Oak Park, IL 60302-2647, USA

Greisinger, Seth (Athlete, Baseball Player, Olympic Athlete)
97 Mariners Cove Rd
Bumpass, VA 23024-4348, USA

Greist, Kim (Actor)
Innovative Artists
1505 10th St
Santa Monica, CA 90401-2805, USA

Grelf, Michael (Director)
La Jolla Playhouse
PO Box 12039
La Jolla, CA 92039-2039, USA

Grenier, Adrian (Actor)
c/o Staff Member *Reckless Productions*
425 Riverside Dr Apt 13D
New York, NY 10025-7732, USA

Grenier, Zach (Actor)
c/o Staff Member *Hartig Hilepo Agency Ltd*
54 W 21st St Rm 610
New York, NY 10010-7344, USA

Grentz, Theresa Shank (Coach)
University of Illinois
Athletic Dept
Champaign, IL 61820, USA

Greschner, Ron (Athlete, Hockey Player)
646 Riversville Rd
Greenwich, CT 06831-2650, USA

Gresham, Bob (Athlete, Football Player)
314 Meadowview Dr Apt 709
Boone, NC 28607-5229, USA

Gresham, Jermaine (Athlete, Football Player)
c/o Ben Dogra *CAA (St. Louis)*
222 S Central Ave Ste 1008
Saint Louis, MO 63105-3509, USA

Gretch, Joel (Actor)
c/o Molly Madden *3 Arts Entertainment (LA)*
9460 Wilshire Blvd Fl 7
Beverly Hills, CA 90212-2713, USA

G. Retcnert, David (Congressman, Politician)
1730 Longworth Hob
Washington, DC 20515-3510, USA

Gretsch, Joel (Actor)
c/o David (Dave) Fleming *Mosaic Media Group*
9200 W Sunset Blvd Ste 10
West Hollywood, CA 90069-3608, USA

Gretzky, Paulina (Actor)
c/o Staff Member *3 Arts Entertainment (LA)*
9460 Wilshire Blvd Fl 7
Beverly Hills, CA 90212-2713, USA

Gretzky, Wayne (Athlete, Hockey Player)
1072 Newbern Ct
Thousand Oaks, CA 91361-5346, USA

Grevey, Kevin (Athlete, Basketball Player)
528 River Bend Rd
Great Falls, VA 22066-2716, USA

Grevioux, Kevin (Actor)
c/o Scott Agostini *William Morris Endeavor (LA)*
9601 Wilshire Blvd
Beverly Hills, CA 90210-5213, USA

Grewal, Alexi (Athlete, Cycler, Olympic Athlete)
1 Echo Canyon Rd
Pagosa Springs, CO 81147-9747, USA

Grey, Dick (Athlete, Baseball Player)
503 S Hampton St
Anaheim, CA 92804-2233, USA

Grey, Jennifer (Actor)
c/o Greg Clark *Untitled Entertainment (LA)*
350 S Beverly Dr Ste 200
Beverly Hills, CA 90212-4819, USA

Grey, Joel (Actor)
c/o Nevin Dolcefino *Innovative Artists (LA)*
1505 10th St
Santa Monica, CA 90401-2805, USA

Grey, Sasha (Actor, Adult Film Star)
PO Box 1480
Studio City, CA 91614-0480, USA

Grey, Skylar (Musician)
c/o Sara Newkirk Simon *William Morris Endeavor (LA)*
9601 Wilshire Blvd
Beverly Hills, CA 90210-5213, USA

Grey, Zena (Actor)
c/o Abby Bluestone *Innovative Artists (LA)*
1505 10th St
Santa Monica, CA 90401-2805, USA

Greyeyes, Michael
3500 W Olive Ave Ste 1400
Burbank, CA 91505-5512

Gribbon, Melissa (Actor)
c/o Dianne Hooper *Starcraft Talent Agency*
265 E Orange Grove Ave Ste D
Burbank, CA 91502-1229, USA

Gribow, Patti
3303 Clerendon Rd
Beverly Hills, CA 90210-1061

Grich, Bobby (Athlete, Baseball Player)
7668 El Camino Real
Ste 104-435
Carlsbad, CA 92009-7932, USA

Grieco, Richard (Actor)
c/o Zack Teperman *ZTPR*
8430 Santa Monica Blvd Ste 203
West Hollywood, CA 90069-4253, USA

Grieder, William (Journalist)
Simon & Schuster
1230 Avenue of the Americas Fl CONC1
New York, NY 10020-1586, USA

Grier, David Alan (Actor, Comedian)
c/o Staff Member *ROAR (LA)*
9701 Wilshire Blvd Fl 8
Beverly Hills, CA 90212-2008, USA

Grier, Marrio (Athlete, Football Player)
826 Almora Dr
Charlotte, NC 28216-3069, USA

Grier, Mike (Athlete, Hockey Player)
72 Stonecrest Dr
Needham, MA 02492-2783

Grier, Pam (Actor)
c/o Harry Gold *TalentWorks (LA)*
3500 W Olive Ave Ste 1400
Burbank, CA 91505-5512, USA

Grier, Rosey (Athlete, Football Player)
1250 4th St Fl 6
Santa Monica, CA 90401-1418, USA

Gries, Jonathan (Jon) (Actor, Director, Producer)
c/o Steve Lovett *Lovett Management*
1327 Brinkley Ave
Los Angeles, CA 90049-3619, USA

Griese, Brian (Athlete, Football Player)
17 Polo Club Dr
Denver, CO 80209-3309, USA

Griese, Robert A (Bob) (Athlete, Football Player, Sportscaster)
12044 SE Birkdale Run
Jupiter, FL 33469-1740, USA

Griesemer, John N (Government Official)
RR 2 Box 204B
Springfield, MO 65802, USA

Grieve, Ben (Athlete, Baseball Player)
6906 Fairway Rd
La Jolla, CA 92037-5619, USA

Grieve, Pierson M (Business Person)
Ecolab Inc
370 Wabasha St N
Ecolab Center
Saint Paul, MN 55102-1349, USA

Grieve, Tom (Athlete, Baseball Player)
PO Box 90111
Attn Broadcast Dept
Arlington, TX 76004-3111, USA

Grieve, Tom (Commentator)
4107 Carnation Dr
Arlington, TX 76016-3922, USA

Griffen, Everson (Athlete, Football Player)
c/o David Dunn *Athletes First, LLC*
23091 Mill Creek Dr
Laguna Hills, CA 92653-1258, USA

Griffey Jr, Ken (Athlete, Baseball Player)
6369 Blu Knight Ln
Windermere, FL 34786-7343, USA

Griffey Sr, Ken (Athlete, Baseball Player)
1102 Portmoor Way
Winter Garden, FL 34787-4619, USA

Griffin, Alfredo (Athlete, Baseball Player)
9731 NW 41st St
Doral, FL 33178-2944, USA

Griffin, Alfredo (Athlete, Baseball Player)
2000 E Gene Autry Way
Attn: Coaching Staff
Anaheim, CA 92806-6143, USA

Griffin, Archie (Athlete, Football Player, Heisman Trophy Winner)
6845 Temperance Point Pl
Westerville, OH 43082-8704, USA

Griffin, Blake (Athlete, Basketball Player)
1333 Pavia Pl
Pacific Palisades, CA 90272-4047, USA

Griffin, Bo (Correspondent, Television Host)
c/o Staff Member *Good Day Live*
10201 W Pico Blvd Bldg 88
20th Century Fox Television
Los Angeles, CA 90064-2606, USA

Griffin, Cedric (Athlete, Football Player)
3015 Garwood St
Austin, TX 78702-3624, USA

Griffin, Cornelius (Athlete, Football Player)
224 Countryside Dr
Troy, AL 36079-9191, USA

Griffin, Courtney (Athlete, Football Player)
6302 N Selland Ave
Fresno, CA 93711-0872, USA

Griffin, Damon (Athlete, Football Player)
1608 Radford Pl
Monrovia, CA 91016-4431, USA

Griffin, David (Athlete, Football Player)
PO Box 1443
Roswell, GA 30077-1443, USA

Griffin, Doug (Athlete, Baseball Player)
15811 El Soneto Dr
Whittier, CA 90603-1446, USA

Griffin, Eddie (Actor, Comedian, Producer)
c/o Dana Sims *ICM Partners (LA)*
10250 Constellation Blvd Fl 7
Los Angeles, CA 90067-6207, USA

Griffin, Eric (Boxer)
PO Box 964
Jasper, TN 37347-0964, USA

Griffin, Forrest (Athlete, Wrestler)
c/o Jervis L Cole
5 E River Park Pl W Ste 203
Fresno, CA 93720-1557, USA

Griffin, Greg (Athlete, Basketball Player)
12051 Bayport St Apt 1-208
1-208
Garden Grove, CA 92840-4404, USA

Griffin, Jim (Athlete, Football Player)
7204 Highway 14
New Iberia, LA 70560-9217, USA

Griffin, John-Ford (Athlete, Baseball Player)
PO Box 1359
Sarasota, FL 34230-1359, USA

Griffin, John W (Athlete, Football Player)
10315 Herons Ridge Dr
Lakeland, TN 38002-8292, USA

Griffin, Kathy (Actor, Comedian, Reality Star)
2955 Passmore Dr
Los Angeles, CA 90068-1716, USA

Griffin, Keith (Athlete, Football Player)
4330 Canada Hills Ct
Waldorf, MD 20602-3106, USA

Griffin, Larry (Athlete, Football Player)
5617 Silchester Ln
Charlotte, NC 28215-5327, USA

Griffin, Leonard (Athlete, Football Player)
PO Box 480
Calhoun, LA 71225-0480, USA

Griffin, Mike (Athlete, Baseball Player)
150 Park Ave
Attn Coaching Staff
Norfolk, VA 23510-2712, USA

Griffin, Mike (Athlete, Baseball Player)
1620 Grove Ave
Woodland, CA 95695-5149, USA

Griffin, Nikki (Actor)
c/o Staff Member *Agency for the Performing Arts (APA-LA)*
405 S Beverly Dr Ste 500
Beverly Hills, CA 90212-4425, USA

Griffin, Patty (Musician, Songwriter, Writer)
Monterey Peninsula Artists
509 Hartnell St
Monterey, CA 93940-2825, USA

Griffin, Paul (Athlete, Basketball Player)
903 Great Tree Dr
San Antonio, TX 78260-7744, USA

Griffin, Ray (Athlete, Football Player)
2304 Somersworth Dr
Columbus, OH 43219-2010, USA

Griffin, Robert P (Politician)
Michigan Supreme Court
3825 Scenic Rdg # 7B
Traverse City, MI 49684-3900, USA

Griffin, Taylor (Athlete, Basketball Player)
c/o Jeff Schwartz *Excel Sports Management (NY)*
1700 Broadway Fl 29
New York, NY 10019-5905, USA

Griffin, Timothy (Congressman, Politician)
1232 Longworth Hob
Washington, DC 20515-2108, USA

Griffin, Tom (Athlete, Baseball Player)
13147 Avenida La Valencia
Poway, CA 92064-1905, USA

Griffin, Tony (Actor, Director, Writer)
c/o Staff Member *Merv Griffin Entertainment*
130 El Camino Dr
Beverly Hills, CA 90212-2700

Griffin, Ty (Athlete, Baseball Player, Olympic Athlete)
7803 N River Shore Dr
Tampa, FL 33604-3903, USA

Griffin, Wade (Athlete, Football Player)
2937 Highway 72
Holly Springs, MS 38635-9512, USA

Griffin, Warren (Warren G) (Actor, Musician)
c/o Portia Scott *Coast to Coast Talent Group*
3350 Barham Blvd
Los Angeles, CA 90068-1404, USA

Griffin, William (W.E.B.) (Writer)
c/o Jeff Gerecke *Gina Maccoby Literary Agency*
PO Box 60
Chappaqua, NY 10514-0060, USA

Griffing, Glynn (Athlete, Football Player)
2318 Irving Pl
Jackson, MS 39211-6133, USA

Griffin III, Robert (Athlete, Football Player)
22553 Creighton Farms Dr
Leesburg, VA 20175-6006, USA

Griffith, Bill (Cartoonist)
Pinhead Productions
PO Box 88
Hadlyme, CT 06439-0088, USA

Griffith, Calvin (Baseball Player)
Minnesota Twins
501 Chicago Ave
Minneapolis, MN 55415-1517, USA

Griffith, Clint (Athlete, Football Player)
878 13th Ave S
Jacksonville Beach, FL 32250-4122, USA

Griffith, Darrell (Athlete, Basketball Player)
PO Box 24841
Louisville, KY 40224-0841, USA

Griffith, Derrell (Athlete, Baseball Player)
201 E Central Blvd
Anadarko, OK 73005-3431, USA

Griffith, H. Morgan (Congressman, Politician)
1108 Longworth Hob
Washington, DC 20515-3809, USA

Griffith, Howard (Athlete, Football Player)
9152 S Clyde Ave
Chicago, IL 60617-3740, USA

Griffith, James (Business Person)
Timken Co
1835 Dueber Ave SW
Canton, OH 44706-2798, USA

Griffith, Melanie (Actor, Producer)
611 S Muirfield Rd
Los Angeles, CA 90005-3832, USA

Griffith, Rhiana (Actor)
c/o Staff Member *Darlene Kaplan Entertainment*
4450 Balboa Ave
Encino, CA 91316-4101, USA

Griffith, Robert (Athlete, Football Player)
3525 Del Mar Heights Rd Unit 331
San Diego, CA 92130-2199, USA

Griffith, Thomas Ian (Actor)
c/o Lou Pitt *Pitt Group, The*
8750 Wilshire Blvd Ste 301
Beverly Hills, CA 90211-2700, USA

Griffith, Thomas Ian (Actor)
Endeavor Talent Agency
9701 Wilshire Blvd Ste 1000
Beverly Hills, CA 90212-2010, USA

Griffith, Wendy (Religious Leader, Television Host)
c/o Staff Member *CBN News*
977 Centerville Tpke
Christian Broadcasting Network
Virginia Beach, VA 23463-1001, USA

Griffith, Yolanda (Basketball Player)
Sacramento Monarchs
1 Sports Pkwy
Arco Arena
Sacramento, CA 95834-2300, USA

Griffiths, Brian (Baseball Player)
16022 SE Goosehollow Dr
Clackamas, OR 97015, USA

Griffiths, Jeremy (Athlete, Baseball Player)
120 Beachdale Dr
Avon Lake, OH 44012-1611, USA

Griffiths, Lucy (Actor)
c/o Larry Taube *Principal Entertainment (LA)*
9255 W Sunset Blvd Ste 500
West Hollywood, CA 90069-3301, USA

Griffiths, Rachel (Actor)
c/o Jodi Gottlieb *Independent Public Relations*
Prefers to be contacted via telephone or email
Los Angeles, CA, USA

Griffiths, Susan
9300 Wilshire Blvd Ste 410
Beverly Hills, CA 90212-3228

Griggs, Acle (Baseball Player)
Birmingham Black Barons
820 Newwau Ave SW
Birmingham, AL 35221, USA

Griggs, Perry (Athlete, Football Player)
1275 Carlysle Park Dr
Lawrenceville, GA 30044-2242, USA

Griggs, William E (Athlete, Football Player)
4923 Barbour Dr
Alexandria, VA 22304-7708, USA

Grigorian, Irina (Figure Skater)
c/o Staff Member *Champions on Ice*
3500 American Blvd W Ste 190
Minneapolis, MN 55431-4431, USA

Grigsby, Benji (Baseball Player)
118 Teakwood Dr SW
Huntsville, AL 35801-3453, USA

Grijalva, Lucy (Writer)
PO Box 1634
Benicia, CA 94510-4634

Grijalva, Victor E (Business Person)
Schlumberger Ltd
277 Park Ave
New York, NY 10172-0003, USA

Grilli, Guido (Athlete, Baseball Player)
250 Sloan Ln
Locust Grove, AR 72550-9000, USA

Grilli, Jason (Athlete, Baseball Player)
9037 Point Cypress Dr
Orlando, FL 32836-5475, USA

Grilli, Steve (Athlete, Baseball Player)
8824 River Rd
Baldwinsville, NY 13027-9227, USA

Grillo, Frank
c/o Chris Huvane *Management 360*
9111 Wilshire Blvd
Beverly Hills, CA 90210-5508, USA

Grim, Robert (Bob) (Athlete, Football Player)
18 NW Saginaw Ave
Bend, OR 97701-1221, USA

Grimaud, Helene (Musician)
I C M Artists
40 W 57th St
New York, NY 10019-4001, USA

Grimes, Brent (Athlete, Football Player)
c/o Ben Dogra *CAA (St. Louis)*
222 S Central Ave Ste 1008
Saint Louis, MO 63105-3509, USA

Grimes, Gary
4578 W 165th St
Lawndale, CA 90260-2805

Grimes, Kareem
c/o Adam Robinson *Southfield Village*
6255 W Sunset Blvd Ste 923
Los Angeles, CA 90028-7410, USA

Grimes, Karolyn (Actor)
PO Box 432
Manchester, WA 98353-0432, USA

Grimes, Martha (Writer)
115 D St SE Apt G6
Washington, DC 20003-1822, USA

Grimes, Randy (Athlete, Football Player)
13214 Halifax St
Houston, TX 77015-2829, USA

Grimes, Scott (Actor)
c/o Adam Levine *Levine Okwu Erickson Management*
2126 N Commonwealth Ave
Los Angeles, CA 90027-2118, USA

Grimes, Tammy (Actor, Musician)
Don Buchwald
10 E 44th St Frnt 1
New York, NY 10017-3654, USA

Grimes, Tinsley (Actor)
c/o Staff Member *Innovative Artists (LA)*
1505 10th St
Santa Monica, CA 90401-2805, USA

Griminelli, Andrea (Musician)
Columbia Artists Mgmt Inc
165 W 57th St
New York, NY 10019-2201, USA

Grimm, Dan (Athlete, Football Player)
2514 Smith Harbour Dr
Denver, NC 28037-8093, USA

Grimm, Russ (Athlete, Coach, Football Coach, Football Player)
2654 E Mead Pi
Chandler, AZ 85249, USA

Grimm, Tim (Actor)
Abrams Artists
9200 W Sunset Blvd Ste 1125
West Hollywood, CA 90069-3610, USA

Grimsley, Jason (Athlete, Baseball Player)
13315 Timberwild Ct
Tomball, TX 77375-2939, USA

Grimsley, Ross (Athlete, Baseball Player)
92 Conewago Ct
Owings Mills, MD 21117-5049, USA

Grimsley, Ross (Athlete, Baseball Player)
Richmond Flying Squirrels
3001 N Boulevard
Richmond, VA 23230-4331, USA

Grinder, Scott (Athlete, Baseball Player)
1323 14th Ave N
Birmingham, AL 35204, USA

Griner, Brittney (Athlete, Basketball Player)
c/o Staff Member *Wasserman Media Group (LA)*
12100 W Olympic Blvd Ste 200
Los Angeles, CA 90064-1075, USA

Griner, Paul (Writer)
Random House
1745 Broadway Frnt 3 # B1
New York, NY 10019-4343, USA

grinnell, todd (Actor)
c/o DEBRA MANNERS *Daniel Hoff Agency*
5455 Wilshire Blvd Ste 1100
Los Angeles, CA 90036-4277, USA

Grinstead, Irish (Musician)
c/o Staff Member *Creative Artists Agency (CAA-LA)*
2000 Avenue of the Stars Ste 100
Los Angeles, CA 90067-4705, USA

Grinstead, LeMisha (Musician)
c/o Staff Member *Creative Artists Agency (CAA-LA)*
2000 Avenue of the Stars Ste 100
Los Angeles, CA 90067-4705, USA

Grinstein, Gerald (Business Person)
Delta Airlines
Hartsfield International Airport
Atlanta, GA 30320, USA

Grisanti, Eugene P (Business Person)
International Flavors
521 W 57th St Fl 9
New York, NY 10019-2960, USA

Grisham, John (Writer)
Oakwood Books
PO Box 1780
Oxford, MS 38655, USA

Grishuk, Pasha
Luzhnetskaia nab. 8
Moscow, RU 11987

Grissom, Marquis (Athlete, Baseball Player)
694 Highway 279
Fayetteville, GA 30214-2607, USA

Grissom, Scott (Race Car Driver)
Grissom Motorsports
395 Sawdust Rd # 2019
Spring, TX 77380-2242, USA

Grissom, Steve (Race Car Driver)
Source International
5901 Orr Rd
Charlotte, NC 28213-6321, USA

Grizzard, George (Baseball Player, Basketball Player)
Champion Lakes
PO Box 288
Bolivar, PA 15923-0288, USA

Groat, Dick (Athlete, Baseball Player)
320 Beech St
Pittsburgh, PA 15218-1406, USA

Grob, Mike (Athlete, Golfer)
2605 Minnesota Ave Unit 202
Billings, MT 59101-4219, USA

Groban, Josh (Musician)
6611 Portshead Rd
Malibu, CA 90265-4259, USA

Groce, Clifton (Clif) (Athlete, Football Player)
1632 Park Pl # B
College Station, TX 77840-3123, USA

Groce, Dejuan (Athlete, Football Player)
2749 Hidden Lake Dr
Grapevine, TX 76051-2402, USA

Groce, Ron (Athlete, Football Player)
3624 5th Ave S
Minneapolis, MN 55409-1329, USA

Grode, Jarrett (Actor)
c/o Ruthanne Secunda *ICM Partners (LA)*
10250 Constellation Blvd Fl 7
Los Angeles, CA 90067-6207, USA

Grodin, Charles
187 Chestnut Hill Rd
Wilton, CT 06897-4108, USA

Groener, Harry (Actor)
c/o Susan Smith *Susan Smith Company, The*
2001 Wilshire Blvd Ste 400
Santa Monica, CA 90403-5686, USA

Groening, Matthew (Matt) (Cartoonist)
c/o Michael A Neidorf *Caplan-Groening Family Foundation*
11400 W Olympic Blvd Ste 590
Los Angeles, CA 90064-1574, USA

Groetzinger Jr, Jon (Business Person)
American Greetings Corp
1 American Rd
Cleveland, OH 44144-2398, USA

Grofe Jr, Ferde
18139 Coastline Dr
Malibu, CA 90265-5738, USA

Groff, Jonathan (Actor)
c/o Tony Lipp *Anonymous Content (LA)*
3532 Hayden Ave
Culver City, CA 90232-2413, USA

Groff, Mike (Race Car Driver)
270 Wigmore Dr
Pasadena, CA 91105-3337, USA

Grogan, John (Writer)
HarperCollins Publishers L.L.C.
53 Glenmaura National Blvd # 300
Moosic, PA 18507-2132, USA

Grogan, Steven J (Steve) (Athlete, Football Player)
6 Country Club Ln
Foxboro, MA 02035-2756, USA

Groh, Al (Coach, Football Coach)
University of Virginia
Athletic Dept
Charlottesville, VA 22903, USA

Groh, Gary (Athlete, Golfer)
331 Signe Ct
Lake Bluff, IL 60044-1219, USA

Grohl, Dave (Musician)
c/o Steve Martin *Nasty Little Man*
110 Greene St Ste 605
New York, NY 10012-3838, USA

Grollman, Rabbi Earl (Religious Leader, Writer)
c/o Staff Member *Beacon Press*
24 Farnsworth St Fl 1
Boston, MA 02210-1297, USA

Groman, Bill (Athlete, Football Player)
7906 Scherzo Ln
Houston, TX 77040-2529, USA

Groman, William (Athlete, Football Player)
7906 Scherzo Ln
Houston, TX 77040-2529, USA

Gronberg, Mathias (Athlete, Golfer)
247 Plymouth Rd
West Palm Beach, FL 33405-3324, USA

Gronkiewicz, Lee (Athlete, Baseball Player)
227 S Marion St Apt D
Columbia, SC 29205-3271, USA

Gronkowski, Rob (Athlete, Football Player)
7 Congdon Cir
Foxboro, MA 02035-4200, USA

Gronman, Tuomas (Athlete, Hockey Player)
66 Mario Lemieux Pl
Pittsburgh, PA 15219-3504, USA

Groom, Buddy (Athlete, Baseball Player)
1991 Saint Andrews Dr
Red Oak, TX 75154-5837, USA

Groom, Sam (Actor)
8730 W Sunset Blvd Ste 440
West Hollywood, CA 90069-2277, USA

Groom, Winston (Writer)
18096 Woodland Dr
Point Clear, AL 36564, USA

Grootegoed, Matt (Athlete, Football Player)
17302 Destry Cir
Huntington Beach, CA 92647-6135, USA

Gros, Earl (Athlete, Football Player)
17424 Airline Hwy Ste 12
Prairieville, LA 70769-3352, USA

Grosek, Michal (Athlete, Hockey Player)
5 Samba Cir
Sandwich, MA 02563-2597

Gross, Al (Athlete, Football Player)
3203 Greenwood St
Stockton, CA 95205-5708, USA

Gross, Alfred E (Athlete, Football Player)
8227 Grandstaff Dr
Sacramento, CA 95823-5970, USA

Gross, Arye
c/o Paul Greenstone *Paul Greenstone Entertainment*
3008 Sorrelwood Dr
San Ramon, CA 94582-5008, USA

Gross, David (Comedian)
c/o Staff Member *United Talent Agency (UTA-LA)*
9336 Civic Center Dr
Beverly Hills, CA 90210-3604, USA

Gross, Don (Athlete, Baseball Player)
1301 Clubhouse Dr
Weidman, MI 48893-8205, USA

Gross, Gabe (Athlete, Baseball Player)
1756 Ravmer Pi
Auburn, AL 36830, USA

Gross, Greg (Athlete, Baseball Player)
802 Hallowell Dr
West Chester, PA 19382-5243, USA

Gross, Henry (Musician)
c/o Pat Horgan *Pat Horgan Talent*
2789 W Main St Ste 5
Wappingers Falls, NY 12590-1524, USA

Gross, Jordan (Athlete, Football Player)
12725 Ninebark Trl
Charlotte, NC 28278-6838, USA

Gross, Kevin (Athlete, Baseball Player)
2058 N Mills Ave
PO Box 144
Claremont, CA 91711-2812, USA

Gross, Kip (Athlete, Baseball Player)
2015 Ridgeview Ct
Redlands, CA 92373-6979, USA

Gross, Lance (Actor)
c/o Kenny Goodman *The Schiff Company*
9220 W Sunset Blvd Ste 106
West Hollywood, CA 90069-3500, USA

Gross, Lee (Athlete, Football Player)
871 Holland Rd
Newton, AL 36352-8035, USA

Gross, Mary (Actor, Comedian)
c/o Staff Member *Pakula/King & Associates*
9229 W Sunset Blvd Ste 315
West Hollywood, CA 90069-3403, USA

Gross, Michael (Actor)
4431 Woodleigh Ln
La Canada Flintridge, CA 91011-3542, USA

Gross, Paul (Actor)
c/o John S Kelly *Bresler Kelly & Associates*
11500 W Olympic Blvd Ste 510
Los Angeles, CA 90064-1527, USA

Gross, Robert (Bob) (Athlete, Basketball Player)
13466 SE Red Rose Ln
Happy Valley, OR 97086-9752, USA

Gross, Terry R (Correspondent)
WHYY-Radio
News Dept
Independence Mall W
Philadelphia, PA 19104, USA

Gross, Wayne (Athlete, Baseball Player)
45 Leonard Ct
Danville, CA 94526-1911, USA

Grosscup, Lee (Athlete, Football Player)
703 Atlantic Ave Apt 360
Alameda, CA 94501-8201, USA

Grossman, Burt (Athlete, Football Player)
2595 Oak Springs Dr
Chula Vista, CA 91915-1551, USA

Grossman, Judith (Athlete, Football Player)
1000 Football Dr
Lake Forest, IL 60045, USA

Grossman, Judith (Writer)
Warren Wilson College
English Dept
Swannanoa, NC 28778, USA

Grossman, Leslie (Actor)
c/o Staff Member *Metropolitan (MTA)*
4526 Wilshire Blvd
Los Angeles, CA 90010-3801, USA

Grossman, Randy (Athlete, Football Player)
204 Ridge Rd
Pittsburgh, PA 15238-1522, USA

Grossman, Rex (Athlete, Football Player)
715 SE 8th St
Delray Beach, FL 33483-5122, USA

Grossman, Rex (Athlete, Football Player)
2552 S Smith Rd
Bloomington, IN 47401-8923, USA

Grosvenor, Gilbert M (Publisher)
National Geographic Society
M N W
Washington, DC 20036, USA

Grote, Jerry (Athlete, Baseball Player)
2608 N Main St Ste B
#21
Belton, TX 76513-1547, USA

Grote, Jerry C. (Athlete, Basketball Player)
4714 W Lapenna Dr
New River, AZ 85087-3054, USA

Grotewold, Jeff (Athlete, Baseball Player)
PO Box 3439
Crestline, CA 92325-3439, USA

Groth, Jeff (Athlete, Football Player)
13824 Driftwood Dr
Carmel, IN 46033-8510, USA

Groth, Johnny (Athlete, Baseball Player)
170 N Ocean Blvd Apt 307
Palm Beach, FL 33480-3931, USA

Grott, Matt (Athlete, Baseball Player)
19431 N Concho Cir
Sun City, AZ 85373-1201, USA

Grottkau, Bob (Athlete, Football Player)
255 Atlantic Dr
Rio Vista, CA 94571-2168, USA

Grottkau, Robert (Athlete, Football Player)
5105 S Muirfield Ln
Spokane, WA 99223-6362, USA

Grouch, Roger K (Astronaut)
Life/Microgravity Sciences Office
Nasa Headquarters
Washington, DC 20546-0001, USA

Groulx, Pierre (Coach, Hockey Player)
156 NW 118th Dr
Coral Springs, FL 33071-8072, USA

Grove, Andrew (Business Person)
Intel Corp
2200 Mission College Blvd
Santa Clara, CA 95054-1549, USA

Groves, Napiera Danielle (Actor)
c/o Christine Thomas *Sweet Mud Group*
648 Broadway # 1002
New York, NY 10012-2348, USA

Grow, Carol (Actor, Model)
c/o Jon Orlando *WNWN Media*
348 Hauser Blvd # PH414
Los Angeles, CA 90036-3276, USA

Grubar, Richard (Athlete, Basketball Player)
1804 Milan Rd
Greensboro, NC 27410-3028, USA

Grubb, John (Athlete, Baseball Player)
6618 Bel Lac Dr
Chester, VA 23831-1431, USA

Grubb, Kevin (Race Car Driver)
c/o Grubb Motorsports
5120 Jefferson Davis Hwy
North Chesterfield, VA 23234-2252, USA

Grubb, Wayne (Race Car Driver)
Grubb Motorsports
5120 Jefferson Davis Hwy
North Chesterfield, VA 23234-2252, USA

Grubbs, Gary (Actor)
Parasigm Agency
10100 Santa Monica Blvd Ste 2500
Los Angeles, CA 90067-4116, USA

Grubbs, Teilor (Actor)
c/o Emily Urbani *Osbrink Talent Agency*
4343 Lankershim Blvd Ste 100
North Hollywood, CA 91602-2705, USA

Gruber, Bob (Athlete, Football Player)
1704 W Call St Apt 107
Tallahassee, FL 32304-4959, USA

Gruber, Jonathan (Director, Writer)
c/o Josh Adler *New Wave Entertainment (LA)*
2660 W Olive Ave
Burbank, CA 91505-4525, USA

Gruber, Kelly (Athlete, Baseball Player)
17718 Linkview Dr
Dripping Springs, TX 78620-2670, USA

Gruber, Paul (Athlete, Football Player)
PO Box 4239
Edwards, CO 81632-4239, USA

Grubnic, Dave (Race Car Driver)
John Mitchell Racing
392 Highway 287
Ennis, MT 59729, USA

Gruden, John (Athlete, Hockey Player)
1287 Essex Dr
Rochester Hills, MI 48307-3139

Gruden, Jon (Athlete, Coach, Football Coach, Football Player)
c/o Bob LaMonte *Professional Sports Representation*
1220 Plumas St
Reno, NV 89509-2745, USA

Grudens, Richard
PO Box 344
Stony Brook, NY 11790-0344

Grudzielanek, Mark (Athlete, Baseball Player)
PO Box 1581
Rancho Santa Fe, CA 92067-1581, USA

Gruen, Sara (Writer)
c/o Staff Member *HarperCollins Publishers*
195 Broadway Fl 2
Cellar 1
New York, NY 10007-3132, USA

Gruenwald, Jim (Athlete, Olympic Athlete, Wrestler)
64 Circle Ave
Wheaton, IL 60187-4024, USA

Gruffudd, Ioan (Actor)
c/o Peg Donegan *Framework Entertainment (LA)*
9057 Nemo St Ste C
West Hollywood, CA 90069-5511, USA

Gruhl, Scott (Athlete, Hockey Player)
8732 Laumic Dr
North Chesterfield, VA 23235-4655

Grum, Clifford J (Business Person)
Temple-Inland Inc
303 S Temple Dr
Diboll, TX 75941-2419, USA

Grumman, Cornelia (Journalist)
Chicago Tribune
435 N Michigan Ave Ste 200
Editorial Dept
Chicago, IL 60611-4024, USA

Grunberg, Greg (Actor)
c/o Susan Calogerakis *SC Management*
9465 Wilshire Blvd Fl 7
Beverly Hills, CA 90212-2606, USA

Grundfest, Joseph A (Government Official)
Stanford University
Law School
Stanford, CA 94305, USA

Grundman, Bernie (Musician)
Bernie Grundman Mastering
1640 N Gower St
Los Angeles, CA 90028-6518, USA

Grundt, Ken (Athlete, Baseball Player)
4814 W Parker Ave
Chicago, IL 60639-1712, USA

Grundy, Hugh (Musician)
Lustig Talent
PO Box 770850
Orlando, FL 32877-0850, USA

Grune, George V (Publisher)
1000 Vicars Landing Way PH 8
Ponte Vedra, FL 32082-3156, USA

Gruneisen, Sam (Athlete, Football Player)
569 Finsbay Ct
Ocoee, FL 34761-5658, USA

Grunfeld, Ernie (Athlete, Basketball Player, Olympic Athlete)
10121 Counselman Rd
Potomac, MD 20854-5021, USA

Grunhard, Tim (Athlete, Football Player)
2005 Arno Rd
Mission Hills, KS 66208-2246, USA

Grunsfeld, John M (Astronaut)
PO Box 279
Highland, MD 20777-0279, USA

Grunwald, Ernie (Actor)
c/o Suzanne (Sue) Wohl *TalentWorks (LA)*
3500 W Olive Ave Ste 1400
Burbank, CA 91505-5512, USA

Grupo Mania (Music Group)
c/o Staff Member *Sony Music Miami*
605 Lincoln Rd Ste 700
Miami Beach, FL 33139-2901, USA

Grupp, Robert (Athlete, Football Player)
305 Hill Ave
Langhorne, PA 19047-2819, USA

Grushin, Dave
200 W Superior St Ste 202
Chicago, IL 60654-3554

Gruttadauria, Mike (Athlete, Football Player)
4250 Swift Rd
Sarasota, FL 34231-6547, USA

Gryboski, Kevin (Athlete, Baseball Player)
127 Castlebrooke Dr
Venetia, PA 15367-1391, USA

Grygiel, George (Athlete, Baseball Player)
451 W Bazille Way
Green Valley, AZ 85614-5270, USA

Grymes, Darrell (Athlete, Football Player)
1737 Minnesota Ave SE Apt 1
Washington, DC 20020-4755, USA

Gryp, Bob (Athlete, Hockey Player)
11 Duren Ave
Woburn, MA 01801-5304

Grzanich, Mike (Athlete, Baseball Player)
176 Holliday Trce
Raymond, MS 39154-9569, USA

Grzebien, Anna (Athlete, Golfer)
c/o Staff Member *Ladies Pro Golf Association (LPGA)*
100 International Golf Dr
Daytona Beach, FL 32124-1092, USA

Grzenda, Joe (Athlete, Baseball Player)
40 Hillcrest Dr
Covington Township, PA 18424-7852, USA

G. Thompson, Bennie (Congressman, Politician)
2466 Rayburn Hob
Washington, DC 20515-3807, USA

Guadagnino, Kathy Baker (Athlete, Golfer)
1535 SW 4th Cir
Boca Raton, FL 33486-4414, USA

Guadagnino, Vinny (Reality Star)
431 Bradley Ave
Staten Island, NY 10314-6945, USA

Guardado, Eddie (Athlete, Baseball Player)
11268 Overlook Pt
Tustin, CA 92782-4314, USA

Guardino, Harry (Actor)
2949 E Via Vaquero Rd
Palm Springs, CA 92262-7941, USA

Guare, John (Writer)
1 Dag Hammarskjold Plz
New York, NY 10017-2201, USA

Guarilia, Gene (Athlete, Basketball Player)
86 Main St
Duryea, PA 18642-1023, USA

Guarini, Justin (Musician)
c/o Jeff Ballard *Jeff Ballard PR*
4814 Lemona Ave
Sherman Oaks, CA 91403-2010, USA

Guarriello, Taimak (Actor)
c/o Staff Member *Chasin Agency, The*
8899 Beverly Blvd Ste 716
Los Angeles, CA 90048-2449, USA

Guaty, Camille (Actor)
c/o Michael Baum *Impression Entertainment*
9229 W Sunset Blvd Ste 700
West Hollywood, CA 90069-3407, USA

Guay, Paul (Athlete, Hockey Player, Olympic Athlete)
34 Kirkbrae Dr
Lincoln, RI 02865-1019

Gubanich, Creighton (Athlete, Baseball Player)
240 Hall St
Phoenixville, PA 19460-3511, USA

Gubelmann, Fiona (Actor)
c/o Brady McKay *Evolution Entertainment (LA)*
9320 Wilshire Blvd Ste 202
Beverly Hills, CA 90212-3217, USA

Guber, Peter (Producer)
Mandaly Entertainment
10202 Washington Blvd # 1070
Culver City, CA 90232-3119, USA

Gubicza, Mark (Athlete, Baseball Player)
11808 Macoda Ln
Chatsworth, CA 91311-1271, USA

Gubler, Matthew Gray (Actor, Director, Writer)
c/o Colton Gramm *Brillstein Entertainment Partners (LA)*
9150 Wilshire Blvd Ste 350
Beverly Hills, CA 90212-3453, USA

Gubner, Gary (Athlete, Olympic Athlete, Weightlifter)
7134 Great Falls Cir
Boynton Beach, FL 33437-0900, USA

Gucciardo, Pat (Athlete, Football Player)
2406 Kenmoore Rd
Maumee, OH 43537-1121, USA

Guccione, Chris (Athlete, Baseball Player)
88 Paloma Ave
Brighton, CO 80601-8791, USA

Guccione, Christopher (Baseball Player)
15362 W Iliff Dr
Denver, CO 80228-6443, USA

Guckert, Elmer (Athlete, Baseball Player)
900 Lincoln Club Dr
Pittsburgh, PA 15237-5092, USA

Gudmundson, Scott (Athlete, Football Player)
11 Guindola Way Apt 268
Hot Springs Village, AR 71909-7128, USA

Gudmundsson, Petur (Athlete, Basketball Player)
2423 Vibrant Oak
San Antonio, TX 78232-2616, USA

Guennel, Joe (Soccer Player)
835 Front Range Rd
Littleton, CO 80120-4005, USA

Gueno, James (Athlete, Football Player)
8173 Drexel Ct
Eden Prairie, MN 55347-2189, USA

Guenther, Johnny (Bowler)
23826 115th Pl W
Woodway, WA 98020-5212, USA

Guerin, Bill (Athlete, Hockey Player, Olympic Athlete)
609 Backbone Rd
Sewickley, PA 15143-1488

Guerin, Bill (Athlete, Hockey Player)
Pittsburgh Penguins
66 Mario Lemieux Pl Ste 2
Pittsburgh, PA 15219-3504

Guerin, Richie (Athlete, Basketball Player)
1355 Bear Island Dr
West Palm Beach, FL 33409-2042, USA

Guerra, Eddie (Actor)
c/o Peter Micelli *Creative Artists Agency (CAA-LA)*
2000 Avenue of the Stars Ste 100
Los Angeles, CA 90067-4705, USA

Guerra, Jackie (Comedian)
c/o Staff Member *Brillstein Entertainment Partners (LA)*
9150 Wilshire Blvd Ste 350
Beverly Hills, CA 90212-3453, USA

Guerra, Juan Luis (Musician)
c/o Staff Member *EMI Music Group (NY)*
150 5th Ave Fl 7
New York, NY 10011-4372, USA

Guerra, Saverio (Actor)
c/o Susan Ferris *Bohemia Group (LA)*
1680 Vine St Ste 412
Los Angeles, CA 90028-8800, USA

Guerra, Vida (Actor, Model)
c/o Staff Member *Britto Agency PR*
90 Franklin St Apt 4N
New York, NY 10013-3489, USA

Guerrero, Diane (Actor)
c/o Josh Taylor *Vamnation Entertainment*
3 Greatmeadow Rd
Locust Valley, NY 11560-1005, USA

Guerrero, Pedro (Athlete, Baseball Player)
10720 NW 66th St Apt 408
Doral, FL 33178-3657, USA

Guerrero, Roberto (Race Car Driver)
PO Box 381
Clay, KY 42404-0381, USA

Guerrero, Vladimir (Athlete, Baseball Player)
5160 E Copa De Oro Dr
Anaheim, CA 92807-3639, USA

Guerrero Coles, Lisa (Actor, Journalist, Sportscaster)
c/o Mike Liotta *True Public Relations*
6725 W Sunset Blvd Ste 470
Los Angeles, CA 90028-7180, USA

Guerrier, Manouschka (Chef)
c/o Jason Pinyan *Artist & Brand Management (LA)*
132 N Laurel Ave
Los Angeles, CA 90048-3512, USA

Guerrier, Matt (Athlete, Baseball Player)
200 Highland View Dr
Birmingham, AL 35242-6874, USA

Guest, Christopher (Actor, Director)
463 Mesa Rd
Santa Monica, CA 90402-1131, USA

Guest, Cornelia (Model)
1419 Donhill Dr
Beverly Hills, CA 90210-2216, USA

Guest, Lance
2269 La Granada Dr
Los Angeles, CA 90068-2723

Guetterman, Lee (Athlete, Baseball Player)
108 1/2 E Broadway St
Lenoir City, TN 37771-2908, USA

Guevara, Carlos (Athlete, Baseball Player)
403 Margaret Ave
Henderson, TX 75654-4343, USA

Guevremont, Jocelyn (Athlete, Hockey Player)
4303 NW 70th Ln
Coral Springs, FL 33065-2130, USA

Guffey, Cary (Actor)
236 Eagle Park Ln
Birmingham, AL 35242, USA

Guffey Jr, John W (Business Person)
Coltec Industries
2550 W Tyvola Rd
Charlotte, NC 28217-4574, USA

Guggemos, Neal (Athlete, Football Player)
8173 Drexel Ct
Eden Prairie, MN 55347-2189, USA

Guggenheim, Marc (Actor)
c/o Eddie Michaels *Insignia Public Relations*
1507 20th St Ste B
Santa Monica, CA 90404-3474, USA

Gugino, Carla (Actor)
c/o Jason Weinberg *Untitled Entertainment (LA)*
350 S Beverly Dr Ste 200
Beverly Hills, CA 90212-4819, USA

Guglielmi, Ralph (Athlete, Football Player)
159 Red Berry Dr
Wallace, NC 28466-2376, USA

Gugliotta, Tom (Athlete, Basketball Player)
992 Wadsworth Dr NW
Atlanta, GA 30318-1654, USA

Guice, Jackson (Cartoonist)
DC Comics
1700 Broadway Fl 6
New York, NY 10019-5905, USA

Guidinger, Jay (Athlete, Basketball Player)
N39W22702 Grandview Dr
Pewaukee, WI 53072-2735, USA

Guidry, Kevin (Athlete, Football Player)
4045 W Briarfield St
Lake Charles, LA 70607-3658, USA

Guidry, Mark
1264 Camelot Ln
Lemont, IL 60439-8505

Guidry, Paul (Athlete, Football Player)
880 Noel Dr
Mount Juliet, TN 37122-1352, USA

Guidry, Ron (Athlete, Baseball Player)
PO Box 666
Scott, LA 70583-0666, USA

Guilbe, Felix (Baseball Player)
Baltimore Elite Giants
Los Cabos Calle Carambala
Ponce, PR 00716, USA

Guilbert, Ann (Actor)
550 Erskine Dr
Pacific Palisades, CA 90272-4247, USA

Guilford, Eric (Athlete, Football Player)
8111 W Wacker Rd Unit 51
Peoria, AZ 85381-4943, USA

Guilfoyle, Kimberly (Television Host)
c/o Staff Member Fox News (NY)
1211 Avenue of the Americas Lowr C1
New York, NY 10036-8705, USA

Guilfoyle, Paul (Actor)
15226 Dickens St
Sherman Oaks, CA 91403-3335, USA

Guill, Juliana (Actor)
c/o Tim Taylor Luber Roklin Management
5815 W Sunset Blvd Ste 206
Los Angeles, CA 90028-6481, USA

Guillaume, Robert (Actor)
c/o Alan David Alan David Management
8840 Wilshire Blvd Ste 200
Beverly Hills, CA 90211-2606, USA

Guillemots (Music Group, Musician)
c/o Staff Member MCT Management
104 W 29th St Rm 1101
New York, NY 10001-5310, USA

Guillen, Carlos
10681 Blue Palm St
Plantation, FL 33324-8231, USA

Guillen, Ozzie (Athlete, Baseball Player)
Florida Marlins
501 Marlins Way
Miami, FL 33125-1121, USA

Guillen, Ozzie (Athlete, Baseball Player)
19462 38th Ct
Golden Beach, FL 33160-2298, USA

Guillerman, John (Director)
309 S Rockingham Ave
Los Angeles, CA 90049-3637, USA

Guillermin, John
309 S Rockingham Ave
Los Angeles, CA 90049-3637

Guillory, Bennet
2082 Pascal St
Santa Rosa, CA 95403-1564

Guillory, Sienna (Actor)
c/o Holly Shakoor Fleischer 42West (LA)
1840 Century Park E Ste 700
Los Angeles, CA 90067-2122, USA

Guillory, Tony (Athlete, Football Player)
2605 Blanchette St
Beaumont, TX 77701-6615, USA

Guinan, Francis
606 N Larchmont Blvd # 309LA
Los Angeles, CA 90004-1321

Guindon, Richard G (Cartoonist)
321 W Lafayette Blvd Lbby
Detroit, MI 48226-2703, USA

Guinee, Tim (Actor)
c/o Jonathan Howard Innovative Artists
(LA)
1505 10th St
Santa Monica, CA 90401-2805, USA

Guiney, Bob (Game Show Host, Reality
Star)
c/o Anthony Embry AE Entertainment
Public Relations
124 Evening Shade Dr
Charleston, SC 29414-9144, USA

Guinn, Skip (Athlete, Baseball Player)
PO Box 911
Stilwell, OK 74960-0911, USA

Guinney, Bob (Reality Star)
c/o Kim Jakwerth Marleah Leslie &
Associates PR
1645 Vine St Apt 712
Los Angeles, CA 90028-8812, USA

Guinta, Frank (Congressman, Politician)
1223 Longworth Hob
Washington, DC 20515-3810, USA

Guion, Letroy (Athlete, Football Player)
c/o Joe Linta JL Sports
1204 Main St Ste 179
Branford, CT 06405-3787, USA

Guirgis, Stephen Adly (Comedian)
c/o Sandra Chang Anonymous Content
(LA)
3532 Hayden Ave
Culver City, CA 90232-2413, USA

Guiry, Thomas (Actor)
c/o Rhonda Price Gersh (NY)
41 Madison Ave
New York, NY 10010-2202, USA

Guisewite, Cathy L (Cartoonist)
4039 Camellia Ave
Studio City, CA 91604-3007, USA

Guite, Ben (Athlete, Hockey Player)
35 Lake Ave
Gray, ME 04039-9793

Guite, Pierre (Athlete, Hockey Player)
96085 Marsh Lakes Dr
Fernandina Beach, FL 32034-0825

Gujral, Namrata
c/o Mike Eistenstadt Amsel, Eisenstadt &
Frazier Talent Agency (AEF)
5055 Wilshire Blvd Ste 860
Los Angeles, CA 90036-6108, USA

Gulager, Clu (Actor)
Clu Gulager Acting
320 Wilshire Blvd
Santa Monica, CA 90401-1315, USA

Gulan, Mike (Athlete, Baseball Player)
4409 Fairway Dr
Steubenville, OH 43953-3305, USA

Gulbis, Natalie (Athlete, Golfer)
30 Strada Principale
Henderson, NV 89011-3603, USA

Gulden, Brad (Athlete, Baseball Player)
15820 Lundstead Rd
Carver, MN 55315-9702, USA

Guliford, Eric (Athlete, Football Player)
8111 W Wacker Rd Unit 51
Peoria, AZ 85381-4943, USA

Gulledge, David (Athlete, Football Player)
304 Roundabout Dr
Trussville, AL 35173-1285, USA

Gullett, Donald E (Don) (Athlete, Baseball
Player)
237 Dotson Ln
South Shore, KY 41175-7879, USA

Gulli, Franco (Musician)
Columbia Artists Mgmt Inc
165 W 57th St
New York, NY 10019-2201, USA

Gullickson, William L (Bill) (Athlete,
Baseball Player)
3 Banchory Ct
Palm Beach Gardens, FL 33418-6811,
USA

Gullikson, Tom (Athlete)
Tim & Tom Gullikson Foundation
8000 Sears Tower
Chicago, IL 60606

Gulliver, Dorothy
28792 Lajos Ln
Valley Center, CA 92082-6107

Gulliver, Glenn (Athlete, Baseball Player)
8123 Cortland Ave
Allen Park, MI 48101-2215, USA

Gulman, Gary (Musician)
c/o Staff Member Paradigm (Monterey)
404 W Franklin St
Monterey, CA 93940-2303, USA

Gulseth, Don (Athlete, Football Player)
100 2nd St SE Apt 202
Minneapolis, MN 55414-2128, USA

Gulutzan, Glen (Athlete, Hockey Player)
Dallas Stars
2601 Avenue of the Stars Ste 100
Frisco, TX 75034-9016

Guman, Michael D (Mike) (Athlete,
Football Player)
3913 Pleasant Ave
Allentown, PA 18103-9773, USA

Gumbel, Bryant C (Sportscaster)
NFL Network
30 Rockefeller Plz Ste 1508
New York, NY 10112-0015, USA

Gumbel, Greg (Sportscaster, Television
Host)
c/o Staff Member CBS Television
51 W 52nd St
New York, NY 10019-6119, USA

Gummer, Grace (Actor)
c/o Michelle Benson 42West (LA)
1840 Century Park E Ste 700
Los Angeles, CA 90067-2122, USA

Gummer, Henry (Musician)
c/o Matthew Berkson Undermountain
Records
843 Tipton Ter
Los Angeles, CA 90042-1253, USA

Gummer, Mamie (Actor)
c/o Michelle Benson 42West (LA)
1840 Century Park E Ste 700
Los Angeles, CA 90067-2122, USA

Gummersall, Devon (Actor)
c/o Peg Donegan Framework
Entertainment (LA)
9057 Nemo St Ste C
West Hollywood, CA 90069-5511, USA

Gummoe, John (Musician)
6812 Apperson St
Tujunga, CA 91042-2018, USA

Gump, Scott (Athlete, Golfer)
11225 Willow Gardens Dr
Windermere, FL 34786-6020, USA

Gumpert, Dave (Athlete, Baseball Player)
68371 Fleetwood Dr
South Haven, MI 49090-8357, USA

Gunderman, Robert (Athlete, Football
Player)
11 Post Brook Rd S
West Milford, NJ 07480-4518, USA

Gunderson, Eric (Athlete, Baseball Player)
19809 SE 10th St
Camas, WA 98607-7273, USA

G Unit (Music Group)
c/o Staff Member Interscope Records (NY)
1755 Broadway
New York, NY 10019-3743, USA

Gunmuddsson, Petur (Athlete, Basketball
Player)
2423 Vibrant Oak
San Antonio, TX 78232-2616, USA

Gunn, Anna (Actor)
c/o Christian Donatelli The Schiff
Company
9220 W Sunset Blvd Ste 106
West Hollywood, CA 90069-3500, USA

Gunn, Chanda (Athlete, Hockey Player,
Olympic Athlete)
74 Rockcroft Rd
Weymouth, MA 02188, USA

Gunn, James (Actor, Director, Writer)
c/o Peter Safran The Safran Company
8748 Holloway Dr
West Hollywood, CA 90069-2327, USA

Gunn, Lance (Athlete, Football Player)
1301 Fernglade
Cedar Park, TX 78613-4562, USA

Gunn, Richard (Actor)
c/o Chris Henze Thruline Entertainment
9250 Wilshire Blvd Ste 100
Ground Floor
Beverly Hills, CA 90212-3343, USA

Gunn, Sean (Actor)
c/o Mitch Clem Shadow Entertainment
655 N Central Ave Fl 17
Glendale, CA 91203-1439, USA

Gunn, Tim (Designer, Reality Star,
Television Host)
c/o CeCe Yorke True Public Relations
6725 W Sunset Blvd Ste 470
Los Angeles, CA 90028-7180, USA

Gunnarsson, Martin (Athlete, Olympic
Athlete, Shooter)
3536 Saint Marys Rd Lot D24
Columbus, GA 31906-4594, USA

Gunnels, Riley (Athlete, Football Player)
606 Wesley Ave
Ocean City, NJ 08226-3856, USA

Gunner, Harry (Athlete, Football Player)
248 Emory Ln
Port Arthur, TX 77642-4769, USA

Guns N' Roses (Music Group)
c/o Staff Member *Geffen Records*
9126 Sunset Blvd
West Hollywood, CA 90069, USA

Gunter, Dan (Actor)
Century Artists
PO Box 59747
Santa Barbara, CA 93150, USA

Gunther, David (Athlete, Basketball Player)
827 Pleasantview Dr
Auburndale, FL 33823-5870, USA

Gunton, Bob (Actor)
34300 Lantern Bay Dr Unit 60
Dana Point, CA 92629-3804, USA

Gunvalson, Vicki (Reality Star)
30021 Tomas Ste 200
Rancho Santa Margarita, CA 92688-2160, USA

Guokas Jr, Matt (Athlete, Basketball Player, Coach)
2410 S 19th St
Philadelphia, PA 19145-4226, USA

Guolla, Steve (Athlete, Hockey Player)
733 Spartan Dr
Rochester Hills, MI 48309-2528

Gupta, Raj (Business Person)
Rohm & Haas Co
100 S Independence Mall W Fl 6
Philadelphia, PA 19106-2320, USA

Gupta, Sanjay (Correspondent, Doctor)
Emory Clinic
550 Peachtree St NE Frnt
Atlanta, GA 30308-2245, USA

Gura, Larry C (Athlete, Baseball Player)
PO Box 94
Litchfield Park, AZ 85340-0094, USA

Guren, Peter (Cartoonist)
Creators Syndicate
737 3rd St
Hermosa Beach, CA 90254-4714, USA

Gurewitz, Brett (Musician)
c/o Staff Member *William Morris Endeavor (LA)*
9601 Wilshire Blvd
Beverly Hills, CA 90210-5213, USA

Gurganus, Alan (Writer)
Vintage/Anchor Publicity
1745 Broadway Fl 20
New York, NY 10019-4640, USA

Gurian, Michael (Writer)
417 W 32nd Ave
Spokane, WA 99203-1777, USA

Gurley, Buck (Athlete, Football Player)
103 Neetle Close Dr
Woodstock, GA 30188-7077, USA

Gurney, Alex (Race Car Driver)
Dan Gurney Racing
2334 S Broadway
Santa Ana, CA 92707-3250, USA

Gurney, Daniel S (Dan) (Race Car Driver)
All-American Racers Inc
2334 S Broadway
Santa Ana, CA 92707-3250, USA

Gurney, Hilda (Horse Racer)
8430 Waters Rd
Moorpark, CA 93021-8715, USA

Gurney, James (Writer)
PO Box 693
Rhinebeck, NY 12572-0693, USA

Gurney, Scott (Actor)
c/o Staff Member *Guttman Associates*
118 S Beverly Dr Ste 201
Beverly Hills, CA 90212-3016, USA

Gurney Jr, Albert R (A R) (Writer)
40 Wellers Bridge Rd
Roxbury, CT 06783-1616, USA

Gurode, Andre (Athlete, Football Player)
15827 Maple Shores Dr
Houston, TX 77044-4485, USA

Gurry, Kick (Actor)
c/o Robert Stein *Robert Stein Management*
PO Box 3797
Beverly Hills, CA 90212-0797, USA

Gursky, Al (Athlete, Football Player)
54 Securda Rd
Reading, PA 19607-2521, USA

Gurwitch, Annabelle (Actor)
Don Buchwald
6500 Wilshire Blvd Ste 2200
Los Angeles, CA 90048-4942, USA

Gusarov, Alexei (Athlete, Hockey Player)
9695 E Kansas Cir Apt 41
Denver, CO 80247-2319

Gusev, Sergei (Athlete, Hockey Player)
16001 Ridley Pl Apt 2-A
Tampa, FL 33647-2050, USA

Gustafson, Derek (Athlete, Hockey Player)
3309 NE 165th Ave
Vancouver, WA 98682-8653

Gustafson, Ed (Athlete, Football Player)
6209 Mineral Point Rd Apt 1007
Madison, WI 53705-4555, USA

Gustafson, Sophie (Athlete, Golfer)
6043 Jamestown Park
Orlando, FL 32819-4435, USA

Gustafson, Steven (Musician)
Agency for Performing Arts
9200 W Sunset Blvd Ste 900
West Hollywood, CA 90069-3604, USA

Gustafsson, Per (Athlete, Hockey Player)
5605 NE 3rd Ave
Fort Lauderdale, FL 33334-1705, USA

Guster (Music Group)
c/o Staff Member *Nettwerk Management (NY)*
345 7th Ave Fl 24
New York, NY 10001-5030, USA

Gustin, Grant (Actor)
c/o Robert Stein *Robert Stein Management*
PO Box 3797
Beverly Hills, CA 90212-0797, USA

Guterman, Lawrence M (Director)
c/o Staff Member *William Morris Endeavor (LA)*
9601 Wilshire Blvd
Beverly Hills, CA 90210-5213, USA

Gutfeld, Greg (Television Host)
c/o Staff Member *Fox News (NY)*
1211 Avenue of the Americas Lowr C1
New York, NY 10036-8705, USA

Guth, Bucky (Athlete, Baseball Player)
202 Morris Dr
Salisbury, MD 21804-7229, USA

Gutherie, Arlo (Actor, Musician)
c/o Dora Whitaker *Whitaker Agency, The*
4924 Vineland Ave
N Hollywood, CA 91601-3847, USA

Gutherie, Jeremy (Athlete, Baseball Player)
1004 Clay St
Ashland, OR 97520-3613, USA

Guthrie, Arlo (Musician, Songwriter)
c/o Annie Guthrie *Rising Son Records*
218 Beach Rd
Clamzo's Court
Washington, MA 01223-9680, USA

Guthrie, Brett (Congressman, Politician)
308 Cannon Hob
Washington, DC 20515-4701, USA

Guthrie, Janet (Race Car Driver)
Janet Guthrie Racing
PO Box 505
Aspen, CO 81612-0505, USA

Guthrie, Jennifer (Actor)
Don Buchwald
6500 Wilshire Blvd Ste 2200
Los Angeles, CA 90048-4942, USA

Guthrie, Jeremy (Athlete, Baseball Player)
6515 Troon Cir
Kansas City, MO 64152-4953, USA

Guthrie, Mark (Athlete, Baseball Player)
3129 Donald Ross Rd E
Sarasota, FL 34240-7628, USA

Guthrie, Savannah (Correspondent)
c/o Michael Glantz *Headline Media Management*
888 7th Ave Ste 503
New York, NY 10106-0501, USA

Gutierrez, Brock (Athlete, Football Player)
1040 Pueblo Pass
Weidman, MI 48893-9322, USA

Gutierrez, Carlos M (Business Person)
Kellogg Co
1 Kellogg Sq
PO Box 3599
Battle Creek, MI 49017-3517, USA

Gutierrez, Franklin (Athlete, Baseball Player)
3180 N Jog Rd Apt 4202
West Palm Bch, FL 33411-7432, USA

Gutierrez, Horacio (Music Group, Musician)
I C M Artists
40 W 57th St
New York, NY 10019-4001, USA

Gutierrez, Jackie (Athlete, Baseball Player)
10631 SW 126th Ave
Miami, FL 33186-3744, USA

Gutierrez, Jennifer (Athlete, Olympic Athlete, Triathlete)
5232 Fullerton Ln
Highlands Ranch, CO 80130-6614, USA

Gutierrez, Ricky (Athlete, Baseball Player)
13803 NW Loth Ct
Pembroke Pines, FL 33028, USA

Gutierrez, Sebastian (Director, Writer)
c/o Craig Brody *Creative Artists Agency (CAA-LA)*
2000 Avenue of the Stars Ste 100
Los Angeles, CA 90067-4705, USA

Gutierrez, Sidney M (Astronaut)
324 Sarah Ln NW
Albuquerque, NM 87114-1026, USA

Gutierrez, Sidney M Colonel (Astronaut)
324 Sarah Ln NW
Albuquerque, NM 87114-1026, USA

Gutman, Roy W (Journalist)
1349 Windy Hill Rd
Mc Lean, VA 22102-2803, USA

Gutschewski, Scott (Basketball Player, Golfer)
20110 Douglas St
Elkhorn, NE 68022-1600, USA

Guttenberg, Steve (Actor)
c/o Staff Member *Binder & Associates*
1465 Lindacrest Dr
Beverly Hills, CA 90210-2519, USA

Gutz, Julie (Athlete, Baseball Player, Commentator)
9940 Gappa Rd
Kabetogama, MN 56669, USA

Guy, Buddy (Music Group, Musician)
Buddy Guy Legends
734 S Wabash Ave
Chicago, IL 60605, USA

Guy, Jasmine (Actor)
c/o Staff Member *Stone Manners Salners Agency (LA)*
6100 Wilshire Blvd Ste 1500
Los Angeles, CA 90048-5110, USA

Guy, Kevan (Athlete, Hockey Player)
10127 S Dunsinane Dr
South Jordan, UT 84095-9066

Guy, Lou (Athlete, Football Player)
2127 Sheffield Dr
Jackson, MS 39211-5851, USA

Guy, Melwood (Athlete, Football Player)
345 Castle St
Lowell, IN 46356-1810, USA

Guy, Ray (Athlete, Football Player)
936 Central Rd SW
Thomson, GA 30824-8278, USA

Guy, Sebastien (Actor)
c/o Staff Member *Acme Talent & Literary (LA)*
1400 Atlantic Ave Ste 274
Long Beach, CA 90813-2013, USA

Guy, William L (Ex-Governor, Politician)
3423 Crocus Ave
Bismarck, ND 58501-3212, USA

Guyer, Cindy (Actor)
c/o Marta Michaud *Cinematic Management*
249 1/2 E 13th St
New York, NY 10003-5602, USA

Guyot, Paul (Actor, Producer, Writer)
c/o Kathy White *Creative Artists Agency (CAA-LA)*
2000 Avenue of the Stars Ste 100
Los Angeles, CA 90067-4705, USA

Guyton, Myron (Athlete, Football Player)
302 Shadow Gln
McDonough, GA 30253-4294, USA

Guzikowski, Aaron (Writer)
c/o Adam Kolbrenner *Madhouse Entertainment*
10390 Santa Monica Blvd Ste 110
Los Angeles, CA 90025-5093, USA

Guzman, Alejandra (Musician)
c/o Staff Member *BMG*
1540 Broadway
New York, NY 10036-4039, USA

Guzman, Cristian (Athlete, Baseball Player)
10727 Cory Lake Dr
Tampa, FL 33647-2725, USA

Guzman, Jose (Athlete, Baseball Player)
4401 Shadycreek Ln
Colleyville, TX 76034-4729, USA

Guzman, Juan (Athlete, Baseball Player)
176 Dockside Cir
Weston, FL 33327-1100, USA

Guzman, Luis (Actor)
Gersh Agency
232 N Canon Dr
Beverly Hills, CA 90210-5302, USA

Guzman, Paloma (Actor)
c/o Jonathan Perry *Agency for the
Performing Arts (APA-LA)*
405 S Beverly Dr Ste 500
Beverly Hills, CA 90212-4425, USA

Guzman, Ryan
c/o Tim Taylor *Luber Roklin Management*
5815 W Sunset Blvd Ste 206
Los Angeles, CA 90028-6481, USA

Guzman, Santiago (Baseball Player)
St Louis Cardinals
1712 N Douty St
Hanford, CA 93230-2155, USA

Guzy, Carol (Journalist, Photographer)
2412 Fort Scott Dr
Arlington, VA 22202-2266, USA

Gwinn, Mary Ann (Journalist)
Seattle Times
Seattle Times Fairview Avenue NAnd John
Street Attn Editorial Dept
Seattle, WA 98111, USA

Gwinn, Ross (Athlete, Football Player)
1736 Washington St
Natchitoches, LA 71457-4926, USA

Gwosdz, Doug (Athlete, Baseball Player)
2108 Rose Rd
Pearland, TX 77581-3844, USA

Gwyn, Marcus (Athlete, Baseball Player)
150 E Elm Cres
Spring, TX 77382-1047, USA

Gwynn, Chris (Athlete, Baseball Player,
Olympic Athlete)
10975 Hillside Rd
Rancho Cucamonga, CA 91737-2458,
USA

Gwynn, Darrell (Race Car Driver)
4850 SW 52nd St Ste 1
Davie, FL 33314-5526, USA

Gyllenhaal, Jake (Actor)
7411 Woodrow Wilson Dr
Los Angeles, CA 90046-1322, USA

Gyllenhaal, Maggie (Actor)
c/o Courtney Kivowitz *The Schiff
Company*
9220 W Sunset Blvd Ste 106
West Hollywood, CA 90069-3500, USA

Gyllenhaal, Stephen G (Director,
Producer, Writer)
c/o Staff Member *William Morris
Endeavor (LA)*
9601 Wilshire Blvd
Beverly Hills, CA 90210-5213, USA

Gym Class Heroes (Music Group)
c/o Bob McLynn *Crush Management*
60-62 E 11th St
7th Floor
New York, NY 10003, USA

GZA (Musician)
c/o Staff Member *The Agency Group
(NYC)*
142 W 57th St Fl 6
New York, NY 10019-3300, USA

H

Haas, Dave (Athlete, Baseball Player)
1826 S Red Oaks St
Wichita, KS 67207-5772, USA

Haas, Eddie (Athlete, Baseball Player,
Coach)
8314 Alpena Way
Louisville, KY 40242-2502, USA

Haas, Hunter (Athlete, Golfer)
4078 Lively Ln
Dallas, TX 75220-1825, USA

Haas, Jay (Athlete, Golfer)
4 Tuscany Ct
Greer, SC 29650-4021, USA

Haas, Jerry (Race Car Driver)
Jerry Haas Motorsports
350 Haas Ln
Fenton, MO 63026-4673, USA

Haas, Lucas (Actor)
Lighthouse
409 N Camden Dr Ste 202
Beverly Hills, CA 90210-4423, USA

Haas, Lukas (Actor)
c/o Jason Weinberg *Untitled
Entertainment (LA)*
350 S Beverly Dr Ste 200
Beverly Hills, CA 90212-4819, USA

Haas, Moose (Athlete, Baseball Player)
4351 E Lariat Ln
Phoenix, AZ 85050-8905, USA

Haas, Robert D (Business Person)
Levi Strauss Assoc
1155 Battery St
San Francisco, CA 94111-1264, USA

Haas, Tommy (Athlete, Tennis Player)
1883 Comstock Ave
Los Angeles, CA 90025-5014, USA

Haase, Andy (Athlete, Football Player)
1508 Bon Homme Richard Dr
Fort Collins, CO 80526-9695, USA

Haayer, Adam (Athlete, Football Player)
2362 Stonecrest Path NW
Prior Lake, MN 55372-4006, USA

Habel, Sarah (Actor)
c/o Everly Lee *Resolution (LA)*
405 S Beverly Dr Ste 500
Beverly Hills, CA 90212-4425, USA

Habib, Brian (Athlete, Football Player)
17235 Sangallo Ln
San Diego, CA 92127-2807, USA

Habscheid, Marc (Athlete, Hockey Player)
6 Sussex Rd
Winchester, MA 01890-3848, USA

Habyan, John (Athlete, Baseball Player)
4 Dorfer Ln
Nesconset, NY 11767-1067, USA

Hachten, Bill (Athlete, Football Player)
6205 Mineral Point Rd Apt 210
Madison, WI 53705-4577, USA

Hachten, William (Athlete, Football
Player)
6205 Mineral Point Rd Apt 210
Madison, WI 53705-4577, USA

Hack, Olivia (Actor)
c/o Bonnie Ventis *Clear Talent Group (LA)*
10950 Ventura Blvd
Studio City, CA 91604-3340, USA

Hack, Shelley (Actor, Model)
1208 Georgina Ave
Santa Monica, CA 90402-2120, USA

Hackbart, Dale (Athlete, Football Player)
2541 Cowley Dr
Lafayette, CO 80026-9175, USA

Hacker, Eric (Athlete, Baseball Player)
526 Shelly Ct
Duncanville, TX 75137-4128, USA

Hacker, Rich (Athlete, Baseball Player)
2900 18th Fairway Dr
Belleville, IL 62220-4840, USA

Hackett, Dino (Athlete, Football Player)
1152 Kearns Hackett Rd
Pleasant Garden, NC 27313-8218, USA

Hackett, D.J. (Athlete, Football Player)
6510 S Delmar Pl
Gilbert, AZ 85298-4061, USA

Hackett, Jeff (Athlete, Hockey Player)
c/o Staff Member *Colorado Avalanche*
1000 Chopper Cir
Pepsi Center
Denver, CO 80204-5805, USA

Hackett, Joey (Athlete, Football Player)
1147 Kearns Hackett Rd
Pleasant Garden, NC 27313-8218, USA

Hackett, Martha (Actor)
Vaughn D Hart
8899 Beverly Blvd Ste 815
Los Angeles, CA 90048-2452, USA

Hackett, Paul (Politician)
Hackett for US Senate
PO Box 43281
Cincinnati, OH 45243-0281, USA

Hackett, Rudy (Athlete, Baseball Player)
10330 Downey Ave Unit 30
Downey, CA 90241-5914, USA

Hackett, Ryan (Race Car Driver)
J&R Supply Corp.
4824 Crain Hwy
White Plains, MD 20695-2858, USA

Hackford, Taylor (Director, Producer,
Writer)
c/o Stan Rosenfield *Stan Rosenfield &
Associates*
2029 Century Park E Ste 1190
Los Angeles, CA 90067-2931, USA

Hackman, Gene (Actor)
1424/1425 Old Sunset Trl
Santa Fe, NM 87501, USA

Hackman, Luther (Athlete, Baseball
Player)
1406 12th Ave N Apt 16G
Columbus, MS 39701-3602, USA

Hackney, Lisa (Basketball Player, Golfer)
c/o Staff Member *Signature Sports Group*
4150 Olson Memorial Hey
Suite 110
Minneapolis, MN 55422, USA

Hackwith, Scott (Music Group, Musician,
Songwriter, Writer)
Overland Productions
156 W 56th St # 500
New York, NY 10019-3800, USA

Haddad, Drew (Athlete, Football Player)
29212 Inverness Dr
Bay Village, OH 44140-1818, USA

Haddad, Janie (Actor)
3018 Gracia St
Los Angeles, CA 90039-2306, USA

Haddix, Margaret (Writer)
c/o Joshua Adams *Adams Literary*
7845 Colony Rd
C4 #215
Charlotte, NC 28226-7681, USA

Haddix, Michael (Athlete, Football Player)
62 Ridgeland Dr
Starkville, MS 39759-4660, USA

Haddix, Wayne (Athlete, Football Player)
8117 S Pole Cvdr
Memphis, TN 38125, USA

Haddock, Karen (Race Car Driver)
Haddock Racing
PO Box 2455
2811 Ocean Hwy.
Shallotte, NC 28459-2455, USA

Haddon, Dayle (Actor, Model)
Hyperion Books
114 5th Ave Fl 13
New York, NY 10011-5690, USA

Haddon, Lawrence (Actor)
14950 Sutton St
Sherman Oaks, CA 91403-4018, USA

Haden, Joe (Athlete, Football Player)
c/o Drew Rosenhaus *Rosenhaus Sports
Representation*
6400 Allison Rd
Miami Beach, FL 33141-4540, USA

Haden, Nate (Actor)
c/o Staff Member *Diverse Talent Group*
9911 W Pico Blvd Ste 340W
Los Angeles, CA 90035-2703, USA

Haden, Nick (Athlete, Football Player)
114 Julianna Dr
Coraopolis, PA 15108-3763, USA

Haden, Patrick C (Pat) (Athlete, Football
Player, Sportscaster)
1525 Wilson Ave
San Marino, CA 91108-2364, USA

Haden Church, Thomas (Actor)
2366 Station C Rd
Vanderpool, TX 78885-8523, USA

Hader, Bill (Actor)
1034 Fiske St
Pacific Palisades, CA 90272-3843, USA

Hadfield, Chris A (Astronaut)
638 Shorewood Dr
Kemah, TX 77565, USA

Hadfield, Chris Colonel (Astronaut)
638 Shorewood Dr
Seabrook, TX 77586-4610, USA

Hadid, Momahed (Business Person)
Hadid Development
11301 W Olympic Blvd Ste 537
Los Angeles, CA 90064-1653, USA

Hadl, John W (Athlete, Football Player)
University of Kansas 1651 Drive Naismith
105 Parrott Athletic Center
Lawrence, KS 66045-0001, USA

Hadley, Brett (Actor)
5070 Woodley Ave
Encino, CA 91436-1411, USA

Hadley, Ron (Athlete, Football Player)
2800 Olympia Fields Ln
Mount Pleasant, SC 29466-9197, USA

Hadnot, James (Athlete, Football Player)
5521 48th St Apt 84
Lubbock, TX 79414-1413, USA

Hadnot, Rex (Athlete, Football Player)
2677 Center Court Dr
Dr
Weston, FL 33332-1833, USA

Haefner, Ruby (Athlete, Baseball Player)
5305 Redstone Dr
Jacksonville, FL 32210-6754, USA

Haegele, Patricia (Publisher)
Good Housekeeping Magazine
300 W 57th St
New York, NY 10019-3741, USA

Haenel, Hal (Athlete, Olympic Athlete, Sailor)
3049 Landa St
Los Angeles, CA 90039-3011, USA

Hafen, Barney (Athlete, Football Player)
1125 Goldenrod Cir
Saint George, UT 84790-7512, USA

Hafer, Fred D (Business Person)
GPU Inc
300 Madison Ave
Morristown, NJ 07960-6169, USA

Haffner, Scott (Athlete, Basketball Player)
5E62 Sweetwater Dr
Noblesville,
IN 46000000000000000000000000000000004000000000000000000000000000000,
USA

Hafner, Travis (Athlete, Baseball Player)
7 Astor Pl
Rocky River, OH 44116-1545, USA

Hafstrom, Mikael (Director)
c/o Robert Newman *William Morris Endeavor (LA)*
9601 Wilshire Blvd
Beverly Hills, CA 90210-5213, USA

Hag, Sid (Actor)
Kathleen Schultz Associates Talent Agency
6442 Coldwater Canyon Ave Ste 206
North Hollywood, CA 91606-1174, USA

Hagan, Cliff (Athlete, Basketball Player)
8839 Lakeside Cir
Vero Beach, FL 32963-4082, USA

Hagan, Derek (Football Player)
830 Madison St Apt 523
Hoboken, NJ 07030-6857, USA

Hagan, Glenn (Athlete, Basketball Player)
34 Roth St
Rochester, NY 14621-5320, USA

Hagan, Mallory (Beauty Pageant Winner)
c/o Lee White *William Morris Endeavor (LA)*
9601 Wilshire Blvd
Beverly Hills, CA 90210-5213, USA

Hagan, Marianne (Actor)
c/o Scott Zimmerman *Evolution Entertainment (LA)*
901 N Highland Ave
Los Angeles, CA 90038-2412, USA

Hagan, Molly (Actor)
c/o Staff Member *Kohner Agency, The*
9300 Wilshire Blvd Ste 555
Beverly Hills, CA 90212-3211, USA

Hagan, Sarah (Actor)
c/o Staff Member *Mark Robert Management*
2208 Patricia Ave
Los Angeles, CA 90064-2318, USA

Hagar, Sammy (Musician, Songwriter)
c/o Irving Azoff *Azoff Music Management*
1100 Glendon Ave Ste 2000
Los Angeles, CA 90024-3524, USA

Hagee, Pastor John (Religious Leader)
John Hagee Ministries
PO Box 1400
San Antonio, TX 78295-1400, USA

Hagel, Chuck (Politician, Senator)
920 Towlston Rd
Mc Lean, VA 22102-1036, USA

Hageman, Fred (Athlete, Football Player)
4700 Carmel Ct
Lawrence, KS 66047-1842, USA

Hagen, Cosma Shiva (Actor)
c/o Nicole Walter *Metro Public Relations*
8383 Wilshire Blvd Ste 208
Beverly Hills, CA 90211-2432, USA

Hagen, Halvor (Athlete, Football Player)
PO Box 911711
Saint George, UT 84791-1711, USA

Hagen, Kevin (Athlete, Baseball Player)
24826 164th Ave SE
Covington, WA 98042-5232, USA

Hager, Bob
4000 Nebraska Ave NW
Washington, DC 20016-2733

Hager, Britt (Athlete, Football Player)
6200 Indian Canyon Dr
Austin, TX 78746-6352, USA

Hager, Jenna Bush (Correspondent)
c/o Staff Member *HarperCollins Publishers*
195 Broadway Fl 2
Cellar 1
New York, NY 10007-3132, USA

Hager, Kristen (Actor)
c/o Shelley Browning *Magnolia Entertainment (LA)*
9595 Wilshire Blvd Ste 601
Beverly Hills, CA 90212-2506, USA

Hager, Robert (Correspondent)
NBC-TV
4001 Nebraska Ave NW
Washington, DC 20016-2795, USA

Hager Twins
PO Box 1516
Champaign, IL 61824-1516

Hagerty, Julie (Actor)
c/o Steven Levy *Framework Entertainment (LA)*
9057 Nemo St Ste C
West Hollywood, CA 90069-5511, USA

Haggans, Clark (Athlete, Football Player)
3165 S Alma School Rd Ste 29-225
Chandler, AZ 85248-3760, USA

Haggard, Merle (Musician, Songwriter)
7691/7733/7735/7737 Silver Bridge Rd
Palo Cedro, CA 96073, USA

Hagge, Marlene (Athlete, Golfer)
PO Box 2212
Palm Desert, CA 92261-2212, USA

Haggerty, Dan (Actor)
c/o Terry Bomar *Blind Squirrel Entertainment*
155 Bent Oak
Royal Palm Beach, FL 33411-8650, USA

Haggerty, Jonathan (Athlete, Football Player)
c/o Staff Member *Synergy Sports, Inc.*
PO Box 800204
Dallas, TX 75380-0204, USA

Haggerty, Sean (Athlete, Hockey Player)
25 Griswold Rd
Rye, NY 10580-1801

Haggerty, Steve (Athlete, Football Player)
3313 E Costilla Ave
Centennial, CO 80122-1849, USA

Haggerty, Tim (Cartoonist)
United Feature Syndicate
PO Box 5610
Cincinnati, OH 45201-5610, USA

Haggins, Odell (Athlete, Football Player)
8125 Blenheim Ln
Tallahassee, FL 32312-6803, USA

Haggins, Raymond (Athlete, Baseball Player)
2825 E Lynchburg Ct
Montgomery, AL 36116-3335, USA

Haggis, Paul (Director, Producer, Writer)
c/o Staff Member *Paul Haggis Productions*
9200 W Sunset Blvd Ste 820
West Hollywood, CA 90069-3603, USA

Hagin, Wayne (Commentator)
2236 Thistle Ridge Cir
Highlands Ranch, CO 80126-2638, USA

Hagin Jr, Kenneth (Religious Leader)
Kenneth Hagin Ministries
PO Box 50126
Tulsa, OK 74150-0126, USA

Hagins, Isaac (Ike) (Athlete, Football Player)
9008 Tudor Dr Apt 105
Tampa, FL 33615-3749, USA

Hagler, Marvin (Boxer)
c/o Valerie Swett *Deutsch Williams*
1 Design Center Pl Ste 600
Boston, MA 02210-2349

Hagner, Meredith (Actor)
c/o James Suskin *James Suskin Management*
2 Charlton St Apt 5K
New York, NY 10014-4970, USA

Hagon, Garrick (Actor)
c/o Staff Member *Coolwaters Productions*
10061 Riverside Dr # 531
Toluca Lake, CA 91602-2560, USA

Hahn, Don (Athlete, Baseball Player)
1046 Boise Dr
Campbell, CA 95008-0306, USA

Hahn, James (Politician)
Mayor's Office
200 N Spring St
Los Angeles, CA 90012-4801, USA

Hahn, Joseph (Music Group)
Artist Group International
9560 Wilshire Blvd Ste 400
Beverly Hills, CA 90212-2442, USA

Hahn, Kathryn (Actor)
c/o Lindsey Porter *Gersh (NY)*
41 Madison Ave
New York, NY 10010-2202, USA

Hahn, Mary Downing (Writer)
c/o Staff Member *Clarion Books*
215 Park Ave S Ste 1101
New York, NY 10003-1626, USA

Hai, Do Thi (Actor)
c/o Barry McPherson *Agency for the Performing Arts (APA-NY)*
135 W 50th St Fl 17
New York, NY 10020-1201, USA

Haid, Charles (Athlete, Baseball Player)
4376 Forman Ave
Toluca Lake, CA 91602-2944, USA

Haigh, Denise (Athlete, Golfer)
198 Barbados Dr
Jupiter, FL 33458-2920, USA

Haight, Mike (Athlete, Football Player)
210 Tartan Dr
North Liberty, IA 52317-8001, USA

Haik, Mac (Athlete, Football Player)
11738 Wood Ln
Houston, TX 77024-5129, USA

Hailer, Bill (Athlete, Baseball Player)
1807 N 1200 St
Brownstown, IL 62418-4426, USA

Hailey, Ken (Athlete, Football Player)
241 Festival Dr
Oceanside, CA 92057-5135, USA

Hailey, Leisha (Actor, Musician, Songwriter)
c/o Geordie Frey *GEF Entertainment*
611 N Cherokee Ave
Los Angeles, CA 90004-1008, USA

Hailey, Oliver
11747 Canton Pl
Studio City, CA 91604-4166

Haill, Gary H (Athlete, Football Player)
6207 Surflanding Ln
Huntington Beach, CA 92648-7507, USA

Haimovitz, Matt (Music Group, Musician)
Columbia Artists Mgmt Inc
165 W 57th St
New York, NY 10019-2201, USA

Haine-Daniels, Audrey (Athlete, Baseball Player, Commentator)
618 Revere Dr
Bay Village, OH 44140-1971, USA

Haines, Byron (Athlete, Football Player)
16625 1st Ave S Apt 202
Burien, WA 98148-1472, USA

Haines, Emily (Musician)
c/o Staff Member *Paradigm (Monterey)*
404 W Franklin St
Monterey, CA 93940-2303, USA

Haines, John (Athlete, Football Player)
1101 Ivean Pearson Rd # G
Lago Vista, TX 78645-5019, USA

Haines, Kris (Athlete, Football Player)
2828 N Talman Ave Unit K
Chicago, IL 60618-7829, USA

Haines, Lee M (Religious Leader)
Wesleyan Church
PO Box 50434
Indianapolis, IN 46250-0434, USA

Haines, Martha (Athlete, Baseball Player, Commentator)
144 Langshire Ct
Florence, KY 41042-3542, USA

Haines, Randa (Director)
1429 Avon Park Ter
Los Angeles, CA 90026-2007, USA

Haines, Sara (Correspondent)
c/o Lou Oppenheim *Headline Media Management*
888 7th Ave Ste 503
New York, NY 10106-0501, USA

Hainsev, Ron (Athlete, Hockey Player)
2154 Wynnton Pt
Duluth, GA 30097-5007

Hainsey, Ron (Athlete, Hockey Player)
Olympic Sports Management
9 Alden Rd
Wellesley Hills, MA 02481-6702, USA

Hair, Harlod (Athlete, Baseball Player)
1645 W 20th St
Jacksonville, FL 32209-4817, USA

Hair, Harold (Athlete, Baseball Player)
1645 W 20th St
Jacksonville, FL 32209-4817, USA

Haire, John E (Business Person)
Highland Capital Partners
1 Broadway Ste 16
Cambridge, MA 02142-1187, USA

Hairston, Alan (Athlete, Basketball Player)
6120 S 125th St
Seattle, WA 98178-3546, USA

Hairston, Carl (Athlete, Football Player)
9023 Gleneagle Dr
Blaine, WA 98230-5720, USA

Hairston, Chris (Athlete, Football Player)
c/o Joe Linta *JL Sports*
1204 Main St 179
Branford, CT 06405-3787, USA

Hairston, Harold (Baseball Player)
Homestead Grays
542 E 107th St
Cleveland, OH 44108-1432, USA

Hairston, John (Johnny) (Athlete, Baseball Player)
4226 NE 22nd Ave
Portland, OR 97211-5757, USA

Hairston, Scott (Athlete, Baseball Player)
4658 S Banning Dr
Gilbert, AZ 85297-5257, USA

Hairston, Stacey (Athlete, Football Player)
2330 Cuba Rd
Wilmington, OH 45177-7156, USA

Hairston Jr, Jerry (Athlete, Baseball Player)
2205 Warwick Way Ste 200
Marriottsville, MD 21104-1632, USA

Hairston Sr, Jerry (Athlete, Baseball Player)
7831 W Peace Pipe Rd
Tucson, AZ 85743-5207, USA

Haise, Fred W
14316 Fm 2354 RR
Baytown, TX 77520, USA

Haise, Jim (Baseball Player)
Washington Senators
2425 Albion Ave
Orlando, FL 32833-3981, USA

Haislip, Marcus (Basketball Player)
Milwaukee Bucks
Bradley Center 1001 N 4th St
Milwaukee, WI 53203, USA

Hajak, Ron
17420 Ventura Blvd # 4
Encino, CA 91316-3827

Hajek, Dave (Athlete, Baseball Player)
5190 Bitterweed Ln
Colorado Springs, CO 80917-1302, USA

Ha Jin (Writer)
Emory University
English Dept
Atlanta, GA 30332-0001, USA

Haji-Sheikh, Ali (Athlete, Football Player)
550 S Spinningwheel Ln
Bloomfield Hills, MI 48304-1318, USA

Hajt, Bill (Athlete, Hockey Player)
215 Old Lyme Dr
Buffalo, NY 14221-2208

Hakim, Az-Zahir (Athlete, Football Player)
210 Canaan Glen Way SW
Atlanta, GA 30331-8055, USA

Hal, Andre (Athlete, Football Player)
c/o Tony Paige *Perennial Sports and Entertainment*
1455 Pennsylvania Ave NW Ste 225
Washington, DC 20004-1026, USA

Halama, John (Athlete, Baseball Player)
7615 Fort Hamilton Pkwy
Brooklyn, NY 11228-2325, USA

Halbert, Charles (Athlete, Basketball Player)
1112 Wildwood Dr
Oak Harbor, WA 98277-8206, USA

Halbert, David (Business Person)
Advance PCS
750 W John Carpenter Fwy Ste 1200
Irving, TX 75039-2507

Halbreich, Kathy (Director, Misc)
Walker Art Center
725 Vineland Pl Ste 1
Minneapolis, MN 55403-1195, USA

Haldeman, Tim (Actor)
4257 Lincoln Ave
Culver City, CA 90232-3217, USA

Haldiman, Phillip (Actor)
Haldi Enterprises
749 E Montebello Ave Unit 129
Phoenix, AZ 85014-2539, USA

Haldorson, Burdette (Athlete, Basketball Player, Olympic Athlete)
2868 Stonewall Hts
Colorado Springs, CO 80909-1735, USA

Hale, Alan Spencer
5476 St Paul Rd
Morristown, NJ 07813

Hale, Barbara (Actor)
PO Box 6061-261
Sherman Oaks, CA 91413, USA

Hale, Bob (Athlete, Baseball Player)
1 N Dee Rd Apt 2B
Park Ridge, IL 60068-2868, USA

Hale, Chanin (Actor)
c/o Staff Member *RRB Consultants*
17300 Ballinger St
Northridge, CA 91325-2005, USA

Hale, Chip (Athlete, Baseball Player)
190 Driftwood Ct
Aptos, CA 95003-5769, USA

Hale, Chris (Athlete, Football Player)
327 E El Sur St
Monrovia, CA 91016-4802, USA

Hale, Dave (Athlete, Football Player)
1204 S Maple St Apt B
Ottawa, KS 66067-3460, USA

Hale, David (Athlete, Hockey Player)
3470 Cortina Dr
Colorado Springs, CO 80918-1814

Hale, Demarlo (Athlete, Baseball Player)
4560 Woodlands Village Dr
Orlando, FL 32835-2717, USA

Hale, John (Athlete, Baseball Player)
2200 Pine St
Bakersfield, CA 93301-3429, USA

Hale, Lucy (Actor)
c/o Elissa Leeds-Fickman *Reel Talent Management*
PO Box 491035
Los Angeles, CA 90049-9035, USA

Hale, Tony (Actor)
c/o Steven Levy *Framework Entertainment (LA)*
9057 Nemo St Ste C
West Hollywood, CA 90069-5511, USA

Hale, walter""chip"" (Athlete, Baseball Player)
7555 E Sabino Vista Dr
Tucson, AZ 85750-2710, USA

Halestorm (Music Group)
c/o Staff Member *In De Goot Entertainment*
119 W 23rd St Ste 609
New York, NY 10011-2594, USA

Haley, Charles J (Athlete, Football Player)
3787 Royal Cove Dr
Dallas, TX 75229-5237, USA

Haley, Dick (Athlete, Football Player)
5248 Shoreline Cir
Sanford, FL 32771-7168, USA

Haley, Jack (Athlete, Basketball Player)
5E9 Ocean Ave
Seal Beach, CA 9E74E, USA

Haley, Jackie Earle (Actor)
c/o Leslie Allan-Rice *Leslie Allan-Rice Management*
1007 Maybrook Dr
Beverly Hills, CA 90210-2715, USA

Haley, Jermaine (Athlete, Football Player)
16806 Heather Knolls Pl
Hamilton, VA 20158-9403, USA

Haley, Katie (Athlete, Golfer)
24312 138th Ave SE
Kent, WA 98042-5168, USA

Haley, Nikki (Governor, Politician)
PO Box 11369
Columbia, SC 29211-1369, USA

Halford, Rob (Music Group)
International Creative Mgmt
40 W 57th St Fl 5
New York, NY 10019-4001, USA

Hali, Tamba (Athlete, Football Player)
13227 Outlook St
Leawood, KS 66209-4022, USA

Haliburton, Ronnie (Athlete, Football Player)
3460 Lake Arthur Dr
Port Arthur, TX 77642-7604, USA

Halicki, Ed (Athlete, Baseball Player)
19605 Paddlewheel Ln
Reno, NV 89521-7850, USA

Halimon, Shaler (Athlete, Basketball Player)
9535 SW Millen Dr
Portland, OR 97224-6510, USA

Halkidis, Bob (Athlete, Hockey Player)
Hal kid is Hockey Training
3419 Lake Park Rd
Indian Trail, NC 28079-6561

Halko, Steve (Athlete, Hockey Player)
124 Crystlewood Ct
Morrisville, NC 27560-7569

Hall, Adam (Athlete, Hockey Player)
1230 Fletcher Ave
Kalamazoo, MI 49006-2432

Hall, Ahmard (Athlete, Football Player)
8402 Cruit Isle
Missouri City, TX 77459-3478, USA

Hall, Alaina Reed (Actor)
10636 Rathburn Ave
Porter Ranch, CA 91326-3127, USA

Hall, Albert (Athlete, Baseball Player)
1628 Spaulding Ishkooda Rd
Birmingham, AL 35211-5520, USA

Hall, Andy (Athlete, Football Player)
4601 Bayview Dr
Fort Lauderdale, FL 33308-5333, USA

Hall, Anthony Michael (Actor)
c/o Staff Member *Morra Brezner Steinberg & Tenenbaum (MBST) Entertainment*
345 N Maple Dr Ste 200
Beverly Hills, CA 90210-5174, USA

Hall, Arsenio (Actor, Musician, Television Host)
c/o Traci Harper *Harper Public Relations*
3940 Laurel Canyon Blvd Ste 1010
Studio City, CA 91604-3709, USA

Hall, Art (Athlete, Football Player)
Cardinal Gibbons High School
4601 Bayview Dr
Fort Lauderdale, FL 33308-5332, USA

Hall, Barbara (Producer, Writer)
c/o Claire Best *Claire Best & Associates*
736 Seward St
Los Angeles, CA 90038-3504, USA

Hall, Bill (Athlete, Baseball Player)
4935 E Berneil Dr
Paradise Valley, AZ 85253-1521, USA

Hall, Bobby
20122 Hall Dr
Brooksville, FL 34601

Hall, Brett A. (Athlete, Hockey Player)
3520 Eben Way
Stillwater, MN 55082-8102, USA

Hall, Bridget (Model)
I M G Models
304 Park Ave S # 1200
New York, NY 10010-4301, USA

Hall, Bruce Michael (Actor)
c/o Jerry Shandrew *Shandrew Public Relations*
1050 S Stanley Ave
Los Angeles, CA 90019-6634, USA

Hall, Bug (Actor)
c/o Laina Cohn *Cohn / Torgan Management*
Prefers to be contacted by telephone or email
Los Angeles, CA, USA

Hall, Carla (Chef, Television Host)
c/o Jonathan Swaden *Creative Artists Agency (CAA-LA)*
2000 Avenue of the Stars Ste 100
Los Angeles, CA 90067-4705, USA

Hall, Chad (Athlete, Football Player)
c/o Chad Speck *Allegiant Athletic Agency*
35 Market Sq Ste 201
Knoxville, TN 37902-1420, USA

Hall, Charlie (Football Player)
602 Lavaca St
Yoakum, TX 77995-4136, USA

Hall, Cory (Athlete, Football Player)
1202 E Swift Ave
Fresno, CA 93704-3836, USA

Hall, Courtney (Athlete, Football Player)
19912 Enslow Dr
Carson, CA 90746-3028, USA

Hall, Dana (Athlete, Football Player)
9730 Diamond St
Yucaipa, CA 92399-2946, USA

Hall, Dante (Athlete)
c/o Staff Member *Kansas City Chiefs*
1 Arrowhead Dr
Kansas City, MO 64129-1651, USA

Hall, Dante (Athlete, Football Player)
13314 Barbstone Dr
Houston, TX 77044-4957, USA

Hall, Darren (Athlete, Baseball Player)
1111 Lexington Ave Apt 1711
Flower Mound, TX 75028-8382, USA

Hall, Darryl (Athlete, Football Player)
21013 E Crestline Cir
Centennial, CO 80015-3619, USA

Hall, Daryl (Music Group, Songwriter)
958/964 Huckleberry Rd
Amenia, NY 12501, USA

Hall, Deangelo (Athlete, Football Player)
5553 Legends Dr
Braselton, GA 30517-4014, USA

Hall, Dean Scott (Race Car Driver)
PO Box 2589
Olympic Valley, CA 96146-2589, USA

Hall, Debi (Actor)
c/o Linda McAlister *Linda McAlister Talent*
100 Oak Ln
Waxahachie, TX 75167-8412, USA

Hall, Deidre (Actor)
1223 Wilshire Blvd # 825
Santa Monica, CA 90403-5406, USA

Hall, Del (Athlete, Hockey Player)
1057 E 6160 S
Salt Lake City, UT 84121-6712

Hall, Delores (Actor, Music Group)
Agency for Performing Arts
485 Madison Ave
New York, NY 10022-5803, USA

Hall, Delton (Athlete, Football Player)
9 Mystic Ct
Greensboro, NC 27406-5724, USA

Hall, Dick (Athlete, Baseball Player)
403 Plumbridge Ct Unit 403
Lutherville Timonium, MD 21093-8131, USA

Hall, Dino (Football Player)
355 Chestnut Neck Rd
Port Republic, NJ 08241-9703, USA

Hall, Donald (Writer)
Eagle Point Farm
Eagle Pond Farm Eagle Pond Road
Wilmot, NH 03287, USA

Hall, Donald J (Business Person)
Hallmark Cards
2501 McGee St
Kansas City, MO 64108-2600, USA

Hall, Donald R (Athlete, Football Player)
355 Chestnut Neck Rd
Port Republic, NJ 08241-9703, USA

Hall, Drew (Athlete, Baseball Player)
4107 Spreading Oaks Ct
Waxhaw, NC 28173-7814, USA

Hall, Edward T (Doctor, Writer)
8 Calle Jacinta
Santa Fe, NM 87508-9561, USA

Hall, Ervin (Erv) (Athlete, Track Athlete)
Citicorp Mortgage
670 Mason Ridge Center Dr
Saint Louis, MO 63141-8573, USA

Hall, Galen (Coach, Football Coach, Football Player)
Pennsylvania State University
198 Bayou Bend Rd
Groveland, FL 34736-3616, USA

Hall, Greff Kaye (Swimmer)
906 3rd St
Mukilteo, WA 98275-1634, USA

Hall, Irma P. (Actor)
3202 O Bannon Dr
Dallas, TX 75224-3239, USA

Hall, James E (Jim) (Race Car Driver)
RR 7 Box 640
Midland, TX 79706, USA

Hall, Jeff (Athlete, Football Player)
2201 Lake Ave Apt 205
Knoxville, TN 37916-2814, USA

Hall, Jerry (Actor, Model)
c/o Staff Member *Ford Models (LA)*
9200 W Sunset Blvd Ste 805
West Hollywood, CA 90069-3603, USA

Hall, Jimmie (Athlete, Baseball Player)
8622 Carter Grove Dr
Elm City, NC 27822-7926, USA

Hall, Joe (Athlete, Baseball Player)
961 Peachers Mill Rd
Clarksville, TN 37042-7629, USA

Hall, Joe B (Basketball Player, Coach)
Central Bank & Trust Co
300 W Vine St Ste 3
Lexington, KY 40507-1666, USA

Hall, Josh (Athlete, Baseball Player)
725 Lake Vista Dr
Forest, VA 24551-1977, USA

Hall, Ken (Football Player)
PO Box 567
Fredericksburg, TX 78624-0567, USA

Hall, Kristen (Musician)
c/o Staff Member *Gail Gellman Management*
23852 Pacific Coast Hwy
Malibu, CA 90265-4876, USA

Hall, Lani (Music Group)
31930 Pacific Coast Hwy
Malibu, CA 90265-2524, USA

Hall, Lemanski (Athlete, Football Player)
185 Carronbridge Way
Franklin, TN 37067-6223, USA

Hall, Leon (Athlete, Football Player)
8386 Kugler Mill Rd
Cincinnati, OH 45243-1331, USA

Hall, Lloyd M Jr (Religious Leader)
Congregation Christian Church Assn
PO Box 1620
Oak Creek, WI 53154, USA

Hall, L Parker (Athlete, Football Player)
4712 Cole Rd
Memphis, TN 38117-4013, USA

Hall, Michael C (Actor, Producer)
2230 Nottingham Ave
Los Angeles, CA 90027-1033, USA

Hall, Monty
519 N Arden Dr
Beverly Hills, CA 90210-3507

Hall, Pooch (Actor)
c/o Mark Turner *Abrams Artists Agency (NY)*
275 7th Ave Fl 26
New York, NY 10001-6708, USA

Hall, Randy (Athlete, Football Player)
PO Box 447
Genesee, ID 83832-0447, USA

Hall, Reamy (Actor)
c/o Gloria Hinojosa *Amsel, Eisenstadt & Frazier Talent Agency (AEF)*
5055 Wilshire Blvd Ste 860
Los Angeles, CA 90036-6108, USA

Hall, Regina (Actor)
c/o Paul Young *Principato/Young Management (LA)*
9465 Wilshire Blvd Ste 900
Beverly Hills, CA 90212-2608, USA

Hall, Rhett (Athlete, Football Player)
15605 Oak Glen Ave
Morgan Hill, CA 95037-8804, USA

Hall, Robert David (Actor)
c/o Cynthia Snyder *Cynthia Snyder Public Relations*
5739 Colfax Ave
N Hollywood, CA 91601-1636, USA

Hall, Samuel (Sam) (Athlete, Swimmer)
5759 Wilcke Way
Dayton, OH 45459-1637, USA

Hall, Shane (Race Car Driver)
Stegall Motorsports
515 Putman Rd
Fountain Inn, SC 29644-1305, USA

Hall, Toby (Athlete, Baseball Player)
3814 Evergreen Oaks Dr
Lutz, FL 33558-5041, USA

Hall, Tom (Athlete, Baseball Player)
3592 Lillian St
Riverside, CA 92504-3609, USA

Hall, Tom (Athlete, Football Player)
75 the Laurels
Enfield, CT 06082-2356, USA

Hall, Tom T (Musician, Songwriter)
Tom T Hall Enterprises
PO Box 1246
Franklin, TN 37065-1246, USA

Hall, Walter (Athlete, Golfer)
271 Orchard Park Dr
Advance, NC 27006-7481, USA

Hall, Willie (Athlete, Football Player)
717 S Hacienda St
Anaheim, CA 92804-2658, USA

Hall, Windlan (Athlete, Football Player)
13609 Pleasant Ln
Burnsville, MN 55337-4547, USA

Halla, Brian L (Business Person)
National Semiconductor
2900 Semiconductor Dr
Santa Clara, CA 95051-0695, USA

Halladay, H Leroy (Roy) (Athlete, Baseball Player)
18509 Council Crest Dr
Odessa, FL 33556-5039, USA

Hall & Oates (Music Group)
c/o Jonathan Wolfson *Wolfson Entertainment*
22201 Ventura Blvd Ste 207
Woodland Hills, CA 91364-1510, USA

Hallberg, Gary (Athlete, Golfer)
12516 Ventana Mesa Cir
Castle Pines, CO 80108-9147, USA

Halldorson, Dan (Athlete, Golfer)
209 South Rd
Cambridge, IL 61238-1429, USA

Hallen, Bob (Athlete, Football Player)
7052 Rushmore Way
Painesville, OH 44077-2301, USA

Haller, Alan (Athlete, Football Player)
1265 Lobelia Ln
Dewitt, MI 48820-7409, USA

Haller, Bill (Baseball Player)
1807 N 1200 St
Brownstown, IL 62418-4426, USA

Haller, Gordon (Athlete)
16 Thetford Dr
Bella Vista, AR 72715-1508, USA

Hallervorden, Dieter (Actor)
Nurnberger Str. 33
Berlin, GE D-107

Hallet, Jim (Athlete, Golfer)
18 Oliver St
South Yarmouth, MA 02664-2902, USA

Hall-Garmes, Ruth (Actor)
432 Alandele Ave
Los Angeles, CA 90036-3153, USA

Halliburton, Jeff (Athlete, Basketball Player)
113 Wake Forest Pl
O Fallon, MO 63368-3786, USA

Hallick, Tom (Actor)
4267 Marina City Dr Unit 404
Marina Del Rey, CA 90292-5810

Halliday, Nathan (Actor)
c/o Sharon Lane *Lane Management Group*
13017 Woodbridge St
Studio City, CA 91604-1431, USA

Hallin, Mats (Athlete, Hockey Player)
c/o Staff Member *Chicago Blackhawks*
1901 W Madison St
Chicago, IL 60612-2459, USA

Hallinan, Joseph T (Journalist)
Random House
1745 Broadway Frnt 3 # B1
New York, NY 10019-4343, USA

Hallion, Tom (Athlete, Baseball Player)
4040 Ormond Rd
Louisville, KY 40207-2036, USA

Hallisay, Brian (Actor)
818 2nd St Apt G
Santa Monica, CA 90403-1668, USA

Hallisey, Caroline (Athlete, Olympic Athlete, Speed Skater)
5 Vine St
Exeter, NH 03833-2308, USA

Halliwell, Geri (Music Group)
c/o Gina Hoffman *PMK/BNC Public Relations (PMK-LA)*
8687 Melrose Ave Ste 8
West Hollywood, CA 90069-5746, USA

Hall Jr, Gary (Athlete, Olympic Athlete, Swimmer)
4335 N Meridian Ave
Miami Beach, FL 33140-2940, USA

Hallman, Tom Jr (Journalist)
Portland Oregonian
1320 SW Broadway
Editorial Dept
Portland, OR 97201-3411, USA

Hallman, Victoria (Actor)
2006 Lombardy Ave
Nashville, TN 37215-1306, USA

Hallock, Ty (Athlete, Football Player)
3676 Hunters Way Dr SE
Ada, MI 49301-8351, USA

Hall Sr, Gary (Athlete, Olympic Athlete, Swimmer)
The Race Club
151 Kahiki Dr
Tavernier, FL 33070-2409, USA

Hallstrom, Lasse (Director)
153 Horizon Ln
Bedford, NY 10506, USA

Hallstrom, Ron (Athlete, Football Player)
PO Box 379
Woodruff, WI 54568-0379, USA

Halpern, Daniel (Writer)
9 Mercer St
Princeton, NJ 08540-6807, USA

Halpern, Jeff (Athlete, Hockey Player)
9212 Sprinklewood Ln
Potomac, MD 20854-2255, USA

Halpin, Luke (Actor)
227 Caddy Rd
Rotonda West, FL 33947-2223, USA

Halsell, James D Colonel (Astronaut)
2101 Nasa Pkwy Spc Centerattn
Houston, TX 77058-3607, USA

Halsell Jr, James D (Astronaut)
257 River Cove Rd
Huntsville, AL 35811-8010, USA

Halstead, Greg (Model, Reality Star)
c/o Anthony Embry *AE Entertainment Public Relations*
124 Evening Shade Dr
Charleston, SC 29414-9144, USA

Halter, Shane (Athlete, Baseball Player)
6501 W 138th Ter Apt 10210
Overland Park, KS 66223-7916, USA

Halterman, Aaron (Athlete, Football Player)
4130 Moss Ridge Ln
Indianapolis, IN 46237-2871, USA

Haluska, Jim (Athlete, Football Player)
3032 S 84th St
Milwaukee, WI 53227-3704, USA

Halverson, Dean (Athlete, Football Player)
3819 Fairmont Ln NW
Olympia, WA 98502-3744, USA

Ham, Darvin (Athlete, Basketball Player)
13E8 Yucatan Dr SE
Rio Rancho, NM 87124, USA

Ham, Jack (Athlete, Football Player)
Jack Ham Enterprises Inc
540 Lindbergh Dr
Coraopolis, PA 15108-2750, USA

Ham, Kenneth T (Astronaut)
19 Plum Hollow Dr
Henderson, NV 89052-6420, USA

Ham, Kenneth T Cdr (Astronaut)
19 Plum Hollow Dr
Henderson, NV 89052-6420, USA

Ham, Tracy (Athlete, Football Player)
164 Cotton Creek Dr
McDonough, GA 30252-9012, USA

Hambrick, Darren (Athlete, Football Player)
38632 Patti Ln
Lacoochee, FL 33537, USA

Hambrick, Troy (Athlete, Football Player)
1103 Pinelane Rd
Columbia, SC 29223-1974, USA

Hambright, Roger (Athlete, Baseball Player)
8709 NE 37th Ave
Vancouver, WA 98665-1065, USA

Hamed, Nihad (Religious Leader)
Islamic Assn in US/Canada
25351 Five Mile Rd
Redford, MI 48239, USA

Hamel, Alan
PO Box 827
Monterey, CA 93942-0827

Hamel, Dean (Athlete, Football Player)
1009 Hawthorne Dr NE
Lenoir, NC 28645-3878, USA

Hamel, Michael A (Astronaut)
1032 Werbel Pl
San Pedro, CA 90731-1166, USA

Hamel, Pierre (Athlete, Hockey Player)
1613 Beechwood Rd
Yadkinville, NC 27055-6604, USA

Hamel, Veronica (Actor, Model)
c/o Staff Member *Cunningham Escott Slevin & Doherty (CESD-LA)*
10635 Santa Monica Blvd Ste 130
Los Angeles, CA 90025-8306, USA

Hamel, William (Religious Leader)
Evangelical Free Church
901 E 78th St
Minneapolis, MN 55420-1300, USA

Hamelin, Bob (Athlete, Baseball Player)
51 Patton Ct SE
Concord, NC 28025-3742, USA

Hamels, Cole (Athlete, Baseball Player)
c/o Jon Orlando *WNWN Media*
348 Hauser Blvd # PH414
Los Angeles, CA 90036-3276, USA

Hamhuis, Dan (Athlete, Hockey Player)
9553 Hampton Reserve Dr
Brentwood, TN 37027-8485, USA

Hamill, Dorothy (Athlete, Figure Skater, Olympic Athlete)
10045 Red Run Blvd Ste 250
Owings Mills, MD 21117-5907, USA

Hamill, Mark (Actor)
c/o Natanya Rose *Danis, Panaro, Nist (DPN)*
9201 W Olympic Blvd
Beverly Hills, CA 90212-4605, USA

Hamilton, Anthony (Musician)
c/o Mark Cheatham *Creative Artists Agency (CAA-NY)*
162 5th Ave Fl 6
New York, NY 10010-6047, USA

Hamilton, Arthur Lee (Athlete, Baseball Player)
4374 Woodley Creek Rd
Jacksonville, FL 32218-9126, USA

Hamilton, Ashley (Actor)
c/o Staff Member *TalentWorks (LA)*
3500 W Olive Ave Ste 1400
Burbank, CA 91505-5512, USA

Hamilton, Ben (Athlete, Football Player)
5240 Golden Ridge Ct
Parker, CO 80134-4546, USA

Hamilton, Bethany (Athlete)
PO Box 863
Hanalei, HI 96714-0863, USA

Hamilton, Bobby Jr (Race Car Driver)
Motorsports Decisions
PO Box 190
Greenbrier, TN 37073-0190, USA

Hamilton, Charles (Musician)
c/o Staff Member *Violator Management*
36 W 25th St Fl 2
New York, NY 10010-2768, USA

Hamilton, Conrad (Athlete, Football Player)
19619 N 35th Pl
Phoenix, AZ 85050, USA

Hamilton, Darrell (Athlete, Football Player)
22 Sunrise Ct
Randallstown, MD 21133-3629, USA

Hamilton, Darryl (Athlete, Baseball Player)
4721 Southwind Dr
Baton Rouge, LA 70816-4738, USA

Hamilton, Dave (Athlete, Baseball Player)
9464 Cherry Hills Ln
San Ramon, CA 94583-3935, USA

Hamilton, Davey (Race Car Driver)
6415 Toledo St
Houston, TX 77008-6236, USA

Hamilton, Derek (Actor)
c/o PJ Shapiro *Ziffren, Brittenham, Branca, Fischer, Gilbert-Lurie, Stiffelman & Cook*
1801 Century Park W Fl 7
Los Angeles, CA 90067-6406, USA

Hamilton, George (Actor)
c/o Jeffrey Lane *Jeffrey Lane & Associates*
8787 Shoreham Dr Apt 1206
West Hollywood, CA 90069-2212, USA

Hamilton, Harry (Athlete, Football Player)
PO Box 986
Lemont, PA 16851-0986, USA

Hamilton, Jack (Athlete, Baseball Player)
Jack's Plaza View Restaurant 245 N Wildwood Dr
Branson, MO 65616, USA

Hamilton, James (Athlete, Football Player)
242 McGirt Rd
Hamlet, NC 28345-9124, USA

Hamilton, Jeff (Athlete, Baseball Player)
2485 Golfview Cir
Fenton, MI 48430-9633, USA

Hamilton, Joe (Athlete, Basketball Player)
9E2 Loveall Ln
Louisville, KY 40223, USA

Hamilton, Joey (Athlete, Baseball Player)
4035 Wellington Mist Pt
Peachtree Corners, GA 30097-2352, USA

Hamilton, Josh (Athlete, Baseball Player)
1215 Perdenalas Trl
Westlake, TX 76262-4820, USA

Hamilton, Keith (Athlete, Football Player)
6 Bonnieview Ln
Towaco, NJ 07082-1289, USA

Hamilton, Laird (Athlete, Producer)
c/o Jane Kachmer *Jane Kachmer Management*
PO Box 2246
Malibu, CA 90265-7246, USA

Hamilton, Laurell K (Writer)
Ma Petite Enterprises, L.L.C.
PO Box 270375
Saint Louis, MO 63127-0375, USA

Hamilton, Lee H (Politician)
Wilson Int'l Schorlars Center
1300 Pennsylvania Ave NW
Washington, DC 20004-3002, USA

Hamilton, Leonard (Basketball Player, Coach)
Florida State University
Athletic Dept
Tallahassee, FL 32306-0001, USA

Hamilton, Linda (Actor)
13717 James Monroe Hwy
Leesburg, VA 20176-5437, USA

Hamilton, Lisa Gay (Actor)
c/o Stacy Boniello *Firm, The*
2049 Century Park E # 2550
Los Angeles, CA 90067-3101, USA

Hamilton, Lynn (Actor)
1042 S Burnside Ave
Los Angeles, CA 90019-6718

Hamilton, Marcus (Actor)
Hank Ketchum Enterprises
PO Box 1997
Monterey, CA 93942-1997, USA

Hamilton, Marcus (Cartoonist)
12225 Ranburne Rd
Mint Hill, NC 28227-5623, USA

Hamilton, Michael (Athlete, Football Player)
6755 Mira Mesa Blvd # 123-227
San Diego, CA 92121-4392, USA

Hamilton, Mike (Athlete, Baseball Player)
1520 Gentle Way
Prosper, TX 75078-9524, USA

Hamilton, Milo (Commentator)
Houston Astros
2001 Holcombe Blvd Unit 901
Houston, TX 77030-4214, USA

Hamilton, Ray (Athlete, Football Player)
PO Box 3233
Windermere, FL 34786-3233, USA

Hamilton, Richard (Athlete, Basketball Player)
c/o Staff Member *Detroit Pistons*
2 Championship Dr
Auburn Hills, MI 48326-1753, USA

Hamilton, Roy Lee (Athlete, Basketball Player)
1644 Del Mar Rd
Oceanside, CA 92057-4910, USA

Hamilton, Ruffin (Athlete, Football Player)
236 Sumac Trl
Woodstock, GA 30188-5154, USA

Hamilton, Scott (Athlete, Figure Skater, Olympic Athlete)
2451 Hidden River Ln
Franklin, TN 37069-6933, USA

Hamilton, Tanya (Director)
c/o Adam Robinson *Southfield Village*
8228 W Sunset Blvd # 190
West Hollywood, CA 90046-2414, USA

Hamilton, Todd (Athlete, Golfer)
2004 Rock Dove Ct
Westlake, TX 76262-9076, USA

Hamilton, Tom (Commentator)
31704 Sailors Cv
Avon Lake, OH 44012-2931, USA

Hamilton, Tom (Musician)
PO Box 67039
Chestnut Hill, MA 02467-0001, USA

Hamilton, Tyler (Artist, Cycler, Olympic Athlete)
40 Cloutmans Ln
Marblehead, MA 01945-1545, USA

Hamilton, Victoria (Actor)
c/o Michael Lazo *Untitled Entertainment (LA)*
350 S Beverly Dr Ste 200
Beverly Hills, CA 90212-4819, USA

Hamilton, Wes
18905 4th Ave N
Minneapolis, MN 55447-3307

Hamilton-Klemperer, Kim
44 W 62nd St Fl 10
New York, NY 10023-7008

Hamiter, Uhuru (Athlete, Football Player)
5737 Hazel Ave
Philadelphia, PA 19143-1910, USA

Hamlin, Brooke (Actor)
c/o Staff Member *Coast to Coast Talent Group*
3350 Barham Blvd
Los Angeles, CA 90068-1404, USA

Hamlin, Denny (Race Car Driver)
Denny Hamlin Racing, Inc
13415 Reese Blvd W
Huntersville, NC 28078-7933, USA

Hamlin, Eugene (Athlete, Football Player)
3571 Silver Farms Ln
Traverse City, MI 49684-8827, USA

Hamlin, Harry (Actor)
3007 Lake Glen Dr
Beverly Hills, CA 90210-1313, USA

Hamlin, Ken (Athlete, Baseball Player)
5242 County Road 413
Mc Millan, MI 49853-9266, USa

Hamlin, Shelley (Athlete, Golfer)
4311 W Ardmore Rd
Laveen, AZ 85339-2112, USA

Hamm, Harold (Business Person)
Continental Resources, Inc
20 N Broadway
Oklahoma City, OK 73102-9213, USA

Hamm, Jon (Actor)
2035 N Catalina St
Los Angeles, CA 90027-1825, USA

Hamm, Mia (Athlete, Olympic Athlete, Soccer Player)
Mia Hamm Foundation
61315th St
Manhattan Beach, CA 90266, USA

Hamm, Morgan (Athlete, Gymnast, Olympic Athlete)
W229S3827 Milky Way Rd
Waukesha, WI 53189-7909, USA

Hamm, Nick (Director)
International Creative Mgmt
10250 Constellation Blvd Fl 1
Los Angeles, CA 90067-6241, USA

Hamm, Paul (Athlete, Gymnast, Olympic Athlete)
c/o Sandy Hamm
W230S3827 Milky Way Rd
Waukesha, WI 53189-7909, USA

Hamm, Pete (Athlete, Baseball Player)
525 Lockhart Gulch Rd
Scotts Valley, CA 95066-3034, USA

Hamm, Richard L (Religious Leader)
Christian Church Disciples of Christ
PO Box 1986
Indianapolis, IN 46206-1986, USA

Hammaker, Atlee (Athlete, Baseball Player)
12740 Manning Ln
Knoxville, TN 37932-1001, USA

Hammarstrom, Inge (Athlete, Hockey Player)
c/o Staff Member *Philadelphia Flyers*
3601 S Broad St Ste 2
First Union Spectrum
Philadelphia, PA 19148-5297, USA

Hammel, Jason
6 Holly Ln
Rehoboth, MA 02769-1437, USA

Hammel, Penny (Athlete, Golfer)
4786 Orchard Ln
Delray Beach, FL 33445-5306, USA

Hammer (Music Group, Musician)
Terrie Williams Agency
1500 Broadway Fl 7
New York, NY 10036-4055, USA

Hammer, AJ (Television Host)
Showbiz Tonight
1 Time Warner Ctr
Cnn
New York, NY 10019-6038, USA

Hammer, Armie (Actor)
c/o Ame Van Iden *PMK/BNC Public Relations (PMK-LA)*
8687 Melrose Ave Ste 8
West Hollywood, CA 90069-5746, USA

Hammer, Jaime (Adult Film Star)
8033 W Sunset Blvd # 535
Los Angeles, CA 90046-2401, USA

Hammer, MC (Actor, Musician, Songwriter)
7683 W Erb Way
Tracy, CA 95304-8792, USA

Hammer, Victor S (Cinematographer)
PO Box 10788
Marina Del Rey, CA 90295-6788, USA

Hammergren, John H (Business Person)
McKesson HBOC Inc
1 Post St Ste 600
San Francisco, CA 94104-5210, USA

Hammer Jr, Jan (Musician)
Elliott Sears Management
7 Dunham Dr
New Fairfield, CT 06812-4022, USA

Hammett, Kirk (Music Group, Musician)
2505 Divisadero St
San Francisco, CA 94115-1119, USA

Hammink, Geert (Athlete, Basketball Player)
2619 Clementon Park Ct
Orlando, FL 32835-6160, USA

Hammock, Robby (Athlete, Baseball Player)
12026 W Leather Ln
Peoria, AZ 85383-5849, USA

Hammon, Ira (Athlete, Football Player)
12901 NE 28th St Apt 347
Vancouver, WA 98682-1290, USA

Hammond, Beresford (Musician)
c/o Jeff Epstein *M.A.G./Universal Attractions*
15 W 36th St Fl 8
New York, NY 10018-7927, USA

Hammond, Bobby (Athlete, Football Player)
2535 Butler St
East Elmhurst, NY 11369-1628, USA

Hammond, Chris (Athlete, Baseball Player)
55 Sneh St
Oxford, AL 36203-0373, USA

Hammond, Darrell (Actor, Comedian)
c/o Geoff Cheddy *Brillstein Entertainment Partners (LA)*
9150 Wilshire Blvd Ste 350
Beverly Hills, CA 90212-3453, USA

Hammond, Donnie (Athlete, Golfer)
8518 Cypress Hollow Ct
Sanford, FL 32771-8119, USA

Hammond, Fred (Music Group)
Face to Face
21421 Hilltop St Ste 20
Southfield, MI 48033-4002, USA

Hammond, Gary (Athlete, Football Player)
5321 Seascape Ln
Plano, TX 75093-4121, USA

Hammond, James T (Religious Leader)
Pentecostal Free Will Baptist Church
PO Box 1568
Dunn, NC 28335-1568, USA

Hammond, John (Music Group, Musician)
c/o Staff Member *Shore Fire Media*
32 Court St Fl 16
Brooklyn, NY 11201-4441, USA

Hammond, Josh (Actor)
c/o Staff Member *Hines and Hunt Entertainment*
1213 W Magnolia Blvd
Burbank, CA 91506-1829, USA

Hammond, Julie (Athlete, Basketball Player)
2943 S Ulster St
Denver, CO 80231-4170, USA

Hammond, Ken (Athlete, Hockey Player)
38325 McDowell Dr
Solon, OH 44139-4686, USA

Hammond, Kim (Athlete, Football Player)
9 Creek Bluff Run
Flagler Beach, FL 32136-5106, USA

Hammond, L Blaine Colonel (Astronaut)
17595 Harvard Ave
Irvine, CA 92614-8516, USA

Hammond, Steve (Athlete, Baseball Player)
11104 Lake Butler Blvd
Windermere, FL 34786-7808, USA

Hammond, Tom (Sportscaster)
NBC-TV
30 Rockefeller Plz Ste 30
New York, NY 10112-0015, USA

Hammonds, Jeffrey (Jeff) (Athlete, Baseball Player, Olympic Athlete)
113 Grand Cove Pl # Pi
Madison, AL 35758-3034, USA

Hammonds, Tom (Athlete, Basketball Player)
4472 New Market Rd
Niceville, FL 32578-4914, USA

Hammons, Roger (Religious Leader)
Primitive Advent Christian Church
6403 Frame Rd
Elkview, WV 25071-7040, USA

Hamner, Earl (Writer)
11575 Amanda Dr
Studio City, CA 91604-4144, USA

Hampson, Justin (Athlete, Baseball Player)
1202 W Main St
Alhambra, IL 62001-2132, USA

Hampson, Ted (Athlete, Hockey Player)
4436 Claremore Dr
Minneapolis, MN 55435-4136, USA

Hampton, Brenda (Producer)
c/o Clifford Gilbert-Lurie *Ziffren, Brittenham, Branca, Fischer, Gilbert-Lurie, Stiffelman & Cook*
1801 Century Park W Fl 7
Los Angeles, CA 90067-6406, USA

Hampton, Casey (Athlete, Football Player)
105 Conover Rd
Pittsburgh, PA 15208-2601, USA

Hampton, Daniel O (Dan) (Athlete, Football Player)
9191 Falling Waters Dr E
Burr Ridge, IL 60527-0716, USA

Hampton, Ike (Baseball Player)
New York Mets
1064 Emma Ln
Nipomo, CA 93444-6660, USA

Hampton, James (Actor)
102 Forest Hill Dr
Roanoke, TX 76262-5522, USA

Hampton, Locksley (Slide) (Music Group, Musician)
Charismic Productions
2604 Mozart Pl NW
Washington, DC 20009-3601, USA

Hampton, Lorenzo (Athlete, Football Player)
1251 Nottoway Trl
Marietta, GA 30066-7811, USA

Hampton, Michael W (Mike) (Athlete, Baseball Player)
8601 N 59th Pl
Paradise Valley, AZ 85253-2212, USA

Hampton, Millard (Athlete, Track Athlete)
201 W Mission St
San Jose, CA 95110-1701, USA

Hampton, Ralph C Jr (Religious Leader)
Free Will Baptist Bible College
3606 W End Ave
Nashville, TN 37205-2403, USA

Hampton, Rodney (Athlete, Football Player)
5603 Grand Floral Blvd
Houston, TX 77041-5563, USA

Hampton, Shanola (Actor)
c/o Elissa Leeds-Fickman *Reel Talent Management*
PO Box 491035
Los Angeles, CA 90049-9035, USA

Hamri, Sanaa
c/o Larry Kennar *Code Entertainment*
9229 W Sunset Blvd Ste 615
West Hollywood, CA 90069-3419, USA

Hamrlik, Roman (Athlete, Hockey Player)
56 Alhambra Dr
Oceanside, NY 11572-5425, USA

Hamulack, Tim (Athlete, Baseball Player)
530 Campbell Rd
York, PA 17402-3335, USA

Hamway, Mark (Athlete, Hockey Player)
2865 Rubbins Rd
Howell, MI 48843-7924, USA

Hamway, Marl (Athlete, Hockey Player)
3758 Loch Bend Dr
Commerce Township, MI 48382-4336, USA

Han, Heejun (Musician)
c/o Staff Member *19 Entertainment (LA)*
9000 W Sunset Blvd Ste 1574
West Hollywood, CA 90069-5817, USA

Hanauer, Terri
8271 Melrose Ave Ste 110
Los Angeles, CA 90046-6800

Hanburger, Christian (Chris) Jr (Athlete, Football Player)
708 Winter Hill Dr
Apex, NC 27502-1376, USA

Hancock, Anthony (Athlete, Football Player)
8233 Corteland Dr
Knoxville, TN 37909-2116, USA

Hancock, Eddie(murphy) (Athlete, Baseball Player)
2104 W 15th St
Pueblo, CO 81003-1126, USA

Hancock, Garry (Athlete, Baseball Player)
2217 Greenhills Dr
Valrico, FL 33596-5215, USA

Hancock, Herbie (Musician)
c/o Bruce Eskowitz *Red Light Management (LA)*
8439 W Sunset Blvd Ste 2
West Hollywood, CA 90069-1925, USA

Hancock, John D (Director)
7355 Fail Rd
La Porte, IN 46350-7108, USA

Hancock, John Lee (Director, Producer, Writer)
c/o David O'Connor *Creative Artists Agency (CAA-LA)*
2000 Avenue of the Stars Ste 100
Los Angeles, CA 90067-4705, USA

Hancock, Lee (Athlete, Baseball Player)
8338 Brentwood Blvd
Brentwood, CA 94513-1113, USA

Hancock, Leroy (Athlete, Baseball Player)
2010 Haywood Ave
Forrest City, AR 72335-4518, USA

Hancock, Mike (Athlete, Football Player)
5513 Coloma Cir
Simi Valley, CA 93063-5029, USA

Hancock, Phillip (Athlete, Golfer)
2800 Blackshear Ave
Pensacola, FL 32503-4874, USA

Hancock, Ryan (Athlete, Baseball Player)
542 W Aiden Ridge Dr
Draper, UT 84020-7305, USA

Hancock, Terri (Athlete, Golfer)
115 Devereux Dr
Athens, GA 30606-1634, USA

Hand, Jon T (Athlete, Football Player)
PO Box 40296
Indianapolis, IN 46240-0296, USA

Hand, Larry (Athlete, Football Player)
4414 Robinhood Rd
Winston Salem, NC 27106-4236, USA

Hand, Rich (Athlete, Baseball Player)
1130 Mission Ln
Argyle, TX 76226-6520, USA

Handelsman, J B (Cartoonist)
New Yorker Magazine
4 Times Sq Fl 22
New York, NY 10036-6592, USA

Handler, Chelsea (Comedian, Television Host)
11011 Anzio Rd
Los Angeles, CA 90077-2201, USA

Handler, Daniel (Actor, Writer)
c/o Esther Newberg *ICM Partners (NY)*
730 5th Ave
New York, NY 10019-4105, USA

Handler, Evan (Actor)
c/o Lenore Zerman *Liberman/Zerman Management*
252 N Larchmont Blvd Ste 200
Los Angeles, CA 90004-3754, USA

Handley, Ray (Athlete, Football Coach, Football Player)
PO Box 355
Glenbrook, NV 89413-0355, USA

Handley, Taylor (Actor)
c/o Booh Schut *Booh Schut Company*
11365 Sunshine Ter
Studio City, CA 91604-3141, USA

Hands, William A (Bill) (Athlete, Baseball Player)
PO Box 334
Orient, NY 11957-0334, USA

Handsome
9255 W Sunset Blvd Ste 200
West Hollywood, CA 90069-3308

Handy, John (Music Group, Musician)
Integrity Talent
PO Box 961
Burlington, MA 01803-5961, USA

Handzus, Michal (Athlete, Hockey Player)
123 29th St
Hermosa Beach, CA 90254-2358, USA

Hanes, Ken
8281 Melrose Ave Ste 200
Los Angeles, CA 90046-6890

Hanescu, Victor (Athlete, Tennis Player)
c/o Staff Member *SFX Sports Management*
5335 Wisconsin Ave NW Ste 850
Washington, DC 20015-2052, USA

Haney, Chris (Athlete, Baseball Player)
PO Box 135
Barboursville, VA 22923-0135, USA

Haney, Hank (Golfer)
Hank Haney Golf Ranch
2791 S Stemmons Fwy
Lewisville, TX 75067-4138, USA

Haney, Larry (Athlete, Baseball Player)
PO Box 157
Barboursville, VA 22923-0157, USA

Haney, Lee (Writer)
Lee Haney Enterprises
105 Trail Point Cir
Fairburn, GA 30213, USA

Haney, Todd (Athlete, Baseball Player)
5404 Pointwood Cir
Waco, TX 76710-1265, USA

Hanford, Dixon (Athlete, Football Player)
1512 Hunters Chase Dr Apt 2C
Westlake, OH 44145-6126, USA

Hangartner, Geoff (Athlete, Football Player)
805 Park Slope Dr
Charlotte, NC 28209-2049, USA

Hangsleben, Alan (Athlete, Hockey Player)
5760 Little Rd
Lothian, MD 20711-9543

Hanie, Caleb (Athlete, Football Player)
2435 Wincrest Dr
Rockwall, TX 75032-7008, USA

Hanifan, Jim (Athlete, Football Coach, Football Player)
1217 Grey Fox Run
Weldon Spring, MO 63304-0307, USA

Hanigan, Ryan
55 Bailey Rd
Andover, MA 01810-4200, USA

Hanke, Christopher (Actor)
c/o Shea Martin *SLATE Public Relations - NY*
307 7th Ave Rm 2401
New York, NY 10001-6019, USA

Hankins, Jay (Athlete, Baseball Player)
26509 E Outer Belt Rd
Greenwood, MO 64034-9387, USA

Hankinson, Ben (Athlete, Hockey Player)
6515 Biscayne Blvd
Minneapolis, MN 55436-1702, USA

Hankinson, Casey (Athlete, Hockey Player)
6615 Parkwood Ln
Minneapolis, MN 55436-1733, USA

Hankinson, Tim (Coach, Soccer Player)
Columbus Crew
2121 Velma Ave
Columbus, OH 43211-2085, USA

Hanks, Colin (Actor)
c/o Christian Donatelli *The Schiff Company*
9220 W Sunset Blvd Ste 106
West Hollywood, CA 90069-3500, USA

Hanks, Merton (Athlete, Football Player)
855 E Davisburg Rd
Holly, MI 48442-8597, USA

Hanks, Sam (Race Car Driver)
17766 Tramonto Dr
Pacific Palisades, CA 90272-3131, USA

Hanks, Tom (Actor, Producer)
c/o Leslee Dart *42West (NYC)*
220 W 42nd St Fl 12
New York, NY 10036-7200, USA

Hanks, Zach (Actor)
c/o Michael Henderson *Heresun Management*
4119 W Burbank Blvd
Burbank, CA 91505-2122, USA

Hankton, Cortez (Athlete, Football Player)
11180 Castlemain Cir W
Jacksonville, FL 32256-4828, USA

Hankton, Karl (Athlete, Football Player)
7024 Indian Ridge Ln
Charlotte, NC 28214-5000, USA

Hanley, Bridget (Actor)
12021 Hesby St
Valley Village, CA 91607-3115

Hanley, Dick (Athlete, Olympic Athlete, Swimmer)
266 Lake Dr
Hurley, WI 54534, USA

Hanley, Kay (Music Group)
c/o Staff Member *Paradigm (Monterey)*
404 W Franklin St
Monterey, CA 93940-2303, USA

Hanley, Richard (Swimmer)
E266 Lake Rd
Ironwood, MI 49938-9736, USA

Hanlon, Glen (Athlete, Hockey Player)
c/o Staff Member *Washington Capitals*
627 N Glebe Rd Ste 850
Arlington, VA 22203-2144, USA

Hann, Judith (Actor)
56 Wood Ln
London, EN W12 7

Hanna, Jack (Activist)
PO Box 400
Powell, OH 43065-0400, USA

Hanna, Jen (Athlete, Golfer)
28 Mandarin Cir
Taylors, SC 29687-6962, USA

Hanna, Jerome (Music Group)
Paramount Entertainment
PO Box 12
Far Hills, NJ 07931-0012, USA

Hanna, Preston (Athlete, Baseball Player)
5555 Mayfair Dr
Pensacola, FL 32506-5390, USA

Hannah, Bob (Baseball Player, Coach)
University of Delaware
Athletic Dept
Newark, DE 19716, USA

Hannah, Charles A (Charley) (Athlete, Football Player)
PO Box 2671
Lutz, FL 33548-2671, USA

Hannah, Daryl (Actor)
c/o Chuck Binder *Binder & Associates*
1465 Lindacrest Dr
Beverly Hills, CA 90210-2519, USA

Hannah, John (Athlete, Football Player)
2407 Hideaway Pl SE
Decatur, AL 35603-5602, USA

Hannah, Travis (Athlete, Football Player)
10807 Lemoli Ave
Inglewood, CA 90303-2023, USA

Hannah, Wayne (Religious Leader)
Fellowship of Grace Brethren Churches
PO Box 386
Winona Lake, IN 46590-0386, USA

Hannahan, Jack (Athlete, Baseball Player)
1995 Bayard Ave
Saint Paul, MN 55116-1214, USA

Hannahs, Gerald (Gerry) (Athlete, Baseball Player)
1411 Andover Rdg
Little Rock, AR 72227-3971, USA

Hannam, Ryan (Athlete, Football Player)
213 S School St
Saint Ansgar, IA 50472-1495, USA

Hannan, Dave (Athlete, Hockey Player)
408 Timberlake Dr
Venetia, PA 15367-1394, USA

Hannan, Jim (Athlete, Baseball Player)
3907 Cherry Hill Way
Annandale, VA 22003-2220, USA

Hannan, Scott (Athlete, Hockey Player)
35 S Bellaire St
Denver, CO 80246-1010, USA

Hannelius, Geneveive (Actor)
c/o Karl Hofheinz *Synergy Talent*
13251 Ventura Blvd Ste 2
Studio City, CA 91604-1838, USA

Hanneman, Craig (Athlete, Football
Player)
4350 Gibson Rd NW
Salem, OR 97304-9547, USA

Hanneman, Steve (Actor)
c/o Staff Member *Abrams Artists Agency
(LA)*
9200 W Sunset Blvd PH 11
West Hollywood, CA 90069-3601, USA

Hannigan, Alyson (Actor)
428 25th St
Santa Monica, CA 90402-3104, USA

Hannigan, Mackenzie (Actor)
c/o Staff Member *Martin Weiss
Management*
PO Box 5656
Santa Monica, CA 90409-5656, USA

Hannigan, Ray (Athlete, Hockey Player)
1717 S Woodland Dr Spc 36
Kalispell, MT 59901-9103, USA

Hannity, Sean (Correspondent)
c/o Staff Member *Fox News (NY)*
1211 Avenue of the Americas Lowr C1
New York, NY 10036-8705, USA

Hannon, Tom (Athlete, Football Player)
17398 Roxbury Ave
Southfield, MI 48075-7609, USA

Hannuia, Dick (Coach, Swimmer)
1021 S Westley Dr
Tacoma, WA 98465-1426, USA

Hanrahan, Don (Athlete, Basketball
Player)
416 Valley Rd
Cos Cob, CT 06807-1622, USA

Hanrahan, Joel (Athlete, Baseball Player)
c/o Larry Reynolds *Reynolds Sports
Management*
3850 Vine St Ste 230
Riverside, CA 92507-4225, USA

Hanratty, Sammi (Actor)
c/o Linda Henrie *Go Talent Management*
12930 Ventura Blvd Ste 904
Studio City, CA 91604-2200, USA

Hanratty, Terrance R (Terry) (Athlete,
Football Player)
31 Gower Rd
New Canaan, CT 06840-6630, USA

Hans, Rollen (Athlete, Basketball Player)
11400 NE 132nd St Apt L104
Kirkland, WA 98034-4749, USA

Hansbrough, Tyler (Athlete, Basketball
Player)
c/o Jeff Schwartz *Excel Sports
Management (NY)*
1700 Broadway Fl 29
New York, NY 10019-5905, USA

Hansell, Greg (Athlete, Baseball Player)
1791 W Prescott Dr
Chandler, AZ 85248-4845, USA

Hansen, Beck (Beck) (Musician,
Songwriter)
c/o John Silva *SAM*
722 Seward St
Los Angeles, CA 90038-3504, USA

Hansen, Bob (Athlete, Baseball Player)
19 N Kelsey Ave
Evansville, IN 47711-6051, USA

Hansen, Bob (Athlete, Basketball Player)
710 36th St
West Des Moines, IA 50265-3166, USA

Hansen, Brendan (Athlete, Olympic
Athlete, Swimmer)
8704 Farmdale Cv
Austin, TX 78749-3439, USA

Hansen, Brian (Athlete, Football Player)
101 W Hazeltine Ln
Sioux Falls, SD 57108-6422, USA

Hansen, Bruce (Athlete, Football Player)
480 N 1100 E
American Fork, UT 84003-1992, USA

Hansen, Chris (Correspondent, Television
Host)
c/o Staff Member *Dateline NBC*
30 Rockefeller Plz
Nbc News
New York, NY 10112-0015, USA

Hansen, Courtney (Actor)
c/o Liza Anderson *Anderson Group Public
Relations*
8060 Melrose Ave Fl 4
Los Angeles, CA 90046-7038, USA

Hansen, Craig (Athlete, Baseball Player)
1180 Washington St Apt 508
Boston, MA 02118-2154, USA

Hansen, David (Dave) (Athlete, Baseball
Player)
9852 Orchard Ln
Villa Park, CA 92861-3105, USA

Hansen, Don (Athlete, Football Player)
3290 Spain Rd
Snellville, GA 30039-8503, USA

Hansen, Frederick M (Fred) (Athlete,
Track Athlete)
201 Vanderpool Ln Apt 12
Houston, TX 77024-6151, USA

Hansen, Gale (Actor)
721 SE 29th Ave
Portland, OR 97214-3027, USA

Hansen, Gunnar (Actor)
PO Box 368
Northeast Harbor, ME 04662-0368, USA

Hansen, Gus (Actor)
c/o Staff Member *Poker Royalty, LLC*
10789 W Twain Ave Ste 200
Las Vegas, NV 89135-3030, USA

Hansen, Guy (Athlete, Baseball Player)
3876 Red Rock St
Las Vegas, NV 89103-2333, USA

Hansen, Jacqueline (Athlete, Track
Athlete)
1133 9th St
Santa Monica, CA 90403-5247, USA

Hansen, Jed (Athlete, Baseball Player)
180 SE Cedar Hill Ln
Shelton, WA 98584-7977, USA

Hansen, Lars (Athlete, Basketball Player)
1230 Horn Ave Apt 504
West Hollywood, CA 90069-2175, USA

Hansen, Mark Victor (Business Person,
Motivational Speaker, Writer)
Mark Victor Hansen and Associates
711 W 17th St Ste D2
Costa Mesa, CA 92627-4344, USA

Hansen, Neil (Race Car Driver)
4018 E 5th Ave
Spokane, WA 99202-5043, USA

Hansen, Peter (Actor)
Stone Manners
6500 Wilshire Blvd # 550
Los Angeles, CA 90048-4920, USA

Hansen, Phil (Athlete, Football Player)
24921 N Melissa Dr
Detroit Lakes, MN 56501-7266, USA

Hansen, Rich (Athlete, Hockey Player)
78 Eatons Neck Rd
Northport, NY 11768-1105, USA

Hansen, Roger (Athlete, Baseball Player)
14618 Kayak Point Rd
Stanwood, WA 98292-5301, USA

Hansen, Ron (Athlete, Baseball Player)
13602 Alliston Dr
Baldwin, MD 21013-9748, USA

Hansen, Roscoe (Athlete, Football Player)
638 Sooy Ln
Absecon, NJ 08201-1325, USA

Hansen, Ryan (Actor)
4123 Van Noord Ave
Studio City, CA 91604-2202, USA

Hansen, Tavis (Athlete, Hockey Player)
3821 51st Ave SW
Seattle, WA 98116-3614, USA

Hansis, Ron (Athlete, Hockey Player)
112 Stegal Cir
Longs, SC 29568-8841

Hansis, Van (Actor)
c/o Kathy Kanner *Kanner Entertainment*
30 W 74th St # PH1
New York, NY 10023-2446, USA

Hanson (Music Group)
1045 W 78th St
Tulsa, OK 74132, USA

Hanson, Curtis (Director, Producer)
c/o David Kramer *United Talent Agency
(UTA-LA)*
9336 Civic Center Dr
Beverly Hills, CA 90210-3604, USA

Hanson, Dave (Athlete, Hockey Player)
304 Timberlake Dr
Venetia, PA 15367-1376

Hanson, Erik (Athlete, Baseball Player)
20333 N 83rd Pl
Scottsdale, AZ 85255-3931, USA

Hanson, Isaac (Musician)
c/o Jeffrey Hasson *Paradigm (Nashville)*
124 12th Ave S Ste 410
Nashville, TN 37203-3170, USA

Hanson, Jason D (Athlete, Football Player)
27272 Ovid Ct
Franklin, MI 48025-1036, USA

Hanson, Jennifer (Musician)
c/o Staff Member *Creative Artists Agency
(CAA-TN)*
401 Commerce St PH
Nashville, TN 37219-2516, USA

Hanson, Joselio (Athlete, Football Player)
2531 Hudspeth St
Inglewood, CA 90303-2432, USA

Hanson, Stan
PO Box 970
Hotchkiss, CO 81419-0970

Hanson, Tommy (Athlete, Baseball Player)
c/o Greg Genske *The Legacy Agency*
500 Newport Center Dr Ste 800
Newport Beach, CA 92660-7008, USA

Hanson, Tracy (Athlete, Golfer)
89 S Atlantic Ave Apt 1403
Ormond Beach, FL 32176-6608, USA

Hanson, Zac (Musician)
c/o Jeffrey Hasson *Paradigm (Nashville)*
124 12th Ave S Ste 410
Nashville, TN 37203-3170, USA

Hanson-Sfingi, Beverly (Athlete, Golfer)
79915 Horseshoe Rd
La Quinta, CA 92253-4309, USA

Hanspard, Byron (Athlete, Football Player)
PO Box 792
Desoto, TX 75123-0792, USA

Hantak, Bob (Athlete, Baseball Player)
526 Summerplace Ct
Saint Louis, MO 63125-5545, USA

Hantla, Bob (Athlete, Football Player)
7815 E Monte Vista Rd
Scottsdale, AZ 85257-2209, USA

Hantla, Robert (Athlete, Football Player)
7815 E Monte Vista Rd
Scottsdale, AZ 85257-2209, USA

Hantuchova, Daniela (Tennis Player)
c/o Staff Member *Women's Tennis
Association (WTA (US))*
1 Progress Plz Ste 1500
St Petersburg, FL 33701-4335, USA

Hanulak, Chet (Athlete, Football Player)
225 Canal Park Dr Apt 6
Salisbury, MD 21804-7266, USA

Hanzal, Martin (Athlete, Hockey Player)
19550 N Grayhawk Dr Unit 1091
Scottsdale, AZ 85255-3993, USA

Hanzlik, Bill (Athlete, Basketball Player,
Olympic Athlete)
5701 Green Oaks Dr
Greenwood Village, CO 80121-1336,
USA

Hape, Patrick (Athlete, Football Player)
105 Sutton Cir
Birmingham, AL 35242-7075, USA

Hapka, Mark (Actor)
c/o Loch Powell *Leverage Management*
3030 Pennsylvania Ave
Santa Monica, CA 90404-4112, USA

Happ, J A (Athlete, Baseball Player)
3832 N Ashland Ave Apt 3S
Chicago, IL 60613-5235, USA

Harang, Aaron (Athlete, Baseball Player)
7828 Sendero Angelica
San Diego, CA 92127-2553, USA

Harang, Aaron (Athlete, Baseball Player)
6411 Glenroy St
San Diego, CA 92120-2713, USA

Harb, Fred (Race Car Driver)
815 E Fairfield Rd
High Point, NC 27263-2353, USA

Harbach, Otto
3455 Congress St
Fairfield, CT 06824-2036

Harbaugh, David (Cartoonist)
1649 Stone Mansion Dr
Sewickley, PA 15143-8600, USA

Harbaugh, Gregory J (Astronaut)
1936 Thornwood Ave
Wilmette, IL 60091-1403, USA

Harbaugh, James (jim) (Athlete, Football Player)
c/o David Dunn *Athletes First, LLC*
23091 Mill Creek Dr
Laguna Hills, CA 92653-1258, USA

Harbaugh, John (Athlete, Coach, Football Coach)
c/o Bryan Harlan *Harlan Sports Management*
400 N Michigan Ave Ste 1016
Chicago, IL 60611-4289, USA

Harbaugh, Robert E (Doctor)
Dartmouth-Hitchcock Medical Center
Surgery Dept
Lebanon, NH 03756, USA

Harbour, David (Actor)
c/o Meg Mortimer *Principal Entertainment (NY)*
1133 Avenue Of The Americas Ste 1621
New York, NY 10036-6710, USA

Harcourt, Ed (Musician)
c/o Staff Member *Paradigm (Monterey)*
404 W Franklin St
Monterey, CA 93940-2303, USA

Hard, Darlene R (Tennis Player)
22924 Erwin St
Woodland Hills, CA 91367-3215, USA

Hardaway, Anfemee (Penny) (Athlete, Basketball Player, Olympic Athlete)
3217 Point Hill Cv
Memphis, TN 38125-8890, USA

Hardaway, Anfernee (Penny) (Athlete, Basketball Player, Olympic Athlete)
3217 Point Hill Cv
Memphis, TN 38125-8890, USA

Hardaway, Tim (Athlete, Basketball Player, Olympic Athlete)
10050 SW 62nd Ave
Miami, FL 33156-3378, USA

Hardeman, Buddy (Athlete, Football Player)
2504 Washington Blvd
Arlington, VA 22201-1118, USA

Hardeman, Don (Athlete, Football Player)
901 S Valley Mills Dr Apt 207-B
Waco, TX 76711-1160, USA

Harden, Bobby (Athlete, Football Player)
5645 NW 117th Ave
Pompano Beach, FL 33076-3617, USA

Harden, James (Athlete, Basketball Player)
c/o Rob Pelinka *Landmark Sports Agency*
881 N Park View Dr
El Segundo, CA 90245-4932, USA

Harden, Marcia Gay (Actor)
God of Carnage
242 W 45th St
Bernard B Jacobs Theater
New York, NY 10036-3901, USA

Harden, Michael (Athlete, Football Player)
7150 Leetsdale Dr Apt 315
Denver, CO 80224-1999, USA

Harden, Mike (Athlete, Football Player)
21512 E Portland Pl
Aurora, CO 80016-2343, USA

Hardenberger, Hahan (Music Group, Musician)
Columbia Artists Mgmt Inc
165 W 57th St
New York, NY 10019-2201, USA

Hardesty, Brandon (Actor)
c/o Brandt Joel *William Morris Endeavor (LA)*
9601 Wilshire Blvd
Beverly Hills, CA 90210-5213, USA

Hardin, Jerry
3033 Vista Crest Dr
Los Angeles, CA 90068-1824

Hardin, Melora (Actor)
c/o Staff Member *Kohner Agency, The*
9300 Wilshire Blvd Ste 555
Beverly Hills, CA 90212-3211, USA

Hardin, Ty (Actor)
2210 87street Ct NW
Gig Harbor, WA 98332, USA

Harding, Daniel (Musician)
c/o Staff Member *ICM Partners (LA)*
10250 Constellation Blvd Fl 7
Los Angeles, CA 90067-6207, USA

Harding, Ian (Actor)
c/o Gina Hoffman *PMK/BNC Public Relations (PMK-LA)*
8687 Melrose Ave Ste 8
West Hollywood, CA 90069-5746, USA

Hardis, Stephen R (Business Person)
Eaton Corp
Eaton Center 1111 Superior Ave
Cleveland, OH 44114, USA

Hardison, Dee (Athlete, Football Player)
756 Belvin Maynard Rd
Harrells, NC 28444-9308, USA

Hardison, Kadeem (Actor)
19743 Valley View Dr
Topanga, CA 90290-3257, USA

Hardman, Cedrick (Athlete, Football Player)
250 Moss St
Laguna Beach, CA 92651-3624, USA

Hardman, Earl
1400 E Carson St
Pittsburgh, PA 15203-1556

Hardnett, Charles (Charlie) (Athlete, Basketball Player, Coach)
1906 Swainsboro Dr
Louisville, KY 40218-2417, USA

Hardrict, Cory (Actor)
c/o Matt Luber *Luber Roklin Management*
5815 W Sunset Blvd Ste 206
Los Angeles, CA 90028-6481, USA

Hardtke, Jason (Athlete, Baseball Player)
6756 Elwood Rd
San Jose, CA 95120-4728, USA

Hardwick, Chris (Actor)
2356 Hollyridge Dr
Los Angeles, CA 90068-3518, USA

Hardwick, Gary C (Director, Producer, Writer)
c/o Bruce Kaufman *ICM Partners (LA)*
10250 Constellation Blvd Fl 7
Los Angeles, CA 90067-6207, USA

Hardwick, Omari (Actor)
c/o Troy Zien *3 Arts Entertainment (LA)*
9460 Wilshire Blvd Fl 7
Beverly Hills, CA 90212-2713, USA

Hardwicke, Catherine (Director)
c/o BeBe Lerner *ID Public Relations (LA)*
7060 Hollywood Blvd Fl 8th
Los Angeles, CA 90028-6021, USA

Hardy, Adrian (Athlete, Football Player)
7530 Kingsport Blvd
New Orleans, LA 70128-2114, USA

Hardy, Alan (Athlete, Basketball Player)
13841 Gratiot Ave
Detroit, MI 48205-2805, USA

Hardy, Bruce A (Athlete, Football Player)
252 W 325 N
Ivins, UT 84738-6132, USA

Hardy, Carroll (Athlete, Baseball Player, Football Player)
1514 Whitehall Dr
Longmont, CO 80504-7971, USA

Hardy, Darrell (Athlete, Basketball Player)
3126 Knoll St
Houston, TX 77080-3011, USA

Hardy, David (Athlete, Football Player)
PO Box 1270
New Waverly, TX 77358-1270, USA

Hardy, Greg (Athlete, Football Player)
c/o Drew Rosenhaus *Rosenhaus Sports Representation*
6400 Allison Rd
Miami Beach, FL 33141-4540, USA

Hardy, James (Athlete, Basketball Player)
1682 E Lakewood Dr
Salt Lake City, UT 84117-7518, USA

Hardy, James (Athlete, Football Player)
c/o Eugene Parker *Maximum Sports Management*
6435 W Jefferson Blvd # 197
Fort Wayne, IN 46804-6203, USA

Hardy, Jeff (Wrestler)
c/o Kerry Rodgerson *World Wrestling Entertainment (WWE)*
1241 E Main St
Titan Towers
Stamford, CT 06902-3520, USA

Hardy, Jim (Athlete, Football Player)
48490 San Vicente St
La Quinta, CA 92253-6253, USA

Hardy, J J (Athlete, Baseball Player)
5070 S Roosevelt St
Tempe, AZ 85282-6599, USA

Hardy, John (Jack) (Athlete, Baseball Player)
1260 NW 192nd Ln
Pembroke Pines, FL 33029-4520, USA

Hardy, Kevin (Athlete, Football Player)
1228 Windsor Harbor Dr
Jacksonville, FL 32225-2651, USA

Hardy, Kevin (Athlete, Football Player)
298 Paraiso Dr
Danville, CA 94526-4950, USA

Hardy, Larry (Athlete, Baseball Player)
7 Jennifer Ct
Roanoke, TX 76262-5402, USA

Hardy, Larry (Athlete, Football Player)
1711 Fairwood Dr
Jackson, MS 39213-7918, USA

HardY, Larry (Athlete, Baseball Player)
17 Jennifer Ct
Roanoke, TX 76262, USA

Hardy, Mark (Athlete, Hockey Player)
121 N Cross St Unit 423
Wheaton, IL 60187-5362, USA

Hardy, Matt (Wrestler)
c/o Kerry Rodgerson *World Wrestling Entertainment (WWE)*
1241 E Main St
Titan Towers
Stamford, CT 06902-3520, USA

Hardy, Rob (Actor)
c/o Adam Robinson *Southfield Village*
8228 W Sunset Blvd # 190
West Hollywood, CA 90046-2414, USA

Hardy, Terry (Athlete, Football Player)
3109 S Rick Dr
Montgomery, AL 36108-3821, USA

Hardy, Tom (Actor)
c/o Mick Sullivan *Creative Artists Agency (CAA-LA)*
2000 Avenue of the Stars Ste 100
Los Angeles, CA 90067-4705, USA

Hare, Eddie (Athlete, Football Player)
802 Walker School Rd
Sugar Land, TX 77479-5807, USA

Hare, Shawn (Athlete, Baseball Player)
1975 Deer Path Trl
Oxford, MI 48371-6062, USA

Haren, Dan (Athlete, Baseball Player)
c/o Joe Urbon *Creative Artists Agency (CAA-NY)*
162 5th Ave Fl 6
New York, NY 10010-6047, USA

Harewood, Dorian (Actor)
c/o Tracy Quinn *Quinn Management*
17328 Ventura Blvd Ste 416
Encino, CA 91316-3904, USA

Hargain, Tony (Athlete, Football Player)
PO Box 116
Fair Oaks, CA 95628-0116, USA

Hargan, Steve (Athlete, Baseball Player)
2502 E Morongo Trl
Palm Springs, CA 92264-4839, USA

Harge, Ira (Athlete, Basketball Player)
328 Yucca Dr NW
Albuquerque, NM 87105-1935, USA

Hargesheimer, Al (Athlete, Baseball Player)
107 N Evanston Ave
Arlington Heights, IL 60004-6617, USA

Hargesheimer, Alan (Athlete, Baseball Player)
107 N Evanston Ave
Arlington Heights, IL 60004-6617, USA

Hargett, Edd (Athlete, Football Player)
379 County Road 222
Nacogdoches, TX 75965-4806, USA

Hargis, Gary (Athlete, Baseball Player)
157 Gemini St
Lompoc, CA 93436-1244, USA

Hargitay, Mariska (Actor)
1357 Broadway # 321
New York, NY 10018-7101, USA

Hargrove, D Michael (Mike) (Athlete, Baseball Player, Coach)
3925 Ramblewood Dr
Richfield, OH 44286-9642, USA

Hargrove, Jim (Athlete, Football Player)
702 W North Ave
Lampasas, TX 76550-1764, USA

Hargrove, Linda (Coach)
Washington Mystics
601 E St NW
Mci Center
Washington, DC 20049-0001, USA

Hargrove, Marion (Writer)
401 Montana Ave # 6
Santa Monica, CA 90403-1303, USA

Harikkala, Tim (Athlete, Baseball Player)
W6132 Everglade Rd
Greenville, WI 54942-8590, USA

Harington, Kit (Actor)
c/o Gene Parseghian *Parseghian Planco LLC*
388 2nd Ave
New York, NY 10010-5616, USA

Haris, Niki (Musician)
c/o Staff Member *Diva Central Inc*
7510 W Sunset Blvd Ste 1445
Los Angeles, CA 90046-3408, USA

Harker, Al (Athlete, Soccer Player)
409 2nd St
Lafayette Hill, PA 19444-1403, USA

Harkey, Mike (Athlete, Baseball Player)
23930 Strange Creek Dr
Diamond Bar, CA 91765-1144, USA

Harkey, Steve (Athlete, Football Player)
6582 Cherry Tree Ln
Atlanta, GA 30328-3319, USA

Harkin, Kenan (Sportscaster)
c/o Staff Member *William Morris Endeavor (LA)*
9601 Wilshire Blvd
Beverly Hills, CA 90210-5213, USA

Harkin, Tom (Politician, Senator)
531 Hart Senate Off Bldg
Washington, DC 20510-0001, USA

Harkins, Brett (Athlete, Hockey Player)
4701 Duhme Rd Apt 1D
Saint Petersburg, FL 33708-2801, USA

Harkleroad, Ashley (Tennis Player)
c/o Jill Smoller *William Morris Endeavor (LA)*
9601 Wilshire Blvd
Beverly Hills, CA 90210-5213, USA

Harkless, Burkley (Athlete, Football Player)
2308 E Windsor Dr
Denton, TX 76209-1447, USA

Harkness, Jerry (Athlete, Basketball Player)
8340 Misty Dr
Indianapolis, IN 46236-9190, USA

Harkrider, Kip (Athlete, Baseball Player, Olympic Athlete)
604 N Sunset St
Carthage, TX 75633-1522, USA

Harlan, Bob (Business Person, Football Executive)
2621 Forestville Dr
Green Bay, WI 54304-1359, USA

Harlan, Kevin (Sportscaster)
CBS-TV
51 W 52nd St
Sprots Dept
New York, NY 10019-6119, USA

Harlicka, Skip (Athlete, Basketball Player)
2643 Saint Marys St
Raleigh, NC 27609-7644, USA

Harlin, Renny (Director, Producer)
Midnight Sun Pictures
8800 W Sunset Blvd # 400
West Hollywood, CA 90069-2105, USA

Harlock, David (Athlete, Hockey Player)
3234 Chamberlain Cir
Ann Arbor, MI 48103-8866, USA

Harlow, Larrv (Athlete, Baseball Player)
26348 W Burnett Rd
Buckeye, AZ 85396-9239, USA

Harlow, Larry (Athlete, Baseball Player)
26348 W Burnett Rd
Buckeye, AZ 85396-9239, USA

Harlow, Pat (Athlete, Football Player)
2308 S Ola Vista
San Clemente, CA 92672-4349, USA

Harlow, Scott (Athlete, Hockey Player)
285 Harvest Ln
Bridgewater, MA 02324-2457, USA

Harman, Jane (Congressman, Politician)
2400 Rayburn Hob
Washington, DC 20515-0536, USA

Harmon, Andrew P (Athlete, Football Player)
1258 Waters Edge Dr
Dayton, OH 45458-3937, USA

Harmon, Andy (Football Player)
1258 Waters Edge Dr
Dayton, OH 45458-3937, USA

Harmon, Angie (Actor)
1901 Wild Holly Ln
Charlotte, NC 28226-5744, USA

Harmon, Chuck (Athlete, Baseball Player)
PO Box 12243
Cincinnati, OH 45212-0243, USA

Harmon, Clarence (Athlete, Football Player)
PO Box 571
Verona, MS 38879-0571, USA

Harmon, Dan (Writer)
c/o Blair Kohan *United Talent Agency (UTA-LA)*
9336 Civic Center Dr
Beverly Hills, CA 90210-3604, USA

Harmon, Duron (Athlete, Football Player)
c/o Brian Levy *Goal Line Football Management*
1025 Kane Concourse Ste 207
Bay Harbor Islands, FL 33154-2118, USA

Harmon, Ed (Football Player)
136 Juniper Hill Rd NE
Albuquerque, NM 87122-1913, USA

Harmon, Joy (Actor)
9901 Poole Ave
Sunland, CA 91040-1335, USA

Harmon, Kelly (Actor, Model)
13224 Old Oak Ln
Los Angeles, CA 90049-2502, USA

Harmon, Manny -
8350 Santa Monica Blvd
West Hollywood, CA 90069-4393

Harmon, Mark (Actor)
c/o Karen Samfilippo *IMPR*
357 S Robertson Blvd
Beverly Hills, CA 90211-3602, USA

Harmon, Merle (Sportscaster)
424 E Lamar Blvd Ste 210
Arlington, TX 76011-3606, USA

Harmon, Michael (Athlete, Football Player)
336 Hayat Loop
Oxford, MS 38655-9017, USA

Harmon, Mike (Race Car Driver)
Donlavey Racing
5011 Old Midlothian Tpke
Richmond, VA 23224-1119, USA

Harmon, Richard (Actor)
c/o Naisha Arnold *Untitled Entertainment (LA)*
350 S Beverly Dr Ste 200
Beverly Hills, CA 90212-4819, USA

Harmon, Robert (Director)
c/o Andrew Ruf *Paradigm (LA)*
360 N Crescent Dr
North Bldg
Beverly Hills, CA 90210-4874, USA

Harmon, Ronnie K (Athlete, Football Player)
13022 218th St
Laurelton, NY 11413-1231, USA

Harmon, Terry (Athlete, Baseball Player)
62 Oakwood Dr
Medford, NJ 08055-8824, USA

Harmon, Tom (Athlete, Baseball Player)
6101 Bon Terra Dr
Austin, TX 78731-3849, USA

Harmon, Winsor
c/o Jerry Shandrew *Shandrew Public Relations*
1050 S Stanley Ave
Los Angeles, CA 90019-6634, USA

Harmonica Rascals, The
4585 N River Rd
Zanesville, OH 43701-7768

Harms, Kristin (Producer)
c/o Staff Member *Creative Artists Agency (CAA-LA)*
2000 Avenue of the Stars Ste 100
Los Angeles, CA 90067-4705, USA

Harnden, Arthur (Art) (Athlete, Olympic Athlete, Track Athlete)
7218 Pepper Ridge Rd
Corpus Christi, TX 78413-5005, USA

Harnes, Robert (Baseball Player)
Chicago Giants
833 E Drexel Sq
Chicago, IL 60615-3705, USA

Harnick, Sheldon (Writer)
122 E 42nd St Fl 31
New York, NY 10168-3100, USA

Harnick, Sheldon
General Delivery
Kirtland Afb, NM 87117-9999, USA

Harnisch, Peter T (Pete) (Athlete, Baseball Player)
35 Bretwood Dr S
Colts Neck, NJ 07722-2402, USA

Harnois, Elisabeth (Actor)
c/o Ted Schachter *Schachter Entertainment*
1157 S Beverly Dr Fl 2
Los Angeles, CA 90035-1119, USA

Harnos, Christine (Actor)
Gersh Agency
232 N Canon Dr
Beverly Hills, CA 90210-5302, USA

Harold, Gale (Actor)
c/o Larry Taube *Principal Entertainment (LA)*
9255 W Sunset Blvd Ste 500
West Hollywood, CA 90069-3301, USA

Harout, Magda (Actor)
20950 Oxnard St Apt 3
Woodland Hills, CA 91367-5227, USA

Harp, George
5456 Youngs Rd
Vernon, NY 13476-4712, USA

Harper, Alvin C (Athlete, Football Player)
501 Harry S Truman Dr Apt 109
Upper Marlboro, MD 20774-2061, USA

Harper, Ben (Musician, Songwriter)
2314 La Mesa Dr
Santa Monica, CA 90402-2331, USA

Harper, Bob (Fitness Expert)
c/o Joyce Sevilla *Entertainment Fusion Group*
6363 Wilshire Blvd Ste 206
Los Angeles, CA 90048-5736, USA

Harper, Brandon (Athlete, Baseball Player)
1612 Iris St
Broomfield, CO 80020-3433, USA

Harper, Brian (Athlete, Baseball Player)
8319 E Shetland Trl
Scottsdale, AZ 85258-1343, USA

Harper, Bruce (Athlete, Football Player)
311 Lindbergh Ave
Closter, NJ 07624-2732, USA

Harper, Bryce (Athlete, Basketball Player)
c/o Scott Boras *Boras Corporation*
3 San Joaquin Plz Ste 100
Newport Beach, CA 92660-5944, USA

Harper, Charles M (Business Person)
6625 State St
Omaha, NE 68152-1633, USA

Harper, Charlie (Athlete, Football Player)
17518 Astrachan Rd
Richmond, TX 77407-2699, USA

Harper, Dave (Athlete, Football Player)
4494 Cedar St
Eureka, CA 95503-8901, USA

Harper, David (Athlete, Football Player)
4494 Cedar St
Eureka, CA 95503-8901, USA

Harper, Dawn (Athlete, Track Athlete)
c/o Staff Member *HS International Sports Management, Inc.*
9871 Irvine Center Dr
Irvine, CA 92618-4361, USA

Harper, Derek (Athlete, Basketball Player)
3EL W 53rd St Apt 14F
New York, NY LEEL9, USA

Harper, Deveron (Athlete, Football Player)
2749 Huntsville St
Kenner, LA 70062-5124, USA

Harper, Donald D W (Don) (Athlete, Diver, Olympic Athlete)
1765 Lynnhaven Dr
Columbus, OH 43221-1409, USA

Harper, Dwayne (Athlete, Football Player)
104 Cue St
Orangeburg, SC 29115-7593, USA

Harper, Gregg (Congressman, Politician)
307 Cq Nnqn Hob
Washington, DC 20515-0001, USA

Harper, Heck
13647 Gaffney Ln Apt 17
Oregon City, OR 97045-8970

Harper, Herschel (Baseball Player)
Negro Baseball Leagues
3302 Hazelwood Dr SW
Atlanta, GA 30311-3038, USA

Harper, Hill (Actor)
c/o Lena Roklin *Luber Roklin Management*
5815 W Sunset Blvd Ste 206
Los Angeles, CA 90028-6481, USA

Harper, Jessica (Actor, Music Group)
15430 Brownwood Pl
Los Angeles, CA 90077-1609, USA

Harper, John
9700 Kessler Ave
Chatsworth, CA 91311-5503

Harper, Mark (Athlete, Football Player)
2162 Albany Ave
Memphis, TN 38108-3011, USA

Harper, Michael (Athlete, Basketball Player)
2387 College Hill Pl
West Linn, OR 97068-1222, USA

Harper, Nick (Athlete, Football Player)
9549 Sanctuary Pl
Brentwood, TN 37027-8499, USA

Harper, Robert (Actor)
Karg/Weissenbach
329 N Wetherly Dr Ste 101
Beverly Hills, CA 90211-1674, USA

Harper, Roger (Athlete, Football Player)
1921 Holburn Ave
Columbus, OH 43207-1683, USA

Harper, Roland (Athlete, Football Player)
207 Grandview Ct
Algonquin, IL 60102-1990, USA

Harper, Roman (Athlete, Football Player)
c/o Pat Dye Jr *SportsTrust Advisors (GA)*
3340 Peachtree Rd NE Fl 16
Atlanta, GA 30326-1000, USA

Harper, Ron (Actor)
c/o Staff Member *Tisherman Gilbert Motley Drozdoski Talent Agency (TGMD)*
6767 Forest Lawn Dr Ste 101
Los Angeles, CA 90068-1027, USA

Harper, Ron (Athlete, Basketball Player)
8934 Brecksville Rd # 417
Brecksville, OH 44141-2318, USA

Harper, Shane (Actor)
c/o Nicole David *William Morris Endeavor (LA)*
9601 Wilshire Blvd
Beverly Hills, CA 90210-5213, USA

Harper, Terry (Athlete, Baseball Player)
2831 Aunt Pitty Pat Ln
Douglasville, GA 30135-2109, USA

Harper, Terry (Athlete, Hockey Player)
PO Box 5227
El Dorado Hills, CA 95762-0005, USA

Harper, Tess (Actor)
c/o David Guc *Vanguard Management Group*
8060 Melrose Ave Fl 4
Los Angeles, CA 90046-7038, USA

Harper, Tommy (Athlete, Baseball Player)
5 Cow Hill Rd
Sharon, MA 02067-2987, USA

Harper, Travis (Athlete, Baseball Player)
3222 Whitings Neck Rd
Martinsburg, WV 25404-1689, USA

Harper, Valerie (Actor)
PO Box 7187
Beverly Hills, CA 90212-7187, USA

Harper, Willie M (Athlete, Football Player)
2525 Berryessa Ct
Tracy, CA 95304-5825, USA

Harpring, Matt (Athlete, Basketball Player)
c/o Staff Member *Utah Jazz*
301 W South Temple
Salt Lake City, UT 84101-1219, USA

Harptones, The
55 W 119th St
New York, NY 10026-1454

Harrah, Colbert D (Toby) (Athlete, Baseball Player, Coach)
316 Leewood Cir
Azle, TX 76020, USA

Harrah, Dennis W (Athlete, Football Player)
925 Rockin One Way
Paso Robles, CA 93446-8433, USA

Harraway, Charley (Athlete, Football Player)
9023 Heritage Sound Dr
Bradenton, FL 34212-3287, USA

Harraway, Charlie (Athlete, Football Player)
9023 Heritage Sound Dr
Bradenton, FL 34212-3287, USA

Harrell, Billy (Athlete, Baseball Player)
253 Mount Hope Dr
Albany, NY 12202-1017, USA

Harrell, Graham (Athlete, Football Player)
c/o Chad Speck *Allegiant Athletic Agency*
35 Market Sq Ste 201
Knoxville, TN 37902-1420, USA

Harrell, James (Athlete, Football Player)
17826 Crystal Preserve Dr
Lutz, FL 33548-6408, USA

Harrell, John (Athlete, Baseball Player)
3218 Denton Ct
Pleasanton, CA 94566-4681, USA

Harrell, Justin (Athlete, Football Player)
c/o Eugene Parker *Maximum Sports Management*
6435 W Jefferson Blvd # 197
Fort Wayne, IN 46804-6203, USA

Harrell, Lucas (Athlete, Baseball Player)
345 Bayberry Dr
Polk City, FL 33868-9345, USA

Harrell, Lynn M (Musician)
I M G Artists
420 W 45th St
New York, NY 10036-3501, USA

Harrell, Sam (Athlete, Football Player)
5758 Hirondel St
Houston, TX 77033-2302, USA

Harrell, Tom (Music Group, Musician)
Joel Chriss
300 Mercer St Apt 3J
New York, NY 10003-6732, USA

Harrell, Willard (Athlete, Football Player)
8 Scarlet Oak Ct
Lake Saint Louis, MO 63367-2143, USA

Harrelson, Bill (Athlete, Baseball Player)
6900 Kimberly Ave
Bakersfield, CA 93308-3923, USA

Harrelson, Brett (Actor)
Agency for Performing Arts
9200 W Sunset Blvd Ste 900
West Hollywood, CA 90069-3604, USA

Harrelson, Derrell M (Bud) (Athlete, Baseball Player, Coach)
357 Ridgefield Rd
Hauppauge, NY 11788-2314, USA

Harrelson, Ken (Commentator)
9006 Shawn Park Pl
Orlando, FL 32819-4830, USA

Harrelson, Woody (Actor)
PO Box 327
Kula, HI 96790-0327, USA

Harrer, Tim (Athlete, Hockey Player)
7030 W 113th St
Minneapolis, MN 55438-2446, USA

Harrick, Jim (Basketball Player, Coach)
Denver Nuggets
1000 Chopper Cir
Pepsi Center
Denver, CO 80204-5805, USA

Harriet, Judy (Actor)
12400 Ventura Blvd
Studio City, CA 91604-2406, USA

Harrigan, Lori (Athlete, Olympic Athlete, Softball Player)
828 Rainbow Rock St
Las Vegas, NV 89123-3121, USA

Harriger, Denny (Athlete, Baseball Player)
902 N Water St
Kittanning, PA 16201-1121, USA

Harring, Laura Elena (Actor, Beauty Pageant Winner)
c/o Jason Priluck *Priluck Company*
1230 Montana Ave Ste 203
Santa Monica, CA 90403-5987, USA

Harrington, Al (Athlete, Basketball Player)
16124 Chancellors Ridge Way
Westfield, IN 46062-7137, USA

Harrington, Bill (Athlete, Baseball Player)
7219 Cleveland School Rd
Garner, NC 27529-8928, USA

Harrington, David (Music Group, Musician)
Kronos Quartet
1235 9th Ave # A
San Francisco, CA 94122-2306, USA

Harrington, Dennis (Athlete, Golfer)
5668 S Rex Rd Ste 101
Stanford Roberts
Memphis, TN 38119-3829, USA

Harrington, Desmond (Actor)
c/o Stephanie Simon *Untitled Entertainment (LA)*
350 S Beverly Dr Ste 200
Beverly Hills, CA 90212-4819, USA

Harrington, Jay (Actor)
c/o Abe Hoch *A Management Company*
9107 Wilshire Blvd Ste 650
Beverly Hills, CA 90210-5544, USA

Harrington, Joey (Athlete, Football Player)
2000 NE 42nd Ave PMB 336
Portland, OR 97213-1399, USA

Harrington, John (Athlete, Hockey Player, Olympic Athlete)
PO Box 7277
Stjohn's University
Collegeville, MN 56321-7277, USA

Harrington, Kevin (Business Person)
As Seen On TV
6 Kentisbury Cir
East Brunswick, NJ 08816-5237, USA

Harrington, Mickev (Athlete, Baseball Player)
135 Scenic Dr
Hattiesburg, MS 39401-8403, USA

Harrington, Mike (Mickey) (Athlete, Baseball Player)
135 Scenic Dr
Hattiesburg, MS 39401-8403, USA

Harrington, Othella (Athlete, Basketball Player)
1602 Rika Pt
Houston, TX 77077-3432, USA

Harrington, Padraig (Golfer)
c/o Staff Member *Pro Golfers Association (PGA) Tour*
112 Tpc Blvd
Ponte Vedra Beach, FL 32082, USA

Harrington, Pat
730 Marzella Ave
Los Angeles, CA 90049-2043

Harrington, Pat Jr (Actor)
730 Marzella Ave
Los Angeles, CA 90049-2043, USA

Harrington, Perry (Athlete, Football Player)
1302 Roxbury Ct
Jackson, MS 39211-6367, USA

Harrington, Robert (Race Car Driver)
2609 Woodshade Ave
New London, NC 28127, USA

Harrington, Scott (Race Car Driver)
920 Ardmore Dr
Louisville, KY 40217-2312, USA

Harris, Al (Athlete, Football Player)
4200 NW 96th Ave
Coral Springs, FL 33065-1518, USA

Harris, Al (Athlete, Football Player)
12 Stone Ridge Dr
South Barrington, IL 60010-9593, USA

Harris, Alonzo (Candy) (Athlete, Baseball Player)
6948 Lisa Dr
Fontana, CA 92336-5772, USA

Harris, Andy (Congressman, Politician)
506 Callinon Hob
Washington, DC 20515-0001, USA

Harris, Antwan (Athlete, Football Player)
7413 Ray Rd
Raleigh, NC 27613-8801, USA

Harris, Archie (Athlete, Football Player)
17 Hawthorne Ct NE
Washington, DC 20017-1014, USA

Harris, Arlen (Athlete, Football Player)
223 Wellsmont Ct
Saint Charles, MO 63304-2326, USA

Harris, Barbara
159 W 53rd St Apt 12D
New York, NY 10019-6068

Harris, Barry (DJ, Music Group,
Musician)
Brad Simon Organization
122 E 57th St # 300
New York, NY 10022-2623, USA

Harris, Bernard A Dr
3411 Erin Knoll Ct
Houston, TX 77059-3716, USA

Harris, Bernard A Jr (Astronaut)
3411 Erin Knoll Ct
Houston, TX 77059-3716, USA

Harris, Billy (Athlete, Baseball Player)
205 Fellowship Dr
Hamlet, NC 28345-3507, USA

Harris, Bishop Barbara
138 Tremont St
Boston, MA 02111-1318

Harris, Bo (Athlete, Football Player)
PO Box 52539
Shreveport, LA 71135-2539, USA

Harris, Boyd (Gail) (Athlete, Baseball
Player)
9008 Weir St
Manassas, VA 20110-4913, USA

Harris, Brendan (Athlete, Baseball Player)
1703 Sun Gazer Dr
Rockledge, FL 32955-6323, USA

Harris, Buddy (Athlete, Baseball Player)
2305 Carol Ln
Norristown, PA 19401-2046, USA

Harris, Callard (Actor)
c/o Amy Slomovits *Evolution
Entertainment (LA)*
901 N Highland Ave
Los Angeles, CA 90038-2412, USA

Harris, Calvin (DJ, Musician)
9342 Sierra Mar Dr
Los Angeles, CA 90069-1737, USA

Harris, Charlaine (Writer)
PO Box 354
Magnolia, AR 71754-0354, USA

Harris, Charles (Bubba) (Athlete, Baseball
Player)
6754 Cr 651
Bushnell, FL 33513-7616, USA

Harris, Chris (Athlete, Basketball Player)
1EE Oakmont Ln Apt 8E8
Clearwater, FL 33756, USA

Harris, Clark (Athlete, Football Player)
c/o Brad Leshnock *BTI Sports Advisors*
170 N Scoville Ave
Oak Park, IL 60302-2647, USA

Harris, Cliff (Athlete, Football Player)
5711 Preston Fairways Dr
Dallas, TX 75252-4956, USA

Harris, Corey (Athlete, Football Player)
933 N Tremont St
Indianapolis, IN 46222-3738, USA

Harris, Cristi Ellen
c/o Staff Member *House of
Representatives, The*
1434 6th St Ste 1
Santa Monica, CA 90401-2527, USA

Harris, Damian (Director)
International Creative Mgmt
10250 Constellation Blvd Fl 1
Los Angeles, CA 90067-6241, USA

Harris, Danielle (Actor)
883 Patriot Dr
B
Moorpark, CA 93021-3359, USA

Harris, Danneel (Actor)
c/o Jason Newman *Untitled Entertainment
(LA)*
350 S Beverly Dr Ste 200
Beverly Hills, CA 90212-4819, USA

Harris, Del (Basketball Coach, Coach)
1134 Osage Cir
Saint George, UT 84790-6810, USA

Harris, Devin (Athlete, Basketball Player)
4875 Gramercy Oaks Dr Apt 253
Dallas, TX 75287-5384, USA

Harris, Donald (Athlete, Baseball Player)
916 Hubert St
Waco, TX 76704-1936, USA

Harris, Duriel (Athlete, Football Player)
3875 San Pablo Rd S Apt 1212
Jacksonville, FL 32224-6819, USA

Harris, Dwayne (Athlete, Football Player)
c/o Chad Speck *Allegiant Athletic Agency*
35 Market Sq Ste 201
Knoxville, TN 37902-1420, USA

Harris, Ed (Actor)
c/o Catherine Olim *PMK/BNC Public
Relations (PMK-LA)*
8687 Melrose Ave Ste 8
West Hollywood, CA 90069-5746, USA

Harris, Emmylou (Musician, Songwriter)
PO Box 158568
Nashville, TN 37215-8568, USA

Harris, Ernest (Athlete, Baseball Player)
1007 46th Street Ensley
Birmingham, AL 35208-1434, USA

Harris, Estelle (Actor)
c/o Joel Dean *TalentWorks (LA)*
3500 W Olive Ave Ste 1400
Burbank, CA 91505-5512, USA

Harris, Franco (Athlete, Football Player)
200 Chaucer Ct S
Sewickley, PA 15143-8726, USA

Harris, Gail (Baseball Player)
New York Giants
9008 Weir St
Manassas, VA 20110-4913, USA

Harris, Gail Robyn (Actor)
Don Gerler
3349 Cahuenga Blvd W Ste 1
Los Angeles, CA 90068-1379, USA

Harris, Greg (Athlete, Baseball Player)
10262 Mardel Dr
Cypress, CA 90630-4100, USA

Harris, Greg (Athlete, Baseball Player)
12613 Richmond Run Dr
Raleigh, NC 27614-6419, USA

Harris, Hernando (Pep) (Athlete, Baseball
Player)
995 Ten Oaks Dr
Lancaster, SC 29720-9039, USA

Harris, Hugh (Athlete, Hockey Player)
9784 Herons Cv
Indianapolis, IN 46280-2787, USA

Harris, Ike (Athlete, Football Player)
Bellsouth Corporation
26 N Waterview Dr
Palm Coast, FL 32137-1619, USA

Harris, Jackie (Athlete, Football Player)
716 W Barraque St
Pine Bluff, AR 71601-4064, USA

Harris, James L (Athlete, Football Player)
9838 Old Baymeadows Rd
Jacksonville, FL 32256-8101, USA

Harris, Jared (Actor)
c/o Amy Guenther *Gateway Management
Company Inc*
860 Via De La Paz Ste F10
Pacific Palisades, CA 90272-3631, USA

Harris, Jay (Cartoonist)
c/o Staff Member *King Features
Syndication*
300 W 57th St Fl 15
New York, NY 10019-5238, USA

Harris, Jeff (Athlete, Baseball Player)
Lake County Captains 35300 Vine St Attn
Eastlake, OH 44095, USA

Harris, Jeremy (Athlete, Football Player)
c/o Don Yee *Yee & Dubin Sports, LLC*
725 S Figueroa St Ste 3085
Los Angeles, CA 90017-5430, USA

Harris, Joe (Athlete, Football Player)
4747 River Rd
Ellenwood, GA 30294-1507, USA

Harris, Joe Frank (Ex-Governor)
712 West Ave
Cartersville, GA 30120-3441, USA

Harris, John (Athlete, Baseball Player)
4404 Derrick Pl
Amarillo, TX 79121-1906, USA

Harris, John (Athlete, Football Player)
270 NW 120th St
Miami, FL 33168-3525, USA

Harris, John (Athlete, Golfer)
4316 Fremont Ave S
Minneapolis, MN 55409-1721, USA

Harris, Jon (Athlete, Football Player)
110 Cedar Ct
Swedesboro, NJ 08085-5054, USA

Harris, Joshua (Actor)
1800 Vine St # 305
Los Angeles, CA 90028-5250, USA

Harris, Juliette (Actor)
c/o Staff Member *It Girl Public Relations*
5301 Beethoven St Ste 220
Los Angeles, CA 90066-7052, USA

Harris, Katherine
c/o Daniel Strone *Trident Media Group
LLC*
41 Madison Ave Fl 36
New York, NY 10010-2257, USA

Harris, Kwame (Athlete, Football Player)
4949 Centennial Blvd
Santa Clara, CA 95054-1229, USA

Harris, Lara (Actor)
c/o Peter Kaiser *Talent House (NY)*
325 W 38th St Rm 605
New York, NY 10018-9642, USA

Harris, Larry (Athlete, Football Player)
41 Alta Ave
Yonkers, NY 10705-1402, USA

Harris, Laura (Actor)
c/o Kami Putnam-Heist *Creative Artists
Agency (CAA-LA)*
2000 Avenue of the Stars Ste 100
Los Angeles, CA 90067-4705, USA

Harris, Lenny (Athlete, Baseball Player)
JD Legends Promotions
10808 Foothill Blvd # 160-454
Attn: Jack Delance
Rancho Cucamonga, CA 91730-3889,
USA

Harris, Leon (Correspondent)
Cable News Network
1050 Techwood Dr NW
News Dept
Atlanta, GA 30318-5695, USA

Harris, Leonard (Athlete, Football Player)
1817 Trilogy Park Dr
Hoschton, GA 30548-6237, USA

Harris, Leotis (Athlete, Football Player)
2815 Stephanie Dr
Little Rock, AR 72206-5421, USA

Harris, Leroy (Athlete, Football Player)
1919 Live Oak St
Savannah, GA 31404-3336, USA

Harris, Lou (Athlete, Football Player)
5606 Windsor Ct
Suitland, MD 20746-4410, USA

Harris, Lucious (Athlete, Basketball
Player)
1149 W 62nd St
Los Angeles, CA 90044-3733, USA

Harris, Major (Athlete, Football Player)
c/o Staff Member *College Football Hall Of
Fame*
233 Peachtree St NE Ste 1400
Atlanta, GA 30303-1507, USA

Harris, Marilyn
217 N San Marino Ave
San Gabriel, CA 91775-2909

Harris, Mel (Actor)
c/o Joanna (Joanie) Burstein *Burstein
Company, The*
15304 W Sunset Blvd Ste 208
Pacific Palisades, CA 90272-3656, USA

Harris, Mike (Athlete, Football Player)
c/o Joe Linta *JL Sports*
1204 Main St Ste 179
Branford, CT 06405-3787, USA

Harris, M L (Athlete, Football Player)
M L Harris Outreach
15589 Apple Valley Rd
Apple Valley, CA 92307-4575, USA

Harris, Moira (Actor)
c/o Staff Member *Creative Artists Agency
(CAA-LA)*
2000 Avenue of the Stars Ste 100
Los Angeles, CA 90067-4705, USA

Harris, Naomie (Actor)
c/o Christina Papadopoulos *Baker
Winokur Ryder Public Relations
(BWR-NY)*
292 Madison Ave Fl 12
New York, NY 10017-6415, USA

Harris, Napoleon (Athlete, Football
Player)
c/o Staff Member *EAG Sports
Management*
909 N Sepulveda Blvd Ste 360
El Segundo, CA 90245-3864, USA

Harris, Neil Patrick (Actor)
c/o Booh Schut *Booh Schut Company*
11365 Sunshine Ter
Studio City, CA 91604-3141, USA

Harris, Nick (Athlete, Football Player)
280 Dover Dr
Walnut Creek, CA 94598-3322, USA

Harris, Niki (Musician)
c/o Stephen Ford *Diva Central Inc*
7510 W Sunset Blvd Ste 1445
Los Angeles, CA 90046-3408, USA

Harris, Odie L Jr (Athlete, Football Player)
821 S Polk St Apt 127
Desoto, TX 75115-7591, USA

Harris, Quentin (Athlete, Football Player)
3013 W Glass Ln
Phoenix, AZ 85041-6366, USA

Harris, Rachael (Actor, Comedian)
c/o Peter Principato *Principato/Young Management (LA)*
9465 Wilshire Blvd Ste 900
Beverly Hills, CA 90212-2608, USA

Harris, Raymont (Athlete, Football Player)
1144 Aroya Ct
New Albany, OH 43054-9205, USA

Harris, Reggie (Athlete, Baseball Player)
100 Guilford Ln Apt 85-3
Waynesboro, VA 22980-1772, USA

Harris, Rickie (Athlete, Football Player)
4225 Mozart Brigade Ln Apt 1
Fairfax, VA 22033-3960, USA

Harris, Robert (Athlete, Football Player)
4533 River Gem Ave
Windermere, FL 34786-3128, USA

Harris, Ronald W (Ronnie) (Boxer)
1365 Glennview St NE
Canton, OH 44721-1916, USA

Harris, Ronnie (Athlete, Football Player)
16911 123rd Pi NE
Bothell, WA 98011, USA

Harris, Ross
6542 Fulcher Ave
North Hollywood, CA 91606-2717

Harris, Ryan (Athlete, Football Player)
c/o Eugene Parker *Maximum Sports Management*
6435 W Jefferson Blvd # 197
Fort Wayne, IN 46804-6203, USA

Harris, Sam (Actor, Music Group, Writer)
c/o Barry Krost *Barry Krost Management*
9220 W Sunset Blvd Ste 106
West Hollywood, CA 90069-3500, USA

Harris, Samantha (Actor)
c/o Siri Garber *Platform Public Relations*
2666 N Beachwood Dr
Los Angeles, CA 90068-2308, USA

Harris, Sean (Athlete, Football Player)
3541 E Coconino Way
Gilbert, AZ 85298-4209, USA

Harris, Sidney (Cartoonist)
302 W 86th St Apt 9A
New York, NY 10024-3154, USA

Harris, Steve (Actor)
c/o Colton Gramm *Brillstein Entertainment Partners (LA)*
9150 Wilshire Blvd Ste 350
Beverly Hills, CA 90212-3453, USA

Harris, Steve (Athlete, Basketball Player)
3005 W Fort Worth St
Broken Arrow, OK 74012-3276, USA

Harris, Susan (Producer)
LaGrange Management
11828 La Grange Ave # 200
Los Angeles, CA 90025-5212, USA

Harris, Ted (Athlete, Hockey Player)
1 Stonegate Ct
Blackwood, NJ 08012-5356, USA

Harris, Thomas (Director, Writer)
c/o Robert (Bob) Bookman *Paradigm (LA)*
2000 Avenue of the Stars
Los Angeles, CA 90067-4700, USA

Harris, Tim (Athlete, Football Player)
81900 Via La Serena
La Quinta, CA 92253-7882, USA

Harris, Tobias (Athlete, Basketball Player)
c/o Henry Thomas *CAA Sports (LA)*
2000 Avenue of the Stars Ste 100
Los Angeles, CA 90067-4705, USA

Harris, Tomas (Writer)
c/o Robert (Bob) Bookman *Paradigm (LA)*
2000 Avenue of the Stars
Los Angeles, CA 90067-4700, USA

Harris, Tommie (Athlete, Football Player)
1000 Football Dr
Lake Forest, IL 60045, USA

Harris, Tony (Athlete, Football Player)
530 Venice Way Apt 6
Inglewood, CA 90302-2841, USA

Harris, Tyrone (Gene) (Athlete, Baseball Player)
1267 NE 16th Ave
Okeechobee, FL 34972-3066, USA

Harris, Vic (Athlete, Baseball Player)
5420 S Garth Ave
Los Angeles, CA 90056-1116, USA

Harris, Walt (Athlete, Football Player)
4103 Shinault Ln
Olive Branch, MS 38654-8039, USA

Harris, Wendell (Athlete, Football Player)
10338 Westwood Ave
Baton Rouge, LA 70809-3268, USA

Harris, William M (Athlete, Football Player)
2118 Laurel Forest Way
Houston, TX 77014-2452, USA

Harris, Willie (Athlete, Baseball Player)
161 Saint Johns Forest Blvd
Saint Johns, FL 32259-4066, USA

Harris, Wilmer (Baseball Player)
Philadelphia Stars
441 Tomlinson Rd Apt F3
Philadelphia, PA 19116-3227, USA

Harris, Wood (Actor)
Gersh Agency
232 N Canon Dr
Beverly Hills, CA 90210-5302, USA

Harris III, James S. (Jimmy Jam) (Musician)
c/o Staff Member *Flyte Tyme Productions*
PO Box 398045
Minneapolis, MN 55439-8045, USA

Harrison, Alvin (Athlete, Track Athlete)
Octagon
7950 Jones Branch Dr
Mc Lean, VA 22102-3302, USA

Harrison, Bob (Athlete, Baseball Player)
16777 Loch Cir
Noblesville, IN 46060-4482, USA

Harrison, Bob (Athlete, Football Player)
3 Westwind Cir
Stamford, TX 79553-6117, USA

Harrison, Brett (Actor)
1539 N Laurel Ave Apt 305
Los Angeles, CA 90046-2591, USA

Harrison, Chris (Actor, Reality Star)
c/o Staff Member *Creative Public Relations*
3385 Oak Glen Dr
Los Angeles, CA 90068-1311, USA

Harrison, Chuck (Athlete, Baseball Player)
222 Buckskin Rd
Abilene, TX 79602-4508, USA

Harrison, Corey (Reality Star)
Gold & Silver Pawn Shop
713 Las Vegas Blvd S
Las Vegas, NV 89101-6755, USA

Harrison, C Richard (Business Person)
Parametric Technology
140 Kendrick St
Needham Heights, MA 02494-2739, USA

Harrison, David (Athlete, Basketball Player)
11593 Larkspur Ln
Carmel, IN 46032-8614, USA

Harrison, Dennis (Athlete, Football Player)
1048 Hickory Hollow Rd
Nashville, TN 37221-1139, USA

Harrison, Dwight (Athlete, Football Player)
5550 Harvest Hill Rd Apt W118
Dallas, TX 75230-1617, USA

Harrison, Glynn (Athlete, Football Player)
485 Huntington Rd Ste 203
Athens, GA 30606-1845, USA

Harrison, Greg (Actor)
c/o Staff Member *Stone Manners Salners Agency (LA)*
6100 Wilshire Blvd Ste 1500
Los Angeles, CA 90048-5110, USA

Harrison, Gregory (Actor)
c/o Steve Himber *Steve Himber Entertainment*
211 S Beverly Dr # 601
Beverly Hills, CA 90212-3807, USA

Harrison, James (Athlete, Football Player)
2525 Matterhorn Dr
Wexford, PA 15090-7963, USA

Harrison, Jenilee (Actor)
JLeeCorp
19528 Ventura Blvd # 365
Tarzana, CA 91356-2917, USA

Harrison, Jerome (Athlete, Football Player)
7500 Paradise Rd Lot 75
San Antonio, TX 78244-2293, USA

Harrison, Jerry (Musician)
Sire/Warner Bros Records
3300 Warner Blvd
Burbank, CA 91505-4694, USA

Harrison, Jim (Athlete, Football Player)
6038 Royal Crk
San Antonio, TX 78239-1614, USA

Harrison, Kathryn (Writer)
Random House
1745 Broadway Frnt 3 # B1
New York, NY 10019-4343, USA

Harrison, Linda (Actor)
9846 Portola Dr
Beverly Hills, CA 90210-1421, USA

Harrison, Lisi (Writer)
c/o Richard Abate *3 Arts Entertainment (NY)*
16 W 22nd St Ste 201
New York, NY 10010-5842, USA

Harrison, Martin (Athlete, Football Player)
6160 S Featherstone Cir
Reno, NV 89511-4349, USA

Harrison, Marvin (Athlete, Football Player)
1223 N 26th St
Philadelphia, PA 19121-4633, USA

Harrison, Matt (Athlete, Baseball Player)
160 LLRVIL Lg Pi
Creedmoor, NC 27522, USA

Harrison, Matthew (Director)
Rigberg Roberts Rugolo
1180 S Beverly Dr Ste 601
Los Angeles, CA 90035-1158, USA

Harrison, (Mya) Marie (Actor)
c/o Melissa Berger *Melissa Berger Public Relations*
613 N West Knoll Dr Apt C
West Hollywood, CA 90069-5200, USA

Harrison, Nolan (Athlete, Football Player)
21805 Omeara Ter Apt 206
Ashburn, VA 20147-6759, USA

Harrison, Randy (Actor, Producer)
c/o Staff Member *Paradigm (LA)*
360 N Crescent Dr
North Bldg
Beverly Hills, CA 90210-4874, USA

Harrison, Reggie (Athlete, Football Player)
1912 Halifax Rd
Woodbridge, VA 22191-2407, USA

Harrison, Rick (Reality Star)
Gold & Silver Pawn Shop
713 Las Vegas Blvd S
Las Vegas, NV 89101-6755, USA

Harrison, Robert (Athlete, Basketball Player)
13405 NW Wax Myrtle Trl
Palm City, FL 34990-4826, USA

Harrison, Rodney (Athlete, Football Player)
2825 Darlington Pointe
Duluth, GA 30097-4318, USA

Harrison, Roric (Athlete, Baseball Player)
18662 MacArthur Blvd Ste 200
Irvine, CA 92612-1285, USA

Harrison, Rorie (Athlete, Baseball Player)
680 Glenneyre St
Laguna Beach, CA 92651-2420, USA

Harrison, Schae
7800 Beverly Blvd # 3371
Los Angeles, CA 90036-2112

Harrison, Tom (Athlete, Baseball Player)
2932 Channing Way
Los Alamitos, CA 90720-4049, USA

Harrison, Tyreo (Athlete, Football Player)
8619 Braun Hill Dr
San Antonio, TX 78254-2301, USA

Harris-Stewart, Luisa (Basketball Player, Olympic Athlete)
1002 Cherry St
Greenwood, MS 38930-6506, USA

Harris-Stewart, Lusia M (Lucy) (Athlete, Basketball Player, Olympic Athlete)
1002 Cherry St
Greenwood, MS 38930-6506, USA

Harrold, Peter (Athlete, Hockey Player)
9385 Baldwin Rd
Mentor, OH 44060-8055, USA

Harron, Mary (Director, Producer, Writer)
c/o Charles Mastropietro *Circle of Confusion (LA)*
8931 Ellis Ave
Los Angeles, CA 90034-3336, USA

Harry, Debbie (Actor, Musician, Songwriter)
c/o Linda Carbone *Press Here Publicity*
138 W 25th St Ste 900
New York, NY 10001-7470, USA

Harry, Deborah (Actor, Musician)
c/o Jason Weinberg *Untitled Entertainment (LA)*
350 S Beverly Dr Ste 200
Beverly Hills, CA 90212-4819, USA

Harry, Emile (Athlete, Football Player)
34 Villa Vista Dr
Brownsville, TX 78520-4649, USA

Harry, Jackee (Actor, Director)
c/o Christopher Barrett *Metropolitan (MTA)*
4526 Wilshire Blvd
Los Angeles, CA 90010-3801, USA

Harsch, Eddie (Musician)
c/o Staff Member *Mitch Schneider Organization (MSO)*
14724 Ventura Blvd Ste 410
Sherman Oaks, CA 91403-3537, USA

Harshman, Jack (Athlete, Baseball Player)
320 Yukon Ter
Georgetown, TX 78633-5098, USA

Harshman, Marv (Athlete, Basketball Player, Coach)
1653 S Geiger St
Tacoma, WA 98465-1509, USA

Hart, Bo (Athlete, Baseball Player)
PO Box 1761
Freedom, CA 95019-1761, USA

Hart, Bob (Bowler)
5740 Laurel Oak Dr
Suwanee, GA 30024-3370, USA

Hart, Christopher
1423 N Martel Ave Apt 4
Los Angeles, CA 90046-4204

Hart, Clinton (Athlete, Football Player)
2894 CR 730
Webster, FL 33597-4084, USA

Hart, Corey (Athlete, Baseball Player)
1445 Lambert Close # 300
Bowling Green, KY 42101, USA

Hart, Dick (Athlete, Football Player)
273 Oarlock Cir
East Syracuse, NY 13057-3123, USA

Hart, Dolores Hart (Actor)
Regina Laudis Abbey
275 Flanders Rd
Bethlehem, CT 06751, USA

Hart, Doris (Tennis Player)
600 Biltmore Way Apt 306
Coral Gables, FL 33134-7528, USA

Hart, Dorothy
43 Martindale Rd
Asheville, NC 28804-1427

Hart, Doug (Athlete, Football Player)
5018 43rd Ave S
Minneapolis, MN 55417-1617, USA

Hart, Dudley (Athlete, Golfer)
5130 Rockledge Dr
Clarence, NY 14031-2442, USA

Hart, Freddie (Music Group, Musician, Songwriter, Writer)
317 N Kenwood St
Burbank, CA 91505-3446, USA

Hart, Gary (Politician)
27925 Troublesome Gulch Rd
Evergreen, CO 80439-9260, USA

Hart, Gary W (Ex-Senator, Politician, Writer)
c/o Staff Member *Henry Holt & Company*
175 5th Ave Ste 400
New York, NY 10010-7726, USA

Hart, Gerry (Athlete, Hockey Player)
10 Parkridge Ct
Huntington, NY 11743-3671, USA

Hart, Harold J (Athlete, Football Player)
1016 Brook View Ave
Atlanta, GA 30340-3842, USA

Hart, Ian (Actor)
c/o Robert Marsala *Wishlab*
2225A Hyperion Ave
Los Angeles, CA 90027-4709, USA

Hart, James V (Director, Producer, Writer)
c/o Jon Levin *Creative Artists Agency (CAA-LA)*
2000 Avenue of the Stars Ste 100
Los Angeles, CA 90067-4705, USA

Hart, James W (Jim) (Athlete, Football Player, Misc)
3141 Dominica Way
Naples, FL 34119-1606, USA

Hart, Jason (Athlete, Baseball Player)
19317 Nestor Ave
Carson, CA 90746-2607, USA

Hart, Jeff (Athlete, Football Player)
1307 SE 14th Ave
Canby, OR 97013-6341, USA

Hart, Jeff (Athlete, Golfer)
105 Guanajuato Ct
Solana Beach, CA 92075-2510, USA

Hart, Jim (Athlete, Football Player)
3141 Dominica Way
Naples, FL 34119-1606, USA

Hart, Jim Ray (Athlete, Baseball Player)
17074 Templeton Ln
Lathrop, CA 95330-8634, USA

Hart, John (Athlete, Baseball Player)
5205 Latrobe Dr
Windermere, FL 34786-8959, USA

Hart, Kevin (Actor, Comedian)
c/o David (Dave) Becky *3 Arts Entertainment (LA)*
9460 Wilshire Blvd Fl 7
Beverly Hills, CA 90212-2713, USA

Hart, Kevin (Athlete, Baseball Player)
5605 Plantation Cir
Plano, TX 75093-4205, USA

Hart, Larry (Athlete, Football Player)
c/o Jordan Woy *Willis and Woy Management*
3030 Olive St Ste 520
Dallas, TX 75219-7629, USA

Hart, Leo (Athlete, Football Player)
1044 Arbor Trce NE
Brookhaven, GA 30319-5378

Hart, Linda (Actor)
c/o Staff Member *Gage Group, The (LA)*
5757 Wilshire Blvd Ste 659
Los Angeles, CA 90036-3682, USA

Hart, Marcy (Athlete, Golfer)
886 Meadowlands Dr
Winston Salem, NC 27107-6026, USA

Hart, Margie
228 S Hudson Ave
Los Angeles, CA 90004-1036

Hart, Mary (Television Host)
9440 Santa Monica Blvd Ste 407
Beverly Hills, CA 90210-4607, USA

Hart, Melissa Joan (Actor)
c/o Staff Member *Hartbreak Films*
14622 Ventura Blvd Ste 102 PMB 435
Sherman Oaks, CA 91403-3662, USA

Hart, Mickey (Music Group, Musician)
c/o Staff Member *The Agency Group (NYC)*
142 W 57th St Fl 6
New York, NY 10019-3300, USA

Hart, Mike (Athlete, Baseball Player)
409 Larkspur Ave
Portage, MI 49002-6243, USA

Hart, Mike (Athlete, Baseball Player)
16552 W Crescent Dr
New Berlin, WI 53151-6514, USA

Hart, Richard (Athlete, Football Player)
273 Oarlock Cir
East Syracuse, NY 13057-3123, USA

Hart, Roxanne
c/o Staff Member *Seven Summits Pictures & Management*
8906 W Olympic Blvd
Ground Floor
Beverly Hills, CA 90211-3550, USA

Hart, Terry J (Astronaut)
PO Box V
Hellertown, PA 18055-0218, USA

Hart, Terry J Dr (Astronaut)
PO Box V
Hellertown, PA 18055-0218, USA

Hart, Tommy (Athlete, Football Player)
3503 Highland Ave
Redwood City, CA 94062-3109, USA

Harte, Houston H (Publisher)
Harte-Hanks Communications
200 Concord Plaza Dr
San Antonio, TX 78216-6943, USA

Hartenstein, Chuck (Athlete, Baseball Player)
10735 Cassia Dr
Austin, TX 78759-6452, USA

Hartenstine, Michael A (Mike) (Athlete, Football Player)
322 Winchester Ct
Lake Bluff, IL 60044-1930, USA

Hartgraves, Dean (Athlete, Baseball Player)
125 E Vista Del Cerro Dr
Tempe, AZ 85281-6641, USA

Hartigan, Mark (Athlete, Hockey Player)
11462 Crow Hassan Park Rd
Hanover, MN 55341-9404, USA

Hartings, Jeff (Athlete, Football Player)
113 Westchester Dr
McKnight, PA 15237-1298, USA

Hartler, Vicky ((Congressman, Politician)
1023 Longworth Hob
Washington, DC 20515-3701, USA

Hartley, Bob (Athlete, Coach, Hockey Player)
13 South Ave SE
Atlanta, GA 30315, USA

Hartley, Frank (Athlete, Football Player)
4022 Fishermans Cove Ct
Lutz, FL 33558-9749, USA

Hartley, Hal (Director)
True Fiction Pictures
39 W 14th St Ste 406
New York, NY 10011-7404, USA

Hartley, Justin (Actor)
c/o Charlotte Burke *ID Public Relations (NY)*
150 W 30th St Fl 19
New York, NY 10001-4119, USA

Hartley, Ken (Athlete, Football Player)
4615 S Bridge Ave
Weslaco, TX 78596-1393, USA

Hartley, Mariette (Actor)
c/o Staff Member *J Michael Bloom*
9255 W Sunset Blvd Ste 710
West Hollywood, CA 90069-3304, USA

Hartley, Mike (Athlete, Baseball Player)
9485 Quail Canyon Rd
El Cajon, CA 92021-6709, USA

Hartley, Nina (Actor, Adult Film Star, Director, Model, Producer)
7095 Hollywood Blvd Ste 648
Los Angeles, CA 90028-8912, USA

Hartley, Ted
524 N Rockingham Ave
Los Angeles, CA 90049-2640

HartleyJ, Bob (Athlete, Hockey Player)
2713 Bonar Hall Path
Duluth, GA 30097-7463, USA

Hartline, Brian (Athlete, Football Player)
c/o Drew Rosenhaus *Rosenhaus Sports Representation*
6400 Allison Rd
Miami Beach, FL 33141-4540, USA

Hartline, Mary (Actor)
c/o Staff Member *Pierce & Shelly*
13775A Mono Way # 220
Sonora, CA 95370-8813, USA

Hartman, J C (Athlete, Baseball Player)
3425 Rosedale St
Houston, TX 77004-6312, USA

Hartman, Kevin (Soccer Player)
Los Angeles Galaxy
1010 Rose Bowl Dr
Pasadena, CA 91103, USA

Hartman, Mike (Athlete, Hockey Player)
PO Box 472405
Charlotte, NC 28247-2405, USA

Hartman, Rhonda (Race Car Driver)
5611 Highway
81 North
Williamston, SC 29697, USA

Hartman, Richard (Race Car Driver)
1340 Keone Cir
Williamston, SC 29697-9245, USA

Hartmann, Robert T (Government Official)
4129 Estate La Grande Princess # C
Christiansted, VI 00820-4280, USA

Hartmann, Thom (Radio Personality, Writer)
c/o Staff Member *Red Wheel / Weiser /Conari*
65 Parker St Ste 7
Newburyport, MA 01950-4600, USA

Hartnell, Scott (Athlete, Hockey Player)
111 Church St
Philadelphia, PA 19106-2209, USA

Hartnett, Josh (Actor)
c/o Suzan Bymel *Management 360*
9111 Wilshire Blvd
Beverly Hills, CA 90210-5508, USA

Harts, Greg (Athlete, Baseball Player)
829 Humphries St SW
Atlanta, GA 30310-2165, USA

Harts, Shaunard (Athlete, Football Player)
5304 Tamarindo Ln
Elk Grove, CA 95758-6821, USA

Hartsfield, Roy (Athlete, Baseball Player)
159 Preserve Pkwy
Ball Ground, GA 30107, USA

Hartshorn, Lawrence (Athlete, Football Player)
627 Langdale Dr
Fort Collins, CO 80526-3941, USA

Hartsock, Ben (Athlete, Football Player)
1274 Wheatley Forest Dr
Brentwood, TN 37027-8342, USA

Hartsock, Desiree (Reality Star)
c/o Staff Member *Next Entertainment*
10200 Riverside Dr Ste 200
Toluca Lake, CA 91602-2539, USA

Hartsock, Jeffrey (Jeff) (Athlete, Baseball Player)
1720 Swannanoa Dr
Greensboro, NC 27410-3932, USA

Hartung, James (Athlete, Gymnast, Olympic Athlete)
6425 Tanglewood Ln
Lincoln, NE 68516-2355, USA

Hartwell, Edgerton (Athlete, Football Player)
2427 Country Valley Ct
North Las Vegas, NV 89030-4702, USA

Hartwell, Erin (Athlete, Cycler, Olympic Athlete)
PO Box 917
Trexlertown, PA 18087-0917, USA

Hartwell, Lisa Wu (Reality Star)
c/o Staff Member *Bravo (NY)*
30 Rockefeller Plz
New York, NY 10112-0015, USA

Hartwig, Carter (Athlete, Football Player)
5539 Fm 762 RR
Richmond, TX 77469-8320, USA

Hartwig, Justin (Athlete, Football Player)
4009 Overland Dr
Lawrence, KS 66049-4122, USA

Hartzell, Paul (Athlete, Baseball Player)
PO Box 2860
Hailey, ID 83333-2860, USA

Hartzog, George B Jr (Government Official)
1643 Chain Bridge Rd
Mc Lean, VA 22101-4329, USA

Haruf, Kent (Writer)
Southern Illinois University
English Dept
Carbondale, IL 62901, USA

Harvey, Anthony (Director)
Arthur Greene
101 Park Ave # 4300
New York, NY 10178-0002, USA

Harvey, Antonio (Athlete, Basketball Player)
59E6 Yaupon Ave
Moss Point, MS 39563, USA

Harvey, Bryan (Athlete, Baseball Player)
152 Windemere Isle Rd
Statesville, NC 28677-2090, USA

Harvey, Claude (Athlete, Football Player)
2918 Dragonwick Dr
Houston, TX 77045-4708, USA

Harvey, David R (Business Person)
Sigme-Aldrich Corp
3050 Spruce St
Saint Louis, MO 63103-2530, USA

Harvey, Don
6310 San Vicente Blvd Ste 520
Los Angeles, CA 90048-5421

Harvey, Donnell (Basketball Player)
Orlando Magic
8701 Maitland Summit Blvd
Waterhouse Center
Orlando, FL 32810-5915, USA

Harvey, Doug (Athlete, Baseball Player)
32398 River Island Dr
Springville, CA 93265-9632, USA

Harvey, H Douglas (Doug) (Athlete, Baseball Player)
32398 River Island Dr
Springville, CA 93265-9632, USA

Harvey, James B (Athlete, Football Player)
3685 Clairice Cv
Memphis, TN 38133-0979, USA

Harvey, Jim (Athlete, Football Player)
3685 Clairice Cv
Memphis, TN 38133-0979, USA

Harvey, Ken (Athlete, Football Player)
19501 Mill Dam Pl
Leesburg, VA 20176-1638, USA

Harvey, Ken (Athlete, Baseball Player)
5012 Grand Ave Apt C
Kansas City, MO 64112-2761, USA

Harvey, Marvin (Athlete, Football Player)
901 Riggins Rd Apt 522
Tallahassee, FL 32308-2202, USA

Harvey, Maurice (Athlete, Football Player)
440 Baldwin Ave Apt 58
Rochester, MI 48307-2126, USA

Harvey, Nancy (Athlete, Golfer)
7006 E Jensen St Unit 62
Mesa, AZ 85207-2833, USA

Harvey, PJ (Musician)
c/o Staff Member *Island Records*
825 8th Ave Rm C2
New York, NY 10019-7472, USA

Harvey, Richard (Athlete, Football Player)
3414 Baltimore Ave
Pascagoula, MS 39581-4236, USA

Harvey, Steve (Actor, Comedian, Television Host)
8330 Jett Ferry Rd
Atlanta, GA 30350-4708, USA

Harvey, Terry (Baseball Player)
US Olympic Team
215 Annandale Dr
Cary, NC 27511-6503, USA

Harvick, Kevin (Race Car Driver)
PO Box 938
Oak Ridge, NC 27310-0938, USA

Harville, Chad (Athlete, Baseball Player)
261 Farmington Rd
Savannah, TN 38372-5635, USA

Harvin, Percy (Athlete, Football Player)
1929 Summit Ridge Rd
Fleming Island, FL 32003-4967, USA

Harwell, Steve (Actor, Music Group)
c/o Staff Member *Creative Artists Agency (CAA-LA)*
2000 Avenue of the Stars Ste 100
Los Angeles, CA 90067-4705, USA

Hasegawa, Shigetoshi (Athlete, Baseball Player)
29 Summer House
Irvine, CA 92603-0211, USA

Haselman, Bill (Athlete, Baseball Player)
14501 SE 85th St
Newcastle, WA 98059-9218, USA

Haselrig, Carlton (Athlete, Football Player)
386 William Penn Ave
Johnstown, PA 15901-1253, USA

Haseltine, Dan (Music Group)
Flood Bumstead McCarthy
1700 Hayes St Ste 304
Nashville, TN 37203-3593, USA

Hasen, Irvin H (Cartoonist)
68 E 79th St Apt E
New York, NY 10075-0224, USA

Hasen, Irwin (Cartoonist)
68 E 9th St Apt E
New York, NY 10003, USA

Hasenmayer, Don (Athlete, Baseball Player)
721 Golf Dr
Warrington, PA 18976-2053, USA

Hasham, Josephine (Athlete, Baseball Player, Commentator)
575 SW 11th St
Miami, FL 33129-1034, USA

Hashimoto, Ryutaro (Politician)
Prime Ministers Office 6-1 Nagata-cho 1 chome Chiyoda-Ku
Birmingham, AL 35214, USA

Hashu, Nick (Athlete, Basketball Player)
1132 S Dover Cir
Anaheim, CA 92805-5944, USA

Haskell, Colleen Marie (Actor)
c/o Andy Cohen *Gersh (LA)*
9465 Wilshire Blvd Ste 600
Beverly Hills, CA 90212-2605, USA

Haskin, Scott (Athlete, Basketball Player)
3924 Wellington Pl
West Linn, OR 97068-3668, USA

Haskins, Clem (Athlete, Basketball Player, Coach)
2632 Roberts Rd
Campbellsville, KY 42718, USA

Haskins, Dennis (Actor)
c/o Arlene Thornton *Arlene Thornton & Associates*
12711 Ventura Blvd Ste 490
Studio City, CA 91604-2477, USA

Haskins, Jon (Athlete, Football Player)
4055 Higel Ave
Sarasota, FL 34242-1138, USA

Haslam, Bill (Governor, Politician)
State Capitol
Nashville, TN 37243-0001, USA

Haslem, Udonis (Athlete, Basketball Player)
1331 Brickell Bay Dr Apt 3311
Miami, FL 33131-3685, USA

Haslett, James D (Jim) (Athlete, Coach, Football Coach, Football Player)
43367 La Belle Pl
Ashburn, VA 20147-5250, USA

Hass, Robert (Writer)
University of California
English Dept
Berkeley, CA 94720-0001, USA

Hassan, Ahmed (Television Host)
3355 Colina Ct
Cameron Park, CA 95682-8138, USA

Hassan, Fred (Business Person)
Schering-Plough Corp
1 Giralda Farms
Madison, NJ 07940-1027, USA

Hassan, Maggie (Governor, Politician)
Office of the Governor
107 N Main St Rm 208
State House
Concord, NH 03301-4990, USA

Hassel, Trenton (Athlete, Baseball Player)
4776 Mickle Ln
Clarksville, TN 37043-8263, U S A

Hasselbach, Harald (Athlete, Football Player)
17919 E Dorado Dr
Centennial, CO 80015-5916, USA

Hasselbeck, Donald W (Don) (Athlete, Football Player)
38 Noon Hill Ave
Norfolk, MA 02056-1145, USA

Hasselbeck, Elisabeth (Reality Star, Television Host)
62 Brookridge Dr
Greenwich, CT 06830-4830, USA

Hasselbeck, Matt (Athlete, Football Player)
130 W 73rd St
Indianapolis, IN 46260-4215, USA

Hasselbeck, Tim (Athlete, Football Player)
38 Noon Hill Ave
Norfolk, MA 02056-1145, USA

Hasselhoff, David (Actor, Musician)
5183 Parkway Calabasas
Calabasas, CA 91302-1481, USA

Hasselhoff, Hayley (Actor, Model)
c/o Liza Anderson *Anderson Group Public Relations*
8060 Melrose Ave Fl 4
Los Angeles, CA 90046-7038, USA

Hassenfeld, Alan G (Business Person)
Hasbro Inc
1027 Newport Ave
Pawtucket, RI 02861-2500, USA

Hassett, Joe (Athlete, Basketball Player)
28 Marigold Cir
North Providence, RI 02904-3891, USA

Hassett, Marilyn (Actor)
8905 Rosewood Ave
West Hollywood, CA 90048-2409, USA

Hassey, Ron (Athlete, Baseball Player)
4751 Main St Attn Ofc
Jupiter, FL 33458-5203, USA

Hassler, Andy (Athlete, Baseball Player)
PO Box 15932
Phoenix, AZ 85060-5932, USA

Hasson, Madelaine (Maddie) (Actor)
c/o Richard Beddingfield *Beddingfield Company, The*
13600 Ventura Blvd Ste B
Sherman Oaks, CA 91423-5050, USA

Hastert, J Dennis (Politician)
PO Box 153
Plano, IL 60545-0153, USA

Hastings, Andre (Athlete, Football Player)
700 N Dobson Rd Unit 37
Chandler, AZ 85224-6940, USA

Hastings, Doc (Congressman, Politician)
1203 Longworth Hob
Washington, DC 20515-3505, USA

Hastings, Don (Actor)
524 W 57th St # 5330
New York, NY 10019-2930, USA

Hastings, Scott (Athlete, Basketball Player)
10210 Ridgegate Cir
Lone Tree, CO 80124-9513, USA

Haston, Kirk (Athlete, Basketball Player)
2600 S Main St
Lobelville, TN 37097, USA

Hasty, James (Athlete, Football Player)
8212 127th Ave SE
Newcastle, WA 98056-9146, USA

Hatalsky, Morris (Athlete, Golfer)
201 S Ocean Grande Dr PH 5
Ponte Vedra Beach, FL 32082-6514, USA

Hatch, Annia (Athlete, Gymnast, Olympic Athlete)
1800 Sans Souci Blvd Apt 239
North Miami, FL 33181-3069, USA

Hatch, Orrin (Politician)
2127 Galloping Way
Vienna, VA 22181-2934, USA

Hatch, Orrin (Senator)
104 Hart Office Building
Washington, DC 20510-0001, USA

Hatch, Richard (Actor, Reality Star)
c/o Michael Kaliski *Omniquest Entertainment (LA)*
1416 N La Brea Ave
Los Angeles, CA 90028-7506, USA

Hatchell, Sylvia (Basketball Player)
University of North Carolina
Athletic Dept
Chapel Hill, NC 27515, USA

Hatcher, Billy (Athlete, Baseball Player)
100 Joe Nuxhall Way
Cincinnati, OH 45202-4109, USA

Hatcher, Chris (Athlete, Baseball Player)
1406 250th St
Audubon, IA 50025-7356, USA

Hatcher, Derian (Athlete, Hockey Player)
3601 S Broad St Ste 2
Attn Coaching Staff
Philadelphia, PA 19148-5250, USA

Hatcher, Derian (Athlete, Hockey Player, Olympic Athlete)
567 Chews Landing Rd
Haddonfield, NJ 08033-3843, USA

Hatcher, Jason (Athlete, Football Player)
c/o Jordan Woy *Willis and Woy Management*
3030 Olive St Ste 520
Dallas, TX 75219-7629, USA

Hatcher, Kevin (Athlete, Hockey Player, Olympic Athlete)
1225 S Water St
Marine City, MI 48039-3600, USA

Hatcher, Mickey (Athlete, Baseball Player)
2000 E Gene Autry Way
Attn Coaching Staff
Anaheim, CA 92806-6143, USA

Hatcher, R Dale (Athlete, Football Player)
906 White Plains Rd
Gaffney, SC 29340-5473, USA

Hatcher, Teri (Actor)
c/o Jeremy Barber *United Talent Agency (UTA-LA)*
9336 Civic Center Dr
Beverly Hills, CA 90210-3604, USA

Hatchett, Derrick (Athlete, Football Player)
7811 Westshire Dr
San Antonio, TX 78227-2760, USA

Hatchett, Judge Glenda (Judge, Reality Star)
c/o Elizabeth Much *Much and House Public Relations*
8075 W 3rd St Ste 500
Los Angeles, CA 90048-4325, USA

Hatchette, Matthew (Athlete, Football Player)
3222 Winding Pine Trl
Longwood, FL 32779-3170, USA

Hatfield, Juliana (Musician, Songwriter)
c/o Staff Member *Concerted Efforts*
PO Box 440326
Somerville, MA 02144-0004, USA

Hathaway, Amy
c/o Beverly Strong *Strong Management*
9350 Wilshire Blvd Ste 224
Beverly Hills, CA 90212-3204, USA

Hathaway, Anne (Actor)
c/o Suzan Bymel *Management 360*
9111 Wilshire Blvd
Beverly Hills, CA 90210-5508, USA

Hathaway, Hilly (Athlete, Baseball Player)
13341 Low Tide Way
Jacksonville, FL 32258-5207, USA

Hathaway, Noah (Actor)
5150 Choppers & Hot Rods
228 Grand Ave
Perryville, MO 63775-1806, USA

Hathaway, Ray (Athlete, Baseball Player)
25 Leisure Mountain Rd
Asheville, NC 28804-1147, USA

Hathcock, Dave (Athlete, Football Player)
417 Rolling Mill Rd
Old Hickory, TN 37138-2137, USA

Hatori, Miho (Music Group)
Billions Corp
833 W Chicago Ave Ste 101
Chicago, IL 60642-8408, USA

Hatosy, Shawn (Actor)
c/o Staff Member *Mary Erickson Management*
2126 N Commonwealth Ave
Los Angeles, CA 90027-2118, USA

Hatteberg, Scott (Athlete, Baseball Player)
802 Berg Ct NW
Gig Harbor, WA 98335-7709, USA

Hatten, Tom (Actor)
1759 Sunset Plaza Dr
Los Angeles, CA 90069-1311, USA

Hatton, Ricky (Athlete, Boxer)
Banner Promotions
PO Box 32368
Philadelphia, PA 19146-0868, USA

Hatton, Vernon (Vern) (Athlete, Basketball Player)
1208 Kannapolis Pl
Lexington, KY 40513-1243, USA

Hattori, Shige (Race Car Driver)
4377 Triple Crown Dr
Concord, NC 28027, USA

Hattori, Shigeaki (Race Car Driver)
Bettenhausen Motorsports
57 Gasoline Aly Ste A
Indianapolis, IN 46222-5932, USA

Hauck, Frederick H (Rick) (Astronaut)
2 Redwood Ln
Falmouth, ME 04105-1368, USA

Hauck, Frederick H ""Rick"" Captain (Astronaut)
2 Redwood Ln
Falmouth, ME 04105-1368, USA

Hauck, Tim (Athlete, Football Player)
460 Great Circle Rd
Nashville, TN 37228-1404, USA

Haudenschild, Jack (Race Car Driver)
Wildchild Designs
628 Maple St
Vermilion, OH 44089, USA

Hauer, Brett (Athlete, Hockey Player)
2921 Branch St
Duluth, MN 55812-2340, USA

Hauer, Rutger (Actor)
c/o Joan Hyler *Hyler Management*
20 Ocean Park Blvd Unit 25
Santa Monica, CA 90405-3590, USA

Hauerwas, Stanley (Religious Leader)
Duke University
Divinity School
Durham, NC 27706, USA

Haughey, Chris (Athlete, Baseball Player)
4117 Stevenson Blvd Apt 283
Fremont, CA 94538-5001, USA

Haught, Gary (Athlete, Baseball Player)
16445 Lynn St
Choctaw, OK 73020-7926, USA

Haughton, Tom
6011 NW 69th Mnr
Parkland, FL 33067-4507, USA

Haun, Darla (Actor)
300 S Raymond Ave Ste 11
Pasadena, CA 91105-2639

Haun, Lindsey (Actor)
c/o Staff Member *Margie Weiner Management*
8205 Santa Monica Blvd Ste 1450
West Hollywood, CA 90046-5967, USA

Hauser, Art (Athlete, Football Player)
2816 Walsh Rd
Cincinnati, OH 45208-3426, USA

Hauser, Cole (Actor)
c/o Michael Gruber *After Dark Management Group*
Prefers to be contacted via telephone
West Hollywood, CA 90069, USA

Hauser, Wings (Actor)
9450 Chivers Ave
Sun Valley, CA 91352-2654, USA

Hausman, Tom (Athlete, Baseball Player)
3165 Westfield Cir
Las Vegas, NV 89121-3332, USA

Hauss, Lenard M (Len) (Athlete, Football Player)
110 Portmere Dr
Jesup, GA 31546-4738, USA

Havelid, Niclas (Athlete, Hockey Player)
Prestige Hocey Group
PO Box 129
Point Roberts, WA 98281-0129, USA

Haven, Annette (Actor)
PO Box 1244
Sausalito, CA 94966-1244

Haven, James (Actor)
c/o Staff Member *Saffron Management*
9171 Wilshire Blvd Ste 441
Beverly Hills, CA 90210-5516, USA

Havens, Brad (Athlete, Baseball Player)
3227 Eden Trl
Brighton, MI 48114-9185, USA

Havens, Frank B (Athlete)
PO Box 55
Harborton, VA 23389-0055, USA

Haverdink, Kevin (Athlete, Football Player)
15844 Prairie Ronde Rd
Schoolcraft, MI 49087-9124, USA

Havers, Nigel (Actor)
c/o John Crosby *John Crosby Management*
1357 N Spaulding Ave
Los Angeles, CA 90046-4009, USA

Havig, Dennis (Athlete, Football Player)
5964 Old Stilesboro Rd NW
Acworth, GA 30101-4304, USA

Havin, Alexa (Actor)
c/o Staff Member *Mattie Management*
1438 N Gower St Ste 57
Los Angeles, CA 90028-8358, USA

Havins, Alexa (Actor)
c/o Noreen Konkle *AKA Talent Agency*
6310 San Vicente Blvd Ste 200
Los Angeles, CA 90048-5488, USA

Havlicek, John (Athlete, Basketball Player)
24 Beech Rd
Weston, MA 02493-1915, USA

Havlish, Jean (Athlete, Baseball Player, Commentator)
PO Box 122
Rockville, MN 56369-0122, USA

Havok, Davey (Musician)
5842 Mendocino Ave
Oakland, CA 94618-1809, USA

Havrilak, Sam (Athlete, Football Player)
1 Trojan Horse Dr
Phoenix, MD 21131-1345, USA

Havrilla, Jo Ann
9751 Old Route 99
Mc Kean, PA 16426

Hawblitzel, Ryan (Athlete, Baseball Player)
9875 Trumpet Vine Loop
New Port Richey, FL 34655-5367, USA

Hawes, Roy (Athlete, Baseball Player)
PO Box 854
Ringgold, GA 30736-0854, USA

Hawes, Steve (Athlete, Basketball Player)
400 W Highland Dr
Seattle, WA 98119-3532, USA

Hawk, Abigail (Actor)
c/o Rosella Olson *Rosella Olson Management*
319 W 105th St Apt 1F
New York, NY 10025-9112, USA

Hawk, AJ (Athlete, Football Player)
8130 Harriott Rd
Dublin, OH 43017-7402, USA

Hawk, Tony (Actor, Athlete, Skateboarder)
Tony Hawk Inc
1611A S Melrose Dr # 362
Vista, CA 92081-5471, USA

Hawke, Ethan (Actor)
247 Dean St
Brooklyn, NY 11217-2202, USA

Hawke, Jason (Adult Film Star)
c/o Staff Member *Diva Central Inc*
7510 W Sunset Blvd Ste 1445
Los Angeles, CA 90046-3408, USA

Hawker, Kari (Actor)
c/o Staff Member *Talent Management Group, Inc.*
512 E 4500 S Ste 200
Salt Lake City, UT 84107-2952, USA

Hawkes, John (Actor)
c/o JB Roberts *Thruline Entertainment*
9250 Wilshire Blvd Ste 100
Ground Floor
Beverly Hills, CA 90212-3343, USA

Hawking, Lucy (Writer)
c/o Staff Member *Simon & Schuster*
1230 Avenue of the Americas Fl CONC1
New York, NY 10020-1586, USA

Hawkins, Alex (Athlete, Football Player)
215 Bonanza Rd
Denmark, SC 29042-9311, USA

Hawkins, Andy (Athlete, Baseball Player)
PO Box 90111
Arlington, TX 76004-3111, USA

Hawkins, Artrell (Athlete, Football Player)
12166 Peak Dr
Cincinnati, OH 45246-1400, USA

Hawkins, Barbara (Music Group)
Superstars Unlimited
PO Box 371371
Las Vegas, NV 89137-1371, USA

Hawkins, Benjamin C (Ben) (Athlete, Football Player)
606 11th Ave
Belmar, NJ 07719-2412, USA

Hawkins, Bill (Athlete, Football Player)
4996 SE Manatee Cove Rd
Stuart, FL 34997-1701, USA

Hawkins, Brad
47 Music Sq E
Nashville, TN 37203-4324

Hawkins, Chauncey (Loon) (Musician)
c/o Mike Esterman *Esterman.Com, LLC*
Prefers to be contacted via email
Baltimore, MD XXXXX, USA

Hawkins, Connie (Athlete, Basketball Player)
2994 E Pony Ct
Gilbert, AZ 85295-3775, USA

Hawkins, Courtney (Athlete, Football Player)
8305 Gale Rd
Goodrich, MI 48438-9436, USA

Hawkins, Edwin (Music Group)
PAZ Entertainment
2041 Locust St
Philadelphia, PA 19103-5613, USA

Hawkins, Frank (Athlete, Football Player)
2300 Alta Dr
Las Vegas, NV 89107-4616, USA

Hawkins, Hersey (Athlete, Basketball Player, Olympic Athlete)
2687 Beacon Hill Dr
West Linn, OR 97068-5614, USA

Hawkins, Laroyce (Actor)
c/o Staff Member *Stewart Talent Agency*
58 W Huron St
Chicago, IL 60654-3806, USA

Hawkins, Latroy (Athlete, Baseball Player)
3521 Amberwood Ln
Prosper, TX 75078-9126, USA

Hawkins, Mike (Athlete, Football Player)
2320 Bordeaux Dr
Bay City, TX 77414-8512, USA

Hawkins, Rip (Athlete, Football Player)
100 Tower Carlile Rd
Devils Tower, WY 82714, USA

Hawkins, Rosa (Music Group)
Superstars Unlimited
PO Box 371371
Las Vegas, NV 89137-1371, USA

Hawkins, Rowena
PO Box 15277
Chattanooga, TN 37415-0277

Hawkins, Sally (Actor)
c/o Staff Member *Block-Korenbrot Public Relations*
6100 Wilshire Blvd Ste 170
Los Angeles, CA 90048-5109, USA

Hawkins, Sophie B (Music Group, Musician, Songwriter, Writer)
Trumpet Swan Productions
520 Washington Blvd # 337
Marina Del Rey, CA 90292, USA

Hawkins, Thomas (Tommy) (Athlete, Basketball Player)
1745 Manzanita Park Ave
Malibu, CA 90265-3013, USA

Hawkins, Todd (Athlete, Hockey Player)
300 Lamoreaux Dr
Elk Rapids, MI 49629-9737, USA

Hawkins, Wayne (Athlete, Football Player)
1 Dogwood Ct
San Ramon, CA 94583-3908, USA

Hawkins, Wynn (Athlete, Baseball Player)
5326 Cottage Dr
Cortland, OH 44410-9521, USA

Hawksworth, Blake (Athlete, Baseball Player)
23 Alcott St
Ladera Ranch, CA 92694-1239, USA

Hawley, Frank (Race Car Driver)
Frank Hawley Drag Racing School
County Road 225
Gainesville, FL 32609, USA

Hawley, Joe (Athlete, Football Player)
c/o Harold C Lewis *National Sports Agency*
15400 Timpaige Dr
Chesterfield, MO 63017-1762, USA

Hawley, Sandy (Jockey)
9625 Merrill Rd
Silverwood, MI 48760-9532, USA

Hawley, Steven (Astronaut)
University of Kansas
3303 Calvin Dr
Lawrence, KS 66049-9003, USA

Hawn, Goldie (Actor, Director, Producer)
1417 Capri Dr
Pacific Palisades, CA 90272-2706, USA

Hawpe, Brad (Athlete, Baseball Player)
2001 Blake St
Denver, CO 80205-2060, USA

Hawthorne, Duane (Athlete, Football Player)
11481 Pineview Crossing Dr
Maryland Heights, MO 63043-5103, USA

Hawthorne, Greg (Athlete, Football Player)
1515 Blair St
Waco, TX 76707-3025, USA

Hax, Carolyn (Writer)
Washington Post
Editorial Dept
1150 15th St NW
Washington, DC 20071-0001, USA

Hay, Jim (Athlete, Hockey Player)
2024 NE 76th Ave
Portland, OR 97213-6020, USA

Hay, Louise L (Writer)
Hay House
PO Box 5100
Carlsbad, CA 92018-5100, USA

Hayashi, Henry
5127 Klump Ave
North Hollywood, CA 91601-3775

Hayashida, Erica (Athlete, Golfer)
1470 NW 107th Ave Ste R
Doral, FL 33172-2735, USA

Haydel, Hal (Athlete, Baseball Player)
304 Lynwood Dr
Houma, LA 70360-6228, USA

Hayden, Aaron (Athlete, Football Player)
504 Stone Oaks Cv
Collierville, TN 38017-9124, USA

Hayden, Gene (Athlete, Baseball Player)
424 W Locust St
Lodi, CA 95240-2018, USA

Hayden, Jim (Publisher)
Philadelphia Inquirer
400 N Broad St
Philadelphia, PA 19130-4099, USA

Hayden, J Michael (Mike) (Ex-Governor, Government Official)
Office Of The Secretary
1020 S Kansas Ave Rm 200
Kansas Dept. of Wildlife & Parks
Topeka, KS 66612-1326, USA

Hayden, John (Race Car Driver)
Hayden Enterprises
107 Flat Ridge Rd
Goodlettsville, TN 37072-8509, USA

Hayden, Leo (Athlete, Football Player)
33 Preston Rd
Columbus, OH 43209-1652, USA

Hayden, Michael (Actor)
H W A Talent
3500 W Olive Ave Ste 1400
Burbank, CA 91505-5512, USA

Hayden, Michael (Politician)
5809 Sagamore Ct
Lawrence, KS 66047-2071, USA

Hayden, Neil Steven (Publisher)
1755 York Ave Apt 19A
New York, NY 10128-6870, USA

Hayden, Nick (Athlete, Football Player)
c/o Brad Leshnock *BTI Sports Advisors*
170 N Scoville Ave
Oak Park, IL 60302-2647, USA

Hayden, Tom (Politician)
152 Wadsworth Ave
Santa Monica, CA 90405-3510, USA

Hayek, Julie
5645 Burning Tree Dr
La Canada Flintridge, CA 91011-2861

Hayek, Peter (Athlete, Hockey Player)
5644 Upton Ave S
Minneapolis, MN 55410-2623, USA

Hayek, Salma (Actor, Model, Producer)
c/o Evelyn O'Neill *Management 360*
9111 Wilshire Blvd
Beverly Hills, CA 90210-5508, USA

Hayes, Amy (Model, Sportscaster)
641 N Hardin Hts
Harrodsburg, KY 40330-9234, USA

Hayes, Ben (Athlete, Baseball Player)
3501 10th St NE
Saint Petersburg, FL 33704-1605, USA

Hayes, Bill (Actor)
4528 Beck Ave
North Hollywood, CA 91602-1904, USA

Hayes, Bill (Athlete, Baseball Player)
24 Willie Mays Plz
San Francisco, CA 94107-2134, USA

Hayes, Billie (Athlete, Football Player)
2876 Avalon St
Riverside, CA 92509-2013, USA

Hayes, Charlie (Athlete, Baseball Player)
22503 Holly Creek Trl
Tomball, TX 77377-3656, USA

Hayes, Chris (Race Car Driver)
R&H Motorsports
10134 6th St Ste G
Rancho Cucamonga, CA 91730-5856, USA

Hayes, Elvin (Athlete, Basketball Player)
PO Box 3688
Santa Clara, CA 95055-3688, USA

Hayes, Erinn (Actor)
4940 Aldama St
Los Angeles, CA 90042-3113, USA

Hayes, Gemma (Musician)
c/o Staff Member *Paradigm (Monterey)*
404 W Franklin St
Monterey, CA 93940-2303, USA

Hayes, Gerald (Athlete, Football Player)
3841 E Windsong Dr
Phoenix, AZ 85048-7916, USA

Hayes, Hunter (Musician)
c/o Rodney Essig *Creative Artists Agency (CAA-TN)*
401 Commerce St PH
Nashville, TN 37219-2516, USA

Hayes, Jarvis (Basketball Player)
Washington Wizards
MCI Center 601 F St NW
Atlanta, DC 30326, USA

Hayes, Jim (Athlete, Basketball Player)
31 Curley St
Long Beach, NY 11561-2705, USA

Hayes, John
1117 Robin Ln
Allentown, NJ 08501, USA

Hayes, Jonathan (Athlete, Football Player)
1231 Obannon Creek Ln
Loveland, OH 45140-6027, USA

Hayes, J P (Athlete, Golfer)
740 Camino Real Ave
El Paso, TX 79922-2010, USA

Hayes, Larry (Athlete, Football Player)
6128 Stonehaven Dr
Nashville, TN 37215-5624, USA

Hayes, Louis S (Music Group, Musician)
PO Box 482
Desoto, TX 75123-0482, USA

Hayes, Mark (Athlete, Golfer)
1014 Saint Andrews Dr
Edmond, OK 73025-2645, USA

Hayes, Mercury (Athlete, Football Player)
138 W Whitney St
Houston, TX 77018-4515, USA

Hayes, Patty (Athlete, Golfer)
3436 Sipsey St
The Villages, FL 32162-6666, USA

Hayes, Ray (Athlete, Football Player)
5000 Laur Rd
North Branch, MI 48461-9782, USA

Hayes, Reggie (Actor)
c/o Staff Member *TalentWorks (LA)*
3500 W Olive Ave Ste 1400
Burbank, CA 91505-5512, USA

Hayes, Rudy (Athlete, Football Player)
354 Red Hill Rd
Pickens, SC 29671-9188, USA

Hayes, Sean (Actor)
4024 Radford Ave
Studio City, CA 91604-2101, USA

Hayes, Steve (Athlete, Basketball Player)
2219 N Imperial Path Ln
Spring, TX 77386-2959, USA

Hayes, Von (Athlete, Baseball Player)
1520 Gulf Blvd Apt 1405
Clearwater Beach, FL 33767-3901, USA

Hayes, Wade (Music Group)
Trey Turner Assoc
40 Music Sq W
Nashville, TN 37203-3206, USA

Hayes, Wendell (Athlete, Football Player)
1935 E 30th St Apt 23
Oakland, CA 94606-3485, USA

Haygood, Herb (Athlete, Football Player)
1735 Central Ave
Sarasota, FL 34234-8410, USA

Hayhoe, Bill (Athlete, Football Player)
6025 Axis Dr
Sparks, NV 89436-7146, USA

Hayhurst, Dirk (Athlete, Baseball Player)
64 Division St
Hudson, OH 44236-3050, USA

Haylett, Alice (Athlete, Baseball Player)
243 Pearl Ave
Lakeland, FL 33815-3737, USA

Hayman, Conway (Athlete, Football Player)
6811 Stiller Dr
Missouri City, TX 77489-3419, USA

Hayman, Fred (Designer, Fashion Designer)
6946 Wildlife Rd
Malibu, CA 90265-4309, USA

Hayman, James (Director)
c/o Staff Member *Creative Artists Agency (CAA-LA)*
2000 Avenue of the Stars Ste 100
Los Angeles, CA 90067-4705, USA

Haymond, Alvin (Athlete, Football Player)
2857 Mantis Dr
San Jose, CA 95148-2136, USA

Haynes, Abner (Athlete, Football Player)
1950 FM 489
Oakwood, TX 75855-8409, USA

Haynes, Betsy (Writer)
5973 Sandhill Cir
The Colony, TX 75056-3678, USA

Haynes, Colton (Actor)
c/o Eric Podwall *Podwall Entertainment*
710 N Orlando Ave Apt 203
Loft 203
West Hollywood, CA 90069-5549, USA

Haynes, Haynes
7200 Sanderling Ct
Carlsbad, CA 92011-5173

Haynes, Heath (Athlete, Baseball Player)
3540 Regal Dr
Lake Havasu City, AZ 86404-2227, USA

Haynes, Jimmy (Athlete, Baseball Player)
516 Riverside Dr
Lagrange, GA 30240-9633, USA

Haynes, Mark (Athlete, Football Player)
220 S Oneida St
Denver, CO 80230-6951, USA

Haynes, Marques (Athlete, Baseball Player)
1300 County Road 4627
Winnsboro, TX 75494-7340, U S A

Haynes, Michael (Athlete, Football Player)
1580 Arbour Glenn Dr
Lawrenceville, GA 30043-7154, USA

Haynes, Michael (Athlete, Football Player)
2375 Saddlesprings Dr
Alpharetta, GA 30004-3254, USA

Haynes, Mike (Athlete, Football Player)
8 Morningside Ln
Westport, CT 06880-3815, USA

Haynes, Mike (Athlete, Football Player)
8141 Santaluz Village Grn S # N
San Diego, CA 92127-2518, USA

Haynes, Nathan (Athlete, Baseball Player)
609 N Ventura St Apt 4
Anaheim, CA 92801-3740, USA

Haynes, Reggie (Athlete, Football Player)
2324 Antiqua Ct
Reston, VA 20191-1706, USA

Haynes, Roy O (Musician)
Ted Kurland
173 Brighton Ave
Allston, MA 02134-2003, USA

Haynes, Todd (Director)
c/o Staff Member *Creative Artists Agency (CAA-LA)*
2000 Avenue of the Stars Ste 100
Los Angeles, CA 90067-4705, USA

Haynes, Verron (Athlete, Football Player)
2500 Northwinds Pkwy Ste 275
Alpharetta, GA 30009-2265, USA

Haynes, Warren (Musician)
c/o Staff Member *Paradigm (Monterey)*
404 W Franklin St
Monterey, CA 93940-2303, USA

Haynes Jr, Cornell (Nelly) (Musician)
c/o Dana Sims *ICM Partners (LA)*
10250 Constellation Blvd Fl 7
Los Angeles, CA 90067-6207, USA

Haynesworth, Albert (Athlete, Football Player)
c/o Chad Speck *Allegiant Athletic Agency*
35 Market Sq Ste 201
Knoxville, TN 37902-1420, USA

Haynie, Jim (Actor)
10100 Santa Monica Blvd Ste 2500
Los Angeles, CA 90067-4116

Haynie, Sandra (Athlete, Golfer)
6 Brookfield Ct
Roanoke, TX 76262-5468, USA

Hays, Harold (Athlete, Football Player)
10410 Ravenswood Rd
Granbury, TX 76049-4543, USA

Hays, Kathryn (Actor)
c/o Staff Member *As The World Turns*
1268 E 14th St
Jc Studios
Brooklyn, NY 11230-5241, USA

Hays, Robert (Actor)
919 Victoria Ave
Venice, CA 90291-3933, USA

Hays, Thomas C (Business Person)
Fortune Brands Inc
300 Tower Pkwy
Lincolnshire, IL 60069-3640, USA

Haysbert, Dennis (Actor)
30400 Morning View Dr
Malibu, CA 90265-3621, USA

Hayter, David (Writer)
c/o Staff Member *Kaplan/Perrone Entertainment*
280 S Beverly Dr Ste 513
Beverly Hills, CA 90212-3908, USA

Hayward, Brian (Athlete, Hockey Player)
2695 E Katella Ave
Attn Broadcast Dept
Anaheim, CA 92806-5904, USA

Hayward, Brian (Athlete, Hockey Player)
7648 E Hollow Oak Rd
Anaheim, CA 92808-1425, USA

Hayward, Brooke
60 E 42nd St Ste 956
New York, NY 10165-0918

Hayward, Casey (Athlete, Football Player)
c/o Scott Smith *XAM Sports*
PO Box 1725
Madison, WI 53701-1725, USA

Hayward, Charles E (Publisher)
Little Brown Co
Time-Life Building
Rockefeller Center
New York, NY 10020, USA

Hayward, Gordon (Athlete, Baseball Player)
76 Brandywine Ct
Brownsburg, IN 46112-1076, U S A

Hayward, Hurley (Race Car Driver)
1445 Ponte Vedra Blvd
Ponte Vedra Beach, FL 32082-4505, USA

Hayward, Kara (Actor)
c/o Christine Tripicchio *Shelter PR*
9350 Wilshire Blvd Ste 450
Beverly Hills, CA 90212-3230, USA

Hayward, Lazar (Athlete, Basketball Player)
c/o Sam Goldfelder *Excel Sports Management (LA)*
9665 Wilshire Blvd Ste 500
Beverly Hills, CA 90212-2312, USA

Hayward, Ray (Athlete, Baseball Player)
5809 112th St
Lubbock, TX 79424-3891, USA

Hayward, Reggie (Athlete, Football Player)
4651 Swilcan Bridge Ln S
Jacksonville, FL 32224-5621, USA

Haywood, Alfred (Athlete, Football Player)
69 Waters Edge Way
Fayetteville, GA 30215-8509, USA

Haywood, Bill (Athlete, Baseball Player)
867 Villa Dr
North Myrtle Beach, SC 29582-2575, USA

Haywood, Spencer (Athlete, Basketball Player, Olympic Athlete)
49447 Plymouth Way
Plymouth, MI 48170-6439, USA

Hayworth, Nan (Congressman, Politician)
1440 Longworth Hob
Washington, DC 20515-0307, USA

Hayworth, Tracy (Athlete, Football Player)
155 Knights Church Rd
Decherd, TN 37324-3279, USA

Hazanavicius, Michael (Director)
c/o Maha Dakhil *Creative Artists Agency (CAA-LA)*
2000 Avenue of the Stars Ste 100
Los Angeles, CA 90067-4705, USA

Haze, Jonathan (Actor)
3636 Woodhill Canyon Rd
Studio City, CA 91604-3658, USA

Hazelton, Major (Athlete, Football Player)
6803 S Crandon Ave
Chicago, IL 60649-1210, USA

Hazen, Maya (Actor)
c/o Adam Griffin *Kritzer Levine Wilkins Entertainment (KLWG)*
11872 La Grange Ave Fl 1
Los Angeles, CA 90025-5283, USA

Hazewood, Drungo (Athlete, Baseball Player)
7991 Westboro Way
Sacramento, CA 95823-4934, USA

Hazzard, Johnny (Adult Film Star)
c/o Staff Member *Diva Central Inc*
7510 W Sunset Blvd Ste 1445
Los Angeles, CA 90046-3408, USA

Hazzard, Shirley (Writer)
200 E 66th St
New York, NY 10065-9175, USA

H. Bishop, Timothy (Congressman, Politician)
306 Cannon Hob
Washington, DC 20515-0303, USA

Head, Don (Athlete, Hockey Player)
15240 NE Knott St
Portland, OR 97230-5280, USA

Head, John (Baseball Player)
Kansas City Monarchs
12677 Tremblewood Dr
Florissant, MO 63033-4729, USA

Head, Roy (Musician)
Texas Sounds Entertainment
2317 Pecan St
Dickinson, TX 77539-4949, USA

Headden, Susan M (Journalist)
Indianapolis Star
130 S Meridian St
Editorial Dept
Indianapolis, IN 46225-1046, USA

Head East (Music Group)
c/o John Domagall *ARM Entertainment*
1257 Arcade St
Saint Paul, MN 55106-2022, USA

Headen, Andy (Athlete, Football Player)
PO Box 821
Liberty, NC 27298-0821, USA

Headey, Lena (Actor)
9255 W Sunset Blvd Ste 600
West Hollywood, CA 90069-3306, USA

Headley, Chase (Athlete, Baseball Player)
1128 Re2ALITV Wav
Knoxville, TN 37923, USA

Headley, Glenne
8942 Wilshire Blvd
Beverly Hills, CA 90211-1908

Headley, Heather (Actor, Musician)
40 W 56th St Apt 5F
New York, NY 10019-3813, USA

Headley, Shari
11226 178th St
Jamaica, NY 11433-4118

Headon, Topper (Musician)
c/o Staff Member *Premier Talent*
3 E 54th St # 1100
New York, NY 10022-3108, USA

Heafner, Vance (Athlete, Golfer)
4513 Edwards Mill Rd Apt A
Raleigh, NC 27612-3779, USA

Heald, Anthony (Actor)
Endeavor Talent Agency
9701 Wilshire Blvd Ste 1000
Beverly Hills, CA 90212-2010, USA

Healey, James
415 S Spalding Dr Unit 306
Beverly Hills, CA 90212-4160

Healy, Chip (Football Player)
1903 Lathan Ct
Nashville, TN 37207-4812, USA

Healy, Don (Athlete, Football Player)
3427 Boca Ciega Dr
Naples, FL 34112-6809, USA

Healy, Fran (Athlete, Baseball Player)
1 Primrose Ln
Holyoke, MA 01040-1523, USA

Healy, Jane E (Journalist)
Orlando Sentinel
633 N Orange Ave Lbby
Editrial Dept
Orlando, FL 32801-1349, USA

Healy, Matthew L. (Matt) (Writer)
c/o Simon Millar *Rumble Media*
1620 Broadway Ste C
Santa Monica, CA 90404-2777, USA

Healy, Patricia (Actor)
Shelter Entertainment
9255 W Sunset Blvd Ste 1010
West Hollywood, CA 90069-3307, USA

Heames, Darin (Actor)
c/o Andrew Stawiarski *ADS Management*
269 S Beverly Dr # 441
Beverly Hills, CA 90212-3851, USA

Heap, Todd (Athlete, Football Player)
7634 E Summit Trail St
Mesa, AZ 85207-7244, USA

Heaphy, Shawn (Athlete, Hockey Player)
73 Lakeview Dr
Charlton, MA 01507-5429, USA

Heard, Amber (Actor)
c/o Geyer Kosinski *Media Talent Group*
9200 W Sunset Blvd Ste 550
West Hollywood, CA 90069-3611, USA

Heard, Garfield (Athlete, Basketball Player)
1735 Peachtree St NE Unit 133
Atlanta, GA 30309-7004, USA

Heard, Herman Jr (Athlete, Football Player)
PO Box 938
Broomfield, CO 80038-0938, USA

Heard, Jerry (Athlete, Golfer)
293 Talowah Rd
Purvis, MS 39475-5047, USA

Heard, John (Actor)
Odyssey Theatre Emsemble
2055 S Sepulveda Blvd
Los Angeles, CA 90025-5621, USA

Hearn, Ed (Athlete, Baseball Player)
5737 Theden St
Shawnee, KS 66218-9199, USA

Hearn, George (Actor, Music Group)
211 S Beverly Dr # 211
Beverly Hills, CA 90212-3807, USA

Hearn, J Woodrow (Religious Leader)
United Methodist Church
PO Box 320
Nashville, TN 37202-0320, USA

Hearn, Tom (Golfer)
Links Mmg
5068 W Plano Pkwy Ste 256
Plano, TX 75093-4441, USA

Hearne, Bill (Music Group, Musician)
Class Act Entertainment
PO Box 160236
Nashville, TN 37216-0236, USA

Hearns, Shane (Athlete, Baseball Player, Olympic Athlete)
8165 Brians Ct
Lambertville, MI 48144-9583, USA

Hearns, Tommy (Boxer)
c/o Staff Member *National Organization of Professional Athletes*
1806 Watermere Ln
Windermere, FL 34786-6121, USA

Hearron, Jeff (Athlete, Baseball Player)
660 E River Rd Apt D
Tucson, AZ 85704-5833, USA

Hearst, Amanda Randolph (Model)
c/o Keya Morgan *Keya Morgan Productions*
PO Box 18447
Beverly Hills, CA 90209-4447, USA

Hearst, Garrison (Athlete, Football Player)
3753 Augusta Hwy
Lincolnton, GA 30817-4402, USA

Hearst, Lydia (Model)
c/o Oren Segal *Radius Entertainment*
9229 W Sunset Blvd Ste 310
West Hollywood, CA 90069-3403, USA

Hearst, Patricia (Writer)
110 5th St
San Francisco, CA 94103-2918

Hearst, Rick (Actor)
Stone Manners
6500 Wilshire Blvd # 550
Los Angeles, CA 90048-4920, USA

Hearst, Victoria
865 Comstock Ave
Los Angeles, CA 90024-2572

Hearst Shaw, Patty (Actor)
51 Upper Station Rd
Garrison, NY 10524-3614, USA

Heart (Musician)
c/o Jeff Frasco *Creative Artists Agency (CAA-LA)*
2000 Avenue of the Stars Ste 100
Los Angeles, CA 90067-4705, USA

Heaslip, Mark (Athlete, Hockey Player)
11 Leland Ct
Chevy Chase, MD 20815-4906, USA

Heater, Don (Athlete, Football Player)
8704 Manchester Ave
Kansas City, MO 64138-4167, USA

Heater, Larry (Athlete, Football Player)
3711 Royal Fern Cir
Las Vegas, NV 89115-1257, USA

Heath, Albert (Tootie) (Music Group, Musician)
Ted Kurland
173 Brighton Ave
Allston, MA 02134-2003, USA

Heath, Bill (Athlete, Baseball Player)
1626 Lake Charlotte Ln
Richmond, TX 77406-7016, USA

Heath, Brandon
c/o Staff Member *Creative Trust, Inc.*
210 Jamestown Park Ste 200
Brentwood, TN 37027-7562, USA

Heath, Carey (Race Car Driver)
Carey Heath Motorsports
12 Worster Rd
Eliot, ME 03903, USA

Heath, Jeff (Athlete, Football Player)
c/o Derrick Fox *Derrick Fox Management*
Prefers to be contacted by telephone
CA, USA

Heath, Kelly (Athlete, Baseball Player)
2249 Portofino Pl Unit 2222
Palm Harbor, FL 34683-7740, USA

Heath, Mike (Athlete, Baseball Player)
10111 Heather Sound Dr
Tampa, FL 33647-2901, USA

Heath, Rodney (Athlete, Football Player)
6673 Red Pine Dr
Liberty Township, OH 45044-8765, USA

Heath, Tommy (Musician)
c/o JD Sobol *Almond Talent Agency*
2600 W Olive Ave Fl 5
Burbank, CA 91505-4572, USA

Heathcock, Jeff (Athlete, Baseball Player)
24962 Calle Vecindad
Lake Forest, CA 92630-2105, USA

Heathcote, Bella (Actor)
c/o Brian Medavoy *Medavoy Management*
10203 Santa Monica Blvd Ste 400
Los Angeles, CA 90067-6405, USA

Heathcote, Jud (Athlete, Basketball Player, Coach)
5418 S Quail Ridge Cir
Spokane, WA 99223-6391, USA

Heathcott, Mike (Athlete, Baseball Player)
12445 E Saddlehorn Trl
Scottsdale, AZ 85259-6125, USA

Heatherly, Eric (Actor)
c/o Staff Member *The Bazel Group Inc*
4636 Lebanon Pike # 308
Hermitage, TN 37076-1316, USA

Heatherton, Erin (Actor)
c/o Maja Chiesi *IMG Models (NY)*
304 Park Ave S Fl 12
New York, NY 10010-4314, USA

Heatherton, Joey (Actor)
14155 Magnolia Blvd
Sherman Oaks, CA 91423-1112, USA

Heaton, Neal (Athlete, Baseball Player)
3 Nursery Ct
East Patchogue, NY 11772-6152, USA

Heaton, Patricia (Actor)
c/o Staff Member *FourBoys Films*
12400 Wilshire Blvd Ste 1275
Los Angeles, CA 90025-1078, USA

Heatwave
6464 W Sunset Blvd Ste 1010
Los Angeles, CA 90028-8012

Heaverlo, Dave (Athlete, Baseball Player)
3720 W Lakeshore Dr
Moses Lake, WA 98837-3003, USA

Hebenton, Andy (Athlete, Hockey Player)
3295 SW Sandalwood Ln
Gresham, OR 97080, USA

Hebenton, Clay (Athlete, Hockey Player)
13457 Whitewater Dr
Poway, CA 92064-5227, USA

Hebert, Ashley (Reality Star)
University Of Pennsylvania
240 S 40th St Ste 1
School of Dental Medicine
Philadelphia, PA 19104-6030, USA

Hebert, Bobby (Athlete, Football Player)
724 Crystal St
New Orleans, LA 70124-3608, USA

Hebert, Bud (Athlete, Football Player)
PO Box 250342
Plano, TX 75025-0342, USA

Hebert, Guy (Athlete, Hockey Player, Olympic Athlete)
8 Gleneagles Dr
Newport Beach, CA 92660-4296, USA

Hebert, Ken (Athlete, Football Player)
7001 Mount Sharp Rd
Wimberley, TX 78676-4245, USA

Hebner, Rich (Richie) (Athlete, Baseball Player)
6 Tetreault Dr
Walpole, MA 02081-2224, USA

Hebron, Vaughn (Athlete, Football Player)
800 Summit Trace Rd
Langhorne, PA 19047-1105, USA

Hebson, Bryan (Athlete, Baseball Player)
1151 Fairmont Ln
Auburn, AL 36830-2105, USA

Heche, Anne (Actor)
c/o Jason Weinberg *Untitled Entertainment (LA)*
350 S Beverly Dr Ste 200
Beverly Hills, CA 90212-4819, USA

Hecht, Albie (Producer, Writer)
c/o Staff Member *Spike TV*
1515 Broadway
New York, NY 10036-8901, USA

Hecht, Jessica (Actor)
c/o Staff Member *Innovative Artists (LA)*
1505 10th St
Santa Monica, CA 90401-2805, USA

Hecht, Jochen (Athlete, Hockey Player)
95 Levin Ln
East Amherst, NY 14051-2243, USA

Hecht-Herskowitz, Gina (Actor)
5930 Foothill Dr
Los Angeles, CA 90068-3524, USA

Heck, Andy (Athlete, Football Player)
11604 Norwood Dr
Leawood, KS 66211-3000, USA

Heck, Bob (Athlete, Football Player)
5060 28th Pl SW
Naples, FL 34116-7620, USA

Heck, Ralph (Athlete, Football Player)
1906 Wicks Ridge Ln
Marietta, GA 30062-6777, USA

Heck, Robert (Athlete, Football Player)
5060 28th Pl SW
Naples, FL 34116-7620, USA

Heckard, Steve (Athlete, Football Player)
671 Glendale Dr
Rock Hill, SC 29732-2309, USA

Heckard, Tae (Actor)
c/o Staff Member *Pakula/King & Associates*
9229 W Sunset Blvd Ste 315
West Hollywood, CA 90069-3403, USA

Heckerling, Amy (Director, Producer)
1330 Schuyler Rd
Beverly Hills, CA 90210-2539, USA

Heckler, Margaret (Politician)
900 N Taylor St Apt 905
Arlington, VA 22203-1885, USA

Heckman, James
4807 S Greenwood Ave
Chicago, IL 60615-1913, USA

Heckscher, August (Writer)
333 E 68th St Apt 8A
New York, NY 10065-5604, USA

Hector, Johnny (Athlete, Football Player)
101 Grandville Dr
Lafayette, LA 70508-6448, USA

Hector, Willie (Athlete, Football Player)
138 Lower Ter
San Francisco, CA 94114-1443, USA

Hedaya, Dan (Actor)
Gersh Agency
232 N Canon Dr
Beverly Hills, CA 90210-5302, USA

Hedberg, Johan (Athlete, Hockey Player)
c/o Jay Grossman *PuckAgency LLC*
555 Pleasantville Rd
North Building, Suite 210
Briarcliff Manor, NY 10510-1955, USA

Hedberg, Randy (Athlete, Football Player)
PO Box 2471
Fargo, ND 58108-2471, USA

Hedderick, Herman (Athlete, Basketball Player)
2021 James St Apt 150
Latrobe, PA 15650-2182, USA

Heder, Jon (Actor, Producer)
c/o Julie Darmody *Mosaic Media Group*
9200 W Sunset Blvd Ste 10
West Hollywood, CA 90069-3608, USA

Hedford, Eric (Music Group, Musician)
Monqui Mgmt
PO Box 5908
Portland, OR 97228-5908, USA

Hedgepeth, Whitney (Athlete, Olympic Athlete, Swimmer)
9801 Westward Dr
Austin, TX 78733-3145, USA

Hedges, Clifton
10475 Crosspoint Blvd
Indianapolis, IN 46256-3386

Hedges, Peter (Director, Writer)
c/o Richard Lovett *Creative Artists Agency (CAA-LA)*
2000 Avenue of the Stars Ste 100
Los Angeles, CA 90067-4705, USA

Hedican, Bret (Athlete, Hockey Player, Olympic Athlete)
290 Las Quebradas
Alamo, CA 94507-1732, USA

Hedington, Tim (Producer)
c/o Staff Member *GK Films*
1411 5th St Ste 200
Santa Monica, CA 90401-2480, USA

Hedison, Alexandra (Actor)
Hedison Photography
PO Box 691636
West Hollywood, CA 90069-9636, USA

Hedison, Bret (Athlete, Hockey Player)
1848 Torrington St
Raleigh, NC 27615-2575, USA

Hedison, David (Actor)
779 Carissa Dr
Royal Palm Beach, FL 33411-3412, USA

Hedlund, Garrett (Actor)
c/o Cynthia Pett-Dante *Brillstein Entertainment Partners (LA)*
9150 Wilshire Blvd Ste 350
Beverly Hills, CA 90212-3453, USA

Hedlund, Mike (Athlete, Baseball Player)
2412 Klinger Rd
Arlington, TX 76016-1143, USA

Hedquist, Julien
c/o Staff Member *IMG*
304 Park Ave S Fl 12
New York, NY 10010-4314, USA

Hedren, Tippi (Actor)
The Roar Foundation
6867 Soledad Canyon Rd
Acton, CA 93510-2221, USA

Hedrick, Chad (Athlete, Olympic Athlete, Speed Skater)
18203 Stockton Springs Dr
Spring, TX 77379-6926, USA

Hedrick, Joan (Writer)
300 Summit St
Hartford, CT 06106-3100, USA

Hedrick, Larry (Race Car Driver)
Larry Hedrick Motorsports
PO Box 511
114 Victory Lane
Statesville, NC 28687-0511, USA

Heenan, Pat (Athlete, Football Player)
10007 Raynor Rd
Silver Spring, MD 20901-2124, USA

Heep, Danny (Athlete, Baseball Player)
18610 Crosstimber
San Antonio, TX 78258-4587, USA

Heeter, Gene (Athlete, Football Player)
11 Symphony Dr
Lake Grove, NY 11755-1313, USA

Heffernan, Bert (Athlete, Baseball Player)
130 Eagle Ct
Locust Grove, VA 22508-5432, USA

Heffernan, Dave (Athlete, Football Player)
8101 SW 79th Ter
Miami, FL 33143, USA

Heffernan, Kevin (Actor, Comedian, Producer, Writer)
Broken Lizard Industries
4000 Warner Blvd Bldg 102
Burbank, CA 91522-0001, USA

Heffner, Bob (Athlete, Baseball Player)
910 N 12th St
Allentown, PA 18102-1102, USA

Heffner, Kyle (Actor)
c/o Melanie Sharp *Sharp Talent*
5538 Willowcrest Ave
North Hollywood, CA 91601-2830, USA

Heffron, John (Actor, Comedian)
c/o Peter Rosegarten *Conversation Company*
1044 Northern Blvd Ste 304
Roslyn, NY 11576-1589, USA

Heffron, Richard T (Director)
c/o Staff Member *Shapiro-Lichtman Talent Agency*
1333 Beverly Green Dr
Los Angeles, CA 90035-1018, USA

Heflin, Bronson (Athlete, Baseball Player)
1004 Pintail Pl
Hendersonville, TN 37075-8897, USA

Heflin, Vince (Athlete, Football Player)
4811 Lake Ontario Way
Bowie, MD 20720-3694, USA

Hefner, Christie (Business Person, Publisher)
Playboy Enterprises
680 N Lake Shore Dr
Chicago, IL 60611-4546, USA

Hefner, Hugh (Producer, Publisher)
Playboy Mansion
10236 Charing Cross Rd
Los Angeles, CA 90024-1815, USA

Hefner, Larry (Athlete, Football Player)
1208 Arboretum Dr
Lewisville, NC 27023-8658, USA

Hefner, Lene (Actor)
15127 Califa St
Van Nuys, CA 91411-3021

Heft, Bob
4098 Green St
Saginaw, MI 48638-6618

Heft, Robert (Bob) (Designer)
PO Box 20404
Saginaw, MI 48602-0404, USA

Hegamin, George (Athlete, Football Player)
601 Snowy Orchid Ln
Desoto, TX 75115-6651, USA

Heger, Rene (Actor)
c/o Jerry Shandrew *Shandrew Public Relations*
1050 S Stanley Ave
Los Angeles, CA 90019-6634, USA

Hegg, Steve (Athlete, Cycler, Olympic Athlete)
3898 Westhaven Dr
Carlsbad, CA 92008-2754, USA

Hegland, Jean (Writer)
5450 Mill Creek Rd
Healdsburg, CA 95448-9760, USA

Hegman, Bob (Athlete, Baseball Player)
3529 NW Winding Woods Dr
Lees Summit, MO 64064-1879, USA

Hegman, Mike (Athlete, Football Player)
2958 Suesand Dr
Memphis, TN 38128-5941, USA

Hehn, Sascha (Actor)
Postfach 100823
Munich, GE D-800

Heidei, James (Athlete, Football Player)
1425 Wisteria Dr
Vicksburg, MS 39180-4756, USA

Heidemann, Jack (Athlete, Baseball Player)
1816 S Salida Del Sol Cir
Mesa, AZ 85202-5529, USA

Heiden, Elizabeth L (Beth) (Athlete, Olympic Athlete, Speed Skater)
915 Swarthmore Ct
Madison, WI 53705-2118, USA

Heiden, Eric (Athlete, Olympic Athlete, Speed Skater)
1219 Cottonwood Ln
Park City, UT 84098-7602, USA

Heiden, Steve (Athlete, Football Player)
415 E Coconino Pl
Chandler, AZ 85249-5315, USA

Heiden, Steve (Athlete, Football Player)
2600 Rushford Vlg
Rushford, MN 55971, USA

Heidmann, Manfred (Actor)
Borbecker Str. 237
Essen, GE D-453

Heidt Jr, Horace (Musician)
4155 Witzel Dr
Sherman Oaks, CA 91423-4613, USA

Heigl, Katherine (Actor, Model)
Jason Heigl Foundation
3450 Cahuenga Blvd W Apt 905
Los Angeles, CA 90068-1594, USA

Heilman, Aaron (Athlete, Baseball Player)
39W272 Sheldon Ln
Geneva, IL 60134-6045, USA

Heim, Val (Athlete, Baseball Player)
1050 Louden St
Superior, NE 68978-2303, USA

Heimbold, Charles A Jr (Business Person)
Bristol-Myers Squibb
345 Park Ave Bsmt LC3
New York, NY 10154-0028, USA

Heimburger, Craig (Athlete, Football Player)
311 Flagstone Dr
Belleville, IL 62221-5821, USA

Heimel, Cynthia (Writer)
Simon & Schuster
1230 Avenue of the Americas Fl CONC1
New York, NY 10020-1586, USA

Heimkreiter, Steve (Athlete, Football Player)
45 Devils Den Apt 208
Fort Thomas, KY 41075-4045, USA

Heimlich, Henry J (Doctor, Physicist)
2347 Bedford Ave # 1D
Cincinnati, OH 45208-2656, USA

Heim-McDaniel, Kay (Athlete, Baseball Player, Commentator)
3390 143rd St W
Rosemount, MN 55068-4057, USA

Heimrath, Jr., Ludwig (Race Car Driver)
26117 34th Ave E
Spanaway, WA 98387-9439, USA

Heimueller, Gorman (Athlete, Baseball Player)
2148 W Glen Ave
Riverton, UT 84065-7079, USA

Heimuli, Lakei (Athlete, Football Player)
1963 W 1870 S
Woods Cross, UT 84087-2181, USA

Heineman, Dave (Governor, Politician)
Office of the Governor
PO Box 94848
Lincoln, NE 68509-4848, USA

Heineman, Ken (Athlete, Football Player)
15982 Serenity Point Ln
Rogers, AR 72756-8615, USA

Heinen, Mike (Athlete, Golfer)
4518 E Meadow Ln
Lake Charles, LA 70605-5318, USA

Heinkel, Don (Athlete, Baseball Player)
412 Deer Creek Dr
Killen, AL 35645-8388, USA

Heinle, Amelia (Actor)
c/o John Carrabino *John Carrabino Management*
5900 Wilshire Blvd Ste 406
Los Angeles, CA 90036-5015, USA

Heinrich, Keith (Athlete, Football Player)
21011 Pricewood Manor Ct
Cypress, TX 77433-2075, USA

Heinrich, Martin (Congressman, Politician)
336 Cannon Hob
Washington, DC 20515-3506, USA

Heins, Shawn (Athlete, Hockey Player)
c/o Staff Member *Sports Personnel Services*
125 Lake St W Ste 200
Wayzata, MN 55391-1573, USA

Heinsohn, Tom (Athlete, Basketball Player, Coach)
PO Box 422
Newton Upper Falls, MA 02464-0002, USA

Heintz, Bob (Athlete, Golfer)
2213 Highland Woods Dr
Dunedin, FL 34698-9407, USA

Heintz, Chris (Athlete, Baseball Player)
7128 Wareham Dr
Tampa, FL 33647-1132, USA

Heintzelman, Tom (Athlete, Baseball Player)
1500 W Rio Salado Pkwy Unit 82
Mesa, AZ 85201-3825, USA

Heinz, Bob (Athlete, Football Player)
6110 W Bluff Ave
Fresno, CA 93722-2385, USA

Heinz, W C (Sportscaster, Writer)
1150 Nichols Hill Rd
Dorset, VT 05251-9536, USA

Heinze, Steve (Athlete, Hockey Player, Olympic Athlete)
4659 La Espada Dr
Santa Barbara, CA 93111-1301, USA

Heise, Bob (Athlete, Baseball Player)
537 Live Oak Dr
Angels Camp, CA 95222, USA

Heiser, Roy (Athlete, Baseball Player)
1038 Grovehill Rd
Halethorpe, MD 21227-3802, USA

Heiserman, Rick (Athlete, Baseball Player)
17252 Adams St
Omaha, NE 68135-3078, USA

Heiskala, Earl (Athlete, Hockey Player)
982 Ocean Ln
Imperial Beach, CA 91932-2420, USA

Heiss Jenkins, Carol (Athlete, Figure Skater, Olympic Athlete)
3183 Regency Pl
Westlake, OH 44145-6735, USA

Heisten, Barrett (Athlete, Hockey Player)
4621 Pavalof St
Anchorage, AK 99507-1016, USA

Heitmann, Eric (Athlete, Football Player)
21511 Grand Hollow Ln
Katy, TX 77450-8809, USA

Heitmeyer, Jayne
4450 W Lakeside Dr Ste 350
Burbank, CA 91505-4064

Heizer, Miles (Actor)
c/o Staff Member *Stein Entertainment Group*
1351 N Crescent Heights Blvd Apt 312
West Hollywood, CA 90046-4549, USA

Hejda, Jan (Athlete, Hockey Player)
9929 Sara Gulch Cir
Parker, CO 80138-7865, USA

Hejduk, Milan (Athlete, Hockey Player)
7895 Forest Keep Cir
Parker, CO 80134-6412, USA

Helberg, Simon (Actor)
2549 N Catalina St
Los Angeles, CA 90027-1132, USA

Held, Carl
1551 E Chevy Chase Dr Unit 313
Glendale, CA 91206-4188

Held, Franklin (Bud) (Athlete, Olympic Athlete, Track Athlete)
13367 Caminito Mar Villa
Del Mar, CA 92014-3613, USA

Held, Mel (Athlete, Baseball Player)
103 Hogan Ln
Bryan, OH 43506-9161, USA

Held, Paul (Athlete, Football Player)
29055 Blue Moon Dr
Menifee, CA 92584-7302, USA

Held, Richard M (Doctor)
Massachusetts Institute of Technology
Psychology Dept
Cambridge, MA 02139, USA

Helde, Annette
8430 Santa Monica Blvd Ste 200
West Hollywood, CA 90069-4253

Heldt, Mike (Athlete, Football Player)
12711 Corral Rd
Tampa, FL 33626-4405, USA

Helfand, Eric (Athlete, Baseball Player)
7314 Jackson Dr
San Diego, CA 92119-2317, USA

Helfer, Tricia (Actor)
c/o Gordon Gilbertson *Gilbertson Management*
1334 3rd Street Promenade Ste 201
Santa Monica, CA 90401-1320, USA

Helford, Bruce (Producer, Writer)
c/o Staff Member *United Talent Agency (UTA-LA)*
9336 Civic Center Dr
Beverly Hills, CA 90210-3604, USA

Helgeland, Brian (Director)
c/o Robert Newman *William Morris Endeavor (LA)*
9601 Wilshire Blvd
Beverly Hills, CA 90210-5213, USA

Helgenberger, Marg (Actor)
c/o Nancy Sanders *Sanders Armstrong Caserta*
2120 Colorado Ave Ste 120
Santa Monica, CA 90404-3561, USA

Heller, Jane (Writer)
1014 Ladera Ln
Santa Barbara, CA 93108-1630, USA

Heller, Jeffrey M (Business Person)
Electronic Data Systems
5400 Legacy Dr
Plano, TX 75024-3199, USA

Heller, Ron (Athlete, Football Player)
538 Stillwater River Rd
Absarokee, MT 59001-6218, USA

Hellerman, Fred (Music Group, Songwriter, Writer)
83 Good Hill Rd
Weston, CT 06883-2802, USA

Hellestrae, Dale (Athlete, Football Player)
4960 E Fellars Dr
Scottsdale, AZ 85254-9634, USA

Hellickson, Russell (Russ) (Athlete, Olympic Athlete, Wrestler)
6893 Lauren Pl
Columbus, OH 43235-2188, USA

Helling, Rick A (Ricky) (Athlete, Baseball Player, Olympic Athlete)
3672 Landings Dr
Excelsior, MN 55331-9709, USA

Hellion
18653 Ventura Blvd # 307
Tarzana, CA 91356-4103

Hellman, Bonnie
1680 Vine St Ste 614
Los Angeles, CA 90028-8833

Hellman, Monte (Director)
8588 Appian Way
Los Angeles, CA 90046-7729, USA

Helluin, Francis (Athlete, Football Player)
3930 Southdown Mandalay Rd
Houma, LA 70360-3001, USA

Helluin, Jerry (Athlete, Football Player)
3930 Southdown Mandalay Rd
Houma, LA 70360-3001, USA

Hellwig, Jim (Athlete, Wrestler)
Ultimate Creations, Inc.
43A County Road 119 N
Santa Fe, NM 87506-7101, USA

Helm, Darren (Athlete, Hockey Player)
c/o Staff Member *Detroit Red Wings*
600 Civic Center Dr
Joe Luis Arena
Detroit, MI 48226-4419, USA

Helm, Peter
1480 S Wild Oaks Dr
Nixa, MO 65714-8269

Helm, Val (Athlete, Baseball Player)
Chicago White Sox
PO Box 423
Superior, NE 68978-0423, USA

Helmerich, Hans C (Business Person)
Helmerich & Payne Inc
Utica & 21st St
Tulsa, OK 74114, USA

Helmerich, Walter H III (Business Person)
Helmerich & Payne Inc
Utica & 21st St
Tulsa, OK 74114, USA

Helmerson, Frans (Music Group, Musician)
Columbia Artists Mgmt Inc
165 W 57th St
New York, NY 10019-2201, USA

Helmond, Katherine (Actor)
2035 Davies Way
Los Angeles, CA 90046-7742, USA

Helms, Ed (Actor, Comedian)
c/o Peter Principato *Principato/Young Management (LA)*
9465 Wilshire Blvd Ste 900
Beverly Hills, CA 90212-2608, USA

Helms, Jimmy (Race Car Driver)
6230 Rock Island Rd
Charlotte, NC 28278-6508, USA

Helms, Susan J (Astronaut)
NASA
2101 Nasa Pkwy Spc Johnsoncenter
Houston, TX 77058-3696, USA

Helms, Susan J Biggen
10824 W Coco Pi
Littleton, CO 80127, USA

Helms, Tommy (Athlete, Baseball Player, Coach)
5427 Bluesky Dr
Cincinnati, OH 45247-7865, USA

Helms, Wes (Athlete, Baseball Player)
9314 Bear Creek Rd
Sterrett, AL 35147-9166, USA

Helmstetter, Shad (Motivational Speaker, Writer)
Goals-On-Line.com Corporate Offices
362 Gulf Breeze Pkwy Ste 104
Gulf Breeze, FL 32561-4492, USA

Helmut
1775 Broadway # 433
New York, NY 10019-1903

Heloise
PO Box 795000
San Antonio, TX 78279-5000

Heloise, (Cruse Evans) (Journalist)
PO Box 795000
San Antonio, TX 78279-5000, USA

Helpern, Joan G (Designer, Fashion Designer)
Joan & David Helpern Inc
46 W 56th St # 200
New York, NY 10019-3882, USA

Helprin, Mark (Writer)
c/o Staff Member *The Wendy Weil Agency, Inc.*
232 Madison Ave Ste 1300
New York, NY 10016-2901, USA

Helton, Barry (Athlete, Football Player)
3325 Clubview Ter
Colorado Springs, CO 80906-4479, USA

Helton, Bill D (Business Person)
New Century Energies
1225 17th St Ste 100
Denver, CO 80202-5518, USA

Helton, Mike (Race Car Driver)
PO Box 2875
Daytona Beach, FL 32120-2875, USA

Helton, RJ (Musician)
PO Box 246
1400 Market Place Blvd
Cumming, GA 30028-0246, USA

Helton, Todd (Athlete, Baseball Player)
Colorado Rockies Foundation 2001 Blake St Unit A
Brighton, CO 80602, USA

Hely, Steve (Actor)
c/o Cori Wellins *William Morris Endeavor (LA)*
9601 Wilshire Blvd
Beverly Hills, CA 90210-5213, USA

Heman, Russ (Athlete, Baseball Player)
5555 Canyon Crest Dr Apt 3D
Riverside, CA 92507-6453, USA

Hemandez, Angel (Baseball Player)
500 Cypress Xing
Wellington, FL 33414-6368, USA

Hemecker, Ralph (Director)
c/o Staff Member *Mythic Films*
225 E Broadway Ste 115B
Glendale, CA 91205-1008, USA

Hemingway, Mariel (Actor, Model)
c/o Tracy Columbus *Columbus & Company Management*
10850 Wilshire Blvd
Los Angeles, CA 90024-4305, USA

Hemingway, Rose (Actor)
c/o Charles Mastropietro *Circle of Confusion (LA)*
8931 Ellis Ave
Los Angeles, CA 90034-3336, USA

Hemingway, Toby (Actor)
c/o Sarah Shyn *3 Arts Entertainment (LA)*
9460 Wilshire Blvd Fl 7
Beverly Hills, CA 90212-2713, USA

Hemme, Christy (Actor)
c/o Liza Anderson *Anderson Group Public Relations*
8060 Melrose Ave Fl 4
Los Angeles, CA 90046-7038, USA

Hemmens, Heather (Actor)
c/o Stephanie Simon *Untitled Entertainment (LA)*
350 S Beverly Dr Ste 200
Beverly Hills, CA 90212-4819, USA

Hemmer, Bill (Correspondent)
c/o Staff Member *Fox News (NY)*
1211 Avenue of the Americas Lowr C1
New York, NY 10036-8705, USA

Hemming, Lindy (Designer, Stylist)
c/o Robert Arakelian *United Talent Agency (UTA-LA)*
9336 Civic Center Dr
Beverly Hills, CA 90210-3604, USA

Hemmis, Paige (Actor, Reality Star)
c/o Staff Member *Extreme Makeover: Home Edition*
9225 W Sunset Blvd # 1100
Endemol Entertainment Usa
West Hollywood, CA 90069-3111, USA

Hemond, Roland (Commentator)
1332 W Edgemont Ave
Phoenix, AZ 85007-1117, USA

Hemond, Scott (Athlete, Baseball Player)
263 Florida Ave
Dunedin, FL 34698-7530, USA

Hemphill., Bret (Athlete, Baseball Player)
1273 Trehowell Dr
Roseville, CA 95678-6110, United States

Hemphill, Darryl (Athlete, Football Player)
10218 Aurora Fld
San Antonio, TX 78245-2622, USA

Hemphill, Joel (Music Group)
Harper Agency
PO Box 144
Goodlettsville, TN 37070-0144, USA

Hemphill, Labreeska (Music Group)
Harper Agency
PO Box 144
Goodlettsville, TN 37070-0144, USA

Hemphill, Richard (Baseball Player)
Kansas City Monarchs
422 Barnes St
Rock Hill, SC 29730-5044, USA

Hempstead, Hessley (Athlete, Football Player)
14823 Dunbeth Dr
Huntersville, NC 28078-3308, USA

Hemric, Dick (Athlete, Basketball Player)
1220 7th St NE
North Canton, OH 44720-2116, USA

Hemsky, Ales (Athlete, Hockey Player)
Jiri Crha Sports Representation
16390 Braeburn Ridge Trl
Delray Beach, FL 33446-9508, USA

Hemsley, Nate (Athlete, Football Player)
26 Roberts Pl
Willingboro, NJ 08046-2514, USA

Hemsley, Stephen J (Business Person)
United HealthCare Corp
9900 Bren Rd E Ste 300W
Opus Center
Hopkins, MN 55343-4402, USA

Hemsworth, Chris (Actor)
7022 Grasswood Ave
Malibu, CA 90265-4247, USA

Hemsworth, Liam (Actor)
c/o Will Ward *ROAR (LA)*
9701 Wilshire Blvd Fl 8
Beverly Hills, CA 90212-2008, USA

Hemus, Solly (Athlete, Baseball Player, Coach)
5100 San Felipe St Unit 194E
Houston, TX 77056-3688, USA

Henao, Zulay (Actor)
c/o Jean-Louis Diamonika *One Entertainment (NY)*
12 W 57th St PH
New York, NY 10019-3900, USA

Henckel von Donnersmarck, Florian (Director)
c/o Craig Gering *Creative Artists Agency (CAA-LA)*
2000 Avenue of the Stars Ste 100
Los Angeles, CA 90067-4705, USA

Hencken, John F (Athlete, Olympic Athlete, Swimmer)
PO Box 2540
Weaverville, NC 28787-2540, USA

Hendershot, Larry (Athlete, Football Player)
6201 W Riviera Dr
Glendale, AZ 85304-2523, USA

Henderson, Alan (Basketball Player)
Atlanta Hawks
190 Marietta St NW Ste 405
Atlanta, GA 30303-2717, USA

Henderson, Anthony (Krayzie Bone) (Musician)
c/o Staff Member *RBC Records*
150 E Olive Ave Ste 114
Burbank, CA 91502-1849, USA

Henderson, Cedric (Athlete, Basketball Player)
1425 Ridenour Blvd NW Apt 7105
Kennesaw, GA 30152-3601, USA

Henderson, Chris (Soccer Player)
Columbus Crew
2121 Velma Ave
Columbus, OH 43211-2085, USA

Henderson, David (Athlete, Basketball Player)
805 Sweet Hollow Ct
Middletown, DE 19709-8645, USA

Henderson, David L (Dave) (Athlete, Baseball Player)
2213 Halleck Ave SW
Seattle, WA 98116-4807, USA

Henderson, Devery (Athlete, Football Player)
835 E Bellevue St
Opelousas, LA 70570, USA

Henderson, Felicia (Writer)
c/o Scott Schwartz *Vision Art Management*
9465 Wilshire Blvd Ste 870
Beverly Hills, CA 90212-2610, USA

Henderson, Florence (Actor, Music Group)
FHB Productions
PO Box 11295
Marina Del Rey, CA 90295-7295, USA

Henderson, Gerald (Athlete, Basketball Player)
185 Birkdale Dr
Blue Bell, PA 19422-3276, USA

Henderson, James A (Business Person)
Cummins Engine Co
PO Box 3005
500 Jackson St
Columbus, IN 47202-3005, USA

Henderson, Jerome (Athlete, Basketball Player)
711 Love Henry Ct
Southlake, TX 76092-6067, USA

Henderson, Jerome (Athlete, Football Player)
11051 Berkely Club Dr Apt 201
Raleigh, NC 27617-8543, USA

Henderson, Joe (Athlete, Baseball Player)
16004 Keno Dr
Horizon City, TX 79928-6526, USA

Henderson, John (Athlete, Football Player)
18130 19th Ave N
Minneapolis, MN 55447-2634, USA

Henderson, John (Athlete, Football Player)
11667 Blackstone River Dr
Jacksonville, FL 32256-2919, USA

Henderson, Josh (Actor)
c/o Michael Baum *Impression Entertainment*
9229 W Sunset Blvd Ste 700
West Hollywood, CA 90069-3407, USA

Henderson, Julie (Model)
596 Broadway # 701
New York, NY 10012-3396, USA

Henderson, Keith (Athlete, Football Player)
PO Box 2754
Cartersville, GA 30120-1696, USA

Henderson, Ken (Athlete, Baseball Player)
228 Valley Ridge Rd
Haverford, PA 19041-2029, USA

Henderson, Kevin (Athlete, Basketball Player)
2955 Champion Way Apt 96
Tustin, CA 92782-1219, USA

Henderson, Logan (Musician)
c/o Remington Franklin *Resolution (LA)*
10250 Constellation Blvd Fl 7
Los Angeles, CA 90067-6207, USA

Henderson, Martin (Actor)
c/o Peter Kiernan *Management 360*
9111 Wilshire Blvd
Beverly Hills, CA 90210-5508, USA

Henderson, Neale (Athlete, Baseball Player)
341 Los Soneto Dr
San Diego, CA 92114-5922, USA

Henderson, Othello (Athlete, Football Player)
PO Box 2113
Cedar Park, TX 78630-2113, USA

Henderson, Paul III (Journalist)
Seattle Times
1000 Denny Way # 5
Editorial Dept
Seattle, WA 98109-5340, USA

Henderson, Reuben (Athlete, Football Player)
3918 Hunters Ridge Dr Apt 4
Lansing, MI 48911-1106, USA

Henderson, Rickey (Athlete, Baseball Player)
10561 Englewood Dr
Oakland, CA 94605-5013, USA

Henderson, Rod (Athlete, Baseball Player)
552 Winter Hill Ln
Lexington, KY 40509-2932, USA

Henderson, Seantrel (Athlete, Football Player)
c/o Joel Segal *Lagardere Unlimited (NYC)*
845 United Nations Plz
New York, NY 10017-3540, USA

Henderson, Steve (Athlete, Baseball Player)
10509 Gretna Green Dr
Tampa, FL 33626-1830, USA

Henderson, Thomas (Athlete, Basketball Player, Olympic Athlete)
6822 Baron Gate Ct
Spring, TX 77379-5094, USA

Henderson, Thomas (Athlete, Football Player)
3106 E 13th St
Austin, TX 78702-2506, USA

Henderson, Thomas
7 Seafield Ln
Westhampton Beach, NY 11978-2714

Henderson, Wymon (Athlete, Football Player)
634 Braidwood Dr NW
Acworth, GA 30101-3529, USA

Henderson, Zachary (Athlete, Football Player)
1817 Sun Valley Ln
Edmond, OK 73034-6867, USA

Henderson III, Joe (Race Car Driver)
1435 W Morehead St # 170
Charlotte, NC 28208-5208, USA

Hendler, Lauri
4034 Stone Canyon Ave
Sherman Oaks, CA 91403-4541

Hendley, Bob (Athlete, Baseball Player)
645 Wimbish Rd
Macon, GA 31210-4328, USA

Hendley, Dick (Athlete, Football Player)
6 Sun Flare Ct
Greer, SC 29650-4419, USA

Hendra, Tony (Writer)
c/o Staff Member *Simon & Schuster*
1230 Avenue of the Americas Fl CONC1
New York, NY 10020-1586, USA

Hendren, Jerry (Athlete, Football Player)
14826 N Chesapeake Ln
Mead, WA 99021-9270, USA

Hendrick, George (Athlete, Baseball Player)
1 Tropicana Dr
Saint Petersburg, FL 33705-1703, USA

Hendricks, Christina (Actor)
c/o Ben Levine *LINK Entertainment*
11872 La Grange Ave Fl 1
Los Angeles, CA 90025-5283, USA

Hendricks, Jon (Music Group)
Virginia Wicks
2737 Edwin Pl
Los Angeles, CA 90046-1031, USA

Hendricks, L H (Baseball Player)
Negro Baseball Leagues
12 Sunset Blvd
Beaufort, SC 29907, USA

Hendricks, Matt (Athlete, Hockey Player)
12410 25th Ave N
Minneapolis, MN 55441-4008, USA

Hendricks, Theodore P (Ted) (Athlete, Football Player)
165 Sunset Way
Miami Springs, FL 33166-5153, USA

Hendrickson, Darby (Athlete, Hockey Player, Olympic Athlete)
317 Washington St
Saint Paul, MN 55102-1609, USA

Hendrickson, Elizabeth (Actor)
c/o Staff Member *Creative Partners Group*
15 Brooks Ave # B
Venice, CA 90291-3226, USA

Hendrickson, Jack (Athlete, Hockey Player)
5118 Griswold Rd
Kimball, MI 48074-2007, USA

Hendrickson, Mark (Athlete, Baseball Player)
1585 Wyndham Dr
York, PA 17403-5925, USA

Hendrickson, Steve (Athlete, Football Player)
210 W 15th Ave
Escondido, CA 92025-5714, USA

Hendrix, Elaine (Actor)
Rigberg Roberts Rugolo
1180 S Beverly Dr Ste 601
Los Angeles, CA 90035-1158, USA

Hendrix, Harville (Writer)
c/o Staff Member *Henry Holt & Company*
175 5th Ave Ste 400
New York, NY 10010-7726, USA

Hendrix, Terri (Musician)
Wilory Records
PO Box 2340
San Marcos, TX 78667-2340, USA

Hendrix, Tim (Athlete, Football Player)
7251 Hamilton Dr
Midlothian, TX 76065-6974, USA

Hendry, Gloria (Actor)
256 S Robertson Blvd
Beverly Hills, CA 90211-2811, USA

Hendry, Jim (Commentator)
1400 S Western Ave
Park Ridge, IL 60068-5062, USA

Hendry, Joel (Athlete, Golfer)
c/o Jim Lehrman *SFX Golf*
36855 W Main St Ste 200
Purcellville, VA 20132-3561, USA

Hendry, Ted (Athlete, Baseball Player)
14740 N 90th Pl
Scottsdale, AZ 85260-2700, USA

Hendryx, Nona (Musician)
Black Rock
6201 Sunset Blvd # 329
Los Angeles, CA 90028, USA

Hendy, John (Athlete, Football Player)
590 N Bayview Ave
Sunnyvale, CA 94085-3633, USA

Henenlotter, Frank (Director)
81 Bedford St Apt 6E
New York, NY 10014-5749, USA

Henery, Alex (Athlete, Football Player)
c/o Neil Cornrich *NC Sports, LLC*
best to contact via email
Columbus, OH 43201, USA

Hengel, Dave (Athlete, Baseball Player)
2642 Kingfisher Ln
Lincoln, CA 95648-8753, USA

Henin-Hardenne, Justine (Tennis Player)
Octagon
7950 Jones Branch Dr
Mc Lean, VA 22102-3302, USA

Henke, Brad (Athlete, Football Player)
4133 Redwood Ave Unit 4006
Los Angeles, CA 90066-5636, USA

Henke, Brad (Actor)
c/o Matt Schwartz *Christopher Wright Management*
930 S Orange Grove Ave
Los Angeles, CA 90036-4457, USA

Henke, Ed (Athlete, Football Player)
11381 Madrone Ct
Auburn, CA 95602-8380, USA

Henke, Karl (Athlete, Football Player)
1180 Bogota Ct
Oxnard, CA 93035-2608, USA

Henke, Nolan (Athlete, Golfer)
1323 Florida Ave
Fort Myers, FL 33901-7707, USA

Henke, Tom (Athlete, Baseball Player)
6200 Saint Francis Dr
Jefferson City, MO 65101-9292, USA

Henkel, Herbert L (Business Person)
Ingersoll-Rand Co
200 Chestnut Ridge Rd
Woodcliff Lake, NJ 07677-7703, USA

Henley, Belth
1350 Avenue of the Americas
New York, NY 10019-4702, USA

Henley, Bob (Athlete, Baseball Player)
11050 Moreland Dr E
Grand Bay, AL 36541-6626, USA

Henley, Carey (Athlete, Football Player)
1611 S Clayton Ave
Chattanooga, TN 37412-1107, USA

Henley, Darryl (Athlete, Football Player)
10178 Woodridge Dr
Rancho Cucamonga, CA 91737-6834, USA

Henley, Don (Musician, Songwriter)
c/o Irving Azoff *Azoff Music Management*
1100 Glendon Ave Ste 2000
Los Angeles, CA 90024-3524, USA

Henley, Gail (Athlete, Baseball Player)
7338 Alta Vis
La Verne, CA 91750-1115, USA

Henley, Garney (Athlete, Football Player)
857 Nebraska Ave SW
SW
Huron, SD 57350-2347, USA

Henley, Patricia
PO Box 259
Battle Ground, IN 47920-0259

Henman, Graham (Director)
Agency for Performing Arts
9200 W Sunset Blvd Ste 900
West Hollywood, CA 90069-3604, USA

Henman, Tim (Tennis Player)
14497 N Dale Mabry Hwy Ste 205
Tampa, FL 33618-2047, USA

Henn, Mark (Animator)
c/o Staff Member *Disney Animation (FL)*
PO Box 10200
Orlando, FL 32830-0200, USA

Henn, Sean (Athlete, Baseball Player)
4747 Kelly Rd
Aledo, TX 76008-4881, USA

Hennagan, Monique (Athlete, Olympic Athlete, Track Athlete)
505 Winter View Way
Stockbridge, GA 30281-7799, USA

Henne, Chad (Athlete, Football Player)
c/o David Dunn *Athletes First, LLC*
23091 Mill Creek Dr
Laguna Hills, CA 92653-1258, USA

Henneman, Brian (Music Group)
Hard Head Productions
180 Varick St Rm 810
New York, NY 10014-5416, USA

Henneman, Mike (Athlete, Baseball Player)
1001 Myers Ave
Frisco, TX 75034-5158, USA

Hennen, Thomas J (Astronaut)
16315 Cascade Caverns Ln
Houston, TX 77044-1240, USA

Hennen, Thomas J Chief (Astronaut)
16315 Cascade Caverns Ln
Houston, TX 77044-1240, USA

Henner, Marilu (Actor)
c/o Rory Rosegarten *Conversation Company*
1044 Northern Blvd Ste 304
Roslyn, NY 11576-1589, USA

Hennessey, Brad (Athlete, Baseball Player)
6657 Brentridge Ln
Lambertville, MI 48144-9374, USA

Hennessey, Wally (Horse Racer)
4141 NW 9th Ct
Coconut Creek, FL 33066-1644, USA

Hennessy, Jill (Actor)
c/o Matthew Saver *Matthew Saver Law Offices*
269 N Beverly Dr
Beverly Hills, CA 90210-5317, USA

Henney, Daniel (Actor)
c/o Brian Medavoy *Medavoy Management*
10203 Santa Monica Blvd Ste 400
Los Angeles, CA 90067-6405, USA

Henney, Jane (Government Official)
Food & Drug Administration
5600 Fishers Ln
Rockville, MD 20852-1750, USA

Hennig, Shelley (Actor)
c/o Allan Grifka *Alchemy Entertainment*
7024 Melrose Ave Ste 420
Los Angeles, CA 90038-3394, USA

Hennigan, Charley (Athlete, Football Player)
3875 Line Ave Apt 107
Shreveport, LA 71106-1160, USA

Hennigan, John (Athlete, Wrestler)
c/o Staff Member *World Wrestling Entertainment (WWE)*
1241 E Main St
Titan Towers
Stamford, CT 06902-3520, USA

Hennigan, Mike (Athlete, Football Player)
456 Loweland Rd
Cookeville, TN 38501-2736, USA

Hennigan, Phil (Athlete, Baseball Player)
PO Box 1212
Center, TX 75935-1212, USA

Henning, Dan (Athlete, Football Coach, Football Player)
116 Meeting Way
Ponte Vedra Beach, FL 32082-3947, USA

Henning, John F Jr (Publisher)
Sunset Magazine
80 Willow Rd
Menlo Park, CA 94025-3691, USA

Henning, Larry
7426 43rd Ave SE
Saint Cloud, MN 56304-9579

Henning, Linda (Actor)
10765 Wrightwood Ln
Studio City, CA 91604-3951, USA

Henning, Paul (Athlete, Hockey Player)
4250 Navajo Ave
Toluca Lake, CA 91602-2914, USA

Henninger, Brian (Athlete, Golfer)
25481 SW Newland Rd
Wilsonville, OR 97070, USA

Henninger, Rick (Athlete, Baseball Player)
98 Park Ln
Pottsboro, TX 75076-3990, USA

Hennings, Chad W (Athlete, Football
Player)
6101 Bay Valley Ct
Flower Mound, TX 75022-5575, USA

Henning-Walker, Anne (Athlete, Olympic
Athlete, Speed Skater)
12359 E Lasalle Pl
Aurora, CO 80014-1921, USA

Hennis, Randy (Athlete, Baseball Player)
1747 Sienna Dr
Melbourne, FL 32934-9030, USA

Henrich, Bobby (Athlete, Baseball Player)
1531 Via Los Coyotes
La Habra, CA 90631-7655, USA

Henrich, Tom
1547 Albino Trl
Dewey, AZ 86327

Henrichs, Jeff (Athlete, Baseball Player)
6192 Riverside Blvd Apt C46
Sacramento, CA 95831-1222, USA

Henrichsen, Brett (DJ)
c/o Len Evans *Project Publicity*
312 W 53rd St Ste 202
New York, NY 10019-5743, USA

Henricks, Jon N (Swimmer)
254 Laurel Ave
Des Plaines, IL 60016, USA

Henricks, Terence Colonel (Astronaut)
1700 Crosswind Dr
Blanco, TX 78606-5896, USA

Henricks, Terence T (Tom) (Astronaut)
Timken Aerospace
PO Box 547
Keene, NH 03431-0547, USA

Henrie, David (Actor)
c/o Jason Weinberg *Untitled
Entertainment (LA)*
350 S Beverly Dr Ste 200
Beverly Hills, CA 90212-4819, USA

Henrikse, Lance (Actor)
c/o Jean-Pierre (JP) Henraux *Henraux
Management*
Prefers to be contacted by telephone
CA, USA

Henriksen, Jan (Horse Racer)
PO Box 176
Crosswicks, NJ 08515-0176, USA

Henrikson, Lance (Actor)
c/o Jeff Witjas *Agency for the Performing
Arts (APA-LA)*
405 S Beverly Dr Ste 500
Beverly Hills, CA 90212-4425, USA

Henriques, Sean Paul (Actor, Musician)
c/o Staff Member *Sosincere Entertainment*
2054 Nostrand Ave Apt 4F
Brooklyn, NY 11210-2526, USA

Henriquez, Ron (Actor)
4906 College View Ave
Los Angeles, CA 90041-1844, USA

Henry, Albert (Athlete, Basketball Player)
2410 N 52nd St
Philadelphia, PA 19131-1409, USA

Henry, Anthony (Athlete, Football Player)
735 N Las Palmas Ave
Los Angeles, CA 90038-3513, USA

Henry, Bill (Athlete, Baseball Player)
2505 Belaire East Ln
Granite Shoals, TX 78654-3108, USA

Henry, Bill (Athlete, Baseball Player)
47 Oyster Landing Ln
Hilton Head Island, SC 29928-3045, USA

Henry, Brad (Politician)
PO Box 156
Shawnee, OK 74802-0156, USA

Henry, Brad (Politician)
Governor's Office
State Capitol Bldg #212
Oklahoma City, OK 73105, USA

Henry, Buck (Actor, Writer)
117 E 57th St
New York, NY 10022-2002, USA

Henry, Buck (Writer)
117 W 57th St
New York, NY 10019-2209, USA

Henry, Butch (Athlete, Baseball Player)
3033 Brandwood Ct
El Paso, TX 79925-5510, USA

Henry, Chris (Athlete, Football Player)
2191 Quaker Ridge Ct
Stockton, CA 95206-4879, USA

Henry, Chuck (Correspondent)
KNBC
3000 W Alameda Ave
Burbank, CA 91523-0002, USA

Henry, Clarence (Forgman) (Music
Group, Songwriter, Writer)
3309 Lawrence St
New Orleans, LA 70114-3230, USA

Henry, Conner (Athlete, Basketball Player)
1122 N College Ave
Claremont, CA 91711-3927, USA

Henry, Dale (Attorney, Hockey Player)
8611 Datapoint Dr Apt 43
San Antonio, TX 78229-5922, USA

Henry, Doug (Athlete, Baseball Player)
2804 Burries Rd
Hartland, WI 53029-8823, USA

Henry, Dwayne (Athlete, Baseball Player)
407 E Hampstead Ct
Middletown, DE 19709-1631, USA

Henry, Gloria (Actor)
849 N Harper Ave
Los Angeles, CA 90046-6803, USA

Henry, Gregg (Actor)
8956 Appian Way
Los Angeles, CA 90046-7737, USA

Henry, J J (Athlete, Golfer)
6901 Sanctuary Ln
Fort Worth, TX 76132-7101, USA

Henry, Joe (Athlete, Baseball Player)
11 Coachlight Dr
Millstadt, IL 62260-1801, USA

Henry, Joe (Music Group, Songwriter,
Writer)
Monterey Peninsula Artists
509 Hartnell St
Monterey, CA 93940-2825, USA

Henry, John (Baseball Player)
Florida Marlins
4698 Sanctuary Ln
Boca Raton, FL 33431-5206, USA

Henry, John (Commentator)
40 Cottage St
Brookline, MA 02445-5938, USA

Henry, Joseph L (Doctor)
60 Marinita Ave
San Rafael, CA 94901-3431, USA

Henry, Joshua (Actor, Musician)
c/o Edie Robb *Station3 (NYC)*
300 W 55th St Apt 5L
New York, NY 10019-5163, USA

Henry, Justin (Actor)
c/o Staff Member *Phoenix Organization,
The*
1990 S Bundy Dr Ste 630
Los Angeles, CA 90025-6140, USA

Henry, Kevin (Athlete, Football Player)
1428 Mill Pointe Ct
Lawrenceville, GA 30043-9111, USA

Henry, Lenny (Actor)
c/o Staff Member *William Morris
Endeavor (LA)*
9601 Wilshire Blvd
Beverly Hills, CA 90210-5213, USA

Henry, Mark (Athlete, Wrestler)
c/o Staff Member *World Wrestling
Entertainment (WWE)*
1241 E Main St
Titan Towers
Stamford, CT 06902-3520, USA

Henry, Mike (Actor)
Pittsburgh Steelers
10803 Blix St Unit 3
North Hollywood, CA 91602-3822, USA

Henry, Piper
1680 Vine St Ste 614
Los Angeles, CA 90028-8833

Henry, Ron (Athlete, Baseball Player)
2160 Downing St Apt 209
Denver, CO 80205-5262, USA

Henry, Steve (Athlete, Football Player)
1907 Darlene Way
Emporia, KS 66801-6024, USA

Henry, Travis (Athlete, Football Player)
6698 S Shawnee Ct
Aurora, CO 80016-2473, USA

Henry, Wally (Athlete, Football Player)
3444 Bernadette Ct Apt A
West Covina, CA 91792-4702, USA

Henry, William H Jr (Producer)
Time-Life Books
Rockefeller Center
New York, NY 10020, USA

Henry, Xavier (Athlete, Basketball Player)
c/o Arn Tellem *Wasserman Media Group
(LA)*
12100 W Olympic Blvd Ste 200
Los Angeles, CA 90064-1075, USA

Hensarling, Jeb (Congressman, Politician)
129 Cannon Hob
Washington, DC 20515-3501, USA

Hensby, Mark (Athlete, Golfer)
20802 N Grayhawk Dr Unit 1024
Scottsdale, AZ 85255-6433, USA

Hensel, Bruce (Doctor)
17526 Tramonto Dr
Pacific Palisades, CA 90272-3127, USA

Hensel, Robert M (Athlete)
wheelierecord@yahoo.com
138 E 3rd St # A
Oswego, NY 13126-2607, USA

Hensick, T J
2950 Charann Dr
Howell, MI 48843-8611, USA

Hensley, Chuck (Athlete, Baseball Player)
2563 S Revolta
Mesa, AZ 85209-6652, USA

Hensley, Clay (Athlete, Baseball Player)
3601 Dogwood Blossom Ct
Pearland, TX 77581-5038, USA

Hensley, Dick (Athlete, Football Player)
6319 Roberto Dr
Huntington, WV 25705-2529, USA

Hensley, Jimmy (Race Car Driver)
2570 Horsepasture Price Rd
Ridgeway, VA 24148-3707, USA

Hensley, John (Actor)
c/o Vincent Cirrincione *Vincent
Cirrincione Associates*
1516 N Fairfax Ave
Los Angeles, CA 90046-2608, USA

Hensley, Kirby J (Religious Leader)
Universal Life Church
601 3rd St
Modesto, CA 95351-3395, USA

Henson, Champ (Athlete, Football Player)
PO Box 3
Ashville, OH 43103-0003, USA

Henson, Darrin Dewitt (Actor)
c/o Adam Griffin *Kritzer Levine Wilkins
Entertainment (KLWG)*
11872 La Grange Ave Fl 1
Los Angeles, CA 90025-5283, USA

Henson, Drew (Athlete, Baseball Player)
3320 W Wallcraft Ave
Tampa, FL 33611-1947, USA

Henson, Elden (Actor)
c/o Chuck Binder *Binder & Associates*
1465 Lindacrest Dr
Beverly Hills, CA 90210-2519, USA

Henson, Gary (Athlete, Football Player)
5032 Vermillion Dr
Castle Rock, CO 80108-9032, USA

Henson, Harold (Athlete, Football Player)
15367 Lockbourne Eastern Rd
Ashville, OH 43103-9476, USA

Henson, John (Actor, Comedian)
c/o Rory Rosegarten *Conversation
Company*
1044 Northern Blvd Ste 304
Roslyn, NY 11576-1589, USA

Henson, John (Athlete, Basketball Player)
c/o Staff Member *Milwaukee Bucks*
1001 N 4th St Ste 1
Milwaukee, WI 53203-1312, USA

Henson, Lisa (Producer)
Columbia Pictures
2400 Riverside Dr
Burbank, CA 91505, USA

Henson, Lou (Basketball Player, Coach)
New Mexico State University
Athletic Dept
Fairacres, NM 88033, USA

Henson, Luther (Athlete, Football Player)
5395 Maple Grove Ave
Blanchester, OH 45107-1533, USA

Henson, Sammie (Athlete, Olympic Athlete, Wrestler)
611 W 5th St
Carrollton, MO 64633-1467, USA

Henson, Taraji P (Actor)
c/o Vincent Cirrincione *Vincent Cirrincione Associates*
1516 N Fairfax Ave
Los Angeles, CA 90046-2608, USA

Henstridge, Elizabeth (Actor)
c/o Amy Slomovits *Evolution Entertainment (LA)*
901 N Highland Ave
Los Angeles, CA 90038-2412, USA

Henstridge, Natasha (Actor, Model)
c/o David (Dave) Fleming *Mosaic Media Group*
9200 W Sunset Blvd Ste 10
West Hollywood, CA 90069-3608, USA

Hentoff, Nat (Writer)
Village Voice 36 Cooper Sq Frnt 1
New York, NY 10003, USA

Henton, Anthony (Athlete, Football Player)
1026 Avenue G
Bessemer, AL 35020-7200, USA

Henton, John (Actor)
c/o Staff Member *Gersh (LA)*
9465 Wilshire Blvd Ste 600
Beverly Hills, CA 90212-2605, USA

Hentrich, Craig (Athlete, Football Player)
9130 Old Smyrna Rd
Brentwood, TN 37027-6116, USA

Hepburn, Cassandra (Actor)
c/o Glenn Hughes III *Gem Entertainment Group*
10920 Wilshire Blvd Ste 150
Los Angeles, CA 90024-3990, USA

Hepburn, Lonnie (Athlete, Football Player)
1875 NW 59th St
Miami, FL 33142-2429, USA

Hepler, Bill (Athlete, Baseball Player)
12518 Fort King Rd
Dade City, FL 33525-5609, USA

Hepple, Alan (Athlete, Hockey Player)
1000 Chopper Cir
Denver, CO 80204-5805, USA

Herb, Marvin (Business Person)
Coca-Cola Bottling Company of Chicago
7400 N Oak Park Ave
Niles, IL 60714-3818

Herbers, Ian (Athlete, Hockey Player)
1135 Ridgeway Rd
Brookfield, WI 53045-2423, USA

Herbert, Doug (Race Car Driver)
4030 Concord Pkwy S
Concord, NC 28027-5024, USA

Herbert, Gary (Governor, Politician)
20 State Capitol
Salt Lake City, UT 84114, USA

Herbert, Holly (Journalist)
Celebrity Justice c/o Warner Bros
4000 Warner Blvd
Burbank, CA 91522-0002, USA

Herbert, Raymond E (Ray) (Athlete, Baseball Player)
9360 Taylors Turn
Stanwood, MI 49346-9686, USA

Herbert, Vincent (Musician, Producer)
c/o Kenny (Kenneth) Meiselas *Grubman Indursky Shire & Meiselas*
152 W 57th St Fl 31
New York, NY 10019-3310, USA

Herd, Carla
8281 Melrose Ave Ste 200
Los Angeles, CA 90046-6890

Herd, Richard (Actor)
PO Box 56297
Sherman Oaks, CA 91413-1297, USA

Heredia, Felix (Athlete, Baseball Player)
PO Box 4842
Hialeah, FL 33014-0842, USA

Heredia, Gil (Athlete, Baseball Player)
Missoula Osprey 412 WAlder St Attn Coaching Staff
Missoula, MT 59802, USA

Heredia, Wilson (Actor)
c/o Sarah Fargo *Paradigm (NY)*
360 Park Ave S Fl 16
New York, NY 10010-1716, USA

Herek, Stephen R (Director)
Endeavor Talent Agency
9701 Wilshire Blvd Ste 1000
Beverly Hills, CA 90212-2010, USA

Herera, Sue (Correspondent, Television Host)
c/o Staff Member *CNBC (Main)*
900 Sylvan Ave
Englewood Cliffs, NJ 07632-3312, USA

Herger, Wally (Congressman, Politician)
242 Cannon Hob
Washington, DC 20515-4322, USA

Hergert, Joe (Athlete, Football Player)
133 Horseshoe Trl
Ormond Beach, FL 32174-8229, USA

Herges, Matt (Athlete, Baseball Player)
21019 N 79th Pl
Scottsdale, AZ 85255, USA

Herjavec, Robert (Business Person, Reality Star)
c/o Monique Moss *Integrated PR*
9025 Wilshire Blvd Ste 400
Beverly Hills, CA 90211-1828, USA

Herkenhoff, Matt (Athlete, Football Player)
PO Box 9
South Haven, MN 55382-0009, USA

Herles, Kathleen (Actor)
c/o Shirley Grant *Shirley Grant Management*
PO Box 866
Teaneck, NJ 07666-0866, USA

Herlihy, Tim (Actor, Comedian)
c/o Staff Member *William Morris Endeavor (LA)*
9601 Wilshire Blvd
Beverly Hills, CA 90210-5213, USA

Herline, Alan (Athlete, Football Player)
610 Post Oak Cir
Brentwood, TN 37027-5189, USA

Herman, Alexis (Politician)
892 Linganore Dr
Mc Lean, VA 22102-2141, USA

Herman, Bill (Athlete, Basketball Player)
200 Laurel Lake Dr Apt 305
Hudson, OH 44236-2156, USA

Herman, Bill (Horse Racer)
478 Sycamore Springs St
Debary, FL 32713-4828, USA

Herman, Dave (Athlete, Football Player)
19 Stephens Ln
Valhalla, NY 10595-1601, USA

Herman, Jerry (Musician)
455 N Palm Dr Apt 3
Beverly Hills, CA 90210-4894, USA

Herman, Micah (Director)
c/o Joanna (Joanie) Burstein *Burstein Company, The*
15304 W Sunset Blvd Ste 208
Pacific Palisades, CA 90272-3656, USA

Herman, Pee-Wee (Actor, Comedian)
PO Box 29373
Los Angeles, CA 90029-0373

Hermann, Mark (Athlete, Football Player)
8525 Tidewater Dr
Indianapolis, IN 46236-8917, USA

Hermannson, Dustin M (Baseball Player)
9002 E Rimrock Dr
Scottsdale, AZ 85255-9133, USA

Hermansen, Chad (Athlete, Baseball Player)
2104 Rhonda Ter
Henderson, NV 89074-0651, USA

Hermanson, Dustin (Athlete, Baseball Player)
9002 E Rimrock Dr
Scottsdale, AZ 85255-9133, USA

Hermeling, Terry (Athlete, Football Player)
717 NW 16th Ave
Portland, OR 97209-2301, USA

Hermida, Jeremy (Athlete, Baseball Player)
3728 Paces Park Cir SE
Smyrna, GA 30080-6874, USA

Hermits s/ Peter Noone, Herman's (Music Group, Musician)
Herman's Hermits Inc
1482 E Valley Rd Ste 515
Santa Barbara, CA 93108-1200, USA

Hern, Tom (Actor)
c/o Simon Millar *Rumble Media*
1620 Broadway Ste C
Santa Monica, CA 90404-2777, USA

Hernandez, Adrian (Athlete, Baseball Player)
1723 Alden Rd Apt 1
Janesville, WI 53545-0886, USA

Hernandez, Angel (Athlete, Baseball Player)
501 Cypress Xing
Wellington, FL 33414-6369, USA

Hernandez, Carlos (Athlete, Baseball Player)
San Diego Padres
PO Box 122000
Attn: Player Development Dept
San Diego, CA 92112-2000, USA

Hernandez, Chuck (Athlete, Baseball Player)
3113 River Cove Dr
Tampa, FL 33614-2828, USA

Hernandez, David (Athlete, Baseball Player)
9618 McKenn L D
Elk Grove, CA 95757, USA

Hernandez, Evelio (Athlete, Baseball Player)
3004 SW 113th Ave
Miami, FL 33165-2228, USA

Hernandez, Felix (Athlete, Baseball Player)
c/o Alan Nero *Octagon (Chicago)*
111 E Wacker Dr Fl 10
Chicago, IL 60601-3713, USA

Hernandez, Jackie (Athlete, Baseball Player)
13390 NE 7th Ave Apt 103
North Miami, FL 33161-7509, USA

Hernandez, Jay (Actor)
United Talent Agency
9336 Civic Center Dr
Beverly Hills, CA 90210-3604, USA

Hernandez, Jeremy (Athlete, Baseball Player)
861 Hemlock Ridge Ct
Simi Valley, CA 93065-5540, USA

Hernandez, Jose (Astronaut)
4915 Cora Post Rd
Lodi, CA 95240-7356, USA

Hernandez, Jose (Athlete, Baseball Player)
22 Calle S
Vega Alta, PR 00692-7073, USA

Hernandez, Keith (Athlete, Baseball Player)
c/o Staff Member *SportsNet New York*
1271 Avenue Of The Americas Bsmt S7
New York, NY 10020-1302, USA

hernandez, keith (Athlete, Baseball Player)
Roosevelt Ave New York Mets 12301 Attn Broadcast Dept
Corona, NY 11368-9993, USA

Hernandez, Leo (Athlete, Baseball Player)
1352 SW 75th Ave
Miami, FL 33144-4422, USA

Hernandez, Livan (Athlete, Baseball Player)
560 Gate Ln
Miami, FL 33137-3361, USA

Hernandez, Matt (Athlete, Football Player)
PO Box 682
Eastpointe, MI 48021-0682, USA

Hernandez, Michel (Athlete, Baseball Player)
18857 Maisons Dr
Lutz, FL 33558-2879, USA

Hernandez, Orlando (Athlete, Baseball Player)
1001 Brickell Bay Dr Ste 1710
Miami, FL 33131-4939, USA

Hernandez, Ramon (Athlete, Baseball Player)
2732 NE 18th St
Ft Lauderdale, FL 33305-3606, USA

Hernandez, Robert J (Business Person)
USX Corp
600 Grant St Ste 153
Pittsburgh, PA 15219-2750, USA

Hernandez, Roberto (Athlete, Baseball Player)
5965 Bayview Cir S
Gulfport, FL 33707-3929, USA

Hernandez, Rudy (Athlete, Baseball Player)
8 Calle Rodriguez Serra
San Juan, PR 00907-1456, USA

Hernandez, Rudy (Athlete, Baseball Player)
Beloit Snappers
PO Box 855
Attn: Coaching Staff
Beloit, WI 53512-0855, USA

Hernandez, Runelvys (Athlete, Baseball Player)
18717 E 24th Street Ct S
Independence, MO 64057-2474, USA

Hernandez, Willie (Athlete, Baseball Player)
PO Box 125
Calle C Buzon
Aguada, PR 00602-0125, USA

Hernandez, Xavier (Athlete, Baseball Player)
3002 E Autumn Run Cir
Sugar Land, TX 77479-2636, USA

Hernandez Colon, Rafael (Ex-Governor)
PO Box 4071
San Juan, PR 00902, USA

Herndon, David (Athlete, Baseball Player)
337 Dusty Ln
Panama City, FL 32409-2203, USA

Herndon, Junior (Athlete, Baseball Player)
1477 Sequoia Ave
Craig, CO 81625-3732, USA

Herndon, Kelly (Athlete, Football Player)
1968 Cambridge St
Twinsburg, OH 44087-2008, USA

Herndon, Larry (Athlete, Baseball Player)
6149 Brunswick Rd
Arlington, TN 38002-6936, USA

Herndon, Mark J (Music Group, Musician)
RR 1 Box 239A
Mentone, AL 35984, USA

Herndon, Ty (Music Group)
PO Box 121858
Nashville, TN 37212-1858, USA

Herr, Matt (Athlete, Hockey Player)
1951 Holly Creek Pl
Concord, CA 94521-1550, USA

Herr, Tom (Athlete, Baseball Player)
1077 Olde Forge Xing
Lancaster, PA 17601-1738, USA

Herren, James (Athlete, Football Player)
224 Monongahela Ave
Glassport, PA 15045-1319, USA

Herrera, Anthony (Athlete, Football Player)
c/o Chad Speck *Allegiant Athletic Agency*
35 Market Sq Ste 201
Knoxville, TN 37902-1420, USA

Herrera, Augustine (Race Car Driver)
Marty Kane Motorsports
PO Box 908
Brea, CA 92822-0908, USA

Herrera, Carolina (Designer, Fashion Designer)
Carolina Herrera Ltd
501 Fashion Ave Fl 17
New York, NY 10018-5911, USA

Herrera, Caroline (Designer, Fashion Designer)
501 Seventh Ave Fl 17
New York, NY 10018, USA

Herrera, Efren (Athlete, Football Player)
861 Atlanta Ct
Claremont, CA 91711-2515, USA

Herrera, Jaime (Congressman, Politician)
1130 Longworth Hob
Washington, DC 20515-0606, USA

Herrera, Johnny (Race Car Driver)
Johnny Herrera Racing Inc
2333 E Southern Ave Unit 1013
Tempe, AZ 85282-7639, USA

Herrera, Kristin (Actor)
c/o Abby Bluestone *Innovative Artists (LA)*
1505 10th St
Santa Monica, CA 90401-2805, USA

Herring, Harold (Athlete, Football Player)
8673 Laurel Dr N
Pinellas Park, FL 33782-4304, USA

Herring, Laura
4702 N 36th St
Phoenix, AZ 85018-3423

Herring, Lynn (Actor)
37900 Road 800
Raymond, CA 93653-9714, USA

Herring-James, Katie (Athlete, Baseball Player, Commentator)
143 Grouse Ridge Rd
Tamaqua, PA 18252-5442, USA

Herrington, John B (Astronaut)
4346 Susie Vw
Colorado Springs, CO 80917-1731, USA

Herrington, John B Cdr (Astronaut)
4346 Susie Vw
Colorado Springs, CO 80917-1731, USA

Herrington, John S (Business Person, Secretary)
Harcourt Brace
525 B St
San Diego, CA 92101-4401, USA

Herrman, Ed (Athlete, Baseball Player)
13153 Tobiasson Rd
Poway, CA 92064-4308, USA

Herrmann, Don (Athlete, Football Player)
PO Box 318
Brookside, NJ 07926-0318, USA

Herrmann, Mark (Athlete, Football Player)
8525 Tidewater Dr
Indianapolis, IN 46236-8917, USA

Herrnstein, John (Athlete, Baseball Player)
603 Seminole Rd
Chillicothe, OH 45601-1547, USA

Herrod, Jeff (Athlete, Football Player)
20129 Tamiami Ave
Tampa, FL 33647-3370, USA

Herron, Bruce (Athlete, Football Player)
8504 S Calumet Ave
Chicago, IL 60619-6026, USA

Herron, Cindy (Music Group)
East West Records
75 Rockefeller Plz # 1200
New York, NY 10019-6908, USA

Herron, Denis (Athlete, Hockey Player)
12841 Marsh Pointe Way
West Palm Beach, FL 33418-6973, USA

Herron, Keith (Athlete, Basketball Player)
5374 Chew Ave Apt G2
Philadelphia, PA 19138-2804, USA

Herron, Tim (Athlete, Golfer)
20440 Linden Rd
Excelsior, MN 55331-9371, USA

Herrscher, Rick (Athlete, Baseball Player)
7714 Marquette St
Dallas, TX 75225-4413, USA

Hersch, Fred (Music Group, Musician)
SRO Artists
PO Box 9532
Madison, WI 53715, USA

Hersh, Earl (Athlete, Baseball Player)
682 Morning Glory Dr
Hanover, PA 17331-7828, USA

Hersh, Kristin (Musician)
c/o Staff Member *Concerted Efforts*
PO Box 440326
Somerville, MA 02144-0004, USA

Hersh, Seymour (Journalist, Writer)
1211 Connecticut Ave NW Ste 320
Washington, DC 20036-2709, USA

Hershey, Barbara (Actor)
c/o Jill Littman *Impression Entertainment*
9229 W Sunset Blvd Ste 700
West Hollywood, CA 90069-3407, USA

Hershey, Erin (Actor)
PO Box 16212
Irvine, CA 92623-6212, USA

Hershey, Maralyn
37337 Green Level Rd
Wakefield, VA 23888-2525

Hershey-Reeser, Esther Anne (Athlete, Baseball Player, Commentator)
3450 Compass Rd
Gap, PA 17527-9006, USA

Hershiser, Orel (Athlete, Baseball Player)
2167 Orchard Mist St
Las Vegas, NV 89135-1563, USA

Herskovitz, Marshall (Producer)
c/o Staff Member *Bedford Falls Company, The*
409 Santa Monica Blvd PH
Santa Monica, CA 90401-2232, USA

Herta, Bryan (Race Car Driver)
Bryan Herta Racing, Inc
26835 Boulder Crest Dr
Stevenson Ranch, CA 91381-0625, USA

Hertel, Rob (Athlete, Football Player)
325 Cordova St Apt 108
Pasadena, CA 91101-4688, USA

Herter, Jason (Athlete, Hockey Player)
5325 Roosevelt Dr
Hermantown, MN 55811-3679, USA

Hertford, Chelsea (Actor)
345 E Tujunga Ave Apt G
Burbank, CA 91502-1339, USA

Hertweck, Neal (Athlete, Baseball Player)
111 Leesburg Ln
Troutman, NC 28166-7600, USA

Hertz, Steve (Athlete, Baseball Player)
10211 SW 96th Ter
Miami, FL 33176-2704, USA

Hertzberg, Daniel (Journalist)
Wall Street Journal
200 Liberty St
Editorial Dept
New York, NY 10281-1003, USA

Hervey, Jason (Actor)
2049 Century Park E Ste 2500
Los Angeles, CA 90067-3127, USA

Hervey, Matt (Athlete, Hockey Player)
38635 Maracaibo Cir W
Palm Springs, CA 92264-0208, USA

Herzfeld, John (Director)
c/o Staff Member *William Morris Endeavor (LA)*
9601 Wilshire Blvd
Beverly Hills, CA 90210-5213, USA

Herzfeld, John M (Director)
Industry Entertainment
955 Carrillo Dr Ste 300
Los Angeles, CA 90048-5400, USA

Herzigova, Eva (Model)
c/o Scott Lipps *One Management*
42 Bond St Apt 2
New York, NY 10012-2428, USA

Herzlinger, Brian (Director)
c/o Naren Desai *Brillstein Entertainment Partners (LA)*
9150 Wilshire Blvd Ste 350
Beverly Hills, CA 90212-3453, USA

Herzog, Arthur III (Writer)
4 E 81st St
New York, NY 10028-0235, USA

Herzog, Roman (Politician)
Schlostrasse Bellevue Spreeweg 1
Berlin, GE D-105, USA

Herzog, Whitey (Athlete, Baseball Player, Coach)
9426 Sappington Estates Dr
Saint Louis, MO 63127-1664, USA

Hesburgh, Father Theodore
1320 Hesburgh Library
South Bend, IN 46566

Hesketh, Joe (Athlete, Baseball Player)
202 Glenridge Rd
East Aurora, NY 14052-2625, USA

Heskin, Kam (Actor)
c/o Susan Calogerakis *SC Management*
9250 Wilshire Blvd
Ground Fl
Beverly Hills, CA 90212-3352, USA

Heslov, Grant (Actor, Director)
14280 Greenleaf St
Sherman Oaks, CA 91423-4012, USA

Hess, Bob (Athlete, Hockey Player)
17926 White Robin Ct
Chesterfield, MO 63005-4968, USA

Hess, Jared (Director, Writer)
Moxie Pictures
2644 30th St Ste 100
Santa Monica, CA 90405-3051, USA

Hess, John B (Business Person)
Amerada Hess Corp
1185 Avenue of the Americas Fl 39
New York, NY 10036-2665, USA

Hess, Sandra (Actor)
3115 Dona Emilia Dr
Studio City, CA 91604-4310, USA

Hesseman, Howard (Actor)
Innovative Artists
1505 10th St
Santa Monica, CA 90401-2805, USA

Hession, Therese (Athlete, Golfer)
3871 Stonesthrow Ln
Hilliard, OH 43026-5712, USA

Hessler, Curtis A (Publisher)
Times-Mirror Co
Times-Mirror Square
Los Angeles, CA 90053, USA

Hessler, Gordon (Director)
8910 Holly Pl
Los Angeles, CA 90046-1836, USA

Hessman, Mike (Athlete, Baseball Player)
524 Saint James Dr
Loris, SC 29569-2550, USA

Hest, Ari (Musician)
c/o Staff Member *Paradigm (Monterey)*
404 W Franklin St
Monterey, CA 93940-2303, USA

Hester, Dan (Athlete, Basketball Player)
13846 N Sunset Dr
Fountain Hills, AZ 85268-3173, USA

Hester, Devin (Athlete, Football Player)
c/o Ashley Smith Becker *Relativity Sports (LA)*
9242 Beverly Blvd Ste 300
Beverly Hills, CA 90210-3728, USA

Hester, Jessie L (Athlete, Football Player)
12813 Pineacre Ct
Wellington, FL 33414-4140, USA

Hester, John (Athlete, Baseball Player)
125 Okoni Ln
Eatonton, GA 31024-1098, USA

Heston, Fraser (Actor)
7990 Briar Summit Dr
Los Angeles, CA 90046-1125, USA

Hetfield, James (Musician)
2020 Union St
San Francisco, CA 94123-4103, USA

Hetki, Johnny (Athlete, Baseball Player)
4004 Stary Dr
Cleveland, OH 44134-5823, USA

Hetrick, Jennifer (Actor)
c/o Staff Member *AKA Talent Agency*
6310 San Vicente Blvd Ste 200
Los Angeles, CA 90048-5488, USA

Hettema, Dave (Athlete, Football Player)
31 Desert Sky Rd SE
Albuquerque, NM 87123-3983, USA

Hetzel, Eric (Athlete, Baseball Player)
2271 Hetzel Rd
Crowley, LA 70526-8318, USA

Hetzel, Fred (Athlete, Basketball Player)
218 Cornwall St NW
Leesburg, VA 20176-2701, USA

Heuring, Lori (Actor)
c/o Holly Shakoor Fleischer *42West (LA)*
1840 Century Park E Ste 700
Los Angeles, CA 90067-2122, USA

Heverly-Williams, Ruth (Baseball Player)
520 Tennis Ave
Ambler, PA 19002-6015, USA

Heveron, Doug (Race Car Driver)
PO Box 250
Denver, NC 28037-0250, USA

Hewett, Christopher
1422 N Sweetzer Ave Apt 110
West Hollywood, CA 90069-1527

Hewett, Howard (Music Group)
GHR Entertainment
6014 N Pointe Pl
Woodland Hills, CA 91367-5500, USA

Hewgley, Claude (Athlete, Football Player)
55 Silvermont Dr
Spring, TX 77382-2007, USA

Hewitt, Angela (Musician)
Cramer/Marder Artists
3436 Springhill Rd
Lafayette, CA 94549-2535, USA

Hewitt, Bill (Athlete, Baseball Player)
923 Vance Jackson Rd Apt 1107
San Antonio, TX 78201-2739, USA

Hewitt, Bob (Tennis Player)
822 Boylston St Ste 203
Chestnut Hill, MA 02467-2504, USA

Hewitt, Christopher (Actor)
154 E 66th St
New York, NY 10065-6643, USA

Hewitt, Jennifer Love (Actor)
575 Erskine Dr
Pacific Palisades, CA 90272-4248, USA

Hewitt, John (Race Car Driver)
Hewitt Racing
37 Hewitt Dr
Troy, NY 12180-8121, USA

Hewitt, Martin (Actor)
1346 Madonna Rd
San Luis Obispo, CA 93405-6504, USA

Hewitt, Paul (Basketball Player, Coach)
Georgia Institute of Technology
Athletic Dept
Atlanta, GA 30332-0001, USA

Hewko, Robert (Athlete, Football Player)
100 Lincoln Rd Apt 634
Miami Beach, FL 33139-2013, USA

Hewlett, David (Actor)
c/o Shelley Browning *Magnolia Entertainment (LA)*
9595 Wilshire Blvd Ste 601
Beverly Hills, CA 90212-2506, USA

Hewlett, Howard (Music Group)
Green Light Talent Agency
PO Box 3172
Beverly Hills, CA 90212-0172, USA

Hewlett, Mark (Reality Star)
c/o Jerry Shandrew *Shandrew Public Relations*
1050 S Stanley Ave
Los Angeles, CA 90019-6634, USA

Hewson, Jack (Athlete, Basketball Player)
114 Tahlequah Ln
Loudon, TN 37774-3143, USA

Hextall, Dennis H (Athlete, Hockey Player)
2631 Harvest Hill Dr
Brighton, MI 48114-8299, USA

Hextall, Ronald (Ron) (Athlete, Hockey Player)
1111 S Figueroa St Ste 3100
Los Angeles, CA 90015-1333, USA

Hey, Virginia (Actor)
c/o Michael Henderson *Heresun Management*
4119 W Burbank Blvd
Burbank, CA 91505-2122, USA

Heydeman, Greg (Athlete, Baseball Player)
702 Ramona Ave
Monterey, CA 93940-5430, USA

Heyer, Kirk (Athlete, Football Player)
4264 Center St
Omaha, NE 68105, USA

Heyer, Shane
345 Toyon Ter
San Marcos, CA 92069-8120, USA

Heyman, Paul (Athlete, Wrestler)
6 Azalea Ct
Scarsdale, NY 10583-3204, USA

Heyward, Cameron (Football Player)
c/o Pat Dye Jr *SportsTrust Advisors (GA)*
3340 Peachtree Rd NE Fl 16
Atlanta, GA 30326-1000, USA

Heyward, Jason (Athlete, Baseball Player)
2443 Crescent Park Ct Apt 1180
Atlanta, GA 30339-6024, USA

Heyward-Bey, Darrius (Athlete, Football Player)
c/o Ben Dogra *CAA (St. Louis)*
222 S Central Ave Ste 1008
Saint Louis, MO 63105-3509, USA

Heywood, Anne (Actor)
9966 Liebe Dr
Beverly Hills, CA 90210-1037, USA

H. Hoyer, Steny (Congressman, Politician)
1705 Longworth Hob
Washington, DC 20515-2005, USA

Hiatt, Jack (Athlete, Baseball Player)
1408 Fisher Rd
Roseburg, OR 97471-8208, USA

Hiatt, John (Music Group, Musician, Songwriter, Writer)
c/o Staff Member *United Talent Agency (UTA-LA)*
9336 Civic Center Dr
Beverly Hills, CA 90210-3604, USA

Hiatt, Phil (Athlete, Baseball Player)
30 Littleton St
Cantonment, FL 32533-6558, USA

Hiatt, Shana (Actor, Model)
c/o Jerry Shandrew *Shandrew Public Relations*
1050 S Stanley Ave
Los Angeles, CA 90019-6634, USA

Hibbard, Greg (Athlete, Baseball Player)
5287 Conifer View Ln
Lakeland, TN 38002-4874, USA

Hibbard, Greg (Athlete, Baseball Player)
Mahoning Valley Scrappers 111 Eastwood Mall Blvd
Attn Coaching Staff
Niles, OH 44446, USA

Hibbert, Edward (Actor)
Gage Group
5757 Wilshire Blvd Ste 659
Los Angeles, CA 90036-3682, USA

Hibbs, Jim (Athlete, Baseball Player)
4659 Foothill Rd
Ventura, CA 93003-1903, USA

Hick', Ray (Athlete, Football Player)
801 Evergreen Dr
Friendswood, TX 77546-4757, USA

Hickam, Homer (Writer)
9532 Hemlock Dr SE
Huntsville, AL 35803-1165, USA

Hickam, Homer H Jr (Writer)
9532 Hemlock Dr SE
Huntsville, AL 35803-1165, USA

Hicke, Ernie (Athlete, Hockey Player)
5287 S Sugarberry Ct
Gilbert, AZ 85298-4657, USA

Hickenbottom, Michael (Wrestler)
c/o Kerry Rodgerson *World Wrestling Entertainment (WWE)*
1241 E Main St
Titan Towers
Stamford, CT 06902-3520, USA

Hickenlooper, John (Governor, Politician)
State Capitol
136 State Capitol
Denver, CO 80203, USA

Hickerson, Bryan (Athlete, Baseball Player)
275 S Hunters Rdg
Warsaw, IN 46582-5645, USA

Hickerson, Gene (Athlete)
4471 Nagel Rd
Avon, OH 44011-2735, USA

Hickey, Bo (Athlete, Football Player)
94 Field Crest Rd
New Canaan, CT 06840-6330, USA

Hickey, Jim (Athlete, Baseball Player)
4297 Sasha Trl
Saint Cloud, FL 34772-8870, USA

Hickey, John Benjamin (Actor)
c/o Sarah Fargo *Paradigm (NY)*
360 Park Ave S Fl 16
New York, NY 10010-1716, USA

Hickey, Maurice (Publisher)
Denver Post
65015th St
Denver, CO 80202, USA

Hickey, William V (Business Person)
Sealed Air Corp
Park 80 E
Saddle Brook, NJ 07663, USA

Hickland, Catherine (Actor)
255 W 84th St Apt 2A
New York, NY 10024-4322, USA

Hickman, Dallas (Athlete, Football Player)
6521 E Dreyfus Ave
Scottsdale, AZ 85254-3915, USA

Hickman, Darryl (Actor)
171 Hermosillo Rd
Santa Barbara, CA 93108-2414, USA

Hickman, Dwayne (Actor)
PO Box 17226
Encino, CA 91416-7226, USA

Hickman, Fred (Sportscaster)
Cable News Network
1050 Techwood Dr NW
Sports Dept
Atlanta, GA 30318-5695, USA

Hickman, Jesse (Athlete, Baseball Player)
2004 Simmons St # A
Alexandria, LA 71301-3739, USA

Hickman, Jim (Race Car Driver)
PO Box 455
Henning, TN 38041-0455, USA

Hickman, Larry (Athlete, Football Player)
5519 Westchester Dr
Tyler, TX 75703-6009, USA

Hickman, Tracy (Writer)
c/o Staff Member *HarperCollins Publishers*
195 Broadway Fl 2
Cellar 1
New York, NY 10007-3132, USA

Hickox, Edwin (Athlete, Baseball Player)
1721 Baron Ct
Port Orange, FL 32128-6789, USA

Hicks, Adam (Actor)
c/o Mona Loring *MLC PR*
7080 Hollywood Blvd Ste 903
Los Angeles, CA 90028-6936, USA

Hicks, Alex (Athlete, Hockey Player)
7511 E Tailspin Ln
Scottsdale, AZ 85255-4632, USA

Hicks, Artis (Athlete, Football Player)
1804 Woods Edge Dr NE
Leesburg, VA 20176-6618, USA

Hicks, Betty (Athlete, Golfer)
669 Canyon View Dr
Laguna Beach, CA 92651-2671, USA

Hicks, Brandon (Athlete, Baseball Player)
4907 Pocahontas Dr
Pasadena, TX 77505-2915, USA

Hicks, Buddy (Athlete, Baseball Player)
1526 N Dixie Downs Rd Unit 26
Saint George, UT 84770-4105, USA

Hicks, Catherine (Actor)
c/o Margrit Polak *Margrit Polak
Management*
1920 Hillhurst Ave Ste 405
Los Angeles, CA 90027-2712, USA

Hicks, Dan (Music Group)
Leslie Wiener
PO Box 245
Sausalito, CA 94966-0245, USA

Hicks, Dan (Sportscaster)
NBC-TV
30 Rockefeller Plz
Sports Dept
New York, NY 10112-0015, USA

Hicks, Dwight (Athlete, Football Player)
PO Box 342
Sierra Madre, CA 91025-0342, USA

Hicks, Eric (Athlete, Football Player)
6714 W 148th Ter
Overland Park, KS 66223-2929, USA

Hicks, Esther (Motivational Speaker,
Writer)
PO Box 690070
San Antonio, TX 78269-0070, USA

Hicks, Jerry (Motivational Speaker,
Writer)
PO Box 690070
San Antonio, TX 78269-0070, USA

Hicks, Jim (Athlete, Baseball Player)
2927 Highland Lakes Dr
Missouri City, TX 77459-4218, USA

Hicks, Jimmy (Musician)
4110 N Shore Dr
West Palm Beach, FL 33407-3202, USA

Hicks, Joe (Athlete, Baseball Player)
2707 Brookmere Rd
Charlottesville, VA 22901-1106, USA

Hicks, Michele (Actor)
c/o Eric Black *Crestview Entertainment*
521 Montana Ave
Santa Monica, CA 90403-1313, USA

Hicks, Michelle (Actor)
c/o Staff Member *Innovative Artists (LA)*
1505 10th St
Santa Monica, CA 90401-2805, USA

Hicks, Robert (Athlete, Football Player)
2544 Hightower Ct NW
Atlanta, GA 30318-7412, USA

Hicks, "Sonny" Osceola (Athlete, Football
Player)
1626 Wood Grove Rd
Memphis, TN 38117, USA

Hicks, Sylvester (Athlete, Football Player)
1891 W Fletcher Run Cir Apt 103
Cordova, TN 38016-2023, USA

Hicks, Taylor (Musician)
1463 Willoughby Cir
Vestavia, AL 35216-2918, USA

Hicks, Thomas O (Commentator)
Texas Rangers
10000 Hollow Way Rd
Dallas, TX 75229-6631, USA

Hicks, Tom (Athlete, Football Player)
43 Timber Trail Dr
Oak Brook, IL 60523-1458, USA

Hicks, Wayne (Athlete, Hockey Player)
7726 E Buteo Dr
Scottsdale, AZ 85255-4656, USA

Hicks, W K (Athlete, Football Player)
10149 Kemp Forest Dr
Houston, TX 77080-2509, USA

Hicks Jr, John C (Athlete, Football Player)
3287 Green Cook Rd
Johnstown, OH 43031-9208, USA

Hidalgo, John (Government Official)
May's Valentine Davenport Moore
1899 L St NW
Washington, DC 20036-3804, USA

Hiddleston, Thomas (Actor)
c/o Jon Rubinstein *Authentic Talent and
Literary Management*
20 Jay St Ste M17
Brooklyn, NY 11201-8300, USA

Hiddleston, Tom (Actor)
c/o Jon Rubinstein *Authentic Talent and
Literary Management*
20 Jay St Ste M17
Brooklyn, NY 11201-8300, USA

Hieb, Richard J (Astronaut)
Allied Signal Tech Services
538 Bright Meadow Dr
Gaithersburg, MD 20878-2190, USA

Hiemstra, Ed (Athlete, Football Player)
100 Hamilton Ct Unit D
Manhattan, MT 59741-8162, USA

Hieronymus, Clara W (Journalist)
50 Spring St
Savannah, TN 38372-1454, USA

Hietala, Brad (Race Car Driver)
85 North St
Enfield, CT 06082-3933, USA

Hietpas, Joe (Athlete, Baseball Player)
611 E Timberline Dr
Appleton, WI 54913-7104, USA

Hi-Five (Music Group)
PO Box 313030
Jamaica, NY 11431-3030, USA

Higdon, Bruce (Cartoonist)
210 Canvasback Ct
Murfreesboro, TN 37130-8855, USA

Higginbotham, Joan E (Astronaut)
1409 Mija Ln
Seabrook, TX 77586-2406, USA

Higgins, Al (Producer)
c/o Staff Member *Creative Artists Agency
(CAA-LA)*
2000 Avenue of the Stars Ste 100
Los Angeles, CA 90067-4705, USA

Higgins, Brian (Congressman, Politician)
2459 Rayburn Hob
Washington, DC 20515-4311, USA

Higgins, Chris (Athlete, Hockey Player)
34 Colgate Dr
Smithtown, NY 11787-2017, USA

Higgins, David (Actor)
c/o Ben Feigin *Anonymous Content (LA)*
3532 Hayden Ave
Culver City, CA 90232-2413, USA

Higgins, Dennis (Athlete, Baseball Player)
1123 Boonville Rd
Jefferson City, MO 65109-0621, USA

Higgins, Earle (Athlete, Basketball Player)
29128 Chateau Ct
Farmington Hills, MI 48334-4112, USA

Higgins, Jack (Cartoonist)
59 Waverly Ave
Clarendon Hills, IL 60514-1236, USA

Higgins, John (Coach, Swimmer)
40 Williams Dr
Annapolis, MD 21401-2265, USA

Higgins, Kevin (Athlete, Baseball Player)
10551 Haywood Dr
Las Vegas, NV 89135-2851, USA

Higgins, Mark (Athlete, Baseball Player)
2999 Abbotts Oak Way
Duluth, GA 30097-2193, USA

Higgins, Mike (Athlete, Basketball Player)
137 48th Ave
Greeley, CO 80634-4307, USA

Higgins, Pam (Athlete, Golfer)
5 Pea Pine Ln
Newport Beach, CA 92660, USA

Higgins, Robert (Business Person)
Fleet Boston Corp
1 Federal St
Boston, MA 02110-2006, USA

Higgins, Rod (Athlete, Basketball Player)
743 Mendenhall Ct
Fort Mill, SC 29715-7852, USA

Higgins, Scott (Athlete, Baseball Player)
3591 Indian Clover St
Plumas Lake, CA 95961-8740, USA

Higgins, Tim (Athlete, Hockey Player)
c/o Staff Member *Chicago Blackhawks*
1901 W Madison St
Chicago, IL 60612-2459, USA

Higginson, Bobby (Athlete, Baseball
Player)
2039 Indian Sky Cir
Lakeland, FL 33813-4859, USA

Higginson, John (Doctor)
16 Sundew Rd
Savannah, GA 31411-2955, USA

Higginson, Torri (Actor)
c/o Staff Member *Sci-FI Channel, The*
100 Universal Plz
Bldg 1280/12
Universal City, CA 91608, USA

Higgs, Kenny (Athlete, Basketball Player)
746 Sargent Dr
Owensboro, KY 42301-8332, USA

Higgs, Mark (Athlete, Football Player)
4650 Lakeside Ter
Davie, FL 33314-4216, USA

Higham, Scott (Journalist)
Washington Post
Editorial Dept
1150 15th St NW
Washington, DC 20071-0001, USA

Highley, Ray (Race Car Driver)
Red Line Racing
1650 Linda Vista Dr
San Marcos, CA 92078-3810, USA

Highsmith, Alonzo (Athlete, Football
Player)
28 Warwick Ln
Missouri City, TX 77459-1904, USA

Highsmith, Don (Athlete, Football Player)
PO Box 664
Piscataway, NJ 08855-0664, USA

High Speed Scene, The (Music Group)
c/o Staff Member *Paradigm (Monterey)*
404 W Franklin St
Monterey, CA 93940-2303, USA

Hightower, Chelsie (Actor)
c/o Cynthia Snyder *Cynthia Snyder Public
Relations*
5739 Colfax Ave
N Hollywood, CA 91601-1636, USA

Hightower, Dont'a (Athlete, Football
Player)
c/o Michael Perrett *SportsTrust Advisors
(GA)*
3340 Peachtree Rd NE Fl 16
Atlanta, GA 30326-1000, USA

Highway 101
PO Box 1547
Goodlettsville, TN 37070-1547

Higuera, Teddy (Athlete, Baseball Player)
1567 S Sycamore Pl
Chandler, AZ 85286-6818, USA

Hiii-Westerman, Joyce (Athlete, Baseball
Player, Commentator)
1565 47th Ave
Kenosha, WI 53144-1289, USA

Hijeulos, Oscar (Writer)
132 E 43rd St
New York, NY 10017-4019, USA

Hikaru, Utada (Musician)
c/o Staff Member *Island Records*
825 8th Ave Rm C2
New York, NY 10019-7472, USA

Hilario, Maybyner (Nene) (Basketball
Player)
Denver Nuggets
1000 Chopper Cir
Pepsi Center
Denver, CO 80204-5805, USA

Hilario, Nene (Athlete, Basketball Player)
c/o Dan Fegan *Relativity Sports (LA)*
9242 Beverly Blvd Ste 300
Beverly Hills, CA 90210-3728, USA

Hilbert, Andy (Athlete, Hockey Player)
419 N Michigan Ave
Howell, MI 48843-1505, USA

Hilbert, Jon (Athlete, Football Player)
8701 Kev Ct
Louisville, KY 40299-1317, USA

Hildebrand, Jeffrey (Business Person)
3780 Willowick Rd
Houston, TX 77019-1116, USA

Hildebrand, Madison (Business Person, Reality Star)
Coldwell Banker
29178 Heathercliff Rd Ste 3
Malibu, CA 90265-4168, USA

Hildebrandt, Greg (Cartoonist)
Dark Horse
10956 SE Main St
Milwaukie, OR 97222-7644, USA

Hilderth, Mark (Actor)
c/o Staff Member *SMS Talent*
8383 Wilshire Blvd Ste 230
Beverly Hills, CA 90211-2436, USA

Hildreth, Eugene A (Doctor)
2000 Cambridge Ave Apt 103
Reading, PA 19610-2723, USA

Hilfiger, Tommy (Designer, Fashion Designer)
Tommy Hilfiger USA
601 W 26th St Rm 500
New York, NY 10001-1142, USA

Hilgenberg, Jay W (Athlete, Football Player)
1296 Kimmer Ct
Lake Forest, IL 60045-3669, USA

Hilgenberg, Joel (Athlete, Football Player)
2027 Ridgeway Dr
Iowa City, IA 52245-3239, USA

Hilgenbrinck, Tad (Actor)
c/o Jonathan Howard *Innovative Artists (LA)*
1505 10th St
Santa Monica, CA 90401-2805, USA

Hilgendorf, Tom (Athlete, Baseball Player)
PO Box 124
Camanche, IA 52730-0124, USA

Hilger, Rusty (Athlete, Football Player)
2625 SW 67th St
Oklahoma City, OK 73159-2735, USA

Hiljus, Erik (Athlete, Baseball Player)
2253 Demaray Dr
Grants Pass, OR 97527-9147, USA

Hill, Aaron (Athlete, Baseball Player)
20749 N 101st St
Scottsdale, AZ 85255-3365, USA

Hill, Aaron (Actor)
c/o Siri Garber *Platform Public Relations*
2666 N Beachwood Dr
Los Angeles, CA 90068-2308, USA

Hill, Al (Athlete, Hockey Player)
4807 Margaret Ln
Harrisburg, PA 17110-3365, United States

Hill, Al (Athlete, Hockey Player)
4807 Margaret Ln
Harrisburg, PA 17110-3365, USA

Hill, Armand (Athlete, Basketball Player)
1626 Laurens Way SW
Atlanta, GA 30311-3718, USA

Hill, Bernard (Actor)
c/o Staff Member *Seven Summits Pictures & Management*
8906 W Olympic Blvd
Ground Floor
Beverly Hills, CA 90211-3550, USA

Hill, Bob (Basketball Coach, Coach)
205 Rio Cordillera
Boerne, TX 78006-5892, USA

Hill, Bobby (Athlete, Baseball Player)
1874 Dry Creek Rd
San Jose, CA 95124-1005, USA

Hill, Brendan (Musician)
c/o Staff Member *ArtistDirect*
9046 Lindblade St
Culver City, CA 90232-2513, USA

Hill, Bruce (Athlete, Football Player)
1919 E Citation Ln
Tempe, AZ 85284-4704, USA

Hill, Calvin (Athlete, Football Player)
10300 Walker Lake Dr
Great Falls, VA 22066-3557, USA

Hill, Carolyn (Athlete, Golfer)
5906 Skimmer Point Blvd S
Gulfport, FL 33707-3938, USA

Hill, Cindy (Athlete, Golfer)
2852 NW 8th St
Fort Lauderdale, FL 33311-6637, USA

Hill, Daniel W (Dan) (Athlete, Football Player)
171 Montrose Dr
Durham, NC 27707-3929, USA

Hill, Dave (Athlete, Baseball Player)
125 Jenny Lind Dr
Hendersonville, NC 28791-1321, USA

Hill, David H (Athlete, Football Player)
921 Clements Cir
Moody, AL 35004-2512, USA

Hill, Derek (Athlete, Football Player)
8939 Gallatin Rd
Pico Rivera, CA 90660-1693, USA

Hill, Donnie (Athlete, Baseball Player)
6 Knob Hl
Laguna Niguel, CA 92677-5903, USA

Hill, Dule (Actor)
c/o Melissa Breaux *Washington Square Arts (LA)*
1041 N Formosa Ave
the Lot Writers Bldg, Room 305
West Hollywood, CA 90046-6703, USA

Hill, Dusty (Music Group, Musician)
Lone Wolf Mgmt
PO Box 163690
Austin, TX 78716-3690, USA

Hill, Eddie (Race Car Driver)
National Hot Rod Association
2035 E Financial Way
Glendora, CA 91741-4602, USA

Hill, Eric (Athlete, Football Player)
5500 Palm Cir
Galveston, TX 77551-5566, USA

Hill, Erica (Television Host)
Prime News Tonight
1 Time Warner Ctr
Cnn
New York, NY 10019-6038, USA

Hill, Faith (Musician)
c/o Coran Capshaw *Red Light Management (VA)*
321 E Main St Ste 500
Charlottesville, VA 22902-3201, USA

Hill, Fred (Athlete, Football Player)
31441 Paseo Riobo
San Juan Capistrano, CA 92675-5524, USA

Hill, Garry (Athlete, Baseball Player)
9602 Willowglen Trl
Charlotte, NC 28215-9767, USA

Hill, Gary (Athlete, Basketball Player, Football Player)
9957 Hickory Hollow Rd
Shawnee, OK 74804-9059, USA

Hill, Geoffrey W (Writer)
Boston University
745 Commonwealth Ave
University Professors
Boston, MA 02215-1401, USA

Hill, Glenallen (Athlete, Baseball Player)
108 Calvin Pl
Santa Cruz, CA 95060-3124, USA

Hill, Grant (Athlete, Basketball Player, Olympic Athlete)
c/o Jim Tanner *Tandem Sports & Entertainment*
2900 Crystal Dr Ste 420
Arlington, VA 22202-3556, USA

Hill, Greg (Athlete, Football Player)
Audio Video Unplugged
126 Oak Lawn Ave
Dallas, TX 75207-6912, USA

Hill, Greg (Athlete, Football Player)
PO Box 43210
Port Hueneme, CA 93044-3210, USA

Hill, Greg L (Athlete, Football Player)
PO Box 43210
Port Hueneme, CA 93044-3210, USA

Hill, Gregory (Director)
c/o Staff Member *Paul Lane Entertainment*
468 N Camden Dr
Beverly Hills, CA 90210-4507, USA

Hill, Ike (Athlete, Football Player)
412 Randolph St
Oak Park, IL 60302-3260, USA

Hill, Jack (Director, Producer, Writer)
5310 Clear Run Dr
Wilmington, NC 28403-1919, USA

Hill, J D (Athlete, Football Player)
2543 N 53rd Dr
Phoenix, AZ 85035-1910, USA

Hill, J.D. (Athlete, Football Player)
1550 S Yucca St
Chandler, AZ 85286-6859, USA

Hill, Jeremy (Athlete, Baseball Player)
10050 Gooding Dr
Dallas, TX 75229-6209, USA

Hill, Jessie (Music Group, Musician)
1210 Caffin Ave
New Orleans, LA 70117, USA

Hill, Jim (Athlete, Football Player)
4120 Parva Ave
Los Angeles, CA 90027-1365, USA

Hill, Jim (Sportscaster)
ABC-TV
77 W 66th St
Sprots Dept
New York, NY 10023-6201, USA

Hill, John S (Athlete, Football Player)
2005 Boyce Bridge Rd
Creedmoor, NC 27522-8023, USA

Hill, Jonah (Actor, Comedian)
c/o Rick Yorn *LBI Entertainment*
2000 Avenue of the Stars
Floor 3, North Tower
Los Angeles, CA 90067-4700, USA

Hill, Jordan (Athlete, Basketball Player)
c/o Bill Duffy *BDA Sports Management (BDA-CA)*
700 Ygnacio Valley Rd Ste 330
Walnut Creek, CA 94596-3838, USA

Hill, Ken (Athlete, Baseball Player)
1360 Shady Oaks Dr
Southlake, TX 76092-4208, USA

Hill, Kenneth (Athlete, Football Player)
121 Hawkins Pl
Boonton, NJ 07005-1127, USA

Hill, Kent (Athlete, Football Player)
630 Hawthorne Pl
Fayetteville, GA 30214-1218, USA

Hill, Kent A (Athlete, Football Player)
630 Hawthorne Pl
Fayetteville, GA 30214-1218, USA

Hill, Kim (Music Group)
Ambassador Artist Agency
PO Box 50358
Nashville, TN 37205-0358, USA

Hill, King (Athlete, Football Player)
7611 Sands Terrace Ln
Spring, TX 77389-2131, USA

Hill, Koyie (Athlete, Baseball Player)
2405 NW 151st St
Edmond, OK 73013-9227, USA

Hill, Koyle (Athlete, Baseball Player)
5216 N Valentine Rd
Park City, KS 67219-2718, USA

Hill, Lauryn (Actor, Musician)
c/o Nicole David *William Morris Endeavor (LA)*
9601 Wilshire Blvd
Beverly Hills, CA 90210-5213, USA

Hill, Madre (Athlete, Football Player)
18 Charleston Ct
Elgin, SC 29045-8521, USA

Hill, Marc (Athlete, Baseball Player)
203 Maple St
Elsberry, MO 63343-1604, USA

Hill, Michael (Commentator)
1293 NW 121st Ave
Plantation, FL 33323-2441, USA

Hill, Mike (Athlete, Golfer)
6750 Jefferson Rd
Brooklyn, MI 49230-9717, USA

Hill, Milt (Athlete, Baseball Player)
2047 Windermere Xing
Cumming, GA 30041-6109, USA

Hill, Pat (Football Player)
California State University
Athletic Dept
Fresno, CA 93740-0001, USA

Hill, Perry (Athlete, Baseball Player)
3726 Thatcher Dr
Rochester Hills, MI 48309-4533, USA

Hill, Randal (Athlete, Football Player)
18101 SW 112th Ave
Miami, FL 33157-5012, USA

Hill, Rich (Athlete, Baseball Player)
17 Spafford Rd
Milton, MA 02186-4408, USA

Hill, Roy (Race Car Driver)
Roy Hill Drag Racing School
4926 Walker Mill Rd
Sophia, NC 27350-9246, USA

Hill, Sean (Athlete, Hockey Player, Olympic Athlete)
2735 E Carob Dr
Chandler, AZ 85286-3118, USA

Hill, Simmie (Athlete, Basketball Player)
1470 Elizabeth Blvd
Pittsburgh, PA 15221-1223, USA

Hill, Steven (Actor)
18 Jill Ln
Monsey, NY 10952-2619, USA

Hill, Tamia (Musician)
c/o Staff Member *HUFF Events and PR*
325 W 38th St Rm 805
New York, NY 10018-9622, USA

Hill, Terence (Actor)
3 Los Pinos Rd
Santa Fe, NM 87507-4300, USA

Hill, Thomas (Tom) (Athlete, Track Athlete)
428 Elmcrest Dr
Norman, OK 73071-7053, USA

Hill, Tony (Athlete, Football Player)
729 Forest Bend Dr
Plano, TX 75025-3205, USA

Hill, Tye (Athlete, Football Player)
c/o Staff Member *Detroit Lions*
222 Republic Dr
Allen Park, MI 48101-3650, USA

Hill, Tyrone (Baseball Player)
Pinnacle
5594 Electric Ave
San Bernardino, CA 92407-2713, USA

Hill, Virgil (Athlete, Boxer)
1618 Santa Gertrudis Loop
Bismarck, ND 58503-0866, USA

Hill, Walter (Director)
836 Greenway Dr
Beverly Hills, CA 90210-3006, USA

Hill, Will (Athlete, Football Player)
c/o Adisa P. Bakari *Dow Lohnes PLLC*
1299 Pennsylvania Ave NW Ste 700
Washington, DC 20004-2431, USA

Hill, Winston (Athlete, Football Player)
101 Lane Dr
Gladewater, TX 75647-5369, USA

Hillan, Patrick (Actor)
11005 Morrison St Apt 206
N Hollywood, CA 91601-3899

Hille, Bertil (Doctor)
10630 Lakeside Ave NE
Seattle, WA 98125-6934, USA

Hillebrand, Gerald (Athlete, Football Player)
23 Madison Cir
Davenport, IA 52806-2812, USA

Hillegas, Shawn (Athlete, Baseball Player)
PO Box 46373
Seattle, WA 98146-0373, USA

Hillen, Bobby (Race Car Driver)
Donlavey Racing
5011 Midlothian Tpke
Richmond, VA 23225, USA

Hillenbrand, Daniel A (Business Person)
Hillenbrand Industries
700 STATE RR 46 E
Batesville, IN 47006, USA

Hillenbrand, Laura (Writer)
c/o Tina Bennett *William Morris Endeavor (NY)*
1325 Avenue of the Americas
New York, NY 10019-6026, USA

Hillenbrand, Shea (Athlete, Baseball Player)
18051 E Happy Rd
Queen Creek, AZ 85142-4952, USA

Hillenburg, Stephen (Steve) (Animator, Producer, Writer)
United Plankton Pictures
11400 W Olympic Blvd Ste 590
Los Angeles, CA 90064-1574, USA

Hiller, Arthur (Director)
1218 Benedict Canyon Dr
Beverly Hills, CA 90210-2728, USA

Hiller, John (Athlete, Baseball Player)
W8085 Becker Dr
Iron Mountain, MI 49801-9385, USA

Hiller, Lee (Journalist)
c/o Staff Member *Artistic Agency*
PO Box 68538
Portland, OR 97268-0538, USA

Hillerman, John (Actor)
1110 Bade St
Houston, TX 77055-7404, USA

Hill Hearth, Amy (Writer)
c/o Staff Member *Trident Media Group LLC*
41 Madison Ave Fl 36
New York, NY 10010-2257, USA

Hilliard, Corey (Athlete, Football Player)
c/o Mitchell Frankel *Impact Sports - Boca Raton*
2799 NW 2nd Ave Ste 203
Boca Raton, FL 33431-6709, USA

Hilliard, Dalton (Athlete, Football Player)
23 Hermitage Dr
Destrehan, LA 70047-3701, USA

Hilliard, Ike (Athlete, Football Player)
c/o Neil Schwartz *Schwartz & Feinsod*
contact via telephone or email
White Plains, NY 10603

Hilliard, Issac (Athlete, Football Player)
8240 SW 164th Ter
Palmetto Bay, FL 33157-3653, USA

Hillier, Randy (Athlete, Hockey Player)
308 Brookhaven Ln
Pittsburgh, PA 15241-2582, USA

Hillin Jr, Bobby (Race Car Driver)
c/o Staff Member *NASCAR*
1801 W Speedway Blvd
Daytona Beach, FL 32114-1243, USA

Hillis, Ali (Actor, Producer)
c/o Staff Member *Pinnacle Public Relations*
8721 Santa Monica Blvd Ste 133
West Hollywood, CA 90069-4507, USA

Hillis, Robert (Rib) (Actor)
c/o John Guglielmetti *Continuum Entertainment*
303 Park Ave S Ste 1220
New York, NY 10010-3601, USA

Hillman, Avriel (Actor)
203 W Comstock St Apt 11
Seattle, WA 98119-3557, USA

Hillman, Chris (Music Group, Musician, Songwriter, Writer)
McMullen Co
433 N Camden Dr Ste 400
Beverly Hills, CA 90210-4408, USA

Hillman, Darnell (Athlete, Basketball Player)
6011 Medora Dr
Indianapolis, IN 46228-1397, USA

Hillman, Dave (Athlete, Baseball Player)
849 Mimosa Dr
Kingsport, TN 37660-2563, USA

Hillman, Eric (Athlete, Baseball Player)
4331 E 23rd Ave
Denver, CO 80207-3156, USA

Hillman, Ronnie (Athlete, Football Player)
c/o Eugene Parker *Maximum Sports Management*
6435 W Jefferson Blvd # 197
Fort Wayne, IN 46804-6203, USA

Hillman, Trey (Athlete, Baseball Player, Coach)
301 Appaloosa Run
Liberty Hill, TX 78642-3862, USA

Hills, Carla (Politician)
3125 Chain Bridge Rd NW
Washington, DC 20016-3411, USA

Hills, Nate (Danja) (Musician, Producer)
8045 Mulholland Dr
Los Angeles, CA 90046-1128, USA

Hillsong (Musician)
c/o Staff Member *Integrity Music*
800 Hillcrest Rd Ste 6
Mobile, AL 36695-3906, USA

Hillton, Dave (Athlete, Baseball Player)
4910 E Sunnyside Dr
Scottsdale, AZ 85254-4671, USA

Hill-Westerman, Joyce (Baseball Player)
1565 47th Ave
Kenosha, WI 53144-1289, USA

Hilmers, David C (Astronaut)
2846 Bellefontaine St
Houston, TX 77025-1610, USA

Hilmers, David C Colonel (Astronaut)
2846 Bellefontaine St
Houston, TX 77025-1610, USA

Hilson, Keri (Musician)
c/o Sherlen Archibald *The Chamber Group*
75 Broad St Ste 2710
New York, NY 10004-2679, USA

Hil St Soul (Music Group)
c/o Staff Member *Paradigm (Monterey)*
404 W Franklin St
Monterey, CA 93940-2303, USA

Hilton, Barron (Business Person, Philanthropist)
Hilton Hotels Corp
7930 Jones Branch Dr Ste 1100
Mc Lean, VA 22102-3313, USA

Hilton, Dave (Athlete, Baseball Player)
4910 E Sunnyside Dr
Scottsdale, AZ 85254-4671, USA

Hilton, Fred (Athlete, Basketball Player)
6169 Mourning Dove Dr
Baton Rouge, LA 70817-1107, USA

Hilton, John J (Athlete, Football Player)
3911 S Fairway Dr
Powhatan, VA 23139-7022, USA

Hilton, Kathy (Reality Star)
c/o Catherine Saxton *The Saxton Group*
535 5th Ave Fl 19
New York, NY 10017-3684, USA

Hilton, Nicky (Designer)
c/o Antranig Balian *Mortar Media*
9465 Wilshire Blvd Ste 300
Beverly Hills, CA 90212-2612, USA

Hilton, Paris (Designer, DJ, Model, Reality Star)
3340 Clerendon Rd
Beverly Hills, CA 90210-1059, USA

Hilton, Perez (Internet Star, Writer)
c/o Ben Russo *EMC / Bowery*
5971 W 3rd St
Los Angeles, CA 90036-2832, USA

Hilton, Rick (Business Person)
Hilton & Hyland
250 N Canon Dr Fl 2
Beverly Hills, CA 90210-5306, USA

Hilton, Roy (Athlete, Football Player)
8332 Merrymount Dr
Windsor Mill, MD 21244-2242, USA

Hilton, T.Y. (Athlete, Football Player)
c/o Erik Burkhardt *Select Sports Group*
2700 Post Oak Blvd Ste 1450
Houston, TX 77056-5785, USA

Hilton, Tyler (Actor)
c/o Victoria Blake *Victoria Blake Management*
23622 Calabasas Rd Ste 230
Calabasas, CA 91302-4109, USA

Hilty, Megan (Actor)
c/o Erica Tuchman *One Entertainment (NY)*
12 W 57th St PH
New York, NY 10019-3900, USA

Hiltz, Nichole (Actor)
c/o Steve Caserta *Sanders Armstrong Caserta*
2120 Colorado Ave Ste 120
Santa Monica, CA 90404-3561, USA

Hiltzik, Michael A (Journalist)
Los Angeles Times
202 W 1st St Ste 500
Editorial Dept
Los Angeles, CA 90012-4401, USA

Hilworth, John (Athlete, Hockey Player)
11084 State Road 37 E
New Haven, IN 46774-9770, USA

HIM (Music Group, Musician)
c/o Tim Edwards *Flowerbooking*
1532 N Milwaukee Ave Ste 201
Chicago, IL 60622-6683, USA

Himelstein, Aaron (Actor)
c/o Paul Brown *New Wave Entertainment (LA)*
2660 W Olive Ave
Burbank, CA 91505-4525, USA

Himes, Dick (Athlete, Football Player)
431 Prairie Ln
Luxemburg, WI 54217-1054, USA

Himes, James (Congressman, Politician)
119 Cannon Hob
Washington, DC 20515-0501, USA

Himes, Larry (Commentator)
6421 W Purdue Ave
Glendale, AZ 85302-2908, USA

Himmelman, Peter (Musician)
230 22nd St
Brentwood, CA 94513, USA

Hincapie, George (Athlete, Cycler, Olympic Athlete)
11 Bella Citta Ct
Greenville, SC 29609-2724, USA

Hinch, AJ (Athlete, Baseball Player)
7010 Fairway Rd
La Jolla, CA 92037-5621, USA

Hinch, A J (Athlete, Baseball Player, Olympic Athlete)
841S Avenida De Las Ondas
La Jolla, CA 92037, USA

Hinchliffe, Brett (Athlete, Baseball Player)
5117 Melbourne St Unit 4204
Punta Gorda, FL 33980-3034, USA

Hinckley, Mike (Athlete, Baseball Player)
132 SW 5th St
Moore, OK 73160-5306, USA

Hinder (Music Group)
Universal Motown Records
1755 Broadway
New York, NY 10019-3743, USA

Hindi, Dion (Race Car Driver)
Hindi Motorsports
1421 Wagon Train Dr SE
Albuquerque, NM 87123-4296, USA

Hindle, Art (Actor)
Buzz Halliday & Assoc
8899 Beverly Blvd # 715
Los Angeles, CA 90048-2412, USA

Hindman, Stan (Athlete, Football Player)
824 Creed Rd
Oakland, CA 94610-1827, USA

Hinds, Aisha (Actor)
c/o Michael Greene *Greene & Associates*
1901 Avenue of the Stars Ste 130
Los Angeles, CA 90067-6030, USA

Hinds, Cirian (Actor)
c/o Staff Member *William Morris Endeavor (LA)*
9601 Wilshire Blvd
Beverly Hills, CA 90210-5213, USA

Hinds, Sam (Athlete, Baseball Player)
2151 Sunnyside Ave Apt 132
Clovis, CA 93611-4045, USA

Hinds, William (Cartoonist)
1301 Spring Oaks Cir
Houston, TX 77055-4703, USA

Hine, Maynard K (Doctor)
1121 W Michigan St
Indianapolis, IN 46202-5211, USA

Hiner, Glen H (Business Person)
Owens-Coming
1 Owens Coming Pkwy
Toledo, OH 43659-0001, USA

Hines, Andre (Athlete, Football Player)
1906 N 44th St
Kansas City, KS 66102-1814, USA

Hines, Ben (Athlete, Baseball Player)
2691 A St
La Verne, CA 91750-4304, USA

Hines, Brendan (Actor)
c/o Steve Caserta *Sanders Armstrong Caserta*
2120 Colorado Ave Ste 120
Santa Monica, CA 90404-3561, USA

Hines, Bruce (Athlete, Baseball Player)
4155 E Fairfield St
Mesa, AZ 85205-5008, USA

Hines, Byron (Race Car Driver)
14010 Marquardt Ave
Santa Fe Springs, CA 90670-5019, USA

Hines, Cheryl (Actor)
1221 Roberto Ln
Los Angeles, CA 90077-2304, USA

Hines, Clint (Race Car Driver)
Hines Racing
8324 140th St W
Taylor Ridge, IL 61284-9769, USA

Hines, Glen Ray (Athlete, Football Player)
861 N Queen Annes Lace Dr
Fayetteville, AR 72704-5106, USA

Hines, Grainger (Actor, Producer)
c/o Marianne Golan *Golan & Blumberg*
6528 W 6th St
Los Angeles, CA 90048-4716, USA

Hines, Mimi (Actor)
2540 S Maryland Pkwy
Las Vegas, NV 89109-1627

Hingsen, Jurgen (Athlete, Track Athlete)
655 Circle Dr
Santa Barbara, CA 93108-1001, USA

Hinkle, Lon (Athlete, Golfer)
PO Box 1347
Bigfork, MT 59911-1347, USA

Hinkle, Marin (Actor)
c/o Staff Member *Innovative Artists (LA)*
1505 10th St
Santa Monica, CA 90401-2805, USA

Hinkle, Robert (Actor)
915 Terrace Dr
Leander, TX 78641-8035, USA

Hinkley, Brent (Actor)
c/o Staff Member *Gage Group, The (LA)*
5757 Wilshire Blvd Ste 659
Los Angeles, CA 90036-3682, USA

Hinn, Benny (Religious Leader)
PO Box 162000
Irving, TX 75016-2000, USA

Hinnant, Michael (Athlete, Football Player)
43 Ashford Way
Schwenksville, PA 19473-1693, USA

Hinojosa, Ruben (Congressman, Politician)
2262 Rayburn Hob
Washington, DC 20515-0703, USA

Hinojosa, Tish (Music Group, Songwriter, Writer)
PO Box 3304
Austin, TX 78764-3304, USA

Hinote, Dan (Athlete, Hockey Player)
200 W Nationwide Blvd Unit 1
Columbus, OH 43215-2561, USA

Hinrich, Kirk (Basketball Player)
c/o Staff Member *Chicago Bulls*
1901 W Madison St
Chicago, IL 60612-2459, USA

Hinrichs, Paul (Athlete, Baseball Player)
1982 Brett Dr
Madisonville, KY 42431-9115, USA

Hinse, Andre (Athlete, Hockey Player)
PO Box 237
Fort Cobb, OK 73038-0237, USA

Hinshaw, Alex (Athlete, Baseball Player)
3367 Yankton Ave
Claremont, CA 91711-2004, USA

Hinshaw, George (Athlete, Baseball Player)
PO Box 4087
Bellflower, CA 90707-4087, USA

Hinske, Eric (Athlete, Baseball Player)
9460 E Sierra Pinta Dr
Scottsdale, AZ 85255-9196, USA

Hinsley, Jerry (Athlete, Baseball Player)
4255 Holliday Ln
Las Cruces, NM 88007-5760, USA

Hinson, Jordan (Actor)
c/o Bonnie Liedtke *Principato/Young Management (LA)*
9465 Wilshire Blvd Ste 900
Beverly Hills, CA 90212-2608, USA

Hinson, Larry (Athlete, Golfer)
Route 4 Box 397
Douglas, GA 31533, USA

Hinson, Roy (Athlete, Basketball Player)
8167 Quail Meadow Way
West Palm Beach, FL 33412-1506, USA

Hinson, Roy (Athlete, Basketball Player)
4272 State Highway 27
Monmouth Junction, NJ 08852, USA

Hinton, Charles R (Athlete, Football Player)
8 Country Squire Rd
Natchez, MS 39120-9314, USA

Hinton, Chris (Athlete, Football Player)
650 Galway Dr
Roswell, GA 30076-5132, USA

Hinton, Christopher J (Chris) (Athlete, Football Player)
5136 Falcon Chase Ln
Atlanta, GA 30342, USA

Hinton, Chuck (Athlete, Football Player)
8 Country Squire Rd
Natchez, MS 39120-9314, USA

Hinton, Chuck (Athlete, Baseball Player)
6330 16th St NW
Washington, DC 20011-8010, USA

Hinton, Darby (Actor)
1267 Bel Air Rd
Los Angeles, CA 90077, USA

Hinton, Eddie (Athlete, Football Player)
34 Auburn Rdg
Spring Branch, TX 78070-6014, USA

Hinton, James David (Actor)
c/o Staff Member *Cunningham Escott Slevin & Doherty (CESD-LA)*
10635 Santa Monica Blvd Ste 130
Los Angeles, CA 90025-8306, USA

Hinton, Jerrika (Actor)
c/o Ingrid Shaw *Shaw Management*
5540 Sylmar Ave Apt 2
Sherman Oaks, CA 91401-5134, USA

Hinton, Jill (Athlete, Golfer)
9503 Ridgefield Rd
Henrico, VA 23229-3929, USA

Hinton, Marcus (Athlete, Football Player)
63 Farrell Breland Rd
Wiggins, MS 39577-9119, USA

Hinton, Rich (Athlete, Baseball Player)
7447 Hawkins Rd
Sarasota, FL 34241-9376, USA

Hinton, Sam (Musician, Songwriter)
1719 Addison St
Berkeley, CA 94703-1501, USA

Hinton, S E (Writer)
8955 Beverly Blvd
West Hollywood, CA 90048-2423, USA

Hintz, Donald C (Business Person)
Entergy Corp
10055 Grogans Mill Rd Ste 150
Spring, TX 77380-1048, USA

Hinzo, Tommy (Athlete, Baseball Player)
308 Elkwood Ave
Imperial Beach, CA 91932-2610, USA

Hipp, I M (Athlete, Football Player)
1216 Hickman Arch
Virginia Beach, VA 23454-5878, USA

Hipp, Paul (Actor)
c/o Staff Member *Stone Manners Salners Agency (LA)*
6100 Wilshire Blvd Ste 1500
Los Angeles, CA 90048-5110, USA

Hipple, Eric (Athlete, Football Player)
7155 Driftwood Dr
Fenton, MI 48430-4304, USA

Hipps, Claude (Athlete, Football Player)
2129 W New Haven Ave Apt 1208
Melbourne, FL 32904-3879, USA

Hirase, Mayumi (Athlete, Golfer)
I M G
1360 E 9th St Ste 100
Cleveland, OH 44114-1730, USA

Hirata-Chalfin, Gail (Athlete, Golfer)
15539 Quiet Oak Dr
Chino Hills, CA 91709-4254, USA

Hire, Kathryn P Cdr (Astronaut)
PO Box 580146
Houston, TX 77258-0146, USA

Hire, Kathryn P (Kay) (Astronaut)
PO Box 580146
Houston, TX 77258-0146, USA

Hirsch, David
6255 W Sunset Blvd # 627
Los Angeles, CA 90028-7403

Hirsch, Emile (Actor)
c/o Sam Maydew *The Collective*
8383 Wilshire Blvd Ste 1050
Beverly Hills, CA 90211-2415, USA

Hirsch, Hallee (Actor, Musician)
c/o Amy Abell *Glick Agency*
1505 10th St
Santa Monica, CA 90401-2805, USA

Hirsch, Judd (Actor)
c/o Joel Rudnick *Paradigm (LA)*
360 N Crescent Dr
North Bldg
Beverly Hills, CA 90210-4874, USA

Hirsch, Laurence E (Business Person)
Centex Corp
2728 N Harwood St Ste 200
Dallas, TX 75201-1579, USA

Hirsch, Lee (Director)
c/o Mark Ross *Paradigm (LA)*
360 N Crescent Dr
North Bldg
Beverly Hills, CA 90210-4874, USA

Hirsch, Stan
16027 Ventura Blvd Ste 206
Encino, CA 91436-2774

Hirsch, Tom (Athlete, Hockey Player)
8469 Zanzibar Ln N
Osseo, MN 55311-1814, USA

Hirschbeck, John (Athlete, Baseball Player)
8730 Raintree Run
Youngstown, OH 44514-2987, USA

Hirschbeck, Mark (Athlete, Baseball Player)
12 Isinglass Ter
Trumbull, CT 06611-4024, USA

Hirschbein, Jonathan (Writer)
c/o Melissa Breaux *Washington Square Arts (LA)*
1041 N Formosa Ave
the Lot Writers Bldg, Room 305
West Hollywood, CA 90046-6703, USA

Hirschbiegel, Oliver (Director)
c/o Tobin Babst *Kaplan/Perrone Entertainment*
9560 Wilshire Blvd Fl 5
Beverly Hills, CA 90212-2401, USA

Hirschfielder, Gerald J (Cinematographer)
425 Ashland St
Ashland, OR 97520-3104, USA

Hirsh, Hallee (Actor)
c/o Staff Member *Dorit Simone Management & Productions*
1010 S Robertson Blvd Ste 11
Los Angeles, CA 90035-1527, USA

Hirson, Alice (Actor)
Halpem Assoc
PO Box 5597
Santa Monica, CA 90409-5597, USA

Hisaishi, Joe (Musician)
c/o Staff Member *Greenspan Artist Management*
8760 W Sunset Blvd
West Hollywood, CA 90069-2206, USA

Hiser, Gene (Athlete, Baseball Player)
1450 Caldwell Ln
Hoffman Estates, IL 60169-1202, USA

Hiskey, Babe (Athlete, Golfer)
4046 Pirates Bch
Galveston, TX 77554-8037, USA

Hisle, Larry E (Athlete, Baseball Player)
2404A N 23rd St
Sheboygan, WI 53083-4447, USA

Hisner, Harley (Athlete, Baseball Player)
4411 Park Place Dr Unit 209
Fort Wayne, IN 46845-8609, USA

Hitchcock, Jimmy (Athlete, Football Player)
616 Briar Patch Ter
Waxhaw, NC 28173-6822, USA

Hitchcock, Ken (Athlete, Hockey Player)
St Louis Blues 1401 Clark
Ave Attn Coaching Staff
Saint Louis, MO 63103, USA

Hitchcock, Michael (Actor)
c/o Staff Member *Gersh (LA)*
9465 Wilshire Blvd Ste 600
Beverly Hills, CA 90212-2605, USA

Hitchcock, Patricia (Actor)
2648 Stafford Rd
Thousand Oaks, CA 91361-5039, USA

Hitchcock, Ray (Athlete, Football Player)
2190 Arcade St
Saint Paul, MN 55109-2572, USA

Hitchcock, Russell (Musician)
Agency for Performing Arts
9200 W Sunset Blvd Ste 900
West Hollywood, CA 90069-3604, USA

Hitchcock, Sterling (Athlete, Baseball Player)
3052 River Lakes Dr
Whitefish, MT 59937-7801, USA

Hitchins, Christopher
2022 Columbia Rd NW Apt 702
Washington, DC 20009-1317

Hite, Shere (Writer)
75 Haywood St Apt 312
Asheville, NC 28801-0075, USA

Hite-James, Kathy (Athlete, Golfer)
38651 Nyasa Dr
Palm Desert, CA 92211-7009, USA

Hitt, Joel (Athlete, Football Player)
800 Founders Pointe Blvd
Franklin, TN 37064-0752, USA

Hitt, Lee (Athlete, Football Player)
4318 N Hall St
Dallas, TX 75219-2731, USA

Hix, William (Athlete, Football Player)
5070 White Dr
Batesville, AR 72501-9138, USA

Hjertstedt, Gabriel (Athlete, Golfer)
100 Sawgrass Corners Dr
Ponte Vedra Beach, FL 32082-3567, USA

Hjorth, Maria (Athlete, Golfer)
608 Henley Cir
Davenport, FL 33896-3072, USA

Hlavac, Jan (Athlete, Hockey Player)
1033 Royal Pass Rd
Tampa, FL 33602-5724, USA

H. Michaud, Michael (Congressman, Politician)
1724 Longworth Hob
Washington, DC 20515-0509, USA

Hnatiuk, Glen (Athlete, Golfer)
8746 Mississippi Run
Weeki Wachee, FL 34613-4046, USA

Hnidy, Shane (Athlete, Hockey Player)
3 Iris
Irvine, CA 92620-2212, USA

Hnilicka, Milan (Athlete, Hockey Player)
1111 S Figueroa St
Los Angeles, CA 90015-1300, USA

Hoag, Jan
855 N Martel Ave
Los Angeles, CA 90046-7561

Hoag, Judith W (Actor)
HWA Talent
3500 W Olive Ave Ste 1400
Burbank, CA 91505-5512, USA

Hoag, Tami (Writer)
c/o Andrea Cirillo *Jane Rotrosen Agency*
318 E 51st St
New York, NY 10022-7803, USA

Hoage, Terrell L (Terry) (Athlete, Football Player)
870 Arbor Rd
Paso Robles, CA 93446-8609, USA

Hoagland, Ashley (Athlete, Golfer)
803 26th Ave W
Palmetto, FL 34221-3576, USA

Hoagland, Edward (Writer)
PO Box 51
Barton, VT 05822-0051, USA

Hoagland, Jahiem (Musician)
c/o Staff Member *Atlantic Records (NY)*
1290 Avenue of the Americas Fl 28
New York, NY 10104-0106, USA

Hoagland, Jimmie L (Jim) (Journalist)
Washington Post
Editorial Dept
1150 15th St NW
Washington, DC 20071-0001, USA

Hoaglin, Fred (Athlete, Coach, Football Coach, Football Player)
7 Governors Rd
Hilton Head, SC 29928-3018, USA

Hoak, Dick (Athlete, Football Player)
162 Crest View Dr
Greensburg, PA 15601-1414, USA

Hoard, Leroy (Athlete, Football Player)
13141 NW 8th Ct
Sunrise, FL 33325-1326, USA

Hoban, Mike (Athlete, Football Player)
1917 Holly Ave
Darien, IL 60561-3518, USA

Hobart, Ken (Athlete, Football Player)
531 18th Ave
Lewiston, ID 83501-3823

Hobart, Nick (Cartoonist)
5632 Indiana Ave
New Port Richey, FL 34652-2333, USA

Hobaugh, Charles O Lt Colonel (Astronaut)
2009 Charter Pointe Ct
League City, TX 77573-9021, USA

Hobaugh, Charles O (Astronaut)
NASA
2101 Nasa Pkwy Spc Johnsoncenter
Houston, TX 77058-3696, USA

Hobaugh, Ed (Athlete, Baseball Player)
243 Port St
Ford City, PA 16226-1733, USA

Hobbie, Glen (Athlete, Baseball Player)
RR 2 Box 234A
Ramsey, IL 62080-9398, USA

Hobbs, Becky (Musician)
Entertainment Artists
2409 21st Ave S Ste 100
Nashville, TN 37212-5317, USA

Hobbs, Ellis (Athlete, Football Player)
8885 Old Southwick Pass
Alpharetta, GA 30022-7137, USA

Hobbs, Jack (Athlete, Baseball Player)
3 Wade Dr
Cherry Hill, NJ 08034-1741, USA

Hobby, Marion (Athlete, Football Player)
708 Nytol Cir
Irondale, AL 35210-2919, USA

Hobel, Mara (Actor)
17 Cunningham Dr
Lagrangeville, NY 12540-6841, USA

Hobgood, CJ (Athlete)
c/o Steven Astephen *Wasserman Media Group - Carlsbad*
2052 Corte Del Nogal
150
Carlsbad, CA 92011-1464, USA

Hobin, Mike
17 Hurlingham Club Rd
Far Hills, NJ 07931-2471

Hoblit, Gregory (Director, Producer)
c/o JC Spink *Benderspink*
8447 Wilshire Blvd Ste 250
Studio E
Beverly Hills, CA 90211-3224, USA

Hobson, Clell L (Butch) (Athlete, Baseball Player)
6302 Catarata St
Bakersfield, CA 93311-9638, USA

Hobson, Mellody (Producer)
c/o Staff Member *DreamWorks SKG*
1000 Flower St
Glendale, CA 91201-3007, USA

Hoch, Carin (Athlete, Golfer)
I M G
1360 E 9th St Ste 100
Cleveland, OH 44114-1730, USA

Hoch, Greg (Horse Racer)
18 Summer Wind Loop
Murrells Inlet, SC 29576-5690, USA

Hoch, Scott (Athlete, Golfer)
8800 Lake Sheen Ct
Orlando, FL 32836-5482, USA

Hochevar, Luke (Athlete, Baseball Player)
11512 Kimball Ln
Knoxville, TN 37934-3951, USA

Hochstein, Lisa (Reality Star)
c/o Jordyn Palos *Persona PR (LA)*
8840 Wilshire Blvd Ste 212
Beverly Hills, CA 90211-2606, USA

Hochstein, Russ (Athlete, Football Player)
43 Massand Rd
North Attleboro, MA 02760-6724, USA

Hock, Dee Ward (Business Person)
Visa International
900 Metro Center Blvd
Foster City, CA 94404-2172, USA

Hockenberry, Chuck (Athlete, Baseball Player)
1546 Birka Ln
Onalaska, WI 54650-2087, USA

Hockenberry, John (Actor, Correspondent, Writer)
c/o Sally Willcox *Creative Artists Agency (CAA-LA)*
2000 Avenue of the Stars Ste 100
Los Angeles, CA 90067-4705, USA

Hockenbery, Chuck (Athlete, Baseball Player)
1546 Birka Ln
Onalaska, WI 54650-2087, USA

Hocking, Dennis (Athlete, Baseball Player)
2592 N Falconer Way
Orange, CA 92867-6493, USA

Hocking, Denny (Athlete, Baseball Player)
1064 S Sundance Dr
Anaheim, CA 92808-2409, USA

Hocking, Justin (Athlete, Hockey Player)
3726 E 52nd Ct
Spokane, WA 99223-8604, USA

Hocott, Brenda (Athlete, Golfer)
261 Cave Ln
San Antonio, TX 78209-2242, USA

Hodder, Kane (Actor)
3701 Senda Calma
Calabasas, CA 91302-3066, USA

Hodder, Kenneth (Religious Leader)
Salvation Army
615 Slaters Ln
Alexandria, VA 22314-1112, USA

Hoddick, Steve (Race Car Driver)
782 Aero Dr
Buffalo, NY 14225-1408, USA

Hodel, Donald (Politician)
2200 Simms Pl
Denver, CO 80215, USA

Hodel, Nathan (Athlete, Football Player)
2411 Goldenrod Way
Wauconda, IL 60084-5087, USA

Hodge, Aldis (Actor)
c/o Matt Luber *Luber Roklin Management*
5815 W Sunset Blvd Ste 206
Los Angeles, CA 90028-6481, USA

Hodge, Daniel A (Dan) (Wrestler)
General Delivery
Perry, OK 73077-9999, USA

hodge, donald
901 Lawrence St NE
Washington, DC 20017-3520, USA

Hodge, Ed (Athlete, Baseball Player)
127 Jewell St
Johnson City, TN 37601-5209, USA

Hodge, Edwin (Actor)
c/o Matt Luber *Luber Roklin Management*
5815 W Sunset Blvd Ste 206
Los Angeles, CA 90028-6481, USA

Hodge, Sedrick (Athlete, Football Player)
120 Victoria Pl
Fayetteville, GA 30214-1176, USA

Hodge, Stephanie (Actor)
Gersh Agency
232 N Canon Dr
Beverly Hills, CA 90210-5302, USA

Hodge, Sue (Actor)
82 Constance Rd Twickenham
Middlesex A, EN TW2 7

Hodge Jr, Kenneth R (Ken) (Athlete, Hockey Player)
7894 Bayou Club Blvd
Seminole, FL 33777-3034, USA

Hodges, Bill (Basketball Player, Coach)
Georgia College
Athletic Dept
Milledgeville, GA 31061, USA

Hodges, Craig (Athlete, Basketball Player)
67 Elm St
Park Forest, IL 60466-1702, USA

Hodges, Eric (Actor)
3800 W Alameda Ave
Burbank, CA 91505-4300

Hodges, Gerald (Athlete, Football Player)
c/o Michael McCartney *Priority Sports & Entertainment - Chicago*
312 N La Salle
Suite 650
Chicago, IL 60610, USA

Hodges, Kevin (Athlete, Baseball Player)
19506 Kuykendahl Rd
Spring, TX 77379-3408, USA

Hodges, Louise (Actor)
31A St George S Rd Leyton
London, EN ELO 5

Hodges, Morris (Athlete, Baseball Player)
404 Park Lake Ter
Helena, AL 35080-3287, USA

Hodges, Morris (Athlete, Baseball Player)
1520 River Haven Ln
Hoover, AL 35244-1259, USA

Hodges, Pat (Actor, Musician)
c/o Staff Member *Diva Central Inc*
7510 W Sunset Blvd Ste 1445
Los Angeles, CA 90046-3408, USA

Hodges, Ron (Athlete, Baseball Player)
55 Hajo Ln
Rocky Mount, VA 24151-6819, USA

Hodges, Trey (Athlete, Baseball Player)
19506 Kuykendahl Rd
Spring, TX 77379-3408, USA

Hodge Sr, Ken (Athlete, Hockey Player)
13 Longfellow Dr
Newburyport, MA 01950-3325, USA

Hodgman, John (Actor)
c/o Jay Gassner *United Talent Agency (UTA-LA)*
9336 Civic Center Dr
Beverly Hills, CA 90210-3604, USA

Hodgson, James D (Politician)
28802 Grayfox St
Malibu, CA 90265-4253, USA

Hodgson, Pat (Athlete, Football Player)
816 Commons Park
Statham, GA 30666-2539, USA

Hodnett, Greg (Race Car Driver)
PO Box 34725
Memphis, TN 38184-0725, USA

Hodo, David (Music Group)
8255 W Sunset Blvd
West Hollywood, CA 90046-2417, USA

Hodson, Tom (Athlete, Football Player)
17938 Crossing Blvd
Baton Rouge, LA 70810-3840, USA

Hoebel, Bret (Reality Star)
c/o Staff Member *Abrams Artists Agency (LA)*
9200 W Sunset Blvd PH 11
West Hollywood, CA 90069-3601, USA

Hoechlin, Tyler (Actor)
c/o Staff Member *Management 360*
9111 Wilshire Blvd
Beverly Hills, CA 90210-5508, USA

Hoegh, Leo (Politician)
1472 W Desert Hills Dr
Green Valley, AZ 85622-8287, USA

Hoelscher, David (Athlete, Football Player)
8931 N Star Fort Loramie Rd
Yorkshire, OH 45388-9750, USA

Hoelscher, Joel (Athlete, Football Player)
8931 N Star Fort Loramie Rd
Yorkshire, OH 45388-9750, USA

Hoelzer, Margaret (Athlete, Olympic Athlete, Swimmer)
4400 Wallingford Ave N Apt 13
Seattle, WA 98103-7544, USA

Hoene, Ohil (Athlete, Hockey Player)
1110 Mississippi Ave
Duluth, MN 55811-4920, USA

Hoene, Phil (Athlete, Hockey Player)
4318 N Linwood Way
Meridian, ID 83646-6363, USA

Hoenig, Michael (Musician)
c/o Staff Member *Gorfaine/Schwartz Agency Inc*
4111 W Alameda Ave Ste 509
Burbank, CA 91505-4171, USA

Hoernig, Otto W Lt Colonel (Astronaut)
12930 Worldgate Dr Ste 700
Herndon, VA 20170-6036, USA

Hoerr, Irv (Race Car Driver)
541 Division St
Campbell, CA 95008-6934, USA

Hoest, Bunny (Cartoonist)
William Hoest Enterprises
27 Watch Way
Lloyd Neck
Lloyd Harbor, NY 11743-9707, USA

Hoeven, john (Politician)
PO Box 2572
Bismarck, ND 58502-2572, USA

Hoey, George (Athlete, Football Player)
4171 Westcliffe Ct
Boulder, CO 80301-1758, USA

Hoey, Jim (Athlete, Baseball Player)
2360 Highway 33
Ste 207
Trenton, NJ 08638, USA

Hofer, Paul (Athlete, Football Player)
7093 Cedardale Rd
Olive Branch, MS 38654-1307, USA

Hoff, Katie (Athlete, Olympic Athlete, Swimmer)
c/o Staff Member *USA Swimming Association*
1 Olympic Plz Bldg 2A
Colorado Springs, CO 80909-5770, USA

Hoff, Philip (Politician)
185 Pine Haven Shores Rd Apt 234
Shelburne, VT 05482-7809, USA

Hoffa, James
2593 Hounds Chase Dr
Troy, MI 48098-2338, USA

Hoffman, Al (Race Car Driver)
Al Hoffman Racing
17818 County Road 450A
Umatilla, FL 32784-9205, USA

Hoffman, Alice (Writer)
32 Lowell Rd
Concord, MA 01742-1707, USA

Hoffman, Barbara (Athlete, Baseball Player, Commentator)
318 E Mill St
Millstadt, IL 62260-1218, USA

Hoffman, Basil (Actor)
26 Aller Ct
Glendale, CA 91206-1701, USA

Hoffman, Dustin (Actor, Director, Producer)
313 N Barrington Ave
Los Angeles, CA 90049-2924, USA

Hoffman, Elizabeth (Actor)
Bauman Assoc
5750 Wilshire Blvd # 473
Los Angeles, CA 90036-3697, USA

Hoffman, Glenn E (Athlete, Baseball Player)
201 S Old Bridge Rd
Anaheim, CA 92808-1326, USA

Hoffman, Guy (Athlete, Baseball Player)
313 Fairway Dr Apt S
Bloomington, IL 61701-8219, USA

Hoffman, Ingrid (Chef, Television Host)
c/o Staff Member *Food Network, The*
1180 Avenue of the Americas Fl 11
New York, NY 10036-8401, USA

Hoffman, Jackie (Actor)
c/o Hannah Roth *Don Buchwald & Associates (LA)*
6500 Wilshire Blvd Ste 2200
Los Angeles, CA 90048-4942, USA

Hoffman, Jamie (Athlete, Baseball Player)
909 N Jefferson St
New Ulm, MN 56073-1433, USA

Hoffman, Jeffrey A Dr (Astronaut)
10 Saint Charles St
Boston, MA 02116-6233, USA

Hoffman, John (Athlete, Football Player)
3303 E Kentucky Ave
Denver, CO 80209-4929, USA

Hoffman, John Robert (Writer)
c/o Rosalie Swedlin *Anonymous Content (LA)*
3532 Hayden Ave
Culver City, CA 90232-2413, USA

Hoffman, Kara (Actor)
c/o Rod Baron *Baron Entertainment*
13848 Ventura Blvd Ste A
Sherman Oaks, CA 91423-3654

Hoffman, Marguerite (Business Person, Philanthropist)
Dallas Museum of Art
1717 N Harwood St
Dallas, TX 75201-2398, USA

Hoffman, Matt (Actor)
c/o Staff Member *Liberation Management*
1412 12th Ave
Los Angeles, CA 90019-4316, USA

Hoffman, Michael (Director)
c/o Doug MacLaren *ICM Partners (LA)*
10250 Constellation Blvd Fl 7
Los Angeles, CA 90067-6207, USA

Hoffman, Reid (Business Person)
LinkedIn
2029 Stierlin Ct
Mountain View, CA 94043-4655, USA

Hoffman, Rick (Actor)
c/o Staff Member *Jeff Morrone Entertainment*
9350 Wilshire Blvd Ste 224
Beverly Hills, CA 90212-3204, USA

Hoffman, Robert (Actor, Dancer)
c/o Michael Baum *Impression Entertainment*
9229 W Sunset Blvd Ste 700
West Hollywood, CA 90069-3407, USA

Hoffman, Toby (Music Group, Musician)
Columbia Artists Mgmt Inc
165 W 57th St
New York, NY 10019-2201, USA

Hoffman, Trevor (Athlete, Baseball Player)
2220 Ocean Frnt
Del Mar, CA 92014-2134, USA

Hoffman, William M (Songwriter, Writer)
190 Prince St
New York, NY 10012-2906, USA

Hoffmann, Frank N (Nordy) (Athlete, Football Player)
400 N Capitol St NW Apt 327
Washington, DC 20001-1511, USA

Hoffmann, Gaby (Actor)
c/o Sue Leibman *Barking Dog Entertainment*
609 Greenwich St Fl 6
New York, NY 10014-3610, USA

Hoffmann, Isabella
6500 Wilshire Blvd Ste 2200
Los Angeles, CA 90048-4942

Hoffmeyer, Bob (Athlete, Hockey Player)
c/o Staff Member *New Jersey Devils*
165 Mulberry St
Continental Arena
Newark, NJ 07102-3607, USA

Hofford, Jim (Athlete, Hockey Player)
63 Filkins St
Fairport, NY 14450-2452, USA

Hoffort, Bruce (Athlete, Hockey Player)
N1778 Hyacinth Ln
Greenville, WI 54942-9005, USA

Hoffpauir, Jarrett (Athlete, Baseball Player)
2043 Viking St
Vidalia, LA 71373-3011, USA

Hoffpauir, Micah (Athlete, Baseball Player)
211 Walnut Cir
Jacksonville, TX 75766-0560, USA

Hoffs, Susanna (Musician)
Bangles Mall
1341 W Fullerton Ave # 180
Chicago, IL 60614-2362, USA

Hofheimer, Charlie (Actor)
c/o Abby Bluestone *Innovative Artists (LA)*
1505 10th St
Santa Monica, CA 90401-2805, USA

Hofmann, Al (Race Car Driver)
PO Box 346
Umatilla, FL 32784-0346, USA

Hofmann, Isabella (Actor)
Don Buchwald
6500 Wilshire Blvd Ste 2200
Los Angeles, CA 90048-4942, USA

Hofmann, Kenneth (Commentator)
Oakland A's
1380 Galaxy Way
Concord, CA 94520-4912, USA

Hofschneider, Marco (Actor)
Progressive Artists Agency
400 S Beverly Dr Ste 216
Beverly Hills, CA 90212-4404, USA

Hofstetter, Steve (Writer)
c/o David Krintzman *Morris Yorn Barnes Levine Krintzman Rubenstein Kohner & Gellman*
2000 Avenue of the Stars Ste 300N
3rd Floor, North Tower
Los Angeles, CA 90067-4704, USA

Hogan, Brooke (Musician, Reality Star)
Brookestar
130 Willadel Dr
Belleair, FL 33756-1942, USA

Hogan, Chris (Actor)
c/o Tim Curtis *William Morris Endeavor (LA)*
9601 Wilshire Blvd
Beverly Hills, CA 90210-5213, USA

Hogan, Chuck (Writer)
c/o Richard Abate *3 Arts Entertainment (NY)*
16 W 22nd St Ste 201
New York, NY 10010-5842, USA

Hogan, Darrell (Athlete, Football Player)
14988 Scenic Loop Rd
Helotes, TX 78023-3701, USA

Hogan, Hulk (Athlete, Wrestler)
1040 Eldorado Ave
Clearwater Beach, FL 33767-1023, USA

Hogan, John (Horse Racer)
4947 State Route 40
Argyle, NY 12809-3468, USA

Hogan, Linda (Actor)
c/o Peter Young *Sovereign Talent Group*
8421 Wilshire Blvd Ste 200
Beverly Hills, CA 90211-3204, USA

Hogan, Linda (Writer)
University of Colorado
English Dept
Boulder, CO 80309-0001, USA

Hogan, Marc (Athlete, Football Player)
3761 Colby St
Pittsburgh, PA 15214-2134, USA

Hogan, Mike (Athlete, Football Player)
11 Walton Creek Dr SW
Rome, GA 30165-7228, USA

Hogan, Nick (Actor, Reality Star)
c/o Darren Prince *Prince Marketing Group*
18 Carillon Cir
Livingston, NJ 07039-2600, USA

Hogan, Paul (Actor)
536 22nd St
Santa Monica, CA 90402-3120, USA

Hogan, Paul (Reality Star)
c/o Staff Member *Acme Talent & Literary (LA)*
1400 Atlantic Ave Ste 274
Long Beach, CA 90813-2013, USA

Hogan, Paul (PJ) (Director, Producer, Writer)
c/o Richard Lovett *Creative Artists Agency (CAA-LA)*
2000 Avenue of the Stars Ste 100
Los Angeles, CA 90067-4705, USA

Hogan, Robert (Actor)
344 W 89th St Apt 1B
New York, NY 10024-2176, USA

Hogan, Terry
130 Willadel Dr
Belleair, FL 33756-1942

Hoganson, Paul (Athlete, Hockey Player)
1070 W Eagle Landing Pl
Tucson, AZ 85737-9230, USA

Hoge, Merril (Athlete, Football Player)
1 Fairway Dr
Southgate, KY 41071-3022, USA

Hogeboom, Gary (Athlete, Football Player)
13635 Hofma Ct
Grand Haven, MI 49417-9669, USA

Hogestyn, Drake (Actor)
28913 W Beach Ln
Malibu, CA 90265-4078, USA

Hoggard, Jay (Music Group, Musician)
Creative Music Consultants
181 Chrystie St # 300
New York, NY 10002-1275, USA

Hogland, Doug (Athlete, Football Player)
1514 4th St
Tillamook, OR 97141-3426, USA

Hogue, Beniot (Athlete, Hockey Player)
488 Village Oaks Ln
Babylon, NY 11702-3124, USA

Hogue, Benoit (Athlete, Hockey Player)
488 Village Oaks Ln
Babylon, NY 11702-3124, USA

Hogue, Stacey
10474 Santa Monica Blvd Ste 380
Los Angeles, CA 90025-6943

Hohensee, Mike (Athlete, Football Player)
6N568 Burr Rd
Saint Charles, IL 60175-6109, USA

Hohlmayer, Alice (Athlete, Baseball Player, Commentator)
5155 Cedarwood Rd Apt 47
Bonita, CA 91902-1946, USA

Hohn, Bill (Athlete, Baseball Player)
1406 Royal Oak Dr
Blue Bell, PA 19422-2166, USA

Hohn, Robert (Athlete, Football Player)
2624 N 78th St
Lincoln, NE 68507-2965, USA

Hoiberg, Fred (Basketball Coach)
2129 Quail Ridge Rd
Ames, IA 50010-9476, USA

Hoiles, Chris (Athlete, Baseball Player)
8688 Jerry City Rd
Wayne, OH 43466-9837, USA

Hoisington, Allan (Athlete, Football Player)
71371 Biskra Rd
Rancho Mirage, CA 92270-4251, USA

Hoke, Chris (Athlete, Football Player)
1709 Shady Knoll Ct
Sewickley, PA 15143-8885, USA

Hoke, Jon (Athlete, Football Player)
813 Cherokee Rd
Lake Forest, IL 60045-3963, USA

Hoku (Musician)
c/o Staff Member *United Talent Agency (UTA-LA)*
9336 Civic Center Dr
Beverly Hills, CA 90210-3604, USA

Holahan, Dennis
9250 Wilshire Blvd Ste 208
Beverly Hills, CA 90212-3344

Holberg, Fred (Athlete, Basketball Player)
2851 Timberview Trl
Chaska, MN 55318-1113, USA

Holbert, Aaron (Athlete, Baseball Player)
32015 Teague Way
Wesley Chapel, FL 33545-1612, USA

Holbert, Ray (Athlete, Baseball Player)
18436 W Palo Verde Ave
Waddell, AZ 85355-4330, USA

Holbrook, Bill (Cartoonist)
c/o Staff Member *King Features Syndication*
300 W 57th St Fl 15
New York, NY 10019-5238, USA

Holbrook, Bill (Cartoonist)
940 Providence Club Dr
Monroe, GA 30656-6214, USA

Holbrook, Hal (Actor)
9100 Hazen Dr
Beverly Hills, CA 90210-1843, USA

Holbrook, Sam (Athlete, Baseball Player)
2620 Sungale Ct
Lexington, KY 40513-1463, USA

Holbrook, Terry (Athlete, Hockey Player)
251 Meriden Rd
Painesville, OH 44077-3733, USA

Holcomb, Corey (Comedian)
c/o Everly Lee *Resolution (LA)*
1801 Century Park E Ste 2300
Los Angeles, CA 90067-2325, USA

Holden, Amanda (Actor)
c/o Melanie Greene *Affirmative Entertainment*
425 N Robertson Blvd
West Hollywood, CA 90048-1735, USA

Holden, Carl (Athlete, Baseball Player)
12755 Henderson Ln
Madison, AL 35756-3327, USA

Holden, Gina (Actor)
c/o Staff Member *The Collective*
8383 Wilshire Blvd Ste 1050
Beverly Hills, CA 90211-2415, USA

Holden, Jennifer
115 S Topanga Canyon Blvd # 153
Topanga, CA 90290-3160

Holden, Joyce (Actor)
444 N El Camino Real Spc 89
Encinitas, CA 92024-1313

Holden, Laurie (Actor)
c/o Jason Newman *Untitled Entertainment (LA)*
350 S Beverly Dr Ste 200
Beverly Hills, CA 90212-4819, USA

Holden, Mari (Athlete, Cycler, Olympic Athlete)
11160 Vista Sorrento Pkwy Apt 302
San Diego, CA 92130-7613, USA

Holden, Mariean (Actor)
L A Talent
8335 W Sunset Blvd Ste 200
Los Angeles, CA 90069-1534, USA

Holden, Mark (Athlete, Hockey Player)
4837 Spruce Pine Way
North Ridgeville, OH 44039-2341, USA

Holden, Robert (Politician)
1937 Windriver Dr
Jefferson City, MO 65101-4375, USA

Holden, Steve (Athlete, Football Player)
1202 N Nevada Way
Mesa, AZ 85203-4323, USA

Holden, Tim (Congressman, Politician)
2417 Rayburn Hob
Washington, DC 20515-3817, USA

Holden, William Wildlife Foundation
PO Box 16637
Beverly Hills, CA 90209-2637

Holden-Reid, Kristen (Actor)
c/o Staff Member *Paradigm (LA)*
360 N Crescent Dr
North Bldg
Beverly Hills, CA 90210-4874, USA

Holden-Ried, Kris (Actor)
c/o Alyssa Beinhaker *MLC PR*
7080 Hollywood Blvd Ste 903
Los Angeles, CA 90028-6936, USA

Holder, Christopher (Actor)
H David Moss
733 Seward St PH
Los Angeles, CA 90038-3503, USA

Holder, Livingston L (Astronaut)
18422 SE 58th St
Issaquah, WA 98027-8618, USA

Holderer, Oskar
2304 Oakwood Ave NW
Huntsville, AL 35810-4408, USA

Holder Jr, Eric H (Government Official)
US Department Of Justice
950 Pennsylvania Ave NW
Washington, DC 20530-0009, USA

Holderness, Joan (Athlete, Baseball Player, Commentator)
1037 Summerwind Dr
Crossville, TN 38571-3691, USA

Holderness, Sue (Actor)
10 Rectory Close Windsor
Berks., EN SL4 5

Holdman, Warrick (Athlete, Football Player)
c/o Fletcher Smith *Blueprint Sports Group*
221 W Jefferson Ave
Naperville, IL 60540-5355, USA

Holdridge, David (Athlete, Baseball Player)
39364 N Parisi Cir
San Tan Valley, AZ 85140-5721, USA

Holdsclaw, Chamique (Basketball Player)
Washington Mystics
601 F St NW
Mcl Center
Washington, DC 20004-1605, USA

Holdsworth, Fred (Athlete, Baseball Player)
13230 Lake Mary Dr
Plainfield, IL 60585-2649, USA

Hole
150 E 58th St Ste 1900
New York, NY 10155-1901

Holecek, John (Athlete, Football Player)
1876 N Wilmot Ave
Chicago, IL 60647-4417, USA

Holgren, Paul H
724 Southwick Cir
Somerdale, NJ 08083-2312, USA

Holiday, Corey (Athlete, Football Player)
302 Oxfordshire Ln
Chapel Hill, NC 27517-6207, USA

Holiday, Debby (Musician)
c/o Staff Member *Diva Central Inc*
7510 W Sunset Blvd Ste 1445
Los Angeles, CA 90046-3408, USA

Holiday, Ron (Athlete, Football Player)
229 Balance Meeting Rd
Peach Bottom, PA 17563-9772, USA

Holik, Bobby (Athlete, Hockey Player)
PO Box 9236
Jackson, WY 83002-9236, USA

Holladay, Robert (Athlete, Football Player)
2369 Timberland Dr NE
Conyers, GA 30207, USA

Holland, Al (Athlete, Baseball Player)
3523 Cove Rd NW
Roanoke, VA 24017-1813, USA

Holland, Al (Athlete, Baseball Player)
3523 Cove Rd NW
Roanoke, VA 24017-1813, USA

Holland, Bill (Race Car Driver)
4790 W 16th St
Indianapolis, IN 46222-2550, USA

Holland, Brad (Athlete, Basketball Player)
6336 Greenhaven Dr
Carlsbad, CA 92009-3084, USA

Holland, Darius (Athlete, Football Player)
13972 Meadowbrook Dr
Broomfield, CO 80020-6148, USA

Holland, Derek (Athlete, Baseball Player)
257 Gregory Dr
Newark, OH 43055-3421, USA

Holland, Dexter (Musician)
Rebel Waltz
31652 2nd Ave
Laguna Beach, CA 92651-8244, USA

Holland, Jamie L (Athlete, Football Player)
Ohio State University
410 Woody Hayes Dr
Attn: Alumni Association
Columbus, OH 43210-1104, USA

Holland, Jennifer (Actor)
c/o Jon Simmons *Simmons & Scott Entertainment*
7942 Mulholland Dr
Los Angeles, CA 90046-1225, USA

Holland, Jennifer (Writer)
c/o Lisa Blum *723 Productions*
2660 W Olive Ave
Burbank, CA 91505-4525, USA

Holland, John (Athlete, Football Player)
3117 Flagstone Dr
Garland, TX 75044-5882, USA

Holland, Johnny (Athlete, Football Player)
4208 Stonebridge Dr
Missouri City, TX 77459-3264, USA

Holland, John R (Religious Leader)
Foursquare Gospel Int'l Church
1910 W Sunset Blvd
Los Angeles, CA 90026-3275, USA

Holland, Josh (Actor)
4533 Willis Ave
Sherman Oaks, CA 91403-2710

Holland, Ken (Athlete, Hockey Player)
19022 Oak Leaf Ln
Northville, MI 48168-3046, USA

Holland, Ken (Athlete, Hockey Player)
600 Civic Center Dr
Attn: General Manager
Detroit, MI 48226-4408, USA

Holland, Paul (Musician)
Variety Artists
1924 Spring St
Paso Robles, CA 93446-1620, USA

Holland, Richard (Actor)
453 Frederick St
San Francisco, CA 94117-2719, USA

Holland, Todd (Director)
c/o David Lonner *Oasis Media Group*
8730 W Sunset Blvd Ste 700
West Hollywood, CA 90069-2249, USA

Holland, Wilbur (Athlete, Basketball Player)
538 Georgia Dr
Columbus, GA 31907-5091, USA

Holland, Willa (Actor)
c/o Ruth Bernstein *Viewpoint Inc (LA)*
8820 Wilshire Blvd Ste 220
Beverly Hills, CA 90211-2622, USA

Holland, Willard R Jr (Business Person)
FirstEnergy Corp
76 S Main St Bsmt
Akron, OH 44308-1890, USA

Hollander, Dan (Figure Skater)
c/o Staff Member *Champions on Ice*
3500 American Blvd W Ste 190
Minneapolis, MN 55431-4431, USA

Hollander, Lorin (Musician)
I C M Artists
40 W 57th St
New York, NY 10019-4001, USA

Hollander, Xaviera
Stadionweg 17
Southwick, MA 01077

Hollander, Zander (Writer)
3805 Yuma St NW
Washington, DC 20016-2213, USA

Hollandsworth, Todd M (Athlete, Baseball Player)
1310 Macalpin Dr
Inverness, IL 60010-6424, USA

Hollas, Donald (Athlete, Football Player)
22015 Gold Leaf Trl
Cypress, TX 77433-4643, USA

Holle, Eric (Athlete, Football Player)
6646 Whitemarsh Valley Walk
Austin, TX 78746-6363, USA

Holle, Gary (Athlete, Baseball Player)
820 5th Ave
Watervliet, NY 12189-3612, USA

Holler, Ed (Athlete, Football Player)
4500 Ivy Hall Dr
Columbia, SC 29206-1229, USA

Holleran, Leslie (Producer)
c/o Staff Member *Laha Films*
137 W 57th St
7th Floor
New York, NY 10019, USA

Holliday, Charles O (Business Person)
E I DuPont de Nemours
1007 Market St
Wilmington, DE 19801, USA

Holliday, Cheryl (Writer)
c/o Staff Member *United Talent Agency (UTA-LA)*
9336 Civic Center Dr
Beverly Hills, CA 90210-3604, USA

Holliday, Fred (Actor)
4610 Forman Ave
Toluca Lake, CA 91602-1617, USA

Holliday, Jennifer (Actor, Music Group)
Universal Attractions
W 57th St #1500
New York, NY 10019, USA

Holliday, Johnny (Commentator)
1500 S Capitol St SE
Attn: Broadcast Dept
Washington, DC 20003-3599, USA

Holliday, Kathy
345 N Maple Dr Ste 397
Beverly Hills, CA 90210-5179

Holliday, Kene
9300 Wilshire Blvd Ste 400
Beverly Hills, CA 90212-3210

Holliday, Matt (Athlete, Baseball Player)
c/o Scott Boras *Boras Corporation*
3 San Joaquin Plz Ste 100
Newport Beach, CA 92660-5944, USA

Holliday, Polly D (Actor, Music Group)
c/o Staff Member *The Blake Agency*
23441 Malibu Colony Rd
Malibu, CA 90265-4640, USA

Hollie, Doug (Athlete, Football Player)
3917 Midvale Ave
Oakland, CA 94602-3940, USA

Hollier, Dwight (Athlete, Football Player)
5012 Woodview Ln
Matthews, NC 28104-8057, USA

Holliman, Earl (Actor)
PO Box 1969
Studio City, CA 91614-0969, USA

Hollimon, Mike (Athlete, Baseball Player)
9922 Glen Canyon Dr
Dallas, TX 75243-4608, USA

Hollimon, Ulysses (Athlete, Baseball Player)
3726 Benton Blvd
Kansas City, MO 64128-2515, USA

Hollings, Ernest (Ex-Senator)
261 Calhoun St Rm 304
Charleston, SC 29401-1378, USA

Hollings, Ernest (Politician)
1415 N Utah St
Arlington, VA 22201-4823, USA

Hollingsworth, Ben (Actor)
c/o Shelley Browning *Magnolia Entertainment (LA)*
9595 Wilshire Blvd Ste 601
Beverly Hills, CA 90212-2506, USA

Hollingsworth, Shawn (Athlete, Football Player)
6 Broyhill Ct
Stafford, VA 22554-7757, USA

Hollinquest, Lamont (Athlete, Football Player)
13709 S San Pedro St
Los Angeles, CA 90061-2619, USA

Hollins, Damon (Athlete, Baseball Player)
1135 Camellia Ln
Suisun City, CA 94585-3804, USA

Hollins, Dave (Athlete, Baseball Player)
3221 Southwestern Blvd
Orchard Park, NY 14127-1230, USA

hollins, Essie (Athlete, Basketball Player)
9102 NW 48th St
Sunrise, FL 33351-5214, USA

Hollins, Lionel (Athlete, Basketball Player, Coach)
7594 Tagg Dr
Germantown, TN 38138-5827, USA

Hollis, Essie (Athlete, Basketball Player)
9102 NW 48th St
Sunrise, FL 33351-5214, USA

Hollis, James (Writer)
5200 Montrose Blvd
Houston, TX 77006-6547, USA

Hollis, Michael (Athlete, Football Player)
24 Falling Waters
Oakland, NJ 07436-2341, USA

Hollister, Dave (Actor, Music Group)
c/o Staff Member *Richard De La Font Agency*
3808 W South Park Blvd
Broken Arrow, OK 74011-1261, USA

Hollister, Ken (Athlete, Football Player)
8772 Linksway Dr
Powell, OH 43065-8299, USA

Hollit, Raye (Zapp) (Actor)
2554 Lincoln Blvd # 638
Marina Del Rey, CA 90292

Holloman, Laurel (Actor)
c/o Tammy Rosen *Sanders Armstrong Caserta*
425 N Robertson Blvd
West Hollywood, CA 90048-1735, USA

Hollomon, Gus (Athlete, Football Player)
2489 County Road 139
Cameron, TX 76520-3614, USA

Holloway, Brenda (Musician)
Universal Attractions
145 W 57th St # 1500
New York, NY 10019-2220, USA

Holloway, Brian (Athlete, Football Player)
742 New York Route 43
Stephentown, NY 12168, USA

Holloway, Johnny (Athlete, Football Player)
1500 W 9th St Apt 5
Lawrence, KS 66044-2462, USA

Holloway, Joseph
25 Broad St Ste 5 PMB 283
Freehold, NJ 07728-1962, USA

Holloway, Josh (Actor)
c/o Jai Khanna *Brillstein Entertainment Partners (LA)*
9150 Wilshire Blvd Ste 350
Beverly Hills, CA 90212-3453, USA

Holloway, Ken (Music Group)
World Class/Berry Mgmt
1848 Tyne Blvd
Nashville, TN 37215-4702, USA

Holloway, Matt (Writer)
c/o Staff Member *Nine Yards Entertainment*
5815 W Sunset Blvd Ste 206
Los Angeles, CA 90028-6481, USA

Hollowell, Matt (Athlete, Baseball Player)
8 Oldwick Rd
Whitehouse Station, NJ 08889-3719, USA

Hollweg, Ryan (Athlete, Hockey Player)
340 Treeline Park Apt 1226
San Antonio, TX 78209-1843, USA

Holly, Buddy Memorial Society
PO Box 6123
Lubbock, TX 79493-6123

Holly, Jeff (Athlete, Baseball Player)
1806 SW Taylors Ferry Rd
Portland, OR 97219-5530, USA

Holly, Lauren (Actor)
c/o Ben Press *Evolution Entertainment (LA)*
6500 Wilshire Blvd Ste 2200
Los Angeles, CA 90048-4942, USA

Holly, Molly (Wrestler)
c/o Staff Member *World Wrestling Entertainment (WWE)*
1241 E Main St
Titan Towers
Stamford, CT 06902-3520, USA

Hollyday, Christopher (Musician)
Ted Kurland
173 Brighton Ave
Allston, MA 02134-2003, USA

Hollywood Undead (Music Group, Musician)
c/o Starr Andreeff *Maple Jam Music Group*
4108 W Riverside Dr Ste 3
Burbank, CA 91505-4143, USA

Holm, Anders (Actor)
c/o Isaac Horne *Avalon Management*
9171 Wilshire Blvd Ste 320
Beverly Hills, CA 90210-5516, USA

Holm, Joan (Bowler)
5829 N Magnolia Ave
Chicago, IL 60660-3415, USA

Holm, Sir Ian (Actor)
46 Albermarle St
London, EN W1X 4

Holm, Steve (Athlete, Baseball Player)
10205 Garden Hwy
Sacramento, CA 95837-9100, USA

Holman, Brad (Athlete, Baseball Player)
8006 W Westlawn Cir
Wichita, KS 67212-7305, USA

Holman, Brian (Athlete, Baseball Player)
23595 W 223rd St
Spring Hill, KS 66083-4029, USA

Holman, C Ray (Business Person)
Mallinckrodt Inc
675 McDonell Blvd
Saint Louis, MO 63134, USA

Holman, Gary (Athlete, Baseball Player)
8073 Camino Montego
Carlsbad, CA 92009-9545, USA

Holman, Marshall (Athlete, Bowler)
3753 Windgate St
Medford, OR 97504-9163, USA

Holman, Rodney (Athlete, Football Player)
41460 Herwig Bluff Rd
Slidell, LA 70461-5040, USA

Holman, Scott (Athlete, Baseball Player)
98 Lauren Ln
Santa Rosa Beach, FL 32459-8304, USA

Holman, Scott (Athlete, Football Player)
4 Comiso
Irvine, CA 92614-0224, USA

Holman, Shawn (Athlete, Baseball Player)
105 Edgewood Rd
Sewickley, PA 15143-9681, USA

Holmberg, Dennis (Athlete, Baseball Player)
2079 Monica Ct
Palm Harbor, FL 34683-5030, USA

Holmberg, Mark (Musician)
MOB Agency
6404 Wilshire Blvd Ste 505
Los Angeles, CA 90048-5507, USA

Holmberg, Rob (Athlete, Football Player)
316 Coppersmith Ln
Strasburg, PA 17579-1021, USA

Holmes, A M (Writer)
Columbia Univesity
English Dept
New York, NY 10027, USA

Holmes, Ashton (Actor)
c/o Jeff Morrone *Intellectual Artists Management*
9350 Wilshire Blvd Ste 224
Beverly Hills, CA 90212-3204, USA

Holmes, Charlie (Athlete, Hockey Player)
7567 NE Meadowmeer Ln
Bainbridge Island, WA 98110-1223, USA

Holmes, Clayton (Athlete, Football Player)
1142 Hollings Ave
Florence, SC 29506-6725, USA

Holmes, Clint (Music Group)
Conversation Co
697 Middle Neck Rd
Great Neck, NY 11023-1216, USA

Holmes, Darren (Athlete, Baseball Player)
1 Emerald Ct
Arden, NC 28704-9594, USA

Holmes, Earl (Athlete, Football Player)
2978 Stonybrook Ct
Tallahassee, FL 32309-2167, USA

Holmes, Eric (Race Car Driver)
Beebe Racing
801 10th St Fl 5-1
Modesto, CA 95354-2311, USA

Holmes, Howdy (Race Car Driver)
301 Barton Shore Dr
Ann Arbor, MI 48105-1025, USA

Holmes, JB (Athlete, Golfer)
7410 Cypress Grove Rd
Orlando, FL 32819-5510, USA

Holmes, Jennifer (Actor)
PO Box 6303
Carmel By The Sea, CA 93921-6303, USA

Holmes, Jerry (Athlete, Football Player)
107 Chatham Ter
Hampton, VA 23666-4105, USA

Holmes, Katie (Actor)
c/o John Carrabino *John Carrabino Management*
5900 Wilshire Blvd Ste 406
Los Angeles, CA 90036-5015, USA

Holmes, Kenneth (Athlete, Football Player)
PO Box 273309
Boca Raton, FL 33427-3309, USA

Holmes, Khaled (Athlete, Football Player)
c/o Joe Panos *Athletes First, LLC*
23091 Mill Creek Dr
Laguna Hills, CA 92653-1258, USA

Holmes, Lamar (Athlete, Football Player)
c/o Bus Cook *Bus Cook Sports, Inc*
1 Willow Bend Dr
Hattiesburg, MS 39402-8552, USA

Holmes, Larry (Boxer)
228 W Canal St
Easton, PA 18042-6244, USA

Holmes, Lester (Athlete, Football Player)
3760 Motor Ave
Los Angeles, CA 90034-6404, USA

Holmes, Pat (Athlete, Football Player)
221 Mack Hollimon Dr
Kerrville, TX 78028-6628, USA

Holmes, Priest (Athlete, Football Player)
c/o Todd France *Five Star Athlete Management*
3500 Lenox Rd NE
Atlanta, GA 30326-4228, USA

Holmes, Rudell (Athlete, Football Player)
1713 Lisa Ave
Vista, CA 92084-3057, USA

Holmes, Rudy (Athlete, Football Player)
2151 Ronda Granada Unit A
Laguna Woods, CA 92637-0718, USA

Holmes, Santonio (Athlete, Football Player)
c/o Peter Miller *Jabez Marketing Group*
516 E 2nd St Ste 3
Boston, MA 02127-1438, USA

Holmes, Susan (Actor, Model)
c/o Jerry Shandrew *Shandrew Public Relations*
1050 S Stanley Ave
Los Angeles, CA 90019-6634, USA

Holmes, Tina (Actor)
c/o Mike Smith *Principal Entertainment (LA)*
9255 W Sunset Blvd Ste 500
West Hollywood, CA 90069-3301, USA

Holmes Norton, Eleanor (Congressman, Politician)
2136 Rayburn Hob
Washington, DC 20515-5100, USA

Holmgren, Michael G (Mike) (Athlete, Coach, Football Coach, Football Player)
17 Shoreby Dr
Cleveland, OH 44108-1161, USA

Holmgren, Paul (Athlete, Coach, Hockey Player)
724 Southwick Cir
Somerdale, NJ 08083-2312, USA

Holmoe, Tom (Athlete, Football Player)
1674 N 1670 W
Provo, UT 84604-7210, USA

Holmquest, Donald L (Astronaut)
205 Princeton Rd
Menlo Park, CA 94025-5217, USA

Holmquest, Donald L Dr (Astronaut)
205 Princeton Rd
Menlo Park, CA 94025-5217, USA

Holmstrom, Carl (Skier)
1703 E 3rd St Apt 101
Duluth, MN 55812-1743, USA

Holmstrom, Peter (Musician)
Monqui Mgmt
PO Box 5908
Portland, OR 97228-5908, USA

Holmstrom, Tomas (Athlete, Hockey Player)
40950 Woodward Ave Ste 303
Bloomfield Hills, MI 48304-5127, USA

Holohan, Pete (Athlete, Football Player)
2945 Curie St
San Diego, CA 92122-4105, USA

Holroyd, Scott (Actor)
c/o Christopher Wright *Christopher Wright Management*
3207 Winnie Dr
Los Angeles, CA 90068-1439, USA

Holt, Chris (Athlete, Baseball Player)
152 Hollywood Dr
Coppell, TX 75019-7302, USA

Holt, Claire (Actor)
c/o Melanie Greene *Affirmative Entertainment*
425 N Robertson Blvd
West Hollywood, CA 90048-1735, USA

Holt, David Lee (Musician)
AristoMedia
1620 16th Ave S
Nashville, TN 37212-2908, USA

Holt, Gary (Athlete, Hockey Player)
5820 S Sorrel Cir
Spokane, WA 99224-8298, USA

Holt, Glenn L (Athlete, Football Player)
North Miami High School
800 NE 137th St
North Miami, FL 33161-3299, USA

Holt, Glynn Dr (Astronaut)
110 Cummington Mall
Boston, MA 02215-2407, USA

Holt, Harry (Athlete, Football Player)
750 E Irvington Rd Apt 1415
Tucson, AZ 85714-3281, USA

Holt, Issac (Athlete, Football Player)
4028 Fairmont Pl
Birmingham, AL 35207-2732, USA

Holt, Issiac (Athlete, Football Player)
4028 Fairmont Pl
Birmingham, AL 35207-2732, USA

Holt, Jim (Athlete, Baseball Player)
150 Judge Sharpe Rd
Graham, NC 27253-8202, USA

Holt, Lester (Correspondent)
NBC-TV
30 Rockefeller Plz
News Dept
New York, NY 10112-0015, USA

Holt, Milton (Athlete, Football Player)
1461 N School St
Honolulu, HI 96817-1915, USA

Holt, Pierce (Athlete, Football Player)
3840 County Road 339
Christoval, TX 76935-3000, USA

Holt, Robert J (Athlete, Football Player)
1332 Williams Ave
Desoto, TX 75115-3182, USA

Holt, Roger (Athlete, Baseball Player)
804 Hilltop St
Fruitland Park, FL 34731-2061, USA

Holt, Sandrine (Actor)
c/o Didi Rea *D2 Management*
9255 W Sunset Blvd Ste 600
West Hollywood, CA 90069-3306, USA

Holt, Torry (Athlete, Football Player)
c/o Mark Lepselter *Maxx Sports & Entertainment*
546 5th Ave Fl 6
New York, NY 10036-5000, USA

Holtgrave, Vern (Athlete, Baseball Player)
389 N 8th St
Breese, IL 62230-1107, USA

Holt Jr, Jack
504 Temple Dr
Harrah, OK 73045, USA

Holt Jr., Rush (Congressman, Politician)
1214 Longworth Hob
Washington, DC 20515-1408, USA

Holt-Kramer, Toni
1229 Santa Monica Blvd
Santa Monica, CA 90404-1705

Holton, Brian (Athlete, Baseball Player)
213 Overcup Loop
Summerville, SC 29483-6969, USA

Holton, Linwood (Politician)
132 Lancaster Dr Apt 426
Irvington, VA 22480-9702, USA

Holton, Mark (Actor)
c/o Staff Member *Gage Group, The (LA)*
5757 Wilshire Blvd Ste 659
Los Angeles, CA 90036-3682, USA

Holton, Michael (Athlete, Basketball Player, Coach)
5822 NW Redfox Dr
Portland, OR 97229-2657, USA

Holtz, Louis L (Lou) (Athlete, Coach, Football Coach, Football Player)
9209 Cromwell Park Pl
Orlando, FL 32827-7005, USA

Holtz, Mike (Athlete, Baseball Player)
620 Robertdale Dr
Duncansville, PA 16635-7524, USA

Holtzman, Jerome (Baseball Player, Writer)
1225 Forest Ave
Evanston, IL 60202-1409, USA

Holtzman, Kenneth D (Ken) (Athlete, Baseball Player)
256 Waterside Dr
Grover, MO 63040-1632, USA

Holtzman, Wayne H (Doctor)
2500 Barton Creek Blvd Apt 1504
Austin, TX 78735-1622, USA

Holub, Dick (Athlete, Basketball Player)
16159 W Wildflower Dr
Surprise, AZ 85374-5048, USA

Holub, E J (Athlete, Football Player)
2311 S County Road 1120
Midland, TX 79706-4942, USA

Holum, Dianne (Athlete, Olympic Athlete, Speed Skater)
2835 W 32nd Ave Apt 89
Denver, CO 80211-3293, USA

Holum, Kirstin (Athlete, Olympic Athlete, Speed Skater)
2835 W 32nd Ave Apt 89
Denver, CO 80211-3293, USA

Holway, Jerome F (Cinematographer)
448 Spruce Dr
Exton, PA 19341-2020, USA

Holy, Steve (Musician)
c/o Staff Member *Paradigm (Nashville)*
124 12th Ave S Ste 410
Nashville, TN 37203-3170, USA

Holyfield, Evander (Athlete, Boxer)
PO Box 143420
Fayetteville, GA 30214-6531, USA

Holz, Gordon (Athlete, Football Player)
730 S Plaza Dr Apt 222
Saint Paul, MN 55120-1575, USA

Holzemer, Mark (Athlete, Baseball Player)
10044 MacAlister Trl
Littleton, CO 80129, USA

Holzer, Kristine (Athlete, Olympic Athlete, Speed Skater)
10410 W Whispering Cliffs Dr
Boise, ID 83704-1911, USA

Holzier, James (Actor)
c/o Bob Willems *Champion Entertainment*
2620 Fountain View Dr Ste 220
Houston, TX 77057-7627, USA

Holzinger, Brian (Athlete, Hockey Player)
1005 Ledgemont Dr
Broadview Heights, OH 44147-4021, USA

Homan, Dennis (Athlete, Football Player)
1950 Charlotte Ct
Florence, AL 35630-6768, USA

Homeier, Skip (Actor, Director)
75381 Desert Valley Ln
Indian Wells, CA 92210-8316, USA

Homfeld, Conrad (Athlete, Horse Racer, Olympic Athlete)
Sandron
11744 Marblestone Ct
Wellington, FL 33414-6041, USA

Honda, Yuka (Music Group)
Billions Corp
833 W Chicago Ave Ste 101
Chicago, IL 60642-8408, USA

Honeycutt, Rick (Athlete, Baseball Player)
207 Forrest Rd
Fort Oglethorpe, GA 30742-3706, USA

Honeycutt, Van B (Business Person)
Computer Sciences Corp
2100 E Grand Ave
El Segundo, CA 90245-5098, USA

Honeycyt (Music Group)
c/o Staff Member *Paradigm (Monterey)*
404 W Franklin St
Monterey, CA 93940-2303, USA

Hong, James (Actor)
c/o Carol Weiss *Stage 9 Talent*
1249 Lodi Pl
Los Angeles, CA 90038-1709, USA

Honig, Donald (Commentator)
2322 Cromwell Hills Dr
Cromwell, CT 06416-1803, USA

Hood, Don (Athlete, Baseball Player)
20753 Charing Cross Cir
Estero, FL 33928-2542, USA

Hood, Estus (Athlete, Football Player)
2105 W Grace St
Kankakee, IL 60901-4590, USA

Hood, Kenneth (Religious Leader)
5799 Bloomfield Ave
Verona, NJ 07044, USA

Hood, Robert
Boys Life Magazine
1325 W Walnut Hill Ln
Editorial Dept
Irving, TX 75038-3008, USA

Hoogstratten, Louise
12451 Mulholland Dr
Beverly Hills, CA 90210-1336

Hook, Chris (Athlete, Baseball Player)
30 Northfield Dr
Florence, KY 41042-8924, USA

Hook, Jay (Athlete, Baseball Player)
PO Box 90
Maple City, MI 49664-0090, USA

Hooker, Fair (Athlete, Football Player)
3728 Rutherford Ct
Inglewood, CA 90305-2244, USA

Hooks, Kevin (Director)
International Creative Mgmt
10250 Constellation Blvd Fl 1
Los Angeles, CA 90067-6241, USA

Hooks, Robert (Actor)
145 N Valley St
Burbank, CA 91505-4036, USA

Hooks, Roland (Athlete, Football Player)
3724 Calgary Dr
Reno, NV 89511-6096, USA

Hoomanawanui, Michael (Athlete, Football Player)
c/o Mark Bartelstein *Priority Sports & Entertainment - Chicago*
312 N La Salle
Suite 650
Chicago, IL 60610, USA

Hoop, Jesca (Musician)
c/o Staff Member *Paradigm (Monterey)*
404 W Franklin St
Monterey, CA 93940-2303, USA

Hooper, Bobby Joe (Athlete, Basketball Player)
825 Ivywood St Apt 4
Dayton, OH 45420-1751, USA

Hooper, C Darrow (Athlete, Olympic Athlete, Track Athlete)
6 Braemore Pl
Dallas, TX 75230-1958, USA

Hooper, Kevin (Athlete, Baseball Player)
2701 Century Dr
Lawrence, KS 66049-2523, USA

Hooper, Lance (Race Car Driver)
204 Lytton St
Chester, WV 26034-1032, USA

Hooper, Tobe
PO Box 5617
Beverly Hills, CA 90209-5617

Hooper, Tom (Director)
c/o Doug MacLaren *ICM Partners (LA)*
10250 Constellation Blvd Fl 7
Los Angeles, CA 90067-6207, USA

Hoopes, Mitch (Athlete, Football Player)
5000 S Murray Blvd Apt F1
Salt Lake City, UT 84123-2674, USA

Hooser, Carroll (Athlete, Basketball Player)
6317 Kings Rd
Lewisville, TX 75077-7314, USA

Hooten, Burt
3619 Granby Ct
San Antonio, TX 78217-4653

Hooten, Leon (Athlete, Baseball Player)
524 S 7th St
Coos Bay, OR 97420-1302, USA

Hootie & The Blowfish (Music Group)
c/o Scott McGhee *McGhee Entertainment*
8730 W Sunset Blvd Ste 175
West Hollywood, CA 90069-2246, USA

Hooton, Burt C (Athlete, Baseball Player)
3619 Granby Ct
San Antonio, TX 78217-4653, USA

Hoover, Alice (Athlete, Baseball Player, Commentator)
340 Roosevelt Ave
Reading, PA 19605-2337, USA

Hoover, Brad (Athlete, Football Player)
2130 Climbing Rose Ln
Matthews, NC 28104-6232, USA

Hoover, Herbert III
200 S Los Robles Ave # 520
Pasadena, CA 91101-2479

Hoover, Houston (Athlete, Football Player)
1216 Mareed Ave
Yazoo City, MS 39194-2831, USA

Hoover, John (Athlete, Baseball Player)
1615 W Fountain Way
Fresno, CA 93705-3331, USA

Hoover, Paul (Athlete, Baseball Player)
307 Baronsway Dr
Cuyahoga Falls, OH 44223-2892, USA

Hoover, Tom (Athlete, Basketball Player)
9 Apple Manor Ln
East Brunswick, NJ 08816-2872, USA

Hoover, Tom (Race Car Driver)
207 Lowry Ave N
Minneapolis, MN 55411-1621, USA

Hoovler, Skip (Athlete, Football Player)
8249 Broad St SW
Pataskala, OH 43062-7831, USA

Hope, Jim (Producer)
c/o Staff Member *William Morris Endeavor (LA)*
9601 Wilshire Blvd
Beverly Hills, CA 90210-5213, USA

Hope, John (Athlete, Baseball Player)
5406 Bayberry Ln
Tamarac, FL 33319-3127, USA

Hope, Leslie (Actor)
c/o Lee Wallman *Wallman Public Relations*
10323 Santa Monica Blvd Ste 109
Los Angeles, CA 90025-5056, USA

Hope, Tamara (Actor)
c/o Matt Schwartz *Christopher Wright Management*
6100 Wilshire Blvd Ste 1170
Los Angeles, CA 90048-5116, USA

Hopkins, Andy (Athlete, Football Player)
2335 Walnut Ridge Dr
Missouri City, TX 77489-5005, USA

Hopkins, Anthony (Actor)
c/o Paul Bloch *Rogers & Cowan PR (LA)*
8687 Melrose Ave Ste 7
West Hollywood, CA 90069-5721, USA

Hopkins, Bernard (Athlete, Boxer)
c/o Staff Member *Golden Boy Promotions*
626 Wilshire Blvd Ste 350
Los Angeles, CA 90017-3581, USA

Hopkins, Bo (Actor)
6628 Ethel Ave
North Hollywood, CA 91606-1018, USA

Hopkins, Bob (Athlete, Basketball Player)
8421 SE 71st St
Mercer Island, WA 98040-5409, USA

Hopkins, DeAndre (Athlete, Football Player)
c/o Hadley Engelhard *Enter-Sports Management*
5 Concourse Pkwy Ste 3000
Atlanta, GA 30328-7106, USA

Hopkins, Demetrius (Boxer)
c/o Staff Member *Top Rank Inc.*
3908 Howard Hughes Pkwy #580
Las Vegas, NV 89109, USA

Hopkins, Don (Athlete, Baseball Player)
PO Box 8817
Benton Harbor, MI 49023-8817, USA

Hopkins, Gail (Athlete, Baseball Player)
120 Canterbury Dr
Parkersburg, WV 26104-8048, USA

Hopkins, Jan (Correspondent)
Cable News Network
1050 Techwood Dr NW
News Dept
Atlanta, GA 30318-5695, USA

Hopkins, Jerry (Athlete, Football Player)
6688 E State Highway 6
Waco, TX 76705-5385, USA

Hopkins, Josh (Actor)
Gersh Agency
232 N Canon Dr
Beverly Hills, CA 90210-5302, USA

Hopkins, Kaitlin (Actor)
19528 Ventura Blvd # 559
Tarzana, CA 91356-2917, USA

Hopkins, Katherine (Actor)
215 S La Cienega Blvd PH
Beverly Hills, CA 90211-3322

Hopkins, Larry (Athlete, Hockey Player)
3012 S Fir Ave
Broken Arrow, OK 74012-7496, USA

Hopkins, Linda (Actor, Musician)
2055 Ivar Ave PH
Los Angeles, CA 90068-3918, USA

Hopkins, Michael S Ltcolonel (Astronaut)
910 White Pine Dr
Friendswood, TX 77546-3570, USA

Hopkins, Stephen
8942 Wilshire Blvd
Beverly Hills, CA 90211-1908

Hopkins, Stephen J (Director)
International Creative Mgmt
10250 Constellation Blvd Fl 1
Los Angeles, CA 90067-6241, USA

Hopkins, Sy (Music Group)
Paramount Entertainment
PO Box 12
Far Hills, NJ 07931-0012, USA

Hopkins, Tamburo (Athlete, Football Player)
2740 Maitland Crossing Way Apt 2208
Orlando, FL 32810-7130, USA

Hopkins, Telma (Actor, Musician)
4122 Don Luis Dr
Los Angeles, CA 90008-4215, USA

Hopkins, Tom (Business Person, Writer)
Tom Hopkins International
7531 E 2nd St
Scottsdale, AZ 85251-4503, USA

Hopkins, Wesley (Athlete, Football Player)
7412 White Oak Rd
Fairfield, AL 35064-2454, USA

Hoppen, Dave (Athlete, Basketball Player)
16341 Webster St
Omaha, NE 68118-2513, USA

Hopper, C Darrow (Athlete, Football Player)
6 Braemore Pl
Dallas, TX 75230-1958, USA

Hopper, Norris (Athlete, Baseball Player)
902 Hampton St
Shelby, NC 28152-6412, USA

Hoppock, Doug (Athlete, Football Player)
13212 W 115th St
Overland Park, KS 66210-3540, USA

Hoppus, Mark (Actor, Musician, Producer)
c/o Geyer Kosinski *Media Talent Group*
9200 W Sunset Blvd Ste 550
West Hollywood, CA 90069-3611, USA

Hopsin, Marcus (Musician, Producer)
Funk Volume
8447 Wilshire Blvd Ste 450
Beverly Hills, CA 90211-3236, USA

Hopson, Dennis (Athlete, Basketball Player)
7229 Donnybrook Dr
Dublin, OH 43017-2403, USA

Horacek, Tony (Athlete, Hockey Player)
71 Clover Pl
Lebanon, PA 17042-9400, USA

Horan, Dennis
32458 Galatina St
Temecula, CA 92592-3881, USA

Horan, James (Actor)
c/o Staff Member *Angel City Talent*
4741 Laurel Canyon Blvd Ste 101
Valley Village, CA 91607-5905, USA

Horan, Machael W (Mike) (Athlete, Football Player)
1232 Edgeview Dr
Santa Ana, CA 92705-2339, USA

Hordges, Cedrick (Athlete, Basketball Player)
237 W 127th St Apt 28
New York, NY 10027-2901, USA

Hordichuk, Darcy (Athlete, Hockey Player)
8237 NW 107th Ter
Parkland, FL 33076-4766, USA

Horford, Al (Athlete, Basketball Player)
c/o Arn Tellem *Wasserman Media Group (LA)*
12100 W Olympic Blvd Ste 200
Los Angeles, CA 90064-1075, USA

Horgan, Joe (Athlete, Baseball Player)
16108 Rim Rd
Edmond, OK 73013-3215, USA

Horgan, Patrick (Actor)
201 E 89th St
New York, NY 10128-3421, USA

Horlen, Joel (Athlete, Baseball Player)
3718 Chartwell Dr
San Antonio, TX 78230-3202, USA

Horn, Don (Athlete, Football Player)
1336 Hazeline Lake Dr
Colorado Springs, CO 80921-4105, USA

Horn, Joe (Athlete, Football Player)
4607 Woodpond Cv
Powder Springs, GA 30127-6020, USA

Horn, Roy (Magician)
Mirage Hotel & Casino
3400 Las Vegas Blvd S
Las Vegas, NV 89109-8907

Horn, Sam (Athlete, Baseball Player)
1305 Narragansett Blvd
Cranston, RI 02905-3825, USA

Horn, Shriley (Music Group)
1007 Towne Ln
Charlottesville, VA 22901-3173, USA

Horn, Thomas (Actor)
c/o Jennifer Allen *Viewpoint Inc (LA)*
8820 Wilshire Blvd Ste 220
Beverly Hills, CA 90211-2622, USA

Hornacek, Jeff (Athlete, Basketball Player)
1360 E 9th St
Cleveland, OH 44114-1737, USA

Hornaday, Ron (Race Car Driver)
Kevin Harvick Inc
PO Box 938
Oak Ridge, NC 27310-0938, USA

Hornbuckle, Alexis (Athlete, Basketball Player)
125 Juniper St
Lake Jackson, TX 77566-5025, USA

Horne, John R (Business Person)
Navistar International
2701 Navistar Dr
Lisle, IL 60532-3637, USA

Horneff, Wil (Actor)
c/o Staff Member *Creative Artists Agency (CAA-LA)*
2000 Avenue of the Stars Ste 100
Los Angeles, CA 90067-4705, USA

Horner, Bob (Athlete, Baseball Player)
209 Steeplechase Dr
Irving, TX 75062-3823, USA

Horner, James (Musician)
c/o Michael Gorfaine *Gorfaine/Schwartz Agency Inc*
4111 W Alameda Ave Ste 509
Burbank, CA 91505-4171, USA

Horner, Sam (Athlete, Football Player)
681 Duck Thurmond Rd
Dawsonville, GA 30534-2811, USA

Hornish Jr, Sam (Race Car Driver)
Penske Racing
200 Penske Way
Mooresville, NC 28115-8022, USA

Hornsby, Bruce (Musician)
PO Box 3545
Williamsburg, VA 23187-3545, USA

Hornsby, Ron (Athlete, Football Player)
2028 Washington St
Franklinton, LA 70438-2533, USA

Hornsby, Russell (Actor)
c/o Leonard Torgan *The Collective*
8383 Wilshire Blvd Ste 1050
Beverly Hills, CA 90211-2415, USA

Hornung, Paul (Athlete, Football Player, Heisman Trophy Winner)
325 W Main St Ste 1116
Waterfront Plaza
Louisville, KY 40202-4255, USA

Horovitz, Adam (King Ad-Rock) (Artist, Music Group, Musician)
c/o Staff Member *William Morris Endeavor (LA)*
9601 Wilshire Blvd
Beverly Hills, CA 90210-5213, USA

Horovitz, Israel A (Writer)
146 W 11th St
New York, NY 10011-8306, USA

Horowitz, Adam
c/o Philip Raskind *William Morris Endeavor (LA)*
9601 Wilshire Blvd
Beverly Hills, CA 90210-5213, USA

Horowitz, David (Correspondent)
Fight Back !
PO Box 49915
Los Angeles, CA 90049-0915, USA

Horowitz, Paul (Doctor, Physicist)
111 Chilton St
Cambridge, MA 02138-6844, USA

Horowitz, Sari (Journalist)
Washington Post
Editorial Dept
1150 15th St NW
Washington, DC 20071-0001, USA

Horowitz, Scott J (Astronaut)
5491 Freestyle Way
Park City, UT 84098-7621, USA

Horowitz, Scott J Colonel (Astronaut)
5491 Freestyle Way
Park City, UT 84098-7621, USA

Horry, Robert (Athlete, Basketball Player)
2126 Countryshire Ln
Richmond, TX 77406-3192, USA

Horsford, Anna Maria (Actor)
PO Box 48082
Los Angeles, CA 90048-0082, USA

Horsley, Jack (Athlete, Olympic Athlete, Swimmer)
608 N Sampson St
Ellensburg, WA 98926-3162, USA

Horsley, Lee A (Actor)
c/o Laura Walsh *Central Artists*
3310 W Burbank Blvd # A
Burbank, CA 91505-2230, USA

Horsman, Vince (Athlete, Baseball Player)
1941 Pinehurst Dr
Clearwater, FL 33763-2228, USA

Horst, Lisa Ann
PO Box 8633
Lancaster, PA 17604-8633

Horstman, Catherine (Athlete, Baseball
Player, Commentator)
39018 Desert Greens Dr E
Palm Desert, CA 92260-1403, USA

Horton, Ethan S (Football Player,
Sportscaster)
4602 Fairvista Dr
Charlotte, NC 28269-1098, USA

Horton, Greg (Athlete, Football Player)
1053 Lytle St
Redlands, CA 92374-6240, USA

Horton, Jonathan (Athlete, Gymnast,
Olympic Athlete)
c/o Staff Member *USA Gymnastics*
132 E Washington St Ste 700
Indianapolis, IN 46204-3674, USA

Horton, Larry (Athlete, Football Player)
215 Emerald St
Harrisburg, PA 17110-1013, USA

Horton, Lawrence (Athlete, Football
Player)
1442 S 13th St
Harrisburg, PA 17104-3107, USA

Horton, Mark (Race Car Driver)
Summit Racing
PO Box 535
Richfield, OH 44286-0535, USA

Horton, Nathan (Athlete, Hockey Player)
The Orr Hockey Group
PO Box 290836
Charlestown, MA 02129-0215, USA

Horton, Peter (Actor)
409 Santa Monica Blvd PH
Santa Monica, CA 90401-2232, USA

Horton, Ray (Athlete, Football Player)
3400 S Water St
Pittsburgh, PA 15203-2349, USA

Horton, Ricky (Athlete, Baseball Player)
16026 Aston Ct
Chesterfield, MO 63005-4575, USA

Horton, Robert (Actor)
5317 Andasol Ave
Encino, CA 91316-2504, USA

Horton, Tony (Athlete, Baseball Player)
17001 Livorno Dr
Pacific Palisades, CA 90272-3232, USA

Horton, Tony (Athlete, Fitness Expert,
Television Host)
BeachBody
3301 Exposition Blvd Fl 3
Santa Monica, CA 90404-5082, USA

Horton, Wes (Athlete, Football Player)
c/o Bruce Tollner *REP 1 Sports Group*
2 Corporate Park Ste 106
Irvine, CA 92606-5103, USA

Horton, Willie (Athlete, Baseball Player)
The Athlete Connection
PO Box 380135
Clinton Township, MI 48038-0060, USA

Horton, Willie(baseball)
15124 Warwick St
Detroit, MI 48223-2293

Horvath, Bronco J (Athlete, Hockey
Player)
27 Oliver St
South Yarmouth, MA 02664-2901, USA

Horvitz, Louis J (Director, Producer)
c/o Bob Gersh *Gersh (LA)*
9465 Wilshire Blvd Ste 600
Beverly Hills, CA 90212-2605, USA

Horwitz, Brian (Athlete, Baseball Player)
5118 E Edgemont Ave
Phoenix, AZ 85008-1642, USA

Horwitz, Tony (Journalist)
Wall Street Journal
200 Liberty St
Editorial Dept
New York, NY 10281-1003, USA

Hosbein, Marion (Athlete, Baseball
Player, Commentator)
1347 Cliff Barnes Dr
Kalamazoo, MI 49009-8329, USA

Hosea, Bobby (Actor)
c/o Sara Schedeen *Metropolitan (MTA)*
4526 Wilshire Blvd
Los Angeles, CA 90010-3801, USA

Hosey, Dwayne (Athlete, Baseball Player)
808 S 91st Cir
Omaha, NE 68114-5132, USA

Hosey, Steve (Athlete, Baseball Player)
2351 W Lorna Linda Ave
Fresno, CA 93711, USA

Hosket, Bill (Athlete, Basketball Player,
Olympic Athlete)
7461 Worthington Galena Rd
Worthington, OH 43085-1529, USA

Hoskins, Derrick (Athlete, Football Player)
10491 Road 842
Philadelphia, MS 39350-8204, USA

Hospodar, Ed (Athlete, Hockey Player)
37 Greythorne Woods Cir
Wayne, PA 19087-4758, USA

Hoss, Clark (Athlete, Football Player)
10305 NE Fox Farm Rd
Dundee, OR 97115-9192, USA

Hosseini, Khaled
c/o Judy Lubershane *Judy Lubershane
Agency*
not available
Boston, MA 02101, USA

Hostak, Al (Boxer)
11501 161st Ave SE
Renton, WA 98059-6145, USA

Hostetler, Dave (Athlete, Baseball Player)
3404 Steeplechase Trl
Arlington, TX 76016-2325, USA

Hostetler, Jeff (Athlete, Football Player)
50 Clay St Ste 410
Morgantown, WV 26501-5932, USA

Hostetter, G Richard (Religious Leader)
Presbyterian Church in America
1852 Century Plz
Atlanta, GA 30345, USA

Hoston, Ricky (Baseball Player)
St Louis Cardinals
16026 Aston Ct
Chesterfield, MO 63005-4575, USA

Hoston, Tony (Baseball Player)
Boston Red Sox
17001 Livorno Dr
Pacific Palisades, CA 90272-3232, USA

Hot Chelle Rae (Music Group)
c/o Staff Member *Jive Records*
550 Madison Ave Fl 6
New York, NY 10022-3211, USA

Hotchkiss, Rob (Musician)
Jon Landau
80 Mason St
Greenwich, CT 06830-5515, USA

Hotchkiss, Rollin D (Doctor, Scientist)
2-4 Rolling Hls
Lenox, MA 01240-2127, USA

Hotchner, Aaron
14 Hillandale Rd
Westport, CT 06880-5225

Hotchner, Aaron Edward (Producer,
Writer)
c/o Staff Member *HarperCollins Publishers*
195 Broadway Fl 2
Cellar 1
New York, NY 10007-3132, USA

Hottelet, Richard C (Correspondent)
120 Chestnut Hill Rd
Wilton, CT 06897-4608, USA

Hottman, Ken (Athlete, Baseball Player)
9537 2nd Ave
Elk Grove, CA 95624-1936, USA

Hoty, Dee
333 W 56th St
New York, NY 10019-3764

Houbregs, Bob (Athlete, Basketball Player)
330 Arledge Ln SW Apt 20F
Olympia, WA 98502-8637, USA

Houda, Doug (Athlete, Hockey Player)
10 Lovell Rd
Lynnfield, MA 01940-1818, USA

Houda, Doug
Boston Bruins
100 Legends Way Ste 250
Attn: Coaching Staff
Boston, MA 02114-1389, USA

Hough, Charlie (Athlete, Baseball Player)
2266 Shadetree Cir
Brea, CA 92821-4423, USA

Hough, Derek (Dancer, Reality Star)
3161 Dona Maria Dr
Studio City, CA 91604-4258, USA

Hough, Jim (Athlete, Football Player)
2440 Christian Dr
Chaska, MN 55318-1993, USA

Hough, Julianne (Dancer, Musician)
PO Box 682425
Park City, UT 84068-2425, USA

Houghton, James (Business Person)
Field 36 Spencer Hill Road
Corning, NY 14830, USA

Houghton, Katherine (Actor)
Ambrosio/Mortimer
165 W 46th St
New York, NY 10036-2501, USA

Hougland, Bill (Athlete, Basketball Player,
Olympic Athlete)
504 Canyon Dr
Lawrence, KS 66049-2400, USA

Houlemard, Michael (Athlete, Baseball
Player)
474 N Daisy Ave
Pasadena, CA 91107-2811, USA

Houlton, D J (Athlete, Baseball Player)
2357 N Campus Ave
Upland, CA 91784-1303, USA

Hounsou, Djimon (Actor, Model,
Producer)
c/o Peter Safran *The Safran Company*
8748 Holloway Dr
West Hollywood, CA 90069-2327, USA

House, Craig (Athlete, Baseball Player)
150 Canterbury Dr
Austin, TX 78737-4549, USA

House, Davon (Athlete, Football Player)
c/o Ken Zuckerman *Priority Sports &
Entertainment - (LA)*
15233 Ventura Blvd Ste 718
Sherman Oaks, CA 91403-2237, USA

House, James
1313 16th Ave S
Nashville, TN 37212-2903

House, J R (Athlete, Baseball Player)
34 River Ridge Trl
Ormond Beach, FL 32174-4340, USA

House, Karen Eliot (Journalist)
1 World Financial Ctr Attn of
New York, NY 10281-1003, USA

House, Karen Ellot (Journalist)
58 Cleveland Ln
Princeton, NJ 08540-3077, USA

House, Kevin (Athlete, Football Player)
4004 Alexander Palm Ct
Tampa, FL 33624-2379, USA

House, Pat (Athlete, Baseball Player)
2554 W Penick Pointe Ct
Meridian, ID 83646-5182, USA

House, Pat (Athlete, Baseball Player)
2053 S White Pine Ln
Boise, ID 83706-4048, USA

House, Stormy
12334 Gorham Ave
Los Angeles, CA 90049-5206

House, Tom (Athlete, Baseball Player)
603 Ranlett Ave
La Puente, CA 91744-4143, USA

House, Yoanna (Model, Television Host)
c/o Staff Member *Style Network*
5750 Wilshire Blvd
Los Angeles, CA 90036-3697, USA

Householder, Paul (Athlete, Baseball
Player)
521 N Swinton Ave
Delray Beach, FL 33444-3969, USA

HouseJ, Eddie (Athlete, Basketball Player)
35 Kings Way
Waltham, MA 02451-9041, USA

House of Pain (Music Group)
c/o Staff Member *William Morris
Endeavor (LA)*
9601 Wilshire Blvd
Beverly Hills, CA 90210-5213, USA

Houser, Huell
450 N Rossmore Ave # 602
Los Angeles, CA 90004-2406

Houser, Jerry (Actor)
4050 Woodman Cyn
Sherman Oaks, CA 91423-4739, USA

Houser, John (Athlete, Football Player)
2197 Creekside Dr
Solvang, CA 93463-2238, USA

Houser, Kevin (Athlete, Football Player)
941 Montclair Cir
Westlake, OH 44145-1445, USA

Houser, Randy (Musician)
c/o Staff Member *Fitzgerald Hartley Co (Nashville)*
1908 Wedgewood Ave
Nashville, TN 37212-3733, USA

Houshmandzadeh, T J (Athlete, Football Player)
16703 Greenbrook Cir
Cerritos, CA 90703-1188, USA

Housie, Wayne (Athlete, Baseball Player)
16530 Colt Way
Moreno Valley, CA 92555-3303, USA

Housley, Phil (Athlete, Hockey Player, Olympic Athlete)
1055 Pine St Apt 430
Nashville, TN 37203-4275, USA

Houston (Adult Film Star)
c/o Staff Member *Atlas Multimedia Inc*
9005 Eton Ave Ste C
Canoga Park, CA 91304-6533, USA

Houston, Allan (Athlete, Basketball Player, Olympic Athlete)
Allan Houston Foundation
350 5th Ave Fl 59
New York, NY 10118-5999, USA

Houston, Andy (Race Car Driver)
835F Williamson Rd # 36
C/O Global Performance Co
Mooresville, NC 28117-8597, USA

Houston, Bobby (Athlete, Football Player)
4640 Vendue Range Dr
Raleigh, NC 27604-5078, USA

Houston, Byron (Athlete, Basketball Player)
16116 Cantera Creek Dr
Edmond, OK 73013-1473, USA

Houston, Cissy (Musician)
The New Hope Baptist Church Youth Choir
106 Sussex Ave
Newark, NJ 07103-3698, USA

Houston, Edwin A (Business Person)
Ryder System Inc
3600 NW 82nd Ave
Doral, FL 33166-6623, USA

Houston, Jarell (J-Boog) (Actor, Musician)
c/o Mike Esterman *Esterman.Com, LLC*
Prefers to be contacted via email
Baltimore, MD XXXXX, USA

Houston, Jim (Athlete, Football Player)
925 Trimble Pl
Northfield, OH 44067-2239, USA

Houston, Justin (Athlete, Football Player)
c/o Chafie Fields *Lagardere Unlimited (NYC)*
845 United Nations Plz
New York, NY 10017-3540, USA

Houston, Kenneth R (Ken) (Athlete, Football Player)
3603 Forest Village Dr
Kingwood, TX 77339-1819, USA

Houston, Lamarr (Athlete, Football Player)
c/o Mitchell Frankel *Impact Sports - Boca Raton*
2799 NW 2nd Ave Ste 203
Boca Raton, FL 33431-6709, USA

Houston, Marques (Batman) (Actor, Musician)
c/o Tyler Grasham *Agency for the Performing Arts (APA-LA)*
405 S Beverly Dr Ste 500
Beverly Hills, CA 90212-4425, USA

Houston, Penelope (Music Group)
Absolute Artists
8490 W Sunset Blvd # 403
West Hollywood, CA 90069-1912, USA

Houston, Thelma (Musician)
c/o Stephen Ford *Diva Central Inc*
7510 W Sunset Blvd Ste 1445
Los Angeles, CA 90046-3408, USA

Houston, Tyler (Athlete, Baseball Player)
325 Pleasant Summit Dr
Henderson, NV 89012-3486, USA

Houston, Wade (Basketball Player, Coach)
University of Tennessee
Athletic Dept
Knoxville, TN 37901, USA

Houston Calls (Music Group)
c/o Staff Member *Drive Thru Records*
3019 Olympic Blvd
Santa Monica, CA 90404-5001, USA

Hovan, Chris (Athlete, Football Player)
17301 Ladera Estates Blvd
Lutz, FL 33548-4817, USA

Hover, Don (Athlete, Football Player)
19 Wolf Creek Rd
Winthrop, WA 98862-9767, USA

Hovind, David J (Business Person)
PACCAR Inc
777 106th Ave NE
Bellevue, WA 98004-5027, USA

Hovis, Guy (Musician)
207 Morningside N
Ridgeland, MS 39157-9755, USA

Hovland, Tim (Athlete, Volleyball Player)
431 Main St
El Segundo, CA 90245-3003, USA

Hovley, Steve (Athlete, Baseball Player)
PO Box 655
Oak View, CA 93022-0655, USA

Hovsepian, Vatche (Religious Leader)
Armenian Church of America West
1201 Vine St
Los Angeles, CA 90038-1695, USA

Howard, Adina (Musician)
International Creative Mgmt
40 W 57th St Fl 5
New York, NY 10019-4001, USA

Howard, Andrew (Actor)
c/o Michelle Czernin von Chudenitz *Popular Press Media Group (PPMG)*
468 N Camden Dr Ste 105A
Beverly Hills, CA 90210-4507, USA

Howard, Arliss (Actor, Director, Writer)
c/o Gene Parseghian *Parseghian Planco LLC*
388 2nd Ave
New York, NY 10010-5616, USA

Howard, Ben (Athlete, Baseball Player)
45 Cross Brook Cv
Jackson, TN 38305-3548, USA

Howard, Bob (Athlete, Football Player)
2444 56th St
San Diego, CA 92105-5012, USA

Howard, Bobby (Athlete, Football Player)
745 Hansell St SE Apt 513
Atlanta, GA 30312-3475, USA

Howard, Brian (Athlete, Basketball Player)
619 Vermont Ave
Fort Walton Beach, FL 32547-3033, USA

Howard, Bruce (Athlete, Baseball Player)
8705 Misty Creek Dr
Sarasota, FL 34241-9562, USA

Howard, Bryce Dallas (Actor)
c/o Peter Kiernan *Management 360*
9111 Wilshire Blvd
Beverly Hills, CA 90210-5508, USA

Howard, Chris (Athlete, Baseball Player)
17 Sea View Ave
Nahant, MA 01908-1548, USA

Howard, Chris (Athlete, Baseball Player)
8655 Jones Rd Apt 301
Jersey Village, TX 77065-5104, USA

Howard, Clark (Radio Personality, Writer)
Newstalk 750 WSB
1601 W Peachtree St NE
Atlanta, GA 30309-2641, USA

Howard, Clint (Actor)
c/o Tiffany Kuzon *Evolution Entertainment (LA)*
901 N Highland Ave
Los Angeles, CA 90038-2412, USA

Howard, Dana (Athlete, Football Player)
228 Oakridge Ct
Fairview Heights, IL 62208-3452, USA

Howard, David (Athlete, Baseball Player)
3321 Mapleridge Dr
Loopapt 111
Lutz, FL 33558-5025, USA

Howard, David (Athlete, Football Player)
5516 E Rosedale St
Fort Worth, TX 76112-6859, USA

Howard, Desmond (Athlete, Football Player, Heisman Trophy Winner)
12206 Mount Overlook Ave
Cleveland, OH 44120-1034, USA

Howard, Doug (Athlete, Baseball Player)
8038 S Deer Creek Rd
Salt Lake City, UT 84121-5762, USA

Howard, Dwight (Athlete, Basketball Player)
2071 Enon Rd SW
Atlanta, GA 30331-7835, USA

Howard, Eddie (Athlete, Football Player)
1130 E Workman Ave
West Covina, CA 91790-2357, USA

Howard, Erik (Athlete, Football Player)
23255 FM 150 W
Driftwood, TX 78619-9155, USA

Howard, Frank (Athlete, Baseball Player, Coach)
24178 Lenah Woods Pl
Aldie, VA 20105-2369, USA

Howard, Frank O (Athlete, Baseball Player)
24178 Lenah Woods Pl
Aldie, VA 20105-2369, USA

Howard, Fred (Athlete, Baseball Player)
250 Lake Lulu Dr
Winter Haven, FL 33880-4461, USA

Howard, Gene (Athlete, Football Player)
11051 Lavender Ave
Fountain Valley, CA 92708-2457, USA

Howard, George (Bowler)
8415 Brookwood Dr
Portage, MI 49024-5209, USA

Howard, George (Musician)
David Rubinson
PO Box 411197
San Francisco, CA 94141-1197, USA

Howard, Greg (Cartoonist)
1900 N Atlantic Ave Apt 604
Daytona Beach, FL 32118-8304, USA

Howard, Greg (Athlete, Basketball Player)
4517 W 16th Pl Apt 2
Los Angeles, CA 90019-5164, USA

Howard, James Newton (Musician)
815 Myrtle Ave
Glendora, CA 91741-3657, USA

Howard, Jan (Music Group)
c/o Staff Member *Tessier-Marsh Talent*
505 Canton Pass
Madison, TN 37115-5449, USA

Howard, Jaye (Athlete, Football Player)
c/o Drew Rosenhaus *Rosenhaus Sports Representation*
6400 Allison Rd
Miami Beach, FL 33141-4540, USA

Howard, Jim (Athlete, Hockey Player)
518 Hamilton St
Ogdensburg, NY 13669-2714, USA

Howard, Joe (Athlete, Football Player)
2501 Joseph Dr
Clinton, MD 20735-4540, USA

Howard, Josh (Athlete, Basketball Player)
PO Box 802851
Dallas, TX 75380-2851, USA

Howard, Joyce
147 Ocean Avenue Ext
Santa Monica, CA 90402-1211

Howard, Juwan (Athlete, Basketball Player)
11714 Bistro Ln
Houston, TX 77082-2726, USA

Howard, Ken (Director)
c/o Diane Perez *Zero Gravity Management*
1531 14th St
Santa Monica, CA 90404-3302, USA

Howard, Kyle (Actor)
c/o Steve Himber *Steve Himber Entertainment*
211 S Beverly Dr # 601
Beverly Hills, CA 90212-3807, USA

Howard, Larry (Athlete, Baseball Player)
207 Innwood Dr
Georgetown, TX 78628-8311, USA

Howard, Lee (Athlete, Baseball Player)
4650 Dulin Rd Spc 203
Fallbrook, CA 92028-8766, USA

Howard, Leo (Actor)
c/o Emily Urbani *Osbrink Talent Agency*
4343 Lankershim Blvd Ste 100
North Hollywood, CA 91602-2705, USA

Howard, Lisa
247 S Beverly Dr # 102
Beverly Hills, CA 90212-3830

Howard, Matt (Athlete, Baseball Player)
45962 Corte Carmello
Temecula, CA 92592-1277, USA

Howard, Mike (Athlete, Baseball Player)
147 Kehle Rd
Madison, MS 39110-7971, USA

Howard, Miki (Musician)
c/o Mike Gardner *Gardener Entertainment*
5683 Hazelcrest Cir
Westlake Village, CA 91362-5426, USA

Howard, Otis (Athlete, Basketball Player)
231 Manhattan Ave
Oak Ridge, TN 37830-7544, USA

Howard, Paige (Actor)
c/o Meredith Wechter *ICM Partners (LA)*
10250 Constellation Blvd Fl 7
Los Angeles, CA 90067-6207, USA

Howard, Paul (Athlete, Football Player)
8502 S Jebel Way
Aurora, CO 80013, USA

Howard, Percy (Athlete, Football Player)
3525 Neely Rd
Memphis, TN 38109-3811, USA

Howard, Rance (Actor)
4286 N Clybourn Ave
Burbank, CA 91505-4002, USA

Howard, Rebecca Lynn (Musician)
c/o Staff Member *Paradigm (Monterey)*
404 W Franklin St
Monterey, CA 93940-2303, USA

Howard, Reggie (Athlete, Baseball Player)
4332 Crimson Leaf Cv
Memphis, TN 38125-2905, USA

Howard, Reggie (Athlete, Football Player)
775 Tucker St
Dyersburg, TN 38024-3791, USA

Howard, Richard (Writer)
23 Waverly Pl Apt 5X
New York, NY 10003-6717, USA

Howard, Robert (Hardcore Holly)
(Wrestler)
c/o Kerry Rodgerson *World Wrestling Entertainment (WWE)*
1241 E Main St
Titan Towers
Stamford, CT 06902-3520, USA

Howard, Ron (Athlete, Football Player)
8508 S 112th St
Seattle, WA 98178-3307, USA

Howard, Ron (Actor, Director, Producer, Writer)
c/o Richard Lovett *Creative Artists Agency (CAA-LA)*
2000 Avenue of the Stars Ste 100
Los Angeles, CA 90067-4705, USA

Howard, Ryan (Athlete, Baseball Player)
1630 Bentshire Ct
Ballwin, MO 63011-4754, USA

Howard, Sherman (Athlete, Football Player)
5125 Thomas Dr
Richton Park, IL 60471-1639, USA

Howard, Sherri (Actor)
c/o Michael Henderson *Heresun Management*
4119 W Burbank Blvd
Burbank, CA 91505-2122, USA

Howard, Sherri (Athlete, Track Athlete)
14059 Bridle Ridge Rd
Sylmar, CA 91342-1060, USA

Howard, Sherry
14059 Bridle Ridge Rd
Sylmar, CA 91342-1060

Howard, Stephen (Athlete, Basketball Player)
3941 Legacy Dr Ste 204 PMB A193
Plano, TX 75023-8331, USA

Howard, Steven (Athlete, Baseball Player)
4712 Shetland Ave
Oakland, CA 94605-5629, USA

Howard, Susan (Actor)
PO Box 1456
Boerne, TX 78006-1456, USA

Howard, Terrence (Actor)
c/o Jon Rubinstein *Authentic Talent and Literary Management*
20 Jay St Ste M17
Brooklyn, NY 11201-8300, USA

Howard, Thomas (Athlete, Baseball Player)
340 Clark St
Middletown, OH 45042-2041, USA

Howard, Tim (Athlete, Soccer Player)
c/o Richard Motzkin *Wasserman Media Group (LA)*
12100 W Olympic Blvd Ste 200
Los Angeles, CA 90064-1075, USA

Howard, Todd (Athlete, Football Player)
17325 Palo Duro Cyn
College Station, TX 77845-4584, USA

Howard, Traylor (Actor)
c/o John Carrabino *John Carrabino Management*
5900 Wilshire Blvd Ste 406
Los Angeles, CA 90036-5015, USA

Howard, Wilbur (Athlete, Baseball Player)
643 Walston Ln
Houston, TX 77060-5846, USA

Howarth, Jim (Athlete, Baseball Player)
2638 Bay Pointe Dr
Biloxi, MS 39531-2757, USA

Howarth, Roger (Actor)
K&H
1212 Avenue of the Americas # 3
New York, NY 10036-1602, USA

Howatt, Garry (Athlete, Hockey Player)
20314 E Bronco Dr
Queen Creek, AZ 85142-6007, USA

Howe, Arthur (Journalist)
Philadelphia Inquirer
400 N Broad St
Editorial Dept
Philadelphia, PA 19130-4099, USA

Howe, Brian (Musician)
c/o Samantha Crisp *Kohner Agency, The*
9300 Wilshire Blvd Ste 555
Beverly Hills, CA 90212-3211, USA

Howe, Delles (Athlete, Football Player)
1907 Crescent Dr
Monroe, LA 71202-3023, USA

Howe, Garry (Athlete, Football Player)
3807 NE Gardenia Ln
Ankeny, IA 50021-9289, USA

Howe, Gordie (Athlete, Hockey Player)
Power Play International
1119 Rochester Rd
Troy, MI 48083-6013, USA

Howe, Marie (Writer)
822 Palmer Rd Apt 2A
Bronxville, NY 10708-3317, USA

Howe, Mark (Athlete, Hockey Player, Olympic Athlete)
9 Inverness Ln
Jackson, NJ 08527-4046, USA

Howe, Marty (Athlete, Hockey Player)
40 Plank Ln
Glastonbury, CT 06033-2523, USA

Howe, Sean (Writer)
c/o Staff Member *HarperCollins Publishers*
195 Broadway Fl 2
Cellar 1
New York, NY 10007-3132, USA

Howe, Tina (Writer)
333 W End Ave
New York, NY 10023-8128, USA

Howe Jr, Arthur H (Art) (Athlete, Baseball Player, Coach)
17214 Calico Peak Way
Cypress, TX 77433-2113, USA

Howell, Alex (Cartoonist)
c/o Staff Member *King Features Syndication*
300 W 57th St Fl 15
New York, NY 10019-5238, USA

Howell, Bailey (Athlete, Basketball Player)
1567 Montgomery Rd
Starkville, MS 39759, USA

Howell, C Thomas (Actor, Director, Producer, Writer)
c/o Jean-Pierre (JP) Henraux *Henraux Management*
Prefers to be contacted by telephone
CA, USA

Howell, Delles (Athlete, Football Player)
910 Stubbs Vinson Rd
Monroe, LA 71203-8349, USA

Howell, Jack (Athlete, Baseball Player)
822 S Lehigh Dr
Tucson, AZ 85710-4741, USA

Howell, Jay (Athlete, Baseball Player)
4560 Colony Pt
Suwanee, GA 30024-3010, USA

Howell, John
8276 Sand Dollar Dr
Windsor, CO 80528-7530, USA

Howell, J P (Athlete, Baseball Player)
1706 11th St Apt 11
Sacramento, CA 95811-6547, USA

Howell, Kanin (Actor)
c/o Brandon Ross *Temptation Management*
1010 S Robertson Blvd Ste 2
Los Angeles, CA 90035-1527, USA

Howell, Ken (Athlete, Baseball Player)
22090 Buckingham Dr
Farmington Hills, MI 48335-5423, USA

Howell, Mike (Athlete, Football Player)
200 Charlotte St
Monroe, LA 71202-3906, USA

Howell, Pat (Athlete, Football Player)
7692 N Kincaid Ave
Fresno, CA 93711-0363, USA

Howell, Patrick (Pat) (Athlete, Baseball Player)
3700 Carlyle Close Apt 974
Mobile, AL 36609-1806, USA

Howell, Roy (Athlete, Baseball Player)
276 El Portal Dr
Pismo Beach, CA 93449-1504, USA

Howell III, Charles (Athlete, Golfer)
c/o Thomas Parker *GPR Sports Management*
11715 Spinnaker Way
Hollywood, FL 33026-1233, USA

Hower, Elizabeth (Actor)
c/o Ken Treusch *Bleecker Street Entertainment*
853 Broadway Ste 1214
New York, NY 10003-4717, USA

Howerdel, Billy (Musician)
4373 Beck Ave
Studio City, CA 91604-2702, USA

Howerton, Glenn (Actor)
c/o Nick Frenkel *3 Arts Entertainment (LA)*
9460 Wilshire Blvd Fl 7
Beverly Hills, CA 90212-2713, USA

Howey, Steve (Actor)
c/o Brian Swardstrom *United Talent Agency (UTA-NYC)*
9601 Wilshire Blvd
Beverly Hills, CA 90210-5213, USA

Howfield, Bobby (Athlete, Football Player)
5529 S Lowell Blvd
Littleton, CO 80123-2840, USA

Howfield, Ian (Athlete, Football Player)
7711 Victory Gallup St
Las Vegas, NV 89131-4123, USA

Howison, Ryan (Athlete, Golfer)
245 Barbados Dr
Jupiter, FL 33458-2927, USA

Howitt, Dann (Athlete, Baseball Player)
5544 141st Ave
Holland, MI 49423-9373, USA

Howitt, Peter (Director)
c/o Stephen Marks *Evolution Entertainment (LA)*
901 N Highland Ave
Los Angeles, CA 90038-2412, USA

Howland, Ben (Basketball Player, Coach)
University of California
Athletic Dept
Los Angeles, CA 90024, USA

Howland, Beth (Actor)
255 Amalfi Dr
Santa Monica, CA 90402-1125, USA

Howle, Paul (Cartoonist)
United Feature Syndicate
PO Box 5610
Cincinnati, OH 45201-5610, USA

Howley, Chuck (Athlete, Football Player)
5234 Ravine Dr
Dallas, TX 75220-2260, USA

Howry, Bobby (Athlete, Baseball Player)
24108 N 73rd Ln
Peoria, AZ 85383-3290, USA

Howry, Keenan (Athlete, Football Player)
4240 Fiesta Way Unit 3
Oceanside, CA 92057-7446, USA

Howze, Leonard Earl (Actor)
c/o Jessica Berlinski *Melissa Prophet Management*
Prefers to be contacted by telephone
CA, USA

Hoy, Peter (Athlete, Baseball Player)
26 Woods Dr
Canton, NY 13617-1061, USA

Hoyda, Dave (Athlete, Hockey Player)
3305 Bahama Dr
Sand Springs, OK 74063-2912, USA

Hoye, James (Athlete, Baseball Player)
12838 Patricia Dr
North Royalton, OH 44133-1024, USA

Hoyem, Steve (Athlete, Football Player)
28 Twilight Blf
Newport Coast, CA 92657-2126, USA

Hoyer, Brian (Athlete, Football Player)
c/o Joe Linta *JL Sports*
1204 Main St Ste 179
Branford, CT 06405-3787, USA

Hoyer, Jed (Commentator)
118 Huntington Ave Apt 206
Boston, MA 02116-5758, USA

Hoying, Bobby (Athlete, Football Player)
9322 Pratolino Villa Dr
Dublin, OH 43016-7375, USA

Hoyt, D LaMarr (Athlete, Baseball Player)
500 Harbison Blvd Apt 1002
Columbia, SC 29212-1719, USA

Hrabosky, Alan T (Al) (Athlete, Baseball Player, Sportscaster)
9 Frontenac Estates Dr
Saint Louis, MO 63131-2613, USA

Hrbek, Kent A (Athlete, Baseball Player)
2611 W 112th St
Minneapolis, MN 55431-3965, USA

Hrdina, Jiri (Athlete, Hockey Player)
c/o Staff Member *Dallas Stars*
2601 Avenue of the Stars Ste 100
Frisco, TX 75034-9016, USA

Hriniak, Walt (Athlete, Baseball Player)
18 Stacy Dr
North Andover, MA 01845-1832, USA

Hrivnak, Gary (Athlete, Football Player)
1508 W Plymouth Dr
Arlington Heights, IL 60004-2847, USA

Hrkac, Tony (Athlete, Hockey Player)
592 N Midvale Blvd
Madison, WI 53705-3238, USA

Hrynewich, Tim (Athlete, Hockey Player)
1132 North Ln
Norton Shores, MI 49441-4684, USA

H. Smith, Christopher (Congressman, Politician)
2373 Rayburn Hob
Washington, DC 20515-3004, USA

Hu, Kelly (Actor)
c/o Cheryl McLean *Creative Public Relations*
3385 Oak Glen Dr
Los Angeles, CA 90068-1311, USA

Huang, Helen (Musician)
I C M Artists
40 W 57th St Fl 19
New York, NY 10019-4001, USA

Huang, James (Actor)
c/o Staff Member *Cunningham Escott Slevin & Doherty (CESD-LA)*
10635 Santa Monica Blvd Ste 130
Los Angeles, CA 90025-8306, USA

Huang, Nina
8007 Highland Trl
Los Angeles, CA 90046-2022

Huang, Ying (Musician)
c/o Staff Member *Sony BMG/Jive Records*
2100 Colorado Ave
Santa Monica, CA 90404-3504, USA

Huard, Bill (Athlete, Hockey Player)
41 Massier Ln
Foothill Ranch, CA 92610-2305, USA

Huard, Brock (Athlete, Football Player)
5840 245th Pl NE
Redmond, WA 98053-2556, USA

Huard, Damon (Athlete, Football Player)
9508 NE 18th St
Clyde Hill, WA 98004-2539, USA

Huard, John (Athlete, Football Player)
40 Vista Dr
S Portland, ME 04106-6894, USA

Huarte, John (Athlete, Football Player, Heisman Trophy Winner)
Arizona Tile
8829 S Priest Dr
Tempe, AZ 85284-1905, USA

Hub (Musician)
William Morris Agency
1325 Avenue of the Americas Bsmt 2
New York, NY 10019-6047, USA

Hubbard, Elizabeth
1505 10th St
Santa Monica, CA 90401-2805

Hubbard, Erica (Actor)
c/o Staff Member *Jenny Delaney Management*
3238 Fond Dr
Encino, CA 91436-4206, USA

Hubbard, Glenn (Athlete, Baseball Player)
1515 Kings Xing
Stone Mountain, GA 30087-1914, USA

Hubbard, Gregg (Hobbie) (Music Group, Musician)
Sawyer Brown Inc
5200 Old Harding Rd
Franklin, TN 37064-9406, USA

Hubbard, Jack
10239 Sorenstam Dr
Trinity, FL 34655-4661, USA

Hubbard, Marvin R (Marv) (Athlete, Football Player)
5804 Dawn View Ct
Castro Valley, CA 94552-1803, USA

Hubbard, Mike (Athlete, Baseball Player)
2552 Brookstone Ln
Henrico, VA 23233-6914, USA

Hubbard, Phil (Athlete, Basketball Player, Olympic Athlete)
5130 Pleasant Forest Dr
Centreville, VA 20120-1248, USA

Hubbard, Ray Wylie (Musician)
c/o Staff Member *Davis McLarty Agency*
4609 Eagle Feather Dr
Austin, TX 78735-6474, USA

Hubbard, Robert (Athlete, Basketball Player)
353 Piper Rd
West Springfield, MA 01089-1757, USA

Hubbard, Trenidad (Athlete, Baseball Player)
4206 Clearwater Ct
Missouri City, TX 77459-1668, USA

Hubbard, Trent (Baseball Player)
Colorado Rockies
2654 E 77th St
Chicago, IL 60649-4725, USA

Hubbert, Brad (Athlete, Football Player)
3100 Landington Dr
Austell, GA 30106-3538, USA

Huber, Jon (Athlete, Baseball Player)
4409 S Angeline St
Seattle, WA 98118-1857, USA

Huber, Kevin (Athlete, Football Player)
c/o Joe Flanagan *BTI Sports Advisors*
170 N Scoville Ave
Oak Park, IL 60302-2647, USA

Huber, Max (Athlete, Football Player)
1047 Riverside Ln
Orem, UT 84097-6601, USA

Huber, Mike (Athlete, Baseball Player)
509 N Hena St
Greenville, IL 62246-1313, USA

Hubert, Janet
10061 Riverside Dr # 204
Toluca Lake, CA 91602-2560

Hubka, Gene (Athlete, Football Player)
62 Neitz Rd Apt 277
Northumberland, PA 17857-9612, USA

Hubley, Season (Actor)
31 Mansfield Ave
Essex Junction, VT 05452-3732, USA

Huckabee, Cooper (Actor)
1800 El Cerrito Pl Apt 34
Los Angeles, CA 90068-3743, USA

Huckabee, Michael (Politician)
756 Blue Mountain Rd
Santa Rosa Beach, FL 32459-5123, USA

Huckabee, Mike (Politician)
756 Blue Mountain Rd
Santa Rosa Beach, FL 32459-5123, USA

Huckaby, Ken (Athlete, Baseball Player)
4490 S Rio Dr
Chandler, AZ 85249-3382, USA

Huckleby, Harlan (Athlete, Football Player)
7473 Franklin Ridge Way
West Bloomfield, MI 48322-4128, USA

Hucles, Angela (Athlete, Olympic Athlete, Soccer Player)
1641 Tether Keep
Virginia Beach, VA 23454-1332, USA

Hucul, Fred (Athlete, Hockey Player)
4550 N Flowing Wells Rd Unit 279
Tucson, AZ 85705-1483, USA

Huddleston, David (Actor)
9200 W Sunset Blvd # 612
West Hollywood, CA 90069-3502, USA

Hudek, John (Athlete, Baseball Player)
John Hudek's All Star Baseball Academy
7603 Shady Way Dr
Sugar Land, TX 77479-6284, USA

Hudepohl, Joe (Athlete, Olympic Athlete, Swimmer)
10437 Greendale Dr
Tampa, FL 33626-5305, USA

Hudgens, Dave (Athlete, Baseball Player)
6002 E Edgemont Ave
Scottsdale, AZ 85257-1049, USA

Hudgens, Vanessa (Actor)
c/o Evan Hainey *Untitled Entertainment (LA)*
350 S Beverly Dr Ste 200
Beverly Hills, CA 90212-4819, USA

Hudis, Mark (Writer)
c/o Staff Member *United Talent Agency (UTA-LA)*
9336 Civic Center Dr
Beverly Hills, CA 90210-3604, USA

Hudler, Jiri (Athlete, Hockey Player)
111 Willits St Apt 502
Birmingham, MI 48009-3332, USA

Hudler, Rex (Athlete, Baseball Player)
9430 W 157th Ct
Overland Park, KS 66221-7818, USA

Hudson, Bill
7023 Birdview Ave
Malibu, CA 90265-4106

Hudson, Bob (Athlete, Football Player)
3408 Dalrock Rd
Rowlett, TX 75088-5538, USA

Hudson, Brett (Actor, Producer, Writer)
c/o Staff Member *William Morris Endeavor (LA)*
9601 Wilshire Blvd
Beverly Hills, CA 90210-5213, USA

Hudson, C B Jr (Business Person)
Torchmark Corp
2001 3rd Ave S
Birmingham, AL 35233-2115, USA

Hudson, Charles (Athlete, Baseball Player)
PO Box 368
Oakwood, TX 75855-0368, USA

Hudson, Charles (Charlie) (Athlete, Baseball Player)
32 W Hooker Ave
Coalgate, OK 74538, USA

Hudson, Chris (Athlete, Football Player)
6361 Moondance Cv
Olive Branch, MS 38654-9060, USA

Hudson, Dave (Athlete, Hockey Player)
5204 Briar Tree Dr
Dallas, TX 75248-6032, USA

Hudson, Emie (Actor)
5711 Hoback Glen Rd
Hidden Hills, CA 91302-1229, USA

Hudson, Ernie (Actor, Producer)
c/o Darryl Marshak *Marshak/Zachary Company, The*
8840 Wilshire Blvd Fl 1
Beverly Hills, CA 90211-2606, USA

Hudson, Garth (Music Group, Musician)
Skyline Music
32 Clayton St
Portland, ME 04103-2250, USA

Hudson, Gary (Actor)
c/o Staff Member *Origin Talent Agency*
4705 Laurel Canyon Blvd Ste 303
Valley Village, CA 91607-5943, USA

Hudson, Gordon (Athlete, Football Player)
12498 S Falls Creek Rd
Riverton, UT 84065-1915, USA

Hudson, Hal (Athlete, Baseball Player)
7548 S US Highway 1
Port St Lucie, FL 34952-1450, USA

Hudson, Haley (Actor)
c/o Staff Member *Weeds*
10880 Wilshire Blvd Ste 1600
Showtime Newtworks (La)
Los Angeles, CA 90024-4117, USA

Hudson, Hugh (Director)
c/o Staff Member *ICM Partners (LA)*
10250 Constellation Blvd Fl 7
Los Angeles, CA 90067-6207, USA

Hudson, James (Doctor)
Harvard Medical School
25 Shattuck St
Psychiatry Dept
Boston, MA 02115-6092, USA

Hudson, Jennifer (Actor, Musician)
8592 Johnston Rd
Burr Ridge, IL 60527-7076, USA

Hudson, Jesse (Athlete, Baseball Player)
341 Albert Lewis Way
Mansfield, LA 71052-5723, USA

Hudson, Joe (Athlete, Baseball Player)
109 Pine Valley Dr
Medford, NJ 08055-9210, USA

Hudson, John (Athlete, Football Player)
3320 Highway 77
Paris, TN 38242-5495, USA

Hudson, Kate (Actor)
780/788 Amalfi Dr
Pacific Palisades, CA 90272, USA

Hudson, Luke (Athlete, Baseball Player)
9912 Aster Cir
Fountain Valley, CA 92708-2309, USA

Hudson, Marvin (Athlete, Baseball Player)
698 Metasville Rd
Washington, GA 30673-2605, USA

Hudson, Orlando (Athlete, Baseball Player)
1416 Pocket Rd
Darlington, SC 29532-8416, USA

Hudson, Ray (Coach, Soccer Player)
DC United
14120 Newbrook Dr
Chantilly, VA 20151-2273, USA

Hudson, Rex (Athlete, Baseball Player)
12451 Cartwright Trl
Ponder, TX 76259-5220, USA

Hudson, Richard S (Athlete, Football Player)
Henry County High School
315 S Wilson St
Attn: Assistant Principal
Paris, TN 38242-5053, USA

Hudson, Robert W (Athlete, Football Player)
3408 Dalrock Rd
Rowlett, TX 75088-5538, USA

Hudson, Rodney (Athlete, Football Player)
c/o Joe Linta *JL Sports*
1204 Main St Ste 179
Branford, CT 06405-3787, USA

Hudson, Sally (Skier)
PO Box 2343
Olympic Valley, CA 96146-2343, USA

Hudson, Tim (Athlete, Baseball Player)
901 Rocky Hills Dr
Auburn, AL 36830-7222, USA

Hudson, Troy (Athlete, Baseball Player)
6040 Earle Brown Dr Ste 4S0
Minneapolis, MN 55430-2514, USA

Hudspeth, Tommy (Athlete, Football Coach, Football Player)
3522 E 71st Pl
Tulsa, OK 74136-5962, USA

Huelskamp, Tim (Congressman, Politician)
126 Cannon Hob
Washington, DC 20515-5401, USA

Huerta, Carlos (Athlete, Football Player)
3060 E Post Rd Ste 110
Las Vegas, NV 89120-4449, USA

Huertas, Jon (Actor, Producer)
c/o Sherry Marsh *Marsh Entertainment*
12444 Ventura Blvd Ste 203
Studio City, CA 91604-2409, USA

Hues, Frankie
2640 NE 135th St Apt 302
North Miami, FL 33181-3540

Huet, Cristobal (Athlete, Hockey Player)
Sports Consulting Group
65 Monroe Ave Ste D
Pittsford, NY 14534-1318, USA

Huff, Aubrey (Athlete, Baseball Player)
14104 Rancho Tierra Trl
San Diego, CA 92130-5234, USA

Huff, Brent (Actor)
c/o Erik Seastrand *William Morris Endeavor (LA)*
9601 Wilshire Blvd
Beverly Hills, CA 90210-5213, USA

Huff, Dann (Musician, Producer)
Dann Huff Productions
10 Music Cir S Fl 2
Nashville, TN 37203-3176, USA

Huff, Gary E (Athlete, Football Player)
3387 Shady Rest Rd
Havana, FL 32333-4869, USA

Huff, Kenneth W (Ken) (Athlete, Football Player)
105 Blackford Ct
Durham, NC 27712-9497, USA

Huff, Marty (Athlete, Football Player)
6700 Keithcrest Dr
Temperance, MI 48182-1231, USA

Huff, Mike (Athlete, Baseball Player)
1580 Sherman Ave Ph 10
Evanston, IL 60201-4498, USA

Huff, Orlando (Athlete, Football Player)
14623 196th Ave SE
Renton, WA 98059-8120, USA

Huff, Sam (Athlete, Football Player, Sportscaster)
Billie Van Pay
PO Box 963
Middleburg, VA 20118-0963, USA

Huff, Shawn
1505 10th St
Santa Monica, CA 90401-2805

Huff, Tanya (Writer)
c/o Staff Member *JABberwocky Literary Agency*
49 W 45th St Ste 1200
New York, NY 10036-4603, USA

Huffington, Arianna (Journalist, Writer)
300 N Carmelina Ave
Los Angeles, CA 90049-2702, USA

Huffington, Michael (Politician, Producer)
3005 45th St NW
Washington, DC 20016-3528, USA

Huffins, Chris (Athlete, Decathlon Athlete, Olympic Athlete)
1319 Wildcliff Pkwy NE
Atlanta, GA 30329-3465, USA

Huffman, Cady
c/o Alan David *Alan David Management*
8840 Wilshire Blvd Ste 200
Beverly Hills, CA 90211-2606, USA

Huffman, Felicity (Actor)
7237 Senalda Rd
Los Angeles, CA 90068-2653, USA

Huffman, Kerry (Athlete, Hockey Player)
5557 Sea Forest Dr Apt 215
New Port Richey, FL 34652-3213, USA

Huffman, Logan (Actor)
c/o Tina Thor *TMT Entertainment Group*
648 Broadway # 1002
New York, NY 10012-2348, USA

Huffman, Phil (Athlete, Baseball Player)
194 Paxton Rd
Rochester, NY 14617-4657, USA

Huffman, Tim (Athlete, Football Player)
3365 Jubilee Trl
Dallas, TX 75229-3810, USA

Hufnagel, John (Athlete, Football Player)
12859 Biggin Church Rd S
Jacksonville, FL 32224-7928, USA

Hufsey, Billy (Actor)
11725 Greystone Pt
Strongsville, OH 44149-9269, USA

Hug, Steve (Athlete, Gymnast, Olympic Athlete)
3813 Hughes Ave
Culver City, CA 90232-2715, USA

Hugasian, Harry (Athlete, Football Player)
Arcadia Gardens
720 W Camino Real Ave
Arcadia, CA 91007-7877, USA

Huggins, Bob (Athlete, Basketball Player, Coach)
207 Beecher Hall
Cincinnati, OH 45221-0001, USA

Hughes, Abby (Athlete, Olympic Athlete, Skier)
c/o Gigi Rock *Heraea Marketing*
10905 E Pear Tree Dr
Cornville, AZ 86325-5523, USA

Hughes, Albert (Director, Producer, Writer)
c/o David Wirtschafter *William Morris Endeavor (LA)*
9601 Wilshire Blvd
Beverly Hills, CA 90210-5213, USA

Hughes, Alfredrick (Athlete, Basketball Player)
5024 S Kildare Ave
Chicago, IL 60632-4543, USA

Hughes, Allen (Director, Producer, Writer)
c/o David Wirtschafter *William Morris Endeavor (LA)*
9601 Wilshire Blvd
Beverly Hills, CA 90210-5213, USA

Hughes, Bobby (Athlete, Baseball Player)
114 Montreal St
Playa Del Rey, CA 90293-7608, USA

Hughes, Bradley (Athlete, Golfer)
204 Easton Ct
Simpsonville, SC 29680-7627, USA

Hughes, Brent (Athlete, Hockey Player)
2211 Settlers Park Loop
Round Rock, TX 78665-4638, USA

Hughes, Brent (Athlete, Hockey Player)
2016 Sweetgum Dr
Hoover, AL 35244-1628, USA

Hughes, Carolyn (Actor, Sportscaster, Television Host)
c/o Staff Member *Fox Sports (LA)*
10201 W Pico Blvd Bldg 101
Los Angeles, CA 90064-2606, USA

Hughes, Danan (Athlete, Football Player)
278 SE Sumpter Ct
Lees Summit, MO 64063-3669, USA

Hughes, David (Athlete, Football Player)
5307 240th Ave NE
Redmond, WA 98053-2543, USA

Hughes, Dennis (Athlete, Football Player)
360 Beechwood Dr
Athens, GA 30606-4010, USA

Hughes, Dustin (Athlete, Baseball Player)
5226 Savannah Pkwy
Southaven, MS 38672-7513, USA

Hughes, Eddie (Athlete, Basketball Player)
4253 Deerfield Hills Rd
Colorado Springs, CO 80916-3506, USA

Hughes, Edward Z (Publisher)
American Heritage Magazine
60 5th Ave
Forbes Building
New York, NY 10011-8868, USA

Hughes, Ernie (Athlete, Football Player)
2116 Camino Brazos
Pleasanton, CA 94566-5811, USA

Hughes, Finola (Actor)
c/o Steven Jensen *Independent Group, The*
6363 Wilshire Blvd Ste 115
Los Angeles, CA 90048-5734, USA

Hughes, Frank John (Actor)
c/o Dan Baron *Agency for the Performing Arts (APA-LA)*
405 S Beverly Dr Ste 500
Beverly Hills, CA 90212-4425, USA

Hughes, Glenn (Musician)
6671 W Sunset Blvd Ste 1585-114
Los Angeles, CA 90028-7116, USA

Hughes, Harry (Politician)
24788 Woods Dr
Denton, MD 21629-2323, USA

Hughes, Howie (Athlete, Hockey Player)
3711 27th Pl W Apt 205
Seattle, WA 98199-2062, USA

Hughes, Irene
500 N Michigan Ave Ste 1039
Chicago, IL 60611-1032

Hughes, Jack (Athlete, Hockey Player)
Beanpot Financial
54 Canal St Ste 350
Boston, MA 02114-2015, USA

Hughes, Jerry (Athlete, Football Player)
c/o Tom Condon *CAA (St. Louis)*
222 S Central Ave Ste 1008
Saint Louis, MO 63105-3509, USA

Hughes, Jim (Athlete, Baseball Player)
530 S Londerry Ln
Anaheim, CA 92807-4654, USA

Hughes, Karen (Government Official)
US Department of State
2201 C St NW
Washington, DC 20520-0099, USA

Hughes, Kate (Athlete, Golfer)
275 Merlot Ln
Saint Albans, MO 63073-1214, USA

Hughes, Kathleen (Actor)
8818 Rising Glen Pl
Los Angeles, CA 90069-1222, USA

Hughes, Keith (Athlete, Baseball Player)
176 Sycamore Rd
Havertown, PA 19083-3508, USA

Hughes, Kim (Athlete, Basketball Player)
2221 Via Cerritos
Palos Verdes Estates, CA 90274-2141, USA

Hughes, Larry (Athlete, Basketball Player)
3 Hanna Ct
Cleveland, OH 44108-1162, USA

Hughes, Macon (Athlete, Football Player)
6141 Avery Dr Apt 7105
Fort Worth, TX 76132-5317, USA

Hughes, Miko (Actor)
Jamieson Assoc
53 Sunrise Rd
Superior, MT 59872, USA

Hughes, Montori (Athlete, Football Player)
c/o Joby Branion *Athletes First, LLC*
23091 Mill Creek Dr
Laguna Hills, CA 92653-1258, USA

Hughes, Pat (Athlete, Football Player)
4 Woodside Dr
Stratham, NH 03885-6549, USA

Hughes, Pat (Athlete, Hockey Player)
8388 Webster Hills Rd
Dexter, MI 48130-9365, USA

Hughes, Pat (Commentator)
13 Fox Trl
Lincolnshire, IL 60069-4010, USA

Hughes, Phil (Athlete, Baseball Player)
c/o Team Member *New York Yankees*
Yankee Stadium
161st St & River Ave
Bronx, NY 10451, USA

Hughes, Randy (Athlete, Football Player)
17608 Cedar Creek Canyon Dr
Dallas, TX 75252-4966, USA

Hughes, Richard H (Dick) (Athlete, Baseball Player)
PO Box 598
Stephens, AR 71764-0598, USA

Hughes, Ryan (Athlete, Hockey Player)
21 Palmerston Pl
Basking Ridge, NJ 07920-2513, USA

Hughes, Sarah (Athlete, Figure Skater, Olympic Athlete)
John Hughes
12 Channel Dr
Great Neck, NY 11024-1212, USA

Hughes, Suzan (Actor)
c/o Staff Member *ICM Partners (LA)*
10250 Constellation Blvd Fl 7
Los Angeles, CA 90067-6207, USA

Hughes, Terry (Athlete, Baseball Player)
107 Woodcreek Dr
Spartanburg, SC 29303-1949, USA

Hughes, Tom (Athlete, Baseball Player)
610 Kimswick Ct
Deer Park, TX 77536-6139, USA

Hughes, Tyrone C (Athlete, Football Player)
4758 Eunice St
New Orleans, LA 70127-3420, USA

Hughes-Fulford, Millie (Astronaut)
Veterans Affairs Dept
4150 Clement St Stop 15INC
Medical Center
San Francisco, CA 94121-1545, USA

Hughes-Fulford, Millie Dr (Astronaut)
1003 Moanakai Rd
Kapaa, HI 96746-1521, USA

Hughley, DL (Actor, Comedian)
c/o Staff Member *Five Timz Productions*
22817 Ventura Blvd Ste 872
Woodland Hills, CA 91364-1202, USA

Hugo, Chad (Musician)
c/o Scott Vener *The Schiff Company*
9220 W Sunset Blvd Ste 106
West Hollywood, CA 90069-3500, USA

Huisman, Justin (Athlete, Baseball Player)
8713 Forest Glen Ct
Saint John, IN 46373-8795, USA

Huisman, Rick (Athlete, Baseball Player)
17W025 Oak Ln
Bensenville, IL 60106-2860, USA

Huismann, Mark (Athlete, Baseball Player)
5751 NW Plantation Ln
Lees Summit, MO 64064-1686, USA

Huizenga, Bill (Congressman, Politician)
1217 Longworth Hob
Washington, DC 20515-4901, USA

Huizenga, H Wayne (Commentator)
1575 Ponce De Leon Dr
Ft Lauderdale, FL 33316-1323, USA

Hulbert, Mike (Athlete, Golfer)
7770 Apple Tree Cir
Orlando, FL 32819-4686, USA

Hulbig, Joe (Athlete, Hockey Player)
11 Bragg Rd
Foxboro, MA 02035-1112, USA

Hulce, Tom (Actor)
2305 Stanley Hills Dr
Los Angeles, CA 90046-1533, USA

Hulcher, Janet
Arnold Palmer Enterprises
9000 Bay Hill Blvd
Orlando, FL 32819-4880, USA

Hulett, Tim (Athlete, Baseball Player)
5706 Wood Ridge Dr
Shreveport, LA 71119-3922, USA

Hull, Bobby (Athlete, Hockey Player)
6916 Lennox Pl
University Park, FL 34201-2256, USA

Hull, Brett (Athlete, Hockey Player, Olympic Athlete)
3520 Eben Way
Stillwater, MN 55082-8102, USA

Hull, Dennis
115 E Maple St
Hinsdale, IL 60521-3730

Hull, Eric (Athlete, Baseball Player)
280 Covey Run
Selah, WA 98942-9605, USA

Hull, Gina (Athlete, Golfer)
479 Arricola Ave
Saint Augustine, FL 32080-4520, USA

Hull, Mike (Athlete, Football Player)
3809 Vista Azul
San Clemente, CA 92672-4543, USA

Hullet, Jamie (Athlete, Golfer)
1153 Lakeview Dr
Mesquite, TX 75149-5813, USA

Hulse, Chuck (Race Car Driver)
7341 Spruce Cir
La Palma, CA 90623-1324, USA

Hulse, David (Athlete, Baseball Player)
1301 Kenwood Dr
San Angelo, TX 76903-7261, USA

Hultgren, Randy (Congressman, Politician)
427 Cannon Hob
Washington, DC 20515-5301, USA

Hultz, Don (Athlete, Football Player)
5078 Pleasant Ridge Rd
Millington, TN 38053-7752, USA

Human League (Music Group)
c/o Staff Member *Performers of the World*
5657 Wilshire Blvd Ste 280
Los Angeles, CA 90036-3755, USA

Humayan, Mark S (Doctor)
Johns Hopkins University
Wilmer Ophthalmology Institute
Baltimore, MD 21218, USA

Humber, Philip (Athlete, Baseball Player)
1646 County Road 114
Carthage, TX 75633-5350, USA

Humbert, John O (Religious Leader)
Christian Church Disciples of Christ
1099 N Meridian St Ste 700
Indianapolis, IN 46204-1036, USA

Humbert, Richard (Athlete, Football Player)
12112 Ashton Park Dr
Glen Allen, VA 23059-7129, USA

Hume, A Britton (Brit) (Correspondent)
1401 N Oak St Apt 608
Arlington, VA 22209-3685, USA

Hume, Brit (Television Host)
c/o Staff Member *Fox News (DC)*
5151 Wisconsin Ave NW Fl 1
Washington, DC 20016-4132, USA

Hume, Kirsty (Model)
c/o Rick Ferrari *LA Models*
7700 W Sunset Blvd Ste 203
Los Angeles, CA 90046-3913, USA

Hume, Tom (Athlete, Baseball Player)
9923 59th St E
Parrish, FL 34219-4467, USA

Humenik, Ed (Athlete, Golfer)
4746 SW Hammock Creek Dr
Palm City, FL 34990-7936, USA

Humes, Edward (Journalist)
Simon & Schuster
1230 Avenue of the Americas Fl CONC1
New York, NY 10020-1586, USA

Humes, Mary-Margaret (Actor)
c/o Lisa Blumenthal *Momentum Talent Management*
13935 Burbank Blvd Apt 102
Van Nuys, CA 91401-5078, USA

Humiston, Mike (Athlete, Football Player)
311 N Richhill St
Waynesburg, PA 15370-1224, USA

Humm, David (Athlete, Football Player)
4301 Via Olivero Ave
Las Vegas, NV 89102-3799, USA

Hummel, Rick (Commentator)
PO Box 270056
Saint Louis, MO 63127-0056, USA

Hummel, Tim (Athlete, Baseball Player)
4528 Church Point Pl
Virginia Beach, VA 23455-4363, USA

Hummer, John (Athlete, Basketball Player)
2640 Baker St
San Francisco, CA 94123-3802, USA

Humperdinck, Engelbert (Actor, Musician, Producer)
c/o Arthur Andelson *Kismet Talent Agency*
3435 Ocean Park Blvd Ste 107
Santa Monica, CA 90405-3320, USA

Humphery, Bobby (Athlete, Football Player)
939 Lee Trevino
San Antonio, TX 78221-3237, USA

Humphrey, Claude (Athlete, Football Player)
3399 Lord Dunmore Cv
Memphis, TN 38134-3089, USA

Humphrey, Gordon J (Ex-Senator, Politician)
78 Garvin Hill Rd
Chichester, NH 03258-6102, USA

Humphrey, Jay (Athlete, Football Player)
408 Endeavor Ct
Rockwall, TX 75032-5772, USA

Humphrey, Paul (Athlete, Football Player)
1120 E Davis Dr Apt 515
Terre Haute, IN 47802-4068, USA

Humphrey, Renee
9300 Wilshire Blvd Ste 555
Beverly Hills, CA 90212-3211

Humphrey, Richard (Athlete, Baseball Player)
26 Player Green Pl
Spring, TX 77382-2021, USA

Humphrey, Richard (Baseball Player)
21 Midland Pl
Morristown, NJ 07960-5064, USA

Humphrey, Ryan (Basketball Player)
Memphis Grizzlies
175 Toyota Plz Ste 150
Memphis, TN 38103-6601, USA

Humphrey, Terry (Athlete, Baseball Player)
7 Oakmont
Trabuco Canyon, CA 92679-4728, USA

Humphreys, Bob (Athlete, Baseball Player)
1803 Oakwood St
Bedford, VA 24523-1217, USA

Humphreys, Mike (Athlete, Baseball Player)
1402 Lost Creek Dr
Desoto, TX 75115-3662, USA

Humphreys, Todd (Race Car Driver)
Humphrey's Race Team
Route #5
Elbridge, NY 13060, USA

Humphries, Jay (Athlete, Basketball Player)
22107 N 37th Ter
Phoenix, AZ 85050-8304, USA

Humphries, Kris (Athlete, Basketball Player)
c/o Liza Anderson *Anderson Group Public Relations*
8060 Melrose Ave Fl 4
Los Angeles, CA 90046-7038, USA

Humphries, Rusty (Radio Personality)
Rusty Humphries Show
225 NE Hillcrest Dr
Grants Pass, OR 97526-3547, USA

Humphries, Stan (Athlete, Football Player)
4100 Chauvin Ln
Monroe, LA 71201-2057, USA

Humphries, Stefan (Athlete, Football Player)
8708 E Redwood Ln
Spokane, WA 99217-9757, USA

Hundley, Mandisa (Musician)
c/o Staff Member *The M Collective*
PO Box 273
Franklin, TN 37065-0273, USA

Hundley, Randy (Athlete, Baseball Player)
Randy Hundley Baseball Camp
1935 S Plum Grove Rd # 5
Rd # 285
Palatine, IL 60067-7258, USA

Hundley, Rod (Hot Rod) (Athlete, Basketball Player, Sportscaster)
1860 E Siggard Dr
Salt Lake City, UT 84106-3870, USA

Hundley, Todd (Athlete, Baseball Player)
21691 W Swan Ct
Kildeer, IL 60047-7211, USA

Hundon, James (Athlete, Football Player)
92 Kenneth Ct
Bay Point, CA 94565-1545, USA

Hundt, Reed E (Government Official)
7215 Delfield St
Chevy Chase, MD 20815-4045, USA

Hung, Sammo (Actor)
c/o Maani Golesorkhi *Bluestone Entertainment*
9000 W Sunset Blvd Ste 700
West Hollywood, CA 90069-5807, USA

Hung, William (Musician, Reality Star)
c/o Mike Esterman *Esterman.Com, LLC*
Prefers to be contacted via email
Baltimore, MD XXXXX, USA

Hunley, Con (Musician)
6406 Spring View Ln
Knoxville, TN 37918-1203, USA

Hunley, Ricky C (Athlete, Football Player)
9617 Stonemasters Dr
Loveland, OH 45140-6210, USA

Hunnam, Charlie (Actor)
c/o Cynthia Pett-Dante *Brillstein Entertainment Partners (LA)*
9150 Wilshire Blvd Ste 350
Beverly Hills, CA 90212-3453, USA

Hunphrey, Bobby (Athlete, Football Player)
4209 Woodbine Ln
Hoover, AL 35226-4122, USA

Hunsicker, Gerald (Commentator)
83 Golden Scroll Cir
Spring, TX 77382-5396, USA

Hunt, Bobby (Athlete, Football Player)
5928 Bentway Dr
Charlotte, NC 28226-8053, USA

Hunt, Bonnie (Actor, Director, Talk Show Host)
415 25th St
Santa Monica, CA 90402-3103, USA

Hunt, Byron (Athlete, Football Player)
PO Box 281
Rutherford, NJ 07070-0281, USA

Hunt, Charlie (Athlete, Football Player)
8700 Nathans Cove Ct
Jacksonville, FL 32256-9536, USA

Hunt, Cletidus (Athlete, Football Player)
7246 Creek Bend Dr
Memphis, TN 38125-3018, USA

Hunt, Courtney (Director, Writer)
c/o Staff Member *William Morris Endeavor (LA)*
9601 Wilshire Blvd
Beverly Hills, CA 90210-5213, USA

Hunt, Crystal (Actor)
c/o Scott Zimmerman *Evolution Entertainment (LA)*
901 N Highland Ave
Los Angeles, CA 90038-2412, USA

Hunt, George (Athlete, Football Player)
40 N Pine Cir
Belleair, FL 33756-1640, USA

Hunt, Helen (Actor)
c/o Stephen Huvane *Slate Public Relations*
9000 W Sunset Blvd Ste 915
West Hollywood, CA 90069-5809, USA

Hunt, James (Politician)
6653D Governor Hunt Rd Apt A
Lucama, NC 27851-9415, USA

Hunt, Jimmy (Actor)
2279 Lansdale Ct
Simi Valley, CA 93065-2530, USA

Hunt, John (Athlete, Football Player)
8 Ulverston Way
Blythewood, SC 29016-8941, USA

Hunt, John R (Religious Leader)
Evangelical Covenant Church
5101 N Francisco Ave
Chicago, IL 60625-3676, USA

Hunt, Kevin (Athlete, Football Player)
11 Royal Ln
Londonderry, NH 03053-2507, USA

Hunt, Lamar (Football Executive, Soccer Player, Tennis Player)
1601 Elm St # 2800
Thanksgiving Tower
Dallas, TX 75201-4701, USA

Hunt, Linda (Athlete, Golfer)
6436 Bella Cir Unit 1105
Boynton Beach, FL 33437-5566, USA

Hunt, Linda (Actor)
c/o Tim Curtis *William Morris Endeavor (LA)*
9601 Wilshire Blvd
Beverly Hills, CA 90210-5213, USA

Hunt, Marsha (Actor)
13131 Magnolia Blvd
Sherman Oaks, CA 91423-1528, USA

Hunt, Peter (Director, Producer)
c/o Dennis Aspland *Aspland Management*
245 W 55th St Ste 1001
New York, NY 10019-5231, USA

Hunt, Randy (Athlete, Baseball Player)
324 Holly Ridge Dr
Montgomery, AL 36109-3904, USA

Hunt, Ray (Business Person)
Hunt Oil Company
1900 N Akard St
Dallas, TX 75201-2300

Hunt, Richard
1017 W Lill Ave
Chicago, IL 60614-2205, USA

Hunt, Ron (Athlete, Baseball Player)
2806 Jackson Rd
Wentzville, MO 63385-4205, USA

Hunt, Sam (Athlete, Football Player)
1708 Eliza St
Nacogdoches, TX 75961-5700, USA

Hunt, Van (Musician)
c/o Staff Member *Creative Artists Agency (CAA-LA)*
2000 Avenue of the Stars Ste 100
Los Angeles, CA 90067-4705, USA

Hunt, Wendy (DJ)
c/o Staff Member *Diva Central Inc*
7510 W Sunset Blvd Ste 1445
Los Angeles, CA 90046-3408, USA

Hunter, Anthony (Athlete, Football Player)
3126 Troy Ave Apt 5
Cincinnati, OH 45213-1313, USA

Hunter, Billy (Athlete, Baseball Player, Coach)
104 E Seminary Ave
Lutherville Timonium, MD 21093-6127, USA

Hunter, Brian (Athlete, Baseball Player)
1440 Kasten Dr
Dolton, IL 60419-2469, USA

Hunter, Brian (Athlete, Baseball Player)
12141 Centralia St Unit 219
Lakewood, CA 90715-1565, USA

Hunter, Buddy (Athlete, Baseball Player)
14467 Penny Dr
Plattsmouth, NE 68048-5121, USA

Hunter, Charlie (Music Group, Musician)
Figurehead Mgmt
3470 19th St
San Francisco, CA 94110-1740, USA

Hunter, Daniel (Athlete, Football Player)
210 N Lakeview Dr
Farmerville, LA 71241-2504, USA

Hunter, Dorothy (Baseball Player)
2607 Miller Ave NW
Grand Rapids, MI 49544-1948, USA

Hunter, Duncan (Congressman, Politician)
223 Cannon Hob
Washington, DC 20515-0003, USA

Hunter, Herman (Athlete, Football Player)
541 Rural Hill Rd
Nashville, TN 37217-4107, USA

Hunter, Holly (Actor)
c/o David Seltzer *Management 360*
9111 Wilshire Blvd
Beverly Hills, CA 90210-5508, USA

Hunter, Jack D
254 Holland Dr
Saint Augustine, FL 32095-8425, USA

Hunter, Jeff (Athlete, Football Player)
3492 Monte Carlo Dr
Augusta, GA 30906-5717, USA

Hunter, Jesse (Music Group, Musician)
Friedman & LaRosa
1334 Lexington Ave
New York, NY 10128, USA

hunter, Jim (Athlete, Baseball Player)
12939 Penshurst Ln
Windermere, FL 34786-6672, USA

Hunter, Jim (Commentator)
3010 Franklins Chance Dr
Fallston, MD 21047-1353, USA

Hunter, Les (Athlete, Basketball Player)
8712 W 92nd St
Overland Park, KS 66212-3817, USA

Hunter, Lindsey
4355 Hickory Ridge Ct
Plymouth, MI 48170-5123

Hunter, Mellisa (Reality Star)
c/o Mike Esterman *Esterman.Com, LLC*
Prefers to be contacted via email
Baltimore, MD XXXXX, USA

Hunter, Montgomery (Athlete, Football Player)
411 Washington St
Dover, OH 44622-1938, USA

Hunter, Patrick (Athlete, Football Player)
880 N David Ct
Chandler, AZ 85226-1659, USA

Hunter, Rachel (Actor, Model)
c/o Chuck Binder *Binder & Associates*
1465 Lindacrest Dr
Beverly Hills, CA 90210-2519, USA

Hunter, Rich (Athlete, Baseball Player)
40490 Corte De Rubi
Murrieta, CA 92562-8410, USA

Hunter, Robert (Politician)
2201 C St NW Dept of
Washington, DC 20520-0099, USA

Hunter, Ronald (Actor)
c/o Barbara Price *Kings Highway Entertainment*
14538 Benefit St Unit 103
Sherman Oaks, CA 91403-5504, USA

Hunter, Scott (Athlete, Football Player)
6386 Dolive Ct
Daphne, AL 36526-7159, USA

Hunter, Stephen (Writer)
Washington Post
Editorial Dept
1150 15th St NW
Washington, DC 20071-0001, USA

Hunter, Steven (Basketball Player)
Orlando Magic
8701 Maitland Summit Blvd
Waterhouse Center
Orlando, FL 32810-5915, USA

Hunter, Tab (Actor, Writer)
PO Box 50308
Santa Barbara, CA 93150-0308, USA

Hunter, Tim (Athlete, Coach, Hockey Player)
c/o Staff Member *San Jose Sharks*
525 W Santa Clara St
San Jose, CA 95113-1500, USA

Hunter, Tim (Director)
c/o Staff Member *Gersh (LA)*
9465 Wilshire Blvd Ste 600
Beverly Hills, CA 90212-2605, USA

Hunter, Tommy (Musician)
c/o Staff Member *Rocklands Entertainment*
1135 Pasadena Ave S Ste 209
South Pasadena, FL 33707-2855, USA

Hunter, Torii (Athlete, Baseball Player)
PO Box 1357
Prosper, TX 75078-1357, USA

Hunter, Trent (Athlete, Hockey Player)
26 MacKay Way
Roslyn, NY 11576-2169, USA

Hunter, Willard (Athlete, Baseball Player)
2562 Poppleton Ave
Omaha, NE 68105-2303, USA

Hunter-Gault, Charlayne (Correspondent)
News Hour Show
2700 S Quincy St Ste 250
Arlington, VA 22206-2222, USA

Hunter-Reay, Ryan (Race Car Driver)
3200 NE 40th Ct
Fort Lauderdale, FL 33308-6416, USA

Hunthausen, Raymond G (Religious Leader)
Catholic Archdiocese of Seattle
910 Marion St
Seattle, WA 98104-1274, USA

Huntington, Neal (Commentator)
332 Rye Gate St
Bay Village, OH 44140-1274, USA

Huntington, Sam (Actor)
c/o Walter Hamada *DMG Entertainment*
3431 Wesley St Ste E
Culver City, CA 90232-2365, USA

Huntington, Samuel P (Politician)
Harvard University
Olin Institute
Political Science Dept
Cambridge, MA 02138, USA

Huntington-Whiteley, Rosie (Actor, Model)
c/o Jeff Speich *Anonymous Content (LA)*
3532 Hayden Ave
Culver City, CA 90232-2413, USA

Huntley, Joni (Athlete, Olympic Athlete, Track Athlete)
7148 SW 4th Ave
Portland, OR 97219-2220, USA

Huntley, Richard (Athlete, Football Player)
6005 Williams Rd Apt A
Charlotte, NC 28215-3606, USA

Huntsman, Stanley H (Coach)
5532 Timbercrest Trl
Knoxville, TN 37909-1837, USA

Huntz, Steve (Athlete, Baseball Player)
3303 Linden Rd Apt 405
Rocky River, OH 44116-4105, USA

Hunwlck, Matt (Athlete, Hockey Player)
37242 Mariano Dr
Sterling Heights, MI 48312-2054, USA

Hunyadfi, Steven (Coach, Swimmer)
838 Ridgewood Dr Apt 12
Fort Wayne, IN 46805-5712, USA

Hunziker, Terry (Designer)
208 3rd Ave S
Seattle, WA 98104-2608, USA

Hupp, Jana Marie (Actor)
c/o Karen Forman *Domain Talent*
9229 W Sunset Blvd Ste 710
West Hollywood, CA 90069-3407, USA

Huppert, Dave (Athlete, Baseball Player)
6732 Stephens Path
Zephyrhills, FL 33542-0652, USA

Hurd, Gale Anne (Producer)
c/o Staff Member *Valhalla Motion Pictures*
3201 Cahuenga Blvd W
Los Angeles, CA 90068-1301, USA

Hurd, Michelle (Actor)
1077 E Santa Anita Ave
Burbank, CA 91501-1509, USA

Hurdle, Clinton M (Clint) (Athlete, Baseball Player, Coach)
9068 Sturbridge Pl
Highlands Ranch, CO 80129-2236, USA

Hurlbut, Linda (Athlete, Golfer)
24741 Calle Conejo
Calabasas, CA 91302-3009, USA

Hurlbut, Mike (Athlete, Hockey Player)
86 Cougar Pt
Massena, NY 13662-3176, USA

Hurley, Bob (Athlete, Basketball Player)
1410 Shoreline Way
Hollywood, FL 33019-5006, USA

Hurley, Chad (Business Person)
YouTube, Inc
901 Cherry Ave
San Bruno, CA 94066-2914, USA

Hurley, Craig (Actor)
c/o Sandie Schnarr *AVO Talent Agency*
5670 Wilshire Blvd Ste 1930
Los Angeles, CA 90036-5603, USA

Hurley, Douglas G (Astronaut)
700 Thomwood Dr
Friendswood, TX 77546, USA

Hurley, Douglas G Ltcol (Astronaut)
1848 Lake Landing Dr
League City, TX 77573-7781, USA

Hurley, Eric (Athlete, Baseball Player)
124 Scotland Yard Blvd
Saint Johns, FL 32259-5912, USA

Hurlic, Philip (Actor)
1105 S Caswell Ave
Compton, CA 90220-3921, USA

Hurns, Allen (Athlete, Football Player)
c/o Drew Rosenhaus *Rosenhaus Sports Representation*
6400 Allison Rd
Miami Beach, FL 33141-4540, USA

Hurran, Nick (Director, Producer)
c/o Geoff Morley *United Talent Agency (UTA-LA)*
9336 Civic Center Dr
Beverly Hills, CA 90210-3604, USA

Hurst, Bill (Athlete, Baseball Player)
15820 SW 88th Ct
Palmetto Bay, FL 33157-2031, USA

Hurst, Bruce (Athlete, Baseball Player)
1080 N Riata St
Gilbert, AZ 85234-3466, USA

Hurst, Grady (Athlete, Football Player)
5810 S 40th St Apt 118
Phoenix, AZ 85040-3965, USA

Hurst, Jackson (Actor)
c/o Staff Member *Lee Peterson and Associates*
78 San Marcos St
Austin, TX 78702-5236, USA

Hurst, James (Athlete, Baseball Player)
5816 Sunnyvalle Dr
Bargersville, IN 46106-8556, USA

Hurst, Jimmy (Athlete, Baseball Player)
901 University Ln
Tuscaloosa, AL 35401-7134, USA

Hurst, Jonathan (Athlete, Baseball Player)
308 Woodburn Creek Rd
Spartanburg, SC 29302-4279, USA

Hurst, Maurice (Athlete, Football Player)
PO Box 431068
Dallas, TX 75343, USA

Hurst, Pat (Athlete, Golfer)
730 Camino Amigo
Danville, CA 94526-2204, USA

Hurst, Rick (Actor)
1230 Horn Ave Apt 401
West Hollywood, CA 90069-2120, USA

Hurst, Ryan (Actor)
5120 Oakdale Ave
Woodland Hills, CA 91364-3630, USA

Hurston, Chuck (Athlete, Football Player)
9360 Prestwick Club Dr
Duluth, GA 30097-2400, USA

Hurt, John (Actor)
c/o John Crosby *John Crosby Management*
1357 N Spaulding Ave
Los Angeles, CA 90046-4009, USA

Hurt, Mary Beth (Actor)
c/o Paul Martino *Martino Management*
149 W 72nd St Apt 1D
New York, NY 10023-3228, USA

Hurt, Robert (Congressman, Politician)
1516 Longworth Hob
Washington, DC 20515-0905, USA

Hurt, William (Actor)
35425 Clamity Creek Ln
Drewsey, OR 97904-5711, USA

Hurtado, Edwin (Athlete, Baseball Player)
Toronto Blue Jays
7219 134th Ct SE
Newcastle, WA 98059-3004, USA

Hurwich, Leo M (Doctor)
University of Pennsylvania
Psychology Dept
Philadelphia, PA 19104, USA

Hurwit, Bruce (Director)
c/o Staff Member *Morra Brezner Steinberg & Tenenbaum (MBST) Entertainment*
345 N Maple Dr Ste 200
Beverly Hills, CA 90210-5174, USA

Hurwitz, Mitchell
c/o Adam Berkowitz *Creative Artists Agency (CAA-LA)*
2000 Avenue of the Stars Ste 100
Los Angeles, CA 90067-4705, USA

Husak, Todd (Athlete, Football Player)
100 N Sepulveda Blvd
El Segundo, CA 90245-4359, USA

Huscroft, Jamie (Athlete, Hockey Player)
3024 38th St SE
Puyallup, WA 98374-1949, USA

Huskey, Robert L (Butch) (Athlete, Baseball Player)
PO Box 996
Apache, OK 73006-0996, USA

Husmann, Ed (Athlete, Football Player)
27266 Orth Ln
Conroe, TX 77385-9087, USA

Huson, Jeff (Athlete, Baseball Player)
10349 Rowlock Way
Parker, CO 80134-9580, USA

Hussey, Matthew (Actor)
c/o Alex Spieller *IMPR*
357 S Robertson Blvd
Beverly Hills, CA 90211-3602, USA

Hussey, Olivia (Actor)
c/o Staff Member *Frozen Flame Entertainment*
8033 W Sunset Blvd Ste 247
Los Angeles, CA 90046-2401, USA

Husted, Dave (Athlete, Bowler)
16231 SE Norma Rd
Portland, OR 97267-5193, USA

Huston, Anjelica (Actor, Director)
c/o Ina Treciokas *Slate Public Relations*
9000 W Sunset Blvd Ste 915
West Hollywood, CA 90069-5809, USA

Huston, Carol (Actor)
10100 Santa Monica Blvd Ste 2500
Los Angeles, CA 90067-4116

Huston, Daniel (Danny) (Actor, Director)
c/o Laina Cohn *Cohn / Torgan Management*
Prefers to be contacted by telephone or email
Los Angeles, CA, USA

Huston, Geoff (Athlete, Basketball Player)
1960 Ellis Ave
Bronx, NY 10472-5006, USA

Huston, Jack (Actor)
c/o Todd Diener *Untitled Entertainment (LA)*
350 S Beverly Dr Ste 200
Beverly Hills, CA 90212-4819, USA

Huston, John (Athlete, Golfer)
322 Magnolia Dr
Clearwater, FL 33756-3836, USA

Hutch, Willie (Athlete, Hockey Player)
225 W 57th St
5th Fir.
New York, NY 10019-2136, USA

Hutcherson, Josh (Actor)
c/o Staff Member *JetLag Productions*
11812 San Vicente Blvd Fl 4
Los Angeles, CA 90049-6625, USA

Hutcherson, Robert (Bobby) (Musician)
Abby Hoffer
223 1/2 E 48th St
New York, NY 10017, USA

Hutchins, Jason (Athlete, Baseball Player)
2401 Stone Castle Cir
College Station, TX 77845-5494, USA

Hutchins, Mel (Athlete, Basketball Player)
350 N El Camino Real Spc 31
Encinitas, CA 92024-2822, USA

Hutchins, Paul (Athlete, Football Player)
7251 S South Shore Dr Apt 20G
Chicago, IL 60649-5783, USA

Hutchins, Sonny (Race Car Driver)
8114 Michael Rd
Henrico, VA 23229-4904, USA

Hutchins, Will (Actor)
PO Box 371
Glen Head, NY 11545-0371, USA

Hutchinson, Andrew (Athlete, Hockey Player)
1350 Dennison Rd
East Lansing, MI 48823-2166, USA

Hutchinson, Anthony (Athlete, Football Player)
124 Bellaire Ct
Bellaire, TX 77401-4219, USA

Hutchinson, Asa (Politician)
1501 N Pierce St Ste 102
Little Rock, AR 72207-5222, USA

Hutchinson, Chad (Athlete, Baseball Player)
1388 Elder Ave
Menlo Park, CA 94025-5566, USA

Hutchinson, Doug (Actor)
United Talent Agency
9336 Civic Center Dr
Beverly Hills, CA 90210-3604, USA

Hutchinson, Doug (Actor)
c/o Ryan Martin *Agency for the Performing Arts (APA-LA)*
405 S Beverly Dr Ste 500
Beverly Hills, CA 90212-4425, USA

Hutchinson, Josh (Actor)
c/o Staff Member *JE Talent*
323 Geary St Ste 302
San Francisco, CA 94102-1820, USA

Hutchinson, Kieran (Actor)
c/o Adam Levine *Levine Okwu Erickson Management*
2126 N Commonwealth Ave
Los Angeles, CA 90027-2118, USA

Hutchinson, Scott (Athlete, Football Player)
726 Forest Glen Ct
Maitland, FL 32751-5109, USA

Hutchinson, Steven (Athlete, Football Player)
404 W Brookfield Dr
Nashville, TN 37205-4408, USA

Hutchinson, Tim (Politician)
1825 I St NW Attn
FL1200PUBPLCY&LAWDEPT
Washington, DC 20006-5403, USA

Hutchison, Doug (Actor)
c/o Ryan Martin *Agency for the Performing Arts (APA-LA)*
405 S Beverly Dr Ste 500
Beverly Hills, CA 90212-4425, USA

Hutchison, Kay Bailey (Politician)
Senate Russell Ofc
Washington, DC 20510-0001, USA

Huther, Bruce (Athlete, Football Player)
1156 N Bonnie Brae St
Denton, TX 76201-2421, USA

Hutson, Brian (Athlete, Football Player)
6077 Arboretum Dr
Frisco, TX 75034-7270, USA

Hutson, Candace (Actor)
3500 W Olive Ave Ste 920
Burbank, CA 91505-5514

Hutson, Herb (Athlete, Baseball Player)
7203 W Sugar Tree Ct
Savannah, GA 31410-2414, USA

Hutson, Tracy (Actor, Reality Star)
c/o Staff Member *Extreme Makeover: Home Edition*
9225 W Sunset Blvd # 1100
Endemol Entertainment Usa
West Hollywood, CA 90069-3111, USA

Hutt, Donald (Athlete, Football Player)
2172 S Tollgate Pl
Boise, ID 83709-2300, USA

Hutter, Mark (Race Car Driver)
Team Rensi Motorsports
6804 Hobson Valley Dr Ste 118
Woodridge, IL 60517-1448, USA

Huttlestone, Daniel (Actor)
c/o Josh Pearl *ICM Partners (NY)*
730 5th Ave
New York, NY 10019-4105, USA

Hutto, Jim (Athlete, Baseball Player)
1317 John Carroll Dr
Pensacola, FL 32504-7114, USA

Hutton, Danny (Music Group, Musician)
2437 Horse Shoe Canyon Rd
Los Angeles, CA 90046-1539, USA

Hutton, Gunilla (Actor)
803 Alston Ln
Santa Barbara, CA 93108-2302, USA

Hutton, Lauren (Actor, Model)
36 Coyote Cir
Ranchos De Taos, NM 87557, USA

Hutton, Pascale (Actor)
c/o Ben Levine *LINK Entertainment*
11872 La Grange Ave Fl 1
Los Angeles, CA 90025-5283, USA

Hutton, Rif (Actor)
c/o Staff Member *Momentum Talent and Literary Agency*
9401 Wilshire Blvd Ste 501
Beverly Hills, CA 90212-2944, USA

Hutton, Timothy (Actor)
75 Cushman Rd
Patterson, NY 12563-2630, USA

Hutton, Tommy (Athlete, Baseball Player)
18 Huntly Dr
Palm Beach Gardens, FL 33418-6812, USA

Hutzler, Brody (Actor)
c/o Staff Member *Pakula/King & Associates*
9229 W Sunset Blvd Ste 315
West Hollywood, CA 90069-3403, USA

Huvane, Kevin (Business Person)
1119 Calle Vista Dr
Beverly Hills, CA 90210-2507, USA

Huxhold, Ken (Athlete, Football Player)
8524 Stone Harbor Ave
Las Vegas, NV 89145-5704, USA

Huxley, Laura (Doctor, Writer)
10636 Whipple St # 1
North Hollywood, CA 91602-2760, USA

Huyck, Willard (Director)
39 Oakmont Dr
Los Angeles, CA 90049-1901, USA

Hwang, David Henry (Writer)
c/o Scott Henderson *Paradigm (LA)*
9601 Wilshire Blvd
Beverly Hills, CA 90210-5213, USA

Hyams, Peter (Director)
PO Box 10
Basking Ridge, NJ 07920-0010, USA

Hyatt, Fred (Athlete, Football Player)
19350 SE 52nd Pl
Morriston, FL 32668-3968, USA

Hyche, Heath (Comedian)
c/o Staff Member *Brillstein Entertainment Partners (LA)*
9150 Wilshire Blvd Ste 350
Beverly Hills, CA 90212-3453, USA

Hyche, Steve (Athlete, Football Player)
2801 Five Oaks Ln
Vestavia, AL 35243-2621, USA

Hyde, Allan (Actor)
c/o Iris Grossman *Paradigm (LA)*
10250 Constellation Blvd Fl 7
Los Angeles, CA 90067-6207, USA

Hyde, Brandon (Athlete, Baseball Player)
9554 Central Park Ave
Evanston, IL 60203-1104, USA

Hyde, Dick (Athlete, Baseball Player)
1506 Cambridge Dr
Champaign, IL 61821-4957, USA

Hyde, Harry
PO Box 291
Harrisburg, NC 28075-0291

Hyder, Greg (Athlete, Basketball Player)
16228 Wato Rd Apt A
Apple Valley, CA 92307-7813, USA

Hyde-White, Alex (Actor)
Borinstein Oreck Bogart
3172 Dona Susana Dr
Studio City, CA 91604-4356, USA

Hyers, Tim (Athlete, Baseball Player)
241 Ridge Rd
Covington, GA 30016-5138, USA

Hyland, Brian (Musician)
Stone Buffalo
PO Box 101
Helendale, CA 92342-0101, USA

Hyland, Robert (Athlete, Football Player)
87 Smith Ave
White Plains, NY 10605-2321, USA

Hyland, Sarah (Actor)
c/o Richard Konigsberg *RKM*
400 N Mansfield Ave
Los Angeles, CA 90036-2622, USA

Hylton, James (Race Car Driver)
15 Avalon Rd
Martin, GA 30557-2551, USA

Hylton, Thomas J (Journalist)
Pottstown Mercury
Editorial Dept
Hanover & Kings Sts
Pottstown, PA 19464, USA

Hyman, B D
PO Box 7107
Charlottesville, VA 22906-7107, USA

Hyman, Dick
223 1/2 E 48th St
New York, NY 10017

Hyman, Earle (Actor)
Manhattan Towers
PO Box 650188
Sterling, VA 20165-0188, USA

Hyman, Fracaswell (Producer)
c/o Staff Member *William Morris Endeavor (LA)*
9601 Wilshire Blvd
Beverly Hills, CA 90210-5213, USA

Hyman, Misty (Athlete, Swimmer)
3826 E Lupine Ave
Phoenix, AZ 85028-2125, USA

Hymes, Randy (Athlete, Football Player)
8108 Hallmark Dr
N Richlnd Hls, TX 76182-8644, USA

Hymowitz, Kay S. (Writer)
Manhattan Institute For Policy Research
52 Vanderbilt Ave Fl 2
New York, NY 10017-3808, USA

Hynd, Noel
c/o Susan Simons *Broder Webb Chervin Silbermann Agency, The (BWCS)*
10250 Constellation Blvd
Los Angeles, CA 90067-6200, USA

Hyndman, Mike (Athlete, Hockey Player)
7143 Bluebell Ct
Lakewood Ranch, FL 34202-4197

Hynes, Dave (Athlete, Hockey Player)
10 Trinity Ct
Wellesley Hills, MA 02481-2505, USA

Hynes, David
10 Trinity Ct
Wellesley Hills, MA 02481-2505

Hynes, Samuel (Writer)
130 Moore St
130 Moore St
Princeton, NJ 08540-3359, USA

Hynoski, Henry (Athlete, Football Player)
PO Box 257
Elysburg, PA 17824-0257, USA

Hyre, John (Business Person)
870 High St Ste 104
Worthington, OH 43085-4141, USA

Hysong, Nick (Athlete, Track Athlete)
10424 N 38th St
Phoenix, AZ 85028-4016, USA

Hyzdu, Adam (Athlete, Baseball Player)
7823 E Red Hawk Cir
Mesa, AZ 85207-1167, USA

Iacavazzi, Cosmo (Athlete, Football Player)
90 Vine St
Taylor, PA 18517-1225, USA

Iacocca, Lee (Business Person)
The Iacocca Foundation
867 Boylston St Fl 6
Boston, MA 02116-2774, USA

Iaconio, Frank (Race Car Driver)
250 US Highway 206
Flanders, NJ 07836-9071, USA

Iacono, Paul (Actor)
c/o Shea Martin *SLATE Public Relations - NY*
307 7th Ave Rm 2401
New York, NY 10001-6019, USA

Iafrate, Al A (Athlete, Hockey Player)
6990 Spring Meadow Ln
Plymouth, MI 48170-5838, USA

Iakovas, Primate Archbishop (Religious Leader)
31 Park Dr
New York, NY 10021, USA

Ian, Janis (Musician)
4501 Granny White Pike
Nashville, TN 37204-4119, USA

Iannucci, Armando (Director)
c/o Chris Simonian *Creative Artists Agency (CAA-LA)*
2000 Avenue of the Stars Ste 100
Los Angeles, CA 90067-4705, USA

Iaquaniello, Mike (Athlete, Football Player)
49105 Plum Tree Dr
Plymouth, MI 48170-3263, USA

Iassonga, Dan (Athlete, Baseball Player)
1501 Bailey Farm Ct SW
Marietta, GA 30064-5281, USA

Iassonga, Daniel (Baseball Player)
5950 N 78th St Unit 159
Scottsdale, AZ 85250-6183, USA

Iavaroni, Marcus (Athlete, Basketball Player)
6308 Starfish Ave
North Port, FL 34291-4525, USA

Ibanez, Raul (Athlete, Baseball Player)
12961 SW 143rd Ter
Miami, FL 33186-8943, USA

Icahn, Carl (Business Person)
Icahn Co
445 Hamilton Ave Ste 1210
White Plains, NY 10601-1833, USA

Ice
11500 W Olympic Blvd Ste 655
Los Angeles, CA 90064-1530

Ice, Vanilla (Musician)
c/o Tommy Quon *TQ Management Agency*
2412 Piedra Dr
Plano, TX 75023-5329, USA

Ice-T (Actor, Musician, Producer, Reality Star)
31A Casta Ln
Edgewater, NJ 07020, USA

Ichaso, Leon (Director)
c/o Michael Pio *Innovative Artists (LA)*
1505 10th St
Santa Monica, CA 90401-2805, USA

Ickes, Harold (Politician)
6215 Tally Ho Ln
Alexandria, VA 22307-1014, USA

Iconic Boyz (Dancer)
14 Wilson Ave Ste 5
Englishtown, NJ 07726-1577, USA

Idle, Eric (Actor, Comedian)
3131 Floye Dr
Los Angeles, CA 90046-1217, USA

Idol, Billy (Musician, Songwriter)
c/o Tony Dimitriades *East End Management*
13721 Ventura Blvd # 2
Sherman Oaks, CA 91423-3023, USA

Ifans, Rhys (Actor)
Endeavor Talent Agency
9701 Wilshire Blvd Ste 1000
Beverly Hills, CA 90212-2010, USA

Ifeachor, Tracy (Actor)
c/o Nicolas Bernheim *NB Management*
1157 S Beverly Dr Fl 2
Los Angeles, CA 90035-1119, USA

Ifeanyi, Israel (Athlete, Football Player)
44733 Ruthron Ave
Lancaster, CA 93536-1431, USA

Ifill, Gwen (Writer)
c/o Staff Member *Doubleday*
1540 Broadway
New York, NY 10036-4039

Iger, Robert A (Business Person)
Walt Disney Co
500 S Buena Vista St
Burbank, CA 91521-0007, USA

Iglesias, Enrique (Musician)
4535 Sabal Palm Rd
Miami, FL 33137-3363, USA

Iglesias, Gabriel (Actor)
c/o Yvette Noel-Schure *Schure Media*
666 Main Rd
Towaco, NJ 07082-6600, USA

Iglesias, Julio (Musician)
7 Indian Creek Island Rd
Indian Creek Village, FL 33154-2903, USA

Iglesias, Tuaquin (Athlete, Football Player)
c/o Chad Speck *Allegiant Athletic Agency*
35 Market Sq Ste 201
Knoxville, TN 37902-1420, USA

Ignasiak, Gary (Athlete, Baseball Player)
1679 S Riverside Ave
Saint Clair, MI 48079-5142, USA

Ignasiak, Mike (Athlete, Baseball Player)
5821 Saline Ann Arbor Rd
Saline, MI 48176-9566, USA

Ignatius, Paul R (Government Official)
3650 Fordham Rd NW
Washington, DC 20016-1906, USA

Ignizo, Mildred (Bowler)
241 Shore Acres Dr
Rochester, NY 14612-5807, USA

Iguodala, Andre (Athlete, Basketball Player)
c/o Rob Pelinka *Landmark Sports Agency*
881 N Park View Dr
El Segundo, CA 90245-4932, USA

Igwebuike, Donald (Athlete, Football Player)
14231 Angelton Ter
Burtonsville, MD 20866-2077, USA

Iha, James (Music Group, Musician)
1245 W Glenlake Ave
Chicago, IL 60660-2503, USA

Ilkin, Tunch (Athlete, Football Player)
2610 Cedarvue Dr
Pittsburgh, PA 15241-2912, USA

Ike, Reverend (Religious Leader)
4140 Broadway
New York, NY 10033-3701, USA

Iken, Monica
c/o Staff Member *William Morris Endeavor (LA)*
9601 Wilshire Blvd
Beverly Hills, CA 90210-5213, USA

Ikola, Willard (Athlete, Hockey Player, Olympic Athlete)
5697 Green Circle Dr Apt 316
Hopkins, MN 55343-9650, USA

Iler, Robert (Actor)
J Mitchell Management
70 W 36th St Ste 1006
C/O Maggie Schuster
New York, NY 10018-8007

Iley, Barbara (Actor)
Paradigm Agency
10100 Santa Monica Blvd Ste 2500
Los Angeles, CA 90067-4116, USA

Ilg, Ray (Athlete, Football Player)
252 Shindagan Rd
Wilmot, NH 03287, USA

Ilgauskas, Zydrunas (Athlete, Basketball Player)
32654 Lake Rd
Avon Lake, OH 44012, USA

Ilgenfritz, Mark (Athlete, Football Player)
742 Sharp Mountain Crk SE
Marietta, GA 30067-5168, USA

Ilitch, Michael (Athlete, Hockey Player)
237670 Woodlynne Dr
Franklin, MI 48025, USA

Ilkin, Tunch (Athlete, Football Player)
1000 Grandview Ave Apt 1103
Pittsburgh, PA 15211-1359, USA

Ilsley, Blaise (Athlete, Baseball Player)
175 Toyota Plz Ste 300
Memphis, TN 38103-2697, USA

Imada, Ryuji (Athlete, Golfer)
16204 Sierra De Avila
Tampa, FL 33613-5221, USA

Imagine Dragons (Music Group)
c/o Hillary Siskind *Interscope Records (LA) - Main*
2220 Colorado Ave
Santa Monica, CA 90404-3506, USA

Imahara, Grant
Mythbusters Beyond Productions
1268 Missouri St
San Francisco, CA 94107-3310, USA

Iman (Actor, Model)
285 Lafayette St # 7DE
New York, NY 10012-3367, USA

Imes, Mo'Nique (Actor, Comedian, Television Host)
c/o Ricky Anderson *Anderson & Smith P.C.*
7322 Southwest Fwy Ste 2010
One Arena Place
Houston, TX 77074-2077, USA

Imhoff, Darrall (Athlete, Basketball Player, Olympic Athlete)
3637 Sterling Woods Dr
Eugene, OR 97408-7201, USA

Imhoff, Darrell (Athlete)
3637 Sterling Woods Dr
Eugene, OR 97408-7201

Imhoff, Gary (Actor)
Samantha Group
300 S Raymond Ave
Pasadena, CA 91105-2620, USA

Imhoff, Martin (Athlete, Football Player)
11224 Corte Playa Azteca
San Diego, CA 92124-4135, USA

Imle, John F Jr (Business Person)
Unocal Corp
2141 Rosecrans Ave
El Segundo, CA 90245-4747, USA

Immelman, Trevor (Athlete, Golfer)
5174 Vardon Dr
Windermere, FL 34786-8960, USA

Immelt, Jeffrey (Business Person)
General Electric Co
705 West Rd
New Canaan, CT 06840-2518, USA

Immerfall, Daniel (Dan) (Speed Skater)
5421 Trempealeau Trl
Madison, WI 53705-4662, USA

Impemba, Mario (Athlete, Baseball Player)
19945 Gallahad Dr
Macomb, MI 48044-1756, USA

Imperato, Carlo
21940 Scallion Dr
Santa Clarita, CA 91350-1636, USA

Imperioli, Michael (Actor)
c/o Tina Thor *TMT Entertainment Group*
648 Broadway # 1002
New York, NY 10012-2348, USA

Imus, Don (Radio Personality)
c/o Staff Member *ICM Partners (LA)*
10250 Constellation Blvd Fl 7
Los Angeles, CA 90067-6207, USA

IMX (Music Group)
c/o Staff Member *Pyramid Entertainment Group*
377 Rector Pl Apt 21A
New York, NY 10280-1439, USA

Inaba, Carrie Ann (Actor, Dancer)
5421 Radford Ave
Valley Village, CA 91607-2213, USA

Inarritu, Alejandro (Actor)
c/o Staff Member *Anonymous Content (LA)*
3532 Hayden Ave
Culver City, CA 90232-2413, USA

Inarritu, Alejandro Gonzalez (Director)
c/o Keleigh Thomas *Sunshine Sachs (LA)*
8409 Santa Monica Blvd
West Hollywood, CA 90069-4209, USA

Incandella, Sal (Race Car Driver)
Indy Racing Regency
5811 W 73rd St
Indianapolis, IN 46278-1743, USA

Incaviglia, Peter J (Pete) (Athlete, Baseball Player)
PO Box 1047
Argyle, TX 76226-1047, USA

Incognito, Richie (Athlete, Football Player)
7340 W Montgomery Rd
Peoria, AZ 85383-5301, USA

Incubus (Music Group)
c/o Marlene Tsuchii *Creative Artists Agency (CAA-LA)*
2000 Avenue of the Stars Ste 100
Los Angeles, CA 90067-4705, USA

Indelicato, Mark (Actor)
c/o Anne Woodward *ROAR (LA)*
9701 Wilshire Blvd Fl 8
Beverly Hills, CA 90212-2008, USA

Indigo Girls (Music Group)
c/o Staff Member *High Road Touring*
751 Bridgeway Fl 2
Sausalito, CA 94965-2174, USA

Infamous Stringdusters, The (Music Group, Musician)
c/o Michael Allenby *The Artist Farm*
100 W South St
1A
Charlottesville, VA 22902-5039, USA

Infante, Lindy (Athlete, Coach, Football Coach, Football Player)
6780 Ala S
Saint Augustine, FL 32080, USA

Infected Mushroom (Music Group)
4373 Irvine Ave
Studio City, CA 91604-2705, USA

ing, Peter (Athlete, Hockey Player)
Fan-Tastic Sports
21021 Heron Way Ste 104
Lakeville, MN 55044-8085, USA

Ingarfield Jr, Earl (Athlete, Hockey Player)
619 Mourning Dove Dr
Sarasota, FL 34236-1903, USA

Inge, Brandon (Athlete, Baseball Player)
3463 Goode Rd
Goode, VA 24556-2289, USA

Ingels, Marty (Actor, Comedian)
c/o Deborah Zucker *Ingels Entertainment*
Suite One Productions
4531 Noeline Way
Encino, CA 91436-2107, USA

Ingelsby, Tom (Athlete, Basketball Player)
1507 Canterbury Ln
Berwyn, PA 19312-1915, USA

Ingersoll, Ralph II (Publisher)
Ingersoll Publications
PO Box 1869
Lakeville, CT 06039-1869, USA

Ingle, Doug (Music Group, Musician)
Entertainment Services Int'l
6400 Pleasant Park Dr
Chanhassen, MN 55317-8804, USA

Inglebright, Jim (Race Car Driver)
Roadrunner Motorsports
4984 Peabody Rd
Fairfield, CA 94533-6552, USA

inglett, joe (Athlete, Baseball Player)
565 Redfield Ln
Copley, OH 44321-2861, USA

Inglis, Bill (Athlete, Hockey Player)
5709 Ozark Dr
Fort Worth, TX 76131-4004, USA

Inglis, Tim (Athlete, Football Player)
105 Crafton Park Ln
Cary, NC 27519-5575, USA

Ingraham, Laura (Radio Personality)
c/o Staff Member *XM Satellite Radio Studios*
1500 Eckington Pl NE
Washington, DC 20002-2128, USA

Ingram, A John (Doctor)
4940 Sullivan Woods Cv
Memphis, TN 38117-2011, USA

Ingram, Brian (Athlete, Football Player)
774 Carlisle Club Dr
Stone Mountain, GA 30083-4708, USA

Ingram, Clint (Athlete, Football Player)
7812 Chase Meadows Dr E
Jacksonville, FL 32256-4641, USA

Ingram, Garey (Athlete, Baseball Player)
PO Box 97389
Pearl, MS 39288-7389, USA

Ingram, Jack (Musician)
16001 Pontevedra Pl
Austin, TX 78738-6031, USA

Ingram, Jack (Race Car Driver)
699 Brevard Rd
Asheville, NC 28806-2229, USA

Ingram, James (Musician)
867 S Muirfield Rd
Los Angeles, CA 90005-3836, USA

Ingram, McKoy (Athlete, Basketball Player)
2301 33rd St
Gulfport, MS 39501-6541, USA

Ingram, Preston (Baseball Player)
Negro Baseball Leagues
174 Douglas St SE
Atlanta, GA 30317-2626, USA

Ingram, Riccardo (Athlete, Baseball Player)
5720 Martin Grove Dr NW
Lilburn, GA 30047-6078, USA

Ingram Jr, Mark (Football Player)
c/o Peter Raskin *The Legacy Agency*
1500 Broadway Ste 2501
New York, NY 10036-4082, USA

Ingrassia, Frank (Horse Racer)
39 Imlaystown Hightstown Rd
Allentown, NJ 08501-2104, USA

Ingrassia, Jacqueline (Horse Racer)
39 Imlaystown Hightstown Rd
Allentown, NJ 08501-2104, USA

Ingrassia, Paul J (Journalist)
111 Division Ave
New Providence, NJ 07974, USA

Ink Spots, The
5100 Dupont Blvd Apt 10A
Fort Lauderdale, FL 33308-4301

Inkster, Juli Simpson (Athlete, Golfer)
23140 Mora Glen Dr
Los Altos, CA 94024-6620, USA

Inman, Dale (Race Car Driver)
142 Holder Inman Rd
Randleman, NC 27317-8044, USA

Inman, Jerry (Athlete, Football Player)
PO Box 1113
Battle Ground, WA 98604-1113, USA

Inman, Joe (Athlete, Golfer)
3599 Tuckers Farm SE
Marietta, GA 30067-5182, USA

Inman, John (Athlete, Golfer)
2210 Chase St
Durham, NC 27707-2228, USA

Inmon, Earl (Athlete, Football Player)
38429 Jamestown St
Umatilla, FL 32784-9519, USA

Innes, Laura (Actor)
2324 La Mesa Dr
Santa Monica, CA 90402-2331, USA

Inniger Jr, Ervin (Athlete, Basketball Player)
311 11th Ave S Apt 101
Fargo, ND 58103-2856, USA

Innis (Musician)
c/o Staff Member *Paradigm (LA)*
360 N Crescent Dr
North Bldg
Beverly Hills, CA 90210-4874, USA

Innis, Jeff (Athlete, Baseball Player)
4920 Woodlong Ln
Cumming, GA 30040-5275, USA

Innis, Roy (Politician)
800 Riverside Dr Apt 6E
New York, NY 10032-7407, USA

Inouye, Lisa (Actor)
c/o Nick Terzian *Nick Terzian Agency (NTA)*
1445 N Stanley Ave Fl 2
Los Angeles, CA 90046-4015, USA

Insane Clown Posse (Music Group, Musician)
c/o Staff Member *William Morris Endeavor (LA)*
9601 Wilshire Blvd
Beverly Hills, CA 90210-5213, USA

Insko, Delmer M (Del) (Horse Racer)
2360 Fischer Rd
South Beloit, IL 61080-9728, USA

Inslee, Jay (Congressman, Politician)
2329 Rayburn Hob
Washington, DC 20515-3218, USA

Insolo, Jimmy (Race Car Driver)
19636 Ermitie St
Canyon Country, CA 91351, USA

Interpol (Music Group)
c/o Darin Harmon *3D Management*
520 S Westgate Ave
Los Angeles, CA 90049-4212, USA

INXS
c/o Michael Moses *Baker Winokur Ryder Public Relations (BWR-LA)*
9100 Wilshire Blvd Ste 500
West Tower Suite 500
Beverly Hills, CA 90212-3426, USA

Iorg, Dane (Athlete, Baseball Player)
5358 W Evergreen Cir
Highland, UT 84003-9476, USA

Iorg, Garth (Athlete, Baseball Player)
1 Brewers Way Stop 4
Milwaukee, WI 53214-3655, USA

Iovine, Jimmy (Business Person, Musician, Producer)
515 S Mapleton Dr
Los Angeles, CA 90024-1810, USA

Iqbal Rashid, Ian (Director)
c/o Staff Member *United Talent Agency (UTA-LA)*
9336 Civic Center Dr
Beverly Hills, CA 90210-3604, USA

Irani, Ray R (Business Person)
Occidental Petroleum
10889 Wilshire Blvd Fl 10
Los Angeles, CA 90024-4213, USA

Irbe, Arturs (Athlete, Hockey Player)
6337 Georgetown Pike
Mc Lean, VA 22101-2209, USA

Ireland, Dan (Director, Producer, Writer)
c/o Staff Member *Gersh (LA)*
9465 Wilshire Blvd Ste 600
Beverly Hills, CA 90212-2605, USA

Ireland, Kathy (Business Person, Model)
Kathy Ireland Worldwide
PO Box 1410
Rancho Mirage, CA 92270-1052, USA

Ireland, Marin (Actor)
c/o Emily Gerson Saines *Brookside Artists Management (NY)*
250 W 57th St Ste 2303
New York, NY 10107-2399, USA

Ireland, Rich (Baseball Player)
181 Glen Dr
Grants Pass, OR 97526-9018, USA

Ireland, Tim (Athlete, Baseball Player)
21001 San Ramon Valley Blvd Ste A4
San Ramon, CA 94583-3454, USA

Iris, Donnie (Music Group, Musician, Songwriter, Writer)
807 Darlington Rd
Beaver Falls, PA 15010-2817, USA

Irizarry, Vincent (Actor)
c/o Staff Member *Bret Adams Agency*
448 W 44th St
New York, NY 10036-5220, USA

Iron Maiden (Music Group)
c/o Staff Member *BMG Chrysalis US*
29 Music Sq E
Nashville, TN 37203-4322, USA

Irons, Gerald (Athlete, Football Player)
30010 E Legends Trail Ct
Spring, TX 77386-2998, USA

Irons, Grant (Athlete, Football Player)
30010 E Legends Trail Ct
Spring, TX 77386-2998, USA

Irons, Jack (Musician)
3460 Decker Canyon Rd
Malibu, CA 90265-2325, USA

Irons, Jeremy (Actor)
c/o Fred Specktor *Creative Artists Agency (CAA-LA)*
2000 Avenue of the Stars Ste 100
Los Angeles, CA 90067-4705, USA

Irons, Max (Actor)
c/o Cindy Guagenti *Baker Winokur Ryder Public Relations (BWR-LA)*
9100 Wilshire Blvd Ste 500
West Tower Suite 500
Beverly Hills, CA 90212-3426, USA

Irons, Robbie (Athlete, Hockey Player)
4227 Cordell Cv
Fort Wayne, IN 46845-8864, USA

Ironside, Michael (Actor, Producer, Writer)
2145 Sunset Crest Dr
Los Angeles, CA 90046-1843, USA

Irrera, Dom (Actor, Comedian)
c/o Jamie Masada *Laugh Factory Management Company*
8001 W Sunset Blvd
Los Angeles, CA 90046-2401, USA

Irsay, Jim (Business Person, Football Executive)
1711 W 116th St
Carmel, IN 46032-6984, USA

Irvan, Ernie (Race Car Driver)
5111 Selkirk Plantation Rd
Trenton, SC 29847, USA

Irvin, Anthony
1 Olympic Plz Bldg 2A
Colorado Springs, CO 80909-5746

Irvin, Byron (Athlete, Basketball Player)
10940 S Parnell Ave
Chicago, IL 60628-3232, USA

Irvin, Cal (Athlete, Baseball Player)
1311 Julian St
Greensboro, NC 27406-2158, USA

Irvin, Daryl (Athlete, Baseball Player)
815 Confederacy Dr
Penn Laird, VA 22846-9633, USA

Irvin, John (Director)
c/o Jack Gilardi *ICM Partners (LA)*
10250 Constellation Blvd Fl 7
Los Angeles, CA 90067-6207, USA

Irvin, Ken (Athlete, Football Player)
8151 Nesbit Ferry Rd
Atlanta, GA 30350-1009, USA

Irvin, Michael (Athlete, Football Player)
2339 Aberdeen Bnd
Carrollton, TX 75007-2040, USA

Irvin, Monte (Athlete, Baseball Player)
1815 Enclave Pkwy Apt 6203
Houston, TX 77077-3669, USA

Irvine, Daryl (Athlete, Baseball Player)
815 Confederacy Dr
Penn Laird, VA 22846-9633, USA

Irvine, George (Athlete, Basketball Player)
PO Box 179
Indianola, WA 98342-0179, USA

Irvine, Jeremy (Actor)
c/o Jessica Kolstad *Relevant*
Prefers to be contacted by telephone or email
CA, USA

Irvine, Paula (Actor)
23852 Pacific Coast Hwy PMB 195
Malibu, CA 90265-4876

Irving, Amy (Actor)
46 Central Park W # 8C
New York, NY 10023, USA

Irving, John (Writer)
c/o Robert (Bob) Bookman *Paradigm (LA)*
2000 Avenue of the Stars
Los Angeles, CA 90067-4700, USA

Irving, Kyrie (Athlete, Basketball Player)
27 Ridgeview Ave
West Orange, NJ 07052-4315, USA

Irving, Nate (Athlete, Football Player)
c/o Fletcher Smith *Blueprint Sports Group*
221 W Jefferson Ave
Naperville, IL 60540-5355, USA

Irving, Stu (Athlete, Hockey Player, Olympic Athlete)
93 Hart St
Beverly, MA 01915-2162, USA

Irving, Terry (Athlete, Football Player)
3205 Avenue R 1/2 Apt 2
Galveston, TX 77550-9651, USA

Irvin Jr, LeRoy (Athlete, Football Player)
2905 Ruby Dr Apt C
Fullerton, CA 92831-3249, USA

Irwin, Bill (Actor, Writer)
20 1st Ave
Nyack, NY 10960-2114, USA

Irwin, Glen (Athlete, Hockey Player)
4024 Chesapeake Ave
Hampton, VA 23669-4632

Irwin, Hale (Athlete, Golfer)
5720 N Saguaro Rd
Paradise Valley, AZ 85253-5237, USA

Irwin, Haley (Athlete, Hockey Player,
Olympic Athlete)
440 Marquette St
Thunder Bay, ON CANAD, USA

Irwin, Heath (Athlete, Football Player)
5530 N 115th St
Longmont, CO 80504-8434, USA

Irwin, Mark (Cinematographer)
1522 Olive St
Santa Barbara, CA 93101-1160, USA

Irwin, Mary (Writer)
3260 Gilcrest Ter
Colorado Springs, CO 80906-4510, USA

Irwin, Tim (Athlete, Football Player)
Law Office Of Tim Irwin
PO Box 2186
Knoxville, TN 37901-2186, USA

Irwin, Tom (Actor)
PO Box 5617
Beverly Hills, CA 90209-5617

Irwin, Tommy (Race Car Driver)
1724 Handley Ave
Winchester, VA 22601-3224, USA

Irwin-Mellencamp, Elaine (Model)
John Caugar Mellencamp
5072 Stevens Rd
Nashville, IN 47448-9484, USA

Isaac, Oscar (Actor, Musician)
c/o Jason Spire *Inspire Entertainment*
315 7th Ave Apt 17E
New York, NY 10001-6011, USA

Isaacks, Levie C (Cinematographer)
6634 Sunnyslope Ave
Van Nuys, CA 91401-1213, USA

Isaacksen, Peter
4635 Placidia Ave
Toluca Lake, CA 91602-1541

Isaacs, Jason (Actor)
c/o Jeff Golenberg *Silver Lining
Entertainment*
421 S Beverly Dr Fl 7
Beverly Hills, CA 90212-4408, USA

Isaacs, Susan (Writer)
Harper Collins Publishers
195 Broadway Fl 2
New York, NY 10007-3132, USA

Isaacson, Walter S (Journalist)
c/o Amanda Urban *ICM Partners (NY)*
730 5th Ave
New York, NY 10019-4105, USA

Isaak, Chris (Actor, Musician, Songwriter)
1655 38th Ave
San Francisco, CA 94122-3001, USA

Isaak, Russell (Business Person)
CPI Corp
1706 Washington Ave
Saint Louis, MO 63103-1717, USA

Isabelle, Katharine (Actor)
c/o Wendy Murphey *LBI Entertainment*
2000 Avenue of the Stars
Floor 3, North Tower
Los Angeles, CA 90067-4700, USA

Isabelle, Katherine (Actor)
c/o Staff Member *IFA Talent Agency*
2000 Avenue Of The Stars
Los Angeles, CA 90067-4700, USA

Isacksen, Peter (Actor)
c/o Staff Member *JWTwo Entertainment*
2425 Olympic Blvd # 200
East Tower
Santa Monica, CA 90404-4030, USA

Isales, Orlando (Athlete, Baseball Player)
14710 SW 106th Ave
Miami, FL 33176-7791, USA

Isbell, Joe Bob (Athlete, Football Player)
1606 Nest Pl
Plano, TX 75093-6030, USA

Isbin, Sharon (Musician)
Columbia Artists Mgmt Inc
165 W 57th St
New York, NY 10019-2201, USA

Iscove, Robert (Director)
16045 Royal Oak Rd
Encino, CA 91436-3913, USA

Isdell, E Neville (Business Person)
Coca-Cola Co
1 Coca Cola Plz NW
310 North Ave NW
Atlanta, GA 30313-2499, USA

Isenbarger, John (Athlete, Football Player)
7808 Somerset Bay Apt C
Indianapolis, IN 46240-3329, USA

Isenhour, Tripp (Athlete, Golfer)
10012 N Fulton Ct
Orlando, FL 32836-3708, USA

Ishida, Jim (Actor)
871 N Vail Ave
Montebello, CA 90640-2432, USA

Ishii, Linda (Athlete, Golfer)
2607 E 3rd St
Los Angeles, CA 90033-4124, USA

Ishikawa, Travis (Athlete, Baseball Player)
1674 Cross Way
San Jose, CA 95125-1216, USA

Ishizaka, Kimishiga (Doctor)
Allergy/Immunology Institute
11149 N Torrey Pines Rd
La Jolla, CA 92037-1009, USA

Ishizaka, Teruko (Doctor)
Good Samaritan Hospital
5601 Loch Raven Blvd
Baltimore, MD 21239-2991, USA

Ishmael, Kemel (Athlete, Football Player)
c/o Drew Rosenhaus *Rosenhaus Sports
Representation*
6400 Allison Rd
Miami Beach, FL 33141-4540, USA

Isler, Jennifer (Athlete, Olympic Athlete,
Sailor)
6828 Country Club Dr
La Jolla, CA 92037-5605, USA

Isley, Ernie (Musician)
403 Sheffield Estate Dr
Saint Louis, MO 63141-8523, USA

Isley, Ronald (Musician)
300 Wyndmoor Terrace Ct
Saint Louis, MO 63141-8021, USA

Isley Brothers (Music Group)
c/o Carleen Donovan *Press Here Publicity*
138 W 25th St Ste 900
New York, NY 10001-7470, USA

Ismail, Qadry (Athlete, Football Player)
1506 Sunningdale Way
Bel Air, MD 21015-2101, USA

Ismail, Raghib R (Rocket) (Athlete,
Football Player)
7423 Marigold Dr
Irving, TX 75063-5505, USA

Isner, John (Athlete, Tennis Player)
17005 Candeleda De Avila
Tampa, FL 33613-5213, USA

Ison, Christopher J (Journalist)
Minneapolis-Saint Paul Star Tribune
425 Portland Ave
Minneapolis, MN 55488-0002, USA

Israel, Steve (Congressman, Politician)
2457 Rayburn Hob
Washington, DC 20515-4313, USA

Isringhausen, Jason (Athlete, Baseball
Player)
7060 N State Route 159
Moro, IL 62067-1622, USA

Issel, Dan (Athlete, Basketball Player,
Coach)
325 E Palace Ave
Santa Fe, NM 87501-2275, USA

Isselbacher, Kurt J (Doctor)
20 Nobscot Rd
Newton Center, MA 02459-1323, USA

Ito, Lance (Attorney, Judge)
Los Angeles Superior Court
825 S Madison Ave
Pasadena, CA 91106-4404, USA

Ito, Robert (Actor)
843 N Sycamore Ave
Los Angeles, CA 90038-3316, USA

Itzin, Gregory (Actor)
Borinstein Oreck Bogart
3172 Dona Susana Dr
Studio City, CA 91604-4356, USA

Iuzzolino, Mike (Athlete, Basketball
Player)
1048 New London Dr
Greensburg, PA 15601-1144, USA

Ivanek, Zeljko
101 W 12th St Apt 18D
New York, NY 10011-8135, USA

Ivanov, Kalina (Actor, Designer)
c/o Sandra Marsh *Sandra Marsh
Management*
6420 Wilshire Blvd Ste 880
Los Angeles, CA 90048-5538, USA

Ivens, Teri (Actor)
c/o Stephen Rice *Pantheon Talent*
1801 Century Park E Ste 1910
Los Angeles, CA 90067-2321, USA

Ivens, Terri (Actor)
c/o Staff Member *Kohner Agency, The*
9300 Wilshire Blvd Ste 555
Beverly Hills, CA 90212-3211, USA

Iver, Bon (Music Group)
c/o Carrie Tolles *Shore Fire Media*
32 Court St Fl 16
Brooklyn, NY 11201-4441, USA

Ivers, Eileen (Athlete, Misc)
Sony Records
2100 Colorado Ave
Santa Monica, CA 90404-3504, USA

Iverson, Allen (Athlete, Basketball Player)
2010 Westbourne Way
Alpharetta, GA 30022-3112, USA

Iverson, Duke (Athlete, Football Player)
616 Elm Dr
Petaluma, CA 94952-1838, USA

Iverson, Portia (Religious Leader)
11312 Highway 75
Plattsmouth, NE 68048-8268, USA

Iverson, Willie (Athlete, Basketball Player)
14789 Rosemary St
Detroit, MI 48213-1539, USA

Ivery, Eddie Lee (Athlete, Football Player)
1080 Wrightsboro Rd
Thomson, GA 30824-7500, USA

Ives, J Atwood (Business Person)
Eastern Enterprises
201 Rivermoor St
West Roxbury, MA 02132-4905, USA

Ivey, Dana (Actor)
Paradigm Agency
10100 Santa Monica Blvd Ste 2500
Los Angeles, CA 90067-4116, USA

Ivey, James
5856 Dahlia Dr Apt 7
Orlando, FL 32807-3261

Ivey, Judith (Actor)
53 W 87th St # 2
New York, NY 10024-3005, USA

Ivey, Royal (Athlete, Basketball Player)
5900 Mosteller Dr Unit 72
Oklahoma City, OK 73112-4608, USA

Ivie, Mike (Athlete, Baseball Player)
PO Box 1565
Loganville, GA 30052-1565, USA

Ivins, Marsha S (Astronaut)
2811 Timber Briar Cir
Houston, TX 77059-2904, USA

Ivlow, John (Athlete, Football Player)
15238 S Poppy Ln
Plainfield, IL 60544-9201, USA

Ivo, Tommy (Race Car Driver)
247 S Orchard Dr
Burbank, CA 91506-2441

Ivory, Elvin (Athlete, Basketball Player)
526 Date Ct
Monrovia, CA 91016-4676, USA

Ivory, Horace O (Athlete, Football Player)
5321 Diaz Ave
Fort Worth, TX 76107-5903, USA

Ivory, James (Athlete, Baseball Player)
3026 Wenonah Park Rd SW
Birmingham, AL 35211-5846, USA

Ivory, James (Director, Producer)
c/o Staff Member *Merchant Ivory
Productions*
PO Box 338
New York, NY 10276-0338, USA

Iwanowski, Mark (Athlete, Football
Player)
523 N 12th St
Reading, PA 19604-2718, USA

Iwerks, Donald W (Business Person)
Iwerks Entertainment
4520 W Valerio St
Burbank, CA 91505-1046, USA

Iwerks, Leslie (Director, Producer)
c/o Scott Agostini *William Morris Endeavor (LA)*
9601 Wilshire Blvd
Beverly Hills, CA 90210-5213, USA

Izibor, Laura (Musician)
c/o Staff Member *Paradigm (Monterey)*
404 W Franklin St
Monterey, CA 93940-2303, USA

Izo, George (Athlete, Football Player)
PO Box 325
Alexandria, VA 22313-0325, USA

Izquierdo, Hank (Athlete, Baseball Player)
12458 71st Pl N
West Palm Beach, FL 33412-1438, USA

Izquierdo, Hansel (Athlete, Baseball Player)
8420 SW 154th Circle Ct Apt 515
Miami, FL 33193-1260, USA

Izturis, Cesar (Athlete, Baseball Player)
375 S 3rd St
Burbank, CA 91502-1364, USA

Izzo, Larry (Athlete, Football Player)
310 W 52nd St Apt 10H
New York, NY 10019-6292, USA

Izzo, Tom (Athlete, Basketball Coach, Basketball Player, Coach)
Michigan State University
Berkowitz Complex, Suite 150
East Lansing, MI 48824, USA

Jablonski, Pat (Athlete, Hockey Player)
18814 Wimbledon Cir
Lutz, FL 33558-5300, USA

Jabs, Matthias (Musician)
c/o Staff Member *The Agency Group (NYC)*
142 W 57th St Fl 6
New York, NY 10019-3300, USA

Jace, Michael (Actor)
c/o Craig Dorfman *Frontline Management*
5670 Wilshire Blvd Ste 1370
Los Angeles, CA 90036-5679, USA

Jack, Eric (Athlete, Football Player)
425 Concert St
Keokuk, IA 52632-5624, USA

Jack, Jarrett (Athlete, Basketball Player)
c/o Jeff Schwartz *Excel Sports Management (NY)*
1700 Broadway Fl 29
New York, NY 10019-5905, USA

Jack Davis, Jack Davis (Cartoonist)
c/o Staff Member *Simon & Schuster*
1230 Avenue of the Americas Fl CONC1
New York, NY 10020-1586, USA

Jacke, Chris (Athlete, Football Player)
1631 Shallow Creek Ct
Green Bay, WI 54313-3963, USA

Jacke, Christoper L (Chris) (Athlete, Football Player)
PO Box 888
Phoenix, AZ 85001-0888, USA

Jackee (Actor)
7250 Franklin Ave Unit 814
Los Angeles, CA 90046-3043, USA

Jacklin, Tony (Athlete, Golfer)
8497 Lindrick Ln
Bradenton, FL 34202-4626, USA

Jackman, Barret (Athlete, Hockey Player)
4924 Pershing Pl
Saint Louis, MO 63108-1202, USA

Jackman, Hugh (Actor)
176 Perry St # 10S
New York, NY 10014-2384, USA

Jacks, Wayne (Race Car Driver)
Wayne Jacks Motorsports
2755 N Lamont St
Las Vegas, NV 89115-4517, USA

Jacks Mannequin (Musician)
c/o Staff Member *Maverick Recording Co (LA)*
3300 Warner Blvd
Burbank, CA 91505-4632, USA

Jackson, Al (Baseball Player)
Pittsburgh Pirates
3221 SE Morningside Blvd
Port Saint Lucie, FL 34952-5919, USA

Jackson, Alan (Musician, Songwriter)
PO Box 121945
Nashville, TN 37212-1945, USA

Jackson, Alfonza (Athlete, Football Player)
2701 Godwin Ln
Pensacola, FL 32526-9047, USA

Jackson, Alfred (Athlete, Football Player)
1811 Kirby Dr
Houston, TX 77019-3415, USA

Jackson, Alvin N (Al) (Athlete, Baseball Player)
3221 SE Morningside Blvd
Port Saint Lucie, FL 34952-5919, USA

Jackson, Anne (Actor)
140 Riverside Dr # 19E
New York, NY 10024-2605, USA

Jackson, Asa (Athlete, Football Player)
c/o Ken Zuckerman *Priority Sports & Entertainment - (LA)*
15233 Ventura Blvd Ste 718
Sherman Oaks, CA 91403-2237, USA

Jackson, Bo (Athlete, Baseball Player)
100 Oak Ridge Dr W
Burr Ridge, IL 60527-6870, USA

Jackson, Bob (Athlete, Football Player)
30608 Salem Dr
Bay Village, OH 44140-1127, USA

Jackson, Bobby (Athlete, Football Player)
47 Tippin Dr
Huntington Station, NY 11746-2130, USA

Jackson, Bobby (Basketball Player)
Sacramento Kings
1 Sports Pkwy
Arco Arena
Sacramento, CA 95834-2301, USA

Jackson, Brandon T (Actor, Producer)
c/o Staff Member *ML Management*
125 W 55th St Fl 8
New York, NY 10019-5369, USA

Jackson, Brian (Athlete, Football Player)
c/o Jordan Woy *Willis and Woy Management*
3030 Olive St Ste 520
Dallas, TX 75219-7629, USA

Jackson, Calvin (Athlete, Football Player)
250 SW 28th Ter
Fort Lauderdale, FL 33312-1285, USA

Jackson, Charles (Athlete, Football Player)
PO Box 888285
Atlanta, GA 30356-0285, USA

Jackson, Cheyenne (Actor)
c/o Stephanie Moyer *SLATE Public Relations - NY*
307 7th Ave Rm 2401
New York, NY 10001-6019, USA

Jackson, Chuck (Athlete, Baseball Player)
15821 SE 175th Pl
Renton, WA 98058-9122, USA

Jackson, Chuck (Musician)
Universal Attractions
225 W 57th St Ste 500
New York, NY 10019-2136, USA

Jackson, Clarence (Athlete, Football Player)
5251 Appleleaf Ct
North Chesterfield, VA 23234-2801, USA

Jackson, Conor (Athlete, Baseball Player)
7301 E 3rd Ave Unit 313
Scottsdale, AZ 85251-4461, USA

Jackson, Curtis (50 Cent) (Musician)
50 Poplar Hill Dr
Farmington, CT 06032-2419, USA

Jackson, Dallas (Producer, Writer)
c/o Staff Member *Davis Entertainment*
150 S Barrington Pl
Los Angeles, CA 90049-3306, USA

Jackson, Damian (Athlete, Baseball Player)
1955 Sunset Dr Unit 81
Escondido, CA 92025-6635, USA

Jackson, Dane (Athlete, Hockey Player)
5887 Pinehurst Ct
Grand Forks, ND 58201-2813, USA

Jackson, Danny (Athlete, Baseball Player)
16332 Larsen St
Overland Park, KS 66062-8520, USA

Jackson, Darrell (Athlete, Baseball Player)
PO Box 4424
Downey, CA 90241-1424, USA

Jackson, Darrell (Athlete, Football Player)
12727 SE 38th St
Bellevue, WA 98006-1235, USA

Jackson, Darrin (Athlete, Baseball Player)
333 W 35th St Attn Dept
Chicago, IL 60616-3621, USA

Jackson, Deanna (Basketball Player)
Indiana Fever
125 S Pennsylvania St
Conseco Fieldhouse
Indianapolis, IN 46204-3610, USA

Jackson, DeSean (Athlete, Football Player)
19400 Santa Rita St
Tarzana, CA 91356-3021, USA

Jackson, Don (Athlete, Hockey Player)
422 E Quivira St
Kechi, KS 67067-8817, USA

Jackson, Doris (Musician)
Nationwide Entertainment
2756 N Green Valley Pkwy
Henderson, NV 89014-2120, USA

Jackson, Earnest (Athlete, Football Player)
407 5th St
Rosenberg, TX 77471-1907, USA

Jackson, Eddie (Bowler)
3961 Glenmore Ave
Cincinnati, OH 45211-3509, USA

Jackson, Edwin (Athlete, Baseball Player)
6955 Setter Dr
Columbus, GA 31909-4803, USA

Jackson, Ernie (Athlete, Football Player)
938 Pisgah N
Eads, TN 38028-9799, USA

Jackson, Frank (Athlete, Football Player)
5904 Gregory Ln
Allen, TX 75002-6710, USA

Jackson, Gildart (Actor)
c/o Chuck Binder *Binder & Associates*
1465 Lindacrest Dr
Beverly Hills, CA 90210-2519, USA

Jackson, Grady (Athlete, Football Player)
PO Box 841
Braselton, GA 30517-0015, USA

Jackson, Grant (Athlete, Baseball Player)
212 Mesa Cir
Pittsburgh, PA 15241-1721, USA

Jackson, Harold (Athlete, Coach, Football Player)
6144 Flight Ave
Los Angeles, CA 90056-1510, USA

Jackson, Harold (Journalist)
Birmingham News
2200 4th Ave N
Editorial Dept
Birmingham, AL 35203-3802, USA

Jackson, Honor (Athlete, Football Player)
384 Wren Dr
Santa Rosa, CA 95401-5852, USA

Jackson, Jack (Athlete, Hockey Player)
12108 Slater St
Overland Park, KS 66213-1557, USA

Jackson, James A (Jim) (Athlete, Basketball Player)
17827 Windflower Way Unit 101
Dallas, TX 75252-5226, USA

Jackson, Janet (Actor, Dancer, Musician)
2469 Ping Dr
Henderson, NV 89074-8314, USA

Jackson, Jaren (Athlete, Basketball Player)
1917 W Main St
Carmel, IN 46032-8831, USA

Jackson, Jarious (Athlete, Football Player)
7423 Marigold Dr
Irving, TX 75063-5505, USA

Jackson, Jeff (Athlete, Baseball Player)
853 S Kingsley Dr Apt D
Los Angeles, CA 90005-4367, USA

Jackson, Jeff (Athlete, Football Player)
1119 Parkview Dr
Griffin, GA 30224-4738, USA

Jackson, Jeremy (Actor, Producer)
c/o Rachel Rothman *Rothman / Andres Entertainment*
4400 Coldwater Canyon Ave Ste 125
Studio City, CA 91604-5040, USA

Jackson, Jermaine (Basketball Player)
Atlanta Hawks
190 Marietta St NW Ste 405
Atlanta, GA 30303-2717, USA

Jackson, Jermaine (Music Group, Musician, Songwriter)
4641 Havenhurst Ave
Encino, CA 91436-3251, USA

Jackson, Jesse (Activist, Politician, Religious Leader)
400 T St NW
Washington, DC 20001-1809, USA

Jackson, Joe (Business Person)
c/o Staff Member *Paradigm (Monterey)*
404 W Franklin St
Monterey, CA 93940-2303, USA

Jackson, john (Athlete, Baseball Player)
PO Box 898
Hodge, LA 71247-0898, USA

Jackson, John (Athlete, Football Player)
8183 Alpine Aster Ct
Liberty Township, OH 45044-1904, USA

Jackson, John David (Boxer)
1022 S State St
Tacoma, WA 98405-3042, USA

Jackson, John (Fabolous) (Musician)
c/o Tammy Brook *FYI Public Relations*
174 5th Ave Ste 404
New York, NY 10010-5964, USA

Jackson, John M (Actor)
JAG
5555 Melrose Ave
Clara Bow #204
Los Angeles, CA 90038-3989, USA

Jackson, Jonathan (Actor)
c/o David Guillod *Intellectual Artists Management*
9560 Wilshire Blvd Fl 5
Beverly Hills, CA 90212-2401, USA

Jackson, Joshua (Actor)
c/o Doug Wald *Anonymous Content (LA)*
3532 Hayden Ave
Culver City, CA 90232-2413, USA

Jackson, Kareem (Athlete, Football Player)
c/o Sean Kiernan *Impact Sports - LA*
11331 Ventura Blvd Ste 1A
Studio City, CA 91604-3147, USA

Jackson, Kate (Actor)
c/o Staff Member *William Morris Endeavor (LA)*
9601 Wilshire Blvd
Beverly Hills, CA 90210-5213, USA

Jackson, Keith (Athlete, Football Player)
1801 Champlin Dr Apt 1707
Little Rock, AR 72223-3987, USA

Jackson, Keith (Race Car Driver)
8941 W Jewell Pl
Lakewood, CO 80227-2388, USA

Jackson, Keith J (Athlete, Football Player)
PO Box 241695
Little Rock, AR 72223-0012, USA

Jackson, Keith M (Sportscaster)
ABC-TV
77 W 66th St Rm 100
New York, NY 10023-6298, USA

Jackson, Ken (Athlete, Baseball Player)
PO Box 613
Waskom, TX 75692-0613, USA

Jackson, Kenny (Athlete, Football Player)
1319 Linn St
State College, PA 16803-3026, USA

Jackson, Kirby (Athlete, Football Player)
3575 Candytuft Run
Auburn, GA 30011-4712, USA

Jackson, Kwame (Business Person, Reality Star)
c/o Staff Member *Mark Burnett Productions*
640 N Sepulveda Blvd
Los Angeles, CA 90049-2108, USA

Jackson, Larron (Athlete, Football Player)
19682 E 63rd Dr
Aurora, CO 80019-2127, USA

Jackson, La Toya (Model, Musician)
c/o Jeffre Phillips *Ja-Tail Enterprises*
8306 Wilshire Blvd Ste 528
Beverly Hills, CA 90211-2304, USA

Jackson, Lauren (Basketball Player)
Seattle Storm
351 Elliott Ave W Ste 500
Key Arena
Seattle, WA 98119-4153, USA

Jackson, Lenzie (Athlete, Football Player)
4524 E La Puente Ave
Phoenix, AZ 85044-1421, USA

Jackson, Leo (Race Car Driver)
PO Box 726
191 Airport Road
Arden, NC 28704-0726, USA

Jackson, Leshon (Athlete, Football Player)
PO Box 957
Haskell, OK 74436-0957, USA

Jackson, Lillian (Baseball Player)
1050 W Camino Velasquez
Green Valley, AZ 85622-4527, USA

Jackson, Luke (Athlete, Basketball Player, Olympic Athlete)
7711 County Road 511
Rosharon, TX 77583-7286, USA

Jackson, Mannie (Athlete, Basketball Player)
Harlem Globetrotters
400 E Van Buren St Ste 300
Phoenix, AZ 85004-0672, USA

Jackson, Mark A (Athlete, Basketball Player, Sportscaster)
17 Winmere Pl
Dix Hills, NY 11746-6553, USA

Jackson, Mark A (Athlete, Football Player)
1480 Lloyd Ct
Wheaton, IL 60189-7368, USA

Jackson, Marlon
4641 Hayvenhurst Ave
Encino, CA 91436-3251

Jackson, Mel (Actor)
c/o Staff Member *Stone Manners Salners Agency (LA)*
6100 Wilshire Blvd Ste 1500
Los Angeles, CA 90048-5110, USA

Jackson, Melvin (Athlete, Football Player)
4345 Enoro Dr
View Park, CA 90008-4870, USA

Jackson, Mervin (Athlete, Basketball Player)
16638 Kildare Ct
Tinley Park, IL 60477-1579, USA

Jackson, Michael (Athlete, Football Player)
14207 128th Pl NE
Kirkland, WA 98034-1575, USA

Jackson, Mick (Director)
1349 Berea Pl
Pacific Palisades, CA 90272-2602, USA

Jackson, Mike (Athlete, Baseball Player)
805 11th Ave Apt 2H
Paterson, NJ 07514-1012, USA

Jackson, Mike (Athlete, Baseball Player)
17214 Oak Dale Dr
Spring, TX 77379-8846, USA

Jackson, Milt (Athlete, Football Player)
5600 John Runge Dr
Sacramento, CA 95835-1713, USA

Jackson, Monte C (Athlete, Football Player)
7646 Westbrook Ave
San Diego, CA 92139-4006, USA

Jackson, Nate (Athlete, Football Player)
11968 E Lake Cir
Greenwood Village, CO 80111-5245, USA

Jackson, Neil (Actor)
c/o Amy Slomovits *Evolution Entertainment (LA)*
901 N Highland Ave
Los Angeles, CA 90038-2412, USA

Jackson, Noah (Athlete, Football Player)
1640 Millburne Rd
Lake Forest, IL 60045-4106, USA

Jackson, Paris (Actor)
c/o Ann Gurrola *Marleah Leslie & Associates PR*
1645 Vine St Apt 712
Los Angeles, CA 90028-8812, USA

Jackson, Peter (Director)
c/o Ken Kamins *Key Creatives*
1800 N Highland Ave Fl 5
Los Angeles, CA 90028-4523, USA

Jackson, Phil (Athlete, Basketball Coach, Basketball Player, Coach)
18942 Medicine Rock Ln
Lakeside, MT 59922-9514, USA

Jackson, Quinton (Rampage) (Athlete, Wrestler)
c/o Staff Member *ROAR (LA)*
9701 Wilshire Blvd Fl 8
Beverly Hills, CA 90212-2008, USA

Jackson, Ralph (Athlete, Basketball Player)
3235 W 111th Pl
Inglewood, CA 90303-2316, USA

Jackson, Randy (Athlete, Baseball Player)
250 Hunnicutt Dr
Athens, GA 30606-1708, USA

Jackson, Randy (Musician, Reality Star)
c/o Jonathan Liebman *Brillstein Entertainment Partners (LA)*
9150 Wilshire Blvd Ste 350
Beverly Hills, CA 90212-3453, USA

Jackson, Randy B (Athlete, Football Player)
747 Musago Run
Lake Mary, FL 32746-2209, USA

Jackson, Ransom (Baseball Player)
Chicago Cubs
250 Hunnicutt Dr
Athens, GA 30606-1708, USA

Jackson, Rebbie (Music Group, Musician, Songwriter, Writer)
4641 Hayvenhurst Ave
Encino, CA 91436-3251, USA

Jackson, Reggie (Athlete, Baseball Player)
c/o Staff Member *Doubleday/ RandomHouse*
1745 Broadway
New York, NY 10019-4640, USA

Jackson, Richard A (Religious Leader)
North Phoenix Baptist Church
5757 N Central Ave
Phoenix, AZ 85012-1397, USA

Jackson, Richard S (Richie) (Athlete, Football Player)
6000 Kingston Ct
New Orleans, LA 70131-5557, USA

Jackson, Rickey (Athlete, Football Player)
3701 Lake Catherine Dr
Harvey, LA 70058-5526, USA

Jackson, Rickey A (Athlete, Football Player)
325 S Barfield Hwy
Pahokee, FL 33476-1929, USA

Jackson, Ron (Athlete, Baseball Player)
1441 Smithfield Park Cir
Pleasant Grove, AL 35127-2641, USA

Jackson, Roy Lee (Athlete, Baseball Player)
8269 Lee Road 54
Auburn, AL 36830-8222, USA

Jackson, Ryan (Athlete, Baseball Player)
2335 Alpine Ave
Sarasota, FL 34239-4117, USA

Jackson, Samuel L (Actor)
c/o Eli Selden *Anonymous Content (LA)*
3532 Hayden Ave
Culver City, CA 90232-2413, USA

Jackson, Sasha (Actor)
c/o Richard Beddingfield *Beddingfield Company, The*
13600 Ventura Blvd Ste B
Sherman Oaks, CA 91423-5050, USA

Jackson, Shar (Actor)
c/o Trisanne Marin *LA Management*
225 E Broadway Ste B104
Glendale, CA 91205-1008, USA

Jackson, Sheldon (Athlete, Football Player)
4466 Teresita Ct
Chino, CA 91710-3929, USA

Jackson, Sherry (Actor)
13082 Mindanao Way Apt 54
Marina Del Rey, CA 90292-8703, USA

Jackson, Sonny (Athlete, Baseball Player)
117 Palm Bay Dr Apt B
Palm Beach Gardens, FL 33418-5790, USA

Jackson, Stephen (Athlete, Basketball Player)
6945 Brazos Ave
Port Arthur, TX 77642-6581, USA

Jackson, Steve (Athlete, Football Player)
3823 Emerald Lake Dr
Missouri City, TX 77459-6540, USA

Jackson, Steve (Athlete, Football Player)
1153 Bergen Pkwy Ste M
Evergreen, CO 80439-9501, USA

Jackson, Steven (Athlete, Football Player)
c/o Eugene Parker *Maximum Sports Management*
6435 W Jefferson Blvd # 197
Fort Wayne, IN 46804-6203, USA

Jackson, Stonewall (Musician, Songwriter)
6007 Cloverland Dr
Brentwood, TN 37027-7607, USA

Jackson, Stoney (Actor)
3151 Cahuenga Blvd W Ste 310
Los Angeles, CA 90068-1768, USA

Jackson, Tarvaris (Athlete, Football Player)
c/o Joel Segal *Lagardere Unlimited (NYC)*
845 United Nations Plz Apt 63D
New York, NY 10017-3538, USA

Jackson, Thomas (Tom) (Athlete, Football Player, Sportscaster)
ESPN-TV
935 Middle St
Sports Dept Espn Plaza
Bristol, CT 06010-1000, USA

Jackson, Tim (Athlete, Football Player)
6501 White Oak Dr
Rowlett, TX 75089-7441, USA

Jackson, Tito (Musician)
25345 Prado De La Felicidad
Calabasas, CA 91302-3651, USA

Jackson, Tracy (Athlete, Basketball Player)
10588 Spotted Horse Ln
Columbia, MD 21044-2214, USA

Jackson, Tre (Athlete, Football Player)
680 Harrison Ave
Peekskill, NY 10566-2219, USA

Jackson, Trina (Athlete, Olympic Athlete, Swimmer)
9271 Saltwater Way
Jacksonville, FL 32256-9606, USA

Jackson, Tyoka (Athlete, Football Player)
16312 Birkdale Dr
Odessa, FL 33556-2802, USA

Jackson, Tyson (Athlete, Football Player)
c/o Ashley Smith Becker *Relativity Sports (LA)*
9242 Beverly Blvd Ste 300
Beverly Hills, CA 90210-3728, USA

Jackson, Verdell (Baseball Player)
Memphis Red Sox
413 Lincoln St
Venice, IL 62090-1117, USA

Jackson, Vernell (Athlete, Baseball Player)
413 Lincoln St
Venice, IL 62090-1117, USA

Jackson, Vestee (Athlete, Football Player)
6554 Eagle Creek Ln
Las Vegas, NV 89156-5945, USA

Jackson, Victoria (Actor, Comedian)
c/o Kim Dorr *Defining Artists Agency*
4370 Tujunga Ave Ste 120
Studio City, CA 91604-2763, USA

Jackson, Victoria (Business Person)
Lola Boutique
110 S Robertson Blvd
Los Angeles, CA 90048-3208, USA

Jackson, Vincent E (Bo) (Athlete, Baseball Player, Football Player)
PO Box 158
Mobile, AL 36601-0158, USA

Jackson, Wanda (Music Group, Musician)
Wanda Jackson Enterprises
8200 S Pennsylvania Ave
Oklahoma City, OK 73159-5202, USA

Jackson, Wardell (Athlete, Basketball Player)
185 Hamilton Ave
Columbus, OH 43203-1478, USA

Jackson, Waverly (Athlete, Football Player)
1231 Halifax St
South Hill, VA 23970-2319, USA

Jackson, Wilbur (Athlete, Football Player)
PO Box 1571
Ozark, AL 36361-1571, USA

Jackson, Willie (Athlete, Football Player)
PO Box 12643
Gainesville, FL 32604-0643, USA

Jackson, Zach (Athlete, Baseball Player)
13612 Matanzas Pl
Lakewood Ranch, FL 34202-5175, USA

Jackson Hoye, Rose (Actor)
c/o Staff Member *Haldeman Business Management*
860 Via De La Paz Ste D3B
Pacific Palisades, CA 90272-5214, USA

Jackson Lee, Sheila (Congressman, Politician)
2160 Rayburn Hob
Washington, DC 20515-0918, USA

Jacob, Ralph (Actor)
c/o Staff Member *Britto Agency PR*
90 Franklin St Apt 4N
New York, NY 10013-3489, USA

Jacobellis, Lindsey (Athlete, Olympic Athlete, Speed Skater)
30684 E Ski Bowl Way
Government Camp, OR 97028-0345, USA

Jacobi, Derek G (Actor)
c/o Staff Member *ICM Partners (LA)*
10250 Constellation Blvd Fl 7
Los Angeles, CA 90067-6207, USA

Jacobs, Allen (Athlete, Football Player)
3050 E Tolcate Ln
Salt Lake City, UT 84121-1545, USA

Jacobs, Ben (Athlete, Football Player)
c/o Derrick Fox *Derrick Fox Management*
Prefers to be contacted by telephone
CA, USA

Jacobs, Brandon (Athlete, Football Player)
153 Eagles Rdg
Alpharetta, GA 30004-8271, USA

Jacobs, Cam (Athlete, Football Player)
5420 Atlantic Vw
Saint Augustine, FL 32080-7148, USA

Jacobs, Dave (Athlete, Football Player)
8388 Glen Eagle Dr
Manlius, NY 13104-9445, USA

Jacobs, Gillian (Actor)
c/o Jill Kaplan *Authentic Talent and Literary Management*
20 Jay St Ste M17
Brooklyn, NY 11201-8300, USA

Jacobs, Glenn (Kane) (Athlete, Wrestler)
790 Locket Ln
Jefferson City, TN 37760-3462, USA

Jacobs, Harry (Athlete, Football Player)
108 Lenora Dr
Hamburg, NY 14075-4710, USA

Jacobs, Irwin M (Business Person)
Qualcomm Inc
5775 Morehouse Dr
San Diego, CA 92121-1714, USA

Jacobs, Jeremy (Business Person)
1300 N Davis Rd
East Aurora, NY 14052-9473, USA

Jacobs, John (Athlete, Golfer)
81080 Shinnecock Hls
La Quinta, CA 92253-8773, USA

Jacobs, Katie (Producer, Writer)
c/o Tony Etz *Creative Artists Agency (CAA-LA)*
2000 Avenue of the Stars Ste 100
Los Angeles, CA 90067-4705, USA

Jacobs, Lawrence-Hilton (Actor)
PO Box 67905
Los Angeles, CA 90067-0905, USA

Jacobs, Marc (Designer, Fashion Designer)
Marc Jacobs
403 Bleecker St
New York, NY 10014-2157, USA

Jacobs, Mike (Athlete, Baseball Player)
2151 Caminito Bartolo Unit 3
Chula Vista, CA 91915-3144, USA

Jacobs, Norman J (Publisher)
Century Publishing Co
990 Grove St Ste 400
Evanston, IL 60201-4302, USA

Jacobs, Proverb (Athlete, Football Player)
4369 Detroit Ave
Oakland, CA 94619-1603, USA

Jacobs, Ray (Athlete, Football Player)
2402 W 5th Ave
Corsicana, TX 75110-4047, USA

Jacobs, Regina (Athlete, Olympic Athlete, Track Athlete)
3209 Wisconsin St
Oakland, CA 94602-4029, USA

Jacobs, Tim (Athlete, Football Player)
7306 Finns Ln
Lanham, MD 20706-1214, USA

Jacobs, Tim (Athlete, Hockey Player)
6516 County Road 301
Parachute, CO 81635-9122, USA

Jacobs-Badini, Jane (Athlete, Baseball Player, Commentator)
1854 4th St
Cuyahoga Falls, OH 44221-3802, USA

Jacobsen, Bucky (Athlete, Baseball Player)
10920 428th Ave SE
North Bend, WA 98045-7963, USA

Jacobsen, Casey (Athlete, Basketball Player)
Phoenix Suns
201 E Jefferson St
Phoenix, AZ 85004-2412, USA

Jacobsen, Peter (Athlete, Golfer)
27771 Marina Pointe Dr
Bonita Springs, FL 34134-0762, USA

Jacobsen, Peter (Athlete, Golfer)
9400 SW Barnes Rd Ste 550
Portland, OR 97225-6690, USA

Jacobsen, Stephanie (Actor)
c/o Christopher Rockwell *Keyword Entertainment*
1051 Cole Ave # B
Los Angeles, CA 90038-2601, USA

Jacobs-Murk, Janet (Athlete, Baseball Player, Commentator)
899 Olentangy Rd
Franklin Lakes, NJ 07417-2811, USA

Jacobson, D D (Bowler)
8261 Rees St
Playa Del Rey, CA 90293-7823, USA

Jacobson, Peter (Actor)
c/o Elizabeth Much *Much and House Public Relations*
8075 W 3rd St Ste 500
Los Angeles, CA 90048-4325, USA

Jacobson, Peter Marc (Actor, Producer, Writer)
c/o Staff Member *New York Nick*
5750 Wilshire Blvd
Los Angeles, CA 90036-3697, USA

Jacoby, Billy
PO Box 46324
Los Angeles, CA 90046-0324

Jacoby, Brook (Athlete, Baseball Player)
100 Joe Nuxhall Way
Cincinnati, OH 45202-4109, USA

Jacoby, Joe (Athlete, Football Player)
2730 Willow Dr
Vienna, VA 22181-5347, USA

Jacoby, Laura
PO Box 46324
Los Angeles, CA 90046-0324

Jacoby, Scott (Actor)
PO Box 461100
Los Angeles, CA 90046-9100, USA

Jacome, Jason (Athlete, Baseball Player)
5115 N Camino Esplendora
Tucson, AZ 85718-6226, USA

Jacot, Christopher (Actor)
c/o Ted Schachter *Schachter Entertainment*
1157 S Beverly Dr Fl 2
Los Angeles, CA 90035-1119, USA

Jacott, Carlos (Actor)
c/o JB Roberts *Thruline Entertainment*
9250 Wilshire Blvd Ste 100
Ground Floor
Beverly Hills, CA 90212-3343, USA

Jacox, Kendyl (Athlete, Football Player)
50 Schubach Dr
Sugar Land, TX 77479-5727, USA

Jacques, Reeves (Athlete, Football Player)
9135 Buffalo Speedway
Houston, TX 77025-4426, USA

Jacquez, Pat (Athlete, Baseball Player)
4430 Annandale Dr
Stockton, CA 95219-1782, USA

Jacquez, Thomas (Tom) (Athlete, Baseball Player)
280 Fell St Apt 410
San Francisco, CA 94102-5174, USA

Jacuzzi, Roy (Business Person)
Jacuzzi Whirlpool Bath
2121 N California Blvd
Walnut Creek, CA 94596-3572, USA

Jadakiss (Artist, Music Group, Musician)
c/o Drew Elliot *Artists International Management (NY)*
333 E 43rd St Apt 115
New York, NY 10017-4822, USA

Jade
c/o Staff Member *Diva Central Inc*
7510 W Sunset Blvd Ste 1445
Los Angeles, CA 90046-3408, USA

Jade, Samantha (Musician)
c/o Staff Member *Jive Records*
550 Madison Ave Fl 6
New York, NY 10022-3211, USA

Jae, Jana
PO Box 35736
Tulsa, OK 74153

Jaeckel, Barry (Athlete, Golfer)
210 Falcon Cv
Brandon, MS 39047-7733, USA

Jaeckel, Paul (Athlete, Baseball Player)
328 W 7th St
Claremont, CA 91711-4313, USA

Jaeger, Andrea (Athlete, Tennis Player)
256 Rancho Milagro Way
Silver Lining Ranch
Hesperus, CO 81326-8750, USA

Jaeger, Jeff T (Athlete, Football Player)
3026 Sahalee Dr W
Sammamish, WA 98074-6304, USA

Jaeger, Sam (Actor)
c/o Steve Dontanville *Circle of Confusion*
(NY)
8931 Ellis Ave
Los Angeles, CA 90034-3336, USA

Jae-sang, Park (PSY) (Musician)
c/o Staff Member *Universal Music Group*
(TN)
401 Commerce St Ste 1100
Nashville, TN 37219-2489, USA

Jaffe, Herold W (Doctor)
Centers for Disease Control
1600 Clifton Rd NE
Atlanta, GA 30329-4018, USA

Jaffe, Marielle (Actor)
c/o Staff Member *Inphenate*
9701 Wilshire Blvd Fl 10
Beverly Hills, CA 90212-2010, USA

Jaffe, Stanley R (Director, Producer)
Lean Building
10202 Washington Blvd
Culver City, CA 90232-3119, USA

Jaffrey, Sakina (Actor)
c/o Marisa Martins *42West (NYC)*
220 W 42nd St Fl 12
New York, NY 10036-7200, USA

Jagendort, Andre T (Doctor)
455 Savage Farm Dr
Ithaca, NY 14850-6522, USA

Jager, Thomas (Tom) (Athlete, Olympic
Athlete, Swimmer)
1416 Chinook St
Moscow, ID 83843-2506, USA

Jager, Tom
64 Ramble Wood Blvd
Tijeras, NM 87059-8004

Jagged Edge (Music Group)
c/o Nancy Josephson *William Morris
Endeavor (LA)*
9601 Wilshire Blvd
Beverly Hills, CA 90210-5213, USA

Jagger, Jade (Business Person)
16th West 19th LLC
752 Pacific St
Brooklyn, NY 11238-3006, USA

Jaglom, Henry (Director)
9165 W Sunset Blvd Ste 300
West Hollywood, CA 90069-3195, USA

Jaguares (Music Group)
c/o Staff Member *BMG*
1540 Broadway
New York, NY 10036-4039, USA

Jaha, John (Athlete, Baseball Player)
9494 SE Chatfield Ct
Happy Valley, OR 97086-9197, USA

Jahan, Marine (Actor, Dancer)
Media Artists Group
6300 Wilshire Blvd Ste 1470
Los Angeles, CA 90048-5200, USA

Jaheim (Musician)
Diane Mill
100 Evergreen Pt # 402
East Orange, NJ 07018, USA

Jahncke, Barton (Athlete, Olympic
Athlete, Sailor)
714 Girod St Apt 2B
New Orleans, LA 70130-3523, USA

Jaitley, Celina (Actor, Beauty Pageant
Winner)
c/o Staff Member *Brillstein Entertainment
Partners (LA)*
9150 Wilshire Blvd Ste 350
Beverly Hills, CA 90212-3453, USA

Jake Locker, Jake
c/o David Dunn *Athletes First, LLC*
23091 Mill Creek Dr
Laguna Hills, CA 92653-1258, USA

Jakeman, Seth (Musician)
c/o Staff Member *Paradigm (Monterey)*
404 W Franklin St
Monterey, CA 93940-2303, USA

Jakes, John (Writer)
445 Meadow Lark Dr
Sarasota, FL 34236-1901, USA

Jakes, TD (Musician, Religious Leader,
Writer)
T.D. Jakes Ministries
PO Box 5390
Dallas, TX 75208-9390, USA

Jakes, Van (Athlete, Football Player)
305 Worthing Ln
McDonough, GA 30253-4244, USA

Jakobson, Maggie (Actor)
c/o Kesha Williams *KW Entertainment*
425 N Robertson Blvd
West Hollywood, CA 90048-1735, USA

Jakopin, John (Athlete, Hockey Player)
57 Samana Dr
Miami, FL 33133-2609, USA

Jakovac, JJ (Athlete, Golfer)
c/o Jim Lehrman *SFX Golf*
36855 W Main St Ste 200
Purcellville, VA 20132-3561, USA

Jakowenko, George (Athlete, Football
Player)
2535 Fenton Pkwy Apt 205
San Diego, CA 92108-6768, USA

Jalbert, Pierre (Actor)
2642 N Beverly Glen Blvd
Los Angeles, CA 90077-2528, USA

Jamal, Ahmad (Music Group, Musician)
Brad Simon Organization
122 E 57th St # 300
New York, NY 10022-2623, USA

Jambor, Agi (Music Group, Musician)
1616 Bolton St
Baltimore, MD 21217-4316, USA

Jamerson, Dave (Athlete, Basketball
Player)
13960 Salsbury Creek Dr
Carmel, IN 46032-8541, USA

James, Aaron (Athlete, Basketball Player)
3057 Orrin Ave
Youngstown, OH 44505-4436, USA

James, Anthony (Actor)
CNA Assoc
1875 Century Park E Ste 2250
Los Angeles, CA 90067-2563, USA

James, Art (Athlete, Baseball Player)
6935 Brown Dr S
Fairburn, GA 30213-3197, USA

James, Bill (Athlete, Baseball Player,
Writer)
625 Ohio St
Lawrence, KS 66044-2357, USA

James, Bill (Sportscaster)
445 Tennessee St
Lawrence, KS 66044-1376, USA

James, Billy (Athlete, Basketball Player)
12 S Sunset Dr
Lexington, IN 47138-8935, USA

James, Bob (Athlete, Baseball Player)
15844 Cindy Ct
Canyon Country, CA 91387-1881, USA

James, Boney (Musician)
c/o Staff Member *Paradigm (Monterey)*
404 W Franklin St
Monterey, CA 93940-2303, USA

James, Bradie (Athlete, Football Player)
838 Dewberry Ln
McKinney, TX 75069-6884, USA

James, Bryton (Athlete, Baseball Player)
4319 Whitsett Ave Apt 5
Studio City, CA 91604-1659, USA

James, Charlie (Athlete, Baseball Player)
3303 Tanglewood Way
Fulton, MO 65251-3981, USA

James, Chris (Athlete, Baseball Player)
1040 County Rd 2707
Alto, TX 75925, USA

James, Chuck (Athlete, Baseball Player)
4840 Golden Dr SW
Mableton, GA 30126, USA

James, Claudis (Athlete, Football Player)
6767 Presidential Dr
Jackson, MS 39213-2427, USA

James, Cleo (Athlete, Baseball Player)
1631 Mesa Ave
Colorado Springs, CO 80906-2917, USA

James, Clifton (Actor)
500 W 43rd St Apt 25D
New York, NY 10036-4336, USA

James, Craig (Athlete, Football Player)
12714 W FM 455
Celina, TX 75009-3959, USA

James, Dalton
303 N Buena Vista St Apt 209
Burbank, CA 91505-3686

James, Delvin (Athlete, Baseball Player)
13355 FM 1878
Nacogdoches, TX 75961-1039, USA

James, Dion (Athlete, Baseball Player)
5 Shelter Point Ct
Sacramento, CA 95831-1415, USA

James, Don (Coach, Football Coach)
7047 Chanticleer Ave SE
Snoqualmie, WA 98065-9785, USA

James, Donald M (Business Person)
Vulcan Materials Co
1200 Urban Center Dr
Vestavia, AL 35242-2545, USA

James, Edgerrin (Athlete, Football Player)
c/o Drew Rosenhaus *Rosenhaus Sports
Representation*
6400 Allison Rd
Miami Beach, FL 33141-4540, USA

James, Forrest (Politician)
21911VY Creek Church Rd
Rutledge, AL 36071, USA

James, G Larry (Athlete, Track Athlete)
Stockton State College
Atheletic Dept
Pomona, NJ 08240, USA

James, Henry (Athlete, Basketball Player)
527 E Leith St
Fort Wayne, IN 46806-1118, USA

James, Ja'Wuan (Athlete, Football Player)
c/o Bill Johnson *SportsTrust Advisors (GA)*
3340 Peachtree Rd NE Fl 16
Atlanta, GA 30326-1000, USA

James, Jesse (Actor)
Austin Speed Shop
3507 Chapman Ln
Austin, TX 78744-1215, USA

James, Jessie (Musician)
c/o Staff Member *Island Records*
825 8th Ave Rm C2
New York, NY 10019-7472, USA

James, John (Actor)
PO Box 9
Cambridge, NY 12816-0009, USA

James, Johnny (Athlete, Baseball Player)
6037 E Larkspur Dr
Scottsdale, AZ 85254-4444, USA

James, John W (Athlete, Football Player)
23108 NE 69th Ave
Melrose, FL 32666-6330, USA

James, Joni (Music Group, Musician)
PO Box 7027
Westchester, IL 60154, USA

James, Joshua (Musician)
c/o Brittany Pearce *Fresh and Clean
Media*
12701 Venice Blvd
Los Angeles, CA 90066-3705, USA

James, Kate (Model)
Men/Women Model Inc
199 Lafayette St Fl 7
New York, NY 10012-4281, USA

James, Kevin (Actor, Comedian)
c/o Staff Member *Hey Eddie*
15374 Dickens St
Sherman Oaks, CA 91403-3007, USA

James, Larry D (Astronaut)
AFELM
USS Space Command
Colorado Springs, CO 80914, USA

James, LeBron (Athlete, Basketball Player)
c/o Keith Estabrook *Estabrook Group LLC*
113 Nassau St Apt 20G
New York, NY 10038-2455, USA

James, Leela (Musician)
c/o Stephanie Mahler *Creative Artists
Agency (CAA-NY)*
162 5th Ave Fl 6
New York, NY 10010-6047, USA

James, Lionel (Athlete, Football Player)
199 Woodbury Dr
Sterrett, AL 35147-8144, USA

James, Michael Raymond (Actor)
c/o Mark Armstrong *Sanders Armstrong
Caserta*
2120 Colorado Ave Ste 120
Santa Monica, CA 90404-3561, USA

James, Mickie (Athlete, Wrestler)
121 Dogwood Ct
Aylett, VA 23009-4136, USA

James, Mike (Athlete, Baseball Player)
115 Austin Ct
Mary Esther, FL 32569-1396, USA

James, Oliver (Actor, Musician)
c/o Staff Member *MPG Management*
1136 Roxbury Dr
Los Angeles, CA 90035-1066, USA

James, Paul (Actor, Producer)
c/o Staff Member *HGTV*
9721 Sherrill Blvd
Knoxville, TN 37932-3330, USA

James, Po (Athlete, Football Player)
1421 Sherman St
Hammond, IN 46320-2208, USA

James, Ralph
205 S Arnaz Dr Apt 4
Beverly Hills, CA 90211-2881

James, Rick (Athlete, Baseball Player)
102 Stoney Creek Dr
Florence, AL 35633-1581, USA

James, Robert (Athlete, Football Player)
1511 N Highland Ave
Murfreesboro, TN 37130-2204, USA

James, Robert (Bob) (Music Group,
Musician, Songwriter, Writer)
Monterey International
200 W Superior St Ste 202
Chicago, IL 60654-6422, USA

James, Roland (Athlete, Football Player)
19 Spring Ln
Sharon, MA 02067-2240, USA

James, Sheila (Actor)
3201 Pearl St
Santa Monica, CA 90405-3106, USA

James, Sheryl (Journalist)
Saint Petersburg Times
490 1st Ave S
Editorial Dept
Saint Petersburg, FL 33701-4223, USA

James, Skip (Athlete, Baseball Player)
14429 Windsor St
Overland Park, KS 66224-3669, USA

James, Sonny (Musician, Songwriter)
c/o Staff Member *William Morris
Endeavor (Nashville)*
1600 Division St Ste 300
Nashville, TN 37203-2755, USA

James, Steve (Director, Producer, Writer)
c/o Paul Canterna *Seven Summits Pictures
& Management*
8906 W Olympic Blvd
Ground Floor
Beverly Hills, CA 90211-3550, USA

James, Tommy (Music Group, Musician)
Aura Entertainment
PO Box 4354
Clifton, NJ 07012-8354, USA

James, Toran (Athlete, Football Player)
RR 3 Box 14-13
Ahoskie, NC 27910, USA

James, Val (Athlete, Hockey Player)
105 S 32nd St
Wyandanch, NY 11798-2613, USA

Jameson, Jenna (Actor, Adult Film Star,
Model)
16722 Baruna Ln
Huntington Beach, CA 92649-3018, USA

Jamieson, Janet (Athlete, Baseball Player,
Commentator)
6324 212th St SW Trlr 3
Lynnwood, WA 98036-7425, USA

Jamiroquai (Music Group)
c/o Staff Member *Nettwerk Management
(LA)*
1545 Wilcox Ace
Suite 200
Los Angeles, CA 90028, USA

Jamison, Antawn (Athlete, Basketball
Player)
Dallas Mavericks
6041 Providence Country Club Dr
Charlotte, NC 28277-2631, USA

Jamison, Jayne (Publisher)
Redbook Magazine
224 W 57th St
New York, NY 10019-3212, USA

Jamison, Jimi (Musician)
4002 Glendale Dr
Memphis, TN 38128-2408, USA

Jamison, Mae
PO Box 580317
Houston, TX 77258-0317

Jamison, Mikki (Actor)
1501 S Latawah St
Spokane, WA 99203-2252, USA

Jamison, Milo
1231 Tennyson St
Manhattan Beach, CA 90266-6956

Jamison, Tim (Athlete, Football Player)
c/o David Dunn *Athletes First, LLC*
23091 Mill Creek Dr
Laguna Hills, CA 92653-1258, USA

Jammer, Quentin (Athlete, Football
Player)
4020 Murphy Canyon Rd
San Diego, CA 92123-4407, USA

Jampolsky, Gerald (Writer)
Celestial Arts
PO Box 7123
Berkeley, CA 94707-0123

Jan & Dean
221 Main St Ste P
Huntington Beach, CA 92648-8119

Janaszak, Steve (Athlete, Hockey Player,
Olympic Athlete)
42 Montrose Ave
Babylon, NY 11702-2626, USA

Jance, J A (Writer)
Avon/William Morrow
1350 Avenue of the Americas
New York, NY 10019-4702, USA

Jande, Marine (Actor)
Gilla Roos
16 W 22nd St Fl 3
New York, NY 10010-5803

Jane, Jesse (Actor, Adult Film Star, Model)
c/o Staff Member *Media Artists Group
(LA)*
8222 Melrose Ave Ste 203
Los Angeles, CA 90046-6838, USA

Jane, Thomas (Actor)
c/o Michael Katcher *Creative Artists
Agency (CAA-LA)*
2000 Avenue of the Stars Ste 100
Los Angeles, CA 90067-4705, USA

Janecyk, Bob (Athlete, Hockey Player)
5973 Pheasant View Dr NE
Ada, MI 49301-8648, USA

Janecyl, Bob (Athlete, Hockey Player)
5973 Pheasant View Dr NE
Ada, MI 49301-8648, USA

Jane's Addiction (Music Group)
c/o Staff Member *William Morris
Endeavor (LA)*
9601 Wilshire Blvd
Beverly Hills, CA 90210-5213, USA

Janeski, Jerry (Athlete, Baseball Player)
28901 Via Buena Vis
San Juan Capistrano, CA 92675-5554,
USA

Janet, Ernest (Athlete, Football Player)
385 Highpoint Ln
Chelan, WA 98816-9579, USA

Janeway, Richard (Doctor)
1941 Georgia Ave
Winston Salem, NC 27104-3103, USA

Jang, Jeong (Athlete, Golfer)
7769 Apple Tree Cir
Orlando, FL 32819-4682, USA

Janik, Doug (Athlete, Hockey Player)
51 Senator Ave
Agawam, MA 01001-2129, USA

Janikowski, Bruce (Athlete, Football
Player)
2716 W 112th St
Leawood, KS 66211-3084, USA

Janis, Byron (Musician)
Phillips Records
810 7th Ave
New York, NY 10019-5818, USA

Janis, Conrad (Actor, Music Group,
Musician)
1434 N Genesee Ave
Los Angeles, CA 90046-3930, USA

Janis, Elizabeth (Actor)
c/o Michael Greenwald *Don Buchwald &
Associates (LA)*
6500 Wilshire Blvd Ste 2200
Los Angeles, CA 90048-4942, USA

Janis, Jeff (Athlete, Football Player)
c/o Jim Ivler *Sportstars Inc*
1350 Avenue of the Americas Fl 28
New York, NY 10019-4702, USA

Janish, Paul (Athlete, Baseball Player)
11926 Deep Woods Dr
Cypress, TX 77429-2741, USA

Janitz, John A (Business Person)
Textron Inc
40 Westminster St Ste 500
Providence, RI 02903-2503, USA

Jankins, Corey (Baseball Player)
Bowman
456 S Church St Apt J1
Lexington, SC 29072-3342, USA

Jankowski, Gene F (Television Host)
American Film Institute
901 15th St NW # 700
Washington, DC 20005-2327, USA

Jankowski, Peter (Producer)
c/o Staff Member *Wolf Films Inc (LA)*
100 Universal City Plz
Universal City, CA 91608-1002, USA

Jannazzo, Izzy (Boxer)
6924 62nd Ave
Middle Village, NY 11379-1120, USA

Janney, Allison (Actor)
c/o Chris Henze *Thruline Entertainment*
9250 Wilshire Blvd Ste 100
Ground Floor
Beverly Hills, CA 90212-3343, USA

Janney, Craig H (Athlete, Hockey Player)
6424 E Exeter Blvd
Scottsdale, AZ 85251-3102, USA

Janotta, Howard (Athlete, Basketball
Player)
18118 Brookwood Frst
San Antonio, TX 78258-4474, USA

Janov, Arthur (Writer)
1205 Abbot Kinney Blvd
Venice, CA 90291-3315, USA

Janowicz, Josh (Actor)
c/o Darren Goldberg *Global Creative*
1051 Cole Ave # B
Los Angeles, CA 90038-2601, USA

Janowitz, Will (Actor)
c/o David Ginsberg *Insight*
PO Box 36359
Los Angeles, CA 90036-0359, USA

Jansen, Dan (Athlete, Olympic Athlete,
Speed Skater)
PO Box 3354
Mooresville, NC 28117-3354, USA

Jansen, Jim (Actor)
c/o Martin Gage *Gage Group, The (LA)*
5757 Wilshire Blvd Ste 659
Los Angeles, CA 90036-3682, USA

Jansen, Raymond A (Publisher)
Newsday Inc
235 Pinelawn Rd
Melville, NY 11747-4250, USA

Janson, Chris (Musician)
c/o Bobby Roberts *Bobby Roberts Agency*
PO Box 1547
Goodlettsville, TN 37070-1547, USA

Janssen, Bill (Athlete, Football Player)
7531 W Rio Rd
Lincoln, NE 68505-2686, USA

Janssen, Cam (Athlete, Hockey Player)
313 Forest Run Dr
Eureka, MO 63025-2119, USA

Janssen, Casey (Athlete, Baseball Player)
232 24th St
Manhattan Beach, CA 90266-4300, USA

Janssen, Dani
2220 Avenue of the Stars Unit 2803
Los Angeles, CA 90067-5686

Janssen, Famke (Actor, Model)
c/o Emily Gerson Saines *Brookside Artists
Management (NY)*
250 W 57th St Ste 2303
New York, NY 10107-2399, USA

Janssen, Frances (Athlete, Baseball Player)
4311 Mayflower Dr
Lafayette, IN 47909-3473, USA

Janssens, Mark (Athlete, Hockey Player)
115 Central Park W Apt 17A
New York, NY 10023-4295, USA

January, Don (Athlete, Golfer)
5006 Village Pl
Dallas, TX 75248-6029, USA

January, Don (Golfer)
4139 Sicily Dr
Frisco, TX 75034, USA

January, Lois (Actor)
PO Box 1233
Beverly Hills, CA 90213-1233, USA

Janzen, Edmund (Religious Leader)
General Conference of Mennonite Brethren
8000 W 21st St N
Wichita, KS 67205-1744, USA

Janzen, Lee (Athlete, Golfer)
9088 Point Cypress Dr
Orlando, FL 32836-5476, USA

Janzen, Marty (Athlete, Baseball Player)
650 N Prince St Attn Coachingstaff
Lancaster, PA 17603-3025, USA

Jaqua, Jon (Athlete, Football Player)
34320 McKenzie View Dr
Eugene, OR 97408-9205, USA

Jaquess, Pete (Athlete, Football Player)
631 Cunningham Ln
El Cajon, CA 92019-3504, USA

Jaramillo, Jason (Athlete, Baseball Player)
6111 Madeline Ln
Caledonia, WI 53108-9557, USA

Jaramillo, Rudy (Athlete, Baseball Player)
3855 Echo Brook Ln
Dallas, TX 75229-5222, USA

Jardine, Alan C (Al) (Musician)
PO Box 36
Big Sur, CA 93920-0036, USA

Jarecki, Andrew (Director, Musician, Producer)
c/o Staff Member *Hit the Ground Running Films*
200 W 57th St Ste 1304
New York, NY 10019-3227, USA

Jarman Jr, Claude (Actor)
16 Tamal Vista Ln
Axminster
Greenbrae, CA 94904-1006, USA

Jarmusch, Jim (Director)
c/o Bart Walker *ICM Partners (LA)*
10250 Constellation Blvd Fl 7
Los Angeles, CA 90067-6207, USA

Jaroncyk, Ryan (Baseball Player)
Bowman
2923 Roseann Ave
Escondido, CA 92027-5306, USA

Jarostchuk, Ilia (Athlete, Football Player)
4 MacArthur Rd
Wellesley, MA 02482-4422, USA

Jarreau, Al (Musician)
c/o Staff Member *Agency for the Performing Arts (APA-LA)*
405 S Beverly Dr Ste 500
Beverly Hills, CA 90212-4425, USA

Jarrell, Tom
77 W 66th St
New York, NY 10023-6201

Jarrett, Dale (Race Car Driver)
1510 46th Ave NE
Hickory, NC 28601-8421, USA

Jarrett, Gary (Athlete, Hockey Player)
9662 E Peak View Rd
Scottsdale, AZ 85262-2352, USA

Jarrett, Jason (Race Car Driver)
Jarrett-Favre Motorsports
2025 Evans St NE
Box 465
Conover, NC 28613, USA

Jarrett, Ned (Race Car Driver)
3182 Ninth Tee Dr
Newton, NC 28658-8725, USA

Jarriel, Thomas E (Tom) (Correspondent)
ABC-TV
77 W 66th St
News Dept
New York, NY 10023-6201, USA

Jarrin, Jaime (Athlete, Baseball Player)
725 La Mirada Ave
San Marino, CA 91108-1729, USA

Jars of Clay (Music Group)
c/o Janet Weir *Red Light Management (LA)*
8439 W Sunset Blvd Ste 2
West Hollywood, CA 90069-1925, USA

Ja Rule (Actor, Musician)
10 Lookout Dr
Saddle River, NJ 07458-3314, USA

Jaru the Damaja (Musician)
William Morris Agency
1325 Avenue of the Americas Bsmt 2
New York, NY 10019-6047, USA

Jarvis, Bruce (Athlete, Football Player)
4153 Issaquah Pine Lake Rd SE
Sammamish, WA 98075-6243, USA

Jarvis, Curtis (Athlete, Football Player)
401 Albert Dr
Gardendale, AL 35071-2588, USA

Jarvis, Graham
15351 Via De Las Olas
Pacific Palisades, CA 90272-4648

Jarvis, James (Athlete, Basketball Player)
PO Box 154
Asotin, WA 99402-0154, USA

Jarvis, Katie (Actor)
c/o Billy Lazarus *United Talent Agency (UTA-LA)*
9336 Civic Center Dr
Beverly Hills, CA 90210-3604, USA

Jarvis, Kevin (Athlete, Baseball Player)
1613 Whispering Hills Dr
Franklin, TN 37069-7242, USA

Jarvis, Lucy
171 W 57th St Apt 8C
New York, NY 10019-2222

Jarvis, Pat (Athlete, Baseball Player)
4201 Providence Ln
Tucker, GA 30084-2630, USA

Jarvis, Ray (Athlete, Baseball Player)
15 Higgins St Apt 106
Smithfield, RI 02917-4033, USA

Jarvis, Ray (Athlete, Football Player)
18320 Taywood Cir Apt 102
Brookfield, WI 53045-5681, USA

Jaso, John (Athlete, Baseball Player)
494 Weldon St
Redding, CA 96001-3642, USA

Jason, Dunn (Athlete, Football Player)
2201 Sweetleaf Ct
Lexington, KY 40513-1376, USA

Jason, Harvey
1280 Sunset Plaza Dr
Los Angeles, CA 90069-1245

Jason, Peter (Actor)
c/o Staff Member *Diverse Talent Group*
9911 W Pico Blvd Ste 340W
Los Angeles, CA 90035-2703, USA

Jason, Sybil (Actor)
19200 Salt Lake Pl # Pi
Porter Ranch, CA 91326-2345, USA

Jason & deMarco (Music Group)
c/o Staff Member *RJN Music!*
8033 W Sunset Blvd # 574
Los Angeles, CA 90046-2401, USA

Jasontek, Rebecca (Athlete, Olympic Athlete, Swimmer)
1201 Retswood Dr
Loveland, OH 45140-8701, USA

Jasper, Edward (Athlete, Football Player)
110 N Price St
Troup, TX 75789-1429, USA

Jaster, Larry (Athlete, Baseball Player)
1105 Mill Creek Dr
Saint Johns, FL 32259-8973, USA

Jastremski, Chet (Athlete, Olympic Athlete, Swimmer)
5064 W September Dr
Bloomington, IN 47404-8994, USA

Jastrow, Terry L (Director)
13201 Old Oak Ln
Los Angeles, CA 90049-2501, USA

Jastrow II, Kenneth M (Business Person)
Temple-Inland Inc
303 S Temple Dr
Diboll, TX 75941-2419, USA

Jata, Paul (Athlete, Baseball Player)
5972 Quartz Valley Dr
Newport, KY 41076-7129, USA

Jauch, Ray (Athlete, Football Player)
5306 Harkey Rd
Waxhaw, NC 28173-8461, USA

Jaugstetter, Robert (Athlete, Olympic Athlete, Rower)
619 Mandeville St Ste 3
New Orleans, LA 70117-8501, USA

Jauron, Dick M (Athlete, Coach, Football Coach, Football Player)
76 Lou Groza Blvd
Berea, OH 44017-1238, USA

Jauss, Dave (Athlete, Baseball Player)
3820 13th Ave SW
Naples, FL 34117-5330, USA

Javerbaum, David (Writer)
c/o Staff Member *3 Arts Entertainment (LA)*
9460 Wilshire Blvd Fl 7
Beverly Hills, CA 90212-2713, USA

Javier, Stan (Athlete, Baseball Player)
11544 NW 43rd Ter
Doral, FL 33178-4235, USA

Javier Galvan Y Fama (Music Group)
c/o Staff Member *Sony Music Miami*
605 Lincoln Rd Ste 700
Miami Beach, FL 33139-2901, USA

Jaworski, Ronald V (Ron) (Athlete, Football Player, Sportscaster)
18 Brookwood Dr
Medford, NJ 08055-8178, USA

Jax, Garth (Athlete, Football Player)
5335 S Valentia Way Apt 137
Greenwood Village, CO 80111-3106, USA

Jay, Bob (Athlete, Hockey Player)
9 Sunnyside Ave
Burlington, MA 01803-4752, USA

Jay, Joey (Athlete, Baseball Player)
7209 Battenwood Ct
Tampa, FL 33615-2023, USA

Jay, Jon (Athlete, Baseball Player)
c/o Nez Balelo *CAA Sports (LA)*
2000 Avenue of the Stars Ste 100
Los Angeles, CA 90067-4705, USA

Jay, Ken (Musician)
Andy Gould Mgmt
9100 Wilshire Blvd Ste 400W
Beverly Hills, CA 90212-3464, USA

Jay, Natalie
6230 Wilshire Blvd Ste 153
Los Angeles, CA 90048-5199

Jay, Ricky (Actor)
Simone
1790 Broadway Ste 1000
New York, NY 10019-1412, USA

Jay, Riemersma (Athlete, Football Player)
3067 Regency Pkwy
Zeeland, MI 49464-6852, USA

Jay, Tony (Actor)
c/o Staff Member *Pakula/King & Associates*
9229 W Sunset Blvd Ste 315
West Hollywood, CA 90069-3403, USA

Jay & The Americans
1045 Pomme De Pin Ln
New Port Richey, FL 34655-5627

Jay & The Techniques
4250 Aia S # D-11
Saint Augustine, FL 32080

Jayne, Billy
8521 Nash Dr
Los Angeles, CA 90046-7705

Jayne, Erika (Musician)
c/o Staff Member *Levine Communications Office*
9100 Wilshire Blvd Ste 540
Beverly Hills, CA 90212-3470, USA

Jay-Z (Musician, Producer)
195 Hudson St # 7ABPH
New York, NY 10013-1813, USA

Jazz Crusaders, The (Music Group)
Universal
225 W 57th St Fl 5
New York, NY 10019-2136

Jazzyfatnastees (Music Group)
c/o Staff Member *Paradigm (Monterey)*
404 W Franklin St
Monterey, CA 93940-2303, USA

Jbara, Gregory (Actor)
c/o Marilyn Szatmary *SMS Talent*
8383 Wilshire Blvd Ste 230
Beverly Hills, CA 90211-2436, USA

JBJ (Musician)
Q Prime
729 7th Ave Ste 1600
New York, NY 10019-6880, USA

J-Bolt (Producer)
Lightning Bolt Entertainment
3342 S Sandhill Rd Ste 9-424
Las Vegas, NV 89121-3414, USA

J. Duncan Jr., John (Congressman, Politician)
2207 Rayburn Hob
Washington, DC 20515-2003, USA

Jeager, Andrea (Athlete, Tennis Player)
3137 Devin Dr
Grand Junction, CO 81504-6057, USA

Jean, Gloria (Actor, Musician)
3844 W Channel Islands Blvd # 166
Oxnard, CA 93035-4001, USA

Jean, Norma (Musician)
22 Skyline Dr
Kimberling City, MO 65686-9658, USA

Jean, Wyclef (Musician)
8 Cameron Rd
Saddle River, NJ 07458-2934, USA

Jean-Baptiste, Marianne (Actor)
c/o Elise Konialian *Untitled Entertainment (NY)*
435 Hudson St Fl 9
New York, NY 10014-3995, USA

Jean-Louis, Jimmy (Actor)
c/o Alex Cole *Elevate Entertainment*
5757 Wilshire Blvd Ste 460
Los Angeles, CA 90036-3658, USA

Jeannotte, Dan (Actor)
c/o Robert Stein *Robert Stein Management*
PO Box 3797
Beverly Hills, CA 90212-0797, USA

Jeanrenaud, Joan (Musician)
Kronos Quartet
1235 9th Ave # A
San Francisco, CA 94122-2306, USA

Jecha, Ralph (Athlete, Football Player)
717 Vinewood Ave
Willow Springs, IL 60480-1523, USA

Jee, Elizabeth (Actor)
Commercials Unlimited
8383 Wilshire Blvd Ste 850
Beverly Hills, CA 90211-2443, USA

Jee, Rupert (Business Person)
Hello Deli
213 W 53rd St
New York, NY 10019-5805

Jeelani, Abdul (Athlete, Basketball Player)
W525 State Road 59
Palmyra, WI 53156-9741, USA

Jeff, Reinke (Athlete, Football Player)
13821 320th St
New Prague, MN 56071-4126, USA

Jeffcoat, Don (Actor)
c/o Staff Member *House of Representatives, The*
1434 6th St Ste 1
Santa Monica, CA 90401-2527, USA

Jeffcoat, James W (Jim) (Athlete, Football Player)
916 Monroe Way
Superior, CO 80027-8179, USA

Jeffcoat, Mike (Athlete, Baseball Player)
4224 Oak Springs Dr
Arlington, TX 76016-4508, USA

Jefferies, Gregg (Athlete, Baseball Player)
20255 Landig Cir
Yorba Linda, CA 92887-3261, USA

Jeffers, Eve Jihan (Actor, Producer)
c/o Amanda Silverman *42West (NYC)*
220 W 42nd St Fl 12
New York, NY 10036-7200, USA

Jeffers, Patrick (Athlete, Football Player)
4514 W Rapid Springs Cv
Austin, TX 78746-1631, USA

Jeffers, Rusty (Athlete)
PO Box 30081
Phoenix, AZ 85046-0081

Jefferson, Al (Athlete, Basketball Player)
c/o Jeff Schwartz *Excel Sports Management (NY)*
1700 Broadway Fl 29
New York, NY 10019-5905, USA

Jefferson, James (Athlete, Football Player)
11220 NE 53rd St
Kirkland, WA 98033-7505, USA

Jefferson, Jeff (Race Car Driver)
752 State Route 410
Naches, WA 98937-9400, USA

Jefferson, John L (Athlete, Football Player)
43590 Merchant Mill Ter
Leesburg, VA 20176-8228, USA

Jefferson, Reggie (Athlete, Baseball Player)
1881 Raymond Tucker Rd
Tallahassee, FL 32311-8793, USA

Jefferson, Richard (Basketball Player)
New Jersey Nets
390 Murray Hill Pkwy
East Rutherford, NJ 07073-2109, USA

Jefferson, Roy (Athlete, Football Player)
PO Box 182
Annandale, VA 22003-0182, USA

Jefferson, Shawn (Athlete, Football Player)
1489 Kellywood Dr
Brentwood, TN 37027-5398, USA

Jefferson, Stan (Athlete, Baseball Player)
2420 Hunter Ave Apt 3E
Bronx, NY 10475-5644, USA

Jefferson, Thad (Athlete, Football Player)
PO Box 1552
Rialto, CA 92377-1552, USA

Jefferson Starship (Music Group)
c/o Staff Member *Mission Control*
15030 Ventura Blvd # 541
Sherman Oaks, CA 91403-5470, USA

Jeffery, Aaron (Actor)
c/o Robert Marsala *Wishlab*
2225A Hyperion Ave
Los Angeles, CA 90027-4709, USA

Jeffery, Alshon (Athlete, Football Player)
c/o Eugene Parker *Maximum Sports Management*
6435 W Jefferson Blvd # 197
Fort Wayne, IN 46804-6203, USA

Jeffires, Haywood (Athlete, Football Player)
2601 Courtyard Ln
Pearland, TX 77584-3000, USA

Jeffre, Justin (Musician)
DAS Communications
83 Riverside Dr
New York, NY 10024-5713, USA

Jeffress, Jeremy
6901 Marlowe Rd
Richmond, VA 23225-4295, USA

Jeffreys, Anne (Actor)
18915 Nordhoff St Ste 5
Northridge, CA 91324-3790, USA

Jeffries, Doug (Adult Film Star)
c/o Staff Member *Diva Central Inc*
7510 W Sunset Blvd Ste 1445
Los Angeles, CA 90046-3408, USA

Jeffries, Fran (Actor)
10160 Cielo Dr
C/O Stanley H.Handman
Beverly Hills, CA 90210-2037, USA

Jeffries, Jared (Basketball Player)
Washington Wizards
601 F St NW
Mcl Centre
Washington, DC 20004-1605, USA

Jeffries, Willie (Athlete, Football Coach)
c/o Staff Member *College Football Hall Of Fame*
233 Peachtree St NE Ste 1400
Atlanta, GA 30303-1507, USA

Jelen, Ben (Musician)
c/o Staff Member *Maverick Recording Co (LA)*
3300 Warner Blvd
Burbank, CA 91505-4632, USA

Jelesky, Tom (Athlete, Football Player)
619 S 19th St
Chesterton, IN 46304-2757, USA

Jelic, Chris (Athlete, Baseball Player)
33 Allegheny Ave Apt 5
Cuddy, PA 15031-9763, USA

Jelks, Greg (Athlete, Baseball Player)
Slippery Rock Sliders
PO Box 501
Attn: Managers Office
Slippery Rock, PA 16057-0501, USA

Jelks, Greg
Philadelphia Phillies
615 Bay Springs Rd
Centre, AL 35960-1212, USA

Jelley, Thomas (Athlete, Football Player)
200 Tabernacle Rd
Black Mountain, NC 28711-7733, USA

Jells, Dietrich (Athlete, Football Player)
2264 Hideaway Point Dr
Little Elm, TX 75068-5983, USA

Jeltz, Steve (Athlete, Baseball Player)
606 W 28th Pl
Lawrence, KS 66046-4620, USA

Jem (Musician)
c/o Seth Friedman *Red Light Management (LA)*
8439 W Sunset Blvd Ste 2
West Hollywood, CA 90069-1925, USA

Jemison, Antawn (Athlete, Basketball Player)
Washington Wizards
601 F St NW
Mcl Centre
Washington, DC 20004-1605, USA

Jemison, Eddie (Actor)
c/o Gabrielle Krengel *Domain Talent*
9229 W Sunset Blvd Ste 710
West Hollywood, CA 90069-3407, USA

Jendresen, Erik (Producer, Writer)
c/o Scott Seidel *William Morris Endeavor (LA)*
9601 Wilshire Blvd
Beverly Hills, CA 90210-5213, USA

Jendrick, Megan (Athlete, Olympic Athlete, Swimmer)
USA Swimming
5315 Park Rd E
Bonney Lake, WA 98391-8980, USA

Jeni, Richard (Comedian)
c/o Staff Member *Agency for the Performing Arts (APA-LA)*
405 S Beverly Dr Ste 500
Beverly Hills, CA 90212-4425, USA

Jenke, Noel (Athlete, Football Player)
17665 Bonnie Ln
Brookfield, WI 53045-7800, USA

Jenkins, A.J. (Athlete, Football Player)
c/o Alan Herman *Sportstars Inc*
1350 Avenue of the Americas Fl 28
New York, NY 10019-4702, USA

Jenkins, Andrew (Actor)
c/o Jon Simmons *Simmons & Scott Entertainment*
7942 Mulholland Dr
Los Angeles, CA 90046-1225, USA

Jenkins, Carter (Actor)
c/o Mary Sanders *inMomentum Management*
14622 Ventura Blvd # 778
Sherman Oaks, CA 91403-3600, USA

Jenkins, Charlie (Athlete, Olympic Athlete, Track Athlete)
12826 Forest Creek Ct
Sykesville, MD 21784-5526

Jenkins, Cullen (Athlete, Football Player)
27 Bonnieview Ln
Towaco, NJ 07082-1266, USA

Jenkins, Daniel (Actor)
S M S Talent
8383 Wilshire Blvd Ste 230
Beverly Hills, CA 90211-2436, USA

Jenkins, David W (Athlete, Figure Skater, Olympic Athlete)
5947 S Atlanta Ave
Tulsa, OK 74105-7545, USA

Jenkins, Dean (Athlete, Hockey Player)
30 Tyngsboro Rd
North Chelmsford, MA 01863-1319, USA

Jenkins, Don (Athlete, Football Player)
49 W Main St
Frostburg, MD 21532-1640, USA

Jenkins, Ed (Athlete, Football Player)
1750 Washington St Ste B1
Boston, MA 02118-1831, USA

Jenkins, Ferguson (Athlete, Baseball Player)
Ferguson Jenkins Foundation
PO Box 664
Lewiston, NY 14092-0664, USA

Jenkins, Fletcher (Athlete, Football Player)
2347 S J St
Tacoma, WA 98405-3831, USA

Jenkins, Geoff (Athlete, Baseball Player)
6683 E Judson Rd
Paradise Valley, AZ 85253-4369, USA

Jenkins, George (Designer, Director)
2402 4th St Apt 10
Santa Monica, CA 90405-3668, USA

Jenkins, Hayes Alan (Athlete, Figure Skater, Olympic Athlete)
3183 Regency Pl
Westlake, OH 44145-6735, USA

Jenkins, Izel (Athlete, Football Player)
5106 Masters Ln N
Wilson, NC 27896-9136, USA

Jenkins, James (Baseball Player)
Cincinnati Indianapolis Clowns
630 Malcolm X Blvd
New York, NY 10037-1247, USA

Jenkins, Jay (Young Jezzy) (Musician)
c/o Laura Wright *Avid Exposure*
1179 W A St Ste 233
Hayward, CA 94541-7006, USA

Jenkins, Jelani (Athlete, Football Player)
c/o Joby Branion *Athletes First, LLC*
23091 Mill Creek Dr
Laguna Hills, CA 92653-1258, USA

Jenkins, Jerry B (Writer)
Tyndale House Publishers
PO Box 80
351 Executive Dr
Wheaton, IL 60187-0080, USA

Jenkins, Kackie (Butch) (Actor)
PO Box 541G
Fairview, NC 28730, USA

Jenkins, Katherine (Musician)
c/o Staff Member *Nettwerk Management (LA)*
1545 Wilcox Ace
Suite 200
Los Angeles, CA 90028, USA

Jenkins, Ken (Actor)
c/o Chris Schmidt *Paradigm (LA)*
360 N Crescent Dr
North Bldg
Beverly Hills, CA 90210-4874, USA

Jenkins, Kerry (Athlete, Football Player)
120 Three Sons Dr
Hoover, AL 35226-2958, USA

Jenkins, Kris (Athlete, Football Player)
309 E Morehead St Apt 622
Charlotte, NC 28202-2310, USA

Jenkins, Loren (Journalist)
Washington Post
Editorial Dept
1150 15th St NW
Washington, DC 20071-0001, USA

Jenkins, Lynn (Congressman, Politician)
1122 Longworth Hob
Washington, DC 20515-3209, USA

Jenkins, Marilyn (Athlete, Baseball Player, Commentator)
1511 Van Auken St SE
Grand Rapids, MI 49508-2511, USA

Jenkins, Mark (Writer)
c/o Staff Member *HarperCollins Publishers*
195 Broadway Fl 2
Cellar 1
New York, NY 10007-3132, USA

Jenkins, MarTay (Athlete, Football Player)
4558 N 153rd Ln
Goodyear, AZ 85395-6303, USA

Jenkins, Patty (Director, Writer)
c/o Michael Sugar *Anonymous Content (LA)*
3532 Hayden Ave
Culver City, CA 90232-2413, USA

Jenkins, Richard (Actor)
c/o Rhonda Price *Gersh (NY)*
41 Madison Ave
New York, NY 10010-2202, USA

Jenkins, Robert (Athlete, Football Player)
2878 Fieldview Ter
San Ramon, CA 94583-1900, USA

Jenkins, Stephan (Music Group, Musician)
c/o Eric Godtland *Eric Godtland Management*
1040 Mariposa St Ste 200
San Francisco, CA 94107-2520, USA

Jenkins, Tom (Athlete, Golfer)
107 Ranch Road 620 S
Lakeway, TX 78734-3942, USA

Jenkins, Walt (Athlete, Football Player)
22570 Thorncliffe St
Southfield, MI 48033-3426, USA

Jenks, Bobby (Athlete, Baseball Player)
8116 E Laurel St
Mesa, AZ 85207-9204, USA

Jenner, Blake (Actor)
c/o David (Dave) Fleming *Mosaic Media Group*
9200 W Sunset Blvd Ste 10
West Hollywood, CA 90069-3608, USA

Jenner, Brody (Reality Star)
6171 Latigo Canyon Rd
Malibu, CA 90265-2820, USA

Jenner, Bruce (Athlete, Decathlon Athlete, Olympic Athlete, Reality Star)
25115 Eldorado Meadow Rd
Hidden Hills, CA 91302-1241, USA

Jenner, Kendall (Model, Reality Star)
25115 Eldorado Meadow Rd
Hidden Hills, CA 91302-1241, USA

Jenner, Kris (Business Person, Reality Star)
25115 Eldorado Meadow Rd
Hidden Hills, CA 91302-1241, USA

Jenner, Kylie (Actor, Model)
c/o Lance Klein *William Morris Endeavor (LA)*
9601 Wilshire Blvd
Beverly Hills, CA 90210-5213, USA

Jenney, Lucinda
1505 10th St
Santa Monica, CA 90401-2805

Jennings, Adam (Athlete, Football Player)
330 Suwanee Ave
Suwanee, GA 30024-6768, USA

Jennings, Brandon (Athlete, Basketball Player)
c/o Bill Duffy *BDA Sports Management (BDA-CA)*
700 Ygnacio Valley Rd Ste 330
Walnut Creek, CA 94596-3838, USA

Jennings, Doug (Athlete, Baseball Player)
PO Box 812692
Boca Raton, FL 33481-2692, USA

Jennings, Doug
Oakland A's
3030 Canterbury Dr
Boca Raton, FL 33434-3348, USA

Jennings, Garth (Director)
c/o Frank Wuliger *Gersh (LA)*
9465 Wilshire Blvd Ste 600
Beverly Hills, CA 90212-2605, USA

Jennings, Grant (Athlete, Hockey Player)
PO Box 190434
Anchorage, AK 99519-0434, USA

Jennings, Greg (Athlete, Football Player)
c/o Eugene Parker *Maximum Sports Management*
6435 W Jefferson Blvd # 197
Fort Wayne, IN 46804-6203, USA

Jennings, Jason (Athlete, Baseball Player)
7978 Stone River Dr
Frisco, TX 75034-7288, USA

Jennings, Jonas (Athlete, Football Player)
123 Davis Rd
Fayetteville, GA 30215-4912, USA

Jennings, Keith (Athlete, Basketball Player)
808 Lakeland Ct
Culpeper, VA 22701-2078, USA

Jennings, Keith (Athlete, Football Player)
119 Axtell Dr
Summerville, SC 29485-3403, USA

Jennings, Ken (Actor)
c/o Staff Member *JEOPARDY!*
10202 Washington Blvd
Culver City, CA 90232-3119

Jennings, Lyfe (Musician)
c/o Staff Member *Sony/RCA Records*
550 Madison Ave Fl 6
New York, NY 10022-3211, USA

Jennings, Lynn (Athlete, Olympic Athlete, Track Athlete)
2124 NW Wilson St
Portland, OR 97210-2316, USA

Jennings, Richard (Athlete, Football Player)
6499 Park Riviera Way
Sacramento, CA 95831-1053, USA

Jennings, Rick (Athlete, Football Player)
442 Sterling Pl Apt 12
Brooklyn, NY 11238-4536, USA

Jennings, Robert B (Doctor)
Duke University
Medical Center
Pathology Dept
Durham, NC 27710-0001, USA

Jennings, Robin (Athlete, Baseball Player)
380 Parkview Dr
Park City, UT 84098-5147, USA

Jennings, Shooter (Musician)
c/o Michael Moses *Baker Winokur Ryder Public Relations (BWR-LA)*
9100 Wilshire Blvd Ste 500
West Tower Suite 500
Beverly Hills, CA 90212-3426, USA

Jennings, Stanford (Athlete, Football Player)
403 G St
Beckley, WV 25801-6613, USA

Jennings, Will (Musician, Songwriter)
c/o Staff Member *Gorfaine/Schwartz Agency Inc*
4111 W Alameda Ave Ste 509
Burbank, CA 91505-4171, USA

Jennings Desmond, Desmond (Athlete, Baseball Player)
2482 Vera Cruz Dr
Birmingham, AL 35235-2233, USA

Jenrette, Richard H (Business Person)
67 E 93rd St
New York, NY 10128-1331, USA

Jenrette, Rita (Writer)
9270 Alden Dr
Beverly Hills, CA 90210, USA

Jens, Salome (Actor)
Badgley Connor Talent
9229 W Sunset Blvd Ste 311
West Hollywood, CA 90069-3403, USA

Jensen, Bob (Athlete, Football Player)
72420 Morningstar Rd
Rancho Mirage, CA 92270-4072, USA

Jensen, Chris (Athlete, Hockey Player)
20310 Enright Way
Farmington, MN 55024-2022, USA

Jensen, David (Athlete, Hockey Player)
65 Cheryl Ln
Holliston, MA 01746-1234, USA

Jensen, Derrick (Athlete, Football Player)
147 Downing St
Panama City Beach, FL 32413-3650, USA

Jensen, Erik (Actor)
2419 Outpost Dr
Los Angeles, CA 90068-2644, USA

Jensen, Flemming (Athlete, Football Player)
9775 S Deer Brook Cir
Sandy, UT 84092-6035, USA

Jensen, Jerry (Athlete, Football Player)
2714 86th St SE
Everett, WA 98208-3548, USA

Jensen, Jim (Athlete, Football Player)
9811 N Oak Knoll Cir
Davie, FL 33324-6406, USA

Jensen, Jim D (Athlete, Football Player)
239 Habitat Cir
Windsor, CO 80550-6197, USA

Jensen, Karen (Actor)
9363 Wilshire Blvd
#212
Beverly Hills, CA 90210, USA

Jensen, Luke (Athlete, Tennis Player)
370 Ferry Lndg
Atlanta, GA 30328-3539, USA

Jensen, Marcus (Athlete, Baseball Player, Olympic Athlete)
19550 N Grayhawk Dr Unit 1134
Scottsdale, AZ 85255-3987, USA

Jensen, Maren (Actor)
Kessler Schneider Co
15260 Ventura Blvd Ste 1040
Sherman Oaks, CA 91403-5345

Jensen, Roger W (Ex-Senator)
3542 Pennyroyal Rd
Port Charlotte, FL 33953-4606, USA

Jensen, Ryan (Athlete, Baseball Player)
13907 Bruyere Ct
San Diego, CA 92129-3127, USA

Jensen, Ryan (Athlete, Football Player)
c/o Michael McCartney *Priority Sports & Entertainment - Chicago*
312 N La Salle
Suite 650
Chicago, IL 60610, USA

Jensen, Steve (Athlete, Hockey Player)
24921 Arena Dr
Deerwood, MN 56444-8780, USA

Jensen Jr, James W (Cinematographer)
28853 Garnet Hill Ct
Agoura Hills, CA 91301-2130, USA

Jent, Chris (Athlete, Basketball Player)
5125 Parkford Cir
Granite Bay, CA 95746-6681, USA

Jeong, Ken (Actor)
c/o Brett Carducci *Sovereign Talent Group*
8421 Wilshire Blvd Ste 200
Beverly Hills, CA 90211-3204, USA

Jeosen, Kevin (Athlete, Baseball Player)
4533 E County Down Dr
Chandler, AZ 85249-7339, USA

Jepsen, Carly Rae (Musician)
c/o Scooter Braun *SB Management*
825 8th Ave Fl 28
New York, NY 10019-7416, USA

Jepsen, Les (Athlete, Basketball Player)
8075 9th Street Way N
Saint Paul, MN 55128-5360, USA

Jepsen, Roger (Politician)
3799 Cadbury Cir Apt 400
Venice, FL 34293-5383, USA

Jeray, Nicole (Athlete, Golfer)
3728 Ridgeland Ave
Berwyn, IL 60402-4020, USA

Jeremiah (Musician)
c/o Staff Member *Siri Music Entertainment*
1324 Lexington Ave
New York, NY 10128-1145, USA

Jeremy, Ron (Actor, Adult Film Star)
c/o Mike Esterman *Esterman.Com, LLC*
Prefers to be contacted via email
Baltimore, MD XXXXX, USA

Jericho, Chris (Athlete, Wrestler)
c/o Michael Braverman *Braverman Bloom Company*
6399 Wilshire Blvd
Los Angeles, CA 90048-5703, USA

Jerkens, H Allen (Horse Racer)
9509 242nd St
Floral Park, NY 11001-3906, USA

Jernigan, Tamara E (Tammy) (Astronaut)
4268 Brindisi Pl
Pleasanton, CA 94566-2238, USA

Jerry, Reichow (Athlete, Football Player)
9 Meredith Dr
Santa Fe, NM 87506, USA

Jervey, Travis (Athlete, Football Player)
22 Sand Dollar Dr
Isle Of Palms, SC 29451-2647, USA

Jerzembeck, Mike (Athlete, Baseball Player)
10625 S Hall Dr
Charlotte, NC 28270-0285, USA

Jessamy, Charles (Athlete, Football Player)
1836 S Shenandoah St
Los Angeles, CA 90035-4327, USA

Jessen, Ruth (Athlete, Golfer)
2823 NE Meadow Pl
Lake Forest Park, WA 98155-5348, USA

Jessie, Tim (Athlete, Football Player)
300 Cherry St Apt 1
Shepherdsville, KY 40165-5971, USA

Jessiman, Hugh (Athlete, Hockey Player)
6008 Highland Dr
Chevy Chase, MD 20815-6612, USA

Jessup, Bill (Athlete, Football Player)
13341 Saint Andrews Dr Unit 137D
Dr Unit 137D
Seal Beach, CA 90740-4139, USA

Jestadt, Garry (Athlete, Baseball Player)
9875 E Larkspur Dr
Scottsdale, AZ 85260-5145, USA

Jester, Virgil (Athlete, Baseball Player)
6784 Benton St
Arvada, CO 80003-4242, USA

Jet (Actor)
c/o Staff Member *Creative Artists Agency (CAA-LA)*
2000 Avenue of the Stars Ste 100
Los Angeles, CA 90067-4705, USA

Jeter, Brad (Race Car Driver)
PO Box 6541
Greenville, SC 29606-6541, USA

Jeter, Derek (Athlete, Baseball Player)
Turn 2 Foundation
215 Park Ave S Ste 1905
Attention: Memorabilia Request
New York, NY 10003-1617, USA

Jeter, Gary (Athlete, Football Player)
3612 Quail Ridge Dr
Plainsboro, NJ 08536-4133, USA

Jeter, Gene (Athlete, Football Player)
2369 Lower Wetumpka Rd
Montgomery, AL 36110-2610, USA

Jeter, John (Athlete, Baseball Player)
113 Bayside Dr
West Monroe, LA 71291-8693, USA

Jeter, Perry (Athlete, Football Player)
772 Lincoln Blvd
Steubenville, OH 43952-3256, USA

Jeter, Shawn (Athlete, Baseball Player)
4287 Walford St
Columbus, OH 43224-2342, USA

Jeter, Tommy (Athlete, Football Player)
2108 Estes Park Rd
Southlake, TX 76092-3835, USA

Jeter, Tony (Athlete, Football Player)
71 S Orange Ave
South Orange, NJ 07079-1715, USA

Jethro Tull (Music Group)
c/o Staff Member *William Morris Endeavor (LA)*
9601 Wilshire Blvd
Beverly Hills, CA 90210-5213, USA

Jetsons (Music Group)
Signature Entertainment
5727 Topanga Canyon Blvd Apt 3
Woodland Hills, CA 91367-4847

Jett, Brent W (Astronaut)
2529 Goldsmith St
Houston, TX 77030-1815, USA

Jett, Jack E (Television Host)
c/o Collin Reno *William Morris Endeavor (LA)*
9601 Wilshire Blvd
Beverly Hills, CA 90210-5213, USA

Jett, James (Athlete, Football Player)
PO Box 430
Kearneysville, WV 25430-0430, USA

Jett, Joan (Musician)
c/o Carianne Laguna Brinkman *Blackheart Records Group*
636 Broadway Ste 1210
New York, NY 10012-2624, USA

Jett, John (Athlete, Football Player)
177 Crowder Point Dr
Reedville, VA 22539-4423, USA

Jetton, Paul (Athlete, Football Player)
70 Breed Rd
Dripping Springs, TX 78620-5466, USA

Jeunet, Jean-Pierre (Director)
International Creative Mgmt
10250 Constellation Blvd Fl 1
Los Angeles, CA 90067-6241, USA

Jewel (Musician, Songwriter)
13741 Farm To Market 914
Stephenville, TX 76401, USA

Jewell, Buddy (Musician)
c/o Staff Member *William Morris Endeavor (Nashville)*
1600 Division St Ste 300
Nashville, TN 37203-2755, USA

Jewett, Bob (Athlete, Football Player)
991 N Shore Dr
Springport, MI 49284-9414, USA

Jewett, Robert (Athlete, Football Player)
991 N Shore Dr
Springport, MI 49284-9414, USA

Jewett, Trent (Athlete, Baseball Player)
330 Sullivan Rd
Glen Morgan, WV 25813-7604, USA

J. Fleischmann, Charles (Congressman, Politician)
511 Cannon Hob
Washington, DC 20515-0607, USA

J. Forbes, Randy (Congressman, Politician)
2438 Rayburn Hob
Washington, DC 20515-3518, USA

J. Heck, Joseph (Congressman, Politician)
132 Cannon Hob
Washington, DC 20515-1006, USA

Jiang, Tian (Musician)
Columbia Artists Mgmt Inc
165 W 57th St
New York, NY 10019-2201, USA

Jiles, Dwayne (Athlete, Football Player)
3712 Churchill Ct
Plano, TX 75075-6119, USA

Jiles, Pam (Athlete, Track Athlete)
2623 Wisteria St
New Orleans, LA 70122-6041

Jiles, Pamela (Pam) (Athlete, Track Athlete)
2623 Wisteria St
New Orleans, LA 70122-6041, USA

Jillette, Penn (Comedian)
7601 W Wigwam Ave
Las Vegas, NV 89113-5409, USA

Jillian, Ann (Actor)
PO Box 57739
Sherman Oaks, CA 91413-2739, USA

Jillson, Jeff (Athlete, Hockey Player)
14 Lincoln Dr
North Smithfield, RI 02896-6955, USA

Jim, Ridlon (Athlete, Football Player)
4468 E Lake Rd
Cazenovia, NY 13035-9214, USA

Jimenez, Joe (Athlete, Golfer)
PO Box 1737
Boerne, TX 78006-6737, USA

Jimenez, Manny (Baseball Player)
Kansas City A's
270 47th St Apt C
San Diego, CA 92102-4874, USA

Jimenez, Miguel Angel (Athlete, Golfer)
Advantage International
1751 Pinnacle Dr Ste 1500
Mc Lean, VA 22102-3833, USA

Jimenez, Ubaldo (Athlete, Baseball Player)
c/o Pat Rooney *SFX Baseball*
400 Skokie Blvd Ste 280
Northbrook, IL 60062-7939, USA

Jimerson, Charlton (Athlete, Baseball Player)
22048 Betlen Way
Castro Valley, CA 94546-6504, USA

Jiminez, Houston (Athlete, Baseball Player)
Asheville Tourists
30 Buchanan Pl
Attn: Coaching Staff
Asheville, NC 28801-4243, USA

Jiminez, Miguel (Athlete, Baseball Player)
128 Post Ave
New York, NY 10034-3432, USA

Jimmy, Deratt
4418 Saddle Run Rd N
Wilson, NC 27896-8406, USA

Jimmy, Keyes (Athlete, Football Player)
5338 Southlake Dr
Milton, FL 32571-7000, USA

Jimmy, Richards (Athlete, Football Player)
733 Vanderbilt Ave
Virginia Beach, VA 23451-3632, USA

Jimmy Eat World (Music Group)
21 W Berridge Ln
Phoenix, AZ 85013-1509, USA

Jimoh, Ade (Athlete, Football Player)
41782 Bristow Manor Dr
Ashburn, VA 20148-8003, USA

Jindal, Bobby (Governor, Politician)
Office of the Governor
PO Box 94004
Baton Rouge, LA 70804-9004, USA

Jindrak, Mark (Wrestler)
2355 Reyer Rd
Auburn, NY 13021

Jinks, Dan (Actor, Producer)
c/o Staff Member *Jinks/Cohen Company*
4000 Warner Blvd Bldg 138
Burbank, CA 91522-0001, USA

Jirsa, Ron (Coach)
University of Georgia
Athletic Dept
Athens, GA 30613, USA

Jirschele, Mike (Athlete, Baseball Player)
186 Robert St
Clintonville, WI 54929-1153, USA

JJ Grey and Mofro (Music Group, Musician)
c/o Jesse Aratow *Madison House Inc.*
4760 Walnut St Ste 106
Boulder, CO 80301-2561, USA

J. Kucinich, Dennis (Congressman, Politician)
2445 Rayburn Hob
Washington, DC 20515-0907, USA

J-Kwon (Musician)
c/o Staff Member *So So Def Recordings Inc*
1350 Spring St NW Ste 750
Atlanta, GA 30309-2870, USA

J. Markey, Edward (Congressman, Politician)
2108 Rayburn Hob
Washington, DC 20515-2107, USA

Joanou, Phil (Actor, Director)
c/o Todd Smith *Todd Smith and Associates*
11835 W Olympic Blvd Ste 640E
Los Angeles, CA 90064-5000, USA

Job, Brian (Swimmer)
PO Box 213
Palo Alto, CA 94302-0213, USA

Jobe, Brandt (Athlete, Golfer)
1077 Harpole Rd E
Argyle, TX 76226-4005, USA

Jobko, William (Athlete, Football Player)
770 Fawn Ct
Loganville, GA 30052-3270, USA

Jobrani, Maz (Actor)
c/o Ray Moheet *Levity Entertainment Group (LEG)*
8675 Washington Blvd Ste 203
Culver City, CA 90232-7486, USA

Joc, Yung (Musician)
100 Rock Creek Trl
Fayetteville, GA 30214-5355, USA

Jochum, Betsy (Athlete, Baseball Player, Commentator)
22997 Brick Rd
South Bend, IN 46628-9719, USA

Jocketty, Walt (Commentator)
520 N and South Rd # AQT304
Saint Louis, MO 63130-3826, USA

Jodat, Jim (Athlete, Football Player)
25032 Mammoth Cir
Lake Forest, CA 92630-2515, USA

Jodie, Brett (Athlete, Baseball Player)
1359 Corley Mill Rd
Lexington, SC 29072-7635, USA

Jodzio, Rick (Athlete, Hockey Player)
23731 Perth Bay
Dana Point, CA 92629-4203

Joe (Musician)
c/o Staff Member *Jive Records*
550 Madison Ave Fl 6
New York, NY 10022-3211, USA

Joe, Billy (Athlete, Football Player)
3964 Butler Springs Way
Hoover, AL 35226-6234, USA

Joe, Devlin ' (Athlete, Football Player)
3715 Schintzius Rd
Eden, NY 14057-9790, USA

Joe, Leon (Athlete, Football Player)
5250 Grand Ave Ste 14
Gurnee, IL 60031-1877, USA

Joe, Reliford (Athlete, Baseball Player)
Kiwanis Club PO Box 1007 Attn
Presidents Office
Douglas, GA 31534, USA

Joe, William (Billy) (Football Player)
Florida A&M University
Athletic Dept
Tallahassee, FL 32307-0001, USA

Joeckel, Luke (Athlete, Football Player)
c/o Ben Dogra *CAA (St. Louis)*
222 S Central Ave Ste 1008
Saint Louis, MO 63105-3509, USA

Joel, Alexa Ray (Musician)
c/o Staff Member *Artist Group International (NY)*
150 E 58th St Fl 19
New York, NY 10155-1900, USA

Joel, Billy (Musician, Songwriter)
211 Elizabeth St Apt 3N
New York, NY 10012-4290, USA

Joel, Katie Lee (Actor)
c/o Jonathan Rosen *William Morris Endeavor (NY)*
1325 Avenue of the Americas
New York, NY 10019-6026, USA

Joel, Phil (Musician)
245 4th Ave S
Franklin, TN 37064-2623, USA

Joel, Piñeiro (Athlete, Baseball Player)
3410 Poinciana Ave
Miami, FL 33133-6525, USA

Joelson, Tsianina (Actor)
c/o Sherry Marsh *Marsh Entertainment*
12444 Ventura Blvd Ste 203
Studio City, CA 91604-2409, USA

Joens, Michael (Writer)
c/o Natasha Kern *Natasha Kern Literary Agency*
PO Box 1069
White Salmon, WA 98672-1069, USA

Joerger, David (Athlete, Basketball Coach, Basketball Player, Coach)
c/o Warren LeGarie *Warren LeGarie Sports Management*
1108 Masonic Ave
San Francisco, CA 94117-2915, USA

Joffee, Roland V (Director, Producer)
c/o Craig Baumgarten *Baumgarten Management*
1447 Cloverfield Blvd Ste 101
Santa Monica, CA 90404-2979, USA

Jogia, Avan (Actor)
c/o Ben Levine *LINK Entertainment*
11872 La Grange Ave
Los Angeles, CA 90025-5282, USA

Jogis, Chris (Athlete)
7 Birch Rd
Larchmont, NY 10538-1526

Johannesen, Glenn (Athlete, Hockey Player)
10 Granby Ct
Derwood, MD 20855-1406, USA

Johannesen, Lena (Athlete)
PO Box 325
Culver City, CA 90232-0325

Johanns, Michael (Politician)
6320 Washington Blvd
Arlington, VA 22205-1906, USA

Johannsen, Jake (Actor, Comedian)
c/o Pam Ellis *Ellis Talent Group*
4705 Laurel Canyon Blvd Ste 300
Valley Village, CA 91607-5901, USA

Johannson, John (Athlete, Hockey Player)
3408 Zenith Ave S
Minneapolis, MN 55416-4622, USA

Johansen, David (Musician)
c/o Nina Nisenholtz *N2N Entertainment*
1230 Montana Ave Ste 203
Santa Monica, CA 90403-5987, USA

Johansen, Iris (Writer)
c/o Author Mail *Bantam-Dell Publishing (NY)*
1745 Broadway
New York, NY 10019-4640, USA

Johansen, Trevor (Athlete, Hockey Player)
6741 N Placita Acebo
Tucson, AZ 85750-1049, USA

Johanssen, David
9200 W Sunset Blvd Ste 900
West Hollywood, CA 90069-3604

Johansson, Calle (Athlete, Hockey Player)
1708 Mayfair Pl
Crofton, MD 21114-2625, USA

Johansson, Ove (Athlete, Football Player)
3511 Goodfellow Ln
Amarillo, TX 79121-1613, USA

Johansson, Paul (Actor)
c/o Gordon Gilbertson *Gilbertson Management*
1334 3rd Street Promenade Ste 201
Santa Monica, CA 90401-1320, USA

Johansson, Per-Ulrik (Athlete, Golfer)
19489 Harbor Rd S
Jupiter, FL 33469-2345, USA

Johansson, Scarlett (Actor)
411 E 53rd St # Phd
New York, NY 10022-5106, USA

Johjima, Kenji (Athlete, Baseball Player)
2412 109th Ave SE
Bellevue, WA 98004-7332, USA

John, Charles (Politician)
131 S Walnut St
Starke, FL 32091-3954, USA

John, Daymond (Business Person, Designer, Reality Star)
FUBU
350 5th Ave Ste 6617
New York, NY 10118-6698, USA

John, Gottfried (Actor)
Elisabethweg 4
Utting, GE D-869

John, John (Politician)
95 Hill Top Dr
East Greenwich, RI 02818-4024, USA

John, Rienstra (Athlete, Football Player)
5056 Briscoglen Dr
Colorado Springs, CO 80906-8612, USA

John, Tommy (Athlete, Baseball Player)
13014 W Palermo Ct
Fort Mill, SC 29707-6485, USA

John, Tylyn (Model)
813 Harbor Blvd # 133
W Sacramento, CA 95691-2201

Johncock, Gordon (Race Car Driver)
8740 Wickert Rd
South Branch, MI 48761-9626, USA

Johnny & The Hurricanes
195 Hannum Ave
Rossford, OH 43460-1109

Johns, Cindy (Actor)
PO Box 369
Arlington, TX 76004-0369

Johns, Doug (Athlete, Baseball Player)
1131 SW 72nd Ave
Plantation, FL 33317-4125, USA

Johns, Freeman (Athlete, Football Player)
906 Sally Cir
Wichita Falls, TX 76301-7230, USA

Johns, Geoff (Producer)
c/o Staff Member *DC Entertainment*
1700 Broadway Frnt 7
New York, NY 10019-5934, USA

Johns, Glynis (Actor)
c/o Staff Member *Marshak/Zachary Company, The*
8840 Wilshire Blvd Fl 1
Beverly Hills, CA 90211-2606, USA

Johns, Keith (Athlete, Baseball Player)
Arkansas Travelers
PO Box 55066
Attn: Coaching Staff
Little Rock, AR 72215-5066, USA

Johns, Lori (Race Car Driver)
PO Box 3667
Corpus Christi, TX 78463-3667, USA

Johns, Marcus (Actor)
c/o Sharon Lane *Lane Management Group*
13017 Woodbridge St
Studio City, CA 91604-1431, USA

Johnson, Aaron (Athlete, Hockey Player)
3810 Gabrielle Dr
Dublin, OH 43016-7281, USA

Johnson, Aaron Perry (Actor)
c/o Cynthia Pett-Dante *Brillstein Entertainment Partners (LA)*
9150 Wilshire Blvd Ste 350
Beverly Hills, CA 90212-3453, USA

Johnson, Abigail (Business Person)
Fidelity Investments
82 Devonshire St # V8C
Boston, MA 02109-3605, USA

Johnson, Adam (Athlete, Baseball Player)
12150 Palomino Ln
Fort Myers, FL 33912-1459, USA

Johnson, Addison (Cartoonist)
c/o Staff Member *King Features Syndication*
300 W 57th St Fl 15
New York, NY 10019-5238, USA

Johnson, Adrian (Athlete, Baseball Player)
8102 Meadville St
Houston, TX 77061-3111, USA

Johnson, Albert (Athlete, Football Player)
3516 Dappled Ridge Way
Pearland, TX 77581-7566, USA

Johnson, Alex (Athlete, Baseball Player)
18425 Bretton Dr
Detroit, MI 48223-1311, USA

Johnson, Alexz (Actor)
c/o Staff Member *William Morris Endeavor (LA)*
9601 Wilshire Blvd Ste 755
Beverly Hills, CA 90210-5227, USA

Johnson, Allen (Athlete, Track Athlete)
Octagon
7950 Jones Branch Dr
Mc Lean, VA 22102-3302, USA

Johnson, Allen (Race Car Driver)
PO Box 926
Greeneville, TN 37744-0926, USA

Johnson, Alonzo (Athlete, Football Player)
PO Box 134
Stanley, NC 28164-0134, USA

Johnson, Amy Jo (Actor)
c/o Joanna (Joanie) Burstein *Burstein Company, The*
15304 W Sunset Blvd Ste 208
Pacific Palisades, CA 90272-3656, USA

Johnson, Andre (Athlete, Football Player)
c/o Kennard McGuire *MS World LLC*
1270 Crabb River Rd Ste 600-104
Richmond, TX 77469-5636, USA

Johnson, Andrew (Athlete, Basketball Player)
1101 Oak Cir
Lansdale, PA 19446-6057, USA

Johnson, Andy (Athlete, Football Player)
PO Box 6828
Athens, GA 30604-6828, USA

Johnson, Anjelah (Actor)
c/o Dave Rath *Generate Management*
8750 Wilshire Blvd Ste 200
Beverly Hills, CA 90211-2707, USA

Johnson, Anne-Marie (Actor)
2522 Silver Lake Ter
Los Angeles, CA 90039-2608, USA

Johnson, Anthony (Athlete, Basketball
Player)
5162 Inwood Pl
Mableton, GA 30126-7612, USA

Johnson, Anthony (Athlete, Football
Player)
534 Magnolia Ave
Saint Johns, FL 32259-9018, USA

Johnson, Arte (Actor, Comedian)
2725 Bottlebrush Dr
Los Angeles, CA 90077-2009, USA

Johnson, Ashley (Actor)
c/o Doreen Wilcox Little *Anonymous
Content (LA)*
3532 Hayden Ave
Culver City, CA 90232-2413, USA

Johnson, Avery (Athlete, Basketball
Coach, Basketball Player, Coach)
5101 Meadowside Ln
Plano, TX 75093-5716

Johnson, Barry (Athlete, Football Player)
1103 Northwind Dr
Reston, VA 20194-1009, USA

Johnson, Bart (Actor)
c/o Matt Luber *Luber Roklin Management*
5815 W Sunset Blvd Ste 206
Los Angeles, CA 90028-6481, USA

Johnson, Bart (Athlete, Baseball Player)
1929 N Newland Ave
Chicago, IL 60707-3308, USA

Johnson, Batsey L (Designer, Fashion
Designer)
Betsey Johnson Co
127 E 9th St Ste 703
Los Angeles, CA 90015-1737, USA

Johnson, Ben (Athlete, Baseball Player)
112 Locksley Dr
Greenwood, SC 29649-9185, USA

Johnson, Bethel (Athlete, Football Player)
1000 Crystal Oak Ln
Arlington, TX 76005-4544, USA

Johnson, Betsey (Designer, Fashion
Designer)
7365 Main St # 204
Stratford, CT 06614-1300, USA

Johnson, Beverly (Actor, Model)
PO Box 1474
Rancho Mirage, CA 92270-1052, USA

Johnson, Bill (Athlete, Baseball Player)
1627 Brady Creek Ln
Richmond, TX 77406-8266, USA

Johnson, Bill (Congressman, Politician)
317 Cannon Hob
Washington, DC 20515-3602, USA

Johnson, Bill (Actor)
c/o Mike Pruitt *Actors Clearinghouse*
501 N 1H35
Austin, TX 78702, USA

Johnson, Bob (Athlete, Football Player)
2 Albion Ln
Cincinnati, OH 45246-4702, USA

Johnson, Bob (Athlete, Hockey Player)
32361 Hearthstone Rd
Farmington Hills, MI 48334-3438

Johnson, Bob D (Athlete, Baseball Player)
650 Caves Hwy
Cave Junction, OR 97523-9820, USA

Johnson, Bob W (Athlete, Baseball Player)
1474 Barclay St
Saint Paul, MN 55106-1406, USA

Johnson, Brad (Athlete, Football Player)
1911 Nellie Gray Ct
Athens, GA 30606-8605, USA

Johnson, Brandon (Athlete, Football
Player)
1541 W Coquina Dr
Gilbert, AZ 85233-7007, USA

Johnson, Brent (Athlete, Hockey Player)
207 Lynhurst Dr
Pittsburgh, PA 15237-1268, USA

Johnson, Brian (Athlete, Baseball Player)
17477 Plaza Del Curtidor Unit 198
San Diego, CA 92128-2274, USA

Johnson, Brian (Musician)
c/o Christopher Dalston *Creative Artists
Agency (CAA-LA)*
2000 Avenue of the Stars Ste 100
Los Angeles, CA 90067-4705, USA

Johnson, Brooks (Coach)
Stanford University
Athletic Dept
Stanford, CA 94305, USA

Johnson, Bryant (Athlete, Football Player)
2963 Springbluff Ln
Buford, GA 30519-4195, USA

Johnson, Bryce (Actor)
c/o Staff Member *Artists Production
Group (APG)*
9348 Civic Center Dr Fl 2
Beverly Hills, CA 90210-3610, USA

Johnson, Buck (Athlete, Basketball Player)
822 Lake Heather Reserve
Birmingham, AL 35242-7614, USA

Johnson, Butch (Athlete, Football Player)
9719 Red Oakes Dr
Highlands Ranch, CO 80126-3595, USA

Johnson, Calvin (Athlete, Football Player)
c/o Bus Cook *Bus Cook Sports, Inc*
1 Willow Bend Dr
Hattiesburg, MS 39402-8552, USA

Johnson, Cam (Athlete, Football Player)
c/o Adisa P. Bakari *Dow Lohnes PLLC*
1299 Pennsylvania Ave NW Ste 700
Washington, DC 20004-2431, USA

Johnson, Carl (Athlete, Football Player)
3420 S Camellia Pl
Chandler, AZ 85248-3866, USA

Johnson, Carolyn Dawn (Musician,
Songwriter)
c/o Staff Member *Creative Artists Agency
(CAA-TN)*
401 Commerce St PH
Nashville, TN 37219-2516, USA

Johnson, Cassie (Athlete, Olympic
Athlete)
412 Birchwood Ct
Saint Paul, MN 55110-1805, USA

Johnson, Cecil (Athlete, Football Player)
1481 NW 103rd St Apt 260
Miami, FL 33147-1409, USA

Johnson, Chad (Athlete, Football Player)
2899 Juniper Ln
Davie, FL 33330-1349, USA

Johnson, Charles (Athlete, Baseball
Player, Olympic Athlete)
12301 NW 7th St
Plantation, FL 33325-1729, USA

Johnson, Charles L (Charley) (Athlete,
Football Player)
c/o Drew Rosenhaus *Rosenhaus Sports
Representation*
6400 Allison Rd
Miami Beach, FL 33141-4540, USA

Johnson, Charles R (Writer)
University of Washington
English Dept
Seattle, WA 98105, USA

Johnson, Charlie W (Athlete, Football
Player)
1400 Willow Ave
Louisville, KY 40204-2506, USA

Johnson, Chris (Actor)
c/o Staff Member *Luber Roklin
Management*
5815 W Sunset Blvd Ste 206
Los Angeles, CA 90028-6481, USA

Johnson, Chris (Athlete, Football Player)
c/o Denise White *EAG Sports
Management*
909 N Sepulveda Blvd Ste 360
El Segundo, CA 90245-3864, USA

Johnson, Chris (Athlete, Golfer)
6210 W Sunset Rd
Tucson, AZ 85743-9581, USA

Johnson, Chuck (Athlete, Football Player)
1203 N Avenue M
Freeport, TX 77541-3611, USA

Johnson, Clark
9560 Wilshire Blvd # 516
Beverly Hills, CA 90212-2427

Johnson, Clay (Athlete, Basketball Player)
9414 NW 86th Ter
Kansas City, MO 64153-1491, USA

Johnson, Clemon (Athlete, Basketball
Player)
3169 Dunbar Ln
Tallahassee, FL 32311-3363, USA

Johnson, Cliff (Athlete, Baseball Player)
9502 Fisherman Prt
Converse, TX 78109-1951, USA

Johnson, Cornelius (Athlete, Football
Player)
603 Dale St
Henrico, VA 23075-1611, USA

Johnson, Craig (Athlete, Hockey Player)
26 Golden Eagle
Irvine, CA 92603-0309, USA

Johnson, Curley (Athlete, Football Player)
5512 Wedgefield Rd
Granbury, TX 76049-4411, USA

Johnson, Curt (Producer, Writer)
c/o Evan Corday *Evolution Entertainment
(LA)*
901 N Highland Ave
Los Angeles, CA 90038-2412, USA

Johnson, Curtis (Athlete, Football Player)
PO Box 70608
Toledo, OH 43607-0608, USA

Johnson, Curtis (Baseball Player)
Kansas City Monarchs
PO Box B-188
Saint Rose, LA 70087, USA

Johnson, Dakota (Actor)
c/o Justin Grey Stone *Management 360*
9111 Wilshire Blvd
Beverly Hills, CA 90210-5508, USA

Johnson, Dane (Athlete, Baseball Player)
2652 Big Pine Dr
Holiday, FL 34691-8761, USA

Johnson, Darius (Athlete, Football Player)
c/o Kennard McGuire *MS World LLC*
1270 Crabb River Rd Ste 600-104
Richmond, TX 77469-5636, USA

Johnson, Darrius (Athlete, Football Player)
402 Thomas St
Terrell, TX 75160-3832, USA

Johnson, Dave (Athlete, Baseball Player)
7101 Mount Vista Rd
Kingsville, MD 21087-1728, USA

Johnson, Dave (Athlete, Baseball Player)
3202 Woodhollow Cir
Abilene, TX 79606-4211, USA

Johnson, Davey (Athlete, Baseball Player,
Coach)
1064 Howell Branch Rd
Winter Park, FL 32789-1004, USA

Johnson, David (Dave) (Athlete, Track
Athlete)
Azusa Pacific University
PO Box 2713
Azusa, CA 91702, USA

Johnson, David W (Business Person)
Campbell Soup Co
1 Campbell Pl
Camden, NJ 08103-1799, USA

Johnson, Demetrios (Athlete, Football
Player)
840 Garonne Dr
Ballwin, MO 63021-5656, USA

Johnson, Dennis (Athlete, Football Player)
PO Box 467
Hawthorne, NJ 07507-0467, USA

Johnson, DerMarr (Basketball Player)
Phoenix Suns
14610 Man 0 War Dr
Bowie, MD 20721, USA

Johnson, Derrick (Athlete, Football Player)
c/o W Vann McElroy *Select Sports Group*
2700 Post Oak Blvd Ste 1450
Houston, TX 77056-5785, USA

Johnson, Dick (Athlete, Baseball Player)
5001 E Main St Lot 762
Mesa, AZ 85205-8172, USA

Johnson, D J (Athlete, Football Player)
3814 Kingsbury Dr
Louisville, KY 40207-4443, USA

Johnson, Don (Athlete, Baseball Player)
1020 NW 9th Ave Apt 903
Portland, OR 97209-3490, USA

Johnson, Don (Actor)
Don Johnson Productions
9633 Santa Monica Blvd Ste 278
Beverly Hills, CA 90210-4401, USA

Johnson, Don (Athlete, Baseball Player)
3935 King Pl
Cincinnati, OH 45223, USA

Johnson, Donnell (Athlete, Football Player)
1792 Temple Ave Apt 1
Atlanta, GA 30337-2723, USA

Johnson, Dwayne (The Rock) (Actor, Athlete, Football Player)
c/o Stephanie Jones *JONESWORKS Inc*
211 E 43rd St Rm 1501
New York, NY 10017-4715, USA

Johnson, Dwight (Athlete, Football Player)
1812 King Cole Dr
Waco, TX 76705-2753, USA

Johnson, Earl (Athlete, Football Player)
340 S Keech St
Daytona Beach, FL 32114-4622, USA

Johnson, Ed (Athlete, Basketball Player)
196 Adobe Ln
Mount Airy, NC 27030-5658, USA

Johnson, Eddie (Athlete, Basketball Player)
Santa Rosa Correctional Institution
5850 E Milton Rd
Milton, FL 32583-7914, USA

Johnson, Elliot (Athlete, Baseball Player)
11 Pee Ram Ct
Durham, NC 27703, USA

Johnson, Eric (Actor)
c/o Jai Khanna *Brillstein Entertainment Partners (LA)*
9150 Wilshire Blvd Ste 350
Beverly Hills, CA 90212-3453, USA

Johnson, Eric (Athlete, Golfer)
893 Chateau Meadows Dr
Eugene, OR 97401-7046, USA

Johnson, Eric (Musician)
Joe Priesnitz Artist Mgmt
PO Box 5249
Austin, TX 78763-5249, USA

Johnson, Erik (Athlete, Baseball Player)
155 Carondelet Plz
#505
San Ramon, CA 94583, USA

Johnson, Ernest
3106 Bowdoin St
Des Moines, IA 50313-4613, USA

Johnson, Ervin (Basketball Player)
Minnesota Timberwolves
8324 Harbortown Pl
Lone Tree, CO 80124-9775, USA

Johnson, Essex (Athlete, Football Player)
1633 E Dimondale Dr
Carson, CA 90746-2914, USA

Johnson, Ezra (Athlete, Football Player)
330 Millhaven Lndg
Fayetteville, GA 30215-8179, USA

Johnson, Footer (Athlete, Baseball Player)
5001 E Main St
Mesa, AZ 85205-8008, USA

Johnson, Frank (Athlete, Baseball Player)
1151 Cypress Hill Ln
Stockton, CA 95206-6245, USA

Johnson, Frank (Athlete, Basketball Player, Coach)
4320 N 40th St
Phoenix, AZ 85018-4105, USA

Johnson, Gary (Athlete, Baseball Player)
50 Tallwood Ct
Atherton, CA 94027-6432, USA

Johnson, Gary E. (Ex-Governor, Politician)
Students For Sensible Drug Policy
1623 Connecticut Ave NW Fl 3
Washington, DC 20009-1098, USA

Johnson, Gary L (Athlete, Football Player)
450 Oliver Rd
Haughton, LA 71037-8942, USA

Johnson, Georgann (Actor)
218 Glenroy Pl
Los Angeles, CA 90049-2420, USA

Johnson, George (Athlete, Football Player)
c/o Brian Levy *Goal Line Football Management*
1025 Kane Concourse Ste 207
Bay Harbor Islands, FL 33154-2118, USA

Johnson, George (Athlete, Golfer)
285 Monarch Village Way
Stockbridge, GA 30281-7764, USA

Johnson, George T (Athlete, Basketball Player)
630 Highland Overlook
Atlanta, GA 30349-3919, USA

Johnson, Greg (Athlete, Hockey Player)
1058 Runyon Rd
Rochester Hills, MI 48306-4522, USA

Johnson, Gregory (Astronaut)
134 NASA Research Center
2100 Brookpark Rd
Attn: Chief - External Programs Division
Cleveland, OH 44134, USA

Johnson, Hailey Noelle (Actor)
c/o Staff Member *TalentWorks (LA)*
3500 W Olive Ave Ste 1400
Burbank, CA 91505-5512, USA

Johnson, Harold (Boxer)
6101 Morris St
Philadelphia, PA 19144-3763, USA

Johnson, Haylie (Actor)
c/o Lin Bickelmann *Encore Artists Management*
3815 W Olive Ave Ste 101
Burbank, CA 91505-4674, USA

Johnson, Holly (Musician)
Lustig Talent
PO Box 770850
Orlando, FL 32877-0850, USA

Johnson, Howard (Athlete, Baseball Player)
8597 SE Coconut St
Hobe Sound, FL 33455-2914, USA

Johnson, Ian (Journalist)
Wall Street Journal
200 Liberty St
Editorial Dept
New York, NY 10281-1003, USA

Johnson, Jack (Athlete, Hockey Player)
48 Malaga Way
Manhattan Beach, CA 90266-7201, USA

Johnson, Jack (Musician)
59-524 Opae Rd
Haleiwa, HI 96712-8646, USA

Johnson, Jake (Actor, Comedian)
c/o Greg Walter *3 Arts Entertainment (LA)*
9460 Wilshire Blvd Fl 7
Beverly Hills, CA 90212-2713, USA

Johnson, James-Michael (Athlete, Football Player)
c/o Scott Smith *XAM Sports*
PO Box 1725
Madison, WI 53701-1725, USA

Johnson, Jamey (Musician)
c/o Staff Member *Webster & Associates PR*
3573 Couchville Pike
Hermitage, TN 37076-4012, USA

Johnson, Jannette (Skier)
PO Box 901
Sun Valley, ID 83353-0901, USA

Johnson, Jarit (Race Car Driver)
1533 Fair Valley Rd
El Cajon, CA 92019-3710, USA

Johnson, Jarret (Athlete, Football Player)
437 Evans Rd
Niceville, FL 32578-4508, USA

Johnson, Jason (Athlete, Football Player)
6821 Eagle Pointe Ln Apt 1F
Indianapolis, IN 46254-4453, USA

Johnson, Jason (Athlete, Baseball Player)
18122 Emerald Bay St
Tampa, FL 33647-3315, USA

Johnson, Jay (Actor, Comedian)
c/o Staff Member *William Morris Endeavor (LA)*
9601 Wilshire Blvd Ste 755
Beverly Hills, CA 90210-5227, USA

Johnson, Jay Kenneth (Actor)
c/o Jeff Morrone *Intellectual Artists Management*
9350 Wilshire Blvd Ste 224
Beverly Hills, CA 90212-3204, USA

Johnson, Jeff (Athlete, Baseball Player)
424 N Hardee St
Durham, NC 27703-2254, USA

Johnson, Jenna (Coach, Swimmer)
University of Tennessee
PO Box 15016
Athletic Dept
Knoxville, TN 37901-5016, USA

Johnson, Jerry (Athlete, Baseball Player)
16670 Espola Rd
Poway, CA 92064-1630, USA

Johnson, Jerry (Athlete, Football Player)
474 SW Meadow Ter
Port Saint Lucie, FL 34984-3545, USA

Johnson, Jesse (Athlete, Football Player)
102 Rosegill Rd
North Chesterfield, VA 23236-2748, USA

Johnson, Jimmie (Race Car Driver)
Jimmie Johnson Fan Club
152 Woodfield Dr
Statesville, NC 28677-2619, USA

Johnson, Jimmy (Cartoonist)
United Feature Syndicate
PO Box 5610
Cincinnati, OH 45201-5610, USA

Johnson, Jimmy (Athlete, Football Coach, Football Player)
656 Amaranth Blvd
Mill Valley, CA 94941-2605, USA

Johnson, J J
648 Broadway Ste 703
New York, NY 10012-2348, USA

Johnson, Joanna (Actor)
c/o Staff Member *William Morris Endeavor (LA)*
9601 Wilshire Blvd Ste 755
Beverly Hills, CA 90210-5227, USA

Johnson, Joe (Athlete, Baseball Player)
14 Evergreen Rd
Plainville, MA 02762-1902, USA

Johnson, Joe (Basketball Player)
c/o Staff Member *Atlanta Hawks*
190 Marietta St NW Ste 405
Atlanta, GA 30303-2717, USA

Johnson, Johari (Actor)
H W A Talent
3500 W Olive Ave Ste 1400
Burbank, CA 91505-5512, USA

Johnson, John (Athlete, Basketball Player)
4751 N 18th St
Milwaukee, WI 53209-6430, USA

Johnson, John (Athlete, Football Player)
133 Plymouth Dr
Lagrange, GA 30240-8537, USA

Johnson, John (Athlete, Golfer)
236 E Hemlock St
Oxnard, CA 93033-3619, USA

Johnson, John Henry (Athlete, Baseball Player)
3345 Delna Dr
Sparks, NV 89431-1408, USA

Johnson, John Henry (Athlete, Baseball Player)
3345 Delna Dr
Sparks, NV 89431-1408, USA

Johnson, Johnny (Athlete, Football Player)
929 Delaware Ave
Santa Cruz, CA 95060-6403, USA

Johnson, Jonathan (Athlete, Baseball Player)
101 Broad Bluff Pt
Irmo, SC 29063-2934, USA

Johnson, Joseph (Athlete, Football Player)
166 Homestead Hills Cir
Winston Salem, NC 27103-6446, USA

Johnson, Junior (Race Car Driver)
3200 Seven Eagles Rd
Charlotte, NC 28210-5938, USA

Johnson, Keith (Athlete, Baseball Player)
PO Box 4122
Park City, UT 84060-4122, USA

Johnson, Kenneth (Athlete, Basketball Player)
1401 N Wheeler Ave
Portland, OR 97227-1831, USA

Johnson, Kenneth (Athlete, Football Player)
1334 NW 42nd St
Miami, FL 33142-4812, USA

Johnson, Kenneth (Athlete, Football Player)
536 E 169th St
Carson, CA 90746-1105, USA

Johnson, Kenny (Actor)
c/o Josh Katz *United Talent Agency (UTA-LA)*
9336 Civic Center Dr
Beverly Hills, CA 90210-3604, USA

Johnson, Kermit (Athlete, Football Player)
518 S El Molino Ave Apt 102
Pasadena, CA 91101-3447, USA

Johnson, Kevin (Baseball Player, Sportscaster)
NBC-TV
30 Rockefeller Plz Lbby 1
Sports Dept
New York, NY 10112-0101, USA

Johnson, Keyshawn (Football Player)
19232 Northfleet Way
Tarzana, CA 91356-5807, USA

Johnson, Kym (Actor)
c/o Siri Garber *Platform Public Relations*
2666 N Beachwood Dr
Los Angeles, CA 90068-2308, USA

Johnson, Lamar (Athlete, Baseball Player)
4105 Sangre Trl
Arlington, TX 76016-2972, USA

Johnson, Lance (Athlete, Baseball Player)
5712 Foxfire Rd
Mobile, AL 36618-2653, USA

Johnson, Landon (Athlete, Football Player)
7556 Fox Chase Dr
West Chester, OH 45069-8685, USA

Johnson, Larry (Athlete, Football Player)
3186 McCutcheon Pl
Columbus, OH 43219-3399, USA

Johnson, Larry (Athlete, Baseball Player)
1905 E Jean St
Tampa, FL 33610-3546, USA

Johnson, Larry D (Basketball Player)
c/o Staff Member *Kansas City Chiefs*
1 Arrowhead Dr
Kansas City, MO 64129-1651, USA

Johnson, Laura
905 Drown Ave
Ojai, CA 93023-1905

Johnson, Lee (Athlete, Football Player)
1173 E McDaniel Cir
Alpine, UT 84004-1231, USA

Johnson, Leon (Athlete, Football Player)
813 Vine Arden Rd
Morganton, NC 28655-2758, USA

Johnson, Leshon (Athlete, Football Player)
15102 Beverly St
Overland Park, KS 66223-3200, USA

Johnson, Levi (Athlete, Football Player)
1202 Craig Dr
Westland, MI 48186-5504, USA

Johnson, Lonnie (Athlete, Football Player)
8500 Amber Ridge Ct
Sanford, FL 32771-8325, USA

Johnson, Lou (Athlete, Baseball Player)
4532 Valley Ridge Ave
View Park, CA 90008-4827, USA

Johnson, Luther (Guitar Jr) (Musician)
c/o Staff Member *Concerted Efforts*
PO Box 440326
Somerville, MA 02144-0004, USA

Johnson, Lynn-Holly (Actor)
Cavaleri
3500 W Olive Ave Ste 300
Burbank, CA 91505-4647, USA

Johnson, Magic (Athlete, Basketball
Player, Olympic Athlete)
12 Beverly Park
Beverly Hills, CA 90210-1540, USA

Johnson, Mamie ""Peanut"" (Athlete,
Baseball Player)
623 14th St NE
Washington, DC 20002-5413, USA

Johnson, Manny (Athlete, Football Player)
c/o Chad Speck *Allegiant Athletic Agency*
35 Market Sq Ste 201
Knoxville, TN 37902-1420, USA

Johnson, Marc (Musician)
A Train Mgmt
PO Box 29242
Oakland, CA 94604-9242, USA

Johnson, Margaret (Athlete, Baseball
Player)
825 Country Club Dr SE Apt 1D
Rio Rancho, NM 87124-2265, USA

Johnson, Mark (Athlete, Baseball Player)
109 Mossy Lake Rd
Perry, GA 31069-9217, USA

Johnson, Mark (Athlete, Baseball Player)
40 Helen Ave
Rye, NY 10580-2447, USA

Johnson, Mark (Athlete, Golfer)
PO Box 2945
Soldotna, AK 99669-2945, USA

Johnson, Mark (Athlete, Hockey Player)
1609 Hidden Hill Dr
Verona, WI 53593-7971, USA

Johnson, Mark (Boxer)
1204 Howison Pl SW
Washington, DC 20024-4132, USA

Johnson, Mark Steven (Director, Writer)
c/o Eddie Michaels *Insignia Public
Relations*
1507 20th St Ste B
Santa Monica, CA 90404-3474, USA

Johnson, Marques (Athlete, Basketball
Player)
5133 Dawn View Pl
Windsor Hills, CA 90043-2006, USA

Johnson, Marvin (Boxer)
5452 Turfway Cir
Indianapolis, IN 46228-2094, USA

Johnson, Maurice (Athlete, Football
Player)
112 Mountainview Rd
Mount Laurel, NJ 08054-4729, USA

Johnson, Michael (Athlete, Track Athlete)
87 Brodea Way
San Rafael, CA 94901-2309, USA

Johnson, Michael (Musician)
Buddy Lee
38 Music Sq E Ste 300
Nashville, TN 37203-4304, USA

Johnson, Mickey (Athlete, Basketball
Player)
3642 W Grenshaw St
Chicago, IL 60624-4207, USA

Johnson, Mike (Athlete, Baseball Player)
124 Isle Verde Way
Palm Beach Gardens, FL 33418-1708,
USA

Johnson, Mike (Athlete, Baseball Player)
20251 State Highway 34
Pelican Rapids, MN 56572-7005, USA

Johnson, Mike (Athlete, Football Player)
c/o Pat Dye Jr *SportsTrust Advisors (GA)*
3340 Peachtree Rd NE Fl 16
Atlanta, GA 30326-1000, USA

Johnson, Mitchell (Athlete, Football
Player)
2764 Unicorn Ln NW
Washington, DC 20015-2234, USA

Johnson, Monica (Writer)
Innovative Artists
1505 10th St
Santa Monica, CA 90401-2805, USA

Johnson, Monte (Athlete, Football Player)
2349 Hurst Dr NE
Atlanta, GA 30305-4232, USA

Johnson, Neil (Athlete, Basketball Player)
821 Plymouth Ln
Virginia Beach, VA 23451-5926, USA

Johnson, Nelson (Writer)
c/o Staff Member *Plexus Publishing, Inc*
143 Old Marlton Pike
Medford, NJ 08055-8750, USA

Johnson, Nic (Race Car Driver)
PTG Racing
441 Victory Rd
Winchester, VA 22602-4567, USA

Johnson, Nick (Athlete, Baseball Player)
8008 Sacramento St
Fair Oaks, CA 95628-7527, USA

Johnson, Norm (Athlete, Football Player)
400 Peachtree Industrial Blvd Apt 1615
Suwanee, GA 30024-6989, USA

Johnson, Norm (Athlete, Hockey Player)
16427 NE Tillamook St
Portland, OR 97230-5534, USA

Johnson, Norm (Athlete, Football Player)
8523 NW Anderson Hill Rd
Silverdale, WA 98383-9353, USA

Johnson, Norman (Musician)
Paramount Entertainment
PO Box 12
Far Hills, NJ 07931-0012, USA

Johnson, Ollie (Athlete, Basketball Player)
15 Shelburne St
Burlington, NJ 08016-4308, USA

Johnson, Ora J (Religious Leader)
General Assn of General Baptists
100 Stinson Dr
Poplar Bluff, MO 63901-8746, USA

Johnson, Paul (Athlete, Hockey Player,
Olympic Athlete)
6373 296th St E
Cannon Falls, MN 55009-9205, USA

Johnson, Paul (Football Coach)
Georgia Tech Athletic Association
150 Bobby Dodd Way NW
Atlanta, GA 30332-2501, USA

Johnson, Penny (Actor)
c/o Mitchell Stubbs *Mitchell K Stubbs &
Assoc (MKS)*
8675 Washington Blvd Ste 203
Culver City, CA 90232-7486, USA

Johnson, Pepper (Athlete, Football Player)
PO Box 1133
Russells Point, OH 43348-1133, USA

Johnson, Pete (Athlete, Football Player)
6304 Misty Cove Ln # in
Columbus, OH 43231-1689, USA

Johnson, Rafer L (Actor, Athlete,
Decathlon Athlete)
4217 Woodcliff Rd
Sherman Oaks, CA 91403-4339, USA

Johnson, Ralph (Athlete, Baseball Player)
PO Box 891262
Tampa, FL 33689-1100, USA

Johnson, Randy (Athlete, Baseball Player)
13509 Sundance Rd
Valley Center, CA 92082-4157, USA

Johnson, Rashad (Athlete, Football Player)
c/o Joel Segal *Lagardere Unlimited (NYC)*
845 United Nations Plz
New York, NY 10017-3540, USA

Johnson, Raylee (Athlete, Football Player)
2010 Black Fox Dr NE
Atlanta, GA 30345-4123, USA

Johnson, Raymond Edward
167 Grieb Rd
Wallingford, CT 06492-2511

Johnson, Ray William (Actor)
c/o David (Dave) Becky *3 Arts
Entertainment (LA)*
9460 Wilshire Blvd Fl 7
Beverly Hills, CA 90212-2713, USA

Johnson, Reed (Athlete, Baseball Player)
30137 Mira Loma Dr
Temecula, CA 92592-2127, USA

Johnson, Reggie (Athlete, Football Player)
17907 Souter Ln
Land O Lakes, FL 34638-7887, USA

Johnson, Rian (Director, Writer)
c/o Brian Dreyfuss *Featured Artists
Agency*
1880 Century Park E Ste 1402
Los Angeles, CA 90067-1630, USA

Johnson, Rob (Athlete, Football Player)
26635 Aracena Dr
Mission Viejo, CA 92691-5105, USA

Johnson, Robert (Business Person)
c/o Staff Member *BET - Black
EntertainmentTelevision (DC)*
1235 W St NE
One Bet Plaza
Washington, DC 20018-1211, USA

Johnson, Robert L (Business Person)
Black Entertainment TV
1900 W Pl NE
Washington, DC 20018-1230, USA

Johnson, Ron (Athlete, Baseball Player)
428 S Maie Ave
Compton, CA 90220-2805, USA

Johnson, Ronald A (Ron) (Athlete,
Football Player)
226 Summit Ave
Summit, NJ 07901-2202, USA

Johnson, Rondin (Athlete, Baseball Player)
1025 S 324th Pl
Federal Way, WA 98003-5930, USA

Johnson, Rontrez (Athlete, Baseball
Player)
1426 NE 18th Pl
Cape Coral, FL 33909-1612, USA

Johnson, Russ (Athlete, Baseball Player,
Olympic Athlete)
3542 Russell Rd
Green Cove Springs, FL 32043-9498, USA

Johnson, Sam (Congressman, Politician)
1211 Longworth Hob
Washington, DC 20515-4303, USA

Johnson, Sammy (Athlete, Football Player)
142 Old Mill Rd Apt B
High Point, NC 27265-1283, USA

Johnson, Scarlett (Actor)
c/o Duncan Millership *William Morris
Endeavor (LA)*
9601 Wilshire Blvd Ste 755
Beverly Hills, CA 90210-5227, USA

Johnson, Shannon (Basketball Player)
Connecticut Sun
Mohegan Sun Arena
Uncasville, CT 06382, USA

Johnson, Shawn (Athlete, Gymnast,
Olympic Athlete)
Chow's Gymnastics
2210 Chows Olympic Ave
West Des Moines, IA 50265-5809, USA

Johnson, Sheila (Business Person)
Washington Mystics
401 9th St NW
Washington, DC 20004-2128, USA

Johnson, Shelly W (Cinematographer)
970 Jimeno Rd
Santa Barbara, CA 93103-2060, USA

Johnson, Spencer (Writer)
Spencer Johnson Partners
825 N 1420 E
Orem, UT 84097-5484, USA

Johnson, Steffond (Athlete, Basketball Player)
10525 Marsh Ln
Dallas, TX 75229-5142, USA

Johnson, Steve (Athlete, Basketball Player)
9715 SW Quail Post Rd
Portland, OR 97219-6363, USA

Johnson, Steve (Race Car Driver)
3760 Mountain View Ln
Vestavia, AL 35223-2227, USA

Johnson, Syl (Musician, Songwriter, Writer)
Blue Sky Artists
761 Washington Ave N
Minneapolis, MN 55401-1101, USA

Johnson, Ted (Athlete, Football Player)
10 Appletree Ln
Wayland, MA 01778-1314, USA

Johnson, Teyo (Athlete, Football Player)
2222 Oak Rd
Lynnwood, WA 98087-6321, USA

Johnson, Thomas (Athlete, Baseball Player)
1611 Constitution Blvd
Rock Hill, SC 29732-3047, USA

Johnson, Tim (Athlete, Baseball Player, Coach)
2700 Van Dorn St
Lincoln, NE 68502-4256, USA

Johnson, Tim (Athlete, Football Player)
21300 Redskin Park Dr
Ashburn, VA 20147-6100, USA

Johnson, Tim (Athlete, Football Player)
2839 Dorell Ave
Orlando, FL 32814-6757, USA

Johnson, Timothy (Correspondent, Doctor)
c/o Staff Member *Good Morning America (NY)*
147 Columbus Ave Fl 6
Abc
New York, NY 10023-6503, USA

Johnson, Tom (Athlete, Baseball Player)
2700 Knox Ave N
Minneapolis, MN 55411-1246, USA

Johnson, Tre (Athlete, Football Player)
680 Harrison Ave
Peekskill, NY 10566-2219, USA

Johnson, Undra (Athlete, Football Player)
9517 Cost Ave Apt 29
Clarksburg, WV 26301-7803, USA

Johnson, Vance (Athlete, Football Player)
491 28 1/4 Rd Apt 3302
Grand Junction, CO 81501-5117, USA

Johnson, Vaughan (Athlete, Football Player)
4915 Arendell St Apt 253
Morehead City, NC 28557-2659, USA

Johnson, Vaughan M (Athlete, Football Player)
5800 Airline Dr
Metairie, LA 70003-3876, USA

Johnson, Vickie (Basketball Player)
c/o Staff Member *New York Liberty*
125 W End Ave # 6
New York, NY 10023-6387, USA

Johnson, Vinnie (Athlete, Basketball Player)
5236 Elmgate Dr
Orchard Lake, MI 48324-3017, USA

Johnson, Wallace (Athlete, Baseball Player)
PO Box 64618
Gary, IN 46401-0618, USA

Johnson, Warren (Race Car Driver)
WJ Enterprises
700 N Price Rd
Sugar Hill, GA 30518-4724, USA

Johnson, Wendy (Race Car Driver)
126 Red Brook Ln
Mooresville, NC 28117-8801, USA

Johnson, Wesley (Athlete, Basketball Player)
PO Box 195
Onamia, MN 56359-0195, USA

Johnson, William A (Billy White Shoes) (Athlete, Football Player)
3701 Whitney Pl
Duluth, GA 30096-3170, USA

Johnson, William B (Business Person)
Ritz-Carlton Hotels
4445 Willard Ave Ste 800
Chevy Chase, MD 20815-3699, USA

Johnson, William H (Athlete, Football Player)
522 E Pleasant Grove Rd
Montgomery, AL 36105-6110, USA

Johnson, William R (Business Person)
H J Heinz Co
PO Box 57
Pittsburgh, PA 15230-0057, USA

Johnson, William W (Athlete, Football Player)
20 Mohawk Rd
Canton, MA 02021-1254, USA

Johnson, Woody (Business Person, Football Executive)
1195 Lamington Rd
Bedminster, NJ 07921-2764, USA

Johnson, Zach (Athlete, Golfer)
PO Box 2336
Cedar Rapids, IA 52406-2336, USA

Johnson-Goodman, Mamie (Peanut) (Athlete, Baseball Player)
618 Southern Ave SE
Washington, DC 20032-3403, USA

Johnson III, Edward (Business Person)
Fidelity Investments
82 Devonshire St # V8C
Boston, MA 02109-3605, USA

Johnson III, Joseph E (Doctor, Physicist)
Philadelphian
2401 Pennsylvania Ave Apt 15C44
Philadelphia, PA 19130-3050, USA

Johnson Jr, Ernie (Sportscaster)
TNT-TV
1050 Techwood Dr NW
Sports Department
Atlanta, GA 30318-5604, USA

Johnson Jr, G Griffith (Government Official)
300 Locust Ave
Annapolis, MD 21401-3329, USA

Johnson Jr, Johnnie (Athlete, Football Player)
PO Box 114
La Grange, TX 78945-0114, USA

Johnson, Jr., Tommy (Race Car Driver)
493 Southpoint Cir
Brownsburg, IN 46112-2203, USA

Johnson Pucci, Gail (Swimmer)
2132 Ward Dr
Walnut Creek, CA 94596-5731, USA

Johnsson, Kim (Athlete, Hockey Player)
5308 Oaklawn Ave
Minneapolis, MN 55424-1309, USA

Johnston, Bernie (Athlete, Hockey Player)
715 Central Park Blvd
Port Orange, FL 32127-7555, USA

Johnston, Brian (Athlete, Football Player)
236 Hideaway Ln
Mooresville, NC 28117-8402, USA

Johnston, Bruce (Musician)
International Creative Mgmt
10250 Constellation Blvd Fl 1
Los Angeles, CA 90067-6241, USA

Johnston, Daryl (Moose) (Athlete, Football Player)
6427 Meadow Rd
Dallas, TX 75230-5142, USA

Johnston, Ed (Athlete, Hockey Player)
c/o Staff Member *Pittsburgh Penguins*
1001 5th Ave
Pittsburgh, PA 15219-6201, USA

Johnston, Freedy (Musician, Songwriter, Writer)
Morebarn Music
30 Hillcrest Ave
Morristown, NJ 07960-5090, USA

Johnston, George (Athlete, Hockey Player)
15604 N Myrtle St # B
Mead, WA 99021-9544, USA

Johnston, Gerald A (Business Person)
McDonnell Douglas Corp
PO Box 516
Saint Louis, MO 63166-0516, USA

Johnston, Gerald E (Business Person)
Clorox Co
1221 Broadway Fl 13th
Oakland, CA 94612-1888, USA

Johnston, J Bennett (Politician)
1330 Connecticut Ave NW Ste 1C
Washington, DC 20036-1724, USA

Johnston, J Bennett Jr (Ex-Senator)
Johnston Assoc
2099 Pennsylvania Ave NW # 1000
Washington, DC 20006-6800, USA

Johnston, Jimmy (Athlete, Golfer)
Pro's Inc
9 S 12th St Fl 3
Richmond, VA 23219-4032, USA

Johnston, Joe (Director)
c/o David Lubliner *William Morris Endeavor (LA)*
9601 Wilshire Blvd Ste 755
Beverly Hills, CA 90210-5227, USA

Johnston, Joel (Athlete, Baseball Player)
2 Outpost Ct
North Potomac, MD 20878-4353, USA

Johnston, John Dennis (Actor)
S D B Partners
315 S Beverly Dr Ste 411
Beverly Hills, CA 90212-4301, USA

Johnston, Ken
6300 Wilshire Blvd # 2110
Los Angeles, CA 90048-5204

Johnston, Kristen (Actor)
c/o Judy Hofflund *Hofflund/Polone*
6300 Wilshire Blvd Ste 1410
Los Angeles, CA 90048-5216, USA

Johnston, Larry (Athlete, Hockey Player)
904 E Liberty St
Milford, MI 48381-2081, USA

Johnston, Lynn (Cartoonist)
Universal Press Syndicate
4520 Main St Ste 340
Kansas City, MO 64111-7705, USA

Johnston, Mark (Athlete, Football Player)
609 Carolyn Ave
Austin, TX 78705-1709, USA

Johnston, Marshall (Athlete, Hockey Player)
3933 Waville Rd NE
Bemidji, MN 56601-8987, USA

Johnston, Nate (Athlete, Basketball Player)
8870 Fontainebleau Blvd Apt 301
Miami, FL 33172-4427, USA

Johnston, Rex D (Athlete, Baseball Player, Football Player)
15117 Illinois Ave
Paramount, CA 90723-4106, USA

Johnston, Sabrina
c/o Staff Member *Diva Central Inc*
7510 W Sunset Blvd Ste 1445
Los Angeles, CA 90046-3408, USA

Johnston, Tom (Musician)
PO Box 359
Sonoma, CA 95476-0359

Johnstone, Jay (Athlete, Baseball Player)
853 Chapea Rd
Pasadena, CA 91107-5656, USA

Johnstone, John (Athlete, Baseball Player)
9330 Clubside Cir Unit 3305
Sarasota, FL 34238-3367, USA

Johnstone, Parker (Race Car Driver)
541 Division St
Campbell, CA 95008-6934, USA

Johnstone, Tony (Athlete, Golfer)
Proserv
5335 Wisconsin Ave NW Ste 850
Washington, DC 20015-2052, USA

Johnstone Jr, John W (Business Person)
467 Carter St
New Canaan, CT 06840-5015, USA

Johnston-Forbes, Cathy (Athlete, Golfer)
5104 Lunar Dr
Kitty Hawk, NC 27949-3958, USA

Johnston Jr, S K (Business Person)
Coca-Cola Enterprises
2500 Windy Ridge Pkwy SE Ste 700
Atlanta, GA 30339-8429, USA

Joiner, Rusty (Actor, Athlete, Model)
c/o Marc Chancer *Origin Talent Agency*
4705 Laurel Canyon Blvd Ste 303
Valley Village, CA 91607-5943, USA

Joiner Jr, Charles (Charlie) (Athlete, Coach, Football Coach, Football Player)
16935 W Bernardo Dr Ste 107
San Diego, CA 92127-1635, USA

Jokinen, Olli (Athlete, Hockey Player)
4401 N Federal Hwy Ste 201
Boca Raton, FL 33431-5164, USA

Joli, France (Musician)
c/o Staff Member *Diva Central Inc*
7510 W Sunset Blvd Ste 1445
Los Angeles, CA 90046-3408, USA

Joliceur, David (Musician)
Famous Artists Agency
250 W 57th St
New York, NY 10107-0001, USA

Jolie, Angelina (Actor, Philanthropist)
c/o Martin Torres *Media Talent Group*
9200 W Sunset Blvd Ste 550
West Hollywood, CA 90069-3611, USA

Jolitz, Evan (Athlete, Football Player)
15 Old Kimball Rd
Brooklyn, CT 06234-1414, USA

Jolley, Gordon (Athlete, Football Player)
1459 Navajo Dr
Saint George, UT 84790-7728, USA

Jolley, Leroy (Horse Racer)
304 Paschal Ave
Franklin Square, NY 11010-2808, USA

Jolley, Lewis (Athlete, Football Player)
2715 Rosegate Ln
Charlotte, NC 28270-0764, USA

Jolley, Willie (Motivational Speaker)
5711 13th St NW
Washington, DC 20011-3547, USA

Jolliff, Howie (Athlete, Basketball Player)
2346 Fallen Oak Cir NE
Massillon, OH 44646-4887, USA

Jolly, Allison (Athlete, Olympic Athlete, Sailor)
27122 Benidorm
Mission Viejo, CA 92692-3405, USA

Jolly, Ken (Athlete, Football Player)
159 Bon Aire Dr
Dallas, TX 75218-1034, USA

Jolovitz, Jenna (Actor, Writer)
c/o Staff Member *Creative Artists Agency (CAA-LA)*
2000 Avenue of the Stars Ste 100
Los Angeles, CA 90067-4705, USA

Joly, Greg (Athlete, Hockey Player)
21 McDonald Dr
Queensbury, NY 12804-6426, USA

Jomdt, L daniel (Business Person)
Walgreen Co
200 Wilmot Rd
Deerfield, IL 60015-4681, USA

Jomphe, Jean-Francois (Athlete, Hockey Player)
6440 Sky Pointe Dr Ste 140
Las Vegas, NV 89131-4048, USA

Jonas, Don (Athlete, Football Player)
1831 Seneca Blvd
Winter Springs, FL 32708-5534, USA

Jonas, Joe (Musician)
c/o Kevin Jonas Sr *The Jonas Group*
4450 W Lakeside Dr Ste 300
Burbank, CA 91505-4007, USA

Jonas, Kevin (Musician)
c/o Kevin Jonas Sr *The Jonas Group*
4450 W Lakeside Dr Ste 300
Burbank, CA 91505-4007, USA

Jonas, Nick (Musician)
c/o Kevin Jonas Sr *The Jonas Group*
4450 W Lakeside Dr Ste 300
Burbank, CA 91505-4007, USA

Jonathan, Wesley (Actor)
c/o Adrienne McWhorter *Abrams Artists Agency (LA)*
9200 W Sunset Blvd PH 11
West Hollywood, CA 90069-3601, USA

Jones, Aaron (Athlete, Football Player)
7677 Torino Ct
Orlando, FL 32835-8195, USA

Jones, Adam (Athlete, Baseball Player)
c/o Staff Member *Baltimore Orioles*
333 W Camden St
Baltimore, MD 21201-2496, USA

Jones, Adam (Athlete, Football Player)
c/o Peter Schaffer *All Pro Sports and Entertainment*
36 Steele St Ste 100
Denver, CO 80206-5709, USA

Jones, Al (Athlete, Baseball Player)
1339 Brussels St
San Francisco, CA 94134-2224, USA

Jones, Alex E (Journalist, Radio Personality)
PO Box 19549
Austin, TX 78760-9549, USA

Jones, Alfred (Boxer)
19303 Patton St
Detroit, MI 48219-2530, USA

Jones, Andruw (Athlete, Baseball Player)
2931 Grey Moss Pass
Duluth, GA 30097-6274, USA

Jones, Angus T (Actor)
c/o Eddie Michaels *Insignia Public Relations*
1507 20th St Ste B
Santa Monica, CA 90404-3474, USA

Jones, Anthony (Athlete, Basketball Player)
44 Hempstead Dr
Newark, DE 19702-7711, USA

Jones, Antonia (Actor)
Buzz Halliday
8899 Beverly Blvd Ste 620
Los Angeles, CA 90048-2428, USA

Jones, Arthur (Athlete, Football Player)
c/o Joe Panos *Athletes First, LLC*
23091 Mill Creek Dr
Laguna Hills, CA 92653-1258, USA

Jones, Asjha (Basketball Player)
Connecticut Sun
Mohegan Sun Arena
Uncasville, CT 06382, USA

Jones, Askia (Athlete, Basketball Player)
3160 SW 132nd Ave
Miramar, FL 33027-3868, USA

Jones, Barry (Athlete, Baseball Player)
411 S Morton Ave
Centerville, IN 47330-1429, USA

Jones, Ben (Athlete, Baseball Player)
1323 Tewkesbury Pl NW
Washington, DC 20012-2921, USA

Jones, Bert (Athlete, Football Player)
1492 Madera St
Ruston, LA 71270-2063, USA

Jones, Bertram H (Bert) (Athlete, Football Player)
PO Box 248
Simsboro, LA 71275-0248, USA

Jones, Bob (Bobby) (Athlete, Baseball Player)
32 Elm St
Rutherford, NJ 07070-1263, USA

Jones, Bobby (Athlete, Baseball Player)
10222 N Whitney Ave
Fresno, CA 93730-4742, USA

Jones, Bobby (Athlete, Baseball Player)
7809 S Oxford Ave
Tulsa, OK 74136-8524, USA

Jones, Bobby (Athlete, Basketball Player, Olympic Athlete)
Charlotte Christian School
7301 Sardis Rd
Charlotte, NC 28270-6063, USA

Jones, Bobby (Athlete, Football Player)
6824 Stewart Sharon Rd
Brookfield, OH 44403-9789, USA

Jones, Booker T (Actor, Musician)
c/o Staff Member *Concerted Efforts*
PO Box 440326
Somerville, MA 02144-0004, USA

Jones, Brad (Athlete, Hockey Player)
c/o Staff Member *International Hockey League*
117 W 4th St
Rochester, MI 48307-2025, USA

Jones, Brandon (Athlete, Football Player)
1070 Randall Rd
Texarkana, TX 75501-2102, USA

Jones, Brent M (Athlete, Football Player, Sportscaster)
756 El Pintado Rd
Danville, CA 94526-1407, USA

Jones, Brian (Athlete, Football Player)
6200 Aviara Dr
Austin, TX 78735-8091, USA

Jones, Buckshot (Race Car Driver)
Buckshot Racing
182 Belue Cir
Boiling Springs, SC 29316-5900, USA

Jones, Calvin (Athlete, Football Player)
301 Crescent Ct Apt 3316
San Francisco, CA 94134-3385, USA

Jones, Calvin (Athlete, Baseball Player)
2815 Butterfield Stage Rd
Lewisville, TX 75077-3181, USA

Jones, Carnetta (Actor)
CunninghamEscottDipene
10635 Santa Monica Blvd Ste 130
Los Angeles, CA 90025-8306, USA

Jones, Cedric (Athlete, Football Player)
48B Rodwell Ave
Greenwich, CT 06830-6121, USA

Jones, Chandler (Athlete, Football Player)
c/o Joe Panos *Athletes First, LLC*
23091 Mill Creek Dr
Laguna Hills, CA 92653-1258, USA

Jones, Charles (Athlete, Basketball Player)
2315 Windsor Ave
Baltimore, MD 21216-3227, USA

Jones, Charles A (Athlete, Basketball Player)
304 Chestnut St
Elizabethtown, KY 42701-9431, USA

Jones, Charlie (Sportscaster)
851 Valparaiso Ave
Menlo Park, CA 94025-4206, USA

Jones, Cherry (Actor)
c/o Scott Henderson *Paradigm (LA)*
9601 Wilshire Blvd Ste 220
Beverly Hills, CA 90210-5205, USA

Jones, Chipper (Athlete, Baseball Player, Olympic Athlete)
c/o Staff Member *Atlanta Braves*
755 Hank Aaron Dr SW
Atlanta, GA 30315-1120, USA

Jones, Chris (Athlete, Baseball Player)
1312 E Thunderhill Pl
Phoenix, AZ 85048-6200, USA

Jones, Chris (Athlete, Baseball Player)
1821 Westward Ho Cir
El Cajon, CA 92021-3721, USA

Jones, Chris T (Athlete, Football Player)
2372 Treasure Isle Dr
West Palm Beach, FL 33410-1312, USA

Jones, Clarence (Athlete, Baseball Player)
2641 Club Dr
Greensboro, GA 30642-3476, USA

Jones, Claude Earl (Actor)
Henderson/Hogan
8285 W Sunset Blvd Ste 1
West Hollywood, CA 90046-2420, USA

Jones, Cleon (Athlete, Baseball Player)
751 Edwards St
Mobile, AL 36610-3334, USA

Jones, Clinton (Athlete, Football Player)
16555 Sherman Way Ste C
Van Nuys, CA 91406-3781, USA

Jones, Cobi (Soccer Player)
501 N Edinburgh Ave
Los Angeles, CA 90048-2309, USA

Jones, Coco (Actor)
c/o Jonathan Shank *Red Light Management (LA)*
8439 W Sunset Blvd Ste 2
West Hollywood, CA 90069-1925, USA

Jones, Collis (Athlete, Basketball Player)
9309 Decatur Pl
Laurel, MD 20723-1821, USA

Jones, Cullen (Athlete, Olympic Athlete, Swimmer)
c/o Staff Member *Premier Management Group (PMG Sports)*
115 Crescent Commons Dr Ste 250
Cary, NC 27518-8134, USA

Jones, Dahntay (Athlete, Basketball Player)
PO Box 9984
Trenton, NJ 08650-2984, USA

Jones, Dale (Athlete, Football Player)
PO Box 2716
Boone, NC 28607-2716, USA

Jones, Dalton (Athlete, Baseball Player)
4688 S Dixon Ln
Liberty, MS 39645-6117, USA

Jones, Damon (Athlete, Football Player)
12690 Copper Springs Rd
Jacksonville, FL 32246-5143, USA

Jones, Damon (Athlete, Basketball Player)
c/o Staff Member *Mark Termini Associates*
Prefers to be contacted via telephone
Cleveland, OH, USA

Jones, Dan (Athlete, Football Player)
5150 SW 20th St
Plantation, FL 33317-5410, USA

Jones, Daniel (Writer)
c/o Staff Member *New York Times*
229 W 43rd St
New York, NY 10036-3982, USA

Jones, Dante (Athlete, Football Player)
326 Partridge Run Dr
Duncanville, TX 75137-3133, USA

Jones, Darryl (Athlete, Baseball Player)
15628 Kings Dr
Meadville, PA 16335-6546, USA

Jones, Darryl (Musician)
Rascoff/Zysblat
110 W 57th St # 300
New York, NY 10019-3319, USA

Jones, Daryl (Politician)
3517 Del Mar Ave
Davie, FL 33328-1340, USA

Jones, Daryll (Athlete, Football Player)
581 N Oakley Dr
Columbus, GA 31906-4369, USA

Jones, Datone (Athlete, Football Player)
c/o Sean Kiernan *Impact Sports - LA*
11331 Ventura Blvd Ste 1A
Studio City, CA 91604-3147, USA

Jones, David D (Athlete, Football Player)
3131 Mockingbird Ln
Dallas, TX 75205-2324, USA

Jones, Davy (Race Car Driver)
TRW Racing
1397 330th St
Adair, IA 50002-8581, USA

Jones, Dax (Athlete, Baseball Player)
10021 W Suddard Pl
Beach Park, IL 60087-1717, USA

Jones, Dean (Actor, Musician)
PO Box 570276
Tarzana, CA 91357-0276, USA

Jones, Dhani (Athlete, Football Player)
20550 Falcons Landing Cir Apt 5403
Sterling, VA 20165-2802, USA

Jones, Dick (Actor)
PO Box 7716
Northridge, CA 91327-7716

Jones, Dickie (Actor)
PO Box 7716
Northridge, CA 91327-7716, USA

Jones, Don (Athlete, Football Player)
8446 Wren Creek Dr
Charlotte, NC 28269-6176, USA

Jones, Donell (Musician)
c/o Ra-Fael Blanco *2R's Entertainment & Media*
601 W 135th St Apt 6E
New York, NY 10031-8304, USA

Jones, Donta (Athlete, Football Player)
4495 Jimmy Greens Pl # Pi
La Plata, MD 20646-5852, USA

Jones, Doug (Actor)
c/o John Zander *Zander Magic*
9068 Priscilla St
Downey, CA 90242-4627, USA

Jones, Doug (Athlete, Baseball Player)
129 E Navilla Pl
Covina, CA 91723-3023, USA

Jones, Dub (Athlete, Football Player)
904 Glendale Dr
Ruston, LA 71270-2346, USA

Jones, Dwight (Athlete, Basketball Player, Olympic Athlete)
28926 Enchanted Dr
Shenandoah, TX 77381-1105, USA

Jones, Earl (Athlete, Basketball Player)
8402 Belding Ct
Brandywine, MD 20613-7107, USA

Jones, Earl (Athlete, Football Player)
3127 Seiler Ct
Naperville, IL 60565-4424, USA

Jones, Earl (Athlete, Track Athlete)
15114 Petoskey Ave
Detroit, MI 48238-2064, USA

Jones, Ed (Athlete, Football Player)
Team Jones, Inc
14232 Marsh Ln PMB 282
Addison, TX 75001-3857, USA

Jones, Eddie (Actor)
Gage Group
5757 Wilshire Blvd Ste 659
Los Angeles, CA 90036-3682, USA

Jones, Eddie (Athlete, Basketball Player)
3400 Paddock Rd
Weston, FL 33331-3520, USA

Jones, E Edward (Religious Leader)
Baptist Convention of America
777 S R L Thornton Fwy Ste 205
Dallas, TX 75203-2970, USA

Jones, Elvin R (Musician)
DL Media
PO Box 2728
Bala Cynwyd, PA 19004-6728, USA

Jones, Ernest (Athlete, Football Player)
17410 SW 109th Ave
Miami, FL 33157-4042, USA

Jones, Evan (Actor)
c/o Susan Curtis *Curtis Talent Management*
9607 Arby Dr
Beverly Hills, CA 90210-1202, USA

Jones, Felicity (Actor)
c/o Erica Gray *Viewpoint Inc (LA)*
8820 Wilshire Blvd Ste 220
Beverly Hills, CA 90211-2622, USA

Jones, Felix (Athlete, Football Player)
c/o Eugene Parker *Maximum Sports Management*
6435 W Jefferson Blvd # 197
Fort Wayne, IN 46804-6203, USA

Jones, Finn (Actor)
c/o Nicolas Bernheim *NB Management*
1157 S Beverly Dr Fl 2
Los Angeles, CA 90035-1119, USA

Jones, Freddie (Athlete, Football Player)
120 Word Ln
Harvest, AL 35749-8800, USA

Jones, Garrett (Athlete, Baseball Player)
1401 S State St Unit 908
Chicago, IL 60605-3626, USA

Jones, Gary (Athlete, Football Player)
3510 Rosedale St
Houston, TX 77004-6406, USA

Jones, Gary (Athlete, Baseball Player)
475 S Westridge Cir
Anaheim, CA 92807-3733, USA

Jones, Glenn (Musician)
Universal Attractions
145 W 57th St # 1500
New York, NY 10019-2220, USA

Jones, Gordon (Athlete, Football Player)
18919 Fishermans Bend Dr
Lutz, FL 33558-9756, USA

Jones, Grace (Actor, Model, Musician)
c/o Staff Member *The Society Management*
156 5th Ave Ste 800
New York, NY 10010-7702, USA

Jones, Greg (Athlete, Baseball Player)
14260 Passage Way
Seminole, FL 33776-1001, USA

Jones, Greg (Athlete, Football Player)
2331 S Fenton Dr
Lakewood, CO 80227-3975, USA

Jones, Greg (Skier)
PO Box 500
Tahoe City, CA 96145-0500, USA

Jones, Gregory M (Athlete, Football Player)
3203 Kirby Ln
Walnut Creek, CA 94598-3908, USA

Jones, Grover (Deacon) (Athlete, Baseball Player)
1015 Goldfinch Ave
Sugar Land, TX 77478-3452, USA

Jones, Hal (Athlete, Baseball Player)
17700 Avalon Blvd Spc 67
Carson, CA 90746-0231, USA

Jones, Hassan (Athlete, Football Player)
1010 Eldridge St
Clearwater, FL 33755-4205, USA

Jones, Hayes W (Athlete, Olympic Athlete, Track Athlete)
408 Stonewood Dr
Peachtree City, GA 30269-6639, USA

Jones, Henry (Hank) (Musician)
Joel Chriss
300 Mercer St Apt 3J
New York, NY 10003-6732, USA

Jones, Homer C (Athlete, Football Player)
416 S Texas St
Pittsburg, TX 75686-1538, USA

Jones, Horace (Athlete, Football Player)
7925 Hobart Ave
Pensacola, FL 32534-4030, USA

Jones, Jack (Musician)
c/o Staff Member *International Ventures*
25115 Avenue Stanford Ste 102
Valencia, CA 91355-4777, USA

Jones, Jacoby (Athlete, Football Player)
c/o Harold C Lewis *National Sports Agency*
15400 Timpaige Dr
Chesterfield, MO 63017-1762, USA

Jones, Jacque (Athlete, Baseball Player, Olympic Athlete)
347 Saint Rita Ct
San Diego, CA 92113-2092, USA

Jones, James (Athlete, Football Player)
20751 W Holt Dr
Buckeye, AZ 85396-7612, USA

Jones, James (Athlete, Football Player)
9481 Highland Oak Dr Unit 1815
Tampa, FL 33647-2518, USA

Jones, James (Athlete, Football Player)
1009 Hunters Creek Dr
Carrollton, TX 75007-1111, USA

Jones, James C (Athlete, Football Player)
1136 S Delano Ct W Apt 814
Chicago, IL 60605-3739, USA

Jones, James Earl (Actor)
Horatio Productions
PO Box 610
Pawling, NY 12564-0610, USA

Jones, James (Jimmy) (Athlete, Basketball Player)
14700 Marvin Ln
Southwest Ranches, FL 33330-3404, USA

Jones, Jamie (Musician)
MPI Talent
9255 W Sunset Blvd Ste 407
West Hollywood, CA 90069-3302, USA

Jones, Janet (Actor)
9100 Wilshire Blvd Ste 1000W
Beverly Hills, CA 90212-3463, USA

Jones, January (Actor)
21017 Mendenhall Ct
Topanga, CA 90290-4484, USA

Jones, Jason (Actor)
c/o Jay Gassner *United Talent Agency (UTA-LA)*
9336 Civic Center Dr
Beverly Hills, CA 90210-3604, USA

Jones, Jason (Athlete, Baseball Player)
1125 Oakview Dr SE
Smyrna, GA 30080-7917, USA

Jones, Jason (Athlete, Football Player)
c/o Michael McCartney *Priority Sports & Entertainment - Chicago*
312 N La Salle
Suite 650
Chicago, IL 60610, USA

Jones, Jeff (Athlete, Baseball Player)
311 White Horse Pike
Haddon Heights, NJ 08035-1704, USA

Jones, Jeff (Athlete, Baseball Player)
51 Emmons Ct
Wyandotte, MI 48192-2553, USA

Jones, Jeff (Coach)
University of Virginia
Athletic Dept
Charlottesville, VA 22903, USA

Jones, Jeffrey (Actor)
7336 Santa Monica Blvd # 691
West Hollywood, CA 90046-6616, USA

Jones, Jenny (Comedian)
c/o Gail Stocker *Gail Stocker Presents*
1025 N Kings Rd Apt 113
West Hollywood, CA 90069-6007, USA

Jones, Jermaine (Athlete, Football Player)
1522 Victor II Blvd
Morgan City, LA 70380-2120, USA

Jones, Jermaine (Musician)
c/o Staff Member *19 Entertainment (LA)*
9000 W Sunset Blvd Ste 1574
West Hollywood, CA 90069-5817, USA

Jones, Jerry (Business Person, Football Executive)
4400 Preston Rd
Dallas, TX 75205-3722, USA

Jones, Jill Marie (Actor)
c/o Peggy Rudman *Identity Talent Agency (ID)*
9107 Wilshire Blvd Ste 500
Beverly Hills, CA 90210-5526, USA

Jones, Jim (Musician)
c/o Gordon MacDonald *Don Buchwald & Associates (LA)*
6500 Wilshire Blvd Ste 2200
Los Angeles, CA 90048-4942, USA

Jones, Jimmie (Athlete, Football Player)
2658 Unicorn Ct
Herndon, VA 20171-2425, USA

Jones, Jimmie (Athlete, Football Player)
204 Moss Dr
Cedar Hill, TX 75104-2398, USA

Jones, Jimmy (Athlete, Baseball Player)
3054 Newcastle Dr
Dallas, TX 75220-1636, USA

Jones, joe (Athlete, Baseball Player)
2411 Carlisle Pl
Sarasota, FL 34231-7013, USA

Jones, Joe (Athlete, Football Player)
1413 Scott Ct
Irving, TX 75060-3703, USA

Jones, Joey (Athlete, Football Player)
4032 Royal Oak Cir
Mountain Brk, AL 35243-5831, USA

Jones, John E (Athlete, Football Player)
19610 100th Ave NE
Bothell, WA 98011-2318, USA

Jones, John Marshall (Actor)
1801 Avenue of the Stars Ste 307
Los Angeles, CA 90067-5905

Jones, Julia (Actor)
c/o Evan Hainey *Untitled Entertainment (LA)*
350 S Beverly Dr Ste 200
Beverly Hills, CA 90212-4819, USA

Jones, Julio (Athlete, Football Player)
c/o Jimmy Sexton *CAA (Memphis)*
6060 Poplar Ave Ste 470
Memphis, TN 38119-0910, USA

Jones, Julius (Athlete, Football Player)
1 N Ocean Blvd Apt 401
Pompano Beach, FL 33062-5726, USA

Jones, June S (Athlete, Coach, Football Coach, Football Player)
6024 Airline Rd
Dallas, TX 75205, USA

Jones, K C (Athlete, Football Player)
1225 Algeria Ave
Coral Gables, FL 33134-2303, USA

Jones, KC (Athlete, Basketball Player)
Basketball Hall of Fame
1000 Hall of Fame Ave Ste 100
Springfield, MA 01105-2545, USA

Jones, K C (Athlete, Basketball Player, Olympic Athlete)
Basketball Hall of Fame 1000 Hall of Fame Ave
1000 Hall of Fame Ave Ste 100
Springfield, MA 01105-2545, USA

Jones, Keith (Athlete, Hockey Player)
c/o Staff Member *Versus Network*
281 Tresser Blvd Fl 9
Stamford, CT 06901-3238, USA

Jones, Keith (Athlete, Hockey Player)
Philadelphia Flyers
3601 S Broad St Ste 2
Attn Broadcast Dept
Philadelphia, PA 19148-5297, USA

Jones, Ken (Athlete, Football Player)
4455 Porter Rd
Niagara Falls, NY 14305-3309, USA

Jones, Kent (Athlete, Golfer)
5108 Coyote Hill Way NW
Albuquerque, NM 87120-1471, USA

Jones, Kim (Athlete, Football Player)
1396 Madison Ave Apt 150
Loveland, CO 80537-3218, USA

Jones, Kimberly (Commentator)
20 Sherry Ln
Saddle Brook, NJ 07663-5935, USA

Jones, Larry (Athlete, Basketball Player)
1442 Cottingham Ct W
Columbus, OH 43209-3144, USA

Jones, Leroy (Athlete, Football Player)
347 Kantor Blvd
Casselberry, FL 32707-5760, USA

Jones, Levi (Athlete, Football Player)
215 E Citation Ln
Tempe, AZ 85284-1403, USA

Jones, Lolo (Athlete, Olympic Athlete, Track Athlete)
Lolo Jones Management
PO Box 82226
C/O Angelia Jefferson
Baton Rouge, LA 70884-2226, USA

Jones, L Q (Actor)
2144 1/2 N Cahuenga Blvd
Los Angeles, CA 90068-2708, USA

Jones, Lynn (Athlete, Baseball Player)
9959 Dicksonburg Rd
Conneautville, PA 16406-1817, USA

Jones, Maggie Elizabeth (Actor)
c/o Jared Schwartz *Caliber Media Company*
5670 Wilshire Blvd Ste 1600
Los Angeles, CA 90036-5659, USA

Jones, Major (Athlete, Basketball Player)
2475 Brandy Mill Rd
Houston, TX 77067-1275, USA

Jones, Malia (Actor, Athlete)
c/o Michelle Henderson *Henderson Represents*
100 Universal City Plz Ste 7152
Universal City, CA 91608-1002, USA

Jones, Marcus (Athlete, Baseball Player)
20375 Longbay Dr
Yorba Linda, CA 92887-3250, USA

Jones, Marcus (Athlete, Football Player)
18701 Pepper Pike
Lutz, FL 33558-5315, USA

Jones, Marilyn (Actor)
Kaplan-Stahler Agency
8383 Wilshire Blvd Ste 923
Beverly Hills, CA 90211-2443, USA

Jones, Marvin (Athlete, Baseball Player)
6900 Lone Pine Ct
Hanahan, SC 29410-4743, USA

Jones, Marvin (Athlete, Football Player)
536 N Biscayne River Dr
Miami, FL 33169-6632, USA

Jones, Marvin M (Athlete, Football Player)
8891 NW 193rd St
Miami, FL 33157, USA

Jones, Matt (Athlete, Football Player)
13838 Bella Riva Ln
Jacksonville, FL 32225-5434, USA

Jones, Maurice (Athlete, Football Player)
34 Pheasant Run Pl
Danville, CA 94506-5819, USA

Jones, Maxine (Musician)
East West Records
75 Rockefeller Plz # 1200
New York, NY 10019-6908, USA

Jones, Merlakia (Basketball Player)
Cleveland Rockers
1 Center Ct
Gund Arena
Cleveland, OH 44115-4001, USA

Jones, Mick (Musician)
Hard to Handle Mgmt
16501 Ventura Blvd Ste 602
Encino, CA 91436-2072, USA

Jones, Mickey (Actor, Musician)
c/o Staff Member *Hervey/Grimes Talent Agency*
3002 Midvale Ave Ste 206
Los Angeles, CA 90034-3418, USA

Jones, Mike (Athlete, Baseball Player)
6761 Atlantic Blvd
Jacksonville, FL 32211-8729, USA

Jones, Mike (Musician)
c/o Staff Member *Warner Bros*
4000 Warner Blvd # 16
Burbank, CA 91522-0002, USA

Jones, Mike A (Athlete, Football Player)
353 Hollywood Rd
Columbia, SC 29212-8400, USA

Jones, Nasir (NAS) (Musician)
c/o Carleen Donovan *Press Here Publicity*
138 W 25th St Ste 900
New York, NY 10001-7470, USA

Jones, Nathan (Actor)
c/o Rick Bassman *Cunningham Escott Slevin & Doherty (CESD-LA)*
10635 Santa Monica Blvd Ste 130
Los Angeles, CA 90025-8306, USA

Jones, Norah (Musician)
166 Amity St
Brooklyn, NY 11201-6202, USA

Jones, Odell (Athlete, Baseball Player)
5831 Opal Ave
Palmdale, CA 93552-3967, USA

Jones, Orlando (Actor)
c/o Chuck Jones *Linasea Corp*
8306 Wilshire Blvd Ste 432
Beverly Hills, CA 90211-2304, USA

Jones, Ozell (Athlete, Basketball Player)
PO Box 1111
Long Beach, CA 90801-1111, USA

Jones, Parnelli (Race Car Driver)
PO Box W
Torrance, CA 90508-0329, USA

Jones, Patrick (Actor)
c/o Staff Member *Martin Weiss Management*
PO Box 5656
Santa Monica, CA 90409-5656, USA

Jones, P. J. (Race Car Driver)
2334 S Broadway # 2186
Santa Ana, CA 92707-3250, USA

Jones, PJ (Race Car Driver)
Patrick Racing
8431 Georgetown Rd
Indianapolis, IN 46268-5628, USA

Jones, Preston (Actor)
c/o Alan Iezman *Shelter Entertainment*
9255 W Sunset Blvd Ste 320
West Hollywood, CA 90069-3313, USA

Jones, Preston (Athlete, Football Player)
116 Hamilton Dr
Anderson, SC 29621-1558, USA

Jones, Quincy (Actor, Musician, Producer)
Quincy Jones Music Publishing
6671 W Sunset Blvd Ste 1574A
Los Angeles, CA 90028-7123, USA

Jones, Randy (Athlete, Baseball Player)
7668 El Camino Real Ste 104-435
Carlsbad, CA 92009-7932, USA

Jones, Randy (Athlete, Hockey Player)
7 Red Fox Trl
Sicklerville, NJ 08081-3709, USA

Jones, Rashida (Actor, Musician)
c/o Jillian Roscoe *ID Public Relations (LA)*
7060 Hollywood Blvd Fl 8th
Los Angeles, CA 90028-6021, USA

Jones, Rees (Athlete, Golfer)
10 Belleclaire Pl
Verona, NJ 07044-5106, USA

Jones, Renee (Actor)
256 S Robertson Blvd # 700
Beverly Hills, CA 90211-2811, USA

Jones, Reshad (Athlete, Football Player)
c/o Joel Segal *Lagardere Unlimited (NYC)*
845 United Nations Plz
New York, NY 10017-3540, USA

Jones, Rich (Athlete, Basketball Player)
101 Luna Way Apt 232
Las Vegas, NV 89145-0187, USA

Jones, Richard T (Actor)
c/o Doug Wald *Anonymous Content (LA)*
3532 Hayden Ave
Culver City, CA 90232-2413, USA

Jones, Richard Timothy
584 Broadway Rm 1009
New York, NY 10012-5239

Jones, Rick (Athlete, Baseball Player)
PO Box 440981
Jacksonville, FL 32222-0010, USA

Jones, Rickie Lee (Musician, Songwriter)
c/o Bruce Solar *Agency Group Ltd, The (LA)*
1880 Century Park E Ste 711
Los Angeles, CA 90067-1618, USA

Jones, Ricky (Athlete, Baseball Player)
PO Box 440981
Jacksonville, FL 32222-0010, USA

Jones, Robert (Athlete, Football Player)
405 Aria Dr
Austin, TX 78738-1741, USA

Jones, Robert (K C) (Athlete, Basketball Player, Coach)
c/o Staff Member *Naismith Memorial Basketball Hall of Fame*
1000 W Columbus Ave
Springfield, MA 01105-2518, USA

Jones, Robin (Athlete, Basketball Player)
16640 Cynthia Ct
Tinley Park, IL 60477-8209, USA

Jones, Rod (Athlete, Football Player)
1121 Angie Ln
Desoto, TX 75115-3873, USA

Jones, Roger (Athlete, Football Player)
712 Trebor Dr
Goodlettsville, TN 37072-2935, USA

Jones, Ron (Athlete, Hockey Player)
301 Brock St
Coppell, TX 75019-3937, USA

Jones, Ronald (Popeye) (Athlete,
Basketball Player)
29 Bass Pond Dr
Frisco, TX 75034-1937, USA

Jones, Rondell (Athlete, Football Player)
421 Competition Rd
Raleigh, NC 27603-1962, USA

Jones, Rosie (Athlete, Golfer)
4895 High Point Rd
Atlanta, GA 30342-2340, USA

Jones, Ross (Athlete, Baseball Player)
4135 Eastridge Cir
Pompano Beach, FL 33064-1847, USA

Jones, Rulon K (Athlete, Football Player)
4003 N 3775 E
Eden, UT 84310, USA

Jones, Ruppert (Athlete, Baseball Player)
7668 El Camino Real Ste 104-435
Carlsbad, CA 92009-7932, USA

Jones, Rushen (Athlete, Football Player)
1803 W Magdalena Ln
Phoenix, AZ 85041-7816, USA

Jones, Sam (Athlete, Basketball Player)
338 S Hampton Club Way
Saint Augustine, FL 32092-1031, USA

Jones, Sean (Athlete, Football Player)
4602 McKeever Ln
Missouri City, TX 77459-6310, USA

Jones, Selwyn (Athlete, Football Player)
11216 Grimes Ave
Pearland, TX 77584-5524, USA

Jones, Shelton (Athlete, Basketball Player)
8112 Lockman Ln
Charlotte, NC 28269-5192, USA

Jones, Shirley (Actor, Musician)
4531 Noeline Way
Encino, CA 91436-2107, USA

Jones, Simon (Actor)
Innovative Artists
1505 10th St
Santa Monica, CA 90401-2805, USA

Jones, Sir Charles
Hep'me Records
3947 Coxs Ferry Rd
Bolton, MS 39041-9519, USA

Jones, Spike (Athlete, Football Player)
3612 Club Dr NW
Kennesaw, GA 30144-2019, USA

Jones, Stacy (Athlete, Baseball Player)
1777 Ponderosa Rd
Attalla, AL 35954-5653, USA

Jones, Star (Actor, Producer, Talk Show
Host)
c/o Tamara Houston *Round Table
Entertainment*
509 N Fairfax Ave Ste 200
Los Angeles, CA 90036-1733, USA

Jones, Sterling (Actor)
c/o Katie Mason *Luber Roklin
Management*
5815 W Sunset Blvd Ste 206
Los Angeles, CA 90028-6481, USA

Jones, Steve (Athlete, Baseball Player)
8116 Kingsdale Dr
Knoxville, TN 37919-7005, USA

Jones, Steve (Athlete, Basketball Player)
8303 Quebec Dr
Houston, TX 77096-1034, USA

Jones, Steve (Football Player)
12774 Fee Fee Rd
Saint Louis, MO 63146-4402, USA

Jones, Tamala (Actor)
c/o Danielle Allman-Del *D2 Management*
9255 W Sunset Blvd Ste 600
West Hollywood, CA 90069-3306, USA

Jones, Taylor (Cartoonist)
Times-Mirror Syndicate
Times-Mirror Square
Los Angeles, CA 90053, USA

Jones, Tebucky (Athlete, Football Player)
55 Brentwood Dr
Avon, CT 06001-3410, USA

Jones, Thomas (Athlete, Football Player)
2742 Clinch Haven Rd
Big Stone Gap, VA 24219-4158, USA

Jones, Thomas D (Astronaut)
10212 Wendover Dr
Vienna, VA 22181-2960, USA

Jones, thomas F (Athlete, Baseball Player)
13846 Atlantic Blvd # APJ509
Jacksonville, FL 32225-3239, USA

Jones, Tim (Athlete, Baseball Player)
30 Chicot Dr
Maumelle, AR 72113-5801, USA

Jones, Tim (Athlete, Baseball Player)
6049 Roloff Way
Orangevale, CA 95662-4544, USA

Jones, Toby (Actor)
c/o Billy Lazarus *United Talent Agency
(UTA-LA)*
9336 Civic Center Dr
Beverly Hills, CA 90210-3604, USA

Jones, Todd B G (Athlete, Baseball Player)
421 Eagle Pointe Dr
Pell City, AL 35128-7266, USA

Jones, Tom (Musician)
Tom Jones Enterprise LLC
1430 Broadway Rm 803
New York, NY 10018-9210, USA

Jones, Tommy Lee (Actor)
PO Box 966
San Saba, TX 76877-0966, USA

Jones, Tony (Athlete, Football Player)
1820 N Brown Rd Ste 40
Lawrenceville, GA 30043-1800, USA

Jones, Tracy (Athlete, Baseball Player)
101 Harbor Green Dr Apt 602
Bellevue, KY 41073-1155, USA

Jones, Ty (Athlete, Hockey Player)
11803 E 20th Ave
Spokane Valley, WA 99206-7002, USA

Jones, Tyler Patrick (Actor)
c/o Barbara Buky *Cosden Morgan Agency*
7080 Hollywood Blvd Ste 1009
Los Angeles, CA 90028-6937, USA

Jones, Victor (Athlete, Football Player)
9710 Sunset Grove Dr
Huntersville, NC 28078-0639, USA

Jones, Victor T (Athlete, Football Player)
PO Box 132241
Dallas, TX 75313-2241, USA

Jones, Vinnie (Actor, Producer)
c/o Alex Cole *Elevate Entertainment*
5757 Wilshire Blvd Ste 460
Los Angeles, CA 90036-3658, USA

Jones, Wali (Athlete, Basketball Player)
3160 SW 132nd Ave
Miramar, FL 33027-3868, USA

Jones, Wallace (Athlete, Basketball Player,
Olympic Athlete)
1509 Mount Rainier Dr
Lexington, KY 40517-3841, USA

Jones, Walter (Athlete, Football Player)
520 Raymond Pl NW
Renton, WA 98057-3432, USA

Jones, Walter Emanuel (Actor)
K & K Entertainment
1498 W Sunset Blvd
Los Angeles, CA 90026-3471, USA

Jones, Wayne (Actor, Comedian)
Smooth Man Productions
206 Belmont Dr
Palatka, FL 32177-6402, USA

Jones, Wilbert (Athlete, Basketball Player)
3360 Idlecreek Way
Decatur, GA 30034-4916, USA

Jones, William A (Dub) (Athlete, Football
Player)
904 Glendale Dr
Ruston, LA 71270-2346, USA

Jones, Willie D (Athlete, Football Player)
4440 Hidden Orchard Ln
Indianapolis, IN 46228-3023, USA

Jones Cox, Vena (Business Person)
Real Life Real Estate
PO Box 58279
Cincinnati, OH 45258-0279, USA

Jones-Doxey, Marilyn (Athlete, Baseball
Player, Commentator)
5058 Red Oak Pi
Bradenton, FL 34207, USA

Jones Girls, The
PO Box 6010
Sherman Oaks, CA 91413-6010

Jones III, Samuel L (Actor)
c/o Staff Member *Abrams Artists Agency
(LA)*
9200 W Sunset Blvd PH 11
West Hollywood, CA 90069-3601, USA

Jones Jr, Robert Trent (Athlete, Golfer)
1900 S Ocean Dr Apt 1612
Fort Lauderdale, FL 33316-3715, USA

Jones Jr, Roy (Actor, Boxer, Producer,
Sportscaster)
c/o Darren Prince *Prince Marketing
Group*
18 Carillon Cir
Livingston, NJ 07039-2600, USA

Jones-Thompson, Marion (Athlete,
Olympic Athlete, Track Athlete)
13532 Utah Flats Dr
Austin, TX 78727-6362, USA

Jong, Erica (Writer)
121 Davis Hill Rd
Weston, CT 06883-2015, USA

Jonrowe, Dee Dee (Athlete)
PO Box 272
Willow, AK 99688-0272, USA

Jonsen, Albert R (Doctor)
University of Washington
Med School
Medical Ethics Dept
Seattle, WA 98195-0001, USA

Jonson, Johnny (Athlete, Football Player)
PO Box 4283
Mooresville, NC 28117-4283, USA

Jonsson, Hans (Athlete, Hockey Player)
Lakasund 1S9
Bonassund, SW 891 7, USA

Jonsson, Jorgen (Athlete, Hockey Player)
2000 E Gene Autry Way
Anaheim, CA 92806-6143, USA

Jonsson, Tomas
Denmark Ice Hockey Union Fodboldens
Hvs DBU Aile 1
Brondbv, DE 260S, USA

Jonze, Spike (Actor, Director)
c/o Staff Member *Dickhouse Productions*
5555 Melrose Ave
Los Angeles, CA 90038-3989, USA

Joost, Henry (Director)
c/o Rowena Arguelles *Creative Artists
Agency (CAA-LA)*
2000 Avenue of the Stars Ste 100
Los Angeles, CA 90067-4705, USA

Jophery, Brown (Athlete, Baseball Player)
3008 W 81st St
Inglewood, CA 90305-1425, USA

Joplin, Josh (Musician)
c/o Staff Member *MCT Management*
104 W 29th St Rm 1101
New York, NY 10001-5310, USA

Jordan, Anthony (Athlete, Football Player)
38 Albemarle St
Rochester, NY 14613-1402, USA

Jordan, Brian (Athlete, Baseball Player)
Brian Jordan Foundation
1429 Orange Shoals Dr
Canton, GA 30115-8554, USA

Jordan, Buford (Athlete, Football Player)
11 Acadia St
Kenner, LA 70065-1001, USA

Jordan, Cameron (Cam) (Football Player)
c/o Doug Hendrickson *Octagon Football*
832 Sansome St Fl 1
San Francisco, CA 94111-1558, USA

Jordan, Claudia (Actor, Television Host)
c/o Laura Wright *Avid Exposure*
1179 W A St Ste 233
Hayward, CA 94541-7006, USA

Jordan, Curtis (Athlete, Football Player)
629 Surfside Ave
Virginia Beach, VA 23451-3658, USA

Jordan, Darin (Athlete, Football Player)
44 Connell Dr
Stoughton, MA 02072-3708, USA

Jordan, Dion (Athlete, Football Player)
c/o Doug Hendrickson *Octagon Football*
832 Sansome St Fl 1
San Francisco, CA 94111-1558, USA

Jordan, Don (Boxer)
5100 2nd Ave
Los Angeles, CA 90043-1951, USA

Jordan, Don D (Business Person)
Reliant Energy
1111 Louisiana St
Houston, TX 77002-5230, USA

Jordan, Eddie (Athlete, Basketball Player)
12620 Tribunal Ln
Potomac, MD 20854-1455, USA

Jordan, Glenn (Director)
9401 Wilshire Blvd Ste 700
Beverly Hills, CA 90212-2944, USA

Jordan, Hamilton (Actor)
The Harry Walker Agency Inc
355 Lexington Ave Fl 21
New York, NY 10017-6603, USA

Jordan, Jeremy (Actor, Musician)
c/o Ted Schachter *Schachter Entertainment*
1157 S Beverly Dr Fl 2
Los Angeles, CA 90035-1119, USA

Jordan, Jim (Congressman, Politician)
1524 Longworth Hob
Washington, DC 20515-2702, USA

Jordan, Kathy (Tennis Player)
114 Walter Hays Dr
Palo Alto, CA 94303-2923, USA

Jordan, Kevin (Athlete, Baseball Player)
127 Ney St
San Francisco, CA 94112-1642, USA

Jordan, Lamont (Athlete, Football Player)
1407 Alberta Dr
District Heights, MD 20747-1902, USA

Jordan, Larry (Athlete, Football Player)
4780 Kirk Rd
Youngstown, OH 44515-5403, USA

Jordan, Laura (Actor)
c/o Matthew Lesher *Insight*
PO Box 36359
Los Angeles, CA 90036-0359, USA

Jordan, Leander (Athlete, Football Player)
1661 Peachtree Cir N
Jacksonville, FL 32207-6423, USA

Jordan, Lee Roy (Athlete, Football Player)
7710 Caruth Blvd
Dallas, TX 75225-8103, USA

Jordan, Le Roy
2425 Burbank St
Dallas, TX 75235-3128

Jordan, Leslie (Actor)
c/o Billy Miller *Billy Miller Management*
8322 Ridpath Dr
Los Angeles, CA 90046-7710, USA

Jordan, Mary (Journalist)
Washington Post
Editorial Dept
1150 15th St NW
Washington, DC 20071-0001, USA

Jordan, Michael (Athlete, Basketball Player, Olympic Athlete)
172 Bears Club Dr
Jupiter, FL 33477-4203, USA

Jordan, Michael B (Actor)
c/o David Schiff *The Schiff Company*
9220 W Sunset Blvd Ste 106
West Hollywood, CA 90069-3500, USA

Jordan, Montell (Musician)
c/o Staff Member *Richard De La Font Agency*
3808 W South Park Blvd
Broken Arrow, OK 74011-1261, USA

Jordan, Neil (Director, Writer)
c/o Staff Member *William Morris Endeavor (LA)*
9601 Wilshire Blvd
Beverly Hills, CA 90210-5213, USA

Jordan, Patty (Athlete, Golfer)
4372 Twilight Ln
Hamburg, NY 14075-1526, USA

Jordan, Randy (Athlete, Football Player)
42742 Mirror Pond Pl
Ashburn, VA 20148-6972, USA

Jordan, Ricardo (Athlete, Baseball Player)
Arcadia Road Prison 13617 SE Highway
70 # B04316
Arcadia, FL 34266, USA

Jordan, Ricky (Athlete, Baseball Player)
965 Moonlit Way
Folsom, CA 95630-7506, USA

Jordan, Scott (Athlete)
1530 Carroll Dr NW Ste 103
Atlanta, GA 30318-3600, USA

Jordan, Scott (Athlete, Baseball Player)
265 Great Oak Dr
Athens, GA 30605-4504, USA

Jordan, Shelby (Athlete, Football Player)
29208 Posey Way
Rancho Palos Verdes, CA 90275-4629, USA

Jordan, Stanley (Musician)
SJ Productions
16845 N 29th Ave # 2000
Phoenix, AZ 85053-3053, USA

Jordan, Steve (Athlete, Football Player)
3848 Newton Way
Pleasanton, CA 94588-8384, USA

Jordan, Tom (Athlete, Baseball Player)
15 Dulce Rd
Santa Fe, NM 87508-8284, USA

Jordan, Tony (Athlete, Football Player)
38 Albemarle St
Rochester, NY 14613-1402, USA

Jordanaires, The
4619 220th Pl
Bayside, NY 11361-3650

Jordanova, Vera (Actor, Model)
c/o Alix Gucovsky *Special Artists Agency*
9200 W Sunset Blvd Ste 410
West Hollywood, CA 90069-3506, USA

Jorden, Tim (Athlete, Football Player)
11402 N 26th Pl
Scottsdale, AZ 85260, USA

Jordison, Joey (Musician)
c/o Staff Member *Gersh (NY)*
41 Madison Ave
New York, NY 10010-2202, USA

Jorgensen, Mike (Athlete, Baseball Player, Coach)
1820 Harbor Mill Dr
Fenton, MO 63026-2653, USA

Jorgensen, Roger (Athlete, Basketball Player)
642 Woodcrest Dr
Pittsburgh, PA 15205-1520, USA

Jorgensen, Ryan (Athlete, Baseball Player)
5 Links Ct
Kingwood, TX 77339-5326, USA

Jorgensen, Terry (Athlete, Baseball Player)
610 N Main St
Luxemburg, WI 54211-1072, USA

Jose, Felix (Athlete, Baseball Player)
9825 Equus Cir
Boynton Beach, FL 33472-4337, USA

Jose, Lind (Baseball Player)
Pittsburgh Pirates
18 Villa Santa
Dorado, PR 00646, USA

Josefowicz, Leila (Musician)
I M G Artists
420 W 45th St
New York, NY 10036-3501, USA

Joseph, Cory (Athlete, Basketball Player)
c/o Rich Paul *Klutch Sports Management*
Prefers to be contacted by telephone
Cleveland, OH, USA

Joseph, Daryl J (Astronaut)
615 Peachtree Ct
Campbell, CA 95008-6353, USA

Joseph, Davin (Athlete, Football Player)
17912 Bimini Isle Ct
Tampa, FL 33647-2782, USA

Joseph, James (Athlete, Football Player)
8942 Stoneridge Pi
Montgomery, AL 36117, USA

Joseph, Jeffrey
400 S Beverly Dr Ste 102
Beverly Hills, CA 90212-4403

Joseph, Kevin (Athlete, Baseball Player)
8826 Lacrosse Dr
Dallas, TX 75231-4826, USA

Joseph, Linval (Athlete, Football Player)
c/o Bill Johnson *SportsTrust Advisors (GA)*
3340 Peachtree Rd NE Fl 16
Atlanta, GA 30326-1000, USA

Joseph, Stephen (Doctor)
New York City Health Department
125 Worth St
New York, NY 10013-4006, USA

Joseph, Vance (Athlete, Football Player)
1995 E Coalton Rd Apt 35-101
Superior, CO 80027-4426, USA

Joseph, William (Musician)
c/o Staff Member *MCT Management*
104 W 29th St Rm 1101
New York, NY 10001-5310, USA

Joseph, William (Athlete, Football Player)
1071 NE 107th St
Miami, FL 33161-7353, USA

Joseph III, Joseph E (Doctor)
University of Michigan
Taubman Center
Ann Arbor, MI 48109, USA

Josephson, Karen (Swimmer)
1923 Junction Dr
Concord, CA 94518-3361, USA

Josephson, Lester (Josey) (Athlete, Football Player)
5388 N Genernatas Dr
Tucson, AZ 85704, USA

Josephson, Sarah (Swimmer)
1923 Junction Dr
Concord, CA 94518-3361, USA

Joshua, Larry (Actor)
c/o Judy Orbach *Judy O Productions*
6136 Glen Holly St
Los Angeles, CA 90068-2338, USA

Joshua, Von (Athlete, Baseball Player)
20922 E Glen Haven Cir
Northville, MI 48167-2465, USA

Jost, Mike (Athlete, Baseball Player)
1068 S Chatfield Pl
Vail, AZ 85641-6748, USA

Jostyn, Jennifer (Actor)
c/o Staff Member *Abrams Artists Agency (LA)*
9200 W Sunset Blvd PH 11
West Hollywood, CA 90069-3601, USA

Josue, Steve (Athlete, Football Player)
18711 NE 3rd Ct Apt 215
Miami, FL 33179-3808, USA

Joswick, Bob (Athlete, Football Player)
5829 W Orlando Cir
Broken Arrow, OK 74011-1153, USA

Joswick, Robert (Athlete, Football Player)
5829 W Orlando Cir
Broken Arrow, OK 74011-1153, USA

Jourdain Jr, Michel (Race Car Driver)
Team Rahal
4601 Lyman Dr
Hilliard, OH 43026-1249, USA

Jourdan, Louis (Actor)
1139 Maybrook Dr
Beverly Hills, CA 90210-2717, USA

Journell, Jimmy (Athlete, Baseball Player)
1511 Eastgate Rd
Springfield, OH 45503-2427, USA

Journey (Music Group)
c/o Peter Grosslight *William Morris Endeavor (LA)*
9601 Wilshire Blvd
Beverly Hills, CA 90210-5213, USA

Jovanovich, Peter W (Publisher)
MacMillan
1177 Avenue of the Americas # 1965
New York, NY 10036-2714, USA

Jovanovski, Ed (Athlete, Hockey Player)
528 E Alexander Palm Rd
Boca Raton, FL 33432-7985, USA

Jovovich, Milla (Actor, Model, Musician)
c/o Jason Weinberg *Untitled Entertainment (LA)*
350 S Beverly Dr Ste 200
Beverly Hills, CA 90212-4819, USA

Jow, Malese (Actor)
c/o Christopher Ledford *Acumen Entertainment Partners*
201 N Hollywood Way Ste 108
Burbank, CA 91505-3477, USA

Jow, Melise (Actor)
c/o Glenn Hughes III *Gem Entertainment Group*
10920 Wilshire Blvd Ste 150
Los Angeles, CA 90024-3990, USA

Joy, Mike (Race Car Driver)
PO Box 1100
Lewisville, NC 27023-1100, USA

Joy, Robert (Actor)
c/o Donna Massetti *SMS Talent*
8383 Wilshire Blvd Ste 230
Beverly Hills, CA 90211-2436, USA

Joyal, Eddie (Athlete, Hockey Player)
6469 Wandermere Dr
San Diego, CA 92120-3214, USA

Joyce, Andrea (Correspondent, Sportscaster)
c/o Staff Member *NBC Sports (NY)*
30 Rockefeller Plz Fl 270E
New York, NY 10112-0299, USA

Joyce, Bob
700 Windgrove Trl
Maitland, FL 32751-5412, USA

Joyce, Delvin (Athlete, Football Player)
355 Trott Cir
Martinsville, VA 24112-7659, USA

Joyce, Duane (Athlete, Hockey Player)
143 W Elm St
Pembroke, MA 02359-2136, USA

Joyce, Elaine (Actor)
724 N Roxbury Dr
Beverly Hills, CA 90210-3212, USA

Joyce, James (Athlete, Baseball Player)
9785 SW 167th Pl
Beaverton, OR 97007-8705, USA

Joyce, Jim (Athlete, Baseball Player)
9785 SW 167th Pl # Pi
Beaverton, OR 97007-8705, USA

Joyce, Joan (Athlete, Golfer)
20024 Back Nine Dr
Boca Raton, FL 33498-4707, USA

Joyce, Kara Lynn (Athlete, Olympic
Athlete, Swimmer)
5973 Cedar Ridge Dr
Ann Arbor, MI 48103-8791, USA

Joyce, Kevin (Athlete, Basketball Player,
Olympic Athlete)
420 W Olive St Apt 9
Long Beach, NY 11561-3128, USA

Joyce, Lisa (Actor)
c/o Staff Member Stone Manners Salners
Agency (LA)
6100 Wilshire Blvd Ste 1500
Los Angeles, CA 90048-5110, USA

Joyce, Matt (Athlete, Football Player)
2932 W Coachman Ave
Tampa, FL 33611-2810, USA

Joyce, Matt (Athlete, Football Player)
6330 E Wilshire Dr
Scottsdale, AZ 85257-1122, USA

Joyce, Mike (Athlete, Baseball Player)
2030 Berkshire Pl
Wheaton, IL 60189-8143, USA

Joyce, William (Artist, Writer)
3302 Centenary Blvd
Shreveport, LA 71104-4504, USA

Joyce, William H (Business Person)
Union Carbide
39 Old Ridgebury Rd
Danbury, CT 06810-5103, USA

Joyeux, Odette
1 Rue Seguier
Carrollton, TX 75006

Joyner, Alrederick (Al) (Athlete, Track
Athlete)
CMG World Wide
8560 W Sunset Blvd
10th Fl Penthouse
West Hollywood, CA 90069-2311, USA

Joyner, Harry (Athlete, Basketball Player)
904 S Lakeview Dr
Payson, AZ 85541-4604, USA

Joyner, Lisa (Television Host)
4202 Klump Ave
N Hollywood, CA 91602-3011, USA

Joyner, Mark (Business Person, Writer)
Mark Joyner Inc
7426 Cherry Ave # 210-150
Fontana, CA 92336-4221, USA

Joyner, Michelle (Actor)
Paradigm Agency
10100 Santa Monica Blvd Ste 2500
Los Angeles, CA 90067-4116, USA

Joyner, Seth (Athlete, Football Player)
5138 N 79th Pi
Scottsdale, AZ 85250, USA

Joyner, Tom (Radio Personality)
PO Box 630495
Irving, TX 75063-0128

Joyner, Wally (Athlete, Baseball Player)
516 E 2800 S
Mapleton, UT 84664-4850, USA

Joyner-Kersee, Jacqueline (Jackie)
(Athlete, Olympic Athlete, Track Athlete)
Women's Sports Foundation
1049 Bristol Manor Dr
Ballwin, MO 63011-5106, USA

Jozwiak, Brian J (Athlete, Coach, Football
Coach, Football Player)
668 Alvarado
North Port, FL 34287-2553, USA

J. Rahall II, Nick (Congressman,
Politician)
2307 Rayburn Hob
Washington, DC 20515-4803, USA

J. Ribble, Reid (Congressman, Politician)
1513 Longworth Hob
Washington, DC 20515-2506, USA

J. Rogers, Mike (Congressman, Politician)
133 Cannon Hob
Washington, DC 20515-2208, USa

J. Rooney, Thomas (Congressman,
Politician)
1529 Qn 9th Hqb
Washington, DC 20515-0001, USA

J. Roskam, Peter (Congressman,
Politician)
227 CA Rtn M Hob
Washington, DC 20515-0001, USA

J. Tiberi, Patrick (Congressman, Politician)
106 Cannon Hob
Washington, DC 20515-3204, USA

Juanes (Musician)
c/o Michel Vega William Morris Endeavor
(Miami)
119 Washington Ave Ste 400
Miami Beach, FL 33139-7202, USA

Juarez, Ricardo (Rocky) (Athlete, Boxer,
Olympic Athlete)
3916 Weems St
Houston, TX 77009-4747, USA

Juchheim, Alwin (Politician)
939 Ave of Pines St
Grenada, MS 38901-4609, USA

Judd, Ashley (Actor)
c/o Annett Wolf WKT Public Relations
(LA)
9350 Wilshire Blvd Ste 450
Beverly Hills, CA 90212-3230, USA

Judd, Cledus T
KOCH Records
22 Harbor Park Dr
Port Washington, NY 11050-4650, USA

Judd, Cris (Actor, Dancer)
c/o Monica Barkett Global Artists Agency
6253 Hollywood Blvd Apt 508
Los Angeles, CA 90028-8251, USA

Judd, Jackie (Correspondent)
ABC-TV
77 W 66th St
News Dept
New York, NY 10023-6201, USA

Judd, Mike (Athlete, Baseball Player)
9805 Shadow Rd
La Mesa, CA 91941-4154, USA

Judd, Naomi (Musician)
c/o Julie Colbert William Morris Endeavor
(LA)
9601 Wilshire Blvd
Beverly Hills, CA 90210-5213, USA

Judd, Wynonna (Musician)
5601 Pinewood Rd
Franklin, TN 37064-9306, USA

Juden, Jeff (Athlete, Baseball Player)
85 Proctor St
Salem, MA 01970-2110, USA

Judge, Christopher (Actor, Writer)
c/o Louisa Spring Louisa Spring
Management
404 Carroll Canal
Venice, CA 90291-4682, USA

Judge, Mike (Actor, Animator, Producer,
Writer)
c/o Staff Member Ternion Pictures
1010 W Martin Luther King Jr Blvd
Austin, TX 78701-1070, USA

Judkins, Jeff (Athlete, Basketball Player)
3471 S 3570 E
Salt Lake City, UT 84109-3243, USA

Judson, Howie (Athlete, Baseball Player)
239 Fairway Cir
Winter Haven, FL 33881-8742, USA

Judson, William (Athlete, Football Player)
652 Sinclair Way
Jonesboro, GA 30238-7962, USA

Jue, Bhawoh (Athlete, Football Player)
21048 Lowry Park Ter Apt 402
Ashburn, VA 20147-6435, USA

Juenger, David (Athlete, Football Player)
790 Cliffside Dr
Chillicothe, OH 45601-2902, USA

Juergensen, Heather (Actor)
c/o Staff Member Generate Management
8750 Wilshire Blvd Ste 200
Beverly Hills, CA 90211-2707, USA

Juicy J (Musician)
411 N Oakhurst Dr Unit 402
Beverly Hills, CA 90210-5607, USA

Jules, Gary (Musician)
c/o Staff Member Paradigm (Monterey)
404 W Franklin St
Monterey, CA 93940-2303, USA

Julian, Fred (Athlete, Football Player)
730 Strawberry Valley Ave NW
Comstock Park, MI 49321-9600, USA

Julian, Janet (Actor)
Borinstein Oreck Bogart
3172 Dona Susana Dr
Studio City, CA 91604-4356, USA

Julian, Jonathan (Actor)
c/o Susan Nathe Nathe & Associates
8281 Melrose Ave Ste 200
Los Angeles, CA 90046-6823, USA

Julian II, Alexander (Designer, Fashion
Designer)
Alexander Julian Inc
323 Florida Hill Rd
Ridgefield, CT 06877-5205, USA

Julich, Bobby (Athlete, Cycler, Olympic
Athlete)
9283 Weeping Willow Pl
Highlands Ranch, CO 80130-4458, USA

Julien, Claude (Athlete, Coach, Hockey
Player)
c/o Staff Member Boston Bruins
100 Legends Way Ste 250
Td Banknorth Garden
Boston, MA 02114-1389, USA

Julien, Max (Actor)
3580 Avenida Del Sol
Studio City, CA 91604-4018, USA

Julio, Jorge (Athlete, Baseball Player)
4032 E Gardenia Ave
Weston, FL 33332-2453, USA

Juma, Kevin (Athlete, Football Player)
12510 107th Avenue Ct E
Puyallup, WA 98374-2793, USA

Jump 5 (Music Group)
c/o Staff Member Bobby Roberts Agency
PO Box 1547
Goodlettsville, TN 37070-1547, USA

Junck, Mary (Publisher)
Baltimore Sun
501 N Calvert St
Baltimore, MD 21278-1000, USA

June, Cato (Athlete, Football Player)
14702 Elberfeld Ct
Upper Marlboro, MD 20774-8966, USA

Junge, Eric (Athlete, Baseball Player)
350 11th Ave Unit 830
San Diego, CA 92101-7479, USA

Junger, Gil (Director, Producer)
c/o Staff Member Creative Artists Agency
(CAA-LA)
2000 Avenue of the Stars Ste 100
Los Angeles, CA 90067-4705, USA

Junger, Sebastian (Writer)
United Talent Agency
9336 Civic Center Dr
Beverly Hills, CA 90210-3604, USA

Jungman, Eric (Actor)
c/o Staff Member Leslie Allan-Rice
Management
1007 Maybrook Dr
Beverly Hills, CA 90210-2715, USA

Jungueira, Bruno (Race Car Driver)
2127 Brickell Ave Apt 3105
Miami, FL 33129-2105, USA

Junior, Ester J (E J) (Athlete, Football
Player)
911 W Summit St
Bolivar, MO 65613-1021, USA

Junior Varsity (Music Group)
Victory Records
346 N Justine St Ste 504
Chicago, IL 60607-1021, USA

Junkin, Abner (Athlete, Football Player)
5 Lakeside Ln
Newport, AR 72112-3948, USA

Junkin, Trey (Athlete, Football Player)
300 Wren St
Winnfield, LA 71483-2662, USA

Junqueira, Bruno (Race Car Driver)
721 Crandon Blvd Apt 308
Key Biscayne, FL 33149-2565, USA

Juppe, Alain (Politician)
57 Rue De Varenne
Paris, FR F-750

Jur, Jeffrey (Cinematographer)
4438 Wortser Ave
Studio City, CA 91604-1432, USA

Jurak, Ed (Athlete, Baseball Player)
3650 S Walker Ave
San Pedro, CA 90731-6046, USA

Juran, Nathan (Director, Writer)
197 Desert Lakes Dr
Rancho Mirage, CA 92270-4053, USA

Jurasik, Peter (Actor)
969 1/2 Manzanita St
Los Angeles, CA 90029-3009, USA

Jurasin, Bobby (Athlete, Football Player)
160 Huron Woods Dr
Marquette, MI 49855-9699, USA

Jurevicius, Joe (Athlete, Football Player)
1779 Berkshire Rd
Gates Mills, OH 44040-9747, USA

Jurewicz, Mike (Athlete, Baseball Player)
7115 N Wyoming Ave
Kansas City, MO 64118-8351, USA

Jurgens, Dan (Cartoonist)
5033 Green Farms Rd
Minneapolis, MN 55436-1091, USA

Jurgensen, Sonny (Athlete, Football Player)
6963 Greentree Dr
Naples, FL 34108-8528, USA

Jurgensmeier-Carroll, Margaret (Athlete, Baseball Player, Commentator)
5245 Rowena Dr
Roscoe, IL 61073-7221, USA

Jurich, Tom (Athlete, Football Player)
14910 Landmark Dr
Louisville, KY 40245-6525, USA

Juriga, James (Athlete, Football Player)
3001 Easton Pl
Saint Charles, IL 60175-5610, USA

Juriga, Jim (Athlete, Football Player)
3001 Easton Pl
Saint Charles, IL 60175-5610, USA

Jurkovic, John (Athlete, Football Player)
2212 June Dr
Schererville, IN 46375-3079, USA

Jurkovic, Mirko (Athlete, Football Player)
68520 Garver Lake Rd
Edwardsburg, MI 49112-9404, USA

Jurow, Martin
5833 Berkshire Ln
Dallas, TX 75209-2403

Jury, Bob (Athlete, Football Player)
2 Sassafras Ln
Greensburg, PA 15601-9023, USA

Just, Walter (Publisher)
Milwaukee Journal
333 W State St
Milwaukee, WI 53203-1309, USA

Juster, Norton (Writer)
259 Lincoln Ave
Amherst, MA 01002-2010, USA

Justice, David (Athlete, Baseball Player)
18570 Old Coach Way
Poway, CA 92064-6651, USA

Justice, Donald R (Writer)
338 Rocky Shore Dr
Iowa City, IA 52246-3836, USA

Justice, Victoria (Actor)
c/o Jonathan Shank *Red Light Management (LA)*
8439 W Sunset Blvd Ste 2
West Hollywood, CA 90069-1925, USA

Justice, William
3832 Chanson Dr
View Park, CA 90043-1602

Justin, Kerry (Athlete, Football Player)
13331 W Marlette Ct
Litchfield Park, AZ 85340-5377, USA

Justin, Paul (Athlete, Football Player)
2529 W Via Perugia
Phoenix, AZ 85086-6631, USA

Just Jinger (Music Group)
c/o Staff Member *Paradigm (Monterey)*
404 W Franklin St
Monterey, CA 93940-2303, USA

Justman, Seth (Musician)
Nick Ben-Meir
652 N Doheny Dr
West Hollywood, CA 90069-5526, USA

Juszczyk, Kyle (Athlete, Football Player)
c/o Joe Linta *JL Sports*
1204 Main St Ste 179
Branford, CT 06405-3787, USA

Jutze, Skip (Athlete, Baseball Player)
3395 Zephyr Ct
Wheat Ridge, CO 80033-5967, USA

Juvenile (Musician)
c/o Staff Member *ICM Partners (LA)*
10250 Constellation Blvd Fl 7
Los Angeles, CA 90067-6207, USA

J. Visclosky, Peter (Congressman, Politician)
2256 Rayburn Hob
Washington, DC 20515-4324, USA

J W, Pirtle (Athlete, Baseball Player)
1205 Carver Dr
Champaign, IL 61820-2412, USA

J. Walz, Timothy (Congressman, Politician)
1722 Longworth Hob
Washington, DC 20515-3008, USA

K

Kaake, Jeff (Actor)
2533 N Carson St # 3105
Carson City, NV 89706-0242, USA

Kaas, Carmen (Model)
Men/Women Model Inc
199 Lafayette St Fl 7
New York, NY 10012-4281, USA

Kaat, Jim (Athlete, Baseball Player)
129 NW 13th St Ste 17
Boca Raton, FL 33432-1635, USA

Kab, Vyto (Athlete, Football Player)
10 Asa St
Montville, NJ 07045-9781, USA

Kaba, Agim (Actor, Producer)
c/o Adam Griffin *Kritzer Levine Wilkins Entertainment (KLWG)*
11872 La Grange Ave Fl 1
Los Angeles, CA 90025-5283, USA

Kabat-Zinn, Jon (Writer)
Sounds True, Inc
413 S Arthur Ave
Louisville, CO 80027-3013, USA

Kacherski, John (Athlete, Football Player)
6860 Macneil Dr
Dublin, OH 43017-7006, USA

Kachowski, Mark (Athlete, Hockey Player)
113 Pine Creek Dr
Venetia, PA 15367-1330, USA

Kaci (Musician)
c/o Staff Member *Curb Records (LA)*
3907 W Alameda Ave Ste 104
Burbank, CA 91505-4359

Kacyvenski, Isaiah (Athlete, Football Player)
1081 Beacon St # 8
Brookline, MA 02446-5610, USA

Kaczmarek, Jane (Actor)
1015 Oak Grove Ave
San Marino, CA 91108-1025, USA

Kaczur, Nick (Athlete, Football Player)
7440 Mystic Ridge Rd
Chagrin Falls, OH 44023-9500, USA

Kadela, Dave (Athlete, Football Player)
9413 Culross Ct
Dublin, OH 43017-9685, USA

Kadish, Lawrence (Horse Racer)
135 Jericho Tpke
Old Westbury, NY 11568-1508, USA

Kadish, Michael S (Mike) (Athlete, Football Player)
7941 Sudbury Ln SE
Ada, MI 49301-9356, USA

Kadison, Joshua (Musician, Songwriter, Writer)
Nick Bode
1265 Electric Ave
Venice, CA 90291-3397, USA

Kadziel, Ron (Athlete, Football Player)
2492 Creek Dr
Park City, UT 84060-6866, USA

Kaeding, Nate (Athlete, Football Player)
1528 1st Ave Unit A
Coralville, IA 52241-1100, USA

Kae-Kazim, Hakeem (Actor)
c/o Staff Member *Rough Diamond Management*
1424 N Kings Rd
West Hollywood, CA 90069-1908, USA

Kaelin, Kato (Actor)
c/o Nicole St. John *Media Artists Group (LA)*
8222 Melrose Ave Ste 203
Los Angeles, CA 90046-6838, USA

Kaepernick, Colin (Athlete, Football Player)
c/o Scott Smith *XAM Sports*
PO Box 1725
Madison, WI 53701-1725, USA

Kaesviharn, Kevin (Athlete, Football Player)
6334 Merrimac Ln N
Osseo, MN 55311-3835, USA

Kafelnikov, Yevgeny A (Tennis Player)
Int'l Mgmt Group
26 Riverside Dr
Rumson, NJ 07760-1048, USA

Kafentzis, Kurt (Athlete, Football Player)
1305 Perkins Ave
Richland, WA 99354-3106, USA

Kafentzis, Mark (Athlete, Football Player)
15912 134th Avenue Ct E
Puyallup, WA 98374-9647, USA

Kaftan, George (Athlete, Basketball Player)
2591 Lantern Light Way
Manasquan, NJ 08736-2247, USA

Kagan, Daryn (Correspondent)
Cable News Network
1050 Techwood Dr NW
News Dept
Atlanta, GA 30318-5695, USA

Kagan, Daryn (Correspondent)
1579 Monroe Dr NE Ste F-134
Atlanta, GA 30324-5039, USA

Kagan, Daryn
Washington Speakers Bureau
1663 Prince St
Alexandria, VA 22314-2818, USA

Kagan, Jeremy Paul (Director)
2024 N Curson Ave
Los Angeles, CA 90046-2210, USA

Kagasoff, Daren (Actor)
c/o John Carrabino *John Carrabino Management*
5900 Wilshire Blvd Ste 406
Los Angeles, CA 90036-5015, USA

Kagen, David (Actor)
6457 Firmament Ave
Van Nuys, CA 91406-6219, USA

Kahane, Jeffrey (Musician)
I M G Artists
420 W 45th St
New York, NY 10036-3501, USA

Kahler, Bob (Athlete, Football Player)
3995 Wellington Pkwy
Palm Harbor, FL 34685-1172, USA

Kahler, Robert (Athlete, Football Player)
3995 Wellington Pkwy
Palm Harbor, FL 34685-1172, USA

Kahn, Joseph (Director, Writer)
c/o Staff Member *HSI Entertainment*
9950 Jefferson Blvd
Culver City, CA 90232-3506, USA

Kahn, Roger (Commentator)
PO Box 556
Stone Ridge, NY 12484-0556, USA

Kahn, Roger (Writer)
280 Marcotte Rd
Kingston, NY 12401-8318, USA

Kahn, Shahid (Business Person)
Flex-N-Gate
1306 E University Ave
Urbana, IL 61802-2093, USA

Kahne, Kasey (Race Car Driver)
c/o Rod Moskowitz *Fuel Sports Management Group*
130 Infield Ct
Mooresville, NC 28117-8026, USA

Kai, Teanna (Adult Film Star)
c/o Staff Member *Atlas Multimedia Inc*
9005 Eton Ave Ste C
Canoga Park, CA 91304-6533, USA

Kaimer, Karl (Athlete, Football Player)
3 Kerr Ave
Lavallette, NJ 08735-2138, USA

Kain, Khalil (Actor)
c/o Staff Member *Envision Entertainment*
8840 Wilshire Blvd Fl 3
Beverly Hills, CA 90211-2606, USA

Kainer, Don (Athlete, Baseball Player)
1923 Sieber Dr
Houston, TX 77017-6201, USA

Kaiser, Bob (Athlete, Baseball Player)
8 Independence Way
Southampton, NJ 08088-9047, USA

Kaiser, Don (Athlete, Baseball Player)
2901 E 12th St
Ada, OK 74820-7259, USA

Kaiser, George B (Business Person)
BOK Financial Corporation
Bank of Oklahoma Tower
PO Box 2300
Tulsa, OK 74192-0001, USA

Kaiser, Jason (Athlete, Football Player)
3885 Cheyenne Pl
Sedalia, CO 80135-8931, USA

Kaiser, Jeff (Athlete, Baseball Player)
26227 James Dr
Grosse Ile, MI 48138-2172, USA

Kaiser, Ken (Athlete, Baseball Player)
56 Holley Sue Ln
Rochester, NY 14626-1170, USA

Kaiser, Natasha (Athlete, Track Athlete)
2601 Hickman Rd
Des Moines, IA 50310-6101, USA

Kaiser, Tim (Producer)
c/o Scott Schwartz *Vision Art Management*
9465 Wilshire Blvd Ste 870
Beverly Hills, CA 90212-2610, USA

Kaiserman, William (Designer, Fashion Designer)
29 W 56th St
New York, NY 10019-3986, USA

Kajlich, Bianca (Actor)
c/o Chris Henze *Thruline Entertainment*
9250 Wilshire Blvd Ste 100
Ground Floor
Beverly Hills, CA 90212-3343, USA

Kaku, Michio (Writer)
c/o Robert Holtz *Kaku Media Inc*
848 N Rainbow Blvd # 3311
Las Vegas, NV 89107-1103, USA

Kalafat, Ed (Athlete, Basketball Player)
1814 Pinehurst Ave
Saint Paul, MN 55116-2117, USA

Kalas, Harry (Sportscaster)
Philadelphia Philies
3308 Chatham Pl
Media, PA 19063-4313, USA

Kalas, Todd (Commentator)
9417 Cavendish Dr Apt 108
Tampa, FL 33626-5173, USA

Kalem, Toni (Actor)
c/o Joy Gorman *Anonymous Content (LA)*
3532 Hayden Ave
Culver City, CA 90232-2413, USA

Kalember, Patricia (Actor)
Innovative Artists
1505 10th St
Santa Monica, CA 90401-2805, USA

Kaler, Jamie (Actor)
c/o Sheila Wenzel *Innovative Artists (LA)*
1505 10th St
Santa Monica, CA 90401-2805, USA

Kaleta, Patrick (Athlete, Hockey Player)
3011 Cloverbank Rd Unit 39
Hamburg, NY 14075-3460, USA

Kalichstein, Joseph (Musician)
I C M Artists
40 W 57th St
New York, NY 10019-4001, USA

Kalikow, Peter S (Publisher)
H J Kalikow Co
101 Park Ave Rm 2500
New York, NY 10178-0075, USA

Kalil, Matt (Athlete, Football Player)
c/o Tom Condon *CAA (St. Louis)*
222 S Central Ave Ste 1008
Saint Louis, MO 63105-3509, USA

Kalil, Ryan (Athlete, Football Player)
c/o Tom Condon *CAA (St. Louis)*
222 S Central Ave Ste 1008
Saint Louis, MO 63105-3509, USA

Kaline, Al (Athlete, Baseball Player)
3613 York Ct
Bloomfield Hills, MI 48301-2058, USA

Kaline, Albert W (Al) (Athlete, Baseball Player)
3613 York Ct
Bloomfield Hills, MI 48301-2058, USA

Kaling, Mindy (Actor, Comedian)
9309 Sierra Mar Dr
Los Angeles, CA 90069-1736, USA

Kalinin, Dmitri (Athlete, Hockey Player)
Puckagency LLC
1 Sunset Dr N
Attn Jay Grossman
Chappaqua, NY 10514-1613, USA

Kalis, Todd A (Athlete, Football Player)
127 Majestic Dr
Mars, PA 16046-5001, USA

kalish, ryan
37 Obre Pl
Shrewsbury, NJ 07702, USA

Kalitta, Connie (Race Car Driver)
American International Airways
1010 James L Hart Pkwy
Ypsilanti, MI 48197-9790, USA

Kalitta, Doug (Race Car Driver)
Kalitta Motorsports
1010 James L Hart Pkwy
Ypsilanti, MI 48197-9790, USA

Kallaugher, Kevin (Kall) (Cartoonist)
Baltimore Sun
501 N Calvert St
Editorial Dept
Baltimore, MD 21278-1000, USA

Kallen, Jackie
c/o Daniel Strone *Trident Media Group LLC*
41 Madison Ave Fl 36
New York, NY 10010-2257, USA

Kallen, Kitty (Musician)
35 Winthrop Pl
Englewood, NJ 07631, USA

Kallir, Lilian (Musician)
Columbia Artists Mgmt Inc
165 W 57th St
New York, NY 10019-2201, USA

Kalmanir, Thomas (Athlete, Football Player)
425 E Shelldrake Cir
Fresno, CA 93730-1230, USA

Kalmbach, Herbert (Politician)
1056 Santiago Dr
Newport Beach, CA 92660-5728, USA

Kalplan, Deborah (Director, Writer)
c/o Staff Member *William Morris Endeavor (LA)*
9601 Wilshire Blvd
Beverly Hills, CA 90210-5213, USA

Kalu, N D (Athlete, Football Player)
3719 Poplar Springs Dr
Missouri City, TX 77459-6722, USA

Kalu, Ndukwe (Athlete, Football Player)
1910 Quail Hollow Dr
Fresno, TX 77545, USA

Kalyan, Adhir (Actor)
1714 Sunset Plaza Dr
Los Angeles, CA 90069-1312, USA

Kamal, Gray (Musician)
William Morris Agency
1325 Avenue of the Americas Bsmt 2
New York, NY 10019-6047, USA

Kamali, Norma (Designer, Fashion Designer)
OMO Norma Kamali
11 W 56th St
New York, NY 10019-3902, USA

Kaman, Chris (Athlete, Basketball Player)
2593 Kenowa Ave SW
Byron Center, MI 49315-9611, USA

Kamana III, John (Athlete, Football Player)
2319 Kapahu St
Honolulu, HI 96813-1443, USA

Kamano, Stacy (Actor)
c/o Staff Member *AKA Talent Agency*
6310 San Vicente Blvd Ste 200
Los Angeles, CA 90048-5488, USA

Kamanu, Lew (Athlete, Football Player)
1822 Alewa Dr
Honolulu, HI 96817-1212, USA

Kamensky, Valeri (Athlete, Hockey Player)
5 Stonehedge Dr S
Greenwich, CT 06831-3219, USA

Kamieniecki, Scott (Athlete, Baseball Player)
7800 Somerhill Ln
Clarkston, MI 48348-4383, USA

Kaminir, Lisa (Actor)
Ellis Talent Group
14241 N Maple Dr
#207
Sherman Oaks, CA 01423, USA

Kaminski, Janusz (Cinematographer)
23801 Calabasas Rd Ste 2004
Calabasas, CA 91302-1565, USA

Kaminski, Kevin (Athlete, Hockey Player)
4560 Venture Dr
Southaven, MS 38671-9719, USA

Kaminski, Larry (Athlete, Football Player)
31423 State Highway 3 NE
Poulsbo, WA 98370-9373, USA

Kaminsky, Yan (Athlete, Hockey Player)
4842 Wildrose Ct NW
Kennesaw, GA 30152-7752, USA

Kamm, Brian (Athlete, Golfer)
479 Barnette Rd
Bluff City, TN 37618-4143, USA

Kammerer, Carl (Athlete, Football Player)
6941 Brooks Rd
Highland, MD 20777-9540, USA

Kamoze, Ini (Musician)
Famous Artists Agency
250 W 57th St
New York, NY 10107-0001, USA

Kampa, Bob (Athlete, Football Player)
2001 Jennifer Dr
Aptos, CA 95003-2840, USA

Kampa, Robert (Athlete, Football Player)
2001 Jennifer Dr
Aptos, CA 95003-2840, USA

Kampman, Aaron (Athlete, Football Player)
2227 Highway 1 NE
Solon, IA 52333-7900, USA

Kanaan, Tony (Race Car Driver)
Andretti Green Racing
7615 Zionsville Rd
Indianapolis, IN 46268-2174, USA

Kanakaredes, Melina (Actor)
c/o Bill Butler *Industry Entertainment*
955 Carrillo Dr Ste 300
Los Angeles, CA 90048-5400, USA

Kanal, Tony (Musician, Songwriter, Writer)
Rebel Waltz Inc
31652 2nd Ave
Laguna Beach, CA 92651-8244, USA

Kanaly, Steve (Actor)
4663 Grand Ave
Ojai, CA 93023-9309, USA

Kanan, Sean
c/o Kim Matuka *Online Talent Group*
Prefers to be contacted via email or telephone
West Hollywood, CA 90069, USA

Kane (Wrestler)
c/o Kerry Rodgerson *World Wrestling Entertainment (WWE)*
1241 E Main St
Titan Towers
Stamford, CT 06902-3520, USA

Kane, Big Daddy (Musician)
c/o Ron Rivlin *Coast II Coast Entertainment*
204 S Beverly Dr Ste 110
Beverly Hills, CA 90212-3800, USA

Kane, Carol (Actor)
c/o Wes Stevens *Vox*
6420 Wilshire Blvd Ste 1080
Los Angeles, CA 90048-5539, USA

Kane, Chelsea (Actor, Musician)
8418 Lookout Mountain Ave
Los Angeles, CA 90046-1551, USA

Kane, Christian (Actor, Musician)
9116 Wonderland Ave
Los Angeles, CA 90046-1858, USA

Kane, Frank ""Red""
2102 Ravinia Dr
Arlington, TX 76012-4444, USA

Kane, John C (Business Person)
Cardinal Health
7000 Cardinal Pl
Dublin, OH 43017-1091, USA

Kane, Jonny (Race Car Driver)
7615 Zionsville Rd
Indianapolis, IN 46268-2174, USA

Kane, Khalil (Actor)
c/o Staff Member *Envision Entertainment*
8840 Wilshire Blvd Fl 3
Beverly Hills, CA 90211-2606, USA

Kane, Nick (Musician)
AstroMedia
1620 16th Ave S
Nashville, TN 37212-2908, USA

Kane, Patrick (Athlete, Hockey Player)
c/o Pat Brisson *Creative Artists Agency*
(CAA-LA)
2000 Avenue of the Stars Ste 100
Los Angeles, CA 90067-4705, USA

Kane, Patrick (Athlete, Hockey Player)
401 N Wabash Ave Unit 33J
Chicago, IL 60611-3637, USA

Kane, Richard (Athlete, Football Player)
2525 Greensboro Pt
Reno, NV 89509-5708, USA

Kane Elson, Marion (Swimmer)
4669 Badger Rd
Santa Rosa, CA 95409-2632, USA

Kanell, Danny (Athlete, Football Player)
32 Sheffield Ln
Avon, CT 06001-3189, USA

Kanellis, Maria (Actor, Wrestler)
c/o Jessica Cohen *JCPR*
9903 Santa Monica Blvd Ste 983
Beverly Hills, CA 90212-1671, USA

Kaneshiro, Takeshi (Actor)
c/o Staff Member *William Morris*
Endeavor (LA)
9601 Wilshire Blvd
Beverly Hills, CA 90210-5213, USA

Kaneswaran, Siva
c/o Scooter Braun *SB Management*
825 8th Ave Fl 28
New York, NY 10019-7416, USA

Kanew, Jeffery R (Director)
c/o Staff Member *Directors Guild of*
America
7920 W Sunset Blvd Ste 600
Los Angeles, CA 90046-3347, USA

Kang, Jimin (Athlete, Golfer)
8539 E Cactus Wren Cir
Scottsdale, AZ 85266-1332, USA

Kang, Sung (Actor)
c/o Scott Schachter *United Talent Agency*
(UTA-LA)
9336 Civic Center Dr
Beverly Hills, CA 90210-3604, USA

Kang, Tim (Actor)
c/o Anna Liza Recto *Vincent Cirrincione*
Associates
1516 N Fairfax Ave
Los Angeles, CA 90046-2608, USA

Kangas-Brody, Jennifer (Athlete, Golfer)
6275 Knob Bend Dr
Grand Blanc, MI 48439-7459, USA

Kanicki, James (Athlete, Football Player)
PO Box 518
Ashtabula, OH 44005-0518, USA

Kanievska, Marek (Director)
International Creative Mgmt
10250 Constellation Blvd Fl 1
Los Angeles, CA 90067-6241, USA

Kann, Peter R (Business Person, Journalist,
Publisher)
Dow Jones Co
200 Liberty St Fl 9
New York, NY 10281-2101, USA

Kann, Stan
570 N Rossmore Ave
Los Angeles, CA 90004-2465

Kanouse, Lyle (Actor)
c/o Staff Member *Gage Group, The (LA)*
5757 Wilshire Blvd Ste 659
Los Angeles, CA 90036-3682, USA

Kansas (Music Group)
c/o Staff Member *Creative Artists Agency*
(CAA-LA)
2000 Avenue of the Stars Ste 100
Los Angeles, CA 90067-4705, USA

Kanter, Paul (Musician)
Ron Rainey Mgmt
315 S Beverly Dr Ste 407
Beverly Hills, CA 90212-4301, USA

Kantor, Secy
5019 Klingle St NW
Washington, DC 20016-2653, USA

Kantrowitz, Adrian (Doctor)
70 Gallogly Rd
Lake Angelus, MI 48326-1227, USA

Kao, Archie (Actor)
c/o Tim Kwok *Convergence Entertainment*
9150 Wilshire Blvd Ste 247
Beverly Hills, CA 90212-3429, USA

Kapadia, Asif (Actor, Director, Writer)
c/o Robert (Bob) Bookman *Paradigm (LA)*
2000 Avenue of the Stars
Los Angeles, CA 90067-4700, USA

Kapele, John (Athlete, Football Player)
45-543 Paleka Rd Apt A
Kaneohe, HI 96744-3413, USA

Kapelos, John (Actor)
c/o Staff Member *McCabe Group, The*
3211 Cahuenga Blvd W Ste 104
Los Angeles, CA 90068-1372, USA

Kapinos, Tom (Producer, Writer)
15960 Alcima Ave
Pacific Palisades, CA 90272-2404, USA

Kapioitas, John (Business Person)
ITT Sheraton Corp
1111 Westchester Ave
West Harrison, NY 10604-3525, USA

Kaplan, Gabe
2732 McConnell Dr
Los Angeles, CA 90064-3405, USA

Kaplan, Jonathan S (Director)
4323 Ben Ave
Studio City, CA 91604-1704, USA

Kaplan, Ken (Athlete, Football Player)
8313 N Fremont Ave
Tampa, FL 33604-2707, USA

Kaplan, Marvin (Actor)
PO Box 1522
Burbank, CA 91507-1522, USA

Kaplan, Steven (Actor)
c/o Ellen Gilbert *Abrams Artists Agency*
(LA)
9200 W Sunset Blvd PH 11
West Hollywood, CA 90069-3601, USA

Kapler, Gabe (Athlete, Baseball Player)
30375 Morning View Dr
Malibu, CA 90265-3618, USA

Kaplon, Al (Actor)
2899 Agoura Rd Ste 172
Westlake Village, CA 91361-3218, USA

Kapono, Jason (Athlete, Basketball Player)
22 Benevolo Dr
Henderson, NV 89011-3134, USA

Kapoor, Ravi (Actor)
c/o Matthew Lesher *Insight*
PO Box 36359
Los Angeles, CA 90036-0359, USA

Kapp, Joseph (Joe) (Athlete, Football
Player)
233 Edelen Ave
Los Gatos, CA 95030-6005, USA

Kapp Horner, Alex (Actor, Producer)
c/o Staff Member *T&A Pictures*
15233 Ventura Blvd Fl 9
Sherman Oaks, CA 91403-2250, USA

Kaptur, Marcy (Congressman, Politician)
2186 Rayburn Hob
Washington, DC 20515-1502, USA

Kapture, Mitzi (Actor)
c/o Rod Baron *Baron Entertainment*
13848 Ventura Blvd Ste A
Sherman Oaks, CA 91423-3654

Karabin, Ladislav (Athlete, Hockey Player)
8907 Russo Rd
Ft. Pierce, FL 349S1, USA

Karamatic, George (Athlete, Football
Player)
982 Donald Way
Santa Maria, CA 93455-5019, USA

Karan, Donna (Designer, Fashion
Designer)
Donna Karan
550 Seventh Ave
New York, NY 10018, USA

Karath, Kym (Actor)
40 Halsey Dr
Old Greenwich, CT 06870-1226, USA

Karatz, Bruce E (Business Person)
Kaufman & Broad Home
10990 Wilshire Blvd Fl 5
Los Angeles, CA 90024-3902, USA

Karcher, Ken (Athlete, Football Player)
PO Box 862
Decatur, MS 39327-0862, USA

Karchner, Matt (Athlete, Baseball Player)
401 E 2nd St
Berwick, PA 18603-4801, USA

Kardashian, Khloe (Actor)
25202 Prado Del Grandioso
Calabasas, CA 91302-3654, USA

Kardashian, Kim (Actor, Model, Reality
Star)
c/o Ina Treciokas *Slate Public Relations*
9000 W Sunset Blvd Ste 915
West Hollywood, CA 90069-5809, USA

Kardashian, Kourtney (Reality Star)
25344 Prado De La Felicidad
Calabasas, CA 91302-3649, USA

Kardashian, Rob (Actor, Reality Star)
c/o Lance Klein *William Morris Endeavor*
(LA)
9601 Wilshire Blvd
Beverly Hills, CA 90210-5213, USA

Karen, James
4455 Los Feliz Blvd Apt 807
Los Angeles, CA 90027-2138

Karim, Reef (Actor)
c/o Staff Member *Daris Hatch*
Management
10027 Rossbury Pl
Los Angeles, CA 90064-4825, USA

Karin, Anna (Actor)
Greene Assoc
7080 Hollywood Blvd Ste 1017
Los Angeles, CA 90028-6937, USA

Karkovice, Ron (Athlete, Baseball Player)
7900 Northlake Pkwy
Orlando, FL 32827-6914, USA

Karl, George (Athlete, Basketball Player)
145 Kearney St
Denver, CO 80220-5924, USA

Karl, George (Coach)
10936 N Port Washington Rd
Mequon, WI 53092-5031, USA

Karl, Jan
5555 Melrose Ave # L
Los Angeles, CA 90038-3989

Karl, Scott (Athlete, Baseball Player)
11765 Costa Blanca Ave
Las Vegas, NV 89138-4556, USA

Karlander, Al (Athlete, Hockey Player)
4940 Deer Ridge Dr N
Carmel, IN 46033-8904, USA

Karlander, Al (Athlete, Hockey Player)
249 W Admiral Way S
Carmel, IN 46032-5152, USA

Karlen, John (Actor)
2940 N Verdugo Rd Unit 202
Glendale, CA 91208-2152, USA

Karlin, Ben (Producer, Writer)
c/o Staff Member *3 Arts Entertainment*
(LA)
9460 Wilshire Blvd Fl 7
Beverly Hills, CA 90212-2713, USA

Karlin, Fred
1187 Coast Village Rd # 1-339
Santa Barbara, CA 93108-2737

Karlis, Rich (Athlete, Football Player)
6740 Ponderosa Dr
Parker, CO 80138-8023, USA

Karloff, Sara
PO Box 2424
Rancho Mirage, CA 92270-1087

Karlson, Kristine (Athlete, Olympic
Athlete, Rower)
4 Pinneo Hill Rd
Hanover, NH 03755-4600, USA

Karlson, Phil
3094 Patricia Ave
Los Angeles, CA 90064-4534

Karlsson, Lena (Musician)
MOB Agency
6404 Wilshire Blvd Ste 505
Los Angeles, CA 90048-5507, USA

Karlzen, Mary (Musician, Songwriter,
Writer)
Little Big Man
155 Avenue of the Americas Rm 700
New York, NY 10013-1507, USA

Karmanos Jr, Peter (Business Person)
Compuware Corp
1 Campus Martius
Detroit, MI 48226-5099, USA

Karn, Richard (Actor)
c/o Staff Member *Stone Manners Salners*
Agency (LA)
6100 Wilshire Blvd Ste 1500
Los Angeles, CA 90048-5110, USA

Karnes, David K (Ex-Senator)
Kutak Rock
1650 Farnam St Fl 2
Omaha Building
Omaha, NE 68102-2186, USA

Karnes, Jay (Actor)
c/o Jonathan Howard *Innovative Artists*
(LA)
1505 10th St
Santa Monica, CA 90401-2805, USA

Karnofsky, Sonny (Athlete, Football
Player)
14801 Nevar Ct
Rancho Murieta, CA 95683-9553, USA

Karns, Christine (Race Car Driver)
Karns Racing
24 Grieson Rd
Honey Brook, PA 19344-9757, USA

Karnuth, Jason (Athlete, Baseball Player)
2822 Helding Park Ct
Katy, TX 77494-8522, USA

Karol, Scott (Producer)
c/o Staff Member *Crystal Sky Pictures*
10203 Santa Monica Blvd Fl 5
Los Angeles, CA 90067-6416, USA

Karolyi, Bela (Athlete, Coach, Olympic
Athlete)
454 Forest Service 200 Rd
Huntsville, TX 77340-2686, USA

Karon, Jan (Writer)
643 Eight Woods Ln
Charlottesville, VA 22903-4676, USA

Karp, Ryan (Athlete, Baseball Player)
8 Fox Run Rd
Medway, MA 02053-2242, USA

Karpa, Dave (Athlete, Hockey Player)
23668 N Lookout Pointe Rd
Port Barrington, IL 60010-1083

Karpatkin, Rhonda H (Publisher)
Consumer Reports Magazine
101 Truman Ave
Yonkers, NY 10703-1057, USA

Karpinski, Keith (Athlete, Football Player)
1803 Sycamore Ave
Royal Oak, MI 48073-5020, USA

Karpluk, Erin (Actor)
c/o Staff Member *ROAR (LA)*
9701 Wilshire Blvd Fl 8
Beverly Hills, CA 90212-2008, USA

Karpowich, Ed (Athlete, Football Player)
PO Box 177
Fallon, NV 89407-0177, USA

Karr, Mary (Writer)
Syracuse University
English Dept
Syracuse, NY 13244-0001, USA

Karras, Louis (Athlete, Football Player)
904 Tulip Cir
Weston, FL 33327-2450, USA

Karras, Ted (Athlete, Football Player)
1122 N Shelby St
Gary, IN 46403-1447, USA

Karros, Eric P (Athlete, Baseball Player)
PO Box 2380
Manhattan Beach, CA 90267-2380, USA

Karsay, Steve (Athlete, Baseball Player)
20244 N 102nd Pl # 1213
Scottsdale, AZ 85255-7151, USA

Karstens, Jeff (Athlete, Baseball Player)
7280 Jamacha Rd
San Diego, CA 92114-3013, USA

Kartheiser, Vincent (Actor)
c/o Evan Hainey *Untitled Entertainment*
(LA)
350 S Beverly Dr Ste 200
Beverly Hills, CA 90212-4819, USA

Kartz, Keith (Athlete, Football Player)
19232 E Hinsdale Ln
Centennial, CO 80016-2147, USA

Karyo, Tcheky (Actor)
c/o Staff Member *Current Entertainment*
9200 W Sunset Blvd Ste 600
West Hollywood, CA 90069-3196, USA

Kasabian, Kamera (Musician)
c/o Staff Member *Paradigm (Monterey)*
404 W Franklin St
Monterey, CA 93940-2303, USA

Kasabov, Anton (Actor)
c/o Scott Karp *The Syndicate*
10203 Santa Monica Blvd Fl 5
Los Angeles, CA 90067-6416, USA

Kasatonov, Alexei (Athlete, Hockey
Player)
153 Eagle Rock Way
Montclair, NJ 07042-1621, USA

Kasay, John (Athlete, Football Player)
8711 Lake Challis Ln
Charlotte, NC 28226-2666, USA

Kasch, Cody (Actor)
c/o Staff Member *ICM Partners (LA)*
10250 Constellation Blvd Fl 7
Los Angeles, CA 90067-6207, USA

Kasch, Max (Actor)
c/o Staff Member *Abrams Artists Agency*
(LA)
9200 W Sunset Blvd PH 11
West Hollywood, CA 90069-3601, USA

Kasdan, Lawrence (Actor, Director,
Producer, Writer)
c/o Staff Member *Kasdan Pictures*
9220 W Sunset Blvd Ste 108
West Hollywood, CA 90069-3500, USA

Kaselowski, Brian (Race Car Driver)
K Auto Motorsports
2790 Auburn Rd
Auburn Hills, MI 48326-3180, USA

Kasem, Jean (Actor)
138 N Mapleton Dr
Los Angeles, CA 90077-3536, USA

Kasem, Kerri (Actor)
c/o Steve Rohr *Lexicon Public Relations*
8430 Santa Monica Blvd Ste 203
West Hollywood, CA 90069-4253, USA

Kash, Daniel (Actor, Director)
c/o Staff Member *Coolwaters Productions*
10061 Riverside Dr # 531
Toluca Lake, CA 91602-2560, USA

Kashkashian, Kim (Musician)
c/o Staff Member *Musicians Corporate
Management*
PO Box 825
Highland, NY 12528-0825, USA

Kashner, Sam (Writer)
c/o Staff Member *Simon & Schuster*
1230 Avenue of the Americas Fl CONC1
New York, NY 10020-1586, USA

Kasich, John (Governor, Politician)
Governor's Office
77 S High St Fl 30
Riffe Center, 30th Floor
Columbus, OH 43215-6117, USA

Kaskade (DJ, Musician)
c/o Barry Taylor *MCT Management*
104 W 29th St Rm 1101
New York, NY 10001-5310, USA

Kasko, Eddie (Athlete, Baseball Player,
Coach)
32 Major Ginter Ct
Richmond, VA 23227-3349, USA

Kasl, Dr. Charlotte (Writer)
Many Roads, One Journey
PO Box 1302
Lolo, MT 59847-1302, USA

Kason, Corinne (Actor)
Lovell Assoc
7095 Hollywood Blvd Ste 1006
Los Angeles, CA 90028-8912, USA

Kasparaitis, Darius (Athlete, Hockey
Player)
16400 NE 30th Ave
N Miami Beach, FL 33160-4133, USA

Kasparaltis, Darius
170 Fairway Landings Dr
Canonsburg, PA 15317-9567

Kasper, Kevin (Athlete, Football Player)
3119 Landore Dr
Naperville, IL 60564-4100, USA

Kasper, Len (Commentator)
445 Drexel Ave
Glencoe, IL 60022-2102, USA

Kasper, Steve (Athlete, Coach, Hockey
Player)
6 Swan Ln
Andover, MA 01810-2844, USA

Kasperek, Dick (Athlete, Football Player)
PO Box 99
Glenn, MI 49416-0099, USA

Kass, Danny (Skier)
PO Box 8549
Mammoth Lakes, CA 93546-8549, USA

Kassebaum, Nancy Landon (Ex-Senator)
US Embassy
Tokyo
Unit 45004 Box 200
Huntsville, AP 37756, USA

Kassebaum-Baker, Nancy (Ex-Senator)
PO Box 8
Huntsville, TN 37756-0008, USA

Kassell, Brad (Athlete, Football Player)
20117 Rancho Cielo Ct
Lago Vista, TX 78645-6046, USA

Kassell, Carl (Correspondent)
National Public Radio
1111 N Capitol St NE
Washington, DC 20002-7502, USA

Kassir, John (Actor)
c/o Vincent Cirrincione *Vincent
Cirrincione Associates*
1516 N Fairfax Ave
Los Angeles, CA 90046-2608, USA

Kassorla, Irene C (Doctor)
908 N Roxbury Dr
Beverly Hills, CA 90210-3020, USA

Kastelic, Ed (Athlete, Hockey Player)
1839 W Muirwood Dr
Phoenix, AZ 85045-1773

Kasten, Robert
1683 31st St NW
Washington, DC 20007-2968, USA

Kaster, Deena (Athlete, Olympic Athlete,
Track Athlete)
1208 Majestic Pines Dr
Mammoth Lakes, CA 93546, USA

Kastor, Deena (Olympic Athlete, Track
Athlete)
PO Box 5068
Mammoth Lakes, CA 93546-5068, USA

Kata, Matt (Athlete, Baseball Player)
563 Treeside Ln
Avon Lake, OH 44012-2748, USA

Katchor, Ben (Cartoonist)
Little Brown
3 Center Plz Ste 100
Boston, MA 02108-2084, USA

Kate, Lauren (Writer)
PO Box 461514
Los Angeles, CA 90046-9514, USA

Kates, Kimberley (Actor)
David Talent
116 S Gardner St
Los Angeles, CA 90036-2718, USA

Kates, Kimberly
3500 W Olive Ave Ste 1400
Burbank, CA 91505-5512

Katic, Stana (Actor)
c/o Staff Member *Sine Timore*
195 S Beverly Dr Ste 400
Beverly Hills, CA 90212-3044, USA

Katims, Jason (Producer)
c/o Staff Member *Creative Artists Agency*
(CAA-LA)
2000 Avenue of the Stars Ste 100
Los Angeles, CA 90067-4705, USA

Katkaveck, Leo (Athlete, Basketball
Player)
1408 Jeremy Ln
Rocky Mount, NC 27803-1516, USA

Katolin, Mike (Athlete, Football Player)
308 Loyola Dr
Aptos, CA 95003-5228, USA

Katsoudas, Stella (Musician, Songwriter,
Writer)
Ashley Talent
2002 Hogback Rd Ste 20
Ann Arbor, MI 48105-9736, USA

Katt, Nicky (Actor)
c/o John Carrabino *John Carrabino
Management*
5900 Wilshire Blvd Ste 406
Los Angeles, CA 90036-5015, USA

Katt, William (Actor)
5860 Le Sage Ave
Woodland Hills, CA 91367-5902, USA

Kattan, Chris (Actor, Comedian)
c/o Evan Hainey *Untitled Entertainment*
(LA)
350 S Beverly Dr Ste 200
Beverly Hills, CA 90212-4819, USA

Kattus, Eric (Athlete, Football Player)
854 Adams Rd
Loveland, OH 45140-7242, USA

Katula, Matt (Athlete, Football Player)
813 Crystal Palace Ct
Owings Mills, MD 21117-2257, USA

Katz, Cindy
Badgley Connor Talent Agency
1680 Vine St Ste 1016
Los Angeles, CA 90028-8800, USA

Katz, Jonathan (Actor, Animator,
Comedian, Producer)
c/o Bonnie Burns *Burns & Burns
Management*
10523 Mars Ln
Los Angeles, CA 90077-3109, USA

Katz, Omri (Actor)
JH Productions
23679 Calabasas Rd # 333
Calabasas, CA 91302-1502, USA

Katz, Ross (Producer)
c/o Staff Member *United Talent Agency
(UTA-LA)*
9336 Civic Center Dr
Beverly Hills, CA 90210-3604, USA

katz, Vera (Politician)
Mayor's Office
1221 SW 4th Ave # 340
City Hall
Portland, OR 97204-1900, USA

Katzenberg, Jeffrey (Business Person)
1025 Loma Vista Dr
Beverly Hills, CA 90210-2620, USA

Katzenmayer, Travis (Baseball Player)
562 N Overland
Mesa, AZ 85207-6670, USA

Katzenmeier, Travis (Athlete, Baseball
Player)
1128 N Mountain Rd
Mesa, AZ 85207-2408, USA

Katzenmoyer, Andy (Athlete, Football
Player)
859 W Main St
Westerville, OH 43081-1224, USA

Kauahi, Kani (Athlete, Game Show Host)
10350 W McDowell Rd Apt 3160
Avondale, AZ 85392-4831, USA

kauffman, bob (Athlete, Basketball Player)
1677 Rivermist Dr SW
Lilburn, GA 30047-2451, USA

Kauffman, Joel (Race Car Driver)
Kitzbradshaw Racing
114 Meadow Hill Cir
Mooresville, NC 28117-8089, USA

Kauffman, Marta (Producer, Writer)
c/o Staff Member *Bright Kauffman Crane
Productions*
4000 Warner Blvd Bldg 750
Burbank, CA 91522-0001

Kaufman, Adam (Actor)
c/o Steven Levy *Framework Entertainment
(LA)*
9057 Nemo St Ste C
West Hollywood, CA 90069-5511, USA

Kaufman, Avy (Actor)
c/o Rick Kurtzman *Creative Artists Agency
(CAA-LA)*
2000 Avenue of the Stars Ste 100
Los Angeles, CA 90067-4705, USA

Kaufman, Bob (Ajax) (Athlete, Basketball
Player)
1677 Rivermist Dr SW
Lilburn, GA 30047-2451, USA

Kaufman, Charlie (Writer)
c/o Sharon Jackson *William Morris
Endeavor (LA)*
9601 Wilshire Blvd
Beverly Hills, CA 90210-5213, USA

Kaufman, Curt (Athlete, Baseball Player)
308 Hillway Dr
Glenwood, IA 51534-1210, USA

Kaufman, Donald (Writer)
c/o Staff Member *United Talent Agency
(UTA-LA)*
9336 Civic Center Dr
Beverly Hills, CA 90210-3604, USA

Kaufman, Joan (Athlete, Baseball Player,
Commentator)
1111 Crystal Spg
San Antonio, TX 78258-6909, USA

Kaufman, Moises (Director)
c/o Patty Detroit *Todd Smith and
Associates*
10250 Constellation Blvd Fl 7
Los Angeles, CA 90067-6207, USA

Kaufman, Napolean (Athlete, Football
Player)
72 Incline Green Ln
Alamo, CA 94507-2334, USA

Kaufman, Napoleon (Athlete, Football
Player)
1913 Via Di Salemo
Pleasanton, CA 94566, USA

Kaufman, Tim (Race Car Driver)
Kaufman Racing
8201 Meade Ave
Burbank, IL 60459-1944, USA

Kaufusi, Steve (Athlete, Football Player)
3018 Comanche Ln
Provo, UT 84604-4344, USA

Kauth, Kathleen (Athlete, Hockey Player,
Olympic Athlete)
13 Hillcrest Ln
Saratoga Springs, NY 12866-8528, USA

Kavana (Musician)
Tony Denton Promotions
19 S Molton Ln
Mayfair
London, EN W1K 5

Kavanagh, Brad (Actor)
c/o Jeff Golenberg *Silver Lining
Entertainment*
421 S Beverly Dr Fl 7
Beverly Hills, CA 90212-4408, USA

Kavanaugh, Ryan (Producer)
c/o Staff Member *Relativity Media*
9242 Beverly Blvd Ste 300
Beverly Hills, CA 90210-3728, USA

Kavandi, Janet L (Astronaut)
3907 Park Circle Way
Houston, TX 77059-3019, USA

Kavner, Julie (Actor)
c/o Paul Martino *Martino Management*
730 5th Ave
New York, NY 10019-4105, USA

Kavovit, Andrew (Actor)
c/o Staff Member *TalentWorks (LA)*
3500 W Olive Ave Ste 1400
Burbank, CA 91505-5512, USA

Kawasaki, Guy (Business Person, Writer)
c/o Staff Member *Keynote Speakers*
2686 Middlefield Rd Ste F
Redwood City, CA 94063-3481, USA

Kay, Bill (Athlete, Football Player)
4266 Waterston Courtyard
Evans, GA 30809-5036, USA

Kay, Dianne (Actor)
1565 Calle Del Estribo
Pacific Palisades, CA 90272-2009, USA

Kay, Jason (Jay) (Musician)
c/o Staff Member *William Morris
Endeavor (LA)*
9601 Wilshire Blvd Ste 1
Beverly Hills, CA 90210-5213, USA

Kay, John (Musician)
Elite Management Corp
2211 Norfolk St Ste 760
Houston, TX 77098-4033, USA

Kay, Michael (Athlete, Baseball Player)
58 Dingletown Rd
Greenwich, CT 06830-3539, USA

Kay, Vanessa (Actor)
c/o Staff Member *Comedy Central (LA)*
2049 Century Park E # 4170
Los Angeles, CA 90067-3101, USA

Kay, William H (Athlete, Football Player)
4266 Waterston Courtyard
Evans, GA 30809-5036, USA

Kaye, David (Actor)
10443 Kling St
Toluca Lake, CA 91602-1529, USA

Kaye, Jonathan (Athlete, Golfer)
328 W El Camino Dr
Phoenix, AZ 85021-5525, USA

Kaye, Judy (Actor, Musician)
Bret Adams
448 W 44th St
New York, NY 10036-5220, USA

Kaye, Justin (Athlete, Baseball Player)
3591 Arville St Unit 302B
Las Vegas, NV 89103-1679, USA

Kaye, Melvina
PO Box 6085
Burbank, CA 91510-6085

Kaye, Thorsten (Actor)
c/o Staff Member *ICM Partners (LA)*
10250 Constellation Blvd Fl 7
Los Angeles, CA 90067-6207, USA

Kayleigh, Layla (Actor, Television Host)
c/o Staff Member *United Talent Agency
(UTA-LA)*
9336 Civic Center Dr
Beverly Hills, CA 90210-3604, USA

Kazan, Lainie (Actor, Musician)
9903 Santa Monica Blvd # 283
Beverly Hills, CA 90212-1671, USA

Kazan, Zoe (Actor)
c/o Jennifer Konawal *Washington Square
Arts (NY)*
310 Bowery Fl 2
New York, NY 10012-2861, USA

Kazanski, Ted (Athlete, Baseball Player)
1544 Dormie Dr
Gladwin, MI 48624-8104, USA

Kazer, Beau
139-A N San Fernando Rd
Burbank, CA 91502

Kazmar, sean
4 Los Llanos
Edgewood, NM 87015, USA

Kazmir, Scott (Athlete, Baseball Player)
9206 Point Park Dr
Houston, TX 77095-2189, USA

KC & The Sunshine Band (Music Group)
c/o Kirt Webster *Webster & Associates PR*
3573 Couchville Pike
Hermitage, TN 37076-4012, USA

K-Ci & JoJo (Music Group)
c/o Staff Member *Devour*
3575 Cahuenga Blvd W Ste 254
Los Angeles, CA 90068-1341, USA

K D, Dunn (Athlete, Football Player)
2264 Colleen Ct
Decatur, GA 30032-7153, USA

K. Davis, Danny (Congressman, Politician)
2159 Rayburn Hob
Washington, DC 20515-2307, USa

Kea, Clarence (Athlete, Basketball Player)
9175 Jennifer St
Beaumont, TX 77707-2727, USA

Keach, James (Actor)
c/o Staff Member *Catfish Productions*
24800 Pacific Coast Hwy
Malibu, CA 90265-4733, USA

Keach, Stacy (Actor)
101 N Robertson Blvd Ste 200
Beverly Hills, CA 90211-2191, USA

Keady, Gene (Coach)
Purdue University
Mackey Arena
West Lafayette, IN 47907, USA

Keagan, Carrie (Television Host)
c/o Staff Member *No Good TV (NGTV)*
9944 Santa Monica Blvd
Beverly Hills, CA 90212-1607, USA

Keaggy, Ian (Musician)
493 Saddle Dr
Nashville, TN 37221-1903, USA

Keaggy, Phil (Musician)
c/o Staff Member *Street Level Artists
Agency*
107 E Center St
Warsaw, IN 46580-2841, USA

Keagle, Greg (Athlete, Baseball Player)
11 Wolcott Dr
Horseheads, NY 14845-1012, USA

Kealey, Steve (Athlete, Baseball Player)
12221 E Zimmerly Ct
Wichita, KS 67207-6579, USA

Kean, Laurel (Athlete, Golfer)
25280 Ojibway Ct
Punta Gorda, FL 33983-6069, USA

Kean, Thomas H (Ex-Governor)
Quad Partners
360 W 31st St Rm 1501
New York, NY 10001-2727, USA

Keanan, Staci (Actor)
c/o Jennifer Goodwin *PMK/BNC Public
Relations (PMK-LA)*
8687 Melrose Ave Ste 8
West Hollywood, CA 90069-5746, USA

Keane, Glen (Animator)
c/o Staff Member *Disney Animation (LA)*
500 S Buena Vista St
Burbank, CA 91521-9500, USA

Keane, Jeff (Cartoonist)
c/o Claudia Smith *King Features
Syndication*
300 W 57th St Fl 15
New York, NY 10019-5238, USA

Keane, Katie Amanda (Actor)
c/o Paul Bennett *PB Management*
6523 W 6th St
Los Angeles, CA 90048-4715, USA

Keane, Kerrie (Actor)
S D B Partners
315 S Beverly Dr Ste 411
Beverly Hills, CA 90212-4301, USA

Keans, Doug (Athlete, Hockey Player)
240 Dartmouth Ave
Spring Hill, FL 34606-5435

Kearney, Bob (Athlete, Baseball Player)
4155 Elizabeth Dr
Stevensville, MI 49127-9530, USA

Kearney, Jim (Athlete, Football Player)
Washington High School
1817 E 59th St
Kansas City, MO 64130-3329, USA

Kearney, Mat (Musician)
c/o Jason Rio *A-Squared Management*
1316 Sherman Ave Ste 215
Evanston, IL 60201-4361, USA

Kearney, Tim (Athlete, Football Player)
2144 Dartmouth Gate Ct
Ballwin, MO 63011-5436, USA

Kearns, Austin (Athlete, Baseball Player)
719 Haverhill Dr
Lexington, KY 40503-3426, USA

Kearns, Michael (Athlete, Basketball Player)
2118 Wilson Ave
Monroe, NC 28110-9168, USA

Kearns, Thomas (Athlete, Basketball Player)
27 Deepwood Rd
Darien, CT 06820-3202, USA

Kearns, Thomas (Athlete, Football Player)
121 Bay Colony Dr
Fort Lauderdale, FL 33308-2024, USA

Kearse, Jevon (Athlete, Football Player)
61 Whitworth Blvd
Nashville, TN 37205-5019, USA

Keaser, Lloyd (Athlete, Olympic Athlete, Wrestler)
43960 Tavern Dr
Ashburn, VA 20147-3905, USA

Keathley, George (Director)
Missouri Repertory Theater
4949 Cherry St
Kansas City, MO 64110-2229, USA

Keating, Bill (Athlete, Football Player)
4810 S Lafayette Ln
Englewood, CO 80113-7011, USA

Keating, Chris (Athlete, Football Player)
741 Canton Ave
Milton, MA 02186-3121, USA

Keating, Dominic (Actor)
c/o Staff Member *Shelter Entertainment*
9255 W Sunset Blvd Ste 320
West Hollywood, CA 90069-3313, USA

Keating, Thomas A (Athlete, Football Player)
3725 W St NW
Washington, DC 20007-1714, USA

Keatley, Greg (Athlete, Baseball Player)
140 Rockridge Ct
Lexington, SC 29072-7970, USA

Keaton, Curtis (Athlete, Football Player)
246 Briarcliff Dr
Kannapolis, NC 28081-7155, USA

Keaton, Diane (Actor, Director, Producer)
c/o Adam Venit *William Morris Endeavor (LA)*
9601 Wilshire Blvd
Beverly Hills, CA 90210-5213, USA

Keaton, Joshua (Josh) (Actor)
c/o Brian Wilkins *Kritzer Levine Wilkins Entertainment (KLWG)*
11872 La Grange Ave Fl 1
Los Angeles, CA 90025-5283, USA

Keaton, Michael (Actor, Director, Producer)
c/o Doug Wald *Anonymous Content (LA)*
3532 Hayden Ave
Culver City, CA 90232-2413, USA

Keats, Ele (Actor)
c/o Rob D'Avola *Rob DAvola & Associates*
9107 Wilshire Blvd Ste 450
Beverly Hills, CA 90210-5535, USA

Kebbel, Arielle (Actor)
c/o Marty Berneman *Precision Entertainment*
465 N Croft Ave
Los Angeles, CA 90048-2508, USA

Kebbell, Toby (Actor)
c/o Samantha Mast *Rogers & Cowan PR (LA)*
8687 Melrose Ave Ste 7
West Hollywood, CA 90069-5721, USA

Kebede, Liya (Model)
c/o Staff Member *IMG Models (NY)*
304 Park Ave S Fl 12
New York, NY 10010-4314, USA

Keb Mo (Musician, Songwriter, Writer)
Monterey International
200 W Superior St Ste 202
Chicago, IL 60654-6422, USA

Keckin, Val (Athlete, Football Player)
8918 Montrose Way
San Diego, CA 92122, USA

Kecman, Dan (Athlete, Football Player)
15308 Georgian Square Ct
Rockville, MD 20853-1822, USA

Keczmer, Dan (Athlete, Olympic Athlete)
PO Box 2883
Brentwood, TN 37024-2883, USA

Keczmer, Don (Athlete, Hockey Player)
8303 Bridle Pl
Brentwood, TN 37027-8128, USA

Kedes, Maureen (Actor)
Tisherman Agency
6767 Forest Lawn Dr # 101
Los Angeles, CA 90068-1027, USA

Keeble, Jerry (Athlete, Football Player)
PO Box 367
Dunnigan, CA 95937-0367, USA

Keeble, John (Musician)
International Talent Group
729 7th Ave Ste 1600
New York, NY 10019-6880, USA

Keedy, Pat (Athlete, Baseball Player)
6308 Mountainview Cir
Gardendale, AL 35071-2088, USA

Keefe, Adam (Athlete, Basketball Player)
15933 Alcima Ave
Pacific Palisades, CA 90272-2405, USA

Keefe, Mike (Cartoonist)
Denver Post
PO Box 1709
Editorial Dept
Denver, CO 80201-1709, USA

Keegan, Andrew (Actor)
c/o Barry McPherson *Agency for the Performing Arts (APA-NY)*
135 W 50th St Fl 17
New York, NY 10020-1201, USA

Keegan, Ed
PO Box 764
Malaga, NJ 08328-0764, USA

Keegan, Kari (Actor)
2042 S Oxford Ave
Los Angeles, CA 90018-1529, USA

Keehne, Virginya (Actor)
Craig Mgmt
125 S Sycamore Ave
Los Angeles, CA 90036-2938, USA

Keeler, Don
24000 Jensen Dr
Canoga Park, CA 91304-3011

Keeler, William H Cardinal (Religious Leader)
National Conference of Catholic Bishops
3211 4th St NE
Washington, DC 20017-1104, USA

Keeling, Charles D (Musician)
Scripps Oceanography Institute
Ritler Hall
9500 Gilman Dr
La Jolla, CA 92093-0001, USA

Keeling, Harold (Athlete, Basketball Player)
6707 Broad Oaks Dr
Richmond, TX 77406-7629, USA

Keelor, Greg (Musician)
c/o Staff Member *ArtistDirect*
9046 Lindblade St
Culver City, CA 90232-2513, USA

Keen, Robert Earl (Musician, Songwriter)
Rosetta
PO Box 2186
Bandera, TX 78003-2186, USA

Keen, Sam (Writer)
16331 Norrbom Rd
Sonoma, CA 95476-4783, USA

Keena, Monica (Actor)
c/o Kieran Maguire *The Arlook Group*
205 S Beverly Dr Ste 209
Beverly Hills, CA 90212-3899, USA

Keenan, Maynard James (Musician)
c/o Staff Member *Virgin Records (NY)*
150 5th Ave Fl 7
New York, NY 10011-4372, USA

Keene, Tommy (Musician, Songwriter, Writer)
Black Park Mgmt
PO Box 107
Sunbury, NC 27979-0107, USA

Keenen, Mary Jo
9200 W Sunset Blvd Ste 1130
West Hollywood, CA 90069-3606

Keener, Catherine (Actor)
c/o Leslie Siebert *Gersh (LA)*
9465 Wilshire Blvd Ste 600
Beverly Hills, CA 90212-2605, USA

Keener, Jeff (Athlete, Baseball Player)
2107 Dewey St
Murphysboro, IL 62966-2451, USA

Keener, Joe (Athlete, Baseball Player)
16915 Glendower Ave
Edwards, CA 93523-3515, USA

Keeslar, Matt (Actor)
c/o Staff Member *Stone Manners Salners Agency (LA)*
6100 Wilshire Blvd Ste 1500
Los Angeles, CA 90048-5110, USA

Keesling, Barbara (Writer)
c/o Staff Member *Random House Publicity*
1745 Broadway Frnt 3
New York, NY 10019-4343, USA

Keeton, Durwood (Athlete, Football Player)
1372 Diamond Gate Pl
El Paso, TX 79936-7841, USA

Keeton, Rickey (Athlete, Baseball Player)
3433 Stathem Ave
Cincinnati, OH 45211-5723, USA

Keflezighi, Meb (Athlete, Olympic Athlete, Track Athlete)
141 Mammoth Knolls Dr
Mammoth Lakes, CA 93546, USA

Keggi, Caroline (Athlete, Golfer)
9228 E Happy Hollow Dr
Scottsdale, AZ 85262-2575, USA

Kehoe, Rick (Athlete, Hockey Player)
1027 Highland Dr
Canonsburg, PA 15317-5227

Keibler, Stacy (Actor, Wrestler)
c/o Stephanie Simon *Untitled Entertainment (LA)*
350 S Beverly Dr Ste 200
Beverly Hills, CA 90212-4819, USA

Keillor, Garrison E (Correspondent, Writer)
A Prairie Home Companion
480 Cedar St
Saint Paul, MN 55101-2217, USA

Keim, Jenny (Swimmer)
R O'Brien
1 Hall of Fame Dr
Swimming Hall of Fame
Fort Lauderdale, FL 33316-1611, USA

Keisler, Randy (Athlete, Baseball Player)
6842 Durango Creek Dr
Magnolia, TX 77354-2749, USA

Keitel, Harvey (Actor)
c/o Toni Howard *ICM Partners (LA)*
10250 Constellation Blvd Fl 7
Los Angeles, CA 90067-6207, USA

Keith, David (Actor, Director)
1449 Spring Pass Way
Knoxville, TN 37919-9044, USA

Keith, Duncan (Athlete, Hockey Player)
1700 W Melrose St
Chicago, IL 60657-1004, USA

Keith, Embray (Athlete, Football Player)
1232 Sunnymede Ave
South Bend, IN 46615-1016, USA

Keith, Louis (Doctor)
250 E Superior St
Chicago, IL 60611-2914, USA

Keith, Sarah (Actor)
c/o Ashley Partington *Abrams Artists Agency (LA)*
9200 W Sunset Blvd PH 11
West Hollywood, CA 90069-3601, USA

Keith, Toby (Musician)
PO Box 8739
Rockford, IL 61126-8739, USA

Keithley, Gary (Athlete, Football Player)
1801 W Westhill Dr
Cleburne, TX 76033-5952, USA

Kekich, Mike (Athlete, Baseball Player)
5314 Canada Vista Pl NW
Albuquerque, NM 87120-2412, USA

Kelce, Travis (Athlete, Football Player)
c/o Adam Heller *Vantage Management Group*
518 Reamer Dr
Carnegie, PA 15106-1845, USA

Kelcher, Louie J (Athlete, Football Player)
10204 Carlotta Cv
Austin, TX 78733-1542, USA

Kelis (Musician)
c/o Tracy Nguyen *Industry Public Relations*
16547 Park Lane Cir
Los Angeles, CA 90049-1184, USA

Kelis (Musician)
30 Vintage Ct
McDonough, GA 30253-4246, USA

Kelis, Kid 'N Play (Music Group)
1650 Broadway Ste 508
New York, NY 10019-6833, USA

Kelker-Kelly, Robert (Actor)
4704 Whitsett Ave
Studio City, CA 91604-1140, USA

Kell, Ayla (Actor)
c/o Scott Zimmerman *Evolution Entertainment (LA)*
901 N Highland Ave
Los Angeles, CA 90038-2412, USA

Kell, Everett (Skeeter) (Athlete, Baseball Player)
1108 Highland Dr
Newport, AR 72112-2628, USA

kell, Everett ""Skeeter"" (Athlete, Baseball Player)
1108 Highland Dr
Newport, AR 72112-2628, USA

Kellar, Mark (Athlete, Football Player)
5514 Oak Gln
Minneapolis, MN 55439-1944, USA

Kelleher, Chris
541 Kitchen Ln
Pittston, PA 18643

Kelleher, Herbert D (Business Person)
144 Thelma Dr
San Antonio, TX 78212-2516, USA

Kelleher, Mick (Athlete, Baseball Player)
1451 Alamo Pintado Rd
Solvang, CA 93463-9757, USA

Keller, Bill (Athlete, Basketball Player)
14602 Scarborough Ln
Noblesville, IN 46062-9729, USA

Keller, Cord (Producer)
c/o Staff Member *Innovative Artists (LA)*
1505 10th St
Santa Monica, CA 90401-2805, USA

Keller, Dave (Athlete, Baseball Player)
6401 S Boston St Unit X201
Greenwood Village, CO 80111-5356, USA

Keller, Dustin (Athlete, Football Player)
c/o Roosevelt Barnes *Maximum Sports Management*
6435 W Jefferson Blvd # 197
Fort Wayne, IN 46804-6203, USA

Keller, Gary (Athlete, Basketball Player)
220 Estado Way NE
Saint Petersburg, FL 33704-3752, USA

Keller, Jason (Race Car Driver)
Progressive Motorsports
201 Rolling Hill Rd
Mooresville, NC 28117-6845, USA

Keller, Joyce (Television Host)
600 Harbor Blvd Unit 905
Weehawken, NJ 07086-6748, USA

Keller, Kalyn (Athlete, Olympic Athlete, Swimmer)
11830 Federalist Way Apt 34
Fairfax, VA 22030-7893, USA

Keller, Klete (Athlete, Olympic Athlete, Swimmer)
13649 Cotesworth Ct
Huntersville, NC 28078-5661, USA

Keller, Kris (Athlete, Baseball Player)
2496 Oakview Dr
Jacksonville, FL 32246-2462, USA

Keller, Larry (Athlete, Football Player)
2933 Five Oaks Ln
Brenham, TX 77833-0089, USA

Keller, Mary Page (Actor)
c/o Staff Member *SMS Talent*
8383 Wilshire Blvd Ste 230
Beverly Hills, CA 90211-2436, USA

Keller, Melissa (Actor)
c/o Margie Weiner *Margie Weiner Management*
8205 Santa Monica Blvd Ste 1450
West Hollywood, CA 90046-5967, USA

Keller, Ralph (Athlete, Hockey Player)
1027 Highland Dr
Canonsburg, PA 15317-5227

Keller, Rita (Baseball Player)
6410 Westchester St
Portage, MI 49024-3276, USA

Keller, Ron (Athlete, Baseball Player)
PO Box 3267
Cashiers, NC 28717-3267, USA

Keller, Thomas (Chef)
French Laundry
6540 Washington St
Yountville, CA 94599-1315, USA

Kellerman, Ernie (Athlete, Football Player)
522 Spice Bush Ln
Chagrin Falls, OH 44023-6735, USA

Kellerman, Faye (Writer)
Karpfinger Agency
357 W 20th St Apt A
New York, NY 10011-4960, USA

Kellerman, Jonathan (Writer)
c/o Brian Pike *Creative Artists Agency (CAA-LA)*
2000 Avenue of the Stars Ste 100
Los Angeles, CA 90067-4705, USA

Kellerman, Max (Actor, Sportscaster)
c/o Staff Member *I, Max*
10201 W Pico Blvd Bldg 101
Fox Sports Television Group
Los Angeles, CA 90064-2606, USA

Kellerman, Sally (Actor)
c/o Chuck Binder *Binder & Associates*
1465 Lindacrest Dr
Beverly Hills, CA 90210-2519, USA

Kellermann, Ernie (Athlete, Football Player)
522 Spice Bush Ln
Chagrin Falls, OH 44023-6735, USA

Kellermeyer, Doug (Athlete, Football Player)
3512 Rock Ridge Rd
Carlsbad, CA 92010-7081, USA

Kelley, Allen (Athlete, Basketball Player, Olympic Athlete)
5900 Longleaf Dr
Lawrence, KS 66049-5801, USA

Kelley, Bill (Athlete, Football Player)
6446 US Highway 69 S
Lone Oak, TX 75453-2242, USA

Kelley, Brian (Athlete, Football Player)
98 Constitution Way
Basking Ridge, NJ 07920-2961, USA

Kelley, David E (Producer, Writer)
c/o Staff Member *David E Kelley Productions*
2900 Olympic Blvd
Santa Monica, CA 90404-4127, USA

Kelley, Dean (Athlete, Basketball Player)
5900 Longleaf Dr
Lawrence, KS 66049-5801, USA

Kelley, Devin (Actor)
c/o Dan Baron *Agency for the Performing Arts (APA-LA)*
405 S Beverly Dr Ste 500
Beverly Hills, CA 90212-4425, USA

Kelley, Dwight (Athlete, Football Player)
1006 Clubview Blvd N
Columbus, OH 43235-1222, USA

Kelley, Earl A (Athlete, Basketball Player)
5900 Longleaf Dr
Lawrence, KS 66049-5801, USA

Kelley, Gaynor N (Business Person)
Perkin-Elmer Corp
710 Bridgeport Ave
Shelton, CT 06484-4794, USA

Kelley, Gordon (Athlete, Football Player)
3101 S Ocean Blvd Apt 126
Highland Beach, FL 33487-2573, USA

Kelley, Ike (Athlete, Football Player)
1006 Clubview Blvd N
Columbus, OH 43235-1222, USA

Kelley, Jack (Athlete, Hockey Player)
PO Box 538
Oakland, ME 04963-0538

Kelley, Jon (Television Host)
c/o Staff Member *Extra (LA)*
1840 Victory Blvd
Telepictures Productions
Glendale, CA 91201-2558, USA

Kelley, Josh (Musician)
c/o Debbie Wilson *Wilspro Management*
P.O. Box 9
New York, NY 10001, USA

Kelley, Kevin (Athlete, Baseball Player)
1311 Quarterpath Ct
Richmond, TX 77406-6502, USA

Kelley, Kitty (Writer)
1228 Eton Ct NW
Washington, DC 20007-3240, USA

Kelley, Malcolm David (Actor)
c/o Nelson Parks *ESI Network*
6310 San Vicente Blvd Ste 340
Los Angeles, CA 90048-5499, United States

Kelley, Manon (Adult Film Star)
PO Box 315
Bellmore, NY 11710-0315, USA

Kelley, Mike (Producer, Writer)
c/o Sonya Rosenfeld *Creative Artists Agency (CAA-LA)*
2000 Avenue of the Stars Ste 100
Los Angeles, CA 90067-4705, USA

Kelley, Nathalie (Actor)
c/o Megan Silverman *William Morris Endeavor (LA)*
9601 Wilshire Blvd
Beverly Hills, CA 90210-5213, USA

Kelley, Rich (Athlete, Basketball Player)
314 Raymundo Dr
Woodside, CA 94062-4129, USA

Kelley, Ryan (Actor)
c/o Staff Member *Much and House Public Relations*
8075 W 3rd St Ste 500
Los Angeles, CA 90048-4325, USA

kelley, shawn (Athlete, Baseball Player)
813 Worlick Way
Chattanooga, TN 37421-8234, USA

Kelley, Sheila (Actor, Producer)
524 Lorraine Blvd
Los Angeles, CA 90020-4732, USA

Kelley, Shelia (Actor)
524 Lorraine Blvd
Los Angeles, CA 90020-4732, USA

Kelley, Steve (Cartoonist)
San Diego Union
350 Camino De La Reina
Editorial Dept
San Diego, CA 92108-3003, USA

Kelley, Tom (Athlete, Baseball Player)
710 11th Ave S
North Myrtle Beach, SC 29582-3754, USA

Kelley, William G (Business Person)
Consolidated Stores
1105 N Market St
Wilmington, DE 19801-1216, USA

Kellin, Kevin (Athlete, Football Player)
PO Box 8485
Saint Petersburg, FL 33738-8485, USA

Kellman, Barnet (Director)
c/o Staff Member *Jackoway Tyerman Wertheimer Austen Mandelbaum Morris & Klein*
1925 Century Park E Fl 22
Los Angeles, CA 90067-2701, USA

Kellner, Catherine (Actor)
c/o Michael Lazo *Untitled Entertainment (LA)*
350 S Beverly Dr Ste 200
Beverly Hills, CA 90212-4819, USA

Kellner, Deborah (Actor)
c/o Jessica (Pilch) Samuel *Sanders Armstrong Caserta*
2120 Colorado Ave Ste 120
Santa Monica, CA 90404-3561, USA

Kellogg, Clark (Athlete, Basketball Player)
5423 Medallion Dr E
Westerville, OH 43082-8691, USA

Kellogg, Jeffrey (Athlete, Baseball Player)
22900 Cherry Hill Ct
Mattawan, MI 49071-9562, USA

Kellogg, Mike (Athlete, Football Player)
7497 Tabor St
Arvada, CO 80005-3283, USA

Kellogg, William S (Business Person)
Kohl's Corp
N56W17000 Ridgewood Dr
Menomonee Falls, WI 53051-7096, USA

Kellum, Marv (Athlete, Football Player)
235 Jamaica Ave
Pittsburgh, PA 15229-1748, USA

Kelly, Annesse (Bowler)
2912 Cape Verde Ln
Las Vegas, NV 89128-7236, USA

Kelly, Arvesta (Athlete, Basketball Player)
1040 Oxford St N
Saint Paul, MN 55103-1246, USA

Kelly, Bob (Athlete, Baseball Player)
4 Millers Way
Old Lyme, CT 06371-1545, USA

Kelly, Bob (Athlete, Hockey Player)
10 Peyton Ct
Marlton, NJ 08053-4700, USA

Kelly, Brendan (Actor)
c/o Staff Member *Allman/Rea
Management*
9255 W Sunset Blvd Ste 600
West Hollywood, CA 90069-3306, USA

Kelly, Brendon John (Actor)
c/o Toni Scheinbaum *C3 Management
Group*
4555 Matilija Ave
Sherman Oaks, CA 91423-2918, USA

Kelly, Brian (Athlete, Football Player)
325 Dark Forest Dr
Chapel Hill, NC 27516-3704, USA

Kelly, Bryan (Athlete, Baseball Player)
5400 Cub Lake Dr
Apopka, FL 32703-1946, USA

Kelly, Clinton
c/o Staff Member *TLC*
10100 Santa Monica Blvd Ste 1500
Los Angeles, CA 90067-4117, USA

Kelly, Dale (Baseball Player)
Toronto Blue Jays
3417 Quail Meadows Dr
Santa Maria, CA 93455-2477, USA

Kelly, Dan (Athlete, Hockey Player)
165 Mulberry St
Harrisburg, NY 17102, USA

Kelly, Daniel-Hugh (Actor)
Innovative Artists
1505 10th St
Santa Monica, CA 90401-2805, USA

Kelly, David Patrick (Actor)
c/o Staff Member *Paradigm (LA)*
360 N Crescent Dr
North Bldg
Beverly Hills, CA 90210-4874, USA

Kelly, Diva Kelly (Athlete, Wrestler)
c/o Staff Member *World Wrestling
Entertainment (WWE)*
1241 E Main St
Titan Towers
Stamford, CT 06902-3520, USA

Kelly, Don (Athlete, Baseball Player)
216 Cliffside Dr
Mars, PA 16046-4802, USA

Kelly, Greg (Correspondent)
Fox News Channel
1211 Avenue of the Americas Lowr C3R
New York, NY 10036-8799, USA

Kelly, Harold (Horse Racer)
440 Tennent Rd
Manalapan, NJ 07726-3410, USA

Kelly, James E (Jim) (Athlete, Football
Player)
Jim Kelly Enterprises, Inc.
1 Regency Ct
Marlton, NJ 08053-4243, USA

Kelly, James M (Jim) (Astronaut)
403 S Northfield St
Mediapolis, IA 52637-9702, USA

Kelly, Jean Louisa (Actor)
c/o Adam Levine *Industry Entertainment*
955 Carrillo Dr Ste 300
Los Angeles, CA 90048-5400, USA

Kelly, Jeff (Athlete, Football Player)
6437 Munke Rd
La Grange, TX 78945-5836, USA

Kelly, Jerry (Athlete, Golfer)
723 Wilder Dr
Madison, WI 53704-6011, USA

Kelly, Joanne (Actor)
c/o Joanna (Joanie) Burstein *Burstein
Company, The*
15304 W Sunset Blvd Ste 208
Pacific Palisades, CA 90272-3656, USA

Kelly, John (Musician)
EMI America Records
6920 W Sunset Blvd
Los Angeles, CA 90028-7010, USA

Kelly, John D (Athlete, Football Player)
816 NE 18th Ave Apt 4
Fort Lauderdale, FL 33304-3005, USA

Kelly, Justin (Actor)
c/o Brad Stokes *Harrison Stokes*
1080 Stearns Dr
Los Angeles, CA 90035-2639, USA

Kelly, Kenny (Athlete, Baseball Player)
1318 Louisiana St
Plant City, FL 33563-5828, USA

Kelly, Kevin (Baseball Player)
1311 Quarterpath Ct
Richmond, TX 77406-6502, USA

Kelly, Leroy (Athlete, Football Player)
91 Club House Dr
Willingboro, NJ 08046-3418, USA

Kelly, Malcolm (Athlete, Football Player)
c/o Chad Speck *Allegiant Athletic Agency*
35 Market Sq Ste 201
Knoxville, TN 37902-1420, USA

Kelly, Mark E (Astronaut)
2121 Barrington Dr
League City, TX 77573, USA

Kelly, Megyn (Correspondent)
c/o Staff Member *Fox News (NY)*
1211 Avenue of the Americas Lowr C1
New York, NY 10036-8705, USA

Kelly, Michael (Actor)
c/o Brian Liebman *Liebman Entertainment*
12 E 46th St Fl 5
New York, NY 10017-2418, USA

Kelly, Mike (Athlete, Baseball Player)
461 W Holmes Ave Unit 388
Mesa, AZ 85210-5150, USA

Kelly, Mike (Athlete, Football Player)
7941 David Kenney Farm Rd
Huntersville, NC 28078-8730, USA

Kelly, Mike (Congressman, Politician)
515 Cannon Hob
Washington, DC 20515-1309, USA

Kelly, Minka (Actor)
c/o Christian Donatelli *The Schiff
Company*
9220 W Sunset Blvd Ste 106
West Hollywood, CA 90069-3500, USA

Kelly, Moira (Actor)
c/o Troy Nankin *Wishlab*
2225A Hyperion Ave
Los Angeles, CA 90027-4709, USA

Kelly, Pat (Athlete, Baseball Player)
1131 Howertown Rd
Catasauqua, PA 18032-1512, USA

Kelly, Pat (Athlete, Baseball Player)
10 Murray St
Bangor, PA 18013, USA

Kelly, Paul (Musician, Songwriter)
c/o Staff Member *Paradigm (Monterey)*
404 W Franklin St
Monterey, CA 93940-2303, USA

Kelly, R (Musician, Songwriter)
1010 W George St
Chicago, IL 60657-4312, USA

Kelly, Richard (Rich) (Director, Writer)
c/o John Campisi *Creative Artists Agency
(CAA-LA)*
2000 Avenue of the Stars Ste 100
Los Angeles, CA 90067-4705, USA

Kelly, Robert (Athlete, Football Player)
1805 Smoky View Cir
Maryville, TN 37801-7830, USA

Kelly, Roberto (Athlete, Baseball Player)
Augusta Greenjackets
1133 Blue Lake Blvd
Arlington, TX 76005-4501, USA

Kelly, Roz (Actor)
5664 Fair Ave Apt 26
North Hollywood, CA 91601-1932

Kelly, Ryan (Athlete, Basketball Player)
c/o Chris Emens *Octagon Home Office*
1751 Pinnacle Dr Fl 15
Mc Lean, VA 22102-3833, USA

Kelly, Scott J (Astronaut)
2121 Barrington Dr
Houston, TX 77058, USA

Kelly, Thomas (Athlete, Basketball Player)
2117 Forge Rd
Santa Barbara, CA 93108-2238, USA

Kelly, Thomas (Athlete, Football Player)
14524 La Mesa Dr
La Mirada, CA 90638-4026, USA

Kelly, Todd (Athlete, Football Player)
237 Gwinhurst Rd
Knoxville, TN 37934-4535, USA

Kelly, Tom (Athlete, Baseball Player,
Coach)
1643 Currie St N
Saint Paul, MN 55119-7160, USA

Kelly, Van (Athlete, Baseball Player)
11 Beauregard Dr
Spencer, NC 28159-1957, USA

Kelly III, Thomas J (Journalist)
PO Box 2208
Sanatoga Branch
Pottstown, PA 19464, USA

Kelm, Larry (Athlete, Football Player)
67 Driftoak Cir
Spring, TX 77381-6632, USA

Kelsay, Chris (Athlete, Football Player)
7790 S 240th St
Gretna, NE 68028-4100, USA

Kelser, Gregory (Athlete, Basketball
Player)
30400 Forest Dr
Franklin, MI 48025-1598, USA

Kelsey, David (Actor)
c/o Staff Member *Select Artists Ltd (CA-
Westside Office)*
1138 12th St Apt 1
Santa Monica, CA 90403-5459, USA

Kelso, Ben (Athlete, Basketball Player)
1877 Midchester Dr
West Bloomfield, MI 48324-1138, USA

Kelso, Bill (Athlete, Baseball Player)
136 NE Briarcliff Rd
Kansas City, MO 64116-4512, USA

Kelso, Mark (Athlete, Football Player)
897 Luther Rd
East Aurora, NY 14052-9764, USA

Kelton, David (Athlete, Baseball Player)
515 Riverside Dr
Lagrange, GA 30240-9635, USA

Kem (Music Group)
c/o Staff Member *Paradigm (Monterey)*
404 W Franklin St
Monterey, CA 93940-2303, USA

Kemmerer, Beatrice (Athlete, Baseball
Player, Commentator)
8437 Carter St
Bremen, IN 46506-9201, USA

Kemmerer, Russ (Athlete, Baseball Player)
6335 Colebrook Dr
Indianapolis, IN 46220-4205, USA

Kemp, Gary (Musician)
International Talent Group
729 7th Ave Ste 1600
New York, NY 10019-6880, USA

Kemp, Jeff (Athlete, Football Player)
8 Chemin Ct
Little Rock, AR 72223-9025, USA

Kemp, Matt (Athlete, Baseball Player)
c/o Staff Member *Los Angeles Dodgers
(LA Dodgers)*
1000 Elysian Park Ave
Los Angeles, CA 90012-1112, USA

Kemp, Perry (Athlete, Football Player)
PO Box 78
Westland, PA 15378-0078, USA

Kemp, Ross (Actor)
EastEnders
BBC Elstree Centre
Clarendon Road
Borehamwood, HE WD6 1

Kemp, Shawn (Athlete, Basketball Player)
18237 Belding Ct
Brandywine, MD 20613, USA

Kemp, Steve (Athlete, Baseball Player)
1428 Colony Plz
Newport Beach, CA 92660-6362, USA

Kempainen, Robert (Athlete, Olympic
Athlete, Track Athlete)
1753 Princeton Ave
Saint Paul, MN 55105-1915, USA

Kemper, Ellie (Actor)
c/o Michael Lasker *Mosaic Media Group*
9200 W Sunset Blvd Ste 10
West Hollywood, CA 90069-3608, USA

Kemper, Victor J (Cinematographer)
Gersh Agency
232 N Canon Dr
Beverly Hills, CA 90210-5302, USA

Kempf, Florian (Athlete, Football Player)
8039 Pine Rd Apt 1
Philadelphia, PA 19111-1808, USA

Kempinska, Charles (Athlete, Football Player)
925 State St
Natchez, MS 39120-3577, USA

Kempner, Patty (Athlete, Olympic Athlete, Swimmer)
1605 Harris Dr
Fort Collins, CO 80524-1041, USA

Kemppel, Nina (Athlete, Olympic Athlete, Track Athlete)
2819 McCollie Ave
Anchorage, AK 99517-1221, USA

Kempthorne, Dirk (Politician)
2081 S White Pine Ln
Boise, ID 83706-4048, USA

Kempton, Tim (Athlete, Basketball Player)
16223 W Cambridge Ave
Goodyear, AZ 85395-2084, USA

Kempton, tin (Athlete, Basketball Player)
16223 W Cambridge Ave
Goodyear, AZ 85395-2084, USA

Ken, Reese
1010 Forest Knoll Ct
Lithia Springs, GA 30122-3639, USA

Kenady, Chris (Athlete, Hockey Player)
5042 Tuxedo Blvd
Mound, MN 55364-9254

Kenan, Sean
77 W 66th St
New York, NY 10023-6201

Kendall, Donald M (Business Person)
PepsiCo Inc
Anderson Hill Road
Purchase, NY 10577, USA

Kendall, Fred (Athlete, Baseball Player)
57575 Johnston Rd
Anza, CA 92539-9646, USA

Kendall, Jason (Athlete, Baseball Player)
11730 Stonehenge Ln
Los Angeles, CA 90077-1302, USA

Kendall, Jeannie (Musician)
Joe Taylor Artist Agency
2802 Columbine Pl
Nashville, TN 37204-3104, USA

Kendall, Pete (Athlete, Football Player)
PO Box 888
Phoenix, AZ 85001-0888, USA

Kendall, Skip (Athlete, Golfer)
8406 Kemper Ln
Windermere, FL 34786-5318, USA

Kendall, Tom (Race Car Driver)
International Motor Sports Assn
1394 Broadway Ave
Braselton, GA 30517-2909, USA

Kenders, Al (Athlete, Baseball Player)
8744 Matilija Ave
Panorama City, CA 91402-3320, USA

Kendrena, Ken (Baseball Player)
4235 Stone Mountain Dr
Chino Hills, CA 91709-6155, USA

Kendrick, Alex (Producer)
c/o Staff Member *Sherwood Pictures*
2201 Whispering Pines Rd
Albany, GA 31707-2421, USA

Kendrick, Anna (Actor)
2421 Creston Way
Los Angeles, CA 90068-2211, USA

Kendrick, Darren (Actor)
c/o Albert Giannelli *Omnium Entertainment Group*
444 N Larchmont Blvd Ste 105
Los Angeles, CA 90004-3030, USA

Kendrick, Frank (Athlete, Basketball Player)
8355 Providence Dr
Fishers, IN 46038-5233, USA

Kendrick, Howard (Athlete, Baseball Player)
8650 E Joshua Tree Ln
Scottsdale, AZ 85250-4923, USA

Kendrick, Kyle (Athlete, Baseball Player)
7475 Wisconsin Ave Ste 600
Bethesda, MD 20814-3492, USA

Kendrick E G, Ken[III] (Athlete, Baseball Player)
3964 E Paradise View Dr
Paradise Valley, AZ 85253-3800, USA

Keneley, Matt (Athlete, Football Player)
25142 Sandia Ct
Laguna Hills, CA 92653-5606, USA

Kener, Kira (Adult Film Star)
Vivid Entertainment
3599 Cahuenga Blvd W Fl 2
Los Angeles, CA 90068-1397, USA

Kenmore, Joan (Actor)
33106 Ocean Rdg
Dana Point, CA 92629-1084, USA

Kenn, Michael L (Mike) (Athlete, Football Player)
360 Bardolier
Alpharetta, GA 30022-5129, USA

Kenna, E Douglas (Doug) (Athlete, Business Person, Football Player)
111 S Saint Joseph St
South Bend, IN 46601-1901, USA

Kennan, Brian (Musician)
PO Box 770850
Lustig Talent
Orlando, FL 32877-0850, USA

Kennard, Derek (Athlete, Football Player)
15849 S 35th Way
Phoenix, AZ 85048-7278, USA

Kennard, Trevor (Athlete, Football Player)
TKM Inc
207 Oxford St
Winnipeg, MB R3M 3H8, USA

Kennard, William (Bill) (Government Official)
Carlyle Group
1001 Pennsylvania Ave NW
Washington, DC 20004-2505, USA

Kennedy, Adam (Athlete, Baseball Player)
5025 Windhill Dr
Riverside, CA 92507-0615, USA

Kennedy, Alan D (Business Person)
Tupperware Corp
PO Box 2353
Orlando, FL 32802-2353, USA

Kennedy, Cortez (Athlete, Football Player)
121 Gary Lynn Dr
Osceola, AR 72370-1709, USA

Kennedy, Courtney (Athlete, Hockey Player, Olympic Athlete)
13 Whispering Hill Rd
Woburn, MA 01801-4781, USA

Kennedy, Dan (Business Person, Writer)
Kennedy Inner Circle Inc
5818 N 7th St # 103
Phoenix, AZ 85014-5806, USA

Kennedy, D James (Religious Leader)
Coral Ridge Presbyterian Church
5554 N Federal Hwy
Fort Lauderdale, FL 33308-3233, USA

Kennedy, Dwayne (Comedian)
c/o Rick Messina *Messina Baker Entertainment*
955 Carrillo Dr Ste 100
Los Angeles, CA 90048-5400, USA

Kennedy, Ethel (Politician)
PO Box 328
Hyannis Port, MA 02647-0328, USA

Kennedy, Eugene (Athlete, Basketball Player)
8218 Westrock Dr
Dallas, TX 75243-6524, USA

Kennedy, George (Actor)
10087 W Wildbranch St
Star, ID 83669-5906, USA

Kennedy, Ian (Athlete, Baseball Player)
c/o Team Member *New York Yankees*
Yankee Stadium
161st St & River Ave
Bronx, NY 10451, USA

Kennedy, James C (Business Person)
Cox Enterprises
1400 Lake Hearn Dr NE
Atlanta, GA 30319-1418, USA

Kennedy, Jamie (Actor, Producer)
c/o Staff Member *Jamie Kennedy Entertainment*
705 W 9th St Apt 702
Los Angeles, CA 90015-1837, USA

Kennedy, Jim (Athlete, Baseball Player)
13940 SW Lisa Ln
Beaverton, OR 97005-4315, USA

Kennedy, Jimmy (Athlete, Football Player)
901 N Broadway
Saint Louis, MO 63101-2800, USA

Kennedy, Joe (Athlete, Basketball Player)
201 43rd St
Virginia Beach, VA 23451-2503, USA

Kennedy, Joey D (Joe) Jr (Journalist)
1635 11th Pl S
Birmingham, AL 35205-5907, USA

Kennedy, John (Athlete, Baseball Player)
2 Rodney Rd
Peabody, MA 01960-3517, USA

Kennedy, John Milton (Actor)
5711 Reseda Blvd # 204
Tarzana, CA 91356-2201, USA

Kennedy, Junior (Athlete, Baseball Player)
6601 Eucalyptus Dr Spc 215
Bakersfield, CA 93306-6844, USA

Kennedy, Kathleen (Producer)
c/o Staff Member *United Talent Agency (UTA-LA)*
9336 Civic Center Dr
Beverly Hills, CA 90210-3604, USA

Kennedy, Ken (Wrestler)
c/o Kerry Rodgerson *World Wrestling Entertainment (WWE)*
1241 E Main St
Titan Towers
Stamford, CT 06902-3520, USA

Kennedy, Kenoy (Athlete, Football Player)
16275 O Conner Ave
Forney, TX 75126-7572, USA

Kennedy, Kevin (Athlete, Baseball Player, Coach, Television Host)
c/o Staff Member *Fox Sports (NY)*
1211 Avenue of the Americas Ste 302
New York, NY 10036-8799, USA

Kennedy, Lan (Athlete, Baseball Player)
2405 Brockton Way
Henderson, NV 89074-5471, USA

Kennedy, Lee (Business Person)
Equifax Inc
1550 Peachtree St NE
Atlanta, GA 30309-2468, USA

Kennedy, Leon Isaac (Actor)
859 N Hollywood Way # 384
Burbank, CA 91505-2814, USA

Kennedy, Lincoln (Athlete, Football Player)
2027 E Minton St
Mesa, AZ 85213-1438, USA

Kennedy, Mimi (Actor)
c/o Todd Justice *Justice & Ponder*
PO Box 480033
Los Angeles, CA 90048-1033, USA

Kennedy, M Peter (Figure Skater)
7650 SE 41st St
Mercer Island, WA 98040-3437, USA

Kennedy, Page (Actor)
c/o Judy Page *Mitchell K Stubbs & Assoc (MKS)*
8675 Washington Blvd Ste 203
Culver City, CA 90232-7486, USA

Kennedy, Ray F (Business Person)
Masco Corp
21001 Van Born Rd
Taylor, MI 48180-1300, USA

Kennedy, Robert F Jr (Attorney)
Pace Environmental Litigation Clinic
78 N Broadway
Pace University School of Law
White Plains, NY 10603-3710, USA

Kennedy, Robert H (Athlete, Football Player)
4906 N 76th Pl
Scottsdale, AZ 85251-1507, USA

Kennedy, Rory (Director, Producer)
7238 Birdview Ave
Malibu, CA 90265-4111, USA

Kennedy, Terrence E (Terry) (Athlete, Baseball Player)
333 N Pennington Dr Unit 23
Chandler, AZ 85224-8266, USA

Kennedy, T Lincoln (Athlete, Football Player)
3917 Spring Garden Pl
Apt 1
Spring Valley, CA 91977, USA

Kennedy, William (Athlete, Basketball Player)
9927 Galleon Dr
West Palm Beach, FL 33411-1807, USA

Kennedy, William J (Athlete, Football Player)
16383 Ronnie Ln
Livonia, MI 48154-2249, USA

Kennedy, William J (Writer)
New York State Writers Institute
Washington Ave
Albany, NY 12222-0001, USA

Kennedy, X Joseph (X J) (Writer)
22 Revere St
Lexington, MA 02420-4424, USA

Kennedy Schlossberg, Caroline (Writer)
ESI Design
111 5th Ave Fl 12
New York, NY 10003-1005, USA

Kennel, Hans
605 Douglas Ln NE
Huntsville, AL 35801-1740, USA

Kenner, Ellen (Radio Personality, Talk Show Host)
PO Box 440
North Scituate, RI 02857-0440, USA

kenner, Kevin (Musician)
Columbia Artists Mgmt Inc
165 W 57th St
New York, NY 10019-2201, USA

Kenney, Art (Athlete, Baseball Player)
3 Timber Ln
North Reading, MA 01864-3016, USA

Kenney, Bill (Athlete, Football Player)
2808 SW Arthur Dr
Lees Summit, MO 64082-4062, USA

Kenney, Jerry (Athlete, Baseball Player)
926 E Windfield Ct
Beloit, WI 53511-6547, USA

Kenney, Stephen F (Steve) (Athlete, Football Player)
1105 Silver Oaks Ct
Raleigh, NC 27614-9359, USA

Kenney, William P (Athlete, Football Player)
14420 W 71st St
Shawnee, KS 66216-3701, USA

Kennibrew, Dee Dee (Musician)
Superstars Unlimited
PO Box 371371
Las Vegas, NV 89137-1371, USA

Kenniff, Sean (Doctor)
6 Madison Ln # 2
Carle Place, NY 11514-1064, USA

Kennison, Eddie (Athlete, Football Player)
14813 Sherwood Rd
Overland Park, KS 66224-3842, USA

Kenny, Shannon (Actor)
c/o Joanna (Joanie) Burstein Burstein Company, The
15304 W Sunset Blvd Ste 208
Pacific Palisades, CA 90272-3656, USA

Kenny, Tom (Actor, Musician, Writer)
c/o Kara Welker Generate Management
8750 Wilshire Blvd Ste 200
Beverly Hills, CA 90211-2707, USA

Kenny G (Musician)
c/o Staff Member Richard De La Font Agency
3808 W South Park Blvd
Broken Arrow, OK 74011-1261, USA

Kenon, Larry (Athlete, Basketball Player)
25057 Toutant Beauregard Rd
San Antonio, TX 78255-3402, USA

Kenseth, Matt (Race Car Driver)
Joe Gibbs Racing
13415 Reese Blvd W
Huntersville, NC 28078-7933, USA

Kensing, Logan (Athlete, Baseball Player)
208 E Bandera Rd
Boerne, TX 78006-2902, USA

Kent, Arthur (Correspondent)
2184 Torringford St
Torrington, CT 06790-2540, USA

Kent, Heather Paige
c/o Justin Grey Stone Management 360
350 S Beverly Dr Ste 200
Beverly Hills, CA 90212-4819, USA

Kent, Jeff (Athlete, Baseball Player)
12006 Pleasant Panorama Vw
Austin, TX 78738-5309, USA

Kent, Joey (Athlete, Football Player)
6409 Eric St NW
Huntsville, AL 35810-1605, USA

Kent, Marjorie
1169 Mary Cir
La Verne, CA 91750-4210

Kent, Steve (Athlete, Baseball Player)
3118 Minthorn Dr
Killeen, TX 76542-1932, USA

Kentucky Headhunters
PO Box 1895
Glasgow, KY 42142-1895, USA

Kenty, Hilmer (Boxer)
Escot Boxing
19260 Bretton Dr
Detroit, MI 48223-1364, USA

Kenville, Bill (Athlete, Basketball Player)
59 Crary Ave
Binghamton, NY 13905-3828, USA

Kenworthy, Dick (Athlete, Baseball Player)
5551 Rue Royale Apt D
Indianapolis, IN 46227-1960, USA

Kenworthy, Gus (Olympic Athlete, Skier)
US Ski And Snowboard Association
1 Victory Ln # 100
Park City, UT 84060-7463, USA

Kenya, Wendi (Actor)
Michael Forman Management
409 N Camden Dr Ste 205
Beverly Hills, CA 90210-4423, USA

Kenyon, Mel (Race Car Driver)
4645 S 25 W
Lebanon, IN 46052, USA

Kenzle, Leila (Actor)
c/o Staff Member Agency for the Performing Arts (APA-LA)
405 S Beverly Dr Ste 500
Beverly Hills, CA 90212-4425, USA

Keo, Shiloh (Athlete, Football Player)
c/o Michael McCartney Priority Sports & Entertainment - Chicago
312 N La Salle
Suite 650
Chicago, IL 60610, USA

Keogan, Murray (Athlete, Hockey Player)
5631 E Superior St
Duluth, MN 55804-2530

Keoghan, Phil (Television Host)
c/o Staff Member ICM Partners (LA)
10250 Constellation Blvd Fl 7
Los Angeles, CA 90067-6207, USA

Keoke, Kimo (Actor)
216 Hermosa Ave Apt 2
Hermosa Beach, CA 90254-5000, USA

Keon, David M (Dave) (Athlete, Hockey Player)
115 Brackenwood Rd
Palm Beach Gardens, FL 33418-9065, USA

Keough, Joe (Athlete, Baseball Player)
110 Binham Hts
Shavano Park, TX 78249-2056, USA

Keough, Marty (Athlete, Baseball Player)
6874 E Nightingale Star Cir
Scottsdale, AZ 85266-7044, USA

Keough, Matt (Athlete, Baseball Player)
12 Shire
Trabuco Canyon, CA 92679-4907, USA

Kepcher, Carolyn (Reality Star)
c/o Staff Member The Apprentice
725 5th Ave
the Trump Co
New York, NY 10022-2519, USA

keppel, Bobby (Athlete, Baseball Player)
1297 Stephenridge Ct
Saint Charles, MO 63304-3405, USA

Keppinger, Jeff (Athlete, Baseball Player)
256 White Marsh Ln
Rotonda West, FL 33947-2171, USA

Kepshire, Kurt (Athlete, Baseball Player)
23244 Salinas Way
Bonita Springs, FL 34135-5374, USA

Ker, Crawford (Athlete, Football Player)
214 Harbor View Ln
Largo, FL 33770-4007, USA

Ker, Joshua (Athlete, Football Player)
2927 Lakeshore Dr
Muskegon, MI 49441, USA

Kerbow, Randall (Athlete, Football Player)
10122 Lost Hollow Ln
Missouri City, TX 77459-2494, USA

Kerbow, Randy (Athlete, Football Player)
3803 Crystal Falls Dr
Missouri City, TX 77459-4249, USA

Kercher, Dick (Athlete, Football Player)
2396 Manzano Loop NE
Rio Rancho, NM 87144-7529, USA

Kercheval, Ken (Actor)
Stephany Hurkos
11935 Kling St Apt 10
Valley Village, CA 91607-5406, USA

Kercheval, Ralph (Athlete, Football Player)
1220 Richmond Rd
Lexington, KY 40502-1614, USA

Kerdyk, Tracy (Athlete, Golfer)
935 S Alhambra Cir
Coral Gables, FL 33146-3805, USA

Kerekorian, Kirk (Business Person)
MGM/UA Communications
2500 Broadway
Santa Monica, CA 90404-3065, USA

Keresztury, Bill (Athlete, Football Player)
8700 Starr Rnch Apt 1204
Boerne, TX 78015-5018, USA

Kerfeld, Charlie (Athlete, Baseball Player)
15402 66th Avenue Ct NW
Gig Harbor, WA 98332-8736, USA

Kerkorian, Kirk (Business Person)
Tracinda Corporation
150 S Rodeo Dr Ste 250
Beverly Hills, CA 90212-2417, USA

Kerkovich, Rob (Actor)
c/o Lorraine Berglund Lorraine Berglund Management
11537 Hesby St
North Hollywood, CA 91601-3618, USA

Kern, Bill (Athlete, Baseball Player)
625 W Green St
Allentown, PA 18102-1601, USA

Kern, Ericca
3972 Barranca Pkwy # J-321
Irvine, CA 92606-1204

Kern, Jim (Athlete, Baseball Player)
6009 Amberwood Ct
Arlington, TX 76016-1001, USA

Kern, Joey (Actor)
c/o Staff Member Paradigm (LA)
360 N Crescent Dr
North Bldg
Beverly Hills, CA 90210-4874, USA

Kern, Rex W (Athlete, Football Player)
2816 Avenida De Autlan
Camarillo, CA 93010-7471, USA

Kernan, Joseph (Politician)
200 W Washington St Ste 226
Indianapolis, IN 46204-2731, USA

Kernek, George (Athlete, Baseball Player)
16423 Cotton Gin Ave
Wayne, OK 73095-3172, USA

Kerner, Ian (Writer)
c/o Staff Member HarperCollins Publishers
195 Broadway Fl 2
Cellar 1
New York, NY 10007-3132, USA

Kerns, Joanna (Actor)
c/o Sean Freidin ICM Partners (LA)
10250 Constellation Blvd Fl 7
Los Angeles, CA 90067-6207, USA

Kerns, Sandra (Actor)
620 Resolano Dr
Pacific Palisades, CA 90272-3032

Kerr, Brook (Actor)
c/o Marty Berneman Precision Entertainment
465 N Croft Ave
Los Angeles, CA 90048-2508, USA

Kerr, Cristie (Athlete, Golfer)
21427 N 102nd St
Scottsdale, AZ 85255, USA

Kerr, Edward (Actor)
9701 Wilshire Blvd Fl 10
Beverly Hills, CA 90212-2010

Kerr, Graham (Chef, Writer)
Kerr Corp
1020 N Sunset Dr
Camano Island, WA 98282-6665, USA

Kerr, Judy (Actor)
350 Paseo De Playa Unit 208
Ventura, CA 93001-2753, USA

Kerr, Kristen (Actor)
c/o Steven Jensen *Independent Group, The*
6363 Wilshire Blvd Ste 115
Los Angeles, CA 90048-5734, USA

Kerr, Miranda (Model)
c/o Aleen Keshishian *Brillstein Entertainment Partners (LA)*
9150 Wilshire Blvd Ste 350
Beverly Hills, CA 90212-3453, USA

Kerr, Pat (Designer, Fashion Designer)
Pat Kerr Inc
200 Wagner Pl PH 2
Memphis, TN 38103-3670, USA

Kerr, Reg (Athlete, Hockey Player)
2291 Birchwood Ln
Northfield, IL 60093-3103, USA

Kerr, Steve (Athlete, Basketball Player)
PO Box 1964
Rancho Santa Fe, CA 92067-1964, USA

Kerr, Tim (Athlete, Coach, Hockey Player)
539 42nd St
Avalon, NJ 08202-1504, USA

Kerr, William T (Business Person)
Meredith Corp
1716 Locust St
Des Moines, IA 50309-3023, USA

Kerrigan, Joseph T (Joe) (Athlete, Baseball Player, Coach)
450 Forest Ln
North Wales, PA 19454-2478, USA

Kerrigan, Marguerite (Athlete, Baseball Player, Commentator)
12179 94th St
Largo, FL 33773-4306, USA

Kerrigan, Nancy (Athlete, Figure Skater, Olympic Athlete)
7 Cedar Ave
Stoneham, MA 02180-2420, USA

Kerrigan, Pamela (Athlete, Golfer)
3205 Tuckers Ln
Hingham, MA 02043-1567, USA

Kerrigan, Ryan (Football Player)
c/o David Dunn *Athletes First, LLC*
23091 Mill Creek Dr
Laguna Hills, CA 92653-1258, USA

Kerry, Alexandra (Actor)
c/o Staff Member *TalentWorks (LA)*
3500 W Olive Ave Ste 1400
Burbank, CA 91505-5512, USA

Kerry, Bob (Ex-Senator)
7602 Pacific St
Omaha, NE 68114-5428, USA

Kerry, John (Politician)
1001 Residence Pl Apt 1
Dulles, VA 20189-1001, USA

Kersee, Bob
1034 S Brentwood Blvd # 1530
Saint Louis, MO 63117-1223

Kersey, Jerome (Athlete, Basketball Player)
24140 SW Petes Mountain Rd
West Linn, OR 97068-4500, USA

Kersey, Merritt (Athlete, Football Player)
17 Ballance Mill Rd
Nottingham, PA 19362-9507, USA

Kersey, Paul (Actor)
c/o Staff Member *TalentWorks (LA)*
3500 W Olive Ave Ste 1400
Burbank, CA 91505-5512, USA

Kersh, David (Musician)
Mark Hybner Entertainment
PO Box 223
Shiner, TX 77984-0223, USA

Kershaw, Clayton (Athlete, Baseball Player)
c/o Staff Member *Los Angeles Dodgers (LA Dodgers)*
1000 Elysian Park Ave
Los Angeles, CA 90012-1112, USA

Kershaw, Doug (Musician)
RR 1 Box 34285
Weld County Road 47
Eaton, CO 80615, USA

Kershaw, Sammy (Musician)
c/o Richard De La Font *Richard De La Font Agency*
3808 W South Park Blvd
Broken Arrow, OK 74011-1261, USA

Kershenbaum, David (Musician, Producer)
19021 Devonport Ln
Tarzana, CA 91356-5800, USA

kerslake, Doug (Athlete, Hockey Player)
2885 Sanford Ave SW
Grandville, MI 49418-1342

Kersten, Wally (Athlete, Football Player)
4604 Longfellow Ave
Minneapolis, MN 55407-3638, USA

Kerwin, Brian (Actor)
c/o Staff Member *Paradigm (LA)*
360 N Crescent Dr
North Bldg
Beverly Hills, CA 90210-4874, USA

Kerwin, Irene (Athlete, Baseball Player, Commentator)
610 W Albany Ave
Peoria, IL 61604-1506, USA

Kerwin, Joseph P (Astronaut)
10411 River Rd
College Station, TX 77845-6719, USA

Kerwin, Lance (Actor)
PO Box 1708
Kapaa, HI 96746-5708, USA

Kerwin, Tom (Athlete, Basketball Player)
283 Salter Path Rd Unit 114
Atlantic Beach, NC 28512-6178, USA

Keseday, Robert (Athlete, Football Player)
57 Linden Ave
Park Ridge, NJ 07656-1254, USA

Keselowski, Brad (Race Car Driver)
c/o Staff Member *Penske Racing South*
200 Penske Way
Mooresville, NC 28115-8022, USA

Keser, Dean (Athlete, Football Player)
202 Rod Cir
Middletown, MD 21769-7826, USA

Kesha (Musician)
933 Forest Acres Ct
Nashville, TN 37220-1803, USA

Keshishian, Alek (Director, Writer)
c/o Aleen Keshishian *Brillstein Entertainment Partners (LA)*
9150 Wilshire Blvd Ste 350
Beverly Hills, CA 90212-3453, USA

Kesler, Ryan (Athlete, Hockey Player)
5982 Pontiac Trl
West Bloomfield, MI 48323-2225

Kessell, Simone (Actor)
c/o Will Ward *ROAR (LA)*
9701 Wilshire Blvd Fl 8
Beverly Hills, CA 90212-2008, USA

Kessinger, Donald E (Don) (Athlete, Baseball Player, Coach)
1306 Pelican Loop
Oxford, MS 38655-7344, USA

Kessinger, Keith (Athlete, Baseball Player)
19002 Water Ridge Cv
Oxford, MS 38655-6058, USA

Kessinger, Ted (Athlete, Football Player)
612 N Washington St
Lindsborg, KS 67456-1516, USA

Kessler, David A (Doctor, Writer)
c/o Phyllis Parsons *The Parsons Company*
1738 Almond Ave
Walnut Creek, CA 94596-4308, USA

Kessler, Glenn (Producer, Writer)
c/o Staff Member *Creative Artists Agency (CAA-LA)*
2000 Avenue of the Stars Ste 100
Los Angeles, CA 90067-4705, USA

Kessler, Ron (Writer)
c/o Staff Member *Trident Media Group LLC*
41 Madison Ave Fl 36
New York, NY 10010-2257, USA

Kessler, Stephen
1120 S Ridgeley Dr
Los Angeles, CA 90019-2528

Kessler, Todd (Producer, Writer)
c/o Staff Member *Creative Artists Agency (CAA-LA)*
2000 Avenue of the Stars Ste 100
Los Angeles, CA 90067-4705, USA

Kester, Rick (Athlete, Baseball Player)
PO Box 623
Gardnerville, NV 89410-0623, USA

Kestner, Boyd (Actor)
Mirisch Agency
1801 Century Park E Ste 1801
Los Angeles, CA 90067-2320, USA

Ketchum, Dave
2318 Waterby St
Westlake Village, CA 91361-1834

Ketchum, Hal (Musician)
602 Wayside Dr
Wimberley, TX 78676-5151

Ketchum, Rai (Musician, Songwriter, Writer)
602 Wayside Dr
Wimberley, TX 78676-5151, USA

Ketola-Lacamera, Helen (Athlete, Baseball Player, Commentator)
907 New York St
Edgewater, FL 32132-2373, USA

Kettle, Roger (Cartoonist)
c/o Staff Member *King Features Syndication*
300 W 57th St Fl 15
New York, NY 10019-5238, USA

Key, Jimmy (Athlete, Baseball Player)
128 Talavera Pl
Palm Beach Gardens, FL 33418-6221, USA

Key, Keegan Michael (Actor)
c/o Joel Zadak *Principato/Young Management (LA)*
9465 Wilshire Blvd Ste 900
Beverly Hills, CA 90212-2608, USA

Key, Larry (Athlete, Football Player)
9661 60th St N
Attn: Church Administrations
Pinellas Park, FL 33782-3206, USA

Key, Sean (Athlete, Football Player)
1505 Elm St Apt 203
Dallas, TX 75201-3517, USA

Key, Ted (Cartoonist)
1694 Glenhardie Rd
Wayne, PA 19087-1004, USA

Key, Wade (Athlete, Football Player)
PO Box 857
Hondo, TX 78861-0857, USA

Keyes, Alan (Politician)
Loyalty to Liberty
PO Box 83759
Gaithersburg, MD 20883-3759, USA

Keyes, Leroy (Athlete, Football Player)
6156 Pleasant Ave
Pennsauken, NJ 08110-3537, USA

Keymah, T'Keyah Crystal (Actor)
121 N San Vicente Blvd
Beverly Hills, CA 90211-2303, USA

Keys, Alicia (Musician, Songwriter)
191 Brayton St
Englewood, NJ 07631-3101, USA

Keys, Brady (Athlete, Football Player)
2931 Banchory Rd
Winter Park, FL 32792-4501, USA

Keys, Rudy (Athlete, Basketball Player)
4308 Ludi Mae Ct
Charlotte, NC 28227-6638, USA

Keys, Tyrone (Athlete, Football Player)
5708 Clouds Peak Dr
Lutz, FL 33558-4974, USA

Keyser, Brian (Athlete, Baseball Player)
411 NE 353rd Ave
Washougal, WA 98671-8969, USA

Keyser, Richard L (Business Person)
WW Grainger Inc
100 Grainger Pkwy
Lake Forest, IL 60045-5202, USA

Keyser Jr, F Ray (Ex-Governor, General)
814 E Keller Ct
Hernando, FL 34442-3373, USA

Keysey, Ken
Rt. 8 Box 477
Eugene, OR 97401

Keyworth, Jon (Athlete, Football Player)
PO Box 36
Taylor, AZ 85939-0036, USA

Khabibulin, Nikolai (Athlete, Hockey Player)
Puckagency LLC
1 Sunset Dr N
Attn Jay Grossman
Chappaqua, NY 10514-1613, USA

Khajag, Barsamian (Religious Leader)
Armenian Church of America
630 2nd Ave
Eastern Diocese
New York, NY 10016-4806, USA

Khaled, DJ (Musician)
c/o Staff Member *5W Public Relations (NY)*
1166 6th Ave Frnt 4
New York, NY 10036-2729, USA

Khali, Simbi (Actor)
Innovative Artists
1505 10th St
Santa Monica, CA 90401-2805, USA

Khalifa, Sam (Athlete, Baseball Player)
1050 N Camino Seco Apt 1044
Tucson, AZ 85710-1770, USA

Khalifa, Wiz (Musician)
30 Virginia Ln
Canonsburg, PA 15317-5802, USA

Khalil, Christel (Actor)
c/o Meredith Fine *Coast to Coast Talent Group*
3350 Barham Blvd
Los Angeles, CA 90068-1404, USA

Khan, Alia (Designer)
Asian Andaz Inc
40 E 34th St Rm 1719
New York, NY 10016-4504, USA

Khan, Chaka (Actor, Musician)
1128 S Point View St
Los Angeles, CA 90035-2619, USA

Khan, Princess Yasmin
146 Central Park W Apt 8D
New York, NY 10023-6297

Kharin, Sergei (Athlete, Hockey Player)
PO Box 3532
Ann Arbor, MI 48106-3532, USA

Khayat, Edward (Eddie) (Athlete, Coach, Football Coach, Football Player)
7813 Haydenberry Cv
Nashville, TN 37221-4675, USA

Khayat, Nadir (RedOne) (Producer)
c/o Alan Melina *New Heights Entertainment*
PO Box 8489
Calabasas, CA 91372-8489, USA

Khayat, Robert (Athlete, Football Player)
PO Box 667
Oxford, MS 38655-0667, USA

K. Hirono, Mazie (Congressman, Politician)
1410 Longworth Hob
Washington, DC 20515-3821, USA

Khmylev, Yuri (Athlete, Hockey Player)
8236 Oakway Ln
Buffalo, NY 14221-2871

Khondji, Darius (Cinematographer)
International Creative Mgmt
10250 Constellation Blvd Fl 1
Los Angeles, CA 90067-6241, USA

Khouri, Callie (Director)
c/o Richard Green *Resolution (LA)*
1801 Century Park E Ste 2300
Los Angeles, CA 90067-2325, USA

Khristich, Dmitri (Athlete, Hockey Player)
5002 N Convent Ln Apt E
Apt E
Philadelphia, PA 19114-3125

Khruschev, Sergei
PO Box 1948
Providence, RI 02912-1948

Kiana (Talk Show Host)
ESPN 2
935 Middle St
Bristol, CT 06010-1099

Kiarostaml, Abbas (Director)
Zeitgeist Films
247 Centre St Rm 203
New York, NY 10013-3216, USA

Kibler, John (Athlete, Baseball Player)
2701 El Camino Real # 205
Palo Alto, CA 94306-1713, USA

Kibrick, Sidney (Actor)
10490 Wilshire Blvd Apt 1901
Los Angeles, CA 90024-4649, USA

Kickinger, Roland (Actor)
c/o Staff Member *Coralie Jr Theatrical Agency*
907 S Victory Blvd
Burbank, CA 91502-2430, USA

Kidd, Carl (Athlete, Football Player)
2317 Peach Tree Dr
Little Rock, AR 72211-4331, USA

Kidd, Dylan (Director)
c/o Staff Member *Creative Artists Agency (CAA-LA)*
2000 Avenue of the Stars Ste 100
Los Angeles, CA 90067-4705, USA

Kidd, Glenna Sue (Athlete, Baseball Player, Commentator)
51 17th St
Logansport, IN 46947-2842, USA

Kidd, Ian (Athlete, Hockey Player)
5107 London Rd
Duluth, MN 55804-2414, USA

Kidd, Jason (Athlete, Basketball Player, Olympic Athlete)
c/o Jeff Schwartz *Excel Sports Management (NY)*
1700 Broadway Fl 29
New York, NY 10019-5905, USA

Kidd, Jodie (Model)
c/o Staff Member *IMG*
304 Park Ave S Fl 12
New York, NY 10010-4314, USA

Kidd, John (Athlete, Football Player)
4204 Moorland Dr
Midland, MI 48640-1906, USA

Kidd, Sue (Baseball Player)
51 17th St
Logansport, IN 46947-2842, USA

Kidd, Warren (Athlete, Basketball Player)
313 River Rd
Harpersville, AL 35078-7014, USA

Kidd, William W (Billy) (Athlete, Olympic Athlete, Skier)
Billy Kidd Racing
2305 Mount Werner Cir
Steamboat Springs, CO 80487-9023, USA

Kidder, Margot (Actor)
c/o Derek Maki *Coolwaters Productions*
10061 Riverside Dr # 531
Toluca Lake, CA 91602-2560, USA

Kidder Lee, Barbara (Skier)
1308 W Highland Ave
Phoenix, AZ 85013-2425, USA

Kidjo, Angelique (Musician)
c/o Staff Member *Red Light Management (LA)*
8439 W Sunset Blvd Ste 2
West Hollywood, CA 90069-1925, USA

Kidman, Nicole (Actor)
c/o Geyer Kosinski *Media Talent Group*
9200 W Sunset Blvd Ste 550
West Hollywood, CA 90069-3611, USA

Kid Rock (Musician)
8979 Ortonville Rd
Clarkston, MI 48348-2844, USA

Kiecker, Dana (Athlete, Baseball Player)
4104 Prairie Ridge Rd
Saint Paul, MN 55123-1625, USA

Kiedis, Anthony (Musician)
8960 St Ives Dr
Los Angeles, CA 90069-1810, USA

Kiefel, Ron (Athlete, Cycler, Olympic Athlete)
3875 Field Dr
Wheat Ridge, CO 80033-4372, USA

Kiefer, Adolph G (Athlete, Coach, Olympic Athlete, Swimmer)
42125 N Hunt Club Rd
Wadsworth, IL 60083-9264, USA

Kiefer, Mark (Athlete, Baseball Player)
11822 Old Fashion Way
Garden Grove, CA 92840-2117, USA

Kiefer, Nicolas (Athlete, Tennis Player)
c/o Staff Member *ATP Tour*
201 Atp Tour Blvd
Ponte Vedra Beach, FL 32082-3211, USA

Kiefer, Steve (Athlete, Baseball Player)
38324 Divot Dr
Beaumont, CA 92223-8093, USA

Kiehl, Stuart (Cinematographer)
4193 Concord Ave
Santa Rosa, CA 95407-6507, USA

Kiel, John (Athlete, Football Player)
12100 Pebblepointe Pass
Carmel, IN 46033-9678, USA

Kielty, Bob (Bobby) (Athlete, Baseball Player)
22961 Blue Bird Dr
Canyon Lake, CA 92587-7555, USA

Kiely, John (Athlete, Baseball Player)
84 Brown St
Brockton, MA 02301-1006, USA

Kiely, Mark
9255 W Sunset Blvd Ste 620
West Hollywood, CA 90069-3303

Kieper, John (Race Car Driver)
15643 NE Siskiyou Ct
Portland, OR 97230-5151, USA

Kier, Udo (Actor)
c/o Richard Schwartz *Richard Schwartz Management*
2934 1/2 N Beverly Glen Cir # 107
Los Angeles, CA 90077-1724, USA

Kieschnick, Brook (Baseball Player)
Chicago Cubs
201 Evans Ave
San Antonio, TX 78209-3721, USA

Kieschnick, Brooks (Athlete, Baseball Player)
210 Joliet Ave Apt A
San Antonio, TX 78209-5230, USA

Kiewel, Jeff (Athlete, Football Player)
9923 E Karst Pl
Tucson, AZ 85748-4566, USA

Kiffin, Irv (Athlete, Basketball Player)
9301 Southern Orchard Rd N
Davie, FL 33328-6989, USA

Kiffin, Lane (Athlete, Football Player)
106 Terraza Pl
Manhattan Beach, CA 90266-6831, USA

Kiffin, Monte (Athlete, Football Player)
6005 Williamsburg Cv
Jonesboro, AR 72404-9636, USA

Kiggens, Lisa (Athlete, Golfer)
1504 Club View Dr
Bakersfield, CA 93309-3541, USA

Kight, Kelvin (Athlete, Football Player)
3748 Bramblevine Cir
Lithonia, GA 30038-2920, USA

Kightlinger, Laura (Actor, Comedian, Producer, Writer)
c/o David Martin *Avalon Management*
9171 Wilshire Blvd Ste 320
Beverly Hills, CA 90210-5516, USA

Kihn, Greg (Musician)
Riot Mgmt
55 Santa Clara Ave Ste 120
Oakland, CA 94610-1375, USA

Kiick, James F (Jim) (Athlete, Football Player)
2900 S University Dr Apt 9112
Davie, FL 33328-1409, USA

Kikuchi, Rinko (Actor)
c/o Staff Member *Creative Artists Agency (CAA-LA)*
2000 Avenue of the Stars Ste 100
Los Angeles, CA 90067-4705, USA

Kilborn, Craig (Talk Show Host)
c/o Shani Rosenzweig *United Talent Agency (UTA-LA)*
9336 Civic Center Dr
Beverly Hills, CA 90210-3604, USA

Kilbourne, Wendy (Actor)
9300 Wilshire Blvd Ste 410
Beverly Hills, CA 90212-3228, USA

Kilburn, Terry (Actor)
Meadowbrook Theatre
Oakland University
Walton & Squirrel
Columbus, MI 48063, USA

Kilcher, Q'Orianka (Actor)
c/o Carlyne Grager *Dramatic Artists Agency*
103 W Alameda Ave Ste 139
Burbank, CA 91502-2253, USA

Kilcullen, Bob (Athlete, Football Player)
400 E Division St
Pilot Point, TX 76258-4510, USA

Kiley, Ariel (Actor)
c/o Gene Parseghian *Parseghian Planco LLC*
388 2nd Ave
New York, NY 10010-5616, USA

Kilgore, Al (Cartoonist)
21655 113th Dr
Queens Village, NY 11429-2617, USA

Kilgore, Jon (Athlete, Football Player)
2422 Glen Oaks Ct NE
Atlanta, GA 30345-3928, USA

Kilgus, Paul (Athlete, Baseball Player)
968 Threewood Cir
Bowling Green, KY 42103-2479, USA

Kilian, Thomas J (Business Person)
Conseco Inc
PO Box 1957
Carmel, IN 46082-1957, USA

Killam, Taran (Actor)
c/o Joel Zadak *Principato/Young Management (LA)*
9465 Wilshire Blvd Ste 900
Beverly Hills, CA 90212-2608, USA

Killeen, Denise (Athlete, Golfer)
803 Golden Wood Trce
Canton, GA 30114-6572, USA

Killeen, Evans (Athlete, Baseball Player)
137 Main St
Westhampton Beach, NY 11978-2607,
USA

Killens, Terry (Athlete, Football Player)
5665 Water Spring Way
Mason, OH 45040-7319, USA

Killett, Charlie (Athlete, Football Player)
114 Forrest Heights Rd
Paris, TN 38242-5749, USA

Kill Hannah (Music Group, Musician)
c/o Staff Member *In De Goot
Entertainment*
119 W 23rd St Ste 609
New York, NY 10011-2594, USA

Killorin, Pat (Athlete, Football Player)
8304 Partridgeberry Dr
Baldwinsville, NY 13027-8946, USA

Killum, Ernie (Athlete, Basketball Player)
PO Box 370832
Decatur, GA 30037-0832, USA

Kilmer, Val (Actor)
c/o Michael Yanni *Michael Yanni*
1642 N Fairfax Ave
Los Angeles, CA 90046-2610, YSA

Kilmer, William O (Billy) (Athlete,
Football Player)
1853 Monte Carlo Way Apt 36
Coral Springs, FL 33071-7829, USA

Kilmore, Chris (Musician)
c/o Staff Member *ArtistDirect*
9046 Lindblade St
Culver City, CA 90232-2513, USA

Kilner, Kevin (Actor)
Innovative Artists
1505 10th St
Santa Monica, CA 90401-2805, USA

Kilpatrick, Carl (Athlete, Basketball
Player)
1928 S 17th St
Tacoma, WA 98405-3210, USA

Kilpatrick, Eric
6330 Simpson Ave Apt 3
North Hollywood, CA 91606-3427

Kilpatrick, Kwame (Politician)
Mayor's Office
2 Woodward Ave Rm 1126
City-County Building
Detroit, MI 48226-3453, USA

Kilrain, Susan L (Astronaut)
4509 Hale Alii Ave
Honolulu, HI 96818-5024, USA

Kilts, James M (Business Person)
Gillette Co
Prudential Tower Building
Boston, MA 02199, USA

Kilzer, Louis C (Lon) (Journalist)
Minneapolis-Saint Paul Star-Tribune
425 Portland Ave
Minneapolis, MN 55488-0002, USA

Kim, Anthony (Athlete, Golfer)
c/o Clarke Jones *IMG (Cleveland)*
1360 E 9th St Ste 100
Cleveland, OH 44114-1730, USA

Kim, Claudia (Actor)
c/o Staff Member *United Talent Agency
(UTA-LA)*
9336 Civic Center Dr
Beverly Hills, CA 90210-3604, USA

Kim, Daniel Dae (Actor)
PO Box 10151
Honolulu, HI 96816-0151, USA

Kim, Jacqueline (Actor)
Innovative Artists
1505 10th St
Santa Monica, CA 90401-2805, USA

Kim, Lil' (Musician)
c/o Michael Schweiger *CEG Management*
520 8th Ave Rm 2001
New York, NY 10018-4166, USA

Kim, Nelli V (Gymnast)
2480 Cobblehill
#A Alocove
Saint Paul, MN 55125, USA

kim, Wendell (Athlete, Baseball Player)
18674 E Aubrey Glen Rd
Queen Creek, AZ 85142-3656, USA

Kim, Yoon-jin (Actor)
c/o Staff Member *William Morris
Endeavor (LA)*
9601 Wilshire Blvd
Beverly Hills, CA 90210-5213, USA

Kim, Young Uck (Musician)
Columbia Artists Mgmt Inc
165 W 57th St
New York, NY 10019-2201, USA

Kim, Yunjin (Actor)
c/o Alex Chaice *Global Creative*
1051 Cole Ave # B
Los Angeles, CA 90038-2601, USA

Kimball, Bobby (Musician)
World Entertainment Assoc
297101 Kinderkamack Rd
#128
Oradell, NJ 07649, USA

Kimball, Bruce (Athlete, Football Player)
41 Spring Rd
Rye, NH 03870-2449, USA

Kimball, Dick (Coach)
1540 Waltham Dr
Ann Arbor, MI 48103-5631, USA

Kimball, Shawn (Athlete, Baseball Player)
75 Black Stream Dr
Levant, ME 04456-4427, USA

Kimball, Toby (Athlete, Basketball Player)
6859 Avenida Avenue
La Jolla, CA 92037, USA

Kimball, Ward
8910 Ardendale Ave
San Gabriel, CA 91775-1906

Kimball-Purdham, Mary Ellen (Athlete,
Baseball Player, Commentator)
15299 S 18th St
Vicksburg, MI 49097-9738, USA

Kimber, Bill (Athlete, Football Player)
7801 Point Meadows Dr Unit 3102
Jacksonville, FL 32256-9145, USA

Kimber, William (Athlete, Football Player)
7801 Point Meadows Dr Unit 3102
Jacksonville, FL 32256-9145, USA

Kimble, Bo (Athlete, Basketball Player)
100 Poe Ct
North Wales, PA 19454-4430, USA

Kimble, Darin (Athlete, Hockey Player)
2660 Cleveland Blvd
Granite City, IL 62040-3436, USA

Kimble, Gregory ""Bo"" (Athlete,
Basketball Player)
100 Poe Ct Unit 83
North Wales, PA 19454-4430, USA

Kimbra (Musician)
c/o Dave Tamaroff *William Morris
Endeavor (LA)*
9601 Wilshire Blvd
Beverly Hills, CA 90210-5213, USA

Kimbrough, Charles (Actor, Musician)
255 Amalfi Dr
Santa Monica, CA 90402-1125, USA

Kimbrough, Elbert (Athlete, Football
Player)
886 W 2nd St
Galesburg, IL 61401-5711, USA

Kimbrough, John (Athlete, Football Player)
2016 Fleming Dr
McKinney, TX 75070-3986, USA

Kimbrough, Stan (Athlete, Basketball
Player)
3922 Elm Ave
Cincinnati, OH 45236-3908, USA

Kimbrough, Tony (Athlete, Football
Player)
4726 Sharp Rd
Sturgis, MS 39769-8939, USA

Kimbrough, Will (Musician)
Cedar Creek Music
164 Dove Creek Rd
Frankfort, KY 40601-8945, USA

Kimm, Bruce (Athlete, Baseball Player,
Coach)
3168 121st St
Amana, IA 52203-8046, USA

Kimmel, Frank (Race Car Driver)
KFPI/Amber Estes
102 Brookshire Dr
Danville, KY 40422-3200, USA

Kimmel, Jerry (Athlete, Football Player)
1411 Colesville Rd
Harpursville, NY 13787-1430, USA

Kimmel, Jimmy (Comedian, Television
Host)
Jimmy Kimmel Live
6834 Hollywood Blvd Ste 600
Los Angeles, CA 90028-6135, USA

Kimmell, Dana (Actor)
26684 Stanford St
Hemet, CA 92544, USA

Kimmins, Kenneth (Actor)
c/o Joanna (Joanie) Burstein *Burstein
Company, The*
15304 W Sunset Blvd Ste 208
Pacific Palisades, CA 90272-3656, USA

Kims of Comedy (Comedian)
c/o Staff Member *Paradigm (Monterey)*
404 W Franklin St
Monterey, CA 93940-2303, USA

Kinard, Billy (Athlete, Football Player)
41 Vail Ln
Watchung, NJ 07069-6149, USA

Kinard, Terry (Athlete, Football Player)
18 Safe Harbor Ave
Pawleys Island, SC 29585-6664, USA

Kincade, Keylon (Athlete, Football Player)
1118 E Park
Lindale, TX 75771-7088, USA

Kincaid, Jamaica (Writer)
College Road
North Bennington, VT 05257, USA

Kincaid, Jim (Athlete, Football Player)
401 Tryon Dr
Goldsboro, NC 27530-9149, USA

Kinchen, Brian (Athlete, Football Player)
19052 E Pinnacle Cir
Baton Rouge, LA 70810-7996, USA

Kinchen, Todd W (Athlete, Football
Player)
247 Guava Dr
Baton Rouge, LA 70808-5031, USA

Kinchla, Chan (Musician)
c/o Staff Member *ArtistDirect*
9046 Lindblade St
Culver City, CA 90232-2513, USA

Kind, Richard (Actor)
c/o Arlene Forster *Forster Entertainment*
12533 Woodgreen St
Los Angeles, CA 90066-2723, USA

Kind, Ron (Congressman, Politician)
1406 Longworth Hob
Washington, DC 20515-4903, USA

Kind, Roslyn (Actor, Musician)
Scott Stander
13707 Riverside Dr
#201
Sherman Oaks, CA 91423, USA

Kindall, Jerry (Athlete, Baseball Player)
7220 E Grey Fox Ln
Tucson, AZ 85750-1377, USA

Kinder, Melvyn (Writer)
c/o Staff Member *Random House*
1540 Broadway
New York, NY 10036-4039, USA

Kinder, Richard D (Business Person)
Kinder and Morgan
500 Dallas St Ste 1000
Houston, TX 77002-4718, USA

Kinderman, Keith (Athlete, Football
Player)
5837 Bradfordville Rd
Tallahassee, FL 32309-6613, USA

Kindig, Howard (Athlete, Football Player)
8740 Bayside Ave
Baton Rouge, LA 70806-7947, USA

Kindle, Greg (Athlete, Football Player)
7606 Heron Park Ct
Humble, TX 77396-2222, USA

Kindrachuk, Orest (Athlete, Hockey
Player)
14044th Ave
Asbury Park, NJ 07712, USA

Kindred, David A (Writer)
Atlanta Constitution
72 Marietta St NW
Editorial Dept
Atlanta, GA 30303-2804, USA

Kindricks, Bill (Athlete, Football Player)
1466 Alma Loop
San Jose, CA 95125-1731, USA

Kiner, Steve (Athlete, Football Player)
112 N Ole Hickory Trl
Carrollton, GA 30117-3509, USA

King, Adrienne (Actor)
c/o Aine Leicht *Horror & Hilarity*
Prefers to be contacted via telephone
Los Angeles, CA 90067, USA

King, Alan (Actor, Producer, Writer)
c/o Lisa Gallant *Gallant Management*
10250 Constellation Blvd Fl 7
Los Angeles, CA 90067-6207, USA

King, Albert (Athlete, Basketball Player)
88 Sturbridge Cir
Wayne, NJ 07470-8402, USA

King, Alton (Athlete, Baseball Player)
16117 Crystal Downs E
Northville, MI 48168-9637, USA

King, Angelo (Athlete, Football Player)
2922 W Royal Ln Apt 2090
Irving, TX 75063-6235, USA

King, BB (Musician)
BB King Road Show Inc
PO Box 26867
Las Vegas, NV 89126-0867, USA

King, Ben E (Musician)
Smiling Clown Music
PO Box 1097
Teaneck, NJ 07666-1097, USA

King, Benjamin (Actor)
c/o Peter Principato *Principato/Young Management (LA)*
9465 Wilshire Blvd Ste 900
Beverly Hills, CA 90212-2608, USA

King, Bernard (Athlete, Basketball Player)
307 Jupiter Hills Dr
Duluth, GA 30097-5900, USA

King, Bernard (Athlete, Football Player)
Hollywood Christian School
1708 N State Road 7
Attn: Athletic Dept
Hollywood, FL 33021-4507, USA

King, Billie Jean (Athlete, Tennis Player)
101 W 79th St PH 1B
New York, NY 10024-6495, USA

King, Bruce (Politician)
9140 E Canyon Terrace Dr
Tucson, AZ 85715-5597, USA

King, Cammie Conlon
c/o Staff Member *Pierce & Shelly*
13775A Mono Way # 220
Sonora, CA 95370-8813, USA

King, Candie (Athlete, Golfer)
2673 Saleroso Dr
Rowland Heights, CA 91748-4364, USA

King, Carlos (Athlete, Football Player)
4016 Enfield Ridge Dr
Cary, NC 27519-2538, USA

King, Carole (Musician)
11684 Ventura Blvd # 273
Studio City, CA 91604-2699, USA

King, Cheryl (Actor)
CLInc Talent
843 N Sycamore Ave
Los Angeles, CA 90038-3316, USA

King, Clyde E (Athlete, Baseball Player, Coach)
103 Stratford Rd
Goldsboro, NC 27534-8971, USA

King, Colbert (Journalist)
Washington Post
Editorial Dept
1150 15th St NW
Washington, DC 20071-0001, USA

King, Curtis (Athlete, Baseball Player)
2538 Beechwood Dr
Vineland, NJ 08361-2932, USA

King, Dan (Athlete, Basketball Player)
4803 Grand Dell Dr
Crestwood, KY 40014-9794, USA

King, Dana (Correspondent)
CBS-TV
524 W 57th St
News Dept
New York, NY 10019-2924, USA

King, Dave (Athlete, Hockey Player)
7748 E Clinton St
Scottsdale, AZ 85260-5582, USA

King, Dave
Phoenix Coyotes
6751 N Sunset Blvd Ste E200
Attn: Coaching Staff
Glendale, AZ 85305-3158, USA

King, David J (Athlete, Football Player)
4365 Riverstone Shls
Ellenwood, GA 30294-6550, USA

King, Diana (Musician)
c/o Stephen Ford *Diva Central Inc*
7510 W Sunset Blvd Ste 1445
Los Angeles, CA 90046-3408, USA

King, Don (Business Person)
c/o Staff Member *Rubenstein Associates Inc*
1345 Avenue of the Americas Fl 30
New York, NY 10105-0109, USA

King, Donald W (Athlete, Football Player)
1621 Fox Hall Rd
Savannah, GA 31406-5005, USA

King, Ed (Athlete, Football Player)
9903 North Blvd
Cleveland, OH 44108-3429, USA

King, Emanuel
PO Box 41
Leroy, AL 36548-0041, USA

King, Eric (Athlete, Baseball Player)
1063 Stanford Dr
Simi Valley, CA 93065-4952, USA

King, Erik (Actor)
c/o Joanna (Joanie) Burstein *Burstein Company, The*
15304 W Sunset Blvd Ste 208
Pacific Palisades, CA 90272-3656, USA

King, Evelyn (Champagne) (Musician)
c/o Stephen Ford *Diva Central Inc*
7510 W Sunset Blvd Ste 1445
Los Angeles, CA 90046-3408, USA

King, Ezell (Athlete, Baseball Player)
PO Box 321154
Houston, TX 77221-1154, USA

King, Frank (Baseball Player)
Negro Baseball Leagues
415 E Rhinehill Rd SE
Atlanta, GA 30315-7403, USA

King, Gayle (Correspondent)
c/o Staff Member *CBS News (NY)*
524 W 57th St Fl 8
New York, NY 10019-2930, USA

King, Gordon (Athlete, Football Player)
2641 Highwood Dr
Roseville, CA 95661-7916, USA

King, Gordon D (Athlete, Football Player)
2641 Highwood Dr
Roseville, CA 95661-7916, USA

King, Graham (Producer)
c/o Joy Fehily *Prime*
9696 Culver Blvd Ste 102
Culver City, CA 90232-2734, USA

King, G Stephen (Athlete, Football Player)
45 Chipping Stone Rd
North Attleboro, MA 02760-4485, USA

King, Hal (Athlete, Baseball Player)
828 Geneva Dr
Oviedo, FL 32765-9503, USA

King, Hogue Maxine (Mick) (Swimmer)
US Air Force Academy
PO Box 155
Usaf Academy, CO 80840-0155, USA

King, Horace (Athlete, Football Player)
900 Autumn Close
Alpharetta, GA 30004-4527, USA

King, Jaime (Actor)
c/o Brad Cafarelli *PMK/BNC Public Relations (PMK-LA)*
8687 Melrose Ave Ste 8
West Hollywood, CA 90069-5746, USA

King, Jean
5510 Cahuenga Blvd
North Hollywood, CA 91601-2919

King, Jeff (Athlete, Baseball Player)
1717 Illinois Ave
Sheboygan, WI 53081-4827, USA

King, Jim (Athlete, Baseball Player)
2402 Heather Lynn Ln
Fayetteville, AR 72701-0455, USA

King, Joe (Athlete, Football Player)
373 Boyd Rd
Hallsville, TX 75650-7003, USA

King, Joey (Actor)
c/o Daniel Spilo *Industry Entertainment*
955 Carrillo Dr Ste 300
Los Angeles, CA 90048-5400, USA

King, John (Correspondent, Television Host)
5003 Belt Rd NW
Washington, DC 20016-4234, USA

King, Kaki (Musician)
c/o Staff Member *Paradigm (Monterey)*
404 W Franklin St
Monterey, CA 93940-2303, USA

King, Kathryn (Katie) (Athlete, Hockey Player, Olympic Athlete)
140 Commonwealth Ave
Attn Womens Ice Hockey Coach
Chestnut Hill, MA 02467-3800, USA

King, Kenny (Athlete, Football Player)
1184 Verde Oaks Ln
Fort Worth, TX 76135-9034, USA

King, Kent Masters (Actor)
c/o Richard Schwartz *Richard Schwartz Management*
2934 1/2 N Beverly Glen Cir # 107
Los Angeles, CA 90077-1724, USA

King, Kevin (Athlete, Baseball Player)
9071 S 105th St E
Braggs, OK 74423-5091, USA

King, Lamar (Athlete, Football Player)
5082 Springhouse Cir
Rosedale, MD 21237-3356, USA

King, Lamnar (Athlete, Football Player)
1453 Browning Dr
Essex, MD 21221-4337, USA

King, Larry (Journalist, Talk Show Host)
707 N Hillcrest Rd
Beverly Hills, CA 90210-3516, USA

King, Linden (Athlete, Football Player)
727 W 7th St Apt 607
Los Angeles, CA 90017-3755, USA

King, Loyd (Athlete, Basketball Player)
118 Wilde Brook Dr
Asheville, NC 28806-1052, USA

King, Michael Patrick (Producer, Writer)
c/o Simon Halls *Slate Public Relations*
9000 W Sunset Blvd Ste 915
West Hollywood, CA 90069-5809, USA

King, Michelle (Producer)
c/o Andy Patman *Paradigm (LA)*
360 N Crescent Dr
North Bldg
Beverly Hills, CA 90210-4874, USA

King, Michel Patrick (Director)
c/o Simon Halls *Slate Public Relations*
9000 W Sunset Blvd Ste 915
West Hollywood, CA 90069-5809, USA

King, Micki (Athlete, Diver, Olympic Athlete)
3S09 Colt Neck Ln
Lexington, KY 40502, USA

King, Morgana (Actor, Musician)
Subrena Artists
330 W 56th St Apt 18M
New York, NY 10019-4222, USA

King, Nellie (Athlete, Baseball Player)
3890 Bigelow Blvd Apt 405
Pittsburgh, PA 15213-1158, USA

King, Patsy
6/70 Hawksburn Rd S Yarra
Victoria, AU 03141

King, Perry (Actor)
3647 Wrightwood Dr
Studio City, CA 91604-3947, USA

King, Ray (Athlete, Baseball Player)
4422 N 153rd Ln
Goodyear, AZ 85395-6302, USA

King, Reggie (Athlete, Basketball Player)
4716 Chouteau St
Shawnee, KS 66226-2300, USA

King, Regina (Actor)
c/o John Carrabino *John Carrabino Management*
5900 Wilshire Blvd Ste 406
Los Angeles, CA 90036-5015, USA

King, Richard L (Business Person)
Albertson's Inc
250 E Parkcenter Blvd
Boise, ID 83706-3999, USA

King, Robert (Producer)
c/o Andy Patman *Paradigm (LA)*
360 N Crescent Dr
North Bldg
Beverly Hills, CA 90210-4874, USA

King, R Stacey (Athlete, Basketball Player)
5340 RR
Lake Zurich, IL 60047-9744, USA

King, Scott (Athlete, Hockey Player)
203 Maple Ave
Hershey, PA 17033-1549, USA

King, Shaun (Business Person)
Upfront Media Group, Inc
135 W 29th St Rm 1102
New York, NY 10001-5159, USA

King, Shaun (Athlete, Football Player)
10116 Caraway Spice Ave
Riverview, FL 33578-7631, USA

King, Shawn Southwick (Actor)
c/o Staff Member *William Morris Endeavor (LA)*
9601 Wilshire Blvd Ste 580
Beverly Hills, CA 90210-5220, USA

King, Stephen (Writer)
c/o *Juliann Eugley*
1380 Hammond St
Bangor, ME 04401-5710, USA

King, Steve (Congressman, Politician)
1131 Longworth Hob
Washington, DC 20515-1008, USA

King, Steven (Athlete, Hockey Player)
55 Chestnut Dr
East Greenwich, RI 02818-2102, USA

King, Tavarres (Athlete, Football Player)
c/o Alan Herman *Sportstars Inc*
1350 Avenue of the Americas Fl 28
New York, NY 10019-4702, USA

King, Ted (Actor, Musician)
c/o Staff Member *Paradigm (LA)*
360 N Crescent Dr
North Bldg
Beverly Hills, CA 90210-4874, USA

King, Tom (Athlete, Basketball Player)
4930 Sea Watch Dr
Fernandina Beach, FL 32034-5741, USA

King, Vania (Athlete, Tennis Player)
c/o John Tobias *Lagardere Unlimited (DC)*
5335 Wisconsin Ave NW Ste 850
Washington, DC 20015-2052, USA

King, Vick (Athlete, Football Player)
255 E 23rd St
Larose, LA 70373-2136, USA

Kingdom, Roger (Athlete, Track Athlete)
146 S Fairmount St Apt 1
Pittsburgh, PA 15206-3580, USA

Kingery, Ellsworth (Athlete, Football Player)
501 Auburn Ave
Monroe, LA 71201-5303, USA

kingery, jeff
6208 S Jamaica Ct
Englewood, CO 80111-5717, USA

Kingery, Mike (Athlete, Baseball Player)
51923 298th St
Grove City, MN 56243-4305, USA

Kingery, Wayne (Athlete, Football Player)
1045 Walters St Apt 411
Lake Charles, LA 70607-4686, USA

King III, Martin Luther (Activist)
Martin Luther King Jr. Center
449 Auburn Ave NE
Atlanta, GA 30312-1503, USA

King Jr, Woodie (Producer)
417 Convent Ave
New York, NY 10031-4213, USA

Kingman, Brian (Athlete, Baseball Player)
2939 E Avalon Dr
Phoenix, AZ 85016-7503, USA

Kingman, Dave (Athlete, Baseball Player)
PO Box 209
Glenbrook, NV 89413-0209, USA

Kingrea, Richard O (Athlete, Football Player)
102 N Bayview St
Fairhope, AL 36532-2505, USA

Kingrea, Rick (Athlete, Football Player)
102 N Bayview St
Fairhope, AL 36532-2505, USA

Kingsale, Gene (Athlete, Baseball Player)
105 Angelfish Ln
Jupiter, FL 33477-7227, USA

King Sisters
10275 S 2505 E
Sandy, UT 84092-4464

Kingsley, Ben (Actor)
2220 Bowmont Dr
Beverly Hills, CA 90210-1807, USA

Kingsley, Patricia (Business Person)
371 Alma Real Dr
Pacific Palisades, CA 90272-4416, USA

Kingsmen, The
1720 N Ross St
Santa Ana, CA 92706-3605

Kings of Convenience (Music Group)
c/o Staff Member *Paradigm (Monterey)*
404 W Franklin St
Monterey, CA 93940-2303, USA

Kings of Leon (Music Group)
c/o Andy Mendelsohn *Vector Management (NYC)*
113 E 55th St
New York, NY 10022-3502, USA

Kingsriter, Doug (Athlete, Football Player)
3118 Saint Johns Dr
Dallas, TX 75205-2938, USA

Kingston, Alex (Actor)
6342 Innsdale Dr
Los Angeles, CA 90068-1624, USA

Kingston, George (Athlete, Hockey Player)
235 W Camino Descanso
Palm Springs, CA 92264-8323, USA

Kingston, Jack (Congressman, Politician)
2372 Rayburn Hob
Washington, DC 20515-0605, USA

Kingston, Kenny
11561 Dona Dorotea Dr
Studio City, CA 91604-4250

Kingston, Maxine Hong (Writer)
University of California
English Dept
Berkeley, CA 94720-0001, USA

Kingston, Sean (Musician)
c/o Joseph Carozza *Epic Records Group*
550 Madison Ave Fl 6
New York, NY 10022-3211, USA

Kingston Trio, The
9410 S 46th St
Phoenix, AZ 85044-7512

Kinkade, Mike (Athlete, Baseball Player)
3802 Broadway
Attn: Coaching Staff
Everett, WA 98201-5032, USA

Kinkade, Mike (Athlete, Baseball Player, Olympic Athlete)
3005 SE Spyglass Dr
Vancouver, WA 98683-3704, USA

Kinley, Heather (Musician)
Epic Records
1211 S Highland Ave
Los Angeles, CA 90019-1734, USA

Kinley, Jennifer (Musician)
Epic Records
1211 S Highland Ave
Los Angeles, CA 90019-1734, USA

Kinleys (Music Group)
PO Box 128501
Nashville, TN 37212-8501, USA

Kinley's, The
PO Box 128501
Nashville, TN 37212-8501

Kinmont, Kathleen (Actor)
9929 Sunset Blvd
#310
West Hollywood, CA 90069, USA

Kinnaman, Joel (Actor)
c/o Shelley Browning *Magnolia Entertainment (LA)*
9595 Wilshire Blvd Ste 601
Beverly Hills, CA 90212-2506, USA

Kinnaman, Melanie (Actor)
1354 N Curson Ave
Los Angeles, CA 90046-4004, USA

Kinnear, Dominic (Coach)
San Jose Earthquakes
3550 Stevens Creek Blvd Ste 200
San Jose, CA 95117-1031, USA

Kinnear, Geordie (Athlete, Hockey Player)
1012 Harrogate Ln
Matthews, NC 28104-6874, USA

Kinnear, Geordie (Athlete, Hockey Player)
Charlotte Checkers
210 E Trade St
Attn: Coaching Staff
Charlotte, NC 28202-2404, USA

Kinnear, Greg (Actor, Comedian)
2280 Mandeville Canyon Rd
Los Angeles, CA 90049-1827, USA

Kinnear III, James W (Business Person)
Ten Standard Forum
PO Box 120
Stamford, CT 06904-0120, USA

Kinnebrew, Larry (Athlete, Football Player)
216 Kingston Ave NE
Rome, GA 30161-5628, USA

Kinney, Dallas (Journalist, Photographer)
13010 Silver Sands Dr
Fort Myers, FL 33913-6934, USA

Kinney, Dennis (Athlete, Baseball Player)
1981 Arundel Rd
Myrtle Beach, SC 29577-5966, USA

Kinney, Erron (Athlete, Football Player)
1103 State Blvd
Franklin, TN 37064-8614, USA

Kinney, Jeff (Athlete, Football Player)
19336 Queens Crescent Way
Monument, CO 80132-8413, USA

Kinney, Jeff (Writer)
c/o Sylvie Rabineau *Rabineau Wachter and Sanford Literary Agency*
522 Wilshire Blvd Ste L
Santa Monica, CA 90401-1445, USA

Kinney, Josh (Athlete, Baseball Player)
588 Uoper Portage Rd
Port Allegany, PA 16743, USA

Kinney, Kathy (Actor)
c/o Billy Miller *Billy Miller Management*
8322 Ridpath Dr
Los Angeles, CA 90046-7710, USA

Kinney, Matt (Athlete, Baseball Player)
12 Owens Way
Hermon, ME 04401-0878, USA

Kinney, Steve (Athlete, Football Player)
229 Cheris Dr
San Jose, CA 95123-1713, USA

Kinney, Taylor (Actor)
264 Mount Hope School Rd
Willow Street, PA 17584-9754, USA

Kinney, Terry (Actor)
Gersh Agency
232 N Canon Dr
Beverly Hills, CA 90210-5302, USA

Kinnunen, Mike (Athlete, Baseball Player)
5818 McKinley Pl N
Seattle, WA 98103-5711, USA

Kinsella, Brian (Athlete, Hockey Player)
1408 Longfellow Dr
Temperance, MI 48182-9296, USA

Kinsella, John P (Swimmer)
PO Box 3067
Sumas, WA 98295-3067, USA

Kinsella, W P
PO Box 3067
Sumas, WA 98295-3067, USA

Kinser, Mark (Race Car Driver)
Mark Kinser Racing
11 Vista Dr
General Delivery
Oolitic, IN 47451-3036, USA

Kinser, Steve (Race Car Driver)
Steve Kinser Racing
280 E Smithville Rd
Bloomington, IN 47401-9251, USA

Kinsey, Angela (Actor)
c/o Staff Member *Jenny Delaney Management*
3238 Fond Dr
Encino, CA 91436-4206, USA

Kinsey, Tarence (Athlete, Basketball Player)
11328 Grand Winthrop Ave
Riverview, FL 33578-4279, USA

Kinski, Nastassja (Actor, Model)
1110 Bel Air Pl
Los Angeles, CA 90077-3002, USA

Kinsler, Ian (Athlete, Baseball Player)
3516 Greenbrier Dr
Dallas, TX 75225-5003, USA

Kinsman, Brent (Actor)
c/o Staff Member *AKA Talent Agency*
6310 San Vicente Blvd Ste 200
Los Angeles, CA 90048-5488, USA

Kinsman, Shane (Actor)
c/o Staff Member *AKA Talent Agency*
6310 San Vicente Blvd Ste 200
Los Angeles, CA 90048-5488, USA

Kinzer, Matt (Athlete, Baseball Player)
6717 Sweetbrier Dr
Fort Wayne, IN 46814-4564, USA

Kinzinger, Adam (Congressman, Politician)
1218 Longworth Hob
Washington, DC 20515-2901, USA

KioKio (DJ)
c/o Staff Member *Diva Central Inc*
7510 W Sunset Blvd Ste 1445
Los Angeles, CA 90046-3408, USA

Kiper Jr, Mel (Sportscaster)
ESPN-TV
935 Middle St
Sports Dept Espn Plaza
Bristol, CT 06010-1000, USA

Kiplinger, Austin H (Publisher)
Montevideo
1680 River Road
Poolesville, MD 20837, USA

Kipp, Fred (Athlete, Baseball Player)
6613 W 126th Ter
Leawood, KS 66209-2599, USA

Kipper, Bob (Athlete, Baseball Player)
PO Box 636
Attn Coaching Staff
Portland, ME 04104-0636, USA

Kipper, Bob (Athlete, Baseball Player)
117 Tuscany Way
Greer, SC 29650-4070, USA

Kipper, Thornton (Athlete, Baseball Player)
4680 W Geronimo St
Chandler, AZ 85226-5306, USA

Kiprusoff, Miikka (Athlete, Hockey Player)
c/o Staff Member *Octagon Sports Representation*
7400 Metro Blvd Ste 280
Minneapolis, MN 55439-2363, USA

Kiraly, Charles F (Karch) (Athlete, Coach, Olympic Athlete, Volleyball Player)
c/o Staff Member *Simon & Schuster*
1230 Avenue of the Americas Fl CONC1
New York, NY 10020-1586, USA

Kirby, Bruce (Actor)
629 N Orlando Ave Apt 3
West Hollywood, CA 90048-2193, USA

Kirby, Durwood (Writer)
PO Box 3454
North Fort Myers, FL 33918-3454, USA

Kirby, Jim (Athlete, Baseball Player)
408 Guethlein Rd
Mount Juliet, TN 37122-4624, USA

Kirby, John (Athlete, Football Player)
586 A St
David City, NE 68632-1939, USA

Kirby, Pete
PO Box 1734
Madison, TN 37116-1734

Kirby, Stuart (Race Car Driver)
832 Broadway Ave
Bowling Green, KY 42101-2538, USA

Kirby, Terry (Athlete, Football Player)
744 Michelle Dr
Newport News, VA 23601-4626, USA

Kirby, Wayne (Athlete, Baseball Player)
333 W Camden St
Attn: Coaching Staff
Baltimore, MD 21201-2496, USA

Kirby, Wayne (Athlete, Baseball Player)
320 Kenya Rd
Las Vegas, NV 89123-1169, USA

Kirby, Will (Reality Star)
c/o Staff Member *Metropolitan (MTA)*
4526 Wilshire Blvd
Los Angeles, CA 90010-3801, USA

Kirchenbauer, Bill
3800 Barham Blvd
Los Angeles, CA 90068-1054

Kirchiro, Bill (Athlete, Football Player)
9889 Fleming Ave
Bethesda, MD 20814-2145, USA

Kirchner, Jamie Lee (Actor)
c/o Maani Golesorkhi *Bluestone Entertainment*
9000 W Sunset Blvd Ste 700
West Hollywood, CA 90069-5807, USA

Kirchner, Mark (Athlete, Football Player)
2629 Newman St
Houston, TX 77098-1403, USA

Kircus, David (Athlete, Football Player)
3880 Banyan Grove Ln Apt 301
Virginia Beach, VA 23462-7478, USA

Kirgo, George (Actor, Writer)
178 N Carmelina Ave
Los Angeles, CA 90049-2737, USA

Kiriazis, Nick (Actor)
c/o Staff Member *Pakula/King & Associates*
9229 W Sunset Blvd Ste 315
West Hollywood, CA 90069-3403, USA

Kirilenko, Andrei (Athlete, Basketball Player)
8 Spruce St Apt 75M
New York, NY 10038-5247, USA

Kirilenko, Maria (Tennis Player)
c/o Staff Member *Women's Tennis Association (WTA (US))*
1 Progress Plz Ste 1500
St Petersburg, FL 33701-4335, USA

Kirk, Bill (Athlete, Baseball Player)
16 Timber Villa
Elizabethtown, PA 17022-9424, USA

Kirk, Justin (Actor)
c/o Lainie Sorkin Becky *Management 360*
9111 Wilshire Blvd
Beverly Hills, CA 90210-5508, USA

Kirk, Rahsaan Roland (Musician)
Atlantic Records
9229 W Sunset Blvd Ste 900
West Hollywood, CA 90069-3410, USA

Kirk, Tammy Jo (Race Car Driver)
732 Peek Rd
Dalton, GA 30721

Kirk, Tara (Athlete, Olympic Athlete, Swimmer)
15 W Montgomery St
Baltimore, MD 21230-3844, USA

Kirk, Walt (Athlete, Basketball Player)
3730 Pennsylvania Ave Apt 302
Dubuque, IA 52002-3785, USA

Kirkconnell, Clare
PO Box 63
Rutherford, CA 94573-0063

Kirke, Jemima (Actor)
c/o Diane McGunigle *The Schiff Company*
9220 W Sunset Blvd Ste 106
West Hollywood, CA 90069-3500, USA

Kirkland, Levon (Athlete, Football Player)
3255 Whitman Way
Tallahassee, FL 32311-3318, USA

Kirkland, Lori (Producer)
c/o Staff Member *Luber Roklin Management*
5815 W Sunset Blvd Ste 206
Los Angeles, CA 90028-6481, USA

Kirkland, Mike (Athlete, Football Player)
3350 N Sassafras Hill Rd
Fayetteville, AR 72703-9640, USA

Kirkland, Mike (Musician)
Bob Flick Productions
300 Vine St Ste 14
Seattle, WA 98121-1465, USA

Kirkland, Niatia (Lil Mama) (Musician)
c/o Laura Pallas *Pallas Management*
5301 Bellaire Ave
Valley Village, CA 91607-2329, US

Kirkland, Wilber (Athlete, Basketball Player)
127 Kimberwick Cir
Glenmoore, PA 19343-1124, USA

Kirkland, Willie (Athlete, Baseball Player)
19374 Northrop St
Detroit, MI 48219-5500, USA

Kirkman, Michael (Athlete, Baseball Player)
171 SW Tina Gin
Lake City, FL 32024, USA

Kirkman, Rick (Cartoonist)
c/o Staff Member *King Features Syndication*
300 W 57th St Fl 15
New York, NY 10019-5238, USA

Kirkman, Robert (Writer)
c/o David Alpert *Circle of Confusion (LA)*
8607 Washington Blvd
Culver City, CA 90232-7441, USA

Kirkpatrick, Chris (Actor, Musician)
c/o Staff Member *Good Guy Entertainment*
3733 Oakfield Dr
Sherman Oaks, CA 91423-4430, USA

Kirkpatrick, David (Director, Producer)
c/o Staff Member *Plymouth Rock Studios*
36 Cordage Park Cir Ste 305
Plymouth, MA 02360-7332, USA

Kirkpatrick, Dre (Athlete, Football Player)
c/o Brian E. Overstreet *E.O. Sports Management*
2211 Norfolk St Ste 210
Houston, TX 77098-4055, USA

Kirkpatrick, Ed (Athlete, Baseball Player)
25703 Compass Way
San Juan Capistrano, CA 92675-4003, USA

Kirkpatrick, Ralph (Musician)
Old Quarry
Guilford, CT 06437, USA

Kirkreit, Daron (Athlete, Baseball Player, Olympic Athlete)
161 Steeplechase Cir
Sanford, FL 32771-9540, USA

Kirksey, Roy (Athlete, Football Player)
204 Williams St
Taylors, SC 29687-2056, USA

Kirkwood, Craig (Actor)
c/o Staff Member *Levine Management*
9028 W Sunset Blvd PH 1
West Hollywood, CA 90069-1830, USA

Kirkwood, Don (Athlete, Baseball Player)
455 W Elmwood Ave
Clawson, MI 48017-1231, USA

Kirllenko, Andrei (Basketball Player)
Utah Jazz
301 W South Temple
Delta Center
Salt Lake City, UT 84101-1219, USA

Kirner, Gary (Athlete, Football Player)
3507 Senasac Ave
Long Beach, CA 90808-2847, USA

Kirouac, Lou (Athlete, Football Player)
3630 Chattahoochee Ct
Duluth, GA 30096-3210, USA

Kirrane, John (Jack) (Athlete, Hockey Player, Olympic Athlete)
3 Country Rd
Chestnut Hill, MA 02467-2912, USA

Kirrene, Joe (Athlete, Baseball Player)
2557 Kilpatrick Ct
San Ramon, CA 94583-1726, USA

Kirschke, Travis (Athlete, Football Player)
10196 Crooked Stick Trl
Lone Tree, CO 80124-8510, USA

kirschner, David (Actor)
c/o Staff Member *William Morris Endeavor (LA)*
9601 Wilshire Blvd
Beverly Hills, CA 90210-5213, USA

Kirschstein, Ruth L (Doctor)
National Institute of Health
9000 Rockville Pike
Bethesda, MD 20892-0002, USA

Kirsebom, Vendela (Model)
c/o Staff Member *TR Management Group*
11740 Wilshire Blvd Apt A2109
Los Angeles, CA 90025-6530, USA

Kirshbaum, Laurence J (Publisher)
Warner Books
Time-Life Building
Rockefeller Center
New York, NY 10020, USA

Kirshbaum, Ralph (Musician)
Columbia Artists Mgmt Inc
165 W 57th St
New York, NY 10019-2201, USA

Kirshner, Mia (Actor)
c/o Daniel (Danny) Sussman *Brillstein Entertainment Partners (LA)*
9150 Wilshire Blvd Ste 350
Beverly Hills, CA 90212-3453, USA

Kirtman, David (Athlete, Football Player)
PO Box 50743
Bellevue, WA 98015-0743, USA

Kiselak, Mike (Athlete, Football Player)
906 Chimney Hill Trl
Southlake, TX 76092-8305, USA

Kiser, Garland (Athlete, Baseball Player)
267 Carr Dr
Blountville, TN 37617-4608, USA

Kiser, Terry (Actor)
Innovative Artists
1505 10th St
Santa Monica, CA 90401-2805, USA

Kison, Bruce (Athlete, Baseball Player)
1403 Riverside Cir
Bradenton, FL 34209, USA

Kisor, Henry (Writer)
2951 Central St Apt 305
Evanston, IL 60201-1295, USA

KISS (Music Group)
c/o Doc McGhee *McGhee Entertainment*
8730 W Sunset Blvd Ste 175
West Hollywood, CA 90069-2246, USA

Kissane, James (Athlete, Basketball Player)
6 Mellen Ln
Wayland, MA 01778-2015, USA

Kissane, Jim (Athlete, Basketball Player)
6 Mellen Ln
Wayland, MA 01778-2015, USA

Kissell, Ed (Athlete, Football Player)
40 Sebbins Pond Dr
Bedford, NH 03110-6630, USA

Kissell, Larry (Congressman, Politician)
1632 Longworth Hob
Washington, DC 20515-2007, USA

Kissel-Lafser, Audrey (Athlete, Baseball
Player, Commentator)
9506 Port Dr
Saint Louis, MO 63123-6530, USA

Kissinger, Henry A (Politician)
350 Park Ave Fl 26
New York, NY 10022-6045, USA

Kitaen, Tawny (Actor)
Talent Group
5670 Wilshire Blvd Ste 820
Los Angeles, CA 90036-5613, USA

Kitchen, Curtis (Athlete, Basketball Player)
343 19th Ave
Seattle, WA 98122-5735, USA

Kitchen, Mike (Athlete, Coach, Hockey
Player)
c/o Staff Member *Florida Panthers*
1 Panther Pkwy
Sunrise, FL 33323-5315, USA

Kitchens, Jimmy (Race Car Driver)
Moy Racing
486 Withrow Rd
Forest City, NC 28043-9693, USA

Kite, Greg (Athlete, Basketball Player)
3060 Seigneury Dr
Windermere, FL 34786-8353, USA

Kite, Jimmy (Race Car Driver)
Blueprint Racing
6800 W 73rd St
Chicago, IL 60638-6024, USA

Kite, Tom (Athlete, Golfer)
907 Terrace Mountain Dr
West Lake Hills, TX 78746-2730, USA

Kitna, Jon (Athlete, Football Player)
18898 Bella Vista Ct
Northville, MI 48168-3534, USA

Kitsch, Taylor (Actor)
c/o Stephanie Simon *Untitled
Entertainment (LA)*
350 S Beverly Dr Ste 200
Beverly Hills, CA 90212-4819, USA

Kitsis, Edward (Eddy) (Producer)
c/o Philip Raskind *William Morris
Endeavor (LA)*
9601 Wilshire Blvd
Beverly Hills, CA 90210-5213, USA

Kitson, Syd (Athlete, Football Player)
7232 Horizon Dr
West Palm Beach, FL 33412-3027, USA

Kitt, A J (Skier)
2437 N Franklin Ave
Louisville, CO 80027-1216, USA

Kittle, Ron (Athlete, Baseball Player)
PO Box 658
Mokena, IL 60448-0658, USA

Kittles, Kerry (Athlete, Basketball Player)
PO Box 641
Franklin Lakes, NJ 07417-0641, USA

Kittles, Tory (Actor)
c/o Matt Luber *Luber Roklin Management*
5815 W Sunset Blvd Ste 206
Los Angeles, CA 90028-6481, USA

Kitzhaber, John (Governor, Politician)
Governor's Office
900 Court St NE Ste 160
State Capitol Building
Salem, OR 97301-4046, USA

Kiyoko, Hayley (Actor)
c/o Staff Member *AKA Talent Agency*
6310 San Vicente Blvd Ste 200
Los Angeles, CA 90048-5488, USA

Kiyosaki, Kim (Business Person, Writer)
CASHFLOW Technologies Inc
4330 N Civic Center Plz Ste 100
Scottsdale, AZ 85251-3529, USA

Kiyosaki, Robert T (Business Person,
Writer)
The Rich Dad Company
4330 N Civic Center Plz Ste 100
Scottsdale, AZ 85251-3529, USA

Klages, Fred (Athlete, Baseball Player)
26240 McDonald Rd
Spring, TX 77380-2495, USA

Klares, John (Athlete, Bowler)
4600 Vegas Dr
Aot 116
Las Vegas, NV 89108-2157, USA

Klasnic, John (Athlete, Football Player)
924 Highland Ave
McKeesport, PA 15133-3920, USA

Klass, Beverly (Athlete, Golfer)
PO Box 244364
Boynton Beach, FL 33424-4364, USA

Klassen, Danny (Athlete, Baseball Player)
5680 SW Pomegranate Way
Palm City, FL 34990-8627, USA

Klatt, Trent (Athlete, Hockey Player)
New York Islanders
1255 Hempstead Tpke
Attn Player Development Dept
Uniondale, NY 11553-1200, USA

Klatt, Trent (Athlete, Hockey Player)
267 SW 12th Ave
Grand Rapids, MN 55744-3487, USA

Klattenhoff, Diego (Actor)
c/o Francis Okwu *Zero Gravity
Management*
6363 Wilshire Blvd Ste 300
Los Angeles, CA 90048-5729, USA

Klaus, Bobby (Athlete, Baseball Player)
10661 Gabacho Dr
San Diego, CA 92124-1404, USA

Klaus, Deita (Actor)
c/o Staff Member *Digigraphics/Dream Girl
World*
4650 Libbit Ave
Encino, CA 91436-2122, USA

Klausing, Chuck (Coach, Football Coach)
2115 Lazor St
Indiana, PA 15701-3463, USA

Klaveno, Mariana
c/o Alan Iezman *Shelter Entertainment*
9255 W Sunset Blvd Ste 320
West Hollywood, CA 90069-3313, USA

Klawitter, Tom (Athlete, Baseball Player)
3220 Dover Ct
Janesville, WI 53546-1956, USA

Klaxons (Music Group)
c/o Staff Member *Paradigm (Monterey)*
404 W Franklin St
Monterey, CA 93940-2303, USA

Klebba, Martin (Actor)
c/o Staff Member *The Stevens Group*
14011 Ventura Blvd Ste 201
Sherman Oaks, CA 91423-5216, USA

Klecko, Joseph E (Joe) (Athlete, Football
Player)
105 Stella Ln
Aston, PA 19014-2741, USA

Klee, Ken (Athlete, Hockey Player)
78 W Ranch Trl
Morrison, CO 80465-9503, USA

Klein, AJ (Athlete, Football Player)
c/o Scott Smith *XAM Sports*
PO Box 1725
Madison, WI 53701-1725, USA

Klein, Calvin (Designer, Fashion Designer)
c/o Staff Member *Calvin Klein Inc*
200 Madison Ave Frnt 3
New York, NY 10016-3903, USA

Klein, Chris (Actor)
c/o Cynthia Pett-Dante *Brillstein
Entertainment Partners (LA)*
9150 Wilshire Blvd Ste 350
Beverly Hills, CA 90212-3453, USA

Klein, Danny (Musician)
Nick Ben-Meir
652 N Doheny Dr
West Hollywood, CA 90069-5526, USA

Klein, Edward
c/o Staff Member *St Martins Press*
175 5th Ave Ste 400
Publicity Dept
New York, NY 10010-7848, USA

Klein, Emilee (Athlete, Golfer)
5350 E Deer Valley Dr Unit 1431
Phoenix, AZ 85054-4131, USA

Klein, Herbert G (Government Official,
Publisher)
Copley Press
350 D Ave
Coronado, CA 92118-1331, USA

Klein, Jennifer (Producer)
c/o Carlos Goodman *Bloom Hergott
Diemer Rosenthal Laviolette Feldman
Schenkman & Goodman*
150 S Rodeo Dr Fl 3
Beverly Hills, CA 90212-2410, USA

Klein, Jenny
201 S Capitol Ave Ste 430
Indianapolis, IN 46225-1026

Klein, Jess (Musician, Songwriter, Writer)
Drake Assoc
177 Woodland Ave
Westwood, NJ 07675-3218, USA

Klein, Joe (Journalist, Writer)
Newsweek Magazine
251 W 57th St
Editorial Dept
New York, NY 10019-1802, USA

Klein, Jonathan (Business Person)
c/o Staff Member *CNN (NY)*
1 Time Warner Ctr
New York, NY 10019-6038, USA

Klein, Lester A (Doctor)
Scripps Clinic
10666 N Torrey Pines Rd
Urology Dept
La Jolla, CA 92037-1092, USA

Klein, Marci (Director, Producer, Writer)
c/o Jeff Jacobs *Creative Artists Agency
(CAA-LA)*
2000 Avenue of the Stars Ste 100
Los Angeles, CA 90067-4705, USA

Klein, Marty (Writer)
2439 Birch St Ste 2
Palo Alto, CA 94306-1946, USA

Klein, Naomi (Producer, Writer)
c/o Staff Member *American Program
Bureau*
1 Gateway Ctr Ste 751
Newton, MA 02458-2817, USA

Klein, Perry (Athlete, Football Player)
30760 Broad Beach Rd
Malibu, CA 90265-2613, USA

Klein, Richard J (Athlete, Football Player)
609 E 2nd St
Pana, IL 62557-1446, USA

Klein, Robert (Actor, Musician)
c/o Rory Rosegarten *Conversation
Company*
1044 Northern Blvd Ste 304
Roslyn, NY 11576-1589, USA

Klein, Robert O (Bob) (Athlete, Football
Player)
15933 Alcima Ave
Pacific Palisades, CA 90272-2405, USA

Klein Borkow, Dana (Producer)
c/o Staff Member *William Morris
Endeavor (LA)*
9601 Wilshire Blvd
Beverly Hills, CA 90210-5213, USA

Kleindienst, Richard
3103 W Crestview Dr
Prescott, AZ 86305-5001

Kleine, Joe (Athlete, Basketball Player,
Olympic Athlete)
53 Hickory Hills Cir
Little Rock, AR 72212-2766, USA

Kleinendorst, Kurt (Athlete, Hockey
Player)
7049 S Village Commons Way
Midvale, UT 84047-4638, USA

Kleinendorst, Scot (Athlete, Hockey
Player)
35387 Lake St
Cohasset, MN 55721-2160, USA

Kleiner, Jeremy (Producer)
c/o Staff Member *Plan B Entertainment*
9150 Wilshire Blvd Ste 350
Beverly Hills, CA 90212-3453, USA

Kleinert, Harold E (Doctor)
225 Abraham Flexner Way Ste 700
Louisville, KY 40202-3868, USA

Kleinsasser, Jim (Athlete, Football Player)
6835 Cardinal Cove Dr
Mound, MN 55364-9535, USA

Kleinsmith, Bruce (Cartoonist)
PO Box 1083
San Juan Bautista, CA 95045-1083, USA

Kleiser, Randal (Director)
3050 Runyon Canyon Rd
Los Angeles, CA 90046-1347, USA

Klemm, Adrian (Athlete, Football Player)
900 W Olympic Blvd Unit 43D
Los Angeles, CA 90015-1395, USA

Klemm, Jay (Athlete, Baseball Player)
47 Choctaw Ridge Rd
Branchburg, NJ 08876-5441, USA

Klemm, Jay (Athlete, Baseball Player)
1605 Airy Hill Ct Unit D
Crofton, MD 21114-2723, USA

Klemm, Jon (Athlete, Hockey Player)
772 Briar Ridge Ct
Castle Pines, CO 80108-8223, USA

Klemm, Jon (Athlete, Hockey Player)
Spokane Chiefs
700 W Mallon Ave
Attn: Coaching Staff
Spokane, WA 99201-2134, USA

Klemmer, John (Musician)
Boardman
10548 Clearwood Ct
Los Angeles, CA 90077-2019, USA

Klensch, Elsa
1050 Techwood Dr NW
Atlanta, GA 30318-5604

Klepper, Jordan (Comedian, Television
Host)
c/o Staff Member *The Daily Show with
Jon Stewart*
733 11th Ave
New York, NY 10019-5051, USA

Klesko, Ryan (Athlete, Baseball Player)
c/o Staff Member *San Diego Padres*
100 Park Blvd
San Diego, CA 92101-7405, USA

Klesla, Rostislav (Athlete, Hockey Player)
6751 N Sunset Blvd # 200
Glendale, AZ 85305-3162, USA

Klesla, Rotislav (Athlete, Hockey Player)
200 W Nationwide Blvd
Columbus, OH 43215-2561, USA

Klett, Peter (Musician)
11410 NE 124th St # 627
Kirkland, WA 98034-4399, USA

Klever, Rocky (Athlete, Football Player)
407 W Edgewood Ave
Linwood, NJ 08221-1709, USA

Klick, Jim (Athlete, Football Player)
4001 E Lake Estates Dr
Davie, FL 33328-3072, USA

Klicullen, Bob (Athlete, Football Player)
400 E Division St
Pilot Point, TX 76258-4510, USA

Klieman, Rikki (Attorney, Commentator)
210 E 65th St Apt 4D
New York, NY 10065-6670, USA

Klima, Petr (Athlete, Hockey Player)
1001 Forest Ln
Bloomfield Hills, MI 48301-4113, USA

Klimchock, Lou (Athlete, Baseball Player)
8876 S Myrtle Ave
Tempe, AZ 85284-3178, USA

Kline, Bobby (Athlete, Baseball Player)
6656 31st Way S
Saint Petersburg, FL 33712-5404, USA

Kline, Jeff (Producer, Writer)
c/o Staff Member *William Morris
Endeavor (LA)*
9601 Wilshire Blvd
Beverly Hills, CA 90210-5213, USA

Kline, John (Congressman, Politician)
2439 Rayburn Hob
Washington, DC 20515-3001, USA

Kline, Kevin (Actor)
26 Wing & Wing
Garrison, NY 10524, USA

Kline, Owen (Actor)
c/o Staff Member *William Morris
Endeavor (LA)*
9601 Wilshire Blvd
Beverly Hills, CA 90210-5213, USA

Kline, Richard (Actor)
c/o Harry Gold *TalentWorks (LA)*
3500 W Olive Ave Ste 1400
Burbank, CA 91505-5512, USA

Kline, Steve (Athlete, Baseball Player)
258 Trutt Rd
Winfield, PA 17889-9304, USA

Kline, Steve (Athlete, Baseball Player)
78 Milledge Rd
Attn: Coaching Staff
Augusta, GA 30904-3022, USA

Kline, Steve (Athlete, Baseball Player)
PO Box 1525
Chelan, WA 98816-1525, USA

Kline-Randall, Maxine (Athlete, Baseball
Player, Commentator)
3751 Milnes Rd
Hillsdale, MI 49242-9313, USA

Klingbeil, Chuck (Athlete, Football Player)
47921 US Highway 41
Houghton, MI 49931-9007, USA

Klingenbeck, Scott (Athlete, Baseball
Player)
6230 Kincora Ct
Cincinnati, OH 45233-4458, USA

Klingler, David (Athlete, Football Player)
3113 N Saddlebrook Ln
Katy, TX 77494-5616, USA

Klingman, Lynzee (Actor)
c/o Staff Member *United Talent Agency
(UTA-LA)*
9336 Civic Center Dr
Beverly Hills, CA 90210-3604, USA

Klink, Joe (Athlete, Baseball Player)
119 Green Heron Ct
Daytona Beach, FL 32119-1303, USA

Klinsmann, Jurgen (Soccer Player)
3419 Via Lido # 600
Newport Beach, CA 92663-3908, USA

Klosowski, Dolores (Baseball Player)
14254 Farnsworth Dr
Sterling Heights, MI 48312-4352, USA

Kloss, Ilana (Athlete, Tennis Player)
World TeamTennis
1776 Broadway Ste 600
New York, NY 10019-2002, USA

Klosterman, Bruce (Athlete, Football
Player)
14194 Deerfield Ct
Dubuque, IA 52003-9414, USA

Klotz, H Louis (Red) (Athlete, Basketball
Player, Coach)
114 S Osborne Ave
Margate City, NJ 08402-2530, USA

Klotz, Jack (Athlete, Football Player)
729 E 25th St
Chester, PA 19013-5229, USA

Klotz, John S (Athlete, Football Player)
729 E 25th St
Chester, PA 19013-5229, USA

Klous, Patricia (Actor)
2539 Benedict Canyon Dr
Beverly Hills, CA 90210-1020, USA

Kloves, Steve (Director, Writer)
c/o David O'Connor *Creative Artists
Agency (CAA-LA)*
2000 Avenue of the Stars Ste 100
Los Angeles, CA 90067-4705, USA

Klueh, Duane (Athlete, Basketball Player)
200 Francis Avenue Ct Apt 211
Terre Haute, IN 47804-1093, USA

Kluer, Duane (Athlete, Basketball Player,
Coach)
252 Francis Avenue Ct
Terre Haute, IN 47804-5101, USA

Kluger, Richard (Writer)
c/o Staff Member *Random House
Publicity*
1745 Broadway Frnt 3
New York, NY 10019-4343, USA

Klugh, Earl (Musician)
c/o Staff Member *Richard De La Font
Agency*
3808 W South Park Blvd
Broken Arrow, OK 74011-1261, USA

Klum, Heidi (Model, Producer, Television
Host)
3384 Stone Ridge Ln
Los Angeles, CA 90077-1740, USA

Klurfeld, Herman
445 Grand Bay Dr Apt 602
Key Biscayne, FL 33149-1909, USA

Klutts, Mickey (Athlete, Baseball Player)
6136 Maple Ave
Lake Isabella, CA 93240-9706, USA

Kluttz, Lonnie (Athlete, Basketball Player)
183 Greenwing Ln
Saint Matthews, SC 29135-8168, USA

Kluwe, Chris (Athlete, Football Player)
6686 Montford Dr
Huntington Beach, CA 92648-6625, USA

Kluzak, Gord (Athlete, Hockey Player)
Boston Bruins
100 Legends Way Ste 250
Attn: Broadcast Dept
Boston, MA 02114-1389, USA

Kluzak, Gord (Athlete, Hockey Player)
770 Boylston St Apt 27C
Boston, MA 02199-7724, USA

Klymaxx (Music Group)
c/o Staff Member *Diva Central Inc*
7510 W Sunset Blvd Ste 1445
Los Angeles, CA 90046-3408, USA

Klyn, Vincent
4200 Ocean View Dr
Malibu, CA 90265-2822

Kmak, Joe (Athlete, Baseball Player)
1021 Hatteras Ct
Foster City, CA 94404-3546, USA

Kmetko, Steve
5670 Wilshire Blvd Ste 200
Los Angeles, CA 90036-5657

Knackert, Brent (Athlete, Baseball Player)
16802 Leafwood Cir
Huntington Beach, CA 92647-4851, USA

Knafelc, Gary (Athlete, Football Player)
2147 Burley Ave
Clermont, FL 34711-5744, USA

Knafelc, Greg (Athlete, Football Player)
1243 Prairie Falcon Trl
Green Bay, WI 54313-7177, USA

Knapp, Alexis (Actor)
c/o Alex Gittelson *Untitled Entertainment
(LA)*
350 S Beverly Dr Ste 200
Beverly Hills, CA 90212-4819, USA

Knapp, Chris (Athlete, Baseball Player)
788 Rich Dr
Oviedo, FL 32765-6447, USA

Knapp, Cleon T (Publisher)
Talewood Corp
10100 Santa Monica Blvd Ste 2000
Los Angeles, CA 90067-4134, USA

Knapp, Jennifer (Musician)
c/o Staff Member *Creative Artists Agency
(CAA-TN)*
401 Commerce St PH
Nashville, TN 37219-2516, USA

Knapp, Lindsay (Athlete, Football Player)
5018 Bruce Ave
Minneapolis, MN 55424-1318, USA

Knapp, Rick (Athlete, Baseball Player)
96131 Long Beach Dr
Fernandina, FL 32034-8716, USA

Knapp, Sebastian (Actor)
c/o Lorraine Berglund *Lorraine Berglund
Management*
11537 Hesby St
North Hollywood, CA 91601-3618, USA

Knapple, Jeff (Athlete, Football Player)
10025 Toluca Lake Ave
Toluca Lake, CA 91602-2923, USA

Knaus, William (Doctor)
*George Washington University
Medical Center*
Washington, DC 20052-0001, USA

Knebel, John A (Politician)
1418 Labumum St
Mc Lean, VA 22101, USA

Kneifel, Chris (Race Car Driver)
6 Timberline Ln
Riverwoods, IL 60015-2443, USA

Knepper, Bob (Athlete, Baseball Player)
2221 Eastwood Dr
Roseville, CA 95747-8879, USA

Knepper, Robert (Actor)
c/o Ben Levine *LINK Entertainment*
11872 La Grange Ave Fl 1
Los Angeles, CA 90025-5283, USA

Knibbs, Darrel (Athlete, Hockey Player)
2236 Surfwood Dr
Muskegon, MI 49441-1162

Knicely, Alan (Athlete, Baseball Player)
700 Three Leagues Rd
McGaheysville, VA 22840-2680, USA

Knickman, Clarence Roy (Athlete, Cycler,
Olympic Athlete)
436 Fallbrook Ave
Newbury Park, CA 91320-4929, USA

Knief, Gayle (Athlete, Football Player)
1825 SE Birchwood Cir
Waukee, IA 50263-8194, USA

Kniffin, Chuck (Athlete, Baseball Player)
420 S Deer Mountain Rd
Florissant, CO 80816, USA

Knight, Billy (Athlete, Basketball Player)
2002 Oglethorpe Dr NE
Brookhaven, GA 30319-2796, USA

Knight, Brandon (Athlete, Baseball Player)
New York Yankees
PO Box 1685
Ventura, CA 93002-1685, USA

Knight, Brevin (Athlete, Basketball Player)
3226 Bedford Ln
Germantown, TN 38139-8043, USA

Knight, Brian (Athlete, Baseball Player)
1123 Stuart St
Helena, MT 59601-2138, USA

Knight, Carlos (Actor)
c/o Ford Englerth *Redrock Entertainment Development*
118 S Cordova St Fl 3
Burbank, CA 91505-4610, USA

Knight, Charles F (Business Person)
Emerson Electric Co
8000 W Florissant Ave # 41000
Saint Louis, MO 63136-1414, USA

Knight, Chris (Musician, Songwriter, Writer)
Rick Alter Mgmt
1018 17th Ave S Ste 12
Nashville, TN 37212-2219, USA

Knight, Christopher (Actor)
1600 Monterey Blvd
Hermosa Beach, CA 90254-2901, USA

Knight, Curt (Athlete, Football Player)
9070 Florence Ave Apt 14
Downey, CA 90240-3442, USA

Knight, David (Athlete, Football Player)
3801 Porter St NW Apt 301
Washington, DC 20016-2947, USA

Knight, Gladys (Musician)
3221 La Mirada Ave
Las Vegas, NV 89120-3011, USA

Knight, Jean (Musician)
Ken Keene Artists
PO Box 1875
Gretna, LA 70054-1875, USA

Knight, Jonathan (Musician)
20 Chase St Fl 2
Danvers, MA 01923-3225, USA

Knight, Jordan (Musician)
c/o Tracy Nguyen *Industry Public Relations*
16547 Park Lane Cir
Los Angeles, CA 90049-1184, USA

Knight, Marcus (Athlete, Football Player)
326 Threatt Ln
Sylacauga, AL 35150-8635, USA

Knight, Marion (Suge) (Actor, Musician, Producer)
c/o Staff Member *Acme Talent & Literary (LA)*
1400 Atlantic Ave Ste 274
Long Beach, CA 90813-2013, USA

Knight, Michael E
1344 Lexington Ave
New York, NY 10128-1507, USA

Knight, Negele (Athlete, Basketball Player)
18624 N 4th Ave
Phoenix, AZ 85027-5665, USA

Knight, Phil (Business Person)
Nike Inc
1 SW Bowerman Dr
Beaverton, OR 97005-0979, USA

Knight, Ray (Athlete, Baseball Player)
1500 S Capitol St SE
Attn: Broadcast Dept
Washington, DC 20003-3599, USA

Knight, Ray (Athlete, Baseball Player)
PO Box 129
Auburn, AL 36831-0129, USA

Knight, Robert M (Bobby) (Athlete, Basketball Player, Coach)
8003 County Road 6910
Lubbock, TX 79407-5760, USA

Knight, Roger (Athlete, Football Player)
929 Flywheel Cir
De Forest, WI 53532-0910, USA

Knight, Ron (Athlete, Basketball Player)
1426 Ellsmere Ave
Los Angeles, CA 90019-3800, USA

Knight, Sandra (Actor)
626 Kaimalino St
Kailua, HI 96734-1613, USA

Knight, Shawn (Athlete, Football Player)
13090 Welcome Way
Reno, NV 89511-8688, USA

Knight, Shirley (Actor)
c/o Martin Gage *Gage Group, The (LA)*
5757 Wilshire Blvd Ste 659
Los Angeles, CA 90036-3682, USA

Knight, Sterling (Actor)
c/o Christopher Rockwell *Keyword Entertainment*
1051 Cole Ave # B
Los Angeles, CA 90038-2601, USA

Knight, Steve (Athlete, Football Player)
4503 Bevington Ln Apt A
Indianapolis, IN 46240-4478, USA

Knight, Steve (Writer)
c/o Staff Member *Creative Artists Agency (CAA-LA)*
2000 Avenue of the Stars Ste 100
Los Angeles, CA 90067-4705, USA

Knight, Summer
PO Box 9786
Marina Del Rey, CA 90295-2186

Knight, Toby (Athlete, Basketball Player)
106 Claywood Dr
Brentwood, NY 11717-5724, USA

Knight, Tom (Athlete, Football Player)
PO Box 888
Phoenix, AZ 85001-0888, USA

Knight, TR (Actor)
c/o Staff Member *Gersh (LA)*
9465 Wilshire Blvd Ste 600
Beverly Hills, CA 90212-2605, USA

Knight, Travis (Athlete, Basketball Player)
3159 Millcreek Rd
Pleasant Grove, UT 84062-8790, USA

Knight, Trevor (Adult Film Star)
c/o Staff Member *Diva Central Inc*
7510 W Sunset Blvd Ste 1445
Los Angeles, CA 90046-3408, USA

Knight, Wayne (Actor)
c/o Staff Member *Agency for the Performing Arts (APA-LA)*
405 S Beverly Dr Ste 500
Beverly Hills, CA 90212-4425, USA

Knight, Wendi (Adult Film Star)
c/o Staff Member *Atlas Multimedia Inc*
9005 Eton Ave Ste C
Canoga Park, CA 91304-6533, USA

Knightlinger, Lauren (Actor)
c/o Peter Principato *Principato/Young Management (LA)*
9465 Wilshire Blvd Ste 900
Beverly Hills, CA 90212-2608, USA

Knighton, Terrance (Athlete, Football Player)
c/o Mitchell Frankel *Impact Sports - Boca Raton*
2799 NW 2nd Ave Ste 203
Boca Raton, FL 33431-6709, USA

Knighton, Zachary (Actor)
c/o Nick Frenkel *3 Arts Entertainment (LA)*
9460 Wilshire Blvd Fl 7
Beverly Hills, CA 90212-2713, USA

Knipple, Bobby (Bowler)
2626 Vuelta Grande Ave
Long Beach, CA 90815-2253, USA

Knipscheer, Fred (Athlete, Hockey Player)
13404 Macaw Pl
Carmel, IN 46033-8964, USA

Knisley, Sam (Athlete, Basketball Player)
14808 Hanover Pike
Upperco, MD 21155-9735, USA

Knobbs, Brian
14804 58th St
North Clearwater, FL 34620

Knoblauch, Chuck (Athlete, Baseball Player)
11702 Forest Glen St
Houston, TX 77024-6414, USA

Knoedler, Justin (Athlete, Baseball Player)
2204 Harbor Lndg
Springfield, IL 62712-9599, USA

Knoff, Kurt (Athlete, Football Player)
11121 Bluestem Ln
Eden Prairie, MN 55347-4732, USA

Knoop, Bobby (Athlete, Baseball Player)
2543 E Mountain Sky Ave
Phoenix, AZ 85048-9516, USA

Knopf, Sascha (Actor, Model)
c/o Bradley Frank *Platform Public Relations*
2666 N Beachwood Dr
Los Angeles, CA 90068-2308, USA

Knopper, Steve (Writer)
3445 W Moncrieff Pl
Denver, CO 80211-3161, USA

Knorr, Micah (Athlete, Football Player)
10391 Whitecrown Cir
Corona, CA 92883-9267, USA

Knorr, Randy (Athlete, Baseball Player)
12134 Bishopsford Dr
Tampa, FL 33626-1319, USA

Knorr, Randy (Athlete, Baseball Player)
Syracuse Chiefs 1 Tex Simone Dr
Attn: Managers Office
Syracuse, NY 13208, USA

Knostman, Richard (Dick) (Athlete, Basketball Player)
346 Crestone Ave
Salida, CO 81201-1521, USA

Knott, Eric (Athlete, Baseball Player)
10200 Independence Pkwy Apt 1303
Plano, TX 75025-8234, USA

Knott, Jon (Athlete, Baseball Player)
1286 Thoreau Cir
Venice, FL 34292-2426, USA

Knotts, Gary (Athlete, Baseball Player)
18 Covey St
Decatur, AL 35603-6021, USA

Knowles, Beyonce (Actor, Musician)
195 Hudson St PH 7AB
New York, NY 10013-1813, USA

Knowles, Darold (Athlete, Baseball Player)
1515 Whisper Wind Ln
Oldsmar, FL 34677-5133, USA

Knowles, Darold (Athlete, Baseball Player)
373 Douglas Ave
Attn: Coaching Staff
Dunedin, FL 34698-7913, USA

Knowles, Harry (Internet Star)
PO Box 180011
Austin, TX 78718-0011, USA

Knowles, Rodney (Athlete, Basketball Player)
3592 Island Dr
N Topsail Beach, NC 28460-8202, USA

Knowles, Solange (Actor, Musician)
c/o Staff Member *Roc Nation*
9348 Civic Center Dr
Beverly Hills, CA 90210-3624, USA

Knowles, Tony (Politician)
1146 S St
Anchorage, AK 99501-4230, USA

Knowlton, Steve R (Skier)
Palmer Yeager Assoc
6600 E Hampden Ave # 210
Denver, CO 80224-3045, USA

Knox, Bill (Athlete, Football Player)
7836 Forest Ave
Gary, IN 46403-2139, USA

Knox, Chuck (Athlete, Football Player)
891 S Walnut St Apt 915
Anaheim, CA 92802-1771, USA

Knox, John (Athlete, Baseball Player)
3701 W Oak Shores Dr
Crossroads, TX 76227-2606, USA

Knox, Kenny (Athlete, Golfer)
3813 Dills Rd
Monticello, FL 32344-4699, USA

Knox, Terence (Actor)
c/o Lin Bickelmann *Encore Artists Management*
3815 W Olive Ave Ste 101
Burbank, CA 91505-4674, USA

Knoxville, Johnny (Actor)
c/o Sean Robinson *LW1*
7257 Beverly Blvd Ste 200
Los Angeles, CA 90036-2567, USA

Knuble, Mike (Athlete, Hockey Player, Olympic Athlete)
K O Sports
501 S Cherry St Ste 580
Attn Kurt Overhardt
Denver, CO 80246-1327, USA

Knudsen, Arthur G (Skier)
5111 Wright Ave Apt 104
Racine, WI 53406-4530, USA

Knudsen, Erik (Actor)
c/o Joanna (Joanie) Burstein *Burstein Company, The*
15304 W Sunset Blvd Ste 208
Pacific Palisades, CA 90272-3656, USA

Knudsen, Kurt (Athlete, Baseball Player)
5155 Patti Jo Dr
Carmichael, CA 95608-0968, USA

Knudson, Mark (Athlete, Baseball Player)
881 W 100th Ave
Northglenn, CO 80260-6255, USA

Knudson, Thomas J (Journalist)
Sacramento Bee
Editorial Dept
21st & Q Sts
Sacramento, CA 95852, USA

Koalska, Matt (Athlete, Hockey Player)
95 Roseavew
Saint Paul, MN 55117, USA

Koart, Matt (Athlete, Football Player)
122 Sonora Ave
Danville, CA 94526-3834, USA

Koba, Jeff
8899 Beverly Blvd # 705
Los Angeles, CA 90048-2412

Koback, Nick (Athlete, Baseball Player)
71 Hopmeadow St Apt 9A-1
Weatogue, CT 06089-9635, USA

Kobel, Kevin (Athlete, Baseball Player)
7650 E Williams Dr Unit 1072
Scottsdale, AZ 85255-4810, USA

Kober, Jeff (Actor)
4544 Ethel Ave
Studio City, CA 91604-1002, USA

Kobza, Jerry (Race Car Driver)
Shenandoah Valley Motorsports
11 S Oak Ln
Waynesboro, VA 22980-5269, USA

Koch, Aaron (Athlete, Football Player)
PO Box 1148
Silverton, OR 97381-0046, USA

Koch, Alan (Athlete, Baseball Player)
1714 Pebble Creek Dr
Prattville, AL 36066-7206, USA

Koch, Alexander (Actor)
c/o Michael Samonte *Sunshine Sachs (LA)*
8409 Santa Monica Blvd
West Hollywood, CA 90069-4209, USA

Koch, Bill (Business Person, Sailor)
Oxbow Corp
1601 Forum Pl Ste 1400
West Palm Beach, FL 33401-8104, USA

Koch, Billy (Athlete, Baseball Player,
Olympic Athlete)
3160 Tusket Ave
North Port, FL 34286-4904, USA

Koch, Carin (Athlete, Golfer)
5231 E Herrera Dr
Phoenix, AZ 85054-7183, USA

Koch, Charles (Business Person)
Charles G Koch Charitable Foundation
655 15th St NW Ste 825
Washington, DC 20005-5718, USA

Koch, David (Business Person)
Koch Family Management
459 Columbus Ave # 216
New York, NY 10024-5129, USA

Koch, Desmond (Des) (Athlete, Football
Player, Track Athlete)
23296 Gilmore St
West Hills, CA 91307-3426, USA

Koch, Gary (Athlete, Golfer)
2934 W Lawn Ave
Tampa, FL 33611-1647, USA

Koch, Gregory M (Greg) (Athlete,
Football Player)
15000 Mansions View Dr Apt 405
Conroe, TX 77384-4341, USA

Koch, Pete (Athlete, Football Player)
866 W 16th St
Newport Beach, CA 92663-2802, USA

Koch, Peter (Actor)
c/o Staff Member *Fly Trap, The*
900 E 1st St Apt 212
Los Angeles, CA 90012-4039, USA

Koch, William (Bill) (Athlete, Olympic
Athlete, Skier)
PO Box 115
Ashland, OR 97520-0004, USA

Kochan, Dieter (Athlete, Hockey Player)
37922 US Highway 41
Chassell, MI 49916-9254, USA

Koch Jr, Howard (Producer)
Producers Guild of America
8530 Wilshire Blvd Ste 400
Beverly Hills, CA 90211-3131, USA

Kochman, Roger (Athlete, Football Player)
521 Beverly Blvd
Upper Darby, PA 19082-3615, USA

Kocourek, Dave (Athlete, Football Player)
1170 Cara Ct
Marco Island, FL 34145-4518, USA

Kocur, Joe (Athlete, Hockey Player)
c/o Staff Member *Detroit Red Wings*
600 Civic Center Dr
Joe Luis Arena
Detroit, MI 48226-4419, USA

Kodjoe, Boris (Actor, Model)
c/o Evan Hainey *Untitled Entertainment
(LA)*
350 S Beverly Dr Ste 200
Beverly Hills, CA 90212-4819, USA

Koecher, Dick (Athlete, Baseball Player)
3310 Grand Cypress Dr Apt 102
Naples, FL 34119-7979, USA

Koechner, David (Actor, Writer)
c/o John Elliott *Mosaic Media Group*
9200 W Sunset Blvd Ste 10
West Hollywood, CA 90069-3608, USA

Koegel, Pete (Athlete, Baseball Player)
301 the Birches
Saugerties, NY 12477-5249, USA

Koegel, Warren (Athlete, Football Player)
Coastal Carolina University
1273 N Fraser St
Georgetown, SC 29440-2853, USA

Koelling, Brian (Athlete, Baseball Player)
20230 Augusta Dr
Lawrenceburg, IN 47025-7370, USA

Koen, Karleen (Writer)
Random House
1745 Broadway Frnt 3 # B1
New York, NY 10019-4343, USA

Koenekamp, Fred (Cinematographer)
9756 Shoshone Ave
Northridge, CA 91325-1831, USA

Koenig, Walter (Actor)
PO Box 4395
Valley Village, CA 91617-0395, USA

Koepfer, Karl (Athlete, Football Player)
2017 Waters Edge Dr
Westlake, OH 44145-6603, USA

Koepp, David (Director, Writer)
c/o Richard Lovett *Creative Artists Agency
(CAA-LA)*
2000 Avenue of the Stars Ste 100
Los Angeles, CA 90067-4705, USA

Koetter, Dirk (Coach, Football Coach)
Arizona State University
Athletic Dept
Tempe, AZ 85287-0001, USA

Koffler, Pamela (Producer)
c/o Staff Member *Killer Films (US)*
526 W 26th St Rm 715
New York, NY 10001-5524, USA

Kofoed, Bart (Athlete, Basketball Player)
10161 Foxhall Dr
Charlotte, NC 28210-7846, USA

Kogan, Theo (Actor, Musician)
Wilhelmina Creative Mgmt
300 Park Ave S # 200
New York, NY 10010-5313, USA

Kogen, Jay (Producer, Writer)
433 Bellagio Ter
Los Angeles, CA 90049-1707, USA

Koger, Gene (Athlete, Baseball Player)
285 Koger Rd
Reidsville, NC 27320-9555, USA

Kogut, Charles (Athlete, Football Player)
210 W 22nd St Ste 110
Oak Brook, IL 60523-4035, USA

Kohan, David (Producer)
c/o Staff Member *KoMut Entertainment*
300 Television Plz
Burbank, CA 91505, USA

Kohan, Jenji (Director, Producer)
c/o Joe Cohen *Creative Artists Agency
(CAA-LA)*
2000 Avenue of the Stars Ste 100
Los Angeles, CA 90067-4705, USA

Koharski, Don (Athlete, Hockey Player)
6946 Old Pasco Rd # 275
Wesley Chapel, FL 33544-3504, USA

Kohl, Ernest (Musician)
c/o Staff Member *Diva Central Inc*
7510 W Sunset Blvd Ste 1445
Los Angeles, CA 90046-3408, USA

Kohl, Herbert (Politician)
929 N Astor St Unit 2708
Milwaukee, WI 53202-3491, USA

Kohlbrand, Joe (Athlete, Football Player)
480 Greenview Rd
Merritt Island, FL 32952-5223, USA

Kohlhaas, Jeannette (Athlete, Golfer)
6287 Battlegate Rd
Jacksonville, FL 32258-9424, USA

Kohlmeier, Ryan (Athlete, Baseball Player)
301 Vine St
Cottonwood Falls, KS 66845-9812, USA

Kohlsaat, Peter (Cartoonist)
5536 Richmond Curv
Minneapolis, MN 55410-2534, USA

Kohn, Alfie (Writer)
c/o Staff Member *Houghton Mifflin
Company (Trade Division)*
222 Berkeley St Fl 8
Boston, MA 02116-3748, USA

Kohrs, Bob (Athlete, Football Player)
2910 E Nance St
Mesa, AZ 85213-1647, USA

Koib, Thomas Claudia A (Coach,
Swimmer)
Stanford University
Athletic Dept
Stanford, CA 94305, USA

Koiv, Kerli (Musician)
c/o Staff Member *Island Def Jam Group*
825 8th Ave Fl 28
New York, NY 10019-7416, USA

Koivu, Mikko (Athlete, Hockey Player)
5500 Halifax Ln
Minneapolis, MN 55424-1439, USA

Kojac, George (Swimmer)
33 Arboles Del Norte
Fort Pierce, FL 34951-2877, USA

Kojis, Don (Athlete, Basketball Player)
8186 Commercial St
La Mesa, CA 91942-2926, USA

Kokkonen, Elissa Lee (Musician)
Columbia Artists Mgmt Inc
165 W 57th St
New York, NY 10019-2201, USA

Kokotakis, Nick
9229 W Sunset Blvd Ste 315
West Hollywood, CA 90069-3403

Kolanko, Mary Lou (Baseball Player)
3109 W Henry Ave
Tampa, FL 33614-5924, USA

Kolat, Cary (Athlete, Olympic Athlete,
Wrestler)
115 Lexington Dr
Chapel Hill, NC 27516-3219, USA

Kolb, Brandon (Athlete, Baseball Player)
2043 Pin Oak Pl
Danville, CA 94506-2119, USA

Kolb, Dan (Athlete, Baseball Player)
PO Box 700
Walnut, IL 61376-0700, USA

Kolb, Danny (Athlete, Baseball Player)
1601 51st Dr
Union Grove, WI 53182-9548, USA

Kolb, Gary (Athlete, Baseball Player)
5143 Hopewell Dr
Charleston, WV 25313-1784, USA

Kolb, Jon (Athlete, Football Player)
44 Hermitage Hills Blvd
Hermitage, PA 16148-5710, USA

Kolb, Kevin (Athlete, Football Player)
4711 Steepleridge Trl
Granbury, TX 76048-5001, USA

Kolber, Suzy (Sportscaster)
ESPN-TV
Sports Dept
ESPN Plaza 935 Middle St
Bristol, CT 06010, USA

Kolden, Scott
8743 Quakertown Ave
Northridge, CA 91324-3229

Kole, Warren (Actor)
c/o Staff Member *D/F Management*
8609 Washington Blvd # 8607
Culver City, CA 90232-7441, USA

Kolen, Mike (Athlete, Football Player)
1613 Manchester Ln
Vestavia, AL 35243-4862, USA

Kolesar, Robert (Athlete, Football Player)
5003 Lincoln Ave
Cleveland, OH 44134-1866, USA

Kolinsky, Sue (Producer)
c/o Staff Member *Innovative Artists (LA)*
1505 10th St
Santa Monica, CA 90401-2805, USA

Kolius, John (Athlete, Olympic Athlete, Sailor)
10804 SE Deck Ct
Hobe Sound, FL 33455-3235, USA

Kollar, Bill (Athlete, Football Player)
4899 Montrose Blvd Apt 605
Houston, TX 77006-6165, USA

Kolodziej, Ross (Athlete, Football Player)
329 Scarlet Cir
Wexford, PA 15090-8688, USA

Kolodziewjski, Chris (Athlete, Football Player)
1123 Sandalwood Dr
Lawrenceville, GA 30043-4621, USA

Kolstad, Dean (Athlete, Hockey Player)
15492 Brooklodge Rd
Hickory Corners, MI 49060-9740, USA

Kolstad, Hal (Athlete, Baseball Player)
15149 Bel Escou Dr
San Jose, CA 95124-5032, USA

Kolsti, Paul (Cartoonist)
Dallas News
Editorial Dept
Communications Center
Dallas, TX 75265, USA

Kolta, Lajos (Cinematographer, Director)
c/o Staff Member *Gersh (LA)*
9465 Wilshire Blvd Ste 600
Beverly Hills, CA 90212-2605, USA

Koltsov, Konstantin (Athlete, Hockey Player)
10395 Forest Bridge Dr
Alpharetta, GA 30022-4528, USA

Komadoski, Neil (Athlete, Hockey Player)
876 Judson Manor Dr
Saint Louis, MO 63141-6057, USA

Koman, Bill (Athlete, Football Player)
5 Upper Ladue Rd
Saint Louis, MO 63124-1677, USA

Koman, Michael (Writer)
c/o Staff Member *ICM Partners (LA)*
10250 Constellation Blvd Fl 7
Los Angeles, CA 90067-6207, USA

Komenich, Nadia (Gymnast)
The Bart Conner Gymnastics Academy
PO Box 720217
Norman, OK 73070-4166, USA

Kometani, Pam (Athlete, Golfer)
4342 Kilauea Ave
Honolulu, HI 96816-5113, USA

Komine, Shane (Athlete, Baseball Player)
641 8th Ave
Honolulu, HI 96816-2109, USA

Kominsky, Cheryl (Bowler)
Ladies Professional Bowling Tour
7200 Harrison Ave # 7171
Rockford, IL 61112-1017, USA

Komisarek, Mike (Athlete, Hockey Player)
Olympic Sports Management
9 Alden Rd
Wellesley Hills, MA 02481-6702, USA

Komisarz, Rachel (Athlete, Olympic Athlete, Swimmer)
9402 Magnolia Ridge Dr Unit 201
Louisville, KY 40291-6756, USA

Komminsk, Brad (Athlete, Baseball Player)
150 Park Ave
Attn Coaching Staff
Norfolk, VA 23510-2712, USA

Komminsk, Brad (Athlete, Baseball Player)
688 Fallside Ln
Westerville, OH 43081-5003, USA

Kompara, John (Athlete, Football Player)
13030 Coldwater Loop
Clermont, FL 34711-8014, USA

Komunyakaa, Yusef (Writer)
900 W State St
Trenton, NJ 08618-5328, USA

Koncak, Jon (Athlete, Basketball Player, Olympic Athlete)
PO Box 10040
Jackson, WY 83002-0040, USA

Koncar, Mark (Athlete, Football Player)
447 N Alpine Blvd
Alpine, UT 84004-1264, USA

Kondia, Tom (Athlete, Basketball Player)
3517 Cleveland Ave
Brookfield, IL 60513-1103, USA

Kondla, Tom (Athlete, Basketball Player)
3517 Cleveland Ave
Brookfield, IL 60513-1103, USA

Konerko, Paul (Athlete, Baseball Player)
8053 E Leaning Rock Rd
Scottsdale, AZ 85266-1645, USA

Koneski, Jr., Walter (Race Car Driver)
Koneski Racing
368 Broezel Ave
Lancaster, NY 14086-1322, USA

Kongos (Music Group)
c/o Corrie Christopher *Paradigm (LA)*
360 N Crescent Dr
North Bldg
Beverly Hills, CA 90210-4874, USA

Konieczny, Doug (Athlete, Baseball Player)
9503 Dundalk St
Spring, TX 77379-4314, USA

Konik, George (Athlete, Hockey Player)
1027 Savannah Rd
Saint Paul, MN 55123-1543, USA

Konitz, Lee (Musician)
Bennett Morgan
1282 RR 376
Wappingers Falls, NY 12590, USA

Konner, Lawrence (Larry) (Writer)
c/o Tom Strickler *William Morris Endeavor (LA)*
9601 Wilshire Blvd
Beverly Hills, CA 90210-5213, USA

Kono, Tommy (Athlete, Olympic Athlete, Weightlifter)
98-2025 Hapaki St
Aiea, HI 96701-1642, USA

Konopasek, Ed (Athlete, Football Player)
2336 Meadowledge Ct
De Pere, WI 54115-8690, USA

Konowalchuk, Steve (Athlete, Hockey Player)
2628 S Adams St
Denver, CO 80210-6232, USA

Konowalchuk, Steve (Athlete, Hockey Player)
Seattle Thunderbirds
625 W James St
Attn: Coaching Staff
Kent, WA 98032-4406, USA

Konrad, Dorothy
10650 Missouri Ave Apt 2
Los Angeles, CA 90025-4815

Konrad, John H (Astronaut)
Hughes Space-Communications Group
PO Box 92919
Los Angeles, CA 90009-2919, USA

Konrad, Rob (Athlete, Football Player)
11884 Windmill Lake Dr
Boynton Beach, FL 33473-7846, USA

Konroyd, Steve (Athlete, Hockey Player)
317 S Park Ave
Hinsdale, IL 60521-4638, USA

Konroyd, Steve (Athlete, Hockey Player)
Chicago Blackhawks
1901 W Madison St
Attn: Broadcast Dept
Chicago, IL 60612-2459, USA

Konstantinov, Vladimir (Athlete, Hockey Player)
6782 Enclave
West Bloomfield, MI 48322-1399, USA

Konuszewski, Dennis (Athlete, Baseball Player)
945 Sue St
Saginaw, MI 48609-4963, USA

Konz, Peter (Athlete, Football Player)
c/o Joe Flanagan *BTI Sports Advisors*
170 N Scoville Ave
Oak Park, IL 60302-2647, USA

Kooistra, Scott (Athlete, Football Player)
106 Overlook Dr
Loveland, OH 45140-6689, USA

Kook, Shannon (Actor)
c/o Jordyn Palos *Persona PR (LA)*
8840 Wilshire Blvd Ste 212
Beverly Hills, CA 90211-2606, USA

Kooks, The (Music Group)
c/o Jonny Kaps *+1 Management and PR*
242 Wythe Ave
Studio 6
Brooklyn, NY 11249-3149, USA

Kool & The Gang (Music Group)
c/o Staff Member *J Bird Entertainment Agency*
4905 S Atlantic Ave
Ponce Inlet, FL 32127-7311, USA

Koonce, George (Athlete, Football Player)
534 Sarah Dr
Fond Du Lac, WI 54935-2826, USA

Koonce, Graham (Athlete, Baseball Player)
1413 Conner Way
Lantana, TX 76226-6991, USA

Koontz, Dean (Astronaut)
PO Box 9529
Newport Beach, CA 92658-9529, USA

Koontz, Ed (Athlete, Football Player)
2860 Blackshear Ave
Pensacola, FL 32503-4874, USA

Kooper, Al (Musician)
Legacy Records
550 Madison Ave Fl 6
New York, NY 10022-3211, USA

Koos, Torin (Athlete, Olympic Athlete, Skier)
1510 Madison St
Wenatchee, WA 98801-1731, USA

Kooser, Ted (Writer)
1820 Branched Oak Rd
Garland, NE 68360-9303, USA

Koosman, Jerry (Athlete, Baseball Player)
2483 State Road 35
Osceola, WI 54020-4216, USA

Kopacz, George (Athlete, Baseball Player)
14150 Somerset Ct
Orland Park, IL 60467-1142, USA

Kopay, Dave (Athlete, Football Player)
2035 Ridgeview Ave
Los Angeles, CA 90041-3018, USA

Kopecky, Tomas (Athlete, Hockey Player)
4401 N Federal Hwy Ste 201
Boca Raton, FL 33431-5164, USA

Kopell, Bernie (Actor)
19413 Olivos Dr
Tarzana, CA 91356-4403, USA

Kopeloff, Eric (Director)
c/o Staff Member *William Morris Endeavor (LA)*
9601 Wilshire Blvd
Beverly Hills, CA 90210-5213, USA

Kopelson, Arnold (Producer)
901 N Roxbury Dr
Beverly Hills, CA 90210-3019, USA

Koper, Herbert (Athlete, Basketball Player)
11707 Rushmore
Oklahoma City, OK 73162-1636, USA

Kopervas, Gary (Cartoonist)
c/o Staff Member *King Features Syndication*
300 W 57th St Fl 15
New York, NY 10019-5238, USA

Kopicki, Joe (Athlete, Basketball Player)
47608 Cheryl Ct
Shelby Township, MI 48315-4708, USA

Kopins, Karen (Actor)
Sutton Barth Vennari
122 Old Mountain Tom Rd
Bantam, CT 06750, USA

Kopit, Arthur (Writer)
240 W 98th St Apt 11B
New York, NY 10025-5516, USA

Kopitar, Anze (Athlete, Hockey Player)
c/o Staff Member *Los Angeles Kings*
1111 S Figueroa St Ste 3100
Los Angeles, CA 90015-1333, USA

Koplitz, Lynne (Actor)
c/o Staff Member *Paradigm (Monterey)*
404 W Franklin St
Monterey, CA 93940-2303, USA

Koplove, Mike (Athlete, Baseball Player)
3235 Chaucer St
Philadelphia, PA 19145-5841, USA

Kopp, Jeff (Athlete, Football Player)
9409 Hannahs Mill Dr Apt 403
Owings Mills, MD 21117-6855, USA

Kopp, Larry (Race Car Driver)
Lary Kopp Racing
5511 McCormick Ave
MacOn, GA 31206, USA

Koppel, Edward J ""Ted"" (Journalist)
10701 Ardnave Pl
Potomac, MD 20854-1261, USA

Koppel, Ted (Correspondent)
10701 Ardnave Pl
Potomac, MD 20854-1261, USA

Koppen, Dan (Athlete, Football Player)
1801 Old Bridge Ln
Bellingham, MA 02019-3134, USA

Koppikar, Isha (Actor)
c/o Staff Member *Canyon Entertainment*
PO Box 256
Palm Springs, CA 92263-0256, USA

Kopple, Barbara J (Director)
Cabin Creek Films
155 Avenue of the Americas
New York, NY 10013-1507, USA

Kopra, Timothy L (Astronaut)
2518 Lakeside Dr
Seabrook, TX 77586-3392, USA

Kopra, Timothy L Lt Colonel (Astronaut)
4912 Cross Creek Ln
League City, TX 77573-6267, USA

Korab, Jerry (Athlete, Hockey Player)
Korab Inc
213 Maison Ct
Palm Beach Gardens, FL 33410-2215, USA

Korach, Ken (Commentator)
1963 Troon Dr
Henderson, NV 89074-1040, USA

Korbut, Olga (Athlete, Gymnast, Olympic Athlete)
16356 N Thompson Peak Pkwy Apt 2024
Scottsdale, AZ 85260-2108, USA

Korcheck, Steve (Athlete, Baseball Player)
6424 98th St E
Bradenton, FL 34202-9769, USA

Korda, Maria
304 N Screenland Dr
Burbank, CA 91505-3805

Korda, Michael V (Writer)
Simon & Schuster/Pocket/Summit
1230 Avenue of the Americas
New York, NY 10020-1513, USA

Korda, Petr (Tennis Player)
4909 61st Avenue Dr W
Bradenton, FL 34210-4041, USA

Korecky, Bobby
11601 4th St N Apt 2502
Saint Petersburg, FL 33716-2745, USA

Koren, Edward B (Cartoonist)
New Yorker Magazine
4 Times Sq Fl 22
Editorial Dept
New York, NY 10036-6592, USA

Koren, Steve (Producer, Writer)
c/o Staff Member *Creative Artists Agency (CAA-LA)*
2000 Avenue of the Stars Ste 100
Los Angeles, CA 90067-4705, USA

Korf, Mia (Actor)
Paradigm Agency
10100 Santa Monica Blvd Ste 2500
Los Angeles, CA 90067-4116, USA

Korloff, Sara (Actor)
Boris Karloff Enterprises
PO Box 2424
Rancho Mirage, CA 92270-1087, USA

Kormann, Peter (Gymnast)
US Olympic Committee
1 Olympic Plz Bldg 4E
Colorado Springs, CO 80909-5760, USA

Korn (Music Group)
c/o Mark Philips *Prospect Park*
1840 Century Park E Ste 1800
Los Angeles, CA 90067-2119, USA

Korn, Jim (Athlete, Hockey Player)
19670 Sweetwater Curv
Excelsior, MN 55331-8113, USA

Kornberg, Hannah (Actor)
c/o Holly Williams *Williams Unlimited*
5010 Buffalo Ave
Sherman Oaks, CA 91423-1414

Kornet, Frank (Athlete, Basketball Player)
71B Brookwood Ter
Nashville, TN 37205-1409, USA

Kornheiser, Tony (Sportscaster, Writer)
Washington Post
Editorial Dept
1150 15th St NW
Washington, DC 20071-0001, USA

Koroll, Cliff (Athlete, Hockey Player)
23W569 Glendale Ter
Roselle, IL 60172-3541, USA

Koromzay, Alix (Actor)
334 Vernon Ave
Venice, CA 90291-2637, USA

Koronka, John (Athlete, Baseball Player)
1403 Loth St
Clermont, FL 34711, USA

Korpan, Richard (Business Person)
Florida Progress Corp
100 Central Ave
Saint Petersburg, FL 33701-3324, USA

Kors, Michael (Designer, Fashion Designer)
Michael Kors Inc
11 W 42nd St
New York, NY 10036-8002, USA

Kors, R J (Athlete, Football Player)
956 Gardenia Way
Corona Del Mar, CA 92625-1546, USA

Korsantiya, Alexander (Musician)
Columbia Artists Mgmt Inc
165 W 57th St
New York, NY 10019-2201, USA

Kortas, Ken (Athlete, Football Player)
466 Brooks Ln
Simpsonville, KY 40067-7419, USA

Korte, Steve (Athlete, Football Player)
1901 Highway 190 Apt 1721
Mandeville, LA 70448-3488, USA

Korver, Kelvin (Athlete, Football Player)
16934 Pella Rd
Adams, NE 68301-7790, USA

Korver, Kyle (Athlete, Basketball Player)
c/o Jeff Schwartz *Excel Sports Management (NY)*
1700 Broadway Fl 29
New York, NY 10019-5905, USA

Kosar Jr, Bernie (Athlete, Football Player)
4280 Winchell Rd
Mantua, OH 44255-9616, USA

Kosberg, Robert (Producer, Writer)
Robert Kosberg Productions
1438 N Gower St Ste 10
Los Angeles, CA 90028-8306, USA

Kosc, Greg (Athlete, Baseball Player)
3465 Hunting Run Rd
Medina, OH 44256-8200, USA

Kosco, Andy (Athlete, Baseball Player)
10324 Springfield Rd
Youngstown, OH 44514-3158, USA

Koshalek, Richard (Director)
Museum of Contemporary Art
250 S Grand Ave
Los Angeles, CA 90012-3021, USA

Koshansky, Joe (Athlete, Baseball Player)
13314 Point Pleasant Dr
Fairfax, VA 22033-3507, USA

Kosier, Kyle (Athlete, Football Player)
8943 E Calle Del Palo Verde
Scottsdale, AZ 85255-8356, USA

Kosins, Gary (Athlete, Football Player)
13895 Ruffner Ln
Sebastian, FL 32958-3418, USA

Kosinski, Joseph (Director)
c/o Bryan Besser *Verve Talent & Literary Agency, LLC*
6310 San Vicente Blvd Ste 100
Los Angeles, CA 90048-5498, USA

Koski, Bill (Athlete, Baseball Player)
1120 Valencia Ct
Modesto, CA 95350-4665, USA

Koski, Tony (Athlete, Basketball Player)
143 King James Dr
South Dennis, MA 02660, USA

Koskie, Corey (Athlete, Baseball Player)
161 Primrose Ln
Hamel, MN 55340-3603, USA

Koskoff, Sarah (Actor)
c/o Cliff Roberts *William Morris Endeavor (LA)*
9601 Wilshire Blvd
Beverly Hills, CA 90210-5213, USA

Koslo, Paul (Actor)
c/o Noreen Savides *323 Talent Management*
PO Box 1005
Lake Hughes, CA 93532-2005, USA

Koslofski, Kevin (Athlete, Baseball Player)
1910 Shore Oak Dr
Decatur, IL 62521-5563, USA

Koslow, Lauren (Actor)
c/o John Crosby *John Crosby Management*
1357 N Spaulding Ave
Los Angeles, CA 90046-4009, USA

Kosmalski, Len (Athlete, Basketball Player)
404 Washington Ave PH 8
Miami Beach, FL 33139-6606, USA

Koss, Stein (Athlete, Football Player)
5219 N Casa Blanca Dr Apt 31
Paradise Valley, AZ 85253-6201, USA

Kosser, Ted (Writer)
1820 Branched Oak Rd
Garland, NE 68360-9303, USA

Kostecki, John (Athlete, Olympic Athlete, Sailor)
2221 Raintree Ct
Rocklin, CA 95765-4653, USA

Koster, Steven J (Cinematographer)
26881 Goya Cir
Mission Viejo, CA 92691-6108, USA

Kostiuk, Mike (Athlete, Football Player)
4500 Dobry Dr Apt 115
Sterling Heights, MI 48314-1228, USA

Kostopoulos, Tom (Athlete, Hockey Player)
8336 Wheatstone Ln
Raleigh, NC 27613-1479, USA

Kostro, Frank (Athlete, Baseball Player)
3161 S Jasmine Way
Denver, CO 80222-7627, USA

Kosugi, Kane (Actor)
c/o Lou Pitt *Pitt Group, The*
8750 Wilshire Blvd Ste 301
Beverly Hills, CA 90211-2700, USA

Koszelak, Stanley N (Astronaut)
1125 Mendocino Way
Redlands, CA 92374-4975, USA

Kotarski, Mike (Athlete, Baseball Player)
31 Grove St
Lexington, MA 02420-1623, USA

Kotb, Hoda (Television Host)
c/o Staff Member *The Today Show*
30 Rockefeller Plz
New York, NY 10112-0015, USA

Kotcheff, W Theodore (Ted) (Director)
Ted Kotcheff Productions
13451 Firth Dr
Beverly Hills, CA 90210-1118, USA

Kotchman, Casey (Athlete, Baseball Player)
8442 125th Ct
Seminole, FL 33776-3200, USA

Koteas, Elias (Actor)
c/o Staff Member *William Morris Endeavor (LA)*
9601 Wilshire Blvd
Beverly Hills, CA 90210-5213, USA

Koterba, Jeff (Cartoonist)
Omaha World Herald
Editorial Dept
14th & Dodge St Wichita
Omaha, NE 68102, USA

Kotero, Apollonia (Actor, Model)
c/o Staff Member *Mary Grady Agency (MGA)*
4400 Coldwater Canyon Ave Ste 135
the Landmark Bldg
Studio City, CA 91604-5038, USA

Kotil, Ariene (Baseball Player)
13045 S 70th Ct
Palos Heights, IL 60463-2107, USA

Kotil, Arlene (Athlete, Baseball Player, Commentator)
13045 S 70th Ct
Palos Heights, IL 60463-2107, USA

Kotite, Richard E (Rich) (Athlete, Coach, Football Coach, Football Player)
241 Fanning St
Staten Island, NY 10314-5309, USA

Kotlarek, Gene (Skier)
4910 Walking Horse Pt
Colorado Springs, CO 80923-1110, USA

Kotlarek, George (Skier)
330 N Arlington Ave Apt 512
Duluth, MN 55811-5127, USA

Kotsay, Mark (Athlete, Baseball Player)
6659 Calle Ponte Bella
Rancho Santa Fe, CA 92091-0208, USA

Kotsonis, Ieronymous (Religious Leader)
Archdiocese of Athens
Hatzichristou 8
Milwaukee, WI 53212, USA

Kotsopoulos, Chris (Athlete, Hockey Player)
1713 Midnight Ln
Stroudsburg, PA 18360-7771, USA

Kottaras, George (Athlete, Baseball Player)
11677 E Del Timbre Dr
Scottsdale, AZ 85259-5908, USA

Kottke, Leo (Musician, Songwriter)
c/o Staff Member *Paradigm (Monterey)*
404 W Franklin St
Monterey, CA 93940-2303, USA

Kotzky, Alex S (Cartoonist)
20317 56th Ave
Oakland Gardens, NY 11364-1641, USA

Kouandjio, Cyrus (Athlete, Football Player)
c/o Bus Cook *Bus Cook Sports, Inc*
1 Willow Bend Dr
Hattiesburg, MS 39402-8552, USA

Koufax, Sandy (Athlete, Baseball Player)
c/o Harlan Werner *Sports Placement Service*
330 W 11th St Apt 105
Los Angeles, CA 90015-3200, USA

Kounen, Jan (Actor, Director, Producer, Writer)
c/o Robert Newman *William Morris Endeavor (LA)*
9601 Wilshire Blvd
Beverly Hills, CA 90210-5213, USA

Kournikova, Anna (Athlete, Tennis Player)
c/o Staff Member *Octagon (VA)*
7231 Forest Ave Ste 103
Richmond, VA 23226-3785, USA

Koutouvides, Niko (Athlete, Football Player)
129 9th Ln
Kirkland, WA 98033-3992, USA

Kouzmanoff, Kevin (Athlete, Baseball Player)
28606 Evergreen Manor Dr
Evergreen, CO 80439-8387, USA

Kovac, Ed (Athlete, Football Player)
2654 Gracewood Ave
Cincinnati, OH 45239-7240, USA

Kovack, Nancy (Actor)
270 Oakmont Dr
Los Angeles, CA 90049, USA

Kovalchick-Roark, Dorothy (Athlete, Commentator, Golfer)
112 Maridale Dr
West Monroe, LA 71291-2350, USA

Kovalchuk, Ilya (Athlete, Hockey Player)
8 Frick Dr
Alpine, NJ 07620, USA

Kovalenko, Alexei (Athlete, Hockey Player)
1 Trimont Ln Apt 2000A
Pittsburgh, PA 15211-1279, USA

Kovalev, Alexei (Athlete, Hockey Player)
Eclipse Sports Management
331 Madison Ave Fl 3
New York, NY 10017-5116, USA

Kovalev, Sergey (Athlete, Boxer)
c/o Egis Klimas *Egis Klimas*
Prefers to be contacted by telephone or email
Edmonds, WA, USA

Kove, Martin (Actor)
c/o Michael Kaliski *Omniquest Entertainment (LA)*
1416 N La Brea Ave
Los Angeles, CA 90028-7506, USA

Kovic, Ron (Writer)
507 N Lucia Ave
Redondo Beach, CA 90277-3009, USA

Kowalczyk, Ed (Musician)
Freedman & Smith
350 W End Ave Apt 1
New York, NY 10024-6818, USA

Kowalczyk, Walt (Athlete, Football Player)
144 W Maryknoll Rd
Rochester Hills, MI 48309-1938, USA

Kowalkowski, Robert (Athlete, Football Player)
2410 Correll Dr
Lake Orion, MI 48360-2258, USA

Kowalkowski, Scott (Athlete, Football Player)
3995 Kelsey Rd
Lake Orion, MI 48360-2516, USA

Kowalski, Ted (Musician)
GEMS
PO Box 1031
Montrose, CA 91021-1031, USA

Kowitz, Brian (Athlete, Baseball Player)
1657 Bullock Cir
Owings Mills, MD 21117-1609, USA

Koy, Ernie (Athlete, Football Player)
PO Box 6
Kenney, TX 77452-0006, USA

Koy, Jo (Comedian)
3600 Berry Dr
Studio City, CA 91604-3852, USA

Koy, Ted (Athlete, Football Player)
1225 County Road 155
Georgetown, TX 78626-1937, USA

Koyama, Debbie (Athlete, Golfer)
118 Tranquila Dr
Camarillo, CA 93012-5174, USA

Koz, Dave (Musician)
c/o Staff Member *Agency for the Performing Arts (APA-LA)*
405 S Beverly Dr Ste 500
Beverly Hills, CA 90212-4425, USA

Kozak, Don (Athlete, Hockey Player)
25911 El Segundo St
Laguna Hills, CA 92653-6201, USA

Kozak, Harley Jane (Actor)
21336 Colina Dr
Topanga, CA 90290, USA

Kozak, Julie (Journalist)
Extra c/o Warner Bros
4000 Warner Blvd
Burbank, CA 91522-0002, USA

Kozak, Les (Athlete, Hockey Player)
1072 Kimbro Dr
Baton Rouge, LA 70808-6042, USA

Kozak, Scott (Athlete, Football Player)
18617 S Grasle Rd
Oregon City, OR 97045-8898, USA

Kozelko, Tom (Athlete, Basketball Player)
6200 Peninsula Dr
Traverse City, MI 49686-1916, USA

Kozer, Sarah (Actor)
8383 Wilshire Blvd Ste 510
C/O Ric Tanner
Beverly Hills, CA 90211-2406, USA

Kozerski, Bruce (Athlete, Football Player)
3088 Waterbury Ct
Edgewood, KY 41017-8124, USA

Kozlicki, Ron (Athlete, Basketball Player)
5002 Hidden Branches Dr
Atlanta, GA 30338-3910, USA

Kozlov, Slava
4934 Powers Ferry Rd
Atlanta, GA 30327-4607, USA

Kozlov, Viktor (Athlete, Hockey Player)
106 W 74th St
Attn Paul Theofanous
New York, NY 10023-2334, USA

Kozlov, Vyacheslav (Athlete, Hockey Player)
4934 Powers Ferry Rd
Atlanta, GA 30327-4607, USA

Kozlova, Anna (Swimmer)
c/o Staff Member *Premier Management Group (PMG Sports)*
115 Crescent Commons Dr Ste 250
Cary, NC 27518-8134, USA

Kozlowski, Ben (Athlete, Baseball Player)
9083 Briarwood Dr
Seminole, FL 33772-2810, USA

Kozlowski, Brian (Athlete, Football Player)
210 Via Ithaca
Newport Beach, CA 92663-4908, USA

Kozlowski, Christine (Beauty Pageant Winner)
PO Box 742
Vicksburg, MS 39181-0742, USA

Kozlowski, Glen (Athlete, Football Player)
455 Belmont Pl Unit 262
Provo, UT 84606-7612, USA

Kozlowski, Linda (Actor)
7022 Grasswood Ave
Malibu, CA 90265-4247, USA

Kozlowski, Mike (Athlete, Football Player)
563 N 2430 W
Provo, UT 84601-7278, USA

Koznick, Kristina (Athlete, Olympic Athlete, Skier)
PO Box 85
Wolcott, CO 81655-0085, USA

Kozol, Jonathan (Writer)
PO Box 145
Byfield, MA 01922-0145, USA

Kraatz, Victor (Figure Skater)
Connecticut Skating Center
300 Alumni Rd
Newington, CT 06111-1868, USA

Kraayeveld, Dave (Athlete, Football Player)
10515 124th Ave NE
Kirkland, WA 98033-4628, USA

Kraemer, Joe (Athlete, Baseball Player)
3212 NE 401st Cir
La Center, WA 98629-5241, USA

Kraft, Greg (Athlete, Golfer)
14820 Rue De Bayonne Apt 302
Clearwater, FL 33762-3029, USA

Kraft, Jonathan (Business Person, Football Executive)
27 Woodland Rd
Chestnut Hill, MA 02467-2318, USA

Kraft, Lindsey (Actor)
c/o Matt Sherman *Medavoy Management*
7510 W Sunset Blvd Ste 1413
Los Angeles, CA 90046-3408, USA

Kraft, Robert (Business Person, Football Executive)
260 Heath St
Chestnut Hill, MA 02467-2823, USA

Kraft, Robert (Musician)
Kraftbox Entertainment
1416 N La Brea Ave
C/O Henson Studios
Los Angeles, CA 90028-7506, USA

Kraft, Ryan (Athlete, Hockey Player)
16219 Hawthorn Path
Lakeville, MN 55044-7573, USA

Kragen, Greg (Athlete, Football Player)
1447 Boulevard Way
Walnut Creek, CA 94595-1303, USA

Kragen, Ken
240 Baroda
Los Angeles, CA 90077

Krahl, Jim (Athlete, Football Player)
514 Rolling Mill Dr
Sugar Land, TX 77498-3072, USA

Krainin, Julian (President)
Krainin Productions
25211 Summerhill Ln
Stevenson Ranch, CA 91381-2262, USA

Krajicek, Lukas (Athlete, Hockey Player)
5319 Fishersound Ln
Apollo Beach, FL 33572-3344, USA

Krajicek, Richard (Tennis Player)
Octagon
7950 Jones Branch Dr
Mc Lean, VA 22102-3302, USA

Krakau, Merv (Athlete, Football Player)
706 Prairie St
Guthrie Center, IA 50115-1711, USA

Krakauer, Jon (Writer)
c/o John Ware *John Ware Literary Agency*
392 Central Park W
New York, NY 10025-5860, USA

Krakoski, Joe (Athlete, Football Player)
1359 Garden Wall Cir
Reston, VA 20194-1979, USA

Krakowski, Jane (Actor, Musician)
c/o Bill Butler *Industry Entertainment*
955 Carrillo Dr Ste 300
Los Angeles, CA 90048-5400, USA

Krall, Gerald (Athlete, Football Player)
9236 Mandell Rd
Perrysburg, OH 43551-3913, USA

Kraly, Steve (Athlete, Baseball Player)
12 Davis Ave
Johnson City, NY 13790-3007, USA

Kramarsky, David (Director, Producer)
1630 Berkeley St Apt 1
Santa Monica, CA 90404-4134, USA

Kramer, Barry (Athlete, Basketball Player)
101 Deanna Ct
Schenectady, NY 12309-1333, USA

Kramer, Billy J (Musician)
Mars Talent
27 L Ambiance Ct
Bardonia, NY 10954-1421, USA

Kramer, Brad (Horse Racer)
2455 Tittabawassee St
Alger, MI 48610-9496, USA

Kramer, Clare (Actor)
c/o Darren Goldberg *Global Creative*
1051 Cole Ave # B
Los Angeles, CA 90038-2601, USA

Kramer, Eric Allen (Actor)
c/o Steve Rodriguez *McGowan Management*
8733 W Sunset Blvd Ste 103
West Hollywood, CA 90069-2241, USA

Kramer, Erik (Athlete, Football Player)
5950 Kingham Ct
Agoura Hills, CA 91301-4436, USA

Kramer, Gerald L (Jerry) (Athlete, Football Player)
11768 Chinden Blvd
Garden City, ID 83714, USA

Kramer, Jack
48900 Avenida El Nido
La Quinta, CA 92253-6232

Kramer, Jana (Actor, Musician)
1008 Norfleet Dr
Nashville, TN 37220-1410, USA

Kramer, Jim (Writer)
c/o Staff Member *3 Arts Entertainment (LA)*
9460 Wilshire Blvd Fl 7
Beverly Hills, CA 90212-2713, USA

Kramer, Joel (Athlete, Basketball Player)
3817 E Highland Ave
Phoenix, AZ 85018-3619, USA

Kramer, Joey (Musician)
105 Cimarron Hills Trl E
Georgetown, TX 78628, USA

Kramer, John A (Jack) (Tennis Player)
231 Glenroy Pl
Los Angeles, CA 90049-2419, USA

Kramer, Kent (Athlete, Football Player)
200 Troon Rd
McKinney, TX 75070-6783, USA

Kramer, Kyle (Athlete, Football Player)
2170 Little Miami Dr
Spring Valley, OH 45370-9789, USA

Kramer, Larry (Activist, Writer)
Gay Men's Health Crisis
446 W 33rd St
New York, NY 10001-2601, USA

Kramer, Paul
20023 Bernist Ave
Torrance, CA 90503-2103

Kramer, Randy (Athlete, Baseball Player)
143 Camino Pacifico
Aptos, CA 95003-5886, USA

Kramer, Stepfanie (Actor, Director, Writer)
c/o Mark Teitelbaum *Teitelbaum Artists Group*
8840 Wilshire Blvd Fl 3
Beverly Hills, CA 90211-2606, USA

Kramer, Steve
1126 N Hollywood Way # 203-A
Burbank, CA 91505-2527

Kramer, Thomas (Tommy) (Athlete, Football Player)
5020 Antler Pass
Bulverde, TX 78163-2338, USA

Kramer, Tom (Athlete, Baseball Player)
10665 Hamilton Ave
Cincinnati, OH 45231-1703, USA

Kramer, Wayne (Musician)
Performers of the World
8901 Melrose Ave # 200
West Hollywood, CA 90069-5605, USA

Kramer-Hartman, Ruth (Athlete, Baseball Player, Commentator)
PO Box 38
Limekiln, PA 19535-0038, USA

Kranchick, Matt (Athlete, Football Player)
579 Crossroad School Rd
Carlisle, PA 17015-9433, USA

Kranek, Ernst
623 W Chino Canyon Rd
Palm Springs, CA 92262-2701

Kranepool, Ed (Athlete, Baseball Player)
177 High Pond Dr
Jericho, NY 11753-2806, USA

Kranitz, Rick (Athlete, Baseball Player)
6344 W Buckskin Trl
Phoenix, AZ 85083-3452, USA

Krantz, Judith (Writer)
166 Groverton Pl
Los Angeles, CA 90077-3732, USA

Kranz, Fran (Actor)
1128 5th Ave
Venice, CA 90291-6342, USA

Kranz, Ken (Athlete, Football Player)
W180n7890 Town Hall Rd Apt B218
Menomonee Falls, WI 53051-4052, USA

Krapek, Karl (Business Person)
United Technologies Corp
United Technologies Building
Hartford, CT 06101, USA

Krasinski, John (Actor)
2410 Crest View Dr
Los Angeles, CA 90046-1407, USA

Krasnoff, Eric (Business Person)
Pall Corp
2200 Northem Blvd
Greenvale, NY 11548, USA

Kratch, Bob (Athlete, Football Player)
1640 Waterbury
Waconia, MN 55387-1244, USA

Kratka, Paul (Actor)
5670 El Camino Real Ste F
Carlsbad, CA 92008-7125, USA

Kratz, Erik (Athlete, Baseball Player)
1840 Manor Dr
Harrisonburg, VA 22801-7625, USA

Kratzert, Bill (Athlete, Golfer)
8130 Merganser Dr
Ponte Vedra Beach, FL 32082-1930, USA

Kraus, Daniel (Athlete, Basketball Player)
10101 Governor Warfield Pkwy Unit 222
Columbia, MD 21044-3322, USA

Krause, Brian (Actor)
c/o Leland LaBarre *Bleu, An Entertainment Company*
5225 Wilshire Blvd Ste 336
Los Angeles, CA 90036-4380, USA

Krause, Chester L (Publisher)
Krause Publications
700 E State St
Iola, WI 54990-0002, USA

Krause, Hemut
15311 Brandonwood Pl
Houston, TX 77069-1538, USA

Krause, Larry (Athlete, Football Player)
N9169 Mill Rd
Summit Lake, WI 54485-9717, USA

Krause, Nick (Actor)
c/o Rebecca Many Rosenberg *Principato/Young Management (LA)*
9465 Wilshire Blvd Ste 900
Beverly Hills, CA 90212-2608, USA

Krause, Paul J (Athlete, Football Player)
18099 Judicial Way N
Lakeville, MN 55044-7105, USA

Krause, Peter (Actor)
c/o Peter Levine *Creative Artists Agency (CAA-LA)*
2000 Avenue of the Stars Ste 100
Los Angeles, CA 90067-4705, USA

Krause, Ryan (Football Player)
3917 S 183rd Ave
Omaha, NE 68130-4221, USA

Krauss, Alison (Musician)
3700 Richland Ave
Nashville, TN 37205-2438, USA

Krauss, Barry (Athlete, Football Player)
5346 Creekbend Dr
Carmel, IN 46033-9194, USA

Krausse, Lew (Athlete, Baseball Player)
12811 NE 186th St
Holt, MO 64048-8956, USA

Krauthammer, Charles (Writer)
Washington Post Writers Group
1150 15th St NW
Washington, DC 20071-0002, USA

Kravec, Ken (Athlete, Baseball Player)
6752 Taeda Dr
Sarasota, FL 34241-9152, USA

Kravits, Jason (Actor)
6310 San Vicente Blvd Ste 520
Los Angeles, CA 90048-5421

Kravitz, Danny (Athlete, Baseball Player)
8810 Route 487
Dushore, PA 18614-8040, USA

Kravitz, Lenny (Musician, Songwriter)
c/o Carleen Donovan *Press Here Publicity*
138 W 25th St Ste 900
New York, NY 10001-7470, USA

Kravitz, Zoe (Actor)
c/o Jillian Neal *Untitled Entertainment (LA)*
350 S Beverly Dr Ste 200
Beverly Hills, CA 90212-4819, USA

Krawczyk, Ray (Athlete, Baseball Player)
10032 Ridgley Dr
Garden Grove, CA 92843-3138, USA

Krayzelburg, Lenny (Athlete, Olympic Athlete, Swimmer)
Octagon
1629 N Crescent Heights Blvd
Los Angeles, CA 90069-1602, USA

Krebbs, John (Race Car Driver)
3232 Amoruso Way
Diamond Ridge
Roseville, CA 95747-9786, USA

Krebs, Art (Race Car Driver)
327 31st St
Gulfport, MS 39507-2341, USA

Krebs, Robert D (Business Person)
Burlington North/Santa Fe
2650 Lou Menk Dr
Fort Worth, TX 76131-2830, USA

Krebs, Susan (Actor)
4704 Tobias Ave
Sherman Oaks, CA 91403-2825, USA

Kregel, Kevin R (Astronaut)
2601 Bay Shore Dr
Seabrook, TX 77586-1690, USA

Krehbiel, Frederick A (Business Person)
Molex Inc
2222 Wellington Ct
Lisle, IL 60532-1682, USA

Krehbiel, John Hammond (Business Person)
Molex Inc.
2222 Wellington Ct
Lisle, IL 60532-1682, USA

Kreider, Dan (Athlete, Football Player)
102 Fawn Hl
Millersville, PA 17551-9758, USA

Kreider, Steve (Athlete, Football Player)
350 Harrow Ln
Blue Bell, PA 19422-3110, USA

Kreischer, Bert (Comedian, Television Host)
c/o Matt Schuler *Levity Entertainment Group (LEG)*
6701 Center Dr W Fl 11
Los Angeles, CA 90045-1535, USA

Kreitling, Richard (Athlete, Football Player)
24017 Trout Lake Rd
Bovey, MN 55709-8548, USA

Krejci, David (Athlete, Hockey Player)
c/o Staff Member *Boston Bruins*
100 Legends Way Ste 250
Td Banknorth Garden
Boston, MA 02114-1389, USA

Kreklow, Wayne (Athlete, Basketball Player)
4001 S Old Mill Creek Rd
Columbia, MO 65203-9635, USA

krels, Jason (Soccer Player)
Dallas Burn
14800 Quorum Dr Ste 300
Dallas, TX 75254-1442, USA

Kremer, Andrea (Sportscaster)
ESPN-TV
Sports Dept
ESPN Plaza 935 Middle St
Bristol, CT 06010, USA

Kremer, Gidon (Musician)
I C M Artists
40 W 57th St
New York, NY 10019-4001, USA

Kremer, Howard (Comedian)
c/o Staff Member *ICM Partners (LA)*
10250 Constellation Blvd Fl 7
Los Angeles, CA 90067-6207, USA

Kremer, Ken (Athlete, Football Player)
6116 Double Eagle Ct
Kansas City, MO 64152-4970, USA

Kremers, Jimmy (Athlete, Baseball Player)
6209 W Orlando St
Broken Arrow, OK 74011-1264, USA

Kremmel, Jim (Athlete, Baseball Player)
3626 Pestana Way
Livermore, CA 94550-3332, USA

Kremser, Karl (Athlete, Football Player)
12204 SW 109th Ct
Miami, FL 33176-4576, USA

Krenchicki, Wayne (Athlete, Baseball Player)
2524 Hawthorne Dr
Beloit, WI 53511-2338, USA

Krenk, Mitch (Athlete, Football Player)
1822 4th Ave
Nebraska City, NE 68410-1822, USA

Krenwinkel, Patricia
#W8314 Bed #MA11U CA Inst. for Women16756 Chino Corona
Frontera, CA 91720

Krenzel, Craig (Athlete, Football Player)
10174 Jerome Rd
Dublin, OH 43017-7606, USA

Krepfle, Keith (Athlete, Football Player)
82 E Butler Dr
Drums, PA 18222-2603, USA

Krerowicz, Mark (Athlete, Football Player)
1425 Luscombe Dr
Toledo, OH 43614-2618, USA

Kresa, Kent (Business Person)
Northrop Grumman Corp
2980 Fairview Park Dr
Falls Church, VA 22042-4511, USA

Kresge, Chris (Athlete, Golfer)
834 Trailwood Dr
Apopka, FL 32712-3217, USA

Kresge, Cliff (Athlete, Golfer)
c/o Jim Lehrman *SFX Golf*
36855 W Main St Ste 200
Purcellville, VA 20132-3561, USA

Kress, Nathan (Actor)
c/o Donna Jeanne Goheen *Young Performers Management*
14431 Ventura Blvd # 506
Sherman Oaks, CA 91423-2606, USA

Kretschmann, Thomas (Director)
c/o Staff Member *United Talent Agency (UTA-LA)*
9336 Civic Center Dr
Beverly Hills, CA 90210-3604, USA

Kreuger, Rick (Athlete, Baseball Player)
4664 Sheldon Ct
Hudsonville, MI 49426-7810, USA

Kreuter, Chad (Athlete, Baseball Player)
2451 Brickell Ave Apt 2J
Miami, FL 33129-2418, USA

Kreutz, Olin (Athlete, Football Player)
750 S Southmeadow Ln
Lake Forest, IL 60045-4836, USA

Kreutzer, Frank (Athlete, Baseball Player)
921 Windwhisper Ln
Annapolis, MD 21403-3486, USA

Kreutzmann, Bill (Musician)
PO Box 1073
San Rafael, CA 94915-1073, USA

Kreviazuk, Chantal (Musician, Songwriter)
c/o Staff Member *Paradigm (Monterey)*
404 W Franklin St
Monterey, CA 93940-2303, USA

Krevis, Al (Athlete, Football Player)
227 Howard St
Northborough, MA 01532-1322, USA

Krewella (Music Group)
c/o Jason Pinyan *Artist & Brand Management (LA)*
132 N Laurel Ave
Los Angeles, CA 90048-3512, USA

Kribel, Joel (Athlete, Golfer)
26254 N 46th St
Phoenix, AZ 85050-8510, USA

Krick, Jaynie (Athlete, Baseball Player, Commentator)
911 Glen Eagle Ln
Fort Wayne, IN 46845-9501, USA

Krickstein, Aaron (Tennis Player)
7559 Fairmont Ct
Boca Raton, FL 33496-5902, USA

Krieg, Dave (Athlete, Football Player)
3353 E Windmere Dr
Phoenix, AZ 85048-5819, USA

Krieg, Jim (Athlete, Football Player)
76690 Lark Ln
Indian Wells, CA 92210-8984, USA

Krieger, Robbie (Musician, Songwriter, Writer)
3011 Ledgewood Dr
Los Angeles, CA 90068-1959, USA

Kriewald, Doug (Athlete, Football Player)
5031 Snow Mesa Dr
Fort Collins, CO 80528-8590, USA

Kriewaldt, Clint (Athlete, Football Player)
320 E Fernwood Ln
Appleton, WI 54913-7651, USA

Krige, Alice (Actor)
c/o Mel McKeon *McKeon-Myones Management*
3500 W Olive Ave Ste 770
Burbank, CA 91505-5527, USA

Krimm, John (Athlete, Football Player)
900 20th Ave S Apt 1506
Nashville, TN 37212-2249, USA

Kring, Tim (Writer)
c/o Richard Abate *3 Arts Entertainment (NY)*
16 W 22nd St Ste 201
New York, NY 10010-5842, USA

Kripke, Eric (Director, Producer, Writer)
c/o Staff Member *Principato/Young Management (LA)*
9465 Wilshire Blvd Ste 900
Beverly Hills, CA 90212-2608, USA

Krisher, Bill (Athlete, Football Player)
5915 Over Downs Dr
Dallas, TX 75230-4044, USA

Kristen, Marta (Actor)
375 Mesa Rd
Santa Monica, CA 90402-1129, USA

Kristien, Dale
691 Country Club Dr
Burbank, CA 91501-1121

Kristina Sisco, Kristina (Actor)
c/o Staff Member *Cohen/Thomas Agency*
1888 N Crescent Heights Blvd
Los Angeles, CA 90069-1647, USA

Kristof, Kathy M (Writer)
Los Angeles Times
202 W 1st St Ste 500
Editorial Dept
Los Angeles, CA 90012-4401, USA

Kristoff, Joe (Bowler)
4290 Meadowview Ct
Columbus, OH 43224-1927, USA

Kristofferson, Kris (Actor, Musician)
3179 Sumac Ridge Rd
Malibu, CA 90265-5127, USA

Kristol, William
6625 Jill Ct
Mc Lean, VA 22101-1613

Krivda, Rick (Athlete, Baseball Player)
112 Dolores Dr
Irwin, PA 15642-5519, USA

Krivokrasov, Sergei (Athlete, Hockey Player)
8505 E Alameda Ave Unit 3329
Denver, CO 80230-6070, USA

Krivsky, Wayne (Commentator)
3841 Gregory Ln
Erlanger, KY 41018-3819, USA

Krizmanich, Jack (Actor)
c/o Mara Santino *Luber Roklin Management*
5815 W Sunset Blvd Ste 206
Los Angeles, CA 90028-6481, USA

Krmpotich, David (Athlete, Olympic Athlete, Rower)
128 Archbishop Dr
Conshohocken, PA 19428-1328, USA

Kroeger, Chad (Musician, Songwriter)
408 Monarch Pl
Lahaina, HI 96761-9070, USA

Kroeger, Josh (Athlete, Baseball Player)
1313 4th Ave N
Clanton, AL 35045-2613

Kroeger, Mike (Musician)
408 Monarch Pl
Lahaina, HI 96761-9070, USA

Kroell, Ronnie (Actor, Model)
c/o Dino May *Dino May Management*
6362 Hollywood Blvd # 422
Los Angeles, CA 90028-6323, USA

Kroenke, Zach (Athlete, Baseball Player)
Double Diamond Sports Management
7640 NW 79th Ave Apt L8
Tamarac, FL 33321-2868, USA

Krofft, Marty (Actor, Producer)
Sid & Marty Krofft Pictures
4024 Radford Ave Studio Cocbscenter
Studio City, CA 91604-2101, USA

Krohn, Jonathan (Writer)
15335 Little Stone Way
Alpharetta, GA 30004-6901, USA

Krol, John Cardinal
222 N 17th St
Philadelphia, PA 19103-1202

Kroll, Alexander S (Alex) (Athlete, Football Player)
581 Whalley Rd
Charlotte, VT 05445-9531, USA

Kroll, Bob (Athlete, Football Player)
344 Golfside Cv
Longwood, FL 32779-4669, USA

Kroll, Gary (Athlete, Baseball Player)
9038 E 40th St
Tulsa, OK 74145-3713, USA

Kroll, Robert L (Athlete, Football Player)
PO Box 8563
Maitland, FL 32751, USA

Krom, Tommy (Athlete, Basketball Player)
519 Briar Hill Rd
Louisville, KY 40206-3009, USA

Kromm, Richard (Rich) (Athlete, Coach, Hockey Player)
1935 Cheyenne Dr
Evansville, IN 47715-7044, USA

Krone, Julie (Horse Racer)
7305 Marine Pi
Carlsbad, CA 92011, USA

Kroner, Gary (Athlete, Football Player)
7330 Buckingham Ct
Boulder, CO 80301-6409, USA

Kronwall, Niklas (Athlete, Hockey Player)
1369 N Glenhurst Dr
Birmingham, MI 48009-1085, USA

Kroon, Marc (Athlete, Baseball Player)
12617 N 56th Pi
Scottsdale, AZ 85254, USA

Kropfelder, Nicholas (Soccer Player)
13803 Lighthouse Ave
Ocean City, MD 21842-4565, USA

Kropp, Tom (Athlete, Basketball Player)
1811 W 41st St
Kearney, NE 68845-8286, USA

Krosney, Alexandra (Actor)
c/o Beverly Strong *Strong Management*
9350 Wilshire Blvd Ste 224
Beverly Hills, CA 90212-3204, USA

Kross, Kayden (Adult Film Star, Model)
c/o Drew Elliot *Artists International Management (NY)*
333 E 43rd St Apt 115
New York, NY 10017-4822, USA

Krough, Jeff (Race Car Driver)
PO Box 602
Kamiah, ID 83536-0602, USA

Krsnich, Rocky (Athlete, Baseball Player)
5701 W 92nd St
Overland Park, KS 66207-2442, USA

KRS-One (Musician)
c/o Sasha Brookner *Heliocentric Public Relations*
5770 W Centinela Ave
Los Angeles, CA 90045-8828, USA

Krstic, Nenad (Basketball Player)
New Jersy Nets
390 Murray Hill Pkwy
East Rutherford, NJ 07073-2109, USA

Kruckei, Marie (Baseball Player)
52128 Woodridge Dr
South Bend, IN 46635-1053, USA

Kruckel, Marie (Athlete, Baseball Player, Commentator)
52128 Woodridge Dr
South Bend, IN 46635-1053, USA

Kruczek, Mike (Athlete, Football Player)
4028 Gilder Rose Pl
Winter Park, FL 32792-9416, USA

Krueger, Bill (Athlete, Baseball Player)
30132 SE Redmond Fall City Rd
Fall City, WA 98024-7104, USA

Krueger, Charles A (Charlie) (Athlete, Football Player)
44 Regency Dr
Clayton, CA 94517-1729, USA

Krueger, Kurt
1221 La Collina Dr
Beverly Hills, CA 90210-2633

Krueger, Phil (Race Car Driver)
8662 Houston Rd
Freetown, IN 47235-9624, USA

Krueger, Rolf (Athlete, Football Player)
6502 Lake Cir
Wallis, TX 77485-8698, USA

Krug, Chris (Athlete, Baseball Player)
PO Box 1350
Wildomar, CA 92595-1350, USA

Krug, Gene (Athlete, Baseball Player)
1327 Baylor Dr
Colorado Springs, CO 80909-3301, USA

Kruger, Hardy (Actor)
PO Box 2450
Palm Springs, CA 92263-2450, USA

Kruger, Lon (Athlete, Basketball Coach, Basketball Player, Coach)
346 W Franklin Rd
Norman, OK 73069-8105, USA

Kruger, Paul (Athlete, Football Player)
c/o Joe Panos *Athletes First, LLC*
23091 Mill Creek Dr
Laguna Hills, CA 92653-1258, USA

Kruk, John (Athlete, Baseball Player)
PO Box 7847
Naples, FL 34101-7847, USA

Kruk, John (Commentator)
935 Middle St Attn Dept
Bristol, CT 06010-1000, USA

Krukow, Mike (Athlete, Baseball Player)
6094 Madbury Ct
San Luis Obispo, CA 93401-8244, USA

Krulwich, Robert (Correspondent)
CBS-TV
524 W 57th St
News Dept
New York, NY 10019-2924, USA

Krumholtz, David (Actor)
c/o Jeff Golenberg *Silver Lining Entertainment*
421 S Beverly Dr Fl 7
Beverly Hills, CA 90212-4408, USA

Krumrie, Tim (Athlete, Football Player)
c/o Staff Member *Kansas City Chiefs*
1 Arrowhead Dr
Kansas City, MO 64129-1651, USA

Krupa, Joanna (Model, Reality Star)
1425 Brickell Ave Apt 42C
Miami, FL 33131-3401, USA

Krupp, Uwe (Athlete, Hockey Player)
2465 Ala Wai Blvd Apt 1204
Honolulu, HI 96815-3453, USA

Kruschen, Jack
PO Box 10143
Canoga Park, CA 91309-1143

Kruscschev, Sergei Dr (Writer)
Brown University
PO Box 1970
Providence, RI 02912-1970, USA

Krushelnyski, Mike (Athlete, Hockey Player)
PO Box 834
Cohoes, NY 12047-0834, USA

Krusiec, Michelle (Actor)
c/o Jennifer Wiley *Framework Entertainment (NY)*
129 W 27th St Fl 12
New York, NY 10001-6206, USA

Krutko, Larry (Athlete, Football Player)
1565 6th St
Waynesburg, PA 15370-1653, USA

Krygier, Todd (Athlete, Hockey Player)
23946 Wintergreen Cir Apt 13
Novi, MI 48374-3681, USA

Krynzel, Dave (Athlete, Baseball Player)
951 Derringer Ln
Henderson, NV 89014-2595, USA

Krypreos, Nick (Athlete, Hockey Player)
9209 Copenhaver Dr
Potomac, MD 20854-3016, USA

Krystkowiak, Larry (Athlete, Basketball Player)
1937 E Siesta Dr
Sandy, UT 84093-6239, USA

Krzysztof, Oliwa (Athlete, Hockey Player)
707 Derzee Ct
Delmar, NY 12054-9645, USA

Krzyzewski, Mike (Athlete, Basketball Player, Coach)
4406 W Cornwallis Rd
Durham, NC 27705-8126, USA

K. Simpson, Michael (Congressman, Politician)
2312 Rayburn Hob
Washington, DC 20515-0102, USA

Kuba, Filip (Athlete, Hockey Player)
17216 Emerald Chase Dr
Tampa, FL 33647-2780, USA

Kubala, Ray (Athlete, Football Player)
3433 Alexandrite Way
Round Rock, TX 78681-2436, USA

Kuban, Bob (Musician)
17626 Lasiandra Dr
Chesterfield, MO 63005-4912, USA

Kubek, Anthony C (Tony) (Athlete, Baseball Player, Sportscaster)
685 Smoky Lake Dr
Phelps, WI 54554-9314, USA

Kubel, Jason (Athlete, Baseball Player)
21031 Ventura Blvd Ste 1000
Woodland Hills, CA 91364-2227, USA

Kubenka, Jeff (Athlete, Baseball Player)
9706 Endcliff
San Antonio, TX 78250-3426, USA

Kuberski, Bob (Athlete, Football Player)
13 Forwood Dr
Garnet Valley, PA 19060-1215, USA

Kuberski, Robert (Athlete, Football Player)
13 Forwood Dr
Garnet Valley, PA 19060-1215, USA

Kuberski, Steve (Athlete, Basketball Player)
91 Lawson Rd
Winchester, MA 01890-3153, USA

Kubiak, Gary (Athlete, Coach, Football Coach, Football Player)
PO Box 350
Plantersville, TX 77363-0350, USA

Kubiak, Leo (Athlete, Basketball Player)
2638 N Prestwick Way
Lecanto, FL 34461-6902, USA

Kubiak, Ted (Athlete, Baseball Player)
11956 Bernardo Plaza Dr
San Diego, CA 92128-2538, USA

Kubik, Brad (Athlete, Football Player)
3025 W Oakhaven Ln
Springfield, MO 65810-1948, USA

Kubin, Larry (Athlete, Football Player)
315 Cannery Ln
Forest Hill, MD 21050-3066, USA

Kubina, Pavel (Athlete, Hockey Player)
1145 81st St S
Saint Petersburg, FL 33707-2726, USA

Kubinski, Tim (Athlete, Baseball Player)
4852 Caballeros Ave
San Luis Obispo, CA 93401-7964, USA

Kubiszvn, Jack (Athlete, Baseball Player)
2306 University Blvd Ste A
Tuscaloosa, AL 35401-1581, USA

Kubiszyn, Jack (Athlete, Baseball Player)
2306 University Blvd Ste A
Tuscaloosa, AL 35401-1581, USA

Kubski, Gil (Athlete, Baseball Player)
7716 Stewart Ave
Los Angeles, CA 90045-1054, USA

Kubski, Gill (Athlete, Baseball Player)
7716 Stewart Ave
Los Angeles, CA 90045-1054, USA

Kucek, Jack (Athlete, Baseball Player)
8220 Blue Heron Ln
Canfield, OH 44406-9134, USA

Kuchar, Matt (Athlete, Golfer)
121 Plantation Cir
Ponte Vedra Beach, FL 32082-3921, USA

Kuchta, Frank (Athlete, Football Player)
5021 Fairlawn Rd
Cleveland, OH 44124-1124, USA

Kuczenski, Bruce (Athlete, Basketball Player)
135 Southshire Dr
Southington, CT 06489-4224, USA

Kuczynski, Betty (Bowler)
4515 Prescott Ave Apt 1B
Lyons, IL 60534-1960, USA

Kudelski, Bob (Athlete, Hockey Player)
3821 E Highway 160
Pagosa Springs, CO 81147-9846, USA

Kudlow, Lawrence (Television Host)
Kudlow & Company
900 Sylvan Ave
Cnbc
Englewood Cliffs, NJ 07632-3312, USA

Kudoh, Youki (Actor)
c/o Vincent Cirrincione *Vincent Cirrincione Associates*
1516 N Fairfax Ave
Los Angeles, CA 90046-2608, USA

Kudrave, David (Race Car Driver)
7918 Zionsville Rd
Indianapolis, IN 46268-1649, USA

Kudrow, Lisa (Actor)
c/o Jennifer Allen *Viewpoint Inc (LA)*
8820 Wilshire Blvd Ste 220
Beverly Hills, CA 90211-2622, USA

Kuechenberg, Robert J (Bob) (Athlete, Football Player)
2519 SW 30th Ter
Fort Lauderdale, FL 33312-4729, USA

Kuechenberg, Rudy (Athlete, Football Player)
2841 NW 73rd Ave
Hollywood, FL 33024-2733, USA

Kuechly, Luke (Athlete, Football Player)
c/o Tom Condon *CAA (St. Louis)*
222 S Central Ave Ste 1008
Saint Louis, MO 63105-3509, USA

Kuehl, Ryan (Athlete, Football Player)
10409 Masters Ter
Potomac, MD 20854-3862, USA

Kuehn, Art (Athlete, Football Player)
19510 NE 185th St
Woodinville, WA 98077-5403, USA

Kuehne, Hank (Athlete, Golfer)
159 Via Condado Way
Palm Beach Gardens, FL 33418-1703, USA

Kuehne, Kelli (Athlete, Golfer)
7211 Oakbluff Dr
Dallas, TX 75254-2736, USA

Kuerten, Gustavo (Tennis Player)
Octagon
7950 Jones Branch Dr
Mc Lean, VA 22102-3302, USA

Kuester, John (Athlete, Basketball Player)
2116 Carpenter Upchurch Rd
Cary, NC 27519-7003, USA

Kufeldt, James (Business Person)
Winn-Dixie Stores
5050 Edgewood Ct
Jacksonville, FL 32254-3699, USA

Kugbila, Edmund (Athlete, Football Player)
c/o Hadley Engelhard *Enter-Sports Management*
5 Concourse Pkwy Ste 3000
Atlanta, GA 30328-7106, USA

Kugler, Pete (Athlete, Football Player)
33 Peach Ct
Marco Island, FL 34145-4728, USA

Kuhaulua, Fred (Athlete, Baseball Player)
89-203 Ualakahiki Pl
Waianae, HI 96792-3937, USA

Kuhlemann, Bill (Race Car Driver)
Summit Racing
PO Box 535
Richfield, OH 44286-0535, USA

Kuhlman, Ron (Actor)
5738 Willis Ave
Van Nuys, CA 91411-3327, USA

Kuhweide, Wilhelm
10031 E Buckskin Trl
Scottsdale, AZ 85255-2338

Kuiper, Duane (Athlete, Baseball Player)
3665 Deer Trail Dr
Danville, CA 94506-6021, USA

Kuiper, Glen (Commentator)
321 Sequoia Ter
Danville, CA 94506-4545, USA

Kukkonen, Lasse (Athlete, Hockey Player)
Puckagency LLC
555 Pleasantville Rd
210N Attn Jay Grossman
Briarcliff Manor, NY 10510-1955, USA

Kukoc, Toni (Athlete, Basketball Player)
1830 Hybernia Dr
Highland Park, IL 60035-5500, USA

Kulbacki, Joe (Football Player)
PO Box 97
Colden, NY 14033-0097, USA

Kulbacki, Joseph (Athlete, Football Player)
9419 S Hill Rd
Boston, NY 14025, USA

Kuleshov, Valery (Musician)
c/o Staff Member *Musicians Corporate Management*
PO Box 825
Highland, NY 12528-0825, USA

Kulich, Vladimir (Actor)
c/o Jeff Goldberg *Jeff Goldberg Management*
817 Monte Leon Dr
Beverly Hills, CA 90210-2629, USA

Kulongoski, Theodore (Politician)
4232 NE Couch St
Portland, OR 97213-1630, USA

Kulpa, Ronald (Athlete, Baseball Player)
1958 Parkland Woods Dr
Maryland Heights, MO 63043-4701, USA

Kumar, Sanjay (Business Person)
Computer Associates Int'l
1 CA Plz
Islandia, NY 11749-7001, USA

Kumble, Roger (Actor, Director, Writer)
c/o Jonathan Berry *3 Arts Entertainment*
(LA)
9460 Wilshire Blvd Fl 7
Beverly Hills, CA 90212-2713, USA

Kume, Mike (Athlete, Baseball Player)
6810 Woodard Rd
Andover, OH 44003-9638, USA

Kumerow, Eric (Athlete, Football Player)
736 Fairview Ln
Bartlett, IL 60103-4566, USA

Kummer, Glenn F (Business Person)
Fleetwood Enterprises
1351 Pomona Rd Ste 230
Corona, CA 92882-7170, USA

Kumpel, Mark (Athlete, Hockey Player,
Olympic Athlete)
22 Oceanwood Dr
Scarborough, ME 04074-8755, USA

Kundla, John (Athlete, Basketball Coach,
Coach)
Main Street Lodge
909 Main St NE Apt 208
Minneapolis, MN 55413-1854, USA

Kunerth, Mark J (Producer, Writer)
c/o Ted Chervin *ICM Partners (LA)*
10250 Constellation Blvd Fl 7
Los Angeles, CA 90067-6207, USA

Kuney, Eva Lee (Actor)
8962 Shale Valley St
Las Vegas, NV 89123-3271, USA

Kunin, Madeleine (Politician)
901 Wake Robin Dr
Shelburne, VT 05482-7583, USA

Kunis, Mila (Actor)
9588 Lime Orchard Rd
Beverly Hills, CA 90210-1316, USA

Kunitz, Chris
1256 Newbury Highland
Bridgeville, PA 15017-2138, USA

Kunitz, Matt (Producer)
c/o Staff Member *William Morris
Endeavor (LA)*
9601 Wilshire Blvd
Beverly Hills, CA 90210-5213, USA

Kunkel, Jeff (Athlete, Baseball Player)
1531 Camino Lago
Irving, TX 75039-3207, USA

Kunkel-Huff, Anna (Baseball Player)
9220 E Fairway Blvd Apt C136
Sun Lakes, AZ 85248-6579, USA

Kunnert, Kevin (Athlete, Basketball Player)
8286 SW Wilderland Ct
Portland, OR 97224-7646, USA

Kuntar, Les (Athlete, Hockey Player)
9721 SW 89th Loop
Ocala, FL 34481-5577, USA

Kuntz, Rusty (Athlete, Baseball Player)
15916 Grant St
Stilwell, KS 66085-6207, USA

Kunz, Eddie (Athlete, Baseball Player)
242 NE 136th Ave
Portland, OR 97230-3345, USA

Kunz, George J (Athlete, Football Player)
8215 Bermuda Rd
Las Vegas, NV 89123-2213, USA

Kunz, Lee (Athlete, Football Player)
4096 Youngfield St
Wheat Ridge, CO 80033-3862, USA

Kunze, Terry (Athlete, Basketball Player)
6931 Halifax Ave N
Minneapolis, MN 55429-1373, USA

Kunzu, Hari (Writer)
EP Dutton
375 Hudson St
New York, NY 10014-3658, USA

Kupchak, Mitch (Athlete, Basketball
Player, Olympic Athlete)
361 Fordyce Rd
Los Angeles, CA 90049-2009, USA

Kupcinet, Kari (Actor)
1660 Mill Trl
Highland Park, IL 60035-1502, USA

Kupec, C J (Athlete, Basketball Player)
6448 River Run
Columbia, MD 21044-6022, USA

Kupets, Courtney (Athlete, Gymnast,
Olympic Athlete)
133 Falling Shoals Dr
Athens, GA 30605-5740, USA

Kupp, Craig (Athlete, Football Player)
609 S 31st Ave
Yakima, WA 98902-4009, USA

Kupp, Jacob (Jake) (Athlete, Football
Player)
4801 Snowmountain Rd
Yakima, WA 98908-2848, USA

Kupper, William P Jr (Publisher)
Business Week
1221 Avenue of the Americas
New York, NY 10020-1001, USA

Kupperman, Joel (Actor)
115 E 9th St Apt 15E
New York, NY 10003-5421, USA

Kurant, Willy (Cinematographer)
Lyons Sheldon Agency
800 S Robertson Blvd Ste 6
Los Angeles, CA 90035-1635, USA

Kuras, Ellen M (Cinematographer)
54 Summit St
Nyack, NY 10960-3726, USA

Kurek, Ralph (Athlete, Football Player)
2373 Lime Pond Rd
South Royalton, VT 05068-4411, USA

Kurisko, Jamie (Athlete, Football Player)
3270 Aldrich Dr
Cumming, GA 30040-5378, USA

Kuriyama, Chiaki (Actor)
c/o Staff Member *Crystal Sky Pictures*
10203 Santa Monica Blvd Fl 5
Los Angeles, CA 90067-6416, USA

Kurkova, Karolina (Model)
c/o Scott Lipps *One Management*
42 Bond St Apt 2
New York, NY 10012-2428, USA

Kurnick, Howie (Athlete, Football Player)
2339 Bretton Dr
Cincinnati, OH 45244-3729, USA

Kurosaki, Ryan (Athlete, Baseball Player)
2024 Fairmont Dr
Benton, AR 72015-3163, USA

Kurosawa, Takuya (Race Car Driver)
Dale Coyne Racing
13400 S Budler Rd
Plainfield, IL 60544-9493, USA

Kurpeikis, Justin (Athlete, Football Player)
246 Varsity Ln
State College, PA 16803-1845, USA

Kurrasch, David B (Business Person)
The Monkey Hook, LLC
31482 Paseo Campeon
San Juan Capo, CA 92675-1828, USA

Kurrasch, Roy (Athlete, Football Player)
2211 Canyon Dr
Los Angeles, CA 90068-2401, USA

Kursinski, Anne (Athlete, Horse Racer,
Olympic Athlete)
107 Spring Hill Rd
Frenchtown, NJ 08825-3019, USA

Kurth, Wallace (Wally) (Actor, Musician)
2143 N Valley Dr
Manhattan Beach, CA 90266-2247, USA

Kurtis, Bill (Television Host)
c/o Staff Member *Kurtis Productions*
400 W Erie St Ste 500
Chicago, IL 60654-5741, USA

Kurtis, Dalene (Actor)
c/o Juliette Harris *It Girl Public Relations*
5301 Beethoven St Ste 220
Los Angeles, CA 90066-7052, USA

Kurtz, Hal (Athlete, Baseball Player)
511 Flat Iron Square Rd
Church Hill, MD 21623-1269, USA

Kurtz, Howard (Television Host)
c/o Staff Member *Fox News (NY)*
1211 Avenue of the Americas Lowr C1
New York, NY 10036-8705, USA

Kurtz, Swoosie (Actor)
c/o Konrad Leh *Creative Talent Group*
1900 Avenue of the Stars Ste 2475
Los Angeles, CA 90067-4512, USA

Kurtzman, Alex (Producer)
c/o BeBe Lerner *ID Public Relations (LA)*
7060 Hollywood Blvd Fl 8th
Los Angeles, CA 90028-6021, USA

Kurtzman, Katy (Actor, Director)
c/o Staff Member *Lynn Production &
Mgmt*
20411 Chapter Dr
Woodland Hills, CA 91364-5612, USA

Kurvers, Tom (Athlete, Hockey Player)
15128 Glen Oak St
Minnetonka, MN 55345-5722, USA

Kurvers, Tom
Tampa Bay Lightning
401 Channelside Dr
Attn: Asst General Manager
Tampa, FL 33602-5400, USA

Kurylenko, Olga (Actor)
c/o Joel Lubin *Creative Artists Agency
(CAA-LA)*
2000 Avenue of the Stars Ste 100
Los Angeles, CA 90067-4705, USA

Kusama, Karyn (Director)
Endeavor Talent Agency
9701 Wilshire Blvd Ste 1000
Beverly Hills, CA 90212-2010, USA

Kusatsu, Clyde (Actor)
Paradign Agency
10100 Santa Monica Blvd Ste 2500
Los Angeles, CA 90067-4116, USA

Kush, Frank (Athlete, Football Player)
113 E Loma Vista Dr
Tempe, AZ 85282-3574, USA

Kush, Rod (Athlete, Football Player)
10111 S 177th St
Omaha, NE 68136-1970, USA

Kushell, Lisa (Actor)
c/o Staff Member *Abrams Artists Agency
(LA)*
9200 W Sunset Blvd PH 11
West Hollywood, CA 90069-3601, USA

Kushner, Dave (Musician)
3276 Longridge Ter
Sherman Oaks, CA 91423-4930, USA

Kushner, Harold S (Writer)
145 Hartford St
Natick, MA 01760-3125

Kushner, Tony (Writer)
c/o Staff Member *Creative Artists Agency
(CAA-LA)*
2000 Avenue of the Stars Ste 100
Los Angeles, CA 90067-4705, USA

Kusnitz, Jared (Actor)
c/o TJ McMurdo *McMurdo Management
& Associates*
1616 N Fuller Ave Apt 313
Los Angeles, CA 90046-3587, USA

Kusnyer, Art (Athlete, Baseball Player)
6598 Taeda Dr
Sarasota, FL 34241-9145, USA

Kutcher, Ashton (Actor, Producer)
9588 Lime Orchard Rd
Beverly Hills, CA 90210-1316, USA

Kutcher, Randy (Athlete, Baseball Player)
3016 Purple Sage Ln
Palmdale, CA 93550-7972, USA

Kuti, Fela (Musician)
Rosebud Agency
PO Box 170429
San Francisco, CA 94117-0429, USA

Kutless (Musician)
c/o Staff Member *William Morris
Endeavor (Nashville)*
1600 Division St Ste 300
Nashville, TN 37203-2755, USA

Kutner, Rob (Writer)
c/o Staff Member *Kaplan-Stahler Agency*
8383 Wilshire Blvd Ste 923
Beverly Hills, CA 90211-2443, USA

Kuttner, Robert (Writer)
c/o Staff Member *Chelsea Green
Publishing*
85 N Main St Ste 120
White River Junction, VT 05001-7135,
USA

Kutyna, Marty (Athlete, Baseball Player)
2255 NW 14th St
Delray Beach, FL 33445-2610, USA

Kutz, Mae
140 Buckingham Ct
Goodlettsville, TN 37072-2146

Kutzler, Jerry (Athlete, Baseball Player)
8415 27th Ave
Kenosha, WI 53143-6232, USA

Kuykendall, Fulton (Athlete, Football
Player)
1497 Rucker Cir
Woodstock, GA 30188-2133, USA

Kuzava, Bob (Athlete, Baseball Player)
1118 Vinewood St
Wyandotte, MI 48192-4945, USA

Kuziel, Bob (Athlete, Football Player)
3375 Walnut Dr
Ellicott City, MD 21043-4351, USA

Kuznetsoff, Alexel (Musician)
Columbia Artists Mgmt Inc
165 W 57th St
New York, NY 10019-2201, USA

Kuzyk, Ken
5 McEnroe Dr
Londonderry, NH 03053-3042, USA

Kuzyk, Mimi (Actor)
Artists Agency
1180 S Beverly Dr Ste 301
Los Angeles, CA 90035-1154, USA

Kvapil, Travis (Race Car Driver)
132 Sagewood Dr
Mooresville, NC 28115-8030, USA

Kvasha, Oleg (Athlete, Hockey Player)
22 Bluff Rd
Glen Cove, NY 11542-1778, USA

Kwalick, Thaddeus J (Ted) (Athlete,
Football Player)
755 Purdue Ct
Santa Clara, CA 95051-5527, USA

Kwan, Jennie (Actor)
Innovative Artists
1505 10th St
Santa Monica, CA 90401-2805, USA

Kwan, Michelle (Athlete, Figure Skater,
Olympic Athlete)
140 N Thurston Ave
Los Angeles, CA 90049-2422, USA

Kwan, Nancy (Actor)
Marlin
252 7th Ave Apt 9P
New York, NY 10001-7340, USA

Kwanten, Ryan (Actor)
c/o Orly Adelson *Orly Adelson
Management*
12304 Santa Monica Blvd Ste 115
Los Angeles, CA 90025-2586, USA

Kwapis, Ken (Comedian, Director,
Producer)
c/o Staff Member *In Cahoots*
4024 Radford Ave
Editorial Bldg 2 #7
Studio City, CA 91604-2101, USA

Kweli, Talib (Musician)
c/o Steve Levine *ICM Partners (LA)*
10250 Constellation Blvd Fl 7
Los Angeles, CA 90067-6207, USA

Kweli, Talieb (Musician)
c/o Steve Levine *ICM Partners (LA)*
10250 Constellation Blvd Fl 7
Los Angeles, CA 90067-6207, USA

Kweller, Ben (Musician)
c/o Staff Member *Paradigm (Monterey)*
404 W Franklin St
Monterey, CA 93940-2303, USA

Kwiatkowski, Joel (Athlete, Hockey
Player)
2020 Tall Pines Dr SE
Grand Rapids, MI 49546-7923, USA

Kwon, Boa (Musician)
c/o Staff Member *Creative Artists Agency
(CAA-LA)*
2000 Avenue of the Stars Ste 100
Los Angeles, CA 90067-4705, USA

Kyle, Aaron (Athlete, Football Player)
14215 Ballantyne Lake Rd Apt 202
Charlotte, NC 28277-3326, USA

Kyle, David L (Business Person)
ONEOK Inc
100 W 5th St Ste Ll
PO Box 871
Tulsa, OK 74103-4298, USA

Kyle, Jason (Athlete, Football Player)
16801 Jetton Rd
Cornelius, NC 28031-7445, USA

Kyle, Richardson (Athlete, Football Player)
3516 Balmar Mews Rd
Baltimore, MD 21211-1471, USA

Kyles, Cedric (Cedric The Entertainer)
(Actor, Comedian, Producer)
22720 La Quilla Dr
Chatsworth, CA 91311-1282, USA

Kyles, Stan (Athlete, Baseball Player)
1587 Foxridge Rd
Rock Hill, SC 29732-9527, USA

Kysar, Jeff (Athlete, Football Player)
570 June St
Rialto, CA 92376-5729, USA

Laaksonen, Antti (Athlete, Hockey Player)
9225 Red Oak Dr
Victoria, MN 55386-4515, USA

Laaveg, Paul (Athlete, Football Player)
PO Box 406
Berryville, VA 22611-0406, USA

Labandeira, Josh (Athlete, Baseball Player)
1337 W Chess Terrace St
Porterville, CA 93257-8889, USA

Labarbera, Jason
8184 E Wingspan Way
Scottsdale, AZ 85255-6504, usa

L'Abbe, Moe (Athlete, Hockey Player)
4520 Golden Triangle Blvd
Fort Worth, TX 76244-6316, USA

Labeaux, Sandy (Athlete, Football Player)
PO Box 3132
San Ramon, CA 94583-8132, USA

LaBeef, Sleepy (Musician)
14469 E Highway 264
Lowell, AR 72745-9212, USA

Labelle, Marc
5705 Eagle Creek Ct
Maineville, OH 45039-7204, USA

LaBelle, Patti (Musician)
c/o Aliya Crawford *W&W PR*
476 Union Ave Ste 2
Middlesex, NJ 08846-1968, USA

LaBeouf, Shia (Actor)
c/o John Crosby *John Crosby Management*
1357 N Spaulding Ave
Los Angeles, CA 90046-4009, USA

Labeque, Katia (Musician)
Columbia Artists Mgmt Inc
165 W 57th St
New York, NY 10019-2201, USA

Labeque, Marielle (Musician)
Columbia Artists Mgmt Inc
165 W 57th St
New York, NY 10019-2201, USA

Labine, Tyler (Actor)
c/o Jason Heyman *Creative Artists Agency
(CAA-LA)*
3500 W Olive Ave Ste 1400
Burbank, CA 91505-5512, USA

Labiosa, David (Actor)
c/o Daryl Kane *Guinan Management*
4942 Vineland Ave Ste 111
North Hollywood, CA 91601-5641, USA

Labonte, Bobby (Race Car Driver)
Petty Enterprises
112 Byers Creek Rd
Mooresville, NC 28117-4376, USA

Labonte, Justin (Race Car Driver)
PO Box 843
Trinity, NC 27370-0843, USA

Labonte, Terry (Race Car Driver)
1100 Clodfelter Rd
Winston Salem, NC 27107-8806, USA

Laborde, Alden J (Business Person)
63 Oriole St
New Orleans, LA 70124-4517, USA

Labounty, Matt (Athlete, Football Player)
360 W 17th Ave
Eugene, OR 97401-3859, USA

Labounty_, Matt (Athlete, Football Player)
360 W 17th Ave
Eugene, OR 97401-3859, USA

Laboy, Travis (Athlete, Football Player)
2709 Arnoldson Ave
San Diego, CA 92122-2109, USA

Labrador, Honey (Actor, Television Host)
c/o Staff Member *Last Bastion
Entertainment*
5226 Parkglen Ave
Windsor Hills, CA 90043-1030, USA

Labrava, David (Actor)
19541 Blackhawk St
Porter Ranch, CA 91326-2210, USA

Labre, Yvon (Athlete, Hockey Player)
7812 Tilmont Ave
Parkville, MD 21234-5539, USA

LaBute, Neil (Director, Writer)
c/o Brad Gross *Brad Gross Agency, The*
161 S Arden Blvd
Los Angeles, CA 90004-3716, USA

Labyorteaux, Matthew (Actor)
10808 Hartsook St
N Hollywood, CA 91601-3914, USA

Labyorteaux, Patrick (Actor)
c/o Kim Dorr *Defining Artists Agency*
4370 Tujunga Ave Ste 120
Studio City, CA 91604-2763, USA

Lacasse, Ryan (Athlete, Football Player)
3 Gaslight Ln
North Easton, MA 02356-2721, USA

Lacefield, Reggie (Athlete, Basketball
Player)
674 Old School House Rd
Middletown, DE 19709-9690, USA

Lacey, Bob (Athlete, Baseball Player)
1717 20th St NW Apt 308
Washington, DC 20009-1114, USA

Lacey, Chonn (Athlete, Football Player)
1314 W Ontario St
Philadelphia, PA 19140-5220, USA

Lacey, Deborah (Actor)
1801 Ave of Stars Ste 1250
Los Angeles, CA 90067-5817, USA

Lacey, Jeff (Boxer)
Gary Shaw Productions LLC
33 Divan Way
Wayne, NJ 07470-5201, USA

Lachance, Michael (Mike) (Race Car
Driver)
183 Sweetmans Ln
Englishtown, NJ 07726, USA

Lachance, Michel (Horse Racer)
183 Sweetmans Ln
Millstone Township, NJ 08535-8107, USA

Lachance, Scott (Athlete, Hockey Player,
Olympic Athlete)
15 Meadow View Ln
Andover, MA 01810-4759, USA

LaChapelle, David (Artist, Photographer)
HSI Productions
601 W 26th St Rm 1420
New York, NY 10001-1136, USA

Lachapelle, Sean (Athlete, Football Player)
9860 Izilda Ct
Sacramento, CA 95829-8167, USA

LaChappelle, Sean P (Athlete, Football
Player)
9860 Izilda Ct
Sacramento, CA 95829-8167, USA

Lachemann, Bill (Athlete, Baseball Player)
208 Riverview Ln
Great Falls, MT 59404-1523, USA

Lachemann, Marcel E (Athlete, Baseball
Player, Coach)
PO Box 1967
Nipomo, CA 93444-1967, USA

Lachemann, Rene G (Athlete, Baseball
Player, Coach)
7500 E Boulders Pkwy Unit 66
Scottsdale, AZ 85266-1212, USA

Lachey, Drew (Musician, Television Host)
c/o Jeremy Katz *Katz Company, The*
1674 Broadway Ste 7E
New York, NY 10019-5888, USA

Lachey, James M (Jim) (Athlete, Football
Player)
1445 Roxbury Rd Apt G
Columbus, OH 43212-3211, USA

Lachey, Nick (Musician, Television Host)
c/o Ken Sunshine *Sunshine Sachs (NY)*
136 Madison Ave Fl 17
New York, NY 10016-6734, USA

Lachowicz, Al (Athlete, Baseball Player)
1000 Sunset Bay Ct
Granbury, TX 76048-1239, USA

Lachowicz, Al (Athlete, Baseball Player)
1000 Sunset Bay Ct
Granbury, TX 76048-1239, USA

Lacina, Corbin (Athlete, Football Player)
130 Otis Ave
Saint Paul, MN 55104-5636, USA

Lackey, Brad (Race Car Driver)
Badco
35 Monument Plz
Pleasant Hill, CA 94523, USA

Lackey, John (Athlete, Baseball Player)
c/o Steve Hilliard *Octagon Home Office*
1751 Pinnacle Dr Fl 15
Mc Lean, VA 22102-3833, USA

Lackey, Mercedes (Writer)
c/o Staff Member *JABberwocky Literary
Agency*
49 W 45th St Ste 1200
New York, NY 10036-4603, USA

Lacock, Pete (Athlete, Baseball Player)
10019 Mackey Cir
Overland Park, KS 66212-3461, USA

Lacorte, Frank (Athlete, Baseball Player)
1667 El Dorado Dr
Gilroy, CA 95020-3754, USA

Lacoss, Mike (Athlete, Baseball Player)
145 County Rd 816
Higdon, AL 35979, USA

La Coste+_a, Banda (Music Group)
c/o Staff Member *BMG*
1540 Broadway
New York, NY 10036-4039, USA

Lacouture, Dan
125 Lakeview Dr
Centerville, MA 02632-1416, USA

Lacroix, Andre J (Athlete, Hockey Player)
115 S Franklin St
Chagrin Falls, OH 44022-3214, USA

Lacroix, Dan
Tampa Bay Lightning
401 Channelside Dr
Attn Coaching Staff
Tampa, FL 33602-5400, USA

lacroix, Eric (Athlete, Hockey Player)
Colorado Avalanche
1000 Chopper Cir
Denver, CO 80204-5805

Lacrosse, Dave (Athlete, Football Player)
1712 Harmon Rd
Conshohocken, PA 19428-1205, USA

Lacy, Alan (Business Person)
Sears Roebuck Co
3333 Beverly Rd
Hoffman Estates, IL 60179-0002, USA

Lacy, Eddie (Athlete, Football Player)
c/o Pat Dye Jr *SportsTrust Advisors (GA)*
3340 Peachtree Rd NE Fl 16
Atlanta, GA 30326-1000, USA

Lacy, Kerry (Athlete, Baseball Player)
145 County Rd 816
Higdon, AL 35979, USA

Lacy, Lee (Athlete, Baseball Player)
Lee Lacy Baseball Academy
6310 Neveda Ave
Apt E420
Woodland Hills, CA 91367, USA

Lacy, Raymon (Athlete, Baseball Player)
2860 State Highway 63 W
Wiergate, TX 75977-9783, USA

Lacy Clay Jr., William (Congressman, Politician)
2418 Rayburn Hob
Washington, DC 20515-1702, USA

Ladd, Andrew (Athlete, Hockey Player)
16821 Crystal Ct
Tinley Park, IL 60477-2779

Ladd, Cheryl (Actor)
PO Box 1329
Santa Ynez, CA 93460-1329, USA

Ladd, David (Actor)
3445 Adina Dr
Los Angeles, CA 90068-1319, USA

Ladd, Diane (Actor)
c/o Scott Hart *Scott Hart Entertainment*
14622 Ventura Blvd # 746
Sherman Oaks, CA 91403-3600, USA

Ladd, Jim (Radio Personality, Writer)
3321 S La Cienega Blvd
Los Angeles, CA 90016-3114, USA

Ladd, Jordan (Actor)
c/o Staff Member *Kritzer Levine Wilkins Entertainment (KLWG)*
11872 La Grange Ave Fl 1
Los Angeles, CA 90025-5283, USA

Ladd, Margaret (Actor)
c/o Staff Member *Abrams Artists Agency (LA)*
9200 W Sunset Blvd PH 11
West Hollywood, CA 90069-3601, USA

Ladd, Pete (Athlete, Baseball Player)
239 Town Farm Rd
New Gloucester, ME 04260-4438, USA

Ladd Jr, Alan
c/o Staff Member *Ladd Company, The*
9465 Wilshire Blvd Ste 910
Beverly Hills, CA 90212-2608, USA

Laden, Nina B
6750 26th Ave NW
Seattle, WA 98117-5828, USA

Ladin, Eric (Actor)
c/o Staff Member *Main Title Entertainment*
8383 Wilshire Blvd Ste 408
Beverly Hills, CA 90211-2435, USA

Ladler, Kenny (Athlete, Football Player)
c/o Scott Smith *XAM Sports*
PO Box 1725
Madison, WI 53701-1725, USA

Ladouceur, L P (Athlete, Football Player)
3807 Prescott Ave Unit B
Dallas, TX 75219-2238, USA

Lady Antebellum (Music Group)
c/o Daniel Miller *Borman Entertainment (TN)*
4322 Harding Pike Ste 429
Nashville, TN 37205-2661, USA

Ladygo, Pete (Athlete, Football Player)
124 Orchard St
Keyser, WV 26726-3153, USA

Ladysmith Black Mambazo (Musician)
326 Ridge Rd Unit D
Cedar Grove, NJ 07009-1636, USA

Laettner, Christian (Athlete, Basketball Player, Olympic Athlete)
1225 Church Rd
Angola, NY 14006-8831, USA

LaFave, Debra
2220 Nichols Rd
Lithia, FL 33547-2230, USA

LaFell, Brandon (Athlete, Football Player)
c/o Brian E. Overstreet *E.O. Sports Management*
2211 Norfolk St Ste 210
Houston, TX 77098-4055, USA

Laffer, Arthur (Doctor)
5375 Exec Sq # 330
La Jolla, CA 92037, USA

Lafferty, James (Actor)
c/o Eric Nelson *Zero Gravity Management (II)*
9255 W Sunset Blvd Ste 1010
West Hollywood, CA 90069-3307, USA

Laffey, Aaron (Athlete, Baseball Player)
32301 Monaco Pl
Avon Lake, OH 44012-2567, USA

Laffite, Jacques (Actor)
Technopole de la Nievre
Magny Cours, FR F-584

LaFleur, Art (Actor)
c/o Joel King *Pakula/King & Associates*
9229 W Sunset Blvd Ste 315
West Hollywood, CA 90069-3403, USA

Lafleur, David (Athlete, Football Player)
3900 Thompson Rd
Sulphur, LA 70665-8901, USA

Lafleur, Greg (Athlete, Football Player)
PO Box 612
Baton Rouge, LA 70821-0612, USA

Lafley, Alan G (Business Person)
Procter & Gamble Co
1 Procter and Gamble Plz
Cincinnati, OH 45202-3393, USA

La Fong, Michelle
3855 Shore Pkwy Apt 1D
Brooklyn, NY 11235-1053

LaFontaine, Patrick (Pat) (Athlete, Hockey Player, Olympic Athlete)
Companions in Courage
PO Box 768
Huntington, NY 11743-0768

Laforest, Pete (Athlete, Baseball Player)
2212 Lansing Ave
Portage, MI 49002-3630, USA

Lafrancois, Roger (Athlete, Baseball Player)
64 Aspinook St
Jewett City, CT 06351-1802, USA

Lafrate, Al (Athlete, Hockey Player)
7975 Five Mile Rd
Livonia, MI 48154, USA

La Frenais, Ian (Director, Producer, Writer)
c/o Bruce Kaufman *ICM Partners (LA)*
10250 Constellation Blvd Fl 7
Los Angeles, CA 90067-6207, USA

LaFrentz, Raef (Athlete, Basketball Player)
PO Box 88
Decorah, IA 52101-0088, USA

Lafton, James D (Athlete, Football Player)
15487 Mesquite Tree Trl
Poway, CA 92064-2286, USA

Laga, Mike (Athlete, Baseball Player)
4 Center Ct
Northampton, MA 01060-3007, USA

Lagace, Jean-Guy (Athlete, Hockey Player)
6420 Ziklag Cir
Birmingham, AL 35235-2160

Lagace, Pierre (Athlete, Hockey Player)
2403 Brooksboro Dr
Erie, PA 16510-4053

Lagana, Jr., Bobby (Race Car Driver)
72 Woodruff Ave
Scarsdale, NY 10583-5126, USA

Lagana, Sr., Bobby (Race Car Driver)
72 Woodruff Ave
Scarsdale, NY 10583-5126, USA

Lagarde, Thomas (Basketball Player, Olympic Athlete)
3809 E Greensboro Chapel Hill Rd
Snow Camp, NC 27349-9841, USA

Lagarde, Tom (Athlete, Basketball Player, Olympic Athlete)
3809 E Greensboro Chapel Hill Rd
Snow Camp, NC 27349-9841, USA

Lagasse, Emeril (Chef)
829 Saint Charles Ave
New Orleans, LA 70130-3715, USA

Lagasse, Jr., Scott (Race Car Driver)
JTG Racing
2668 Peachtree Rd
Statesville, NC 28625-8252, USA

Lagatd, Bernar (Athlete, Olympic Athlete, Track Athlete)
9121 E Cottonwood Ct
Tucson, AZ 85749-9783, USA

Lagattuta, Bill (Correspondent)
CBS-TV
7800 Beverly Blvd
News Dept
Los Angeles, CA 90036-2112, USA

Lagedrost, Kelly (Athlete, Golfer)
10011 Kimbrough Dr
Brooksville, FL 34601-5260, USA

Lageman, Jeff (Athlete, Football Player)
2907 Forest Cir
Jacksonville, FL 32257-5617, USA

Lagerfelt, Caroline (Actor)
8730 W Sunset Blvd Ste 480
West Hollywood, CA 90069-2277, USA

Lago, David (Actor)
c/o Mark Robert *Mark Robert Management*
2208 Patricia Ave
Los Angeles, CA 90064-2318, USA

Lagod, Chet (Athlete, Football Player)
7016 Rocky Trl
Chattanooga, TN 37421-5213, USA

Lagrand, Morris (Athlete, Football Player)
4419 Ellenwood Ave
Saint Louis, MO 63116-1521, USA

LaGravenese, Richard (Director, Producer, Writer)
c/o Erwin Stoff *3 Arts Entertainment (LA)*
9460 Wilshire Blvd Fl 7
Beverly Hills, CA 90212-2713, USA

Lagrone, John (Athlete, Football Player)
1416 Marigold St
Borger, TX 79007-6440, USA

Lagrossa, Stephanie (Reality Star)
c/o Jamie Lopez
3400 Beacon Ave S
the Actors Group
Seattle, WA 98144-6702, USA

Lagrow, Lerrin (Athlete, Baseball Player)
12271 E Turquoise Ave
Scottsdale, AZ 85259-5105, USA

Lahaie, Dick (Race Car Driver)
Drag Racing HOF
13700 SW 16th Ave
Ocala, FL 34473-3970, USA

Lahair, Bryan (Athlete, Baseball Player)
13712 W Country Gables Dr
Surprise, AZ 85379-8335, USA

LaHaye, Tim (Writer)
Tyndale House Publishers
PO Box 80
351 Executive Dr
Wheaton, IL 60187-0080, USA

Lahgenbrunner, Jamie (Athlete, Hockey Player)
94233 Warloe Shore Ln
Moose Lake, MN 55767-6713, USA

Lahiri, Jhumpa (Writer)
Houghton Mifflin
222 Berkeley St # 700
Boston, MA 02116-3748, USA

Lahood, Mike (Athlete, Football Player)
23816 S Bronze Dr
Sun Lakes, AZ 85248-0851, USA

Lahoud, Joe (Athlete, Baseball Player)
263 Saw Pit Hill Rd
Woodbury, CT 06798-2614, USA

Lahti, Christine (Actor, Director)
23924 Long Valley Rd
Hidden Hills, CA 91302-2421, USA

Lahti, Jeff (Athlete, Baseball Player)
4632 Tyler Dr
Hood River, OR 97031-9742, USA

Laidlaw, Scott (Athlete, Football Player)
302 Sand Oak Blvd
Panama City Beach, FL 32413-4681, USA

Laidlaw, Tom (Athlete, Hockey Player)
Laidlaw Sports Management
32 Ridge Blvd
Port Chester, NY 10573-2120

Lail, Leah (Actor)
c/o Staff Member *Diverse Talent Group*
9911 W Pico Blvd Ste 340W
Los Angeles, CA 90035-2703, USA

Laimbeer, Bill (Athlete, Basketball Player)
470 Gray Ct
Marco Island, FL 34145-1939, USA

Laine, Skylar (Musician)
c/o Staff Member *19 Entertainment (LA)*
9000 W Sunset Blvd Ste 1574
West Hollywood, CA 90069-5817, USA

Laird, Bruce (Athlete, Football Player)
20 Stoneridge Ct
Baltimore, MD 21239-1339, USA

Laird, Gerald (Athlete, Baseball Player)
13735 E Yucca St
Scottsdale, AZ 85259-4641, USA

Laird, Melvin R (Politician)
16676 Bobcat Dr
Fort Myers, FL 33908-4325, USA

Laird, Peter (Cartoonist)
351 Pleasant St Ste B
Northampton, MA 01060-3998, USA

Laird, Ron (Athlete, Olympic Athlete, Track Athlete)
4706 Diane Dr
Ashtabula, OH 44004-4636, USA

Laird, Ronald (Ron) (Athlete, Track Athlete)
4706 Diane Dr
Ashtabula, OH 44004-4636, USA

LaJoie, Jon (Comedian)
c/o Trevor Engelson *Underground Management*
447 S Highland Ave
Los Angeles, CA 90036-3530, USA

LaJoie, Randy (Race Car Driver)
Phoenix Racing
S Industrial Park #7
Mooresville, NC 28115, USA

Lajoie, Bill (Baseball Player)
Detroit Tigers
456 Yacht Harbor Dr
Osprey, FL 34229-9744, USA

Lakatos, Josh (Athlete, Olympic Athlete, Shooter)
955 SW Summit View Dr
Portland, OR 97225-6179, USA

Lake, Antwan (Athlete, Football Player)
1032 Bluebell Dr
Dacula, GA 30019-7855, USA

Lake, Carnell A (Athlete, Football Player)
PO Box 55048
Irvine, CA 92619-5048, USA

Lake, Don (Actor, Writer)
c/o Gayle Divine *Divine Management*
3822 Latrobe St
Los Angeles, CA 90031-1446

Lake, Oliver E (Musician)
DL Media
PO Box 2728
Bala Cynwyd, PA 19004-6728, USA

Lake, Ricki (Actor, Talk Show Host)
3205 Sumac Ridge Rd
Malibu, CA 90265-5129, USA

Lake, Sanoe (Actor)
c/o Staff Member *Luber Roklin Management*
5815 W Sunset Blvd Ste 206
Los Angeles, CA 90028-6481, USA

Lake, Steve (Athlete, Baseball Player)
5415 N Pajaro Ct
Litchfield Park, AZ 85340-3302, USA

Laker, Tim (Athlete, Baseball Player)
325 Spring Breeze Ct
Simi Valley, CA 93065-6719, USA

Lakin, Christine (Actor)
c/o Gordon Gilbertson *Gilbertson Management*
1334 3rd Street Promenade Ste 201
Santa Monica, CA 90401-1320, USA

Lalaine (Actor, Musician)
c/o Peter Young *Sovereign Talent Group*
8421 Wilshire Blvd Ste 200
Beverly Hills, CA 90211-3204, USA

La Lanne, Jack (Athlete)
430 Quintana Rd
Morro Bay, CA 93442-1937, USA

La Lanne, Jack
430 Quintana Rd # 151
Morro Bay, CA 93442-1937

Lalas, Alexi (Athlete, Soccer Player)
1641 8th St
Manhattan Beach, CA 90266-6352, USA

La Ley (Music Group)
c/o Staff Member *United Talent Agency (UTA-LA)*
9336 Civic Center Dr
Beverly Hills, CA 90210-3604, USA

LaLiberte, Nicole (Actor)
c/o Allan Mindel *Framework Entertainment (LA)*
9057 Nemo St Ste C
West Hollywood, CA 90069-5511, USA

Lalive, Caroline (Athlete, Olympic Athlete, Skier)
30 Blue Sage Circle Steamboat
Steamboat Springs, CO 80487, USA

Lally, Bob (Athlete, Football Player)
2716 182nd St
Redondo Beach, CA 90278-3931, USA

Lalonde, Donny
2554 Lincoln Blvd # 729
Venice, CA 90291-5043

Lalonde, Larry (Musician)
Figurehead Mgmt
3470 19th St
San Francisco, CA 94110-1740, USA

Lalor, Mike (Athlete, Hockey Player)
51 Meadowbrook Rd
Needham, MA 02492-1913

Lam, Derek (Designer)
Derek Lam
764 Madison Ave Frnt 1
New York, NY 10065-6550, USA

Lamar, Chuck (Commentator)
2250 Kent Pi
Clearwater, FL 33764, USA

Lamar, Dwight (Bo) (Athlete, Basketball Player)
103 Claire St
Lafayette, LA 70507-4803, USA

Lamar, Kendrick (Musician)
c/o Staff Member *Interscope Records (NY)*
1755 Broadway
New York, NY 10019-3743, USA

LaMarr, Phil (Actor, Comedian)
c/o Staff Member *Sanders Armstrong Caserta*
2120 Colorado Ave Ste 120
Santa Monica, CA 90404-3561, USA

Lamas, A J (Actor)
c/o Ryan Daly *Zero Gravity Management*
1531 14th St
Santa Monica, CA 90404-3302, USA

Lamb, Brad (Athlete, Football Player)
6460 Chase Dr
Mentor, OH 44060-3606, USA

Lamb, David (Athlete, Baseball Player)
603 Hampshire Rd Apt 465
Westlake Village, CA 91361-2307, USA

Lamb, John (Athlete, Baseball Player)
PO Box 2
Sharon, CT 06069-0002, USA

Lamb, Mike (Athlete, Baseball Player)
17 Meadow Wood Dr
Trabuco Canyon, CA 92679-4737, USA

Lamb, Ray (Athlete, Baseball Player)
3 Corte Tallista
San Clemente, CA 92673-6863, USA

Lamb, Wally (Writer)
c/o Staff Member *HarperCollins Publishers*
195 Broadway Fl 2
Cellar 1
New York, NY 10007-3132, USA

Lamberg, Adam (Actor)
c/o Stephanie Davis *Wet Dog Entertainment*
9460 Wilshire Blvd Fl 7
Beverly Hills, CA 90212-2713, USA

Lambert, Adam (Musician)
c/o Staff Member *Direct Management Group*
8332 Melrose Ave
West Hollywood, CA 90069-5420, USA

Lambert, Chris (Athlete, Baseball Player)
1072 Cilley Rd
Manchester, NH 03103-2908, USA

Lambert, Christopher (Actor, Producer, Writer)
c/o Gerry Harrington *Brillstein Entertainment Partners (LA)*
9150 Wilshire Blvd Ste 350
Beverly Hills, CA 90212-3453, USA

Lambert, Dan (Athlete, Hockey Player)
7375 E Wingspan Way
Scottsdale, AZ 85255-4758

Lambert, Dion (Athlete, Football Player)
11157 Sunburst St
Sylmar, CA 91342-6628, USA

Lambert, Frank (Athlete, Football Player)
15610 Early Bird Cir
Saint Paul, MN 55124-7847, USA

Lambert, Gordon (Athlete, Football Player)
PO Box 11
Pageton, WV 24871-0011, USA

Lambert, Jack (Athlete, Football Player)
PO Box 512
Worthington, PA 16262-0512, USA

Lambert, Jerry
PO Box 25371
Charlotte, NC 28229-5371

Lambert, John (Athlete, Basketball Player)
884 Dolphin Dr
Danville, CA 94526-1826, USA

Lambert, Lane (Athlete, Hockey Player)
Nashville Predators
501 Broadway
Nashville, TN 37203-3980

Lambert, L W
Rt. #1
Olin, NC 28860, USA

Lambert, Mary (Musician)
c/o JD Sobol *Almond Talent Agency*
2600 W Olive Ave Fl 5
Burbank, CA 91505-4572, USA

Lambert, Miranda (Musician)
c/o Staff Member *Shopkeeper Management*
918 19th Ave S
Nashville, TN 37212-2108, USA

Lambert, Sheila (Basketball Player)
Charlotte Sting
100 Hive Dr
Charlotte, NC 28217-4524, USA

Lamberti, Pasquale (Athlete, Football Player)
8 Wellington Ave
Everett, MA 02149-1818, USA

Lamb Of God (Music Group, Musician)
c/o Larry Mazer *Entertainment Services Unlimited*
1000 Main St Ste 303
Voorhees, NJ 08043-4633, USA

Lamborn, Doug (Congressman, Politician)
437 Cannon Hob
Washington, DC 20515-1902, USA

Lambros, Andy
9310 Topanga Canyon Blvd # 125
Chatsworth, CA 91311-5713

Lamby, Dick (Athlete, Hockey Player, Olympic Athlete)
3 Ocean Ave
Salem, MA 01970-5456

Lamelin, Stephanie (Actor)
c/o Katie Mason *Luber Roklin Management*
5815 W Sunset Blvd Ste 206
Los Angeles, CA 90028-6481, USA

Lamkin, Kathy (Actor)
c/o Linda McAlister *Linda McAlister Talent*
100 Oak Ln
Waxahachie, TX 75167-8412, USA

Lamm, Julie
PO Box B
Aspen, CO 81612-7402

Lamm, Richard D (Politician)
University of Denver
W Center Ave For Public Policy
Denver, CO 80219, USA

Lamm, Robert (Musician)
Air Tight Mgmt
115 West Rd
Winsted, CT 06098-2301, USA

Lammens, Hank (Athlete, Hockey Player)
11 Hilltop Rd
Norwalk, CT 06854-5001

Lammons, Pete (Athlete, Football Player)
5006 E Fallen Bough Dr
Houston, TX 77041-7887, USA

Lamonica, Darryl (Athlete, Football Player)
8796 N 6th St
Fresno, CA 93720-1711, USA

Lamonica, Daryle (Athlete, Football Player)
8796 N 6th St
Fresno, CA 93720-1711, USA

Lamont, Gene W (Athlete, Baseball Player, Coach)
5194 Siesta Woods Dr
Sarasota, FL 34242-1457, USA

LaMontagne, Ray (Musician)
c/o Staff Member *Paradigm (Monterey)*
404 W Franklin St
Monterey, CA 93940-2303, USA

Lamoriello, Lou (Athlete, Hockey Player)
6D Cove Ln N
North Bergen, NJ 07047-6237

LaMorte, Robia (Actor)
c/o Rob D'Avola *Rob DAvola & Associates*
9107 Wilshire Blvd Ste 450
Beverly Hills, CA 90210-5535, USA

Lamott, Anne (Writer)
c/o Steven Barclay *Steven Barclay Agency*
12 Western Ave
Petaluma, CA 94952-2907, USA

LaMotta, Jake (Boxer)
3598 Yacht Club Dr Apt 503
Miami, FL 33180-4010, USA

Lamp, Dennis (Athlete, Baseball Player)
2 Enterprise Apt 6311
Aliso Viejo, CA 92656-8003, USA

Lamp, Jeff (Athlete, Basketball Player)
4971 Credit River Dr
Savage, MN 55378-4610, USA

Lampa, Rachael
25 Music Sq W
Nashville, TN 37203-3205

Lampanelli, Lisa (Comedian)
1053 Fairfield Beach Rd
Fairfield, CT 06824-6561, USA

Lampard, Keith (Athlete, Baseball Player)
6124 Highway 6 N
Houston, TX 77084-1304, USA

Lamparski, Richard (Writer)
4202 Calle Real Apt 245
Santa Barbara, CA 93110-4081, USA

Lampert, Edward S (Business Person)
ESL Investments Inc
200 Greenwich Ave
Greenwich, CT 06830-2506, USA

Lampert, Zohra (Actor)
Don Buchwald
6500 Wilshire Blvd Ste 2200
Los Angeles, CA 90048-4942, USA

Lamphear, Dan (Athlete, Football Player)
669 Bent Ridge Ln
Barrington, IL 60010-6604, USA

Lampkin, Tom (Athlete, Baseball Player)
3810 SE 153rd Ct
Vancouver, WA 98683-5313, USA

Lampley, Jim (Sportscaster)
c/o Staff Member *Crystal Spring Productions*
9713 Santa Monica Blvd Ste 214
Beverly Hills, CA 90210-4229, USA

Lampley, Jimmy (Athlete, Basketball Player)
3197 Balsam Cv
Memphis, TN 38127-7483, USA

Lamplugh, Ian (Athlete, Baseball Player)
1830 Fairburn Dr
Victoria Bc, V8 CANAD, USA

Lampman, Bryce (Athlete, Hockey Player)
5217 Castlewood Ln NW
Rochester, MN 55901-2078

Lampman, Mike (Athlete, Hockey Player)
7007 Hawaii Kai Dr Apt D22
Honolulu, HI 96825-3141

Lampton, Michael (Astronaut)
University of California
Space Science Laboratory
Berkeley, CA 94720-0001, USA

La Mura, Mark
6399 Wilshire Blvd Ste 414
Los Angeles, CA 90048-5716

Lanasa, Katherine (Actor, Dancer)
17 Jib St
Marina Del Rey, CA 90292-5908, USA

Lanbros, Andy
9040 Topanga Canyon Blvd # 200
Canoga Park, CA 91304-1435

Lancaster, Amber
c/o Cindy Guagenti *Baker Winokur Ryder Public Relations (BWR-LA)*
9100 Wilshire Blvd Ste 500
West Tower Suite 500
Beverly Hills, CA 90212-3426, USA

Lancaster, Les (Athlete, Baseball Player)
PO Box 1105
Dothan, AL 36302-1105, USA

Lancaster, Mark (Horse Racer)
195 Mill Ln W
Columbus, NJ 08022-1941, USA

Lancaster, Neal (Athlete, Golfer)
6 Quail Run
Smithfield, NC 27577, USA

Lancaster, Penny (Actor)
c/o Staff Member *Special Artists Agency*
9200 W Sunset Blvd Ste 410
West Hollywood, CA 90069-3506, USA

Lancaster, Sarah (Actor)
c/o Amanda Glazer *Kohner Agency, The*
9300 Wilshire Blvd Ste 555
Beverly Hills, CA 90212-3211, USA

Lance, Dirk (Musician)
c/o Staff Member *ArtistDirect*
9046 Lindblade St
Culver City, CA 90232-2513, USA

Lance, Gary (Athlete, Baseball Player)
212 Sunset Cir
Prosperity, SC 29127-8426, USA

Lance, Leonard (Congressman, Politician)
426 Cannon Hob
Washington, DC 20515-3813, USA

Lancellotti, Rick (Athlete, Baseball Player)
5190 Thompson Rd
Clarence, NY 14031-1127, USA

Lancelotti, Rick (Athlete, Baseball Player)
5190 Thompson Rd
Clarence, NY 14031-1127, USA

Land, Tammi
c/o Staff Member *Osbrink Talent Agency*
4343 Lankershim Blvd Ste 100
North Hollywood, CA 91602-2705, USA

Landaker, Dave (Baseball Player)
Topps
3593 Buffum St
Simi Valley, CA 93063-3215, USA

Landau, Jon (Director, Producer, Writer)
c/o Staff Member *LightStorm Entertainment*
1600 Rosecrans Ave
Manhattan Beach, CA 90266-3708, USA

Landau, Juliet (Actor)
Miss Juliet Productions
PO Box 2792
Los Angeles, CA 90078-2792

Landau, Martin (Actor)
c/o Rona Menashe *Guttman Associates*
118 S Beverly Dr Ste 201
Beverly Hills, CA 90212-3016, USA

Landeau, Aleksia (Actor)
c/o Staff Member *Metropolitan (MTA)*
4526 Wilshire Blvd
Los Angeles, CA 90010-3801, USA

Landecker, Amy (Actor)
c/o Lisa Sharon Goldberg *Lisa Sharon Goldberg*
88 Leonard St Apt 607
New York, NY 10013-3495, USA

Landecker, John Records
MAGIC 104.3 WJMK
180 N Stetson Ave Ste 900
Prudential 2 Building
Chicago, IL 60601-6728

Lander, David L (Actor)
c/o Staff Member *Arlene Thornton & Associates*
12711 Ventura Blvd Ste 490
Studio City, CA 91604-2477, USA

Lander, Natalie (Actor)
c/o Scott Zimmerman *Evolution Entertainment (LA)*
901 N Highland Ave
Los Angeles, CA 90038-2412, USA

Landers, Amy (Actor)
c/o Staff Member *Badgley-Connor-King*
9229 W Sunset Blvd Ste 311
West Hollywood, CA 90069-3403, USA

Landers, Andy (Coach)
University of Georgia
310 Athletic Dept
Athens, GA 30602-0001, USA

Landers, Audrey (Actor, Musician)
688 Eagle Watch Ln
Osprey, FL 34229-9356, USA

Landers, Judy (Actor)
3933 Losillias Dr
Sarasota, FL 34238-4537, USA

Landers, Kristy (Actor)
c/o Gregory (Greg) Redlitz *Robert Thorne Company*
5315 Laurel Canyon Blvd Ste 203
Valley Village, CA 91607-4918, USA

Landers, Robert (Athlete, Golfer)
PO Box 497
Azle, TX 76098-0497, USA

Landes, Michael (Actor)
c/o Jason Weinberg *Untitled Entertainment (LA)*
350 S Beverly Dr Ste 200
Beverly Hills, CA 90212-4819, USA

Landesberg, Sylven (Athlete, Basketball Player)
c/o Jeff Schwartz *Excel Sports Management (NY)*
1700 Broadway Fl 29
New York, NY 10019-5905, USA

Landestoy, Rafael (Athlete, Baseball Player)
13564 SW 177th Ter
Miami, FL 33177-7777, USA

Landeta, Sean (Athlete, Football Player)
PO Box 422
Manhasset, NY 11030-0422, USA

Landey, Nina (Actor)
c/o Staff Member *Bauman Redanty & Shaul Agency*
5757 Wilshire Blvd
Suite 473
Beverly Hills, CA 90212, USA

Landi, Sal (Actor)
c/o Craig Mobbs *AKA Talent Agency*
6310 San Vicente Blvd Ste 200
Los Angeles, CA 90048-5488, USA

Landis, Bill (Athlete, Baseball Player)
525 E Sycamore Dr
Hanford, CA 93230-1443, USA

Landis, Floyd (Athlete)
Ouch Pro Cycling Team
3530 Grand Ave Ste 4
Oakland, CA 94610-2036, USA

Landis, Jim (Athlete, Baseball Player)
203 Alchemy Way
Napa, CA 94558-7214, USA

Landis, John D (Director)
c/o Abram Nalibotsky *Gersh (LA)*
9465 Wilshire Blvd Ste 600
Beverly Hills, CA 90212-2605, USA

Lando, Joe (Actor)
c/o Staff Member *Metropolitan (MTA)*
4526 Wilshire Blvd
Los Angeles, CA 90010-3801, USA

Landon, Bruce (Athlete, Hockey Player)
250 Dewey St
West Springfield, MA 01089-1606

Landon, Jennifer (Actor)
c/o Jamie Freed *Paris Hilton Entertainment*
2934 1/2 N Beverly Glen Cir # 383
Los Angeles, CA 90077-1724, USA

Landon, R Kirk (Business Person)
Lennar
700 NW 107th Ave Ste 115
Miami, FL 33172-3128, USA

Landon Jr, Michael (Actor, Director, Producer, Writer)
c/o Staff Member *Believe Pictures*
2 Saint Elias
Trabuco Canyon, CA 92679-3413, USA

Landreaux, Ken (Athlete, Baseball Player)
JD Legends Promotions
10808 Foothill Blvd # 160-454
Rancho Cucamonga, CA 91730-3889,
USA

Landres, Paul
5343 Amestoy Ave
Encino, CA 91316-2613

Landri, Derek (Athlete, Football Player)
125 Crestwood Ln
Buffalo, NY 14221-1462, USA

Landrieu, Mary (Politician)
405 E Capitol St SE
Washington, DC 20003-3810, USA

Landrieu, Moon (Politician)
4301 S Prieur St
New Orleans, LA 70125-5125, USA

Landrith, Hobie (Athlete, Baseball Player)
1462 Nome Ct
Sunnyvale, CA 94087-4264, USA

Landrum, Bill (Athlete, Baseball Player)
840 Silverpoint Rd
Chapin, SC 29036-7963, USA

Landrum, Ced (Athlete, Baseball Player)
2425 Hillview Dr
Fort Worth, TX 76119-2722, USA

Landrum, Joe (Athlete, Baseball Player)
715 Sharpe Rd
Columbia, SC 29203-9347, USA

Landrum, Mike (Athlete, Football Player)
88 Raybourn Rd
Sumrall, MS 39482-3926, USA

Landrum, Tito (Athlete, Baseball Player)
428 E 58th St Apt Grd
New York, NY 10022-2362, USA

Landry, Ali (Actor, Model)
c/o Staff Member *Reel Talent Management*
PO Box 491035
Los Angeles, CA 90049-9035, USA

Landry, Dawan (Athlete, Football Player)
309 Kennedy St
Ama, LA 70031, USA

Landry, Gregory P (Greg) (Athlete, Coach, Football Coach, Football Player)
133 Melanie Ln
Troy, MI 48098-1707, USA

Landry, Troy (Reality Star)
Choot Em Enterprises
506 Renwick Blvd
Berwick, LA 70342-3212, USA

Landsberger, Mark (Athlete, Basketball Player)
1702 8th Ave SE
Saint Cloud, MN 56304-2104, USA

Landsburg, Valerie (Actor)
22745 Chamera Ln
Topanga, CA 90290-4006, USA

Landsee, Bob (Athlete, Football Player)
1861 Corinth Dr
Sun Prairie, WI 53590-3551, USA

Landsee, Robert (Athlete, Football Player)
1861 Corinth Dr
Sun Prairie, WI 53590-3551, USA

Landy, Leonard (Actor)
78229 Kistler Way
Palm Desert, CA 92211-2725, USA

Landzaat, Andre
7500 Devista Dr
Los Angeles, CA 90046-1712

Lane, Abbe (Actor, Musician)
500 Bel Air Rd
Los Angeles, CA 90077-3817, USA

Lane, Barry (Athlete, Golfer)
I M G
1360 E 9th St Ste 100
Cleveland, OH 44114-1730, USA

Lane, Cristy (Musician)
PO Box 654
Madison, TN 37116-0654, USA

Lane, Diane (Actor)
c/o Joan Hyler *Hyler Management*
20 Ocean Park Blvd Unit 25
Santa Monica, CA 90405-3590, USA

Lane, Dick (Athlete, Baseball Player)
2717 Legend Dr
Las Vegas, NV 89134-8829, USA

Lane, Garcia (Athlete, Football Player)
1095 Great Oak Dr Apt F
Columbus, OH 43213-4517, USA

Lane, Gord (Athlete, Hockey Player)
5656 Vantage Point Rd
Columbia, MD 21044-2613

Lane, Jason (Athlete, Baseball Player)
8930 Oak Grove Ave
Sebastopol, CA 95472-2460, USA

Lane, Jerome (Athlete, Basketball Player)
1500 Marion Ave Apt 509
Akron, OH 44313-7628, USA

Lane, Johnny
5048 Casa Dr
Tarzana, CA 91356-4422

Lane, Kenneth Jay (Designer, Fashion Designer)
Kenneth Jay Lane Inc
20 W 37th St Fl 9
New York, NY 10018-7367, USA

Lane, Lilas (Actor)
c/o Peter Himberger *Impact Artists Group LLC*
42 Hamilton Ter
New York, NY 10031-6403, USA

Lane, MacArthur (Athlete, Football Player)
3238 Knowland Ave
Oakland, CA 94619-2630, USA

Lane, Marvin (Marv) (Athlete, Baseball Player)
40164 Gulliver Dr
Sterling Heights, MI 48310-1729, USA

Lane, Max (Athlete, Football Player)
16 Strong St
Newburyport, MA 01950-2411, USA

Lane, Melvin B (Publisher)
99 Tallwood Ct
Atherton, CA 94027-6431, USA

Lane, Mike (Cartoonist)
Baltimore Sun
501 N Calvert St
Editorial Dept
Baltimore, MD 21278-1000, USA

Lane, Nathan (Actor, Musician)
c/o Simon Halls *Slate Public Relations*
9000 W Sunset Blvd Ste 915
West Hollywood, CA 90069-5809, USA

Lane, Skip (Athlete, Business Person, Football Player)
14 Roosevelt Rd
Westport, CT 06880-6840, USA

Lane, Tory (Actor, Adult Film Star, Model)
c/o Staff Member *LA Direct Models*
5535 Balboa Blvd Ste 103
Encino, CA 91316-1575, USA

Laneuville, Eric (Actor)
5138 W Slauson Ave
Los Angeles, CA 90056-1641, USA

Lang, Andrew (Athlete, Basketball Player)
1048 Woodruff Plantation Pkwy SE
Marietta, GA 30067-9106, USA

Lang, Antonio (Athlete, Basketball Player)
2255 Barretts Ln
Mobile, AL 36617-2734, USA

Lang, Chip (Athlete, Baseball Player)
132 Westminster Dr
Pittsburgh, PA 15229-3165, USA

Lang, Gene (Athlete, Football Player)
11526 Azalea Trce
Gulfport, MS 39503-8398, USA

Lang, Helmut (Designer, Fashion Designer)
Helmut Lang New York
819 Washington St
New York, NY 10014-1405, USA

Lang, Jack (Writer)
4 Barry Dr
E Northport, NY 11731-1307, USA

Lang, Jonny (Musician)
Blue Sky Artists
761 Washington Ave N
Minneapolis, MN 55401-1101, USA

Lang, June (Actor)
12756 Kahlenberg Ln
Valley Village, CA 91607-2919, USA

Lang, Katherine Kelly (Actor, Model)
The Bold and The Beautiful""
7800 Beverly Blvd Ste 3371
Bell-Phillip Television Productions Inc
Los Angeles, CA 90036-2112, USA

Lang, KD (Actor, Musician)
1314 NW Irving St Apt 714 PMB 714
Portland, OR 97209-2728, USA

Lang, Kenard (Athlete, Football Player)
2628 Glen Forest Dr
Apopka, FL 32712-5034, USA

Lang, Lang (Musician)
c/o Staff Member *Columbia Artists Mgmt Inc*
1790 Broadway Fl 6
New York, NY 10019-1537, USA

Lang, Le-Lo (Athlete, Football Player)
19436 E Maplewood Pl
Aurora, CO 80016-3868, USA

Lang, T.J. (Athlete, Football Player)
c/o Michael McCartney *Priority Sports & Entertainment - Chicago*
312 N La Salle
Suite 650
Chicago, IL 60610, USA

Langbo, Arnold G (Business Person)
Kellogg Co
1 Kellogg Sq
PO Box 3599
Battle Creek, MI 49017-3517, USA

Langdon, Brooke
1180 S Beverly Dr Ste 608
Los Angeles, CA 90035-1158

Langdon, Sue Ane (Actor)
4618 Park Mirasol
Calabasas, CA 91302-1731, USA

Langdon, Sue Ann (Actor)
4618 Park Mirasol
Calabasas, CA 91302-1731, USA

Lange, Allison
3500 W Olive Ave Ste 1400
Burbank, CA 91505-5512

Lange, Artie (Actor)
c/o Richard Abate *3 Arts Entertainment (NY)*
16 W 22nd St Ste 201
New York, NY 10010-5842, USA

Lange, Bonnie
PO Box 3827
Beverly Hills, CA 90212-0827

Lange, Detective Tom
12021 Wilshire Blvd # 846
Los Angeles, CA 90025-1206

Lange, Dick (Athlete, Baseball Player)
39744 Salvatore Dr
Sterling Heights, MI 48313-5165, USA

Lange, Eric (Actor)
c/o Devon Jackson *Trademark Talent*
144 S Beverly Dr Ste 404
Beverly Hills, CA 90212-3022, USA

Lange, Jessica (Actor)
c/o Jason Weinberg *Untitled Entertainment (LA)*
350 S Beverly Dr Ste 200
Beverly Hills, CA 90212-4819, USA

Lange, Niklaus (Actor)
c/o Staff Member *Schumacher Management*
2018 Glendon Ave
Los Angeles, CA 90025-6324, USA

Lange, Ted (Actor)
c/o Staff Member *Connor Ankrum & Associates*
1680 Vine St Ste 916
Los Angeles, CA 90028-8838, USA

Langehorne, Reggie (Athlete, Football Player)
12260 Smiths Neck Rd
Carrollton, VA 23314-3802, USA

Langella, Frank (Actor)
c/o Toni Howard *ICM Partners (LA)*
10250 Constellation Blvd Fl 7
Los Angeles, CA 90067-6207, USA

Langenbrunner, Jamie (Athlete, Hockey Player, Olympic Athlete)
94096 Warloe Shore Ln
Moose Lake, MN 55767-6711

Langencamp, Reather (Actor)
156 F St SE
Washington, DC 20003-2603, USA

Langenkamp, Heather (Actor)
c/o Harrison Cheung *Harrison Cheung & Associates*
11617 Natrona Dr
Austin, TX 78759-4123, USA

Langer, AJ (Actor)
c/o Michael Valeo *Valeo Entertainment*
8581 Santa Monica Blvd Ste 570
West Hollywood, CA 90069-4120, USA

Langer, Bernhard (Athlete, Golfer)
3667 Princeton Pl
Boca Raton, FL 33496-2711, USA

Langer, James J (Jim) (Athlete, Football Player)
14280 Wolfram St NW
Anoka, MN 55303-4563, USA

Langer, Robert (Doctor)
Massachusetts Institute of Technology
Chem Engineer Dept
Cambridge, MA 02139, USA

Langerhans, Ryan (Athlete, Baseball Player)
18911 Angel Mountain Dr
Leander, TX 78641-3805, USA

Langevin, Dave (Athlete, Hockey Player)
1090 W Circle Ct
Saint Paul, MN 55118-4148

Langevin, Jim (Politician)
Jim Langevin for Congress
181 Knight St Ste A
Warwick, RI 02886-1296, USA

Langfeld, Josh (Athlete, Hockey Player)
13050 Linnet St NW
Minneapolis, MN 55448-7078

Langford, Jevon (Athlete, Football Player)
1 Paul Brown Stadium
Cincinnati, OH 45202-3418, USA

Langford, Rick (Athlete, Baseball Player)
8330 9th Avenue Ter NW
Bradenton, FL 34209-9678, USA

Langham, C Antonio (Athlete, Football Player)
PO Box 232
Town Creek, AL 35672-0232, USA

Langham, Franklin (Athlete, Golfer)
PO Box 3428
Peachtree City, GA 30269-7428, USA

Langham, Wallace (Actor)
10264 Rochester Ave
Los Angeles, CA 90024-5331, USA

Langham, Wally (Actor)
c/o Josh Katz *United Talent Agency (UTA-LA)*
9336 Civic Center Dr
Beverly Hills, CA 90210-3604, USA

Langhorne, Reggie (Athlete, Football Player)
12260 Smiths Neck Rd
Carrollton, VA 23314-3802, USA

Langkow, Daymond (Athlete, Hockey Player)
11549 E Cochise Dr
Scottsdale, AZ 85259-4904

Langley, Neva (Beauty Pageant Winner)
6300 Rivoli Dr
Macon, GA 31210-1459, USA

Langley, Roger (Skier)
Broad St
Barre, MA 01005, USA

Langlois, Lisa (Actor)
c/o Staff Member *Leavitt Talent Group*
8222 Melrose Ave Ste 203
Los Angeles, CA 90046-6838, USA

Langlois Jr, Albert (Athlete, Hockey Player)
2473 Crest View Dr
Los Angeles, CA 90046-1406

Langone, Kenneth (Business Person)
Invemed Associates
375 Park Ave Ste 2205
New York, NY 10152-0189, USA

Langston, J William (Doctor)
Parkinson's Foundation
2444 Moorpark Ave
San Jose, CA 95128, USA

Langston, Mark E (Athlete, Baseball Player)
56 Golden Eagle
Irvine, CA 92603-0309, USA

Langston, Murray (Actor, Comedian)
Entertainment Alliance
PO Box 4734
Santa Rosa, CA 95402-4734, USA

Langton, Brooke (Actor)
Rigberg Roberts Rugolo
1180 S Beverly Dr Ste 601
Los Angeles, CA 90035-1158, USA

Langton, Brooke (Actor)
c/o Mark Measures *Kazarian, Measures, Ruskin & Associates (LA)*
11969 Ventura Blvd Fl 3
Studio City, CA 91604-2630, USA

Lanier, Bob (Athlete, Basketball Player, Coach)
Bob Lanier Enterprises Inc.
5403 N 118th Ct
Milwaukee, WI 53225-3087, USA

Lanier, Harold C (Hal) (Athlete, Baseball Player, Coach)
3270 Countryside View Dr
Saint Cloud, FL 34772-7050, USA

Lanier, Ken (Athlete, Football Player)
24583 E Hoover Pl Unit A
Aurora, CO 80016-7317, USA

Lanier, Lorenzo (Rimp) (Athlete, Baseball Player)
4515 E Frontenac Dr
Cleveland, OH 44128-5004, USA

Lanier, Lorenzo ""Rimp"" (Athlete, Baseball Player)
4515 E Frontenac Dr
Cleveland, OH 44128-5004, USA

Lanier, Willie E (Athlete, Football Player)
2911 E Brigstock Rd
Midlothian, VA 23113-3905, USA

Lankford, Frank (Athlete, Baseball Player)
104 Lakeview Ave NE
Atlanta, GA 30305-3725, USA

Lankford, Kim (Actor)
6071 US 64
Bloomfield, NM 87413-9551, USA

Lankford, Paul (Athlete, Football Player)
3838 Biggin Church Rd W
Jacksonville, FL 32224-7984, USA

Lankford, Ray (Athlete, Baseball Player)
1520 Lake Whitney Dr
Windermere, FL 34786-6041, USA

Lannetta, Chris
7422 E 7th Ave Unit 14
Denver, CO 80230-6230, USA

Lanois, Daniel (Actor, Musician)
c/o Staff Member *Paradigm (Monterey)*
404 W Franklin St
Monterey, CA 93940-2303, USA

Ianotta, Howard (Athlete, Basketball Player)
18118 Brookwood Frst
San Antonio, TX 78258-4474, USA

Lanphear, Dan (Athlete, Football Player)
669 Bent Ridge Ln
Barrington, IL 60010-6604, USA

Lansberry, Ross (Athlete, Hockey Player)
32610 Big Springs Rd
Acton, CA 93510-1501

Lansbury, Angela (Actor, Musician)
635 N Bonhill Rd
Los Angeles, CA 90049-2301, USA

Lansbury, David (Actor)
Don Buchwald
6500 Wilshire Blvd Ste 2200
Los Angeles, CA 90048-4942, USA

Lansdale, Joe R
199 County Road 508
Nacogdoches, TX 75961-0170, USA

Lansford, Alex (Athlete, Football Player)
PO Box 905
Lampasas, TX 76550-0007, USA

Lansford, Carney (Athlete, Baseball Player)
2001 Blake St
Denver, CO 80205-2060, USA

Lansford, Jody (Athlete, Baseball Player)
5730 San Lorenzo Dr
San Jose, CA 95123-2967, USA

Lansford, Mike (Athlete, Football Player)
6200 E Canyon Rim Rd Ste 205
Anaheim, CA 92807-4340, USA

Lansing, Mike (Athlete, Baseball Player)
9691 Sun Meadow St
Highlands Ranch, CO 80129-6925, USA

Lansing, Sherry (Producer)
10741 Levico Way
Los Angeles, CA 90077-1918, USA

Lanter, Matt (Actor)
4112 Alcove Ave
Studio City, CA 91604-2347, USA

Lantz, Stu (Athlete, Basketball Player)
5270 Mount Burnham Dr
San Diego, CA 92111-3948, USA

Lanz, David (Musician)
c/o Narada
4650 N Port Washington Rd
Milwaukee, WI 53212-1077, USA

Lanza, Charles (Athlete, Football Player)
19 Snowberry Ct
Cockeysville, MD 21030-1954, USA

Lanza, Suzanne
345 N Maple Dr Ste 397
Beverly Hills, CA 90210-5179

La Oreja de Van Gogh (Music Group)
c/o Staff Member *Sony Music Miami*
605 Lincoln Rd Ste 700
Miami Beach, FL 33139-2901, USA

Laoretti, Larry (Athlete, Golfer)
712 Baytree Dr
Titusville, FL 32780-2310, USA

LaPage, Paul (Governor, Politician)
Office of the Governor
1 State House Sta
Augusta, ME 04333-0001, USA

LaPaglia, Anthony (Actor)
c/o Jennifer Allen *Viewpoint Inc (LA)*
8820 Wilshire Blvd Ste 220
Beverly Hills, CA 90211-2622, USA

LaPaglia, Jonathan
1505 10th St
Santa Monica, CA 90401-2805

Lapaine, Daniel (Actor)
Envision Entertainment
409 Santa Monica Blvd
Santa Monica, CA 90401-2378, USA

Laperriere, Ian (Athlete, Hockey Player)
C A A Sports
2000 Avenue of the Stars Fl 3
Los Angeles, CA 90067-4704, USA

Laperriere, J Jacques H (Athlete, Coach, Hockey Player)
6 Governors Ct
Palm Beach Gardens, FL 33418-7159

Laperrlere, Jacques
New Jersey Devils
165 Mulberry St
Newark, NJ 07102-3607

Lapham, Bill (Athlete, Football Player)
136 S 52nd St
West Des Moines, IA 50265-2895, USA

Lapham, Dave (Athlete, Football Player)
8254 Sunfish Ln
Maineville, OH 45039-8978, USA

Lapine, James E (Director, Writer)
c/o Staff Member *Judi Farkas Management*
926 S Longwood Ave
Los Angeles, CA 90019-1752, USA

Lapira, Liza (Actor)
c/o Eric Nelson *Zero Gravity Management (II)*
9255 W Sunset Blvd Ste 1010
West Hollywood, CA 90069-3307, USA

Lapka, Myron (Athlete, Football Player)
3982 Hemway Ct
Simi Valley, CA 93063-2848, USA

La Placa, Alison (Actor)
c/o Staff Member *Marshak/Zachary Company, The*
8840 Wilshire Blvd Fl 1
Beverly Hills, CA 90211-2606, USA

LaPlaca, Alison (Actor)
1614 Argyle Ave
Los Angeles, CA 90028-6408, USA

LaPlanche, Rosemary (Actor)
13914 Hartsook St
Sherman Oaks, CA 91423-1210, USA

LaPlante, Lynda (Writer)
Random House
1745 Broadway Frnt 3 # B1
New York, NY 10019-4343, USA

Lapoint, Dave (Athlete, Baseball Player)
11704 Stonewood Gate Dr
Riverview, FL 33579-4025, USA

Lapointe, Claude (Athlete, Hockey Player)
105 Runnymede Dr
Lansdale, PA 19446-6366

Lapointe, Martin (Athlete, Hockey Player)
317 Washington St
Saint Paul, MN 55102-1609

Lapointe, Ron (Athlete, Football Player)
940 E Haverford Rd
Bryn Mawr, PA 19010-3845, USA

LaPorte, Danny (Race Car Driver)
949 Via Del Monte
Palos Verdes Estates, CA 90274-1615, USA

Lappalainen, Markku (Musician)
Island Def Jam Records
8920 W Sunset Blvd # 200
West Hollywood, CA 90069-1832, USA

Lappas, Steve (Coach)
Villanova University
Athletic Dept
Villanova, PA 19085, USA

Lappe, Frances Moore (Writer)
989 Market St
San Francisco, CA 94103-1708, USA

Lappin, Peter (Athlete, Hockey Player)
1258 Meadows Rd
Geneva, IL 60134-3214

LaPraed, Ronald (Ron) (Musician)
Management Assoc
1920 Benson Ave
Saint Paul, MN 55116-3214, USA

Lara, Joe (Actor)
c/o Peter Giagni *Peter Giagni Management*
8981 W Sunset Blvd Ste 103
West Hollywood, CA 90069-1850, USA

Laraway, Jack (Athlete, Football Player)
5250 Fox Hollow Dr Apt 530
Naples, FL 34104-5191, USA

Lardner Jr, George (Journalist)
Washington Post
Editorial Dept
1150 15th St NW
Washington, DC 20071-0001, USA

Lardon, Brad (Athlete, Golfer)
17334 Sioux Springs Dr
College Station, TX 77845-4589, USA

Laredo, Ruth (Musician)
I C M Artists
40 W 57th St
New York, NY 10019-4001, USA

Larena, John (Designer)
c/o Staff Member *Mirisch Agency*
8840 Wilshire Blvd Ste 100
Beverly Hills, CA 90211-2606, USA

Laresca, Vincent (Actor)
c/o Brandy Gold *TalentWorks (LA)*
3500 W Olive Ave Ste 1400
Burbank, CA 91505-5512, USA

Larese, York (Athlete, Basketball Player)
30 Revere Beach Pkwy Apt 702
Medford, MA 02155-5163, USA

Large, Storm (Musician)
The Dowd Agency
444 Park Ave S PH
New York, NY 10016-7321, USA

Largent, Steve (Athlete, Football Player)
37420 S 4210 Rd
Inola, OK 74036-5643, USA

Larionov, Igor (Athlete, Hockey Player)
2025 Quarton Rd
Bloomfield Hills, MI 48301-2320

Larish, Jeff (Baseball Player)
26912 N 52nd Gln
Phoenix, AZ 85083-6305

Lark, Maria (Actor)
c/o Staff Member *Frontier Booking International*
1560 Broadway Ste 1110
New York, NY 10036-1537, USA

Larkin, Andy (Athlete, Baseball Player)
2844 E Flower St
Gilbert, AZ 85298-5754, USA

Larkin, Barry (Athlete, Baseball Player)
5410 Osprey Isle Ln
Orlando, FL 32819-4015, USA

Larkin, Barry L (Athlete, Baseball Player, Olympic Athlete)
5410 Osprey Isle Ln
Orlando, FL 32819-4015, USA

Larkin, Gene (Athlete, Baseball Player)
7475 Flying Cloud Dr Apt 556
Eden Prairie, MN 55344-3834, USA

Larkin, Pat (Athlete, Baseball Player)
23400 Canzonet St
Woodland Hills, CA 91367-6013, USA

Larkin, Patty (Musician, Songwriter, Writer)
SRO Artists
6629 University Ave Ste 206
Middleton, WI 53562-3037, USA

Larkin, Sheila
9229 W Sunset Blvd Ste 311
West Hollywood, CA 90069-3403

Larkin, Stephen (Athlete, Baseball Player)
9178 Solon Dr
Cincinnati, OH 45242-4616, USA

Larner, Stevan (Cinematographer)
1209 Ballard Canyon Rd
Solvang, CA 93463-9716, USA

Larocca, Greg (Athlete, Baseball Player)
14 Tinker Rd
Bedford, NH 03110-4429, USA

Laroche, Adam (Athlete, Baseball Player)
1735 E Oak St
Fort Scott, KS 66701-1841, USA

Laroche, Andy
842 195th St
Fort Scott, KS 66701-8790

Laroche, Dave (Athlete, Baseball Player)
842 195th St
Fort Scott, KS 66701-8790, USA

LaRosa, Julius (Musician)
67 Sycamore Ln
Irvington, NY 10533-1933, USA

Larose, Claude (Athlete, Hockey Player)
5060 NW 54th St
Coconut Creek, FL 33073-3713, USA

Larose, Dan (Athlete, Football Player)
4873 N Raymond Rd
Luther, MI 49656-9503, USA

Larose, Guy (Athlete, Hockey Player)
5 Tip Cart Rd
Sutton, MA 01590-4801

Larose, John (Athlete, Baseball Player)
99 Roland St
Cumberland, RI 02864-5515, USA

Larose, Vic (Athlete, Baseball Player)
2908 E Sylvia St
Phoenix, AZ 85032-7135, USA

LaRouche, Lyndon
15820 Round Top Ln
Round Hill, VA 20141

Larouche, Pierre (Athlete, Hockey Player)
1005 Cherry Hill Dr
Presto, PA 15142-1550

LaRouche Jr, Lyndon H (Politician)
18520 Round Top Ln
Round Hill, VA 20141-2052, USA

La Roux (Musician)
c/o Marty Diamond *Paradigm (NY)*
360 Park Ave S Fl 16
New York, NY 10010-1716, USA

Larrieux, Amel (Musician)
Bliss Life
2114 Pico Blvd # B
Santa Monica, CA 90405-1718, USA

Larroquette, John (Actor)
139 Union Jack Mall
Marina Del Rey, CA 90292-7295, USA

Larry, Rentz (Athlete, Football Player)
2 Grove Isle Dr Apt 1504
Miami, FL 33133-4112, USA

Larry, Wendy (Coach)
Old Dominion University
Athletic Dept
Norfolk, VA 23529-0001, USA

Larry Sanitsky, Larry Sanitsky (Producer)
c/o Nancy Josephson *William Morris Endeavor (LA)*
9601 Wilshire Blvd
Beverly Hills, CA 90210-5213, USA

Larsen, Blaine (Musician)
c/o Staff Member *Paradigm (Monterey)*
404 W Franklin St
Monterey, CA 93940-2303, USA

Larsen, Don (Athlete, Baseball Player)
PO Box 2863
Hayden, ID 83835-2863, USA

Larsen, Gary L (Athlete, Football Player)
4317 San Juan St NE
Lacey, WA 98516-6277, USA

Larsen, Larry (Actor)
24680 Road N
Cortez, CO 81321-9302, USA

Larsen, Paul E (Religious Leader)
Evangelical Convenant Church
5101 N Francisco Ave
Chicago, IL 60625-3676, USA

Larsen, Ralph S (Business Person)
Johnson & Johnson
1 Johnson and Johnson Plz
New Brunswick, NJ 08933-0002, USA

Larson, Bill (Athlete, Football Player)
1365 Redwood Dr
Windsor, CO 80550-4603, USA

Larson, Brandon (Athlete, Baseball Player)
8922 Rich Way
San Antonio, TX 78251-2971, USA

Larson, Brie (Actor)
3935 Rhodes Ave
Studio City, CA 91604-2405, USA

Larson, Bruce (Race Car Driver)
PO Box 71
Dauphin, PA 17018-0071, USA

Larson, Dan (Athlete, Baseball Player)
797 Oxen St
Paso Robles, CA 93446-4656, USA

Larson, Darrell
8380 Melrose Ave # 207
West Hollywood, CA 90069-5422

Larson, Gary (Cartoonist)
Universal Press Syndicate
4520 Main St Ste 340
Kansas City, MO 64111-7705, USA

Larson, Gerald (Jerry Lacy) (Actor)
c/o Staff Member *Sutton Barth & Vennari Inc*
5900 Wilshire Blvd Ste 700
Los Angeles, CA 90036-5009, USA

Larson, Greg (Athlete, Football Player)
PO Box 393
Nisswa, MN 56468-0393, USA

Larson, Jack (Actor)
449 N Skyewiay Rd
Los Angeles, CA 90049-2844, USA

Larson, Jay (Musician)
c/o Staff Member *Paradigm (Monterey)*
404 W Franklin St
Monterey, CA 93940-2303, USA

Larson, Jill (Actor)
Innovative Artists
1505 10th St
Santa Monica, CA 90401-2805, USA

Larson, Kent (Adult Film Star)
c/o Staff Member *Diva Central Inc*
7510 W Sunset Blvd Ste 1445
Los Angeles, CA 90046-3408, USA

Larson, Kurt (Athlete, Football Player)
N66W35796 W Spring Hollow Cir
Oconomowoc, WI 53066-6211, USA

Larson, Kyle (Athlete, Football Player)
4809 Summitt Rd
Kearney, NE 68845-1677, USA

Larson, Lance (Athlete, Olympic Athlete, Swimmer)
18592 Medford Ave
Santa Ana, CA 92705-2737, USA

Larson, Lyndon (Athlete, Football Player)
4117 E Encanto St
Mesa, AZ 85205-5121, USA

Larson, Lynn (Athlete, Football Player)
12209 N 66th St
Scottsdale, AZ 85254-4521, USA

Larson, Paul (Athlete, Football Player)
3718 W Harding Rd
Turlock, CA 95380-9217, USA

Larson, Pete (Athlete, Football Player)
3901 N Ridgeview Rd
Arlington, VA 22207-4664, USA

Larson, Peter N (Business Person)
Brunswick Corp
1 N Field Ct
Lake Forest, IL 60045-4811, USA

Larson, Reed (Athlete, Hockey Player)
14334 Fairway Dr
Eden Prairie, MN 55344-1955

Larson, Rick (Congressman, Politician)
108 Cannon Hob
Washington, DC 20515-0914, USA

Larson, Sarah (Model)
c/o Kenya Knight *Nous Model Management*
117 N Robertson Blvd
Los Angeles, CA 90048-3101, USA

Larson, Shana (Producer, Writer)
c/o Lucy Stille *Agency for the Performing Arts (APA-NY)*
360 N Crescent Dr
North Bldg
Beverly Hills, CA 90210-4874, USA

Larson, Ted (Athlete, Football Player)
c/o Anthony J. Agnone *Eastern Athletic Services*
11350 McCormick Rd
Suite 800 - Executive Plaza
Hunt Valley, MD 21031-1002, USA

Larson, William H (Athlete, Football Player)
1365 Redwood Dr
Windsor, CO 80550-4603, USA

Larson, Wolf (Actor)
10600 Holman Ave Apt 1
Los Angeles, CA 90024-5931, USA

Larson-Pessolano, Becky (Athlete, Golfer)
121 Manor Ct
Springfield, MA 01118-2449, USA

Larsson, Dean (Athlete, Golfer)
Advantage International
1751 Pinnacle Dr Ste 1500
Mc Lean, VA 22102-3833, USA

Larter, Al
6100 Wilshire Blvd Ste 1170
Los Angeles, CA 90048-5116

Larter, Ali (Actor)
2501 Astral Dr
Los Angeles, CA 90046-1705, USA

LaRue, Chi Chi (Director, DJ)
c/o Staff Member *Diva Central Inc*
7510 W Sunset Blvd Ste 1445
Los Angeles, CA 90046-3408, USA

LaRue, Eva (Actor, Television Host)
c/o Marv Dauer *Marv Dauer Management*
2236 The Terrace
Los Angeles, CA 90049-1171, USA

La Rue, Florence
4300 Louise Ave
Encino, CA 91316-3916

LaRue, Florence (Actor, Musician)
c/o Konrad Leh *Creative Talent Group*
1900 Avenue of the Stars Ste 2475
Los Angeles, CA 90067-4512, USA

Larue, Jason (Athlete, Baseball Player)
35 Jones Cemetary Rd
Kendalia, TX 78027-1924, USA

Larue, Renee (Adult Film Star)
c/o Staff Member *Atlas Multimedia Inc*
9005 Eton Ave Ste C
Canoga Park, CA 91304-6533, USA

Larussa, Tonv (Baseball Player)
338 Golden Meadow Pl # Pi
Alamo, CA 94507-2711

LaRussa, Tony (Athlete, Baseball Player, Coach)
Tony LaRussa's Animal Rescue Foundation
PO Box 30215
Walnut Creek, CA 94598-9215, USA

LaRusso, Vincent
419 Park Ave S Rm 1009
New York, NY 10016-8410

Larv, Frank (Baseball Player)
11813 Baseball Dr
Northport, AL 35475-4908

Lary, Frank (Athlete, Baseball Player)
11813 Baseball Dr
Northport, AL 35475-4908, USA

Lary, R Yale (Athlete, Football Player)
6366 Lansdale Rd
Fort Worth, TX 76116-1622, USA

LaSalle, Denise (Musician)
CAI Entertainment Agency
PO Box 9267
Jackson, MS 39286-9267, USA

LaSalle, Eriq (Actor, Director)
PO Box 2369
Beverly Hills, CA 90213-2369, USA

Lasardo, Robert (Actor)
c/o Staff Member *SMS Talent*
8383 Wilshire Blvd Ste 230
Beverly Hills, CA 90211-2436, USA

La Scala, Nancy (Actor)
c/o Victor Kruglov *Victor Kruglov Talent Management*
6565 W Sunset Blvd Ste 200
Los Angeles, CA 90028-7219, USA

Lascher, David (Actor)
c/o Staff Member *Vanguard Management Group*
8060 Melrose Ave Fl 4
Los Angeles, CA 90046-7038, USA

Lash, Bill (Skier)
17438 Bothell Way NE Unit C305
Bothell, WA 98011-1965, USA

Lash, Jim (Athlete, Football Player)
597 Van Everett Ave
Akron, OH 44306-2418, USA

Lashar, Tim (Athlete, Football Player)
609 Waterwood Dr
Norman, OK 73072-4368, USA

Lashay, Gia (Adult Film Star)
GL Productions
PO Box 70741
Sunnyvale, CA 94086-0741, USA

Lasher, Fred (Athlete, Baseball Player)
446 Woodland Dr
Strum, WI 54770-7819, USA

Lashley, Nick (Musician)
1034 Garfield Ave
Venice, CA 90291-4935, USA

Lasker, Deedee (Athlete, Golfer)
1665 Chamisal Ct
Carlsbad, CA 92011-5031, USA

Lasker, Greg (Athlete, Football Player)
412 Sturgis Rd
Conway, AR 72034-9261, USA

Las Ketchup (Music Group)
c/o Staff Member *Sony Music Miami*
605 Lincoln Rd Ste 700
Miami Beach, FL 33139-2901, USA

Laskey, Bill (Athlete, Baseball Player)
PO Box 1556
Burlingame, CA 94011-1556, USA

Laskey, Bill (Athlete, Football Player)
PO Box 734
3257 N Manitou Trl
Leland, MI 49654-0734, USA

Laskey, Frank (Athlete, Football Player)
584 Battle Branch Vista Dr
Franklin, NC 28734-8548, USA

Laskoski, Gary (Athlete, Hockey Player)
10 Summit Vw
Goshen, NY 10924-5713

Laskowski, John (Athlete, Basketball Player)
3930 E Stonegate Dr
Bloomington, IN 47401-9800, USA

Lasky, Scott (Sportscaster)
c/o Staff Member *Maxx Sports & Entertainment*
546 5th Ave Fl 6
New York, NY 10036-5000, USA

Laslavic, Jim (Athlete, Football Player)
648 A Ave
Coronado, CA 92118-2205, USA

Lasorda, Tommy (Athlete, Baseball Player, Coach)
1473 W Maxzim Ave
Fullerton, CA 92833-4611, USA

Lasse, Dick (Athlete, Football Player)
111 Windcrest Ct
Beaver Falls, PA 15010-1178, USA

Lasse, Richard S (Athlete, Football Player)
111 Windcrest Ct
Beaver Falls, PA 15010-1178, USA

Lasser, Louise (Actor, Comedian)
200 E 71st St Apt 20C
New York, NY 10021-0472, USA

Lasseter, John (Animator, Director)
c/o Staff Member *Pixar Animation Studios*
1200 Park Ave
Emeryville, CA 94608-3677, USA

Lassetter, Don (Athlete, Baseball Player)
PO Box 326
Lyon, MS 38645-0326, USA

Lassez, Sarah (Actor)
Innovative Artists
1505 10th St
Santa Monica, CA 90401-2805, USA

Lassic, Derrick (Athlete, Football Player)
353 Shawnee Indian Ct
Suwanee, GA 30024, USA

Lassick, Sydney
2734 Bellevue Ave
Los Angeles, CA 90026-3882

Lassiter, Amanda (Basketball Player)
Minnesota Lunx
600 1st Ave N
Target Center
Minneapolis, MN 55403-1400, USA

Lassiter, Ike (Athlete, Football Player)
2812 Rawson St
Oakland, CA 94619-3348, USA

Lassiter, Isaac (Athlete, Football Player)
2812 Rawson St
Oakland, CA 94619-3348, USA

Lassiter, Kwamie (Athlete, Football Player)
1222 W Sunrise Pl
Chandler, AZ 85248-3741, USA

Last Vegas (Music Group)
c/o Ben Epand *10th Street Entertainment (LA)*
700 N San Vicente Blvd Ste G410
West Hollywood, CA 90069-5060, USA

Laswell, Greg (Musician)
c/o Jena Vuylsteke *Vanguard Records*
11400 W Olympic Blvd Ste 1450
Los Angeles, CA 90064-1649, USA

Latarte, Steve (Race Car Driver)
18420 Nantz Rd
Cornelius, NC 28031-8614, USA

Lateef (Music Group, Musician)
c/o Staff Member *Madison House Inc.*
4760 Walnut St Ste 106
Boulder, CO 80301-2561, USA

Latham, Bill (Athlete, Baseball Player)
211 Magnolia St
Trussville, AL 35173-1307, USA

Latham, Chris (Athlete, Baseball Player)
7357 Marbury St
Las Vegas, NV 89166-5261, USA

Latham, Louise (Actor)
300 Hot Springs Rd
Santa Barbara, CA 93108-2037, USA

Latham, Tom (Congressman, Politician)
2217 Rayburn Hob
Washington, DC 20515-4904, USA

Lathan, Sanaa (Actor)
c/o Philip Grenz *ICM Partners (LA)*
10250 Constellation Blvd Fl 7
Los Angeles, CA 90067-6207, USA

Lathan, Stan (Director, Producer, Writer)
c/o Staff Member *Simmons Lathan Media Group*
6100 Wilshire Blvd Ste 1111
Los Angeles, CA 90048-5198, USA

Lathon, Lamar L (Athlete, Football Player)
23 Westpoint Dr
Missouri City, TX 77459-6331, USA

Latifah, Queen (Actor, Musician)
9125 Alto Cedro Dr
Beverly Hills, CA 90210-1800, USA

Latimer, Cody (Athlete, Football Player)
c/o Ed Wasielewski *EMG Sports - PA*
PO Box 22371
Philadelphia, PA 19110-2371, USA

Latimer, Don (Athlete, Football Player)
562 S Kalispell Way
Aurora, CO 80017-2112, USA

Latimore (Musician)
Rodgers Redding
1048 Tattnall St
Macon, GA 31201-1537, USA

Latimore, Joseph
1505 10th St
Santa Monica, CA 90401-2805

Latin, Jerry (Athlete, Football Player)
2312 Clover Ave
Rockford, IL 61102-3412, USA

Latman, Barry (Athlete, Baseball Player)
2726 Shelter Island Dr
P.O. Box 519
San Diego, CA 92106-2731, USA

Laton, Gary (Race Car Driver)
Gary Laton Motorsports
4011 Hands Mill Hwy
York, SC 29745-9647, USA

Latreille, Phil (Athlete, Hockey Player)
360 Park St
Menasha, WI 54952-3428

Lattanzi, Chloe (Musician)
c/o Staff Member *Innovative Artists (NY)*
235 Park Ave S Fl 7
New York, NY 10003-1405, USA

Lattimore, Brian (Athlete, Football Player)
1790 Santa Blas Walk Apt 503
Saint Louis, MO 63138-1950, USA

Lattimore, Jamari (Athlete, Football Player)
c/o Anthony J. Agnone *Eastern Athletic Services*
11350 McCormick Rd
Suite 800 - Executive Plaza
Hunt Valley, MD 21031-1002, USA

Lattimore, Kenny (Actor)
c/o Sara Ramaker *Paradigm (LA)*
360 N Crescent Dr
North Bldg
Beverly Hills, CA 90210-4874, USA

Lattin, David (Athlete, Basketball Player)
8230 Twin Tree Ln
Houston, TX 77071-2918, USA

Lattisaw, Stacy (Musician)
9537 Fort Foote Rd
Ft Washington, MD 20744-5726, USA

Lattlmore, Kenny (Musician)
Rhythm Jazz Entertainment Group
4465 Don Milagro Dr
Los Angeles, CA 90008-2831, USA

Lattner, Johnny (Athlete, Football Player, Heisman Trophy Winner)
1700 Riverwoods Dr Apt 503
Melrose Park, IL 60160-1617, USA

Latzke, Paul (Athlete, Football Player)
232 Spring St
Santa Cruz, CA 95060-2522, USA

Laude, Bill (Athlete, Baseball Player)
662 Franklin Ave
Frankfort, IL 60423-1206, USA

Lauder, Leonard A (Business Person)
Estee Lauder Companies
767 5th Ave Bsmt 1
New York, NY 10153-0003, USA

Lauder, Ronald (Business Person)
Estee Lauder Companies
767 5th Ave Bsmt 1
New York, NY 10153-0003, USA

Laudner, Tim (Athlete, Baseball Player)
PO Box 10
Hamel, MN 55340-0010, USA

Lauen, Michel (Athlete, Hockey Player)
5901 Laurel Ave Apt 130
Minneapolis, MN 55416-1069, USA

Lauer, Andrew (Actor)
3018 3rd St
Santa Monica, CA 90405-5410, USA

Lauer, Andy (Actor)
c/o Andrea Pett-Joseph *Brillstein Entertainment Partners (LA)*
9150 Wilshire Blvd Ste 350
Beverly Hills, CA 90212-3453, USA

Lauer, Bonnie (Athlete, Golfer)
525 Via Laguna Vis
San Luis Obispo, CA 93405-4757, USA

Lauer, Matt (Correspondent)
2301 Deerfield Rd
Sag Harbor, NY 11963-2016, USA

Laufenberg, Brandon (Athlete, Football Player)
5917 Azalea Ln
Dallas, TX 75230-3403, USA

Laughlin, Craig (Athlete, Hockey Player)
2217 Mount Tabor Rd
Gambrills, MD 21054-1801

Laughlin, Craig (Athlete, Hockey Player)
Washington Capitals
627 N Glebe Rd Ste 850
Arlington, VA 22203-2144

Laughlin, John (Actor)
Laughlin Enterprises
13116 Albers St
Sherman Oaks, CA 91401-6002, USA

Laughlin, Teresa (TC) (Actor, Designer)
TC Laughlin Design Group Inc
8 Larchmont Ave
Larchmont, NY 10538-4220, USA

Laughlin, Jr., Mike (Race Car Driver)
Laughlin Racing
114 Pride Dr
Simpsonville, SC 29681-3298, USA

Laukkanen, Janne (Athlete, Hockey Player)
401 Channelside Dr
Tampa, FL 33602-5400, USA

Laundry, LaRon (Athlete, Football Player)
c/o Joel Segal *Lagardere Unlimited (NYC)*
845 United Nations Plz Apt 53A
New York, NY 10017-3536, USA

Lauper, Cyndi (Musician, Songwriter)
c/o Lisa Barbaris *So What Management*
890 W End Ave Apt 1A
New York, NY 10025-3520, USA

Laurance, Ashley (Actor)
c/o Leland LaBarre *Bleu, An Entertainment Company*
5225 Wilshire Blvd Ste 336
Los Angeles, CA 90036-4380, USA

Laurance, Dale (Business Person)
Occidental Petroleum
10889 Wilshire Blvd Fl 10
Los Angeles, CA 90024-4213, USA

Laurance, Matthew (Actor)
1951 Hillcrest Rd
Los Angeles, CA 90068-3116, USA

Laurel, Rich (Athlete, Basketball Player)
706 Antelope Way
Kissimmee, FL 34759-4212, USA

Lauren, Joy (Actor)
c/o Mary Sanders *inMomentum Management*
14622 Ventura Blvd # 778
Sherman Oaks, CA 91403-3600, USA

Lauren, Ralph (Designer, Fashion Designer)
Polo Ralph Lauren Corp
867 Madison Ave
New York, NY 10021-4103, USA

Lauren, Tammy (Actor)
Gage Group
5757 Wilshire Blvd Ste 659
Los Angeles, CA 90036-3682, USA

Laurente, Dennis (Boxer)
c/o Staff Member *Top Rank Inc.*
3908 Howard Hughes Pkwy
#580
Las Vegas, NV 89109, USA

Laurents, Arthur (Writer)
608 Northville Tpke
Riverhead, NY 11901-4717, USA

Laurer, Joanie (Chyna) (Actor, Wrestler)
c/o Mike Esterman *Esterman.Com, LLC*
Prefers to be contacted via email
Baltimore, MD XXXXX, USA

Lauria, Dan (Actor)
c/o Harry Gold *TalentWorks (LA)*
3500 W Olive Ave Ste 1400
Burbank, CA 91505-5512, USA

Lauria, Matt (Actor)
c/o Jillian Roscoe *ID Public Relations (LA)*
7060 Hollywood Blvd Fl 8th
Los Angeles, CA 90028-6021, USA

Laurie, Greg (Religious Leader)
Harvest Christian Fellowship Church
6115 Arlington Ave
Riverside, CA 92504-1999, USA

Laurie, Harry (Athlete, Basketball Player)
540 Bramhall Ave Apt 3
Jersey City, NJ 07304-2323, USA

Laurie, Piper (Actor)
c/o Neil Bagg *Don Buchwald & Associates (LA)*
6500 Wilshire Blvd Ste 2200
Los Angeles, CA 90048-4942, USA

Laurinaitis, James (Athlete, Football Player)
11 Sherwyn Ln
Saint Louis, MO 63141-7821, USA

Laurita, Jacqueline (Reality Star)
322 Water View Dr
Franklin Lakes, NJ 07417-2954, USA

Lauro, Lindore (Athlete, Football Player)
111 Scott Dr
New Castle, PA 16105-3101, USA

Laut, David (Athlete, Olympic Athlete)
421 Eastwood Dr
Oxnard, CA 93030-4014, USA

Lautenschlaeger, Fred (Athlete, Football Player)
612 Breton Pl
Arnold, MD 21012-1536, USA

Lauterstein, Alex (DJ)
c/o Staff Member *Diva Central Inc*
7510 W Sunset Blvd Ste 1445
Los Angeles, CA 90046-3408, USA

Lautner, Taylor (Actor)
c/o Peter Kiernan *Management 360*
9111 Wilshire Blvd
Beverly Hills, CA 90210-5508, USA

Lauzerique, George (Athlete, Baseball Player)
601 Oleaster Ave
Wellington, FL 33414-8197, USA

Lavalais, Chad (Athlete, Football Player)
3460 Tupelo Trl
Auburn, GA 30011-4601, USA

Lavallee, Kevin (Athlete, Hockey Player)
1210 Butterfly Ct
Marco Island, FL 34145-2308

Lavalliere, Mike (Athlete, Baseball Player)
216 81st St W
Bradenton, FL 34209-2154, USA

Lavarre, Mark
2028 Walters Ave
Northbrook, IL 60062-4526

Lavelle, Gary (Athlete, Baseball Player)
1100 Worthington Ct
Virginia Beach, VA 23464-5855, USA

Lavelle, James (DJ, Musician)
c/o Joel Zimmerman *William Morris Endeavor (NY)*
1325 Avenue of the Americas
New York, NY 10019-6026, USA

Lavender, Brian (Athlete, Hockey Player)
11585 Decatur St Apt C
Denver, CO 80234-3567

Lavender, Jay (Producer)
c/o Staff Member *Principato/Young Management (LA)*
9465 Wilshire Blvd Ste 900
Beverly Hills, CA 90212-2608, USA

Lavender, Jody (Race Car Driver)
Jody Lavender Racing
PO Box 1527
Hartsville, SC 29551-1527, USA

Lavender, Joseph (Athlete, Football Player)
1215 Alma St
Glendale, CA 91202-2014, USA

Laver, Rodney G (Rod) (Tennis Player)
PO Box 4798
Hilton Head Island, SC 29938-4798, USA

Lavery, Sean (Dancer)
New York City Ballet
Lincoln Center Plaza
New York, NY 10023, USA

Lavigne, Avril (Musician, Songwriter)
c/o Nicole Perna *Baker Winokur Ryder Public Relations (BWR-LA)*
9100 Wilshire Blvd Ste 500
West Tower Suite 500
Beverly Hills, CA 90212-3426, USA

Lavin, Bernice E (Business Person)
Alberto-Culver
800 Sylvan Ave
Englewood Cliffs, NJ 07632-3201, USA

Lavin, Leonard H (Business Person)
Alberto-Culver
800 Sylvan Ave
Englewood Cliffs, NJ 07632-3201, USA

Lavin, Linda (Actor, Musician)
c/o Staff Member *Lavin Entertainment Group*
200 Central Park S Apt 8N
New York, NY 10019-1595, USA

Lavin, TJ (Athlete, Television Host)
c/o Staff Member *Dragon Talent*
8444 Wilshire Blvd PH
Beverly Hills, CA 90211-3200, USA

Laviolette, Peter (Athlete, Hockey Player)
Philadelphia Flyers
3601 S Broad St Ste 2
Philadelphia, PA 19148-5297

Laviolette, Peter (Athlete, Coach, Hockey Player, Olympic Athlete)
7000 Firehouse Rd
Longboat Key, FL 34228-1138

Lavoie, Dominic (Athlete, Hockey Player)
5081 Garlenda Dr
El Dorado Hills, CA 95762-5456

Lavon, Peaches (Musician)
c/o Janice Gaffney *Butterscotch Castle*
535 Geary St Apt 612
San Francisco, CA 94102-1635, USA

LaVoo, George (Director, Producer, Writer)
c/o Jon Rubinstein *Authentic Talent and Literary Management*
20 Jay St Ste M17
Brooklyn, NY 11201-8300, USA

LaVorgna, Adam (Actor)
c/o Beverly Strong *Strong Management*
9350 Wilshire Blvd Ste 224
Beverly Hills, CA 90212-3204, USA

Lavoy, Robert (Athlete, Basketball Player)
613 Wood Rd
Seffner, FL 33584-5446, USA

Law, Jude (Actor)
c/o Rick Yorn *LBI Entertainment*
2000 Avenue of the Stars
Floor 3, North Tower
Los Angeles, CA 90067-4700, USA

Law, Ron (Baseball Player)
Cleveland Indians
3 Mountainview Rd
Greenwood Village, CO 80111-1736,
USA

Law, Rudy (Athlete, Baseball Player)
JD Legends Promotions
PO Box 107
Hawthorne, CA 90251-0107, USA

Law, Ty (Athlete, Football Player)
10862 Hawks Vista St
Plantation, FL 33324-8206, USA

Law, Vance (Athlete, Baseball Player)
1547 W 1970 N
Provo, UT 84604-4708, USA

Law, Vern (Athlete, Baseball Player)
1718 N 1050 W
Provo, UT 84604-1159, USA

Lawanson, Ruth (Athlete, Olympic
Athlete, Volleyball Player)
8081 Highland Flume Cir
Reno, NV 89523-8985, USA

Lawford, Christopher (Actor)
c/o Christine Holder *Zero Gravity
Management (II)*
9255 W Sunset Blvd Ste 1010
West Hollywood, CA 90069-3307, USA

Lawler, Jerry (Athlete, Wrestler)
415 Saint Nick Dr
Memphis, TN 38117-4115, USA

Lawler, Steve (DJ, Musician)
c/o Joel Zimmerman *William Morris
Endeavor (NY)*
1325 Avenue of the Americas
New York, NY 10019-6026, USA

Lawless, Burton (Athlete, Football Player)
2035 Oak Glen Dr
Mc Gregor, TX 76657-3455, USA

Lawless, Lucy (Actor)
Lawlessinc
16030 Ventura Blvd Ste 380
Encino, CA 91436-2778, USA

Lawless, Paul
4231 N Winfield Scott Plz Ste 1
Scottsdale, AZ 85251-3912

Lawless, Renee (Actor)
c/o Siri Garber *Platform Public Relations*
2666 N Beachwood Dr
Los Angeles, CA 90068-2308, USA

Lawless, Tom (Athlete, Baseball Player)
734 E Port Ave Attn Managersofc
Corpus Christi, TX 78401-1006, USA

Lawrence, Andrew (Actor)
c/o Staff Member *Kass Management*
501 Santa Monica Blvd Ste 604
Santa Monica, CA 90401-2467, USA

Lawrence, Bill (Writer)
c/o Staff Member *Broder Webb Chervin
Silbermann Agency, The (BWCS)*
10250 Constellation Blvd
Los Angeles, CA 90067-6200, USA

Lawrence, Braxton Janice (Basketball
Player)
Cleveland Rockers
1 Center Ct
Gund Arena
Cleveland, OH 44115-4001, USA

Lawrence, Brian (Athlete, Baseball Player)
3379 County Rd 1132
Linden, TX 75563, USA

Lawrence, Carol (Actor)
12337 Ridge Cir
Los Angeles, CA 90049-1183, USA

Lawrence, David Jr (Publisher)
Miami Herald
PO Box 3028
Livonia, MI 48151-3028, USA

Lawrence, Don (Athlete, Football Player)
12620 Cedar St
Leawood, KS 66209-3167, USA

Lawrence, Francis (Actor)
c/o Gretchen Rush *Hansen, Jacobson,
Teller, Hoberman, Newman, Warren &
Richman*
450 N Roxbury Dr Fl 8
Beverly Hills, CA 90210-4222, USA

Lawrence, Francis (Director)
c/o Erwin Stoff *3 Arts Entertainment (LA)*
9460 Wilshire Blvd Fl 7
Beverly Hills, CA 90212-2713, USA

Lawrence, Henry (Athlete, Football
Player)
2110 2nd Ave E
Palmetto, FL 34221-3310, USA

Lawrence, Jennifer (Actor)
PO Box 6509
Louisville, KY 40206-0509, USA

Lawrence, Joe (Athlete, Baseball Player)
4358 Poydras St
Lake Charles, LA 70605-4400, USA

Lawrence, Joey (Actor)
4521 Park Marbella
Calabasas, CA 91302-2535, USA

Lawrence, Kent (Athlete, Football Player)
150 Charter Ct
Athens, GA 30605-4628, USA

Lawrence, Linda
4926 Commonwealth Ave
La Canada Flintridge, CA 91011-2514

Lawrence, Mark (Athlete, Hockey Player)
49754 Churchill St
Mattawan, MI 49071-7805

Lawrence, Martin (Actor, Comedian)
15999 High Knoll Rd
Encino, CA 91436-3426, USA

Lawrence, Matthew (Actor)
c/o Robbie Kass *Kass Management*
501 Santa Monica Blvd Ste 604
Santa Monica, CA 90401-2467, USA

Lawrence, Nigel (Musician)
c/o Staff Member *Paradigm (Monterey)*
404 W Franklin St
Monterey, CA 93940-2303, USA

Lawrence, Rolland (Athlete, Football
Player)
317 Sugarcreek Dr
Franklin, PA 16323-5641, USA

Lawrence, Russell (Actor)
7800 Beverly Blvd # 3305
Los Angeles, CA 90036-2112

Lawrence, Sean (Athlete, Baseball Player)
336 S Poplar Ave
Elmhurst, IL 60126-3565, USA

Lawrence, Sharon (Actor, Producer)
c/o David Lust *Rogers & Cowan PR (LA)*
8687 Melrose Ave Ste 7
West Hollywood, CA 90069-5721, USA

Lawrence, Steve (Musician)
944 Pinehurst Dr
Las Vegas, NV 89109-1569, USA

Lawrence, Tracy (Musician, Songwriter)
c/o Greg Oswald *William Morris
Endeavor (Nashville)*
1600 Division St Ste 300
Nashville, TN 37203-2755, USA

Lawrence, Vicki (Actor, Musician)
6000 Lido Ln
Long Beach, CA 90803-4105, USA

Lawrence, Wendy B (Astronaut)
National Reconnaissance Office
14675 Lee Rd
Chantilly, VA 20151-1715, USA

Lawrence, Wendy B Captain (Astronaut)
6225 Argyle St
Ferndale, WA 98248-8995, USA

Laws, Hubert
1078 S Ogden Dr
Los Angeles, CA 90019-6501

Laws, Ronnie (Musician)
c/o Staff Member *Pyramid Entertainment
Group*
377 Rector Pl Apt 21A
New York, NY 10280-1439, USA

Lawson, Ana Maria (Beauty Pageant
Winner)
PO Box 59064
Potomac, MD 20859-9064, USA

Lawson, Bianca (Actor)
c/o Tiffany Kuzon *Evolution Entertainment
(LA)*
901 N Highland Ave
Los Angeles, CA 90038-2412, USA

Lawson, Doyle (Musician)
c/o Staff Member *Paradigm (Monterey)*
404 W Franklin St
Monterey, CA 93940-2303, USA

Lawson, Josh (Actor, Writer)
c/o Gabriel Cohen *Management 360*
9111 Wilshire Blvd
Beverly Hills, CA 90210-5508, USA

Lawson, Kara (Basketball Player)
c/o Staff Member *Sacramento Monarchs*
1 Sports Pkwy
Arco Arena
Sacramento, CA 95834-2300, USA

Lawson, Ken (Ken L) (Actor)
c/o Staff Member *Agency West
Entertainment*
6255 W Sunset Blvd Ste 908
Los Angeles, CA 90028-7410, USA

Lawson, Maggie (Actor)
2401 Canyon Dr
Los Angeles, CA 90068-2413, USA

Lawson, Manny (Athlete, Football Player)
c/o Neil Schwartz *Schwartz & Feinsod*
contact via telephone or email
White Plains, NY 10603

Lawson, Nevin (Athlete, Football Player)
c/o Jordan Woy *Willis and Woy
Management*
3030 Olive St Ste 520
Dallas, TX 75219-7629, USA

Lawson, Richard (Actor)
8840 Wilshire Blvd # 200
Beverly Hills, CA 90211-2606, USA

Lawson, Steve (Athlete, Baseball Player)
PO Box 5630
Brookings, OR 97415-0120, USA

Lawson, Ty
c/o Ashley Smith Becker *Relativity Sports
(LA)*
9242 Beverly Blvd Ste 300
Beverly Hills, CA 90210-3728, USA

Lawson, William (Athlete, Baseball Player)
8800 E McClellan St
Tucson, AZ 85710-4419, USA

Lawston, Marlene (Actor)
c/o Victoria Kress *Don Buchwald &
Associates (NY)*
10 E 44th St Frnt 1
New York, NY 10017-3654, USA

Lawton, Brian (Athlete, Hockey Player)
5012 Oak Bend Ln
Minneapolis, MN 55436-1167

Lawton, Jonathan (J.F.) (Writer)
c/o Sara Bottfeld *Industry Entertainment*
955 Carrillo Dr Ste 300
Los Angeles, CA 90048-5400, USA

Lawton, Marcus (Athlete, Baseball Player)
15354 Dellwood Cv
Gulfport, MS 39503-2718, USA

Lawton, Mary (Cartoonist)
Chronicle Features
901 Mission St
San Francisco, CA 94103-2905, USA

Lawton, Matthew (Matt) (Athlete,
Baseball Player)
27264 Bethel Rd
Saucier, MS 39574-9020, USA

Lax, John (Athlete, Hockey Player)
3 Greendale Ln
Harwich, MA 02645, USA

Laxalt, Paul (Ex-Governor, Ex-Senator,
Politician)
750 9th St NW Ste 750
#750
Washington, DC 20001-4589, USA

Laxdal, Derek
4147 E Aphrodite Dr
Boise, ID 83716-7059

Laxton, Bill (Athlete, Baseball Player)
261 Mansion Ave
Audubon, NJ 08106-1529, USA

Laxton, Brett (Athlete, Baseball Player)
13216 Montrose South Dr
Denham Springs, LA 70726-7447, USA

Laxton, Gordie (Athlete, Hockey Player)
2843 Big Timber Dr NE
Grand Rapids, MI 49525-3018

Layden, Frank (Basketball Coach, Coach)
241 N Vine St Apt 1204W
Salt Lake City, UT 84103-1938, USA

Layman, Jason (Athlete, Football Player)
163 New Center Rd
Sevierville, TN 37876-2167, USA

Layne, Jerry (Athlete, Baseball Player)
2323 Cypress Gardens Blvd
Winter Haven, FL 33884-2120, USA

Layne, Shontelle (Musician)
c/o Carl Sturken *SRC - Street Records
Corporation*
Universal - Motown
1755 Broadway New Media
New York, NY 10019, USA

Layton, Dennis (Athlete, Basketball
Player)
872 S 14th St
Newark, NJ 07108-1320, USA

Lazar, Danny (Athlete, Baseball Player)
8444 Oakwood Ave
Munster, IN 46321-1915, USA

Lazar, Laurence (Religious Leader)
Romanian Orthodox Episcopate
2522 Grey Tower Rd
Jackson, MI 49201-9120, USA

Lazard, Justin (Actor)
9350 Wilshire Blvd Ste 324
Beverly Hills, CA 90212-3206

Lazaro, Jeff (Athlete, Hockey Player)
6422 Memphis St
New Orleans, LA 70124-3151

Lazaroff, Barbara
805 N Sierra Dr
Beverly Hills, CA 90210-2644

Lazarus, Lisa (Actor, Beauty Pageant
Winner)
c/o Mike Esterman *Esterman.Com, LLC*
Prefers to be contacted via email
Baltimore, MD XXXXX, USA

Lazarus, Mell (Cartoonist)
Creators Syndicate
737 3rd St
Hermosa Beach, CA 90254-4714, USA

Lazarus, Shelly (Business Person)
Ogilvy & Mather Worldwide
309 W 49th St
New York, NY 10019-7316, USA

Lazenby, George (Actor)
c/o Staff Member *Hervey/Grimes Talent
Agency*
3002 Midvale Ave Ste 206
Los Angeles, CA 90034-3418, USA

Lazetich, Bill (Athlete, Football Player)
3840 Rimrock Rd Apt 2100
Billings, MT 59102-0153, USA

Lazetich, Pete (Athlete, Football Player)
185 Martin St
Reno, NV 89509-2827, USA

Lazier, Buddy (Race Car Driver)
Dreyer & Reinbold Racing
9375 Whitley Dr
Indianapolis, IN 46240-1349, USA

Lazier, Jacques (Race Car Driver)
5485 Carriage Pl
Rancho Cucamonga, CA 91737-1801,
USA

Lazier, Robert (Buddy) (Race Car Driver)
130 Gasoline Aly
Indianapolis, IN 46222-3965, USA

Lazlo, Viktor (Actor)
56 Rue De Lisbonne
Paris, FR F-750

Lazorko, Jack (Athlete, Baseball Player)
1360 Meandering Way
Rockwall, TX 75087-2309, USA

Ibbetson, Bruce (Athlete, Olympic
Athlete, Rower)
424 San Bernardino Ave
Newport Beach, CA 92663-4811, USA

L. Berman, Howard (Congressman,
Politician)
2221 Rayburn Hob
Washington, DC 20515-0528, USA

L. Boswell, Leonard (Congressman,
Politician)
1026 Longworth Hob
Washington, DC 20515-4319, USA

L. Braley, Bruce (Congressman, Politician)
1727 Longworth Hob
Washington, DC 20515-1007, USA

L. Delauro, Rosa (Congressman,
Politician)
2413 Rayburn Hob
Washington, DC 20515-0512, USA

Le, Cung (Actor)
c/o Scott Karp *The Syndicate*
10203 Santa Monica Blvd Fl 5
Los Angeles, CA 90067-6416, USA

Leabu, Tristan Lake (Actor)
LA Talent
7700 W Sunset Blvd Ste 203
C/O Tracy Dwyer
Los Angeles, CA 90046-3913, USA

Leach, Brent
150 Pleasant Grove Dr
Brandon, MS 39042-2617

Leach, Jalal (Athlete, Baseball Player)
1855 Trinity Way
West Sacramento, CA 95691-5194, USA

Leach, Reggie (Athlete, Hockey Player)
906 Clydesdale Dr
Bear, DE 19701-2205

Leach, Rick (Athlete, Baseball Player)
593 Layman Creek Cir
Grand Blanc, MI 48439-1384, USA

Leach, Robin (Producer, Television Host)
c/o James Weir *Anderson Group Public
Relations*
8060 Melrose Ave Fl 4
Los Angeles, CA 90046-7038, USA

Leach, Sheryl (Animator)
Lyons Group
300 E Bethany Rd
Allen, TX 75002, USA

Leach, Steve (Athlete, Hockey Player,
Olympic Athlete)
21 Goodrich Rd
Wolfeboro, NH 03894-4225

Leach, Terry (Athlete, Baseball Player)
2135 SW Locks Rd
Stuart, FL 34997-7011, USA

Leachman, Cloris (Actor)
c/o Juliet Green *Juliet Green Management*
9025 Wilshire Blvd Ste 400
Beverly Hills, CA 90211-1828, USA

Leadbetter, Kelly (Athlete, Golfer)
14729 Augustine Rd
Orlando, FL 32832-6520, USA

Leadon, Bernie (Musician)
2000 Glen Echo Rd Ste 105
Nashville, TN 37215-2857, USA

Leaf, Ryan (Athlete, Football Player)
1020 35th Ave NE
Great Falls, MT 59404-1210, USA

League, Brandon (Athlete, Baseball
Player)
72385 Lake Heather Heights Ct
Dunedin, FL 34698, USA

Leah, Rachelle (Actor, Athlete)
c/o Ivo Fischer *William Morris Endeavor
(LA)*
9601 Wilshire Blvd
Beverly Hills, CA 90210-5213, USA

Leahy, Bob (Athlete, Football Player)
2701 Rosedale Dr
Monroe, LA 71201-3068, USA

Leahy, Gerry (Athlete, Football Player)
5129 Oakridge Dr
Beaverton, MI 48612-8591, USA

Leahy, Pat (Athlete, Hockey Player)
1 Bristol Dr
Duxbury, MA 02332-4117

Leahy, Patrick (Politician, Senator)
31 Green Acres Dr
Burlington, VT 05408-2415, USA

Leak, Jennifer (Actor)
James D'Auria Associates
PO Box 2219
Amagansett, NY 11930-2219, USA

Leak, Justice (Actor)
c/o Staff Member *People Store*
645 Lambert Dr NE
Atlanta, GA 30324-4125, USA

Leake, Brett (Comedian)
3561 Leatherwood Ln
Maidens, VA 23102-2025, USA

Leakes, NeNe (Actor, Reality Star)
c/o Steven Grossman *Untitled
Entertainment (LA)*
350 S Beverly Dr Ste 200
Beverly Hills, CA 90212-4819, USA

Leaks, Manny (Athlete, Basketball Player)
9912 North Blvd
Cleveland, OH 44108-3430, USA

Leaks Jr, Roosevelt (Athlete, Football
Player)
11525 Glen Falloch Ct
Austin, TX 78754-5807, USA

Leal, Sharon (Actor, Musician)
c/o Scott Wexler *Brillstein Entertainment
Partners (LA)*
9150 Wilshire Blvd Ste 350
Beverly Hills, CA 90212-3453, USA

Leanderson, Matthew (Athlete, Olympic
Athlete, Rower)
1301 N Highlands Pkwy Apt 110
Tacoma, WA 98406-2182, USA

LeAnn, Summer (Actor)
c/o Rebecca Wood *Triple Threat*
7070 W Sunset Blvd Ste 126
Los Angeles, CA 90028-7521, USA

Lear, Harold (Athlete, Basketball Player)
8960 E Gail Rd
Scottsdale, AZ 85260-6146, USA

Lear, Norman (Director, Producer, Writer)
c/o Staff Member *Act III Communications*
100 N Crescent Dr Ste 120
Beverly Hills, CA 90210-5427, USA

Learned, Michael (Actor)
1600 N Beverly Dr
Beverly Hills, CA 90210-2316, USA

Leary, Denis (Actor, Comedian, Producer)
c/o Staff Member *Apostle Pictures*
568 Broadway Rm 601
New York, NY 10012-3260, USA

Leary, Ronald (Athlete, Football Player)
c/o Adisa P. Bakari *Dow Lohnes PLLC*
1299 Pennsylvania Ave NW Ste 700
Washington, DC 20004-2431, USA

Leary, Tim (Athlete, Baseball Player)
2461 Santa Monica Blvd Ste D
Santa Monica, CA 90404-2137, USA

Leatherdale, Douglas W (Business Person)
Saint Paul Companies
385 Washington St
Saint Paul, MN 55102-1396, USA

Leavell, Allen (Athlete, Basketball Player)
7007 Windy Pines Dr
Spring, TX 77379-4733, USA

Leavell, Chuck (Musician)
Charlane Plantation
665 Charlane Dr
Dry Branch, GA 31020-5256, USA

Leavelle, James
5701 Drexel Dr
Garland, TX 75043-5417, USA

Leavenworth, Scotty (Actor)
c/o Susan Curtis *Curtis Talent
Management*
9607 Arby Dr
Beverly Hills, CA 90210-1202, USA

Leaves (Music Group)
c/o Staff Member *Paradigm (Monterey)*
404 W Franklin St
Monterey, CA 93940-2303, USA

Leavitt, Allan (Athlete, Football Player)
2261 Royal Fern Ln S
Jacksonville, FL 32223-1875, USA

Leavitt, Michael O (Ex-Governor,
Politician)
Leavitt Partners
229 S Main St
Ste 2300
Salt Lake City, UT 84111-2203, USA

Leavitt, Phil (Musician)
GEMS
PO Box 1031
Montrose, CA 91021-1031, USA

Leavy, Jon (Race Car Driver)
Leavy Racing Enterprises
7700 NW 37th Ave
Miami, FL 33147-4423, USA

LeBaron, Edward W (Eddie) Jr (Athlete,
Football Player)
7524 Pineridge Ln
Fair Oaks, CA 95628-4854, USA

Lebda, Brett (Athlete, Hockey Player)
557 Chatham Cir
Buffalo Grove, IL 60089-3343

LeBeau, Becky
9461 Charleville Blvd # 602
Beverly Hills, CA 90212-3017

LeBeau, C Richard (Dick) (Athlete,
Coach, Football Player)
10405 Stone Ct
Montgomery, OH 45242-5128, USA

LeBeauf, Sabrina (Actor)
735 Kappock St Apt 6F
Bronx, NY 10463-4629, USA

LeBel, B Harper (Athlete, Football Player)
3379 Scadlock Ln
Sherman Oaks, CA 91403-4914, USA

Leber, Ben (Athlete, Football Player)
5 Bridge Ln
Minneapolis, MN 55424-1224, USA

LeBlanc, Christian LeBlanc (Actor)
c/o Staff Member *The Young and The
Restless*
7800 Beverly Blvd Ste 3305
Los Angeles, CA 90036-2112, USA

LeBlanc, Jean-Paul (Athlete, Hockey
Player)
120 Gadwall Ln
Manlius, NY 13104-9679

LeBlanc, Matt (Actor)
c/o Cindy Guagenti *Baker Winokur Ryder Public Relations (BWR-LA)*
9100 Wilshire Blvd Ste 500
West Tower Suite 500
Beverly Hills, CA 90212-3426, USA

Leblanc, Ray (Athlete, Hockey Player)
3070 19th Pi SW
Largo, FL 33774

LeBlanc, Wade (Baseball Player)
1477 Mary Carla Ln
Lake Charles, LA 70605-7196

Lebo, Jeff (Athlete, Basketball Player)
500 Hidden Lake Way
Santa Rosa Beach, FL 32459-0200, USA

LeBoeuf, Raymond W (Business Person)
PPG Industries
1 Ppg Pl Ste 800
Pittsburgh, PA 15222-5432, USA

Le Bon, Charlotte (Actor)
c/o Ali Benmohamed *United Talent Agency (UTA-LA)*
9336 Civic Center Dr
Beverly Hills, CA 90210-3604, USA

Leboutillier, Peter (Athlete, Hockey Player)
35 Wandsworth Bridge Way
Lutherville Timonium, MD 21093-3963

Lebowitz, Fran (Writer)
Random House
1745 Broadway Frnt 3 # B1
New York, NY 10019-4343, USA

LeBrock, Kelly (Actor, Model)
Bartels Co
PO Box 57593
Sherman Oaks, CA 91413-2593, USA

Lebron, Juan (Baseball Player)
Bowman
PO Box 242
Arroyo, PR 00714-0242, USA

Lecaine, Bill (Athlete, Hockey Player)
5078 Stonecrop Cir
Castle Rock, CO 80109-8493

Lecause, Carl (Horse Racer)
124 Asbury Ave
Freehold, NJ 07728-8187, USA

Lechler, Shane (Athlete, Football Player)
2115 Countryshire Ln
Richmond, TX 77406-3192, USA

Lechner, Ed (Athlete, Football Player)
6305 Burnham Cir Apt 122
Inver Grove Heights, MN 55076-1665, USA

Lechter, Sharon L (Writer)
Cashflow Technologies
4330 N Civic Center Plz Ste 100
Scottsdale, AZ 85251-3529, USA

Leckey, Nick (Athlete, Football Player)
302 Terrace Trl W
Lake Quivira, KS 66217-8697, USA

Leckner, Eric (Athlete, Basketball Player)
608 27th St
Manhattan Beach, CA 90266-2231, USA

Leckonby, William (Athlete, Football Player)
PO Box 1006
Bethlehem, PA 18016-1006, USA

LeClair, James M (Jim) (Athlete, Football Player)
32 4th Ave NE
Mayville, ND 58257-1226, USA

Leclair, Jim (Athlete, Football Player)
600 Plymouth Way
Burlingame, CA 94010-2733, USA

Le Clair, John (Athlete, Hockey Player)
208 Turnbridge Cir
Haverford, PA 19041, USA

Leclair, John (Athlete, Hockey Player, Olympic Athlete)
108 Tunbridge Cir
Haverford, PA 19041-1058

Leclaire, Pascal (Athlete, Hockey Player)
250 Daniel Burnham Sq
Square #250
Columbus, OH 43215-2689, USA

LeClerc, Jean (Actor)
19 W 44th St Ste 1500
New York, NY 10036-6101, USA

Leclerc, Katie (Actor)
c/o Stephanie Moy *Luber Roklin Management*
5815 W Sunset Blvd Ste 206
Los Angeles, CA 90028-6481, USA

Leclerc, Mike (Athlete, Hockey Player)
473 Abbie Way
Costa Mesa, CA 92627-3162

Leclerc, Roger (Athlete, Football Player)
257 Elm St
Agawam, MA 01001-2444, USA

LeClere, Jennifer
5601 Navigation Blvd
Houston, TX 77011-1105

Lecomte, Benoit (Swimmer)
Cross Atlantic Swimming Challenge
3005 S Lamar Blvd # D109-353
Austin, TX 78704-8864, USA

Lecount, Terry (Athlete, Football Player)
1288 Branchfield Ct
Riverdale, GA 30296-2148, USA

Lecroy, Matt (Athlete, Baseball Player, Olympic Athlete)
PO Box 2148
Woodbridge, VA 22195-2148, USA

Ledbetter, Monte (Athlete, Football Player)
340 Sawgrass Dr
Valdosta, GA 31602-1477, USA

Ledee, Ricky (Athlete, Baseball Player)
PO Box 22024
Hilton Head, SC 29925-2024, USA

Leder, Mimi (Director)
c/o Sara Bottfeld *Industry Entertainment*
955 Carrillo Dr Ste 300
Los Angeles, CA 90048-5400, USA

Ledesma, Aaron (Athlete, Baseball Player)
13820 Cherry Creek Dr
Charleston, SC ?941, USA

Ledet, Joshua (Musician)
c/o Staff Member *19 Entertainment (LA)*
9000 W Sunset Blvd Ste 1574
West Hollywood, CA 90069-5817, USA

Ledford, Judith
11365 Ventura Blvd Ste 100
Studio City, CA 91604-3148

Ledingham, Walt (Athlete, Hockey Player)
5421 Glenwood St
Duluth, MN 55804-1333, USA

Leduc, Bob (Athlete, Hockey Player)
385 Buxton St
Harrisville, RI 02830-1704

Leduc-Alverson, Noella (Athlete, Baseball Player, Commentator)
5 Leonard Ave
Leonardo, NJ 07737-1536, USA

Ledyard, Courtney (Athlete, Football Player)
419 Miller Ave
Freeport, NY 11520-6112, USA

Ledyard, Grant (Athlete, Hockey Player)
5072 Old Goodrich Rd
Clarence, NY 14031-1515

Lee, Alexandra (Actor)
c/o Staff Member *Loeb & Loeb (Office 1)*
10100 Santa Monica Blvd Ste 2200
Los Angeles, CA 90067-4120, USA

Lee, Amy (Musician)
135 Joralemon St
Brooklyn, NY 11201-4007, USA

Lee, Ang (Director, Producer, Writer)
206 Hommocks Rd
Larchmont, NY 10538-3915, USA

Lee, Anthonia W (Amp) (Athlete, Football Player)
990 Brickyard Rd
Chipley, FL 32428-4346, USA

Lee, Barbara (Congressman, Politician)
2267 Rayburn Hob
Washington, DC 20515-4202, USA

Lee, Beverly (Musician)
Bevi Corp
PO Box 100
Clifton, NJ 07015-0100, USA

Lee, Bill (Athlete, Baseball Player)
305 Common View Dr
Craftsbury, VT 05826-9779, USA

Lee, Blake (Actor)
c/o Eric Kranzler *Management 360*
9111 Wilshire Blvd
Beverly Hills, CA 90210-5508, USA

Lee, Bobby (Actor)
c/o Staff Member *Gersh (LA)*
9465 Wilshire Blvd Ste 600
Beverly Hills, CA 90212-2605, USA

Lee, Bracken (Politician)
PO Box 58371
Salt Lake City, UT 84158-0371, USA

Lee, Brandon (Adult Film Star)
c/o Staff Member *Diva Central Inc*
7510 W Sunset Blvd Ste 1445
Los Angeles, CA 90046-3408, USA

Lee, Brenda (Musician)
306 Elberta St
Nashville, TN 37210-4930, USA

Lee, Briana (Adult Film Star)
8033 W Sunset Blvd # 851
Los Angeles, CA 90046-2401, USA

Lee, Butch (Athlete, Basketball Player)
2045 Story Ave Apt 3P
Bronx, NY 10473-2030, USA

Lee, Carl (Athlete, Football Player)
1 Stonegate Dr
Hurricane, WV 25526-9217, USA

Lee, Carlos (Athlete, Baseball Player)
1400 N 11th Ave
Melrose Park, IL 60160-3524, USA

Lee, Chang-Rae (Writer)
International Creative Mgmt
40 W 57th St Fl 5
New York, NY 10019-4001, USA

Lee, Charles R (Business Person)
GTE Corp
1255 Corporate Dr
Irving, TX 75038-2562, USA

Lee, Christopher (Congressman, Politician)
1711 Longworth Hob
Washington, DC 20515-1201, USA

Lee, Cliff (Athlete, Baseball Player)
c/o Darek Braunecker *Braunecker Sports Counseling*
226 Trelon Cir
Little Rock, AR 72223-3920, USA

Lee, Clyde (Athlete, Basketball Player)
1118 Crater Hill Dr
Nashville, TN 37215-4510, USA

Lee, Corey (Athlete, Baseball Player)
278 Lancashire Run
Smithfield, NC 27577-8025, USA

Lee, C.S. (Actor, Director)
c/o Andrew Tetenbaum *ATA Management*
12 Desbrosses St
New York, NY 10013-1704, USA

Lee, David (Actor)
c/o Paula Rosenberg *ICA Talent*
818 12th St Apt 9
Santa Monica, CA 90403-1727, USA

Lee, David (Athlete, Baseball Player)
56 Terrace Dr
Pittsburgh, PA 15205-4312, USA

Lee, David (Athlete, Basketball Player)
c/o Mark Bartelstein *Priority Sports & Entertainment - Chicago*
312 N La Salle
Suite 650
Chicago, IL 60610, USA

Lee, David A (Athlete, Football Player)
2518 N Waverly Dr
Bossier City, LA 71111-5940, USA

Lee, Debra (Business Person, Producer)
c/o Staff Member *BET - Black EntertainmentTelevision (DC)*
1235 W St NE
One Bet Plaza
Washington, DC 20018-1211, USA

Lee, Denise (Actor)
c/o Terry Loftis *Verve Communications Group*
325 N Saint Paul St Ste 2360
Dallas, TX 75201-3824, USA

Lee, Derek (Athlete, Baseball Player)
3576 Brittany Way
El Dorado Hills, CA 95762-3952, USA

Lee, Derek (Athlete, Baseball Player)
8834 Liatris Dr
Frankfort, IL 60423-1742, USA

Lee, Derrek
First Touch Foundation
5098 Foothills Blvd # 3-492
Roseville, CA 95747-6526

Lee, Dickey (Musician)
Mars Talent
27 L Ambiance Ct
Bardonia, NY 10954-1421, USA

Lee, Don (Athlete, Baseball Player)
PO Box 147
Kearny, AZ 85137-0103, USA

Lee, Doug (Athlete, Basketball Player)
10770 Procyon St
Las Vegas, NV 89141-8844, USA

Lee, Dwight (Athlete, Football Player)
PO Box 480397
New Haven, MI 48048-0397, USA

Lee, Ed (Athlete, Hockey Player)
6 Normand St Apt D
Bristol, RI 02809-4719

Lee, Edward (Athlete, Football Player)
1781 Verbena St NW
Washington, DC 20012-1048, USA

Lee, Edward (Writer)
Necro Publications/Bedlam Press
PO Box 540298
Orlando, FL 32854-0298, USA

Lee, Eugene (Actor)
c/o Vincent Cirrincione *Vincent Cirrincione Associates*
1516 N Fairfax Ave
Los Angeles, CA 90046-2608, USA

Lee, Eunice (Musician)
Columbia Artists Mgmt Inc
165 W 57th St
New York, NY 10019-2201, USA

Lee, Grandma (Actor, Comedian)
Lee Strong
626 Staffordshire Dr
Jacksonville, FL 32225, USA

Lee, Gregory (Athlete, Basketball Player)
8077 Wild Flower Way
San Diego, CA 92120-1622, USA

Lee, Harper (Writer)
McIntosh & Otis
353 Lexington Ave Rm 1500
New York, NY 10016-0900, USA

Lee, Harper (Writer)
PO Box 278
Monroeville, AL 36461-0278, USA

Lee, Homer & The Braschler's
PO Box 1408
Branson, MO 65615-1408

Lee, Jack R (Athlete, Football Player)
6306 Mid Pines Dr
Houston, TX 77069-1346, USA

Lee, Jacky (Athlete, Football Player)
6306 Mid Pines Dr
Houston, TX 77069-1346, USA

Lee, James Kyson (Actor)
c/o Staff Member *Kass Management*
501 Santa Monica Blvd Ste 604
Santa Monica, CA 90401-2467, USA

Lee, Jared B (Cartoonist)
Jared B Lee Studio
2942 Hamilton Rd
Lebanon, OH 45036-8857, USA

Lee, Jason (Actor, Producer, Writer)
c/o Gay Ribisi *Ribisi Entertainment*
3278 Wilshire Blvd Apt 702
Los Angeles, CA 90010-1425, USA

Lee, Jason Scott (Actor)
c/o Cynthia Shelton-Droke *Sweet Mud Group*
648 Broadway # 1002
New York, NY 10012-2348, USA

Lee, Jenny (Athlete, Golfer)
c/o Staff Member *Ladies Pro Golf Association (LPGA)*
100 International Golf Dr
Daytona Beach, FL 32124-1092, USA

Lee, Joe (Business Person)
Darden Restaurants
5900 Lake Ellenor Dr
Orlando, FL 32809-4618, USA

Lee, Jonna (Actor)
8721 W Sunset Blvd Ste 103
West Hollywood, CA 90069-2271, USA

Lee, Julia (Actor)
c/o Staff Member *Privilege Talent Agency*
PO Box 260860
Encino, CA 91426-0860, USA

Lee, Kathy
204 Rivers Edge Ln
Sevierville, TN 37862-5213

Lee, Keith (Athlete, Basketball Player)
11653 Metz Pl
Eads, TN 38028-6912, USA

Lee, Kurk (Athlete, Basketball Player)
2745 Scarborough Cir
Windsor Mill, MD 21244-8024, USA

Lee, Larry (Athlete, Football Player)
PO Box 3889
Highland Park, MI 48203-0889, USA

Lee, Laura
155 N Beverwyck Pmb 245
Lake Hiawatha, NJ 07034

Lee, Laurie Ann (Athlete, Baseball Player, Commentator)
19528 Cohasset St
Reseda, CA 91335-2436, USA

Lee, Lela (Actor)
c/o Marilyn Szatmary *SMS Talent*
8383 Wilshire Blvd Ste 230
Beverly Hills, CA 90211-2436, USA

Lee, Leron (Athlete, Baseball Player)
8150 Warren Ct
Granite Bay, CA 95746-9576, USA

Lee, Lloyd (Athlete, Football Player)
11062 Harbor Bay Dr
Fishers, IN 46040-9483, USA

Lee, London (Actor)
1650 Broadway Ste 1410
New York, NY 10019-6957

Lee, Malcolm D (Actor, Director, Writer)
c/o Adam Kanter *Paradigm (LA)*
2000 Avenue of the Stars Ste 1000N
Los Angeles, CA 90067-4734, USA

Lee, Mark (Athlete, Football Player)
20005 9th Ave W
Lynnwood, WA 98036-7195, USA

Lee, Mark (Athlete, Baseball Player)
130 N Rosemont St
Amarillo, TX 79106-5214, USA

Lee, Mark (Athlete, Baseball Player)
3580 Brunswick Dr
Colorado Springs, CO 80920-7338, USA

Lee, Mark C (Astronaut)
4574 Bishops Ct
Middleton, WI 53562-2326, USA

Lee, Mark C Colonel (Astronaut)
79 S Player Crest Cir
Spring, TX 77382-1809, USA

Lee, Marqise (Athlete, Football Player)
c/o Andrew Kessler *Athletes First, LLC*
23091 Mill Creek Dr
Laguna Hills, CA 92653-1258, USA

Lee, Michele (Actor)
c/o Irvin Arthur *Park Avenue Talent*
1560 Broadway # 1100
New York, NY 10036-1537, USA

Lee, Michelle (Actor)
141 N Gunston Dr
Los Angeles, CA 90049-2012, USA

Lee, Mike (Athlete, Baseball Player)
1790 Calmin Dr
Fallbrook, CA 92028-4303, USA

Lee, Raphael C (Doctor)
Massachusetts Institute Technology
Engineering Dept
Cambridge, MA 02139, USA

Lee, Reggie (Actor)
c/o Adam Griffin *Kritzer Levine Wilkins Entertainment (KLWG)*
11872 La Grange Ave Fl 1
Los Angeles, CA 90025-5283, USA

Lee, Rex (Actor)
c/o Marc Hamou *Thruline Entertainment*
9250 Wilshire Blvd Ste 100
Ground Floor
Beverly Hills, CA 90212-3343, USA

Lee, Robert M (Athlete, Football Player)
363 Parker Ave
San Francisco, CA 94118-4235, USA

Lee, Robinne (Actor)
c/o Darren Goldberg *Global Creative*
1051 Cole Ave # B
Los Angeles, CA 90038-2601, USA

Lee, Rock (Athlete, Basketball Player)
4616 Blackfoot Ave
San Diego, CA 92117-6230, USA

Lee, Ron (Athlete, Basketball Player)
35788 Woodridge Ct
Farmington Hills, MI 48335-2206, USA

Lee, Ronnie (Athlete, Football Player)
139 Shady Trl
Mc Gregor, TX 76657-3768, USA

Lee, RonReaco
c/o Brett Carella *Lab, The*
5540 Hollywood Blvd # 200
Los Angeles, CA 90028-6808, USA

Lee, Russell (Athlete, Basketball Player)
1457 Smokehouse Ln
Stone Mountain, GA 30088-3312, USA

Lee, Ruta (Actor)
2623 Laurel Canyon Blvd
Los Angeles, CA 90046-1106, USA

Lee, Sammy (Athlete, Diver, Olympic Athlete)
16537 Harbour Ln
Huntington Beach, CA 92649-2105, USA

Lee, Samuel (Sammy) (Coach)
16537 Harbour Ln
Huntington Beach, CA 92649-2105, USA

Lee, Sandra (Chef, Television Host)
c/o Staff Member *Food Network, The*
1180 Avenue of the Americas Fl 11
New York, NY 10036-8401, USA

Lee, Sean (Athlete, Football Player)
c/o Michael McCartney *Priority Sports & Entertainment - Chicago*
312 N La Salle
Suite 650
Chicago, IL 60610, USA

Lee, Shannon (Actor)
c/o Steven Younger *Myman Greenspan Fineman Fox Rosenberg & Light*
11601 Wilshire Blvd Ste 2200
Los Angeles, CA 90025-1758, USA

Lee, Sheryl (Actor)
c/o Daniel (Danny) Sussman *Brillstein Entertainment Partners (LA)*
9150 Wilshire Blvd Ste 350
Beverly Hills, CA 90212-3453, USA

Lee, Spike (Director, Producer)
c/o Staff Member *40 Acres & A Mule Filmworks Inc (NY)*
75 S Elliott Pl
Brooklyn, NY 11217-1207, USA

Lee, Stan (Cartoonist, Publisher)
Marvel Entertainment
1440 S Sepulveda Blvd # 114
Los Angeles, CA 90025-3458, USA

Lee, Steven (Television Host)
c/o Staff Member *Travel Channel*
1 Discovery Pl
Silver Spring, MD 20910-3354, USA

Lee, Sung Hi
c/o Staff Member *TalentWorks (LA)*
3500 W Olive Ave Ste 1400
Burbank, CA 91505-5512, USA

Lee, Terry (Athlete, Baseball Player)
4650 Wendover St
Eugene, OR 97404-1348, USA

Lee, Tommy (Musician)
c/o David Weise *David Weise and Associates*
16000 Ventura Blvd Ste 600
Encino, CA 91436-2753, USA

Lee, Tony (Actor)
c/o Dave Phillips *Edmonds Management*
1635 N Cahuenga Blvd Fl 5
Los Angeles, CA 90028-6201, USA

Lee, Travis (Athlete, Baseball Player, Olympic Athlete)
PO Box 1572
Rancho Santa Fe, CA 92067-1572, USA

Lee, Vernon R (Religious Leader)
Wyatt Baptist Church
4621 W Hillsboro St
El Dorado, AR 71730-6768, USA

Lee, Vincent (Baseball Player)
Baltimore Black Sox
3228 Avondale Ave
Baltimore, MD 21215-4702, USA

Lee, William Gregory (Actor)
c/o Jeff Witjas *Agency for the Performing Arts (APA-LA)*
405 S Beverly Dr Ste 500
Beverly Hills, CA 90212-4425, USA

Lee, Willie James (Athlete, Baseball Player)
400 5th Way
Birmingham, AL 35214-5706, USA

Lee, Zeph (Athlete, Football Player)
7417 1/2 S Normandie Ave
Los Angeles, CA 90044-2468, USA

Leech, Allen (Actor)
c/o Vanessa Pereira *Artists Independent Management (LA)*
1522 2nd St
Santa Monica, CA 90401-2303, USA

Leech, Beverly
9150 Wilshire Blvd Ste 175
Beverly Hills, CA 90212-3450

Leede, Ed (Athlete, Basketball Player)
307 Roca Pl
Castle Rock, CO 80108-9020, USA

Lee-Dries, Dolores (Athlete, Baseball
Player, Commentator)
1950 Barcelona Rd SW
Deming, NM 88030-8552, USA

Lee Fincher, Stephen (Congressman,
Politician)
1118 Longworth Hob
Washington, DC 20515-1011, USA

Lee-Harmon, Annabelle (Baseball Player)
960 Senate St
Costa Mesa, CA 92627-3332, USA

Lee-Hom, Wang (Actor)
c/o Bryan Lourd *Creative Artists Agency*
(CAA-LA)
2000 Avenue of the Stars Ste 100
Los Angeles, CA 90067-4705, USA

Leek, Gene (Athlete, Baseball Player)
4055 Hamilton St Apt 5
San Diego, CA 92104-6108, USA

Leen, Bill (Musician)
William Morris Agency
2100 W End Ave Ste 1000
Nashville, TN 37203-5240, USA

Leeper, Dave (Athlete, Baseball Player)
23997 Kaleb Dr
Corona, CA 92883-9385, USA

Leerhsen, Erica (Actor)
c/o Staff Member *Kritzer Levine Wilkins*
Entertainment (KLWG)
11872 La Grange Ave Fl 1
Los Angeles, CA 90025-5283, USA

Leese, Howard (Musician)
219 2nd Ave N
#333
Seattle, WA 98109, USA

Leestma, David C (Astronaut)
4314 Lake Grove Dr
Seabrook, TX 77586-4114, USA

Leestma, David C Captain (Astronaut)
4314 Lake Grove Dr
Seabrook, TX 77586-4114, USA

Leetch, Brian (Athlete, Hockey Player)
40 Battery St PH 12
Boston, MA 02109-1907

Leetch, Brian J (Athlete, Hockey Player,
Olympic Athlete)
c/o Staff Member *PuckAgency LLC*
555 Pleasantville Rd
North Building, Suite 210
Briarcliff Manor, NY 10510-1955, USA

Leetsma, David C
2101 Nasa Pkwy
Houston, TX 77058-3607, USA

Leetzow, Max (Athlete, Football Player)
4744 E Caley Pi
Littleton, CO 80121, USA

Leeuwenburg, Jay (Athlete, Football
Player)
6268 S Coventry Ln W
Littleton, CO 80123-6756, USA

Leeves, Jane (Actor)
c/o Molly Madden *3 Arts Entertainment*
(LA)
9460 Wilshire Blvd Fl 7
Beverly Hills, CA 90212-2713, USA

Lefcourt, Peter (Actor)
c/o Staff Member *Creative Artists Agency*
(CAA-LA)
2000 Avenue of the Stars Ste 100
Los Angeles, CA 90067-4705, USA

Lefebvre, Jim (Athlete, Baseball Player,
Coach)
10160 E Whispering Wind Dr
Scottsdale, AZ 85255-3007, USA

Lefebvre, Joe (Athlete, Baseball Player)
12 Blake St
Concord, NH 03301-4010, USA

Lefebvre, Ryan (Commentator)
622 N Winnebago Dr
Greenwood, MO 64034-9419, USA

Lefebvre, Sylvain (Athlete, Hockey Player)
1000 Chopper Cir
Denver, CO 80204-5805

Lefevre, Rachelle (Actor)
c/o Pearl Hanan *Pearl Hanan*
Management
7775 W Sunset Blvd Ste 118
Los Angeles, CA 90046-3911, USA

Lefferts, Craig (Athlete, Baseball Player)
Stockton Ports 404 W Fremont St Attn
Coaching Staff
Stockton, CA 95203, USA

Lefkowitz, Louis (Politician)
575 Park Ave
New York, NY 10065-7332, USA

Leflore, Ron (Athlete, Baseball Player)
6263 93rd Ter N Apt 4206
Pinellas Park, FL 33782-4640, USA

LeFrak, Richard (Business Person)
LeFrak
40 W 57th St Fl 23
New York, NY 10019-4011, USA

Leftwich, Byron (Athlete, Football Player)
1725 Catherine Fran Dr
Accokeek, MD 20607-3231, USA

Leftwich, Phil (Athlete, Baseball Player)
15819 S 31st St
Phoenix, AZ 85048-7775, USA

Legace, Jean-Guy (Athlete, Hockey
Player)
126 Casa Grande Ln
Santa Rosa Beach, FL 32459-3162, USA

Legace, Manny (Athlete, Hockey Player)
40708 Village Oaks
Novi, MI 48375-4464

Legend, John (Actor, Musician)
3023 Longdale Ln
Los Angeles, CA 90068-1833, USA

Legette, Burnie (Athlete, Football Player)
1118 Doyle Pl
Colorado Springs, CO 80915-2327, USA

Legette, Tyrone (Athlete, Football Player)
1304 Hancock St
Columbia, SC 29205-4850, USA

Legg, Greg (Athlete, Baseball Player)
2 Stadium Way
Lakewood, NJ 08701-4536, USA

Leggat, Ashley (Actor)
c/o Staff Member *Walt Disney Co, The*
(Buena Vista Motion Picture Group)
500 S Buena Vista St
Burbank, CA 91521-0007

Leggatt, Ian (Athlete, Golfer)
9726 E Mountain Spring Rd
Scottsdale, AZ 85255-6640, USA

Legge, Katherine (Race Car Driver)
307 Park Ave
Chardon, OH 44024-1311, USA

Leggero, Natasha (Actor)
c/o Geoff Cheddy *Brillstein Entertainment*
Partners (LA)
9150 Wilshire Blvd Ste 350
Beverly Hills, CA 90212-3453, USA

Leggett, Dave (Athlete, Football Player)
1655 Lewis Ridge Vw
Colorado Springs, CO 80907-7171, USA

Leggett, Jay (Actor, Producer, Writer)
c/o Lenore Zerman *Liberman/Zerman*
Management
252 N Larchmont Blvd Ste 200
Los Angeles, CA 90004-3754, USA

Legler, Tim (Athlete, Basketball Player)
275 82nd St
Stone Harbor, NJ 08247-1707, USA

Legrand, Michel (Musician)
c/o Staff Member *Kraft-Engel Management*
15233 Ventura Blvd Ste 200
Sherman Oaks, CA 91403-2244, USA

Legrande, Larry (Athlete, Baseball Player)
1331 Leon St NW
Roanoke, VA 24017-6011, USA

Legree, Lance (Athlete, Football Player)
25 Ardmore Ave
Clifton, NJ 07012-1807, USA

LeGros, James (Actor)
5850 W Highway 22
Wilson, WY 83014, USA

Leguin, Ursula (Writer)
PO Box 278
Milford, PA 18337-0278, USA

LeGuin, Ursula K (Writer)
PO Box 10541
Portland, OR 97296-0541, USA

Leguizamo, John (Actor, Comedian,
Producer)
c/o Jeff Golenberg *Silver Lining*
Entertainment
421 S Beverly Dr Fl 7
Beverly Hills, CA 90212-4408, USA

Legwand, David (Athlete, Hockey Player)
37700 Lakeshore Dr
Harrison Township, MI 48045-2849

Lehan, Michael (Athlete, Football Player)
418 Madison Ave S
Hopkins, MN 55343-8469, USA

Lehane, Dennis (Writer)
341 Kerrville South Dr
Kerrville, TX 78028-8770, USA

Lehew, Jim (Athlete, Baseball Player)
3086 Fairview Rd
Grantsville, MD 21536-2239, USA

Lehman, Manny (DJ)
c/o Len Evans *Project Publicity*
312 W 53rd St Ste 202
New York, NY 10019-5743, USA

Lehman, Tom (Athlete, Golfer)
9820 E Thompson Peak Pkwy Unit 704
Scottsdale, AZ 85255-6656, USA

Lehmann, Edie (Actor)
24844 Malibu Rd
Malibu, CA 90265-4617, USA

Lehmann, Michael (Director, Producer)
c/o Staff Member *Industry Entertainment*
955 Carrillo Dr Ste 300
Los Angeles, CA 90048-5400, USA

Lehmkuhl, Reichen (Model, Reality Star,
Writer)
c/o Mara Santino *Luber Roklin*
Management
5815 W Sunset Blvd Ste 206
Los Angeles, CA 90028-6481, USA

Lehne, Fredric (Actor)
c/o Staff Member *Bauman Redanty &*
Shaul Agency
5757 Wilshire Blvd
Suite 473
Beverly Hills, CA 90212, USA

Lehr, John (Actor, Producer, Writer)
c/o Staff Member *William Morris*
Endeavor (LA)
9601 Wilshire Blvd
Beverly Hills, CA 90210-5213, USA

Lehr, Justin (Athlete, Baseball Player)
35 Harvest Wind Pl
Spring, TX 77382-3602, USA

Lehr, Zella (Musician)
1961 NE 31st St
Lighthouse Point, FL 33064-7643, USA

Lehrer, Jim (Journalist, Television Host,
Writer)
c/o Jim Griffin *Paradigm (NY)*
360 Park Ave S Fl 16
New York, NY 10010-1716, USA

Lehrman, Logan (Actor)
c/o Joseph (Joe) Rice *Abrams Artists*
Agency (LA)
9200 W Sunset Blvd PH 11
West Hollywood, CA 90069-3601, USA

Lehtinen, Jere (Athlete, Hockey Player)
968 Gibbs Xing
Coppell, TX 75019-6395, USA

Lehto, JJ (Race Car Driver)
Hogan Racing LLC
3473 Rider Trl S
Earth City, MO 63045-1110, USA

Lehtonen, Kari (Athlete, Hockey Player)
6331 Deloache Ave
Dallas, TX 75225-2816

Lehuep, John (Athlete, Football Player)
205 Bud Nalley Dr
Easley, SC 29642-3578, USA

Lehvonen, Hank (Athlete, Hockey Player)
4000 N Federal Hwy Ste 207
Boca Raton, FL 33431-4527, USA

Lei, Kaylani (Actor, Adult Film Star,
Model)
c/o Gina Rodriguez *GR Media*
Prefers to be contacted via telephone or
email
Reseda, CA 91335, USA

Leibman, Ron (Actor)
22 Kinnicut Rd
Pound Ridge, NY 10576-1800, USA

Leibovitz, Annie (Artist, Photographer)
443 W 18th St # 4
Annie Leibovitz Photography
New York, NY 10011-3817, USA

Leibowitz, Barry (Athlete, Basketball
Player)
3900 Galt Ocean Dr Apt 912
Ft Lauderdale, FL 33308-6630, USA

Leibrandt, Charlie (Athlete, Baseball
Player)
1235 Stuart Rdg
Alpharetta, GA 30022-6364, USA

Leicester, Jon (Athlete, Baseball Player)
17151 Corbina Ln Apt 112
Huntington Beach, CA 92649-5168, USA

Leick, Hudson (Actor)
c/o Staff Member *Geddes Agency, The*
1203 Greenacre Ave
West Hollywood, CA 90046-5707, USA

Leifer, Carol (Actor, Comedian)
c/o Lori Jonas *Jonas Public Relations*
240 26th St Ste 3
Santa Monica, CA 90402-2542, USA

Leigeb, Brian (Football Player)
c/o Team Member *Oakland Raiders*
1220 Harbor Bay Pkwy
Alameda, CA 94502-6570, USA

Leigh, Barbara (Actor)
GRA
9320 Wilshire Blvd Ste 302
Beverly Hills, CA 90212-3218, USA

Leigh, Chyler (Actor)
c/o Joanna (Joanie) Burstein *Burstein Company, The*
15304 W Sunset Blvd Ste 208
Pacific Palisades, CA 90272-3656, USA

Leigh, Danni (Musician)
c/o Bridget Bauer *Bismeaux Productions*
PO Box 463
Austin, TX 78767-0463, USA

Leigh, Jennifer Jason (Actor)
c/o Cari Ross *Balance Public Relations*
2212 Linda Flora Dr
Los Angeles, CA 90077-1411, USA

Leigh, Regina (Musician)
Bobby Roberts
909 Meadowlark Ln
Goodlettsville, TN 37072-2309, USA

Leighton, Brad (Race Car Driver)
c/o Staff Member *NASCAR*
1801 W Speedway Blvd
Daytona Beach, FL 32114-1243, USA

Leighton, GB (Musician)
c/o Staff Member *Paradigm (Monterey)*
404 W Franklin St
Monterey, CA 93940-2303, USA

Leighton, Laura (Actor)
3357 Ledgewood Dr
Los Angeles, CA 90068-1619, USA

Leija, James (Jesse) (Athlete, Boxer)
154 Octavia Pl
San Antonio, TX 78214-1236, USA

Leiker, Tony (Athlete, Football Player)
411 E 21st St
Hays, KS 67601-2805, USA

Leimkuehler, Paul (Business Person, Skier)
351 Darbys Run
Bay Village, OH 44140-2968, USA

Leinart, Matt (Athlete, Football Player, Heisman Trophy Winner)
6966 Turf Dr
Huntington Beach, CA 92648-1546, USA

Leiper, Dave (Athlete, Baseball Player)
13082 N 103rd St
Scottsdale, AZ 85260-7272, USA

Leipheimer, Levi (Athlete, Cycler, Olympic Athlete)
1755 Crystal Springs Ct
Santa Rosa, CA 95404-1095, USA

Leister, John (Athlete, Baseball Player)
304 Devon Dr
Saint Louis, MI 48880-9427, USA

Leisure, David (Actor)
26807 Fairlain Dr
Valencia, CA 91355-4961, USA

Leitch, Donovan
8794 Lookout Mountain Ave
Los Angeles, CA 90046-1859

Leitch, Matthew (Actor)
c/o Colleen Schlegel *Artist Management*
5670 Wilshire Blvd Ste 1370
Los Angeles, CA 90036-5679, USA

Leiter, Al (Athlete, Baseball Player)
181 E 90th St Apt 9B
New York, NY 10128-2389, USA

Leiter, Alois T (Al) (Athlete, Baseball Player)
New York Yankees
161st Street & River Ave
Attn: Broadcast Dept
Bronx, NY 10451, USA

Leiter, Ken (Athlete, Hockey Player)
30098 Warley Ct
Novi, MI 48377-2191, USA

Leiter, Mark (Athlete, Baseball Player)
121 Carriage Way
Forked River, NJ 08731-5843, USA

Leith, Virginia (Actor)
37621 Melrose Dr
Cathedral City, CA 92234-7840, USA

Leitner, Ted (Commentator)
PO Box 8926
Rancho Santa Fe, CA 92067-8926, USA

Leius, Scott (Athlete, Baseball Player)
12620 42nd Pl N
Minneapolis, MN 55442-2344, USA

Lekakis, Paul (Musician)
c/o Staff Member *Diva Central Inc*
7510 W Sunset Blvd Ste 1445
Los Angeles, CA 90046-3408, USA

Lekang, Anton (Skier)
47 Pratt St
Winsted, CT 06098-2025, USA

Lelbrandt, Charlie (Athlete, Baseball Player)
Cincinnati Reds
1235 Stuart Rdg
Alpharetta, GA 30022-6364, USA

Lelliott, Jeremy (Actor)
c/o Joan Green *Joan Green Management*
1836 Courtney Ter
Los Angeles, CA 90046-2106, USA

L. Ellmers, Renee (Congressman, Politician)
1533 Longworth Hob
Washington, DC 20515-3302

Lemaire, Jacques (Athlete, Hockey Player)
PO Box 1207
Palmetto, FL 34220-1207

Lemaire, Jacques G (Athlete, Coach, Hockey Player)
803 Riviera Dunes Way
Palmetto, FL 34221-7125, USA

Lemanczyk, Dave (Athlete, Baseball Player)
24 Lehigh Ct
Rockville Centre, NY 11570-2016, USA

Lemaster, Denny (Athlete, Baseball Player)
4833 Carlene W R L SW
Lilburn, GA 30047, USA

Lemaster, Denny (Athlete, Baseball Player)
1909 Indian Rd
Lincolnton, GA 30817-3805, USA

Lemaster, Frank (Athlete, Football Player)
PO Box 159
Birchrunville, PA 19421-0159, USA

Lemaster, Johnnie (Athlete, Baseball Player)
PO Box 943
Paintsville, KY 41240-0943, USA

Lemaster, Jr., Ron (Race Car Driver)
3705 Brandon Rd
Huntington, WV 25704-1107, USA

Le Mat, Paul (Actor)
6300 Wilshire Blvd Ste 1460
Los Angeles, CA 90048-5200, USA

Lemay, Dick (Athlete, Baseball Player)
12960 Ridgeview Dr
Platte City, MO 64079-7704, USA

Lembeck, Michael (Actor, Director)
23852 Pacific Coast Hwy # 355
Malibu, CA 90265-4876, USA

Lemche, Kris (Actor)
c/o Brian Wilkins *Kritzer Levine Wilkins Entertainment (KLWG)*
11872 La Grange Ave Fl 1
Los Angeles, CA 90025-5283, USA

Lemelin, Reggie (Athlete, Hockey Player)
10 Benevento Cir
Peabody, MA 01960-1268

Lemieux, Alain (Athlete, Hockey Player)
113 Wyngate Rd
Coraopolis, PA 15108-1028

Lemieux, Claude (Athlete, Hockey Player)
720 Manhattan Ave
Manhattan Bch, CA 90266-5653

Lemieux, Jean (Athlete, Hockey Player)
113 Wyngate Rd
Coraopolis, PA 15108-1028

Lemieux, Joseph H (Business Person)
Owens-Illinois Inc
1 Seagate
Toledo, OH 43604-1558, USA

LeMieux, Kathryn (Cartoonist)
c/o Staff Member *King Features Syndication*
300 W 57th St Fl 15
New York, NY 10019-5238, USA

Lemieux, Mario (Athlete, Hockey Player)
Mario Lemieux Foundation
816 5th Ave Fl 6
Pittsburgh, PA 15219-4765, USA

Lemke, Cheryl (Television Host)
WOWT-TV
3501 Farnam St
Omaha, NE 68131-3301, USA

Lemke, Mark (Athlete, Baseball Player)
3 Olena Dr
Whitesboro, NY 13492-2103, USA

Lemme, Steve (Comedian)
c/o Staff Member *United Talent Agency (UTA-LA)*
9336 Civic Center Dr
Beverly Hills, CA 90210-3604, USA

Lemmerman, Bruce (Athlete, Football Player)
621 Silverado Way
Eagle Point, OR 97524-9011, USA

Lemmon, Chris (Actor)
80 Murray Dr
South Glastonbury, CT 06073-2435, USA

Lemmon, Christopher (Actor)
80 Murray Dr
S Glastonbury, CT 06073-2435, USA

Lemmons, Kasi (Actor, Director)
c/o Frank Wuliger *Gersh (LA)*
9465 Wilshire Blvd Ste 600
Beverly Hills, CA 90212-2605, USA

Lemon, Chet (Athlete, Baseball Player)
38150 Timberlane Dr
Umatilla, FL 32784-9302, USA

Lemon, Cleo (Athlete, Football Player)
1525 Harrington Park Dr
Jacksonville, FL 32225-4919, USA

Lemon, Don (Correspondent, Journalist)
c/o Staff Member *N.S. Bienstock*
250 W 57th St Ste 333
New York, NY 10107-0302, USA

Lemon, Meadowlark (Actor, Athlete, Basketball Player)
6501 E Greenway Pkwy Ste 102
Scottsdale, AZ 85254-2066, USA

Lemon, Mike (Athlete, Football Player)
455 Whitree Ln
Chesterfield, MO 63017-2450, USA

Lemond, Greg (Athlete, Cycler, Olympic Athlete)
3000 Willow Dr
Hamel, MN 55340-9799, USA

Lemonds, Dave (Athlete, Baseball Player)
1501 Aringill Ln
Matthews, NC 28104-8049, USA

Lemongelio, Mark (Baseball Player)
Houston Astros
13437 S 47th St
Phoenix, AZ 85044-4833, USA

Lemongello, Mark (Athlete, Baseball Player)
13437 S 47th St
Phoenix, AZ 85044-4833, USA

Lemonis, Marcus (Business Person)
Camping World
650 Three Springs Rd
Bowling Green, KY 42104-7561, USA

Lemon Jelly (Music Group)
c/o Staff Member *Paradigm (Monterey)*
404 W Franklin St
Monterey, CA 93940-2303, USA

Lemos, Richie (Boxer)
18658 Klum Pl
Rowland Heights, CA 91748-4850, USA

Lenard, Voshon (Athlete, Basketball Player)
22694 Nottingham Ln
Southfield, MI 48033-3393, USA

Lenarduzzi, Mike (Athlete, Hockey Player)
18165 Pine Ridge Dr
Prairieville, LA 70769-3455

Lendl, Ivan (Athlete, Tennis Player)
400 5 1/2 Mile Rd
Goshen, CT 06756-1032, USA

Lenehan, Nancy (Actor)
c/o Meghan Schumacher *Meghan Schumacher Management*
13351D Riverside Dr # 387
Sherman Oaks, CA 91423-2508, USA

L. Engel, Eliot (Congressman, Politician)
2161 Rayburn Hob
Washington, DC 20515-2206, USA

Lengies, Vanessa (Actor)
c/o Joanna (Joanie) Burstein *Burstein Company, The*
15304 W Sunset Blvd Ste 208
Pacific Palisades, CA 90272-3656, USA

Lenhardt, Don (Athlete, Baseball Player)
13317 Woodlake Village Ct W
Saint Louis, MO 63141-6071, USA

Lenk, Tom (Actor)
c/o Bernard Kira *Vanguard Management Group*
8060 Melrose Ave Fl 4
Los Angeles, CA 90046-7038, USA

Lenkaitis, Bill (Athlete, Football Player)
26 Rose Court Way
East Walpole, MA 02032-1185, USA

Lenkaitis, William E (Athlete, Football Player)
26 Rose Court Way
East Walpole, MA 02032-1185, USA

Lennix, Harry (Actor)
c/o Staff Member *Creative Artists Agency (CAA-LA)*
2000 Avenue of the Stars Ste 100
Los Angeles, CA 90067-4705, USA

Lennon, Cynthia (Artist, Writer)
c/o Staff Member *Crown Publishers*
1745 Broadway
New York, NY 10019-4640, USA

Lennon, Diane (Musician)
1984 State Highway 165
Branson, MO 65616-8936, USA

Lennon, Janet (Musician)
223 Devonshire Dr
Branson, MO 65616-3489, USA

Lennon, Kathy (Musician)
Overlook Dr
#10
Branson, MO 65616, USA

Lennon, Patrick (Athlete, Baseball Player)
60 Meister Blvd
Freeport, NY 11520-5938, USA

Lennon, Peggy (Musician)
1984 State Highway 165
Branson, MO 65616-8936, USA

Lennon, Richard G (Religious Leader)
Archdiocese of Boston
2121 Commonwealth Ave
Brighton, MA 02135-3101, USA

Lennon, Sean (Musician)
Dakota Hotel
1 W 72nd St Apt 78
New York, NY 10023-3425, USA

Lennon, Thomas (Actor, Producer, Writer)
c/o Peter Principato *Principato/Young Management (LA)*
9465 Wilshire Blvd Ste 900
Beverly Hills, CA 90212-2608, USA

Lennox, Kai (Actor)
c/o Gabrielle Allabashi *Ellis Talent Group*
4705 Laurel Canyon Blvd Ste 300
Valley Village, CA 91607-5901, USA

Lenny, Rick H. (Business Person)
Hershey Foods
100 Crystal A Dr Unit 8
Hershey, PA 17033-9702, USA

Leno, Jay (Actor, Comedian, Talk Show Host)
PO Box 7885
Burbank, CA 91510-7885, USA

Lenon, Paris (Athlete, Football Player)
1505 Taylor St
Lynchburg, VA 24504-3437, USA

Lenox, Adriane (Actor)
c/o Staff Member *Leading Artists*
145 W 45th St Rm 1000
New York, NY 10036-4032, USA

Lentine, Jim (Athlete, Baseball Player)
1066 Calle Del Cerro Unit 1411
San Clemente, CA 92672-6075, USA

Lentinen, Jere (Athlete, Hockey Player)
2601 Avenue of the Stars
Frisco, TX 75034-9015, USA

Lentz, Jack (Athlete, Football Player)
11809 Lake House Ct
North Palm Beach, FL 33408-3321, USA

Lentz, Leary (Athlete, Basketball Player)
1309 Whispering Pines Dr
Houston, TX 77055-6854, USA

Lenz, Kay (Actor)
5916 Filaree Hts
Malibu, CA 90265-3721, USA

Lenz, Kim (Musician, Songwriter, Writer)
Mark Pucia Media
5000 Oak Bluff Ct
Atlanta, GA 30350-1069, USA

Lenz, Nicole (Actor)
c/o Victor Del Toro *Elite Model Management (LA)*
345 N Maple Dr Ste 176
Beverly Hills, CA 90210-5193, USA

Lenz, Rick (Actor)
12955 Calvert St
Van Nuys, CA 91401-3206, USA

Leo, Jim (Athlete, Hockey Player)
201 Old Oak Pl
Thurmont, MD 21788, USA

Leo, Melissa (Actor)
832 Peak Rd
Stone Ridge, NY 12484-5260, USA

Leon
1180 S Beverly Dr Ste 608
Los Angeles, CA 90035-1158

Leon, Carlos
4519 Cockerham Dr
Los Angeles, CA 90027-1223

Leon, Eddie (Athlete, Baseball Player)
5285 N Strada De Rubino
Tucson, AZ 85750-6043, USA

Leon, Kenny (Actor, Director, Producer)
True Colors Theatre Company
887 W Marietta St NW Ste J102
Atlanta, GA 30318-5266, USA

Leon, Lourdes (Actor, Designer)
c/o Liz Rosenberg *Liz Rosenberg Media*
1650 Broadway
505A
New York, NY 10019-6833, USA

Leonard, Bob (Slick) (Athlete, Basketball Player, Coach)
1241 Hillcrest Dr
Carmel, IN 46033-2343, USA

Leonard, Brian (Athlete, Football Player)
20 Countryside Court Dr
Gouverneur, NY 13642-4306, USA

Leonard, Dennis (Athlete, Baseball Player)
4102 SW Evergreen St
Blue Springs, MO 64015-9713, USA

Leonard, Gary (Athlete, Basketball Player)
2406 Ridgefield Rd
Columbia, MO 65203-1532, USA

Leonard, James (Athlete, Football Player)
RR 332 Box 349
Mullica Hill, NY 10862, USA

Leonard, Jeffrey (Athlete, Baseball Player)
Reno Silver Sox
205 Redfield Pkwy Ste 201
Attn: Manager's Office
Reno, NV 89509-6572, USA

Leonard, Jim (Athlete, Football Player)
119 Cress Rd
Santa Cruz, CA 95060-1001, USA

Leonard, Joshua (Actor)
c/o Laina Cohn *Cohn / Torgan Management*
Prefers to be contacted by telephone or email
Los Angeles, CA, USA

Leonard, Justin (Athlete, Golfer)
3700 Euclid Ave
Dallas, TX 75205-3162, USA

Leonard, Mark (Athlete, Baseball Player)
22042 Hibiscus Dr
Cupertino, CA 95014-0109, USA

Leonard, Robert Sean (Actor)
c/o Scott Henderson *Paradigm (LA)*
9601 Wilshire Blvd
Beverly Hills, CA 90210-5213, USA

Leonard, Robert (Slick) (Athlete, Basketball Coach, Basketball Player, Coach)
5398 Baltimore Ct
Carmel, IN 46033-8882, USA

Leonard, Sugar Ray (Athlete, Boxer, Olympic Athlete)
PO Box 1149
Pacific Palisades, CA 90272-1149, USA

Leonard, Wayne (Business Person)
Entergy Corp
10055 Grogans Mill Rd Ste 150
Spring, TX 77380-1048, USA

Leonard-Linehan, Rhoda (Athlete, Baseball Player, Commentator)
84 Bruce Rd
Norwood, MA 02062-3103, USA

Leone, Justin (Athlete, Baseball Player)
5965 Kevin Way
Las Vegas, NV 89149-3348, USA

Leone, Sunny (Adult Film Star)
c/o Staff Member *Vivid Entertainment*
3599 Cahuenga Blvd W Fl 2
Los Angeles, CA 90068-1397, USA

Leonetti, Jean-Baptiste (Director)
c/o Jerome Duboz *William Morris Endeavor (LA)*
9601 Wilshire Blvd
Beverly Hills, CA 90210-5213, USA

Leonetti, John R (Cinematographer)
1605 Avenida Salvador
San Clemente, CA 92672-3266, USA

Leonetti, Matthew (Cinematographer)
1362 Bella Oceana Vis
Pacific Palisades, CA 90272-2359, USA

Leong, Page (Actor)
C N A Assoc
1925 Century Park E Ste 750
Los Angeles, CA 90067-2708, USA

Leonhard, Dave (Athlete, Baseball Player)
87 Corning St
Beverly, MA 01915-3732, USA

Leonhard, Jim (Athlete, Football Player)
c/o Scott Smith *XAM Sports*
PO Box 1725
Madison, WI 53701-1725, USA

Leoni, Tea (Actor, Producer)
190 Riverside Dr # 8C/8D
New York, NY 10024-1008, USA

Leonidas, Stephanie (Actor)
c/o Andrew Rogers *ICM Partners (LA)*
10250 Constellation Blvd Fl 7
Los Angeles, CA 90067-6207, USA

Leonskaja, Elisabeth (Musician)
Columbia Artists Mgmt Inc
165 W 57th St
New York, NY 10019-2201, USA

Leopold, Bobby (Athlete, Football Player)
801 Beckleymeade Ave Apt 1116
Dallas, TX 75232-5225, USA

Leopold, Jordan (Athlete, Hockey Player, Olympic Athlete)
Octagon Athlete Representation
8000 Norman Center Dr
Dr Ste 400
Minneapolis, MN 55437-1178, USA

Leopold, Tom (Comedian)
c/o Staff Member *Gersh (LA)*
9465 Wilshire Blvd Ste 600
Beverly Hills, CA 90212-2605, USA

Lepage, Kevin (Race Car Driver)
618 Rice Hill Rd
Franklin, VT 05457-9821, USA

Lepchenko, Varvara (Athlete, Tennis Player)
1362 Doe Trail Rd
Allentown, PA 18104-2053, USA

Lepcio, Ted (Athlete, Baseball Player)
263 Greenlodge St
Dedham, MA 02026-6400, USA

Lepley, Tyler (Actor)
c/o Siri Garber *Platform Public Relations*
2666 N Beachwood Dr
Los Angeles, CA 90068-2308, USA

Lepore, Amanda (Actor, Model)
c/o Bill Coleman *Peace Bisquit*
963 Kent Ave Apt E3
Brooklyn, NY 11205-4469, USA

Leppard, Raymond J
Indianapolis Symphony
32 E Washington St Ste 600
Indianapolis, IN 46204-2919, USA

Lepperd, Thomas (Athlete, Baseball Player)
5962 Wistful Vista Dr
West Des Moines, IA 50266-2864, USA

Leppert, Don (Athlete, Baseball Player)
9226 Rami Ave
Columbus, OH 43240-2158, USA

Leppert, Don (Athlete, Baseball Player)
1630 Epping Forest Dr
Southaven, MS 38671-8849, USA

Lepsis, Matt (Athlete, Football Player)
4904 Pecan Hill Rd
McKinney, TX 75070-5246, USA

Lequia-Barker, Joan (Athlete, Baseball Player, Commentator)
3236 34th St SW
Grandville, MI 49418-1905, USA

L'Erario, Joe
7700 Wisconsin Ave
Bethesda, MD 20814-3578

Lerch, Randy (Athlete, Baseball Player)
19490 Monterey St
Morgan Hill, CA 95037-2606, USA

Lerche, Sondre (Musician)
c/o Staff Member *Paradigm (Monterey)*
404 W Franklin St
Monterey, CA 93940-2303, USA

Lerew, Anthony (Athlete, Baseball Player)
6 Summer Dr
Dillsburg, PA 17019-9544, USA

Lerman, Logan (Actor)
c/o Mara Buxbaum *ID Public Relations (LA)*
7060 Hollywood Blvd Fl 8th
Los Angeles, CA 90028-6021, USA

Lerner, Harriet (Writer)
c/o Staff Member *HarperCollins Publishers*
10 E 53rd St Fl 8
Cellar 1
New York, NY 10022-5076, USA

Lerner, Michael (Actor)
Innovative Artists
1505 10th St
Santa Monica, CA 90401-2805, USA

Leroux, Nicolette (Athlete, Golfer)
4786 Orchard Ln
Delray Beach, FL 33445-5306, USA

Leroy, Emarlos (Athlete, Football Player)
10135 Gate Pkwy N Apt 1014
Jacksonville, FL 32246-8262, USA

LeRoy, Gloria (Actor)
Shelly & Pierce
13775A Mono Way # 220
Sonora, CA 95370-8813, USA

Les, Jim (Athlete, Basketball Player)
4030 Shadybrook Ct
Granite Bay, CA 95746-8839, USA

Les, Jim (Athlete, Basketball Player)
4030 Shadvbrooke Ct
Granite Bay, CA 95746, USA

Lesane, Jimmy (Athlete, Football Player)
3629 Coronado Rd
Windsor Mill, MD 21244-3848, USA

Lesar, David (Business Person)
Halliburton Co
500 N Akard St Ste 3600
Lincoln Plaza
Dallas, TX 75201-3328, USA

Leschin, Luisa (Producer, Writer)
c/o Staff Member *William Morris Endeavor (LA)*
9601 Wilshire Blvd
Beverly Hills, CA 90210-5213, USA

Lesh, Phil (Musician)
c/o Jonathan Levine *Paradigm (Monterey)*
404 W Franklin St
Monterey, CA 93940-2303, USA

Lesher, Brian (Athlete, Baseball Player)
217 Vassar Dr
Newark, DE 19711-3158, USA

Leskanic, Curt (Athlete, Baseball Player)
2032 Alaqua Dr
Longwood, FL 32779-3116, USA

Lesko, Matthew (Writer)
HiRise Promotions Inc
1555 N Dearborn Pkwy Fl 25
C/O Kim McCoy
Chicago, IL 60610-1448, USA

Lesley, Brad (Athlete, Baseball Player)
13131 Moorpark St Apt 401
Sherman Oaks, CA 91423-3301, USA

Leslie, Conor (Actor)
c/o Katie Rhodes *Untitled Entertainment (LA)*
350 S Beverly Dr Ste 200
Beverly Hills, CA 90212-4819, USA

Leslie, Ed (Actor, Wrestler)
c/o Nick Cordasco *Prince Marketing Group*
18 Carillon Cir
Livingston, NJ 07039-2600, USA

Leslie, Fred W (Astronaut)
2038 Springhouse Rd SE
Huntsville, AL 35802-1890, USA

Leslie, Joan (Actor)
2228 N Catalina St
Los Angeles, CA 90027-1127, USA

Leslie, Lisa (Athlete, Basketball Player, Model, Olympic Athlete)
5639 S La Cienega Blvd
Los Angeles, CA 90056-1333, USA

Leslie, Robbie (DJ)
c/o Staff Member *Diva Central Inc*
7510 W Sunset Blvd Ste 1445
Los Angeles, CA 90046-3408, USA

Leslie, Rose (Actor)
c/o Heather Nunn *Anonymous Content (LA)*
3532 Hayden Ave
Culver City, CA 90232-2413, USA

Leslie, Ryan (Musician)
c/o Chris Chambers *The Chamber Group*
75 Broad St Ste 2710
New York, NY 10004-2679, USA

Lesnar, Brock (Athlete, Wrestler)
c/o Drew Elliot *Artists International Management (NY)*
333 E 43rd St Apt 115
New York, NY 10017-4822, USA

Lesniak, John (Race Car Driver)
47 Industrial Park Access Rd # 198
Middlefield, CT 06455-1263, USA

Lesnie, Andrew (Cinematographer)
c/o Wayne Fitterman *United Talent Agency (UTA-LA)*
9336 Civic Center Dr
Beverly Hills, CA 90210-3604, USA

Lessard, Rick (Athlete, Hockey Player)
125 Chocolay River Trl
Marquette, MI 49855-9589

Lessard, Stefan (Musician)
333 37th Ave E
Seattle, WA 98112-4934, USA

Lesseos, Mimi (Actor, Athlete)
2484 Vista Del Monte Dr
Acton, CA 93510-1899, USA

Lester, Adrian (Actor)
c/o William Baylock *Seven Summits Pictures & Management*
8906 W Olympic Blvd
Ground Floor
Beverly Hills, CA 90211-3550, USA

Lester, Bill (Race Car Driver)
6224 View Crest Dr
Oakland, CA 94619-3717, USA

Lester, Jon (Athlete, Baseball Player)
3575 Ridgewood Rd NW
Atlanta, GA 30327-2419, USA

Lester, Ketty (Actor, Musician)
5931 Comey Ave
Los Angeles, CA 90034-2213, USA

Lester, Mark L (Director)
17268 Camino Yatasto
Pacific Palisades, CA 90272, USA

Lester, Richard (Dick) (Director)
c/o Staff Member *Creative Artists Agency (CAA-LA)*
2000 Avenue of the Stars Ste 100
Los Angeles, CA 90067-4705, USA

Lester, Robert (Athlete, Football Player)
c/o Pat Dye Jr *SportsTrust Advisors (GA)*
3340 Peachtree Rd NE Fl 16
Atlanta, GA 30326-1000, USA

Lester, Ron (Actor)
c/o David Bradley *Bradley Entertainment*
PO Box 3182
Cocoa, FL 32924-3182, USA

Lester, Ronnie (Athlete, Basketball Player)
4841 NW 16th Ter
Boca Raton, FL 33431-3317, USA

Lester, Tim (Athlete, Football Player)
1160 Bream Dr
Alpharetta, GA 30004-4411, USA

Lester, Tom
c/o Gary Moore *Gary Moore Management*
55 Karen Dr
Greenville, SC 29607-1207, USA

Lesueur, Emily (Athlete, Olympic Athlete, Swimmer)
2208 E Nora St
Mesa, AZ 85213-1562, USA

Lesure, James (Actor)
1535 Merriman Dr
Glendale, CA 91202-1212, USA

Letbetter, R Steve (Business Person)
Reliant Energy
1111 Louisiana St
Houston, TX 77002-5230, USA

Leterrier, Louis (Director)
c/o Guymon Casady *Management 360*
9111 Wilshire Blvd
Beverly Hills, CA 90210-5508, USA

Letho, JJ (Race Car Driver)
Champion Racing
3101 Center Port Cir
Pompano Beach, FL 33064-2104, USA

Le Tigre (Music Group)
Esther Creative Group
32 E 31st St Frnt A
C/O Tom Sarig
New York, NY 10016-6881, USA

Letlow, W R (Russ) (Athlete, Football Player)
1876 Thelma Dr
San Luis Obispo, CA 93405-6238, USA

Letner, Robert (Athlete, Football Player)
6515 Patty Ln
Harrison, TN 37341-6987, USA

Leto, Jared (Actor)
c/o Jason Weinberg *Untitled Entertainment (LA)*
350 S Beverly Dr Ste 200
Beverly Hills, CA 90212-4819, USA

Letowski, Trevor (Athlete, Hockey Player)
3612 Lion Ridge Ct
Raleigh, NC 27612-4235, USA

Letscher, Matt (Actor)
c/o Nancy Sanders *Sanders Armstrong Caserta*
2120 Colorado Ave Ste 120
Santa Monica, CA 90404-3561, USA

Lett, Clifford (Athlete, Basketball Player)
7067 Rampart Way
Pensacola, FL 32505-3478, USA

Lett, Jim (Athlete, Baseball Player)
26 Philoah Farm
Winfield, WV 25213-9456, USA

Lett, Leon (Athlete, Football Coach, Football Player)
ULM Athletics
308 Warhawk Way
Monroe, LA 71209-0001, USA

Letterle, Daniel (Actor)
c/o Geordie Frey *GEF Entertainment*
611 N Cherokee Ave
Los Angeles, CA 90004-1008, USA

Letterman, David (Comedian, Talk Show Host)
Late Show with David Letterman
1697 Broadway Fl 11
New York, NY 10019-5904, USA

Lettermen, The
9255 W Sunset Blvd Ste 407
West Hollywood, CA 90069-3302

Letts, Tracy (Actor, Writer)
c/o Staff Member *Dewalt & Musik Management*
623 N Parish Pl
Burbank, CA 91506-1701, USA

Leung, Ken (Actor)
c/o Paul Hilepo *Hartig Hilepo Agency Ltd*
54 W 21st St Rm 610
New York, NY 10010-7344, USA

Levandowski, Leo (Athlete, Football Player)
1823 Twin House Rd
Oxford, PA 19363-3918, USA

Levang, Neil (Actor)
15630 Condor Ridge Rd
Canyon Country, CA 91387-3979, USA

Levangie, Gigi (Writer)
c/o David Lubliner *William Morris Endeavor (LA)*
9601 Wilshire Blvd
Beverly Hills, CA 90210-5213, USA

Level 42 (Music Group, Musician)
c/o Guy Richard *Agency Group Ltd, The (LA)*
1880 Century Park E Ste 711
Los Angeles, CA 90067-1618, USA

Levellers (Music Group)
c/o Staff Member *Paradigm (Monterey)*
404 W Franklin St
Monterey, CA 93940-2303, USA

Levels, Dwayne (Athlete, Football Player)
3614 Colonial Ave
Dallas, TX 75215-3640, USA

Levendis, George (Business Person)
c/o Staff Member *Syco Television*
9830 Wilshire Blvd Fl 3
Beverly Hills, CA 90212-1804, USA

Levene, Keith (Musician)
c/o Staff Member *Taang! Records*
3715 Ocean Front Walk
San Diego, CA 92109-7107, USA

Levenick, Dave (Athlete, Football Player)
8570 SW Sea Captain Dr
Stuart, FL 34997-9122, USA

Levens, Dorsey (Athlete, Football Player)
4249 Olde Mill Ln NE
Atlanta, GA 30342-3400, USA

Levenseller, Mike (Athlete, Football Player)
1570 SW Wadleigh Dr
Pullman, WA 99163-2049, USA

Levenstein, John (Comedian)
c/o Staff Member *ICM Partners (LA)*
10250 Constellation Blvd Fl 7
Los Angeles, CA 90067-6207, USA

Lever, Don (Athlete, Hockey Player)
247 Quail Hollow Ln
East Amherst, NY 14051-1633

Lever, Lafayette (Athlete, Basketball Player)
1702 W Lynx Way
Chandler, AZ 85248-5425, USA

Leverette, Otis (Athlete, Football Player)
716 N Lee St
Americus, GA 31719-3093, USA

Levering, Kate (Actor)
c/o Staff Member *Forward Entertainment*
9255 W Sunset Blvd Ste 805
West Hollywood, CA 90069-3305, USA

Leverington, Shelby
1801 Avenue of the Stars Ste 1250
Los Angeles, CA 90067-5817

Leveritt, Mara (Writer)
c/o Staff Member *St Martins Press*
175 5th Ave Ste 400
Publicity Dept
New York, NY 10010-7848, USA

Le Vert
110-112 Lantoga Rd # D
Wayne, PA 19087

Levert, Eddie (Musician)
c/o Staff Member *Associated Booking Corp*
PO Box 800137
Miami, FL 33280-0137, USA

Levesque, Joanna (Jojo) (Musician)
c/o Diana Levesque *Momma D's Management*
151 Lafayette St Rm 6
New York, NY 10013-3617, USA

Levesque, Paul (Triple H) (Athlete, Wrestler)
c/o Kerry Rodgerson *World Wrestling Entertainment (WWE)*
1241 E Main St
Titan Towers
Stamford, CT 06902-3520, USA

Levet, Thomas (Athlete, Golfer)
12041 Captains Lndg
North Palm Beach, FL 33408-2501, USA

Levi, Alan J. (Actor)
c/o Debbee Klein *Paradigm (LA)*
360 N Crescent Dr
North Bldg
Beverly Hills, CA 90210-4874, USA

Levi, Wayne (Athlete, Golfer)
17 Ironwood Rd
New Hartford, NY 13413-3902, USA

Levi, Zachary (Actor)
c/o Tej Bhatia Herring *Rogers & Cowan PR (LA)*
8687 Melrose Ave Ste 7
West Hollywood, CA 90069-5721, USA

LeVias, Jerry (Athlete, Football Player)
1626 Park St
Houston, TX 77019-5326, USA

Levieva, Margarieta (Actor)
c/o Shani Rosenzweig *United Talent Agency (UTA-LA)*
9336 Civic Center Dr
Beverly Hills, CA 90210-3604, USA

Levieva, Margarita (Actor)
100 Hudson St Apt 5A
New York, NY 10013-3039, USA

Levin, Carl (Politician)
1017 E Capitol St SE
Washington, DC 20003-3905, USA

Levin, Drake (Musician)
Paradise Artists
108 E Matilija St
Ojai, CA 93023-2639, USA

Levin, Harvey (Journalist, Television Host)
TMZ
4000 Warner Blvd
Burbank, CA 91522-0001, USA

Levin, Mark (Radio Personality, Talk Show Host)
WPLJ-FM Radio
2 Pennsylvania Plz # 1700
New York, NY 10121, USA

Levin Downey, Susan (Producer)
c/o Peter Micelli *Creative Artists Agency (CAA-LA)*
2000 Avenue of the Stars Ste 100
Los Angeles, CA 90067-4705, USA

Levine, Adam (Musician)
c/o Carleen Donovan *Press Here Publicity*
138 W 25th St Ste 900
New York, NY 10001-7470, USA

Levine, Alan (Athlete, Baseball Player)
10916 E Paradise Dr
Scottsdale, AZ 85259-7007, USA

Levine, Irene (Writer)
Chicago Tribune
435 N Michigan Ave Ste 200
C/O Travel
Chicago, IL 60611-4024, USA

Levine, James
Boston Symphony Orchestra
301 Massachusetts Ave
Boston, MA 02115-4511, USA

Levine, Jerry (Actor, Director)
c/o Staff Member *Rain Management Group (RMG)*
1631 21st St
Santa Monica, CA 90404-3914, USA

Levine, Jonathan (Director)
c/o Ragna Nervik *The Ragna Nervik Company*
Prefers to be contacted via telephone
Los Angeles, CA, USA

Levine, Ken (Writer)
c/o Staff Member *Broder Webb Chervin Silbermann Agency, The (BWCS)*
10250 Constellation Blvd Fl 17
Los Angeles, CA 90067-6217, USA

Levine, Michael (Business Person)
Levine Communications
9100 Wilshire Blvd Ste 540E
Beverly Hills, CA 90212-3470, USA

Levine, Philip (Writer)
4549 N Van Ness Blvd
Fresno, CA 93704-3727, USA

Levine, Samm (Actor, Producer)
c/o Melanie Marquez *M4 Publicity*
11684 Ventura Blvd # 213
Studio City, CA 91604-2699, USA

Levine, Samuel A (Actor)
c/o Staff Member *Badgley-Connor-King*
9229 W Sunset Blvd Ste 311
West Hollywood, CA 90069-3403, USA

Levine, S Robert (Business Person)
Cabletron Systems
PO Box 5005
Rochester, NH 03866, USA

Levine, Ted (Actor)
c/o Robbie Kass *Kass Management*
501 Santa Monica Blvd Ste 604
Santa Monica, CA 90401-2467, USA

Levingston, Cliff (Basketball Player)
Denver Nuggets
1000 Chopper Cir
Pepsi Center
Denver, CO 80204-5805, USA

LevinIra, Ira (Writer)
40 E 49th St
New York, NY 10017, USA

Levins, Scott (Athlete, Hockey Player)
815 Covered Bridge Dr
Delaware, OH 43015-3193, USA

Levinsohn, Gary (Producer)
c/o Staff Member *Mutual Film Company*
3535 Hayden Ave Ste 340
Culver City, CA 90232-2462, USA

Levinson, Barry (Actor, Director, Producer, Writer)
104 Wooster St Apt 2N
New York, NY 10012-3870, USA

Levinson, Chris (Writer)
c/o Staff Member *William Morris Endeavor (LA)*
9601 Wilshire Blvd
Beverly Hills, CA 90210-5213, USA

Levinson, Jay Conrad (Business Person, Writer)
Guerilla Marketing Intl
3700 S Westport Ave # 2994
Sioux Falls, SD 57106-6360, USA

Levis, Jesse (Athlete, Baseball Player)
1219 Highland Ave
Fort Washington, PA 19034-1605, USA

Levis, Patrick (Actor)
c/o Staff Member *Defining Artists Agency*
4370 Tujunga Ave Ste 120
Studio City, CA 91604-2763, USA

Levitas, Andrew (Actor)
c/o Justin Grey Stone *Management 360*
350 S Beverly Dr Ste 200
Beverly Hills, CA 90212-4819, USA

Levitt, Chad (Athlete, Football Player)
104 Towanda Ave
Elkins Park, PA 19027-2932, USA

Levitt, Gene
9200 W Sunset Blvd PH 25
West Hollywood, CA 90069-3601

Levrault, Allen (Athlete, Baseball Player)
PO Box 1316
Westport, MA 02790-0694, USA

Levy, Eugene (Actor, Director)
c/o Ben Feigin *Anonymous Content (LA)*
3532 Hayden Ave
Culver City, CA 90232-2413, USA

Levy, Jane (Actor)
c/o Joanna (Joanie) Burstein *Burstein Company, The*
15304 W Sunset Blvd Ste 208
Pacific Palisades, CA 90272-3656, USA

Levy, Kenneth (Business Person)
KLA-Tencor Corp
160 Rio Robles
San Jose, CA 95134-1813, USA

Levy, Marv (Coach, Football Coach, Football Player)
2550 N Lakeview Ave Unit N1101
Chicago, IL 60614-8191, USA

Levy, Mary (Athlete, Football Player)
2550 N Lakeview Ave Unit N1101
Chicago, IL 60614-8191, USA

Levy, Michael R (Publisher)
Texas Monthly Magazine
PO Box 1569
Austin, TX 78767-1569, USA

Levy, Peter (Cinematographer)
International Creative Mgmt
10250 Constellation Blvd Fl 1
Los Angeles, CA 90067-6241, USA

Levy, Shawn (Actor, Director)
c/o Amanda Lundberg *42West (NYC)*
220 W 42nd St Fl 12
New York, NY 10036-7200, USA

Levy, William (Actor, Model)
c/o Gladys Gonzalez *John Carrabino Management*
5900 Wilshire Blvd Ste 406
Los Angeles, CA 90036-5015, USA

Levya, Danell (Athlete, Gymnast, Olympic Athlete)
Universal Gymnastics
13439 SW 131st St
Miami, FL 33186-5818, USA

Lewallyn, Dennis (Athlete, Baseball Player)
2900 Breckenridge Dr
Pensacola, FL 32526-2903, USA

Lewin, Josh (Commentator)
601 N Park Blvd Apt 508
Grapevine, TX 76051-6908, USA

Lewinsky, Monica
7250 Franklin Ave Unit 908
Los Angeles, CA 90046-3044, USA

Lewis, Aaron (Musician)
Staind/Elektra Records
75 Rockefeller Plz Bsmt 2
New York, NY 10019-6931

Lewis, Albert R (Athlete, Football Player)
3532 Macedonia Rd
Centreville, MS 39631-3634, USA

Lewis, Al (Grandpa) (Actor)
PO Box 277
New York, NY 10044-0205, USA

Lewis, Ananda (Actor)
c/o Marvet Britto *Britto Agency PR*
90 Franklin St Apt 4N
New York, NY 10013-3489, USA

Lewis, Ashton (Race Car Driver)
Lewis Motorsports
4317 Triple Crown Dr SW
Concord, NC 28027-8978, USA

Lewis, Barbara (Musician)
Hello Stranger Productions
PO Box 300488
Casselberry, FL 32730-0488, USA

Lewis, Bill (Coach, Football Coach)
Georgia Institute of Technology
8701 S Hardy Dr
Tempe, AZ 85284-2800, USA

Lewis, Bob (Athlete, Basketball Player)
63910 E Squash Blossom Ln
Tucson, AZ 85739-1264, USA

Lewis, Bobby (Musician)
Lustig Talent
PO Box 770850
Orlando, FL 32877-0850, USA

Lewis, Brooke (Actor)
c/o Staff Member *Coolwaters Productions*
10061 Riverside Dr # 531
Toluca Lake, CA 91602-2560, USA

Lewis, Bubba (Actor)
c/o Ryan Daly *Zero Gravity Management*
1531 14th St
Santa Monica, CA 90404-3302, USA

Lewis, Carl (Actor, Athlete, Olympic Athlete, Track Athlete)
528 Palisades Dr
Pacific Palisades, CA 90272-2844, USA

Lewis, Chad (Athlete, Football Player)
4529 N 100 W
Provo, UT 84604-5511, USA

Lewis, Charlotte (Athlete, Basketball Player, Olympic Athlete)
2814 N Sheridan Rd
Peoria, IL 61604-2716, USA

Lewis, Clea (Actor)
1659 S Highland Ave
Los Angeles, CA 90019-5540, USA

Lewis, Colby (Athlete, Baseball Player)
15730 Strebor Dr
Bakersfield, CA 93314-9257, USA

Lewis, Crystal (Musician)
Proper Mgmt
PO Box 150867
Nashville, TN 37215-0867, USA

Lewis, Damione (Athlete, Football Player)
9601 Gato Del Sol Ct
Waxhaw, NC 28173-0113, USA

Lewis, Dan (Athlete, Football Player)
460 S Park St
Detroit, MI 48215-4108, USA

Lewis, Darren (Athlete, Football Player)
641 Seabeach Rd
Dallas, TX 75232-4842, USA

Lewis, Darryl (Athlete, Football Player)
2441 S Nadine St Apt 1
West Covina, CA 91792-3562, USA

Lewis, Dave (Athlete, Coach, Hockey Player)
2040 Ranch Rd
Holly, MI 48442-8027

Lewis, Dave (Athlete, Football Player)
14015 Tahiti Way Apt 111
Marina Del Rey, CA 90292-6507, USA

Lewis, Dave (Athlete, Hockey Player)
Carolina Hurricanes
1400 Edwards Mill Rd
Raleigh, NC 27607-3624

Lewis, David Levering (Writer)
Rutgers University
History Dept
New Brunswick, NJ 08903, USA

Lewis, David R (Athlete, Football Player)
406 142nd St
Ocean City, MD 21842-5602, USA

Lewis, Dawnn (Actor)
c/o Staff Member *Gage Group, The (LA)*
5757 Wilshire Blvd Ste 659
Los Angeles, CA 90036-3682, USA

Lewis, D D (Athlete, Football Player)
1624 Northcrest Dr
Plano, TX 75075-8749, USA

Lewis, D D (Athlete, Football Player)
2530 Dolly Wright St
Houston, TX 77088-7528, USA

Lewis, Dion (Athlete, Football Player)
10 Twiller St
Albany, NY 12209-2128, USA

Lewis, Drew (Business Person, Politician, Secretary)
PO Box 70
Lederach, PA 19450-0070, USA

Lewis, Emmanuel (Actor)
859 Highway 92 N
Fayetteville, GA 30214-1364, USA

Lewis, Frank (Athlete, Football Player)
118 Presque Isle Dr
Houma, LA 70363-3828, USA

Lewis, Freddie (Athlete, Basketball Player)
4122 Illinois Ave NW
Washington, DC 20011-5950, USA

Lewis, Garry (Athlete, Football Player)
1000 Alcorn Dr Apt 737
Lorman, MS 39096-7500, USA

Lewis, Gary (Athlete, Football Player)
1225 Town Center Dr Apt 3007
Pflugerville, TX 78660-7867, USA

Lewis, Gary (Athlete, Football Player)
10610 59th Ave S
Seattle, WA 98178-2406, USA

Lewis, Geoffrey (Actor, Writer)
c/o Joel Stevens *Joel Stevens Entertainment*
5627 Allott Ave
Van Nuys, CA 91401-4502, USA

Lewis, Glenn (Musician)
c/o Staff Member *Creative Artists Agency (CAA-LA)*
2000 Avenue of the Stars Ste 100
Los Angeles, CA 90067-4705, USA

Lewis, Grady (Athlete, Basketball Player)
2398 E Camelback Rd Ste 400
Phoenix, AZ 85016-9011

Lewis, Huey (Actor, Musician)
c/o Bob Brown *Bob Brown Management*
PO Box 779
Mill Valley, CA 94942-0779, USA

Lewis, Jamal (Athlete, Football Player)
75 Summit Ave
Newark, NJ 07112-1210, USA

Lewis, Jason (Actor)
c/o Alissa Vradenburg *Untitled Entertainment (LA)*
350 S Beverly Dr Ste 200
Beverly Hills, CA 90212-4819, USA

Lewis, Jazmin
c/o Daniel Spilo *Industry Entertainment*
955 Carrillo Dr Ste 300
Los Angeles, CA 90048-5400, USA

Lewis, Jeff (Athlete, Football Player)
230 N 2nd St Trlr 6
Berthoud, CO 80513-1327, USA

Lewis, Jeff (Designer, Reality Star)
1946 N Gramercy Pl
Los Angeles, CA 90068-3615, USA

Lewis, Jenifer (Actor)
c/o Arnold M Preston *Preston Entertainment Inc*
8033 W Sunset Blvd # 7250
Los Angeles, CA 90046-2401

Lewis, Jenna (Reality Star)
c/o Juliette Harris *It Girl Public Relations*
5301 Beethoven St Ste 220
Los Angeles, CA 90066-7052, USA

Lewis, Jensen (Athlete, Baseball Player)
5311 Salem Rd
Cincinnati, OH 45230-1327, USA

Lewis, Jermaine (Athlete, Football Player)
4919 Pleasant Grove Rd
Reisterstown, MD 21136-3913, USA

Lewis, Jerry (Actor, Comedian, Director)
c/o Staff Member *Jerry Lewis Films Inc*
2820 W Charleston Blvd # D33
Las Vegas, NV 89102-1942, USA

Lewis, Jerry (Congressman, Politician)
2112 Rayburn Hob
Washington, DC 20515-0541, USA

Lewis, Jerry Lee (Musician)
1595 Malone Rd
Nesbit, MS 38651-9310, USA

Lewis, Jim (Athlete, Baseball Player)
5062 Big Rock St
Jackson, MI 49201-8126, USA

Lewis, Jim (Athlete, Baseball Player)
5311 Hansel Ave Apt D12
Orlando, FL 32809-3415, USA

Lewis, J L (Athlete, Golfer)
2504 Orleans Dr
Cedar Park, TX 78613-4727, USA

Lewis, John (Congressman, Politician)
343 Cannon Hob
Washington, DC 20515-1005, USA

Lewis, John (Race Car Driver)
524 El Cerrito Ave
Hillsborough, CA 94010-6822, USA

Lewis, Johnny (Athlete, Baseball Player)
7710 Fiesta Dr
Pensacola, FL 32534-4515, USA

Lewis, Jon Peter (Musician, Reality Star)
PO Box 533
Newbury Park, CA 91319-0533, USA

Lewis, Juliette (Actor)
305 E Valencia Ave Apt E
Burbank, CA 91502-2654, USA

Lewis, Karen (Writer)
c/o James Sarnoff *The Sarnoff Company Inc*
10 Universal City Plz # 2000
Universal City, CA 91608-1002, USA

Lewis, Kendrick (Athlete, Football Player)
c/o Bus Cook *Bus Cook Sports, Inc*
1 Willow Bend Dr
Hattiesburg, MS 39402-8552, USA

Lewis, Kevin (Athlete, Football Player)
4417 Roy St
Orlando, FL 32812-7350, USA

Lewis, Leona (Actor, Musician)
2668 Astral Dr
Los Angeles, CA 90046-1708, USA

Lewis, Marcedes (Athlete, Football Player)
3725 Bouton Dr
Lakewood, CA 90712-3822, USA

Lewis, Mark (Athlete, Baseball Player)
1753 Cleveland Ave
Hamilton, OH 45013-5114, USA

Lewis, Mark (Athlete, Football Player)
PO Box 11021
Spring, TX 77391-1021, USA

Lewis, Marvin (Coach, Football Coach)
Cincinnati Bengals
1 Paul Brown Stadium
Cincinnati, OH 45202-3492, USA

Lewis, Michael (Writer)
c/o Matthew Snyder *Creative Artists Agency (CAA-LA)*
2000 Avenue of the Stars Ste 100
Los Angeles, CA 90067-4705, USA

Lewis, Mike (Athlete, Basketball Player)
490 Windsor Park Rd
Kernersville, NC 27284-7013, USA

Lewis, Mike (Athlete, Football Player)
3350 Blodgett St
Houston, TX 77004-6305, USA

Lewis, Mo (Athlete, Baseball Player)
4210 Blackhawk Meadow Ct
Danville, CA 94506-5862, USA

Lewis, Mo (Athlete, Football Player)
3280 Northside Pkwy NW Apt 314
Atlanta, GA 30327-2260, USA

Lewis, Monica (Musician)
Lang
1100 Alta Loma Rd Apt 16A
West Hollywood, CA 90069-2441, USA

Lewis, Nate (Athlete, Football Player)
3374 Brooksong Way
Dacula, GA 30019-1199, USA

Lewis, Phill (Actor)
c/o Gregg A Klein *AKA Talent Agency*
6310 San Vicente Blvd Ste 200
Los Angeles, CA 90048-5488, USA

Lewis, Ralph (Athlete, Basketball Player)
3004 Maryannes Ct
North Wales, PA 19454-2024, USA

Lewis, Ramsey (Musician)
c/o Ted Kurland *Ted Kurland Associates*
173 Brighton Ave
Allston, MA 02134-2003, USA

Lewis, Rashard (Basketball Player)
Seattle SuperSonics
351 Elliott Ave W Ste 500
Seattle, WA 98119-4153, USA

Lewis, Ray (Athlete, Football Player)
c/o David Dunn *Athletes First, LLC*
23091 Mill Creek Dr
Laguna Hills, CA 92653-1258, USA

Lewis, Richard (Actor, Comedian)
c/o Mike Eistenstadt *Amsel, Eistenstadt & Frazier Talent Agency (AEF)*
5055 Wilshire Blvd Ste 860
Los Angeles, CA 90036-6108, USA

Lewis, Richard J (Producer)
c/o Carel Cutler *ICM Partners (LA)*
10250 Constellation Blvd Fl 7
Los Angeles, CA 90067-6207, USA

Lewis, Richie (Athlete, Baseball Player)
13209 E County Road 700 S
Losantville, IN 47354-9514, USA

Lewis, Robert (Athlete, Basketball Player)
3656 Bay Dr
Edgewater, MD 21037-4143, USA

Lewis, Rommie (Athlete, Basketball Player)
5511 Mountville Rd
Adamstown, MD 21710-9612, USA

Lewis, Ron (Athlete, Football Player)
12821 Haverford Rd W Apt 1
Jacksonville, FL 32218-4879, USA

Lewis, Scott (Athlete, Baseball Player)
238 Camellia Ln
Costa Mesa, CA 92627-1803, USA

Lewis, Shane (Race Car Driver)
209 Ridge Rd
Jupiter, FL 33477-9660, USA

Lewis, Sherman (Athlete, Football Player)
45822 Bristol Cir
Novi, MI 48377-3900, USA

Lewis, Thaddaeus (Athlete, Football Player)
c/o Drew Rosenhaus *Rosenhaus Sports Representation*
6400 Allison Rd
Miami Beach, FL 33141-4540, USA

Lewis, Thomas (Athlete, Football Player)
13634 N 12th Pl
Phoenix, AZ 85022-4968, USA

Lewis, Tim (Athlete, Football Player)
2938 Major Ridge Trl
Duluth, GA 30097-4985, USA

Lewis, Travis (Athlete, Football Player)
c/o Erik Burkhardt *Select Sports Group*
2700 Post Oak Blvd Ste 1450
Houston, TX 77056-5785, USA

Lewis, Vicki (Actor, Comedian)
c/o Staff Member *Stone Manners Salners Agency (LA)*
6100 Wilshire Blvd Ste 1500
Los Angeles, CA 90048-5110, USA

Lewis, Will (Athlete, Football Player)
1980 Seattle Seahawks
Sammamish, WA 98074, USA

Lewis, W Paul (Race Car Driver)
3408 Bristol Hwy
Johnson City, TN 37601-1320, USA

Lewis III, Leo (Athlete, Football Player)
1301 White Oak Ln
Columbia, MO 65203-1927, USA

Lewis III, Randy (Race Car Driver)
4101 Big Ranch Rd
Napa, CA 94558-1406, USA

Lewis-Moore, Kapron (Athlete, Football Player)
c/o David Lee *Players Rep Sports Management*
34208 Aurora Rd
#250
Solon, OH 44139, USA

Lewit-Nirenberg, Julie (Publisher)
Mademoiselle Magazine
350 Madison Ave
New York, NY 10017-3700, USA

Ley, Terry (Athlete, Baseball Player)
32270 Stone Rd
Warren, OR 97053-9744, USA

Leyden, Paul (Actor)
c/o Rhonda Price *Gersh (NY)*
41 Madison Ave
New York, NY 10010-2202, USA

Leyland, Jim (Athlete, Baseball Player, Coach)
261 Tech Rd
Pittsburgh, PA 15205-1734, USA

Leyritz, Jim (Athlete, Baseball Player)
11060 Cameron Ct Apt 304
Davie, FL 33324-4188, USA

Leyva, Nick (Athlete, Baseball Player, Coach)
1098 Tilghman Rd
Chesterbrook, PA 19087-5878, USA

Leyva, Victor (Athlete, Football Player)
17690 Road 320
Springville, CA 93265-9635, USA

Lezak, Jason (Athlete, Olympic Athlete, Swimmer)
c/o Evan Morgenstein *Premier Management Group (PMG Sports)*
115 Crescent Commons Dr Ste 250
Cary, NC 27518-8134, USA

Lezcano, Carlos (Athlete, Baseball Player)
3870 S Dew Drop Ln
Gilbert, AZ 85297-8033, USA

Lezcano, Sixto (Athlete, Baseball Player)
7828 Bardmoor Hill Cir
Orlando, FL 32835-8158, USA

LFO (Musician)
Evolution Talent Agency
1776 Broadway Fl 15
New York, NY 10019-2002

L. Fudge, Marcia (Congressman, Politician)
1019 Longworth Hob
Washington, DC 20515-3012, USA

Ignasiak, Gary (Athlete, Baseball Player)
3084 Angelus Dr
Waterford, MI 48329-2506, USA

Ignizio, Mildred (Bowler)
241 Shore Acres Dr
Rochester, NY 14612-5807, USA

L. Hanna, Richard (Congressman, Politician)
319 Cajimon Hob
Washington, DC 20515-0001, USA

L. Hastings, Alcee (Congressman, Politician)
2353 Rayburn Hob
Washington, DC 20515-3811, USA

Li, Gong (Actor, Model)
c/o Julie Moore *The J-Line Group Inc*
8671 Wilshire Blvd Fl 4
Beverly Hills, CA 90211-2926, USA

Li, Jet (Actor)
c/o Steve Chasman *Current Entertainment*
9200 W Sunset Blvd Ste 600
West Hollywood, CA 90069-3196, USA

Li, Yiyun (Writer)
c/o Richard Abate *3 Arts Entertainment (NY)*
16 W 22nd St Ste 201
New York, NY 10010-5842, USA

Liars (Music Group)
c/o David T Viecelli *Billions Corporation, The*
833 W Chicago Ave Ste 101
Chicago, IL 60642-8408, USA

Liars Inc (Music Group)
c/o Staff Member *Foodchain Records*
4212 W Sunset Blvd
Los Angeles, CA 90029-2110, USA

Libby, Jeff (Athlete, Hockey Player)
24 Foxwell Dr
Scarborough, ME 04074-7608, USA

Liber, Jon (Baseball Player)
Pittsburgh Pirates
2805 Churchbell Ct
Mobile, AL 36695-2528, USA

Liberace, Dora
1775 E Tropicana Ave
Las Vegas, NV 89119-6529

Libertini, Richard (Actor)
2313 McKinley Ave
Venice, CA 90291-4623, USA

Liberty, Marcus (Athlete, Basketball Player)
3923 N Drake Ave
Chicago, IL 60618-3205, USA

Liberty, Richard
225 SW 6th St
Dania, FL 33004-3943

Libett, Nick (Athlete, Hockey Player)
4272 N McNay Ct
West Bloomfield, MI 48323-2839

Liboiron, Landon (Actor)
c/o Kimberlin Dalehite *Magnolia Entertainment (LA)*
9595 Wilshire Blvd Ste 601
Beverly Hills, CA 90212-2506, USA

Libran, Frankie (Athlete, Baseball Player)
PO Box 312
Mayaguez, PR 00681-0312, USA

Licad, Cecile (Musician)
Columbia Artists Mgmt Inc
165 W 57th St
New York, NY 10019-2201, USA

Licht, Jeremy (Actor)
4355 Clybourn Ave
Toluca Lake, CA 91602-2906, USA

Lichtenberg, Byron K (Astronaut)
5701 Impala South Rd
Athens, TX 75752-6053, USA

Lichtenberg, Byron K Dr (Astronaut)
570LLMPALA South Rd
Athens, TX 75752, USA

Lichtenberger, H W (Business Person)
Praxair Inc
39 Old Ridgebury Rd
Danbury, CT 06810-5103, USA

Lichtenstein, Harvey (Music Group)
Brooklyn Academy of Music
30 Lafayette Ave
Brooklyn, NY 11217-1486, USA

Lichti, Todd (Athlete, Basketball Player)
2331 Holly View Dr
Martinez, CA 94553-3375, USA

Lick, Dennis A (Athlete, Football Player)
6140 S Knox Ave
Chicago, IL 60629-5424, USA

Lickert, John (Athlete, Baseball Player)
PO Box 279
North Scituate, RI 02857-0279, USA

Lickliter, Frank (Athlete, Golfer)
846 S Main St
Franklin, OH 45005-2731, USA

Licon, Jeffrey (Actor)
c/o Katie Mason *Luber Roklin Management*
5815 W Sunset Blvd Ste 206
Los Angeles, CA 90028-6481, USA

Lidback, Jenny (Athlete, Golfer)
1130 Graystone Xing
Alpharetta, GA 30005-7436, USA

Liddell, Chuck (Iceman) (Athlete, Wrestler)
c/o Staff Member *UFC*
PO Box 26959
Las Vegas, NV 89126-0959, USA

Liddell, Dave (Athlete, Baseball Player)
2631 Preakness Way
Norco, CA 92860-4201, USA

Liddington, Bob (Athlete, Hockey Player)
2538 E Sahuaro Dr
Phoenix, AZ 85028-2538

Liddle, Steve (Athlete, Basketball Player)
437 Heath Pi
Smyrna, TN 37167, USA

Liddy, Edward M (Business Person)
Allstate Corp
2775 Sanders Rd
Allstate Plaza
Northbrook, IL 60062-6110, USA

Liddy, G Gordon (Actor)
9112 Riverside Dr
Fort Washington, MD 20744-6863, USA

Lidge, Brad (Athlete, Baseball Player)
4833 Front St Ste A
Castle Rock, CO 80104-7901, USA

Lidster, Doug (Athlete, Hockey Player)
312 Homestead Blvd Unit 203
Lynden, WA 98264-9162

Lidstrom, Niklas (Attorney, Hockey Player)
47725 Bellagio Dr
Northville, MI 48167-9803

Liebenstein, Todd (Athlete, Football Player)
4486 Chain O Lakes Rd
Eagle River, WI 54521, USA

Liebensteuin, Todd (Athlete, Football Player)
4486 Chain O Lakes Rd
Eagle River, WI 54521-8856, USA

Lieber, Jon (Athlete, Baseball Player)
3060 Isle of Palms Dr W
Mobile, AL 36695-2576, USA

Lieber, Larry (Cartoonist)
c/o Staff Member *King Features Syndication*
300 W 57th St Fl 15
New York, NY 10019-5238, USA

Lieber, Paul (Actor)
c/o Margrit Polak *Margrit Polak Management*
1920 Hillhurst Ave Ste 405
Los Angeles, CA 90027-2712, USA

Lieber, Rob (Writer)
c/o Staff Member *ICM Partners (LA)*
10250 Constellation Blvd Fl 7
Los Angeles, CA 90067-6207, USA

Lieberman, Joseph I (Politician, Senator)
392LLVY Terrace Ct NW
Washington, DC 20007, USA

Lieberman, Nancy (Athlete, Basketball Player)
5756 Quebec Ln
Plano, TX 75024-2904, USA

Lieberman, Wendy
PO Box 5617
Beverly Hills, CA 90209-5617

Lieberman-cline, Nancy (Athlete, Basketball Player, Olympic Athlete)
2636 Creekway Dr
Carrollton, TX 75010-4227, USA

Liebert, Ottmar (Musician)
Jones & O'Malley
10123 Camarillo St
Toluca Lake, CA 91602-1601, USA

Lieberthal, Michael S (Mike) (Athlete, Baseball Player)
1740 Larkfield Ave
Westlake Village, CA 91362-4245, USA

Liebeskind, John (Doctor)
University of California Medical Center
Surgery Dept
Los Angeles, CA 90024, USA

Liebesman, Jonathan (Director)
617 N Fuller Ave
Los Angeles, CA 90036-1938, USA

Liebman, David (Musician)
1541 Brislin Rd
Stroudsburg, PA 18360-7689, USA

Liebowitz, Fran
205 W 57th St
New York, NY 10019-2105

Liebrich, Barbara (Athlete, Baseball Player)
16608 N 51st St
Scottsdale, AZ 85254-1063, USA

Liefeld, Bob (Cartoonist)
16780 Oak Burl Dr
Yorba Linda, CA 92886-1654, USA

Liefeld, Rob (Artist, Cartoonist)
1942 University Ave Ste 305
Berkeley, CA 94704-1244, USA

Liefer, Jeff (Athlete, Baseball Player)
1116 W Bay Ave
Newport Beach, CA 92661-1017, USA

Lien, Jennifer (Actor)
9932 Lemon Ave
Rancho Cucamonga, CA 91737-3621, USA

Lienhard, Bill (Athlete, Basketball Player, Olympic Athlete)
1320 Lawrence Ave
Lawrence, KS 66049-2938, USA

Lietzke, Bruce (Athlete, Golfer)
PO Box 177
Larue, TX 75770-0177, USA

Lifehouse (Music Group)
c/o Dave Klein *Creative Artists Agency (CAA-LA)*
2000 Avenue of the Stars Ste 100
Los Angeles, CA 90067-4705, USA

Life On Repeat (Music Group, Musician)
c/o Steve Taylor *Anthem Artist Management*
9048 Woodland Trl
Alpharetta, GA 30009-8758, USA

Lifford, Tina (Actor)
c/o Nancy Sanders *Sanders Armstrong Caserta*
2120 Colorado Ave Ste 120
Santa Monica, CA 90404-3561, USA

Lifvendahl, Harold R (Publisher)
Orlando Sentinel
633 N Orange Ave Lbby
Orlando, FL 32801-1349, USA

Light, John (Actor)
c/o Arlene Forster *Forster Entertainment*
12533 Woodgreen St
Los Angeles, CA 90066-2723, USA

Light, Judith (Actor)
c/o Bob Gersh *Gersh (LA)*
9465 Wilshire Blvd Ste 600
Beverly Hills, CA 90212-2605, USA

Light, Matt (Athlete, Football Player)
261 East St
Foxboro, MA 02035-3023, USA

Lightfoot, Leonard
446 S Orchard Dr
Burbank, CA 91506-2738

Ligon, Bill (Athlete, Basketball Player)
PO Box 1432
Gallatin, TN 37066-1432, USA

Ligon, Tom
227 Waverly Pl Apt 1A
New York, NY 10014-2410

Ligtenberg, Kerry (Athlete, Baseball Player)
9274 Albright Ct
Inver Grove Heights, MN 55077-4546, USA

Lil' Cease (Musician)
Famous Artists Agency
250 W 57th St
New York, NY 10107-0001, USA

Liles, Kevin (Business Person)
512 Fashion Ave Rm 4100
New York, NY 10018-4741, USA

Lil' J (Actor, Musician, Television Host)
c/o Staff Member *Thruline Entertainment*
9250 Wilshire Blvd Ste 100
Ground Floor
Beverly Hills, CA 90212-3343, USA

Lilja, Andreas (Athlete, Hockey Player)
6501 N Federal Hwy Ste 2
Boca Raton, FL 33487-3137

Lilja, George (Athlete, Football Player)
8 Driftwood Dr
Warren, PA 16365-3380, USA

Lil Jon (Musician)
c/o David Wirtschafter *William Morris Endeavor (LA)*
9601 Wilshire Blvd Ste 220
Beverly Hills, CA 90210-5205, USA

Lillard, Bill (Bowler)
5418 Imogene St
Houston, TX 77096-2206, USA

Lillard, Damian (Athlete, Basketball Player)
c/o Aaron Goodwin *Goodwin Sports Management*
121 Lakeside Ave Ste 100B
Seattle, WA 98122-6587, USA

Lillard, Matthew (Actor, Producer)
c/o Melissa Kates *Viewpoint Inc (LA)*
8820 Wilshire Blvd Ste 220
Beverly Hills, CA 90211-2622, USA

Lilley, John (Athlete, Hockey Player)
25 Curtis St
Wakefield, MA 01880-5109, USA

Lillibridge, Brent (Athlete, Baseball Player)
14631 43rd Dr SE
Snohomish, WA 98296-6993, USA

Lillien, Lisa (Writer)
c/o Bill Stankey *Westport Entertainment Associates*
1120 W State Route 89a
Sedona, AZ 86336-5759, USA

Lilliquist, Derek (Athlete, Baseball Player)
226 10th Ave
Vero Beach, FL 32962-2819, USA

Lillis, Bob (Athlete, Baseball Player, Coach)
5107 Cherry Tree Ln
Orlando, FL 32819-3848, USA

Lillis, Charles M (Business Person)
MediaOne Group
188 Inverness Dr W
Englewood, CO 80112-5205, USA

Lilly, Bob (Athlete, Football Player)
104 Aster Cir
Georgetown, TX 78633-4537, USA

Lilly, Evangeline (Actor)
c/o David Miner *3 Arts Entertainment (LA)*
9460 Wilshire Blvd Fl 7
Beverly Hills, CA 90212-2713, USA

Lilly, Ted (Athlete, Baseball Player)
1305 W Waveland Ave
Chicago, IL 60613-3720, USA

Lilly, Theodore (Baseball Player)
Montreal Expos
PO Box 257
Bass Lake, CA 93604-0257, USA

Lilly, Tony (Athlete, Football Player)
13815 Holly Forest Dr
Manassas, VA 20112-3864, USA

Lilly-Heavey, Kristine (Athlete, Olympic Athlete, Soccer Player)
359 Grove St
Needham, MA 02492-1009, USA

Lillywhite, Verl (Athlete, Football Player)
1828 N Barkley
Mesa, AZ 85203-2702, USA

Lil Wayne (Musician)
94 Lagorce Cir
Miami Beach, FL 33141-4520, USA

Lily, Morgan (Actor)
c/o Casey Crawford *Origin Talent Agency*
4705 Laurel Canyon Blvd Ste 303
Valley Village, CA 91607-5943, USA

Lilyholm, Len (Athlete, Hockey Player, Olympic Athlete)
2850 S Ocean Blvd Apt 113
Palm Beach, FL 33480-6242, USA

Lim, Kwan Hi
1660 Piikoi St Apt E
Honolulu, HI 96822-2719

Lim, Phillip (Designer)
Phillip Lim Retail LLC
304 Hudson St Fl 8
8th Floor N
New York, NY 10013-1015, USA

Lim, Siew-Ai (Athlete, Golfer)
304 Morning Sun Dr
Birmingham, AL 35242-2912, USA

Lima, Adriana (Actor, Model)
c/o Chris Kiely *Marilyn Model Management*
32 Union Sq E PH
New York, NY 10003-3209, USA

Lima, Devin (Actor)
LFO/BMG Records
8750 Wilshire Blvd
Beverly Hills, CA 90211-2703

Lima, Floriana (Actor)
c/o Adam Levine *Industry Entertainment*
955 Carrillo Dr Ste 300
Los Angeles, CA 90048-5400, USA

Liman, Doug (Director, Producer, Writer)
c/o Adam Kanter *Paradigm (LA)*
2000 Avenue of the Stars
Los Angeles, CA 90067-4700, USA

Limato, Ed
456 S Plymouth Blvd
Los Angeles, CA 90020-4708

Limbaugh, Rush (Politician)
PO Box 2795
Palm Beach, FL 33480-2795, USA

Limbrick, Garrett (Athlete, Football Player)
PO Box 472
Hempstead, TX 77445-0472, USA

Lime, Yvonne (Actor)
Fedderson
6135 E McDonald Dr
Paradise Valley, AZ 85253-5222, USA

Limelighters, The
11761 E Speedway Blvd
Tucson, AZ 85748-2017

Limelights
11761 E Speedway Blvd
Tucson, AZ 85748-2017

Limos, Tiffany (Actor)
c/o Staff Member *Paradigm (LA)*
360 N Crescent Dr
North Bldg
Beverly Hills, CA 90210-4874, USA

Lin, Cho-Laing (Musician)
5404 John Dreaper Dr
Houston, TX 77056-4231

Lin, Cho-Liang (Musician)
Hilliard School
60 Lincoln Center Plz
New York, NY 10023-6588, USA

Lin, Jeremy (Linsanity) (Athlete, Basketball Player)
c/o Roger Montgomery *Montgomery Sports Group*
19141 Stone Oak Pkwy
San Antonio, TX 78258-3366, USA

Lin, Justin (Director)
c/o Rowena Arguelles *Creative Artists Agency (CAA-LA)*
2000 Avenue of the Stars Ste 100
Los Angeles, CA 90067-4705, USA

Lin, Yu Ping (Athlete, Golfer)
1000 S Romney Dr
Walnut, CA 91789-4804, USA

Lincecum, Tim (Athlete, Baseball Player)
c/o Rick Thurman *Beverly Hills Sports Council*
131 S Rodeo Dr Ste 100
Beverly Hills, CA 90212-2439, USA

Lincicome, Brittany (Athlete, Golfer)
8664 Longwood Dr
Seminole, FL 33777-1309, USA

Lincoln, Andrew (Actor)
c/o Shea Martin *SLATE Public Relations - NY*
307 7th Ave Rm 2401
New York, NY 10001-6019, USA

Lincoln, Blanche (Politician)
3942 27th Rd N
Arlington, VA 22207-5242, USA

Lincoln, Brad (Athlete, Baseball Player)
331 S Shanks St
Clute, TX 77531-4622, USA

Lincoln, Craig (Athlete, Diver, Olympic Athlete)
20930 Almazan Rd
Woodland Hills, CA 91364-5501, USA

Lincoln, Howard (Commentator)
Seattle Mariners
6 Holly Hill Dr
Mercer Island, WA 98040-5326, USA

Lincoln, Jeremy (Athlete, Football Player)
71 Broadway Apt 20A
New York, NY 10006-2612, USA

Lincoln, Keith P (Athlete, Football Player)
550 SE Crestview St
Pullman, WA 99163-2257, USA

Lincoln, Lar Park
8899 Beverly Blvd Ste 510
Los Angeles, CA 90048-2449

Lincoln, Michael (Mike) (Athlete, Baseball Player)
8269 Moss Oak Ave
Citrus Heights, CA 95610-0763, USA

Lind, Adam (Athlete, Baseball Player)
6520 Turf Way
Anderson, IN 46013-9588, USA

Lind, DeDe
PO Box 1712
Boca Raton, FL 33429-1712

Lind, Don L (Astronaut)
51 N 376 E
Smithfield, UT 84335-1111, USA

Lind, Don L Dr (Astronaut)
51 N 376 E
Smithfield, UT 84335-1111, USA

Lind, Emily Alyn (Actor)
c/o Penny Vizcarra *Integrated PR*
9025 Wilshire Blvd Ste 400
Beverly Hills, CA 90211-1828, USA

Lind, Jack (Athlete, Baseball Player)
6132 E Redmont Dr
Mesa, AZ 85215-0878, USA

Lind, Joan (Athlete)
240 Euclid Ave
Long Beach, CA 90803-6020, USA

Lind, Jose (Athlete, Baseball Player)
18 Brisas Del Plata
Dorado, PR 00646-5123, USA

Lindahl, David (Business Person)
PHP Inc
75 Old High St
Whitman, MA 02382-1143

Lindahl, George III (Business Person)
Union Pacific Resources
PO Box 1330
Houston, TX 77251-1330, USA

Lindberg, Chad (Actor)
c/o Staff Member *Michael Black Management*
9701 Wilshire Blvd Fl 10
Beverly Hills, CA 90212-2010, USA

Lindbergh, Reeve (Writer)
839 Tripp Ln
St Johnsbury, VT 05819-8507, USA

Lindelind, Liv (Model)
PO Box 1029
Frazier Park, CA 93225-1029, USA

Lindell, Rian (Athlete, Football Player)
8221 233rd Pl NE
Redmond, WA 98053-1985, USA

Lindelof, Damon (Producer, Writer)
c/o Ted Miller *Creative Artists Agency (CAA-LA)*
2000 Avenue of the Stars Ste 100
Los Angeles, CA 90067-4705, USA

Lindeman, Jim (Athlete, Baseball Player)
2250 W Golf Rd Apt 207
Hoffman Estates, IL 60169-1112, USA

Lindemann, Tony (Bowler)
6250 Roosevelt Blvd Lot 80
Clearwater, FL 33760-2583, USA

Lindemulder, Janine (Adult Film Star)
c/o Staff Member *Vivid Entertainment*
3599 Cahuenga Blvd W Fl 2
Los Angeles, CA 90068-1397, USA

Linden, Eric (Athlete, Hockey Player)
1 Pattison Pl
Philadelphia, PA 19148, USA

Linden, Hal (Actor)
c/o Staff Member *Stone Manners Talent & Literary (NY)*
900 Broadway Ste 803
New York, NY 10003-1229, USA

Linden, Todd (Athlete, Baseball Player)
7825 NW Anderson Hill Rd
Silverdale, WA 98383-9313, USA

Linden, Walt (Athlete, Baseball Player)
4432 Harvey Ave
Western Springs, IL 60558-1645, USA

Lindenlaub, Karl W (Cinematographer)
3021 Nichols Canyon Rd
Los Angeles, CA 90046-1242, USA

Lindenmann, Tony (Bowler)
35096 Jefferson Ave Apt 216
Harrison Township, MI 48045-3275, USA

Linder, Brandon (Athlete, Football Player)
c/o Alan Herman *Sportstars Inc*
1350 Avenue of the Americas Fl 28
New York, NY 10019-4702, USA

Linder, Kate (Actor)
c/o Sandra Siegal *Siegal Company, The*
9025 Wilshire Blvd Ste 400
Beverly Hills, CA 90211-1828, USA

Lindh, Hilary (Skier)
PO Box 33036
Juneau, AK 99803-3036, USA

Lindholm, Mikael (Athlete, Hockey Player)
Norra Abyggebyvagen 44
Gavle, 80 SWEDE

Lindhome, Riki (Actor, Director, Writer)
c/o Mary Ellen Mulcahy *Framework Entertainment (LA)*
9057 Nemo St Ste C
West Hollywood, CA 90069-5511, USA

Lindig, Bill M (Business Person)
Sysco Corp
1390 Enclave Pkwy
Houston, TX 77077-2099, USA

Lindland, Matt (Athlete, Olympic Athlete, Wrestler)
26501 SE Mattson Ln
Eagle Creek, OR 97022-9606, USA

Lindley, Christina (Model)
Lindley Enterprises
114 Rhine Dr
Madison, TN 37115-3561, USA

Lindley, Leta (Athlete, Golfer)
104 Alegria Way
Palm Beach Gardens, FL 33418-1722, USA

Lindley, Ryan (Athlete, Football Player)
c/o Bruce Tollner *REP 1 Sports Group*
2 Corporate Park Ste 106
Irvine, CA 92606-5103, USA

Lindo, Delroy (Actor)
c/o Brian Swardstrom *United Talent Agency (UTA-NYC)*
888 7th Ave Fl 38
New York, NY 10106-3899, USA

Lindsay, Bill (Athlete, Hockey Player)
Florida Panthers
1 Panther Pkwy
Sunrise, FL 33323-5315

Lindsay, Bill (Athlete, Hockey Player)
700 NW 7th Ave
Boca Raton, FL 33486-3518

Lindsay, Everett (Athlete, Football Player)
101 Wildwood Beach Rd Apt
Beachaptrdwildwood PMB 13.101
Saint Paul, MN 55115-1662, USA

Lindsay, Mort
6970 Fernhill Dr
Malibu, CA 90265-4239

Lindsay, R B Theodore (Ted) (Athlete, Hockey Player)
2598 Invitational Dr
Oakland, MI 48363-2453, USA

Lindsay, Ted (Athlete, Hockey Player)
25981NVITATIONAL Dr
Oakland, MI 48363

Lindsey, Bill (Athlete, Baseball Player)
1317 Winterberry Dr
Reidsville, NC 27320-7154, USA

Lindsey, Dale (Athlete, Football Player)
4020 Murphy Canyon Rd
San Diego, CA 92123-4407, USA

Lindsey, Doug (Athlete, Baseball Player)
2410 Silver Spur Ln
Leander, TX 78641-7883, USA

Lindsey, Hub (Athlete, Football Player)
1320 Frebis Ave
Columbus, OH 43206-3717, USA

Lindsey, James E (Athlete, Football Player)
1165 E Joyce Blvd
Fayetteville, AR 72703-5183, USA

Lindsey, Jim
1165 E Joyce Blvd
Fayetteville, AR 72703-5183, USA

Lindsey, Rodney (Rod) (Athlete, Baseball Player)
610 Comanchee Dr Lot 43
Opelika, AL 36804-6500, USA

Lindsey, Steven W (Athlete, Football Player)
1327 County Road 123
Water Valley, MS 38965-6114, USA

Lindsey, Steven W Colonel (Astronaut)
3217 W Yarrow Cir
Superior, CO 80027-6021, USA

Lindsey, Terry (Athlete, Football Player)
324 W Brookdale Pl
Fullerton, CA 92832-1426, USA

Lindsey, Tracy
651 N Kilkea Dr
Los Angeles, CA 90048-2213

Lindsley, Blake (Actor)
Gold Marshak Liedtke
3500 W Olive Ave Ste 1400
Burbank, CA 91505-5512, USA

Lindstrom, Charlie (Chuck) (Athlete, Baseball Player)
PO Box 486
Atlanta, IL 61723-0486, USA

Lindstrom, Chris (Athlete, Football Player)
70 Dudley Hill Rd
Dudley, MA 01571-5924, USA

Lindstrom, David (Dave) (Athlete, Football Player)
13209 Woodson St
Leawood, KS 66209-3817, USA

Lindstrom, Jack (Cartoonist)
United Feature Syndicate
PO Box 5610
Cincinnati, OH 45201-5610, USA

Lindstrom, Jon (Actor)
c/o Staff Member *Gilbertson Management*
1334 3rd Street Promenade Ste 201
Santa Monica, CA 90401-1320, USA

Lindstrom, Matt (Athlete, Baseball Player)
316 Mohawk Ave
Rexburg, ID 83440-2227, USA

Lindstrom, Pia (Journalist)
30 Rockefeller Plz Ste 700
New York, NY 10112-0015, USA

Lindvall, Angela (Actor, Model)
c/o Siri Garber *Platform Public Relations*
2666 N Beachwood Dr
Los Angeles, CA 90068-2308, USA

Line, Bill (Athlete, Football Player)
6048 Plumas St Apt E
Reno, NV 89519-6024, USA

Line, Lorie (Musician)
Lorie Line
PO Box 400
Mound, MN 55364-0400, USA

Linebrink, Scott (Athlete, Baseball Player)
2100 County Road 156
Granger, TX 76530-5328, USA

Lineger, Jerry (Astronaut)
c/o Staff Member *Washington Speakers Bureau*
1663 Prince St
Alexandria, VA 22314-2818, USA

Linehan, Scott (Athlete, Football Player)
6315 Westchester Dr
Dallas, TX 75205-1668, USA

Linenger, Jerry M (Astronaut)
550 S Stony Point Rd
Suttons Bay, MI 49682-9575, USA

Linenger, Jerry M Dr (Astronaut)
550 S Stony Point Rd
Suttons Bay, MI 49682-9575, USA

Lines, Dick (Athlete, Baseball Player)
1716 Pebble Beach Ln
Lady Lake, FL 32159-2238, USA

Liney, John (Cartoonist)
c/o Staff Member *King Features
Syndication*
300 W 57th St Fl 15
New York, NY 10019-5238, USA

Ling (Model)
I M G Models
304 Park Ave S # 1200
New York, NY 10010-4301, USA

Ling, Bai (Actor)
c/o Matt Luber *Luber Roklin Management*
5815 W Sunset Blvd Ste 206
Los Angeles, CA 90028-6481, USA

Ling, Lisa (Correspondent, Journalist)
234 Alta Ave
Santa Monica, CA 90402-2728, USA

Lingenfelter, Bob (Football Player)
Cleveland Browns
53144 865 Rd
Plainview, NE 68769-2505, USA

Lingenfelter, John (Race Car Driver)
Summit Racing
PO Box 535
Richfield, OH 44286-0535, USA

Lingenfelter, Steve (Athlete, Basketball
Player)
17378 Ithaca Ct
Lakeville, MN 55044-8742, USA

Lingle, Linda (Politician)
520 Lunalilo Home Rd Unit 8425
Honolulu, HI 96825-1760, USA

Lingmerth, Goran (Athlete, Football
Player)
624 Enfield Ct
Delray Beach, FL 33444-1749, USA

Lingner, Adam (Athlete, Football Player)
8395 Norwood Ln N
Maple Grove, MN 55369-3058, USA

Linhart, Anton (Athlete, Football Player)
13 Summer Run Ct
Lutherville Timonium, MD 21093-4346,
USA

Linhart, Carl (Athlete, Baseball Player)
2647 Delmar Ave
Granite City, IL 62040-3439, USA

Linhart, Toni (Athlete, Football Player)
13 Summer Run Ct
Lutherville Timonium, MD 21093-4346,
USA

Liniak, Cole (Athlete, Baseball Player)
PO Box 235625
Encinitas, CA 92023-5625, USA

Linke, Paul (Actor)
Zealous Artists
139 S Beverly Dr Ste 225
Beverly Hills, CA 90212-3028, USA

Linkert, Lo (Artist, Cartoonist)
9541 Lenore Dr
Garden Grove, CA 92841-4925, USA

Linklater, Hamish (Actor)
c/o Leanne Coronel *Coronel Group*
1100 Glendon Ave Fl 17
Los Angeles, CA 90024-3588, USA

Linklater, Hamish (Actor)
c/o Hildy Gottlieb *ICM Partners (LA)*
10250 Constellation Blvd Fl 7
Los Angeles, CA 90067-6207, USA

Linklater, Richard (Director, Producer,
Writer)
Detour Filmproduction
PO Box 13351
Austin, TX 78711-3351, USA

Linkletter, Nicole (Model)
c/o Staff Member *Elite Model
Management (NY)*
245 5th Ave Fl 24
New York, NY 10016-8728, USA

Linley, Cody (Actor)
c/o Staff Member *Reel Talent
Management*
PO Box 491035
Los Angeles, CA 90049-9035, USA

Linn, Jack (Athlete, Football Player)
8418 Trillium Rd
Fort Myers, FL 33967-3486, USA

Linn, Teri Ann (Actor)
Sutton Barth Vennari
5900 Wilshire Blvd Ste 100
Los Angeles, CA 90036-5007, USA

Linn-Baker, Mark (Actor)
27702 Fairweather St
Canyon Country, CA 91351-2925, USA

Linne, Aubrey (Athlete, Football Player)
4606 Lanham St
Midland, TX 79705-3213, USA

Linne, Larry (Athlete, Football Player)
6861 Pumpkin Ridge Dr
Windsor, CO 80550-7015, USA

Linneha, Richard M Dr (Astronaut)
16802 Hartwood Way
Houston, 77 TX, USA

Linnehan, Richard M (Astronaut)
1501 Copperfield Pkwy Apt 216
College Sta, TX 77845-4678, USA

Linney, Laura (Actor)
c/o Aleen Keshishian *Brillstein
Entertainment Partners (LA)*
9150 Wilshire Blvd Ste 350
Beverly Hills, CA 90212-3453, USA

Linnin, Chris (Athlete, Football Player)
1037 Purple Sage Loop
Castle Rock, CO 80104-7846, USA

Linsalata, Joe (Athlete, Baseball Player)
4017 Washington St
Hollywood, FL 33021-7349, USA

Linseman, Ken (Athlete, Hockey Player)
1070 Ocean Blvd
Hampton, NH 03842-1500

Linskey, Mike (Baseball Player)
Bowman
18826 Polo Meadow Dr
Humble, TX 77346-8121, USA

Linson, Art (Director, Producer)
Art Linson Productions
Warner Bros
4000 Warner Blvd
Burbank, CA 91522-0001, USA

Lintel, Michelle (Actor)
c/o John Paradise *The Paradise Group*
PO Box 69451
West Hollywood, CA 90069-0451, USA

Linteris, Gregory T (Astronaut)
US Commerce Dept
Fire Science Division
Gaithersburg, MD 20899-0001, USA

Linteris, Gregory T Dr (Astronaut)
15325 Turkey Foot Rd
Gaithersburg, MD 20878-3640, USA

Linton, Doug (Athlete, Baseball Player)
201 Ellison St
Rochester, NY 14609-4047, USA

Lintz, Larry (Athlete, Baseball Player)
8529 Sun Sprite Way
Elk Grove, CA 95624-3816, USA

Linville, Joanne (Actor)
345 N Maple Dr # 302
Beverly Hills, CA 90210-3869, USA

Linz, Alex D (Actor)
Innovative Artists
1505 10th St
Santa Monica, CA 90401-2805, USA

Linz, Phil (Athlete, Baseball Player)
20 Rocky Rapids Rd
Stamford, CT 06903-3131, USA

Linzy, Frank (Athlete, Baseball Player)
38947 E 151st St S
Coweta, OK 74429-8550, USA

Liotta, Ray (Actor)
c/o Beth Holden-Garland *Untitled
Entertainment (LA)*
350 S Beverly Dr Ste 200
Beverly Hills, CA 90212-4819, USA

Lipetri, Angelo (Athlete, Baseball Player)
150 Yoakum Ave
Farmingdale, NY 11735-5034, USA

Lipinski, Ann Marie (Journalist)
Chicago Tribune
435 N Michigan Ave Ste 200
Editorial Dept
Chicago, IL 60611-4024, USA

Lipinski, Daniel (Congressman, Politician)
1717 Longworth Hob
Washington, DC 20515-1901, USA

Lipinski, Tara (Actor, Athlete, Figure
Skater, Olympic Athlete)
41 Surfsong Rd
Johns Island, SC 29455-5753, USA

Lipnicki, Jonathan (Actor)
c/o Jason Egenberg *United Talent Agency
(UTA-LA)*
9336 Civic Center Dr
Beverly Hills, CA 90210-3604, USA

Lippett, Ronnie (Athlete, Football Player)
610 Foundry St
South Easton, MA 02375-1318, USA

Lippincott, Philip E (Business Person)
Campbell Soup Co
Campbell Place
Camden, NJ 08103, USA

Lipps, Lisa (Adult Film Star)
Moonlite Bunny Ranch
69 Moonlight Rd
Mound House, NV 89706-7048, USA

Lipps, Louis (Athlete, Football Player)
132 Ruth St
Pittsburgh, PA 15211-2308, USA

Lipski, Bob (Athlete, Baseball Player)
1 Snook St
Scranton, PA 18505-2865, USA

Lipson, D Herbert (Publisher)
Philadelphia Magazine
1500 Walnut St
Philadelphia, PA 19102-3523, USA

Lipton, Bruce (Motivational Speaker)
2574 Pine Flat Rd
Santa Cruz, CA 95060-9497, USA

Lipton, Holly (Musician)
c/o Staff Member *Charles Rapp Enterprises
Inc*
88 Pine St Ste 2601
New York, NY 10005-1826, USA

Lipton, James (Actor, Producer, Television
Host)
c/o Staff Member *James Lipton
Productions*
120A E 23rd St Fl 3A
New York, NY 10010-4516, USA

Lipton, Peggy (Actor, Writer)
c/o Staff Member *St Martins Press*
175 5th Ave Ste 400
Publicity Dept
New York, NY 10010-7848, USA

Lipton, Robert (Actor)
c/o Staff Member *Judy Fox Personal
Talent Management*
Prefers to be contacted via telephone
West Hollywood, CA 90069, USA

Lipuma, Chris (Athlete, Hockey Player)
16032 Crystal Creek Dr Apt 1B
Orland Park, IL 60462-5355

Liquor, Shirley Q (Comedian)
c/o Stephen Ford *Diva Central Inc*
7510 W Sunset Blvd Ste 1445
Los Angeles, CA 90046-3408, USA

Liquori, Martin (Marty) (Athlete, Olympic
Athlete, Sportscaster, Track Athlete)
2915 NW 58th Blvd
Gainesville, FL 32606-8517, USA

Liriano, Francisco (Athlete, Baseball
Player)
2900 Thomas Ave S
Minneapolis, MN 55416-4477, USA

Liriano, Nelson (Athlete, Baseball Player)
Burlington Royals
PO Box 1143
Burlington, NC 27216-1143, USA

Lisbe, Mike (Writer)
c/o Brian Sher *Category 5 Entertainment*
300 71st St Ste 620
Miami Beach, FL 33141-3089, USA

Lisbon, Don (Athlete, Football Player)
PO Box 495
Grove City, PA 16127-0495, USA

Lisch, Russell (Athlete, Football Player)
206 Country Club Ln
Belleville, IL 62223-1910, USA

Lisch, Rusty (Athlete, Football Player)
206 Country Club Ln
Belleville, IL 62223-1910, USA

Liscio, Patti (Golfer)
7803 Glenneagle Dr
Dallas, TX 75248-2335, USA

Liscio, Tony (Athlete, Football Player)
10348 Trailcliff Dr
Dallas, TX 75238-1556, USA

Lisi, Rick (Athlete, Baseball Player)
143 Pinto Rd
Rogers, AR 72756-7148, USA

Lisitsa, Valentina (Musician)
Columbia Artists Mgmt Inc
165 W 57th St
New York, NY 10019-2201, USA

Liska, Stephen (Actor)
c/o Larry Metzger *Grant Savic Kopaloff & Associates*
6399 Wilshire Blvd Ste 414
Los Angeles, CA 90048-5716, USA

Liske, Pete (Athlete, Football Player)
13225 E Copper River Ln
Spokane, WA 99206-7063, USA

Liss, Joe (Actor)
c/o Scott Howard *Howard Entertainment*
16530 Ventura Blvd Ste 305
Encino, CA 91436-4594, USA

Lissie (Musician)
c/o Staff Member *Paradigm (Monterey)*
404 W Franklin St
Monterey, CA 93940-2303, USA

List, Peyton (Actor)
c/o Abby Bluestone *Innovative Artists (LA)*
1505 10th St
Santa Monica, CA 90401-2805, USA

List, Robert (Politician)
50 W Liberty St # 210
Reno, NV 89501-1940, USA

Listach, Pat (Athlete, Baseball Player)
Chicago Cubs
1060 W Addison St Ste 1
Chicago, IL 60613-4398

Listach, Pat (Athlete, Baseball Player)
6030 Durande Dr
Baton Rouge, LA 70820-5421, USA

Lister, Alton (Athlete, Basketball Player)
5413 Kirkridge Pl
Garland, TX 75044-4633, USA

Lister Jr, Tommy (Tiny Zeus) (Actor)
c/o Staff Member *Cindy Cowan Entertainment*
8265 W Sunset Blvd Ste 205
West Hollywood, CA 90046-2470, USA

Listopad, Ed (Athlete, Football Player)
6719 Roberts Ave
Dundalk, MD 21222-1053, USA

Lit (Music Group)
c/o Ruta Seopetys *Sepetys Entertainment Group*
5543 Edmondson Pike Ste 8A
Nashville, TN 37211-5808, USA

Lithgow, John (Actor)
c/o Mandi Warren *Viewpoint Inc (NYC)*
109 W 27th St Rm 6B
New York, NY 10001-6208, USA

Litsch, Jesse (Athlete, Baseball Player)
6948 80th Tern
Pinellas Park, FL 33781, USA

Littell, Mark (Athlete, Baseball Player)
27358 N 88th Ln
Peoria, AZ 85383-4853, USA

Litterell, Brian (Musician)
The Firm
9100 Wilshire Blvd Ste 100W
Beverly Hills, CA 90212-3435, USA

Little, Bernie (Race Car Driver)
PO Box 194
Novi, MI 48376-0194, USA

Little, Bryan (Athlete, Baseball Player)
4766 Tiffany Park Cir
Bryan, TX 77802-5822, USA

Little, Chad (Race Car Driver)
8718 Statesville Rd
Charlotte, NC 28269-2622, USA

Little, Dwight H (Director)
c/o Robert Lazar *Resolution (LA)*
1801 Century Park E Ste 2300
Los Angeles, CA 90067-2325, USA

Little, Everett (Athlete, Football Player)
5219 Kingsbury St
Houston, TX 77021-3724, USA

Little, Floyd D (Athlete, Football Player)
33207 Pacific Hwy S
Federal Way, WA 98003-6442, USA

Little, George (Athlete, Football Player)
1805 Powers St
McKeesport, PA 15132-5150, USA

Little, Grady (Athlete, Baseball Player)
13115 Odell Hejg Heights Dr
Charlotte, NC 28227, USA

Little, Jack (Athlete, Football Player)
PO Box 23528
Waco, TX 76702-3528, USA

Little, Jeff (Athlete, Baseball Player)
5711 W Camper Rd
Genoa, OH 43430-9300, USA

Little, Larry C (Athlete, Coach, Football Player)
14761 SW 169th Ln
Miami, FL 33187-1745, USA

Little, Leonard (Athlete, Football Player)
c/o Chad Speck *Allegiant Athletic Agency*
35 Market Sq Ste 201
Knoxville, TN 37902-1420, USA

Little, Mark (Athlete, Baseball Player)
28014 Moss Fern Dr
Katy, TX 77494-3240, USA

Little, Milton (Musician)
Camil Productions
6606 Solitary Ave
Las Vegas, NV 89110, USA

Little, Rich (Actor, Comedian)
c/o David Martin *David Martin Management*
13849 Riverside Dr
Sherman Oaks, CA 91423-2426, USA

Little, Sally (Athlete, Golfer)
3210 S Ocean Blvd Apt 702
Highland Beach, FL 33487-2597, USA

Little, Scott (Athlete, Baseball Player)
1321 Rosebud Dr
Jackson, MO 63755-1086, USA

Little, Steven (Musician)
Premier Talent
3 E 54th St # 1100
New York, NY 10022-3108, USA

Little, Tony
12750 59th Way N
Clearwater, FL 33760-3906, USA

Little, W Grady (Athlete, Baseball Player, Coach)
13115 Odell Heights Dr
Charlotte, NC 28227-4390, USA

Little, William (Athlete, Baseball Player)
7161 Chevy Chase
Memphis, TN 38125-2610, USA

Little Big Town (Music Group)
c/o Jason Owen *Sandbox Entertainment*
54 Music Sq E Ste 200
Nashville, TN 37203-4360, USA

Little Eva
1161 NW 76th Ave
Plantation, FL 33322-5120

Littlefield, David (Commentator)
105 Spenser Ln
Sewickley, PA 15143-8725, USA

Littlefield, John (Actor)
c/o Judy Orbach *Judy O Productions*
6136 Glen Holly St
Los Angeles, CA 90068-2338, USA

Littlefield, John (Athlete, Baseball Player)
1935 Ramar Rd
Bullhead City, AZ 86442-6949, USA

Littlefield, Warren (Producer)
815 Brooktree Rd
Pacific Palisades, CA 90272-3904, USA

Littleford, Beth (Actor)
c/o Alex Spieller *IMPR*
357 S Robertson Blvd
Beverly Hills, CA 90211-3602, USA

Little JJ (Actor)
c/o Charles King *William Morris Endeavor (LA)*
9601 Wilshire Blvd
Beverly Hills, CA 90210-5213, USA

Littlejohn, Dennis (Athlete, Baseball Player)
6813 Klamath Way Apt D
Bakersfield, CA 93309-7899, USA

Little Man Tate (Music Group)
c/o Staff Member *Paradigm (Monterey)*
404 W Franklin St
Monterey, CA 93940-2303, USA

Little Ones, The (Music Group)
c/o Jason Colton *Red Light Management (VA)*
321 E Main St Ste 500
Charlottesville, VA 22902-3201, USA

Littler, Gene (Athlete, Golfer)
PO Box 1949
Rancho Santa Fe, CA 92067-1949, USA

Little Richard (Musician)
c/o William (Bill) Sobel *Edelstein Laird & Sobel*
9255 W Sunset Blvd Ste 800
West Hollywood, CA 90069-3320, USA

Little River Band
9850 Sandalfoot Blvd # 458
Boca Raton, FL 33428-6645

Littles, Gene (Athlete, Basketball Player)
6421 E Beck Ln
Scottsdale, AZ 85254-2005, USA

Littleton, Larry (Athlete, Baseball Player)
1076 Dunbarton Trce NE
Atlanta, GA 30319-2674, USA

Littleton, Wes (Athlete, Baseball Player)
14770 W Laurel Ln
Surprise, AZ 85379-6309, USA

Littman, David (Athlete, Hockey Player)
3761 Spring House Ct SE
Marietta, GA 30067-4929

Littman, Jonathan (Producer)
c/o Staff Member *Creative Artists Agency (CAA-LA)*
2000 Avenue of the Stars Ste 100
Los Angeles, CA 90067-4705, USA

Litton, Bruce (Race Car Driver)
Bruce Litton Racing
PO Box 34174
Indianapolis, IN 46234-0174, USA

Litton, Greg (Athlete, Baseball Player)
785 Farmington Rd
Pensacola, FL 32504-7079, USA

Littrell, Brian (Musician)
c/o Johnny Wright *Wright Entertainment Group*
PO Box 590009
Orlando, FL 32859-0009, USA

Liu, Lucy (Actor)
c/o Mary Ellen Mulcahy *Framework Entertainment (LA)*
9057 Nemo St Ste C
West Hollywood, CA 90069-5511, USA

Liu, Matthew Stephen
10635 Santa Monica Blvd Ste 130
Los Angeles, CA 90025-8306

Liu, Nancy
9057-C Nemo St
West Hollywood, CA 90069

Liuget, Corey (Football Player)
c/o Tony Fleming *Impact Sports - LA*
11331 Ventura Blvd Ste 1A
Studio City, CA 91604-3147, USA

Liukin, Nastia (Athlete, Gymnast, Olympic Athlete)
c/o Joann Mignano *Krupp Kommunications*
59 W 19th St Rm 4C
New York, NY 10011-4245, USA

Liut, Mike (Athlete, Hockey Player)
26011 German Mill Rd
Franklin, MI 48025-1139

Live (Music Group)
c/o Staff Member *Paradigm (Monterey)*
404 W Franklin St
Monterey, CA 93940-2303, USA

Lively, Blake (Actor)
c/o Justin Grey Stone *Management 360*
9111 Wilshire Blvd
Beverly Hills, CA 90210-5508, USA

Lively, Bud (Athlete, Baseball Player)
8605 Esslinger Ct SE
Huntsville, AL 35802-3640, USA

Lively, Eric (Actor)
c/o Justin Grey Stone *Management 360*
350 S Beverly Dr Ste 200
Beverly Hills, CA 90212-4819, USA

Lively, Robyn (Actor)
7825 Shady Cove Ave
Burbank, CA 91504-1036, USA

Livermore, Ann (Business Person)
Hewlett-Packard Co
300 Hanover St
Palo Alto, CA 94304, USA

Livers, Virgil (Athlete, Football Player)
234 Johnson Ct
Tulare, CA 93274-3199, USA

Living Colour
6201 Sunset Blvd # 329
Los Angeles, CA 90028

Livingston, Andrew (Athlete, Football Player)
650 E Century Ave
Gilbert, AZ 85296-1118, USA

Livingston, Andy (Athlete, Football Player)
650 E Century Ave
Gilbert, AZ 85296-1118, USA

Livingston, Barry (Actor)
11310 Blix St
North Hollywood, CA 91602-1209, USA

Livingston, Bruce (Athlete, Football Player)
511 25th Ave W
Bradenton, FL 34205-8264, USA

Livingston, Mike (Athlete, Football Player)
8181 Monrovia St
Lenexa, KS 66215-2728, USA

Livingston, Robert L Jr (Politician)
Livingston Group
499 S Capitol St SW Ste 600
Washington, DC 20003-4037, USA

Livingston, Ron (Actor)
Rigberg Roberts Rugolo
1180 S Beverly Dr Ste 601
Los Angeles, CA 90035-1158, USA

Livingston, Shaun (Basketball Player)
Los Angeles Clippers
1111 S Figueroa St Ste 1100
Staples Center
Los Angeles, CA 90015-1345, USA

Livingston, Stanley (Actor)
PO Box 1782
Studio City, CA 91614-0782, USA

Livingston, Warren (Athlete, Football Player)
308 E Malibu Dr
Tempe, AZ 85282-5304, USA

Livingstone, Bob (Athlete, Football Player)
1625 Bluebird Ln
Munster, IN 46321-3322, USA

Livingstone, Scott (Athlete, Baseball Player)
3504 Sunrise Ranch Rd
Southlake, TX 76092-2082, USA

L. Jackson Jr., Jesse (Congressman, Politician)
2419 Rayburn Hob
Washington, DC 20515-1302, USA

Ljungberg, Fredrik (Model, Soccer Player)
c/o Noelle Keshishian Jenner Communications
8687 Melrose Ave Ste 8
West Hollywood, CA 90069-5746, USA

Llamosa, Carlos (Soccer Player)
New England Revolution
1 Patriot Pl
Cmgi Field
Foxboro, MA 02035-1388, USA

LL Cool J (Actor, Musician)
LL COOL J Inc.
6311 Romaine St
Los Angeles, CA 90038-2617, USA

Llewellyn, John A (Astronaut)
University of South Florida
4202 E Fowler Ave Stop U30329
Tampa, FL 33620-9951, USA

Llewellyn, John Dr (Astronaut)
141140th Ave E
Saint Petersburg, FL 33708, USA

Llewelyn, Doug (Actor)
8075 W 3rd St # 303
Los Angeles, CA 90048-4318

Lloyd, Arroyn (Actor)
c/o Michael Bircumshaw Water Street Management
5225 Wilshire Blvd Ste 615
Los Angeles, CA 90036-4350, USA

Lloyd, Brandon (Athlete, Football Player)
21109 E 50th Street Ct S
Blue Springs, MO 64015-2254, USA

Lloyd, Christopher (Actor)
c/o Andy Freedman Andrew J Freedman Personal Management
20 Ironsides St Apt 18
Marina Del Rey, CA 90292-5958, USA

Lloyd, Danny (Athlete, Football Player)
6025 Miwok Dr
San Jose, CA 95123-4113, USA

Lloyd, Dave (Athlete, Football Player)
24432 County Road 3107
Gladewater, TX 75647-8842, USA

Lloyd, Earl (Athlete, Basketball Coach, Basketball Player, Coach)
15 Pineridge Ct
Crossville, TN 38558-6532, USA

Lloyd, Emily Ann (Actor)
c/o Staff Member United Talent Agency (UTA-LA)
9336 Civic Center Dr
Beverly Hills, CA 90210-3604, USA

Lloyd, Eric (Actor)
c/o Mark Schumacher Schumacher Management
2018 Glendon Ave
Los Angeles, CA 90025-6324, USA

Lloyd, Gary (Race Car Driver)
Thee Dixon Racing
410 Marly Dr
Durham, NC 27703-5641, USA

Lloyd, Georgina (Writer)
Bantam Books
1540 Broadway
New York, NY 10036-4039, USA

Lloyd, Graeme (Athlete, Baseball Player)
455 Oceanview Ave
Palm Harbor, FL 34683-1816, USA

Lloyd, Greg (Athlete, Football Player)
154 Highland Park Dr
McDonough, GA 30252-2970, USA

Lloyd, Jake (Actor)
Osbrink Talent
4343 Lankershim Blvd # 100
North Hollywood, CA 91602-2705, USA

Lloyd, Madison (Actor)
Osbrink Talent
4343 Lankershim Blvd # 100
North Hollywood, CA 91602-2705, USA

Lloyd, Norman (Actor)
c/o Staff Member The Marion Rosenberg Office
8428 Melrose Pl Ste B
West Hollywood, CA 90069-5300, USA

Lloyd, Sabrina (Actor)
c/o Rachel Sheedy Resolution (LA)
10 E 44th St
New York, NY 10017-3601, USA

Lloyd, Sam (Actor)
c/o Staff Member Heidi Rotbart Management
1810 Malcolm Ave Apt 207
Los Angeles, CA 90025-7610, USA

Lloyd, Scott (Athlete, Basketball Player)
6838 Alexander Dr
Dallas, TX 75214-3208, USA

Lloyd, Tony (Athlete, Baseball Player)
6536 Cherokee Dr
Fairfield, AL 35064-1703, USA

Lloyd, Walt (Cinematographer)
22287 Mulholland Hwy # 393
Calabasas, CA 91302-5157, USA

Llyod, Tony (Baseball Player)
Birmingham Black Barons
6536 Cherokee Dr
Fairfield, AL 35064-1703, USA

LMFAO (Music Group)
c/o Johnny Maroney Moodswing 360
60 E 11th St Fl 7
New York, NY 10003-6022, USA

L. Mica, John (Congressman, Politician)
2187 Rayburn Hob
Washington, DC 20515-4609, USA

Immerfall, Dan (Athlete, Olympic Athlete, Speed Skater)
5421 Trempealeau Trl
Madison, WI 53705-4662, USA

Impe, Ed Van (Athlete, Hockey Player)
Philadelphia Flyers
3601 S Broad St Ste 2
Philadelphia, PA 19148-5297

Impemba, Mario (Commentator)
19945 Gallahad Dr
Macomb, MI 48044-1756, USA

Imus, Don (Journalist)
16 West Ave
Darien, CT 06820-4401, USA

Inhofe, James (Politician)
117 4th St SE
Washington, DC 20003-1002, USA

L. Noem, Kristi (Congressman, Politician)
226 Cannon Hob
Washington, DC 20515-3818, USA

Loaf, Meat (Actor, Musician, Producer)
c/o Michael Greene Greene & Associates
1901 Avenue of the Stars Ste 130
Los Angeles, CA 90067-6030, USA

Loaiza, Esteban (Athlete, Baseball Player)
2155 Corte Vis Apt 55
Chula Vista, CA 91915-4124, USA

Loar, John (Producer)
c/o Staff Member Red Bird Cinema
PO Box 846
166 Montair Dr
Danville, CA 94526-0846, USA

Lobdell, Erinn (Reality Star)
2472 N Bremen St
Milwaukee, WI 53212-3036, USA

Lobenstein, Bill (Athlete, Football Player)
3272 Deerfield Rd
Deerfield, WI 53531-9733, USA

Lobenstein, William (Athlete, Football Player)
3272 Deerfield Rd
Deerfield, WI 53531-9733, USA

Lo Bianco, Tony
c/o Staff Member Artists Only Management
10203 Santa Monica Blvd
Los Angeles, CA 90067-6405, USA

LoBiondo, Frank (Congressman, Politician)
2427 Rayburn Hob
Washington, DC 20515-0524, USA

Lobo, Rebecca (Athlete, Basketball Player, Olympic Athlete)
PO Box 734
Granby, CT 06035-0734, USA

Loc, Tone (Music Group)
c/o Staff Member M.A.G./Universal Attractions
15 W 36th St Fl 8
New York, NY 10018-7927, USA

Loc, Tone
7932 Hillside Ave
Los Angeles, CA 90046-2122

Locane, Amy (Actor)
c/o Staff Member Don Buchwald & Associates (LA)
6500 Wilshire Blvd Ste 2200
Los Angeles, CA 90048-4942, USA

Loceff, Michael (Producer)
c/o Staff Member Luber Roklin Management
5815 W Sunset Blvd Ste 206
Los Angeles, CA 90028-6481, USA

Locher, Dick
435 N Michigan Ave
Chicago, IL 60611-4066

Lochmueller, Robert (Athlete, Basketball Player)
18 William Tell Blvd
Tell City, IN 47586-2030, USA

Lochner, Philip R Jr (Business Person, Government Official)
Time Warner Inc
1 Time Warner Ctr Bsmt B
New York, NY 10019-6010, USA

Lochte, Ryan (Athlete, Olympic Athlete, Swimmer)
2701 NW 23rd Blvd Apt F219
Gainesville, FL 32605-5949, USA

Lock, Don (Athlete, Baseball Player)
11725 W Alderny Ct Unit 42
Wichita, KS 67212-6510, USA

Lockbaum, Gordie (Athlete, Football Player)
35 Brookshire Rd
Worcester, MA 01609-1251, USA

Locke, Bobby (Athlete, Baseball Player)
194 Eighty Acres Rd
Dunbar, PA 15431-2274, USA

Locke, Bruce (Actor)
5670 Wilshire Blvd Ste 820
Los Angeles, CA 90036-5613

Locke, Chuck (Athlete, Baseball Player)
2525 Brownwood Ct
Poplar Bluff, MO 63901-2657, USA

Locke, Gary (Politician)
Unit 7300 Box 10
DPO, AP 96521-0010, USA

Locke, Kimberley (Actor, Musician)
c/o Mark Measures Kazarian, Measures, Ruskin & Associates (LA)
11969 Ventura Blvd Fl 3
Studio City, CA 91604-2630, USA

Locke, Larry (Baseball Player)
Cleveland Indians
155 Eighty Acres Rd Apt 2
Dunbar, PA 15431-2275, USA

Locke, Ron (Athlete, Baseball Player)
11140 Caravel Cir Apt 102
Fort Myers, FL 33908-3996, USA

Locke, Sonda (Actor)
c/o Staff Member *David Shapira &
Associates*
193 N Robertson Blvd
Beverly Hills, CA 90211-2103, USA

Locke, Sondra (Actor)
7465 Hillside Ave
Los Angeles, CA 90046-2228, USA

Locke, Spencer (Actor)
c/o Sharon Lane *Lane Management Group*
13017 Woodbridge St
Studio City, CA 91604-1431, USA

Locke, Tembi (Actor)
c/o Bob McGowan *McGowan
Management*
8733 W Sunset Blvd Ste 103
West Hollywood, CA 90069-2241, USA

Locker, Bob (Athlete, Baseball Player)
1705 Durston Rd
Bozeman, MT 59715-2734, USA

Lockerman, Brad
300 S Raymond Ave Ste 11
Pasadena, CA 91105-2639

Lockett, Frank (Athlete, Football Player)
2705 Cerritas Via
Harvey, LA 70058-2936, USA

Lockett, Kevin (Athlete, Football Player)
1319 W Xyler St
Tulsa, OK 74127-2717, USA

Lockhart, Anne (Actor)
c/o Linda McAlister *Linda McAlister
Talent*
100 Oak Ln
Waxahachie, TX 75167-8412, USA

Lockhart, Eugene (Athlete, Football
Player)
2215 High Country Dr
Carrollton, TX 75007-1701, USA

Lockhart, Ian (Athlete, Basketball Player)
Q25 Calle Excelsa
Yauco, PR 00698-3172, USA

Lockhart, June (Actor)
c/o Staff Member *Agency for the
Performing Arts (APA-LA)*
405 S Beverly Dr Ste 500
Beverly Hills, CA 90212-4425, USA

Lockhart, Keith (Athlete, Baseball Player)
3330 McKinley Point Dr
Dacula, GA 30019-1599, USA

Lockhart, Keith
Boston Pops Orchestra
301 Massachusetts Ave
Symphony Hall
Boston, MA 02115-4557, USA

Lockhart, Paul S (Astronaut)
3142 Pleasant Cove Ct
Houston, TX 77059-3232, USA

Lockhart, Paul S Lt Colonel (Astronaut)
PSC 802 Box 74
FPO, AE 09608-0001, USA

Lockington, David
Cramer/Marder Artists
3436 Springhill Rd
Lafayette, CA 94549-2535, USA

Locklear, Gene (Athlete, Baseball Player)
1811 Penasco Rd
El Cajon, CA 92019-3708, USA

Locklear, Heather (Actor)
c/o Daniel (Danny) Sussman *Brillstein
Entertainment Partners (LA)*
9150 Wilshire Blvd Ste 350
Beverly Hills, CA 90212-3453, USA

Locklear, Sean (Athlete, Football Player)
700 1st St Apt 16J
Hoboken, NJ 07030-8827, USA

Locklin, Kerry (Athlete, Football Player)
2087 E Emilie Ave
Fresno, CA 93730-4731, USA

Locklin, Stu (Athlete, Baseball Player)
532 Carfax Pl SW
Albuquerque, NM 87121-2273, USA

Lockwood, Gary (Actor)
1065 E Loma Alta Dr
Altadena, CA 91001-1507, USA

Lockwood, Scott (Athlete, Football Player)
870 West Ln
Estes Park, CO 80517-9624, USA

Lockwood, Skip (Athlete, Baseball Player)
47 John Druce Ln
Wrentham, MA 02093-1390, USA

Loder, Kevin (Athlete, Basketball Player)
505 W 4th St
Mishawaka, IN 46544-1818, USA

Loder, Kurt (Journalist, Television Host)
c/o Staff Member *MTV News*
1515 Broadway Fl 29
New York, NY 10036-8901, USA

Lodge, Roger (Actor, Television Host)
c/o Michelle Bega *Rogers & Cowan PR
(LA)*
8687 Melrose Ave Ste 7
West Hollywood, CA 90069-5721, USA

Lodish, Mike (Athlete, Football Player)
1150 Trailwood Path Apt D
Bloomfield Hills, MI 48301-1742, USA

Loduca, Paul (Athlete, Baseball Player)
3227 Medaris Ln
San Antonio
San Antonio, TX 78258-1624, USA

Lodwick, Todd (Athlete, Olympic Athlete,
Skier)
907 Merritt Steamboat
Steamboat Springs, CO 80487, USA

Loe, Harald A (Doctor)
National Dental Research Institute
9000 Rockville Pike
Bethesda, MD 20892-0001, USA

Loe, Kameron (Athlete, Baseball Player)
17530 Ventura Blvd Ste 201
Encino, CA 91316-3889, USA

Loeb, Jerome T (Business Person)
May Department Stores
611 Olive St Ste 2076
Saint Louis, MO 63101-1721, USA

Loeb, Lisa (Musician, Songwriter)
c/o Alix Gucovsky *Special Artists Agency*
9200 W Sunset Blvd Ste 410
West Hollywood, CA 90069-3506, USA

Loeber, Jerry (Athlete, Baseball Player)
578 Bayville Rd
Locust Valley, NY 11560-1211, USA

Loebsak, David (Congressman, Politician)
1527 Longworth Hob
Washington, DC 20515-4316, USA

Loehr, Bet (Actor)
c/o Staff Member *Coast to Coast Talent
Group*
3350 Barham Blvd
Los Angeles, CA 90068-1404, USA

Loehr, Bret (Actor)
c/o Staff Member *Coast to Coast Talent
Group*
3350 Barham Blvd
Los Angeles, CA 90068-1404, USA

Loewen, Adam (Athlete, Baseball Player)
12302 N 136th Pl # Pi
Scottsdale, AZ 85259-2311, USA

Loewen, Darcy (Athlete, Hockey Player)
11605 Cabo Del Verde Ave
Las Vegas, NV 89138-6063

Loewer, Carlton (Athlete, Baseball Player)
PO Box 3590
Alpine, WY 83128-0590, USA

Lofgren, Nils (Musician, Songwriter,
Writer)
Vision Music
7422 E Berridge Ln
Scottsdale, AZ 85250-4625, USA

Lofgren, Zoe (Congressman, Politician)
1401 Longworth Hob
Washington, DC 20515-4005, USA

Loftin, Lennie (Actor)
c/o Scott Zimmerman *Evolution
Entertainment (LA)*
901 N Highland Ave
Los Angeles, CA 90038-2412, USA

Lofton, Cirroc (Actor)
c/o Staff Member *Innovative Artists (LA)*
1505 10th St
Santa Monica, CA 90401-2805, USA

Lofton, Fred C (Religious Leader)
Progressive National Baptist Convention
601 50th St NE
Washington, DC 20019-5498, USA

Lofton, James (Athlete, Baseball Player)
14103 Cerise Ave Apt 18
Hawthorne, CA 90250-8843, USA

Lofton, James D (Athlete, Football Player)
13177 Via Mesa Dr
San Diego, CA 92129-2287, USA

Lofton, Kenny (Athlete, Baseball Player)
PO Box 68473
Tucson, AZ 85737-8473, USA

Lofton, Oscar (Athlete, Football Player)
823 Oak Hollow Dr
Hammond, LA 70401-8260, USA

logan, bob (Athlete, Hockey Player)
11 White Pine Rd
Amherst, MA 01002-3467

Logan, Chuck (Athlete, Football Player)
2526 Lawndale Ave
Evanston, IL 60201-1158, USA

Logan, Daniel (Actor)
c/o Staff Member *Entertainment Legends
Management*
1100 Irvine Blvd # 66
Tustin, CA 92780-3529, USA

Logan, Dave (Athlete, Hockey Player)
142 Acorn Ln
Shelburne, VT 05482-7330

Logan, Dick (Athlete, Football Player)
475 Chapple Hill Dr NE
North Canton, OH 44720-1775, USA

Logan, Don (Publisher)
Time Inc
Time-Life Building
Rockefeller Center
New York, NY 10020, USA

Logan, Ernie (Athlete, Football Player)
609 Francis Ct
Spring Lake, NC 28390-3006, USA

Logan, Exavier (Nook) (Athlete, Baseball
Player)
19410 Creek Bend Dr
Spring, TX 77388-3095, USA

Logan, Jack (Musician)
William Morris Agency
1325 Avenue of the Americas Bsmt 2
New York, NY 10019-6047, USA

Logan, James K (Athlete, Football Player)
US Court of Appeals
1608 Stowers Dr
Dothan, AL 36305-6336, USA

Logan, Jerry (Athlete, Football Player)
1624 Hillcrest Dr
Graham, TX 76450-4702, USA

Logan, John (Producer, Writer)
c/o David O'Connor *Creative Artists
Agency (CAA-LA)*
2000 Avenue of the Stars Ste 100
Los Angeles, CA 90067-4705, USA

Logan, Johnny (Athlete, Baseball Player)
6115 W Cleveland Ave
Milwaukee, WI 53219-2653, USA

Logan, Marc (Athlete, Football Player)
2501 Glascow Ln
Lexington, KY 40511-9126, USA

Logan, Melissa (Musician)
K Records
924 Jefferson St SE
#101
Olympia, WA 98501, USA

Logan, Randy (Athlete, Football Player)
330 W Fornance St
Norristown, PA 19401-2906, USA

Logan, Tom (Director)
PO Box 10547
Costa Mesa, CA 92627-0190, USA

Logano, Joey (Race Car Driver)
c/o Jeremy Troiano *MCG Sports*
122 Saint Albans Ln Ste D
Davidson, NC 28036-6513, USA

Logg, Charles (Athlete, Olympic Athlete,
Rower)
3634 Shady Oak Trl
Gainesville, GA 30506-4542, USA

Loggia, Robert (Actor)
c/o Steve Lovett *Lovett Management*
1327 Brinkley Ave
Los Angeles, CA 90049-3619, USA

Loggins, Kenny (Musician, Songwriter)
1100 Calle Malaga
Santa Barbara, CA 93109-1138, USA

Logue, Donal (Actor)
c/o Perri Kipperman *Kipperman Management*
345 7th Ave Rm 503
New York, NY 10001-5054, USA

Logue, Karina (Actor)
c/o Justin Evans *The Independent Group*
6363 Wilshire Blvd Ste 115
Los Angeles, CA 90048-5734, USA

Lohan, Ali (Actor)
c/o Glenn Gulino *G2 Entertainment LLC*
1 Columbus Pl Apt S25E
New York, NY 10019-8208, USA

Lohan, Dina (Reality Star)
c/o Gina Rodriguez *GR Media*
Prefers to be contacted via telephone or email
Reseda, CA 91335, USA

Lohan, Lindsay (Actor)
c/o Staff Member *Wishnow Ross Warsazsky & Company*
16130 Ventura Blvd Ste 320
Encino, CA 91436-2595, USA

Lohan, Michael (Reality Star)
c/o Gina Rodriguez *GR Media*
Prefers to be contacted via telephone or email
Reseda, CA 91335, USA

Lohaus, Brad (Athlete, Basketball Player)
55 Tartan Dr
North Liberty, IA 52317-8002, USA

Lohman, Alison (Actor)
c/o Nicole King *Management 360*
9111 Wilshire Blvd
Beverly Hills, CA 90210-5508, USA

Lohmann, Katie (Actor)
c/o Giovanni Elmore *WNWN Media*
348 Hauser Blvd # PH414
Los Angeles, CA 90036-3276, USA

Lohmeyer, Eddie (Horse Racer)
63 Red Valley Rd
Cream Ridge, NJ 08514-2007, USA

Lohmiller, Chip (Athlete, Football Player)
PO Box 810
Crosslake, MN 56442-0810, USA

Lohr, Aaron (Actor)
c/o Beth Rosner *Beth Rosner Management*
15 Stuyvesant Oval
New York, NY 10009-2011, USA

Lohr, Bob (Athlete, Golfer)
8225 Breeze Cove Ln
Orlando, FL 32819-5078, USA

Lohrke, Jack (Athlete, Baseball Player)
2817 Lucena Dr
San Jose, CA 95132-2244, USA

Lohse, Kyle (Athlete, Baseball Player)
7852 Corte De Luz
San Diego, CA 92127-2555, USA

Loiola, Jose (Athlete, Volleyball Player)
1141 2nd St
Manhattan Beach, CA 90266-6834, USA

Loiseau, Shawn (Athlete, Football Player)
c/o Adam Heller *Vantage Management Group*
518 Reamer Dr
Carnegie, PA 15106-1845, USA

Loiselle, Claude (Athlete, Hockey Player)
7 Orchard Dr
Queensbury, NY 12804-6206

Loiselle, Rich (Athlete, Baseball Player)
560 Timber Dr
Harvard, IL 60033-7823, USA

Loken, Kristanna (Actor)
c/o Staff Member *ICM Partners (LA)*
10250 Constellation Blvd Fl 7
Los Angeles, CA 90067-6207, USA

Lokey, Lorey (Business Person)
Business Wire
44 Montgomery St Fl 39
San Francisco, CA 94104-4812, USA

Lolich, Mickey (Athlete, Baseball Player)
6252 Robin Hl
Washington, MI 48094-2186, USA

Lolich, Ron (Athlete, Baseball Player)
7055 SW Dogwood Pl
Portland, OR 97225-1571, USA

Lollar, Tim (Athlete, Baseball Player)
16626 W Bayaud Dr
Golden, CO 80401-6577, USA

Loman, Doug (Athlete, Baseball Player)
25 Lincoln St
Bakersfield, CA 93305-3412, USA

Lomas, Mark (Athlete, Football Player)
PO Box 17781
Irvine, CA 92623-7781, USA

Lomasney, Steve (Athlete, Baseball Player)
7 Arnold Rd
Peabody, MA 01960-5203, USA

Lomax, Melanie
5900 Wilshire Blvd
Los Angeles, CA 90036-5013

Lomax, Neil V (Athlete, Football Player)
13090 Knaus Rd
Lake Oswego, OR 97034-1590, USA

Lombard, George (Athlete, Baseball Player)
2275 Rhinehill Rd SE
Atlanta, GA 30315-7413, USA

Lombard, Karina (Actor, Model)
EOS Entertainment Corporation
1209 N Orange St
Wilmington, DE 19801-1120, USA

Lombard, Louise (Actor)
c/o Lena Roklin *Luber Roklin Management*
5815 W Sunset Blvd Ste 206
Los Angeles, CA 90028-6481, USA

Lombardi, Leigh (Actor)
c/o Staff Member *Abrams Artists Agency (NY)*
275 7th Ave Fl 26
New York, NY 10001-6708, USA

Lombardi, Louis (Actor)
c/o Erik Kritzer *LINK Entertainment*
11872 La Grange Ave Fl 1
Los Angeles, CA 90025-5283, USA

Lombardi, Phil (Athlete, Baseball Player)
26440 Brooks Cir
Stevenson Ranch, CA 91381-1417, USA

Lombardo, John (Musician)
Agency for Performing Arts
9200 W Sunset Blvd Ste 900
West Hollywood, CA 90069-3604, USA

Lombardozzi, Domenick (Actor)
c/o Michael Garnett *Leverage Management*
3030 Pennsylvania Ave
Santa Monica, CA 90404-4112, USA

Lombardozzi, Steve (Athlete, Baseball Player)
12404 Hall Shop Rd
Fulton, MD 20759-9746, USA

Lomenda, Michael (Actor)
c/o Siri Garber *Platform Public Relations*
2666 N Beachwood Dr
Los Angeles, CA 90068-2308, USA

Lomma, Jonathan
1120 S Washington Ave
Scranton, PA 18505-1532

Lommi, Tony (Musician)
Red Light Communications
3305 Lobban Pl
Charlottesville, VA 22903-7069, USA

Lomon, Kevin (Athlete, Baseball Player)
13397 Morris Loop
Cameron, OK 74932-2173, USA

Lonborg, Jim (Athlete, Baseball Player)
498 First Parish Rd
Scituate, MA 02066-3201, USA

London, Antonio (Athlete, Football Player)
108 Oak Forest Way
Pelham, AL 35124-2516, USA

London, Carolyn (Producer)
c/o Staff Member *Bankable Productions*
226 W 26th St Fl 4
New York, NY 10001-6700, USA

London, Jason (Actor)
c/o Staff Member *Levine Okwu Erickson Management*
2126 N Commonwealth Ave
Los Angeles, CA 90027-2118, USA

London, Jeremy (Actor, Director, Producer)
c/o Jean-Pierre (JP) Henraux *Henraux Management*
Prefers to be contacted by telephone
CA, USA

London, Lauren (Actor)
c/o John Carrabino *John Carrabino Management*
5900 Wilshire Blvd Ste 406
Los Angeles, CA 90036-5015, USA

London, Lisa (Actor, Model)
8949 W Sunset Blvd Ste 201
West Hollywood, CA 90069-1806, USA

London, Michael (Producer)
c/o Staff Member *Groundswell Productions / Michael Landon Productions*
9350 Wilshire Blvd Ste 324
Beverly Hills, CA 90212-3206, USA

London, Rick (Cartoonist)
c/o Staff Member *Artistic Licensing Agency*
240 Central Ave Apt 224
Hot Springs, AR 71901-3541, USA

London, Stacy (Reality Star, Television Host)
c/o Staff Member *TLC*
10100 Santa Monica Blvd Ste 1500
Los Angeles, CA 90067-4117, USA

Loneker, Keith (Athlete, Football Player)
56 W Lincoln Ave
Roselle Park, NJ 07204-1358, USA

Lonergan, Kenneth (Director, Writer)
c/o John Buzzetti *William Morris Endeavor (NY)*
1325 Avenue of the Americas
New York, NY 10019-6026, USA

Lonergan, Kenneth (Writer)
c/o Staff Member *William Morris Endeavor (LA)*
9601 Wilshire Blvd
Beverly Hills, CA 90210-5213, USA

Lonestar (Music Group)
c/o Gary Borman *Moir / Borman Entertainment*
1250 6th St Ste 401
Santa Monica, CA 90401-1638, USA

Lonetto, Sarah (Baseball Player)
26560 Burg Rd Apt 132
Warren, MI 48089-3594, USA

Loney, James (Athlete, Baseball Player)
c/o Joe Urbon *Creative Artists Agency (CAA-NY)*
162 5th Ave Fl 6
New York, NY 10010-6047, USA

Loney, Troy (Athlete, Hockey Player)
4245 Glasgow Rd
Valencia, PA 16059-1729

Long, Bill (Athlete, Baseball Player)
7699 Dimmick Rd
West Chester, OH 45241-1166, USA

Long, Billy (Congressman, Politician)
1541 Longworth Hob
Washington, DC 20515-3806, USA

Long, Bishop Eddie (Religious Leader)
New Birth
6400 Woodrow Rd
Lithonia, GA 30038-2437, USA

Long, Bob (Athlete, Baseball Player)
3646 Willow Lake Cir
Chattanooga, TN 37419-1459, USA

Long, Bob (Athlete, Football Player)
PO Box 245
Ashland, PA 17921-0245, USA

Long, Bob (Athlete, Football Player)
1413 W Via De La Gloria
Green Valley, AZ 85622-5007, USA

Long, Bob (Athlete, Football Player)
630 N 4th St Unit 614
Milwaukee, WI 53203-2809, USA

Long, Carl (Athlete, Baseball Player)
401 Duggins Dr
Kinston, NC 28501-8211, USA

Long, Carson (Athlete, Football Player)
1618 Walnut St
Ashland, PA 17921-1724, USA

Long, Charles F (Chuck) II (Athlete, Football Player)
2425 N MacArthur Blvd
Oklahoma City, OK 73127-1605, USA

Long, Chris (Athlete, Football Player)
c/o Steve Rosner *16W Marketing LLC*
75 Union Ave Ste 2
Rutherford, NJ 07070-1212, USA

Long, Chuck (Athlete, Football Coach, Football Player)
1651 Naismith Dr
Lawrence, KS 66045-4069, USA

Long, Dallas (Athlete, Olympic Athlete, Track Athlete)
PO Box 355
Whitefish, MT 59937-0355, USA

Long, Dave (Athlete, Football Player)
309 16th St
Marion, IA 52302-4356, USA

Long, David L (Publisher)
Sports Illustrated Magazine
Rockefeller Center
New York, NY 10020, USA

Long, Dennis (Denny) (Soccer Player)
RR 5
Poplar Bluff, MO 63901, USA

Long, Don (Athlete, Baseball Player)
747 Puget Ln
Edmonds, WA 98020-2643, USA

Long, Elizabeth Valk (Business Person)
J.M. Smucker Co
1 Strawberry Ln
Orrville, OH 44667-1298, USA

Long, Grant (Athlete, Basketball Player)
8501 Morton Taylor Rd
Belleville, MI 48111-5313, USA

Long, Howie (Actor, Football Player,
Sportscaster)
c/o Jack Gilardi *ICM Partners (LA)*
10250 Constellation Blvd Fl 7
Los Angeles, CA 90067-6207, USA

Long, Jackie (Actor)
c/o Tammy Brook *FYI Public Relations*
174 5th Ave Ste 404
New York, NY 10010-5964, USA

Long, Jeoff (Athlete, Baseball Player)
11 Flower Ct
Lakeside Park, KY 41017-2102, USA

Long, Jessica (Athlete, Swimmer)
c/o Peter Carlisle *Octagon Olympics &
Action Sports*
15 Lund Rd # 10
Saco, ME 04072-1806, USA

Long, Joey (Athlete, Baseball Player)
5541 Kiser Lake Rd
Conover, OH 45317-9643, USA

Long, John (Athlete, Basketball Player)
11976 Hunt St
Romulus, MI 48174-3830, USA

Long, Justin (Actor)
c/o Rhonda Price *Gersh (NY)*
41 Madison Ave Ste 1504
New York, NY 10010-2242, USA

Long, Kevin (Athlete, Baseball Player)
8540 E Via Montoya
Scottsdale, AZ 85255-4936, USA

Long, Kevin (Athlete, Baseball Player)
6 Southpine Ct
Columbia, SC 29212-2918, USA

Long, Khari (Athlete, Football Player)
4405 Call Field Rd
Wichita Falls, TX 76308-2445, USA

Long, Kyle (Athlete, Football Player)
c/o Marvin Demoff *Morris Yorn Barnes
Levine Krintzman Rubenstein Kohner &
Gellman*
2000 Avenue of the Stars Ste 300N
3rd Floor, North Tower
Los Angeles, CA 90067-4704, USA

Long, Mark (Reality Star)
c/o Staff Member *MTV Networks (LA)*
2600 Colorado Ave
Santa Monica, CA 90404-3519

Long, Matt (Actor)
c/o Robert Glennon *Authentic Talent and
Literary Management*
20 Jay St Ste M17
Brooklyn, NY 11201-8300, USA

Long, Mel (Athlete, Football Player)
837 Imani Cir
Toledo, OH 43604-8425, USA

Long, Nia (Actor)
2065 Outpost Dr
Los Angeles, CA 90068-3725, USA

Long, Rien (Athlete, Football Player)
460 Great Circle Rd
Nashville, TN 37228-1404, USA

Long, Rob (Producer)
c/o Brett Loncar *Creative Artists Agency
(CAA-LA)*
2000 Avenue of the Stars Ste 100
Los Angeles, CA 90067-4705, USA

Long, Robert M (Business Person)
Longs Drug Stores
141 N Civic Dr
Walnut Creek, CA 94596-3815, USA

Long, Rocky (Athlete, Football Player)
San Dego State University
5500 Campanile Dr
San Diego, CA 92182-0003, USA

Long, Ryan (Athlete, Baseball Player)
5618 Duval St
Bradenton, FL 34203-8088, USA

Long, Scott (Actor, Reality Star)
c/o Staff Member *Big Brother*
4146 Lankershim Blvd Ste 300
Arnold Shapiro Productions
North Hollywood, CA 91602-2878, USA

Long, Shelley (Actor)
PO Box 45530
Los Angeles, CA 90045-0530, USA

Long, Terrance (Athlete, Baseball Player)
6248 Sycamore Dr
Montgomery, AL 36117-4568, USA

Long, Tim (Athlete, Football Player)
16410 Hawfield Farms Rd Unit 925
Charlotte, NC 28277-0484, USA

Long, William Ivey (Designer)
International Creative Mgmt
40 W 57th St Fl 5
New York, NY 10019-4001, USA

Longet, Claudine (Actor)
Ronald D Austin
6000 E Hopkins
Aspen, CO 81611, USA

Longfield, William (Business Person)
CR Bard Inc
730 Central Ave
New Providence, NJ 07974-1199, USA

Longley, Clint (Athlete, Football Player)
13602 Camino De Oro Ct
Corpus Christi, TX 78418-6910, USA

Longmire, Sam (Athlete, Football Player)
3220 W Ina Rd Apt 15103
Tucson, AZ 85741-2170, USA

Longmire, Tony (Athlete, Baseball Player)
419 Fleming Ave E
Vallejo, CA 94591-4030, USA

Longo, Cody (Actor)
c/o Mara Santino *Luber Roklin
Management*
5815 W Sunset Blvd Ste 206
Los Angeles, CA 90028-6481, USA

Longo, Lenny (Musician)
Texas Sounds
PO Box 1644
Dickinson, TX 77539-1644, USA

Longo, Tom (Athlete, Football Player)
2 Donna Ln
Wayne, NJ 07470-2711, USA

Longo, Tony (Actor)
24 Westwind St
Marina Del Rey, CA 90292-7135

Longoria, Eva (Actor)
c/o Liza Anderson *Anderson Group Public
Relations*
8060 Melrose Ave Fl 4
Los Angeles, CA 90046-7038, USA

Longoria, Evan (Athlete, Baseball Player)
c/o Staff Member *Tampa Bay Devil Rays*
1 Tropicana Dr
Tropicana Field
Saint Petersburg, FL 33705-1703, USA

Long-View (Music Group)
c/o Staff Member *Paradigm (Monterey)*
404 W Franklin St
Monterey, CA 93940-2303, USA

Longwell, Ryan (Athlete, Football Player)
9748 Green Island Cv
Windermere, FL 34786-8953, USA

Lonneke (Model)
Pauline's Talent Corp
379 W Broadway # 502
New York, NY 10012-5121, USA

Lonow, Claudia (Comedian)
c/o Staff Member *ICM Partners (LA)*
10250 Constellation Blvd Fl 7
Los Angeles, CA 90067-6207, USA

Lonsberry, Ross (Athlete, Hockey Player)
32610 Big Springs Rd
Acton, CA 93510-1501, USA

Lonsdale, Gordon (Cinematographer,
Director)
4513 W 10600 N
Highland, UT 84003-9552, USA

Lonsdale, Michael (Actor)
25 Rue De General-Foy
Paris, FR F-750

Look, Bruce (Athlete, Baseball Player)
PO Box 332
Elk Rapids, MI 49629-0332, USA

Look, Dean (Athlete, Baseball Player)
80 Victorian Hills Dr
Okemos, MI 48864-3160, USA

Look, Dean Z (Athlete, Baseball Player)
80 Victorian Hills Dr
Okemos, MI 48864-3160, USA

Looker, Dane (Athlete, Football Player)
7213 41st Avenue Ct E
Tacoma, WA 98443-1811, USA

Lookinland, Mike (Actor)
PO Box 9968
Salt Lake City, UT 84109-0968, USA

Loomis, Robbie (Race Car Driver)
Hendrick Racing
4414 Pappa Joe Hendrtck Blvd
Charlotte, NC 28262, USA

Loomis, Rod (Actor)
5114 Vineland Ave
North Hollywood, CA 91601-3814

Loon (Musician)
c/o Mike Esterman *Esterman.Com, LLC*
Prefers to be contacted via email
Baltimore, MD XXXXX, USA

Looney, Brian (Athlete, Baseball Player)
188 Romulus Rd
Cheshire, CT 06410-3535, USA

Looney, Don (Athlete, Football Player)
8955 Reata Place Trl
Benbrook, TX 76126-1650

Looney, Shelley (Athlete, Hockey Player,
Olympic Athlete)
78 W Oakwood Pl # 1
Buffalo, NY 14214-2338, USA

Looper, Aaron (Athlete, Baseball Player)
1405 Manchester Dr
Shawnee, OK 74804-2327, USA

Looper, Braden (Athlete, Baseball Player,
Olympic Athlete)
11711 Sandstone Ct
Frankfort, IL 60423-8866, USA

Loose, John W (Business Person)
Coming Corp
Houghton Park
Corning, NY 14831-0001, USA

Looseleaf, Victoria
144 S Doheny Dr Apt 304
Los Angeles, CA 90048-2939

Lopasky, Bill (Athlete, Football Player)
476 Jackson Rd
Dallas, PA 18612-3073, USA

Lopasky, William (Athlete, Football
Player)
Huntsville Ceasetown Rd
Dallas, PA 18612, USA

Lopata, Stan (Athlete, Baseball Player)
421 Freedom Blvd
Coatesville, PA 19320-1559, USA

Loper, Daniel (Athlete, Football Player)
115 Stillwater Trl
Hendersonville, TN 37075-4305, USA

Lopes, Davey (Athlete, Baseball Player)
Los Angeles Dodgers
1000 Elysian Park Ave Attn Coachingstaff
Dodgertown, CA 90090-1112, USA

Lopes, Davey (Athlete, Baseball Player)
309 San Elijo St
San Diego, CA 92106-3455, USA

Lopes, Lisa
1505 10th St
Santa Monica, CA 90401-2805

Lopez, Adamari (Actor)
c/o Staff Member *Telemundo*
2470 W 8th Ave
Hialeah, FL 33010-2000, USA

Lopez, Albie (Athlete, Baseball Player)
698 E Park Ave
Gilbert, AZ 85234-5894, USA

Lopez, Arturo (Athlete, Baseball Player)
1425 Tobias Dr SE
Washington, DC 20020-2953, USA

Lopez, Danny (Little Red) (Boxer)
16531 Aquamarine Ct
Chino Hills, CA 91709-4644, USA

Lopez, Feliciano (Athlete, Tennis Player)
IMG Center
1360 E 9th St Ste 100
Cleveland, OH 44114-1730, USA

Lopez, Felipe (Athlete, Baseball Player)
11171 Sun Center Dr Ste 290
Rancho Cordova, CA 95670-6190, USA

Lopez, George (Actor, Comedian,
Producer, Talk Show Host)
2349 N Catalina St
Los Angeles, CA 90027-1128, USA

Lopez, Hector (Athlete, Baseball Player)
11415 Faldo Ct
Hudson, FL 34667, USA

Lopez, Israel (Cachao) (Musician)
c/o Staff Member *Paradigm (Monterey)*
404 W Franklin St
Monterey, CA 93940-2303, USA

Lopez, Javier (Athlete, Baseball Player)
c/o Barry Meister *Meister Sports Management*
770 Lake Cook Rd Ste 300
Deerfield, IL 60015-4920, USA

Lopez, Javy (Athlete, Baseball Player)
4644 Whitestone Way
Suwanee, GA 30024-7380, USA

Lopez, Jennifer (Actor, Musician)
25067 Jim Bridger Rd
Hidden Hills, CA 91302-1128, USA

Lopez, Juan (Athlete, Baseball Player)
1451 Lavilla Ct
Deltona, FL 32725-4759, USA

Lopez, Luis (Athlete, Baseball Player)
636 40th St
Brooklyn, NY 11232-3108, USA

Lopez, Luis (Athlete, Baseball Player)
Greenville Drive
945 S Main St Attn Coachingstaff
Greenville, SC 29601-3334, USA

Lopez, Luis (Athlete, Baseball Player)
1701 Pleasant Run Rd
Carrollton, TX 75006-7537, USA

Lopez, Lynda (Television Host)
c/o Staff Member *Style Network*
5750 Wilshire Blvd
Los Angeles, CA 90036-3697, USA

Lopez, Mario (Actor, Television Host)
c/o Mark Schulman *3 Arts Entertainment (LA)*
9460 Wilshire Blvd Fl 7
Beverly Hills, CA 90212-2713, USA

Lopez, Mickey (Athlete, Baseball Player)
17430 SW 117th Ave
Miami, FL 33177-2203, USA

Lopez, Raul (Basketball Player)
Utah Jazz
301 W South Temple
Delta Center
Salt Lake City, UT 84101-1219, USA

Lopez, Rodrigo (Baseball Player)
Baltimore Orioles
333 W Camden St
Oriole Park
Baltimore, MD 21201-2496, USA

Lopez, Sal (Actor, Musician)
c/o Ivan De Paz *DePaz Management*
2011 N Vermont Ave
Los Angeles, CA 90027-1931, USA

Lopez, Sergi (Actor)
c/o Staff Member *ICM Partners (LA)*
10250 Constellation Blvd Fl 7
Los Angeles, CA 90067-6207, USA

Lopez, Steven (Athlete)
PO Box Bix
Sugar Land, TX 77487, USA

Lopez, Trini (Actor, Musician)
1139 Abrigo Rd
Palm Springs, CA 92262-4101, USA

Lopienski, Tom (Athlete, Football Player)
128 Blackberry Dr
Hudson, OH 44236-4701, USA

Lopitalier, Phil (Athlete, Baseball Player)
231 N Kings Ave
Massapequa, NY 11758-3325, USA

Lopresti, Pete (Athlete, Hockey Player)
5100 Tifton Dr
Minneapolis, MN 55439-1457

Loquasto, Santo (Designer)
Paradigm Agency
10100 Santa Monica Blvd Ste 2500
Los Angeles, CA 90067-4116, USA

Lorch, Karl (Athlete, Football Player)
92-861 Palailai St
Kapolei, HI 96707-1239, USA

Lord, Albert L (Business Person)
SLM Holding Corp
11600 American Dream Way
Reston, VA 20190-4758, USA

Lord, Jammal (Athlete, Football Player)
17011 Cedar Plz Apt 7B
Omaha, NE 68130-2368, USA

Lord, Marjorie (Actor)
1110 Maytor Pl
Beverly Hills, CA 90210-2600, USA

Lorde (Musician)
c/o Tom Windish *The Windish Agency*
1658 N Milwaukee Ave # 211
Chicago, IL 60647-6905, USA

Lords, Traci
c/o Staff Member *Juliet Green Management*
9025 Wilshire Blvd Ste 400
Beverly Hills, CA 90211-1828, USA

Loren, Josie (Actor)
c/o Ellen Meyer *Ellen Meyer Management*
8899 Beverly Blvd Ste 612
Los Angeles, CA 90048-2429, USA

Loren, Veronica (Actor)
c/o Staff Member *International Artists PR & Talent Management*
3010 Wilshire Blvd # 594
Los Angeles, CA 90010-1103, USA

Lorentz, Jim (Athlete, Hockey Player)
2555 Staley Rd
Grand Island, NY 14072-2040

Lorenz, Danny (Athlete, Hockey Player)
Kent Valley Ice Centre 6015 S 240th St
Kent, WA 98032

Lorenz, Ericka (Athlete, Olympic Athlete, Water Polo Player)
2604 Fulton St
Berkeley, CA 94704-3229, USA

Lorenz, Lee (Cartoonist)
PO Box 131
Easton, CT 06612-0131, USA

Lorenzen, Fred (Race Car Driver)
906 Burr Oak Ct
Oak Brook, IL 60523-1514, USA

Lorenzo, Blas (Actor)
PO Box 2127
Los Angeles, CA 90078-2127

Lorenzo, Francisco (Boxer)
c/o Staff Member *Top Rank Inc.*
3908 Howard Hughes Pkwy #580
Las Vegas, NV 89109, USA

Loretta, Mark (Athlete, Baseball Player)
PO Box 9505
Rancho Santa Fe, CA 92067-4505, USA

Lorey, Dean (Writer)
25540 Colette Way
Calabasas, CA 91302-3149

Loria, Christopher (Gus) (Astronaut)
1420 Marina Bay Dr Apt 620
Kemah, TX 77565-2277, USA

Loria, Christopher J Lt Colonel (Astronaut)
1420 Marina Bay Dr Apt 620
Kemah, TX 77565-2277, USA

Loria, Jeffrey (Baseball Player)
Florida Marlins
44 Cocoanut Row Unit 407-B
Palm Beach, FL 33480-4069, USA

loria, jeffrey (Commentator)
19 E 72nd St Apt 14C
New York, NY 10021-4193, USA

Lorick, Tony (Athlete, Football Player)
349 Burney Ln
Kerrville, TX 78028-8074, USA

Lorig, Khatuna (Athlete, Olympic Athlete)
c/o Staff Member *USA Archery*
1 Olympic Plz
Colorado Springs, CO 80909-5780, USA

Loring, Gloria (Actor, Musician)
PO Box 1243
Cedar Glen, CA 92321-1243, USA

Loring, Lynn (Actor)
4910 Petit Ave
Encino, CA 91436-1131, USA

Lorraine, Andrew (Athlete, Baseball Player)
10436 E Acoma Dr
Scottsdale, AZ 85255-1711, USA

Lorraine, Andrew (Athlete, Baseball Player)
Everett Aquasox
3802 Broadway Attn Coachingstaff
Everett, WA 98201-5032, USA

Lorre, Chuck (Producer, Writer)
c/o Pam Wilson *Ink Media Corp*
25465 Doyle Ct
Stevenson Ranch, CA 91381-1550, USA

Lorthridge, Ryan (Athlete, Basketball Player)
PO Box 68693
Jackson, MS 39286-8693, USA

Lortie, Louis (Musician)
Cramer/Marder Artists
3436 Springhill Rd
Lafayette, CA 94549-2535, USA

Loscutoff, James (Jim) (Athlete, Basketball Player, Coach)
166 Jenkins Rd
Andover, MA 01810-2304, USA

Los Lagos, Banda (Music Group)
c/o Staff Member *Sony Music Miami*
605 Lincoln Rd Ste 700
Miami Beach, FL 33139-2901, USA

Los Lobos (Music Group)
c/o Staff Member *Paradigm (Monterey)*
404 W Franklin St
Monterey, CA 93940-2303, USA

Los Lonely Boys (Music Group)
Loophole Entertainment
PO Box 162045
Austin, TX 78716-2045, USA

Losman, J P (Athlete, Football Player)
70 Oakland Pi
Buffalo, NY 14222, USA

Los Rabanes (Music Group)
c/o Staff Member *Sony Music Miami*
605 Lincoln Rd Ste 700
Miami Beach, FL 33139-2901, USA

Los Sementales de Nuevo Leon (Music Group)
c/o Staff Member *Sony Music Miami*
605 Lincoln Rd Ste 700
Miami Beach, FL 33139-2901, USA

Los Super Reyes (Music Group, Musician)
c/o Staff Member *Warner Music International (WMI-USA)*
75 Rockefeller Plz
New York, NY 10019-6908, USA

Lost Boys
1775 Broadway # 433
New York, NY 10019-1903

Lostprophets (Music Group)
c/o Staff Member *Sony Music International*
550 Madison Ave Fl 6
New York, NY 10022-3211, USA

Lothamer, Ed (Athlete, Football Player)
14545 W 183rd St
Olathe, KS 66062-9192, USA

Lott, John (Athlete, Football Player)
14 E Oakwood Hills Dr
Chandler, AZ 85248-6200, USA

Lott, Phil (Producer)
c/o Staff Member *ICM Partners (LA)*
10250 Constellation Blvd Fl 7
Los Angeles, CA 90067-6207, USA

Lott, Ronald M (Ronnie) (Sportscaster)
Fox-TV
PO Box 900
Sports Dept
Beverly Hills, CA 90213-0900, USA

Lott, Ronnie (Athlete, Football Player)
11342 Canyon View Cir
Cupertino, CA 95014-4838, USA

Lott, Thomas (Athlete, Football Player)
3617 Sailmaker Ln
Plano, TX 75023-3712, USA

Lott, Trent (Politician, Senator)
2401 Pennsylvania Ave NW Apt 806
Washington, DC 20037-1735, USA

Lotti, Helmut (Actor)
Bevrijdingstraat 39
Turnhout, BE 02300

Lotulelei, Star (Athlete, Football Player)
c/o Bruce Tollner *REP 1 Sports Group*
2 Corporate Park Ste 106
Irvine, CA 92606-5103, USA

Lotz, Anne Graham (Religious Leader)
AnGel Ministries
3246 Lewis Farm Rd
Raleigh, NC 27607-6723, USA

Louboutin, Christian (Designer)
Christian Louboutin
306 W 38th St Fl 12
New York, NY 10018-8404, USA

Louchiey, Corey (Athlete, Football Player)
8 Misty Creek Ln
Greenville, SC 29611-7718, USA

Loucks, Scott (Athlete, Baseball Player)
1801 Viola Dr
Sierra Vista, AZ 85635-2149, USA

Loucks, Vernon R Jr (Business Person)
Baxter International
1 Baxter Pkwy
Deerfield, IL 60015-4658, USA

Louden, Stephanie (Athlete, Golfer)
621 Verbena Ln
Frisco, TX 75034-8849, USA

Louderback, Tom (Athlete, Football Player)
PO Box 6879
Oakland, CA 94603-0879, USA

Louganis, Greg (Athlete, Diver, Olympic Athlete)
PO Box 16598
Beverly Hills, CA 90209-2598, USA

Loughery, Kevin (Athlete, Basketball Player, Coach)
1091 Byrnwyck Rd NE
Brookhaven, GA 30319-1666, USA

Loughlin, Lori (Actor)
c/o Joanna (Joanie) Burstein *Burstein Company, The*
15304 W Sunset Blvd Ste 208
Pacific Palisades, CA 90272-3656, USA

Loughlin, Mary Anne (Correspondent)
WTBS-TV News Dept
1050 Techwood Dr NW
Atlanta, GA 30318-5695, USA

Louis, Lance (Athlete, Football Player)
c/o Ryan Tollner *REP 1 Sports Group*
2 Corporate Park Ste 106
Irvine, CA 92606-5103, USA

Louisa, Maria (Model)
Next Model Mgmt
23 Watts St
New York, NY 10013, USA

Louis-Dreyfus, Julia (Actor, Comedian)
535 Alma Real Dr
Pacific Palisades, CA 90272-4420, USA

Louise, Tina (Actor, Musician)
310 E 46th St Apt 24G
New York, NY 10017-3031, USA

Louiso, Todd (Actor)
S M S Talent
8383 Wilshire Blvd Ste 230
Beverly Hills, CA 90211-2436, USA

Loukas, Angelo (Athlete, Football Player)
1535 Robin Rd
Bannockburn, IL 60015-1852, USA

Loun, Don (Athlete, Baseball Player)
9095 Wexford Dr
Vienna, VA 22182-2152, USA

Louris, Gary (Musician, Songwriter, Writer)
Sussman Assoc
700 12th Ave S Unit 201
Nashville, TN 37203-3329, USA

Lousma, Jack R (Astronaut)
310 Twin Springs Rd N
Kerrville, TX 78028-8603, USA

Lousma, Jack R Colonel (Astronaut)
310 Twin Springs Rd N
Kerrville, TX 78028-8603, USA

Loux, Shane (Athlete, Baseball Player)
4134 E Cherrywood Pl
Chandler, AZ 85249-5416, USA

Lovato, Demi (Actor)
c/o Kevin Jonas Sr *The Jonas Group*
4450 W Lakeside Dr Ste 300
Burbank, CA 91505-4007, USA

Love, Courtney (Musician, Songwriter)
250 W 10th St
New York, NY 10014-2976, USA

Love, Darlene (Actor, Musician)
Greater Talent
437 5th Ave Ste 8A
New York, NY 10016-2205, USA

Love, Duval (Athlete, Football Player)
8985 Yuba River Ave
Fountain Valley, CA 92708-6346, USA

Love, Faizon (Actor)
c/o Paula Rosenberg *ICA Talent*
818 12th St Apt 9
Santa Monica, CA 90403-1727, USA

Love, Ian (Musician)
c/o Staff Member *Paradigm (Monterey)*
404 W Franklin St
Monterey, CA 93940-2303, USA

Love, Kevin (Athlete, Basketball Player)
1950 Egan Way
Lake Oswego, OR 97034-2728, USA

Love, Loni (Actor, Comedian)
c/o Valerie Allen *Valerie Allen PR*
2452 Chelsea Pl
Santa Monica, CA 90404-2037, USA

Love, Mike (Musician)
969 Fairview Blvd
Incline Village, NV 89451, USA

Love, Patricia (Writer)
c/o Author Mail *Bantam-Dell Publishing (NY)*
1745 Broadway
New York, NY 10019-4640, USA

Love, Randy (Athlete, Football Player)
2202 Fairlands Dr
Garland, TX 75040-1158, USA

Love, Sean (Athlete, Football Player)
121 Hunter St
Tamaqua, PA 18252-2405, USA

Love, Stan (Athlete, Basketball Player)
1950 Egan Way
Lake Oswego, OR 97034-2728, USA

Love, Stanley G (Astronaut)
4315 Indian Sunrise Ct
Houston, TX 77059-5582, USA

Love, Stanley G Dr (Astronaut)
4315 Indian Sunrise Ct
Houston, TX 77059-5582, USA

Love III, Davis (Athlete, Golfer)
Love Golf Design
100 Brunswick Ave
Saint Simons Island, GA 31522-2605, USA

Lovelace, Alan (Astronaut)
10960 S Tropical Trl
Merritt Island, FL 32952-7014, USA

Lovelace, Vance (Athlete, Baseball Player)
5608 12th Ave S
Tampa, FL 33619-3756, USA

Lovelady, Edwin (Athlete, Football Player)
2707 Glenwood Pkwy
Chattanooga, TN 37404-1712, USA

Loveless, Patty (Musician, Songwriter)
c/o Staff Member *William Morris Endeavor (LA)*
9601 Wilshire Blvd
Beverly Hills, CA 90210-5213, USA

Lovell, James A Captain (Astronaut)
964 Lake Rd
Lake Forest, IL 60045-2223, USA

Lovell, James A, Jr (Astronaut)
Lovell Communications
PO Box 49
Lake Forest, IL 60045-0049, USA

Lovell, Jaqueline (Sara Saint James) (Actor, Adult Film Star)
c/o Staff Member *Martin and Donalds*
2131 Hollywood Blvd Ste 304
Hollywood, FL 33020-6751, USA

Lovell, Jim (Astronaut)
Lovell Communications
PO Box 49
Lake Forest, IL 60045-0049, USA

Lovell, Marilyn
7840 Torreyson Dr
Los Angeles, CA 90046-1229

Lovellette, Clyde (Athlete, Basketball Player, Olympic Athlete)
8 Woodspoint Cir
North Manchester, IN 46962-9123, USA

Lovemark, Jaime (Athlete, Golfer)
16449 La Via Feliz
Rancho Santa Fe, CA 92067, USA

Lovering, David (Musician)
720 Montecito Dr
Los Angeles, CA 90031-1432, USA

Loverne, David (Athlete, Football Player)
2307 Amber Falls Dr
Rocklin, CA 95765-4200, USA

Lovetere, John (Athlete, Football Player)
445 Old Statesville Rd
Watertown, TN 37184-4827, USA

Lovett, Lyie (Musician, Songwriter, Writer)
Haber Corp
1016 17th Ave S # 1
Nashville, TN 37212-2202, USA

Lovett, Lyle (Musician)
c/o Ken Levitan *Vector Management*
PO Box 120479
Nashville, TN 37212-0479, USA

Lovett, Ruby (Musician)
Myers Media
PO Box 378
Canton, NY 13617, USA

Lovett, Steve (Actor)
c/o Steve Lovett *Lovett Management*
1327 Brinkley Ave
Los Angeles, CA 90049-3619, USA

Lovibond, Ophelia (Actor)
c/o Brantley Brown *Schachter Entertainment*
1157 S Beverly Dr Fl 2
Los Angeles, CA 90035-1119, USA

Loviglio, Jay (Athlete, Baseball Player)
23 3rd Ave
East Islip, NY 11730-2015, USA

Loville, Derek (Athlete, Football Player)
3020 E Camelback Rd Ste 213
Phoenix, AZ 85016-4423, USA

Lovine, Vicki
c/o Daniel Strone *Trident Media Group LLC*
41 Madison Ave Fl 36
New York, NY 10010-2257, USA

Lovin' Spoonful
Duryea Entertainment
35 White Birch Rd
Ridgefield, CT 06877-5620, USA

Lovitz, Jon (Actor, Comedian, Producer, Writer)
c/o Chuck Binder *Binder & Associates*
1465 Lindacrest Dr
Beverly Hills, CA 90210-2519, USA

Lovrich, Pete (Athlete, Baseball Player)
19626 Beechnut Dr
Mokena, IL 60448-9333, USA

Lovullo, Torey (Athlete, Baseball Player)
32108 Sailview Ln
Westlake Village, CA 91361-3619, USA

Lovuolo, Frank (Athlete, Football Player)
6 Pleasant Ct
Binghamton, NY 13905-1516, USA

Low, G David (Astronaut)
Orbital Science Group
45101 Warp Dr
Sterling, VA 20166-6874, USA

Low, Reed (Athlete, Hockey Player)
1869 Pomme Rd
Arnold, MO 63010-2453

Lowder, Kyle (Actor)
c/o Michael P Levine *Levine Management*
9028 W Sunset Blvd PH 1
West Hollywood, CA 90069-1830, USA

Lowdermilk, R Kirk (Athlete, Football Player)
8080 Apollo Rd NE
Kensington, OH 44427-9626, USA

Lowe, Chad (Actor)
c/o David Rose *Innovative Artists (LA)*
1505 10th St
Santa Monica, CA 90401-2805, USA

Lowe, Cortland (Athlete, Golfer)
713 Taylor Ridge Rd
Winston Salem, NC 27106-5075, USA

Lowe, Derek (Athlete, Baseball Player)
12711 Terabella Way
Fort Myers, FL 33912-0910, USA

Lowe, Gary (Athlete, Football Player)
16940 Lauderdale Ave
Beverly Hills, MI 48025-5549, USA

Lowe, Lloyd (Athlete, Football Player)
8805 Deerwood Dr
Rowlett, TX 75088-4809, USA

lowe, Mark
11922 NW 39th Ct
Vancouver, WA 98685-2780, USA

Lowe, Nick (Musician, Songwriter, Writer)
MVO Ltd
307 7th Ave Rm 807
New York, NY 10001-6066, USA

Lowe, Paul (Athlete, Football Player)
5134 Logan Ave
San Diego, CA 92114-6221, USA

Lowe, QV
125 Palomino Ln
Wetumpka, AL 36093-2103, USA

Lowe, Rob (Actor)
PO Box 5038
Santa Barbara, CA 93150-5038, USA

Lowe, Sean (Athlete, Baseball Player)
802 Oak Dr
Mesquite, TX 75149-4028, USA

Lowe, Sean
c/o Matt Kirschner *Talent Resources*
124 E 36th St Ste A
New York, NY 10016-3402, USA

Lowe, Sidney (Athlete, Basketball Player, Coach)
2631 Wallingford Rd
Winston Salem, NC 27101-1923, USA

Lowe, Stephanie (Athlete, Golfer)
2004 Delancey Dr
Norman, OK 73071-3872, USA

Lowe, Woodrow (Athlete, Coach, Football Player)
Jackson-Olin High School
PO Box 988
Alabaster, AL 35007-2054, USA

Loweecey, Alice (Writer)
c/o Staff Member *Midnight Ink*
2143 Wooddale Dr
Saint Paul, MN 55125-2989, USA

Lowell, Carey (Actor)
c/o Sue Leibman *Barking Dog Entertainment*
609 Greenwich St Fl 6
New York, NY 10014-3610, USA

Lowell, Charlie (Musician)
Flood Burnstead McCready McCarthy
1700 Hayes St Ste 304
Nashville, TN 37203-3593, USA

Lowell, Christopher (Designer, Television Host)
The Christopher Lowell Show
2800 Olympic Blvd Fl 2
Santa Monica, CA 90404-4101, USA

Lowell, Mike (Athlete, Baseball Player)
620 Santurce Ave
Coral Gables, FL 33143-6360, USA

Lowell, Scott
6500 Wilshire Blvd Ste 2200
Los Angeles, CA 90048-4942

L. Owens, William (Congressman, Politician)
431 Cannon Hob
Washington, DC 20515-1603, USA

Lowenstein, Evan (Actor, Musician)
c/o Ruthanne Secunda *ICM Partners (LA)*
10250 Constellation Blvd Fl 7
Los Angeles, CA 90067-6207, USA

Lowenstein, Jaron (Actor, Musician)
c/o Ruthanne Secunda *ICM Partners (LA)*
10250 Constellation Blvd Fl 7
Los Angeles, CA 90067-6207, USA

Lowenstein, John (Athlete, Baseball Player)
7017 Via Locanda Ave
Las Vegas, NV 89131-0114, USA

Lowery, Devon (Baseball Player)
11611 Ragan Elizabeth Ct
Charlotte, NC 28278-4001, USA

Lowery, Dwight (Athlete, Football Player)
c/o Frank Bauer *Sun West Sports*
7883 N Pershing Ave
Stockton, CA 95207-1749, USA

Lowery, Nick (Athlete, Football Player)
8416 E Via De Jardin
Scottsdale, AZ 85258-3207, USA

Lowery, Steve (Athlete, Golfer)
379 Woodward Ct
Birmingham, AL 35242-6041, USA

Lowery, Terrell (Athlete, Baseball Player)
3565 Antigua Pl
West Sacramento, CA 95691-5822, USA

Lowes, Katie (Actor)
c/o David Sweeney *Sweeney Entertainment*
6253 Hollywood Blvd Apt 201
Los Angeles, CA 90028-8248, USA

Lown, Bernard (Doctor)
Lown Cardiovascular Group
21 Longwood Ave
Brookline, MA 02446-5239, USA

Lown, Turk (Athlete, Baseball Player)
1106 Van Buren St
Pueblo, CO 81004-2832, USA

Lowndes, Jessica (Actor)
c/o Jeff Witjas *Agency for the Performing Arts (APA-LA)*
405 S Beverly Dr Ste 500
Beverly Hills, CA 90212-4425, USA

Lowrie, Jed
2958 N Evergreen St
Buckeye, AZ 85396-7783, USA

Lowry, Calvin (Athlete, Football Player)
66 Daughtrey Ave Apt 203
Waco, TX 76706-1675, USA

Lowry, Lois (Writer)
9 Whipple Farm Ln
Falmouth, ME 04105-1898, USA

Lowry, Mark
MLP Inc
PO Box 1405
Hendersonville, TN 37077-1405, USA

Lowry, Noah (Athlete, Baseball Player)
1237 Eagle Dr
Windsor, CA 95492-9798, USA

Low Stars (Music Group)
c/o Staff Member *Paradigm (Monterey)*
404 W Franklin St
Monterey, CA 93940-2303, USA

Loynd, Mike (Athlete, Baseball Player)
952 Pompano Dr
Jupiter, FL 33458-4311, USA

Lozada, Evelyn (Actor, Reality Star)
c/o Matt Kirschner *Talent Resources*
124 E 36th St Ste A
New York, NY 10016-3402, USA

Lozado, Willie (Athlete, Baseball Player)
3032 Shagbark Trl
Sellersburg, IN 47172-9117, USA

Lozano, Conrad (Musician)
Gold Mountain
3575 Cahuenga Blvd W Ste 450
Los Angeles, CA 90068-1364, USA

Lozano, Karyme (Actor)
c/o Ivan De Paz *DePaz Management*
2011 N Vermont Ave
Los Angeles, CA 90027-1931, USA

L. Richmond, Cedric (Congressman, Politician)
415 Cannon Hob
Washington, DC 20515-2211, USA

L. Rush, Bobby (Congressman, Politician)
2268 Rayburn Hob
Washington, DC 20515-0502, USA

Isikoff, Michael (Writer)
123 Main St # A
Irvington, NY 10533-1718, USA

Lu, Cindy (Actor)
c/o Kim Matuka *Online Talent Group*
Prefers to be contacted via email or telephone
West Hollywood, CA 90069, USA

Lu, Edward T (Ed) (Astronaut)
12332 Kosich Pl
Saratoga, CA 95070-3575, USA

Lu, Lisa
1737 N Orange Grove Ave
Los Angeles, CA 90046-2131

Lubanski, Ed (Bowler)
5326 Christi Dr
Warren, MI 48091-4195, USA

Lubezki, Emmanuel (Cinematographer)
c/o Julia Kole *Jacob & Kole Agency, The*
522 Wilshire Blvd Ste H
Santa Monica, CA 90401-1445, USA

Lubich, Bronko (Wrestler)
3146 Whitemarsh Cir
Dallas, TX 75234-2239, USA

Lubin, Arthur
5737 Newcastle Ave
Encino, CA 91316-1054

Lubin, Steven (Musician)
State University of New York
School of Arts
Purchase, NY 10577, USA

Lubischer, Steve (Athlete, Football Player)
6 Fiore Ct
Oceanport, NJ 07757-1405, USA

Lublin, Nancy (Business Person)
Do Something
24 Union Sq E # 32
New York, NY 10003-3201, USA

Lubratich, Steve (Athlete, Baseball Player)
24 Sackett Rd
Lee, NH 03861-6616, USA

Lubsen, Chip (Athlete, Olympic Athlete, Rower)
13215 Stable
Herndon, VA 20171, USA

Luc, Tone (Actor, Musician)
Headline Talent
1650 Broadway Ste 508
New York, NY 10019-6833, USA

Lucado, Max (Religious Leader, Writer)
Oak Hills Church of Christ
6929 Camp Bullis Rd
San Antonio, TX 78256-2334, USA

Lucas, Craig (Director, Producer, Writer)
c/o Staff Member *Gersh (LA)*
9465 Wilshire Blvd Ste 600
Beverly Hills, CA 90212-2605, USA

Lucas, Dan (Athlete, Hockey Player)
609 Forest Ave
Portland, ME 04101-1515

Lucas, Dick (Athlete, Football Player)
1269 Estate Dr
West Chester, PA 19380-1258, USA

Lucas, Erin (Actor, Reality Star)
c/o Staff Member *Creative Management Entertainment Group (CMEG)*
2050 S Bundy Dr Ste 280
Los Angeles, CA 90025-6128, USA

Lucas, Gary (Athlete, Baseball Player)
1511 High St
Rice Lake, WI 54868-1874, USA

Lucas, George (Business Person, Director, Producer)
c/o Staff Member *LucasFilm Ltd*
5858 Lucas Valley Rd
Nicasio, CA 94946-9703, USA

Lucas, Geralyn (Writer)
1349 Lexington Ave Apt 4D
New York, NY 10128-1514, USA

Lucas, Isabel (Actor)
1810 Arteique Rd
Topanga, CA 90290-4248, USA

Lucas, Jerry (Athlete, Basketball Player, Olympic Athlete)
Dr Memorabilia
231 E 2nd St
Chillicothe, OH 45601-2612, USA

Lucas, Jessica (Actor)
c/o Staff Member *Thruline Entertainment*
9250 Wilshire Blvd Ste 100
Ground Floor
Beverly Hills, CA 90212-3343, USA

Lucas, John (Athlete, Basketball Player)
21 Pin Oak Estates Ct
Bellaire, TX 77401-4225, USA

Lucas, Josh (Actor)
8459 Ridpath Dr
Los Angeles, CA 90046-7711, USA

Lucas, Ken (Athlete, Football Player)
1108 Stamps Cv
Cleveland, MS 38732-4014, USA

Lucas, Matt (Actor, Producer, Writer)
c/o Kevin McLaughlin *Baker Winokur Ryder Public Relations (BWR-LA)*
9100 Wilshire Blvd Ste 500
West Tower Suite 500
Beverly Hills, CA 90212-3426, USA

Lucas, Michael (Adult Film Star, Director)
Lucas Entertainment
589 8th Ave Fl 2
New York, NY 10018-3097, USA

Lucas, Ray (Athlete, Football Player)
415 Davis Ave
Harrison, NJ 07029-1509, USA

Lucas, Richard J (Richie) (Athlete, Football Player)
1855 Hamilton Ave
Tyrone, PA 16686-2366, USA

Lucas, Tim (Athlete, Football Player)
5081 S Florence Dr
Greenwood Village, CO 80111-3613, USA

Lucas, William (Government Official)
Justice Department
Constitution & 10th NW
Washington, DC 20530-0001, USA

Lucca, Lou (Baseball Player)
Topps
10211 Willow Bend Cir Apt 1B
Charlotte, NC 28210-8424, USA

Lucchesi, Frank (Athlete, Baseball Player, Coach)
4703 Mill Creek Dr
Colleyville, TX 76034-3646, USA

Lucchesini, Andrea (Musician)
Arts Management Group
1133 Broadway Ste 1025
New York, NY 10010-7985, USA

Lucci, Mike (Athlete, Football Player)
3184 Middlebelt Rd
West Bloomfield, MI 48323-1937, USA

Lucci, Susan (Actor)
c/o Fran Curtis *Rogers & Cowan PR (NY)*
919 3rd Ave Fl 18
New York, NY 10022-3902, USA

Lucci, Vince Sr (Bowler)
1182 Queens Way
West Chester, PA 19382, USA

Luce, Derrel (Athlete, Football Player)
4112 Green Oak Dr
Waco, TX 76710-1440, USA

Luce, Don
67 Tartan Ln
Buffalo, NY 14221-2616

Luce, Don
Philadelphia Flyers
3601 S Broad St Ste 2
Philadelphia, PA 19148-5297

Luce, Henry III (Publisher)
Mill Hill Road
Mill Neck, NY 11765, USA

Luce, Lew (Athlete, Football Player)
850 Symphony Isles Blvd
Apollo Beach, FL 33572-2764, USA

Luce, William (Bill) (Writer)
PO Box 370
Depoe Bay, OR 97341-0370, USA

Lucero (Musician)
c/o Staff Member *Sony Music Miami*
605 Lincoln Rd Ste 700
Miami Beach, FL 33139-2901, USA

Lucey, Dorothy (Actor, Correspondent, Television Host)
c/o Staff Member *Good Day Live*
10201 W Pico Blvd Bldg 88
20th Century Fox Television
Los Angeles, CA 90064-2606, USA

Luchento, Tom (Horse Racer)
3 Hedge Row Ct
Columbus, NJ 08022-1129, USA

Luchsinger, Susie (Musician)
Psalms Ministries
PO Box 990
Atoka, OK 74525-0990, USA

Lucic, Milan (Athlete, Hockey Player)
50 Fleet St Ste 301
Boston, MA 02109-1129, USA

Lucid, Shannon W (Astronaut, Physicist)
1622 Gunwale Rd
Houston, TX 77062-4538, USA

Lucid, Shannon W Dr (Astronaut)
1622 Gunwale Rd
Houston, TX 77062-4538, USA

Lucier, Lou (Athlete, Baseball Player)
7 Jaclyn Rae Dr
Millbury, MA 01527-3372, USA

Lucier, Wayne (Athlete, Football Player)
13 Jana Rd
Salem, NH 03079-2261, USA

Lucin, Arthur
5737 Newcastle Ave
Encino, CA 91316-1054

Lucio, Shannon (Actor)
c/o Justin Grey Stone *Management 360*
350 S Beverly Dr Ste 200
Beverly Hills, CA 90212-4819, USA

Luck, Andrew (Athlete, Football Player)
925 Riverview Dr
Morgantown, WV 26505-4633, USA

Luck, Oliver (Athlete, Football Player)
925 Riverview Dr
Morgantown, WV 26505-4633, USA

Luck, Terry (Athlete, Football Player)
334 N Brooke Dr
Canton, GA 30115-3002, USA

Luckenbill, Laurence
PO Box 636
Cross River, NY 10518-0636

Luckett, Letoya (Actor)
c/o Everly Lee *Resolution (LA)*
1801 Century Park E Ste 2300
Los Angeles, CA 90067-2325, USA

Luckhurst, Mick (Athlete, Football Player)
103 Pierrepont Isle
Duluth, GA 30097-5908, USA

Luckinbill, Laurence (Actor)
RR 3
Katonah, NY 10536, USA

Luckinbill, Lawrence (Actor)
PO Box 330
Georgetown, CT 06829-0330, USA

Luckinbill, Thad (Actor)
370 Aderno Way
Pacific Palisades, CA 90272-3344, USA

Lucking, William (Actor)
c/o Staff Member *Twentieth Century Artists*
15760 Ventura Blvd Ste 700
Encino, CA 91436-3016, USA

Lucky, Lillian (Baseball Player)
243 Owens St
Niles, MI 49120-4150, USA

Lucky, Mike (Athlete, Football Player)
10550 E Sanger Ave
Mesa, AZ 85212-8067, USA

Lucroy, Jonathan (Athlete, Baseball Player)
9 Huntington Rd Apt 10-E
Scarsdale, NY 10583-2039

Lucy, Donny (Athlete, Baseball Player)
2328 Via Del Aquacate
Fallbrook, CA 92028-9697, USA

Luczo, Stephen J (Business Person)
Seagate Technology
215 El Pueblo Rd
Scotts Valley, CA 95066-4229, USA

Ludacris (Actor, Musician, Producer)
3683 Demooney Rd
Atlanta, GA 30349, USA

Ludaker, Dave (Baseball Player)
3593 Buffum St
Simi Valley, CA 93063-3215, USA

Luddington, Camilla (Actor)
c/o Tracy Steinsapir *Main Title Entertainment*
8383 Wilshire Blvd Ste 408
Beverly Hills, CA 90211-2435, USA

Luddy, Barbara
119 Sultan Ave
Capitol Heights, MD 20743-1954

Ludes, John T (Business Person)
Fortune Brands Inc
300 Tower Pkwy
Lincolnshire, IL 60069-3640, USA

Ludington, Ronald (Athlete, Figure Skater, Olympic Athlete)
611 Thompson Station Rd
Newark, DE 19711-7505, USA

Ludlum, Robert (Actor)
c/o Ben Smith *ICM Partners (LA)*
10250 Constellation Blvd Fl 7
Los Angeles, CA 90067-6207, USA

Ludwick, Eric (Athlete, Baseball Player)
7146 Madarang Ave
Las Vegas, NV 89178-8002, USA

Ludwick, Ryan (Athlete, Baseball Player)
511 County Road 262
Georgetown, TX 78633-1950, USA

Ludwig, Alexander (Actor)
c/o Guido Giordano *ICM Partners (LA)*
10250 Constellation Blvd Fl 7
Los Angeles, CA 90067-6207, USA

Ludwig, Craig (Athlete, Hockey Player)
8401 Albritton Dr
Frisco, TX 75034-7702, USA

Ludwig, Ken (Writer)
c/o Peter Franklin *William Morris Endeavor (NY)*
1325 Avenue of the Americas
New York, NY 10019-6026, USA

Luebber, Steve (Athlete, Baseball Player)
3302 Moorhead Dr
Joplin, MO 64804-5323, USA

Luebbers, Larry (Athlete, Baseball Player)
2045 Timberwyck Ln
Burlington, KY 41005-2500, USA

Luebke, Cory (Athlete, Baseball Player)
2190 Oak St
Maria Stein, OH 45860-9509, USA

Lueck, Bill (Athlete, Football Player)
409 E Bird Ln
Litchfield Park, AZ 85340-4214, USA

Luecken, Rick (Athlete, Baseball Player)
2902 Fontana Dr
Houston, TX 77043-1305, USA

Luetkemeyer, Blaine (Congressman, Politician)
1740 Longworth Hob
Washington, DC 20515-3503, USA

Luft, Joey (Actor)
108 E Matilija St
Ojai, CA 93023-2639

Luft, Lorna (Actor, Musician)
280 Coldwater Canyon Dr
Beverly Hills, CA 90210, USA

Lugar, Richard (Politician, Senator)
7841 Old Dominion Dr
Mc Lean, VA 22102-2425, USA

Lugavere, Max (Television Host)
c/o Rob Levy *Untitled Entertainment (LA)*
350 S Beverly Dr Ste 200
Beverly Hills, CA 90212-4819, USA

Lugbill, Jon (Athlete, Olympic Athlete)
American Cance Assn
2422 Grove Ave
Richmond, VA 23220-4416, USA

Luger, Lex (Athlete, Wrestler)
c/o Staff Member *World Wrestling Entertainment (WWE)*
1241 E Main St
Titan Towers
Stamford, CT 06902-3520, USA

Lugo, Julio (Athlete, Baseball Player)
1555 Gants Cir
Kissimmee, FL 34744-6459, USA

Lugo, Ruddy (Athlete, Baseball Player)
1555 Gants Cir
Kissimmee, FL 34744-6459, USA

Lugosi Jr, Bela
520 N Central Ave Ste 800
Glendale, CA 91203-3962, USA

Lui, Stephen
10635 Santa Monica Blvd Ste 130
Los Angeles, CA 90025-8306

luis, isaac (Athlete, Baseball Player)
PO Box 1167
Carolina, PR 00986-1167, USA

Luisi, Caesar (Actor)
c/o Christopher Smith *Paradigm (LA)*
360 N Crescent Dr
North Bldg
Beverly Hills, CA 90210-4874, USA

Luisi, James
22562 Seaver Ct
Santa Clarita, CA 91350-1389

Lujack, Johnny (Athlete, Football Player, Heisman Trophy Winner)
6321 Crow Valley Dr
Bettendorf, IA 52722-6219, USA

Lujan, Ben Ray (Congressman, Politician)
330 Cannon Hob
Washington, DC 20515-4302, USA

Lujan, Manuel Jr (Politician, Secretary)
Manuel Lujan Agencies
PO Box 90756
Albuquerque, NM 87199-0756, USA

Lukachyk, Rob (Athlete, Baseball Player)
100 High St
Woodbridge, NJ 07095-3018, USA

Lukacs, John (Writer)
c/o Staff Member *Simon & Schuster*
1230 Avenue of the Americas Fl CONC1
New York, NY 10020-1586, USA

Lukas, D Wayne (Coach)
5242 Katella Ave # 103
Los Alamitos, CA 90720-2820, USA

Lukas, DWayne (Horse Racer)
1034 Oak Canyon Ln
Glendora, CA 91741-2256, USA

Lukas, D Wayne (Race Car Driver)
5699 Happy Canyon Rd
Santa Ynez, CA 93460-9741, USA

Lukasiewicz, Mark (Athlete, Baseball Player)
8035 Fir Dr
Clay, NY 13041-8646, USA

Lukather, Steve (Musician)
Fitzgerald-Hartley
34 N Palm St Ste 100
Ventura, CA 93001-2610, USA

Luke (Musician)
Richard Walters
1800 Argyle Ave # 408
Los Angeles, CA 90028-5253, USA

Luke, Derek (Actor)
c/o Cindy Guagenti *Baker Winokur Ryder Public Relations (BWR-LA)*
9100 Wilshire Blvd Ste 500
West Tower Suite 500
Beverly Hills, CA 90212-3426, USA

Luke, John A Jr (Business Person)
Westvaco Corp
299 Park Ave Fl 13
New York, NY 10171-3800, USA

Luke, Matt (Athlete, Baseball Player)
5262 Eucalyptus Hill Rd
Yorba Linda, CA 92886-4209, USA

Luke, Steve (Athlete, Football Player)
812 Bluffview Dr
Columbus, OH 43235-1728, USA

Luke, Tommy (Athlete, Football Player)
116 W Shore Dr
Saltillo, MS 38866-5745

Luke, Triandos (Athlete, Football Player)
217 Highgrove Ln
Aston, PA 19014-1481, USA

Luken, Tom (Athlete, Football Player)
4708 Virginia Ln
Minneapolis, MN 55424-1763, USA

Lukens, Max L (Business Person)
Baker Hughes Inc
3900 Essex Ln
Houston, TX 77027-5133, USA

Luker, Rebecca (Actor)
c/o Staff Member William Morris
Endeavor (LA)
9601 Wilshire Blvd
Beverly Hills, CA 90210-5213, USA

Luketic, Robert (Actor)
c/o Paul Nelson Mosaic Media Group
9200 W Sunset Blvd Ste 10
West Hollywood, CA 90069-3608, USA

Lukin, Matt (Musician)
Legends of 21st Century
7 Trinity Row
Florence, MA 01062-1931, USA

Lukowich, Brad (Athlete, Hockey Player)
3400 Craig Dr Apt 721
McKinney, TX 75070-4513

Lulabel & Scottie
PO Box 171132
Nashville, TN 37217-8132

lulo, Ken (Horse Racer)
165 Prospect St Fl 2
Passaic, NJ 07055-5160, USA

Lum, Mike (Athlete, Baseball Player)
3476 Cochise Dr SE
Atlanta, GA 30339-4324, USA

Lumbly, Carl (Actor)
c/o Karen Forman Domain Talent
9229 W Sunset Blvd Ste 710
West Hollywood, CA 90069-3407, USA

Lumenti, Ralph (Athlete, Baseball Player)
9 Tomaso Rd
Milford, MA 01757-2224, USA

Lumineers, The (Music Group)
c/o Jim Merlis Big Hassle Media
40 Exchange Pl Ste 1900
New York, NY 10005-2714, USA

Lumley, Dave (Athlete, Hockey Player)
PO Box 610
Murfreesboro, AR 71958-0610

Lumpkin, Elgin (Ginuwine) (Musician)
c/o Michael Irving Emancipated Talent
215 Clinton St
Brooklyn, NY 11201, USA

Lumpkin, Sean (Athlete, Football Player)
4708 Virginia Ln
Minneapolis, MN 55424-1763, USA

Lumpp, Ray (Athlete, Basketball Player,
Olympic Athlete)
21 Hewlett Dr
East Williston, NY 11596-2003, USA

Luna, Barbara (Actor)
18026 Rodarte Way
Encino, CA 91316-4370, USA

Luna-Hill, Betty (Baseball Player)
19887 Red Feather Rd
Apple Valley, CA 92307-5514, USA

Lunar, Fernando (Athlete, Baseball Player)
3125 Zuni Pl
Alamogordo, NM 88310-4029, USA

Lunatics, St (Musician)
c/o Staff Member Team Lunatics (MO)
4246 Forest Park Ave Ste 2C
Saint Louis, MO 63108-2811, USA

Lund, Gordy (Athlete, Baseball Player)
1602 S Harvard Ave
Arlington Heights, IL 60005-3517, USA

Lund, Katia (Director)
c/o Sandra Lucchesi Gersh (LA)
9465 Wilshire Blvd Ste 600
Beverly Hills, CA 90212-2605, USA

Lunday, James (Actor)
c/o Staff Member TLC
10100 Santa Monica Blvd Ste 1500
Los Angeles, CA 90067-4117, USA

Lunday, Kenneth (Athlete, Football Player)
1419 W Locust St
Durant, OK 74701-3458, USA

Lunde, Martin (Arn Anderson) (Athlete,
Wrestler)
10520 Wynyates Ln
Charlotte, NC 28270-2504, USA

Lunden, Joan (Correspondent, Producer)
32 Orchard Hill Ln
Greenwich, CT 06831-3626, USA

Lundgren, Dolph (Actor)
c/o Craig Baumgarten Baumgarten
Management
1447 Cloverfield Blvd Ste 101
Santa Monica, CA 90404-2979, USA

Lundgren, Terry (Business Person)
Federated Department Stores
151 W 34th St
New York, NY 10001-2101, USA

Lundholm, Mark (Actor, Comedian)
c/o Staff Member William Morris
Endeavor (LA)
9601 Wilshire Blvd
Beverly Hills, CA 90210-5213, USA

Lundquist, Dave (Athlete, Baseball Player)
714 12th Ave NE
Hickory, NC 28601-2707, USA

Lundquist, David (Athlete, Baseball
Player)
Hickory Crawdads
PO Box 1268
Attn: Coaching Staff
Hickory, NC 28603-1268, USA

Lundquist, Steve (Athlete, Olympic
Athlete, Swimmer)
246 Northwind Dr
Stockbridge, GA 30281-6216, USA

Lundquist, Verne (Sportscaster)
NBC-TV
1710 Natches Way
Steamboat Springs, CO 80487-9004, USA

Lundqvist, Alex (Model)
c/o Robyn Bluestone Robyn Bluestone
Management
11021 73rd Rd Apt 4G
Forest Hills, NY 11375-6316, USA

Lundqvist, Henrik (Athlete, Hockey
Player)
225 W 83rd St Apt 20G
New York, NY 10024-4964, USA

Lundstedt, Tom (Athlete, Baseball Player)
8645 Hunters Way
Saint Paul, MN 55124-9430, USA

Lundy, Carmen (Musician)
Abby Hoffer
223 1/2 E 48th St
New York, NY 10017, USA

Lundy, Jessica (Actor)
c/o Staff Member Metropolitan (MTA)
4526 Wilshire Blvd
Los Angeles, CA 90010-3801, USA

Luner, Jaime (Actor)
Martin Hurwitz
427 N Canon Dr Ste 215
Beverly Hills, CA 90210-4840, USA

Luner, Jamie (Actor)
c/o Marty Berneman Precision
Entertainment
465 N Croft Ave
Los Angeles, CA 90048-2508, USA

Lunke, Hilary (Athlete, Golfer)
11701 Broad Oaks Dr
Austin, TX 78759-3713, USA

Lunn, Bob (Athlete, Golfer)
PO Box 1495
Woodbridge, CA 95258-1495, USA

Lunsford, Scott (Actor)
c/o Robert Yaffee Infinity Management
7923 Hollywood Blvd
Los Angeles, CA 90046-2611, USA

Lunsford, Stephen (Actor)
c/o Bonnie Liedtke Principato/Young
Management (LA)
9465 Wilshire Blvd Ste 900
Beverly Hills, CA 90212-2608, USA

Lunsford, Trey (Athlete, Baseball Player)
3955 Nail Rd
Southaven, MS 38672-6739, USA

Luongo, Chris (Athlete, Hockey Player)
245 Concord Dr
Madison, AL 35758-8148, USA

Luongo, Roberto (Athlete, Hockey Player)
7280 Lemon Grass Dr
Parkland, FL 33076-3950, USA

Lupberger, Edwin A (Business Person)
Entergy Corp
10055 Grogans Mill Rd Ste 150
Spring, TX 77380-1048, USA

Lupica, Mike (Writer)
87 Bald Hill Rd
New Canaan, CT 06840-2404, USA

Luplow, Al (Baseball Player)
4250 Lakecress Dr E
Saginaw, MI 48603-1687, USA

Luplow, Al (Athlete, Baseball Player)
4250 Lakecress Dr E
Saginaw, MI 48603-1687, USA

Lupo, Frank (Producer, Writer)
c/o Stephen Marks Evolution
Entertainment (LA)
901 N Highland Ave
Los Angeles, CA 90038-2412, USA

LuPone, Patti (Actor, Musician)
c/o Iris Grossman Paradigm (LA)
360 N Crescent Dr
North Bldg
Beverly Hills, CA 90210-4874, USA

Lupul, Jaffrey (Athlete, Hockey Player)
600 1/2 36th St
Newport Beach, CA 92663-6203, USA

Lupus, Peter (Actor)
2401 S 24th St # 110
Phoenix, AZ 85034-6806, USA

Lurie, Alison (Writer)
159 Sapsucker Woods Rd
Ithaca, NY 14850-1923, USA

Lurie, Alison (Writer)
Cornell University
English Dept
Ithaca, NY 14850, USA

Lurie, Jeffrey (Business Person, Football
Executive)
312 Llanfair Rd
Wynnewood, PA 19096-1216, USA

Lurie, Rod (Director)
7550 Mulholland Dr
Los Angeles, CA 90046-1239, USA

Lurtsema, Bob (Athlete, Football Player)
16920 Judicial Rd
Lakeville, MN 55044-8975, USA

Lusader, Scott (Athlete, Baseball Player)
4169 Bold Mdws
Oakland Township, MI 48306-4701, USA

Lusby, Vaughn (Athlete, Football Player)
4011 N Belt Line Rd Apt 928
Irving, TX 75038-8419, USA

Luscinski, Jim (Athlete, Football Player)
49 Pleasant St
Pembroke, MA 02359-2302, USA

Luse, Bernadette (Athlete, Golfer)
2528 Reading Dr
Orlando, FL 32804-4938, USA

Lush, Mike (Athlete, Football Player)
287 Blue Sage Dr
Allentown, PA 18104-8202, USA

Lusha, Masiela (Actor, Producer)
Illuminary Films
7046 Hollywood Blvd
Los Angeles, CA 90028-6008, USA

Lusk, Herbert (Athlete, Football Player)
71 Palomar Real
Campbell, CA 95008-4206, USA

Lustig, Aaron (Actor)
c/o Staff Member House of
Representatives, The
1434 6th St Ste 1
Santa Monica, CA 90401-2527, USA

Lustig, William (Producer)
15016 Marble Dr
Sherman Oaks, CA 91403-4521, USA

Lutes, Eric (Actor)
c/o Kate Edwards Grand View
Management
578 Washington Blvd # 688
Marina Del Rey, CA 90292-5442, USA

Luther, Bobbi Sue (Actor, Model)
c/o Staff Member Paradigm (LA)
360 N Crescent Dr
North Bldg
Beverly Hills, CA 90210-4874, USA

Luther, Ed (Athlete, Football Player)
30486 Le Prt
Laguna Niguel, CA 92677-5537, USA

Luttrell, Rachel (Actor)
c/o Staff Member SMS Talent
8383 Wilshire Blvd Ste 230
Beverly Hills, CA 90211-2436, USA

Lutui, Taitusi ""Deuce"" (Athlete, Football
Player)
3829 N Stone Gully
Mesa, AZ 85207-1101, USA

Lutz, Bob (Tennis Player)
101 Via Ensueno
San Clemente, CA 92672-2456, USA

Lutz, Joleen (Actor)
H David Moss
733 Seward St PH
Los Angeles, CA 90038-3503, USA

Lutz, Kellan (Actor)
2821 Dell Ave
Venice, CA 90291-4546, USA

Lutz, Robert A (Business Person)
3600 Green Ct Ste 720
Ann Arbor, MI 48105-1570, USA

Luu, Chan (Designer)
818 S Broadway Fl 6
Los Angeles, CA 90014-3224, USA

Luuloa, Keith (Athlete, Baseball Player)
30905 Young Dove St
Menifee, CA 92584-8358, USA

LuValle, James (Athlete, Track Athlete)
1174 Los Altos Ave Apt 160
Los Altos, CA 94022-1062, USA

Luvana, Carmen (Adult Film Star)
c/o Adam & Eve Productions
9445 De Soto Ave
Chatsworth, CA 91311-4920, USA

Luyties, Ricci (Athlete, Olympic Athlete, Volleyball Player)
University of California - San Diego
2215 Hartford St
San Diego, CA 92110-2336, USA

Luz, Franc
606 N Larchmont Blvd Ste 309
Los Angeles, CA 90004-1309

Luzinski, Greg (Athlete, Baseball Player)
25680 Streamlet Ct
Bonita Springs, FL 34135-7829, USA

Luzinski, Ryan (Athlete, Baseball Player)
25680 Streamlet Ct
Bonita Springs, FL 34135-7829, USA

Ivey, James (Cartoonist)
5840 Dahlia Dr Apt 7
Orlando, FL 32807-3251, USA

Iwamura, Akinori (Athlete, Baseball Player)
623 Saxony Blvd
Saint Petersburg, FL 33716-1297, USA

L. Watt, Melvin (Congressman, Politician)
2304 Rayburn Hob
Washington, DC 20515-4206, USA

Lyden, Mitch (Athlete, Baseball Player)
6055 NW 72nd Ct
Parkland, FL 33067-2441, USA

Lydman, Toni (Athlete, Hockey Player)
6035 Corinne Ln
Clarence Center, NY 14032-9510, USA

Lydon, James (Jimmy) (Actor)
3538 Lomacitas Ln
Bonita, CA 91902-1105, USA

Lydon, John (Johnny Rotten) (Musician)
31962 Pacific Coast Hwy
Malibu, CA 90265-2506, USA

Lydon, Malcolm (Astronaut)
684 E Pelham Rd NE
Atlanta, GA 30324-5202, USA

Lydy, Scott (Athlete, Baseball Player)
4278 S Leoma Ln
Chandler, AZ 85249-4782, USA

Lye, Mark (Athlete, Golfer)
4610 Via Cappello
Bonita Springs, FL 34134-4954, USA

Lyfe (Musician)
c/o Staff Member Sony/RCA Records
550 Madison Ave Fl 6
New York, NY 10022-3211, USA

Lyght, Todd (Athlete, Football Player)
302 Salter St
Philadelphia, PA 19147-4275, USA

Lyle, Garry (Athlete, Football Player)
222 Beach Dr NE
Saint Petersburg, FL 33701-3414, USA

Lyle, George (Athlete, Hockey Player)
33754 N 69th St
Scottsdale, AZ 85266-7014, USA

Lyle, Jarrod (Athlete, Golfer)
c/o Jim Lehrman SFX Golf
36855 W Main St Ste 200
Purcellville, VA 20132-3561, USA

Lyle, Kami (Musician, Songwriter, Writer)
DS Mgmt
2814 12th Ave S Ste 202
Nashville, TN 37204-2513, USA

Lyle, Keith (Athlete, Football Player)
9615 Maypan Pl
Seminole, FL 33777-4906, USA

Lyle, Sandy (Athlete, Golfer)
4905 Duck Creek Ln
Ponte Vedra Beach, FL 32082-3023, USA

Lyle, Sparky (Athlete, Baseball Player)
17 Signal Hill Dr
Voorhees, NJ 08043-2948, USA

Lyles, Lester (Athlete, Football Player)
6315 14th St NW
Washington, DC 20011-8003, USA

Lyles, Robert (Athlete, Football Player)
PO Box 1075
Jackson, MS 39215-1075, USA

Lyman, Arthur
508 Kaanini St
Hilo, HI 96720-2751

Lyman, Dorothy
c/o Staff Member Stone Manners Salners Agency (LA)
6100 Wilshire Blvd Ste 1500
Los Angeles, CA 90048-5110, USA

Lyman, Dustin (Athlete, Football Player)
501 W Spruce St
Louisville, CO 80027-2209

Lymon, Frankie
1650 Broadway Ste 508
New York, NY 10019-6833

Lyn, Mai
190 W Kern Ave
Mc Farland, CA 93250-1349

Lynch, Claire
1 Camp St
Cambridge, MA 02140-1103

Lynch, Cynthia (Athlete, Wrestler)
4205 Bridlepath Pl
Louisville, KY 40245-1971, USA

Lynch, David (Director)
David Lynch Foundation
216 E 45th St Fl 13
New York, NY 10017-3304, USA

Lynch, Dustin (Musician)
c/o Staff Member William Morris Endeavor (Nashville)
1600 Division St Ste 300
Nashville, TN 37203-2755, USA

Lynch, Ed (Athlete, Baseball Player)
7832 E Parkview Ln
Scottsdale, AZ 85255-2704, USA

Lynch, Evanna (Actor)
c/o Ricky Rollins Schumacher Management
2018 Glendon Ave
Los Angeles, CA 90025-6324, USA

Lynch, Fran (Athlete, Football Player)
14295 Lipan St
Westminster, CO 80023-8435, USA

Lynch, George (Basketball Player)
5930 Royal Ln Ste E
Dallas, TX 75230-3896, USA

Lynch, Holly (Actor)
c/o Scott Karp The Syndicate
10203 Santa Monica Blvd Fl 5
Los Angeles, CA 90067-6416, USA

Lynch, Jair (Athlete, Gymnast, Olympic Athlete)
9207 Three Oaks Dr
Silver Spring, MD 20901-3363, USA

Lynch, James E (Jim) (Athlete, Football Player)
1009 W 67th St
Kansas City, MO 64113-1916, USA

Lynch, Jane (Actor)
10866 Wilshire Blvd Fl 10
Los Angeles, CA 90024-4350, USA

Lynch, Jennifer (Director, Producer)
1894 El Cerrito Pl
Los Angeles, CA 90068-3781, USA

Lynch, Jessica (Beauty Pageant Winner)
c/o Staff Member Miss New York City Scholarship Organization
35 E 19th St Fl 2
New York, NY 10003-1313, USA

Lynch, John (Football Player)
c/o Staff Member Denver Broncos
13655 Broncos Pkwy
Englewood, CO 80112-4151, USA

Lynch, John Carroll (Actor)
c/o James Suskin James Suskin Management
2 Charlton St Apt 5K
New York, NY 10014-4970, USA

Lynch, Kelly (Actor, Model)
c/o Tiffany Kuzon Evolution Entertainment (LA)
901 N Highland Ave
Los Angeles, CA 90038-2412, USA

Lynch, Marshawn (Athlete, Football Player)
2100 Lake Washington Blvd N Apt C101
Renton, WA 98056-1450, USA

Lynch, Peg
304 11th St Box 339
Becket, MA 01223

Lynch, Richard (Actor)
Richard Sindell
1910 Holmby Ave Apt 1
Los Angeles, CA 90025-5936, USA

Lynch, Ross (Actor)
c/o Nils Larsen Principato/Young Management (LA)
9465 Wilshire Blvd Ste 900
Beverly Hills, CA 90212-2608, USA

Lynde, Janice (Actor)
c/o David Moore Moore Artist's Management
310 Washington Blvd Ste 117
Marina Del Rey, CA 90292-5149, USA

Lyndon, Frank (Musician)
Paramount Entertainment
PO Box 12
Far Hills, NJ 07931-0012, USA

Lyne, Adrian (Director)
9876 Beverly Grove Dr
Beverly Hills, CA 90210-2120, USA

Lynette, Lady (Actor)
11979 Rochester Ave Apt 6
Los Angeles, CA 90025-2136, USA

Lynley, Carol (Actor)
Don gerler
3349 Cahuenga Blvd W Ste 1
Los Angeles, CA 90068-1379, USA

Lynn, Anthony (Athlete, Football Player)
512 Paddock Ln
Celina, TX 75009-4643, USA

Lynn, Betty (Actor)
The Surry Arts Council
PO Box 141
218 Rockford St
Mount Airy, NC 27030-0141, USA

Lynn, Cheryl (Actor, Musician)
c/o Jeff Epstein M.A.G./Universal Attractions
15 W 36th St Fl 8
New York, NY 10018-7927, USA

Lynn, Eleanor (Actor)
136 Longford Dr
South San Francisco, CA 94080-1039, USA

Lynn, Fred (Athlete, Baseball Player)
7336 El Fuerte St
Carlsbad, CA 92009-6409, USA

Lynn, Janet (Athlete, Olympic Athlete, Speed Skater)
4215 Marsh Ave
Rockford, IL 61114-6143, USA

Lynn, Johnnie (Athlete, Football Player)
20 Descanso Dr Unit 1110
San Jose, CA 95134-1840, USA

Lynn, Johnny (Athlete, Football Player)
1031 Fair Oaks Ave
Alameda, CA 94501-3921, USA

Lynn, Jonathan (Director)
c/o Mike Marcus Echo Lake Management
421 S Beverly Dr Fl 8
Beverly Hills, CA 90212-4408, USA

Lynn, Keith (Race Car Driver)
Schnitz Racing
222 N 3rd St
Decatur, IN 46733-1377, USA

Lynn, Loretta (Musician, Songwriter)
44 Hurricane Mills Rd
Hurricane Mills, TN 37078-2147, USA

Lynn, Meredith Scott (Actor)
Rigberg Roberts Rugolo
1180 S Beverly Dr Ste 601
Los Angeles, CA 90035-1158, USA

Lynn, Na'im (Comedian)
c/o Jeff Witjas *Agency for the Performing Arts (APA-LA)*
405 S Beverly Dr Ste 500
Beverly Hills, CA 90212-4425, USA

Lynn, Salomon Janet (Figure Skater)
PO Box 1026
Haymarket, VA 20168-8026, USA

Lynn, Therese
PO Box 6057
Hoboken, NJ 07030-7201

Lynn Allen, Ginger (Actor, Adult Film Star, Model)
5965 Nora Lynn Dr
Woodland Hills, CA 91367-1056, USA

Lynn Chadwick, Aimee (Actor)
c/o Melanie Sharp *Sharp Talent*
5538 Willowcrest Ave
North Hollywood, CA 91601-2830, USA

Lynne, Bobbe
22732 Foothill Rd # 6
Hayward, CA 94541

Lynne, Shelby (Musician, Songwriter, Writer)
c/o Staff Member *William Morris Endeavor (LA)*
9601 Wilshire Blvd
Beverly Hills, CA 90210-5213, USA

Lynskey, Melanie (Actor)
c/o Susan Smith *Susan Smith Company, The*
2001 Wilshire Blvd Ste 400
Santa Monica, CA 90403-5686, USA

Lynyrd Skynyrd (Music Group)
c/o Staff Member *Vector Management*
PO Box 120479
Nashville, TN 37212-0479, USA

Lyn-Z (Musician)
3820 San Rafael Ave
Los Angeles, CA 90065-3225, USA

Lyon, Brandon (Athlete, Baseball Player)
526 W 8th S
Preston, ID 83263-1459, USA

Lyon, Sue (Actor)
1244 Havenhurst Dr
West Hollywood, CA 90046-4911, USA

Lyon, William (Business Person, General)
William Lyon Co
4695 Macarthur Ct # 8
Newport Beach, CA 92660-1882, USA

Lyonne, Natasha (Actor, Producer)
c/o Sara Planco *Viewpoint Inc (NYC)*
109 W 27th St Rm 6B
New York, NY 10001-6208, USA

Lyons, Barry (Athlete, Baseball Player)
527 Front Beach Dr Apt 71
Ocean Springs, MS 39564-4942, USA

Lyons, Bill (Athlete, Baseball Player)
811 Tomahawk
Heyworth, IL 61745-9309, USA

Lyons, Brooke (Actor)
c/o Staff Member *Burstein Company, The*
15304 W Sunset Blvd Ste 208
Pacific Palisades, CA 90272-3656, USA

Lyons, Curt (Athlete, Baseball Player)
124 Virginia Dr
Richmond, KY 40475-8631, USA

Lyons, Elena (Actor)
c/o Brian McCabe *Venture IAB*
3211 Cahuenga Blvd W Ste 104
Los Angeles, CA 90068-1372, USA

Lyons, Jeffrey (Journalist)
205 W 57th St Apt 5DD
New York, NY 10019-2112, USA

Lyons, Lamar (Athlete, Football Player)
3726 Bluff Pl
San Pedro, CA 90731-7006, USA

Lyons, Marty (Athlete, Football Player)
8 White Pine Ct
Smithtown, NY 11787-1199, USA

Lyons, Mitchell W (Mitch) (Athlete, Football Player)
8344 Woodcrest Dr NE
Rockford, MI 49341-8507, USA

Lyons, Phyllis
9171 Wilshire Blvd Ste 441
Beverly Hills, CA 90210-5516

Lyons, Robert F (Actor)
1801 Ave of Stars Ste 1250
Los Angeles, CA 90067-5817, USA

Lyons, Steve (Athlete, Baseball Player)
JD Legends Promotions
3012th St
Hermosa Beach, CA 90254, USA

Lyons, Thomas L (Athlete, Football Player)
2814 Drummond Pt SE
Atlanta, GA 30339-5332, USA

Lysacek, Evan (Figure Skater)
Toyota Sports Center
555 N Nash St
El Segundo, CA 90245-2818, USA

Lysander, Rick (Athlete, Baseball Player)
12667 Gaillon Ct
San Diego, CA 92128-6179, USA

Lysiak, Tom (Athlete, Hockey Player)
1050 Cedar Grove Rd
Buckhead, GA 30625-1818, USA

Lyte, MC (Musician)
c/o Judy Page *Mitchell K Stubbs & Assoc (MKS)*
8675 Washington Blvd Ste 203
Culver City, CA 90232-7486, USA

Lythgoe, Nigel (Producer)
Nigel Lythgoe Productions
11766 Wilshire Blvd Fl 9
Los Angeles, CA 90025-6548, USA

Lytle, Jason
c/o Staff Member *Paradigm (Monterey)*
404 W Franklin St
Monterey, CA 93940-2303, USA

Lytle, Matt (Athlete, Football Player)
4602 Irish Creek Rd
Bernville, PA 19506-8346, USA

Lytle, Roland (Athlete, Football Player)
10409 Highway 159 E
Bellville, TX 77418-8631, USA

Lyttle, Jim (Athlete, Baseball Player)
751 Camino Lakes Cir
Boca Raton, FL 33486-6961, USA

Lyttle, Kevin (Musician)
c/o Mike Esterman *Esterman.Com, LLC*
Prefers to be contacted via email
Baltimore, MD XXXXX, USA

Izauierdo, Hansel (Athlete, Baseball Player)
10003 NW 9th Street Cir Apt 9-17
Miami, FL 33172-5181, USA

Izturis, Cesar (Athlete, Baseball Player)
7901 Hispanola Ave Apt 607
North Bay Village, FL 33141-4153, USA

M2M (Music Group)
c/o Staff Member *Creative Artists Agency (CAA-LA)*
2000 Avenue of the Stars Ste 100
Los Angeles, CA 90067-4705, USA

Ma, Tzi (Actor)
Greene & Associates
526 N Larchmont Blvd # 201
Los Angeles, CA 90004-1300

Ma, Yo-Yo (Musician)
54 Highland St
Cambridge, MA 02138-3332, USA

Maarleveld, John (Athlete, Football Player)
42 Carlton Pl
Rutherford, NJ 07070-1120, USA

Maas, Alex
6962 Wildlife Rd
Malibu, CA 90265-4309

Maas, Bill (Athlete, Football Player)
653 NE Shoreline Dr
Lees Summit, MO 64064-1382, USA

Maas, Kevin (Athlete, Baseball Player)
17672 Hillside Ct
Castro Valley, CA 94546-1403, USA

Maas, William T (Bill) (Athlete, Football Player)
PO Box 2175
Lees Summit, MO 64063-7175, USA

Mabeus, Chris (Athlete, Baseball Player)
2417 Canberra Ave
Henderson, NV 89052-4945, USA

Mabius, Eric (Actor)
c/o Geordie Frey *GEF Entertainment*
611 N Cherokee Ave
Los Angeles, CA 90004-1008, USA

Mably, Luke (Actor)
c/o Stephanie Ritz *William Morris Endeavor (LA)*
9601 Wilshire Blvd
Beverly Hills, CA 90210-5213, USA

Mabon, Lee (Athlete, Baseball Player)
2084 Vollintine Ave
Memphis, TN 38107-4700, USA

Mabra, Ron (Athlete, Football Player)
155 Thornton Ct
Fayetteville, GA 30214-3830, USA

Mabrey, Sunny (Actor)
c/o Chris Schmidt *Paradigm (LA)*
360 N Crescent Dr
North Bldg
Beverly Hills, CA 90210-4874, USA

Mabrey, Vicki (Correspondent, Journalist)
c/o Staff Member *Nightline*
1717 Desales St NW
Washington, DC 20036-4401, USA

Mabry, John (Athlete, Baseball Player)
715 Bellerive Manor Dr
Saint Louis, MO 63141-6084, USA

Mabus, Raymond (Politician)
325 N Pitt St
Alexandria, VA 22314-2508, USA

Mac, Fleetwood (Music Group)
c/o Rick Canny *Sanctuary Artist Management*
8750 Wilshire Blvd Ste 200
Beverly Hills, CA 90211-2707, USA

MacAfee Sr, Ken (Athlete, Football Player)
26 W Elm Ter
Brockton, MA 02301-3629, USA

Macallan, Jes (Actor)
c/o Stephanie Moy *Luber Roklin Management*
5815 W Sunset Blvd Ste 206
Los Angeles, CA 90028-6481, USA

Macaluso, mike (Basketball Player)
1054 Cypress Way
Castle Rock, CO 80108-3465, USA

Macat, Julio G (Cinematographer)
Gersh Agency
232 N Canon Dr
Beverly Hills, CA 90210-5302, USA

MacBeth, Lois
4095 Athenian Way
View Park, CA 90043-1617

Macc, Willie (Actor)
Charles Belk Management
8939 S Sepulveda Blvd # 110-240
C/O Charles Belk
Los Angeles, CA 90045-3631, USA

Maccarone, Sam (Director)
c/o David Krintzman *Morris Yorn Barnes Levine Krintzman Rubenstein Kohner & Gellman*
2000 Avenue of the Stars Ste 300N
3rd Floor, North Tower
Los Angeles, CA 90067-4704, USA

Macchio, Ralph (Actor)
c/o Jennifer Merlino *Untitled Entertainment (LA)*
350 S Beverly Dr Ste 200
Beverly Hills, CA 90212-4819, USA

Maccormack, Frank (Athlete, Baseball Player)
2 Schmidts Pl
Secaucus, NJ 07094-4110, USA

Macdissi, Peter (Actor)
c/o Melissa Stone *42West (LA)*
1840 Century Park E Ste 700
Los Angeles, CA 90067-2122, USA

MacDonald, Ann-Marie (Writer)
c/o Staff Member *Simon & Schuster*
1230 Avenue of the Americas Fl CONC1
New York, NY 10020-1586, USA

Macdonald, Bob (Athlete, Baseball Player)
522 Harbor Grove Cir
Safety Harbor, FL 34695-4977, USA

MacDonald, C Parker (Athlete, Hockey Player)
3 Miller Rd
Northford, CT 06472-1424, USA

MacDonald, Jeffrey (Athlete, Football Player)
9334 Cody Dr
Broomfield, CO 80021-5325, USA

MacDonald, Kelly (Actor)
c/o Emily Yomtobian *PMK/BNC Public Relations (PMK-LA)*
8687 Melrose Ave Ste 8
West Hollywood, CA 90069-5746, USA

MacDonald, Lowell (Athlete, Hockey Player)
178 Amblewood Ln
Naples, FL 34105-7147, USA

MacDonald, Mark (Athlete, Football Player)
19178 Echo Ln
Farmington, MN 55024-9184, USA

Macdonald, Norm (Actor, Comedian)
c/o Marc Gurvitz *Brillstein Entertainment Partners (LA)*
9150 Wilshire Blvd Ste 350
Beverly Hills, CA 90212-3453, USA

MacDonald, Ryan
10801 Connecticut Ave
Kensington, MD 20895-2134

Macdougal, Mike (Athlete, Baseball Player)
2429 N Travis
Mesa, AZ 85207-2539, USA

MacDowell, Andie (Actor)
28745 Josephine Creek Rd
Huson, MT 59846-9679, USA

Macek, Don (Athlete, Football Player)
3615 Monte Real
Escondido, CA 92029-7911, USA

Macfadyen, Angus (Actor)
c/o Bradley Kramer *Kramer Management*
5699 Kanan Rd # 275
Agoura Hills, CA 91301-3358, USA

Macfadyen, Matthew (Actor)
c/o Hylda Queally *Creative Artists Agency (CAA-LA)*
2000 Avenue of the Stars Ste 100
Los Angeles, CA 90067-4705, USA

MacFarlane, Luke (Actor)
c/o Bonnie Bernstein *ICM Partners (NY)*
730 5th Ave
New York, NY 10019-4105, USA

Macfarlane, Mike (Athlete, Baseball Player)
14909 Alhambra St
Overland Park, KS 66224-3905, USA

MacFarlane, Seth (Actor, Director)
1542 Tower Grove Dr
Beverly Hills, CA 90210-2142, USA

MacGraw, Ali (Actor)
c/o Alan Nevins *Renaissance Literary & Talent*
PO Box 17379
Beverly Hills, CA 90209-3379, USA

MacGregor, Jeff (Actor, Writer)
c/o Katherine Herring *HarperCollins Publishers*
195 Broadway Fl 2
Cellar 1
New York, NY 10007-3132, USA

MacGregor, Joanna C (Musician)
Columbia Artists Mgmt Inc
165 W 57th St
New York, NY 10019-2201, USA

MacGregor, Katherine (Actor)
23388 Mulholland Dr
Woodland Hills, CA 91364-2733, USA

MacGuigan, Garth (Athlete, Hockey Player)
3600 Hoya Dr Apt 223
Arlington, TX 76015-3429, USA

Mach, Brian (Athlete, Hockey Player)
8715 Osprey Ln
Chanhassen, MN 55317-8565, USA

Macha, Ken (Athlete, Baseball Player, Coach)
1118 Winnie Way
Latrobe, PA 15650-9080, USA

Macha, Mike (Athlete, Baseball Player)
PO Box 3844
Victoria, TX 77903-3844, USA

Machado, J P (Athlete, Football Player)
710 Butterfly Ln
Weldon Spring, MO 63304-7899, USA

Machado, Justina (Actor)
c/o Danielle Allman-Del *D2 Management*
9255 W Sunset Blvd Ste 600
West Hollywood, CA 90069-3306, USA

Machado, Mario
5750 Briarcliff Rd
Los Angeles, CA 90068-3633

Machado, Robert (Athlete, Baseball Player)
c/o Derek Reynolds *Doyle & McKean*
23586 Calabasas Rd Ste 209
Calabasas, CA 91302-1318, USA

Machado-Van Sant, Helene (Athlete, Baseball Player, Commentator)
1221 Marion Ave
San Bernardino, CA 92407-1217, USA

Machemehl, Chuck (Baseball Player)
809 Charlotte Dr
McKinney, TX 75071-6081, USA

Machemer, Dave (Athlete, Baseball Player)
2159 Alpine Ct
Stevensville, MI 49127-9554, USA

Machida, Lyoto (Athlete, Boxer)
c/o Staff Member *UFC*
PO Box 26959
Las Vegas, NV 89126-0959, USA

Macht, Gabriel (Actor)
4077 Woking Way
Los Angeles, CA 90027-1323, USA

Macht, Stephen (Actor)
248 S Rodeo Dr
Beverly Hills, CA 90212-3804, USA

Macias, Jose (Athlete, Baseball Player)
c/o Staff Member *Stockton Ports*
404 W Fremont St
Banner Island Ballpark
Stockton, CA 95203-2806, USA

macieod, Bill (Athlete, Baseball Player)
14 Heritage Way
Marblehead, MA 01945-2332, USA

Macinnis, AL
1401 Clark Ave
Attn: Vp, Hockey Operations
Saint Louis, MO 63103-2700, USA

Macinnis, Allan (Athlete, Hockey Player)
1132 Highland Pointe Dr
Saint Louis, MO 63131-1408, USA

MacIntosh, Craig (Cartoonist)
3403 W 28th St
Minneapolis, MN 55416-4302, USA

MacIntyre, Colin (Musician)
c/o Staff Member *Paradigm (Monterey)*
404 W Franklin St
Monterey, CA 93940-2303, USA

Macio (Musician)
c/o Staff Member *Paradigm (Monterey)*
404 W Franklin St
Monterey, CA 93940-2303, USA

Maciver, Norm (Athlete, Hockey Player)
2119 Ponderosa Cir
Duluth, MN 55811-1960, USA

Mack, Alex (Athlete, Football Player)
c/o Marvin Demoff *Morris Yorn Barnes Levine Krintzman Rubenstein Kohner & Gellman*
2000 Avenue of the Stars Ste 300N
3rd Floor, North Tower
Los Angeles, CA 90067-4704, USA

Mack, Allison (Actor)
c/o Sheila Wenzel *Innovative Artists (LA)*
1505 10th St
Santa Monica, CA 90401-2805, USA

Mack, Bill (Athlete, Football Player)
51910 N Shoreham Ct
South Bend, IN 46637-1357, USA

Mack, Bill (Radio Personality)
Bill Mack Country, Inc.
PO Box 8777
Fort Worth, TX 76124-0777, USA

Mack, Cedric (Athlete, Football Player)
116 Chestnut St
Lake Jackson, TX 77566-5526, USA

Mack, Elbert (Athlete, Football Player)
c/o Brian Levy *Goal Line Football Management*
1025 Kane Concourse Ste 207
Bay Harbor Islands, FL 33154-2118, USA

Mack, J Kevin (Athlete, Football Player)
29359 Hummingbird Cir
Westlake, OH 44145-5287, USA

Mack, Lonnie (Musician)
Concerted Efforts
59 Parsons St
West Newton, MA 02465-2137, USA

Mack, Quinn (Athlete, Baseball Player)
35324 Marsh Ln
Wildomar, CA 92595-9019, USA

Mack, Rico (Athlete, Football Player)
1200 RR MACK Rd
Statham, GA 30666-3140, USA

Mack, Sam (Athlete, Basketball Player)
8142S S Prairie Park Pl
Chicago, IL 60619, USA

Mack, Shane (Athlete, Baseball Player, Olympic Athlete)
35324 Marsh Ln
Wildomar, CA 92595-9019, USA

Mack, Stacey (Athlete, Football Player)
1431 19th St
Orlando, FL 32805-4415, USA

Mack, Thomas (Tom) (Athlete, Football Player)
52 Grand Miramar Dr
Henderson, NV 89011-2202, USA

Mack, Tony (Baseball Player)
California Angels
431 Rogers Rd Apt 18
Lexington, KY 40505-1932, USA

Mack, Tremain (Athlete, Football Player)
4016 Burton Pl W
Seattle, WA 98199-1554, USA

Mack, Warner (Musician)
National Talent Agency
2260 E Apple Ave
Muskegon, MI 49442-4369, USA

Mack, William (Athlete, Football Player)
51910 N Shoreham Ct
South Bend, IN 46637-1357, USA

Mackall, Michelle (Athlete, Golfer)
2057 Oxford Ave
Cardiff By The Sea, CA 92007-1719, USA

Mackanin, Pete (Athlete, Baseball Player, Coach)
11563 E Bronco Trl
Scottsdale, AZ 85255-8243, USA

MacKasey, Blair (Athlete, Hockey Player)
317 Washington St
Attn Dir Player Personnel
Saint Paul, MN 55102-1609, USA

Mackay, David (Director)
Gersh Agency
232 N Canon Dr
Beverly Hills, CA 90210-5302, USA

Mackay, Harvey (Business Person, Writer)
Mackay Envelope Corp
2100 Elm St SE
Minneapolis, MN 55414-2597, USA

MacKenney, Tamara
4935 Parkers Mill Rd
Lexington, KY 40513-9760

Mackenroth, Jack (Designer, Reality Star)
c/o Steve Glick *Glick Agency*
1321 7th St Ste 203
Santa Monica, CA 90401-1631, USA

MacKenzie, Aaron (Athlete, Hockey Player)
1510 Zamia Ave Apt 202
Boulder, CO 80304-4434, USA

MacKenzie, Benjamin (Actor)
c/o Staff Member *Management 360*
9111 Wilshire Blvd
Beverly Hills, CA 90210-5508, USA

Mackenzie, Brock (Athlete, Golfer)
c/o Jim Lehrman *SFX Golf*
36855 W Main St Ste 200
Purcellville, VA 20132-3561, USA

Mackenzie, Gordy (Athlete, Baseball Player)
36535 Micro Racetrack Rd
Fruitland Park, FL 34731-5163, USA

MacKenzie, J C
3500 W Olive Ave Ste 1400
Burbank, CA 91505-5512, USA

Mackenzie, Ken (Athlete, Baseball Player)
15 Fair St
Guilford, CT 06437-2601, USA

MacKenzie, Patch
3500 W Olive Ave Ste 1400
Burbank, CA 91505-5512

Mackenzie, Will (Athlete, Golfer)
35 Laurel Oaks Cir
Jupiter, FL 33469-2757, USA

Mackey, Cindy (Athlete, Golfer)
1190 Millstone Run
Watkinsville, GA 30677-7762, USA

Mackey, Kyle (Athlete, Football Player)
136 Brookwood Dr
Silsbee, TX 77656-8912, USA

Mackey, Louis (Athlete, Football Player)
7002 Winter Blossom Dr
Humble, TX 77346-3387, USA

Mackey, Malcolm (Athlete, Basketball Player)
309 Montrose Dr
McDonough, GA 30253-4257, USA

Mackie, Anthony (Actor)
c/o Jason Spire *Inspire Entertainment*
315 7th Ave Apt 17E
New York, NY 10001-6011, USA

Mackie, Bob (Fashion Designer)
Bob Mackie Design Group, Ltd
230 Park Ave Rm 446
New York, NY 10169-0499, USA

MacKinnon, Gillies (Director)
c/o Patty Detroit *Todd Smith and Associates*
10250 Constellation Blvd Fl 7
Los Angeles, CA 90067-6207, USA

Macklemore (Musician)
1935 10th Ave E
Seattle, WA 98102-4252, USA

Macklin, David (Athlete, Football Player)
16042 S 14th Dr
Phoenix, AZ 85045-0613, USA

Macklin, Rudy (Athlete, Basketball Player)
10749 Hillgate Ave
Baton Rouge, LA 70810-7067, USA

Macknowski, John (Athlete, Basketball Player)
1920 Garnet Ln
Dandridge, TN 37725-4428, USA

Mackovic, John (Athlete, Football Coach, Football Player)
79295 Rancho La Quinta Dr
La Quinta, CA 92253-6217, USA

Mackowiak, Rob (Athlete, Baseball Player)
2414 W Superior St
Chicago, IL 60612-1214, USA

Mackrides, Bill (Athlete, Football Player)
1060 Beverly Ln
Newtown Square, PA 19073-2736, USA

Mackrides, William (Athlete, Football Player)
1060 Beverly Ln
Newtown Square, PA 19073-2736, USA

MacLachian, Kyle (Actor)
Industry Entertainment
955 Carrillo Dr Ste 300
Los Angeles, CA 90048-5400, USA

MacLachlan, Kyle (Actor)
c/o David Seltzer *Management 360*
9111 Wilshire Blvd
Beverly Hills, CA 90210-5508, USA

MacLachlan, Patricia (Writer)
21 Unquomonk Rd
Williamsburg, MA 01096-9718, USA

MacLaine, Shirley (Actor, Writer)
Maclaine Enterprises
PO Box 33950
Santa Fe, NM 87594-3950, USA

MacLean, Don (Athlete, Basketball Player)
216 Los Padres Dr
Thousand Oaks, CA 91361-1333, USA

MacLean, Doug (Coach)
330 Tucker Dr
Worthington, OH 43085-3030, USA

MacLean, John (Athlete, Coach, Hockey Player)
44 Old Farm Rd
Basking Ridge, NJ 07920-3309, USA

Maclean, Paul (Athlete, Hockey Player)
41544 Glade Rd
Canton, MI 48187-3770, USA

Macleay, Lachlan (Astronaut)
5105 Saddleback Hts
Colorado Springs, CO 80923-1113, USA

MacLeish, Rick (Athlete, Hockey Player)
5612 Bay Ave
Ocean City, NJ 08226-1000, USA

Maclellan, Brian (Athlete, Hockey Player)
627 N Glebe Rd Ste 850
Attn Dir Player Personnel
Arlington, VA 22203-2144, USA

Macleod, Bill (Athlete, Baseball Player)
14 Heritage Way
Marblehead, MA 01945-2332, USA

MacLeod, Gavin (Actor)
70070 Frank Sinatra Dr Apt 7
Rancho Mirage, CA 92270-2538, USA

MacLeod, John (Basketball Coach, Coach)
4610 E Fanfol Dr
Phoenix, AZ 85028-5206, USA

Macleod, Pat (Athlete, Hockey Player)
904 Birchwood Dr
Lebanon, OH 45036-1431, USA

Macleod, Tom (Athlete, Football Player)
15412 N Hazard Rd
Spokane, WA 99208-8289, USA

Maclin, Jeremy (Athlete, Football Player)
c/o Jim Steiner *CAA (St. Louis)*
222 S Central Ave Ste 1008
Saint Louis, MO 63105-3509, USA

Maclin, Lonnie (Athlete, Baseball Player)
9635 Meeks Blvd
Saint Louis, MO 63132-1507, USA

MacManus, Tristan (Dancer)
c/o Staff Member *Dancing With The Stars*
500 S Buena Vista St
Burbank, CA 91521-0001, USA

Macmillan, Duncan L. (Business Person)
Bloomberg L.P.
731 Lexington Ave Fl LL2
New York, NY 10022-1346, USA

MacMillan, John (Athlete, Hockey Player)
2672 W Conifer Dr
Eagle, ID 83616-4667, USA

MacMillan, Shannon (Soccer Player)
Portland University
Athletic Dept
Portland, OR 97203, USA

MacMurray, Jamie (Race Car Driver)
211 Milford Cir
Mooresville, NC 28117, USA

Macnee, Patrick (Actor)
PO Box 1853
Rancho Mirage, CA 92270-1081, USA

MacNeil, Karen (Writer)
Karen MacNeil & Company
1335 Main St Ste 109
Saint Helena, CA 94574-1940, USA

MacNeil, Robert (Correspondent, Writer)
c/o Staff Member *Penguin Press HC*
375 Hudson St Bsmt 3
New York, NY 10014-7465, USA

Macneil, Robert (Journalist)
2700 S Quincy St
Arlington, VA 22206-2242, USA

MacNichol, Peter (Actor)
International Creative Mgmt
10250 Constellation Blvd Fl 1
Los Angeles, CA 90067-6241, USA

MacNicol, Peter (Actor)
c/o Ron West *Thruline Entertainment*
9250 Wilshire Blvd Ste 100
Ground Floor
Beverly Hills, CA 90212-3343, USA

Macoherson, Harry (Athlete, Baseball Player)
971 Bay Vista Blvd
Englewood, FL 34223-2405, USA

Macomber, Debbie (Writer)
c/o Irene Goodman *Irene Goodman Literary Agency*
27 W 24th St Ste 700B
New York, NY 10010-4105, USA

Macomber, Dick (Horse Racer)
6720 NW 28th Ter
Fort Lauderdale, FL 33309-1320, USA

Macomber, George B H (Skier)
1 Design Center Pl Ste 600
Boston, MA 02210-2349, USA

Macon, Eddie (Athlete, Football Player)
28661 Highpoint Ave
Moreno Valley, CA 92555-7002, USA

Macosko, Anna (Athlete, Golfer)
304 Earl Dr
Kerrville, TX 78028-7019, USA

MacPhail, Andy (Baseball Player)
Chicago Cubs
1080 Sunset Rd
Winnetka, IL 60093-3625, USA

Macphail, Andy (Commentator)
12403 Hunters Gin
Owings Mills, MD 21117, USA

MacPherson, Dick (Athlete, Football Coach, Football Player)
6202 the Hamlet
Jamesville, NY 13078-9785, USA

Macpherson, Elle (Model)
c/o Michael McConnell *Mavrick Artists Agency*
6100 Wilshire Blvd Ste 550
Los Angeles, CA 90048-5164, USA

Macpherson, Harry (Athlete, Baseball Player)
9000 Ibis Way # 108
Venice, FL 34292-3084, USA

Macpherson, Wendy (Bowler)
PO Box 93433
Henderson, NV 89009-3433, USA

Mac Quayle (DJ)
c/o Staff Member *Diva Central Inc*
7510 W Sunset Blvd Ste 1445
Los Angeles, CA 90046-3408, USA

Macrae, Scott (Athlete, Baseball Player)
1164 Forest Brook Ct
Marietta, GA 30068-2827, USA

MacTavish, Craig (Athlete, Coach, Hockey Player)
2301 Ravine Way
Attn: Coaching Staff
Glenview, IL 60025-7627, USA

Maculan, Tim (Actor)
c/o Christopher Black *Opus Entertainment*
5225 Wilshire Blvd Ste 905
Los Angeles, CA 90036-4353, USA

Macwhorter, Keith (Athlete, Baseball Player)
75 Martin St
Rehoboth, MA 02769-2114, USA

Macy, Kyle (Athlete, Basketball Player)
3320 Overbrook Dr
Lexington, KY 40502-3352, USA

Macy, William H (Actor)
7237 Senalda Rd
Los Angeles, CA 90068-2653, USA

Madball (Musician)
c/o Paul Gourlie *Agency Group Ltd, The (LA)*
1880 Century Park E Ste 711
Los Angeles, CA 90067-1618, USA

Maddalena, Julie (Actor)
c/o Staff Member *Tisherman Gilbert Motley Drozdoski Talent Agency (TGMD)*
6767 Forest Lawn Dr Ste 101
Los Angeles, CA 90068-1027, USA

Madden, Beezie (Athlete, Horse Racer, Olympic Athlete)
3980 Stone Bridge Rd
Cazenovia, NY 13035-9535, USA

Madden, Benji (Musician)
2265 Nichols Canyon Rd
Los Angeles, CA 90046-1730, USA

Madden, David (Writer)
Louisiana State University
US Civil War Center
Baton Rouge, LA 70803-0001, USA

Madden, Diane (Dancer)
Trisha Brown Dance Co
211 W 61st St
New York, NY 10023-7832, USA

Madden, D S (Religious Leader)
American Baptist Assn
4605 N State Line Ave
Texarkana, TX 75503-2916, USA

Madden, Joe (Athlete, Baseball Player)
2515 S Ysabella Ave
Tampa, FL 33629-6238, USA

Madden, Joel (Musician)
8305 Lookout Mountain Ave
Los Angeles, CA 90046-1548, USA

Madden, John (Athlete, Hockey Player)
6990 Long Leaf Dr
Parkland, FL 33076-3946, USA

Madden, John (Athlete, Football Coach, Football Player, Sportscaster)
5955 Coronado Ln
Pleasanton, CA 94588-8518, USA

Madden, Mike (Athlete, Baseball Player)
4733 Frankfort Way
Denver, CO 80239-5922, USA

Madden, Morris (Athlete, Baseball Player)
105 Jennings St
Laurens, SC 29360-3317, USA

Madden, Steve (Designer)
Steve Madden Ltd
5216 Barnett Ave
Sunnyside, NY 11104-1018, USA

Maddix, Raydell (Athlete, Baseball Player)
3724 E North Bay St
Tampa, FL 33610-7959, USA

Maddock, Robert (Athlete, Football Player)
3541 Geranium Ave
Corona Del Mar, CA 92625-1673, USA

Maddon, Joe (Athlete, Baseball Player, Coach)
2560 N Lindsay Rd Unit 32
Mesa, AZ 85213-1520, USA

Maddow, Rachel (Journalist, Radio Personality)
c/o Staff Member *MSNBC*
30 Rockefeller Plz
New York, NY 10112-0015, USA

Maddox, Bob (Athlete, Football Player)
7612 Colson Dr
Louisville, KY 40220-3358, USA

Maddox, Elliott (Athlete, Baseball Player)
980 Coral Ridge Dr Apt 104
Coral Springs, FL 33071-4148, USA

Maddox, Garry (Athlete, Baseball Player)
312 Wynne Ln
Penn Valley, PA 19072-1338, USA

Maddox, Jerry (Athlete, Baseball Player)
20647 Thundersky Cir
Riverside, CA 92508-3177, USA

Maddox, Mark (Athlete, Football Player)
PO Box 3922
Chandler, AZ 85244-3922, USA

Maddox, Robert (Athlete, Football Player)
7612 Colson Dr
Louisville, KY 40220-3358, USA

Maddox, Tommy (Athlete, Football Player)
2541 Morgan Ln
Roanoke, TX 76262-5042, USA

Maddux, Greg (Athlete, Baseball Player)
20 Painted Feather Way
Las Vegas, NV 89135-7855, USA

Maddux, Mike (Athlete, Baseball Player)
PO Box 90111
Arlington, TX 76004-3111, USA

Madekwe, Ashley (Actor)
c/o Staff Member *Silver Lining Entertainment*
421 S Beverly Dr Fl 7
Beverly Hills, CA 90212-4408, USA

Madeley, Darrin (Athlete, Hockey Player)
Lake Forest Academy 1500 W Kennedy Rd
Lake Forest, IL 60045, USA

Mader, Rebecca (Actor)
c/o Paul Nelson *Mosaic Media Group*
9200 W Sunset Blvd Ste 10
West Hollywood, CA 90069-3608, USA

Maderos, George (Athlete, Football Player)
12 Spinnaker Way
Chico, CA 95926-1627, USA

Madigan, Amy (Actor)
c/o Staff Member *Industry Entertainment*
955 Carrillo Dr Ste 300
Los Angeles, CA 90048-5400, USA

Madigan, Connie (Athlete, Hockey Player)
7655 NE Alameda St
Portland, OR 97213-5931, USA

Madigan, John W (Business Person, Publisher)
Tribune Co
435 N Michigan Ave Ste 1800
Chicago, IL 60611-4030, USA

Madigan, Kathleen (Comedian)
c/o Michael O'Brien *Michael OBrien Entertainment*
Prefers to be contacted by telephone or email
New York, NY 10012, USA

Madigan, Sam (Athlete, Football Player)
3685 Heron Ridge Ln
Weston, FL 33331-3711, USA

Madill, Jeff (Athlete, Hockey Player)
8601 N Hickory St Apt 1103
Kansas City, MO 64155-4134, USA

Madise, Adrian (Athlete, Football Player)
1561 Drury Dr
Dallas, TX 75232-1939, USA

Madison, Bailee (Actor)
c/o Chris Rossi *Core Public Relations Group*
4401 Wilshire Blvd Fl 4
Los Angeles, CA 90010-3703, USA

Madison, Holly (Model, Reality Star)
3626 Regal Pl
Los Angeles, CA 90068-1230, USA

Madison, Martha (Actor)
c/o Jason Egenberg *United Talent Agency (UTA-LA)*
9336 Civic Center Dr
Beverly Hills, CA 90210-3604, USA

Madison, Sam (Athlete, Football Player)
13153 SW 25th Pl # Pi
Davie, FL 33325-5140, USA

Madison, Sarah Danielle (Actor)
c/o Connie Tavel *Forward Entertainment*
9255 W Sunset Blvd Ste 805
West Hollywood, CA 90069-3305, USA

Madison, Scotti (Athlete, Baseball Player)
5397 Thornapple Ln NW
Acworth, GA 30101-7886, USA

Madison, Scotty (Athlete, Baseball Player)
5397 Thornapple Ln NW
Acworth, GA 30101-7886, USA

Madkins, Gerald (Athlete, Basketball Player)
528 W 8th St
Merced, CA 95341-6023, USA

Madlock, Bill (Athlete, Baseball Player)
104 Prairie Ave
Highwood, IL 60040-1714, USA

Madoff, Bernard (Bernie) (Business Person)
Butner Low FCI
PO Box 999
Butner, NC 27509-0999, USA

Madonna (Actor, Dancer, Musician, Songwriter)
152 E 81st St
New York, NY 10028-1804, USA

Madore, Joe (Race Car Driver)
Jam Motorsports
400 S Vermont Ave Ste 125
Oklahoma City, OK 73108-1025, USA

Madrid, Alex (Athlete, Baseball Player)
PO Box 1974
Saint Johns, AZ 85936-1974, USA

Madrigal, Al (Actor, Comedian)
c/o Geoff Cheddy *Brillstein Entertainment Partners (LA)*
9150 Wilshire Blvd Ste 350
Beverly Hills, CA 90212-3453, USA

Madrigali, Jeff (Athlete, Olympic Athlete, Sailor)
6212 Green Bower Ln
Clinton, WA 98236, USA

Madritsch, Bobby (Athlete, Baseball Player)
8628 Linder Ave
Burbank, IL 60459-2928, USA

Madrugada (Music Group)
c/o Staff Member *Paradigm (Monterey)*
404 W Franklin St
Monterey, CA 93940-2303, USA

Madsen, mark (Basketball Player)
4223 Vintage Cir
Provo, UT 84604-5693, USA

Madsen, Michael (Actor)
c/o Chuck Binder *Binder & Associates*
1465 Lindacrest Dr
Beverly Hills, CA 90210-2519, USA

Madsen, Virgina (Actor)
c/o Katie Rhodes *Untitled Entertainment (LA)*
350 S Beverly Dr Ste 200
Beverly Hills, CA 90212-4819, USA

Madsen, Virginia (Actor)
c/o Katie Rhodes *Untitled Entertainment (LA)*
350 S Beverly Dr Ste 200
Beverly Hills, CA 90212-4819, USA

Madson, Michael (Actor)
The Firm
9100 Wilshire Blvd Ste 100W
Beverly Hills, CA 90212-3435, USA

Madson, Ryan (Athlete, Baseball Player)
1204 Suncast Ln Ste 2
El Dorado Hills, CA 95762-9665, USA

Maduro, Calvin (Athlete, Baseball Player)
793 Springdale Dr
Millersville, MD 21108-1435, USA

Maegle, Dick (Athlete, Football Player)
4207 Deforest Ridge Cir
Katy, TX 77494-4444, USA

Maese, Joe (Athlete, Football Player)
3409 Springhurst Ct
Reisterstown, MD 21136-4419, USA

Maestro, Mia (Actor)
c/o Pamela Kohl *3 Arts Entertainment (LA)*
9460 Wilshire Blvd Fl 7
Beverly Hills, CA 90212-2713, USA

Maffay, Peter (Actor)
Klenzestr. 1
Tutzing, GE D-823

Maffett, Debra
1525 McGavock St
Nashville, TN 37203

Maffett, Debra Sue (Debbie) (Beauty Pageant Winner)
1525 McGavock St
Nashville, TN 37203, USA

Maffia, Roma (Actor)
c/o Staff Member *Stone Manners Salners Agency (LA)*
6100 Wilshire Blvd Ste 1500
Los Angeles, CA 90048-5110, USA

Maga, Mickey (Actor)
123 Jasper St Spc 24
Encinitas, CA 92024-2069, USA

Magadan, Dave (Athlete, Baseball Player)
3733 Johnathon Ave
Palm Harbor, FL 34685-3605, USA

Magallanes, Ever (Athlete, Baseball Player)
834 Governor St
Costa Mesa, CA 92627-3342, USA

Magee, Alex (Athlete, Football Player)
c/o Roosevelt Barnes *Maximum Sports Management*
6435 W Jefferson Blvd # 197
Fort Wayne, IN 46804-6203, USA

Magee, Andrew (Andy) (Athlete, Golfer)
6100 E Huntress Dr
Paradise Valley, AZ 85253-4217, USA

Magee, Calvin (Athlete, Football Player)
1985 2320 Comanche Trl
Grand Prairie, TX 75052, USA

Magee, Dave (Horse Racer)
5S350 Deer Ridge Path
Big Rock, IL 60511-9777, USA

Magee, Wendell (Athlete, Baseball Player)
6500 Muskogee Cv
Leeds, AL 35094-3868, USA

Maggard, Dave (Athlete, Track Athlete)
University of Houston
Athletic Dept
Houston, TX 77204-0001, USA

Maggart, Brandon (Actor)
8730 W Sunset Blvd Ste 480
West Hollywood, CA 90069-2277

Maggart, Garett (Actor)
c/o Staff Member *SDB Partners Inc*
315 S Beverly Dr Ste 411
Beverly Hills, CA 90212-4301, USA

Maggert, Jeff (Athlete, Golfer)
62 W Bracebridge Cir
Spring, TX 77382-2539, USA

Maggette, Corey (Basketball Player)
Los Angeles Clippers
1111 S Figueroa St Ste 1100
Staples Center
Los Angeles, CA 90015-1345, USA

Maggs, Darryl (Athlete, Hockey Player)
20918 E US Highway 24
Woodland Park, CO 80863-8002, USA

Maggs, Don (Athlete, Football Player)
8665 Indigo Trl
Mentor, OH 44060-1574, USA

Magilton, Gerald E (Jerry) (Astronaut)
Marlin Marietta Astro Space
100 Campus Dr
Newtown, PA 18940-1784, USA

Magilton, Gerard (Astronaut)
313 Saint James Dr
Langhorne, PA 19047-1634, USA

Maginnes, John (Athlete, Golfer)
612 Topwater Ln
Greensboro, NC 27455-3458, USA

Magliozzi, Ray (Television Host)
c/o Staff Member *Car Talk Plaza*
Harvard St Apt 3500
Cambridge, MA 02138-4117, USA

Magliozzi, Tom (Actor, Television Host)
c/o Staff Member *Car Talk Plaza*
Harvard St Apt 3500
Cambridge, MA 02138-4117, USA

Magnante, Mike (Athlete, Baseball Player)
5305 Via Quinto
Newbury Park, CA 91320-6937, USA

Magnus, Edie (Correspondent)
NBC-TV
30 Rockefeller Plz
News Dept
New York, NY 10112-0015, USA

Magnus, Johnny (Actor)
c/o Staff Member *Cassell-Levy Inc*
6032 Wilkinson Ave
North Hollywood, CA 91606-4516, USA

Magnus, Sandra H (Sandy) (Astronaut)
11771 Arbor Glen Way
Reston, VA 20194-1582, USA

Magnuson, Ann
1317 Maltman Ave
Los Angeles, CA 90026-6224

Magnussen, Jan (Race Car Driver)
5294 Winder Hwy
Braselton, GA 30517-1709, USA

Magowan, Peter (Commentator)
San Francisco Giants
2100 Washington St
San Francisco, CA 94109-2845, USA

Magrane, Joe (Athlete, Baseball Player)
601 Channelside Walk Way Apt 1431
Tampa, FL 33602-6741, USA

Magrane, Shannon (Musician)
c/o Staff Member *19 Entertainment (LA)*
9000 W Sunset Blvd Ste 1574
West Hollywood, CA 90069-5817, USA

Magrann, Tom (Athlete, Baseball Player)
910 N 31st Ct
Hollywood, FL 33021-5509, USA

Magrath, Kelly (Race Car Driver)
Jim Dunn Racing
840 Kallin Ave
Long Beach, CA 90815-5004, USA

Magrini, Pete (Athlete, Baseball Player)
2402 Rancho Cabeza Dr
Santa Rosa, CA 95404-2326, USA

Magro, Ronnie (Fist Pump) (Reality Star)
c/o Matt Cohen *IAG Entertainment & Sports*
5189 Argonne Ct
San Diego, CA 92117-1054, USA

Magruder, Chris (Athlete, Baseball Player)
1114 N High Desert Dr
Deer Park, WA 99006-5009, USA

Magsamen, Sandra (Artist, Writer)
Orchard Books/Scholastic
557 Broadway
New York, NY 10012-3962, USA

Maguire, Gregory (Writer)
HarperCollins Children's Books
1350 Avenue of the Americas
New York, NY 10019-4702, USA

Maguire, Paul L (Athlete, Football Player, Sportscaster)
707 Ocean Blvd
Isle Of Palms, SC 29451-2136, USA

Maguire, Richard W (Cinematographer)
605 Summer Mesa Dr
Las Vegas, NV 89144-1502, USA

Maguire, Sean (Actor)
c/o Staff Member *The Management Company*
2030 Pinehurst Rd
Los Angeles, CA 90068-3732, USA

Maguire, Tobey (Actor)
c/o Darin Friedman *Management 360*
9111 Wilshire Blvd
Beverly Hills, CA 90210-5508, USA

Maguson, Keith A (Athlete, Hockey Player)
265 King Muir Rd
Lake Forest, IL 60045-2034, USA

Magyar, Derek (Actor)
c/o Staff Member *Wilkins Management*
12200 W Olympic Blvd Ste 400
Los Angeles, CA 90064-1047, USA

Mahaffey, Art (Athlete, Baseball Player)
3140 W Tilghman St
PO Box 261
Allentown, PA 18104-4222, USA

Mahaffey, John (Athlete, Golfer)
594 Sawdust Rd Unit 229
Spring, TX 77380-2215, USA

Mahaffey, Randy (Athlete, Basketball Player)
25 Berkeley Rd
Avondale Estates, GA 30002-1468, USA

Mahaffey, Valerie (Actor)
c/o Steven Muller *Innovative Artists (LA)*
1505 10th St
Santa Monica, CA 90401-2805, USA

Mahaffey, Valerio
121 N San Vicente Blvd
Beverly Hills, CA 90211-2303

Mahal, Taj (Musician, Songwriter, Writer)
c/o Staff Member *Red Light Management (LA)*
8439 W Sunset Blvd Ste 2
West Hollywood, CA 90069-1925, USA

Mahalic, Drew (Athlete, Football Player)
2114 SW Sunset Dr
Portland, OR 97239-2066, USA

Mahan, Hunter (Athlete, Golfer)
24 Lake View Dr
Trabuco Canyon, CA 92679-5119, USA

Mahan, Larry
PO Box 41
Center Point, TX 78010-0041

Mahan, Lawrence (Larry) (Rodeo Rider)
PO Box 119
Sunset, TX 76270-0119, USA

Mahar, kevin (Baseball Player)
2506 E Wheeler St
Midland, MI 48642-3178, USA

Maharidge, Date D (Writer)
Stanford University
Communications Dept
Stanford, CA 94305, USA

Maharis, George (Actor)
9401 Wilshire Blvd Ste 700
700
Beverly Hills, CA 90212-2944, USA

Mahay, Ron (Athlete, Baseball Player)
1825 N Rose St
Burbank, CA 91505-1317, USA

Mahe, Reno (Athlete, Football Player)
2619 Knollbrook Ln
Spring, TX 77373-9130, USA

Maher, Bill (Talk Show Host)
c/o Marc Gurvitz *Brillstein Entertainment Partners (LA)*
9150 Wilshire Blvd Ste 350
Beverly Hills, CA 90212-3453, USA

Maher, Sean
c/o Staff Member *Gersh (LA)*
9465 Wilshire Blvd Ste 600
Beverly Hills, CA 90212-2605, USA

Maheu, Robert (Government Official, Misc)
2140 Vista Famosa Ct
Las Vegas, NV 89123-4304, USA

Mahfouz, Robbie (Athlete, Football Player)
181 Belle Terre Blvd
Covington, LA 70433-4734, USA

Mahlberg, Greg (Athlete, Baseball Player)
5100 N Placita Del Lazo
Tucson, AZ 85750-1535, USA

Mahler, Mickey (Athlete, Baseball Player)
7911 Quirt St
San Antonio, TX 78227-2636, USA

Mahlum, Eric (Athlete, Football Player)
17794 NW Solano Ct
Portland, OR 97229-2210, USA

Mahogany, Kevin (Actor, Musician)
Ted Kurland
173 Brighton Ave
Allston, MA 02134-2003, USA

Maholm, Paul (Athlete, Baseball Player)
135 Wild Mdws
Hattiesburg, MS 39402-8108, USA

Mahomes, Pat (Baseball Player)
Minnesota Twins
3110 Oleander Dr
Tyler, TX 75707-2000, USA

Mahon, Sean (Actor)
c/o Staff Member *McCabe Group, The*
3211 Cahuenga Blvd W Ste 104
Los Angeles, CA 90068-1372, USA

Mahone, Austin (Musician)
PO Box 409009
Fort Lauderdale, FL 33340-9009, USA

Mahoney, Brian (Athlete, Basketball Player)
96 Greystone Rd
Rockville Centre, NY 11570-4515, USA

Mahoney, Dan (Writer)
13 Swan Ln
Levittown, NY 11756-3921, USA

Mahoney, David L (Business Person)
McKesson HBOX Inc
1 Post St
San Francisco, CA 94104-5203, USA

Mahoney, Jim (Athlete, Baseball Player)
345 Hawthorne Ave # 2
Apt R19
Hawthorne, NJ 07506-1244, USA

Mahoney, John (Actor)
c/o Staff Member *Martino Management*
149 W 72nd St Apt 1D
New York, NY 10023-3228, USA

Mahoney, Marie (Athlete, Baseball Player, Commentator)
207 Birdsall St
Houston, TX 77007-8107, USA

Mahoney, Marle (Baseball Player)
207 Birdsall St
Houston, TX 77007-8107, USA

Mahoney, Mike (Athlete, Baseball Player)
PO Box 875
Waukee, IA 50263-0875, USA

Mahony, Cardinal Roger
1531 W 9th St
Los Angeles, CA 90012

Mahorn, Rick (Athlete, Basketball Player)
3091 Mapleridge Ct
Rochester Hills, MI 48309-4505, USA

Mahovlich, Peter (Athlete, Hockey Player)
116 Farr Ln
Queensbury, NY 12804-1989, USA

Mahre, Phil (Athlete, Olympic Athlete, Skier)
4114 122nd St NE
Marysville, WA 98271-8572, USA

Mahre, Phil
PO Box 100
Park City, UT 84060-0100, USA

Mahre, Steve (Athlete, Olympic Athlete, Skier)
7610 W Chestnut Ave
Yakima, WA 98908-1553, USA

Maida, Adam J Cardinal (Religious Leader)
Archdiocese of Detroit
1234 Washington Blvd Ste 1
Detroit, MI 48226-1800, USA

Maida, Raine (Musician)
c/o Staff Member *Paradigm (Monterey)*
404 W Franklin St
Monterey, CA 93940-2303, USA

Maiden-Naccarato, Jeanne (Bowler)
1 N Stadium Way Apt 4
Tacoma, WA 98403-3154, USA

Maidlow, Steve (Athlete, Football Player)
1311 Garfield Ave
Springfield, OH 45504-1430, USA

Maier, Mitch (Baseball Player)
435 Amelia Cir
South Lyon, MI 48178-8211, USA

Maietta, Mike (Race Car Driver)
154 Pleasant Hill Rd
Scarborough, ME 04074-7119, USA

Mailhot, Jacques (Athlete, Hockey Player)
30 Green Terrace Cv
Austin, TX 78734-5713

Mailhouse, Robert (Actor)
1623 N Dillon St
Los Angeles, CA 90026-1203, USA

Maillard, Carol (Musician)
Sweet Honey Agency
PO Box 600099
Newtonville, MA 02460-0001, USA

Maine, John (Athlete, Baseball Player)
13825 Island Dr
Huntersville, NC 28078-8903, USA

Maine, scott (Baseball Player)
9365 SW 94th Loop
Ocala, FL 34481-4607, USA

Maines, Natalie (Musician)
c/o Simon Renshaw *Strategic Artist Management*
1100 Glendon Ave Ste 1000
Los Angeles, CA 90024-3514, USA

Mair, Adam (Athlete, Hockey Player)
25 San Fernando Ln
East Amherst, NY 14051-2235, USA

Mairena, Oswaldo (Athlete, Baseball Player)
160 E 6th Pl # Pi
Mesa, AZ 85201-5068, USA

Maisel, Lucian (Actor)
c/o Marc Hamou *Thruline Entertainment*
9250 Wilshire Blvd Ste 100
Ground Floor
Beverly Hills, CA 90212-3343, USA

Maisky, Mischa M (Musician)
Columbia Artists Mgmt Inc
165 W 57th St
New York, NY 10019-2201, USA

Maisonneuve, Brian (Soccer Player)
Columbus Crew
2121 Volman Ave
Columbus, OH 43211, USA

Maitland, Jack (Athlete, Football Player)
3079 N Palm Aire Dr
Pompano Beach, FL 33069-3457, USA

Majerle, Dan (Athlete, Basketball Player, Olympic Athlete)
3901 E Rancho Dr
Paradise Valley, AZ 85253-5024, USA

Majewski, Gary (Athlete, Baseball Player)
1103 Chamboard Ln
Houston, TX 77018-3212, USA

Majewski, Val (Athlete, Baseball Player)
890 Oakley Dr
Freehold, NJ 07728-8237, USA

Majkowski, Don (Athlete, Football Player)
1593 Bayhill Dr
Duluth, GA 30097-5980, USA

Majoli, Iva (Tennis Player)
27 Framingham Ln
Pittsford, NY 14534-1047, USA

Major, Bruce
15 Evergreen Ln
Topsfield, MA 01983-1431, USA

Major, Clarence L (Writer)
University of California
English Dept
Voorhies Hall
Davis, CA 95616, USA

Majoras, Deborah (Government Official)
Federal Trade Commission
Pennsylvania Ave & 6th St NW
Washington, DC 20580-0001, USA

Majorino, Tina (Actor)
5333 Via Pisa
Newbury Park, CA 91320-7007, USA

Majors, Austin
Major Minors
3940 Laurel Canyon Blvd # 177
Studio City, CA 91604-3709

Majors, Bobby (Athlete, Football Player)
9625 Post Oak Ter
Ooltewah, TN 37363-8023, USA

Majors, John I (Johnny) (Athlete, Coach, Football Coach, Football Player)
4207 Beechwood Rd
Knoxville, TN 37920-6011, USA

Majors, Lee (Actor)
1831 Rocking Horse Dr
Simi Valley, CA 93065-5913, USA

Majtyka, Roy (Baseball Player)
2082 Orangeside Rd
Palm Harbor, FL 34683-3340, USA

Majumder, Shaun (Actor, Comedian, Musician)
3524 Cazador St
Los Angeles, CA 90065-3405, USA

Makar, Jimmy (Race Car Driver)
131 Ridgecliff Dr
Statesville, NC 28677-9000, USA

Makarov, Sergei (Athlete, Hockey Player)
4072 Teale Ave
San Jose, CA 95117-3432, USA

Make Good Your Escape (Music Group)
c/o Staff Member Paradigm (Monterey)
404 W Franklin St
Monterey, CA 93940-2303, USA

Maker, Marvin (Horse Racer)
RR 1 Box 201
Pemberton, NJ 08068, USA

Makings, Elizabeth (Athlete, Golfer)
10063 E San Bernardo Dr
Scottsdale, AZ 85258-5665, USA

Makinson, Jessica (Comedian)
c/o Staff Member Berwick & Kovacik
6300 Wilshire Blvd Ste 1410
Los Angeles, CA 90048-5216, USA

Makkena, Wendy (Actor)
c/o Staff Member Schumacher
Management
2018 Glendon Ave
Los Angeles, CA 90025-6324, USA

Mako (Actor)
6477 Peppertree Ln
Somis, CA 93066-9758, USA

Makowski, Tom (Athlete, Baseball Player)
8760 Krager Hill Rd
Little Valley, NY 14755-9784, USA

Makowsky, Bruce (Designer)
77 Beverly Park Ln
Beverly Hills, CA 90210-1571, USA

Maksudian, Mike (Athlete, Baseball Player)
12148 E San Simeon Dr
Scottsdale, AZ 85259-6049, USA

Malakar, Sanjaya (Musician, Reality Star)
c/o Staff Member SUM Company
10736 Jefferson Blvd # 140
Culver City, CA 90230-4933, USA

Malakhov, Vladimir (Athlete, Hockey Player)
PO Box 420536
Kissimmee, FL 34742-0536, USA

Malakian, Daron (Musician)
Velvet Hammer
9911 W Pico Blvd Ste 350
Los Angeles, CA 90035-2730, USA

Malamala, Siupeli (Athlete, Football Player)
122 110th Ave SE
Bellevue, WA 98004-6332, USA

Malandrino, Catherine (Designer, Fashion Designer)
468 Broome St
New York, NY 10013-2611, USA

Malandro, Kristina (Actor)
2518 Cardigan Ct
Los Angeles, CA 90077-1337, USA

Malanowski-Marlowe, Jean (Baseball Player)
100 Smallacombe Dr # 205-24
Scranton, PA 18508-2650, USA

Malarchuk, Clint (Athlete, Hockey Player)
1308 Myers Dr
Gardnerville, NV 89410-6166, USA

Malarkey, Michael (Actor)
c/o Matt Goldman Silver Lining
Entertainment
421 S Beverly Dr Fl 7
Beverly Hills, CA 90212-4408, USA

Malaska, Mark (Athlete, Baseball Player)
3823 Cumberland Dr
Youngstown, OH 44515-4610, USA

Malchow, Tom (Athlete, Olympic Athlete, Swimmer)
10220 NW Edgewood Dr
Portland, OR 97229-7617, USA

Malco, Romany (Actor)
c/o Staff Member Mosaic Media Group
9200 W Sunset Blvd Ste 10
West Hollywood, CA 90069-3608, USA

Malcomson, Paula (Actor, Producer)
c/o Sean Fay Kritzer Levine Wilkins
Entertainment (KLWG)
11872 La Grange Ave Fl 1
Los Angeles, CA 90025-5283, USA

Maldonado, Candy (Athlete, Baseball Player)
HC 2 Box 16800
Arecibo, PR 00612-9396, USA

Malek, Rami (Actor)
c/o Kyle Fritz Kyle Fritz Management
6325 Heather Dr
Los Angeles, CA 90068-1633, USA

Maler, Jim (Athlete, Baseball Player)
7542 NW 23rd St
Hollywood, FL 33024-1035, USA

Maley, David (Athlete, Hockey Player)
1366 Norelius Ct
San Jose, CA 95120-3849, USA

Malick, Terrence (Director, Producer)
c/o Roeg Sutherland Creative Artists
Agency (CAA-LA)
2000 Avenue of the Stars Ste 100
Los Angeles, CA 90067-4705, USA

Malick, Wendie (Actor, Model)
c/o Nevin Dolcefino Innovative Artists
(LA)
1505 10th St
Santa Monica, CA 90401-2805, USA

malicki-Sanchez, Keram (Actor)
c/o Tiffany Kuzon Evolution Entertainment
(LA)
901 N Highland Ave
Los Angeles, CA 90038-2412, USA

Malik, Marek (Athlete, Hockey Player)
919 Anchorage Rd
Tampa, FL 33602-5755, USA

Malil, Shelley (Actor)
c/o Mark Measures Kazarian, Measures,
Ruskin & Associates (LA)
11969 Ventura Blvd Fl 3
Studio City, CA 91604-2630, USA

Malina, Josh
2262 Cloverfield Blvd
Santa Monica, CA 90405-1821

Malina, Joshua (Actor, Producer)
c/o David Ginsberg Insight
PO Box 36359
Los Angeles, CA 90036-0359, USA

Malinchak, Bill (Athlete, Football Executive)
6422 NW 65th Way
Parkland, FL 33067-1503, USA

Malinger, Ross
6212 Banner Ave
Los Angeles, CA 90038-2802

Malizia, Mike (Athlete, Golfer)
570 SE Southwood Trl
Stuart, FL 34997-6367, USA

Malkin, Evgenl (Athlete, Hockey Player)
66 Mario Lemieux Pl
Pittsburgh, PA 15219-3504, USA

Malkin, Laurence (Writer)
c/o Josh Kesselman Thruline
Entertainment
9250 Wilshire Blvd Ste 100
Ground Floor
Beverly Hills, CA 90212-3343, USA

Malkin, Michelle (Correspondent)
445C E Cheyenne Mountain Blvd # 415
Colorado Springs, CO 80906-4506, USA

Malkmus, Bobby (Athlete, Baseball Player)
400 Wallingford Ter
Union, NJ 07083-7328, USA

Malkmus, Stephen (Actor)
3535 E Burnside St
Portland, OR 97214-2052, USA

Malkovich, John (Actor)
c/o Liz Mahoney ID Public Relations (LA)
7060 Hollywood Blvd Fl 8th
Los Angeles, CA 90028-6021, USA

Mallard, Josh (Athlete, Football Player)
175 International Dr
Athens, GA 30605-6617, USA

Mallard, Wesly (Athlete, Football Player)
6073 SW 67th Pl
Portland, OR 97223-7613, USA

Mallee, John (Athlete, Baseball Player)
7426 Hamlin St
Schererville, IN 46375-3454, USA

Mallet, Jeff (Horse Racer)
1375 Chinquapin Rd
Southampton, PA 18966-4609, USA

Mallett, Jerry (Athlete, Baseball Player)
4070 Cascade Trl
Mc Gregor, TX 76657-4102, USA

Mallett, Ronnie (Athlete, Football Player)
711 Gallup St
Jennings, LA 70546-6319, USA

Mallett, Ryan (Athlete, Football Player)
c/o David Dunn Athletes First, LLC
23091 Mill Creek Dr
Laguna Hills, CA 92653-1258, USA

Mallette, Brian (Athlete, Baseball Player)
1179 Lowery Fire House Rd
Glenwood, GA 30428-2214, USA

Mallick, Fran (Athlete, Football Player)
88 Scott Swamp Rd Apt 138
Farmington, CT 06032-2995, USA

Mallicoat, Rob (Athlete, Baseball Player)
13025 NE 70th Dr
Kirkland, WA 98033-8302, USA

Mallinger, John (Athlete, Golfer)
2020 N Beverly Plz
Long Beach, CA 90815-2882, USA

Mallon, Meg (Athlete, Golfer)
219 Palm Trl
Delray Beach, FL 33483-5526, USA

Mallon, Thomas (Writer)
801 25th St NW
Washington, DC 20037-2209, USA

Mallory, Carole (Actor)
2300 5th Ave
New York, NY 10037-1610, USA

Mallory, Irvin (Athlete, Football Player)
3 Paula Ln
Waterford, CT 06385-1521, USA

Mallory, John (Athlete, Football Player)
33C Medford Rd
Whiting, NJ 08759-3844, USA

Mallory, Larry (Athlete, Football Player)
1911 Stonebrook Dr
Arlington, TX 76012-5707, USA

Mallory, Rick (Athlete, Football Player)
920 W Emerson St
Seattle, WA 98119-1419, USA

Mallory, Sheldon (Athlete, Baseball Player)
21353 Old North Church Rd
Frankfort, IL 60423-3016, USA

Malloy, Bob (Athlete, Baseball Player)
1904 San Carlos Ave
Allen, TX 75002-2626, USA

Malloy, Dannel (Governor, Politician)
State Capitol
210 Capitol Ave Ste 1
Hartford, CT 06106-1562, USA

Malloy, Marty (Athlete, Baseball Player)
PO Box 1644
Chiefland, FL 32644-1644, USA

Malloy, Matt (Actor)
c/o Mark A. Schlegel Cornerstone Talent Agency
37 W 20th St Ste 1007
New York, NY 10011-3714, USA

Malloy, Robert (Pete Hamil) (Actor, Writer)
c/o Staff Member ICM Partners (LA)
10250 Constellation Blvd Fl 7
Los Angeles, CA 90067-6207, USA

Malloy, Tommy
1687 Amsterdam Ave
Merrick, NY 11566-2516

Malloys, The (Music Group)
c/o Staff Member Creative Artists Agency (CAA-LA)
2000 Avenue of the Stars Ste 100
Los Angeles, CA 90067-4705, USA

Maloff, Sam (Designer)
PO Box 8051
Rancho Cucamonga, CA 91701-0051, USA

Malone, Brendan (Coach)
Indiana Pacers
125 S Pennsylvania St
Conseco Fieldhouse
Indianapolis, IN 46204-3610, USA

Malone, Chuck (Athlete, Baseball Player)
310 Liberty St
Marked Tree, AR 72365-2209, USA

Malone, Dorothy (Actor)
PO Box 7287
Dallas, TX 75209-0287, USA

Malone, Greg (Athlete, Hockey Player)
1771 Waterford Ct
Pittsburgh, PA 15241-3150, USA

Malone, Jeff (Athlete, Basketball Player)
415 Lee Road 313
Smiths Station, AL 36877-3168, USA

Malone, Jena (Actor)
c/o Allison Band Gersh (LA)
9465 Wilshire Blvd Ste 600
Beverly Hills, CA 90212-2605, USA

Malone, John (Business Person)
Liberty Media
12300 Liberty Blvd
Englewood, CO 80112-7009

Malone, Karl (Athlete, Basketball Player, Olympic Athlete)
105 W Charter St
Farmerville, LA 71241-2841, USA

Malone, Kevin (Commentator)
PO Box 770
Santa Monica, CA 90406-0770, USA

Malone, Maicel (Athlete, Olympic Athlete, Track Athlete)
4064 Bothwell Ter
Tallahassee, FL 32317-8545, USA

Malone, Mike (Athlete, Basketball Coach, Basketball Player, Coach)
c/o Staff Member Sacramento Kings
1 Sports Pkwy
Sacramento, CA 95834-2301

Malone, Moses (Athlete, Basketball Player)
310 S Keswick Ct
Sugar Land, TX 77478-3952, USA

Malone, Patricia (Business Person)
c/o Staff Member Gucci America
50 Hartz Way
Secaucus, NJ 07094-2420, USA

Malone, Ryan (Athlete, Hockey Player)
Octagon Sports Management
7950 Jones Branch Dr
Mc Lean, VA 22102-3302, USA

Malone, Shannon (Actor, Television Host)
c/o Jerry Shandrew Shandrew Public Relations
1050 S Stanley Ave
Los Angeles, CA 90019-6634, USA

Malone, Van (Athlete, Football Player)
4921 W Briarcreek Dr
Stillwater, OK 74074-2092, USA

Maloney, Dave (Athlete, Hockey Player)
1 Lockwood Ave
Old Greenwich, CT 06870-1707, USA

Maloney, Don (Athlete, Hockey Player)
60 Cambridge Dr
Greenwich, CT 06831-4134, USA

Maloney, Jim (Athlete, Baseball Player)
9722 Groffs Mill Dr Ste 107
Unit 102
Owings Mills, MD 21117-6341, USA

Maloney, Sean (Athlete, Baseball Player)
244 Pheasant Run
Saunderstown, RI 02874-2033, USA

Maloof, Adrienne (Business Person, Reality Star)
c/o Shaila Arora Arora/Wasserman Entertainment Media
23679 Calabasas Rd Ste 633
Calabasas, CA 91302-1502, USA

Maloof, Gavin (Business Person)
c/o Staff Member Sacramento Kings
1 Sports Pkwy
Sacramento, CA 95834-2301

Maloof, Mary Lou Metzger (Musician)
5100 Stern Ave
Sherman Oaks, CA 91423-1244, USA

Maloof Jr, George (Business Person)
Palms Casino Resort
4321 W Flamingo Rd
Las Vegas, NV 89103-3903, USA

Maloog, Jack (Athlete, Baseball Player)
3140 S Vista Dr
Chandler, AZ 85248-3728, USA

Malrena, Oswaldo (Baseball Player)
Chicago Cubs
2510 W Rio Salado Pkwy
Mesa, AZ 85201-3603, USA

Maltais, Steve (Athlete, Hockey Player)
646 Country Club Dr
Itasca, IL 60143-1681, USA

Maltbie, Roger (Athlete, Golfer)
179 Longmeadow Dr
Los Gatos, CA 95032-5655, USA

Maltby, Kirk (Athlete, Hockey Player)
58 Putnam Pl
Grosse Pointe Shores, MI 48236-1224, USA

Maltin, Leonard (Journalist)
13835 Chandler Blvd
Sherman Oaks, CA 91401-5815, USA

Maltin, Leonard (Correspondent)
c/o Staff Member Entertainment Tonight (ET)
4024 Radford Ave
Studio City, CA 91604-2101, USA

Malzone, Frank (Athlete, Baseball Player)
16 Aletha Rd
Needham, MA 02492-4302, USA

Mamas & The Papas, The
61 Purchase St Ste 2
Rye, NY 10580-3059

Mambo, Kevin (Actor)
3500 W Olympic Blvd # 1400
Burbank, CA 91505

Mamet, David (Writer)
2 Northfield Plz Ste 200
Northfield, IL 60093-1272, USA

Mamet, Zosia (Actor)
c/o Sarah Shyn 3 Arts Entertainment (LA)
9460 Wilshire Blvd Fl 7
Beverly Hills, CA 90212-2713, USA

Mamoa, Jason (Actor)
c/o Jeff Witjas Agency for the Performing Arts (APA-LA)
405 S Beverly Dr Ste 500
Beverly Hills, CA 90212-4425, USA

Mana (Music Group)
c/o Staff Member Creative Artists Agency (CAA-LA)
2000 Avenue of the Stars Ste 100
Los Angeles, CA 90067-4705, USA

Manafort, Jason (Race Car Driver)
414 New Britain Ave
Plainville, CT 06062-2065, USA

Manahan, Austin (Athlete, Baseball Player)
21150 N Tatum Blvd Apt 2079
Phoenix, AZ 85050-7209, USA

Manca, Massimo (Athlete, Football Player)
3867 Miriam Dr
Doylestown, PA 18902-9176, USA

Manchester, Melissa (Musician)
c/o Peter Varano AVO Talent Agency
5670 Wilshire Blvd Ste 1930
Los Angeles, CA 90036-5603, USA

Mancina, Mark (Actor)
c/o Staff Member Gorfaine/Schwartz Agency Inc
4111 W Alameda Ave Ste 509
Burbank, CA 91505-4171, USA

Mancini, Ray
13900 Marquesas Way Apt 3435
Marina Del Rey, CA 90292-6054

Mancuso, Gail (Director, Producer)
c/o Matthew Labov Forefront Media
8500 Melrose Ave Ste 205
West Hollywood, CA 90069-5169, USA

Mancuso, Nick (Actor)
c/o Joel Dean TalentWorks (LA)
3500 W Olive Ave Ste 1400
Burbank, CA 91505-5512, USA

Mancuso Jr, Frank (Producer)
c/o Staff Member FGM Entertainment
201 N Canon Dr # 328
Beverly Hills, CA 90210

Mandan, Robert
Jim Moore & Associates
16700 Celtic St
Granada Hills, CA 91344-5109

Mandarich, Tony (Athlete, Football Player)
5450 E Deer Valley Dr Unit 4004
Phoenix, AZ 85054-8115, USA

Mandel, Howie (Comedian, Game Show Host, Television Host)
c/o Michael Rotenberg 3 Arts Entertainment (LA)
9460 Wilshire Blvd Fl 7
Beverly Hills, CA 90212-2713, USA

Mandelbaum, Michael (Writer)
Basic Books
250 W 57th St Fl 15
New York, NY 10107-1307, USA

Mandich, Dan (Athlete, Hockey Player)
9075 Hyland Creek Cir
Minneapolis, MN 55437-1907, USA

Mandley, Pete (Athlete, Football Player)
2925 E Cathy Dr
Gilbert, AZ 85296-8873, USA

Mandrell, Barbara (Musician)
B.M.I.F.C.
PO Box 620
Hendersonville, TN 37077-0620, USA

Mandrell, Louise (Actor)
c/o Staff Member Morris Artists Management
818 19th Ave S
Nashville, TN 37203-3202, USA

Mandvi, Aasif (Actor)
c/o Lillian LaSalle LaSalle Holland
141 W 28th St Rm 300
New York, NY 10001-6187, USA

Mandylor, Costas (Actor)
c/o Staff Member Evolution Entertainment (LA)
901 N Highland Ave
Los Angeles, CA 90038-2412, USA

Mandylor, Louis (Actor)
c/o Erik Kritzer LINK Entertainment
11872 La Grange Ave Fl 1
Los Angeles, CA 90025-5283, USA

Mane, Tyler (Actor)
c/o Lesa Kirk Open Entertainment
1051 Cole Ave Ste B
Los Angeles, CA 90038-2601, USA

Manell, George (Race Car Driver)
5455 Polaris Ave
Las Vegas, NV 89118-2421, USA

Manery, Kris (Athlete, Hockey Player)
48568 Quail Run Dr S
Plymouth, MI 48170-5717, USA

Manery, Randy (Athlete, Hockey Player)
7119 Massey Rd
Waxhaw, NC 28173-7406

Maness, James (Athlete, Football Player)
1001 Jarvis Ln
Azle, TX 76020-3321, USA

Manetti, Larry (Actor)
4615 Winnetka
Woodland Hills, CA 91364

Manfra, Fred (Commentator)
3001 Lyndebrooke Ct
Fallston, MD 21047-1362, USA

Manganiello, Joe (Actor)
10960 Wilshire Blvd Ste 1900
Los Angeles, CA 90024-3805, USA

Manges, Mark (Athlete, Football Player)
701 White Ave
Cumberland, MD 21502-3816, USA

Mangieri, Dino (Athlete, Football Player)
108 Lamport Blvd Apt 3C
Staten Island, NY 10305-3629, USA

Mangini, Eric (Athlete, Football Player)
59 Moss ln
Brewster, MA 02631, USA

Mangione, Chuck (Musician)
476 Hampton Blvd
Rochester, NY 14612-4227

Mangold, James Allen (Director, Producer, Writer)
c/o Bo Morrison *Block-Korenbrot Public Relations*
6100 Wilshire Blvd Ste 170
Los Angeles, CA 90048-5109, USA

Mangold, Nick (Athlete, Football Player)
361 Shunpike Rd
Chatham, NJ 07928-1634, USA

Mangual, Angel (Baseball Player)
Pittsburgh Pirates
1406 R Del Valle
Ponce, PR 00728, USA

Mangual, Pepe (Athlete, Baseball Player)
2325 Calle Tabonuco
Urb Los Caobos
Ponce, PR 00716-2712, USA

Mangum, John (Athlete, Football Player)
150 Summerwood Dr
Pearl, MS 39208-9074, USA

Mangum, Jonathan (Actor)
c/o Staff Member *Shapiro/West & Associates*
141 El Camino Dr Ste 205
Beverly Hills, CA 90212-2786, USA

Mangum, Kris (Athlete, Football Player)
16720 Krishna Ln
Charlotte, NC 28277-1638, USA

Manheim, Camryn (Actor, Producer)
c/o Peg Donegan *Framework Entertainment (LA)*
9057 Nemo St Ste C
West Hollywood, CA 90069-5511, USA

Manic Street Preachers (Music Group)
c/o Staff Member *Paradigm (Monterey)*
404 W Franklin St
Monterey, CA 93940-2303, USA

Manilow, Barry (Musician)
c/o Garry Kief *Stiletto Entertainment*
8295 S La Cienega Blvd
Inglewood, CA 90301-1521, USA

Manis, Randy (Producer)
c/o Staff Member *Killer Films (US)*
526 W 26th St Rm 715
New York, NY 10001-5524, USA

Manjia, Nicki (Musician)
c/o Staff Member *Motown Records (NY)*
1755 Broadway Fl 7
New York, NY 10019-3743, USA

Mankiewicz, Frank
The Wyoming Columbia Rd. NW
Washington, DC 20009

Mankiewicz, Tom
10850 Wilshire Blvd Ste 730
Los Angeles, CA 90024-4325

Mankins, Logan (Athlete, Football Player)
1 Jeffrey Dr
North Attleboro, MA 02760-2761, USA

Mankowski, Phil (Athlete, Baseball Player)
11 Concord Dr
Orchard Park, NY 14127-3907, USA

Manley, Dexter (Athlete, Football Player)
PO Box 25049
Washington, DC 20027-8049, USA

Manley, Elizabeth (Figure Skater)
Marco Enterprises
74830 Velie Way Ste A
Palm Desert, CA 92260-7954, USA

Manley, Joe (Athlete, Football Player)
3365 County Road 92
Rogersville, AL 35652-2736, USA

Manley, Leon (Athlete, Football Player)
1207 Knollpark Cir
Austin, TX 78758-3815, USA

Mann, Aimee (Musician)
Girlie Action Media And Marketing
243 W 30th St Fl 12
New York, NY 10001-2812, USA

Mann, Almee (Musician, Songwriter, Writer)
Michael Hausman Mgmt
511 Avenue of the Americas # 197
New York, NY 10011-8436, USA

Mann, Art (Producer, Television Host)
HDNet Films
122 Hudson St Fl 5
New York, NY 10013-2355, USA

Mann, Carol (Athlete, Golfer)
6 Cape Chestnut Dr
Spring, TX 77381-2978, USA

Mann, Catherine
10806 Waring Pl
Charlotte, NC 28277-2765

Mann, Charles (Athlete, Football Player)
40741 Carry Back Ln
Leesburg, VA 20176-6306, USA

Mann, David W (Religious Leader)
10550 S 200 W
Columbia City, IN 46725-9618, USA

Mann, Errol (Athlete, Football Player)
5521 Bonanza Pl
Missoula, MT 59808-9386, USA

Mann, Gabriel (Actor)
c/o Van Johnson *Van Johnson Company*
10250 Constellation Blvd Ste 2320
Los Angeles, CA 90067-6256, USA

Mann, Garbriel (Actor)
United Talent Agency
9336 Civic Center Dr
Beverly Hills, CA 90210-3604, USA

Mann, H Thompson (Athlete, Swimmer)
23 Pleasant St Apt 501
Newburyport, MA 01950-2634, USA

Mann, Jim (Athlete, Baseball Player)
197 N Franklin St Apt 1
Holbrook, MA 02343-1111, USA

Mann, Jimmy (Athlete, Hockey Player)
1538 Scio Ridge Rd
Ann Arbor, MI 48103-8991

Mann, Leslie (Actor)
239 N Bristol Ave
Los Angeles, CA 90049-2603, USA

Mann, Marvin L (Business Person)
Lexmark International
740 W New Circle Rd
Lexington, KY 40511-1876, USA

Mann, Michael K (Actor, Director, Producer, Writer)
c/o Staff Member *Forward Pass Inc*
12233 W Olympic Blvd Ste 340
Los Angeles, CA 90064-1092

Mann, Monroe (Actor, Producer, Writer)
c/o Staff Member *Loco Dawn Films, LLC*
499 Seventh Ave
12th Floor North
New York, NY 10018, USA

Mann, Robert (Athlete, Football Player)
515 SW Hampton Ct
Port Saint Lucie, FL 34986-2022, USA

Mann, Shelley I (Swimmer)
1301 S Scott St # 638S
Arlington, VA 22204-6205, USA

Mann, Tamela (Actor, Musician)
c/o Staff Member *Capital Entertainment*
1201 N St NW # A5
Washington, DC 20005-5115, USA

Mann, Terrence V (Actor)
c/o Steve Stone *Cornerstone Talent Agency*
37 W 20th St Ste 1007
New York, NY 10011-3714, USA

Mannelly, Patrick (Athlete, Football Player)
1128 Kildare Ave
Libertyville, IL 60048-1203, USA

Manners, Miss
1651 Harvard St NW
Washington, DC 20009-3702

Mannheim Steamroller (Music Group)
9120 Mormon Bridge Rd
Omaha, NE 68152-1937, USA

Manning, Aaron (Athlete, Football Player)
6906 27th Ave
Kenosha, WI 53143-5214, USA

Manning, Archie (Athlete, Football Player)
1420 1st St
New Orleans, LA 70130-5713, USA

Manning, Charlie (Athlete, Baseball Player)
PO Box 964
Winter Haven, FL 33882-0964, USA

Manning, Danny (Athlete, Basketball Player, Olympic Athlete)
205 Running Ridge Rd
Lawrence, KS 66049-2180, USA

Manning, Eli (Athlete, Football Player)
c/o Alan Zucker *Excel Sports Management (LA)*
1360 E 9th St Ste 100
Cleveland, OH 44114-1730, USA

Manning, Jim (Athlete, Baseball Player)
41 Fox Run Dr
Weaverville, NC 28787-8307, USA

Manning, Peyton (Athlete, Football Player)
The Peyback Foundation
6325 Guilford Ave Ste 201
Indianapolis, IN 46220-1741, USA

Manning, Rick (Athlete, Baseball Player)
PO Box 5485
Carefree, AZ 85377-5485, USA

Manning, Taryn (Actor, Musician)
13331 Moorpark St Apt 311
Sherman Oaks, CA 91423-3950, USA

Manning, Wade (Athlete, Football Player)
5133 Malaya St
Denver, CO 80249-8548, USA

Mannion, Pace (Athlete, Basketball Player)
4190 S Achilles Dr
Salt Lake City, UT 84124-3266, USA

Mannix, Ernie (Musician)
c/o Staff Member *Greenspan Artist Management*
8760 W Sunset Blvd
West Hollywood, CA 90069-2206, USA

Manoa, Tim (Athlete, Football Player)
1285 Boardman Canfield Rd
Youngstown, OH 44512-4058, USA

Manoff, Dinah (Actor)
Innovative Artists
1505 10th St
Santa Monica, CA 90401-2805, USA

Manon, Julio (Athlete, Baseball Player)
4726 15th Ave S
Saint Petersburg, FL 33711-2328, USA

Manoogian, RIchard A (Business Person)
Masco Corp
2100 Van Born Rd
Taylor, MI 48180, USA

Manor, Brison (Athlete, Football Player)
285 Spruce St
Bridgeton, NJ 08302-3347, USA

Manos, Sam (Athlete, Football Player)
1424 E Normandy Blvd
Deltona, FL 32725-8408, USA

Manoukian, Don (Athlete, Football Player)
5405 Mae Anne Ave
Reno, NV 89523-1813, USA

Manrique, Fred (Baseball Player)
Toronto Blue Jays
1775 SW 2nd Ave
Boca Raton, FL 33432-7230, USA

Mansell, Kevin (Business Person)
Kohl's Corp
N56W17000 Ridgewood Dr
Menomonee Falls, WI 53051-7096, USA

Mansfield, Mike (Ex-Senator, Senator)
1101 Pennsylvania Ave NW Ste 900
Washington, DC 20004-2514, USA

Mansfield, Von (Athlete, Football Player)
3530 194th St
Homewood, IL 60430-4325, USA

Mansfield-Kelley, Marie (Athlete, Baseball Player, Commentator)
9 Eastland Rd
Jamaica Plain, MA 02130-4616, USA

Mansolino, Doug (Athlete, Baseball Player)
110 Tecumseh Ln
Loudon, TN 37774-3138, USA

Manson, Dave (Athlete, Hockey Player)
211 Cowboys Pkwy
Irving, TX 75063-5931, USA

Manson, Marilyn (Musician)
3401 Troy Dr
Los Angeles, CA 90068-1435, USA

Manson, Shirley (Musician)
c/o Staff Member *Untitled Entertainment*
(LA)
350 S Beverly Dr Ste 200
Beverly Hills, CA 90212-4819, USA

Mant, Cathy (Athlete, Golfer)
326 Broadmoor Way
McDonough, GA 30253-4291, USA

Mantador, Steve (Athlete, Hockey Player)
6301 Osprey Ter
Coconut Creek, FL 33073-2624, USA

Mantegna, Joe (Actor, Producer, Writer)
c/o Jack Gilardi *ICM Partners (LA)*
10250 Constellation Blvd Fl 7
Los Angeles, CA 90067-6207, USA

Mantei, Matt (Athlete, Baseball Player)
4709 Chicago Path
Stevensville, MI 49127-9356, USA

Mantenuto, Michael (Actor)
c/o Kim Hodgert *Creative Artists Agency*
(CAA-LA)
2000 Avenue of the Stars Ste 100
Los Angeles, CA 90067-4705, USA

Mantha, Mo
8423 Tally Ho Rd
Lutherville Timonium, MD 21093-4725

Mantha, Moe (Athlete, Hockey Player,
Olympic Athlete)
1538 Scio Ridge Rd
Ann Arbor, MI 48103-8991, USA

Manthey, Jerri (Actor)
PO Box 801507
Santa Clarita, CA 91380-1507

Mantilla, Felix (Athlete, Baseball Player)
6973 N Tacoma St
Milwaukee, WI 53224-4759, USA

Mantis, Nick (Athlete, Basketball Player)
2344 Autumn Dr
Crown Point, IN 46307, USA

Mantle, Anthony (Cinematographer)
c/o Staff Member *ICM Partners (LA)*
10250 Constellation Blvd Fl 7
Los Angeles, CA 90067-6207, USA

Mantley, John
4121 Longridge Ave
Sherman Oaks, CA 91423-4335

Manto, Jeff (Athlete, Baseball Player)
725 Radcliffe St
Bristol, PA 19007-5223, USA

Mantooth, Randolph (Actor)
c/o Staff Member *Stone Manners Salners*
Agency (LA)
6100 Wilshire Blvd Ste 1500
Los Angeles, CA 90048-5110, USA

Mantranga, Jonah (Musician)
c/o Staff Member *Paradigm (Monterey)*
404 W Franklin St
Monterey, CA 93940-2303, USA

Mantreola, Patricia
c/o Staff Member *BMG*
1540 Broadway
New York, NY 10036-4039, USA

Mantz, Michael R (Astronaut)
1188 W 18th St
San Pedro, CA 90731-3810, USA

Mantzoukas, Jason (Actor)
c/o Christie Smith *Mosaic Media Group*
9200 W Sunset Blvd Ste 10
West Hollywood, CA 90069-3608, USA

Manucci, Dan (Athlete, Football Player)
6326 N 14th St
Phoenix, AZ 85014-1431, USA

Manuel, Barry (Athlete, Baseball Player)
805 Oak St
Mamou, LA 70554-2715, USA

Manuel, Charles F (Chuck) (Baseball
Player)
2931 Plantation Rd
Winter Haven, FL 33884-1233, USA

Manuel, Charlie (Athlete, Baseball Player,
Coach)
2931 Plantation Rd
Winter Haven, FL 33884-1233, USA

Manuel, E J (Athlete, Football Player)
c/o Malik Hafeez Shareef *Dimensional*
Sports, Inc.
3148 Circle Dr SW
Roanoke, VA 24018-2110, USA

Manuel, Jay (Reality Star, Television Host)
c/o Lisa Shotland *Creative Artists Agency*
(CAA-LA)
2000 Avenue of the Stars Ste 100
Los Angeles, CA 90067-4705, USA

Manuel, Jerry (Athlete, Baseball Player,
Coach)
5556 Ridge Park Dr
Loomis, CA 95650-9400, USA

Manuel, Lionel (Athlete, Football Player)
827 E Cedar Dr
Chandler, AZ 85249-3319, USA

Manuel, Marquand (Athlete, Football
Player)
3672 Churchill Downs Dr
Davie, FL 33328-1307, USA

Manumaleuna, Brandon (Athlete, Football
Player)
1218 Koleeta Dr
Harbor City, CA 90710-1824, USA

Manusky, Greg (Athlete, Football Player)
11537 Willow Springs Dr
Zionsville, IN 46077-7830, USA

Manville, Dick (Athlete, Baseball Player)
1436 Lake Francis Dr
Apopka, FL 32712-2007, USA

Manwaring, Kirt (Athlete, Baseball Player)
San Francisco Giants
20 Prospect Rdg
Horseheads, NY 14845-7988, USA

Manwaring, Kurt D (Athlete, Baseball
Player)
20 Prospect Rdg
Horseheads, NY 14845-7988, USA

Manza, Ralph
550 Hygeia Ave
Encinitas, CA 92024-2601

Manzanillo, Josias (Athlete, Baseball
Player)
4445 SW 160th Ave Apt 101
Hollywood, FL 33027-5745, USA

Manzella, Tommy (Athlete, Baseball
Player)
3213 Veronica Dr
Chalmette, LA 70043-3555, USA

Manzi, Catello (Horse Racer)
1 Hickory Ln
Freehold, NJ 07728-1588, USA

Manzi, Louis (Horse Racer)
4036 Grace Ave
Bronx, NY 10466-2210, USA

Manzi, Rocco (Horse Racer)
730 Chip Ave
Pompano Beach, FL 33069-1175, USA

Manziel, Johnny (Athlete, Football Player)
c/o Erik Burkhardt *Select Sports Group*
2700 Post Oak Blvd Ste 1450
Houston, TX 77056-5785, USA

Manzo, Caroline (Business Person, Reality
Star)
709 Saber Ct
Franklin Lakes, NJ 07417-2931, USA

Manzo, Dina (Business Person, Reality
Star)
705 Ewing Ave
Franklin Lakes, NJ 07417-2228, USA

Manzullo, Donald (Congressman,
Politician)
2228 Rayburn Hob
Washington, DC 20515-1316, USA

Mapa, Alec (Actor)
c/o Stephen Ford *Diva Central Inc*
7510 W Sunset Blvd Ste 1445
Los Angeles, CA 90046-3408, USA

Mapes, Cliff
PO Box 872
Pryor, OK 74362-0872

Maple, Eddie (Horse Racer)
25 Spartina Cres
Bluffton, SC 29910-4702, USA

Maple, Eddie (Race Car Driver)
420 Fair Hill Dr # 1
Elkton, MD 21921-2573, USA

Maples, Marla (Actor)
c/o Alec Shankman *Abrams Artists*
Agency (LA)
9200 W Sunset Blvd PH 11
West Hollywood, CA 90069-3601, USA

Maponga, Stansly (Athlete, Football
Player)
c/o Bus Cook *Bus Cook Sports, Inc*
1 Willow Bend Dr
Hattiesburg, MS 39402-8552, USA

Mapother, William (Actor)
c/o Brian Medavoy *Medavoy*
Management
10203 Santa Monica Blvd Ste 400
Los Angeles, CA 90067-6405, USA

Mar, Marcela (Actor)
c/o Luis Balaguer *Latin World*
Entertainment Agency (LWE)
3470 NW 82nd Ave
Doral, FL 33122-1024, USA

Mara, Kate (Actor)
c/o Jennifer Allen *Viewpoint Inc (LA)*
8820 Wilshire Blvd Ste 220
Beverly Hills, CA 90211-2622, USA

mara, Paul
48472 Meadow Ct
Plymouth, MI 48170-3204

Marachuk, Steve
568 Hana Hwy
Paia, HI 96779-8133

Marak, Paul (Athlete, Baseball Player)
1211 Comanche Trl
Alamogordo, NM 88310-4010, USA

Maran, Josie (Actor)
c/o Darren Goldberg *Global Creative*
1051 Cole Ave # B
Los Angeles, CA 90038-2601, USA

Marangi, Gary (Athlete, Football Player)
26 Morton St
Port Jefferson Station, NY 11776-4013,
USA

Maraniss, David (Journalist)
Washington Post
Editorial Dept
1150 15th St NW
Washington, DC 20071-0001, USA

Marano, Laura (Actor)
c/o Jennifer Millar *Paradigm (LA)*
360 N Crescent Dr
North Bldg
Beverly Hills, CA 90210-4874, USA

Marano, Vanessa (Actor)
c/o Elizabeth Much *Much and House*
Public Relations
8075 W 3rd St Ste 500
Los Angeles, CA 90048-4325, USA

Maratos, Terry (Actor)
c/o Staff Member *Cage Group, The*
14724 Ventura Blvd Ste 505
Sherman Oaks, CA 91403-3505

Maratos-Flier, Elftheria (Doctor)
Joslin Diabetes Center
1 Joslin Pl
Boston, MA 02215-5394, USA

Marble, Roy (Athlete, Basketball Player)
1355 Wagon Wheel Ln
Grand Blanc, MI 48439-4863, USA

Marbley, Harlan (Athlete, Boxer, Olympic
Athlete)
6113 Parkview Ln
Clinton, MD 20735-3850, USA

Marbury, Joseph (Athlete, Baseball Player)
1472 21st St N
Birmingham, AL 35234-2708, USA

Marbury, Kerry (Athlete, Football Player)
1201 Locust Ave
Fairmont, WV 26554-2451, USA

Marbury, Rendon (Athlete, Baseball
Player)
1472 21st St N
Birmingham, AL 35234-2708, USA

Marbury, Stephan (Athlete, Basketball
Coach, Olympic Athlete)
2940 W 31st St Apt 4G
Brooklyn, NY 11224-1734, USA

Marbury, Stephon (Athlete, Basketball
Player, Olympic Athlete)
2940 W 31st St Apt 4G
Brooklyn, NY 11224-1734, USA

Marbut, Robert G (Publisher)
Argyle Communications
100 NE Loop
#1400
San Antonio, TX 78216, USA

Marcelino, Mario
1418 N Highland Ave # 102
Los Angeles, CA 90028-7611

March, Forbes (Actor)
c/o Staff Member *Innovative Artists (LA)*
1505 10th St
Santa Monica, CA 90401-2805, USA

March, Joan
Whale Rock Ranch Rd.
Ojai, CA 93023

March, Little Peggy (Musician)
Cape Entertainment
1161 NW 76th Ave
Plantation, FL 33322-5120, USA

March, Peggy
1161 NW 76th Ave
Plantation, FL 33322-5120

March, Stephanie (Actor)
c/o Erica Tarin *ID Public Relations (LA)*
7060 Hollywood Blvd Fl 8th
Los Angeles, CA 90028-6021, USA

Marchant, Kenny (Congressman, Politician)
1110 Longworth Hob
Washington, DC 20515-3401, USA

Marchant, Todd (Athlete, Hockey Player, Olympic Athlete)
10448 Caribou Way
Tustin, CA 92782-1470, USA

Marchette, Josh
6500 Wilshire Blvd Ste 2200
Los Angeles, CA 90048-4942

Marchetti, Gino J (Athlete, Football Player)
324 Devon Way
West Chester, PA 19380-6825, USA

Marchibroda, Ted (Athlete, Football Player)
90 Orchard Point Dr
Weems, VA 22576-2648, USA

Marchinko, Jhoni (Producer)
c/o Staff Member *United Talent Agency (UTA-LA)*
9336 Civic Center Dr
Beverly Hills, CA 90210-3604, USA

Marchiol, Ken (Athlete, Football Player)
6489 S Olathe St # 5
Centennial, CO 80016-1052, USA

Marchlewski, Frank (Athlete, Football Player)
428 Toledo Dr
New Kensington, PA 15068-3315, USA

Marciano, David (Actor)
c/o Staff Member *Don Buchwald & Associates (LA)*
6500 Wilshire Blvd Ste 2200
Los Angeles, CA 90048-4942, USA

Marciano, Rob (Television Host)
c/o Staff Member *Entertainment Tonight (ET)*
4024 Radford Ave
Studio City, CA 91604-2101, USA

Marcil, Vanessa (Actor)
c/o Becky Poliakoff *aTa Management (LA)*
2508 N Vermont Ave
Los Angeles, CA 90027-1243, USA

Marcille, Eva Pigford (Actor, Model, Reality Star)
c/o Jerome Martin *Jerome Martin Management*
1655 N Cherokee Ave
2nd Floor
Los Angeles, CA 90028, USA

Marciniak, Ron (Athlete, Football Player)
2222 Hopespring Loop
The Villages, FL 32162-7044, USA

Marcinko, Richard (Writer)
c/o Kimberly Witherspoon *Inkwell Management*
521 5th Ave Fl 10
New York, NY 10175-1099, USA

Marcis, Dave (Race Car Driver)
Marcis Auto Racing
10 Greenleaf Rd
Arden, NC 28704, USA

Marco, Gian (Musician)
c/o Staff Member *Creative Artists Agency (CAA-LA)*
2000 Avenue of the Stars Ste 100
Los Angeles, CA 90067-4705, USA

Marcol, Czeslaw C (Chester) (Athlete, Football Player)
PO Box 466
Dollar Bay, MI 49922-0466, USA

Marcontell, Ed (Athlete, Football Player)
PO Box 884
Rusk, TX 75785-0884, USA

Marcos (Musician)
East West America Records
75 Rockefeller Plz
New York, NY 10019-6908, USA

Marcotte, Don (Athlete, Hockey Player)
12 Cote St
Amesbury, MA 01913-3804, USA

Marcovicci, Andrea (Actor, Musician)
Donald Smith Promotions
1640 E 48th St
#14U
New York, NY 10017, USA

Marcum, Art (Writer)
c/o Staff Member *Nine Yards Entertainment*
5815 W Sunset Blvd Ste 206
Los Angeles, CA 90028-6481, USA

Marcum, Shaun (Athlete, Baseball Player)
1413 Jill Ln
Excelsior Springs, MO 64024-9790, USA

Marcus, Bernard (Business Person)
Marcus Foundation
2455 Paces Ferry Rd SE Bldg C
Atlanta, GA 30339-1834, USA

Marcus, John (Race Car Driver)
PO Box 1018
Talladega, AL 35161-1018, USA

Marcus, Sparky (Actor)
910 Arlene Ct
Yreka, CA 96097-2744, USA

Marcus, Trula M (Actor)
The Agency
1800 Avenue of the Stars Ste 400
Los Angeles, CA 90067-4206, USA

Marder, Barry
c/o Daniel Strone *Trident Media Group LLC*
41 Madison Ave Fl 36
New York, NY 10010-2257, USA

Marderian, Greg (Athlete, Football Player)
1400 Barton Rd Apt 1701
Redlands, CA 92373-1404, USA

Mardones, Benny (Musician)
Tony Cee
PO Box 410
Utica, NY 13503-0410, USA

Mare, Olindo (Athlete, Football Player)
5 Serenity Dr
Mandeville, LA 70471-6764, USA

Maree, Sydney (Athlete, Track Athlete)
2 Braxton Rd
Bryn Mawr, PA 19010-1029, USA

Marek, Marcus (Athlete, Football Player)
26 Nora Ct
New Ipswich, NH 03071-3504, USA

Maren, Elizabeth (Actor)
PO Box 90010
San Diego, CA 92169-2010, USA

Maren, Jerry (Actor)
PO Box 90010
San Diego, CA 92169-2010, USA

Marentette, Leo (Athlete, Baseball Player)
33606 Beechwood St
Westland, MI 48185-3002, USA

Margalit, Israela (Musician)
Columbia Artists Mgmt Inc
165 W 57th St
New York, NY 10019-2201, USA

Margarita, Henry R (Athlete, Football Player)
4 Drury Ln
Stoneham, MA 02180-3205, USA

Margavage, Dave (Athlete, Football Player)
474 Woodview Dr
Lexington, KY 40515-5945, USA

Margera, Bam (Actor, Producer, Writer)
PO Box 671
Westtown, PA 19395-0671, USA

Margera, Vincent (Actor)
c/o Mike Esterman *Esterman.Com, LLC*
Prefers to be contacted via email
Baltimore, MD XXXXX, USA

Margerum, Ken (Athlete, Football Player)
494 Riverview Dr
Capitola, CA 95010-2778, USA

Margo, Philip (Musician)
American Mgmt
19948 Mayall St
Chatsworth, CA 91311-3522, USA

Margolin, Phillip (Writer)
c/o Jean V Naggar *Jean Naggar Literary Agency*
216 E 75th St Ste 1E
New York, NY 10021-2921, USA

Margolis, Cindy (Actor, Model)
c/o Glenn Gulino *G2 Entertainment LLC*
1 Columbus Pl Apt S25E
New York, NY 10019-8208, USA

Margolis, Jonathan (Director)
c/o Gary Castaldo *Real Deal Management*
353 S Reeves Dr
Beverly Hills, CA 90212-4551, USA

Margolis, Mark (Actor)
c/o Van Johnson *Van Johnson Company*
10250 Constellation Blvd Ste 2320
Los Angeles, CA 90067-6256, USA

Margoneri, Joe (Athlete, Baseball Player)
341 Turkeytown Rd
West Newton, PA 15089-1850, USA

Margot, Sandra (Athlete, Wrestler)
PO Box 1168
Studio City, CA 91614-0168, USA

Margret, Ann (Actor, Dancer, Musician)
2707 Benedict Canyon Dr
Beverly Hills, CA 90210-1024, USA

Margulies, Donald (Writer)
Yale University
English Dept
New Haven, CT 06520, USA

Mariano, Jarah (Model)
c/o Staff Member *IMG Models (NY)*
304 Park Ave S Fl 12
New York, NY 10010-4314, USA

Marichal, Juan (Athlete, Baseball Player)
9458 NW 54th Doral Circle Ln
Doral, FL 33178-2048, USA

Marie, Ann (Actor)
1608 N Cahuenga Blvd # 354
Los Angeles, CA 90028-6202, USA

Marie, Constance (Actor)
c/o Rachael Reiss *Prime*
9696 Culver Blvd Ste 102
Culver City, CA 90232-2734, USA

Marie, Lisa (Actor, Model)
c/o Chris Forberg *LA Models*
555 W 25th St
New York, NY 10001-5542, USA

Marienthal, Eli (Actor)
c/o Lisa Gallant *Gallant Management*
10250 Constellation Blvd Fl 7
Los Angeles, CA 90067-6207, USA

Marienthal, Eric (Musician)
15030 Ventura Blvd # 710
Sherman Oaks, CA 91403-5470, USA

Marillion (Musician)
c/o Staff Member *Paradigm (Monterey)*
404 W Franklin St
Monterey, CA 93940-2303, USA

Marimow, William K (Journalist)
440 S Broad St Unit 1602
Philadelphia, PA 19146-4909, USA

Marin, Jack (Athlete, Basketball Player)
3909 Regent Rd
Durham, NC 27707-5311, USA

Marin, Mindy (Director)
c/o Jeremy Plager *Creative Artists Agency (CAA-LA)*
2000 Avenue of the Stars Ste 100
Los Angeles, CA 90067-4705, USA

Marin, Richard A (Cheech) (Actor, Comedian)
c/o Ben Feigin *Anonymous Content (LA)*
3532 Hayden Ave
Culver City, CA 90232-2413, USA

Marin, Rosario (Government Official, Writer)
Fuerza, Inc.
1340 E McWood St
West Covina, CA 91790-5320, USA

Marinaro, Ed (Athlete, Football Player)
1466 N Doheny Dr
Los Angeles, CA 90069-1143, USA

Marinelli, Rod (Athlete, Football Player)
1981 W Southmeadow Ln
Lake Forest, IL 60045-4831, USA

Marini, Gilles (Actor, Model)
c/o Vikram Dhawer *Authentic Talent and Literary Management*
20 Jay St Ste M17
Brooklyn, NY 11201-8300, USA

Marinin, Maxim (Figure Skater)
c/o Staff Member *Champions on Ice*
3500 American Blvd W Ste 190
Minneapolis, MN 55431-4431, USA

Marino, Cathy (Athlete, Golfer)
6313 Willowdale Dr
Plano, TX 75093-7802, USA

Marino, Dan (Football Player)
c/o Staff Member *Miami Dolphins*
7500 SW 30th St
Davie, FL 33314-1020, USA

Marino, Ken (Actor)
I F A Talent Agency
8730 W Sunset Blvd Ste 490
West Hollywood, CA 90069-2248, USA

Marino, Stephen (Athlete, Golfer)
203 Evergrene Pkwy Unit 18-B
Palm Beach Gardens, FL 33410-1508,
USA

Marino, Tom (Congressman, Politician)
410 Cannon Hob
Washington, DC 20515-4402, USA

Marinovich, Marv (Athlete, Football
Player)
1/2 Santa Margarita Pkwy
Rancho Santa Margarita, CA 92688, USA

Marinovich, Todd (Athlete, Football
Player)
132 E Balboa Blvd
Newport Beach, CA 92661-1118, USA

Marinucci, Chris (Athlete, Hockey Player)
30300 Laplant Rd
Grand Rapids, MN 55744-6062

Mario (Musician)
c/o Staff Member *J Erving Group*
555 Whitehall St SW Apt N
Atlanta, GA 30303-3715, USA

Mario, Ernest (Business Person)
ALZA Corp
1950 Charleston Rd
Mountain View, CA 94043-1218, USA

Marion, Brock (Athlete, Football Player)
24051 Schultz Rd NE
Aurora, OR 97002-9652, USA

Marion, Frank (Athlete, Football Player)
27416 SW 143rd Ave
Homestead, FL 33032-8867, USA

Marion, Fred (Athlete, Football Player)
10032 Oak Quarry Dr
Orlando, FL 32832-5645, USA

Marion, Jerry (Athlete, Football Player)
12411 Riverfront Park Dr
Bakersfield, CA 93311-5112, USA

Marion, Shawn (Athlete, Basketball
Player)
5434 E Cannon Dr
Paradise Valley, AZ 85253-1155, USA

Maris, Ada
10100 Santa Monica Blvd Ste 2500
Los Angeles, CA 90067-4116

Mariucci, Steve (Athlete, Football Player)
15940 Romita Ct
Monte Sereno, CA 95030-3092, USA

Mariye, Lily (Director, Writer)
c/o Staff Member *Bauman Redanty &
Shaul Agency*
5757 Wilshire Blvd
Suite 473
Beverly Hills, CA 90212, USA

Mark, Albert J (Beauty Pageant Winner)
Miss American Pageant
1325 Broadway
Atlantic City, NJ 08401, USA

Mark, Greg (Athlete, Football Player)
2920 Washington St
Miami, FL 33133-3825, USA

Mark, Marky
63 Pilgrim Rd
Braintree, MA 02184-6003

Mark, Reed (Athlete, Football Player)
3724 Falcon Way
Saint Paul, MN 55123-2491, USA

Mark, Reuben (Business Person)
Colgate-Palmolive Co
300 Park Ave Fl 8
New York, NY 10022-7499, USA

Markakis, Nick (Athlete, Baseball Player)
949 Piney Hill Rd
Monkton, MD 21111-1426, USA

Markbreit, Jerry (Athlete, Football Player)
9739 Keystone Ave
Skokie, IL 60076-1136, USA

Markell, Jack (Governor, Politician)
Governor's Office
150 Martin Luther King Jr Blvd S Ste 2
Dover, DE 19901-3637, USA

Markell, John
7540 Spring Mill Dr
Canal Winchester, OH 43110-8831

Marker, Steve (Musician)
Borman Entertainment
1250 6th St Ste 401
Santa Monica, CA 90401-1638, USA

Markgraf-Sobrero, Kathryn (Athlete,
Olympic Athlete, Soccer Player)
5055 N Cumberland Blvd
Milwaukee, WI 53217-5745, USA

Mark Green, Mark
c/o *Brewco Motorsports Inc*
PO Box 3453
Dana Point, CA 92629-8453, USA

Markham, Dale (Athlete, Football Player)
1832 Valley Dr
Bismarck, ND 58503-0195, USA

Markham, Monte (Actor)
PO Box 36
Malibu, CA 90265-0036, USA

Markie, Biz (Actor, Musician)
c/o Ron Rivlin *Coast II Coast
Entertainment*
204 S Beverly Dr Ste 110
Beverly Hills, CA 90212-3800, USA

Markland, Jeff (Athlete, Football Player)
1135 Thornfield Ln
Las Vegas, NV 89123-0828, USA

Markle, Meghan (Actor)
c/o Pearl Servat *PMK/BNC Public
Relations (PMK-LA)*
8687 Melrose Ave Ste 8
West Hollywood, CA 90069-5746, USA

Markle, Peter F (Director)
7510 W Sunset Blvd # 509
Los Angeles, CA 90046-3408, USA

Markov, Danny (Athlete, Hockey Player)
17875 Collins Ave Apt 3402
Sunny Isles Beach, FL 33160-2718, USA

Markovich, Mark (Athlete, Football
Player)
9825 N Townsend Dr
Peoria, IL 61615-1389, USA

Markowitz, Barry (Cinematographer)
225 W 83rd St Apt 20G
New York, NY 10024-4964, USA

Markowitz, Robert (Director, Producer)
11521 Amanda Dr
Studio City, CA 91604-4144, USA

Marks, Chandler
PO Box 184
Franklin, TN 37065-0184

Marks, John (Athlete, Hockey Player)
2733 47th St S Apt 205
Fargo, ND 58104-8539

Marks, Sean
2702 Circle Dr
Newport Beach, CA 92663-5619

Marks, Sen'Derrick (Athlete, Football
Player)
c/o Hadley Engelhard *Enter-Sports
Management*
5 Concourse Pkwy Ste 3000
Atlanta, GA 30328-7106, USA

Markwart, Nevin (Athlete, Hockey Player)
24 Old Barn Rd
Hanover, MA 02339-3504

Marlatt, Harvey (Athlete, Basketball
Player)
10145 Lakeview Dr
Atlanta, MI 49709-9224, USA

Marleau, Patrick (Athlete, Hockey Player)
12021 Magnolia Ct
Saratoga, CA 95070-5386

Marley, Damian (Musician)
c/o Staff Member *Red Light Management
(LA)*
8439 W Sunset Blvd Ste 2
West Hollywood, CA 90069-1925, USA

Marlin, Sterling (Race Car Driver)
Phoenix Racing
195 Jones Rd
Spartanburg, SC 29307-5448, USA

Marling, Laura (Musician)
c/o Linda Carbone *Press Here Publicity*
138 W 25th St Ste 900
New York, NY 10001-7470, USA

Marlohe, Berenice (Actor)
c/o Andy Coleman *ICM Partners (LA)*
10250 Constellation Blvd Fl 7
Los Angeles, CA 90067-6207, USA

Marlowe, Andrew (Producer, Writer)
c/o Guymon Casady *Management 360*
9111 Wilshire Blvd
Beverly Hills, CA 90210-5508, USA

Marlowe, Marion (Actor)
2475 N Haskell Dr Apt 407
Tucson, AZ 85716-2613, USA

Marlowe, Scott
6399 Wilshire Blvd Ste 414
Los Angeles, CA 90048-5716

Marmol, Carlos (Athlete, Baseball Player)
3786 W Pippin St
Chicago, IL 60652-1347, USA

Marnie, Larry (Coach, Football Coach)
Arizona State University
Athletic Dept
Tempe, AZ 85287-0001, USA

Marohn, James (Horse Racer)
700 Birchwood Dr
Westbury, NY 11590-5807, USA

Marohn, William D (Business Person)
Whirlpool Corp
2000 N State St
RR 63
Benton Harbor, MI 49022, USA

Marolewski, Fred (Athlete, Baseball
Player)
15705 W Waterford Ln
Manhattan, IL 60442-8160, USA

Maron, Marc (Comedian)
c/o Staff Member *United Talent Agency
(UTA-LA)*
9336 Civic Center Dr
Beverly Hills, CA 90210-3604, USA

Marone, Lou (Athlete, Baseball Player)
10851 Carbet Pl
San Diego, CA 92124-2042, USA

Maroney, Kelli (Actor, Producer)
c/o Staff Member *Bohemia Group (LA)*
1680 Vine St Ste 412
Los Angeles, CA 90028-8800, USA

Maroney, Laurence (Athlete, Football
Player)
12560 Grandview Forest Dr
Saint Louis, MO 63127-0030, USA

Maroney, McKayla (Athlete, Gymnast)
c/o Staff Member *William Morris
Endeavor (LA)*
9601 Wilshire Blvd
Beverly Hills, CA 90210-5213, USA

Maroon 5 (Music Group)
c/o Brian Manning *Creative Artists Agency
(CAA-LA)*
2000 Avenue of the Stars Ste 100
Los Angeles, CA 90067-4705, USA

Maroth, Mike (Athlete, Baseball Player)
2333 Pesaro Cir
Ocoee, FL 34761-5006, USA

Maroto, Enrique (Athlete, Baseball Player)
701 NW 136th Ave
Miami, FL 33182-2291, USA

Maroulis, Constantine (Musician)
c/o Paul Reisman *Abrams Artists Agency
(NY)*
275 7th Ave Fl 26
New York, NY 10001-6708, USA

Marquardt, Bridget (Model, Reality Star)
c/o Jonathan Stone *SW PR Shop*
7083 Hollywood Blvd
Los Angeles, CA 90028-8901, USA

Marques, Tarso (Race Car Driver)
Payton-Coyne Racing
13400 S Budler Rd
Plainfield, IL 60544-9493, USA

Marquette, Chris (Actor)
c/o Ashley Franklin *Thruline
Entertainment*
9250 Wilshire Blvd Ste 100
Ground Floor
Beverly Hills, CA 90212-3343, USA

Marquez, Alfonso (Athlete, Baseball
Player)
PO Box 413
Arbuckle, CA 95912-0413, USA

Marquez, Alfonso (Baseball Player)
4102 S Skyline Ct
Gilbert, AZ 85297-9668, USA

Marquez, Jeff (Athlete, Baseball Player)
801 Rio Grande Dr
Vacaville, CA 95687-4343, USA

Marquis, Jason (Athlete, Baseball Player)
300 Vogel Ave
Staten Island, NY 10309-2905, USA

Marrero, Eli (Athlete, Baseball Player)
10230 SW 64th St
Miami, FL 33173-2807, USA

Marriott, Evan (Reality Star)
c/o Mike Esterman *Esterman.Com, LLC*
Prefers to be contacted via email
Baltimore, MD XXXXX, USA

Marriott, J Willard Jr (Business Person)
Marriott International
10400 Fernwood Rd
Bethesda, MD 20817-1102, USA

Marriott, Richard E (Business Person)
Host Marriott Corp
10400 Fernwood Rd
Bethesda, MD 20817-1118, USA

Marrone, Doug (Athlete, Football Player)
Georgia Tech
790 Lebrun Rd
Buffalo, NY 14226-4216, USA

Marrow, Tracy (Ice T) (Musician)
c/o Jorge Hinojosa *Jorge Hinojosa*
6606 Maryland Dr
Los Angeles, CA 90048-4614, USA

Mars, Bruno (Musician)
7979 Mulholland Dr
Los Angeles, CA 90046-1224, USA

Mars, Jacqueline (Business Person)
Mars Inc
6885 Elm St Ste 1
Mc Lean, VA 22101-6038, USA

Mars, John (Business Person)
Mars Inc
6885 Elm St Ste 1
Mc Lean, VA 22101-6038, USA

Mars, Mick (Musician)
c/o Staff Member *HarperCollins Publishers*
195 Broadway Fl 2
Cellar 1
New York, NY 10007-3132, USA

Marsalis, Branford (Musician)
Wilkins Mgmt
323 Broadway
Cambridge, MA 02139-1801, USA

Marsalis, James (Athlete, Football Player)
101 Royal Oak Ln
Kathleen, GA 31047-2149, USA

Marsalis, Wynton (Musician)
c/o Staff Member *Creative Artists Agency (CAA-LA)*
2000 Avenue of the Stars Ste 100
Los Angeles, CA 90067-4705, USA

Marsan, Edward (Eddie) (Actor)
c/o Marsha McManus *Principal Entertainment (LA)*
9255 W Sunset Blvd Ste 500
West Hollywood, CA 90069-3301, USA

Marsden, James (Actor)
4218 Warner Blvd
Burbank, CA 91505-4041, USA

Marsden, Matthew (Actor)
c/o Paul Nelson *Mosaic Media Group*
9200 W Sunset Blvd Ste 10
West Hollywood, CA 90069-3608, USA

Marsh, Doug (Athlete, Football Player)
629 Forest Ave
Saint Louis, MO 63135-2050, USA

Marsh, Frank (Athlete, Baseball Player)
304 Bay Shore Ave Apt 426
Mobile, AL 36607-2059, USA

Marsh, Graham (Golfer)
112 Pga Tour Blvd
Ponte Vedra Beach, FL 32082-3046, USA

Marsh, Henry (Athlete, Track Athlete)
General Delivery
Bountiful, UT 84010, USA

Marsh, Julian (DJ)
c/o Staff Member *Diva Central Inc*
7510 W Sunset Blvd Ste 1445
Los Angeles, CA 90046-3408, USA

Marsh, Linda (Actor)
170 W End Ave Apt 22P
22P
New York, NY 10023-5414, USA

Marsh, Marian (Actor)
PO Box 1
Palm Desert, CA 92261-0001, USA

Marsh, Michael (Mike) (Athlete, Track Athlete)
2425 Holly Hall St Apt 152
Houston, TX 77054-3996, USA

Marsh, Mike
2847 Indian Trail Dr
Missouri City, TX 77489

Marsh, Miles L (Business Person)
Fort James Corp
1919 S Broadway
Green Bay, WI 54304-4905, USA

Marsh, Peter (Athlete, Hockey Player)
210 Coe Rd
Clarendon Hills, IL 60514-1002, USA

Marsh, Randy (Athlete, Baseball Player)
559 Palmer Ct
Crestview Hills, KY 41017-3482, USA

Marsh, Robert T (Business Person, General)
20550 Falcons Landing Cir Apt 5106
Sterling, VA 20165-3586, USA

Marsh, Thomas (Tom) (Athlete, Baseball Player)
9140 Summerfield Rd
Temperance, MI 48182-9757, USA

Marshall, Albert L (Ben) (Athlete, Hockey Player)
9603 166th Street Ct E
Puyallup, WA 98375-2203, USA

Marshall, Amanda (Musician)
c/o Staff Member *Creative Artists Agency (CAA-LA)*
2000 Avenue of the Stars Ste 100
Los Angeles, CA 90067-4705, USA

Marshall, Arthur (Athlete, Football Player)
4821 Rocky Shoals Cir
Evans, GA 30809-7042, USA

Marshall, Brandon (Athlete, Football Player)
16710 Stratford Ct
Southwest Ranches, FL 33331-1358, USA

Marshall, Brian (Musician)
Agency Group
1776 Broadway Ste 430
New York, NY 10019-2002, USA

Marshall, Burchard (Athlete, Baseball Player)
60 Crouch Ave Apt C12B
Norwich, CT 06360-7329, USA

Marshall, Carolyn M (Religious Leader)
United Methodist Church
204 N Newlin St
Veedersburg, IN 47987-1358, USA

Marshall, Chan (Cat Power) (Actor, Musician)
c/o Oren Segal *Radius Entertainment*
9229 W Sunset Blvd Ste 310
West Hollywood, CA 90069-3403, USA

Marshall, Chan (Cat Power) (Musician)
c/o Staff Member *Matador Records (NY)*
304 Hudson St Rm 701
New York, NY 10013-1012, USA

Marshall, Charles (Athlete, Football Player)
4605 Preston Bend Dr
Arlington, TX 76016-1970, USA

Marshall, Chuck (Athlete, Football Player)
11215 Ponderosa Ln
Franktown, CO 80116-9306, USA

Marshall, Dave (Athlete, Baseball Player)
4802 E Centralia St
Long Beach, CA 90808-1312, USA

Marshall, David (Athlete, Football Player)
2740 Towne Village Dr
Duluth, GA 30097-7614, USA

Marshall, Donny (Athlete, Basketball Player)
410 N 63rd St
Seattle, WA 98103-5526, USA

Marshall, Donyell (Athlete, Basketball Player)
55 Ridgecreek Trl
Chagrin Falls, OH 44022-2379, USA

Marshall, Ed (Athlete, Football Player)
7010 Monarch St
Corpus Christi, TX 78413-4328, USA

Marshall, Elaine (Politician)
North Carolina Secretary Of State
PO Box 25128
Raleigh, NC 27611-5128, USA

Marshall, Frank (Director, Producer)
c/o Staff Member *Kennedy/Marshall Company*
619 Arizona Ave # 2
Santa Monica, CA 90401-1609, USA

Marshall, F Ray (Politician)
PO Box Y
Austin, TX 78713-8925, USA

Marshall, Garry K (Actor, Director)
c/o Michelle Bega *Rogers & Cowan PR (LA)*
8687 Melrose Ave Ste 7
West Hollywood, CA 90069-5721, USA

Marshall, Grant (Athlete, Hockey Player)
29 Garside Ave
Wayne, NJ 07470-2410

Marshall, James (Actor)
1833 Rutgers Dr
Thousand Oaks, CA 91360-5021, USA

Marshall, James (Horse Racer)
700 Anderson Rd
Jackson, NJ 08527-5340, USA

Marshall, James L (Jim) (Athlete, Football Player)
5258 Brookleigh Dr
Byram, MS 39272-6009, USA

Marshall, Jason
59 Clermont
Newport Coast, CA 92657-1082

Marshall, Jim (Athlete, Baseball Player, Coach)
19700 N 76th St Apt 1091
Scottsdale, AZ 85255-4587, USA

Marshall, Jim (Athlete, Football Player)
4241 Basswood Rd
Minneapolis, MN 55416-3848, USA

Marshall, Johnston (Athlete, Hockey Player)
Carolina Hurricanes
1400 Edwards Mill Rd
Attn Dir Pro Scouting
Raleigh, NC 27607-3624, USA

Marshall, Keith (Athlete, Baseball Player)
334 Beckwith Rd
Pine City, NY 14871, USA

Marshall, Ken (Actor)
Marshall Artists
345 N Maple Dr # 302
Beverly Hills, CA 90210-3869, USA

Marshall, Larry (Athlete, Football Player)
4605 SW Hickory Ln
Blue Springs, MO 64015-4524, USA

Marshall, Leonard (Athlete, Football Player)
PO Box 272016
Boca Raton, FL 33427-2016, USA

Marshall, Michael G (Mike) (Athlete, Baseball Player)
38324 Jendral Ave
Zephyrhills, FL 33542-7830, USA

Marshall, Mike (Athlete, Baseball Player)
6505 Amposta Dr
El Paso, TX 79912-2422, USA

Marshall, Patricia
969 Hilgard Ave Apt 401
Los Angeles, CA 90024-3078

Marshall, Paula (Actor)
6361 Innsdale Dr
Los Angeles, CA 90068-1623, USA

Marshall, Penny (Actor, Director)
c/o Staff Member *Parkway Productions*
7095 Hollywood Blvd Ste 1009
Los Angeles, CA 90028-8912, USA

Marshall, Peter (Television Host)
16714 Oak View Dr
Encino, CA 91436-3238, USA

Marshall, Rob (Director)
Moxie Pictures
2644 30th St Ste 100
Santa Monica, CA 90405-3051, USA

Marshall, Sean (Athlete, Baseball Player)
6515 N Kilbourn Ave
Lincolnwood, IL 60712-3436, USA

Marshall, Theda (Athlete, Baseball Player)
708 E Phillips Dr N
Littleton, CO 80122-2864, USA

Marshall, Thurgood (Politician)
6546 28th St N
Arlington, VA 22213-1207, USA

Marshall, Tom (Athlete, Basketball Player)
9548 Mariners Cove Ln
Fort Myers, FL 33919-4592, USA

Marshall, Vester (Athlete, Basketball Player)
2204 1st Ave Apt 201
Seattle, WA 98121-1600, USA

Marshall, Warren (Athlete, Football Player)
10108 Clairbourne Pl
Raleigh, NC 27615-1323, USA

Marshall, Whit (Athlete, Football Player)
57 Putnam Dr NW
Atlanta, GA 30342-4411, USA

Marshall, Wilber B (Athlete, Football Player)
4553 Sir Page Ln
Titusville, FL 32796-1444, USA

Marshall, Willard
204 Main St
Fort Lee, NJ 07024-5702

Marshall, Willie (Athlete, Hockey Player)
2110 Acorn Ct
Lebanon, PA 17042-5769

Marshall Green, Logan (Actor)
c/o Nick Frenkel 3 Arts Entertainment (LA)
9460 Wilshire Blvd Fl 7
Beverly Hills, CA 90212-2713, USA

Marshall Tucker Band
100 W Putnam Ave
Greenwich, CT 06830-5361

Marshburn, Thomas H Dr (Astronaut)
11607 Ivory Creek Dr
Pearland, TX 77584-8223, USA

Marson, Lou (Athlete, Baseball Player)
1680 Glendola Rd
Wall Township, NJ 07719-4506, USA

Marsonek, Sam (Athlete, Baseball Player)
712 Welton Rd
Lutz, FL 33548-5039, USA

Marsters, James (Actor)
c/o Jenni Weinman Patricola Lust PR
9171 Wilshire Blvd Ste 441
Beverly Hills, CA 90210-5516, USA

Marston, Joshua (Director, Writer)
c/o Cliff Roberts William Morris Endeavor
(LA)
9601 Wilshire Blvd
Beverly Hills, CA 90210-5213, USA

Marston, Natalie Elizabeth (Actor)
c/o Shepard Smith Luber Roklin
Management
1608 Argyle Ave
Los Angeles, CA 90028-6408, USA

Marston, Nathanial (Actor)
c/o Staff Member Donegan Entertaiment
129 W 27th St Fl 12
New York, NY 10001-6206, USA

Marston, Nathaniel (Actor)
c/o Staff Member One Life to Live
56 W 66th St
New York, NY 10023-6225, USA

Marta, Lynn (Actor)
c/o Staff Member Bobby Ball Talent
Agency
3500 W Olive Ave Ste 300
Burbank, CA 91505-4647, USA

Marte, Judy (Actor)
c/o Michael Cooper Creative Artists
Agency (CAA-LA)
2000 Avenue of the Stars Ste 100
Los Angeles, CA 90067-4705, USA

Martel, Arlene (Actor)
2109 S Wilbur Ave
Walla Walla, WA 99362-9048, USA

Martell, Donna
PO Box 3335
Granada Hills, CA 91394-0335

Martemucci, Anna (Director)
c/o Chad Hamilton Anonymous Content
(LA)
3532 Hayden Ave
Culver City, CA 90232-2413, USA

Martha, Paul (Athlete, Football Player)
6464 Dwane Ave
San Diego, CA 92120-3925, USA

Marti, Benita (Actor)
c/o Staff Member Select Artists Ltd (CA-
Valley Office)
PO Box 4359
Burbank, CA 91503-4359, USA

Martika (Musician)
Entertainment Artists
2409 21st Ave S Ste 100
Nashville, TN 37212-5317, USA

Martin, Aaron (Athlete, Football Player)
3605 Seth Ct
Springdale, MD 20774-5408, USA

Martin, Al (Athlete, Baseball Player)
510 N Alma School Rd Unit 302
Mesa, AZ 85201-5445, USA

Martin, Al (Athlete, Baseball Player)
11000 N 77th Pl Unit 1005
Scottsdale, AZ 85260-5599, USA

Martin, Amos (Athlete, Football Player)
2605 Bradford Commons Dr Unit 103
Louisville, KY 40299-6189, USA

Martin, Ann (Correspondent)
KCBS-TV
6121 W Sunset Blvd
News Dept
Los Angeles, CA 90028-6442, USA

Martin, Ann M (Writer)
c/o Staff Member Scholastic Entertainment
557 Broadway
New York, NY 10012-3962, USA

Martin, Babe (Athlete, Baseball Player)
114 N Holloway Rd
Ballwin, MO 63011-3205, USA

Martin, Billy (Athlete, Football Player)
PO Box 2969
Cumming, GA 30028-6513, USA

Martin, Billy (Musician)
c/o Brian Greenbaum Creative Artists
Agency (CAA-LA)
2000 Avenue of the Stars Ste 100
Los Angeles, CA 90067-4705, USA

Martin, Blanche (Athlete, Football Player)
1621 Stoney Point Dr
Lansing, MI 48917-1409, USA

Martin, Bob (Athlete, Basketball Player)
16036 N 11th Ave Unit 1092
Phoenix, AZ 85023-8206, USA

Martin, Bob (Athlete, Football Player)
14200 N 27th St
Davey, NE 68336-3638, USA

Martin, Boris "Babe" (Athlete, Baseball
Player)
5660 N Kolb Rd Apt 150
Tucson, AZ 85750-3204

Martin, Brian (Athlete)
1123 66th St
Emeryville, CA 94608-1133, USA

Martin, Casey (Athlete, Golfer)
University of Oregon
2727 Leo Harris Pkwy
Attn: Athletic Dept
Eugene, OR 97401-8835, USA

Martin, Casey
PO Box 109601
Palm Beach Gardens, FL 33410-9601

Martin, Chris (Actor)
c/o Barry McPherson Agency for the
Performing Arts (APA-NY)
135 W 50th St Fl 17
New York, NY 10020-1201, USA

Martin, Chris (Athlete, Football Player)
c/o Jeff Lynch Sports Management
Worldwide
1100 NW Glisan St Ste 2B
Portland, OR 97209-3064, USA

Martin, Chris (Musician)
28815 Grayfox St
Malibu, CA 90265-4252, USA

Martin, Christy (Boxer)
2015 University Heights Ln
Charlotte, NC 28213-4071, USA

Martin, Cuonzo (Athlete, Basketball
Player)
4315 Thistlewood Way
Knoxville, TN 37919-7884, USA

Martin, Curtis (Athlete, Football Player)
100 Hilton Ave Apt PH-1
Garden City, NY 11530-1564, USA

Martin, Dave (Athlete, Football Player)
9306 E Berry Ave
Greenwood Village, CO 80111-3509,
USA

Martin, Dave (Chef)
c/o Staff Member Magical Elves Inc
453 S Spring Street Ste
Los Angeles, CA 90013, USA

Martin, David (Correspondent)
CBS-TV
2020 M St NW
News Dept
Washington, DC 20036-3368, USA

Martin, Deana (Actor)
144 Welford Ln
Branson, MO 65616-3418, USA

Martin, Demetri (Actor, Comedian)
c/o Jason Heyman Creative Artists Agency
(CAA-LA)
3500 W Olive Ave Ste 1400
Burbank, CA 91505-5512, USA

Martin, Don (Athlete, Football Player)
1003 Hilltop Dr
Carrollton, MO 64633-1909, USA

Martin, Doug (Athlete, Golfer)
1406 Meadowlake Way
Union, KY 41091-7118, USA

Martin, Duane (Actor)
22401 S Summit Ridge Cir
Chatsworth, CA 91311-2682, USA

Martin, Ed (Baseball Player)
Philadelphia Stars
6666 Brookmont Ter Apt 407
Nashville, TN 37205-4622, USA

Martin, Ed F (Actor)
c/o Steven Neibert Imperium 7 Talent
Agency
5455 Wilshire Blvd Ste 1706
Los Angeles, CA 90036-4217, USA

Martin, Eric (Athlete, Football Player)
111 Windfall Pl
Clinton, MS 39056-6072, USA

Martin, Eric Band
PO Box 5952
San Francisco, CA 94101

Martin, Gene (Athlete, Baseball Player)
133 Winchester Dr
Leesburg, GA 31763-5064, USA

Martin, George (Athlete, Football Player)
50 Cheshire Ln
Ringwood, NJ 07456-2743, USA

Martin, George R R (Writer)
103 San Salvador Ln
Santa Fe, NM 87501-1739, USA

Martin, Graham Patrick (Actor)
c/o Evan Hainey Untitled Entertainment
(LA)
350 S Beverly Dr Ste 200
Beverly Hills, CA 90212-4819, USA

Martin, Greg (Musician)
Mitchell Fox Mgmt
212 3rd Ave N Ste 301
Nashville, TN 37201-1632, USA

Martin, Helen
1440 N Fairfax Ave Apt 109
West Hollywood, CA 90046-3939

Martin, Henry R (Cartoonist)
1382 Newtown Langhorne Rd # G206
Newtown, PA 18940-2418, USA

Martin, Ingle (Athlete, Football Player)
320 Red Feather Ln
Brentwood, TN 37027-4771, USA

Martin, James G (Ex-Governor, Politician)
McGuire Woods Consulting
PO Box 32861
Charlotte, NC 28232-2861, USA

Martin, J C (Athlete, Baseball Player)
112 Oakmont Ct
Advance, NC 27006-7097, USA

Martin, Jerry (Athlete, Baseball Player)
109 Chelton Ct
Columbia, SC 29212-8522, USA

Martin, Jesse L (Actor)
c/o Bob McGowan McGowan
Management
8733 W Sunset Blvd Ste 103
West Hollywood, CA 90069-2241, USA

Martin, Joe (Cartoonist)
Weederman Grafix
C/O Neatly Chiseled Features
1870 Loramoor Lane
Lake Geneva, WI 53147, USA

Martin, John (Athlete, Baseball Player)
2037 SW Stratford Way
Palm City, FL 34990-2033, USA

Martin, Judith (Miss Manners) (Journalist)
1651 Harvard St NW
Washington, DC 20009-3702, USA

Martin, Justin (Actor)
c/o Ellen Meyer Ellen Meyer Management
8899 Beverly Blvd Ste 612
Los Angeles, CA 90048-2429, USA

Martin, Kellie (Actor)
c/o William Mercer Thruline
Entertainment
9250 Wilshire Blvd Ste 100
Ground Floor
Beverly Hills, CA 90212-3343, USA

Martin, Kelvin (Athlete, Football Player)
44 Veranda Ln
Colleyville, TX 76034-2926, USA

Martin, Kenyon (Athlete, Basketball
Player)
924 Bentwater Pkwy
Cedar Hill, TX 75104-8269, USA

Martin, Keshawn (Athlete, Football Player)
c/o Bruce Tollner *REP 1 Sports Group*
2 Corporate Park Ste 106
Irvine, CA 92606-5103, USA

Martin, Kevin (Athlete, Basketball Player)
c/o Dan Fegan *Relativity Sports (LA)*
9242 Beverly Blvd Ste 300
Beverly Hills, CA 90210-3728, USA

Martin, Larue (Athlete, Basketball Player)
1236 Harvest Ln
University Park, IL 60484-3320, USA

Martin, Lynn M (Politician, Secretary)
171 Willabay Dr
Williams Bay, WI 53191-9673, USA

Martin, Madeleine (Actor)
c/o Jill Fritzo *PMK/BNC Public Relations (PMK-NY)*
622 3rd Ave Fl 8
New York, NY 10017-6707, USA

Martin, Maria (Actor)
c/o Staff Member *Select Artists Ltd (CA-Valley Office)*
PO Box 4359
Burbank, CA 91503-4359, USA

Martin, Mark (Athlete, Hockey Player)
5887 SE Riverboat Dr
Stuart, FL 34997-1511, USA

Martin, Mark (Race Car Driver)
c/o Staff Member *Hendrick Motorsports*
4400 Papa Joe Hendrick Blvd
Charlotte, NC 28262-5703, USA

Martin, Max (Producer)
882 N Doheny Dr
West Hollywood, CA 90069-4821, USA

Martin, Meaghan Jette (Actor)
c/o Myrna Lieberman *Myrna Lieberman Management*
3001 Hollyridge Dr
Los Angeles, CA 90068-1951, USA

Martin, Medeski (Musician)
c/o Staff Member *Paradigm (Monterey)*
404 W Franklin St
Monterey, CA 93940-2303, USA

Martin, Mike (Athlete, Baseball Player)
7904 Waterfalls Ave
Las Vegas, NV 89128-6709, USA

Martin, Norberto (Athlete, Baseball Player)
Helena Brewers
PO Box 6756
Attn: Coaching Staff
Helena, MT 59604-6756, USA

Martin, Ray (Athlete, Baseball Player)
22 Washington St Ste 5
Norwell, MA 02061-1732, USA

Martin, Renie (Athlete, Baseball Player)
509 Little Eagle Ct
Valrico, FL 33594-3973, USA

Martin, Ricky (Actor, Dancer, Musician)
170 E End Ave # 7AB
New York, NY 10128-7600, USA

Martin, Rod (Athlete, Football Player)
312 Highland Ave
Manhattan Bch, CA 90266-6437, USA

Martin, Roland (Correspondent)
c/o Tosha Whitten Griggs *FrontPage Firm, The*
6442 Coldwater Canyon Ave Ste 202
North Hollywood, CA 91606-1160, USA

Martin, Rudolf (Actor)
c/o Amanda Glazer *Kohner Agency, The*
9300 Wilshire Blvd Ste 555
Beverly Hills, CA 90212-3211, USA

Martin, Rudolph (Actor)
c/o Staff Member *Treusch/Erickson Associates*
8955 Norma Pl
West Hollywood, CA 90069-4818, USA

Martin, Sammy (Athlete, Football Player)
114 Summit Dr
Carriere, MS 39426-7665, USA

Martin, Sandy (Actor)
CNA Assoc
1875 Century Park E Ste 2250
Los Angeles, CA 90067-2563, USA

Martin, Sherrod (Athlete, Football Player)
c/o Hadley Engelhard *Enter-Sports Management*
5 Concourse Pkwy Ste 3000
Atlanta, GA 30328-7106, USA

Martin, Steve (Actor, Comedian, Producer, Writer)
c/o Allison Elbl *ID Public Relations (LA)*
7060 Hollywood Blvd Fl 8th
Los Angeles, CA 90028-6021, USA

Martin, Sylvia Wene (Bowler)
2701 Clark Towers Ct Apt 125
Las Vegas, NV 89102-5855, USA

Martin, Terry (Athlete, Hockey Player)
185 Hampton Hill Dr
Buffalo, NY 14221-5842, USA

Martin, Todd (Athlete, Olympic Athlete, Tennis Player)
156 Coach Lamp Way
Ponte Vedra Beach, FL 32082-1904, USA

Martin, Tom (Athlete, Baseball Player)
8001 Surf Dr
Panama City, FL 32408-8530, USA

Martin, Tony (Athlete, Football Player)
1198 B Green Rd
Boston, GA 31626-2010, USA

Martin, Wayne (Athlete, Football Player)
PO Box 4
Cherry Valley, AR 72324-0004, USA

Martin, Zack (Athlete, Football Player)
c/o Tom Condon *CAA (St. Louis)*
222 S Central Ave Ste 1008
Saint Louis, MO 63105-3509, USA

Martin Chase, Deborah (Debra) (Producer)
c/o Staff Member *William Morris Endeavor (LA)*
9601 Wilshire Blvd
Beverly Hills, CA 90210-5213, USA

Martindale, Margo (Actor)
c/o Andrew Freedman *Andrew Freedman Public Relations*
9127 Thrasher Ave
Los Angeles, CA 90069-1144, USA

Martindale, Wink (DJ, Television Host)
5744 Newcastle Ln
Calabasas, CA 91302-3117, USA

Martinek, Radek (Athlete, Hockey Player)
64 Hope Dr
Plainview, NY 11803-5650, USA

Martinez, A (Actor)
PO Box 6387
Malibu, CA 90264-6387, USA

Martinez, Alfredo (Athlete, Baseball Player)
2346 Thomas St
Los Angeles, CA 90031-2820, USA

Martinez, Anais (Musician)
Univision Music Group
5820 Canoga Ave Ste 300
Woodland Hills, CA 91367-6564, USA

Martinez, Angela (Television Host)
c/o Staff Member *Abrams Artists Agency (LA)*
9200 W Sunset Blvd PH 11
West Hollywood, CA 90069-3601, USA

Martinez, Angie (Musician)
395 Hudson St Fl 7
New York, NY 10014-7452, USA

Martinez, Benito (Actor)
c/o Ro Diamond *SDB Partners Inc*
315 S Beverly Dr Ste 411
Beverly Hills, CA 90212-4301, USA

Martinez, Billy Joe (Actor)
c/o Linda McAlister *Linda McAlister Talent*
100 Oak Ln
Waxahachie, TX 75167-8412, USA

Martinez, Buck (Athlete, Baseball Player, Coach)
10315 Long Beach Blvd
Long Beach Township, NJ 08008-3135, USA

Martinez, Carmelo (Athlete, Baseball Player)
32 Brisas Del Plata
Dorado, PR 00646-5118, USA

Martinez, Chito (Athlete, Baseball Player)
100 Legacy Barn
Dr Apt 101
Collierville, TN 38017, USA

Martinez, Constantino (Tino) (Athlete, Baseball Player)
324 Blanca Ave
Tampa, FL 33606-3630, USA

Martinez, Dave (Athlete, Baseball Player)
3315 Enterprise Rd E
Safety Harbor, FL 34695-5307, USA

Martinez, Edgar (Athlete, Baseball Player)
3036 249th Ave SE
Sammamish, WA 98075-9421, USA

Martinez, Fred (Baseball Player)
California Angels
2346 Thomas St
Los Angeles, CA 90031-2820, USA

Martinez, Greg (Athlete, Baseball Player)
1596 Palora Ave
Las Vegas, NV 89169-2504, USA

Martinez, J Dennis (Athlete, Baseball Player)
9400 SW 63rd Ct
Miami, FL 33156-1817, USA

Martinez, Jose (Athlete, Baseball Player)
14601 SW 33rd Ct
Miramar, FL 33027-3729, USA

Martinez, Jose Rene (J R) (Actor, Reality Star)
c/o Cynthia Snyder *Cynthia Snyder Public Relations*
5739 Colfax Ave
N Hollywood, CA 91601-1636, USA

Martinez, Mel (Politician)
140 W Fawsett Rd
Winter Park, FL 32789-6016, USA

Martinez, Natalie (Actor)
c/o Sean Fay *Kritzer Levine Wilkins Entertainment (KLWG)*
11872 La Grange Ave Fl 1
Los Angeles, CA 90025-5283, USA

Martinez, Olivier (Actor)
c/o David Unger *Resolution (LA)*
1801 Century Park E Ste 2300
Los Angeles, CA 90067-2325, USA

Martinez, Patrice (Actor)
c/o Staff Member *Select Artists Ltd (CA-Valley Office)*
PO Box 4359
Burbank, CA 91503-4359, USA

Martinez, Pedro (Athlete, Baseball Player)
3029 Birkdale
Weston, FL 33332-1813, USA

Martinez, Pedro A (Baseball Player)
186 Fairmount Ave
Hyde Park, MA 02136-3506, USA

Martinez, Robert (Bob) (Ex-Governor, Politician)
100 N Tampa St Ste 4100
Tampa, FL 33602-3642, USA

Martinez, Silvio (Athlete, Baseball Player)
4914 103rd St Fl 2
Corona, NY 11368-3121, USA

Martinez, Susana (Governor, Politician)
Office of the Governor
490 Old Santa Fe Trl Ste 400
Santa Fe, NM 87501-2704, USA

Martinez, Tino (Athlete, Baseball Player, Olympic Athlete)
324 Blanca Ave
Tampa, FL 33606-3630, USA

Martinez, Tippy (Athlete, Baseball Player)
1524 Dellsway Rd
Towson, MD 21286-5901, USA

martinez, Victor (Athlete, Baseball Player)
10157 Tavistock Rd
Orlando, FL 32827-7054, USA

Martini, Max (Actor, Director)
c/o Vera Mihailovich *Forward Entertainment*
9255 W Sunset Blvd Ste 805
West Hollywood, CA 90069-3305, USA

Martinkovic, John (Athlete, Football Player)
1001 Ernst Dr
Green Bay, WI 54304-2205, USA

Martins, Joao Carlos (Musician)
c/o Staff Member *Musicians Corporate Management*
PO Box 825
Highland, NY 12528-0825, USA

Martins, Steve (Athlete, Hockey Player)
22475 N Linden Dr
Lake Barrington, IL 60010-5956

Martinson, Leslie
2288 Coldwater Canyon Dr
Beverly Hills, CA 90210-1756

Martinson, Lestie H (Director)
2288 Coldwater Canyon Dr
Beverly Hills, CA 90210-1756, USA

Martinson, Steve (Athlete, Hockey Player)
1500 Autumnmist Dr
Allen, TX 75002-4969

Martlin, Marlee (Actor)
10340 Santa Monica Blvd
Los Angeles, CA 90025-6904, USA

Marton, Katalin (Kati) (Writer)
c/o Amanda Urban *ICM Partners (NY)*
730 5th Ave Ste 700
New York, NY 10019-4121, USA

Marts, Lonnie (Athlete, Football Player)
13459 Nottingham Knoll Ct
Jacksonville, FL 32225-4925, USA

Marty, Martin E (Religious Leader)
175 E Delaware Pl Apt 8508
Chicago, IL 60611-7750, USA

Marty, Mike (Coach, Football Coach)
Saint Louis Rams
901 N Broadway
Saint Louis, MO 63101-2800, USA

Martyn, Bob (Athlete, Baseball Player)
PO Box 778
Pacific City, OR 97135-0778, USA

Martz, Gary (Athlete, Baseball Player)
525 Sage Hills Dr
Wenatchee, WA 98801-2466, USA

Martz, Judy (Politician)
119092 Juniper Acres Rd
Butte, MT 59750-9705, USA

Martz, Mike (Athlete, Football Coach,
Football Player)
222 Republic Dr
Allen Park, MI 48101-3650, USA

Martz, Randy (Athlete, Baseball Player)
211 HI Pointe Pl
East Alton, IL 62024-1641, USA

Martzke, Rudy (Writer)
USA Today
1000 Wilson Blvd Ste 600
Editorial Dept
Arlington, VA 22209-3906, USA

Maruyama, Karen (Actor)
c/o Staff Member *Halpern Management*
PO Box 5042
Santa Monica, CA 90409-5042, USA

Maruyama, Shigeki (Athlete, Golfer)
15210 Antelo Pl
Los Angeles, CA 90077-1634, USA

Marvaso, Tommy (Athlete, Football
Player)
2 W Melrose St
Chevy Chase, MD 20815-4244, USA

Marve, Eugene (Athlete, Football Player)
4516 W Lamb Ave
Tampa, FL 33629-6530, USA

Marvel, Elizabeth (Actor)
c/o Robert Glennon *Authentic Talent and
Literary Management*
20 Jay St Ste M17
Brooklyn, NY 11201-8300, USA

Marvelettes, The (Music Group)
9936 Majorca Pl
Boca Raton, FL 33434-3714, USA

Marx, Gilda (Designer, Fashion Designer)
Gilda Marx Industries
11755 Exposition Blvd
Los Angeles, CA 90064-1338, USA

Marx, Greg (Athlete, Football Player)
18629 Jamestown Cir
Northville, MI 48168-1834, USA

Marx, Jeffrey A (Journalist)
Lexington Herald-Leader
Editorial Dept
Main & Midland
Lexington, KY 40507, USA

Marx, Richard (Musician, Songwriter)
700 Arbor Dr
Lake Bluff, IL 60044-1352, USA

Marx, Timothy (Producer)
c/o Staff Member *ICM Partners (LA)*
10250 Constellation Blvd Fl 7
Los Angeles, CA 90067-6207, USA

Maryland, Russell (Athlete, Football
Player)
1330 Eagle Bnd
Southlake, TX 76092-9406, USA

Mary Mary (Music Group)
c/o Richard De La Font *Richard De La
Font Agency*
3808 W South Park Blvd
Broken Arrow, OK 74011-1261, USA

Marzich, Andy (Bowler)
1421 Cravens Ave Apt 318
Torrance, CA 90501-2734, USA

Masak, Ron (Actor)
5350 Seabreeze Way
Oxnard, CA 93035-1048, USA

Masakayan, Liz (Athlete, Volleyball
Player)
2864 Palomino Cir
La Jolla, CA 92037-7066, USA

Masaoka, Onan (Athlete, Baseball Player)
1323 Auwae Rd
Hilo, HI 96720-6906, USA

Mascaras, Mil
200 W 16th St # 10
New York, NY 10011-6165

Mascolo, Joseph (Actor)
c/o Staff Member *Bold and The Beautiful,
The*
7800 Beverly Blvd # 3371
Los Angeles, CA 90036-2112

Mase (Musician)
c/o Staff Member *Bad Boy Worldwide
Entertainment*
1440 Broadway Fl 19
New York, NY 10018-2301, USA

Masekela, Hugh (Musician)
c/o Staff Member *Opus 3 Artists*
5670 Wilshire Blvd Ste 1790
Los Angeles, CA 90036-5627, USA

Masekela, Sal (Television Host)
c/o Staff Member *ROAR (LA)*
9701 Wilshire Blvd Fl 8
Beverly Hills, CA 90212-2008, USA

MaShay, Pepper (Actor, Musician)
c/o Staff Member *Diva Central Inc*
7510 W Sunset Blvd Ste 1445
Los Angeles, CA 90046-3408, USA

Mashburn, Jamal (Athlete, Basketball
Player)
5625 Pine Tree Dr
Miami Beach, FL 33140-2149, USA

Mashburn, Jesse (Athlete, Track Athlete)
8520 S Pennsylvania Ave
Oklahoma City, OK 73159-5226, USA

Mashore, Clyde (Athlete, Baseball Player)
590 Valmore Pl
Brentwood, CA 94513-6909, USA

Mashore, Damon (Athlete, Baseball
Player)
240 Eagle Glen Ln
Eagle, ID 83616-4938, USA

Masiello, Tony (Politician)
Mayor's Office
65 Niagara Sq Rm 201
City Hall
Buffalo, NY 14202-3392, USA

Maslany, Tatiana (Actor)
c/o Shelley Browning *Magnolia
Entertainment (LA)*
9595 Wilshire Blvd Ste 601
Beverly Hills, CA 90212-2506, USA

Maslow, James (Actor, Musician)
c/o Liza Anderson *Anderson Group Public
Relations*
8060 Melrose Ave Fl 4
Los Angeles, CA 90046-7038, USA

Maslowski, Matt (Athlete, Football Player)
22281 Destello
Mission Viejo, CA 92691-1525, USA

Mason, Anthony (Athlete, Basketball
Player)
9 Brownstone Way Apt 308
Englewood, NJ 07631-1216, USA

Mason, Bob (Athlete, Hockey Player)
Minnesota Wild
317 Washington St
Saint Paul, MN 55102-1667

Mason, Bob (Athlete, Hockey Player,
Olympic Athlete)
9549 Yukon Aves
Minneapolis, MN 55438, USA

Mason, Bobbie Ann (Writer)
PO Box 518
Lawrenceburg, KY 40342-0518, USA

Mason, Chris (Athlete, Hockey Player)
PO Box 12465
Saint Louis, MO 63132-0165, USA

Mason, Dave (Athlete, Football Player)
37 Jackson Ave
Winchester, VA 22601-4933, USA

Mason, Dave (Musician, Songwriter)
3130 E Ojai Ave
Ojai, CA 93023-9319, USA

Mason, Derrick (Athlete, Football Player)
8665 Ritchboro Rd
District Heights, MD 20747-2658, USA

Mason, Don (Athlete, Baseball Player)
8 Fawn Rd
South Yarmouth, MA 02664-1808, USA

Mason, Glen (Coach, Football Coach)
University of Minnesota
Athletic Dept
Minneapolis, MN 55455, USA

Mason, Hank (Athlete, Baseball Player)
5004 W Leyburn Ct Apt 102
Henrico, VA 23228-4852, USA

Mason, Jackie (Actor, Comedian)
World According to Me
146 W 57th St Apt 68D
New York, NY 10019-0079, USA

Mason, Jim (Athlete, Baseball Player)
11410 Queens Way
Theodore, AL 36582-8312, USA

Mason, Laurence (Actor)
c/o Mara Santino *Luber Roklin
Management*
5815 W Sunset Blvd Ste 206
Los Angeles, CA 90028-6481, USA

Mason, Lindsey (Athlete, Football Player)
3 Elwell Ct
Randallstown, MD 21133-4307, USA

Mason, Marilyn
27 Glen Oak Ct
Medford, OR 97504-7671

Mason, Marlyn (Actor, Musician)
27 Glen Oak Ct
Medford, OR 97504-7671, USA

Mason, Marsha (Actor)
c/o Alexa Pagonas *Michael Black
Management*
9701 Wilshire Blvd Fl 10
Beverly Hills, CA 90212-2010, USA

Mason, Marty (Athlete, Baseball Player)
8255 SE Angelina Ct
Hobe Sound, FL 33455-8948, USA

Mason, Mike (Athlete, Baseball Player)
2711 Piper Ridge Ln
Excelsior, MN 55331-7803, USA

Mason, Roger (Athlete, Baseball Player)
4587 Stover Rd
Bellaire, MI 49615-9046, USA

Mason, Ron (Coach)
Michigan State University
Athletic Dept
Detroit, MI 48224, USA

Mason, Stephen (Musician, Songwriter)
c/o Janet Weir *Red Light Management
(LA)*
8439 W Sunset Blvd Ste 2
West Hollywood, CA 90069-1925, USA

Mason, Sully
4043 Irving Pl
Culver City, CA 90232-2963

Mason, Tom (Actor)
870 Heights Pl
Oyster Bay, NY 11771-1122, USA

Mason, Tommy (Athlete, Football Player)
PO Box 8506
Newport Beach, CA 92658-8506, USA

Mason, Vince (Musician)
Famous Artists Agency
250 W 57th St
New York, NY 10107-0001, USA

Mason, Willy (Musician)
c/o Staff Member *Paradigm (Monterey)*
404 W Franklin St
Monterey, CA 93940-2303, USA

Mason, Zachary (Producer, Writer)
c/o Staff Member *Farrar, Straus and
Giroux*
18 W 18th St Fl 7
New York, NY 10011-4675, USA

Mason Dixon
PO Box 214
Flint, TX 75762-0214

Mass, Wayne (Athlete, Football Player)
71 Eagle View Dr
Durango, CO 81303-6686, USA

Massa, Gordon (Athlete, Baseball Player)
8255 Bonanza Ln
Cincinnati, OH 45255-2504, USA

Massaquoi, Jonathan (Athlete, Football
Player)
c/o Bus Cook *Bus Cook Sports, Inc*
1 Willow Bend Dr
Hattiesburg, MS 39402-8552, USA

Massaro, Ashley (Wrestler)
c/o Kerry Rodgerson *World Wrestling Entertainment (WWE)*
1241 E Main St
Titan Towers
Stamford, CT 06902-3520, USA

Masse, Bill (Baseball Player)
US Olympic Team
2501 Amherst Ct Apt 25A
Boynton Beach, FL 33436-9017, USA

Massen, Osa
10501 Wilshire Blvd Unit 704
Los Angeles, CA 90024-6321

Massenburg, Tony (Athlete, Basketball Player)
13265 Tony Ln
Stony Creek, VA 23882-3209, USA

Masset, Andrew
11635 Huston St
North Hollywood, CA 91601-4315

Masset, Nick (Athlete, Baseball Player)
14575 W Mountain View Blvd Unit 11107
Surprise, AZ 85374-8674, USA

Massey, Debbie (Athlete, Golfer)
PO Box 116
Cheboygan, MI 49721-0116, USA

Massey, Kent (Athlete, Olympic Athlete, Sailor)
4085 Foothill Rd
Carpinteria, CA 93013-3093, USA

Massey, Kyle (Actor)
Boy-O-Boy Entertainment
PO Box 6811
Riverdale, GA 30296, USA

Massey, Robert (Athlete, Football Player)
9617 Worley Dr
Charlotte, NC 28215-7529, USA

Massiah, Corinne (Actor)
c/o Judy Landis *Judy Landis Management*
Prefers to be contacted by telephone or email
Thousand Oaks, CA 91362, USA

Massie, Bobby (Athlete, Football Player)
c/o Neil Schwartz *Schwartz & Feinsod*
contact via telephone or email
White Plains, NY 10603

Massie, Giddeon (Athlete, Cycler, Olympic Athlete)
PO Box 31
Zionhill, PA 18981-0031, USA

Massie, Rick (Athlete, Football Player)
238 Doyle Ave
Paris, KY 40361-1223, USA

Massie, Robert K (Writer)
52 W Clinton Ave
Irvington, NY 10533-2130, USA

Massie, Toby (Race Car Driver)
Massie Flying Hillbilly Racing
3862 N 2450 East Rd
Le Roy, IL 61752-9498, USA

Massimino, Michael J (Astronaut)
15814 Elk Park Ln
Houston, TX 77062-4775, USA

Massimino, Rollie (Coach)
18578 Es Ferland Ct
Jupiter, FL 33469, USA

Massive Attack (Music Group)
c/o Steve Martin *Nasty Little Man*
110 Greene St Ste 605
New York, NY 10012-3838, USA

Massoglia, Chris (Actor)
c/o Sandra Chang *Anonymous Content (LA)*
3532 Hayden Ave
Culver City, CA 90232-2413, USA

Mast, Dick (Athlete, Golfer)
15831 Tower View Dr
Clermont, FL 34711-9381, USA

Mast, Rick (Race Car Driver)
4909 Stough Rd SW
Concord, NC 28027-8969, USA

Mastandrea, Katlin (Actor)
c/o DebraLynn Findon *Discover Inc Management*
11425 Moorpark St
North Hollywood, CA 91602-2009, USA

Masteller, Dan (Athlete, Baseball Player)
28 Palm Ct
Menlo Park, CA 94025-5755, USA

Masters, Ben (Actor)
c/o Staff Member *SMS Talent*
8383 Wilshire Blvd Ste 230
Beverly Hills, CA 90211-2436, USA

Masters, Billy (Athlete, Football Player)
501 SW Silverspur Cir
Lees Summit, MO 64081-2482, USA

Masters, Margie (Athlete, Golfer)
8440 E Hazeltine Ln
Tucson, AZ 85710-7161, USA

Masterson, Christopher (Chris) Kennedy (Actor)
c/o Staff Member *United Talent Agency (UTA-LA)*
9336 Civic Center Dr
Beverly Hills, CA 90210-3604, USA

Masterson, Connie (Athlete, Golfer)
4004 Island Bay Cir
Sanford, FL 32771-6344, USA

Masterson, Danny (Actor, Producer)
2151 Hollyridge Dr
Los Angeles, CA 90068-3514, USA

Masterson, Fay (Actor)
c/o Francis Okwu *Zero Gravity Management*
6363 Wilshire Blvd Ste 300
Los Angeles, CA 90048-5729, USA

Masterson, Justin (Athlete, Baseball Player)
4095 White Oak Dr
Beavercreek, OH 45432-1927, USA

Masterson, Lisa (Talk Show Host)
Masterson MD
1333 Ocean Ave Ste A
Santa Monica, CA 90401-1001, USA

Masterson, Mary Stuart (Actor)
c/o John Carrabino *John Carrabino Management*
5900 Wilshire Blvd Ste 406
Los Angeles, CA 90036-5015, USA

Masterson, Peter (Director, Producer, Writer)
1165 5th Ave # 15A
New York, NY 10029-6931, USA

Masterson, Sean (Actor, Writer)
c/o Melanie Truhett *Messina Baker Entertainment*
955 Carrillo Dr Ste 100
Los Angeles, CA 90048-5400, USA

Mastny, Tom (Athlete, Baseball Player)
302 Lochleven Ct
Grovetown, GA 30813-5830, USA

Mastodon (Music Group, Musician)
c/o Jon Goldwater *Pinnacle Entertainment*
30 Glenn St
White Plains, NY 10603-3254, USA

Maston, Le'shai (Athlete, Football Player)
7856 Overridge Dr
Dallas, TX 75232-4316, USA

Mastracchio, Richard A
1910 Hillside Oak Ln
Houston, TX 77062-3663, USA

Mastracchio, Richard A (Rick) (Astronaut)
1423 Roden Blvd
Sheppard Afb, TX 76311-1378, USA

Mastrangelo, Carlo (Musician)
Paramount Entertainment
PO Box 12
Far Hills, NJ 07931-0012, USA

Mastrantonio, Mary Elizabeth (Actor, Musician)
International Creative Mgmt
10250 Constellation Blvd Fl 1
Los Angeles, CA 90067-6241, USA

Mastrogiacomo, Gina (Actor)
Pakula/King
9229 W Sunset Blvd Ste 315
West Hollywood, CA 90069-3403, USA

Mastroianni, Darin (Athlete, Baseball Player)
4248 Yosemite Ave S
Minneapolis, MN 55416-3125, USA

Mastronardi, Alessandra (Actor)
c/o Staff Member *Creative Artists Agency (CAA-LA)*
2000 Avenue of the Stars Ste 100
Los Angeles, CA 90067-4705, USA

Mastrov, Mark (Sportscaster)
c/o Staff Member *William Morris Endeavor (LA)*
9601 Wilshire Blvd
Beverly Hills, CA 90210-5213, USA

Masur, Andy (Commentator)
1931 W Patterson Ave
Chicago, IL 60613-3523, USA

Masur, Richard (Actor)
10340 Santa Monica Blvd
Los Angeles, CA 90025-6904, USA

Matalin, Mary (Journalist, Talk Show Host, Writer)
Gaslight Inc
325 Fishers Rd
Maurertown, VA 22644-2760, USA

Matan, Bill (Athlete, Football Player)
1660 Peachtree St NW Apt 6109
Atlanta, GA 30309-2485, USA

Matarazzo, Heather (Actor)
c/o Kieran Maguire *The Arlook Group*
205 S Beverly Dr Ste 209
Beverly Hills, CA 90212-3899, USA

Matarazzo, Len (Athlete, Baseball Player)
2715 Carlisle St
New Castle, PA 16105-1714, USA

Matchbox 20 (Music Group)
c/o Michael Lippman *Lippman Entertainment*
23586 Calabasas Rd Ste 208
Calabasas, CA 91302-1361, USA

Matchett, Kari (Actor)
c/o Staff Member *Brillstein Entertainment Partners (LA)*
9150 Wilshire Blvd Ste 350
Beverly Hills, CA 90212-3453, USA

Matchick, Tom (Athlete, Baseball Player)
7700 Pilliod Rd
Holland, OH 43528-8077, USA

Matenopoulos, Debbie (Actor, Producer)
c/o Staff Member *Fifteen Minutes (LA)*
8436 W 3rd St Ste 650
Los Angeles, CA 90048-4131, USA

Matheny, Jim (Athlete, Football Player)
6850 N Pira Ave
Meridian, ID 83646-4953, USA

Matheny, Mike (Athlete, Baseball Player)
460 Old Wolfrum Rd
Weldon Spring, MO 63304-7804, USA

Mathers, Jerry (Actor)
23965 Via Aranda
Valencia, CA 91355-3112, USA

Mathers, Marshall (Eminem) (Musician)
5760 Winkler Mill Rd
Rochester Hills, MI 48306-2153, USA

Matherson, Tim (Actor, Director)
246 Miramar Ave
Santa Barbara, CA 93108-2628, USA

Matheson, Chris (Writer)
c/o Rima Greer *Above the Line Agency*
468 N Camden Dr Ste 200
Beverly Hills, CA 90210-4507, USA

Matheson, Jim (Congressman, Politician)
2434 Rayburn Hob
Washington, DC 20515-0305, USA

Matheson, Tim (Actor, Director)
c/o Michael Nilon *Kritzer Levine Wilkins Entertainment (KLWG)*
11872 La Grange Ave Fl 1
Los Angeles, CA 90025-5283, USA

Mathews, Byron (Baseball Player)
557 Golfwood Dr
Ballwin, MO 63021-6316, USA

Mathews, Carole (Actor)
39668 Old Spring Rd
Murrieta, CA 92563-5550, USA

Mathews, F David (Politician, Secretary)
200 Commons Rd
Dayton, OH 45459-2788, USA

Mathews, Greg (Athlete, Baseball Player)
25242 Via Lido
Cir Apt H
Laguna Niguel, CA 92677-7307, USA

Mathews, Harlan (Senator)
420 Hunt Club Rd
Nashville, TN 37221-4310, USA

Mathews, Nelson (Athlete, Baseball Player)
211 E Crestview Dr
Columbia, IL 62236-1203, USA

Mathews, Ray (Athlete, Football Player)
PO Box 108
Harrisville, PA 16038-0108, USA

Mathews, Rick (Athlete, Baseball Player)
2007 Golfview Cir
Centerville, IA 52544-8937, USA

Mathews, Ross (Comedian, Correspondent, Television Host)
c/o Staff Member *E! Entertainment Television (LA)*
5750 Wilshire Blvd Ste 500
Los Angeles, CA 90036-3635, USA

Mathews, T J (Athlete, Baseball Player)
211 E Crestview Dr
Columbia, IL 62236-1203, USA

Mathias, Buster Jr (Boxer)
4409 Carol Ave SW
Wyoming, MI 49519-4519, USA

Mathias, Carl (Athlete, Baseball Player)
567 Long Ln
Oley, PA 19547-9009, USA

Mathias, Ric (Athlete, Football Player)
13753 Cardinal Point Trl
Verona, WI 53593

Mathieson, Jim (Athlete, Hockey Player)
88 Shaws Mill Rd
Gorham, ME 04038-2231

Mathieson, John (Director)
c/o Spyros Skouras *The Skouras Agency*
1149 3rd St Ste 300
Santa Monica, CA 90403-7201, USA

Mathieu, Marquis (Athlete)
113 W Lake Shore Dr
Hallandale, FL 33009-6026

Mathieu, Philip (Musician)
Lindy S MArtin Mgmt
5 Loblolly Ct
Executive Suite
Pinehurst, NC 28374-9349, USA

Mathis, Alonzo (Gorilla Zoe) (Musician)
c/o Staff Member *Atlantic Records (NY)*
1290 Avenue of the Americas Fl 28
New York, NY 10104-0106, USA

Mathis, Bill (Athlete, Football Player)
43 W Paces Dr NW
Atlanta, GA 30327, USA

Mathis, Clint (Soccer Player)
c/o Lyle Yorks *James Grant Sports Ltd (USA)*
3233 M St NW
Washington, DC 20007-3556, USA

Mathis, Evan (Athlete, Football Player)
11938 N 113th Pl # Pi
Scottsdale, AZ 85259-3131, USA

Mathis, Jeff (Athlete, Baseball Player)
4420 Spring Valley Dr
Marianna, FL 32448-5414, USA

Mathis, Johnny (Musician)
1469 Stebbins Ter
Los Angeles, CA 90069-1340, USA

Mathis, Rashean (Athlete, Football Player)
26200 Marsh Landing Pkwy
Ponte Vedra Beach, FL 32082-1224, USA

Mathis, Robert (Athlete, Football Player)
c/o Hadley Engelhard *Enter-Sports Management*
5 Concourse Pkwy Ste 3000
Atlanta, GA 30328-7106, USA

Mathis, Ron (Athlete, Baseball Player)
1441 Wagner St
Houston, TX 77007-3721, USA

Mathis, Samantha (Actor)
c/o Courtney Kivowitz *The Schiff Company*
9220 W Sunset Blvd Ste 106
West Hollywood, CA 90069-3500, USA

Mathis, Terance (Athlete, Football Player)
3415 Camellia Ln
Suwanee, GA 30024-5348, USA

Mathis Jr, Buster
4409 Carol Ave SW
Wyoming, MI 49519-4519, USA

Mathison, Bruce (Athlete, Football Player)
1228 E Squawbush Pl
Phoenix, AZ 85048-4450, USA

Mathison, Cameron (Actor)
c/o Marcia Hurwitz *Innovative Artists (LA)*
1505 10th St
Santa Monica, CA 90401-2805, USA

Mathison, Camerson (Actor)
c/o Staff Member *Innovative Artists (LA)*
1505 10th St
Santa Monica, CA 90401-2805, USA

Mathison, Melissa (Writer)
655 Macculloch Dr
Los Angeles, CA 90049-2024, USA

Matias, John (Athlete, Baseball Player)
98-1616 Hoolauae St
Aiea, HI 96701-1801, USA

Matiko, Marie (Actor)
c/o Staff Member *Sovereign Talent Group*
8421 Wilshire Blvd Ste 200
Beverly Hills, CA 90211-3204, USA

Matisyahu (Musician)
c/o Carla Sacks *Sacks and Co*
423 W 14th St Ste 3F
New York, NY 10014-1028, USA

Matkevich, Mark (Actor)
c/o Staff Member *Glasser/Black Management*
283 Cedarhurst Ave
Cedarhurst, NY 11516-1671, USA

Matlack, Jon (Athlete, Baseball Player)
2495 Sawdust Rd
Aot 1101
Spring, TX 77380-3354, USA

Matlack-Sagrati, Ruth (Athlete, Baseball Player, Commentator)
1086 Bristol Pike Apt 312
Bensalem, PA 19020-5664, USA

Matlin, Marlee (Actor, Producer)
c/o Staff Member *Solo One Productions*
8149 Santa Monica Blvd Ste 279
West Hollywood, CA 90046-4912, USA

Matos, Francisco (Athlete, Baseball Player)
Arkansas Travelers
PO Box 55066
Coaching Staff
Little Rock, AR 72215-5066, USA

Matos, Julius (Athlete, Baseball Player)
8725 Braxton Dr
Hudson, FL 34667-6947, USA

Matranga, Dave (Athlete, Baseball Player)
303 N Park Ln
Orange, CA 92867-7640, USA

Matricaria, Ronald (Business Person)
Saint Jude Medical Inc
1 Lillehei Plz
Saint Paul, MN 55117-1799, USA

Matsik, George A (Business Person)
Ball Corp
10 Longs Peak Dr
Broomfield, CO 80021-2510, USA

Matson, April (Actor)
c/o Jennifer Millar *Paradigm (LA)*
9200 W Sunset Blvd PH 11
West Hollywood, CA 90069-3601, USA

Matson, J Randel (Randy) (Athlete, Track Athlete)
1002 Park Pl
College Station, TX 77840-3008, USA

Matson, Pat (Athlete, Football Player)
987 Village Circle Dr
Greenwood, IN 46143-8465, USA

Matson, Randy (Athlete, Olympic Athlete, Track Athlete)
1002 Park Pl
College Station, TX 77840-3008, USA

Matsos, Arch (Athlete, Football Player)
1410 Coventry Close St
East Lansing, MI 48823-2419, USA

Matsos, Archie (Athlete, Football Player)
1410 Coventry Close St
East Lansing, MI 48823-2419, USA

Matsuda, Naomi (Actor)
c/o Staff Member *AKA Talent Agency*
6310 San Vicente Blvd Ste 200
Los Angeles, CA 90048-5488, USA

Matsuda, Seiko (Actor, Musician)
Propaganda Films Mgmt
1741 Ivar Ave
Los Angeles, CA 90028-5105, USA

Matsui, Hideki (Athlete, Baseball Player)
119 W 72nd St # 306
New York, NY 10023-3201, USA

Matsui, Kaz (Athlete, Baseball Player)
229 N Almont Dr
Beverly Hills, CA 90211-1615, USA

Matsui, Keiko (Musician)
Ted Kurland
173 Brighton Ave
Allston, MA 02134-2003, USA

Matsukisa, Nobuyaki (Nobu) (Chef)
c/o Staff Member *Verve Entertainment*
5900 Wilshire Blvd Ste 1720
Los Angeles, CA 90036-5021, USA

Matsushita, Hiro (Race Car Driver)
1600 Avenida Salvador
San Clemente, CA 92672-3265, USA

Matsuzaka, Daisuke (Athlete, Baseball Player)
c/o Scott Boras *Boras Corporation*
3 San Joaquin Plz Ste 100
Newport Beach, CA 92660-5944, USA

Matt and Kim (Music Group)
c/o Staff Member *Right On PR*
4010 Cherrywood Rd
Austin, TX 78722-1222, USA

Matte, Thomas R (Tom) (Athlete, Football Player)
11309 Old Carriage Rd
Glen Arm, MD 21057-9422, USA

Mattea, Kathy (Actor, Musician)
866 Sage Dr
Pleasant Grove, UT 84062-2019, USA

Mattei, Frank (Musician)
Joe Taylor Mgmt
PO Box 1017
Blackwood, NJ 08012-0837, USA

Mattek-Sands, Bethanie (Athlete, Tennis Player)
c/o Staff Member *CMPR*
1600 Rosecrans Ave Bldg 3
Manhattan Beach, CA 90266-3708, USA

Mattes, Ron (Athlete, Football Player)
135 Thoroughbred Cir
Lexington, VA 24450-3675, USA

Mattes, Troy (Athlete, Baseball Player)
2932 Lexington St
Sarasota, FL 34231-6118, USA

Matteson, Troy (Athlete, Golfer)
6518 Old Shadburn Ferry Rd
Buford, GA 30518-1138, USA

Matteucci, Matt (Athlete, Hockey Player)
4282 W Timberwood Dr
Traverse City, MI 49686-3844

Matthews, Al (Athlete, Football Player)
19541 Diablo Dr
Pflugerville, TX 78660-5088, USA

Matthews, Aubrey (Athlete, Football Player)
15 Saint Charles Pl
Madison, MS 39110-9593, USA

Matthews, Bill (Athlete, Football Player)
32 Olde Farm Rd
South Easton, MA 02375-1438, USA

Matthews, Bo (Athlete, Football Player)
10053 Vine Ct
Thornton, CO 80229-2385, USA

Matthews, Bruce R (Athlete, Football Player)
1565 Lost Hollow Dr
Brentwood, TN 37027-8608, USA

Matthews, Chris (Television Host)
c/o Staff Member *MSNBC*
30 Rockefeller Plz Fl 31
New York, NY 10112-3199, USA

Matthews, Clay (Athlete, Football Player)
6068 Canterbury Dr
Agoura Hills, CA 91301-4131, USA

Matthews, Clay (Athlete, Football Player)
c/o David Dunn *Athletes First, LLC*
23091 Mill Creek Dr
Laguna Hills, CA 92653-1258, USA

Matthews, Dakin (Actor)
c/o Staff Member *McCabe Group, The*
3211 Cahuenga Blvd W Ste 104
Los Angeles, CA 90068-1372, USA

Matthews, Dave (Musician, Songwriter)
28929 Bison Ct
Malibu, CA 90265-4203, USA

Matthews, DeLane (Actor)
Don Buchwald
5500 Wilshire Blvd # 2200
Los Angeles, CA 90036-3802, USA

Matthews, Denny (Commentator)
11816 Norwood Dr
Leawood, KS 66211-3006, USA

Matthews, Gary N (Athlete, Baseball Player)
1542 W Jackson Blvd
Chicago, IL 60607-5304, USA

Matthews, Ian (Musician)
Geoffrey Blumenauer
11846 Balboa Blvd # 204
Granada Hills, CA 91344-2753, USA

Matthews, Kevin (Athlete, Football Player)
c/o David Dunn *Athletes First, LLC*
23091 Mill Creek Dr
Laguna Hills, CA 92653-1258, USA

Matthews, Liesel (Actor)
c/o Staff Member *Creative Artists Agency (CAA-LA)*
2000 Avenue of the Stars Ste 100
Los Angeles, CA 90067-4705, USA

Matthews, Mike (Athlete, Baseball Player)
3657 Winged Foot Cir
Green Cove Springs, FL 32043-8023, USA

Matthews, Pat Stanley (Actor)
210 Stanton St
Walla Walla, WA 99362-2058, USA

Matthews, Rishard (Athlete, Football Player)
c/o Kennard McGuire *MS World LLC*
1270 Crabb River Rd Ste 600-104
Richmond, TX 77469-5636, USA

Matthews, Shane (Athlete, Football Player)
848 NW 136th St
Newberry, FL 32669-3329, USA

Matthews, Steve (Athlete, Football Player)
1464 Yarnell Station Blvd
Knoxville, TN 37932-2676, USA

Matthews, Vincent (Vince) (Athlete, Track Athlete)
6755 193rd Ln
Fresh Meadows, NY 11365, USA

Matthews Jr, Gary (Athlete, Baseball Player)
1231 Dolphin Ter
Corona Del Mar, CA 92625-1726, USA

Matthies, Nina (Athlete, Coach, Volleyball Player)
Pepperdine University
24255 Pacific Coast Hwy
Athletic Dept
Malibu, CA 90263-3999, USA

Matthiesen, David H Dr (Astronaut)
3770 E Surrey Ct
Rocky River, OH 44116-4206, USA

Mattiace, Len (Athlete, Golfer)
12803 Hunt Club Rd N
Jacksonville, FL 32224, USA

Mattingly, Don (Athlete, Baseball Player)
8720 Whetstone Rd
Evansville, IN 47725-1444, USA

Mattingly, Mack F (Politician, Senator)
4315 10th St
East Beach
Saint Simons Island, GA 31522-3004, USA

Mattingly, Thomas K Radm (Astronaut)
1500 Quail St Spc 103
Newport Beach, CA 92660-2732, USA

Mattos, Grant (Athlete, Football Player)
1392 Miller Pl
Los Angeles, CA 90069-1423, USA

Mattson, Riley (Athlete, Football Player)
12 Coconut Grove Ln
Lahaina, HI 96761-8735, USA

Mattson, Robin (Actor)
Stan Kamens Mgmt
7772 Torreyson Dr
Los Angeles, CA 90046-1227, USA

Mattson-Baumgart, Jacqueline (Athlete, Baseball Player, Commentator)
4814 W Fillmore Dr
Milwaukee, WI 53219-2364, USA

Mattsson, Helena (Actor)
c/o Liza Anderson *Anderson Group Public Relations*
8060 Melrose Ave Fl 4
Los Angeles, CA 90046-7038, USA

Matula, Rick (Athlete, Baseball Player)
1817 Chapel Heights Dr
Wharton, TX 77488-4459, USA

Matusz, Brian (Athlete, Baseball Player)
4654 E Quien Sabe Way
Cave Creek, AZ 85331-2149, USA

Matuszek, Len (Athlete, Baseball Player)
10326 Deerfield Rd
Cincinnati, OH 45242-5105, USA

Matvichuk, Richard (Athlete, Hockey Player)
8 Chapel Hill Ct
Cedar Grove, NJ 07009-1302, USA

Matzdorf, Pat (Athlete, Track Athlete)
1252 Bainbridge Dr
Naperville, IL 60563-2065, USA

Mauch, Billy & Bobby
538 W Northwest Hwy Unit C
Palatine, IL 60067-8695

Mauch, Billy (Bill) (Actor)
538 W Northwest Hwy Unit C
Palatine, IL 60067-8695

Mauck, Carl (Athlete, Football Player)
2129 Winthrop Hill Rd
Argyle, TX 76226-2103, USA

Mauck, Matt (Athlete, Football Player)
3 Coral Pl
Greenwood Village, CO 80111-3457, USA

Mauer, Joe (Athlete, Baseball Player)
671 Lexington Pkwy N
Saint Paul, MN 55104-2025, USA

Maugham, R H (Religious Leader)
Christian & Missionary Alliance
PO Box 35000
Colorado Springs, CO 80935-3500, USA

Maulden, Jerry L (Business Person)
Entergy Corp
10055 Grogans Mill Rd Ste 150
Spring, TX 77380-1048, USA

Mauldin, Greg (Athlete, Hockey Player)
58 Balancing Rock Dr
Holliston, MA 01746-3416

Mauldin, William H (Cartoonist)
Loomis-Watkins Agency
150 E 35th St
New York, NY 10016-4102

Maule, Brad (Actor)
c/o Hank Hedland *Opus Entertainment*
5225 Wilshire Blvd Ste 905
Los Angeles, CA 90036-4353, USA

Maurer, Andy (Athlete, Football Player)
30 Perrydale Ave
Medford, OR 97501-2037, USA

Maurer, Dave (Athlete, Baseball Player)
6845 Lake Harrison Cir
Chanhassen, MN 55317-4589, USA

Maurer, Rob (Athlete, Baseball Player)
3114 E Gum St
Evansville, IN 47714-2614, USA

Maurice, Paul (Athlete, Hockey Player)
Carolina Hurricanes
1400 Edwards Mill Rd
Raleigh, NC 27607-3624

Maurice, Paul (Athlete, Hockey Player)
3032 Cone Manor Ln
Raleigh, NC 27613-6604

Mauriello, Julianna Rose (Actor)
c/o Nancy Carson *Carson-Adler Agency*
250 W 57th St Ste 2128
New York, NY 10107-2104, USA

Mauriello, Ralph (Athlete, Baseball Player)
4241 Persimmon St
Moorpark, CA 93021-3515, USA

Maurier, Claire
Il rue de la Montague-le-Breuil
Thousand Oaks, CA 91360

Maurin, Laurence (Skier)
PO Box 1980
West Bend, WI 53095-7980, USA

Maury, Duncan (Athlete, Football Player)
1554 Fallbrook Ave
Clovis, CA 93611-7348, USA

Mauser, Tim (Athlete, Baseball Player)
114 Shadow Creek Ln
Aledo, TX 76008-3111, USA

Mauti, Michael (Athlete, Football Player)
c/o Michael McCartney *Priority Sports & Entertainment - Chicago*
312 N La Salle
Suite 650
Chicago, IL 60610, USA

Mauti, Rich (Athlete, Football Player)
304 Plantation Dr
Mandeville, LA 70471-1502, USA

Maven, Max
PO Box 1298
La Mesa, CA 91944-1298

Mawae, Kevin J (Athlete, Football Player)
19414 Old Perkins Rd E
Baton Rouge, LA 70810-6030, USA

Maxa, Rudy (Radio Personality, Television Host)
SavTrav Productions, Inc.
400 Spring St Apt 240
Saint Paul, MN 55102-4448, USA

Maxcy, Brian (Athlete, Baseball Player)
982 Cobble Creek Dr
Hoover, AL 35226-2867, USA

Maxey, Caty (Designer)
c/o Staff Member *Mirisch Agency*
8840 Wilshire Blvd Ste 100
Beverly Hills, CA 90211-2606, USA

Maxey, Marlon (Athlete, Basketball Player)
9013 S Blackstone Ave
Chicago, IL 60619-7909, USA

Maxey, Virginia
16414 Pick Pl
Riverside, CA 92504-5645

Maxie, Brett (Athlete, Football Player)
131 Guineveres Retreat
Franklin, TN 37067-6486, USA

Maxie, Larry (Athlete, Baseball Player)
296 Verdugo Way
Upland, CA 91786-7138, USA

Maxson, Alvin (Athlete, Football Player)
17377 E Adriatic Pl Apt S302
Aurora, CO 80013-5130, USA

Maxvill, Dal (Athlete, Baseball Player, Commentator)
1115 Eagle Creek Rd
Chesterfield, MO 63005-6606, USA

Maxwell, Brad (Athlete, Hockey Player)
27285 Natchez Ave
Elko New Market, MN 55020-9563, USA

Maxwell, Cedric (Athlete, Basketball Player)
151 Tremont St Apt 25R
Apt 25R
Boston, MA 02111-1123, USA

Maxwell, Charlie (Athlete, Baseball Player)
730 Mapleview Dr
Paw Paw, MI 49079-1185, USA

Maxwell, Dobie (Comedian)
333 W North Ave # 343
Chicago, IL 60610-1293, USA

Maxwell, Frank (Politician)
Federation of TV-Radio Artists
260 Madison Ave
New York, NY 10016-2401, USA

Maxwell, Jacqui (Actor)
c/o Karen Goldberg *Inphenate*
9701 Wilshire Blvd Fl 10
Beverly Hills, CA 90212-2010, USA

Maxwell, Jason (Athlete, Baseball Player)
406 Hicks Rd
Nashville, TN 37221-2002, USA

Maxwell, John (Business Person, Writer)
The John Maxwell Company
2170 Satellite Blvd Ste 195
Duluth, GA 30097-4971, USA

Maxwell, Kevin (Athlete, Hockey Player)
16 Morton Ln
West Hartford, CT 06117-1427

Maxwell, Monica (Athlete, Basketball Player)
1108 Quaise Moor W
Antioch, TN 37013-4943, USA

Maxwell, Ronald F (Director, Writer)
c/o Staff Member *Phoenix Organization, The*
1990 S Bundy Dr Ste 630
Los Angeles, CA 90025-6140, USA

Maxwell, Tommy (Athlete, Football Player)
1634 Rockview Dr
Granbury, TX 76049-5733, USA

Maxwell, Vernon (Athlete, Basketball Player)
2601 NW 23rd Blvd Apt 170
Gainesville, FL 32605-5954, USA

Maxwell, Vernon (Athlete, Football Player)
1955 E Citation Ln
Tempe, AZ 85284-4708, USA

May, Alan (Athlete, Hockey Player)
c/o Staff Member *Boston Bruins*
100 Legends Way Ste 250
Td Banknorth Garden
Boston, MA 02114-1389, USA

May, Alan (Athlete, Hockey Player)
Washington Capitals
627 N Glebe Rd Ste 850
Arlington, VA 22203-2144

May, Bob (Athlete, Golfer)
420 Grand Augusta Ln
Las Vegas, NV 89144-4300, USA

May, Brad (Athlete, Hockey Player)
9167 E Mountain Spring Rd
Scottsdale, AZ 85255-9151

May, Carlos (Athlete, Baseball Player)
6102 Amherst Pl
Matteson, IL 60443-1988, USA

May, Chad (Athlete, Football Player)
1300 S Jesse St
Chandler, AZ 85286-1142, USA

May, Darrell (Athlete, Baseball Player)
3315 Windsor Rd
Austin, TX 78703-2263, USA

May, David (Actor)
c/o Staff Member *Cunningham Escott
Slevin & Doherty (CESD-LA)*
10635 Santa Monica Blvd Ste 130
Los Angeles, CA 90025-8306, USA

May, Dean (Athlete, Football Player)
5337 Pine Bark Ln
Wesley Chapel, FL 33543-4456, USA

May, Deborah (Actor)
Artists Agency
1180 S Beverly Dr Ste 301
Los Angeles, CA 90035-1154, USA

May, Deems (Athlete, Football Player)
3922 Ayscough Rd
Charlotte, NC 28211-3470, USA

May, Derrick (Athlete, Baseball Player)
2 Jaymar Blvd
Newark, DE 19702-2877, USA

May, Don (Athlete, Basketball Player)
PO Box 331
Lake Ariel, PA 18436-0331, USA

May, Don (Athlete, Basketball Player)
1128 Colwick Dr
Dayton, OH 45420-2206, USA

May, Donald
733 Seward St
Los Angeles, CA 90038-3503

May, Elaine (Actor, Director, Writer)
c/o Staff Member *William Morris
Endeavor (LA)*
9601 Wilshire Blvd
Beverly Hills, CA 90210-5213, USA

May, Lee (Athlete, Baseball Player)
5533 Hill and Dale Dr
Cincinnati, OH 45213-2615, USA

May, Mark E (Football Player,
Sportscaster)
c/o Staff Member *ESPN (Main)*
935 Middle St
Espn Plaza
Bristol, CT 06010-1000, USA

May, Milt (Athlete, Baseball Player)
2200 Manatee Ave W
Bradenton, FL 34205-5430, USA

May, Ray (Athlete, Football Player)
1921 Wellington Rd
Los Angeles, CA 90016-1822, USA

May, Robert (Producer)
c/o Staff Member *SenArt Films*
555 W 25th St Fl 4
New York, NY 10001-5542, USA

May, Rudy (Athlete, Baseball Player)
PO Box 84
Friant, CA 93626-0084, USA

may, Scott (Athlete, Baseball Player)
4904 Boynton Ct
Tampa, FL 33625-6622, USA

May, Scott (Athlete, Basketball Player,
Olympic Athlete)
2001 E Hillside Dr
Bloomington, IN 47401-6203, USA

May, Suzanne (Actor)
c/o Staff Member *Frontline Management*
5670 Wilshire Blvd Ste 1370
Los Angeles, CA 90036-5679, USA

Mayasich, John (Athlete, Hockey Player)
801 McKinley Ave Apt 108
Eveleth, MN 55734-1476

Maybank, Anthuan (Athlete, Olympic
Athlete, Track Athlete)
171 N Porter St
Elgin, IL 60120-4476, USA

Mayberry, Doug (Athlete, Football Player)
PO Box 1390
Williams, CA 95987-1390, USA

Mayberry, Jermane (Athlete, Football
Player)
201 Town Center Ln Apt 1402
Keller, TX 76248-2162, USA

Mayberry, John C (Athlete, Baseball
Player)
11115 W 121st Ter
Overland Park, KS 66213-1945, USA

Mayberry, Lee (Athlete, Basketball Player)
4115 E 36th St N
Tulsa, OK 74115-1709, USA

Mayberry, Tony (Athlete, Football Player)
15704 Cochester Rd
Tampa, FL 33647-1100, USA

Mayberry, Jr., John (Athlete, Baseball
Player)
11115 W 121st Ter
Overland Park, KS 66213-1945, USA

Maybin, Cameron (Athlete, Baseball
Player)
85 Brompton Rd
Arden, NC 28704-8607, USA

Maybury, John (Director)
c/o Staff Member *William Morris
Endeavor (LA)*
9601 Wilshire Blvd
Beverly Hills, CA 90210-5213, USA

Maydan, Dan (Business Person)
Applied Materials
3050 Bowers Ave
Santa Clara, CA 95054-3298, USA

Mayer, Ed (Athlete, Baseball Player)
440 Oakland Ave
Corte Madera, CA 94925, USA

Mayer, Gene (Tennis Player)
115 South St
Glenn Dale, MD 20769, USA

Mayer, Gil (Athlete, Hockey Player)
85 Woodland St
Lincoln, RI 02865-2804

Mayer, John (Musician, Songwriter)
162 Pine Creek Rd
Livingston, MT 59047-9119, USA

Mayer, Marissa (Business Person)
Yahoo! Inc.
701 First Ave
Sunnyvale, CA 94089-1019, USA

Mayer, Pat
6417 Livernois Rd
Troy, MI 48098-1542

Mayer, Phil
Rt. 9 Box 715-M
Yakima, WA 98901

Mayer, Shawn (Athlete, Football Player)
378 Zion Rd
Hillsborough, NJ 08844-2512, USA

Mayer, Travis (Skier)
37050 Williams St
Steamboat Springs, CO 80487, USA

Mayers, Jamal (Athlete, Hockey Player)
9800 Countryshire Pl
Saint Louis, MO 63141-7914, USA

Mayes, Alonzo (Athlete, Football Player)
3000 SE 56th St
Oklahoma City, OK 73135-1620, USA

Mayes, clyde
502 Dove Tree Rd
Greenville, SC 29615-4434, USA

Mayes, David (Athlete, Football Player)
3018 Kingsley Rd
Shaker Heights, OH 44122-2816, USA

Mayes, Derrick (Athlete, Football Player)
3335 N Keystone Ave
Indianapolis, IN 46218-2075, USA

Mayes, Rob (Actor)
c/o Christina Gualazzi *Silver Lining
Entertainment*
8383 Wilshire Blvd Ste 1050
Beverly Hills, CA 90211-2415, USA

Mayes, Rueben (Athlete, Football Player)
610 SE Edge Knoll Dr
Pullman, WA 99163-2447, USA

Mayes, Tharon
29 Winnett St
Hamden, CT 06517-2720, USA

Mayes, Wendell
1504 Bel Air Rd
Los Angeles, CA 90077-3022

Mayfair, Billy (Athlete, Golfer)
PO Box 25490
Scottsdale, AZ 85255-0108, USA

Mayfield, Corey (Athlete, Football Player)
3412 Lark Meadow Way
Dallas, TX 75287-6007, USA

Mayfield, Jeremy (Race Car Driver)
Jeremy Mayfield Fan Club
PO Box 3998
Mooresville, NC 28117-3998, USA

Mayhew, Lauren (Actor)
c/o David Eisenberg *Protege
Entertainment*
710 E Angeleno Ave
Burbank, CA 91501-2213, USA

Mayhew, Martin (Athlete, Football Player)
4035 Sonnet Dr
Tallahassee, FL 32303-2225, USA

Maynard, Aaron (Race Car Driver)
33 Lake Rd
Milton, VT 05468-3513

Maynard, Andrew (Boxer)
Mike Trainer
3922 Fairmont Ave
Bethesda, MD 20814, USA

Maynard, Brad (Athlete, Football Player)
284 Milford Cir
Mooresville, NC 28117-7001, USA

Maynard, Emily (Reality Star)
3025 Greystone Dr
Morgantown, WV 26508-8600, USA

Maynard, Emily (Reality Star)
c/o Liza Anderson *Anderson Group Public
Relations*
8060 Melrose Ave Fl 4
Los Angeles, CA 90046-7038, USA

Maynard, Mimi (Actor)
Badgley Connor Talent
9229 W Sunset Blvd Ste 311
West Hollywood, CA 90069-3403, USA

Maynard, Mujaahid (Athlete, Olympic
Athlete, Wrestler)
23372 E Chenango Pl
Aurora, CO 80016-5394, USA

Mayne, Brent (Athlete, Baseball Player)
1863 Parkglen Cir
Costa Mesa, CA 92627-4506, USA

Mayne, Kenny (Sportscaster)
ESPN-TV
935 Middle St
Sports Dept Espn Plaza
Bristol, CT 06010-1000, USA

Mayne, Lew (Athlete, Football Player)
403 Freeman Ave
Daingerfield, TX 75638-2410, USA

Mayne, Roy (Race Car Driver)
24 Reynolds Rd
Sumter, SC 29150-3221, USA

Maynor, Asa
PO Box 1641
Beverly Hills, CA 90213-1641

Maynor, Stephanie (Athlete, Golfer)
6213 Three Apple Downs
Columbia, MD 21045-7419, USA

mayo, 0 J
3576 Golf Walk Cir
Memphis, TN 38125-8908, USA

Mayo, Jackie (Athlete, Baseball Player)
94 7 Auiwsta Dr
Youngstown, OH 44512, USA

Mayo, Itzhak Ltcolonel
2101 Nasa Pkwy Spc Centerbldg
Houston, TX 77058-3607, USA

Mayo, Ron (Athlete, Football Player)
3995 Warner Ave Apt D2
Hyattsville, MD 20784-2054, USA

Mayock, Michael (Athlete, Football
Player)
607 Georges Ln
Ardmore, PA 19003-1905, USA

Mayock, Mike (Athlete, Football Player)
607 Georges Ln
Ardmore, PA 19003-1905, USA

Mayotte, Tim (Athlete, Olympic Athlete,
Tennis Player)
2430 Beacon St Unit 201
Chestnut Hill, MA 02467-1466, USA

Mayotte, Timothy S (Tim) (Tennis Player)
SFX Sports Group
2665 S Bayshore Dr # 602
Miami, FL 33133-5448, USA

Mayron, Melanie (Actor, Director)
1435 N Ogden Dr
Los Angeles, CA 90046-3906, USA

Mays, Alvoid (Athlete, Football Player)
3903 Cape Vista Dr
Bradenton, FL 34209-6725, USA

Mays, Damon (Athlete, Football Player)
12705 N 57th Dr
Glendale, AZ 85304-1884, USA

Mays, David (Business Person)
2690 Cobb Pkwy SE Ste A5-304
Smyrna, GA 30080-3001, USA

Mays, Jayma (Actor)
2317 Richland Ave
Los Angeles, CA 90027-1343, USA

Mays, Jeryn (Actor)
28318 Birdie St
Moreno Valley, CA 92555-6358, USA

Mays, Joe (Athlete, Baseball Player)
7620 205th St E
Bradenton, FL 34202-8304, USA

Mays, Lyle (Musician)
Ted Kurland
173 Brighton Ave
Allston, MA 02134-2003, USA

Mays, Melinda (Race Car Driver)
2221 Peachtree Rd NE # D-440
Atlanta, GA 30309-1148, USA

Mays, Rueben
7306 172nd St SW
Edmonds, WA 98026-5121

Mays, Stafford (Athlete, Football Player)
2235 W Viewmont Way W
Seattle, WA 98199-3951, USA

Mays, Taylor (Athlete, Football Player)
c/o David Dunn *Athletes First, LLC*
23091 Mill Creek Dr
Laguna Hills, CA 92653-1258, USA

Mays, Willie (Athlete, Baseball Player)
Say Hey Foundation
PO Box 2410
Menlo Park, CA 94026-2410, USA

Maysey, Matt (Athlete, Baseball Player)
10190 Katy Fwy Ste 350
Houston, TX 77043-5239, USA

May-Treanor, Misty (Athlete, Olympic Athlete, Volleyball Player)
1440 Coral Ridge Dr
Coral Springs, FL 33071-5433, USA

Mayweather Jr, Floyd (Athlete, Boxer)
4720 Laguna Vista St
Las Vegas, NV 89147-6043, USA

Mazar, Debi (Actor)
c/o Peg Donegan *Framework Entertainment (LA)*
9057 Nemo St Ste C
West Hollywood, CA 90069-5511, USA

Mazarella, Jacqueline (Actor)
c/o Tony Martinez *Kazarian, Measures, Ruskin & Associates (LA)*
8981 W Sunset Blvd Ste 101
West Hollywood, CA 90069-1850, USA

Mazaroski, William S (Bill) (Baseball Player)
RR 6 Box 130
Greensburg, PA 15601, USA

Maze, Krista (Race Car Driver)
PO Box 7791
Huntington Beach, CA 92615-7791, USA

Mazeroski, Bill (Athlete, Baseball Player)
281 Walton Tea Room Rd
Greensburg, PA 15601-6406, USA

Mazur, Jay (Athlete, Hockey Player)
148 Elderberry Dr
South Portland, ME 04106-6890

Mazur, John (Athlete, Football Coach, Football Player)
672 Cornwallis Dr
Mount Laurel, NJ 08054-3217, USA

Mazur, Monet (Actor)
c/o Marsha McManus *Principal Entertainment (LA)*
9255 W Sunset Blvd Ste 500
West Hollywood, CA 90069-3301, USA

Mazurek, Fred (Athlete, Football Player)
2019 E Catamaran Dr
Gilbert, AZ 85234-2821, USA

Mazzanti, Geno (Athlete, Football Player)
1644 S Colorado St Apt 204
Greenville, MS 38703-7261, USA

Mazzanti, Jerry (Athlete, Football Player)
1712 S Lakeshore Dr
Lake Village, AR 71653-1573, USA

Mazzara, Glen (Producer)
c/o Staff Member *Creative Artists Agency (CAA-LA)*
2000 Avenue of the Stars Ste 100
Los Angeles, CA 90067-4705, USA

Mazzaro, Vin (Athlete, Baseball Player)
133 Brigantine Blvd
Waretown, NJ 08758-2675, USA

Mazzello, Joseph (Actor)
46691 Mission Blvd # 536
Fremont, CA 94539-7994

Mazzetti, Tim (Athlete, Football Player)
2 N La Salle St Ste 800
Chicago, IL 60602-3785, USA

Mazzie, Marin (Actor, Musician)
J Michael Bloom
233 Park Ave S # 1000
New York, NY 10003-1606, USA

Mazzilli, Lee L (Athlete, Baseball Player, Coach)
67 Stonehedge Dr S
Greenwich, CT 06831-3220, USA

Mazzone, Leo (Athlete, Baseball Player)
4518 Mystique Wayne
Roswell, GA 30075, USA

Mbatha-Raw, Gugu (Actor)
c/o Meg Mortimer *Principal Entertainment (NY)*
1133 Avenue Of The Americas Ste 1621
New York, NY 10036-6710, USA

Mbenga, D J (Athlete, Basketball Player)
6112 Winton St
Dallas, TX 75214-2636, USA

M. Bilirakis, Gus (Congressman, Politician)
407 Cannon Hob
Washington, DC 20515-3901, USA

McAdam, Gary
34 Meadow Ln
Portland, ME 04103-3727

McAdams, Bob (Athlete, Football Player)
271 S French Broad Ave
Asheville, NC 28801-3956, USA

McAdams, Carl (Athlete, Football Player)
206 E Main St
Antlers, OK 74523-3256, USA

McAdams, Carl (Athlete, Football Player)
HC 82 Box 526
Atoka, OK 74525, USA

McAddley, Jason (Athlete, Football Player)
3600 S Tower Ave
Chandler, AZ 85286-2692, USA

McAdoo, Bob (Athlete, Basketball Player, Coach)
17843 Lake Azure Way
Boca Raton, FL 33496-1047, USA

McAfee, John (Business Person)
McAfee Inc
2821 Mission College Blvd
Santa Clara, CA 95054-1838, USA

McAfee, Ken
8 Deerfield Dr
Medfield, MA 02052-1318

McAfee, Pat (Athlete, Football Player)
c/o Roosevelt Barnes *Maximum Sports Management*
6435 W Jefferson Blvd # 197
Fort Wayne, IN 46804-6203, USA

McAillister-Morton, Susie (Athlete, Golfer)
40241 Club View Dr
Rancho Mirage, CA 92270-3527, USA

McAleese, Peter (Producer)
c/o Lisa Helsing *Lenhoff Lenhoff & Lenhoff*
830 Palm Ave
West Hollywood, CA 90069-4009

McAleney, Ed (Athlete, Football Player)
PO Box 2415
S Portland, ME 04116-2415, USA

McAlister, Chris (Athlete, Football Player)
8206 Pumpkin Hill Ct
Pikesville, MD 21208-1872, USA

McAlister, James E (Athlete, Football Player, Track Athlete)
155 Glorieta St
Pasadena, CA 91103-3018, USA

McAllister, Chris (Athlete, Hockey Player)
162 Eastlawn St
Fairfield, CT 06824-6480

McAllister, Deuce (Athlete, Football Player)
c/o Staff Member *Philadelphia Eagles*
1 Novacare Way
Philadelphia, PA 19145-5996, USA

McAlpine, Chris (Athlete, Hockey Player)
4390 Reiland Ln
Saint Paul, MN 55126-3131

McAlpine, Donald M (Cinematographer)
377 Placer Creek Ln
Henderson, NV 89014-4560, USA

McAnally, Ernie (Athlete, Baseball Player)
PO Box 492
Mt Pleasant, TX 75456-0492, USA

McAnally, Mac (Musician, Songwriter)
c/o Staff Member *Paradigm (Monterey)*
404 W Franklin St
Monterey, CA 93940-2303, USA

McAnally, Ron (Race Car Driver)
Motorsports HOF
191 Union Ave
Saratoga Springs, NY 12866-3513, USA

McAnany, Jim (Athlete, Baseball Player)
1723 Cochran St Apt G
Simi Valley, CA 93065-2174, USA

McAndrew, James (Race Car Driver)
Team Matthew Inc
PO Box 743
Duncan, SC 29334-0743, USA

McAndrew, Jamie (Athlete, Baseball Player)
9620 E Diamond Rim Dr
Scottsdale, AZ 85255-3330, USA

McAndrew, Jim (Athlete, Baseball Player)
16540 E El Lago Blvd Unit 41
Fountain Hills, AZ 85268-4732, USA

McAneeley, Ted (Athlete, Hockey Player)
234 Aikane St
Kailua, HI 96734-1603, USA

McAnulty, Paul (Athlete, Baseball Player)
921 Palomar Way
Oxnard, CA 93033-5111, USA

McArdle, Andrea (Actor, Musician)
Edd Kalehoff
301 W 45th St Apt 4D
New York, NY 10036-3825, USA

McArdle, John (Athlete, Baseball Player)
6640 Lynford St
Philadelphia, PA 19149-2124, USA

McArthur, Alex (Actor)
9443 Hillrose St
Sunland, CA 91040-1716, USA

McArthur, Kevin (Athlete, Football Player)
3817 Meredith Ln
Balch Springs, TX 75180-5017, USA

McArthur, K Megan (Astronaut)
103 Harborcrest Dr
Seabrook, TX 77586-4601, USA

McArthur, William S (Bill) Jr (Astronaut)
14503 Sycamore Lake Rd
Houston, TX 77062-2245, USA

McArthur, William S Colonel (Astronaut)
NASA Johnson Space Center 2101 Nasa Pkwy Atn Safety and Mission Assurance
Houston, TX 77058, USA

McAtee, Jud (Athlete, Hockey Player)
54 Bada10NA Dr
Hot Springs Village, AR 71909, USA

McAuley, Alphonso (Actor)
c/o David (Dave) Fleming *Mosaic Media Group*
9200 W Sunset Blvd Ste 10
West Hollywood, CA 90069-3608, USA

McAuley, Jordan (Business Person, Writer)
Contact Any Celebrity
8721 Santa Monica Blvd
W Hollywood, CA 90069-4507, USA

McAuliffe, Callan (Actor)
c/o Nicholas Bogner *Affirmative Entertainment*
425 N Robertson Blvd
West Hollywood, CA 90048-1735, USA

McAuliffe, Dick (Athlete, Baseball Player)
32 Worthington Dr
Farmington, CT 06032-1493, USA

McAvoy, James (Actor)
c/o Meredith O'Sullivan *42West (LA)*
1840 Century Park E Ste 700
Los Angeles, CA 90067-2122, USA

McBain, Diane (Actor)
20185 Canyon View Dr # 1
Canyon Country, CA 91351-5734, USA

McBain, Jason (Athlete, Hockey Player)
17558 SW 104th Ave
Tualatin, OR 97062-8605

McBath, Mike (Athlete, Football Player)
5044 Sailwind Cir
Orlando, FL 32810-1839, USA

McBean, Al (Athlete, Baseball Player)
PO Box 4475
St Thomas, VI 00801, USA

McBee, Rives (Athlete, Golfer)
1504 Canyon Oaks Dr
Irving, TX 75061-2116, USA

McBeth, Marcus (Athlete, Baseball Player)
583 W Thompson Pl
Chandler, AZ 85286-7049, USA

McBratney, Sam (Writer)
c/o Staff Member *HarperCollins Publishers*
195 Broadway Fl 2
Cellar 1
New York, NY 10007-3132, USA

McBrayer, Jack
c/o Jo Yao *United Talent Agency*
(UTA-LA)
9336 Civic Center Dr
Beverly Hills, CA 90210-3604, USA

McBriar, Mat (Athlete, Football Player)
223 Ocean St
Solana Beach, CA 92075-1118, USA

McBride, Bake (Athlete, Baseball Player)
4077 Reliant Cir
Owensboro, KY 42301-0024, USA

McBride, Chi (Actor)
c/o Sam Maydew *The Collective*
8383 Wilshire Blvd Ste 1050
Beverly Hills, CA 90211-2415, USA

McBride, Danny (Actor)
8027 Briar Summit Dr
Los Angeles, CA 90046-1126, USA

McBride, Jeff (Magician)
McBride Magin
3132 Shadowridge Ave
Las Vegas, NV 89120-3467, USA

McBride, Jon A (Astronaut)
Image Development Group
1018 Kanawha Blvd E Ste 901
Charleston, WV 25301-2800, USA

McBride, Jon A Captain (Astronaut)
2705 N Indian River Dr
Cocoa, FL 32922-7075, USA

McBride, Ken (Athlete, Baseball Player)
3446 Cypress Cir
Westlake, OH 44145-4409, USA

McBride, Macay (Athlete, Baseball Player)
608 McDonald Rd
Sylvania, GA 30467-5718, USA

McBride, Martina (Musician)
c/o Jake Basden *Big Machine Records*
1219 16th Ave S
Nashville, TN 37212-2901, USA

McBride, Melissa (Actor)
c/o Staff Member *Kitty Bundy*
Management
3155 Roswell Rd NE Ste 220
Atlanta, GA 30305-1837, USA

McBride, Oscar (Athlete, Football Player)
34 Platinum Cir
Ladera Ranch, CA 92694-1348, USA

Mcbride, Susan (Writer)
6 Ladue Crest Ln
Saint Louis, MO 63124-1543, USA

McBride, Turk (Athlete, Football Player)
c/o Eugene Parker *Maximum Sports*
Management
6435 W Jefferson Blvd # 197
Fort Wayne, IN 46804-6203, USA

McBroom, Amanda (Musician,
Songwriter, Writer)
167 Fairview Rd
Ojai, CA 93023-9537, USA

McCabe, Frank (Athlete, Basketball
Player, Olympic Athlete)
6712 N White Fir Dr
Edwards, IL 61528-9424, USA

McCabe, Joe (Athlete, Baseball Player)
3003 Gardens Blvd
Naples, FL 34105-6647, USA

McCabe, Kayleen (Reality Star)
c/o Brian Samuels *Evolution Entertainment*
(LA)
901 N Highland Ave
Los Angeles, CA 90038-2412, USA

McCabe, Marcia (Actor)
1990 Broadway Box 417 Ansonia Sta
New York, NY 10023

McCabe, Zia (Musician)
Mongui Mgmt
PO Box 5908
Portland, OR 97228-5908, USA

McCafferty, Donald F (Don) Jr (Coach,
Football Coach)
167 E Shore Rd
Halesite, NY 11743-1128, USA

McCaffrey, Mike (Athlete, Football Player)
6040 N Nantucket Ave
Fresno, CA 93704-1620, USA

McCain, Edwin (Songwriter, Writer)
c/o Cass Scripps *Buddy Lee Attractions*
Inc
38 Music Sq E Ste 300
Nashville, TN 37203-4304, USA

McCain, John (Politician)
U.S. Senate
2211 E Camelback Rd Unit 1105
Phoenix, AZ 85016-9059, USA

McCain, Meghan
U.S. Senate
241 Russell
Senate Office Bldg
Washington, DC 20510-0001, USA

McCall, Brian (Athlete, Baseball Player)
550 Tremont Ave
Greensburg, PA 15601-4263, USA

McCall, Don (Athlete, Football Player)
16830 Kingsbury St Apt 131
Granada Hills, CA 91344-6465, USA

McCall, Joe (Athlete, Football Player)
1011 SW 100th Ter
Pembroke Pines, FL 33025-3619, USA

McCall, John "windy" (Athlete, Baseball
Player)
32 N Stone Ave # 4
Tucson, AZ 85701-1458, USA

McCall, Larry (Athlete, Baseball Player)
354 Justice Ridge Rd
Candler, NC 28715-9576, USA

McCall, Mitzi (Actor)
c/o Staff Member *Cunningham Escott*
Slevin & Doherty (CESD-LA)
10635 Santa Monica Blvd Ste 130
Los Angeles, CA 90025-8306, USA

McCall, Reese (Athlete, Football Player)
1311 1st Ave N
Bessemer, AL 35020-5602, USA

McCallany, Holt (Actor)
c/o David (Dave) Fleming *Mosaic Media*
Group
9200 W Sunset Blvd Ste 10
West Hollywood, CA 90069-3608, USA

McCallister, Blaine (Athlete, Golfer)
1878 Epping Forest Way S
Jacksonville, FL 32217-2670, USA

McCall Smith, Alexander (Writer)
c/o Staff Member *Random House*
1540 Broadway
New York, NY 10036-4039, USA

McCallum, David (Actor)
40 E 62nd St Apt 9W
New York, NY 10065-8093, USA

McCallum, Napoleon (Athlete, Football
Player)
314 Doe Run Cir
Henderson, NV 89012-2700, USA

McCambridge, Mercedes (Astronaut)
210932 Pleasant Park Dr
Conifer, CO 80433, USA

McCament, Randy (Athlete, Baseball
Player)
15038 N 60th Dr
Glendale, AZ 85306-3273, USA

McCandless, Bruce (Astronaut)
21852 Pleasant Park Rd
Conifer, CO 80433-6802, USA

McCandless, Bruce Captain (Astronaut)
21932 Pleasant Park Rd
Conifer, CO 80433-6802, USA

McCanlies, Tim (Director, Producer,
Writer)
c/o Lindsay Williams *The Gotham Group*
Inc
9255 W Sunset Blvd Ste 515
West Hollywood, CA 90069-3308, USA

McCann, Brendan (Athlete, Basketball
Player)
3599 Shinnecock Ln
Green Cove Springs, FL 32043-8028, USA

McCann, Brian (Athlete, Baseball Player)
869 Big Horn Holw
Suwanee, GA 30024-1764, USA

McCann, Chuck (Actor, Comedian)
2941 Briar Knoll Dr
Los Angeles, CA 90046-1122, USA

McCann, Lila (Musician)
c/o Rick Shipp *William Morris Endeavor*
(Nashville)
1600 Division St Ste 300
Nashville, TN 37203-2755, USA

McCann, Michelle
1200 Singer Dr
Riviera Beach, FL 33404-2765

McCann, Tim (Director)
c/o Jennifer Konawal *Washington Square*
Arts (NY)
41 Madison Ave
New York, NY 10010-2202, USA

McCants, Darnerien (Athlete, Football
Player)
43847 Chadwick Ter
Ashburn, VA 20148-3154, USA

McCants, Keith (Athlete, Football Player)
919 Selma Smith Ct Apt D
Tampa, FL 33605-4952, USA

McCants, Mel (Athlete, Basketball Player)
6404 Somis Way
Sacramento, CA 95828-1523, USA

McCants, Rashad (Athlete, Basketball
Player)
c/o Jeff Schwartz *Excel Sports*
Management (NY)
1700 Broadway Fl 29
New York, NY 10019-5905, USA

McCardell, Keenan (Athlete, Football
Player)
4918 Newpoint Dr
Fresno, TX 77545-9200, USA

McCareins, Justin (Athlete, Football
Player)
7707 Andes Ln
Parkland, FL 33067-2300, USA

McCarren, Larry (Athlete, Football Player)
520 W Chickadee Ln
Green Bay, WI 54313-5039, USA

McCarrick, Theodore E Cardinal
(Religious Leader)
Archdiocesan Pastoral Center
5001 Eastern Ave
Washington, DC 20017, USA

McCarroll, Jay (Fashion Designer)
c/o Nancy Kane *Kane & Associates*
319 N Venice Blvd
Venice, CA 90291-4598, USA

McCarron, Chris (Horse Racer)
1372 Sugar Maple Ln
Lexington, KY 40511-2325, USA

McCarron, Chris
PO Box 861
Sierra Madre, CA 91025-0861

McCarron, Christopher (Chris) (Jockey)
Dun Roamin
318 N Terrace View Dr
Monrovia, CA 91016-1570, USA

McCarron, Scott (Athlete, Golfer)
1835 Manzanita Cir
Reno, NV 89509-5260, USA

McCarry, Charles (Writer)
Random House
1745 Broadway Frnt 3 # B1
New York, NY 10019-4343, USA

McCartan, Jack (Athlete, Hockey Player,
Olympic Athlete)
15504 Almond Ln
Eden Prairie, MN 55347-2554, USA

McCarter, Andre (Athlete, Basketball
Player)
3257 Kibbe Ct
Lawrenceville, GA 30044-3263, USA

McCarter, Willie (Athlete, Basketball
Player)
1123 Buckingham St SW
Wyoming, MI 49509-2832, USA

McCarter Sisters
PO Box 121551
Nashville, TN 37212-1551

McCarthy, Andrew (Actor)
c/o Emily Gerson Saines *Brookside Artists*
Management (NY)
250 W 57th St Ste 2303
New York, NY 10107-2399, USA

McCarthy, Bill (Athlete, Football Player)
1640 Walnut Ave
Winter Park, FL 32789-2036, USA

McCarthy, Brandon (Athlete, Baseball
Player)
34457 N Legend Trail Pkwy Unit 1018
Pkwy Unit 1018
Scottsdale, AZ 85262-4428, USA

McCarthy, Carolyn (Congressman, Politician)
2346 Rayburn Hob
Washington, DC 20515-3507, USA

McCarthy, Cormac (Writer)
c/o Amanda Urban *ICM Partners (NY)*
730 5th Ave
New York, NY 10019-4105, USA

McCarthy, Dan (Athlete, Hockey Player)
1346 Wolf Hill Rd
Cheshire, CT 06410-1739

McCarthy, Greg (Athlete, Baseball Player)
56 Wakelee Avenue Ext
Shelton, CT 06484-3954, USA

McCarthy, Jenny (Actor, Model, Television Host)
c/o Judi Brown *Levity Entertainment Group (LEG)*
6701 Center Dr W Fl 11
Los Angeles, CA 90045-1535, USA

McCarthy, Joey (Race Car Driver)
McCarthy/Pritchard Motorsports
PO Box 1494
Dover, NJ 07802-1494, USA

McCarthy, John (Athlete, Basketball Player)
1350 Union Rd Apt 2F
Apt 2F
West Seneca, NY 14224-2940, USA

McCarthy, Julianna (Actor)
Stone Manners
6500 Wilshire Blvd # 550
Los Angeles, CA 90048-4920, USA

McCarthy, Kevin (Athlete, Hockey Player)
Philadelphia Flyers
3601 S Broad St Ste 2
Philadelphia, PA 19148-5297

McCarthy, Kevin (Congressman, Politician)
326 Cannon Hob
Washington, DC 20515-0529, USA

McCarthy, Kevin (Athlete, Hockey Player)
1139 Warf Rd
Lexington, NC 27292-1929, USA

McCarthy, Melissa (Actor)
c/o Courtney Kivowitz *The Schiff Company*
9220 W Sunset Blvd Ste 106
West Hollywood, CA 90069-3500, USA

McCarthy, Nobu
9229 W Sunset Blvd Ste 311
West Hollywood, CA 90069-3403

McCarthy, Norma (Actor)
818385 Mead Lane Slu Box 9063
Victorville, CA 92392

McCarthy, Shawn (Athlete, Football Player)
300 N Lakeshore Rd
Payson, AZ 85541-6220, USA

McCarthy, Timothy
8686 Butterfield Ln
Orland Park, IL 60462-1492

McCarthy, Tom (Athlete, Baseball Player)
PO Box 38
Limington, ME 04049-0038, USA

McCarthy, Tom (Director)
c/o Rhonda Price *Gersh (NY)*
41 Madison Ave
New York, NY 10010-2202, USA

McCarthy, Tom (Commentator)
2229 Union Blvd
Allentown, PA 18109, USA

McCarthy-Miller, Beth (Director, Producer)
c/o Dan Rabinow *ICM Partners (LA)*
10250 Constellation Blvd Fl 7
Los Angeles, CA 90067-6207, USA

McCartney, Jesse (Musician)
c/o Sherry Kondor *Good Noize Entertainment*
12129 Maxwellton Rd
Studio City, CA 91604-3623, USA

McCartney, Ron (Athlete, Football Player)
10722 Bell Valley Dr
Knoxville, TN 37934-5098, USA

McCarty, Chris
9105 Carmelita Ave Apt 101
Beverly Hills, CA 90210-3543

McCarty, Darren
33 Laguna Ct
Manhattan Beach, CA 90266-7207

McCarty, Darren (Athlete)
c/o Staff Member *Detroit Red Wings*
600 Civic Center Dr
Joe Luis Arena
Detroit, MI 48226-4419, USA

McCarty, David (Athlete, Baseball Player)
110 Waldo Ave
Piedmont, CA 94611-3943, USA

McCarty, Mary (Baseball Player)
9455 N Genesee Rd
Mount Morris, MI 48458-9734, USA

McCarty, Walter (Athlete, Basketball Player)
840 Winter St
Waltham, MA 02451-1433, USA

McCarver, J Timothy (Tim) (Athlete, Baseball Player, Sportscaster)
5825 Riegels Harbor Rd
Sarasota, FL 34242-1779, USA

McCarver, Shonna
13280 Northwest Fwy # F-252
Houston, TX 77040-6029

McCarver, Tim (Athlete, Baseball Player)
San Francisco Giants
5825 Riegels Harbor Rd
Sarasota, FL 34242-1779, USA

McCary, Michael (Musician)
Southpaw Entertainment
10675 Santa Monica Blvd
Los Angeles, CA 90025-4807, USA

McCashin, Constance (Actor)
66 Fountain St
West Newton, MA 02465-3023, USA

McCaskill, Kirk E (Athlete, Baseball Player)
1738 Oxford Ave
Cardiff By The Sea, CA 92007-1633, USA

McCaskill, Ted (Athlete, Hockey Player)
4101 E Columbine Dr
Phoenix, AZ 85032-7403

McCatty, Steve (Athlete, Baseball Player)
1075 Woodbriar Dr
Oxford, MI 48371-6069, USA

McCauley, Don (Athlete, Football Player)
1005 Tuscany Dr
Hillsborough, NC 27278-7690, USA

McCauley, Herb (Horse Racer)
69 Horseshoe Ct
Oceanport, NJ 07757-1170, USA

McCauley, Wes (Athlete, Hockey Player)
251 Elderberry Dr
South Portland, ME 04106-7810

McCay, Peggy (Actor)
2714 Carmar Dr
Los Angeles, CA 90046-1009, USA

McChesney, Robert (Bob) (Writer)
1103 S Douglas Ave
Urbana, IL 61801-4934, USA

McCkorkle, Kevin (Actor)
c/o Peter Himberger *Impact Artists Group LLC*
42 Hamilton Ter
New York, NY 10031-6403, USA

McClain, Antoine (Athlete, Football Player)
c/o Joe Linta *JL Sports*
1204 Main St Ste 179
Branford, CT 06405-3787, USA

McClain, Cady (Actor)
c/o Marnie Sparer *Innovative Artists (LA)*
1505 10th St
Santa Monica, CA 90401-2805, USA

McClain, Charly (Musician)
John Lentz
PO Box 198888
Nashville, TN 37219-8888, USA

McClain, China Anne (Actor)
c/o Chris Rossi *Core Public Relations Group*
4401 Wilshire Blvd Fl 4
Los Angeles, CA 90010-3703, USA

McClain, Dewey (Athlete, Football Player)
1032 Flagg Way
Lawrenceville, GA 30044-3354, USA

McClain, Eugene (Athlete, Baseball Player)
828 W 8th St
Chester, PA 19013-3712, USA

McClain, Joe (Athlete, Baseball Player)
1370 Milligan Hwy
Johnson City, TN 37601-5518, USA

McClain, Katrina (Athlete, Basketball Player, Olympic Athlete)
Naismith HOF
PO Box 40893
North Charleston, SC 29423-0893, USA

McClain, Robert (Athlete, Football Player)
c/o Ed Wasielewski *EMG Sports - PA*
PO Box 22371
Philadelphia, PA 19110-2371, USA

McClain, Rolando (Athlete, Football Player)
c/o Pat Dye Jr *SportsTrust Advisors (GA)*
3340 Peachtree Rd NE Fl 16
Atlanta, GA 30326-1000, USA

McClain, Scott (Athlete, Baseball Player)
660 Golden Gate Pt Apt 61
Sarasota, FL 34236-6645, USA

McClain, Ted (Athlete, Basketball Player)
104 Eaton Ct
Nashville, TN 37218-1003, USA

McClairen, Jack (Athlete, Football Player)
1337 Idlewild Dr
Daytona Beach, FL 32114-1614, USA

McClairen, Jack (Cy) (Coach, Football Coach)
Pittsburgh Steelers
1337 Idlewild Dr
Daytona Beach, FL 32114-1614, USA

McClanahan, Brent (Athlete, Football Player)
1100 Sayword Ct
Bakersfield, CA 93312-5750, USA

McClanahan, Randy (Athlete, Football Player)
8107 W Via Del Sol
Peoria, AZ 85383-2142, USA

McClanahan, Rob (Athlete, Hockey Player, Olympic Athlete)
3310 Watertown Rd
Long Lake, MN 55356-9207, USA

McClard, Bill (Athlete, Football Player)
149 N Pleasant Ridge Dr
Rogers, AR 72756-0702, USA

McClarnon, Zahn (Actor)
c/o Gloria Hinojosa *Amsel, Eisenstadt & Frazier Talent Agency (AEF)*
5055 Wilshire Blvd Ste 860
Los Angeles, CA 90036-6108, USA

McClary, Thomas (Tom) (Athlete, Football Player)
Management Assoc
PO Box 701341
Dallas, TX 75370-1341, USA

McCleary, Norris (Athlete, Football Player)
115 Ferguson Dr
Kings Mountain, NC 28086-9727, USA

McClellan, Beverly (Musician)
c/o Stephen Ford *Diva Central Inc*
7510 W Sunset Blvd Ste 1445
Los Angeles, CA 90046-3408, USA

McClellan, Kyle (Athlete, Baseball Player)
253 Fox Haven Dr
O Fallon, MO 63368-6584, USA

McClellan, Lloyd (Athlete, Baseball Player)
1082 Mission Hills Ct
Chesterton, IN 46304-9605, USA

McClellan, Paul (Athlete, Baseball Player)
PO Box 2115
Napa, CA 94558-0211, USA

McClellan, Scott (Government Official, Writer)
c/o Staff Member *Public Affairs*
250 W 57th St Fl 15
New York, NY 10107-1307

McClellan, Zach (Athlete, Baseball Player)
4262 W Geranium Ln
Bloomington, IN 47404-1440, USA

McClelland, Dave (Race Car Driver)
980 Eilinita Ave
Glendale, CA 91208-1128, USA

McClelland, Kevin (Athlete, Hockey Player)
Wichita Thunder
505 W Maple St # 100
Wichita, KS 67213-4616

McClelland, Kevin
1993 Bayfront Dr
Windsor, CO 80550-3589

McClelland, Melissa (Musician)
c/o Staff Member *Paradigm (Monterey)*
404 W Franklin St
Monterey, CA 93940-2303, USA

McClelland, Tim (Athlete, Baseball Player)
5405 Woodland Ave
West Des Moines, IA 50266-7259, USA

McClellin, Shea (Athlete, Football Player)
c/o Bruce Tollner *REP 1 Sports Group*
2 Corporate Park Ste 106
Irvine, CA 92606-5103, USA

McClenathan, Cory (Race Car Driver)
PO Box 1602
Lake Havasu City, AZ 86405-1602, USA

McClendon, Jacques (Athlete, Football Player)
c/o Tony Paige *Perennial Sports and Entertainment*
1455 Pennsylvania Ave NW Ste 225
Washington, DC 20004-1026, USA

McClendon, Lloyd (Athlete, Baseball Player, Coach)
1082 Mission Hills Ct
Chesterton, IN 46304-9605, USA

McClendon, Reiley (Actor)
c/o Staff Member *Kritzer Levine Wilkins Entertainment (KLWG)*
11872 La Grange Ave Fl 1
Los Angeles, CA 90025-5283, USA

McClendon, Sarah
3133 Connecticut Ave NW Apt 215
Washington, DC 20008-5105

McClendon, Skip (Athlete, Football Player)
1456 E Pecos Rd Apt 3063
Gilbert, AZ 85295-1790, USA

McClendon, Willie (Athlete, Football Player)
575 Cativo Dr SW
Atlanta, GA 30311-2107, USA

McCleon, Dexter (Athlete, Football Player)
1901 Post Oak Blvd Apt 509
Houston, TX 77056-3926, USA

McClintock, Eddie (Actor)
c/o Richard Beddingfield *Beddingfield Company, The*
13600 Ventura Blvd Ste B
Sherman Oaks, CA 91423-5050, USA

McClintock, Jessica (Designer, Fashion Designer)
Jessica McClintock Co
2307 Broadway St
San Francisco, CA 94115-1233, USA

McClintock, Tom (Congressman, Politician)
428 Cannon Hob
Washington, DC 20515-4308, USA

McClinton, Curtis (Athlete, Football Player)
11714 Jefferson St
McClinton Development Company
Kansas City, MO 64114-5580, USA

McClinton, Delbert (Musician)
c/o Staff Member *Alligator Records*
PO Box 60234
Chicago, IL 60660-0234, USA

McCloskey, Jack (Basketball Player)
Minnesota Timberwolves
600 1st Ave N
Target Center
Minneapolis, MN 55403-1400, USA

McCloskey, Leigh
6032 Philip Ave
Malibu, CA 90265-3747

McCloskey, Leigh J (Actor)
6032 Philip Ave
Malibu, CA 90265-3747, USA

McCloskey, Mike (Athlete, Football Player)
108 Summer Ridge Dr
Lansdale, PA 19446-6707, USA

McCloskey, Pete (Politician)
2200 Geng Rd
Palo Alto, CA 94303-3358, USA

McCloskey, Rep (Politician)
580 Mountain Home Rd
Woodside, CA 94062-2515

McCloskey-Rogers, Gloria (Athlete, Baseball Player, Commentator)
PO Box 512
Macon, MO 63552-0512, USA

McCloud, George (Athlete, Basketball Player)
19501 W Country Club Dr # AT1603
Aventura, FL 33180-2471, USA

McCloud, Tyrus (Athlete, Football Player)
2850 NW 8th St
Pompano Beach, FL 33069-2139, USA

McCloughan, Dave (Athlete, Football Player)
121 Sweet Clover Ct
Loveland, CO 80537-3426, USA

McCloughan, Kent (Athlete, Football Player)
2241 Woody Creek Cir
Loveland, CO 80538-5333, USA

McClover, Darrell (Athlete, Football Player)
6120 SW 19th St
Pompano Beach, FL 33068-4911, USA

McClover, Stanley (Athlete, Football Player)
4720 Buckminister Ct
Charlotte, NC 28269-8173, USA

McClung, Seth (Athlete, Baseball Player)
13588 Park Blvd
Seminole, FL 33776-3432, USA

McClure, Bob (Athlete, Baseball Player)
1137 SE Conference Cir
Stuart, FL 34997-7638, USA

McClure, Bryton (Actor)
c/o Jeff Witjas *Agency for the Performing Arts (APA-LA)*
405 S Beverly Dr Ste 500
Beverly Hills, CA 90212-4425, USA

McClure, Eric (Race Car Driver)
Rensi Hamilton Racing
4011 Hands Mill Hwy
York, SC 29745-9647, USA

McClure, Larry (Race Car Driver)
Morgan-McClure Racing
26502 Newbanks Rd
Abingdon, VA 24210-7500, USA

McClure, Marc
3574 E Bogert Trl
Palm Springs, CA 92264-9623

McClure, Molly
12456 Ventura Blvd Ste 1
Studio City, CA 91604-2484

McClure, Tane (Actor)
Don Gerler
3349 Cahuenga Blvd W Ste 1
Los Angeles, CA 90068-1379, USA

McClurg, Edie
9229 W Sunset Blvd Ste 315
West Hollywood, CA 90069-3403

McClurkin, Donnie (Musician)
c/o Staff Member *The Alliance Agency*
1035 Bates Ct
Hendersonville, TN 37075-8864, USA

McCluskey, David (Athlete, Football Player)
22 Tannassee Ln NW Apt E8
Rome, GA 30165, USA

McCole Bartusiak, Skye (Actor)
c/o Mitchell Gossett *Cunningham Escott Slevin & Doherty (CESD-LA)*
10635 Santa Monica Blvd Ste 130
Los Angeles, CA 90025-8306, USA

McColl, Bill (Football Player)
Chicago Bears
5166 Chelsea St
La Jolla, CA 92037-7908, USA

McCollough, David (Writer)
445 Park Ave
New York, NY 10022-2606, USA

McCollum, Andy (Athlete, Football Player)
120 Bluffs Pl
Eureka, MO 63025-3195, USA

McCollum, Betty (Congressman, Politician)
1714 Longworth Hob
Washington, DC 20515-2203, USA

McColm, Matt (Actor)
c/o Bob Read *ReBar Management*
10061 Riverside Dr # 722
Toluca Lake, CA 91602-2560

McColms, Matt (Actor)
c/o Staff Member *Agency for the Performing Arts (APA-LA)*
405 S Beverly Dr Ste 500
Beverly Hills, CA 90212-4425, USA

McComas, Brian (Musician)
c/o Staff Member *Leon Medica Management*
187 Hidden Lake Rd
Hendersonville, TN 37075-5528, USA

McComb, Jeremy (Musician)
c/o Staff Member *Paradigm (Monterey)*
404 W Franklin St
Monterey, CA 93940-2303, USA

McComb, Joanne (Athlete, Baseball Player, Commentator)
105 Nottingham Rd
Bloomsburg, PA 17815-3021, USA

McCombs, Red (Business Person, Football Executive)
825 Contour Dr
San Antonio, TX 78212-1700, USA

McConathy, John (Athlete, Basketball Player)
2320 Belmont Blvd
Bossier City, LA 71111-2427, USA

McConaughey, Matthew (Actor)
3210 Hillbilly Ln
Austin, TX 78746-1707, USA

McConkey, Phil (Athlete, Football Player)
1856 Viking Way
La Jolla, CA 92037-3354, USA

McConneii-Serio, Suzie (Athlete, Basketball Player, Olympic Athlete)
2590 Rossmoor Dr
Pittsburgh, PA 15241-2584, USA

McConnell, Dave (Race Car Driver)
Dave McConnell Racing
101 Lantern Cir
Canonsburg, PA 15317-3654, USA

McConnell, John P (Business Person)
Worthington Industries
200 W Old Wilson Bridge Rd
Worthington, OH 43085-2247, USA

McConnell, Mitch (Politician)
2318 Dundee Rd
Louisville, KY 40205-2070, USA

McConnell, Page (Musician)
c/o Staff Member *Paradigm (Monterey)*
404 W Franklin St
Monterey, CA 93940-2303, USA

McConnell, Robert M G (Rob) (Musician)
Thomas Cassidy
11761 E Speedway Blvd
Tucson, AZ 85748-2017, USA

McConnell, Sam (Athlete, Baseball Player)
301 McKinley St
Middletown, OH 45042-3256, USA

McConnell-Serio, Suzie (Athlete, Basketball Player)
2590 Rossmoor Dr
Pittsburgh, PA 15241-2584, USA

McCoo, Marilyn (Actor, Musician)
PO Box 7905
Beverly Hills, CA 90212-7905, USA

McCook, John (Actor)
10245 Briarwood Dr
Los Angeles, CA 90077-2521, USA

McCool, Bill (Athlete, Baseball Player)
9250 SE 121st Loop
Summerfield, FL 34491-9477, USA

McCool, Billy (Athlete, Baseball Player)
9250 SE 121st Loop
Summerfield, FL 34491-9477, USA

McCool, Michelle (Wrestler)
c/o Kerry Rodgerson *World Wrestling Entertainment (WWE)*
1241 E Main St
Titan Towers
Stamford, CT 06902-3520, USA

McCord, Alex (Reality Star)
c/o Staff Member *Bravo (NY)*
30 Rockefeller Plz
New York, NY 10112-0015, USA

McCord, AnnaLynne (Actor)
c/o Gary Mantoosh *Baker Winokur Ryder Public Relations (BWR-LA)*
9100 Wilshire Blvd Ste 500
West Tower Suite 500
Beverly Hills, CA 90212-3426, USA

McCord, Bob (Athlete, Hockey Player)
11540 Donley Dr
Parker, CO 80138-8027, USA

McCord, Clinton (Athlete, Baseball Player)
1821 Knowles St
Nashville, TN 37208-2438, USA

McCord, Darris (Athlete, Football Player)
6160 W Surrey Rd
Bloomfield Hills, MI 48301-1661, USA

McCord, Gary (Athlete, Golfer)
15215 N Kierland Blvd Unit 738
Scottsdale, AZ 85254-8224, USA

McCord, Keith (Athlete, Basketball Player)
1609 Five Acre Rd
Dolomite, AL 35061-1036, USA

McCord, Kent
c/o Staff Member *Tisherman Gilbert Motley Drozdoski Talent Agency (TGMD)*
6767 Forest Lawn Dr Ste 101
Los Angeles, CA 90068-1027, USA

McCord, Mack (Race Car Driver)
Gorilla AA/FA
PO Box 2608
Phoenix, AZ 85002-2608, USA

McCord, Quentin (Athlete, Football Player)
4194 Berwick Farm Dr
Duluth, GA 30096-2597, USA

McCord, Susie (Race Car Driver)
Gorilla AA/FA
PO Box 2608
Phoenix, AZ 85002-2608, USA

McCormack, Don (Athlete, Baseball Player)
866 Glenfield Dr
Palm Harbor, FL 34684-3218, USA

McCormack, Eric (Actor)
10155 Valley Spring Ln
Toluca Lake, CA 91602-2929, USA

McCormack, Mary (Actor)
PO Box 67335
Los Angeles, CA 90067-0335, USA

McCormack, Patty (Actor)
c/o Kurt Patino *Patino Management Company*
2600 W Olive Ave Fl 5
Burbank, CA 91505-4572, USA

McCormack, Will (Actor)
c/o Greg Clark *Untitled Entertainment (LA)*
350 S Beverly Dr Ste 200
Beverly Hills, CA 90212-4819, USA

McCormick, Carolyn (Actor)
Bresler Kelly Assoc
11500 W Olympic Blvd Ste 510
Los Angeles, CA 90064-1527, USA

McCormick, Kelly
PO Box 250
Seal Beach, CA 90740-0250

McCormick, Len (Athlete, Football Player)
PO Box 19764
Houston, TX 77224-9764, USA

McCormick, Malcolm (Mac Miller) (Musician)
c/o Zach Quillen *The Agency Group (NYC)*
142 W 57th St Fl 6
New York, NY 10019-3300, USA

McCormick, Maureen (Actor, Musician)
c/o Debra Goldfarb *Rebel Entertainment Partners*
5700 Wilshire Blvd Ste 456
Los Angeles, CA 90036-3648, USA

McCormick, Mike (Athlete, Baseball Player)
22250 Market St
Cornelius, NC 28031-3000, USA

McCormick, Pat (Athlete, Diver, Olympic Athlete)
92 Riversea Rd
Seal Beach, CA 90740-5971, USA

McCormick, Sierra (Actor)
c/o Oren Segal *Radius Entertainment*
9229 W Sunset Blvd Ste 301
West Hollywood, CA 90069-3417, USA

McCormick, Tim (Athlete, Basketball Player)
2S00 Leroy Ln
West Bloomfield, MI 48324, USA

McCormick, Tom (Athlete, Football Player)
6241 Woodcreek Dr
Citrus Heights, CA 95621-6119, USA

McCornack, Bill (Race Car Driver)
McCornack Racing
PO Box 12265
Lexington, KY 40582-2265, USA

McCorvey, Kez (Athlete, Football Player)
3313 SW 173rd Ter
Miramar, FL 33029-1641, USA

McCorvey, Norma (Attorney)
11343 Cactus Ln
Dallas, TX 75238-3805, USA

McCorvey, Norma
12730 Thomas Sumter St
San Antonio, TX 78233-4630

McCosh, Shawn (Athlete, Hockey Player)
18992 N 74th Dr
Glendale, AZ 85308-5668

McCouch, Grayson
c/o Dan Baron *Agency for the Performing Arts (APA-LA)*
405 S Beverly Dr Ste 500
Beverly Hills, CA 90212-4425, USA

McCourt, Frank (Business Person)
22426 Pacific Coast Hwy
Malibu, CA 90265-5033, USA

McCourt, Malachy (Actor, Writer)
c/o Marc Bass *Beacon Talent Agency*
170 Apple Ridge Rd
Woodcliff Lake, NJ 07677-8149, USA

McCoury, Del (Musician)
c/o Staff Member *Paradigm (Monterey)*
404 W Franklin St
Monterey, CA 93940-2303, USA

McCovey, Willie (Athlete, Baseball Player)
PO Box 620342
Redwood City, CA 94062-0342, USA

McCown, Josh (Athlete, Football Player)
10417 Mahonia St Unit 102
Charlotte, NC 28277-3962, USA

McCown, Luke (Athlete, Football Player)
30963 US Highway 69 N
Rusk, TX 75785-1720, USA

McCoy, Charlie (Musician)
PO Box 50455
Nashville, TN 37205-0455, USA

McCoy, Colt (Athlete, Football Player)
c/o Jordan Bazant *The Legacy Agency*
1500 Broadway Ste 2501
New York, NY 10036-4082, USA

McCoy, Gerald (Athlete, Football Player)
c/o Kelli Masters *Kelli Masters Management*
100 N Broadway Ste 1700
Oklahoma City, OK 73102-9211, USA

McCoy, Larry (Athlete, Baseball Player)
5758 Highway 139
Greenway Ar, 72 USA, USA

McCoy, LeRon (Athlete, Football Player)
761 Cattail Dr
Harrisburg, PA 17111-3395, USA

McCoy, LisaRaye (Actor)
c/o Staff Member *The Forum Entertainment Group*
10940 Wilshire Blvd Ste 1600
Los Angeles, CA 90024-3910, USA

McCoy, Mark
7120 Hawthorn Ave Apt 18
Los Angeles, CA 90046-3280

McCoy, Matt (Actor)
Artists Agency
1180 S Beverly Dr Ste 301
Los Angeles, CA 90035-1154, USA

McCoy, Mike (Athlete, Football Player)
2224 Cotton Gin Row
Jefferson, GA 30549-8819, USA

McCoy, Neal (Musician)
c/o Joey Lee *William Morris Endeavor (Nashville)*
1600 Division St Ste 300
Nashville, TN 37203-2755, USA

McCoy, Sandra (Actor)
c/o Cole Harris *Pantheon Talent*
1801 Century Park E Ste 1910
Los Angeles, CA 90067-2321, USA

McCoy, Tony (Athlete, Football Player)
PO Box 836
Groveland, FL 34736-0836, USA

McCracken, Paul (Athlete, Basketball Player)
914 Westwood Blvd Apt 256
Los Angeles, CA 90024-2905, USA

McCracken, Quinton (Athlete, Baseball Player)
27911 Walsh Crossing Dr
Katy, TX 77494-1751, USA

McCrane, Paul (Actor)
VOX
6420 Wilshire Blvd Ste 1080
Los Angeles, CA 90048-5539, USA

McCrary, Bill (Athlete, Baseball Player)
2 Escocia Ln
Hot Springs Village, AR 71909-7604, USA

McCrary, Darius (Actor)
19518 Branding Iron Rd
Walnut, CA 91789-4212, USA

McCrary, Fred (Athlete, Football Player)
134 Grandmar Chase
Canton, GA 30115-6408, USA

McCrary, Joel (Actor)
c/o Holly Shelton *Precision Entertainment*
465 N Croft Ave
Los Angeles, CA 90048-2508, USA

McCrary, Michael (Athlete, Football Player)
9907 Chase Hill Ct
Vienna, VA 22182-1427, USA

McCrary, Prentice (Athlete, Football Player)
5414 E Dolphin Cir
Mesa, AZ 85206-2225, USA

McCraw, Tommy (Athlete, Baseball Player)
3142 SE Monte Vista Ct
Port Saint Lucie, FL 34952-6062, USA

McCray, Bobby (Athlete, Football Player)
c/o Staff Member *EAG Sports Management*
909 N Sepulveda Blvd Ste 360
El Segundo, CA 90245-3864, USA

McCray, Kelcie (Athlete, Football Player)
c/o Pat Dye Jr *SportsTrust Advisors (GA)*
3340 Peachtree Rd NE Fl 16
Atlanta, GA 30326-1000, USA

McCray, Nikki (Athlete, Basketball Player, Olympic Athlete)
4278 Fox Hills Dr
Louisville, TN 37777-5105, USA

McCray, Prentice (Athlete, Football Player)
2109 N Argonaut St
Stockton, CA 95204-6201, USA

McCray, Rick (Race Car Driver)
McCray Racing
28746 Glenheather Dr
Highland, CA 92346-5357, USA

McCray, Rodney (Athlete, Baseball Player)
45365 Horseshoe Cir
Canton, MI 48187-5042, USA

McCray, Rodney (Athlete, Basketball Player)
33 Bonita Vista Rd
Mount Vernon, NY 10552-1301, USA

McCreary, Bill
4318 Highcrest Dr Apt 1
Brighton, MI 48116-9798

McCreary, Bob (Athlete, Football Player)
1473 Knolls Dr
Newton, NC 28658-9452, USA

McCreary, Tex
PO Box 405
Mill Neck, NY 11765-0405

McCreary, Sr., Bill (Athlete, Hockey Player)
3979 Broadmoor Ct
Howell, MI 48843-7464

McCree, Marlon (Athlete, Football Player)
15590 Camden Pl
San Diego, CA 92131-4318, USA

McCreery, Scotty (Musician)
c/o Becky Gardenhire *William Morris Endeavor (Nashville)*
1600 Division St Ste 300
Nashville, TN 37203-2755, USA

McCrills, John W (Writer)
McCrillis & Eldredge Insurance
17 Depot St
Newport, NH 03773-1533, USA

McCrory, Bob (Athlete, Baseball Player)
30 Rebecca Ln
Hattiesburg, MS 39402-8224, USA

McCrory, Milton (Milt) (Boxer)
Escot Boxing Enterprises
19244 Bretton Dr
Detroit, MI 48223-1364, USA

McCrory, Pat (Governor, Politician)
Office of the Governor
20301 Mail Service Ctr
Raleigh, NC 27699-0300, USA

McCrudden, Ian (Actor)
c/o Josh Silver *Silver Mine Entertainment*
6705 W Sunset Blvd
Los Angeles, CA 90028-7107, USA

McCullers, Dale (Athlete, Football Player)
1613 Tupelo Dr
Waycross, GA 31501-5054, USA

McCullers, Lance (Athlete, Baseball Player)
3309 Hoedt Ro
Tampa, FL 33618, USA

McCulley, Michael J (Astronaut)
365 Private Road 652
Bay City, TX 77414-2451, USA

McCulley, Michael J Captain (Astronaut)
100 Yacht Haven Dr
Cocoa Beach, FL 32931-2627, USA

McCulloch, Ed (Race Car Driver)
Schumacher Racing
22424 Masters Dr
Friant, CA 93626-9793, USA

McCullouch, Earl (Athlete, Football
Player)
2108 Santa Fe Ave Apt 15
Long Beach, CA 90810-3546, USA

McCullough, Bob (Athlete, Football
Player)
2225 Deerfield Ln
Helena, MT 59601-8643, USA

McCullough, David (Actor)
c/o Staff Member *Creative Artists Agency
(CAA-LA)*
2000 Avenue of the Stars Ste 100
Los Angeles, CA 90067-4705, USA

McCullough, David (Writer)
Janklow & Nesbit Assoc
445 Park Ave Fl 13
New York, NY 10022-8628, USA

McCullough, Earl (Athlete, Football
Player, Track Athlete)
2108 Santa Fe Ave
Long Beach, CA 90810-3546, USA

McCullough, Julian (Musician)
c/o Staff Member *Paradigm (Monterey)*
404 W Franklin St
Monterey, CA 93940-2303, USA

McCullough, Julie (Actor)
c/o Hillard Elkins *Elkins Entertainment*
8306 Wilshire Blvd Ste 438
Beverly Hills, CA 90211-2304, USA

McCullough, Kimberly
9229 W Sunset Blvd Ste 315
West Hollywood, CA 90069-3403

McCullough, Mike (Athlete, Golfer)
6334 E Evening Glow Dr
Scottsdale, AZ 85266-7339, USA

McCullough, Rich (Athlete, Football
Player)
910 Cypress Station Dr Apt 506
Houston, TX 77090-1516, USA

McCullough, Shanna
7920 Alabama Ave
Canoga Park, CA 91304-4907

McCullough, Wayne (Athlete, Boxer)
11756 Culver Blvd
Los Angeles, CA 90066-6381, USA

McCullum, Sam (Athlete, Football Player)
7701 88th Pl SE
Mercer Island, WA 98040-5746, USA

McCully, Kilmer (Doctor)
Veteran Affairs Med Center
Pathology Dept
Davis Park
Providence, RI 02908, USA

McCumber, Josh (Athlete, Golfer)
2121 Sea Hawk Dr
Ponte Vedra Beach, FL 32082-1683, USA

McCumber, Mark (Athlete, Golfer,
Sportscaster)
527 Le Master Dr
Ponte Vedra Beach, FL 32082-2312, USA

McCune, Don (Bowler)
3551 Coventry Gardens Dr
Las Vegas, NV 89135-2838, USA

McCurdy, Cindy (Golfer)
18 Cottage Dr
Newnan, GA 30265-5513, USA

McCurdy, Jennette (Actor)
3912 Big Oak Dr
Studio City, CA 91604-3846, USA

McCurry, Jeff (Athlete, Baseball Player)
3726 Dumbarton St
Houston, TX 77025-2422, USA

McCurry, Mike (Journalist, Politician)
Cable News Network
1050 Techwood Dr NW
News Dept
Atlanta, GA 30318-5695, USA

McCusker, Jim (Athlete, Football Player)
209 N Main St
Jamestown, NY 14701-5209, USA

McCutchen, Andrew (Athlete, Baseball
Player)
6895 Bushnell Dr
Lakeland, FL 33813-3738, USA

McCutchen, Daniel (Athlete, Baseball
Player)
310 Texas Country Dr
New Braunfels, TX 78132-4429, USA

McCutcheon, Brian (Athlete, Hockey
Player)
133 Iradell Rd
Ithaca, NY 14850-9265

McCutcheon, Darwin (Athlete, Hockey
Player)
PO Box 5556
Vail, CO 81658-5556, USA

McCutcheon, Daylon (Athlete, Football
Player)
4393 Hiwassee
Claremont, CA 91711-8320, USA

McCutcheon, Dayton (Athlete, Football
Player)
901 Golden Springs Dr # F-G
Diamond Bar, CA 91765-1181, USA

McCutcheon, Lawrence (Athlete, Football
Player)
16721 Sims Ln Apt C
Huntington Beach, CA 92649-3360, USA

McCutcheon, Linda (Publisher)
AARP Publications
Director's Office
601 E St NW
Washington, DC 20049-0001, USA

McDaniel, Ed (Athlete, Football Player)
13111 Brenwood Trl
Hopkins, MN 55343-6801, USA

McDaniel, James (Actor)
c/o Craig Shapiro *ICM Partners (LA)*
10250 Constellation Blvd Fl 7
Los Angeles, CA 90067-6207, USA

McDaniel, Jeremy (Athlete, Football
Player)
25 Pickwick Pl
Greensboro, NC 27407-2732, USA

McDaniel, John (Cinematographer,
Musician, Producer)
c/o Glenn Daniels *Glenn Daniels Arts
Management*
123 Cliff Rd W
Wading River, NY 11792-1239, USA

McDaniel, John (Athlete, Football Player)
586 Janney Rd
Ohatchee, AL 36271-5213, USA

McDaniel, Lecharls (Athlete, Football
Player)
12844 Starwood Ln
San Diego, CA 92131-4210, USA

McDaniel, Lindy (Athlete, Baseball Player)
1095 Meadow Hill Dr
Lavon, TX 75166-1262, USA

McDaniel, Lindy
Rt. #2 Box 353A
Hollis, OK 73550

McDaniel, Orlando (Athlete, Football
Player)
1012 N Goos Blvd
Lake Charles, LA 70601-1866, USA

McDaniel, Randall C (Athlete, Football
Player)
20405 Manor Rd
Excelsior, MN 55331-9470, USA

McDaniel, Terry (Athlete, Baseball Player)
1441 E 75th St
Kansas City, MO 64131-1867, USA

McDaniel, Terry (Athlete, Football Player)
730 Shenandoah
Cedar Hill, TX 75104-1242, USA

McDaniel, Xavier (Athlete, Basketball
Player)
2 Oakmist Ct
Blythewood, SC 29016-8707, USA

McDaniels, Darryl (Darryl M) (Music
Group, Musician)
Entertainment Artists
2409 21st Ave S Ste 100
Nashville, TN 37212-5317, USA

McDaniels, Jim
515 Coombs Dr Apt H2
Bowling Green, KY 42101-1134, USA

McDaniels, Pellom (Athlete, Football
Player)
186 Ridgeland Ave
Decatur, GA 30030-2054, USA

McDavid, Ray (Athlete, Baseball Player)
1245 Market St Apt 1348
San Diego, CA 92101-7358, USA

McDermott, Alice (Writer)
Farrar Straus Giroux
19 Union Sq W
New York, NY 10003-3304, USA

McDermott, Charlie (Actor)
c/o Adam Griffin *Kritzer Levine Wilkins
Entertainment (KLWG)*
11872 La Grange Ave Fl 1
Los Angeles, CA 90025-5283, USA

McDermott, Dean (Actor)
c/o Danielle Iturbe *Flutie Entertainment
(LA)*
2105 Colorado Ave Ste 106
Santa Monica, CA 90404-3503, USA

McDermott, Dylan (Actor, Director)
c/o Geyer Kosinski *Media Talent Group*
9200 W Sunset Blvd Ste 550
West Hollywood, CA 90069-3611, USA

McDermott, Edward A (Government
Official)
875 E Camino Real
Lake House South
Boca Raton, FL 33432-6356, USA

McDermott, Jim (Congressman, Politician)
1035 Longworth Hob
Washington, DC 20515-4707, USA

McDermott, R Terrance (Terry) (Speed
Skater)
5078 Chain Bridge Rd
Bloomfield Hills, MI 48304-3727, USA

McDermott, Shane
200 W 57th St Ste 900
New York, NY 10019-3211

McDermott, Terry (Athlete, Baseball
Player)
7205 Sunlight Peak Dr NE
Rio Rancho, NM 87144-7508, USA

McDill, Allen (Athlete, Baseball Player)
244 Richwoods Rd
Arkadelphia, AR 71923-8836, USA

McDivitt, James
9146 Cherry Ave
Rapid City, MI 49676-8624

McDivitt, James A Brig Gen (Astronaut)
3530 E Calle Puerta De Acero
Tucson, AZ 85718-6000, USA

McDivitt, James A (Jim) (Astronaut,
General)
3530 E Calle Puerta De Acero
Tucson, AZ 85718-6000, USA

McDole, Ron (Athlete, Football Player)
158 Jackson Pl
Middletown, VA 22645-4005, USA

McDonagh, John Michael (Director,
Writer)
c/o Jeremy Barber *United Talent Agency
(UTA-LA)*
9336 Civic Center Dr
Beverly Hills, CA 90210-3604, USA

McDonald, Audra (Actor, Musician)
c/o David Kalodner *William Morris
Endeavor (NY)*
1325 Avenue of the Americas
New York, NY 10019-6026, USA

McDonald, Ben (Athlete, Baseball Player,
Olympic Athlete)
8780 Henderson Rd
Denham Springs, LA 70726-6705, USA

McDonald, Bruce (Director, Producer)
c/o Bill Douglass *Paradigm (LA)*
360 N Crescent Dr
North Bldg
Beverly Hills, CA 90210-4874, USA

McDonald, Christopher
c/o Daniel (Danny) Sussman *Brillstein
Entertainment Partners (LA)*
9150 Wilshire Blvd Ste 350
Beverly Hills, CA 90212-3453, USA

McDonald, Country Joe (Musician)
PO Box 7054
Berkeley, CA 94707-0054, USA

McDonald, Darnell (Athlete, Baseball
Player)
542 W Windsor Ave Frnt
Phoenix, AZ 85003-1062, USA

McDonald, Darnell (Athlete, Football
Player)
13551 Bentley Cir
Woodbridge, VA 22192-4336, USA

McDonald, Dave (Athlete, Baseball
Player)
2545 SE 3rd St
Pompano Beach, FL 33062-5401, USA

McDonald, Devon (Athlete, Football Player)
10812 Green Meadow Pl # Pi
Indianapolis, IN 46229-3530, USA

McDonald, Donzell (Athlete, Baseball Player)
3225 Scranton St
Aurora, CO 80011-1827, USA

McDonald, Gerry
41st Rd
Wethersfield, CT 06109

McDonald, Glenn (Athlete, Basketball Player)
2135 Vuelta Grande Ave
Long Beach, CA 90815-3562, USA

McDonald, Heather (Actor)
c/o Alex Spieller *IMPR*
357 S Robertson Blvd
Beverly Hills, CA 90211-3602, USA

McDonald, Jiggs (Sportscaster)
8331 Arborfield Ct
Fort Myers, FL 33912-4684, USA

McDonald, John (Athlete, Baseball Player)
411 Tilden Rd
Scituate, MA 02066-2124, USA

McDonald, Keith (Athlete, Baseball Player)
5162 E Greensboro Ln
Anaheim, CA 92807-4612, USA

McDonald, Michael (Musician, Songwriter)
64 Wai Kulu Pl
Lahaina, HI 96761-5713, USA

McDonald, Michael James (Actor, Director, Writer)
c/o Staff Member *3 Arts Entertainment (LA)*
9460 Wilshire Blvd Fl 7
Beverly Hills, CA 90212-2713, USA

McDonald, Mike (Athlete, Football Player)
1067 E Angeleno Ave
Burbank, CA 91501-1420, USA

McDonald, Miriam (Actor)
c/o Brantley Brown *Schachter Entertainment*
1157 S Beverly Dr Fl 2
Los Angeles, CA 90035-1119, USA

McDonald, Paul (Athlete, Football Player)
1815 Tradewinds Ln
Newport Beach, CA 92660-3810, USA

McDonald, Ramos (Athlete, Football Player)
11620 Audelia Rd Apt 715
Dallas, TX 75243-5686, USA

McDonald, Ricardo (Athlete, Football Player)
425 E 25th St
Paterson, NJ 07514-2306, USA

McDonald, Richie (Musician)
PO Box 128648
Nashville, TN 37212, USA

McDonald, Roderick
982 Walglen Ct
San Jose, CA 95136-1463, USA

McDonald, Thomas F (Tommy) (Athlete, Football Player)
537 W Valley Forge Rd
King Of Prussia, PA 19406-1568, USA

McDonald, Tim (Athlete, Attorney, Football Player)
208 Stone Creek Ct
Whippany, NJ 07981-2507, USA

McDonell, Thomas (Actor)
c/o Annabel Gualazzi *William Morris Endeavor (LA)*
9601 Wilshire Blvd
Beverly Hills, CA 90210-5213, USA

McDonnell, Bob (Governor, Politician)
1111 E Broad St
State Capitol
Richmond, VA 23219-1934, USA

McDonnell, Joe (Athlete, Hockey Player)
Detroit Red Wings
600 Civic Center Dr
Detroit, MI 48226-4419

McDonnell, John F (Business Person)
McDonnell Douglas Corp
PO Box 516
Saint Louis, MO 63166-0516, USA

McDonnell, Mary (Actor)
c/o Perri Kipperman *Kipperman Management*
345 7th Ave Rm 503
New York, NY 10001-5054, USA

McDonnell, Patrick (Cartoonist)
c/o Staff Member *King Features Syndication*
300 W 57th St Fl 15
New York, NY 10019-5238, USA

McDonnell, Stephen (Business Person)
Applegate
750 US Highway 202 Ste 300
Bridgewater, NJ 08807-5530, USA

McDonough, Hubie (Athlete, Hockey Player)
Manchester Monarchs
555 Elm St Ste 3
Manchester, NH 03101-2535

McDonough, Hubie (Athlete, Hockey Player)
65 Holmes Dr
Manchester, NH 03104-2890, USA

McDonough, Mary (Actor)
6858 Cantaloupe Ave
Van Nuys, CA 91405-4148, USA

McDonough, Neal (Actor)
453 S Las Palmas Ave
Los Angeles, CA 90020-4815, USA

McDonough, Neil (Actor)
Rigberg Robert Rugolo
1180 S Beverly Dr Ste 601
Los Angeles, CA 90035-1158, USA

McDonough, Patrick (Athlete, Cycler, Olympic Athlete)
64 Myrtle St Apt 2
Boston, MA 02114-4577, USA

McDonough, Sean (Sportscaster)
ABC-TV
77 W 66th St
Sports Dept
New York, NY 10023-6201, USA

McDorman, Jake (Actor)
c/o Elissa Leeds-Fickman *Reel Talent Management*
PO Box 491035
Los Angeles, CA 90049-9035, USA

McDormand, Frances (Actor)
23 Rafael Ave
Bolinas, CA 94924, USA

McDougal, Mike (Athlete, Hockey Player)
2892 Tanglewood Dr
Kimball, MI 48074-1535

McDougal, Susan
350 S Grand Ave Ste 3900
Los Angeles, CA 90071-3410

McDougale, Stockar (Athlete, Football Player)
15 Bradford Ct
Dearborn, MI 48126-4170, USA

McDougall, Charles (Writer)
c/o Staff Member *Industry Entertainment*
955 Carrillo Dr Ste 300
Los Angeles, CA 90048-5400, USA

McDougall, Ian (Producer)
c/o Staff Member *Gersh (LA)*
9465 Wilshire Blvd Ste 600
Beverly Hills, CA 90212-2605, USA

McDougall, Marshall (Athlete, Baseball Player)
213 Bell Branch Ln
Saint Johns, FL 32259-4438, USA

McDowel, Michael (Race Car Driver)
20310 Chartwell Center Dr
Cornelius, NC 28031-5253, USA

McDowell, Bubba (Athlete, Football Player)
6353 Richmond Ave
Houston, TX 77057-5964, USA

McDowell, Dagen (Correspondent)
c/o Staff Member *Fox Business Network (NY)*
1211 Avenue of the Americas Fl 15
New York, NY 10036-8705, USA

McDowell, Frank (Doctor)
100 N Kalaheo Ave Apt F
Kailua, HI 96734-2306, USA

McDowell, Jack (Athlete, Baseball Player)
1141 Lynbrook Dr
Charlotte, NC 28211-4255, USA

McDowell, Malcolm (Actor)
c/o Staff Member *Dontanville/Frattaroli (D/F)*
270 Lafayette St Ste 402
New York, NY 10012-3327, USA

McDowell, Michael (Race Car Driver)
Michael Waltrip Racing
20310 Chartwell Center Dr
Cornelius, NC 28031-5253, USA

McDowell, Oddibe (Athlete, Baseball Player)
5240 SW 18th St
West Park, FL 33023-3157, USA

McDowell, Roger (Athlete, Baseball Player)
2690 Pete Shaw Rd
Marietta, GA 30066-2224, USA

McDowell, Ronnie (Musician)
c/o Bobby Roberts *Bobby Roberts Agency*
PO Box 1547
Goodlettsville, TN 37070-1547, USA

McDowell, Sam (Athlete, Baseball Player)
12902 Brown Bark Trl
Clermont, FL 34711-7646, USA

McDsyes, Antonio (Athlete, Basketball Player)
979 County Road 473
Meridian, MS 39301-9636, USA

McDuffie, George (Athlete, Football Player)
819 Independence Rd
Toledo, OH 43607-2529, USA

McDuffie, Otis J (O J) (Athlete, Football Player)
1333 NW 121st Ave
Plantation, FL 33323-2438, USA

McDuffie, Robert (Musician)
Columbia Artists Mgmt Inc
165 W 57th St
New York, NY 10019-2201, USA

McDyess, Antonio (Athlete, Basketball Player, Olympic Athlete)
979 County Road 473
Meridian, MS 39301-9636, USA

McEachern, Shawn (Athlete, Hockey Player, Olympic Athlete)
71 Beach St
Marblehead, MA 01945-2957, USA

McEldowney, Brooke (Cartoonist)
United Feature Syndicate
PO Box 5610
Cincinnati, OH 45201-5610, USA

McElhenney, Rob (Actor)
c/o Nick Frenkel *3 Arts Entertainment (LA)*
9460 Wilshire Blvd Fl 7
Beverly Hills, CA 90212-2713, USA

McElhenny, Hugh (Athlete, Football Player)
3013 Via Venezia
Henderson, NV 89052-3802, USA

McElhone, Natascha (Actor)
c/o Christina Papadopoulos *Baker Winokur Ryder Public Relations (BWR-NY)*
292 Madison Ave Fl 12
New York, NY 10017-6415, USA

McElligott, Sarah (Actor)
c/o Monica Barkett *Global Artists Agency*
6253 Hollywood Blvd Apt 508
Los Angeles, CA 90028-8251, USA

McElman, Andy (Athlete, Hockey Player)
260 Beach Dr
Algonquin, IL 60102-2502

McElmury, Jim (Athlete, Hockey Player, Olympic Athlete)
9122 78th St S
Cottage Grove, MN 55016-2211, USA

McElroy, Chuck (Athlete, Baseball Player)
1049 Nederland Ave
Port Arthur, TX 77640-4338, USA

McElroy, Hugh (Athlete, Football Player)
3899 Fonville Ave
Beaumont, TX 77705-2207, USA

McElroy, Leeland (Athlete, Football Player)
23003 Blackwater Rd
San Antonio, TX 78258-2559, USA

McElroy, Reggie (Athlete, Football Player)
30661 Pheasant Dr
Lebanon, MO 65536-7249, USA

McElroy, Vann (Athlete, Football Player)
HC 34 Box 1011
Uvalde, TX 78801, USA

McElwain, Jason (Sportscaster)
c/o Staff Member *William Morris Endeavor (LA)*
9601 Wilshire Blvd
Beverly Hills, CA 90210-5213, USA

McEnaney, Will (Athlete, Baseball Player)
169 Roycourt Cir
Royal Palm Beach, FL 33411-8295, USA

McEnroe, John (Athlete, Tennis Player)
28000 Sea Lane Dr
Malibu, CA 90265-4325, USA

McEntee, Gerald W (Politician)
State County Municipal Employees Union
1625 L St NW
Washington, DC 20036-5665, USA

McEntire, Reba (Musician)
c/o Narvel Blackstock Starstruck
Entertainment
40 Music Sq W
Nashville, TN 37203-3206, USA

McEwen, Craig (Athlete, Football Player)
1610 Hilton Head Ct Apt 1265
El Cajon, CA 92019-4578, USA

McEwen, Mark (Correspondent)
CBS TV
51 W 52nd St
News Dept
New York, NY 10019-6119, USA

McEwen, Mike
3712 N Peniel Ave
Bethany, OK 73008-3441

McEwen, Tom (Race Car Driver)
Motorsports HOF
PO Box 194
Novi, MI 48376-0194, USA

McEwen, Tom (Writer)
Tampa Tribune
202 S Parker St
Editorial Dept
Tampa, FL 33606-2395, USA

McEwing, Joe (Athlete, Baseball Player)
309 Cricket Ct
Yardley, PA 19067-5794, USA

McFadden, Cynthia (Correspondent,
Journalist, Television Host)
c/o Staff Member Nightline
1717 Desales St NW
Washington, DC 20036-4401, USA

McFadden, Darren (Athlete, Football
Player)
c/o Michael Conley BDA Sports
Management (BDA-CA)
700 Ygnacio Valley Rd Ste 330
Walnut Creek, CA 94596-3838, USA

McFadden, Davenia (Actor)
c/o Felicia Sager Sager Management
260 S Beverly Dr Ste 205
Beverly Hills, CA 90212-3812, USA

McFadden, Gates (Actor)
c/o Marcia Hurwitz Innovative Artists (LA)
1505 10th St
Santa Monica, CA 90401-2805, USA

McFadden, Leon (Athlete, Baseball Player)
8617 S 10th Ave
Inglewood, CA 90305-2346, USA

McFadden, Paul (Athlete, Football Player)
7395 Christopher Dr
Youngstown, OH 44514-2563, USA

McFadin, Bud
1467 Albrecht Rd
Victoria, TX 77905

McFall, Dan (Athlete, Hockey Player)
475 N Williston Rd
Williston, VT 05495-9572

McFarland, Anthony (Athlete, Football
Player)
7733 Still Lakes Dr
Odessa, FL 33556-2262, USA

McFarland, Jim (Athlete, Football Player)
5102 S 90th St
Lincoln, NE 68526-9627, USA

McFarland, Kay (Athlete, Football Player)
7394 S Monaco St
Centennial, CO 80112-1528, USA

McFarland, Kirsten (Writer)
c/o Staff Member ICM Partners (LA)
10250 Constellation Blvd Fl 7
Los Angeles, CA 90067-6207, USA

McFarland, Mike (Race Car Driver)
PO Box 330
Mooresville, NC 28115-0330, USA

McFarlane, Andrew (Actor)
c/o Staff Member Jeff Morrone
Entertainment
9350 Wilshire Blvd Ste 224
Beverly Hills, CA 90212-3204, USA

McFarlane, Robert C (Government
Official)
2010 Prospect St NW
Washington, DC 20037, USA

McFarlane, Todd (Cartoonist)
Todd McFarlane Entertainment
1711 W Greentree Rd Ste 208
Tempe, AZ 85284-2717, USA

McFaull, David (Athlete, Olympic Athlete,
Sailor)
109 Poloke Pl
Honolulu, HI 96822-5007, USA

McFayden, Brian (Actor)
c/o Babette Perry IMG (LA)
2049 Century Park E Ste 2460
Los Angeles, CA 90067-3126, USA

McFerrin, Bobby (Actor, Songwriter,
Writer)
Original Artists
400 E 52nd St Ph W
New York, NY 10022-6410, USA

Mcfly (Music Group)
c/o Staff Member Universal Music Group
(UMG - LA)
2220 Colorado Ave
Santa Monica, CA 90404-3506, USA

McG (Director, Producer)
Wonderland Sound and Vision
8739 W Sunset Blvd
West Hollywood, CA 90069-2205, USA

McGaffigan, Andy (Athlete, Baseball
Player)
6243 Forestwood Dr E
Lakeland, FL 33811-2402, USA

McGahee, Willis (Athlete, Football Player)
1 Bills Dr
Orchard Park, NY 14127-2237, USA

McGahey, Kathleen (Athlete, Hockey
Player, Olympic Athlete)
7427 W 81st St
Los Angeles, CA 90045-2303, USA

McGann, Michelle (Athlete, Golfer)
1200 Singer Dr
Riviera Beach, FL 33404-2765, USA

McGarity, Wane (Athlete, Football Player)
4622 Lavender Ln
San Antonio, TX 78220-2511, USA

McGarrahan, Scott (Athlete, Football
Player)
6636 W William Cannon Dr
Austin, TX 78735-8529, USA

McGarrigle, Anne (Musician)
c/o Staff Member Concerted Efforts
PO Box 440326
Somerville, MA 02144-0004, USA

McGarry, John (Athlete, Football Player)
5725 S Woodlawn Ave
Chicago, IL 60637-1602, USA

McGarry, Kelly (Actor)
c/o Staff Member Heresun Management
4119 W Burbank Blvd
Burbank, CA 91505-2122, USA

McGarry, Steve (Cartoonist)
United feature Syndicate
PO Box 5610
Cincinnati, OH 45201-5610, USA

McGaughey, Shug (Horse Racer)
20941 NE 38th Ave
Miami, FL 33180-3783, USA

McGaw, Patrick (Actor)
Banner Entertainment
8265 W Sunset Blvd Ste 200
West Hollywood, CA 90046-2470, USA

McGee, Ben (Athlete, Football Player)
35 Castle Cv
Jackson, MS 39212-3448, USA

McGee, Herb (Athlete, Basketball Player)
PO Box 67
Southeastern, PA 19399-0067, USA

McGee, Jake (Athlete, Baseball Player)
6126 Yeats Manor Dr
Tampa, FL 33616-1325, USA

McGee, Michael B (Mike) (Athlete,
Football Player)
University Of South California
2 Medical Park Rd Ste 502
Columbia, SC 29203-6876, USA

McGee, Pamela (Pam) (Basketball Player)
Los Angeles Sparks
1111 S Figueroa St
Staples Center
Los Angeles, CA 90015-1300, USA

McGee, Stephen (Athlete, Football Player)
c/o Staff Member Dallas Cowboys
1 Cowboys Pkwy
Irving, TX 75063-4999, USA

McGee, Tim (Athlete, Football Player)
4226 Maxwell Dr
Mason, OH 45040-6504, USA

McGee, Tony (Athlete, Football Player)
170 Tana Dr
Fayetteville, GA 30214-7539, USA

McGee, Trina (Actor)
c/o Stephen Rice Pantheon Talent
1801 Century Park E Ste 1910
Los Angeles, CA 90067-2321, USA

McGee, Willie (Athlete, Baseball Player)
300 Stone View Ct
Martinez, CA 94553-9644, USA

McGeever, John (Athlete, Football Player)
3479 Norwich Dr
Vestavia, AL 35243-2128, USA

McGehee, Kevin (Athlete, Baseball Player)
8639 Rid11EMONT Dr
Pineville, LA 71360, USA

McGehee, Robby (Race Car Driver)
17879 Wild Horse Creek Rd
Chesterfield, MO 63005-3621, USA

McGeorge, Missie (Athlete, Golfer)
1836 Willow Springs Ct
Haslet, TX 76052-2856, USA

McGeorge, Rich (Athlete, Football Player)
2200 Trail Wood Dr
Durham, NC 27705-1305, USA

McGhee, Carla (Athlete, Basketball
Player, Olympic Athlete)
1664 N Virginia St
Reno, NV 89557-0001, USa

McGhee, George C (Government Official)
12 Eastman St
Saint Augustine, FL 32084-0325, USA

McGhee-Anderson, Kathleen (Producer)
c/o Staff Member Creative Artists Agency
(CAA-LA)
2000 Avenue of the Stars Ste 100
Los Angeles, CA 90067-4705, USA

McGiinchy, Kevin (Athlete, Baseball
Player)
388 Medford St
Malden, MA 02148-7209, USA

McGilberry, Randy (Athlete, Baseball
Player)
2110 Foxford St
Cantonment, FL 32533-6851, USA

McGill, Billy (Athlete, Basketball Player)
5129 W 58th Pl
Los Angeles, CA 90056-1601, USA

McGill, Bob (Athlete, Hockey Player)
Toronto Maple Leafs
400-40 Bay St
Toronto, ON M5J 2X2

McGill, Bruce (Actor)
c/o Scott Manners Stone Manners Salners
Agency (LA)
6100 Wilshire Blvd Ste 1500
Los Angeles, CA 90048-5110, USA

McGill, Everett (Actor)
c/o Staff Member William Morris
Endeavor (LA)
9601 Wilshire Blvd
Beverly Hills, CA 90210-5213, USA

McGill, Jill (Athlete, Golfer)
6756 Inverness Ln
Dallas, TX 75214-2518, USA

McGill, Karmeeleyah (Athlete, Football
Player)
1626 N Greenwood Ave
Clearwater, FL 33755, USA

McGill, Mike (Athlete, Football Player)
8930 Louis Ct
Saint John, IN 46373-9708, USA

McGill, Paul (Actor)
c/o Jill Fritzo PMK/BNC Public Relations
(PMK-NY)
622 3rd Ave Fl 8
New York, NY 10017-6707, USA

McGill, Ryan (Athlete, Hockey Player)
958 Yoeman Hall Rd
Kalispell, MT 59901-7610

McGillin, Howard (Actor)
c/o Staff Member Cunningham Escott
Slevin & Doherty (CESD-LA)
10635 Santa Monica Blvd Ste 130
Los Angeles, CA 90025-8306, USA

McGillis, Kelly (Actor, Producer)
37 Southern Scenic Hts
Hendersonville, NC 28792-2318, USA

McGillivray, Scott (Television Host)
c/o Staff Member *HGTV*
9721 Sherrill Blvd
Knoxville, TN 37932-3330, USA

McGinest, Willie (Athlete, Football Player)
4132 Prado De Las Cabras
Calabasas, CA 91302-3627, USA

McGinley, John C (Actor)
Innovative Artists
1505 10th St
Santa Monica, CA 90401-2805, USA

McGinley, Ted (Actor)
c/o Mark Teitelbaum *Teitelbaum Artists Group*
8840 Wilshire Blvd Fl 3
Beverly Hills, CA 90211-2606, USA

McGinn, Dan (Athlete, Baseball Player)
1309 S 189th Ct
Omaha, NE 68130-2842, USA

McGinnis, Dave (Athlete, Coach, Football Coach, Football Player)
Arizona Cardinals
PO Box 888
Phoenix, AZ 85001-0888, USA

McGinnis, George (Athlete, Basketball Player)
811E Bounty Ct
Indianapolis, IN 46236, USA

McGinnis, Joe (Writer)
Janklow & Nesbit
445 Park Ave Fl 13
New York, NY 10022-8628, USA

McGinnis, Russ (Athlete, Baseball Player)
15444 Artesian Spring Rd
San Diego, CA 92127-5736, USA

McGinty, Damian (Actor)
c/o Paul Lyttle *Twenty Four Seven PR*
Prefers to be contacted via telephone or email
Los Angeles, CA, USA

McGirt, James (Buddy) (Boxer)
195 Suffolk Ave
Brentwood, NY 11717-4205, USA

McGiver, Boris (Actor)
c/o Staff Member *Harden-Curtis Associates*
214 W 29th St Rm 1203
New York, NY 10001-5754, USA

McGlinchy, Kevin (Athlete, Baseball Player)
10 West St
Malden, MA 02148-5311, USA

McGlockin, Jon (Athlete, Basketball Player)
5281 State Rd
#83
Hartland, WI 53029, USA

McGlocklin, Jon
5281 State Road 83
Hartland, WI 53029-9306, USA

McGlothin, Pat (Athlete, Baseball Player)
1454 Kenesaw Ave
Knoxville, TN 37919-7749, USA

McGlynn, Dennis (Race Car Driver)
Dover Downs Speedway
PO Box 843
Dover, DE 19903-0843, USA

McGlynn, Dick (Athlete, Hockey Player)
38 Rock Glen Rd
Medford, MA 02155-1946, USA

McGlynn, Dick (Athlete, Hockey Player, Olympic Athlete)
38 Rock Glen Rd
Medford, MA 02155-1946, USA

McGlynn, Mike (Athlete, Football Player)
c/o Michael Perrett *SportsTrust Advisors (GA)*
3340 Peachtree Rd NE Fl 16
Atlanta, GA 30326-1000, USA

McGlynn, Ryan (Race Car Driver)
Raynard McGlynn Motorsports
92 Allen St
Nanticoke, PA 18634-1127, USA

McGonigal, Kelly (Motivational Speaker)
c/o Staff Member *The Leigh Bureau*
92 E Main St Ste 200
Somerville, NJ 08876-2319, USA

McGoon, Dwight C (Doctor)
211 2nd St NW Apt 2016
Rochester, MN 55901-3101, USA

McGovern, Elizabeth (Actor)
c/o Staff Member *Anonymous Content (LA)*
3532 Hayden Ave
Culver City, CA 90232-2413, USA

McGovern, Jim (Athlete, Golfer)
900 Amaryllis Ave
Oradell, NJ 07649-1302, USA

McGovern, Maureen (Actor, Musician)
MM Productions Inc
12087 Evergreen St NW
C/O Jennifer Howe
Minneapolis, MN 55448-2433, USA

McGovern, Rob (Athlete, Football Player)
419 E 57th St Apt 2D
New York, NY 10022-3176, USA

McGowan, Charles E (Religious Leader)
Presbyterian Church in America
1852 Century Pl NE Ste 201
Atlanta, GA 30345-4305, USA

McGowan, Dustin (Athlete, Baseball Player)
6869 Roberts Rd
Tallahassee, FL 32309-9279, USA

McGowan, Michael (Director)
c/o Bill Douglass *Paradigm (LA)*
360 N Crescent Dr
North Bldg
Beverly Hills, CA 90210-4874, USA

McGowan, Pat (Athlete, Golfer)
PO Box 88
Southern Pines, NC 28388-0088, USA

McGowan, Rose (Actor)
7561 Devista Dr
Los Angeles, CA 90046-1711, USA

McGrady, Michael (Actor)
c/o Staff Member *Main Title Entertainment*
8383 Wilshire Blvd Ste 408
Beverly Hills, CA 90211-2435, USA

McGrady, Tracy (Athlete, Basketball Player)
23 Beacon Hl
Sugar Land, TX 77479-2551, USA

McGrath, Alister (Writer)
c/o Staff Member *HarperCollins Publishers*
195 Broadway Fl 2
Cellar 1
New York, NY 10007-3132, USA

McGrath, Doug (Director)
c/o Staff Member *ICM Partners (LA)*
10250 Constellation Blvd Fl 7
Los Angeles, CA 90067-6207, USA

McGrath, Douglas (Actor, Director, Writer)
c/o Staff Member *Creative Artists Agency (CAA-LA)*
2000 Avenue of the Stars Ste 100
Los Angeles, CA 90067-4705, USA

McGrath, Eugene R (Business Person)
Consolidated Edison
4 Irving Pl
New York, NY 10003-3502, USA

McGrath, Mark (Musician, Television Host)
c/o John Marx *William Morris Endeavor (LA)*
9601 Wilshire Blvd
Beverly Hills, CA 90210-5213, USA

McGrath, Mike (Bowler)
63 W Napa Dr
Petaluma, CA 94954-1336, USA

McGraw, Dr Phil (Doctor, Talk Show Host)
1407 Davies Dr
Beverly Hills, CA 90210-2027, USA

McGraw, Harold W Jr (Publisher)
McGraw-Hill Inc
2 Penn Plz Fl 5
New York, NY 10121-0600, USA

McGraw, Jay (Writer)
c/o Staff Member *The Dr. Phil Show*
5555 Melrose Ave
Mae West Bldg
Los Angeles, CA 90038-3989, USA

McGraw, Melinda (Actor)
c/o Staff Member *McKeon-Myones Management*
3500 W Olive Ave Ste 770
Burbank, CA 91505-5527, USA

McGraw, Mike (Athlete, Football Player)
PO Box 529
Medicine Bow, WY 82328, USA

McGraw, Tim (Musician)
c/o Coran Capshaw *Red Light Management (VA)*
321 E Main St Ste 500
Charlottesville, VA 22902-3201, USA

McGraw, Tom (Athlete, Baseball Player)
11300 NE 379th St
La Center, WA 98629-4307, USA

McGraw III, Harold W (Business Person, Publisher)
McGraw-Hill Inc
2 Penn Plz Fl 5
New York, NY 10121-0600, USA

McGreevey, James (Politician)
109A Green St
Woodbridge, NJ 07095-2910, USA

McGregor, Ewan (Actor)
c/o Megan Moss Pachon *ID Public Relations (LA)*
7060 Hollywood Blvd Fl 8th
Los Angeles, CA 90028-6021, USA

McGregor, Gilbert (Athlete, Basketball Player)
5815 Maylandia Rd
Charlotte, NC 28269-1396, USA

McGregor, Scott (Athlete, Baseball Player)
1514 Providence Rd # A
Towson, MD 21286-1523, USA

McGrew, Reggie (Athlete, Football Player)
1247 Lakeside Dr Apt 2039
Sunnyvale, CA 94085-1008, USA

McGriff, Elton (Athlete, Basketball Player)
4011 Shoreline Dr
Dallas, TX 75233-3709, USA

McGriff, Fred (Athlete, Baseball Player)
16314 Millan De Avila
Tampa, FL 33613-1089, USA

McGriff, Hershel (Race Car Driver)
General Delivery
Green Valley, AZ 85622, USA

McGriff, Lee (Athlete, Football Player)
3501 W University Ave Ste A
Gainesville, FL 32607-2465, USA

McGriff, Terry (Athlete, Baseball Player)
2905 Langston Dr
Fort Pierce, FL 34946-1180, USA

McGriff, Tery (Athlete, Baseball Player)
2905 Langston Dr
Fort Pierce, FL 34946-1180, USA

McGriff, Travis (Athlete, Football Player)
5910 NW 19th Pl
Gainesville, FL 32605-3246, USA

McGruder, Aaron (Cartoonist)
Universal Press Syndicate
4520 Main St Ste 340
Kansas City, MO 64111-7705, USA

McGuane III, Thomas F (Writer)
410 S 3rd Ave
Bozeman, MT 59715-5251, USA

McGuigan, Frank (Athlete, Football Player)
2715 Willits Rd
Philadelphia, PA 19114-3410, USA

McGuinn, Roger (Musician)
c/o Staff Member *Shore Fire Media*
32 Court St Fl 16
Brooklyn, NY 11201-4441, USA

McGuire, Allie
4 Tanglewood Ln
Winchester, MA 01890-3376

McGuire, Betty (Actor)
H David Moss
733 Seward St PH
Los Angeles, CA 90038-3503, USA

McGuire, Bill (Athlete, Baseball Player)
17209 L St
Omaha, NE 68135, USA

McGuire, Christine (Musician)
100 Rancho Cir
Las Vegas, NV 89107-4600, USA

McGuire, Kevin E (Athlete, Basketball Player)
20 Blue Jay Ln
Saint Paul, MN 55127-2015, USA

Mcguire, Maeve
c/o Staff Member *Gage Group, The (LA)*
5757 Wilshire Blvd Ste 659
Los Angeles, CA 90036-3682, USA

McGuire, Marcy (Actor)
681 Red Arrow Trl
Palm Desert, CA 92211-7427, USA

McGuire, Mickey (Athlete, Baseball Player)
1521 Middle Park Dr
Dayton, OH 45414-1500, USA

McGuire, Phyllis (Musician)
7373 N Scottsdale Rd Ste A130
Paradise Valley, AZ 85253-3522, USA

McGuire, Ryan (Athlete, Baseball Player)
10 Atwater
Irvine, CA 92602-2028, USA

McGuire, Walter E (Gene) (Athlete, Football Player)
3229 Country Club Dr
Lynn Haven, FL 32444-5125, USA

McGuire, William Biff (Actor)
McKenrick
1443 Pandora Ave
Los Angeles, CA 90024-5164, USA

McGuire, William W (Business Person)
United HealthCare Corp
9900 Bren Rd E Ste 300W
Opus Center
Hopkins, MN 55343-4402, USA

McGuire-Leveque, Sarah (Athlete, Golfer)
2433 S 15th St
Springfield, IL 62703-3644, USA

McGuire Sisters (Music Group)
c/o Stan Scottland *Stan Scottland Entertainment*
701 Fallsgrove Dr Apt 407
Rockville, MD 20850-8710, USA

McGwire, Mark (Athlete, Baseball Player, Olympic Athlete)
700 Clark Ave
Saint Louis, MO 63102-1727, USA

McHale, Christina (Athlete, Tennis Player)
c/o Staff Member *Women's Tennis Association (WTA (US))*
1 Progress Plz Ste 1500
St Petersburg, FL 33701-4335, USA

Mchale, Joel (Actor, Television Host)
c/o James Dolin *Sonesta Entertainment*
150 Ocean Park Blvd Unit 423
Santa Monica, CA 90405-3574, USA

McHale, Kevin (Actor)
c/o Jamie Malone *MC Talent Management*
4821 Lankershim Blvd # F329
N Hollywood, CA 91601-4538, USA

McHale, Kevin (Athlete, Basketball Player)
20 Blue Jay Ln
Saint Paul, MN 55127-2015, USA

McHattie, Stephen (Actor)
c/o Christopher Wright *Christopher Wright Management*
3207 Winnie Dr
Los Angeles, CA 90068-1439, USA

McHenry, Vance (Athlete, Baseball Player)
2396 Brown St
Durham, CA 95938-9620, USA

M. Christensen, Donna (Congressman, Politician)
1510 Longworth Hob
Washington, DC 20515-5501, USA

McHugh, Heather (Writer)
University of Washington
English Dept
PO Box 35330
Seattle, WA 98195-0001, USA

McHugh, Mike (Athlete, Hockey Player)
945 Parish Pl
Hummelstown, PA 17036-8986

Mcilhargey, Jack (Athlete, Hockey Player)
2120 Birch St
Point Roberts, WA 98281-9507

Mcilhenny, Don (Athlete, Football Player)
8505 Edgemere Rd Apt 101
Dallas, TX 75225-3520, USA

Mcilravy, Lincoln (Athlete, Olympic Athlete)
4220 210th St NE
Solon, IA 52333-9657, USA

McIlvaine, Jim (Athlete, Basketball Player)
Camp Anokijig
Camp Anokijig W5639 Anokijig Ln
Plymouth,
WI 53000000000000000000000000000000000000000000000000
USA

McIlvaine, Joe (Commentator)
106 Stoney Brook Blvd
Newtown Square, PA 19073-3974, USA

McInerney, Jay (Actor, Writer)
c/o Doug MacLaren *ICM Partners (LA)*
10250 Constellation Blvd Fl 7
Los Angeles, CA 90067-6207, USA

McInnis, Hugh (Athlete, Football Player)
290 Rockwell Church Rd NE
Winder, GA 30680-3039, USA

Mcinnis, Jeffrey (Athlete, Basketball Player)
34E4 Lazy Day Ln
Charlotte, NC 28269, USA

McInnis, Marty (Athlete, Hockey Player, Olympic Athlete)
21 Peter Hobart Dr
Hingham, MA 02043-3751, USA

McIntosh, Bill (Athlete, Golfer)
2222 Faye Dr
Ann Arbor, MI 48103-3415, USA

McIntosh, Chris (Athlete, Football Player)
4937 Bear Mountain Dr
Evergreen, CO 80439-5606, USA

McIntosh, Damion (Athlete, Football Player)
1221 SW Summit Crossing Dr
Lees Summit, MO 64081-3264, USA

McIntosh, Joe (Athlete, Baseball Player)
9120 SE 54th St
Mercer Island, WA 98040-5148, USA

McIntosh, Tim (Athlete, Baseball Player)
1815 S Talbott Pl
Waynesboro, VA 22980-2250, USA

McIntosh Slaughter, Louise (Congressman, Politician)
2469 Rayburn Hob
Washington, DC 20515-3228, USA

McIntyre, Guy (Athlete, Football Player)
257 Arrowhead Way
Hayward, CA 94544-6649, USA

McIntyre, Joe (Actor)
c/o Gina Rugolo *Rugolo Entertainment*
195 S Beverly Dr Ste 400
Beverly Hills, CA 90212-3044, USA

McIntyre, Joey (Musician)
c/o Jason Gutman *Gersh (NY)*
41 Madison Ave
New York, NY 10010-2202, USA

Mcintyre, Larry (Athlete, Hockey Player)
PO Box 546
Bixby, OK 74008-0546

McIntyre, Mike (Congressman, Politician)
2133 Rayburn Hob
Washington, DC 20515-2102, USA

McIntyre, Secedrick (Athlete, Football Player)
4801 Tannery Ave
Tampa, FL 33624-4533, USA

McIntyre, Vonda (Writer)
PO Box 31041
Seattle, WA 98103-1041, USA

McIver, Everett (Athlete, Football Player)
1205 Avignon Dr SW
Conyers, GA 30094-8406, USA

McIver, Rose (Actor)
c/o Kimberlin Dalehite *Magnolia Entertainment (LA)*
9595 Wilshire Blvd Ste 601
Beverly Hills, CA 90212-2506, USA

McIvor, Richard (Athlete, Football Player)
PO Box 148
Fort Davis, TX 79734-0148, USA

Mc.Julien, Paul (Athlete, Football Player)
12111 Gibbens Rd
Baton Rouge, LA 70807-1602, USA

McJulien, Paul (Athlete, Football Player)
527 Whitney Dr
Newberg, OR 97132-2294, USA

McKagen, Duff
8647 Edwin Dr
Los Angeles, CA 90046-1047

McKay, Adam (Actor, Director, Writer)
c/o Jimmy Miller *Mosaic Media Group*
9200 W Sunset Blvd Ste 10
West Hollywood, CA 90069-3608, USA

McKay, Bob (Athlete, Football Player)
4110 Bluffridge Dr
Austin, TX 78759-7354, USA

McKay, Cody (Athlete, Baseball Player)
6033 E Long Shadow Trl
Scottsdale, AZ 85266-8207, USA

McKay, Dave (Athlete, Baseball Player)
9702 E La Posada Cir
Scottsdale, AZ 85255-3716, USA

McKay, Gardner (Actor, Director, Writer)
1040 Lunalilo St PH 2
Honolulu, HI 96822-5712, USA

McKay, John (Athlete, Football Player)
16601 Calle Haleigh
Pacific Palisades, CA 90272-1968, USA

McKay, Mhairi (Athlete, Golfer)
898 W Ashbourne Dr
Eagle, ID 83616-6433, USA

McKay, Nellie (Actor)
c/o Staff Member *Kid Logic*
156 Liberty St Apt 12
Little Ferry, NJ 07643-1768, USA

McKay, Peggy (Actor)
8811 Wonderland Ave
Los Angeles, CA 90046-1851, USA

McKay, Randy (Athlete, Hockey Player)
44640 US Highway 41
Chassell, MI 49916-9102

McKay, Ross (Athlete, Hockey Player)
1401 Thornwood Dr
Downers Grove, IL 60516-1224

McKay, Tom (Actor)
c/o Jason Spire *Inspire Entertainment*
315 7th Ave Apt 17E
New York, NY 10001-6011, USA

McKean, Eddy (Race Car Driver)
Enerjetix Motors
20520 E 1st Ave
Greenacres, WA 99016-8617, USA

McKean, Jim (Athlete, Baseball Player)
740 Sand Pine Dr NE
Saint Petersburg, FL 33703-3181, USA

McKean, Michael (Actor, Comedian)
3202 Club Dr
Los Angeles, CA 90064-4812, USA

McKee, Bonnie (Musician)
15353 SE 49th Pl
Bellevue, WA 98006-3652, USA

McKee, Jay (Athlete, Hockey Player)
20 Douglas Ln
Elma, NY 14059-9022

McKee, Jay (Athlete, Hockey Player)
Rochester Americans
1 War Memorial Sq Ste 228
Rochester, NY 14614-2192

McKee, Lonette (Actor)
New Artist Group
131 W 35th St Fl 8
C/O Keith Perkins
New York, NY 10001-2111, USA

McKee, Lucky (Director)
9300 Wilshire Blvd Ste 555
Beverly Hills, CA 90212-3211, USA

McKee, Maria (Musician)
Eleven Thirty
449 Trollingwood Rd # A
Haw River, NC 27258-8750, USA

McKee, Mike (Athlete, Hockey Player)
55 Ballard St
Newton Center, MA 02459-1230

McKee, Rogers (Athlete, Baseball Player)
409 Forest Hill Dr
Shelby, NC 28150-5520, USA

McKee, Todd (Actor)
611 N Flores St Apt 2
West Hollywood, CA 90048-2134, USA

McKeehan, Pat
PO Box 486
Louisville, TN 37777-0486

McKeel, Walt (Athlete, Baseball Player)
7669 NC Highway 58 N
Stantonsburg, NC 27883-8635, USA

McKeever, Vito (Athlete, Football Player)
6823 Coral Reef St
Lake Worth, FL 33467-7635, USA

McKellar, Danica (Actor)
c/o Matt Sherman *Medavoy Management*
10203 Santa Monica Blvd Ste 400
Los Angeles, CA 90067-6405, USA

McKellen, Ian (Actor)
c/o Chris Andrews *Creative Artists Agency (CAA-LA)*
2000 Avenue of the Stars Ste 100
Los Angeles, CA 90067-4705, USA

McKeller, Keith (Athlete, Football Player)
1972 Waccamaw Path
Winston Salem, NC 27127-9433, USA

McKelvey, Rob (Athlete, Golfer)
1814 Duke Rd
Atlanta, GA 30341-4853, USA

McKelvin, Leodis (Athlete, Football Player)
c/o Hadley Engelhard *Enter-Sports Management*
5 Concourse Pkwy Ste 3000
Atlanta, GA 30328-7106, USA

McKendry, Alex (Athlete, Hockey Player)
151 Courthouse Rd
Franklin Square, NY 11010-2913, USA

McKendry, Chris (Commentator, Journalist, Sportscaster)
57 Hermit Ln
Westport, CT 06880-1125, USA

McKenna, Alex (Actor)
c/o Staff Member *Grey Media Group*
16848 Charmel Ln
Pacific Palisades, CA 90272-2216, USA

McKenna, Aline Brosh (Writer)
c/o Todd Feldman *Creative Artists Agency (CAA-LA)*
2000 Avenue of the Stars Ste 100
Los Angeles, CA 90067-4705, USA

McKenna, Andrew J (Business Person)
McDonald's Corp
1 Kroc Dr
1 McDonald's Plaza
Oak Brook, IL 60523-2275, USA

McKenna, David (Dave) (Musician)
Thomas Cassidy
11761 E Speedway Blvd
Tucson, AZ 85748-2017, USA

McKenna, Kevin (Athlete, Basketball Player)
3068 Cimarron Pl
Eugene, OR 97405-1751, USA

McKenney, Donald H (Don) (Athlete, Hockey Player)
16 Edgewater Dr
Norton, MA 02766-2123

McKennon, Keith R (Business Person)
5434 E Lincoln Dr
Paradise Valley, AZ 85253-4118, USA

McKenry, Michael (Athlete, Baseball Player)
8364 David Tippit Way
Knoxville, TN 37931-4478, USA

McKenzie, Benjamin (Actor)
c/o David Seltzer *Management 360*
9111 Wilshire Blvd
Beverly Hills, CA 90210-5508, USA

McKenzie, Bill (Athlete, Hockey Player)
2812 Harborside Way
Southport, NC 28461-8373

McKenzie, Constance
3360 Barham Blvd
Los Angeles, CA 90068-1473

McKenzie, Forrest (Athlete, Basketball Player)
2516 S Laurelwood
Santa Ana, CA 92704-5439, USA

McKenzie, Jacqueline (Actor)
c/o Brett Carella *Lab, The*
5540 Hollywood Blvd # 200
Los Angeles, CA 90028-6808, USA

McKenzie, Jim (Athlete, Hockey Player)
9266 Chevoit Dr
Brentwood, TN 37027-6138

McKenzie, John (Athlete, Hockey Player)
144 Marble St Apt 104
Stoneham, MA 02180-2714

McKenzie, Kareem (Athlete, Football Player)
131 Desilvio Dr
Sicklerville, NJ 08081-3400, USA

McKenzie, Raleigh (Athlete, Football Player)
715 Huntsman Pl
Herndon, VA 20170-3160, USA

McKenzie, Reggie (Athlete, Football Player)
411 Carta Rd
Knoxville, TN 37914-3619, USA

McKenzie, Reginald (Reggie) (Athlete, Football Player)
13853 Trumbull St
Highland Park, MI 48203-3073, USA

McKenzie, Stan (Athlete, Basketball Player)
PO Box 1508
Ellicott City, MD 21041-1508, USA

McKenzie, Vashti (Religious Leader)
Payne Memorial Church
1714 Madison Ave # 16
Baltimore, MD 21217-3750, USA

McKeon, Doug (Actor)
c/o Raymond Miller *Archetype*
1608 Argyle Ave
Los Angeles, CA 90028-6408, USA

McKeon, Jack (Athlete, Baseball Player, Coach)
1529 Charleigh Ct
Elon, NC 27244-9770, USA

McKeon, Joel (Athlete, Baseball Player)
1901 Pierce St Apt 7
Hollywood, FL 33020-4047, USA

McKeon, Lindsey (Actor)
c/o Robbie Kass *Kass Management*
501 Santa Monica Blvd Ste 604
Santa Monica, CA 90401-2467, USA

McKeon, Matt (Soccer Player)
Kansas City Wizards
2 Arrowhead Dr
Kansas City, MO 64129, USA

McKeon, Nancy (Actor)
PO Box 6778
Burbank, CA 91510-6778, USA

McKeown, Bob (Correspondent)
CBS-TV
51 W 52nd St
News Dept
New York, NY 10019-6119, USA

McKernan, John (Ex-Governor, Politician)
Education Management Corporation
77 Sanderson Rd
Cumberland Foreside, ME 04110-1436, USA

McKey, Derrick (Athlete, Basketball Player)
8 Woodard Pl
Zionsville, IN 46077-8189, USA

McKibben, Bill (Writer)
c/o Staff Member *Simon & Schuster*
1230 Avenue of the Americas Fl CONC1
New York, NY 10020-1586, USA

McKibben, Mike (Athlete, Football Player)
2523 Forest Brook Dr
Pittsburgh, PA 15241-2586, USA

McKibbin, Nikki (Actor, Musician)
c/o JD Sobol *Almond Talent Agency*
2600 W Olive Ave Fl 5
Burbank, CA 91505-4572, USA

McKidd, Kevin (Actor)
7750 Woodrow Wilson Dr
Los Angeles, CA 90046-1212, USA

McKie, Aaron (Athlete, Basketball Player)
14EE Youngs Ford Rd
Gladwyne, PA 19035, USA

McKie, Jason (Athlete, Football Player)
1008 Vineyard Dr
Gurnee, IL 60031-5100, USA

McKim, Peggy (Actor)
15801 Wyandotte St Unit 111
Van Nuys, CA 91406-3181, USA

McKinley, Alvin (Athlete, Football Player)
2792 Elkins Lk
Huntsville, TX 77340, USA

McKinley, Dennis (Athlete, Football Player)
150 McKinley Rd
Mc Cool, MS 39108-4220, USA

McKinley, Robin (Writer)
Writer's House
Writer's House Inc 21 W 26th St Fl1
New York, NY 10010, USA

McKinley-Uselmann, Therese (Athlete, Baseball Player, Commentator)
1644 N Greenwood Ave
Park Ridge, IL 60068-1215, USA

McKinnely, Phil (Athlete, Football Player)
585 Edgehill Pl
Alpharetta, GA 30022-7006, USA

McKinney, Carlton (Athlete, Basketball Player)
310 E 4th Ave
Nixon, TX 78140-2939, USA

Mckinney, Demetria
c/o Staff Member *Serendipity Entertainment*
1041 N Formosa Ave Ste 206A
West Hollywood, CA 90046-6703, USA

Mckinney, Frank (Business Person)
PO Box 388
Boynton Beach, FL 33425-0388, USA

McKinney, Gil (Actor)
c/o Steven Levy *Framework Entertainment (LA)*
9057 Nemo St Ste C
West Hollywood, CA 90069-5511, USA

McKinney, Greg
1800 Avenue of the Stars Ste 400
Los Angeles, CA 90067-4206

McKinney, Jack (Basketball Coach, Coach)
St Joseph's University
5600 City Ave
Hawk's Hall of Fame
Philadelphia, PA 19131-1376, USA

McKinney, Kurt
9200 W Sunset Blvd Ste 1130
West Hollywood, CA 90069-3606

McKinney, Mark (Actor)
c/o Staff Member *William Morris Endeavor (LA)*
9601 Wilshire Blvd
Beverly Hills, CA 90210-5213, USA

McKinney, Odis (Athlete, Football Player)
23126 Collins St
Woodland Hills, CA 91367-4225, USA

McKinney, Rich (Athlete, Baseball Player)
2495 E Peterson Rd
Troy, OH 45373-7790, USA

McKinney, Royce (Athlete, Football Player)
1930 N Beech Daly Rd
Dearborn Heights, MI 48127-3462, USA

McKinney, Seth (Athlete, Football Player)
2403 Crown Ct
College Station, TX 77845-2006, USA

McKinney, Steve (Athlete, Football Player)
2403 Crown Ct
College Station, TX 77845-2006, USA

McKinney, Tamara (Athlete, Olympic Athlete, Skier)
4935 Parkers Mill Rd
Lexington, KY 40513-9760, USA

McKinnie, Bryant (Athlete, Football Player)
101 SW 117th Ave Apt 308
Pembroke Pines, FL 33025-4914, USA

McKinnie, Silas (Athlete, Football Player)
22875 Summer House Ct Apt 205
Novi, MI 48375-4582, USA

McKinnis, Hugh (Athlete, Football Player)
4759 NW El Camino Blvd
Bremerton, WA 98312-1101, USA

McKinnney, Kurt (Actor)
5003 Tilden Ave Unit 206
Sherman Oaks, CA 91423-1747, USA

McKinnney, Richard (Rick) (Athlete)
7659 Kavooras Dr
Sacramento, CA 95831-4207, USA

McKinney, Tamara (Skier)
4935 Parkers Mill Rd
Lexington, KY 40513-9760, USA

McKinnon, Dan (Athlete, Hockey Player)
610 E River Dr
Warroad, MN 56763, USA

McKinnon, Dennis (Athlete, Football Player)
PO Box 47661
Chicago, IL 60647-7212, USA

McKinnon, Kate (Comedian)
c/o Brian Steinberg *Principato/Young Management (NY)*
261 Madison Ave Fl 9
New York, NY 10016-2311, USA

McKinnon, Ray (Actor)
Judy Schoen
606 N Larchmont Blvd Ste 309
Los Angeles, CA 90004-1309, USA

McKinnon, Ronald (Athlete, Football Player)
1063 Grand Oaks Dr
Bessemer, AL 35022-7237, USA

McKinny, Laura Hart
3224 Nottingham Rd
Winston Salem, NC 27104-1839

McKnight, Brian (Musician, Songwriter)
c/o Ann Gurrola *Marleah Leslie & Associates PR*
1645 Vine St Apt 712
Los Angeles, CA 90028-8812, USA

McKnight, Ira (Athlete, Baseball Player)
8417 Laurel Valley Dr
Indianapolis, IN 46250-3906, USA

McKnight, James (Athlete, Football Player)
16705 Berkshire Ct
Southwest Ranches, FL 33331-1331, USA

McKnight, Jeff (Athlete, Baseball Player)
3296 Highway 92 W
Bee Branch, AR 72013-8937, USA

McKnight, Joe (Athlete, Football Player)
c/o David Dunn *Athletes First, LLC*
23091 Mill Creek Dr
Laguna Hills, CA 92653-1258, USA

McKnight, Lauren (Actor)
c/o Mia Hansen *MLC PR*
7080 Hollywood Blvd Ste 903
Los Angeles, CA 90028-6936, USA

McKnight, Scotty (Athlete, Football Player)
15 Manchester Ct
Trabuco Canyon, CA 92679-4724, USA

McKnight, Ted (Athlete, Football Player)
10148 Locust St
Kansas City, MO 64131-4222, USA

McKnight, Tom (Athlete, Golfer)
340 Good Hope Rd
Okatie, SC 29909-3107, USA

McKnight, Tony (Athlete, Baseball Player)
406 Dundee Rd
Texarkana, AR 71854-9768, USA

McKoy, Bill (Athlete, Football Player)
4713 Legacy Cove Ln
Mableton, GA 30126-2580, USA

McKuen, Rod (Musician, Songwriter, Writer)
1155 Angelo Dr
Beverly Hills, CA 90210-2703, USA

McKyer, Tim (Athlete, Football Player)
11201 Golden Dr
Charlotte, NC 28216-5624, USA

Mclachlan, Murray (Athlete, Hockey Player)
16 Oneida Ct
Chester Springs, PA 19425-2934

McLain, Denny (Athlete, Baseball Player)
PO Box 868
Brighton, MI 48116-0868, USA

McLain, Kevin (Athlete, Football Player)
2551 State St Ste 222
Carlsbad, CA 92008-1682, USA

McLane, Drayton (Baseball Player, Commentator)
Houston Astros
100 N Apache Dr
Temple, TX 76504-2863, USA

McLane, James P (Jimmy) Jr (Swimmer)
85 Pinckney St
Boston, MA 02114-4303, USA

McLaren, John (Athlete, Baseball Player, Coach)
Seattle Mariners
7942 W Briden Ln
Peoria, AZ 85383-1016, USA

Mclaren, Kyle (Athlete, Hockey Player)
6582 Skyfarm Dr
San Jose, CA 95120-4542

Mclaughlin, Ann (Politician, Secretary)
390 Sopris Mountain Ranch Rd
Basalt, CO 81621-9178, USA

McLaughlin, Bo (Athlete, Baseball Player)
536 N Grand
Mesa, AZ 85201-5031, USA

McLaughlin, Byron (Baseball Player)
Seattle Mariners
7030 Alamitos Ave
San Diego, CA 92154-4764, USA

McLaughlin, Carol (Musician)
Columbia Artists Mgmt Inc
165 W 57th St
New York, NY 10019-2201, USA

Mclaughlin, Dan (Commentator)
45 Ballas Ct
Saint Louis, MO 63131-3000, USA

McLaughlin, Jake (Actor)
c/o Miles Levy *James/Levy Management Inc*
3500 W Olive Ave Ste 1470
Burbank, CA 91505-5514, USA

McLaughlin, Joe (Athlete, Football Player)
65 Pells Fishing Rd
Brewster, MA 02631-2104, USA

McLaughlin, Joey (Athlete, Baseball Player)
1611 S Troost Ave
Tulsa, OK 74120-6615, USA

McLaughlin, John (Athlete, Football Player)
5415 Kansas St
Houston, TX 77007-1101, USA

McLaughlin, John (Government Official)
Central Intelligence Agency
Deputy Director's Office
Washington, DC 20505-0001, USA

McLaughlin, John J (Television Host)
The McLaughlin Group
1717 Rhode Island Ave NW Ste 640
Oliver Productions Inc
Washington, DC 20036-3025, USA

McLaughlin, Mike (Race Car Driver)
PO Box 5532
Mooresville, NC 28117-0532, USA

McLean, Barney (Athlete, Skier)
13724 W 58th Pl
Arvada, CO 80004-3734, USA

McLean, Don (Musician, Songwriter, Writer)
c/o Jim Lenz *Paradise Artists*
108 E Matilija St
Ojai, CA 93023-2639, USA

McLean, Greg (Director)
c/o Staff Member *William Morris Endeavor (LA)*
9601 Wilshire Blvd
Beverly Hills, CA 90210-5213, USA

McLean, James (Athlete, Golfer)
c/o Jim Lehrman *SFX Golf*
36855 W Main St Ste 200
Purcellville, VA 20132-3561, USA

Mclean, Jeff (Athlete, Hockey Player)
47 Iron Bottom Ln
Daniel Island, SC 29492-8415

McLean, Kirk (Athlete, Hockey Player)
Colorado Avalanche
1000 Chopper Cir
Denver, CO 80204-5805

McLean, Rene (Musician)
Brad Simon Organization
122 E 57th St # 300
New York, NY 10022-2623, USA

McLean, Ron (Athlete, Football Player)
761 Fairmont Ave
Santa Maria, CA 93455-3250, USA

McLean, Scott (Athlete, Football Player)
375 Bear Ln
Lake Placid, FL 33852-4411, USA

McLeary, Marty (Athlete, Baseball Player)
106 Copperas Ct
Murfreesboro, TN 37128-3668, USA

Mclellan, Todd (Athlete, Hockey Player)
San Jose Sharks
525 W Santa Clara St
San Jose, CA 95113-1500

Mclellan, Zoe (Actor)
c/o Mandi Warren *Viewpoint Inc (NYC)*
109 W 27th St Rm 6B
New York, NY 10001-6208, USA

McLemore, Dana (Athlete, Football Player)
125 Seagate Dr
San Mateo, CA 94403-4930, USA

McLemore, LaMonte (Musician)
Sterling/Winters
10877 Wilshire Blvd # 15
Los Angeles, CA 90024-4341, USA

McLemore, Mark (Athlete, Baseball Player)
533 S White Chapel Blvd
Southlake, TX 76092-7316, USA

McLemore, Mark (Athlete, Baseball Player)
7965 Eagle View Ln
Granite Bay, CA 95746-7333, USA

McLendon-Covey, Wendi (Actor)
c/o John Carrabino *John Carrabino Management*
5900 Wilshire Blvd Ste 406
Los Angeles, CA 90036-5015, USA

Mcleod, Al (Athlete, Hockey Player)
8021 N 14th Ave
Phoenix, AZ 85021-5631

McLeod, George (Athlete, Basketball Player)
834 Greenpark Dr
Houston, TX 77079-4502, USA

McLeod, Jimmy (Athlete, Hockey Player)
6404 SE 23rd Ave Apt 413
Portland, OR 97202-5458, USA

McLeod, Robert D (Athlete, Football Player)
600 Spring Creek Rd
Brenham, TX 77833-8159, USA

McLerie, Allyn Ann (Actor, Dancer)
3344 Campanil Dr
Santa Barbara, CA 93109-1017, USA

McLerran, Joshua (Actor)
c/o Staff Member *The Craze Agency*
9176 S 300 W Ste 3
Sandy, UT 84070-2564, USA

McInally, Pat (Athlete, Football Player)
19321 Ocean Heights Ln
Huntington Beach, CA 92648-7514, USA

McLouth, Nate (Athlete, Baseball Player)
5476 Olds Ln
Whitehall, MI 49461-9355, USA

McIvor, Rick (Athlete, Football Player)
PO Box 148
Fort Davis, TX 79734-0148, USA

McMahan, Jack (Athlete, Baseball Player)
131 Forest View Cir
Hot Springs National Park,
AR 71913-6557, USA

McMahon, Art (Athlete, Football Player)
319 Stearns St Unit 32
Carlisle, MA 01741-1898, USA

McMahon, James R (Jim) (Athlete, Football Player)
22431 N Violetta Dr
Scottsdale, AZ 85255-4428, USA

McMahon, Jenna (Actor)
PO Box 5033
Carmel By The Sea, CA 93921-5033, USA

McMahon, Julian (Actor, Producer)
c/o Monique Moss *Integrated PR*
9025 Wilshire Blvd Ste 400
Beverly Hills, CA 90211-1828, USA

McMahon, Mike (Athlete, Football Player)
313 Oak Grove Ct
Wexford, PA 15090-9570

McMahon, Shane (Wrestler)
c/o Kerry Rodgerson *World Wrestling Entertainment (WWE)*
1241 E Main St
Titan Towers
Stamford, CT 06902-3520, USA

McMahon, Stephanie (Wrestler)
c/o Kerry Rodgerson *World Wrestling Entertainment (WWE)*
1241 E Main St
Titan Towers
Stamford, CT 06902-3520, USA

McMahon, Vince (Business Person)
47 Hurtingham Dr
Greenwich, CT 06831, USA

McMahon, Jr., Mike (Athlete, Hockey Player)
1475 Saint Clair Ave # 1
Saint Paul, MN 55105-2340, USA

McMakin, John (Athlete, Football Player)
PO Box 863
Anacortes, WA 98221-0863, USA

McManus, Brandon (Athlete, Football Player)
c/o Drew Rosenhaus *Rosenhaus Sports Representation*
6400 Allison Rd
Miami Beach, FL 33141-4540, USA

McManus, Don (Actor)
c/o Staff Member *Principal Entertainment (LA)*
9255 W Sunset Blvd Ste 500
West Hollywood, CA 90069-3301, USA

McManus, Doyle (Journalist)
LA Times
202 W 1st St Ste 500
Los Angeles, CA 90012-4401, USA

McManus, Jim (Athlete, Baseball Player)
2352 Hopkins Mill Rd
Duluth, GA 30096-4524, USA

McManus, Michaela (Actor)
2111 Ames St
Los Angeles, CA 90027-2902, USA

McMartin, John (Actor, Musician)
Artists Agency
1180 S Beverly Dr Ste 301
Los Angeles, CA 90035-1154, USA

McMath, Herb (Athlete, Football Player)
1515 E Glenn Ave
Springfield, IL 62703-3725, USA

McMath, Jimmy (Athlete, Baseball Player)
3321 22nd St
Tuscaloosa, AL 35401-5203, USA

McMichael, Greg (Athlete, Baseball Player)
240 Parkside Club Ct
Duluth, GA 30097-7847, USA

McMichael, Randy (Athlete, Football Player)
281 Athens Ave
Athens, GA 30601-2003, USA

McMichael, Steve D (Athlete, Football Player)
644 Wild Indigo Ave
Romeoville, IL 60446-3973, USA

McMillan, Audray (Athlete, Football Player)
1230 Hahlo St
Houston, TX 77020-7340, USA

McMillan, Caroline (Athlete, Golfer)
7525 E Phantom Way
Scottsdale, AZ 85255-4622, USA

McMillan, Caroline (Athlete, Golfer)
5101 N Casa Blanca Dr Unit 206
Paradise Valley, AZ 85253-6984, USA

McMillan, Eddie (Athlete, Football Player)
6204 222nd St SW
Mountlake Terrace, WA 98043-2530, USA

McMillan, Erik (Athlete, Football Player)
17209 Chesterfield Airport Rd # 308
Chesterfield, MO 63005-1423, USA

McMillan, Ernie (Athlete, Football Player)
14816 Sycamore Manor Ct
Chesterfield, MO 63017-5535, USA

McMillan, Nate (Athlete, Basketball Player, Coach)
c/o Lonnie Cooper *Career Sports and Entertainment*
150 Interstate North Pkwy SE Ste 100
Atlanta, GA 30339-2101, USA

McMillan, Randy (Athlete, Football Player)
6832 Hayley Ridge Way Unit D
Baltimore, MD 21209-5206, USA

McMillan, Susan Carpenter
1744 Oak Ln
San Marino, CA 91108-1021

McMillan, Terry (Writer)
PO Box 378
Pasadena, CA 91102-0378, USA

McMillan, Todd (Athlete, Football Player)
6113 W Spur Dr
Phoenix, AZ 85083-6531, USA

McMillan, Tommy (Athlete, Baseball Player)
712 Spring Lake Rd
Thomasville, GA 31792-8605, USA

McMillen, Robert (Athlete, Olympic Athlete, Track Athlete)
5708 Golden West Ave
Temple City, CA 91780-2503, USA

McMillen, Tom (Athlete, Basketball Player, Olympic Athlete)
1103 S Carolina Ave SE
Washington, DC 20003-2205, USA

McMillian, Audray G (Athlete, Football Player)
1230 Hahlo St
Houston, TX 77020-7340, USA

McMillian, Jim (Athlete, Basketball Player)
179E Polo Rd
Winston Salem, NC 27105, USA

McMillian, Mark (Athlete, Football Player)
13820 S 44th St
Phoenix, AZ 85044-4849, USA

McMillian, Michael (Actor)
c/o Abby Bluestone *Innovative Artists (LA)*
1505 10th St
Santa Monica, CA 90401-2805, USA

McMillin, James R (Athlete, Football Player)
7985 Westview Dr
Lakewood, CO 80214-4541, USA

McMillon, Billy (Athlete, Baseball Player)
1516 Lost Creek Dr
Columbia, SC 29212-2859, USA

McMonagle, Donald R (Astronaut)
7737 E Shadow Vista Ct
Tucson, AZ 85750-0742, USA

McMonagle, Donald R Colonel (Astronaut)
7737 E Shadow Vista Ct
Tucson, AZ 85750-0742, USA

McMorris, Cathy (Congressman, Politician)
2421 Rayburn Hob
Washington, DC 20515-2902, USA

McMullen, Kathy (Athlete, Golfer)
526 Harrison St
Emmaus, PA 18049-2314, USA

McMullen, Ken (Athlete, Baseball Player)
10 Estaban Dr
Camarillo, CA 93010-1610, USA

McMullen, Kirk (Athlete, Football Player)
4108 County Line Rd
Macedon, NY 14502-9386, USA

McMurray, Jamie (Race Car Driver)
c/o Rod Moskowitz *Fuel Sports Management Group*
130 Infield Ct
Mooresville, NC 28117-8026, USA

McMurray, Sam
11500 W Olympic Blvd Ste 510
Los Angeles, CA 90064-1527

McMurray, W Grant (Religious Leader)
Reorganized Church of Latter Day Saints
PO Box 1059
Independence, MO 64051-0559, USA

McMurtry, Craig (Athlete, Baseball Player)
2835 Bottoms East Rd
Troy, TX 76579-3008, USA

McMurtry, Greg (Athlete, Football Player)
755 Oak Point Ln
Madison Heights, MI 48071-1940, USA

McMurtry, James (Musician, Songwriter, Writer)
High Road
751 Bridgeway Fl 2
Sausalito, CA 94965-2174, USA

McMurtry, Larry (Writer)
PO Box 552
Archer City, TX 76351-0552, USA

McNab, Mercedes (Actor)
c/o Jason Egenberg *United Talent Agency (UTA-LA)*
9336 Civic Center Dr
Beverly Hills, CA 90210-3604, USA

McNab, Peter (Athlete, Hockey Player)
10311 Rancho Montecito Dr
Parker, CO 80138-7862

McNab, Peter (Athlete, Hockey Player)
Colorado Avalanche
1000 Chopper Cir
Denver, CO 80204-5805

McNabb, Dexter (Athlete, Football Player)
1449 Pat Tillman St
De Pere, WI 54115-7529, USA

McNabb, Donovan (Athlete, Football Player)
421 Seneca Rd
Great Falls, VA 22066-1114, USA

McNair, Kelly (Actor)
c/o Staff Member *GVA Talent Agency Inc*
8981 W Sunset Blvd Ste 101
West Hollywood, CA 90069-1850, USA

McNairy, Mark (Designer)
c/o Jason Hodes *William Morris Endeavor (NY)*
1325 Avenue of the Americas
New York, NY 10019-6026, USA

McNairy, Scoot (Actor)
c/o Mia Hansen *MLC PR*
7080 Hollywood Blvd Ste 903
Los Angeles, CA 90028-6936, USA

McNally, Kevin (Actor)
c/o Mark A. Schlegel *Cornerstone Talent Agency*
37 W 20th St Ste 1007
New York, NY 10011-3714, USA

McNally, Terrence (Writer)
c/o Jonathan Lomma *William Morris Endeavor (LA)*
9601 Wilshire Blvd
Beverly Hills, CA 90210-5213, USA

McNamara, Bob (Athlete, Football Player)
4909 Prescott Cir
Minneapolis, MN 55436-1011, USA

McNamara, Brian (Actor)
c/o Staff Member *Pathway Entertainment*
1739 Berkeley St Ste 110C
Santa Monica, CA 90404-4155, USA

McNamara, Eileen (Journalist)
Boston Globe
135 William T Morrissey Blvd # T
Editorial Dept
Dorchester, MA 02125-3310, USA

McNamara, Jim (Baseball Player)
San Francisco Giants
15317 Surrey House Way
Centreville, VA 20120-1196, USA

McNamara, John (Athlete, Baseball Player, Coach)
1206 Beech Hill Rd
Brentwood, TN 37027-5530, USA

McNamara, John F (Athlete, Baseball Player)
15317 Surrey House Way
Centreville, VA 20120-1196, USA

McNamara, Julianne L (Actor, Gymnast)
Barry Axelrod
2236 Encinitas Blvd Ste A
Encinitas, CA 92024-4353, USA

McNamara, Julie (Business Person)
c/o Staff Member *CBS Paramount Network Television*
4024 Radford Ave
Cbs Studios
Studio City, CA 91604-2190, USA

McNamara, Katherine (Actor)
c/o Bonnie Liedtke *Principato/Young Management (LA)*
9465 Wilshire Blvd Ste 900
Beverly Hills, CA 90212-2608, USA

McNamara, Mark
PO Box 134
Strawberry, CA 95375-0134, USA

McNamara, Melissa (Athlete, Golfer)
7715 S Quebec Ave
Tulsa, OK 74136-8104, USA

McNamara, William (Actor)
c/o Frederick Levy *Management 101*
11271 Ventura Blvd # 102
Studio City, CA 91604-3136, USA

McNanie, Sean (Athlete, Football Player)
261 26th St
Del Mar, CA 92014-2016, USA

McNaught, Judith (Writer)
Pocket Books
1230 Avenue of the Americas Fl CONC1
New York, NY 10020-1586, USA

McNaughton, John D (Director)
1370 N Milwaukee Ave
Chicago, IL 60622-9107, USA

McNeal, Donald (Don) (Athlete, Football Player)
3311 Toledo Plz
Coral Gables, FL 33134-6483, USA

McNeal, Travis (Athlete, Football Player)
4707 40th Pi N
Birmingham, AL 35217, USA

McNealey, Christopher (Athlete, Basketball Player)
30 Shady Oak Ct
Danville, CA 94506-6145, USA

McNealy, Rusty (Athlete, Baseball Player)
3301 Bozeman St
Sacramento, CA 95838-4105, USA

McNealy, Scott (Business Person)
Sun Microsystems
4150 Network Cir
Santa Clara, CA 95054-1778, USA

McNeely, Jeff (Athlete, Baseball Player)
405 Everette St
Monroe, NC 28112-5622, USA

McNeice, Ian (Actor)
c/o Renee Jennett *Renee Jennett Management*
5757 Wilshire Blvd Ste 473
Los Angeles, CA 90036-3632, USA

McNeil, Clifton (Athlete, Football Player)
1001 Westbury Dr
Mobile, AL 36609-3336, USA

McNeil, Emanuel (Athlete, Football Player)
15335 Park Row Apt 402
Houston, TX 77084-2893, USA

McNeil, Frederick A (Fred) (Athlete, Football Player)
9667 W Olympic Blvd Apt 5
Beverly Hills, CA 90212-3745, USA

McNeil, Freeman (Athlete, Football Player)
52 Dunlop Rd
Huntington, NY 11743-3934, USA

McNeil, Gerald (Athlete, Football Player)
215 Haven Brook Ln
Richmond, TX 77406-3494, USA

McNeil, Kate (Actor)
1743 N Dillon St
Los Angeles, CA 90026-1113, USA

McNeil, Lori (Tennis Player)
Int'l Mgmt Group
1 Erieview Plz
1360 E 9th St #1300
Cleveland, OH 44114-1738, USA

McNeil, Mike (Athlete, Hockey Player)
1723 Bader Ave
South Bend, IN 46617-2521, USA

McNeil, Pat (Athlete, Football Player)
7135 Elliott Dr
Dallas, TX 75227-1806, USA

McNeil, Ryan (Athlete, Football Player)
4702 Avenue Q
Fort Pierce, FL 34947-7049, USA

McNeill, Fred (Athlete, Football Player)
801 E Walnut St Apt 1502
Pasadena, CA 91101-5608, USA

McNeill, Mike (Athlete, Hockey Player)
52425 Spring Wood Ct
Granger, IN 46530-7438

McNeill, Robert (Athlete, Basketball Player)
1318 Wooded Way
Wayne, PA 19ELE, USA

McNeill, Rod (Athlete, Football Player)
1048 S Magnolia Ave
West Covina, CA 91791-3730, USA

McNeill, Tom (Athlete, Football Player)
31019 Torrey Rd
Waller, TX 77484-9354, USA

McNeill, W Donald (Don) (Tennis Player)
2165 15th Ave
Vero Beach, FL 32960-3435, USA

McNell, Rufus (Baseball Player)
Indianapolis Clowns
205 Heard St
Kinston, NC 28501-5850, USA

McNerney, Jerry (Congressman, Politician)
1210 Longworth Hob
Washington, DC 20515-1311, USA

McNertney, Jerry (Athlete, Baseball Player)
112410th St
Nevada, IA 50201, USA

McNichol, Brian (Athlete, Baseball Player)
14830 Darbydale Ave
Woodbridge, VA 22193-2765, USA

McNichol, Kristy (Actor)
c/o Staff Member Good Guy Entertainment
3733 Oakfield Dr
Sherman Oaks, CA 91423-4430, USA

McNichols, Stephen (Politician)
6481 S Kearney Cir
Centennial, CO 80111-4315, USA

McNorton, Bruce (Athlete, Football Player)
PO Box 672
Bloomfield Hills, MI 48303-0672, USA

McNown, Cade (Athlete, Football Player)
200 Lorraine Blvd
Los Angeles, CA 90004-3812, USA

McNulty, Bill (Athlete, Baseball Player)
32716 74th Avenue Ct E
Eatonville, WA 98328-8967, USA

McNulty, Carl (Athlete, Basketball Player)
212 Westmoreland Dr E
Kokomo, IN 46901-5155, USA

McNutt, Marvin (Athlete, Football Player)
c/o Adisa P. Bakari *Dow Lohnes PLLC*
1299 Pennsylvania Ave NW Ste 700
Washington, DC 20004-2431, USA

McPartlin, Ant (Television Host)
c/o Kevin McLaughlin *Baker Winokur Ryder Public Relations (BWR-LA)*
9100 Wilshire Blvd Ste 500
West Tower Suite 500
Beverly Hills, CA 90212-3426, USA

McPartlin, Ryan (Actor)
c/o Miles Levy *James/Levy Management Inc*
3500 W Olive Ave Ste 1470
Burbank, CA 91505-5514, USA

McPartlnad, Marian M (Musician)
Abby Hoffer
223 1/2 E 48th St
New York, NY 10017, USA

McPeak, Holly (Athlete, Volleyball Player)
1400 the Strand
Manhattan Beach, CA 90266-4731, USA

McPhail, Coleman (Athlete, Football Player)
104 Flagstone Ct
Chapel Hill, NC 27517-8381, USA

McPhail, Jerris (Athlete, Football Player)
1820 Lake Glen Dr
Fuquay Varina, NC 27526-6951, USA

McPhee, George (Athlete, Hockey Player)
Washington Capitals
627 N Glebe Rd Ste 850
Arlington, VA 22203-2144

McPhee, George (Athlete, Hockey Player)
6723 Landon Ln
Bethesda, MD 20817-5639

McPhee, John A (Writer)
475 Drakes Corner Rd
Princeton, NJ 08540-7516, USA

McPhee, Katharine (Musician, Reality Star)
c/o Gregory Harrison *Artist and Athlete Co.*
2110 Main St Ste 302
Santa Monica, CA 90405-2276, USA

McPhee, Pernell (Athlete, Football Player)
c/o Bus Cook *Bus Cook Sports, Inc*
1 Willow Bend Dr
Hattiesburg, MS 39402-8552, USA

McPherson, Dallas (Athlete, Baseball Player)
133 Shellbark Dr
McDonough, GA 30252-1622, USA

McPherson, Don (Athlete, Football Player)
3 Salem Ridge Dr
Huntington, NY 11743-3016, USA

McPherson, James (Writer)
Little Brown And Company
3 centre plz ste 100
Boston, MA 02108, USA

McPherson, John (Cartoonist)
Universal Press Syndicate
4520 Main St Ste 340
Kansas City, MO 64111-7705, USA

McPherson, Kristy (Athlete, Golfer)
c/o Staff Member *Gaylord Sports Management*
13845 N Northsight Blvd Ste 200
Scottsdale, AZ 85260-3609, USA

McPherson, Miles (Athlete, Football Player)
12088 Avenida Sivrita
San Diego, CA 92128-4546, USA

McQuagg, Sam (Race Car Driver)
8886 Hamilton Rd
Midland, GA 31820, USA

McQuarrie, Christopher (Director, Producer)
c/o Ken Kamins *Key Creatives*
1800 N Highland Ave Fl 5
Los Angeles, CA 90028-4523, USA

McQuarters, R W (Athlete, Football Player)
1548 E 54th St N
Tulsa, OK 74126-2811, USA

McQueen, Chad (Actor, Producer)
15260 Ventura Blvd Ste 1750
Sherman Oaks, CA 91403-5336, USA

McQueen, Cozell (Athlete, Basketball Player)
100 E Charing Cross
Cary, NC 27513-3024, USA

McQueen, Mike (Athlete, Baseball Player)
30 Boulder Dr
Batesville, AR 72501-9492, USA

Mcqueen, Sam (Race Car Driver)
8866 Hamilton Rd
Midland, GA 31820, USA

McQueen, Steven R (Actor)
c/o Risa Shapiro *The Schiff Company*
9220 W Sunset Blvd Ste 106
West Hollywood, CA 90069-3500, USA

McQuilken, Kim (Athlete, Football Player)
801 Moore Rd
Newnan, GA 30263-5220, USA

McRae, Bennie (Athlete, Football Player)
532 W 143rd St Apt 63
New York, NY 10031-6518, USA

McRae, Brian (Athlete, Baseball Player)
6721 W 121st St
Leawood, KS 66209-2003, USA

McRae, Charles (Athlete, Football Player)
247 John H McConnell Blvd
Columbus, OH 43215-2669, USA

McRae, Frank (Actor)
Marshak/Zachary Company
8840 Wilshire Blvd Fl 1
Beverly Hills, CA 90211-2606, USA

McRae, Gord (Athlete, Hockey Player)
8168 S Wabash Ct
Centennial, CO 80112-3329

McRae, Hal (Athlete, Baseball Player, Coach)
519 Sand Crane Ct
Bradenton, FL 34212-6203, USA

McRae, Jerrold (Athlete, Football Player)
4306 Drexel Way
Atlanta, GA 30346-1965, USA

McRae, Mo (Actor)
c/o Staff Member *Harrison Stokes*
1080 Stearns Dr
Los Angeles, CA 90035-2639, USA

McRae, Tom (Musician)
c/o Staff Member *Paradigm (Monterey)*
404 W Franklin St
Monterey, CA 93940-2303, USA

McRaney, Gerald (Actor)
4270 Farmdale Ave
Studio City, CA 91604-2733, USA

McReynolds, Jesse (Musician)
J&J Music
PO Box 1385
Gallatin, TN 37066-1385, USA

McReynolds, Kevin (Athlete, Baseball Player)
2 Country Pl
Roland, AR 72135-9763, USA

McReynolds, Larry (Race Car Driver)
123 Mystic Lake Loop
Mooresville, NC 28117-6000, USA

McReynolds, Madison (Actor)
c/o Bonnie Ventis *Clear Talent Group (LA)*
10950 Ventura Blvd
Studio City, CA 91604-3340, USA

McRoy, Spike (Athlete, Golfer)
15019 Collier Dr SE
Huntsville, AL 35803-3631, USA

McShane, Jamie (Actor)
c/o Staff Member *Select Artists Ltd (CA-Westside Office)*
1138 12th St Apt 1
Santa Monica, CA 90403-5459, USA

McShane, Jennifer (Jenny) (Actor)
c/o Laura Pallas *Pallas Management*
5301 Bellaire Ave
Valley Village, CA 91607-2329, US

McShann, James C (Jay) (Musician)
Ozark Talent
718 Schwarz Rd
Lawrence, KS 66049-4506, USA

McShera, Sophie (Actor)
c/o Mark Armstrong *Sanders Armstrong Caserta*
2120 Colorado Ave Ste 120
Santa Monica, CA 90404-3561, USA

McSorley, Gerard (Actor)
c/o Staff Member *Insight*
PO Box 36359
Los Angeles, CA 90036-0359, USA

McSorley, Marty (Athlete, Hockey Player)
3301 the Strand
Hermosa Beach, CA 90254-2053

McSwain, Chuck (Athlete, Football Player)
PO Box 603
Caroleen, NC 28019-0603, USA

McSwain, Rod (Athlete, Football Player)
5393 Stonewood Dr
Hickory, NC 28602-5578, USA

McSween, Don (Athlete, Hockey Player)
4954 Glen Meadow Ct SE
Grand Rapids, MI 49546-7927

McSween, John (Athlete, Hockey Player)
4954 Glen Meadows Ct St
Grand Rapids, MI 49546, USA

McTaggart, Jim (Athlete, Hockey Player)
Seattle Thunderbirds
625 W James St
Kent, WA 98032-4406

McTeigue, James (Director)
c/o Lawrence Mattis *Circle of Confusion (NY)*
8931 Ellis Ave
Los Angeles, CA 90034-3336, USA

McTiernan, John C (Director)
The Firm
9100 Wilshire Blvd Ste 100W
Beverly Hills, CA 90212-3435, USA

McVay, John (Athlete, Football Coach, Football Player)
7300 Sierra Dr
Granite Bay, CA 95746-6957, USA

McVeigh, John (Athlete, Football Player)
1404 W Beach Dr
Panama City, FL 32401-1927, USA

McVey, Robert (Athlete, Hockey Player, Olympic Athlete)
3333 NE 34th St Apt 1522
Fort Lauderdale, FL 33308-6914, USA

McVicar, Daniel (Actor)
1704 Oak St
Santa Monica, CA 90405-4804, USA

McVie, Christine (Actor, Musician)
c/o Staff Member *Sugaroo! LLC*
3650 Helms Ave
Culver City, CA 90232-2417, USA

McVie, John (Musician, Songwriter)
3124 Noela Dr
Honolulu, HI 96815-4515, USA

McVie, Tom (Athlete, Hockey Player)
19517 SE 26th Way
Camas, WA 98607-8818

McWashington, Shawn (Athlete, Football Player)
3400 S King St
Seattle, WA 98144-2653, USA

McWatters, Bill (Athlete, Football Player)
3300 Thornway Dr
Columbus, OH 43231-6199, USA

McWilliams, David (Football Executive, Football Player)
University of Texas
Athletic Dept
Austin, TX 78712, USA

McWilliams, Eric (Athlete, Basketball Player)
5301 Talbot Rd S Apt C101
Renton, WA 98055-8278, USA

McWilliams, John (Athlete, Football Player)
4540 E Blue Spruce Ln
Gilbert, AZ 85298-4637, USA

McWilliams, Larry (Athlete, Baseball Player)
5113 Park Road 21
Cleburne, TX 76033-8390, USA

MDO (Music Group)
c/o Staff Member *Sony Music Miami*
605 Lincoln Rd Ste 700
Miami Beach, FL 33139-2901, USA

Meacham, Bobby (Athlete, Baseball Player)
20610 Prince Creek Dr
Katy, TX 77450-4908, USA

Meacham, Mildred (Athlete, Baseball Player, Commentator)
6053 Wilora Lake Rd Rm 301
Charlotte, NC 28212-2850, USA

Meacham, Rusty (Athlete, Baseball Player)
1906 Eden Glen Ln
Pearland, TX 77581-1700, USA

Mead, Amber (Actor)
c/o Courtney Kivowitz *The Schiff Company*
9220 W Sunset Blvd Ste 106
West Hollywood, CA 90069-3500, USA

Mead, Charlie (Athlete, Baseball Player)
7482 Svl Box
Victorville, CA 92395-5157, USA

Mead, John (Athlete, Football Player)
10567 Westwood Dr Unit 2
Sister Bay, WI 54234-9030, USA

Mead, Matt (Governor, Politician)
State Capitol
200 W 24th St
Cheyenne, WY 82002-0001, USA

Mead, Richelle (Writer)
c/o Staff Member *Kensington Publishing Corp.*
119 W 40th St
New York, NY 10018-2500, USA

Meade, Carl J (Astronaut)
5711 Bienveneda Ter
Palmdale, CA 93551-1189, USA

Meade, Carl J Colonel (Astronaut)
15013 Live Oak Springs Canyon Rd
Canyon Country, CA 91387-4804, USA

Meade, Glenn (Writer)
Saint Martin's Press
175 5th Ave Ste 400
New York, NY 10010-7848, USA

Meade, Julia
101O Fifth Ave
New York, NY 10003

Meade, Robin (Television Host)
CNN Headline News
100 International Blvd NW
Atlanta, GA 30303, USA

Meador, Eddle D (Ed) (Athlete, Football Player)
1085 Red Mill Rd
Natural Bridge, VA 24578-4199, USA

Meadows, Brian (Athlete, Baseball Player)
117 Ingram Dr
Troy, AL 36079-2983, USA

Meadows, Jayne (Actor)
16185 Woodvale Rd
Encino, CA 91436-3448, USA

Meadows, Louie (Athlete, Baseball Player)
110 Heavens Ln
Maysville, NC 28555-9479, USA

Meadows, Stephen (Actor)
1760 Courtney Ave
Los Angeles, CA 90046-2103, USA

Meadows, Tim (Actor, Comedian)
c/o Geoff Cheddy *Brillstein Entertainment Partners (LA)*
9150 Wilshire Blvd Ste 350
Beverly Hills, CA 90212-3453, USA

Meads, Dave (Athlete, Baseball Player)
3220 Cypress Way
Santa Rosa, CA 95405-7512, USA

Meads, Johnny (Athlete, Football Player)
9419 Pine Lilly Ct
Navarre, FL 32566-2865, USA

Meagher, Mary T (Athlete, Olympic Athlete, Swimmer)
404 Vanderwall
Peachtree City, GA 30269-3335, USA

Mealey, Rondell (Athlete, Football Player)
2952 N Nobile St
Paulina, LA 70763-2523, USA

Meals, Gerald (Baseball Player)
2164 Shamrock Arbor Dr
Salem, OH 44460-7639, USA

Meals, Gerry (Athlete, Baseball Player)
2164 Shamrock Arbor Dr
Salem, OH 44460-7639, USA

Meamber, Tim (Athlete, Football Player)
3410 Grant St
Vancouver, WA 98660-1823, USA

Meaney, Colm (Actor)
11921 Laurel Hills Rd
Studio City, CA 91604-3726, USA

Meaney, Kevin (Actor, Comedian)
c/o Tom Ingengo *OmniPop Talent Group (NY)*
260 N Broadway Ste 5
Hicksville, NY 11801-2935, USA

Means, Jimmy (Race Car Driver)
Jimmy Means Racing
102 Greenbriar Dr
Forest City, NC 28043, USA

Means, Marianne (Journalist)
2555 Pennsylvania Ave NW Apt 902
Washington, DC 20037-1637, USA

Means, Natrone J (Athlete, Football Player)
14602 Greenpoint Ln
Huntersville, NC 28078-2624, USA

Means, Winslow (Athlete, Basketball Player)
1336 Arch St
Zanesville, OH 43701-5714, USA

Meara, Anne (Actor, Comedian)
c/o Staff Member *Innovative Artists (LA)*
1505 10th St
Santa Monica, CA 90401-2805, USA

Meares, Pat (Athlete, Baseball Player)
8405 E Bridlewood St
Wichita, KS 67206-4408, USA

Mears, Casey (Race Car Driver)
c/o Staff Member *Valvoline*
PO Box 14000
Lexington, KY 40512-4000, USA

Mears, Clint (Race Car Driver)
Team Mears
416 Fairview Rd
Bakersfield, CA 93307-5516, USA

Mears, Derek (Actor)
c/o Staff Member *Kazarian, Measures, Ruskin & Associates (LA)*
11969 Ventura Blvd Fl 3
Studio City, CA 91604-2630, USA

Mears, Gary (Musician)
12170 Country Rd 215
Tyler, TX 75707, USA

Mears, Rick (Race Car Driver)
204 Spyglass Ln
Jupiter, FL 33477-4091, USA

Mears, Roger (Race Car Driver)
PO Box 520
Terrell, NC 28682-0520, USA

Mears, Walter R (Journalist)
Associated Press
2021 K St NW
Editorial Dept
Washington, DC 20006-1003, USA

Mebane, Brandon (Athlete, Football Player)
2310 SE 2nd Ct
Renton, WA 98056-8871, USA

Mecchi, Irene (Actor)
c/o Staff Member *William Morris Endeavor (LA)*
9601 Wilshire Blvd
Beverly Hills, CA 90210-5213, USA

Mechalides, Louie (Race Car Driver)
8 Davis St
Tyngsboro, MA 01879-1606, USA

Meche, Gil (Athlete, Baseball Player)
PO Box 932
Scott, LA 70583-0932, USA

Mechlowicz, Scott (Actor)
c/o Eric Kranzler *Management 360*
9111 Wilshire Blvd
Beverly Hills, CA 90210-5508, USA

Mechoso, Julio Oscar (Actor)
c/o Staff Member *Gage Group, The (LA)*
5757 Wilshire Blvd Ste 659
Los Angeles, CA 90036-3682, USA

Mecir, Jim (Athlete, Baseball Player)
21219 W Creekside Dr
Kildeer, IL 60047-7847, USA

Mecklenburg, Karl (Football Player)
6372 S Zenobia Ct
Littleton, CO 80123-6740, USA

Mecko, Joe (Athlete, Baseball Player)
2219 Templeton Dr
Arlington, TX 76006-5769, USA

Medak, Peter (Director)
c/o Jon Brown *Ensemble Entertainment*
10474 Santa Monica Blvd Ste 380
Los Angeles, CA 90025-6943, USA

Medavoy, Mike (Producer)
9540 Oak Pass Rd
Beverly Hills, CA 90210-1230, USA

Medders, Brandon (Athlete, Baseball Player)
9732 Charolais Dr
Tuscaloosa, AL 35405-9771, USA

Meddick, Jim (Cartoonist)
United Feature Syndicate
PO Box 5610
Cincinnati, OH 45201-5610, USA

Meddine, Raya (Actor)
c/o Audrey Caan *Audrey Caan Management*
8665 Burton Way Apt 520
Los Angeles, CA 90048-3995, USA

Medearis, Angela Shelf (Chef, Writer)
c/o Staff Member *Diva Productions, Inc*
PO Box 91625
Austin, TX 78709-1625, USA

Medeiros, Glenn (Musician)
PO Box 8
Lawai, HI 96765-0008, USA

Mediate, Rocco (Athlete, Golfer)
c/o Staff Member *Lagardere Unlimited (AZ)*
13845 N Northsight Blvd Ste 200
Scottsdale, AZ 85260-3609, USA

Medich, George Doc (Athlete, Baseball Player)
3007 Woodfield Dr
Aliquippa, PA 15001-1163, USA

Medina, Luis (Athlete, Baseball Player)
2021 E Barkwood Rd
Phoenix, AZ 85048-4246, USA

Medina, Rafael (Baseball Player)
Florida Marlins
2964 Peachtree Rd Apt 330
Hialeah, FL 33015, USA

Medlen, Kris (Athlete, Baseball Player)
6633 Sutherland St
Abilene, TX 79606-1635, USA

Medley, Bill (Musician)
c/o Staff Member *William Morris Endeavor (LA)*
9601 Wilshire Blvd
Beverly Hills, CA 90210-5213, USA

Medlin, Dan (Athlete, Football Player)
712 Guilford Rd
Jamestown, NC 27282-9764, USA

Medlocke, Rickey (Musician)
15138 Portside Dr
Fort Myers, FL 33908-1893, USA

Medrano, Frank (Actor)
c/o Kate Ward *Ward Agency*
1617 N El Centro Ave Ste 15
Los Angeles, CA 90028-6429, USA

Medress, Henry (Musician)
Brothers Mgmt
141 Dunbar Ave
Fords, NJ 08863-1551, USA

Medved, David (Journalist)
8501 SE 82nd St
Mercer Island, WA 98040-5642, USA

Medved, Michael (Radio Personality, Writer)
c/o Staff Member *Greater Talent Network Inc*
437 5th Ave Ste 8A
New York, NY 10016-2205, USA

Medved, Ron (Athlete, Football Player)
6615 239th Ave E
Buckley, WA 98321-9422, USA

Medvedenko, Stanislav (Athlete, Basketball Player)
5721 S Crescent Park Apt 404
Playa Vista, CA 90094-4002, USA

Medvin, Scott (Athlete, Baseball Player)
673 Lynbrook Ave
Tonawanda, NY 14150-7309, USA

Mee, Darnell (Athlete, Basketball Player)
1742 Cave Mill Rd Apt B
Bowling Green, KY 42104-6370, USA

Meehan, Greg (Athlete, Football Player)
1084 Cheshire Hills Ct
Westlake Village, CA 91361-1475, USA

Meehan, Patrick (Congressman, Politician)
613 Cannon Hob
Washington, DC 20515-0003, USA

Meehan, Thomas E (Musician, Writer)
Brook House
Obtuse Road
Newtown, CT 06470, USA

Meek, Carrie (Politician)
6830 NW 28th Ave
Miami, FL 33147-6766, USA

Meek, Jeffrey
c/o Anne Geddes *Geddes Agency, The*
1203 Greenacre Ave
West Hollywood, CA 90046-5707, USA

Meeke, Brent (Athlete, Hockey Player)
11331 Whitetail Run St NW
Bolivar, OH 44612-9230

Meeks, Aaron (Actor)
c/o Staff Member *Showtime Networks (LA)*
10880 Wilshire Blvd Ste 1600
Los Angeles, CA 90024-4117, USA

Meeks, Bob (Athlete, Football Player)
PO Box 29734
Denver, CO 80229-0734, USA

Meeler, Phil (Athlete, Baseball Player)
PO Box 595
Zebulon, NC 27597-0595, USA

Meely, Cliff (Athlete, Basketball Player)
457 Grove Ave
Valparaiso, IN 46385-4240, USA

Meents, Scott (Athlete, Basketball Player)
4231 155th Pl SE
Bellevue, WA 98006-2579, USA

Meese (Music Group)
c/o Staff Member *Red Light Management (LA)*
8439 W Sunset Blvd Ste 2
West Hollywood, CA 90069-1925, USA

Meese, edwin (Politician)
1800 Old Meadow Rd Apt 810
Mc Lean, VA 22102-1813, USA

Meester, Brad (Athlete, Football Player)
7644 Chipwood Ln
Jacksonville, FL 32256-2338, USA

Meester, Leighton (Actor)
c/o Loch Powell *Leverage Management*
3030 Pennsylvania Ave
Santa Monica, CA 90404-4112, USA

Meeuwsen, Terry (Religious Leader, Television Host)
c/o 700 Club *Christian Broadcasting Network (CBN)*
977 Centerville Tpke
Virginia Beach, VA 23463-1001, USA

Me First And The Gimme Gimmes (Music Group)
c/o Staff Member *Fat Wreck Chords*
PO Box 193690
San Francisco, CA 94119-3690, USA

Meggett, Dave (Athlete, Football Player)
Lieber Correctional Institute
PO Box 205
Scdc Id: 00343610
Ridgeville, SC 29472-0205, USA

Meggysey, Dave (Athlete, Football Player)
2528 Benvenue Ave
Berkeley, CA 94704-3031, USA

Megrew, Mike (Athlete, Baseball Player)
25 Karen Dr
Hope Valley, RI 02832-1267, USA

Mehl, Lance A (Athlete, Football Player)
44920 Kacsmar Estates Dr
Saint Clairsville, OH 43950-9454, USA

Mehra, Smirti (Athlete, Golfer)
4038 Greystone Dr
Clermont, FL 34711-7197, USA

Mehta, Shailesh J (Business Person)
Providian Financial Corp
201 Mission St Ste 1875
San Francisco, CA 94105-8118, USA

Mehta, Ved (Writer)
139 E 79th St Fl 12
New York, NY 10075-0378, USA

Meier, Dave (Athlete, Baseball Player)
523 W Stuart Ave
Fresno, CA 93704-1430, USA

Meier, Richard A (Designer)
Richard Meier Partners
475 10th Ave Fl 6
New York, NY 10018-1179, USA

Meier, Shad (Athlete, Football Player)
4001 Skyline Dr
Nashville, TN 37215-2318, USA

Meiias, Roman (Athlete, Baseball Player)
27325 Terrytown Rd
Sun City, CA 92586-5220, United States

Meijer, Doug (Business Person)
Meijer Inc
2929 Walker Ave NW
Grand Rapids, MI 49544-9428, USA

Meijer, Hank (Business Person)
Meijer Inc
2929 Walker Ave NW
Grand Rapids, MI 49544-9428, USA

Meiko (Musician)
c/o Michael Moses *Baker Winokur Ryder Public Relations (BWR-LA)*
9100 Wilshire Blvd Ste 500
West Tower Suite 500
Beverly Hills, CA 90212-3426, USA

Meilinger, Steve (Athlete, Football Player)
719 Camino Dr
Lexington, KY 40502-2776, USA

Meineke, Don (Athlete, Basketball Player)
1266 Westcliff Ct
Dayton, OH 45409-1144, USA

Meinhold, Carl (Athlete, Basketball Player)
5 Courtleigh Pl
Reading, PA 19606-2941, USA

Meira, Vitor (Race Car Driver)
Team Rahel
4601 Lyman Dr
Hilliard, OH 43026-1249, USA

Meirelles, Fernando (Director, Producer)
c/o Staff Member *William Morris Endeavor (LA)*
9601 Wilshire Blvd
Beverly Hills, CA 90210-5213, USA

Meisenhelder, Glen (Race Car Driver)
Glen-Ken
77 Peros Dr
Agawam, MA 01001-3533, USA

Meisner, Greg (Athlete, Football Player)
419 Glenmeade Rd
Greensburg, PA 15601-1170, USA

Meisner, Randy (Musician)
3706 Eureka Dr
Studio City, CA 91604-3104, USA

Meissner, Kimmie (Figure Skater)
Office of Public Relations
105 E Main St
the Academy Building
Newark, DE 19716-0799, USA

Mejias, Roman (Athlete, Baseball Player)
27325 Terrytown Rd
Sun City, CA 92586-5220, USA

Mekka, Eddie (Actor)
Cosden Morgan
129 W Wilson St Ste 202
Costa Mesa, CA 92627-1586, USA

Mel, Renfro (Athlete, Football Player)
8211 Hunnicut Rd
Dallas, TX 75228-5930, USA

Melancon, Mei (Actor)
c/o Lena Roklin *Luber Roklin Management*
5815 W Sunset Blvd Ste 206
Los Angeles, CA 90028-6481, USA

Melander, Jon (Athlete, Football Player)
8255 Kelzer Pond Dr
Victoria, MN 55386-4500, USA

Melanie (Musician, Songwriter, Writer)
53 Baymont St # 5
Clearwater Beach, FL 33767-1705, USA

Melby, Russ (Athlete, Football Player)
8208 Spanish Meadows Ave
Las Vegas, NV 89131-1447, USA

Melcher, John (Politician)
2519 Wylie Ave
Missoula, MT 59802-3260, USA

Melchiondo, Mickey (Music Group, Musician)
100 Kiltie Dr
New Hope, PA 18938-1405, USA

Melchionni, Bill (Athlete, Basketball Player)
ne Bay Tree Ct
Naples, FL 34100000000, USA

Melchionni, Gary (Athlete, Basketball Player)
1040 Grandview Blvd
Lancaster, PA 17601-5108, USA

Melchior, Ib (Writer)
8228 Marmont Ln
Los Angeles, CA 90069-1624, USA

Melchoir, Tracy Lindsay
c/o Michael Bruno *The Michael Bruno Group*
13576 Cheltenham Dr
Sherman Oaks, CA 91423-4818, USA

Mele, Sam (Athlete, Baseball Player, Coach)
340 Adams St
Quincy, MA 02169-1702, USA

Melek, Temara (Musician)
c/o Staff Member *Creative Artists Agency (CAA-LA)*
2000 Avenue of the Stars Ste 100
Los Angeles, CA 90067-4705, USA

Melendez, John (Actor, Writer)
c/o Staff Member *Chapter 2 Productions*
3500 W Olive Ave Ste 300
Burbank, CA 91505-4647, USA

Melendez, John (Musician)
c/o Staff Member *Paradigm (Monterey)*
404 W Franklin St
Monterey, CA 93940-2303, USA

Melendez, Kiki (Musician)
c/o Staff Member *Paradigm (Monterey)*
404 W Franklin St
Monterey, CA 93940-2303, USA

Melendez, Lisette (Musician)
Famous Artists Agency
250 W 57th St
New York, NY 10107-0001, USA

Melendez, Ron
12533 Woodgreen St
Los Angeles, CA 90066-2723

Meler, Dave (Baseball Player)
Minnesota Twins
523 W Stuart Ave
Fresno, CA 93704-1430, USA

Melges, Harry (Athlete, Olympic Athlete, Sailor)
N2007 N Lakeshore Dr
Fontana, WI 53125-1179, USA

Melhuse, Adam (Athlete, Baseball Player)
248 Almond St
San Luis Obispo, CA 93405-2302, USA

Melillo, Kevin (Athlete, Baseball Player)
9101 Clerkenwell Dr
Waxhaw, NC 28173-6786, USA

Mellanby, Scott (Athlete, Hockey Player)
St Louis Blues
1401 Clark Ave
Saint Louis, MO 63103-2700

Mellanby, Scott (Athlete, Hockey Player)
2548 Town and Country Ln
Saint Louis, MO 63131-1121

Mellekas, John (Athlete, Football Player)
498 Broadway
Newport, RI 02840-1440, USA

Mellenby, Scott (Athlete, Hockey Player)
2548 Town and Country Ln
Saint Louis, MO 63131-1121, USA

Mellencamp, John (Musician, Songwriter)
PO Box 6777
Bloomington, IN 47407-6777, USA

Mellette, Aaron (Athlete, Football Player)
c/o Adisa P. Bakari *Dow Lohnes PLLC*
1299 Pennsylvania Ave NW Ste 700
Washington, DC 20004-2431, USA

Mello, Tamara (Actor)
c/o Brandy Gold *TalentWorks (LA)*
3500 W Olive Ave Ste 1400
Burbank, CA 91505-5512, USA

Mellons, Ken (Musician)
c/o Staff Member *Buddy Lee Attractions Inc*
38 Music Sq E Ste 300
Nashville, TN 37203-4304, USA

Mellor, Tom (Athlete, Hockey Player, Olympic Athlete)
48 4th Ave
Weymouth, MA 02188-3710

Melnick, Bruce E (Astronaut)
Boeing Aerospace
PO Box 21233
Orlando, FL 32815-0233, USA

Melnick, Bruce E Cdr (Astronaut)
5530 Clipper Ct
New Port Richey, FL 34652-3006, USa

Melnick, Daniel (Producer)
1123 Sunset Hills Rd
West Hollywood, CA 90069-1756, USA

Melniker, Benjamin (Producer)
Batfilm Productions
123 W 44th St # 10-K
New York, NY 10036-4089, USA

Melnyk, Steve (Athlete, Golfer)
5015 Pirates Cove Rd
Jacksonville, FL 32210-8309, USA

Meloan, Jon (Athlete, Baseball Player)
16903 W 83rd St
Lenexa, KS 66219-8100, USA

Meloche, Gilles (Athlete, Hockey Player)
Pittsburgh Penguins
66 Mario Lemieux Pl Ste 2
Pittsburgh, PA 15219-3504

Meloche, Gilles (Athlete, Hockey Player)
401 Church Hill Rd
Venetia, PA 15367-1142

Melody (Musician)
c/o Staff Member *Sony Music Miami*
605 Lincoln Rd Ste 700
Miami Beach, FL 33139-2901, USA

Meloff, Chris (Athlete, Hockey Player)
8568 NW 52nd Pl
Coral Springs, FL 33067-2839, USA

Meloni, Christopher (Actor)
627 N Palm Dr
Beverly Hills, CA 90210-3414, USA

Melrose, Barry J (Athlete, Coach, Hockey Player)
10 Windy Ridge Rd
Glens Falls, NY 12801-2473

Melroy, Pamela A (Astronaut)
3605 14th St N
Arlington, VA 22201-4926, USA

Melroy, Pamela A Colonel (Astronaut)
3605 14th St N
Arlington, VA 22201-4926, USA

Melton, Bill (Athlete, Baseball Player)
9609 E Roadrunner Dr
Scottsdale, AZ 85262-1444, USA

Melton, Dave (Athlete, Baseball Player)
72 Cherry Ridge Ct
San Jose, CA 95136-3635, USA

Melton, Henry (Athlete, Football Player)
c/o Jordan Woy *Willis and Woy Management*
3030 Olive St Ste 520
Dallas, TX 75219-7629, USA

Meluskey, Mitch (Athlete, Baseball Player)
26 Meadowbrook Rd
Yakima, WA 98903-9505, USA

Melvill, Michael W (Astronaut)
24120 Jacaranda Dr
Tehachapi, CA 93561-8309, USA

Melvin, Bob (Athlete, Baseball Player, Coach)
8711 E Pinnacle Peak Rd
Scottsdale, AZ 85255-3517, USA

Melvin, Donnie
45 Overlook Ter Apt 3J
New York, NY 10033-2208

Melvin, Doug (Commentator)
4111 W Stonefield Rd
Mequon, WI 53092-2770, USA

Melvin, Leland D (Astronaut)
805 Main St Apt 809201
Lynchburg, VA 24504-1553, USA

Melvin, Rachel (Actor)
c/o Anne Woodward *ROAR (LA)*
9701 Wilshire Blvd Fl 8
Beverly Hills, CA 90212-2008, USA

Melvoin, Wendy (Actor)
c/o Rick Jacobellis *First Artists Management*
4764 Park Granada Ste 210
Calabasas, CA 91302-3333, USA

Member, Tim (Athlete, Football Player)
3410 Grant St
Vancouver, WA 98660-1823, USA

Members, Swollen (Music Group, Musician)
c/o Staff Member *Agency Group Ltd, The (LA)*
1880 Century Park E Ste 711
Los Angeles, CA 90067-1618, USA

Memmel, Chellsie (Athlete, Gymnast, Olympic Athlete)
PO Box 510474
New Berlin, WI 53151-0474, USA

Men, Baha (Music Group)
Evolution Talent
1776 Broadway Fl 15
New York, NY 10019-2002

Menafee, Cornell (Athlete, Football Player)
403 Elm Ct
Opelika, AL 36801-6423, USA

Menaker, Mitchell G
5062 Isleworth Country Club Dr
Windermere, FL 34786-8920, USA

Menard, Hillary ""Minnie"" (Athlete, Hockey Player)
1908 NW 126th St # 2A
Clive, IA 50325-8164

Menard, Paul (Race Car Driver)
18432 Harbor Light Blvd
Cornelius, NC 28031-7795, USA

Menard Jr, John (Business Person)
Menard Inc
4777 Menard Dr
Eau Claire, WI 54703-9604, USA

Mench, Kevin (Athlete, Baseball Player)
1305 Danbury Parks Dr
Keller, TX 76248-5271, USA

Mencia, Carlos (Actor)
c/o Tim Sarkes *Brillstein Entertainment Partners (LA)*
9150 Wilshire Blvd Ste 350
Beverly Hills, CA 90212-3453, USA

Mendelsohn, Ben (Actor)
1957 Rockford Rd
Los Angeles, CA 90039-3128, USA

Mendenhall, John (Athlete, Football Player)
PO Box 235
Cullen, LA 71021-0235, USA

Mendenhall, Ken (Athlete, Football Player)
1708 S Rankin St
Edmond, OK 73013-5128, USA

Mendenhall, Ted
12907 Papago Dr
Poway, CA 92064-4513, USA

Mendes, Eva (Actor)
c/o David Seltzer *Management 360*
9111 Wilshire Blvd
Beverly Hills, CA 90210-5508, USA

Mendes, Jonna (Athlete, Olympic Athlete, Track Athlete)
PO Box 92
Nixon, NV 89424-0092, USA

Mendes, Sam (Director)
532 W 22nd St Apt 5A
New York, NY 10011-1117, USA

Mendez, Carlos (Athlete, Baseball Player)
755 Braves Blvd NE
Rome, GA 30161-2983, USA

Mendez, Lazaro (DJ Laz) (Radio Personality)
Power 96
194 NW 187th St
Miami, FL 33169-4050, USA

Mendler, Bridgit (Actor)
c/o Elaine Lively *LA Entertainment*
1375 S San Fernando Blvd
Suite 505
Burbank, CA 91504, USA

Mendoza, Dayana (Beauty Pageant Winner)
c/o Chris Rossi *Core Public Relations Group*
4401 Wilshire Blvd Fl 4
Los Angeles, CA 90010-3703, USA

Mendoza, Jessica (Athlete)
Amateur Softball Association (USA Softball)
2801 NE 50th St
Oklahoma City, OK 73111-7203, USA

Mendoza, Linda (Director)
c/o Staff Member *Creative Artists Agency (CAA-LA)*
2000 Avenue of the Stars Ste 100
Los Angeles, CA 90067-4705, USA

Mendoza, Mike (Athlete, Baseball Player)
14207 S 20th St
Phoenix, AZ 85048-4519, USA

Mendoza, Minnie (Athlete, Baseball Player)
2866 Charlotte Dr
Murrells Inlet, SC 29576-8481, USA

Mendoza, Ramiro (Athlete, Baseball Player)
PO Box 7027
Brandon, FL 33508-6017, USA

Mendoza, Reynol (Baseball Player)
2408 2nd St
Eagle Pass, TX 78852-4119, USA

Mendoza, Zuleyka Rivera (Beauty Pageant Winner)
c/o Richie Walls *International Talent Agency (ITA)*
10 Nbc Universal Studios Plz
20th Floor
Universal City, CA 91608, USA

Mendte, Larry
330 Bob Hope Dr
Burbank, CA 91505-4751

Menechino, Frank (Athlete, Baseball Player)
522 Arlene St
Staten Island, NY 10314-3818, USA

Menendez, Erik
1878449 Csp-Sac Box 290066
Represa, CA 95671-0001, USA

Menendez, Lyle
California Correctional Institute
#1887106
CCI-Box 1031
Tehachapi, CA 93581, USA

Menendez, Tony (Athlete, Baseball Player)
18730 NW 48th Ct
Miami Gardens, FL 33055-2536, USA

Meneses, Alex (Actor)
c/o Cindy Schultzel-Ambers *Art/Work Entertainment*
5900 Wilshire Blvd Ste 1720
Los Angeles, CA 90036-5021, USA

Meneses, Antonio (Musician)
Columbia Artists Mgmt Inc
165 W 57th St
New York, NY 10019-2201, USA

Menew (Music Group, Musician)
c/o Staff Member *REDCORE MUSIC GROUP*
520 8th Ave Rm 2001
New York, NY 10018-4166, USA

Mengatti, John
8322 Beverly Blvd # 200
Los Angeles, CA 90048-2600

Mengelt, John (Athlete, Basketball Player)
1270 Breckenridge Ct
Lake Forest, IL 60045-3875, USA

Menhart, Paul (Athlete, Baseball Player)
725 Kelsall Dr
Richmond Hill, GA 31324-7707, USA

Menheer-Zoromapal, Marie (Baseball Player)
8871 Lake Marion Creek Rd
Haines City, FL 33844-2004, USA

Menke, Denis (Athlete, Baseball Player)
1246 Berkshire Ln
Tarpon Springs, FL 34688-7626, USA

Mennell, Laura (Actor)
c/o Craig Schneider *Pinnacle Public Relations*
8721 Santa Monica Blvd Ste 133
West Hollywood, CA 90069-4507, USA

Menninga, Chris (Race Car Driver)
Conquest Racing
5062 W 79th St
Indianapolis, IN 46268-1645, USA

Meno, Chorepiscopus John (Religious Leader)
771 Cedarwood Ct
Stanley, NC 28164-6846, USA

Menon, Krishnan (Actor)
c/o Jai Khanna *Brillstein Entertainment Partners (LA)*
9150 Wilshire Blvd Ste 350
Beverly Hills, CA 90212-3453, USA

Menounos, Maria (Actor, Correspondent)
c/o Staff Member *Extra (LA)*
1840 Victory Blvd
Telepictures Productions
Glendale, CA 91201-2558, USA

Mensah, Peter (Actor)
c/o Cheri Barner *Artist Management*
1118 15th St Apt 1
Santa Monica, CA 90403-5580, USA

Mentez, Chris (Musician)
Arsisanian Assoc
6671 W Sunset Blvd Ste 1502
Los Angeles, CA 90028-7235, USA

Menudo
2895 Biscayne Blvd # 455
Miami, FL 33137-4537

Men Women & Children (Music Group)
c/o Staff Member *Paradigm (Monterey)*
404 W Franklin St
Monterey, CA 93940-2303, USA

Menzel, Idina (Actor, Musician)
c/o Heather Reynolds *One Entertainment (NY)*
12 W 57th St PH
New York, NY 10019-3900, USA

Menzies, LaNeah (Starshell) (Actor, Musician)
c/o Karyanne Tencer *Tencer and Associates*
411 N Oakhurst Dr Unit 411
Beverly Hills, CA 90210-5609, USA

Menzies, Peter G Jr (Cinematographer)
903 Tahoe Blvd
#802
Incline Village, NV 89451, USA

Meola, Tony (Soccer Player)
488 Forest St
Kearny, NJ 07032-3623, USA

Meoli, Christian (Actor)
c/o Brian McCabe *Venture IAB*
3211 Cahuenga Blvd W Ste 104
Los Angeles, CA 90068-1372, USA

Meoli, Rudy (Athlete, Baseball Player)
1211 San Gabriel Ave
Henderson, NV 89002-9402, USA

Meraz, Alex (Actor)
c/o Jeb Brandon *Kritzer Levine Wilkins Entertainment (KLWG)*
11872 La Grange Ave Fl 1
Los Angeles, CA 90025-5283, USA

Merbold, Ulf D Dr (Astronaut)
Am Sonnenhang 4
Siegburg, GE D-537, USA

Mercado, Orlando (Athlete, Baseball Player)
5292 Bishop St Apt 10
Cypress, CA 90630-3082, USA

Merced, Orlando (Athlete, Baseball Player)
PO Box 190494
San Juan, PR 00919-0494, USA

Mercein, Chuck (Athlete, Football Player)
746 Mamaroneck Ave Apt 1320
Mamaroneck, NY 10543-1989, USA

Mercer, Mark (Athlete, Baseball Player)
10607 Penn Ave S
Minneapolis, MN 55431-3445, USA

Mercer, Mike (Athlete, Football Player)
64463 McGrath Rd
Bend, OR 97701-8830, USA

Mercer, Ron (Athlete, Basketball Player)
San Antonio Spurs
1843 Glenhill Dr
Lexington, KY 40502-2817, USA

Merchant, Andy (Athlete, Baseball Player)
PO Box 8
Malcolm, AL 36556-0008, USA

Merchant, Natalie (Musician, Songwriter)
124 Cherry Hill Rd
Accord, NY 12404-5241, USA

Merchant, Stephen (Actor, Director, Producer, Writer)
c/o Staff Member *William Morris Endeavor (LA)*
9601 Wilshire Blvd
Beverly Hills, CA 90210-5213, USA

Mercilus, Whitney (Athlete, Football Player)
c/o Sean Howard *Octagon Football*
832 Sansome St Fl 1
San Francisco, CA 94111-1558, USA

Mercker, Kent (Athlete, Baseball Player)
8690 Hawick Ct N
Dublin, OH 43017-9618, USA

Mercurio, Nicole (Actor)
Innovative Artists
1505 10th St
Santa Monica, CA 90401-2805, USA

Mercurio, Steven
Columbia Artists Mgmt Inc
165 W 57th St
New York, NY 10019-2201, USA

Mercurio, Tara (Actor)
c/o Aaron Ray *The Collective*
8383 Wilshire Blvd Ste 1050
Beverly Hills, CA 90211-2415, USA

Mercy Me (Music Group, Musician)
c/o Scott Bickell *Brickhouse Entertainment*
106 Mission Ct Ste 1202
Franklin, TN 37067-6484, USA

Meredith, Cla (Athlete, Baseball Player)
3807 Kensington Ave
Richmond, VA 23221-2009, USA

Meredith, Greg (Athlete, Hockey Player)
111 W 67th St Apt 36A
New York, NY 10023-5960

Meredith, james (Politician)
929 Meadowbrook Rd
Jackson, MS 39206-5945, USA

Meredith, Jamon (Athlete, Football Player)
c/o Michael Perrett *SportsTrust Advisors (GA)*
3340 Peachtree Rd NE Fl 16
Atlanta, GA 30326-1000, USA

Meredith, William (Writer)
Connecticut College
PO Box 1498
New London, CT 06320, USA

Merediz, Olga (Actor)
c/o Staff Member *Cyd LeVin & Associates*
Prefers to be contacted by telephone or email
Burbank, CA 91501, USA

Mereszczak, Laryssa (Athlete, Volleyball Player)
c/o Gigi Rock *Heraea Marketing*
10905 E Pear Tree Dr
Cornville, AZ 86325-5523, USA

Meridith, Ron (Athlete, Baseball Player)
308 Via Promesa
San Clemente, CA 92673-6820, USA

Merila, Mark (Athlete, Baseball Player)
3730 Union Terrace Ln N
Minneapolis, MN 55441-2425, USA

Meriweather, Lee (Actor, Beauty Pageant Winner)
12139 Jeanette Pl
Granada Hills, CA 91344-2336, USA

Meriwether, Chick (Baseball Player)
2409 Seifried St
Nashville, TN 37208-1344, USA

Meriwether, Chuck (Athlete, Baseball Player)
2409 Seifried St
Nashville, TN 37208-1344, USA

Meriwether, Lee (Actor)
c/o Scott Stander *Scott Stander & Associates*
13701 Riverside Dr Ste 201
Sherman Oaks, CA 91423-2447, USA

Meriwether, Porter (Athlete, Basketball Player)
8137 S Saint Lawrence Ave
Chicago, IL 60619-5007, USA

Merkens, Guido (Athlete, Football Player)
1238 Elkins Lk
Huntsville, TX 77340-7321, USA

Merkerson, S Epatha (Actor)
c/o Jillian Roscoe *ID Public Relations (LA)*
7060 Hollywood Blvd Fl 8th
Los Angeles, CA 90028-6021, USA

Merkin, Daphne (Writer)
c/o Staff Member *New York Times*
229 W 43rd St
New York, NY 10036-3982, USA

Merkosky, Glenn (Athlete, Hockey Player)
113 Farr Ln
Queensbury, NY 12804-1996

Merlin, Jan (Actor)
347 N California St
Burbank, CA 91505-3508, USA

Merlo, James L (Athlete, Football Player)
1547 E Starpass Dr
Fresno, CA 93730-3448, USA

Merloni, Lou (Athlete, Baseball Player)
207 Quail Run
Marshfield, MA 02050-2066, USA

Meron, Neil (Producer)
c/o Staff Member *William Morris Endeavor (LA)*
9601 Wilshire Blvd
Beverly Hills, CA 90210-5213, USA

Merovich, Pete (Soccer Player)
945 Spruce St
Pittsburgh, PA 15234-2127, USA

Merrick, Dawn
8281 Melrose Ave Ste 200
Los Angeles, CA 90046-6890

Merrick, Robert (Athlete, Olympic Athlete, Sailor)
470 Sea Meadow Dr
Portsmouth, RI 02871-3935, USA

Merrill, Carl (Stump) (Athlete, Baseball Player, Coach)
18 Merrymeeting Dr
Topsham, ME 04086-1839, USA

Merrill, Casey (Athlete, Football Player)
78395 Avenue 41
Bermuda Dunes, CA 92203-1008, USA

Merrill, Dina (Actor)
Sue Siegel
405 E 54th St Apt 12A
New York, NY 10022-5159, USA

Merrill, Mark (Athlete, Football Player)
782 Mimosa Ln
Saint Paul, MN 55112-2520, USA

Merriman, Brent (Athlete, Baseball Player)
4101 E Baseline Rd Apt 915
Gilbert, AZ 85234-9113, USA

Merriman, Brett (Athlete, Baseball Player)
13828 E Lupine Ave
Scottsdale, AZ 85259-3718, USA

Merriman, Ryan (Actor)
c/o Beth Holden-Garland *Untitled Entertainment (LA)*
350 S Beverly Dr Ste 200
Beverly Hills, CA 90212-4819, USA

Merriman, Shawne (Athlete, Football Player)
c/o David Dunn *Athletes First, LLC*
23091 Mill Creek Dr
Laguna Hills, CA 92653-1258, USA

Merriott, Ronald (Athlete, Diver, Olympic Athlete)
1182 Kilbery Ln
North Aurora, IL 60542-4601, USA

Merritt, David (Athlete, Football Player)
479 Hartford Dr
Nutley, NJ 07110-3944, USA

Merritt, Jim (Athlete, Baseball Player)
2095 Aspen Dr
Hemet, CA 92545-8160, USA

Merritt, Lloyd (Athlete, Baseball Player)
4703 Wlld Iris Dr
Apt 301
Myrtle Beach, SC 29577, USA

Merritt, Tift (Musician)
c/o Staff Member *Red Light Management (LA)*
8439 W Sunset Blvd Ste 2
West Hollywood, CA 90069-1925, USA

Merriweather, Daniel (Musician)
c/o Staff Member *Allido*
19 Mercer St Apt 5
New York, NY 10013-2757, USA

Merriweather, Mike (Athlete, Football Player)
PO Box 8351
Stockton, CA 95208-0351, USA

Merten, Lauri (Athlete, Golfer)
1010 Del Harbour Dr
Delray Beach, FL 33483-6510, USA

Mertens, Jerry (Athlete, Football Player)
465 Woodside Dr
Woodside, CA 94062-2375, USA

Meruelo, Alex (Business Person)
36 Indian Creek Island Rd
Indian Creek Village, FL 33154-2901, USA

Merullo, Lennie (Athlete, Baseball Player)
159 Summer Ave
Reading, MA 01867-2825, USA

Merullo, Matt (Athlete, Baseball Player)
8 Fox Run Rd
Madison, CT 06443-2052, USA

Merwin, John D (Ex-Governor)
PO Box 1029
Hudson, OH 44236-6229, USA

Merwin, William Stanley (Writer)
Farleigh Dickinson University Press
285 Madison Ave
Madison, NJ 07940-1099, USA

Merz, Curt (Athlete, Football Player)
1111 W Seminole St
Springfield, MO 65807-2551, USA

Merz, Sue (Athlete, Hockey Player, Olympic Athlete)
5 Douglas Dr
Greenwich, CT 06831-3612, USA

Mesa, Jose (Athlete, Baseball Player)
13080 SW 52nd St
Miramar, FL 33027-5453, USA

Meschery, Tom (Athlete, Basketball Player)
710 Commons Dr
Sacramento, CA 95825-6643, USA

Meseroll, Mark (Athlete, Football Player)
450 Roger Dr
Salisbury, NC 28147-8878, USA

Mesina Stanley, Dianne (Producer)
c/o Staff Member *United Talent Agency (UTA-LA)*
9336 Civic Center Dr
Beverly Hills, CA 90210-3604, USA

Meskill, Thomas (Politician)
218 Stony Mill Ln
East Berlin, CT 06023-1042, USA

Mesner, Bruce (Athlete, Football Player)
6881 Lions Head Ln
Boca Raton, FL 33496-5955, USA

Messenger, Randy (Athlete, Baseball Player)
455 Market St Ste 2240
San Francisco, CA 94105-2446, USA

Messer, Dale (Athlete, Football Player)
5449 N Brooks Ave
Fresno, CA 93711-2914, USA

Messerschmidt, J Alexander (Andy) (Baseball Player)
200 Lagunita Dr
Soquel, CA 95073-9594, USA

Messer Simms, Leah (Reality Star)
c/o Lindsay Rielly *Continuum Entertainment*
303 Park Ave S Ste 1220
New York, NY 10010-3601, USA

Messersmith, Andy (Athlete, Baseball Player)
200 Lagunita Dr
Soquel, CA 95073-9594, USA

Messina, Chris (Actor)
c/o Jon Rubinstein *Authentic Talent and Literary Management*
20 Jay St Ste M17
Brooklyn, NY 11201-8300, USA

Messina, Jim (Musician)
c/o Staff Member *Agency for the Performing Arts (APA-LA)*
405 S Beverly Dr Ste 500
Beverly Hills, CA 90212-4425, USA

Messina, Jo Dee (Musician, Songwriter)
1572 Old Hillsboro Rd # 74
Franklin, TN 37069-9135, USA

Messing, Debra (Actor)
c/o Molly Madden *3 Arts Entertainment (LA)*
9460 Wilshire Blvd Fl 7
Beverly Hills, CA 90212-2713, USA

Messner, Johnny (Actor)
c/o Staff Member *McKeon-Myones Management*
3500 W Olive Ave Ste 770
Burbank, CA 91505-5527, USA

Mestnik, Frank (Athlete, Football Player)
730 Eagles Mere Ct
Alpharetta, GA 30005-4233, USA

Mestrik, Frank (Athlete, Football Player)
730 Eagles Mere Ct
Alpharetta, GA 30005-4233, USA

Meszaros, Andrej (Athlete, Hockey Player)
58 1/2 Martinique Ave
Tampa, FL 33606-4039

Metallica (Music Group)
c/o Cliff Burnstein *Q Prime Inc*
729 7th Ave Ste 1600
New York, NY 10019-6880, USA

Metaxas, Eric (Writer)
c/o Staff Member *HarperCollins Publishers*
195 Broadway Fl 2
Cellar 1
New York, NY 10007-3132, USA

Metcalf, Eric Q (Athlete, Football Player)
5112 S Fountain St
Seattle, WA 98178-2114, USA

Metcalf, Laurie (Actor)
Steppenwolf Theatre Company
1650 N Halsted St
Chicago, IL 60614-5530, USA

Metcalf, Mark (Actor)
c/o Staff Member *Peter Strain & Associates Inc (LA)*
5455 Wilshire Blvd Ste 1812
Los Angeles, CA 90036-4268, USA

Metcalf, Shelby (Coach)
Texas A & M University
Athletic Dept
College Station, TX 77843-0001, USA

Metcalf, Terrance R (Terry) (Athlete, Football Player)
5112 S Fountain St
Seattle, WA 98178-2114, USA

Metcalf, Terrence (Athlete, Football Player)
1524 Jackson Ave E Unit 9
Oxford, MS 38655-4024, USA

Metcalf, Tom (Athlete, Baseball Player)
1390 Wisconsin River Dr
Port Edwards, WI 54469-1042, USA

Metcalf, Travis (Athlete, Baseball Player)
610 Tenna Lorna Ct
Dallas, TX 75208, USA

Metcalfe, Burt
11800 Brookdale Ln
Studio City, CA 91604-4203

Metcalfe, Jesse (Actor)
1642 N Crescent Heights Blvd
Los Angeles, CA 90069-1649, USA

Metcalfe, Mike (Athlete, Baseball Player)
9 Cottage Pl
Ashland, NH 03217-4370, USA

Metcalfe, Scott (Athlete, Hockey Player)
36 Town Pump Cir
Spencerport, NY 14559-9734

Metcalf-Lindenburger, Dorothy M (Astronaut)
2235 Water Way
Seabrook, TX 77586-2814, USA

Metesh, Bernice (Athlete, Baseball Player, Commentator)
1210 Kelly Ave
Joliet, IL 60435-4251, USA

Metheny, Pat (Musician)
c/o Ted Kurland *Ted Kurland Associates*
173 Brighton Ave
Allston, MA 02134-2003, USA

Metrano, Art (Actor)
131 N Croft Ave Apt 402
Los Angeles, CA 90048-3472, USA

Metric (Music Group)
c/o Staff Member *Paradigm (Monterey)*
404 W Franklin St
Monterey, CA 93940-2303, USA

Metrolis, Norma (Baseball Player)
175 Sea Dunes Dr
Melbourne Beach, FL 32951-3313, USA

Metropolit, Glen (Athlete, Hockey Player)
1070 Redwine Cove Rd SW
Dalton, GA 30720-4954

Metro Station (Music Group, Musician)
c/o Staff Member *Sony Music Entertainment*
555 Madison Ave
New York, NY 10022-3301, USA

Metta World Peace (Athlete, Basketball Player)
5617 Ridge Park Dr
Loomis, CA 95650-9487, USA

Metwally, Omar (Actor)
c/o James Suskin *James Suskin Management*
2 Charlton St Apt 5K
New York, NY 10014-4970, USA

Metzelaars, Pete (Athlete, Football Player)
292 Point Carpenter Rd
Fort Mill, SC 29707-6875, USA

Metzenbaum, Howard M (Senator)
Consumer Federation of America
1424 16th St NW
Washington, DC 20036-2211, USA

Metzger, Butch (Athlete, Baseball Player)
641 Rivergate Way
Sacramento, CA 95831-3345, USA

Metzger, Clarence (Butch) (Athlete, Baseball Player)
641 Rivergate Way
Sacramento, CA 95831-3345, USA

Metzger, Roger (Athlete, Baseball Player)
3560 Bluebonnet Blvd
Brenham, TX 77833-7180, USA

Metzig, Bill (Athlete, Baseball Player)
221 Chuck Wagon Rd
Lubbock, TX 79404-1903, USA

Metzler, Jim
6300 Wilshire Blvd # 2110
Los Angeles, CA 90048-5204

Meulens, Hensley (Athlete, Baseball Player)
Inidianapolis Indians
555 Mission Rock St
San Francisco, CA 94158-2119, USA

Meunier-Lebouc, Patricia (Athlete, Golfer)
152 Porto Vecchio Way
Palm Beach Gardens, FL 33418-6223, USA

Mewes, Jason (Actor)
c/o Andrew Weitz *William Morris Endeavor (LA)*
9601 Wilshire Blvd
Beverly Hills, CA 90210-5213, USA

Mewhort, Jack (Athlete, Football Player)
c/o Michael McCartney *Priority Sports & Entertainment - Chicago*
312 N La Salle
Suite 650
Chicago, IL 60610, USA

Meyer, Bess
PO Box 5617
Beverly Hills, CA 90209-5617

Meyer, Bob (Athlete, Baseball Player)
24446 Caswell Ct
Laguna Niguel, CA 92677-7008, USA

Meyer, Bob
PO Box 57
Edwards, CA 93523-0057, USA

Meyer, Breckin (Actor)
c/o Ashley Franklin *Thruline Entertainment*
9250 Wilshire Blvd Ste 100
Ground Floor
Beverly Hills, CA 90212-3343, USA

Meyer, Brian (Athlete, Baseball Player)
33 Bank St
Medford, NJ 08055-2635, USA

Meyer, Dan (Athlete, Baseball Player)
11540 Marsh Creek Rd
Clayton, CA 94517-9759, USA

Meyer, Daniel J (Business Person)
Milacron Inc
2090 Florence Ave Ste 100
Cincinnati, OH 45206-2489, USA

Meyer, Debbie (Athlete, Olympic Athlete,
Swimmer)
PO Box 2076
Carmichael, CA 95609-2076, USA

Meyer, Dina (Actor)
c/o Stephen (Steve) LaManna *Innovative
Artists (LA)*
1505 10th St
Santa Monica, CA 90401-2805, USA

Meyer, Jerome J (Business Person)
Tektronix Inc
26600 SW Parkway Ave
Wilsonville, OR 97070-9297, USA

Meyer, Joey (Athlete, Baseball Player)
392 Kaimake Loop
Kailua, HI 96734-2019, USA

Meyer, John (Athlete, Football Player)
2085 Lost Dauphin Rd
De Pere, WI 54115-1605, USA

Meyer, Joyce (Religious Leader)
Joyce Meyers Ministries
PO Box 655
Fenton, MO 63026-0655, USA

Meyer, Nicholas (Director, Producer,
Writer)
c/o Alan Gasmer *Alan Gasmer
Management Company*
10877 Wilshire Blvd Ste 603
Los Angeles, CA 90024-4348, USA

Meyer, Ron (Athlete, Football Player)
628 18th St
Windom, MN 56101-1102, USA

Meyer, Ron (Business Person, Producer)
c/o Staff Member *NBC Universal (LA)*
100 Universal City Plz
Universal City, CA 91608-1002, USA

Meyer, Scott (Athlete, Baseball Player)
9311 E Calle De Valle Dr
Scottsdale, AZ 85255-4303, USA

Meyer, Stephenie (Writer)
c/o Jodi Reamer *Writers House*
21 W 26th St
New York, NY 10010-1083, USA

Meyer Maguire, Jennifer (Designer)
230 N Carmelina Ave
Los Angeles, CA 90049-2726, USA

Meyer-Petrovic, Anna (Athlete, Baseball
Player, Commentator)
1125 N Nema Ave
Tucson, AZ 85712-4723, USA

Meyer Reyes, Deborah E (Debbie)
(Swimmer)
PO Box 2076
Carmichael, CA 95609-2076, USA

Meyers, Anne Akiko (Musician)
ICM Artists
40 W 57th St
New York, NY 10019-4001, USA

Meyers, Ari (Actor)
c/o Holly Lebed *Holly Lebed Personal
Management*
10535 Wilshire Blvd Apt 808
Los Angeles, CA 90024-4556, USA

Meyers, Augie (Musician)
Encore Talent
2137 Zercher Rd
San Antonio, TX 78209-1194, USA

Meyers, Chad (Athlete, Baseball Player)
7636 Leawood St
Papillion, NE 68046-4207, USA

Meyers, Dave (Athlete, Basketball Player)
40629 Carmelita Cir
Temecula, CA 92591-1609, USA

Meyers, David (Dave) (Director)
c/o Ramses Ishak *United Talent Agency
(UTA-LA)*
9336 Civic Center Dr
Beverly Hills, CA 90210-3604, USA

Meyers, Josh (Comedian)
c/o April Lim *Global Artists Agency*
6253 Hollywood Blvd Apt 508
Los Angeles, CA 90028-8251, USA

Meyers, Krystal (Musician)
5902 Parham Rd
Franklin, TN 37064-9220, USA

Meyers, Nancy (Director)
c/o Jeff Berg *Resolution (LA)*
1801 Century Park E Ste 2300
Los Angeles, CA 90067-2325, USA

Meyers, Patricia (Athlete, Golfer)
2784 Moran Dr
Waldorf, MD 20601-2604, USA

Meyers, Seth (Actor, Comedian)
302 W 12th St Apt 12G
New York, NY 10014-6033, USA

Meyers-Drysdale, Ann (Athlete, Basketball
Player, Olympic Athlete)
235 W Main St
Los Gatos, CA 95030-6818, USA

Mezei, Branislav (Athlete, Hockey Player)
8017 Laurel Ridge Ct
Delray Beach, FL 33446-9537

Mezzogiorno, Giovanna (Actor)
c/o Estelle Lasher *Lasher Group*
1133 Avenue Of The Americas Ste 1621
New York, NY 10036-6710, USA

Mfume, Kweisi (Politician)
4805 Mount Hope Dr
Baltimore, MD 21215-3206, USA

MGK (Machine Gun Kelly) (Musician)
c/o Dana Sims *ICM Partners (LA)*
10250 Constellation Blvd Fl 7
Los Angeles, CA 90067-6207, USA

MGMT (Music Group)
c/o Staff Member *Columbia Records*
550 Madison Ave
New York, NY 10022-3211

M. Grijalva, Raul (Congressman,
Politician)
1511 Longworth Hob
Washington, DC 20515-4330, USA

M. Hall, Ralph (Congressman, Politician)
2405 Rayburn Hob
Washington, DC 20515-4304, USA

M. Honda, Michael (Congressman,
Politician)
1713 Longworth Hob
Washington, DC 20515-0515, USA

MIA (Musician)
c/o Todd Jacobs *William Morris Endeavor
(LA)*
9601 Wilshire Blvd
Beverly Hills, CA 90210-5213, USA

Miadich, Bart (Athlete, Baseball Player)
17841 Hillside Dr
Lake Oswego, OR 97034-7525, USA

Mialik, Larry (Athlete, Football Player)
21 Arboredge Way
Fitchburg, WI 53711-7214, USA

Miami Sound Machine
6205 Bird Rd
Miami, FL 33155-4823

Miano, Rich (Athlete, Football Player)
Miano Sports Bar
7168 Makaa St
Honolulu, HI 96825-3103, USA

Micech, Phil (Athlete, Football Player)
3029 N 91st St
Milwaukee, WI 53222-4620, USA

Miceli, Dan (Athlete, Baseball Player)
8520 Bowden Way
Windermere, FL 34786-5306, USA

Miceli, Joe
189 Vanderbilt Ave
Brentwood, NY 11717-2518

Micell, Justine (Actor)
Don Buchwald
6500 Wilshire Blvd Ste 2200
Los Angeles, CA 90048-4942, USA

Micelotta, Mickey (Athlete, Baseball
Player)
3266 Jog Park Dr
Greenacres, FL 33467-2014, USA

Micelotta, Robert P ""Mickey"" (Athlete,
Baseball Player)
3616 Via De Leoni Ave
Henderson, NV 89052-8739, USA

Michael, Archbishop (Religious Leader)
Antiochian Orthodox Christian Church
358 Mountain Rd
Englewood, NJ 07631-3798, USA

Michael, Bob (Politician)
1029 N Glenwood Ave
Peoria, IL 61606-1007

Michael, Gene (Athlete, Baseball Player,
Coach, Commentator)
55 Kelleys Trl
Oldsmar, FL 34677-1919, USA

Michael, George (Musician, Songwriter)
c/o Michael Lippman *Lippman
Entertainment*
23586 Calabasas Rd Ste 208
Calabasas, CA 91302-1361, USA

Michael, Kevin (Musician)
c/o Staff Member *Paradigm (Monterey)*
404 W Franklin St
Monterey, CA 93940-2303, USA

Michael Carroll, Jason (Musician)
c/o Staff Member *Creative Artists Agency
(CAA-TN)*
401 Commerce St PH
Nashville, TN 37219-2516, USA

Michael E Captain, Lopez-Aiegria
(Astronaut)
_1_8715 Point Lookout Dr
Houston, TX 77058, USA

Michaels, Al (Commentator)
401 S Bristol Ave
Los Angeles, CA 90049-3820, USA

Michaels, Al
47 W 66th St
New York, NY 10023-6201

Michaels, Alan R (Al) (Sportscaster)
ABC-TV
77 W 66th St
Sports Dept
New York, NY 10023-6201, USA

Michaels, Bret (Musician, Reality Star)
c/o Joann Mignano *Krupp
Kommunications*
59 W 19th St Rm 4C
New York, NY 10011-4245, USA

Michaels, Chad (Impersonator)
c/o Stephen Ford *Diva Central Inc*
7510 W Sunset Blvd Ste 1445
Los Angeles, CA 90046-3408, USA

Michaels, Fern (Writer)
1006 S Main St
Summerville, SC 29483-4231, USA

Michaels, Jason (Athlete, Baseball Player,
Coach)
10317 Carroll Cove Pl
Tampa, FL 33612-6508, USA

Michaels, Jillian (Fitness Expert, Reality
Star)
5924 Bonsall Dr
Malibu, CA 90265-3821, USA

Michaels, Lorne (Producer, Writer)
c/o Staff Member *Broadway Video
Entertainment*
5555 Melrose Ave
Dressing Room Bldg #105
Los Angeles, CA 90038-3989

Michaels, Louis A (Lou) (Athlete, Football
Player)
69 Grace St
Kingston, PA 18704-3040, USA

Michaels, Marilyn
185 W End Ave Apt 22M
New York, NY 10023-5549

Michaels, Mia (Dancer)
c/o Tim O'Brien *Clear Talent Group (LA)*
10950 Ventura Blvd
Studio City, CA 91604-3340, USA

Michaels, Shawn (Wrestler)
*Shawn Michaels' MacMillan River
Adventures*
43445 Business Park Dr Ste 103
Temecula, CA 92590-3670, USA

Michaels, Tammy Lynn (Actor)
c/o Marcel Pariseau *True Public Relations*
6725 W Sunset Blvd Ste 470
Los Angeles, CA 90028-7180, USA

Michaels, Walter (Walt) (Athlete, Coach,
Football Player, Football Player)
12 Birch Ave
Wilkes Barre, PA 18705-2208, USA

Michaelsen, Kari (Actor)
Kazarian/Spencer
11365 Ventura Blvd Ste 100
Studio City, CA 91604-3148, USA

Michaelson, Ingrid (Musician)
c/o Patrick Confrey *Sunshine Sachs (NY)*
136 Madison Ave Fl 17
New York, NY 10016-6734, USA

Michalak, Chris (Athlete, Baseball Player)
1108 Mockingbird Ln
Keller, TX 76248-2903, USA

Michalek, Zbynek (Athlete, Hockey
Player)
9290 E Thompson Peak Pkwy Unit 102
Scottsdale, AZ 85255-4523, USA

Michalik, Art (Athlete, Football Player)
33400 Gafford Rd
Wildomar, CA 92595-8293, USA

Michalka, Aly (Actor, Musician)
c/o Hilary Hansen *PMK/BNC Public Relations (PMK-LA)*
8687 Melrose Ave Ste 8
West Hollywood, CA 90069-5746, USA

Michalka, Amanda (Musician)
c/o Staff Member *Lynda Goodfriend Management*
338 S Beachwood Dr
Burbank, CA 91506-2713, USA

Micheaux, Larry (Athlete, Basketball Player)
2914 Calender Lake Dr
Missouri City, TX 77459-3920, USA

Micheaux, Nicki (Actor)
c/o Charlton Blackburne *A Management Company*
9107 Wilshire Blvd Ste 650
Beverly Hills, CA 90210-5544, USA

Micheel, Shaun (Athlete, Golfer)
3100 Kenney Dr
Germantown, TN 38139-8041, USA

Michel, Alex (Reality Star)
260 W 54th St Apt 17A
New York, NY 10019-5542, USA

Michel, F Curtis (Astronaut)
2101 University Blvd
Houston, TX 77030-1218, USA

Michel, F Curtis Dr (Astronaut)
2101 University Blvd
Houston, TX 77030-1218, USA

Michel, Mike (Athlete, Football Player)
5248 Lafayette St
Ventura, CA 93003-4218, USA

Michel, Robert (Politician)
2112 Rayburn Hob
Washington, DC 20515-0541, USA

Michele, Chrisette (Musician)
c/o Mark Siegel *ICM Partners (LA)*
10250 Constellation Blvd Fl 7
Los Angeles, CA 90067-6207, USA

Michele, Lea (Actor, Musician)
c/o Jason Weinberg *Untitled Entertainment (LA)*
350 S Beverly Dr Ste 200
Beverly Hills, CA 90212-4819, USA

Michele, Michael (Actor)
c/o Staff Member *A Management Company*
9107 Wilshire Blvd Ste 650
Beverly Hills, CA 90210-5544, USA

Micheletti, Joe (Athlete, Hockey Player)
143 Rolling Hills Rd
Thornwood, NY 10594-1821

Micheletti, Joe (Athlete, Hockey Player)
New York Rangers
2 Penn Plz Fl 22
New York, NY 10121-2299

Micheletti, Pat (Athlete, Hockey Player)
832 Ivy Ln
Saint Paul, MN 55123-2425

Michelle, Candice (Actor, Model)
c/o Jerry Donato *Abraxas Talent Agency*
4260 Troost Ave Apt 1
Studio City, CA 91604-2882, USA

Michelle, Sheley (Actor)
c/o Mike Simpson *William Morris Endeavor (LA)*
9601 Wilshire Blvd
Beverly Hills, CA 90210-5213, USA

Michelmore, Lawrence (Government Official)
4924 Sentinel Dr
Bethesda, MD 20816-3590, USA

Michels, John (Athlete, Football Player)
39 Meadow Brook Pl
Spring, TX 77382-1234, USA

Michels, John (Athlete, Football Player)
4544 Alveo Rd
La Canada Flintridge, CA 91011-3703, USA

Michner, Andy (Race Car Driver)
PO Box 24697
Indianapolis, IN 46224-0697, USA

Michos, Anastas N (Cinematographer)
Gersh Agency
232 N Canon Dr
Beverly Hills, CA 90210-5302, USA

Mickal, Abe (Athlete, Football Player, Physicist)
774 Topaz St
New Orleans, LA 70124-3624, USA

Mickell, Darren (Athlete, Football Player)
9250 Chelsea Dr
Miramar, FL 33025-3803, USA

Mickelson, Ed (Athlete, Baseball Player)
1532 Charlemont Dr
Chesterfield, MO 63017-4604, USA

Mickelson, Phil (Athlete, Golfer)
c/o Steve Loy *Gaylord Sports Management*
13845 N Northsight Blvd Ste 200
Scottsdale, AZ 85260-3609, USA

Mickens, Glenn (Athlete, Baseball Player)
5920 Kini Pl
Kapaa, HI 96746-8938, USA

Mickey, Joey (Athlete, Football Player)
6213 Canyon Dr
Oklahoma City, OK 73105-6415, USA

Mickolio, Kam (Athlete, Baseball Player)
4579 Danube Ln
Bozeman, MT 59718-8094, USA

Micucci, Kate (Actor)
c/o Christie Smith *Mosaic Media Group*
9200 W Sunset Blvd Ste 10
West Hollywood, CA 90069-3608, USA

Middendorf, Dave (Athlete, Football Player)
PO Box 525
Port Orchard, WA 98366-0525, USA

Middendorf, Max (Athlete, Hockey Player)
1917 E Daley Ln
Phoenix, AZ 85024-2470

Middendorf, Tracy (Actor)
PO Box 480410
Los Angeles, CA 90048-1410, USA

Middlebrook, Jason (Athlete, Baseball Player)
3103 Eaneswood Dr
Austin, TX 78746-6716, USA

Middlebrook, Lindsay (Athlete, Hockey Player)
2060 Flamingo Dr
Florissant, MO 63031-3516

Middlebrooks, Charley (Athlete, Baseball Player)
Indianapolis Clowns
528 Rigby St NE
Marietta, GA 30060-1703, USA

Middlebrooks, Willie (Athlete, Football Player)
18775 SW 78th Ct
Cutler Bay, FL 33157-7404, USA

Middleton, Rick (Athlete, Hockey Player)
PO Box 1161
Hampton, NH 03843-1161

Middleton, Terdell (Athlete, Football Player)
1893 Prospect St
Memphis, TN 38106-7645, USA

Middleton-Gentry, Ruth (Baseball Player)
28 Grandview Hts
Hamilton, IN 46742, USA

Midkiff, Dale (Actor)
c/o John Frazier *Amsel, Eisenstadt & Frazier Talent Agency (AEF)*
5055 Wilshire Blvd Ste 860
Los Angeles, CA 90036-6108, USA

Midler, Bette (Actor, Musician)
c/o Larry Brezner *Morra Brezner Steinberg & Tenenbaum (MBST) Entertainment*
345 N Maple Dr Ste 200
Beverly Hills, CA 90210-5174, USA

Midori (Musician)
Midori Foundation
850 7th Ave Ste 705
New York, NY 10019-5438, USA

Mieczko, A J (Athlete, Hockey Player)
295 Central Park W Apt 9G
New York, NY 10024-3023, USA

Mieczko, AJ (Athlete, Hockey Player, Olympic Athlete)
3 Hinckley Ln
Nantucket, MA 02554-2006, USA

Mielke, Gary (Athlete, Baseball Player)
1718 Orchid Dr S
North Mankato, MN 56003-1435, USA

Mientkiewicz, Doug (Athlete, Baseball Player, Olympic Athlete)
125 Bawiew Isle Dr
Islamorada, FL 33036, USA

Mierkowicz, Ed (Athlete, Baseball Player)
1349 Hollins Hall Ln
Troy, MI 48085-6742, USA

Mieske, Matt (Athlete, Baseball Player)
2199 E Bombay Rd
Midland, MI 48642-8351, USA

Miggins, Larry (Athlete, Baseball Player)
2405 Kingston St
Houston, TX 77019-6603, USA

Mighty Mighty Bosstones (Music Group)
c/o Staff Member *Paradigm (Monterey)*
404 W Franklin St
Monterey, CA 93940-2303, USA

Migliazzo, Paul (Athlete, Football Player)
605 W 68th Ter
Kansas City, MO 64113-1954, USA

Migliore, Richard (Horse Racer)
48 Killearn Rd
Millbrook, NY 12545-6216, USA

Migliore, Richard (Race Car Driver)
420 Fair Hill Dr # 1
Elkton, MD 21921-2573, USA

Mignola, Mike (Cartoonist)
c/o Staff Member *Dark Horse Entertainment*
1438 N Gower St Ste 28
Los Angeles, CA 90028-8306, USA

Miguel (Musician)
c/o Troy Carter *Atom Factory/Coalition Media Group*
1630 Colorado Ave
Santa Monica, CA 90404, USA

Mihm, Chris (Athlete, Basketball Player)
Celeland Cavallers
47E8 Peace Pipe Path
Austin, TX 78746, USA

Mihok, Dash (Actor)
c/o Alex Spieller *IMPR*
357 S Robertson Blvd
Beverly Hills, CA 90211-3602, USA

Mikan, Larry (Athlete, Basketball Player)
891 Carmona Ct
Chula Vista, CA 91910-8012, USA

Mike, Dennery (Athlete, Football Player)
6419 Oakley St
Philadelphia, PA 19111-5218, USA

Mikel, Liz (Actor)
c/o Terry Loftis *Verve Communications Group*
325 N Saint Paul St Ste 2360
Dallas, TX 75201-3824, USA

Mike-Mayer, Istvan (Steve) (Athlete, Football Player)
681 Lincoln Ave
Glen Rock, NJ 07452-2519, USA

Mike-Mayer, Nicholas (Nick) (Athlete, Football Player)
681 Lincoln Ave
Glen Rock, NJ 07452-2519, USA

Mike Rizzo, Mike (DJ)
c/o Staff Member *Diva Central Inc*
7510 W Sunset Blvd Ste 1445
Los Angeles, CA 90046-3408, USA

Mikeska, Russ (Athlete, Football Player)
100 Spirit Run
Eatonton, GA 31024-5035, USA

Mike Will Made It (Musician)
c/o Vinny Kumar *Keniley Kumar Law*
2 Ravinia Dr Ste 500
Atlanta, GA 30346-2105, USA

Mikita, Stan (Athlete, Hockey Player)
4770 Pebble Brook Dr
Oldsmar, FL 34677-4848, USA

Mikita, Valerie (Actor)
c/o Staff Member *The Stevens Group*
14011 Ventura Blvd Ste 201
Sherman Oaks, CA 91423-5216, USA

Mikkelsen, Mads (Actor)
c/o Theresa Peters *United Talent Agency (UTA-LA)*
9336 Civic Center Dr
Beverly Hills, CA 90210-3604, USA

Miklich, William (Athlete, Football Player)
Highway 106
Dousman, WI 53118, USA

Miklos, Arpad (Adult Film Star)
c/o Staff Member *Diva Central Inc*
7510 W Sunset Blvd Ste 1445
Los Angeles, CA 90046-3408, USA

Miko, Izabella (Actor)
c/o Kesha Williams *KW Entertainment*
425 N Robertson Blvd
West Hollywood, CA 90048-1735, USA

Mikol, Jim (Athlete, Hockey Player)
17350 SE 82nd Roslyn Ct
The Villages, FL 32162-2881

Mikolajczyk, Ron (Athlete, Football Player)
18323 Oakde Rd
Odessa, FL 33556, USA

Mikolajewski, Pete (Athlete, Football Player)
2520 Singing Vista Way
El Cajon, CA 92019-2740, USA

Miksis, Al (Athlete, Basketball Player)
522 E Algonquin Rd Apt 203
Schaumburg, IL 60173-3801, USA

Mikulski, Barbara (Politician)
3704 N Charles St Unit 1003
Baltimore, MD 21218-2325, USA

Mikulski, Barbara (Senator)
212 W Main St Ste 200
Salisbury, MD 21801-5106, USA

Mikvy, Bill (Athlete, Basketball Player)
586 Linton Hill Rd
Newtown, PA 18940-1204, USA

Milacki, Bob (Athlete, Baseball Player)
PO Box 15050
Reading, PA 19612-5050, USA

Milan, Don (Athlete, Football Player)
PO Box 126
Gardnerville, NV 89410-0126, USA

Milandro, Kristina
2518 Cardigan Ct
Los Angeles, CA 90077-1337

Milani, Denise
Periscope Media
60027 Via St
Cathedral City, CA 92234, USA

Milano, Alyssa (Actor)
Peace By Peace Productions
14757 Royal Way
Truckee, CA 96161-1179, USA

Milbourne, Larry (Athlete, Baseball Player)
747 Yale Ter
Vineland, NJ 08360-5818, USA

Milbrett, Tiffeny (Athlete, Olympic Athlete, Soccer Player)
1902 SW Broadleaf Dr
Portland, OR 97219-6375, USA

Milburn, Darryl (Athlete, Football Player)
270 E Harding St
Baton Rouge, LA 70802-7323, USA

Milburn, Glyn (Athlete, Football Player)
11900 Courtleigh Dr Apt 505
Los Angeles, CA 90066-6588, USA

Milbury, Mike (Athlete, Coach, Hockey Player)
61 Edwardel Rd
Needham, MA 02492-4001

Milbury, Mike (Athlete, Hockey Player)
Boston Bruins
100 Legends Way Ste 250
Boston, MA 02114-1389

Milchan, Arnon (Producer)
c/o Staff Member *New Regency Pictures*
10201 W Pico Blvd Bldg 12
Los Angeles, CA 90064-2606, USA

Milchin, Mike (Athlete, Baseball Player, Olympic Athlete)
13118 Bellaria Cir
Windermere, FL 34786-7401, USA

Milem, John (Athlete, Football Player)
PO Box 5236
Salisbury, NC 28147, USA

Miles, Aaron (Athlete, Baseball Player)
1716 San Jose Dr
Antioch, CA 94509-4217, USA

Miles, Carl (Athlete, Baseball Player)
3710 S Lenoir St
Columbia, MO 65201-5463, USA

Miles, Darius (Athlete, Basketball Player)
1906 Llewellyn Rd
Belleville, IL 62223-7904, USA

Miles, Don (Athlete, Baseball Player)
400 Central Ave
Palacios, TX 77465-2000, USA

Miles, Eddie (Athlete, Football Player)
960 NW 48th Ave
Coconut Creek, FL 33063-4631, USA

Miles, Jeromy (Athlete, Football Player)
c/o Joe Linta *JL Sports*
1204 Main St Ste 179
Branford, CT 06405-3787, USA

Miles, Jim (Athlete, Baseball Player)
134 Moores Creek Rd
Maben, MS 39750-5532, USA

Miles, Joanna (Actor)
2062 Vine St Apt 5
Los Angeles, CA 90068-3928, USA

Miles, John (Baseball Player)
Chicago American Giants
4130 Treehouse Dr
San Antonio, TX 78222-3510, USA

Miles, John ""Mule"" (Athlete, Baseball Player)
4130 Treehouse Dr
San Antonio, TX 78222-3510, USA

Miles, John R (Jack) (Writer)
4 Wharton Ct
Irvine, CA 92617-4108, USA

Miles, Les (Football Coach)
LSU Athletic Department
Attn Coach Miles
PO Box 25095
Baton Rouge, LA 70894, USA

Miles, Mark (Athlete, Tennis Player)
Assn of Tennis Pros
200 Tournament Players Rd
Ponte Vedra Beach, FL 32082, USA

Miles, Ostell (Athlete, Football Player)
9400 W 11th Ave
Lakewood, CO 80215-3001, USA

Miles, Sylvia (Actor)
c/o Staff Member *Agency for the Performing Arts (APA-LA)*
405 S Beverly Dr Ste 500
Beverly Hills, CA 90212-4425, USA

Miles, Vera (Actor)
PO Box 1599
Palm Desert, CA 92261-1599, USA

Miles-Clark, Jearl (Athlete, Track Athlete)
J J Clark
University of Florida
Athletic Dept
Gainesville, FL 32604, USA

Miley, Dave (Athlete, Baseball Player, Coach)
235 Montage Mountain Rd
Moosic, PA 18507-1765, USA

Milgliore, Richard (Race Car Driver)
420 Fair Hill Dr # 1
Elkton, MD 21921-2573, USA

Milhoan, Michael (Actor)
c/o Staff Member *Sanders Armstrong Caserta*
2120 Colorado Ave Ste 120
Santa Monica, CA 90404-3561, USA

Mili, Itula (Athlete, Football Player)
6648 W Sunset Hills Ct
Highland, UT 84003-3759, USA

Milian, Christina (Actor)
c/o Carmen Milian *Milian Management*
16830 Ventura Blvd Ste 501
Encino, CA 91436-1717, USA

Milian, Marilyn (Judge, Television Host)
The Peoples Court
401 5th Ave
New York, NY 10016-3317, USA

Milicevic, Ivana (Actor, Model)
c/o Staff Member *One Talent Management*
3680 1/2 Fredonia Dr
Los Angeles, CA 90068-1208, USA

Milicic, Darko
5460 Whitehall Blvd
Oakland Township, MI 48306-2277

Milinchik, Joe (Athlete, Football Player)
9329 Barker Rd
New Hill, NC 27562-9795, USA

Milinichik, Joe (Athlete, Football Player)
653 Ryan Dr
Allentown, PA 18103-3683, USA

Militano, Mark (Athlete, Figure Skater, Olympic Athlete)
10940 Johnson St NE
Minneapolis, MN 55434-3777, USA

Militello, Sam (Athlete, Baseball Player)
3217 W Saint John St
Tampa, FL 33607-2127, USA

Milius, John F (Director, Writer)
888 Linda Flora Dr
Los Angeles, CA 90049-1629, USA

Mill, Andy (Athlete, Olympic Athlete, Skier)
69 Danielson Dr
Aspen, CO 81611-9707, USA

Millan, Cesar (Television Host)
Cesar Millan Inc
3003 N San Fernando Blvd
Burbank, CA 91504-2525, USA

Millan, Felix (Athlete, Baseball Player)
G16 Calle Camarero
Carolina, PR 00987-8523, USA

Millar, Jeff (Cartoonist)
1301 Spring Oaks Cir
Houston, TX 77055-4703, USA

Millar, Jeffrey L (Jeff) (Cartoonist)
1301 Spring Oaks Cir
Houston, TX 77055-4703, USA

Millar, Kevin (Athlete, Baseball Player)
40 Hartz Way Ste 10
Secaucus, NJ 07094-2403, USA

Millar, Miles (Writer)
c/o Staff Member *Millar/Gough Ink*
3800 Barham Blvd Ste 503
Los Angeles, CA 90068-1042, USA

Millard, Bryan (Athlete, Football Player)
507 Sabine St Apt 1001
Austin, TX 78701-4188, USA

Millard, Keith (Athlete, Football Player)
5685 Maymont Ln
Dublin, CA 94568-7407, USA

Millbern, David (Actor)
c/o Staff Member *Barry Krost Management*
9220 W Sunset Blvd Ste 106
West Hollywood, CA 90069-3500, USA

Millcic, Darko (Basketball Player)
Detroit Pistons
2 Championship Dr
Palace
Auburn Hills, MI 48326-1753, USA

Milledge, Lastings (Athlete, Baseball Player)
11114 Sailbrooke Dr
Riverview, FL 33579-7074, USA

Millegan, Eric (Actor)
c/o Peter Young *Sovereign Talent Group*
8421 Wilshire Blvd Ste 200
Beverly Hills, CA 90211-3204, USA

Millen, Corey (Athlete, Hockey Player, Olympic Athlete)
1206 Doddridge Ave
Cloquet, MN 55720-2323, USA

Millen, Hugh (Athlete, Football Player)
6836 Cascade Ave SE
Snoqualmie, WA 98065-9725, USA

Millen, Matt (Athlete, Football Player)
PO Box 196
Durham, PA 18039-0196, USA

Miller, Aaron (Athlete, Hockey Player, Olympic Athlete)
147 Appletree Point Rd
Burlington, VT 05408-2446

Miller, Aaron David (Writer)
c/o Staff Member *Random House*
1540 Broadway Ste 1010
New York, NY 10036-4083, USA

Miller, Abby Lee (Dancer, Reality Star)
Abby Lee Miller Dance Company
7123 Saltsburg Rd
Pittsburgh, PA 15235-2252, USA

Miller, Alan (Athlete, Football Player)
3118 Erie Dr
Orchard Lake, MI 48324-1512, USA

Miller, Alan (Journalist)
Los Angeles Times
202 W 1st St Ste 500
Editorial Dept
Los Angeles, CA 90012-4401, USA

Miller, Alice (Athlete, Golfer)
2 Log Church Rd
Wilmington, DE 19807-1724, USA

Miller, Allan (Actor)
Douglas Gorman Rothacker Wilhelm
1501 Broadway Ste 703
New York, NY 10036-5501, USA

Miller, Allison (Actor)
c/o Staff Member *Beth Goldstein Management*
4433 Colbath Ave Apt 34
Sherman Oaks, CA 91423-3527, USA

Miller, Andre (Basketball Player)
Denver Nuggets
1000 Chopper Cir
Pepsi Center
Denver, CO 80204-5805, USA

Miller, Andrew (Athlete, Baseball Player)
Detroit Tigers Foundation
581 Marmora Ave
Tampa, FL 33606-3823, USA

Miller, Anthony
325 S San Dimas Canyon Rd Apt 108
San Dimas, CA 91773-3064, USA

Miller, Anthony (Athlete, Basketball
Player)
1083 Superior St
Benton Harbor, MI 49022-5310, USA

Miller, Beatrice (Actor, Musician)
c/o Rachel Altman *Abrams Artists Agency*
(NY)
275 7th Ave Fl 26
New York, NY 10001-6708, USA

Miller, Bennett (Director)
c/o Leslee Dart *42West (NYC)*
220 W 42nd St Fl 12
New York, NY 10036-7200, USA

Miller, Bill (Athlete, Baseball Player)
PO Box 2681
Aptos, CA 95001-2681, USA

Miller, Bill (Race Car Driver)
4895 Convair Dr
Carson City, NV 89706-0492, USA

Miller, Billy (Athlete, Football Player)
3957 Skelton Canyon Cir
Westlake Village, CA 91362-4230, USA

Miller, Billy (Actor)
c/o Staff Member *James/Levy Management*
Inc
3500 W Olive Ave Ste 1470
Burbank, CA 91505-5514, USA

Miller, Billy (Athlete, Football Player)
465 Cosmos Ct
Thousand Oaks, CA 91360-1427, USA

Miller, Bob (Athlete, Baseball Player)
17397 Glenmore
Redford, MI 48240-2127, USA

Miller, Bob (Athlete, Baseball Player)
3133 Coventry Dr
Waterford, MI 48329-3213, USA

Miller, Bob (Athlete, Hockey Player)
1429 Main St
Marshfield, MA 02050-2072

Miller, BobG
1702 Keirn Trl
Saint Charles, IL 60174

Miller, Bode (Athlete, Olympic Athlete,
Skier)
65 Easton Valley Rd
Franconia, NH 03580-5412, USA

Miller, Brad (Athlete, Basketball Player)
Sacramento Kings
5960 Via De La Rosa
Granite Bay, CA 95746-9040, USA

Miller, Brad (Congressman, Politician)
1127 Longworth Hob
Washington, DC 20515-3219, USA

Miller, Brandon (Race Car Driver)
Childress Racing
PO Box 1189
236 Industrial Dr.
Welcome, NC 27374-1189, USA

Miller, Bruce (Athlete, Baseball Player)
2126 Parkland Dr
Fort Wayne, IN 46825-3929, USA

Miller, Buddy (Musician)
Mark Pucci Media
5000 Oak Bluff Ct
Atlanta, GA 30350-1069, USA

Miller, Calvin (Athlete, Football Player)
1602 Fairfield Dr
Stillwater, OK 74074-2331, USA

Miller, C Arden (Doctor)
500 Oak Is
Chapel Hill, NC 27516-0439, USA

Miller, Carl (Athlete, Football Player)
PO Box 773
Crowley, TX 76036-0773, USA

Miller, Charles D (Business Person)
Avery Dennison Corp
207 N Goode Ave Fl 6
Glendale, CA 91203-1364, USA

Miller, Cheryl (Athlete, Basketball Player,
Olympic Athlete)
3206 Ellington Dr
Los Angeles, CA 90068-1741, USA

Miller, Cheryl D (Athlete, Basketball
Player, Coach)
3206 Ellington Dr
Los Angeles, CA 90068-1741, USA

Miller, Chris (Athlete, Football Player)
2114 Elkhorn Dr
Eugene, OR 97408-1203, USA

Miller, Chris (Director)
c/o Joy Fehily *Prime*
9696 Culver Blvd Ste 102
Culver City, CA 90232-2734, USA

Miller, Christa (Actor)
c/o Jill Littman *Impression Entertainment*
9229 W Sunset Blvd Ste 700
West Hollywood, CA 90069-3407, USA

Miller, Chryste Gaines (Athlete, Olympic
Athlete, Track Athlete)
5408 E Saddleridge Ln
Lithonia, GA 30038-3976, USA

Miller, Coco (Basketball Player)
Washington Mystics
601 F St NW
Mcl Center
Washington, DC 20004-1605, USA

Miller, Corey (Athlete, Football Player)
2528 Crofton Way
Columbia, SC 29223-2299, USA

Miller, Corky (Athlete, Baseball Player)
1115 7th St
Calimesa, CA 92320-1013, USA

Miller, C Ray (Religious Leader)
United Brethren in Christ
302 Lake St
Huntington, IN 46750-9711, USA

Miller, Damian (Athlete, Baseball Player)
N1276 Wuensch Rd
La Crosse, WI 54601-2655, USA

Miller, Dan (Musician)
Trans Continental Records
7380 W Sand Lake Rd # 350
Orlando, FL 32819-5248, USA

Miller, Darrell (Athlete, Baseball Player)
21159 Via Alisa
Yorba Linda, CA 92887-2510, USA

Miller, Dave (Cartoonist)
1401 Folkstone
Edmond, OK 73034-3305, USA

Miller, dave
2401 Ontario St
Cleveland, OH 44115-4003

Miller, David (Cartoonist)
167 Tremont St
Rehoboth, MA 02769-2818, USA

Miller, Denise (Actor, Producer)
c/o Richard Sindell *Bob Waters Agency*
9301 Wilshire Blvd Ste 300
Beverly Hills, CA 90210-6119, USA

Miller, Dennis (Actor, Comedian)
c/o Marc Gurvitz *Brillstein Entertainment*
Partners (LA)
9150 Wilshire Blvd Ste 350
Beverly Hills, CA 90212-3453, USA

Miller, Denny (Actor)
9612 Gavin Stone Ave
Las Vegas, NV 89145-8626, USA

Miller, Dyar (Athlete, Baseball Player)
8816 Admirals Bay Dr
Indianapolis, IN 46236-9292, USA

Miller, Eddie (Athlete, Baseball Player)
1819 Alfreda Blvd
San Pablo, CA 94806-4715, USA

Miller, Eddie (Athlete, Football Player)
1503 Summerwood Dr
Clarkston, GA 30021-3096, USA

Miller, Frank (Actor, Writer)
c/o Staff Member *Shapiro-Lichtman Talent*
Agency
1333 Beverly Green Dr
Los Angeles, CA 90035-1018, USA

Miller, Frank (Cartoonist)
Dark House Publishing
10956 SE Main St
Milwaukie, OR 97222-7644, USA

Miller, Fred (Athlete, Football Player)
7143 Sawmill Trl
Houston, TX 77040-1830, USA

Miller, Fred D (Athlete, Football Player)
1945 Hillary Dr
Westminster, MD 21157-3478, USA

Miller, George (Congressman, Politician)
2205 Rayburn Hob
Washington, DC 20515-0507, USA

Miller, Glenn Birthplace Society
PO Box 61
Clarinda, IA 51632-0061

Miller, Glenn (Orchestra)
605 Crescent Executive Ct Ste 300
Lake Mary, FL 32746-2133

Miller, Jack (Politician)
11507 Orilla Del Rio Pl
Temple Terrace, FL 33617-2624, USA

Miller, Jack (Race Car Driver)
Arizona Motorsports
30 Gasoline Aly Ste F
Indianapolis, IN 46222-3900, USA

Miller, Jamir (Athlete, Football Player)
331 Grenadine Way
Hercules, CA 94547-2048, USA

Miller, Jason (Writer)
10000 Santa Monica Blvd Ste 305
Los Angeles, CA 90067, USA

Miller, Jason (Mayhem) (Athlete)
c/o Jeff Sussman *Jeff Sussman*
Management
15374 Dickens St Fl 2
Sherman Oaks, CA 91403-3007

Miller, Jay (Athlete, Hockey Player)
175 Chester St
North Falmouth, MA 02556-2302

Miller, Jeff (Congressman, Politician)
2416 Rayburn Hob
Washington, DC 20515-1301, USA

Miller, Jeff
1301 Spring Oaks Cir
Houston, TX 77055-4703

Miller, Jeremy (Actor)
21240 Ficus Dr Unit 204
Newhall, CA 91321-4423, USA

Miller, Jim (Athlete, Football Player)
PO Box 863
Ripley, MS 38663-0863, USA

Miller, Jody (Musician)
PO Box 413
Blanchard, OK 73010-0413, USA

Miller, Joel McKinnon (Actor)
c/o Michael Greene *Greene & Associates*
1901 Avenue of the Stars Ste 130
Los Angeles, CA 90067-6030, USA

Miller, Joey (Race Car Driver)
Country Joe Racing
22222 Dodd Blvd
Lakeville, MN 55044-8553, USA

Miller, John (Athlete, Baseball Player)
13443 Old Annapolis Rd
Mount Airy, MD 21771-7732, USA

Miller, John (Athlete, Baseball Player)
5105 River Ave Apt A
Newport Beach, CA 92663-2415, USA

Miller, John (Correspondent)
ABC-TV
77 W 66th St
News Dept
New York, NY 10023-6201, USA

Miller, Johnny (Athlete, Golfer)
PO Box 970488
Orem, UT 84097-0488, USA

Miller, Johnny (Athlete, Football Player)
94 Beach St
Revere, MA 02151-5006, USA

Miller, Jon (Baseball Player,
Commentator, Sportscaster)
San Francisco Giants
401 Nevada Ave
Moss Beach, CA 94038-9643, USA

Miller, Jonny Lee (Actor)
c/o Ina Treciokas *Slate Public Relations*
9000 W Sunset Blvd Ste 915
West Hollywood, CA 90069-5809, USA

Miller, Josh (Athlete, Football Player)
16 Summer Heights Dr
Franklin, MA 02038-2365, USA

Miller, J Ronald (Religious Leader)
Int'l Community Churches Council
21116 Washington Pkwy
Frankfort, IL 60423-3112, USA

Miller, Julie (Musician, Songwriter,
Writer)
Mark Pucci Media
5000 Oak Bluff Ct
Atlanta, GA 30350-1069, USA

Miller, Justin (Athlete, Baseball Player)
22715 Anza Ave
Torrance, CA 90505-3420, USA

Miller, Justin (Athlete, Football Player)
c/o Eugene Parker *Maximum Sports*
Management
6435 W Jefferson Blvd # 197
Fort Wayne, IN 46804-6203, USA

Miller, Keith (Athlete, Baseball Player)
10510 Terra Lago Dr
West Palm Beach, FL 33412-3026, USA

Miller, Keith (Athlete, Baseball Player)
1831 W Alamosa Dr
Terrell, TX 75160-0811, USA

Miller, Keith (Politician)
3705 Arctic Blvd
Anchorage, AK 99503-5774, USA

Miller, Keith H (Ex-Governor)
3705 Arctic Blvd
Anchorage, AK 99503-5774, USA

Miller, Kelly (Athlete, Hockey Player)
3783 Chippendale Cir
Okemos, MI 48864-3861

Miller, Kelly (Basketball Player)
Indiana Fever
3763 Chippendale Cir
Okemos, MI 48864, USA

Miller, Kenny
5312 Eagle Lake Dr
Palm Beach Gardens, FL 33418-1539

Miller, Kevin (Athlete, Hockey Player,
Olympic Athlete)
4243 Redbud Trl
Williamston, MI 48895-9103

Miller, Kip (Athlete, Hockey Player)
2558 Lupine Ct
Okemos, MI 48864-3366

Miller, Kristen (Actor)
Lighthouse
409 N Camden Dr Ste 202
Beverly Hills, CA 90210-4423, USA

Miller, Lamar (Athlete, Football Player)
c/o Drew Rosenhaus *Rosenhaus Sports
Representation*
6400 Allison Rd
Miami Beach, FL 33141-4540, USA

Miller, Larry (Actor, Comedian)
c/o Staff Member *Brillstein Entertainment
Partners (LA)*
9150 Wilshire Blvd Ste 350
Beverly Hills, CA 90212-3453, USA

Miller, Larry (Athlete, Baseball Player)
3205 E Desert Cove Ave
Phoenix, AZ 85028-2735, USA

Miller, Larry (Athlete, Football Player)
3 Cour De La Reine
Palos Hills, IL 60465-2405, USA

Miller, Larry
311 Mulberry St
Catasauqua, PA 18032-1825, USA

Miller, Lemmie (Athlete, Baseball Player)
Rockford Riverhawks
4503 Interstate Blvd
Attn: Coaching Staff
Loves Park, IL 61111-5700, USA

Miller, Lennox (Athlete, Track Athlete)
2120 Pinecrest Dr
Altadena, CA 91001-2121, USA

Miller, Linda G
242 Conway Ave
Los Angeles, CA 90024-2602, USA

Miller, LW (Race Car Driver)
Miller Racing
206 Performance Rd
Mooresville, NC 28115-9591, USA

Miller, Marisa (Actor, Model)
c/o Zoe Lee *Cartel Management*
665 Lillian Way
Los Angeles, CA 90004-1107, USA

Miller, Mark (Athlete, Football Player)
6020 Poling Rd
Lima, OH 45807-9492, USA

Miller, Mark (Musician)
Sawyer Brown Inc
5200 Old Harding Rd
Franklin, TN 37064-9406, USA

Miller, Matt (Athlete, Baseball Player)
9600 Quaker Ave Unit 10
Lubbock, TX 79424-5116, USA

Miller, Matt (Athlete, Football Player)
112 Briarwood Dr # 2
Ithaca, NY 14850-1900, USA

Miller, McKaley (Actor)
c/o Kelly-Marie Smith *Brilliant Public
Relations*
6260 W 3rd St Apt 425
Los Angeles, CA 90036-7610, USA

Miller, Michael (Athlete, Football Player)
2337 Kellar Ave
Flint, MI 48504-7102, USA

Miller, Mike (Athlete, Basketball Player)
24752 Eagle Pointe
Columbia Station, OH 44028-8924, USA

Miller, Nancy (Writer)
c/o Michael Donkis *Prime*
9696 Culver Blvd Ste 102
Culver City, CA 90232-2734, USA

Miller, Nate (Boxer)
1214 Allengrove St
Philadelphia, PA 19124-2904, USA

Miller, Nicole J (Designer, Fashion
Designer)
780 Madison Ave Frnt 1
New York, NY 10065-6108, USA

Miller, Norm (Athlete, Baseball Player)
835 Royal Ln
Jacksonville, OR 97530-9457, USA

Miller, Oliver (Athlete, Basketball Player)
2912 S Meadow Dr
Fort Worth, TX 76133-7214, USA

Miller, Omar Benson (Actor)
c/o Stephen Tenenbaum *Morra Brezner
Steinberg & Tenenbaum (MBST)
Entertainment*
345 N Maple Dr Ste 200
Beverly Hills, CA 90210-5174, USA

Miller, Paul (Athlete, Baseball Player)
252 Redbud Ln
Batavia, IL 60510-3623, USA

Miller, Paul (Athlete, Hockey Player)
5 Celtic Ave
Billerica, MA 01821-1203

Miller, Penelope Ann (Actor)
c/o Stephanie Simon *Untitled
Entertainment (LA)*
350 S Beverly Dr Ste 200
Beverly Hills, CA 90212-4819, USA

Miller, Percy (P Miller) (Master P) (Actor,
Musician)
c/o Holly Davis-Carter *Releve*
6255 W Sunset Blvd Ste 908
Los Angeles, CA 90028-7410, USA

Miller, Randy (Athlete, Baseball Player)
22523 Oak Mist Ln
Katy, TX 77494-2256, USA

Miller, Raymond (Ray) (Athlete, Baseball
Player, Coach)
PO Box 41
New Athens, OH 43981-0041, USA

Miller, Reggie (Athlete, Basketball Player,
Olympic Athlete)
3785 Puerco Canyon Rd
Malibu, CA 90265-4551, USA

Miller, Reginald W (Reggie) (Athlete,
Basketball Player)
3785 Puerco Canyon Rd
Malibu, CA 90265-4551, USA

Miller, Rick (Athlete, Baseball Player)
12790 Silverthorn Ct
Bonita Springs, FL 34135-2452, USA

Miller, Robert
Capitol Complex
Carson City, NV 89710, USA

Miller, Robert M (Athlete, Football Player)
8475 Knox Rd
Clarkston, MI 48348-1721, USA

Miller, Robert N (Red) (Athlete, Coach,
Football Coach, Football Player)
3841 S Narcissus Way
Denver, CO 80237-1239, USA

Miller, Robin (Chef)
c/o Staff Member *Food Network, The*
1180 Avenue of the Americas Fl 11
New York, NY 10036-8401, USA

Miller, Rod (Athlete, Baseball Player)
413 Cabarton Rd
Cascade, ID 83611-5004, USA

Miller, Romeo (Musician)
c/o Morgan Terrelle *Carman Hall
Entertainment*
1600 Rosecrans Ave
Media Center Bldg 4th Fl
Manhattan Beach, CA 90266-3708, USA

Miller, Roy (Athlete, Football Player)
c/o Michael McCartney *Priority Sports &
Entertainment - Chicago*
312 N La Salle
Suite 650
Chicago, IL 60610, USA

Miller, Ryan (Athlete, Hockey Player)
700 Walbert Dr
East Lansing, MI 48823

Miller, Scott (Athlete, Football Player)
26432 Charford Way
Lake Forest, CA 92630-6520, USA

Miller, Shannon (Athlete, Gymnast,
Olympic Athlete)
Shannon Miller Lifestyle
4311 Salisbury Rd
Jacksonville, FL 32216-6123, USA

Miller, Shauna (Writer)
c/o Jordyn Palos *Persona PR (LA)*
8840 Wilshire Blvd Ste 212
Beverly Hills, CA 90211-2606, USA

Miller, Shawn (Athlete, Football Player)
3070 W Old Highway Rd
Morgan, UT 84050-9307, USA

Miller, Stephanie (Comedian, Television
Host)
KTLK AM 1150
3400 W Olive Ave Ste 550
Burbank, CA 91505-5544, USA

Miller, Steve (Musician, Songwriter)
PO Box 12680
Seattle, WA 98111-4680, USA

Miller, Stu (Athlete, Baseball Player)
3701 Ocaso Ct
Cameron Park, CA 95682-8961, USA

Miller, Stuart L (Stu) (Baseball Player)
St Louis Cardinals
3701 Ocaso Ct
Cameron Park, CA 95682-8961, USA

Miller, Tangi (Actor)
c/o Adam Robinson *Southfield Village*
8228 W Sunset Blvd # 190
West Hollywood, CA 90046-2414, USA

Miller, Terry (Athlete, Football Player)
9015 W 2nd Ave
Stillwater, OK 74074-6775, USA

Miller, TJ (Actor, Comedian)
c/o David (Dave) Becky *3 Arts
Entertainment (LA)*
9460 Wilshire Blvd Fl 7
Beverly Hills, CA 90212-2713, USA

Miller, Travis (Athlete, Baseball Player)
269 Lakengren Dr
Eaton, OH 45320-2943, USA

Miller, Trever (Athlete, Baseball Player)
24155 Hideout Trl
Land O Lakes, FL 34639-8111, USA

Miller, Ty (Actor)
c/o Staff Member *Tedesco Management*
Prefers to be contacted via telephone
West Hollywood, CA 90069, USA

Miller, Valarie Rae
3500 W Olive Ave Ste 1400
Burbank, CA 91505-5512

Miller, Von (Athlete, Football Player)
c/o David Dunn *Athletes First, LLC*
23091 Mill Creek Dr
Laguna Hills, CA 92653-1258, USA

Miller, Wade (Athlete, Baseball Player)
12 Woods Way
Reading, PA 19610-1199, USA

Miller, Warren (Athlete, Hockey Player)
937 21st Ave N
South Saint Paul, MN 55075-1316, USA

Miller, Wentworth (Actor)
1802 N Kenmore Ave
Los Angeles, CA 90027-4008, USA

Miller, Wiley (Artist, Cartoonist)
107 Pebblestump Pt
Peachtree City, GA 30269-1645, USA

Miller, William (Athlete, Baseball Player)
PO Box 2681
Aptos, CA 95001-2681, USA

Miller, Willie T (Athlete, Football Player)
6290 Walnut Dr
Pinson, AL 35126-6423, USA

Miller, Zach (Athlete, Football Player)
c/o Tom Condon *CAA (St. Louis)*
222 S Central Ste 1008
Saint Louis, MO 63105-3509, USA

Miller, Zell (Government Official,
Politician)
709 Miller St
Young Harris, GA 30582-4019, USA

Millett, Kate (Writer)
20 Old Overlook Rd
Poughkeepsie, NY 12603-6220, USA

Millette, Joe (Athlete, Baseball Player)
759 Solana Dr
Lafayette, CA 94549-5206, USA

Millhauser, Steven (Writer)
235 Caroline St
Saratoga Springs, NY 12866-3505, USA

Milliard, Ralph (Baseball Player)
101 Runaway Bay Dr Apt 304
Virginia Beach, VA 23452-8157

Milligan, Randy (Athlete, Baseball Player)
6905 Real Princess Ln
Gwynn Oak, MD 21207-4577, USA

Millikan, Joe (Race Car Driver)
4671 Bull Creek Rd
Franklinville, NC 27248, USA

Milliken, William (Politician)
6103 Peninsula Dr
Traverse City, MI 49686-1913, USA

Millionaires (Music Group)
c/o Jonathan Daniel *Crush Management*
60-62 E 11th St
7th Floor
New York, NY 10003, USA

Millman, Dan (Writer)
PO Box 6148
San Rafael, CA 94903-0148, USA

Millner, eddie
491 Stambaugh Ave
Columbus, OH 43207-2565

Millns, James (Athlete, Figure Skater,
Olympic Athlete)
7603 Dunbridge Dr
Odessa, FL 33556-2259, USA

Millns, Jim (Athlete, Figure Skater,
Olympic Athlete)
16306 Doune Ct
Tampa, FL 33647-2761, USA

Milloy, Lawyer (Athlete, Football Player)
1 Bills Dr
Orchard Park, NY 14127-2237, USA

Mills, Alan (Athlete, Baseball Player)
1811 Bellgrove St
Lakeland, FL 33805-2523, USA

Mills, Alley (Actor)
444 Carroll Canal
Venice, CA 90291-4682, USA

Mills, Bill (Athlete, Baseball Player)
4344 Commercial St
Port Charlotte, FL 33953-5945, USA

Mills, Billy (Athlete, Olympic Athlete,
Track Athlete)
c/o Staff Member *Billy Mills Speakers
Bureau, The*
7760 Winding Way # 723
Fair Oaks, CA 95628-5735, USA

Mills, Brad (Athlete, Baseball Player)
723 N 22nd Pi
Mesa, AZ 85213, USA

Mills, Chris (Athlete, Basketball Player)
2223 Camden Ave
Los Angeles, CA 90064-1905, USA

Mills, Curtis (Athlete, Track Athlete)
328 Lake St
Lufkin, TX 75904, USA

Mills, Dick (Athlete, Baseball Player)
10345 E Desert Cove Ave
Scottsdale, AZ 85260-6304, USA

Mills, Donna (Actor)
c/o Staff Member *Darlene Kaplan
Entertainment*
4450 Balboa Ave
Encino, CA 91316-4101, USA

Mills, Eddie (Actor)
c/o Staff Member *Peter Strain &
Associates Inc (LA)*
5455 Wilshire Blvd Ste 1812
Los Angeles, CA 90036-4268, USA

Mills, Ernie (Athlete, Football Player)
21246 SW Plantation St
Dunnellon, FL 34431-3482, USA

Mills, Hayley (Actor)
c/o Alan Willig *Don Buchwald &
Associates (NY)*
10 E 44th St Frnt 1
New York, NY 10017-3654, USA

Mills, John Henry (Athlete, Football
Player)
755 Bahia Cir
Ocala, FL 34472-8831, USA

Mills, Jordan (Athlete, Football Player)
6500 Wilshire Blvd Ste 2200
Los Angeles, CA 90048-4942

Mills, Judson (Actor)
c/o Dino May *Dino May Management*
6362 Hollywood Blvd # 422
Los Angeles, CA 90028-6323, USA

Mills, Juliet (Actor, Writer)
442 Montana Cir
Ojai, CA 93023-1621, USA

Mills, Kyle (Writer)
c/o Staff Member *Vanguard Press*
387 Park Ave S Fl 12
New York, NY 10016-8810, USA

Mills, Leigh Ann (Athlete, Golfer)
1919 W Carmen St
Tampa, FL 33606-1225, USA

Mills, Mary (Athlete, Golfer)
310 S Ocean Blvd Apt 106
Boca Raton, FL 33432-6207, USA

Mills, Mike (Musician)
c/o Staff Member *ICM Partners (LA)*
10250 Constellation Blvd Fl 7
Los Angeles, CA 90067-6207, USA

Mills, Noah (Actor, Model)
c/o Melissa Stone *42West (LA)*
1840 Century Park E Ste 700
Los Angeles, CA 90067-2122, USA

Mills, Pete (Football Player)
Buffalo Bills
27 Langfield Dr
Buffalo, NY 14215-3321, USA

Mills, Stephanie (Actor, Musician)
Associated Booking Corp
1995 Broadway # 501
New York, NY 10023-5882, USA

Mills, Terry (Athlete, Basketball Player)
Indiana Pacers
37840 Scott Pine Dr
New Boston, MI 48164-9190, USA

Mills, William M (Billy) (Athlete, Track
Athlete)
7760 Winding Way
Fair Oaks, CA 95628-5735, USA

Mills, Zach (Actor)
c/o Judy Savage *Savage Agency*
6212 Banner Ave
Los Angeles, CA 90038-2802, USA

millwood, Kevin
1204 Suncast Ln Ste 2
El Dorado Hills, CA 95762-9665

Millwood, Kevin A (Athlete, Baseball
Player)
1204 Suncast Ln Ste 2
El Dorado Hills, CA 95762-9665, USA

Milner, Brian (Athlete, Baseball Player)
11825 Elko Ln
Fort Worth, TX 76108-4783, USA

Milner, Eddie (Athlete, Baseball Player)
491 Stambaugh Ave
Columbus, OH 43207-2565, USA

Milner, Martin (Actor)
3106 Azahar St
Carlsbad, CA 92009-8362, USA

Milonakis, Andy (Actor)
c/o Jason Cunningham *Paradigm (LA)*
360 N Crescent Dr
North Bldg
Beverly Hills, CA 90210-4874, USA

Milos, Sofia (Actor)
Sofia Milos Fan Club
8950 W Olympic Blvd
P.O. Box 173
Beverly Hills, CA 90211-3561, USA

Milsap, Ronnie (Musician, Songwriter)
806 N Curtiswood Ln
Nashville, TN 37204-4314, USA

Milsome, Doug (Cinematographer)
Simth/Gosnell/Nicholson
PO Box 1156
Studio City, CA 91614-0156, USA

Milstead, Charles (Football Player)
Houston Oilers
14414 Sandalin Dr
Cypress, TX 77429-1861, USA

Milstead, Rod (Athlete, Football Player)
11815 Brookeville Landing Ct
Bowie, MD 20721-4502, USA

Milteer, Lee (Business Person, Writer)
Lee Milteer Inc.
2100 Thoroughgood Rd
Virginia Beach, VA 23455-4015, USA

Milton, DeLisha (Basketball Player)
Los Angeles Sparks
1111 S Figueroa St
Staples Center
Los Angeles, CA 90015-1300, USA

Milton, Eric (Athlete, Baseball Player)
1133 Asquith Dr
Arnold, MD 21012-2153, USA

Mimbs, Michael (Athlete, Baseball Player)
2761 Mimbs Rd
Alamo, GA 30411-2502, USA

Mimbs, Mike (Basketball Player)
950 Huntcliffe Ct
Macon, GA 31210-7553, USA

Mims, Madeline Manning (Athlete, Track
Athlete)
7477 E 48th St # 83-4
Tulsa, OK 74145-6679, USA

Minaj, Nicki (Musician)
c/o Holly Shakoor Fleischer *42West (LA)*
1840 Century Park E Ste 700
Los Angeles, CA 90067-2122, USA

Minarcin, Rudy (Athlete, Baseball Player)
1037 1st St
Vandergrift, PA 15690-1007, USA

Minarik, Henry (Athlete, Football Player)
1001 N Linda Ln Apt A
Lake City, MI 49651-9227, USA

Minaya, Omar (Athlete, Baseball Player,
Commentator)
c/o Staff Member *San Diego Padres*
100 Park Blvd
San Diego, CA 92101-7405, USA

Minchey, Nate (Athlete, Baseball Player)
2008 Baxter Ln
Franklin, TN 37069-8111, USA

Minchin, Tim (Actor, Comedian)
5606 Green Oak Dr
Los Angeles, CA 90068-2504, USA

Mincy, Charles (Athlete, Football Player)
2227 W 24th St Apt 7
Los Angeles, CA 90018-1944, USA

Mincy, Purnell (Baseball Player)
Philadelphia Stars
127 W 96th St Apt 160
New York, NY 10025-6427, USA

Mindell, Earl (Writer)
Hay House
PO Box 5100
Carlsbad, CA 92018-5100

Mindless Behavior (Music Group)
c/o Troy Carter *Atom Factory/Coalition
Media Group*
1630 Colorado Ave
Santa Monica, CA 90404, USA

Minear, Tim (Director, Writer)
c/o Lawrence Shuman *Shuman Company*
3815 Hughes Ave Fl 4
Culver City, CA 90232-2715, USA

Mineo, Gordon (Race Car Driver)
Flash Gordon Racing
214 Windy Ln
Rockwall, TX 75087-8005, USA

Miner, Harold (Athlete, Basketball Player)
5067 Mountain Foliage Dr
Las Vegas, NV 89148-1438, USA

Miner, Steve (Director)
1137 2nd St Ste 103
Santa Monica, CA 90403-5069, USA

Miner, Zack (Baseball Player)
108 Glencullen Cir
Jupiter, FL 33458-6534

Minervini, Craig (Athlete, Baseball Player)
229 Cameron Dr
Weston, FL 33326-3515, USA

Minetto, Craig (Athlete, Baseball Player)
1809 Lakeshore Dr
Lodi, CA 95242-4230, USA

Ming, Tsai (Chef)
Food Network
1180 Avenue of the Americas Ste 1220 #
1200
New York, NY 10036-8406, USA

Ming, Yao (Athlete, Basketball Player)
430 Thamer Ln
Houston, TX 77024-6946, USA

Mingenbach, Louise (Designer)
c/o Wayne Fitterman *United Talent
Agency (UTA-LA)*
9336 Civic Center Dr
Beverly Hills, CA 90210-3604, USA

Minghella, Max (Actor)
c/o Tony Lipp *Anonymous Content (LA)*
3532 Hayden Ave
Culver City, CA 90232-2413, USA

Ming-Na, Wen (Actor)
c/o Troy Nankin *Wishlab*
2225A Hyperion Ave
Los Angeles, CA 90027-4709, USA

Mingo, Gene (Athlete, Football Player)
5701 E Colorado Ave
Denver, CO 80224-2102, USA

Mingori, Steve (Athlete, Baseball Player)
8841 N Congress Ave Apt 637
Kansas City, MO 64153-1914, USA

Mingus, Charles
484 W 43rd St Apt 43S
New York, NY 10036-6327

Ming Wang, Chien (Athlete, Baseball
Player)
c/o Team Member *New York Yankees*
Yankee Stadium
161st St & River Ave
Bronx, NY 10451, USA

Miniefield, Kevin (Athlete, Football
Player)
1030 Lakehurst Dr
Waukegan, IL 60085-8232, USA

Mink, Rep (Politician)
PO Box 50144
Honolulu, HI 96850-5544

Minka (Adult Film Star)
USP Entertainment Inc
8635 W Sahara Ave # 564
Las Vegas, NV 89117-5858, USA

Minkoff, Rob (Director, Producer)
c/o Rand Holston *Paradigm (LA)*
2000 Avenue of the Stars
Los Angeles, CA 90067-4700, USA

Minnelli, Liza (Actor, Musician, Producer)
150 E 69th St Apt 21G
New York, NY 10021-5722, USA

Minnick, Don (Athlete, Baseball Player)
215 Bernard Rd
Rocky Mount, VA 24151-2243, USA

Minniear, Randy (Athlete, Football Player)
739 Westport Rd
Easton, CT 06612-1537, USA

Minniefield, Dick (Athlete, Basketball
Player)
10902 Little Gap Ct
Sugar Land, TX 77498-0946, USA

Minniefield, Dirk
10902 Little Gap Ct
Sugar Land, TX 77498-0946

Minnifield, Frank (Athlete, Football
Player)
4809 Chaffey Ln
Lexington, KY 40515-1166, USA

Minnillo, Vanessa (Actor, Television Host)
c/o Melissa Raubvogel *Baker Winokur
Ryder Public Relations (BWR-NY)*
292 Madison Ave Fl 12
New York, NY 10017-6415, USA

Minogue, Kylie (Dancer, Musician)
c/o Staff Member *Roc Nation*
9348 Civic Center Dr
Beverly Hills, CA 90210-3624, USA

Minor, Blas (Athlete, Baseball Player)
7139 Dean St
Winton, CA 95388-9766, USA

Minor, Claudie (Athlete, Football Player)
730 17th St Ste 520
Denver, CO 80202-3539, USA

Minor, Damon (Athlete, Baseball Player)
6000 Airline Dr
Metairie, LA 70003-4373, USA

Minor, Gerry (Athlete, Hockey Player)
6516 Jackson Dr
San Diego, CA 92119-3309

Minor, Greg (Athlete, Basketball Player)
6543 Merrick Landing Blvd
Blvd
Windermere, FL 34786-7351, USA

Minor, Kory (Athlete, Football Player)
1402 W Farlington St
West Covina, CA 91790-3354, USA

Minor, Larry (Race Car Driver)
PO Box 398
San Jacinto, CA 92581-0398, USA

Minor, Lincoln (Athlete, Football Player)
5036 Coldwater Canyon Ave Apt 104
Sherman Oaks, CA 91423-1603, USA

Minor, Mark (Athlete, Basketball Player)
5693 Muldoon Ct
Dublin, OH 43016-4334, USA

Minor, Mike (Baseball Player)
4036 Cottonwood Ct
Lewisburg, TN 37091-6693

Minor, Rickey (Musician)
c/o Staff Member *William Morris
Endeavor (LA)*
9601 Wilshire Blvd
Beverly Hills, CA 90210-5213, USA

Minor, Ronald R (Religious Leader)
Pentecostal Church of God
PO Box 211866
Bedford, TX 76095-8866, USA

Minor, Ryan (Athlete, Baseball Player)
PO Box 1557
Salisbury, MD 21802-1557, USA

Minor, Shane (Musician)
ESP Mgmt
838 N Doheny Dr Apt 302
West Hollywood, CA 90069-4849, USA

Minor, Travis (Athlete, Football Player)
PO Box 1635
Hallandale, FL 33008-1635, USA

Minoso, Minnie (Basketball Player,
Coach)
3700 N Lake Shore Dr Apt 303
Chicago, IL 60613-4244, USA

Minoso, Minnle (Athlete, Baseball Player)
3700 N Lake Shore Dr Apt 303
Chicago, IL 60613-4244, USA

Minow, Newton (Journalist)
375 Palos Rd
Glencoe, IL 60022-1951, USA

Minow, Newton N (Government Official)
179 E Lake Shore Dr # 15W
Chicago, IL 60611-1340, USA

Minshall, Jim (Athlete, Baseball Player)
225 Marv Ingles Hwy
Melbourne, KY 41059, USA

Minshew, Alicia (Actor)
c/o Seth Greenky *Green Key Mgmt (NY)*
251 W 89th St Apt 4A
New York, NY 10024-1713, USA

Mint Condition (Musician)
c/o Staff Member *Green Light Talent
Agency*
PO Box 3172
Beverly Hills, CA 90212-0172, USA

Minter, Barry (Athlete, Football Player)
2626 Garcitas Crk
Richmond, TX 77406-1961, USA

Minter, Cedric (Athlete, Football Player)
5653 E Bay Trail Ct
Boise, ID 83716-7031, USA

Minter, Kelly (Actor)
c/o John Ly *John Ly Agency*
1601 N Gower St Ste 202
Los Angeles, CA 90028-7598, USA

Minter, Kevin (Athlete, Football Player)
c/o Joel Segal *Lagardere Unlimited (NYC)*
845 United Nations Plz
New York, NY 10017-3540, USA

Minter, Kristin (Actor)
c/o Charles Silver *SMS Talent*
8383 Wilshire Blvd Ste 230
Beverly Hills, CA 90211-2436, USA

Minter, Mike (Athlete, Football Player)
1557 Morton St
Lincoln, NE 68521-5638, USA

Minton, Greg (Athlete, Baseball Player)
1042 E Driftwood Dr
Tempe, AZ 85283-2014, USA

Minton, Madge Rutherford
6431 N Oxford St
Indianapolis, IN 46220-2244, USA

Mintz, Shiomo (Musician)
I C M Artists
40 W 57th St
New York, NY 10019-4001, USA

Mintz, Steve (Athlete, Baseball Player)
Fort Myers Miracle 14400 Six Mile
Cypress Pkwy A
Fort Myers, FL 33912, USA

Mintz-Plasse, Christopher (Actor)
21236 Velicata St
Woodland Hills, CA 91364-3256, USA

Minutelli, Gino (Athlete, Baseball Player)
3305 Foxtrot Ct
Spring Hill, TN 37174-7116, USA

Mio, Eddie (Athlete, Hockey Player)
PO Box 252745
West Bloomfield, MI 48325-2745

Mira, George (Athlete, Football Player)
19225 SW 128th Ct
Miami, FL 33177-4222, USA

Mirabella, Erin (Athlete, Cycler, Olympic
Athlete)
914 N Idaho St
La Habra, CA 90631, USA

Mirabella, Paul (Athlete, Baseball Player)
125 Jenks Rd
Morristown, NJ 07960-8701, USA

Mirabelli, Doug (Athlete, Baseball Player)
9788 Edgewood Ave
Traverse City, MI 49685-8173, USA

Miracles, The
141 Dunbar Ave
Fords, NJ 08863-1551

Miraldi, Dean (Athlete, Football Player)
14015 Live Oak Ln
Grass Valley, CA 95945-9509, USA

Miranda, Christianne (Musician,
Songwriter, Writer)
c/o Staff Member *Kult Records*
38 W 36th St Fl 3
New York, NY 10018-8078, USA

Miranda, Lin-Manuel (Actor)
c/o Brian Liebman *Liebman Entertainment*
12 E 46th St Fl 5
New York, NY 10017-2418, USA

Miranda, Patricia (Wrestler)
*Stanford Wrestling - Department of
Athletics*
Stanford University
Arrillaga Family Sports Center
Stanford, CA 94305, USA

Miranda, Willie
5502 Whitwood Rd
Baltimore, MD 21206-3748

Mirchoff, Beau (Actor)
c/o Scott Fish *Velocity Entertainment
Partners*
5455 Wilshire Blvd Ste 802
Los Angeles, CA 90036-4271, USA

Mirer, Rick (Athlete, Football Player)
PO Box 3422
Rancho Santa Fe, CA 92067-3422, USA

Mirich, Rex (Athlete, Football Player)
620 W Yaqui Dr
Tucson, AZ 85704-3742, USA

Mirikitani, Janice (Writer)
Glide Memorial United Methodist Church
330 Ellis St
San Francisco, CA 94102-2735, USA

Mirisch, Walter M (Producer)
647 Warner Ave
Los Angeles, CA 90024-2566, USA

Mirkin, David (Actor, Director)
c/o David Gersh *Gersh (LA)*
9465 Wilshire Blvd Ste 600
Beverly Hills, CA 90212-2605, USA

Mirnyi, Max (Athlete, Tennis Player)
c/o Staff Member *ATP Tour*
201 Atp Tour Blvd
Ponte Vedra Beach, FL 32082-3211, USA

Mironov, Boris (Athlete, Hockey Player)
110 E Parsonage Way
Manalapan, NJ 07726-7949

Mirra, Dave (Athlete)
Wasserman Media Group, LLC
12100 W Olympic Blvd Ste 400
Los Angeles, CA 90064-1052, USA

Mirren, Helen (Actor, Director, Producer)
c/o Melissa Sun *Stan Rosenfield &
Associates*
2029 Century Park E Ste 1190
Los Angeles, CA 90067-2931, USA

Misaka, Walt (Athlete, Basketball Player)
173 Aruba Dr
Saratoga Springs, UT 84045-5115, USA

Misaka, Wataru "Wat"
288 E 2450 S
Bountiful, UT 84010-5638

Misch, Patrick (Athlete, Baseball Player)
366 E Krista Way
Tempe, AZ 85284-1445, USA

Mischak, Bob (Athlete, Football Player)
73 Brookwood Rd Unit 12
Orinda, CA 94563-3310, USA

Mischka, Badgley (Designer, Fashion
Designer)
525 Seventh Ave Fl 14
New York, NY 10018, USA

Mischke, Carl H (Religious Leader)
1034 Buena Vista Dr
Sun Prairie, WI 53590-2031, USA

Misi, Koa (Athlete, Football Player)
c/o Ken Zuckerman *Priority Sports & Entertainment - (LA)*
15233 Ventura Blvd Ste 718
Sherman Oaks, CA 91403-2237, USA

Misiano, Christopher (Director)
c/o Staff Member *Creative Artists Agency (CAA-LA)*
2000 Avenue of the Stars Ste 100
Los Angeles, CA 90067-4705, USA

Misiano, Vincent (Director)
c/o Staff Member *Creative Artists Agency (CAA-LA)*
2000 Avenue of the Stars Ste 100
Los Angeles, CA 90067-4705, USA

Misko, John (Athlete, Football Player)
33252 Tule Oak Dr
Springville, CA 93265-9636, USA

Misner, Ivan (Business Person)
BNI
545 College Commerce Way
Upland, CA 91786-4377, USA

Missick, Dorian (Actor)
c/o Myrna Jacoby *MJ Management*
130 W 57th St Apt 11A
New York, NY 10019-3311, USA

Missing Persons
11935 Laurel Hills Rd
Studio City, CA 91604-3726

Miss Teen USA
6420 Wilshire Blvd
Los Angeles, CA 90048-5502

Mistler, John (Athlete, Football Player)
9799 E Hidden Green Dr
Scottsdale, AZ 85262-3611, USA

Mistry, Jimi (Actor)
c/o Staff Member *William Morris Endeavor (LA)*
9601 Wilshire Blvd
Beverly Hills, CA 90210-5213, USA

Misuraca, Mike (Athlete, Baseball Player)
250 N College Park Dr Apt F26
Upland, CA 91786-9467, USA

Mitchell, Aaron (Athlete, Football Player)
3613 Frankford Rd Apt 738
Dallas, TX 75287-6142, USA

Mitchell, Andrea (Correspondent, Journalist)
2710 Chain Bridge Rd NW
Washington, DC 20016-3404, USA

Mitchell, Basil (Athlete, Football Player)
806 Baker Ave
Mount Pleasant, TX 75455-4846, USA

Mitchell, Betsy (Athlete, Olympic Athlete, Swimmer)
Laurel High School
1 Lyman Cir Ofc Athletic
Beachwood, OH 44122-2110, USA

Mitchell, Beverley (Actor)
c/o Barry McPherson *Agency for the Performing Arts (APA-NY)*
135 W 50th St Fl 17
New York, NY 10020-1201, USA

Mitchell, Beverly (Actor)
c/o Staff Member *Forster Entertainment*
12533 Woodgreen St
Los Angeles, CA 90066-2723, USA

Mitchell, Bill (Athlete, Hockey Player)
13 Exeter Rd
Perrysburg, OH 43551-3117

Mitchell, Bobby (Athlete, Baseball Player)
14661 Thebes St
San Diego, CA 92129-1629, USA

Mitchell, Bobby (Athlete, Baseball Player)
8697 Tiogawoods Dr
Sacramento, CA 95828-5116, USA

Mitchell, Bobby (Athlete, Football Player)
450 Blue Beech Way
Chesapeake, VA 23320-3812, USA

Mitchell, Bobby (Athlete, Golfer)
435 Wimbish Dr
Danville, VA 24541-5823, USA

Mitchell, Brandon (Athlete, Football Player)
806 Schlessinger St
Abbeville, LA 70510-7050, USA

Mitchell, Brian (Athlete, Football Player)
137 Lamplighter Dr
Morgantown, WV 26508-8649, USA

Mitchell, Brian (Actor)
5307B Wilkinson Ave Unit 20
Valley Village, CA 91607-2464, USA

Mitchell, Brian (Athlete, Football Player)
5435 Chandley Farm Cir
Centreville, VA 20120-1240, USA

Mitchell, Brian Stokes (Actor, Musician)
243 W 98th St Apt 5C
New York, NY 10025-5566, USA

Mitchell, Charlie (Athlete, Baseball Player)
5017 Hasty Dr
Nashville, TN 37211-5345, USA

Mitchell, Charlie (Athlete, Football Player)
6300 Seward Park Ave S
Seattle, WA 98118-3055, USA

Mitchell, Craig (Athlete, Baseball Player)
PO Box 174
Elk, CA 95432-0174, USA

Mitchell, Dale (Athlete, Football Player)
1837 Tanner Ave SW
Canton, OH 44706-2623, USA

Mitchell, Darryl (Actor)
c/o Staff Member *Forster Entertainment*
12533 Woodgreen St
Los Angeles, CA 90066-2723, USA

Mitchell, Daryl (Chill) (Actor)
c/o Jenny Delaney *Jenny Delaney Management*
3238 Fond Dr
Encino, CA 91436-4206, USA

Mitchell, Donald (Athlete, Football Player)
5620 Minner Dr
Beaumont, TX 77708-4515, USA

Mitchell, Earl (Athlete, Football Player)
c/o Brad Leshnock *BTI Sports Advisors*
170 N Scoville Ave
Oak Park, IL 60302-2647, USA

Mitchell, Edgar D (Astronaut)
PO Box 540037
Greenacres, FL 33454-0037, USA

Mitchell, Edgar D Captain (Astronaut)
PO Box 540037
Greenacres, FL 33454-0037, USA

Mitchell, Elizabeth (Actor)
c/o Ben Levine *LINK Entertainment*
11872 La Grange Ave Fl 1
Los Angeles, CA 90025-5283, USA

Mitchell, Elvis (Producer, Radio Personality, Writer)
KCRW
1900 Pico Blvd
Santa Monica, CA 90405-1628, USA

Mitchell, Freddie (Athlete, Football Player)
606 N Brunnell Pkwy
Lakeland, FL 33815-1258, USA

Mitchell, George (Politician)
151 Crandon Blvd Apt 110
Key Biscayne, FL 33149-1529, USA

Mitchell, George J (Politician, Senator)
DLA Piper Rudnick Gray Cary
1251 Avenue of the Americas Ste C2-75
New York, NY 10020-0073, USA

Mitchell, Jeff (Athlete, Football Player)
12151 Roseland Dr
New Port Richey, FL 34654-6323, USA

Mitchell, Jeff (Athlete, Hockey Player)
Suburban Hockey Schools
23995 Freeway Park Dr Ste 200
Farmington Hills, MI 48335-2829

Mitchell, Jessie (Baseball Player)
Birmingham Black Barons
1964 Cherry Ave
Birmingham, AL 35214-1802, USA

Mitchell, Jim H (Athlete, Football Player)
120 Twin Creek Ter
Forest, VA 24551-1328, USA

Mitchell, John (Athlete, Baseball Player)
5017 Hasty Dr
Nashville, TN 37211-5345, USA

mitchell, John (Athlete, Basketball Player)
1708 Castleberry Way
Birmingham, AL 35214-4826, USA

Mitchell, John Cameron (Actor, Director)
c/o Richie Jackson *Jackson Group Entertainment*
400 W 12th St Apt 5C
New York, NY 10014-1861, USA

Mitchell, Johnny (Athlete, Football Player)
8721 S Normal Ave
Chicago, IL 60620-2119, USA

Mitchell, Kawika (Athlete, Football Player)
971 N Lake Sybelia Dr
Maitland, FL 32751-4811, USA

Mitchell, Keith (Athlete, Baseball Player)
731 S 42nd St
San Diego, CA 92113-1813, USA

Mitchell, Kel (Actor)
c/o Staff Member *Nine Yards Entertainment*
5815 W Sunset Blvd Ste 206
Los Angeles, CA 90028-6481, USA

Mitchell, Ken (Athlete, Football Player)
4313 Cityview Dr
Plano, TX 75093-3236, USA

Mitchell, Kevin (Athlete, Baseball Player)
3869 Ocean View Blvd
San Diego, CA 92113-1736, USA

Mitchell, Larry (Athlete, Baseball Player)
1040 Preston Ave
Charlottesville, VA 22903-2109, USA

Mitchell, Leroy (Athlete, Football Player)
6598 Pinewood Dr
Parker, CO 80134-6356, USA

Mitchell, Luke (Actor)
c/o Gabriel Cohen *Management 360*
9111 Wilshire Blvd
Beverly Hills, CA 90210-5508, USA

Mitchell, Lydell D (Athlete, Football Player)
702 Reservoir St
Baltimore, MD 21217-4632, USA

Mitchell, Mack (Athlete, Football Player)
1200 Maynard St
Diboll, TX 75941-2602, USA

Mitchell, Maia (Actor, Musician)
c/o Peter McGrath *Station3 (LA)*
1051 Cole Ave Ste B
Los Angeles, CA 90038-2601, USA

Mitchell, Mike (Director)
c/o Gregory McKnight *Creative Artists Agency (CAA-LA)*
2000 Avenue of the Stars Ste 100
Los Angeles, CA 90067-4705, USA

Mitchell, Murray (Athlete, Basketball Player)
101 N Upper Broadway St Apt 403
Corpus Christi, TX 78401-2755, USA

Mitchell, Paul (Athlete, Baseball Player)
23 Carr Rd
Berlin, MA 01503-1116, USA

Mitchell, Pete (Athlete, Football Player)
100 Paddock Pl
Ponte Vedra Beach, FL 32082-3957, USA

Mitchell, Radha (Actor)
2722 6th St
Santa Monica, CA 90405-4406, USA

Mitchell, Rick (DJ)
c/o Staff Member *Diva Central Inc*
7510 W Sunset Blvd Ste 1445
Los Angeles, CA 90046-3408, USA

Mitchell, Robert (Athlete, Baseball Player)
Cleveland Buckeyes
2009 Elmwood Ave
Tampa, FL 33605-6625, USA

Mitchell, Roger (Athlete, Football Player)
Chaminade-Madonna College Prep
500 E Chaminade Dr
Hollywood, FL 33021-5853, USA

Mitchell, Roger (Director, Producer)
c/o Beth Swofford *Creative Artists Agency (CAA-LA)*
2000 Avenue of the Stars Ste 100
Los Angeles, CA 90067-4705, USA

Mitchell, Roland (Athlete, Football Player)
PO Box 5701
Lake Charles, LA 70606-5701, USA

Mitchell, Roy (Athlete, Hockey Player)
14449 W Stockwell St
Boise, ID 83713-0949

Mitchell, Russ (Correspondent, Television Host)
c/o Staff Member *CBS News (NY)*
524 W 57th St Fl 8
New York, NY 10019-2930, USA

Mitchell, Sam (Athlete, Basketball Player, Coach)
73 Smokerise Pt
Peachtree City, GA 30269-4068, USA

Mitchell, Sasha (Actor)
c/o Kathy McComb *Kathy McComb Management*
10630 1/2 Landale St
North Hollywood, CA 91602-2317, USA

Mitchell, Scott (Athlete, Football Player)
5060 Franklin Rd
Bloomfield Hills, MI 48302-2614, USA

Mitchell, Shareen (Actor)
J Michael Bloom
9255 W Sunset Blvd Ste 710
West Hollywood, CA 90069-3304, USA

Mitchell, Sharon
1122 White Rock Dr
Dixon, IL 61021-9049

Mitchell, Shay (Actor)
c/o Tej Bhatia Herring *Rogers & Cowan PR (LA)*
8687 Melrose Ave Ste 7
West Hollywood, CA 90069-5721, USA

Mitchell, Silas Weir (Actor)
2340 Ronda Vista Dr
Los Angeles, CA 90027-4644, USA

Mitchell, Steve (Actor)
c/o Staff Member *Select Artists Ltd (CA-Westside Office)*
1138 12th St Apt 1
Santa Monica, CA 90403-5459, USA

Mitchell, Susan (Writer)
Florida Atlantic University
English Dept
Boca Raton, FL 33431, USA

Mitchell, Todd (Athlete, Basketball Player)
4134 Emmajean Rd
Toledo, OH 43607-1015, USA

Mitchell, Tom (Athlete, Football Player)
1421 SW 49th Ter
Cape Coral, FL 33914-6934, USA

Mitchell, Vernessa (Musician)
c/o Staff Member *Diva Central Inc*
7510 W Sunset Blvd Ste 1445
Los Angeles, CA 90046-3408, USA

Mitchum, Carrie (Actor)
Camden ITG Talent
1501 Main St Ste 204
Venice, CA 90291-3699, USA

Mitra, Rhona (Actor)
c/o Jason Weinberg *Untitled Entertainment (LA)*
350 S Beverly Dr Ste 200
Beverly Hills, CA 90212-4819, USA

Mitre, Sergio (Athlete, Baseball Player)
1443 Blairwood Ave
Chula Vista, CA 91913-2960, USA

Mitrione, Matt (Athlete, Football Player)
729 Toddsbury Ln
Richmond, IN 47374-7152, USA

Mitte, RJ (Actor)
c/o Stewart Strunk *Main Title Entertainment*
8383 Wilshire Blvd Ste 408
Beverly Hills, CA 90211-2435, USA

Mitterwald, George (Athlete, Baseball Player)
5314 Kenyon Rd
Orlando, FL 32810-1714, USA

Mitts, Heather (Soccer Player)
US Soccer/ Heather Mitts
18400 Avalon Blvd Ste 500
Carson, CA 90746-2183, USA

Mitz, Alonzo (Athlete, Football Player)
2609 NE 4th St Apt 216
Renton, WA 98056-4053, USA

Mitzelfeld, Jim (Journalist)
969 N Lebanon St
Arlington, VA 22205-1455, USA

Mivelaz, Betty (Bowler)
1543 Grand Ave
Medford, OR 97504-5304, USA

Mix, Bryant (Athlete, Football Player)
37 Greenwood Plantation Rd
Natchez, MS 39120-8946, USA

Mix, Ronald J (Ron) (Athlete, Football Player)
2317 Caminito Recodo
San Diego, CA 92107-1529, USA

Mix, Steve (Athlete, Basketball Player)
25743 Willowbend Rd
Perrysburg, OH 43551-9787, USA

Mixon, Katy (Actor)
c/o Larry Taube *Principal Entertainment (LA)*
9255 W Sunset Blvd Ste 500
West Hollywood, CA 90069-3301, USA

Mixon, Ken (Athlete, Football Player)
3225 E Quayside Dr
Hollywood, FL 33026-3788, USA

Mixon, Wayne (Politician)
2219 Demeron Rd
Tallahassee, FL 32308-0943, USA

Mixson, J Wayne (Ex-Governor)
2219 Demeron Rd
Tallahassee, FL 32308-0943, USA

Miza, Ola L
211 Hartwood Dr
Gadsden, AL 35901-6228, USA

Mize, Larry (Athlete, Golfer)
106 Graystone Ct
Columbus, GA 31904-4300, USA

Mizerock, John (Athlete, Baseball Player, Coach)
2297 Juneau Rd
Punxsutawney, PA 15767-9428, USA

Mizrahi, Isaac (Fashion Designer, Television Host)
Isaac Mizrahi Studio
475 10th Ave Fl 4
New York, NY 10018-1120, USA

Mizrahie, Barbara (Athlete, Golfer)
7419 Floranada Way
Delray Beach, FL 33446-2374, USA

M. Landry, Jeffrey (Congressman, Politician)
206 Cannon Hob
Washington, DC 20515-3801, USA

M. Levin, Sander (Congressman, Politician)
1236 Longworth Hob
Washington, DC 20515-2503, USA

Mlicki, Dave (Athlete, Baseball Player)
5350 Reserve Dr
Dublin, OH 43017-8404, USA

Mlkvy, Bill (Athlete, Basketball Player)
586 Linton Hill Rd
Newtown, PA 18940-1204, USA

Mlneta, Norman (Politician)
1631 Cliff Dr
Edgewater, MD 21037-4922, USA

Mlnner, Ruth (Politician)
1056 Church Hill Rd
Milford, DE 19963-5539, USA

M. Lowey, Nita (Congressman, Politician)
2365 Rayburn Hob
Washington, DC 20515-2308, USA

M. Lumis, Cynthia (Congressman, Politician)
113 Cannon Hob
Washington, DC 20515-3512, USA

Mmahat, Kevin (Athlete, Baseball Player)
5500 Erlanger Rd
Kenner, LA 70065-1534, USA

Moakler, Shanna (Actor, Model, Reality Star)
3890 Prado De La Mariposa
Calabasas, CA 91302-3605, USA

Moala, Fili (Athlete, Football Player)
c/o Eric Kaufman *Premier Sports Management*
16133 Ventura Blvd Ste 500
Encino, CA 91436-2402, USA

Moates, Dave (Athlete, Baseball Player)
7906 4th Ave W
Bradenton, FL 34209-3254, USA

Moats, David (Journalist)
Rutland Herald
PO Box 668
Editorial Dept
Rutland, VT 05702-0668, USA

Mobb Deep (Music Group)
c/o Staff Member *Interscope Records (NY)*
1755 Broadway
New York, NY 10019-3743, USA

Mobley, Cuttino (Athlete, Basketball Player)
11706 Empress Oaks Ct
Houston, TX 77082-6842, USA

Mobley, Mary Ann (Actor, Beauty Pageant Winner)
2751 Hutton Dr
Beverly Hills, CA 90210-1215, USA

Mobley, Singor (Athlete, Football Player)
2123 US Highway 80 E
Mesquite, TX 75150-5549, USA

Moceanu, Dominique (Gymnast)
211 Walden Ridge Dr
Hinckley, OH 44233-9001, USA

Mochrie, Dottie (Athlete, Golfer)
15 Blazing Star Trl
Landrum, SC 29356-3305, USA

Mock, Garrett (Athlete, Baseball Player)
13850 Maisemore Rd
Houston, TX 77015-2303, USA

Mock, Janet (Writer)
c/o Andrea Smith *Simon & Schuster*
1230 Avenue of the Americas Fl CONC1
New York, NY 10020-1586, USA

Mockett, Cathy (Athlete, Golfer)
1601 Antigua Way
Newport Beach, CA 92660-4345, USA

Moczynski, Betty (Athlete, Baseball Player, Commentator)
4912 S 19th St Apt B
Milwaukee, WI 53221-2830, USA

Modano, Mike (Athlete, Hockey Player, Olympic Athlete)
10114 E Hualapai Dr
Scottsdale, AZ 85255-7167, USA

Modean, Jayne (Actor)
1030 Winsor Ave
Piedmont, CA 94610-1104, USA

Modell, Frank (Cartoonist)
115 Three Mile Crse
Guilford, CT 06437-2522, USA

Modell, Frank (Cartoonist)
295 Central Park W Apt 11E
New York, NY 10024-3023, USA

Modernaires, The
11761 E Speedway Blvd
Tucson, AZ 85748-2017

Modin, Fredrik (Athlete, Hockey Player)
8955 Dunn Ct
Dublin, OH 43017-8880, USA

Modine, Matthew (Actor, Director, Producer)
420 W 25th St Apt 9C
New York, NY 10001-6554, USA

Modry, Jaroslav (Athlete, Hockey Player)
1481 E Palm Ave
El Segundo, CA 90245-3327

Modzelewski, Ed (Athlete, Football Player)
PO Box 4207
Sedona, AZ 86340-4207, USA

Modzelewski, Richard B (Dick) (Athlete, Football Player)
1 Pier Pt
New Bern, NC 28562-8820, USA

Moe (Music Group)
c/o Staff Member *Paradigm (Monterey)*
404 W Franklin St
Monterey, CA 93940-2303, USA

moe. (Music Group)
45 Hadlock Rd
Falmouth, ME 04105-2559, USA

Moe, Douglas E (Doug) (Athlete, Basketball Player)
13 Arnold Palmer
San Antonio, TX 78257-1722, USA

Moe, Tommy (Athlete, Olympic Athlete, Skier)
1556 Hidden Ln
Anchorage, AK 99501-4916, USA

Moe, Tommy
2138 Churchill Dr
Anchorage, AK 99517-1389

Moegle, Dickey (Athlete, Football Player)
4207 Deforest Ridge Cir
Katy, TX 77494-4444, USA

Moehler, Brian (Athlete, Baseball Player)
4492 Belvedere Pl SE
Marietta, GA 30067-4066, USA

Moe-Humphreys, Karen (Swimmer)
505 Augusta Dr
Moraga, CA 94556-3004, USA

Moeller, Chad (Athlete, Baseball Player)
11058 E Raintree Dr
Scottsdale, AZ 85255-1809, USA

Moeller, Dennis (Athlete, Baseball Player)
2324 Ridgemont Dr
Birmingham, AL 35244-1219, USA

Moeller, Edward (Athlete, Basketball Player)
1011 Kelton Cottage Way
Morrisville, NC 27560-7031, USA

Moeller, Joe (Athlete, Baseball Player)
1505 Avenida De Nogales
San Clemente, CA 92672-9464, USA

Moeller, Ralf (Actor)
c/o Chuck Binder *Binder & Associates*
1465 Lindacrest Dr
Beverly Hills, CA 90210-2519, USA

Moeller, Ron (Athlete, Baseball Player)
7355 Appleridge Ct
Cincinnati, OH 45247-5055, USA

Moennig, Katherine (Actor)
8462 Wyndham Rd
Los Angeles, CA 90046-1538, USA

Moers, Walter (Writer)
c/o Staff Member *The Overlook Press*
141 Wooster St
New York, NY 10012-3163, USA

Moesta-Anderson, Rebecca (Writer)
Anderzone
PO Box 767
Monument, CO 80132-0767, USA

Moffat, Donald (Actor)
c/o Staff Member *Jenny Delaney Management*
3238 Fond Dr
Encino, CA 91436-4206, USA

Moffat, Katherine (Kitty) (Actor)
Henderson/Hogan
8285 W Sunset Blvd Ste 1
West Hollywood, CA 90046-2420, USA

Moffat, Mike (Athlete, Hockey Player)
17 Riverbend Rd
Markham, ON L3R 1K4

Moffat, Steven (Writer)
c/o Charlie Ferraro *United Talent Agency (UTA-LA)*
9336 Civic Center Dr
Beverly Hills, CA 90210-3604, USA

Moffatt, Katy (Musician, Songwriter, Writer)
PO Box 334
O Fallon, IL 62269-0334, USA

Moffet, Jane (Athlete, Baseball Player, Commentator)
501 Tidewater Ave
Rio Grande, NJ 08242-2807, USA

Moffett, D W (Actor)
Three Arts Entertainment
9460 Wilshire Blvd Ste 700
Beverly Hills, CA 90212-2713, USA

Moffett, James R (Business Person)
Freeport-McMoRan Inc
1615 Poydras St Ste 300
New Orleans, LA 70112-5404, USA

Moffett, Randy
110 Lakeover Dr
Athens, GA 30607-2046

Moffett, Tim (Athlete, Football Player)
115 County Road 213
Oxford, MS 38655-8855, USA

Moffitt, Randy (Athlete, Baseball Player)
1725 Baltic Ave
Prescott, AZ 86301-6501, USA

Mofford, Ian (Athlete, Football Player)
PO Box 1158
Waitsfield, VT 05673-1158, USA

Mofford, Rose (Ex-Governor)
330 W Maryland Ave Unit 104
Phoenix, AZ 85013-1340, USA

Mogilevsky, Evgeny (Musician)
Columbia Artists Mgmt Inc
165 W 57th St
New York, NY 10019-2201, USA

Mogilny, Alexander (Athlete, Hockey Player)
24146 Malibu Rd
Malibu, CA 90265-4610, USA

Mohacsi, Mary (Bowler)
15445 Sunset St
Livonia, MI 48154-3215, USA

MoHair (Music Group)
c/o Staff Member *Paradigm (Monterey)*
404 W Franklin St
Monterey, CA 93940-2303, USA

Mohamed, Mike (Athlete, Football Player)
c/o Doug Hendrickson *Octagon Football*
832 Sansome St Fl 1
San Francisco, CA 94111-1558, USA

Mohler, Mike (Athlete, Baseball Player)
1627 S Shirley Ave
Gonzales, LA 70737-3917, USA

Mohler, R Albert
Southern Baptist Theological Seminary
Office of the President
2825 Lexington Rd
Louisville, KY 40280-0001, USA

Mohoney, John (Actor)
International Creative Mgmt
10250 Constellation Blvd Fl 1
Los Angeles, CA 90067-6241, USA

Mohoney, Roger (Cartoonist)
c/o Staff Member *King Features Syndication*
300 W 57th St Fl 15
New York, NY 10019-5238, USA

Mohony, Roger Cardinal (Religious Leader)
Archdiocese of Los Angeles
3424 Wilshire Blvd
Los Angeles, CA 90010-2241, USA

Mohorcic, Dale (Athlete, Baseball Player)
15501 Rockside Rd
Maple Heights, OH 44137-3948, USA

Mohr, Chris (Athlete, Football Player)
PO Box 1232
Thomson, GA 30824-1232, USA

Mohr, Dustan (Athlete, Baseball Player)
103 Parkwood Dr
Hattiesburg, MS 39402-2217, USA

Mohr, Jay (Actor, Comedian)
737 El Medio Ave
Pacific Palisades, CA 90272-3452, USA

Mohr, Todd (Musician)
Morris Bliessner
1658 York St
Denver, CO 80206-1410, USA

Moiler, Randy (Athlete, Hockey Player)
3950 NW 23rd Ter
Boca Raton, FL 33431-5405

Moisan, Bill (Athlete, Baseball Player)
PO Box 41
Newton, NH 03858-0041, USA

Moise, Patty (Race Car Driver)
Atkins Motorsports
222 Raceway Dr
Mooresville, NC 28117-6510, USA

Moiseyev, Jack (Horse Racer)
499 Scotland Dr
Jackson, NJ 08527-1188, USA

Mojsiejenko, Ralf (Athlete, Football Player)
11334 Baldwin Rd
Bridgman, MI 49106-9727, USA

Mojslejenko, Ralf (Athlete, Football Player)
11334 Baldwin Rd
Bridgman, MI 49106-9727, USA

Mok, Karen (Actor)
c/o Staff Member *Creative Artists Agency (CAA-LA)*
2000 Avenue of the Stars Ste 100
Los Angeles, CA 90067-4705, USA

Mok, Ken (Director, Producer)
c/o Steve Wohl *Paradigm (LA)*
360 N Crescent Dr
North Bldg
Beverly Hills, CA 90210-4874, USA

Mokeski, Paul (Athlete, Basketball Player)
4004 Crestwood Dr
Carrollton, TX 75007-1645, USA

Mokosak, Carl (Athlete, Hockey Player)
8073 Rum Creek Trl NE
Rockford, MI 49341-8222

Mokri, Amir (Cinematographer)
c/o Staff Member *Montana Artists Agency*
16133 Ventura Blvd Ste 620
Encino, CA 91436-2404, USA

Mol, Gretchen (Actor)
c/o John Carrabino *John Carrabino Management*
5900 Wilshire Blvd Ste 406
Los Angeles, CA 90036-5015, USA

Molale, Brandon (Actor)
c/o Staff Member *DDC Entertainment*
2305 Marshallfield Ln
Redondo Beach, CA 90278-4467, USA

Molden, Alex (Athlete, Football Player)
2030 Wellington Dr
West Linn, OR 97068-3653, USA

Mole, Fenton (Athlete, Baseball Player)
738 Glen Eagle Ct
Danville, CA 94526-6209, USA

Moler, Jason (Athlete, Baseball Player, Olympic Athlete)
2918 Ranch Road 620 N Apt 281
Austin, TX 78734-2269, USA

Molina, Alfred (Actor)
c/o Joan Hyler *Hyler Management*
20 Ocean Park Blvd Unit 25
Santa Monica, CA 90405-3590, USA

Molina, Beniie (Athlete, Baseball Player)
6475 E Crabtree Pl
Yuma, AZ 85365-1115, USA

Molina, Gabe (Athlete, Baseball Player)
5531 E 118th Ave
Denver, CO 80233-1855, USA

Molina, Islay (Izzy) (Athlete, Baseball Player)
369 Atwater St
Port Charlotte, FL 33954-2904, USA

Molina, Jose (Athlete, Baseball Player)
c/o Team Member *New York Yankees*
Yankee Stadium
161st St & River Ave
Bronx, NY 10451, USA

Molina, Izzy (Athlete, Baseball Player)
18132 NW 19th St
Pembroke Pines, FL 33029-3026, USA

Molina, Morio
PO Box 12406
La Jolla, CA 92039-2406, USA

Molinari, Susan (Politician)
3 Friendship Dr Unit A-3
West Bridgewater, MA 02379-1266, USA

Molinaro, Al (Actor)
1530 Arboles Dr
Glendale, CA 91207-1204, USA

Molinaro, Bob (Athlete, Baseball Player)
1 Harbourside Dr Apt 2312
Delray Beach, FL 33483-5170, USA

Molitor, Paul L (Athlete, Baseball Player, Coach)
c/o Staff Member *John Boggs & Associates*
5675 Ruffin Rd Ste 350
San Diego, CA 92123-1398, USA

Moll, Richard (Actor)
1119 Amalfi Dr
Pacific Palisades, CA 90272-4031, USA

Mollen, Jenny (Actor)
2515 Benedict Canyon Dr
Beverly Hills, CA 90210-1020, USA

Moller, Randy (Athlete, Hockey Player)
Florida Panthers
1 Panther Pkwy
Sunrise, FL 33323-5315

Molloy, Irene
PO Box 5617
Beverly Hills, CA 90209-5617

Moloney, Janel (Actor)
c/o Staff Member *Gersh (LA)*
9465 Wilshire Blvd Ste 600
Beverly Hills, CA 90212-2605, USA

Moloney, Michael (Actor, Reality Star)
c/o Staff Member *Extreme Makeover: Home Edition*
9225 W Sunset Blvd # 1100
Endemol Entertainment Usa
West Hollywood, CA 90069-3111, USA

Moloney, Rich (Athlete, Baseball Player)
125 Mallard Way
Waltham, MA 02452-8117, USA

Momaday, N Scott (Writer)
University of Arizona
English Dept
Tucson, AZ 85721-0001, USA

Momaday, N scott (Writer)
1600E Univ Dept 1600E
Tucson, AZ 85721-0001, USA

Momoa, Jason (Actor)
c/o Jeff Witjas *Agency for the Performing Arts (APA-LA)*
405 S Beverly Dr Ste 500
Beverly Hills, CA 90212-4425, USA

Momolu-Briggs, Korto (Fashion Designer)
Art Scene and Art Market
200 E 3rd St
Little Rock, AR 72201-1608, USA

Momsen, Robert (Athlete, Football Player)
4730 Glendale Ave Apt 102
Toledo, OH 43614-1974, USA

Momsen, Taylor (Actor, Musician)
c/o John Stratton *DAS Communications*
83 Riverside Dr
New York, NY 10024-5713, USA

Monacelli, Amieto (Bowler)
Professional Bowlers Assn
55 E Jackson Blvd Ste 401
Chicago, IL 60604-4307, USA

Monaco, Kelly (Actor)
c/o Alejandra Cristina *Ace PR*
4122 Sunnyslope Ave
Sherman Oaks, CA 91423-4308, USA

Monae, Janelle (Musician)
c/o Cara Donatto *Atlantic Records (LA)*
3400 W Olive Ave Fl 2
Burbank, CA 91505-5538, USA

Monaghan, Dominic (Actor)
c/o Jeff Raymond *Rogers & Cowan PR (LA)*
8687 Melrose Ave Ste 7
West Hollywood, CA 90069-5721, USA

Monaghan, Kris (Athlete, Golfer)
54 Golf Course Dr
Ranchos De Taos, NM 87557-7914, USA

Monaghan, Marjorie
2109 S Wilbur Ave
Walla Walla, WA 99362-9048, USA

Monaghan, Michelle (Actor)
c/o Frank Frattaroli *Circle of Confusion (LA)*
8931 Ellis Ave
Los Angeles, CA 90034-3336, USA

Monaghan, Thomas L
3001 Earhart
Ann Arbor, MI 48105, USA

Monaghan, Tom (Business Person)
The Ave Maria Foundation
PO Box 373
One Ave Maria Dr
Ann Arbor, MI 48106-0373, USA

Monahan, Dan (Actor)
c/o Helene Sokol *Cuzzins Management*
499 N Canon Dr
Beverly Hills, CA 90210-4887, USA

Monahan, David (Actor, Director)
c/o Staff Member *Metropolitan (MTA)*
4526 Wilshire Blvd
Los Angeles, CA 90010-3801, USA

Monahan, Hartland (Athlete, Hockey Player)
624 Stickley Oak Way
Woodstock, GA 30189-3781

Monahan, Patrick (Musician)
Jon Landau
18806 SE 42nd St
Issaquah, WA 98027-9366, USA

Monahan, Shane (Athlete, Baseball Player)
624 Stickley Oak Way
Woodstock, GA 30189-3781, USA

Monbouauette, Bill (Athlete, Baseball Player)
46 Doonan St
Medford, MA 02155-1333, USA

Monbouquette, William C (Bill) (Athlete, Baseball Player)
6B Heron Cir
Gloucester, MA 01930-1484, USA

Monchak, Alex (Al) (Athlete, Baseball Player)
7414 8th Ave W
Bradenton, FL 34209-3425, USA

Moncrief, Donte (Athlete, Football Player)
c/o Joel Segal *Lagardere Unlimited (NYC)*
845 United Nations Plz
New York, NY 10017-3540, USA

Moncrief, Sidney (Athlete, Basketball Player)
9842 Audelia Rd Apt 1109
Dallas, TX 75238-1968, USA

Moncrieff, Karen (Actor)
c/o Brad Gross *Brad Gross Agency, The*
161 S Arden Blvd
Los Angeles, CA 90004-3716, USA

Mondale, Walter (Politician)
600 S 2nd St Apt 405
Minneapolis, MN 55401-2162, USA

Mondale, Walter F (President, Senator, Vice President)
50 S 6th St Ste 1500
Minneapolis, MN 55402-1498, USA

Monday, Kenny (Athlete, Olympic Athlete, Wrestler)
4703 Enchanted Bay Blvd
Arlington, TX 76016-5334, USA

Monday, Rick (Athlete, Baseball Player)
811 Gayfeather Ln
Vero Beach, FL 32963-2048, USA

Monday, Robert J (Rick) (Baseball Player, Sportscaster)
811 Gayfeather Ln
Vero Beach, FL 32963-2048, USA

Mondesi, Raul (Athlete, Baseball Player)
Los Angeles Dodgers
1169 Old Phillips Rd
Glendale, CA 91207-1153, USA

Monds, Wonderful (Athlete, Baseball Player)
665 NW Fairhaven Dr
Port St Lucie, FL 34983-1079, USA

Monet, Daniella (Actor)
c/o Staff Member *LA Entertainment*
1375 S San Fernando Blvd
Suite 505
Burbank, CA 91504, USA

Money, Don (Athlete, Baseball Player)
282 Old Forest Rd
Vineland, NJ 08360-1667, USA

Money, Eddie (Musician)
c/o Josh Humiston *Agency for the Performing Arts (APA-LA)*
405 S Beverly Dr Ste 500
Beverly Hills, CA 90212-4425, USA

Money, Eric (Athlete, Basketball Player)
457 S Harvard Ave
Tucson, AZ 85710-4630, USA

Moneyham, Bill (Baseball Player)
Oakland A's
5731 White Crane Rd
Merced, CA 95340, USA

Monfort, Charles (Athlete, Baseball Player)
PO Box G
Greeley, CO 80632, USA

Monge, Sid (Athlete, Baseball Player)
10 Lilah Ln
Reading, MA 01867-1075, USA

Monger, Matt (Athlete, Football Player)
1306 N Douglas Dr
Claremore, OK 74017-4623, USA

Monheit, Jane (Musician)
c/o Cynthia B. Herbst *American International Artists*
356 Pine Valley Rd
Hoosick Falls, NY 12090-3859, USA

Monica (Musician)
c/o Cara Lewis *Creative Artists Agency (CAA-NY)*
162 5th Ave Fl 6
New York, NY 10010-6047, USA

Monin, Clarence V (President)
Locomotive Engineers Brotherhood
1370 Ontario St
Cleveland, OH 44113-1701, USA

Moniz, Wendy (Actor)
c/o Nancy Sanders *Sanders Armstrong Caserta*
2120 Colorado Ave Ste 120
Santa Monica, CA 90404-3561, USA

Monk, Arthur (Art) (Athlete, Football Player, Sportscaster)
10896 Lake Windermere Dr
Great Falls, VA 22066-1528, USA

Monk, Debra (Actor)
Gage Group
315 W 57th St Frnt 4H
New York, NY 10019-3158, USA

Monk, Quincy (Athlete, Football Player)
104 White Oak Blvd Apt 104
Jacksonville, NC 28546-4539, USA

Monk, Sophie (Actor)
c/o Jenni Weinman *Patricola Lust PR*
9171 Wilshire Blvd Ste 441
Beverly Hills, CA 90210-5516, USA

Monk Jr, Thelonious
173 Brighton Ave
Allston, MA 02134-2003, USA

Monroe, Craig (Athlete, Baseball Player)
4123 Lynn Dr
Texarkana, TX 75503-2816, USA

Monroe, Earl (Athlete, Basketball Player)
1925 Adam Clayton Powell Jr Blvd Apt 6D
Jr Blvd Apt 60
New York, NY 10026-2214, USA

Monroe, Larry (Athlete, Baseball Player)
725 N Hundley St
Hoffman Estates, IL 60169-4559, USA

Monroe, Lola (Model, Musician)
c/o Staff Member *New Era Agency, The*
Prefers to be contacted via telephone or email
Atlanta, GA, USA

Monroe, Maika (Actor)
c/o Lena Roklin *Luber Roklin Management*
5815 W Sunset Blvd Ste 206
Los Angeles, CA 90028-6481, USA

Monroe, Meredith (Musician)
c/o Ame Van Iden *PMK/BNC Public Relations (PMK-LA)*
8687 Melrose Ave Ste 8
West Hollywood, CA 90069-5746, USA

Monroe, Mircea (Actor)
c/o Tiffany Kuzon *Evolution Entertainment (LA)*
901 N Highland Ave
Los Angeles, CA 90038-2412, USA

Monroe, Rodney (Athlete, Basketball Player)
892 Forest Glen Ln
Wellington, FL 33414-6328, USA

Monroe, Zach (Athlete, Baseball Player)
1 Sandalwood Ln
Bartonville, IL 61607-2145, USA

Monsilovich, Larry (Athlete, Football Player)
35 Alice Ln
Oxford, PA 19363-1025, USA

Monson, Dan (Basketball Player, Coach)
University of Minnesota
Bierman Athletic Building
Minneapolis, MN 55455, USA

Monsters, The (Music Group)
c/o Staff Member *Paradigm (Monterey)*
404 W Franklin St
Monterey, CA 93940-2303, USA

Mont, Tommy (Athlete, Football Player)
15414 W Sky Hawk Dr
Sun City West, AZ 85375-6511, USA

Montador, Steve (Athlete, Hockey Player)
5857 NW 122nd Ter
Coral Springs, FL 33076-4012, USA

Montag, Holly (Reality Star)
c/o Anna Babbitt *New Wave Entertainment (LA)*
2660 W Olive Ave
Burbank, CA 91505-4525, USA

Montague, Ed (Athlete, Baseball Player)
1521 Cherrywood Dr
San Mateo, CA 94403-3903, USA

Montague, John (Athlete, Baseball Player)
6001 Vineyard Ln
Montgomery, AL 36117-5003, USA

Montalban, Paolo (Actor)
c/o Staff Member *Innovative Artists (LA)*
1505 10th St
Santa Monica, CA 90401-2805, USA

Montalbano, Chuck (Athlete, Golfer)
4725 Farmdale Ave
North Hollywood, CA 91602-1109, USA

Montalvo, Rafael (Athlete)
Hudson Valley Renegades
PO Box 661
Attn: Coaching Staff
Fishkill, NY 12524-0661, USA

Montana, French (Musician)
c/o Staff Member *Mizay Entertainment*
Prefers to be contacted via telephone
Atlanta, GA, USA

Montana, Joe (Athlete, Football Player)
9010 Franz Valley Rd
Calistoga, CA 94515-9552, USA

Montanez, Luis (Athlete, Baseball Player)
5745 SW 34th St
Miami, FL 33155-4912, USA

Montanez, Willie (Athlete, Baseball Player)
HC 5 Box 52020
Caguas, PR 00725-9201, USA

Montano, Sumalee (Actor)
c/o Kim Dorr *Defining Artists Agency*
4370 Tujunga Ave Ste 120
Studio City, CA 91604-2763, USA

Monte, Chante
c/o Staff Member *William Morris Endeavor (NY)*
1325 Avenue of the Americas
New York, NY 10019-6026, USA

Montefusco, John (Athlete, Baseball Player)
1 Oakdale Dr Apt 3D
Middletown, NJ 07748-2124, USA

Monteith, Kelly (Comedian)
PO Box 11669
Knoxville, TN 37939-1669

Monteleone, Rich (Athlete, Baseball Player)
441 Lucerne Ace
Tampa, FL 33606, USA

Montermini, Andrea (Race Car Driver)
434 E Main St
Brownsburg, IN 46112-1419, USA

Montero, Agustin (Athlete, Baseball Player)
4600 Parkview Dr
McCullom Lake, IL 60050-2455, USA

Montero, Gabriela (Musician)
c/o Staff Member *Paradigm (Monterey)*
404 W Franklin St
Monterey, CA 93940-2303, USA

Montero, Miguel (Athlete, Baseball Player)
6630 N Desert Fairways Dr
Paradise Valley, AZ 85253-3333, USA

Monterola, Pablo (Musician)
c/o Staff Member *BMG*
1540 Broadway
New York, NY 10036-4039, USA

Montevecchi, Liliane (Musician)
Buzz Halliday
8899 Beverly Blvd Ste 620
Los Angeles, CA 90048-2428, USA

Montez, Chris
6671 W Sunset Blvd Ste 1502
Los Angeles, CA 90028-7235

Montgomerv, Jeff (Athlete, Baseball Player)
3701 W 140th St
Overland Park, KS 66224-8406, USA

Montgomery, Alton (Athlete, Football Player)
925 Meriwether St Apt B
Griffin, GA 30224-4025, USA

Montgomery, Anthony (Actor)
c/o Jerry Shandrew *Shandrew Public Relations*
1050 S Stanley Ave
Los Angeles, CA 90019-6634, USA

Montgomery, Belinda (Actor)
Epstein-Wyckoff
280 S Beverly Dr Ste 400
Beverly Hills, CA 90212-3904, USA

Montgomery, Bob (Athlete, Baseball Player)
2 Parkway Dr
Saugus, MA 01906-1957, USA

Montgomery, Chase (Race Car Driver)
Tomar Motorsports
232 Main St
Box 68
Peterson, IA 51047, USA

Montgomery, Chuck (Actor)
c/o Staff Member *Don Buchwald & Associates (LA)*
6500 Wilshire Blvd Ste 2200
Los Angeles, CA 90048-4942, USA

Montgomery, Cleo (Athlete, Football Player)
404 Dakota Trl
Irving, TX 75063-4547, USA

MontgomerY, David (Athlete, Baseball Player)
8525 Ardmore Ave
Glenside, PA 19038-8454, USA

Montgomery, Delmonico (Athlete, Football Player)
3011 Pecan Way Ct
Richmond, TX 77406-6902, USA

Montgomery, Dorothy (Baseball Player)
2621 Berkley Dr
Chattanooga, TN 37415-5701, USA

Montgomery, Eddie (Musician)
c/o Staff Member *Hallmark Direction Company*
713 18th Ave S
Nashville, TN 37203-3214, USA

Montgomery, Grady (Athlete, Baseball Player)
Baltimore Elite Giants
11904 Fort Washington Rd
Fort Washington, MD 20744-5908, USA

Montgomery, James P (Jim) (Athlete, Olympic Athlete, Swimmer)
3 Castlecreek Ct
Dallas, TX 75225-1808, USA

Montgomery, Jeff (Athlete, Baseball Player)
2713 W 116th St
Leawood, KS 66211-3025, USA

Montgomery, Jim (Athlete, Hockey Player)
PO Box 357
Dubuque, IA 52004-0357, USA

Montgomery, John Michael (Musician)
c/o John Dorris Sr *Hallmark Direction Company*
713 18th Ave S
Nashville, TN 37203-3214, USA

Montgomery, Lisa Kennedy (Actor)
Game Show Network
10202 Washington Blvd
Culver City, CA 90232-3119, USA

Montgomery, Marv (Athlete, Football Player)
1509 S Macon St
Aurora, CO 80012-5140, USA

Montgomery, Melba (Musician)
Joe Taylor Artist Agency
2802 Columbine Pl
Nashville, TN 37204-3104, USA

Montgomery, Mike (Athlete, Football Player)
5150 Miller Ave
Dallas, TX 75206-6419, USA

Montgomery, Mike (Basketball Player, Coach)
Golden State Warriors
1001 Broadway
Oakland, CA 94607-4019, USA

Montgomery, Monty (Athlete, Baseball Player)
807 Corn Tassel Trl
Martinsville, VA 24112-5601, USA

Montgomery, Poppy (Actor)
12323 23rd Helena Dr
Los Angeles, CA 90049-3943, USA

Montgomery, Ray (Athlete, Baseball Player)
3107 S Webber Ct
Pearland, TX 77584-9418, USA

Montgomery, Ryan (Royce da 5'9) (Musician)
c/o Peter Schwartz *The Agency Group (NYC)*
142 W 57th St Fl 6
New York, NY 10019-3300, USA

Montgomery, Steve (Athlete, Baseball Player)
13731 Mercado Dr
Del Mar, CA 92014-3415, USA

Montgomery, Wilbert (Athlete, Football Player)
45990 Tournament Dr
Northville, MI 48168-8498, USA

Montgomery Jr, Dan (Actor)
c/o Karyn Spencer *Peter Strain & Associates Inc (LA)*
5455 Wilshire Blvd Ste 1812
Los Angeles, CA 90036-4268, USA

Montiel, Fernando (Boxer)
c/o Staff Member *Top Rank Inc.*
3908 Howard Hughes Pkwy
#580
Las Vegas, NV 89109, USA

Montiel, H Pierre
102 W 73rd St
New York, NY 10023-3047, USA

Montler, Mike (Athlete, Football Player)
479 Tiara Vista Dr
Grand Junction, CO 81507-8716, USA

montovo, Charlie (Athlete, Baseball Player)
202 Stoneridge Dr
Duson, LA 70529-3951, USA

Montoya, Al (Athlete, Hockey Player)
2410 Indian Ridge Dr
Glenview, IL 60026-1030, USA

Montoya, Al (Athlete, Hockey Player)
2 Penn Plz
New York, NY 10121-0101, USA

Montoya, Juan Pablo (Race Car Driver)
Ganassi Racing
8500 Westmoreland Dr NW
Concord, NC 28027-7571, USA

Montoya, Rebeka (Actor)
c/o Alan Iezman *Shelter Entertainment*
9255 W Sunset Blvd Ste 320
West Hollywood, CA 90069-3313, USA

Montoyo, Jose Carlos (Charlie) (Athlete, Baseball Player)
438 Summer Sails Dr
Valrico, FL 33594-8021, USA

Montreuil, Allan (Athlete, Baseball Player)
2016 Laurel Ave
Gretna, LA 70056-5232, USA

Montross, Eric (Athlete, Basketball Player)
4668 S NC Highway 150
Lexington, NC 27295-8026, USA

Montsho, Este (Musician)
William Morris Agency
1325 Avenue of the Americas Bsmt 2
New York, NY 10019-6047, USA

Montville, Leigh (Writer)
Boston Globe
Editorial Dept
135 WT Morrissey Blvd
Dorchester, MA 02125, USA

Monty Q (DJ)
c/o Staff Member *Diva Central Inc*
7510 W Sunset Blvd Ste 1445
Los Angeles, CA 90046-3408, USA

Monzikova, Anya (Actor)
c/o Greg Meyer *Meyer Management Group (MMG)*
1901 Avenue of the Stars Ste 365
Los Angeles, CA 90067-6025, USA

Moock, Joe (Athlete, Baseball Player)
12432 Pecos Ave
Greenwell Springs, LA 70739-3039, USA

Moodie, Janice (Athlete, Golfer)
10746 Woodchase Cir
Orlando, FL 32836-5870, USA

Moody, Eric (Athlete, Baseball Player)
336 Gleneagle Cir
Irmo, SC 29063-8432, USA

Moody, Keith M (Athlete, Football Player)
4632 Riverview Ct
Tracy, CA 95377-8288, USA

Moody, Lynne (Actor)
8708 Skyline Dr
Los Angeles, CA 90046-1422, USA

Moody, Orville (Athlete, Golfer)
9221 Chesapeake Ln
McKinney, TX 75071-6039, USA

Moody, Ritchie (Baseball Player)
1696 Rockleigh Rd
Dayton, OH 45458-6048, USA

Moody-Luckhurst, Terri (Athlete, Golfer)
103 Pierrepont Isle
Duluth, GA 30097-5908, USA

Moog, Andy (Athlete, Hockey Player)
109 Sunrise Dr
Coppell, TX 75019-3691, USA

Moomaw, Donn D (Athlete, Football Player)
3124 Corda Dr
Los Angeles, CA 90049-1104, USA

Moon, Philip
449 N Highland Ave
Los Angeles, CA 90036-2627

Moon, Wallace W (Wally) (Athlete, Baseball Player)
702 Ellen Lee Ct
Bryan, TX 77802-1146, USA

Moon, Wally
3801 E Crest Dr Apt 6401
Bryan, TX 77802-5715

Moon, Warren (Athlete, Football Player)
24610 NE 126th St
Duvall, WA 98019-9006, USA

Mooney, Debra (Actor)
c/o Mike Smith *Principal Entertainment (LA)*
9255 W Sunset Blvd Ste 500
West Hollywood, CA 90069-3301, USA

Mooney, Ed (Athlete, Football Player)
4105 63rd St
Lubbock, TX 79413-5023, USA

Mooney, John (Musician)
Intrepid Artists
1300 Baxter St Ste 130
Midtown Plaza
Charlotte, NC 28204-3807, USA

Mooney, Paul (Actor)
c/o Staff Member *Simon & Schuster*
1230 Avenue of the Americas Fl CONC1
New York, NY 10020-1586, USA

Mooneyham, Bill (Athlete, Baseball Player)
5731 White Crane Rd
Atwater, CA 95301-8573, USA

Mooneyhan, Bill (Athlete, Baseball Player)
5731 White Crane Rd
Atwater, CA 95301-8573, USA

Moonves, Leslie (Business Person, Producer)
22432 Pacific Coast Hwy
Malibu, CA 90265-5033, USA

Moon Zombie, Sherrie (Actor)
8491 W Sunset Blvd # 125
West Hollywood, CA 90069-1911, USA

Moore, Abra (Musician)
Haber Corp
16830 Ventura Blvd Ste 501
Encino, CA 91436-1731, USA

Moore, Adam (Athlete, Baseball Player)
2030 County Rd 2260
Mineola, TX 75773, USA

Moore, Andre (Athlete, Basketball Player)
12137 S Justine St
Chicago, IL 60643-5443, USA

Moore, Ann S (Publisher)
People Magazine
Publisher's Office
Time & Life Building
New York, NY 10020, USA

Moore, Arch (Politician)
PO Box 11247
Charleston, WV 25339-1247, USA

Moore, Archie (Athlete, Baseball Player)
201 Courtland Rd
Indiana, PA 15701-3202, USA

Moore, Balor (Athlete, Baseball Player)
901 W Viejo Dr
Friendswood, TX 77546-5836, USA

Moore, Barry (Athlete, Baseball Player)
6702 Conifer Cir
Indian Trail, NC 28079-7588, USA

Moore, Bill (Billy) (Athlete, Baseball Player)
10849 Mirador Dr
Rancho Cucamonga, CA 91737-6991, USA

Moore, Billie (Athlete, Basketball Player, Coach)
2247 Meadow Ln
Fullerton, CA 92831-2122, USA

Moore, Bob (Athlete, Baseball Player)
2500 Wellington Rd
Los Angeles, CA 90016-3034, USA

Moore, Bobby (Athlete, Baseball Player)
3703 Hyde Park Ave
Cincinnati, OH 45209-2321, USA

Moore, Brad (Athlete, Baseball Player)
3135 Challenger Point Dr
Loveland, CO 80538-7222, USA

Moore, Brandon (Athlete, Football Player)
15010 S 47th St
Phoenix, AZ 85044-6889, USA

Moore, Brent (Athlete, Football Player)
137 Wild Horse Valley Dr
Novato, CA 94947-3615, USA

Moore, Bud (Race Car Driver)
PO Box 2916
Spartanburg, SC 29304-2916, USA

Moore, Chante (Musician, Songwriter)
c/o Staff Member *Shanachie Entertainment*
37 E Clinton St
Newton, NJ 07860-1870, USA

Moore, Charlie (Athlete, Baseball Player)
342 County Road 276
Cullman, AL 35057-4976, USA

Moore, Chris (Producer)
c/o Staff Member *LivePlanet*
11150 Santa Monica Blvd Ste 1200
Los Angeles, CA 90025-3386, USA

Moore, Christina (Actor)
c/o Paul Rosicker *Gersh (LA)*
9465 Wilshire Blvd Ste 600
Beverly Hills, CA 90212-2605, USA

Moore, Christopher (Chris) (Director, Producer)
c/o Staff Member *William Morris Endeavor (LA)*
9601 Wilshire Blvd
Beverly Hills, CA 90210-5213, USA

Moore, Christopher (Lil Twist) (Musician)
c/o Cortez Bryant *Blueprint Group*
555 Washington Ave Ste 240
Miami Beach, FL 33139-6639, USA

Moore, Corwin (Writer)
c/o Staff Member *Creative Artists Agency (CAA-LA)*
2000 Avenue of the Stars Ste 100
Los Angeles, CA 90067-4705, USA

Moore, Darla (Business Person)
Rainwater, Inc
777 Main St Ste 2250
Fort Worth, TX 76102-5308, USA

Moore, Darryl (Athlete, Football Player)
503 High St
Minden, LA 71055-3698, USA

Moore, Dave (Football Player)
c/o Team Member *Tampa Bay Buccaneers*
1 Buccaneer Pl
Tampa, FL 33607-5701, USA

Moore, Dayton (Athlete, Baseball Player)
2508 W 118th St
Leawood, KS 66211-3032, USA

Moore, Demi (Actor)
c/o Jason Weinberg *Untitled Entertainment (LA)*
350 S Beverly Dr Ste 200
Beverly Hills, CA 90212-4819, USA

Moore, Derland P (Athlete, Football Player)
1917 Madison St
Mandeville, LA 70448-5840, USA

Moore, Derrick (Athlete, Football Player)
3164 Jackson Creek Dr
Stockbridge, GA 30281-5688, USA

Moore, Dick (Cartoonist)
Dick Moore Assoc
1560 Broadway
New York, NY 10036-1537, USA

Moore, Dickie
150 W End Ave Apt 26C
New York, NY 10023-5743

Moore, Dorothy (Musician)
Sirius Entertainment
13531 Clairmont Way Unit 8
Oregon City, OR 97045-4249, USA

Moore, Earl
215 W End Blvd
Winston Salem, NC 27101

Moore, Eric P (Athlete, Football Player)
2225 Lindsay Ln
Florissant, MO 63031-5626, USA

Moore, Gary (Athlete, Baseball Player)
7985 Roundrock Rd
Dallas, TX 75248-5341, USA

Moore, George E (Doctor)
12048 Black Hawk Dr
Conifer, CO 80433-7137, USA

Moore, Gwen (Congressman, Politician)
2245 Rayburn Hob
Washington, DC 20515-2001, USA

Moore, Harold G General (Writer)
585 Moores Mill Rd
Auburn, AL 36830-6027, USA

Moore, Henry (Athlete, Football Player)
2200 Pleasure Dr
Bryant, AR 72019-6365, USA

Moore, Herman J (Athlete, Football Player)
4840 N Adams Rd Ste 503
Rochester, MI 48306-1415, USA

Moore, Jackie (Athlete, Basketball Player)
2721 Laurel Valley Ln
Arlington, TX 76006-4019, USA

Moore, Jackie (Musician)
T-Best Talent Agency
508 Honey Lake Ct
Danville, CA 94506-1237, USA

Moore, Jacqueline (Wrestler)
15030 Ventura Blvd Ste 525
Sherman Oaks, CA 91403-5470, USA

Moore, James R ""Red"" (Athlete, Baseball Player)
1886 Ravenwood Way NE
Atlanta, GA 30329-2734, USA

Moore, Jeffrey B (Athlete, Football Player)
4055 Delgate Cv
Memphis, TN 38125-2718, USA

Moore, Jerald (Athlete, Football Player)
1806 Sabine Ln
Richmond, TX 77406-7940, USA

Moore, Jerry (Athlete, Football Player)
401 Ivory Dr
Little Rock, AR 72205-2640, USA

Moore, Joe
2410 Memorial Dr # 3C
Bryan, TX 77802-2851

Moore, Joel David (Actor)
Coattails Entertainment
11271 Ventura Blvd Ste 434
Studio City, CA 91604-3136, USA

Moore, John (Director, Producer, Writer)
c/o Rowena Arguelles *Creative Artists Agency (CAA-LA)*
2000 Avenue of the Stars Ste 100
Los Angeles, CA 90067-4705, USA

Moore, Julianne (Actor)
c/o Evelyn O'Neill *Management 360*
9111 Wilshire Blvd
Beverly Hills, CA 90210-5508, USA

Moore, Junior (Athlete, Baseball Player)
3728 Wall Ave
Richmond, CA 94804-3346, USA

Moore, Justin (Musician)
c/o Jake Basden *Big Machine Records*
1219 16th Ave S
Nashville, TN 37212-2901, USA

Moore, Kellen (Athlete, Football Player)
c/o David Dunn *Athletes First, LLC*
23091 Mill Creek Dr
Laguna Hills, CA 92653-1258, USA

Moore, Kelly (Race Car Driver)
PO Box 1210
Scarborough, ME 04070-1210, USA

Moore, Kelvin (Athlete, Baseball Player)
75 Stoney Point Ter
Covington, GA 30014-7070, USA

Moore, Kelvin (Athlete, Football Player)
1564 W 110th Pl
Los Angeles, CA 90047-4915, USA

Moore, Kenya (Beauty Pageant Winner, Reality Star)
c/o Gloria Hinojosa *Amsel, Eisenstadt & Frazier Talent Agency (AEF)*
5055 Wilshire Blvd Ste 860
Los Angeles, CA 90036-6108, USA

Moore, Kerwin (Athlete, Baseball Player)
18137 Goddard St
Detroit, MI 48234-4404, USA

Moore, Kip (Musician)
c/o Shawn McSpadden *Red Light Management (TN)*
PO Box 159310
Nashville, TN 37215-9310, USA

Moore, Leonard E (Lenny) (Athlete, Football Player)
8815 Stonehaven Rd
Randallstown, MD 21133-4223, USA

Moore, Leroy (Athlete, Football Player)
842 Golf Dr Apt 201
Pontiac, MI 48341-2385, USA

Moore, Lloyd (Race Car Driver)
857 Hillside Dr
Frewsburg, NY 14738-9619, USA

Moore, Lorrie (Writer)
University of Wisconsin
English Dept
Madison, WI 53706, USA

Moore, Lowes
21 Hutchinson Blvd
Mount Vernon, NY 10552-2509, USA

Moore, Lucille (Baseball Player)
6450 Miami Cir
South Bend, IN 46614-6480, USA

Moore, Mandy (Actor, Musician)
c/o Jon Leshay *Storefront Entertainment*
647 N Martel Ave Ste 102
Los Angeles, CA 90036-1930, USA

Moore, Manfred (Athlete, Football Player)
330 N Hayworth Ave
Los Angeles, CA 90048-2702, USA

Moore, Marcus (Athlete, Baseball Player)
PO Box 5144
Richmond, CA 94805-0144, USA

Moore, Mary (Athlete, Baseball Player)
4225 Lake Grove Ct
White Lake, MI 48383-1528, USA

Moore, Mary Tyler (Actor)
510 E 86th St Apt 21A
New York, NY 10028-7509, USA

Moore, Matt (Athlete, Football Player)
c/o G. Lynn Lashbrook *Sports Management Worldwide*
1100 NW Glisan St Ste 2B
Portland, OR 97209-3064, USA

Moore, McNeil (Athlete, Football Player)
3150 Canterbury Ln
Port Neches, TX 77651-6217, USA

Moore, Melanie
3500 W Olive Ave Ste 920
Burbank, CA 91505-5514

Moore, Melba (Actor, Musician)
Artist Services Inc
1017 O St NW # B
Washington, DC 20001-4229, USA

Moore, Melissa Anne (Actor)
PO Box 55
Versailles, KY 40383-0055, USA

Moore, Michael (Director)
c/o Ari Emanuel *William Morris Endeavor (LA)*
9601 Wilshire Blvd
Beverly Hills, CA 90210-5213, USA

Moore, Mike (Athlete, Baseball Player)
1472 E Calle De Caballos
Tempe, AZ 85284-2406, USA

Moore, Mindy (Athlete, Golfer)
36 Black Hickory Way
Ormond Beach, FL 32174-5704, USA

Moore, Moulty (Athlete, Football Player)
806 Darby Ln
Brooksville, FL 34601-3137, USA

Moore, Nathanlel (Nat) (Athlete, Football Player)
20041 E Oakmont Dr
Hialeah, FL 33015-2048, USA

Moore, Otis (Baseball Player)
Pittsburgh Pirates
2923 178th Dr Apt 3
Hammond, IN 46323, USA

Moore, Patrick (Athlete, Golfer)
4638 E Dartmouth St
Mesa, AZ 85205-6324, USA

Moore, Paul (Bud) (Race Car Driver)
PO Box 2916
Spartanburg, SC 29304-2916, USA

Moore, Rachel (Actor, Model)
c/o Staff Member *WNWN Media*
348 Hauser Blvd # PH414
Los Angeles, CA 90036-3276, USA

Moore, Rahim (Athlete, Football Player)
c/o Sean Kiernan *Impact Sports - LA*
11331 Ventura Blvd Ste 1A
Studio City, CA 91604-3147, USA

Moore, Ralph (Musician)
Denon Records
135 W 50th St # 1915
New York, NY 10020-1201, USA

Moore, Red (Baseball Player)
Atlanta Black Crackers
2450 Perry Blvd NW
Atlanta, GA 30318-8809, USA

Moore, Rob (Athlete, Football Player)
1 River Pl Apt 2306
New York, NY 10036-4379, USA

Moore, Robert A (Athlete, Football Player)
1906 E Gate Dr
Stone Mountain, GA 30087-1947, USA

Moore, Robert R (Athlete, Football Player)
20 Sally Ann Rd
Orinda, CA 94563-3525, USA

Moore, Roger (Actor, Director)
c/o Tom Chasin *Chasin Agency, The*
8899 Beverly Blvd Ste 716
Los Angeles, CA 90048-2449, USA

Moore, Ron (Athlete, Football Player)
5730 Oakwood St
Spencer, OK 73084, USA

Moore, Ronald D (Producer, Writer)
c/o Brett Loncar *Creative Artists Agency (CAA-LA)*
2000 Avenue of the Stars Ste 100
Los Angeles, CA 90067-4705, USA

Moore, Sam (Musician)
I'ma Da Wife Enterprises
7119 E Shea Blvd # 109-436
#109-436
Scottsdale, AZ 85254-6107, USA

Moore, Scott (Athlete, Baseball Player)
3503 Orange Ave
Long Beach, CA 90807-4828, USA

Moore, Scotty (Musician)
5340 Simpkins Rd
Whites Creek, TN 37189-9061, USA

Moore, Shawn (Athlete, Football Player)
573 Brookfield Dr
Centreville, MD 21617-2397, USA

Moore, Shemar (Actor)
727 Esplanade Unit 102
Redondo Beach, CA 90277-4638, USA

Moore, Sterling (Athlete, Football Player)
c/o Jordan Woy *Willis and Woy Management*
3030 Olive St Ste 520
Dallas, TX 75219-7629, USA

Moore, Tamara
Phoenix Mercury
201 E Jefferson St
American West Arena
Phoenix, AZ 85004-2412, USA

Moore, Terry (Actor)
c/o Budd Burton Moss *Burton Moss*
10533 Strathmore Dr
Los Angeles, CA 90024-2540, USA

Moore, Toby (Actor)
c/o Staff Member *Sanders Armstrong Caserta*
2120 Colorado Ave Ste 120
Santa Monica, CA 90404-3561, USA

Moore, Tom (Athlete, Football Player)
1038 Forest Harbor Dr
Hendersonville, TN 37075-9649, USA

Moore, Tommy (Athlete, Baseball Player)
PO Box 336
Pioneertown, CA 92268-0336, USA

Moore, Tracy (Athlete, Basketball Player)
12116 E 37th Pl
Tulsa, OK 74146-3104, USA

Moore, Trey (Athlete, Baseball Player)
PO Box 11636
College Station, TX 77842-1636, USA

Moore, William (Athlete, Football Player)
c/o Ken Landphere *Octagon Football*
832 Sansome St Fl 1
San Francisco, CA 94111-1558, USA

Moore, Zach (Athlete, Football Player)
c/o Blake Baratz *The Institute for Athletes*
3600 Minnesota Dr Ste 550
Minneapolis, MN 55435-7925, USA

Moore, Zeke (Athlete, Football Player)
3422 Prudence Dr
Houston, TX 77045-5718, USA

Moore Capito, Shelley (Congressman, Politician)
2443 Rayburn Hob
Washington, DC 20515-4705, United States

Moorehead, Emery (Athlete, Football Player)
1005 Sussex Dr
Northbrook, IL 60062-3328, USA

Moore Jr, Charles (Athlete, Track Athlete)
PO Box 175
Laporte, PA 18626-0175, USA

Moore (Paxson), Melanie Deanne (Actor)
c/o Melisa Spamer *Domain Talent*
9229 W Sunset Blvd Ste 710
West Hollywood, CA 90069-3407, USA

Moorer, Allison (Actor, Musician, Songwriter, Writer)
TKO Artist Mgmt
1107 17th Ave S
Nashville, TN 37212-2203, USA

Moores, John (Athlete, Baseball Player)
8022 Oxfordshire Dr
Spring, TX 77379-4665, USA

Moore-Warner, Eleanor (Athlete, Baseball Player)
2172 Kinney Ave NW
Grand Rapids, MI 49534-1160, USA

Moore-Watkins, Pauline (Actor)
4077 Sunset Dr Apt 202
Lake Oswego, OR 97035-4391, USA

Mooring, John (Athlete, Football Player)
1901 Pat Booker Rd
Universal City, TX 78148-3438, USA

Moorman, Dorothea Johnson
2400 E Howell St Apt I
Seattle, WA 98122-3070, USA

Moorman, Mo (Athlete, Football Player)
9641 Shelbyville Rd
Simpsonville, KY 40067-6506, USA

Moorse, Kiki (Musician)
K Records
924 Jefferson St SE
#101
Olympia, WA 98501, USA

MOP (Music Group)
c/o Staff Member *Interscope Records (NY)*
1755 Broadway
New York, NY 10019-3743, USA

Mora, Gene (Cartoonist)
United Feature Syndicate
PO Box 5610
Cincinnati, OH 45201-5610, USA

Mora, Melvin (Athlete, Baseball Player)
2316 Willow Vale Dr
Fallston, MD 21047-1502, USA

Mora, Philippe (Director)
Altman Co
9255 W Sunset Blvd Ste 901
West Hollywood, CA 90069-3306, USA

Mora, Sergio (Reality Star)
c/o Staff Member *The Contender*
Nbc Entertainment
3000 W. Alameda Ave #5366
Burbank, CA 91523-0001, USA

Morabito, Rocky (Journalist, Photographer)
3036 Gilmore St
Jacksonville, FL 32205, USA

Morabito, Tim (Athlete, Football Player)
PO Box 152
Garnerville, NY 10923-0152, USA

Moraga, David (Athlete, Baseball Player)
608 Peach Ct
Fairfield, CA 94534-1522, USA

Mora Jr, James E (Jim) (Coach, Football Coach)
c/o Bob LaMonte *Professional Sports Representation*
1220 Plumas St
Reno, NV 89509-2745, USA

Morales, Esai (Actor)
c/o Jai Khanna *Brillstein Entertainment Partners (LA)*
9150 Wilshire Blvd Ste 350
Beverly Hills, CA 90212-3453, USA

Morales, Esal (Actor)
7527 Woodrow Wilson Dr
Los Angeles, CA 90046-1324, USA

Morales, Jerry (Athlete, Baseball Player, Coach)
Washington Nationals
2400 E Capitol St NE
Attn: Coaching Staff
Washington, DC 20003-1734, USA

Morales, Jose M (Athlete, Baseball Player)
17411 Fosgate Rd
Montverde, FL 34756-3002, USA

Morales, Kendry (Athlete, Baseball Player)
c/o Staff Member *Los Angeles Dodgers (LA Dodgers)*
1000 Elysian Park Ave
Los Angeles, CA 90012-1112, USA

Morales, Natalie (Actor)
c/o Vincent Nastri *Bleecker Street Entertainment*
853 Broadway Ste 1214
New York, NY 10003-4717, USA

Morales, Natalie (Correspondent)
c/o Staff Member *NBC News (NY)*
30 Rockefeller Plz
New York, NY 10112-0015, USA

Morales, Pedro (Athlete, Wrestler)
118 Willry St
Woodbridge, NJ 07095-2414, USA

Morales, P Pablo (Swimmer)
University of Nebraska
Athletic Dept
Lincoln, NE 68588, USA

Morales, Rich (Athlete, Baseball Player)
1650 Rosita Rd
Pacifica, CA 94044-4431, USA

Morales, Willie (Athlete, Baseball Player)
5001 W Camino Del Desierto
Tucson, AZ 85745-9119, USA

Moran, Al (Athlete, Baseball Player)
34134 Banbury St
Farmington Hills, MI 48331-2216, USA

Moran, Al (Athlete, Baseball Player)
34134 Banbury St
Farmington Hills, MI 48331-2216, USA

Moran, Bill (Athlete, Baseball Player)
200 Shore Dr
Portsmouth, VA 23701-1241, USA

Moran, Billy (Athlete, Baseball Player)
PO Box 82
Luthersville, GA 30251-0082, USA

Moran, Carl (Baseball Player)
Chicago White Sox
200 Shore Dr
Portsmouth, VA 23701-1241, USA

Moran, Erin (Actor)
2860 Bishopgate Dr NE
New Salisbury, IN 47161-9715, USA

Moran, Ian (Athlete, Hockey Player)
PO Box 1462
Duxbury, MA 02331-1462, USA

Moran, John (Religious Leader)
Missionary Church
PO Box 9127
Fort Wayne, IN 46899-9127, USA

Moran, Ian (Athlete, Hockey Player)
PO Box 1462
Duxbury, MA 02331-1462, USA

Moran, Nick (Actor)
c/o Staff Member *Diverse Talent Group*
9911 W Pico Blvd Ste 340W
Los Angeles, CA 90035-2703, USA

Moran, Richard J (Rich) (Athlete, Football Player)
7252 Mimosa Dr
Carlsbad, CA 92011-5149, USA

Moran, Sean (Athlete, Football Player)
13577 W 84th Dr
Arvada, CO 80005-5825, USA

Moran, Tony (DJ)
c/o Len Evans *Project Publicity*
312 W 53rd St Ste 202
New York, NY 10019-5743, USA

Morandini, Mickey (Athlete, Baseball Player, Olympic Athlete)
148 Smithbridge Rd
Glen Mills, PA 19342-1425, USA

Moranis, Rick (Actor)
c/o Troy Bailey *Bailey Brand Management*
1017 Ocean Ave Apt G
Santa Monica, CA 90403-3526, USA

Morasca, Jenna (Reality Star)
M Morasca
172 5th Ave Apt 6C
New York, NY 10010-5906, USA

Morath, Max (Musician)
Producers Inc
1186 N 56th St
Tampa, FL 33617, USA

Moravec, Ivan (Musician)
Cramer/Marder Artists
3436 Springhill Rd
Lafayette, CA 94549-2535, USA

Morcott, Southwood J (Business Person)
Dana Corp
PO Box 1000
Toledo, OH 43697-1000, USA

Mordecai, Mike (Athlete, Baseball Player)
10 Cross Creek Ln
Dothan, AL 36303-9320, USA

More, Camilla (Actor)
Sharon Kemp
477 S Robertson Blvd
#204
Beverly Hills, CA 90211, USA

More, Jayson (Athlete, Hockey Player)
9532 Thoroughbred Way
Brentwood, TN 37027-8922, USA

Moreau, Doug (Athlete, Football Player)
5875 Highland Rd
Baton Rouge, LA 70808-6559, USA

Moreau, Marguerite (Actor)
c/o Graciella Sanchez *One Talent Management*
3680 1/2 Fredonia Dr
Los Angeles, CA 90068-1208, USA

Morehead, Dave (Athlete, Baseball Player)
13872 Glenmere Dr
Santa Ana, CA 92705-2812, USA

Moreino, Joe (Athlete, Football Player)
25 Gemini Dr Apt 2M
East Providence, RI 02914-4039, USA

Moreira, Airto (Musician)
A Train Mgmt
PO Box 29242
Oakland, CA 94604-9242, USA

Morejon, Dan (Athlete, Baseball Player)
22625 SW 207th Ave
Miami, FL 33170-4846, USA

Moreland, Keith (Athlete, Baseball Player)
4209 Hidden Canyon Cv
Austin, TX 78746-1256, USA

Morello, Tom (Musician)
GAS Entertainment
8935 Lindblade St
Culver City, CA 90232-2438, USA

Moreno, Arturo "Arte" (Business Person)
c/o Staff Member *Los Angeles Angels Of Anaheim*
2000 E Gene Autry Way
Angels Stadium of Anaheim
Anaheim, CA 92806-6143, USA

Moreno, Azucar (Music Group)
c/o Staff Member *Sony Music Miami*
605 Lincoln Rd Ste 700
Miami Beach, FL 33139-2901, USA

Moreno, Catalina Sandino (Actor)
c/o Staff Member *Creative Artists Agency (CAA-LA)*
2000 Avenue of the Stars Ste 100
Los Angeles, CA 90067-4705, USA

Moreno, Jaime (Musician)
New York/New Jersey Mtrostars
1 Harmon Plz # 300
Secaucus, NJ 07094-2803, USA

Moreno, Jaime (Race Car Driver)
252 Montclaire Cir
Fort Lauderdale, FL 33326, USA

Moreno, Knowshon (Athlete, Football Player)
c/o Tom Condon *CAA (St. Louis)*
222 S Central Ave Ste 1008
Saint Louis, MO 63105-3509, USA

Moreno, Lea (Actor)
4739 Lankershim Blvd
North Hollywood, CA 91602-1803

Moreno, Moses (Athlete, Football Player)
11627 Lakeside Ave
Lakeside, CA 92040-1614, USA

Moreno, Orber (Athlete, Baseball Player)
4833 Kingston Cir
Kissimmee, FL 34746-5102, USA

Moreno, Rita (Actor)
7027 Devon Way
Berkeley, CA 94705-1722, USA

Moreno, Roberto (Race Car Driver)
Herdez Competition
57 Gasoline Aly Ste A
Indianapolis, IN 46222-5932, USA

Moresco, Robert (Actor, Director, Producer, Writer)
c/o Chris Silberman *ICM Partners (LA)*
10250 Constellation Blvd Fl 7
Los Angeles, CA 90067-6207, USA

Moresco, Tim (Athlete, Football Player)
2413 Pond Rd
Duluth, GA 30096-6002, USA

Moret, Rogelio (Roger) (Athlete, Baseball Player)
HC 1 Box 5225
Guaynabo, PR 00971, USA

Moretti, Fabrizio (Musician)
114 E 13th St Apt 8C
New York, NY 10003-5354, USA

Moretz, Chloe Grace (Actor)
c/o Andrew Dunlap *William Morris Endeavor (LA)*
9601 Wilshire Blvd
Beverly Hills, CA 90210-5213, USA

Morey, Bill (Actor)
Kazarian/Spencer
11365 Ventura Blvd Ste 100
Studio City, CA 91604-3148, USA

Morfogen, George (Actor)
c/o Staff Member *Gersh (LA)*
9465 Wilshire Blvd Ste 600
Beverly Hills, CA 90212-2605, USA

Morgado, Arnold (Athlete, Football Player)
1750 Kaahumanu St
Apt 53-C
Pearl City, HI 96782, USA

Morgado, Diogo (Actor)
c/o Liza Anderson *Anderson Group Public Relations*
8060 Melrose Ave Fl 4
Los Angeles, CA 90046-7038, USA

Morgan, Alex (Athlete, Soccer Player)
c/o Dan Levy *Wasserman Media Group (NC)*
4208 Six Forks Rd Ste 1020
Raleigh, NC 27609-5738, USA

Morgan, Angelique (Reality Star)
c/o Anthony Embry *AE Entertainment Public Relations*
124 Evening Shade Dr
Charleston, SC 29414-9144, USA

Morgan, Barbara R (Astronaut)
2996 S Rookery Ln
Boise, ID 83706-5484, USA

Morgan, Bill (Writer)
c/o Staff Member *Da Capo Press*
44 Farnsworth St Fl 3
Boston, MA 02210-1223, USA

Morgan, Bobby (Athlete, Baseball Player)
3004 Stonybrook Rd
Oklahoma City, OK 73120-5716, USA

Morgan, Bobby (Athlete, Baseball Player)
3004 Stonybrook Rd
Oklahoma City, OK 73120-5716, USA

Morgan, Brit (Actor)
c/o Jessica Cohen *JCPR*
9903 Santa Monica Blvd Ste 983
Beverly Hills, CA 90212-1671, USA

Morgan, Chad (Actor)
c/o Staff Member *SMS Talent*
8383 Wilshire Blvd Ste 230
Beverly Hills, CA 90211-2436, USA

Morgan, Cindy (Actor, Comedian)
PO Box 677
Boynton Beach, FL 33425-0677, USA

Morgan, Craig (Musician)
c/o Staff Member *William Morris Endeavor (Nashville)*
1600 Division St Ste 300
Nashville, TN 37203-2755, USA

Morgan, Dan (Athlete, Football Player)
3627 212th Pl SE
Sammamish, WA 98075-9211, USA

Morgan, Debbi (Actor)
c/o Elissa Leeds-Fickman *Reel Talent Management*
PO Box 491035
Los Angeles, CA 90049-9035, USA

Morgan, Debelah (Musician)
DAS Communications
83 Riverside Dr
New York, NY 10024-5713, USA

Morgan, Derrick (Athlete, Football Player)
26826 Morgan Run
Westlake, OH 44145-7404, USA

Morgan, Donald M (Cinematographer)
15826 Mayall St
North Hills, CA 91343-1415, USA

Morgan, Frank (Musician)
Integrity Talent
PO Box 961
Burlington, MA 01803-5961, USA

Morgan, Gil (Athlete, Golfer)
PO Box 806
Edmond, OK 73083-0806, USA

Morgan, Glen (Director, Producer, Writer)
c/o Staff Member *William Morris Endeavor (LA)*
9601 Wilshire Blvd
Beverly Hills, CA 90210-5213, USA

Morgan, James C (Business Person)
Applied Materials
3050 Bowers Ave
Santa Clara, CA 95054-3298, USA

Morgan, Jane (Musician)
63 North St
Kennebunkport, ME 04046-6024, USA

Morgan, Jaye P (Actor, Musician)
1185 La Grange Ave
Newbury Park, CA 91320-5316, USA

Morgan, Jeffrey Dean (Actor)
97 W Pine Rd
Staatsburg, NY 12580-5405, USA

Morgan, Joe (Athlete, Baseball Player, Coach)
15 Oak Hill Dr
Walpole, MA 02081-2713, USA

Morgan, Joe (Athlete, Baseball Player)
1988 Mgr Boston Red Sox
Walpole, MA 02081, USA

Morgan, Joseph (Actor)
c/o Richard Konigsberg *RKM*
400 N Mansfield Ave
Los Angeles, CA 90036-2622, USA

Morgan, Josh (Athlete, Football Player)
c/o Joel Segal *Lagardere Unlimited (NYC)*
845 United Nations Plz
New York, NY 10017-3540, USA

Morgan, Kevin (Athlete, Baseball Player)
325 Yearling Rd Lot 10
Duson, LA 70529-3117, USA

Morgan, Larry (Race Car Driver)
5399 Horn S Hill Rd
Newark, OH 43055, USA

Morgan, Lorrie (Actor, Musician)
c/o Staff Member *Webster & Associates PR*
3573 Couchville Pike
Hermitage, TN 37076-4012, USA

Morgan, Marabel (Writer)
Total Woman Inc
1300 NW 167th St Ste 3
Miami, FL 33169-5787, USA

Morgan, Michelle (Actor)
c/o Staff Member *Levine Okwu Erickson Management*
2126 N Commonwealth Ave
Los Angeles, CA 90027-2118, USA

Morgan, Mike (Athlete, Baseball Player)
PO Box 681130
Park City, UT 84068-1130, USA

Morgan, Mike (Cartoonist)
Creators Syndicate
5777 W Century Blvd Ste 1700
Los Angeles, CA 90045-5671, USA

Morgan, Munden (Athlete, Basketball Player)
4361 Mill Creek Rd
Winston Salem, NC 27106-2921, USA

Morgan, Peter (Director, Producer, Writer)
c/o Jeremy Barber *United Talent Agency (UTA-LA)*
9336 Civic Center Dr
Beverly Hills, CA 90210-3604, USA

Morgan, Piers (Journalist, Television Host)
706 Walden Dr
Beverly Hills, CA 90210-3125, USA

Morgan, Quincy (Athlete, Football Player)
4654 N Jupiter Rd Apt 1411
Garland, TX 75044-8820, USA

Morgan, Rob (Race Car Driver)
Morgan DollarMotorsports
Hwy 81 South
Box 646
Hennessey, OK 73742, USA

Morgan, Robert (Politician)
1362 Keith Hills Rd
Lillington, NC 27546-8264, USA

Morgan, Robert B (Senator)
Morgan and Gilchrist
101 E Front St
Lillington, NC 27546-6683, USA

Morgan, Shelly Taylor (Actor)
Pakula/King
9229 W Sunset Blvd Ste 315
West Hollywood, CA 90069-3403, USA

Morgan, Sonja (Reality Star)
c/o Michael Schweiger *CEG Management*
520 8th Ave Rm 2001
New York, NY 10018-4166, USA

Morgan, Stanley D (Athlete, Football Player)
PO Box 383048
Germantown, TN 38183-3048, USA

Morgan, Tracy (Actor, Comedian)
275 Truman Dr
Cresskill, NJ 07626-1723, USA

Morgan, Trevor (Actor)
c/o Beverly Strong *Strong Management*
9350 Wilshire Blvd Ste 224
Beverly Hills, CA 90212-3204, USA

Morgan, Vanessa (Actor)
c/o Vincent Cirrincione *Vincent Cirrincione Associates*
1516 N Fairfax Ave
Los Angeles, CA 90046-2608, USA

Morgan, Walter (Athlete, Golfer)
15536 Fishermans Rest Ct
Cornelius, NC 28031-7646, USA

Morgenthau, Robert (Politician)
1 Hogan Pl
New York, NY 10013-4311, USA

Morgridge, John P (Business Person)
Cisco Systems
170 W Tasman Dr
San Jose, CA 95134-1706, USA

Morhardt, Moe (Athlete, Baseball Player)
219 Spencer Hill Rd
Winsted, CT 06098-2214, USA

Mori, Barbara (Actor)
c/o Jared Schwartz *Caliber Media Company*
5670 Wilshire Blvd Ste 1600
Los Angeles, CA 90036-5659, USA

Moriarty, Cathy (Actor)
c/o Brian Liebman *Liebman Entertainment*
12 E 46th St Fl 5
New York, NY 10017-2418, USA

Moriarty, Michael (Actor)
200 W 58th St Apt 3B
New York, NY 10019-1477, USA

Moriarty, Mike (Athlete, Baseball Player)
5 E Oleander Dr
Mount Laurel, NJ 08054-3601, USA

Moriarty, Tom (Athlete, Football Player)
28800 Fairmount Blvd
Cleveland, OH 44124-4542, USA

Morimoto, Masaharu (Chef)
88 10th Ave Lbby L2
New York, NY 10011-4760, USA

Morin, Alan (Athlete, Golfer)
139 Jay Ct
Royal Palm Beach, FL 33411-1723, USA

Morin, Lee M Captain (Astronaut)
10 Marys Creek Ln
Friendswood, TX 77546-3492, USA

Morin, Lee M E (Astronaut)
10 Marys Creek Ln
Friendswood, TX 77546-3492, USA

Morison, Patricia (Actor, Musician)
Craig Mgmt
125 S Sycamore Ave
Los Angeles, CA 90036-2938, USA

Morissette, Alanis (Musician, Songwriter, Writer)
c/o Dvora Vener Englefield *42West (LA)*
1840 Century Park E Ste 700
Los Angeles, CA 90067-2122, USA

Moritz, Brett (Athlete, Football Player)
613 Cameron Ridge Ct
Parkton, MD 21120-8906, USA

Moritz, Louisa (Actor)
405 S Cliffwood Ave
Los Angeles, CA 90049-3827

Moritz, Neal (Producer)
1606 N Beverly Dr
Beverly Hills, CA 90210-2316, USA

Morkis, Dorothy (Athlete, Horse Racer, Olympic Athlete)
17 Farm St
Dover, MA 02030-2303, USA

Morlan, John (Athlete, Baseball Player)
3290 Belgreen Dr
Grove City, OH 43123-8297, USA

Morland, David (Athlete, Golfer)
5531 Oxford Moor Blvd
Windermere, FL 34786-7012, USA

Morman, Alvin (Athlete, Baseball Player)
117 Philadelphia Dr
Rockingham, NC 28379-8607, USA

Morman, Russ (Athlete, Baseball Player)
1800 Tulare St
Fresno, CA 93721-2505, USA

Mormon, Russ (Athlete, Baseball Player)
1200 SW Stonecreek Dr
Blue Springs, MO 64015-8806, USA

Morneau, Justin (Athlete, Baseball Player)
1829 Forestview Ln N
Minneapolis, MN 55441-4105, USA

Mornell, Sara
9300 Wilshire Blvd Ste 555
Beverly Hills, CA 90212-3211

Mornhinweg, Marty (Athlete, Football Coach, Football Player)
25 Spencer Dr
Morristown, NJ 07960-3539, USA

Morning After Girls, The (Music Group)
c/o Staff Member *Paradigm (Monterey)*
404 W Franklin St
Monterey, CA 93940-2303, USA

Morningstar, Darren (Athlete, Basketball Player)
1515 W Ingomar Rd
Pittsburgh, PA 15237-1644, USA

Morogiello, Dan (Athlete, Baseball Player)
99 Distillery Rd
Whitehouse Station, NJ 08889-3005, USA

Moronko, Jeff (Athlete, Baseball Player)
10711 Girvan Ln
Richmond, TX 77407-2102, USA

Moroski, Mike (Athlete, Football Player)
1808 Everett St
Caldwell, ID 83605-5050, USA

Morozov, Aleksey (Athlete, Hockey Player)
c/o Staff Member *Pittsburgh Penguins*
1001 5th Ave
Pittsburgh, PA 15219-6201, USA

Morphine
48 Laight St
New York, NY 10013-2156

Morrell, David (Writer)
c/o Staff Member *Vanguard Press*
387 Park Ave S Fl 12
New York, NY 10016-8810, USA

Morris, Ashley Austin (Actor)
c/o Rob Kolker *Red Letter Entertainment*
242 W 36th St Frnt 3
New York, NY 10018-8977, USA

Morris, Betty (Bowler)
225 Lemming Dr
Reno, NV 89523-9662, USA

Morris, Betty (Bowler)
2169 Donovan Dr
Lincoln, CA 95648-2967, USA

Morris, Byron (Bam) (Athlete, Football Player)
251 NE 4th St
Cooper, TX 75432-1833, USA

Morris, Charles R. (Writer)
The Century Foundation
1333 H St NW Fl 10
Washington, DC 20005-4746, USA

Morris, Chris (Athlete, Basketball Player)
3097 Milford Chase SW
Marietta, GA 30008-6883, USA

Morris, Colleen
8271 Melrose Ave Ste 110
Los Angeles, CA 90046-6800

Morris, Danny (Athlete, Baseball Player)
802 E Main St
Petersburg, IN 47567-1232, USA

Morris, Darius (Athlete, Basketball Player)
c/o Brian Dyke *Shibumi Sports*
4771 Sweetwater Blvd # 228
Sugar Land, TX 77479-3121, USA

Morris, Donnie Joe (Athlete, Football Player)
1414 NW 13th Ave
Amarillo, TX 79107-1604, USA

Morris, Doug (Business Person)
c/o Staff Member *Universal Music Group (UMG - LA)*
2220 Colorado Ave
Santa Monica, CA 90404-3506, USA

Morris, Dwaine (Athlete, Football Player)
4002 Kilkenny Dr
Baton Rouge, LA 70814-7525, USA

Morris, Errol (Director)
c/o Staff Member *Block-Korenbrot Public Relations*
6100 Wilshire Blvd Ste 170
Los Angeles, CA 90048-5109, USA

Morris, Eugene (Athlete, Football Player)
11315 SW 243rd Ter
Homestead, FL 33032-7125, USA

Morris, Garrett (Actor, Comedian)
12067 Guerin St Unit 103
Studio City, CA 91604-4762, USA

Morris, Gary (Musician)
Gary Morris Productions
PO Box 176
Chromo, CO 81128-0176, USA

Morris, Hal (Athlete, Baseball Player)
2000 E Gene Autry Way
Anaheim, CA 92806-6143, USA

Morris, Heather (Actor)
c/o Jennifer Merlino *Untitled Entertainment (LA)*
350 S Beverly Dr Ste 200
Beverly Hills, CA 90212-4819, USA

Morris, Isaiah (Athlete, Basketball Player)
4308 W Cermak Rd
Chicago, IL 60623-2901, USA

Morris, Jack (Athlete, Baseball Player)
1 Twins Way Attn Dept
Minneapolis, MN 55403-1418, USA

Morris, Jason (Athlete, Olympic Athlete)
575 Swaggertown Rd
Schenectady, NY 12302-9628, USA

Morris, Jim (Athlete, Baseball Player)
2216 Rock Creek Dr
Kerrville, TX 78028-6502, USA

Morris, John (Athlete, Baseball Player)
2645 Elm Dr
North Bellmore, NY 11710-1303, USA

Morris, John (Athlete, Baseball Player)
5538 E Paradise Ln
Scottsdale, AZ 85254-1165, USA

Morris, Johnny (Athlete, Football Player)
753 Shoreline Rd
Lake Barrington, IL 60010-3825, USA

Morris, Jon (Athlete, Football Player)
16 Gail St
Chelmsford, MA 01824-3510, USA

Morris, Julian (Actor)
c/o Jai Khanna *Brillstein Entertainment Partners (LA)*
9150 Wilshire Blvd Ste 350
Beverly Hills, CA 90212-3453, USA

Morris, Kathryn (Actor)
c/o David (Dave) Fleming *Mosaic Media Group*
9200 W Sunset Blvd Ste 10
West Hollywood, CA 90069-3608, USA

Morris, Keith (Musician)
International Creative Mgmt
10250 Constellation Blvd Fl 1
Los Angeles, CA 90067-6241, USA

Morris, Lamorne (Actor)
c/o Naomi Odenkirk *Odenkirk Provissiero Entertainment*
1936 N Bronson Ave
Raleigh Studios
Los Angeles, CA 90068-5602, USA

Morris, Marianne (Athlete, Golfer)
360 Tamarack Trl
Springboro, OH 45066-1471, USA

Morris, Matt (Athlete, Baseball Player)
397 Old Jupiter Beach Rd
Jupiter, FL 33477-5034, USA

Morris, Matt (Musician)
c/o Staff Member *William Morris Endeavor (LA)*
9601 Wilshire Blvd
Beverly Hills, CA 90210-5213, USA

Morris, Mitch (Actor)
c/o Benjamin Tappan *Tappan Entertainment*
8324 Fountain Ave Apt C
West Hollywood, CA 90069-2916, USA

Morris, Nathan (Musician)
c/o Staff Member *Southpaw Entertainment*
1710 N Fuller Ave Apt 323
Los Angeles, CA 90046-3064, USA

Morris, Phil (Race Car Driver)
Blue RidgeMotorsports
32 E Side Hwy
Waynesboro, VA 22980-7011, USA

Morris, Phil (Actor)
704 Strand
Manhattan Beach, CA 90266, USA

Morris, Ron (Athlete, Olympic Athlete, Track Athlete)
330 S Reese Pl
Burbank, CA 91506-2724, USA

Morris, Sarah Ann (Actor)
c/o Staff Member *TalentWorks (LA)*
3500 W Olive Ave Ste 1400
Burbank, CA 91505-5512, USA

Morris, Sarah Jane (Actor)
c/o Melissa Stone *42West (LA)*
1840 Century Park E Ste 700
Los Angeles, CA 90067-2122, USA

Morris, Wanya (Musician)
c/o Staff Member *Creative Artists Agency (CAA-LA)*
2000 Avenue of the Stars Ste 100
Los Angeles, CA 90067-4705, USA

Morris, Warren (Athlete, Baseball Player, Olympic Athlete)
1215 Wilshire Dr
Alexandria, LA 71303-3141, USA

Morris, Wayna (Musician)
c/o Staff Member *Southpaw Entertainment*
1710 N Fuller Ave Apt 323
Los Angeles, CA 90046-3064, USA

Morris, Wayne (Athlete, Football Player)
5715 Old Ox Rd
Dallas, TX 75241-2118, USA

Morris, Wingerter Pam (Swimmer)
PO Box 14381
New Bern, NC 28561-4381, USA

Morrison, Adam (Athlete, Basketball Player)
309 W Brierwood Ave
Spokane, WA 99218-2507, USA

Morrison, Allan E (Athlete, Football Player)
2303 Reading Hills Ave
Henderson, NV 89052-5836, USA

Morrison, Christopher (Mink) (Director)
c/o Staff Member *ICM Partners (LA)*
10250 Constellation Blvd Fl 7
Los Angeles, CA 90067-6207, USA

Morrison, Dan (Athlete, Baseball Player)
13120 Plantation Ter
Seminole, FL 33776-2430, USA

Morrison, Darryl (Athlete, Football Player)
22607 Blue Elder Ter Unit 302
Ashburn, VA 20148-4811, USA

Morrison, Don (Athlete, Football Player)
PO Box 432
Wolfe City, TX 75496-0432, USA

Morrison, Dwight (Athlete, Basketball Player)
6112 E Singletree St
Apache Junction, AZ 85119-9548, USA

Morrison, Felton (Baseball Player)
Philadelphia Stars
3860 N Bouvier St
Philadelphia, PA 19140-3528, USA

Morrison, Fred (Athlete, Football Player)
38189 Greywalls Dr
Murrieta, CA 92562-3058, USA

Morrison, James (Actor)
c/o Mitch Clem *Shadow Entertainment*
655 N Central Ave Fl 17
Glendale, CA 91203-1439, USA

Morrison, Jennifer (Actor)
c/o John Carrabino *John Carrabino Management*
5900 Wilshire Blvd Ste 406
Los Angeles, CA 90036-5015, USA

Morrison, Jim (Athlete, Baseball Player)
Philadelphia Phillies
2300 El Jobean Rd
Port Charlotte, FL 33948-1120, USA

Morrison, Kirk (Athlete, Football Player)
c/o Staff Member *EAG Sports Management*
909 N Sepulveda Blvd Ste 360
El Segundo, CA 90245-3864, USA

Morrison, Matthew (Actor)
c/o Evelyn Karamanos *Relevant*
9350 Wilshire Blvd Ste 450
Beverly Hills, CA 90212-3230, USA

Morrison, Mike (Athlete, Basketball Player)
113 Rivanna Ln
Greenville, SC 29607-5488, USA

Morrison, Patricia (Musician)
400 Hauser Blvd Apt 9L
Los Angeles, CA 90036-5571, USA

Morrison, Robert S (Bob) (Business Person)
Quaker Oats Co
Quaker Tower
PO Box 049001
Chicago, IL 60604, USA

Morrison, Shelley (Actor)
1209 S Alfred St
Los Angeles, CA 90035-2569, USA

Morrison, Temuera (Actor)
c/o Staff Member *Abrams Artists Agency (LA)*
9200 W Sunset Blvd PH 11
West Hollywood, CA 90069-3601, USA

Morrison, Toni (Nobel Prize Laureate, Writer)
The Lewis Center For The Arts - Creative Writing
6 New S
Princeton, NJ 08544-0001, USA

Morrison, Toni (Writer)
185 Nassau St
Princeton, NJ 08544-2003, USA

Morrison, Van (Musician, Songwriter)
c/o Staff Member *Monterey International*
PO Box 297
Carmel By The Sea, CA 93921-0297, USA

Morrison-Gamberdella, Ester (Baseball Player)
3179 Pleasant Creek Rd
Rogue River, OR 97537-9803, USA

Morrison-Gamberdella, Esther (Athlete, Baseball Player)
3179 Pleasant Creek Rd
Rogue River, OR 97537-9803, USA

Morriss, Guy (Athlete, Football Player)
812 Andover Ct
Bowling Green, KY 42104-5457, USA

Morrissette, Billy (Actor, Director, Writer)
c/o Brian Inerfeld *Protocol Entertainment (LA)*
8899 Beverly Blvd Ste 803
Los Angeles, CA 90048-2451, USA

Morrissey (Musician)
c/o Todd Jacobs *William Morris Endeavor (LA)*
9601 Wilshire Blvd
Beverly Hills, CA 90210-5213, USA

Morrissey, Jim (Athlete, Football Player)
48 Fox Trl
Lincolnshire, IL 60069-4012, USA

Morrone, Joe (Coach, Football Coach)
University of Connecticut
Athletic Dept
Storrs Mansfield, CT 06269-0001, USA

Morrow, Bobby (Athlete, Olympic Athlete, Track Athlete)
2022 Elmwood Dr
Harlingen, TX 78550-8078, USA

Morrow, Bobby Joe (Athlete, Track Athlete)
PO Box 9
Beeville, TX 78104-0009, USA

Morrow, Brandon (Athlete, Baseball Player)
3638 N 51st Dr
Phoenix, AZ 85033, USA

Morrow, Brenden (Athlete, Hockey Player)
3528 Centenary Ave
Dallas, TX 75225-5013, USA

Morrow, Bruce (Cousin Brucie) (Radio Personality)
c/o Staff Member *Sirius/XM Satellite Radio*
1221 Avenue of the Americas Fl 19
New York, NY 10020-1011, USA

Morrow, Harold (Athlete, Football Player)
3390 US Highway 82
Maplesville, AL 36750-5112, USA

Morrow, Jo (Actor)
17000 Ramsey Rd
White City, OR 97503-8525, USA

Morrow, Joshua (Actor)
c/o Marv Dauer *Marv Dauer Management*
2236 The Terrace
Los Angeles, CA 90049-1171, USA

Morrow, Ken (Athlete, Hockey Player)
1255 Hempstead Tpke
Attn Dir Pro Scouting
Uniondale, NY 11553-1260, USA

Morrow, Ken (Athlete, Hockey Player, Olympic Athlete)
6732 R-Bnticello Dr
Kansas City, MO 64152, USA

Morrow, Mari (Actor)
c/o David Ziff *Cunningham Escott Slevin & Doherty (CESD-LA)*
10635 Santa Monica Blvd Ste 130
Los Angeles, CA 90025-8306, USA

Morrow, Rob (Actor)
c/o Judy Hofflund *Hofflund/Polone*
6300 Wilshire Blvd Ste 1410
Los Angeles, CA 90048-5216, USA

Morse, Cathy (Athlete, Golfer)
6228 Celadon Cir
West Palm Beach, FL 33418-1436, USA

Morse, David (Actor)
Yvette Bikoff
1040 1st Ave # 1126
New York, NY 10022-2991, USA

Morse, David (Musician)
Agency for Performing Arts
9200 W Sunset Blvd Ste 900
West Hollywood, CA 90069-3604, USA

Morse, David E (Publisher)
Christian Science Monitor
1 Norway Park
Publisher's Office
Hyde Park, MA 02136-4016, USA

Morse, John (Athlete, Golfer)
9291 17 Mile Rd
Marshall, MI 49068-9755, USA

Morse, Mike (Athlete, Baseball Player)
417 NW 97th Ave
Plantation, FL 33324-7075, USA

Morse, Ray
989 NW Spruce Ave Apt 207
Corvallis, OR 97330-2173

Morse, Robert (Actor)
13830 Davana Ter
Sherman Oaks, CA 91423-4216, USA

Morse, Steve (Athlete, Football Player)
32743 Weybridge St
Fulshear, TX 77441-4132, USA

Morstead, Thomas (Athlete, Football Player)
c/o W Vann McElroy *Select Sports Group*
2700 Post Oak Blvd Ste 1450
Houston, TX 77056-5785, USA

Mortensen, Chris (Sportscaster)
ESPN-TV
935 Middle St
Sports Dept Espn Plaza
Bristol, CT 06010-1000, USA

Mortensen, Clayton (Athlete, Baseball Player)
1340 Fairview Ave
Rexburg, ID 83440-5078, USA

Mortensen, J D (Doctor)
Cardipulmonics Inc
5060 W Amelia Earhart Dr
Salt Lake City, UT 84116-2800, USA

Mortensen, Viggo (Actor)
c/o Lynn Rawlins *Rawlins Company*
5967 Oak Meadow Pl
Oak Park, CA 91377-1123, USA

Mortimer, Emily (Actor)
c/o Aleen Keshishian *Brillstein Entertainment Partners (LA)*
9150 Wilshire Blvd Ste 350
Beverly Hills, CA 90212-3453, USA

Mortimer, Tinsley (Reality Star)
c/o Jan Planit *Planit Management*
11 E 26th St
New York, NY 10010-1402, USA

Mortita, Pat (Noriyuki) (Actor)
6399 Wilshire Blvd # 444
Los Angeles, CA 90048-5703, USA

Morton, Alicia (Actor)
c/o Staff Member *William Morris Endeavor (LA)*
9601 Wilshire Blvd
Beverly Hills, CA 90210-5213, USA

Morton, Charie (Athlete, Baseball Player)
5122 Sea Forest Dr
Johns Island, SC 29455-5450, USA

Morton, Craig (Athlete, Football Player)
9850 N 73rd St Unit 2037
Scottsdale, AZ 85258-1032, USA

Morton, Genevieve (Model)
c/o Lisa Benson *IMG Models (NY)*
304 Park Ave S Fl 12
New York, NY 10010-4314, USA

Morton, Guy (Athlete, Baseball Player)
567 Femdale Ave
Vermilion, OH 44089, USA

Morton, Joe (Actor)
c/o Jay Kane *TalentWorks (NY)*
220 E 23rd St Ste 400
New York, NY 10010-4669, USA

Morton, John (Athlete, Football Player)
39991 Purmice Dr
Cassel, CA 96016, USA

Morton, Johnnie (Athlete, Football Player)
2911 Oakwood Ln
Torrance, CA 90505-7121, USA

Morton, Kevin (Athlete, Baseball Player)
12 Glen Pines Ln
Norwalk, CT 06850-1800, USA

Morton, Kristopher (Colt) (Athlete, Baseball Player)
3245 Santa Barbara Dr
Wellington, FL 33414-7267, USA

Morton, Richard (Athlete, Basketball Player)
1111 Gilman Ave
San Francisco, CA 94124-3622, USA

Morton, Samantha (Actor)
c/o Troy Nankin *Wishlab*
2225A Hyperion Ave
Los Angeles, CA 90027-4709, USA

Moschitta Jr, John
11601 Dunstan Way Apt 206
Los Angeles, CA 90049-4300, USA

Moschitto, Ross (Athlete, Baseball Player)
1200 Warburton Ave Apt 47
Yonkers, NY 10701-1062, USA

Moscoso, Guillermo (Athlete, Baseball Player)
3667 Victoria Manor Dr Apt 103
Lakeland, FL 33805-2989, USA

Moscow, David (Actor)
c/o Robert Stein *Robert Stein Management*
PO Box 3797
Beverly Hills, CA 90212-0797, USA

Mosebar, Donald H (Don) (Athlete, Football Player)
1713 Walnut Ave
Manhattan Beach, CA 90266-5016, USA

Moseby, Lloyd (Athlete, Baseball Player)
9140 Los Lagos Cir S
Granite Bay, CA 95746-5842, USA

Mosel, Tad (Writer)
149 E Side Dr Apt 26-B
Concord, NH 03301-5410, USA

Moseley, Dustin (Athlete, Baseball Player)
3 Bluestem Cv
Little Rock, AR 72211-4484, USA

Moseley, John (Athlete, Football Player)
408 Manor Dr
Columbia, MO 65203-1734, USA

Moseley, Jonny (Athlete, Olympic Athlete, Skier)
167 Trinidad Dr
Belvedere Tiburon, CA 94920-1037, USA

Moseley, Mark (Athlete, Football Player)
7250 Middle Rd
Middletown, VA 22645-2121, USA

Moseley, William (Actor)
c/o David Guillod *Intellectual Artists Management*
10585 Santa Monica Blvd Ste 135
Los Angeles, CA 90025-6392, USA

Moselle, Dominic (Athlete, Football Player)
2019 Hammond Ave
Superior, WI 54880-2751, USA

Moser, Casey (Athlete, Baseball Player)
9013 FM 368 N
Iowa Park, TX 76367-5341, USA

Moser, Rick (Athlete, Football Player)
1616 Esplanada Ave
Apt 10
Redondo Beach, CA 90277, USA

Moses, Billy E
409 N Camden Dr Ste 202
Beverly Hills, CA 90210-4423, USA

Moses, Dezman (Athlete, Football Player)
c/o Blake Baratz *The Institute for Athletes*
3600 Minnesota Dr Ste 550
Minneapolis, MN 55435-7925, USA

Moses, Ed (Athlete)
c/o Staff Member *Premier Management Group (PMG Sports)*
115 Crescent Commons Dr Ste 250
Cary, NC 27518-8134, USA

Moses, Edwin (Athlete, Olympic Athlete, Track Athlete)
1184 Daventry Way NE
Atlanta, GA 30319-4547, USA

Moses, Haven C (Athlete, Football Player)
1140 Cherokee St Unit 640
Denver, CO 80204-3684, USA

Moses, Jerry (Athlete, Baseball Player)
8 Hickory Ln
Ipswich, MA 01938-1080, USA

Moses, John (Athlete, Baseball Player)
734 E Port Ave Attn Coachingstaff
Corpus Christi, TX 78401-1006, USA

Moses, Kim (Producer)
c/o Staff Member *William Morris Endeavor (LA)*
9601 Wilshire Blvd
Beverly Hills, CA 90210-5213, USA

Moses, Mark (Actor)
c/o Leanne Coronel *Coronel Group*
1100 Glendon Ave Fl 17
Los Angeles, CA 90024-3588, USA

Moses, Rick (Actor, Musician)
Calder Agency
19919 Redwing St
Woodland Hills, CA 91364-2620, USA

Mosher, Gregory D (Director, Producer)
c/o Patrick Herold *Helen Merrill Ltd*
295 Lafayette St Ste 915
New York, NY 10012-2700, USA

Moskau, Paul (Athlete, Baseball Player)
5041 N Apache Hills Trl
Tucson, AZ 85750-5912, USA

Moskovitz, Dustin (Business Person)
Asana
1550 Bryant St Ste 800
San Francisco, CA 94103-4859, USA

Mosler, John (Athlete, Football Player)
12604 Cambridge Rd
Leawood, KS 66209-1327, USA

Mosley, C.J. (Athlete, Football Player)
c/o Jimmy Sexton *CAA (Memphis)*
6060 Poplar Ave Ste 470
Memphis, TN 38119-0910, USA

Mosley, J Brooke (Religious Leader)
1604 Foulkeways
Gwynedd, PA 19436-1033, USA

Mosley, Michael (Actor)
c/o Laurie Smith *Smith Talent Group*
77 Gold St
Brooklyn, NY 11201-1228, USA

Mosley, Mike (Athlete, Football Player)
109 Heritage Hill Rd
Wimberley, TX 78676-5632, USA

Mosley, Roger E (Actor)
4470 W Sunset Blvd # 107-342
Los Angeles, CA 90027-6302, USA

Mosley, Sugar Shane (Boxer)
c/o Larry O. Williams Jr. *Williams Talent Agency*
1438 N Gower St Ste 43
Los Angeles, CA 90028-8362, USA

Mosley, Timothy (Timbaland) (Musician, Producer)
c/o David Zedeck *Creative Artists Agency (CAA-NY)*
162 5th Ave Fl 6
New York, NY 10010-6047, USA

Mosley, Walter (Writer)
c/o Bruce Miller *Washington Square Arts (NY)*
310 Bowery Fl 2
New York, NY 10012-2861, USA

Mosquera, Julio (Athlete, Baseball Player)
1419 Stone Creek Dr
Tarpon Springs, FL 34689-3045, USA

Moss, Carrie-Anne (Actor)
c/o Staff Member *William Morris Endeavor (LA)*
9601 Wilshire Blvd
Beverly Hills, CA 90210-5213, USA

Moss, Damian (Athlete, Baseball Player)
1877 GA Highway 19 S
Dublin, GA 31021-1480, USA

Moss, Eddie (Athlete, Football Player)
15404 Eagle Estates Ln
Florissant, MO 63034-1616, USA

Moss, Elisabeth (Actor)
c/o Gay Ribisi *Ribisi Entertainment*
3278 Wilshire Blvd Apt 702
Los Angeles, CA 90010-1425, USA

Moss, Elza (Religious Leader)
Primitive Advent Christian Church
6403 Frame Rd
Elkview, WV 25071-7040, USA

Moss, Geoffrey (Cartoonist)
315 E 68th St Apt 9F
New York, NY 10065-5603, USA

Moss, Lance (Race Car Driver)
Moss Motorsports
100 W First St
Dallas, NC 28034, USA

Moss, Les (Athlete, Baseball Player, Coach)
420 Tullis Ave
Longwood, FL 32750-5535, USA

Moss, Paige (Actor)
c/o Staff Member *Marshak/Zachary Company, The*
8840 Wilshire Blvd Fl 1
Beverly Hills, CA 90211-2606, USA

Moss, Perry (Athlete, Basketball Player)
165 Columbia Dr
Amherst, MA 01002-3107, USA

Moss, Perry (Athlete, Football Player, Golfer)
5660 S Lakeshore Dr Apt 505
Shreveport, LA 71119-4038, USA

Moss, Randy (Athlete, Football Player)
c/o Chafie Fields *Lagardere Unlimited (NYC)*
845 United Nations Plz Apt 88A
New York, NY 10017-3539, USA

Moss, Roland (Athlete, Football Player)
411 Camelot Dr
Salisbury, NC 28144-9416, USA

Moss, Ronn (Actor)
2401 Nottingham Ave
Los Angeles, CA 90027-1036, USA

Moss, Santana (Athlete, Football Player)
18619 SW 50th Ct
Miramar, FL 33029-6245, USA

Moss, Zefross (Athlete, Football Player)
126 Kensington Dr
Madison, AL 35758-7844, USA

Mosser, Jonell (Musician)
Phil Mayo Co
PO Box 304
Bomoseen, VT 05732-0304, USA

Mossi, Don (Athlete, Baseball Player)
23250 Canyon Ln
Caldwell, ID 83607-7709, USA

Mossman, Doug
999 Kalapaki St
Honolulu, HI 96825-2707

Most, Don (Actor)
c/o Brian Ronalds *Dark Falls PR*
Prefers to be contacted by telephone or
email
Los Angeles, CA 90046, USA

Mostardo, Rich (Athlete, Football Player)
3376 Summit Rd
Ravenna, OH 44266-9015, USA

Mostow, Jonathan (Director)
Creative Artists Agency
9830 Wilshire Blvd
Beverly Hills, CA 90212-1804, USA

Mota, Andres (Athlete, Baseball Player)
PO Box 2820
Toluca Lake, CA 91610-0820, USA

Mota, Andy (Athlete, Baseball Player)
9068 NW 50th Ct
Coral Springs, FL 33067-1933, USA

Mota, Bethany (Internet Star)
c/o Jennifer Abel *PMK/BNC Public
Relations (PMK-LA)*
8687 Melrose Ave Ste 8
West Hollywood, CA 90069-5746, USA

Mota, Guillermo (Athlete, Baseball Player)
c/o Staff Member *Los Angeles Dodgers
(LA Dodgers)*
1000 Elysian Park Ave
Los Angeles, CA 90012-1112, USA

Mota, Jose (Athlete, Baseball Player)
19058 E La Crosse St
Glendora, CA 91741-1918, USA

Mota, Manny (Athlete, Baseball Player)
1000 Elysian Park Ave
Los Angeles, CA 90012-1112, USA

Mote, Bobby (Rodeo Rider)
6510 SW King Ln
Culver, OR 97734-9670, USA

Mote, Kelley (Athlete, Football Player)
41121 Ocean View Dr
Avon, NC 27915, USA

Moten, Mike (Athlete, Football Player)
706 Loomis Ave
Daytona Beach, FL 32114-4724, USA

Mother Mother (Music Group)
c/o Staff Member *Paradigm (Monterey)*
404 W Franklin St
Monterey, CA 93940-2303, USA

Mothersbaugh, Mark (Musician)
8766 Appian Way
Los Angeles, CA 90046-7733, USA

Motion City Soundtrack (Music Group)
Asquared Management
2336 W Belmont Ave
Chicago, IL 60618-6423, USA

Motley, Darryl (Athlete, Baseball Player)
10800 W 65th St
Shawnee, KS 66203-3810, USA

Motley Crue (Music Group)
c/o Frank Cimler *10th Street
Entertainment (LA)*
700 N San Vicente Blvd Ste G410
West Hollywood, CA 90069-5060, USA

Mott, John C (Athlete, Football Player)
215 Thistledown Ln
Hamilton, MT 59840-9153, USA

Mott, Steve (Athlete, Football Player)
7018 N Highfield Dr
Birmingham, AL 35242-7239, USA

Mott, Stewart R (Politician)
515 Madison Ave
New York, NY 10022-5403, USA

Motta, Dick (Basketball Coach, Coach)
423 Highway 89
Fish Haven, ID 83287-5109, USA

Motta, Zeke (Athlete, Football Player)
c/o Joe Flanagan *BTI Sports Advisors*
170 N Scoville Ave
Oak Park, IL 60302-2647, USA

Mottau, Mike (Athlete, Hockey Player)
57 Herring Weir Rd
Duxbury, MA 02332-3304, USA

Mottola, Chad (Athlete, Baseball Player)
4040 Oak St
Orlando, FL 32814-6129, USA

Mottola, Greg (Director, Writer)
c/o Staff Member *United Talent Agency
(UTA-LA)*
9336 Civic Center Dr
Beverly Hills, CA 90210-3604, USA

Mottola, Thomas (Tommy) (Business
Person)
c/o Staff Member *Mottola Company, The*
745 5th Ave # 800
New York, NY 10151-0099, USA

Motton, Curt (Athlete, Baseball Player)
19903 Quiet Valley Ct
Parkton, MD 21120-8917, USA

Mouawad, Jerry (Director)
Imago Theater
PO Box 15182
Portland, OR 97293-5182, USA

Mouchawar, Alan (Athlete, Olympic
Athlete, Water Polo Player)
30982 Steeplechase Dr
San Juan Capistrano, CA 92675-1928,
USA

Mould, Bob (Musician, Songwriter,
Writer)
c/o Staff Member *High Road Touring*
751 Bridgeway Fl 2
Sausalito, CA 94965-2174, USA

Moulton, Sara (Chef, Television Host)
c/o Staff Member *Grand Productions*
2811 Champion Rd
Naperville, IL 60564-4958, USA

Mounce, Tony (Athlete, Baseball Player)
3901 W 46th Ave
Kennewick, WA 99337-2781, USA

Mounsey, Tara (Athlete, Hockey Player,
Olympic Athlete)
22 Forge Pond Unit B
Canton, MA 02021-2990, USA

Mount, Anson (Actor)
c/o Emily Gerson Saines *Brookside Artists
Management (NY)*
250 W 57th St Ste 2303
New York, NY 10107-2399, USA

Mount, Rick (Athlete, Basketball Player)
904 Hopkins Rd
Lebanon, IN 46052-1436, USA

Mount, Thomas H (Tom) (Producer)
c/o Staff Member *Mount Film Company*
9245 Cordell Dr
Los Angeles, CA 90069-1753, USA

Mourning, Alonzo (Athlete, Basketball
Player, Olympic Athlete)
33 Arvida Pkwy
Miami, FL 33156-2310, USA

Mouse, Mickey Club
PO Box 10200
Orlando, FL 32830-0200

Mouton, James (Athlete, Baseball Player)
4710 Lakeside Meadow Ct
Missouri City, TX 77459-1630, USA

Mouton, Leslie (Journalist)
1333 Northland Dr
Saint Paul, MN 55120-1345

Mouton, Lyle (Athlete, Baseball Player)
4101 Auston Way
Palm Harbor, FL 34685-4014, USA

Moverman, Oren (Director)
c/o Staff Member *William Morris
Endeavor (LA)*
9601 Wilshire Blvd
Beverly Hills, CA 90210-5213, USA

Movessian, Victoria (Viki) (Athlete,
Hockey Player)
17 Webb St
Lexington, MA 02420-2219, USA

Movita
2766 Motor Ave
Los Angeles, CA 90064-3436

Movsessian, Vicki (Athlete, Hockey
Player, Olympic Athlete)
1 Pine Tree Ln
Lincoln, RI 02865-4569, USA

Mowatt, Ezekial (Athlete, Football Player)
245 Prospect Ave Apt 2B
Hackensack, NJ 07601-2571, USA

Mowers, Mark (Athlete, Hockey Player)
10 Pollock Dr
Middleton, MA 01949-1747, USA

Mowerson, Robert (Swimmer)
2601 Kenzie Ter Apt 324
Minneapolis, MN 55418-4239, USA

Mowrey, Dude (Musician)
Joe Taylor Artist Agency
2802 Columbine Pl
Nashville, TN 37204-3104, USA

Mowry, Tahj (Actor)
c/o Jason Egenberg *United Talent Agency
(UTA-LA)*
9336 Civic Center Dr
Beverly Hills, CA 90210-3604, USA

Mowry, Tamera (Actor, Producer)
c/o Tracy Steinsapir *Main Title
Entertainment*
8383 Wilshire Blvd Ste 408
Beverly Hills, CA 90211-2435, USA

Mowry-Hardrict, Tia (Actor)
c/o Adam Griffin *Kritzer Levine Wilkins
Entertainment (KLWG)*
11872 La Grange Ave Fl 1
Los Angeles, CA 90025-5283, USA

Moxness, Barbara (Athlete, Golfer)
5512 Mirror Lakes Dr
Minneapolis, MN 55436-2037, USA

Moyer, Jamie (Athlete, Baseball Player)
2426 32nd Ave W
Seattle, WA 98199-3202, USA

Moyer, Ken (Athlete, Football Player)
3896 Magma Ct
Mason, OH 45040-2896, USA

Moyer, Paul (Correspondent)
12742 Highwood St
Los Angeles, CA 90049-2624, USA

Moyer, Stephen (Actor)
c/o Lena Roklin *Luber Roklin
Management*
5815 W Sunset Blvd Ste 206
Los Angeles, CA 90028-6481, USA

Moyers, Bill (Journalist)
151 Central Park W Apt Sn
New York, NY 10023-1577, USA

Moyers, Bill D (Correspondent)
c/o Staff Member *HarperCollins Publishers*
195 Broadway Fl 2
Cellar 1
New York, NY 10007-3132, USA

Moylan, Peter
1889 Point River Dr
Duluth, GA 30097-7957, USA

Moyle, Allan (Director, Writer)
c/o Staff Member *Wisdom Literary*
287 S Robertson Blvd Ste 258
Beverly Hills, CA 90211-2810, USA

Moynahan, Bridget (Actor, Model)
c/o Andrea Pett-Joseph *Brillstein
Entertainment Partners (LA)*
9150 Wilshire Blvd Ste 350
Beverly Hills, CA 90212-3453, USA

Moynihan, Bobby (Actor, Comedian)
c/o Staff Member *Odenkirk Provissiero
Entertainment*
1936 N Bronson Ave
Raleigh Studios
Los Angeles, CA 90068-5602, USA

Moynihan, Christopher (Actor)
c/o Ron West *Thruline Entertainment*
9250 Wilshire Blvd Ste 100
Ground Floor
Beverly Hills, CA 90212-3343, USA

Mozeliak, John (Athlete, Baseball Player)
5 Maryhill Dr
Saint Louis, MO 63124-1368, USA

Mozo, Rebecca (Actor)
c/o Staff Member *Insight*
PO Box 36359
Los Angeles, CA 90036-0359, USA

M. Palazzo, Steven (Congressman,
Politician)
331 Cannon Hob
Washington, DC 20515-0901, USA

Mraz, Jason (Musician, Songwriter)
c/o Bill Silva *Bill Silva Management*
8255 Santa Monica Blvd
Los Angeles, CA 90046, USA

Mrazovich, Chuck (Athlete, Basketball
Player)
7260 W 12th Ave
Hialeah, FL 33014-4618, USA

Mr Big (Music Group, Musician)
c/o Tim Heyne *Union Entertainment
Group*
1323 Newbury Rd Ste 104
Newbury Park, CA 91320-3679, USA

Mrosko, Robert (Athlete, Football Player)
2874 Coleridge Rd
Cleveland, OH 44118-3544, USA

Mrozik, Rick
2234 Kelly Ave
Cloquet, MN 55720-2224, USA

Muccino, Gabriele (Director)
c/o Jason Weinberg *Untitled
Entertainment (LA)*
350 S Beverly Dr Ste 200
Beverly Hills, CA 90212-4819, USA

Mucha, Barb (Athlete, Golfer)
5922 Crystal View Dr
Orlando, FL 32819-4207, USA

Muchlinski, Mike (Athlete, Baseball
Player)
3004 183rd St SE
Bothell, WA 98012-9323, USA

Muckalt, Bill (Athlete, Hockey Player)
1400 Townsend Dr
Houghton, MI 49931-1200, USA

Muckensturm, Jerry (Athlete, Football
Player)
4209 Hickory Ln
Jonesboro, AR 72401-8430, USA

Muckier, John (Athlete, Hockey Player)
387 Wood Acres Dr
East Amherst, NY 14051-1660, USA

Mudcrutch (Music Group)
c/o Staff Member *Warner Bros Records
(LA)*
PO Box 6868
Burbank, CA 91510-6868, USA

Mudd, Howard E (Athlete, Coach,
Football Player)
311 W Walnut St
Indianapolis, IN 46202-3163, USA

Mudd, Jodie (Athlete, Golfer)
3512 Mildred Dr
Louisville, KY 40216-4341, USA

Mudd, Roger (Journalist)
7167 Old Dominion Dr
Mc Lean, VA 22101-2705, USA

Mudd, Roger H (Correspondent)
7167 Old Dominion Dr
Mc Lean, VA 22101-2705, USA

Mudge, Nancy (Athlete, Baseball Player)
23019 County Road 1
Elk River, MN 55330-9437, USA

Mudra, Darrell (Coach, Football Coach)
424 Tiger Hammock Rd
Crawfordville, FL 32327-1470, USA

Mudrock, Phil (Athlete, Baseball Player)
2548 E 6600 S
Salt Lake City, UT 84121-2346, USA

Mudvayne (Music Group)
c/o Chuck Toler *Anger Management*
6907 University Ave # 199
Middleton, WI 53562-2767, USA

Muelhaupt Jr, Chuck (Athlete, Football
Player)
3615 Oak Creek Pl
West Des Moines, IA 50265-6424, USA

Muelier, Charles W (Business Person)
Ameren Corp
1901 Chouteau Ave
Saint Louis, MO 63103-3085, USA

Mueller, Bill (Athlete, Baseball Player)
570 W Canyon Wav
Chandler, AZ 85248, USA

Mueller, Brooke (Actor)
c/o Howard Bragman *Fifteen Minutes (LA)*
8436 W 3rd St Ste 650
Los Angeles, CA 90048-4131, USA

Mueller, Les (Athlete, Baseball Player)
5520 Vogel Pl
Millstadt, IL 62260-2744, USA

Mueller, Vance (Athlete, Football Player)
8141 Damico Dr
El Dorado Hills, CA 95762-5482, USA

Mueller, Willard (Willie) (Athlete,
Baseball Player)
2320 Tolbert Ln
West Bend, WI 53090-1234, USA

Mueller-Bajda, Dolores (Baseball Player)
2913 N Linder Ave
Chicago, IL 60641-4812, USA

Mueller-Stahl, Armin (Actor)
c/o ZBF
Ordensmeisterstr. 15-16
Berlin, GE D-120

Muellner, William (Athlete, Football
Player)
727 Sherwood Rd
La Grange Park, IL 60526-1545, USA

Muhammad, Elijah
7351 S Stony Island Ave
Chicago, IL 60649-3106

Muhammad, Muhsin (Athlete, Football
Player)
c/o Staff Member *Golden Peak Sports &
Entertainment LLC*
11352 Haswell Dr
Parker, CO 80134-7548, USA

Muhammad, Wallace D (Religious
Leader)
American Muslim Mission
7351 S Stony Island Ave
Chicago, IL 60649-3106, USA

Muhlbach, Don (Athlete, Football Player)
c/o David Dunn *Athletes First, LLC*
23091 Mill Creek Dr
Laguna Hills, CA 92653-1258, USA

Muir, Roger
10 Drewid Hill Ave
Methuen, MA 01844

Mukai, Chiaki Naito (Astronaut)
100 Cyberonics Blvd Ste 201
Houston, TX 77058-2074, USA

Mukherjee, Bharati (Writer)
130 Rivoli St
San Francisco, CA 94117-4341, USA

Mulaney, John (Actor, Comedian)
c/o David (Dave) Becky *3 Arts
Entertainment (LA)*
9460 Wilshire Blvd Fl 7
Beverly Hills, CA 90212-2713, USA

Mularkey, Mike (Athlete, Football Coach,
Football Player)
1719 Beach Ave
Atlantic Beach, FL 32233-5838, USA

Mulcahy, Anne
Xerox Corp
800 Long Ridge Rd
Stamford, CT 06902-1227, USA

Mulcahy, J Patrick (Business Person)
Raiston Purina Co
Checkerboard Square
Saint Louis, MO 63164-0001, USA

Mulcahy, Russell (Director)
c/o Staff Member *Agency for the
Performing Arts (APA-LA)*
405 S Beverly Dr Ste 500
Beverly Hills, CA 90212-4425, USA

Muldaur, Maria (Musician, Songwriter,
Writer)
Piedmont Talent
PO Box 680006
Charlotte, NC 28216-0001, USA

Mulder, Karen (Model)
c/o Staff Member *Metropolitan Modeling
Agency*
5 Union Sq W Ste 500
New York, NY 10003-3306, USA

Mulder, Mark (Athlete, Baseball Player)
10295 E Cholla St
Scottsdale, AZ 85260-6038, USA

Muldoon, Leslie L (Doctor)
Oregon Health Sciences University
Neurology Dept
Portland, OR 97201, USA

Muldoon, Patrick (Actor, Model)
27652 Eastvale Rd
Palos Verdes Peninsula, CA 90274-4023,
USA

Muldoon, Paul B (Writer)
Princeton University
Creative Writing Program
Princeton, NJ 08544-0001, USA

Mulgrew, Kate (Actor)
c/o Lisa Loosemore *Viking Entertainment*
445 W 23rd St Ste 1A
New York, NY 10011-1445, USA

Mulhern, Matt (Actor)
Gold Marshak Liedtke
3500 W Olive Ave Ste 1400
Burbank, CA 91505-5512, USA

Mulhern, Ryan (Athlete, Hockey Player)
19 Beachview Ter
Middletown, RI 02842-5904, USA

Mulholland, Terry (Athlete, Baseball
Player)
PO Box 96
Paulden, AZ 86334-0096, USA

Mulitalo, Edwin (Athlete, Football Player)
110 Santa Barbara Ave
Daly City, CA 94014-1045, USA

Mulkerin, Ted (Writer)
c/o Staff Member *William Morris
Endeavor (LA)*
9601 Wilshire Blvd
Beverly Hills, CA 90210-5213, USA

Mulkey, Chris (Actor)
Paradigm Agency
10100 Santa Monica Blvd Ste 2500
Los Angeles, CA 90067-4116, USA

Mulkey-Robertson, Kim (Basketball
Player, Coach)
Baylor University
Athletic Dept
Waco, TX 76798, USA

Mull, Clay (Athlete, Olympic Athlete,
Speed Skater)
4344 S New Hope Rd
Gastonia, NC 28056-8454, USA

Mull, Martin (Actor)
338 S Chadbourne Ave
Los Angeles, CA 90049-3709, USA

Mullady, Tom (Athlete, Football Player)
2855 Crooked Oak Dr
Germantown, TN 38138-7614, USA

Mullally, Megan (Actor, Musician)
c/o Carrie Gordon *42West (NYC)*
220 W 42nd St Fl 12
New York, NY 10036-7200, USA

Mullan, Peter (Writer)
c/o Staff Member *ICM Partners (LA)*
10250 Constellation Blvd Fl 7
Los Angeles, CA 90067-6207, USA

Mullane, Richard M Colonel (Astronaut)
1301 Las Lomas Rd NE
Albuquerque, NM 87106-4527, USA

Mullane, Richard M (Mike) (Astronaut)
1301 Las Lomas Rd NE
Albuquerque, NM 87106-4527, USA

Mullaney, Mark (Athlete, Football Player)
13490 Essex Ct
Eden Prairie, MN 55347-1710, USA

Mullavey, Greg (Actor)
1818 Thayer Ave Apt 303
Los Angeles, CA 90025-4965, USA

Mullavy, Greg
1818 Thayer Ave Apt 303
Los Angeles, CA 90025-4965

Mullen, Brian (Athlete, Hockey Player)
124 Berkeley Cir
Basking Ridge, NJ 07920-2023, USA

Mullen, Ford (Moon) (Athlete, Baseball
Player)
20420 Marine Dr Apt B19
Stanwood, WA 98292-6154, USA

Mullen, Joe (Athlete, Hockey Player)
3601 S Broad St Ste 2
Attn Coaching Staff
Philadelphia, PA 19148-5250, USA

Mullen, Josep P (Joey) (Athlete, Hockey
Player)
36 Friends Ln
South Dennis, MA 02660-2549, USA

Mullen, Nicole (Musician)
c/o Staff Member *Word Records*
25 Music Sq W
Nashville, TN 37203-3205, USa

Mullen, Rodney (Athlete, Skateboarder)
Almost Skateboards
225 S Aviation Blvd
El Segundo, CA 90245-4604, USA

Mullen, Scott (Athlete, Baseball Player)
73 Walling Grove Rd
Beaufort, SC 29907-1067, USA

Mullen, Tom (Athlete, Football Player)
292 Burnt Pine Dr
Naples, FL 34119-9750, USA

Mullen, Tony (Race Car Driver)
22207 26th Ave E
Bradenton, FL 34211-9139, USA

Muller, Herta (Writer)
c/o Staff Member *Henry Holt & Company*
175 5th Ave Ste 400
New York, NY 10010-7726, USA

Muller, Kirk (Athlete, Hockey Player)
1001 N 4th St Ste 3
Attn: Coaching Staff
Milwaukee, WI 53203-1314, USA

Muller, Lisel (Writer)
LSU Press
PO Box 25053
Baton Rouge, LA 70894, USA

Muller, Marcia (Writer)
Mysterious Press
1271 Avenue of the Americas
Warner Books
New York, NY 10020-1300, USA

Muller, Robby (Cinematographer)
Smith/Gosnell/Nicholson
PO Box 1156
Studio City, CA 91614-0156, USA

Mulligan, Carey (Actor)
c/o Jessica Kolstad *Relevant*
9350 Wilshire Blvd Ste 450
Beverly Hills, CA 90212-3230, USA

Mulligan, Gerry (Writer)
c/o Staff Member *3 Arts Entertainment (LA)*
9460 Wilshire Blvd Fl 7
Beverly Hills, CA 90212-2713, USA

Mulligan, Sean (Athlete, Baseball Player)
24474 Eastgate
Diamond Bar, CA 91765-4626, USA

Mulligan, Wayne (Athlete, Football Player)
2410 the Haul Over
Johns Island, SC 29455-6103, USA

Mulliken, William (Bill) (Swimmer)
4216 N Keeler Ave
Chicago, IL 60641-2271, USA

Mullin, Chris (Athlete, Basketball Player, Olympic Athlete)
116 Laurelwood Dr
Danville, CA 94506-1408, USA

Mullin, J Stanley (Skier)
Sheppard Mullin Richter Hampton
333 S Hope St Fl 43
Los Angeles, CA 90071-1422, USA

Mulliniks, Rance (Athlete, Baseball Player)
2614 S Peppertree St
Visalia, CA 93277-5507, USA

Mullins, Eric (Athlete, Football Player)
3249 Parkwood Dr
Houston, TX 77021-1136, USA

Mullins, Fran (Athlete, Baseball Player)
9226 Ritenour Ct
Lone Tree, CO 80124-8971, USA

Mullins, Gerry (Athlete, Football Player)
1108 Mohawk Rd
Mc Donald, PA 15057-2552, USA

Mullins, Greg (Athlete, Baseball Player)
PO Box 443
Florahome, FL 32140-0443, USA

Mullins, Jeff (Athlete, Basketball Player, Olympic Athlete)
8866 N Sea Oaks Way Apt 202
Vero Beach, FL 32963-4195, USA

Mullins, Shawn (Musician, Songwriter, Writer)
High Road
751 Bridgeway Fl 2
Sausalito, CA 94965-2174, USA

Mullins, Terry (Race Car Driver)
105 Artesia Dr
Oak Ridge, TN 37830-7818, USA

Mulloy, Gardner (Tennis Player)
800 NW 9th Ave
Miami, FL 33136-3006, USA

Muloin, Wayne (Athlete, Hockey Player)
2991 Hayes St
Avon, OH 44011-2178, USA

Mulroney, Dermot (Actor)
c/o Stephen Huvane *Slate Public Relations*
9000 W Sunset Blvd Ste 915
West Hollywood, CA 90069-5809, USA

Mulva, James J (Business Person)
Conoco/Philips Inc
600 N Dairy Ashford Rd
Houston, TX 77079-1100, USA

Mulvaney, Mick (Congressman, Politician)
1004 Longworth Hob
Washington, DC 20515-1703, USA

Mulvenna, Glenn (Athlete, Hockey Player)
1480 Kilrush Dr
Ormond Beach, FL 32174-2882, USA

Mulvey, Grant (Athlete, Hockey Player)
491 S Hampshire Ave
Elmhurst, IL 60126-4105, USA

Mulvey, Kevin (Athlete, Baseball Player)
24 Eric Ct
Parlin, NJ 08859-1159, USA

Mulvey, Paul (Athlete, Hockey Player)
8009 Oak Hollow Ln
Fairfax Station, VA 22039-2651, USA

Mulvey, Peter (Musician)
c/o Staff Member *Young / Hunter Management*
350 Massachusetts Ave # 230
Arlington, MA 02474-6713, USA

Mumba, Samantha (Actor, Musician)
c/o Jeff Morrone *Intellectual Artists Management*
10585 Santa Monica Blvd Ste 135
Los Angeles, CA 90025-6392, USA

Mumley, Nick (Athlete, Football Player)
1432 Audubon Dr
Columbus, IN 47203-1432, USA

Mumphord, Lloyd (Athlete, Football Player)
2316 Mumphord St
Victoria, TX 77901-7750, USA

Mumphrey, Jerry (Athlete, Baseball Player)
7709 FM 850
Tyler, TX 75705-2135, USA

Mumy, Bill (Actor)
11333 Moorpark St
PO Box 433
North Hollywood, CA 91602-2618, USA

Mumy, Liliana (Actor)
c/o Meredith Fine *Coast to Coast Talent Group*
3350 Barham Blvd
Los Angeles, CA 90068-1404, USA

Munchak, Michael A (Mike) (Athlete, Football Player)
9155 Saddlebow Dr
Brentwood, TN 37027-6060, USA

Muncrief, Kevin (Athlete, Golfer)
939 S Flood Ave
Norman, OK 73069-4504, USA

Mundae, Misty (Actor)
PO Box 447
Ringwood, NJ 07456-0447

Mundie, Craig (Business Person)
3 Centerpointe Dr Ste 300
Waggener Edstrom Worldwide - Rapid Response Team
Lake Oswego, OR 97035-8663

Muni, Craig (Athlete, Hockey Player)
37 Greenbriar Dr
Lancaster, NY 14086-1037, USA

Muniz, Frankie (Actor)
c/o Jeff Kolodny *Paradigm (LA)*
360 N Crescent Dr
North Bldg
Beverly Hills, CA 90210-4874, USA

Muniz, Manuel (Athlete, Baseball Player)
PO Box 6301
Caguas, PR 00726-6301, USA

Munk, Chris (Athlete, Basketball Player)
14 Hillview Ct
San Francisco, CA 94124-2487, USA

Munn, Allison (Actor)
c/o Steve Caserta *Sanders Armstrong Caserta*
2120 Colorado Ave Ste 120
Santa Monica, CA 90404-3561, USA

Munn, Jeff (Athlete, Baseball Player)
7055 S Kachina Dr
Tempe, AZ 85283-4268, USA

Munn, Olivia (Actor, Talk Show Host)
c/o David (Dave) Fleming *Mosaic Media Group*
9200 W Sunset Blvd Ste 10
West Hollywood, CA 90069-3608, USA

Munnerlyn, Captain (Athlete, Football Player)
c/o Hadley Engelhard *Enter-Sports Management*
5 Concourse Pkwy Ste 3000
Atlanta, GA 30328-7106, USA

Munninghoff, Scott (Athlete, Baseball Player)
866 Laverty Ln
Cincinnati, OH 45230-3558, USA

Munos, Maria (Television Host)
c/o Staff Member *Entertainment Tonight (ET)*
4024 Radford Ave
Studio City, CA 91604-2101, USA

Munoz, Bobby (Athlete, Baseball Player)
9040 NW 20th St
Pembroke Pines, FL 33024-3211, USA

Munoz, M Anthony (Athlete, Football Player, Sportscaster)
6529 Irwin Simpson Rd
Mason, OH 45040-9285, USA

Munoz, Mike (Athlete, Baseball Player)
1000 Carroll Meadows Ct
Southlake, TX 76092-3830, USA

Munoz, Oscar (Athlete, Baseball Player)
14161 Leaning Pine Dr
Miami Lakes, FL 33014-2512, USA

Munro, Lochlyn (Actor)
International Creative Mgmt
10250 Constellation Blvd Fl 1
Los Angeles, CA 90067-6241, USA

Munro, Peter (Athlete, Baseball Player)
4311 Westmoreland St
Little Neck, NY 11363-1943, USA

Munroe, George (Athlete, Basketball Player)
870 United Nations Plz Apt 13E
New York, NY 10017-1824, USA

Munson, Eric (Athlete, Baseball Player)
2640 Becker Ct
Dubuque, IA 52001-1607, USA

Munson, John (Musician)
Monterey Peninsula Artists
509 Hartnell St
Monterey, CA 93940-2825, USA

Munter, Leilani (Race Car Driver)
Maia Motorsports
PO Box 3355
Memphis, NC 38117, USA

Munter, Scott (Athlete, Baseball Player)
13024 Jessie Ave
Omaha, NE 68164-1375, USA

Muppets, The
PO Box 20750
New York, NY 10023-1488

Mura, Steve (Athlete, Baseball Player)
31892 Old Oak Rd
Trabuco Canyon, CA 92679-3245, USA

Muransky, Ed (Athlete, Football Player)
16221 Villarreal De Avila
Tampa, FL 33613-1083, USA

Murchison, Ira (Athlete, Track Athlete)
10113 S Sangamon St
Chicago, IL 60643-2228, USA

Murchison, Lee (Athlete, Football Player)
1061 N Pilgrim St
Stockton, CA 95205-4112, USA

Murciano, Jr, Enrique (Actor)
c/o Ilene Feldman *LBI Entertainment*
2000 Avenue of the Stars
Floor 3, North Tower
Los Angeles, CA 90067-4700, USA

Murdoch, Rupert (Business Person, Publisher)
1 Madison Ave
New York, NY 10010-3603, USA

Murdoch, Sarah (Actor)
c/o Staff Member *William Morris Endeavor (LA)*
9601 Wilshire Blvd
Beverly Hills, CA 90210-5213, USA

Murdoch, Stuart (Musician, Songwriter, Writer)
Legends of 21st Century
7 Trinity Row
Florence, MA 01062-1931, USA

Murdock, David H (Business Person)
Dole Food Company
PO Box 5700
Westlake Village, CA 91359-5700, USA

Murdock, George P (Doctor)
Wynnewood Plaza
#107
Wynnewood, PA 19096, USA

Murdock, Guy (Athlete, Football Player)
106 Medinah Ln
Tower Lakes, IL 60010-1350, USA

Murdock, Rupert (Publisher)
1330 Angelo Dr
Beverly Hills, CA 90210-2016, USA

Murdock, Shirley (Musician)
Millennium Entertainment Group
1319 5th Ave N
Nashville, TN 37208-2725, USA

Muresan, Georghe (Actor, Basketball Player)
New Jersey Nets
390 Murray Hill Pkwy
East Rutherford, NJ 07073-2109, USA

Muresan, Gheorghe
10913 Burbank Dr
Potomac, MD 20854-1559

Murgatroyd, Peta (Dancer)
c/o Staff Member *Continuum Entertainment*
303 Park Ave S Ste 1220
New York, NY 10010-3601, USA

Muris, Timothy (Government Official)
Federal Trade Commission
Pennsylvania Ave & 6th St NW
Washington, DC 20580-0001, USA

Murkowsk, Frank (Politician)
232 S Carolina Ave SE
Washington, DC 20003-1940, USA

Murkowski, Lisa (Politician)
232 S Carolina Ave SE
Washington, DC 20003-1940, USA

Murley, Matt (Athlete, Hockey Player)
32 Hialeah Dr
Troy, NY 12182-9770, USA

Murphey, Michael Martin (Musician, Songwriter, Writer)
Wildfire Productions
PO Box 450
Ranchos De Taos, NM 87557-0450, USA

Murphy, Ben (Actor)
2690 Rambla Pacifico
Malibu, CA 90265-3423, USA

Murphy, Bill (Athlete, Football Player)
Excel Communications
6411 SW 25th St
Miramar, FL 33023-2829, USA

Murphy, Billy (Athlete, Baseball Player)
5309 66th Avenue Ct W
University Place, WA 98467-2231, USA

Murphy, Bob (Athlete, Golfer)
12005 Dunes Rd
Boynton Beach, FL 33436-5508, USA

Murphy, Bob (Baseball Player, Sportscaster)
New York Mets
220 Coral Cay Ter
Palm Beach Gardens, FL 33418-4003, USA

Murphy, Calvin (Athlete, Basketball Player)
8218 Cliffshire Ct
Houston, TX 77083-6526, USA

Murphy, Carolyn (Model)
c/o Staff Member *IMG World (NY)*
200 5th Ave Bsmt 7
New York, NY 10010-3312, USA

Murphy, Caryle M (Journalist)
Washington Post
Editorial Dept
1150 15th St NW
Washington, DC 20071-0001, USA

Murphy, Charles Q (Actor)
c/o Lorrie Bartlett *ICM Partners (LA)*
10250 Constellation Blvd Fl 7
Los Angeles, CA 90067-6207, USA

Murphy, Charles S (Government Official)
100 Bluff View Dr Apt 503C
Belleair Bluffs, FL 33770-1376, USA

Murphy, Cillian (Actor)
c/o Craig Bankey *Craig Bankey Public Relations*
9350 Wilshire Blvd Ste 450
Beverly Hills, CA 90212-3230, USA

Murphy, Dale (Athlete, Baseball Player)
467 Aspen Ridge Ln
Alpine, UT 84004-1223, USA

Murphy, Dan (Athlete, Baseball Player)
19661 Symeron Rd
Apple Valley, CA 92307-4736, USA

Murphy, Daniel
2878 Dickie Ct
Jacksonville, FL 32216-5397, USA

Murphy, Danny (Actor)
c/o Staff Member *Kazarian, Measures, Ruskin & Associates (LA)*
11969 Ventura Blvd Fl 3
Studio City, CA 91604-2630, USA

Murphy, Danny (Athlete, Baseball Player)
120 N Ocean Blvd Aot S-4
Delray Beach, FL 33483-7013, USA

Murphy, David (Athlete, Baseball Player)
3708 Sunrise Ranch Rd
Southlake, TX 76092-2055, USA

Murphy, David Lee (Musician)
c/o Staff Member *Agency for the Performing Arts (APA-LA)*
405 S Beverly Dr Ste 500
Beverly Hills, CA 90212-4425, USA

Murphy, Dennis A (Athlete, Hockey Player)
22790 Kentfield St
Grand Terrace, CA 92313-5763, USA

Murphy, Dick (Athlete, Baseball Player)
6890 Connie Dr
Avon, IN 46123-8532, USA

Murphy, Donna (Actor, Musician)
Gerson Saines
250 W 57th St Ste 2303
New York, NY 10107-2399, USA

Murphy, Donnie (Athlete, Baseball Player)
10449 E Helm Dr
Scottsdale, AZ 85255-8578, USA

Murphy, Dwayne (Athlete, Baseball Player)
1811 S Karen Dr
Chandler, AZ 85286-6350, USA

Murphy, Ed (Basketball Player, Coach)
University of Mississippi
Smith Coliseum
University, MS 38677, USA

Murphy, Eddie (Actor, Comedian)
19 Beverly Park Cir
Beverly Hills, CA 90210, USA

Murphy, Erin (Actor)
c/o Staff Member *James/Levy Management Inc*
3500 W Olive Ave Ste 1470
Burbank, CA 91505-5514, USA

Murphy, Gord (Athlete, Hockey Player)
Florida Panthers
1 Panther Pkwy
Attn: Coaching Staff
Sunrise, FL 33323-5315, USA

Murphy, Gord (Athlete, Hockey Player)
10041 Cartgate Ct
Dublin, OH 43017-8865, USA

Murphy, Joe (Athlete, Hockey Player)
10292 Horton Rd
Goodrich, MI 48438-9473, USA

Murphy, Lawrence T (Larry) (Athlete, Hockey Player)
Detroit Red Wings
600 Civic Center Dr
Detroit, MI 48226-4419, USA

Murphy, Mark (Athlete, Football Player)
736 Michigan Ave
Evanston, IL 60202-2512, USA

Murphy, Mark H (Musician)
Prince/SF Productions
1450 Southgate Ave Apt 206
Daly City, CA 94015-4021, USA

Murphy, Mark S (Athlete, Football Player)
1020 Ruby St NW
Hartville, OH 44632-9651, USA

Murphy, Mary (Athlete, Golfer)
1069 Meda St
Memphis, TN 38104-5819, USA

Murphy, Mary (Dancer, Reality Star)
Champion Ballroom Academy
3580 5th Ave
San Diego, CA 92103-5017, USA

Murphy, Michael Martin
4077 State Highway 14
Ranchos De Taos, NM 87557

Murphy, Rob (Athlete, Baseball Player)
PO Box 1996
Stuart, FL 34995-1996, USA

Murphy, Roisin (Musician)
c/o Staff Member *Spectrum*
9107 Wilshire Blvd Ste 450
Beverly Hills, CA 90210-5535, USA

Murphy, Ron (Athlete, Basketball Player)
14800 Hanover Pike
Upperco, MD 21155-9735, USA

Murphy, Rosemary (Actor)
220 E 73rd St
New York, NY 10021-4319, USA

Murphy, Ryan (Producer)
Ryan Murphy Productions
5555 Melrose Ave
Chevalier Bldg
Los Angeles, CA 90038-3989, USA

Murphy, Sean (Athlete, Golfer)
1004 June Pl
Lovington, NM 88260-4521, USA

Murphy, Terry (Journalist)
77 W 66th St
New York, NY 10023-6201, USA

Murphy, Tim (Congressman, Politician)
322 Cannon Hob
Washington, DC 20515-4602, USA

Murphy, Tod (Athlete, Basketball Player)
23 Parsons Hill Rd
Wenham, MA 01984-1823, USA

Murphy, Tom (Athlete, Baseball Player)
26561 Via Sacramento
Capistrano Beach, CA 92624-1337, USA

Murphy, Tommy (Athlete, Baseball Player)
45 Cedar Cir
Boynton Beach, FL 33436-9117, USA

Murphy, Troy (Basketball Player)
404 W Mountain Rd
Sparta, NJ 07871-3532, USA

Murray, Aaron (Athlete, Football Player)
c/o Pat Dye Jr *SportsTrust Advisors (GA)*
3340 Peachtree Rd NE Fl 16
Atlanta, GA 30326-1000, USA

Murray, Aj (Athlete, Baseball Player)
2154 E 4500 S
Vernal, UT 84078-9207, USA

Murray, Bill (Actor, Comedian)
1414 Thompson Ave
Sullivans Island, SC 29482-9760, USA

Murray, Bob (Athlete, Hockey Player)
Anaheim Ducks
2695 E Katella Ave
Attn: General Manager
Anaheim, CA 92806-5904, USA

Murray, Bob (Athlete, Hockey Player)
445 S Bridge View Dr
Anaheim, CA 92808-1346, USA

Murray, Brain Doyle (Actor)
Abrams Artists
9200 W Sunset Blvd Ste 1125
West Hollywood, CA 90069-3610, USA

Murray, Calvin (Athlete, Baseball Player, Olympic Athlete)
17434 Courtney Pine Cir
Spring, TX 77379-8505, USA

Murray, Chad Michael (Actor)
5327 Coldwater Canyon Ave Apt C
Sherman Oaks, CA 91401-6141, USA

Murray, Chad Micheal (Actor)
c/o JoAnne Colonna *Brillstein Entertainment Partners (LA)*
9150 Wilshire Blvd Ste 350
Beverly Hills, CA 90212-3453, USA

Murray, Cherry A (Business Person, Physicist)
700 Mountain Ave
New Providence, NJ 07974-1208, USA

Murray, Dale (Athlete, Baseball Player)
5695 FM 2718
Yorktown, TX 78164-1939, USA

Murray, Dan (Athlete, Baseball Player)
4312 W 78th St
Prairie Village, KS 66208-4352, USA

Murray, Dan (Athlete, Football Player)
9 Washington Rd
Ogdensburg, NJ 07439-1036, USA

Murray, David K (Musician)
Joel Chriss
300 Mercer St Apt 3J
New York, NY 10003-6732, USA

Murray, DeMarco (Athlete, Football Player)
4848 Lemmon Ave Ste 100-504
Dallas, TX 75219-1400, USA

Murray, Don (Actor)
1201 La Patera Canyon Rd
Goleta, CA 93117-1548, USA

Murray, Doug (Cartoonist)
Marvel Comic Group
10 E 40th St # 900
New York, NY 10016-0200, USA

Murray, Eddie C (Athlete, Baseball Player)
15609 Bronco Dr
Canyon Country, CA 91387-4717, USA

Murray, Edward P (Eddie) (Athlete,
Football Player)
1070 Forest Bay Dr
Waterford, MI 48328-4284, USA

Murray, Glen (Athlete, Hockey Player)
1320 Loth St
Manhattan Beach, CA 90266, USA

Murray, Glenn (Athlete, Baseball Player)
2 Spalding St
Nashua, NH 03060-4737, USA

Murray, Heath (Athlete, Baseball Player)
2605 Greenlawn Dr
Troy, OH 45373-4362, USA

Murray, Jaime (Actor)
c/o Lena Roklin *Luber Roklin
Management*
5815 W Sunset Blvd Ste 206
Los Angeles, CA 90028-6481, USA

Murray, Joe (Athlete, Football Player)
12900 Ridgemoor Dr
Prospect, KY 40059-8195, USA

Murray, Joel
PO Box 5617
Beverly Hills, CA 90209-5617

Murray, Jonathan (Producer)
c/o Staff Member *Bunim/Murray
Productions*
6007 Sepulveda Blvd
Van Nuys, CA 91411-2502, USA

Murray, Keith (Artist, Musician)
Famous Artists Agency
250 W 57th St
New York, NY 10107-0001, USA

Murray, Larry (Athlete, Baseball Player)
3200 Round Hill Dr
Hayward, CA 94542-2122, USA

Murray, Margaret (Baseball Player)
1320 S Desert Meadows Cir Apt 3109
Green Valley, AZ 85614-1832, USA

Murray, Marty (Athlete, Hockey Player)
1301 34th Ave SW
Minot, ND 58701-7221, USA

Murray, Matt (Athlete, Baseball Player)
109 Greenwood Ave
Swampscott, MA 01907-2124, USA

Murray, Michael (Musician)
4436 Zeller Rd
Columbus, OH 43214-2620, USA

Murray, Mike (Athlete, Hockey Player)
4942 Fragrant Cloud Ln
Knoxville, TN 37918-8143, USA

Murray, Patty (Government Official,
Senator)
154 Russell Senate Office Building
Washington, DC 20510-0001, USA

Murray, Patty (Politician)
2419 8th Ave N Apt 301
Seattle, WA 98109-2285, USA

Murray, Peg (Actor)
800 Lighthouse Rd
Southold, NY 11971-2301, USA

Murray, Randy (Athlete, Hockey Player)
1016 68 Ave SW Ste 200
Calgary, AB T2V 4J2

Murray, Rem (Athlete, Hockey Player)
60593 Balmoral Way
Rochester, MI 48306-2064, USA

Murray, Rich (Athlete, Baseball Player)
435 E 108th St
Los Angeles, CA 90061-2507, USA

Murray, Rob (Athlete, Hockey Player)
Alaska Aces
724 E 15th Ave
Attn: Coaching Staff
Anchorage, AK 99501-5462, USA

Murray, Sean (Actor)
c/o Al Onorato *Unified Management*
4231 W National Ave
Burbank, CA 91505-4022, USA

Murray, Terence R (Terry) (Athlete,
Hockey Player)
11 Kirkwood Rd
Scarborough, ME 04074-9456, USA

Murray, terry (Athlete, Hockey Player)
Los Angeles Kings
1111 S Figueroa St Ste 3100
Attn Coaching Staff
Los Angeles, CA 90015-1333, USA

Murray, Tracy (Athlete, Basketball Player)
25519 Brassie Ln
La Verne, CA 91750-5918, USA

Murray, Troy (Athlete, Hockey Player)
409 6th Ave
La Grange, IL 60525-2439, USA

Murray, Troy (Athlete, Hockey Player)
Chicago Blackhawks
1901 W Madison St
Attn: Broadcast Dept
Chicago, IL 60612-2459, USA

Murray, Ty (Athlete, Rodeo Rider)
13741 Farm To Market 914
Stephenville, TX 76401, USA

Murray-Leslie, Alex (Musician)
K Records
924 Jefferson St SE
#101
Olympia, WA 98501, USA

Murrey, Dorie (Athlete, Basketball Player)
230 NE 178th St
Shoreline, WA 98155-3500, USA

Murro, Noam (Director)
c/o Staff Member *Management 360*
9111 Wilshire Blvd
Beverly Hills, CA 90210-5508, USA

Murtagh, Kate (Actor)
5104 Greenbush Ave
Sherman Oaks, CA 91423-1508, USA

Murton, Matt (Athlete, Baseball Player)
2304 Silver Palm Dr Apt 302
Kissimmee, FL 34747-2738, USA

Musberger, Brent
47 W 66th St
New York, NY 10023-6201

Musburger, Brent (Sportscaster)
286 Locha Dr
Jupiter, FL 33458-7733, USA

Muscarello, Carl
720 NW 71st Ave
Plantation, FL 33317-1125

Muse (Music Group)
c/o Cliff Burnstein *Q Prime Inc*
1140 Broadway Rm 1505
New York, NY 10001-7503, USA

Muser, Tony (Athlete, Baseball Player,
Coach)
11222 Martha Ann Dr
Los Alamitos, CA 90720-2956, USA

Musgrave, Bill (Athlete, Football Player)
2712 Pinebloom Way
Duluth, GA 30097-4094, USA

Musgrave, F Story (Astronaut)
8572 Sweetwater Trl
Kissimmee, FL 34747-1519, USA

Musgrave, F Story Dr (Astronaut)
8572 Sweetwater Trl
Kissimmee, FL 34747-1519, USA

Musgrave, Mandy (Actor)
c/o Adam Levine *Levine Okwu Erickson
Management*
2126 N Commonwealth Ave
Los Angeles, CA 90027-2118, USA

Musgrave, Spain (Athlete, Football Player)
9727 Mount Pisgah Rd Apt 811
Silver Spring, MD 20903-2011, USA

Musgrave, Ted (Race Car Driver)
175 Lakeside Dr E
Port Orange, FL 32128-6620, USA

Musgraves, Dennis (Athlete, Baseball
Player)
17100 N Highway 124
Centralia, MO 65240-3830, USA

Musgraves, Kacey (Musician)
c/o Staff Member *Sandbox Entertainment*
54 Music Sq E Ste 200
Nashville, TN 37203-4360, USA

Musgrove, Spain (Athlete, Football Player)
2350 Deckman Ln
Silver Spring, MD 20906-2266, USA

Music, The (Music Group)
c/o Staff Member *Paradigm (Monterey)*
404 W Franklin St
Monterey, CA 93940-2303, USA

Musiq (Musician)
Def Soul Records
825 8th Ave # 2700
New York, NY 10019-7416, USA

Musiq Soulchild (Music Group)
c/o Staff Member *Paradigm (Monterey)*
404 W Franklin St
Monterey, CA 93940-2303, USA

Musk, Elon (Business Person)
SpaceX
1 Rocket Rd
Hawthorne, CA 90250-6844, USA

Musker, John (Animator, Director)
c/o Staff Member *Creative Artists Agency
(CAA-LA)*
2000 Avenue of the Stars Ste 100
Los Angeles, CA 90067-4705, USA

Musselman, Jeff (Athlete, Baseball Player)
1842 Port Tiffin Pl
Newport Beach, CA 92660-7121, USA

Musselman, Ron (Athlete, Baseball Player)
5313 Autumn Dr
Wilmington, NC 28409-5701, USA

Musselwhite, Charlie (Musician)
c/o Kevin Morrow *Morrow Management*
5003 Westpark Dr Unit 102
North Hollywood, CA 91601-3612, USA

Musser, Neal (Athlete, Baseball Player)
6140 NW Gaylord Ter
Port Saint Lucie, FL 34986-3766, USA

Mussill, Barney (Athlete, Baseball Player)
912 Moorland Dr
Grosse Pointe Woods, MI 48236-1131,
USA

Mussina, Mike (Athlete, Baseball Player)
737 White Church Rd
Muncy, PA 17756-8004, USA

Musso, John (Athlete, Football Player)
242 E 3rd St
Hinsdale, IL 60521-4221, USA

Musso, Mitchel (Actor)
c/o Elissa Leeds-Fickman *Reel Talent
Management*
PO Box 491035
Los Angeles, CA 90049-9035, USA

Musson, Ron (Race Car Driver)
Motorsports HOF
PO Box 194
Novi, MI 48376-0194, USA

Must (Music Group)
c/o Staff Member *Wind-up Records*
72 Madison Ave Fl 8
New York, NY 10016-8731, USA

Mustaf, Jerrod (Athlete, Basketball Player)
7724 Hanover Pkwy Apt 302
Greenbelt, MD 20770-2625, USA

Mustafa, Isaiah (Actor)
c/o Siri Garber *Platform Public Relations*
2666 N Beachwood Dr
Los Angeles, CA 90068-2308, USA

Mustaine, Dave (Musician)
ESP Mgmt
838 N Doheny Dr Apt 302
West Hollywood, CA 90069-4849, USA

Muster, Brad (Athlete, Football Player)
2017 Stony Oak Ct
Santa Rosa, CA 95403-0912, USA

Muster, Thomas (Tennis Player)
370 Felter Ave
Hewlett, NY 11557-1132, USA

Musto, Michael (Writer)
Village Voice
80 Maiden Ln Rm 2105
New York, NY 10038-4893

Mutchnick, Max (Producer)
c/o Staff Member *KoMut Entertainment*
300 Television Plz
Burbank, CA 91505, USA

Muth, Ellen (Actor)
c/o Barbara Gale *Envoy Entertainment*
2637 Centinela Ave Apt 8
Santa Monica, CA 90405-3162, USA

Muth, Rene (Coach)
Pennsylvania State University
Athletic Dept
University Park, PA 16802, USA

Mutis, Jeff (Athlete, Baseball Player)
630 E Wyoming St
C/O Thomas Mutis
Allentown, PA 18103-3536, USA

Mutombo, Dikembe (Athlete, Basketball Player)
4787 Northside Dr
Atlanta, GA 30327-4551, USA

Mutscheller, Jim (Athlete, Football Player)
12350 Rosslare Ridge Rd Unit 102
Lutherville Timonium, MD 21093-8233, USA

Muxworthy, Jake (Actor)
c/o Staff Member *United Talent Agency (UTA-LA)*
9336 Civic Center Dr
Beverly Hills, CA 90210-3604, USA

Muzzatti, Jason (Athlete, Hockey Player)
4581 Dunmorrow Dr
Okemos, MI 48864-1256, USA

M. Velazquez, Nydia (Congressman, Politician)
2302 Rayburn Hob
Washington, DC 20515-4801, USA

Mwine, Ntare (Actor)
c/o August Kammer *TalentWorks (LA)*
3500 W Olive Ave Ste 1400
Burbank, CA 91505-5512, USA

Mya (Actor, Musician)
c/o Stephen Ford *Diva Central Inc*
7510 W Sunset Blvd Ste 1445
Los Angeles, CA 90046-3408, USA

My Chemical Romance (Music Group)
c/o Matt Galle *Paradigm (NY)*
360 Park Ave S Fl 16
New York, NY 10010-1716, USA

Mycoskie, Blake (Business Person)
c/o Elise Freimuth *PMK/BNC Public Relations (PMK-LA)*
8687 Melrose Ave Ste 8
West Hollywood, CA 90069-5746, USA

Myer, Steve (Athlete, Football Player)
23709 S Harmony Way
Chandler, AZ 85248-6022, USA

Myers, A Maurice (Business Person)
Waste Management Inc
1001 Fannin St Ste 4000
Houston, TX 77002-6711, USA

Myers, Anne M (Religious Leader)
Church of the Brethren
1451 Dundee Ave
Elgin, IL 60120-1694, USA

Myers, Billie
PO Box 12198
Miami, FL 33101-2198

Myers, Brett (Athlete, Baseball Player)
312 S Pimlico St
Saint Augustine, FL 32092-3003, USA

Myers, Chris (Athlete, Football Player)
c/o Drew Rosenhaus *Rosenhaus Sports Representation*
6400 Allison Rd
Miami Beach, FL 33141-4540, USA

Myers, Cynthia (Actor, Model)
PO Box 10
Llano, CA 93544-0010, USA

Myers, Danny (Race Car Driver)
Childress Racing
PO Box 1189
Industrial Dr
Welcome, NC 27374-1189, USA

Myers, Dave (Athlete, Baseball Player)
4221 71st Avenue Ct NW
Gig Harbor, WA 98335-6517, USA

Myers, Dee Dee (Actor, Writer)
c/o Ari Greenburg *William Morris Endeavor (LA)*
9601 Wilshire Blvd
Beverly Hills, CA 90210-5213, USA

Myers, Frank (Athlete, Football Player)
6603 Spring Branch Dr
Krum, TX 76249-7022, USA

Myers, Greg (Athlete, Baseball Player)
7917 Brasado Way
Riverside, CA 92508-8719, USA

Myers, Jack (Athlete, Football Player)
25 Biltmore Ln
Menlo Park, CA 94025-6686, USA

Myers, Jimmy (Athlete, Baseball Player)
1312 NW 14th Pl
Moore, OK 73170-1461, USA

Myers, Lisa (Correspondent)
NBC-TV
4001 Nebraska Ave NW
News Dept
Washington, DC 20016-2795, USA

Myers, Margaret J (Dee Dee) (Government Official)
Equal Time Show
1233 20th St NW Ste 302
Cbs-Tv
Washington, DC 20036-2482, USA

Myers, Mike (Actor, Comedian)
c/o Ina Treciokas *Slate Public Relations*
9000 W Sunset Blvd Ste 915
West Hollywood, CA 90069-5809, USA

Myers, Mike (Athlete, Baseball Player)
337 High Ridge Way
Castle Pines, CO 80108-3422, USA

Myers, Pete (Athlete, Basketball Player)
PO Box 101242
Chicago, IL 60610-8903, USA

Myers, Randy (Athlete, Baseball Player)
15525 NE Caples Rd
Brush Prairie, WA 98606-8504, USA

Myers, Robert (Bob) (Athlete)
c/o Staff Member *SFX Sports Management*
5335 Wisconsin Ave NW Ste 850
Washington, DC 20015-2052, USA

Myers, Rochelle (Writer)
3827 California St
San Francisco, CA 94118-1501, USA

Myers, Roderick (Rod) (Athlete, Baseball Player)
1816 S 3rd St
Conroe, TX 77301-5131, USA

Myers, Rodney (Rod) (Athlete, Baseball Player)
229 E Tanya Rd
Phoenix, AZ 85086-9253, USA

Myers, Russell (Cartoonist)
Tribune Media Services
435 N Michigan Ave Ste 1500
Chicago, IL 60611-4012, USA

Myers, Tikalsky Linda (Skier)
RR 5 Box 2651
Santa Fe, NM 87506, USA

Myers, Tom (Athlete, Football Player)
6015 Rapid Creek Ct
Kingwood, TX 77345-1954, USA

Myers Jr, Harry J (Publisher)
46 W Ranch Trl
Morrison, CO 80465-9504, USA

Myrah, Don (Athlete, Cycler, Olympic Athlete)
5291 Kentfield Dr
San Jose, CA 95124-5524, USA

Myrick, Daniel (Director)
Artisan Entertainment
2700 Colorado Ave
Santa Monica, CA 90404-3553, USA

Myrin, Arden (Actor)
c/o Steve Caserta *Sanders Armstrong Caserta*
2120 Colorado Ave Ste 120
Santa Monica, CA 90404-3561, USA

Myron, Vicki (Writer)
c/o Staff Member *Grand Central Publishing*
237 Park Ave
C/O Author Mail: (Author's Name)
New York, NY 10017-3140, USA

Myrow, Brian (Athlete, Baseball Player)
621 Crystal Brook Dr
Saginaw, TX 76179-0939, USA

Myrtle, Chip (Athlete, Football Player)
6010 S Lima Way
Englewood, CO 80111-5813, USA

Myslinski, Tom (Athlete, Football Player)
2842 Forest Lake Dr
Westlake, OH 44145-1780, USA

Mysterio, Rey (Wrestler)
c/o Kerry Rodgerson *World Wrestling Entertainment (WWE)*
1241 E Main St
Titan Towers
Stamford, CT 06902-3520, USA

Mystic (Music Group, Musician)
c/o Staff Member *General Entertainment*
PO Box 91868
Atlanta, GA 30364-1868, USA

Mystics
The88 Anador St.
Staten Island, NY 10303

Mystikal (Musician)
c/o Staff Member *ICM Partners (LA)*
10250 Constellation Blvd Fl 7
Los Angeles, CA 90067-6207, USA

Na, Li (Athlete, Tennis Player)
c/o Max Eisenbud *IMG Miami*
1500 S Douglas Rd # 230
Coral Gables, FL 33134-4108, USA

Nabe, Ricky (Actor)
c/o Staff Member *Envision Entertainment*
8840 Wilshire Blvd Fl 3
Beverly Hills, CA 90211-2606, USA

Naber, Jofin P (Swimmer)
PO Box 50107
Pasadena, CA 91115-0107, USA

Naber, John (Athlete, Olympic Athlete, Swimmer)
PNaber And Associates Inc PO Box 50107 O Box 50107
Pasadena, CA 91115, USA

Nabers, Drayton Jr (Business Person)
Protective Life Corp
2801 Highway 280 S Ofc
Birmingham, AL 35223-2488, USA

Nabholz, Chris (Athlete, Baseball Player)
2030 W Market St
Pottsville, PA 17901-1917, USA

Nabokov, Evgeni (Athlete, Hockey Player)
5763 Poppy Hills Pl # Pi
San Jose, CA 95138-2243, USA

Nabors, Jim (Actor, Musician)
PO Box 6364
Honolulu, HI 96816, USA

Nabors, Richard (Athlete, Football Player)
1625 Brighton Ct
Beaumont, TX 77706-3220, USA

Naccarato, Vin (Musician)
Paramount Entertainment
PO Box 12
Far Hills, NJ 07931-0012, USA

Nachamkin, Boris (Athlete, Basketball Player)
350 E 62nd St Apt 5J
New York, NY 10065-8261, USA

Nachbaur, Don (Athlete, Hockey Player)
671 Clermont Dr
Richland, WA 99352-9519, USA

Nachmanoff, Jeffrey (Director)
1963 Canyon Dr
Los Angeles, CA 90068-3604, USA

Nacincik, John (Athlete, Basketball Player)
591 Sawgrass Bridge Rd
Venice, FL 34292-4483, USA

Nadal, Rafael (Athlete, Tennis Player)
c/o Staff Member *ATP Tour*
201 Atp Tour Blvd
Ponte Vedra Beach, FL 32082-3211, USA

Nada Surf (Music Group)
c/o Staff Member *Paradigm (Monterey)*
404 W Franklin St
Monterey, CA 93940-2303, USA

Nadeau, Jerry (Race Car Driver)
192 Apple Hill Rd
Troutman, NC 28166-9570, USA

Nadel, Barbara (Writer)
c/o Staff Member *St Martins Press*
175 5th Ave Ste 400
Publicity Dept
New York, NY 10010-7848, USA

Nadel, Eric (Sportscaster)
10612 De Bercy Ct
Dallas, TX 75229-5331, USA

Nader, Michael (Actor)
28 E 10th St
New York, NY 10003-6201, USA

Nader, Ralph (Activist, Writer)
53 Hillside Ave
Winsted, CT 06098-1531, USA

Nadler, Jerrold (Congressman, Politician)
2334 Rayburn Hob
Washington, DC 20515-3208, USA

Nady, Xavier (Athlete, Baseball Player)
15671 Via Santa Pradera
San Diego, CA 92131-4314, USA

Naegle, Sue (Business Person)
HBO Entertainment
2500 Broadway Ste 400
Santa Monica, CA 90404-3176, USA

Naehring, Tim (Athlete, Baseball Player)
7300 Pinehurst Dr
Cincinnati, OH 45244-3272, USA

Naeole, Chris (Athlete, Football Player)
1314 Charter Ct E
Jacksonville, FL 32225-2658, USA

Nafziger, Dana A (Athlete, Football Player)
251 El Dorado Way
Pismo Beach, CA 93449-1535, USA

Nagahama, Kazu (Actor)
c/o Staff Member *Ology Entertainment*
9151 W Sunset Blvd
West Hollywood, CA 90069-3106, USA

Nagel, Craig (Athlete, Football Player)
222 Woodcrest Dr
Loveland, OH 45140-7772, USA

Nagel, Steven R (Astronaut)
3801 Eagle View Ct
Columbia, MO 65203-1064, USA

Nagelson, Russ (Rusty) (Athlete, Baseball Player)
4 Carriage Ct
Little Rock, AR 72211-2280, USA

Nageotte, Clint (Athlete, Baseball Player)
4700 Morningside Dr
Cleveland, OH 44109-4560, USA

Nagl, Miriam (Athlete, Golfer)
2120 Harbourside Dr Unit 616
Longboat Key, FL 34228-4261, USA

Nagle, Browning (Athlete, Football Player)
PO Box 436946
Louisville, KY 40253-6946, USA

Nagler, Gern (Athlete, Football Player)
73595 Agave Ln
Palm Desert, CA 92260-6685, USA

Nagobads, George (Athlete, Hockey Player)
5180 Circle Dr
Minneapolis, MN 55439-1401, USA

Nagra, Parminder (Actor)
2445 Lyric Ave
Los Angeles, CA 90027-4654, USA

Nagy, Charles (Athlete, Baseball Player, Olympic Athlete)
60 Robin Rd
Westbury, NY 11590-1104, USA

Nagy, Ladislav (Athlete, Hockey Player)
10628 E Meadowhill Dr
Scottsdale, AZ 85255-1734, USA

Nagy, Mike (Athlete, Baseball Player)
24 Nial Ra Ln
West Yarmouth, MA 02673, USA

Nagy, Steve (Athlete, Baseball Player)
2205 NE Ridgewood Dr
Poulsbo, WA 98370-8529, USA

Nahan, Stu (Sportscaster)
11274 Canton Dr
Studio City, CA 91604-4154, USA

Nahorodny, Bill (Athlete, Baseball Player)
1948 Rainbow Dr
Clearwater, FL 33765-3564, USA

Nahrgang, Jim (Athlete, Hockey Player)
14531 E Golden Eagle Blvd
Fountain Hills, AZ 85268-1221, USA

Naifeh, Steven W (Writer)
335 Sumter St SE
Aiken, SC 29801-4661, USA

Nail, David (Musician)
5180 Regent Dr
Nashville, TN 37220-1940, USA

Nailon, Lee (Athlete, Basketball Player)
1532 N Evergreen Ln Apt 4
Wichita, KS 67212-6222, USA

Naimoli, Vincent (Baseball Player)
Tampa Bay Devil Rays
16616 Villalenda De Avila
Tampa, FL 33613-5200, USA

Nair, Mira (Director)
c/o Staff Member *Mirabai Films*
27 W 24th St Ste 403
New York, NY 10010-3287, USA

Najarian, John S (Doctor)
University of Minnesota
Health Center
Surgery Dept
Minneapolis, MN 55455, USA

Najee (Musician)
Associated booking Corp
1995 Broadway # 501
New York, NY 10023-5882, USA

Najera, Eduardo (Basketball Player)
c/o Staff Member *Dallas Mavericks*
2909 Taylor St
Dallas, TX 75226-1909, USA

Najera, Rick (Actor)
c/o Michelle Grant *Grant Management*
1158 26th St # 414
Santa Monica, CA 90403-4698, USA

Najimy, Kathy (Actor, Comedian)
c/o Erica Tuchman *One Entertainment (NY)*
12 W 57th St PH
New York, NY 10019-3900, USA

Nakama, Keo (Swimmer)
1344 9th Ave
Honolulu, HI 96816-2615, USA

Nakano, Shinji (Race Car Driver)
Fernandez Racing
6950 Guion Rd # 51
Indianapolis, IN 46268-2576, USA

Naked, Bif (Musician)
Crazed Mgmt
PO Box 779
New Hope, PA 18938-0779, USA

Nalder, Eric C (Journalist)
Seattle Times
1000 Denny Way # 5
Editorial Dept
Seattle, WA 98109-5340, USA

Nalen, Tom (Athlete, Football Player)
PO Box 4864
Englewood, CO 80155-4864, USA

Nalick, Anna (Musician)
Lippman Entertainment
23586 Calabasas Rd Ste 208
Calabasas, CA 91302-1361, USA

Nall, Benita Krista (Actor)
c/o Staff Member *Main Title Entertainment*
8383 Wilshire Blvd Ste 408
Beverly Hills, CA 90211-2435, USA

Nall, N Anita (Swimmer)
PO Box 872505
Tempe, AZ 85287-2505, USA

Nalle, Karen Dotrice (Actor)
501 Sadie Rd
Topanga, CA 90290-3432, USA

Nam, Leonardo (Actor)
c/o Staff Member *Overbrook Entertainment*
10202 Washington Blvd
Culver City, CA 90232-3119, USA

Namath, Joe (Actor, Athlete, Football Player)
Joe Namath Camp
PO Box 515
Old Saybrook, CT 06475-0515, USA

Namestnikov, Evgeny (Athlete, Hockey Player)
3110 Bay Front Ct
Waterford, MI 48328-1696, USA

Na-Ming
9903 Santa Monica Blvd # 575
Beverly Hills, CA 90212-1671

Nance, John J (Writer)
4512 S 8th St
Tacoma, WA 98405-1208, USA

Nance, Shane (Athlete, Baseball Player)
3403 Harbour Breeze Ln
Pearland, TX 77584-7958, USA

Nance, Todd (Musician)
Brown Cat Inc
400 Foundry St
Athens, GA 30601-2623, USA

Nancy, Ted L
c/o Daniel Strone *Trident Media Group LLC*
41 Madison Ave Fl 36
New York, NY 10010-2257, USA

Nanne, Lou (Athlete, Hockey Player, Olympic Athlete)
6982 Tupa Dr
Minneapolis, MN 55439-1641, USA

Nantucket
250 N Kepler Rd Deland
Flint, CA 33724

Nantz, Jim (Sportscaster)
2919 Rosemary Park Ln
Houston, TX 77082-6806, USA

Napier, Hugo
2207 N Beachwood Dr
Los Angeles, CA 90068-2903

Naples, Al (Athlete, Baseball Player)
99 Nickerson Rd
Orleans, MA 02653-3314, USA

Napoleon, Ed (Athlete, Baseball Player)
1312 73rd St NW
Bradenton, FL 34209-1155, USA

Napoli, Mike (Athlete, Baseball Player)
c/o Staff Member *Los Angeles Dodgers (LA Dodgers)*
1000 Elysian Park Ave
Los Angeles, CA 90012-1112, USA

Naponic, Robert (Athlete, Football Player)
10807 Timberglen Dr
Houston, TX 77024-6808, USA

Naragon, Hal (Athlete, Baseball Player)
1521 Hagey Dr
Barberton, OH 44203-7724, USA

Narain, Nicole (Actor)
8033 W Sunset Blvd # 224
Los Angeles, CA 90046-2401

Naranjo, Monica (Musician)
c/o Staff Member *Sony Music Miami*
605 Lincoln Rd Ste 700
Miami Beach, FL 33139-2901, USA

Nardelli, Michael (Actor)
2241 Sunset Plaza Dr
Los Angeles, CA 90069-1206, USA

Nardini, Thomas (Tom) (Actor)
139 Beach Ave
Madison, CT 06443-2854, USA

Narducci, Katherine
2843 Waterbury Ave
Bronx, NY 10461-6150

Narducci, Tim (Musician)
Artists Group International
9560 Wilshire Blvd Ste 400
Beverly Hills, CA 90212-2442, USA

Narita, Hiro (Cinematographer)
2262 Magnolia Ave
Petaluma, CA 94952-1631, USA

Narita, Richard
8831 Sunset Blvd # 304
West Hollywood, CA 90069

Narron, Jerry (Athlete, Baseball Player, Coach)
304 Ashworth Dr
Goldsboro, NC 27530-5563, USA

Narron, Sam (Athlete, Baseball Player)
101 Mill Pi
Goldsboro, NC 27534, USA

Narveson, Chris (Athlete, Baseball Player)
5525 E Thomas Rd Unit Hl
Phoenix, AZ 85018-8126, USA

Narz, Jack (Television Host)
1906 Beverly Pl
Beverly Hills, CA 90210, USA

Nas (Musician)
30 Vintage Ct
McDonough, GA 30253-4246, USA

Nash, Charles F (Cotton) (Athlete, Basketball Player)
600 Summershade Cir
Lexington, KY 40502-2723, USA

Nash, Dick (Musician)
EMI Music
1750 Vine St
Capital Records
Los Angeles, CA 90028-5209, USA

Nash, Graham (Musician, Songwriter)
709 E Colorado Blvd Ste 220
Pasadena, CA 91101-2125, USA

Nash, Jamia Simone (Actor)
c/o Staff Member *Carson-Adler Agency*
250 W 57th St Ste 2128
New York, NY 10107-2104, USA

Nash, Jim (Athlete, Baseball Player)
4383 White Surrey Dr NW
Kennesaw, GA 30144-5106, USA

Nash, Joe (Athlete, Football Player)
29 Vermont St
West Roxbury, MA 02132-2336, USA

Nash, Kate (Musician)
c/o Margrit Polak *Margrit Polak Management*
1920 Hillhurst Ave Ste 405
Los Angeles, CA 90027-2712, USA

Nash, Keisha
344 E 59th St
New York, NY 10022-1593

Nash, Kevin (Wrestler)
c/o Andrew Stawiarski *ADS Management*
269 S Beverly Dr # 441
Beverly Hills, CA 90212-3851, USA

Nash, Leigh (Musician)
c/o Staff Member *Paradigm (Monterey)*
404 W Franklin St
Monterey, CA 93940-2303, USA

Nash, Niecy (Actor, Television Host)
19400 Kinzie St
Northridge, CA 91324-1622, USA

Nash, Noreen (Actor)
719 N Maple Dr
Beverly Hills, CA 90210-3480, USA

Nash, Richard
6024 Agapanthus Pl
Woodland Hills, CA 91367-7200

Nash, Rick (Athlete, Hockey Player)
c/o Staff Member *Columbus Blue Jackets*
200 W Nationwide Blvd Ste Level
Nationwide Arena
Columbus, OH 43215-2564, USA

Nash, Robert (Athlete, Basketball Player)
659 Kahiau Loop
Honolulu, HI 96821-2539, USA

Nash, Steve (Athlete, Basketball Player)
2903 Manhattan Ave
Manhattan Beach, CA 90266-2050, USA

Nash, Terius (The-Dream) (Musician)
c/o Staff Member *Island Def Jam Group*
825 8th Ave Fl 28
New York, NY 10019-7416, USA

Nash, Tyson (Athlete, Hockey Player)
17751 N 92nd Way
Scottsdale, AZ 85255-6025, USA

Nash, Tyson (Athlete, Hockey Player)
Phoenix Coyotes
6751 N Sunset Blvd Ste E200
Attn: Broadcast Dept
Glendale, AZ 85305-3158, USA

Nash, Wyatt (Actor)
c/o Atil Singh *Principal Entertainment (LA)*
9255 W Sunset Blvd Ste 500
West Hollywood, CA 90069-3301, USA

Nasland, Markus (Athlete, Hockey Player)
800 Griffiths Way
Vancouver, BC V6B 6G1, USA

Naslund, Ron (Athlete, Hockey Player, Olympic Athlete)
2600 Cheyenne Cir
Hopkins, MN 55305-2309, USA

Nasreddine, Alain (Athlete, Hockey Player)
35 Brians Pl
Wilkes Barre, PA 18702-7864, USA

Nasser, Jacques A (Business Person)
One Equity Partners
1st National Plz
Chicago, IL 60607, USA

Nassetta, Christopher (Business Person)
10410 Bellagio Rd
Los Angeles, CA 90077-3819, USA

Nassif, Paul (Doctor, Reality Star)
Spalding Drive Cosmetic Surgery & Dermatology
120 S Spalding Dr Ste 315
Beverly Hills, CA 90212-1836, USA

Nastu, Phil (Athlete, Baseball Player)
52 Stratfield Pl
Bridgeport, CT 06606-4002, USA

Natal, Bob (Athlete, Baseball Player)
3913 Cockrill Dr
McKinney, TX 75070-2413, USA

Natali, Vincenzo (Director)
c/o Philip Raskind *William Morris Endeavor (LA)*
9601 Wilshire Blvd
Beverly Hills, CA 90210-5213, USA

Natalie (Musician)
c/o Staff Member *Motown Records (NY)*
1755 Broadway Fl 7
New York, NY 10019-3743, USA

Nater, Swen (Athlete, Basketball Player)
4125 248th Ct SE
Issaquah, WA 98029-5754, USA

Nathan, Joe (Athlete, Baseball Player)
5235 Bent River Blvd
Knoxville, TN 37919-9352, USA

Nathan, Joseph A (Business Person)
Compuware Corp
1 Campus Martius
Detroit, MI 48226-5099, USA

Nathan, Tony C (Athlete, Coach, Football Coach, Football Player)
15110 Dunbarton Pl
Miami Lakes, FL 33016-1415, USA

Nathaniel (Popp), Bishop (Religious Leader)
Romanian Orthodox Episcopate
2522 Grey Tower Rd
Jackson, MI 49201-9120, USA

Nathanson, Jeff (Writer)
c/o Staff Member *United Talent Agency (UTA-LA)*
9336 Civic Center Dr
Beverly Hills, CA 90210-3604, USA

Nathanson, Matt (Musician)
70 Nebraska St
San Francisco, CA 94110-5719, USA

Nathanson, Roy (Musician)
Brad Simon Organization
122 E 57th St # 300
New York, NY 10022-2623, USA

Nation, Joey (Athlete, Baseball Player)
716 E Hillcrest Ln
Mustang, OK 73064-4262, USA

Natividad, Kitten (Actor)
c/o Siouxzan Perry *Girlwerks Management*
3395 E Camino Rojos
Palm Springs, CA 92262-5417, USA

Natowich, Andrew (Athlete, Football Player)
24 Lexington Ave
Brattleboro, VT 05301-6626, USA

Natsios, Andrew (Government Official)
US International Development Agency
320 21st NW
Washington, DC 20523-0002, USA

Natt, Calvin (Athlete, Basketball Player)
25201 E Indore Dr
Aurora, CO 80016-2189, USA

Nattiel, Ricky (Athlete, Football Player)
835 NW 119th St
Gainesville, FL 32606-0449, USA

Natural (Musician)
Official International Fan Club
PO Box 5097
Bellingham, WA 98227-5097, USA

Natyshak, Mike (Athlete, Hockey Player)
2005 Mount Vernon Ave
Toledo, OH 43607-1545, USA

Naudet, Jules (Producer)
c/o Staff Member *William Morris Endeavor (LA)*
9601 Wilshire Blvd
Beverly Hills, CA 90210-5213, USA

Nauert, Paul (Athlete, Baseball Player)
1201 Steeple Run
Lawrenceville, GA 30043-6354, USA

Naughton, David (Actor)
69930 Pomegranate Ln
Cathedral City, CA 92234-1728, USA

Naughton, James (Actor)
127 Valley Forge Rd
Weston, CT 06883-1914, USA

Naughton, Laurie (Actor)
c/o Bruce Smith *OmniPop Talent Group (LA)*
4605 Lankershim Blvd Ste 201
North Hollywood, CA 91602-1874, USA

Naughton, Naturi (Musician)
c/o Matt Luber *Luber Roklin Management*
5815 W Sunset Blvd Ste 206
Los Angeles, CA 90028-6481, USA

Naulis, Willie (Basketball Player)
Chuck & Willie's Auto Agency
13900 Hawthorne Blvd
Hawthorne, CA 90250, USA

Naulls, Willie (Athlete, Basketball Player)
6501 Orange St Apt 201
Los Angeles, CA 90048-4765, USA

Naulty, Dan (Athlete, Baseball Player)
23705 Via Del Rio
Yorba Linda, CA 92887-2717, USA

Naumenko, Gregg (Athlete, Hockey Player)
991 S Prospect Ave
Elmhurst, IL 60126-5030, USA

Naumoff, Paul (Athlete, Football Player)
932 Mohawk St
Columbus, OH 43206-2633, USA

Naum-Parker, Dorothy (Baseball Player)
2620 Bridlecreek Ln
Galesburg, IL 61401-5547, USA

Nause, Martha (Athlete, Golfer)
13206 Patterson Trl
Minocqua, WI 54548, USA

Nauta, Kate (Actor)
c/o Ben Press *Evolution Entertainment (LA)*
6500 Wilshire Blvd Ste 2200
Los Angeles, CA 90048-4942, USA

Nava, Daniel (Athlete, Baseball Player)
315 T Francis St
Redwood City, CA 94062, USA

Nava, Gregory (Director)
International Creative Mgmt
10250 Constellation Blvd Fl 1
Los Angeles, CA 90067-6241, USA

Navaira, Emilio (Musician)
c/o Staff Member *William Morris Endeavor (LA)*
9601 Wilshire Blvd
Beverly Hills, CA 90210-5213, USA

Navarez, Alfred (Musician)
MPI Talent
9255 W Sunset Blvd Ste 407
West Hollywood, CA 90069-3302, USA

Navarro, Dave (Musician)
1645 Vine St Apt 509
Los Angeles, CA 90028-8810, USA

Navarro, Dioner (Athlete, Baseball Player)
13243 Pike Lake Dr
Riverview, FL 33579-4039, USA

Navarro, Guillermo J (Cinematographer)
Lyons Sheldon Prosnit Agency
800 S Robertson Blvd Ste 6
Los Angeles, CA 90035-1635, USA

Navarro, Jaime (Athlete, Baseball Player)
8100 Oak Park Rd
Orlando, FL 32819-3266, USA

Navarro, Juan Carlos (Athlete, Basketball Player)
10545 Ashglen Cir S
Collierville, TN 38017-3660, USA

Navarro, Julio (Athlete, Baseball Player)
10-32 Calle 3
Santa Rosa
Bayamon, PR 00959-6612, USA

Navarro, Tito (Athlete, Baseball Player)
556 Calle Creuz
San Juan, PR 00923-1826, USA

Navayne, Kevin (Actor)
c/o Talon Outlaw *Outlaw Management Group*
9777 Wilshire Blvd Ste 918
Beverly Hills, CA 90212-1902, USA

Navies, Hannibal (Athlete, Football Player)
2891 Grey Moss Pass
Duluth, GA 30097-6272, USA

Navis, Hannibal (Athlete, Football Player)
4616 Rustling Woods Dr
Denver, NC 28037-5600, USA

Navratilova, Martina (Tennis Player)
2555 Collins Ave Apt 1711
Miami Beach, FL 33140-4777, USA

Naylor, Gloria (Writer)
One Way Productions
PO Box 2436
Key West, FL 33045-2436, USA

Naymenko, Gregg (Athlete)
2695 E Katella Ave
Anaheim, CA 92806-5904

Nayyar, Kunal (Actor)
c/o Jason Kim *Lovett Management*
1327 Brinkley Ave
Los Angeles, CA 90049-3619, USA

Nazarian, Sam (Business Person)
SBE Entertainment
5900 Wilshire Blvd Ste 3100
Los Angeles, CA 90036-5030, USA

N. Cicilline, David (Congressman, Politician)
128 Cannon Hob
Washington, DC 20515-1102, USA

Ndegeocello, Me'Shell (Musician)
Monetary Peninsula Artists
509 Hartnell St
Monterey, CA 93940-2825, USA

Ndegeocello, Michelle (Musician)
c/o Staff Member *Paradigm (Monterey)*
404 W Franklin St
Monterey, CA 93940-2303, USA

N'Dour, Youssou (Musician)
c/o Staff Member *Nonesuch Records*
75 Rockefeller Plz Fl 8
New York, NY 10019-6908, USA

Neagle, Denny (Athlete, Baseball Player)
2018 Haverford Dr
Crownsville, MD 21032-2234, USA

Neal, Blaine (Athlete, Baseball Player)
256 Dowdy Dr
Gibbstown, NJ 08027-1175, USA

Neal, Craig (Athlete, Basketball Player)
122 Wellesley Dr NE
Albuquerque, NM 87106-2129, USA

Neal, Curley (Athlete, Basketball Player)
1275 Regency Pl
Lake Mary, FL 32746-4339, USA

Neal, Doris (Athlete, Baseball Player)
477 NW 7th Ave
Webster, FL 33597-4746, USA

Neal, Dylan (Actor)
c/o Sara Schedeen *Metropolitan (MTA)*
4526 Wilshire Blvd
Los Angeles, CA 90010-3801, USA

Neal, Edwin (Actor)
501 W Powell Ln
Austin, TX 78753-5978, USA

Neal, Elise (Actor)
407 W 7th St Apt 329
San Pedro, CA 90731-3264, USA

Neal, Fred (Curly) (Basketball Player)
PO Box 915415
Longwood, FL 32791-5415, USA

Neal, Lloyd (Athlete, Basketball Player)
905 NE Mariners Loop
Portland, OR 97211-1574, USA

Neal, Lorenzo (Athlete, Football Player)
PO Box 4917
Fresno, CA 93744-4917, USA

Neal, Mike (Athlete, Football Player)
c/o Eugene Parker *Maximum Sports Management*
6435 W Jefferson Blvd # 197
Fort Wayne, IN 46804-6203, USA

Neal, Philip M (Business Person)
Avery Dennison Corp
207 N Goode Ave Fl 6
Glendale, CA 91203-1364, USA

Neal, T Daniel (Dan) (Athlete, Football Player)
711 Homestead Blvd
Louisville, KY 40207-3630, USA

Neale, Gary L (Business Person)
Northern Indiana Service
801 E 86th Ave
Merrillville, IN 46410-6271, USA

Neale, Harry (Athlete, Hockey Player)
224 Quail Hollow Ln
East Amherst, NY 14051-1634, USA

Nealon, Kevin (Actor, Comedian)
16105 Northfield St
Pacific Palisades, CA 90272-4263, USA

Nealy, Eddie (Athlete, Basketball Player)
702 Lightstone Dr
San Antonio, TX 78258-2305, USA

Neame, Christopher (Actor)
Borinstein Oreck Bogart
3172 Dona Susana Dr
Studio City, CA 91604-4356, USA

Near, Holly (Actor, Musician, Songwriter, Writer)
PO Box 236
Ukiah, CA 95482-0236, USA

Nearing, Merna (Baseball Player)
21079 W Good Hope Rd Apt D-1
Lannon, WI 53046, USA

Neary, Robert (Actor, Director)
c/o Lin Bickelmann *Encore Artists Management*
3815 W Olive Ave Ste 101
Burbank, CA 91505-4674, USA

Neaton, Pat (Athlete, Hockey Player)
3519 Olde Dominion Dr # 2
Brighton, MI 48114-4942, USA

Nebel, Dorothy Hoyt (Skier)
5340 Balfor Dr
Virginia Beach, VA 23464-2441, USA

Necciai, Ron (Athlete, Baseball Player)
6261 Overlook Ln
Belle Vernon, PA 15012-3928, USA

Nechaev, Victor (Athlete, Hockey Player)
1806 Twin Palms Dr
San Marino, CA 91108-2555, USA

Neck, Tommy (Athlete, Football Player)
2107 Marie Pl
Monroe, LA 71201-3413, USA

Neckar, Stanislav (Athlete, Hockey Player)
10255 Waterside Oaks Dr
Tampa, FL 33647-3194, USA

Necker, Stanislav (Athlete, Hockey Player)
10255 Waterside Oaks Dr
Tampa, FL 33647-3194, USA

Ned, Derrick (Athlete, Football Player)
430 Charles St
Eunice, LA 70535-4904, USA

Nedeljakova, Barbara (Actor)
Beverly Hecht Agency
6320 Canoga Ave Fl 15
C/O Robert Depp
Woodland Hills, CA 91367-2563, USA

Nedney, Joe (Athlete, Football Player)
121 Lauren Cir
Scotts Valley, CA 95066-3836, USA

Nedomansky, Vaclav (Athlete, Hockey Player)
32650 Nantasket Dr Apt 87
Rancho Palos Verdes, CA 90275-5850, USA

Nedorost, Vaclav (Athlete, Hockey Player)
1 Panther Pkwy
Sunrise, FL 33323-5315, USA

Needham, Col (Business Person)
Internet Movie Database
410 Terry Ave N
Seattle, WA 98109-5210, USA

Needham, Connie (Actor)
26234 Kingsington Ln
Laguna Hills, CA 92653-8220, USA

Needham, James J (Business Person)
1500 Brecknock Rd Apt 103
Greenport, NY 11944-3119, USA

Needham, Tracey (Actor)
c/o Tony Chargin *Ovation Management*
12028 National Blvd
Los Angeles, CA 90064-3542, USA

Neel, Roy (Politician)
3307 Northampton St NW
Washington, DC 20015-1652, USA

Neel, Troy (Athlete, Baseball Player)
2613 Farleigh Ln
Cedar Park, TX 78613-4334, USA

Neely, Cam (Athlete, Hockey Player)
76 Davison Dr
Lincoln, MA 01773-2216, USA

Neely, Cam (Athlete, Hockey Player)
100 Legends Way Ste 250
Attn Office of the President
Boston, MA 02114-1390, United States

Neely, Gina (Chef, Television Host)
Neelys Barbeque
PO Box 771684
Memphis, TN 38177-1684, USA

Neely, Pat (Chef, Television Host)
Neelys Barbque
PO Box 771634
Memphis, TN 38177-1634, USA

Neely, Ralph E (Athlete, Football Player)
6943 Sperry St
Dallas, TX 75214-2855, USA

Neely, Rumy (Fashion Designer, Internet Star, Writer)
c/o Lori Sale *Artist & Brand Management (LA)*
132 N Laurel Ave
Los Angeles, CA 90048-3512, USA

Neeman, Cal (Athlete, Baseball Player)
93 Champagne Dr
Lake Saint Louis, MO 63367-1604, USA

Neeson, Liam (Actor)
111 W 67th St Apt 28F # 28D/ PMB 28E/
New York, NY 10023-5956, USA

Neff, Bob (Athlete, Football Player)
2 Crestview
Athens, TX 75751-2932, USA

Neff, Francine I (Government Official)
PO Box 1498
Pena Blanca, NM 87041-1498, USA

Neff, Lucas (Actor)
c/o Jason Weinberg *Untitled Entertainment (LA)*
350 S Beverly Dr Ste 200
Beverly Hills, CA 90212-4819, USA

Neff, Steve (Bowler)
3655 S Suncoast Blvd
Homosassa, FL 34448-2625, USA

Negoesco, Stephen (Coach)
University of San Francisco Athletic Dept
San Francisco, CA 94117, USA

Negray, Ron (Athlete, Baseball Player)
587 W Nimisila Rd
New Franklin, OH 44319-4616, USA

Negreanu, Daniel (Actor)
PO Box 416
2251 North Rampart Blvd
Las Vegas, NV 89125-0416, USA

Negron, Chuck (Musician)
c/o Staff Member *Mitch Schneider Organization (MSO)*
14724 Ventura Blvd Ste 410
Sherman Oaks, CA 91403-3537, USA

Negron, Taylor (Actor, Comedian)
8968 Lloyd Pl
West Hollywood, CA 90069-5503, USA

Nehemiah, Renaldo (Athlete, Football Player)
1751 Pinnacle Dr Ste 1500
Mc Lean, VA 22102-3833, USA

Neibauer, Gary (Athlete, Baseball Player)
146 Delta Ave
Bismarck, ND 58504-6655, USA

Neibhors, William (Athlete, Football Player)
1904 Chippendale Dr SE
Huntsville, AL 35801-1309, USA

Neidert, John (Athlete, Football Player)
4731 Placid Cir
Sarasota, FL 34231-6486, USA

Neidich, Charles (Musician)
Colbert Artists
307 7th Ave Rm 2006
New York, NY 10001-6099, USA

Neidlinger, Jim (Athlete, Baseball Player)
139 Sunset Dr
Burlington, VT 05408-1910, USA

Neiger, Al (Athlete, Baseball Player)
213 Pinehurst Rd
Wilmington, DE 19803-3125, USA

Neil, Ray (Baseball Player)
Ethiopian Clowns
250 N Wells Ave Apt 511
Benton Harbor, MI 49022, USA

Neil, Vince (Musician)
4980 Mountain Creek Dr
Las Vegas, NV 89148-1439, USA

Neill, Mary Gardner (Director)
Seattle Art Museum
Volunteer Park
Seattle, WA 98112, USA

Neill, Mike (Athlete, Baseball Player, Olympic Athlete)
17 Cape May Pt
Greensboro, NC 27455-1363, USA

Neill, Noel (Actor)
2295 Belgrade St
Metropolis, IL 62960-6825, USA

Neill, Rolfe (Publisher)
Charlotte News-Observer
600 S Tryon St
Charlotte, NC 28202-1842, USA

Neill, William M (Athlete, Football Player)
34 Gibbs Dr
Wayne, NJ 07470-4103, USA

Neils, Steve (Athlete, Football Player)
1329 Waterford Rd
Saint Paul, MN 55125-2366, USA

Neilson-Bell, Sandra (Swimmer)
3101 Mistyglen Cir
Austin, TX 78746-7811, USA

Neis, Reagan Dale (Actor)
c/o Susan Curtis *Curtis Talent Management*
9607 Arby Dr
Beverly Hills, CA 90210-1202, USA

Neison, Chuck (Athlete, Baseball Player)
8681 Carriage Hill Draw
Savage, MN 55378-2366, USA

Neitling, Marissa (Actor)
c/o Andrew Edwards *Wishlab*
2225A Hyperion Ave
Los Angeles, CA 90027-4709, USA

Nelkin, Stacey (Actor)
2770 Hutton Dr
Beverly Hills, CA 90210-1216

Nelligan, Kate (Actor)
c/o Gary Gersh *Innovative Artists (NY)*
235 Park Ave S Fl 7
New York, NY 10003-1405, USA

Nelly (Musician)
17329 Hidden Valley Dr
Eureka, MO 63025-2231, USA

Nelms, Michael (Mike) (Athlete, Football Player)
11331 Fawn Lake Pkwy
Spotsylvania, VA 22551-4665, USA

Nelsen, Bill (Athlete, Football Player)
13512 Dornoch Dr
Orlando, FL 32828-8802, USA

Nelson
15003 Greenleaf St
Sherman Oaks, CA 91403-4006

Nelson, Al (Athlete, Football Player)
660 Boas St Apt 918
Harrisburg, PA 17102-1323, USA

Nelson, Andy (Athlete, Football Player)
12251 Manor Rd
Glen Arm, MD 21057-9542, USA

Nelson, Ben (Politician)
9738 Fieldcrest Dr
Omaha, NE 68114-4933, USA

Nelson, Bob (Baseball Player)
Baltimore Orioles
18110 Langford Ln
Forney, TX 75126-8173, USA

Nelson, Brad (Athlete, Baseball Player)
1405 210th St
Algona, IA 50511-7076, USA

Nelson, Bry (Athlete, Baseball Player)
11 Campden Hill Rd
Sherwood, AR 72120-6536, USA

Nelson, Charles L (Athlete, Football Player)
3028 162nd Pl SE
Mill Creek, WA 98012-7848, USA

Nelson, Charlie (Athlete, Baseball Player, Olympic Athlete)
11205 Kinsley St
Eden Prairie, MN 55344-1826, USA

Nelson, Cindy (Athlete, Olympic Athlete, Skier)
PO Box 1699
0171 Larkspur Lane
Vail, CO 81658-1699, USA

Nelson, Colette (Fitness Expert, Model)
PO Box 1122
Seaford, NY 11783-0078, USA

Nelson, Craig T (Actor)
28872 Boniface Dr
Malibu, CA 90265-4206, USA

Nelson, Darrin (Athlete, Football Player)
215 Marianne Ct
Mountain View, CA 94040-3283, USA

Nelson, Dave (Athlete, Baseball Player)
12213 Clubhouse Dr
Lakewood Ranch, FL 34202-2098, USA

Nelson, Deborah (Journalist)
Seattle Times
1000 Denny Way # 5
Editorial Dept
Seattle, WA 98109-5340, USA

Nelson, Dennis (Athlete, Football Player)
6098 E 2370 St
Kewanee, IL 61443-8529, USA

Nelson, Derrie (Athlete, Football Player)
7790 S Marian Rd
Hastings, NE 68901-7564, USA

Nelson, Diane (Horse Racer)
24 S Howell Ave
Farmingville, NY 11738-1116, USA

Nelson, Dick (Athlete, Baseball Player)
102 N Maple St
Enfield, CT 06082-3958, USA

Nelson, Don
2284 S Kihei Rd
Kihei, HI 96753-8632, USA

Nelson, Donald A (Nellie) (Basketball Player, Coach)
Dallas Mavericks
2909 Taylor St
Dallas, TX 75226-1909, USA

Nelson, Drew (Actor)
c/o Staff Member *Select Artists Ltd (CA-Westside Office)*
1138 12th St Apt 1
Santa Monica, CA 90403-5459, USA

Nelson, Ed (Athlete, Football Player)
7647 Westlake Rd
Sterlington, LA 71280-3231, USA

Nelson, Gene (Athlete, Baseball Player)
160 Habersham Landing Dr
Demorest, GA 30535-4867, USA

Nelson, George D (Astronaut)
AAAS Project
1200 New York Ave NW Ste 100
Washington, DC 20005-3929, USA

Nelson, George D Dr (Astronaut)
1543 Toledo Ct
Bellingham, WA 98229-5375, USA

Nelson, Gunnar (Musician)
14 S Douglas Ave
Nashville, TN 37204, USA

Nelson, Haywood "Butch" (Athlete, Football Player)
697 Salter Rd
Luverne, AL 36049-5749, USA

Nelson, Jameer (Athlete, Basketball Player)
c/o Staff Member *Cornerstone Management*
944 County Line Rd
Bryn Mawr, PA 19010-2502, USA

Nelson, James E (Religious Leader)
Baha i Faith
536 Sheridan Rd
Wilmette, IL 60091-2891, USA

Nelson, Jamie (Athlete, Baseball Player)
Princeton Devil Rays
1602 Spring Creek Ave
Springdale, AR 72764-7847, USA

Nelson, Jeff (Athlete, Baseball Player)
6525 Douglas Ave SE
Snoqualmie, WA 98065-9467, USA

Nelson, Jeff (Athlete, Hockey Player)
249 Simon Rd
Waldoboro, ME 04572-5716, USA

Nelson, Jimmy
10404 Greenhaven Pkwy
Brecksville, OH 44141-1625

Nelson, Joe (Athlete, Baseball Player)
2407 Azure Cir
West Palm Beach, FL 33410-2521, USA

Nelson, John Allen (Actor)
c/o Cynthia Booth *Resolution (LA)*
6253 Hollywood Blvd Apt 508
Los Angeles, CA 90028-8251, USA

Nelson, Jordy (Athlete, Football Player)
9471 Fairview Church Rd
Riley, KS 66531-9677, USA

Nelson, Judd (Actor)
9206 Cordell Dr
Los Angeles, CA 90069-1720, USA

Nelson, Karl (Athlete, Football Player)
10 Grand St
Westwood, NJ 07675-1644, USA

Nelson, Kent C (Business Person)
United Parcel Service
55 Glenlake Pkwy
Atlanta, GA 30328-3498, USA

Nelson, Kirsten (Actor)
5237 Bluebell Ave
Valley Village, CA 91607-2339, USA

Nelson, Larry (Athlete, Golfer)
438 Langley Oaks Dr SE
Marietta, GA 30067-4981, USA

Nelson, Lee (Athlete, Football Player)
23 Lindley Ave NW
Marietta, GA 30064-2185, USA

Nelson, Lori (Actor)
19558 Pine Valley Ave
Porter Ranch, CA 91326-1408, USA

Nelson, Marilyn Carison (Business Person)
Carlson Companies
PO Box 59159
Carlson Parkway
Minneapolis, MN 55459-8200, USA

Nelson, Mary (Athlete, Baseball Player)
4222 Katrina Ln
San Antonio, TX 78222-2712, USA

Nelson, Matthew (Musician)
205 Saddlebridge Ln
Franklin, TN 37069-4316, USA

Nelson, Mel (Athlete, Baseball Player)
27420 Fisher St
Highland, CA 92346-3251, USA

Nelson, Richard (Baseball Player)
104 Montgomery Ln
Perryville, AR 72126-8114, USA

Nelson, Ricky (Baseball Player)
Seattle Mariners
2599 E Desert Broom Pl
Chandler, AZ 85286-2464, USA

Nelson, Rob (Athlete, Baseball Player)
312 Alta Vista Ave
South Pasadena, CA 91030-3502, USA

Nelson, Roger (Athlete, Baseball Player)
4113 Limerick Dr
Lake Wales, FL 33859-5748, USA

Nelson, Ron (Athlete, Basketball Player)
1550 Eagle Ridge Ln NE
Albuquerque, NM 87122-1187, USA

Nelson, Scott (Athlete, Baseball Player)
811 Overlook Dr
Coshocton, OH 43812-9107, USA

Nelson, Shane (Athlete, Football Player)
559 Carmel Dr
Sandia, TX 78383-5678, USA

Nelson, Terry (Athlete, Football Player)
3393 Highway 51 N
Arkadelphia, AR 71923-8584, USA

Nelson, Tim Blake (Actor, Director)
c/o Amy Guenther *Gateway Management Company Inc*
860 Via De La Paz Ste F10
Pacific Palisades, CA 90272-3631, USA

Nelson, Todd (Athlete, Hockey Player)
Oklahoma City Barons
501 N Walker Ave Ste 140
Attn Coaching Staff
Oklahoma City, OK 73102-1233, USA

Nelson, Tracy (Actor)
c/o Scott Carlson *Scott Carlson Entertainment*
5739 Bucknell Ave
Valley Village, CA 91607-1301, USA

Nelson, William (Bill) (Politician)
3000 Rocky Point Rd
Malabar, FL 32950-4613, USA

Nelson, Willie (Musician, Songwriter)
21910 Shotts Dr
Spicewood, TX 78669-2251, USA

Nelson Jr, J Bryon (Golfer)
Fairway Ranch
RR 2 Box 5 Litsey Road
Roanoke, TX 76262, USA

Nelson-Walker, Doris (Baseball Player)
7887 N 16th St Unit 129
Phoenix, AZ 85020-4453, USA

Nemchinov, Sergei (Athlete, Hockey Player)
14 Cornell Pl
Rye, NY 10580-3206, USA

Nemcova, Petra (Model)
c/o Michael Samonte *Sunshine Sachs (LA)*
8409 Santa Monica Blvd
West Hollywood, CA 90069-4209, USA

Nemec, Corin (Actor)
859 N Hollywood Way # 104
Burbank, CA 91505-2814, USA

Nemechek, Joe (Race Car Driver)
Ginn Racing
128 S Iredell Industrial Park Rd
Mooresville, NC 28115-7128, USA

Nemechek, III, Joseph Frank (Race Car Driver)
128 S Iredell Industrial Park Rd
Mooresville, NC 28115-7128, USA

Nemelka, Richard (Athlete, Basketball Player)
6108 S 1300 E
Salt Lake City, UT 84121, USA

Nen, Dick (Athlete, Baseball Player)
48 Via Barcaza
Trabuco Canyon, CA 92679-4831, USA

Nen, Robb (Athlete, Baseball Player)
JD Legends Promotions
10808 Foothill Blvd # 160-454
Rancho Cucamonga, CA 91730-3889, USA

Nenez, Clemente (Baseball Player)
6433 Blackberry Pl
Riverside, CA 92505-2205, USA

Neon Trees (Music Group)
c/o Staff Member *In De Goot Entertainment*
119 W 23rd St Ste 609
New York, NY 10011-2594, USA

N*E*R*D (Music Group)
c/o Staff Member *Paradigm (Monterey)*
404 W Franklin St
Monterey, CA 93940-2303, USA

NERD (Music Group)
c/o Amanda Silverman *42West (NYC)*
220 W 42nd St Fl 12
New York, NY 10036-7200, USA

Neri, Francesca (Actor)
c/o Philip Button *William Morris Endeavor (LA)*
9601 Wilshire Blvd
Beverly Hills, CA 90210-5213, USA

Nero, Franco ((Actor)
c/o Camilla Fluxman-Pines *Muse Management*
2001 Wilshire Blvd Ste 250
Santa Monica, CA 90403-5681, USA

Nero, Haley (Actor)
c/o Staff Member *Charlie's Talent Agency*
1350 Old Skokie Rd Ste 202
Highland Park, IL 60035-3058, USA

Nero, Peter (Musician)
202 Hidden Acres Ln
Media, PA 19063-1666, USA

Nershi, Bill (Musician)
1002 County Road 99
Nederland, CO 80466, USA

Nerud, John (Horse Racer)
19 Pound Hollow Rd # A
Glen Head, NY 11545-2209, USA

Nesbit, Jamar (Athlete, Football Player)
4083 Richmond Park Dr E
Jacksonville, FL 32224-2223, USA

Nesbitt-Wisham, Mary (Athlete, Baseball Player)
PO Box 194
Hollister, FL 32147-0194, USA

Neserovic, Radoslav (Basketball Player)
San Antonio Spurs
1 at and T Center Pkwy
Alamodome
San Antonio, TX 78219-3604, USA

Neshek, Pat (Athlete, Baseball Player)
6745 Angeles Rd
Melbourne Beach, FL 32951-3856, USA

Nesher, Avi (Director)
Gersh Agency
232 N Canon Dr
Beverly Hills, CA 90210-5302, USA

Nesic, Alex (Actor)
c/o Staff Member *Principato/Young Management (LA)*
9465 Wilshire Blvd Ste 900
Beverly Hills, CA 90212-2608, USA

Nesmith, Michael (Musician)
13 Sleepy Hollow Dr
Carmel Valley, CA 93924-9017, USA

Nespoli, Paolo (Astronaut)
2011 Dawn Crest Ct
League City, TX 77573-3931, USA

Nespral, Jackie (Correspondent)
NBC-TV
30 Rockefeller Plz
News Dept
New York, NY 10112-0015, USA

Ness, Rick (Musician)
Metropolitan Entertainment Group
2 Penn Plz # 2600
New York, NY 10121-0101, USA

Nessen, Ronald H (Ron) (Politician)
1835 K St NW Ste 805
Washington, DC 20006-1203, USA

Nesterenko, Eric (Athlete, Hockey Player)
PO Box 1025
Vail, CO 81658-1025, USA

Netherland, Joseph H (Business Person)
FMC Corp
200 E Randolph St
Chicago, IL 60601-6436, USA

Netherton, Tom (Musician)
Germantown Performing Arts Centre
1801 Exeter Rd
Germantown, TN 38138-2934, USA

Netolicky, Bob (Athlete, Basketball Player)
PO Box 531
Carmel, IN 46082-0531, USA

Nettles, Doug (Athlete, Football Player)
13105 Quail Creek Ct
Silver Spring, MD 20904-3588, USA

Nettles, Graig (Athlete, Baseball Player)
4255 Parris Dr
Lenoir City, TN 37772-3947, USA

Nettles, Jennifer (Musician)
5443 Leipers Creek Rd
Franklin, TN 37064-9284, USA

Nettles, Jim (Athlete, Baseball Player)
4632 N Darien Dr
Tacoma, WA 98407-1212, USA

Nettles, Jim (Athlete, Football Player)
3817 Mandeville Canyon Rd
Los Angeles, CA 90049-1027, USA

Nettles, Morris (Athlete, Baseball Player)
551 1/2 San Juan Ave
Venice, CA 90291-5643, USA

Neu, Mike (Athlete, Baseball Player)
406 Fraga Ct
Martinez, CA 94553-6812, USA

Neubeck, Francis G (Astronaut)
4702 Arnold Loop
Las Vegas, NV 89115-2370, USA

Neubert, Keith (Actor)
10000 Santa Monica Blvd # 305
Los Angeles, CA 90067

Neufeld, Ryan (Athlete, Football Player)
625 Spring Hill Dr
Morgan Hill, CA 95037-4814, USA

Neugebauer, Nick (Athlete, Baseball Player)
777 W Chandler Blvd Apt 2363
Chandler, AZ 85225-2529, USA

Neugebauer, Randy (Congressman, Politician)
1424 Kibgwirth Hob
Washington, DC 20515-0001, USA

Neuheisel, Richard (Rick) (Athlete, Coach, Football Coach, Football Player)
3601 Winding Creek Rd
Sacramento, CA 95864-1530, USA

Neumann, Liselotte (Athlete, Golfer)
11003 Muirfield Dr
Rancho Mirage, CA 92270-1431, USA

Neumark, Julie
900 E 1st St Apt 314
Los Angeles, CA 90012-4039

Neumeier, Dan (Athlete, Baseball Player)
N2635 County Road V
Lodi, WI 53555-1568, USA

Neustadt, Richard (Politician)
1010 Memorial Dr
Cambridge, MA 02138-4859, USA

Neuwirth, Bebe (Actor)
25 Richard Ct
Princeton, NJ 08540-3802, USA

Neverett, Tim (Sportscaster)
320 Saddlebrook Rd
Gibsonia, PA 15044-7809, USA

Nevett, Elijah (Athlete, Football Player)
931 30th St N
Bessemer, AL 35020-3565, USA

Neville, Aaron (Musician)
3 Bleu Lake Dr
Covington, LA 70435-8408, USA

Neville, Arthel (Correspondent, Television Host)
1840 Victory Blvd
Glendale, CA 91201-2558, USA

Neville, Bill (Cartoonist)
511 Valleybrook Dr
Jamestown, NC 27282-8822, USA

Neville, Cyril (Musician)
60432 Dixie Ranch Rd
Slidell, LA 70460-4034, USA

Neville, David (Designer)
Rag & Bone
425 W 13th St Ofc 2
New York, NY 10014-1123, USA

Neville, Katherine (Writer)
PO Box 788
Warrenton, VA 20188-0788, USA

Neville, Thomas O (Athlete, Football Player)
PO Box 11175
Montgomery, AL 36111-0175, USA

Nevin, Brooke (Actor)
c/o Suzanne (Sue) Wohl *TalentWorks (LA)*
3500 W Olive Ave Ste 1400
Burbank, CA 91505-5512, USA

Nevin, Phil (Athlete, Baseball Player, Olympic Athlete)
18795 Heritage Dr
Poway, CA 92064-6643, USA

Nevins, Claudette (Actor)
Gold Marshak Liedtke
3500 W Olive Ave Ste 1400
Burbank, CA 91505-5512, USA

Nevins, Sheila (Business Person, Producer)
c/o Staff Member *Home Box Office (HBO-LA)*
2500 Broadway Ste 400
Santa Monica, CA 90404-3176, USA

Nevis, Drake (Athlete, Football Player)
c/o Pat Dye Jr *SportsTrust Advisors (GA)*
3340 Peachtree Rd NE Fl 16
Atlanta, GA 30326-1000, USA

Nevitt, Chuck (Athlete, Basketball Player)
3124 Cartwright Dr
Raleigh, NC 27612-2113, USA

Newark, Samantha (Musician)
c/o Arlene Thornton *Arlene Thornton & Associates*
12711 Ventura Blvd Ste 490
Studio City, CA 91604-2477, USA

Newbern, George (Actor)
c/o Tiffany Kuzon *Evolution Entertainment (LA)*
901 N Highland Ave
Los Angeles, CA 90038-2412, USA

Newberry, Bob (Race Car Driver)
key Prts Racing
5835 Mariaville Rd
Schenectady, NY 12306, USA

Newberry, Jeremy (Athlete, Football Player)
2525 Sunset Rd
Brentwood, CA 94513-2895, USA

Newberry, Thomas (Tom) (Athlete, Football Player)
224 Tarpon St
Tavernier, FL 33070-2534, USA

Newbill, Ivano (Athlete, Basketball Player)
3877 6th Ave
Los Angeles, CA 90008-1918, USA

Newble, Ira
41617 Cummings Ln
Novi, MI 48377-2851, USA

Newbrough, Ashley (Actor)
c/o William Mercer *Thruline Entertainment*
9250 Wilshire Blvd Ste 100
Ground Floor
Beverly Hills, CA 90212-3343, USA

Newcomb, Jonathan (Publisher)
35 Pierrepont St
Brooklyn, NY 11201-3359, USA

Newcomb, Mike (Radio Personality)
OnSecondThought
4927 E Palo Brea Ln
Cave Creek, AZ 85331-5995, USA

Newcombe, Don (Athlete, Baseball Player)
c/o Karen Newcombe
1448 Young St Apt 1108
Honolulu, HI 96814-1861, USA

Newcombe, John (Athlete, Tennis Player)
325 Mission Valley Rd
New Braunfels, TX 78132-3629, USA

Newcomer, Carrie (Musician)
PO Box 5653
Bloomington, IN 47407-5653, USA

New Edition (Music Group)
c/o Amy Malone *GIC Public Relations*
Prefers to be contacted via email or telephone
West Hollywood, CA 90069, USA

Newell, Alex (Actor, Musician)
c/o Jordyn Palos *Persona PR (LA)*
8840 Wilshire Blvd Ste 212
Beverly Hills, CA 90211-2606, USA

Newell, James
20519 Rodax St
Winnetka, CA 91306-1530

Newell, Rick (Athlete, Hockey Player)
5223 N 24th St
Phoenix, AZ 85016-3590, USA

Newell, Tom (Athlete, Baseball Player)
9525 Cordoba Blvd
Sparks, NV 89441-5569, USA

Newfield, Heidi (Musician)
1010 16th Ave S Unit 203
Nashville, TN 37212-2347, USA

Newfield, Marc (Athlete, Baseball Player)
1717 N Los Robles Ave
Pasadena, CA 91104-1051, USA

New Grass Revival
PO Box 128037
Nashville, TN 37212-8037

Newhan, David (Athlete, Baseball Player)
2125 Walnut Ln
Vista, CA 92084-7716, USA

Newhan, Ross (Sportscaster)
2678 Harvest Crest Ln
Corona, CA 92881-3572, USA

Newhart, Bob (Actor, Comedian)
420 Amapola Ln
Los Angeles, CA 90077-3411, USA

Newhauser, Don (Athlete, Baseball Player)
321 Sheryl Dr
Deltona, FL 32738-8441, USA

Newhouse, Bob
6847 Truxton Dr
Dallas, TX 75231-5717

Newhouse, Donald E (Publisher)
Advance Publications
950 W Fingerboard Rd
Staten Island, NY 10305-1453, USA

Newhouse, Fredrick (Fred) (Athlete, Track
Athlete)
3003 Pine Lake Trl
Houston, TX 77068-1435, USA

Newhouse, Marshall (Athlete, Football
Player)
c/o Jordan Woy *Willis and Woy
Management*
3030 Olive St Ste 520
Dallas, TX 75219-7629, USA

Newhouse Jr, Samuel I (Publisher)
Advance Publications
950 W Fingerboard Rd
Staten Island, NY 10305-1453, USA

New Kids on the Block (NKOTB) (Music
Group)
c/o Staff Member *Interscope Records (LA)
- Main*
2220 Colorado Ave
Santa Monica, CA 90404-3506, USA

Newkirk, Ingrid (Activist)
PETA
501 Front St
Norfolk, VA 23510-1009, USA

Newland, Bob (Athlete, Football Player)
3895 Vine Maple St
Eugene, OR 97405-4494, USA

Newlin, Mike (Athlete, Basketball Player)
1414 Horseshoe Dr
Sugar Land, TX 77478-3464, USA

Newman, Al (Athlete, Baseball Player)
Newmie's Rewards
15240 Fairlawn Shores Trl SE
Prior Lake, MN 55372-1940, USA

Newman, Alan (Athlete, Baseball Player)
24 Rice Ln
Dry Prong, LA 71423-8742, USA

Newman, Alec (Actor)
c/o Laina Cohn *Cohn / Torgan
Management*
Prefers to be contacted by telephone or
email
Los Angeles, CA, USA

Newman, Barry (Actor)
c/o Tom Chasin *Chasin Agency, The*
8899 Beverly Blvd Ste 716
Los Angeles, CA 90048-2449, USA

Newman, Edward K (Ed) (Athlete,
Football Player)
10100 SW 140th St
Miami, FL 33176-6685, USA

Newman, James H (Astronaut)
Naval Post Graduate School
1 University Cir
Attn Nasa Visiting Professor
Monterey, CA 93943-5098, USA

Newman, Jeff (Athlete, Baseball Player,
Coach)
10133 N 103rd St
Scottsdale, AZ 85258-4953, USA

Newman, Johnny (Athlete, Basketball
Player)
Dallas Mavericks
3720 Favero Rd
Henrico, VA 23233-7037, USA

Newman, Josh (Athlete, Baseball Player)
67 Michaela Dr
Wheelersburg, OH 45694-8204, USA

Newman, Kevin (Correspondent)
ABC-TV
77 W 66th St
News Dept
New York, NY 10023-6201, USA

Newman, Kyle (Director)
c/o Staff Member *Fire Thief Films*
13801 Ventura Blvd
Sherman Oaks, CA 91423-3603, USA

Newman, Laraine (Actor, Comedian)
10480 Ashton Ave
Los Angeles, CA 90024-5137, USA

Newman, Loraine (Comedian)
c/o Staff Member *TalentWorks (LA)*
3500 W Olive Ave Ste 1400
Burbank, CA 91505-5512, USA

Newman, Nell (Business Person)
Newman's Own Organics
246 Post Rd E Ste 308
Westport, CT 06880-3615, USA

Newman, Phyllis (Actor, Musician)
c/o Judy Katz *Judy Katz PR*
1745 Broadway Fl 17
New York, NY 10019-4642, USA

Newman, Randy (Musician, Songwriter)
1610 San Remo Dr
Pacific Palisades, CA 90272-2741, USA

Newman, Ray (Athlete, Baseball Player)
584 Vista Dr
Murrells Inlet, SC 29576-9029, USA

Newman, Ryan (Actor)
c/o Gladys Gonzalez *John Carrabino
Management*
5900 Wilshire Blvd Ste 406
Los Angeles, CA 90036-5015, USA

Newman, Ryan (Race Car Driver)
298/318 Jennings Rd
Statesville, NC 28625, USA

Newman, Terence (Athlete, Football
Player)
1 Cowboys Pkwy
Irving, TX 75063-4924, USA

Newman, Thomas (Actor)
c/o Staff Member *Chasen & Company*
8899 Beverly Blvd Ste 405
Los Angeles, CA 90048-2431, USA

Newmar, Julie (Actor)
204 S Carmelina Ave
Los Angeles, CA 90049-3952, USA

Newmark, Craig
354 Shotwell St
San Francisco, CA 94110-1325, USA

Newmark, Dave (Athlete, Basketball
Player)
545 Pierce St Apt 2301
Albany, CA 94706-1065, USA

New Order (Music Group, Musician)
c/o Staff Member *Warner Bros Records
(NY)*
75 Rockefeller Plz
New York, NY 10019-6908, USA

New Radicals
c/o Staff Member *MCA Records (LA)*
2220 Colorado Ave
Santa Monica, CA 90404-3506, USA

New Rascals, The
PO Box 1821
Ojai, CA 93024-1821

New Riders of the Purple Sage
PO Box 3773
San Rafael, CA 94912-3773

Newsboys (Music Group)
Sparrow Records
PO Box 5010
Brentwood, TN 37024-5010, USA

Newsom, David (Actor)
Innovative Artists
1505 10th St
Santa Monica, CA 90401-2805, USA

Newsom, Gavin (Politician)
Mayor's Office
400 S Van Ness Ave
City Hall
San Francisco, CA 94103-3630, USA

Newsome, Billy (Athlete, Football Player)
PO Box 2001
Shreveport, LA 71166-2001, USA

Newsome, Harry (Athlete, Football
Player)
531 Manor Rd
Cheraw, SC 29520, USA

Newsome, Ozzie (Athlete, Football
Player)
6 Padonia Woods Ct
Cockeysville, MD 21030-1744, USA

Newsome, Paula (Actor)
15044 Martha St
Van Nuys, CA 91411-3223, USA

Newsome, Timothy A (Athlete, Football
Player)
7005 Quartermile Ln
Dallas, TX 75248-1447, USA

Newsome, Vince (Athlete, Football Player)
5308 Woodnote Ln
Columbia, MD 21044-5707, USA

Newson, Warren (Athlete, Baseball
Player)
13232 Padre Ave
Fort Worth, TX 76244-4326, USA

New Song (Music Group)
c/o Staff Member *VanLiere-Wilcox*
251 2nd Ave S
Franklin, TN 37064-2659, USA

Newsted, Jason (Musician)
205 Alamo View Pl
Walnut Creek, CA 94595-2600, USA

Newton, Becki (Actor)
c/o Nicole King *Management 360*
9111 Wilshire Blvd
Beverly Hills, CA 90210-5508, USA

Newton, Bill (Athlete, Basketball Player)
2902 Manitou Park Dr
Rochester, IN 46975-8936, USA

Newton, Cam (Athlete, Football Player,
Heisman Trophy Winner)
c/o Bus Cook *Bus Cook Sports, Inc*
1 Willow Bend Dr
Hattiesburg, MS 39402-8552, USA

Newton, C M (Athlete, Basketball Player,
Coach)
9160 Enterprise Ave NE
Tuscaloosa, AL 35406-1042, USA

Newton, John Haymes (Actor)
c/o Staff Member *Pakula/King &
Associates*
9229 W Sunset Blvd Ste 315
West Hollywood, CA 90069-3403, USA

Newton, Jon (Business Person)
American General Corp
2929 Allen Pkwy Ste 3800
Houston, TX 77019-2155, USA

Newton, Juice (Musician, Songwriter)
4289 Kerwood Ct
San Diego, CA 92130-2136, USA

Newton, Nate (Athlete, Football Player)
1921 White Oak Clearing
Southlake, TX 76092-6929, USA

Newton, Robert L (Athlete, Football
Player)
11500 NE 76th St Apt A-353
Vancouver, WA 98662-3901, USA

Newton, Thandie (Actor)
c/o Jillian Roscoe *ID Public Relations (LA)*
7060 Hollywood Blvd Fl 8th
Los Angeles, CA 90028-6021, USA

Newton, Tom (Athlete, Football Player)
169 Park Rd
Rochester, NY 14622-1217, USA

Newton, Wayne (Actor, Musician)
6629 S Pecos Rd
Las Vegas, NV 89120-2809, USA

Newton-John, Olivia (Actor, Musician,
Producer)
c/o Mark Hartley *Fitzgerald-Hartley Co
(Ventura)*
34 N Palm St Ste 100
Ventura, CA 93001-2610, USA

New York Yankees
Yankee Stadium
161st & Riv
Bronx, NY 10451, USA

Ne-Yo (Musician)
40 Club Ct
Alpharetta, GA 30005-7422, USA

Nezelek, Andy (Athlete, Baseball Player)
5707 Long Cove Rd
Midlothian, VA 23112-2450, USA

Ngata, Haloti (Athlete, Football Player)
c/o Michael McCartney *Priority Sports &
Entertainment - Chicago*
312 N La Salle
Suite 650
Chicago, IL 60610, USA

Ngata, Haoti (Athlete, Football Player)
c/o Staff Member *Baltimore Ravens*
1 Winning Dr
Owings Mills, MD 21117-4776, USA

Nguyen, Dat (Athlete, Football Player)
3610 Spears Rd
Houston, TX 77066-4117, USA

Nguyen, Dustin (Actor)
1051 S Dunsmuir Ave
Los Angeles, CA 90019-6755, USA

Nguyen, Navia (Actor)
c/o Michael Greenwald *Don Buchwald &
Associates (LA)*
6500 Wilshire Blvd Ste 2200
Los Angeles, CA 90048-4942, USA

Niccol, Andrew (Director, Producer,
Writer)
c/o Richard Green *Resolution (LA)*
1801 Century Park E Ste 2300
Los Angeles, CA 90067-2325, USA

Nichol, Joseph McGinty (McG)
(Musician, Producer, Writer)
c/o Staff Member *Wonderland Sound and Vision*
8739 W Sunset Blvd
W Hollywood, CA 90069-2205, USA

Nichol, Scott (Athlete, Hockey Player)
2270 Lansford Ave
San Jose, CA 95125-4023, USA

Nicholas, Denise (Actor)
932 S Longwood Ave
Los Angeles, CA 90019-1752, USA

Nicholas, Eric (Writer)
c/o Staff Member *Gersh (LA)*
9465 Wilshire Blvd Ste 600
Beverly Hills, CA 90212-2605, USA

Nicholas, J D (Musician)
Management Assoc
1920 Benson Ave
Saint Paul, MN 55116-3214, USA

Nicholas, Peter M (Business Person)
Boston Scientific Corp
100 Boston Scientific Way
Marlborough, MA 01752-1234, USA

Nicholas, Stephen (Football Player)
c/o Chad Speck *Allegiant Athletic Agency*
35 Market Sq Ste 201
Knoxville, TN 37902-1420, USA

Nicholas, Thomas Ian (Actor)
11934 Hartsook St
Valley Village, CA 91607-3103, USA

Nicholas Jr, Nicholas J (Publisher)
Pluggers Inc
1000 SW Broadway # 1850
Portland, OR 97205-3035, USA

Nicholas(Smisko), Bishop (Religious Leader)
American Carpatho
312 Garfield St
Johnstown, PA 15906-2122, USA

Nicholls, Bernie (Athlete, Hockey Player)
17101 Planters Row
Addison, TX 75001-5039, USA

Nicholls, Paul (Actor)
c/o Staff Member *IFA Talent Agency*
2000 Avenue Of The Stars
Los Angeles, CA 90067-4700, USA

Nichols, Austin (Actor)
c/o Joan Green *Joan Green Management*
1836 Courtney Ter
Los Angeles, CA 90046-2106, USA

Nichols, Bobby (Athlete, Golfer)
8681 Glenlyon Ct
Fort Myers, FL 33912-2408, USA

Nichols, Carl (Athlete, Baseball Player)
901 E Artesia Blvd
Compton, CA 90221-5356, USA

Nichols, Dr. Michael (Writer)
c/o Staff Member *Guilford Press*
72 Spring St
New York, NY 10012-4019, USA

Nichols, Hamilton J (Athlete, Football Player)
11015 Kirkmead Dr
Houston, TX 77089-3116, USA

Nichols, Joe (Musician)
7410 Macallan Cv
Tyler, TX 75703-0942, USA

Nichols, John (Writer)
c/o Staff Member *The New Press*
120 Wall St Fl 31
New York, NY 10005-4007, USA

Nichols, Kenwood C (Business Person)
Champion Int'l Corp
1 Champion Plz
Stamford, CT 06921-0001, USA

Nichols, Larry (Designer)
Moleculon Research Corp
139 Main St
Cambridge, MA 02142-1530, USA

Nichols, Lorrie (Bowler)
1251 Lexington Dr
Algonquin, IL 60102-2065, USA

Nichols, Marisol (Actor)
c/o Michael Baum *Impression Entertainment*
9229 W Sunset Blvd Ste 700
West Hollywood, CA 90069-3407, USA

Nichols, Mark (Athlete, Football Player)
5905 Penn Station Ln
Bakersfield, CA 93311-9016, USA

Nichols, Mark (Race Car Driver)
Henderson Motosports
532 E Main St
Abingdon, VA 24210-3410, USA

Nichols, Mike (Comedian, Director)
Friends in Deed Inc
594 Broadway Rm 706
New York, NY 10012-3257, USA

Nichols, Nichelle (Actor)
23281 Leonora Dr
Woodland Hills, CA 91367-6038, USA

Nichols, Nicole (Business Person)
c/o Staff Member *OWN: The Oprah Winfrey Network*
5700 Wilshire Blvd Ste 120
Los Angeles, CA 90036-3644, USA

Nichols, Rachel (Actor)
c/o Peter Kiernan *Management 360*
9111 Wilshire Blvd
Beverly Hills, CA 90210-5508, USA

Nichols, Reid (Athlete, Baseball Player)
Milwaukee Brewers
17547 W East Wind Ave
Goodyear, AZ 85338-5840, USA

Nichols, Rod (Athlete, Baseball Player)
1570 Elk Trail Dr
Helena, MT 59601-9633, USA

Nichols, Stephen (Actor)
11664 National Blvd # 116
Los Angeles, CA 90064-3802, USA

Nicholson, Bruce
PO Box 2573
Georgetown, SC 29442-2573

Nicholson, Dave (Athlete, Baseball Player)
15316 Lakepoint Dr
Benton, IL 62812-4676, USA

Nicholson, Don (Dyno) (Race Car Driver)
604 E Vista Del Playa Ave
Orange, CA 92865-3436, USA

Nicholson, Jack (Actor)
12758 Mulholland Dr
Beverly Hills, CA 90210-1329, USA

Nicholson, Jim (Athlete, Football Player)
91-845 Kauwili St
Ewa Beach, HI 96706-2854, USA

Nicholson, Jim (Government Official, Secretary)
412 Russell Senate Office Building
Washington, DC 20510-0001, USA

Nicholson, Julianne (Actor)
c/o Courtney Kivowitz *The Schiff Company*
9220 W Sunset Blvd Ste 106
West Hollywood, CA 90069-3500, USA

Nicholson, Kathrin
9057-A Nemo St
West Hollywood, CA 90069

Nichting, Chris (Athlete, Baseball Player)
7151 Gracely Dr
Cincinnati, OH 45233-1019, USA

Nickelback (Music Group)
c/o John Greenberg *Union Entertainment Group*
1323 Newbury Rd Ste 104
Newbury Park, CA 91320-3679, USA

Nickel Creek (Music Group)
c/o Staff Member *William Morris Endeavor (Nashville)*
1600 Division St Ste 300
Nashville, TN 37203-2755, USA

Nickells, Bruce (Horse Racer)
PO Box 5009
Lighthouse Point, FL 33074-5009, USA

Nickens, David (Race Car Driver)
604 E Vista Del Playa Ave
Orange, CA 92865-3436, USA

Nickerson, Denice (Actor)
4292 S Salida Way Unit 1
Aurora, CO 80013-3289, USA

Nickerson, Denise (Actor)
6853 S Ivy Way # 7-301
C/O Frann Harrison
Englewood, CO 80112-6205, USA

Nickerson, Hardy O (Athlete, Football Player)
1820 Melvin Rd
Oakland, CA 94602-2025, USA

Nickerson Jr, Donald A (Religious Leader)
Episcopal Church
815 2nd Ave Bsmt
New York, NY 10017-4594, USA

Nickla, Ed (Athlete, Football Player)
21 Ida Ln
North Babylon, NY 11703-1403, USA

Nicklaus, Gary
112 Tpc Blvd
Ponte Vedra Beach, FL 32082

Nicklaus, Jack (Athlete, Golfer)
11396/11397/11406 Old Harbour Rd
N Palm Beach, FL 33408, USA

Nickle, Doug (Athlete, Baseball Player)
19440 Victoria Ct
Sonoma, CA 95476-3829, USA

Nickles, Don (Politician)
903 Centrillion Dr
Mc Lean, VA 22102-1443, USA

Nicks, Carl (Athlete, Basketball Player)
10200 Yosemite Ln
Indianapolis, IN 46234-9821, USA

Nicks, Hakeem (Athlete, Football Player)
c/o Tom Condon *CAA (St. Louis)*
222 S Central Ave Ste 1008
Saint Louis, MO 63105-3509, USA

Nicks, Orlando (Athlete, Basketball Player)
10200 Yosemite Ln
Indianapolis, IN 46234-9821, USA

Nicks, Regina (Musician)
Bobby Roberts
909 Meadowlark Ln
Goodlettsville, TN 37072-2309, USA

Nicks, Stevie (Musician)
468 Chautauqua Blvd
Pacific Palisades, CA 90272-4406, USA

Nickson, Julia (Actor)
Elkins Entertainment
8306 Wilshire Blvd # 438
Beverly Hills, CA 90211-2304, USA

Nickulas, Eric (Athlete, Hockey Player)
616 Huckins Neck Rd
Centerville, MA 02632-1440, USA

Nico & Vinz (Music Group)
c/o Keith Sarkisian *William Morris Endeavor (LA)*
9601 Wilshire Blvd
Beverly Hills, CA 90210-5213, USA

Nicol, Lesley (Actor)
c/o Patty Freedman *Andrew Freedman Public Relations*
9127 Thrasher Ave
Los Angeles, CA 90069-1144, USA

Nicol, Steve (Coach, Football Coach)
New England Revolution
1 Patriot Pl
Cmgi Field
Foxboro, MA 02035-1388, USA

Nicole, Britt (Musician)
c/o Amy Fogleman *Creative Trust, Inc.*
210 Jamestown Park Ste 200
Brentwood, TN 37027-7562, USA

Nicole, Kaylan (Adult Film Star)
9800D Topanga Canyon Blvd # 3252
Chatsworth, CA 91311-4005, USA

Nicolet, Danielle (Actor)
c/o Lena Roklin *Luber Roklin Management*
5815 W Sunset Blvd Ste 206
Los Angeles, CA 90028-6481, USA

Nicol-Fox, Helen (Athlete, Baseball Player)
432 E Cornell Dr
Tempe, AZ 85283-1908, USA

Nicollier, Claude (Astronaut)
20 Leeward Ln
Houston, TX 77058-4212, USA

Nicolucci, Guy (Writer)
c/o Staff Member *Gersh (LA)*
9465 Wilshire Blvd Ste 600
Beverly Hills, CA 90212-2605, USA

Nicosia, Steve (Athlete, Baseball Player)
5735 Wylmoor
Norcross, GA 30093-4181, USA

Nied, David (Athlete, Baseball Player)
211 Masters Ln
Midlothian, TX 76065-7209, USA

Niedenfuer, Tom (Athlete, Baseball Player)
3933 Losillias Dr
Sarasota, FL 34238-4537, USA

Nieder, William H (Bill) (Athlete, Track Athlete)
PO Box 310
Mountain Ranch, CA 95246-0310, USA

Niehaus, Dave (Sportscaster)
Seattle Mariners
PO Box 4100
Safeco Field
Seattle, WA 98194-0100, USA

Niehaus, David (Athlete, Baseball Player)
18406 NW Montreux Dr
Issaquah, WA 98027-7817, USA

Niehaus, Ralph (Athlete, Football Player)
7219 E Nathan St
Mesa, AZ 85207-0822, USA

Niehaus, Steve (Athlete, Football Player)
114 Siebenthaler Ave
Cincinnati, OH 45215-3716, USA

Niekamp, Jim (Athlete, Hockey Player)
3511 E Cochise Dr
Phoenix, AZ 85028-3924, USA

Niekamp, Ted (Athlete, Hockey Player)
3511 E Cochise Dr
Phoenix, AZ 85028-3924, USA

Niekro, Lance (Athlete, Baseball Player)
3822 Cheverly Dr E
Lakeland, FL 33813-1203, USA

Niekro, Phil (Athlete, Baseball Player)
6382 Nichols Rd
Flowery Branch, GA 30542-2619, USA

Niel, Steve (Actor)
c/o Laura Walsh *Central Artists*
3310 W Burbank Blvd # A
Burbank, CA 91505-2230, USA

Nielsen, Brigitte (Actor, Model)
3374 Floyd Ter
Los Angeles, CA 90068-1448, USA

Nielsen, Connie (Actor)
c/o Estelle Lasher *Lasher Group*
1133 Avenue Of The Americas Ste 1621
New York, NY 10036-6710, USA

Nielsen, Gifford (Athlete, Football Player)
10 Sarahs Cv
Sugar Land, TX 77479-2449, USA

Nielsen, Jeff (Athlete, Hockey Player)
6113 Birchcrest Dr
Minneapolis, MN 55436-2627, USA

Nielsen, Jerry (Athlete, Baseball Player)
4631 Kewanee St
Fair Oaks, CA 95628-6219, USA

Nielsen, Lonnie (Athlete, Golfer)
6 Marlwood Ln
Palm Beach Gardens, FL 33418-6805,
USA

Nielsen, Rick (Musician)
4 Jacoby Pl
Rockford, IL 61107-1817, USA

Nielsen, Scott (Athlete, Baseball Player)
2898 E Valley View Ave
Salt Lake City, UT 84117-5550, USA

Niemann, Jeff (Athlete, Baseball Player)
5922 Jason St
Houston, TX 77074-7742, USA

Niemann, Randy (Athlete, Baseball Player)
1585 SW Harbour Isles Cir
Port Saint Lucie, FL 34986-3403, USA

Niemann, Richard (Athlete, Basketball
Player)
7911 Stanford Ave
Saint Louis, MO 63130-3613, USA

Niemi, Lisa (Actor)
c/o Staff Member *Atria Books*
1230 Avenue of the Americas
New York, NY 10020-1513, USA

Niemiec-Konwinski, Dolly (Athlete,
Baseball Player)
1821 Spring Meadow Ct SE
Caledonia, MI 49316-9154, USA

Nies, Eric (Actor, Model, Reality Star)
c/o Staff Member *Bunim/Murray
Productions*
6007 Sepulveda Blvd
Van Nuys, CA 91411-2502, USA

Niese, Jonathon
2054 Driftwood Ln
Oregon, OH 43616-4470, USA

Nieson, Chuck (Athlete, Baseball Player)
31923 Trails End Rd
Clinton, MN 56225-5163, USA

Nieto, Tom (Athlete, Baseball Player)
22446 Eagles Watch Dr
Land O Lakes, FL 34639-6759, USA

Nieuwendyk, Joe (Athlete, Hockey Player)
2840 Dyer St
Dallas, TX 75205-1906, USA

Nieuwendyk, Joe (Athlete, Hockey Player)
2601 Avenue of the Stars Ste 100
Attn: General Manager
Frisco, TX 75034-9016, USA

Nieves, Juan (Athlete, Baseball Player,
Coach)
Chicago White Sox
333 W 35th St
Attn: Coaching Staff
Chicago, IL 60616-3621, USA

Nieves, Melvin (Athlete, Baseball Player)
6131 7 Lks W
West End, NC 27376-9320, USA

Nigam, Anjul (Actor)
c/o Lisa DiSante-Frank *DiSante Frank &
Company*
10061 Riverside Dr # 377
Toluca Lake, CA 91602-2560, USA

Nigam, Sonu (Musician)
c/o Linda Jones *The Mass Appeal*
11607 Burbank Blvd Ste A
North Hollywood, CA 91601-2345, USA

Nigh, George P (Ex-Governor)
2946 NW 160th St
Edmond, OK 73013-1464, USA

Nighswander, Nicholas (Athlete, Football
Player)
PO Box 46
Burgoon, OH 43407-0046, USA

Nightingale, Maxine (Musician)
c/o Stephen Ford *Diva Central Inc*
7510 W Sunset Blvd Ste 1445
Los Angeles, CA 90046-3408, USA

Nighy, Bill (Actor)
c/o Chris Andrews *Creative Artists Agency
(CAA-LA)*
2000 Avenue of the Stars Ste 100
Los Angeles, CA 90067-4705, USA

Niittymaki, Antero (Athlete, Hockey
Player)
1751 Pinnacle Dr Ste 1500
Mc Lean, VA 22102-3833, USA

Nikkanen, Kurt (Musician)
Columbia Artists Mgmt Inc
165 W 57th St
New York, NY 10019-2201, USA

Niklas, Jan (Actor)
Konigsberger Str. 20
Munich, GE D-819

Nikolishin, Andrei (Athlete, Hockey
Player)
105 Bloomfield Ave
Hartford, CT 06105-1007, USA

Nilan, Chris (Athlete, Hockey Player)
577 Adams St Unit D
Milton, MA 02186-5636, USA

Niland, John H (Athlete, Football Player)
16058 Chalfont Ct
Dallas, TX 75248-3547, USA

Niles, Nicholas H (Publisher)
Sporting News Publishing Co
1212 N Lindbergh Blvd
Saint Louis, MO 63132, USA

Niles, Prescott (Musician)
Artists & Audience Entertainment
PO Box 35
Pawling, NY 12564-0035, USA

Nill, Jim (Athlete, Hockey Player)
20847 Dundee St
Novi, MI 48375, USA

Nill, Jim (Athlete, Hockey Player)
Detroit Red Wings 600 Civic Center Dr
Attn: Asst General Manager
Novi, MI 48375, USA

Nilsmark, Catrin (Athlete, Golfer)
187 Commodore Dr
Jupiter, FL 33477-4007, USA

Nilsson, Kent (Athlete, Hockey Player)
9034 Crichton Wood Dr
Orlando, FL 32819-4836, USA

Nimmons, Ernest (Baseball Player)
Indianapolis Clowns
2658 Collins Dr
Lorain, OH 44053-1142, USA

Nimoy, Leonard (Actor, Director,
Photographer)
801 Stone Canyon Rd
Los Angeles, CA 90077-2911, USA

Nimphius, Kurt (Athlete, Basketball
Player)
750 Dry Creek Rd
Sedona, AZ 86336-3621, USA

Nimziki, Joe (Director)
Paradigm Agency
10100 Santa Monica Blvd Ste 2500
Los Angeles, CA 90067-4116, USA

Nine (9) Inch Nails (Music Group)
c/o Jim Guerinot *Rebel Waltz Inc*
31652 2nd Ave
Laguna Beach, CA 92651-8244, USA

Ninedays (Music Group)
c/o Staff Member *Epic Records Group*
550 Madison Ave Fl 6
New York, NY 10022-3211, USA

Ninowski, Jim (Athlete, Football Player)
2715 Melcombe Cir Apt 302
Troy, MI 48084-3453, USA

Nipar, Yvette (Actor)
Irv Schechter
9300 Wilshire Blvd Ste 410
Beverly Hills, CA 90212-3228, USA

Nipp, Maury (Athlete, Football Player)
631 E Michelle St
West Covina, CA 91790-5146, USA

Nipper, Al (Athlete, Baseball Player)
401 White Birch Valley Ct
Chesterfield, MO 63017-2457, USA

Nippert, Dustin (Athlete, Baseball Player)
PO Box 8540
Stockton, CA 95208-0540, USA

Nippert, Merlin (Athlete, Baseball Player)
1015 N Michigan Ave
Mangum, OK 73554-1820, USA

Nischwitz, Ron (Athlete, Baseball Player)
6790 Garber Rd
Dayton, OH 45415-1504, USA

Nish, Wayne (Chef)
405 E 58th St
New York, NY 10022-2302, USA

Nishikori, Kei (Athlete, Tennis Player)
5618 Title Row Dr
Bradenton, FL 34210-4072, USA

Nishilori, Kei (Athlete, Tennis Player)
5618 Title Row Dr
Bradenton, FL 34210-4072, USA

Nishkian, Byron (Skier)
150 4th St PH
San Francisco, CA 94130-2201, USA

Nispel, Marcus (Director)
2125 Rockledge Rd
Los Angeles, CA 90068-3135, USA

Nissalke, Tom (Basketball Coach, Coach)
3075 E Kennedy Dr Apt 406
Salt Lake City, UT 84108-2200, USA

Nissen, Steve (Doctor)
2200 Devonshire Dr
Cleveland, OH 44106-4607, USA

Nitkowski, C J (Athlete, Baseball Player)
205 Townsend Ln
Alpharetta, GA 30004-2553, USA

Nittmo, Bjorn (Athlete, Football Player)
201 E Jefferson St
Phoenix, AZ 85004-2412, USA

Nitty Gritty Dirt Band (Music Group)
c/o Staff Member *Paradigm (Monterey)*
404 W Franklin St
Monterey, CA 93940-2303, USA

Nitz, Leonard (Athlete, Cycler, Olympic
Athlete)
5515 Ruhkala Rd
Rocklin, CA 95677-3117, USA

Nitzkowski, Monte (Athlete, Olympic
Athlete, Swimmer)
7041 Seal Cir
Huntington Beach, CA 92648-3035, USA

Niven, Barbara
Gail Abbott Management
10926 Bluffside Dr Unit 26
Studio City, CA 91604-3347, USA

Niven, Kip (Actor)
8109 Sagamore Rd
Leawood, KS 66206-1232, USA

Niven, Laurence (Larry) (Writer)
136 El Camino Dr
Beverly Hills, CA 90212-2705, USA

Niven Jr, David (Actor, Producer)
1100 Alta Loma Rd Apt 1004
West Hollywood, CA 90069-2439, USA

Nivola, Alessandro (Actor)
c/o William Choi *Management 360*
9111 Wilshire Blvd
Beverly Hills, CA 90210-5508, USA

Niwa, Gail (Musician)
Siegel Artist Mgmt
1416 Hinman Ave
Evanston, IL 60201-5324, USA

Nix, Jimmy (Race Car Driver)
520 SE 30th St Ste 6
Oklahoma City, OK 73129-4900, USA

Nix, John L (Athlete, Football Player)
2278 Lindsey Ct
Fallbrook, CA 92028-5304, USA

Nix, Kent (Athlete, Football Player)
2732 Colonial Pkwy
Fort Worth, TX 76109-1211, USA

Nix, Laynce (Athlete, Baseball Player)
1506 Princeton Ave
Midland, TX 79701-5762, USA

Nix, Matt (Writer)
c/o Staff Member *William Morris Endeavor (LA)*
9601 Wilshire Blvd
Beverly Hills, CA 90210-5213, USA

Nixey, Troy (Director)
c/o Gary Ungar *Exile Entertainment*
732 El Medio Ave
Pacific Palisades, CA 90272-3451, USA

Nix III, Louis (Athlete, Football Player)
c/o Todd France *Five Star Athlete Management*
3500 Lenox Rd NE
Atlanta, GA 30326-4228, USA

Nixon, Agnes (Producer, Writer)
774 Conestoga Rd
Bryn Mawr, PA 19010-1257, USA

Nixon, Cynthia (Actor)
10 Bleecker St Apt 3B
New York, NY 10012-2436, USA

Nixon, Derek Lee (Actor, Producer, Writer)
c/o Staff Member *Mark Robert Management*
2208 Patricia Ave
Los Angeles, CA 90064-2318, USA

Nixon, Donell (Athlete, Baseball Player)
Seattle Mariners
2681 Mount Olive Rd
Whiteville, NC 28472-6863, USA

Nixon, Jay (Governor, Politician)
Office of Governor
PO Box 720
Jefferson City, MO 65102-0720, USA

Nixon, Jeff (Athlete, Football Player)
549 Linwood Ave
Buffalo, NY 14209-1403, USA

Nixon, Kimberley (Actor)
c/o Larry Taube *Principal Entertainment (LA)*
9255 W Sunset Blvd Ste 500
West Hollywood, CA 90069-3301, USA

Nixon, Marni (Actor, Musician)
315 W End Ave Apt 2A
New York, NY 10023-8174, USA

Nixon, Norm (Athlete, Basketball Player)
Nixon and Associates
607 Marguerita Ave
Santa Monica, CA 90402-1919, USA

Nixon, Otis (Athlete, Baseball Player)
1000 Montage Way Apt 1814
Atlanta, GA 30341-6071, USA

Nixon, Russ (Athlete, Baseball Player)
4265 N Tee Pee Ln
Las Vegas, NV 89129-2628, USA

Nixon, Torran (Athlete, Football Player)
3265 Thorn St
San Diego, CA 92104-4754, USA

Nixon, Trot (Athlete, Baseball Player)
1023 Ocean Ridge Dr
Wilmington, NC 28405-5287, USA

Nixon-Eisenhower, Julie (Politician)
255 Foxall Ln
Berwyn, PA 19312-1843, USA

Niziolek, Robert (Athlete, Football Player)
206 Brome Ave
Lafayette, CO 80026-1738, USA

Niznik, Stephanie (Actor)
15263 Mulholland Dr
Los Angeles, CA 90077-1620, USA

Noah, Joakim (Athlete, Basketball Player)
712 W Schubert Ave
Chicago, IL 60614-1507, USA

Noah, John (Athlete, Hockey Player, Olympic Athlete)
3315 W Prairiewood Dr S
Fargo, ND 58103-4666, USA

Noah, Trevor (Comedian)
c/o Matthew Blake *Creative Artists Agency (CAA-LA)*
2000 Avenue of the Stars Ste 100
Los Angeles, CA 90067-4705, USA

Noah, Yannick (Athlete, Coach, Musician, Tennis Player)
230 Central Park S
New York, NY 10019-1409, USA

Nobilo, Frank (Athlete, Golfer)
10209 Atterbury Ct
Orlando, FL 32827-7041, USA

Nobis, Thomas H (Tommy) Jr (Athlete, Football Executive, Football Player)
40 S Battery Pl
Atlanta, GA 30342-2443, USA

Noble, Brandon (Athlete, Football Player)
2154 Ferncroft Ln
Chester Springs, PA 19425-3846, USA

Noble, Brian (Athlete, Football Player)
3664 Via Certaldo Ave
Henderson, NV 89052-0511, USA

Noble, James (Actor)
113 Ledgebrook Dr
Norwalk, CT 06854-1070, USA

Noble, John (Actor)
c/o Nicolas Bernheim *NB Management*
8906 W Olympic Blvd
Ground Floor
Beverly Hills, CA 90211-3550, USA

Noble, Karen (Athlete, Golfer)
36 Edgewood Rd
Chatham, NJ 07928-2002, USA

Noble, Reginald (Redman) (Musician)
c/o Greg Weiss *Vanguard Management Group (NY)*
220 5th Ave PH West
New York, NY 10001-7745, USA

Noble, Samantha (Actor)
c/o David Rudy *Armada Partners*
PO Box 64547
Los Angeles, CA 90064-0547, USA

Noblitt, Niles L (Business Person)
Biomet Inc
PO Box 587
Airport Industrial Park
Warsaw, IN 46581-0587, USA

Noboa, Junior (Athlete, Baseball Player)
Arizona Diamondbacks
PO Box 2095
Attn: Director, Latin American Ops
Phoenix, AZ 85001-2095, USA

Noce, Paul (Athlete, Baseball Player)
942 W Maumee St
Adrian, MI 49221-1916, USA

Nocioni, Andres
2281 Royal Ridge Dr
Northbrook, IL 60062-8608, USA

Nock, George (Athlete, Football Player)
1025 Nine North Dr Ste H
Alpharetta, GA 30004-3951, USA

Nodell, Mart (Cartoonist)
117 Lake Irene Dr
West Palm Beach, FL 33411-2266, USA

No Doubt (Music Group)
c/o Irving Azoff *Azoff Music Management*
1100 Glendon Ave Ste 2000
Los Angeles, CA 90024-3524, USA

Noel, Alyson (Writer)
14 Monarch Bay Plz
#186
Dana Point, CA 92629, USA

Noel, Chris (Actor)
6815 Lake Ave
West Palm Beach, FL 33405-4525, USA

Noel, Claude (Athlete, Hockey Player)
4361 Bridgeside Pl
New Albany, OH 43054-7053, USA

Noel, Don (Race Car Driver)
PO Box 2757
Lake Isabella, CA 93240-2757, USA

Noel, Philip W (Politician)
20403 Wildcat Run Dr
Estero, FL 33928-2014, USA

Nogle, Donald (Athlete, Football Player)
1248 Calle Christopher
Encinitas, CA 92024-5519, United States

Noguchi, Soichi (Astronaut)
100 Cyberonics Blvd Ste 201
Houston, TX 77058-2074, USA

Nogulich, Natalia (Actor)
11841 Kiowa Ave Apt 7
Los Angeles, CA 90049-6016

Nogulich, Natalija (Actor)
11841 Kiowa Ave Apt 7
Los Angeles, CA 90049-6016, USA

Noji, Minae (Actor)
c/o Steven Jensen *Vincent Cirrincione Associates*
8332 Melrose Ave
West Hollywood, CA 90069-5420, USA

Nojima, Minoru (Musician)
John Gingrich Mgmt
PO Box 515
New York, NY 10023, USA

Nokelainen, Petteri (Athlete, Hockey Player)
c/o Staff Member *Boston Bruins*
100 Legends Way Ste 250
Td Banknorth Garden
Boston, MA 02114-1389, USA

Nokes, Matt (Athlete, Baseball Player)
22S5 Oxford Ave
Cardiff By The Sea, CA 92007, USA

Nolan, Christopher (Director, Writer)
2121 Canyon Dr
Los Angeles, CA 90068-3608, USA

Nolan, Deanna (Basketball Player)
Detroit Shock
2 Championship Dr
Palace
Auburn Hills, MI 48326-1753, USA

Nolan, Gary (Athlete, Baseball Player)
9025 Alpine Peaks Ave
Las Vegas, NV 89147-7819, USA

Nolan, Graham (Cartoonist)
162 Godfrey Ter
East Aurora, NY 14052-2040, USA

Nolan, Joe (Athlete, Baseball Player)
9515 Alix Dr
Saint Louis, MO 63123-7101, USA

Nolan, Jonathan (Producer)
c/o Jeff Gorin *William Morris Endeavor (LA)*
9601 Wilshire Blvd Ste GL25
Beverly Hills, CA 90210-5217, USA

Nolan, Kathleen (Actor)
c/o Staff Member *House of Representatives, The*
1434 6th St Ste 1
Santa Monica, CA 90401-2527, USA

Nolan, Nolan (Athlete, Football Player)
1400 Zillock Rd Ofc
San Benito, TX 78586-9730, USA

Nolan, Owen (Athlete, Hockey Player)
17110 Cooper Hill Dr
Davenport, CA 95017, USA

Nolan, Tom
1335 N Ontario St
Burbank, CA 91505-1910

Nolasco, Amaury (Actor)
c/o Evan Hainey *Untitled Entertainment (LA)*
350 S Beverly Dr Ste 200
Beverly Hills, CA 90212-4819, USA

Nolasco, Ricky (Athlete, Baseball Player)
3370 NE 190th St Apt 1812
Miami, FL 33180-2417, USA

Nold, Dick (Athlete, Baseball Player)
715 Athens St
San Francisco, CA 94112-3513, USA

Nolen, Paul (Athlete, Basketball Player)
480 Pecan Dr
Burleson, TX 76028-6308, USA

Noles, Dickie (Athlete, Baseball Player)
15 Hidden Valley Rd
Aston, PA 19014-2513, USA

Nolfi, George (Director)
c/o David Wirtschafter *William Morris Endeavor (LA)*
9601 Wilshire Blvd Ste GL25
Beverly Hills, CA 90210-5217, USA

Nolin, Gena Lee (Actor)
c/o David Rose *Innovative Artists (LA)*
1505 10th St
Santa Monica, CA 90401-2805, USA

Nolte, Eric (Athlete, Baseball Player)
2388S Noelle Ave
Hemet, CA 92544, USA

Nolte, Nick (Actor, Producer)
6173 Bonsall Dr
Malibu, CA 90265-3824, USA

Nolting, Paul F (Religious Leader)
Church of Lutheran Confession
620 E 50th St
Loveland, CO 80538-1838, USA

Nomellini, Leo
906 Avalon Ave
San Francisco, CA 94112-2134

Nomina, Tom (Athlete, Football Player)
731 N Namaqua Ave
Loveland, CO 80537-4401, USA

Nomo, Hideo (Athlete, Baseball Player)
11746 Stonehenge Ln
Los Angeles, CA 90077-1302, USA

Noonan, Brian (Athlete, Hockey Player)
262 W Eggleston Ave Apt F
Elmhurst, IL 60126-3885, USA

Noonan, Chris (Director)
c/o Craig Gering *Creative Artists Agency*
(CAA-LA)
2000 Avenue of the Stars Ste 100
Los Angeles, CA 90067-4705, USA

Noonan, Danny (Athlete, Football Player)
1 Cowboys Pkwy
Irving, TX 75063-4924, USA

Noonan, Karl (Athlete, Football Player)
7149 Oxford Hunt Dr
Stanley, NC 28164-6803, USA

Noonan, Peggy (Writer)
Reagan Books
10 E 53rd St
New York, NY 10022-5244, USA

Noone, Kathleen (Actor)
130 W 42nd St Ste 1804
New York, NY 10036-7902, USA

Noone, Peter (Actor, Musician)
2140 Ten Acre Rd
Santa Barbara, CA 93108-2227, USA

Noory, George (Radio Personality)
WOR News Talk Radio 710
111 Broadway Fl 3
New York, NY 10006-2012, USA

Norcross, Clayton
951 Galloway St
Pacific Palisades, CA 90272-3850

Nordbrook, Tim (Athlete, Baseball Player)
14018 Blenheim Rd N
Phoenix, MD 21131-1830, USA

Norden, Tommy (Actor)
34 Bal Bay Dr
Bal Harbour, FL 33154-1349, USA

Nordgren, Fred (Athlete, Football Player)
1385 Ranier Loop NW
Salem, OR 97304-2081, USA

Nordhagen, Wayne (Athlete, Baseball
Player)
2S896 Ramillo Way
Valencia, CA 91355, USA

Nordlander, Mattias (Musician)
MOB Agency
6404 Wilshire Blvd Ste 505
Los Angeles, CA 90048-5507, USA

Nordling, Jeffrey (Actor)
245 Spencer St
Glendale, CA 91202-1813, USA

Nordmann, Robert (Athlete, Basketball
Player)
12711 Isle Royale Dr
Dewitt, MI 48820-8622, USA

Nordquist, Helen (Athlete, Baseball
Player)
PO Box 474
Alton, NH 03809-0474, USA

Nordquist, Mark (Athlete, Football Player)
3495 Seacrest Dr
Carlsbad, CA 92008-2039, USA

Nordsieck, Kenneth H (Astronaut)
2807 Ridge Rd
Madison, WI 53705-5223, USA

Noren, Irv (Athlete, Baseball Player)
3154 Camino Crest Dr
Oceanside, CA 92056-3613, USA

Norgaard, Chloe (Model)
c/o Staff Member *One Management*
42 Bond St Apt 2
New York, NY 10012-2428, USA

Norgard, Erik C (Athlete, Football Player)
404 Winterthur Way
Highlands Ranch, CO 80129-5662, USA

Noriander, John (Basketball Player)
801 9th St N Apt 102
Virginia, MN 55792-2393, USA

Norick, Lance (Race Car Driver)
6306 S Macdill Ave Apt 1724
Tampa, FL 33611-5059, USA

Noriega, Carlos I (Astronaut)
4630 Silhouette Dr
Katy, TX 77493-8099, USA

Noriega, Carlos L Lt Colonel (Astronaut)
4630 Silhouette Dr
Katy, TX 77493-8099, USA

Noris, Joe (Athlete, Hockey Player)
1111 Via Carolina
La Jolla, CA 92037-6254, USA

Norman, Dan (Athlete, Baseball Player)
430 McBroom Ave
Barstow, CA 92311-5538, USA

Norman, Edie Jo (Bowler)
3544 Mariner Blvd
Spring Hill, FL 34609-2487, USA

Norman, Fred (Athlete, Baseball Player)
5921 Monnett Rd
Julian, NC 27283-9187, USA

Norman, Greg (Athlete, Golfer)
2041 Vista Pkwy Ste L
West Palm Beach, FL 33411-6758, USA

Norman, Jessye (Musician)
c/o Staff Member *Columbia Artists Mgmt
Inc*
1790 Broadway Fl 6
New York, NY 10019-1537, USA

Norman, Joe (Athlete, Football Player)
1526 Saunders Dr
Wooster, OH 44691-1558, USA

Norman, Ken (Athlete, Basketball Player)
19020 Kedzie Ave
Homewood, IL 60430-4359, USA

Norman, Les (Athlete, Baseball Player)
1401 Dogwood Dr
Greenwood, MO 64034-8671, USA

Norman, Marsha (Writer)
375 Greenwich St # 700
New York, NY 10013-2376, USA

Norman, Nelson (Athlete, Baseball Player)
3282 Fairfax Ave NE
Palm Bay, FL 32905-5915, USA

Norman, Pettis (Athlete, Football Player)
1430 Bar Harbor Cir
Dallas, TX 75232-3010, USA

Norman, Steve (Musician)
International Talent Group
729 7th Ave Ste 1600
New York, NY 10019-6880, USA

Norman, Tim (Reality Star)
Sweetie Pie's
3643 Delmar Blvd
Saint Louis, MO 63110, USA

Norman, Todd (Athlete, Football Player)
27517 Via Montoya
San Juan Capistrano, CA 92675-5364,
USA

Norona, David (Actor)
c/o Staff Member *Kohner Agency, The*
9300 Wilshire Blvd Ste 555
Beverly Hills, CA 90212-3211, USA

Noronen, Mika (Athlete, Hockey Player)
65 S Autumn Dr
Rochester, NY 14626, USA

Norrena, Fredrik (Athlete, Hockey Player)
1751 Barrington Rd
Columbus, OH 43221-3838, USA

Norris, Aaron (Director, Producer)
C/O Henry Holmes
2450 Colorado Ave Ste 400
Santa Monica, CA 90404-3575, USA

Norris, Chuck (Actor, Producer, Writer)
696 S Golf Dr
Naples, FL 34102-5353, USA

Norris, Daran (Actor)
812 N Rose St
Burbank, CA 91505-2733, USA

Norris, Darran (Actor)
c/o Staff Member *ICM Partners (LA)*
10250 Constellation Blvd Fl 7
Los Angeles, CA 90067-6207, USA

Norris, Dean (Actor)
c/o Keith Addis *Industry Entertainment*
955 Carrillo Dr Ste 300
Los Angeles, CA 90048-5400, USA

Norris, Dwayne (Athlete, Hockey Player)
850 Eastlake Ct
Oxford, MI 48371-6802, USA

Norris, Jim (Athlete, Baseball Player)
6375 Oak Hollow Dr
Burleson, TX 76028-2839, USA

Norris, John (Journalist, Television Host)
c/o Staff Member *MTV News*
1515 Broadway Fl 29
New York, NY 10036-8901, USA

Norris, Martyn (Athlete, Basketball Player)
18943 Crescent Bay Dr
Houston, TX 77094-3329, USA

Norris, Michele (Correspondent)
ABC-TV
5010 Creston St
News Dept
Hyattsville, MD 20781-1216, USA

Norris, Mike (Athlete, Baseball Player)
6228 Ridgemont Dr
Oakland, CA 94619-3725, USA

Norris, Paul J (Business Person)
WR Grace Co
7500 Grace Dr
Columbia, MD 21044-4029, USA

Norris, Terry (Boxer)
Don King Productions
968 Pinehurst Dr
Las Vegas, NV 89109-1569, USA

Norris, Tim (Athlete, Golfer)
1604 Little Kitten Ave
Manhattan, KS 66503-7500, USA

Norrish, Rod (Athlete, Hockey Player)
3516 Amherst Ave
Dallas, TX 75225-7419, USA

Norseth, Mike (Athlete, Football Player)
9774 S Jameson Point Cv
Sandy, UT 84092-4200, USA

North, Andy (Athlete, Golfer)
3289 High Point Rd
Madison, WI 53719, USA

North, Billy (Athlete, Baseball Player)
5523 106th Ave NE
Kirkland, WA 98033-7413, USA

North, Heather (Actor)
12996 Galewood St
Studio City, CA 91604-4045, USA

North, Jay (Actor)
290 NE 1st Ave
Lake Butler, FL 32054-1202, USA

North, J J
PO Box 614
Bloomfield, NJ 07003-0614, USA

North, Lowell (Athlete, Olympic Athlete,
Sailor)
333 San Antonio Ave
San Diego, CA 92106-3546, USA

North, Oliver L (Politician)
c/o Staff Member *Fox News (NY)*
1211 Avenue of the Americas Lowr C1
New York, NY 10036-8705, USA

North, Peter (Adult Film Star)
c/o Staff Member *Vivid Entertainment*
3599 Cahuenga Blvd W Fl 2
Los Angeles, CA 90068-1397, USA

Northam, Jeremy (Actor)
c/o Chris Andrews *Creative Artists Agency*
(CAA-LA)
2000 Avenue of the Stars Ste 100
Los Angeles, CA 90067-4705, USA

Northcutt, Dennis (Athlete, Football
Player)
13761 Saxon Lake Dr S
Jacksonville, FL 32225-2680, USA

Northey, Scott (Athlete, Baseball Player)
9920 Bankside Dr
Roswell, GA 30076-3735, USA

Northrop, Wayne (Actor)
37900 Road 800
Raymond, CA 93653-9714, USA

Northrup, Wayne
21919 Canon Dr
Topanga, CA 90290-4336

Northrup, MD, Christiane (Writer)
Empowering Women's Wisdom
PO Box 199
Yarmouth, ME 04096-0199, USA

Northway, Douglas (Doug) (Swimmer)
3239 E 3rd St Unit C
Tucson, AZ 85716-4231, USA

Norton, Brad (Athlete, Hockey Player)
26856 N 90th Dr
Peoria, AZ 85383-4639, USA

Norton, Bryan (Athlete, Golfer)
4001 W 105th St Apt 244
Overland Park, KS 66207-4032, USA

Norton, Corin (Actor)
c/o Staff Member *Bruce Heller and Associates*
3272 Motor Ave
Los Angeles, CA 90034-3772, USA

Norton, Edward (Actor)
360 N Martel Ave
Los Angeles, CA 90036-2516, USA

Norton, Gale (Politician)
6645 S Quemoy Cir
Aurora, CO 80016-2686, USA

Norton, Greg (Athlete, Baseball Player)
1618 Marie Loop
Auburn, AL 36830-6713, USA

Norton, James A (Athlete, Football Player)
201 S Elliott Ave Unit 14
Wenatchee, WA 98801-6325, USA

Norton, James C (Athlete, Football Player)
PO Box 495997
Garland, TX 75049-5997, USA

Norton, Jeff (Athlete, Hockey Player, Olympic Athlete)
110 Humphreys Ln
Duxbury, MA 02332-4846, USA

Norton, Jerry (Athlete, Football Player)
6901 Chevy Chase Ave
Dallas, TX 75225-2416, USA

Norton, Judy (Actor)
c/o Karen Renna *Karen Renna & Associates*
PO Box 4227
Burbank, CA 91503-4227, USA

Norton, Peter (Designer)
225 Arizona Ave # 200W
Santa Monica, CA 90401-1243, USA

Norton, Phil (Athlete, Baseball Player)
677 County Road 3772
Queen City, TX 75572-7947, USA

Norton, Richard (Actor)
c/o Ray Cavaleri *Cavaleri & Associates*
3500 W Olive Ave Ste 300
Burbank, CA 91505-4647, USA

Norton, Rick (Athlete, Football Player)
901 W Mahoney St
Plant City, FL 33563-4435, USA

Norton, Tom (Athlete, Baseball Player)
4900 Southwood Dr
Sheffield Lake, OH 44054-1559, USA

Norton, Virginia (Bowler)
11706 Mindanao St
Cypress, CA 90630-5662, USA

Norton Jr, Ken (Athlete, Coach, Football Coach, Football Player)
Seattle Seahawks
800 Occidental Ave S Ste 200
Coaching Staff
Seattle, WA 98134-1200, USA

Norvell, Jay (Athlete, Football Player)
2166 Clinton Ave
Alameda, CA 94501-4945, USA

Norville, Deborah (Journalist)
c/o Rick Hersh *Celebrity Consultants LLC*
3340 Ocean Park Blvd Ste 1030
Santa Monica, CA 90405-3259, USA

Norwell, Andrew (Athlete, Football Player)
c/o Adam Heller *Vantage Management Group*
518 Reamer Dr
Carnegie, PA 15106-1845, USA

Norwich, Craig (Athlete, Hockey Player)
66 9th St E Unit 2711
Saint Paul, MN 55101-2282, USA

Norwood, Brandy (Actor, Musician)
23463 Park Colombo
Calabasas, CA 91302-2814, USA

Norwood, Jerious (Football Player)
c/o Staff Member *Atlanta Falcons*
4400 Falcon Pkwy
Flowery Branch, GA 30542-3176, USA

Norwood, Jordan (Athlete, Football Player)
c/o Peter Schaffer *All Pro Sports and Entertainment*
36 Steele St Ste 100
Denver, CO 80206-5709, USA

Norwood, Lee (Athlete, Hockey Player)
1409 SE 20th Ct
Cape Coral, FL 33990-3898, USA

Norwood, Ray J (Actor, Musician)
c/o Staff Member *Defining Artists Agency*
4370 Tujunga Ave Ste 120
Studio City, CA 91604-2763, USA

Norwood, Robin (Writer)
c/o Staff Member *Simon & Schuster*
1230 Avenue of the Americas Fl CONC1
New York, NY 10020-1586, USA

Norwood, Scott (Athlete, Football Player)
42923 Shelbourne Sq
Chantilly, VA 20152-2097, USA

Norwood, Willie (Athlete, Basketball Player)
15710 Halldale Ave Apt C
Gardena, CA 90247-3838, USA

Norwood, Willie (Athlete, Baseball Player)
225 Gunsmoke Dr
Diamond Bar, CA 91765-1257, USA

Nosek, Randy (Athlete, Baseball Player)
15485 Knobhill Dr
Linden, MI 48451-8716, USA

Noseworthy, Jack
955 Carrillo Dr Ste 300
Los Angeles, CA 90048-5400

Nosseck, Noel (Director)
1435 San Ysidro Dr
Beverly Hills, CA 90210-2108, USA

Nossek, Joe (Athlete, Baseball Player)
630 Sunrise Dr
Amherst, OH 44001-1659, USA

Notaro, Phyllis (Bowler)
11123 Maritime Ct
Wellington, FL 33449-8364, USA

Notebaert, Richard (Business Person)
Quest Communications
1801 California St Ste 900
Denver, CO 80202-2609, USA

Noth, Chris (Actor)
13656 Oak Canyon Ave
Sherman Oaks, CA 91423-4723, USA

Nothstein, Marty (Athlete, Cycler, Olympic Athlete)
1019 Village Round
Allentown, PA 18106-9779, USA

Notley, Alice (Writer)
c/o Staff Member *Wesleyan University Press*
215 Long Ln
Middletown, CT 06457-4073, USA

Noto, Lucio A (Business Person)
Mobil Corp
3225 Gallows Rd
Fairfax, VA 22037-0003, USA

Nott, Tara (Athlete, Olympic Athlete, Weightlifter)
9516 Hayes St
Overland Park, KS 66212-5029, USA

Nottingham, Don (Athlete, Football Player)
PO Box 459
Belleview, FL 34421-0459, USA

Nottingham, Robert
4348 Coldwater Canyon Ave Apt B
Studio City, CA 91604-5016

Nottle, Ed (Athlete, Baseball Player)
7527 Midway Dr
Evansville, IN 47711-6300, USA

Nouri, Michael (Actor)
c/o Joanna (Joanie) Burstein *Burstein Company, The*
15304 W Sunset Blvd Ste 208
Pacific Palisades, CA 90272-3656, USA

Noury, Alain
Soyans s/Crest
, FR 26400

Nova, Nikki (Actor)
4331 E Baseline Rd Ste B105
PO Box 431
Gilbert, AZ 85234-2960, USA

Novack, K J (Business Person)
America Online
22000 Aol Way
Sterling, VA 20166-9302, USA

Novack, William
3 Ashton Ave
Newton Center, MA 02459-1526

Novak, BJ (Actor, Comedian)
c/o Kevin McLaughlin *Baker Winokur Ryder Public Relations (BWR-LA)*
9100 Wilshire Blvd Ste 500
West Tower Suite 500
Beverly Hills, CA 90212-3426, USA

Novak, David C (Business Person)
Tricon Global Restaurants
1441 Gardiner Ln
Louisville, KY 40213-1914, USA

Novak, Jack (Athlete, Football Player)
201 Adams
Georgetown, TX 78628-3680, USA

Novak, Kim (Actor)
13777 Agate Rd
Eagle Point, OR 97524-6567, USA

Novakovic, Bojana (Actor)
2607 Nichols Canyon Rd
Los Angeles, CA 90046-1343, USA

Novello, Antonia Dr (Politician)
1110 SW Ivanhoe Blvd Apt 14
Orlando, FL 32804-6370, USA

Novello, Don
PO Box 245
Fairfax, CA 94978-0245

Novello, Don (Fr Guido Sarducci) (Actor, Comedian)
Elizabeth Rush Agency
82 Cumberland Ave
Verona, NJ 07044-2105, USA

Noveskey, Matt (Musician)
Ashley Talent
2002 Hogback Rd Ste 20
Ann Arbor, MI 48105-9736, USA

Novoa, Rafael (Athlete, Baseball Player)
3420 N 47th Way
Phoenix, AZ 85018-6014, USA

Novoselic, Krist (Activist, Musician)
3105 S Lucile St
Seattle, WA 98108-3032, USA

Novoselsky, Brent (Athlete, Football Player)
405 Marvins Way
Buffalo Grove, IL 60089-6419, USA

Novotna, Jana (Tennis Player)
7834 Montvale Way
Mc Lean, VA 22102-2028, USA

Nowak, Lisa M (Astronaut)
17123 Parsley Hawthorne Ct
Houston, TX 77059, USA

Nowak, Lisa M Cdr (Astronaut)
17123 Parsley Hawthorne Ct
Houston, TX 77059-3231, USA

Nowak, Peter (Coach, Soccer Player)
DC United
14120 Newbrook Dr
Chantilly, VA 20151-2273, USA

Nowak, Tim (Athlete, Hockey Player)
7081 Blackberry Ct
Easton, MD 21601-4767, USA

Nowatzke, Tom (Athlete, Football Player)
4335 Diuble Rd
Ann Arbor, MI 48103-9606, USA

Nowicki, Tom (Actor)
c/o Staff Member *Davis Management*
4111 Lankershim Blvd
North Hollywood, CA 91602-2828

Nowitzki, Dirk (Athlete, Basketball Player)
10735 Strait Ln
Dallas, TX 75229-5428, USA

Noxon, Marti (Writer)
c/o Staff Member *William Morris Endeavor (LA)*
9601 Wilshire Blvd
Beverly Hills, CA 90210-5213, USA

Noyce, Phillip (Director)
6666 Whitley Ter
Los Angeles, CA 90068-3221, USA

Noyd, R Allen (Religious Leader)
General Council
1294 Rutledge Rd
Christian Church
Transfer, PA 16154-2226, USA

Nucci, Danny (Actor)
6361 Innsdale Dr
Los Angeles, CA 90068-1623, USA

Nugent, Eddie
PO Box 1266
New York, NY 10150-1266

Nugent, Kevin (Athlete, Hockey Player)
86 Glen Dr
New Canaan, CT 06840-3636, USA

Nugent, Mike (Athlete, Football Player)
c/o Ken Harris *Optimum Sports Management*
3225 S Macdill Ave Ste 330
Tampa, FL 33629-8171, USA

Nugent, Nelle (Producer)
Foxboro Entertainment
234 W 44th St Ste 1005
New York, NY 10036-3909, USA

Nugent, Ted (Musician)
2424 Coopers Crossing Rd
China Spring, TX 76633-3121, USA

Numeroff, Laura Joffe (Writer)
c/o Staff Member *HarperCollins Publishers*
195 Broadway Fl 2
Cellar 1
New York, NY 10007-3132, USA

Numminen, Teppo (Athlete, Hockey Player)
5975 Tipperary Mnr
Clarence Center, NY 14032-9509, USA

Numminen, Teppo (Athlete, Hockey Player)
Buffalo Sabres 1 Seymour H Knox III Plz Ste 1
Attn: Coaching Staff
Buffalo, NY 14203, USA

Nunes, Devin (Congressman, Politician)
1013 Longworth Hob
Washington, DC 20515-0004, USA

Nunez, Abraham (Athlete, Baseball Player)
Pittsburgh Pirates
2863 Post Rock Dr
Tarpon Springs, FL 34688-7311, USA

Nunez, Chris (Reality Star)
c/o Adena Chawke *Greenlight Management and Production*
9713 Santa Monica Blvd Ste 219
Beverly Hills, CA 90210-4215, USA

Nunez, Edwin (Athlete, Baseball Player)
2618 E Locust Dr
Chandler, AZ 85286-2721, USA

Nunez, Oscar (Actor)
c/o Bruce Smith *OmniPop Talent Group (LA)*
4605 Lankershim Blvd Ste 201
North Hollywood, CA 91602-1874, USA

Nunez, Victor (Director)
Paul Kohner
9300 Wilshire Blvd Ste 555
Beverly Hills, CA 90212-3211, USA

Nunez, Vladimir (Athlete, Baseball Player)
1205 Park Pass Way
Suwanee, GA 30024-4514, USA

Nunez Jr, Miguel A (Actor)
PO Box 570518
Tarzana, CA 91357-0518, USA

Nunley, Frank (Athlete, Football Player)
2131 Mulberry Cir
San Jose, CA 95125-4647, USA

Nunley, Jeremy (Athlete, Football Player)
1595 Little Hurricane Rd
Winchester, TN 37398-4229, USA

Nunn, Samuel A (Sam) (Politician)
781 Marietta St NW
Atlanta, GA 30318-5750, USA

Nunn, Teri (Musician)
MOB Agency
6404 Wilshire Blvd Ste 505
Los Angeles, CA 90048-5507, USA

Nunn, Terri (Actor)
11275 Highridge Ct
Santa Rosa Valley, CA 93012-8299, USA

Nunnally, Jon (Athlete, Baseball Player)
36550 Chester Rd Apt 504
Avon, OH 44011-1098, USA

Nunnari, Talmadge (Athlete, Baseball Player)
2811 Park St
Jacksonville, FL 32205-8016, USA

Nunnelee, Alan (Congressman, Politician)
1432 Longworth Hob
Washington, DC 20515-1505, USA

Nunnery, R B (Athlete, Football Player)
3276 Claude Smith Rd
Magnolia, MS 39652-9534, USA

Nurding, Louise (Actor)
42 Colwith Rd
London, EN W6 9E

Nussbaum, Joe (Actor, Director)
5837 Balcom Ave
Encino, CA 91316-1106, USA

Nussmeier, Doug (Athlete, Football Player)
28493 SW Meadows Loop
Wilsonville, OR 97070-6779, USA

Nutt, Dennis (Athlete, Basketball Player)
704 Magnolia Dr
Arkadelphia, AR 71923-4109, USA

Nutter, David (Director)
911 El Medio Ave
Pacific Palisades, CA 90272-2418, USA

Nutting, Ed (Athlete, Football Player)
607 Ashford Pkwy
Atlanta, GA 30338-5534, USA

Nutting, Robert (Sportscaster)
366 Oglebay Dr
Wheeling, WV 26003-1624, USA

Nutzie, Futzie (Artist, Cartoonist)
PO Box 325
Aromas, CA 95004-0325, USA

Nuveman, Stacey (Athlete, Olympic Athlete, Softball Player)
2801 NE 50th St # Usa
Oklahoma City, OK 73111-7203, USA

Nuwer, Hank (Journalist, Writer)
PO Box 31
Fairland, IN 46126-0031, USA

Nuyen, France (Actor)
c/o Budd Burton Moss *Burton Moss*
10533 Strathmore Dr
Los Angeles, CA 90024-2540, USA

Nwosu, Julius (Athlete, Basketball Player)
12436 Park Regency P1
Rd Apt 1122
San Antonio, TX 78230, USA

Nyad, Diana (Athlete, Olympic Athlete, Swimmer)
870 5th Ave
Los Angeles, CA 90005-3522, USA

Nyberg, Karen L (Astronaut)
1848 Lake Landing Dr
League City, TX 77573-7781, USA

Nyberg, Karen L Dr (Astronaut)
1848 Lake Landing Dr
League City, TX 77573-7781, USA

Nye, Blaine (Athlete, Football Player)
702 Marshall St Ste 200
Redwood City, CA 94063-1823, USA

Nye, Erie (Business Person)
Texas Utilities Co
1601 Bryan St
Energy Plaza
Dallas, TX 75201-3431, USA

Nye, Naomi Shihab (Writer)
c/o Staff Member *HarperCollins Children's Books*
1350 Avenue of the Americas
New York, NY 10019-4702, USA

Nye, Rich (Athlete, Baseball Player)
40W2S7 Seavey Rd
Batavia, IL 60510, USA

Nye, Ryan (Athlete, Baseball Player)
3603 Tpc Dr
Alma, AR 72921-8600, USA

Nyers, Dick (Athlete, Football Player)
5174 Sanibel Dr
Columbus, IN 47203-8361, USA

Nykoluk, Mike (Athlete, Hockey Player)
47 Bennington Dr Apt 2
Naples, FL 34104-6553, USA

Nylander, Michael (Athlete, Hockey Player)
726 S Monroe St
Hinsdale, IL 60521-4320, USA

Nyman, Chris (Athlete, Baseball Player)
1700 Happy Creek Rd
Front Royal, VA 22630-6438, USA

Nyman, Jerry (Athlete, Baseball Player)
114 N Parkwood Ln
Payson, AZ 85541-4357, USA

Nyman, Nyls (Athlete, Baseball Player)
PO Box 236
Susanville, CA 96130-0236, USA

Nyong'o, Lupita (Actor)
c/o Didi Rea *D2 Management*
9255 W Sunset Blvd Ste 600
West Hollywood, CA 90069-3306, USA

Nyquist, Ryan (Athlete)
c/o Staff Member *Wasserman Media Group - Carlsbad*
2052 Corte Del Nogal
150
Carlsbad, CA 92011-1464, USA

Nystrom, Bob (Athlete, Hockey Player)
475 Berry Hill Rd
Oyster Bay, NY 11771, USA

Nystrom, Eric (Athlete, Hockey Player)
475 Berry Hill Rd
Oyster Bay, NY 11771, USA

Nystrom, Lee (Athlete, Football Player)
18411 Priory Ave
Minnetonka, MN 55345-2459, USA

Nyvell, Vic (Athlete, Football Player)
P.O. Box 159C
Kilgore, TX 75663, USA

O, Karen (Musician)
Yeah Yeah Yeahs
249 Metropolitan Ave
Brooklyn, NY 11211-4009, USA

Oakenfold, Paul (DJ, Musician)
6901 Oporto Dr
Los Angeles, CA 90068-2638, USA

Oakes, Don (Athlete, Football Player)
101 Aftons Meadow Rd
Vinton, VA 24179-9701, USA

Oakes, Summer Rayne (Model)
59 Grand St
Brooklyn, NY 11249-4110, USA

Oakley, Charles (Athlete, Basketball Player)
700 Park Regency P1
NE Apt 1105
Atlanta, GA 30326, USA

Oak Ridge Boys (Music Group)
Oak Ridge Boys, Inc.
88 New Shackle Island Rd
Hendersonville, TN 37075-2393, USA

O.A.R. (Music Group)
c/o Dave Roberge *Red Light Management (NY)*
44 Wall St Fl 22
New York, NY 10005-2401, USA

OAR (Music Group)
c/o Dave Roberge *Red Light Management (NY)*
44 Wall St Fl 22
New York, NY 10005-2401, USA

Oates, Adam (Athlete, Hockey Player)
165 Mulberry St
Attn Coaching Staff
Newark, NJ 07102-3607, USA

Oates, Adam R (Athlete, Hockey Player)
114 Lighthouse Dr
Jupiter, FL 33469-3511, USA

Oates, Bart S (Athlete, Football Player, Sportscaster)
2 Silverbrook Rd
Morristown, NJ 07960-8003, USA

Oates, John (Musician)
1214 Woody Creek Rd
Woody Creek, CO 81656, USA

Oates, Joyce Carol (Writer)
Princeton University
English Dept
Princeton, NJ 08540, USA

Oats, Carleton (Athlete, Football Player)
10605 E Coralbell Ave
Mesa, AZ 85208-7442, USA

Oatway, Devin
10635 Santa Monica Blvd Ste 130
Los Angeles, CA 90025-8306

Obama, Barack (Politician, President)
1600 Pennsylvania Ave NW
the White House
Washington, DC 20500-0005, USA

Obama, Michelle (Politician)
1600 Pennsylvania Ave NW
the White House
Washington, DC 20500-0005, USA

Obando, Sherman (Athlete, Baseball Player)
7037 Coral Cove Dr
Orlando, FL 32818-2866, USA

O'Bannon, Dan (Director)
c/o Staff Member *Agency for the Performing Arts (APA-LA)*
405 S Beverly Dr Ste 500
Beverly Hills, CA 90212-4425, USA

O'Bannon, Ed (Athlete, Basketball Player)
1387 Minuet St
Henderson, NV 89052-6454, USA

O'Bannon, Ed (Basketball Player)
11930 Agnes St
Cerritos, CA 90703-6902, USA

O'Bard, Ronnie (Athlete, Football Player)
28 Cuervo
Rancho Santa Margarita, CA 92688-4916, USA

Obee, Duncan (Athlete, Football Player)
4488 283rd St
Toledo, OH 43611-1864, USA

Obeidallah, Dean (Comedian)
338 E 70th St Apt 3A
New York, NY 10021-8682, USA

Oben, Roman (Athlete, Football Player)
11476 Creekstone Ln
San Diego, CA 92128-6325, USA

Oberding, Mark (Basketball Player)
4131 Cliff Oaks St
San Antonio, TX 78229-3536, USA

Oberer, Angela (Actor, Producer)
PO Box 4122
Los Angeles, CA 90078-4122, USA

Oberg, Tom (Athlete, Football Player)
280 Avery St
Ashland, OR 97520-2202, USA

Oberholser, Arron (Golfer)
c/o Staff Member *Pro Golfers Association (PGA) Tour*
112 Tpc Blvd
Ponte Vedra Beach, FL 32082, USA

Oberkfell, Ken (Athlete, Baseball Player)
1335 W Welsford Dr
Spring, TX 77386-2599, USA

Oberlin, David W (Government Official)
800 Independence Ave SW # 814
Washington, DC 20591-0001, USA

Obermeyer, Klaus F (Designer, Fashion Designer)
Sport Obermeyer
115 Aspen Airport Business Ctr
Aspen, CO 81611-2502, USA

Obermueller, Wes (Athlete, Baseball Player)
7031 27th Ave
Newhall, IA 52315-9600, USA

O'Berry, Mike (Athlete, Baseball Player)
5977 S Fork Dr
Hoover, AL 35244-5466, USA

Oberst, Conner (Musician)
c/o Chloe Walsh *Press Here Publicity*
138 W 25th St Ste 900
New York, NY 10001-7470, USA

Oberst, Conor (Musician)
c/o Brian Young *KillerMoxie Management*
5890 W Jefferson Blvd Ste J
Los Angeles, CA 90016-3161, USA

Oberto, Fabricio (Athlete, Basketball Player)
230 W Superior St Ste 510
Chicago, IL 60654-3584, USA

O'Boyle, Maureen (Television Host)
WBTV News 3
1 Julian Price Pl
Charlotte, NC 28208-5211, USA

Obradors, Jacqueline (Actor)
c/o Todd Eisner *Innovative Artists (LA)*
405 S Beverly Dr Ste 500
Beverly Hills, CA 90212-4425, USA

O'Bradovich, Ed (Athlete, Football Player)
235 N Smith St Apt 207
Palatine, IL 60067-8503, USA

Obregon, Ana (Actor)
Paul Kohner
9300 Wilshire Blvd Ste 555
Beverly Hills, CA 90212-3211, USA

O'Brian, Hugh (Actor)
Hugh O'Brian Youth Foundation
31255 Cedar Valley Dr Ste 327
Westlake Village, CA 91362-7140, USA

O'Brien, Austin (Actor)
Gersh Agency
232 N Canon Dr
Beverly Hills, CA 90210-5302, USA

O'Brien, Bob (Athlete, Baseball Player)
1243 E Jamestown Dr
Fresno, CA 93720-4079, USA

O'Brien, Carl (Cubby) (Actor)
2530 Independence Ave Apt 2J
Bronx, NY 10463-6236, USA

O'Brien, Cathy (Athlete, Track Athlete)
19 Foss Farm Rd
Durham, NH 03824-2927, USA

O'Brien, Charlie (Athlete, Baseball Player)
4932 E 38th Pl
Tulsa, OK 74135-5529, USA

O'Brien, Conan (Comedian, Talk Show Host)
Conaco
4000 Warner Blvd Bldg 2
Burbank, CA 91522-0001, USA

O'Brien, Cubby
2839 N Surrey Dr
Carrollton, TX 75006-4800

O'Brien, Dan (Athlete, Baseball Player)
4978 Southpointe Pkwy
Monroe, MI 48161-4522, USA

O'Brien, Dan (Athlete, Decathlon Athlete, Olympic Athlete)
9420 N 87th St
Scottsdale, AZ 85258-1901, USA

O'Brien, David (Athlete, Football Player)
61 Colony Rd
Jupiter, FL 33469-3507, USA

OBrien, Dylan (Actor)
c/o Liz York *Principal Entertainment (LA)*
9255 W Sunset Blvd Ste 500
West Hollywood, CA 90069-3301, USA

O'Brien, Ed (Musician)
Nasty Little Man
72 Spring St # 1100
New York, NY 10012-4019, USA

O'Brien, Emily (Actor)
c/o Beverly Strong *Strong Management*
9350 Wilshire Blvd Ste 224
Beverly Hills, CA 90212-3204, USA

O'Brien, Jim (Athlete, Football Player)
413 Bethany St
Thousand Oaks, CA 91360-2025, USA

O'Brien, Jim (Basketball Player, Coach)
Philadelphia 76er's
3601 S Broad St Ste 6
1 Union Center
Philadelphia, PA 19148-5250, USA

O'Brien, John (Writer)
2 Columbine Pl
Delran, NJ 08075-2860, USA

O'Brien, Johnny (Athlete, Baseball Player)
2405 N 75th St
Seattle, WA 98103-4959, USA

O'Brien, Kenneth J (Ken) Jr (Athlete, Football Player)
201 Manhattan Ave
Manhattan Beach, CA 90266-6439, USA

O'Brien, Margaret (Actor)
1250 La Peresa Dr
Thousand Oaks, CA 91362-2229, USA

O'Brien, Mark (Business Person)
Pulte Corp
10 N Martingale Rd Ste 400
Schaumburg, IL 60173-2411, USA

O'Brien, Miles (Television Host)
c/o Staff Member *CNN (NY)*
1 Time Warner Ctr
New York, NY 10019-6038, USA

O'Brien, Pat (Sportscaster, Television Host)
c/o Bruce Kaufman *ICM Partners (LA)*
10250 Constellation Blvd Fl 7
Los Angeles, CA 90067-6207, USA

O'Brien, Pete (Athlete, Baseball Player)
5509 Montclair Dr
Colleyville, TX 76034-5028, USA

O'Brien, Ron (Coach)
80450 Overseas Hwy Apt 401
Islamorada, FL 33036-3751, USA

O'Brien, Scott (Athlete, Football Player)
12690 Overlook Mountain Dr
Charlotte, NC 28216-6726, USA

O'Brien, Soledad (Correspondent, Television Host)
c/o Eric Ortner *Spivak Management / Laff Mobb Enterprises*
6222 Wilshire Blvd Ste 240
Los Angeles, CA 90048-5159, USA

O'Brien, Syd (Athlete, Baseball Player)
10189 Hemlock St
Rancho Cucamonga, CA 91730-3023, USA

O'Brien, Tim (Athlete, Track Athlete)
17 Partride Ln
Boxford, MA 01921, USA

O'Brien, Tina (Actor)
c/o Martin Spencer *Paradigm (LA)*
2000 Avenue of the Stars Ste 1200
Los Angeles, CA 90067-4711, USA

O'Brien, Trever (Actor)
c/o Faras Rabadi *Emerald Talent Group*
10 Universal City Plz Fl 20
Universal City, CA 91608-1002, USA

O'Brien, Trevor (Actor)
c/o Staff Member *Abrams Artists Agency (LA)*
9200 W Sunset Blvd PH 11
West Hollywood, CA 90069-3601, USA

O'Bryan, Sean (Actor)
c/o Staff Member *Alan Siegel Entertainment*
9200 W Sunset Blvd Ste 407
West Hollywood, CA 90069-3511, USA

Obst, Lynda (Producer)
c/o Staff Member *Lynda Obst Productions*
5555 Melrose Ave Rm 210
Los Angeles, CA 90038-3996

O'Callahan, Jack (Athlete, Hockey Player, Olympic Athlete)
101 Linden Ave
Glencoe, IL 60022-2144, USA

O'Callahan, John (Athlete, Football Player)
361A La Perle Ln
Costa Mesa, CA 92627-3757, USA

Ocasek, Ric (Musician, Songwriter)
75 Altamont Rd
Millbrook, NY 12545-6149, USA

Ocean, Frank (Musician)
c/o Mara Buxbaum *ID Public Relations (LA)*
7060 Hollywood Blvd Fl 8th
Los Angeles, CA 90028-6021, USA

Ocean Colour Scene (Music Group)
c/o Staff Member *Paradigm (Monterey)*
404 W Franklin St
Monterey, CA 93940-2303, USA

Oceansize (Music Group)
c/o Staff Member *Paradigm (Monterey)*
404 W Franklin St
Monterey, CA 93940-2303, USA

Ochoa, Alex (Athlete, Baseball Player)
14526 NW 83rd Psge
Hialeah, FL 33016-5726, USA

Ochoa, Ellen (Astronaut)
4515 Sterling Wood Way
Houston, TX 77059-3153, USA

Ochoa, Ellen Dr (Astronaut)
4515 Sterling Wood Way
Houston, TX 77059-3153, USA

Ochoa, Lorena (Golfer)
c/o Staff Member *Ladies Pro Golf Association (LPGA)*
100 International Golf Dr
Daytona Beach, FL 32124-1092, USA

Ochoa, Raymond (Actor)
c/o Robin Spitzer *Origin Talent Agency*
4705 Laurel Canyon Blvd Ste 303
Valley Village, CA 91607-5943, USA

Ochoa, Ryan (Actor)
c/o Kelly-Marie Smith *Brilliant Public Relations*
PO Box 703
Wildomar, CA 92595-0703, USA

Ochocinco, Chad (Athlete, Football Player)
c/o Drew Rosenhaus *Rosenhaus Sports Representation*
6400 Allison Rd
Miami Beach, FL 33141-4540, USA

Ochowicz, Elli (Athlete, Olympic Athlete, Speed Skater)
945 Hutchinson Ave
Palo Alto, CA 94301-3440, USA

Ochowicz, James (Athlete, Cycler, Olympic Athlete)
945 Hutchinson Ave
Palo Alto, CA 94301-3440, USA

Ochowicz, Sheila Young (Athlete, Olympic Athlete, Speed Skater)
945 Hutchinson Ave
Palo Alto, CA 94301-3440, USA

Ochse, Alyshia (Actor)
c/o Yoni Ovadia *Ovadia Talent*
Prefers to be contacted by telephone or email
Los Angeles, CA 90028, USA

Ockels, Wubbo J Dr (Astronaut)
ESTEC Postbus 299
Code ADM-RE
Noordwijk, NL NETHE, USA

O'Connell, Charlie (Actor)
c/o Staff Member *Artistry Management*
340 N Camden Dr Ste 302
Beverly Hills, CA 90210-5116, USA

O'Connell, Deirdre (Actor)
c/o Marty Berneman *Precision Entertainment*
465 N Croft Ave
Los Angeles, CA 90048-2508, USA

O'Connell, Jerry (Actor)
23062 Mulholland Hwy
Calabasas, CA 91302-2050, USA

O'Connell, Maura (Musician)
Maura O'Connell Mgmt
4222 Lindawood Dr
Nashville, TN 37215-3208, USA

O'Connell, Mike (Athlete, Hockey Player)
17 Border St
Cohasset, MA 02025-2020, USA

O'Connell, Mike (Athlete, Hockey Player)
1111 S Figueroa St Ste 3100
Attn: Pro Development Dept
Los Angeles, CA 90015-1333, USA

O'Connell, William (Actor)
5835 Mineral Spring Rd
Suffolk, VA 23438-9462, USA

O'Connolly, James (Astronaut)
1305 Lafayette Dr
Alexandria, VA 22308-1107, USA

O'Connor, Brian (Athlete, Baseball Player)
3054 Inwood Dr
Cincinnati, OH 45241-3101, USA

O'Connor, Bryan D (Astronaut)
2615 Gadsby Pl
Alexandria, VA 22311-4929, USA

O'Connor, Bryan D Colonel (Astronaut)
1305 Lafayette Dr
Alexandria, VA 22308-1107, USA

O'Connor, Frances (Actor)
c/o Staff Member *Creative Artists Agency (CAA-LA)*
2000 Avenue of the Stars Ste 100
Los Angeles, CA 90067-4705, USA

O'Connor, Gavin (Director)
c/o Simon Halls *Slate Public Relations*
9000 W Sunset Blvd Ste 915
West Hollywood, CA 90069-5809, USA

O'Connor, Glynnis (Actor)
c/o Staff Member *Bauman Redanty & Shaul Agency*
5757 Wilshire Blvd
Suite 473
Beverly Hills, CA 90212, USA

O'Connor, Jack (Athlete, Baseball Player)
PO Box 430
Yucca Valley, CA 92286-0430, USA

O'Connor, Mark (Musician)
CM Mgmt
5749 Lanyan Dr
Woodland Hills, CA 91367, USA

O'Connor, Mary (Athlete, Basketball Player, Olympic Athlete)
60 Romanock Pl
Fairfield, CT 06825-7240, USA

O'Connor, Maryanne (Basketball Player)
60 Romanock Pl
Fairfield, CT 06825-7240, USA

O'Connor, Michael (Athlete, Baseball Player)
c/o Staff Member *Washington Nationals*
1500 S Capitol St SE
Washington, DC 20003-3599, USA

O'Connor, Patrick (Actor)
c/o Staff Member *Select Artists Ltd (CA-Westside Office)*
1138 12th St Apt 1
Santa Monica, CA 90403-5459, USA

O'Connor, Renee (Actor)
c/o Staff Member *Grant Management*
1158 26th St # 414
Santa Monica, CA 90403-4698, USA

O'Connor, Sandra Day (Attorney)
United States Supreme Court
11th St NE
PO Box 8795
Washington, DC 20543-0001, USA

O'Connor, Tim (Actor)
PO Box 458
Nevada City, CA 95959-0458, USA

O'Conor, John (Musician)
Columbia Artists Mgmt Inc
165 W 57th St
New York, NY 10019-2201, USA

O'Day, Aubrey (Musician)
c/o Steven Grossman *Untitled Entertainment (LA)*
8383 Wilshire Blvd Ste 1050
Beverly Hills, CA 90211-2415, USA

O'Day, Darren (Athlete, Baseball Player)
8728 Timber Oak Ln
Laurel, MD 20723-5907, USA

ODB (Musician)
Famous Artists Agency
250 W 57th St
New York, NY 10107-0001, USA

O'Dea, Judith (Actor)
PO Box 3566
Flagstaff, AZ 86003-3566, USA

Odegard, Vickie (Golfer)
112 Ashford Dr
Bridgeport, WV 26330-1138, USA

Odelein, Lyle (Athlete, Hockey Player)
12569 Winding Hollow Ln
Frisco, TX 75033-3497, USA

Odeleln, Lyle (Athlete, Hockey Player)
12569 Winding Hollow Ln
Frisco, TX 75033-3497

O'Dell, Billy (Athlete, Baseball Player)
225 Odell Rd
Newberry, SC 29108-9250, USA

Odell, Bob H (Athlete, Coach, Football Coach, Football Player)
911 Stenton Pl
Ocean City, NJ 08226-4343, USA

O'Dell, Jennifer (Actor)
c/o Scott Hart *Scott Hart Entertainment*
14622 Ventura Blvd # 746
Sherman Oaks, CA 91403-3600, USA

O'Dell, Nancy (Television Host)
3477 Lombardy Rd
Pasadena, CA 91107-5649, USA

O'Dell, Stewart (Athlete, Football Player)
3532 State Road 144
Mooresville, IN 46158, USA

O'Dell, Tawni (Writer)
Viking Press
375 Hudson St
New York, NY 10014-3658, USA

O'Dell, Tony
417 N Griffith Park Dr
Burbank, CA 91506-2031

Oden, Beverly (Athlete, Olympic Athlete, Volleyball Player)
4631 Lockhaven Cir
Irvine, CA 92604-2336, USA

Oden, Derrick (Athlete, Football Player)
1805 S Barkley Dr
Mobile, AL 36606-1151, USA

Oden, Greg (Athlete)
c/o Staff Member *BDA Sports Management (BDA-CA)*
700 Ygnacio Valley Rd Ste 330
Walnut Creek, CA 94596-3838, USA

Odenkirk, Bob (Actor)
2320 Alto Oak Dr
Los Angeles, CA 90068-2510, USA

Odessa, Devon (Actor)
c/o Staff Member *Vincent Cirrincione Associates*
1516 N Fairfax Ave
Los Angeles, CA 90046-2608, USA

Odom, Cliff (Athlete, Football Player)
6708 Marthas Vineyard Dr
Arlington, TX 76001-5508, USA

Odom, Jason (Athlete, Football Player)
11506 Joshuas Bend Dr
Tampa, FL 33612-5071, USA

Odom, John Lee (Blue Moon) (Athlete, Baseball Player)
10343 Slater Ave Apt 204
Fountain Valley, CA 92708-4783, USA

Odom, Lamar (Athlete, Basketball Player)
19011 Ashurst Ln
Tarzana, CA 91356-5825, USA

Odom, Steve (Athlete, Football Player)
1482 Lincoln St
Berkeley, CA 94702-1247, USA

Odomes, Nathaniel B (Nate) (Athlete, Football Player)
900 Quail Creek Dr
Columbus, GA 31907-6536, USA

Odoms, Riley M (Athlete, Football Player)
834 1/2 Staffordshire Rd
Stafford, TX 77477, USA

O'Donahue, Pat (Athlete, Football Player)
1524 Wheeler Rd Unit D
Madison, WI 53704-7048, USA

O'Donis, Colby (Musician)
c/o Juliette Harris *It Girl Public Relations*
5301 Beethoven St Ste 220
Los Angeles, CA 90066-7052, USA

O'Donnell, Andrew (Athlete, Basketball Player)
3310 Lincoln Ave
Allentown, PA 18103-7917, USA

O'Donnell, Annie (Actor)
Capital Artists
6404 Wilshire Blvd Ste 950
Los Angeles, CA 90048-5529, USA

O'Donnell, Charles (Chuck) (Bowler)
7354 Forest Haven Est
Saint Louis, MO 63123-2101, USA

O'Donnell, Chris (Actor)
14915 Camarosa Dr
Pacific Palisades, CA 90272-4428, USA

O'Donnell, George (Athlete, Baseball Player)
220 N Pittsburg Lndg
Springfield, IL 62711-7960, USA

O'Donnell, Jake (Athlete, Baseball Player)
12223 SE Birkdale Run
Jupiter, FL 33469-1746, USA

O'Donnell, James Michael (Baseball Player)
204 N Diamond St
Clifton Heights, PA 19018-1507, USA

O'Donnell, Joe (Athlete, Football Player)
447 Bodley Cres
Milan, MI 48160-1206, USA

O'Donnell, Keir (Actor)
c/o Tom Parziali *Visionary Entertainment*
1558 N Stanley Ave
Los Angeles, CA 90046-2711, USA

O'Donnell, Lawrence (Producer, Writer)
c/o Ari Emanuel *William Morris Endeavor (LA)*
9601 Wilshire Blvd
Beverly Hills, CA 90210-5213, USA

O'Donnell, Neil K (Athlete, Football Player)
PO Box 403
New Vernon, NJ 07976-0403, USA

O'Donnell, Pat (Athlete, Football Player)
c/o Drew Rosenhaus *Rosenhaus Sports Representation*
6400 Allison Rd
Miami Beach, FL 33141-4540, USA

O'Donnell, Rosie (Actor, Comedian, Talk Show Host)
115 E Allendale Rd
Saddle River, NJ 07458-3009, USA

O'Donnell, Sean
3550 Sarasota Golf Club Blvd
Sarasota, FL 34240-9318

O'Donnell, William (Bill) (Horse Racer)
569 Penn Est
East Stroudsburg, PA 18301-9062, USA

O'Donoghue, Colin (Actor)
c/o Allan Grifka *Alchemy Entertainment*
7024 Melrose Ave Ste 420
Los Angeles, CA 90038-3394, USA

O'Donoghue, John (Athlete, Baseball Player)
10107 Summerfield Dr
Denham Springs, LA 70726-1583, USA

O'Donoghue, John (Athlete, Baseball Player)
5246 Far Oak Cir
Sarasota, FL 34238-3304, USA

O'Donoghue, Neil (Athlete, Football Player)
1118 Flushing Ave
Clearwater, FL 33764-4906, USA

O'Donohue, Jessica (Actor)
c/o Dan Cotoia *Letnom Management*
1776 Broadway Fl 9
New York, NY 10019-2002, USA

O'Dowd, Anna Mae (Athlete, Baseball Player)
1179 Pelzer Ave
The Villages, FL 32162-8691, USA

O'Dowd, Chris (Actor)
713 N Alta Vista Blvd
Los Angeles, CA 90046-7601, USA

Odrick, Jared (Athlete, Football Player)
c/o Eugene Parker *Maximum Sports Management*
6435 W Jefferson Blvd # 197
Fort Wayne, IN 46804-6203, USA

O'Driscoll, Martha (Actor)
22 Indian Creek Island Rd
Indian Creek Village, FL 33154-2904, USA

Oedekerk, Steve (Actor, Director, Producer, Writer)
O Entertainment
31872 Camino Capistrano Ste 100
San Juan Capistrano, CA 92675-3249, USA

Oefelein, William A (Astronaut)
1205 Hawkhill Dr
Friendswood, TX 77546-7811, USA

Oefelein, William A Cdr (Astronaut)
Adventure Write
PO Box 872241
Wasilla, AK 99687-2241, USA

Oelkers, Bryan (Athlete, Baseball Player)
3404 Taylor Ave
Bridgeton, MO 63044-3055, USA

Oenish, Dean (Doctor)
Preventive Medical Research Institute
900 Bridgeway # 204
Sausalito, CA 94965-2100, USA

Oester, Ron (Athlete, Baseball Player)
3776 9 Mile Tobasco Rd
Cincinnati, OH 45255-5232, USA

Oetiker, Phil (Cinematographer)
422 10th St
Brooklyn, NY 11215-4009, USA

Offerdahl, John A (Athlete, Football Player)
2749 NE 37th Dr
Fort Lauderdale, FL 33308-6326, USA

Offerman, Jose (Athlete, Baseball Player)
10720 Moorpark St
North Hollywood, CA 91602-2723, USA

Offerman, Nick (Actor)
1775 Stone Canyon Rd
Los Angeles, CA 90077-1914, USA

Office, Rowland (Athlete, Baseball Player)
1028 Lake Glen Way
Sacramento, CA 95822-3224, USA

Offishall, Kardinal (Musician)
c/o Staff Member *MCA Records (LA)*
2220 Colorado Ave
Santa Monica, CA 90404-3506, USA

Offspring, The (Music Group)
c/o Jim Guerinot *Rebel Waltz Inc*
31652 2nd Ave
Laguna Beach, CA 92651-8244, USA

O'Flaherty, Eric (Athlete, Baseball Player)
2608 W Lake Sammamish Pkwy NE
Redmond, WA 98052-5915, USA

Of Mice and Men (Music Group)
c/o Eric Rushing *The Artery Foundation*
PO Box 160451
Sacramento, CA 95816-0451, USA

Ogden, Bud (Athlete, Basketball Player)
3324 S 4th St
Springfield, IL 62703-4619, USA

Ogden, Joanne (Baseball Player)
200 1/2 W Cypress St
Glendale, CA 91204-2660, USA

Ogden, Jonathan (Athlete, Football Player)
14 Corral De Tierra Pl
Henderson, NV 89052-6705, USA

Ogden, Margaret (Writer)
4621 N 28th St
Tacoma, WA 98407-4617, USA

Ogden, Ray (Athlete, Football Player)
202 Anderson Dr
Brunswick, GA 31520-1612, USA

Ogea, Chad (Athlete, Baseball Player)
3233 Plantation Ct
Baton Rouge, LA 70820-5753, USA

Ogilvie, Lana (Model)
c/o Michael Flutie *MFO*
17 Little West 12th St
Studio 333
New York, NY 10014-1301, USA

Ogilvy, Geoff (Golfer)
c/o Staff Member *Pro Golfers Association (PGA) Tour*
112 Tpc Blvd
Ponte Vedra Beach, FL 32082, USA

Ogle, Brett (Golfer)
Advantage International
1751 Pinnacle Dr Ste 1500
Mc Lean, VA 22102-3833, USA

Oglive, Benjamin A (Ben) (Athlete, Baseball Player)
1012 E Sandpiper Dr
Tempe, AZ 85283-2021, USA

Oglivie, Ben (Athlete, Baseball Player)
1012 E Sandpiper Dr
Tempe, AZ 85283-2021, USA

O'Grady, Gail (Actor)
c/o Alan lezman *Shelter Entertainment*
9255 W Sunset Blvd Ste 320
West Hollywood, CA 90069-3313, USA

O'Grady, Scott
3519 Wallingford Ave N # 2
Seattle, WA 98103-9057, USA

O'Grady, Sean (Boxer)
Adoreable Promotions
PO Box 9
Bay City, MI 48707-0009, USA

Ogrin, David (Athlete, Golfer)
1074 Running Riv
New Braunfels, TX 78130-2429, USA

Ogrodnick, John (Athlete, Hockey Player)
37034 Aldgate Ct
Farmington Hills, MI 48335-5402, USA

Ogunleye, Adewale (Athlete, Football Player)
19113 NW 23rd Ct
Pembroke Pines, FL 33029-5336, USA

Oh, Sandra (Actor)
1943 N Van Ness Ave
Los Angeles, CA 90068-3624, USA

Oh, Soon-Teck (Actor)
5091 N Fresno St Ste 130
Fresno, CA 93710-7617, USA

O'Hair, Sean (Athlete, Golfer)
c/o Staff Member *Pro Golfers Association (PGA) Tour*
112 Tpc Blvd
Ponte Vedra Beach, FL 32082, USA

O'Hanlon, Bill (Writer)
c/o Staff Member *Loretta Barrett Books, Inc.*
101 5th Ave Fl 11
New York, NY 10003-1008, USA

O'Hanlon, Francis (Athlete, Basketball Player)
27 W Wayne Ave
Easton, PA 18042-1662, USA

O'Hara, Catherine (Actor, Comedian)
575 Hanley Ave
Los Angeles, CA 90049-1922, USA

O'Hara, David (Actor)
c/o Tammy Rosen *Sanders Armstrong Caserta*
425 N Robertson Blvd
West Hollywood, CA 90048-1735, USA

O'Hara, Jamie
1025 16th Ave S Ste 200
Nashville, TN 37212-2343

O'Hara, Jenny (Actor)
8663 Wonderland Ave
Los Angeles, CA 90046-1452, USA

O'Hara, Kelli (Actor)
c/o Erica Tuchman *One Entertainment (NY)*
12 W 57th St PH
New York, NY 10019-3900, USA

O'Hara, Paige (Actor)
2406 Legacy Island Cir
Henderson, NV 89074-6155, USA

O'Hara, Shaun (Athlete, Football Player)
c/o Anthony J. Agnone *Eastern Athletic Services*
11350 McCormick Rd
Suite 800 - Executive Plaza
Hunt Valley, MD 21031-1002, USA

O'Hara, Terrence J (Director)
Armstrong/Hirsch
1888 Century Park E Ste 1800
Los Angeles, CA 90067-1722, USA

O'Hare, Denis (Actor)
c/o Shea Martin *SLATE Public Relations - NY*
307 7th Ave Rm 2401
New York, NY 10001-6019, USA

Oher, Michael (Athlete, Football Player)
c/o Raphael Berko *Media Artists Group (LA)*
8222 Melrose Ave Ste 203
Los Angeles, CA 90046-6838, USA

Ohl, Don (Athlete, Basketball Player)
2 E Lockhaven Ct
Edwardsville, IL 62025-3703, USA

Ohlendorf, Ross (Athlete, Baseball Player)
2300 Barton Creek Blvd Apt 40
Austin, TX 78735-1687, USA

Ohlsson, Garrick (Musician)
International Creative Mgmt
10250 Constellation Blvd Fl 1
Los Angeles, CA 90067-6241, USA

Ohman, Will (Athlete, Baseball Player)
4346 N Desert Oasis Cir
Mesa, AZ 85207-7246, USA

Ohme, Kevin (Athlete, Baseball Player)
806 Starlifter Ln
Valrico, FL 33594-2978, USA

Ohno, Apolo (Athlete, Olympic Athlete, Speed Skater)
2201 Century Hl
Los Angeles, CA 90067-3536, USA

O'Hurley, John (Actor)
1710 Monte Cielo Ct
Beverly Hills, CA 90210-2422, USA

Oimeon, Casper (Skier)
540 S Mountain Ave
Ashland, OR 97520-3242, USA

Oja, Kim (Actor)
c/o Staff Member *Gage Group, The (LA)*
5757 Wilshire Blvd Ste 659
Los Angeles, CA 90036-3682, USA

Ojala, Kirt (Athlete, Baseball Player)
1902 Forest Lake Dr SE
Grand Rapids, MI 49546-8234, USA

O'Jays, The (Music Group, Musician)
c/o Toby Ludwig *21st Century Artists Inc.*
853 Broadway Ste 1214
New York, NY 10003-4717, USA

Ojeda, Augie (Athlete, Baseball Player)
5351 W Morgan Pl
Chandler, AZ 85226-8613, USA

Ojeda, Augle (Athlete, Baseball Player)
9402 Dorothy Ave
South Gate, CA 90280-5106, USA

Ojeda, Bob (Athlete, Baseball Player)
20 Somerset Dr
Rumson, NJ 07760-1101, USA

Ojeda, Miguel (Baseball Player)
c/o Staff Member *San Diego Padres*
100 Park Blvd
San Diego, CA 92101-7405, USA

Oka, Masi (Actor, Writer)
c/o Ilan Breil *Mosaic Media Group*
9200 W Sunset Blvd Ste 10
West Hollywood, CA 90069-3608, USA

Okafor, Alex (Athlete, Football Player)
c/o Andrew Kessler *Athletes First, LLC*
23091 Mill Creek Dr
Laguna Hills, CA 92653-1258, USA

Okafor, Emeka (Athlete, Basketball Player)
c/o Jeff Schwartz *Excel Sports Management (NY)*
1700 Broadway Fl 29
New York, NY 10019-5905, USA

Okajima, Hideki (Athlete, Baseball Player)
4 Liberty St
Framingham, MA 01702-8435, USA

Okamoto, Ayako (Golfer)
22627 Ladeene Ave
Torrance, CA 90505-3438, USA

Okazake, Kenji (Race Car Driver)
840 Kallin Ave
Long Beach, CA 90815-5004, USA

O'Keefe, Jodie Lyn (Actor)
11717 Landale St
Valley Village, CA 91607-4118, USA

O'Keefe, Michael (Actor)
c/o Staff Member *Paradigm (LA)*
360 N Crescent Dr
North Bldg
Beverly Hills, CA 90210-4874, USA

O'Keefe, Miles (Actor)
c/o Alexandra Karrys *Divine Management*
117 N Orlando Ave
Los Angeles, CA 90048-3403, USA

O'Keefe, Paul
225 W 83rd St # 9-5
New York, NY 10024-4952

O'Keefe, Richard (Athlete, Basketball Player)
31 Corte Ortega Apt 7
Greenbrae, CA 94904-1992, USA

O'Keefe, Stuart (Chef)
c/o Jason Pinyan *Artist & Brand Management (LA)*
132 N Laurel Ave
Los Angeles, CA 90048-3512, USA

O'Keefe, Tommy (Athlete, Basketball Player)
8250 Singing Wood Ct
Spotsylvania, VA 22553-3518, USA

O'Kelley, Tricia (Actor)
10545 Sarah St
Toluca Lake, CA 91602-1513, USA

Okeniyi, Dayo (Actor)
c/o Kanica Suy *Sweeney Entertainment*
6253 Hollywood Blvd Apt 201
Los Angeles, CA 90028-8248, USA

Okerlund, Todd (Athlete, Hockey Player, Olympic Athlete)
3264 N Clanton St
Buckeye, AZ 85396-7709, USA

Okobi, Chukky (Athlete, Football Player)
15 Baker Rd
Hamden, CT 06514-3703, USA

Okolowicz, Jeff (Musician)
Living Eye Productions
PO Box 12956
Rochester, NY 14612-0956, USA

Okolowicz, Ted (Musician)
Living Eye Productions
PO Box 12956
Rochester, NY 14612-0956, USA

Okoniewski, Steve (Athlete, Football Player)
2691 Hillside Heights Dr
Green Bay, WI 54311-6774, USA

Okonma, Tyler (The Creator) (Musician)
Diystro, Llc
410 N Fairfax Ave
Los Angeles, CA 90036-1717, USA

O'Koren, Mike (Athlete, Basketball Player)
12 Danbury Ct
Township Of Washington, NJ 07676-4350, USA

Okoye, Amobi (Athlete, Football Player)
2431 Sara Ridge Ln
Katy, TX 77450-5377, USA

Okoye, Christian E (Athlete, Football Player)
10082 Big Pine Dr
Rancho Cucamonga, CA 91737-4247, USA

Okposo, Kyle (Athlete, Hockey Player)
17 Kensington Cir
Manhasset, NY 11030-4103

Okrent, Daniel (Sportscaster)
645 W End Ave Apt 12F
New York, NY 10025-7354, USA

Okrie, Len (Athlete, Baseball Player)
2636 Burke Ln
Fayetteville, NC 28306-2629, USA

Okumura, Tomohiro (Musician)
Jecklin Assoc
2717 Nichols Ln
Davenport, IA 52803-3620, USA

Okungbowa, Tony (DJ)
1863 Preston Ave
Los Angeles, CA 90026-1825, USA

Okur, Mehmet
1387 E Perrys Hollow Rd
Salt Lake City, UT 84103-4263, USA

Olajuwon, Hakeem (Athlete, Basketball Player, Olympic Athlete)
1305 N Horseshoe Dr
Sugar Land, TX 77478-3428, USA

Olander, Jim (Athlete, Baseball Player)
13876 E Fiery Dawn Dr
Vail, AZ 85641-6456, USA

Olander, Jimmy (Musician)
3020 Jubilee Ridge Rd
Franklin, TN 37069-4777, USA

Olandt, Ken (Actor)
Gold Marshak Liedtke
3500 W Olive Ave Ste 1400
Burbank, CA 91505-5512, USA

Olay, Ruth (Musician)
3100 Neilson Way Apt 216
Santa Monica, CA 90405-5329, USA

Olberding, Mark (Athlete, Basketball Player)
403 Geddington
Shavano Park, TX 78249-2091, USA

Olberman, Bob (Athlete, Football Player)
4486 Dobbs Xing
Marietta, GA 30068-2714, USA

Olbermann, Keith (Sportscaster, Television Host)
200 E 69th St Apt 40B
New York, NY 10021-5747, USA

Olczyk, Ed (Athlete, Hockey Player, Olympic Athlete)
4581 Pamela Ct
Long Grove, IL 60047-5271, USA

Olczyk, Eddie (Athlete, Hockey Player)
Chicago Blackhawks
1901 W Madison St
Chicago, IL 60612-2459

Olczyk, Eddie
4581 Pamela Ct
Long Grove, IL 60047-5271

Old Crow Medicine Show (Music Group)
c/o Staff Member *Paradigm (Monterey)*
404 W Franklin St
Monterey, CA 93940-2303, USA

Olde, Jeff (Director, Producer)
c/o Staff Member *VH1 Television*
1515 Broadway
New York, NY 10036-8901, USA

Oldenburg, Richard E (Director)
447 E 57th St Apt 9A
New York, NY 10022-3172, USA

Oldendorf, William (Doctor)
University of California
Medical Center
Neurology Dept
Los Angeles, CA 90024, USA

Olderman, Murray (Sportscaster)
28 La Costa Dr
Rancho Mirage, CA 92270-1611, USA

Oldershaw, Kelsey (Actor)
c/o Darren Goldberg *Global Creative*
1051 Cole Ave # B
Los Angeles, CA 90038-2601, USA

Oldham, John (Athlete, Baseball Player)
1845 Anne Way
San Jose, CA 95124-6137, USA

Oldham, John (Athlete, Basketball Player)
2127 Sycamore Dr
Bowling Green, KY 42104-3868, USA

Oldham, Tasha (Director)
c/o Jerry Shandrew *Shandrew Public Relations*
1050 S Stanley Ave
Los Angeles, CA 90019-6634, USA

Oldham, Todd (Designer, Fashion Designer)
c/o Staff Member *Creative Artists Agency (CAA-LA)*
2000 Avenue of the Stars Ste 100
Los Angeles, CA 90067-4705, USA

Oldis, Bob (Athlete, Baseball Player)
306 Virginia Dr
Iowa City, IA 52245-1639, USA

Oldman, Gary (Actor, Director, Producer)
2338 Observatory Ave
Los Angeles, CA 90027-1336, USA

Olds, Bill (Athlete, Football Player)
7414 Pohick Rd
Lorton, VA 22079-1518, USA

Olds, Gabriel (Actor)
c/o Darryl Marshak *Marshak/Zachary Company, The*
8840 Wilshire Blvd Fl 1
Beverly Hills, CA 90211-2606, USA

Olds, Sharon (Writer)
New York University
58 W 10th St Ste 303
Attn: English Department
New York, NY 10011-8702, USA

Olds, Wally (Athlete, Hockey Player, Olympic Athlete)
7343 Colfax Ave S
Minneapolis, MN 55423-3022, USA

Oleary, Dan (Athlete, Football Player)
3088 Joslyn Rd
Cleveland, OH 44111-1555, USA

O'Leary, George (Coach, Football Coach)
Central Florida University
Athletic Dept
Orlando, FL 32918, USA

O'Leary, John (Actor)
Gage Group
5757 Wilshire Blvd Ste 659
Los Angeles, CA 90036-3682, USA

O'Leary, John (Athlete, Football Player)
4819 N 160th St
Omaha, NE 68116-8038, USA

O'Leary, Kevin (Business Person, Reality Star)
Electronic Arts Inc
209 Redwood Shores Pkwy
Redwood City, CA 94065-1175, USA

O'Leary, Marrissa (Actor)
c/o Staff Member *Select Artists Ltd (CA-Valley Office)*
PO Box 4359
Burbank, CA 91503-4359, USA

O'Leary, Matthew (Actor)
c/o Brian Swardstrom *United Talent Agency (UTA-NYC)*
9601 Wilshire Blvd
Beverly Hills, CA 90210-5213, USA

O'Leary, Michael (Actor)
242 Bellevue Ave
Montclair, NJ 07043-1344, USA

O'Leary, Troy (Athlete, Baseball Player)
1060 W Norwood St
Rialto, CA 92377-8220, USA

O'Leary, William (Actor)
c/o Staff Member *Coast to Coast Talent Group*
3350 Barham Blvd
Los Angeles, CA 90068-1404, USA

Olejnik, Craig (Actor)
c/o Robert Stein *Robert Stein Management*
PO Box 3797
Beverly Hills, CA 90212-0797, USA

Olerich, Dave (Athlete, Football Player)
12260 Galice Rd
Merlin, OR 97532-9725, USA

Olerud, John (Athlete, Baseball Player)
PO Box 606
Medina, WA 98039-0606, USA

Olesz, Rostislav (Athlete, Hockey Player)
8687 Melrose Ave Ste 7
West Hollywood, CA 90069-5721

Olevsky, Julian (Musician)
68 Blue Hills Rd
Amherst, MA 01002-2220, USA

Oleynick, Frank (Athlete, Basketball Player)
1164 Brooklawn Ave
Bridgeport, CT 06604-1206, USA

Oleynik, Larisa (Actor)
216 San Juan Ave
Venice, CA 90291-3730, USA

Oliceira, Ana Cristina (Actor)
c/o Clifford Gilbert-Lurie *Ziffren, Brittenham, Branca, Fischer, Gilbert-Lurie, Stiffelman & Cook*
1801 Century Park W Fl 7
Los Angeles, CA 90067-6406, USA

Olin, Ken (Actor)
c/o Staff Member *Creative Artists Agency (CAA-LA)*
2000 Avenue of the Stars Ste 100
Los Angeles, CA 90067-4705, USA

Olin, Lena (Actor)
153 Horizon Ln
Bedford, NY 10506, USA

Olin, Lina (Actor)
c/o Staff Member *Industry Entertainment*
955 Carrillo Dr Ste 300
Los Angeles, CA 90048-5400, USA

Olin, Roxy (Actor)
c/o Katie Mason *Luber Roklin Management*
5815 W Sunset Blvd Ste 206
Los Angeles, CA 90028-6481, USA

Olinger, Marilyn (Baseball Player)
6451 Far Hills Ave
Dayton, OH 45459-2725, USA

Olinski, Harry (Athlete, Football Player)
3205 Furman Blvd
Louisville, KY 40220-1949, USA

Oliphant, Patrick B (Cartoonist)
Universal Press Syndicate
4520 Main St Ste 340
Kansas City, MO 64111-7705, USA

Oliu, Ingrid (Actor)
c/o Staff Member *Cunningham Escott Slevin & Doherty (CESD-LA)*
10635 Santa Monica Blvd Ste 130
Los Angeles, CA 90025-8306, USA

Oliva, Tony (Athlete, Baseball Player)
1 Twins Way
Attn Alumni Association
Minneapolis, MN 55403-1418, USA

Olivares, Ed (Athlete, Baseball Player)
HC 2 Box 12887
San German, PR 00683, USA

Olivares, Omar (Athlete, Baseball Player)
PO Box 1328
San German, PR 00683-1328, USA

Olivares, Ruben (Boxer)
Geno Productions
PO Box 113
Montebello, CA 90640-0113, USA

Olivas, John D (Astronaut)
595 36th St
Manhattan Beach, CA 90266-3409, USA

Olivas, John D Dr (Astronaut)
595 36th St
Manhattan Beach, CA 90266-3409, USA

Olive, Jason (Actor, Model)
c/o Cory Richman *Liebman Entertainment*
12 E 46th St Fl 5
New York, NY 10017-2418, USA

Olive, John (Athlete, Basketball Player)
8652 Harjoan Ave
San Diego, CA 92123-3445, USA

Oliveira, Elmar (Musician)
Cramer/Marder Artists
3436 Springhill Rd
Lafayette, CA 94549-2535, USA

Oliver, Al (Athlete, Baseball Player)
PO Box 1466
Portsmouth, OH 45662-1466, USA

Oliver, Albert (Al) (Athlete, Baseball Player)
PO Box 1466
Portsmouth, OH 45662-1466, USA

Oliver, Bilal (Musician)
c/o Staff Member *Creative Artists Agency (CAA-LA)*
2000 Avenue of the Stars Ste 100
Los Angeles, CA 90067-4705, USA

Oliver, Bob (Athlete, Baseball Player)
1716 G St
Rio Linda, CA 95673-4534, USA

Oliver, Christian (Actor)
7211 Mulholland Dr
Los Angeles, CA 90068-2031, USA

Oliver, Clancy (Athlete, Football Player)
233 Springview
Irvine, CA 92620-1970, USA

Oliver, Daniel (Government Official)
Heritage Foundation
214 Massachusetts Ave NE Bsmt
Washington, DC 20002-4999, USA

Oliver, Darren (Athlete, Baseball Player)
1804 Larkspur Ct
Southlake, TX 76092-3572, USA

Oliver, Dave (Athlete, Baseball Player)
1709 Timberlake Cir
Lodi, CA 95242-4283, USA

Oliver, Dean (Race Car Driver)
21386 Notus Rd
Greenleaf, ID 83626-8940, USA

Oliver, Hubie (Athlete, Football Player)
136 Blake St
Elyria, OH 44035-5422, USA

Oliver, Joe (Athlete, Baseball Player)
4137 Bounce Dr
Orlando, FL 32812-8147, USA

Oliver, Kristine (Musician)
349 Stable Rd
Franklin, TN 37069-4527, USA

Oliver, Louis (Athlete, Football Player)
5082 SW 167th Ave
Miramar, FL 33027-4910, USA

Oliver, Mary (Writer)
Molly Malone Cook Agency
PO Box 1071
Sweet Briar, VA 24595-1071, USA

Oliver, Murray C (Athlete, Hockey Player)
5505 McGuire Rd
Minneapolis, MN 55439-1342

Oliver, Nate (Athlete, Baseball Player)
4403 Oak Hill Rd
Oakland, CA 94605-4632, USA

Oliver, Pam (Sportscaster)
Fox-TV
205 E 67th St
Sports Dept
New York, NY 10065-6089, USA

Oliver, Ron (Director, Writer)
c/o Mark Itkin *William Morris Endeavor (LA)*
9601 Wilshire Blvd Ste GF1
Beverly Hills, CA 90210-5231, USA

Oliver, Winslow (Athlete, Football Player)
2027 Summerall Ct
Richmond, TX 77406-6737, USA

Oliveras, Mako (Athlete, Baseball Player)
PO Box 8717
Bayamon, PR 00960-8717, USA

Oliveres, Rubin (Actor)
PO Box 113
Montebello, CA 90640-0113

Olivia (Musician)
c/o Staff Member *Interscope Records (LA) - Main*
2220 Colorado Ave
Santa Monica, CA 90404-3506, USA

Olivieri, Dawn (Actor)
c/o Joel Stevens *Joel Stevens Entertainment*
5627 Allott Ave
Van Nuys, CA 91401-4502, USA

Olivo, America (Actor)
PO Box 54228
Cincinnati, OH 45254-0228, USA

Olivo, Joey (Boxer)
9628 Poinciana St
Pico Rivera, CA 90660-4242, USA

Olivo, Karen (Actor)
c/o Brian Liebman *Liebman Entertainment*
12 E 46th St Fl 5
New York, NY 10017-2418, USA

Olivo, Miguel (Athlete, Baseball Player)
10004 Plaza De Oro Dr
Oakdale, CA 95361-9235, USA

Olivor, Jane (Music Group, Musician)
Ed Keane
32 Saint Edward Rd
Boston, MA 02128-1263, USA

Olkewicz, Neal (Athlete, Football Player)
5706 English Ct
Bethesda, MD 20817-6258, USA

Olkewicz, Walter (Actor)
Gold Marshak Liedtke
3500 W Olive Ave Ste 1400
Burbank, CA 91505-5512, USA

Oller, Tony (Actor, Musician)
c/o Evan Bogart *Boardwalk Entertainment Company, The*
1149 N Gower St # 205
Los Angeles, CA 90038-1801, USA

Ollie, Kevin (Athlete, Basketball Player)
210 Thompson St
South Glastonbury, CT 06073-2915, USA

Ollie, mack (Athlete, Basketball Player)
4023 N Grandview Dr
Peoria, IL 61614-6624, USA

Ollom, Jim (Athlete, Baseball Player)
10916 27th Ave SE
Everett, WA 98208-7807, USA

Olmedo, Alex (Tennis Player)
5067 Woodley Ave
Encino, CA 91436-1472, USA

Olmo, Luis (Athlete, Baseball Player)
620 Calle Jose Ramon Figueroa
San Juan, PR 00907-3928, USA

Olmos, Edward James (Actor)
5300 Encino Ave
Encino, CA 91316-2526, USA

Olmstead, Chris Von Saltza (Athlete, Olympic Athlete, Swimmer)
520 Crocker Rd
Sacramento, CA 95864-5608, USA

Olmstead, Matt (Producer)
c/o Staff Member *ICM Partners (LA)*
10250 Constellation Blvd Fl 7
Los Angeles, CA 90067-6207, USA

Olmsted, Al (Athlete, Baseball Player)
1008 Pinecone Trl
Florissant, MO 63031-7436, USA

Olmsted, Al (Athlete, Baseball Player)
1008 Pinecone Trl
Florissant, MO 63031-7436, USA

O'Loughlin, Gerald
PO Box 340832
Pacoima, CA 91334-0832

O'Loughlin, Gerald S (Actor)
23388 Mulholland Dr # 204
Woodland Hills, CA 91364-2733, USA

Olowaonkandi, Michael (Basketball Player)
c/o Staff Member *Los Angeles Clippers*
1111 S Figueroa St Ste 1100
Los Angeles, CA 90015-1345, USA

Olowokandi, Michael (Athlete, Basketball Player)
Minnesota Timberwolves
10061 SW 60th Ct
Miami, FL 33156-1980, USA

Olsavsky, Bill (Athlete, Football Player)
132 Walnut Ave
Saint Clairsville, OH 43950-1702, USA

Olsavsky, Jerry (Athlete, Football Player)
92 Lake Shore Dr
Youngstown, OH 44511-3552, USA

Olsen, Andrew (Baseball Player)
555 4th St N
Saint Petersburg, FL 33701-2301, USA

Olsen, Andy (Athlete, Baseball Player)
555 4th St N
Saint Petersburg, FL 33701-2301, USA

Olsen, Ashley (Actor)
c/o Nicole Caruso *Relevant*
584 Broadway Rm 310
New York, NY 10012-5246, USA

Olsen, Bud (Athlete, Basketball Player)
1602 Gardiner Ln Apt 130
Louisville, KY 40205-2761, USA

Olsen, Darryl (Athlete, Hockey Player)
3632 S Elk Mountain Rd Apt 314
Magna, UT 84044-2771

Olsen, Elizabeth (Actor)
c/o Cynthia Pett-Dante *Brillstein Entertainment Partners (LA)*
9150 Wilshire Blvd Ste 350
Beverly Hills, CA 90212-3453, USA

Olsen, Eric Christian (Actor)
238 Quadro Vecchio Dr
Pacific Palisades, CA 90272-3112, USA

Olsen, Greg (Athlete, Football Player)
c/o Drew Rosenhaus *Rosenhaus Sports Representation*
6400 Allison Rd
Miami Beach, FL 33141-4540, USA

Olsen, Gregory (Astronaut, Business Person)
Sensors Unlimited
3490 US Highway 1 Ste 12
Princeton, NJ 08540-5920, USA

Olsen, Kevin (Athlete, Baseball Player)
3353 Dales Dr
Norco, CA 92860-2281, USA

Olsen, Mary-Kate (Actor, Designer)
c/o Steven Kavovit *Thruline Entertainment*
9250 Wilshire Blvd Ste 100
Ground Floor
Beverly Hills, CA 90212-3343, USA

Olsen, Mike (Race Car Driver)
PO Box 427
Main St.
North Haverhill, NH 03774-0427, USA

Olsen, Phil (Athlete, Football Player)
112 Hitching Post Rd
Bozeman, MT 59715-8027, USA

Olsen, Scott (Athlete, Baseball Player)
2991 NE 185th St Apt 1701
Miami, FL 33180-2904, USA

Olsen, Stanford (Musician, Opera Singer)
c/o Staff Member *Columbia Artists Mgmt Inc*
1790 Broadway Fl 6
New York, NY 10019-1537, USA

Olshansky, Igor (Athlete, Football Player)
200 Peacock Dr
San Rafael, CA 94901-8334, USA

Olson, Allen (Politician)
International Joint Commission
28736 160th Ave SW
Crookston, MN 56716-8844, USA

Olson, Benji (Athlete, Football Player)
2211 Old Natchez Trce
Franklin, TN 37069-1904, USA

Olson, Bree (Actor, Adult Film Star, Model)
PO Box 10471
Fort Wayne, IN 46852-0471, USA

Olson, Candice (Designer)
Divine Design
2760 Mornington Dr NW
Atlanta, GA 30327-1216, USA

Olson, Greg (Athlete, Baseball Player)
18592 Saint Mellion Pl
Eden Prairie, MN 55347-3487, USA

Olson, Gregg (Athlete, Baseball Player)
1996 Port Nelson Pl
Newport Beach, CA 92660-6618, USA

Olson, Harold (Athlete, Football Player)
1012 Keystone Ln
Clemson, SC 29631-2026, USA

Olson, James (Actor)
250 W 57th St Ste 803
New York, NY 10107-0800, USA

Olson, Kaitlin (Actor)
c/o Amy Slomovits *Evolution Entertainment (LA)*
901 N Highland Ave
Los Angeles, CA 90038-2412, USA

Olson, Karl (Athlete, Baseball Player)
1417 Pin Oak Dr
Gardnerville, NV 89410-7388, USA

Olson, Lute (Athlete, Basketball Player, Coach)
5831 E Finisterra
Tucson, AZ 85750-1008, USA

Olson, Mark (Musician, Songwriter, Writer)
Sussman Assoc
700 12th Ave S Unit 201
Nashville, TN 37203-3329, USA

Olson, Nancy (Actor)
945 N Alpine Dr
Beverly Hills, CA 90210-2946, USA

Olson, Peter (Congressman, Politician)
312 Cannon Hob
Washington, DC 20515-3207, USA

Olson, Richard E (Business Person)
Champion Int'l Corp
1 Champion Plz
Stamford, CT 06921-0001, USA

Olson, Tim (Athlete, Baseball Player)
601 Moss Cliff Cir
McKinney, TX 75071-7629, USA

Olson, Weldon (Athlete, Hockey Player, Olympic Athlete)
2623 Goldenrod Ln
Findlay, OH 45840-1025, USA

Olssen, Lance (Athlete, Football Player)
5222 E Timberwood Dr
Newburgh, IN 47630-3014, USA

Olstead, Renee (Musician)
c/o Beverly Strong *Strong Management*
9350 Wilshire Blvd Ste 224
Beverly Hills, CA 90212-3204, USA

Olwine, Ed (Athlete, Baseball Player)
1010 Chestnut Cir
Greenville, OH 45331-1079, USA

Olympia (Music Group, Musician)
c/o Staff Member *Equal Vision Records*
PO Box 38202
Albany, NY 12203-8202, USA

Olyphant, Timothy (Actor)
776 Glenmont Ave
Los Angeles, CA 90024-3202, USA

O'Malley, Bryan Lee (Writer)
c/o Staff Member *Oni Press*
1305 SE M L King Blvd Ste A
Portland, OR 97214-3457, USA

O'Malley, Jim (Athlete, Football Player)
238 S Berryline Cir
Spring, TX 77381-4824, USA

O'Malley, Joe (Athlete, Football Player)
1701 Cairnbrook Dr
Montgomery, AL 36106-3042, USA

O'Malley, Martin (Governor, Politician)
Office of the Governor
100 State Cir
Annapolis, MD 21401-1924, USA

O'Malley, Mike (Actor, Director, Writer)
547 N Cahuenga Blvd
Los Angeles, CA 90004-1101, USA

O'Malley, Peter (Baseball Player)
326 S Hudson Ave
Los Angeles, CA 90020-4804, USA

O'Malley, Sean Patrick (Religious Leader)
Archdiocese of Boston
2121 Commonwealth Ave
Brighton, MA 02135-3101, USA

O'Malley, Thomas D (Business Person)
Tosco Corp
1700 E Putnam Ave # 500
Old Greenwich, CT 06870-1366, USA

O'Malley, Tom (Athlete, Baseball Player)
89 Carriage S Cl
Montoursville, PA 17754, USA

Omar, Don (Musician)
45 Ann Arbor Pl
Closter, NJ 07624-1538, USA

O'Mara, Jason (Actor)
c/o Michael (Mike) Jelline *United Talent Agency (UTA-LA)*
9336 Civic Center Dr
Beverly Hills, CA 90210-3604, USA

O'Mara, Mark (Horse Racer)
629 Laurel Cove Ct Apt 205
Orlando, FL 32825-3220, USA

Omar & The Howlers
PO Box 93
Austin, TX 78767-0093

Omarion (Actor)
c/o Christopher Stokes *Ultimate Group, The*
6320 Canoga Ave # 420
Woodland Hills, CA 91367-2526, USA

Omartian, Stormie (Writer)
c/o Staff Member *Harvest House Publisher*
990 Owen Loop N
Eugene, OR 97402-9173, USA

O. Matsui, Doris (Congressman, Politician)
222 Cannon Hob
Washington, DC 20515-3517, USA

O'Meara, Mark (Athlete, Golfer)
6060 Parkland Blvd Ste 100
Cleveland, OH 44124-4225, USA

O'Meara, Peter (Actor)
c/o Staff Member *ROAR (LA)*
9701 Wilshire Blvd Fl 8
Beverly Hills, CA 90212-2008, USA

OMG Girlz (Music Group, Musician)
c/o Staff Member *Interscope Records (LA) - Main*
2220 Colorado Ave
Santa Monica, CA 90404-3506, USA

Omidyar, Pierre (Business Person)
eBay
2145 Hamilton Ave
San Jose, CA 95125-5905, USA

Ommanney, Catherine (Reality Star)
c/o Staff Member *Bravo (NY)*
30 Rockefeller Plz
New York, NY 10112-0015, USA

Omundson, Timothy (Actor)
c/o Michael Bircumshaw *Water Street Management*
5225 Wilshire Blvd Ste 615
Los Angeles, CA 90036-4350, USA

On, Richard (Music Group)
c/o Sid Craig *Craig Management*
125 S Sycamore Ave
Los Angeles, CA 90036-2938, USA

Onanian, Edward (Religious Leader)
Diocese of Armenian Church
630 2nd Ave
New York, NY 10016-4806, USA

Onarati, Peter (Actor)
Liberman Zerman
252 N Larchmont Blvd Ste 200
Los Angeles, CA 90004-3754, USA

Ondetti, Miguel A
79 Hemlock Cir
Princeton, NJ 08540-5405, USA

Ondrasik, John (Musician, Songwriter)
c/o Staff Member *Paradigm (NY)*
360 Park Ave S Fl 16
New York, NY 10010-1716, USA

O'neal, Blair (Athlete, Golfer)
c/o Eddie Smith *Gaylord Sports Management*
13845 N Northsight Blvd Ste 200
Scottsdale, AZ 85260-3609, USA

O'Neal, Griffin (Actor)
21368 Pacific Coast Hwy
Malibu, CA 90265-5203, USA

O'Neal, Jamie (Musician, Songwriter, Writer)
Fitzgerald Hartley
19078 Wedgewood Ave
Nashville, TN 37212, USA

O'Neal, Jermaine (Athlete, Basketball Player)
c/o Arn Tellem *Wasserman Media Group (LA)*
12100 W Olympic Blvd Ste 200
Los Angeles, CA 90064-1075, USA

O'Neal, Leslie C (Athlete, Football Player)
5617 Adobe Falls Rd Unit A
San Diego, CA 92120-4654, USA

O'Neal, Randy (Athlete, Baseball Player)
10015 Honey Tree Ct
Orlando, FL 32836-5937, USA

O'Neal, Ryan (Actor)
21368 Pacific Coast Hwy
Malibu, CA 90265-5203, USA

O'Neal, Shaquille (Athlete, Basketball Player, Olympic Athlete)
9927 Giffin Ct
Windermere, FL 34786-8932, USA

O'Neal, Shaunie (Actor, Reality Star)
c/o Nathan Habben *Prestige Talent Agency*
8421 Wilshire Blvd Ste 200
Beverly Hills, CA 90211-3204, USA

O'Neal, Steve (Athlete, Football Player)
2914 Coronado Dr
College Station, TX 77845-7716, USA

O'Neal, Tatum (Actor)
c/o Miles Levy *James/Levy Management Inc*
3500 W Olive Ave Ste 1470
Burbank, CA 91505-5514, USA

O'Neil, Edward W (Athlete, Football Player)
943 Robin Rd
Buffalo, NY 14228-1029, USA

O'Neil, Lawrence (Director)
International Creative Mgmt
10250 Constellation Blvd Fl 1
Los Angeles, CA 90067-6241, USA

O'Neil, Ron
10100 Santa Monica Blvd Ste 2500
Los Angeles, CA 90067-4116

O'Neil, Tricia (Actor)
c/o Staff Member *David Shapira & Associates*
193 N Robertson Blvd
Beverly Hills, CA 90211-2103, USA

O'Neil, Warren (Baseball Player)
Detroit Stars
258 Terrace Park
Rochester, NY 14619-2443, USA

O'Neill, Ed (Actor)
c/o Marc Gurvitz *Brillstein Entertainment Partners (LA)*
9150 Wilshire Blvd Ste 350
Beverly Hills, CA 90212-3453, USA

O'Neill, Jennifer (Actor, Model)
Jennifer O'Neill Ministries
30 Hillenglade Dr
Nashville, TN 37207-1797, USA

O'Neill, Kevin (Athlete, Football Player)
1363 Masters Dr
Metamora, MI 48455-8701, USA

O'Neill, Michael (Actor)
c/o Staff Member *Mitchell K Stubbs & Assoc (MKS)*
8675 Washington Blvd Ste 203
Culver City, CA 90232-7486, USA

O'Neill, Paul (Athlete, Baseball Player)
7785 Hartford Hill Ln
Montgomery, OH 45242-4347, USA

O'Neill, Paul H (Politician)
3 Von Lent Pl
Pittsburgh, PA 15232-1444, USA

OneRepublic (Music Group)
c/o Ron Laffitte *Red Light Management (LA)*
8439 W Sunset Blvd Ste 2
West Hollywood, CA 90069-1925, USA

Onesti, Larry (Athlete, Football Player)
5476 E James Rd
Bloomington, IN 47408-9402, USA

Onkotz, Dennis (Athlete, Football Player)
551 Brush Valley Rd
Boalsburg, PA 16827-1018, USA

Oñ, Tommy (Director)
c/o Staff Member *William Morris Endeavor (LA)*
9601 Wilshire Blvd
Beverly Hills, CA 90210-5213, USA

O'Nora, Brian (Athlete, Baseball Player)
5265 Nashua Dr
Youngstown, OH 44515-5174, USA

O'Nora, Brian (Baseball Player)
4294 Maureen Dr
Youngstown, OH 44511-1014, USA

Onorati, Peter
c/o Kay Liberman *Liberman/Zerman Management*
252 N Larchmont Blvd Ste 200
Los Angeles, CA 90004-3754, USA

Ontiveros, Steve (Athlete, Baseball Player)
9970 E Charter Oak Rd
Scottsdale, AZ 85260-5138, USA

Ontiveros, Steve (Athlete, Baseball Player)
18061 N 87th Dr Unit 2127
Peoria, AZ 85382-3073, USA

Ontkean, Michael (Actor)
PO Box 51
Kilauea, HI 96754-0051, USA

Oosterhouse, Carter (Television Host)
c/o Robert Flutie *Flutie Entertainment (LA)*
2105 Colorado Ave Ste 106
Santa Monica, CA 90404-3503, USA

Opalinski-Harrer, Janice (Athlete, Volleyball Player)
Women's Pro Volleyball Assn
3653 Diamond Head Cir
Honolulu, HI 96815-4430, USA

Operator (Music Group)
c/o Staff Member *Agency Group Ltd, The (LA)*
1880 Century Park E Ste 711
Los Angeles, CA 90067-1618, USA

Opie, John D (Business Person)
General Electric Co
3135 Easton Tpke
Fairfield, CT 06828-0001, USA

Oppegard, Peter (Athlete, Figure Skater, Olympic Athlete)
8 Veranda
Newport Coast, CA 92657-1632, USA

Oppenheimer, Allan (Actor)
200 N Swall Dr Unit 405
Beverly Hills, CA 90211-4727, USA

Oppenheimer, Deborah (Producer)
c/o Staff Member *United Talent Agency (UTA-LA)*
9336 Civic Center Dr
Beverly Hills, CA 90210-3604, USA

O'Pry, Sean (Model)
c/o Staff Member *VNY Model Management*
928 Broadway Ste 700
New York, NY 10010-8136, USA

Opry, Tonya
1525 E Noble Ave # 160
Visalia, CA 93292-3043

Oquendo, Jose (Athlete, Baseball Player)
357 SE Ashley Oaks Way
Stuart, FL 34997-2806, USA

O'Quinn, Danny (Race Car Driver)
O'Quinn Motorsports
PO Box 1342
Coeburn, VA 24230-1342, USA

O'Quinn, Terry (Actor)
Innovative Artists
1505 10th St
Santa Monica, CA 90401-2805, USA

Oquist, Mike (Athlete, Baseball Player)
1910 Raton Ave
La Junta, CO 81050-3427, USA

Ora, Rita (Musician)
c/o Jana Fleishman *Roc Nation*
9348 Civic Center Dr Fl 3
Beverly Hills, CA 90210-3600, USA

Orakpo, Brian (Athlete, Football Player)
c/o Tom Condon *CAA (St. Louis)*
222 S Central Ave Ste 1008
Saint Louis, MO 63105-3509, USA

Orange, Walter (Clyde) (Music Group, Musician)
Management Assoc
1920 Benson Ave
Saint Paul, MN 55116-3214, USA

Orbit, William (Musician)
c/o Staff Member *Creative Artists Agency (CAA-LA)*
2000 Avenue of the Stars Ste 100
Los Angeles, CA 90067-4705, USA

Orci, Roberto (Producer)
c/o Risa Gertner *Creative Artists Agency (CAA-LA)*
2000 Avenue of the Stars Ste 100
Los Angeles, CA 90067-4705, USA

Ordaz, Luis (Athlete, Baseball Player)
130 N Division St
Attn: Coaching Staff
Auburn, NY 13021-1707, USA

Ordonez, Magglio (Athlete, Baseball Player)
181 Nurmi Dr
Fort Lauderdale, FL 33301-1404, USA

Ordonez, Rey (Athlete, Baseball Player)
1000 SE 9th Ave
Hialeah, FL 33010-5810, USA

Orduna, Joe (Athlete, Football Player)
15 Grant
Irvine, CA 92620-3354, USA

O'Ree, William E (Willie) (Athlete, Hockey Player)
7961 Anders Cir
La Mesa, CA 91942-2304, USA

O'Regan, Tom (Athlete, Hockey Player)
31 Cleveland Rd
Needham, MA 02492-3005

O'Reilly, Bill (Television Host)
33 Shore Dr
Manhasset, NY 11030-1018, USA

O'Reilly, Cyril (Actor)
Stone Manners
6500 Wilshire Blvd # 550
Los Angeles, CA 90048-4920, USA

O'Reilly, Terry (Athlete, Coach, Hockey Player)
PO Box 5544
Salisbury, MA 01952-0544, USA

Oremans, Miriam (Tennis Player)
Octagon
7950 Jones Branch Dr
Mc Lean, VA 22102-3302, USA

Orend, Jack R
1808 N Van Ness Ave
Los Angeles, CA 90028-5674, USA

Orendi, Ron
6323 Salem Park Cir
Mechanicsburg, PA 17050-2839

Orenstein, Andrew (Producer)
c/o Staff Member *United Talent Agency (UTA-LA)*
9336 Civic Center Dr
Beverly Hills, CA 90210-3604, USA

Oreskaband (Music Group)
c/o Staff Member *Paradigm (Monterey)*
404 W Franklin St
Monterey, CA 93940-2303, USA

Orgy (Music Group)
c/o Staff Member *Creative Artists Agency (CAA-LA)*
2000 Avenue of the Stars Ste 100
Los Angeles, CA 90067-4705, USA

Oriard, Michael (Athlete, Football Player)
3010 NW McKinley Dr
Corvallis, OR 97330-1138, USA

Orie, Kevin (Athlete, Baseball Player)
6 Ppg Pl Ste 300
Pi Ste 600
Pittsburgh, PA 15222-5406, USA

O'Riordan, Dolores (Musician)
c/o Danny Goldberg *Gold Village Entertainment*
37 W 17th St Ste 7W
New York, NY 10011-5525, USA

Orland, Frank J (Doctor)
519 Jackson Blvd
Forest Park, IL 60130-1807, USA

Orlando, Bo (Athlete, Football Player)
1360 Armstrong Rd
Bethlehem, PA 18017-1002, USA

Orlando, Gates (Athlete, Hockey Player)
252 Bennington Hills Ct
West Henrietta, NY 14586-9765

Orlando, Tony (Musician)
c/o David Brokaw *Brokaw Company, The*
9255 W Sunset Blvd Ste 804
West Hollywood, CA 90069-3305, USA

Orleans, Joan (Musician)
PO Box 2596
New York, NY 10009-8923, USA

Orlenko, Oksana (Actor)
c/o Staff Member *Sharp Entertainment*
1515 Broadway
New York, NY 10036-8901, USA

Orlich, Dan (Athlete, Football Player)
1030 Porter Cir
Reno, NV 89509-2349, USA

Orlov, Yuri
Cornell Univ.Newman Lab.
Ithaca, NY 14853

Orlovsky, Dan (Athlete, Football Player)
c/o David Dunn *Athletes First, LLC*
23091 Mill Creek Dr
Laguna Hills, CA 92653-1258, USA

Orman, Suze (Business Person, Television Host)
Suze Orman Financial Group
2000 Powell St Ste 1605
Emeryville, CA 94608-1861, USA

Ormond, Julia (Actor)
c/o Staff Member *Creative Partners Group*
15 Brooks Ave # B
Venice, CA 90291-3226, USA

Ormond, Paul (Business Person)
Manor Care Inc
333 N Summit St Ste 100
Toledo, OH 43604-2617, USA

Orms, Barry (Athlete, Basketball Player)
500 N Rossmore Ave Apt 403
Los Angeles, CA 90004-2437, USA

Orndorff, Paul (Athlete, Wrestler)
135 Pamela Ct
Fayetteville, GA 30214-4309, USA

Ornish, Dean (Doctor, Writer)
Preventative Medicine Research Institue
7 Miller Ave
Sausalito, CA 94965-2039, USA

Ornstein, Michael (Actor)
c/o Eric Nelson *Zero Gravity Management (II)*
9255 W Sunset Blvd Ste 1010
West Hollywood, CA 90069-3307, USA

Ornston, David E. (Producer)
Salvatore/Ornston Productions
5650 Camellia Ave
North Hollywood, CA 91601-1710, USA

Oropesa, Eddie (Athlete, Baseball Player)
15757 SW 102nd St
Miami, FL 33196-5420, USA

Orosco, Jesse (Athlete, Baseball Player)
16242 Winecreek Rd
San Diego, CA 92127-3733, USA

Orosz, Tom (Athlete, Football Player)
425 1/2 5th St
Fairport Harbor, OH 44077-5629, USA

O'Rourke, Charles C (Athlete, Football Player)
220 Bedford St Apt 7A
Bridgewater, MA 02324-3123, USA

O'Rourke, Charlie (Athlete, Baseball Player)
15612 N Little Spokane Dr
Spokane, WA 99208-8527, USA

O'Rourke, PJ (Actor)
c/o Missy Malkin *Brillstein Entertainment Partners (LA)*
9150 Wilshire Blvd Ste 350
Beverly Hills, CA 90212-3453, USA

O'Rourke, P.J. (Athlete, Hockey Player)
1 Cherry Ln
Georgetown, MA 01833-1112, USA

O'Rourke, Tom (Actor)
c/o Staff Member *Law & Order: SVU*
100 Universal City Plz Bldg 2252
Universal City, CA 91608-1002, USA

Orpik, Brooks (Athlete, Hockey Player)
Sports Management
51 Nathaniel Pl
Englewood, NJ 07631-2736, USA

Orr, Bobby (Athlete, Hockey Player)
6413 Mullin St
Jupiter, FL 33458-6666, USA

Orr, Christopher (Actor)
c/o Staff Member *3 Arts Entertainment (LA)*
9460 Wilshire Blvd Fl 7
Beverly Hills, CA 90212-2713, USA

Orr, Gregory (Writer)
University Of Virginia
PO Box 400121
Charlottesville, VA 22904-4121, USA

Orr, James E (Athlete, Football Player)
3104 Glynn Ave
Brunswick, GA 31520, USA

Orr, Kay (Politician)
1610 Brent Blvd
Lincoln, NE 68506-1866, USA

Orr, Louis (Athlete, Basketball Player, Coach)
1333 Pine Valley Dr
Bowling Green, OH 43402-5207, USA

Orr, Terrence S (Dancer)
American Ballet Theatre
890 Broadway Fl 3
New York, NY 10003-1278, USA

Orr, Terry (Athlete, Football Player)
2710 Kellogg Ave
Dallas, TX 75216-3250, USA

Orrall, Robert Ellis (Musician)
3 E 54th St # 1400
New York, NY 10022-3108, USA

Orr-Cahall, Christina (Director)
Norton Gallery of Art
1451 S Olive Ave
West Palm Beach, FL 33401-7198, USA

Orrico, Stacie (Musician)
c/o Staff Member *Creative Artists Agency
(CAA-LA)*
2000 Avenue of the Stars Ste 100
Los Angeles, CA 90067-4705, USA

Orr III, James E (Business Person)
UNUMProvident Corp
2211 Congress St
Portland, ME 04122-0003, USA

Orr Jr, James E (Jim) (Athlete, Football
Player)
3104 Glynn Ave
Brunswick, GA 31520, USA

Orser, Leland (Actor)
c/o Kami Putnam-Heist *Creative Artists
Agency (CAA-LA)*
2000 Avenue of the Stars Ste 100
Los Angeles, CA 90067-4705, USA

Orsin, Raymond (Cartoonist)
Cleveland Plain Dealer
1801 Superior Ave E
Cleveland, OH 44114-2198, USA

Orsino, John (Athlete, Baseball Player)
301 187th St
Sunny Isles Beach, FL 33160-2410, USA

Orsulak, Joe (Athlete, Baseball Player)
29 Keansburg Rd
Parsippany, NJ 07054-3508, USA

Orta, Jorge (Athlete, Baseball Player)
1201 Heather Hill Cres
Flossmoor, IL 60422-1425, USA

Ortega, Bill (Athlete, Baseball Player)
4635 NW 95th Ave
Doral, FL 33178-2091, USA

Ortega, Gaspar
38 Branhaven Dr
East Haven, CT 06513-2005

Ortega, Jeannie (Musician)
Hollywood Records
500 S Buena Vista St
Burbank, CA 91521-0002, USA

Ortega, Keith (Athlete, Football Player)
142 Lucille St
Lake Charles, LA 70601-8423, USA

Ortega, Kenny (Actor, Director, Producer)
c/o Andy Patman *Paradigm (LA)*
360 N Crescent Dr
North Bldg
Beverly Hills, CA 90210-4874, USA

Ortega, Phil (Athlete, Baseball Player)
307 Leighton Dr
Ventura, CA 93001-1556, USA

Ortega, Ralph (Athlete, Football Player)
10465 SW 124th St
Miami, FL 33176-4721, USA

Ortenzio, Frank (Athlete, Baseball Player)
2357 Oak Forest Dr
Jacksonville Beach, FL 32250-2942, USA

Ortiz, Adalberto (Junior) (Athlete,
Baseball Player)
161 Kinchafoonee Creek Rd
Leesburg, GA 31763-4903, USA

Ortiz, Ana (Actor)
c/o Geordie Frey *GEF Entertainment*
611 N Cherokee Ave
Los Angeles, CA 90004-1008, USA

Ortiz, David (Athlete, Baseball Player)
278 Peterlynn Dr
Wrightstown, WI 54180-1089, USA

Ortiz, Javier (Athlete, Baseball Player)
19520 SW 39th Ct
Miramar, FL 33029-2736, USA

Ortiz, John (Actor)
c/o Mark Armstrong *Sanders Armstrong
Caserta*
2120 Colorado Ave Ste 120
Santa Monica, CA 90404-3561, USA

Ortiz, Louis (Baseball Player)
1683 La Verde Dr
San Marcos, CA 92078-5223, USA

Ortiz, Luis (Athlete, Baseball Player)
6408 Rogers Dr
North Richland Hills, TX 76182-4807,
USA

Ortiz, Manuel
1 Hall of Fame Dr
Canastota, NY 13032-1175

Ortiz, Russ (Athlete, Baseball Player)
2601 N Val Vista Dr
Mesa, AZ 85213-1719, USA

Ortiz, Shalim (Actor)
c/o Irene Marie *Irene Marie Management
Group*
PO Box 398115
Miami Beach, FL 33239-8115, USA

Ortiz, Tito (Athlete, Boxer)
c/o Liam Collopy *Levine Communications
Office*
9100 Wilshire Blvd Ste 540
Beverly Hills, CA 90212-3470, USA

Ortiz, Victor (Athlete, Boxer)
c/o Staff Member *Dancing With The Stars*
500 S Buena Vista St
Burbank, CA 91521-0001, USA

Ortmann, Charles (Athlete, Football
Player)
4 River Birch Ln
Savannah, GA 31411-2847, USA

Ortmeier, Dan (Athlete, Baseball Player)
933 Southwood Dr
Lewisville, TX 75077-6434, USA

Ortmeyer, Jed
1421 S 52nd St
Omaha, NE 68106-2303

Ortner, Bev (Bowler)
PO Box 436
Odebolt, IA 51458-0436, USA

Orton, Beth (Musician)
c/o Beth Holden-Garland *Untitled
Entertainment (LA)*
350 S Beverly Dr Ste 200
Beverly Hills, CA 90212-4819, USA

Orton, John (Athlete, Baseball Player)
2929 E Dublin St
Gilbert, AZ 85295-0403, USA

Orton, Kyle (Football Player)
c/o Staff Member *Chicago Bears*
1000 Football Dr
Lake Forest, IL 60045, USA

Orton, Randy (Athlete, Wrestler)
c/o Kerry Rodgerson *World Wrestling
Entertainment (WWE)*
1241 E Main St
Titan Towers
Stamford, CT 06902-3520, USA

Oruche, Phina (Actor)
c/o Staff Member *Bauman Redanty &
Shaul Agency*
5757 Wilshire Blvd
Suite 473
Beverly Hills, CA 90212, USA

Orvella, Chad (Athlete, Baseball Player)
1205 N 27th Pl
Renton, WA 98056-1472, USA

Orvick, George M (Religious Leader)
Evangelical Lutheran Synod
6 Browns Ct
Mankato, MN 56001-6121, USA

Orvis, Herb (Athlete, Football Player)
22146 E Phillips Pl
Aurora, CO 80016-7236, USA

O'Sadnick, Craig (Athlete, Football Player)
10 Huntington Forest Ct E
Saint Charles, MO 63301-0490, USA

Osborn, Danny (Athlete, Baseball Player)
5061 W 73rd Ave
Westminster, CO 80030-5122, USA

Osborn, David V (Dave) (Athlete,
Football Player)
18067 Judicial Way S
Lakeville, MN 55044-8895, USA

Osborn, Jim (Athlete, Football Player)
4 Canyon Ct
Algonquin, IL 60102-6306, USA

Osborn, John Jay (Writer)
14 Fair Oaks St
San Francisco, CA 94110-2209, USA

Osborn, Kassidy (Musician)
LGB Media
1228 Pineview Ln
Nashville, TN 37211-7422, USA

Osborn, Kelsi (Musician)
LGB Media
1228 Pineview Ln
Nashville, TN 37211-7422, USA

Osborn, Kristyn (Musician, Songwriter,
Writer)
LGB Media
1228 Pineview Ln
Nashville, TN 37211-7422, USA

Osborne, Barrie M (Director, Producer)
c/o Staff Member *Emerald City
Productions*
9777 Wilshire Blvd Ste 550
Beverly Hills, CA 90212-1905, United
States

Osborne, Burl (Religious Leader)
Salvation Army
799 Bloomfield Ave
Verona, NJ 07044-1367, USA

Osborne, Donovan (Athlete, Baseball
Player)
1651 Brightstone Ct
Reno, NV 89521-4049, USA

Osborne, Jeffrey (Musician, Songwriter,
Writer)
Entertainment Artists
2409 21st Ave S Ste 100
Nashville, TN 37212-5317, USA

Osborne, Joan (Musician, Songwriter)
c/o Staff Member *Paradigm (Monterey)*
404 W Franklin St
Monterey, CA 93940-2303, USA

Osborne, Mary Pope (Writer)
c/o Matthew Snyder *Creative Artists
Agency (CAA-LA)*
2000 Avenue of the Stars Ste 100
Los Angeles, CA 90067-4705, USA

Osborne, Richard (Athlete, Football
Player)
418 Tango Dr
San Antonio, TX 78216-3564, USA

Osborne, Tom (Athlete, Football Coach,
Football Player)
5400 Trotter Rd
Lincoln, NE 68516-3419, USA

Osbourne, Jack (Reality Star)
4451 Lemp Ave
North Hollywood, CA 91602-1919, USA

Osbourne, Kelly (Musician)
1500 San Ysidro Dr
Beverly Hills, CA 90210-2111, USA

Osbourne, Ozzy (Musician, Songwriter)
10990 Wilshire Blvd Fl 8
Los Angeles, CA 90024-3918, USA

Osbourne, Sharon (Business Person,
Reality Star, Talk Show Host)
c/o Melissa Raubvogel *Baker Winokur
Ryder Public Relations (BWR-NY)*
292 Madison Ave Fl 12
New York, NY 10017-6415, USA

Osburn, Pat (Athlete, Baseball Player)
208 64th Street Ct NW
Bradenton, FL 34209-1625, USA

Osby, Greg (Musician)
Bridge Agency
2600 John F Kennedy Blvd Apt 1H
Jersey City, NJ 07306-6068, USA

Oseary, Guy (Business Person, Producer)
c/o Staff Member *Untitled Entertainment
(LA)*
350 S Beverly Dr Ste 200
Beverly Hills, CA 90212-4819, USA

Osemele, Kelechi (Athlete, Football
Player)
c/o David Dunn *Athletes First, LLC*
23091 Mill Creek Dr
Laguna Hills, CA 92653-1258, USA

Osgood, Chris (Athlete, Hockey Player)
1445 Penniman Ave
Plymouth, MI 48170-1036, USA

O'Shea, Danny (Athlete, Hockey Player)
1425 County Road 110 N
Mound, MN 55364-8921

O'Shea, Terry (Athlete, Football Player)
506 Amberson Pl
Greensburg, PA 15601-8684, USA

Osher, John (Business Person)
Maltz Jupiter Theatre
1001 E Indiantown Rd
Board of Directors
Jupiter, FL 33477-5110, USA

Oshodin, Willie (Athlete, Football Player)
8134 Murray Hill Dr
Fort Washington, MD 20744-4416, USA

Osiecki, Mark (Athlete, Hockey Player)
1233 Scenic Ridge Dr
Verona, WI 53593-2270

Osiecki, Sandy (Athlete, Football Player)
11 Bryan Cir
Seymour, CT 06483-3676, USA

Osik, Keith (Athlete, Baseball Player)
5 Pal Ct
Shoreham, NY 11786-2352, USA

Osinski, Dan (Athlete, Baseball Player)
9723 W Amber Trl
Sun City, AZ 85351-1346, USA

Oslin, K T (Musician)
Moress-Nanas-Hart
704 18th Ave S
Nashville, TN 37203-3215, USA

Osment, Emily (Actor)
c/o Kim Jakwerth *Marleah Leslie &
Associates PR*
1645 Vine St Apt 712
Los Angeles, CA 90028-8812, USA

Osment, Haley Joel (Actor)
c/o Meredith Fine *Coast to Coast Talent
Group*
3350 Barham Blvd
Los Angeles, CA 90068-1404, USA

Osmond, Cliff (Actor, Director)
15515 W Sunset Blvd Unit 210
Pacific Plsds, CA 90272-3530, USA

Osmond, Donny (Actor, Musician,
Producer)
Donny Osmond Entertainment
1329 S 800 E
Orem, UT 84097-7737, USA

Osmond, Ken (Actor)
9863 Wornom Ave
Sunland, CA 91040-1535, USA

Osmond, Marie (Actor, Musician)
1391 Quiet River Ave
Henderson, NV 89012-7219, USA

Osorio, Jorge Federico (Musician)
Columbia Artists Mgmt Inc
165 W 57th St
New York, NY 10019-2201, USA

Osrin, Raymond H (Cartoonist)
Cleveland Plain Dealer
1801 Superior Ave E
Editorial Dept
Cleveland, OH 44114-2198, USA

Oss, Arnold (Athlete, Hockey Player,
Olympic Athlete)
25601 N Abajo Dr
Rio Verde, AZ 85263-7219, USA

Ossana, Diana (Producer, Writer)
c/o Adam Shulman *Anonymous Content
(LA)*
3532 Hayden Ave
Culver City, CA 90232-2413, USA

Ostaseski, Frank (Director)
Zen Hospice Project
273 Page St
San Francisco, CA 94102-5616, USA

Osteen, Claude W (Athlete, Baseball
Player)
2313 Duncan Perry Rd
Grand Prairie, TX 75050-2039, USA

Osteen, Darrell (Athlete, Baseball Player)
73400 Desert Greens Dr N
Palm Desert, CA 92260-1208, USA

Osteen, Joel (Religious Leader, Writer)
Lakewood Church
3700 Southwest Fwy
Houston, TX 77027-7514, USA

Oster, Bill (Athlete, Baseball Player)
56 Little Neck Rd
Centerport, NY 11721-1617, USA

Osterbrock, Donald E
120 Woodside Ave
Santa Cruz, CA 95060-3422, USA

Osterhage, Jeff (Actor)
7309 Santa Barbara St
Carlsbad, CA 92011-4638, USA

Ostertag, Greg (Athlete, Basketball Player)
7401 Cobblestone Ct
McKinney, TX 75070-5073, USA

Osting, Jimmy (Athlete, Baseball Player)
927 Lakeside Dr
Taylorsville, KY 40071-9271, USA

Ostlund, Ruben (Director)
c/o Jerome Duboz *William Morris
Endeavor (LA)*
9601 Wilshire Blvd
Beverly Hills, CA 90210-5213, USA

Ostroski, Gerald (Athlete, Football Player)
6926 E 115th Pl S
Bixby, OK 74008-8248, USA

Ostrosky, Beth (Actor, Model)
c/o Staff Member *Don Buchwald &
Associates (NY)*
10 E 44th St Frnt 1
New York, NY 10017-3654, USA

Ostrum, Peter (Actor)
6065 Duncan Rd
Glenfield, NY 13343-4021, USA

O'Sullivan, Chris (Athlete, Hockey Player)
114 Elmer Rd
Dorchester Center, MA 02124-5034

O'Sullivan, Dan (Athlete, Basketball
Player)
33 Crescent Ave
Summit, NJ 07901-1902, USA

Osuna, Antonio (Athlete, Baseball Player)
10345 W Olympic Blvd
Los Angeles, CA 90064-2524, USA

Oswald, Mark (Race Car Driver)
Championship Quest Motorsports
237B N Hollywood Rd
Houma, LA 70364-2807, USA

Oswald, Paul (Athlete, Football Player)
521 Cambridge Ct
Alpharetta, GA 30005-4216, USA

Oswald, Stephen S (Astronaut)
NASA
2101 Nasa Pkwy Spc Johnsoncenter
Houston, TX 77058-3696, USA

Oswald, Stephen S Rear Admiral
(Astronaut)
1102 Fugate St
Houston, TX 77009-5016, USA

Oswalt, Patton (Actor, Comedian)
3241 Lowry Rd
Los Angeles, CA 90027-2206, USA

Oswalt, Roy (Athlete, Baseball Player,
Olympic Athlete)
292 Jenny Penn Rd
Crawford, MS 39743-2000, USA

Osweiler, Brock (Athlete, Football Player)
c/o Jimmy Sexton *CAA (Memphis)*
6060 Poplar Ave Ste 470
Memphis, TN 38119-0910, USA

Oszajca, John (Musician)
Interscope Records
2220 Colorado Ave
Santa Monica, CA 90404-3506, USA

Otanez, Willis (Athlete, Baseball Player)
7904 March Brown Ave
Las Vegas, NV 89149-5101, USA

Otellini, Paul (Business Person)
Intel Corp
2200 Mission College Blvd
Santa Clara, CA 95054-1549, USA

Otep (Musician)
c/o Staff Member *Zen Media Group*
272 Grand St Ste B
Brooklyn, NY 11211-4796, USA

Oteri, Cheri (Actor, Comedian)
c/o Lori Sale *Artist & Brand Management
(LA)*
132 N Laurel Ave
Los Angeles, CA 90048-3512, USA

Otero, Ricky (Athlete, Baseball Player)
126 Calle Sorbona
Urb University Gardens
San Juan, PR 00927, USA

Othenin-Girard, Dominque (Director)
327 S Church Ln
Los Angeles, CA 90049-3057, USA

Othick, Trent (Producer)
c/o Staff Member *Creative Artists Agency
(CAA-LA)*
2000 Avenue of the Stars Ste 100
Los Angeles, CA 90067-4705, USA

Otis, Amos J (Athlete, Baseball Player)
8930 Tiger Shale Way
Las Vegas, NV 89123-3132, USA

Otis, James L (Jim) (Athlete, Football
Player)
14795 Greenleaf Valley Dr
Chesterfield, MO 63017-5542, USA

O'Toole, Annette (Actor)
3202 Club Dr
Los Angeles, CA 90064-4812, USA

O'Toole, Dennis (Denny) (Athlete,
Baseball Player)
9105 Royal Oak Ln
Union, KY 41091-8806, USA

O'Toole, Jim (Athlete, Baseball Player)
1010 Lanette Dr
Cincinnati, OH 45230-3616, USA

O-Town (Music Group)
c/o Mona Loring *MLC PR*
7080 Hollywood Blvd Ste 903
Los Angeles, CA 90028-6936, USA

Otsuka, Akinori (Athlete, Baseball Player)
891 Fairway Dr
Boulder City, NV 89005-3609, USA

Otsuki, Tamayo (Actor)
Patterson Assoc
20318 Hiawatha St
Chatsworth, CA 91311-2553, USA

Ott, Billy (Athlete, Baseball Player)
132 W Nyack Way
West Nyack, NY 10994-2202, USA

Ott, Ed (Athlete, Baseball Player)
3164 New London Rd
Forest, VA 24551-1814, USA

Otten, Jim (Athlete, Baseball Player)
1539 E Hale St
Mesa, AZ 85203-3819, USA

Otten, Mac (Athlete, Basketball Player)
1772 Ridgewood Dr NE
Atlanta, GA 30307-1164, USA

Otter, C.L. (Butch) (Governor, Politician)
Office of the Governor
PO Box 83720
Boise, ID 83720-0003, USA

Ottinger, LD (Race Car Driver)
1021 Scarlet Rd
Newport, TN 37821-7520, USA

Otto, August J (Gus) (Athlete, Football
Player)
8 Cool Meadows Dr
Ballwin, MO 63011-3883, USA

Otto, Bob (Athlete, Football Player)
1713 Guthrie Dr
Las Vegas, NV 89117-9000, USA

Otto, Dave (Athlete, Baseball Player)
1383 Shady Ln
Wheaton, IL 60187-3722, USA

Otto, James (Musician)
c/o Dan Anderson *Red Light Management
(TN)*
PO Box 159310
Nashville, TN 37215-9310, USA

Otto, James E (Jim) (Athlete, Football
Player)
100 Estates Dr
Auburn, CA 95602, USA

Otto, Michael (Business Person)
Spiegel Inc
3500 Lacey Rd
Downers Grove, IL 60515-5422, USA

Oubre, Louis (Athlete, Football Player)
11008 Curran Blvd
New Orleans, LA 70127-1408, USA

Oudin, Melanie (Athlete, Tennis Player)
c/o Sam Duvall *Lagardere Unlimited (DC)*
5335 Wisconsin Ave NW Ste 850
Washington, DC 20015-2052, USA

Ouellette, Phil (Athlete, Baseball Player)
7421 Poppy St
Corona, CA 92881-3739, USA

Oureiro, Natalia (Musician)
c/o Staff Member *BMG*
1540 Broadway
New York, NY 10036-4039, USA

Outkast (Music Group)
c/o Sara Newkirk Simon *William Morris
Endeavor (LA)*
9601 Wilshire Blvd
Beverly Hills, CA 90210-5213, USA

Outlar, Jesse (Sportscaster)
1252 Stephens St SW
Lilburn, GA 30047-4354, USA

Outlaw, Charles (Bo) (Athlete, Basketball
Player)
7716 Belvoir Dr
Orlando, FL 32835-8185, USA

Outlaw, Travis (Athlete, Basketball Player)
c/o Bill Duffy *BDA Sports Management
(BDA-CA)*
700 Ygnacio Valley Rd Ste 330
Walnut Creek, CA 94596-3838, USA

Outman, Josh (Athlete, Baseball Player)
5273 Seasonbrooks Ln
Imperial, MO 63052-4012, USA

OV7 (Music Group)
c/o Staff Member *Sony Music Miami*
605 Lincoln Rd Ste 700
Miami Beach, FL 33139-2901, USA

Ovechkin, Alexander (Athlete, Hockey Player)
6301 Osprey Ter
Coconut Creek, FL 33073-2624, USA

Overall, Park (Actor)
33150 Drill Rd
Santa Clarita, CA 91390-4698, USA

Overbay, Lyle (Athlete, Baseball Player)
4907 101st Ln SW
Olympia, WA 98512-7521, USA

Overbeck, Carla (Athlete, Olympic Athlete, Soccer Player)
205 Zapata Ln
Chapel Hill, NC 27517-7742, USA

Overgard, Robert M (Religious Leader)
Church of Lutheran Brethren
PO Box 655
Fergus Falls, MN 56538-0655, USA

Overgard, William (Cartoonist)
United Feature Syndicate
PO Box 5610
Cincinnati, OH 45201-5610, USA

Overhauser, Chad (Athlete, Football Player)
8303 N No Pac Expy
Suite 425B
Austin, TX 78759, USA

Overleese, Joanne (Baseball Player)
849 Coach Blvd
La Jolla, CA 92037, USA

Overman, Ion
c/o Staff Member *GVA Talent Agency Inc*
8981 W Sunset Blvd Ste 101
West Hollywood, CA 90069-1850, USA

Overmyer, Eric (Writer)
c/o Rob Kenneally *Creative Artists Agency (CAA-LA)*
2000 Avenue of the Stars Ste 100
Los Angeles, CA 90067-4705, USA

Overstreet, Chord (Actor, Musician)
3076 Durand Dr
Los Angeles, CA 90068-1910, USA

Overstreet, Paul (Musician, Songwriter, Writer)
White Horse Enterprises
475 Annex Ave
Nashville, TN 37209-2747, USA

Overstreet, Tommy (Musician)
c/o Robert Metzgar *Capitol Management Group*
330 Franklin Rd
Brentwood, TN 37027-3280, USA

Overstreet, Will (Athlete, Football Player)
106 Avondale St
Jackson, MS 39216, USA

Overton, Kelly (Actor)
c/o Staff Member *Management 360*
9111 Wilshire Blvd
Beverly Hills, CA 90210-5508, USA

Overton, Rick (Actor)
c/o Staff Member *Sutton Barth & Vennari Inc*
5900 Wilshire Blvd Ste 700
Los Angeles, CA 90036-5009, USA

Overy, Mike (Athlete, Baseball Player)
3010 N 152nd Ln
Goodyear, AZ 85395-8636, USA

Ovitz, Michael S (Business Person)
457 N Rockingham Ave
Los Angeles, CA 90049-2637, USA

Owchinko, Bob (Athlete, Baseball Player)
15111 N Hayden Rd # 160-357
Scottsdale, AZ 85260-2581, USA

Owen, Clive (Actor)
c/o Staff Member *42West (NYC)*
220 W 42nd St Fl 12
New York, NY 10036-7200, USA

Owen, Dave (Athlete, Baseball Player)
1921 FM 3136
Cleburne, TX 76031-8792, USA

Owen, Edwyn (Bob) (Athlete, Hockey Player)
3630 SW Stratford Rd
Topeka, KS 66604-2544, USA

Owen, Jake (Musician)
1254 Webb Ridge Rd
Kingston Springs, TN 37082-8171, USA

Owen, Larry (Athlete, Baseball Player)
3497 River Narrows Rd
Hilliard, OH 43026-7833, USA

Owen, Randy Y (Musician)
PO Box 529
Fort Payne, AL 35968, USA

Owen, Rena (Actor, Model)
c/o Michael Greene *Greene & Associates*
1901 Avenue of the Stars Ste 130
Los Angeles, CA 90067-6030, USA

Owen, Spike (Athlete, Baseball Player)
11211 Musket Rim St
Austin, TX 78738-6613, USA

Owen, Tom (Athlete, Football Player)
PO Box 3
Albany, OK 74721-0003, USA

Owens, Al (Baseball Player)
Nashville Elite Giants
63 Bluff Ave
La Grange, IL 60525-2507, USA

Owens, Billy (Athlete, Basketball Player)
608 Canary Dr
Carlisle, PA 17013-8768, USA

Owens, Brig (Athlete, Football Player)
6902 Lupine Ln
Mc Lean, VA 22101-1578, USA

Owens, Buddy (Athlete, Baseball Player)
63 Bluff Ave
La Grange, IL 60525-2507, USA

Owens, Burgess (Athlete, Football Player)
1155 E Sunset Dunes Way
Draper, UT 84020-5676, USA

Owens, Charles W (Tinker) (Athlete, Football Player)
2547 McGee Dr
Norman, OK 73072-6704, USA

Owens, Chris (Actor)
c/o Jerry Shandrew *Shandrew Public Relations*
1050 S Stanley Ave
Los Angeles, CA 90019-6634, USA

Owens, Chris (Athlete, Football Player)
c/o Frank Bauer *Sun West Sports*
7883 N Pershing Ave
Stockton, CA 95207-1749, USA

Owens, Cotton (Race Car Driver)
Cotton Owens Garage
7065 White Ave
Spartanburg, SC 29303-2058, USA

Owens, Craig (Musician)
c/o Staff Member *Equal Vision Records*
PO Box 38202
Albany, NY 12203-8202, USA

Owens, Dan (Athlete, Football Player)
280 Selkirk Ln
Duluth, GA 30097-8043, USA

Owens, Darrick (Athlete, Football Player)
610 Cypress St
Raceland, LA 70394-2817, USA

Owens, Eric (Athlete, Baseball Player)
22431 N 54th St
Phoenix, AZ 85054-7210, USA

Owens, Gary (DJ)
17856 Via Vallarta
Encino, CA 91316-4345, USA

Owens, Henry (Athlete, Baseball Player)
4944 SW 140th Ct
Miami, FL 33175-4806, USA

Owens, Jackson (Athlete, Baseball Player)
PO Box 6046
Decatur, IL 62524-6046, USA

Owens, Jayhawk (Athlete, Baseball Player)
273 Warwick Pl
Castle Pines, CO 80108-8823, USA

Owens, Jim (Athlete, Baseball Player)
1426 Ramada Dr
Houston, TX 77062-5908, USA

Owens, Joe (Athlete, Football Player)
2754 Highway 13 N
Columbia, MS 39429-8634, USA

Owens, Kem (Musician)
c/o Staff Member *The Paradise Group*
PO Box 69451
West Hollywood, CA 90069-0451, USA

Owens, Lorenzo (Musician)
c/o Staff Member *Paradigm (Monterey)*
404 W Franklin St
Monterey, CA 93940-2303, USA

Owens, Luke (Athlete, Football Player)
2970 Richmond Rd
Beachwood, OH 44122-3248, USA

Owens, Mel (Athlete, Football Player)
1230 Market St Apt 504
San Francisco, CA 94102-4801, USA

Owens, Morris (Athlete, Football Player)
3010 W Yorkshire Dr Apt 1114
Phoenix, AZ 85027-3919, USA

Owens, Rawleigh C (R C) (Athlete, Football Player)
626 E Yosemite Ave
Manteca, CA 95336-5826, USA

Owens, Steve (Athlete, Football Player, Heisman Trophy Winner)
3700 W Robinson St Ste 230
Norman, OK 73072-3639, USA

Owens, Terrell (Athlete, Football Player)
4658 Longridge Ave
Sherman Oaks, CA 91423-3220, USA

Owens, Terry (Athlete, Football Player)
2524 Poovey Rd SE
Decatur, AL 35603-5624, USA

Owens, Tom (Athlete, Basketball Coach)
19788 Wildwood Dr
West Linn, OR 97068-2252, USA

Owens, William (Politician)
14111 Vance Jackson Rd Apt 9306
San Antonio, TX 78249-1999, USA

Owensby, Earl (Actor)
1056 Old Springs Rd
Shelby, NC 28152, USA

Owings, Jim (Athlete, Football Player)
961 Chestnut St SE Ste 107
Gainesville, GA 30501-6902, USA

Owings, Micah (Athlete, Baseball Player)
2219 Sidney Drive Dr NE
Gainesville, GA 30506, USA

Owl City (Music Group, Musician)
c/o Sonia Aneja *Stunt Company*
20 Jay St Ste 208
Brooklyn, NY 11201-8319, USA

Ownbey, Rick (Athlete, Baseball Player)
PO Box 1063
Bonsall, CA 92003-1063, USA

Oxenberg, Catherine (Actor)
c/o Staff Member *Power Entertainment*
9100 Wilshire Blvd Ste 700
Beverly Hills, CA 90212-3423, USA

Oyakawa, Yoshinobu (Yoshi) (Swimmer)
4171 Hutchinson Rd
Cincinnati, OH 45248-2219, USA

Oye, Erlend (Musician)
c/o Staff Member *Paradigm (Monterey)*
404 W Franklin St
Monterey, CA 93940-2303, USA

Oyelowo, David (Actor)
6025 Calvin Ave
Tarzana, CA 91356-1114, USA

Oyelowo, Jessica (Actor)
6025 Calvin Ave
Tarzana, CA 91356-1114, USA

Oz, Daphne (Television Host)
c/o Jill Fritzo *PMK/BNC Public Relations (PMK-NY)*
622 3rd Ave Fl 8
New York, NY 10017-6707, USA

Oz, Dr Mehmet (Doctor, Talk Show Host)
14 Edgewater Rd
Cliffside Park, NJ 07010-2805, USA

Oz, Frank R (Director)
c/o David O'Connor *Creative Artists Agency (CAA-LA)*
2000 Avenue of the Stars Ste 100
Los Angeles, CA 90067-4705, USA

Oz, Lisa (Writer)
14 Edgewater Rd
Cliffside Park, NJ 07010-2805, USA

Ozaki, Masashi (Golfer)
Bridgestone Sports
14230 Lochridge Blvd Ste G
Covington, GA 30014-4953, USA

Ozio, David (Bowler)
6110 Barrington Ave
Beaumont, TX 77706-7381, USA

Ozolinsh, Sandis (Athlete, Hockey Player)
701 Golf Club Dr
Castle Rock, CO 80108-8359

Ozomatli (Music Group)
c/o Amy Blackman *Tsunami Entertainment*
2525 Hyperion Ave
Los Angeles, CA 90027-3316, USA

Ozsan, Hal (Actor)
c/o Staff Member *Overbrook Entertainment*
10202 Washington Blvd
Culver City, CA 90232-3119, USA

Ozzie, Raymond (Ray) (Designer)
33 Harbor St
Manchester, MA 01944-1461, USA

Paavola, Rodney (Athlete, Hockey Player)
General Delivery
Hancock, MI 49930-9999, USA

Pablo Cruise
PO Box 770850
Orlando, FL 32877-0850

Pacar, Johnny (Actor)
c/o Matt Goldman *Silver Lining
Entertainment*
421 S Beverly Dr Fl 7
Beverly Hills, CA 90212-4408, USA

Pace, Dominic (Actor)
c/o Budd Burton Moss *Burton Moss*
10533 Strathmore Dr
Los Angeles, CA 90024-2540, USA

Pace, Judy (Actor)
4139 S Cloverdale Ave
Los Angeles, CA 90008-1034, USA

Pace, Justin (Actor)
c/o Todd Justice *Justice & Ponder*
PO Box 480033
Los Angeles, CA 90048-1033, USA

Pace, Lee (Actor)
c/o Joe Machota *Creative Artists Agency
(CAA-NY)*
162 5th Ave Fl 6
New York, NY 10010-6047, USA

Pace, Orlando (Athlete, Football Player)
355 Galahad Ct
Saint Charles, MO 63304, USA

Pacella, John (Athlete, Baseball Player)
1500 Abbotsford Green Dr
Powell, OH 43065-8938, USA

Pacheco, Ferdie (Sportscaster)
4151 Gate Ln
Miami, FL 33137-3319, USA

Pacillo, Pat (Athlete, Baseball Player,
Olympic Athlete)
8 Rocky Glen Way
Lebanon, NJ 08833-4611, USA

Pacino, Al (Actor)
89 Corbett Ln
Palisades, NY 10964-1603, USA

Paciorek, Jim (Athlete, Baseball Player)
9641 E Waters Edge Pl
Tucson, AZ 85749-7901, USA

Paciorek, John (Athlete, Baseball Player)
8400 Huntington Dr
San Gabriel, CA 91775-1154, USA

Paciorek, Tom (Athlete, Baseball Player)
2389 Broad Creek Dr
Stone Mountain, GA 30087-3755, USA

Pacioretty, Max (Athlete, Hockey Player)
589 Oenoke Rdg
New Canaan, CT 06840-3613

Packard, Kelly (Actor, Model)
c/o Michael Valeo *Valeo Entertainment*
8581 Santa Monica Blvd Ste 570
West Hollywood, CA 90069-4120, USA

Packard, Scott (Athlete, Baseball Player)
135 Eastview Dr
Horseheads, NY 14845-2548, USA

Packer, Billy (Sportscaster)
105 Fescue Dr
Advance, NC 27006, USA

Packer, David (Actor)
c/o Staff Member *Creative Artists Agency
(CAA-LA)*
2000 Avenue of the Stars Ste 100
Los Angeles, CA 90067-4705, USA

Packer, Erica (Model, Musician)
11004 Bellagio Pl
Los Angeles, CA 90077-3217, USA

Packer Jr, William E. (Producer)
Rainforest Films
323A Edgewood Ave SE
Atlanta, GA 30312-4003, USA

Packwocd, Bob (Ex-Senator, Senator)
2201 Wisconsin Ave NW Ste C120
Washington, DC 20007-4114, USA

Pacquet, Fernand (Horse Racer)
7563 S State Road 7
Lake Worth, FL 33449-6701, USA

Pacquiao, Manny (Athlete, Boxer)
Wild Card Boxing Gym
1123 Vine St Ste 14A
Los Angeles, CA 90038-1670, USA

Pacula, Joanna (Actor)
Chuck Binder
1465 Lindacrest Dr
Beverly Hills, CA 90210-2519, USA

Padalecki, Jared (Actor)
c/o Daniel Spilo *Industry Entertainment*
955 Carrillo Dr Ste 300
Los Angeles, CA 90048-5400, USA

Paddio, Gerald (Athlete, Basketball
Player)
5112 Morris St
Las Vegas, NV 89122-7063, USA

Paddock, John (Athlete, Hockey Player)
Philadelphia Flyers
3601 S Broad St Ste 2
Philadelphia, PA 19148-5297

Padgett, Jason (Actor)
c/o Staff Member *GVA Talent Agency Inc*
8981 W Sunset Blvd Ste 101
West Hollywood, CA 90069-1850, USA

Padilla, Douglas (Doug) (Athlete, Track
Athlete)
182 N 555 W
Orem, UT 84057-1937, USA

Padilla, Vicente (Athlete, Baseball Player)
2112 Royal Dominion Ct
Arlington, TX 76006-4836, USA

Padjen, Gary (Athlete, Football Player)
9314 Tower Bridge Rd Apt B
Indianapolis, IN 46240-5434, USA

Paea, Stephen (Athlete, Football Player)
c/o David Dunn *Athletes First, LLC*
23091 Mill Creek Dr
Laguna Hills, CA 92653-1258, USA

Paek, Jim (Athlete, Hockey Player)
7360 Crystal View Dr SE
Caledonia, MI 49316-7981

Paek, Jim (Athlete, Hockey Player)
Grand Rapids Griffins
130 Fulton St W Ste 111
Grand Rapids, MI 49503-2682

Paepke, Dennis (Athlete, Baseball Player)
4560 Trieste Dr
Carlsbad, CA 92010-3741, USA

Paepke, Jack (Athlete, Baseball Player)
158 Steffy Rd
Ramona, CA 92065-3523, USA

Paes, Leander (Athlete, Tennis Player)
c/o Staff Member *ATP Tour*
201 Atp Tour Blvd
Ponte Vedra Beach, FL 32082-3211, USA

Paetkau, David (Actor)
c/o Marty Berneman *Precision
Entertainment*
465 N Croft Ave
Los Angeles, CA 90048-2508, USA

Paetsch, Nathan (Athlete, Hockey Player)
324 Tennyson Ter
East Amherst, NY 14051

Paez, Jorge (Maromero) (Boxer)
233 Paulin Ave
Calexico, CA 92231-2615, USA

Paffrath, Amy (Actor)
c/o Scott Karp *The Syndicate*
10203 Santa Monica Blvd Fl 5
Los Angeles, CA 90067-6416, USA

Pagac, Fred (Athlete, Football Player)
1 Bills Dr
Orchard Park, NY 14127-2237, USA

Pagan, Reo (Baseball Player)
Negro Baseball Leagues
280 Creekview Trl
Fayetteville, GA 30214-7230, USA

Page, Alan C (Athlete, Football Player,
Judge)
Page Education Foundation
PO Box 581254
Minneapolis, MN 55458-1254, USA

Page, Bettle (Model)
JL Swanson
PO Box 56176
Chicago, IL 60656-0176, USA

Page, Corey (Actor)
Agency for Performing Arts
9200 W Sunset Blvd Ste 900
West Hollywood, CA 90069-3604, USA

Page, Ellen (Actor)
2521 Astral Dr
Los Angeles, CA 90046-1705, USA

Page, Erika (Actor)
Progressive Artists Agency
400 S Beverly Dr Ste 216
Beverly Hills, CA 90212-4404, USA

Page, Greg (Boxer)
Don King Promotions
968 Pinehurst Dr
Las Vegas, NV 89109-1569, USA

Page, Harrison (Actor)
S D B Partners
315 S Beverly Dr Ste 411
Beverly Hills, CA 90212-4301, USA

Page, Kimberly (Actor)
c/o Staff Member *The Paradise Group*
PO Box 69451
West Hollywood, CA 90069-0451, USA

Page, Larry (Business Person)
Google Inc
1600 Amphitheatre Pkwy
Mountain View, CA 94043-1351, USA

Page, Mike (Athlete, Baseball Player)
599 Briarcliff Dr
Woodruff, SC 29388-2326, USA

Page, Murriel (Basketball Player)
Washington Mystics
601 F St NW
Mcl Center
Washington, DC 20004-1605, USA

Page, Pierre (Athlete, Coach, Hockey
Player)
2000 E Gene Autry Way
Anaheim, CA 92806-6143, USA

Page, Sam (Actor)
c/o Lena Roklin *Luber Roklin
Management*
5815 W Sunset Blvd Ste 206
Los Angeles, CA 90028-6481, USA

Page, Solomon (Athlete, Football Player)
9302 Vista Cir
Irving, TX 75063-5060, USA

Page, Steven (Musician)
c/o Larry Webman *Paradigm (NY)*
360 Park Ave S Fl 16
New York, NY 10010-1716, USA

Page, Tim (Journalist)
Washington Post
Editorial Dept
1150 15th St NW
Washington, DC 20071-0001, USA

Pagel, Karl (Athlete, Baseball Player)
2698 N Ellis St
Chandler, AZ 85224-1777, USA

Pagel, Mike (Athlete, Football Player)
3263 Millstone Creek Rd
Lancaster, SC 29720-6923, USA

Paget, Debra (Actor)
411 Kari Ct
Houston, TX 77024-6804, USA

Pagett, Dana (Athlete, Basketball Player)
120 Yale Ln
Seal Beach, CA 90740-2522, USA

Paggi, Nicole (Actor)
c/o Kenny Goodman *The Schiff Company*
9220 W Sunset Blvd Ste 106
West Hollywood, CA 90069-3500, USA

Paglia, Camile (Writer)
c/o Staff Member *Random House
Publicity*
1745 Broadway Frnt 3
New York, NY 10019-4343, USA

Paglia, Camille (Writer)
University of the Arts
320 S Broad St
Humanities Dept
Philadelphia, PA 19102-4994, USA

Pagliarulo, Michael T (Mike) (Athlete,
Baseball Player)
11 Fieldstone Dr
Winchester, MA 01890-3257, USA

Pagliei, Joe (Athlete, Football Player)
7 Pine Ridge Ct
Sewell, NJ 08080-3648, USA

Pagnozzi, Matt (Athlete, Baseball Player)
1710 W Park Ave
Chandler, AZ 85224-9002, USA

Pagnozzi, Thomas A (Tom) (Athlete,
Baseball Player)
3288 E Piper Gin
Fayetteville, AR 72703, USA

Pagnucco, Chris (Athlete, Football Player)
937 W Belden Ave
Chicago, IL 60614-3239, USA

Pahlsson, Samuel (Athlete, Hockey Player)
9429 Tartan Ridge Blvd
Dublin, OH 43017-8924

Pahukoa, Jeff (Athlete, Football Player)
20191 Cape Coral Ln
Huntington Beach, CA 92646-8514, USA

Paich, David (Musician)
Fitzgerald-Hartley
34 N Palm St Ste 100
Ventura, CA 93001-2610, USA

Paiement, Rosaire (Athlete, Hockey Player)
3351 S Palm Aire Dr Apt 301
Pompano Beach, FL 33069-4254

Paige, Colleen (Business Person)
Colleen Paige, LLC
PO Box 2061
Kingston, WA 98346-2061, USA

Paige, Janis (Actor)
1700 Rising Glen Rd
Los Angeles, CA 90069-1230, USA

Paige, Peter (Actor)
c/o Suzanne (Sue) Wohl *TalentWorks (LA)*
3500 W Olive Ave Ste 1400
Burbank, CA 91505-5512, USA

Paige, Rod (Politician, Secretary)
Education Department
14022 Hampton Cove Dr
Houston, TX 77077-2142, USA

Paige, Tarah (Actor)
c/o Michael Henderson *Heresun Management*
4119 W Burbank Blvd
Burbank, CA 91505-2122, USA

Pailes, William A (Astronaut)
411 S Cedar Ridge Cir
Robinson, TX 76706-5681, USA

Paille, Daniel (Athlete, Hockey Player)
90 Autumn Creek Ln
East Amherst, NY 14051-2918

Paine, Chris
c/o Eddie Michaels *Insignia Public Relations*
1507 20th St Ste B
Santa Monica, CA 90404-3474, USA

Paine, Horner (Athlete, Football Player)
2021 Coast Guard Dr
Stafford, VA 22554-2513, USA

Paine, John (Musician)
Bob Flick Productions
300 Vine St Ste 14
Seattle, WA 98121-1465, USA

Painter, John Mark (Musician)
Michael Dixon Mgmt
119 Pebble Creek Rd
Franklin, TN 37064-5525, USA

Painter, Lance (Athlete, Baseball Player)
3561 E Loma Vista St
Gilbert, AZ 85295-3479, USA

Painter, Vinston (Athlete, Football Player)
c/o Neil Schwartz *Schwartz & Feinsod*
contact via telephone or email
White Plains, NY 10603

Paisley, Brad (Musician)
2223 N Berrys Chapel Rd
Franklin, TN 37069-6610, USA

Pak, Se Ri (Golfer)
8836 Elliotts Ct
Orlando, FL 32836-5027, USA

Pakeledinaz, Martin (Designer)
Gersh Agency
232 N Canon Dr
Beverly Hills, CA 90210-5302, USA

Palacios, Rey (Athlete, Baseball Player)
183 Kings Gate S
Rochester, NY 14617-5439, USA

Palahniuk, Chuck (Writer)
c/o Howard Sanders *United Talent Agency (UTA-LA)*
9336 Civic Center Dr
Beverly Hills, CA 90210-3604, USA

Palance, Holly (Actor)
2753 Roscomare Rd
Los Angeles, CA 90077-1632

Palatella, Lou (Athlete, Football Player)
1532 Kennewick Dr
Sunnyvale, CA 94087-4158, USA

Palau, Doug (Producer)
c/o Staff Member *William Morris Endeavor (LA)*
9601 Wilshire Blvd
Beverly Hills, CA 90210-5213, USA

Palazzari, Doug (Athlete, Hockey Player)
616 Michigan Ave W
Gilbert, MN 55741-5136, USA

Palazzi, Togo (Athlete, Basketball Player)
84 Framingham Rd
Southborough, MA 01772-1268, USA

Paldridge, Curt (Athlete, Football Player)
2820 Country Club Ln
Dekalb, IL 60115-4922, USA

Palelei, Lonnie (Athlete, Football Player)
1808 SW Chief Cir
Blue Springs, MO 64015-5420, USA

Palermo, Olivia (Reality Star)
c/o Barbara Saint-Aime *Platform Public Relations*
2666 N Beachwood Dr
Los Angeles, CA 90068-2308, USA

Palermo, Steve (Athlete, Baseball Player)
5102 W 143rd Ter
Overland Park, KS 66224-3746, USA

Palesh, Shirley (Athlete, Baseball Player)
120 Grand Ave Apt 307
Wausau, WI 54403-7209, USA

Palffy, Zigmund (Athlete, Hockey Player)
HK 36 Skalica Clementisova SO
Skalica, 90 SLOVA

Palicki, Adrianne (Actor)
c/o Michael Sugar *Anonymous Content (LA)*
3532 Hayden Ave
Culver City, CA 90232-2413, USA

Palin, Bristol (Reality Star)
BSMP
711 H St Ste 620
Anchorage, AK 99501-3454, USA

Palin, Sarah (Ex-Governor, Politician)
1140 W Parks Hwy
Wasilla, AK 99654-6910, USA

Pall, Donn (Athlete, Baseball Player)
155 Wellington Dr
Bloomingdale, IL 60108-3012, USA

Pall, Gloria (Actor, Model)
Showgirl Press
12814 Victory Blvd
North Hollywood, CA 91606-3013

Palladino, Eric (Actor)
1204 Moncado Dr
Glendale, CA 91207-1830, USA

Palladino, Erik (Actor)
c/o Andrew Tetenbaum *ATA Management*
12 Desbrosses St
New York, NY 10013-1704, USA

Palli, Anne-Marie (Golfer)
4510 N Alta Hacienda Dr
Phoenix, AZ 85018-2004, USA

Pallone, Dave (Athlete, Baseball Player)
4420 Dickason Ave Apt 1135
Dallas, TX 75219-6642, USA

Pallone Jr., Frank (Congressman, Politician)
237 Cannon Hob
Washington, DC 20515-0526, USA

Pally, Adam (Actor)
3808 Mound View Ave
Studio City, CA 91604-3630, USA

Palmeiro, Orlando (Athlete, Baseball Player)
11991 SW 103rd Ter
Miami, FL 33186-2654, USA

Palmeiro, Rafael C (Athlete, Baseball Player)
5216 Reims Ct
Colleyville, TX 76034-5574, USA

Palmer, Amanda (Musician)
c/o Staff Member *High Road Touring*
751 Bridgeway Fl 2
Sausalito, CA 94965-2174, USA

Palmer, Arnold (Athlete, Golfer)
9000 Bay Hill Blvd
Orlando, FL 32819-4880, USA

Palmer, Ashlee (Athlete, Football Player)
c/o Drew Rosenhaus *Rosenhaus Sports Representation*
6400 Allison Rd
Miami Beach, FL 33141-4540, USA

Palmer, Betsy (Actor)
c/o Brad LeMack *Lemack & Company Management*
2275 Huntington Dr Ste 552
San Marino, CA 91108-2640, USA

Palmer, Carson (Athlete, Football Player, Heisman Trophy Winner)
8885 Whisperinghill Dr
Cincinnati, OH 45242-4670, USA

Palmer, C R (Business Person)
Rowan Companies
2800 Post Oak Blvd
Transco Tower
Houston, TX 77056-6100, USA

Palmer, David (Athlete, Baseball Player)
5090 Oak Nut Ct
Stone Mountain, GA 30087-3290, USA

Palmer, David (Athlete, Football Player)
527 Carlton Pl
Birmingham, AL 35214-1331, USA

Palmer, Dean (Athlete, Baseball Player)
3943 Old Mill Run
Tallahassee, FL 32312-1086, USA

Palmer, Gery (Athlete, Football Player)
6411 E Irish Pl
Centennial, CO 80112-2404, USA

Palmer, Gregg (Actor)
5726 Graves Ave
Encino, CA 91316-1441

Palmer, Jesse (Athlete, Football Player, Reality Star)
c/o Staff Member *San Francisco 49ers*
4949 Centennial Blvd
Santa Clara, CA 95054-1254, USA

Palmer, Jim (Athlete, Baseball Player)
4 Route 385
Catskill, NY 12414-5028, USA

Palmer, Keke (Actor)
c/o Shannon Barr *Rogers & Cowan PR (LA)*
8687 Melrose Ave Ste 7
West Hollywood, CA 90069-5721, USA

Palmer, Lowell (Athlete, Baseball Player)
5640 Hemlock St
Sacramento, CA 95841-2316, USA

Palmer, Matt (Athlete, Baseball Player)
c/o Staff Member *Los Angeles Dodgers (LA Dodgers)*
1000 Elysian Park Ave
Los Angeles, CA 90012-1112, USA

Palmer, Mitch (Athlete, Football Player)
14420 Cypress Pt
Poway, CA 92064-6600, USA

Palmer, Peter (Actor)
PO Box 482
Simpsonville, KY 40067-0482, USA

Palmer, Ralph (Baseball Player)
Chicago American Giants
PO Box 25065
Lansing, MI 48909-5065, USA

Palmer, Richard H (Athlete, Football Player)
14420 Cypress Pt
Poway, CA 92064-6600, USA

Palmer, Rob (Athlete, Hockey Player)
3812 Sepulveda Blvd Ste 310
Torrance, CA 90505-2481

Palmer, Sandra (Athlete, Golfer)
498 Peralta Ave
Long Beach, CA 90803-2218, USA

Palmer, Scott (Athlete, Football Player)
7408 Lady Suzannes Ct
Austin, TX 78729-7793, USA

Palmer, Teresa (Actor)
3174 Deronda Dr
Los Angeles, CA 90068-1608, USA

Palmer, Walter (Athlete, Basketball Player)
87 South St
Rockport, MA 01966-1924, USA

Palmieri, Eddie (Musician)
Berkeley Agency
2608 9th St Ste 301
Berkeley, CA 94710-2556, USA

Palmieri, Paul (Religious Leader)
Church of Jesus Christ
6th & Lincoln Sts
Monongahela, PA 15063, USA

Palminteri, Chazz (Actor)
34 Stone Paddock Pl
Bedford, NY 10506-1058, USA

Palomino, Carlos (Boxer)
14242 Burbank Blvd # 8
Sherman Oaks, CA 91401-4937, USA

Palone, Dave (Horse Racer)
100 Quarry Rd
Washington, PA 15301-9563, USA

Paltrow, Gwyneth (Actor)
c/o Zack Morgenroth *Brillstein Entertainment Partners (LA)*
9150 Wilshire Blvd Ste 350
Beverly Hills, CA 90212-3453, USA

Paltrow, Jake (Director)
c/o John Lesher *William Morris Endeavor (LA)*
9601 Wilshire Blvd
Beverly Hills, CA 90210-5213, USA

Palumba, Joe (Athlete, Football Player)
927 Old Garth Rd
Charlottesville, VA 22901-1937, USA

Paly, Bar (Actor)
c/o David Gardner *Principato/Young Management (LA)*
9465 Wilshire Blvd Ste 900
Beverly Hills, CA 90212-2608, USA

Palys, Stan (Athlete, Baseball Player)
11150 167th Pl N
Jupiter, FL 33478-6151, USA

Pampling, Rod (Golfer)
4709 Rangewood Dr
Flower Mound, TX 75028-1695, USA

Panabaker, Danielle (Actor)
c/o Lainie Sorkin Becky *Management 360*
9111 Wilshire Blvd
Beverly Hills, CA 90210-5508, USA

Panabaker, Kay (Actor)
c/o Lena Roklin *Luber Roklin Management*
5815 W Sunset Blvd Ste 206
Los Angeles, CA 90028-6481, USA

Panagaris, Orianthi (Musician)
c/o Sterling McIlwaine *19 Entertainment (LA)*
9000 W Sunset Blvd Ste 1574
West Hollywood, CA 90069-5817, USA

Pancake, Sam (Actor)
c/o Joel King *Pakula/King & Associates*
9229 W Sunset Blvd Ste 315
West Hollywood, CA 90069-3403, USA

Panch, Marvin (Race Car Driver)
1648 Taylor Rd # 406
Port Orange, FL 32128-6753, USA

Pancholy, Maulik (Actor)
c/o Staff Member *ROAR (LA)*
9701 Wilshire Blvd Fl 8
Beverly Hills, CA 90212-2008, USA

Pandolfo, Jay (Athlete, Hockey Player)
Pro-Athletes Management
3 Meadowcroft Rd
Burlington, MA 01803-1019, USA

Panetta, Leon E (Government Official, Politician)
15 Panetta Rd
Carmel Valley, CA 93924-9452, USA

Panettiere, Hayden (Actor)
c/o Emily Gerson Saines *Brookside Artists Management (NY)*
250 W 57th St Ste 2303
New York, NY 10107-2399, USA

Pang, Darren (Athlete, Hockey Player)
7439 Washington Ave
Saint Louis, MO 63130-4050

Pang, Darren (Athlete, Hockey Player)
St Louis Blues
1401 Clark Ave
Saint Louis, MO 63103-2700

Pang, May
1619 3rd Ave Apt 9D
New York, NY 10128-3937

Pang, Qing (Figure Skater)
c/o Staff Member *Champions on Ice*
3500 American Blvd W Ste 190
Minneapolis, MN 55431-4431, USA

Panic, Milan (Business Person, Prime Minister)
1050 Arden Rd
Pasadena, CA 91106-4004, USA

Panic at the Disco (Music Group)
c/o *Fueled by Ramen*
PO Box 1803
Tampa, FL 33601-1803, USA

Panichas, George A (Writer)
PO Box AB
College Park, MD 20741-3025, USA

Panjabi, Archie (Actor)
c/o Angelique ONeil *Angelique ONeil Enterprises*
200 Riverside Blvd
Suite 401 at Trump Place
New York, NY 10069-0901, USA

Pankewicz, Greg (Athlete, Hockey Player)
209 Oak St
Windsor, CO 80550-5437

Pankey, Irv (Athlete, Football Player)
348 Walker St
Aberdeen, MD 21001-3543, USA

Pankin, Stuart (Actor)
1288 Bienevenda Ave
Pacific Palisades, CA 90272, USA

Pankovits, Jim (Athlete, Baseball Player)
6014 Catalina Dr Unit 115
North Myrtle Beach, SC 29582-8388, USA

Pankow, James (Musician)
3826 Bowsprit Cir
Westlake Village, CA 91361-3814, USA

Pankow, John (Actor)
Gersh Agency
232 N Canon Dr
Beverly Hills, CA 90210-5302, USA

Panos, Joe (Athlete, Football Player)
360 Rustic Ln
Hartland, WI 53029-2286, USA

Panozzo, Chuck (Musician)
c/o Sterling Bacon *TBA Artist Management (Atlanta)*
1111 Alderman Dr Ste 285
Alpharetta, GA 30005-5433, USA

Panteleev, Grigori (Athlete, Hockey Player)
5 Commonwealth Rd
Natick, MA 01760-1526

Panther, Jim (Athlete, Baseball Player)
7936 Tiger Palm Way
Fort Myers, FL 33966-6447, USA

Pantoja, Arnie (Actor)
c/o Julie Balfour *AKA Talent Agency*
6310 San Vicente Blvd Ste 200
Los Angeles, CA 90048-5488, USA

Pantoliano, Joe (Actor)
c/o Devon Jackson *Trademark Talent*
144 S Beverly Dr Ste 404
Beverly Hills, CA 90212-3022, USA

Paolini, Christopher (Writer)
c/o Staff Member *Random House*
1540 Broadway
New York, NY 10036-4039, USA

Paolo, Connor (Actor)
c/o Michael Gagliardo *PMK/BNC Public Relations (PMK-NY)*
622 3rd Ave Fl 8
New York, NY 10017-6707, USA

Papa, Greg (Athlete, Baseball Player)
11 San Andreas Dr
Danville, CA 94506-2035, USA

Papa, John (Athlete, Baseball Player)
275 Mary Ave
Stratford, CT 06614-5329, USA

Papa, Tom (Comedian)
c/o Josh Pearl *ICM Partners (NY)*
730 5th Ave
New York, NY 10019-4105, USA

Papach, George (Athlete, Football Player)
5454 Hohman Ave
Hammond, IN 46320-1931, USA

Papa Doo Run Run
PO Box 255
Cupertino, CA 95015-0255

Papajohn, Michael (Actor)
c/o Monique Moss *Integrated PR*
8060 Melrose Ave Fl 4
Los Angeles, CA 90046-7038, USA

Papale, Vince (Athlete, Football Player)
2219 S 15th St
Philadelphia, PA 19145-3920, USA

Papamichael, Phedon M (Cinematographer)
Innovative Artists
1505 10th St
Santa Monica, CA 90401-2805, USA

Papa Roach (Music Group)
c/o Frank Cimler *10th Street Entertainment (LA)*
700 N San Vicente Blvd Ste G410
West Hollywood, CA 90069-5060, USA

Papazian, Martin (Marty) (Actor)
c/o Lin Bickelmann *Encore Artists Management*
3815 W Olive Ave Ste 101
Burbank, CA 91505-4674, USA

Papazian, Marty (Actor)
c/o Lin Bickelmann *Encore Artists Management*
3815 W Olive Ave Ste 101
Burbank, CA 91505-4674, USA

Papazian, Robert (Producer)
c/o Gene Schwam *Hanson & Schwam Public Relations*
9350 Wilshire Blvd Ste 315
Beverly Hills, CA 90212-3206

Pape, Ken (Athlete, Baseball Player)
2127 Green Creek St
San Antonio, TX 78232-3913, USA

Papelbon, Jonathan (Athlete, Baseball Player)
127 Wild Mdws
Hattiesburg, MS 39402-8108, USA

Papi, Stan (Athlete, Baseball Player)
1111 W Sierra Madre Ave
Fresno, CA 93705-0433, USA

Papis, Max (Race Car Driver)
Max Papis Racing
112 Byers Creek Rd
Mooresville, NC 28117-4376, USA

Papit, Johnny (Athlete, Football Player)
29 Sellers Ave
Lexington, VA 24450-1930, USA

Papoose (Musician)
c/o Staff Member *Violator Management*
36 W 25th St Fl 2
New York, NY 10010-2768, USA

Pappas, Brenden (Athlete, Golfer)
5770 SW 42nd Pl
Ocala, FL 34474-9516, USA

Pappas, Deane (Athlete, Golfer)
4409 Stoney Dr
Jonesboro, AR 72404-9571, USA

Pappas, Erik (Athlete, Baseball Player)
10248 S Seeley Ave
Chicago, IL 60643, USA

Pappas, George (Bowler)
21108 Blakely Shores Dr
Cornelius, NC 28031-6606, USA

Pappas, Milt (Athlete, Baseball Player)
502 Highlington Ct
Beecher, IL 60401-3576, USA

Pappin, James J (Jim) (Athlete, Hockey Player)
4052 Villa Quintana
Yorba Linda, CA 92886-8676, USA

Paquette, Craig (Athlete, Baseball Player)
16626 S Magenta Rd
Phoenix, AZ 85048-2073, USA

Paquin, Anna (Actor)
c/o JoAnne Colonna *Brillstein Entertainment Partners (LA)*
9150 Wilshire Blvd Ste 350
Beverly Hills, CA 90212-3453, USA

Paquin, Kit (Actor)
c/o Staff Member *Trilogy Talent*
13425 Ventura Blvd Fl 2
Sherman Oaks, CA 91423-3974, USA

Paradis, Vanessa (Actor, Model, Musician)
7760 Woodrow Wilson Dr
Los Angeles, CA 90046-1212, USA

Paradise, Bob (Athlete, Hockey Player, Olympic Athlete)
1303 Beechwood Pl
Saint Paul, MN 55116-2202, USA

Parahia, Murray (Musician)
I M G Artists
420 W 45th St
New York, NY 10036-3501, USA

Paramore (Music Group)
c/o Ken Fermaglich *The Agency Group (NYC)*
142 W 57th St Fl 6
New York, NY 10019-3300, USA

Paraseghian, Ara
51767 Oakbrook Ct
Granger, IN 46530-8731

Parazaider, Walter (Musician)
Front Line Mgmt
8900 Wilshire Blvd Ste 300
Beverly Hills, CA 90211-1959, USA

Parazynski, Scott E (Astronaut)
2015 Wroxton Rd
Houston, TX 77005-1654, USA

Parcells, Duane C (Bill) (Athlete, Coach, Football Coach, Football Player)
340 S US Highway 1
Jupiter, FL 33477-5928, USA

Parchem, Aaron (Athlete, Figure Skater, Olympic Athlete)
364 N Vista
Auburn Hills, MI 48326-1446, USA

Pardo, Al (Athlete, Baseball Player)
908 Hillary Cir
Lutz, FL 33548-5052, USA

Pardo, Jimmy (Comedian)
c/o Bruce Smith *OmniPop Talent Group (LA)*
4605 Lankershim Blvd Ste 201
North Hollywood, CA 91602-1874, USA

Pardue, Kip (Actor)
c/o Jason Newman *Untitled Entertainment (LA)*
350 S Beverly Dr Ste 200
Beverly Hills, CA 90212-4819, USA

Pardus, Dan (Race Car Driver)
Jim & Judie Motorsports
4345 Motorsports Dr SW
Concord, NC 28027-8977, USA

Pare, Jessica (Actor)
c/o Nick Frenkel *3 Arts Entertainment (LA)*
9460 Wilshire Blvd Fl 7
Beverly Hills, CA 90212-2713, USA

Pare, Michael (Actor)
c/o John Ferriter *Octagon Entertainment*
8687 Melrose Ave Ste 7
West Hollywood, CA 90069-5721, USA

Parekh, Kal (Actor)
c/o Jenn Lederer *AFST Management*
350 W 43rd St Apt 32G
New York, NY 10036-6476, USA

Parent, Bernie (Athlete, Hockey Player)
Offices of Bernie Parent
125 N Route 73
West Berlin, NJ 08091-9225, USA

Parent, Gail
2001 Mandeville Canyon Rd
Los Angeles, CA 90049-2226

Parent, Mark (Athlete, Baseball Player)
8829 Midview Dr
Palo Cedro, CA 96073-8635, USA

Parent, Monique (Actor, Model)
PO Box 3458
Ventura, CA 93006-3458, USA

Paretsky, Sara N (Writer)
5831 S Blackstone Ave
Chicago, IL 60637-1855, USA

Pargo, Jannero (Athlete, Basketball Player)
3280 Timberwood Ln
Riverwoods, IL 60015-2418, USA

Parham, Gus (Athlete, Football Player)
Taylor Made Office Systems
4294 El Camino Real
Los Altos, CA 94022-1048, USA

Parilla, Jennifer (Athlete, Gymnast, Olympic Athlete)
21822 Rushford Dr
Lake Forest, CA 92630-6503, USA

Parilla, Lana (Actor)
c/o Liza Anderson *Anderson Group Public Relations*
8060 Melrose Ave Fl 4
Los Angeles, CA 90046-7038, USA

Parilli, Vito (Babe) (Athlete, Coach, Football Coach, Football Player)
8060 E Girard Ave Apt 218
Denver, CO 80231-4414, USA

Paris, Bubba (Athlete, Football Player)
225 S Sonrisa St
Tracy, CA 95391-3004, USA

Paris, Clarke (Race Car Driver)
Crave Racing
PO Box 972
Harvey, LA 70059-0972, USA

Paris, Kelly (Athlete, Baseball Player)
42 Warwick Cir Apt 111
Clover, SC 29710-7812, USA

Paris, Mica (Musician)
Richard Walters
1800 Argyle Ave # 408
Los Angeles, CA 90028-5253, USA

Paris, Twila (Musician, Songwriter, Writer)
Proper Mgmt
PO Box 150867
Nashville, TN 37215-0867, USA

Parise, JP (Athlete, Hockey Player)
3814 Raspberry Ridge Rd NW
Prior Lake, MN 55372-1120

Parise, Robert L (Basketball Player)
20 Stonybrook Rd Apt 1
Framingham, MA 01702-5997, USA

Parise, Ronald A (Astronaut)
15419 Good Hope Rd
Silver Spring, MD 20905-4129, USA

Parise, Vanessa (Actor)
c/o Lara Rosenstock *Lara Rosenstock Management*
8371 Blackburn Ave Apt 1
Los Angeles, CA 90048-4245, USA

Parish, Robert (Athlete, Basketball Player)
6609 Virgo Dr
Shreveport, LA 71119-5015, USA

Parisi, Siobhan
c/o Staff Member *Carry Company, The*
3875 Wilshire Blvd Ste 402
Los Angeles, CA 90010-3209, USA

Parisot, Dean (Director)
c/o Staff Member *3 Arts Entertainment (LA)*
9460 Wilshire Blvd Fl 7
Beverly Hills, CA 90212-2713, USA

Parisse, Annie (Actor)
c/o Stephen Hirsch *Gersh (NY)*
41 Madison Ave Fl 32
New York, NY 10010-2283, USA

Park, Alyssa (Musician)
Columbia Artists Mgmt Inc
165 W 57th St
New York, NY 10019-2201, USA

Park, Chan Ho (Athlete, Baseball Player)
c/o Team Member *New York Yankees*
Yankee Stadium
161st St & River Ave
Bronx, NY 10451, USA

Park, D Bradford (Brad) (Athlete, Coach, Hockey Player)
100 Legends Way Ste 250
Boston, MA 02114-1390, USA

Park, Ernie (Athlete, Football Player)
3160 Private Road 1101
Clyde, TX 79510-4905, USA

Park, Joon (Actor)
c/o Susan Yoo *Susan Yoo*
Prefers to be contacted via telephone
Los Angeles, CA, USA

Park, Linda (Actor)
c/o Ro Diamond *SDB Partners Inc*
315 S Beverly Dr Ste 411
Beverly Hills, CA 90212-4301, USA

Park, Linkin (Music Group)
c/o Michael Arfin *Artist Group International (NY)*
150 E 58th St Fl 19
New York, NY 10155-1900, USA

Park, Maximo (Musician)
c/o Kirk Sommer *William Morris Endeavor (LA)*
9601 Wilshire Blvd Fl 3
Beverly Hills, CA 90210-5219, USA

Park, Patrick (Musician)
c/o Staff Member *Red Light Management (LA)*
8439 W Sunset Blvd Ste 2
West Hollywood, CA 90069-1925, USA

Park, Ray (Actor)
c/o Dino May *Dino May Management*
6362 Hollywood Blvd # 422
Los Angeles, CA 90028-6323, USA

Park, Richard (Athlete, Hockey Player)
6416 Vista Pacifica
Rancho Palos Verdes, CA 90275-5896

Park, Steve (Race Car Driver)
261 Indian Trl
Mooresville, NC 28117-8968, USA

Parke, Evan Dexter (Actor)
c/o Staff Member *McCabe Group, The*
3211 Cahuenga Blvd W Ste 104
Los Angeles, CA 90068-1372, USA

Parkening, Christopher (Musician)
IMG Artists
420 W 45th St
New York, NY 10036-3501, USA

Parker, Andrea (Actor)
c/o Dan Baron *Agency for the Performing Arts (APA-LA)*
405 S Beverly Dr Ste 500
Beverly Hills, CA 90212-4425, USA

Parker, Anthony (Athlete, Football Player)
1054 E Geneva Dr
Tempe, AZ 85282-3805, USA

Parker, Anthony (Basketball Player)
Orlando Magic
8701 Maitland Summit Blvd
Waterhouse Center
Orlando, FL 32810-5915, USA

Parker, Bob (Skier)
408 Camino Don Miguel
Santa Fe, NM 87505-5948, USA

Parker, Brant J (Cartoonist)
901 Glenwood Blvd
Waynesboro, VA 22980-3409, USA

Parker, Caryl Mack (Musician)
Scream Marketing
PO Box 120053
Nashville, TN 37212-0053, USA

Parker, Christian (Athlete, Baseball Player)
10101 Mesa Arriba Ave NE
Albuquerque, NM 87111-4962, USA

Parker, Clay (Athlete, Baseball Player)
6614 Brickston St
Hixson, TN 37343-2593, USA

Parker, Corey (Actor)
Muse Mgmt
429 Santa Monica Blvd # 520
Santa Monica, CA 90401-3401, USA

Parker, Craig (Actor)
c/o Joe Smith *ICM Partners (LA)*
10250 Constellation Blvd Fl 7
Los Angeles, CA 90067-6207, USA

Parker, Dave (Athlete, Baseball Player)
2047 Seymour Ave
Cincinnati, OH 45237-4721, USA

Parker, Franklin (Writer)
Western Carolina University
Education & Psychology Dept
Cullowhee, NC 28723, USA

Parker, Hank Jr (Race Car Driver)
MRO
5555 Concord Pkwy S Ste 405
Concord, NC 28027-4622, USA

Parker, Jack Jr (Horse Racer)
38 Lea Ct
Frederica, DE 19946-1985, USA

Parker, Jack Sr (Horse Racer)
127 Roosevelt Ave
Westwood, NJ 07675-2316, USA

Parker, Jameson (Actor)
1604 N Vista St
Los Angeles, CA 90046-2818, USA

Parker, Jeff (Athlete, Hockey Player)
2018 Riviera Ave S
Lakeland, MN 55043-9419

Parker, Lara (Actor)
PO Box 1254
Topanga, CA 90290-1254, USA

Parker, Larry (Athlete, Football Player)
15903 San Marco Pl
Bakersfield, CA 93314-6650, USA

Parker, Lu
12222 Vance Jackson Rd Apt 734
San Antonio, TX 78230-5941

Parker, Maceo (Musician)
109 W Newark Ave
Wildwood, NJ 08260-1038

Parker, Mary-Louise (Actor)
c/o Jillian Roscoe *ID Public Relations (LA)*
7060 Hollywood Blvd Fl 8th
Los Angeles, CA 90028-6021, USA

Parker, Molly (Actor)
c/o Staff Member *Dontanville/Frattaroli (D/F)*
270 Lafayette St Ste 402
New York, NY 10012-3327, USA

Parker, Nate (Actor)
c/o Samantha Hill *WKT Public Relations (LA)*
9350 Wilshire Blvd Ste 450
Beverly Hills, CA 90212-3230, USA

Parker, Nathanial
10100 Santa Monica Blvd Ste 2500
Los Angeles, CA 90067-4116

Parker, Nicole (Actor)
c/o Mark Rousso *New Wave Entertainment (LA)*
2660 W Olive Ave
Burbank, CA 91505-4525, USA

Parker, Nicole Ari (Actor)
c/o Maani Golesorkhi *Bluestone Entertainment*
9000 W Sunset Blvd Ste 700
West Hollywood, CA 90069-5807, USA

Parker, Noelle
9300 Wilshire Blvd Ste 555
Beverly Hills, CA 90212-3211

Parker, Orlando (Athlete, Football Player)
4402 Chatham Pl
Montgomery, AL 36108-4902, USA

Parker, Paula Jai (Actor)
c/o Leonard Torgan *The Collective*
8383 Wilshire Blvd Ste 1050
Beverly Hills, CA 90211-2415, USA

Parker, Rick (Athlete, Baseball Player)
2641 NE 74th St
Kansas City, MO 64119-5349, USA

Parker, Riddick (Athlete, Football Player)
11226 NE 68th St Apt 212-B
Kirkland, WA 98033-7181, USA

Parker, Robert (Astronaut)
NASA
2101 Nasa Pkwy Spc Johnsoncenter
Houston, TX 77058-3696, USA

Parker, Robert (Athlete, Basketball Player)
7947 S Chappel Ave
Chicago, IL 60617-1052, USA

Parker, Robert A Dr (Astronaut)
5316 Godbey Dr
La Canada Flintridge, CA 91011-1833,
USA

Parker, Sarah Jessica (Actor, Producer)
c/o Ina Treciokas *Slate Public Relations*
9000 W Sunset Blvd Ste 915
West Hollywood, CA 90069-5809, USA

Parker, Scott (Athlete, Hockey Player)
1950 W Wolfensberger Ct
Castle Rock, CO 80109-9699

Parker, Sean (Business Person)
45 W 18th St Fl 7
New York, NY 10011-4655, USA

Parker, T Jefferson (Writer)
c/o Staff Member *Trident Media Group
LLC*
41 Madison Ave Fl 36
New York, NY 10010-2257, USA

Parker, Tony (Athlete, Basketball Player)
c/o Steve Heumann *CAA Sports (LA)*
2000 Avenue of the Stars Ste 100
Los Angeles, CA 90067-4705, USA

Parker, Trey (Actor, Animator, Director,
Producer)
311 N Rockingham Ave
Los Angeles, CA 90049-2635, USA

Parker, Vaughn (Athlete, Football Player)
2500 6th Ave Unit 107
San Diego, CA 92103-6629, USA

Parker, Wes (Athlete, Baseball Player)
Los Angeles Dodgers
1000 Elysian Park Ave
Attn: Community Relations Dept
Dodgertown, CA 90090-1112, USA

Parker, Willie (Athlete, Football Player)
9327 Kai Dr
Beach City, TX 77523-2333, USA

Parker Jr, Ray (Musician)
c/o Staff Member *Performers of the World*
5657 Wilshire Blvd Ste 280
Los Angeles, CA 90036-3755, USA

Parkhill, Barry (Athlete, Basketball Player)
3429 Cesford Grange
Keswick, VA 22947-9127, USA

Parkhurst, Heather
8383 Wilshire Blvd # 954
Beverly Hills, CA 90211-2425

Parkhurst, Heather Elizabeth (Actor)
8491 W Sunset Blvd # 440
West Hollywood, CA 90069-1911, USA

Parkins, Barbara
6399 Wilshire Blvd Ste 414
Los Angeles, CA 90048-5716

Parkinson, Bradford W (Business Person)
2780 Volley Cir
Meadow Vista, CA 95722-9530, USA

Parkinson, Roger P (Publisher)
Minneapolis Star Tribune
425 Portland Ave
Minneapolis, MN 55488-0002, USA

Parks, Catherine (Actor)
1144 N Vista St Apt 2
West Hollywood, CA 90046-5629, USA

Parks, Cherokee (Athlete, Basketball
Player)
PO Box 11525
Las Vegas, NV 89111-1525, USA

Parks, Chris (Athlete, Wrestler)
c/o Staff Member *TNA Wrestling*
209 10th Ave S Ste 302
Nashville, TN 37203-0730, USA

Parks, Dallas (Athlete, Baseball Player)
3353 Pittman Grove Church Rd
Raeford, NC 28376-6012, USA

Parks, David W (Dave) (Athlete, Football
Player)
6629 Southpoint Dr
Dallas, TX 75248-2221, USA

Parks, Derek (Athlete, Baseball Player)
7828 Day Creek Blvd Apt 1414
Act 1214
Rancho Cucamonga, CA 91739-8581,
USA

Parks, Maxie (Athlete, Track Athlete)
4545 E Norwich Ave
Fresno, CA 93726-2726, USA

Parks, Michael (Actor)
11684 Ventura Blvd # 476
Studio City, CA 91604-2699, USA

Parks, Phaedra (Attorney, Reality Star)
3070 Montclair Cir SE
Smyrna, GA 30080-3797, USA

Parks, Suzan-Lori (Actor, Writer)
c/o Staff Member *Creative Artists Agency
(CAA-LA)*
2000 Avenue of the Stars Ste 100
Los Angeles, CA 90067-4705, USA

Parks-Young, Barbara (Athlete, Baseball
Player)
5078 Edinboro Ln
Wilmington, NC 28409-8518, USA

Parlavecchio, Chet (Athlete, Football
Player)
178 Brooklake Rd
Florham Park, NJ 07932-2707, USA

Parlen, Megan (Actor)
c/o Staff Member *Cunningham Escott
Slevin & Doherty (CESD-LA)*
10635 Santa Monica Blvd Ste 130
Los Angeles, CA 90025-8306, USA

Parlow, Cindy (Athlete, Olympic Athlete,
Soccer Player)
2611 English Hill Dr
Murfreesboro, TN 37130-1433, USA

Parmalee, Bernie (Athlete, Football
Player)
14695 Heatherton Dr
Granger, IN 46530-4212, USA

Parmele, Jalen (Athlete, Football Player)
c/o Bruce Tollner *REP 1 Sports Group*
2 Corporate Park Ste 106
Irvine, CA 92606-5103, USA

Parmenter, Skip (Athlete, Football Player)
34881 Seagrass Plantation Ln34881
Seagrass Plantation Ln
Dagsboro, DE 19939, USA

Parmet, Philip (Cinematographer)
1080 S Hayworth Ave
Los Angeles, CA 90035-2602, USA

Parnell, Bobby (Athlete, Baseball Player)
2265 Barger Rd
Salisbury, NC 28146-5049, USA

Parnell, Chris (Actor)
2281 Moreno Dr
Los Angeles, CA 90039-3049, USA

Parnell, Lee Roy (Musician)
PO Box 23451
Nashville, TN 37202-3451, USA

Parnell, LeRoy
PO Box 23451
Nashville, TN 37202-3451

Parnell, Peter (Writer)
c/o Staff Member *United Talent Agency
(UTA-LA)*
9336 Civic Center Dr
Beverly Hills, CA 90210-3604, USA

Parnell, Sean (Governor, Politician)
Alaska State Capitol Building
PO Box 110001
Juneau, AK 99811-0001, USA

Parnevik, Jesper (Golfer)
17553 SE Conch Bar Ave
Jupiter, FL 33469-1709, USA

Parodi, Starr (Musician)
c/o Staff Member *Evolution Music
Partners*
1680 Vine St Ste 500
Los Angeles, CA 90028-8800, USA

Paronto, Chad (Athlete, Baseball Player)
617 Benedict Rd
Pittsfield, MA 01201-2899, USA

Parque, jim (Athlete, Baseball Player)
3142 Halverson Way
Roseville, CA 95661-4038, USA

Parque, Jim (Athlete, Baseball Player,
Olympic Athlete)
4109 Crystal Ridge Dr SE
Puyallup, WA 98372-5214, USA

Parr, Jerry S
4529 38th St NW
Washington, DC 20016-1827, USA

Parr, Todd (Writer)
c/o Staff Member *Suppertime
Entertainment*
21300 Oxnard St Ste 100
Woodland Hills, CA 91367-5059, USA

Parra, Derek (Athlete, Olympic Athlete,
Speed Skater)
US Speedskating
14927 S Treseder St
Draper, UT 84020-3403, USA

Parra, Manny (Athlete, Baseball Player)
c/o Joe Urbon *Creative Artists Agency
(CAA-NY)*
162 5th Ave Fl 6
New York, NY 10010-6047, USA

Parrack, Jim (Actor)
c/o Jamie Harhay Skinner *IMPR*
357 S Robertson Blvd
Beverly Hills, CA 90211-3602, USA

Parrella, John (Athlete, Football Player)
108 E Park St
Marquette, MI 49855-3625, USA

Parrett, Jeff (Athlete, Baseball Player)
722 Seattle Dr
Lexington, KY 40503-2127, USA

Parrett, William (Business Person)
Deloitte Touche Tohmatsu
433 Country Club Rd W
New Canaan, CT 06840-3604, USA

Parrilla, Lana (Actor)
c/o Scott Wexler *Brillstein Entertainment
Partners (LA)*
9150 Wilshire Blvd Ste 350
Beverly Hills, CA 90212-3453, USA

Parriott, James (Director)
c/o Jamie Mandelbaum *Jackoway
Tyerman Wertheimer Austen
Mandelbaum Morris & Klein*
1925 Century Park E Fl 22
Los Angeles, CA 90067-2701, USA

Parris, Fred (Musician)
Paramount Entertainment
PO Box 12
Far Hills, NJ 07931-0012, USA

Parris, Gary (Athlete, Football Player)
5170 9th St
Vero Beach, FL 32966-2841, USA

Parris, Jonathan (Athlete, Baseball Player)
23127 128th Rd
Springfield Gardens, NY 11413-1310,
USA

Parris, Steve (Athlete, Baseball Player)
403 Rookery Ct
Joliet, IL 60431-2820, USA

Parrish, Bernard J (Bernie) (Athlete,
Football Player)
140A Torns Creek Rd
Eastanollee, GA 30538, USA

Parrish, Hunter (Actor)
c/o Lainie Sorkin Becky *Management 360*
9111 Wilshire Blvd
Beverly Hills, CA 90210-5508, USA

Parrish, John (Athlete, Baseball Player)
5673 Strasburg Rd
Atglen, PA 19310-1743, USA

Parrish, Lance M (Athlete, Baseball
Player)
1101 Chateau Ln
Nashville, TN 37215-4505, USA

Parrish, Larry A (Athlete, Baseball Player,
Coach)
1269 Blakely Hwy
Fort Gaines, GA 39851-4029, USA

Parrish, Lemar (Athlete, Football Player)
733 Schumate Chapel Rd
Jefferson City, MO 65109-0515, USA

Parrish, Mark (Athlete, Hockey Player,
Olympic Athlete)
15525 51st Ave N
Minneapolis, MN 55446-2220, USA

Parro, Dave (Athlete, Hockey Player)
820 3rd Ave
Hershey, PA 17033-1903

Parros, George (Athlete, Hockey Player)
PO Box 905
Hermosa Beach, CA 90254-0905, USA

Parros, Peter (Actor)
PO Box 3055
West Orange, NJ 07052-0655, USA

Parrot, Andrew
Jonathan Wentworth
5 Lockwood Rd
Scarsdale, NY 10583-5301, USA

Parrott, Mike (Athlete, Baseball Player)
PO Box 1264
Lyons, CO 80540-1264, USA

Parry, Craig (Golfer)
5139 Latrobe Dr
Windermere, FL 34786-8916, USA

Parry, Edward (Athlete, Basketball Player)
7201 1st St
Cottrellville, MI 48039-2801, USA

Parseghian, Ara (Coach, Football Coach,
Sportscaster)
51767 Oakbridge Ct
Mentone, IN 46539, USA

Parseghian, Gregory (Business Person)
Federal Home Loan Mortgage
8200 Jones Branch Dr
Mc Lean, VA 22102-3107, USA

Parsons, Alan (Musician)
c/o Staff Member *The Agency Group
(NYC)*
142 W 57th St Fl 6
New York, NY 10019-3300, USA

Parsons, Bill (Athlete, Baseball Player)
322 Karen Ave Unit 3901
Las Vegas, NV 89109-0453, USA

Parsons, Bob (Athlete, Football Player)
1098 Stanton Rd
Lake Zurich, IL 60047-1746, USA

Parsons, Casey (Athlete, Baseball Player)
17214 E Galactica Ct
Greenacres, WA 99016-7766, USA

Parsons, Estelle (Actor)
924 W End Ave Apt T5
New York, NY 10025-3543, USA

Parsons, Jim (Actor)
c/o Marsha McManus *Principal
Entertainment (LA)*
9255 W Sunset Blvd Ste 500
West Hollywood, CA 90069-3301, USA

Parsons, Johnny (Race Car Driver)
Brian Bollinger CMG
10500 Crosspoint Blvd
Indianapolis, IN 46256-3331, USA

Parsons, Nathan (Actor)
c/o Staff Member *Creative Partners Group*
15 Brooks Ave # B
Venice, CA 90291-3226, USA

Parsons, Phil (Athlete, Race Car Driver)
18801 Coveside Ln
Cornelius, NC 28031-5250, USA

Parsons, Robert (Bob)
Go Daddy
14455 N Hayden Rd Ste 219
Scottsdale, AZ 85260-6993, USA

Parsons, Tom (Athlete, Baseball Player)
7106 Lorraine Ave NW
North Canton, OH 44720-8832, USA

Parsons-Zipay, Suzanne (Athlete, Baseball
Player)
2310 Englewood Rd
Englewood, FL 34223-6333, USA

Partee, Dennis (Athlete, Football Player)
103 Denise Dr
Marshall, TX 75672-8403, USA

Parten, Ty (Athlete, Football Player)
23217 N 71st Dr
Glendale, AZ 85310-5868, USA

Partlow, Hope (Musician)
c/o Staff Member *Virgin Records (NY)*
150 5th Ave Fl 7
New York, NY 10011-4372, USA

Parton, Dolly (Actor, Musician,
Songwriter)
Dollywood Co
2700 Dollywood Parks Blvd
Pigeon Forge, TN 37863-4101, USA

Parton, Stella (Musician)
PO Box 120871
Nashville, TN 37212-0871, USA

Partridge, Rick (Athlete, Football Player)
707 Reeder Rd
Paramus, NJ 07652-3721, USA

Pasanella, Marco (Designer)
Pasanella Co
45 W 18th St
New York, NY 10011-4609, USA

Pasarell, Charles (Tennis Player)
78200 Miles Ave
Indian Wells, CA 92210-6803, USA

Pascal, Adam (Actor)
c/o Staff Member *Paradigm (LA)*
360 N Crescent Dr
North Bldg
Beverly Hills, CA 90210-4874, USA

Pascal, Pedro (Actor)
c/o Jason Weinberg *Untitled
Entertainment (LA)*
350 S Beverly Dr Ste 200
Beverly Hills, CA 90212-4819, USA

Paschal, Doug (Athlete, Football Player)
8702 Thornbury Pl
Waxhaw, NC 28173-7157, USA

Paschall, Bill (Athlete, Baseball Player)
7926 Windspray Dr
Summerfield, NC 27358-9715, USA

Paschall, Jim (Race Car Driver)
RR 2 Box 450
Denton, NC 27239, USA

Pascrell Jr., Bill (Congressman, Politician)
2370 Rayburn Hob
Washington, DC 20515-0906, USA

Pascual, Camilo (Athlete, Baseball Player)
4625 SW 82nd Pl
Miami, FL 33155-5453, USA

Pascucci, Val (Athlete, Baseball Player)
11163 James Pl
Cerritos, CA 90703-6450, USA

Pasdar, Adrian (Actor)
c/o Leigh Brillstein *Resolution (LA)*
10250 Constellation Blvd Fl 7
Los Angeles, CA 90067-6207, USA

Pashnick, Larry (Athlete, Baseball Player)
506 Highland St
Wyandotte, MI 48192-2433, USA

Pasian, Karina (Musician)
c/o Staff Member *Island Def Jam Group*
825 8th Ave Fl 28
New York, NY 10019-7416, USA

Pasillas, Jose (Musician)
c/o Staff Member *ArtistDirect*
9046 Lindblade St
Culver City, CA 90232-2513, USA

Pasin, Dave (Athlete)
787 Holly Oak Dr
Palo Alto, CA 94303-4143

Paslawski, Greg (Athlete, Hockey Player)
10 Topping Ln
Saint Louis, MO 63131-1901, USA

Pasley, Kevin (Athlete, Baseball Player)
2701 Lancaster Dr
Sun City Center, FL 33573-6517, USA

Pasqua, Dan (Athlete, Baseball Player)
10423 Capistrano
Moreno Valley, CA 92557, USA

Pasquale, Edward (Athlete, Hockey
Player)
101 Marietta St NW Ste 1900
Atlanta, GA 30303-2771, USA

Pasquale, Steven (Actor)
c/o Staff Member *Overbrook
Entertainment*
10202 Washington Blvd
Culver City, CA 90232-3119, USA

Pasqualini, Tony (Actor)
c/o Sandra Joseph *SLJ Management*
833 N Edinburgh Ave Unit 203
Los Angeles, CA 90046-6947, USA

Pasqualino, Luke (Actor)
c/o Brantley Brown *Schachter
Entertainment*
1157 S Beverly Dr Fl 2
Los Angeles, CA 90035-1119, USA

Pasqualoni, Paul (Coach, Football Coach)
Syracuse University
Athletic Dept
Syracuse, NY 13244-0001, USA

Pasquesi, Anthony (Athlete, Football
Player)
463 N Clubview Ct
Addison, IL 60101-2998, USA

Pasquesi, David (Actor)
c/o Mark Teitelbaum *Teitelbaum Artists
Group*
8840 Wilshire Blvd Fl 3
Beverly Hills, CA 90211-2606, USA

Pasquin, John (Director)
c/o Staff Member *Paradox Productions*
801 Tarcuto Way
Los Angeles, CA 90077-3216, USA

Pass, Patrick (Athlete, Football Player)
4 Spruce Pond Rd
Franklin, MA 02038-2500, USA

Passaglia, Martin (Athlete, Basketball
Player)
7377 Capay Ave
Orland, CA 95963-9687, USA

Passer, Ivan (Director)
c/o Staff Member *Innovative Artists (LA)*
1505 10th St
Santa Monica, CA 90401-2805, USA

Passion Pit (Music Group)
c/o Staff Member *Foundations Artist
Management*
307 7th Ave Rm 403
New York, NY 10001-6081, USA

Passions, The
141 Dunbar Ave
Fords, NJ 08863-1551

Passmore, Christi (Race Car Driver)
GAP Roofing
Rt. 3
Box 6870
Pryor, OK 74361, USA

Passmore, Matt (Actor)
c/o Jordan Tilzer *ROAR (LA)*
9701 Wilshire Blvd Fl 8
Beverly Hills, CA 90212-2008, USA

Passos, Rosa (Musician)
c/o Staff Member *Concord Music Group,
Inc*
900 N Rohlwing Rd
Itasca, IL 60143-1161, USA

Pastan, Linda (Writer)
11710 Beall Mountain Rd
Potomac, MD 20854-1105, USA

Pasternak, Harley (Fitness Expert)
732 N Fuller Ave
Los Angeles, CA 90046-7505, USA

Pasternak, Michael (Actor)
c/o Craig Wyckoff *Epstein Wyckoff Corsa
Ross (LA)*
11350 Ventura Blvd Ste 100
Studio City, CA 91604-3140, USA

Pastor, Ed (Congressman, Politician)
2465 Rayburn Hob
Washington, DC 20515-0304, USA

Pastore, Frank (Athlete, Baseball Player)
1542 Francis Way
Upland, CA 91786-2353, USA

Pastore, Vincent (Actor)
PO Box 207
Bronx, NY 10464-0207, USA

Pastorini Jr, Darite A (Dan) (Athlete,
Football Player)
1316 Stanford St
Houston, TX 77019-4327, USA

Pastornicky, Cliff (Athlete, Baseball
Player)
4815 50th Ave W
Bradenton, FL 34210-4907, USA

Pat, Dunsmore (Athlete, Football Player)
21301 Whispering Dr
Lenexa, KS 66220-3212, USA

Pataki, Governor George E (Ex-Governor,
Politician)
Chadbourne & Parke, LLP
1017 Route 9D
Garrison, NY 10524-3636, USA

Pataky, Elsa (Actor)
7022 Grasswood Ave
Malibu, CA 90265-4247, USA

Patchett, Ann (Writer)
Parnassus Books
3900 Hillsboro Pike Ste 14
Nashville, TN 37215-2714, USA

Pate, Bob (Athlete, Baseball Player)
10447 Sagecrest Dr
Moreno Valley, CA 92557-3036, USA

Pate, Cynthia (Beauty Pageant Winner)
Future Productions
7907 Stafford Trl
Savage, MN 55378-4308, USA

Pate, Jerry (Golfer)
5 Hyde Park Rd
Pensacola, FL 32503-5830, USA

Pate, Rupert (Athlete, Football Player)
428 Shadowbrook Dr
Burlington, NC 27215-4775, USA

Pate, Steve (Golfer)
1034 Brookview Ave
Westlake Village, CA 91361-1623, USA

Patek, Freddie (Athlete, Baseball Player)
5408 NE Wedgewood Ln
Ln
Lees Summit, MO 64064-1220, USA

Patera, Dennis (Athlete, Football Player)
61535 S Highway 97 Apt 9512
Bend, OR 97702-2154, USA

Patera, George (Athlete, Football Player)
7305 172nd St SW
Edmonds, WA 98026-5121, USA

Patera, John A (Jack) (Athlete, Coach,
Football Coach, Football Player)
82 Osprey Dr
Cle Elum, WA 98922, USA

Patera, Ken (Athlete, Olympic Athlete,
Weightlifter)
6932 Stratford Draw
Saint Paul, MN 55125-2413, USA

Patera, Pavel (Athlete, Hockey Player)
175 Kellogg Blvd W
Xcel Enegy Arena
Saint Paul, MN 55102-1206, USA

Paterra, Greg (Athlete, Football Player)
305 Douglas Ave
Elizabeth, PA 15037-1724, USA

Paterra, Herb (Athlete, Football Player)
3696 Woodmonte Dr
Rochester, MI 48306-4799, USA

Paterson, Joe (Athlete, Hockey Player)
Adirondack Phantoms
1 Civic Center Plz
Glens Falls, NY 12801-4532

Paterson, Joe (Athlete, Hockey Player)
49 Sullivan Pl
Lake George, NY 12845-4334

Paterson, Katherine (Writer)
70 Wildersburg Cmn
Barre, VT 05641-9761, USA

Paterson, Rick (Athlete, Hockey Player)
2695 E Katella Ave
Anaheim, CA 92806-5904

Patey, Larry (Athlete, Hockey Player)
2713 Autumn Run Ct
Chesterfield, MO 63005-7001

Pathon, Jerome (Athlete, Football Player)
4827 Eagles Watch Ln
Indianapolis, IN 46254-9531, USA

Patillo, Maria
6300 Wilshire Blvd # 2110
Los Angeles, CA 90048-5204

Patinkin, Mandy (Actor, Musician)
535 W 110th St # 12CE
New York, NY 10025-2086, USA

Patitz, Tatjana (Model)
c/o Gordon Rael *JV Entertainment*
5455 Wilshire Blvd Ste 2114
Los Angeles, CA 90036-4290, USA

Patric, Jason (Actor, Producer)
c/o Michael Nilon *Kritzer Levine Wilkins
Entertainment (KLWG)*
11872 La Grange Ave Fl 1
Los Angeles, CA 90025-5283, USA

Patrick, Bronswell (Athlete, Baseball
Player)
3202 Morton Ln
Greenville, NC 27834-4930, USA

Patrick, Craig (Athlete, Coach, Hockey
Player)
113 Royston Rd
Pittsburgh, PA 15238-2311, USA

Patrick, Danica (Race Car Driver)
Danica Racing
12985 N 119th St
Scottsdale, AZ 85259-2735, USA

Patrick, Deval (Governor, Politician)
Office of the Governor
24 Beacon St Ste 280
Boston, MA 02133-1010, USA

Patrick, Frank (Athlete, Football Player)
5689 SW 98th St
Denton, NE 68339-3346, USA

Patrick, Glenn (Athlete, Hockey Player)
637 Lakeside Dr
Harveys Lake, PA 18618-3128

Patrick, Ian (Actor)
c/o Monique Moss *Integrated PR*
9025 Wilshire Blvd Ste 400
Beverly Hills, CA 90211-1828, USA

Patrick, James (Athlete, Hockey Player)
9123 Chapel Valley Rd
Dallas, TX 75220-5029

Patrick, James (Athlete, Hockey Player)
Buffalo Sabres
1 Seymour H Knox III Plz Ste 1
Buffalo, NY 14203-3096

Patrick, John (Writer)
PO Box 2386
St Thomas, VI 00801, USA

Patrick, Marcus (Actor)
c/o Staff Member *Gar Lester Agency*
11026 Ventura Blvd Ste 10
Studio City, CA 91604-3598, USA

Patrick, Nicholas J M (Astronaut)
13708 NE 32nd Pl
Bellevue, WA 98005-1401, USA

Patrick, Richard (Musician)
c/o Jamie Talbot *Sanctuary Artist
Management*
8750 Wilshire Blvd Ste 200
Beverly Hills, CA 90211-2707, USA

Patrick, Robert (Actor, Producer)
c/o Susan Patricola *Patricola Lust PR*
9171 Wilshire Blvd Ste 441
Beverly Hills, CA 90210-5516, USA

Patrick, Robert (Race Car Driver)
Patrick Racing
PO Box 3366
College Station
Fredericksburg, VA 22402-3366, USA

Patrick, Tera (Adult Film Star)
14813 Huston St
Sherman Oaks, CA 91403-1608, USA

Patrick, Thomas M (Business Person)
Peoples Energy Corp
130 E Randolph St Ste 300
Chicago, IL 60601-6203, USA

Patridge, Audrina (Actor, Reality Star)
c/o David (Dave) Fleming *Mosaic Media
Group*
9200 W Sunset Blvd Ste 10
West Hollywood, CA 90069-3608, USA

Patrone, Shana
209 10th Ave S Ste 229
Nashville, TN 37203-0721

Patten, Joel (Athlete, Football Player)
12 W Bayard St
Fenwick Island, DE 19944-4502, USA

Patterson, Bob (Athlete, Baseball Player)
1093 7th Street Blvd SE
Hickory, NC 28602-4342, USA

Patterson, Carly (Athlete, Gymnast,
Olympic Athlete)
PO Box 1280
Angel Fire, NM 87710-1280, USA

Patterson, Cordarrelle (Athlete, Football
Player)
c/o Joby Branion *Athletes First, LLC*
23091 Mill Creek Dr
Laguna Hills, CA 92653-1258, USA

Patterson, Corey (Athlete, Baseball Player)
1115 Gordon Combs Rd NW
Marietta, GA 30064-1225, USA

Patterson, Danny (Athlete, Baseball
Player)
13944 E Yucca St
Scottsdale, AZ 85259-4638, USA

Patterson, Daryl (Athlete, Baseball Player)
20145 Tollhouse Rd
Clovis, CA 93619-9760, USA

Patterson, Dave (Athlete, Baseball Player)
8425 Evanston Ave
Raytown, MO 64138-3346, USA

Patterson, Dennis (Athlete, Hockey
Player)
46808 Glengarry Blvd
Canton, MI 48188-3056

Patterson, Don (Athlete, Football Player)
1558 Halisport Lake Dr NW
Kennesaw, GA 30152-4072, USA

Patterson, Elvis V (Athlete, Football
Player)
3939 Alberta St
Houston, TX 77021-4009, USA

Patterson, Gary (Cartoonist)
Patterson International
25208 Malibu Rd
Malibu, CA 90265-4635, USA

Patterson, Gil (Athlete, Baseball Player)
19705 Gunn Hwy
Odessa, FL 33556-4517, USA

Patterson, James (Business Person, Writer)
James Patterson Entertainment
10 Red Horse Hl
Sharon, CT 06069-2464, USA

Patterson, Jarrod (Athlete, Baseball
Player)
405 6th St N
Clanton, AL 35045-2823, USA

Patterson, Jeff (Athlete, Baseball Player)
27825 Tamara Dr
Yorba Linda, CA 92887-5843, USA

Patterson, John (Athlete, Baseball Player)
PO Box 27881
Tempe, AZ 85285-7881, USA

Patterson, John (Athlete, Baseball Player)
2709 Country Club Dr
Orange, TX 77630-2142, USA

Patterson, John M (Ex-Governor)
Court of Judiciary
PO Box 30155
Montgomery, AL 36103, USA

Patterson, Katerine (Writer)
70 Wildersburg Cmn
Barre, VT 05641-9761, USA

Patterson, Ken (Athlete, Baseball Player)
9100 Aspen Dr
Woodway, TX 76712-8771, USA

Patterson, Lorna (Actor)
23852 Pacific Coast Hwy # 355
Malibu, CA 90265-4876, USA

Patterson, Marne (Actor)
c/o Matthew Lesher *Insight*
PO Box 36359
Los Angeles, CA 90036-0359, USA

Patterson, Marnette (Actor)
c/o Matthew Lesher *Insight*
PO Box 36359
Los Angeles, CA 90036-0359, USA

Patterson, Melody (Actor)
MILLER SPECIALTIES
141 Sunny Ln
Reeds Spring, MO 65737-9606, USA

Patterson, Mike (Athlete, Baseball Player)
19306 Chamblee Ave
Cerritos, CA 90703-6751, USA

Patterson, Neva
11870 Santa Monica Blvd Ste 106
Los Angeles, CA 90025-5276

Patterson, Reggie (Athlete, Baseball
Player)
PO Box 401
Bessemer, AL 35021-0401, USA

Patterson, Richard North (Writer)
PO Box 183
West Tisbury, MA 02575-0183, USA

Patterson, Ross (Actor)
c/o Gina Hoffman *PMK/BNC Public
Relations (PMK-LA)*
8687 Melrose Ave Ste 8
West Hollywood, CA 90069-5746, USA

Patterson, Scott (Athlete, Baseball Player)
148 Tall Maple Ct
Freeburg, IL 62243-4078, USA

Patterson, Scott (Actor)
c/o Laina Cohn *Cohn / Torgan
Management*
Prefers to be contacted by telephone or
email
Los Angeles, CA, USA

Patterson, Todd (Race Car Driver)
Todd Racing
PO Box 338
920 Industrial Rd.
Augusta, KS 67010-0338, USA

Patterson, Willie (Baseball Player)
New York Cubans
409 Tuscaloosa Ave SW Apt 7
Birmingham, AL 35211-1457, USA

Patterson, Worthy (Athlete, Basketball
Player)
2091 Kerwood Ave
Los Angeles, CA 90025-6006, USA

Pattillo, Linda (Correspondent)
Cable News Network
820 1st St NE Ste 1000
News Dept
Washington, DC 20002-4363, USA

Pattin, Marty (Athlete, Baseball Player)
3401 Sweetgrass Ct
Lawrence, KS 66049-4245, USA

Pattinson, Robert (Actor)
12001 Crest Ct
Beverly Hills, CA 90210-1474, USA

Pattison, Mark (Athlete, Football Player)
3828 48th Ave NE
Seattle, WA 98105-5227, USA

Patton, Candice (Actor)
c/o Vincent Cirrincione *Vincent Cirrincione Associates*
1516 N Fairfax Ave
Los Angeles, CA 90046-2608, USA

Patton, Donovan (Actor)
c/o Staff Member *Glasser/Black Management*
283 Cedarhurst Ave
Cedarhurst, NY 11516-1671, USA

Patton, Eric (Athlete, Football Player)
23732 San Esteban Dr
Mission Viejo, CA 92691-3346, USA

Patton, Marvcus (Athlete, Football Player)
12994 Wyckland Dr
Clifton, VA 20124-2053, USA

Patton, Mel (Athlete, Olympic Athlete, Track Athlete)
2312 Via Del Aquacate
Fallbrook, CA 92028-9697, USA

Patton, Melvin (Mel) (Athlete, Track Athlete)
2312 Via Del Aquacate
Fallbrook, CA 92028-9697, USA

Patton, Paula (Actor, Director)
1568 Blue Jay Way
Los Angeles, CA 90069-1215, USA

Patton, Sean (Actor)
c/o Dave Rath *Generate Management*
8750 Wilshire Blvd Ste 200
Beverly Hills, CA 90211-2707, USA

Patton, Tom (Athlete, Baseball Player)
577 Daisy Dr
New Holland, PA 17557-8708, USA

Patton, Troy (Athlete, Baseball Player)
c/o Staff Member *Baltimore Orioles*
333 W Camden St
Baltimore, MD 21201-2496, USA

Patton, Virginia (Actor)
2205 Melrose Ave
Ann Arbor, MI 48104-4069, USA

Patton, Will (Actor)
c/o Kate Edwards *Grand View Management*
578 Washington Blvd # 688
Marina Del Rey, CA 90292-5442, USA

Patty, Sandi (Musician)
5701 NW 163rd Ter
Edmond, OK 73013-9435, USA

Patu, Saul (Athlete, Football Player)
6001 S Hazel St
Seattle, WA 98178-2450, USA

Patulski, Walter G (Walt) (Athlete, Football Player)
420 Kimber Rd
Syracuse, NY 13224-1836, USA

Paul, Aaron (Actor)
8247 Roxbury Rd
Los Angeles, CA 90069-1629, USA

Paul, Adrian (Actor, Director, Producer)
15059 Rayneta Dr
Sherman Oaks, CA 91403-4427, USA

Paul, Alan (Music Group, Musician)
Columbia/CBS Records
1801 Century Park W
Los Angeles, CA 90067-6409, USA

Paul, Alexandra (Actor)
8475 Brier Dr
Los Angeles, CA 90046-1907, USA

Paul, Billy (Musician)
8215 Winthrop St
Philadelphia, PA 19136-1914, USA

Paul, Chris (Athlete, Basketball Player)
749 Fountain Brook Ln
Lewisville, NC 27023-8371, USA

Paul, Christi (Correspondent)
Cable News Network
1050 Techwood Dr NW
News Dept
Atlanta, GA 30318-5695, USA

Paul, Emily (Actor)
c/o Simon Millar *Rumble Media*
1620 Broadway Ste C
Santa Monica, CA 90404-2777, USA

Paul, Henry (Music Group, Musician)
Vector Mgmt
1607 17th Ave S
Nashville, TN 37212-2812, USA

Paul, Jarrad (Actor)
c/o JC Spink *Benderspink*
8447 Wilshire Blvd Ste 250
Studio E
Beverly Hills, CA 90211-3224, USA

Paul, Josh (Athlete, Baseball Player)
28751 Windover St
Wesley Chapel, FL 33545-4378, USA

Paul, Markus (Athlete, Football Player)
2673 Mill Run Blvd
Kissimmee, FL 34744-3020, USA

Paul, Mike (Athlete, Baseball Player)
5121 N Circulo Sobrio
Tucson, AZ 85718-6037, USA

Paul, Robert (Figure Skater)
10675 Rochester Ave
Los Angeles, CA 90024-5009, USA

Paul, Ron (Politician)
c/o Andrew Stuart *Stuart Agency, The*
260 W 52nd St Apt 24C
New York, NY 10019-5836, USA

Paul, Vinnie (Musician)
c/o Staff Member *Zen Media Group*
272 Grand St Ste B
Brooklyn, NY 11211-4796, USA

Paul, Whitney (Athlete, Football Player)
6802 Thornwild Rd
Missouri City, TX 77489-2649, USA

Paul, Xavier (Athlete, Baseball Player)
2637 5th St
Slidell, LA 70458-4105, USA

Paul & Paula
7251 Lowell Dr # 200
Overland Park, KS 66204-1840

Pauley, David (Athlete, Baseball Player)
19839 N 45th Ave
Glendale, AZ 85308-7389, USA

Pauley, Jane (Journalist)
c/o Wayne Kabak *WSK Management, LLC*
888 7th Ave Ste 503
New York, NY 10106-0501, USA

Paulino, Felipe (Athlete, Baseball Player)
12312 Evening Bay Dr
Pearland, TX 77584-8827, USA

Paulino, Ronny (Athlete, Baseball Player)
8012 Wiles Rd
Coral Springs, FL 33067-2072, USA

Paul Jr, John (Race Car Driver)
44 Musdogee Rd
Atlanta, GA 30305, USA

Paulk, Charlie (Athlete, Basketball Player)
5750 Friars Rd Apt 102
San Diego, CA 92110-1833, USA

Paulk, Jeff (Athlete, Football Player)
7751 S Bonarden Ln
Tempe, AZ 85284-1569, USA

Paulo (DJ)
c/o Staff Member *Diva Central Inc*
7510 W Sunset Blvd Ste 1445
Los Angeles, CA 90046-3408, USA

Paulsen, Erik (Congressman, Politician)
127 Cannon Hob
Washington, DC 20515-0904, USA

Paulson, Brandon (Athlete, Olympic Athlete, Wrestler)
4165 120th Ave NW
Minneapolis, MN 55433-1611, USA

Paulson, Carl (Golfer)
137 Royal Creek Dr
Lexington, SC 29072-7099, USA

Paulson, Dainard (Athlete, Football Player)
700 W Goodlander Rd
Selah, WA 98942-8740, USA

Paulson, Dennis (Golfer)
1872 Shadetree Dr
San Marcos, CA 92078-0902, USA

Paulson, John (Business Person)
Paulson & CO
590 Madison Ave Fl 29
New York, NY 10022-2524, USA

Paulson, Richard L (Business Person)
Potlatch Corp
601 W Riverside Ave Ste 1100
Spokane, WA 99201-0644, USA

Paulson, Sarah (Actor)
c/o Perri Kipperman *Kipperman Management*
345 7th Ave Rm 503
New York, NY 10001-5054, USA

Paultz, Billy (Athlete, Basketball Player)
1941 Waters Edge Ln
Seabrook, TX 77586-2599, USA

Paulusma, Polly (Musician)
c/o Staff Member *Paradigm (Monterey)*
404 W Franklin St
Monterey, CA 93940-2303, USA

Paup, Bryce E (Athlete, Football Player)
3110 Pendleton Dr
Cedar Falls, IA 50613-1636, USA

Pausini, Laura (Musician)
c/o Staff Member *Creative Artists Agency (CAA-LA)*
2000 Avenue of the Stars Ste 100
Los Angeles, CA 90067-4705, USA

Pavano, Carl (Athlete, Baseball Player)
110 Playa Rienta Way Apt 23C
Palm Beach Gardens, FL 33418-6210, USA

Pavelich, Mark (Athlete, Hockey Player, Olympic Athlete)
19 E Norwood Shrs
Lutsen, MN 55612, USA

Pavelich, Marty (Athlete, Hockey Player)
PO Box 160448
Big Sky, MT 59716-0448

Pavelka, Jake (Reality Star)
c/o Susan Haber *Haber Entertainment*
434 S Canon Dr Apt 204
Beverly Hills, CA 90212-4501, USA

Pavelski, Joe (Athlete, Hockey Player)
1724 Peregrino Way
San Jose, CA 95125-4536

Paven, Corey
2515 McKinney Ave Ste 930
Dallas, TX 75201-1921

Pavese, Jim (Athlete, Hockey Player)
65 Whittier Dr
Kings Park, NY 11754-2339

Pavia, Joe (Horse Racer)
1600 SW 3rd St
Pompano Beach, FL 33069-3102, USA

Pavia, Ria
3500 W Olive Ave Ste 1400
Burbank, CA 91505-5512

Pavin, Corey (Golfer)
4332 Gilbert Ave
Dallas, TX 75219-2908, USA

Pavlas, David (Dave) (Athlete, Baseball Player)
PO Box 1224
Shiner, TX 77984-1224, USA

Pavletich, Don (Athlete, Baseball Player)
13645 Adelaide Ln
Brookfield, WI 53005-4965, USA

Pavlick, Greg (Athlete, Baseball Player)
936 Pinellas Bavwav
S Unit TH8
Saint Petersburg, FL 33715, USA

Pavlik, Kelly (Boxer)
Top Rank Inc
3908 Howard Hughes Pkwy # 580
Las Vegas, NV 89109, USA

Pavlik, Roger (Athlete, Baseball Player)
622 Beaver Bend Rd
Houston, TX 77037-2004, USA

Pavlovic, Aleksandar (Basketball Player)
Utah Jazz
301 W South Temple
Delta Center
Salt Lake City, UT 84101-1219, USA

Pawelczyk, James A Dr (Astronaut)
2047 Pine Cliff Rd
State College, PA 16801-2405, USA

Pawelczyk, James A (Jim) (Astronaut)
NASA
2101 Nasa Pkwy Spc Johnsoncenter
Houston, TX 77058-3696, USA

Pawlenty, Tim (Politician)
4117 Countrvview Dr
Saint Paul, MN 55123, USA

Pawloski, Stan (Athlete, Baseball Player)
413 Maryjoe Way
Warrington, PA 18976-1695, USA

Pawlowski, John (Athlete, Baseball Player)
257 Mill Branch Way
North Augusta, SC 29860-8622, USA

Pawuk, Mark (Race Car Driver)
PO Box 535
Richfield, OH 44286-0535, USA

Paxson, Jim (Athlete, Basketball Player)
8500 N Sendero Tres M # M
Paradise Valley, AZ 85253-8116, USA

Paxson, Jim (Athlete, Basketball Player)
3225 Southdale Dr Apt 1
Dayton, OH 45409-1130, USA

Paxson, John (Athlete, Basketball Player, Misc)
125 Boardman Ct
Lake Bluff, IL 60044-2454, USA

Paxton, Bill (Actor)
c/o Jillian Roscoe *ID Public Relations (LA)*
7060 Hollywood Blvd Fl 8th
Los Angeles, CA 90028-6021, USA

Paxton, Mike (Athlete, Baseball Player)
1432 Brayhill Cv
Collierville, TN 38017-3978, USA

Paxton, Sara (Actor)
22729 Brenford St
Woodland Hills, CA 91364-4906, USA

Paxton, Tom (Music Group, Musician, Songwriter, Writer)
Fleming Tamulevich Assoc
733 N Main St
Ann Arbor, MI 48104-1030, USA

Payette, Julie (Astronaut)
Space Agency
12175 Shenandoah Rd
Middletown, CA 95461-7707, USA

Paymer, David (Actor)
327 19th St
Santa Monica, CA 90402-2409, USA

Payne, Alexander (Actor, Director, Producer)
Ad Hominem
506 Santa Monica Blvd Ste 400
Santa Monica, CA 90401-2412, USA

Payne, Allen (Actor)
c/o Staff Member *Harrison Stokes*
1080 Stearns Dr
Los Angeles, CA 90035-2639, USA

Payne, Barbara (Athlete, Baseball Player)
15897 W Desert Meadow Dr
Surprise, AZ 85374-5636, USA

Payne, Bruce (Actor)
c/o Gordon Gilbertson *Gilbertson Management*
1334 3rd Street Promenade Ste 201
Santa Monica, CA 90401-1320, USA

Payne, Davis (Athlete, Hockey Player)
1704 Harkness St
Manhattan Beach, CA 90266-4228

Payne, Freda (Music Group, Musician)
c/o Staff Member *Diva Central Inc*
7510 W Sunset Blvd Ste 1445
Los Angeles, CA 90046-3408, USA

Payne, Julie (Actor)
c/o Staff Member *Pakula/King & Associates*
9229 W Sunset Blvd Ste 315
West Hollywood, CA 90069-3403, USA

Payne, Kenny (Athlete, Basketball Player)
1968 General Warfield Way
Lexington, KY 40505-4836, USA

Payne, Kherington (Actor)
c/o Staff Member *Luber Roklin Management*
5815 W Sunset Blvd Ste 206
Los Angeles, CA 90028-6481, USA

Payne, Rod (Athlete, Football Player)
9622 Stonemasters Dr
Loveland, OH 45140-6209, USA

Payne, Scherrie-
433 N Camden Dr Ste 400
Beverly Hills, CA 90210-4408

Payne, Seth (Athlete, Football Player)
5004 Chestnut St
Bellaire, TX 77401-3412, USA

Payne, Steve (Athlete, Hockey Player)
1307 89th St
New Richmond, WI 54017-6958

Payne, Tom (Actor)
c/o Beth Holden-Garland *Untitled Entertainment (LA)*
350 S Beverly Dr Ste 200
Beverly Hills, CA 90212-4819, USA

Payne, Waylon (Actor, Musician)
c/o Ben Feigin *Anonymous Content (LA)*
3532 Hayden Ave
Culver City, CA 90232-2413, USA

Pays, Amanda (Actor)
11955 Addison St
Valley Village, CA 91607-3106, USA

Payton, Christian (Actor)
c/o Staff Member *William Morris Endeavor (LA)*
9601 Wilshire Blvd
Beverly Hills, CA 90210-5213, USA

Payton, Eddie (Athlete, Football Player)
2656 Hemingway Cir
Jackson, MS 39209-7026, USA

Payton, Gary (Athlete, Basketball Player, Olympic Athlete)
2745 S Monte Cristo Way
Las Vegas, NV 89117-2974, USA

Payton, Gary E (Astronaut)
2367 Diamond Creek Dr
Colorado Springs, CO 80921-2916, USA

Payton, Gary E Colonel (Astronaut)
2367 Diamond Creek Dr
Colorado Springs, CO 80921-2916, USA

Payton, Jay (Athlete, Baseball Player)
2002 Wild Waters Dr
Raleigh, NC 27614-7636, USA

Payton, JoMarie (Actor)
c/o Gar Lester *Gar Lester Agency*
11026 Ventura Blvd Ste 10
Studio City, CA 91604-3598, USA

payton, khary (Actor)
c/o Theodore B Gekis *Gekis Management*
4217 Verdugo View Dr
Los Angeles, CA 90065-4317, USA

Payton, Nicholas (Musician)
Management Ark
116 Village Blvd Ste 200
Princeton, NJ 08540-5700, USA

Payton, Sean (Football Coach, Football Player)
c/o Jamie Fritz *Fritz Martin Management*
1801 Avenue of the Stars Ste 250
Los Angeles, CA 90067-5914, USA

Pazienda, Vinnie
64 Waterman Ave
Cranston, RI 02910-4522

Pazienza, Vinny (Boxer)
c/o Darren Prince *Prince Marketing Group*
18 Carillon Cir
Livingston, NJ 07039-2600, USA

Pazik, Mike (Athlete, Baseball Player)
8413 Comanche Ct
Bethesda, MD 20817-4533, USA

P. Bilbray, Brian (Congressman, Politician)
2410 Rayburn Hob
Washington, DC 20515-0504, USA

PC Quest
PO Box 720423
Norman, OK 73070-4310

P. Duffy, Sean (Congressman, Politician)
1208 Longworth Hob
Washington, DC 20515-0604, USA

Peace, Terry (Actor)
PO Box 74
Allison Park, PA 15101-0074, USA

Peace, Warren (Baseball Player)
Newark Eagles
27921 NC Highway 903
Robersonville, NC 27871-8904, USA

Peaches and Herb (Music Group)
c/o Staff Member *M.A.G./Universal Attractions*
15 W 36th St Fl 8
New York, NY 10018-7927, USA

Peake, Don (Musician)
c/o Mike Rosen *Working Artists Agency*
13525 Ventura Blvd
Sherman Oaks, CA 91423-3801

Peake, Pat (Athlete, Hockey Player)
327 Hecht Dr
Madison Heights, MI 48071-2890

Peaker, E J (Actor)
4935 Densmore Ave
Encino, CA 91436-1537, USA

Peaks, Pandora (Adult Film Star)
Photo Clubs
6011 Winterpointe Ln Apt 201
Raleigh, NC 27606-2278, USA

Pear, Dave (Athlete, Football Player)
3126 199th Ave SE
Sammamish, WA 98075-9652, USA

Pearce, Colby (Athlete, Cycler, Olympic Athlete)
755 Hawthorn Ave
Boulder, CO 80304-2139, USA

Pearce, Frank (Business Person)
Blizzard Entertainment
PO Box 18979
Irvine, CA 92623-8979, USA

Pearce, Josh (Athlete, Baseball Player)
2607 Draper Rd
Yakima, WA 98903-9216, USA

Pearce, Richard I (Director)
240 Bentley Cir
Los Angeles, CA 90049-2414, USA

Pearce, Stevan (Congressman, Politician)
2432 Rayburn Hob
Washington, DC 20515-2402, USA

Pearce, Steve (Athlete, Baseball Player)
7109 Twelve Oaks Dr
Lakeland, FL 33813-5672, USA

Pearcy, James W (Athlete, Football Player)
PO Box 609
Cobbs Creek, VA 23035-0609, USA

Pearl, Barry (Actor)
c/o Staff Member *Coolwaters Productions*
10061 Riverside Dr # 531
Toluca Lake, CA 91602-2560, USA

Pearl Jam (Music Group)
c/o Nicole Vandenberg *Vandenberg Communications*
1900 S Corgiat Dr
Seattle, WA 98108-2817, USA

Pearlman, Steve
c/o Sean Freidin *ICM Partners (LA)*
10250 Constellation Blvd Fl 7
Los Angeles, CA 90067-6207, USA

Pearlman, Zack (Actor)
c/o Paul Young *Principato/Young Management (LA)*
9465 Wilshire Blvd Ste 900
Beverly Hills, CA 90212-2608, USA

Pearlstine, Norman (Writer)
c/o Lynn Nesbit *Janklow & Nesbit Associates*
445 Park Ave Fl 13
New York, NY 10022-8628, USA

Pears, Erik (Athlete, Football Player)
c/o Jeff Sperbeck *The Novo Agency*
3201 Danville Blvd Ste 295
Alamo, CA 94507-1978, USA

Pearson, Albie (Athlete, Baseball Player)
55473 Oakhill
La Quinta, CA 92253-4730, USA

Pearson, Barry (Athlete, Football Player)
85 Westledge Rd
West Simsbury, CT 06092-2327, USA

Pearson, Corey (Actor)
c/o Colton Gramm *Brillstein Entertainment Partners (LA)*
9150 Wilshire Blvd Ste 350
Beverly Hills, CA 90212-3453, USA

Pearson, David (Race Car Driver)
290 Burnett Rd
Boiling Springs, SC 29316-5934, USA

Pearson, Drew (Athlete, Football Player)
3721 Mount Vernon Way
Plano, TX 75025-3729, USA

Pearson, Durk
PO Box 1067
Hollywood, FL 33022

Pearson, Jason (Athlete, Baseball Player)
2373 Sunset Dr
Freeport, IL 61032-8348, USA

Pearson, Jayice (Athlete, Football Player)
721 SW Winterhill Ln
Lees Summit, MO 64081-2676, USA

Pearson, Larry (Race Car Driver)
Buckshot Racing
182 Belue Cir
Boiling Springs, SC 29316-5900, USA

Pearson, Preston (Athlete, Football Player)
9104 Moss Farm Ln
Dallas, TX 75243-7429, USA

Pearson, Scott (Athlete, Hockey Player)
114 Lauren Ln
Brunswick, GA 31525-9579

Pearson, Terry (Athlete, Baseball Player)
3010 Wisteria Ln
Northport, AL 35473-8165, USA

Pearson-Tesseine, Dolly (Baseball Player)
1510A Canterbury Trl
Mount Pleasant, MI 48858-4002, USA

Pease, Patsy (Actor)
10710 Walnut Springs Dr Apt 1615
Charlotte, NC 28277-0731

Peatros, Maurice (Athlete, Baseball Player)
Homestead Grays
8633 Copper Mine Ave
Las Vegas, NV 89129-7630, USA

Peavy, Jake (Athlete, Baseball Player)
927 County Road 4
Catherine, AL 36728-3516, USA

Peay, Francis (Athlete, Football Player)
7351 Overbrook Dr
Saint Louis, MO 63121-2533, USA

Peca, Michael (Athlete, Hockey Player)
5152 Rockledge Dr
Clarence, NY 14031-2442

Peca, Michael (Athlete, Hockey Player)
Buffalo Junior Sabres
1615 Amherst Manor Dr
Buffalo, NY 14221-2040

Peck, Austin (Actor)
The Michael Bruno Group Los Angeles
13576 Cheltenham Dr
Sherman Oaks, CA 91423-4818, USA

Peck, Ethan (Actor)
c/o Stephanie Ritz *William Morris Endeavor (LA)*
9601 Wilshire Blvd
Beverly Hills, CA 90210-5213, USA

Peck, J Eddie (Actor)
28354 Linda Vista St
Canyon Country, CA 91387-3198, USA

Peck, Josh (Actor)
c/o Sam Maydew *The Collective*
8383 Wilshire Blvd Ste 1050
Beverly Hills, CA 90211-2415, USA

Peck, Richard (Writer)
c/o Staff Member *Scholastic Entertainment*
557 Broadway
New York, NY 10012-3962, USA

Peck, Tom (Race Car Driver)
Peckie's Auto Body Repair
417 E North St
Mc Connellsburg, PA 17233-1141, USA

Pecota, Bill (Athlete, Baseball Player)
332 NE Warrington Ct
Lees Summit, MO 64064-1605, USA

Pedersen, Allen (Athlete, Hockey Player)
2261 Fieldcrest Dr
Colorado Springs, CO 80921-4000, USA

Pedersen, Monica (Designer, Television Host)
c/o Staff Member *HGTV*
9721 Sherrill Blvd
Knoxville, TN 37932-3330, USA

Pedersen, Tilly Scott (Actor)
c/o George Englund *George Englund Jr Management*
11661 San Vicente Blvd Ste 609
Los Angeles, CA 90049-5114, USA

Pederson, Barry (Athlete, Hockey Player)
16 Cutting Rd
Swampscott, MA 01907-1602, USA

Pederson, Barry (Athlete, Hockey Player)
Boston Bruins
100 Legends Way Ste 250
Boston, MA 02114-1389

Pederson, Mark (Athlete, Hockey Player)
151 Equestrian Ln
Kalispell, MT 59901-8050

Pederson, Stu (Athlete, Baseball Player)
45 Alannah Ct
Palo Alto, CA 94303-3009, USA

Pederson, Tom (Athlete, Hockey Player)
3140 Bay Rd
Redwood City, CA 94063-3907

Pedrad, Nasim (Comedian)
c/o Michael Rotenberg *3 Arts Entertainment (LA)*
9460 Wilshire Blvd Fl 7
Beverly Hills, CA 90212-2713, USA

Pedre, Jorge (Athlete, Baseball Player)
7894 Bellflower Dr
Buena Park, CA 90620, USA

Pedregon, Frank (Race Car Driver)
6174 Cabernet Pl
Rancho Cucamonga, CA 91737-6968, USA

Pedriaue, Al (Athlete, Baseball Player)
10382 E Oakbrook St
Tucson, AZ 85747-5967, USA

Pedrigue, Al (Athlete, Baseball Player)
10382 E Oakbrook St
Tucson, AZ 85747-5967, USA

Pedrique, Al (Athlete, Baseball Player, Coach)
10382 E Oakbrook St
Tucson, AZ 85747-5967, USA

Pedroia, Dustin (Athlete, Baseball Player)
c/o Seth Levinson *A.C.E.S*
188 Montague St Fl 6
Brooklyn, NY 11201-3609, USA

Peebles, Danny (Athlete, Football Player)
12205 Fieldmist Dr
Raleigh, NC 27614-7539, USA

Peek, Richard (Athlete, Basketball Player)
15631 State Highway 31 W
Tyler, TX 75709-3335, USA

Peeler, Anthony (Athlete, Basketball Player)
4502 E 48th St
Kansas City, MO 64130-2231, USA

Peeples, George (Athlete, Basketball Player)
1032 Loma Lisa Ln
Arcadia, CA 91006-2218, USA

Peeples, Nathaniel (Athlete, Baseball Player)
Kansas City Monarchs
536 Lipford St
Memphis, TN 38112-2934, USA

Peeples, Nia (Actor)
c/o Staff Member *Stone Manners Salners Agency (LA)*
6100 Wilshire Blvd Ste 1500
Los Angeles, CA 90048-5110, USA

Peet, Amanda (Actor)
1228 N Wetherly Dr
Los Angeles, CA 90069-1816, USA

Peet, Lizzie (Actor)
4623 Ambrose Ave Apt 1
Los Angeles, CA 90027-1935, USA

Peete, Calvin (Golfer)
128 Garden Gate Dr
Ponte Vedra Beach, FL 32082-3668, USA

Peete, Rodney (Athlete, Football Player, Television Host)
5056 Chicopee Ave
Encino, CA 91316-2508, USA

Peeters, Pete (Athlete, Hockey Player)
2695 E Katella Ave
Anaheim, CA 92806-5904

Peets, Brian (Athlete, Football Player)
5361 Auburn Blvd
Sacramento, CA 95841-2805, USA

Pegler, Luke (Actor)
c/o Will Ward *ROAR (LA)*
9701 Wilshire Blvd Fl 8
Beverly Hills, CA 90212-2008, USA

Pegram, Erric (Athlete, Football Player)
2030 Chicopee Ave
Encino, CA 91316, USA

Peguero, Julio (Athlete, Baseball Player)
1500 State Road 1
Socorro, NM 87801-5093, USA

Pegues, Steve (Athlete, Baseball Player)
362 Presidents Dr
Pontotoc, MS 38863-2322, USA

Peguese, Willis (Athlete, Football Player)
Hialeah-Miami Lakes High School
7977 W 12th Ave
Hialeah, FL 33014-3595, USA

Peil, Mary Beth (Actor)
c/o Lindsay Porter *Gersh (NY)*
41 Madison Ave
New York, NY 10010-2202, USA

Peirce, Kimberly (Director, Producer, Writer)
c/o Staff Member *Creative Artists Agency (CAA-LA)*
2000 Avenue of the Stars Ste 100
Los Angeles, CA 90067-4705, USA

Peirsol, Aaron (Athlete, Olympic Athlete, Swimmer)
1748 Plaza Del Norte
Newport Beach, CA 92661-1416, USA

Peirson, John (Athlete, Hockey Player)
3 Steepletree Ln
Wayland, MA 01778-3912

Peizerat, Gwendal (Figure Skater)
c/o Staff Member *Champions on Ice*
3500 American Blvd W Ste 190
Minneapolis, MN 55431-4431, USA

Pelaez, Alex (Athlete, Baseball Player)
1501 Oleander Ave
Chula Vista, CA 91911-5623, USA

Peldon, Ashley (Actor)
c/o Pamela Wagner *Metropolitan (MTA)*
4526 Wilshire Blvd
Los Angeles, CA 90010-3801, USA

Peldon, Courtney (Actor)
c/o Steve Rodriguez *McGowan Management*
8733 W Sunset Blvd Ste 103
West Hollywood, CA 90069-2241, USA

Pelfrey, Mike (Athlete, Baseball Player)
2336 N Rosemont Cir
Wichita, KS 67228-8074, USA

Pelfrey, Raymond (Athlete, Football Player)
1301 Summit St
Portsmouth, OH 45662-3719, USA

Peli, Oren (Director)
c/o Michael Esola *William Morris Endeavor (LA)*
9601 Wilshire Blvd
Beverly Hills, CA 90210-5213, USA

Pelikan, Lisa (Actor)
c/o Peter Giagni *Premier Talent Group*
1749 N Sycamore Ave Apt 15
Los Angeles, CA 90028-8612, USA

Pell, Claybourne (Ex-Senator, Senator)
45 Ledge Rd
Newport, RI 02840-4257, USA

Pellegrini, Robert
1731 Route 9 Unit 97
Ocean View, NJ 08230-1388

Pellegrino, Mark (Actor)
c/o Mary Ellen Mulcahy *Framework Entertainment (LA)*
9057 Nemo St Ste C
West Hollywood, CA 90069-5511, USA

Pellerin, Scott (Athlete, Hockey Player)
10 Dunraven Rd
Windham, NH 03087-1263

Pelletier, Jean-Marc (Athlete, Hockey Player)
83 Canterbury Cir
East Longmeadow, MA 01028-5705

Pelletier, Marcel (Athlete, Hockey Player)
2129 Old Marlton Pike
Cherry Hill, NJ 08003-1302

Pelley, Scott (Correspondent, Journalist)
5 Peach Hill Rd
Darien, CT 06820-2821, USA

Pellington, Mark (Director, Producer)
c/o Staff Member *3 Arts Entertainment (LA)*
9460 Wilshire Blvd Fl 7
Beverly Hills, CA 90212-2713, USA

Pellow, Kit (Athlete, Baseball Player)
1229 W Bluegrass Rd
Nixa, MO 65714-8058, USA

Pelluer, Steve (Athlete, Football Player)
1306 177th Ave NE
Bellevue, WA 98008-3208, USA

Peloffy, Andre (Athlete, Hockey Player)
PO Box 2382
Morehead City, NC 28557-2382

Pelosi, Nancy (Congressman, Politician)
235 Cannon Hob
Washington, DC 20515-1314, USA

Pelphrey, Tom (Actor)
c/o Cyrena Esposito *Cyrena Esposito Management*
437 W 48th St Apt D
New York, NY 10036-1285, USA

Peltier, Dan (Athlete, Baseball Player)
1643 Oak Hill Dr
Hastings, MN 55033-5000, USA

Peltier, Leonard (Writer)
c/o Staff Member *St Martins Press*
175 5th Ave Ste 400
Publicity Dept
New York, NY 10010-7848, USA

Peltonen, Ville (Athlete, Hockey Player)
12210 NW 71st St
Parkland, FL 33076-4601, USA

Peltz, Nicola (Actor)
c/o Cynthia Pett-Dante *Brillstein Entertainment Partners (LA)*
9150 Wilshire Blvd Ste 350
Beverly Hills, CA 90212-3453, USA

Peluce, Meeno (Actor)
2445 Metzler Dr
Los Angeles, CA 90031-2830, USA

The Celebrity Black Book 2015

Peluso, Mike (Athlete, Hockey Player)
3456 Fairfax Ln
Saint Paul, MN 55129-9342

Peluso, Mike (Athlete, Hockey Player)
6111 Magnolia Dr
Bismarck, ND 58503-9311

Pelzer, Dave (Writer)
PO Box 131
The Sea Ranch, CA 95497-0131

Pember, Dave (Athlete, Baseball Player)
1013 Sandy Springs Rd NW
Rd NW
Huntsville, AL 35806-2411, USA

Pemberton, Brock (Athlete, Baseball Player)
1402 N Elm St
Owasso, OK 74055-4926, USA

Pemberton, Rudy (Athlete, Baseball Player)
PO Box 602
Imperial, PA 15126-0602, USA

Pena, Alejandro (Athlete, Baseball Player)
PO Box 4414
Suwanee, GA 30024-9002, USA

Pena, Brayan (Athlete, Baseball Player)
14217 SW 102nd St
Miami, FL 33186-6970, USA

Pena, Carlos (Athlete, Baseball Player)
8157 Via Bella Notte
Orlando, FL 32836-7705, USA

Pena, Carlos (Musician)
c/o Glenn Hughes III *Gem Entertainment Group*
10920 Wilshire Blvd Ste 150
Los Angeles, CA 90024-3990, USA

Peña, Elizabeth (Actor, Director)
c/o Staff Member *Rugolo Entertainment*
195 S Beverly Dr Ste 400
Beverly Hills, CA 90212-3044, USA

Pena, Federico (Politician)
362 Detroit St Unit A
Denver, CO 80206-4377, USA

Pena, Federico Secy
3517 Sterling Ave
Alexandria, VA 22304-1834, USA

Pena, Hipolito (Athlete, Baseball Player)
11412 Park Blvd
Seminole, FL 33772-4620, USA

Pena, Jim (Athlete, Baseball Player)
3228 E Silverwood Dr
Phoenix, AZ 85048-7257, USA

Pena, Juan (Athlete, Baseball Player)
4940 NW 179th St
Miami Gardens, FL 33055-3244, USA

Pena, Michael (Actor)
c/o Eric Kranzler *Management 360*
9111 Wilshire Blvd
Beverly Hills, CA 90210-5508, USA

Pena, Orlando (Athlete, Baseball Player)
1750 W 46th St Apt 416
Hialeah, FL 33012-2849, USA

Pena, Ramiro (Athlete, Baseball Player)
c/o Team Member *New York Yankees*
Yankee Stadium
161st St & River Ave
Bronx, NY 10451, USA

Pena, Robert (Athlete, Football Player)
77 John Parker Rd
East Falmouth, MA 02536-5116, USA

Pena, Tony (Athlete, Baseball Player, Coach)
New York Yankees
161st Street & River Ave
Attn: Coaching Staff
Bronx, NY 10451, USA

Pena, Willy Mo (Athlete, Baseball Player)
27520 Breakers Dr
Wesley Chapel, FL 33544-6667, USA

Pena, Wily Mo (Athlete, Baseball Player)
27520 Breakers Dr
Wesley Chapel, FL 33544-6667, USA

Penaranda, Jairo (Athlete, Football Player)
2023 Lloyd Ctr
Portland, OR 97232-1314, USA

PenaVega, Alexa (Actor)
c/o John Carrabino *John Carrabino Management*
5900 Wilshire Blvd Ste 406
Los Angeles, CA 90036-5015, USA

Pence, Hunter (Athlete, Baseball Player)
25344 Fm 2100 RR
Huffman, TX 77336-4102, USA

Pence, Josh (Actor)
c/o Sandra Chang *Anonymous Content (LA)*
3532 Hayden Ave
Culver City, CA 90232-2413, USA

Pence, Mike (Congressman, Politician)
100 Cannon Hob
Washington, DC 20515-2802, USA

Pence, Mike (Governor, Politician)
Office of the Governor
200 W Washington St Ste 206
Indianapolis, IN 46204-2731, USA

Penchion, Bob (Athlete, Football Player)
315 County Road 266
Town Creek, AL 35672-3939, USA

Pender, Jerry Lee (Athlete, Basketball Player)
PO Box 6073
Wilson, NC 27894-6073, USA

Pender, Mel (Athlete, Olympic Athlete, Track Athlete)
2330 Goodwood Blvd SE
Smyrna, GA 30080-8207, USA

Pendleton, Austin (Actor)
155 E 76th St
New York, NY 10021-2810

Pendleton, Karen (Actor)
7328 N Fruit Ave
Fresno, CA 93711-0717, USA

Pendleton, Terry (Athlete, Baseball Player)
2998 Grey Moss Pass
Duluth, GA 30097, USA

Penfold, James (Model)
c/o Staff Member *DNA Model Management*
555 W 25th St Fl 6
New York, NY 10001-5542, USA

Penghlis, Thaao (Actor)
c/o Christopher Barrett *Metropolitan (MTA)*
4526 Wilshire Blvd
Los Angeles, CA 90010-3801, USA

Penguins, The
24210 E East Fork Rd Spc 9
Azusa, CA 91702-6249

Penhaligon, Susan (Actor)
109 Jermyn St
London, EN SW1

Penhall, Bruce (Race Car Driver)
PO Box 5625
Norco, CA 92860-8021, USA

Peniche, Kari Ann (Actor)
c/o Ted Maier *Maier Management*
11870 Santa Monica Blvd Ste 106
Los Angeles, CA 90025-5276, USA

Penick, Trevor (Musician)
Trans Continental Records
7380 W Sand Lake Rd # 350
Orlando, FL 32819-5248, USA

Penikett, Tahmoh (Actor)
c/o Robert Stein *Robert Stein Management*
PO Box 3797
Beverly Hills, CA 90212-0797, USA

Peniston, CeCe (Musician)
c/o Staff Member *Diva Central Inc*
7510 W Sunset Blvd Ste 1445
Los Angeles, CA 90046-3408, USA

Peniston, Ce Ce (Musician)
250 W 57th St # 821
New York, NY 10107-0001

Penn, Chris (Athlete, Football Player)
PO Box 123
S Coffeyville, OK 74072-0123, USA

Penn, Dylan (Actor)
c/o Heather Nunn *Anonymous Content (LA)*
3532 Hayden Ave
Culver City, CA 90232-2413, USA

Penn, Hayden (Athlete, Baseball Player)
PO Box 2364
Walnut Creek, CA 94595-0364, USA

Penn, Jesse (Athlete, Football Player)
8420 Wildcreek Dr
Plano, TX 75025-4150, USA

Penn, Kal (Actor, Producer)
c/o Daniel Spilo *Industry Entertainment*
955 Carrillo Dr Ste 300
Los Angeles, CA 90048-5400, USA

Penn, Michael (Musician)
c/o Staff Member *Kraft-Engel Management*
15233 Ventura Blvd Ste 200
Sherman Oaks, CA 91403-2244, USA

Penn, Sean (Actor, Director)
28965 Grayfox St
Malibu, CA 90265-4254, USA

Penn, Shannon (Athlete, Baseball Player)
1548 Jonathan Ave # 2
Cincinnati, OH 45207-1449, USA

Penna, Angel (Horse Racer)
17 Chestnut H
Roslyn, NY 11576, USA

Penn & Teller (Comedian, Magician)
c/o Glenn Alai *Star Price Productions*
3555 W Reno Ave Ste L
Las Vegas, NV 89118-1609, USA

Pennell, Larry
15516 W Sunset Blvd Apt 101
Pacific Palisades, CA 90272-3542

Penner, Jonathan (Actor)
c/o Staff Member *Modus Entertainment*
8569 Holloway Dr Apt 1
West Hollywood, CA 90069-6918, USA

Penney, Rick
1901 75th St SE
Everett, WA 98203-6843, USA

Penniman, Michael (Mika) (Musician)
c/o Jbeau Lewis *Creative Artists Agency (CAA-LA)*
2000 Avenue of the Stars Ste 100
Los Angeles, CA 90067-4705, USA

Penniman, Micheal (Mika) (Musician)
c/o Jbeau Lewis *Creative Artists Agency (CAA-LA)*
2000 Avenue of the Stars Ste 100
Los Angeles, CA 90067-4705, USA

Pennington, Ann (Actor)
701 N Oakhurst Dr
Beverly Hills, CA 90210-3532

Pennington, Art (Athlete, Baseball Player)
Chicago American Giants
922 5th St SE Apt E5
Cedar Rapids, IA 52401-2440, USA

Pennington, Brad (Athlete, Baseball Player)
7220 E State Road 160
Salem, IN 47167-7856, USA

Pennington, Chad (Athlete, Football Player)
c/o Tom Condon *CAA (St. Louis)*
222 S Central Ave Ste 1008
Saint Louis, MO 63105-3509, USA

Pennington, Cliff (Athlete, Hockey Player)
9960 5th St N Apt 203
Saint Petersburg, FL 33702-2200

Pennington, Janice (Actor, Model)
PO Box 11402
Beverly Hills, CA 90213-4402, USA

Pennington, Julia
PO Box 5617
Beverly Hills, CA 90209-5617

Pennington, T Durwood (Athlete, Football Player)
480 Peninsula Rd
Gainesville, GA 30506-1705, USA

Pennington, Ty (Reality Star, Television Host)
2554 Lincoln Blvd # 660
Venice, CA 90291-5043, USA

Pennison, Jay (Athlete, Football Player)
3007 W Autumn Run Cir
Sugar Land, TX 77479-2624, USA

Pennock, Chris (Actor)
25150 1/2 Malibu Rd
Malibu, CA 90265-4639, USA

Pennv, Brad (Athlete, Baseball Player)
25071 Abercrombie Ln
Calabasas, CA 91302-2360, USA

Penny, Brad (Athlete, Baseball Player)
25071 Abercrombie Ln
Calabasas, CA 91302-2360, USA

Penny, Joe (Actor)
c/o Staff Member *Geddes Agency, The*
1203 Greenacre Ave
West Hollywood, CA 90046-5707, USA

Penny, Roger P (Business Person)
Bethlehem Steel
1170 8th Ave
Bethlehem, PA 18018-2255, USA

Penny, Sudney (Actor)
Baker/Winokur/Ryder
9100 Wilshire Blvd Ste 600
Beverly Hills, CA 90212-3494, USA

Penny, Sydney (Actor)
c/o Bob McGowan *McGowan Management*
8733 W Sunset Blvd Ste 103
West Hollywood, CA 90069-2241, USA

Pennyfeather, Will (Athlete, Baseball Player)
333 Rector St Apt 6D
Perth Amboy, NJ 08861-4277, USA

Penny's
3220 Altura Ave Apt 106
La Crescenta, CA 91214-3304

Pennywell, Carlos (Athlete, Football Player)
3729 Clover Dr
Arcadia, LA 71001-3628, USA

Pennywell, Robert (Athlete, Football Player)
1523 Staring Ln
Baton Rouge, LA 70810-1458, USA

Penot, Jacques (Actor)
9 Rue De L Isly
Paris, FR F-750

Penrose, Craig R (Athlete, Football Player)
1609 Camino Way
Woodland, CA 95695-5517, USA

Penske, Roger (Race Car Driver)
Penske Racing
2555 S Telegraph Rd
Bloomfield Hills, MI 48302-0974, USA

Pensky, Robert (Writer)
236 Bay State Rd Attn Dept
Boston, MA 02215-1403, USA

Pentecost, Del (Actor)
c/o Staff Member *Paradigm (LA)*
360 N Crescent Dr
North Bldg
Beverly Hills, CA 90210-4874, USA

Penthouse Pets
277 Park Ave
New York, NY 10172-0003

Pentland, Jeff (Athlete, Baseball Player)
1032 N Cherry
Mesa, AZ 85201-3208, USA

Pentz, Gene (Athlete, Baseball Player)
207 Rainbow Dr
Johnstown, PA 15904-2253, USA

People, Village (Music Group, Musician)
c/o Staff Member *William Morris Endeavor (LA)*
9601 Wilshire Blvd
Beverly Hills, CA 90210-5213, USA

Pepin, Jacques (Chef)
214 Durham Rd
Madison, CT 06443-2451, USA

Pepitone, Joe (Athlete, Baseball Player)
32 Lois Ln
Farmingdale, NY 11735-6003, USA

Peplowski, Mike (Athlete, Basketball Player)
4110 Harris Rd
Williamston, MI 48895-9204, USA

Peppas, June (Athlete, Baseball Player)
1700 NE Indian River Dr Apt 302
Jensen Beach, FL 34957-5860, USA

Pepper, Barry (Actor)
c/o Nancy Mccarty Iannios *Nancy Iannois Public Relations*
PO Box 430
Signal Mountain, TN 37377-0430, USA

Pepper, Cynthia (Actor)
219 Friendly Ct
Henderson, NV 89052-5660

Pepper, Don (Athlete, Baseball Player)
7 Beckenham Ln
Greenville, SC 29609-6023, USA

Pepper, Dottie (Golfer)
108 Micco Cir
Jupiter, FL 33458-7730, USA

Pepper, Laurin (Athlete, Baseball Player)
8932 Davis St
Ocean Springs, MS 39564-3633, USA

Peppers, Julius (Athlete, Football Player)
173 Rehoboth Ln
Mooresville, NC 28117-6711, USA

Peppler, Mary Jo (Athlete, Volleyball Player)
Bridge Volleyball Club
2390 Boswell Rd Ste 400
Chula Vista, CA 91914-3541, USA

Perabo, Piper (Actor)
c/o Tina Thor *TMT Entertainment Group*
648 Broadway # 1002
New York, NY 10012-2348, USA

Peralta, Jhonny (Athlete, Baseball Player)
12970 Woodlark Ln
Saint Louis, MO 63131-1314, USA

Peranoski, Ron (Baseball Player)
Los Angeles Dodgers
4800 Highway A1a Apt 307
Vero Beach, FL 32963-1230, USA

Perayra, Marianela (Television Host)
c/o Mike Esterman *Esterman.Com, LLC*
Prefers to be contacted via email
Baltimore, MD XXXXX, USA

Percival, Mac (Athlete, Football Player)
6710 Flowermound Dr
Sugar Land, TX 77479-6000, USA

Percival, Troy E (Athlete, Baseball Player)
2127 Century Ave
Riverside, CA 92506-4653, USA

Perconte, Jack (Athlete, Baseball Player)
6197 Hinterlong Ct
Lisle, IL 60532-2818, USA

Perdue, Sonny (Ex-Governor, Politician)
217 Houston Dr
Bonaire, GA 31005, USA

Perdue, Will (Athlete, Basketball Player)
6310 Innisbrook Dr
Prospect, KY 40059-9223, USA

Peregrym, Missy (Actor)
c/o Jai Khanna *Brillstein Entertainment Partners (LA)*
9150 Wilshire Blvd Ste 350
Beverly Hills, CA 90212-3453, USA

Perelman, Ronald O (Business Person)
MacAndrews & Forbes
35 E 62nd St
New York, NY 10065-8014, USA

Perelman, Vadim (Director)
c/o Simon Millar *Rumble Media*
1620 Broadway Ste C
Santa Monica, CA 90404-2777, USA

Peretti, Jonah (Business Person)
BuzzFeed, Inc
200 5th Ave Ste 804
New York, NY 10010-3087, USA

Perez, Atanasio (Athlete, Baseball Player)
1717 N Bayshore Dr
Miami, FL 33132-1180, USA

Perez, Chris (Musician)
Big FD Entertainment
301 Arizona Ave Ste 200
Santa Monica, CA 90401-1364, USA

Perez, Danny (Athlete, Baseball Player)
10511 Cuesta Brava Ln
El Paso, TX 79935-2210, USA

Perez, Eddie (Athlete, Baseball Player)
615 Rose Creek Cir
Duluth, GA 30097-7895, USA

Perez, Eduardo (Athlete, Baseball Player)
113 Calle Las Flores
San Juan, PR 00911-2298, USA

Perez, George (Athlete, Baseball Player)
711 S Old Stage Rd
Cave Junction, OR 97523-9362, USA

Perez, Hugo (Soccer Player)
22018 Newbridge Dr
Lake Forest, CA 92630-6511, USA

Perez, Luiz (Louie) (Musician)
Gold Mountain
3575 Cahuenga Blvd W Ste 450
Los Angeles, CA 90068-1364, USA

Perez, Manny (Actor, Producer, Writer)
c/o Scott Zimmerman *Evolution Entertainment (LA)*
901 N Highland Ave
Los Angeles, CA 90038-2412, USA

Perez, Marty (Athlete, Baseball Player)
30 Willowick Dr
Lithonia, GA 30038-1722, USA

Perez, Mike (Athlete, Baseball Player)
10538 Hc 1
Penuelas, PR 00624-9890, USA

Perez, Neifi (Athlete, Baseball Player)
43515 Blacksmith Sq Apt 106
Ashburn, VA 20147-4637, USA

Perez, Odalis A (Baseball Player)
Los Angeles Dodgers
1000 Elysian Park Ave
Stadium
Los Angeles, CA 90012-1112, USA

Perez, Oliver (Baseball Player)
c/o Scott Boras *Boras Corporation*
3 San Joaquin Plz Ste 100
Newport Beach, CA 92660-5944, USA

Perez, Rosie (Actor, Producer)
c/o Jon Rubinstein *Authentic Talent and Literary Management*
20 Jay St Ste M17
Brooklyn, NY 11201-8300, USA

Perez, Scott (Cartoonist)
DC Comics
1700 Broadway Fl 6
New York, NY 10019-5905, USA

Perez, Timothy Paul (Actor)
Badgley Connor Talent
9229 W Sunset Blvd Ste 311
West Hollywood, CA 90069-3403, USA

Perez, Tony (Athlete, Baseball Player, Coach)
1717 N Bayshore Dr # A-2735
Miami, FL 33132-1180, USA

Perez, Yorkis (Athlete, Baseball Player)
3303 Potter St
Philadelphia, PA 19134-1404, USA

Perez-Brown, Maria (Producer)
c/o Staff Member *William Morris Endeavor (LA)*
9601 Wilshire Blvd
Beverly Hills, CA 90210-5213, USA

Perezchica, Tony (Athlete, Baseball Player)
79220 Victoria Dr
La Quinta, CA 92253-4274, USA

Perez de Tagle, Anna Maria (Actor)
c/o Beverly Strong *Strong Management*
9350 Wilshire Blvd Ste 224
Beverly Hills, CA 90212-3204, USA

Perez de Tagle, Anna Marie (Actor)
c/o Beverly Strong *Strong Management*
9350 Wilshire Blvd Ste 224
Beverly Hills, CA 90212-3204, USA

Perez Limon, Iyari (Actor)
c/o Mitchell Stubbs *Mitchell K Stubbs & Assoc (MKS)*
8675 Washington Blvd Ste 203
Culver City, CA 90232-7486, USA

Pergine, John (Athlete, Football Player)
5 Jody Dr
Plymouth Meeting, PA 19462-2625, USA

Perishers, The (Music Group)
c/o Staff Member *Paradigm (Monterey)*
404 W Franklin St
Monterey, CA 93940-2303, USA

Perisho, Matt (Athlete, Baseball Player)
728 W Aloe Pl
Chandler, AZ 85248-4402, USA

Perkins, Broderick (Athlete, Baseball Player)
5367 San Vincente Blvd
Apt 237
Spring Valley, CA 91977, USA

Perkins, Bruce (Athlete, Football Player)
19014 E Ryan Rd
Queen Creek, AZ 85142-6877, USA

Perkins, Cecil (Athlete, Baseball Player)
711 Cushwa Rd
Martinsburg, WV 25403-1228, USA

Perkins, Dan (Athlete, Baseball Player)
1509 Kenan St NW
Wilson, NC 27893-2252, USA

Perkins, Elivs (Musician)
c/o Staff Member *Paradigm (Monterey)*
404 W Franklin St
Monterey, CA 93940-2303, USA

Perkins, Elizabeth (Actor)
c/o Leslie Siebert *Gersh (LA)*
9465 Wilshire Blvd Ste 600
Beverly Hills, CA 90212-2605, USA

Perkins, Glen (Athlete, Baseball Player)
19775 Jersey Ave
Lakeville, MN 55044-9435, USA

Perkins, John (Writer)
c/o Paul Fedorko *Trident Media Group LLC*
41 Madison Ave Fl 36
New York, NY 10010-2257, USA

Perkins, Kathleen Rose (Actor)
c/o Devon Jackson *Trademark Talent*
144 S Beverly Dr Ste 404
Beverly Hills, CA 90212-3022, USA

Perkins, Kendrick (Athlete, Basketball Player)
8522 Haven Trl # 1
Tomball, TX 77375-2650, USA

Perkins, Lucian (Journalist, Photographer)
3103 17th St NW
Washington, DC 20010-2701, USA

Perkins, Millie (Actor)
2511 Canyon Dr
Los Angeles, CA 90068-2415, USA

Perkins, Oz
7720 W Sunset Blvd
Los Angeles, CA 90046-3962

Perkins, Sam (Athlete, Basketball Player)
14901 Bellbrook Dr
Dallas, TX 75254-7673, USA

Perkins, Tex (Musician)
Stack/Polydor Records
70 Universal City Plz
Universal City, CA 91608-1011, USA

Perkins, Warren (Athlete, Basketball
Player)
717 Fairfield Ave
Gretna, LA 70056-7625, USA

Perkins, W Ray (Athlete, Coach, Football
Coach, Football Player)
57 Honors Ln
Hattiesburg, MS 39402-7100, USA

Perkoff, Gerald T (Doctor)
1235 Alimingo Dr
Indianapolis, IN 46260-4054, USA

Perkowski, Harry (Athlete, Baseball
Player)
211 McGinnis St
Beckley, WV 25801-5725, USA

Perks, Craig (Golfer)
321 Thibodeaux Dr
Lafayette, LA 70503-4444, USA

Perl, Frank J (Cinematographer)
5020 Biloxi Ave
North Hollywood, CA 91601-4140, USA

Perles, George (Athlete, Football Coach,
Football Player)
6153 W Longview Dr
East Lansing, MI 48823-9739, USA

Perlich, Max (Actor)
c/o Staff Member *Metropolitan (MTA)*
4526 Wilshire Blvd
Los Angeles, CA 90010-3801, USA

Perlick-Keating, Edythe (Baseball Player)
3051 S Palm Aire Dr Bldg 34
Pompano Beach, FL 33069-4277, USA

Perlman, Jon (Athlete, Baseball Player)
3225 Bryn Mawr Dr
Dallas, TX 75225-7646, USA

Perlman, Lawrence (Business Person)
Ceridian Corp
3311 E Old Shakopee Rd
Minneapolis, MN 55425-1640, USA

Perlman, Phil
439 S Catalina Ave Apt 102
Pasadena, CA 91106-3343

Perlman, Rhea (Actor, Producer)
8665 Burton Way Apt 507
Los Angeles, CA 90048-3995, USA

Perlman, Ron (Actor)
4025 Cromwell Ave
Los Angeles, CA 90027-1351, USA

Perlmutter, Ed (Congressman, Politician)
1221 Longworth Hob
Washington, DC 20515-0517, USA

Perlozzo, Sam (Athlete, Baseball Player,
Coach)
18101 Emerald Bay St
Tampa, FL 33647-3316, USA

Pernandez, Mervyn (Athlete, Football
Player)
1546 Morning Star Dr
Morgan Hill, CA 95037-9033, USA

Pernice Jr, Tom (Golfer)
c/o Staff Member *Pro Golfers Association
(PGA) Tour*
112 Tpc Blvd
Ponte Vedra Beach, FL 32082, USA

Perot, Henry Ross (Business Person)
c/o Staff Member *Perot Group*
2300 W Plano Pkwy
Plano, TX 75075-8427, USA

Perot, Pete (Athlete, Football Player)
2401 Hillside Rd
Ruston, LA 71270-2093, USA

Perot Jr, Henry Ross (Business Person)
c/o Staff Member *Perot Group*
2300 W Plano Pkwy
Plano, TX 75075-8427, USA

Perranoski, Ron (Athlete, Baseball Player)
4800 Highway A1A Apt 307
Vero Beach, FL 32963-1230, USA

Perreau, Gigi (Actor)
18411 Hatteras St Unit 120
Tarzana, CA 91356-1962, USA

Perreault, Gilbert (Gil) (Athlete, Hockey
Player)
Buffalo Sabres
1 Seymour H Knox III Plz Ste 1
Buffalo, NY 14203-3096

Perret, Craig (Horse Racer)
4149 Palomar Blvd
Lexington, KY 40513-1316, USA

Perretta, Ralph (Athlete, Football Player)
1305 Calle Scott
Encinitas, CA 92024-5532, USA

Perrette, Pauley (Actor)
c/o Steven Jang *SDB Partners Inc*
315 S Beverly Dr Ste 411
Beverly Hills, CA 90212-4301, USA

Perriman, Brett (Athlete, Football Player)
PO Box 83337
Conyers, GA 30013-8019, USA

Perrin, Benny (Athlete, Football Player)
28646 Olde Stone Rd NW
Madison, AL 35756-4257, USA

Perrin, Eric (Athlete, Hockey Player)
408 Colemans Run
Woodstock, GA 30188-5328

Perrin, Lonnie (Athlete, Football Player)
7809 Green St
Clinton, MD 20735-1973, USA

Perrin, Philippe (Astronaut)
11923 Mighty Redwood Dr
Houston, TX 77059-5542, USA

Perrin, Philippe Colonel (Astronaut)
11923 Mighty Redwood Dr
Houston, TX 77059-5542, USA

Perrine, Valerie (Actor)
c/o Lynda Bensky *Bensky Entertainment*
15021 Ventura Blvd Ste 343
Sherman Oaks, CA 91403-2442, USA

Perrineau Jr, Harold (Actor, Producer)
c/o Stacy Abrams *Abrams Entertainment*
5225 Wilshire Blvd Ste 515
Los Angeles, CA 90036-4349, USA

Perron, Jean (Coach)
5 Thomas Mellon Cir
San Francisco, CA 94134-2501, USA

Perrotta, Tom (Writer)
Saint Martin's Press
175 5th Ave Ste 400
New York, NY 10010-7848, USA

Perry, Barbara
6926 La Presa Dr
Los Angeles, CA 90068-3103

Perry, Barry W (Business Person)
Engelhard Corp
101 Wood Ave S
Iselin, NJ 08830-2749, USA

Perry, Chan (Athlete, Baseball Player)
788 NE County Road 353
Mayo, FL 32066-5450, USA

Perry, Chris (Athlete, Football Player)
c/o Eugene Parker *Maximum Sports
Management*
6435 W Jefferson Blvd # 197
Fort Wayne, IN 46804-6203, USA

Perry, Chris (Athlete, Golfer)
170 Valley Run Dr
Powell, OH 43065-9454, USA

Perry, Darren (Athlete, Football Player)
6451 Pinehurst Ln
Mason, OH 45040-2051, USA

Perry, Ed (Athlete, Football Player)
1583 SW 161st Ave
Pembroke Pines, FL 33027-5140, USA

Perry, Elliott (Athlete, Basketball Player)
3306 Darby Dan Cv
Germantown, TN 38138-8260, USA

Perry, Felton (Actor)
PO Box 931359
Los Angeles, CA 90093-1359, USA

Perry, Gaylord (Athlete, Baseball Player)
PO Box 489
Spruce Pine, NC 28777-0489, USA

Perry, Gerald (Athlete, Baseball Player)
1348 Waterford Green Close
Marietta, GA 30068-2919, USA

Perry, Gerald (Athlete, Football Player)
2940 Dell Dr
Columbia, SC 29209-4906, USA

Perry, Gerald E (Athlete, Football Player)
336 5th St
Manhattan Beach, CA 90266-5712, USA

Perry, Herb (Athlete, Baseball Player)
978 N Fletcher Ave
Mayo, FL 32066-4506, USA

Perry, Jeff (Actor)
c/o Staff Member *Steppenwolf Films*
813 Gaffield Pl
Evanston, IL 60201-2803, USA

Perry, Jim (Athlete, Baseball Player)
155 Printers Ln
New London, NC 28127-8104, USA

Perry, Joe (Musician, Songwriter)
1405 Tremont St
Duxbury, MA 02332-3711, USA

Perry, John Bennett (Actor)
Judy Schoen
606 N Larchmont Blvd Ste 309
Los Angeles, CA 90004-1309, USA

Perry, Katy (Musician)
7302 Mulholland Dr
Los Angeles, CA 90046-1342, USA

Perry, Kenny (Golfer)
418 Quail Ridge Rd
Franklin, KY 42134-9650, USA

Perry, Kimberly (Musician)
c/o Jake Basden *Big Machine Records*
1219 16th Ave S
Nashville, TN 37212-2901, USA

Perry, Leon (Athlete, Football Player)
RR 1 Box 195A
Gloster, MS 39638, USA

Perry, Linda (Musician, Producer)
Custard Records
9615 Brighton Way Ste 300
Beverly Hills, CA 90210-5118, USa

Perry, Luke (Actor)
453 S Las Palmas Ave
Los Angeles, CA 90020-4815, USA

Perry, Matthew (Actor)
25438 Malibu Rd
Malibu, CA 90265-4622, USA

Perry, Michael Dean (Athlete, Football
Player)
PO Box 221771
Charlotte, NC 28222-1771, USA

Perry, Neil (Musician)
c/o Jake Basden *Big Machine Records*
1219 16th Ave S
Nashville, TN 37212-2901, USA

Perry, Nick (Athlete, Football Player)
c/o Joe Panos *Athletes First, LLC*
23091 Mill Creek Dr
Laguna Hills, CA 92653-1258, USA

Perry, Pat (Athlete, Baseball Player)
1115 W Franklin St
Taylorville, IL 62568-2037, USA

Perry, Rachel (Actor)
c/o Staff Member *Envision Entertainment*
8840 Wilshire Blvd Fl 3
Beverly Hills, CA 90211-2606, USA

Perry, Richard (Musician, Producer)
1575 Carla Rdg
Beverly Hills, CA 90210-2501, USA

Perry, Rick (Governor, Politician)
1010 Colorado St
Austin, TX 78701-2334, USA

Perry, Rod (Athlete, Football Player)
PO Box 532551
Indianapolis, IN 46253-2551, USA

Perry, Ryan (Athlete, Baseball Player)
12360 N Feather Song Ave
Marana, AZ 85658-4697, USA

Perry, Scott (Athlete, Football Player)
2807 Graysby Ave
San Pedro, CA 90732-4607, USA

Perry, Steve (Director, Producer)
c/o Staff Member *DH1 Studios*
8730 W Sunset Blvd Fl 6
West Hollywood, CA 90069-2210, USA

Perry, Steve (Musician)
c/o Lee Phillips *Manatt Phelps & Phillips
LLP*
11355 W Olympic Blvd Fl 2
Los Angeles, CA 90064-1656, USA

Perry, Todd (Athlete, Football Player)
13805 Brittle Rd
Alpharetta, GA 30004-3577, USA

Perry, Tyler (Actor, Director, Producer, Writer)
4110 Paces Ferry Rd NW
Atlanta, GA 30327-3012, USA

Perry, Vernon (Athlete, Football Player)
PO Box 3
Jackson, MS 39205-0003, USA

Perry, William (Politician)
620 Sand Hill Rd Apt 421E
Palo Alto, CA 94304-2079, USA

Perry, William (Refrigerator) (Athlete, Football Player)
349 Kershaw St NE
Aiken, SC 29801-4432, USA

Perry, Wilmont (Athlete, Football Player)
1757 W River Rd
Franklinton, NC 27525-8293, USA

Perry, Yvonne (Actor)
As World Turns Show
524 W 57th St
Cbs-Tv
New York, NY 10019-2930, USA

Perryman, Jim (Athlete, Football Player)
2345 Southwood Dr
Pittsburgh, PA 15241-3344, USA

Perryman, Robert (Athlete, Football Player)
PO Box 8543
Haverhill, MA 01835-0985, USA

Persoff, Nahemiah (Actor)
5670 Moonstone Beach Dr
Cambria, CA 93428-2210, USA

Persoff, Nehemiah (Actor)
5670 Moonstone Beach Dr
Cambria, CA 93428-2210, USA

Person, Chuck (Athlete, Basketball Player)
2301 S Garfield Dr
Indianapolis, IN 46203-4218, USA

Person, Robert (Athlete, Baseball Player)
25 Bellerive Acres
Saint Louis, MO 63121-4328, USA

Person, Wesley (Athlete, Basketball Player)
PO Box 481
Brantley, AL 36009-0481, USA

Persons, Peter (Golfer)
1153 Saint Andrews Dr
Macon, GA 31210-4760, USA

Peruzovic, Josip (Actor, Wrestler)
c/o Nick Cordasco *Prince Marketing Group*
18 Carillon Cir
Livingston, NJ 07039-2600, USA

Pervical, Troy (Baseball Player)
California Angels
2127 Century Ave
Riverside, CA 92506-4653, USA

Perzanowski, Stan (Athlete, Baseball Player)
PO Box 133
New Park, PA 17352-0133, USA

Perzigian, Jerry (Producer, Writer)
c/o Joseph Cohen *Creative Artists Agency (CAA-LA)*
2000 Avenue of the Stars Ste 100
Los Angeles, CA 90067-4705, USA

Pesce, P J (Director, Writer)
c/o Jordan Bayer *Original Artists (LA)*
9465 Wilshire Blvd Ste 870
Beverly Hills, CA 90212-2610, USA

Pesci, Joe (Actor)
91 Pershing Blvd
Lavallette, NJ 08735-2832, USA

Pescow, Donna (Actor)
8267 Paseo Canyon Dr
Malibu, CA 90265, USA

Pesi, Gino Anthony (Actor)
c/o Loch Powell *Leverage Management*
3030 Pennsylvania Ave
Santa Monica, CA 90404-4112, USA

Pesonen, Richard (Athlete, Football Player)
2032 Fairview Ln
The Villages, FL 32162-7032, USA

Pestano, Vinnie (Athlete, Baseball Player)
740 S Crown Pointe Dr
Anaheim, CA 92807-4758, USA

Petagine, Roberto (Athlete, Baseball Player)
1123 Obispo Ave
Coral Gables, FL 33134-3557, USA

Petcka, Joe (Actor)
c/o Marta Michaud *Cinematic Management*
249 1/2 E 13th St
New York, NY 10003-5602, USA

Peter, Philipp (Race Car Driver)
Dorricott Racing
29103 Arnold Dr
Sonoma, CA 95476-9761, USA

Peterek, Jeff (Athlete, Baseball Player)
8073 Elm Valley Rd
Three Oaks, MI 49128-9552, USA

Peterffy, Thomas (Business Person)
Interactive Brokers LLC
1 Pickwick Plz Ste 100
Greenwich, CT 06830-5531, USA

Peterman, Melissa (Actor, Television Host)
2609 Waverly Dr
Los Angeles, CA 90039-2724, USA

Peter Paul & Mary (Music Group, Musician)
121 Mount Hermon Way
Ocean Grove, NJ 07756-1443

Peters, Andrew (Athlete, Hockey Player)
107 Huntington Ct
Buffalo, NY 14221-5354, USA

Peters, Anthony L (Tony) (Athlete, Football Player)
2402 Boston St
Muskogee, OK 74401-5233, USA

Peters, Barbara (Director)
1118 Magnolia Blvd
North Hollywood, CA 91601, USA

Peters, Bernadette (Actor, Musician)
c/o Jeff Hunter *William Morris Endeavor (NY)*
1325 Avenue of the Americas
New York, NY 10019-6026, USA

Peters, Bob (Coach)
Bernidji State University
Athletic Dept
Bemidji, MN 56601, USA

Peters, Caleigh (Musician)
c/o Siri Garber *Platform Public Relations*
2666 N Beachwood Dr
Los Angeles, CA 90068-2308, USA

Peters, Charlie (Writer)
c/o Todd Feldman *Creative Artists Agency (CAA-LA)*
2000 Avenue of the Stars Ste 100
Los Angeles, CA 90067-4705, USA

Peters, Chris (Athlete, Baseball Player)
613 Chessbriar Dr
Bethel Park, PA 15102-1531, USA

Peters, Clarke (Actor)
c/o Staff Member *Writers and Artists Group Intl (NY)*
360 Park Ave # 16
New York, NY 10022-5909, USA

Peters, Dan (Musician)
Legends of 21st Century
7 Trinity Row
Florence, MA 01062-1931, USA

Peters, Evan (Actor)
c/o Tim Taylor *Luber Roklin Management*
5815 W Sunset Blvd Ste 206
Los Angeles, CA 90028-6481, USA

Peters, Gary (Athlete, Baseball Player)
7121 N Serenoa Dr
Sarasota, FL 34241-9271, USA

Peters, Gretchen (Musician, Songwriter, Writer)
Gretchen Peters Management
PO Box 331242
Nashville, TN 37203-7512, USA

Peters, Hank (Baseball Player)
3407 S Ocean Blvd Apt 8D
Highland Beach, FL 33487-4714, USA

Peters, Jason (Athlete, Football Player)
11611 Secretariat Dr
Walton, NE 68461-9804, USA

Peters, Jim (Athlete, Hockey Player)
60 Main St
Essex Junction, VT 05452-3145

Peters, Jon (Producer)
c/o Staff Member *Peters Entertainment*
21731 Ventura Blvd Ste 300
Woodland Hills, CA 91364-1851, USA

Peters, Marjorie (Athlete, Baseball Player)
4081 S 122nd St
Milwaukee, WI 53228-1823, USA

Peters, Mike (Cartoonist)
PO Box 957
Bradenton, FL 34206-0957, USA

Peters, Ralph (Writer)
c/o Scott Miller *Trident Media Group LLC*
41 Madison Ave Fl 36
New York, NY 10010-2257, USA

Peters, Ray (Athlete, Baseball Player)
11013 Southerland Dr
Denton, TX 76207-8687, USA

Peters, Rick (Actor)
c/o Patricia (Patty) Woo *Patty Woo Management*
8906 W Olympic Blvd
Beverly Hills, CA 90211-3550, USA

Peters, Rick (Athlete, Baseball Player)
43977 W Juniper Ave
Maricopa, AZ 85138-4072, USA

Peters, Roberta (Actor, Opera Singer)
19356 Cedar Glen Dr
Boca Raton, FL 33434-5129, USA

Peters, Russell (Actor)
c/o Paul Canterna *Seven Summits Pictures & Management*
8906 W Olympic Blvd
Ground Floor
Beverly Hills, CA 90211-3550, USA

Peters, Steve (Athlete, Baseball Player)
12400 Ladonna Dr
Oklahoma City, OK 73170-1026, USA

Peters, Timothy (Race Car Driver)
BHR
PO Box 1708
Mount Juliet, TN 37121-1708, USA

Peters, Tom (Business Person)
Tom Peters Group
555 Hamilton Ave
Palo Alto, CA 94301-2015, USA

Peters, Volney (Athlete, Football Player)
325 Lancaster Rd
Walnut Creek, CA 94595-1760, USA

Petersen, Chris (Athlete, Baseball Player)
242 Timberland Ave
Longwood, FL 32750-6159, USA

petersen, jim (Athlete, Basketball Player)
14794 Summer Oaks Dr
Wayzata, MN 55391-2230, USA

Petersen, Kurt (Athlete, Football Player)
5520 Linmore Ln
Plano, TX 75093-7619, USA

Petersen, Loy (Athlete, Basketball Player)
475 NE Meadowlark Ln
Madras, OR 97741-9063, USA

Petersen, Melvin (Athlete, Basketball Player)
1412 Princeton Ct Apt C
Wheaton, IL 60189-7535, USA

Petersen, Pat
1634 Veteran Ave
Los Angeles, CA 90024-5517

Petersen, Patty (Actor)
60 Kennedy St
Camarillo, CA 93010, USA

Petersen, Robert E (Publisher)
Petersen Publishing Co
6420 Wilshire Blvd Ste 100
Los Angeles, CA 90048-5540, USA

Petersen, Stewart
PO Box 64
Cokeville, WY 83114-0064

Petersen, Ted (Athlete, Football Player)
323 Ridge Point Cir Apt 32A
Bridgeville, PA 15017-1566, USA

Petersen, Toby (Athlete, Hockey Player)
103 Pleasantview Ave
Longmeadow, MA 01106-1021

Petersen, William (Actor, Producer)
c/o Staff Member *High Horse Films*
25135 Anza Dr
Stage 5
Valencia, CA 91355-3416, USA

Petersen, Wolfgang (Director)
c/o Staff Member *Radiant Productions*
914 Montana Ave Fl 2
Santa Monica, CA 90403-1505, USA

Petersmark, Brett (Athlete, Football Player)
2082 Pennsbury Ln
Hanover Park, IL 60133-6715, USA

Peterson, Adam (Athlete, Baseball Player)
5610 NE 33rd Ave
Vancouver, WA 98663, USA

Peterson, Adrian L. (Athlete, Football Player)
c/o Michael Lartigue *CAA (St. Louis)*
222 S Central Ave Ste 1008
Saint Louis, MO 63105-3509, USA

Peterson, Anthony (Athlete, Football Player)
3717 Bloxham Ct
Atlanta, GA 30341-4601, USA

Peterson, Anthony (Boxer)
c/o Staff Member *Top Rank Inc.*
3908 Howard Hughes Pkwy
#580
Las Vegas, NV 89109, USA

Peterson, Ben (Athlete, Olympic Athlete, Wrestler)
205 Dewey Ave
Watertown, WI 53094-3915, USA

Peterson, Brent (Athlete, Hockey Player)
724 Glen Oaks Dr
Franklin, TN 37067-1345

Peterson, Buzz (Coach)
University of Tennessee
Athletic Dept
Knoxville, TN 37996-0001, USA

Peterson, Cal (Athlete, Football Player)
22646 Ingomar St
Canoga Park, CA 91304-4622, USA

Peterson, David C (Journalist, Photographer)
4805 Pinehurst Ct
Pleasant Hill, IA 50327-0959, USA

Peterson, Debbi (Musician)
Bangles Mall
1341 W Fullerton Ave # 180
Chicago, IL 60614-2362, USA

Peterson, Donald H
427 Pebblebrook Dr
El Lago, TX 77586-6012, USA

Peterson, Donald H Colonel (Astronaut)
427 Pebblebrook Dr
El Lago, TX 77586-6012, USA

Peterson, Donald R (Astronaut)
Aerospace Operations Consultants
427 Pebblebrook Dr
El Lago, TX 77586-6012, USA

Peterson, Fritz (Athlete, Baseball Player)
c/o Staff Member *LightSide Books*
PO Box 265
Windber, PA 15963-0265, USA

Peterson, Harding (Hardy) (Athlete, Baseball Player)
2822 Sherbrooke Ln Apt C
Palm Harbor, FL 34684-2545, USA

Peterson, Jessie Lee (Radio Personality, Television Host)
PO Box 35090
Los Angeles, CA 90035-0090, USA

Peterson, John (Wrestler)
457 19th Ave
Comstock, WI 54826-9746, USA

Peterson, Kyle (Athlete, Baseball Player)
13253 Hamilton St
Omaha, NE 68154-5293, USA

Peterson, Larry (Race Car Driver)
Bales Motorsports
PO Box 4098
107 Bennett St.
Sidney, OH 45365-4098, USA

Peterson, Maggie
3310 W Warm Springs Rd
Las Vegas, NV 89118-5229

peterson, melvin (Athlete, Basketball Player)
1412 Princeton Ct Apt C
Wheaton, IL 60189-7535, USA

Peterson, Michael (Athlete, Football Player)
PO Box 904
Alachua, FL 32616-0904, USA

Peterson, Mike (Athlete, Olympic Athlete, Rower)
7321 Elbow Ln
Philadelphia, PA 19119-2810, USA

Peterson, Morris (Athlete, Basketball Player)
909 Lafayette St Apt 12
New Orleans, LA 70113-1041, USA

Peterson, Patrick (Athlete, Baseball Player)
c/o Patrick William Lawlor *Galaxy Sports*
811 E Hillsboro Blvd
Deerfield Beach, FL 33441-3521, USA

Peterson, Patrick (Athlete, Football Player)
c/o Denise White *EAG Sports Management*
909 N Sepulveda Blvd Ste 360
El Segundo, CA 90245-3864, USA

Peterson, Peter G (Politician)
345 Park Ave Bsmt LB4
New York, NY 10154-3001, USA

Peterson, Seth (Actor)
6125 Fulton Ave Apt 31
Van Nuys, CA 91401-3108, USA

Peterson, Todd (Athlete, Football Player)
3249 Chatham Rd NW
Atlanta, GA 30305-1101, USA

Peterson, Vicki (Musician)
Bangles Mall
1341 W Fullerton Ave # 180
Chicago, IL 60614-2362, USA

Peterson, William (Actor)
c/o Steve Dontanville *Circle of Confusion (NY)*
8931 Ellis Ave
Los Angeles, CA 90034-3336, USA

Peterson, William W (Athlete, Football Player)
6014 Chandler Dr
San Diego, CA 92117-3302, USA

Peterson-Fox, Betty Jean (Athlete, Baseball Player)
PO Box 280
110 E North St
Wyanet, IL 61379-0280, USA

Peterson-Parker, Katie (Golfer)
527 Henkel Cir
Winter Park, FL 32789-5127, USA

Pete Stark, Fortney (Congressman, Politician)
239 Cannon Hob
Washington, DC 20515-0513, USA

Petievich, Gerald (Producer, Writer)
c/o Brian Lipson *William Morris Endeavor (LA)*
9601 Wilshire Blvd
Beverly Hills, CA 90210-5213, USA

Petit, Michel (Athlete, Hockey Player)
129 Latches Ln
Media, PA 19063-5309

Petitbon, John (Athlete, Football Player)
3804 N Labarre Rd
Metairie, LA 70002-1817, USA

Petitbon, Richie (Athlete, Football Coach, Football Player)
9628 Percussion Way
Vienna, VA 22182-3334, USA

Petitgout, Luke (Athlete, Football Player)
267 Prospect St
Ridgewood, NJ 07450-5121, USA

Petke, Mike (Soccer Player)
DC United
14120 Newbrook Dr
Chantilly, VA 20151-2273, USA

Petkovic, Andrea (Athlete, Tennis Player)
c/o Staff Member *Women's Tennis Association (WTA (US))*
1 Progress Plz Ste 1500
St Petersburg, FL 33701-4335, USA

Petkovsek, Mark (Athlete, Baseball Player)
5575 Duff St
Beaumont, TX 77706-6307, USA

Petraglia, Johnny (Bowler)
25 Turnbridge Ct
Jackson, NJ 08527-6412, USA

Petralli, Geno (Athlete, Baseball Player)
604 E Anderson St
Weatherford, TX 76086-5704, USA

Petras, Ernestine (Athlete, Baseball Player)
5 Greenwood Ave
Haskell, NJ 07420-1417, USA

Petree, Andy (Race Car Driver)
Petree Racing
PO Box 325
908 Upward Rd.
East Flat Rock, NC 28726-0325, USA

Petrenko, Victor (Figure Skater)
c/o Staff Member *Champions on Ice*
3500 American Blvd W Ste 190
Minneapolis, MN 55431-4431, USA

Petrenko, Viktor (Figure Skater)
International Skating Center
1375 Hopmeadow St
Simsbury, CT 06070-1423, USA

Petrey, Dan
1808 Cartlen Dr
Placentia, CA 92870-2734

Petrich, Bob (Athlete, Football Player)
1391 Silverberry Ct
El Cajon, CA 92019-2835, USA

Petrick, Ben (Athlete, Baseball Player)
1553 NE Jackson School Rd
Hillsboro, OR 97124-2425, USA

Petrick, Billy (Athlete, Baseball Player)
201 Boulder Dr
Morris, IL 60450-3331, USA

Petrie, Donald (Director)
c/o Alan Gasmer *Alan Gasmer Management Company*
10877 Wilshire Blvd Ste 603
Los Angeles, CA 90024-4348, USA

Petrie, Geoff (Athlete, Basketball Player)
3675 Holly Hill Ln
Loomis, CA 95650-8818, USA

Petrocelli, Americo P (Rico) (Athlete, Baseball Player)
37 Green Heron Ln
Nashua, NH 03062-2239, USA

Petrone, Shana (Musician)
c/o Staff Member *Creative Artists Agency (CAA-TN)*
401 Commerce St PH
Nashville, TN 37219-2516, USA

Petrone, Shana (Musician)
Creative Artists Agency
3310 W End Ave Ste 500
Nashville, TN 37203-1087, USA

Petroni, Michael (Director)
United Talent Agency
9336 Civic Center Dr
Beverly Hills, CA 90210-3604, USA

Petroske, John (Athlete, Hockey Player)
PO Box 366
Side Lake, MN 55781-0366, USA

Petrovic, Tim (Golfer)
12708 Tradition Dr
Dade City, FL 33525-8240, USA

Petrovicky, Robert (Athlete, Hockey Player)
20944 Island Sound Cir Unit 106
Estero, FL 33928-8996

Petrucci, John (Musician)
c/o Staff Member *Agency Group Ltd, The (LA)*
1880 Century Park E Ste 711
Los Angeles, CA 90067-1618, USA

Petry, Dan (Athlete, Baseball Player)
The Athletic Connection
PO Box 380135
Clinton Township, MI 48038-0060, USA

Petryna-Mullins, Doreen (Athlete, Baseball Player)
1104 Somonauk St
Sycamore, IL 60178-2521, USA

Pet Shop Boys (Music Group)
c/o Staff Member *Creative Artists Agency (CAA-LA)*
2000 Avenue of the Stars Ste 100
Los Angeles, CA 90067-4705, USA

Pett, Joel (Cartoonist)
Lexington Herald-Leader
1010 W New Circle Rd
Lexington, KY 40511-1839, USA

Pettee, Roger (Athlete, Football Player)
5714 Tortoise Pl
Apollo Beach, FL 33572-3355, USA

Pettersson, Carl (Athlete, Golfer)
1604 Dogwood View Ln
Raleigh, NC 27614-7989, USA

Pettibon, Richard A (Richie) (Athlete, Football Player)
9628 Percussion Way
Vienna, VA 22182-3334, USA

Pettibone, Jay (Athlete, Baseball Player)
5112 Via Marcos
Yorba Linda, CA 92887-2530, USA

Pettie, Jim (Athlete, Hockey Player)
81 Kirk Rd
Rochester, NY 14612-3301

Petties, Neal (Athlete, Football Player)
767 Jewell Dr
San Diego, CA 92113-2731, USA

Pettiford, Valarie
c/o Jeff Morrone *Intellectual Artists Management*
9350 Wilshire Blvd Ste 224
Beverly Hills, CA 90212-3204, USA

Pettigrew, Brandon (Athlete, Football Player)
c/o Sean Howard *Octagon Football*
832 Sansome St Fl 1
San Francisco, CA 94111-1558, USA

Pettigrew, Gary (Athlete, Football Player)
1107 W 33rd Ave
Spokane, WA 99203-1403, USA

Pettinato, Rachelle (Actor)
c/o Staff Member *Select Artists Ltd (CA-Westside Office)*
1138 12th St Apt 1
Santa Monica, CA 90403-5459, USA

Pettini, Joe (Athlete, Baseball Player)
112 Logan Ct
Bethany, WV 26032-2016, USA

Pettis, Gary (Athlete, Baseball Player)
3129 Crestline Ct
Antioch, CA 94531-6640, USA

Pettis, Madison (Actor)
c/o Alissa Vradenburg *Untitled Entertainment (LA)*
350 S Beverly Dr Ste 200
Beverly Hills, CA 90212-4819, USA

Pettis, Madsion (Actor)
c/o Alissa Vradenburg *Untitled Entertainment (LA)*
350 S Beverly Dr Ste 200
Beverly Hills, CA 90212-4819, USA

Pettit, Bob (Athlete, Basketball Player)
7 Garden Ln
New Orleans, LA 70124-1024, USA

Pettit, Donald R (Astronaut)
2014 Country Ridge Dr
Houston, TX 77062-3636, USA

Pettit, Paul (Athlete, Baseball Player)
928 Sarazen St
Hemet, CA 92543, USA

Pettit Jr, Robert L (Bob) (Basketball Player)
7 Garden Ln
New Orleans, LA 70124-1024, USA

Pettitte, Andy (Athlete, Baseball Player)
c/o Team Member *New York Yankees*
Yankee Stadium
161st St & River Ave
Bronx, NY 10451, USA

Pettway, Kenneth (Athlete, Football Player)
2631 Via Verona
Lancaster, CA 93535-2853, USA

Petty, Kyle (Race Car Driver)
135 Longfield Dr
Mooresville, NC 28115-7342, USA

Petty, Lori (Actor)
c/o Mark J. Holder *Zero Gravity Management*
1531 14th St
Santa Monica, CA 90404-3302, USA

Petty, Maurice (Race Car Driver)
248 Branson Mill Rd
Randleman, NC 27317-8007, USA

Petty, Richard (Race Car Driver)
Richard Petty Museum
311 Branson Mill Rd
Randleman, NC 27317-8008, USA

Pettyfer, Alex (Actor)
c/o Simon Halls *Slate Public Relations*
9000 W Sunset Blvd Ste 915
West Hollywood, CA 90069-5809, USA

Pettyiohn, Adam (Athlete, Baseball Player)
4626 W Addisyn Ct
Visalia, CA 93291-9150, USA

Pettyjohn, Adam (Athlete, Baseball Player)
717 Westwood Dr
Exeter, CA 93221-1438, USA

Pevec, Katja (Actor)
c/o Anne Woodward *ROAR (LA)*
9701 Wilshire Blvd Fl 8
Beverly Hills, CA 90212-2008, USA

Pevey, Marty (Athlete, Baseball Player)
158 Nightwind Trce
Acworth, GA 30101-5981, USA

Peviani, Bob (Athlete, Football Player)
25262 Northrup Dr
Laguna Hills, CA 92653-5223, USA

Peyton, Brad (Director)
c/o Staff Member *William Morris Endeavor (LA)*
9601 Wilshire Blvd
Beverly Hills, CA 90210-5213, USA

Pezzano, Chuck (Bowler)
27 Mountainside Ter
Clifton, NJ 07013-1107, USA

Pfann, George R (Athlete, Coach, Football Coach, Football Player)
120 Warwick Pl
Ithaca, NY 14850-1731, USA

Pfeiffer, Dedee (Actor, Model)
c/o David Rose *Innovative Artists (LA)*
1505 10th St
Santa Monica, CA 90401-2805, USA

Pfeiffer, Michelle (Actor)
c/o Suzan Bymel *Management 360*
9111 Wilshire Blvd
Beverly Hills, CA 90210-5508, USA

Pfeil, Bobby (Athlete, Baseball Player)
2358 Pheasant Run Cir
Stockton, CA 95207-5210, USA

Pfeil, Mark (Golfer)
2565 Chelsea Rd
Palos Verdes Estates, CA 90274-4309, USA

Pfister, Dan (Athlete, Baseball Player)
1436 NW 9th St
Dania, FL 33004-2332, USA

Pflug, Jo Ann (Actor)
PO Box 3292
Jupiter, FL 33469-1004, USA

P. Frelinghuysen, Rodney (Congressman, Politician)
2369 Rayburn Hob
Washington, DC 20515-3225, USA

Pfund, Lee (Athlete, Baseball Player)
130 Windsor Park Dr Apt C214
Carol Stream, IL 60188-1998, USA

Pfund, Randy (Basketball Coach, Coach)
31906 Village Green Blvd
Apt 1206
Warrenville, IL 60555-5904, USA

P. Gibson, Christopher (Chris) (Congressman, Politician)
502 Cannon Hob
Washington, DC 20515-1003, USA

Phair, Liz (Actor, Musician, Songwriter)
c/o Jason Weinberg *Untitled Entertainment (LA)*
350 S Beverly Dr Ste 200
Beverly Hills, CA 90212-4819, USA

Phair, Lyle (Athlete, Hockey Player)
16256 Winchester Dr
Northville, MI 48168-2347

Phaneuf, Al (Athlete, Football Player)
5376 Pepper Brush Cv
Apopka, FL 32703-1971, USA

Phegley, Roger (Athlete, Basketball Player)
43 Timberlane Dr
Morton, IL 61550-1146, USA

Pheil, Anna (Actor)
c/o Scott Zimmerman *Evolution Entertainment (LA)*
901 N Highland Ave
Los Angeles, CA 90038-2412, USA

Phelan, Jack (Athlete, Basketball Player)
6404 21st Ave W Apt H502
Bradenton, FL 34209-7878, USA

Phelan, Jim (Athlete, Basketball Player)
16579 Old Emmitsburg Rd
Emmitsburg, MD 21727-8927, USA

Phelos, Travis (Athlete, Baseball Player)
PO Box 336
Wheaton, MO 64874-0336, USA

Phelps, Brian (Actor)
1265 Coldwater Canyon Dr
Beverly Hills, CA 90210-2419

Phelps, Doug (Musician)
Mitchell Fox Mgmt
212 3rd Ave N Ste 301
Nashville, TN 37201-1632, USA

Phelps, Jaycie (Athlete, Gymnast, Olympic Athlete)
Jaycie Phelps Athletic Center
3802A N 600 W
Greenfield, IN 46140-9642, USA

Phelps, Josh (Athlete, Baseball Player)
1503 Regal Mist Loop
Trinity, FL 34655-4974, USA

Phelps, Kelly Joe (Athlete, Football Player)
Fleming/Tamulevich Assoc
8782 Brooks Creek Dr Apt 1516
Cincinnati, OH 45249-3001, USA

Phelps, Ken (Athlete, Baseball Player)
6030 E Foothill Dr N
Paradise Valley, AZ 85253-3070, USA

Phelps, Michael (Athlete, Olympic Athlete, Swimmer)
PO Box 65239
Baltimore, MD 21209-0239, USA

Phelps, Richard (Athlete)
c/o Staff Member *ESPN (Main)*
935 Middle St
Espn Plaza
Bristol, CT 06010-1000, USA

Phelps, Richard F (Digger) (Coach)
ESPN-TV
Sports Dept
ESPN Plaza 935 Middle St
Bristol, CT 06010, USA

Phelps, Tommy (Athlete, Baseball Player)
4418 Pawnee Path
Valrico, FL 33594-5529, USA

Phelps, Travis (Athlete, Baseball Player)
PO Box 336
Wheaton, MO 64874-0336, USA

Phelps Jr, Ashton (Publisher)
New Orleans Times-Picayune
3800 Howard Ave
New Orleans, LA 70125-1429, USA

Phenix, Perry Lee (Athlete, Football Player)
4849 Frankford Rd Apt 715
Dallas, TX 75287-5309, USA

Phifer, Mekhi (Actor)
c/o Emily Gerson Saines *Brookside Artists Management (NY)*
250 W 57th St Ste 2303
New York, NY 10107-2399, USA

Phifer, Roman Z (Athlete, Football Player)
PO Box 83215
Los Angeles, CA 90083-0215, USA

Philbin, Gerry (Athlete, Football Player)
5527 N Military Trl Apt 1406
Boca Raton, FL 33496-3494, USA

Philbin, Regis (Television Host)
101 W 67th St Apt 51A
New York, NY 10023-5953, USA

Philbrick, Denise (Golfer)
5364 Carnegie Loop
Livermore, CA 94550-7136, USA

Philcox, Todd (Athlete, Football Player)
1201 1st St N Apt 703
Jacksonville Beach, FL 32250-8205, USA

Philip, Primate (Religious Leader)
Antiochian Orthodox Christian Church
358 Mountain Rd
Englewood, NJ 07631-3798, USA

Philippoussis, Mark (Tennis Player)
Octagon
7950 Jones Branch Dr
Mc Lean, VA 22102-3302, USA

Philipps, Busy (Actor)
c/o Julie Darmody *Mosaic Media Group*
1840 Century Park E Ste 1700
Los Angeles, CA 90067-2118, USA

Philips, brandon (Athlete, Baseball Player)
586 Rowland Rd
Stone Mountain, GA 30083-4573, USA

Philips, Chuck (Journalist)
Los Angeles Times
202 W 1st St Ste 500
Editorial Dept
Los Angeles, CA 90012-4401, USA

Philips, Emo (Actor)
c/o Staff Member *OmniPop Talent Group (LA)*
4605 Lankershim Blvd Ste 201
North Hollywood, CA 91602-1874, USA

Philips, Gina (Actor)
c/o Erik Kritzer *LINK Entertainment*
11872 La Grange Ave Fl 1
Los Angeles, CA 90025-5283, USA

Phillios, Jason (Athlete, Baseball Player)
7111 Defranzo Loop
Fort George G Meade, MD 20755-4053, USA

Phillipoff, Harold (Athlete, Hockey Player)
446 Harrison St
Sumas, WA 98295-9613, USA

Phillippe, Ryan (Actor)
704 Desiree Way
Hockessin, DE 19707-9331, USA

Phillips, Bijou (Actor, Model, Musician)
2151 Hollyridge Dr
Los Angeles, CA 90068-3514, USA

Phillips, Bill (Writer)
High Point Media LLC
10100 Santa Monica Blvd Ste 1300
Los Angeles, CA 90067-4114, USA

Phillips, Bobbie (Actor)
The Kelly Agency
3001 Heavenly Ridge St
Thousand Oaks, CA 91362-1178, USA

Phillips, Brandon (Athlete, Baseball Player)
586 Rowland Rd
Stone Mountain, GA 30083-4573, USA

Phillips, Caryl (Writer)
Amherst College
English Dept
Amherst, MA 01002, USA

Phillips, Chynna (Actor, Musician)
1007 Montana Ave # 230
Santa Monica, CA 90403-1603, USA

Phillips, Connie Anne (Business Person)
Conde Nast
4 Times Sq Fl 22
New York, NY 10036-6561, USA

Phillips, Davey (Athlete, Baseball Player)
42 Lily Pond Ln
Weldon Spring, MO 63304-0542, USA

Phillips, David (Producer)
Corner of the Sky
1724 N Highland Ave Apt 328
Los Angeles, CA 90028-4417, USA

Phillips, Eddie (Athlete, Baseball Player)
1261 S Brookview
Springfield, MO 65809-2293, USA

Phillips, Eddie Lee (Athlete, Basketball Player)
800 McCary St SW
Birmingham, AL 35211-2944, USA

Phillips, Ethan (Actor)
c/o Donald Spradlin *Essential Talent Management*
6399 Wilshire Blvd Ste 401
Los Angeles, CA 90048-5716, USA

Phillips, Gary (Athlete, Basketball Player)
729 Country Club Dr
Kerrville, TX 78028-2781, USA

Phillips, Gene (Athlete, Basketball Player)
4630 Eldon Run
San Antonio, TX 78247-5520, USA

Phillips, Gersha (Designer)
c/o Staff Member *Paradigm (LA)*
360 N Crescent Dr
North Bldg
Beverly Hills, CA 90210-4874, USA

Phillips, Glasgow (Director)
c/o Brett Hansen *United Talent Agency (UTA-LA)*
9336 Civic Center Dr
Beverly Hills, CA 90210-3604, USA

Phillips, Graham (Actor)
c/o Dannielle Thomas *Untitled Entertainment (LA)*
350 S Beverly Dr Ste 200
Beverly Hills, CA 90212-4819, USA

Phillips, Grant Lee (Musician)
c/o Staff Member *Paradigm (Monterey)*
404 W Franklin St
Monterey, CA 93940-2303, USA

Phillips, Jack (Athlete, Baseball Player)
721 May Rd
Potsdam, NY 13676-3244, USA

Phillips, James (Red) (Athlete, Football Player)
1948 Wicker Point Rd
Alexander City, AL 35010-6504, USA

Phillips, Jason (Athlete, Baseball Player)
140 Mountain Rd
Montoursville, PA 17754-7858, USA

Phillips, Jason (Athlete, Baseball Player)
1777 Tara Way
San Marcos, CA 92078-1081, USA

Phillips, Jason (Athlete, Football Player)
3001 N Boulevard
Richmond, VA 23230-4331, USA

Phillips, Jeffrey
8436 W 3rd St # 740
Los Angeles, CA 90048-4163

Phillips, Jess (Athlete, Football Player)
2820 San Antonio St
Beaumont, TX 77701-8036, USA

Phillips, Jim (Athlete, Football Player)
67 Lakeview Dr Unit 10D
Alexander City, AL 35010-6292, USA

Phillips, Joe (Athlete, Football Player)
425 Barker Ave
Oregon City, OR 97045-3449, USA

Phillips, John (Coach)
University of Tulsa
Athletic Dept
Tulsa, OK 74104, USA

Phillips, John L (Astronaut)
154 Canoe Cove Ln
Sandpoint, ID 83864-7968, USA

Phillips, Joseph C
8730 W Sunset Blvd Ste 480
West Hollywood, CA 90069-2277, USA

Phillips, J R (Athlete, Baseball Player)
22410 N 74th St
Glendale, AZ 85310-5670, USA

Phillips, Kevin (Actor)
c/o Todd Eisner *Innovative Artists (LA)*
405 S Beverly Dr Ste 500
Beverly Hills, CA 90212-4425, USA

Phillips, Kirk (Athlete, Football Player)
2103 E Alma Ave
Sherman, TX 75090-4008, USA

Phillips, Lawrence (Athlete, Football Player)
PO Box 4430
Lancaster, CA 93539-4430, USA

Phillips, Lou Diamond (Actor)
c/o JB Roberts *Thruline Entertainment*
9250 Wilshire Blvd Ste 100
Ground Floor
Beverly Hills, CA 90212-3343, USA

Phillips, Loyd (Athlete, Football Player)
General Delivery
Springdale, AR 72764-9999, USA

Phillips, Mackenzie (Actor)
c/o Geneva Bray *GVA Talent Agency Inc*
8981 W Sunset Blvd Ste 101
West Hollywood, CA 90069-1850, USA

Phillips, Mel (Athlete, Football Player)
6368 Milk Wagon Ln
Miami Lakes, FL 33014-6083, USA

Phillips, Michelie (Actor, Musician)
c/o Marc Chancer *Origin Talent Agency*
4705 Laurel Canyon Blvd Ste 303
Valley Village, CA 91607-5943, USA

Phillips, Michelle (Actor)
c/o Merritt Blake *The Blake Agency*
23441 Malibu Colony Rd
Malibu, CA 90265-4640, USA

Phillips, Mike (Athlete, Baseball Player)
3322 Ridgefield St
Irving, TX 75062-4157, USA

Phillips, Paul (Athlete, Baseball Player)
507 N Mine Ave
Demopolis, AL 36732, USA

Phillips, Phillip (Musician)
c/o Brett Radin *19 Entertainment*
8560 W Sunset Blvd Fl 9
West Hollywood, CA 90069-2339, USA

Phillips, Ricky (Musician)
c/o Sterling Bacon *TBA Artist Management (Atlanta)*
1111 Alderman Dr Ste 285
Alpharetta, GA 30005-5433, USA

Phillips, Sam (Musician, Songwriter, Writer)
Prager & Fenton
12424 Wilshire Blvd Ste 1000
Los Angeles, CA 90025-1071, USA

Phillips, Scott (Musician)
Agency Group
1776 Broadway Ste 430
New York, NY 10019-2002, USA

Phillips, Shaun (Athlete, Football Player)
c/o Staff Member *EAG Sports Management*
909 N Sepulveda Blvd Ste 360
El Segundo, CA 90245-3864, USA

Phillips, steve (Sportscaster)
148 Mather St
Wilton, CT 06897-5011, USA

Phillips, Stone (Correspondent)
c/o Staff Member *Dateline NBC*
30 Rockefeller Plz Ste 4350
Nbc News
New York, NY 10112-4399, USA

Phillips, Stu (Musician)
654 Long Hollow Pike
Goodlettsville, TN 37072-3449, USA

Phillips, Tari (Basketball Player)
New York Liberty
125 W End Ave # 6
Madison Square Garden
New York, NY 10023-6387, USA

Phillips, Taylor (Athlete, Baseball Player)
594 Mein Mitchell Rd
Hiram, GA 30141-5810, USA

Phillips, Ted (Business Person, Football Executive)
125 E Ellis Ave
Libertyville, IL 60048-1957, USA

Phillips, Teresa (Basketball Player, Coach)
Tennessee State University
Athletic Dept
Nashville, TN 37209, USA

Phillips, Todd (Actor, Director, Producer, Writer)
c/o Todd Feldman *Creative Artists Agency (CAA-LA)*
2000 Avenue of the Stars Ste 100
Los Angeles, CA 90067-4705, USA

Phillips, Tony (Athlete, Baseball Player)
13341 E Cochise Rd
Scottsdale, AZ 85259-5442, USA

Phillips, Wade (Athlete, Coach, Football Coach, Football Player)
311 Chapel Belle Ln
Houston, TX 77024-5038, USA

Phillips, Warren H (Publisher)
Bridge Works Publications
PO Box 1798
Bridgehampton, NY 11932-1798, USA

Phillips-Bannister, Kristie (Gymnast)
KPAC Gymnastics
2809 Amity Hill Rd
Statesville, NC 28677-9744, USA

Phillips, Craig, and Dean (Musician)
c/o Staff Member *INO Records*
210 Jamestown Park Ste 100
Brentwood, TN 37027-7570, USA

Phillopusis, Mark (Tennis Player)
c/o Staff Member *Octagon (VA)*
7950 Jones Branch Dr
Mc Lean, VA 22102-3302, USA

Philyaw, Charles (Athlete, Football Player)
3929 Eileen Ln
Shreveport, LA 71109-1921, USA

Philyaw, Dino (Athlete, Football Player)
3164 Arrowhead St
Eugene, OR 97404-3858, USA

Phinney, Davis (Athlete, Cycler, Olympic Athlete)
470 Juniper Ave
Boulder, CO 80304-1716, USA

Phipps, Michael E (Mike) (Athlete, Football Player)
2748 NE 25th St
Lighthouse Point, FL 33064-8308, USA

Phipps, Ogden M (Horse Racer)
1486 N Lake Way
Palm Beach, FL 33480-3031, USA

Phipps, Sam
2346 Walgrove Ave
Los Angeles, CA 90066-3504

Phish (Music Group)
c/o Patrick Jordan *Red Light Management (VA)*
321 E Main St Ste 500
Charlottesville, VA 22902-3201, USA

Phoebus, Thomas H (Tom) (Athlete, Baseball Player)
2822 SW Lakemont Pl
Palm City, FL 34990-6094, USA

Phoenix, Beth (Wrestler)
c/o Kerry Rodgerson *World Wrestling Entertainment (WWE)*
1241 E Main St
Titan Towers
Stamford, CT 06902-3520, USA

Phoenix, Joaquin (Actor)
8301 Mulholland Dr
Los Angeles, CA 90046, USA

Phoenix, Nikki (Adult Film Star, Model)
c/o Staff Member *ATMLA*
22020 Clarendon St Ste 300
Woodland Hills, CA 91367-6333, USA

Phoenix, Rain (Actor)
c/o Josh Taylor *Val's Artist Management*
3 Greatmeadow Rd
Locust Valley, NY 11560-1005, USA

Phoenix, Steve (Athlete, Baseball Player)
11212 Horizon Hills Dr
El Cajon, CA 92020-8231, USA

Phoenix, Summer (Actor)
2054 Laughlin Park Dr
Los Angeles, CA 90027-1712, USA

Physioc, Steve (Sportscaster)
17285 Antioch Rd
Stilwell, KS 66085-8877, USA

Piatkowski, Eric (Athlete, Basketball Player)
9211 N 46th St
Phoenix, AZ 85028-5516, USA

Piatkowski, Walt (Athlete, Basketball Player)
20233 C St
Omaha, NE 68130-5064, USA

Piatt, Adam (Athlete, Baseball Player)
1808 SE 37th Ter
Cape Coral, FL 33904-5036, USA

Piatt, Doug (Athlete, Baseball Player)
102 5th St
Aliquippa, PA 15001-2409, USA

Piazza, Mike (Athlete, Baseball Player)
1401 W 27th St
Miami Beach, FL 33140-4208, USA

Piazza, Vincent (Actor)
c/o Rhonda Price *Gersh (NY)*
41 Madison Ave
New York, NY 10010-2202, USA

Picard, Alexandre (Athlete, Hockey Player)
200 W Nationwide Blvd
Arena
Columbus, OH 43215-2561, USA

Picard, Geoffrey (Athlete, Olympic Athlete, Rower)
2020 W Lake Blvd
Tahoe City, CA 96145, USA

Picard, Robert (Athlete, Hockey Player)
4718 Grand Cypress Cir N
Coconut Creek, FL 33073-2337

Picardo, Robert (Actor)
c/o Peter Young *Sovereign Talent Group*
8421 Wilshire Blvd Ste 200
Beverly Hills, CA 90211-3204, USA

Picatto, Alexandra (Actor)
c/o Kari Estrin *Paradigm (LA)*
360 N Crescent Dr
North Bldg
Beverly Hills, CA 90210-4874, USA

Piccard, Noel
3636 Wilmington Ave
Saint Louis, MO 63116-3218, USA

Picciolo, Rob (Athlete, Baseball Player)
11773 Invierno Dr
San Diego, CA 92124-2814, USA

Picco, Giandomenico
1 United Nations Plz
New York, NY 10017-3515

Piccone, Lou (Athlete, Football Player)
49 S Youngs Rd
Buffalo, NY 14221-7024, USA

Piccone, Robin (Designer, Fashion Designer)
Piccone Apparel Corp
1424 Washington Blvd
Venice, CA 90291, USA

Pichardo, Hipolito (Athlete, Baseball Player)
21218 Saint Andrews Blvd Apt 305
Boca Raton, FL 33433-2435, USA

Pichler, David (Athlete, Diver, Olympic Athlete)
9346 SW 1st St
Plantation, FL 33324-2449, USA

Pichler, Joseph A (Business Person)
Kroger Co
1014 Vine St Ste 1000
Cincinnati, OH 45202-1119, USA

Pichlikova, Lenka (Actor)
101 Knickerbocker Ave
Stamford, CT 06907-2520, USA

Pickard, Nancy (Writer)
4020 W 94th Ter Apt 211
Prairie Village, KS 66207-2756, USA

Pickel, William (Bill) (Athlete, Football Player)
9 Autumn Ridge Rd
South Salem, NY 10590-1103, USA

Pickens, Bruce (Athlete, Football Player)
2811 Wickeford Mill Dr
Buford, GA 30519-7611, USA

Pickens, Carl M (Athlete, Football Player)
623 Terrace Ave
Murphy, NC 28906, USA

Pickens, Madeleine (Business Person)
Saving America's Mustangs
2683 Via De La Valle # G313
Del Mar, CA 92014-1911, USA

Pickens, Robert (Athlete, Football Player)
790 Sudbury Rd
Atlanta, GA 30328-1410, USA

Pickens, T Boone (Business Person)
8117 Preston Rd Ste 260
Dallas, TX 75225-6321, USA

Pickens Jr, James (Actor)
c/o Christopher Wright *Christopher Wright Management*
3207 Winnie Dr
Los Angeles, CA 90068-1439, USA

Pickering, Calvin (Baseball Player)
Baltimore Orioles
201 Tanglewood Pl Apt 305
Irvine, FL 92604, USA

Pickering, Jeff (Cartoonist)
c/o Staff Member *King Features Syndication*
300 W 57th St Fl 15
New York, NY 10019-5238, USA

Pickett, Cecil "Ricky" (Athlete, Baseball Player)
168 Deer Creek Dr
Aledo, TX 76008-3900, USA

Pickett, Cindy (Actor)
c/o Andrew Howard *Incognito Management*
9440 Santa Monica Blvd Ste 302
Beverly Hills, CA 90210-4614, USA

Pickett, Jay
24801 Eilat St
Woodland Hills, CA 91367-1036

Pickett, Rex
c/o Daniel Strone *Trident Media Group LLC*
41 Madison Ave Fl 36
New York, NY 10010-2257, USA

Pickett, Ricky (Athlete, Baseball Player)
1017 Wood Ridge Dr
Azle, TX 76020-3759, USA

Pickett, Ryan (Athlete, Football Player)
901 N Broadway
Saint Louis, MO 63101-2800, USA

Pickford, Kevin (Athlete, Baseball Player)
6006 N Harcourt Dr
Coeur D Alene, ID 83815-8473, USA

Pickford, Mary Foundation
9171 Wilshire Blvd # 512
Beverly Hills, CA 90210-5530

Pickler, Kellie (Musician)
4102 Sneed Rd
Nashville, TN 37215-2304, USA

Pickles, Christina (Actor)
137 S Westgate Ave
Los Angeles, CA 90049-4222, USA

Pickren, Bradley (Actor)
c/o Philip Marcus *Clear Talent Group (LA)*
10950 Ventura Blvd
Studio City, CA 91604-3340, USA

Pickren, Spencer (Actor)
c/o Philip Marcus *Clear Talent Group (LA)*
10950 Ventura Blvd
Studio City, CA 91604-3340, USA

Pico, Jeff (Athlete, Baseball Player)
2862 Wingfield Ave
Chico, CA 95928-8940, USA

Picone, Mario (Athlete, Baseball Player)
8876 Bay 16th St Fl 2
Brooklyn, NY 11214-5902, USA

Picou, James (Horse Racer)
8961 S Hollybrook Blvd Apt 104
Pembroke Pines, FL 33025-1313, USA

Picoult, Jodi (Writer)
38 Goodfellow Rd
Hanover, NH 03755-4800, USA

Pictor, Bruce (Musician)
Variety Artists
1924 Spring St
Paso Robles, CA 93446-1620, USA

Piedmont, Matt (Director, Producer, Writer)
c/o Simon Millar *Rumble Media*
1620 Broadway Ste C
Santa Monica, CA 90404-2777, USA

Pied Pipers, The
25 Cobble Creek Dr Rd Box 1
Tannersville, PA 18372

Piedra, Jorge (Athlete, Baseball Player)
5608 Fairfax Dr
Frisco, TX 75034-5927, USA

Pierce, Adrienne (Musician)
c/o Staff Member *Paradigm (Monterey)*
404 W Franklin St
Monterey, CA 93940-2303, USA

Pierce, Antonio (Athlete, Football Player, Sportscaster)
c/o Andy Elkin *Creative Artists Agency (CAA-LA)*
2000 Avenue of the Stars Ste 100
Los Angeles, CA 90067-4705, USA

Pierce, David Hyde (Actor)
c/o Chris Kanarick *ID Public Relations (NY)*
150 W 30th St Fl 19
New York, NY 10001-4119, USA

Pierce, Ed (Athlete, Baseball Player)
543 Crestview Dr
Glendora, CA 91741-2942, USA

Pierce, Jack (Athlete, Baseball Player)
1002 Cortez St
Laredo, TX 78040-6237, USA

Pierce, Jeff (Athlete, Baseball Player)
1046 Lantern Ln
Circle Pines, MN 55014-1335, USA

Pierce, Jeffrey (Actor)
c/o Gary Pearl *Pearl Pictures & Management*
10956 Weyburn Ave Ste 200
Los Angeles, CA 90024-2835, USA

Pierce, Jill (Actor)
Extreme Team Productions
15941 Harlem Ave # 319
Tinley Park, IL 60477-1609, USA

Pierce, John (Musician)
c/o Staff Member *Paradigm (Monterey)*
404 W Franklin St
Monterey, CA 93940-2303, USA

Pierce, Jonathan (Musician)
Muse Assoc
330 Franklin Rd # 135-8
Brentwood, TN 37027-3280, USA

Pierce, Lincoln (Cartoonist)
United Feature Syndicate
PO Box 5610
Cincinnati, OH 45201-5610, USA

Pierce, Paul (Athlete, Basketball Player)
25201 Prado Del Misterio
Calabasas, CA 91302-3600, USA

Pierce, Ron (Horse Racer)
15 Deer Trail Dr
Millstone Township, NJ 08510-1509, USA

Pierce, Stack (Actor)
Haeggstrom Office
11288 Ventura Blvd # 620
Studio City, CA 91604-3187, USA

Pierce, Tamora (Writer)
612 Westcott St
Syracuse, NY 13210-2536, USA

Pierce, Tony (Athlete, Baseball Player)
6119 Brittany Ct
Columbus, GA 31909-4247, USA

Pierce, Wendell (Actor)
c/o Alex Spieller *IMPR*
357 S Robertson Blvd
Beverly Hills, CA 90211-3602, USA

Pierce, W William (Billy) (Athlete, Baseball Player)
1321 Baileys Crossing Dr
Lemont, IL 60439-8540, USA

Pierces, The (Music Group)
c/o Staff Member *Paradigm (Monterey)*
404 W Franklin St
Monterey, CA 93940-2303, USA

Pierce The Veil (Music Group, Musician)
c/o Heather Gonzales *Fearless Records*
13772 Goldenwest St # 545
Westminster, CA 92683-3123, USA

Piercy, Marge (Writer)
PO Box 1473
Wellfleet, MA 02667-1473, USA

Pieri, Damon (Athlete, Football Player)
1120 W Tuckey Ln
Phoenix, AZ 85013-1049, USA

Pierpoint, Eric (Actor)
2199 Topanga Skyline Dr
Topanga, CA 90290-4050, USA

Pierre, Juan (Athlete, Baseball Player)
6148 NW 65th Ter
Parkland, FL 33067-1553, USA

Piers, Julie (Golfer)
5019 SW Hammock Creek Dr
Palm City, FL 34990-7909, USA

Piersall, James A (Jimmy) (Athlete, Baseball Player)
1105 Oakview Dr
Wheaton, IL 60187-3026, USA

Piersoll, Chris (Athlete, Baseball Player)
4417 Groveland Ave
Sarasota, FL 34231-7557, USA

Pierson, Geoff (Actor)
Ambrosio/Mortimer
165 W 46th St
New York, NY 10036-2501, USA

Pierson, John (Athlete, Hockey Player)
3 Steepletree Ln
Wayland, MA 01778-3912, USA

Pierson, Kate (Musician)
Direct Management Group
8332 Melrose Ave # 2
West Hollywood, CA 90069-5420, USA

Pierson, Pete (Athlete, Football Player)
19130 Beckett Dr
Odessa, FL 33556-2274, USA

Pierzynski, Anthony J (AJ) (Athlete, Baseball Player)
2139 N Clifton Ave
Chicago, IL 60614-4115, USA

Pieterse, Sasha (Actor)
c/o Ryan Martin *Agency for the Performing Arts (APA-LA)*
405 S Beverly Dr Ste 500
Beverly Hills, CA 90212-4425, USA

Pietkiewicz, Stan (Athlete, Basketball Player)
2213 Venetian Way
Winter Park, FL 32789-1215, USA

Pietrus, Mickael (Basketball Player)
Golden State Warriors
1001 Broadway
Oakland, CA 94607-4019, USA

Pietrus, Mikael
PO Box 2874
Windermere, FL 34786-2874, USA

Pietruski Jr, John M (Business Person)
27 Paddock Ln
Colts Neck, NJ 07722-1266, USA

Pietrzak, Jim (Athlete, Football Player)
9800 4th St N Ste 400
Saint Petersburg, FL 33702-2464, USA

Pietz, Amy (Actor)
c/o Scott Howard *Howard Entertainment*
16530 Ventura Blvd Ste 305
Encino, CA 91436-4594, USA

Pifferini, Bob Sr (Athlete, Football Player)
4160 Jade St Spc 65
Capitola, CA 95010-3922, USA

Pignatano, Joe (Athlete, Baseball Player)
150 78th St
Brooklyn, NY 11209-2914, USA

Pignatiello, Carmen (Athlete, Baseball Player)
4087 Milford Ln
Aurora, IL 60504-2059, USA

Pignatiellp, Carmen (Athlete, Baseball Player)
4087 Milford Ln
Aurora, IL 60504-2059, USA

Pi-Gonzalez, Amaury (Sportscaster)
4940 Adagio Ct
Fremont, CA 94538-3201, USA

Pigott, Mark C (Business Person)
PACCAR Inc
777 106th Ave NE
Bellevue, WA 98004-5027, USA

Pigott, Sebastian (Actor)
c/o Andrew Edwards *Wishlab*
2225A Hyperion Ave
Los Angeles, CA 90027-4709, USA

Pike, Gary (Musician)
10031 Benares Pl
Sun Valley, CA 91352-4207, USA

Pike, Jim (Musician)
MPI Talent Agency
9255 W Sunset Blvd Ste 407
West Hollywood, CA 90069-3302, USA

Pike, Rosamund (Actor)
c/o Shelley Browning *Magnolia Entertainment (LA)*
9595 Wilshire Blvd Ste 601
Beverly Hills, CA 90212-2506, USA

Pikser, Jeremy (Actor)
c/o Margaret Riley *Brillstein Entertainment Partners (LA)*
9150 Wilshire Blvd Ste 350
Beverly Hills, CA 90212-3453, USA

Pilarczyk, Daniel E (Religious Leader)
100 E 8th St Fl 8
Cincinnati, OH 45202-2129, USA

Pilares, Kealoha (Athlete, Football Player)
c/o Ryan Morgan *MAG Sports Agency*
8222 Melrose Ave Fl 2
Los Angeles, CA 90046-6825, USA

Pileggi, Mitch (Actor)
c/o Joel King *Pakula/King & Associates*
9229 W Sunset Blvd Ste 315
West Hollywood, CA 90069-3403, USA

Piligian, Craig (Producer)
c/o Staff Member *William Morris Endeavor (LA)*
9601 Wilshire Blvd
Beverly Hills, CA 90210-5213, USA

Pilkey, Dav (Writer)
Scholastic Press
555 Broadway
New York, NY 10012-3919, USA

Pilkey, Dave (Writer)
7406 Summer Trail Dr
Sugar Land, TX 77479-6232, USA

Pill, Alison (Actor)
c/o Joanna (Joanie) Burstein *Burstein Company, The*
15304 W Sunset Blvd Ste 208
Pacific Palisades, CA 90272-3656, USA

Pilla, Anthony M (Religious Leader)
Catholic Bishops National Conference
3211 4th St NE
Washington, DC 20017-1104, USA

Pillath, Roger (Athlete, Football Player)
N3623 Lepinsky Rd
Peshtigo, WI 54157-9403, USA

Piller, Zach (Athlete, Football Player)
3907 Dunleer Ct
Tallahassee, FL 32309-2630, USA

Pillers, Lawrence (Athlete, Football Player)
4305 Hanging Moss Rd
Jackson, MS 39206-4719, USA

Pillow, Ray (Musician)
900 Harpeth Trace Dr
Nashville, TN 37221-3114, USA

Pilotdrift (Music Group)
c/o Staff Member *Paradigm (Monterey)*
404 W Franklin St
Monterey, CA 93940-2303, USA

Pimental, Nancy (Actor, Writer)
c/o Staff Member *William Morris Endeavor (LA)*
9601 Wilshire Blvd
Beverly Hills, CA 90210-5213, USA

Pimentel, Miguel (Musician)
c/o Mark Pitts *Bystorm Entertainment*
550 Madison Ave Fl 10
New York, NY 10022-3211, USA

Pincay, Laffit (Horse Racer)
719 Carriage House Dr
Arcadia, CA 91006-2010, USA

Pinchak, Jimmy (Jax) (Actor)
c/o Staff Member *Agency for the Performing Arts (APA-LA)*
405 S Beverly Dr Ste 500
Beverly Hills, CA 90212-4425, USA

Pinchot, Bronson (Actor)
10061 Riverside Dr
Toluca Lake, CA 91602-2560, USA

Pinckney, Ed (Athlete, Basketball Player)
3350 SW 27th Ave Apt 1202
Miami, FL 33133-5326, USA

Pinckney, Sandra (Chef, Television Host)
c/o Staff Member *Food Network, The*
1180 Avenue of the Americas Fl 11
New York, NY 10036-8401, USA

Pinder, Cyril (Athlete, Football Player)
7137 S Luella Ave
Chicago, IL 60649-2511, USA

Pine, Chris (Actor)
c/o John Carrabino *John Carrabino Management*
5900 Wilshire Blvd Ste 406
Los Angeles, CA 90036-5015, USA

Pine, Courtney (Musician)
Elizabeth Rush Agency
100 Park St Apt 4
Montclair, NJ 07042-2996, USA

Pine, Phillip (Actor)
3972 Acapulco Ave
Las Vegas, NV 89121-6104, USA

Pine, Robert (Actor)
4212 Ben Ave
Studio City, CA 91604-2021, USA

Pineda, Allan (Apl. de. ap) (Musician)
c/o William Derella *DAS Communications*
83 Riverside Dr
New York, NY 10024-5713, USA

Pinero, Joel (Athlete, Baseball Player)
9406 Lake Washington Blvd NE
Bellevue, WA 98004-5409, USA

Pingel, John S (Athlete, Football Player)
80 Celestial Way Apt 203
Juno Beach, FL 33408-2314, USA

Pinger, Mark (Swimmer)
5201 Orduna Dr Apt 6
Coral Gables, FL 33146-2655, USA

Pingree, Chellie (Congressman, Politician)
1318 Longworth Hob
Washington, DC 20515-4332, USA

Piniella, Louis V (Lou) (Athlete, Baseball Player, Coach)
705 Berrocales De Avila
Tampa, FL 33613-1099, USA

Pink, Steve
c/o Gabrielle (Gaby) Morgerman *William Morris Endeavor (LA)*
9601 Wilshire Blvd
Beverly Hills, CA 90210-5213, USA

Pinkel, Gary (Coach, Football Coach)
University of Missouri
Athletic Dept
Columbia, MO 64211, USA

Pinkett, Allen (Athlete, Football Player)
2026 Tuam St
Houston, TX 77004-1349, USA

Pinkett Smith, Jada (Actor, Producer)
1401/1405/1409 Cold Canyon Rd
Calabasas, CA 91302, USA

Pinkins, Tonya (Actor)
Innovative Artists
1505 10th St
Santa Monica, CA 90401-2805, USA

Pink (P!nk) (Musician)
c/o Roger Davies *RDWM America*
1158 26th St Ste 564
Santa Monica, CA 90403-4698, USA

Pinkston, Rob (Actor)
c/o Staff Member *Mark Robert Management*
2208 Patricia Ave
Los Angeles, CA 90064-2318, USA

Pinkston, Ryan (Actor)
c/o Staff Member *Morra Brezner Steinberg & Tenenbaum (MBST) Entertainment*
345 N Maple Dr Ste 200
Beverly Hills, CA 90210-5174, USA

Pinkston, Todd (Athlete, Football Player)
1 Novacare Way
Philadelphia, PA 19145-5900, USA

Pinmonkey (Music Group)
c/o Staff Member *William Morris Endeavor (Nashville)*
1600 Division St Ste 300
Nashville, TN 37203-2755, USA

Pinner, Artose (Athlete, Football Player)
102 Big Blue Ct
Hopkinsville, KY 42240-2600, USA

Pinney, Ray (Athlete, Football Player)
6529B NE Windermere Rd
Seattle, WA 98105-2057, USA

Pino, Danny (Actor)
c/o Geordie Frey *GEF Entertainment*
611 N Cherokee Ave
Los Angeles, CA 90004-1008, USA

Pinone, John (Athlete, Basketball Player)
108 Riverview Rd
Glastonbury, CT 06033-3140, USA

Pinsent, Gordon (Actor)
c/o Steve Lovett *Lovett Management*
1327 Brinkley Ave
Los Angeles, CA 90049-3619, USA

Pinsky, Dr. Drew (Doctor, Reality Star, Television Host)
2050 Huntington Dr Ste D
S Pasadena, CA 91030-4900, USA

Pinsky, Robert N (Writer)
Boston University
236 Bay State Rd Attn Dept
Boston, MA 02215-1403, USA

Pinson, Julie (Actor)
13576 Cheltenham Dr
Sherman Oaks, CA 91423-4818, USA

Pinson, Vada
710 31st St
Oakland, CA 94609-2925

Pintauro, Danny (Actor)
c/o Arnold M Preston *Preston Entertainment Inc*
8033 W Sunset Blvd # 7250
Los Angeles, CA 90046-2401

Piotrowski, Tom (Athlete, Basketball Player)
80 Clarks Landing Rd
Port Republic, NJ 08241-9741, USA

Piper, Rowdy Roddy (Actor, Athlete, Wrestler)
Flying Noodles Inc.
13110 SW Whitmore Rd
Roderic Toombs
Hillsboro, OR 97123-9073, USA

Pipes, Leah (Actor)
c/o Jason Newman *Untitled Entertainment (LA)*
350 S Beverly Dr Ste 200
Beverly Hills, CA 90212-4819, USA

Pipettes, The (Music Group)
c/o Staff Member *Paradigm (Monterey)*
404 W Franklin St
Monterey, CA 93940-2303, USA

Pippen, Scottie (Athlete, Basketball Player, Olympic Athlete)
2571 Del Lago Dr
Fort Lauderdale, FL 33316-2303, USA

Pippig, Uta (Athlete, Olympic Athlete, Track Athlete)
Postfach 1249
Ellsworth, PA 15331, USA

Pirae, Marcus Jean (Actor)
c/o Tom Parziali *Visionary Entertainment*
1558 N Stanley Ave
Los Angeles, CA 90046-2711, USA

Pirates of the Mississippi
PO Box 17087
Nashville, TN 37217-0087

Pires, Alexandre (Musician)
c/o Staff Member *BMG*
1540 Broadway
New York, NY 10036-4039, USA

Pires, Mary Joao (Musician)
Columbia Artists Mgmt Inc
165 W 57th St
New York, NY 10019-2201, USA

Pirie, Lockwood (Athlete, Olympic Athlete, Sailor)
5644 Ravenspur Dr Apt 319
Rancho Palos Verdes, CA 90275-3585, USA

Pirkl, Greg (Athlete, Baseball Player)
6822 Emerald Bay Ln
Indianapolis, IN 46237-5063, USA

Pirner, Dave (Musician, Songwriter, Writer)
Monterey Peninsula Artists
509 Hartnell St
Monterey, CA 93940-2825, USA

Piro, Stephanie (Cartoonist)
PO Box 605
Hampton, NH 03843-0605, USA

Pirok, Pauline (Athlete, Baseball Player)
13636 86th Ave
Orland Park, IL 60462-1612, USA

Pirri, Jim
9300 Wilshire Blvd Ste 555
Beverly Hills, CA 90212-3211

Pirtle, Gerry (Athlete, Baseball Player)
30306 E 59th St S
Broken Arrow, OK 74014-8434, USA

Pirus, Alex (Athlete, Hockey Player)
15W222 Concord St
Elmhurst, IL 60126-5326

Pisarcik, Joe (Athlete, Football Player)
27 Compass Cir
Mount Laurel, NJ 08054-6106, USA

Pisarkiewicz, Steve (Athlete, Football Player)
2550 Citrus Tower Blvd Apt 10206
Clermont, FL 34711-6839, USA

Pisciotta, Marc (Athlete, Baseball Player)
867 Village Greene NW
Marietta, GA 30064-4749, USA

Piscopo, Joe (Actor, Comedian)
c/o Staff Member *Niad Management*
15021 Ventura Blvd Ste 860
Sherman Oaks, CA 91403-2442, USA

Piskula, Grace (Athlete, Baseball Player)
415 Cherry Hill Dr
Mount Pleasant, WI 53406-3523, USA

Pistone, Tom (Race Car Driver)
7858 Old Concord Rd
Charlotte, NC 28213, USA

Pitbull (Musician)
c/o Leslie Zigel *Ziglaw*
4500 Biscayne Blvd Ste 201
Miami, FL 33137-3227, USA

Pitchford, Dean
1701 Queens Ct
Los Angeles, CA 90069-1431

Pitcock, Joan (Golfer)
341 E Lester Ave
Fresno, CA 93720-1615, USA

Pitillo, Maria (Actor)
c/o Jonathan Howard *Innovative Artists (LA)*
1505 10th St
Santa Monica, CA 90401-2805, USA

Pitino, Rick (Basketball Coach, Coach)
212 Mockingbird Gardens Dr
Louisville, KY 40207-5711, USA

Pitlick, Lance (Athlete, Hockey Player)
5010 Shenandoah Ln N
Minneapolis, MN 55446-2120

Pitlock, Skip (Athlete, Baseball Player)
215 Prospect St
Seguin, TX 78155-6018, USA

Pitoc, John Paul (Actor)
c/o Amy Slomovits *Evolution Entertainment (LA)*
9320 Wilshire Blvd Ste 202
Beverly Hills, CA 90212-3217, USA

Pitoc, J P
1836 Courtney Ter
Los Angeles, CA 90046-2106, USA

Pitou, Penny
100 Potter Hill Rd
Gilford, NH 03249-6802, USA

Pitou Zimmerman, Penny (Skier)
560 Sanborn Rd
Sanbornton, NH 03269-2401, USA

Pitt, Brad (Actor, Producer)
c/o Staff Member *Plan B Entertainment*
9150 Wilshire Blvd Ste 350
Beverly Hills, CA 90212-3453, USA

Pitt, Eugene (Musician)
Paramount Entertainment
PO Box 12
Far Hills, NJ 07931-0012, USA

Pitt, Michael (Actor)
c/o Jason Weinberg *Untitled Entertainment (LA)*
350 S Beverly Dr Ste 200
Beverly Hills, CA 90212-4819, USA

Pitta, Dennis (Athlete, Football Player)
c/o David Dunn *Athletes First, LLC*
23091 Mill Creek Dr
Laguna Hills, CA 92653-1258, USA

Pittaro, Chris (Athlete, Baseball Player)
42 Pintinalli Dr
Trenton, NJ 08619-1558, USA

Pittman, Charles (Athlete, Basketball Player)
16286 N 29th Dr
Phoenix, AZ 85053-3004, USA

Pittman, Danny (Football Player)
New York Giants
University of Wyoming Attn Alumni Association
Laramie, WY 82071, USA

Pittman, Joe (Athlete, Baseball Player)
809 McKinnon Dr
Columbus, GA 31907-6508, USA

Pittman, R F (Publisher)
Tampa Tribune
202 S Parker St
Tampa, FL 33606-2395, USA

Pittman, Sheldon (Race Car Driver)
Morgan McClure Racing
26502 Newbanks Rd
Abingdon, VA 24210-7500, USA

Pitts, Chester (Athlete, Football Player)
c/o Staff Member *EAG Sports Management*
909 N Sepulveda Blvd Ste 360
El Segundo, CA 90245-3864, USA

Pitts, Frank (Athlete, Football Player)
8249 S Laredo Ave
Baton Rouge, LA 70811-4055, USA

Pitts, Gaylen (Athlete, Baseball Player)
214 Rocky Bluff Ln
Mountain Home, AR 72653-7186, USA

Pitts, Greg
c/o Amy Slomovits *Evolution Entertainment (LA)*
9320 Wilshire Blvd Ste 202
Beverly Hills, CA 90212-3217, USA

Pitts, Hugh (Athlete, Football Player)
3612 Short St
Greenville, TX 75401-3900, USA

Pitts, Jacob (Actor)
c/o Robert Stein *Robert Stein Management*
PO Box 3797
Beverly Hills, CA 90212-0797, USA

Pitts, John (Athlete, Football Player)
4899 W Tyson St
Chandler, AZ 85226-2909, USA

Pitts, Robert (R C) (Athlete, Basketball Player)
12655 E Millburn Ave
Baton Rouge, LA 70815-6827, USA

Pitts, Ron (Athlete, Football Player)
3811 Davids Rd
Agoura Hills, CA 91301-3643, USA

Pitts, Ron (Sportscaster)
Fox TV
205 E 67th St
Sports Dept
New York, NY 10065-6089, USA

Pitts, Tyrone S (Religious Leader)
Progressive National Baptist Convention
601 50th St NE
Washington, DC 20019-5498, USA

Pittsley, Jim (Athlete, Baseball Player)
5 Old Woods Rd
Du Bois, PA 15801-8711, USA

Pivec, Dave (Athlete, Football Player)
1288 Fenwick Garth
Arnold, MD 21012-2107, USA

Piven, Jeremy (Actor)
c/o Jon Rubinstein *Authentic Talent and Literary Management*
20 Jay St Ste M17
Brooklyn, NY 11201-8300, USA

Pivonka, Michal (Athlete, Hockey Player)
8312 Grand Estuary Trl Unit 102
Bradenton, FL 34212-4264

Pixies (Music Group, Musician)
c/o John Branigan *William Morris Endeavor (LA)*
9601 Wilshire Blvd
Beverly Hills, CA 90210-5213, USA

Pizarro, Artur (Musician)
c/o Staff Member *Musicians Corporate Management*
PO Box 825
Highland, NY 12528-0825, USA

Pizarro, Juan (Athlete, Baseball Player)
2262 Ave Borinquen
San Juan, PR 00915-4421, USA

Pizzo, Angelo (Director, Producer, Writer)
c/o David Greenblatt *Greenlit*
1800 N Highland Ave Ste 500
Los Angeles, CA 90028-4527, USA

Place, Marcella (Athlete, Hockey Player, Olympic Athlete)
1091 Oak Hill Rd
Lafayette, CA 94549-3136, USA

Place, Mary Kay (Actor)
c/o Staff Member *Gersh (LA)*
9465 Wilshire Blvd Ste 600
Beverly Hills, CA 90212-2605, USA

Plager, Bob (Athlete, Hockey Player)
St Louis Blues
1401 Clark Ave
Saint Louis, MO 63103-2700

Plager, Robert B (Bob) (Athlete, Coach, Hockey Player)
362 Branchport Dr
Chesterfield, MO 63017-2902

Plainic, Zoran (Basketball Player)
New Jersey Nets
390 Murray Hill Pkwy
East Rutherford, NJ 07073-2109, USA

Plain White T's (Music Group)
c/o Sharrin Summers *Hollywood Records*
500 S Buena Vista St
Burbank, CA 91521-0002, USA

Plakson, Suzie (Actor)
302 N La Brea Ave # 363
Los Angeles, CA 90036-2518, USA

Plana, Tony (Actor)
c/o Todd Eisner *Innovative Artists (LA)*
405 S Beverly Dr Ste 500
Beverly Hills, CA 90212-4425, USA

Plan B (Music Group)
c/o Staff Member *Paradigm (Monterey)*
404 W Franklin St
Monterey, CA 93940-2303, USA

Plank, Doug (Athlete, Football Player)
12622 E Paradise Dr
Scottsdale, AZ 85259-3455, USA

Plank, Ed (Eddie) (Athlete, Baseball Player)
1353 Leawood Rd
Englewood, FL 34223-1714, USA

Plank, Kevin (Business Person)
Under Armour, Inc.
1020 Hull St Ste 300
Baltimore, MD 21230-5358, USA

Plank, Raymond (Business Person)
Apache Corp
2000 Post Oak Blvd Ste B100
Houston, TX 77056-4428, USA

Plante, Bruce (Cartoonist)
Chattanooga Times
100 E 11th St Ste 400
Editorial Dept
Chattanooga, TN 37402-4214, USA

Plante, Dan (Athlete, Hockey Player)
5 Gillingham Ct
Algonquin, IL 60102-6285

Plante, Derek (Athlete, Hockey Player)
5325 Roosevelt Dr
Hermantown, MN 55811-3679

Plante, William M (Correspondent)
CBS-TV
2020 M St NW
News Dept
Washington, DC 20036-3368, USA

Plantenberg, Erik (Athlete, Baseball Player)
1846 Creekside Dr NE
Owatonna, MN 55060-3973, USA

Plantery, Mark (Athlete, Hockey Player)
ON182 Alexander Dr
Geneva, IL 60134

Plantier, Phil (Athlete, Baseball Player)
PO Box 122000
San Diego, CA 92112-2000, USA

Planutis, Jerry (Athlete, Football Player)
3776 Stadium Dr
Bridgman, MI 49106-9789, USA

Plaskett, Thomas G (Business Person)
5215 N O Connor Blvd Ste 1070
Irving, TX 75039-3738, USA

Platov, Yevgeni (Dancer)
Connecticut Skating Center
300 Alumni Rd
Newington, CT 06111-1868, USA

Platt, Howard (Actor)
9200 W Sunset Blvd Ste 1130
West Hollywood, CA 90069-3606, USA

Platt, Kenneth A (Doctor)
11435 Quivas Way
Denver, CO 80234-2620, USA

Platt, Lewis E (Lew) (Business Person)
Hewlett-Packard Co
3000 Hanover St
Palo Alto, CA 94304-1185, USA

Platt, Oliver (Actor, Producer)
c/o Carrie Byalick *I/D PR (NY)*
150 W 30th St Fl 19
New York, NY 10001-4119, USA

Platters
2756 N Green Valley Pkwy # 449
Henderson, NV 89014-2120

Platts, Todd (Congressman, Politician)
2455 Rayburn Hob
Washington, DC 20515-2401, USA

Playboy Playmates
2112 Broadway
Santa Monica, CA 90404-2912

Player, Gary J (Athlete, Golfer)
635 Garden Market Dr
Travelers Rest, SC 29690-7111, USA

Player, Scott (Athlete, Football Player)
115 Averley Way
Saint Johns, FL 32259-8221, USA

Playfair, Jim (Athlete, Hockey Player)
Phoenix Coyotes
6751 N Sunset Blvd Ste E200
Glendale, AZ 85305-3158

Playfair, Larry (Athlete, Hockey Player)
724 Ransom Rd
Grand Island, NY 14072-1464

Playfair, Larry (Athlete, Hockey Player)
Buffalo Sabres
1 Seymour H Knox III Plz Ste 1
Buffalo, NY 14203-3096

Plaza, Aubrey (Actor)
c/o Greg Walter *3 Arts Entertainment (LA)*
9460 Wilshire Blvd Fl 7
Beverly Hills, CA 90212-2713, USA

Pleasant, Anthony (Athlete, Football Player)
PO Box 23238
Overland Park, KS 66283-0238, USA

Pleasant, Reggie (Athlete, Football Player)
8270 Milford Plantation Rd
Pinewood, SC 29125-9249, USA

Pleau, Larry (Athlete, Hockey Player, Olympic Athlete)
12 Atlantic Ave
Seabrook, NH 03874-4803

Pleau, Larry (Athlete, Hockey Player)
St Louis Blues
1401 Clark Ave
Saint Louis, MO 63103-2700

Pleis, Bill (Athlete, Baseball Player)
16744 4th Ave NE
Bradenton, FL 34212-5510, USA

Plemons, Jesse (Actor)
c/o Staff Member *Simmons & Scott Entertainment*
7942 Mulholland Dr
Los Angeles, CA 90046-1225, USA

Plenty, Patty
1350 E Flamingo Rd # 150
Las Vegas, NV 89119-5263

Plesac, Dan (Athlete, Baseball Player)
40 Hartz Way Ste 1
Secaucus, NJ 07094-2403, USA

Pleshette, John (Actor)
2643 Creston Dr
Los Angeles, CA 90068-2207, USA

Pless, Rance (Athlete, Baseball Player)
5528 Asheville Hwy
Greeneville, TN 37743-2287, USA

Pletcher, Eidon (Cartoonist)
210 Canberra Ct
Slidell, LA 70458-1520, USA

Plett, Willi (Athlete, Hockey Player)
2701 Timbercreek Cir
Roswell, GA 30076-8805

Plews, Herb (Athlete, Baseball Player)
350 Ponca Pl
Boulder, CO 80303-3828, USA

Plimpton, Calvin H (Doctor)
Downstate Medical Center
450 Clarkson Ave
Brooklyn, NY 11203-2098, USA

Plimpton, Martha (Actor)
c/o Jill Littman *Impression Entertainment*
9229 W Sunset Blvd Ste 700
West Hollywood, CA 90069-3407, USA

Plodinec, Tim (Athlete, Baseball Player)
23251 Gilmore St
West Hills, CA 91307-3427, USA

Ploeger, Kurt (Athlete, Football Player)
6451 E Nance St
Mesa, AZ 85215-1608, USA

Plotkin, Stanley A (Musician)
3940 Delancey St
Philadelphia, PA 19104-4107, USA

Plouffe, Trevor (Baseball Player)
11437 Vineland Ct
Porter Ranch, CA 91326-4178

Plum, Milton R (Milt) (Athlete, Football Player)
1104 Oakside Ct
Raleigh, NC 27609-3596, USA

Plum, Ted (Athlete, Football Player)
17 Laurel Hill Dr
Cherry Hill, NJ 08003-2658, USA

Plumb, Eve (Actor)
c/o Mark Measures *Kazarian, Measures, Ruskin & Associates (LA)*
11969 Ventura Blvd Fl 3
Studio City, CA 91604-2630, USA

Plumer, Patricia (PattiSue) (Athlete, Track Athlete)
USA Track & Field
4341 Starlight Dr
Indianapolis, IN 46239-1473, USA

Plumlee, Mason (Athlete, Basketball Player)
c/o Mark Bartelstein *Priority Sports & Entertainment - Chicago*
312 N La Salle
Suite 650
Chicago, IL 60610, USA

Plummer, Bill (Athlete, Baseball Player, Coach)
52171 Sageway Dr
Redding, CA 96003, USA

Plummer, Christopher (Actor, Musician)
49 Wampum Hill Rd Ste 480
Weston, CT 06883-1228, USA

Plummer, Garry (Athlete, Basketball Player)
2119 Arthur Ave Apt 1
Belmont, CA 94002-1661, USA

Plummer, Gary (Athlete, Basketball Player)
2119 Arthur Ave
Belmont, CA 94002-1660, USA

Plummer, Gary (Athlete, Football Player)
10374 Rue Chamberry
San Diego, CA 92131-2212, USA

Plummer, Glenn (Actor)
c/o Brian Wilkins *Kritzer Levine Wilkins Entertainment (KLWG)*
11872 La Grange Ave Fl 1
Los Angeles, CA 90025-5283, USA

Plummer, Scotty
909 Parkview Ave
Lodi, CA 95242-2347

Plunk, Eric (Athlete, Baseball Player)
9520 Pats Point Dr
Corona, CA 92883-5068, USA

Plunkett, Jim (Athlete, Football Player, Heisman Trophy Winner)
51 Kilroy Way
Atherton, CA 94027-5405, USA

Plunkett, Maryann
10 E 44th St
New York, NY 10017-3601

Plunkett, Warren (Athlete, Football Player)
25150 N Windy Walk Dr Unit 30
Scottsdale, AZ 85255-8106, USA

Plushenko, Evgeni (Figure Skater)
c/o Staff Member *Champions on Ice*
3500 American Blvd W Ste 190
Minneapolis, MN 55431-4431, USA

Plus One (Music Group)
c/o Teresa Davis *Paradigm (Nashville)*
124 12th Ave S Ste 410
Nashville, TN 37203-3170, USA

Ply, Bobby (Athlete, Football Player)
8616 Ash Ave
Raytown, MO 64138-3431, USA

Plympton, Jeff (Athlete, Baseball Player)
8 Robin St
Plainville, MA 02762-1522, USA

P. McGovern, James (Congressman, Politician)
438 Cannon Hob
Washington, DC 20515-0519, USA

P. McKeon, Howard H (Congressman, Politician)
2184 Rayburn Hob
Washington, DC 20515-2701, USA

PM Dawn (Music Group)
Raw Shack
857 Atlantic Ave Apt 5
Brooklyn, NY 11238-2797, USA

P. Moran, James (Congressman, Politician)
2239 Rayburn Hob
Washington, DC 20515-4608, USA

Poapst, Steve (Athlete, Hockey Player)
502 Kelly Ct
Lombard, IL 60148-3115

Poapst, Steve (Athlete, Hockey Player)
Rockford Icehogs
300 Elm St
Rockford, IL 61101-1238

Pochman, Owen (Athlete, Football Player)
7405 91st Ave SE
Mercer Island, WA 98040-5805, USA

Pochmara, Brian (Athlete, Hockey Player)
38191 E Horseshoe Dr
Clinton Township, MI 48036-1727

Pocoroba, Biff (Athlete, Baseball Player)
2700 Forest Dr
Melbourne, FL 32901-6827, USA

POD (Music Group)
c/o Staff Member *Paradigm (Monterey)*
404 W Franklin St
Monterey, CA 93940-2303, USA

Podein, Shjon (Athlete, Hockey Player)
4350 Browndale Ave
Minneapolis, MN 55424-1012

Podell, Eyal (Actor)
c/o Samantha Crisp *Kohner Agency, The*
9300 Wilshire Blvd Ste 555
Beverly Hills, CA 90212-3211, USA

Podeswa, Jeremy (Director, Writer)
c/o Jennifer Levine *Untitled Entertainment (LA)*
350 S Beverly Dr Ste 200
Beverly Hills, CA 90212-4819, USA

Podewell, Cathy (Actor)
17328 S Crest Dr
Los Angeles, CA 90035, USA

Podloski, Ray (Athlete, Hockey Player)
1622 Kerr Rd NW
Sumas, WA 98295, USA

Podolak, Edward J (Ed) (Athlete, Football Player)
PO Box 2000
Basalt, CO 81621-2000, USA

Podres, Johnny (Athlete, Baseball Player)
1 Colonial Ct
Queensbury, NY 12804-1912, USA

Podsednik, Scott (Athlete, Baseball Player)
c/o Staff Member *Chicago White Sox*
U.S. Cellular Field
333 Wes 35th St
Chicago, IL 60616, USA

Poe, Dontari (Athlete, Football Player)
c/o Jimmy Sexton *CAA (Memphis)*
6060 Poplar Ave Ste 470
Memphis, TN 38119-0910, USA

Poe, Gregory (Designer, Fashion Designer)
Dutch Courage
1950 S Santa Fe Ave
Los Angeles, CA 90021-2928, USA

Poe, Johnnie (Athlete, Football Player)
222 Autumn Pine Dr
Fairview Hts, IL 62208-2960, USA

Poe, Richard
10 Prospect Park SW Apt 17
Brooklyn, NY 11215-5937

Poe, Ted (Congressman, Politician)
320 Cannon Hob
Washington, DC 20515-0603, USA

Poehler, Amy (Actor, Comedian)
c/o David (Dave) Becky *3 Arts Entertainment (LA)*
9460 Wilshire Blvd Fl 7
Beverly Hills, CA 90212-2713, USA

Poepping, Mike (Athlete, Baseball Player)
13047 230th Ave
Pierz, MN 56364-1563, USA

Poff, John (Athlete, Baseball Player)
2786 Mishler Rd
Mio, MI 48647-9505, USA

Pogue, David (Correspondent)
c/o Staff Member *CNBC (Main)*
900 Sylvan Ave
Englewood Cliffs, NJ 07632-3312, USA

Pohl, Dan (Golfer)
3424 E Suncrest Ct
Phoenix, AZ 85044-3506, USA

Pohl, Don (Golfer)
3424 E Suncrest Ct
Phoenix, AZ 85044-3506, USA

Pohl, Frederick (Writer)
855 S Harvard Dr
Palatine, IL 60067-7026, USA

Pohl, Johnny (Athlete, Hockey Player)
1790 Deephaven Dr
Saint Paul, MN 55129-6230

Pohlad, Carl (Baseball Player, Business Person)
c/o Staff Member *Minnesota Twins*
Metrodome
34 Kirby Punkett Place
Minneapolis, MN 55415, USA

Poimboeuf, Lance (Athlete, Football Player)
309 Fairfield Dr
Thibodaux, LA 70301-3721, USA

Poindexter, Anthony (Athlete, Football Player)
RR 3 Box 128
Forest, VA 24551, USA

Poindexter, Buster (Musician)
c/o Nina Nisenholtz *N2N Entertainment*
1230 Montana Ave Ste 203
Santa Monica, CA 90403-5987, USA

Poindexter, Christian H (Business Person)
Constellation Energy Group
39 W Lexington St
Baltimore, MD 21201-3910, USA

Poindexter, John M
10 Barrington Fare
Rockville, MD 20850-3001, USA

Pointer, Aaron (Athlete, Baseball Player)
4902 N Scenic View Ln
Tacoma, WA 98407-1365, USA

Pointer, Anita (Musician)
12060 Crest Ct
Beverly Hills, CA 90210-1348, USA

Pointer, Bonnie (Musician)
T-Best Talent Agency
508 Honey Lake Ct
Danville, CA 94506-1237, USA

Pointer, Priscilla (Actor)
c/o Staff Member *William Morris Endeavor (LA)*
9601 Wilshire Blvd
Beverly Hills, CA 90210-5213, USA

Pointer, Priscilla (Musician)
213 16th St
Santa Monica, CA 90402-2215, USA

Point of Grace (Music Group)
c/o David Breen *The Breen Agency*
25 Music Sq W
Nashville, TN 37203-3205, USA

Poirier, Mark (Writer)
c/o Rowena Arguelles *Creative Artists Agency (CAA-LA)*
2000 Avenue of the Stars Ste 100
Los Angeles, CA 90067-4705, USA

Poitier, Sidney (Actor)
1718 Angelo Dr
Beverly Hills, CA 90210-2722, USA

Polaha, Kristoffer (Actor)
c/o Paul Rosicker *Gersh (LA)*
9465 Wilshire Blvd Ste 600
Beverly Hills, CA 90212-2605, USA

Polamalu, Troy (Athlete, Football Player)
135 Windwood Dr
Wexford, PA 15090-8502, USA

Polanco, Placido (Athlete, Baseball Player)
8950 SW 63rd Ct
Miami, FL 33156-1830, USA

Polano, Nick (Athlete, Hockey Player)
16981 Birchwood Dr
Northville, MI 48168-4422, USA

Polanski, Roman (Director)
c/o Jeff Berg *Resolution (LA)*
1801 Century Park E Ste 2300
Los Angeles, CA 90067-2325, USA

Polansky, Abraham
135 S McCarty Dr PH 4
Beverly Hills, CA 90212-2257

Polansky, Mark (Astronaut)
15906 Meadowside Dr
Houston, TX 77062-4761, USA

Polcovich, Kevin (Athlete, Baseball Player)
3 Beardsley St
Auburn, NY 13021-2809, USA

Poldberg, Brian
1119 Cachelin Dr
Carter Lake, IA 51510-1233

Pole, Dick (Athlete, Baseball Player)
5124 Marsh Field Ln
Sarasota, FL 34235-7014, USA

Polee, Dwayne (Athlete, Basketball Player)
1169 E 60th St
Los Angeles, CA 90001-1117, USA

Poletiek, Noah (Actor)
c/o Staff Member *Protege Entertainment*
710 E Angeleno Ave
Burbank, CA 91501-2213, USA

Polic, Henry II (Actor)
Sutton Barth Vennari
5900 Wilshire Blvd Ste 100
Los Angeles, CA 90036-5007, USA

Polich, Mike (Athlete, Hockey Player)
825 3rd St NE
Osseo, MN 55369-1409

Polish, Mark (Actor, Producer, Writer)
c/o Sean Elliott *Authentic Talent and Literary Management*
20 Jay St Ste M17
Brooklyn, NY 11201-8300, USA

Polish, Michael (Director)
27676 Emerald Bay Ln
Bigfork, MT 59911, USA

Polishchuk, Oleksiy (Figure Skater)
c/o Staff Member *Champions on Ice*
3500 American Blvd W Ste 190
Minneapolis, MN 55431-4431, USA

Polito, Jon (Actor)
c/o Mary Ellen Mulcahy *Framework Entertainment (LA)*
9057 Nemo St Ste C
West Hollywood, CA 90069-5511, USA

Politte, Cliff (Athlete, Baseball Player)
6306 Sprig Oak Ct Apt C
Saint Louis, MO 63128-4336, USA

Poliziani, Dan (Athlete, Hockey Player)
5533 Clark Rd
Conesus, NY 14435-9549

Polizzi, Nicole (Snooki) (Reality Star)
13 Rohn St
East Hanover, NJ 07936-3651, USA

Pollack, Daniel (Musician)
University of Southern California
Music Dept
Los Angeles, CA 90089-0001, USA

Pollack, Frank (Athlete, Football Player)
907 Hillcrest Trl
Southlake, TX 76092-8439, USA

Pollack, Jim (Actor)
Ericka Wain
1418 N Highland Ave # 102
Los Angeles, CA 90028-7611, USA

Pollack, Kevin (Actor)
c/o Annett Wolf *WKT Public Relations (LA)*
9350 Wilshire Blvd Ste 450
Beverly Hills, CA 90212-3230, USA

Pollak, Kevin (Actor, Comedian)
c/o Staff Member *Red Bird Cinema*
11601 Wilshire Blvd Ste 2200
Los Angeles, CA 90025-1758, USA

Pollak, Mike (Athlete, Football Player)
c/o Ken Zuckerman *Priority Sports & Entertainment - (LA)*
15233 Ventura Blvd Ste 718
Sherman Oaks, CA 91403-2237, USA

Pollan, Michael (Writer)
c/o Steven Barclay *Steven Barclay Agency*
12 Western Ave
Petaluma, CA 94952-2907, USA

Pollan, Tracy (Actor)
c/o Bob Gersh *Gersh (LA)*
9465 Wilshire Blvd Ste 600
Beverly Hills, CA 90212-2605, USA

Pollard, Bob (Athlete, Football Player)
8987 Washington Blvd
Beaumont, TX 77707-2814, USA

Pollard, Frank (Athlete, Football Player)
1526 N 12th St
Waco, TX 76707-2320, USA

Pollard, Marcus (Athlete, Football Player)
2991 Cameo Dr
Carmel, IN 46032-9313, USA

Pollard, Michael J (Actor)
520 S Burnside Ave Apt 12A
Los Angeles, CA 90036-3956, USA

Pollard, Scot (Athlete, Basketball Player)
10560 Chatham Ct
Carmel, IN 46032-8301, USA

Pollard, Tiffany (New York) (Actor, Reality Star)
c/o Chuck Binder *Binder & Associates*
1465 Lindacrest Dr
Beverly Hills, CA 90210-2519, USA

Pollari, Joey (Actor)
c/o Nancy Kremer *Nancy Kremer Management*
4545 Morse Ave
Studio City, CA 91604-1008, USA

Polley, Dale (Athlete, Baseball Player)
107 Redding Rd
Georgetown, KY 40324-1078, USA

Polley, Sarah (Actor, Director, Writer)
c/o Frank Frattaroli *Circle of Confusion (LA)*
8931 Ellis Ave
Los Angeles, CA 90034-3336, USA

Pollitt-Deschaine, Alice (Athlete, Baseball Player)
9140 Silver Strand Rd
Levering, MI 49755-9103, USA

Pollock, Alex J (Business Person)
Federal Home Loan Bank
111 E Wacker Dr
Chicago, IL 60601-3713, USA

Polo, Ana Maria (Actor)
c/o Staff Member *Telemundo*
2470 W 8th Ave
Hialeah, FL 33010-2000, USA

Polo, Teri (Actor)
c/o Bob McGowan *McGowan Management*
8733 W Sunset Blvd Ste 103
West Hollywood, CA 90069-2241, USA

Polo, Terri (Actor)
c/o Staff Member *United Talent Agency (UTA-LA)*
9336 Civic Center Dr
Beverly Hills, CA 90210-3604, USA

Polofsky, Gordon (Athlete, Football Player)
802 N Ocean Blvd
North Myrtle Beach, SC 29582-2840, USA

Polone, Gavin (Producer)
c/o Staff Member *William Morris Endeavor (LA)*
9601 Wilshire Blvd
Beverly Hills, CA 90210-5213, USA

Poloni, John (Athlete, Baseball Player)
1714 Polo Club Dr
Tarpon Springs, FL 34689-8013, USA

Polow Da Don (Musician)
c/o Laura Wright *Avid Exposure*
1179 W A St Ste 233
Hayward, CA 94541-7006, USA

Polowski, Larry (Athlete, Football Player)
365 E Brookhollow Dr
Boise, ID 83706-6730, USA

Polson, Ralph (Athlete, Basketball Player)
3846 S Eagle Ln
Spokane Valley, WA 99206-6351, USA

Polynice, Olden (Athlete, Basketball Player)
PO Box 220339
Newhall, CA 91322-0339, USA

Polyphonic Spree, The (Music Group)
c/o Staff Member *Paradigm (Monterey)*
404 W Franklin St
Monterey, CA 93940-2303, USA

Pomers, Scarlett
c/o Rhonda Boudreaux *Rhonda Boudreaux Publicity*
Prefers to be contacted via telephone
Oakland, CA 00900, USA

Pominville, Jason (Athlete, Hockey Player)
3509 W 55th St
Edina, MN 55410-2306

Pompeo, Ellen (Actor)
c/o John Carrabino *John Carrabino Management*
5900 Wilshire Blvd Ste 406
Los Angeles, CA 90036-5015, USA

Pompeo, Mike (Congressman, Politician)
107 Cannon Hob
Washington, DC 20515-0902, USA

Ponazecki, Joe (Actor)
Don Buchwald
10 E 44th St Frnt 1
New York, NY 10017-3654, USA

Ponce, Carlos (Athlete, Baseball Player)
590 Kingsbury Ct
Wellington, FL 33414-3919, USA

Ponce, Carlos (Musician)
c/o Staff Member *William Morris Endeavor (LA)*
9601 Wilshire Blvd
Beverly Hills, CA 90210-5213, USA

Ponce, LuAnne (Actor)
Gold Marshak Liedtke
3500 W Olive Ave Ste 1400
Burbank, CA 91505-5512, USA

Ponce, Walter (Musician)
Columbia Artists Mgmt Inc
165 W 57th St
New York, NY 10019-2201, USA

Poncino, Larry (Athlete, Baseball Player)
2954 N Calle Ladera
Tucson, AZ 85715-3202, USA

Pond, Lennie (Race Car Driver)
4301 Caronado Dr
Chester, VA 23831-4502, USA

Pond, Matt (Musician)
c/o Staff Member *Paradigm (Monterey)*
404 W Franklin St
Monterey, CA 93940-2303, USA

Ponder, Christian (Football Player)
c/o Jimmy Sexton *CAA (Memphis)*
6060 Poplar Ave Ste 470
Memphis, TN 38119-0910, USA

Ponder, Dave (Athlete, Football Player)
1818 Sandalwood Ln
Grapevine, TX 76051-7344, USA

Ponder, Samantha Steele (Sportscaster)
c/o Nick Khan *Creative Artists Agency (CAA-LA)*
2000 Avenue of the Stars Ste 100
Los Angeles, CA 90067-4705, USA

Pondexter, Cliff (Athlete, Basketball Player)
1135 W Stuart Ave
Fresno, CA 93711-2040, USA

Pondexterok, Cliff
1135 W Stuart Ave
Fresno, CA 93711-2040, USA

Ponikarovsky, Alexei (Athlete, Hockey Player)
645 29th St
Manhattan Beach, CA 90266-2232

Ponson, Sidney (Athlete, Baseball Player)
443 Hendricks Isle Slip 2
Fort Lauderdale, FL 33301-5740, USA

Pontes, Marcos (Astronaut)
16807 Soaring Forest Dr
Houston, TX 77059-4002, USA

Pontes, Marcos Major (Astronaut)
16807 Soaring Forest Dr
Houston, TX 77059-4002, USA

Pontius, Chris (Actor, Writer)
c/o Beth Holden-Garland *Untitled Entertainment (LA)*
350 S Beverly Dr Ste 200
Beverly Hills, CA 90212-4819, USA

Ponty, Jean-Luc (Musician)
10340 Santa Monica Blvd
Los Angeles, CA 90025-6904, USA

Ponzini, Anthony (Actor)
Gold Marshak Liedtke
3500 W Olive Ave Ste 1400
Burbank, CA 91505-5512, USA

Pook, Chris (Race Car Driver)
Championship Auto Racing
5350 Lakeview Parkway South Dr
Indianapolis, IN 46268-5129, USA

Pool, David (Athlete, Football Player)
460 Vista Glen Dr
Cincinnati, OH 45246-2366, USA

Pool, John L (Doctor)
4104 Corbin Hall Ln
Fredericksburg, VA 22408-9534, USA

Poole, Bob (Athlete, Football Player)
7802 Shadyvilla Ln
Houston, TX 77055, USA

Poole, George B (Athlete, Football Player)
PO Box 278
Gloster, MS 39638-0278, USA

Poole, Jim (Athlete, Baseball Player)
605 Falls Lake Dr
Alpharetta, GA 30022-8059, USA

Poole, Keith (Athlete, Football Player)
4700 S Fulton Ranch Blvd Unit 61
Chandler, AZ 85248-5036, USA

Poole, Larry (Athlete, Football Player)
15803 Sea Oats Pl
Tampa, FL 33624-1629, USA

Poole, Nathan (Athlete, Football Player)
8686 Longwood St
San Diego, CA 92126-3654, USA

Poole, Oliver (Athlete, Football Player)
PO Box 184
Gloster, MS 39638-0184, USA

Poole, Tyrone (Athlete, Football Player)
3415 Rivers Call Blvd
Atlanta, GA 30339-5662, USA

Poole, William (Government Official)
Federal Reserve Bank
137 Frontenac Frst
Saint Louis, MO 63131-3220, USA

Pooley, Don (Athlete, Golfer)
5251 N Camino Sumo
Tucson, AZ 85718-6047, USA

Pooley, Paul (Athlete, Hockey Player)
51029 Broken Wood Ct
Granger, IN 46530-4816

Poots, Imogen (Actor)
c/o Elan Ruspoli *Creative Artists Agency (CAA-LA)*
2000 Avenue of the Stars Ste 100
Los Angeles, CA 90067-4705, USA

Pop, Iggy (Musician)
14150 SW 68th Ave
Palmetto Bay, FL 33158-1311, USA

Popcorn, Faith (Journalist)
Brain Reserve
1 Dag Hammarskjold Plz Fl 9
885 Second Avenue Fl 16
New York, NY 10017-2201, USA

Pope, Bucky (Athlete, Football Player)
7 Bunker Hill Dr
Washington Crossing, PA 18977-1415, USA

Pope, Carly (Actor, Producer)
c/o Ben Levine *LINK Entertainment*
11872 La Grange Ave Fl 1
Los Angeles, CA 90025-5283, USA

Pope, Cassadee (Musician)
c/o Jake Basden *Big Machine Records*
1219 16th Ave S
Nashville, TN 37212-2901, USA

Pope, Eddie (Soccer Player)
New York/New Jersey MetroStars
1 Harmon Plz # 300
Secaucus, NJ 07094-2803, USA

Pope, Edwin (Sportscaster)
Miami Herald Editorial Dept
1 Herald Plz
Miami, FL 33132-1609, USA

Pope, Marquez (Athlete, Football Player)
110 Avila St
San Francisco, CA 94123-2010, USA

Pope, Monsanto (Athlete, Football Player)
312 13th St NW Apt 10
Charlottesville, VA 22903-2754, USA

Pope, Odeon (Musician)
Brad Simon Organization
122 E 57th St # 300
New York, NY 10022-2623, USA

Pope, Rosie (Reality Star)
Rosie Pope Maternity
55 Warren St Frnt 1
New York, NY 10007-1165, USA

Pope, Willie (Baseball Player)
Homestead Grays
7616 Bennett St
Pittsburgh, PA 15208-1602, USA

Popeil, Ron (Business Person)
192 Monte Cielo Dr
Beverly Hills, CA 90210, USA

Popein, Larry (Athlete, Hockey Player)
80-650 Harrington Rd
Kamloops, BC V2B 6T7

popfinger, Bill (Horse Racer)
6205 Bay Club Dr Apt 1
Fort Lauderdale, FL 33308-1521, USA

popfinger, Frank (Horse Racer)
52 Cambridge Ave
Garden City, NY 11530-5125, USA

Popiel, Jan (Athlete, Hockey Player)
17214 Lakeway Park
Tomball, TX 77375-8398, USA

Popiel, Poul P (Athlete, Hockey Player)
2501 Peppermill Ridge Dr
Chesterfield, MO 63005-6707

Popoff, A Jay (Musician)
Sepetys Entertainment
1223 Wilshire Blvd # 804
Santa Monica, CA 90403-5406, USA

Popoff, Frank P (Business Person)
Dow Chemical
2030 Dow Ctr
Midland, MI 48674-2030, USA

Popovich, Gregg (Athlete, Basketball Coach, Basketball Player, Coach)
41 Vineyard Dr
San Antonio, TX 78257-1236, USA

Popovich, Milt (Athlete, Football Player)
1355 Dewey Blvd
Butte, MT 59701-3415, USA

Popovich, Paul (Athlete, Baseball Player)
2604 Woodlawn Rd
Northbrook, IL 60062-5951, USA

Popowich, Paul (Actor)
c/o Mark Schumacher Schumacher Management
2018 Glendon Ave
Los Angeles, CA 90025-6324, USA

Popp, Nathaniel (Religious Leader)
Romanian Orthodox Episcopate
PO Box 309
Grass Lake, MI 49240-0309, USA

Popper, John (Musician)
c/o Staff Member ArtistDirect
9046 Lindblade St
Culver City, CA 90232-2513, USA

Poppycock, Prince (Musician)
c/o Stephen Ford Diva Central Inc
7510 W Sunset Blvd Ste 1445
Los Angeles, CA 90046-3408, USA

Popson, Dave (Athlete, Basketball Player)
82 Fall St
Ashley, PA 18706-2709, USA

Poquette, Ben (Athlete, Basketball Player)
17917 N Shore Estates Rd
Spring Lake, MI 49456-9114, USA

Poquette, Tom (Athlete, Baseball Player)
3411 Ridgeway Dr
Eau Claire, WI 54701-8142, USA

Porcaro, Steve (Musician)
Fitzgeraid-Hartley
34 N Palm St
Ventura, CA 93001-2600, USA

Porcello, Rick (Baseball Player)
PO Box 27
Oldwick, NJ 08858-0027

Porch, Colleen (Actor)
c/o Vincent Cirrincione Vincent Cirrincione Associates
1516 N Fairfax Ave
Los Angeles, CA 90046-2608, USA

Porcher, Robert (Athlete, Football Player)
PO Box 691464
Orlando, FL 32869-1464, USA

Porizkova, Paulina (Actor, Model)
75 Altamont Rd
Millbrook, NY 12545-6149, USA

Pork Tornado (Music Group)
c/o Staff Member Paradigm (Monterey)
404 W Franklin St
Monterey, CA 93940-2303, USA

Port, Chris (Athlete, Football Player)
452 Walnut St
New Orleans, LA 70118-4932, USA

Port, Michael (Sportscaster)
4459 S Franks Pl
Gilbert, AZ 85297-9484, USA

Port, Whitney (Reality Star)
c/o Nicole Perez-Krueger PMK/BNC Public Relations (PMK-LA)
8687 Melrose Ave Ste 8
West Hollywood, CA 90069-5746, USA

Portale, Carl (Publisher)
Elle Magazine
1633 Broadway
Hachette Filipacchi
New York, NY 10019-6708, USA

Porter, Adina (Actor)
c/o Heidi Ifft Bamboo Management
17 Buccaneer St
Marina Del Rey, CA 90292-5103, USA

Porter, Alan (Athlete, Baseball Player)
4 Park Rd
Ambler, PA 19002-1119, USA

Porter, Andrew (Athlete, Baseball Player)
4881 Linscott Pl Apt 1
Los Angeles, CA 90016-5422, USA

Porter, Billy (Musician)
c/o Staff Member Gersh (LA)
9465 Wilshire Blvd Ste 600
Beverly Hills, CA 90212-2605, USA

Porter, Bob (Athlete, Baseball Player)
771 Pueblo Ave
Napa, CA 94558-3546, USA

Porter, Chuck (Athlete, Baseball Player)
9321 Snyder Ln
Perry Hall, MD 21128-9414, USA

Porter, Colin (Athlete, Baseball Player)
245 E Sunburst Cir
Tucson, AZ 85704-7325, USA

Porter, Dan (Athlete, Baseball Player)
40275 Colony Dr
Murrieta, CA 92562-5514, USA

Porter, Daryl (Athlete, Football Player)
9053 W Sunrise Blvd
Plantation, FL 33322-5218, USA

Porter, Doug (Athlete, Football Player)
PO Box 588
Grambling, LA 71245-0588, USA

Porter, Gregory (Actor)
c/o Staff Member Wehmann Models/ Talent Inc
1128 Harmon Pl Ste 202
Minneapolis, MN 55403-2055, USA

Porter, Gregory (Musician)
c/o Paul Ewing Wingsmusic Entertainment, Inc
Prefers to be contacted via email or telephone
NY, USA

Porter, Jack (Athlete, Football Player)
1027 County Road 1530
Rush Springs, OK 73082-2416, USA

Porter, Jay (Athlete, Baseball Player)
9677 Heather Cir W
Palm Beach Gardens, FL 33410-5467, USA

Porter, Jean (Actor)
200 Glenwood Cir Apt 717
Monterey, CA 93940-6750, USA

Porter, Jody (Musician)
MOB Agency
6404 Wilshire Blvd Ste 505
Los Angeles, CA 90048-5507, USA

Porter, Joey (Athlete, Football Player)
c/o Staff Member Pittsburgh Steelers
3400 S Water St
Pittsburgh, PA 15203-2358, USA

Porter, Lee (Athlete, Golfer)
1604 Birch Ln
Greensboro, NC 27408-6500, USA

Porter, Marina Oswald
1850 Wfm Rd 550
Rockwall, TX 75087

Porter, Marquis (Bo) (Athlete, Baseball Player)
1500 S Capitol St SE Attn Coachr
Washington, DC 20003-3599, USA

Porter, Randy (Race Car Driver)
Laughlin Racing
113 Pride Dr
Simpsonville, SC 29681, USA

Porter, Rufus (Athlete, Football Player)
8 to 80
2555 Eldridge Pkwy # 1321
Houston, TX 77082, USA

Porter, Scott (Actor)
c/o Staff Member Brillstein Entertainment Partners (LA)
9150 Wilshire Blvd Ste 350
Beverly Hills, CA 90212-3453, USA

Porter, Sean (Athlete, Football Player)
c/o Adisa P. Bakari Dow Lohnes PLLC
1299 Pennsylvania Ave NW Ste 700
Washington, DC 20004-2431, USA

Porter, Terry (Basketball Player, Coach)
Milwaukee Bucks
1001 N 4th St Ste 1
Bradley Center
Milwaukee, WI 53203-1312, USA

Porter, Tracy (Athlete, Football Player)
c/o Roosevelt Barnes Maximum Sports Management
6435 W Jefferson Blvd # 197
Fort Wayne, IN 46804-6203, USA

Porterfield, Ellary Hume (Actor)
c/o Marv Dauer Marv Dauer Management
2236 The Terrace
Los Angeles, CA 90049-1171, USA

Porterfield, Garry (Athlete, Football Player)
7621 S Harvard Pl
Tulsa, OK 74136-8000, USA

Porter-King, Mary Bea (Golfer)
6412 Kalama Rd
Kapaa, HI 96746-8633, USA

Portilla, Jose (Athlete, Football Player)
8831 E Quill St
Mesa, AZ 85207-9706, USA

Portis, Charles (Writer)
7417 Kingwood Rd
Little Rock, AR 72207-1734, USA

Portis, Clinton (Athlete, Football Player)
3510 NE 156th Ave
Gainesville, FL 32609-8895, USA

Portishead (Music Group)
c/o Frank Riley High Road Touring
751 Bridgeway Fl 2
Sausalito, CA 94965-2174, USA

Portland, Rene (Coach)
Pennsylvania State University
Greenberg Complex
University Park, PA 16802, USA

Portman, Natalie (Actor)
5200 Linwood Dr
Los Angeles, CA 90027-1753, USA

Portman, Robert (Athlete, Basketball Player)
2107 Cedar St
San Carlos, CA 94070-4753, USA

Portugal, Mark (Athlete, Baseball Player)
67 Serpentine Rd
Warren, RI 02885-1812, USA

Portugal. The Man (Music Group, Musician)
c/o Matt Hickey High Road Touring
751 Bridgeway Fl 2
Sausalito, CA 94965-2174, USA

Poryes, Michael (Producer, Writer)
c/o Debbee Klein Paradigm (LA)
360 N Crescent Dr
North Bldg
Beverly Hills, CA 90210-4874, USA

Porzio, Mike (Athlete, Baseball Player)
PO Box 2242
Westport, CT 06880-0242, USA

Posada, Jorge (Athlete, Baseball Player)
300 E 77th St Apt 11B
New York, NY 10075-2484, USA

Posada, Jorge (Baseball Player)
9335 Balada St
Coral Gables, FL 33156-2333

Posada, Leo (Athlete, Baseball Player)
8200 Grand Canal Dr
Miami, FL 33144-3538, USA

Pose, Scott (Athlete, Baseball Player)
1216 Kintail Dr
Raleigh, NC 27613-8121, USA

Posehn, Brian (Comedian)
c/o Dave Rath Generate Management
8750 Wilshire Blvd Ste 200
Beverly Hills, CA 90211-2707, USA

Posen, Zac (Designer, Reality Star)
1979 Pleasant View Rd
C/O Susan Posen
Coopersburg, PA 18036-9054, USA

Poses, Frederic M (Business Person)
AlliedSignal Inc
PO Box 4000
Morristown, NJ 07962, USA

Posey, Bill (Congressman, Politician)
120 Cannon Hob
Washington, DC 20515-2106, USA

Posey, Buster (Athlete, Baseball Player)
137 Leland Ferrell Dr
Leesburg, GA 31763-4559, USA

Posey, DeVier (Athlete, Football Player)
c/o Michael Perrett SportsTrust Advisors (GA)
3340 Peachtree Rd NE Fl 16
Atlanta, GA 30326-1000, USA

Posey, Gerald (Buster) (Athlete, Baseball Player)
137 Leland Ferrell Dr
Leesburg, GA 31763-4559, USA

Posey, James (Athlete, Basketball Player)
4671 E 153rd St
Cleveland, OH 44128-3014, USA

Posey, Parker (Actor)
c/o Frank Frattaroli Circle of Confusion (LA)
8931 Ellis Ave
Los Angeles, CA 90034-3336, USA

Posey, Sam (Race Car Driver)
Low Road
Sharon, CT 06069, USA

Posey, Tyler (Actor)
c/o Sarah Shyn 3 Arts Entertainment (LA)
9460 Wilshire Blvd Fl 7
Beverly Hills, CA 90212-2713, USA

Posluszny, Paul (Athlete, Football Player)
c/o Michael McCartney *Priority Sports & Entertainment - Chicago*
312 N La Salle
Suite 650
Chicago, IL 60610, USA

Posner, Mike (Musician)
c/o Jamie Abzug *Sony/RCA Records*
550 Madison Ave Fl 6
New York, NY 10022-3211, USA

Posner, Vladimir
1125 16th St NW
Washington, DC 20036-4801

Post, Avery D (Religious Leader)
80 Lyme Rd Apt 246
Hanover, NH 03755-1246, USA

Post, Markie (Actor)
c/o Staff Member *Insight*
PO Box 36359
Los Angeles, CA 90036-0359, USA

Post, Richard (Athlete, Football Player)
1812 Rickey Canyon Rd
Rice, WA 99167-9754, USA

Post, Sandra (Golfer)
Ladies Pro Golf Assn
100 International Golf Dr
Daytona Beach, FL 32124-1082, USA

Post, William (Business Person)
Pinnacle West Capital
400 E Van Buren St Ste 700
PO Box 52132
Phoenix, AZ 85004-0673, USA

Postaer, Staffan (Writer)
c/o David Krintzman *Morris Yorn Barnes Levine Krintzman Rubenstein Kohner & Gellman*
2000 Avenue of the Stars Ste 300N
3rd Floor, North Tower
Los Angeles, CA 90067-4704, USA

Postell, Lavor (Athlete, Basketball Player)
2008 Murray Hill Ln
Albany, GA 31707-3268, USA

Postema, Pam (Baseball Player)
171 Garver Rd
Mansfield, OH 44903-9056, USA

Poster, Steve (Cinematographer)
Smith/Gosnell/Nicholson
PO Box 1156
Studio City, CA 91614-0156, USA

Post III, Glen F (Business Person)
Centurytel Inc
100 Century Park Dr
Monroe, LA 71203, USA

Postlewait, Kathy (Golfer)
111 Saint Johns Landing Dr
Winter Springs, FL 32708-6501, USA

Postrel, Virginia (Writer)
c/o Staff Member *Simon & Schuster*
1230 Avenue of the Americas Fl CONC1
New York, NY 10020-1586, USA

Pote, Lou (Athlete, Baseball Player)
10601 Orchard Ln
Chicago Ridge, IL 60415-1864, USA

Poteat, Hank (Athlete, Football Player)
4107 Buxmont Rd
Marlton, NJ 08053-8510, USA

Potente, Franka (Actor)
c/o Ashley Franklin *Thruline Entertainment*
9250 Wilshire Blvd Ste 100
Ground Floor
Beverly Hills, CA 90212-3343, USA

Pothier, Brian (Athlete, Hockey Player)
437 Neck Rd
Rochester, MA 02770-1709, USA

Poti, Tom (Athlete, Hockey Player, Olympic Athlete)
2 Honey Locust Ln
Sandwich, MA 02563-2700

Potter, Carol
c/o Staff Member *Pakula/King & Associates*
9229 W Sunset Blvd Ste 315
West Hollywood, CA 90069-3403, USA

Potter, Chris (Musician)
c/o Louise Holland *Vision Arts Management*
16 Clint Finger Rd
Saugerties, NY 12477-4360, USA

Potter, Cindy
1189 Ragley Hall Rd NE
Atlanta, GA 30319

Potter, Cynthia (Athlete, Diver, Olympic Athlete)
2628 Winding Ln NE
Atlanta, GA 30319-3232, USA

Potter, Cynthia (Cindy) (Sportscaster, Swimmer)
1188 Ragley Hall Rd NE
Atlanta, GA 30319-2512, USA

Potter, Dan M (Religious Leader)
21 Forest Dr
Albany, NY 12205-2521, USA

Potter, John (Government Official)
US Postal Service
475 Lenfant Plz SW
Washington, DC 20260-0004, USA

Potter, Lauren (Actor)
c/o Patrick Welborn *Kazarian, Measures, Ruskin & Associates (LA)*
11969 Ventura Blvd Fl 3
Studio City, CA 91604-2630, USA

Potter, Mike (Athlete, Baseball Player)
21582 Archer Cir
Huntington Beach, CA 92646-8017, USA

Potter, Mike (Race Car Driver)
1318 E Lakeview Dr
Johnson City, TN 37601-2312, USA

Potter, Monica (Actor)
c/o Christian Donatelli *The Schiff Company*
9220 W Sunset Blvd Ste 106
West Hollywood, CA 90069-3500, USA

Potter, Ryan (Actor)
c/o Karen Renna *Karen Renna & Associates*
PO Box 4227
Burbank, CA 91503-4227, USA

Potter, Scott (Athlete, Baseball Player)
1637 Cordova Ave
Daytona Beach, FL 32117-1708, USA

Potter, Steve (Athlete, Football Player)
750 SE 7th Ave
Pompano Beach, FL 33060-9502, USA

Pottinger, Stanley (Writer)
c/o Staff Member *St Martins Press*
175 5th Ave Ste 400
Publicity Dept
New York, NY 10010-7848, USA

Potts, Annie (Actor, Producer)
16 S Oakland Ave
Pasadena, CA 91101-2043, USA

Potts, Cliff (Actor)
PO Box 131
Topanga, CA 90290-0131, USA

Potts, MC
818 18th Ave S
Nashville, TN 37203-6663

Potts, Mike (Athlete, Baseball Player)
60418th St
Butner, NC 27509, USA

Potts, Roosevelt (Athlete, Football Player)
2800 Crystal St Apt J-4
Anderson, IN 46012-1446, USA

Potts, Sarah-Jane (Actor)
c/o Staff Member *Anonymous Content (LA)*
3532 Hayden Ave
Culver City, CA 90232-2413, USA

Potts, Tony (Television Host)
c/o Access Hollywood *KNBC (LA)*
3000 W Alameda Ave
Burbank, CA 91523-0002, USA

Potvin, Felix (Athlete, Hockey Player)
40 Grove St Ste 430
Wellesley, MA 02482-7774, USA

Potvin, Jean R (Athlete, Hockey Player)
24 Longwood Dr
Huntington Station, NY 11746-4716

Pough, Ernest (Athlete, Football Player)
2141 Buckman St
Jacksonville, FL 32206-4124, USA

Poul, Alan (Producer)
1544 N Sierra Bonita Ave
Los Angeles, CA 90046-2812, USA

Poulin, Dave (Athlete, Coach, Hockey Player)
16771 Orchard Ridge Ct
Granger, IN 46530-5916

Poulin, Rene (Horse Racer)
147 Alden St
Wallington, NJ 07057-1433, USA

Poulsen, Ken (Athlete, Baseball Player)
PO Box 1699
Oakhurst, CA 93644-1699, USA

Poulson, Josh (Actor)
c/o Staff Member *William Morris Endeavor (LA)*
9601 Wilshire Blvd
Beverly Hills, CA 90210-5213, USA

Poulter, Ian (Athlete, Golfer)
9791 Covent Garden Dr
Orlando, FL 32827-7066, USA

Pouncey, Mike (Football Player)
c/o Joel Segal *Lagardere Unlimited (NYC)*
845 United Nations Plz
New York, NY 10017-3540, USA

Pound, The Dog
8942 Wilshire Blvd
Beverly Hills, CA 90211-1908

Pounder, CCH (Actor)
c/o Richard Hoffman *Warren Cowan & Associates PR*
8899 Beverly Blvd Ste 918
Los Angeles, CA 90048-2427, USA

Poundstone, Paula (Actor, Comedian)
c/o Bonnie Burns *Burns & Burns Management*
10523 Mars Ln
Los Angeles, CA 90077-3109, USA

Pousette, Lena (Actor)
Atkins Assoc
8040 Ventura Canyon Ave
Panorama City, CA 91402-6313, USA

Povich, Maury (Journalist)
The Maury Show
1 W 72nd St Apt 4
New York, NY 10023-3414, USA

Povitsky, Esther (Little Esther) (Comedian, Internet Star)
c/o Lee Kernis *Brillstein Entertainment Partners (LA)*
9150 Wilshire Blvd Ste 350
Beverly Hills, CA 90212-3453, USA

Powe, Jerrell (Athlete, Football Player)
c/o Bus Cook *Bus Cook Sports, Inc*
109 Cornerstone Rd
Hattiesburg, MS 39402-8232, USA

Powe, Karl (Athlete, Football Player)
PO Box 160961
Mobile, AL 36616-1961, USA

Powell, Alonzo (Athlete, Baseball Player)
2502 S Tyler St Attn Coachingstaff
Tacoma, WA 98405-1051, USA

Powell, Andre (Athlete, Football Player)
N50W16962 Maple Crest Ln
Menomonee Falls, WI 53051-6689, USA

Powell, Art (Athlete, Football Player)
25221 Via Lido
Laguna Niguel, CA 92677-7307, USA

Powell, Arthur (Art) (Athlete, Football Player)
25221 Via Lido
Laguna Niguel, CA 92677-7307, USA

Powell, Brittany
145 S Fairfax Ave Ste 310
Los Angeles, CA 90036-2176

Powell, Brittney (Actor, Model)
c/o Mike Eistenstadt *Amsel, Eisenstadt & Frazier Talent Agency (AEF)*
5055 Wilshire Blvd Ste 860
Los Angeles, CA 90036-6108, USA

Powell, Charley (Athlete, Football Player)
4119 Aralia Rd
Altadena, CA 91001-3701, USA

Powell, Cincy (Athlete, Basketball Player)
1515 Hard Rock Rd Apt 212
Irving, TX 75061-3786, USA

Powell, Clifton (Actor)
c/o Christopher Black *Opus Entertainment*
5225 Wilshire Blvd Ste 905
Los Angeles, CA 90036-4353, USA

Powell, Colin (Politician)
1317 Ballantrae Farm Dr
Mc Lean, VA 22101-3028, USA

Powell, Cristen (Race Car Driver)
3072 Patricia Ave
Los Angeles, CA 90064-4504, USA

Powell, Dante (Athlete, Baseball Player)
5715 E Walton St
Long Beach, CA 90815-1325, USA

Powell, Dennis (Athlete, Baseball Player)
1743 Eastgate Ave
Upland, CA 91784-9211, USA

Powell, Dick (Athlete, Baseball Player)
2864 Hunt Valley Dr
Glenwood, MD 21738-9639, USA

Powell, Drew (Actor)
c/o Billy Miller *Billy Miller Management*
8322 Ridpath Dr
Los Angeles, CA 90046-7710, USA

Powell, Dwane (Cartoonist)
PO Box 191
Raleigh, NC 27602-9150, USA

Powell, Glen (Actor)
c/o Richard Konigsberg *RKM*
400 N Mansfield Ave
Los Angeles, CA 90036-2622, USA

Powell, Hosken (Athlete, Baseball Player)
1289 Tamara Dr
Pensacola, FL 32504-6642, USA

Powell, Jane (Actor)
150 W End Ave Apt 26C
New York, NY 10023-5743, USA

Powell, Jay (Athlete, Baseball Player)
155 Butler Dr
Ridgeland, MS 39157-9779, USA

Powell, Jeremy (Athlete, Baseball Player)
3022 W Summit Walk Ct
Anthem, AZ 85086-1012, USA

Powell, Jesse (Musician)
c/o Staff Member *Pyramid Entertainment Group*
377 Rector Pl Apt 21A
New York, NY 10280-1439, USA

Powell, John (Athlete, Olympic Athlete)
5545 Sobb Ave
Las Vegas, NV 89118-3422, USA

Powell, John G (Athlete, Track Athlete)
John Powell Assoc
10445 Mary Ave
Cupertino, CA 95014-1348, USA

Powell, John W (Boog) (Athlete, Baseball Player)
Boog's Barbeque
333 W Camden St
Baltimore, MD 21201-2496, USA

Powell, Landon (Athlete, Baseball Player)
104 Meyers Dr
Greenville, SC 29605-1923, USA

Powell, Leroy (Athlete, Baseball Player)
PO Box 4036
Muscle Shoals, AL 35662-4036, USA

Powell, Marvin (Athlete, Football Player)
10411 Harborbluff Way
Tampa, FL 33615-3658, USA

Powell, Michael K (Government Official)
Federal Communications Commission
1919 M St NW
Washington, DC 20554-0001, USA

Powell, Michael (Mike) (Athlete, Track Athlete)
Team Powell
PO Box 8000-354
Rancho Cucamonga, CA 91701, USA

Powell, Mike
1751 Pinnacle Dr Ste 1500
Mc Lean, VA 22102-3833

Powell, Monroe (Musician)
Personality Presents
880 E Sahara Ave # 101
Las Vegas, NV 89104-3002, USA

Powell, Nicole (Basketball Player)
Charlotte Sting
100 Hive Dr
Charlotte, NC 28217-4524, USA

Powell, Paul (Athlete, Baseball Player)
5254 E Enrose St
Mesa, AZ 85205-5484, USA

Powell, Randolph
2644 Highland Ave
Santa Monica, CA 90405-4402

Powell, Ross (Athlete, Baseball Player)
PO Box 6407
McKinney, TX 75071-5111, USA

Powell, Susan (Actor)
6333 Bryn Mawr Dr
Los Angeles, CA 90068-2808, USA

Powell, Ted (Athlete, Football Player)
308 Hodder Ln
Henrico, VA 23075-2510, USA

Powell, William (Baseball Player)
Birmingham Black Barons
5516 Avenue I
Birmingham, AL 35208-3011, USA

Powell Jobs, Laurene (Business Person)
2101 Waverley St
Palo Alto, CA 94301-3955, USA

Powell Jr, D Duane (Cartoonist)
215 S McDowell St
Raleigh, NC 27601-1331, USA

Power, Dave (Actor)
c/o Steven Siebert *Lighthouse Entertainment*
9220 W Sunset Blvd Ste 200
West Hollywood, CA 90069-3501, USA

Power, J D (Dave) (Business Person)
J D Power Associates
2625 Townsgate Rd Ste 100
Westlake Village, CA 91361-5737, USA

Power, Taryn (Actor)
522 1/2 S Main St
Viroqua, WI 54665-2058, USA

Power, Ted (Athlete, Baseball Player)
Louisville Bats 401 E Main St Attn: Coaching Staf
Louseville, K 40707, USA

Power, Udana
1962 N Beachwood Dr Apt 202
Los Angeles, CA 90068-4073

Powers, Alexandra (Actor)
United Talent Agency
9336 Civic Center Dr
Beverly Hills, CA 90210-3604, USA

Powers, Clyde (Athlete, Football Player)
17 S Point Ct
Bluffton, SC 29910-6132, USA

Powers, James B (Religious Leader)
American Baptist Assn
4605 N State Line Ave
Texarkana, TX 75503-2916, USA

Powers, Jeff (Athlete)
USA Water Polo
2124 Main St Ste 210
Huntington Beach, CA 92648-2405, USA

Powers, Ross (Athlete, Olympic Athlete, Snowboarder)
c/o Peter Carlisle *Octagon Olympics & Action Sports*
15 Lund Rd # 10
Saco, ME 04072-1806, USA

Powers, Stefanie (Actor)
c/o Jeffrey Lane *Jeffrey Lane & Associates*
8787 Shoreham Dr Apt 1206
West Hollywood, CA 90069-2212, USA

Powers, Warren (Athlete, Football Player)
3909 Lausanne Rd
Randallstown, MD 21133-4511, USA

Powers, Warren A (Athlete, Football Player)
14742 Thornbird Manor Pkwy
Chesterfield, MO 63017-2497, USA

Powis, Lynn (Athlete, Hockey Player)
2669 S Columbine St
Denver, CO 80210-6441

Powley, Bel (Actor)
c/o Brantley Brown *Schachter Entertainment*
1157 S Beverly Dr Fl 2
Los Angeles, CA 90035-1119, USA

Powlus, Ron (Athlete, Football Player)
1012 Ruthann Dr
Berwick, PA 18603-2426, USA

Powter, Daniel (Musician)
c/o Staff Member *Paradigm (Monterey)*
404 W Franklin St
Monterey, CA 93940-2303, USA

Poyer, Jordan (Athlete, Football Player)
c/o Ryan Morgan *MAG Sports Agency*
8222 Melrose Ave Fl 2
Los Angeles, CA 90046-6825, USA

Poynter, Dougie (Musician)
c/o Staff Member *Universal Music Group (UMG - LA)*
2220 Colorado Ave
Santa Monica, CA 90404-3506, USA

Pozderac, Phil (Athlete, Football Player)
2193 Carmel Dr
Carrollton, TX 75006-2814, USA

Pozdnykova, Tatyana (Athlete, Track Athlete)
4151 NW 43rd St
Gainesville, FL 32606-4582, USA

Prado, Edgar (Horse Racer)
c/o Staff Member *HarperCollins Publishers*
195 Broadway Fl 2
Cellar 1
New York, NY 10007-3132, USA

Prady, Bill (Producer)
10063 Toluca Lake Ave
Toluca Lake, CA 91602-2941, USA

Praed, Michael
11500 W Olympic Blvd Ste 510
Los Angeles, CA 90064-1527

Prall, Willie (Athlete, Baseball Player)
3 Pheasant Run
Kinnelon, NJ 07405-3022, USA

Prange, Laurie
1519 Sargent Pl
Los Angeles, CA 90026

Prangley, Chris
c/o Jeff Morrone *Intellectual Artists Management*
9350 Wilshire Blvd Ste 224
Beverly Hills, CA 90212-3204, USA

Prappas, Ted (Race Car Driver)
3072 Patricia Ave
Los Angeles, CA 90064-4504, USA

Pras (Musician)
DAS Communications
83 Riverside Dr
New York, NY 10024-5713, USA

Prather, Joan (Actor)
31647 Sea Level Dr
Malibu, CA 90265-2633, USA

Pratt, Andy (Athlete, Baseball Player)
1244 Gardenia Ln
Prescott, AZ 86305-6749, USA

Pratt, Awadagin (Musician)
Cramer/Marder Artists
3436 Springhill Rd
Lafayette, CA 94549-2535, USA

Pratt, Chris (Actor)
7651 Willow Glen Rd
Los Angeles, CA 90046-1656, USA

Pratt, Deborah (Actor, Producer, Writer)
c/o Staff Member *Hirsch Wallerstein Hayum Matlof & Fishman*
10100 Santa Monica Blvd Fl 23
Los Angeles, CA 90067-4003, USA

Pratt, Heidi Montag (Musician, Reality Star)
c/o Kyell Thomas *Octagon Entertainment*
8687 Melrose Ave Ste 7
West Hollywood, CA 90069-5721, USA

Pratt, Judson
8745 Oak Park Ave
Sherwood Forest, CA 91325-3211

Pratt, Keri Lynn (Actor)
c/o Steve Caserta *Sanders Armstrong Caserta*
2120 Colorado Ave Ste 120
Santa Monica, CA 90404-3561, USA

Pratt, Kyla (Actor)
c/o Judy Landis *Judy Landis Management*
625 E Thousand Oaks Blvd # 279
Thousand Oaks, CA 91360, USA

Pratt, Kyle (Actor)
c/o Staff Member *Acme Talent & Literary (LA)*
1400 Atlantic Ave Ste 274
Long Beach, CA 90813-2013, USA

Pratt, Mary (Athlete, Baseball Player)
1000 Southern Artery Apt 219
Quincy, MA 02169-8500, USA

Pratt, Michael (Athlete, Basketball Player)
14603 Landon Ct
Louisville, KY 40245-4190, USA

Pratt, Nolan (Athlete, Hockey Player)
Springfield Falcons
45 Falcons Way
Springfield, MA 01103-1742

Pratt, Robert (Athlete, Football Player)
320 Greenway Ln
Richmond, VA 23226-1632, USA

Pratt, Spencer (Reality Star)
c/o Adam Gelvan *William Morris Endeavor (LA)*
9601 Wilshire Blvd
Beverly Hills, CA 90210-5213, USA

Pratt, Stephanie (Reality Star)
c/o Leslie Allan-Rice *Leslie Allan-Rice Management*
1007 Maybrook Dr
Beverly Hills, CA 90210-2715, USA

Pratt, Susan C (Actor)
7 Old Pound Rd
Pound Ridge, NY 10576-1737, USA

Pratt, Todd (Athlete, Baseball Player)
5950 Dorset Bridge Rd
Douglasville, GA 30135-6014, USA

Pratt, Victoria (Actor)
c/o Gordon Gilbertson *Gilbertson Management*
1334 3rd Street Promenade Ste 201
Santa Monica, CA 90401-1320, USA

Prebola, Gene (Athlete, Football Player)
24 Hayward Rd
Sparta, NJ 07871-3119, USA

Precourt, Charles J (Astronaut)
1960 Shoshone Dr
Ogden, UT 84403-4655, USA

Precourt, Charles J Colonel (Astronaut)
1960 Shoshone Dr
Ogden, UT 84403-4655, USA

Preece, Steve (Athlete, Football Player)
2723 NW Monte Vista Ter
Portland, OR 97210-3338, USA

Pregenzer, John (Athlete, Baseball Player)
80 Red Top Rd
Wibaux, MT 59353-9168, USA

Pregulman, Merv (Athlete, Football Player)
4 Cherokee Blvd Apt 517
Chattanooga, TN 37405-4904, USA

Preissing, Tom (Athlete, Hockey Player)
9481 Vista Hill Ln
Lone Tree, CO 80124-8459

Prejean, Helen Sister (Writer)
317 Bonnabel Blvd
Metairie, LA 70005-3740, USA

Prejean, Patrick (Actor)
B5 135 Poissonniere
Paris, FR F-750

Preki (Soccer Player)
Kansas City Wizards
2 Arrowhead Dr
Kansas City, MO 64129, USA

Prendergast, John (Writer)
c/o Joe Veltre *Gersh (NY)*
41 Madison Ave
New York, NY 10010-2202, USA

Prentiss, Paula (Actor, Comedian)
719 Foothill Rd
Beverly Hills, CA 90210-3437, USA

Prepon, Laura (Actor)
c/o Paul Brown *New Wave Entertainment (LA)*
2660 W Olive Ave
Burbank, CA 91505-4525, USA

Prescott, Jon (Actor)
c/o Miles Levy *James/Levy Management Inc*
3500 W Olive Ave Ste 1470
Burbank, CA 91505-5514, USA

Presko, Joe (Athlete, Baseball Player)
1612 NE 77th Ter
Kansas City, MO 64118-1939, USA

Presley, Alex (Baseball Player)
10000 Ferry Creek Dr
Shreveport, LA 71106-8406, USA

Presley, Brian (Actor)
c/o Nikki Joel *ICM Partners (LA)*
10250 Constellation Blvd Fl 7
Los Angeles, CA 90067-6207, USA

Presley, Jim (Athlete, Baseball Player)
333 W Camden St Attn Coaching
Baltimore, MD 21201-2496, USA

Presley, Priscilla (Actor, Producer, Writer)
1167 Summit Dr
Beverly Hills, CA 90210-2251, USA

Presley, Richard (Musician)
c/o Staff Member *William Morris Endeavor (LA)*
9601 Wilshire Blvd
Beverly Hills, CA 90210-5213, USA

Presley, Wayne (Athlete, Hockey Player)
1339 Kingsway Dr
Highland, MI 48356-1165

Pressel, Morgan (Athlete, Golfer)
c/o Chris Armstrong *Wasserman Media Group (LA)*
12100 W Olympic Blvd Ste 200
Los Angeles, CA 90064-1075, USA

Pressey, Paul (Athlete, Basketball Player, Coach)
782 Haddonstone Cir
Lake Mary, FL 32746-5603, USA

Pressler, Larry L (Politician)
2812 Davis Ave
Alexandria, VA 22302-2507, USA

Pressler, Menahem M J (Musician)
Melvin Kaplan
115 College St Ste 3
Burlington, VT 05401-8428, USA

Pressley, Dominic (Athlete, Basketball Player)
1406 Whooping Ct
Upper Marlboro, MD 20774-7086, USA

Pressley, Harold (Athlete, Basketball Player)
6470 Matheny Way
Citrus Heights, CA 95621-4839, USA

Pressley, Paul (Athlete, Basketball Player)
Pressliz Inc
600 County Road 4694
Timpson, TX 75975, USA

Pressley, Robert (Race Car Driver)
6 Forestdale Dr
Asheville, NC 28803-1811, USA

Pressly, Jaime (Actor)
4233 Woodcliff Rd
Sherman Oaks, CA 91403-4339, USA

Pressman, Edward R (Producer)
Edward Pressman Films
130 El Camino Dr
Beverly Hills, CA 90212-2700, USA

Pressman, Lawrence (Actor)
15033 Encanto Dr
Sherman Oaks, CA 91403-4409, USA

Pressman, Michael (Actor, Director, Producer)
c/o Judy Hofflund *Hofflund/Polone*
6300 Wilshire Blvd Ste 1410
Los Angeles, CA 90048-5216, USA

Pressman, Sally (Actor)
c/o Staff Member *Abrams Artists Agency (LA)*
9200 W Sunset Blvd PH 11
West Hollywood, CA 90069-3601, USA

Presswood, Hank (Athlete, Baseball Player)
1445 W 71st Pi
Chicago, IL 60636, USA

Presswood, Henry (Baseball Player)
Cincinnati Buckeyes
1445 W 71st Pl
Chicago, IL 60636-3961, USA

Presta, Peter (DJ)
c/o Len Evans *Project Publicity*
312 W 53rd St Ste 202
New York, NY 10019-5743, USA

Prestel, Jim (Athlete, Football Player)
6150 Hurricane Ct
Parker, CO 80134-5704, USA

Preston, Carrie (Actor)
c/o Steve Caserta *Sanders Armstrong Caserta*
2120 Colorado Ave Ste 120
Santa Monica, CA 90404-3561, USA

Preston, Cynthia (Actor)
c/o Charles Silver *SMS Talent*
8383 Wilshire Blvd Ste 230
Beverly Hills, CA 90211-2436, USA

Preston, Douglas (Writer)
c/o Staff Member *Tom Doherty Associates, LLC*
175 5th Ave
New York, NY 10010-7703, USA

Preston, J A (Actor)
Paradigm Agency
10100 Santa Monica Blvd Ste 2500
Los Angeles, CA 90067-4116, USA

Preston, Kelly (Actor)
735 N Bonhill Rd
Los Angeles, CA 90049-2303, USA

Preston, Ray (Athlete, Football Player)
688 Colin Dr
Avon, IN 46123-9683, USA

Prestridge, Luke (Athlete, Football Player)
17802 Island Spring Ln
Tomball, TX 77377-8155, USA

Prettyman, Tristan (Musician)
c/o Staff Member *Paradigm (Monterey)*
404 W Franklin St
Monterey, CA 93940-2303, USA

Pretty Ricky (Music Group)
c/o Staff Member *Atlantic Records (NY)*
1290 Avenue of the Americas Fl 28
New York, NY 10104-0106, USA

Preus, David W (Religious Leader)
2481 Como Ave
Saint Paul, MN 55108-1445, USA

Previte, Richard (Business Person)
Advanced Micro Devices
1 Amd Pl
PO Box 3453
Sunnyvale, CA 94085-3905, USA

Prevost, Josette (Actor)
Tisherman Agency
6767 Forest Lawn Dr # 101
Los Angeles, CA 90068-1027, USA

Prew, Augustus (Actor)
c/o Brantley Brown *Schachter Entertainment*
1157 S Beverly Dr Fl 2
Los Angeles, CA 90035-1119, USA

Prew, William A (Business Person, Swimmer)
30600 Telegraph Rd Ste 3110
Bingham Farms, MI 48025-4589, USA

Price, AJ (Athlete, Basketball Player)
c/o Jeff Schwartz *Excel Sports Management (NY)*
1700 Broadway Fl 29
New York, NY 10019-5905, USA

Price, Alan (Musician, Songwriter, Writer)
Lustig Talent
PO Box 770850
Orlando, FL 32877-0850, USA

Price, Brent (Athlete, Basketball Player)
1111 W Wynona Ave
Enid, OK 73703-6909, USA

price, Bryan (Baseball Player, Coach)
10987 N 122nd St
Scottsdale, AZ 85259

Price, Charles W (Athlete, Football Player)
3712 43rd St
Lubbock, TX 79413-3036, USA

Price, David (Baseball Player)
450 Knights Run Ave Unit 1004
Tampa, FL 33602-5806

Price, Elex (Athlete, Football Player)
2833 Newport St
Jackson, MS 39213-5335, USA

Price, Ferne (Baseball Player)
40 Jackson Blvd
Greencastle, IN 46135-1964, USA

Price, Frederick K C (Religious Leader)
Crenshaw Christian Church
7901 S Vermont Ave
Los Angeles, CA 90044-3531, USA

Price, Hillary (Cartoonist)
221 Pine St # 4G3
Florence, MA 01062-1267, USA

Price, James G (Doctor)
12205 Mohawk Rd
Leawood, KS 66209-2137, USA

Price, Jim (Athlete, Baseball Player)
2100 Woodward Ave
Detroit, MI 48201-3470, USA

Price, Joe (Athlete, Baseball Player)
6460 Harrison Ave Ste 201
Cincinnati, OH 45247-7958, USA

Price, Kelly (Musician)
JL Ent
18653 Ventura Blvd # 340
Tarzana, CA 91356-4103, USA

Price, Lindsay (Actor)
3220 Tahoe Pl
Los Angeles, CA 90068-1657, USA

Price, Lloyd (Musician, Songwriter, Writer)
95 Horseshoe Hill Rd
Pound Ridge, NY 10576-1636, USA

Price, Lonny (Actor)
c/o Joy Gorman *Anonymous Content (LA)*
3532 Hayden Ave
Culver City, CA 90232-2413, USA

Price, Marc (Actor)
8444 Magnolia Dr
Los Angeles, CA 90046-1932, USA

Price, Marvin (Athlete, Baseball Player)
Chicago American Giants
2425 E 71st St
Chicago, IL 60649-2612, USA

Price, Megyn (Actor)
c/o Leslie Allan-Rice *Leslie Allan-Rice Management*
1007 Maybrook Dr
Beverly Hills, CA 90210-2715, USA

Price, MIke (Athlete, Basketball Player)
4415 Thornleigh Dr
Indianapolis, IN 46226-2165, USA

Price, Mike (Coach, Football Coach)
University of Texas
Athletic Dept
El Paso, TX 79968-0001, USA

Price, Mitchell (Athlete, Football Player)
3935 Thousand Oaks Dr Apt 1506
San Antonio, TX 78217-1877, USA

Price, Molly (Actor)
c/o Stephen Hirsch *Gersh (NY)*
41 Madison Ave
New York, NY 10010-2202, USA

Price, Nick (Golfer)
Nick Price Group Inc
900 S US Hwy Ste 1 PMB 5
Jupiter, FL 33477, USA

Price, Peerless (Athlete, Football Player)
5658 Legends Club Cir
Braselton, GA 30517-6029, USA

Price, Phoebe (Actor)
Pmodelmanagement
24200 Albers St
Woodland Hills, CA 91367-5704, USA

Price, S H (Publisher)
Newsweek Inc
251 W 57th St
New York, NY 10019-1802, USA

Price, Terry (Athlete, Football Player)
59 Fieldstone Dr
South Glastonbury, CT 06073-3717, USA

Price, Tom (Congressman, Politician)
403 Cannon Hob
Washington, DC 20515-1807, USA

Price, Willard D
PO Box 2783
Laguna Hills, CA 92654-2783, USA

Price, W Mark (Basketball Player)
Georgia Institute of Technology
Athletic Dept
Atlanta, GA 30332-0001, USA

Price-Bunch, Ashil (Golfer)
1629 Country Club Dr
Morristown, TN 37814-3316, USA

Priddy, Bob (Athlete, Baseball Player)
1347 State Ave Apt 201
Coraopolis, PA 15108-2012, USA

Priddy, Bob (Athlete, Basketball Player)
Lazy Arrow Ranch
PO Box 3169
Boys Ranch, TX 79010-3169, USA

Priddy, Nancy (Actor)
11223 Sunshine Ter
Studio City, CA 91604-3123, USA

Pride, Charley (Baseball Player)
Memphis Red Sox
PO Box 670507
Dallas, TX 75367-0507, USA

Pride, Charlie (Musician)
CECCA Productions
PO Box 670507
Dallas, TX 75367-0507, USA

Pride, Curtis (Athlete, Baseball Player)
1288 Lake Breeze Dr
Wellington, FL 33414-7953, USA

Pride, Dicky (Athlete, Golfer)
1214 Belleaire Cir
Orlando, FL 32804-6706, USA

Pride, Lynn (Basketball Player)
Minnesota Lynx
600 1st Ave N
Target Center
Minneapolis, MN 55403-1400, USA

Pride, Mack (Baseball Player)
Kansas City Monarchs
3305 Pierce St
Wheat Ridge, CO 80033-6333, USA

Pridemore, Tom (Athlete, Football Player)
3935 Poplar Springs Rd
Gainesville, GA 30507-8618, USA

Pridie, Jason (Baseball Player)
4475 E Campbell Ct
Gilbert, AZ 85234-7643

Pridy, Todd (Athlete, Baseball Player)
3430 Scenic Dr
Napa, CA 94558-4239, USA

Priesand, Sally J (Religious Leader)
10 Wedgewood Cir
Eatontown, NJ 07724-1203, USA

Priest, Eddie (Athlete, Baseball Player)
445 Ballard Rd
Altoona, AL 35952-6227, USA

Priest, Judas (Music Group, Musician)
c/o Troy Blakely *Agency for the
Performing Arts (APA-LA)*
405 S Beverly Dr Ste 500
Beverly Hills, CA 90212-4425, USA

Priest, Maxi (Musician)
Virgin Records
150 5th Ave Fl 7
New York, NY 10011-4372, USA

Priestley, Jason (Actor, Race Car Driver)
c/o JB Roberts *Thruline Entertainment*
9250 Wilshire Blvd Ste 100
Ground Floor
Beverly Hills, CA 90212-3343, USA

Priestley, Jr, Thomas (Director,
Photographer)
c/o Jay Gilbert *Broder Webb Chervin
Silbermann Agency, The (BWCS)*
10250 Constellation Blvd
Los Angeles, CA 90067-6200, USA

Prieto, Ariel (Athlete, Baseball Player)
Vermont Lake Monsters 1 King Street
Ferry Dock Attn
Burlington, VT 05401, USA

Prieto, Chris (Athlete, Baseball Player)
PO Box 10911
Eugene, OR 97440-2911, USA

Prieto, Rodrigo (Cinematographer)
PO Box 3338
Beverly Hills, CA 90212-0338, USA

Primeau, Keith (Athlete, Hockey Player)
2 Danforth Dr
Voorhees, NJ 08043-3947

Primus (Music Group)
c/o Ken Weinstein *Big Hassle Media*
40 Exchange Pl Ste 1900
New York, NY 10005-2714, USA

Primus, Barry (Actor)
2735 Creston Dr
Los Angeles, CA 90068-2209

Prince (Musician)
7021 Galpin Blvd
Chanhassen, MN 55317, USA

Prince, Angel (Dancer)
Prince Dance
PO Box 1991
Honokaa, HI 96727-1832, USA

Prince, Clayton
3500 W Olive Ave Ste 1400
Burbank, CA 91505-5512

Prince, Don (Baseball Player)
11143 James B White Hwy S
Whiteville, NC 28472-6419, USA

Prince, Faith (Actor, Musician)
Innovative Artists
1505 10th St
Santa Monica, CA 90401-2805, USA

Prince, Harold S (Hal) (Director,
Producer)
Harold Prince Organization
10 Rockefeller Plz Ste 1104
New York, NY 10020-1972, USA

Prince, Jonathan (Actor)
723 N Elm Dr
Beverly Hills, CA 90210-3422, USA

Prince, Karim (Actor)
3313 1/2 Barham Blvd
Los Angeles, CA 90068-1450

Prince, Larry L (Business Person)
Genuine Parts Co
2999 Circle 75 Pkwy SE
Atlanta, GA 30339-3050, USA

Prince, Tayshaun (Athlete, Basketball
Player)
8866 Prestancia Cv S
Memphis, TN 38125-1734, USA

Prince, Tom (Athlete, Baseball Player)
6816 10th Ave NW
Bradenton, FL 34209-1209, USA

Prince-Bythewood, Gina (Director,
Producer, Writer)
c/o Ava DuVernay *The DuVernay Agency*
Prefers to be contact via telephone or
email
West Hollywood, CA 90069, USA

Princess Ann Claire (Actor, Musician,
Royalty)
c/o Staff Member *Love Is In The Heir*
5750 Wilshire Blvd
E! Entertainment Television
Los Angeles, CA 90036-3697, USA

Principal, Victoria (Actor, Business
Person, Producer)
c/o Alan Iezman *Shelter Entertainment*
9255 W Sunset Blvd Ste 320
West Hollywood, CA 90069-3313, USA

Principe, Dom (Athlete, Football Player)
300 N Highway A1A Apt E303
Jupiter, FL 33477-4542, USA

Principi, Anthony (Politician)
Veteran Affairs Department
24710 New Post Rd
Saint Michaels, MD 21663-2308, USA

Prine, Andrew (Actor)
3364 Longridge Ave
Sherman Oaks, CA 91423, USA

Prine, John (Musician, Songwriter, Writer)
Al Bunetta Mgmt
33 Music Sq W Ste 102B
Nashville, TN 37203-6607, USA

Pringle, Joan (Actor)
Gold Marshak Liedtke
3500 W Olive Ave Ste 1400
Burbank, CA 91505-5512, USA

Pringley, Mike (Athlete, Football Player)
6344 Mimosa Cir
Tucker, GA 30084-1946, USA

Prinz, Bret (Athlete, Baseball Player)
15471 N 88th Ave
Peoria, AZ 85382-3789, USA

Prinze Jr, Freddie (Actor)
2435 Mandeville Canyon Rd
Los Angeles, CA 90049-1235, USA

Prinzi, Frank (Cinematographer)
571 W 113th St
#24
New York, NY 10025, USA

Prioleau, Pierson (Athlete, Football Player)
2221 Santee River Rd
Saint Stephen, SC 29479-3844, USA

Prior, Anthony (Athlete, Football Player)
3861 Lofton Pl
Riverside, CA 92501-1809, USA

Prior, Mark (Athlete, Baseball Player)
4340 Altamirano Way
San Diego, CA 92103-1004, USA

Prior, Tom (Actor)
c/o Eric Podwall *Podwall Entertainment*
710 N Orlando Ave Apt 203
Loft 203
West Hollywood, CA 90069-5549, USA

Priory, Richard B (Business Person)
Duke Energy Co
526 S Church St
Charlotte, NC 28202-1802, USA

Pritchard, Barry (Musician)
Lustig Talent
PO Box 770850
Orlando, FL 32877-0850, USA

Pritchard, Buddy (Athlete, Baseball
Player)
507 E Sunny Hills Rd
Fullerton, CA 92835-1357, USA

Pritchard, Kevin (Athlete, Basketball
Player)
10492 Mission Park Ave
Las Vegas, NV 89135-1047, USA

Pritchard, Michael (Athlete, Football
Player)
1041 Collingtree St
Las Vegas, NV 89145-8513, USA

Pritchard, Ron (Athlete, Football Player)
495 E Coconino Dr
Chandler, AZ 85249-5302, USA

Pritchett, Chris (Athlete, Baseball Player)
959 Fir Tree Pl
Carlsbad, CA 92011-3926, USA

Pritchett, Kelvin (Athlete, Football Player)
4765 Guilford Forest Dr SW
Atlanta, GA 30331-7395, USA

Pritchett, Stanley (Athlete, Football
Player)
523 Monteagle Trce
Stone Mountain, GA 30087-4937, USA

Pritchett, Wes (Athlete, Football Player)
1194 Brookgate Way NE
Atlanta, GA 30319-2877, USA

Pritikin, Greg (Director)
c/o Staff Member *Anonymous Content
(LA)*
3532 Hayden Ave
Culver City, CA 90232-2413, USA

Pritkin, Roland I (Doctor)
4128 Grove Ave
Berwyn, IL 60402-4435, USA

Pritko, Steve (Athlete, Football Player)
328 Chanticlair Dr
Apex, NC 27502-9623, USA

Probst, Jeff (Game Show Host, Reality Star, Television Host)
3171 Brookdale Rd
Studio City, CA 91604-4208, USA

Prochnow, Jurgen (Actor)
c/o Staff Member *ICM Partners (LA)*
10250 Constellation Blvd Fl 7
Los Angeles, CA 90067-6207, USA

Procter, Emily (Actor)
c/o Brad Slater *William Morris Endeavor (LA)*
9601 Wilshire Blvd
Beverly Hills, CA 90210-5213, USA

Proctor, Bob (Writer)
LifeSuccess Productions, LLC
8900 E Pinnacle Peak Rd Ste D240
Scottsdale, AZ 85255-3651, USA

Proctor, Charles N (Skier)
100 Lockewood Ln Apt 238
Scotts Valley, CA 95066-3959, USA

Proctor, David (Baseball Player)
Bowman
5517 SW 23rd St
Topeka, KS 66614-1727, USA

Proctor, James (Jim) (Athlete, Baseball Player)
2 Westmoreland Pl
Saint Louis, MO 63108-1228, USA

Proctor, Scott (Athlete, Baseball Player)
428 NE Bayberry Ln
Jensen Beach, FL 34957, USA

Prodigy (Music Group)
c/o Staff Member *Maverick Recording Co (LA)*
3300 Warner Blvd
Burbank, CA 91505-4632, USA

P. Roe, David (Congressman, Politician)
419 Cannon Hob
Washington, DC 20515-0908, USA

Proehl, Ricky (Athlete, Football Player)
8214 Drakeview Ct
Charlotte, NC 28270-9553, USA

Professor, Griff (Actor, Musician)
c/o Staff Member *William Morris Endeavor (LA)*
9601 Wilshire Blvd
Beverly Hills, CA 90210-5213, USA

Profit, Gene (Athlete, Football Player)
PO Box 41033
Bethesda, MD 20824-1033, USA

Profit, Mel (Athlete, Football Player)
PO Box 4155
Redondo Beach, CA 90277-1750, USA

Project 86 (Music Group)
c/o Staff Member *Paradigm (Monterey)*
404 W Franklin St
Monterey, CA 93940-2303, USA

Prokop, Matt (Actor)
c/o Margot Menzel *Evolution Entertainment (LA)*
9111 Wilshire Blvd
Beverly Hills, CA 90210-5508, USA

Proly, Mike (Athlete, Baseball Player)
112 Country Mist Dr
Greer, SC 29651-1919, USA

Pronger, Sean (Athlete, Hockey Player)
290 Magnolia St
Costa Mesa, CA 92627-2826

Proops, Greg (Actor)
c/o Lee Kernis *Brillstein Entertainment Partners (LA)*
9150 Wilshire Blvd Ste 350
Beverly Hills, CA 90212-3453, USA

Prophet, Billy (Musician)
Paramount Entertainment
PO Box 12
Far Hills, NJ 07931-0012, USA

Prophet, Elizabeth Clare (Religious Leader)
Church Universal & Triumphant
PO Box A
Livingston, MT 59047, USA

Prophet, Ronnie (Actor)
1227 Saxon Dr
Nashville, TN 37215-4426

Propp, Brian (Athlete, Hockey Player)
2320 Riverton Rd
Cinnaminson, NJ 08077-3719

Props, Rene (Actor)
Agency for Performing Arts
9200 W Sunset Blvd Ste 900
West Hollywood, CA 90069-3604, USA

Prosch, Jay (Athlete, Football Player)
c/o Bill Johnson *SportsTrust Advisors (GA)*
3340 Peachtree Rd NE Fl 16
Atlanta, GA 30326-1000, USA

Prospal, Vaclav (Athlete, Hockey Player)
17 S Treasure Dr
Tampa, FL 33609-3508, USA

Prospal, Vactav (Athlete, Hockey Player)
401 Channelside Dr
Ice Palace
Tampa, FL 33602-5400, USA

Prosper, Sandra (Actor)
c/o Staff Member *Mitchell K Stubbs & Assoc (MKS)*
8675 Washington Blvd Ste 203
Culver City, CA 90232-7486, USA

Prosser, Robert (Religious Leader)
Cumberland Presbyterian Church
1978 Union Ave
Memphis, TN 38104-4134, USA

Proulx, Brooklynn (Actor)
c/o Christopher Rockwell *Keyword Entertainment*
1051 Cole Ave # B
Los Angeles, CA 90038-2601, USA

Prout, Bob (Athlete, Football Player)
23102 N Shepard Rd
Chillicothe, IL 61523-9035, USA

Prout, Brian (Musician)
Oreamcatcher Artists Mgmt
2908 Poston Ave
Nashville, TN 37203-1312, USA

Prout, Kirsten (Actor)
c/o Allan Grifka *Alchemy Entertainment*
7024 Melrose Ave Ste 420
Los Angeles, CA 90038-3394, USA

Proval, David (Actor)
c/o Andrew Howard *Incognito Management*
9440 Santa Monica Blvd Ste 302
Beverly Hills, CA 90210-4614, USA

Provence, Andrew (Athlete, Football Player)
224 Providence Rd
Fayetteville, GA 30215-2844, USA

Provenza, Paul (Actor)
c/o Peter Golden *Golden Entertainment West*
10921 Wilshire Blvd
Los Angeles, CA 90024-3906, United States

Provenzano, Chris (Director, Writer)
c/o David Ginsberg *Insight*
PO Box 36359
Los Angeles, CA 90036-0359, USA

Provost, Jon
627 Montclair Dr
Santa Rosa, CA 95409-2833

Prowse, David (Actor)
c/o Nick Cordasco *Prince Marketing Group*
18 Carillon Cir
Livingston, NJ 07039-2600, USA

Proyas, Alex (Director)
International Creative Mgmt
10250 Constellation Blvd Fl 1
Los Angeles, CA 90067-6241, USA

Prudhomme, Don (Race Car Driver)
1232 Distribution Way
Vista, CA 92081-8816, USA

Prudhomme, Paul (Chef)
527 Mandeville St
New Orleans, LA 70117-8627, USA

Pruett, Harold
8904 Wonderland Ave
Los Angeles, CA 90046-1854

Pruett, Jeanne (Musician, Songwriter)
Joe Taylor Artists Agency
PO Box 279
Williamstown, NJ 08094-0279, USA

Pruett, Scott (Race Car Driver)
Rocket Sports
3400 West Rd
East Lansing, MI 48823-7309, USA

Pruitt, Gregory D (Greg) (Athlete, Football Player)
13851 Larchmere Blvd
Cleveland, OH 44120-1349, USA

Pruitt, James (Athlete, Football Player)
PO Box 432301
Miami, FL 33243-2301, USA

Pruitt, Jason (Baseball Player)
Topps
320 Clark Dr Apt 101
Summerfield, NC 27358, USA

Pruitt, Jordan (Musician)
c/o Thor Bradwell *LBI Entertainment*
9601 Wilshire Blvd
Beverly Hills, CA 90210-5213, USA

Pruitt, Ron (Athlete, Baseball Player)
3632 Turnberry Dr
Medina, OH 44256-6827, USA

Pruitt Jr, Basil A (Doctor)
US Army Institute of Surgical Research
Jbsa Ft Sam Houston, TX 78234, USA

Pryce, Travor (Athlete, Football Player)
13655 Broncos Pkwy
Englewood, CO 80112-4150, USA

Pryor, Chris (Athlete, Hockey Player)
Philadelphia Flyers
3601 S Broad St Ste 2
Philadelphia, PA 19148-5297

Pryor, Chris (Athlete, Hockey Player)
6877 Macbeth Ct
Saint Paul, MN 55125-2409

Pryor, David H (Politician)
502 Bellwood Dr
Paragould, AR 72450-3865, USA

Pryor, Greg (Athlete, Baseball Player)
9726 W 115th Ter
Overland Park, KS 66210-2927, USA

Pryor, Kelli (Writer)
c/o Andrea Simon *Andrea Simon Entertainment*
4230 Woodman Ave
Sherman Oaks, CA 91423-4334, USA

Pryor, Mark (Politician)
2200 Andover Ct Apt 901
Little Rock, AR 72227-3982, USA

Pryor, Nicholas (Actor)
PO Box 849
Hampstead, NC 28443-0849, USA

Pryor, Rain (Actor, Producer)
2709 Hanson Ave Apt 2A
Baltimore, MD 21209-3997, USA

Przybilla, Joel (Athlete, Basketball Player)
104 Oakview Cir
Monticello, MN 55362-8973, USA

Psaltis, Jim (Athlete, Football Player)
23115 Samuel St Apt 23
Torrance, CA 90505-3850, USA

Psy (Musician)
10490 Wilshire Blvd Apt 403
Los Angeles, CA 90024-4647, USA

Psycho, Les (Musician)
c/o Staff Member *The Agency Group (NYC)*
142 W 57th St Fl 6
New York, NY 10019-3300, USA

Ptacek, Bob (Athlete, Football Player)
648 Deptford Ave
Dayton, OH 45429-5941, USA

Ptak, Frank (Business Person)
Illinois Tool Works
3600 W Lake Ave
Glenview, IL 60026-5811, USA

Public Enemy (Music Group, Musician)
c/o Walter F. Leaphart Jr *Creamworks*
8391 Beverly Blvd Ste 352
Los Angeles, CA 90048-2633, USA

Pucci, Ben (Athlete, Football Player)
8502 Timber West St
San Antonio, TX 78250-4209, USA

Pucci, Bert (Publisher)
Los Angeles Magazine
1888 Century Park E
Los Angeles, CA 90067-1702, USA

Puck, Wolfgang (Chef)
707 N Faring Rd
Los Angeles, CA 90077-3524, USA

Puckett, Gary (Musician, Songwriter, Writer)
10710 Seminole Blvd Ste 3
Largo, FL 33778-3316, USA

Pudi, Danny (Actor, Comedian)
2026 Rose Villa St
Pasadena, CA 91107-5043, USA

Puemer, John P (Publisher)
Chicago Tribune
435 N Michigan Ave Ste 200
Chicago, IL 60611-4024, USA

Puerner, John P (Publisher)
Los Angeles Times
202 W 1st St Ste 500
Editorial Dept
Los Angeles, CA 90012-4401, USA

Puett, Tommy (Actor)
16621 Cerulean Ct
Chino Hills, CA 91709-4690, USA

Puetz, Garry (Athlete, Football Player)
1779 Robinson Rd
Dahlonega, GA 30533-6119, USA

Puffer, Brandon (Athlete, Baseball Player)
1546 Haynie Bnd
Round Rock, TX 78665-1216, USA

Pugh, Daniel Patrick (Dan Patrick)
(Sportscaster)
c/o Staff Member *Simon & Schuster*
1230 Avenue of the Americas Fl CONC1
New York, NY 10020-1586, USA

Pugh, Larry (Football Player)
RR 4
New Castle, PA 16101, USA

Pugh, Lewis Gordon (Sportscaster)
c/o Staff Member *William Morris Endeavor (LA)*
9601 Wilshire Blvd
Beverly Hills, CA 90210-5213, USA

Pugh, Tim (Athlete, Baseball Player)
7906 N 125th East Cir
Owasso, OK 74055-3539, USA

Pugh Jr, Jethro (Athlete, Football Player)
329 E Colorado Blvd Apt 505
Dallas, TX 75203-1257, USA

Pugliese, Charles (Producer)
c/o Staff Member *Killer Films (US)*
526 W 26th St Rm 715
New York, NY 10001-5524, USA

Pugsley, Don (Actor)
c/o Hazel Shallon *Shallon Star Management*
14320 Ventura Blvd # 624
Sherman Oaks, CA 91423-2717, USA

Puhl, Terry (Athlete, Baseball Player)
918 Gondola St
Sugar Land, TX 77478-3414, USA

Puig, Rich (Athlete, Baseball Player)
4216 Mill Valle Yct
Tampa, FL 33618, USA

Pujols, Albert (Athlete, Baseball Player)
102 Grand Meridien Frst
Chesterfield, MO 63005-4980, USA

Pujols, Luis B (Athlete, Baseball Player, Coach)
2 Townsend St Apt 2-613
San Francisco, CA 94107-2061, USA

Pulcini, Robert (Director)
c/o Staff Member *Creative Artists Agency (CAA-LA)*
2000 Avenue of the Stars Ste 100
Los Angeles, CA 90067-4705, USA

Puleo, Charlie (Athlete, Baseball Player)
3202 Miser Station Rd
Louisville, TN 37777-3604, USA

Pulford, Robert J (Bob) (Athlete, Hockey Player)
78 Coventry Rd
Northfield, IL 60093-3117

Pulido, Carlos (Athlete, Baseball Player)
55 SE 6th St Apt 2001
Miami, FL 33131-2564, USA

Pullard, Anthony (Athlete, Basketball Player)
3518 Monroe St
Lake Charles, LA 70607-3204, USA

Pulliam, Harvey (Athlete, Baseball Player)
2400 Shady Willow Ln Unit 2C
Brentwood, CA 94513-5393, USA

Pulliam, Keshia Knight (Actor)
c/o Everly Lee *Resolution (LA)*
1801 Century Park E Ste 2300
Los Angeles, CA 90067-2325, USA

Pullman, Bill (Actor, Director)
c/o Staff Member *One Talent Management*
3680 1/2 Fredonia Dr
Los Angeles, CA 90068-1208, USA

Pulman, Bill (Actor, Director, Producer)
c/o Graciella Sanchez *One Talent Management*
3680 1/2 Fredonia Dr
Los Angeles, CA 90068-1208, USA

Pulos, Jenni (Reality Star)
c/o Staff Member *All Moxie*
8322 Beverly Blvd Ste 303A
Los Angeles, CA 90048-2665, USA

Pulp (Music Group)
c/o Staff Member *Paradigm (Monterey)*
404 W Franklin St
Monterey, CA 93940-2303, USA

Pulsipher, Bill (Athlete, Baseball Player)
10 Woodbine Ln
East Moriches, NY 11940-1413, USA

Pumpkins, Penelope (Adult Film Star)
1247 14th St # 104
Santa Monica, CA 90404, USA

Pumple, Rich (Athlete, Hockey Player)
2110 SE 11th Ave
Cape Coral, FL 33990-4606, USA

Punch, Lucy (Actor)
c/o Christian Donatelli *The Schiff Company*
9220 W Sunset Blvd Ste 106
West Hollywood, CA 90069-3500, USA

Punsley, Bernard (Actor)
1415 Granvia Altemeia
Palos Verdes Peninsula, CA 90274, USA

Punto, Nick (Athlete, Baseball Player)
19550 N Grayhawk Dr Unit 1122
Scottsdale, AZ 85255-3986, USA

Puppa, Daren (Athlete, Hockey Player)
4526 Cheval Blvd
Lutz, FL 33558-5331

Puppies, The
15476 NW 77th Ct # 286
Hialeah, FL 33016-5823

Pupunu, Alfred (Athlete, Football Player)
415 Conestoga Dr
Moscow, ID 83843-5028, USA

Purcell, Dominic (Actor)
c/o Beth Holden-Garland *Untitled Entertainment (LA)*
350 S Beverly Dr Ste 200
Beverly Hills, CA 90212-4819, USA

Purcell, Herman (Athlete, Baseball Player)
Cleveland Buckeyes
1031 Cass Ave SE
Grand Rapids, MI 49507-1119, USA

Purcell, Lee (Actor)
11101 Provence Ln
Tujunga, CA 91042-1263, USA

Purcell, Patrick B (Publisher)
Boston Herald
1 Herald St
Boston, MA 02118, USA

Purcell, Sarah (Actor)
4437 Alla Rd Unit 6
Marina Del Rey, CA 90292-6330, USA

Purcey, David (Athlete, Baseball Player)
4339 Highlander Dr
Dallas, TX 75287-6842, USA

Purdee, Nathan (Actor)
56 W 66th St
New York, NY 10023-6225, USA

Purdin, John (Athlete, Baseball Player)
4942 Southgate Pkwy
Myrtle Beach, SC 29579-4147, USA

Purdy, Ted (Athlete, Golfer)
5600 N 4th St
Phoenix, AZ 85012-1305, USA

Purefoy, James (Actor)
c/o JoAnne Colonna *Brillstein Entertainment Partners (LA)*
9150 Wilshire Blvd Ste 350
Beverly Hills, CA 90212-3453, USA

Pure Reason Revolution (Music Group)
c/o Staff Member *Paradigm (Monterey)*
404 W Franklin St
Monterey, CA 93940-2303, USA

Purim, Flora (Musician)
A Train Mgmt
PO Box 29242
Oakland, CA 94604-9242, USA

Purkey, Bob (Athlete, Baseball Player)
5559 Steeplechase Ct
Bethel Park, PA 15102-4501, USA

Purpura, Tim (Baseball Player)
206 Hays Ct
Colleyville, TX 76034-7612, USA

Purtzer, Tom (Golfer)
10529 N 106th Pl
Scottsdale, AZ 85258-9214, USA

Purvis, Jeff (Race Car Driver)
1157 Dunbar Cave Rd
Clarksville, TN 37043-2045, USA

Pushor, Jamie (Athlete, Hockey Player)
29 Jay Rd W
Lake George, NY 12845-4426

Puskaric, Joseph (Athlete, Baseball Player)
201 West Dr N Apt 14
Marshall, MI 49068-1484, USA

Puskarioc, Joseph (Baseball Player)
429 35th St
McKeesport, PA 15132-7226, USA

Pussycat Dolls (Music Group)
c/o Staff Member *William Morris Endeavor (LA)*
9601 Wilshire Blvd
Beverly Hills, CA 90210-5213, USA

Pustari, Rit (Race Car Driver)
Pustari-Goodrich Racing
4 Taft St # 82
Norwalk, CT 06854-4279, USA

Pustovyi, Yarolslav Dr (Astronaut)
2101 Nasa Pkwy Spc Centerbldg
Houston, TX 77058-3607, USA

Putch, John (Actor)
3972 Sunswept Dr
Studio City, CA 91604-2330, USA

Putman, Earl (Athlete, Football Player)
PO Box 18091
Munds Park, AZ 86017-8091, USA

Putman, Ed (Athlete, Baseball Player)
PO Box 3366
Mesquite, NV 89024-3366, USA

Putman, Pat (Baseball Player)
Texas Rangers
2311 Carrell Rd
Fort Myers, FL 33901-8012, USA

Putnam, David (Actor, Producer)
c/o Staff Member *Enigma Productions*
429 Santa Monica Blvd Ste 700
Santa Monica, CA 90401-3435, USA

Putnam, Duane (Athlete, Football Player)
1545 Magnolia Ave
Ontario, CA 91762-5335, USA

Putnam, Pat (Athlete, Baseball Player)
4040 Staley Rd
Fort Myers, FL 33905-6410, USA

Putti, Frank (Athlete, Baseball Player)
1981 Downing Pl
Palm Harbor, FL 34683-5727, USA

Putz, J J (Athlete, Baseball Player)
2425 NE Ivy Way
Issaquah, WA 98029-7621, USA

Putzier, Jeb (Athlete, Baseball Player)
2641 W 131st Ter
Leawood, KS 66209-1923, USA

Puz, Craig A (Astronaut)
S313 Devils Head Cir
Golden, CO 80403, USA

Pyburn, Jack (Athlete, Football Player)
1197 Peachtree St NE Ste 533A
Atlanta, GA 30361-3508, USA

Pye, Eddie (Athlete, Baseball Player)
307 Polk St
Columbia, TN 38401-4453, USA

Pyeatt, John (Johnny) (Athlete, Football Player)
18374 E Via De Palmas
Queen Creek, AZ 85242, USA

Pyecha, John (Athlete, Baseball Player)
107 Nottingham Dr
Chapel Hill, NC 27517-6569, USA

Pyfrom, Shawn (Actor)
c/o Eric Podwall *Podwall Entertainment*
710 N Orlando Ave Apt 203
Loft 203
West Hollywood, CA 90069-5549, USA

Pygram, Wayne (Actor)
c/o Bob Knotek *McCann - Knotek Associates*
8539 W Sunset Blvd Ste 4-136
West Hollywood, CA 90069-2334, USA

Pyle, Michael J (Mike) (Athlete, Football Player)
2436 Saranac Ct
Glenview, IL 60026-1042, USA

Pyle, Missi (Actor)
c/o Mel McKeon *McKeon-Myones Management*
3500 W Olive Ave Ste 770
Burbank, CA 91505-5527, USA

Pyle, Missy (Actor)
Paradigm Agency
10100 Santa Monica Blvd Ste 2500
Los Angeles, CA 90067-4116, USA

Pyle, Palmer (Athlete, Football Player)
2487 Potter Rd E
Traverse City, MI 49696-8572, USA

Pyne, George F (Athlete, Football Player)
123 Congress St
Milford, MA 01757-2006, USA

Pyott, David E I (Business Person)
Allergan Inc
2525 Dupont Dr
Irvine, CA 92612-1599, USA

Pyper-Ferguson, John (Actor)
c/o Adena Chawke *Greenlight Management and Production*
9713 Santa Monica Blvd Ste 219
Beverly Hills, CA 90210-4215, USA

Pyznarski, Tim (Athlete, Baseball Player)
10716 Austin Ave
Chicago Ridge, IL 60415-2224, USA

Q, Maggie (Actor, Model)
12979 Blairwood Dr
Studio City, CA 91604-4031, USA

Qaiyum, Gregory (GQ) (Actor)
c/o Sandra Joseph *SLJ Management*
833 N Edinburgh Ave Unit 203
Los Angeles, CA 90046-6947, USA

Qin, Shaobo (Actor)
c/o Don Hughes *IAI Presentations*
PO Box 4
Pismo Beach, CA 93448-0004, USA

Q-Tip (Musician)
251 Marietta St
Englewood Cliffs, NJ 07632-1644, USA

Quackenbush, Bill
54 Danielle Ct
Lawrence Township, NJ 08648-1452

Quade, John (Actor)
Alex Brewis
12429 Laurel Terrace Dr
Studio City, CA 91604-2402, USA

Quade, Mike (Athlete, Baseball Player)
823 Hadleigh Pass
Westfield, IN 46074-5900, USA

Quaerna, Jerry (Athlete, Football Player)
1211 Pheasant Ct
Lake Geneva, WI 53147-1077, USA

Quaid, Dennis (Actor)
c/o Cara Tripicchio *Shelter PR*
9350 Wilshire Blvd Ste 450
Beverly Hills, CA 90212-3230, USA

Quaid, Jack (Actor)
c/o Tony Lipp *Anonymous Content (LA)*
3532 Hayden Ave
Culver City, CA 90232-2413, USA

Quaid, Randy (Actor)
PO Box 17372
Beverly Hills, CA 90209-3372, USA

Quaintance, Rachel (Comedian)
c/o Bruce Smith *OmniPop Talent Group (LA)*
4605 Lankershim Blvd Ste 201
North Hollywood, CA 91602-1874, USA

Qualls, Chad (Athlete, Baseball Player)
8416 Big View Dr
Austin, TX 78730-1534, USA

Qualls, DJ (Actor)
c/o Staff Member *Principato/Young Management (LA)*
9465 Wilshire Blvd Ste 900
Beverly Hills, CA 90212-2608, USA

Qualls, Jim (Athlete, Baseball Player)
410 N County Road 950
Sutter, IL 62373-5021, USA

Qualters, Tom (Athlete, Baseball Player)
235 Mallard Rd
Somerset, PA 15501-7023, USA

Quan, Samantha (Actor)
c/o Vincent Cirrincione *Vincent Cirrincione Associates*
1516 N Fairfax Ave
Los Angeles, CA 90046-2608, USA

Quance, Kristine (Athlete, Olympic Athlete, Swimmer)
1320 Moncado Dr
Glendale, CA 91207-1832, USA

Quann, Megan (Athlete, Olympic Athlete, Swimmer)
3516 109th Street Ct NW
Gig Harbor, WA 98332-8991, USA

Quarashi (Musician)
c/o Staff Member *Creative Artists Agency (CAA-LA)*
2000 Avenue of the Stars Ste 100
Los Angeles, CA 90067-4705, USA

Quarles, Kelcy (Athlete, Football Player)
c/o Eugene Parker *Maximum Sports Management*
6435 W Jefferson Blvd # 197
Fort Wayne, IN 46804-6203, USA

Quarles, Shelton (Athlete, Football Player)
17019 Candeleda De Avila
Tampa, FL 33613-5213, USA

Quarless, Andrew (Athlete, Football Player)
c/o Peter Schaffer *All Pro Sports and Entertainment*
36 Steele St Ste 100
Denver, CO 80206-5709, USA

Quarterflash
5410 SW MacAdam Ave Ste 280
Portland, OR 97239-3825

Quasthoff, Thomas (Musician)
Cramer/Marser Artists
3436 Springhill Rd
Lafayette, CA 94549-2535, USA

Quayle, Dan (Politician)
c/o Laura Minter
6224 N 61st Pl # Pi
Paradise Valley, AZ 85253-4212, USA

Qubein, Nido (Business Person)
Creative Services Inc
806 Westchester Dr
806 Westchester Dr
High Point, NC 27262-7347, USA

Quddus (Television Host)
c/o Mike Esterman *Esterman.Com, LLC*
Prefers to be contacted via email
Baltimore, MD XXXXX, USA

Queen, Ida (Musician)
Traditional Arts Services
16045 36th Ave NE
Lake Forest Park, WA 98155-6623, USA

Queen, Jeff (Athlete, Football Player)
1367 Temple Heights Dr
Oceanside, CA 92056-2210, USA

Queen, Konga (Actor, Wrestler)
PO Box 5050
Carson, CA 90749-5050, USA

Queens of the Stone Age (Music Group)
c/o Staff Member *Creative Artists Agency (CAA-LA)*
2000 Avenue of the Stars Ste 100
Los Angeles, CA 90067-4705, USA

Queensryche (Music Group)
c/o Staff Member *Monterey International (Chicago)*
200 W Superior St Ste 202
Chicago, IL 60654-6422, USA

Quenneville, Joel (Athlete, Coach, Hockey Player)
835 S Park Ave
Hinsdale, IL 60521-4569

Quenneville, Joel (Athlete, Hockey Player)
Chicago Blackhawks
1901 W Madison St
Chicago, IL 60612-2459

Quentin, Carlos (Athlete, Baseball Player)
1223 Crestview Dr
Cardiff By The Sea, CA 92007-1400, USA

Querrey, Sam (Athlete, Tennis Player)
532 Regents Gate Dr
Henderson, NV 89012-7234, USA

Query, Jeff (Athlete, Football Player)
8440 N Sam Houston Pkwy E Apt 911
Humble, TX 77396-2972, USA

Questlove (Musician)
Motown Records
6255 W Sunset Blvd
Los Angeles, CA 90028-7403, USA

Questrom, Allen I (Business Person)
J C Penney Co
6501 Legacy Dr
Plano, TX 75024-3698, USA

Quezada, Steven Michael (Actor)
c/o Gloria Hinojosa *Amsel, Eisenstadt & Frazier Talent Agency (AEF)*
5055 Wilshire Blvd Ste 860
Los Angeles, CA 90036-6108, USA

Quick, Clarence E (Musician, Songwriter, Writer)
376 Quincy St
Brooklyn, NY 11216-1502, USA

Quick, James E (Jim) (Actor)
PO Box 12760
Scottsdale, AZ 85267-2760, USA

Quick, Jim (Athlete, Baseball Player)
PO Box 1127
Camino, CA 95709-1127, USA

Quick, Jonathan (Athlete, Hockey Player)
c/o Staff Member *Los Angeles Kings*
1111 S Figueroa St Ste 3100
Los Angeles, CA 90015-1333, USA

Quick, Michael A (Mike) (Athlete, Football Player)
13 Slab Branch Ct
Marlton, NJ 08053-5407, USA

Quick, Rebecca (Talk Show Host)
900 Sylvan Ave
Squawk Box
Englewood Cliffs, NJ 07632-3312, USA

Quick, Richard (Coach, Swimmer)
Stanford University
Athletic Dept
Stanford, CA 94305, USA

Quicksilver (Music Group)
c/o Staff Member *Paradigm (Monterey)*
404 W Franklin St
Monterey, CA 93940-2303, USA

Quie, Al (Politician)
100 Promenade Ave Apt 228
Wayzata, MN 55391-4557, USA

Quie, Albert H (Al) (Ex-Governor)
100 Promenade Ave Apt 228
Wayzata, MN 55391-4557, USA

Quiet Riot
2002 Hogback Rd Ste 20
Ann Arbor, MI 48105-9736

Quigley, Dana (Athlete, Golfer)
2670 Tecumseh Dr
West Palm Beach, FL 33409-7421, USA

Quigley, Linnea (Actor)
2608 N Ocean Blvd Ste 1 PMB 126
Pompano Beach, FL 33062-2955, USA

Quigley, Mary T (Actor)
Velvet Ears, Inc
11845 Kling St
Valley Village, CA 91607-4009, USA

Quigley, Mike (Congressman, Politician)
3742 W Irving Park Rd
Chicago, IL 60618-3116, USA

Quigley, Philip J (Phil) (Business Person)
Pacific Telesis Group
130 Keamy St
San Francisco, CA 94108, USA

Quik, D J (Musician)
International Creative Mgmt
10250 Constellation Blvd Fl 1
Los Angeles, CA 90067-6241, USA

Quilici, Frank (Athlete, Baseball Player, Coach)
3413 E 126th St
Burnsville, MN 55337-3440, USA

Quillan, Frederick (Fred) (Athlete, Football Player)
2050 Carmel Ave
Eugene, OR 97401-7222, USA

Quinaz, Victor (Director)
c/o Chad Hamilton *Anonymous Content (LA)*
3532 Hayden Ave
Culver City, CA 90232-2413, USA

Quindlen, Anna (Writer)
c/o Amanda Urban *ICM Partners (NY)*
730 5th Ave
New York, NY 10019-4105, USA

Quinlan, Kathleen (Actor)
PO Box 6728
Malibu, CA 90264-6728, USA

Quinlan, Maeve (Actor)
c/o Staff Member *Main Title Entertainment*
8383 Wilshire Blvd Ste 408
Beverly Hills, CA 90211-2435, USA

Quinlan, Maive
1123 N Flores St Apt 5
West Hollywood, CA 90069-2969

Quinlan, Robb (Athlete, Baseball Player)
5875 Upland Ln N
Minneapolis, MN 55446-4535, USA

Quinlan, Sally (Athlete, Golfer)
2621 Colina Vista Loop # A
Austin, TX 78750, USA

Quinlan, Tom (Athlete, Baseball Player)
1061 Sterling St S
Saint Paul, MN 55119-5972, USA

Quinlan, William D (Bill) (Athlete, Football Player)
393 Mount Vernon St
Lawrence, MA 01843-3103, USA

Quinn, Aidan (Actor)
40 Highland Ave
Palisades, NY 10964-1600, USA

Quinn, Aileen (Actor)
c/o David Moss *David Moss Company, The*
733 Seward St PH
Los Angeles, CA 90038-3503, USA

Quinn, Brady (Athlete, Football Player)
c/o Team Member *Cleveland Browns*
76 Lou Groza Blvd
Berea, OH 44017-1269, USA

Quinn, Brandon (Actor)
c/o Ben Feigin *Anonymous Content (LA)*
3532 Hayden Ave
Culver City, CA 90232-2413, USA

Quinn, Brian (Coach, Soccer Player)
San Jose Earthquakes
3550 Stevens Creek Blvd Ste 200
San Jose, CA 95117-1031, USA

Quinn, Chris
13000 SW 92nd Ave Apt B311
Miami, FL 33176-5756, USA

Quinn, Colin (Actor, Comedian)
c/o Staff Member *Agency for the Performing Arts (APA-LA)*
405 S Beverly Dr Ste 500
Beverly Hills, CA 90212-4425, USA

Quinn, Colleen (Actor)
Bauman Assoc
5750 Wilshire Blvd # 473
Los Angeles, CA 90036-3697, USA

Quinn, Dan (Athlete, Hockey Player)
1049 Vintner Blvd
Palm Beach Gardens, FL 33410-1526

Quinn, Danny (Actor)
c/o Michael Greenwald *Don Buchwald & Associates (LA)*
6500 Wilshire Blvd Ste 2200
Los Angeles, CA 90048-4942, USA

Quinn, David W (Business Person)
Centex Corp
2728 N Harwood St Ste 200
Dallas, TX 75201-1579, USA

Quinn, DeClan (Cinematographer)
22 Cherry Ave
Cornwall On Hudson, NY 12520-1506, USA

Quinn, Ed (Actor)
c/o Staff Member *Burstein Company, The*
15304 W Sunset Blvd Ste 208
Pacific Palisades, CA 90272-3656, USA

Quinn, Glenn (Actor)
Sanders Armstrong Management
2120 Colorado Ave Ste 120
Santa Monica, CA 90404-3561, USA

Quinn, Jane Bryant (Journalist)
Newsweek Magazine
251 W 57th St
Editorial Dept
New York, NY 10019-1802, USA

Quinn, Mark (Athlete, Baseball Player)
1013 S Dancove Dr
West Covina, CA 91791-3720, USA

Quinn, Martha (Actor, Model)
28890 Hampton Pl
Malibu, CA 90265-4235, USA

Quinn, Mike (Athlete, Football Player)
10703 Del Monte Dr
Houston, TX 77042-2326, USA

Quinn, Molly (Actor)
c/o Ellen Meyer *Ellen Meyer Management*
8899 Beverly Blvd Ste 612
Los Angeles, CA 90048-2429, USA

Quinn, Pat (Governor, Politician)
Office of the Governor
207 State House
Springfield, IL 62706-0001, USA

Quinn, Robert (Football Player)
c/o Carl Carey *Champion Pro Consulting Group*
3547 Ruth St
Houston, TX 77004-5515, USA

Quinn, Sally (Journalist)
3014 N St NW
Washington, DC 20007-3404, USA

Quinn, Stephen (Athlete, Football Player)
783 1375N Ave
Mount Sterling, IL 62353-1069, USA

Quinnett, Brian (Athlete, Basketball Player)
862 Indian Hills Dr
Moscow, ID 83843-9373, USA

Quinney, Ken (Athlete, Hockey Player)
5423 Rebecca Rd
Las Vegas, NV 89130-1703

Quinones, John (Correspondent)
c/o Staff Member *ABC News*
77 W 66th St Fl 3
New York, NY 10023-6201, USA

Quinones, John (Television Host)
c/o Staff Member *ABC TV (NY)*
77 W 66th St
New York, NY 10023-6201, USA

Quinones, Luis (Athlete, Baseball Player)
5821 Calle San Bruno
Urb Santa Teresita
Ponce, PR 00730-4443, USA

Quinones, Rey (Athlete, Baseball Player)
216 Calle Ronda
San Juan, PR 00926-2351, USA

Quint, Deron (Athlete, Hockey Player)
21154 N 36th Pl # Pi
Phoenix, AZ 85050-8386

Quintana, Chela (Golfer)
Ladies Pro Golf Assn
100 International Golf Dr
Daytona Beach, FL 32124-1082, USA

Quintanilla, Omar (Athlete, Baseball Player)
12457 Paseo De Arco Ct
El Paso, TX 79928-5669, USA

Quintero, Humberto
12201 Mossy Trail Ct
Pearland, TX 77584-4558, USA

Quintin, J F (Athlete, Hockey Player)
6821 Oak St
Kansas City, MO 64113-2476

Quinto, Zachary (Actor)
4019 Cumberland Ave
Los Angeles, CA 90027-1507, USA

Quirico, Rafael (Athlete, Baseball Player)
2901 N Dale Mabry Hwy Apt 2103
Tampa, FL 33607-2483, USA

Quirk, Art (Athlete, Baseball Player)
2 Ensign Ln
Stonington, CT 06378-2944, USA

Quirk, James P (Jamie) (Athlete, Baseball Player)
501 Crawford St Ste 400
Houston, TX 77002-2113, USA

Quist, Janet (Model)
13446 Poway Rd # 239
Poway, CA 92064-4714, USA

Quitones, John (Correspondent)
ABC-TV
77 W 66th St
News Dept
New York, NY 10023-6201, USA

Quivers, Robin (Radio Personality, Talk Show Host)
6 Long Beach Blvd
Long Beach Township, NJ 08008-6142, USA

Qulgley, Brett (Golfer)
127 Sandpiper Cir
Jupiter, FL 33477-8434, USA

Qulgley, Dana (Golfer)
2670 Tecumseh Dr
West Palm Beach, FL 33409-7421, USA

Quon, Di (Actor)
c/o Loch Powell *Leverage Management*
3030 Pennsylvania Ave
Santa Monica, CA 90404-4112, USA

R

R5 (Music Group, Musician)
c/o Stella Alex *Savage Agency*
6212 Banner Ave
Los Angeles, CA 90038-2802, USA

Raab, Chris (Actor)
c/o Staff Member *Haber Entertainment*
434 S Canon Dr Apt 204
Beverly Hills, CA 90212-4501, USA

Raab, Marc (Athlete, Football Player)
1211 Cuyamaca Ave
Spring Valley, CA 91977-4610, USA

Raabe, Brian (Athlete, Baseball Player)
38760 Kost Trl
North Branch, MN 55056-6722, USA

Raaurn, Gustav (Skier)
PO Box 700
Mercer Island, WA 98040-0700, USA

Raba, Robert (Athlete, Football Player)
16066 Acre St
North Hills, CA 91343-4822, USA

Rabb, John (Athlete, Baseball Player)
8614 Hooper Ave
Los Angeles, CA 90002-1143, USA

Rabe, Charlie (Athlete, Baseball Player)
6059 E Sierra Blanca St
Mesa, AZ 85215-7753, USA

Rabe, Josh (Athlete, Baseball Player)
1800 College Ave
Attn: Mens Baseball Head Coa
Quincy, IL 62301-2670, USA

Rabe, Lily (Actor)
c/o Peg Donegan *Framework Entertainment (LA)*
9057 Nemo St Ste C
West Hollywood, CA 90069-5511, USA

Rabelo, Mike (Athlete, Baseball Player)
1231 Robinswood Ct S
Lakeland, FL 33813-2271, USA

Rabinowitz, Dorothy (Journalist)
Wall Street Journal
200 Liberty St
Editorial Dept
New York, NY 10281-1003, USA

Rabkin, Mitchell T (Doctor)
Beth Israel Deaconess Medical Center
330 Brookline Ave
Boston, MA 02215-5491, USA

Raburn, Ryan (Athlete, Baseball Player)
14546 Sweat Loop Rd
Wimauma, FL 33598-5004, USA

Rachal, Latorio (Athlete, Football Player)
3266 Golden Ave
Long Beach, CA 90806-1208, USA

Rachin, Julian (Musician)
Columbia Artists Mgmt Inc
165 W 57th St
New York, NY 10019-2201, USA

Rachins, Alan (Actor)
c/o Mark Teitelbaum *Teitelbaum Artists Group*
8840 Wilshire Blvd Fl 3
Beverly Hills, CA 90211-2606, USA

Racicot, Marc F (Politician)
28013 Swan Cove Dr
Bigfork, MT 59911-7846, USA

Racicot, Pierre (Athlete, Hockey Player)
828 Hampton Ct
Weston, FL 33326-2917

Racine, Bruce (Athlete, Hockey Player)
35 S Ridge Meadows Ln
Troy, MO 63379-6306

Rackers, Neil (Athlete, Football Player)
945 Shady Path Ct
Saint Peters, MO 63376-3898, USA

Rackley, David (Athlete, Baseball Player)
2515 Coatsdale Ln
Matthews, NC 28104-5167, USA

Rackley, Derek (Athlete, Football Player)
5659 Legends Club Cir
Braselton, GA 30517-6029, USA

Rackley, Luther (Athlete, Basketball Player)
36 W 128th St Apt 2
New York, NY 10027-3100, USA

Rackley, Marv (Athlete, Baseball Player)
512 S Bibb St
Westminster, SC 29693-2134, USA

Raczka, Mike (Athlete, Baseball Player)
72 Foley Dr
Southington, CT 06489-4400, USA

Radachowsky, George (Athlete, Football Player)
87 Merrimac St
Danbury, CT 06810-6463, USA

Radcliffe, Daniel (Actor)
c/o Scott Boute *Scott Boute Publicity*
529 W 42nd St Apt 5A
New York, NY 10036-6228, USA

Rade, John (Athlete, Football Player)
611 Deertrail Dr
Hailey, ID 83333-8731, USA

Rademacher, Bill (Athlete, Football Player)
PO Box 11
Haslett, MI 48840-0011, USA

Rademacher, Ingo (Actor)
667 Santa Clara Ave
Venice, CA 90291-3445, USA

Rademacher, Pete (Athlete, Boxer, Olympic Athlete)
5585 River Styx Rd
Medina, OH 44256-8786, USA

Rademacher, T Peter (Pete) (Boxer)
5585 River Styx Rd
Medina, OH 44256-8786, USA

Rader, Dave (Athlete, Baseball Player)
2660 Sunset Hls
Escondido, CA 92025-7850, USA

Rader, Douglas L (Doug) (Athlete, Baseball Player, Coach)
PO Box 2768
Stuart, FL 34995-2768, USA

Rader, Stanley
360 Waverly Dr
Pasadena, CA 91105-1820

Radford, Mark (Athlete, Basketball Player)
5160 NE Wistaria Dr
Portland, OR 97213-2557, USA

Radford, Wayne (Athlete, Basketball Player)
4660 Running Brook Ter
Greenwood, IN 46143-9254, USA

Radigan, Terry (Musician, Songwriter)
Frank Callan Corp
209 10th Ave S Ste 322
Nashville, TN 37203-0744, USA

Radin, Joshua
c/o Debbie Wilson Wilspro Management
P.O. Box 9
New York, NY 10001, USA

Radinsky, Scott (Athlete, Baseball Player)
1605 E Hillcrest Dr Unit B
Thousand Oaks, CA 91362-2647, USA

Radison, Dan (Athlete, Baseball Player)
116 SE 20th Ave
Deerfield Beach, FL 33441-4521, USA

Radke, Brad W (Athlete, Baseball Player)
413 S Paloma Pl
Tampa, FL 33609-3711, USA

Radloff, Wayne (Athlete, Football Player)
60 S Sea Pines Dr
Hilton Head Island, SC 29928-4063, USA

Radlosky, Rob (Athlete, Baseball Player)
1219 W Broward St
Lantana, FL 33462-3013, USA

Radmanovich, Ryan (Athlete, Baseball Player)
25 Ware Ave
West Hartford, CT 06119-1532, USA

Radnor, Josh (Actor)
c/o Carrie Byalick I/D PR (NY)
150 W 30th St Fl 19
New York, NY 10001-4119, USA

Radojevic, Danilo (Dancer)
American Ballet Theatre
890 Broadway Fl 3
New York, NY 10003-1278, USA

Radosevich, George (Athlete, Football Player)
414 Shaffer Ave
Elizabeth, PA 15037-1840, USA

Radovich, Frank (Athlete, Basketball Player)
121 Lakewood Dr
Statesboro, GA 30458-9041, USA

Rady, Michael (Actor)
c/o Kasra Ajir Velocity Entertainment Partners
5455 Wilshire Blvd Ste 802
Los Angeles, CA 90036-4271, USA

Radziwill, Carole (Journalist, Reality Star, Writer)
c/o Staff Member Bravo (NY)
30 Rockefeller Plz
New York, NY 10112-0015, USA

Rae, Cassidy (Actor)
SDB Partners Inc
315 S Beverly Dr Ste 411
C/O Ro Diamond
Beverly Hills, CA 90212-4301, USA

Rae, Charlotte (Actor)
10790 Wilshire Blvd Apt 903
Los Angeles, CA 90024-4478, USA

Rae, Emily (Actor)
c/o Pamela Kohl 3 Arts Entertainment (LA)
9460 Wilshire Blvd Fl 7
Beverly Hills, CA 90212-2713, USA

Rae, Mike (Athlete, Football Player)
18541 Auburn Ave
Santa Ana, CA 92705-2704, USA

Rae, Odessa (Actor)
547 N Kings Rd # 401
West Hollywood, CA 90048-6005, USA

Rae, Savannah Paige
c/o Sarah Shyn 3 Arts Entertainment (LA)
9460 Wilshire Blvd Fl 7
Beverly Hills, CA 90212-2713, USA

Raekwon (Musician)
c/o Drew Elliot Artists International Management (NY)
333 E 43rd St Apt 115
New York, NY 10017-4822, USA

Raether, Hal (Athlete, Baseball Player)
6105 Lincoln Dr Apt 133
Minneapolis, MN 55436-1619, USA

Rafalski, Brian (Athlete, Hockey Player, Olympic Athlete)
20 Holton Ln
Essex Fells, NJ 07021-1709, USA

Rafelson, Bob (Director)
1543 Dog Team Road
1022 Palm Ave # 3
New Haven, VT 05472, USA

Rafferty, Sarah (Actor)
c/o Charlton Blackburne A Management Company
9107 Wilshire Blvd Ste 650
Beverly Hills, CA 90210-5544, USA

Rafferty, Tom (Athlete, Football Player)
1526 Mount Gilead Rd
Keller, TX 76262-7358, USA

Raffo, Al (Athlete, Baseball Player)
330 Pleasant View Cir
Jasper, TN 37347-7242, USA

Rafko, Kaye Lani Rae
4932 Frary Ln
Monroe, MI 48161-9708

Rafshoon, Gerald
3028 Q St NW
Washington, DC 20007-3080

Raftery, Erin (Actor)
c/o Rachel Rothman Rothman / Andres Entertainment
4400 Coldwater Canyon Ave Ste 125
Studio City, CA 91604-5040, USA

Ragan, Dave (Athlete, Golfer)
Dave Ragan Inc
PO Box 1131
Harrisburg, NC 28075-1131, USA

Ragan, David (Race Car Driver)
c/o Staff Member NASCAR
1801 W Speedway Blvd
Daytona Beach, FL 32114-1243, USA

Rage Against The Machine (Music Group, Musician)
c/o Don Muller William Morris Endeavor (LA)
9601 Wilshire Blvd Ste 700
Beverly Hills, CA 90210-5211, USA

Rager, Roger (Race Car Driver)
1680 64th St SW Unit 1
Pequot Lakes, MN 56472-2239, USA

Raggio, Brady (Athlete, Baseball Player)
10653 Rue D Azur
Reno, NV 89511-4308, USA

Raggio, Lisa
9300 Wilshire Blvd Ste 410
Beverly Hills, CA 90212-3228

Ragland, Tom (Athlete, Baseball Player)
20201 Greenlawn St
Detroit, MI 48221-1187, USA

Raglin, Floyd (Athlete, Football Player)
2701 Alister Ave
Tustin, CA 92782-0934, USA

Ragnarsson, Marcus (Athlete, Hockey Player)
Hallonstigen 2
Bjorklinge, S- SWEDE

Ragogna, Mike (Musician, Producer)
204 E Madison Ave
Fairfield, IA 52556-3641, USA

Ragsdale, William (Actor)
Innovative Artists
1505 10th St
Santa Monica, CA 90401-2805, USA

Rahal, Bashar (Actor)
c/o Victor Kruglov Victor Kruglov Talent Management
6565 W Sunset Blvd Ste 200
Los Angeles, CA 90028-7219, USA

Rahal, Bobby
1903 N Howe St
Chicago, IL 60614-5127

Rahal, Robert W (Bobby) (Race Car Driver)
Team Rahal Racing
5 New Albany Farms Rd
New Albany, OH 43054-9000, USA

Rahlves, Daron (Athlete, Olympic Athlete, Skier)
11655 Mount Rose View Dr
Truckee, CA 96161, USA

Rahm, Kevin (Actor)
3 Arts Entertainment
9460 Wilshire Blvd Ste 700
Beverly Hills, CA 90212-2713, USA

Rahman, A.R. (Bollywood, Composer)
c/o Sam Schwartz Gorfaine/Schwartz Agency Inc
4111 W Alameda Ave Ste 509
Burbank, CA 91505-4171, USA

Rahner, Robert (Horse Racer)
2000 Boyle Rd Apt 8D
Selden, NY 11784-1235, USA

Rahyel, Bobby (Race Car Driver)
934 Crescent Blvd
Glen Ellyn, IL 60137-4255, USA

Rahzel (Musician)
c/o Staff Member The Agency Group (NYC)
142 W 57th St Fl 6
New York, NY 10019-3300, USA

Raible, Steve (Athlete, Football Player)
2721 1st Ave Unit 1002
Seattle, WA 98121-3521, USA

Raich, Eric (Athlete, Baseball Player)
3963 Edward Dr
Brunswick, OH 44212-1509, USA

Raichle, Marcus E (Doctor)
Washington University
Medical School
Neurology Dept
Saint Louis, MO 63130, USA

Raider-Wexler, Victor (Actor)
c/o Lorraine Berglund Lorraine Berglund Management
11537 Hesby St
North Hollywood, CA 91601-3618, USA

Raiken, Sherwin (Athlete, Basketball Player)
2400 McClellan Ave Apt 120B
Pennsauken, NJ 08109-4629, USA

Railsback, Steve (Actor)
11684 Ventura Blvd # 581
Studio City, CA 91604-2699, USA

Raimi, Sam (Writer)
c/o Richard Lovett Creative Artists Agency (CAA-LA)
2000 Avenue of the Stars Ste 100
Los Angeles, CA 90067-4705, USA

Raimondi, Ben (Athlete, Football Player)
5 Grandview Dr
Holmdel, NJ 07733-2007, USA

Rain, Steve (Athlete, Baseball Player)
20320 E Crestline Dr
Walnut, CA 91789-4605, USA

Rainer, Wali (Athlete, Football Player)
4715 Monaco Dr
Sandston, VA 23150-3205, USA

Raines, Cristina
6399 Wilshire Blvd Ste 414
Los Angeles, CA 90048-5716

Raines, Mike (Athlete, Football Player)
8116 Amber Ct
Montgomery, AL 36117-6978, USA

Raines, Tim (Athlete, Baseball Player)
1242 Saint Albans Loop
Lake Mary, FL 32746-1978, USA

Raines, Tony (Race Car Driver)
Front Row Motorsports
3536 Denver Dr
Denver, NC 28037-7217, USA

Rainey, Chuck (Athlete, Baseball Player)
6484 Del Cerro Blvd
San Diego, CA 92120-4804, USA

Rainey, Matt (Journalist)
Star-Ledger
1 Star Ledger Plz Ste 1
Editorial Dept
Newark, NJ 07102-1227, USA

Rains, Dan (Athlete, Football Player)
2509 Wigwam Rd
Aliquippa, PA 15001-4340, USA

Rains, Luce (Actor, Producer)
c/o Andrew Stawiarski *ADS Management*
269 S Beverly Dr # 441
Beverly Hills, CA 90212-3851, USA

Rainwater, G L (Business Person)
Ameren Corp
1901 Chouteau Ave
Saint Louis, MO 63103-3085, USA

Rainwater, Gregg (Actor)
PO Box 291836
Los Angeles, CA 90029-8836, USA

Raiola, Angela (Big Ang) (Reality Star)
c/o Michael Schweiger *CEG Management*
520 8th Ave Rm 2001
New York, NY 10018-4166, USA

Raisa, Francia (Actor)
c/o Faras Rabadi *Emerald Talent Group*
10 Universal City Plz Fl 20
Universal City, CA 91608-1002, USA

Raisman, Alexandra (Athlete, Gymnast)
c/o Peter Carlisle *Octagon Olympics & Action Sports*
15 Lund Rd # 10
Saco, ME 04072-1806, USA

Raisman, Aly (Athlete, Gymnast, Olympic Athlete)
Brestyan's American Gymnastics Club
13 Ray Ave
Burlington, MA 01803-4720, USA

Raitt, Bonnie L (Musician, Songwriter, Writer)
PO Box 626
Los Angeles, CA 90078-0626, USA

Raji, B.J. (Athlete, Football Player)
c/o David Dunn *Athletes First, LLC*
23091 Mill Creek Dr
Laguna Hills, CA 92653-1258, USA

Rajisich, Dave (Athlete, Baseball Player)
1605 N Main St
Flagstaff, AZ 86004-4917, USA

Rajsich, Dave (Athlete, Baseball Player)
1605 N Main St
Flagstaff, AZ 86004-4917, USA

Rajsich, Gary (Athlete, Baseball Player)
8940 Sahalee Ct
Pasadena, MD 21122-6678, USA

Rajsich, Rhonda (Athlete)
c/o Gigi Rock *Heraea Marketing*
10905 E Pear Tree Dr
Cornville, AZ 86325-5523, USA

Rajskub, Mary Lynn (Actor, Writer)
c/o Christie Smith *Mosaic Media Group*
9200 W Sunset Blvd Ste 10
West Hollywood, CA 90069-3608, USA

Rakers, Aaron (Athlete, Baseball Player)
553 W 3rd St
Trenton, IL 62293-1013, USA

Rakers, Jason (Athlete, Baseball Player)
547 Hickory Hollow Dr
Canfield, OH 44406-1052, USA

Rakestraw, Larry (Athlete, Football Player)
2462 Welford Ct
Suwanee, GA 30024-3130, USA

Rakestraw, Wilbur (Race Car Driver)
2609 Marietta Hwy
Ridgeland, GA 39157, USA

Raki, Laya (Actor)
Atkins Assoc
8040 Ventura Canyon Ave
Panorama City, CA 91402-6313, USA

Rakim (Musician)
Padell Nadell Fine Wineberger
156 W 56th St # 400
New York, NY 10019-3800, USA

Rakoczy, Gregg (Athlete, Football Player)
2679 NW 42nd St
Boca Raton, FL 33434-2565, USA

Rakos, Shawn (Athlete, Baseball Player)
23405 Fiske Rd E
Orting, WA 98360, USA

Rales, Steven M (Business Person, Producer)
c/o Staff Member *Indian Paintbrush*
2308 Broadway
Santa Monica, CA 90404-2916, USA

Rall, J Edward (Doctor)
3947 Baltimore St
Kensington, MD 20895-3913, USA

Rall, Ted (Cartoonist)
Chronicle Features
901 Mission St
San Francisco, CA 94103-2905, USA

Rall, Tommy (Dancer)
777 Enchanted Way
Pacific Palisades, CA 90272-2819, USA

Ralston, Bob (Actor)
17027 Tennyson Pl
Granada Hills, CA 91344-1225

Ralston, Dennis (Tennis Player)
2005 San Vincente Dr
Concord, CA 94519-1018, USA

Ralston, John R (Athlete, Coach, Football Coach, Football Player)
8245 Claret Ct
San Jose, CA 95135-1415, USA

Ralston, Steve (Soccer Player)
New England Revolution
1 Patriot Pl
Cmgi Field
Foxboro, MA 02035-1388, USA

Ram, C Venkata (Doctor)
Texas Southwestern Medical Center
5323 Harry Hines Blvd # Y8322
Dallas, TX 75390-7208, USA

Ramage, Rob (Athlete, Hockey Player)
16127 Wilson Manor Dr
Chesterfield, MO 63005-4583, USA

Ramamurthy, Sendhil (Actor)
c/o Mary Erickson *Levine Okwu Erickson Management*
2126 N Commonwealth Ave
Los Angeles, CA 90027-2118, USA

Rama Rau, Santha (Writer)
496 Leedsville Rd
Amenia, NY 12501-5820, USA

Ramazzott, Eros (Musician)
c/o Staff Member *Universal Music Publishing Group (Latin)*
420 Lincoln Rd Ste 200
Miami Beach, FL 33139-3014, USA

Rambin, Leven (Actor)
c/o Rhonda Price *Gersh (NY)*
41 Madison Ave
New York, NY 10010-2202, USA

Rambis, Kurt (Athlete, Basketball Player)
20 Chatham
Manhattan Beach, CA 90266-7225, USA

Rambo, David L (Religious Leader)
Christian & Missionary Alliance
PO Box 35000
Colorado Springs, CO 80935-3500, USA

Rambo, John (Athlete, Track Athlete)
1847 Myrtle Ave
Long Beach, CA 90806-5613, USA

Rambola, Tony (Musician)
c/o Staff Member *William Morris Endeavor (LA)*
9601 Wilshire Blvd
Beverly Hills, CA 90210-5213, USA

Ramenofsky, Marilyn (Athlete, Olympic Athlete, Swimmer)
2909 Anza Ave
Davis, CA 95616-0215, USA

Ramey, Louis (Actor, Comedian)
Top Draw Entertainment
10839 Union Tpke
Forest Hills, NY 11375-6823, USA

Ramini, TJ (Actor)
c/o Joel King *Pakula/King & Associates*
9229 W Sunset Blvd Ste 315
West Hollywood, CA 90069-3403, USA

Ramirez, Alex (Athlete, Baseball Player)
PO Box 880
Winter Haven, FL 33882-0880, USA

Ramirez, Allan (Athlete, Baseball Player)
8 Line Drive Rd
Victoria, TX 77905-5414, USA

Ramirez, Aramis (Athlete, Baseball Player)
1440 N Lake Shore Dr Apt 10EG
Chicago, IL 60610-1626, USA

Ramirez, Cierra (Actor)
c/o Thomas Richards *Corsa Agency, The*
11704 Wilshire Blvd Ste 204
Los Angeles, CA 90025-1510, USA

Ramirez, Dania (Actor, Producer)
c/o Jeff Morrone *Intellectual Artists Management*
9350 Wilshire Blvd Ste 224
Beverly Hills, CA 90212-3204, USA

Ramirez, Edgar (Actor)
c/o Jill Littman *Impression Entertainment*
9229 W Sunset Blvd Ste 700
West Hollywood, CA 90069-3407, USA

Ramirez, Efren (Actor)
c/o Staff Member *James/Levy Management Inc*
3500 W Olive Ave Ste 1470
Burbank, CA 91505-5514, USA

Ramirez, Erasmo (Athlete, Baseball Player)
3605 S Parton St
Santa Ana, CA 92707-4824, USA

Ramirez, Hanley (Athlete, Baseball Player)
2903 Lake Ridge Ln
Weston, FL 33332-2505, USA

Ramirez, Horacio (Athlete, Baseball Player)
850 Cox Rd
Roswell, GA 30075-1018, USA

Ramirez, Manny (Athlete, Baseball Player)
13737 NW 18th Ct
Pembroke Pines, FL 33028-2602, USA

Ramirez, Mario (Athlete, Baseball Player)
HC 3 Box 14107
Yauco, PR 00698, USA

Ramirez, Michael P (Mike) (Cartoonist)
Los Angeles Times
202 W 1st St Ste 500
Editorial Dept
Los Angeles, CA 90012-4401, USA

Ramirez, Milt (Athlete, Baseball Player)
7 Calle Tulio Larrinaga
Urb Ramirez De Arellano
Mayaguez, PR 00682-2447, USA

Ramirez, Rafael (Baseball Player)
5701 NW 3rd St
Miami, FL 33126-4705, USA

Ramirez, Sara (Actor)
c/o Staff Member *Mitchell K Stubbs & Assoc (MKS)*
8675 Washington Blvd Ste 203
Culver City, CA 90232-7486, USA

Ramirez, Twiggy (Musician)
c/o Staff Member *Mitch Schneider Organization (MSO)*
14724 Ventura Blvd Ste 410
Sherman Oaks, CA 91403-3537, USA

Ramm, Haley (Actor)
c/o Wendi Niad *Niad Management*
15021 Ventura Blvd Ste 860
Sherman Oaks, CA 91403-2442, USA

Ramo, Simon (Business Person)
9200 W Sunset Blvd Ste 401
W Hollywood, CA 90069-3506, USA

Ramones, The (Music Group)
c/o Gary Kurfirst *Kurfirst/Blackwell Management*
88 Laight St Frnt 1
New York, NY 10013-2071

Ramon Gaspar, Henderson (Athlete, Baseball Player)
205 Cedar Run Dr
Douglassville, PA 19518-8707, USA

Ramos, Bobby (Athlete, Baseball Player)
12301 SW 76th St
Miami, FL 33183-3601, USA

Ramos, Cesar (Athlete, Baseball Player)
8371 Tele11RAOH Rd
Pico Rivera, CA 90660, USA

Ramos, Constance (Connie) (Actor, Reality Star)
c/o Staff Member *Extreme Makeover: Home Edition*
9225 W Sunset Blvd # 1100
Endemol Entertainment Usa
West Hollywood, CA 90069-3111, USA

Ramos, John (Athlete, Baseball Player)
4214 W Leona St
Tampa, FL 33629-7714, USA

Ramos, Jorge (Actor)
c/o Staff Member *Univision*
605 3rd Ave Fl 12
New York, NY 10158-0034, USA

Ramos, Ken (Athlete, Baseball Player)
9 Lronbrid11E Ln
Pueblo, CO 81001, USA

Ramos, Mario (Athlete, Baseball Player)
20228 Mustang Island Cir
Pflugerville, TX 78660-7720, USA

Ramos, Moises (Reality Star)
c/o Staff Member *Fly on the Wall*
5219 Craner Ave
North Hollywood, CA 91601-3311, USA

Ramos, Nathalia (Actor)
c/o Loch Powell *Leverage Management*
3030 Pennsylvania Ave
Santa Monica, CA 90404-4112, USA

Ramos, Pedro (Athlete, Baseball Player)
6637 W 22nd Ln
Hialeah, FL 33016-3916, USA

Ramos, Sarah (Actor)
c/o Doug Wald *Anonymous Content (LA)*
3532 Hayden Ave
Culver City, CA 90232-2413, USA

Ramos, Tab (Athlete, Soccer Player)
Tab Ramos Soccer Programs
17 Blair Rd
Matawan, NJ 07747-1242, USA

Ramsay, Anne
c/o Todd Eisner *Innovative Artists (LA)*
405 S Beverly Dr Ste 500
Beverly Hills, CA 90212-4425, USA

Ramsay, Bruce
9150 Wilshire Blvd Ste 350
Beverly Hills, CA 90212-3453

Ramsay, Craig (Athlete, Hockey Player)
Florida Panthers
1 Panther Pkwy
Sunrise, FL 33323-5315

Ramsay, Craig (Athlete, Coach, Hockey Player)
10602 Plantation Bay Dr
Tampa, FL 33647-3319

Ramsay, Gordon (Chef, Reality Star)
One Potato Two Potato
1950 Sawtelle Blvd Ste 310
Los Angeles, CA 90025-7073, USA

Ramsay, Laymon (Baseball Player)
Chicago American Giants
2417 Princeton Ave SW
Birmingham, AL 35211-3144, USA

Ramsay, Lynne (Cinematographer, Director, Writer)
c/o Jon Rubinstein *Authentic Talent and Literary Management*
20 Jay St Ste M17
Brooklyn, NY 11201-8300, USA

Ramsay, Robert (Athlete, Baseball Player)
214 N Roosevelt St
Moscow, ID 83843-3602, USA

Ramsay, Tana (Chef, Writer)
c/o Staff Member *HarperCollins Publishers*
195 Broadway Fl 2
Cellar 1
New York, NY 10007-3132, USA

Ramsbottom, Nancy (Golfer)
2216 Parkers Hill Dr
Maidens, VA 23102-2243, USA

Ramsey, Bill (Athlete, Baseball Player)
6301 Village Grove Dr
Memphis, TN 38115-8119, USA

Ramsey, Boniface (Writer)
c/o Staff Member *New City Press*
202 Comforter Blvd
Hyde Park, NY 12538-2977, USA

Ramsey, Cal (Athlete, Basketball Player)
New York University
181 Mercer St Ofc
New York, NY 10012-1501, USA

Ramsey, Chuck (Athlete, Football Player)
17519 Martel Rd
Lenoir City, TN 37772-4235, USA

Ramsey, David (Actor)
c/o Staff Member *Agency for the Performing Arts (APA-LA)*
405 S Beverly Dr Ste 500
Beverly Hills, CA 90212-4425, USA

Ramsey, Derrick (Athlete, Football Player)
1801 Barwick Dr
Lexington, KY 40505-2546, USA

Ramsey, Fernando (Athlete, Baseball Player)
2501 Sandy Trl
Keller, TX 76248-8490, USA

Ramsey, Frank (Athlete, Basketball Player, Coach)
PO Box 363
Madisonville, KY 42431-0007, USA

Ramsey, Gerrard (Athlete, Football Player)
4102 US Highway 411 S
Maryville, TN 37801-9148, USA

Ramsey, Laura (Actor)
c/o Michael Nilon *Kritzer Levine Wilkins Entertainment (KLWG)*
11872 La Grange Ave Fl 1
Los Angeles, CA 90025-5283, USA

Ramsey, Logan
12923 Killion St
Sherman Oaks, CA 91401-5421

Ramsey, Marion (Actor)
c/o Aine Leicht *Horror & Hilarity*
Prefers to be contacted via telephone
Los Angeles, CA 90067, USA

Ramsey, Mary (Musician)
Agency for Performing Arts
9200 W Sunset Blvd Ste 900
West Hollywood, CA 90069-3604, USA

Ramsey, Michael (Mike) (Athlete, Hockey Player)
445 W 79th St
Chanhassen, MN 55317-4505, USA

Ramsey, Mike (Athlete, Baseball Player)
PO Box 262
Harlem, GA 30814-0262, USA

Ramsey, Mike (Athlete, Baseball Player)
11564 92nd Way
Largo, FL 33773-4606, USA

Ramsey, Mike (Athlete, Hockey Player, Olympic Athlete)
6362 Oxbow Bnd
Chanhassen, MN 55317-9109

Ramsey, Nate (Athlete, Football Player)
1938 Cambridge St
Philadelphia, PA 19130-1508, USA

Ramsey, Ray (Athlete, Basketball Player)
1721 N Albany St
Springfield, IL 62702-3122, USA

Ramsey, Tom (Athlete, Football Player)
4999 Beauchamp Ct
San Diego, CA 92130-2742, USA

Ramsey, Wes (Actor)
c/o Robert Attermann *Abrams Artists Agency (NY)*
9200 W Sunset Blvd PH 11
West Hollywood, CA 90069-3601, USA

Ramson, Eason (Athlete, Football Player)
1000 Claudia Ct Apt 39
Antioch, CA 94509-3440, USA

Rancic, Bill (Business Person, Reality Star)
12218 Octagon St
Los Angeles, CA 90049-2337, USA

Rancic, Giuliana (Reality Star, Television Host)
12218 Octagon St
Los Angeles, CA 90049-2337, USA

Rancid (Music Group, Musician)
c/o Staff Member *Leave Home Booking*
1400 S Foothill Dr Ste 34
Salt Lake City, UT 84108-2392, USA

Rand, Reese Mary (Athlete, Track Athlete)
6650 Los Gatos Rd
Atascadero, CA 93422-3608, USA

Randa, Joe (Athlete, Baseball Player)
6436 Ensley Ln
Mission Hills, KS 66208-1932, USA

Randall, Alice (Writer)
c/o Staff Member *Houghton Mifflin Company (Trade Division)*
222 Berkeley St Fl 8
Boston, MA 02116-3748, USA

Randall, Anne (Model)
10526 W Tropicana Cir
Sun City, AZ 85351-2218, USA

Randall, Bob (Athlete, Baseball Player)
2105 Hillview Dr
Manhattan, KS 66502-1942, USA

Randall, Claire (Religious Leader)
10015 W Royal Oak Rd Apt 1214
Sun City, AZ 85351-3164, USA

Randall, Frankie (Boxer)
355 Fish Hatchery Rd
#02
Morristown, TN 37813, USA

Randall, James (Sap) (Athlete, Baseball Player)
158 Heather Ln
Ruston, LA 71270-1165, USA

Randall, Jon (Musician)
Joe's Garage
4405 Belmont Park Ter
Nashville, TN 37215-3609, USA

Randall, Josh (Actor)
I F A Talent Agency
8730 W Sunset Blvd Ste 490
West Hollywood, CA 90069-2248, USA

Randall, Kikkan (Athlete, Olympic Athlete, Track Athlete)
8601 Pioneer Dr
Anchorage, AK 99504-4215, USA

Randall, Mark (Athlete, Basketball Player)
10476 Lynx Bay
Lone Tree, CO 80124-9549, USA

Randall, Maurice (Race Car Driver)
426 Sumpter St # 606
Charlotte, MI 48813-1120, USA

Randall, Rebel (Actor)
PO Box 1405
Riverside, CA 92502-1405, USA

Randall, Scott (Athlete, Baseball Player)
785 Grey Eagle Cir N
Colorado Springs, CO 80919-1605, USA

Randall, Tom (Athlete, Football Player)
2521 Park Vista Cir
Ames, IA 50014-4568, USA

Randall Johnson, Nicole (Actor)
c/o Paul Brown *New Wave Entertainment (LA)*
2660 W Olive Ave
Burbank, CA 91505-4525, USA

Randazzo, Mike (Actor, Talk Show Host)
3469 W Stones Crossing Rd
C/O Mike Randazzo
Greenwood, IN 46143-8564, USA

Randazzo, Tony (Athlete, Baseball Player)
2462 Los Alamos Ct
Las Cruces, NM 88011-1657, USA

Randie, John (Athlete, Football Player)
PO Box 489
Harrisonburg, VA 22803-0489, USA

Randle, Betsy
9300 Wilshire Blvd Ste 555
Beverly Hills, CA 90212-3211

Randle, Ervin (Athlete, Football Player)
900 Spring Creek Dr
Grapevine, TX 76051-8269, USA

Randle, John (Athlete, Football Player)
c/o Gary Uberstine *Premier Sports Management*
16133 Ventura Blvd Ste 500
Encino, CA 91436-2402, USA

Randle, Joseph (Athlete, Football Player)
c/o Erik Burkhardt *Select Sports Group*
2700 Post Oak Blvd Ste 1450
Houston, TX 77056-5785, USA

Randle, Kirk (Kirko Bangz) (Musician)
c/o Staff Member *Warner Bros Records (LA)*
PO Box 6868
Burbank, CA 91510-6868, USA

Randle, Lenny (Athlete, Baseball Player)
39461 Cozumel Ct
Murrieta, CA 92563-2552, USA

Randle, Lynda (Musician)
5565 NW Barry Rd
PO Box 236
Kansas City, MO 64154-1408, USA

Randle, Tate (Athlete, Football Player)
495 Koebig Rd
Seguin, TX 78155-0327, USA

Randle, Ulmo (Sonny) (Athlete, Football Player)
PO Box 487
Harrisonburg, VA 22803-0487, USA

Randolph, Alvin (Athlete, Football Player)
319 Roble Ave
Redwood City, CA 94061-3732, USA

Randolph, Carl (Musician)
David Levin Mgmt
200 W 57th St Ste 308
New York, NY 10019-3211, USA

Randolph, Jackson H (Business Person)
Cinergy Corp
139 E 4th St
Cincinnati, OH 45202-4003, USA

Randolph, Jay (Baseball Player)
1420 Lindgate Dr
Saint Louis, MO 63122-2340, USA

Randolph, Joyce (Actor)
295 Central Park W Apt 18A
New York, NY 10024-3024

Randolph, Judson G (Doctor)
111 Michigan Ave NW
Washington, DC 20010-2916, USA

Randolph, Robert (Musician)
c/o Coran Capshaw *Red Light Management (VA)*
321 E Main St Ste 500
Charlottesville, VA 22902-3201, USA

Randolph, Sam (Golfer)
1305 Briar Ridge Dr
Keller, TX 76248-8376, USA

Randolph, Stephen (Athlete, Baseball Player)
3706 Apache Forest Dr
Austin, TX 78739-4418, USA

Randolph, Willie L (Athlete, Baseball Player, Coach)
715 Jenny Trl
Franklin Lakes, NJ 07417-2907, USA

Randolph, Zach (Athlete, Basketball Player)
c/o Staff Member *Memphis Grizzlies*
191 Beale St
Memphis, TN 38103-3715, USA

Randy, Duncan (Athlete, Football Player)
4240 Foster Dr
Des Moines, IA 50312-2542, USA

Randy Rogers Band (Music Group, Musician)
c/o Joey Lee *William Morris Endeavor (Nashville)*
1600 Division St Ste 300
Nashville, TN 37203-2755, USA

Raney, Catherine (Athlete, Olympic Athlete, Speed Skater)
5800 Chaseview Rd
Nashville, TN 37221-4115, USA

Rangel, Charles B (Politician)
74 W 132nd St Apt 4A
New York, NY 10037-3313

Ranger, Bruce (Horse Racer)
2205 S Cypress Bend Dr Apt 705
Pompano Beach, FL 33069-4459, USA

Ranger, Doug (Songwriter, Writer)
New Frontier Mgmt
1921 Broadway
Nashville, TN 37203-2719, USA

Ranheim, Paul (Athlete, Hockey Player)
7131 Oak Pointe Curv
Minneapolis, MN 55438-3403, USA

Rankin, Ian (Writer)
c/o Staff Member *St Martins Press*
175 5th Ave Ste 400
Publicity Dept
New York, NY 10010-7848, USA

Rankin, Judy (Golfer)
2715 Racquet Club Dr
Midland, TX 79705-7432, USA

Rankin, Kenny (Musician, Songwriter)
c/o Staff Member *Variety Artists International Inc*
1924 Spring St
Paso Robles, CA 93446-1620, USA

Rankin, Kevin (Actor)
c/o Dominic Friesen *Bridge and Tunnel Communications*
9157 W Sunset Blvd Ste 205
West Hollywood, CA 90069-3167, USA

Rankin Jr, Alfred M (Business Person)
NACCO Industries
5875 Landerbrook Dr Ste 300
Cleveland, OH 44124-4069, USA

Ranks, Shabba (Musician)
c/o Clifton Dillon *Shang Artist Management*
222 NE 27th St
Miami, FL 33137-4522, USA

Rannells, Andrew (Actor, Musician)
c/o Christie Smith *Mosaic Media Group*
9200 W Sunset Blvd Ste 10
West Hollywood, CA 90069-3608, USA

Ransey, Kelvin (Athlete, Basketball Player)
3195 Monterey Dr
Tupelo, MS 38801-6817, USA

Ransom, Cody (Athlete, Baseball Player)
2168 E Maplewood St
Gilbert, AZ 85297-1140, USA

Ransom, Derrick (Athlete, Football Player)
6521 Sparrowood Ct
Indianapolis, IN 46236-8122, USA

Ransom, Jeff (Athlete, Baseball Player)
2131 Curtis St
Berkeley, CA 94702-1815, USA

Ransone, James (Actor)
c/o Kimberlin Dalehite *Magnolia Entertainment (LA)*
9595 Wilshire Blvd Ste 601
Beverly Hills, CA 90212-2506, USA

Raoul, Dale (Actor)
c/o Staff Member *JC Robbins Management*
865 S Sherbourne Dr
Los Angeles, CA 90035-1809, USA

Rapace, Noomi (Actor)
c/o Shelley Browning *Magnolia Entertainment (LA)*
9595 Wilshire Blvd Ste 601
Beverly Hills, CA 90212-2506, USA

Rapada, Clay (Athlete, Baseball Player)
37224 Summerglen Ave
Murrieta, CA 92563-5070, USA

Rapaport, Michael (Actor)
c/o Suzan Bymel *Management 360*
9111 Wilshire Blvd
Beverly Hills, CA 90210-5508, USA

Raphael (Actor)
Kaduri Agency
16125 NE 18th Ave
North Miami Beach, FL 33162-4749, USA

Raphael, June Diane (Actor, Writer)
c/o Jon Rubinstein *Authentic Talent and Literary Management*
20 Jay St Ste M17
Brooklyn, NY 11201-8300, USA

Raphael, Sally Jessy (Journalist)
616 Quaker Hill Rd
Pawling, NY 12564-3321, USA

Raposo, Greg (Actor, Musician)
PO Box 434
Glen Head, NY 11545-0434

Rapp, Anthony (Actor)
c/o Elise Konialian *Untitled Entertainment (NY)*
435 Hudson St Fl 9
New York, NY 10014-3995, USA

Rapp, Pat (Athlete, Baseball Player)
2554 Pete Seay Rd
Sulphur, LA 70663-9377, USA

Rapp, Vern (Athlete, Baseball Player, Coach)
1559 Redwing Ln
Broomfield, CO 80020-0614, USA

Rappaport, Jill (Correspondent)
c/o Staff Member *Simon & Schuster*
1230 Avenue of the Americas Fl CONC1
New York, NY 10020-1586, USA

Rappaport, Sheeri (Actor)
c/o Paul Greenstone *Paul Greenstone Entertainment*
3008 Sorrelwood Dr
San Ramon, CA 94582-5008, USA

Rapping 4-Tay (Musician)
Richard Walters
1800 Argyle Ave # 408
Los Angeles, CA 90028-5253, USA

Rapuano, Ed (Athlete, Baseball Player)
10815 Japonica Ct
Boca Raton, FL 33498-4839, USA

Rarick, Cindy (Golfer)
PO Box 30001
Tucson, AZ 85751-0001, USA

Rasa Don (Musician)
William Morris Agency
1325 Avenue of the Americas Bsmt 2
New York, NY 10019-6047, USA

Rasby, Walter (Athlete, Football Player)
6413 Brookbury Ct
Charlotte, NC 28226-6131, USA

Rascal Flatts (Music Group)
c/o Jake Basden *Big Machine Records*
1219 16th Ave S
Nashville, TN 37212-2901, USA

Rasche, David (Actor)
c/o Brian Liebman *Liebman Entertainment*
12 E 46th St Fl 5
New York, NY 10017-2418, USA

Rascoe, Robert (Bobby) (Athlete, Basketball Player)
523 Sumpter Ave
Bowling Green, KY 42101-3750, USA

Rash, Jim (Actor)
c/o Jeff Morrone *Intellectual Artists Management*
10585 Santa Monica Blvd Ste 135
Los Angeles, CA 90025-6392, USA

Rash, Steve (Director)
c/o Staff Member *Gersh (LA)*
9465 Wilshire Blvd Ste 600
Beverly Hills, CA 90212-2605, USA

Rashad, Ahmad (Athlete, Football Player)
13220 Verdun Dr
Palm Beach Gardens, FL 33410-1472, USA

Rashad, Condola (Actor)
c/o Emily Gerson Saines *Brookside Artists Management (NY)*
250 W 57th St Ste 2303
New York, NY 10107-2399, USA

Rashad, Phylicia (Actor)
25 Magnolia Ave
Mount Vernon, NY 10553-1209, USA

Rasheeda (Musician)
c/o Staff Member *ICM Partners (LA)*
10250 Constellation Blvd Fl 7
Los Angeles, CA 90067-6207, USA

Rashid, Karim (Designer)
357 W 17th St Fl 2
New York, NY 10011-5060, USA

Rask, Tuuka (Athlete, Hockey Player)
19 Pier 7 Unit 19
Charlestown, MA 02129-4225

Raskin, Alex (Journalist)
Los Angeles Times
202 W 1st St Ste 500
Editorial Dept
Los Angeles, CA 90012-4401, USA

Rasley, Rocky (Athlete, Football Player)
1918 S Mills Ave Apt 4
Lodi, CA 95242-4475, USA

Rasmus, Colby (Athlete, Baseball Player)
3110 Newsome Rd
Phenix City, AL 36870-2827, USA

Rasmussen, Blair (Athlete, Basketball Player)
9810 SE 35th Pl
Mercer Island, WA 98040-3150, USA

Rasmussen, Dennis (Athlete, Baseball Player)
PO Box 547341
Orlando, FL 32854-7341, USA

Rasmussen, Eric (Athlete, Baseball Player)
237 SW 45th St
Cape Coral, FL 33914-5907, USA

Rasmussen, Erik (Athlete, Hockey Player)
5124 Clear Spring Ct
Minnetonka, MN 55345-4309

Rasmussen, Eris (Athlete, Baseball Player)
237 SW 45th St
Cape Coral, FL 33914-5907, USA

Rasmussen, Randy (Athlete, Football Player)
81 Grumman Hill Rd
Wilton, CT 06897-4508, USA

Rasmussen, Randy (Athlete, Football Player)
3990 114th Ln NW
Minneapolis, MN 55433-2506, USA

Rasmussen, Wayne (Athlete, Football Player)
PO Box 756
Brandon, SD 57005-0756, USA

Rassas, Nick (Athlete, Football Player)
PO Box 227
Moose, WY 83012-0227, USA

Rasuk, Victor (Actor)
c/o Katherine Atkinson *Washington Square Arts (LA)*
1041 N Formosa Ave
the Lot Writers Bldg, Room 305
West Hollywood, CA 90046-6703, USA

Ratchford, Jeremy (Actor)
Paradigm Agency
10100 Santa Monica Blvd Ste 2500
Los Angeles, CA 90067-4116, USA

Ratchuk, Peter (Athlete, Hockey Player)
218 Ruskin Rd
Buffalo, NY 14226-4256

Ratelle, Jean (Athlete, Hockey Player)
1200 Salem St Apt 111
Lynnfield, MA 01940-1595

Rath, Fred (Athlete, Baseball Player)
7308 Pelican Island Dr
Tampa, FL 33634-7470, USA

Rath, Gary (Athlete, Baseball Player)
15433 Meadow Brook Ct
Gulfport, MS 39503-9465, USA

Rath, Meaghan (Actor)
c/o Jim Hess *Silver Lining Entertainment*
421 S Beverly Dr Fl 7
Beverly Hills, CA 90212-4408, USA

Rathbone, Jackson (Actor)
4373 Irvine Ave
Studio City, CA 91604-2705, USA

Rather, Bo (Athlete, Football Player)
7728 La Jessica Cir
Kalamazoo, MI 49009-7542, USA

Rather, Dan (Journalist)
Dan Rather Reports
45 E 80th St Apt 26A
New York, NY 10075-0189, USA

Rathje, Mike (Athlete, Hockey Player)
14850 Blossom Hill Rd
Los Gatos, CA 95032-4901

Rathman, Tom (Athlete, Football Player)
222 Republic Dr
Allen Park, MI 48101-3650, USA

Ratican, Tim (Race Car Driver)
TNT Motorsports
929 Jacaranda Dr
Lady Lake, FL 32159-5110, USA

Ratigan, Brian (Athlete, Football Player)
51702 Ashton Ct
Granger, IN 46530-8747, USA

Ratkowski, Ray (Athlete, Football Player)
9510 Evergreen St
Silver Spring, MD 20901-2932, USA

Ratleff, Ed (Athlete, Basketball Player,
Olympic Athlete)
4202 Paseo De Oro
Cypress, CA 90630-3420, USA

Ratliff, Don (Athlete, Football Player)
9048 Bay Hill Blvd
Orlando, FL 32819-4880, USA

Ratliff, Gene (Athlete, Baseball Player)
315 Southern Walk Cir
Gray, GA 31032-4528, USA

Ratliff, Jon (Athlete, Baseball Player)
289 Boughton Hill Rd
Honeoye Falls, NY 14472-9706, USA

Ratliff, Theo (Athlete, Basketball Player)
118E Mount Paran Rd NW
Atlanta, GA 30327, USA

Ratliffe, Paul (Athlete, Baseball Player)
78 Campton Pl
Laguna Niguel, CA 92677-4734, USA

Ratner, Brett (Director)
c/o Richard Lovett *Creative Artists Agency
(CAA-LA)*
2000 Avenue of the Stars Ste 100
Los Angeles, CA 90067-4705, USA

Ratner, Ellen (Actor, Radio Personality)
c/o Judy Orbach *Judy O Productions*
6136 Glen Holly St
Los Angeles, CA 90068-2338, USA

Ratnoff, Oscar D (Doctor)
1801 Chestnut Hills Dr Apt 1A
Cleveland, OH 44106-4619, USA

Ratser, Dmitri (Musician)
Naxim Gershunoff
1401 NE 9th St Apt 38
Fort Lauderdale, FL 33304-4412, USA

Ratt (Music Group)
WBS, Inc
11684 Ventura Blvd # 675
Studio City, CA 91604-2699, USA

Ratzenberger, John (Actor)
Shelter Entertainment
9255 W Sunset Blvd Ste 1010
West Hollywood, CA 90069-3307, USA

Ratzer, Steve (Athlete, Baseball Player)
91 Lake Linden Dr
Bluffton, SC 29910-6419, USA

Rau, Doug (Athlete, Baseball Player)
1615 Treasure Oaks Dr
Katy, TX 77450-5088, USA

Rauch, Bob (Athlete, Baseball Player)
10700 N La Reserve Dr Apt 5202
Tucson, AZ 85737-9083, USA

Rauch, Jon (Athlete, Baseball Player,
Olympic Athlete)
14081 N Old Forest Trl
Oro Valley, AZ 85755-5789, USA

Rauch, Melissa (Actor)
c/o Brad Petrigala *Brillstein Entertainment
Partners (LA)*
9150 Wilshire Blvd Ste 350
Beverly Hills, CA 90212-3453, USA

Raudman, Bob (Athlete, Baseball Player)
PO Box 8675
Jackson, WY 83002-8675, USA

Raudman, Craig (Race Car Driver)
Dave Reed Racing/AMI
6145 Northbelt Pkwy Ste F
Norcross, GA 30071-2972, USA

Rauner-Harrington, Helen (Baseball
Player)
2027 Kentucky Ave
Fort Wayne, IN 46805-4442, USA

Raup, David M (Musician)
423 Johnson Dr
Washington Island, WI 54246-9169, USA

Rausse, Errol (Athlete, Hockey Player)
338 Rosslare Dr
Arnold, MD 21012-3014

Rautins, Andy (Athlete, Basketball Player)
c/o Bill Duffy *BDA Sports Management
(BDA-CA)*
700 Ygnacio Valley Rd Ste 330
Walnut Creek, CA 94596-3838, USA

Rautins, Leo (Athlete, Basketball Player)
202 Litchfield Dr
Syracuse, NY 13224-2023, USA

Rautzhan, Lance (Athlete, Baseball Player)
2472 Covington Dr
Myrtle Beach, SC 29579-3123, USA

Raven, Eddy (Musician, Songwriter,
Writer)
Great American Talent
PO Box 2476
Hendersonville, TN 37077-2476, USA

Raven, Marion (Musician)
c/o Frank Cimler *10th Street
Entertainment (LA)*
700 N San Vicente Blvd Ste G410
West Hollywood, CA 90069-5060, USA

Ravensberg, Robert (Athlete, Football
Player)
636 Sherwood Dr
Saint Louis, MO 63119-3754, USA

Raver, Kim (Actor)
c/o David (Dave) Fleming *Mosaic Media
Group*
9200 W Sunset Blvd Ste 10
West Hollywood, CA 90069-3608, USA

Ravlich, Matt (Athlete, Hockey Player)
15 Appletree Ln
Dalton, MA 01226-1351

Ravotti, Eric (Athlete, Football Player)
6000 Christopher Wren Dr Apt 117
Wexford, PA 15090-7364, USA

Rawat, Navi (Actor)
c/o Jai Khanna *Brillstein Entertainment
Partners (LA)*
9150 Wilshire Blvd Ste 350
Beverly Hills, CA 90212-3453, USA

Rawis, Betsy (Golfer)
501 Country Club Dr
Wilmington, DE 19803-2430, USA

Rawley, Shane (Athlete, Baseball Player)
4587 Cherrybark Ct
Sarasota, FL 34241-9213, USA

Rawlings, David (Musician)
PO Box 60007
Nashville, TN 37206-0007, USA

Rawlings, Richard (Business Person,
Reality Star)
2330 Merrell Rd
Dallas, TX 75229-4405, USA

Rawls, Betsy (Athlete, Golfer)
4618 Sylvanus Dr
Wilmington, DE 19803-4814, USA

Rawls, Elizabeth E (Betsy) (Golfer)
501 Country Club Dr
Wilmington, DE 19803-2430, USA

Rawls, Sam (Cartoonist)
c/o Staff Member *King Features
Syndication*
300 W 57th St Fl 15
New York, NY 10019-5238, USA

Rawson, Anna (Athlete, Golfer, Model)
c/o Jeff Chilcoat *Sterling Sports
Management, LLC*
7650 Rivers Edge Dr Ste 100
Columbus, OH 43235-1342, USA

Ray, Amy (Musician, Songwriter)
c/o Staff Member *High Road Touring*
751 Bridgeway Fl 2
Sausalito, CA 94965-2174, USA

Ray, Bobby (B.o.B.) (Musician)
2352 Old Ivey Walk
Stone Mountain, GA 30087-2757, USA

Ray, Chris (Athlete, Baseball Player)
15311 Winding Creek Dr
Tampa, FL 33613-1217, USA

Ray, Darrol (Athlete, Football Player)
13000 Doriath Way
Oklahoma City, OK 73170-2108, USA

Ray, David (Athlete, Football Player)
6962 Bridgewater Dr
Huntington Beach, CA 92647-4023, USA

Ray, Dipierro (Athlete, Football Player)
10542 Fremont Pike Apt 256
Perrysburg, OH 43551-3367, USA

Ray, Ear (Athlete, Basketball Player)
446 N Lowell St
Casper, WY 82601-2147, USA

Ray, Earl (Athlete, Basketball Player)
446 N Lowell St
Casper, WY 82601-2147, USA

Ray, Eddie (Athlete, Football Player)
5319 Avondale Dr
Sugar Land, TX 77479-3814, USA

Ray, Fred Olen (Director)
PO Box 3563
Van Nuys, CA 91407-3563, USA

Ray, Greg (Race Car Driver)
Access Motorsports
8227 Northwest Blvd Ste 300
Indianapolis, IN 46278-1386, USA

Ray, James Arthur (Business Person)
James Ray International
5927 Balfour Ct Ste 104
Carlsbad, CA 92008-7376, USA

Ray, John (Athlete, Football Player)
10 Ranger Ln
South Charleston, WV 25309, USA

Ray, Johnny (Athlete, Baseball Player)
20618 Laverton Dr
Katy, TX 77450-1914, USA

Ray, Ken (Athlete, Baseball Player)
8952 W Electra Ln
Peoria, AZ 85383-1404, USA

Ray, Larry (Athlete, Baseball Player)
26 Masters Place Cv
Maumelle, AR 72113-7018, USA

Ray, Lisa (Actor)
c/o Dannielle Thomas *Untitled
Entertainment (LA)*
350 S Beverly Dr Ste 200
Beverly Hills, CA 90212-4819, USA

Ray, Marguerite (Actor)
1329 N Vista St Apt 106
Los Angeles, CA 90046-4833, USA

Ray, Rachael (Chef, Talk Show Host)
22 Costellos Dr
Lake Luzerne, NY 12846-3120, USA

Ray, Rob (Athlete, Hockey Player)
289 Sausalito Dr
East Amherst, NY 14051-1472

Ray, Rob (Athlete, Hockey Player)
Buffalo Sabres
1 Seymour H Knox III Plz Ste 1
Buffalo, NY 14203-3096

Ray, Robert D (Ex-Governor)
3522 Grand Ave Unit 421
Des Moines, IA 50312-4340, USA

Ray, Sugar (Music Group)
c/o Staff Member *Pinnacle Entertainment*
30 Glenn St
White Plains, NY 10603-3254, USA

Ray, Terry (Athlete, Football Player)
42559 Angel Wing Way
Ashburn, VA 20148-5635, USA

Ray, Vanessa (Actor)
c/o Randi Goldstein *Gersh (NY)*
41 Madison Ave
New York, NY 10010-2202, USA

Raybon, Marty (Musician)
Hallmark Direction
15 Music Sq W
Nashville, TN 37203-6200, USA

Raydon, Curt (Athlete, Baseball Player)
PO Box 5124
Jasper, TX 75951-7701, USA

Raye, Collin (Musician)
c/o Dave Fowler *Nashville Artist
Management*
Prefers to be contacted via telephone
Nashville, TN, USA

Raye, Lisa (Actor)
c/o Susan Haber *Haber Entertainment*
434 S Canon Dr Apt 204
Beverly Hills, CA 90212-4501, USA

Rayford, Floyd (Athlete, Baseball Player)
1621 NE Waldo Rd # 56
Gainesville, FL 32609-3900, USA

Rayl, James (Athlete, Basketball Player)
58 Rideout Rd
Hollis, NH 03049-6110, USA

Raymer, Cory (Athlete, Football Player)
46629 Hampshire Station Dr
Sterling, VA 20165-7395, USA

Raymond, Corey (Athlete, Football Player)
106 Carter St
New Iberia, LA 70560-6214, USA

Raymond, Craig (Athlete, Basketball Player)
4617 N 265 E
Provo, UT 84604-5403

Raymond, Jeff
8687 Melrose Ave
West Hollywood, CA 90069-5701, USA

Raymond, Lisa (Tennis Player)
Octagon
7950 Jones Branch Dr
Mc Lean, VA 22102-3302, USA

Raymond, Mistral (Athlete, Football Player)
c/o Adam Heller *Vantage Management Group*
518 Reamer Dr
Carnegie, PA 15106-1845, USA

Raymond, Usher (Dancer, Musician)
Usher's New Look
3700 Crestwood Pkwy NW Ste 460
Duluth, GA 30096-5553, USA

Raymonde, Tania (Actor)
c/o Katie Rhodes *Untitled Entertainment (LA)*
350 S Beverly Dr Ste 200
Beverly Hills, CA 90212-4819, USA

Raymund, Monica (Actor)
c/o Kyle Luker *The Group Entertainment*
115 W 29th St Rm 1102
New York, NY 10001-5106, USA

Rayner, Chuck (Actor)
c/o Laraine Golden *Main Line Models & Talent*
1215 W Baltimore Pike Ste 9
Media, PA 19063-5540, USA

Ray Newman, Jaime (Actor)
c/o Joanna (Joanie) Burstein *Burstein Company, The*
15304 W Sunset Blvd Ste 208
Pacific Palisades, CA 90272-3656, USA

Raynis, Richard (Producer)
c/o Staff Member *Creative Artists Agency (CAA-LA)*
2000 Avenue of the Stars Ste 100
Los Angeles, CA 90067-4705, USA

Raynor, Bruce (Politician)
Unite
275 7th Ave Fl 11
New York, NY 10001-6708, USA

Raynr, David (Actor, Director, Producer)
c/o Simon Millar *Rumble Media*
1620 Broadway Ste C
Santa Monica, CA 90404-2777, USA

Raz, Kavi (Actor)
c/o Staff Member *Almond Talent Agency*
8217 Beverly Blvd Ste 8
Los Angeles, CA 90048-4534, USA

Raza, S Atiq (Business Person)
Advanced Micro Devices
1 Amd Pl
Sunnyvale, CA 94085-3905, USA

Raz B (Actor, Musician)
c/o Mike Esterman *Esterman.Com, LLC*
Prefers to be contacted via email
Baltimore, MD XXXXX, USA

Raziano, Barry (Athlete, Baseball Player)
1315 4th St
Kenner, LA 70062-7311, USA

R. Carter, John (Congressman, Politician)
409 Cannon Hob
Washington, DC 20515-0911, USA

R. Conseco, Francisco (Congressman, Politician)
1339 Longworth Hob
Washington, DC 20515-1202, USA

Rea, Connie (Athlete, Basketball Player)
13 Marina Dr
Winter Haven, FL 33881-9710, USA

Rea, Stephen (Actor, Writer)
c/o Sue Leibman *Barking Dog Entertainment*
609 Greenwich St Fl 6
New York, NY 10014-3610, USA

Read, Amy (Athlete, Golfer)
7301 Barbaradale Cir
Las Vegas, NV 89146, USA

Read, James (Actor)
c/o Staff Member *Pakula/King & Associates*
9229 W Sunset Blvd Ste 315
West Hollywood, CA 90069-3403, USA

Read, Nicolas (Actor)
c/o Carlo Capomazza *Capocom Entertainment*
8917 Cynthia St Apt 3
West Hollywood, CA 90069-4427, USA

Read, Richard (Journalist)
Portland Oregonian
1320 SW Broadway
Editorial Dept
Portland, OR 97201-3411, USA

Readdy, William F (Bill) (Astronaut)
NASA
2101 Nasa Pkwy Spc Johnsoncenter
Houston, TX 77058-3696, USA

Readdy, William F Captain (Astronaut)
1818 S Lynn St
Arlington, VA 22202-1619, USA

Reading, John (Musician)
14321 Draft Horse Ln
Wellington, FL 33414-1020, USA

Read-Martin, Dolly (Actor)
30765 Pacific Coast Hwy Ste 103
Malibu, CA 90265-3643

Ready, Randy (Athlete, Baseball Player)
4410 Enfield Dr
Dallas, TX 75220-6406, USA

Reagan, Bernice Johnson (Musician)
American University
History Dept
Washington, DC 20016, USA

Reagan, Michael (Radio Personality, Writer)
c/o Staff Member *Premiere Speakers Bureau*
109 International Dr Ste 300
Franklin, TN 37067-1764, USA

Reagan, Nancy (Politician)
10880 Wilshire Blvd Ste 870
Los Angeles, CA 90024-4109, USA

Reagan, Ron (Journalist)
2612 28th Ave W
Seattle, WA 98199-3320, USA

Reagins, Tony (Baseball Player)
8220 E Blackwillow Cir Apt 104
Anaheim, CA 92808-1904, USA

Reagor, Montae (Athlete, Football Player)
1511 Drexel Dr
Waxahachie, TX 75165-4409, USA

Real, Roxanne (Musician)
Headline Talent
1650 Broadway Ste 508
New York, NY 10019-6833, USA

Real, Terrence (Writer)
Real Relational Solutions
754 Massachusetts Ave
Arlington, MA 02476-4712, USA

Reali, Tony (Sportscaster, Television Host)
c/o Staff Member *CAA Sports (LA)*
2000 Avenue of the Stars Ste 100
Los Angeles, CA 90067-4705, USA

Ream, Charles (Athlete, Football Player)
8366 Thistle Ln Apt A
Liberty Township, OH 45044-8557, USA

Reames, Britt (Athlete, Baseball Player)
806 Dalton Rd
Seneca, SC 29678-3722, USA

Reamon, Tommy (Athlete, Football Player)
709 Galahad Dr
Newport News, VA 23608-1807, USA

Reams, Leroy (Athlete, Baseball Player)
PO Box 6575
Oakland, CA 94603-0575, USA

Reardon, Jeff (Athlete, Baseball Player)
130 Thornton Dr
Palm Beach Gardens, FL 33418-8087, USA

Reardon, John (Actor)
c/o Courtney Kivowitz *The Schiff Company*
9220 W Sunset Blvd Ste 106
West Hollywood, CA 90069-3500, USA

Reaser, Elizabeth (Actor)
c/o Perri Kipperman *Kipperman Management*
345 7th Ave Rm 503
New York, NY 10001-5054, USA

Reason, Rex (Actor)
Roadside Productions
20105 Rhapsody Rd
Walnut, CA 91789-3533, USA

Reason, Rhodes (Actor)
PO Box 503
Gladstone, OR 97027-0503, USA

Reasoner, Marty (Athlete, Hockey Player)
5250 Winlane Dr
Bloomfield Hills, MI 48302-2960

Reasons, Gary P (Athlete, Football Player)
17029 Hardwood Pl
Edmond, OK 73012-9121, USA

Reaugh, Daryl (Athlete, Hockey Player)
Dallas Stars
2601 Avenue of the Stars Ste 100
Frisco, TX 75034-9016

reaugh, daryl (Athlete, Hockey Player)
3400 Saint Johns Dr
Dallas, TX 75205-2906

Reaves, Ken (Athlete, Football Player)
413 Oakside Dr SW
Atlanta, GA 30331-3724, USA

Reaves, Shawn (Actor)
c/o Claudia Black *Glasser/Black Management*
283 Cedarhurst Ave
Cedarhurst, NY 11516-1671, USA

Reaves, Stephanie (Race Car Driver)
Rapid Motorsports Inc
PO Box 55
Bar Mills, ME 04004-0055, USA

Reaves, T Johnson (John) (Athlete, Coach, Football Coach, Football Player)
5716 Bayshore Blvd
Tampa, FL 33611-4726, USA

Reavis, Dave (Athlete, Football Player)
5495 S Newport Cir
Greenwood Village, CO 80111-1601, USA

Reavis, Phil (Athlete, Olympic Athlete)
41 School St
Somerville, MA 02143-1721, USA

Rebagliati, Ross
1 Erieview Plz # 1300
Cleveland, OH 44114-1738

Rebardo, Joe (Musician)
Billy Paul Mgmt
8215 Winthrop St
Philadelphia, PA 19136-1914, USA

Rebel Emergency (Music Group)
c/o Staff Member *Paradigm (Monterey)*
404 W Franklin St
Monterey, CA 93940-2303, USA

Reberger, Frank (Athlete, Baseball Player)
PO Box 439056
San Ysidro, CA 92143-9056, USA

Reboulet, Jeff (Athlete, Baseball Player)
Horizon Wealth Management
8280 Ymca Plaza Dr Bldg 5
Baton Rouge, LA 70810-0927, USA

Rebowe, Rusty (Athlete, Football Player)
656 Pine St
Norco, LA 70079-2136, USA

Rebraca, Zeljko (Athlete, Basketball Player)
1550 8th St
Manhattan Beach, CA 90266-6351, USA

Recari, Beatriz (Athlete, Golfer)
c/o Staff Member *Ladies Pro Golf Association (LPGA)*
100 International Golf Dr
Daytona Beach, FL 32124-1092, USA

Recasner, Eldridge (Athlete, Basketball Player)
6159 164th Ave SE
Bellevue, WA 98006-5613, USA

Recchi, Mark (Athlete, Hockey Player)
The Orr Hockey Group
PO Box 290836
Charlestown, MA 02129-0215, USA

Recher, Dave (Athlete, Football Player)
970 E Devon Dr
Gilbert, AZ 85296-3620, USA

Rechichar, Albert (Bert) (Athlete, Football Player)
141 W McClain Rd
Belle Vernon, PA 15012-3507, USA

Reckell, Peter (Actor)
c/o Staff Member *Rebel Entertainment Partners*
5700 Wilshire Blvd Ste 456
Los Angeles, CA 90036-3648, USA

Reckless Kelly (Music Group)
c/o Staff Member *Paradigm (Monterey)*
404 W Franklin St
Monterey, CA 93940-2303, USA

Records, Max (Actor)
c/o Ara Keshishian *Creative Artists Agency (CAA-LA)*
2000 Avenue of the Stars Ste 100
Los Angeles, CA 90067-4705, USA

Rector, Jeff (Actor)
10153 1/2 Riverside Dr
North Hollywood, CA 91602-2561, USA

Red Alert, Kool DJ (Musician)
c/o Staff Member *Violator Management*
36 W 25th St Fl 2
New York, NY 10010-2768, USA

Redbone, Leon (Musician)
Red Shark Inc
2169 Aquetong Rd
New Hope, PA 18938-1148, USA

Redd, Michael (Athlete, Basketball Player)
2 Crescent Pond
New Albany, OH 43054-9081, USA

Redden, Barry (Athlete, Football Player)
PO Box 6501
Katy, TX 77491-6501, USA

Reddick, Cat (Athlete, Olympic Athlete, Soccer Player)
2620 Altadena Rd
Vestavia, AL 35243-4500, USA

Reddick, Eldon "Pokey" (Athlete, Hockey Player)
7794 Briana Renee Way
Las Vegas, NV 89123-0447

Reddick, Josh (Athlete, Baseball Player)
103 Oak St
Rincon, GA 31326-5453, USA

Reddick, Lance (Actor, Musician)
12024 Sarah St
Valley Village, CA 91607-4131, USA

Redding, Cory (Athlete, Football Player)
c/o Kennard McGuire *MS World LLC*
1270 Crabb River Rd Ste 600-104
Richmond, TX 77469-5636, USA

Redding, Juli
PO Box 1806
Beverly Hills, CA 90213-1806

Redding, Tim (Athlete, Baseball Player)
8882 Squire Trl
Bellevue, MI 49021-9566, USA

Reddout, Frank (Athlete, Basketball Player)
379 Niblick Cir
Winter Haven, FL 33881-9572, USA

Reddy, Helen (Musician)
c/o Staff Member *T-Best Talent Agency*
508 Honey Lake Ct
Danville, CA 94506-1237, USA

Redfern, Pete (Athlete, Baseball Player)
12516 Haddon Ave
Sylmar, CA 91342-3636, USA

Redfield, James (Actor, Producer, Writer)
3584 Pelham Pkwy
Pelham, AL 35124-2034, USA

Redfield, Joe (Athlete, Baseball Player)
307 Glenview Cir
Woodway, TX 76712-3141, USA

Redford, Blair (Actor)
c/o Matt Fletcher *Greene & Associates*
1901 Avenue of the Stars Ste 130
Los Angeles, CA 90067-6030, USA

Redford, Jamie (Producer)
c/o Jim Ehrich *Rothman Brecher*
9250 Wilshire Blvd Ste 400
Beverly Hills, CA 90212-3397, USA

Redford, Paul (Producer, Writer)
c/o Cori Wellins *William Morris Endeavor (LA)*
9601 Wilshire Blvd
Beverly Hills, CA 90210-5213, USA

Redford, Robert (Actor, Director)
The Redford Center
PO Box 29144
San Francisco, CA 94129-0144, USA

Redgrave, Vanessa (Actor)
c/o Nicole Caruso *Relevant*
584 Broadway Rm 310
New York, NY 10012-5246, USA

Red-Horse, Valerie (Actor, Director, Producer, Writer)
c/o Staff Member *Suite A Management Talent & Literary Agency*
120 El Camino Dr Ste 202
Beverly Hills, CA 90212-2723, USA

Red Hot Chili Peppers (Music Group)
c/o Cliff Burnstein *Q Prime Inc*
729 7th Ave Ste 1600
New York, NY 10019-6880, USA

Redick, JJ (Athlete, Basketball Player)
2919 Toro Canyon Rd
Austin, TX 78746-2450, USA

Reding, Juli (Actor)
PO Box 1806
Beverly Hills, CA 90213-1806, USA

Redman, Brian (Race Car Driver)
10945 Scott Mill Rd
Jacksonville, FL 32223-6514, USA

Redman, Joshua (Race Car Driver)
Wilkins Management
323 Broadway
Cambridge, MA 02139-1801, USA

Redman, Julian "Tike" (Athlete, Baseball Player)
1109 Lauren Way NW
Acworth, GA 30101-3887, USA

Redman, Magdalen (Athlete, Baseball Player)
N7780 Vicksburg Way Apt D
Oconomowoc, WI 53066-2016, USA

Redman, Mark (Athlete, Baseball Player)
6818 E 109th St
Tulsa, OK 74133-7153, USA

Redman, Michele (Golfer)
3410 Queensland Ln N
Minneapolis, MN 55447-1153, USA

Redman, Prentice (Athlete, Baseball Player)
14248 Manchester Rd Ste F Dr Apt K
Ballwin, MO 63011-4515, USA

Redman, Susle (Golfer)
137 SW Saratoga Ave
Port Saint Lucie, FL 34953-5974, USA

Redmann, Teal (Actor)
c/o Amy Abell *Glick Agency*
1505 10th St
Santa Monica, CA 90401-2805, USA

Redmayne, Eddie (Actor)
c/o Gene Parseghian *Parseghian Planco LLC*
388 2nd Ave
New York, NY 10010-5616, USA

Redmon, Glenn (Athlete, Baseball Player)
PO Box 2171
Riverview, FL 33568-2171, USA

Redmond, Marge (Actor)
Abrams Artists
9200 W Sunset Blvd Ste 1125
West Hollywood, CA 90069-3610, USA

Redmond, Markus (Actor)
c/o Staff Member *Gersh (LA)*
9465 Wilshire Blvd Ste 600
Beverly Hills, CA 90212-2605, USA

Redmond, Marlon (Athlete, Basketball Player)
441 Oak St
San Francisco, CA 94102-5609, USA

Redmond, Michael E (Mickey) (Athlete, Hockey Player)
30699 Harlincin Ct
Franklin, MI 48025-1521, USA

Redmond, Mickey (Athlete, Hockey Player)
Detroit Red Wings
600 Civic Center Dr
Detroit, MI 48226-4419

Redmond, Mike (Athlete, Baseball Player)
13506 S Bluegrouse Ln
Spokane, WA 99224-8523, USA

Redmond, Rudy (Athlete, Football Player)
17091 Melrose St
Southfield, MI 48075-4260, USA

Redmond, Wayne (Athlete, Baseball Player)
18061 Sussex St
Detroit, MI 48235-2835, USA

Rednikova, Yekaterina (Actor)
358 N Gardner St
C/O Larry Hummel
Los Angeles, CA 90036-5721, USA

Redstone, Sumner (Business Person)
c/o Staff Member *Viacom Entertainment Group*
5555 Melrose Ave
Los Angeles, CA 90038-3989

Redus, Gary (Athlete, Baseball Player)
2202 Mallard Ln SE
Decatur, AL 35601-6759, USA

Redwine, Jarvis J (Athlete, Football Player)
2707 W 79th St
Inglewood, CA 90305-1033, USA

Redwine, Tim
3518 Cahuenga Blvd W # 200
Los Angeles, CA 90068-1304

Reece, Beasley (Athlete, Football Player, Sportscaster)
17 Stirling Way
Lumberton, NJ 08048-5207, USA

Reece, Bob (Athlete, Baseball Player)
3106 Castlewood Cir
Pollock Pines, CA 95726-9522, USA

Reece, Carmen (Musician)
c/o Mark Feist *Real MF Ltd*
22425 Ventura Blvd # 179
Woodland Hills, CA 91364-1524, USA

Reece, Daniel (Danny) (Athlete, Football Player)
6565 Crescent Park W Apt 402
Playa Vista, CA 90094-2286, USA

Reece, Dave (Athlete, Hockey Player)
138 Peaked Rock Rd
Wakefield, RI 02879-2384

Reece, Gabrielle (Athlete, Model, Volleyball Player)
c/o Lisa Shotland *Creative Artists Agency (CAA-LA)*
2000 Avenue of the Stars Ste 100
Los Angeles, CA 90067-4705, USA

Reece, John (Athlete, Football Player)
5927 Cape Hatteras Dr
Houston, TX 77041-5911, USA

Reece, Thomas L (Business Person)
Dover Corp
280 Park Ave
New York, NY 10017-1216, USA

Reed, Alvin (Athlete, Football Player)
3910 Abbeywood Dr
Pearland, TX 77584-4943, USA

Reed, Alyson (Actor)
c/o Christopher Black *Opus Entertainment*
5225 Wilshire Blvd Ste 905
Los Angeles, CA 90036-4353, USA

Reed, Andre D (Athlete, Football Player)
16 Gypsy Ln
East Aurora, NY 14052-2108, USA

Reed, Ben
c/o Staff Member *AKA Talent Agency*
6310 San Vicente Blvd Ste 200
Los Angeles, CA 90048-5488, USA

Reed, Bob (Athlete, Baseball Player)
42519 Lake Hospitality Ln
Altoona, FL 32702-9584, USA

Reed, Brooks (Athlete, Football Player)
c/o Ken Zuckerman *Priority Sports & Entertainment - (LA)*
15233 Ventura Blvd Ste 718
Sherman Oaks, CA 91403-2237, USA

Reed, Bruce (Writer)
c/o Staff Member *Public Affairs Books*
1094 Flex Dr
Jackson, TN 38301-5070, USA

Reed, Crystal (Actor)
c/o Staff Member *Main Title Entertainment*
8383 Wilshire Blvd Ste 408
Beverly Hills, CA 90211-2435, USA

Reed, Darren (Athlete, Baseball Player)
8101 Santa Ana Rd
Ventura, CA 93001-9723, USA

Reed, Dizzy (Musician)
c/o Joel Miller *Albion Entertainment*
24331 Hatteras St
Woodland Hills, CA 91367, USA

Reed, Ed (Athlete, Football Player)
1 Winning Dr
Owings Mills, MD 21117-4776, USA

Reed, Eddie (Athlete, Baseball Player)
Memphis Red Sox
708 8th Ave S
Great Falls, MT 59405-2052, USA

Reed, Eric (Musician)
Joel Chriss
300 Mercer St Apt 3J
New York, NY 10003-6732, USA

Reed, Hub (Athlete, Basketball Player)
46601 Garretts Lake Rd
Shawnee, OK 74804-9494, USA

Reed, Jack (Athlete, Baseball Player)
PO Box 97
Silver City, MS 39166-0097, USA

Reed, Jeff (Athlete, Baseball Player)
17688 Sylvan Hill Rd
Elizabethton, TN 37643, USA

Reed, Jeremy (Athlete, Baseball Player)
4819 N 35th St
Phoenix, AZ 85018-3476, USA

Reed, Jerry (Athlete, Baseball Player)
13964 106th Ave
Largo, FL 33774-4543, USA

Reed, Jim (Race Car Driver)
8 Cutler Ln
Garrison, NY 10524-3919, USA

Reed, Jody (Athlete, Baseball Player)
19153 E Briarwood Dr
Centennial, CO 80016-2161, USA

Reed, Joe (Athlete, Football Player)
106 Whitechapel Ct
Cedar Park, TX 78613-3219, USA

Reed, Johnny (Musician)
Jackson Artists
7251 Lowell Dr # 200
Overland Park, KS 66204-1840, USA

Reed, Josh (Athlete, Football Player)
124 Allegro Ave
Duson, LA 70529-3349, USA

Reed, Keith (Athlete, Baseball Player)
513A S Main St
Rolesville, NC 27571-9666, USA

Reed, Kira
PO Box 251255
Los Angeles, CA 90025-9755

Reed, Margaret
524 W 57th St # 5330
New York, NY 10019-2930

Reed, Mark A (Doctor)
Yale University
Electrical Engineering Dept
PO Box 2157
New Haven, CT 06520, USA

Reed, Nikki (Actor)
3369 Charleston Way
Los Angeles, CA 90068-1415, USA

Reed, Oscar (Athlete, Football Player)
700 Elizabeth Ln
Minneapolis, MN 55411-3340, USA

Reed, Pamela (Actor)
Innovative Artists
1505 10th St
Santa Monica, CA 90401-2805, USA

Reed, Peyton (Actor, Director, Producer)
c/o Staff Member Moxie Pictures
2644 30th St Ste 100
Santa Monica, CA 90405-3051, USA

Reed, Priscilla (Musician)
153 Rue De Grande
Brentwood, TN 37027-8011, USA

Reed, Rex (Journalist)
Dakota Hotel
1 W 72nd St Apt 86
New York, NY 10023-3425, USA

Reed, Richard A (Rick) (Baseball Player)
Pittsburgh Pirates
86 Private Dr 8323
Proctorville, OH 45669, USA

Reed, Rick (Athlete, Baseball Player)
4938 Crestone Way
Rochester, MI 48306-1682, USA

Reed, Robert (Athlete, Football Player)
21 Wells St Apt 412
Saratoga Springs, NY 12866-1214, USA

Reed, Ronald L (Ron) (Athlete, Baseball
Player, Basketball Player)
2613 Cliffview Dr SW
Lilburn, GA 30047-4794, USA

Reed, Royce (Actor)
*c/o Dominic Friesen Bridge and Tunnel
Communications*
9157 W Sunset Blvd Ste 205
West Hollywood, CA 90069-3167, USA

Reed, Shanna (Actor)
1327 Brinkley Ave
Los Angeles, CA 90049-3619, USA

Reed, Steve (Athlete, Baseball Player)
5335 Pine Ridge Rd
Golden, CO 80403-8030, USA

Reed, Thomas C (Government Official)
Quaker Hill Development Corp
PO Box 2240
Healdsburg, CA 95448-2240, USA

Reed, Tom (Congressman, Politician)
1037 Longworth Hob
Washington, DC 20515-0542, USA

Reed, Tony (Athlete, Football Player)
14068 Mount Tabor Rd
Odessa, MO 64076-7109, USA

Reed, Walter
3400 Paul Sweet Rd Unit B209
Santa Cruz, CA 95065-1552

Reed, Willis (Athlete, Basketball Player,
Football Player)
176 Three Ponds Rd
Ruston, LA 71270, USA

Reed Jr, Alan
3455 Laurelvale Dr
Studio City, CA 91604-4135, USA

Reeds, Mark (Athlete, Hockey Player)
7823 Cardinal Ridge Ct
Saint Louis, MO 63119-5014, USA

Reedus, Norman (Actor)
*c/o JoAnne Colonna Brillstein
Entertainment Partners (LA)*
9150 Wilshire Blvd Ste 350
Beverly Hills, CA 90212-3453, USA

Reehl, Robert (Race Car Driver)
13434 Lambert Rd
Whittier, CA 90605-2454, USA

Reekie, Joe (Athlete, Hockey Player)
13210 Waterford Run Dr
Riverview, FL 33569-5733

Reep, Jon (Actor, Comedian)
c/o Kara Welker Generate Management
8750 Wilshire Blvd Ste 200
Beverly Hills, CA 90211-2707, USA

Rees, John (Musician)
TPA
PO Box 124
Round Corner, NS 02158, USA

Rees, Roger (Actor)
Innovative Artists
1505 10th St
Santa Monica, CA 90401-2805, USA

Reese, Brian Adrian (Cassidy) (Musician)
c/o Greg Cohen Amalgam Management
705 Town Blvd NE Apt 510
Atlanta, GA 30319-3082, USA

Reese, Calvin (Pokey) (Athlete, Baseball
Player)
12416 Sylvan Oak Way
Charlotte, NC 28273-4728, USA

Reese, Della (Actor, Musician)
c/o Lynda Bensky Bensky Entertainment
15021 Ventura Blvd Ste 343
Sherman Oaks, CA 91403-2442, USA

Reese, Eddie (Coach, Swimmer)
University of Texas
Athletic Dept
Austin, TX 78712, USA

Reese, Guy (Athlete, Football Player)
2409 Cardinal Way
McKinney, TX 75070-5966, USA

Reese, Izell (Athlete, Football Player)
10270 Willeo Creek Trce
Roswell, GA 30075-3269, USA

Reese, Jeff (Athlete, Hockey Player)
856 Longwood Cir
Haddonfield, NJ 08033-1069

Reese, Kevin (Athlete, Baseball Player)
1221 Willow St
San Diego, CA 92106-2538, USA

Reese, Rich (Athlete, Baseball Player)
PO Box 2339
Carefree, AZ 85377-2339, USA

Reese, Steve (Athlete, Football Player)
1146 Parkwood Trce
Stone Mountain, GA 30083-2485, USA

Reeser, Autumn (Actor)
*c/o Staff Member Kritzer Levine Wilkins
Entertainment (KLWG)*
11872 La Grange Ave Fl 1
Los Angeles, CA 90025-5283, USA

Reeser, Morgan (Athlete, Olympic
Athlete, Sailor)
1948 Coral Gardens Dr
Wilton Manors, FL 33306-1334, USA

Reeser, Robert (Horse Racer)
139 Barksdale Ct
Milford, DE 19963-4174, USA

Reeves, Bryant (Athlete, Basketball Player)
116458 S 4710 Rd
Muldrow, OK 74948-6882, USA

Reeves, Dan (Athlete, Football Player)
785 W Conway Dr NW
Atlanta, GA 30327-3633, USA

Reeves, Diane
PO Box 66
Englishtown, NJ 07726-0066

Reeves, Dianne (Musician)
PO Box 66
Englishtown, NJ 07726-0066, USA

Reeves, Julie
PO Box 300
Russell, KY 41169-0300

Reeves, Keanu (Actor)
Arch Motorcycle Company LLC
1801 Century Park E Ste 2160
32160
Los Angeles, CA 90067-2343, USA

Reeves, Khalid (Athlete, Basketball Player)
11519 140th St
Jamaica, NY 11436-1018, USA

Reeves, Martha (Musician)
14608 Annapolis Dr
Sterling Hts, MI 48313-3616, USA

Reeves, Melissa (Actor)
6520 Platt Ave # 634
West Hills, CA 91307-3218

Reeves, Perrey (Actor)
2101 Broadview Ter
Los Angeles, CA 90068-3124, USA

Reeves, Ronna
5114 Albert Dr
Brentwood, TN 37027-6810

Reeves, Scott (Actor)
6520 Platt Ave # 634
West Hills, CA 91307-3218, USA

Reeves, Stevie (Race Car Driver)
CAA Performance Group
218 Chestnut Ave
Kannapolis, NC 28081, USA

Reeves, Teri (Actor)
*c/o Paul Brown New Wave Entertainment
(LA)*
2660 W Olive Ave
Burbank, CA 91505-4525, USA

Reeves, Walter (Athlete, Football Player)
5013 Lincoln Oaks Dr S Apt 1805
Fort Worth, TX 76132-2250, USA

Refaeli, Bar (Actor, Model)
c/o Scott Lipps One Management
42 Bond St Apt 2
New York, NY 10012-2428, USA

Reffner, Bryan (Race Car Driver)
Phelon Motors
2063 University Pkwy
Aiken, SC 29801-6343, USA

Regaibuto, Joe (Actor)
724 24th St
Santa Monica, CA 90402-3138, USA

Regalado, Rudy (Athlete, Baseball Player)
PO Box 475
Borrego Springs, CA 92004-0475, USA

Regalbuto, Joe
724 24th St
Santa Monica, CA 90402-3138

Regan, Brian (Actor, Comedian)
*c/o Rory Rosegarten Conversation
Company*
1044 Northern Blvd Ste 304
Roslyn, NY 11576-1589, USA

Regan, Bridget (Actor)
*c/o Staff Member TMT Entertainment
Group*
648 Broadway # 1002
New York, NY 10012-2348, USA

Regan, Chris (Writer)
c/o Staff Member Gersh (LA)
9465 Wilshire Blvd Ste 600
Beverly Hills, CA 90212-2605, USA

Regan, Donald T
240 McLaws Cir Ste 142
Williamsburg, VA 23185-6429, USA

Regan, Judith (Talk Show Host, Writer)
c/o Staff Member *Regan Media*
10100 Santa Monica Blvd Fl 10
Los Angeles, CA 90067-4003, USA

Regan, Laura (Actor)
c/o Ethan Salter *Greene & Associates*
1901 Avenue of the Stars Ste 130
Los Angeles, CA 90067-6030, USA

Regan, Phil (Athlete, Baseball Player, Coach)
1687 SW Harbour Isles Cir # 6
Port St Lucie, FL 34986-3405, USA

Regbo, Toby (Actor)
c/o Brantley Brown *Schachter Entertainment*
1157 S Beverly Dr Fl 2
Los Angeles, CA 90035-1119, USA

Regeher, Robyn (Athlete, Football Player)
1721 Monterey Blvd
Hermosa Beach, CA 90254-2905, USA

Regehr, Duncan (Actor)
2501 Main St
Santa Monica, CA 90405, USA

Regen, Elizabeth (Actor)
c/o Mark Measures *Kazarian, Measures, Ruskin & Associates (LA)*
11969 Ventura Blvd Fl 3
Studio City, CA 91604-2630, USA

Reger, John (Athlete, Football Player)
9919 SW 42nd Rd
Gainesville, FL 32608-7103, USA

Reger, Nate (Writer)
c/o Staff Member *ICM Partners (LA)*
10250 Constellation Blvd Fl 7
Los Angeles, CA 90067-6207, USA

Reggio, Godfrey (Director)
Regional Education Institute
PO Box 2404
Santa Fe, NM 87504-2404, USA

Reghi, Mike (Baseball Player)
9344 Saybrook Dr
North Ridgeville, OH 44039-8748, USA

Regier, Darcy (Athlete, Hockey Player)
8362 Black Walnut Dr
East Amherst, NY 14051-1561

Regier, Darcy (Athlete, Hockey Player)
Buffalo Sabres
1 Seymour H Knox III Plz Ste 1
Buffalo, NY 14203-3096

Regilio, Nick (Athlete, Baseball Player)
6505 Raham Ct
Port Orange, FL 32128-6069, USA

Regine (Business Person)
502 Park Ave
New York, NY 10022-1108, USA

Register, Steven (Athlete, Baseball Player)
2606 Weston St
Auburn, AL 36832-3670, USA

Regner, Tom (Athlete, Football Player)
2231 Big Trail Cir
Reno, NV 89521-8957, USA

Rehberg, Denny (Congressman, Politician)
2448 Rayburn Hob
Washington, DC 20515-3227, USA

Rehberg, Scott (Athlete, Football Player)
1153 Thistle Ln
Lebanon, OH 45036-7788, USA

Rehder, Tom (Athlete, Football Player)
730 Monarch Ln
Nipomo, CA 93444-9418, USA

Rehm, Diane (Radio Personality)
c/o Staff Member *National Public Radio (NPR)*
1111 N Capitol St NE
Washington, DC 20002-7502, USA

Rehm, Fred (Athlete, Basketball Player)
19340A Stonehedge Dr
Brookfield, WI 53045-3665, USA

Rehm, Jack D (Publisher)
19 Neponset Ave # 9A
Old Saybrook, CT 06475-3107, USA

Rehn, Trista (Reality Star)
42 W Meadow Dr
Vail, CO 81657-5705, USA

Rehr, Frank (Cartoonist)
United Feature Syndicate
PO Box 5610
Cincinnati, OH 45201-5610, USA

Rehrer-Carteaux, Rita (Athlete, Baseball Player)
3210 Kenwood Ave
Fort Wayne, IN 46805-2932, USA

Reich, Frank M (Athlete, Football Player)
5348 Chelsea St
La Jolla, CA 92037-7912, USA

Reich, Jason (Writer)
c/o Staff Member *Kaplan-Stahler Agency*
8383 Wilshire Blvd Ste 923
Beverly Hills, CA 90211-2443, USA

Reich, John (Director)
724 Bohemia Pkwy
Sayville, NY 11782-3300, USA

Reich, Robert (Politician)
1230 Bonita Ave
Berkeley, CA 94709-1923, USA

Reichard, Daniel
c/o Jeff Morrone *Intellectual Artists Management*
9350 Wilshire Blvd Ste 224
Beverly Hills, CA 90212-3204, USA

Reichardt, Rick (Athlete, Baseball Player)
2605 NW 90th Ter
Gainesville, FL 32606-6742, USA

Reichenbach, Mike (Athlete, Football Player)
2230 Cloverly Cir
Jamison, PA 18929-1555, USA

Reichert, Bill (Race Car Driver)
Bar's Leak Racing
203 S Gould St
Owosso, MI 48867-3249, USA

Reichert, Dan (Athlete, Baseball Player)
6620 Glass Ridge Dr
Lincoln, NE 68526-9752, USA

Reichert, Jack F (Business Person)
580 Douglas Dr
Lake Forest, IL 60045-3342, USA

Reichman, Judith (Doctor, Writer)
2080 Century Park E Ste 1009
Los Angeles, CA 90067-2013, USA

Reichow, Garet N (Athlete, Football Player)
PO Box 822
Tesuque, NM 87574-0822, USA

Reichs, Kathy (Writer)
c/o Jennifer Rudolph Walsh *William Morris Endeavor (NY)*
1325 Avenue of the Americas
New York, NY 10019-6026, USA

Reid, Antonio (L.A.) (Producer)
836 Sagg Main St
Sagaponack, NY 11962, USA

Reid, Caraun (Athlete, Football Player)
c/o Michael McCartney *Priority Sports & Entertainment - Chicago*
312 N La Salle
Suite 650
Chicago, IL 60610, USA

Reid, Christopher (Actor)
c/o Rod Baron *Baron Entertainment*
13848 Ventura Blvd Ste A
Sherman Oaks, CA 91423-3654

Reid, Daphne (Actor)
New Millenium
1 New Millennium Dr
Petersburg, VA 23805-8907, USA

Reid, Don S (Musician, Songwriter, Writer)
American Major Talent
8747 Highway 304
Hernando, MS 38632-8445, USA

Reid, Dorice (Athlete, Baseball Player)
1165 Via Santa Paulo
Vista, CA 92081-6332, USA

Reid, Douglas (Race Car Driver)
Doug Reid Racing
1217 24th Ave
Bessemer, AL 35023-3667, USA

Reid, Elliott
11201 Ventura Blvd
Studio City, CA 91604-3136, USA

Reid, Harold (Musician, Songwriter, Writer)
1004 E Beverley St
Staunton, VA 24401-3503, USA

Reid, Harry (Politician)
1155 23rd St NW Apt 2E
Washington, DC 20037-3302, USA

Reid, Jah (Athlete, Football Player)
c/o Derrick Fox *Derrick Fox Management*
Prefers to be contacted by telephone
CA, USA

Reid, Jesse (Athlete, Baseball Player)
2641 Carey Station Rd
Greensboro, GA 30642-2625, USA

Reid, Joe (Athlete, Football Player)
651 Shady Hollow St
Houston, TX 77056-1635, USA

Reid, Joy-Ann (Correspondent)
NBCU
30 Rockefeller Plz Fl 270E
New York, NY 10112-0044, USA

Reid, J R (Athlete, Basketball Player)
121 Cemetary St
Chester, SC 29706-1620, USA

Reid, Michael B (Mike) (Athlete, Football Player)
825 Overton Ln
Nashville, TN 37220-1515, USA

Reid, Michael Eric (Actor)
c/o Rita Berger *Rita B Management*
10063 Riverside Dr # 2763
Toluca Lake, CA 91602-2515, USA

Reid, Mike (Athlete, Football Player)
PO Box 362
Pacolet, SC 29372-0362, USA

Reid, Mike (Golfer)
935 E 80 N
Orem, UT 84097-4978, USA

Reid, Ogden
Ophir Hill
Purchase, NY 10577

Reid, Scott (Athlete, Baseball Player)
525 E Cathedral Rock Dr
Phoenix, AZ 85048-1803, USA

Reid, Stephen E (Steve) (Athlete, Doctor, Football Player)
1784 Locust St
Des Plaines, IL 60018-2234, USA

Reid, Tara (Actor)
c/o Matt Luber *Luber Roklin Management*
5815 W Sunset Blvd Ste 206
Los Angeles, CA 90028-6481, USA

Reid, Tim (Actor, Director)
New Millenium
1 New Millennium Dr
Petersburg, VA 23805-8907, USA

Reid, Tom (Athlete, Hockey Player)
317 Washington St
Saint Paul, MN 55102-1609

Reid, Tom (Athlete, Hockey Player)
603 Hawthorne Woods Dr
Saint Paul, MN 55123-3052

Reid, William J (Athlete, Football Player)
315 Ramona St
Palo Alto, CA 94301-1440, USA

Reierson, Dave (Athlete, Hockey Player)
99 Grand Ave
Grand Haven, MI 49417-2408

Reiff, Riley (Athlete, Football Player)
c/o Neil Cornrich *NC Sports, LLC*
best to contact via email
Columbus, OH 43201, USA

Reifsnyder, Robert H (Bob) (Athlete, Football Player)
4 Helm Ct
Berlin, MD 21811-1836, USA

Reightler, Kenneth S Captain (Astronaut)
1602 Honeysuckle Ridge Ct
Annapolis, MD 21401-6425, USA

Reightler Jr, Kenneth S (Astronaut)
1602 Honeysuckle Ridge Ct
Annapolis, MD 21401-6425, USA

Reihner, George (Athlete, Football Player)
1010 Electric St
Scranton, PA 18509-1951, USA

Reil, Shannen
Murray State University
PO Box 661
West Van Lear, KY 41268-0661, USA

Reilly, Gabrielle (Model)
PO Box 3145
Shawnee, KS 66203-0145, USA

Reilly, Jennifer
345 N Maple Dr Ste 397
Beverly Hills, CA 90210-5179

Reilly, John (Actor)
c/o Peter Young *Sovereign Talent Group*
8421 Wilshire Blvd Ste 200
Beverly Hills, CA 90211-3204, USA

Reilly, John C (Actor)
c/o Peg Donegan *Framework Entertainment (LA)*
9057 Nemo St Ste C
West Hollywood, CA 90069-5511, USA

Reilly, Kevin (Athlete, Football Player)
Webster Farms
521 Rothbury Rd
Wilmington, DE 19803-2439, USA

Reilly, Mike (Athlete, Baseball Player)
131 Smithfield Rd
Battle Creek, MI 49015-3545, USA

Reilly, Mike (Athlete, Football Player)
708 Loretto Ct
Dubuque, IA 52003-7813, USA

Reilly, Rick (Writer)
891 14th St Unit 2601
Denver, CO 80202-3272, USA

Reilly, William K (Government Official)
Stanford University
International Studies Institute
Stanford, CA 94305, USA

Reilly II, James F (Astronaut)
15903 Lake Lodge Dr
Houston, TX 77062-4745, USA

Reimer, Kevin (Athlete, Baseball Player)
1797 W 28th Ave Apt 250
Apache Junction, AZ 85120-9504, USA

Reimer, Roland (Religious Leader)
mennonite Brethren Churches Conference
8000 W 21st St N
Wichita, KS 67205-1744, USA

Reimers, Bruce (Athlete, Football Player)
2206 W River Dr
Humboldt, IA 50548-2638, USA

Reimold, Nolan (Athlete, Baseball Player)
1315 Oaklanding Ln
Fleming Island, FL 32003-9017, USA

Rein, Andrew (Athlete, Olympic Athlete, Wrestler)
31 Acorn Dr
Hawthorn Woods, IL 60047-7408, United States

Reina (Musician)
c/o Staff Member *Diva Central Inc*
7510 W Sunset Blvd Ste 1445
Los Angeles, CA 90046-3408, USA

Reineke, Chad (Athlete, Baseball Player)
1904 Tanglewood Dr
Defiance, OH 43512-3638, USA

Reiner, Alysia (Actor)
c/o Charlie Roina *Persona PR (NYC)*
1 Little West 12th St
New York, NY 10014-1302, USA

Reiner, Carl (Actor, Director)
c/o Staff Member *Clear Productions*
9171 Wilshire Blvd Ste 350
Beverly Hills, CA 90210-5523, USA

Reiner, ex-DA Ira
1290 Sunset Plaza Dr
Los Angeles, CA 90069-1245

Reiner, John (Cartoonist)
Parade Magazine
30 Nathan Hale Dr Apt 71B
Huntington, NY 11743-7034, USA

Reiner, Rob (Actor, Director)
23704 Malibu Colony Rd
Malibu, CA 90265-6629, USA

Reinfeldt, Mike (Athlete, Football Player)
2014 Waterstone Dr
Franklin, TN 37069-7197, USA

Reinhard, Bill (Athlete, Football Player)
43683 Old Troon Ct
Indio, CA 92201-8910, USA

Reinhardt, Doug (Athlete, Baseball Player, Reality Star)
c/o Liza Anderson *Anderson Group Public Relations*
8060 Melrose Ave Fl 4
Los Angeles, CA 90046-7038, USA

Reinhart, Haley (Musician, Reality Star)
Alex Theatre
216 N Brand Blvd
Glendale, CA 91203-2610, USA

Reinhold, Judge (Actor, Director)
17 La Vega
Lamy, NM 87540-9768, USA

Reininger, Travis (Athlete, Baseball Player)
464 Hunter Ct
Brighton, CO 80601-4360, USA

Reinking, Ann (Actor, Dancer, Director)
International Creative Mgmt
40 W 57th St Fl 5
New York, NY 10019-4001, USA

Reinprecht, Steven (Athlete, Hockey Player)
45 S Garfield St
Denver, CO 80209-3115

Reinsdorf, Jerry (Baseball Player)
Chicago White Sox
40 E Elm St
Chicago, IL 60611-1016, USA

Reirden, Todd (Athlete, Hockey Player)
Pittsburgh Penguins
66 Mario Lemieux Pl Ste 2
Pittsburgh, PA 15219-3504

Reirden, Todd (Athlete, Hockey Player)
45 S Garfield St
Denver, CO 80209-3115

Reis, Tommy (Athlete, Baseball Player)
15456 SW 15th Terrace Rd
Ocala, FL 34473-8862, USA

Reiser, Paul (Actor, Producer)
c/o Mark Rousso *New Wave Entertainment (LA)*
2660 W Olive Ave
Burbank, CA 91505-4525, USA

Reiser, Robbie (Race Car Driver)
Reiser Motorsports
142 Points End Dr
Mooresville, NC 28117-7303, USA

Reiser, Rock
9014 Melrose Ave
West Hollywood, CA 90069-5610

Reitenour, Megan (Race Car Driver)
c/o Gigi Rock *Heraea Marketing*
10905 E Pear Tree Dr
Cornville, AZ 86325-5523, USA

Reith, Brian (Athlete, Baseball Player)
9706 54th Ct E
Parrish, FL 34219-4440, USA

Reitherman, Bruce (Cinematographer, Producer, Writer)
c/o Staff Member *Pandion Enterprises, Inc.*
2287 Whitney Ave
Summerland, CA 93067, USA

Reitman, Ivan (Director, Producer)
900 Cold Springs Rd
Santa Barbara, CA 93108-1009, USA

Reitman, Jason (Director)
c/o BeBe Lerner *ID Public Relations (LA)*
7060 Hollywood Blvd Fl 8th
Los Angeles, CA 90028-6021, USA

Reitman, Joe (Actor)
c/o Suzanne (Sue) Wohl *TalentWorks (LA)*
3500 W Olive Ave Ste 1400
Burbank, CA 91505-5512, USA

Reitsma, Chris (Athlete, Baseball Player)
6050 Jim Davis Rd
Parrish, FL 34219-9363, USA

Reitz, Bruce (Doctor)
Johns Hopkins Hospital
600 N Wolfe St # 100
Baltimore, MD 21287-0005, USA

Reitz, Ken (Athlete, Baseball Player)
1704 Carbine Ln
Saint Charles, MO 63303-1104, USA

Rekar, Bryan (Athlete, Baseball Player)
4326 Waterville Ave
Wesley Chapel, FL 33543-7037, USA

Reklow, Jesse (Cartoonist)
2415 College Ave Apt 20
Berkeley, CA 94704-2458, USA

Relaford, Desmond (Athlete, Baseball Player)
11334 Aston Hall Dr
Jacksonville, FL 32246-0646, USA

Relch, Steve (Baseball Player)
US Olympic Team
28 Scofield Hill Rd
Washington Depot, CT 06794-1012, USA

Reld, Andy (Athlete, Football Coach, Football Player)
1215 Page Ter
Villanova, PA 19085-2132, USA

Relient K (Music Group, Musician)
c/o Kevin Spellman *Vector Management (LA)*
1100 Glendon Ave Ste 2000
Los Angeles, CA 90024-3524, USA

Reliford, Charlie (Athlete, Baseball Player)
1509 Cypress St
Ashland, KY 41101-3624, USA

Rell, M Jodi (Politician)
18 Andover Ct
Brookfield, CT 06804-2715, USA

Rellford, Richard (Athlete, Basketball Player)
28 Balfour Rd W
Palm Beach Gardens, FL 33418-7090, USA

R.E.M. (Music Group)
170 College Ave
Athens, GA 30601-2805, US

Remar, James (Actor)
409 N Camden Dr Ste 202
Beverly Hills, CA 90210-4423, USA

Rembert, Johnny (Athlete, Football Player)
2564 Willow Creek Dr
Fleming Island, FL 32003-8375, USA

Remigino, Lindy (Athlete, Olympic Athlete, Track Athlete)
22 Paris Ln
Newington, CT 06111-1628, USA

Remini, Leah (Actor)
PO Box 15669
North Hollywood, CA 91615-5669, USA

Remlinger, Mike (Athlete, Baseball Player)
18331 N 93rd Way
Scottsdale, AZ 85255-6048, USA

Remmen, Larry (Horse Racer)
319 Marshall St
Ridgewood, NJ 07450-3320, USA

Remmen, Ray (Horse Racer)
PO Box 446
Lodi, NJ 07644-0446, USA

Remmert, Dennis (Athlete, Football Player)
3933 Briarwood Dr
Cedar Falls, IA 50613-7508, USA

Remnick, David (Writer)
c/o Robert (Bob) Bookman *Paradigm (LA)*
2000 Avenue of the Stars
Los Angeles, CA 90067-4700, USA

Remo, Ken
121 S Orange Dr
Los Angeles, CA 90036-3012

Remy, Gerald P (Jerry) (Athlete, Baseball Player)
1403 Wisteria Way
Wayland, MA 01778-2850, USA

Renard, Mercedes (Actor)
c/o Evan Hainey *Untitled Entertainment (LA)*
350 S Beverly Dr Ste 200
Beverly Hills, CA 90212-4819, USA

Renault, Dennis (Cartoonist)
Sacramento Bee
Editorial Dept
21st & Q Sts
Sacramento, CA 95852, USA

Renbourn, John (Musician)
Folklore Inc
PO Box 7003
Santa Monica, CA 90406-7003, USA

Rencher, Terrence (Athlete, Basketball Player)
2001 S Mo Pac Expy Apt 1932
Austin, TX 78746-7593, USA

Rendell, Edward (Politician)
3425 Warden Dr
Philadelphia, PA 19129-1417, USA

Rene, Chris
c/o Staff Member *FanManager, LLC*
PO Box 5881
Sherman Oaks, CA 91413-5881, USA

Renfree, Sean (Athlete, Football Player)
c/o Eric Metz *Lock Metz Milanovic LLC*
6900 E Camelback Rd Ste 600
Scottsdale, AZ 85251-8044, USA

Renfro, Leonard (Athlete, Football Player)
8893 E 24th Pl Unit 103
Denver, CO 80238-2839, USA

Renfro, Mike (Athlete, Football Player)
PO Box 93073
Southlake, TX 76092-1073, USA

Renfroe, Jay (Producer)
c/o Staff Member *Renegade 83 Entertainment*
5700 Wilshire Blvd Fl 6
Los Angeles, CA 90036-3659, USA

Renfroe, Laddie (Athlete, Baseball Player)
236 Hickory Ln
Batesville, MS 38606-9339, USA

Rengel, Mike (Athlete, Football Player)
6500 W Mansfield Ave Unit 4
Denver, CO 80235-3049, USA

Renick, Rick (Athlete, Baseball Player)
7320 Hawkins Rd
Sarasota, FL 34241-9375, USA

Renis, Tony (Musician)
Ischia Global
501 Deep Valley Dr Fl 1
Rolling Hills Estates, CA 90274-7605,
USA

Renko, Steven (Steve) (Athlete, Baseball
Player)
15812 W 136th St
Olathe, KS 66062-5310, USA

Renna, Bill (Athlete, Baseball Player)
1476 Lesher Ct
San Jose, CA 95125-3936, USA

Renna, Eugene A (Business Person)
Mobil Corp
3225 Gallows Rd
Fairfax, VA 22037-0003, USA

Renna, Patrick (Actor)
c/o Staff Member *Karen Renna &
Associates*
PO Box 4227
Burbank, CA 91503-4227, USA

Rennebohm, J Fred (Religious Leader)
Congregational Christian Churches Assn
PO Box 1620
Oak Creek, WI 53154, USA

Renner, Jeremy (Actor)
107 Delfern Dr
Los Angeles, CA 90077-3542, USA

Rennert, Dutch (Baseball Player)
156 N Churchill Dr
St Augustine, FL 32086-4172, USA

Rennert, Dutch (Athlete, Baseball Player)
145 N Churchill Dr
Saint Augustine, FL 32086-4180, USA

Reno, Jack
PO Box 1001
Florence, KY 41022-1001

Reno, Janet (Politician)
11200 N Kendall Dr
Miami, FL 33176-1108, USA

Reno, Jean (Actor)
c/o Amy Guenther *Gateway Management
Company Inc*
860 Via De La Paz Ste F10
Pacific Palisades, CA 90272-3631, USA

Rensberger, Scott (Journalist)
914 7th St NE
Washington, DC 20002-3612, USA

Renteria, Edgar (Athlete, Baseball Player)
5640 Collins Ave Apt 2C
Miami Beach, FL 33140-2436, USA

Renteria, Rich (Athlete, Baseball Player)
930 Pacific Hills Pt Apt B103
Colorado Springs, CO 80906-8407, USA

Renteria, Rick (Athlete, Baseball Player)
1700 S Araby Dr Apt 72
Palm Springs, CA 92264-6816, USA

Rentie, Caesar (Athlete, Football Player)
7614 Fallen Antler Pl
Arlington, TX 76002-4320, USA

Rentzel, Lance (Athlete, Football Player)
12104 Monument Dr Apt 354
Fairfax, VA 22033-4053, USA

Renvall, Johan (Dancer)
American Ballet Theatre
890 Broadway Fl 3
New York, NY 10003-1278, USA

Reo, Don (Producer)
c/o Debbee Klein *Paradigm (LA)*
360 N Crescent Dr
North Bldg
Beverly Hills, CA 90210-4874, USA

Repeta, Nina (Actor)
Gage Group
5757 Wilshire Blvd Ste 659
Los Angeles, CA 90036-3682, USA

Repko, Jason (Athlete, Baseball Player)
93005 E Chelsea Rd
Kennewick, WA 99338-8906, USA

Repoz, Roger (Athlete, Baseball Player)
930 Whitewater Dr
Fullerton, CA 92833-2194, USA

Rerych, Stephen (Athlete, Olympic
Athlete, Swimmer)
1142 Ridgewood Dr
Point Pleasant, WV 25550-3578, USA

Resch, Chico (Athlete, Hockey Player)
PO Box 207
1171 Dahler Ave
Emily, MN 56447-0207, USA

Resch, Glenn "Chico" (Athlete, Hockey
Player)
607 8th St
Lyndhurst, NJ 07071-3105

Resch, Glenn "Chico" (Athlete, Hockey
Player)
New Jersey Devils
165 Mulberry St
Newark, NJ 07102-3607

Resop, Chris (Athlete, Baseball Player)
2152 Harlans Run
Naples, FL 34105-8518, USA

Resor, Helen (Athlete, Hockey Player,
Olympic Athlete)
22 N Stanwich Rd
Greenwich, CT 06831-2841, USA

Ressler, Glenn E (Athlete, Football Player)
1524 Woodcreek Dr
Mechanicsburg, PA 17055-6766, USA

Ressler, Robert
PO Box 187
Spotsylvania, VA 22553-0187

Reston, James (Journalist)
4714 Hunt Ave
Chevy Chase, MD 20815-5423, USA

Restovich, Michael (Athlete, Baseball
Player)
710 11th St SW
Rochester, MN 55902-6339, USA

Retherford, Dave (Athlete, Football
Player)
68 Pine Lake Dr
Atlanta, GA 30327-4934, USA

Retta (Actor, Comedian)
c/o Sam Maydew *The Collective*
8383 Wilshire Blvd Ste 1050
Beverly Hills, CA 90211-2415, USA

Rettenmund, Merv (Athlete, Baseball
Player)
655 India St Unit 123
San Diego, CA 92101-6738, USA

Retton, Mary Lou (Athlete, Gymnast)
Michael Suttle Business Management
23427 Fairway Valley Ln
Katy, TX 77494-2021, USA

Retzer, Ken (Athlete, Baseball Player)
13638 N Newcastle Dr Apt 148
Sun City, AZ 85351-2593, USA

Retzlaff, Palmer (Pete) (Athlete, Football
Player)
669 New Rd
Gilbertsville, PA 19525-9613, USA

Reuben, Gloria (Actor)
c/o Staff Member *Untitled Entertainment
(LA)*
350 S Beverly Dr Ste 200
Beverly Hills, CA 90212-4819, USA

Reubens, Paul (Actor, Comedian)
PO Box 29373
Los Angeles, CA 90029-0373, USA

Reuschel, Paul (Athlete, Baseball Player)
1143 Stacy Ln
Macomb, IL 61455-2646, USA

Reuschel, Ricky E (Rick) (Athlete, Baseball
Player)
PO Box 143
Renfrew, PA 16053-0143, USA

Reuss, Jerry (Athlete, Baseball Player)
c/o Staff Member *JD Legends Promotions*
10808 Foothill Blvd Ste 160-454
Rancho Cucamonga, CA 91730-3889,
USA

Reuten, Thekla (Actor)
c/o Paula Rosenberg *ICA Talent*
818 12th St Apt 9
Santa Monica, CA 90403-1727, USA

Reutershan, Randy (Athlete, Football
Player)
4 Indian Field Ct
Mahwah, NJ 07430-2243, USA

Reutimann, David (Race Car Driver)
6910 Wire Rd
Zephyrhills, FL 33542-1656, USA

Reveiz, Fuad (Athlete, Football Player)
2160 Lakeside Centre Way Ste 250
Knoxville, TN 37922-0201, USA

Revenig, Todd (Athlete, Baseball Player)
2412 E Prescott Pl
Chandler, AZ 85249-2946, USA

Revere, Ben (Athlete, Baseball Player)
108 White Oak Dr
Richmond, KY 40475-8619, USA

Revering, Dave (Athlete, Baseball Player)
4976 N Mesquite Dr
Saint George, UT 84770-5442, USA

Revill, Clive (Actor)
15029 Encanto Dr
Sherman Oaks, CA 91403-4409, USA

Revis, Darrelle (Athlete, Football Player)
c/o Neil Schwartz *Schwartz & Feinsod*
contact via telephone or email
White Plains, NY 10603

Revolution Mother (Music Group,
Musician)
c/o Staff Member *Velvet Hammer*
9014 Melrose Ave
West Hollywood, CA 90069-5610, USA

Revs, The (Music Group)
c/o Staff Member *Paradigm (Monterey)*
404 W Franklin St
Monterey, CA 93940-2303, USA

Rex (Musician)
Concrete Mgmt
361 W Broadway # 200
New York, NY 10013-2209, USA

Rex, Simon (Actor, Television Host)
c/o Katie Mason *Luber Roklin
Management*
5815 W Sunset Blvd Ste 206
Los Angeles, CA 90028-6481, USA

Rey, Reynaldo (Actor, Comedian, Writer)
Starwil Talent
433 N Camden Dr Ste 400
Beverly Hills, CA 90210-4408, USA

Reyburn, Daniel (Athlete, Baseball Player)
514 Maplegrove Dr
Franklin, TN 37064-5124, USA

Reyes, Anthony (Athlete, Baseball Player)
8929 Watson Ave
Whittier, CA 90605-2035, USA

Reyes, Carlos (Athlete, Baseball Player)
7205 N Cortez Ave
Tampa, FL 33614-2638, USA

reyes, Jo-Jo (Athlete, Baseball Player)
9554 Paradise Pl
Riverside, CA 92508-8007, USA

Reyes, Jose (Athlete, Baseball Player)
24 Stone Hill Dr S
Manhasset, NY 11030-4426, USA

Reyes, Judy (Actor)
c/o Leonard Torgan *The Collective*
8383 Wilshire Blvd Ste 1050
Beverly Hills, CA 90211-2415, USA

Reyes, Lalo (Actor)
c/o Paul Uvanitte *ProActive Management
Group (PMG)*
10944 Bluffside Dr Apt 213
Studio City, CA 91604-3362, USA

Reyes, Senen (Sen Dog) (Actor,
Composer, Musician)
c/o Randy Cabrera *Venture IAB*
3211 Cahuenga Blvd W Ste 104
Los Angeles, CA 90068-1372, USA

Reyes, Silvestre (Congressman, Politician)
2210 Rayburn Hob
Washington, DC 20515-3221, USA

Reyes Jr, Ernie
12561 Willard St
N Hollywood, CA 91605-1244, USA

Reymundo, Alex (Comedian)
c/o Alex D'Andrea *Edmonds Management*
1635 N Cahuenga Blvd Fl 5
Los Angeles, CA 90028-6201, USA

Reynolds, Archie (Athlete, Baseball
Player)
1828 Pinecrest Dr
Tyler, TX 75701-5006, USA

Reynolds, Bob (Athlete, Baseball Player)
2203 62nd Ave E Apt 7-201
Unit K1
Tacoma, WA 98424-3528, USA

Reynolds, Burt (Actor, Director)
c/o Erik Kritzer *LINK Entertainment*
11872 La Grange Ave Fl 1
Los Angeles, CA 90025-5283, USA

Reynolds, Craig (Athlete, Baseball Player)
4210 Hidden Links Ct
Kingwood, TX 77339-5308, USA

Reynolds, Debbie (Actor, Musician)
6514 Lankershim Blvd
N Hollywood, CA 91606-2409, USA

Reynolds, Don (Athlete, Baseball Player)
6035 NE 35th Pl
Portland, OR 97211-7358, USA

Reynolds, Ed (Athlete, Football Player)
173 Moyer Rd
Stoneville, NC 27048-8462, USA

Reynolds, Garett (Athlete, Football Player)
c/o Chad Speck *Allegiant Athletic Agency*
35 Market Sq Ste 201
Knoxville, TN 37902-1420, USA

Reynolds, Gene (Actor, Producer)
2034 Castilian Dr
Los Angeles, CA 90068-2609, USA

Reynolds, Harold (Athlete, Baseball Player)
2890 NW Angelica Dr
Corvallis, OR 97330-3619, USA

Reynolds, Harry (Butch) (Athlete, Track Athlete)
Advantage International
1025 Thomas Jefferson St NW # 450
Washington, DC 20007-5201, USA

Reynolds, Jack (Athlete, Football Player)
11480 SW 102nd St
Miami, FL 33176-2588, USA

Reynolds, Jamai (Athlete, Football Player)
PO Box 10628
Green Bay, WI 54307-0628, USA

Reynolds, Jamal (Athlete, Football Player)
31 Sellers Dr
Q
Crawfordville, FL 32327-0595, USA

Reynolds, James (Actor)
1925 Hanscom Dr
South Pasadena, CA 91030-4009, USA

Reynolds, James (Baseball Player)
708 Highpoint Dr
Rocky Hill, CT 06067-1088, USA

Reynolds, Jerry O (Coach)
Sacramento Kings
1 Sports Pkwy
Arco Arena
Sacramento, CA 95834-2301, USA

Reynolds, Jim (Athlete, Baseball Player)
708 Highpoint Dr
Rocky Hill, CT 06067-1088, USA

Reynolds, Ken (Athlete, Baseball Player)
182 Greenwood St
Marlborough, MA 01752-3307, USA

Reynolds, Kevin (Director, Writer)
c/o Mike Simpson *William Morris Endeavor (LA)*
9601 Wilshire Blvd
Beverly Hills, CA 90210-5213, USA

Reynolds, Mark (Athlete, Baseball Player)
10960 Wilshire Blvd Fl 5
Los Angeles, CA 90024-3708, USA

Reynolds, Patti
PO Box 530
Fontana, WI 53125-0530

Reynolds, Randolph N (Business Person)
Reynolds Metal Co
6601 W Broad St
PO Box 27003
Richmond, VA 23230-1723, USA

Reynolds, Ricky (Athlete, Football Player)
17223 Tiffany Shore Dr
Lutz, FL 33549-7621, USA

Reynolds, Robert (Musician)
AristoMedia
1620 16th Ave S
Nashville, TN 37212-2908, USA

Reynolds, Ronn (Athlete, Baseball Player)
1410 N Armour St
Wichita, KS 67206-1128, USA

Reynolds, Roxy (Actor)
c/o Staff Member *Sosincere Entertainment*
2054 Nostrand Ave Apt 4F
Brooklyn, NY 11210-2526, USA

Reynolds, Ryan (Actor)
c/o Meredith O'Sullivan *42West (LA)*
1840 Century Park E Ste 700
Los Angeles, CA 90067-2122, USA

Reynolds, Shane (Athlete, Baseball Player)
129 E Shore Rd
Monroe, LA 71203-8857, USA

Reynolds, Sheldon (Musician)
Great Scott Productions
137 N Wetherly Dr Apt 403
Los Angeles, CA 90048-2866, USA

Reynolds, Tom (Athlete, Baseball Player)
640 Jinks Crossing Rd
Bainbridge, GA 39819-1334, USA

Reynolds Booth, Nancy (Skier)
3197 Padaro Ln
Carpinteria, CA 93013-1115, USA

Reynoso, Armando (Athlete, Baseball Player)
PO Box 442
Scottsdale, AZ 85252-0442, USA

Rezendes, Dave (Race Car Driver)
3 Sammys Ln
Assonet, MA 02702-1101, USA

Reznor, Trent (Musician)
1663 Summitridge Dr
Beverly Hills, CA 90210-1605, USA

Rhames, Ving (Actor)
c/o Steven Muller *Innovative Artists (LA)*
1505 10th St
Santa Monica, CA 90401-2805, USA

Rhea, Caroline (Actor, Comedian)
c/o Jonathan Howard *Innovative Artists (LA)*
1505 10th St
Santa Monica, CA 90401-2805, USA

Rheams, Leonta (Athlete, Football Player)
1712 W Jackson St
Tyler, TX 75701-1209, USA

Rheaume, Manon (Athlete, Hockey Player)
Manon Rheaume Foundation
PO Box 701816
Plymouth, MI 48170-0971

Rheinecker, John (Athlete, Baseball Player)
100 Jefferson Dr
Waterloo, IL 62298-1551, USA

Rhett, Alicia (Actor)
PO Box 700
Charleston, SC 29402-0700, USA

Rhett, Errict (Athlete, Football Player)
6 NW 108th Ter
Plantation, FL 33324-1560, USA

Rhimes, Shonda (Producer, Writer)
c/o Staff Member *Shondaland*
4151 Prospect Ave Fl 4
Los Angeles, CA 90027-4524, USA

Rhine, Kendall (Athlete, Baseball Player)
624E State Route 127 N
Alto Pass, IL 62905, USA

Rhinehart, Coby (Athlete, Football Player)
3206 Walker Dr
Richardson, TX 75082-2451, USA

Rhine Sr, Kendall (Athlete, Basketball Player)
6240 State Route 127 N
Alto Pass, IL 62905-3230, USA

Rhino, Randy (Athlete, Football Player)
6295 River Shore Pkwy
Atlanta, GA 30328-3746, USA

Rhoades, George
1478 Mecklenburg Rd
Ithaca, NY 14850-9301, USA

Rhoades, Kerry (Football Player)
c/o Team Member *New York Jets*
1 Jets Dr
Florham Park, NJ 07932-1215, USA

Rhoda, Hilary (Model)
c/o Staff Member *IMG*
304 Park Ave S Fl 12
New York, NY 10010-4314, USA

Rhode, Kim (Athlete, Olympic Athlete, Shooter)
11640 Hemlock St
El Monte, CA 91732-1410, USA

Rhoden, Rick (Athlete, Baseball Player)
1253 Killarney Dr
Ormond Beach, FL 32174-2828, USA

Rhodes, Arthur (Athlete, Baseball Player)
14114 Phoenix Rd
Phoenix, MD 21131-1020, USA

Rhodes, Cynthia (Actor, Dancer)
15260 Ventura Blvd Ste 2100
Sherman Oaks, CA 91403-5360, USA

Rhodes, Damian (Athlete, Hockey Player)
9665 Little Mountain Rd
Mentor, OH 44060-8049

Rhodes, Donnelly (Actor)
Gold Marshak Liedtke
3500 W Olive Ave Ste 1400
Burbank, CA 91505-5512, USA

Rhodes, Eugene (Athlete, Basketball Player)
132 N Peterson Ave Apt 7
Louisville, KY 40206-2340, USA

Rhodes, Harry (Athlete, Baseball Player)
7207 S Evans Ave
Chicago, IL 60619-1224, USA

Rhodes, Karl (Athlete, Baseball Player)
8600 Fawnmeadow Ln
Cincinnati, OH 45242-4524, USA

Rhodes, Lou (Musician)
c/o Staff Member *Paradigm (Monterey)*
404 W Franklin St
Monterey, CA 93940-2303, USA

Rhodes, Philip (Musician)
William Morris Agency
2100 W End Ave Ste 1000
Nashville, TN 37203-5240, USA

Rhodes, Randi (Radio Personality)
c/o Myles Peterson *Premiere Radio Network*
1270 Avenue Of The Americas Fl 14
New York, NY 10020-1702, USA

Rhodes, Ray (Athlete, Coach, Football Coach, Football Player)
1507 Juliet Dr
Allen, TX 75013-5816, USA

Rhodes, Richard L (Writer)
Janklow & Nesbit
445 Park Ave Fl 13
New York, NY 10022-8628, USA

Rhodes, Richard Lee (Writer)
c/o Staff Member *Simon & Schuster*
1230 Avenue of the Americas Fl CONC1
New York, NY 10020-1586, USA

Rhodes, Rodrick (Athlete, Basketball Player)
PO Box 17704
Sugar Land, TX 77496-7704, USA

Rhomberg, Kevin (Athlete, Baseball Player)
9692 Executive Ct
Mentor, OH 44060-8721, USA

Rhome, Gerald B (Jerry) (Athlete, Coach, Football Coach, Football Player)
3883 Morning Meadow Ln
Buford, GA 30519-4383, USA

Rhone, Earriest C (Ernie) (Athlete, Football Player)
3603 Potomac Ave
Texarkana, TX 75503-3519, USA

Rhone, Sylvia (Business Person)
Elektra Entertainment Group
75 Rockefeller Plz Fl 15
New York, NY 10019-6908

Rhude, Kellan (Actor)
c/o Staff Member *Diverse Talent Group*
9911 W Pico Blvd Ste 340W
Los Angeles, CA 90035-2703, USA

Rhyan, Dick (Golfer)
111 Camp Dr
Georgetown, TX 78633-4874, USA

Rhymer, Don (Writer)
c/o David Kramer *United Talent Agency (UTA-LA)*
9336 Civic Center Dr
Beverly Hills, CA 90210-3604, USA

Rhymes, Busta (Musician)
c/o Ron Rivlin *Coast II Coast Entertainment*
204 S Beverly Dr Ste 110
Beverly Hills, CA 90212-3800, USA

Rhymes, Buster (Athlete, Football Player)
17120 NW 37th Ave
Miami Gardens, FL 33056-4112, USA

Rhymes, Will (Athlete, Baseball Player)
6914 9th Ct E
Sarasota, FL 34243-1211, USA

Rhys, Matthew (Actor)
c/o Suzan Bymel *Management 360*
9111 Wilshire Blvd
Beverly Hills, CA 90210-5508, USA

Rhys, Paul (Actor)
Gersh Agency
232 N Canon Dr
Beverly Hills, CA 90210-5302, USA

Rhys, Phillip (Actor)
c/o Joe Vance *Domain Talent*
9229 W Sunset Blvd Ste 710
West Hollywood, CA 90069-3407, USA

Rhys-Davies, John (Actor)
3428 Oak Glen Dr
Los Angeles, CA 90068-1314, USA

Rhys-Meyers, Jonathan (Actor)
c/o Stacy O'Neil *Brillstein Entertainment Partners (LA)*
9150 Wilshire Blvd Ste 350
Beverly Hills, CA 90212-3453, USA

Rhythm Syndicate
6255 W Sunset Blvd Ste 2100
Los Angeles, CA 90028-7422

Ribant, Dennis (Athlete, Baseball Player)
46 Sidra Cv
Newport Coast, CA 92657-2115, USA

Ribbs, Willy (Race Car Driver)
Craftsman
1801 W Speedway Blvd
Daytona Beach, FL 32114-1215, USA

Ribeiro, Alfonso (Actor)
c/o Konrad Leh *Creative Talent Group*
1900 Avenue of the Stars Ste 2475
Los Angeles, CA 90067-4512, USA

Ribeiro, Andre (Race Car Driver)
4192 Weaver Ct
Hilliard, OH 43026, USA

Ribeiro, Mike (Athlete, Hockey Player)
1034 Founders Ridge Ln
Mc Lean, VA 22102-2040

Ribisi, Giovanni (Actor)
c/o Eric Kranzler *Management 360*
9111 Wilshire Blvd
Beverly Hills, CA 90210-5508, USA

Ribisi, Marissa (Actor)
4121 Wilshire Blvd Apt 415
Los Angeles, CA 90010-3525, USA

Ricard, Alan (Athlete, Football Player)
10306 Ripple Lake Dr
Houston, TX 77065-4087, USA

Ricardo, Benny (Athlete, Football Player)
3012 Harding Way
Costa Mesa, CA 92626-2846, USA

Ricardo Y Alberto (Music Group)
c/o Staff Member *Sony Music Miami*
605 Lincoln Rd Ste 700
Miami Beach, FL 33139-2901, USA

Ricca, John (Athlete, Football Player)
4 Fairfax Ct Apt 22
Chevy Chase, MD 20815-6522, USA

Riccelli, Frank (Athlete, Baseball Player)
PO Box 5102
Syracuse, NY 13220-5102, USA

Ricci, Christina (Actor)
c/o David Seltzer *Management 360*
9111 Wilshire Blvd
Beverly Hills, CA 90210-5508, USA

Ricci, Chuck (Athlete, Baseball Player)
125 Oak Holw
Williamsburg, VA 23188-8919, USA

Ricci, Mike (Athlete, Hockey Player)
286 Mountain Laurel Ln
Los Gatos, CA 95032-5740

Rice, Andy (Athlete, Football Player)
801 N Main St
Hallettsville, TX 77964-2321, USA

Rice, Anne (Writer)
9 Monte Carlo Way
Kenner, LA 70065-2028, USA

Rice, Bobby G
505 Canton Pass
Madison, TN 37115-5449, USA

Rice, Buddy (Race Car Driver)
Team Rahal
4601 Lyman Dr
Hilliard, OH 43026-1249, USA

Rice, Christopher (Writer)
1239 1st St
New Orleans, LA 70130-5708, USA

Rice, Condoleezza (Government Official)
Stanford University
616 Serra St Ste 123
Freeman Spogli Institute for International
Studies
Stanford, CA 94305-6013, USA

Rice, Elizabeth (Actor)
c/o Steven Warren *Hansen, Jacobson,
Teller, Hoberman, Newman, Warren &
Richman*
450 N Roxbury Dr Fl 8
Beverly Hills, CA 90210-4222, USA

Rice, Gene D (Religious Leader)
Church of God
PO Box 2430
Cleveland, TN 37320-2430, USA

Rice, Gigi (Actor)
14951 Alva Dr
Pacific Palisades, CA 90272-4402, USA

Rice, Glen (Athlete, Basketball Player)
8920 SW 162nd Ter
Palmetto Bay, FL 33157-3556, USA

Rice, Glen
9492 Doral Blvd
Miami, FL 33178

Rice, Glenn (Athlete, Basketball Player)
4835 SW 82nd St
Miami, FL 33143-8603, USA

Rice, James E (Jim) (Athlete, Baseball
Player)
35 Bobby Jones Dr
Andover, MA 01810-2880, USA

Rice, Jerry (Athlete, Football Player)
c/o Jim Steiner *CAA (St. Louis)*
222 S Central Ave Ste 1008
Saint Louis, MO 63105-3509, USA

Rice, John (Athlete, Baseball Player)
8901 S Leavitt St
Chicago, IL 60643-6427, USA

Rice, Ken (Athlete, Football Player)
10619 Big Canoe
Big Canoe, GA 30143-5130, USA

Rice, Larry (Race Car Driver)
1150 Forest
Brownsburg, IN 46112, USA

Rice, Norman B (Politician)
Mayor's Office
600 4th Ave
Municipal Building
Seattle, WA 98104-1850, USA

Rice, Pat (Athlete, Baseball Player)
4090 Zurich Dr
Colorado Springs, CO 80920-7521, USA

Rice, Ray (Athlete, Football Player)
c/o Deb Poquette *Prestige Lifestyle
Management*
1300 Saint Michaels Rd
Mount Airy, MD 21771-3228, USA

Rice, Regina (Actor, Producer)
c/o Staff Member *Temptation
Management*
1010 S Robertson Blvd Ste 2
Los Angeles, CA 90035-1527, USA

Rice, Ron (Athlete, Football Player)
22880 Twyckingham Way
Southfield, MI 48034-6260, USA

Rice, Simeon (Athlete, Football Player)
371 Channelside Walk Way Unit 401
Tampa, FL 33602-6767, USA

Rice, Tony (Athlete, Football Player)
PO Box 6455
South Bend, IN 46660-6455, USA

Rice-Hughes, Donna
PO Box 888
Fairfax, VA 22038-0888

Rich, Adam (Actor)
4814 Lemona Ave
Sherman Oaks, CA 91403-2010, USA

Rich, Allan (Actor)
225 E 57th St Apt 1Q
New York, NY 10022-2857, USA

Rich, Christopher (Actor)
Bresler Kelly Assoc
11500 W Olympic Blvd Ste 510
Los Angeles, CA 90064-1527, USA

Rich, Clayton (Doctor)
University of Oklahoma
Health Services Center
Oklahoma City, OK 73190-0001, USA

Rich, Denise (Musician)
IGD Music & Media
785 5th Ave
New York, NY 10022-1608

Rich, Elaine
500 S Sepulveda Blvd Fl 4
Los Angeles, CA 90049-3550

Rich, John (Musician)
c/o Dale Morris *Morris Artists
Management*
818 19th Ave S
Nashville, TN 37203-3202, USA

Rich, Katie
10100 Santa Monica Blvd # 2490
Los Angeles, CA 90067

Rich, Matty
9560 Wilshire Blvd Ste 500
Beverly Hills, CA 90212-2401

Rich, Randy (Athlete, Baseball Player)
9421 Eagle Springs Ct
Roseville, CA 95747-6316, USA

Rich, Richie (Fashion Designer)
MAC Cosmetics
575 Broadway Fl 2
New York, NY 10012-3230, USA

Rich, Tony (Musician)
Prestige
220 E 23rd St Ste 303
New York, NY 10010-4676, USA

Richard, Chris (Athlete, Baseball Player)
11389 Ironwood Rd
San Diego, CA 92131-1916, USA

Richard, Clayton (Athlete, Baseball
Player)
3551 Eisenhower Rd
Lafayette, IN 47905-4108, USA

Richard, Deb (Golfer)
125 Hidden Cove Ln
Ponte Vedra Beach, FL 32082-2154, USA

Richard, James Rodney (J R) (Athlete,
Baseball Player)
5615 Chimney Rock Rd Apt 338
Houston, TX 77081-1957, USA

Richard, J R (Athlete, Baseball Player)
Mary Olive Baptist Church
2804 McGowen St
Attn Associate Pastor
Houston, TX 77004-1658, USA

Richard, Lee (Athlete, Baseball Player)
1621 14th St
Port Arthur, TX 77640-4482, USA

Richard, Pierre
6 Rue De Vieux-Moulin
Charlotte, NC 28230

Richard, Ruth (Athlete, Baseball Player)
880 Allentown Rd
Sellersville, PA 18960-1000, USA

Richard III, Oliver G (Business Person)
Columbia Energy Group
200 Civic Center Dr
Columbus, OH 43215-4138, USA

Richards, Ariana (Actor)
Don Buchwald
6500 Wilshire Blvd Ste 2200
Los Angeles, CA 90048-4942, USA

Richards, Bob (Athlete, Olympic Athlete,
Track Athlete)
100 Old Steinbeck Rd
Waco, TX 76708-5233, USA

Richards, Bob (Doctor)
1616 Estates Dr
Woodway, TX 76712-2208, USA

Richards, Bobby (Athlete, Football Player)
2881 Fairplay Rd
Rutledge, GA 30663-2000, USA

Richards, Brad (Athlete, Hockey Player)
401 N Wabash Ave Unit 80A
Chicago, IL 60611-3990

Richards, Charles (Writer)
c/o David Hahn *Planned Television Arts*
1110 2nd Ave Rm 303
New York, NY 10022-2021, USA

Richards, Curvin (Athlete, Football Player)
11000 Gatesden Dr Apt 1311
Tomball, TX 77377-8706, USA

Richards, David R (Athlete, Football
Player)
4209 San Carlos St
Dallas, TX 75205-2049, USA

Richards, DeLeon (Actor, Musician)
c/o Staff Member *Britto Agency PR*
90 Franklin St Apt 4N
New York, NY 10013-3489, USA

Richards, Denise (Actor)
23726 Long Valley Rd
Hidden Hills, CA 91302-2408, USA

Richards, Duane (Athlete, Baseball Player)
PO Box 54
Palestine, OH 45352-0054, USA

Richards, Emelie
PO Box 7052
Arlington, VA 22207-0052

Richards, Evan
1800 Avenue of the Stars Ste 400
Los Angeles, CA 90067-4206

Richards, Fred (Athlete, Baseball Player)
1760 Dodge Dr NW
Warren, OH 44485-1823, USA

Richards, Garrett (Athlete, Baseball
Player)
433 NW 14th St
Oklahoma City, OK 73103-3510, USA

Richards, Gene (Athlete, Baseball Player)
1468 Normandy Dr
Chula Vista, CA 91913-3903, USA

Richards, Golden (Athlete, Football Player)
7274 S Winesap Ct
Salt Lake City, UT 84121-4439, USA

Richards, Howard (Athlete, Football Player)
PSC 98 Box 30
Dpo, AE 09830, USA

Richards, James B (Athlete, Football Player)
733 Vanderbilt Ave
Virginia Beach, VA 23451-3632, USA

Richards, J August (Actor)
PO Box 99
China Spring, TX 76633-0099, USA

Richards, J R (Musician)
William Morris Agency
1325 Avenue of the Americas Bsmt 2
New York, NY 10019-6047, USA

Richards, Keith (Musician)
1 5th Ave Apt 18A
New York, NY 10003-4317, USA

Richards, Kim (Actor, Reality Star)
c/o Bette Smith *Bette Smith Management*
499 N Canon Dr
Beverly Hills, CA 90210-4887, USA

Richards, Kyle (Actor, Reality Star)
Kyle by Alene Too
9647 Brighton Way
Beverly Hills, CA 90210-5109, USA

Richards, Lou
2467 Brighton Dr # 2-B
Valencia, CA 91355

Richards, Michael (Actor, Comedian)
c/o Staff Member *Untitled Entertainment (NY)*
435 Hudson St Fl 9
New York, NY 10014-3995, USA

Richards, Paul W (Astronaut)
NASA
605 First St
Annapolis, MD 21403-3321, USA

Richards, Renee (Tennis Player)
1604 Union St
San Francisco, CA 94123-4507, USA

Richards, Richard N (Astronaut)
NASA
2101 Nasa Pkwy Spc Johnsoncenter
Houston, TX 77058-3696, USA

Richards, Richard N Captain (Astronaut)
3317 Las Palmas St
Houston, TX 77027-6345, USA

Richards, Robert E (Bob) (Athlete, Track Athlete)
1616 Estates Dr
Woodway, TX 76712-2208, USA

Richards, Rusty (Athlete, Baseball Player)
8210 Mattwood Dr
Richmond, TX 77406-4306, USA

Richards, Sanya (Athlete, Olympic Athlete)
c/o Lowell Taub *Creative Artists Agency (CAA-NY)*
162 5th Ave Fl 6
New York, NY 10010-6047, USA

Richards, Stephanie (Actor)
H David Moss
733 Seward St PH
Los Angeles, CA 90038-3503, USA

Richards, Todd (Athlete, Hockey Player)
Columbus Blue Jackets
200 W Nationwide Blvd Unit 1
Columbus, OH 43215-2564

Richards, Todd (Athlete, Hockey Player)
5208 107th Ave N
Minneapolis, MN 55443-5902

Richards, Warren J
9075 S 700 E Apt 109
Sandy, UT 84070-2445, USA

Richardson, Al (Athlete, Football Player)
3003 Mary Ashley Ct SE
Conyers, GA 30013-6419, USA

Richardson, Antonio (Athlete, Football Player)
c/o Eugene Parker *Maximum Sports Management*
6435 W Jefferson Blvd # 197
Fort Wayne, IN 46804-6203, USA

Richardson, Bill (Politician)
1058 Encantado Dr
Santa Fe, NM 87501-1086, USA

Richardson, Bucky (Athlete, Football Player)
PO Box 79266
Houston, TX 77279-9266, USA

Richardson, Cameron (Actor)
c/o Staff Member *United Talent Agency (UTA-LA)*
9336 Civic Center Dr
Beverly Hills, CA 90210-3604, USA

Richardson, Cheryl (Actor)
749 Fair Oaks Dr
Alamo, CA 94507-1457, USA

Richardson, Cliff (Athlete, Basketball Player)
6236 Radiance Blvd E # 2
Fife, WA 98424-3868, USA

Richardson, Clint (Athlete, Basketball Player)
12E7 9th Ave NW
Puyallup, WA 98371, USA

Richardson, Damien (Athlete, Football Player)
1300 E Cromwell Ave Apt 102
Fresno, CA 93720-2628, USA

Richardson, Dan (Musician)
c/o Staff Member *The Agency Group (NYC)*
142 W 57th St Fl 6
New York, NY 10019-3300, USA

Richardson, Dot (Athlete, Olympic Athlete, Softball Player)
1120 W Lakeshore Dr
Clermont, FL 34711-2936, USA

Richardson, Eliot
1100 Crest Ln
Mc Lean, VA 22101-1815

Richardson, Eric (Athlete, Football Player)
509 Ely Blvd S
Petaluma, CA 94954-3813, USA

Richardson, Gloster (Athlete, Football Player)
9143 S Euclid Ave
Chicago, IL 60617-3749, USA

Richardson, Gordie (Athlete, Baseball Player)
23 Saint Paul Church Rd
Colquitt, GA 39837-6829, USA

Richardson, Grady (Athlete, Football Player)
3633 Mentone Ave Apt 203
Los Angeles, CA 90034-5659, USA

Richardson, Greg (Boxer)
382 Camden Ave
Youngstown, OH 44505-4845, USA

Richardson, Hamilton (Tennis Player)
870 United Nations Plz
New York, NY 10017-1807, USA

Richardson, Huey (Athlete, Football Player)
2 Duncan Ct
Mahwah, NJ 07430-3183, USA

Richardson, Jake (Actor)
c/o Meredith Fine *Coast to Coast Talent Group*
3350 Barham Blvd
Los Angeles, CA 90068-1404, USA

Richardson, Jason (Athlete, Basketball Player)
c/o Dan Fegan *Relativity Sports (LA)*
9242 Beverly Blvd Ste 300
Beverly Hills, CA 90210-3728, USA

Richardson, Jay (Athlete, Football Player)
c/o Eugene Parker *Maximum Sports Management*
6435 W Jefferson Blvd # 197
Fort Wayne, IN 46804-6203, USA

Richardson, Jeff (Athlete, Baseball Player)
47 Kuester Lk
Grand Island, NE 68801-8609, USA

Richardson, Jeffrey (Jeff) (Athlete, Baseball Player)
11779 W Fordson Dr
Marana, AZ 85653-7722, USA

Richardson, Jerome ""Pooh"" (Athlete, Basketball Player)
23434 Sherman Way
West Hills, CA 91307-1426, USA

Richardson, Jerry (Business Person, Football Executive)
6245 N Shore Dr # A14
Nebo, NC 28761-8604, USA

Richardson, John (Athlete, Football Player)
3053 Eagles Claw Ave
Thousand Oaks, CA 91362-1771, USA

Richardson, Kevin (Musician)
c/o Johnny Wright *Wright Entertainment Group*
PO Box 590009
Orlando, FL 32859-0009, USA

Richardson, Kevin Michael (Actor)
c/o Anita Haeggstrom *Arts & Letters Entertainment*
1800 Century Park E # 1600
Los Angeles, CA 90067-1501, USA

Richardson, Kristin (Actor)
c/o Brady McKay *Evolution Entertainment (LA)*
9320 Wilshire Blvd Ste 202
Beverly Hills, CA 90212-3217, USA

Richardson, LaTanya (Actor, Producer)
c/o Staff Member *Paradigm (LA)*
360 N Crescent Dr
North Bldg
Beverly Hills, CA 90210-4874, USA

Richardson, Laura (Congressman, Politician)
1330 Longworth Hob
Washington, DC 20515-0402, USA

Richardson, Michael Ray (Athlete, Basketball Player)
5012 SW Oxford Pl
Lawton, OK 73505-0827, USA

Richardson, Mike (Athlete, Football Player)
1619 W Caldwell St
Compton, CA 90220-4333, USA

Richardson, Mike (Athlete, Football Player)
7310 Covewood Dr
Garland, TX 75044-2624, USA

Richardson, Mike (Producer)
c/o Staff Member *Dark Horse Entertainment*
1438 N Gower St Ste 28
Los Angeles, CA 90028-8306, USA

Richardson, Nolan (Coach)
2539 E Joyce Blvd
Fayetteville, AR 72703-4553, USA

Richardson, Patricia (Actor)
c/o Jonathan Howard *Innovative Artists (LA)*
1505 10th St
Santa Monica, CA 90401-2805, USA

Richardson, Quentin (Basketball Player)
Los Angeles Clippers
1111 S Figueroa St Ste 1100
Staples Center
Los Angeles, CA 90015-1345, USA

Richardson, Robert (Cinematographer)
c/o Spyros Skouras *The Skouras Agency*
1149 3rd St Ste 300
Santa Monica, CA 90403-7201, USA

Richardson, Robert (Race Car Driver)
R3 Motorsports
3685 NC 152 W
China Grove, NC 28023-6771, USA

Richardson, Robert C (Bobby) (Athlete, Baseball Player)
47 Adams Ave
Sumter, SC 29150-4037, USA

Richardson, Sean (Athlete, Football Player)
c/o Ryan Tollner *REP 1 Sports Group*
2 Corporate Park Ste 106
Irvine, CA 92606-5103, USA

Richardson, Terry (Artist, Director, Photographer)
c/o Brian Young *Untitled Entertainment (LA)*
350 S Beverly Dr Ste 200
Beverly Hills, CA 90212-4819, USA

Richardson, Trent (Athlete, Football Player)
c/o Jimmy Sexton *CAA (Memphis)*
6060 Poplar Ave Ste 470
Memphis, TN 38119-0910, USA

Richardson, W Franklyn (Religious Leader)
National Baptist Convention
52 S 6th Ave
Mount Vernon, NY 10550-3005, USA

Richardson, Willie (Athlete, Football Player)
5928 Waverly Dr
Jackson, MS 39206-2503, USA

Richardson-Whitfield, Salli (Actor)
c/o Craig Dorfman *Frontline Management*
5670 Wilshire Blvd Ste 1370
Los Angeles, CA 90036-5679, USA

Richardt, Mike (Athlete, Baseball Player)
3236 W Western Ave
Fresno, CA 93722-4843, USA

Richelmy, Lorenzo (Actor)
c/o Andrew Cannava *United Talent Agency (UTA-LA)*
9336 Civic Center Dr
Beverly Hills, CA 90210-3604, USA

Richert, Nate (Actor)
c/o Iris Burton *Iris Burton Agency*
10100 Santa Monica Blvd Ste 1300
Los Angeles, CA 90067-4114, USA

Richert, Pete (Athlete, Baseball Player)
80 La Cerra Dr
Rancho Mirage, CA 92270-3811, USA

Richeson, Ray (Athlete, Football Player)
1348 Willoughby Rd
Vestavia, AL 35216-2906, USA

Richey, Cliff (Tennis Player)
2936 Cumberland Dr
San Angelo, TX 76904-6163, USA

Richey, Jennifer (Actor)
c/o Staff Member *Cunningham Escott Slevin & Doherty (CESD-LA)*
10635 Santa Monica Blvd Ste 130
Los Angeles, CA 90025-8306, USA

Richey, Nancy (Tennis Player)
2936 Cumberland Dr
San Angelo, TX 76904-6163, USA

Richey, Wade (Athlete, Football Player)
207 Bayonne Dr
Lafayette, LA 70507-3243, USA

Richie, Lionel (Musician, Songwriter)
Lionel Richie Productions, Inc.
2850 Ocean Park Blvd Ste 300
Santa Monica, CA 90405-6216, USA

Richie, Nicole (Designer, Reality Star)
8305 Lookout Mountain Ave
Los Angeles, CA 90046-1548, USA

Richie, Rob (Athlete, Baseball Player)
1835 Meadowvale Way
Sparks, NV 89431-2949, USA

Richman, Adam (Television Host)
c/o Eileen Stringer *Rain Management Group (RMG)*
1631 21st St
Santa Monica, CA 90404-3914, USA

Richman, Caryn (Actor)
1805 Via Arriba
Palos Verdes Estates, CA 90274-1236, USA

Richman, Jonathan (Actor, Musician)
High Road
751 Bridgeway Fl 2
Sausalito, CA 94965-2174, USA

Richman, Peter Mark (Actor)
5114 Del Moreno Dr
Woodland Hills, CA 91364-2426, USA

Richmond, Branscombe (Actor)
PO Box 881095
Pukalani, HI 96788-1095, USA

Richmond, Mitch (Athlete, Basketball Player, Olympic Athlete)
25374 Prado De La Felicidad
Calabasas, CA 91302-3649, USA

Richmond, Steve (Athlete, Hockey Player)
Washington Capitals
627 N Glebe Rd Ste 850
Arlington, VA 22203-2144

Richmond, Steve (Athlete, Hockey Player)
21290 W Pepper Dr
Lake Zurich, IL 60047-8046

Richmond, Tequan (Actor)
c/o Temple Poteat *AMP Live Entertainment*
3727 W Magnolia Blvd # 446
Burbank, CA 91505-2818, USA

Richt, Mark (Coach, Football Coach)
University of Georgia
PO Box 1472
Athletic Dept
Athens, GA 30603-1472, USA

Richter, Al (Athlete, Baseball Player)
3810 Atlantic Ave Apt 703
Virginia Beach, VA 23451-2736, USA

Richter, Andy (Actor, Comedian)
c/o Tim Sarkes *Brillstein Entertainment Partners (LA)*
9150 Wilshire Blvd Ste 350
Beverly Hills, CA 90212-3453, USA

Richter, Barry (Athlete, Hockey Player, Olympic Athlete)
PO Box 259408
Madison, WI 53725-9408, USA

Richter, Dave (Athlete, Hockey Player)
16910 Trenton Ln
Eden Prairie, MN 55347-3377

Richter, Frank (Athlete, Football Player)
734 Creekside Dr
Leesburg, GA 31763-4804, USA

Richter, James A (Jim) (Athlete, Football Player)
8620 Bournemouth Dr
Raleigh, NC 27615-2008, USA

Richter, Jason James (Actor)
United Talent Agency
9336 Civic Center Dr
Beverly Hills, CA 90210-3604, USA

Richter, John (Athlete, Basketball Player)
2740 Narcissa Rd
Plymouth Meeting, PA 19462-1107, USA

Richter, Les (Race Car Driver)
c/o Staff Member *NASCAR*
1801 W Speedway Blvd
Daytona Beach, FL 32114-1243, USA

Richter, Mike (Athlete, Hockey Player, Olympic Athlete)
61 Cutler Rd
Greenwich, CT 06831-2508

Richter, Pat V (Athlete, Football Executive, Football Player)
833 Kings Way
Madison, WI 53704-6046, USA

Richter, Sonja (Actor)
c/o Toni Howard *ICM Partners (LA)*
10250 Constellation Blvd Fl 7
Los Angeles, CA 90067-6207, USA

Richwine, Maria (Actor)
Abrams-Rubaloff Lawrence
8075 W 3rd St # 303
Los Angeles, CA 90048-4318, USA

Rickards, Ashley (Actor)
c/o Ben Levine *LINK Entertainment*
11872 La Grange Ave Fl 1
Los Angeles, CA 90025-5283, USA

Rickards, Emily Bett (Actor)
c/o Allan Grifka *Alchemy Entertainment*
7024 Melrose Ave Ste 420
Los Angeles, CA 90038-3394, USA

Ricker, Robert S (Religious Leader)
Baptists Conference
2002 S Arlington Heights Rd
Arlington Heights, IL 60005-4102, USA

Ricketts, Dave (Athlete, Baseball Player)
12860 Polo Parc Dr
Saint Louis, MO 63146-1504, USA

Ricketts, Tom (Athlete, Football Player)
720 Warrendale Bayne Rd
Wexford, PA 15090-7492, USA

Rickey, Dixon (Athlete, Football Player)
908 Country Creek Ln
Red Oak, TX 75154-3902, USA

Rickles, Don (Actor, Comedian)
10249 Century Woods Dr
Los Angeles, CA 90067-6312, USA

Rickman, Alan (Actor, Producer)
c/o Judy Hofflund *Hofflund/Polone*
6300 Wilshire Blvd Ste 1410
Los Angeles, CA 90048-5216, USA

Rickon-Mitchell, Kelly (Athlete, Olympic Athlete, Rower)
3120 Goldsmith St
San Diego, CA 92106-1419, USA

Ricks, Lawrence (Athlete, Football Player)
6417 Timbermill Way
Reynoldsburg, OH 43068-4327, USA

Ricks, Mikhael (Athlete, Football Player)
5024 Lincoln St
Hollywood, FL 33021-5256, USA

Rico, Alfredo (Fred) (Athlete, Baseball Player)
7720 Ensign Ave
Sun Valley, CA 91352-4451, USA

Rida, Flo (Musician)
14401 Sunset Ln
Southwest Ranches, FL 33330-3409, USA

Ridder, P Anthony (Business Person, Publisher)
Knight-Ridder Inc
50 W San Fernando St
San Jose, CA 95113-2429, USA

Riddick, Steve (Athlete, Olympic Athlete, Track Athlete)
PO Box 1000
Petersburg, VA 23804-1000, USA

Riddick, Theo (Athlete, Football Player)
c/o Joe Flanagan *BTI Sports Advisors*
170 N Scoville Ave
Oak Park, IL 60302-2647, USA

Riddleberger, Denny (Athlete, Baseball Player)
9525 SW 84th Ter Unit C
Ocala, FL 34481-8212, USA

Riddoch, Greg (Athlete, Baseball Player, Coach)
703 Windflower Dr
Longmont, CO 80504-2770, USA

Rider, Amy (Actor)
c/o Amy Slomovits *Evolution Entertainment (LA)*
9320 Wilshire Blvd Ste 202
Beverly Hills, CA 90212-3217, USA

Rider, Isiah
PO Box 121R
Montchanin, DE 19710, USA

Rider, Isiah (J R) (Athlete, Basketball Player)
P.O. Box 121R
Montchanin, DE 19710, USA

Riders In The Sky
38 Music Sq E Ste 300
Nashville, TN 37203-4304

Riders of the Purple Sage
PO Box 1987
Studio City, CA 91614-0987

Ridge, Houston (Athlete, Football Player)
7027 Benson Ave
San Diego, CA 92114-5908, USA

Ridge, Thomas (Politician)
5315 Woodlawn Ave
Chevy Chase, MD 20815-6635, USA

Ridgeley, Andrew (Musician)
8800 W Sunset Blvd # 401
West Hollywood, CA 90069-2105, USA

Ridgeway, Angle (Golfer)
c/o Staff Member *Pro Golfers Association (PGA) Tour*
112 Tpc Blvd
Ponte Vedra Beach, FL 32082, USA

Ridgeway, Frank (Cartoonist)
c/o Staff Member *King Features Syndication*
300 W 57th St Fl 15
New York, NY 10019-5238, USA

Ridge, Elston (Athlete, Football Player)
5317 Wilkinson Ave
Valley Village, CA 91607-2412, USA

Ridgley, Bob (Actor)
20th Century Artists
4605 Lankershim Blvd Ste 305
North Hollywood, CA 91602-1875, USA

Ridgway, Dave (Athlete, Football Player)
5875 W State Highway 250
Paris Crossing, IN 47270-9785, USA

Ridgway, Jeff (Athlete, Baseball Player)
9041 Parlor Dr
Ladson, SC 29456-5528, USA

Ridings, Tag (Athlete, Golfer)
2040 Bantry Dr
Keller, TX 76262-9001, USA

Ridker, Paul (Doctor)
Brigham & Women's Hospital
75 Francis St
Boston, MA 02115-6106, USA

Ridlehuber, Preston (Athlete, Football Player)
720 Serramonte Dr
Marietta, GA 30068-4674, USA

Ridley, Curt (Athlete, Hockey Player)
722 E Grubb Dr
Mesquite, TX 75149-7502

Ridley, John (Director, Producer, Writer)
c/o Missy Malkin *Brillstein Entertainment Partners (LA)*
9150 Wilshire Blvd Ste 350
Beverly Hills, CA 90212-3453, USA

Ridlon, James A (Athlete, Football Player)
8006 E Lake Rd
Cazenovia, NY 13035, USA

Ridnour, Luke (Basketball Player)
Seattle SuperSonics
351 Elliott Ave W Ste 500
Seattle, WA 98119-4153, USA

Ridzik, Steve (Athlete, Baseball Player)
7008 11th Ave W
Bradenton, FL 34209-4066, USA

Riedling, John (Athlete, Baseball Player)
2118 Homestead Ln
Franklin, TN 37064-1177, USA

Riegel, Eden (Actor, Musician)
c/o Leigh Brillstein Resolution (LA)
10250 Constellation Blvd Fl 7
Los Angeles, CA 90067-6207, USA

Riegert, Peter (Actor)
c/o John S Kelly Bresler Kelly &
Associates
11500 W Olympic Blvd Ste 510
Los Angeles, CA 90064-1527, USA

Riegger, John (Golfer)
768 Tossa De Mar Ave
Henderson, NV 89002-6536, USA

Riegle, Bruce (Horse Racer)
300 W Main St
Greenville, OH 45331-1432, USA

Riegle, Gene (Coach, Horse Racer)
818 Chestnut Cir
Greenville, OH 45331-1075, USA

Riegle Jr, Donald W (Business Person, Ex-
Senator, Senator)
APCO Worldwide
700 12th St NW Ste 800
Washington, DC 20005-3949, USA

Riehle, Richard (Actor)
Abrams Artists
9200 W Sunset Blvd Ste 1125
West Hollywood, CA 90069-3610, USA

Rieker, Rich (Athlete, Baseball Player)
1223 Grey Fox Run
Weldon Spring, MO 63304-0307, USA

Rieker, Richard (Baseball Player)
5337 Foxshire Ct
Orlando, FL 32819-3824, USA

Rienstra, John (Athlete, Football Player)
PO Box 2447
Frisco, CO 80443-2447, USA

Riepe, James S (Business Person)
T Rowe Price Assoc
100 E Pratt St Ste 310
Baltimore, MD 21202-1065, USA

Riesenberg, Doug (Athlete, Football
Player)
7275 SW Deerhaven Dr
Corvallis, OR 97333-9314, USA

Riesgo, Nikco (Damon) (Athlete, Baseball
Player)
29625 Bermuda Ln
Southfield, MI 48076-1663, USA

Riesgraf, Beth (Actor)
c/o Matthew Lesher Insight
PO Box 36359
Los Angeles, CA 90036-0359, USA

Riessen, Marty (Tennis Player)
PO Box 5444
Santa Barbara, CA 93150-5444, USA

Ries-Zillmer, Ruth (Baseball Player)
133 Adeline St
Walworth, WI 53184, USA

Rieves, Charles (Athlete, Football Player)
3107 Long Bay Ct
Houston, TX 77059-3720, USA

Rieves, Charley (Athlete, Football Player)
3107 Long Bay Ct
Houston, TX 77059-3720, USA

Rife, Rikki
520 Washington Blvd # 924
Marina Del Rey, CA 90292

Riff
PO Box 7257
Paterson, NJ 07509-7257

Rifkin, Adam (Actor, Director, Writer)
c/o Simon Millar Rumble Media
1620 Broadway Ste C
Santa Monica, CA 90404-2777, USA

Rifkin, Ron (Actor, Musician)
c/o Marcia Hurwitz Innovative Artists (LA)
1505 10th St
Santa Monica, CA 90401-2805, USA

Rigali, Justin F Cardinal (Religious Leader)
Archdiocese
222 N 17th St
Philadelphia, PA 19103-1295, USA

Rigazio, Donald (Athlete, Hockey Player,
Olympic Athlete)
2412 Glenmary Ave Apt 1
Louisville, KY 40204-2158, USA

Rigby, Amy (Musician, Songwriter, Writer)
Press Network
1229 17th Ave S
Nashville, TN 37212-2801, USA

Rigby, Brad (Athlete, Baseball Player)
3161 Cecelia Dr
Apopka, FL 32703-7815, USA

Rigby, Cathy (Athlete, Gymnast, Olympic
Athlete)
McCoy Rigby Dance Academy
22601 La Palma Ave Ste 105
Yorba Linda, CA 92887-6711, USA

Rigby, Paul (Cartoonist)
119 Monterey Pointe Dr
Palm Beach Gardens, FL 33418-5811,
USA

Rigdon, Paul (Athlete, Baseball Player)
9231 Coxwell Ct
Jacksonville, FL 32221-1378, USA

Riggan, Jerrod (Athlete, Baseball Player)
PO Box 1019
Brewster, WA 98812-1019, USA

Riggans, Shawn (Athlete, Baseball Player)
5700 Hancock Rd
Southwest Ranches, FL 33330-3006, USA

Riggins, John (Athlete, Football Player)
Schulte Sports Marketing
7272 Wisconsin Ave Ste 300
Bethesda, MD 20814-4858, USA

Riggins, Mark (Athlete, Baseball Player)
101 Arbor Dr
Murray, KY 42071-6835, USA

Riggio, Dominic (Athlete, Football Player)
4621 Mandalay Ave
Royal Oak, MI 48073-1623, USA

Riggio, Leonard (Business Person)
Barnes & Noble Inc
122 5th Ave Fl 2
New York, NY 10011-5693, USA

Riggle, Bob (Athlete, Football Player)
55 Waynesburg Rd
Washington, PA 15301-3224, USA

Riggle, Rob (Actor)
c/o Peter Principato Principato/Young
Management (LA)
9465 Wilshire Blvd Ste 900
Beverly Hills, CA 90212-2608, USA

Riggleman, James D (Jim) (Athlete,
Baseball Player, Coach)
14950 Gulf Blvd Apt 1003
Madeira Beach, FL 33708-2047, USA

Riggs, Adam (Athlete, Baseball Player)
26 Pebble Hollow Ct
Spring, TX 77381-4803, USA

Riggs, Chandler (Actor)
c/o Joanna (Joanie) Burstein Burstein
Company, The
15304 W Sunset Blvd Ste 208
Pacific Palisades, CA 90272-3656, USA

Riggs, Gerald (Athlete, Football Player)
566 Elizabeth Crest Rd
Chattanooga, TN 37421-4622, USA

Riggs, Gerald (Athlete, Football Player)
2574 Bright Ct
Decatur, GA 30034-2245, USA

Riggs, Jim (Athlete, Football Player)
15 Dellany Ct
Greer, SC 29651-6857, USA

Riggs, Ransom (Writer)
c/o Staff Member Heroes and Villains
Entertainment
1041 N Formosa Ave
Formosa Bldg, Suite 202
West Hollywood, CA 90046-6703, USA

Riggs, Scott (Race Car Driver)
MBV/MB2 Motorsports
7065 Zephr Pl NW
Concord, NC 29028, USA

Riggs, Thron (Athlete, Football Player)
2645 E Southern Ave Apt A496
Tempe, AZ 85282-7791, USA

Righetti, Amanda (Actor, Producer)
c/o David (Dave) Fleming Mosaic Media
Group
9200 W Sunset Blvd Ste 10
West Hollywood, CA 90069-3608, USA

Righetti, David A (Dave) (Athlete,
Baseball Player)
552 Magdalena Ave
Los Altos Hills, CA 94024-5233, USA

Righteous Bros (Music Group)
c/o Staff Member William Morris
Endeavor (LA)
9601 Wilshire Blvd
Beverly Hills, CA 90210-5213, USA

Rightnowar, Ron (Athlete, Baseball
Player)
8926 Stonybrook Blvd
Sylvania, OH 43560-8906, USA

Rights, Graham H (Religious Leader)
Moravian Church Southern Province
459 S Church St
Winston Salem, NC 27101-5314, USA

Rigoli, Joe (Athlete, Baseball Player)
117 Metro Trl
Hopatcong, NJ 07843-1554, USA

Rigsby, Donald (Musician)
Donald Rigsby Group, Inc
2774 Golf Lake Dr
Plant City, FL 33566-0952, USA

Rihanna (Musician)
932 Rivas Cyn
Pacific Palisades, CA 90272-3957, USA

Rijker, Lucia (Actor)
c/o Harlan Werner Sports Placement
Service
330 W 11th St Apt 105
Los Angeles, CA 90015-3200, USA

Rijo, Jose (Athlete, Baseball Player)
2127 Brickell Ave Apt 2101
Miami, FL 33129-2146, USA

Rikaart, Greg (Actor)
c/o Kyle Fritz Kyle Fritz Management
6325 Heather Dr
Los Angeles, CA 90068-1633, USA

Riker, Robin (Actor)
c/o Staff Member Don Buchwald &
Associates (LA)
6500 Wilshire Blvd Ste 2200
Los Angeles, CA 90048-4942, USA

Riker, Tom (Athlete, Basketball Player)
600 Fines Creek Rd
Clyde, NC 28721-9183, USA

Riklis, Meshulam (Business Person)
Riklis Family Corp
2901 Las Vegas Blvd S
Las Vegas, NV 89109-1933, USA

Riles, Ernest (Athlete, Baseball Player)
221 Asante Dr
Ellenwood, GA 30294-3187, USA

Riley, Amber (Actor)
c/o Scooter Braun SB Management
825 8th Ave Fl 28
New York, NY 10019-7416, USA

Riley, Boots (Musician)
c/o Danny Goldberg Gold Village
Entertainment
37 W 17th St Ste 7W
New York, NY 10011-5525, USA

Riley, Chris (Athlete, Golfer)
2625 Barbaradale Cir
Las Vegas, NV 89146-5160, USA

Riley, Elaine (Actor)
405 N Bay Frnt
Newport Beach, CA 92662-1047, USA

Riley, Eric (Athlete, Basketball Player)
6601 Sands Point Dr Apt 4
Houston, TX 77074-3731, USA

Riley, Forbes (Actor)
c/o Staff Member Cohen Entertainment
964 Hancock Ave Apt 305
West Hollywood, CA 90069-4091, USA

Riley, George (Athlete, Baseball Player)
451 Basket Rd
Oley, PA 19547-9245, USA

Riley, H John Jr (Business Person)
Cooper Industries
600 Travis St Ste 5400
Houston, TX 77002-2909, USA

Riley, Jack (Athlete, Hockey Player,
Olympic Athlete)
PO Box 1070
Sandwich, MA 02563-1070, USA

Riley, Jack (Actor)
c/o Staff Member House of
Representatives, The
1434 6th St Ste 1
Santa Monica, CA 90401-2527, USA

Riley, James (Athlete, Football Player)
2201 Cardinal Dr
Edmond, OK 73013-7635, USA

Riley, Jeannie (Musician)
1003 Lakeview Dr
Brenham, TX 77833-4755, USA

Riley, Ken (Athlete, Football Player)
1865 E Gibbons St
Bartow, FL 33830-6712, USA

Riley, Kevin (Alex Riley) (Actor, Athlete, Wrestler)
3808 Villas Del Sol Ct
Tampa, FL 33609-4440, USA

Riley, Madison (Actor)
c/o Mona Loring *MLC PR*
7080 Hollywood Blvd Ste 903
Los Angeles, CA 90028-6936, USA

Riley, Matt (Athlete, Baseball Player)
3007 Everleigh Pl
Spring Hill, TN 37174-2766, USA

Riley, Michael
9200 W Sunset Blvd Ste 900
West Hollywood, CA 90069-3604

Riley, Mike (Coach, Football Coach)
Oregon State University
Athletic Dept
Corvallis, OR 97331, USA

Riley, Pat (Athlete, Basketball Coach, Basketball Player, Coach)
800 S Pointe Dr # B
Miami Beach, FL 33139-7163, USA

Riley, Raven (Actor)
Evil Motion Pictures
Prefers to be contacted via email
Phoenix, AZ 85066, USA

Riley, Robert (Politician)
742 County Road 5
Ashland, AL 36251-5533, USA

Riley, Ruth (Athlete)
3777 Lapeer Rd
Auburn Hills, MI 48326-1733

Riley, Steve (Athlete, Football Player)
PO Box 2723
Park City, UT 84060-2723, USA

Riley, Teddy (Musician, Songwriter)
Future Enterprise Records
70 Universal City Plz
Universal City, CA 91608-1011, USA

Riley, Victor (Athlete, Football Player)
136 Sandy Oak Ln
Gaston, SC 29053-8775, USA

Rimando, Nick (Soccer Player)
DC United
2400 E Capitol St NE Ste 1
Rfk Stadium
Washington, DC 20003-1738, USA

Rimer, Jeff (Sportscaster)
5454 Waxen Dr
Dublin, OH 43016-8372, USA

Rimes, LeAnn (Musician)
5565 Bonneville Rd
Hidden Hills, CA 91302-1202, USA

Rimington, Dave (Athlete, Football Player)
222 Riverside Dr # 11-D
New York, NY 10025-6809, USA

Rimmel, James E (Religious Leader)
Evangelical Presbyterian Church
26049 5 Mile Rd
Redford, MI 48239-3235, USA

Rinaldi, Kathy (Tennis Player)
Advantage International
1025 Thomas Jefferson St NW # 450
Washington, DC 20007-5201, USA

Rinaldi, Rich (Athlete, Basketball Player)
1117 Perry Ln
Collegeville, PA 19426-1067, USA

Rinaldo, Benjamin (Skier)
Ski World
2680 Buena Park Dr
Studio City, CA 91604, USA

Rincon, Andy (Athlete, Baseball Player)
5425 Los Toros Ave
Pico Rivera, CA 90660-3038, USA

Rincon, Juan (Athlete, Baseball Player)
5150 Lincoln Dr
Minneapolis, MN 55436-1010, USA

Rincon, Ricardo (Baseball Player)
c/o Staff Member *Oakland Athletics*
7000 Coliseum Way Ste 3
Oakland, CA 94621-1992, USA

Rinearson, Peter M (Journalist)
Seattle Times
1000 Denny Way # 5
Editorial Dept
Seattle, WA 98109-5340, USA

Rineer, Jeff (Athlete, Baseball Player)
325 W Charlotte St
Millersville, PA 17551-9515, USA

Ring, Bob (Athlete, Hockey Player)
28 St Simons Dr
Bluffton, SC 29910-6151

Ring, Royce (Athlete, Baseball Player)
2860 Aber St
San Diego, CA 92117-2422, USA

Ringer, Robert J (Motivational Speaker, Writer)
c/o Staff Member *The Harry Walker Agency*
355 Lexington Ave Fl 21
New York, NY 10017-6603, USA

Ringolsby, Tracy (Baseball Player)
1526 Fox Chase Rd
Cheyenne, WY 82009-8396, USA

Ringwald, Molly (Actor)
217 E 85th St Apt 18
New York, NY 10028-3091, USA

Rini, Mary (Athlete, Baseball Player)
37592 Charter Oaks Blvd
Clinton Township, MI 48036-2422, USA

Rinker, Larry (Golfer)
1615 Woodland Ave
Winter Park, FL 32789-2774, USA

Rinna, Lisa (Actor)
3007 Lake Glen Dr
Beverly Hills, CA 90210-1313, USA

Rinne, Pekka (Athlete, Hockey Player)
Puckagency LLC
1 Sunset Dr N
Attn Jay Grossman
Chappaqua, NY 10514-1613, USA

Rintoul, Steve (Golfer)
17506 Osprey Manor Way
Lithia, FL 33547-5044, USA

Riordan, Marjorie
1833 Pelham Ave
Los Angeles, CA 90025-4713

Riordan, Mike (Athlete, Basketball Player)
Riordan's Saloon
14E Inwood Rd
Stevensville, MD 21666, USA

Riordan, Richard J (Politician)
Bingham McCutchen
355 S Grand Ave Ste 4400
Los Angeles, CA 90071-3106, USA

Rios, Alberto (Writer)
Arizona State University
English Dept
Tempe, AZ 85287-0001, USA

Rios, Alexis (Baseball Player)
Yale Field
252 Derby Ave
West Haven, CT 06516, USA

Rios, Armando (Athlete, Baseball Player)
790 Ridenhour Cir
Orlando, FL 32809-7158, USA

Rios, Brandon (Boxer)
c/o Staff Member *Top Rank Inc.*
3908 Howard Hughes Pkwy
#580
Las Vegas, NV 89109, USA

Rios, Danny (Athlete, Baseball Player)
2523 W 9th Ln
Hialeah, FL 33010-1225, USA

Rios, Emily (Actor)
c/o Staff Member *Kass Management*
501 Santa Monica Blvd Ste 604
Santa Monica, CA 90401-2467, USA

Ripa, Kelly (Actor, Talk Show Host)
Live with Kelly & Michael
7 Lincoln Sq Fl 5
Wabc-Tv
New York, NY 10023-7219, USA

Ripert, Eric (Chef)
Le Bernardin
787 7th Ave Fl CONC1
New York, NY 10019-8103, USA

Ripken, Billy (Athlete, Baseball Player)
Major League Baseball Network
900 Mount Soma Ct
Fallston, MD 21047-1935, USA

Ripken Jr, Cal (Athlete, Baseball Player)
Cal Ripken Foundation
1427 Clarkview Rd Ste 100
Baltimore, MD 21209-0030, USA

Ripley, Alexandra (Writer)
24 Ripley St
Newport News, VA 23603-1305, USA

Ripley, Alice (Actor, Musician)
c/o Staff Member *Douglas Gorman Rothacker & Wilhelm Inc*
1501 Broadway Ste 703
New York, NY 10036-5501, USA

Ripley, Allen (Athlete, Baseball Player)
50 Dunham St
Attleboro, MA 02703-3052, USA

Rippelmeyer, Ray (Athlete, Baseball Player)
104 Eagle Ct
Waterloo, IL 62298-3158, USA

Rippey, Rodney Allan (Actor)
3941 Veselich Ave # 4-251
Los Angeles, CA 90039-1461, USA

Rippey, Rodney Allen
3939 Veselich Ave # 351
Los Angeles, CA 90039-1460

Rippley, Steve (Athlete, Baseball Player)
3900 Galt Ocean Dr Apt 1406
Fort Lauderdale, FL 33308-6606, USA

Risebrough, Doug (Athlete, Coach, Hockey Player)
5809 Schaefer Rd
Minneapolis, MN 55436-1115

Risher, Alan (Athlete, Football Player)
17732 Highland Rd Ste G
Baton Rouge, LA 70810-3846, USA

Risien, Cody L (Athlete, Football Player)
12060 Lake Ave Apt 401
Lakewood, OH 44107-1865, USA

Risinger, Earlene (Baseball Player)
334 Aurora St SE
Grand Rapids, MI 49507-3124, USA

Riske, Alison (Athlete, Tennis Player)
c/o Staff Member *Women's Tennis Association (WTA (US))*
1 Progress Plz Ste 1500
St Petersburg, FL 33701-4335, USA

Riske, David (Athlete, Baseball Player)
2771 Culloden Ave
Henderson, NV 89044-0233, USA

Risley, Bill (Athlete, Baseball Player)
1160 Prim Rose Cir
Greenwood, AR 72936-3066, USA

Rispoli, Michael (Actor)
c/o Staff Member *Gersh (LA)*
9465 Wilshire Blvd Ste 600
Beverly Hills, CA 90212-2605, USA

Rissling, Gary (Athlete, Hockey Player)
717 Paige Cir
Bel Air, MD 21014-5258, USA

Rissmiller, Pat (Athlete, Hockey Player)
276 Brackett St Apt 2R
Portland, ME 04102-3239

Rissmiller, Ray (Athlete, Football Player)
114 Iken Cir
Goose Creek, SC 29445-7148, USA

Rist, Robbie
PO Box 867
Woodland Hills, CA 91365-0867

Ristorucci, Lisa (Actor)
Progressive Artists Agency
400 S Beverly Dr Ste 216
Beverly Hills, CA 90212-4404, USA

Ritch, Michael (Race Car Driver)
David & Wright Motorsports
2730 Zion Church Rd
Concord, NC 28025-7027, USA

Ritcher, James A (Jim) (Athlete, Football Player)
8620 Bournemouth Dr
Raleigh, NC 27615, USA

Ritchie, Guy (Director, Producer, Writer)
c/o Staff Member *Anonymous Content (LA)*
3532 Hayden Ave
Culver City, CA 90232-2413, USA

Ritchie, Jay (Athlete, Baseball Player)
8275 Highway 52
Rockwell, NC 28138-8545, USA

Ritchie, Jill (Actor)
c/o Staff Member *Rugolo Entertainment*
195 S Beverly Dr Ste 400
Beverly Hills, CA 90212-3044, USA

Ritchie, Jon (Football Player)
c/o Staff Member *Philadelphia Eagles*
1 Novacare Way
Philadelphia, PA 19145-5996, USA

Ritchie, Todd (Athlete, Baseball Player)
114 Hulan Dr
Kerens, TX 75144-6046, USA

Ritchie, Wally (Athlete, Baseball Player)
417 Robert Cir
Santa Clara, UT 84765-5617, USA

Ritchie Family, The
4100 W Flagler St # B-2
Coral Gables, FL 33134-1612

Ritchson, Alan (Actor)
c/o Gayle Divine *Divine Management*
3822 Latrobe St
Los Angeles, CA 90031-1446

Ritger, Dick (Bowler)
804 Valley View Dr
River Falls, WI 54022-2724, USA

Rittenhouse, Lenore (Golfer)
295 Bellhaven Dr
Whispering Pines, NC 28327-7133, USA

Ritter, Huntley (Actor, Producer)
c/o Sheila Wenzel *Innovative Artists (LA)*
1505 10th St
Santa Monica, CA 90401-2805, USA

Ritter, Jason (Actor)
c/o Joanna (Joanie) Burstein *Burstein Company, The*
15304 W Sunset Blvd Ste 208
Pacific Palisades, CA 90272-3656, USA

Ritter, Josh (Musician)
c/o Darius Zelkha *Tough Love Artist Management*
660 York St Ste 205
San Francisco, CA 94110-2102, USA

Ritter, Krysten (Actor)
c/o Nancy Sanders *Sanders Armstrong Caserta*
2120 Colorado Ave Ste 120
Santa Monica, CA 90404-3561, USA

Ritter, Lawrence (Baseball Player)
424 W End Ave Apt 6D
New York, NY 10024-5777, USA

Ritter, Reggie (Athlete, Baseball Player)
1564 Estep Rd
Donaldson, AR 71941-8987, USA

Ritter, Tyson (Musician)
c/o Jack Ketsoyan *EMC / Bowery*
5971 W 3rd St
Los Angeles, CA 90036-2832, USA

Ritts, Jim (Golfer, Television Host)
Ladies Pro Golf Assn
100 International Golf Dr
Daytona Beach, FL 32124-1082, USA

Rittwage, Jim (Athlete, Baseball Player)
23931 Columbus Rd
Bedford, OH 44146-2969, USA

Ritz, David
c/o Daniel Strone *Trident Media Group LLC*
41 Madison Ave Fl 36
New York, NY 10010-2257, USA

Ritz, Kevin (Athlete, Baseball Player)
68559 8th Street Rd
Cambridge, OH 43725-9568, USA

Ritzenhaler, Henry Leon
1617 Pearson Rd
Paradise, CA 95969-6029

Ritzman, Alice (Golfer)
614 S Foys Lake Dr
Kalispell, MT 59901-7440, USA

Riutta, Bruce (Athlete, Hockey Player, Olympic Athlete)
1320 Crystal Cove Trl Apt 3
Green Bay, WI 54311-4293, USA

Riva, Diana Maria (Actor)
c/o Amy Guenther *Gateway Management Company Inc*
860 Via De La Paz Ste F10
Pacific Palisades, CA 90272-3631, USA

Rivas, Daniel Louis (Actor)
c/o Paul Santana *Agency for the Performing Arts (APA-LA)*
405 S Beverly Dr Ste 500
Beverly Hills, CA 90212-4425, USA

Rivera, Alex (Baseball Player)
21228 Shell Valley Rd
Edmonds, WA 98026-7346, USA

Rivera, Chita (Actor, Dancer, Musician)
c/o Staff Member *William Morris Endeavor (LA)*
9601 Wilshire Blvd
Beverly Hills, CA 90210-5213, USA

Rivera, David (Congressman, Politician)
417 Cannon Hob
Washington, DC 20515-1013, USA

Rivera, Emilio (Actor)
4637 Willowcrest Ave
North Hollywood, CA 91602-1464, USA

Rivera, Geraldo (Journalist, Television Host)
c/o Jim Griffin *Paradigm (NY)*
360 Park Ave S Fl 16
New York, NY 10010-1716, USA

Rivera, Jerry (Musician)
c/o Staff Member *BMG*
1540 Broadway Ste 1010
New York, NY 10036-4083, USA

Rivera, Jim (Athlete, Baseball Player)
6151 Bissot Blvd
Fort Wayne, IN 46835-7706, USA

Rivera, Jose (Producer, Writer)
c/o Rick Berg *Code Entertainment*
9229 W Sunset Blvd Ste 615
West Hollywood, CA 90069-3419, USA

Rivera, Juan (Athlete, Baseball Player)
c/o Staff Member *Los Angeles Dodgers (LA Dodgers)*
1000 Elysian Park Ave
Los Angeles, CA 90012-1112, USA

Rivera, Luis (Athlete, Baseball Player)
16 Calle Lazaro Ramos
Cidra, PR 00739-3424, USA

Rivera, Lupillo (Music Group)
c/o Staff Member *Sony Music Miami*
605 Lincoln Rd Ste 700
Miami Beach, FL 33139-2901, USA

Rivera, Mariano (Athlete, Baseball Player)
147 Anderson Hill Rd
Purchase, NY 10577-2007, USA

Rivera, Maxwell (Musician)
c/o Staff Member *Shore Fire Media*
32 Court St Fl 16
Brooklyn, NY 11201-4441, USA

Rivera, Mike (Athlete, Baseball Player)
1051 Wood Cv
Kissimmee, FL 34743-7800, USA

Rivera, Naya (Actor)
3722 Effingham Pl
Los Angeles, CA 90027-1428, USA

Rivera, Ron (Athlete, Football Player)
9212 Heydon Hall Cir
Charlotte, NC 28210-6063, USA

Rivera, Ximena Sarinana (Musician)
c/o Staff Member *Warner Bros Music*
4000 Warner Blvd
Burbank, CA 91522-0002

Rivera-Drew, Malaya (Actor)
8777 Lookout Mountain Ave
Los Angeles, CA 90046-1861, USA

Rivero, Jorge (Actor)
H David Moss
733 Seward St PH
Los Angeles, CA 90038-3503, USA

Rivers, David (Athlete, Basketball Player)
10509 Greensprings Dr
Tampa, FL 33626-1724, USA

Rivers, Glenn (Doc) (Athlete, Basketball Coach, Basketball Player, Coach)
5 Isle of Sicily
Winter Park, FL 32789-1505, USA

Rivers, Jamie (Athlete, Football Player)
4006 Lindell Blvd
Saint Louis, MO 63108-3202, USA

Rivers, Johnny (Musician, Songwriter, Writer)
3141 Coldwater Canyon Ln
Beverly Hills, CA 90210-1250, USA

Rivers, Keith (Athlete, Football Player)
c/o David Dunn *Athletes First, LLC*
23091 Mill Creek Dr
Laguna Hills, CA 92653-1258, USA

Rivers, Marcellus (Athlete, Football Player)
12003 Eden Ln
Frisco, TX 75033-1146, USA

Rivers, Melissa (Talk Show Host)
c/o Elizabeth Much *Much and House Public Relations*
8075 W 3rd St Ste 500
Los Angeles, CA 90048-4325, USA

Rivers, Mickey (Athlete, Baseball Player)
M D M Sports Marketing
218 Washington Ave Apt C14
Attn: David Ratner
Cedarhurst, NY 11516-1510, USA

Rivers, Philip (Athlete, Football Player)
4020 Murphy Canyon Rd
San Diego, CA 92123-4407, USA

Rivers, Reggie (Athlete, Football Player)
5003 E Weaver Pl
Centennial, CO 80121-3520, USA

Rivers, Wayne (Athlete, Hockey Player)
2821 San Ardo Way
Belmont, CA 94002-1341

Riverside, Vincent
c/o Melanie Sharp *Sharp Talent*
5538 Willowcrest Ave
North Hollywood, CA 91601-2830, USA

Rives, Don (Athlete, Football Player)
PO Box 553
Wheeler, TX 79096-0553, USA

Rivlin, Alice M (Government Official)
2842 Chesterfield Pl NW
Washington, DC 20008-1015, USA

Rizzo, Anthony (Athlete, Baseball Player)
Anthony Rizzo Family Foundation
6574 N State Rd
#201
Pompano Beach, FL 33073, USA

Rizzo, Jack (Athlete, Football Player)
1105 Forest Trails Dr
Castle Pines, CO 80108-8280, USA

Rizzo, Jerry (Athlete, Basketball Player)
2548 126th St Apt 1
Flushing, NY 11354-1126, USA

Rizzo, Joe (Athlete, Football Player)
6131 Dorsett Pl
Wilmington, NC 28403-0128, USA

Rizzo, Joe (Horse Racer)
5 Berkshire Dr
Howell, NJ 07731-2355, USA

Rizzo, John R (Athlete, Football Player)
1105 Forest Trails Dr
Castle Pines, CO 80108-8280, USA

Rizzo, Patti (Golfer)
2455 Provence Cir
Weston, FL 33327-1303, USA

Rizzo, Rizzo (DJ)
c/o Len Evans *Project Publicity*
312 W 53rd St Ste 202
New York, NY 10019-5743, USA

Rizzo, Rob (Race Car Driver)
Rizzo Racing
700 Main St
East Greenwich, RI 02818-3541, USA

Rizzo, Todd (Athlete, Baseball Player)
7 Williamsburg Ct
Sewell, NJ 08080-3230, USA

Rizzo-Depardon, Patti (Golfer)
1008 SE 5th Ct
Ft Lauderdale, FL 33301-3004, USA

Rizzotti, Jennifer (Basketball Player, Coach)
University of Hartford
Athletic Dept
West Hartford, CT 06117, USA

Rizzs, Rick (Sportscaster)
4008 243rd Pi SE
Issaquah, WA 98029, USA

R. Keating, William (Congressman, Politician)
315 Cannon Hob
Washington, DC 20515-0101, USA

R. Labrador, Raul (Congressman, Politician)
1523 Longworth Hob
Washington, DC 20515-4003, USA

R. Langevin, James (Congressman, Politician)
109 Cannon Hob
Washington, DC 20515-3902, USA

Roa, Joe (Athlete, Baseball Player)
677 E Brickley Ave
Hazel Park, MI 48030-1270, USA

Roach, Andy (Athlete, Hockey Player)
PO Box 488
Mattawan, MI 49071-0488

Roach, Jason (Athlete, Baseball Player)
12295 SE Birkdale Run
Jupiter, FL 33469-1746, USA

Roach, Jay (Director, Producer, Writer)
c/o Staff Member *Everyman Pictures*
3000 Olympic Blvd Ste 1500
Santa Monica, CA 90404-5073, USA

Roach, John (Athlete, Football Player)
4101 San Carlos St
Dallas, TX 75205-2047, USA

Roach, Mel (Athlete, Baseball Player)
4131 Southaven Rd
Richmond, VA 23235-1026, USA

Roache, Linus (Actor)
c/o Staff Member *William Morris Endeavor (LA)*
9601 Wilshire Blvd
Beverly Hills, CA 90210-5213, USA

Roaches, Carl (Athlete, Football Player)
1314 Twining Oaks Ln
Missouri City, TX 77489-2110, USA

Roaf, William L (Willie) (Athlete, Football Player)
1900 E 38th Ave
Pine Bluff, AR 71601-7280, USA

Roan, Michael (Athlete, Football Player)
11275 Green Valley Rd
Sebastopol, CA 95472-9771, USA

Roan, Oscar (Athlete, Football Player)
9 Pringle Ln
Rockwall, TX 75087-8004, USA

Roark, Anastasia (Actor)
c/o Nicole Chabot *Re: Group*
815 Broadway St Ste 2
Venice, CA 90291-3407, USA

Roarke, Mike (Athlete, Baseball Player)
940 Quaker Ln Apt 2302
East Greenwich, RI 02818-5085, USA

Roath, Stephen D (Business Person)
Longs Drug Stores
141 N Civic Dr
Walnut Creek, CA 94596-3815, USA

Robach, Amy (Correspondent)
100 John St Ph 3402
New York, NY 10038-0073, USA

Robards, Jake (Actor)
c/o Staff Member *Don Buchwald & Associates (NY)*
10 E 44th St Frnt 1
New York, NY 10017-3654, USA

Robards, Sam (Actor)
Rigberg Roberts Rugolo
1180 S Beverly Dr Ste 601
Los Angeles, CA 90035-1158, USA

Robb, Annasophia (Actor)
c/o Alissa Vradenburg *Untitled Entertainment (LA)*
350 S Beverly Dr Ste 200
Beverly Hills, CA 90212-4819, USA

Robb, Charles (Politician)
612 Chain Bridge Rd
Mc Lean, VA 22101-1810, USA

Robb, Lynda Johnson (Politician)
612 Chain Bridge Rd
Mc Lean, VA 22101-1810, USA

Robb, Riddick (Athlete, Football Player)
101 Hearthstone Dr
Woodstock, GA 30189-5263, USA

Robbers on High Street (Music Group)
c/o Staff Member *Paradigm (Monterey)*
404 W Franklin St
Monterey, CA 93940-2303, USA

Robbie, Margot (Actor)
c/o Chris Huvane *Management 360*
9111 Wilshire Blvd
Beverly Hills, CA 90210-5508, USA

Robbie, Timothy J (Tim) (Football Executive)
Miami Dolphins
7500 SW 30th St
Davie, FL 33314-1020, USA

Robbins, Anthony (Tony) (Motivational Speaker, Writer)
Robbins Research International Inc
9888 Carroll Centre Rd Ste 100
San Diego, CA 92126-4581, USA

Robbins, Austin (Athlete, Football Player)
4627 Hilltop Ter SE
Washington, DC 20019-7837, USA

Robbins, Barret (Athlete, Football Player)
5151 Stallion Cir
Huntingtn Bch, CA 92649-3607, USA

Robbins, Brian (Director)
c/o Staff Member *Tollin/Robbins Management*
4130 Cahuenga Blvd Ste 305
Toluca Lake, CA 91602-2847, USA

Robbins, Bruce (Athlete, Baseball Player)
5504 W Shoreline Ter
Muncie, IN 47304-6095, USA

Robbins, Deanna (Actor)
630 N Keystone St
Burbank, CA 91506-1922, USA

Robbins, Doug (Athlete, Baseball Player, Olympic Athlete)
7655 W Randolph County Line
Williamsburg, IN 47393-9500, USA

Robbins, Jake (Athlete, Baseball Player)
14208 Castle Abbey Ln
Charlotte, NC 28277-1612, USA

Robbins, John (Writer)
c/o Staff Member *Red Wheel / Weiser /Conari*
65 Parker St Ste 7
Newburyport, MA 01950-4600, USA

Robbins, Kelly (Golfer)
1025 Lincoln Dr
Weidman, MI 48893-9365, USA

Robbins, Lizz (Model)
c/o Mike Esterman *Esterman.Com, LLC*
Prefers to be contacted via email
Baltimore, MD XXXXX, USA

Robbins, Randy (Athlete, Football Player)
1131 E Valle Vista Dr
Nogales, AZ 85621-1229, USA

Robbins, Tim (Actor, Director)
820 Nowita Pl
Venice, CA 90291, USA

Robbins, Tom (Writer)
PO Box 338
La Conner, WA 98257-0338, USA

Robbins, Tootie (Athlete, Football Player)
6712 W Shannon St
Chandler, AZ 85226-1669, USA

Robelot, Jane (Correspondent)
CBS-TV
51 W 52nd St
News Dept
New York, NY 10019-6119, USA

Roberge, Bert (Athlete, Baseball Player)
267 Sunderland Dr
Auburn, ME 04210-9232, USA

Roberson, Antoinette (Musician)
c/o Staff Member *Diva Central Inc*
7510 W Sunset Blvd Ste 1445
Los Angeles, CA 90046-3408, USA

Roberson, Chris (Athlete, Baseball Player)
10626 Liberty Bell Dr
Tampa, FL 33647-3656, USA

Roberson, Irvin (Bo) (Athlete, Football Player, Track Athlete)
820 N Raymond Ave Apt 47
Pasadena, CA 91103-3151, USA

Roberson, James (Athlete, Football Player)
417 Labarre Ct
Saint Johns, FL 32259-4024, USA

Roberson, James W (Cinematographer)
PO Box 121013
Big Bear Lake, CA 92315-8948, USA

Roberson, Kevin (Athlete, Baseball Player)
1565 E North Port Rd
Decatur, IL 62526-2823, USA

Roberson, Rick (Athlete, Basketball Player)
635 W West Ave
Fullerton, CA 92832-2120, USA

Roberson, Sid (Athlete, Baseball Player)
1005 Rio Lindo Dr
Jacksonville, FL 32207-5249, USA

Roberts, Alfredo (Athlete, Football Player)
20406 Donegal Ln
Strongsville, OH 44149-0960, USA

Roberts, Allene (Actor)
7703 Carlton Dr SW
Huntsville, AL 35802-2934, USA

Roberts, Bert C Jr (Business Person)
MCI WorldCom Inc
500 Clinton Pkwy
Clinton, MS 39056-4032, USA

Roberts, Bret (Actor)
c/o Scott Karp *The Syndicate*
10203 Santa Monica Blvd Fl 5
Los Angeles, CA 90067-6416, USA

Roberts, Brian (Athlete, Baseball Player)
4712 Higel Ave
Sarasota, FL 34242-1208, USA

Roberts, Brian L (Business Person)
Comcast
1500 Market St Fl 33E
Philadelphia, PA 19102-2131, USA

Roberts, Bruce (Musician, Songwriter, Writer)
c/o Staff Member *Gorfaine/Schwartz Agency Inc*
4111 W Alameda Ave Ste 509
Burbank, CA 91505-4171, USA

Roberts, Cokie (Correspondent, Journalist)
5315 Bradley Blvd
Bethesda, MD 20814-1244, USA

Roberts, Dale (Athlete, Baseball Player)
206 Berry Ave
Versailles, KY 40383-1457, USA

Roberts, Dallas (Actor)
c/o Marnie Briskin *Circle of Confusion (NY)*
8931 Ellis Ave
Los Angeles, CA 90034-3336, USA

Roberts, Danny (Reality Star)
c/o Staff Member *Heffner Management*
80 Vine St Apt 203
Seattle, WA 98121-1369, USA

Roberts, Dave (Athlete, Baseball Player)
6937 Laurel Valley Dr
Fort Worth, TX 76132-4461, USA

Roberts, Dave (Athlete, Baseball Player)
9705 Sam Bass Trl
Fort Worth, TX 76244-6092, USA

Roberts, Dave (Athlete, Baseball Player)
1208 Crestview Dr
Cardiff By The Sea, CA 92007-1400, USA

Roberts, Dave (Athlete, Baseball Player)
San Diego Padres
PO Box 122000
Attn Coaching Staff
San Diego, CA 92112-2000, USA

Roberts, David (Athlete, Hockey Player)
Telemus Capital Partners
Ann Arbor, MI 48104

Roberts, David (Dave) (Athlete, Track Athlete)
14310 SW 73rd Ave
Archer, FL 32618-2914, USA

Roberts, Doris (Actor)
6225 Quebec Dr
Los Angeles, CA 90068-2219, USA

Roberts, Doug (Athlete, Hockey Player)
PO Box 1011
Old Lyme, CT 06371-0999, USA

Roberts, Emma (Actor)
c/o David Sweeney *Sweeney Entertainment*
6253 Hollywood Blvd Apt 201
Los Angeles, CA 90028-8248, USA

Roberts, Eric (Actor)
c/o Mark Teitelbaum *Teitelbaum Artists Group*
8840 Wilshire Blvd Fl 3
Beverly Hills, CA 90211-2606, USA

Roberts, Fred (Athlete, Basketball Player)
463 Knight Cir
Alpine, UT 84004-1259, USA

Roberts, Gary (Athlete, Hockey Player)
12348 NW 69th Ct
Parkland, FL 33076-3334

Roberts, Gordie (Athlete, Hockey Player)
3965 Yorktown Ln N
Minneapolis, MN 55441-1427, USA

Roberts, Grant (Athlete, Baseball Player)
1299 Vista Captain Dr
El Cajon, CA 92020, USA

Roberts, Jake (Actor, Writer)
PO Box 3859
Stamford, CT 06905

Roberts, James A (Jim) (Athlete, Coach, Hockey Player)
137 Ridgecrest Dr
Chesterfield, MO 63017-2653

Roberts, J D (Athlete, Football Coach, Football Player)
6708 Trevi Ct
Oklahoma City, OK 73116-2604, USA

Roberts, Joe (Athlete, Basketball Player)
4100 Redwood Rd Ste 10
Oakland, CA 94619-2363, USA

Roberts, John D (J D) (Athlete, Coach, Football Player)
6708 Trevi Ct
Oklahoma City, OK 73116-2604, USA

Roberts, Julia (Actor)
c/o Franklin Latt *Creative Artists Agency (CAA-LA)*
2000 Avenue of the Stars Ste 100
Los Angeles, CA 90067-4705, USA

Roberts, Julie (Musician)
c/o Staff Member *Creative Artists Agency (CAA-LA)*
2000 Avenue of the Stars Ste 100
Los Angeles, CA 90067-4705, USA

Roberts, Larry (Race Car Driver)
MR Motorsports
PO Box 194
Novi, MI 48376-0194, USA

Roberts, Leon (Athlete, Baseball Player)
4711 Chapel Springs Ct
Arlington, TX 76017-1204, USA

Roberts, Leonard (Actor)
c/o Lena Roklin *Luber Roklin Management*
5815 W Sunset Blvd Ste 206
Los Angeles, CA 90028-6481, USA

Roberts, Leonard (Business Person)
Tandy Corp
300 Trinity Campus Cir
Fort Worth, TX 76102-1964, USA

Roberts, Leonard (Athlete, Baseball Player)
1027 Waterford Dr
Dallas, TX 75218-2845, USA

Roberts, Leon (Bip) (Athlete, Baseball Player)
3569 Rosincress Dr
San Ramon, CA 94582-5078, USA

Roberts, Loren (Athlete, Golfer)
8429 Orchard Hill Dr
Germantown, TN 38138-6297, USA

Roberts, Louie
2401 12th Ave S
Nashville, TN 37204-2415

Roberts, Lynn
42 Vespers Way
Okatie, SC 29909-6216, USA

Roberts, Marcus (Musician)
Columbia Artists Mgmt Inc
165 W 57th St
New York, NY 10019-2201, USA

Roberts, Marvin (Athlete, Basketball Player)
21 Shadow Mountain Dr
Logan, UT 84321-6757, USA

Roberts, Mica (Musician)
c/o Curt Motley *Paradigm (Nashville)*
124 12th Ave S Ste 410
Nashville, TN 37203-3170, USA

Roberts, Michael D (Actor)
c/o Staff Member *Karen Renna & Associates*
PO Box 4227
Burbank, CA 91503-4227, USA

Roberts, Nora (Writer)
19239 Burnside Bridge Rd
Keedysville, MD 21756-1603, USA

Roberts, Pat (Politician)
2203 Whiteoaks Dr
Alexandria, VA 22306-2436, USA

Roberts, Ralph J (Business Person)
Comcast Corp
1500 Market St Fl 11E
Philadelphia, PA 19102-2107, USA

Roberts, Randy (Actor)
14220 Winterset Dr
Greenwell Springs, LA 70739-3275, USA

Roberts, Randy (Actor)
Ryan Artists, Inc
239 NW 13th Ave Ste 215
C/O Mary Dangerfield
Portland, OR 97209-2927, USA

Roberts, Rick
9150 Wilshire Blvd Ste 350
Beverly Hills, CA 90212-3453

Roberts, Robin (Sportscaster, Television Host)
c/o Staff Member *Good Morning America (NY)*
147 Columbus Ave Fl 6
Abc
New York, NY 10023-6503, USA

Roberts, Rodney (Race Car Driver)
MR Motorsports
PO Box 92826
Lakeland, FL 33804-2826, USA

Roberts, Ryan (Athlete, Baseball Player)
6017 Avalon St
North Richland Hills, TX 76180-5593, USA

Roberts, Shawn (Actor)
c/o Staff Member *Christopher Wright Management*
3207 Winnie Dr
Los Angeles, CA 90068-1439, USA

Roberts, Stanley (Athlete, Basketball Player)
1192 Congaree Rd
Hopkins, SC 29061-9704, USA

Roberts, Steven
5315 Bradley Blvd
Bethesda, MD 20814-1244

Roberts, Tanya (Actor)
c/o Jay Schwartz *Jay D Schwartz & Associates*
6767 Forest Lawn Dr Ste 211
Los Angeles, CA 90068-1051, USA

Roberts, Thomas (Journalist, Television Host)
c/o Staff Member *MSNBC*
30 Rockefeller Plz Fl 31
New York, NY 10112-3199, USA

Roberts, Tiffany (Athlete, Olympic Athlete, Soccer Player)
2772 Ascot Dr
San Ramon, CA 94583-2504, USA

Roberts, Tim (Athlete, Football Player)
3930 Minnow Rd
Rex, GA 30273-1536, USA

Roberts, Tony (Actor)
970 Park Ave # 8N
New York, NY 10028-0324, USA

Roberts, Trish (Athlete, Basketball Player, Olympic Athlete)
218 Carver Dr
Monroe, GA 30655-1814, USA

Roberts, Vicki (Actor)
c/o Arthur Andelson *Kismet Talent Agency*
3435 Ocean Park Blvd Ste 107
Santa Monica, CA 90405-3320, USA

Roberts, Walter (Athlete, Football Player)
268 Kenbrook Cir
San Jose, CA 95111-3262, USA

Roberts, William H (Athlete, Football Player)
18520 NW 67th Ave Apt 141
Hialeah, FL 33015-3302, USA

Roberts, Willie (Athlete, Baseball Player)
11476 Emuness Rd
Jacksonville, FL 32218, USA

Roberts, Willis (Athlete, Baseball Player)
11478 Vera Dr
Jacksonville, FL 32218-4064, USA

Roberts, Xavier (Business Person, Designer)
PO Box 1438
Cleveland, GA 30528-0027, USA

Robertson, Alvin (Athlete, Basketball Player, Olympic Athlete)
6515 Amber Oak
San Antonio, TX 78249-1586, USA

Robertson, Andre (Athlete, Baseball Player)
2229 Cross Ln
Orange, TX 77630-2561, USA

Robertson, Bob (Athlete, Baseball Player)
10015 Shinnamon Dr SW
Cumberland, MD 21502-6149, USA

Robertson, Bob (Athlete, Football Player)
411 Belle Monti Ct
Aptos, CA 95003-5208, USA

Robertson, Brittany (Britt) (Actor)
c/o Francis Okwu *Zero Gravity Management*
6363 Wilshire Blvd Ste 300
Los Angeles, CA 90048-5729, USA

Robertson, Connor (Athlete, Baseball Player)
2201 Champions Cir
Franklin, TN 37064-2870, USA

Robertson, Daryl (Athlete, Baseball Player)
52 W Princeton Dr
Midvale, UT 84047-7514, USA

Robertson, David (Athlete, Baseball Player)
c/o Team Member *New York Yankees*
Yankee Stadium
161st St & River Ave
Bronx, NY 10451, USA

Robertson, Davis (Dancer)
Joffrey Ballet
70 E Lake St Ste 1300
Chicago, IL 60601-7458, USA

Robertson, DeWayne (Athlete, Football Player)
1000 Fulton Ave
Hempstead, NY 11550-1030, USA

Robertson, Don (Athlete, Baseball Player)
5715 W Monte Vista Rd
Phoenix, AZ 85035-3626, USA

Robertson, Geordie (Athlete, Hockey Player)
1 Scarborough Park
Rochester, NY 14625-1363

Robertson, Gordon (Religious Leader, Television Host)
c/o 700 Club *Christian Broadcasting Network (CBN)*
977 Centerville Tpke # 317
Virginia Beach, VA 23463-1001, USA

Robertson, Isiah (Athlete, Football Player)
PO Box 1405
Mabank, TX 75147-1405, USA

Robertson, Jason (Jase) (Reality Star)
Duck Commander
117 Kings Ln
West Monroe, LA 71292-9430, USA

Robertson, Jenny (Actor)
Shelter Entertainment
9255 W Sunset Blvd Ste 1010
West Hollywood, CA 90069-3307, USA

Robertson, Jerry (Race Car Driver)
Quick Time Motorsports
124 N 325 W # 58-6
Hurricane, UT 84737-2041, USA

Robertson, Jim (Athlete, Baseball Player)
11315 Trilogy Pkwy NE Apt 110
Redmond, WA 98053-8900, USA

Robertson, Kathleen (Actor)
c/o Staff Member *Jeff Morrone Entertainment*
9350 Wilshire Blvd Ste 224
Beverly Hills, CA 90212-3204, USA

Robertson, Kimmy (Actor)
Commercials Unlimited
8383 Wilshire Blvd Ste 850
Beverly Hills, CA 90211-2443, USA

Robertson, Korie
The Duck Commander
104 Yellowood Dr
West Monroe, LA 71291-9450, USA

Robertson, Lisa
1365 Enterprise Dr
West Chester, PA 19380-5959

Robertson, Marcus A (Athlete, Football Player)
3218 Cypress Point Dr
Missouri City, TX 77459-3634, USA

Robertson, Mike (Athlete, Baseball Player)
2626 E Viking Rd
Las Vegas, NV 89121-4114, USA

Robertson, Nate (Athlete, Baseball Player)
7918 W 53rd St N
Maize, KS 67101-9185, USA

Robertson, Oscar (Athlete, Basketball Player, Olympic Athlete)
621 Tusculum Ave
Cincinnati, OH 45226-1771, USA

Robertson, Pat (Religious Leader, Television Host)
PO Box 64303
Virginia Beach, VA 23467-4303, USA

Robertson, Phil (Reality Star)
Duck Commander
117 Kings Ln
West Monroe, LA 71292-9430, USA

Robertson, Rich (Athlete, Baseball Player)
32202 Sandwedge Dr
Waller, TX 77484-9017, USA

Robertson, Rich (Athlete, Baseball Player)
1201 Crescent Ter
Sunnyvale, CA 94087-2855, USA

Robertson, Robbie (Musician)
c/o Staff Member *Special Artists Agency*
9200 W Sunset Blvd Ste 410
West Hollywood, CA 90069-3506, USA

Robertson, Robbie (Musician, Songwriter, Writer)
323 14th St
Santa Monica, CA 90402-2113, USA

Robertson, Si (Reality Star)
335 Philpot Rd
West Monroe, LA 71292-2649, USA

Robertson, Willie (Business Person, Reality Star)
Duck Commander
117 Kings Ln
West Monroe, LA 71292-9430, USA

Robes, Ernest C (Bill) (Skier)
3 Mile Rd
Etna, NH 03750, USA

Robey, Nickell (Athlete, Football Player)
c/o Kelli Masters *Kelli Masters Management*
100 N Broadway Ste 1700
Oklahoma City, OK 73102-9211, USA

Robey, Rick (Athlete, Basketball Player)
330 Lanai Ct
Louisville, KY 40245-3976, USA

Robidas, Stephane (Athlete, Hockey Player)
3216 Wellshire Ct
Plano, TX 75093-3458

Robidoux, Billy Joe (Athlete, Baseball Player)
2 King George Dr
Ware, MA 01082-9799, USA

Robie, Jarod (Race Car Driver)
Robie Racing
232 Chester Rd
Candia, NH 03034-2607, USA

Robins, Oliver (Actor, Director)
c/o Dawn Goodson *Genius Talent Management*
342 1/2 N Genesee Ave
Los Angeles, CA 90036-2261, USA

Robinson, Aldrick (Athlete, Football Player)
c/o Jordan Woy *Willis and Woy Management*
3030 Olive St Ste 520
Dallas, TX 75219-7629, USA

Robinson, Alexia
3500 W Olive Ave Ste 920
Burbank, CA 91505-5514

Robinson, Allen (Athlete, Football Player)
c/o Eugene Parker *Maximum Sports Management*
6435 W Jefferson Blvd # 197
Fort Wayne, IN 46804-6203, USA

Robinson, Andrea (Actor)
c/o Alan Saffron *Saffron Management*
9171 Wilshire Blvd Ste 441
Beverly Hills, CA 90210-5516, USA

Robinson, Andrew (Actor)
2671 Byron Pl
Los Angeles, CA 90046-1021, USA

Robinson, Ann (Actor)
1357 Elysian Park Dr
Los Angeles, CA 90026-3407, USA

Robinson, Bo (Athlete, Football Player)
6311 Barberry Ave
Denton, TX 76208-5895, USA

Robinson, Brooks (Athlete, Baseball Player)
PO Box 1168
Baltimore, MD 21203-1168, USA

Robinson, Bruce (Athlete, Baseball Player)
1310 Dellcrest Ln
La Jolla, CA 92037-5207, USA

Robinson, Bruce (Director)
c/o Rand Holston *Paradigm (LA)*
2000 Avenue of the Stars
Los Angeles, CA 90067-4700, USA

Robinson, Bumper (Actor)
c/o David Altman *Altman Greenfield & Selvaggi*
200 Park Ave S Ste 8
New York, NY 10003-1503, United States

Robinson, Charles
10000 Santa Monica Blvd # 305
Los Angeles, CA 90067

Robinson, Charles Knox
10637 Burbank Blvd
North Hollywood, CA 91601-2512

Robinson, Chip (Race Car Driver)
PO Box 476
Oldwick, NJ 08858-0476, USA

Robinson, Chris (Director)
c/o Peter Safran *The Safran Company*
8748 Holloway Dr
West Hollywood, CA 90069-2327, USA

Robinson, Chris (Musician)
921 24th St
Santa Monica, CA 90403-2105, USA

Robinson, Christina (Actor)
c/o Bill Perlman *Perlman Management Group*
PO Box 2939
Beverly Hills, CA 90213-2939, USA

Robinson, Claire (Chef)
c/o Norman Aladjem *Levity Entertainment Group (LEG)*
6701 Center Dr W Fl 11
Los Angeles, CA 90045-1535, USA

Robinson, Clarence (Arnie) (Athlete, Track Athlete)
2904 Ocean View Blvd
San Diego, CA 92113-1336, USA

Robinson, Cliff (Athlete, Basketball Player)
98 S Bardsbrook Cir
Spring, TX 77382-2858, USA

Robinson, Clifford (Athlete, Basketball Player)
702 Sandia Pl
Franklin Lakes, NJ 07417-2120, USA

Robinson, Craig (Actor)
c/o Mark Schulman *3 Arts Entertainment (LA)*
9460 Wilshire Blvd Fl 7
Beverly Hills, CA 90212-2713, USA

Robinson, Craig (Athlete, Baseball Player)
648 Picketts Mill Dr
Shreveport, LA 71115-3862, USA

Robinson, Daniel (Baseball Player)
10889 Dauphine St
Shreveport, LA 71106-8524, USA

Robinson, Dave (Athlete, Baseball Player)
6140 Camino Del Rincon
San Diego, CA 92120-3112, USA

Robinson, David (Athlete, Basketball Player)
PO Box 691207
San Antonio, TX 78269-1207, USA

Robinson, David M (Athlete, Basketball Player)
Ship Mates, Inc.
24165 Ih-I O W
San Antonio, TX 78257, USA

Robinson, Dawn (Actor, Musician)
c/o Jonathan Clardy *CN Publicity*
9107 Wilshire Blvd Ste 450
Beverly Hills, CA 90210-5535, USA

Robinson, Denard (Athlete, Football Player)
c/o Michael Perrett *SportsTrust Advisors (GA)*
3340 Peachtree Rd NE Fl 16
Atlanta, GA 30326-1000, USA

Robinson, Dewey (Athlete, Baseball Player)
1388 Cottonwood Trl
Sarasota, FL 34232-3437, USA

Robinson, Don (Athlete, Baseball Player)
1215 86th Ct NW
Bradenton, FL 34209-9307, USA

Robinson, Earl (Athlete, Baseball Player)
1675 7th St Unit 24121
Oakland, CA 94623-6037, USA

Robinson, Eddie (Athlete, Baseball Player)
6104 Cholla Dr
Fort Worth, TX 76112-1105, USA

Robinson, Elizabeth
12706 E Pacific Cir # 202
Aurora, CO 80014

Robinson, Emily (Musician)
c/o Staff Member *Creative Artists Agency (CAA-LA)*
2000 Avenue of the Stars Ste 100
Los Angeles, CA 90067-4705, USA

Robinson, Emily Erwin (Athlete, Football Player)
4400 Falcon Pkwy
Flowery Branch, GA 30542-3176, USA

Robinson, Fatima
Fatima
8306 Wilshire Blvd PMB 833
Beverly Hills, CA 90211-2304, USA

Robinson, Floyd (Athlete, Baseball Player)
PO Box 152419
San Diego, CA 92195-2419, USA

Robinson, Frank (Athlete, Baseball Player, Coach)
15557 Aqua Verde Dr
Los Angeles, CA 90077-1503, USA

Robinson, Frank (Athlete, Football Player)
15401 E Wyoming Dr Unit C
Aurora, CO 80017-4727, USA

Robinson, Gerald (Athlete, Football Player)
4708 Scarborough Pl
Stone Mountain, GA 30087-4104, USA

Robinson, Gerell (Athlete, Football Player)
c/o Michael McCartney *Priority Sports & Entertainment - Chicago*
312 N La Salle
Suite 650
Chicago, IL 60610, USA

Robinson, Glenn (Basketball Player, Coach)
Franklin & Marshall College
Athletic Dept
Lancaster, PA 17604, USA

Robinson, Jackie (Athlete, Basketball Player)
10595 Riva Grande Ct
Las Vegas, NV 89135-2455, USA

Robinson, Jacob (Baseball Player)
Chicago American Giants
1300 Giddings Ave SE
Grand Rapids, MI 49506-3216, USA

Robinson, James (Baseball Player)
Philadelphia Stars
65 W 96th St Apt 22G
New York, NY 10025-6533, USA

Robinson, Janice (Musician)
c/o Staff Member *Diva Central Inc*
7510 W Sunset Blvd Ste 1445
Los Angeles, CA 90046-3408, USA

Robinson, Jay (Actor)
1610 Post St Ste 210
San Francisco, CA 94115-3600, USA

Robinson, Jeff (Athlete, Baseball Player)
5317 W 158th Pl
Overland Park, KS 66224-3616, USA

Robinson, Jeff (Athlete, Baseball Player)
27 Weber Ln
Trabuco Canyon, CA 92679-5235, USA

Robinson, Jerry (Athlete, Football Player)
1408 Fairoaks Ct
Merced, CA 95340-2341, USA

Robinson, John A (Athlete, Coach, Football Coach, Football Player)
6991 Goldstone Rd
Carlsbad, CA 92009-1711, USA

Robinson, Johnny N (Athlete, Football Player)
3209 S Grand St
Monroe, LA 71202-5225, USA

Robinson, Josh (Athlete, Football Player)
c/o Drew Rosenhaus *Rosenhaus Sports Representation*
6400 Allison Rd
Miami Beach, FL 33141-4540, USA

Robinson, Julie Anne (Director)
c/o Leslie Maskin *United Talent Agency (UTA-LA)*
9336 Civic Center Dr
Beverly Hills, CA 90210-3604, USA

Robinson, Keith (Actor)
c/o Staff Member *Stone Manners Salners Agency (LA)*
6100 Wilshire Blvd Ste 1500
Los Angeles, CA 90048-5110, USA

Robinson, Keith (Musician)
c/o Staff Member *Paradigm (NY)*
360 Park Ave S Fl 16
New York, NY 10010-1716, USA

Robinson, Kenneth (Government Official)
c/o Staff Member *Washington Speakers Bureau*
1663 Prince St
Alexandria, VA 22314-2818, USA

Robinson, Kerry (Athlete, Baseball Player)
133 Vlasis Dr
Ballwin, MO 63011-3055, USA

Robinson, Khiry (Athlete, Football Player)
c/o Adam Heller *Vantage Management Group*
518 Reamer Dr
Carnegie, PA 15106-1845, USA

Robinson, Kim Stanley (Writer)
c/o Vince Gerardis *Grok! Studio*
Prefers to be contacted via email or telephone
Los Angeles, CA, USA

Robinson, Koren (Athlete, Football Player)
12 Henry Ave
Belmont, NC 28012-3930, USA

Robinson, Larry (Athlete, Hockey Player)
New Jersey Devils
165 Mulberry St
Newark, NJ 07102-3607

Robinson, Larry (Athlete, Coach, Hockey Player)
10709 Winding Stream Way
Bradenton, FL 34212-5255

Robinson, Laura (Actor)
Henderson/Hogan
8285 W Sunset Blvd Ste 1
West Hollywood, CA 90046-2420, USA

Robinson, Leon (Leon) (Actor, Producer)
c/o Leo Bozzuto *Inphenate*
9701 Wilshire Blvd Fl 10
Beverly Hills, CA 90212-2010, USA

Robinson, Leroy
1183 Broad Rd
Tignall, GA 30668-1205, USA

Robinson, Marcus (Athlete, Football Player)
PO Box 1924
Fort Valley, GA 31030-1924, USA

Robinson, Mark (Athlete, Football Player)
303 Pennsylvania Ave
Palm Harbor, FL 34683-5222, USA

Robinson, Marnia (Writer)
c/o Staff Member *North Atlantic Books*
2526 Martin Luther King Jr Way
Berkeley, CA 94704-2607, USA

Robinson, Matt (Athlete, Football Player)
12374 Mandarin Rd
Jacksonville, FL 32223-1892, USA

Robinson, Nichole (Actor)
c/o Tiffany Kuzon *Evolution Entertainment (LA)*
901 N Highland Ave
Los Angeles, CA 90038-2412, USA

Robinson, Oliver (Athlete, Basketball Player)
9640 Eastpointe Cir
Birmingham, AL 35217-5202, USA

Robinson, Patrick (Athlete, Football Player)
Cincinnati Bengals
3875 N Advantage Way Dr Apt 104
Memphis, TN 38128-7239, USA

Robinson, Patrick (Designer, Fashion Designer)
Gap
1 Harrison St Fl 4
San Francisco, CA 94105-6131, USA

Robinson, Paul (Athlete, Football Player)
1303 W 26th St
Safford, AZ 85546-3721, USA

Robinson, Rachel (Baseball Player)
The Jackie Robinson Foundation
75 Varick St Frnt 2
New York, NY 10013-1947

Robinson, Rafael (Athlete, Football Player)
6203 Wynbrook Dr
Randolph, NJ 07869-1287, USA

Robinson, Randall
1744 R St NW
Washington, DC 20009-2410

Robinson, Rich (Musician)
c/o Staff Member *Paradigm (Monterey)*
404 W Franklin St
Monterey, CA 93940-2303, USA

Robinson, Richard D (Dave) (Athlete, Football Player)
212 Kenwood Ave
Akron, OH 44313-6309, USA

Robinson, Rob (Athlete, Hockey Player)
23466 Greening Dr
Novi, MI 48375-3225

Robinson, Robinson (Director)
c/o Peter Safran *The Safran Company*
8748 Holloway Dr
West Hollywood, CA 90069-2327, USA

Robinson, Ron (Athlete, Baseball Player)
3128 E Race Ave
Visalia, CA 93292-6858, USA

Robinson, Ronnie (Athlete, Basketball Player)
4169 S Germantown Rd
Memphis, TN 38125-2624, USA

Robinson, Rumeal (Athlete, Basketball Player)
3645 Brushy Wood Dr
Loganville, GA 30052-5481, USA

Robinson, Sam (Athlete, Basketball Player)
130 W Harcourt St
Long Beach, CA 90805-2124, USA

Robinson, Sammy (Baseball Player)
Detroit Stars
503 Umatilla St SE
Grand Rapids, MI 49507-1218, USA

Robinson, Sandra Dee (Actor)
c/o Vincent Cirrincione *Vincent Cirrincione Associates*
1516 N Fairfax Ave
Los Angeles, CA 90046-2608, USA

Robinson, Shaun (Correspondent)
c/o Susan Haber *Haber Entertainment*
434 S Canon Dr Apt 204
Beverly Hills, CA 90212-4501, USA

Robinson, Shawna (Race Car Driver)
Shawna Robinson Racing
PO Box 1858
New Smyrna Beach, FL 32170-1858, USA

Robinson, Shelton (Athlete, Football Player)
18725 20th Dr SE
Bothell, WA 98012-8721, USA

Robinson, Stephen K (Astronaut)
286 Cottage Cir
Davis, CA 95616-4674, USA

Robinson, Ted (Sportscaster)
c/o Lou Oppenheim *Headline Media Management*
888 7th Ave Ste 503
New York, NY 10106-0501, USA

Robinson, Trayvon (Athlete, Baseball Player)
1455 W 97th St
Los Angeles, CA 90047-3934, USA

Robinson, V Gene (Religious Leader)
Saint Paul's Church
21 Centre St
Concord, NH 03301-6301, USA

Robinson, Wayne (Athlete, Football Player)
9550 Campo Rd Apt 45.
Spring Valley, CA 91977-1244, USA

Robinson, Wendy Raquel (Actor)
c/o Patricia (Patty) Woo *Patty Woo Management*
8906 W Olympic Blvd
Beverly Hills, CA 90211-3550, USA

Robinson, Wilbert (Athlete, Basketball Player)
2124 Bedell Rd
Grand Island, NY 14072-1652, USA

Robinson, William (Smokey) (Musician, Producer, Songwriter, Writer)
Smokey Robinson Foundation
385 S Lemon Ave Ste E181
Walnut, CA 91789-2727, USA

Robinson, Zuleikha (Actor)
c/o Daniel Spilo *Industry Entertainment*
955 Carrillo Dr Ste 300
Los Angeles, CA 90048-5400, USA

Robinson-Peete, Holly (Actor)
5056 Chicopee Ave
Encino, CA 91316-2508, USA

Robisch, Dave (Athlete, Basketball Player)
1401 Guemes Ct
Springfield, IL 62702-6400, USA

Robiskie, Terry (Athlete, Football Player)
40 River Mountain Ln
Chagrin Falls, OH 44022-2064, USA

Robison, Br5an (Athlete, Football Player)
c/o W Vann McElroy *Select Sports Group*
2700 Post Oak Blvd Ste 1450
Houston, TX 77056-5785, USA

Robison, Bruce (Musician, Songwriter, Writer)
Artists Envoy Agency
1016 16th Ave S Apt 101
Nashville, TN 37212-2315, USA

Robison, Charlie (Musician, Songwriter)
c/o Staff Member *Paradigm (Monterey)*
404 W Franklin St
Monterey, CA 93940-2303, USA

Robison, Paula (Musician)
18 Allison Ave
Staten Island, NY 10306-2806, USA

Robison, Tommy (Athlete, Football Player)
711 Biscayne Dr
Mansfield, TX 76063-3236, USA

Robitaille, Luc (Athlete, Hockey Player)
Los Angeles Kings
1111 S Figueroa St Ste 3100
Los Angeles, CA 90015-1333

Robitaille, Luc (Athlete, Hockey Player)
370 25th St
Santa Monica, CA 90402-2522

Robitaille, Mike (Athlete, Hockey Player)
Buffalo Sabres
1 Seymour H Knox III Plz Ste 1
Buffalo, NY 14203-3096

Robl, Harold (Athlete, Football Player)
W1089 County Road C
Gleason, WI 54435-9472, USA

Robles, Mike (Producer)
ICM
8942 Wilshire Blvd
Beverly Hills, CA 90211-1908

Robson, Tom (Athlete, Baseball Player)
8902 E Hercules Ct
Sun Lakes, AZ 85248-9005, USA

Robson, Wade (Dancer)
c/o Andrew Jacobs *McDonald/Selznick Assoc (MSA)*
1611A N El Centro Ave
Los Angeles, CA 90028, USA

Robuck, Nicolas (Nic) (Actor)
c/o Margot Menzel *Evolution Entertainment (LA)*
901 N Highland Ave
Los Angeles, CA 90038-2412, USA

Roby, Bradley (Athlete, Football Player)
c/o Michael Perrett *SportsTrust Advisors (GA)*
3340 Peachtree Rd NE Fl 16
Atlanta, GA 30326-1000, USA

Roby, Courtney (Athlete, Football Player)
c/o Peter Schaffer *All Pro Sports and Entertainment*
36 Steele St Ste 100
Denver, CO 80206-5709, USA

Roby, Martha (Congressman, Politician)
414 Cannon Hob
Washington, DC 20515-1801, USA

Rocca, Constantino (Golfer)
Golf Products International
5719 Lake Lindero Dr
Agoura Hills, CA 91301-1444, USA

Rocca, Costentino (Golfer)
Golf Projects International
5719 Lake Lindero Dr
Agoura Hills, CA 91301-1444, USA

Rocca, Mo (Correspondent)
c/o Don Epstein *Greater Talent Network Inc*
437 5th Ave Ste 8A
New York, NY 10016-2205, USA

Rocca, Peter (Swimmer)
534 Hazel Ave
San Bruno, CA 94066-4228, USA

Rocco, Alex (Actor)
c/o Staff Member *Bresler Kelly & Associates*
11500 W Olympic Blvd Ste 510
Los Angeles, CA 90064-1527, USA

Rocha, Coco (Musician)
c/o Christina Neuman *Full Picture Management (NYC)*
915 Broadway Fl 20
New York, NY 10010-7131, USA

Rocha, Kali (Actor)
c/o Katie Rhodes *Untitled Entertainment (LA)*
350 S Beverly Dr Ste 200
Beverly Hills, CA 90212-4819, USA

Roche, Alden (Athlete, Football Player)
1082 Farragut St
New Orleans, LA 70114-2810, USA

Roche, Brian (Athlete, Football Player)
1358 Oak Tree Cir
Chino Hills, CA 91709-2231, USA

Roche, John (Athlete, Basketball Player)
191 Clayton Ln Unit 303
Denver, CO 80206-5679, USA

Roche, Sebastian (Actor)
c/o Mary Ellen Mulcahy *Framework Entertainment (LA)*
9057 Nemo St Ste C
West Hollywood, CA 90069-5511, USA

Rochefort, Normand (Athlete, Hockey Player)
1530 Burgos Dr
Sarasota, FL 34238-2706

Rochester, Paul (Athlete, Football Player)
218 Evans Dr
Jacksonville Beach, FL 32250-2631, USA

Rochford, Mike (Athlete, Baseball Player)
926 N 0 St
Lake Worth, FL 33460, USA

Rochon, Debbie (Actor)
PO Box 1299
New York, NY 10009-8958

Rochon, Frank (Athlete, Hockey Player)
PO Box 212
Lake Harmony, PA 18624-0212, USA

Rochon, Lela (Actor)
3332 Clerendon Rd
Beverly Hills, CA 90210-1059, USA

Rock (Actor, Wrestler)
World Wrestling Entertainment
1241 E Main St
Titan Towers
Stamford, CT 06902-3520, USA

Rock, Angela (Athlete, Volleyball Player)
University of California - SB
Athletic Dept
1210 Cheadle Hall
Santa Barbara, CA 93106-0001, USA

Rock, Chris (Actor, Comedian, Director, Producer)
64 Margo Way
Alpine, NJ 07620, USA

Rock, Pete
Reach Global
3500 Rose Crest Ln
Fairfax, VA 22033-1635, USA

Rock, Tony (Comedian)
c/o Staff Member *New Wave Entertainment (LA)*
2660 W Olive Ave
Burbank, CA 91505-4525, USA

Rock, Walt (Athlete, Football Player)
1030 Highams Ct
Woodbridge, VA 22191-1445, USA

Rock City (Music Group, Musician)
c/o Noel Palm *Element Talent Agency*
120 S Vignes St Apt 202
Los Angeles, CA 90012-4336, USA

Rockefeller, Jay (Politician, Senator)
531 Hart Senate Office Building
Washington, DC 20510-0001, USA

Rockefeller, Margaretta (Happy)
(Politician)
630 Bedford Rd
Tarrytown, NY 10591-1202, USA

Rockefeller, Sharon Percy
1940 Shepherd St NW
Washington, DC 20011

Rocker, David (Athlete, Football Player)
3833 Seton Hall Dr
Decatur, GA 30034-5540, USA

Rocker, John (Athlete, Baseball Player)
1223 Manor Oaks Ct
Atlanta, GA 30338-2756, USA

Rockett, Pat (Athlete, Baseball Player)
17107 Eagle Hollow Dr
San Antonio, TX 78248-1553, USA

Rockett, Rikki (Musician)
c/o Staff Member *HK Management (LA)*
10866 Wilshire Blvd Ste 200
Los Angeles, CA 90024-4350, USA

Rockford, Jim (Athlete, Football Player)
1829 Camden St
Springfield, IL 62702-3201, USA

Rockwell, Martha (Coach, Skier)
Dartmouth College
PO Box 9
Hanover, NH 03755-0009, USA

Rockwell, Nancy (Athlete, Baseball Player)
54658 County Road 101
Elkhart, IN 46514-8967, USA

Rockwell, Robert
18428 Coastline Dr
Malibu, CA 90265-5707

Rockwell, Sam (Actor)
c/o Liz Mahoney *ID Public Relations (LA)*
7060 Hollywood Blvd Fl 8th
Los Angeles, CA 90028-6021, USA

Rocky, ASAP (Musician)
c/o Theola Borden *RCA Records (NY)*
550 Madison Ave Fl 6
New York, NY 10022-3211, USA

Rodan, Jay (Actor)
c/o Staff Member *William Morris Endeavor (LA)*
9601 Wilshire Blvd
Beverly Hills, CA 90210-5213, USA

Rodas, Rich (Athlete, Baseball Player)
6877 Bergano Pl
Rancho Cucamonga, CA 91701-8606, USA

Roday, James (Actor, Writer)
16-20 W 19th St # 8D
New York, NY 10011, USA

Rodd, Marcia (Actor)
11738 Moorpark St Apt C
Studio City, CA 91604-2116, USA

Roddick, Andy (Athlete, Tennis Player)
9709 Angelwylde Dr
Austin, TX 78733-6513, USA

Roden, Holland (Actor)
c/o Heather Nunn *Anonymous Content (LA)*
3532 Hayden Ave
Culver City, CA 90232-2413, USA

Rodenhauser, Mark (Athlete, Football Player)
1451 Charlotte Hwy
York, SC 29745-8947, USA

Rodenhiser, Dick (Athlete, Hockey Player, Olympic Athlete)
186 State St
Framingham, MA 01702-2462, USA

Roder, Mirro (Athlete, Football Player)
181 Herrick Rd
Riverside, IL 60546-2045, USA

Roderick, Brande (Actor, Model)
c/o Shannon Barr *Rogers & Cowan PR (LA)*
8687 Melrose Ave Ste 7
West Hollywood, CA 90069-5721, USA

Rodgers, Aaron (Athlete, Football Player)
2360 Crown Pointe Blvd
Suamico, WI 54173-8083, USA

Rodgers, Bill (Athlete, Olympic Athlete, Track Athlete)
Bill Rodgers Running Center 1 N Market St Ste 353
Boston, MA 02109, USA

Rodgers, Del (Athlete, Football Player)
3112 Yosemite Park Way
Elk Grove, CA 95758-4687, USA

Rodgers, Derrick (Athlete, Football Player)
15222 SW 52nd St
Miramar, FL 33027-3691, USA

Rodgers, Jimmie (Musician)
42230 Sandy Bay Rd
Bermuda Dunes, CA 92203-1394, USA

Rodgers, Jimmy (Basketball Coach, Coach)
4995 Marsh Turtle Trl Unit 101
Estero, FL 33928-3943, USA

Rodgers, Johnny (Athlete, Football Player, Heisman Trophy Winner)
PO Box 11172
Omaha, NE 68111-0172, USA

Rodgers, Marion Elizabeth (Writer)
c/o Staff Member *Library of America, The*
14 E 60th St Ste 1101
New York, NY 10022-7115, USA

Rodgers, Michael (Actor)
c/o Adam Levine *Levine Okwu Erickson Management*
2126 N Commonwealth Ave
Los Angeles, CA 90027-2118, USA

Rodgers, Nile (Musician)
9 Covlee Dr
Westport, CT 06880-6406, USA

Rodgers, Phil (Golfer)
Eddle Elias Enterprises
4067 N Shore Dr
Akron, OH 44333-8305, USA

Rodgers, Richard (Athlete, Football Player)
c/o Frank Bauer *Sun West Sports*
7883 N Pershing Ave
Stockton, CA 95207-1749, USA

Rodgers, Robert ""Buck"" (Athlete, Baseball Player)
216 Iris Ave
Corona Del Mar, CA 92625-3226, USA

Rodgers, Robert (Buck) (Athlete, Baseball Player, Coach)
216 Iris Ave
Corona Del Mar, CA 92625-3226, USA

Rodgers, Roscoe (Horse Racer)
7834 N Music Mountain Ln
Prescott Valley, AZ 86315-9085, USA

Rodgers-Cromartie, Dominique (Athlete, Football Player)
c/o Eugene Parker *Maximum Sports Management*
6435 W Jefferson Blvd # 197
Fort Wayne, IN 46804-6203, USA

Rodina, Irina (Athlete)
13243 Fiji Way # 7
Marina Del Rey, CA 90292-7079, USA

Rodman, Dennis (Athlete, Basketball Player)
Rodman Group
4910 Campus Dr
Newport Beach, CA 92660-2119, USA

Rodman, Judy (Musician, Songwriter)
308 Cody Hill Pl
Nashville, TN 37211-7927, USA

Rodrigues, Bienvenido (Athlete, Baseball Player)
PO Box 42
Santa Isabel, PR 00757-0042, USA

Rodrigues, Blenvenido (Baseball Player)
Chicago American Giants
PO Box 42
Santa Isabel, PR 00757-0042, USA

Rodriguez, Adam (Actor)
c/o Abe Hoch *A Management Company*
9107 Wilshire Blvd Ste 650
Beverly Hills, CA 90210-5544, USA

Rodriguez, Alex (A-Rod) (Athlete, Baseball Player)
c/o Guy Oseary *Untitled Entertainment (LA)*
350 S Beverly Dr Ste 200
Beverly Hills, CA 90212-4819, USA

Rodriguez, Anthony (Golfer)
13602 Summer Glen Dr
San Antonio, TX 78247-3510, USA

Rodriguez, Carlos (Athlete, Baseball Player)
7562 Burgstresser Ct
Canal Winchester, OH 43110-8432, USA

Rodriguez, Eddie (Athlete, Baseball Player)
4320 N Elias St
Mesa, AZ 85215, USA

Rodriguez, Edwin (Athlete, Baseball Player)
7901 30th Ave N
Saint Petersburg, FL 33710-1151, USA

Rodriguez, Ellie (Athlete, Baseball Player)
1787 Calle Astromelia
San Juan, PR 00926-7222, USA

Rodriguez, Francisco (Athlete, Baseball Player)
c/o Staff Member *New York Mets*
Shea Stadium
123-01 Roosevelt Avenue
Corona, NY 11368, USA

Rodriguez, Freddy (Actor)
c/o Robbie Kass *Kass Management*
501 Santa Monica Blvd Ste 604
Santa Monica, CA 90401-2467, USA

Rodriguez, Genesis (Actor)
c/o Ivan De Paz *DePaz Management*
2011 N Vermont Ave
Los Angeles, CA 90027-1931, USA

Rodriguez, Henry (Athlete, Baseball Player)
295 Wadsworth Ave Apt 3F
New York, NY 10040-4416, USA

Rodriguez, Ivan (Pudge) (Athlete, Baseball Player)
15530 SW 70th Ter
Miami, FL 33193-2127, USA

Rodriguez, Jai (Actor, Television Host)
c/o Van Johnson *Van Johnson Company*
10250 Constellation Blvd Ste 2320
Los Angeles, CA 90067-6256, USA

Rodriguez, Javier (Actor)
c/o Staff Member *Select Artists Ltd (CA-Valley Office)*
PO Box 4359
Burbank, CA 91503-4359, USA

Rodriguez, Johnny
PO Box 23162
Nashville, TN 37202-3162

Rodriguez, Jose Luis (El Puma) (Musician)
c/o Staff Member *BMG*
1540 Broadway
New York, NY 10036-4039, USA

Rodriguez, Juan (Chi Chi) (Athlete)
Eddie Elias Enterprises
3916 Clock Pointe Trl Ste 101
Stow, OH 44224-2932

Rodriguez, Maggie (Television Host)
c/o Staff Member CBS News (NY)
524 W 57th St Fl 8
New York, NY 10019-2930, USA

Rodriguez, Michelle (Actor)
c/o Jason Weinberg Untitled
Entertainment (LA)
350 S Beverly Dr Ste 200
Beverly Hills, CA 90212-4819, USA

Rodriguez, Paul (Actor)
c/o Barry Katz Barry Katz Entertainment
10100 Santa Monica Blvd Ste 2485
Los Angeles, CA 90067-4011, USA

Rodriguez, Raini (Actor)
c/o Susan Osser Susan Osser Talent
Company
Prefers to be contacted via telephone and
email
Los Angeles, CA, USA

Rodriguez, Ramon (Actor)
c/o Allan Grifka Alchemy Entertainment
7024 Melrose Ave Ste 420
Los Angeles, CA 90038-3394, USA

Rodriguez, Rich (Athlete, Baseball Player)
96 Glenbrook Rd Apt 24
Stamford, CT 06902-2926, USA

Rodriguez, Rick (Athlete, Baseball Player)
7000 Coliseum Way Ste 3
Oakland, CA 94621-1917, USA

Rodriguez, Rico (Actor)
c/o Traci Harper Harper Public Relations
3940 Laurel Canyon Blvd Ste 1010
Studio City, CA 91604-3709, USA

Rodriguez, Robert (Director, Producer)
c/o Robert Newman William Morris
Endeavor (LA)
9601 Wilshire Blvd
Beverly Hills, CA 90210-5213, USA

Rodriguez, Steve (Athlete, Baseball
Player)
28905 Bardell Dr
Agoura Hills, CA 91301-2133, USA

Rodriguez, Vic (Athlete, Baseball Player)
2796 Via Piazza Loop
Fort Myers, FL 33905-5562, USA

Rodriguez, Wandy (Athlete, Baseball
Player)
2501 Still Bay St
Pearland, TX 77584-8289, USA

Rodriquez, Paul (Skateboarder)
Plan B Skateboards
121 Waterworks Way Ste 100
Irvine, CA 92618-3110, USA

Roe, Billy (Race Car Driver)
9595 E Sunnyside Dr
Scottsdale, AZ 85260-7115, USA

Roe, Elwin (Preacher) (Athlete, Baseball
Player)
204 Wildwood Ter
West Plains, MO 65775-2548, USA

Roe, Rocky (Athlete, Baseball Player)
2033 Stefano Ct
Mount Dora, FL 32757-6511, USA

Roe, Tommy
PO Box 26037
Minneapolis, MN 55426-0037

Roebuck, Daniel (Actor)
c/o Leslie Allan-Rice Leslie Allan-Rice
Management
1007 Maybrook Dr
Beverly Hills, CA 90210-2715, USA

Roebuck, Ed (Athlete, Baseball Player)
3434 Warwood Rd
Lakewood, CA 90712-3751, USA

Roedel, Herb (Athlete, Football Player)
4810 201st St
Oakland Gardens, NY 11364-1012, USA

Roemer, Charles ""Buddy"" (Ex-Governor,
Politician)
4200 Saint Peter St
New Orleans, LA 70119-4618, USA

Roemer, Sarah (Actor, Model)
c/o Staff Member Luber Roklin
Management
5815 W Sunset Blvd Ste 206
Los Angeles, CA 90028-6481, USA

Roenick, Jeremy (Athlete, Hockey Player,
Olympic Athlete)
Roenicklife LLC
8912 E Pinnacle Peak Rd Ste F9-661
Scottsdale, AZ 85255-3615, USA

Roenicke, Gary (Athlete, Baseball Player)
11023 Rough and Ready Rd
Rough And Ready, CA 95975-9750, USA

Roenicke, Josh (Athlete, Baseball Player)
8130 Santa Rosa Ct
Sarasota, FL 34243-3000, USA

Roenicke, Ron (Athlete, Baseball Player)
787 Avenida Salvador
San Clemente, CA 92672-2369, USA

Roeper, Lindsey
Palms Playboy Club
4321 W Flamingo Rd
Las Vegas, NV 89103-3903, USA

Roerig, Zach (Actor)
c/o Loch Powell Leverage Management
3030 Pennsylvania Ave
Santa Monica, CA 90404-4112, USA

Roesler, Mike (Athlete, Baseball Player)
12033 Fallen Leaf Ct
Fort Wayne, IN 46845-8992, USA

Roessler, Pat (Athlete, Baseball Player)
4910 Hidden Oaks Trl
Sarasota, FL 34232-3040, USA

Roethlisberger, Ben (Athlete, Football
Player)
2213 Chardonnay Cir
Gibsonia, PA 15044-7401, USA

Roethlisberger, Fred (Athlete, Gymnast,
Olympic Athlete)
W9920 710th Ave
River Falls, WI 54022-4017, USA

Roffe-Steinrotter, Diann (Athlete,
Olympic Athlete, Skier)
248 N 29th St
Camp Hill, PA 17011-2904, USA

Rogan, Joe (Comedian)
c/o Ivo Fischer William Morris Endeavor
(LA)
9601 Wilshire Blvd
Beverly Hills, CA 90210-5213, USA

Rogas, Dan (Athlete, Football Player)
2352 Evalon St
Beaumont, TX 77702-1310, USA

Rogen, Seth (Actor)
c/o Marsha McManus Principal
Entertainment (LA)
9255 W Sunset Blvd Ste 500
West Hollywood, CA 90069-3301, USA

Roger, Elena (Musician)
c/o Bill Butler Industry Entertainment
955 Carrillo Dr Ste 300
Los Angeles, CA 90048-5400, USA

Roger, John (Religious Leader)
John Roger Foundation
2101 Wilshire Blvd
Santa Monica, CA 90403-5744, USA

Rogers, Bill (Golfer)
710 Patterson Ave
San Antonio, TX 78209-5637, USA

Rogers, Chad (Business Person, Reality
Star)
Hilton & Hyland
250 N Canon Dr
Beverly Hills, CA 90210-5322, USA

Rogers, Da'Rick (Athlete, Football Player)
c/o Joby Branion Athletes First, LLC
23091 Mill Creek Dr
Laguna Hills, CA 92653-1258, USA

Rogers, Dennis (Athlete)
c/o Staff Member Big Machine Media
780 3rd Ave Rm 1500
New York, NY 10017-2172, USA

Rogers, George (Athlete, Football Player,
Heisman Trophy Winner)
1007 Lofty Pine Dr
Columbia, SC 29212-2037, USA

Rogers, Greg (Writer)
PO Box 414
McAlester, OK 74502-0414, USA

Rogers, Harold (Congressman, Politician)
2406 Rayburn Hob
Washington, DC 20515-1705, USA

Rogers, Jackie (Race Car Driver)
5731 Camellia Ln
Wilmington, NC 28409-5801, USA

Rogers, Jamar (Musician)
c/o Stephen Ford Diva Central Inc
7510 W Sunset Blvd Ste 1445
Los Angeles, CA 90046-3408, USA

Rogers, Jane
1485 S Beverly Dr Apt 8
Los Angeles, CA 90035-3021

Rogers, Jimmy (Athlete, Baseball Player)
16175 Timbers Dr
Oklahoma City, OK 73165-6549, USA

Rogers, Kenny (Musician)
Kenny Rogers Productions
103 Paradise Dr
Hendersonville, TN 37075-4201, USA

Rogers, Kenny (Athlete, Baseball Player)
1730 Ottinger Rd
Roanoke, TX 76262, USA

Rogers, Kevin (Athlete, Baseball Player)
604 Douglas Ave
Cleveland, MS 38732-2026, USA

Rogers, Lamarr (Baseball Player)
1240 Spring Green Ln
Burnsville, MN 55306-6413, USA

Rogers, Melody
2051 Nichols Canyon Rd
Los Angeles, CA 90046-1727

Rogers, Mike (Congressman, Politician)
324 Cannon Hob
Washington, DC 20515-4301, USA

Rogers, Mimi (Actor)
c/o Jason Shapiro Silver Lining
Entertainment
421 S Beverly Dr Fl 7
Beverly Hills, CA 90212-4408, USA

Rogers, Reg (Actor)
c/o Staff Member Brookside Artists
Management (NY)
250 W 57th St Ste 2303
New York, NY 10107-2399, USA

Rogers, Sharon (Model)
PO Box 5785
Lacey, WA 98509-5785, USA

Rogers, Stephen D (Steve) (Baseball
Player)
3746 S Madison Ave
Tulsa, OK 74105-3016, USA

Rogers, Steve (Athlete, Baseball Player)
949 W 115th St S
Jenks, OK 74037-2071, USA

Rogers, Suzanne (Actor)
11266 Canton Dr
Studio City, CA 91604-4154, USA

Rogers, Tracy (Athlete, Football Player)
1011 Tam O Shanter Dr
Bakersfield, CA 93309-2451, USA

Rogers, Wayne (Actor)
11828 La Grange Ave
Los Angeles, CA 90025-5212, USA

Roges, Al (Athlete, Basketball Player)
6217 Scenic Ave
Los Angeles, CA 90068-2914, USA

Roggeman, Tom (Athlete, Football Player)
51267 Pembridge Ct
Granger, IN 46530-8306, USA

Roggenburk, Garry (Athlete, Baseball
Player)
33550 Streamview Dr
Avon, OH 44011-2597, USA

Roggin, Fred
3000 W Alameda Ave
Burbank, CA 91523-0001

Rogodzinski, Mike (Athlete, Baseball
Player)
1 Emlyn Ct
Clementon, NJ 08021-4871, USA

Rogow, Stan (Producer)
c/o Staff Member ICM Partners (LA)
10250 Constellation Blvd Fl 7
Los Angeles, CA 90067-6207, USA

Rogue Wave (Music Group)
c/o Staff Member Paradigm (Monterey)
404 W Franklin St
Monterey, CA 93940-2303, USA

Roh, Craig (Athlete, Football Player)
c/o Blake Baratz The Institute for Athletes
3600 Minnesota Dr Ste 550
Minneapolis, MN 55435-7925, USA

Rohde, Bruce (Business Person)
ConAgra Inc
1 Conagra Dr
Omaha, NE 68102-5003, USA

Rohde, Dave (Athlete, Baseball Player)
1707 Port Barmouth Pl
Newport Beach, CA 92660-5314, USA

Rohde, David (Journalist)
229 W 43rd St
New York, NY 10036-3982, USA

Rohde, Kristen (Actor)
c/o Staff Member *Gersh (LA)*
9465 Wilshire Blvd Ste 600
Beverly Hills, CA 90212-2605, USA

Rohde, Len (Athlete, Football Player)
100 W El Camino Real Ste 76
Mountain View, CA 94040-2679, USA

Rohde, Lisa (Athlete, Olympic Athlete, Rower)
9807 Whitethorn Dr
Charlotte, NC 28277-9029, USA

Rohlinger, Ryan (Athlete, Baseball Player)
634 Ridge Rd
West Bend, WI 53095-3845, USA

Rohloff, Jon (Athlete, Hockey Player)
4435 Starwood Ct
Reno, NV 89519-7925

Rohloff, Kenneth (Athlete, Basketball Player)
121 Willow Pond Dr
Morehead City, NC 28557-2618, USA

Rohloff, Todd (Athlete, Hockey Player)
PO Box 690
Grand Rapids, MN 55744-0690

Rohm, Elisabeth (Actor)
c/o Katie Mason *Luber Roklin Management*
5815 W Sunset Blvd Ste 206
Los Angeles, CA 90028-6481, USA

Rohm, Elizabeth (Actor)
c/o Katie Mason *Luber Roklin Management*
5815 W Sunset Blvd Ste 206
Los Angeles, CA 90028-6481, USA

Rohn, Dan (Athlete, Baseball Player)
2406 Arthur Ct
Traverse City, MI 49685-7411, USA

Rohner, Clayton (Actor)
6924 Treasure Trl
Los Angeles, CA 90068-1838

Rohr, Bill (Athlete, Baseball Player)
67545 S Lae Una Dr
Cathedral City, CA 92234, USA

Rohr, Les (Athlete, Baseball Player)
3914 Palisades Park Dr
Billings, MT 59102-0134, USA

Rohrbacher, Dana (Congressman, Politician)
2300 Rayburn Hob
Washington, DC 20515-2212, USA

Rohrer, Jeff (Athlete, Football Player)
3201 Executive Cir
Dallas, TX 75234-3764, USA

Rohrmeier, Dan (Athlete, Baseball Player)
1029 Ede Etree Ln
Cincinnati, OH 45238, USA

Roig, Tony (Athlete, Baseball Player)
16508 S Cheney Spokane Rd
Cheney, WA 99004-8659, USA

Roiz, Sasha (Actor)
c/o Pearl Hanan *Pearl Hanan Management*
7775 W Sunset Blvd Ste 118
Los Angeles, CA 90046-3911, USA

Roizman, Owen (Cinematographer)
17533 Magnolia Blvd
Encino, CA 91316, USA

Rojas, Euky (Athlete, Baseball Player)
6042 SW 163rd Ave
Miami, FL 33193-6010, USA

Rojas, Geoffrey (Prince Royce) (Musician)
c/o Miles Gidaly *William Morris Endeavor (NY)*
1325 Avenue of the Americas
New York, NY 10019-6026, USA

Rojas, Goffrey (Prince Royal) (Musician)
c/o Michael Vega *William Morris Endeavor (Miami)*
119 Washington Ave Ste 400
Miami Beach, FL 33139-7202, USA

Rojas, Mel (Athlete, Baseball Player)
15645 Collins Ave Apt 802
North Miami Beach, FL 33160-4790, USA

Rojas, Nydia (Musician)
Silverlight Entertainment
9171 Wilshire Blvd Ste 426
Beverly Hills, CA 90210-5516, USA

Rojas, Octavio R (Cookie) (Athlete, Baseball Player, Coach)
19195 Mystic Pointe Dr Apt 3002
Aventura, FL 33180-4502, USA

Rojcewicz, Susan (Athlete, Basketball Player, Olympic Athlete)
30 Via Encina
Monterey, CA 93940-6112, USA

Rojeski, Shawn (Athlete, Olympic Athlete)
510 11th St NW
Chisholm, MN 55719-1157, USA

Roker, Al (Correspondent, Television Host)
c/o Staff Member *The Today Show*
30 Rockefeller Plz
New York, NY 10112-0015, USA

Rokita, Todd (Congressman, Politician)
236 Cannon Hob
Washington, DC 20515-0503, USA

Roland, Ed (Musician, Songwriter, Writer)
Spivak Entertainment
11845 W Olympic Blvd Ste 1125
Los Angeles, CA 90064-5096, USA

Roland, Jim (Athlete, Baseball Player)
1802 Arbor Way Dr
Shelby, NC 28150-6166, USA

Roland, Johnny E (Athlete, Coach, Football Player)
8701 S Hardy Dr
Tempe, AZ 85284-2800, USA

Rolen, Scott (Athlete, Baseball Player)
721 Key Royale Dr
Holmes Beach, FL 34217-1231, USA

Roles-Williams, Barbara (Athlete, Figure Skater, Olympic Athlete)
3790 Leisure Ln
Las Vegas, NV 89103-2323, USA

Rolison, Nathan (Nate) (Athlete, Baseball Player)
118 County Rd 3709
Enterprise, MS 39330, USA

Rolle, Butch (Athlete, Football Player)
17822 NW 15th St
Pembroke Pines, FL 33029-3134, USA

Roller, David E (Athlete, Football Player)
1404 Bristol Trce
Alpharetta, GA 30022-1080, USA

Rollin, Betty (Correspondent, Writer)
67 Park Ave
New York, NY 10016-2557, USA

Rolling Stones (Music Group)
c/o Fran Curtis *Rogers & Cowan PR (LA)*
8687 Melrose Ave Ste 7
West Hollywood, CA 90069-5721, USA

Rollins, Ed
c/o Staff Member *William Morris Endeavor (LA)*
9601 Wilshire Blvd
Beverly Hills, CA 90210-5213, USA

Rollins, Henry (Musician, Songwriter)
c/o Tiffany Kuzon *Evolution Entertainment (LA)*
901 N Highland Ave
Los Angeles, CA 90038-2412, USA

Rollins, Jerry (Athlete, Hockey Player)
14062 Caminito Vistana
San Diego, CA 92130-3719, USA

Rollins, Jimmy (Athlete, Baseball Player)
120 Fox Chase Ct
Swedesboro, NJ 08085-3043, USA

Rollins, John (Golfer)
8703 Playground Ct
North Chesterfield, VA 23237-2378, USA

Rollins, Kenneth (Athlete, Basketball Player, Olympic Athlete)
1497 N County Road 175 W Lot 1
Greencastle, IN 46135-9239, USA

Rollins, Phil (Athlete, Basketball Player)
221 Norbourne Blvd
Louisville, KY 40207-3922, USA

Rollins, Rich (Athlete, Baseball Player)
4146 Evergreen Ln
Richfield, OH 44286-9592, USA

Rollins, Rose (Actor)
c/o David Sweeney *Sweeney Entertainment*
6253 Hollywood Blvd Apt 201
Los Angeles, CA 90028-8248, USA

Rollins, Wayne (Tree) (Athlete, Basketball Player, Coach)
PO Box 1209
Apopka, FL 32704-1209, USA

Rolls, Damian (Athlete, Baseball Player)
11112 Shadybrook Dr
Tampa, FL 33625-5708, USA

Roloff, Matt
23985 NW Grossen Dr
Hillsboro, OR 97124-8149

Roloson, Dwayne (Athlete, Hockey Player)
Global Hockey Consultants
470 Atlantic Ave Fl 3
Attn Mark Witkin
Boston, MA 02210-2230, USA

Rolston, Brian (Athlete, Hockey Player, Olympic Athlete)
Sports Consulting Group
65 Monroe Ave Ste D
Pittsford, NY 14534-1318, USA

Roman, Bill (Athlete, Baseball Player)
1720 Yale Ct
Lake Forest, IL 60045-5117, USA

Roman, Dan (Baseball Player)
10313 Arran Ct
Huntersville, NC 28078-7021, USA

Roman, John (Athlete, Football Player)
13 Mendham Rd
Bernardsville, NJ 07924, USA

Roman, Lauren
170 Flanders Drakestown Rd
Flanders, NJ 07836-4014

Roman, Phil
10635 Riverside Dr
North Hollywood, CA 91602-2341

Roman, Tami (Actor, Reality Star)
c/o Shakim Compere *Flavor Unit Entertainment*
155 Morgan St
Jersey City, NJ 07302-2932, USA

Romanek, Mark (Director)
c/o Staff Member *Creative Artists Agency (CAA-LA)*
2000 Avenue of the Stars Ste 100
Los Angeles, CA 90067-4705, USA

Romanetti, Ray (Horse Racer)
227 S Spring Valley Rd
Canonsburg, PA 15317-2823, USA

Romanick, Ron (Athlete, Baseball Player)
17108 E Kingstree Blvd Apt 1
Fountain Hills, AZ 85268-5556, USA

Romaniszyn, Jim (Athlete, Football Player)
619 Amy Lee Cir
Port Orange, FL 32127-7542, USA

Romano, Andy (Actor)
c/o Staff Member *Golan & Blumberg*
6528 W 6th St
Los Angeles, CA 90048-4716, USA

Romano, Christy Carlson (Actor)
c/o Staff Member *American Way Productions*
PO Box 166
Milford, CT 06460-0166, USA

Romano, Jason (Athlete, Baseball Player)
1411 Willow Oak Cir
Bradenton, FL 34209-7822, USA

Romano, Johnny (Athlete, Baseball Player)
160 W Pago Pago Dr
Naples, FL 34113-8616, USA

Romano, Larry (Actor)
Gold Marshak Liedtke
3500 W Olive Ave Ste 1400
Burbank, CA 91505-5512, USA

Romano, Mike (Athlete, Baseball Player)
1202 N Lee Rd
Covington, LA 70433-1738, USA

Romano, Pete (Cinematographer)
HydroFlex Inc
5335 McConnell Ave
Los Angeles, CA 90066-7025, USA

Romano, Ray (Actor, Comedian, Producer, Writer)
5225 Encino Ave
Encino, CA 91316-2525, USA

Romano, Tom (Athlete, Baseball Player)
1266 Penora St
Depew, NY 14043-4512, USA

Romanos, John J (Jack) Jr (Publisher)
Pocket Books
1230 Avenue of the Americas Fl CONC1
New York, NY 10020-1586, USA

Romanov, Stephanie (Actor)
c/o Staff Member *Diverse Talent Group*
9911 W Pico Blvd Ste 340W
Los Angeles, CA 90035-2703, USA

Romanowski, Bill (Athlete, Football Player)
3706 Mt Diablo Blvd Ste 200
Lafayette, CA 94549-3638, USA

Romansky, Monroe J (Doctor)
5600 Wisconsin Ave Apt 110
Chevy Chase, MD 20815-4409, USA

Romantics, The
1924 Spring St
Paso Robles, CA 93446-1620

Romanus, Richard (Actor)
Chasin Agency
8899 Beverly Blvd Ste 716
Los Angeles, CA 90048-2449, USA

Romanus, Robert (Actor)
c/o Melanie Sharp *Sharp Talent*
5538 Willowcrest Ave
North Hollywood, CA 91601-2830, USA

Roman Waugh, Ric (Director)
2967 E 3rd St
Los Angeles, CA 90033-4108, USA

Romar, Lorenzo (Athlete, Basketball
Player)
4408 164th Ln SE
Bellevue, WA 98006-8946, USA

Rombough, Doug (Athlete, Hockey
Player)
10434 Sunrise Lakes Blvd Apt 303
Sunrise, FL 33322-5961

Romby, Bob (Baseball Player)
Baltimore Elite Giants
38 Holman Mill Rd
Cumberland, VA 23040-2804, USA

Rome, Jim (Actor)
c/o Jeff Jacobs *Creative Artists Agency
(CAA-LA)*
2000 Avenue of the Stars Ste 100
Los Angeles, CA 90067-4705, USA

Rome, Jim (Sportscaster)
3801 Marfield Ave
Tarzana, CA 91356-5812, USA

Rome, Stan (Athlete, Football Player)
4489 Green Island Rd
Valdosta, GA 31602-0870, USA

Romer, Roy R (Ex-Governor, Politician)
Strong American Schools
4861 County Rd 43
Bailey, CO 80421, USA

Romero, Celino (Musician)
Columbia Artists Mgmt Inc
165 W 57th St
New York, NY 10019-2201, USA

Romero, Danny Jr (Boxer)
800 Salida Sandia SW
Albuquerque, NM 87105-7607, USA

Romero, Ed (Athlete, Baseball Player)
1380 Wood Row Way
Wellington, FL 33414-9082, USA

Romero, George
c/o Staff Member *Gersh (LA)*
9465 Wilshire Blvd Ste 600
Beverly Hills, CA 90212-2605, USA

Romero, J.C (Athlete, Baseball Player)
140 Augusta Ct
Fairhope, AL 36532-6352, USA

Romero, Mandy (Athlete, Baseball Player)
19280 SW 216th St
Miami, FL 33170-1214, USA

Romero, Ned (Actor)
19438 Lassen St
Northridge, CA 91324-1121, USA

Romero, Randy (Horse Racer)
7124 La Highway 343
Kaplan, LA 70548-6103, USA

Romero, Richard (Actor)
c/o Staff Member *Select Artists Ltd (CA-
Valley Office)*
PO Box 4359
Burbank, CA 91503-4359, USA

Romijn, Rebecca (Actor, Model)
23062 Mulholland Hwy
Calabasas, CA 91302-2050, USA

Romine, Alton (Athlete, Football Player)
286 Highway 79
Phil Campbell, AL 35581-6314, USA

Romine, Andrew (Athlete, Baseball
Player)
22701 Fernwood St
Lake Forest, CA 92630-3612, USA

romine, Austin (Athlete, Baseball Player)
22701 Fernwood St
Lake Forest, CA 92630-3612, USA

Romine, Kevin (Athlete, Baseball Player)
22701 Fernwood St
Lake Forest, CA 92630-3612, USA

Romine, Paul (Race Car Driver)
Aerolite Racing
3645 Developers Rd
Indianapolis, IN 46227-3521, United
States

Rominger, Kent V (Astronaut)
2714 E Bridgeport Ave
Salt Lake City, UT 84121-5603, USA

Rominger, Kent V Captain (Astronaut)
2714 E Bridgeport Ave
Salt Lake City, UT 84121-5603, USA

Rominski, Dale (Athlete, Hockey Player)
32043 Staman Ct
Farmington Hills, MI 48336-1861

Romita Sr., John (Artist, Cartoonist)
11301 W Olympic Blvd # 587
Los Angeles, CA 90064-1653, USA

Romney, Ann (Politician)
6730 Silver Lake Dr
Park City, UT 84060-5155, USA

Romney, Mitt (Business Person, Politician)
2151 E 5340 S
Salt Lake City, UT 84117-7632, USA

Romo, Sergio (Athlete, Baseball Player)
6331 E Crabtree Pl
Yuma, AZ 85365-1111, USA

Romo, Tony (Athlete, Football Player)
PO Box 141809
Irving, TX 75014-1809, USA

Ron, Duncan (Athlete, Football Player)
500 N Fountain Ave
Springfield, OH 45504-2539, USA

Ronan, Ed (Athlete, Hockey Player)
15 Opal Cir
Franklin, MA 02038-4624

Ronan, Len (Athlete, Hockey Player)
2006 SW Eastwood Ave
Gresham, OR 97080-5751, USA

Ronan, Marc (Athlete, Baseball Player)
5603 S Chadwick Dr
Rogers, AR 72758-8223, USA

Ronan, Saoirse (Actor)
c/o Staff Member *Creative Artists Agency
(CAA-LA)*
2000 Avenue of the Stars Ste 100
Los Angeles, CA 90067-4705, USA

Rondeau, Pete (Race Car Driver)
PO Box 1918
Biddeford, ME 04005-1918, USA

Rondo, Rajon (Athlete, Basketball Player)
c/o Bill Duffy *BDA Sports Management
(BDA-CA)*
700 Ygnacio Valley Rd Ste 330
Walnut Creek, CA 94596-3838, USA

Rondon, Gilberto (Gil) (Athlete, Baseball
Player)
13281 Ramona Dr
Garden Grove, CA 92843-2626, USA

Ronettes, The
855 E Twain Ave # 123411
Las Vegas, NV 89169-0819

Roney, Matt (Athlete, Baseball Player)
1809 Nighthawk Ct
Edmond, OK 73034-6110, USA

Ronney, Paul D (Astronaut)
613 Ranchito Rd
Monrovia, CA 91016-3733, USA

Ronney, Paul D Dr (Astronaut)
613 Ranchito Rd
Monrovia, CA 91016-3733, USA

Ronning, Cliff (Athlete, Hockey Player)
317 Washington St
Saint Paul, MN 55102-1609, USA

Rono, Peter (Athlete, Track Athlete)
Mount Saint Mary's College
Athletic Dept
Emmitsburg, MD 21727, USA

Ronson, Len (Athlete, Hockey Player)
2006 SW Eastwood Ave
Gresham, OR 97080-5751

Ronson, Mark (Musician)
c/o Jenn Tolman *Paradigm (LA)*
360 N Crescent Dr
North Bldg
Beverly Hills, CA 90210-4874, USA

Ronson, Samantha (DJ, Musician)
3012 Bentley Ct
Santa Monica, CA 90405-5626, USA

Ronstadt, Linda (Musician)
c/o Brian Dubin *Artist Brand Alliance*
11 E 86th St Fl 9
New York, NY 10028-0501, USA

Ronty, Paul (Athlete, Hockey Player)
2300 Commonwealth Ave Apt 3-4
Auburndale, MA 02466-1796

Roof, Gene (Athlete, Baseball Player)
175 Spring Valley Dr
Paducah, KY 42003-8894, USA

Roof, Michael (Actor)
c/o Staff Member *3 Arts Entertainment
(LA)*
9460 Wilshire Blvd Fl 7
Beverly Hills, CA 90212-2713, USA

Roof, Phil (Athlete, Baseball Player)
1301 Pillar Chase
Paducah, KY 42001-6137, USA

Rook, Jerry (Athlete, Basketball Player)
Route 9 Box 124L
Jonesboro, AR 72404, USA

Rook, Susan (Correspondent)
Cable News Network
1050 Techwood Dr NW
News Dept
Atlanta, GA 30318-5695, USA

Rooker, Jim (Athlete, Baseball Player)
2378 Windchime Dr
Jacksonville, FL 32224-2016, USA

Rooker, Michael (Actor)
8330 McGroarty St
Sunland, CA 91040-3208, USA

Roomes, Rolando (Athlete, Baseball
Player)
3067 Meadow Brook Dr
Saint Paul, MN 55125-4307, USA

Roomful of Blues (Music Group,
Musician)
c/o Staff Member *Concerted Efforts*
PO Box 440326
Somerville, MA 02144-0004, USA

Rooney, Art (Horse Racer)
1190 Washington Rd
Pittsburgh, PA 15228-1817, USA

Rooney, Dan (Football Executive)
940 N Lincoln Ave
Pittsburgh, PA 15233-1814, USA

Rooney, Jim (Soccer Player)
New England Revolution
1 Patriot Pl
Cmgi Field
Foxboro, MA 02035-1388, USA

Rooney, Joe Don (Musician)
LGB Media
1228 Pineview Ln
Nashville, TN 37211-7422, USA

Rooney, Pat (Athlete, Baseball Player)
400 Skokie Blvd Ste 280
Northbrook, IL 60062-7939, USA

Rooney, Patrick W (Business Person)
Cooper Tire & Rubber Co
Lima & Western Aves
Findlay, OH 45840, USA

Rooney, Steve (Athlete, Hockey Player)
5 Helen Dr
Canton, MA 02021-2404

Rooney, Timothy (Horse Racer)
810 Central Park Ave
Yonkers, NY 10704, USA

Rooney II, Art (Business Person, Football
Executive)
1300 Inverness Ave
Pittsburgh, PA 15217-1156, USA

Roop, Richard (Business Person)
Bottom Line Results Inc
743 Goldhills Pl S # 239
Woodland Park, CO 80863, USA

Roopenian, Mark (Athlete, Football
Player)
358 Charles River Rd
Watertown, MA 02472-2737, USA

Roos, Don (Actor, Producer)
c/o Steve Rabineau *United Talent Agency
(UTA-LA)*
9336 Civic Center Dr
Beverly Hills, CA 90210-3604, USA

Rooster (Music Group)
c/o Staff Member *BMG*
1540 Broadway
New York, NY 10036-4039, USA

Rooster, The Red
PO Box 3859
Stamford, CT 06905

Root, Bonnie (Actor)
c/o Tracy Steinsapir *Main Title Entertainment*
8383 Wilshire Blvd Ste 408
Beverly Hills, CA 90211-2435, USA

Root, Stephen (Steven) (Actor)
c/o Jai Khanna *Brillstein Entertainment Partners (LA)*
9150 Wilshire Blvd Ste 350
Beverly Hills, CA 90212-3453, USA

Roots, The (Music Group)
c/o Cara Lewis *Creative Artists Agency (CAA-NY)*
162 5th Ave Fl 6
New York, NY 10010-6047, USA

Roper, Dee Dee (Spinderella) (Musician)
Nest Plateau Records
1650 Broadway # 1130
New York, NY 10019-6833, USA

Roper, John (Athlete, Baseball Player)
519 John Roper Ave
Raeford, NC 28376-2211, USA

Roper, John (Athlete, Football Player)
4213 Alice St
Houston, TX 77021-4903, USA

Rosa, Rosa
6640 W Sunset Blvd # 110
Los Angeles, CA 90028-7104

Rosales, Adam (Athlete, Baseball Player)
1900 Woodland Ave
Park Ridge, IL 60068-1911, USA

Rosales, Jenny (Athlete, Golfer)
265 S Vine St
Anaheim, CA 92805-4128, USA

Rosales, Leo
952 N Ardmore Ave Apt 7
Los Angeles, CA 90029-3389, USA

Rosario, Jimmy (Athlete, Baseball Player)
PO Box 9020739
San Juan, PR 00902-0739, USA

Rosario, Mel (Athlete, Baseball Player)
205 Round Tree Ct
Egg Harbor Township, NJ 08234-7910, USA

Rosario, Santiago (Athlete, Baseball Player)
Kansas City A's
PO Box 561238
Guayanilla, PR 00656-3238, USA

Rosas, Cesar (Musician, Songwriter, Writer)
Monterey International
200 W Superior St Ste 202
Chicago, IL 60654-6422, USA

Rosburg, Bob (Golfer)
49425 Avenida Club La Quinta
La Quinta, CA 92253-2703, USA

Rose, Adam (Actor)
c/o Steven Siebert *Lighthouse Entertainment*
9220 W Sunset Blvd Ste 200
West Hollywood, CA 90069-3501, USA

Rose, Amber (Actor)
30 Virginia Ln
Canonsburg, PA 15317-5802, USA

Rose, Anika Noni (Actor)
c/o David Williams *David Williams Management*
9614 W Olympic Blvd Apt F
Beverly Hills, CA 90212-3761, USA

Rose, Axl (Musician, Songwriter, Writer)
5055 Latigo Canyon Rd
Malibu, CA 90265-2812, USA

Rose, Barry (Athlete, Football Player)
1761 W White Ash Dr
Balsam Lake, WI 54810-2416, USA

Rose, Bobby (Athlete, Baseball Player)
2713 Highview Dr
Bullhead City, AZ 86429-5928, USA

Rose, Brian (Athlete, Baseball Player)
5 Ashland St
South Dartmouth, MA 02748-3211, USA

Rose, Charlie (Television Host)
Rose Communications
499 Park Ave # 1500
New York, NY 10022-1240, USA

Rose, Chris (Television Host)
c/o Staff Member *Best Damned Sports Show Period, The*
10201 W Pico Blvd
Fox Sports Net
Los Angeles, CA 90064-2606, USA

Rose, Clarence (Golfer)
405 Walnut Creek Dr
Goldsboro, NC 27534-8995, USA

Rose, Cristine (Actor)
c/o Staff Member *SMS Talent*
8383 Wilshire Blvd Ste 230
Beverly Hills, CA 90211-2436, USA

Rose, Derrick (Athlete, Basketball Player)
c/o BJ Armstrong *Wasserman Media Group (LA)*
12100 W Olympic Blvd Ste 200
Los Angeles, CA 90064-1075, USA

Rose, Don (Athlete, Baseball Player)
16254 Palomino Mesa Way
San Diego, CA 92127-4445, USA

Rose, Donovan (Athlete, Football Player)
103 Lenox Ct
Yorktown, VA 23693-5501, USA

Rose, Emily (Actor)
c/o Connie Tavel *Forward Entertainment*
9255 W Sunset Blvd Ste 805
West Hollywood, CA 90069-3305, USA

Rose, Felipe (Musician)
1 Vanada Dr
Neptune, NJ 07753-2540, USA

Rose, George (Athlete, Football Player)
712 Indian Mound Rd
Brunswick, GA 31525-2124, USA

Rose, Howie (Baseball Player)
5 Turret Ln
Woodbury, NY 11797-1021, USA

Rose, Jalen (Athlete, Basketball Player)
4512 Orchard Trail Ct
Orchard Lake, MI 48324-3039, USA

Rose, Jamie (Actor)
c/o Staff Member *Marshak/Zachary Company, The*
8840 Wilshire Blvd Fl 1
Beverly Hills, CA 90211-2606, USA

Rose, Jessica (Actor)
c/o Brad Marks *Blue Five Media*
1550 17th St
Santa Monica, CA 90404-3402, USA

Rose, Joe (Athlete, Football Player)
3293 SW 138th Way
Davie, FL 33330-4664, USA

Rose, John (Cartoonist)
95 Laurel St
Harrisonburg, VA 22801-2732, USA

Rose, Justin (Golfer)
c/o Staff Member *Pro Golfers Assoc of America (PGA)*
112 Tpc Blvd
Ponte Vedra Beach, FL 32082, USA

Rose, Katy (Musician)
c/o Staff Member *Paradigm (Monterey)*
404 W Franklin St
Monterey, CA 93940-2303, USA

Rose, Ken (Athlete, Football Player)
1736 Bronzewood Ct
Newbury Park, CA 91320-4546, USA

Rose, Lee (Director, Producer)
c/o Staff Member *Broder Webb Chervin Silbermann Agency, The (BWCS)*
10250 Constellation Blvd Ste 1700
Los Angeles, CA 90067-6253, USA

Rose, Lucy (Musician)
c/o Staff Member *ICM Partners (LA)*
10250 Constellation Blvd Fl 7
Los Angeles, CA 90067-6207, USA

Rose, Malik (Athlete, Basketball Player)
1318 Greystone Rdg
San Antonio, TX 78258-4406, USA

Rose, Marie (Actor)
6916 Chisholm Ave
Van Nuys, CA 91406-5111, USA

Rose, Matthew (Business Person)
Burlington North/Santa Fe
2650 Lou Menk Dr
Fort Worth, TX 76131-2830, USA

Rose, Mauri (Race Car Driver)
International Motorsports
PO Box 1018
Talladega, AL 35161-1018, USA

Rose, Pete (Athlete, Baseball Player, Coach)
7434 McLennan Ave
Van Nuys, CA 91406-2716, USA

Rose, Peter H (Business Person)
Krytek Corp
2 Centennial Dr
Peabody, MA 01960-7911, USA

Rose, Shayna (Actor)
Rough Diamond Productions
1424 N Kings Rd
C/O Bill Kravitz
West Hollywood, CA 90069-1908, USA

Rose, Sherrie (Actor, Model)
1758 Laurel Canyon Blvd
Los Angeles, CA 90046-2134, USA

Rosecrans, James (Athlete, Football Player)
210 Houston Ave
Syracuse, NY 13224-1754, USA

Rosegarten, Rory (Producer)
c/o Staff Member *William Morris Endeavor (LA)*
9601 Wilshire Blvd
Beverly Hills, CA 90210-5213, USA

Rose Jr, Pete (Athlete, Baseball Player)
3921 Legendary Ridge Ln
Cleves, OH 45002-2395, USA

Roselli, Bob (Athlete, Baseball Player)
100 Clydesdale Way
Roseville, CA 95678-6032, USA

Rosello, Dave (Athlete, Baseball Player)
160 Calle La Paz
Urb Bo Paris
Mayaguez, PR 00680-5441, USA

Rosema, Roger (Athlete, Football Player)
2131 Deer Hollow Dr SE
Grand Rapids, MI 49508-8777, USA

Rosemont, Romy (Actor)
c/o Tracy Steinsapir *Main Title Entertainment*
8383 Wilshire Blvd Ste 408
Beverly Hills, CA 90211-2435, USA

Rosen, Albert L (Al) (Athlete, Baseball Player)
15 Mayfair Dr
Rancho Mirage, CA 92270-2586, USA

Rosen, Andrew (Business Person)
Theory
38 Gansevoort St
New York, NY 10014-1502, USA

Rosen, Beatrice (Actor)
c/o Staff Member *Inspire Entertainment*
315 7th Ave Apt 17E
New York, NY 10001-6011, USA

Rosen, Nathaniel (Musician)
282 Cabrini Blvd Apt 4J
New York, NY 10040-3679, USA

Rosen, Sam (Actor)
c/o Staff Member *Brookside Artists Management (NY)*
250 W 57th St Ste 2303
New York, NY 10107-2399, USA

Rosenbaum, Michael (Actor)
c/o Jason Newman *Untitled Entertainment (LA)*
350 S Beverly Dr Ste 200
Beverly Hills, CA 90212-4819, USA

Rosenberg, Alan
PO Box 5617
Beverly Hills, CA 90209-5617

Rosenberg, Alyse (Producer)
c/o Staff Member *The Alpern Group*
15645 Royal Oak Rd
Encino, CA 91436-3905, USA

Rosenberg, Craig (Director, Writer)
c/o Staff Member *Firm, The*
2049 Century Park E # 2550
Los Angeles, CA 90067-3101, USA

Rosenberg, Joel C (Writer)
Beverly Rykerd Public Relations
PO Box 88180
C/O Beverly Rykerd
Colorado Springs, CO 80908-8180, USA

Rosenberg, Michael (Producer)
c/o Staff Member *Imagine Films Entertainment*
9465 Wilshire Blvd
7th Floor
Los Angeles, CA 90067, USA

Rosenberg, Scott (Writer)
c/o David O'Connor *Creative Artists Agency (CAA-LA)*
2000 Avenue of the Stars Ste 100
Los Angeles, CA 90067-4705, USA

Rosenberg, Steve (Athlete, Baseball Player)
2430 NE 35th St
Lighthouse Point, FL 33064-8155, USA

Rosenberg, Steven A (Doctor)
10104 Iron Gate Rd
Potomac, MD 20854-4728, USA

Rosenberg, Stuart (Director)
4438 Romero Dr
Tarzana, CA 91356-5512, USA

Rosenberg, Tina (Writer)
New School for Social Research
World Policy Institute
New York, NY 10011, USA

Rosenblatt, Dana (Boxer)
30 Cleveland Rd
Chestnut Hill, MA 02467, USA

Rosenbluth, Leonard (Lennie) (Athlete, Basketball Player)
123 Priestly Creek Dr
Chapel Hill, NC 27514-5432, USA

Rosenbohm, Jim (Baseball Player)
9513 Bedford Ave
Omaha, NE 68134-4607, USA

Rosenburg, Saul A (Doctor)
Stanford University
Oncology Division
Stanford, CA 94305, USA

Rosenfels, Sage (Athlete, Football Player)
110 Ferndale St
Bellaire, TX 77401-5325, USA

Rosenfelt, David (Writer)
c/o Staff Member *St Martins Press*
175 5th Ave Ste 400
Publicity Dept
New York, NY 10010-7848, USA

Rosengarten, David (Writer)
PO Box 20459
New York, NY 10025-1520, USA

Rosenman, Howard (Producer)
c/o Staff Member *Marshak/Zachary Company, The*
8840 Wilshire Blvd Fl 1
Beverly Hills, CA 90211-2606, USA

Rosenmeyer, Grant (Actor)
c/o Staff Member *DreamWorks SKG*
1000 Flower St
Glendale, CA 91201-3007, USA

Rosenthal, A M (Journalist)
229 W 43rd St Attn Dept
New York, NY 10036-3982, USA

Rosenthal, Amy Krouse (Writer)
Crown Publishing Group
1745 Broadway Fl 17
New York, NY 10019-4642, USA

Rosenthal, David S (Director, Writer)
1801 Century Park E Ste 2160
Los Angeles, CA 90067-2343

Rosenthal, Dick (Athlete, Basketball Player)
33108 Lake Forest Ct
Niles, MI 49120-7794, USA

Rosenthal, Gay (Producer)
c/o Mark Schulman *3 Arts Entertainment (LA)*
9460 Wilshire Blvd Fl 7
Beverly Hills, CA 90212-2713, USA

Rosenthal, Jane (Producer)
c/o Staff Member *Tribeca Productions*
375 Greenwich St Fl 7
New York, NY 10013-2379, USA

Rosenthal, Mark D (Writer)
c/o Tom Strickler *William Morris Endeavor (LA)*
9601 Wilshire Blvd
Beverly Hills, CA 90210-5213, USA

Rosenthal, Mike (Athlete, Football Player)
3701 Senate Ct
Valencia, PA 16059-3917, USA

Rosenthal, Philip (Producer)
c/o Adam Berkowitz *Creative Artists Agency (CAA-LA)*
2000 Avenue of the Stars Ste 100
Los Angeles, CA 90067-4705, USA

Rosenthal, Richard L (Rick) (Director, Producer)
c/o Staff Member *Whitewater Films*
11264 La Grange Ave
Los Angeles, CA 90025-5514, USA

Rosenthal, Sean (Athlete, Volleyball Player)
USA Volleyball
4065 Sinton Rd Ste 100
Colorado Springs, CO 80907-5093, USA

Rosenthal, Wayne (Athlete, Baseball Player)
10224 Allamanda Blvd
Palm Beach Gardens, FL 33410-5206, USA

Rosenzweig, Barney (Producer)
2311 Fisher Island Dr
Miami Beach, FL 33109-0086, USA

Roses, Allen D (Doctor)
Duke University
Medical Center
Bryan Research Center
Durham, NC 27706, USA

Rosewoman, Michele (Musician)
Abby Hoffer
223 1/2 E 48th St
New York, NY 10017, USA

Rosi, Francesco
Via Gregoriana 36
Rome, IT 1-001

Rosin, Walter L (Religious Leader)
Lutheran Church Missouri Synod
1333 S Kirkwood Rd
Saint Louis, MO 63122-7295, USA

Roskos, John (Athlete, Baseball Player)
PO Box 45514
Rio Rancho, NM 87174-5514, USA

Ros-Lehtinen, Ileana (Congressman, Politician)
2206 Rayburn Hob
Washington, DC 20515-2504, USA

Rosman, Mackenzie (Actor)
c/o Kanica Suy *Sweeney Entertainment*
6253 Hollywood Blvd Apt 201
Los Angeles, CA 90028-8248, USA

Rosnes, Renee (Musician)
Integrity Talent
PO Box 961
Burlington, MA 01803-5961, USA

Ross, Aaron (Athlete, Football Player)
c/o Denise White *EAG Sports Management*
909 N Sepulveda Blvd Ste 360
El Segundo, CA 90245-3864, USA

Ross, Ben (Director)
United Talent Agency
9336 Civic Center Dr
Beverly Hills, CA 90210-3604, USA

Ross, Betsy (Sportscaster)
ESPN-TV
Sports Dept
ESPN Plaza 935 Middle St
Bristol, CT 06010, USA

Ross, Bob (Athlete, Baseball Player)
862 Bergamo Ave
San Jacinto, CA 92583-2967, USA

Ross, Brian (Correspondent)
c/o Staff Member *ABC News*
77 W 66th St Fl 3
New York, NY 10023-6201, USA

Ross, Charlotte (Actor)
c/o Liza Anderson *Anderson Group Public Relations*
8060 Melrose Ave Fl 4
Los Angeles, CA 90046-7038, USA

Ross, Chelcie (Actor)
c/o Staff Member *Geddes Agency, The*
1203 Greenacre Ave
West Hollywood, CA 90046-5707, USA

Ross, Cody (Athlete, Baseball Player)
21469 N 83rd St
Scottsdale, AZ 85255-6473, USA

Ross, Dave (Athlete, Baseball Player)
2604 Antietam Trl
Tallahassee, FL 32312-4841, USA

Ross, David (Athlete, Baseball Player)
2548 Halleck Ln
Tallahassee, FL 32312-7566, USA

Ross, David A (Director)
Whitney Museum of American Art
99 Gansevoort St
New York, NY 10014-1404, USA

Ross, Dennis (Congressman, Politician)
404 Cannon Hob
Washington, DC 20515-2245, USA

Ross, Diana (Actor, Musician)
65 Meadow Wood Dr
Greenwich, CT 06830-7016, USA

Ross, Don (Athlete)
PO Box 981
Venice, CA 90294-0981, USA

Ross, Evan (Actor, Musician)
c/o Adam Griffin *Kritzer Levine Wilkins Entertainment (KLWG)*
11872 La Grange Ave Fl 1
Los Angeles, CA 90025-5283, USA

Ross, Fairbanks Anne (Swimmer)
10 Grandview Ave
Troy, NY 12180-2113, USA

Ross, Gary (Athlete, Baseball Player)
1729 Cuadro Vis
San Marcos, CA 92078-2102, USA

Ross, Gary (Director, Producer, Writer)
c/o Staff Member *Larger Than Life Productions*
100 Universal City Plz Bldg 5138
Universal City, CA 91608-1002

Ross, George (Business Person, Reality Star)
c/o Staff Member *The Apprentice*
725 5th Ave Bsmt A
the Trump Co
New York, NY 10022-2519, USA

Ross, Heather (Musician)
HER Productions
11313 Marjory Ave
Tampa, FL 33612-5633, USA

Ross, Jeffrey (Actor, Comedian)
c/o Amy Zvi *Thruline Entertainment*
9250 Wilshire Blvd Ste 100
Ground Floor
Beverly Hills, CA 90212-3343, USA

Ross, Jeremy (Athlete, Football Player)
c/o Joe Linta *JL Sports*
1204 Main St Ste 179
Branford, CT 06405-3787, USA

Ross, Jerry L (Astronaut)
NASA
2101 Nasa Pkwy Spc Johnsoncenter
Houston, TX 77058-3696, USA

Ross, Jerry L Colonel (Astronaut)
301 Gleneagles Dr
Friendswood, TX 77546-5634, USA

Ross, Jim (Athlete, Wrestler)
605 Shadow View Ct
Norman, OK 73072-4827, USA

Ross, Karie (Sportscaster)
ESPN-TV
Sports Dept
ESPN Plaza 935 Middle St
Bristol, CT 06010, USA

Ross, Katharine (Actor)
33050 Pacific Coast Hwy
Malibu, CA 90265-2300

Ross, Kevin (Athlete, Football Player)
146 High St
Woodbury, NJ 08096-2304, USA

Ross, Liberty (Actor)
c/o Stephanie Simon *Untitled Entertainment (LA)*
350 S Beverly Dr Ste 200
Beverly Hills, CA 90212-4819, USA

Ross, Lonny (Actor)
c/o Ashley Franklin *Thruline Entertainment*
9250 Wilshire Blvd Ste 100
Ground Floor
Beverly Hills, CA 90212-3343, USA

Ross, Louis (Athlete, Football Player)
4283 Booker St
Orlando, FL 32811-4662, USA

Ross, Marion (Actor)
4230 Natoma Ave
Woodland Hills, CA 91364-5623, USA

Ross, Mark (Athlete, Baseball Player)
2617 E Big View Dr
Oro Valley, AZ 85755-1938, USA

Ross, Mike (Congressman, Politician)
2436 Rayburn H B
Washington, DC 20515-0001, USA

Ross, Rick (Musician)
794 Evander Holyfield Hwy
Fairburn, GA 30213, USA

Ross, Robert J (Bobby) (Coach, Football Coach)
US Millitary Academy
Athletic Dept
West Point, NY 10996, USA

Ross, Ryan (Actor)
c/o Staff Member *Vincent Cirrincione Associates*
1516 N Fairfax Ave
Los Angeles, CA 90046-2608, USA

Ross, Scott (Athlete, Football Player)
303 Lake View Dr Unit D
Montgomery, TX 77356-5782, USA

Ross, Stan
1410 N Gardner St
Los Angeles, CA 90046-4142

Ross, Stephen M (Business Person)
Related Companies
60 Columbus Cir Fl 19
New York, NY 10023-5802, USA

Ross, Tracee Ellis (Actor)
c/o Jill Littman *Impression Entertainment*
9229 W Sunset Blvd Ste 700
West Hollywood, CA 90069-3407, USA

Ross, Willie (Athlete, Football Player)
1100 S Hamilton Ave
Chicago, IL 60612-4207, USA

Ross, Yolanda (Actor)
c/o Brian Liebman *Liebman Entertainment*
12 E 46th St Fl 5
New York, NY 10017-2418, USA

Rossdale, Gavin (Actor, Musician)
c/o Cynthia Pett-Dante *Brillstein
Entertainment Partners (LA)*
9150 Wilshire Blvd Ste 350
Beverly Hills, CA 90212-3453, USA

Rosselli, Jimmy
344 Paterson Plank Rd
Jersey City, NJ 07307-1051

Rosselli, Joe (Athlete, Baseball Player)
3827 Dixon Ct
Simi Valley, CA 93063-2834, USA

Rossellini, Isabella (Actor)
c/o Cindy Schultzel-Ambers *Art/Work
Entertainment*
5900 Wilshire Blvd Ste 1720
Los Angeles, CA 90036-5021, USA

Rossen, Daniel (Musician)
c/o Sam Kirby *William Morris Endeavor
(NY)*
1325 Avenue of the Americas
New York, NY 10019-6026, USA

Rossi, Gretchen (Reality Star)
c/o Marki Costello *Creative Management
Entertainment Group (CMEG)*
2050 S Bundy Dr Ste 280
Los Angeles, CA 90025-6128, USA

Rossi, Luigi Francis (Shorty) (Actor)
Shorty's Pit Bull Rescue
12405 Venice Blvd Ste 7
Los Angeles, CA 90066-3803, USA

Rossi, Theo (Actor)
c/o Michael Greene *Greene & Associates*
1901 Avenue of the Stars Ste 130
Los Angeles, CA 90067-6030, USA

Rossi, Tony (Ray) (Actor)
c/o Kristene Wallis *Wallis Agency*
210 N Pass Ave Ste 205
Burbank, CA 91505-3936, USA

Rossio, Terry (Writer)
c/o Brian Siberell *Creative Artists Agency
(CAA-LA)*
2000 Avenue of the Stars Ste 100
Los Angeles, CA 90067-4705, USA

Rossovich, Rick
PO Box 5617
Beverly Hills, CA 90209-5617

Rossovich, Tim (Athlete, Football Player)
19811 Wildwood West Dr
Penn Valley, CA 95946-9547, USA

Rossum, Allen (Athlete, Football Player)
2520 Johnson Dr
Mesquite, TX 75181-4619, USA

Rossum, Emmy (Actor, Musician)
c/o Christian Donatelli *The Schiff
Company*
9220 W Sunset Blvd Ste 106
West Hollywood, CA 90069-3500, USA

Rossy, Rico (Athlete, Baseball Player)
A7 Calle Atenas
Bayamon, PR 00959-4928, USA

Rostosky, Pete (Athlete, Football Player)
637 E McMurray Rd
Canonsburg, PA 15317-3430, USA

Rostow, Walt
5103 Valley Oak Dr
Austin, TX 78731-5408

Rote, Kyle
24700 Deepwater Point Dr Unit 14
Saint Michaels, MD 21663-2327

Rote, Tobin
7590 Lighthouse Rd
Port Hope, MI 48468-9760

Rote Jr, Kyle
6075 Poplar Ave # 920
Memphis, TN 38119-4740, USA

Rotem, Jonathan (J.R.) (Producer)
c/o Zach Katz *Beluga Heights
Management*
5225 Wilshire Blvd Ste 336
Los Angeles, CA 90036-4380, USA

Roth, Andrea (Actor)
c/o Adam Levine *Industry Entertainment*
955 Carrillo Dr Ste 300
Los Angeles, CA 90048-5400, USA

Roth, Arnold (Cartoonist)
9 Ebony Ct
Brooklyn, NY 11229-5939, USA

Roth, David Lee (Musician)
c/o Garry Buck *Monterey International*
PO Box 297
Carmel By The Sea, CA 93921-0297, USA

Roth, Doug (Athlete, Basketball Player)
9975 Spillway Cir Apt 201
Cordova, TN 38016-7152, USA

Roth, Ed (Race Car Driver)
The Rat Fink
377 E 100th N
Manti, UT 84642, USA

Roth, Eli (Producer, Writer)
c/o Simon Halls *Slate Public Relations*
9000 W Sunset Blvd Ste 915
West Hollywood, CA 90069-5809, USA

Roth, Ellaine (Baseball Player)
872 Goguac St W
Springfield, MI 49015-1737, USA

Roth, Eric (Writer)
c/o Staff Member *Creative Artists Agency
(CAA-LA)*
2000 Avenue of the Stars Ste 100
Los Angeles, CA 90067-4705, USA

Roth, Matt
PO Box 5617
Beverly Hills, CA 90209-5617

Roth, Philip (Writer)
c/o Andrew Wylie *The Andrew Wylie
Agency*
250 W 57th St Ste 2114
New York, NY 10107-2114, USA

Roth, Rachel (Actor)
c/o Justine Hunt *Hines and Hunt
Entertainment*
1213 W Magnolia Blvd
Burbank, CA 91506-1829, USA

Rothemund, Marc (Director)
c/o Daniel J Talbot *ICM Partners (LA)*
10250 Constellation Blvd Fl 7
Los Angeles, CA 90067-6207, USA

Rothenberg, Irv (Athlete, Basketball
Player)
6600 Capistrano Beach Trl
Delray Beach, FL 33446-5664, USA

Rothman, John
9229 W Sunset Blvd Ste 710
West Hollywood, CA 90069-3407

Rothman, Les (Athlete, Basketball Player)
11854 Fountainside Cir
Boynton Beach, FL 33437, USA

Rothrock, Cynthia
561 Calle Arroyo
Thousand Oaks, CA 91360-2506

Rothrock, Ray (Business Person)
Venrock
3340 Hillview Ave
Palo Alto, CA 94304-1276, USA

Rothschild, Larry (Athlete, Baseball
Player, Coach)
4508 W Culbreath Ave
Tampa, FL 33609-4206, USA

Rothstein, Ron (Athlete, Basketball Coach,
Basketball Player, Coach)
60 Edgewater Dr Apt 4E
Coral Gables, FL 33133-6971, USA

Rotimi (Actor, Dancer, Musician)
c/o Brian Sher *Category 5 Entertainment*
300 71st St Ste 620
Miami Beach, FL 33141-3089, USA

Rottino, Vinny (Athlete, Baseball Player)
4939 Crystal Spg
Racine, WI 53406-1526, USA

Rouen, Amy Van Dyken (Athlete,
Olympic Athlete, Swimmer)
20343 N Hayden Rd Ste 105
Scottsdale, AZ 85255-3876, USA

Rouen, Tom (Athlete, Football Player)
19947 N 84th St
Scottsdale, AZ 85255, USA

Roughan, Howard (Writer)
c/o Jennifer Rudolph Walsh *William
Morris Endeavor (NY)*
1325 Avenue of the Americas
New York, NY 10019-6026, USA

Rougier, Michael
RR 3
Vergennes, VT 05491, USA

Rouillard, Richard
11750 W Sunset Blvd Apt 117
Los Angeles, CA 90049-2904

Roulston, Tom (Athlete, Hockey Player)
5500 N Woodlawn St
Kechi, KS 67067-9052, USA

Roumel, Katie (Producer)
c/o Staff Member *Killer Films (US)*
526 W 26th St Rm 715
New York, NY 10001-5524, USA

Rounds, Michael (Governor, Politician)
2418 Whispering Shores Dr
Fort Pierre, SD 57532-2403, USA

Roundtree, Raleigh (Athlete, Football
Player)
2001 Roosevelt Dr
Augusta, GA 30904-5021, USA

Roundtree, Richard (Actor)
7120 Hayvenhurst Ave Ste 409
Van Nuys, CA 91406-3813, USA

Rounsaville, Gene (Athlete, Baseball
Player)
537 Red Rome Ln
Brentwood, CA 94513-2689, USA

Rountree, Mary (Athlete, Baseball Player)
8204 NW 80th St
Tamarac, FL 33321-1627, USA

Rourke, Jim (Athlete, Football Player)
466 Plymouth St
Abington, MA 02351-1842, USA

Rourke, Mickey (Actor)
1203 Washington Ave
Miami Beach, FL 33139-4613, USA

Rouse, Curtis (Athlete, Football Player)
710 Heatherhurst Ct
Clarksville, TN 37043-7221, USA

Rouse, Jeff (Athlete, Olympic Athlete,
Swimmer)
993 Vernon Berry Ln
Tracy, CA 95376-6708, USA

Rouse, mike (Athlete, Baseball Player)
4580 Big Branch Rd
Shingle Spgs, CA 95682-7511, USA

Rouse, Mitch (Actor)
c/o David (Dave) Becky *3 Arts
Entertainment (LA)*
9460 Wilshire Blvd Fl 7
Beverly Hills, CA 90212-2713, USA

Rousey, Ronda (Athlete, Olympic Athlete,
Wrestler)
c/o Brad Slater *William Morris Endeavor
(LA)*
9601 Wilshire Blvd
Beverly Hills, CA 90210-5213, USA

Roush, Jack (Race Car Driver)
Roush Racing
4202 Roush Pl NW
Concord, NC 28027-7112, USA

Rouson, Lee (Athlete, Football Player)
20 Main St
Flanders, NJ 07836-9112, USA

Roussel, Tom (Athlete, Football Player)
13 Heron Ln
Mandeville, LA 70471-6739, USA

Rousset, Christophe (Musician)
Trawick Artists
1926 Broadway
New York, NY 10023-6915, USA

Roustabouts, The
PO Box 25371
Charlotte, NC 28229-5371

Routh, Brandon (Actor)
c/o Stewart Strunk *Main Title
Entertainment*
8383 Wilshire Blvd Ste 408
Beverly Hills, CA 90211-2435, USA

Roux, Nick (Actor)
c/o Todd Diener *Untitled Entertainment
(LA)*
350 S Beverly Dr Ste 200
Beverly Hills, CA 90212-4819, USA

Rove, Karl (Government Official)
1111 New Hampshire Ave NW # 600
Washington, DC 20037, USA

Roven, Charles (Producer)
c/o Mara Buxbaum *ID Public Relations (LA)*
7060 Hollywood Blvd Fl 8th
Los Angeles, CA 90028-6021, USA

Rowan, Carl T
3116 Fessenden St NW
Washington, DC 20008-2029, USA

Rowan, Kelly (Actor, Producer)
c/o British (Brit) Reece *PMK/BNC Public Relations (PMK-LA)*
8687 Melrose Ave Ste 8
West Hollywood, CA 90069-5746, USA

Rowand, Aaron (Athlete, Baseball Player)
34 Meadowhawk Ln
Las Vegas, NV 89135-5201, USA

Rowdon, Wade (Athlete, Baseball Player)
230 Crooked Tree Trl
Deland, FL 32724-3426, USA

Rowe, Bob (Athlete, Football Player)
16304 Downey Terrace Ct
Ballwin, MO 63011-1915, USA

Rowe, Brad (Actor, Producer, Writer)
1327 Brinkley Ave
Los Angeles, CA 90049-3619, USA

Rowe, Dave (Athlete, Football Player)
372 Broken Arrow Trl
Boone, NC 28607-6535, USA

Rowe, John W (Business Person)
Aetna Inc
151 Farmington Ave
Hartford, CT 06156-0002, USA

Rowe, John W (Business Person)
Unicom Corp
10 S Dearborn St
Chicago, IL 60603-2300, USA

Rowe, Ken (Athlete, Baseball Player)
127 Morgan Lake Ln
Dallas, GA 30157-8115, USA

Rowe, Maggie (Comedian)
c/o Staff Member *ICM Partners (LA)*
10250 Constellation Blvd Fl 7
Los Angeles, CA 90067-6207, USA

Rowe, Mike (Television Host)
c/o Mary Sullivan *A Professional Law Corporation*
201 Santa Monica Blvd
Santa Monica, CA 90401-2214, USA

Rowe, Misty (Actor)
2193 River Rd
Egg Harbor City, NJ 08215-4745, USA

Rowe, Patrick (Athlete, Football Player)
6259 Alderley St
San Diego, CA 92114-6715, USA

Rowe, Ray (Athlete, Football Player)
11443 Westonhill Dr
San Diego, CA 92126-1450, USA

Rowe, Red
79 Margarita Ave
Camarillo, CA 93012-8113

rowe, Tom (Athlete, Hockey Player)
38 Holly Hill Dr
Amherst, NH 03031-1627

Rowe-Jackson, Debbie
435 N Roxbury Dr
Beverly Hills, CA 90210-5027

Rowell, Victoria (Actor)
c/o Tracy Christian *TCA/Jed Root*
6500 Wilshire Blvd Ste 2200
Los Angeles, CA 90048-4942, USA

Rowland, Betty (Dancer)
125 N Barrington Ave Apt 103
Los Angeles, CA 90049-2949, USA

Rowland, Brad (Athlete, Football Player)
3389 Lazy Acres Ln
The Villages, FL 32163-2485, USA

Rowland, Dave
PO Box 121089
Nashville, TN 37212-1089

Rowland, Derrick (Athlete, Basketball Player)
3 Island View Rd
Cohoes, NY 12047-4929, USA

Rowland, John (Ex-Governor, Politician)
98 Leonard Rd
Middlebury, CT 06762-3603, USA

Rowland, Justin (Athlete, Football Player)
1919 NW Loop 410 Ste 200
San Antonio, TX 78213-2325, USA

Rowland, Kelly (Musician)
c/o Marcus Grant *The Collective*
8383 Wilshire Blvd Ste 1050
Beverly Hills, CA 90211-2415, USA

Rowland, Landon H (Business Person)
Kansas City Southern
PO Box 219335
Kansas City, MO 64121-9335, USA

Rowland, Mike (Athlete, Baseball Player)
12104 E Mescal St
Scottsdale, AZ 85259-4230, USA

Rowland, Rich (Athlete, Baseball Player)
91 Clark Ave
Cloverdale, CA 95425-3918, USA

Rowland, Rodney (Actor, Model)
c/o Sandy Oroumieh *Rothman / Andres Entertainment*
4400 Coldwater Canyon Ave Ste 125
Studio City, CA 91604-5040, USA

Rowland, Troy (Producer)
c/o Susan Curtis *Curtis Talent Management*
9607 Arby Dr
Beverly Hills, CA 90210-1202, USA

Rowlands, Gena (Actor)
c/o Lou Pitt *Pitt Group, The*
8750 Wilshire Blvd Ste 301
Beverly Hills, CA 90211-2700, USA

Rowlands, Sherry
5055 Seminary Rd
Alexandria, VA 22311-2034

Rowley, Cynthia (Designer, Fashion Designer)
498 Fashion Ave
New York, NY 10018-6798, USA

Rowley, Elwood R (Athlete, Football Player)
14468 Bayou Terrace Dr
Saint Amant, LA 70774-3833, USA

Rowser, John (Athlete, Football Player)
17564 Alta Vista Dr
Southfield, MI 48075-1936, USA

Roxburgh, Richard (Actor, Music Group)
c/o Sandra Chang *Anonymous Content (LA)*
3532 Hayden Ave
Culver City, CA 90232-2413, USA

Roy, Andre (Athlete, Hockey Player)
17352 Emerald Chase Dr
Tampa, FL 33647-3517, USA

Roy, Arundhati (Writer)
c/o Kimberly Witherspoon *Inkwell Management*
521 5th Ave
New York, NY 10175-0003, USA

Roy, Brandon (Athlete, Basketball Player)
c/o Arn Tellem *Wasserman Media Group (LA)*
12100 W Olympic Blvd Ste 200
Los Angeles, CA 90064-1075, USA

Roy, Deep (Actor)
c/o Victor Kruglov *Victor Kruglov Talent Management*
6565 W Sunset Blvd Ste 200
Los Angeles, CA 90028-7219, USA

Roy, Derek (Athlete, Hockey Player)
100 Rivermist Dr
Buffalo, NY 14202-4300

Roy, Drew (Actor)
c/o Mark Armstrong *Sanders Armstrong Caserta*
2120 Colorado Ave Ste 120
Santa Monica, CA 90404-3561, USA

Roy, John (Actor, Comedian)
c/o Gabrielle Krengel *Domain Talent*
9229 W Sunset Blvd Ste 710
West Hollywood, CA 90069-3407, USA

Roy, Patricia (Athlete, Baseball Player)
201 E Amkey Way
Carmel, IN 46032-5170, USA

Roy, Rachel (Fashion Designer)
The Jones Group Inc
180 Rittenhouse Cir
Bristol, PA 19007-1618, USA

Roy, Stephane (Race Car Driver)
Hammerhead Racing
7026 E Aster Dr
Scottsdale, AZ 85254-5327, USA

Royal, Billy Joe (Musician, Songwriter, Writer)
1306 Patterson St
Morehead City, NC 28557-4100, USA

Royal, Robert (Athlete, Football Player)
43268 Hill Head Pl
Leesburg, VA 20176-3902, USA

Royals, Mark (Athlete, Football Player)
4035 Courtside Way
Tampa, FL 33618-2748, USA

Royals, Reggie (Athlete, Basketball Player)
PO Box 742
Tulsa, OK 74101-0742, USA

Royal Underground (Music Group)
c/o Jill Siegel *10th Street Entertainment (LA)*
700 N San Vicente Blvd Ste G410
West Hollywood, CA 90069-5060, USA

Roybal-Allard, Lucille (Congressman, Politician)
2330 Rayburn Hob
Washington, DC 20515-0534, USA

Royce, Mike (Comedian)
c/o Staff Member *United Talent Agency (UTA-LA)*
9336 Civic Center Dr
Beverly Hills, CA 90210-3604, USA

Roye, Orpheus (Athlete, Football Player)
26403 Primrose Ln
Westlake, OH 44145-5491, USA

Royer, Stan (Athlete, Baseball Player)
9301 Christopher Lake Dr
Columbia, IL 62236-3458, USA

Roylance, Juanita (Baseball Player)
PO Box 282
Lorida, FL 33857-0282, USA

Roylance, Pamela
221 S Gale Dr Unit 403
Beverly Hills, CA 90211-5409

Royster, Jeron K (Jerry) (Athlete, Baseball Player, Coach)
36000 Portofino Cir Apt 114
Palm Beach Gardens, FL 33418-1284, USA

Royster, Mazio (Athlete, Football Player)
15529 Cardiff Ln
Victorville, CA 92394-1592, USA

Royster, Willie (Athlete, Baseball Player)
229 55th St NE
Washington, DC 20019-6737, USA

Rozalla (Musician)
c/o Staff Member *Diva Central Inc*
7510 W Sunset Blvd Ste 1445
Los Angeles, CA 90046-3408, USA

Rozelle, Pete (Athlete, Football Player)
23800 Valley Oak Ct
Newhall, CA 91321-3746, USA

Rozema, Dave (Athlete, Baseball Player)
1560 N Renaud Rd
Grosse Pointe Woods, MI 48236-1763, USA

Rozier, Clifford (Athlete, Basketball Player)
PO Box 1194
Palmetto, FL 34220-1194, USA

Rozier, Mike (Athlete, Football Player, Heisman Trophy Winner)
9 Hidden Hollow Ln
Sicklerville, NJ 08081-3910, USA

Roznovsky, Vic (Athlete, Baseball Player)
266 W Bluff Ave
Fresno, CA 93711-6930, USA

Rozon, Tim (Actor)
c/o Pearl Hanan *Pearl Hanan Management*
7775 W Sunset Blvd Ste 118
Los Angeles, CA 90046-3911, USA

Rozumek, Dave (Athlete, Football Player)
18 Old Rockingham Rd
Salem, NH 03079-2111, USA

Rozzell, Aubrey (Athlete, Football Player)
PO Box 844
Quitman, MS 39355-0844, USA

R. Pierluisi, Pedro (Congressman, Politician)
1213 Longworth Hob
Washington, DC 20515-1313, USA

R. Pitts, Joseph (Congressman, Politician)
420 Carmon Hob
Washington, DC 20515-0001, USA

R. Rothman, Stevan (Congressman, Politician)
2303 Rayburn Hob
Washington, DC 20515-0920, USA

R. Rothman, Steven (Congressman, Politician)
2303 Rayburn Hob
Washington, DC 20515-0920, USA

R. Royce, Edward (Congressman, Politician)
2185 Rayburn Hob
Washington, DC 20515-1405, USA

R. Tipton, Scott (Congressman, Politician)
218 Cannon Hob
Washington, DC 20515-2803, USA

R. Turner, Michael (Congressman, Politician)
2454 Rayburn Hob
Washington, DC 20515-1312, USA

Ruah, Daniela (Actor)
c/o Samantha Hill *WKT Public Relations (LA)*
9350 Wilshire Blvd Ste 450
Beverly Hills, CA 90212-3230, USA

Rubalcaba, Gonzalo (Musician)
Eardrums Music
5930 NW 201st St
Miami, FL 33105, USA

Rubel, Fran (Director, Producer)
c/o Staff Member *Kuzui Enterprises*
8225 Santa Monica Blvd
West Hollywood, CA 90046-5912, USA

Ruben, Joseph P (Joe) (Director)
250 W 57th St # 1905
New York, NY 10107-0001, USA

Rubens, Larry (Athlete, Football Player)
611 Waterside Cir
Andersonville, TN 37705-2123, USA

Rubenstein, Ann (Correspondent)
NBC-TV
30 Rockefeller Plz
News Dept
New York, NY 10112-0015, USA

Rubenstein, David (Business Person)
Carlyle Group
1001 Pennsylvania Ave NW Ste 220S
Washington, DC 20004-2573, USA

Ruberto, Sonny (Athlete, Baseball Player)
207 Ambridge Ct
204
Chesterfield, MO 63017-9506, USA

Rubick, Rob (Athlete, Football Player)
1571 Stonewood Dr
Lapeer, MI 48446-4200, USA

Rubin, Amy (Actor)
Hervey/Grimes
PO Box 64249
Los Angeles, CA 90064-0249, USA

Rubin, Chanda (Athlete, Olympic Athlete, Tennis Player)
708 S Saint Antoine St
Lafayette, LA 70501-5740, USA

Rubin, Chandra (Tennis Player)
708 S Saint Antoine St
Lafayette, LA 70501-5740, USA

Rubin, Gloria (Actor)
c/o Leigh Brillstein *Resolution (LA)*
10250 Constellation Blvd Fl 7
Los Angeles, CA 90067-6207, USA

Rubin, Leigh (Cartoonist)
Creators Syndicate
737 3rd St
Hermosa Beach, CA 90254-4714, USA

Rubin, Rick (Musician, Producer)
c/o Staff Member *American Recordings*
3300 Warner Blvd
Burbank, CA 91505-4632, USA

Rubin, Vanessa (Musician)
Joel Chriss
300 Mercer St Apt 3J
New York, NY 10003-6732, USA

Rubinek, Saul (Actor)
Gersh Agency
232 N Canon Dr
Beverly Hills, CA 90210-5302, USA

Rubinoff, Marla (Actor)
c/o Staff Member *John Glenn Harding Management*
7004 Oakwood Ave
Los Angeles, CA 90036-2660, USA

Rubins, Kathleen Dr (Astronaut)
2300 Halls Creek Ct
Friendswood, TX 77546-2539, USA

Rubinstein, John (Actor)
4417 Leydon Ave
Woodland Hills, CA 91364-4847, USA

Rubinstein, Zeida (Actor)
The Agency
1800 Avenue of the Stars Ste 400
Los Angeles, CA 90067-4206, USA

Rubin-Vega, Daphne (Actor)
c/o Jeremy Katz *Katz Company, The*
1674 Broadway Ste 7E
New York, NY 10019-5888, USA

Rubio, Marco (Senator)
B40A Dirksen Senate Office Bldg
Washington, DC 20510-0001, USA

Rubio, Paulina (Musician)
c/o Rick Canny *Sanctuary Artist Management*
8750 Wilshire Blvd Ste 200
Beverly Hills, CA 90211-2707, USA

Rubio, Ricky (Athlete, Basketball Player)
c/o Dan Fegan *Relativity Sports (LA)*
9242 Beverly Blvd Ste 300
Beverly Hills, CA 90210-3728, USA

Ruby & The Romantics
1650 Broadway Ste 508
New York, NY 10019-6833

Rucchin, Steve (Athlete, Hockey Player)
614 Acacia Ave
Corona Del Mar, CA 92625-1907

Rucci, Todd (Athlete, Football Player)
5 Southview Ln
Lititz, PA 17543-8205, USA

Ruccolo, Richard (Actor)
ER Talent
301 W 53rd St Apt 4K
New York, NY 10019-5768, USA

Rucinski, Mike (Athlete, Hockey Player)
5175 Pinetum Trl
Brighton, MI 48114-9076

Rucinski, Mike (Athlete, Hockey Player)
11980 Cape Cod Ln
Huntley, IL 60142-8168

Ruck, Alan (Actor)
c/o Lisa Lieberman *Innovative Artists (NY)*
235 Park Ave S Fl 7
New York, NY 10003-1405, USA

Rucka, Leo (Athlete, Football Player)
814 Crosby Dayton Rd
Crosby, TX 77532-5803, USA

Ruckelshaus, William D (Business Person, Government Official, Politician)
PO Box 76
Medina, WA 98039-0076, USA

Rucker, Darius (Musician)
c/o Scott McGhee *McGhee Entertainment*
8730 W Sunset Blvd Ste 175
West Hollywood, CA 90069-2246, USA

Rucker, Dave (Athlete, Baseball Player)
18602 Piper Pl
Yorba Linda, CA 92886-2559, USA

Rucker, Michael (Athlete, Football Player)
3039 Kings Manor Dr
Matthews, NC 28104-6868, USA

Rucker, Reggie (Athlete, Football Player)
26300 Village Ln Apt 303
Beachwood, OH 44122-8520, USA

Rucker, Reginald J (Reggie) (Athlete, Football Player)
3128 Richmond Rd
Beachwood, OH 44122-3249, USA

Rudd, Delaney (Athlete, Basketball Player)
422 Chesham Dr
Kernersville, NC 27284-7017, USA

Rudd, Dwayne (Athlete, Football Player)
PO Box 273309
Boca Raton, FL 33427-3309, USA

Rudd, John (Athlete, Basketball Player)
4440 Sweet Bay Dr
Lake Charles, LA 70611-3240, USA

Rudd, Paul (Actor)
95 Horatio St Apt 7K
New York, NY 10014-1590, USA

Rudd, Ricky (Race Car Driver)
Entertainment Market
124 Summerville Dr
Mooresville, NC 28115-7864, USA

Rudd, Xavier (Musician)
c/o Staff Member *Paradigm (Monterey)*
404 W Franklin St
Monterey, CA 93940-2303, USA

Ruddock, Donovan (Razor) (Boxer)
7379 NW 34th St
Lauderhill, FL 33319-4962, USA

Ruddy, Al
1601 Clear View Dr
Beverly Hills, CA 90210-2010

Ruddy, Albert (Producer)
1601 Clear View Dr
Beverly Hills, CA 90210-2010, USA

Ruddy, Tim (Athlete, Football Player)
PO Box 268553
Fort Lauderdale, FL 33326-8553, USA

Rudelsky, Seth (Actor, Radio Personality)
On Broadway - Sirius
1221 Avenue of the Americas
New York, NY 10020-1001, USA

Ruder, Bill
9494 Wicklow Dr
Brentwood, TN 37027-3539, USA

Rudi, Joseph O (Joe) (Athlete, Baseball Player)
PO Box 425
Baker City, OR 97814-0425, USA

Rudie, Evelyn (Actor)
Santa Monica Playhouse
7514 Hollywood Blvd
Los Angeles, CA 90046-2814, USA

Rudin, Scott (Producer)
Scott Rudin Productions
120 W 45th St Ste 1001
New York, NY 10036-4031, USA

Rudis-Bestudik, Mary (Baseball Player)
4333 Deeboyar Ave
Lakewood, CA 90712-3703, USA

Rudnay, Jack (Athlete, Football Player)
7219 Whipperwill Rd
Versailles, MO 65084-4033, USA

Rudner, Rita (Actor, Comedian)
331 Monarch Bay Dr
Dana Point, CA 92629-3408, USA

Rudnick, Paul (Writer)
c/o Robert (Bob) Bookman *Paradigm (LA)*
2000 Avenue of the Stars
Los Angeles, CA 90067-4700, USA

Rudnick, Tim (Athlete, Football Player)
1516 Heather Ln
Des Plaines, IL 60018-1400, USA

Rudolph, Alan
15760 Ventura Blvd Fl 16
Encino, CA 91436-3027

Rudolph, Alan S (Director)
International Creative Mgmt
10250 Constellation Blvd Fl 1
Los Angeles, CA 90067-6241, USA

Rudolph, Ben (Athlete, Football Player)
561 E General Gorgas Dr
Mobile, AL 36617-3036, USA

Rudolph, Coleman (Athlete, Football Player)
412 Billings Farm Ln
Canton, GA 30115, USA

Rudolph, Council (Athlete, Football Player)
8310 Lago Vista Dr
Tampa, FL 33614-2769, USA

Rudolph, Ken (Athlete, Baseball Player)
1317 W Sands Ct
Gilbert, AZ 85233-6637, USA

Rudolph, Kyle (Athlete, Football Player)
c/o David Dunn *Athletes First, LLC*
23091 Mill Creek Dr
Laguna Hills, CA 92653-1258, USA

Rudolph, Larry (Producer)
c/o Staff Member *ReignDeer Entertainment*
100 Glendon Ave
Suite 1100
Los Angeles, CA 90024, USA

Rudolph, Maya (Actor)
4900 Casa Dr
Tarzana, CA 91356-3941, USA

Rudometkin, John (Athlete, Basketball Player)
6181 Wise Rd
Newcastle, CA 95658-9231, USA

Rudzinski, Paul (Athlete, Football Player)
3216 Delahaut St
Green Bay, WI 54301-1551, USA

Rue, Sara (Actor)
c/o Alan David *Alan David Management*
8840 Wilshire Blvd Ste 200
Beverly Hills, CA 90211-2606, USA

Ruebel, Matt (Athlete, Baseball Player)
7509 W Augusta Blvd
Yorktown, IN 47396-9354, USA

Ruegamer, Grey (Athlete, Football Player)
PO Box 70155
Las Vegas, NV 89170-0155, USA

Ruehl, Mercedes (Actor)
c/o Jonathan Howard *Innovative Artists (LA)*
1505 10th St
Santa Monica, CA 90401-2805, USA

Ruelas, Gabriel (Gabe) (Athlete, Boxer)
1119 S Hudson Ave
Los Angeles, CA 90019-1807, USA

Ruell, Aaron (Actor, Director, Writer)
c/o Staff Member *Brillstein Entertainment Partners (LA)*
9150 Wilshire Blvd Ste 350
Beverly Hills, CA 90212-3453, USA

Rueter, Kirk (Athlete, Baseball Player)
46 Pheasant Ridge Ct
Nashville, IL 62263-5845, USA

Ruether, Mike (Athlete, Football Player)
23014 Gardner Dr
Alpharetta, GA 30009-2179, USA

Ruettgers, Ken (Athlete, Football Player)
16897 Golden Stone Dr
Sisters, OR 97759-9696, USA

Ruettgers, Michael C (Business Person)
ECM Corp
35 Parkway Dr
Hopkinton, MA 01748, USA

Ruettiger, Daniel (Rudy) (Athlete, Football Player)
293 Goldstar St
Henderson, NV 89012-0104, USA

Ruff, Lindy (Athlete, Coach, Hockey Player)
5006 Winding Ln
Clarence, NY 14031-1500, USA

Ruff, Lindy (Athlete, Hockey Player)
Buffalo Sabres
1 Seymour H Knox III Plz Ste 1
Buffalo, NY 14203-3096

Ruffalo, Mark (Actor)
c/o Aleen Keshishian *Brillstein Entertainment Partners (LA)*
9150 Wilshire Blvd Ste 350
Beverly Hills, CA 90212-3453, USA

Ruffcorn, Scott (Athlete, Baseball Player)
2137 Barton Hills Dr
Austin, TX 78704-4659, USA

Ruffin, Bruce (Athlete, Baseball Player)
4808 Pyrenees Pass
Austin, TX 78738-4020, USA

Ruffin, Jimmy
102 Ryders Ln
East Brunswick, NJ 08816-1328

Ruffin, Johnny (Athlete, Baseball Player)
4229 Trumpworth Ct
Valrico, FL 33596-8494, USA

Ruffner, Barry (Athlete, Football Player)
134 Frogtown Rd
New Alexandria, PA 15670-3080, USA

Ruffner, Paul (Athlete, Basketball Player)
4508 Brookshire Dr
Provo, UT 84604-5245, USA

Rufus
7250 Beverly Blvd Ste 200
Los Angeles, CA 90036-2560

Ruge, John A (Cartoonist)
240 Bronxville Rd Apt B4
Bronxville, NY 10708-2800, USA

Ruggiano, Justin (Athlete, Baseball Player)
153 Falcon Point Dr
Rockwall, TX 75032-8651, USA

Ruggiero, Angela (Athlete, Hockey Player, Olympic Athlete)
Shade Global
171 W 57th St Apt 8A
New York, NY 10019-2222, USA

Ruhman, Chris (Athlete, Football Player)
13206 Vinery Ct
Cypress, TX 77429-5195, USA

Ruivivar, Anthony Michael (Actor)
c/o Nick Collins *Gersh (LA)*
9465 Wilshire Blvd Ste 600
Beverly Hills, CA 90212-2605, USA

Ruiz, Chico (Athlete, Baseball Player)
267 Calle Tapia
San Juan, PR 00912-4201, USA

Ruiz, John (Boxer)
John Ruiz Inc
PO Box 2581
Taunton, MA 02780-0980, USA

Rukavina, Terry (Baseball Player)
6676 Washington Cir
Franklin, OH 45005-5521, USA

Ruklick, Joe (Athlete, Basketball Player)
1300 Central St Apt 302
Evanston, IL 60201-1678, USA

Ruland, Jeff (Athlete, Basketball Player)
38 Glen Lake Dr
Medford, NJ 08055-3104, USA

Rule, Bob (Athlete, Basketball Player)
4303 Kansas Ave
Riverside, CA 92507-5153, USA

Rule, Gordon (Athlete, Football Player)
27712 N 130th Ave
Peoria, AZ 85383-2862, USA

Rulin, Olesya (Actor)
c/o Brian Medavoy *Medavoy Management*
10203 Santa Monica Blvd Ste 400
Los Angeles, CA 90067-6405, USA

Rullo, Jerry (Athlete, Basketball Player)
3EE Brookline Blvd
Havertown, PA 19083, USA

Rumble, Darren (Athlete, Hockey Player)
Seattle Thunderbirds
625 W James St
Kent, WA 98032-4406

Rumer (Music Group, Musician)
c/o Christian Bernhardt *Agency Group Ltd, The (LA)*
1880 Century Park E
Los Angeles, CA 90067-1600, USA

Rummells, Dave (Golfer)
1820 Harbor Blvd
Kissimmee, FL 34744-6623, USA

Rumsey, Janet (Athlete, Baseball Player)
7830 W County Road 80 N
Greensburg, IN 47240-7910, USA

Rumsfeld, Donald (Business Person)
1718 M St NW # 366
Washington, DC 20036-4504, USA

Runager, Max (Athlete, Football Player)
PO Box 37971
Rock Hill, SC 29732-0534, USA

Runco, Mario Lt Cmdr (Astronaut)
207 Lakeshore Dr
Seabrook, TX 77586-6128, USA

Rundgren, Todd (Musician)
c/o Staff Member *The Agency Group (NYC)*
142 W 57th St Fl 6
New York, NY 10019-3300, USA

Rundles, Rich (Athlete, Baseball Player)
2103 Creekside Way
Jefferson City, TN 37760-1707, USA

Run DMC (Music Group)
c/o Tracey Miller *Tracey Miller & Associates*
2610 Fire Rd
Egg Harbor Township, NJ 08234-9551, USA

Runga, Bic (Musician)
c/o Staff Member *Paradigm (Monterey)*
404 W Franklin St
Monterey, CA 93940-2303, USA

Runge, Brian (Athlete, Baseball Player)
8225 E County Dr
El Cajon, CA 92021-8826, USA

Runge, Paul (Athlete, Baseball Player)
1719 W Community Dr
Jupiter, FL 33458-8218, USA

Runge, Paul (Athlete, Baseball Player)
8225 E County Dr
El Cajon, CA 92021-8826, USA

Runnells, Tom (Athlete, Baseball Player, Coach)
6045 Settlers Ridge Cir
Sylvania, OH 43560-9474, USA

Runnels, Terri (Model, Wrestler)
11520 NW 8th Ln
Gainesville, FL 32606-0408, USA

Runnels, Jr, Virgil (Dusty Rhodes) (Athlete, Wrestler)
c/o Staff Member *World Wrestling Entertainment (WWE)*
1241 E Main St
Titan Towers
Stamford, CT 06902-3520, USA

RunningWolf, Myrton (Actor)
c/o Tracey Mapes *Imperium 7 Talent Agency*
5455 Wilshire Blvd Ste 1706
Los Angeles, CA 90036-4217, USA

Runyan, Jon (Congressman, Politician)
1239 Longworth Hob
Washington, DC 20515-3213, USA

Runyan, Jon (Athlete, Football Player)
262 Mount Laurel Rd
Mount Laurel, NJ 08054, USA

Runyan, Marla (Athlete, Olympic Athlete, Track Athlete)
42 Royal St
Watertown, MA 02472-2766, USA

Runyan, Sean (Athlete, Baseball Player)
1958 Bermuda Pointe Dr
Haines City, FL 33844-2413, USA

Runyon, Jennifer (Actor)
5922 SW Amberwood Ave
Corvallis, OR 97333-2702, USA

RuPaul (Impersonator, Musician, Reality Star)
RuCo Inc
332 Bleecker St # F-22
New York, NY 10014-2980, USA

Rupe, Josh (Athlete, Baseball Player)
225 Arrowfield Rd
Virginia Beach, VA 23454-4300, USA

Rupe, Ryan (Athlete, Baseball Player)
5338 Pine Wood Hills Ct
Spring, TX 77386-3801, USA

Rupp, Debra Jo (Actor)
c/o Staff Member *Christopher Wright Management*
3207 Winnie Dr
Los Angeles, CA 90068-1439, USA

Rupp, Duane (Athlete, Hockey Player)
2446 McMonagle Ave
Pittsburgh, PA 15216-2705, USA

Rupp, Michael (Athlete, Hockey Player)
1936 Medford Sq
Hilliard, OH 43026

Ruppersberger, C. A. (Congressman, Politician)
2453 Rayburn Hob
Washington, DC 20515-3514, USA

Ruprecht, Tom (Writer)
c/o Staff Member *3 Arts Entertainment (LA)*
9460 Wilshire Blvd Fl 7
Beverly Hills, CA 90212-2713, USA

Rusch, Glendon (Athlete, Baseball Player)
6428 Chaffee St
Tujunga, CA 91042-2811, USA

Rusch, Kristine Kathryn (Writer)
PO Box 479
Lincoln City, OR 97367-0479, USA

Rush, Barbara (Actor)
1709 Tropical Ave
Beverly Hills, CA 90210, USA

Rush, Cathy (Athlete, Basketball Player)
2433 Linden Dr
Havertown, PA 19083-1651, USA

Rush, Deborah (Actor)
c/o Rhonda Price *Gersh (NY)*
41 Madison Ave
New York, NY 10010-2202, USA

Rush, Geoffrey (Actor)
c/o Stan Rosenfield *Stan Rosenfield & Associates*
2029 Century Park E Ste 1190
Los Angeles, CA 90067-2931, USA

Rush, Jerry (Athlete, Football Player)
17536 Oak Dr
Detroit, MI 48221-2747, USA

Rush, Joshua (Actor)
c/o Susan Curtis *Curtis Talent Management*
9607 Arby Dr
Beverly Hills, CA 90210-1202, USA

Rush, Kareem (Athlete, Basketball Player)
2805 E 62nd St
Kansas City, MO 64130-3745, USA

Rush, Mathew (Adult Film Star)
c/o Staff Member *Diva Central Inc*
7510 W Sunset Blvd Ste 1445
Los Angeles, CA 90046-3408, USA

Rush, Matthew (Actor, Adult Film Star)
c/o Staff Member *Diva Central Inc*
7510 W Sunset Blvd Ste 1445
Los Angeles, CA 90046-3408, USA

Rush, Merrilee (Musician)
21458 NE Redmond Fall City Rd
Redmond, WA 98053-8227, USA

Rush, Odeya (Actor)
c/o Ruth Bernstein *Viewpoint Inc (LA)*
8820 Wilshire Blvd Ste 220
Beverly Hills, CA 90211-2622, USA

Rush, Robert J (Athlete, Football Player)
8201 Scruggs Dr
Germantown, TN 38138-6119, USA

Rush, Rudy (Comedian)
c/o Staff Member *ICM Partners (LA)*
10250 Constellation Blvd Fl 7
Los Angeles, CA 90067-6207, USA

Rush, Sarah (Actor)
c/o Staff Member *Acme Talent & Literary (LA)*
1400 Atlantic Ave Ste 274
Long Beach, CA 90813-2013, USA

Rush, Tom (Musician)
Maple Hill Productions Inc
PO Box 1570
Wilson, WY 83014-1570, USA

Rushen, Patrice
PO Box 6278
Altadena, CA 91003-6278, USA

Rushford, Jim (Athlete, Baseball Player)
45 W Camino Presidio Quemado
Sahuarita, AZ 85629-8842, USA

Rushing, Marion (Athlete, Football Player)
358 Bathon Dr
Pinckneyville, IL 62274-3335, USA

Ruskin, Scott (Athlete, Baseball Player)
387 Saint Johns Golf Dr
Saint Augustine, FL 32092-1082, USA

Ruskowski, Terry (Athlete, Hockey Player)
7000 Langmuir Dr
McKinney, TX 75071-4604, USA

Rusler, Robert
c/o Staff Member *Ellis Talent Group*
4705 Laurel Canyon Blvd Ste 300
Valley Village, CA 91607-5901, USA

Russ, Steve (Athlete, Football Player)
PO Box 817
Buffalo, NY 14224-0817, USA

Russ, Tim (Actor, Director)
7336 Santa Monica Blvd # 711
West Hollywood, CA 90046-6616, USA

Russell, Adam (Athlete, Baseball Player)
627 Mariner Vlg
Huron, OH 44839-1004, USA

Russell, Andy (Athlete, Football Player)
625 Liberty Ave Ste 3100
Pittsburgh, PA 15222-3115, USA

Russell, Austin ""Chumlee"" (Reality Star)
24040 Camino Del Avion
A127
Dana Point, CA 92629-4005, USA

Russell, Betsy (Actor)
c/o Mark Burg *Evolution Entertainment (LA)*
901 N Highland Ave
Los Angeles, CA 90038-2412, USA

Russell, Bill (Athlete, Baseball Player, Coach)
27982 Red Pine Ct
Valencia, CA 91354-1888, USA

Russell, Bill (Athlete, Basketball Player, Olympic Athlete)
9415 SE 52nd St
Mercer Island, WA 98040-4723, USA

Russell, Brenda (Actor, Musician)
c/o Seth Keller *SKM Artist Management*
PO Box 25906
Los Angeles, CA 90025-0906, USA

Russell, Brian (Athlete, Football Player)
20 Laguna Pl
Long Beach, CA 90803-4435, USA

Russell, Bryon
455E E Thousand Oaks Blvd Ste 1EE
Thousand Oaks, CA 91362, USA

Russell, Campy (Athlete, Basketball Player)
66 Earlmoor Blvd
Pontiac, MI 48341-2816, USA

Russell, Cazzie (Athlete, Basketball Player)
Savannah College of Art and Design
425 W Montgomery Xrd
Live Oak Community Church
Savannah, GA 31406-3310, USA

Russell, Chuck (Director)
c/o Robert Stein *Paradigm (LA)*
360 N Crescent Dr
North Bldg
Beverly Hills, CA 90210-4874, USA

Russell, David O (Actor, Director, Producer)
c/o Nikki Weiss *Nikki Weiss & Co.*
4646 Saloma Ave
Sherman Oaks, CA 91403-2511, USA

Russell, Fred (Sportscaster)
226 Ensworth Pl
Nashville, TN 37205-1922, USA

Russell, JaMarcus (Athlete, Football Player)
2325 River Forest Rd
Mobile, AL 36605-4440, USA

Russell, James (Athlete, Baseball Player)
2325 Oak Knoll Dr
Colleyville, TX 76034-4478, USA

Russell, Jeannie (Actor)
101923 Riverside Dr
N Hollywood, CA 91602, USA

Russell, Jeff (Athlete, Baseball Player)
2325 Oak Knoll Dr
Colleyville, TX 76034-4478, USA

Russell, John (Athlete, Baseball Player, Coach)
8004 Grand Estuary Trl Unit 103
Trl Unit 103
Bradenton, FL 34212-4256, USA

Russell, Johnny
PO Box 740091
San Diego, CA 92174-0091

Russell, Keri (Actor)
c/o Joanna (Joanie) Burstein *Burstein Company, The*
15304 W Sunset Blvd Ste 208
Pacific Palisades, CA 90272-3656, USA

Russell, Kimberly (Actor)
11617 Laurelwood Dr
Studio City, CA 91604-3818

Russell, Kurt (Actor, Producer, Writer)
c/o Michael Cooper *Creative Artists Agency (CAA-LA)*
2000 Avenue of the Stars Ste 100
Los Angeles, CA 90067-4705, USA

Russell, Leon (Musician)
Leon Russell Records
PO Box 7044
Overland Park, KS 66207-0044, USA

Russell, Leonard (Athlete, Football Player)
497 Saint Louis Ave Apt 102
Long Beach, CA 90814-3363, USA

Russell, Mark (Politician)
PO Box 9904
Washington, DC 20016-8904, USA

Russell, Mark
3201 33rd Pl NW
Washington, DC 20008-3304

Russell, Phil (Athlete, Hockey Player)
590 Wind Drift Ln
Spring Lake, MI 49456-2168

Russell, Rubin (Athlete, Basketball Player)
PO Box Bix
Grand Prairie, TX 75054, USA

Russell, T E
8271 Melrose Ave Ste 110
Los Angeles, CA 90046-6800, USA

Russell, Theresa (Actor)
c/o Scott Zimmerman *Evolution Entertainment (LA)*
901 N Highland Ave
Los Angeles, CA 90038-2412, USA

Russell, Twan (Athlete, Football Player)
11201 NW 8th St
Plantation, FL 33325-1508, USA

Russert, Luke (Correspondent)
c/o Staff Member *NBC Nightly News*
30 Rockefeller Plz # 300S
New York, NY 10112-0015, USA

Russo, Deanna (Actor)
c/o Cheryl McLean *Creative Public Relations*
3385 Oak Glen Dr
Los Angeles, CA 90068-1311, USA

Russo, James (Actor)
c/o Staff Member *United Talent Agency (UTA-LA)*
9336 Civic Center Dr
Beverly Hills, CA 90210-3604, USA

Russo, Joe (Director, Producer, Writer)
c/o Staff Member *United Talent Agency (UTA-LA)*
9336 Civic Center Dr
Beverly Hills, CA 90210-3604, USA

Russo, John
218 Euclid Ave
Glassport, PA 15045-1331

Russo, Patricia (Business Person)
Lucent Technologies Inc
600 Mountain Ave
New Providence, NJ 07974-2008, USA

Russo, Rene (Actor, Model)
c/o John Crosby *John Crosby Management*
1357 N Spaulding Ave
Los Angeles, CA 90046-4009, USA

Rust, Paul (Actor)
c/o Christie Smith *Mosaic Media Group*
9200 W Sunset Blvd Ste 10
West Hollywood, CA 90069-3608, USA

Rust, Rod (Athlete, Football Coach, Football Player)
1 W 13th St
Ocean City, NJ 08226-2945, USA

Rusteck, Dick (Athlete, Baseball Player)
13470 Peters Rd
Lake Oswego, OR 97035-1333, USA

Rutan, Elbert L (Burt) (Designer)
6383 E Dewey Cir
Coeur D Alene, ID 83814-7918, USA

Rutan, Richard G (Dick) (Designer)
2833 Delmar Ave
Mojave, CA 93501-1113, USA

Rutgens, Joe (Athlete, Football Player)
227 W Devlin St
Spring Valley, IL 61362-1923, USA

Ruth, Lauren (Cartoonist)
PO Box 200206
New Haven, CT 06520-0206, USA

Ruth, Mike (Athlete, Football Player)
17 Rock Ridge Dr
Atkinson, NH 03811-5117, USA

Rutherford, Jim (Athlete, Hockey Player)
2542 Village Manor Way
Raleigh, NC 27614-8099, USA

Rutherford, Jim (Athlete, Hockey Player)
Carolina Hurricanes
1400 Edwards Mill Rd
Raleigh, NC 27607-3624

Rutherford, Johnny (Athlete, Baseball Player)
802 Helston Rd
Bloomfield Hills, MI 48304-2016, USA

Rutherford, Johnny (Race Car Driver)
4919 Black Oak Ln
River Oaks, TX 76114-2933

Rutherfurd, Emily (Actor)
c/o Chris Schmidt *Paradigm (LA)*
360 N Crescent Dr
North Bldg
Beverly Hills, CA 90210-4874, USA

Ruthven, Dick (Athlete, Baseball Player)
13480 Providence Lake Dr
Alpharetta, GA 30004-7510, USA

Rutigliano, Sam (Athlete, Coach, Football Coach, Football Player)
9671 Metcalf Rd
Willoughby, OH 44094-9744, USA

Rutkowski, Ed (Athlete, Football Player)
47 Brenton Ln
Hamburg, NY 14075-4327, USA

Rutkowski, Ken (Business Person, Radio Personality)
Business Rockstars, LLC
604 Arizona Ave
Santa Monica, CA 90401-1610, USA

Rutland, Reggie (Athlete, Football Player)
4265 Jailette Rd
Atlanta, GA 30349-1881, USA

Rutledge, Jeffrey R (Jeff) (Athlete, Coach, Football Coach, Football Player)
6102 W Gary Dr
Chandler, AZ 85226-1193, USA

Rutledge, Johnny (Athlete, Football Player)
948 SW Avenue J
Belle Glade, FL 33430-4232, USA

Rutschman, Adolph (Ad) (Coach, Football Coach)
2142 NW Pinehurst Dr
McMinnville, OR 97128-2426, USA

Ruttan, Susan (Actor)
c/o Christopher Black *Opus Entertainment*
5225 Wilshire Blvd Ste 905
Los Angeles, CA 90036-4353, USA

Rutten, Bas (Actor, Athlete, Wrestler)
c/o Chandra Keyes *Jeff Sussman Management*
15374 Dickens St Fl 2
Sherman Oaks, CA 91403-3007

Ruttman, Joe (Race Car Driver)
c/o Staff Member *NASCAR*
1801 W Speedway Blvd
Daytona Beach, FL 32114-1243, USA

Ruud, Tom (Athlete, Football Player)
1821 S 33rd St
Lincoln, NE 68506-1905, USA

Ruuska, Percy Sylvia (Swimmer)
4216 College View Way
Carmichael, CA 95608, USA

Ruzek, Roger (Athlete, Football Player)
921 Warwick St
Bedford, TX 76022-7856, USA

Ruzicka, Vladimir (Athlete, Hockey
Player)
17 Highland Ct
Needham, MA 02492-3149, USA

R. Wolf, Frank (Congressman, Politician)
241 Cannon Hob
Washington, DC 20515-4610, USA

Ryal, Mark (Athlete, Baseball Player)
307 Fairway Dr
Perkins, OK 74059-4421, USA

Ryal, Rusty (Athlete, Baseball Player)
307 Fairway Dr
Perkins, OK 74059-4421, USA

Ryan, Amy (Actor)
c/o Jennifer Wiley *Framework
Entertainment (NY)*
129 W 27th St Fl 12
New York, NY 10001-6206, USA

Ryan, Arthur F (Business Person)
Prudential Insurance
751 Broad St
Prudential Plaza
Newark, NJ 07102-3714, USA

Ryan, B J (Athlete, Baseball Player)
4014 Wisteria Ln
Benton, LA 71006-9368, USA

Ryan, B J (Athlete, Baseball Player)
1211 Perdenalas Trl
Westlake, TX 76262-4820, USA

Ryan, Blanchard (Actor)
c/o Staff Member *Jeff Morrone
Entertainment*
9350 Wilshire Blvd Ste 224
Beverly Hills, CA 90212-3204, USA

Ryan, Buddy (Athlete, Football Coach,
Football Player)
819 Abingdon Ln
Shelbyville, KY 40065-6310, USA

Ryan, Dave (Musician)
c/o Staff Member *The Agency Group
(NYC)*
142 W 57th St Fl 6
New York, NY 10019-3300, USA

Ryan, Debble (Comedian)
University of Virginia
Athletic Dept
PO Box 3785
Charlottesville, VA 22903, USA

Ryan, Debby (Actor)
c/o Michael Hepburn *Industry
Entertainment*
955 Carrillo Dr Ste 300
Los Angeles, CA 90048-5400, USA

Ryan, Dusty (Athlete, Baseball Player)
3906 Menton Ct
Merced, CA 95348-9537, USA

Ryan, Ed (Horse Racer)
PO Box 6249
Freehold, NJ 07728-6249, USA

Ryan, Frank (Athlete, Football Player)
PO Box 185
Grafton, VT 05146-0185, USA

Ryan, Jay (Athlete, Baseball Player)
1232 Rocky River Rd W
Charlotte, NC 28213-5034, USA

Ryan, Jeri (Actor)
c/o David Lust *Rogers & Cowan PR (LA)*
8687 Melrose Ave Ste 7
West Hollywood, CA 90069-5721, USA

Ryan, Ken (Athlete, Baseball Player)
45 Tanager Rd
Seekonk, MA 02771-2707, USA

Ryan, Lee (Actor)
c/o Jack Gilardi *ICM Partners (LA)*
10250 Constellation Blvd Fl 7
Los Angeles, CA 90067-6207, USA

Ryan, Lisa Dean (Actor)
c/o Staff Member *Pakula/King &
Associates*
9229 W Sunset Blvd Ste 315
West Hollywood, CA 90069-3403, USA

Ryan, Logan (Athlete, Football Player)
c/o Neil Schwartz *Schwartz & Feinsod*
contact via telephone or email
White Plains, NY 10603

Ryan, Marisa (Actor)
c/o Bob McGowan *McGowan
Management*
8733 W Sunset Blvd Ste 103
West Hollywood, CA 90069-2241, USA

Ryan, Mark (Actor)
c/o Staff Member *Starfish PR*
PO Box 7000-54
Redondo Beach, CA 90277, USA

Ryan, Matt (Athlete, Football Player)
c/o Ben Dogra *CAA (St. Louis)*
222 S Central Ave Ste 1008
Saint Louis, MO 63105-3509, USA

Ryan, Max (Actor)
c/o Erik Kritzer *LINK Entertainment*
11872 La Grange Ave Fl 1
Los Angeles, CA 90025-5283, USA

Ryan, Meg (Actor)
c/o Stephen Huvane *Slate Public
Relations*
9000 W Sunset Blvd Ste 915
West Hollywood, CA 90069-5809, USA

Ryan, Michael (Athlete, Baseball Player)
521 Water St
Indiana, PA 15701-1927, USA

Ryan, Michelle (Actor)
c/o Philip Grenz *ICM Partners (LA)*
10250 Constellation Blvd Fl 7
Los Angeles, CA 90067-6207, USA

Ryan, Mike (Athlete, Baseball Player)
592 Stoneham Rd
Wolfeboro, NH 03894-4711, USA

Ryan, Mitchell (Actor)
30355 Mulholland Hwy
Agoura Hills, CA 91301-3117, USA

Ryan, Nolan (Athlete, Baseball Player)
The Nolan Ryan Foundation
2925 S Bypass 35
Alvin, TX 77511, USA

Ryan, Pat (Athlete, Football Player)
6930 Old Kent Dr
Knoxville, TN 37919-7472, USA

Ryan, Patrick G (Business Person)
Aon Corp
200 E Randolf St
Chicago, IL 60601, USA

Ryan, Paul (Congressman, Politician)
20 S Main St Ste 10
Janesville, WI 53545-3959, USA

Ryan, Rex (Athlete, Football Coach)
c/o David Dunn *Athletes First, LLC*
23091 Mill Creek Dr
Laguna Hills, CA 92653-1258, USA

Ryan, Rob (Athlete, Baseball Player)
12402 N Division St
Spokane, WA 99218-1930, USA

Ryan, Roz (Actor)
c/o Staff Member *Gage Group, The (LA)*
5757 Wilshire Blvd Ste 659
Los Angeles, CA 90036-3682, USA

Ryan, Ryan (Actor)
c/o Staff Member *Warner Bros Television
Production*
4000 Warner Blvd
Burbank, CA 91522-0002

Ryan, Shawn (Producer)
c/o Staff Member *ICM Partners (LA)*
10250 Constellation Blvd Fl 7
Los Angeles, CA 90067-6207, USA

Ryan, Thomas M (Business Person)
CVS Corp
1 Cvs Dr
Woonsocket, RI 02895-6184, USA

Ryan, Tim (Congressman, Politician)
1421 Longworth Hob
Washington, DC 20515-4703, USA

Ryan, Tim E (Athlete, Football Player)
1159 Calle Ventura
San Jose, CA 95120-5503, USA

Ryan, Timothy T (Tim) (Athlete, Football
Player)
4901 Sugar Creek Dr
Evansville, IN 47715-7744, USA

Ryan, Tom K (Cartoonist)
North American Syndicate
235 E 45th St
New York, NY 10017-3305, USA

Ryans, Larry (Athlete, Football Player)
110 Brookfield Dr
Greenwood, SC 29646-8501, USA

Rybska, Agnieszka (Music Group,
Musician)
RPM Music Productions
130 W 57th St Apt 9D
New York, NY 10019-3311, USA

Rychlec, Tom (Athlete, Football Player)
71 Round Hill Rd
Southington, CT 06489-3645, USA

Ryckman, Billy (Athlete, Football Player)
PO Box 60804
Lafayette, LA 70596-0804, USA

rycroft, Mark (Athlete, Hockey Player)
2746 S Grant St
Englewood, CO 80113-1611

Rycroft, Melissa (Actor)
c/o Susan Madore *Guttman Associates*
118 S Beverly Dr Ste 201
Beverly Hills, CA 90212-3016, USA

Ryczek, Dan (Athlete, Football Player)
3714 Monitor Pl
Olney, MD 20832-2248, USA

Ryczek, Paul (Athlete, Football Player)
9335 Scott Rd
Roswell, GA 30076-3416, USA

Rydalch, Ron (Athlete, Football Player)
500 E Durfee St
Grantsville, UT 84029-9514, USA

Rydell, Bobby (Actor, Music Group,
Musician)
917 Bryn Mawr Ave
Penn Valley, PA 19072-1524, USA

Rydell, Christopher (Actor)
911 N Sweetzer Ave Apt C
West Hollywood, CA 90069-4368, USA

Rydell, Mark (Director)
Concourse Productions
3110 Main St Ste 220
Santa Monica, CA 90405-5353, USA

Ryder, JoJo (Actor, Producer, Writer)
c/o Staff Member *Untouchable J
Productions*
9300 Civic Center Dr # 202
Beverly Hills, CA 90210-3604, USA

Ryder, Mark (Actor)
c/o Andrew Kurland *ICM Partners (LA)*
10250 Constellation Blvd Fl 7
Los Angeles, CA 90067-6207, USA

Ryder, Michael (Athlete, Hockey Player)
c/o Staff Member *Boston Bruins*
100 Legends Way Ste 250
Td Banknorth Garden
Boston, MA 02114-1389, USA

Ryder, Mitch (Music Group, Musician)
Entertainment Services Int'l
6400 Pleasant Park Dr
Chanhassen, MN 55317-8804, USA

Ryder, Nick (Athlete, Football Player)
14 Ridgeway
Goshen, NY 10924-1408, USA

Ryder, Thomas O (Publisher)
Reader's Digest Assn
PO Box 100
Pleasantville, NY 10570-0100, USA

Ryder, Winona (Actor)
2526 Union St
San Francisco, CA 94123-3833, USA

Ryders, Ruff (Music Group)
c/o Staff Member *M.A.G./Universal
Attractions*
15 W 36th St Fl 8
New York, NY 10018-7927, USA

Rydman, Blaine (Athlete, Hockey Player)
132 Wintergreen Rd
Winston Salem, NC 27107-1754, USA

Rydze, Richard (Athlete, Diver, Olympic
Athlete)
915 Penn Ave Apt 1011
Pittsburgh, PA 15222-3831, USA

Ryerson, Ann
935 Gayley Ave
Los Angeles, CA 90024-2805

Ryerson, Gary (Athlete, Baseball Player)
1059 Terrace Crst
El Cajon, CA 92019-3129, USA

Ryff, Frankie
2055 McGraw Ave
Bronx, NY 10462-8014

Ryknow (Musician)
c/o Staff Member *The Agency Group* (NYC)
142 W 57th St Fl 6
New York, NY 10019-3300, USA

Rylan, Marcy (Actor)
c/o Marnie Sparer *Innovative Artists (LA)*
1505 10th St
Santa Monica, CA 90401-2805, USA

Rymer, Charlie (Golfer)
225 Magnolia St
Windermere, FL 34786-8635, USA

Rymsha, Andy (Athlete, Hockey Player)
8144 Huntington Rd
Huntington Woods, MI 48070-1654

Rypien, Mark (Race Car Driver)
8817 N Warren St
Spokane, WA 99208-4346, USA

Ryun, Jim (Athlete, Olympic Athlete, Track Athlete)
132 D St SE
Washington, DC 20003-1810, USA

RZA (Artist, Director, Musician)
c/o Holly Shakoor Fleischer *42West (LA)*
1840 Century Park E Ste 700
Los Angeles, CA 90067-2122, USA

Rzepczynski, Marc (Athlete, Baseball Player)
5415 Christopher Dr
Yorba Linda, CA 92887-5851, USA

Rzeznik, Johnny (Musician)
c/o Staff Member *William Morris Endeavor (LA)*
9601 Wilshire Blvd
Beverly Hills, CA 90210-5213, USA

S, Kimberley
c/o Staff Member *Diva Central Inc*
7510 W Sunset Blvd Ste 1445
Los Angeles, CA 90046-3408, USA

S, Kimberly (DJ)
c/o Len Evans *Project Publicity*
312 W 53rd St Ste 202
New York, NY 10019-5743, USA

s, Mel (Athlete, Baseball Player)
270 Home Run Dr
West Columbia, WV 25287-8692, USA

S, Robin (Musician)
c/o Stephen Ford *Diva Central Inc*
7510 W Sunset Blvd Ste 1445
Los Angeles, CA 90046-3408, USA

Saadiq, Raphael (Musician)
c/o Marty Diamond *Paradigm (NY)*
360 Park Ave S Fl 16
New York, NY 10010-1716, USA

Saalfeld, Kelly (Athlete, Football Player)
444 N 185th Ct Apt 307
Elkhorn, NE 68022-7936, USA

Saari, Roy A (Swimmer)
PO Box 7086
Mammoth Lakes, CA 93546-7086, USA

Saarloos, Kirk (Athlete, Baseball Player)
2518 Stadium Dr
Fort Worth, TX 76109-1369, USA

Saban, Haim (Business Person, Producer)
61 Beverly Park
Beverly Hills, CA 90210-1569, USA

Saban, Nick (Athlete, Football Coach, Football Player)
1549 Sharlo Ave
Baton Rouge, LA 70820-4553, USA

Sabara, Daryl (Actor)
c/o Katie Rhodes *Untitled Entertainment (LA)*
350 S Beverly Dr Ste 200
Beverly Hills, CA 90212-4819, USA

Sabathia, CC (Athlete, Baseball Player)
PO Box 30
Alpine, NJ 07620-0030, usa

Sabatini, Gabriela (Tennis Player)
151 Crandon Blvd Apt 1123
Key Biscayne, FL 33149-1566, USA

Sabatino, Joe (Actor)
c/o Melanie Sharp *Sharp Talent*
5538 Willowcrest Ave
North Hollywood, CA 91601-2830, USA

Sabatino, Michael (Actor)
13538 Valleyheart Dr N
Sherman Oaks, CA 91423-3124, USA

Sabato Jr, Antonio (Actor, Model)
c/o Tracy Steinsapir *Main Title Entertainment*
8383 Wilshire Blvd Ste 408
Beverly Hills, CA 90211-2435, USA

Sabb, Dwayne (Athlete, Football Player)
26 Marie Rd
Fords, NJ 08863-1306, USA

Sabbatini, Rory (Athlete, Golfer)
2939 Crockett St Apt 348
Fort Worth, TX 76107-2957, USA

Sabean, Brian (Baseball Player)
12 Solana Ct
Belmont, CL 94NN2, USA

Sabel, Erik (Athlete, Baseball Player)
4609 Haven Ct
W Lafayette, IN 47906-5600, USA

Sabelle (Music Group, Musician, Songwriter, Writer)
Sarmast Entertainment
241 W 36th St Apt 2R
New York, NY 10018-7541, USA

Saberhagen, Bret W (Athlete, Baseball Player)
Make a Difference Foundation
22817 Ventura Blvd Ste 474
Woodland Hills, CA 91364-1202, USA

Sabihy, Kyle (Actor)
c/o Dino May *Dino May Management*
6362 Hollywood Blvd # 422
Los Angeles, CA 90028-6323, USA

Sabiston Jr, David C (Doctor)
622 Cedar Club Cir
Chapel Hill, NC 27517-7215, USA

Sablan, Gregorio (Congressman, Politician)
423 Cannon Hob
Washington, DC 20515-4305, USA

Sabo, Christopher A (Chris) (Athlete, Baseball Player)
7455 Stonemeadow Ln
Montgomery, OH 45242-6305, USA

Sabo-Dusanko, Julie (Baseball Player)
7702 E Doubletree Ranch Rd Ste 150
Scottsdale, AZ 85258-2130, USA

Sabourin, Bob (Athlete, Hockey Player)
7400 Hogan Rd Apt 219
Jacksonville, FL 32216-1608

Sabuda, Robert (Writer)
155 W 72nd St Rm 401
New York, NY 10023-3250, USA

Sacchi, Robert (Actor)
203 N Gramercy Pl
Los Angeles, CA 90004-4021

Sacco, David (Athlete, Hockey Player, Olympic Athlete)
3 Bishop Ln
Middleton, MA 01949-1697, USA

Sacco, Joe (Athlete, Hockey Player)
Colorado Avalanche
1000 Chopper Cir
Denver, CO 80204-5805

Sacco, Joe (Athlete, Hockey Player, Olympic Athlete)
c/o Staff Member *Fantagraphics Books*
7563 Lake City Way NE
Seattle, WA 98115-4218, USA

Saccomanno, Mark
4711 Spicewood Springs Rd Unit 141
Austin, TX 78759-8428, USA

Sachs, Richard (Doctor)
6 Saint Ronan Ter
New Haven, CT 06511-2315, USA

Sachs, William (Director)
3739 Montuso Pl
Encino, CA 91436-4001, USA

Sack, Kevin (Journalist)
Los Angeles Times
202 W 1st St Ste 500
Editorial Dept
Los Angeles, CA 90012-4401, USA

Sack, Steve (Cartoonist)
Minneapolis Star-Tribune
425 Portland Ave
Minneapolis, MN 55488-0002, USA

Sackhoff, Katee (Actor)
c/o Leland LaBarre *Bleu, An Entertainment Company*
5225 Wilshire Blvd Ste 336
Los Angeles, CA 90036-4380, USA

Sackinsky, Brian (Athlete, Baseball Player)
5310 Humboldt Dr
Rocklin, CA 95765-4807, USA

Sacks, Greg (Race Car Driver)
6092 Sabal Creek Blvd
Port Orange, FL 32128-7131, USA

Sacks, Oliver W (Doctor, Writer)
2 Horatio St Apt 3G
New York, NY 10014-1638, USA

Sacramone, Alicia (Athlete, Gymnast, Olympic Athlete)
c/o Staff Member *USA Gymnastics*
132 E Washington St Ste 700
Indianapolis, IN 46204-3674, USA

Sacre, Robert (Athlete, Basketball Player)
c/o Keith Kreiter *Edge Sports International*
75 Tri State Intl Ste 180
Lincolnshire, IL 60069-4422, USA

Sadat, Madame Jehan
2310 Decatur Pl NW
Washington, DC 20008-4010

Sadecki, Raymond M (Ray) (Athlete, Baseball Player)
4237 E Clovis Ave
Mesa, AZ 85206-1945, USA

Sadek, Mike (Athlete, Baseball Player)
6741 Quartz Mine Rd
Mountain Ranch, CA, 95246-9748, USA

Sadik, Nafis (Government Official)
United Nations Population Fund
220 E 42nd St
New York, NY 10017-5806, USA

Sadler, Billy (Athlete, Baseball Player)
236 Llnverness Dr
Pensacola, FL 32503, USA

Sadler, Carl (Athlete, Baseball Player)
2752 Morgan Whiddon Rd
Perry, FL 32347-8702, USA

Sadler, Donnie (Athlete, Baseball Player)
802 Sadler Rd
Valley Mills, TX 76689-4499, USA

Sadler, Elliott (Race Car Driver)
108 Conway Ct
Mooresville, NC 28117-6052, USA

Sadler, Hermie (Race Car Driver)
PO Box 32
Emporia, VA 23847-0032, USA

Sadler, Ray (Athlete, Baseball Player)
4423 Lake Shore Villa Dr
Waco, TX 76710-1448, USA

Sadler, William (Actor)
c/o James Suskin *James Suskin Management*
2 Charlton St Apt 5K
New York, NY 10014-4970, USA

Sadoski, Thomas (Actor)
c/o Howard Axel *TMT Entertainment Group*
648 Broadway # 1002
New York, NY 10012-2348, USA

Sadowski, Bob (Athlete, Baseball Player)
26 Barrington Ct
Sharpsburg, GA 30277-1849, USA

Sadowski, Bob (Athlete, Baseball Player)
1465 Creekside Dr
High Ridge, MO 63049-1314, USA

Sadowski, Jim (Athlete, Baseball Player)
696 Sloop Rd
Pittsburgh, PA 15237-4164, USA

Sadowski, Jonathan (Actor)
c/o Siri Garber *Platform Public Relations*
2666 N Beachwood Dr
Los Angeles, CA 90068-2308, USA

Sadowsky, Clint (Athlete, Baseball Player)
2801 Tropicana Ave
Norman, OK 73071-1711, USA

Saenz, Chris (Athlete, Baseball Player)
7919 N Rondure Loop
Tucson, AZ 85743-7413, USA

Safer, Morley (Journalist)
c/o *60 Minutes CBS News (NY)*
524 W 57th St Fl 8
New York, NY 10019-2930, USA

Saferight, Harry (Baseball Player)
2321 Wadebridge Rd
Midlothian, VA 23113-3839, USA

Saffell, Tom (Athlete, Baseball Player)
19240 Olympia St
Porter Ranch, CA 91326-2962, USA

Saffiotti, Umberto (Doctor)
5114 Wissioming Rd
Bethesda, MD 20816-2259, USA

Safina, Dinara (Athlete, Tennis Player)
c/o Staff Member *Women's Tennis Association (WTA (US))*
1 Progress Plz Ste 1500
St Petersburg, FL 33701-4335, USA

Safka, Melanie (Musician)
Two Story Records, Inc
53 Baymont St
Clearwater Beach, FL 33767-1705, USA

Safran Foer, Jonathan (Writer)
c/o Geoffrey Sanford *Rabineau Wachter & Sanford Literary*
522 Wilshire Blvd Ste L
Santa Monica, CA 90401-1445, USA

Safuto, Dominick (Randy) (Music Group, Musician)
PO Box 656507
Fresh Meadows, NY 11365-6507, USA

Safuto, Frank (Music Group, Musician)
PO Box 656507
Fresh Meadows, NY 11365-6507, USA

Sagal, Jean (Actor)
Progressive Artists Agency
400 S Beverly Dr Ste 216
Beverly Hills, CA 90212-4404, USA

Sagal, Katey (Actor)
c/o Belle Zwerdling *B and B Management*
9696 Culver Blvd Ste 110
Culver City, CA 90232-2737, USA

Sagal, Liz (Actor)
c/o Staff Member *Gersh (LA)*
9465 Wilshire Blvd Ste 600
Beverly Hills, CA 90212-2605, USA

Saganiuk, Rocky (Athlete, Hockey Player)
12909 Norwich St
Plainfield, IL 60585-7908

Sagansky, Jeff
145 Ocean Avenue Ext
Santa Monica, CA 90402-1211

Sage, Halston (Actor)
c/o Nick Styne *Creative Artists Agency (CAA-LA)*
2000 Avenue of the Stars Ste 100
Los Angeles, CA 90067-4705, USA

Sage, William (Actor)
Gersh Agency
232 N Canon Dr
Beverly Hills, CA 90210-5302, USA

Sagely, Floyd (Athlete, Football Player)
181 Wildflower Pl W
Edwards, CO 81632, USA

Sagemiller, Melissa (Actor)
c/o Leslie Siebert *Gersh (LA)*
9465 Wilshire Blvd Ste 600
Beverly Hills, CA 90212-2605, USA

Sager, A J (Athlete, Baseball Player)
10310 Belmont Meadows Ln
Perrysburg, OH 43551-6403, USA

Sager, Carole Bayer (Musician, Songwriter)
10761 Bellagio Rd
Los Angeles, CA 90077-3731, USA

Saget, Bob (Actor)
c/o Daniel (Danny) Sussman *Brillstein Entertainment Partners (LA)*
9150 Wilshire Blvd Ste 350
Beverly Hills, CA 90212-3453, USA

Sagmoen, Marc (Athlete, Baseball Player)
19715 1st Pl SW
Normandy Park, WA 98166-4007, USA

Sagnier, Ludivine (Actor)
c/o Jon Rubinstein *Authentic Talent and Literary Management*
20 Jay St Ste M17
Brooklyn, NY 11201-8300, USA

Sagona, Katie (Actor)
Wilhelmina Creative Mgmt
300 Park Ave S # 200
New York, NY 10010-5313, USA

Sahagun, Elena (Actor)
Artists Agency
1180 S Beverly Dr Ste 301
Los Angeles, CA 90035-1154, USA

Sahara Hotnights (Music Group)
c/o Staff Member *Paradigm (Monterey)*
404 W Franklin St
Monterey, CA 93940-2303, USA

Sahgal, Ajay (Actor, Producer, Writer)
c/o Nicole Clemens *ICM Partners (LA)*
10250 Constellation Blvd Fl 7
Los Angeles, CA 90067-6207, USA

Sahl, Mort (Actor, Comedian)
1441 3rd Ave Apt 12C
New York, NY 10028-1976, USA

Said, Boris (Race Car Driver)
32675 Schoolcraft Rd
Livonia, MI 48150-1604, USA

Said III, Boris (Race Car Driver)
441 Victory Rd
Winchester, VA 22602-4567, USA

Saidock, Tom (Athlete, Football Player)
20316 Old Colony Rd
Dearborn Heights, MI 48127-2758, USA

Sailors, Kenny (Ken) (Athlete, Basketball Player)
571E Howe Ln
Laramie, WY 82070, USA

Saindon, Pat (Athlete, Football Player)
PO Box 264
Helena, AL 35080-0264, USA

Saint, Eva Marie (Actor)
c/o Joel Dean *TalentWorks (LA)*
3500 W Olive Ave Ste 1400
Burbank, CA 91505-5512, USA

Saint, Silva (Adult Film Star)
c/o Staff Member *Atlas Multimedia Inc*
9005 Eton Ave Ste C
Canoga Park, CA 91304-6533, USA

Saint, Sylvia
Suze.net
26500 Agoura Rd # 389
Calabasas, CA 91302-1952

Sainte-Marie, Buffy (Musician, Songwriter)
RR 1 Box 368
Kapaa, HI 96746, USA

Saipe, Mike (Athlete, Baseball Player)
4191 Combe Way
San Diego, CA 92122-2511, USA

Sajak, Pat (Game Show Host)
c/o Staff Member *PAT Productions*
10202 Washington Blvd
Robert Young Bldg, Suite 2000
Culver City, CA 90232-3119, USA

Sajko, Kristina (Model)
Karin Models
6 W 14th St Ste 3
New York, NY 10011-7506, USA

Sakamoto, Soichi (Coach, Swimmer)
768 McCully St
Honolulu, HI 96826-5908, USA

Sakata, Lenn (Athlete, Baseball Player)
San Jose Giants
6770 Hawaii Kai Dr Apt 609
Honolulu, HI 96825-1529, USA

Sakharov, Alik (Cinematographer)
6050 Kennedy Blvd E Apt 4D
West New York, NJ 07093-3932, USA

Saks, Gene (Actor, Director)
International Creative Mgmt
40 W 57th St Fl 5
New York, NY 10019-4001, USA

Sala, Richard (Cartoonist)
3131 College Ave
Berkeley, CA 94705-2740, USA

Salaam, Abdul (Athlete, Football Player)
11153 Embassy Dr
Cincinnati, OH 45240-3005, USA

Salaam, Ephraim (Athlete, Football Player)
c/o Staff Member *EAG Sports Management*
909 N Sepulveda Blvd Ste 360
El Segundo, CA 90245-3864, USA

Salaam, Rashaan (Athlete, Football Player, Heisman Trophy Winner)
2191 Enterprise St
Superior, CO 80027-4433, USA

Salahi, Michaele (Reality Star)
c/o Staff Member *Bravo (NY)*
30 Rockefeller Plz
New York, NY 10112-0015, USA

Salanda, Zoe (Actor)
c/o Andrea Pett-Joseph *Brillstein Entertainment Partners (LA)*
9150 Wilshire Blvd Ste 350
Beverly Hills, CA 90212-3453, USA

Salans, Lester B (Doctor)
Sandoz Research Institute
RR 10
East Hanover, NJ 07936, USA

Salas, Mark (Athlete, Baseball Player)
1302 6th St SE
Ruskin, FL 33570-5308, USA

Salata, Paul (Athlete, Football Player)
3723 Birch St Ste 11
Newport Beach, CA 92660-2614, USA

Salata, Sheri (Producer)
c/o Staff Member *OWN: The Oprah Winfrey Network*
5700 Wilshire Blvd Ste 120
Los Angeles, CA 90036-3644, USA

Salazar, Alberto (Athlete, Olympic Athlete, Track Athlete)
1 SW Bowerman Dr
Beaverton, OR 97005-0979, USA

Salazar, Arion (Musician)
Eric Godtland Mgmt
5715 Claremont Ave # C
Oakland, CA 94618-1279, USA

Salazar, Eliseo (Race Car Driver)
701 S Girls School Rd
Indianapolis, IN 46231-3132, USA

Salazar, Luis (Athlete, Baseball Player)
20808 Cabrillo Way
Boca Raton, FL 33428-1201, USA

Saldana, Theresa (Actor)
c/o Staff Member *Leavitt Talent Group*
8222 Melrose Ave Ste 203
Los Angeles, CA 90046-6838, USA

Saldana, Zoe (Actor)
2320 St George St
Los Angeles, CA 90027-3204, USA

Saldanha, Carlos (Animator, Director)
c/o Staff Member *Blue Sky Studios*
1 American Ln Ste 210
Greenwich, CT 06831-2563, USA

Saldi, Jay (Athlete, Football Player)
303 Donley Ct
Southlake, TX 76092-5940, USA

Saleaumua, Dan (Athlete, Football Player)
8234 Marshall Dr
Overland Park, KS 66214-1537, USA

Saleen, Steve
Saleen Inc.
76 Fairbanks
Irvine, CA 92618-1602, USA

Salem, Dahlia (Actor)
c/o Robert (Rob) Gomez *Precision Entertainment*
465 N Croft Ave
Los Angeles, CA 90048-2508, USA

Salem, Harvey (Athlete, Football Player)
25 Menlo Pl
Berkeley, CA 94707-1532, USA

Salemi, Sam (Athlete, Football Player)
2971 Delaware Ave
Buffalo, NY 14217-2353, USA

Salenger, Meredith (Actor)
c/o Scott Zimmerman *Evolution Entertainment (LA)*
901 N Highland Ave
Los Angeles, CA 90038-2412, USA

Salerno-Sonnenberg, Nadja (Musician)
Columbia Artists Mgmt Inc
165 W 57th St
New York, NY 10019-2201, USA

Sales, Nykesha (Basketball Player)
Connecticut Sun
Mohegan Sun Arena
Uncasville, CT 06382, USA

Saleski, Don (Athlete, Hockey Player)
1800 N Ridley Creek Rd
Media, PA 19063-4529, USA

Salgado, Michael (Musician)
c/o Staff Member *Sony Music Miami*
605 Lincoln Rd Ste 700
Miami Beach, FL 33139-2901, USA

Saliba, Metropolitan Primate Philip (Religious Leader)
Antiochian Orthodox Christian Diocese
358 Mountain Rd
Englewood, NJ 07631-3798, USA

Saliers, Emily (Musician, Songwriter, Writer)
c/o Staff Member *Russell Carter Artists*
567 Ralph McGill Blvd NE
Atlanta, GA 30312-1110, USA

Salinas, Dixie Carter (Producer)
TNA Wrestling, LLC
209 10th Ave S Ste 302
Nashville, TN 37203-0730, USA

Salinas, Maria Elena (Actor)
c/o Staff Member *Univision*
605 3rd Ave Fl 12
New York, NY 10158-0034, USA

Salinger, Diane (Actor)
c/o Robert Depp *Beverly Hecht Agency*
6320 Canoga Ave Fl 15
Woodland Hills, CA 91367-2563, USA

Salinger, Matt (Actor)
Bresler Kelly Assoc
11500 W Olympic Blvd Ste 510
Los Angeles, CA 90064-1527, USA

Salisbury, Sean (Athlete, Football Player)
8616 Pauline St
Plano, TX 75024-6877, USA

Salise, Steve (Congressman, Politician)
429 Cannon Hob
Washington, DC 20515-3202, USA

Salkeld, Roger (Athlete, Baseball Player)
27824 Ridgegrove Dr
Santa Clarita, CA 91350-1747, USA

Salles, Gualter (Race Car Driver)
Dale Coyne Racing
13400 S Budler Rd
Plainfield, IL 60544-9493, United States

Salles, Walter (Director, Producer)
c/o Staff Member *William Morris Endeavor (LA)*
9601 Wilshire Blvd
Beverly Hills, CA 90210-5213, USA

Salley, John (Athlete, Basketball Player, Television Host)
Black Folk Entertainment
Salley Foundation
1ees2 Shana Way
Elk Grove, CA 95757, USA

Salling, Mark (Actor)
c/o Jason Solomon *Full Circle Management*
4932 Lankershim Blvd Ste 202
North Hollywood, CA 91601-4452, USA

Sally, Jerome (Athlete, Football Player)
4107 Roxbury Ct
Columbia, MO 65203-6832, USA

Salmon, Brad (Athlete, Baseball Player)
11102 Herschel Loop
Daphne, AL 36526-6648, USA

Salmon, Tim (Athlete, Baseball Player)
6061 E Sunnyside Dr
Scottsdale, AZ 85254-4977, USA

Salmons, John (Basketball Player)
Philadelphia 76ers
909 Waverly Rd
Bryn Mawr, PA 19010-1930, USA

Salo, Tommy (Athlete, Hockey Player)
Leksands IF Ishockey
PO Box 118
Leksand, S- SWEDE

Salome, Angel (Athlete, Baseball Player)
2153 Amsterdam Ave Apt 15
New York, NY 10032-2530, USA

Salomon, Mikael (Cinematographer)
c/o Patrick Hughes *Intellectual Artists Management*
10585 Santa Monica Blvd Ste 135
Los Angeles, CA 90025-6392, USA

Salonen, Brian (Athlete, Football Player)
2801 S Russell St Ste 33
Missoula, MT 59801-7914, USA

Salopek, Paul (Journalist)
Chicago Tribune
435 N Michigan Ave Ste 200
Editorial Dept
Chicago, IL 60611-4024, USA

Salt, Jennifer (Actor, Writer)
c/o Emily Rose *Mosaic Media Group*
9200 W Sunset Blvd Ste 10
West Hollywood, CA 90069-3608, USA

Saltalamacchia, Jarrod (Athlete, Baseball Player)
2095 Windsock Way
Wellington, FL 33414-8304, USA

Salter, Bryant (Athlete, Football Player)
16810 SW 88th Ct
Palmetto Bay, FL 33157-4537, USA

Salter, Hans
3658 Woodhill Canyon Rd
Studio City, CA 91604-3658

Salt-N-Pepa (Music Group)
c/o Stephen Ford *Diva Central Inc*
7510 W Sunset Blvd Ste 1445
Los Angeles, CA 90046-3408, USA

Salva, Victor (Director)
c/o Staff Member *Gersh (LA)*
9465 Wilshire Blvd Ste 600
Beverly Hills, CA 90212-2605, USA

Salvador, Bryce (Athlete, Hockey Player)
422 Lenox Ave
Westfield, NJ 07090-2140

Salvador, Henri
6 Place Vendome
Addison, TX 75001

Salvadori, Al (Athlete, Basketball Player)
787 Lindsay Rd
Carnegie, PA 15106-3845, USA

Salvail, Eve (DJ)
c/o Len Evans *Project Publicity*
312 W 53rd St Ste 202
New York, NY 10019-5743, USA

Salvatore, Robert Anthony (R.A.) (Writer)
c/o Staff Member *Random House*
1540 Broadway
New York, NY 10036-4039, USA

Salvino, Carmen (Bowler)
65 Stevens Dr
Schaumburg, IL 60173-2176, USA

Sam, Michael (Athlete, Football Player)
c/o Cameron Weiss *Empire Athletes*
2200 Colorado Ave Apt 729
Santa Monica, CA 90404-5534, USA

Samaras, Lucas (Artist, Photographer)
Pace Gallery
32 E 57th St Fl 4
New York, NY 10022-2530, USA

Samardzija, Jeff (Athlete, Baseball Player)
3351 N Southoort Ave
Chicago, IL 60657, USA

Samberg, Andy (Actor)
c/o Julie Darmody *Mosaic Media Group*
9200 W Sunset Blvd Ste 10
West Hollywood, CA 90069-3608, USA

Sambito, Joe (Athlete, Baseball Player)
23 Modesto
Irvine, CA 92602-0929, USA

Samcoff, Ed (Athlete, Baseball Player)
8153 Maderia Port Ln
Fair Oaks, CA 95628-2833, USA

Samford, Ron (Athlete, Baseball Player)
2174 Kessler Ct
Dallas, TX 75208-2948, USA

Sammartino, Bruno (Wrestler)
413 Goldsmith Rd
Pittsburgh, PA 15237-3723, USA

Sammel, Richard (Actor)
c/o Catherine Olim *PMK/BNC Public Relations (PMK-LA)*
8687 Melrose Ave Ste 8
West Hollywood, CA 90069-5746, USA

Sammie (Actor)
c/o Staff Member *Green Light Talent Agency*
PO Box 3172
Beverly Hills, CA 90212-0172, USA

Sammons, Clint (Athlete, Baseball Player)
732 King Sword Ct SE
Mableton, GA 30126-6437, USA

Samms, Emma (Actor)
2934 1/2 N Beverly Glen Cir # 417
Los Angeles, CA 90077-1724, USA

Sammy, Sugar (Actor)
c/o Jodi Lieberman *Parallel Entertainment*
9420 Wilshire Blvd Ste 250
Beverly Hills, CA 90212-3151, USA

Samotsvetov, Anatoly (Athlete, Hockey Player)
501 Broadway
Nashville, TN 37203-3980, USA

Sampen, Bill (Athlete, Baseball Player)
11 Carnaby Ct
Brownsburg, IN 46112-8834, USA

Sample, Billy (Athlete, Baseball Player)
10 Pascack Rd
Township Of Washington,
NJ 07676-5116, USA

Samples, Keith (Director, Producer, Writer)
c/o Rob Kenneally *Creative Artists Agency (CAA-LA)*
2000 Avenue of the Stars Ste 100
Los Angeles, CA 90067-4705, USA

Sampleton, Lawrence (Athlete, Football Player)
2900 Bunny Run
Austin, TX 78746-1702, USA

Sampras, Pete (Athlete, Olympic Athlete, Tennis Player)
2552 Via Anita
Palos Verdes Estates, CA 90274-1011

Sampson, Benj (Athlete, Baseball Player)
8312 Flat Rock Ct
North Richland Hills, TX 76182-8471, USA

Sampson, Chris (Athlete, Baseball Player)
2926 Brahman Dr
Manvel, TX 77578-3266, USA

Sampson, Gary (Athlete, Hockey Player, Olympic Athlete)
PO Box 231985
Anchorage, AK 99523-1985, USA

Sampson, Greg (Athlete, Football Player)
3286 Highland Dr
Carlsbad, CA 92008-1918, USA

Sampson, Kelvin (Basketball Player, Coach)
University of Oklahoma
Lloyd Noble Complex
Norman, OK 73019-0001, USA

Sampson, Ralph L Jr (Athlete, Basketball Player, Coach)
530 Myrtle St
Harrisonburg, VA 22802-4725, USA

Sampson, Robert (Actor)
20th Century Artists
4605 Lankershim Blvd Ste 305
North Hollywood, CA 91602-1875, USA

Sams, Dean (Musician)
c/o Staff Member *Borman Entertainment (TN)*
4322 Harding Pike Ste 429
Nashville, TN 37205-2661, USA

Sams, Jeffrey D (Actor)
c/o Toni Benson *Thirdhill Entertainment*
195 S Beverly Dr Ste 400
Beverly Hills, CA 90212-3044, USA

Sams, Judy (Golfer)
5704 Whistlewood Cir
Sarasota, FL 34232-6016, USA

Sams, Russell (Actor)
c/o Jon Simmons *Simmons & Scott Entertainment*
7942 Mulholland Dr
Los Angeles, CA 90046-1225, USA

Samson, Savanna (Adult Film Star)
c/o Natalie Oliveras
118 Fullerton St # 149
New York, NY 10038, USA

Samsonov, Sergei (Athlete, Hockey Player)
2896 Croftshire Ct
Rochester, MI 48306-4925

Sam the Sham (Musician)
6123 Old Brunswick Rd
Arlington, TN 38002-5928, USA

Samuel, Amado (Athlete, Baseball Player)
1931 Yale Dr
Louisville, KY 40205-2038, USA

Samuel, Juan (Athlete, Baseball Player)
19712 Maddelena Cir
Fort Myers, FL 33967-0537, USA

Samuel, Skinner (Politician)
111NDIAN Hill Rd
Winnetka, IL 60093, USA

Samuel, Xavier (Actor)
c/o David Seltzer *Management 360*
9111 Wilshire Blvd
Beverly Hills, CA 90210-5508, USA

Samuels, Chris (Athlete, Football Player)
18303 Oakhampton Dr
Houston, TX 77084-3260, USA

Samuels, Dale (Athlete, Football Player)
2401 Kayla Dr
Waukesha, WI 53188-8021, USA

Samuels, Jack (Athlete, Baseball Player)
840 Vista Cir
Brea, CA 92821-2317, USA

Samuels, Roger (Athlete, Baseball Player)
4865 Tampico Way
San Jose, CA 95118-2348, USA

Samuels, Ron
PO Box 1690
Rancho Mirage, CA 92270-1058

Samuels, Skyler (Actor)
c/o Aleen Keshishian *Brillstein Entertainment Partners (LA)*
9150 Wilshire Blvd Ste 350
Beverly Hills, CA 90212-3453, USA

Samuelson, Joan Benoit (Athlete, Olympic Athlete, Track Athlete)
95 Lower Flying Point Rd
Freeport, ME 04032-6305, USA

Samuelson, Kjell (Athlete, Hockey Player)
7 Knottingham Dr
Voorhees, NJ 08043-3930, USA

Samuelsson, Kjell (Athlete, Hockey Player)
10 Simsbury Dr
Voorhees, NJ 08043-3949, USA

Samuelsson, Marcus (Chef, Reality Star)
c/o Andrew Chason *The Legacy Agency*
1500 Broadway Ste 2501
New York, NY 10036-4082, USA

Samuelsson, Mikael (Athlete, Hockey
Player)
Puckagency LLC
1 Sunset Dr N
Attn Rick Komarow
Chappaqua, NY 10514-1613, USA

Samuelsson, Ulf (Athlete, Hockey Player)
3 Orchard Dr
Rye, NY 10580-3323, USA

Samyn, Jean-Luc (Horse Racer)
57 Shore Rd
Manhasset, NY 11030-1323, USA

Sanabria, Marilyn (Actor)
c/o Laura Walsh *Central Artists*
3310 W Burbank Blvd # A
Burbank, CA 91505-2230, USA

Sanada, Hiroyuki (Actor)
c/o William Choi *Management 360*
9111 Wilshire Blvd
Beverly Hills, CA 90210-5508, USA

San Basilio, Paloma (Music Group)
c/o Staff Member *Sony Music Miami*
605 Lincoln Rd Ste 700
Miami Beach, FL 33139-2901, USA

Sanborn, David (Musician)
c/o Staff Member *ICM Partners (LA)*
10250 Constellation Blvd Fl 7
Los Angeles, CA 90067-6207, USA

Sanches, Brian (Athlete, Baseball Player)
9020 Taylor Cir
Orange, TX 77630-8828, USA

Sanchez, Aaron (Chef)
c/o Andrew Chason *The Legacy Agency*
1500 Broadway Ste 2501
New York, NY 10036-4082, USA

Sanchez, Alex (Athlete, Baseball Player)
1400 Mellissa Cir
Antioch, CA 94509-6301, USA

Sanchez, Claudio (Musician)
2375 US-6
Middletown, NY 10940, USA

Sanchez, Duaner (Athlete, Baseball
Player)
56748 Eastvue Dr
Osceola, IN 46561-9468, USA

Sanchez, Eduardo (Director)
c/o Staff Member *Elements Entertainment*
312 W 5th St Apt 815
Los Angeles, CA 90013-1750, USA

Sanchez, Elena (Actor)
c/o Siri Garber *Platform Public Relations*
2666 N Beachwood Dr
Los Angeles, CA 90068-2308, USA

Sanchez, Freddy (Athlete, Baseball Player)
2494 E Cloud Dr
Chandler, AZ 85249-3777, USA

Sanchez, Gaby (Athlete, Baseball Player)
5621 SW 130th Pi
Miami, FL 33183, USA

Sanchez, Humberto (Athlete, Baseball
Player)
1064 Glenraven Ln
Clermont, FL 34711-9011, USA

Sanchez, Israel (Athlete, Baseball Player)
5444 N Spaulding Ave Apt 2
Chicago, IL 60625-4608, USA

Sanchez, Jessica (Musician)
c/o Staff Member *19 Entertainment (LA)*
9000 W Sunset Blvd Ste 1574
West Hollywood, CA 90069-5817, USA

Sanchez, Juan (Pepe) (Basketball Player)
c/o Staff Member *Detroit Pistons*
2 Championship Dr
Auburn Hills, MI 48326-1753, USA

Sanchez, Kiele (Actor)
c/o Daniel Spilo *Industry Entertainment*
955 Carrillo Dr Ste 300
Los Angeles, CA 90048-5400, USA

Sanchez, Lauren (Actor)
c/o Janet Heng *William Morris Endeavor
(LA)*
9601 Wilshire Blvd
Beverly Hills, CA 90210-5213, USA

Sanchez, Linda (Congressman, Politician)
2423 Rayburn Hob
Washington, DC 20515-3812, USA

Sanchez, Loretta (Congressman,
Politician)
1114 Longworth Hob
Washington, DC 20515-5001, USA

Sanchez, Lupe (Athlete, Football Player)
29070 Road 68
Visalia, CA 93277-9436, USA

Sanchez, Marco (Actor)
c/o Tim Stone *Stone Manners Salners
Agency (LA)*
6100 Wilshire Blvd Ste 1500
Los Angeles, CA 90048-5110, USA

Sanchez, Mark (Athlete, Football Player)
c/o David Dunn *Athletes First, LLC*
23091 Mill Creek Dr
Laguna Hills, CA 92653-1258, USA

Sanchez, Rey (Athlete, Baseball Player)
788 Calle Pampero
San Juan, PR 00924-1772, USA

Sanchez, Roselyn (Actor)
c/o Lena Roklin *Luber Roklin
Management*
5815 W Sunset Blvd Ste 206
Los Angeles, CA 90028-6481, USA

Sanctus Real (Music Group, Musician)
c/o Dan Spencer *Flat-Out Management*
1800 Blair Blvd
Nashville, TN 37212-5004, USA

Sand, Paul (Actor)
Paradigm Agency
10100 Santa Monica Blvd Ste 2500
Los Angeles, CA 90067-4116, USA

Sand, Shauna
c/o Staff Member *Acme Talent & Literary
(LA)*
1400 Atlantic Ave Ste 274
Long Beach, CA 90813-2013, USA

Sand, Todd (Figure Skater)
2973 Harbor Blvd # 468
Costa Mesa, CA 92626-3912, USA

Sanda, Dominique (Actor)
201 Rue Du Faubourg St Honore
Paris, FR F-750

Sandbeck, Cal (Athlete, Hockey Player)
PO Box 129
La Veta, CO 81055-0129, USA

Sandberg, Jared (Athlete, Baseball Player)
4275 NE 125th St
Seattle, WA 98125-4635, USA

Sandberg, Ryne (Athlete, Baseball Player)
26 Biltmore Est
Phoenix, AZ 85016-2823, USA

Sandberg, Sheryl (Business Person)
Facebook
1 Hacker Way Bldg 10
Menlo Park, CA 94025-1456, USA

Sande, Emeli (Musician)
c/o Ambrosia Healy *The Fun Star*
8439 W Sunset Blvd Ste 2
West Hollywood, CA 90069-1925, USA

Sandelin, Scott (Athlete, Hockey Player)
4880 Adrian Ln
Hermantown, MN 55811-3904

Sandeno, Kaitlin (Athlete, Olympic
Athlete, Swimmer)
c/o Staff Member *Premier Management
Group (PMG Sports)*
115 Crescent Commons Dr Ste 250
Cary, NC 27518-8134, USA

Sander, Casey
c/o Jeffrey Leavitt *Leavitt Talent Group*
8222 Melrose Ave Ste 203
Los Angeles, CA 90046-6838, USA

Sander, Ian (Producer)
c/o Staff Member *William Morris
Endeavor (LA)*
9601 Wilshire Blvd
Beverly Hills, CA 90210-5213, USA

Sander, Mark (Athlete, Football Player)
4930 NW 83rd Ave
Lauderhill, FL 33351-5553, USA

Sanderman, Bill (Athlete, Football Player)
Tahoma Meadows Bed & Breakfast
PO Box 203
Homewood, CA 96141-0203, USA

Sanders, Anthony (Athlete, Baseball
Player)
7881 E McGee Mountain Rd
Tucson, AZ 85750-7406, USA

Sanders, Barry (Athlete, Football Player,
Heisman Trophy Winner)
c/o Rhiannon Ellis *Moves Management*
108 Hill Ave
Orlando, FL 32801-2030, USA

Sanders, Beverly (Actor)
12218 Morrison St
Valley Village, CA 91607-3627, USA

Sanders, Bill (Cartoonist)
PO Box 661
Milwaukee, WI 53201-0661, USA

Sanders, Bobby (Baseball Player)
Birmingham Black Barons
24799 Lake Shore Blvd Apt 712
Euclid, OH 44123-4246, USA

Sanders, Charles A (Charlie) (Athlete,
Coach, Football Coach, Football Player)
3418 Palm Aire Ct
Rochester Hills, MI 48309-1040, USA

Sanders, Chris (Director)
c/o Rob Carlson *William Morris Endeavor
(LA)*
9601 Wilshire Blvd
Beverly Hills, CA 90210-5213, USA

Sanders, Christoph (Actor)
c/o Beverly Strong *Strong Management*
9350 Wilshire Blvd Ste 224
Beverly Hills, CA 90212-3204, USA

Sanders, Daryl (Athlete, Football Player)
9220 Shawnee Trl
Powell, OH 43065-5012, USA

Sanders, David (Athlete, Baseball Player)
10411 S Ellen St
Mulvane, KS 67110-9374, USA

Sanders, Deion (Athlete, Baseball Player)
2314 Sunset Ridge Cir
Cedar Hill, TX 75104-4547, USA

Sanders, Doug (Golfer)
1311 Nantucket Dr
Houston, TX 77057-1907, USA

Sanders, Eric D (Athlete, Football Player)
9325 Tailey Cir
Duluth, GA 30097-2451, USA

Sanders, James (Baseball Player)
Kansas City Monarchs
1001 43rd Place Ensley
Birmingham, AL 35208-1402, USA

Sanders, Jay O (Actor)
165 W 46th St Ste 409
New York, NY 10036-2522, USA

Sanders, Jeff (Athlete, Basketball Player)
PO Box 374
South Holland, IL 60473-0374, USA

Sanders, John (Athlete, Baseball Player)
3004 Cheshire Ct
Woodstock, GA 30189-6690, USA

Sanders, John M (Athlete, Football Player)
520 Old Whitfield Rd
Pearl, MS 39208-5512, USA

Sanders, Ken (Athlete, Baseball Player)
12141 Parkview Ln
Hales Corners, WI 53130-2341, USA

Sanders, Mariene (Correspondent)
WNET-TV
356 W 58th St
News Dept
New York, NY 10019-1804, USA

Sanders, Marlene
175 Riverside Dr
New York, NY 10024-1616

Sanders, Orban (Athlete, Football Player)
3520 NW Ferris Ave
Lawton, OK 73505-6104, USA

Sanders, Pharoah (Musician)
Joel Chriss
300 Mercer St Apt 3J
New York, NY 10003-6732, USA

Sanders, Pilar (Actor)
c/o Staff Member *Kim Dawson Agency,
The*
1645 N Stemmons Fwy Ste B
Dallas, TX 75207-3444, USA

Sanders, Reggie
225 Ashepoo Creek Dr
Myrtle Beach, SC 29579-8228, USA

Sanders, Robert J (Athlete, Football
Player)
115 Hyacinth St
Metairie, LA 70005-4217, USA

Sanders, Rupert (Director)
c/o Guymon Casady *Management 360*
9111 Wilshire Blvd
Beverly Hills, CA 90210-5508, USA

Sanders, Scott G (Athlete, Baseball Player)
315 Belmont Dr
Thibodaux, LA 70301-2908, USA

Sanders, Summer (Athlete, Olympic Athlete, Swimmer)
731 Martingale Ln
Park City, UT 84098-7559, USA

Sanders, Terry Wayne (Homer Lee) (Actor)
PO Box 1570
Branson, MO 65615-1570, USA

Sanders, Thomas (Athlete, Football Player)
72 S Fiore Pkwy
Vernon Hills, IL 60061-3269, USA

Sanders, Thomas ""Satch"" (Athlete, Basketball Player, Misc)
PO Box 505
Sturbridge, MA 01566-0505, USA

Sanderson, Cael (Wrestler)
Steve Sanderson
1380 N Valley Hills Blvd
Heber City, UT 84032-1111, USA

Sanderson, Derek (Athlete, Hockey Player)
Howland Captital Management
75 Federal St Ste 1100
Boston, MA 02110-1911, USA

Sanderson, Geoff (Athlete, Hockey Player)
New York Islanders
1255 Hempstead Tpke
Uniondale, NY 11553-1200, USA

Sanderson, Reggie (Athlete, Football Player)
160 Mara Ave
Ventura, CA 93004-1513, USA

Sanderson, Scott (Athlete, Baseball Player)
945 Newcastle Dr
Lake Forest, IL 60045-4928, USA

Sanderson, William (Actor)
c/o Lori DeWaal *Lori DeWaal & Associates PR*
7080 Hollywood Blvd Ste 515
Los Angeles, CA 90028-6932, USA

Sandford, Ed (Athlete, Hockey Player)
18 Clearwater Rd
Winchester, MA 01890-4011

Sandit, Tom (Athlete)
540 S Ashland Ave
La Grange, IL 60525-2811

Sandler, Adam (Actor, Comedian)
1422/1436 Capri Dr
Pacific Palisades, CA 90272, USA

Sandler, Elliott (Race Car Driver)
Cox Marketing
149-B Rolling Hills Rd
Mooresville, NC 28117, USA

Sandlock, Mike (Athlete, Baseball Player)
81 Bible St
Cos Cob, CT 06807-2109, USA

Sandlund, Debra (Actor)
Innovative Artists
1505 10th St
Santa Monica, CA 90401-2805, USA

Sandoval, Arturo (Musician)
4706 Granada Blvd
Coral Gables, FL 33146-1250, USA

Sandoval, Brian (Governor, Politician)
State Capitol
101 N Carson St Ste 6
Carson City, NV 89701-4786, USA

Sandoval, Miguel (Actor)
Paradigm Agency
10100 Santa Monica Blvd Ste 2500
Los Angeles, CA 90067-4116, USA

Sandoval, Sonny (Musician)
East West America Records
75 Rockefeller Plz
New York, NY 10019-6908, USA

Sandow, Nick (Actor)
c/o Tina Thor *TMT Entertainment Group*
648 Broadway # 1002
New York, NY 10012-2348, USA

Sandrich, Jay (Director)
c/o Staff Member *Creative Artists Agency (CAA-LA)*
2000 Avenue of the Stars Ste 100
Los Angeles, CA 90067-4705, USA

Sands, Charlie (Athlete, Baseball Player)
4740 Stratford Ct Apt 1603
Naples, FL 34105-6689, USA

Sands, Jerry (Athlete, Baseball Player)
121 Christian St
Clayton, NC 27527-7519, USA

Sands, Julian (Actor)
1287 Ozeta Ter
West Hollywood, CA 90069-1835, USA

Sands, Tommy (Actor, Musician)
Green Linnet
916 19th Ave S
Nashville, TN 37212-2108, USA

Sands-Ferguson, Sarah Jane (Athlete, Baseball Player)
338 Rohrsburg Rd
Orangeville, PA 17859-9108, USA

Sandt, Tommy (Athlete, Baseball Player)
3736 Eleanor Ct
Lake Oswego, OR 97035-4454, USA

Sandusky, Alexander B (Alex) (Athlete, Football Player)
22 Floral Ave
Key West, FL 33040-6243, USA

Sandusky, Jerry (Football Coach)
SCI Greene Maximum Security Prison
175 Progress Dr
Waynesburg, PA 15370-8082, USA

Sandusky, Mike (Athlete, Football Player)
2786 Amberwood Ct
Naples, FL 34120-7520, USA

Sandvoss, Steve (Actor)
c/o Joan Hyler *Hyler Management*
20 Ocean Park Blvd Unit 25
Santa Monica, CA 90405-3590, USA

Sandy, Baby (Sandra Magee)
6846 Haywood St
Tujunga, CA 91042-2850

Sandy, Gary (Actor)
PO Box 818
Cynthiana, KY 41031-0818, USA

Sandy B (Musician)
Atlantic Entertainment Group
2922 Atlantic Ave Ste 200
Atlantic City, NJ 08401-6337, USA

Sandy Jr, Alomar (Baseball Player)
4635 Prestwick Xing
Westlake, OH 44145-5073, USA

Sanford, Chance (Athlete, Baseball Player)
15028 Bardwell Ln
Frisco, TX 75035-0412, USA

Sanford, Ed (Athlete, Hockey Player)
18 Clearwater Rd
Winchester, MA 01890-4011

Sanford, Jack
2300 Presidential Way
West Palm Beach, FL 33401-1510

Sanford, Leo (Athlete, Football Player)
3044 Gorton Rd
Shreveport, LA 71119-3606, USA

Sanford, Lucius M (Athlete, Football Player)
8745 Carriage Hills Dr
Columbia, MD 21046, USA

Sanford, Mark (Politician)
800 Richland St
Columbia, SC 29201-2327, USA

Sanford, Meredith (Athlete)
8528 MS Highway 389
Starkville, MS 39759-6593

Sanford, Mo (Athlete, Baseball Player)
8528 MS Highway 389
Starkville, MS 39759-6593, USA

Sanford, Rick (Athlete, Football Player)
514 River Camp Dr
Lexington, SC 29072-8292, USA

Sanford, Ron (Athlete, Basketball Player)
3129 Santana Ln
Plano, TX 75023-3630, USA

Sangare, Oumou (Musician)
c/o Staff Member *Concerted Efforts*
PO Box 440326
Somerville, MA 02144-0004, USA

Sanger, Stephan W (Business Person)
General Mills Inc
1 General Mills Blvd
PO Box 1113
Minneapolis, MN 55426-1348, USA

SanGiacomo, Laura (Actor)
c/o Staff Member *Rugolo Entertainment*
195 S Beverly Dr Ste 400
Beverly Hills, CA 90212-3044, USA

Sangster, Thomas (Actor)
c/o Duncan Millership *William Morris Endeavor (LA)*
9601 Wilshire Blvd
Beverly Hills, CA 90210-5213, USA

Sanguillen, Manny (Athlete, Baseball Player)
2838 SW 4th St
Boynton Beach, FL 33435-7902, USA

Sannes, Amy (Athlete, Olympic Athlete, Speed Skater)
143 W Pleasant Lake Rd
Saint Paul, MN 55127-2630, USA

Sano, Roya A (Religious Leader)
United Methodist Church
PO Box 320
Nashville, TN 37202-0320, USA

Sansom, Chip (Cartoonist)
PO Box 5610
Cincinnati, OH 45201-5610, USA

Santana, Ava (Actor)
c/o Claudia Speicher *New Orleans Talent Agency*
7458 Palmer Rd
Greens Fork, IN 47345-9720, USA

Santana, Carlos (Musician, Songwriter)
27 Skybird Ct
Las Vegas, NV 89135-7865, USA

Santana, Johan (Athlete, Baseball Player)
10471 Via Lombardia Ct
Miromar Lakes, FL 33913-7782, USA

Santana, Juelz (Musician)
c/o Staff Member *Island Def Jam Group*
825 8th Ave Fl 28
New York, NY 10019-7416, USA

Santana, Manuel (Tennis Player)
International Tennis Hall of Fame
194 Bellevue Ave
Newport, RI 02840-3586, USA

Santana, Rafael (Athlete, Baseball Player)
3220 SE 1st Ave
Cape Coral, FL 33904-4103, USA

Santangelo, F P (Athlete, Baseball Player)
3602 Rocky Ridge Way
El Dorado Hills, CA 95762-4432, USA

Santaolalla, Gustavo (Musician)
c/o Robert Messinger *First Artists Management*
4764 Park Granada Ste 210
Calabasas, CA 91302-3333, USA

Santa Rosa, Gilberto (Musician)
c/o Staff Member *Richard De La Font Agency*
3808 W South Park Blvd
Broken Arrow, OK 74011-1261, USA

Santerre, Andy (Race Car Driver)
5254 Pitt Rd So
Harrisburg, NC 28075, United States

Santiago, Benito R (Athlete, Baseball Player)
610 W Las Olas Blvd Apt 1212W
Fort Lauderdale, FL 33312-7129, USA

Santiago, Carlos (Baseball Player)
New York Cubans
7 Calle Archilla Cabrera
Mayaguez, PR 00680-3302, USA

Santiago, Daniel (Basketball Player)
c/o Staff Member *Phoenix Suns*
201 E Jefferson St
Phoenix, AZ 85004-2412, USA

Santiago, Eddie (Musician)
c/o Staff Member *Sony Music Miami*
605 Lincoln Rd Ste 700
Miami Beach, FL 33139-2901, USA

Santiago, Jose (Athlete, Baseball Player)
690 Calle Cesar Gonzalez Apt 2108
San Juan, PR 00918-3906, USA

Santiago, Ray (Actor)
c/o Scott Zimmerman *Evolution Entertainment (LA)*
901 N Highland Ave
Los Angeles, CA 90038-2412, USA

Santiago, Rodiney (Model, Reality Star)
c/o Staff Member *Mega Models (Miami)*
420 Lincoln Rd Ste 408
Miami Beach, FL 33139-3015, USA

Santiago, Victor (Nore) (Musician)
c/o Staff Member *Violator Management*
36 W 25th St Fl 2
New York, NY 10010-2768, USA

Santiago-Hudson, Ruben (Actor)
c/o Vincent Cirrincione *Vincent Cirrincione Associates*
1516 N Fairfax Ave
Los Angeles, CA 90046-2608, USA

Santini, Geo (Director)
c/o Kieran Maguire *The Arlook Group*
205 S Beverly Dr Ste 209
Beverly Hills, CA 90212-3899, USA

Santo & Johnny
217 Edgewood Ave
Clearwater, FL 33755-5702

Santo Domingo, Rafael (Athlete, Baseball
Player)
PO Box 21
Orocovis, PR 00720-0021, USA

Santorelli, Frank (Actor)
c/o Mitch Smelkinson *Stone, Meyer,
Genow, Smelkinson and Binder*
9665 Wilshire Blvd Ste 500
Beverly Hills, CA 90212-2312, USA

Santorini, Al (Athlete, Baseball Player)
69 Foxwood Rd
Lakewood, NJ 08701-5730, USA

Santorini, AL (Athlete, Baseball Player)
69 Foxwood Rd
Lakewood, NJ 08701-5730, USA

Santoro, Rodrigo (Actor)
c/o Aleen Keshishian *Brillstein
Entertainment Partners (LA)*
9150 Wilshire Blvd Ste 350
Beverly Hills, CA 90212-3453, USA

Santorum, Rick (Politician)
PO Box 609
Great Falls, VA 22066-0609, USA

Santos, Al (Actor)
c/o Staff Member *Don Buchwald &
Associates (LA)*
6500 Wilshire Blvd Ste 2200
Los Angeles, CA 90048-4942, USA

Santos, Anthony (Romeo) (Musician)
c/o John Reilly *Rogers & Cowan PR (LA)*
8687 Melrose Ave Ste 7
West Hollywood, CA 90069-5721, USA

Santos, Carlos (Comedian)
c/o Mohammed Ali *Aligned Entertainment*
201 Wilshire Blvd Fl 2
Santa Monica, CA 90401-1219, USA

Santos, Joe (Actor)
c/o Mike Eistenstadt *Amsel, Eisenstadt &
Frazier Talent Agency (AEF)*
5055 Wilshire Blvd Ste 860
Los Angeles, CA 90036-6108, USA

Santos, Jose (Horse Racer)
1055 Papaya St
Hollywood, FL 33019-4842, USA

Santos, Omir (Athlete, Baseball Player)
2252 Viehman Trl
Kissimmee, FL 34746-2211, USA

Santos, Rey-Phillip (Actor)
c/o Staff Member *Dramatic Artists Agency*
103 W Alameda Ave Ste 139
Burbank, CA 91502-2253, USA

Santos, Rick (Race Car Driver)
S&S Automotive
14127 Washington Ave
San Leandro, CA 94578-3324, USA

Santos, Sergio (Athlete, Baseball Player)
746 Cienaga Dr
Fullerton, CA 92835-1224, USA

Santos de Oliveira, Alessandra (Basketball
Player)
Washington Mystics
601 F St NW
Mci Center
Washington, DC 20004-1605, USA

Santovenia, Nelson (Athlete, Baseball
Player)
14642 SW 141st Ct
Miami, FL 33186-7260, USA

Sanu, Mohamed (Athlete, Football Player)
c/o Michael McCartney *Priority Sports &
Entertainment - Chicago*
312 N La Salle
Suite 650
Chicago, IL 60610, USA

Sanz, Horatio (Actor)
c/o David (Dave) Becky *3 Arts
Entertainment (LA)*
9460 Wilshire Blvd Fl 7
Beverly Hills, CA 90212-2713, USA

Sanzenbacher, Dane (Athlete, Football
Player)
c/o Joe Flanagan *BTI Sports Advisors*
170 N Scoville Ave
Oak Park, IL 60302-2647, USA

Saper, Clifford (Doctor)
Beth Israel Hospital
330 Brookline Ave
Neurology Dept
Boston, MA 02215-5491, USA

Saperstein, David (Director, Producer,
Writer)
c/o Staff Member *Fran Saperstein
Organization*
Marina Del Rey, CA 90292, USA

Sapienza, Al
10474 Santa Monica Blvd Ste 380
Los Angeles, CA 90025-6943

Sapienza, Americo (Athlete, Football
Player)
6 Forenza Rd
Peabody, MA 01960-3732, USA

Saplenza, Al (Actor)
PO Box 691240
West Hollywood, CA 90069-9240, USA

Saporta, Gabe (Musician)
c/o Staff Member *Fueled By Ramen*
PO Box 1803
Tampa, FL 33601-1803, USA

Sapp, Bob (Actor)
c/o Blake Bandy *Kritzer Levine Wilkins
Entertainment (KLWG)*
11872 La Grange Ave Fl 1
Los Angeles, CA 90025-5283, USA

Sapp, Carolyn
1840 41st Ave # 102-227
Capitola, CA 95010-2513

Sapp, Marvin (Musician)
c/o Staff Member *M.A.G./Universal
Attractions*
15 W 36th St Fl 8
New York, NY 10018-7927, USA

Sapp, Ricky (Athlete, Football Player)
c/o Carl Carey *Champion Pro Consulting
Group*
3547 Ruth St
Houston, TX 77004-5515, USA

Sapp, Theron (Athlete, Football Player)
892 N Belair Rd
Evans, GA 30809-4222, USA

Sapp, Warren (Athlete, Football Player)
c/o Drew Rosenhaus *Rosenhaus Sports
Representation*
6400 Allison Rd
Miami Beach, FL 33141-4540, USA

Sappleton, Wayne (Athlete, Basketball
Player)
8040 N Nob Hill Rd Apt 205
Tamarac, FL 33321-7410, USA

Saprykin, Oleg (Athlete, Hockey Player)
15802 N 71st St Unit 451
Scottsdale, AZ 85254-7118

Sara, Mia (Actor)
c/o Andy Freedman *Andrew J Freedman
Personal Management*
20 Ironsides St Apt 18
Marina Del Rey, CA 90292-5958, USA

Sarachan, Dave (Coach, Soccer Player)
Chicago Fire
980 N Michigan Ave Ste 1998
Chicago, IL 60611-7504, USA

Sarafian, Richard C (Actor, Director,
Writer)
c/o Staff Member *Leavitt Talent Group*
8222 Melrose Ave Ste 203
Los Angeles, CA 90046-6838, USA

Sarahyba, Daniella (Model)
c/o Staff Member *IMG Models (NY)*
304 Park Ave S Fl 12
New York, NY 10010-4314, USA

Saralegui, Cristina (Correspondent)
c/o Staff Member *Creative Artists Agency
(CAA-LA)*
2000 Avenue of the Stars Ste 100
Los Angeles, CA 90067-4705, USA

Sarandon, Chris (Actor)
c/o Miles Levy *James/Levy Management
Inc*
3500 W Olive Ave Ste 1470
Burbank, CA 91505-5514, USA

Sarandon, Susan (Actor, Producer)
820 Nowita Pl
Venice, CA 90291, USA

Sarazen-Smith, Dorothy (Baseball Player)
4774 Eagle Crest Dr
Madison, WI 53704-6426, USA

Sarbanes, Paul (Politician)
320 Suffolk Rd
Baltimore, MD 21218-2521, USA

Sarcev, Ursula
PO Box 25738
Los Angeles, CA 90025-0738

Sardinha, Bronson (Athlete, Baseball
Player)
156 Kuulei Rd
Kailua, HI 96734-2718, USA

Sardinha, Dane (Athlete, Baseball Player)
156 Kuulei Rd
Kailua, HI 96734-2718, USA

Sare, Chris
21100 Erwin St
Woodland Hills, CA 91367-3712

Sarfate, Dennis (Athlete, Baseball Player)
78 W Powell Way
Chandler, AZ 85248-5210, USA

Sargent, Fran
3208 SE Braemar Way
Port Saint Lucie, FL 34952-6034, USA

Sargent, Gary (Athlete, Hockey Player)
9624 Power Dam Rd NE
Bemidji, MN 56601-7414

Sargent, Joseph (Director, Producer)
27432 Latigo Bay View Dr
Malibu, CA 90265-2865, USA

Sargent, Ronald L (Business Person)
Staples Inc
PO Box 9265
Framingham, MA 01701-9265, USA

Sargent, Wallace
400 S Berkeley Ave
Pasadena, CA 91107-5062, USA

Sarich, Cory (Athlete, Hockey Player)
19322 Autumn Woods Ave
Tampa, FL 33647-3249, USA

Sark, Eari (Athlete, Football Player)
8656 W Bowling Green Ln NW
Lancaster, OH 43130-7857, USA

Sarkisian, Alex (Athlete, Football Player)
1604 E 142nd St
East Chicago, IN 46312-3008, USA

Sarmiento, Manny (Athlete, Baseball
Player)
14904 Southfork Dr
Tampa, FL 33624-2322, USA

Sarna, Craig (Athlete, Hockey Player)
1375 Brown Rd S
Wayzata, MN 55391-9316, USA

Sarner, Craig (Athlete, Hockey Player,
Olympic Athlete)
3607 E Gillespie Ln
Odessa, TX 79765-8612, USA

Sarni, Vincent A (Baseball Player, Misc)
Pittsburgh Pirates
115 Federal St Ste 115B
Pnc Park
Pittsburgh, PA 15212-5740, USA

Sarnoff, William (Publisher)
Warner Publishing Inc
1325 Avenue of the Americas
New York, NY 10019-6026, USA

Sarratt, Charles (Athlete, Football Player)
5812 Oak Tree Rd
Edmond, OK 73025-2620, USA

Sarsgaard, Peter (Actor)
c/o Jon Rubinstein *Authentic Talent and
Literary Management*
20 Jay St Ste M17
Brooklyn, NY 11201-8300, USA

Sartain, Gailard (Actor)
c/o Michael Livingston *Artists Agency Inc
(LA)*
8255 W Sunset Blvd
West Hollywood, CA 90046-2417, USA

Sarver, Bruce (Race Car Driver)
Bruce Sarver Racing
4550 Coffee Rd # 1-A
Bakersfield, CA 93308-5023, USA

Sarzo, Rudy
1155 N La Cienega Blvd Apt 506
West Hollywood, CA 90069-2437

Sasaki, Kazuhiro (Baseball Player)
Seattle Mariners
PO Box 4100
Safeco Field
Seattle, WA 98194-0100, USA

Sassano, C E (Business Person)
Bausch & Lomb
1 Bausch and Lomb Pl
Rochester, NY 14604-2799, USA

Sasser, Grant (Athlete, Hockey Player)
1949 SE Orient Dr Apt B
Gresham, OR 97080-7228

Sasser, Jason (Athlete, Basketball Player)
4211 Tiffany Trl
Grand Prairie, TX 75052-2823, USA

Sasser, Mackey (Athlete, Baseball Player)
19 Harrington Ln
Dothan, AL 36305-9732, USA

Sasser, Rob (Athlete, Baseball Player)
1004 Delta River Way
Knightdale, NC 27545-7326, USA

Sasso, Will (Actor, Comedian)
c/o Staff Member *Lord Mucker Entertainment*
839 E Orange Grove Ave
Burbank, CA 91501-1404, USA

Sastre, Ines (Actor)
c/o Brad Schenck *Paradigm (LA)*
360 N Crescent Dr
North Bldg
Beverly Hills, CA 90210-4874, USA

Satan, Miroslav (Athlete, Hockey Player)
46 Kettlepond Rd
Jericho, NY 11753-1158

Satcher, Dr L Robert (Astronaut)
4813 Beech St
Bellaire, TX 77401-3403, USA

Satcher, Leslie (Music Group, Musician, Songwriter, Writer)
Warner Bros Records
3300 Warner Blvd
Burbank, CA 91505-4694, USA

Sather, Glen (Athlete, Coach, Hockey Player)
77380 Vista Rosa
La Quinta, CA 92253-2586, USA

Satra, Sonia (Actor)
Innovative Artists
1505 10th St
Santa Monica, CA 90401-2805, USA

Satre, Philip G (Business Person)
Harrah's Entertainment
1023 Cherry Rd
Memphis, TN 38117-5423, USA

Satriano, Tom (Athlete, Baseball Player)
5320 Otis Ave
Tarzana, CA 91356-4214, USA

Satterfield, Paul (Actor)
PO Box 6945
Beverly Hills, CA 90212-6945, USA

Satterwhite, Howard (Athlete, Football Player)
3418 Action Ln
San Antonio, TX 78210-3402, USA

Saturday, Jeff (Athlete, Football Player)
3045 Camp Branch Rd
Buford, GA 30519-4460, USA

Saubert, Jean M (Skier)
147 Harbor Heights Blvd
Bigfork, MT 59911-3739, USA

Saucier, Frank (Athlete, Baseball Player)
1615 S Bryan St Apt 9
Amarillo, TX 79102-2326, USA

Saucier, Kevin (Athlete, Baseball Player)
2316 Silversides Loop
Pensacola, FL 32526-1509, USA

Sauderbeck, Scott (Athlete, Baseball Player)
3919 Riverview Blvd
Bradenton, FL 34209-2000, USA

Sauer, Craig (Athlete, Football Player)
PO Box 1079
Crosslake, MN 56442-1079, USA

Sauer, Kurt (Athlete, Hockey Player)
7610 E Rose Garden Ln
Scottsdale, AZ 85255-4789

Sauerbeck, Scott (Athlete, Baseball Player)
1904 8th St W
Palmetto, FL 34221-4346, USA

Sauers, Gene (Golfer)
9 Judsons Ct
Savannah, GA 31410-1060, USA

Saul, April (Journalist)
Philadelphia Inquirer
400 N Broad St
Editorial Dept
Philadelphia, PA 19130-4099, USA

Saul, Frank ""Pep""
23 Queensbridge Dr
East Hanover, NJ 07936-3563, USA

Saul, Jim (Athlete, Baseball Player)
2405 Osborne St
Bristol, VA 24201-2322, USA

Saul, John (Writer)
Grade A Entertainment
368 N La Cienega Blvd
Los Angeles, CA 90048-1949, USA

Saul, John
Robin Straus
229 E 79th St
New York, NY 10075-0866

Saul, John W III (Writer)
The Firm
9100 Wilshire Blvd Ste 100W
Beverly Hills, CA 90212-3435, USA

Saul, Ralph S (Business Person)
1400 Waverly Rd Apt B145
Gladwyne, PA 19035-1264, USA

Saul, Stephanie (Journalist)
Newsday
235 Pinelawn Rd
Editorial Dept
Melville, NY 11747-4250, USA

Sauli, Daniel (Actor)
c/o James Suskin *James Suskin Management*
2 Charlton St Apt 5K
New York, NY 10014-4970, USA

Sauls, Don (Religious Leader)
Pentecostal Free Will Baptist Church
PO Box 1568
Dunn, NC 28335-1568, USA

Saulters, Glynn (Athlete, Basketball Player, Olympic Athlete)
240 Country Ln
Quitman, LA 71268-1226, USA

Saum, Sherri (Actor)
c/o Christian Donatelli *The Schiff Company*
9220 W Sunset Blvd Ste 106
West Hollywood, CA 90069-3500, USA

Saunders, Bernie (Athlete, Hockey Player)
150 Pinecrest Dr Hastings on
Hastings On Hudson, NY 10706-3702

Saunders, Dennis (Athlete, Baseball Player)
2854 Rosewood St
Trenton, MI 48183-3602, USA

Saunders, Doug (Athlete, Baseball Player)
10580 Parkington Ln Unit A
Highlands Ranch, CO 80126-6748, USA

Saunders, Doug
43 Saint Kitts
Dana Point, CA 92629-4130

Saunders, George (Writer)
Random House
1745 Broadway Frnt 3 # B1
New York, NY 10019-4343, USA

Saunders, Joe (Athlete, Baseball Player)
4426 N Los Vecinos Dr
Phoenix, AZ 85018-3232, USA

Saunders, John (Cartoonist)
c/o Staff Member *King Features Syndication*
300 W 57th St Fl 15
New York, NY 10019-5238, USA

Saunders, John (Sportscaster)
ESPN-TV
Sports Dept
ESPN Plaza 935 Middle St
Bristol, CT 06010, USA

Saunders, John R (Race Car Driver)
Watkins Glen Speedway
PO Box 500F
Watkins Glen, NY 14891, USA

Saunders, Lori (Actor)
Lori's Friends
99 La Vuelta Rd
Santa Barbara, CA 93108-2621, USA

Saunders, Phillip (Flip) (Basketball Coach, Coach)
395 Calamus Cir
Hamel, MN 55340-9228, USA

Saunders, Rachel (Beauty Pageant Winner)
203 Bocage Dr
Dothan, AL 36303-2944, USA

Saunders, Tony (Athlete, Baseball Player)
1067 Vena Ln
Pasadena, MD 21122-1861, USA

Saunders, Townsend (Athlete, Olympic Athlete, Wrestler)
733 Chantilly Dr
Sierra Vista, AZ 85635-4733, USA

Sauter, Jay (Race Car Driver)
4L5-D River Hwy
Box 278
Mooresville, NC 28115, USA

Sauter, Johnny (Race Car Driver)
Richard Childress Racing
236 Industrial Dr
Welcome, NC 27374, USA

Sauveur, Rich (Athlete, Baseball Player)
3312 47th Ave E
Bradenton, FL 34203-3947, USA

Savage, Adam (Television Host)
Behr Abramson Kaller
9701 Wilshire Blvd Ste 800
Beverly Hills, CA 90212-2033, USA

Savage, Andrea (Actor, Producer, Writer)
c/o Julie Darmody *Mosaic Media Group*
9200 W Sunset Blvd Ste 10
West Hollywood, CA 90069-3608, USA

Savage, Ann (Actor)
1541 N Hayworth Ave Apt 203
Los Angeles, CA 90046-3333, USA

Savage, Ben (Actor)
c/o Staff Member *Abrams Artists Agency (LA)*
9200 W Sunset Blvd PH 11
West Hollywood, CA 90069-3601, USA

Savage, Bob (Athlete, Baseball Player)
95 Raycrest Dr
Randolph, NH 03593-5213, USA

Savage, Brian (Athlete, Hockey Player)
8030 E Whistling Wind Way
Scottsdale, AZ 85255-6480, USA

Savage, Chad (Adult Film Star)
c/o Staff Member *Diva Central Inc*
7510 W Sunset Blvd Ste 1445
Los Angeles, CA 90046-3408, USA

Savage, Chantay (Music Group, Musician)
Famous Artists Agency
250 W 57th St
New York, NY 10107-0001, USA

Savage, Dan (Writer)
The Stranger
1535 11th Ave Fl 3
Seattle, WA 98122-3933, USA

Savage, Don (Athlete, Basketball Player)
53 Park Edge # Le
Berkeley Heights, NJ 07922-1281, USA

Savage, Fred (Actor)
c/o Andy Elkin *Creative Artists Agency (CAA-LA)*
2000 Avenue of the Stars Ste 100
Los Angeles, CA 90067-4705, USA

Savage, Herschel (Adult Film Star)
c/o Staff Member *Vivid Entertainment*
3599 Cahuenga Blvd W Fl 2
Los Angeles, CA 90068-1397, USA

Savage, Jack (Athlete, Baseball Player)
821 2nd Ave Unit 8285
Sheppard Afb, TX 76311-2772, USA

Savage, John (Actor)
5584 Bonneville Rd
Hidden Hills, CA 91302-1201, USA

Savage, Michael (Radio Personality)
110 Pacific Ave # 135
San Francisco, CA 94111-1962, USA

Savage, Reggie (Athlete, Hockey Player)
601 Grassy Stone Dr
Winter Garden, FL 34787-2421

Savage, Stephanie (Producer, Writer)
c/o Staff Member *Wonderland Sound and Vision*
8739 W Sunset Blvd
W Hollywood, CA 90069-2205, USA

Savage, Ted (Athlete, Baseball Player)
1510 Mallard Landing Ct
Chesterfield, MO 63017-5588, USA

Savage, Tom (Athlete, Football Player)
c/o Neil Schwartz *Schwartz & Feinsod*
contact via telephone or email
White Plains, NY 10603

Savage, Tracie
6212 Banner Ave
Los Angeles, CA 90038-2802

Savant, Doug (Actor)
3357 Ledgewood Dr
Los Angeles, CA 90068-1619, USA

Savard, Marc (Athlete, Hockey Player)
c/o Staff Member *Boston Bruins*
100 Legends Way Ste 250
Td Banknorth Garden
Boston, MA 02114-1389, USA

Save Ferris (Music Group)
c/o Staff Member *Epic Records Group*
550 Madison Ave Fl 6
New York, NY 10022-3211, USA

Saverine, Bob (Athlete, Baseball Player)
228 Slice Dr
Stamford, CT 06907-1137, USA

Saverson, Henry (Baseball Player)
Detroit Stars
1726 Benjamin Ave NE
Grand Rapids, MI 49505-5434, USA

Saves the Day (Music Group)
c/o Richard Egan *Hard 8 Management*
1709 19th Ave S
Nashville, TN 37212-3701, USA

Savidge, Jennifer (Actor)
c/o Staff Member *TalentWorks (LA)*
3500 W Olive Ave Ste 1400
Burbank, CA 91505-5512, USA

Saving Jane
9423 Old Forest Ln
Loveland, OH 45140-1065, USA

Savini, Tom
311 Taylor St
Pittsburgh, PA 15224-1862

Savitt, Dick
19 E 80th St Apt 11B
New York, NY 10075-0170

Savitt, Richard (Dick) (Tennis Player)
19 E 80th St Apt 11B
New York, NY 10075-0170, USA

Savoie, Matt (Athlete, Figure Skater,
Olympic Athlete)
1026 N Maplewood Ave
Peoria, IL 61606-1034, USA

Savoretti, Jack (Musician)
c/o Michael Moses *Baker Winokur Ryder
Public Relations (BWR-LA)*
9100 Wilshire Blvd Ste 500
West Tower Suite 500
Beverly Hills, CA 90212-3426, USA

Savoy, Gene
643 Ralston St
Reno, NV 89503-4436

Savransky, Moe (Athlete, Baseball Player)
128 Dorset D
Boca Raton, FL 33434-3076, USA

Savre, Danielle (Actor)
c/o Adam Griffin *Kritzer Levine Wilkins
Entertainment (KLWG)*
11872 La Grange Ave Fl 1
Los Angeles, CA 90025-5283, USA

Sawa, Devon (Actor)
23705 Park Belmonte
Calabasas, CA 91302-1606, USA

Sawalha, Nadia (Talk Show Host)
BBC
Broadcasting House
Portland Place
London, UK W1A 1

Sawyer, Alan (Athlete, Basketball Player)
117 San Juan Dr
Sequim, WA 98382-9326, USA

Sawyer, Daine (Correspondent)
147 Columbus Ave # 300
New York, NY 10023-6503, USA

Sawyer, Diane (Journalist)
77 W 66th St
New York, NY 10023-6201, USA

Sawyer, Elton (Race Car Driver)
Akins Motorsports
185 McKenzie Rd
Mooresville, NC 28115-7976, USA

Sawyer, Forrest (Correspondent)
NBC-TV
30 Rockefeller Plz
News Dept
New York, NY 10112-0015, USA

Sawyer, John (Athlete, Football Player)
23637 Sunnyside Ln
Zachary, LA 70791-6118, USA

Sawyer, Ken (Athlete, Football Player)
40 S Quaker Ln
Hyde Park, NY 12538-2620, USA

Sawyer, Kevin (Athlete, Hockey Player)
519 S Lucille Ct
Spokane Valley, WA 99216-0827, USA

Sawyer, Paul (Race Car Driver)
Richmond International Raceway
600 E Laburnum Ave
Richmond, VA 23222-2207, USA

Sawyer, Rick (Athlete, Baseball Player)
1201 Calle Extrano
Bakersfield, CA 93309-7116, USA

Sawyer, Robert E (Religious Leader)
Moravian Church Southern Province
459 S Church St
Winston Salem, NC 27101-5314, USA

Sawyer, Talance (Athlete, Football Player)
6150 Brookhaven Dr
Bastrop, LA 71220-1878, USA

Sawyer Brown (Music Group)
c/o Staff Member *Paradigm (Nashville)*
124 12th Ave S Ste 410
Nashville, TN 37203-3170, USA

Sax, Dave (Athlete, Baseball Player)
3352 Eaton Dr
Roseville, CA 95661-7907, USA

Sax, Steve (Athlete, Baseball Player)
201 Wesley Ct
Roseville, CA 95661-7913, USA

Saxon, Edward (Producer)
c/o Staff Member *Creative Artists Agency
(CAA-LA)*
2000 Avenue of the Stars Ste 100
Los Angeles, CA 90067-4705, USA

Saxon, James E (Athlete, Football Player)
RR 3 Box 34X
Beaufort, SC 29906, USA

Saxon, James E (Jimmy) (Athlete, Football
Player)
1 Mulberry Ln
West Lake Hills, TX 78746-4321, USA

Saxon, John (Actor)
2432 Banyan Dr
Los Angeles, CA 90049-1240, USA

Saxon, Mike (Athlete, Football Player)
660 W Peninsula Dr
Coppell, TX 75019-6801, USA

Saxton, Brian (Athlete, Football Player)
3604 Tudor Dr
Pompton Plains, NJ 07444-1141, USA

Saxton, Jimmy (Athlete, Football Player)
1 Mulberry Ln
West Lake Hills, TX 78746-4321, USA

Saxton, Johnny (Boxer)
1710 4th Ave N
Crystal Palms
Lake Worth, FL 33460-2874, USA

Saxton, Shirley Childress (Music Group,
Musician)
Sweet Honey Agency
PO Box 600099
Newtonville, MA 02460-0001, USA

Say, Peggy
438 Lake Shore Dr
Cadiz, KY 42211

Sayers, Gale (Athlete, Football Player)
852 Coving Dr
Lawrence, KS 66049-7846, USA

Sayles, John (Director)
210 13th St
Hoboken, NJ 07030-4435, USA

Sayre, Anne
1268 E 14th St
Brooklyn, NY 11230-5241

Sbarge, Raphael (Actor)
c/o Tracy Steinsapir *Main Title
Entertainment*
8383 Wilshire Blvd Ste 408
Beverly Hills, CA 90211-2435, USA

Sbranti, Ron (Athlete, Football Player)
2925 Roosevelt Ln
Antioch, CA 94509-5040, USA

Scaasi, Arnold (Designer, Fashion
Designer)
16 E 52nd St
New York, NY 10022-5306, USA

Scacchi, Greta (Actor)
c/o Susan Smith *Susan Smith Company,
The*
2001 Wilshire Blvd Ste 400
Santa Monica, CA 90403-5686, USA

Scaduto, Al (Cartoonist)
571 Swanson Cres
Milford, CT 06461-2735, USA

Scadyac, Tom (Director)
c/o Staff Member *Creative Artists Agency
(CAA-LA)*
2000 Avenue of the Stars Ste 100
Los Angeles, CA 90067-4705, USA

Scafa, Bob (Baseball Player)
US Olympic Team
2090 Milton Ave
Park Ridge, IL 60068-2320, USA

Scaggs, Boz (Musician, Songwriter)
c/o Craig Fruin *HK Management (LA)*
10866 Wilshire Blvd Ste 200
Los Angeles, CA 90024-4350, USA

Scagliotti-Smith, Allison (Actor)
4358 W Kling St
Burbank, CA 91505-3724, USA

Scalabrine, Brian
176 Vernal Dr
Alamo, CA 94507-1242, USA

Scales, Bobby (Athlete, Baseball Player)
142 Blaze
Irvine, CA 92618-1507, USA

Scales, Charlie (Athlete, Football Player)
4035 Vistaview St
West Mifflin, PA 15122-2134, USA

Scales, DeWayne
8505 Sikorski Ln
Dallas, TX 75228-5446, USA

Scales, Dwight (Athlete, Football Player)
6112 Roosevelt Cir NW
Huntsville, AL 35810-1634, USA

Scales, Greg (Athlete, Football Player)
4118 Carnation Dr
Winston Salem, NC 27105-3219, USA

Scales, Hurles (Athlete, Football Player)
600 N Adams St
Amarillo, TX 79107-5068, USA

Scalia, Antonin (Attorney)
6713 Wemberly Way
Mc Lean, VA 22101-1529, USA

Scalia, Jack (Actor)
6200 Kentland Ave
Woodland Hills, CA 91367-1721, USA

Scalians, Bret (Musician)
Media Five Entertainment
3005 Brodhead Rd Ste 170
Bethlehem, PA 18020-9426, USA

Scalzitti, Will (Baseball Player)
19321 SW 61st St
Ft Lauderdale, FL 33332-3354, USA

Scalzo, Tony (Musician)
c/o Staff Member *Russell Carter Artists*
567 Ralph McGill Blvd NE
Atlanta, GA 30312-1110, USA

Scaminace, Joseph M (Business Person)
Sherwin-Williams Co
101 W Prospect Ave Ste 1020
Cleveland, OH 44115-1075, USA

Scamurra, Peter (Athlete, Hockey Player)
15 Guinevere Ct
Getzville, NY 14068-1194

Scancarelli, Jim (Cartoonist)
Mark J Cohen
PO Box 1892
Santa Rosa, CA 95402-1892, USA

Scanlan, Bob (Athlete, Baseball Player)
3020 N 14th St Apt 118A
Phoenix, AZ 85014-5686, USA

Scanlon, Pat (Athlete, Baseball Player)
7400 Portland Ave
Minneapolis, MN 55423-4343, USA

Scarbath, John C (Jack) (Athlete, Football
Player)
736 Calvert Rd
Rising Sun, MD 21911-2332, USA

Scarber, Sam (Athlete, Football Player)
12209 Crewe St
North Hollywood, CA 91605-5609, USA

Scarbery, Randy (Athlete, Baseball Player)
5010 E Lewis Ave
Fresno, CA 93727-2418, USA

Scarborough, Joe (Congressman,
Journalist, Television Host)
370 Wahackme Rd
New Canaan, CT 06840-3936, USA

Scarce, Mac (Athlete, Baseball Player)
1664 Cedar Bluff Way
Marietta, GA 30062-3236, USA

Scarf, Maggie (Writer)
c/o Camille McDuffie *Goldberg McDuffie
Communications*
250 Park Ave Fl 7
New York, NY 10177-0799, USA

Scarface (Musician)
c/o Staff Member *American Talent Agency*
153 W 27th St Ste 300
New York, NY 10001-6259, USA

Scarfe, Jonathan
4739 Lankershim Blvd
North Hollywood, CA 91602-1803

Scarpati, Joseph H (Athlete, Football Player)
32 Lexington Cir
Marlton, NJ 08053-3860, USA

Scarpelli, Glenn (Actor)
20 San Remo Ct
Sedona, AZ 86336-5963, USA

Scarpitto, Bob (Athlete, Football Player)
123 White Oaks Ln
Carmel Valley, CA 93924-9650, USA

Scarry, Mike (Athlete, Football Player)
7430 Lake Breeze Dr Apt 104
Fort Myers, FL 33907-8058, USA

Scarsone, Steve (Athlete, Baseball Player)
22008 N 36th St
Phoenix, AZ 85050-7389, USA

Scarwid, Diana (Actor)
PO Box 3614
Savannah, GA 31414-3614, USA

Scatchard, Dave (Athlete, Hockey Player)
215 Orchard Valley Dr
Harriman, TN 37748-4698

Scates, Al (Coach, Volleyball Player)
UCLA
PO Box 24044
Athletic Dept - Volleyball
Los Angeles, CA 90024-0044, USA

Scelba-Shorte, Mercedes (Reality Star)
c/o Staff Member *Ty Ty Baby Productions*
8346 W 3rd St # 650
Los Angeles, CA 90048-4311, USA

Scelzi, Gary (Race Car Driver)
Alen Johnson Racing
2772 S Cherry Ave
Fresno, CA 93706-5424, USA

Scerbo, Cassie (Actor)
c/o Adam Griffin *Kritzer Levine Wilkins Entertainment (KLWG)*
11872 La Grange Ave Fl 1
Los Angeles, CA 90025-5283, USA

Schaaf, Fred (Athlete, Baseball Player)
3911 Lake Saint George Dr
Palm Harbor, FL 34684-4220, USA

Schaal, Paul (Athlete, Baseball Player)
68-1962 Puu Nui St
Waikoloa, HI 96738-5238, USA

Schaal, Wendy (Actor)
Gage Group
5757 Wilshire Blvd Ste 659
Los Angeles, CA 90036-3682, USA

Schaap, Dick
77 W 66th St
New York, NY 10023-6201

Schabarum, Pete (Athlete, Football Player)
46170 E Eldorado Dr
Indian Wells, CA 92210-8633, USA

Schacher, Mel (Musician)
Lustig Talent
PO Box 770850
Orlando, FL 32877-0850, USA

Schacht, Henry B (Business Person)
Lucent Technologies Inc
600 Mountain Ave
New Providence, NJ 07974-2008, USA

Schachter, Blanche (Baseball Player)
145 Berkeley Pl
Brooklyn, NY 11217-3603, USA

Schachter, Steven (Director, Writer)
c/o Staff Member *Ken Gross Management*
12135 Stanwood Dr
Los Angeles, CA 90066-1052, USA

Schachter Sisters
182-06 Midland Park Blvd
Jamaica, NY 11432

Schacker, Hal (Athlete, Baseball Player)
4609 N Matanzas Ave
Tampa, FL 33614-6652, USA

Schade, Frank (Athlete, Basketball Player)
825 Nicolet Ave
Oshkosh, WI 54901-1635, USA

Schade, Molly (Actor)
c/o Aron Giannini *United Talent Agency (UTA-LA)*
8383 Wilshire Blvd Ste 1050
Beverly Hills, CA 90211-2415, USA

Schadler, Ben
300 NW Ilwaco Ct
Camas, WA 98607-7956, USA

Schadler, Jay (Correspondent)
c/o Staff Member *Primetime*
147 Columbus Ave
New York, NY 10023-6503, USA

Schadt, James P (Publisher)
Reader's Digest Assn
Reader's Digest Road
Pleasantville, NY 10570, USA

Schaech, Johnathon (Actor)
6234 Holly Mont Dr
Los Angeles, CA 90068-3308, USA

Schaefer, Bob (Athlete, Baseball Player, Coach)
9070 Old Hickory Cir
Fort Myers, FL 33912-6844, USA

Schaefer, Don (Athlete, Football Player)
286 Birch Pkwy
Wyckoff, NJ 07481-2831, USA

Schaefer, Jeff (Athlete, Baseball Player)
2110 Woodbend Trl
Fort Mill, SC 29708-8343, USA

Schaefer, Roberto (Cinematographer)
Innovative Artists
1505 10th St
Santa Monica, CA 90401-2805, USA

Schaefer, Sara (Actor, Comedian)
c/o Rebecca Sides Capellan *ID Public Relations (NY)*
150 W 30th St Fl 19
New York, NY 10001-4119, USA

Schaefer, Yvonne Maria (Actor, Producer)
YMC Films
343 E 76th St
New York, NY 10021-2404, USA

Schaeffer, Billy
7 Ames Pl
Huntington Station, NY 11746-4701, USA

Schaeffer, Danny (Athlete, Baseball Player)
Round Rock Express
3400 E Palm Valley Blvd
Attn: Coaching Staff
Round Rock, TX 78665-3906, USA

Schaeffer, Eric (Actor, Director)
c/o Norman Aladjem *Levity Entertainment Group (LEG)*
6701 Center Dr W Fl 11
Los Angeles, CA 90045-1535, USA

Schaeffer, George
1040 Woodland Dr
Beverly Hills, CA 90210-2936

Schaeffer, Leonard (Business Person)
Quintiles
4820 Emperor Blvd
Durham, NC 27703-8426, USA

Schaeffer, Mark (Athlete, Baseball Player)
18261 Parthenia St
Northridge, CA 91325-3303, USA

Schaefzel, John R (Writer)
2 Bay Tree Ln
Bethesda, MD 20816-1046, USA

Schafer, Edward (Politician)
4426 Carrie Rose Ln S
Fargo, ND 58104-6818, USA

Schafer, Jordan (Athlete, Baseball Player)
80 Pine Forest Dr
Haines City, FL 33844-9710, USA

Schaffel, Lewis (Basketball Player, Misc)
Miami Heat
601 Biscayne Blvd
American Airlines Arena
Miami, FL 33132-1801, USA

Schaffer, Eric (Music Group, Musician)
Kennedy Center for Performing Arts
Washington, DC 20011, USA

Schaffer, Jimmie (Athlete, Baseball Player)
655 Birch Ter
Coopersburg, PA 18036-2407, USA

Schaffermoth, Joe (Athlete, Baseball Player)
20 Marion Ave
Berkeley Heights, NJ 07922-1260, USA

Schaffernoth, Joe (Athlete, Baseball Player)
20 Marion Ave
Berkeley Heights, NJ 07922-1260, USA

Schafrath, Dick (Athlete, Football Player)
704 Ashland Rd
Mansfield, OH 44905-2536, USA

Schalder, Ben (Athlete, Basketball Player)
808 Bauer Dr
San Carlos, CA 94070-3614, USA

Schall, Benny (Athlete, Basketball Player)
4305 Robinhood Ln
Toledo, OH 43623-2537, USA

Schall, Gene (Athlete, Baseball Player)
1582 Bromley Dr
Harleysville, PA 19438-3056, USA

Schaller, Cliff (Athlete, Baseball Player)
1978 3847 Powner Rd
Cincinnati, OH 45248, USA

Schaller, Willie (Soccer Player)
3283 S Indiana St
Lakewood, CO 80228-5499, USA

Schallert, William (Actor)
Distinguished Character
14920 Ramos Pl
Pacific Palisades, CA 90272-4460, USA

Schallock, Art (Athlete, Baseball Player)
749 Crocus Dr
Sonoma, CA 95476-8325, USA

Schamehorn, Kevin (Athlete, Hockey Player)
5536 Stoney Brook Rd
Kalamazoo, MI 49009-7703

Schanberg, Sydney H (Journalist)
PO Box 236
Rifton, NY 12471-0236, USA

Schank, Roger C (Doctor, Scientist)
Northwestern University
Learning Sciences Institute
Evanston, IL 60201, USA

Schankweiler, Scott (Athlete, Football Player)
11 Bartley Ct
Nottingham, MD 21236-2428, USA

Schanz, Heidi (Actor)
Gersh Agency
232 N Canon Dr
Beverly Hills, CA 90210-5302, USA

Schapker, Alison (Producer, Writer)
c/o Ilan Breil *Mosaic Media Group*
9200 W Sunset Blvd Ste 10
West Hollywood, CA 90069-3608, USA

Schapp, Dick (Sportscaster)
ESPN-TV
Sports Dept
ESPN Plaza 935 Middle St
Bristol, CT 06010, USA

Schar, Dwight (Business Person)
NVR Inc
7601 Lewinsville Rd Ste 300
Mc Lean, VA 22102-2835, USA

Schattinger, Jeff (Athlete, Baseball Player)
PO Box 134
Lake Arrowhead, CA 92352-0134, USA

Schatz, Donny (Race Car Driver)
Schatz Motorsports
4510 19th Ave S
Fargo, ND 58103-0802, USA

Schatzberg, Jerry N (Director)
c/o Staff Member *ICM Partners (LA)*
10250 Constellation Blvd Fl 7
Los Angeles, CA 90067-6207, USA

Schatzeder, Dan (Athlete, Baseball Player)
186 River Mist Dr
Oswego, IL 60543-8358, USA

Schaub, Matt (Athlete, Football Player)
c/o David Dunn *Athletes First, LLC*
23091 Mill Creek Dr
Laguna Hills, CA 92653-1258, USA

Schaum, Greg (Athlete, Football Player)
4303 Piney Park Rd
Perry Hall, MD 21128-9524, USA

Schauman, Wilhelm (Athlete, Golfer)
c/o Jim Lehrman *SFX Golf*
36855 W Main St Ste 200
Purcellville, VA 20132-3561, USA

Schayes, Danny (Athlete, Basketball Player)
8586 E Krail St
Scottsdale, AZ 85250-4931, USA

Schayes, Dolph (Athlete, Basketball Player)
200 Polk St
Denver, CO 80239, USA

Schayes, Wendy Lucero (Athlete, Diver, Olympic Athlete)
8586 E Krail St
Scottsdale, AZ 85250-4931, Usa

Schechkter, Tomas (Race Car Driver)
5101 Decatur Blvd Ste P
Indianapolis, IN 46241-9529, USA

Scheckter, Tomas (Race Car Driver)
11412 Divers Cove Ct
Indianapolis, IN 46236-8601, USA

Schecter, Leroy (Business Person)
55 Passaic Ave
Kearny, NJ 07032-1103, USA

Schedeen, Anne (Actor)
c/o Tom Markley *Metropolitan Talent Agency*
5405 Wilshire Blvd # 218
Los Angeles, CA 90036-4203, USA

Scheer-Demme, Amanda (Business Person, Producer)
c/o Staff Member *Thrive Music*
1024 N Orange Dr
Los Angeles, CA 90038-2336, USA

Scheffer, Aaron (Athlete, Baseball Player)
1351 Sharon St
Westland, MI 48186-5044, USA

Scheffler, Tony (Football Player)
c/o Staff Member *Denver Broncos*
13655 Broncos Pkwy
Englewood, CO 80112-4151, USA

Schefft, Jen (Reality Star)
3650 N Magnolia Ave
Chicago, IL 60613-3821, USA

Scheib, Carl (Athlete, Baseball Player)
2922 Old Ranch Rd
San Antonio, TX 78217-5858, USA

Scheibel, Arnold B (Doctor)
100 Bay Pl Apt 804
Oakland, CA 94610-4443, USA

Scheid, Rich (Athlete, Baseball Player)
1 Hancock Ct
Hightstown, NJ 08520-2722, USA

Schein, Philip S (Doctor)
6212 Robinwood Rd
Bethesda, MD 20817-6115, USA

Scheinblum, Richie (Athlete, Baseball Player)
1308 Woodstock Dr
Palm Harbor, FL 34684-2246, USA

Schell, Ronnie
Angel City Talent
4741 Laurel Canyon Blvd Ste 101
Valley Village, CA 91607-5905, USA

Schellen, Mark (Athlete, Football Player)
320 Shorewood Ln
Waterloo, NE 68069-9717, USA

Schellenbach, Kate (Musician)
Metropolitan Entertainment
2 Penn Plz # 2600
New York, NY 10121-0101, USA

Schellhase, Dave (Athlete, Basketball Player)
862 Walnut Rdg E
Logansport, IN 46947-3965, USA

Schelmerding, Kirk (Race Car Driver)
Childress Racing
PO Box 1189
Industrial Dr
Welcome, NC 27374-1189, USA

Schemansky, Norbert (Athlete, Olympic Athlete, Weightlifter)
24826 New York St
Dearborn, MI 48124-4485, USA

Schembechler, Bo
1904 Boulder Dr
Ann Arbor, MI 48104-4164

Schembechler, Glenn E (Bo) Jr (Athlete, Coach, Football Player)
1904 Boulder Dr
Ann Arbor, MI 48104-4164, USA

Schemling, Bill
PO Box 11308
Portland, OR 97211-0308

Schenert, Turk (Athlete, Football Player)
239 Willow Ave
Pompton Lakes, NJ 07442-2443, USA

Schenkenberg, Markus (Actor, Model)
c/o Maury DiMauro *Innovative Artists (LA)*
235 Park Ave S Fl 10
New York, NY 10003-1405, USA

Schenker, Nathan (Athlete, Football Player)
26400 George Zeiger Dr Apt 116
Beachwood, OH 44122-7511, USA

Schenkkan, Robert F (Writer)
Dramatist Guild
1501 Broadway Ste 701
New York, NY 10036-5505, USA

Schenkman, Eric (Musician)
DAS Communications
84 Riverside Dr
New York, NY 10024-5723, USA

Schepisi, Fred (Director)
c/o Staff Member *William Morris Endeavor (LA)*
9601 Wilshire Blvd
Beverly Hills, CA 90210-5213, USA

Scherbo, Vitali (Gymnast)
8308 Aqua Spray Ave
Las Vegas, NV 89128-7432, USA

Scherbo, Vitaly
8308 Aqua Spray Ave
Las Vegas, NV 89128-7432

Scherer, Bernard (Athlete, Football Player)
PO Box 5201
Carmel By The Sea, CA 93921-5201, USA

Scherman, Fred (Athlete, Baseball Player)
7454 S Tipp Cowlesville Rd
Tipp City, OH 45371-8351, USA

Scherrer, Bill (Athlete, Baseball Player)
4155 E Rockledge Rd
Phoenix, AZ 85044-6770, USA

Scherza, Chuck (Athlete, Hockey Player)
22 Gentry Way
North Scituate, RI 02857-1545

Scherzer, Max (Athlete, Baseball Player)
534 Glenfield Ridge Ct
Chesterfield, MO 63017-2728, USA

Scherzinger, Nicole (Actor, Musician)
c/o British (Brit) Reece *PMK/BNC Public Relations (PMK-LA)*
8687 Melrose Ave Ste 8
West Hollywood, CA 90069-5746, USA

Scheuring, Paul (Director)
c/o Adam Berkowitz *Creative Artists Agency (CAA-LA)*
2000 Avenue of the Stars Ste 100
Los Angeles, CA 90067-4705, USA

Schevill, James (Writer)
1309 Oxford St
Berkeley, CA 94709-1424, USA

Schieffer, Bob (Journalist)
c/o Richard Leibner *N.S. Bienstock*
250 W 57th St Ste 333
New York, NY 10107-0302, USA

Schierholtz, Nate (Athlete, Baseball Player)
7500 E Deer Valley Rd Unit 118
Scottsdale, AZ 85255-4867, USA

Schiff, Andras (Musician)
Shirley Kirshbaum
711 W End Ave Apt 5KN
New York, NY 10025-0100, USA

Schiff, Mark (Actor, Comedian)
Gail Stocker Presents
1025 N Kings Rd Apt 113
West Hollywood, CA 90069-6007, USA

Schiff, Richard (Actor, Director)
c/o Michael Garnett *Leverage Management*
3030 Pennsylvania Ave
Santa Monica, CA 90404-4112, USA

Schiff, Robin (Writer)
c/o Staff Member *Broder Webb Chervin Silbermann Agency, The (BWCS)*
10250 Constellation Blvd
Los Angeles, CA 90067-6200, USA

Schiffer, Eric (Writer)
6965 El Camino Real Ste 105
Pmb 517
Carlsbad, CA 92009-4101

Schiffer, Michael (Writer)
c/o Greg Weiss *Vanguard Management Group (NY)*
220 5th Ave PH West
New York, NY 10001-7745, USA

Schiffner, Travis (Actor)
c/o Staff Member *Bohemia Group (LA)*
1680 Vine St Ste 412
Los Angeles, CA 90028-8800, USA

Schifrin, Lalo (Musician)
710 N Hillcrest Rd
Beverly Hills, CA 90210-3517, USA

Schiller, Lawrence J (Director, Writer)
5430 Oakdale Ave
Woodland Hills, CA 91364-2611, USA

Schilling, Chuck (Athlete, Baseball Player)
907 Caroline St
New Bern, NC 28560-1804, USA

Schilling, Curtis (Curt) M (Athlete, Baseball Player)
3 Sturbridge Rd
Medfield, MA 02052-1442, USA

Schilling, Taylor (Actor)
c/o Molly Madden *3 Arts Entertainment (LA)*
9460 Wilshire Blvd Fl 7
Beverly Hills, CA 90212-2713, USA

Schilling, William
626 N Valley St
Burbank, CA 91505-3147

Schimberg, Henry R (Business Person)
Coca-Cola Enterprises
2500 Windy Ridge Pkwy SE Ste 700
Atlanta, GA 30339-8429, USA

Schindler, Steve (Athlete, Football Player)
6109 Willow Springs Dr
Morrison, CO 80465-2133, USA

Schinkel, Kenneth (Ken) (Athlete, Hockey Player)
19927 Beaulieu Ct
Fort Myers, FL 33908-4832, USA

Schino, Dominic (Producer)
c/o Staff Member *Magic Touch Records*
1215 36th Ave Apt 4E
#4-E
Astoria, NY 11106-4736, USA

Schipper, Ron (Coach, Football Coach)
1088 Fountain View Cir Unit 1
Holland, MI 49423-5620, USA

Schiraldi, Calvin (Athlete, Baseball Player)
9108 Tweed Berwick Dr
Austin, TX 78750-3554, USA

Schirinowskij, Wladmir
Sokolnitscheskij wal 38-114
Moscow, RU 10711

Schirripa, Steve (Actor)
c/o Brad Stokes *Harrison Stokes*
501 Santa Monica Blvd Ste 604
Santa Monica, CA 90401-2467, USA

Schisgal, Murray J (Writer)
International Creative Mgmt
40 W 57th St Fl 5
New York, NY 10019-4001, USA

Schissler, Les (Bowler)
3060 E Bridge St Lot 20
Brighton, CO 80601-2718, USA

Schlamme, Thomas (Actor)
c/o Rosalie Swedlin *Anonymous Content (LA)*
3532 Hayden Ave
Culver City, CA 90232-2413, USA

Schlatter, Charlie (Actor)
638 Lindero Canyon Rd # 322
Oak Park, CA 91377-5457, USA

Schlatter, George
400 Robert Ln
Beverly Hills, CA 90210-2632

Schlegel, Ernie (Bowler)
13300 SE Angus St
Vancouver, WA 98683-6694, USA

Schleinzer, Markus (Director)
c/o Doug MacLaren *ICM Partners (LA)*
10250 Constellation Blvd Fl 7
Los Angeles, CA 90067-6207, USA

Schleper, Sarah (Athlete, Olympic Athlete)
595 Stone Creek Dr
Avon, CO 81620, usa

Schlereth, Daniel (Athlete, Baseball Player)
9479 S Shadow Hill Cir
Lone Tree, CO 80124-5484, USA

Schlereth, Mark (Athlete, Football Player)
c/o Lou Oppenheim *Headline Media Management*
888 7th Ave Ste 503
New York, NY 10106-0501, USA

Schlesinger, Adam (Music Group, Musician, Songwriter, Writer)
MOB Agency
6404 Wilshire Blvd Ste 505
Los Angeles, CA 90048-5507, USA

Schlesinger, Bill (Athlete, Baseball Player)
4230 Glenway Ave Apt 2
Deer Park, OH 45236-3646, USA

Schlesinger, Cory (Athlete, Football Player)
36 Bradford Ct
Dearborn, MI 48126-4169, USA

Schlesinger, Iliza (Comedian)
c/o Staff Member *Gersh (LA)*
9465 Wilshire Blvd Ste 600
Beverly Hills, CA 90212-2605, USA

Schlesinger, James (Politician)
The Mitre Corporation
7515 Colshire Dr Attn: Chairman's Office
Mc Lean, VA 22102, USA

Schlesinger, Rudy (Athlete, Baseball Player)
5708 Abelia Ct
Cincinnati, OH 45213-2434, USA

Schlessinger, Laura (Radio Personality, Writer)
PO Box 8120
Van Nuys, CA 91409-8120, USA

Schlichting, Travis (Athlete, Baseball Player)
2202 Parkland Cv
Round Rock, TX 78681-4086, USA

Schlitter, Brian (Athlete, Baseball Player)
912 S Greenwood Ave
Park Ridge, IL 60068-4544, USA

Schlopy, Erik (Athlete, Olympic Athlete, Skier)
731 Martingale Ln
Park City, UT 84098-7559, USA

Schloredt, Robert S (Bob) (Athlete, Football Player)
1827 N 167th St
Shoreline, WA 98133-5505, USA

Schlossberg, Edwin (Writer)
The John F Kennedy Presidential Library & Museum
Columbia Point
Dorchester, NY 02125

Schlossberg, Katie (Actor)
Talent Group
6300 Wilshire Blvd Ste 2100
Los Angeles, CA 90048-5282, USA

Schlossberg, Katie (Actor)
Talent Group
5670 Wilshire Blvd Ste 820
Los Angeles, CA 90036-5613, USA

Schlosser, Eric (Writer)
c/o Staff Member *Houghton Mifflin*
215 Park Ave S Fl 12
New York, NY 10003-1621, USA

Schlueter, Dale (Athlete, Basketball Player)
15555 SW Harcourt Ter
Portland, OR 97224-5234, USA

Schmack, Brian (Athlete, Baseball Player)
504 E Wye Mesa
Brookings, SD 57006-4534, USA

Schmautz, Bobby (Athlete, Hockey Player)
19866 N 90th Ave
Peoria, AZ 85382-8678, USA

Schmelz, Al (Athlete, Baseball Player)
3166 E Morrison Ranch Pkwy
Gilbert, AZ 85296-9465, USA

Schmelz, Al (Athlete, Baseball Player)
3166 E Morrison Ranch Pkwy
Gilbert, AZ 85296-9465, USA

Schmemann, Serge (Journalist)
229 W 43rd St
Attn Editorial Dept
New York, NY 10036-3982, USA

Schmich, Mary (Journalist)
Chicago Tribune
435 N Michigan Ave Ste 200
Chicago, IL 60611-4024, USA

Schmid, Dave
17173 Rayen St
Sherwood Forest, CA 91325-2908

Schmid, Sigi (Coach, Soccer Player)
Los Angeles Galaxy
1010 Rose Bowl Dr
Pasadena, CA 91103, USA

Schmidgall, Jennifer (Athlete, Hockey Player, Olympic Athlete)
3640 Wooddale Ave S Unit 103
Minneapolis, MN 55416-5157, USA

Schmidt, Bob (Athlete, Football Player)
4315 Twilight Ln
Hamburg, NY 14075-1526, USA

Schmidt, Bob (Athlete, Baseball Player)
9 Hardwood Dr
Saint Charles, MO 63303-5942, USA

Schmidt, Curt (Athlete, Baseball Player)
4025 Chara Ln
Billings, MT 59105-5659, USA

Schmidt, Dave (Athlete, Baseball Player)
7172 N Serenoa Dr
Sarasota, FL 34241-9270, USA

Schmidt, Dave (Athlete, Baseball Player)
26636 Portales Ln
Mission Viejo, CA 92691-5122, USA

Schmidt, Eric (Business Person)
c/o Staff Member *Google Inc*
1600 Amphitheatre Pkwy
Mountain View, CA 94043-1351, USA

Schmidt, Freddy (Athlete, Baseball Player)
128 Constitution Ave
Wind Gap, PA 18091-1119, USA

Schmidt, Hank (Athlete, Football Player)
4641 Mission Bell Ln
La Mesa, CA 91941-5450, USA

Schmidt, Jason (Athlete, Baseball Player)
6539 E Cheney Dr
Paradise Valley, AZ 85253-3511, USA

Schmidt, Jean (Congressman, Politician)
2464 Rayburn Hob
Washington, DC 20515-4603, USA

Schmidt, Jeff (Athlete, Baseball Player)
1028 Seminole Hwy
Madison, WI 53711-3021, USA

Schmidt, Joseph P (Joe) (Athlete, Football Coach, Football Player)
226 Norcliff Dr
Bloomfield Hills, MI 48302-1556, USA

Schmidt, Kathryn (Kate) (Athlete, Track Athlete)
1008 Dexter St
Los Angeles, CA 90042-2248, USA

Schmidt, Kendall (Musician)
11700 W Charleston Blvd # 170-131
Las Vegas, NV 89135-1573, USA

Schmidt, Kenneth (Actor)
c/o Staff Member *Coast to Coast Talent Group*
3350 Barham Blvd
Los Angeles, CA 90068-1404, USA

Schmidt, Kevin (Actor)
c/o David Eisenberg *Protege Entertainment*
710 E Angeleno Ave
Burbank, CA 91501-2213, USA

Schmidt, Maarten
California Lnstitue of Technology 1200
California Blvd Dept 105-24
Pasadena, CA 91125-0001, USA

Schmidt, Mike (Athlete, Baseball Player)
c/o Staff Member *National Baseball Hall of Fame*
PO Box 590
Cooperstown, NY 13326-0590, USA

Schmidt, Milton C (Milt) (Athlete, Hockey Player)
10 Longwood Dr Unit 376
Westwood, MA 02090-1144, USA

Schmidt, Richard (Doctor)
University of Pennsylvania
3400 Spruce St
Philadelphia, PA 19104-4238, USA

Schmidt, Roy (Athlete, Football Player)
1844 Highpoint Rd
Snellville, GA 30078-2802, USA

Schmidt, Sam (Race Car Driver)
Treadway Racing
6017 W 7th St
Indianapolis, IN 46278, USA

Schmidt, Steve (Race Car Driver)
Schmidt Racing
8405 E 30th St
Indianapolis, IN 46219-1411, USA

Schmidt, Terry (Athlete, Football Player)
10910 Double Island Rd
Green Mtn, NC 28740-6029, USA

Schmidt, William (Bill) (Athlete, Track Athlete)
1809 Devonwood Ct
Knoxville, TN 37922-6233, USA

Schmidt, Wrenn (Actor)
c/o Dale Davis *Davis Spylios Management*
244 W 54th St Ste 707
New York, NY 10019-5515

Schmidt-Nielsen, Knut (Doctor)
Kuke University
Zoology Dept
Durham, NC 27706, USA

Schmidtt, Harrison (Ex-Senator, Senator)
PO Box 90730
Albuquerque, NM 87199-0730, USA

Schmidt-Weitzman, Violet (Athlete, Baseball Player)
225 S Mill St
Mishawaka, IN 46544-2002, USA

Schmiesing, Joe (Athlete, Football Player)
19460 County 2
Sauk Centre, MN 56378-4624, USA

Schmit, Timothy B (Musician)
William Morris Agency
1325 Avenue of the Americas Bsmt 2
New York, NY 10019-6047, USA

Schmitt, Dr H Harrison (Astronaut)
PO Box 90730
Albuquerque, NM 87199-0730, USA

Schmitt, Harrison H (Jack) (Astronaut, Ex-Senator)
PO Box 90730
Albuquerque, NM 87199-0730, USA

Schmitt, John (Athlete, Football Player)
2 Mayflower Rd
Glen Head, NY 11545-3120, USA

Schmock, Jonathan (Actor)
c/o Judy Orbach *Judy O Productions*
6136 Glen Holly St
Los Angeles, CA 90068-2338, USA

Schmoeller, David (Director)
3910 Woodhill Ave
Las Vegas, NV 89121-6245, USA

Schmoll, Steve (Athlete, Baseball Player)
4758 Chastain Dr
Melbourne, FL 32940-1274, USA

Schnabel, Julian (Artist, Director)
c/o Bart Walker *ICM Partners (LA)*
10250 Constellation Blvd Fl 7
Los Angeles, CA 90067-6207, USA

Schnabel, Marco (Director)
c/o Staff Member *3 Arts Entertainment (LA)*
9460 Wilshire Blvd Fl 7
Beverly Hills, CA 90212-2713, USA

Schnarch, David (Writer)
c/o Staff Member *HarperCollins Publishers*
195 Broadway Fl 2
Cellar 1
New York, NY 10007-3132, USA

Schnarre, Monika (Actor, Model)
Alex Stevens
137 N Larchmont Blvd # 259
Los Angeles, CA 90004-3704, USA

Schneck, Dave (Athlete, Baseball Player)
3891 Lehigh Dr
Northampton, PA 18067-9771, USA

Schneck, Mike (Athlete, Football Player)
110 Three Degree Rd
Allison Park, PA 15101, USA

Schneider, Andrew (Journalist)
c/o Richard Weitz *William Morris Endeavor (LA)*
9601 Wilshire Blvd
Beverly Hills, CA 90210-5213, USA

Schneider, Bob (Musician)
c/o Paul Nugent *Rainmaker Artists*
10925 Estate Ln Ste 124
Dallas, TX 75238-5168, USA

Schneider, Brian (Athlete, Baseball Player)
130 Playa Rienta Way
Palm Beach Gardens, FL 33418-6210, USA

Schneider, Cory (Athlete, Hockey Player)
12 Preston Ct
Swampscott, MA 01907-1650

Schneider, Dan (Athlete, Baseball Player)
PO Box 2421
Tubac, AZ 85646-2421, USA

Schneider, Dan (Producer, Writer)
c/o Staff Member *William Morris Endeavor (LA)*
9601 Wilshire Blvd
Beverly Hills, CA 90210-5213, USA

Schneider, Fred (Musician, Songwriter)
c/o Staff Member *Direct Management Group*
8332 Melrose Ave
West Hollywood, CA 90069-5420, USA

Schneider, Howie (Cartoonist)
United Feature Syndicate
PO Box 5610
Cincinnati, OH 45201-5610, USA

Schneider, Jeff (Athlete, Baseball Player)
268 Pin Oak Dr
Geneseo, IL 61254-1944, USA

Schneider, John (Actor, Musician)
c/o Staff Member *The Michael Gursey Company*
1482 E Valley Rd Ste 112
Santa Barbara, CA 93108-1200, USA

Schneider, Kurt Hugo (Internet Star, Musician)
c/o Zachary Druker *William Morris Endeavor (LA)*
9601 Wilshire Blvd
Beverly Hills, CA 90210-5213, USA

Schneider, Mathieu (Athlete, Hockey Player)
122 Cross St Apt C303
Westerly, RI 02891-2477, USA

Schneider, Max (Actor)
c/o Jeff Golenberg *Silver Lining Entertainment*
421 S Beverly Dr Fl 7
Beverly Hills, CA 90212-4408, USA

Schneider, Paul (Actor)
c/o Jillian Roscoe *ID Public Relations (LA)*
7060 Hollywood Blvd Fl 8th
Los Angeles, CA 90028-6021, USA

Schneider, Rob (Actor, Comedian, Producer, Writer)
c/o Lisa Blum *723 Productions*
2660 W Olive Ave
Burbank, CA 91505-4525, USA

Schneider, William ""Buzz"" (Athlete, Hockey Player)
5656 Turtle Lake Rd
Saint Paul, MN 55126-4769, USA

Schneider, William (Buzz) (Athlete, Hockey Player, Olympic Athlete)
5656 Turtle Lake Rd
Saint Paul, MN 55126-4769, USA

Schneiderman, Leon (Musician)
The Alliance for Democracy
PO Box 540115
Waltham, MA 02454-0115, USA

Schnelker, Bob (Coach)
Philadelphia Eagles
85 Silver Oaks Cir Apt 6102
Naples, FL 34119-4665, USA

Schnellenberger, Howard (Athlete, Coach, Football Coach, Football Player)
118 SE 25th Ave
Boynton Beach, FL 33435-7622, USA

Schnetzer, Ben (Actor)
c/o Rhonda Price *Gersh (NY)*
41 Madison Ave
New York, NY 10010-2202, USA

Schnetzer, Stephen (Actor)
c/o Matthew Sullivan *Sullivan Talent Group*
305 W 105th St Apt 3B
New York, NY 10025-9116, USA

Schnitker, Mike (Athlete, Football Player)
PO Box 968
Conifer, CO 80433-0968, USA

Schnittker, Richard (Dick) (Athlete, Basketball Player)
203 E Las Granadas
Green Valley, AZ 85614-2233, USA

Schochet, Bob (Cartoonist)
6 Sunset Rd
Highland Mills, NY 10930, USA

Schock, Aaron (Congressman, Politician)
328 Cannon Hob
Washington, DC 20515-0543, USA

Schock, Gina (Musician)
PO Box 720160
San Francisco, CA 94172-0160, USA

Schock, Ron (Athlete, Hockey Player)
1360 Whalen Rd
Penfield, NY 14526-1918, USA

Schoeffling, Michael (Actor)
413 Crestmont Dr
Newfoundland, PA 18445-5203, USA

Schoelen, Jill (Actor)
Gold Marshak Liedtke
3500 W Olive Ave Ste 1400
Burbank, CA 91505-5512, USA

Schoen, Gerry (Athlete, Baseball Player)
13 Santa Fe
Prescott, AZ 86305-5068, USA

Schoen, Max H (Doctor)
123 Wellfleet Cir
Folsom, CA 95630-6541, USA

Schoen, Tom (Athlete, Football Player)
437 W Belmont Ave Apt 13
Chicago, IL 60657-4756, USA

Schoendienst, Red (Athlete, Baseball Player, Coach)
1105 Jo Carr Dr
Chesterfield, MO 63017-8401, USA

Schoene, Russ (Athlete, Basketball Player)
6319 189th Pl NE Unit 103
Redmond, WA 98052-8582, USA

Schoeneweis, Scott (Athlete, Baseball Player)
14420 E Kern Ct
Fountain Hills, AZ 85268-6383, USA

Schoenfeld, Jim (Athlete, Coach, Hockey Player)
45 W 60th St Apt 18D
New York, NY 10023-7944

Schoenfeld, Jim (Athlete, Hockey Player)
New York Rangers
2 Penn Plz Fl 22
New York, NY 10121-2299

Schoenfield, Al (Athlete, Swimmer)
75 Santa Rosa St
San Luis Obispo, CA 93405-1819, USA

Schoenfield, Dana (Swimmer)
7734 E Lakeview Trl
Orange, CA 92869-2446, USA

Schoenke, Raymond F (Athlete, Football Player)
21151 Woodfield Rd
Gaithersburg, MD 20882-4847, USA

Schofield, Annabel (Actor)
Special Artists Agency
345 N Maple Dr # 302
Beverly Hills, CA 90210-3869, USA

Schofield, Dick (Athlete, Baseball Player)
17148 Windsor Crest Blvd
Glencoe, MO 63038-1392, USA

Schofield, Dwight (Athlete, Hockey Player)
9024 Cardinal Ter
Saint Louis, MO 63144-1103

Scholes, Clarke (Athlete, Olympic Athlete, Swimmer)
20671 Wedgewood Dr
Grosse Pointe Woods, MI 48236-1560, USA

Schollander, Don (Athlete, Olympic Athlete, Swimmer)
3576 Lakeview Blvd
Lake Oswego, OR 97035-5544, USA

Schollander, Donald A (Don) (Swimmer)
3576 Lakeview Blvd
Lake Oswego, OR 97035-5544, USA

Scholten, Jim (Music Group, Musician)
Sawyer Brown Inc
5200 Old Harding Rd
Franklin, TN 37064-9406, USA

Scholtz, Bob (Athlete, Football Player)
6721 S 71st East Ave
Tulsa, OK 74133-1818, USA

Scholtz, Bruce (Athlete, Football Player)
6636 W William Cannon Dr Apt 1718
Austin, TX 78735-8549, USA

Scholz, Tom (Musician)
c/o Gail Parenteau *Parenteau Guidance*
132 E 35th St # 3J
New York, NY 10016-3892, USA

Schon, Kyra (Actor)
930 N Sheridan Ave
Pittsburgh, PA 15206-2261, USA

Schon, Neal (Musician)
c/o Howard Nelson Cromwell
LLEWMORC Media & Production Agency
2300 Good Hope Rd SE Apt 320
Washington, DC 20020-5115, USA

Schon, Neil (Musician)
c/o Staff Member *William Morris Endeavor (LA)*
9601 Wilshire Blvd
Beverly Hills, CA 90210-5213, USA

Schoofs, Mark (Journalist)
Village Voice
32 Cooper Sq
Editorial Dept
New York, NY 10003-7117, USA

Schooler, Mike (Athlete, Baseball Player)
10846 Poplar St Apt 114
Loma Linda, CA 92354-2222, USA

Schools, Dave (Musician)
11230 Occidental Rd
Sebastopol, CA 95472-9650, USA

Schoon, Milton (Athlete, Basketball Player)
1218 Blaine Ave
Janesville, WI 53545-1834, USA

Schoonmaker, Jerry (Athlete, Baseball Player)
8343 Schreiber Dr
Munster, IN 46321-1829, USA

Schorer, Jane (Journalist)
Des Moines Register
PO Box 957
Editorial Dept
Des Moines, IA 50306-0957, USA

Schorr, Bill (Cartoonist)
United Feature Syndicate
PO Box 5610
Cincinnati, OH 45201-5610, USA

Schott, Stephen (Baseball Player)
Oakland A's
12330 Hilltop Dr
Los Altos Hills, CA 94024-5218, USA

Schott, Steve (Baseball Player)
12330 Hilltop Dr
Los Altos Hills, CA 94024-5218

Schottenheimer, Marty (Athlete, Football Coach, Football Player)
19825 N Cove Rd Ste B
Cornelius, NC 28031-6446, USA

Schourek, Pete (Athlete, Baseball Player)
14917 Cub Run Park Dr
Centreville, VA 20120-1234, USA

Schrader, Ken (Race Car Driver)
Ken Schrader Racing Incorporated
PO Box 5430
Concord, NC 28027-1507, USA

Schrader, Kurt (Congressman, Politician)
314 Cannon Hob
Washington, DC 20515-0404, USA

Schrader, Maria (Actor)
c/o Joel Kleinman *Baier/Kleinman International*
3575 Cahuenga Blvd W Ste 500
Los Angeles, CA 90068-1344, USA

Schrader, Paul (Actor, Director, Writer)
c/o Johnnie Planco *Parseghian Planco LLC*
388 2nd Ave
New York, NY 10010-5616, USA

Schram, Bitty (Actor)
c/o Robert Marsala *Wishlab*
2225A Hyperion Ave
Los Angeles, CA 90027-4709, USA

Schram, Jessy (Actor)
14900 Magnolia Blvd
Sherman Oaks, CA 91403-1330, USA

Schramka, Paul (Athlete, Baseball Player)
W180N9923 Riversbend Cir W
Germantown, WI 53022-4656, USA

Schramm, David (Actor)
3521 Berry Dr
Studio City, CA 91604-3882, USA

Schreiber, Adam (Athlete, Football Player)
2520 River Summit Dr
Duluth, GA 30097-2255, USA

Schreiber, Avery
6399 Wilshire Blvd Ste 414
Los Angeles, CA 90048-5716

Schreiber, Larry (Athlete, Football Player)
388 Albion Ave
Woodside, CA 94062-3603, USA

Schreiber, Liev (Actor)
427 Washington St # 2EW
New York, NY 10013-1735, USA

Schreiber, Martin J (Ex-Governor)
2700 S Shore Dr Unit B
Milwaukee, WI 53207-2366, USA

Schreiber, Ted (Athlete, Baseball Player)
116 Nantucket Is
Centerville, GA 31028-8547, USA

Schremmer, Patty (Golfer)
714 Siesta Key Cir
Sarasota, FL 34242-1250, USA

Schremp, Bob (Athlete, Football Player)
24576 Creekview Dr
Laguna Hills, CA 92653-4209, USA

Schremp, Rob (Athlete, Hockey Player)
303 Phillips St
Fulton, NY 13069-1514

Schrempf, Detlef (Athlete, Basketball Player, Olympic Athlete)
9735 NE 1st St
Bellevue, WA 98004-5413, USA

Schrenk, Steve (Athlete, Baseball Player)
14325 San Paolo Ln
Charlotte, NC 28277-3378, USA

Schreyer, Cindy (Golfer)
18 Cottage Dr
Newnan, GA 30265-5513, USA

Schrieber, Paul (Athlete, Baseball Player)
9179 N 102nd St
Scottsdale, AZ 85258-5704, USA

Schrimshaw, Nevin S (Doctor)
Sandwich Notch Farm
Campton, NH 03223, USA

Schroder, Bob (Athlete, Baseball Player)
2810 Jefferson Dr
Hattiesburg, MS 39402-2047, USA

Schroder, Chris (Athlete, Baseball Player)
4016 Valley Creek Rd
Edmond, OK 73034-8455, USA

Schroder, Jochen (Actor)
Postfach 10 23 46
Bochum, GE D-447

Schroder, Ricky (Actor)
21914 Gold Stone Rd
Topanga, CA 90290-4106, USA

Schroeder, Barbet (Director, Producer)
8033 W Sunset Blvd # 51
Los Angeles, CA 90046-2401, USA

Schroeder, Bill (Athlete, Baseball Player)
4760 S Providence Dr
New Berlin, WI 53146-4012, USA

Schroeder, Carly (Actor)
c/o Beverly Strong *Strong Management*
9350 Wilshire Blvd Ste 224
Beverly Hills, CA 90212-3204, USA

Schroeder, Dorsey (Race Car Driver)
2314 Channelview Dr
Osage Beach, MO 65065-4902, USA

Schroeder, Gene (Athlete, Football Player)
918 Aaron Ct
Crown Point, IN 46307-7593, USA

Schroeder, Jay (Athlete, Football Player)
502 Hampton Rd
Burbank, CA 91504-2405, USA

Schroeder, Jeret (Race Car Driver)
529 Old Mill Rd
Millersville, MD 21108-1327, USA

Schroeder, Jim (Bowler)
3 Greenhaven Ter
Tonawanda, NY 14150-5503, USA

Schroeder, John (Athlete, Golfer)
PO Box 2768
Del Mar, CA 92014-5768, USA

Schroeder, Kenneth L (Business Person)
KLA-Tencor Corp
160 Rio Robles
San Jose, CA 95134-1813, USA

Schroeder, Patricia S (Politician)
c/o Staff Member *21st Century Speakers*
1352 Lake Ave
Gouldsboro, PA 18424, USA

Schroeder, Paul W (Writer)
University of Illinois
810 S Wright St
History Dept
Urbana, IL 61801-3644, USA

Schroeder, Steven A (Doctor, Misc)
10 Paseo Mirasol
Bel Tiburon, CA 94920-2021, USA

Schroeder, Terry (Athlete, Coach)
4901 Lewis Rd
Agoura Hills, CA 91301-2453, USA

Schroll, William (Athlete, Football Player)
1640 Oakley Dr
Baton Rouge, LA 70806-8623, USA

Schrom, Ken (Athlete, Baseball Player)
1002 Black Diamond Ct
Portland, TX 78374-4162, USA

Schroy, Ken (Athlete, Football Player)
79 Russell Rd
Garden City, NY 11530-1933, USA

Schruefer, John J (Doctor)
Georgetown University Hospital
Ob-Gyn Dept
Washington, DC 20007, USA

Schu, Rick (Athlete, Baseball Player)
2013 Driftwood Cir
El Dorado Hills, CA 95762-3744, USA

Schubb, Mark
9744 Wilshire Blvd Ste 308
Beverly Hills, CA 90212-1813

Schubert, Eric (Athlete, Football Player)
722 Homestead Ave
Maybrook, NY 12543-1308, USA

Schubert, Mark (Coach, Swimmer)
PO Box 479
Surfside, CA 90743-0479, USA

Schubert, Steve (Athlete, Football Player)
7 Douglas Dr
Candia, NH 03034-2304, USA

Schuck, John (Actor)
1501 Broadway Ste 703
New York, NY 10036-5501, USA

Schueler, Ron (Athlete, Baseball Player)
3108 E San Juan Ave
Phoenix, AZ 85016-3725, USA

Schuerholz, John (Baseball Player)
Atlanta Braves
1025 Royal Dr
Canonsburg, PA 15317-5004, USA

Schuessler, Jack (Business Person)
Wendy's International
4288 W Dublin Granville Rd
Dublin, OH 43017-2093, USA

Schuh, Harry F (Athlete, Football Player)
2309 Massey Rd
Memphis, TN 38119-6516, USA

Schuh, Jeff (Athlete, Football Player)
5550 Vagabond Ln N
Minneapolis, MN 55446-1323, USA

Schuhmacher, John (Athlete, Football
Player)
8226 Garrison Point Dr
Houston, TX 77040-6061, USA

Schul, Bob (Athlete, Olympic Athlete,
Track Athlete)
320 Wisteria Dr
Oakwood, OH 45419-3553, USA

Schuldt, Travis (Actor)
c/o Robert Marsala *Wishlab*
2225A Hyperion Ave
Los Angeles, CA 90027-4709, USA

Schuler, Carolyn (Swimmer)
26552 Via Del Sol
Mission Viejo, CA 92691-6125, USA

Schuler, Dave (Athlete, Baseball Player)
17210 Chatham St
Lewes, DE 19958-7229, USA

Schull, Rebecca (Actor)
Writers & Artists
8383 Wilshire Blvd # 550
Beverly Hills, CA 90211-2425, USA

Schuller, Robert (Religious Leader)
Crystal Cathedral Ministries
12921 Lewis St
Garden Grove, CA 92840-6207, USA

Schullstrom, Erik (Athlete, Baseball
Player)
1425 Court St
Alameda, CA 94501-3145, USA

Schulman, Ariel (Director)
c/o Rowena Arguelles *Creative Artists
Agency (CAA-LA)*
2000 Avenue of the Stars Ste 100
Los Angeles, CA 90067-4705, USA

Schult, Art (Athlete, Baseball Player)
48 Marie Ct
Wappingers Falls, NY 12590-6518, USA

Schulte, Greg (Baseball Player)
Arizona Diamondbacks
20723 N 56th Ave
Glendale, AZ 85308-6276, USA

Schulte, Richard (Athlete, Football Player)
1216 N Kenneth Pl
Chandler, AZ 85226-7210, USA

Schulters, Lance (Athlete, Football Player)
594 Grant Ave
Roselle, NJ 07203-2911, USA

Schultz, Barney (Athlete, Baseball Player)
790 Woodlane Rd
Beverly, NJ 08010-1902, USA

Schultz, Bill (Athlete, Football Player)
10302 Lakeland Dr
Fishers, IN 46037-9323, USA

Schultz, Boomer (Race Car Driver)
Schultz Sports Marketing
PO Box 8648
South Lake Tahoe, CA 96158-1648, USA

Schultz, Buddy (Athlete, Baseball Player)
5729 E Sandy Ln
Scottsdale, AZ 85254-4361, USA

Schultz, Dave (Athlete, Hockey Player)
1001 Harbour Cv
Somers Point, NJ 08244-2809, USA

Schultz, Dave (Race Car Driver)
2365 Lazy River Ln
Fort Myers, FL 33905-2242, USA

Schultz, Dwight (Actor)
23210 Beaumont St
Valencia, CA 91354-2139, USA

Schultz, Ed (Radio Personality)
The Ed Schultz Show
417 38th St S Ste F
Fargo, ND 58103-6508, USA

Schultz, Frederick H (Government
Official)
PO Box 1200
Jacksonville, FL 32201, USA

Schultz, George (Athlete, Baseball Player)
400 Fern Brook Ln # 218
Mount Laurel, NJ 08054-9542, USA

Schultz, Howard (Business Person)
Starbucks Corp
2401 Utah Ave S Ste 1
Seattle, WA 98134-1498, USA

Schultz, John (Athlete, Football Player)
503 Skyline Dr
Vestal, NY 13850-5321, USA

Schultz, John (Director)
c/o Staff Member *Creative Artists Agency
(CAA-LA)*
2000 Avenue of the Stars Ste 100
Los Angeles, CA 90067-4705, USA

Schultz, Kurt (Athlete, Football Player)
5075 Rockledge Dr
Clarence, NY 14031-2426, USA

Schultz, Michael A (Director)
Chrystalite Productions
PO Box 1940
Santa Monica, CA 90406-1940, USA

Schultze, Charles L (Government Official)
Brookings Institute
1775 Massachusetts Ave NW
Washington, DC 20036-2103, USA

Schulz, Jeff (Athlete, Baseball Player)
931 Greengate Ct
Evansville, IN 47715-7180, USA

Schulz, Jody (Athlete, Football Player)
222 Schulz Ln
Chester, MD 21619-2658, USA

Schulz, Kurt (Athlete, Football Player)
5130 Rockledge Dr
Clarence, NY 14031-2442, USA

Schulze, Don (Athlete, Baseball Player)
1851 N Brinton Ave
Dixon, IL 61021-8262, USA

Schulze, Matt (Actor)
c/o David Gardner *Principato/Young
Management (LA)*
9465 Wilshire Blvd Ste 900
Beverly Hills, CA 90212-2608, USA

Schulze, Paul (Actor)
c/o Staff Member *Kyle Fritz Management*
6325 Heather Dr
Los Angeles, CA 90068-1633, USA

Schulze, Richard (Business Person)
Best Buy Co
7601 Penn Ave S
Minneapolis, MN 55423-3683, USA

Schumacher, Gregg (Athlete, Football
Player)
104 Surfview Dr Apt 2108
Palm Coast, FL 32137-2348, USA

Schumacher, Joel (Director)
Greenfield & Selvaggi
11766 Wilshire Blvd Ste 1610
Los Angeles, CA 90025-6565, USA

Schumacher, Kelly (Basketball Player)
Indiana Fever
125 S Pennsylvania St
Conseco Fieldhouse
Indianapolis, IN 46204-3610, USA

Schumacher, Kurt (Athlete, Football
Player)
673 Northfield Ln
Harleysville, PA 19438-1698, USA

Schumaker, Jared (Skip) (Athlete, Baseball
Player)
6 Starlight Isle
Ladera Ranch, CA 92694-1466, USA

Schuman, Allan L (Business Person)
Ecolab Inc
370 Wabasha St N
Ecolab Center
Saint Paul, MN 55102-1349, USA

Schuman, Melissa (Actor)
c/o Staff Member *Kazarian, Measures, Ruskin & Associates (LA)*
11969 Ventura Blvd Fl 3
Studio City, CA 91604-2630, USA

Schuman, Tom (Musician)
PO Box 435
Highland Mills, NY 10930-0435, USA

Schumer, Amy (Comedian)
c/o Jimmy Miller *Mosaic Media Group*
9200 W Sunset Blvd Ste 10
West Hollywood, CA 90069-3608, USA

Schumer, Charles (Politician)
9 Prospect Park W Apt Lob
Brooklyn, NY 11215-1763, USA

Schur, Michael (Writer)
c/o Staff Member *3 Arts Entertainment (LA)*
9460 Wilshire Blvd Fl 7
Beverly Hills, CA 90212-2713, USA

Schurig, Roger (Athlete, Basketball Player)
1031 Brookside
Greensboro, GA 30642-6814, USA

Schurr, Wavne (Athlete, Baseball Player)
10030W 500 S
Hudson, IN 46747, USA

Schurr, Wayne (Athlete, Baseball Player)
10030 W 500 S
Hudson, IN 46747-9705, USA

Schussler Florenza, Elisabeth (Writer)
Notre Dame University
Theology Dept
Notre Dame, IN 46556, USA

Schutz, Carl (Athlete, Baseball Player)
PO Box 162
French Settlement, LA 70733-0162, USA

Schutz, Susan Polis (Writer)
Blue Mountain Arts Inc
PO Box 4549
Boulder, CO 80306-4549, USA

Schuur, Diane (Music Group, Musician)
Paul Canter Enterprises
33042 Ocean Rdg
Dana Point, CA 92629-1078, USA

Schwab, Charles (Business Person)
PO Box 620070
Redwood City, CA 94062-0070, USA

Schwab, Corey (Athlete, Hockey Player)
San Jose Sharks
525 W Santa Clara St
San Jose, CA 95113-1500

Schwab, Corey (Athlete, Hockey Player)
20633 76th Ave SE
Snohomish, WA 98296-5169

Schwab, John J (Doctor)
6217 Innes Trace Rd
Louisville, KY 40222-6008, USA

Schwabe, Mike (Athlete, Baseball Player)
13341 Presidio Pl
Tustin, CA 92782-8608, USA

Schwall, Don (Athlete, Baseball Player)
741 Wolverine Rd
Gibsonia, PA 15044, USA

Schwantz, Jim (Athlete, Football Player)
1047 W Chatham Dr
Palatine, IL 60067-5817, USA

Schwartz, Ben (Actor)
c/o Staff Member *Haven Entertainment*
8111 Beverly Blvd Ste 201
Los Angeles, CA 90048-4531, USA

Schwartz, Don (Athlete, Football Player)
19410 NE Redmond Rd
Redmond, WA 98053, USA

Schwartz, Ivan E (Producer)
c/o Staff Member *Greater Cleveland Film Commission*
812 Huron Rd E Ste 390
Cleveland, OH 44115-1145, USA

Schwartz, Josh (Producer, Writer)
3556 Lowry Rd
Los Angeles, CA 90027-1434, USA

Schwartz, Kevin (Race Car Driver)
606A Performance Rd
Mooresville, NC 28115-9595, USA

Schwartz, Lloyd (Journalist)
27 Pennsylvania Ave
Somerville, MA 02145-2217, USA

Schwartz, Neil J (Actor)
3044 Pearl Harbor Dr
Las Vegas, NV 89117-0925, USA

Schwartz, Randy (Athlete, Baseball Player)
757 El Rancho Dr
El Cajon, CA 92019-1141, USA

Schwartz, Scott (Actor)
Baseball Cards, Movie Collectibles Etc
21144 Ventura Blvd
Woodland Hills, CA 91364-2103, USA

Schwartzman, Jason (Actor)
c/o Matthew Labov *Forefront Media*
8500 Melrose Ave Ste 205
West Hollywood, CA 90069-5169, USA

Schwartzman, Robert (Actor)
c/o Joanne Wiles *ICM Partners (LA)*
10250 Constellation Blvd Fl 7
Los Angeles, CA 90067-6207, USA

Schwarz, Jeff (Athlete, Baseball Player)
912 Club Dr
Palm Beach Gardens, FL 33418-7065, USA

Schwarzbein, Diana (Doctor, Writer)
Health Communications
3201 SW 15th St
Deerfield Beach, FL 33442-8157, USA

Schwarzenegger, Arnold (Actor, Politician)
3110 Main St Ste 300
Santa Monica, CA 90405-5354, USA

Schwarzman, Stephen (Steve) (Business Person)
The Blackstone Group
345 Park Ave Ste 1100
New York, NY 10154-1703, USA

Schwarzman, Steve (Business Person)
Blackstone Group
345 Park Ave Ste 1100
New York, NY 10154-1703, USA

Schwedes, Gerhard (Athlete, Football Player)
PO Box 570
Clayton, NY 13624-0570, USA

Schwedes, Scott (Athlete, Football Player)
6871 Claret Cir
Fayetteville, NY 13066-1048, USA

Schweickart, Rusty (Astronaut)
B612 Foundation
2440 W El Camino Real Ste 300
Mountain View, CA 94040-1498, USA

Schweiker, Richard S (Politician)
8890 Windy Ridge Way
Mc Lean, VA 22102-1558, USA

Schweikert, David (Congressman, Politician)
1205 Longworth Hob
Washington, DC 20515-1704, USA

Schweikert, J E (Religious Leader)
Old Roman Catholic Church
4200 N Kedvale Ave
Chicago, IL 60641-2215, USA

Schweitz, John (Athlete, Basketball Player)
813 Smith Dr
Florence, SC 29501-5979, USA

Schwentke, Robert (Writer)
c/o Jennifer Davisson Killoran *LBI Entertainment*
2000 Avenue of the Stars
Floor 3, North Tower
Los Angeles, CA 90067-4700, USA

Schwimmer, David (Actor)
c/o Eric Kranzler *Management 360*
9111 Wilshire Blvd
Beverly Hills, CA 90210-5508, USA

Schwimmer, Lacey-Mae (Actor)
c/o Tiffany Kuzon *Evolution Entertainment (LA)*
901 N Highland Ave
Los Angeles, CA 90038-2412, USA

Schwinden, Ted (Ex-Governor)
18811 N 19th Ave Apt 3022
Phoenix, AZ 85027-5283, USA

Schypinski, Jerry (Athlete, Baseball Player)
13610 Kingsville Dr
Sterling Heights, MI 48312-4134, USA

Scialfa, Patty (Music Group, Musician)
c/o Staff Member *Sony Music International*
550 Madison Ave Fl 6
New York, NY 10022-3211, USA

Sciarra, John M (Athlete, Football Player)
404 Morning Star Ln
Newport Beach, CA 92660-5711, USA

Sciascia, Leonardo
Viale Scaduto 10/B
Palermo, IT 1-901

Scifres, Steve (Athlete, Football Player)
2026 Northglen Dr
Colorado Springs, CO 80909-1629, USA

Sciole, Jennifer (Actor, Producer)
c/o Steve Honig *Honig Company, The*
4804 Laurel Canyon Blvd Ste 828
Valley Village, CA 91607-3717, USA

Scioli, Brad (Football Player)
Indianapolis Colts
5433 Bay Harbor Dr
Indianapolis, IN 46254-4510, USA

Sciorra, Annabella (Actor)
c/o Sarah Fargo *Paradigm (NY)*
360 Park Ave S Fl 16
New York, NY 10010-1716, USA

Scioscia, Michael L (Mike) (Athlete, Baseball Player, Coach)
1915 Falling Star Ave
Westlake Village, CA 91362-5284, USA

Scissor Sisters (Music Group)
c/o Darin Harmon *3D Management*
520 S Westgate Ave
Los Angeles, CA 90049-4212, USA

Sciutto, Nellie (Actor)
c/o Ted Schachter *Schachter Entertainment*
1157 S Beverly Dr Fl 2
Los Angeles, CA 90035-1119, USA

S Club 7 (Music Group)
c/o Staff Member *Creative Artists Agency (CAA-LA)*
2000 Avenue of the Stars Ste 100
Los Angeles, CA 90067-4705, USA

Scobee, Josh (Athlete, Football Player)
c/o Ken Harris *Optimum Sports Management*
3225 S Macdill Ave Ste 330
Tampa, FL 33629-8171, USA

Scofield, Dean
12304 Santa Monica Blvd Ste 104
Los Angeles, CA 90025-2586

Scofield, Dino (Actor)
3330 Barham Blvd Ste 103
Los Angeles, CA 90068-1476, USA

Scofield, John (Musician)
Ted Kurland
173 Brighton Ave
Allston, MA 02134-2003, USA

Scoggins, Matt (Swimmer)
4900 Calhoun Canyon Loop
Austin, TX 78735-6417, USA

Scoggins, Tracy (Actor)
c/o Staff Member *Bette Smith Management*
499 N Canon Dr
Beverly Hills, CA 90210-4887, USA

Scola, Luis
5819 E Mountain View Rd
Paradise Valley, AZ 85253-1746, USA

Scolari, Peter (Actor)
c/o Staff Member *Peter Strain & Associates Inc (LA)*
5455 Wilshire Blvd Ste 1812
Los Angeles, CA 90036-4268, USA

Scolnick, Edward M (Doctor, Scientist)
1201 Magnolia Dr
Wayland, MA 01778-2848, USA

Scolnik, Glenn (Athlete, Football Player)
301 Willowgate Dr
Indianapolis, IN 46260-1476, USA

Sconiers, Daryl (Athlete, Baseball Player)
15985 Hibiscus St
Fontana, CA 92335-4460, USA

Scooters, The
15190 Encanto Dr
Sherman Oaks, CA 91403-4410

Scorpions (Music Group)
c/o Steve Martin *The Agency Group (NYC)*
142 W 57th St Fl 6
New York, NY 10019-3300, USA

Scorsese, Martin (Director)
c/o Staff Member *Sikelia Productions*
121 E 64th St
New York, NY 10065-7004, USA

Scorsese, Nicolette (Actor)
c/o Gregory (Greg) Mayo *Orange Grove Group, The*
12178 Ventura Blvd Ste 205
Studio City, CA 91604-2540, USA

Scorupco, Izabella (Actor, Model, Music Group, Musician)
c/o Anne Woodward *ROAR (LA)*
9701 Wilshire Blvd Fl 8
Beverly Hills, CA 90212-2008, USA

Scott, Adam (Actor)
c/o Jason Weinberg *Untitled Entertainment (LA)*
350 S Beverly Dr Ste 200
Beverly Hills, CA 90212-4819, USA

Scott, Alvin (Athlete, Basketball Player)
5786 W Townley Ave
Glendale, AZ 85302-4612, USA

Scott, Arthur (Athlete, Football Player)
634 U St
Kng Of Prussa, PA 19406-2702, USA

Scott, Ashley (Actor)
c/o Mary Putnam Greene *MPG Management*
9150 Wilshire Blvd Ste 350
Beverly Hills, CA 90212-3453, USA

Scott, Austin (Congressman, Politician)
516 Cannon Hob
Washington, DC 20515-2601, USA

Scott, Bo (Athlete, Football Player)
1301 Fountain Ln
Apt 1
Columbus, OH 43213, USA

Scott, Bobby (Athlete, Football Player)
14273 Northshore Dr
Lenoir City, TN 37772-4207, USA

Scott, Byron (Athlete, Basketball Player, Coach)
7505 Hannum Ave
Culver City, CA 90230-6162, USA

Scott, Camilla
23773 Via Canon Unit 201
Newhall, CA 91321-4632

Scott, Campbell (Actor)
6 Westwoods Road 1
Sharon, CT 06069-2225, USA

Scott, Captain E Winston (Astronaut)
150 W University Blvd Attn
Deancllgofaeronautics
Florida Institute of Technology
Melbourne, FL 32901-6982, USA

Scott, Carlos (Athlete, Football Player)
RR 1 Box 346
Hempstead, TX 77445, USA

Scott, Chad (Athlete, Football Player)
18526 Reliant Dr
Gaithersburg, MD 20879-5421, USA

Scott, Chris (Athlete, Football Player)
c/o Chad Speck *Allegiant Athletic Agency*
35 Market Sq Ste 201
Knoxville, TN 37902-1420, USA

Scott, Chuck (Athlete, Football Player)
875 Landover Xing
Suwanee, GA 30024-3045, USA

Scott, Clarence (Athlete, Football Player)
216 Sisson Ave NE
Atlanta, GA 30317-1422, USA

Scott, Clyde L (Smackover) (Athlete, Football Player, Track Athlete)
707 Pleasant Valley Dr Unit 29
Little Rock, AR 72227-2162, USA

Scott, Colonel David (Astronaut)
6033 W Century Blvd Ste 400
Scott Science and Technology Inc
Los Angeles, CA 90045-6416, USA

Scott, Coltin
195 S Beverly Dr Ste 400
Beverly Hills, CA 90212-3044

Scott, Dale (Athlete, Baseball Player)
1283 SW Cardinell Dr
Portland, OR 97201-3114, USA

Scott, Darnay (Athlete, Football Player)
13151 Scabard Pl
San Diego, CA 92128-4055, USA

Scott, Darryl (Athlete, Baseball Player)
4026 E Hamblin Dr
Phoenix, AZ 85050-8712, USA

Scott, Dave (Athlete, Football Player)
3151 Robindale Rd
Decatur, GA 30034-4962, USA

Scott, David (Congressman, Politician)
225 Cannon Hob
Washington, DC 20515-3002, USA

Scott, David
1300 Manhattan Ave Apt B
Manhattan Beach, CA 90266-4776

Scott, David R (Astronaut)
Merces
30 Hackamore Ln Ste 1
Vc Johnson
Bell Canyon, CA 91307-1065, USA

Scott, Dennis (Athlete, Basketball Player)
9832 Laurel Valley Dr
Windermere, FL 34786-8911, USA

Scott, Dick (Athlete, Baseball Player)
7399 E Cortez Rd
Scottsdale, AZ 85260-5432, USA

Scott, Dick (Athlete, Baseball Player)
166 Sunset Ln
Cairo, GA 39828-6737, USA

Scott, Donnie (Athlete, Baseball Player)
6042 114th Ter N
Pinellas Park, FL 33782-2018, USA

Scott, Donovan (Actor)
Talent Group
6300 Wilshire Blvd Ste 2100
Los Angeles, CA 90048-5282, USA

Scott, Dougray (Actor)
c/o Staff Member *Dontanville/Frattaroli (D/F)*
270 Lafayette St Ste 402
New York, NY 10012-3327, USA

Scott, Dragos (Athlete, Football Player)
1750 Pacific Beach Dr
San Diego, CA 92109-6047, USA

Scott, Edward (Politician)
4708 Yarrow Ct
Williamsburg, VA 23188-2427, USA

Scott, Edward (Baseball Player)
Indianapolis Clowns
720 Kasserine Pass
Mobile, AL 36609-6430, USA

Scott, Emmet (Writer)
c/o Staff Member *New English Review*
PO Box 158397
Nashville, TN 37215-8397, USA

Scott, Eric
11934 River Grove Ct
Moorpark, CA 93021-3105

Scott, Freddie L (Athlete, Football Player)
PO Box 197
Coahoma, MS 38617-0197, USA

Scott, Gary (Athlete, Baseball Player)
25 W Elm St Apt 47
Greenwich, CT 06830-6448, USA

Scott, Gavin (Writer)
c/o Jordan Bayer *Original Artists (LA)*
9465 Wilshire Blvd Ste 870
Beverly Hills, CA 90212-2610, USA

Scott, Geoffrey
1126 N Hollywood Way # 203-A
Burbank, CA 91505-2527

Scott, Herbert (Athlete, Football Player)
605 Rawhide Ct
Plano, TX 75023-4753, USA

Scott, H Lee Jr (Business Person)
Wal-Mart Stores
702 SW 8th St
Bentonville, AR 72712-6209, USA

Scott, Jack (Music Group, Musician, Songwriter, Writer)
34039 Coachwood Dr
Sterling Heights, MI 48312-5617, USA

Scott, Jacob E (Jake) Jr (Athlete, Football Player)
PO Box 857
Hanalei, HI 96714-0857, USA

Scott, James (Actor)
c/o Sandra Siegal *Siegal Company, The*
9025 Wilshire Blvd Ste 400
Beverly Hills, CA 90211-1828, USA

Scott, James (Athlete, Football Player)
10127 Chisholm Trl
Dallas, TX 75243-2511, USA

Scott, Jill (Actor, Musician)
11558 Morrison St
N Hollywood, CA 91601-4343, USA

scott, joe b (Athlete, Baseball Player)
1749 Netherwood Ave
Memphis, TN 38114-1932, USA

Scott, John (Athlete, Baseball Player)
917 S Pearl Ave
Compton, CA 90221-4320, USA

Scott, John (Athlete, Football Player)
1583 N Ellen Ave
Decatur, IL 62526, USA

Scott, Judson (Actor)
10000 Santa Monica Blvd # 305
Los Angeles, CA 90067

Scott, Kathryn Leigh (Actor)
3236 Bennett Dr
Los Angeles, CA 90068-1702, USA

Scott, Kevin B (Athlete, Football Player)
2335 Cascade St
Milpitas, CA 95035-7807, USA

Scott, Klea (Actor)
c/o Staff Member *Epstein Wyckoff Corsa Ross (LA)*
11350 Ventura Blvd Ste 100
Studio City, CA 91604-3140, USA

Scott, Lary R (Business Person)
Carolina Freight Corp
PO Box 1000
Cherryville, NC 28021-1000, USA

Scott, Lew (Athlete, Football Player)
317 Woodward Ave SE
Atlanta, GA 30312-2123, USA

Scott, Lindsay (Athlete, Football Player)
214 N Troup St
Valdosta, GA 31601-5738, USA

Scott, Lizabeth (Actor)
8277 Hollywood Blvd
Los Angeles, CA 90069-1611, USA

Scott, Lorna (Actor)
c/o Staff Member *Kjar and Associates*
10153 1/2 Riverside Dr
Toluca Lake, CA 91602-2561, USA

Scott, Luke (Athlete, Baseball Player)
1245 Arredondo Grant Rd
De Leon Springs, FL 32130-3719, USA

Scott, Melody Thomas (Actor)
12068 Crest Ct
Beverly Hills, CA 90210-1354, USA

Scott, Michael W (Mike) (Athlete, Baseball Player)
28355 Chat Dr
Laguna Niguel, CA 92677-1384, USA

Scott, Patricia (Athlete, Baseball Player)
3000 Riggs Rd Apt 105
Erlanger, KY 41018-3048, USA

Scott, Randy (Athlete, Football Player)
1440 Woodland Lake Dr
Snellville, GA 30078-2097, USA

Scott, Ray (Basketball Player, Coach)
Colonial Life Insurance
33200 Schoolcraft Rd
Livonia, MI 48150-1643, USA

Scott, Reid (Actor)
c/o Bridget Smith *Impression Entertainment*
9229 W Sunset Blvd Ste 700
West Hollywood, CA 90069-3407, USA

Scott, Reppert (Athlete, Football Player)
3133 N Bass Lake Rd
Eagle River, WI 54521-9150, USA

Scott, Richard U (Dick) (Athlete, Football Player)
1042 Blueberry Ln
Chambersburg, PA 17202-7567, USA

Scott, Rick (Governor, Politician)
Office of Governor Rick Scott
State of Florida, the Capitol
400 S. Monroe St.
Tallahassee, FL 32399-0001, USA

Scott, Ridley (Director)
c/o Simon Halls *Slate Public Relations*
9000 W Sunset Blvd Ste 915
West Hollywood, CA 90069-5809, USA

Scott, Robert (Baseball Player)
New York Black Yankees
236 W Grand St Apt A2
Elizabeth, NJ 07202-1280, USA

Scott, Rodney (Athlete, Baseball Player)
4206 Priscilla Ave
Indianapolis, IN 46226-3334, USA

Scott, Ron (Athlete, Hockey Player)
8822 Madeleine Dr
Baldwinsville, NY 13027-8916

Scott, Sean (Athlete, Football Player)
3217 Boise St
Berkeley, CA 94702-2607, USA

Scott, Seann William (Actor, Producer)
c/o Christina Papadopoulos *Baker Winokur Ryder Public Relations (BWR-NY)*
292 Madison Ave Fl 12
New York, NY 10017-6415, USA

Scott, Stephen (Musician)
Bridge Agency
2600 John F Kennedy Blvd Apt 1H
Jersey City, NJ 07306-6068, USA

Scott, Steven M (Steve) (Athlete, Track Athlete)
4106 La Portalada Dr
Carlsbad, CA 92010-2805, USA

Scott, Stuart
c/o Staff Member *ESPN (Main)*
935 Middle St
Espn Plaza
Bristol, CT 06010-1000, USA

Scott, Thomas C (Tom) (Athlete, Football Player)
3259 Kirkwood Ct
Keswick, VA 22947, USA

Scott, Tighe (Race Car Driver)
RD #1 - Box 1847
First St.
Saylorsburg, PA 18353, United States

Scott, Tim (Athlete, Baseball Player)
956 W Julia Way
Hanford, CA 93230-8552, USA

Scott, Tim (Congressman, Politician)
1117 Longwortij Hob
Washington, DC 20515-0001, USA

Scott, Todd (Athlete, Football Player)
5605 Avenue P
Galveston, TX 77551-5028, USA

Scott, Tom (Athlete, Football Player)
350 Portico Way Apt 310
Charlottesville, VA 22911-8486, USA

Scott, Tom (Athlete, Football Player)
1012 Peed Dr Apt 8
Greenville, NC 27834-7063, USA

Scott, Tom (Musician)
Performers of the World
8901 Melrose Ave # 200
West Hollywood, CA 90069-5605, USA

Scott, Tom Everett (Actor)
c/o John Carrabino *John Carrabino Management*
5900 Wilshire Blvd Ste 406
Los Angeles, CA 90036-5015, USA

Scott, Tony (Athlete, Baseball Player)
156 Oakwood Ave
Spartanburg, SC 29302-1602, USA

Scott, Trevor (Athlete, Football Player)
c/o Dave Butz *Sportstars Inc*
1350 Avenue of the Americas Fl 28
New York, NY 10019-4702, USA

Scott, Walter (Athlete, Football Player)
1991 Edgefield Rd
Trenton, SC 29847-2435, USA

Scott, Willard (Television Host)
c/o Staff Member *NBC News (NY)*
30 Rockefeller Plz
New York, NY 10112-0015, USA

Scott, William (Politician)
9229 Arlington Blvd Apt 250
Fairfax, VA 22031-2543, USA

Scott, William Lee
c/o Daniel Spilo *Industry Entertainment*
955 Carrillo Dr Ste 300
Los Angeles, CA 90048-5400, USA

Scott, Willie (Athlete, Football Player)
1123 Long St
Newberry, SC 29108-4231, USA

Scott, Winston E (Astronaut)
PO Box 1192
Cape Canaveral, FL 32920-1192, USA

Scotti, Benjamin (Athlete, Football Player)
715 N Beverly Dr
Beverly Hills, CA 90210-3321, USA

Scotti, Nick (Actor, Musician)
c/o Elise Konialian *Untitled Entertainment (NY)*
435 Hudson St Fl 9
New York, NY 10014-3995, USA

Scott Kay, Dominic (Actor)
c/o Rich Hueners *Paradigm (LA)*
360 N Crescent Dr
North Bldg
Beverly Hills, CA 90210-4874, USA

Scotto, Rosanna (Correspondent)
WNYW TV
205 E 67th St
New York, NY 10065-6089, USA

Scottoline, Lisa (Writer)
Harper Collins Publishers
195 Broadway Fl 2
New York, NY 10007-3132, USA

Scott Thomas, Kristin (Actor)
c/o Mara Buxbaum *ID Public Relations (LA)*
7060 Hollywood Blvd Fl 8th
Los Angeles, CA 90028-6021, USA

Scotty K (DJ)
c/o Staff Member *Diva Central Inc*
7510 W Sunset Blvd Ste 1445
Los Angeles, CA 90046-3408, USA

Scovell, Nell (Producer)
c/o Staff Member *William Morris Endeavor (LA)*
9601 Wilshire Blvd
Beverly Hills, CA 90210-5213, USA

Scoville, Darrel (Athlete, Hockey Player)
18 Landmark Rd
Scarborough, ME 04074-8482

Scowcroft, Brent (Politician)
350 Park Ave # 2600
New York, NY 10022-6022, USA

Scrafford, Kirk (Athlete, Football Player)
19400 US Highway 93 N
Florence, MT 59833-5914, USA

Scranton, Jim (Athlete, Baseball Player)
27519 Hammack Ave
Perris, CA 92570-7071, USA

Scranton, Nancy (Golfer)
15820 Sanctuary Dr
Tampa, FL 33647-1075, USA

Scratch (Artist, Musician)
William Morris Agency
1325 Avenue of the Americas Bsmt 2
New York, NY 10019-6047, USA

Scream3 (Music Group)
c/o Staff Member *Wind-up Records*
72 Madison Ave Fl 8
New York, NY 10016-8731, USA

Scremin, Claudio (Athlete, Hockey Player)
84 Littlebrook Ln
Eliot, ME 03903-1512

Scribner, Bucky (Athlete, Football Player)
512 Georgina Ave
Santa Monica, CA 90402, USA

Scribner, Rick (Race Car Driver)
8904 Amerigo Ave
Orangevale, CA 95662-4612, USA

Scrimm, Angus (Actor)
PO Box 5193
North Hollywood, CA 91616-5193, USA

Scrimshaw, Nevin S (Doctor)
PO Box 330
Sandwich Mountain Farm
Campton, NH 03223-0330, USA

Scripps, Charles E (Publisher)
10 Grandin Ln
Cincinnati, OH 45208-3304, USA

S. Critz, Mark (Congressman, Politician)
1022 Longworth Hob
Washington, DC 20515-4902, USA

Scrivener, Chuck (Athlete, Baseball Player)
1766 Hazel St
Birmingham, MI 48009-6892, USA

Scroggins, Tracy (Athlete, Football Player)
2026 Willow Leaf Dr
Rochester Hills, MI 48309-3730, USA

Scruggs, Eugene (Baseball Player)
Detroit Stars
618 Dawson Ter NW
Huntsville, AL 35811-1782, USA

Scruggs, Randy (Musician)
McLachlan Scruggs
2821 Bransford Ave
Nashville, TN 37204-3101, USA

Scruggs, Tony (Athlete, Baseball Player)
11621 Braddock Dr Apt 17
Culver City, CA 90230-5175, USA

Scudder, Scott (Athlete, Baseball Player)
38 Fernwood Dr
Texarkana, TX 75503-1652, USA

Scuderi, Rob (Athlete, Hockey Player)
Sports Consulting Group
65 Monroe Ave Ste D
Pittsford, NY 14534-1318, USA

Scudero, Joe (Athlete, Football Player)
11811 Mandy Ln
Manassas, VA 20112-3134, USA

Scully, John (Athlete, Football Player)
3500 Bankview Dr
Joliet, IL 60431-4804, USA

Scully, Vin (Sportscaster)
c/o Staff Member *Los Angeles Dodgers (LA Dodgers)*
1000 Elysian Park Ave
Los Angeles, CA 90012-1112, USA

Scurry, Briana (Athlete, Olympic Athlete, Soccer Player)
11610 137th Ave N
Dayton, MN 55327-9730, USA

Scurti, John (Actor)
c/o Jennifer Konawal *Washington Square Arts (NY)*
41 Madison Ave
New York, NY 10010-2202, USA

Scutaro, Marco (Athlete, Baseball Player)
19877 E Country Club Dr Apt 3503
Miami, FL 33180-4812, USA

Sczurek, Stan (Athlete, Football Player)
689 Beaver Ridge Trl
Broadview Heights, OH 44147-1972, USA

Sea, Daniela (Actor)
c/o Hannah Roth *Don Buchwald & Associates (LA)*
6500 Wilshire Blvd Ste 2200
Los Angeles, CA 90048-4942, USA

Seabol, Scott (Athlete, Baseball Player)
427 Cedar Dr
Elizabeth, PA 15037-2167, USA

Seabron, Malcolm (Athlete, Football Player)
10418 Cliffwood Dr
Houston, TX 77035-3702, USA

Seabrook, Andrea (Correspondent)
c/o Staff Member *National Public Radio (NPR)*
1111 N Capitol St NE
Washington, DC 20002-7502, USA

Seabrook, Brent (Athlete, Hockey Player)
3323 N Hoyne Ave
Chicago, IL 60618-6243

Seacrest, Ryan (Producer, Radio Personality, Television Host)
c/o Melissa Stone *42West (LA)*
1840 Century Park E Ste 700
Los Angeles, CA 90067-2122, USA

Seaforth Hayes, Susan (Actor)
4528 Beck Ave
North Hollywood, CA 91602-1904, USA

Seagal, Steven (Actor)
c/o Carlos Keyes *Red Entertainment Agency*
505 8th Ave Rm 1004
New York, NY 10018-6529, USA

Seagrave, Jocelyn (Actor)
c/o Gregg Steiner *Perspective Film*
15030 Ventura Blvd
Sherman Oaks, CA 91403-5470, USA

Seagraves, Ralph (Race Car Driver)
RR 10 Box 413
Winston Salem, NC 27127, USA

Seagren, Bob (Athlete, Olympic Athlete, Track Athlete)
International City Racing
10545 Humbolt St
Attn: Ceo
Los Alamitos, CA 90720-5401, USA

Seal (Musician)
12759 Chalon Rd
Los Angeles, CA 90049-1250, USA

Seal, Paul (Athlete, Football Player)
21599 Hidden Rivers Dr N
Southfield, MI 48075-6110, USA

Seale, John C (Cinematographer)
Mirisch Agency
1801 Century Park E
Los Angeles, CA 90067-2302, USA

Seale, Johnnie (Athlete, Baseball Player)
1941 County Road 207
Durango, CO 81301-7700, USA

Seale, Sam (Athlete, Football Player)
1818 Da Gama Ct
Escondido, CA 92026-1729, USA

Sealey, Tom (Athlete, Basketball Player)
316 Fountain Ave
Brooklyn, NY 11208-4302, USA

Seals, Brady
2100 W End Ave Ste 1000
Nashville, TN 37203-5240

Seals, Bruce (Athlete, Basketball Player)
29 2nd St
Malden, MA 02148-1953, USA

Seals, George (Athlete, Football Player)
1101 1st St Unit 204
Coronado, CA 92118-1496, USA

Seals, Ray (Athlete, Football Player)
664 NW Shaw Gln
Lake City, FL 32055-0408, USA

Seals & Croft (Music Group)
c/o Staff Member *4STAR Entertainment LLC*
1675 York Ave Apt 32C
New York, NY 10128-6905, USA

Sealy, Tom (Athlete, Basketball Player)
387 Classon Ave
Brooklyn, NY 11238-1307, USA

Seaman, Kim (Athlete, Baseball Player)
4900 Main St
Moss Point, MS 39563-2735, USA

Sean, Jay (Musician)
c/o David Zedeck *Creative Artists Agency (CAA-NY)*
162 5th Ave Fl 6
New York, NY 10010-6047, USA

Sean, SeanMahan (Athlete, Football Player)
4202 E 116th Pl # Pi
Tulsa, OK 74137-6120, USA

Seanez, Rudy (Athlete, Baseball Player)
1422 McCabe Cove Rd
El Centro, CA 92243-9741, USA

Searage, Ray (Athlete, Baseball Player)
9737 Pine Lake Trl
Saint Petersburg, FL 33708-3571, USA

Searchers, The
2514 Build America Dr
Hampton, VA 23666-3223

Searcy, Leon (Athlete, Football Player)
3841 Biggin Church Rd W
Jacksonville, FL 32224-7985, USA

Searcy, Nick (Actor)
c/o Joseph (Joe) Rice *Abrams Artists Agency (LA)*
9200 W Sunset Blvd PH 11
West Hollywood, CA 90069-3601, USA

Searcy, Steve (Athlete, Baseball Player)
5112 Gouffon Rd
Knoxville, TN 37918-9319, USA

Searfoss, Colonel A Richard (Astronaut)
25101 Bear Valley Rd
Tehachapi, CA 93561-8311, USA

Searfoss, Richard A (Astronaut)
24480 Silver Creek Way
Tehachapi, CA 93561-8399, USA

Searle, Jackie
7214 Chestwood Dr
Tujunga, CA 91042

Searles, Kyle (Actor)
c/o Loch Powell *Leverage Management*
3030 Pennsylvania Ave
Santa Monica, CA 90404-4112, USA

Sears, Brian (Horse Racer)
83 Osprey Ct
Secaucus, NJ 07094-2934, USA

Sears, Jay (Horse Racer)
750 NW 30th Ave Apt A
Delray Beach, FL 33445-2077, USA

Sears, Ken (Athlete, Basketball Player)
40 Cutter Dr
Watsonville, CA 95076-2229, USA

Sears, Teddy (Actor)
c/o Sandy Erickson *Vic Ramos Management*
337 E 13th St Apt 6
New York, NY 10003-5852, USA

Sears, Todd (Athlete, Baseball Player)
513 NW Chapel Dr
Ankeny, IA 50023-1420, USA

Sears, Dr, William
34761 Doheny Pl
Capistrano Beach, CA 92624-1713

Sease, Marvin
Malaco Music Group
PO Box 9287
Jackson, MS 39286-9287, USA

Seaver, Tom (Athlete, Baseball Player)
1761 Diamond Mountain Rd
Calistoga, CA 94515-9672, USA

Seaward, Tracey (Producer)
c/o Staff Member *ICM Partners (LA)*
10250 Constellation Blvd Fl 7
Los Angeles, CA 90067-6207, USA

Seay, Bobby (Athlete, Baseball Player, Olympic Athlete)
1591 Oak Cir N
Sarasota, FL 34232-3478, USA

Seay, Laura (Actor)
c/o Susan Smith *Susan Smith Company, The*
2001 Wilshire Blvd Ste 400
Santa Monica, CA 90403-5686, USA

Seay, Mark (Athlete, Football Player)
2866 Muscupiabe Dr
San Bernardino, CA 92405-3060, USA

Seay, Virgil (Athlete, Football Player)
5611 Fort Corloran Dr
Burke, VA 22015-2112, USA

Sebaldt, Maria (Actor)
Geranienstr. 3
Grunwald, GE D-820

Sebastian, John (Musician)
11 Music Hill Rd
Woodstock, NY 12498-2238, USA

Sebastian, Toby (Actor)
c/o Bridget Smith *Impression Entertainment*
9229 W Sunset Blvd Ste 700
West Hollywood, CA 90069-3407, USA

Sebelius, Kathleen (Politician)
Health/Human Services Dept
200 Independence Ave SW
Washington, DC 20201-0007, USA

Sebesky, Don (Musician)
c/o Staff Member *Bennett Morgan & Associates*
1022 Route 376 Ste 4
Wappingers Falls, NY 12590-6372, USA

Sebold, Alice (Writer)
c/o Steven Barclay *Steven Barclay Agency*
12 Western Ave
Petaluma, CA 94952-2907, USA

Sebra, Bob (Athlete, Baseball Player)
20 Misners Trl
Ormond Beach, FL 32174-8531, USA

Secada, Jon (Musician)
c/o Susan Haber *Haber Entertainment*
434 S Canon Dr Apt 204
Beverly Hills, CA 90212-4501, USA

Secor, Kyle (Actor)
Brillstein/Grey
9150 Wilshire Blvd Ste 350
Beverly Hills, CA 90212-3453, USA

Secord, Al (Athlete, Hockey Player)
950 Ginger Ct
Southlake, TX 76092-6063

Secord, John (Music Group, Musician)
Making Texas Music
PO Box 1013
Old Putnam Bank Building
Putnam, TX 76469-1013, USA

Secord, Richard (Politician)
Thermal Imaging
108 Windlake Ct
Niceville, FL 32578-4804, USA

Secrest, Charles (Baseball Player)
215 Orchard Grove Ave
Lewistown, PA 17044, USA

Secret Machines (Music Group)
c/o Mike Luba *Madison House Inc.*
4760 Walnut St Ste 106
Boulder, CO 80301-2561, USA

Secrets, No (Music Group)
Official International Fan Club
PO Box 5247
Bellingham, WA 98227-5247, USA

Secrist, Don (Athlete, Baseball Player)
5851 Park Rd
Pinckneyville, IL 62274-2513, USA

Secules, Scott (Athlete, Football Player)
3909 Royal Palms Ct
Dallas, TX 75244-7261, USA

Secunda, Andrew (Writer)
c/o Staff Member *United Talent Agency (UTA-LA)*
9336 Civic Center Dr
Beverly Hills, CA 90210-3604, USA

Seda, Jon (Actor)
c/o Adam Schweitzer *ICM Partners (NY)*
730 5th Ave
New York, NY 10019-4105, USA

Sedaka, Neil (Musician)
Sedaka Music
201 E 66th St Apt 3N
New York, NY 10065-6454, USA

Sedar, Ed (Athlete, Baseball Player)
8 S Lake Ave
Third Lake, IL 60030-8431, USA

Sedaris, Amy (Actor)
c/o Sarah Fargo *Paradigm (NY)*
360 Park Ave S Fl 16
New York, NY 10010-1716, USA

Sedaris, David (Comedian, Writer)
c/o Staff Member *Little, Brown & Co.*
466 Lexington Ave Lbby 15
New York, NY 10017-3165, USA

Seddon, Dr Rhea M (Astronaut)
1709 Shagbark Trl
Murfreesboro, TN 37130-1136, USA

Seddon, Margaret Rhea (Astronaut)
1709 Shagbark Trl
Murfreesboro, TN 37130-1136, USA

Seddon, M Rhea
1709 Shagbark Trl
Murfreesboro, TN 37130-1136, USA

Sedelmaier, Joe (Cartoonist)
Sedelmaier Film Productions
858 W Armitage Ave # 267
Chicago, IL 60614-4370, USA

Sedgwick, Bill (Race Car Driver)
33056 Acklins Ave
Acton, CA 93510-1747, USA

Sedgwick, Kyra (Actor)
2800 Glendower Ave
Los Angeles, CA 90027-1119, USA

Sedgworth, Bill
1811 Volusia Ave
Daytona Beach, FL 32114

Sedlacek, Shawn (Athlete, Baseball Player)
11008 W 131st St
Overland Park, KS 66213-3659, USA

Sedoris, Chris (Athlete, Football Player)
119 Edgewood Way
Pewee Valley, KY 40056-9132, USA

Seduction (Music Group)
c/o Staff Member *Diva Central Inc*
7510 W Sunset Blvd Ste 1445
Los Angeles, CA 90046-3408, USA

See, Carolyn (Writer)
17339 Tramonto Dr Apt 303
Pacific Palisades, CA 90272-3149, USA

See, Larry (Athlete, Baseball Player)
1913 W Remington Dr
Chandler, AZ 85286-6231, USA

See, Marshall (Athlete, Basketball Player)
1138 S Canal Cir
Camp Verde, AZ 86322-7014, USA

Seebold, Bill (Race Car Driver)
Motorsports HOF
PO Box 193
Novi, MI 48376-0193, USA

Seegal, Denise (Business Person)
Liz Claiborne Inc
1441 Broadway
New York, NY 10018-1905, USA

Seeger, Michael
PO Box 1592
Lexington, VA 24450-1592, USA

Seehorn, Rhea (Actor)
c/o Randi Ross *Epstein Wyckoff Corsa Ross (LA)*
11350 Ventura Blvd Ste 100
Studio City, CA 91604-3140, USA

Seelbach, Chris (Athlete, Baseball Player)
302 Fort Howell Dr
Hilton Head, SC 29926-2764, USA

Seelbach, Chuck (Athlete, Baseball Player)
13800 Fairhill Rd Apt 501
Cleveland, OH 44120-5510, USA

Seelenfreund, Alan (Business Person)
McKesson HBOC Inc
1 Post St
San Francisco, CA 94104-5203, USA

Seeley, Andrew (Actor, Musician)
c/o Ellen Drantch-Billet *EDB Management*
1953 Barry Ave
Los Angeles, CA 90025-5381, USA

Seely, Jeannie (Music Group, Musician, Songwriter, Writer)
c/o Staff Member *Tessier-Marsh Talent*
505 Canton Pass
Madison, TN 37115-5449, USA

Seerman, Jamie (Jaymay) (Musician)
c/o Lee Scheinbaum *Halfpipe Entertainment*
PO Box 10534
Beverly Hills, CA 90213-3534, USA

Seether (Music Group)
c/o Staff Member *Wind-up Records*
72 Madison Ave Fl 8
New York, NY 10016-8731, USA

Sefcik, Kevin (Athlete, Baseball Player)
16921 Steeplechase Pkwy
Orland Park, IL 60467-8769, USA

Sefolosha, Thabo (Athlete, Basketball Player)
910 Colony Dr
Salisbury, MD 21804-8758, USA

Sega, Dr M Ronald
1700 W Plum St Apt 54B
Fort Collins, CO 80521-3802, USA

Segal, Fred (Designer, Fashion Designer)
Fred Segal Jeans
8100 Melrose Ave
Los Angeles, CA 90046-7091, USA

Segal, George (Actor)
c/o Abe Hoch *A Management Company*
9107 Wilshire Blvd Ste 650
Beverly Hills, CA 90210-5544, USA

Segal, George (Horse Racer)
750 Michigan Ave
US Trotting Association
Columbus, OH 43215-1107, USA

Segal, Jonathan
PO Box 3059
Forreston, IL 61030

Segal, Peter (Director, Producer, Writer)
c/o Adam Kanter *Paradigm (LA)*
2000 Avenue of the Stars
Los Angeles, CA 90067-4700, USA

Segall, Pamela (Actor)
c/o Staff Member *Meghan Schumacher Management*
13351D Riverside Dr # 387
Sherman Oaks, CA 91423-2508, USA

Segel, Jason (Actor, Producer)
c/o Stacy Abrams *Abrams Entertainment*
5225 Wilshire Blvd Ste 515
Los Angeles, CA 90036-4349, USA

Segelke, Herman (Athlete, Baseball Player)
PO Box 2513
Antioch, CA 94531-2513, USA

Seger, Bob (Musician, Songwriter)
3841 Laplaya Ln
Orchard Lake, MI 48324-2940, USA

Segreti, Donald (Politician)
387 Timber Ridge Dr
Bartlett, IL 60103-6605, USA

Segrist, Kal (Athlete, Baseball Player)
3813 55th St
Lubbock, TX 79413-4619, USA

Segui, David V (Athlete, Baseball Player)
2740 N 131st St
Kansas City, KS 66109-3365, USA

Segui, Diego P (Athlete, Baseball Player)
13421 Leavenworth Rd
Kansas City, KS 66109-3351, USA

Seguignol, Fernando (Athlete, Baseball Player)
3517 Turenne Way
Wellington, FL 33449-8061, USA

Segura, Francisco (Pancho) (Tennis Player)
Rancho La Costa Hotel & Spa
7690 Camino Real
Carlsbad, CA 92009, USA

Segura, Pancho
. La Costa Hotel
Carlsbad, CA 92009

Seguso, Robert (Athlete, Olympic Athlete, Tennis Player)
3904 Bayside Ct
Bradenton, FL 34210-4107, USA

Sehorn, Jason (Athlete, Football Player)
1901 Wild Holly Ln
Charlotte, NC 28226-5744, USA

Seibel, Phil (Athlete, Baseball Player)
PO Box 317
Driftwood, TX 78619-0317, USA

Seibert, Kurt (Athlete, Baseball Player)
141 Greenridge Rd
Clover, SC 29710-8940, USA

Seidel, Frederick (Writer)
c/o Staff Member *Farrar, Straus and Giroux*
18 W 18th St Fl 7
New York, NY 10011-4675, USA

Seidel, Guenter (Athlete, Horse Racer, Olympic Athlete)
2108 Oxford Ave
Cardiff By The Sea, CA 92007-1820, USA

Seidel, Kelly
8441 Balboa Blvd Apt 36
Northridge, CA 91325-4096

Seidel, Martie (Music Group, Musician)
Senior Mgmt
9465 Wilshire Blvd
Beverly Hills, CA 90212-2612, USA

Seidelman, Susan (Director)
Michael Shedler
225 W 34th St Ste 1012
New York, NY 10122-1012, USA

Seidenberg, Dennis (Athlete, Hockey Player)
20073 N 85th Pl
Scottsdale, AZ 85255-6301

Seidenberg, Ivan G (Business Person)
1095 Avenue of the Americas
Bell Atlantic Corp
New York, NY 10036-6797, USA

Seidler, David (Writer)
c/o Jeff Aghassi *Jeff Aghassi Management*
2810 S Bedford St
Los Angeles, CA 90034-2523, USA

Seidman, L William (Business Person, Government Official)
1025 Connecticut Ave NW Ste 800
Washington, DC 20036-5419, USA

Seifert, Bill (Race Car Driver)
17007 Jetton Rd
Cornelius, NC 28031-7449, United States

Seifert, George G (Athlete, Coach, Football Coach, Football Player, Sportscaster)
1276 Estate Dr
Los Altos, CA 94024-6100, USA

Seifert, Mike (Athlete, Football Player)
1605 E Bristlecone Dr
Hartland, WI 53029-8655, USA

Seifert, Mike (Athlete, Football Player)
N5610 Lac Verde Cir
Green Lake, WI 54941-9702, USA

Seiheimer, Rick (Athlete, Baseball Player)
401 Hickory Hollow Ln
Brenham, TX 77833-9240, USA

Seikaly, Rony (Athlete, Basketball Player)
2301 Lake Ave
Miami Beach, FL 33140-4539, USA

Seilheimer, Rick (Athlete, Baseball Player)
401 Hickory Hollow Ln
Brenham, TX 77833-9240, USA

Seiling, Ric (Athlete, Hockey Player)
37 Quail Ln
Rochester, NY 14624-1066

Seinfeld, Evan (Actor, Adult Film Star, Musician)
14813 Huston St
Sherman Oaks, CA 91403-1608, USA

Seinfeld, Jerry (Actor, Comedian)
330/332 Further Ln
Amagansett, NY 11930, USA

Seinfeld, Jessica (Chef)
2971 Bellmore Ave
Bellmore, NY 11710-4313, USA

Seiple, Larry (Athlete, Football Player)
1361 W Golfview Dr
Pembroke Pines, FL 33026-3112, USA

Seitzer, Kevin (Athlete, Baseball Player)
Mac-N-Seitz
13705 Holmes Rd
Kansas City, MO 64145-1591, USA

Seixas, E Victor (Vic) Jr (Tennis Player)
8 Harbor Point Dr Apt 207
Mill Valley, CA 94941-3241, USA

Seixas, Vic
8 Harbor Point Dr Apt 207
Mill Valley, CA 94941-3241

Seka
1122 White Rock Dr
Dixon, IL 61021-9049

Selby, Bill (Athlete, Baseball Player)
228 Eunice Bonner Rd
Waynesboro, MS 39367-9474, USA

Selby, David (Actor)
International Creative Mgmt
10250 Constellation Blvd Fl 1
Los Angeles, CA 90067-6241, USA

Seldin, Donald W (Doctor)
Texas Southwestern Medical Center
5323 Harry Hines Blvd
Dallas, TX 75390-7208, USA

Sele, Aaron H (Athlete, Baseball Player)
11 Honors Dr
Newport Beach, CA 92660-4287, USA

Seles, Monica (Athlete, Olympic Athlete, Tennis Player)
2895 Dick Wilson Dr
Sarasota, FL 34240-8729, USA

Self, Bill (Athlete, Basketball Player, Coach)
Bill Self's Assists Foundation
1651 Naismith Dr
Lawrence, KS 66045-4069, USA

Self, Todd (Athlete, Baseball Player)
10238 Cardiff Dr
Keithville, LA 71047-8980, USA

Selfridge, Andy (Athlete, Football Player)
3400 Dunscroft Ct
Keswick, VA 22947-9141, USA

Selig, Bud (Baseball Player, Misc)
Baseball Commissioner's Office
1480 E Standish Pl
Milwaukee, WI 53217-1958, USA

Seligman, Martin E P (Doctor)
University of Pennsylvania
Psychology Dept
Philadelphia, PA 19104, USA

Selig-Prieb, Wendy (Baseball Player)
Milwaukee Brewers
6620 N Lake Dr
Milwaukee, WI 53217-4245, USA

Selivanov, Alexander (Athlete, Hockey Player)
4003 W Tacon St
Tampa, FL 33629-8544

Selkoe, Dennis J (Doctor)
Brigham & Women's Hospital
221 Longwood Ave
Boston, MA 02115-5817, USA

Selleca, Connie (Actor)
c/o Chuck Binder *Binder & Associates*
1465 Lindacrest Dr
Beverly Hills, CA 90210-2519, USA

Selleck, Tom (Actor, Producer)
c/o Staff Member *WKT Public Relations (LA)*
9350 Wilshire Blvd Ste 450
Beverly Hills, CA 90212-3230, USA

Sellers, Brad (Athlete, Basketball Player)
682 Arbor Way
Aurora, OH 44202-9113, USA

Sellers, Franklin (Religious Leader)
Reformed Episcopal Church
2001 Frederick Rd
Catonsville, MD 21228-5511, USA

Sellers, Goldie (Athlete, Football Player)
13425 Braun Rd
Golden, CO 80401-1646, USA

Sellers, Jeff (Athlete, Baseball Player)
833 S 224th Ln
Buckeye, AZ 85326-5593, USA

Sellers, Justin (Athlete, Baseball Player)
7640 NW 79th Ave Apt L8
Tamarac, FL 33321-2868, USA

Sellers, Larry (Actor)
c/o Vaughn Hart *Vaughn Hart & Associates*
12304 Santa Monica Blvd Ste 111
Los Angeles, CA 90025-2586, USA

Sellers, Michael (Actor, Producer, Writer)
c/o Staff Member *Quantum Entertainment*
209 E Alameda Ave Ste 203
Burbank, CA 91502-2674, USA

Sellers, Mike (Athlete, Football Player)
7526 Tottenham Dr
White Plains, MD 20695-4437, USA

Sellers, Piers J (Astronaut)
16011 Craighurst Dr
Houston, TX 77059-6424, USA

Sellers, Ron F (Athlete, Football Player)
129 Via Palacio
Palm Bch Gdns, FL 33418-6212, USA

Sellers, Shane (Horse Racer)
425 New Orleans Ave
Lake Arthur, LA 70549-4120, USA

Sellers, Victoria
1927 Vista Del Mar St
Los Angeles, CA 90068-4004

Sells, Dave (Athlete, Baseball Player)
700 Blue Ridge Ln
Vacaville, CA 95688-2023, USA

Selmon, Dewey W (Athlete, Football Player)
2725 S Berry Rd
Norman, OK 73072-6908, USA

Selmon, Lucious (Athlete, Coach, Football Player)
1 Alltel Stadium Pl
Jacksonville, FL 32202-1917, USA

Seltz, Rolland (Basketball Player)
3328 Oswego Heights Rd
Saint Paul, MN 55126, USA

Seltz, Rollie (Athlete, Basketball Player)
3328 Owasso Heights Rd
Saint Paul, MN 55126-4149, USA

Seltzer, David (Director, Producer, Writer)
c/o Dan Aloni *William Morris Endeavor (LA)*
9601 Wilshire Blvd
Beverly Hills, CA 90210-5213, USA

Selvie, George (Athlete, Football Player)
c/o Drew Rosenhaus *Rosenhaus Sports Representation*
6400 Allison Rd
Miami Beach, FL 33141-4540, USA

Selvy, Frank (Athlete, Baseball Player)
212 Vintage Ave
Greenville, SC 29607-3153, USA

Selvy, Franklin D (Frank) (Athlete, Basketball Player)
206 Honey Horn Dr
Simpsonville, SC 29681-5814, USA

Selway, Phil (Musician)
8017 Fareholm Dr
Los Angeles, CA 90046-2114, USA

Selwyn, Zach (Actor)
c/o Kenny Goodman *The Schiff Company*
9220 W Sunset Blvd Ste 106
West Hollywood, CA 90069-3500, USA

Selzer, Richard (Doctor, Writer)
88 Notch Hill Rd Apt 154
North Branford, CT 06471-1848, USA

Selznick, Albie
2800 Neilson Way
Santa Monica, CA 90405-4025

Selznick, Brian (Writer)
c/o Jason Dravis *Monteiro Rose Dravis Agency*
4370 Tujunga Ave Ste 145
Studio City, CA 91604-2788, USA

Semak, Alexander (Athlete, Hockey Player)
305 W 13th St Apt 1J
New York, NY 10014-1223

Sembello, Michael (Musician, Songwriter)
105 Shad Row Ste B
Piermont, NY 10968-3001, USA

Sember, Mike (Athlete, Baseball Player)
285 S Country Club Blvd
Boca Raton, FL 33487-2326, USA

Semchuk, Thomas "Brandy" (Athlete, Hockey Player)
8944 N Garden Ave
Fresno, CA 93720-5371

Semel, David (Director)
c/o Staff Member *3 Arts Entertainment (LA)*
9460 Wilshire Blvd Fl 7
Beverly Hills, CA 90212-2713, USA

Semel, Terry (Business Person)
Windsor Media Investments
10877 Wilshire Blvd
Los Angeles, CA 90024-4341, USA

Semin, Alexander (Athlete, Hockey Player)
2600 Village Manor Way
Raleigh, NC 27614-8097

Seminara, Frank (Athlete, Baseball Player)
8029 Harbor View Ter
Brooklyn, NY 11209-2822, USA

Semiz, Teata (Bowler)
3131 Kennedy Blvd
North Bergen, NJ 07047-2379, USA

Semiz, Teata (Bowler)
27 Burnside Pl
Haskell, NJ 07420-1003, USA

Semler, Dean (Cinematographer, Director)
4260 Arcola Ave
Toluca Lake, CA 91602-2902, USA

Sempe, Jean-Jacques (Cartoonist)
4 Rue De Moulin-Vert
Paris, FR F-750, USA

Semproch, Ray (Athlete, Baseball Player)
4220 Buechner Ave
Cleveland, OH 44109-5035, USA

Sena, Dominic (Director)
c/o Robert Newman *William Morris Endeavor (LA)*
9601 Wilshire Blvd Ste 560
Beverly Hills, CA 90210-5220, USA

Sena, Suzanne
6310 San Vicente Blvd Ste 200
Los Angeles, CA 90048-5488

Sendejo, Andrew (Athlete, Football Player)
c/o Erik Burkhardt *Select Sports Group*
2700 Post Oak Blvd Ste 1450
Houston, TX 77056-5785, USA

Sendlein, Lyle (Athlete, Football Player)
c/o Eric Metz *Lock Metz Milanovic LLC*
6900 E Camelback Rd Ste 600
Scottsdale, AZ 85251-8044, USA

Sendlein, Robin (Athlete, Football Player)
14737 E Mark Ln
Scottsdale, AZ 85262-7814, USA

Senior, Peter (Golfer)
c/o Staff Member *Pro Golfers Association (PGA) Tour*
112 Tpc Blvd
Ponte Vedra Beach, FL 32082, USA

Senneker, Bob (Race Car Driver)
PO Box 140984
Grand Rapids, MI 49514-0984, USA

Sennett, Susan (Actor)
1201 Oak Ave
Manhattan Beach, CA 90266-5125, USA

Senser, Joe (Athlete, Football Player)
Joe Senser's Sports Grill
4217 W 80th St
Minneapolis, MN 55437, USA

Sensiba, Dave (Race Car Driver)
Throop Motorsports Racing
2775 Horseshoe Dr SW
Wyoming, MI 49418-9309, USA

Sensibaugh, Mike (Athlete, Football Player)
18414 Woodlands Terrace Dr
Glencoe, MO 63038-1829, USA

Senske, Sara (Race Car Driver)
Lynx Racing
5806 Saloma Ave
Van Nuys, CA 91411-3017, USA

Senter, Marc (Actor)
c/o Jennifer Shoucair Weaver *S/W PR Shop*
7083 Hollywood Blvd
Los Angeles, CA 90028-8901, USA

Seoane, Manny (Athlete, Baseball Player)
8912 Southbay Dr
Tampa, FL 33615-2770, USA

Septimus, Jake (Producer)
c/o Staff Member *Creative Artists Agency (CAA-LA)*
2000 Avenue of the Stars Ste 100
Los Angeles, CA 90067-4705, USA

Sepulveda, Charlie (Musician)
Ralph Mercado Mgmt
568 Broadway # 608
New York, NY 10012-3225, USA

Serafini, Dan (Athlete, Baseball Player)
430 Alamosa Dr
Sparks, NV 89441-8583, USA

Serafini, Ron (Athlete, Hockey Player)
Morgan and Milzow Realty
25 S Main St
Clarkston, MI 48346-1525, USA

Serafinowitz, Peter (Actor, Producer, Writer)
c/o Peter Principato *Principato/Young Management (LA)*
9465 Wilshire Blvd Ste 900
Beverly Hills, CA 90212-2608, USA

Serano, Greg (Actor)
c/o Erik Kritzer *LINK Entertainment*
11872 La Grange Ave Fl 1
Los Angeles, CA 90025-5283, USA

Serendipity Singers, The (Music Group)
349 S Main St
Wauconda, IL 60084-1966

Sergei, Ivan (Actor)
c/o Joanna (Joanie) Burstein *Burstein Company, The*
15304 W Sunset Blvd Ste 208
Pacific Palisades, CA 90272-3656, USA

Serig, Jennifer (Designer, Fashion Designer)
c/o Staff Member *Perception Public Relations LLC*
3940 Laurel Canyon Blvd Ste 169
Studio City, CA 91604-3709, USA

Seriki, Hakeem (Chamillionaire) (Musician)
c/o Sara Ramaker *Paradigm (LA)*
360 N Crescent Dr
North Bldg
Beverly Hills, CA 90210-4874, USA

Serkin, Peter A (Musician)
Manne Music College
150 W 85th St
New York, NY 10024-4402, USA

Serkis, Andy (Actor)
c/o Larry Taube *Principal Entertainment (LA)*
9255 W Sunset Blvd Ste 500
West Hollywood, CA 90069-3301, USA

Serlenga, Nikki (Athlete, Olympic Athlete, Soccer Player)
1489 Hawthorne Ave NW
Atlanta, GA 30309-2229, USA

Sermon, Eric (Musician)
Richard Walters
1800 Argyle Ave # 408
Los Angeles, CA 90028-5253, USA

Serna, Diego (Soccer Player)
Los Angeles Galaxy
1010 Rose Bowl Dr
Pasadena, CA 91103, USA

Serna, Paul (Athlete, Baseball Player)
32421 Outrigger Way
Laguna Niguel, CA 92677-4219, USA

Serna, Pepe (Actor)
127 Ruby Ave
Newport Beach, CA 92662-1125, USA

Serowik, Jeff (Athlete, Hockey Player)
371 Davisville Rd
East Falmouth, MA 02536-7085

Serra, Eduardo (Cinematographer)
c/o Staff Member *United Talent Agency (UTA-LA)*
9336 Civic Center Dr
Beverly Hills, CA 90210-3604, USA

Serrano, Jimmy (Athlete, Baseball Player)
2943 E Erika Ct
Grand Junction, CO 81504-6963, USA

Serrano, Juan (Musician)
Prince/SF Productions
1450 Southgate Ave Apt 206
Daly City, CA 94015-4021, USA

Serrano, Nestor (Actor)
c/o Danielle Galiana-Allman *InnerAct Entertainment*
141 S Barrington Ave Ste E
Los Angeles, CA 90049-3314, USA

Serratos, Christian (Actor)
c/o Christina Karakasidis *Thruline Entertainment*
9250 Wilshire Blvd Ste 100
Ground Floor
Beverly Hills, CA 90212-3343, USA

Serum, Gary (Athlete, Baseball Player)
10525 Hidden Oaks Ln N
Champlin, MN 55316-3045, USA

Servais, Scott (Athlete, Baseball Player, Olympic Athlete)
4409 Triple Eagle Trl
Larkspur, CO 80118-5744, USA

Server, Josh (Actor)
c/o Mike Eistenstadt *Amsel, Eisenstadt & Frazier Talent Agency (AEF)*
5055 Wilshire Blvd Ste 860
Los Angeles, CA 90036-6108, USA

Servia, Oriol (Race Car Driver)
PWR Racing
4001 Methanol Ln
Indianapolis, IN 46268-4855, USA

Service, Scott (Athlete, Baseball Player)
7959 Gaines Rd
Cincinnati, OH 45247-3419, USA

Sesame Street
1 Lincoln Plz
New York, NY 10023-7129

Sessions, Jeff (Politician)
208 Justice Ct NE Apt A
Washington, DC 20002-5788, USA

Sessions, Pete (Congressman, Politician)
2233 Rayburn Hob
Washington, DC 20515-4501, USA

Sessions, Ronnie (Musician)
540 Gunson Ridge Rd
Cumberland City, TN 37050-4301, USA

Sessions, William (Politician)
3920 Argyle Ter NW
Washington, DC 20011-5329, USA

Sestero, Greg (Actor, Director)
c/o Staff Member *Simon & Schuster*
1230 Avenue of the Americas Fl CONC1
New York, NY 10020-1586, USA

Setari, Robert (Actor)
c/o Patty Stevens *Vessel Entertainment*
10989 Bluffside Dr Apt 3210
Studio City, CA 91604-4407

Seth, Joshua (Actor)
c/o Staff Member *Sutton Barth & Vennari Inc*
5900 Wilshire Blvd Ste 700
Los Angeles, CA 90036-5009, USA

Settle, John (Athlete, Football Player)
8109 Dog Leg Dr
Presto, PA 15142-1583, USA

Settle, Matthew (Actor)
c/o Jeb Brandon *Kritzer Levine Wilkins Entertainment (KLWG)*
11872 La Grange Ave Fl 1
Los Angeles, CA 90025-5283, USA

Settles, Tawambi (Athlete, Football Player)
4204 Rogers Rd
Chattanooga, TN 37411-3244, USA

Setzer, Brian (Music Group, Musician)
c/o Staff Member *William Morris Endeavor (LA)*
9601 Wilshire Blvd
Beverly Hills, CA 90210-5213, USA

Setzer, Dennis (Race Car Driver)
PO Box 665
Dawsonville, GA 30534-0013, USA

Setzler, Steve (Athlete, Football Player)
1S767 Hemlock Ct
Saint Paul, MN 55124, USA

Seubert, Rich (Athlete, Football Player)
D1891 County Road C
Stratford, WI 54484-9330, USA

Seurer, Frank (Athlete, Football Player)
16168 S Brookfield St
Olathe, KS 66062-3927, USA

Sevani, Adam (Actor)
c/o Christian Donatelli *The Schiff Company*
9220 W Sunset Blvd Ste 106
West Hollywood, CA 90069-3500, USA

Sevcik, John (Athlete, Baseball Player)
10202 River Plantation Dr
Austin, TX 78747-1119, USA

Sevendust (Music Group)
c/o Staff Member *TVT Records*
23 E 4th St Fl 3
New York, NY 10003-7023, USA

Severance, Joan (Actor)
PO Box 282
Carbondale, CO 81623-0282, USA

Severinsen, Al (Athlete, Baseball Player)
133 Warren Ave
Mystic, CT 06355-2136, USA

Severinsen, Carl H (Doc) (Musician)
PO Box 4066
Burbank, CA 91503-4066, USA

Severson, Jeff (Athlete, Football Player)
20625 Sierra Elena
Murrieta, CA 92562-8817, USA

Severson, Kimberly (Athlete, Horse Racer, Olympic Athlete)
631 Dobby Creek Rd
Scottsville, VA 24590-3026, USA

Severson, Rich (Athlete, Baseball Player)
781 Spring Flowers Trl
Brandon, FL 33511-5993, USA

Severyn, Brent (Athlete, Hockey Player)
4521 Avebury Dr
Plano, TX 75024-7358

Sevier, Corey (Actor)
c/o Sheila Wenzel *Innovative Artists (LA)*
1505 10th St
Santa Monica, CA 90401-2805, USA

Sevigny, Chloe (Actor)
9 Prospect Park W Apt 2C
Brooklyn, NY 11215-1737, USA

Sevsec, Pedro (Actor)
c/o Staff Member *Telemundo*
2470 W 8th Ave
Hialeah, FL 33010-2000, USA

Sevy, Jeff (Athlete, Football Player)
5890 Arcadia Ave
Loomis, CA 95650-8734, USA

Sewell, Rufus (Actor)
c/o Gene Parseghian *Parseghian Planco LLC*
388 2nd Ave
New York, NY 10010-5616, USA

Sewell, Steve (Athlete, Football Player)
15918 E Crestridge Pl
Centennial, CO 80015-4219, USA

Sewell, Terri (Congressman, Politician)
1133 Longworth Hob
Washington, DC 20515-3201, USA

Sex Pistols
c/o Mitch Schneider *Mitch Schneider Organization (MSO)*
14724 Ventura Blvd Ste 410
Sherman Oaks, CA 91403-3537, USA

Sexsmith, Ron (Musician)
c/o Staff Member *Paradigm (Monterey)*
404 W Franklin St
Monterey, CA 93940-2303, USA

Sexson, Richie (Athlete, Baseball Player)
2828 NW Lakemont Dr
Bend, OR 97701-7031, USA

Sexto, Camilo (Musician)
c/o Staff Member *BMG*
1540 Broadway
New York, NY 10036-4039, USA

Sexton, Brent (Actor)
c/o Staff Member *Greene & Associates*
1901 Avenue of the Stars Ste 130
Los Angeles, CA 90067-6030, USA

Sexton, Chris (Athlete, Baseball Player)
7030 Baytowne Dr
Cincinnati, OH 45247-5097, USA

Sexton, Dan (Athlete, Hockey Player)
7683 133rd St W
Saint Paul, MN 55124-7617

Sexton, Jimmy (Athlete, Baseball Player)
2680 Baxter Rd
Wilmer, AL 36587-8225, USA

Sexton III, Brendan (Actor)
c/o Staff Member *Gersh (LA)*
9465 Wilshire Blvd Ste 600
Beverly Hills, CA 90212-2605, USA

Seyfried, Amanda (Actor)
3140 Tighlman St # B
PMB 216
Allentown, PA 18104, USA

Seyfried, Gordon (Athlete, Baseball Player)
56428 Lowe Ave
Yucca Valley, CA 92284-1740, USA

Seymour, Cara (Actor)
c/o Vanessa Pereira *Artists Independent Management (LA)*
1522 2nd St
Santa Monica, CA 90401-2303, USA

Seymour, Carolyn (Actor)
Chasin Agency
8899 Beverly Blvd Ste 716
Los Angeles, CA 90048-2449, USA

Seymour, Jane (Actor, Producer)
c/o Staff Member *Catfish Productions*
23852 Pacific Coast Hwy Ste 313
Malibu, CA 90265-4876, USA

Seymour, John (Senator)
239 S Helix Ave Unit 26
Solana Beach, CA 92075-1868, USA

Seymour, John (Politician)
239 S Helix Ave Unit 26
Solana Beach, CA 92075-1868, USA

Seymour, Paul (Athlete, Football Player)
4188 Shoals Dr
Okemos, MI 48864-3431, USA

Seymour, Paul C (Athlete, Football Player)
4188 Shoals Dr
Okemos, MI 48864-3431, USA

Seymour, Richard (Athlete, Football Player)
c/o Eugene Parker *Maximum Sports Management*
6435 W Jefferson Blvd # 197
Fort Wayne, IN 46804-6203, USA

Seymour, Stephanie (Model)
385 Taconic Rd
Greenwich, CT 06831-2828, USA

Seymour, Terri (Actor)
c/o Ivo Fischer *William Morris Endeavor (LA)*
9601 Wilshire Blvd
Beverly Hills, CA 90210-5213, USA

Seynhaeve, Ingrid
111 E 22nd St # 200
New York, NY 10010-5400

Shaback, Nick (Athlete, Basketball Player)
3019 49th St Apt 2N
Astoria, NY 11103-1315, USA

Shabala, Adam (Athlete, Baseball Player)
18527 W Surprise Farms Loop N
Surprise, AZ 85388-1848, USA

Shackelford, Brian (Athlete, Baseball Player)
2812 N Birch St
McAlester, OK 74501-2412, USA

Shackelford, Don (Athlete, Football Player)
PO Box 1468
Lansdale, PA 19446, USA

shackelford, ray (Athlete, Baseball Player)
716 El Toro Rd
Ojai, CA 93023-1756, USA

Shackelford, Ted (Actor)
12305 Valleyheart Dr
Studio City, CA 91604-1643, USA

Shackleford, Brian (Athlete, Baseball Player)
2812 N Birch St
McAlester, OK 74501-2412, USA

Shackleford, Charles (Athlete, Basketball Player)
107 E Peyton Ave Apt 5H
Kinston, NC 28501-4375, USA

Shackleton, Simon (Elite Force) (Musician)
c/o Staff Member *Beatport*
2399 Blake St Ste 170
Denver, CO 80205-2187, USA

Shackouls, Bobby S (Business Person)
Burlington Resources
5051 Westheimer Rd
Houston, TX 77056-5622, USA

Shadic-Campbell, Lillian (Athlete, Baseball Player)
61 Bloody Hill Rd
Craryville, NY 12521-5101, USA

Shadow (DJ)
Quannum Projects LLC
690 5th St # 208
San Francisco, CA 94107-1517, USA

Shadyac, Tom (Director)
c/o Dan Aloni *William Morris Endeavor (LA)*
9601 Wilshire Blvd
Beverly Hills, CA 90210-5213, USA

Shafer, Martin (Business Person)
c/o Staff Member *Castle Rock Entertainment*
335 N Maple Dr Ste 175
Beverly Hills, CA 90210-3867, USA

Shafer, Matthew (Uncle Kracker) (Music Group, Musician)
c/o Jeff Kwatinetz *Prospect Park*
1840 Century Park E Ste 1800
Los Angeles, CA 90067-2119, USA

Shafer, R Donald (Religious Leader)
Brethren in Christ Church
431 Grantham Rd
Mechanicsburg, PA 17055-5812, USA

Shaffer, Akiva (Director, Writer)
c/o Staff Member *Mosaic Media Group*
9200 W Sunset Blvd Ste 10
West Hollywood, CA 90069-3608, USA

Shaffer, Atticus (Actor)
c/o Linda Defilippo *D.C. Talent Management*
Prefers to be contacted via email or telephone
West Hollywood, CA 90069, USA

Shaffer, David H (Publisher)
MacMillan
175 5th Ave
New York, NY 10010-7703, USA

Shaffer, Lee (Athlete, Basketball Player)
3822 Nottaway Rd
Durham, NC 27707-5421, USA

Shaffer, Paul (Musician)
Worldwide Pants
1697 Broadway
Ed Sullivan Theatre
New York, NY 10019-5904, USA

Shaffer, Peter (Writer)
Lantz
200 W 57th St Ste 503
New York, NY 10019-3211, USA

Shaggy (Radio Personality)
c/o Staff Member *WPKX*
1331 Main St Ste 4
Springfield, MA 01103-1621, USA

Shah, Kiran (Actor)
c/o Michael Henderson *Heresun Management*
4119 W Burbank Blvd
Burbank, CA 91505-2122, USA

Shahan, Gil (Musician)
ICM Artists
40 W 57th St
New York, NY 10019-4001, USA

Shahans, Shirley Bridges (Race Car Driver)
1400 Colorado St
Boulder City, NV 89005-2436, USA

Shaheen, Jeanne (Politician)
73 Perkins Rd
Madbury, NH 03823-7612, USA

Shahi, Sarah (Actor)
c/o Laura Myones *McKeon-Myones Management*
3500 W Olive Ave Ste 770
Burbank, CA 91505-5527, USA

Shahidi, Yara (Actor)
c/o Laura Ackerman *Persona PR (LA)*
8840 Wilshire Blvd Ste 212
Beverly Hills, CA 90211-2606, USA

Shakar, Martin (Actor)
118 E 37th St
New York, NY 10016-3025, USA

Shake, Christi (Model)
c/o Mike Esterman *Esterman.Com, LLC*
Prefers to be contacted via email
Baltimore, MD XXXXX, USA

Shakira (Musician)
c/o Joseph Carozza *Epic Records Group*
550 Madison Ave Fl 6
New York, NY 10022-3211, USA

Shakur, Kula
39A Gramercy Park N Apt 1C
New York, NY 10010-6312

Shalala, Donna (Politician)
11355 Four Fillies Rd
Miami, FL 33156-4241, USA

Shalamar
707 18th Ave S
Nashville, TN 37203-3214

Shales, Tom
1650 Kirby Rd
Mc Lean, VA 22101-3209

Shalhoub, Tony (Actor)
248 S Van Ness Ave
Los Angeles, CA 90004-3921, USA

Shal-Houd, Tony
9560 Wilshire Blvd # 516
Beverly Hills, CA 90212-2427

Shalim (Musician)
c/o Staff Member *Sony Music Miami*
605 Lincoln Rd Ste 700
Miami Beach, FL 33139-2901, USA

Shallow, Parvati (Reality Star)
c/o Ken Jacobson *Ken Jacobson Management*
Preferred to be contacted by phone or email
Woodland Hills, CA 91367, USA

Shamrock, Ken (Actor, Athlete, Wrestler)
c/o Staff Member *UFC*
PO Box 26959
Las Vegas, NV 89126-0959, USA

Shamsky, Art (Athlete, Baseball Player)
PO Box 1400
New York, NY 10163-1400, USA

Shanahan, Brendan (Athlete, Hockey Player)
47 Saquatucket Bluffs Rd
Harwich Port, MA 02646-2510

Shanahan, Greg (Athlete, Baseball Player)
3883 E St
Eureka, CA 95503-6026, USA

Shanahan, Mike (Athlete, Coach, Football Coach, Football Player)
20 Cherry Hills Farm Dr
Englewood, CO 80113-7165, USA

Shand, David (Athlete, Hockey Player)
213 E Michigan Ave
Saline, MI 48176-1554

Shandling, Garry (Actor, Comedian)
1745 Correa Way
Los Angeles, CA 90049-2201, USA

Shane, Bob (Music Group, Musician)
9410 S 46th St
Phoenix, AZ 85044-7512, USA

Shange, Ntozake (Writer)
c/o Staff Member *Simon & Schuster*
1230 Avenue of the Americas Fl CONC1
New York, NY 10020-1586, USA

Shangri-La's, The
27 L Ambiance Ct
Bardonia, NY 10954-1421

Shanice (Musician)
Richard Walters
1800 Argyle Ave # 408
Los Angeles, CA 90028-5253, USA

Shank, Harvey (Athlete, Baseball Player)
201 E Jefferson St
Phoenix, AZ 85004-2412, USA

Shank, Michael (Race Car Driver)
Michael Shank Racing
1386 Fields Ave
Columbus, OH 43211-2635, USA

Shankle, Joel (Athlete, Olympic Athlete, Track Athlete)
16181 Berryvale Ln
Culpeper, VA 22701-5530, USA

Shankman, Adam (Dancer, Director)
c/o BeBe Lerner *ID Public Relations (LA)*
7060 Hollywood Blvd Fl 8th
Los Angeles, CA 90028-6021, USA

Shanks, Michael (Actor, Director, Writer)
c/o Francis Okwu *Zero Gravity Management*
1531 14th St
Santa Monica, CA 90404-3302, USA

Shanley, Jim (Athlete, Football Player)
4 Brookside Dr
Apt D
Walla Walla, WA 99362, USA

Shanley, John Patrick (Director, Writer)
c/o Staff Member *Creative Artists Agency (CAA-LA)*
2000 Avenue of the Stars Ste 100
Los Angeles, CA 90067-4705, USA

Shannon (Music Group, Musician)
Big Mgmt
226 5th Ave
New York, NY 10001-7706, USA

Shannon (Musician)
c/o Staff Member *Diva Central Inc*
7510 W Sunset Blvd Ste 1445
Los Angeles, CA 90046-3408, USA

Shannon, Carver (Athlete, Football Player)
6005 S La Cienega Blvd
Los Angeles, CA 90056-1523, USA

Shannon, Darryl (Athlete, Hockey Player)
18 Landings Dr
Buffalo, NY 14228-1479

Shannon, June (Mama June) (Reality Star)
PO Box 72
Mc Intyre, GA 31054-0072, USA

Shannon, Mem (Musician, Songwriter)
1048 Hesper Ave
Metairie, LA 70005-1552, USA

Shannon, Michael (Actor)
c/o Bryna Rifkin *ID Public Relations (LA)*
7060 Hollywood Blvd Fl 8th
Los Angeles, CA 90028-6021, USA

Shannon, Michael E (Business Person)
Ecolab Inc
370 Wabasha St N
Ecolab Center
Saint Paul, MN 55102-1349, USA

Shannon, Mike (Athlete, Baseball Player)
Mike Shannon's Steaks And Seafood
3104 Southwick St
Saint Charles, MO 63301-1191, USA

Shannon, Molly (Actor, Comedian)
c/o Steven Levy *Framework Entertainment (LA)*
9057 Nemo St Ste C
West Hollywood, CA 90069-5511, USA

Shannon, Randy (Athlete, Football Player)
7420 SW 107th Ave Apt 7-207
Miami, FL 33173-2970, USA

Shannon, Vicellous (Actor)
c/o Tony Chargin *Ovation Management*
12028 National Blvd
Los Angeles, CA 90064-3542, USA

Shantz, Robert C (Bobby) (Athlete, Baseball Player)
152 E Mount Pleasant Ave
Ambler, PA 19002-4209, USA

Shapar, Howard K (Government Official)
PO Box 30242
Bethesda, MD 20824-0242, USA

Shapiro, Dani (Writer)
Random House
1745 Broadway Frnt 3 # B1
New York, NY 10019-4343, USA

Shapiro, Debbie (Actor)
Agency for Performing Arts
9200 W Sunset Blvd Ste 900
West Hollywood, CA 90069-3604, USA

Shapiro, Jim (Actor)
Legislative Office Building Room 4028
Hartford, CT 06106, USA

Shapiro, Karl (Writer)
211 W 106th St Apt 11C
New York, NY 10025-3688, USA

Shapiro, Mark (Commentator)
70 Winding River Trl
Chagrin Falls, OH 44022-3607, USA

Shapiro, Mary L (Government Official)
Securities & Exchange Commission
450 5th St NW
Washington, DC 20549-0001, USA

Shapiro, Mel (Writer)
University of California
Theater Film/TV Dept
Los Angeles, CA 90024, USA

Shapiro, Neal (Horse Racer)
296 Sharon Rd
Trenton, NJ 08691-2313, USA

Shapiro, Rami (Rabbi) (Writer)
c/o Staff Member *SkyLight Paths Publishing*
PO Box 237
Woodstock, VT 05091-0237, USA

Shapiro, Richard & Esther
617 N Alta Dr
Beverly Hills, CA 90210-3503

Shapiro, Robert (Attorney)
Christensen, Glaser, Fink, Jacobs, Glaser, Weil and Shapiro
10250 Constellation Blvd Fl 19
Los Angeles, CA 90067-6219, USA

Shapiro, Robert
2590 Wallingford Dr
Beverly Hills, CA 90210-1073, USA

Sharapova, Maria (Athlete, Tennis Player)
c/o Staff Member *IMG Academy*
5500 34th St W
Bradenton, FL 34210-3506, USA

Share, Charlie (Athlete, Baseball Player)
12922 Twin Meadows Ct
Saint Louis, MO 63146-1803, USA

Share, Charlie (Chuck) (Athlete, Basketball Player)
12922 Twin Meadows Ct
Saint Louis, MO 63146-1803, USA

Sharkey, Ed (Athlete, Football Player)
3615 Russell Rd
Centralia, WA 98531-1666, USA

Sharkey, Jack (Writer)
39927 Chippewa Cir
Murrieta, CA 92562-4109, USA

Sharma, Barbara (Actor)
PO Box 29125
Los Angeles, CA 90029-0125, USA

Sharma, Chris (Athlete)
c/o Staff Member *Sanuk Climbing Team*
9600 Toledo Way
Irvine, CA 92618-1808, USA

Sharma, Suraj (Actor)
c/o Jennifer Plante *SLATE Public Relations - NY*
307 7th Ave Rm 2401
New York, NY 10001-6019, USA

Sharman, Daniel (Actor)
c/o Justin Grey Stone *Management 360*
9111 Wilshire Blvd
Beverly Hills, CA 90210-5508, USA

Sharockman, Ed (Athlete, Football Player)
8955 Thomas Ln
Saint Paul, MN 55125-7603, USA

Sharon, Dick (Athlete, Baseball Player)
1143 N 31st St
Billings, MT 59101-0132, USA

Sharp, Bill (Athlete, Baseball Player)
2244 Thornwood Ave
Wilmette, IL 60091-1454, USA

Sharp, Dee Dee (Musician)
William W Witherspoon Esq.
PO Box 7
C/O Dione Larue
Lakehurst, NJ 08733-0007, USA

Sharp, Kevin (Musician)
Rising Star
1415 River Landing Way
Woodstock, GA 30188-5345, USA

Sharp, Leslie (Actor)
International Creative Mgmt
10250 Constellation Blvd Fl 1
Los Angeles, CA 90067-6241, USA

Sharp, Linda K (Coach)
Phoenix Mercury
201 E Jefferson St
American West Arena
Phoenix, AZ 85004-2412, USA

Sharp, Marsha (Coach)
Texas Tech University
Athletic Dept
Lubbock, TX 79409, USA

Sharp, Preston (Actor, Reality Star)
c/o Staff Member *Extreme Makeover: Home Edition*
9225 W Sunset Blvd # 1100
Endemol Entertainment Usa
West Hollywood, CA 90069-3111, USA

Sharp, Scott (Race Car Driver)
Fernandez Racing
6950 Guion Rd # 51
Indianapolis, IN 46268-2576, United States

Sharpe, Luis (Athlete, Football Player)
Arizona State Prison
PO Box 3939
Doc #122301
Kingman, AZ 86402-3939, USA

Sharpe, Rochelle P (Journalist)
94 Dudley St # 2
Brookline, MA 02445-5937, USA

Sharpe, Shannon (Athlete, Football Player)
867 Carlton Rdg NE
Atlanta, GA 30342-4346, USA

Sharpe, Sterling (Athlete, Football Player)
81 Running Fox Rd
Columbia, SC 29223-3052, USA

Sharper, Darren (Athlete, Football Player)
11613 Heverley Ct
Glen Allen, VA 23059-4829, USA

Sharper, Jamie (Athlete, Football Player)
11613 Heverley Ct
Glen Allen, VA 23059-4829, USA

Sharples, Jeff (Athlete, Hockey Player)
2504 Mahaila Cir
Henderson, NV 89074-5909

sharpless, Josh (Athlete, Baseball Player)
3214 Apache Rd
Pittsburgh, PA 15241-1114, USA

Sharpton, Al (Activist, Religious Leader)
National Action Network
106 W 145th St Frnt
New York, NY 10039-4138, USA

Shasky, John (Athlete, Basketball Player)
1755 S Benson Rd
Frankfort, KY 40601-7649, USA

Shatner, Melanie (Actor)
Henderson/Hogan
8285 W Sunset Blvd Ste 1
West Hollywood, CA 90046-2420, USA

Shatner, William (Actor)
3674 Berry Dr
Studio City, CA 91604-3852, USA

Shatraw, David
c/o Staff Member *Stone Manners Salners Agency (LA)*
6100 Wilshire Blvd Ste 1500
Los Angeles, CA 90048-5110, USA

Shattuck, Kim (Musician)
International Creative Mgmt
40 W 57th St Fl 5
New York, NY 10019-4001, USA

Shattuck, Molly (Reality Star)
c/o Staff Member *Fox Broabasting Company*
PO Box 900
Beverly Hills, CA 90213-0900

Shattuck, Shari (Actor, Writer)
4142 Big Tujunga Canyon Rd
Tujunga, CA 91042-1010

Shaud, Grant (Actor)
8738 Appian Way
Los Angeles, CA 90046-7733, USA

Shaughnessy, Charles (Actor)
c/o Staff Member *Marshak/Zachary Company, The*
8840 Wilshire Blvd Fl 1
Beverly Hills, CA 90211-2606, USA

Shaunessy, Scott (Athlete, Hockey Player)
1 Treetop Ln
Duxbury, MA 02332-4123

Shave, Jon (Athlete, Baseball Player)
851 Parkview Pl W
Fernandina Beach, FL 32034-4633, USA

Shavelson, Mel
11947 Sunshine Ter
Studio City, CA 91604-3708

Shaver, Billy Joe (Musician, Songwriter)
c/o Staff Member *Class Act Entertainment*
PO Box 160236
Nashville, TN 37216-0236, USA

Shaver, Helen (Actor)
Innovative Artists
1505 10th St
Santa Monica, CA 90401-2805, USA

Shaver, Jeff (Athlete, Baseball Player)
9651 E Clinton St
Scottsdale, AZ 85260-6209, USA

Shaw, Anthony (Director)
c/o Staff Member *Corymore Productions*
100 Universal City Plz # 2372A
Universal City, CA 91608-1002

Shaw, Bernard (Journalist)
5801 Nicholson Ln Apt 1516
Rockville, MD 20852-5727, USA

Shaw, Brad (Athlete, Hockey Player)
514 Iron Lantern Dr
Ballwin, MO 63011-2726

Shaw, Brad (Athlete, Hockey Player)
St Louis Blues
1401 Clark Ave
Saint Louis, MO 63103-2700

Shaw, Brewster H Colonel (Astronaut)
3519 Rice Blvd
Houston, TX 77005-2937, USA

Shaw, Brian (Athlete, Basketball Coach, Basketball Player, Coach)
c/o Staff Member *Denver Nuggets*
1000 Chopper Cir
Denver, CO 80204-5805, USA

Shaw, Bryant (Athlete, Football Player)
1851 N Greenville Ave Apt 4208
Richardson, TX 75081-1617, USA

Shaw, Carolyn Hagner (Publisher)
Social Register
2620 P St NW
Washington, DC 20007-3062, USA

Shaw, Dennis (Athlete, Football Player)
14844 Priscilla St
San Diego, CA 92129-1525, USA

Shaw, Don (Athlete, Baseball Player)
857 Waterford Villas Dr
Lake Saint Louis, MO 63367-2574, USA

Shaw, Eric (Athlete, Football Player)
3450 Wallingford Ct
Lexington, KY 40503-4332, USA

Shaw, Fiona (Actor)
c/o Brian Swardstrom *United Talent Agency (UTA-NYC)*
888 7th Ave
New York, NY 10106-0001, USA

Shaw, Frances (Actor)
c/o Justin Deanda *ICM Partners (LA)*
10250 Constellation Blvd Fl 7
Los Angeles, CA 90067-6207, USA

Shaw, Jeffrey L (Jeff) (Athlete, Baseball Player)
1215 Storybrook Dr
Washington Court House,
OH 43160-2608, USA

Shaw, Kim (Actor)
c/o Marilyn Glasser *Glasser/Black Management*
283 Cedarhurst Ave
Cedarhurst, NY 11516-1671, USA

Shaw, Lindsey (Actor)
c/o Pat Cutler *Cutler Management*
13043 W Sunset Blvd
Los Angeles, CA 90049-2527, USA

Shaw, Mariena (Musician)
Berkeley Agency
2608 9th St Ste 301
Berkeley, CA 94710-2556, USA

Shaw, Pete (Athlete, Football Player)
25052 Pappas Rd
Ramona, CA 92065-4920, USA

Shaw, Robert (Athlete, Football Player)
487 Old Coach Rd Apt D
Westerville, OH 43081-1392, USA

Shaw, Robert (Athlete, Football Player)
4013 Centenary Ave
Dallas, TX 75225-5430, USA

Shaw, Scott (Journalist)
20771 Lake Rd
Rocky River, OH 44116-1335, USA

Shaw, Sedrick (Athlete, Football Player)
1007 Waller St
Austin, TX 78702-2632, USA

Shaw, Stan (Actor)
Innovative Artists
1505 10th St
Santa Monica, CA 90401-2805, USA

Shaw, Tim
5315 River Ave
Newport Beach, CA 92663-2208

Shaw, Timothy A (Tim) (Swimmer)
5315 River Ave
Newport Beach, CA 92663-2208, USA

Shaw, Todd (Too Short) (Musician)
c/o David Weintraub *DWE Talent*
Prefers to be contacted via telephone
CA, USA

Shaw, Tommy (Musician, Songwriter)
914 Overton Lea Rd
Nashville, TN 37220-1503, USA

Shaw, Victoria (Musician, Songwriter, Writer)
PO Box 58175
Nashville, TN 37205-8175, USA

Shaw, Vinessa (Actor)
Industry Entertainment
955 Carrillo Dr Ste 300
Los Angeles, CA 90048-5400, USA

Shaw, William L (Billy) (Athlete, Football Player)
3427 Old Rothell Rd
Toccoa, GA 30577, USA

Shaw Jr, Brewster H (Astronaut)
3519 Rice Blvd
Houston, TX 77005-2937, USA

Shawkat, Alia (Actor, Producer)
c/o Michelle Theodat *Kipperman Management*
345 7th Ave Rm 503
New York, NY 10001-5054, USA

Shawn, Wallace (Actor, Writer)
c/o Christopher Black *Opus Entertainment*
5225 Wilshire Blvd Ste 905
Los Angeles, CA 90036-4353, USA

Shay, Jerry (Athlete, Football Player)
81 E Shasta St
Chula Vista, CA 91910-6127, USA

Shaye, Lin (Actor)
Paul Kohner
9300 Wilshire Blvd Ste 555
Beverly Hills, CA 90212-3211, USA

Shaye, Skyler (Actor)
c/o Dorothy Koster *Crystal Sky/Artists Only Management*
10203 Santa Monica Blvd Fl 5
Los Angeles, CA 90067-6416, USA

Shea, Charity (Actor)
c/o Scott Karp *The Syndicate*
10203 Santa Monica Blvd Fl 5
Los Angeles, CA 90067-6416, USA

Shea, Dan (Actor)
c/o Staff Member *Talent Plus*
275 Union Blvd Apt 1700
Saint Louis, MO 63108-1246, USA

Shea, Eric (Actor)
27710 Jubilee Run Rd
Pearblossom, CA 93553-3439, USA

Shea, Jere (Actor)
SMS Talent
8383 Wilshire Blvd Ste 230
Beverly Hills, CA 90211-2436, USA

Shea, Katt (Actor)
International Creative Mgmt
10250 Constellation Blvd Fl 1
Los Angeles, CA 90067-6241, USA

Shea, Pat (Athlete, Football Player)
1175 Evergreen Dr
Encinitas, CA 92024-3918, USA

Shea, Steve (Athlete, Baseball Player)
1 Shepherds Ln
North Hampton, NH 03862-2133, USA

Shea, Terry (Coach, Football Coach)
San Jose State University
Athletic Dept
San Jose, CA 95192-0001, USA

Sheaffer, Danny (Athlete, Baseball Player)
165 Savannah Ln
Mount Airy, NC 27030-8688, USA

Shealy, Ryan (Athlete, Baseball Player)
2168 NE 63rd Ct
Fort Lauderdale, FL 33308-1335, USA

Shear, Jules (Actor, Musician, Songwriter, Writer)
c/o Staff Member *Concerted Efforts*
PO Box 440326
Somerville, MA 02144-0004, USA

Shear, Rhonda (Actor, Comedian, Model)
J Cast Productions
2550 Greenvalley Rd
Los Angeles, CA 90046-1438, USA

Sheard, Jabaal (Athlete, Football Player)
c/o Drew Rosenhaus *Rosenhaus Sports Representation*
6400 Allison Rd
Miami Beach, FL 33141-4540, USA

Sheard, Kiera Kiki (Musician)
c/o Staff Member *EMI Gospel*
PO Box 5085
Brentwood, TN 37024-5085, USA

Shearer, Harry (Actor, Comedian)
c/o Melanie Greene *Affirmative Entertainment*
425 N Robertson Blvd
West Hollywood, CA 90048-1735, USA

Shearer, S Bradford (Brad) (Athlete, Football Player)
1909B Lakeshore Dr Apt B
Austin, TX 78746-2904, USA

Shearin, Joe (Athlete, Football Player)
3533 Stanford Ave
Dallas, TX 75225-7402, USA

Shearn, Tom (Athlete, Baseball Player)
18504 Copper Grassland Way
Pflugerville, TX 78660-4051, USA

Shears, Jake (Musician)
3606 Amesbury Rd
Los Angeles, CA 90027-1304, USA

Shears, Larry (Athlete, Football Player)
355 Cammel St
Mobile, AL 36610-3529, USA

Sheckler, Ryan (Actor, Skateboarder)
c/o Nick Styne *Creative Artists Agency (CAA-LA)*
2000 Avenue of the Stars Ste 100
Los Angeles, CA 90067-4705, USA

Shedd, Kenny (Athlete, Football Player)
342 Oleander St
Brentwood, CA 94513-6351, USA

Shedden, Doug (Athlete, Hockey Player)
7 E Main St
Stony Point, NY 10980-1615

Sheedy, Ally (Actor)
c/o Bill Veloric *Innovative Artists (NY)*
235 Park Ave S Fl 7
New York, NY 10003-1405, USA

Sheehan, Doug (Actor)
Innovative Artists
1505 10th St
Santa Monica, CA 90401-2805, USA

Sheehan, Jeremiah J (Business Person)
Reynolds Metals Co
6601 W Broad St
PO Box 27003
Richmond, VA 23230-1723, USA

Sheehan, Neil (Journalist)
4505 Klingle St NW
Washington, DC 20016-3580, USA

Sheehan, Patrick (Golfer)
485 Graham Ave
Oviedo, FL 32765-8702, USA

Sheehan, Patty (Golfer)
c/o Staff Member *Ladies Pro Golf Association (LPGA)*
100 International Golf Dr
Daytona Beach, FL 32124-1092, USA

Sheehan, Susan (Writer)
4505 Klingle St NW
Washington, DC 20016-3580, USA

Sheehy, Neil (Athlete, Hockey Player)
Sheehy Hockey LLC
7760 France Ave S Ste 1100
Minneapolis, MN 55435-5930

Sheehy, Tim (Athlete, Hockey Player, Olympic Athlete)
4 Boswell Ln
Southborough, MA 01772-1763, USA

Sheelor, Willie (Baseball Player)
Chicago American Giants
152 Beaumont Ave
Kannapolis, NC 28083-6501, USA

Sheen, Charles (Actor)
Jeffrey Ballard
4814 Lemara Ave
Sherman Oaks, CA 91403, USA

Sheen, Charlie (Actor)
c/o Staff Member *Estevez Sheen Productions*
99 S Raymond Ave # 601
Pasadena, CA 91105-2046, USA

Sheen, Martin (Actor)
c/o Staff Member *Estevez Sheen Productions*
99 S Raymond Ave # 601
Pasadena, CA 91105-2046, USA

Sheen, Michael (Actor, Producer)
c/o Tammy Rosen *Sanders Armstrong Caserta*
425 N Robertson Blvd
West Hollywood, CA 90048-1735, USA

Sheen, Ramon
6916 Dume Dr
Malibu, CA 90265-4227

Sheerer, Gary (Athlete)
1557 Country Club Dr
Los Altos, CA 94024-5908, USA

Sheets, Andy (Athlete, Baseball Player)
104 Villaggio Dr
Lafayette, LA 70508-6795, USA

Sheets, Ben (Athlete, Baseball Player, Olympic Athlete)
105 E Shore Rd
Monroe, LA 71203-8857, USA

Sheets, Larry (Athlete, Baseball Player)
1411 Chippendale Rd
Lutherville Timonium, MD 21093-1608, USA

Sheffer, Craig (Actor)
5699 Kanan Rd # 275
Agoura Hills, CA 91301-3358, USA

Sheffield, Fred (Athlete, Basketball Player)
11664 McDougall
Tustin, CA 92782-3345, USA

Sheffield, Gary A (Athlete, Baseball Player)
922 Anchorage Rd
Tampa, FL 33602-5754, USA

Sheffield, Johnny
834 1st Ave
Chula Vista, CA 91911-1451

Sheffield, Lois (Athlete, Baseball Player)
227 Jones St
Wellington, OH 44090-1062, USA

Sheffield, Tony (Baseball Player)
PO Box 164
Tullahoma, TN 37388-0164, USA

Sheffield, William J (Bill) (Ex-Governor)
PO Box 911476
Anchorage, AK 99509, USA

Shefft, Jen (Reality Star)
c/o Mike Esterman *Esterman.Com, LLC*
Prefers to be contacted via email
Baltimore, MD XXXXX, USA

Shehee, Rashaan (Athlete, Football Player)
6120 Bay Club Ct
Bakersfield, CA 93312-6212, USA

Sheibler, Jim
PO Box 60
Venice, CA 90294-0060

Sheik, Duncan (Musician, Songwriter, Writer)
Nonesuch Records
75 Rockefeller Plz
New York, NY 10019-6908, USA

Sheila E (Musician)
Ofoove Ent
1005 N Alfred St Apt 2
Los Angeles, CA 90069-4757, USA

Sheindlin, Judith (Judge Judy) (Judge, Television Host)
Big Ticket Television
5800 W Sunset Blvd
C/O Ktla Studios
Los Angeles, CA 90028-6607, USA

Sheiner, David S (Actor)
1827 Veteran Ave Apt 19
Los Angeles, CA 90025-4567, USA

Shelby, John (Athlete, Baseball Player)
2232 Broadhead Pl
Lexington, KY 40515-1147, USA

Shelby, Richard (Politician)
1414 High Forest Dr N
Tuscaloosa, AL 35406-2152, USA

Sheldon, Bob (Athlete, Baseball Player)
3013 River Lakes Dr
Whitefish, MT 59937-7801, USA

Sheldon, Jack (Musician)
7095 Hollywood Blvd Ste 617
Los Angeles, CA 90028-8912, USA

Sheldon, Rollie (Athlete, Baseball Player)
614 NE Coronado Ave
Lees Summit, MO 64063-2522, USA

Sheldon, Scott (Athlete, Baseball Player)
5768 Lightstone Ln
League City, TX 77573-1897, USA

Shell, Arthur (Art) (Athlete, Coach, Football Coach, Football Player)
4319 Rilea Way Apt 2
Oakland, CA 94605-3765, USA

Shell, Donnie (Athlete, Football Player)
2945 Shandon Rd
Rock Hill, SC 29730-9521, USA

Shell, Todd (Athlete, Football Player)
4222 E McLellan Cir Unit 15
Mesa, AZ 85205-3119, USA

Shellenback, Jim (Athlete, Baseball Player)
10627 Dreamy Ln
Parker, AZ 85344-7576, USA

Shellenbeck, Jim (Athlete, Baseball Player)
10627 Dreamy Ln
Parker, AZ 85344-7576, USA

Shellenberger, Michael (Activist, Writer)
The Breakthrough Institute
436 14th St Ste 820
Oakland, CA 94612-2726, USA

Shelley, Carole (Actor)
c/o Steve Stone *Cornerstone Talent Agency*
37 W 20th St Ste 1007
New York, NY 10011-3714, USA

Shelley, Jody (Athlete, Hockey Player)
9533 Sunset Dr
Powell, OH 43065-9605

Shelley, Rachel (Actor)
c/o Kesha Williams *KW Entertainment*
425 N Robertson Blvd
West Hollywood, CA 90048-1735, USA

Shelly, Randy (Actor)
c/o Ellen Gilbert *Abrams Artists Agency (LA)*
9200 W Sunset Blvd PH 11
West Hollywood, CA 90069-3601, USA

Shelmerdine, Kirk (Race Car Driver)
Kirk Shelmerdine Racing
PO Box 1133
Welcome, NC 27374-1133, United States

Shelton, Angela V (Comedian)
c/o Staff Member *Gekis Management*
4217 Verdugo View Dr
Los Angeles, CA 90065-4317, USA

Shelton, Ben (Athlete, Baseball Player)
1192 Clarence Ave Unit 11
Oak Park, IL 60304-2169, USA

Shelton, Blake (Musician)
23 Governors Way
Brentwood, TN 37027-8926, USA

Shelton, Chris (Athlete, Baseball Player)
6382 S Shady Grove Cir
Salt Lake City, UT 84121-6508, USA

Shelton, Craig (Athlete, Basketball Player)
8618 Leslie Ave
Glenarden, MD 20706-1528, USA

Shelton, Deborah (Actor)
c/o Marc Bass *Beacon Talent Agency*
170 Apple Ridge Rd
Woodcliff Lake, NJ 07677-8149, USA

Shelton, Derek (Athlete, Baseball Player)
203 46th Avenue St
Saint Petersburg, FL 33706, USA

Shelton, L J (Athlete, Football Player)
650 Carrotwood Ter
Plantation, FL 33324-8240, USA

Shelton, Lonnie (Athlete, Basketball Player)
3883 Union Ave Apt 5
Bakersfield, CA 93305-2444, USA

Shelton, Marley (Actor)
c/o Jason Weinberg *Untitled Entertainment (LA)*
350 S Beverly Dr Ste 200
Beverly Hills, CA 90212-4819, USA

Shelton, Richard (Athlete, Football Player)
6367 Raw Hyde Trl N
Jacksonville, FL 32210-3821, USA

The Celebrity Black Book 2015

Shelton, Ricky Van (Musician, Songwriter)
PO Box 111
Woodlawn, VA 24381-0111, USA

Shelton, Ronald W (Director)
c/o Staff Member *William Morris Endeavor (LA)*
9601 Wilshire Blvd
Beverly Hills, CA 90210-5213, USA

Shelton, Samantha (Actor)
c/o Staff Member *Innovative Artists (LA)*
1505 10th St
Santa Monica, CA 90401-2805, USA

Shembo, Prince (Athlete, Football Player)
c/o Adisa P. Bakari *Dow Lohnes PLLC*
1299 Pennsylvania Ave NW Ste 700
Washington, DC 20004-2431, USA

Shemin, Robert (Business Person, Writer)
Robert Shemin Inc
7965 S 700 E
C/O Preig
Sandy, UT 84070-0256, USA

Shen, Parry (Actor)
c/o Staff Member *Lichtman/Salners Company*
12216 Moorpark St
Studio City, CA 91604-5228, USA

Shenandoah (Music Group)
PO Box 680956
Franklin, TN 37068-0956, USA

Shenandoh, Joanne (Musician, Songwriter, Writer)
Oneida Nation Territory
PO Box 450
Oneida, NY 13421-0450, USA

Shenkman, Ben (Actor)
2 Charlton St Apt 5K
New York, NY 10014-4970, USA

Shepard, Dax (Actor, Reality Star, Writer)
c/o Staff Member *Baker Winokur Ryder Public Relations (BWR-LA)*
9100 Wilshire Blvd Ste 500
West Tower Suite 500
Beverly Hills, CA 90212-3426, USA

Shepard, Devon (Producer, Writer)
c/o Staff Member *Agency for the Performing Arts (APA-LA)*
405 S Beverly Dr Ste 500
Beverly Hills, CA 90212-4425, USA

Shepard, Jean (Musician)
Billy Deaton Talent
1214 16th Ave S
Nashville, TN 37212-2902, USA

Shepard, Judy (Activist)
The Matthew Shepard Foundation
301 Thelma Dr # 512
Casper, WY 82609-2325, USA

Shepard, Kenny Wayne (Musician)
c/o Staff Member *Richard De La Font Agency*
3808 W South Park Blvd
Broken Arrow, OK 74011-1261, USA

Shepard, Kiki (Actor)
c/o Staff Member *Cunningham Escott Slevin & Doherty (CESD-LA)*
10635 Santa Monica Blvd Ste 130
Los Angeles, CA 90025-8306, USA

Shepard, Samuel (Sam) (Actor, Writer)
c/o Judy Boals *Judy Boals Talent & Literary Agency*
307 W 38th St Rm 812
New York, NY 10018-3533, USA

Shepard, Sara (Writer)
c/o Andy McNicol *William Morris Endeavor (NY)*
1325 Avenue of the Americas
New York, NY 10019-6026, USA

Shepard, Vonda (Actor, Musician, Songwriter)
1114 Harvard St
Santa Monica, CA 90403-4710, USA

Sheperd, Ben (Musician)
9198 NE Hidden Cove Rd
Bainbridge Island, WA 98110-4106, USA

Sheperd, Morgan (Race Car Driver)
57 Rhody Creek Loop
Stuart, VA 24171-3011, USA

Shepherd, Ashton (Musician)
c/o Nicole Zeller *P.L.A. Media*
1303 16th Ave S Ste A
Nashville, TN 37212-2929, USA

Shepherd, Cybill (Actor)
4355 Bergamo Dr
Encino, CA 91436-3303, USA

Shepherd, Gannon (Athlete, Football Player)
5818 Alvaton Ct
Peachtree Corners, GA 30092-3901, USA

Shepherd, Keith (Athlete, Baseball Player)
2201 Parnell Ave
Fort Wayne, IN 46805-3338, USA

Shepherd, Morgan (Race Car Driver)
PO Box 623
Conover, NC 28613-0623, USA

Shepherd, Ron (Athlete, Baseball Player)
5821 FM 349
Kilgore, TX 75662-6905, USA

Shepherd, Sherri (Actor, Comedian, Talk Show Host)
c/o Staff Member *The View*
320 W 66th St
New York, NY 10023-6304, USA

Shepherd, Sherrie (Cartoonist)
United Feature Syndicate
PO Box 5610
Cincinnati, OH 45201-5610, USA

Shepherd, William M (Astronaut)
18623 Prince William Ln
Houston, TX 77058-4224, USA

Shepherd, William M Captain (Astronaut)
25 Piscataqua Dr
Newington, NH 03801-7816, USA

Shepis, Tiffany (Actor)
c/o Michael J Roberts *D-Mentd Entertainment*
Prefers to be contact via email or telephone
Wilmington, NC, USA

Sheppard, Delia (Actor, Model)
c/o Cheryl Murphy *Spectrum*
9107 Wilshire Blvd Ste 450
Beverly Hills, CA 90210-5535, USA

Sheppard, Julian (Comedian)
c/o Staff Member *Gersh (LA)*
9465 Wilshire Blvd Ste 600
Beverly Hills, CA 90212-2605, USA

Sheppard, Kelvin (Athlete, Football Player)
c/o Todd France *Five Star Athlete Management*
3500 Lenox Rd NE
Atlanta, GA 30326-4228, USA

Sheppard, Mike (Coach, Football Coach)
University of New Mexico
Athletic Dept
Albuquerque, NM 87131-0001, USA

Sheppard, Ray (Athlete, Hockey Player)
19110 Fox Landing Dr
Boca Raton, FL 33434-5156

Sheppard, William Morgan (Actor)
c/o Bri Franchot *Franchot Management*
PO Box 48890A
Los Angeles, CA 90048-0971, USA

Sher, Eden (Actor)
c/o Adam Griffin *Kritzer Levine Wilkins Entertainment (KLWG)*
11872 La Grange Ave Fl 1
Los Angeles, CA 90025-5283, USA

Sher, Stacey (Business Person, Producer)
3661 Alomar Dr
Sherman Oaks, CA 91423-4946, USA

Shera, Mark (Actor)
PO Box 15717
Beverly Hills, CA 90209-1717, USA

Sherba, John (Musician)
Kronos Quartet
1235 9th Ave # A
San Francisco, CA 94122-2306, USA

Sherbedgia, Rade (Actor)
Innovative Artists
1505 10th St
Santa Monica, CA 90401-2805, USA

Sherer, Dave (Athlete, Football Player)
4212 Colgate Ave
Dallas, TX 75225-6603, USA

Sherffius, John (Cartoonist)
Saint Louis Post Dispatch
900 N Tucker Blvd
Editorial Dept
Saint Louis, MO 63101-1099, USA

Sheridan, Bonnie (Musician)
c/o Mike Eistenstadt *Amsel, Eisenstadt & Frazier Talent Agency (AEF)*
5055 Wilshire Blvd Ste 860
Los Angeles, CA 90036-6108, USA

Sheridan, Bonnie Bramlett (Actor, Musician)
18011 Martha St
Encino, CA 91316-1052, USA

Sheridan, Dave C (Actor, Writer)
c/o Kara Welker *Generate Management*
8750 Wilshire Blvd Ste 200
Beverly Hills, CA 90211-2707, USA

Sheridan, Jamey (Actor)
c/o Daniel (Danny) Sussman *Brillstein Entertainment Partners (LA)*
9150 Wilshire Blvd Ste 350
Beverly Hills, CA 90212-3453, USA

Sheridan, Lisa (Actor)
c/o Joanna (Joanie) Burstein *Burstein Company, The*
15304 W Sunset Blvd Ste 208
Pacific Palisades, CA 90272-3656, USA

Sheridan, Liz (Actor)
11333 Moorpark St # 427
North Hollywood, CA 91602-2618

Sheridan, Neill (Athlete, Baseball Player)
5161 Mathewson Ct
Antioch, CA 94531-9135, USA

Sheridan, Nicole (Adult Film Star)
c/o Staff Member *Atlas Multimedia Inc*
9005 Eton Ave Ste C
Canoga Park, CA 91304-6533, USA

Sheridan, Nicollette (Actor)
c/o Nicole Perna *Baker Winokur Ryder Public Relations (BWR-LA)*
9100 Wilshire Blvd Ste 500
West Tower Suite 500
Beverly Hills, CA 90212-3426, USA

Sheridan, Pat (Athlete, Baseball Player)
31654 Taft St
Wayne, MI 48184-2234, USA

Sheridan, Rondell (Actor)
Gail Stocker Presents
1025 N Kings Rd Apt 113
West Hollywood, CA 90069-6007, USA

Sheridan, Tye (Actor)
c/o Emily Rose *Mosaic Media Group*
9200 W Sunset Blvd Ste 10
West Hollywood, CA 90069-3608, USA

Sherk, Jerry M (Athlete, Football Player)
1518 Orangeview Dr
Encinitas, CA 92024-4747, USA

Sherlock, Glenn (Athlete, Baseball Player)
9152 E Mountain Spring Rd
Scottsdale, AZ 85255-9149, USA

Sherlock, Nancy J (Astronaut)
NASA
2101 Nasa Pkwy Spc Johnsoncenter
Houston, TX 77058-3696, USA

Sherlock, Nancy J (Astronaut)
2003 Morning Tide Ln
League City, TX 77573-6640, USA

Sherlock-Currie, Nancy
2101 Nasa Pkwy
Houston, TX 77058-3607, USA

Sherman, Allie (Athlete, Football Coach, Football Player)
136 E 55th St Apt 12H
New York, NY 10022-4523, USA

Sherman, Anthony (Athlete, Football Player)
c/o Alan Herman *Sportstars Inc*
1350 Avenue of the Americas Fl 28
New York, NY 10019-4702, USA

Sherman, Bobby (Actor, Musician)
1870 Sunset Plaza Dr
Los Angeles, CA 90069-1314, USA

Sherman, Brad (Congressman, Politician)
2242 Rayburn Hob
Washington, DC 20515-1001, USA

Sherman, Brent (Race Car Driver)
Atkins Motorsports
222 Raceway Dr
Mooresville, NC 28117-6510, USA

Sherman, Darrell (Athlete, Baseball Player)
7450 Northrop Dr Apt 323
Riverside, CA 92508-5012, USA

Sherman, Edgar A (Coach, Football Coach)
681 Nancy Ln
Newark, OH 43055-4333, USA

Sherman, Heath (Athlete, Football Player)
2785 County Road 247
Wharton, TX 77488-5554, USA

Sherman, Mike (Athlete, Coach, Football Coach, Football Player)
161 Uncle Barneys Rd
West Dennis, MA 02670-2326, USA

Sherman, Richard (Athlete, Football Player)
c/o Jamie Fritz *Fritz Martin Management*
1801 Avenue of the Stars Ste 250
Los Angeles, CA 90067-5914, USA

Sherman, Rod (Athlete, Football Player)
PO Box 4551
Incline Village, NV 89450-4551, USA

Sherman, Saul (Athlete, Football Player)
1313 N Wood St # 2
Chicago, IL 60622-3204, USA

Sherman-Palladino, Amy (Director, Producer, Writer)
c/o Staff Member *Creative Artists Agency (CAA-LA)*
2000 Avenue of the Stars Ste 100
Los Angeles, CA 90067-4705, USA

Sherod, Edmund (Athlete, Basketball Player)
519 Montvale Ave
Richmond, VA 23222-3020, USA

Shero-Witiuk, Doris (Athlete, Baseball Player)
11821 N Hemlock St
Spokane, WA 99218-2718, USA

Sherr, Lynn (Correspondent)
c/o Staff Member *American Program Bureau*
1 Gateway Ctr Ste 751
Newton, MA 02458-2817, USA

Sherrard, Michael W (Mike) (Athlete, Football Player)
5661 Colodny Dr
Agoura Hills, CA 91301-2217, USA

Sherrill, Dennis (Athlete, Baseball Player)
1691 Tolley Ter SE
Palm Bay, FL 32909-8831, USA

Sherrill, George (Athlete, Baseball Player)
1442 E Vine Meadow Cir
Salt Lake City, UT 84121-1785, USA

Sherrill, Jackie W (Coach, Football Coach)
Mississippi State University
Athletic Dept
Mississippi State, MS 39762, USA

Sherrill, Tim (Athlete, Baseball Player)
PO Box 812
Harrison, AR 72602-0812, USA

Sherrod, Derek (Football Player)
c/o Adisa P. Bakari *Dow Lohnes PLLC*
1299 Pennsylvania Ave NW Ste 700
Washington, DC 20004-2431, USA

Sherry, Norm (Athlete, Baseball Player, Coach)
4383 Nobel Dr Unit 89
San Diego, CA 92122-1575, USA

Sherry, Paul H (Religious Leader)
United Church of Christ
700 Prospect Ave E
Cleveland, OH 44115-1100, USA

Sherwin, Tim (Athlete, Football Player)
6 Mill Rd
Latham, NY 12110-1184, USA

Sherwood, Brad (Actor, Producer)
c/o Erik Kritzer *LINK Entertainment*
11872 La Grange Ave Fl 1
Los Angeles, CA 90025-5283, USA

Shesol, Jeff (Cartoonist)
Creators Syndicate
737 3rd St
Hermosa Beach, CA 90254-4714, USA

Shetty, Reshma (Actor)
c/o Smith (Stevie) Stephanie *Station3 (NYC)*
300 W 55th St Apt 5L
New York, NY 10019-5163, USA

Shevchenko, Arkady N (Politician)
Alfred Knopf/Ballantine/Fawcett Publishers
201 E 50th St
New York, NY 10022-7703

Shields, Ben (Actor)
10965 Fruitland Dr Apt 102
Studio City, CA 91604-4601, USA

Shields, Billy (Athlete, Football Player)
12701 Treeridge Ter
Poway, CA 92064-6426, USA

Shields, Brooke (Actor, Model)
36 Lewis St
Southampton, NY 11968-5004, USA

Shields, James (Athlete, Baseball Player)
PO Box 9671
Rancho Santa Fe, CA 92067-4671, USA

Shields, Lebron (Athlete, Football Player)
1405 82nd Ave Lot 31
Vero Beach, FL 32966-8792, USA

Shields, Sam (Athlete, Football Player)
c/o Drew Rosenhaus *Rosenhaus Sports Representation*
6400 Allison Rd
Miami Beach, FL 33141-4540, USA

Shields, Samona (Samantha Strong) (Adult Film Star)
3324 Castle Heights Ave
Los Angeles, CA 90034-2729, USA

Shields, Scott (Athlete, Football Player)
16139 Pine Valley Dr
Northville, MI 48168-9655, USA

Shields, Steve (Athlete, Baseball Player)
3049 Posey Rd
Gadsden, AL 35903-6807, USA

Shields, Steve (Athlete, Hockey Player)
8558 Holloway Dr Apt 208
West Hollywood, CA 90069-2466

Shields, Steve (Athlete, Hockey Player)
Michigan Tech University Athletics
1400 Townsend Dr
Houghton, MI 49931-1295

Shields, Tommy (Athlete, Baseball Player)
518 N Elm St
Lititz, PA 17543-1312, USA

Shields, Tyler (Cinematographer)
c/o Eric Podwall *Podwall Entertainment*
710 N Orlando Ave Apt 203
Loft 203
West Hollywood, CA 90069-5549, USA

Shields, Will H (Athlete, Football Player)
13125 W 127th Pl
Overland Park, KS 66213-3846, USA

Shiell, Jason (Athlete, Baseball Player)
301 Sting Ray Ct
Guyton, GA 31312-6592, USA

Shiely, John S (Business Person)
Briggs & Stratton
PO Box 702
Milwaukee, WI 53201-0702, USA

Shifflett, Garland (Athlete, Baseball Player)
1095 Cody St
Lakewood, CO 80215-4818, USA

Shifflett, Steve (Athlete, Baseball Player)
24004 E 172nd St
Pleasant Hill, MO 64080-7582, USA

Shifty, Shellshock (Musician)
Q Prime
729 7th Ave Ste 1600
New York, NY 10019-6880, USA

Shih, Wen Yann (Actor)
c/o Vincent Cirrincione *Vincent Cirrincione Associates*
1516 N Fairfax Ave
Los Angeles, CA 90046-2608, USA

Shiley, Newhouse Jean (Athlete, Track Athlete)
1100 Sunnybrae Ave
Chatsworth, CA 91311, USA

Shilling, Curt (Baseball Player)
c/o Staff Member *Boston Red Sox*
4 Yawkey Way
Boston, MA 02215-3496, USA

Shimada, Yoko (Actor)
7245 Hillside Ave Apt 415
Los Angeles, CA 90046-2342

Shimerman, Armin (Actor)
Innovative Artists
1505 10th St
Santa Monica, CA 90401-2805, USA

Shimkis, Joanna
9255 Doheny Rd
West Hollywood, CA 90069-3201

Shimkus, Joanna (Actor)
c/o Staff Member *Creative Artists Agency (CAA-LA)*
2000 Avenue of the Stars Ste 100
Los Angeles, CA 90067-4705, USA

Shimkus, John (Congressman, Politician)
2452 Rayburn Hob
Washington, DC 20515-1009, USA

Shimmerman, Armin (Actor)
c/o Staff Member *Innovative Artists (LA)*
1505 10th St
Santa Monica, CA 90401-2805, USA

Shimono, Sab (Actor)
12711 Ventura Blvd Ste 440
Studio City, CA 91604-2456, USA

Shinall, Zak (Athlete, Baseball Player)
16605 Sell Cir
Huntington Beach, CA 92649-3299, USA

Shindle, Kate
2 Convention Blvd Ste 1000
Atlantic City, NJ 08401-4137

Shiner, Dick (Athlete, Football Player)
6683 Terrace Way
Harrisburg, PA 17111-7057, USA

Shines, Anthony (Razor) (Athlete, Baseball Player)
11508 Herb Cv
Austin, TX 78750-3671, USA

Shinn, Christopher (Comedian)
c/o Staff Member *Gersh (LA)*
9465 Wilshire Blvd Ste 600
Beverly Hills, CA 90212-2605, USA

Shinn, George (Business Person)
New Orleans/Oklahoma City Hornets
210 Park Ave Ste 1850
Oklahoma Tower
Oklahoma City, OK 73102-5636, USA

Shinners, John (Athlete, Football Player)
N120W1495 Freistadt Road
Germantown, WI 53022, USA

Shinoda, Mike (Musician)
Artist Group International
9560 Wilshire Blvd Ste 400
Beverly Hills, CA 90212-2442, USA

Shiny Toy Guns (Music Group)
c/o Staff Member *Paradigm (Monterey)*
404 W Franklin St
Monterey, CA 93940-2303, USA

Shipka, Kiernan (Actor)
c/o Alexandra Crotin *42West (LA)*
1840 Century Park E Ste 700
Los Angeles, CA 90067-2122, USA

Shipler, David K (Journalist)
4005 Thornapple St
Chevy Chase, MD 20815-5037, USA

Shipley, A.Q. (Athlete, Football Player)
c/o Eric Metz *Lock Metz Milanovic LLC*
6900 E Camelback Rd Ste 600
Scottsdale, AZ 85251-8044, USA

Shipley, Craig (Athlete, Baseball Player)
Boston Red Sox
4 Yawkey Way
Attn: V.P. Scouting Dept
Boston, MA 02215-3496, USA

Shipley, Joe (Athlete, Baseball Player)
23 Park Dr
Saint Charles, MO 63303-3607, USA

Shipley, Julie (Race Car Driver)
M&S Management
13904 Fiji Way Apt 242
Marina Del Rey, CA 90292-6925, USA

Shipman, Clarie (Correspondent)
ABC-TV
77 W 66th St
News Dept
New York, NY 10023-6201, USA

Shipman, Kim (Golfer)
239 Texas Dr
Hideaway, TX 75771-5030, USA

Shipp, Jackie (Athlete, Football Player)
3117 Trails Ct
Norman, OK 73072-7459, USA

Shipp, Jerry (Athlete, Basketball Player, Olympic Athlete)
PO Box 370
Kingston, OK 73439-0370, USA

Shipp, John Wesley (Actor)
c/o Janette Anderson *Janette Anderson Entertainment*
9682 Via Torino
Burbank, CA 91504-1410, USA

Shipp, William (Athlete, Football Player)
3920 Camellia Dr
Mobile, AL 36693-2814, USA

Shire, Talia (Actor, Director)
10730 Bellagio Rd
Los Angeles, CA 90077-3730, USA

Shirelles, The
PO Box 100
Clifton, NJ 07015-0100

Shires, Jim (Athlete, Hockey Player)
161 Hubbard Rd
Woodstock, GA 30188-5036

Shirk, Gary (Athlete, Football Player)
PO Box 287
Laporte, PA 18626-0287, USA

Shirley, Bart (Athlete, Baseball Player)
5757 S Staples St Apt 4208
Corpus Christi, TX 78413-3752, USA

Shirley, Bob (Athlete, Baseball Player)
761 W 13th St
Tulsa, OK 74127-9162, USA

Shirley, J Dallas (Referee)
5324 Pommel Dr
Mount Airy, MD 21771-8124, USA

Shirley, Steve (Athlete, Baseball Player)
9200 James Pl NE
Albuquerque, NM 87111-3323, USA

Shiver, Sanders (Athlete, Football Player)
9217 Christo Ct
Owings Mills, MD 21117-3596, USA

Shivers, Roy (Athlete, Football Player)
2067 Hidden Hollow Ln
Henderson, NV 89012-3203, USA

Shlomi, Vince (Offer) (Director)
1680 Michigan Ave Ste 700
Miami Beach, FL 33139-2551, USA

Shoals, Roger (Athlete, Football Player)
365 Righters Mill Rd
Gladwyne, PA 19035-1542, USA

Shobert, Bubba (Race Car Driver)
5235 95th St
Lubbock, TX 79424-4409, USA

Shocked, Michelle (Musician)
Skyline Music
28 Union St
Whitefield, NH 03598-3503, USA

Shockey, Jeremy (Athlete, Football Player)
c/o Traci Harper *Harper Public Relations*
3940 Laurel Canyon Blvd Ste 1010
Studio City, CA 91604-3709, USA

Shockley, Costen (Athlete, Baseball Player)
403 Wilson St
Georgetown, DE 19947-2340, USA

Shockley, Jeremy (Football Player)
New York Giants
Giants Stadium
East Rutherford, NJ 07073, USA

Shockley, William (Actor)
6345 Balboa Blvd Ste 375
Encino, CA 91316-5238, USA

Shoebottom, Bruce (Athlete, Hockey Player)
40 Woodfield Dr
Scarborough, ME 04074-8437

Shoeffling, Michael
PO Box 2563
Canyon Country, CA 91386-2563

Shoemaker, Bill
250 W Main St # 1820
Lexington, KY 40507-1714

Shoemaker, Craig (Actor)
c/o Staff Member *Osbrink Talent Agency*
4343 Lankershim Blvd Ste 100
North Hollywood, CA 91602-2705, USA

Shoemaker, John (Race Car Driver)
American Eagle Racing
3305 Horseshoe Dr
Sacramento, CA 95821-1717, USA

Shoemate, C Richard (Business Person)
Bestfoods
700 Sylvan Ave
International Plaza
Englewood Cliffs, NJ 07632-3150, USA

Shofner, Delbert M (Del) (Athlete, Football Player)
1665 Del Mar Ave
San Marino, CA 91108-2621, USA

Shofner, James (Jim) (Athlete, Football Coach, Football Player)
9620 Champions Dr
Granbury, TX 76049-4447, USA

Shoji, Dave (Coach)
University of Hawaii
Athletic Dept
Hilo, HI 96720, USA

Shoop, Ron
PO Box 92
Rural Valley, PA 16249-0092

Shopay, Tom (Athlete, Baseball Player)
10145 NW 19th St
Doral, FL 33172-2529, USA

Shoppach, Kelly (Athlete, Baseball Player)
15358 Briarcrest Cir
Fort Myers, FL 33912-6359, USA

Shore, David (Producer, Writer)
c/o Lawrence Shuman *Shuman Company*
3815 Hughes Ave Fl 4
Culver City, CA 90232-2715, USA

Shore, Howard (Actor, Composer, Musician)
c/o Staff Member *Columbia Artists Mgmt Inc*
1790 Broadway Fl 6
New York, NY 10019-1537, USA

Shore, Pauly (Actor, Comedian)
c/o Staff Member *Landing Patch Productions*
8491 W Sunset Blvd # 700
West Hollywood, CA 90069-1911, USA

Shore, Roberta (Actor)
PO Box 71639
Salt Lake City, UT 84171-0639

Shores, Del (Producer, Writer)
Del Shores Productions
8581 Santa Monica Blvd # 560
West Hollywood, CA 90069-4120, USA

Shorr, Lonnie
707 18th Ave S
Nashville, TN 37203-3214

Short, Bill (Athlete, Baseball Player)
2975 57th St
Sarasota, FL 34243-2434, USA

Short, Brandon (Athlete, Football Player)
1717 Sumac St
McKeesport, PA 15132-5470, USA

Short, Columbus (Actor)
Great Picture Show
12400 Wilshire Blvd Ste 1275
Los Angeles, CA 90025-1078, USA

Short, Eugene (Athlete, Basketball Player)
8111 Fondren Lake Dr
Houston, TX 77071-3610, USA

Short, Kawann (Athlete, Football Player)
c/o Joel Segal *Lagardere Unlimited (NYC)*
845 United Nations Plz Apt 24D
New York, NY 10017-3532, USA

Short, Martin (Actor, Comedian, Musician)
15907 Alcima Ave
Pacific Palisades, CA 90272-2405, USA

Short, Purvis (Athlete, Basketball Player)
8111 Fondren Lake Dr
Houston, TX 77071-3610, USA

Short, Rick (Athlete, Baseball Player)
3021 Forsythe Ct
Peoria, IL 61614-1119, USA

Shorter, Frank (Athlete, Olympic Athlete, Track Athlete)
558 Utica Ct
Boulder, CO 80304-0773, USA

Shortridge, Stephen (Actor)
3304 E Sky Harbor Dr
Coeur D Alene, ID 83814-9494, USA

Shortridge, Steve (Actor)
1707 Clear View Dr
Beverly Hills, CA 90210-2012, USA

Shorts, Cecil (Athlete, Football Player)
c/o Ryan Tollner *REP 1 Sports Group*
2 Corporate Park Ste 106
Irvine, CA 92606-5103, USA

Shorts, Peter (Athlete, Football Player)
810 S Cedar Point Dr
Anaheim, CA 92808-1680, USA

Shostakovich, Maxim D (Musician)
PO Box 273
Jordanville, NY 13361-0273, USA

Shou, Robin (Actor)
Paradigm Agency
10100 Santa Monica Blvd Ste 2500
Los Angeles, CA 90067-4116, USA

Shouse, Brian (Athlete, Baseball Player)
3121 W Summerbend Ct
Peoria, IL 61615-8879, USA

Shouse, Dexter (Athlete, Basketball Player)
4523 E Rhonda Dr
Phoenix, AZ 85018-7223, USA

Shout Out Louds (Music Group)
c/o Staff Member *Paradigm (Monterey)*
404 W Franklin St
Monterey, CA 93940-2303, USA

Show, Frida (Actor)
c/o Kim Matuka *Online Talent Group*
Prefers to be contacted via email or telephone
West Hollywood, CA 90069, USA

Show, Grant (Actor)
17 Jib St
Marina Del Rey, CA 90292-5908, USA

Showalter III, William N (Buck) (Athlete, Baseball Player, Coach)
9736 Hathaway St
Dallas, TX 75220-2114, USA

Showder, Lisa (Race Car Driver)
1650 E Golf Rd
Schaumburg, IL 60196-0001, USA

Shreve, Susan R (Writer)
3506 35th St NW
Washington, DC 20016-3114, USA

Shribman, David M (Journalist)
Boston Globe
1130 Connecticut Ave NW Ste 520
Editorial Dept
Washington, DC 20036-3943, USA

Shrider, Richard (Athlete, Basketball Player)
6666 Morning Sun Rd
Oxford, OH 45056-8843, USA

Shriner, Kin (Actor)
Don Buchwald
6500 Wilshire Blvd Ste 2200
Los Angeles, CA 90048-4942, USA

Shriner, Wil (Television Host)
5313 Quakertown Ave
Woodland Hills, CA 91364-3542, USA

Shriver, Anthony
100 SE 2nd St # 1990
Miami, FL 33131-2100

Shriver, Bobby (Activist, Attorney, Journalist)
3032 Wilshire Blvd
Santa Monica, CA 90403-2302, USA

Shriver, Loren J (Astronaut)
2513 Nimbus Dr
Estes Park, CO 80517-8105, USA

shriver, Loren J Colonel (Astronaut)
2513 Nimbus Dr
Estes Park, CO 80517-8105, USA

Shriver, Maria (Correspondent, Television Host)
3110 Main St Ste 300
Santa Monica, CA 90405-5354, USA

Shriver, Mark (Motivational Speaker)
Save the Children
54 Wilton Rd
Westport, CT 06880-3108, USA

Shriver, Pam (Athlete, Olympic Athlete, Tennis Player)
Pam Shriver Tennis Challenge
14524 Dover Rd
Reisterstown, MD 21136-3877, USA

Shriver, R
1325 G St NW Ste 500
Washington, DC 20005-3136, USA

Shrontz, Frank A (Business Person)
2949 81st Pl SE # P
Mercer Island, WA 98040-3059, USA

Shrowder, Lisa (Race Car Driver)
1650 E Golf Rd
Schaumburg, IL 60196-0001, USA

Shroyer, Sonny (Actor)
12725 Ventura Blvd Ste F
Studio City, CA 91604-2437, USA

Shtalenkov, Mikhail (Athlete, Hockey Player)
7 Faenza
Newport Coast, CA 92657-1602

Shuchuk, Gary (Athlete, Hockey Player)
5713 Lancashier Ct
Fitchburg, WI 53711-6504

Shue, Andrew (Actor)
c/o Jimmy Darmody *Creative Artists Agency (CAA-LA)*
2000 Avenue of the Stars Ste 100
Los Angeles, CA 90067-4705, USA

Shue, Elisabeth (Actor)
c/o David Seltzer *Management 360*
9111 Wilshire Blvd
Beverly Hills, CA 90210-5508, USA

Shue, Gene (Athlete, Basketball Player, Coach)
4338 Redwood Ave Unit 303
Marina Del Rey, CA 90292-7648, USA

Shuey, Paul (Athlete, Baseball Player)
5252 Mill Dam Rd
Wake Forest, NC 27587-6386, USA

Shugart, Clyde (Athlete, Football Player)
6368 Heronwalk Dr
Gulf Breeze, FL 32563-7024, USA

Shugarts, Bret (Athlete, Football Player)
18823 Forest Bend Creek Way
Spring, TX 77379-5510, USA

Shukovsky, Joel (Writer)
Shukovsky-English Ent
4024 Radford Ave
Studio City, CA 91604-2101, USA

Shula, David D (Dave) (Athlete, Coach, Football Coach, Football Player)
10805 Indian Trl
Cooper City, FL 33328-5509, USA

Shula, Don (Athlete, Coach, Football Coach, Football Player)
16 Indian Creek Island Rd
Indian Creek Village, FL 33154-2904, USA

Shula, Mike (Athlete, Coach, Football Coach, Football Player)
19140 Peninsula Club Dr
Cornelius, NC 28031-5122, USA

Shuler, Heath (Athlete, Football Player)
Shuler Real Estate
8550 Kingston Pike
Knoxville, TN 37919-5353, USA

Shuler, Joseph Heath (Congressman, Politician)
229 69 Non Hob
Washington, DC 20515-0001, USA

Shuler, Mickey C (Athlete, Football Player)
c/o Scott Smith *XAM Sports*
PO Box 1725
Madison, WI 53701-1725, USA

Shulock, John (Athlete, Baseball Player)
4180 5th St SW
Vero Beach, FL 32968-3909, USA

Shultz, George (Politician)
776 Dolores St
Stanford, CA 94305-8428, USA

Shultz, George P (Politician, Secretary)
Hoover Institute
Stanford University
Stanford, CA 94305, USA

Shumaker, Anthony (Athlete, Baseball Player)
2213 Jefferson St
Paducah, KY 42001-3108, USA

Shuman-Juransinski, Amy (Baseball Player)
424 Douglass St
Wyomissing, PA 19610-2906, USA

Shumate, John (Athlete, Basketball Player, Coach)
16406 S 12th Pl
Phoenix, AZ 85048-4045, USA

Shumate, Rachel (Actor)
c/o Sean Fay *Kritzer Levine Wilkins Entertainment (KLWG)*
11872 La Grange Ave Fl 1
Los Angeles, CA 90025-5283, USA

Shum Jr., Harry (Actor, Dancer, Musician)
3415 Primera Ave
Los Angeles, CA 90068-1551, USA

Shumlin, Peter (Governor, Politician)
Pavilion Office Bldg
109 State St Fl 5
Montpelier, VT 05609-0001, USA

Shumpert, Terry (Athlete, Baseball Player)
8432 Fairview Ct
Lone Tree, CO 80124-3181, USA

Shust, Aaron (Musician)
c/o Mitch White *Moose Management*
Prefers to be contacted via telephone
Nashville, TN, USA

Shuster, Bill (Congressman, Politician)
204 Cannon Hob
Washington, DC 20515-3816, USa

Shutan, Jan (Actor)
3115 Deep Canyon Dr
Beverly Hills, CA 90210-1035, USA

Shutt, Byron (Athlete, Hockey Player)
29723 Lake Rd
Bay Village, OH 44140-1277, USA

Shutt, Steve (Athlete, Coach, Hockey Player)
7814 Heritage Grand Pl
Bradenton, FL 34212-3261, USA

Shuttz, George P
776 Dolores St
Stanford, CA 94305-8428, USA

Shut Up Stella (Music Group)
c/o Staff Member *Paradigm (Monterey)*
404 W Franklin St
Monterey, CA 93940-2303, USA

Shy, Les (Athlete, Football Player)
1022 W Bogey Ln
Palatine, IL 60067-2392, USA

Shyamalan, M Night (Director, Producer, Writer)
c/o Staff Member *Night Chronicles*
1800 Century Park E
C/O Media Rights Capital
Los Angeles, CA 90067-1501, USA

Shydner, Ritch (Comedian)
c/o Daniel Strone *Trident Media Group LLC*
41 Madison Ave Fl 36
New York, NY 10010-2257, USA

Shyer, Charles R (Director, Writer)
227 N Glenroy Ave
Los Angeles, CA 90049-2417, USA

Shys, The (Music Group)
c/o Staff Member *Paradigm (Monterey)*
404 W Franklin St
Monterey, CA 93940-2303, USA

Sia, Beau (Actor)
c/o Staff Member *Creative Artists Agency (CAA-LA)*
2000 Avenue of the Stars Ste 100
Los Angeles, CA 90067-4705, USA

Sias, John B (Publisher)
Chronicle Publishing Co
901 Mission St
San Francisco, CA 94103-2905, USA

Sibbett, Jane (Actor)
c/o John Carrabino *John Carrabino Management*
5900 Wilshire Blvd Ste 406
Los Angeles, CA 90036-5015, USA

Sibert, Sam (Athlete, Basketball Player)
4615 Enchanted Bay Blvd
Arlington, TX 76016-5331, USA

Sibley, David (Actor)
c/o Staff Member *Select Artists Ltd (CA-Westside Office)*
1138 12th St Apt 1
Santa Monica, CA 90403-5459, USA

Sibley, Mark (Athlete, Basketball Player)
334 E McKenna Ct
Elmhurst, IL 60126-5361, USA

Sichting, Jerry (Basketball Player)
3190 N Country Club Rd
Martinsville, IN 46151-7929, USA

Siddiqui, Aamera (Actor)
c/o Staff Member *NUTS*
820 Lilac Dr N Ste 101
Minneapolis, MN 55422-4754, USA

Siddons, Anne (Writer)
60 Church St
Charleston, SC 29401-2558, USA

Siddons, Anne R (Writer)
767 Vermont Rd
Atlanta, GA 30319, USA

Siddons, Ann Rivers (Writer)
60 Church St
Charleston, SC 29401-2558

Sider, Harvey R (Religious Leader)
Brethren in Christ Church
431 Grantham Rd
Mechanicsburg, PA 17055-5812, USA

Sidewalk Prophets (Music Group, Musician)
c/o Scott Bickell *Brickhouse Entertainment*
106 Mission Ct Ste 1202
Franklin, TN 37067-6484, USA

Sidgmore, John (Business Person)
WorldCom
500 Clinton Center Dr Ste 2400
Clinton, MS 39056-5674, USA

Sidibe, Gabourey (Gabby) (Actor)
c/o Jill Kaplan *Authentic Talent and Literary Management*
20 Jay St Ste M17
Brooklyn, NY 11201-8300, USA

Sidney, Dainon (Athlete, Football Player)
605 Lakemeade Pt
Old Hickory, TN 37138-2588, USA

Sidney, Rice (Athlete, Football Player)
11931 Tiffany Ln
Eden Prairie, MN 55344-5384, USA

Sidran, Ben (Race Car Driver)
Go Jazz
PO Box 2023
Madison, WI 53701-2023, USA

Sidransky, David (Doctor, Scientist)
Baylor Medical Center
1200 Moursand Ave
Houston, TX 77030, USA

Siebel, Jennifer (Actor, Producer)
Girl's Club Entertainment
San Francisco, CA, USA

Sieber, Christopher (Actor)
c/o Richard Fisher *Abrams Artists Agency (NY)*
275 7th Ave Fl 26
New York, NY 10001-6708, USA

Siebern, Norm (Athlete, Baseball Player)
2006 Palo Alto Ave
Lady Lake, FL 32159-9211, USA

Siebert, Paul (Athlete, Baseball Player)
1711 Acker St
Orlando, FL 32837-6588, USA

Siebert, Sonny
2583 Brush Creek Rd
Saint Louis, MO 63129-5601, USA

Siebert, Wilfred C (Sonny) (Athlete, Baseball Player)
2555 Brush Creek Rd
Saint Louis, MO 63129-5601, USA

Siebler, Dwight (Athlete, Baseball Player)
4646 N 79th St
Omaha, NE 68134-3328, USA

Siebold, Pete
1624 Flight Line
Mojave, CA 93501-1663, USA

Siega, Marcos (Director)
c/o Staff Member *William Morris Endeavor (LA)*
9601 Wilshire Blvd
Beverly Hills, CA 90210-5213, USA

Siegal, Bernard (Writer)
61 0X Bow Ln
Woodbridge, CT 06525

Siegal, Jay (Music Group, Musician)
Brothers Mgmt
141 Dunbar Ave
Fords, NJ 08863-1551, USA

Siegal, John (Football Player)
Chicago Bears
Harvey's Bt
Harveys Lake, PA 18618, USA

Siegel, Barry (Journalist)
Los Angeles Times
202 W 1st St Ste 500
Editorial Dept
Los Angeles, CA 90012-4401, USA

Siegel, Bernie (Doctor, Writer)
61 Ox Bow Ln
Woodbridge, CT 06525-1525, USA

Siegel, Eric (Actor)
c/o Mickey Berman *United Talent Agency (UTA-LA)*
9336 Civic Center Dr
Beverly Hills, CA 90210-3604, USA

Siegel, Herbert J (Business Person)
Chris-Craft Industries
767 5th Ave
New York, NY 10153-0023, USA

Siegel, Ira T (Publisher)
16589 Senterra Dr
Delray Beach, FL 33484-6986, USA

Siegel, Jake (Actor)
c/o Staff Member *JC Robbins Management*
865 S Sherbourne Dr
Los Angeles, CA 90035-1809, USA

Siegel, Janis (Musician)
International Creative Mgmt
40 W 57th St Fl 5
New York, NY 10019-4001, USA

Siegel, L Pendleton (Business Person)
Potlatch Corp
601 W Riverside Ave Ste 1100
Spokane, WA 99201-0644, USA

Siegel, Norman (Attorney)
Committee for Norman Siegel
260 Madison Ave
New York, NY 10016-2401, USA

Siegel, Robert C (Correspondent)
c/o Gregory McKnight *Creative Artists Agency (CAA-LA)*
2000 Avenue of the Stars Ste 100
Los Angeles, CA 90067-4705, USA

Siegel, Ron (Chef)
Charles Nob Hill 1250 Jones St
San Francisco, CA 94109, USA

Siemaszko, Casey (Actor)
Gersh Agency
232 N Canon Dr
Beverly Hills, CA 90210-5302, USA

Siemaszko, Nina (Actor)
c/o David Rose *Innovative Artists (LA)*
1505 10th St
Santa Monica, CA 90401-2805, USA

Sieminski, Chuck (Athlete, Football Player)
5000 Village Way Apt 406
Marcus Hook, PA 19061-6857, USA

Siemon, Jeffrey G (Jeff) (Athlete, Football Player)
5401 Londonderry Rd
Minneapolis, MN 55436-1026, USA

Sienkiewicz, Troy (Athlete, Football Player)
186 Darcy Ave
Goose Creek, SC 29445-6664, USA

Sierchio, Tom (Actor, Writer)
c/o Alan Gasmer *Alan Gasmer Management Company*
10877 Wilshire Blvd Ste 603
Los Angeles, CA 90024-4348, USA

Siering, Lauri (Swimmer)
3829 Rotterdam Ave
Modesto, CA 95356-0739, USA

Sierra, Jessica (Musician)
c/o *Network Solutions*
PO Box 447
Herndon, VA 20172-0447, USA

Sierra, Pedro (Athlete, Baseball Player)
Indianapolis Clowns
3604 Whitehall Ct
Mays Landing, NJ 08330-3241, USA

Sierra, Ruben A (Athlete, Baseball Player)
12355 SW 51st St
Miami, FL 33175-5506, USA

Sierra, Rubin
1 Res Jard Selles Apt 2501
San Juan, PR 00924-2964

Sievers, Eric (Athlete, Football Player)
11550 Great Falls Way
Great Falls, VA 22066-1148, USA

Sievers, Gary (Actor)
c/o Staff Member *Dani's Agency*
434 E Southern Ave
Tempe, AZ 85282-5216, USA

Sievers, Roy E (Athlete, Baseball Player)
11505 Bellefontaine Rd
Saint Louis, MO 63138-1706, USA

Siff, Maggie (Actor)
c/o James Suskin *James Suskin Management*
2 Charlton St Apt 5K
New York, NY 10014-4970, USA

Sifford, Charlie (Athlete, Golfer)
7540 Sanctuary Cir
Brecksville, OH 44141-3195, USA

Sigel, Beanie (Musician)
International Creative Mgmt
10250 Constellation Blvd Fl 1
Los Angeles, CA 90067-6241, USA

Sigel, Jay (Golfer)
1284 Farm Rd
Berwyn, PA 19312-2000, USA

Sigel, Tom (Cinematographer)
International Creative Mgmt
10250 Constellation Blvd Fl 1
Los Angeles, CA 90067-6241, USA

Sigholtz, Bob
5425 Shirley Ave
Tarzana, CA 91356-2910

Sigler, Jamie-Lynn (Actor)
c/o Glenn Gulino *G2 Entertainment LLC*
1 Columbus Pl Apt S25E
New York, NY 10019-8208, USA

Sigman, Stan (Business Person)
Cingular Creative Mgmt
5565 Glenridge Connector
Atlanta, GA 30342-4756, USA

Sigur Ros (Music Group)
c/o Staff Member *Paradigm (Monterey)*
404 W Franklin St
Monterey, CA 93940-2303, USA

Sikahema, Vai (Athlete, Football Player)
28 Abington Rd
Mount Laurel, NJ 08054-4720, USA

Sikes, Alfred C (Government Official)
3214 Kirwans Neck Rd
Church Creek, MD 21622-1323, USA

Sikes, Cynthia (Actor)
10500 Rocca Pl
Los Angeles, CA 90077-2904, USA

Sikharulidze, Anton (Figure Skater)
Ice House Skating Rink
111 Midtown Bridge Approac
Hackensack, NJ 07601-7505, USA

Sikich, Mike P (Athlete, Football Player)
702 Tudor Dr
Janesville, WI 53546-2001, USA

Sikking, James B (Actor)
258 S Carmelina Ave
Los Angeles, CA 90049-3957, USA

Sikma, Jack (Athlete, Basketball Player)
9125 NE 21st Pl
Clyde Hill, WA 98004-2437, USA

Sikora, Joe (Actor)
c/o Myrna Jacoby *MJ Management*
130 W 57th St Apt 11A
New York, NY 10019-3311, USA

Sikora, Nicole (Athlete, Golfer)
Westchester Golf Range
701 Dobbs Ferry Rd
White Plains, NY 10607-1744, USA

Sikorski, Brian (Athlete, Baseball Player)
17930 Wexford St
Roseville, MI 48066-4630, USA

Silas, James (Athlete, Basketball Player)
6800 Thistle Hill Way
Austin, TX 78754-5800, USA

Silas, Paul (Athlete, Basketball Player, Coach)
2463 Peninsula Shores Ct
Denver, NC 28037-7655, USA

Silatolu, Amini (Athlete, Football Player)
c/o Bruce Tollner *REP 1 Sports Group*
2 Corporate Park Ste 106
Irvine, CA 92606-5103, USA

Silberling, Bradley (Brad) (Director, Producer)
c/o Jimmy Miller *Mosaic Media Group*
9200 W Sunset Blvd Ste 10
West Hollywood, CA 90069-3608, USA

Silbermann, Jake (Actor)
c/o Robyn Ziegler *Robyn Ziegler Management*
143 W 29th St Ste 1103
New York, NY 10001-5134, USA

Silberstein, Diane Wichard (Publisher)
New Yorker Magazine
4 Times Sq Fl 22
Publisher's Office
New York, NY 10036-6592, USA

Sileo, Dan (Athlete, Football Player)
46 Woodland Dr Apt 203
Vero Beach, FL 32962-3782, USA

Silia, Felix (Actor)
8927 Snowden Ave
Arleta, CA 91331-6115, USA

Silk (Artist, Musician)
c/o Staff Member *Faa*
250 W 57th St Fl 15
New York, NY 10107-1307, USA

Silk, Anna (Actor)
c/o Abe Hoch *A Management Company*
9107 Wilshire Blvd Ste 650
Beverly Hills, CA 90210-5544, USA

Silk, Dave (Athlete, Hockey Player, Olympic Athlete)
7 Whiting Ln
Hingham, MA 02043-4019

Silla, Felix (Actor)
5313 Magenta Ct
Las Vegas, NV 89108-2305, USA

Sillas, Karen (Actor)
PO Box 725
Wading River, NY 11792-0725, USA

Siller, Eugenio (Actor)
c/o Tom Harrison *Diverse Talent Group*
9911 W Pico Blvd Ste 340W
Los Angeles, CA 90035-2703, USA

Silliman, Ron (Writer)
262 Orchard Rd
Paoli, PA 19301-1116, USA

Sills, Douglas (Actor, Musician)
Gold Marshak Liedike
3500 W Olive Ave Ste 1400
Burbank, CA 91505-5512, USA

Silva, Anderson (Athlete, Wrestler)
c/o Staff Member *Black House Team Nogueira*
7550 Miramar Rd Ste 330
San Diego, CA 92126-4217, USA

Silva, Daniel (Writer)
3512 Winfield Ln NW
Washington, DC 20007-2344

Silva, Henry (Actor)
8747 Clifton Way Apt 305
Beverly Hills, CA 90211-2125, USA

Silva, Jason (Television Host)
c/o Rob Levy *Untitled Entertainment (LA)*
350 S Beverly Dr Ste 200
Beverly Hills, CA 90212-4819, USA

Silva, Jose (Athlete, Baseball Player)
401 Pappan Dr
Imperial, PA 15126-1192, USA

Silva, Zack (Actor)
Valeo Entertainment
8265 W Sunset Blvd Ste 103
C/O Michael Dean Valeo
West Hollywood, CA 90046-2433, USA

Silver, Edward J (Religious Leader)
Bible Way Church
5118 Clarendon Rd
Brooklyn, NY 11203-5329, USA

Silver, Harvey (Actor)
c/o Staff Member *Anonymous Content (LA)*
3532 Hayden Ave
Culver City, CA 90232-2413, USA

Silver, Jeffrey (Producer)
c/o Staff Member *Outlaw Productions*
9350 Civic Center Dr Ste 100
Beverly Hills, CA 90210-3629, USA

Silver, Joan Macklin (Director)
Silverfilm Productions
510 Park Ave Apt 9B
New York, NY 10022-6640, USA

Silver, Joel (Producer)
c/o Staff Member *Silver Pictures*
4000 Warner Blvd Bldg 90
Burbank, CA 91522-0001

Silver, Michael B
9229 W Sunset Blvd Ste 315
West Hollywood, CA 90069-3403, USA

Silvera, Charlie (Athlete, Baseball Player)
1240 Manzanita Dr
Millbrae, CA 94030-2934, USA

Silverberg, Robert (Writer)
c/o *Tom Doherty Associates, LLC*
175 5th Ave
New York, NY 10010-7703, USA

Silverbush, Lori (Actor)
c/o Brantley Brown *Schachter Entertainment*
1157 S Beverly Dr Fl 2
Los Angeles, CA 90035-1119, USA

Silverio, Luis (Athlete, Baseball Player)
3130 NW 89th Ter
Kansas City, MO 64154-1835, USA

Silverman, Al (Publisher)
411 E 53rd St
16H
New York, NY 10022-5106, USA

Silverman, Benjamin (Producer)
c/o Staff Member *NBC Universal (LA)*
100 Universal City Plz
Universal City, CA 91608-1002, USA

Silverman, Fred
1642 Mandeville Canyon Rd
Los Angeles, CA 90049-2524

Silverman, Henry R (Business Person)
Cendant Corp
9 W 57th St Fl 39
New York, NY 10019-2701, USA

Silverman, Jerry (Horse Racer)
3888 Meadow Ln
Hollywood, FL 33021-2645, USA

Silverman, Jonathan (Actor)
c/o Beth Holden-Garland *Untitled Entertainment (LA)*
350 S Beverly Dr Ste 200
Beverly Hills, CA 90212-4819, USA

Silverman, Sarah (Actor, Comedian)
c/o Amy Zvi *Thruline Entertainment*
9250 Wilshire Blvd Ste 100
Ground Floor
Beverly Hills, CA 90212-3343, USA

Silverstein, Elliott (Director)
Gersh Agency
232 N Canon Dr
Beverly Hills, CA 90210-5302, USA

Silverstone, Alicia (Actor)
8777 Wonderland Ave
Los Angeles, CA 90046-1849, USA

Silversun Pickups (Music Group, Musician)
c/o Cliff Burnstein *Q Prime Inc*
729 7th Ave Ste 1600
New York, NY 10019-6880, USA

Silvestri, Dave (Athlete, Baseball Player, Olympic Athlete)
15511 Country Mill Ct
Chesterfield, MO 63017-5148, USA

Silvstedt, Victoria (Actor, Model)
c/o Liza Anderson *Anderson Group Public Relations*
8060 Melrose Ave Fl 4
Los Angeles, CA 90046-7038, USA

Simas, Bill (Athlete, Baseball Player)
1890 E Warwick Ave
Fresno, CA 93720-5633, USA

Sime, Dave (Athlete, Olympic Athlete, Track Athlete)
9140 Bay Dr
Surfside, FL 33154-3112, USA

Simhan, Meera (Actor)
Bamboo Management
17 Buccaneer St
C/O Heidi L Ifft
Marina Del Rey, CA 90292-5103, USA

Simic, Charles (Writer)
PO Box 192
Strafford, NH 03884-0192, USA

Simien, Tracy (Athlete, Football Player)
3219 Sumac Dr
Pearland, TX 77584-8069, USA

Simien, Wayne (Basketball Player)
c/o Staff Member *Miami Heat*
601 Biscayne Blvd
American Airlines Arena
Miami, FL 33132-1801, USA

Simkus, Arnold (Athlete, Football Player)
4248 Chicago Rd
Warren, MI 48092-1471, USA

Simmonds, Sara (Actor)
c/o Steven Jensen *Independent Group, The*
6363 Wilshire Blvd Ste 115
Los Angeles, CA 90048-5734, USA

Simmons, Arthur (Baseball Player)
Kansas City Monarchs
27 158th Pl Apt 2W
Calumet City, IL 60409-4945, USA

Simmons, Bob (Athlete, Football Player)
16040 Chalfont Cir
Dallas, TX 75248-3544, USA

Simmons, Brian (Athlete, Baseball Player)
226 Village Dr
Canonsburg, PA 15317-2367, USA

Simmons, Brian (Athlete, Football Player)
9240 Liberty Hill Ct
Cincinnati, OH 45242-4663, USA

Simmons, Canary (Athlete, Football Player)
13531 Lyndonville Dr
Houston, TX 77041-4804, USA

Simmons, Curtis T (Curt) (Athlete, Baseball Player)
200 Park Rd
Ambler, PA 19002-1121, USA

Simmons, Dan (Writer)
c/o Michael Prevett *The Gotham Group Inc*
9255 W Sunset Blvd Ste 515
West Hollywood, CA 90069-3308, USA

Simmons, Daniel (Diggy Simmons) (Musician)
c/o Daniel Kim *Creative Artists Agency (CAA-LA)*
2000 Avenue of the Stars Ste 100
Los Angeles, CA 90067-4705, USA

Simmons, Earl (DMX) (Actor, Musician)
142 McLain St
Mount Kisco, NY 10549-4932, USA

Simmons, Ed (Athlete, Football Player)
PO Box 6632
Kennewick, WA 99336-0639, USA

Simmons, Gary (Athlete, Hockey Player)
2624 Inverness Dr
Lake Havasu City, AZ 86404-1373

Simmons, Gene (Business Person, Musician, Reality Star)
Gene Simmons Company
PO Box 16075
Beverly Hills, CA 90209-2075, USA

Simmons, Grant (Athlete, Basketball Player)
7274 E Costilla Pl
Centennial, CO 80112-1111, USA

Simmons, Hubert (Baseball Player)
Baltimore Elite Giants
3247 Sonia Trl
Ellicott City, MD 21043-3273, USA

Simmons, Jaason (Actor)
Gilbertson & Kincaid Mgmt
1330 4th St
Santa Monica, CA 90401-1302, USA

Simmons, Jason (Athlete, Football Player)
2828 Spring St
Pittsburgh, PA 15210-2675, USA

Simmons, Jeff (Race Car Driver)
Team Green
7615 Zionsville Rd
Indianapolis, IN 46268-2174, USA

Simmons, Jerry (Athlete, Football Player)
2233 S King Dr
Chicago, IL 60616-1415, USA

Simmons, JK (Actor)
c/o Stephen Hirsh *Gersh (NY)*
41 Madison Ave
New York, NY 10010-2202, USA

Simmons, Johnny (Actor)
c/o Ruth Bernstein *Viewpoint Inc (LA)*
8820 Wilshire Blvd Ste 220
Beverly Hills, CA 90211-2622, USA

Simmons, Joseph (Rev Run) (Actor, Producer)
Rush Philanthropic Arts Foundation
6 Half Moon Ln
43rd Floor
Prt Washingtn, NY 11050-1204, USA

Simmons, Kimora Lee (Designer, Fashion Designer)
c/o Staff Member *Phat Fashions LLC*
512 Seventh Ave
New York, NY 10018, USA

Simmons, Lionel (Athlete, Basketball Player)
108 Wellesley Ct
Mount Laurel, NJ 08054-5133, USA

Simmons, Lionel J (Athlete, Basketball Player)
108 Wellesley Ct
Mount Laurel, NJ 08054-5133, USA

Simmons, Lon (Sportscaster)
165 Pierce St Apt 443
Daly City, CA 94015-1999, USA

Simmons, Nelson (Athlete)
4445 Rosebud Ln Apt B
La Mesa, CA 91941-6255, USA

Simmons, Richard (Fitness Expert)
c/o Tom Estey *Tom Estey Publicity*
144 E 22nd St Apt 1B
New York, NY 10010-6333, USA

Simmons, Richard P (Business Person)
Allegheny Teledyne
1000 6 Ppg Pl
Pittsburgh, PA 15222, USA

Simmons, Russell (Producer)
1354 N Doheny Dr
Los Angeles, CA 90069-1725, USA

Simmons, Shadia (Actor)
265 GA Highway 30 W
Americus, GA 31719-8502, USA

Simmons, Stacey (Athlete, Football Player)
1780 Harbor Dr
Clearwater, FL 33755-1828, USA

Simmons, Ted L (Athlete, Baseball Player)
PO Box 26
Chesterfield, MO 63006-0026, USA

Simmons, Todd (Baseball Player)
39778 Pinedale Way
Murrieta, CA 92562-6719, USA

Simmons, Tony (Athlete, Football Player)
366 Grand Ave Apt 319
Oakland, CA 94610-4840, USA

Simmons, Vanessa (Model)
c/o Staff Member *Ford Models (LA)*
9200 W Sunset Blvd Ste 805
West Hollywood, CA 90069-3603, USA

Simmons, Victor (Athlete, Football Player)
PO Box 2992
Chicago, IL 60690-2992, USA

Simms, Chris (Football Player)
c/o Team Member *Tampa Bay Buccaneers*
1 Buccaneer Pl
Tampa, FL 33607-5701, USA

Simms, Larry (Actor)
1043 Keeho Marina
Honolulu, HI 96819, USA

Simms, Mike (Athlete, Baseball Player)
118 Via Monte Picayo
San Clemente, CA 92673-6600, USA

Simms, Molly (Actor)
c/o Alissa Vradenburg *Untitled Entertainment (LA)*
350 S Beverly Dr Ste 200
Beverly Hills, CA 90212-4819, USA

Simms, Philip (Phil) (Athlete, Football Player, Sportscaster)
930 Old Mill Rd
Franklin Lakes, NJ 07417-1906, USA

Simo, Brian (Race Car Driver)
28033 Arnold Dr
EC-2
Sonoma, CA 95476-9710, USA

Simollardes, Drew (Musician)
David Levin Mgmt
200 W 57th St Ste 308
New York, NY 10019-3211, USA

Simon, Bob (Correspondent)
c/o 60 Minutes *CBS News (NY)*
524 W 57th St Fl 8
New York, NY 10019-2930, USA

Simon, Corey (Athlete, Football Player)
9010 Winged Foot Dr
Tallahassee, FL 32312-4000, USA

Simon, Daniella (Designer)
Daniella Fashions, Inc
315 W 70th St Apt 8I
New York, NY 10023-3512, USA

Simon, David (Actor, Producer, Writer)
c/o Staff Member *Creative Artists Agency (CAA-LA)*
2000 Avenue of the Stars Ste 100
Los Angeles, CA 90067-4705, USA

Simon, Dick (Race Car Driver)
Dick Simon Racing
24896 Sea Crest Dr
Dana Point, CA 92629-1923, USA

Simon, George W (Astronaut)
PO Box 62
Sunspot, NM 88349-0062, USA

Simon, James (Athlete, Football Player)
8501 SW 103rd Ave
Gainesville, FL 32608-7206, USA

Simon, Neil (Writer)
1836 Deerfield Rd
Water Mill, NY 11976-2109, USA

Simon, Paul (Musician, Songwriter)
82 Brookwood Ln
New Canaan, CT 06840-3101, USA

Simon, Roger M (Writer)
Baltimore Sun
1627 K St NW
Editorial Dept
Washington, DC 20006-1702, USA

Simon, Salem (Athlete, Football Player)
2245 Sheridan Rd
Evanston, IL 60201-2918, USA

Simon, Sam (Director)
c/o Andy Patman *Paradigm (LA)*
360 N Crescent Dr
North Bldg
Beverly Hills, CA 90210-4874, USA

Simon, Scott (Correspondent)
NBC-TV
30 Rockefeller Plz Fl 2
News Dept
New York, NY 10112-0037, USA

Simon, Todd (Athlete, Hockey Player)
Morrell Wine Bar and Cafe
1 Rockefeller Plz
New York, NY 10020-2003

Simone, Hannah (Actor)
c/o Jodi Gottlieb *Independent Public Relations*
Prefers to be contacted via telephone or email
Los Angeles, CA, USA

Simoneau, Mark (Athlete, Football Player)
17 Waterview Dr
Sicklerville, NJ 08081-1683, USA

Simoneau, Yves (Director, Producer, Writer)
c/o Adam Levine *Levine Okwu Erickson Management*
2126 N Commonwealth Ave
Los Angeles, CA 90027-2118, USA

Simonetti, Frank (Athlete, Hockey Player)
33 Perkins St
Stoneham, MA 02180-4345

Simonini, Edward (Ed) (Athlete, Football Player)
3825 E 66th St
Tulsa, OK 74136-2820, USA

Simons, Doug (Athlete, Baseball Player)
1988 Mount Olive Rd
Lookout Mountain, GA 30750-4746, USA

Simons, James (Business Person)
Renaissance Technologies
600 Route 25A
East Setauket, NY 11733-1235, USA

Simons, James (Producer)
c/o Staff Member *Paradigm (LA)*
360 N Crescent Dr
North Bldg
Beverly Hills, CA 90210-4874, USA

Simons, Lawrence B (Government Official)
Powell Goldstein Frazier
1001 Pennsylvania Ave NW
Washington, DC 20004-2505, USA

Simons, Timothy (Actor)
c/o Ben Curtis *Brillstein Entertainment Partners (LA)*
9150 Wilshire Blvd Ste 350
Beverly Hills, CA 90212-3453, USA

Simonson, Dave (Athlete, Football Player)
408 1st St SW
Austin, MN 55912-3254, USA

Simontacchi, Jason (Athlete, Baseball Player)
7300 Summer Manor Dr
Saint Louis, MO 63129-5700, USA

Simpkins, Dickey (Athlete, Basketball Player)
6401 Sail Pointe Ln
Hixson, TN 37343-3196, USA

Simple Kid (Music Group)
c/o Staff Member *Paradigm (Monterey)*
404 W Franklin St
Monterey, CA 93940-2303, USA

Simple Plan (Music Group)
c/o Staff Member *Creative Artists Agency (CAA-LA)*
2000 Avenue of the Stars Ste 100
Los Angeles, CA 90067-4705, USA

Simpson, Alan (Politician)
1201 Sunshine Ave
Cody, WY 82414-4228, USA

Simpson, Alan K (Senator)
1201 Sunshine Ave
PO Box 270
Cody, WY 82414-4228, USA

Simpson, Arnelle
11661 San Vicente Blvd # 632
Los Angeles, CA 90049-5103

Simpson, Bill (Athlete, Football Player)
5732 Huntley Ave
Garden Grove, CA 92845-2040, USA

Simpson, Carl (Athlete, Football Player)
12106 Parkview Ln
Alpharetta, GA 30005-5418, USA

Simpson, Carole (Correspondent)
ABC-TV
77 W 66th St
News Dept
New York, NY 10023-6201, USA

Simpson, Cody (Musician)
PO Box 1766
Studio City, CA 91614-0766, USA

Simpson, Dick (Athlete, Baseball Player)
PO Box 3593
Culver City, CA 90231-3593, USA

Simpson, Duke (Athlete, Baseball Player)
78340 Willowrich Dr
Palm Desert, CA 92211-1309, USA

Simpson, Herbert (Athlete, Baseball Player)
Birmingham Black Barons
1462 Farragut St
New Orleans, LA 70114-2818, USA

Simpson, Jason
11661 San Vicente Blvd # 632
Los Angeles, CA 90049-5103

Simpson, Jessica (Designer, Musician)
5535 Dixon Trail Rd
Hidden Hills, CA 91302-1185, USA

Simpson, Jimmi (Actor)
c/o Staff Member *ROAR (LA)*
9701 Wilshire Blvd Fl 8
Beverly Hills, CA 90212-2008, USA

Simpson, Joe (Producer)
1351 Palisades Beach Rd
Santa Monica, CA 90401-1015, USA

Simpson, Joe (Athlete, Baseball Player)
4681 Jefferson Township Ln
Marietta, GA 30066-1737, USA

Simpson, John (Horse Racer)
51 High Rock Rd N
Hanover, PA 17331-9454, USA

Simpson, Juliene (Athlete, Basketball Player, Olympic Athlete)
PO Box 1267
Stroudsburg, PA 18360-4267, USA

Simpson, Juliene Brazinski (Athlete, Basketball Player)
PO Box 1267
Stroudsburg, PA 18360-4267, USA

Simpson, Keith (Athlete, Football Player)
20710 Castle Bend Dr
Katy, TX 77450-4911, USA

Simpson, Ralph (Athlete, Basketball Player)
5185 Fraser St
Denver, CO 80239, USA

Simpson, Reid (Athlete, Hockey Player)
340 W Superior St Apt 1210
Chicago, IL 60654-6190

Simpson, Scott (Athlete, Golfer)
15778 Paseo Hermoso
Poway, CA 92064-2164, USA

Simpson, Suzi (Actor, Model)
24338 El Toro Rd # E315
Laguna Woods, CA 92637-2776, USA

Simpson, Terry (Coach)
Anaheim Mighty Ducks
2000 E Gene Autry Way
Anaheim, CA 92806-6143, USA

Simpson, Wayne K (Athlete, Baseball Player)
330 E Collamer Dr
Carson, CA 90746-1139, USA

Simpson, Webb (Athlete, Golfer)
c/o Thomas Parker *GPR Sports Management*
11715 Spinnaker Way
Hollywood, FL 33026-1233, USA

Simpson, William (Writer)
c/o Staff Member *HarperCollins Publishers*
195 Broadway Fl 2
Cellar 1
New York, NY 10007-3132, USA

Simpson Sr, John F (Race Car Driver)
Mount Morris Star Route
Waynesburg, PA 15370, USA

Simpson-Wentz, Ashlee (Actor, Musician)
3767 Reklaw Dr
Studio City, CA 91604-3830, USA

Sims, Al (Athlete, Hockey Player)
4215 Winding Way Dr
Fort Wayne, IN 46835-1466

Sims, Barry (Athlete, Football Player)
369 Golden Grass Dr
Alamo, CA 94507-2788, USA

Sims, Billy R (Athlete, Football Player)
PO Box 3147
Coppell, TX 75019-9147, USA

Sims, Darryl (Athlete, Football Player)
PO Box 379
Mc Farland, WI 53558-0379, USA

Sims, Dion (Athlete, Football Player)
c/o Alan Herman *Sportstars Inc*
1350 Avenue of the Americas Fl 28
New York, NY 10019-4702, USA

Sims, Duane (Duke) (Athlete, Baseball Player)
10509 Shoalhaven Dr
Las Vegas, NV 89134-7425, USA

Sims, Duane ""Duke"" (Athlete, Baseball Player)
10509 Shoalhaven Dr
Las Vegas, NV 89134-7425, USA

Sims, Greg (Athlete, Baseball Player)
6700 Rancho Pico Way
Sacramento, CA 95828-1325, USA

Sims, Heath (Athlete, Olympic Athlete, Wrestler)
1027 Pearl St Apt 4
La Jolla, CA 92037-5162, USA

Sims, Keith (Athlete, Football Player)
2920 Luckie Rd
Weston, FL 33331-3005, USA

Sims, Ken (Athlete, Football Player)
4898 Converse Ave
East Saint Louis, IL 62207-2533, USA

Sims, Kenneth W (Athlete, Football Player)
PO Box 236
Kosse, TX 76653-0236, USA

Sims, Molly (Actor, Model)
43 S Breeze Dr
East Hampton, NY 11937-8468, USA

Sims, Rob (Athlete, Football Player)
c/o Joel Segal *Lagardere Unlimited (NYC)*
845 United Nations Plz Apt 39B
New York, NY 10017-3533, USA

Sims, Robert (Athlete, Basketball Player)
915 Highland Ave Apt 3
Duarte, CA 91010-1935, USA

Simses, Kate (Actor)
c/o Ken Treusch *Bleecker Street Entertainment*
853 Broadway Ste 1214
New York, NY 10003-4717, USA

Sinatra, Nancy (Actor, Musician)
c/o Thomas De Lorenzo *SmartPR*
8033 W Sunset Blvd Ste 1033
Los Angeles, CA 90046-2401, USA

Sinatra, Ray
1234 8th Pl
Las Vegas, NV 89104-1555

Sinatra Jr, Frank (Musician)
c/o Seth Shomes *Day After Day Productions*
436 1st St Ste 102
Solvang, CA 93463-3710, USA

Sinatro, Matt (Athlete, Baseball Player)
2619 239th Ave SE
Sammamish, WA 98075-9442, USA

Sinbad (Actor, Comedian)
6520 Platt Ave # 814
West Hills, CA 91307-3218, USA

Sinceno, Kaseem (Athlete, Football Player)
168B Bradford Ct
Mount Laurel, NJ 08054-3705, USA

Sinclair, Harry (Director, Writer)
c/o Ken Kamins *ICM Partners (LA)*
10250 Constellation Blvd Fl 7
Los Angeles, CA 90067-6207, USA

Sinclair, Michael (Athlete, Football Player)
1914 Pannell St
Houston, TX 77020-2339, USA

Sindelar, Jerry
213 Prospect Hill Rd
Horseheads, NY 14845

Sindelar, Joan (Baseball Player)
504 W Sunland Ave
Phoenix, AZ 85041-4822, USA

Sindelar, Joey (Golfer)
18 Prospect Rdg
Horseheads, NY 14845-7988, USA

Sinden, Harry (Athlete, Hockey Player)
9 Olde Village Dr
Winchester, MA 01890-2213

Sinden, Harry (Athlete, Hockey Player)
Boston Bruins
100 Legends Way Ste 250
Boston, MA 02114-1389

Sinegal, James (Business Person)
Costco Wholesale Corp
999 Lake Dr
Issaquah, WA 98027-8990, USA

Singer, Bryan (Director)
c/o Staff Member *Bad Hat Harry Productions*
4000 Warner Blvd Bldg 200
Burbank, CA 91522-0001, USA

Singer, Lori (Actor)
Chuck Binder
1465 Lindacrest Dr
Beverly Hills, CA 90210-2519, USA

Singer, Marc (Actor)
11218 Canton Dr
Studio City, CA 91604-4154, USA

Singer, Ramona (Designer, Reality Star)
c/o Staff Member *CEG Talent*
251 W 39th St Fl 7
New York, NY 10018-3171, USA

Singer, William R (Bill) (Athlete, Baseball Player)
1119 Mallard Marsh Dr
Osprey, FL 34229-6810, USA

Singh, Tjinder (Musician)
Legends of 21st Century
7 Trinity Row
Florence, MA 01062-1931, USA

Singh, Vijay (Golfer)
1275 Ponte Vedra Blvd
Ponte Vedra Beach, FL 32082-4402, USA

Singletary, Daryl
1000 18th Ave S
Nashville, TN 37212-2105

Singletary, Mike (Athlete, Coach, Football
Coach, Football Player)
c/o Bob LaMonte *Professional Sports
Representation*
1220 Plumas St
Reno, NV 89509-2745, USA

Singletary, Tony (Director)
c/o Staff Member *Agency for the
Performing Arts (APA-LA)*
405 S Beverly Dr Ste 500
Beverly Hills, CA 90212-4425, USA

Singleton, Chris (Athlete, Baseball Player)
2038 Town Manor Ct
Dacula, GA 30019-3247, USA

Singleton, Chris (Athlete, Football Player)
42599 W Sunland Dr
Maricopa, AZ 85138-1632, USA

Singleton, Duane (Athlete, Baseball
Player)
191 MacDonough St
Brooklyn, NY 11216-2507, USA

Singleton, Isaac (Actor)
c/o Jason Mellerstig *Artist International
Management (LA)*
9595 Wilshire Blvd Fl 9
Beverly Hills, CA 90212-2512, USA

Singleton, John D (Director, Producer,
Writer)
c/o Staff Member *Creative Artists Agency
(CAA-LA)*
2000 Avenue of the Stars Ste 100
Los Angeles, CA 90067-4705, USA

Singleton, Kenneth W (Kenny) (Athlete,
Baseball Player)
10 Sparks Farm Rd
Sparks Glencoe, MD 21152-9300, USA

Singleton, Margie (Musician)
PO Box 567
Hendersonville, TN 37077-0567, USA

Sinisalo, Ilkka (Athlete, Hockey Player)
6221 Main St
Voorhees, NJ 08043-4629

Sinise, Gary (Actor)
c/o Marc Gurvitz *Brillstein Entertainment
Partners (LA)*
9150 Wilshire Blvd Ste 350
Beverly Hills, CA 90212-3453, USA

Sinn, Pearl (Golfer)
132 21st Pl
Manhattan Beach, CA 90266-4402, USA

Sinner, George (Politician)
1013th St N
Moorhead, MN 56560, USA

Sinner, George A (Ex-Governor)
101 3rd St N
Moorhead, MN 56560-1952, USA

Sinnott, John (Athlete, Football Player)
9 Primrose Ln
North Providence, RI 02904-3840, USA

Siouxsie & The Banshees
1325 Avenue of the Americas
New York, NY 10019-6026

Sipchen, Bob (Journalist)
Los Angeles Times
202 W 1st St Ste 500
Editorial Dept
Los Angeles, CA 90012-4401, USA

Sipe, Brian W (Athlete, Football Player)
17 E H St
Encinitas, CA 92024-3616, USA

Sipin, John (Athlete, Baseball Player)
455 Ponza Ln
Soquel, CA 95073-9528, USA

Sipos, Shaun (Actor)
c/o Sheila Wenzel *Innovative Artists (LA)*
1505 10th St
Santa Monica, CA 90401-2805, USA

Sipp, Tony (Athlete, Baseball Player)
3976 River Pine Dr
Moss Point, MS 39563, USA

Sippy Cups, The (Music Group)
c/o Staff Member *Paradigm (Monterey)*
404 W Franklin St
Monterey, CA 93940-2303, USA

Siragusa, Tony (Athlete, Football Player)
349 Ashwood Ave
Kenilworth, NJ 07033-2056, USA

Sir Douglas Quintet
59 Parsons St
Newtonville, MA 02160

Sires, Albin (Congressman, Politician)
2342 Rayburn Hob
Washington, DC 20515-3603, USA

Sirhan, Sirhan
#B21014Corcoran State Prison Box 8800
Corcoran, CA 93212

Siriano, Christian (Designer, Reality Star)
260 W 35th St
New York, NY 10001-2503, USA

Sirico, Tony (Actor)
c/o Bob McGowan *McGowan
Management*
8733 W Sunset Blvd Ste 103
West Hollywood, CA 90069-2241, USA

Siri Singh Sahib (Religious Leader)
Sikh
PO Box 351149
Los Angeles, CA 90035-9549, USA

Sir Mix-a-Lot (Musician)
16727 SE Lake Holm Rd
Auburn, WA 98092-5926, USA

Sirmon, Peter (Athlete, Football Player)
5255 McGavock Rd
Brentwood, TN 37027-5197, USA

Sirotka, Mike (Athlete, Baseball Player)
4200 Scotland St Apt 839
Houston, TX 77007-7553, USA

Sirtis, Marina (Actor)
c/o Alan Saffron *Saffron Management*
9171 Wilshire Blvd Ste 441
Beverly Hills, CA 90210-5516, USA

Sisco, Andrew (Athlete, Baseball Player)
25324 176th Ave SE
Covington, WA 98042-6709, USA

Sisco, Steve (Athlete, Baseball Player)
630 San Doval Pl
Thousand Oaks, CA 91360-1314, USA

Sisemore, Jerald G (Jerry) (Athlete,
Football Player)
17301 Whippoorwill Trl
Lago Vista, TX 78645-9734, USA

Sisk, Bradford (Producer)
c/o Staff Member *Bankable Productions*
226 W 26th St Fl 4
New York, NY 10001-6700, USA

Sisk, Doug (Athlete, Baseball Player)
2141 E Trails End Dr
Belfair, WA 98528-9546, USA

Sisk, John (Athlete, Football Player)
7814 W Wisconsin Ave
Milwaukee, WI 53213-3420, USA

Sisk, Tommie (Athlete, Baseball Player)
164 E 4635 N
Provo, UT 84604-5447, USA

Sisko, David (Race Car Driver)
2125 Linden Hwy
Hohenwald, TN 38462-2375, USA

Sislen, Myrna (Musician)
Lindy Martin Mgmt
5 Loblolly Ct
Pinehurst, NC 28374-9349, USA

Sisman, Adam (Writer)
c/o Staff Member *Penguin Press HC*
375 Hudson St Bsmt 3
New York, NY 10014-7465, USA

Sissel, George A (Business Person)
Ball Corp
10 Longs Peak Dr
Broomfield, CO 80021-2510, USA

Sissi (Actor)
c/o Staff Member *Univision*
605 3rd Ave Fl 12
New York, NY 10158-0034, USA

Sisson, Doug (Athlete, Baseball Player)
1821 Matts Ln
Watkinsville, GA 30677-4862, USA

Sisson, Scott (Athlete, Football Player)
902 Ravenwood Way
Canton, GA 30115-6421, USA

Sissons, Kimber (Actor)
412 Amaz Dr
#204
Los Angeles, CA 90048, USA

Sister Hazel (Music Group)
c/o Staff Member *Sixthman*
83 Walton St NW
Atlanta, GA 30303-2179, USA

Sisto, Jeremy (Actor)
7674 Willow Glen Rd
Los Angeles, CA 90046-1609, USA

Sistrunk, Manny (Athlete, Football Player)
1601 Jarvis Ave
Oxon Hill, MD 20745-3243, USA

Sistrunk, Otis (Athlete, Football Player)
PO Box 372
Dupont, WA 98327-0372, USA

Sites, Brian (Actor)
c/o Staff Member *Innovative Artists (LA)*
1505 10th St
Santa Monica, CA 90401-2805, USA

Sites, James W (Producer)
American Legion Magazine
700 N Pennsylvania St
Indianapolis, IN 46204-1172, USA

Sitkovetsky, Dmitry (Musician)
Columbia Artists Mgmt Inc
165 W 57th St
New York, NY 10019-2201, USA

Sitter, Charles R (Business Person)
Exxon Corp
5959 Las Colinas Blvd
Irving, TX 75039-2298, USA

Sittler, Darrell (Athlete, Hockey Player)
84 Buttonwood Ct
East Amherst, NY 14051-1644, USA

Sitton, Charles (Athlete, Basketball Player)
3035 SW Homesteader Rd
West Linn, OR 97068-9612, USA

Sivad, Darryl (Actor)
c/o Staff Member *Leavitt Talent Group*
8222 Melrose Ave Ste 203
Los Angeles, CA 90046-6838, USA

Sivan, Santosh (Cinematographer,
Director, Writer)
c/o Staff Member *Paradigm (LA)*
360 N Crescent Dr
North Bldg
Beverly Hills, CA 90210-4874, USA

Siwy, Jim (Athlete, Baseball Player)
6919 April Wind Ave
Las Vegas, NV 89131-0119, USA

Six Shooter
PO Box 53
Portland, TN 37148-0053

Sixthman (Music Group, Musician)
158 Moreland Ave SE
Atlanta, GA 30316-1676, USA

Sixx
9255 W Sunset Blvd Ste 200
West Hollywood, CA 90069-3308

Sixx, Nikki (Musician)
Royal Underground
2532 White Rd
Irvine, CA 92614-6236, USA

Sizemore, Grady (Athlete, Baseball
Player)
1951 W 26th St Apt 512
Cleveland, OH 44113-3467, USA

Sizemore, Marge
1951 Bottlebrush Dr
Melbourne, FL 32935-4783, USA

Sizemore, Matt (Adult Film Star)
c/o Staff Member *Diva Central Inc*
7510 W Sunset Blvd Ste 1445
Los Angeles, CA 90046-3408, USA

Sizemore, Ted (Athlete, Baseball Player)
14030 Conway Rd
Chesterfield, MO 63017-3402, USA

Sizemore, Tom (Actor)
c/o Staff Member *Evolution Entertainment
(LA)*
901 N Highland Ave
Los Angeles, CA 90038-2412, USA

Sjostrom, Fredrik (Athlete, Hockey Player)
18362 N 94th Pl
Scottsdale, AZ 85255

Skaalen, Jim (Athlete, Baseball Player)
2608 El Aguila Ln
Carlsbad, CA 92009-4332, USA

Skabo, Paul
529 Nevada St
Sausalito, CA 94965-1613, USA

Skaggs, Dave (Athlete, Baseball Player)
11131 Arlington Ave
Riverside, CA 92505-2148, USA

Skaggs, Jim (Athlete, Football Player)
421 Falcon Ridge Rd
Ellensburg, WA 98926-5037, USA

Skaggs, Ricky (Actor, Musician)
c/o Bobby Cudd *Paradigm (Nashville)*
124 12th Ave S Ste 410
Nashville, TN 37203-3170, USA

Skala, Brian T (Actor)
c/o Staff Member *Osbrink Talent Agency*
4343 Lankershim Blvd Ste 100
North Hollywood, CA 91602-2705, USA

Skalde, Jarrod (Athlete, Hockey Player)
2454 Beaufort Ave
Virginia Beach, VA 23455-1376, USA

Skalski, Joe (Athlete, Baseball Player)
15546 Drexel Ave
Dolton, IL 60419-2750, USA

Skarda, Randy (Athlete, Hockey Player)
26885 Noble Rd
Excelsior, MN 55331-8239

Skarsgard, Alexander (Actor)
5699 Holly Oak Dr
Los Angeles, CA 90068-2521, USA

Skarsgard, Gustaf (Actor)
c/o Jim Dempsey *Paradigm (LA)*
360 N Crescent Dr
North Bldg
Beverly Hills, CA 90210-4874, USA

Skarsten, Rachel (Actor)
c/o Steve Lovett *Lovett Management*
1327 Brinkley Ave
Los Angeles, CA 90049-3619, USA

Skaugstad, Daryle (Athlete, Football
Player)
17216 NE 195th St
Woodinville, WA 98072, USA

Skaugstad, Dave (Athlete, Baseball Player)
16222 Monterey Ln Spc 274
Huntington Beach, CA 92649-2248, USA

Skayskal, Wayne
PO Box 191
Tampa, FL 33601-0191

Skeels, Mark (Baseball Player)
1835 Hilton Head Rd
El Cajon, CA 92019-4472, USA

Skeen, Archie (Baseball Player)
2685 N 4275 W
Ogden, UT 84404-9074, USA

Skeet, DJ Skeet (DJ)
c/o Ron Laffitte *Red Light Management
(LA)*
8439 W Sunset Blvd Ste 2
West Hollywood, CA 90069-1925, USA

Skeeters, The (Music Group)
c/o Staff Member *Paradigm (Monterey)*
404 W Franklin St
Monterey, CA 93940-2303, USA

Skelton, Mike (Writer)
c/o Jon Huddle *United Talent Agency
(UTA-LA)*
9336 Civic Center Dr
Beverly Hills, CA 90210-3604, USA

Skerritt, Tom (Actor)
c/o Amy Weiss *Brillstein Entertainment
Partners (LA)*
9150 Wilshire Blvd Ste 350
Beverly Hills, CA 90212-3453, USA

Skibinski, Joe (Athlete, Football Player)
1515 Barrington Rd Apt 220
Hoffman Estates, IL 60169-1076, USA

Skidmore, Paul (Athlete, Hockey Player)
469W 760 N
Santaquin, UT 84655

Skidmore, Roe (Athlete, Baseball Player)
964 E Marlin Dr
Decatur, IL 62521-5549, USA

Skid Row (Music Group)
720 E Palisade Ave
Englewood Cliffs, NJ 07632-3053, USA

Skiles, Scott (Athlete, Basketball Player)
3975 S Inverness Farm Rd
Bloomington, IN 47401-9190, USA

Skillet (Music Group)
c/o Zach Kelm *Q Management Group*
PO Box 273
Franklin, TN 37065-0273, USA

Skinner, Al (Athlete, Basketball Player)
145 Great Plain Ave
Wellesley, MA 02482-7211, USA

Skinner, Jeff (Athlete, Hockey Player)
c/o Darren Ferris *ARC Sports Group*
PO Box 290836
Charlestown, MA 02129-0215, USA

Skinner, Joel P (Athlete, Baseball Player,
Coach)
275 Pamilla Cir
Avon Lake, OH 44012-1973, USA

Skinner, Jonty (Coach, Swimmer)
University of Alabama
Athletic Dept
Tuscaloosa, AL 35487-0001, USA

Skinner, Mike (Race Car Driver)
Mike Skinner Enterprises
3685 Highway
152 W
China Grove, NC 28023, USA

Skinner, Robert R (Bob) (Athlete, Baseball
Player, Coach)
1576 Diamond St
San Diego, CA 92109-3050, USA

Skinner, Samuel K (Business Person,
Secretary)
Commonwealth Edison
PO Box 767
1 First National Plaza
Chicago, IL 60690-0767, USA

Skinner, Sonny (Golfer)
114 Northlake Dr
Sylvester, GA 31791-3909, USA

Skinner, Val (Golfer)
44 Bridge Ave
Bay Head, NJ 08742-4747, USA

Skinny Puppy (Music Group, Musician)
c/o Jeremy Holgersen *The Agency Group
(NYC)*
142 W 57th St Fl 6
New York, NY 10019-3300, USA

Skizas, Lou (Athlete, Baseball Player)
1125 Baytowne Dr Apt 18
Champaign, IL 61822-6903, USA

Skladany, John (Athlete, Football Player)
541 Wilmington Cir
Oviedo, FL 32765-6988

Skladany, Thomas E (Tom) (Athlete,
Football Player)
6666 Highland Lakes Pl
Westerville, OH 43082-8703, USA

Sklar, Jason (Comedian, Sportscaster)
8522 Edwin Dr
Los Angeles, CA 90046-1028, USA

Sklar, Randy (Comedian, Sportscaster)
2310 Kenilworth Ave
Los Angeles, CA 90039-3042, USA

Skok, Craig (Athlete, Baseball Player)
981 Slash Pine Way
Lawrenceville, GA 30043-3465, USA

Skoll, Jeff (Business Person, Producer)
Skoll Foundation
250 University Ave Ste 200
Palo Alto, CA 94301-1738, USA

Skolnik, Michael (Business Person)
c/o Staff Member *Article 19 Films*
247 Centre St Ste 7W
New York, NY 10013-3216, USA

Skoog, Meyer (Whitey) (Athlete,
Basketball Player, Coach)
1545 Aspen Dr
Saint Peter, MN 56082-1586, USA

Skoog, Myer (Athlete, Baseball Player)
1302 W Traverse Rd Apt 203
Saint Peter, MN 56082-1748, USA

Skoronski, Bob (Athlete, Football Player)
3907 Signature Dr
Middleton, WI 53562-2388, USA

Skorupan, John P (Athlete, Football
Player)
142 Crossing Ridge Trl
Cranberry Township, PA 16066-6512,
USA

Skoula, Martin (Athlete, Hockey Player)
2441 Sheridan Aves
Minneapolis, MN 55405

Skov, Glen (Athlete, Hockey Player)
3898 Timber Ridge Ct
Palm Harbor, FL 34685-3127

Skrepenak, Greg (Athlete, Football Player)
Hyders Total Fitnbess Center
400 Middle Rd
Nanticoke, PA 18634-3821, USA

Skribble (DJ)
c/o Len Evans *Project Publicity*
312 W 53rd St Ste 202
New York, NY 10019-5743, USA

Skrillex (DJ, Musician)
c/o Ryan Downey *Blood Company*
PO Box 46851
Los Angeles, CA 90046-0851, USA

Skrine, Buster (Athlete, Football Player)
c/o Alan Herman *Sportstars Inc*
1350 Avenue of the Americas Fl 28
New York, NY 10019-4702, USA

Skrmetta, Matt (Athlete, Baseball Player)
527 Siena Ct
Satellite Beach, FL 32937-2991, USA

Skrovan, Steve (Comedian)
c/o Staff Member *William Morris
Endeavor (LA)*
9601 Wilshire Blvd
Beverly Hills, CA 90210-5213, USA

Skrudland, Brian (Athlete, Hockey Player)
Florida Panthers
1 Panther Pkwy
Sunrise, FL 33323-5315

Skrypnk, Metropolitan Mstyslav S
(Religious Leader)
Ukranian Orthodox Church
PO Box 445
South Bound Brook, NJ 08880-0445, USA

Skube, Bob (Athlete, Baseball Player)
7135 W Foothill Dr
Glendale, AZ 85310-5817, USA

Skufca, Scott (Race Car Driver)
5903 Reynolds Rd
Mentor On The Lake, OH 44060-3033,
USA

Skuza, Dean (Race Car Driver)
650 Ken Mar Industrial Pkwy
Broadview Heights, OH 44147-2918,
USA

Sky, Jennifer (Actor)
12533 Woodgreen St
Los Angeles, CA 90066-2723, USA

Sky, Nina (Music Group, Musician)
c/o Tammy Brook *FYI Public Relations*
174 5th Ave Ste 404
New York, NY 10010-5964, USA

Skye, Azura (Actor)
c/o Brian Wilkins *Kritzer Levine Wilkins
Entertainment (KLWG)*
11872 La Grange Ave Fl 1
Los Angeles, CA 90025-5283, USA

Skye, Ione (Actor)
c/o Mike Packenham *Concrete
Entertainment*
468 N Camden Dr # 200
Beverly Hills, CA 90210-4507, USA

Sky Eats Airplane (Music Group,
Musician)
c/o Brigitte Wright *Brigitte Wright
Management*
1674 Broadway Fl 3
New York, NY 10019-5861, USA

Slaby, Lou (Athlete, Football Player)
6 Elder Pl
Denville, NJ 07834-9312, USA

Slack, Reggie (Athlete, Football Player)
5973 Queen St
Milton, FL 32570-3574, USA

Slack, Reggie
6653 Walker St
Milton, FL 32570-6672, USA

Slade, Bernard N (Writer)
345 N Saltair Ave
Los Angeles, CA 90049-2914, USA

Slade, Chris (Athlete, Football Player)
4810 Ivy Ridge Dr SE Unit 201
Atlanta, GA 30339-1352, USA

Slade, David (Director)
c/o Keith Redmon *Anonymous Content
(LA)*
3532 Hayden Ave
Culver City, CA 90232-2413, USA

Slade, Jeff (Athlete, Basketball Player)
5354 Farmington Rd
Toledo, OH 43623-2636, USA

Slade, Mark (Actor)
38 Joppa Rd
Worcester, MA 01602-2230, USA

Slagle, James R
13630 Barryknoll Ln
Houston, TX 77079-5928, USA

Slagle, Roger (Athlete, Baseball Player)
7560 George Nash Rd
White House, TN 37188-5101, USA

Slagle, Tim (Race Car Driver)
2824 Dorr Ave Ste E
Fairfax, VA 22031-1516, USA

Slaney, John (Athlete, Hockey Player)
Portland Pirates
94 Free St
Portland, ME 04101-3920

Slaney, John (Athlete, Hockey Player)
11 Hunts Point Rd
Cape Elizabeth, ME 04107-2926

Slaney, Mary Decker (Athlete, Olympic Athlete, Track Athlete)
87141 Kellmore St
Eugene, OR 97402-9128, USA

Slash (Musician)
PO Box 57593
Sherman Oaks, CA 91413-2593, USA

Slaten, Doug (Athlete, Baseball Player)
233 Rennie Ave
Venice, CA 90291-2645, USA

Slater, Bob (Baseball Player)
4322 Avenida Rio Del Oro
Yorba Linda, CA 92886-3011, USA

Slater, Christian (Actor)
3618 Saint Gaudens Rd
Miami, FL 33133-6533, USA

Slater, Jackie (Athlete, Football Player)
PO Box 6411
Orange, CA 92863-6411, USA

Slater, Kelly (Actor, Athlete)
Quiksilver Inc
15202 Graham St
Huntington Beach, CA 92649-1109, USA

Slater, Mark (Athlete, Football Player)
10545 Rome Ave
Young America, MN 55397-9468, USA

Slater, Matthew (Athlete, Football Player)
c/o Ryan Tollner *REP 1 Sports Group*
2 Corporate Park Ste 106
Irvine, CA 92606-5103, USA

Slater, Ryan
3500 W Olive Ave Ste 1400
Burbank, CA 91505-5512

Slater, Suzanne
10000 Riverside Dr Ste 10
Toluca Lake, CA 91602-2537

Slaton, Jim (Athlete, Baseball Player)
4082 N Arbor Ln
Buckeye, AZ 85396-3603, USA

Slaton, Mike (Athlete, Football Player)
7691 Park Village Rd
San Diego, CA 92129-4514, USA

Slaton, Tony (Athlete, Football Player)
122 E Childs Ave
Merced, CA 95341-6346, USA

Slaught, Don (Athlete, Baseball Player)
27 Middleridge Ln S
Rolling Hills, CA 90274-4055, USA

Slaughter (Music Group)
c/o Staff Member *Artist Representation & Management*
1257 Arcade St
Saint Paul, MN 55106-2022

Slaughter, Frank (Doctor)
Box 14 Ortega Station
Jacksonville, FL 32210, USA

Slaughter, J Mack (Actor)
c/o Jeff Golenberg *Silver Lining Entertainment*
421 S Beverly Dr Fl 7
Beverly Hills, CA 90212-4408, USA

Slaughter, Mickey (Athlete, Football Player)
1402 Mesa Ave
Ruston, LA 71270-2032, USA

Slaughter, Stering (Athlete, Baseball Player)
742 E Avenida Sierra Madre
Gilbert, AZ 85296-1108, USA

Slaughter, Sterling (Athlete, Baseball Player)
742 E Avenida Sierra Madre
Gilbert, AZ 85296-1108, USA

Slaughter, Webster (Athlete, Football Player)
3706 Rory Ct
Missouri City, TX 77459-6662, USA

Slavin, Randall (Actor)
Gold Marshak Liedtke
3500 W Olive Ave Ste 1400
Burbank, CA 91505-5512, USA

Slavitt, David R (Writer)
35 West St Apt 5
Cambridge, MA 02139-1723, USA

Slay, Brandon (Wrestler)
6155 Lehman Dr
Colorado Springs, CO 80918-3456, USA

Slay, Darius (Athlete, Football Player)
c/o Eugene Parker *Maximum Sports Management*
6435 W Jefferson Blvd # 197
Fort Wayne, IN 46804-6203, USA

Slayback, Bill (Athlete, Baseball Player)
25710 Armstrong Cir Unit E
Stevenson Ranch, CA 91381-2336, USA

Slayer (Music Group)
c/o Rick Sales *Rick Sales Entertainment Group*
5355 Cartwright Ave
North Hollywood, CA 91601-3481, USA

Slayton, Bobby (Comedian)
c/o Sherry Marsh *Marsh Entertainment*
12444 Ventura Blvd Ste 203
Studio City, CA 91604-2409, USA

Sleater, Lou (Athlete, Baseball Player)
12 Bandon Ct Unit 102
Lutherville Timonium, MD 21093-7504, USA

Sledd, William L (Internet Star)
PO Box 3714
Paducah, KY 42002-3714, USA

Sledge, Kathy (Musician)
c/o Staff Member *Webster & Associates PR*
3573 Couchville Pike
Hermitage, TN 37076-4012, USA

Sledge, Leroy (Athlete, Football Player)
6036 Golden Gate Cir
Dallas, TX 75241-5258, USA

Sledge, Percy (Musician)
c/o Terry Shields
9430 Palmetto Ln
Shreveport, LA 71118-4012, USA

Sledge, Termel (Athlete, Baseball Player)
30041 Medford Pl
Castaic, CA 91384-4565, USA

Sledge, Terrmel (Athlete, Baseball Player)
30041 Medford Pl
Castaic, CA 91384-4565, USA

Sleepy Jackson, The (Music Group)
c/o Staff Member *Paradigm (Monterey)*
404 W Franklin St
Monterey, CA 93940-2303, USA

Slegr, Jirl (Athlete, Hockey Player)
1 Fleetcenter Pl
Boston, MA 02114-1300, USA

Slezak, Erika (Actor)
International Creative Mgmt
40 W 57th St Fl 5
New York, NY 10019-4001, USA

Slice, Kimbo (Athlete, Wrestler)
c/o Raphael Berko *Media Artists Group (LA)*
8222 Melrose Ave Ste 203
Los Angeles, CA 90046-6838, USA

Slichter, Jacob (Musician)
Monterey Peninsula Artists
509 Hartnell St
Monterey, CA 93940-2825, USA

Slick, Grace (Musician, Songwriter)
5956 Kanan Dume Rd
Malibu, CA 90265-4027, USA

Slick, Rick (Musician)
Famous Artists Agency
250 W 57th St
New York, NY 10107-0001, USA

Slider, Rac (Athlete, Baseball Player)
123 County Rd 3306
De Kalb, TX 75559, USA

Slightly Stoopid (Music Group)
c/o Jon Phillips *Silverback Professional Artist Management*
9469 Jefferson Blvd Ste 101
Culver City, CA 90232-2915, USA

Slipknot (Musician)
c/o Staff Member *The Agency Group (NYC)*
142 W 57th St Fl 6
New York, NY 10019-3300, USA

Sliwa, Curtis
215 E 96th St
New York, NY 10128-3835, USA

Sliwinska, Edyta (Dancer, Reality Star)
c/o Bob Knotek *McCann - Knotek Associates*
8539 W Sunset Blvd Ste 4-136
West Hollywood, CA 90069-2334, USA

Sloan (Music Group)
c/o Staff Member *Paradigm (Monterey)*
404 W Franklin St
Monterey, CA 93940-2303, USA

Sloan, David (Athlete, Football Player)
10898 E Butherus Dr
Scottsdale, AZ 85255-1848, USA

Sloan, Ed (Musician)
216 Lincoln St
West Columbia, SC 29170-1812, USA

Sloan, Gerald E (Jerry) (Basketball Player, Coach)
300 S Washington St
Mc Leansboro, IL 62859-1141, USA

Sloan, Holly Goldberg (Director)
Sanford-Beckett-Skouras
1015 Gayley Ave Ste 300
Los Angeles, CA 90024-3440, USA

Sloan, Jerry (Athlete, Basketball Player)
13103 S Riverbendview Cv
Riverton, UT 84065-6262, USA

Sloan, P F (Musician, Songwriter, Writer)
All the Best
PO Box 164
Cedarhurst, NY 11516-0164, USA

Sloan, Stephen C (Steve) (Coach, Football Coach, Football Player)
University of Central Florida
Athletic Dept
Orlando, FL 32816-0001, USA

Sloane, Carol (Musician)
c/o Jerry Kravat *Park Avenue Talent*
1560 Broadway # 1100
New York, NY 10036-1537, USA

Sloane, Lindsay (Actor)
c/o Ron West *Thruline Entertainment*
9250 Wilshire Blvd Ste 100
Ground Floor
Beverly Hills, CA 90212-3343, USA

Sloat, Micah (Actor)
c/o Alex Cole *Elevate Entertainment*
5757 Wilshire Blvd Ste 460
Los Angeles, CA 90036-3658, USA

Sloatman, Lala
11917 Vose St
North Hollywood, CA 91605-5750

Slobodyanik, Alexander (Musician)
Columbia Artists Mgmt Inc
165 W 57th St
New York, NY 10019-2201, USA

Slocum, Brian (Athlete, Baseball Player)
435 Steinway Rd
Saddle Brook, NJ 07663-5913, USA

Slocum, Heath (Golfer)
5640 Keystone Rd
Pensacola, FL 32504-8416, USA

Slocum, Ron (Athlete, Baseball Player)
34641 Elmwood Ln
Yucaipa, CA 92399-6842, USA

Slocumb, Heathcliff (Heath) (Athlete, Baseball Player)
1045 Arthur St
Uniondale, NY 11553-3103, USA

Slosburg, Phil (Athlete, Football Player)
9896 Bustleton Ave Apt B317
Philadelphia, PA 19115-5234, USA

Slotnick, Joey (Actor)
Gersh Agency
232 N Canon Dr
Beverly Hills, CA 90210-5302, USA

Slotnick, R Nathan (Doctor)
825 Fairfax Ave
Norfolk, VA 23507-1914, USA

Slovin, Eric (Writer)
c/o Staff Member *Principato/Young Management (LA)*
9465 Wilshire Blvd Ste 900
Beverly Hills, CA 90212-2608, USA

Slowes, Charles (Baseball Player, Sportscaster)
Tampa Bay Devil Rays
3936 Mimosa Pl
Palm Harbor, FL 34685-3674, USA

Slowey, Kevin (Athlete, Baseball Player)
1748 Quigg Dr
Pittsburgh, PA 15241-2023, USA

Sloyan, James (Actor)
920 Kagawa St
Pacific Palisades, CA 90272-3833, USA

Sluby, Tom (Athlete, Basketball Player)
39 Poplar St
Ramsey, NJ 07446-1535, USA

Sluman, Jeff (Golfer)
808 McKinley Ln
Hinsdale, IL 60521-4831, USA

Slusarski, Joe (Athlete, Baseball Player, Olympic Athlete)
8701 Ken Aaron Ct
Austin, TX 78717-5489, USA

Slutskaya, Irina (Figure Skater)
c/o Staff Member *Champions on Ice*
3500 American Blvd W Ste 190
Minneapolis, MN 55431-4431, USA

Smaby, Matt (Athlete, Hockey Player)
5037 Newton Aves
Minneapolis, MN 55419

Smagala, Stan (Athlete, Football Player)
13155 Meadow Hill Ln
Lemont, IL 60439-6743, USA

Smail, Doug (Athlete, Hockey Player)
23550 Pondview Pl
Golden, CO 80401-9353

Smajstria, Craig (Athlete, Baseball Player)
2520 Creeks Edge Dr
Pearland, TX 77581-4488, USA

Smajstrla, Craig (Athlete, Baseball Player)
2520 Creeks Edge Dr
Pearland, TX 77581-4488, USA

Small, Aaron (Athlete, Baseball Player)
775 Loudon Rd
Loudon, TN 37774-6705, USA

Small, Jim (Athlete, Baseball Player)
7960 Island Ln
Stanwood, MI 49346-8920, USA

Small, Mark (Athlete, Baseball Player)
10605 229th Pl SW
Edmonds, WA 98020-6151, USA

Small, Mary
165 W 66th St
New York, NY 10023-6508

Small, Marya (Actor)
CL Inc
843 N Sycamore Ave
Los Angeles, CA 90038-3316, USA

Small, Torrance (Athlete, Football Player)
66 Chateau Mouton Dr
Kenner, LA 70065-1903, USA

Smalley, Roy (Athlete, Baseball Player)
6319 Timber Trl
Minneapolis, MN 55439-1049, USA

Smalls, Joan (Model)
c/o Vanessa Gringer *IMG Models (NY)*
304 Park Ave S Fl 12
New York, NY 10010-4314, USA

Smallwood, Dwana (Dancer)
Alvin Ailey American Dance Foundation
211 W 61st St # 300
New York, NY 10023-7832, USA

Smallwood, Richard (Music Group, Musician)
Sierra Mgmt
1035 Bates Ct
Hendersonville, TN 37075-8864, USA

Smart, Amy (Actor)
9500 Tullis Dr
Beverly Hills, CA 90210-1748, USA

Smart, Erinn (Athlete, Olympic Athlete)
201 S 18th St Apt 301
Philadelphia, PA 19103-5920, USA

Smart, J D (Athlete, Baseball Player)
1325 Lost Creek Blvd
Austin, TX 78746-6331, USA

Smart, Jean (Actor)
17351 Rancho St
Encino, CA 91316-3946, USA

Smart, Keith (Athlete, Basketball Player, Coach)
6071 Round Hill Dr
Dublin, CA 94568-8814, USA

Smart, Pamela
#93G0356 Bedford Hills Corr. Fac.
Bedford Hills, NY 10507

Smashing Pumpkins (Music Group)
c/o Irving Azoff *Azoff Music Management*
1100 Glendon Ave Ste 2000
Los Angeles, CA 90024-3524, USA

Smash Mouth (Music Group, Musician)
c/o Staff Member *Creative Artists Agency (CAA-LA)*
2000 Avenue of the Stars Ste 100
Los Angeles, CA 90067-4705, USA

Smear, Steve (Athlete, Football Player)
1701 Tree House Ct
Annapolis, MD 21401-6539, USA

Smeaton, Bruce
585 Nepean Highway Carrum
Victoria, AU 03197

Smedsmo, Dale (Athlete, Hockey Player)
609 3rd St NE
Roseau, MN 56751-1201, USA

Smedvig, Rolf (Musician)
Columbia Artists Mgmt Inc
165 W 57th St
New York, NY 10019-2201, USA

Smeenge, Joel (Athlete, Football Player)
9148 Sugarland Dr
Jacksonville, FL 32256-9611, USA

Smehlik, Richard (Athlete, Hockey Player)
8824 Hearthstone Dr
East Amherst, NY 14051-2354

Smerek, Don (Athlete, Football Player)
1298 Valhalla Dr
Denver, NC 28037-5503, USA

Smerlas, Fred (Athlete, Football Player)
11 Saddle Ridge Rd
Sudbury, MA 01776-2770, USA

Smid, Ladislav (Athlete, Hockey Player)
2000 E Gene Autry Way
Anaheim, CA 92806-6143, USA

Smidt, Eric (Business Person)
60 Beverly Park
Beverly Hills, CA 90210-1544, USA

Smigel, Irwin (Doctor)
Smigel Research
635 Madison Ave
New York, NY 10022-1009, USA

Smigel, Robert (Actor, Writer)
c/o Staff Member *Creative Artists Agency (CAA-LA)*
2000 Avenue of the Stars Ste 100
Los Angeles, CA 90067-4705, USA

Smigelsky, Dave (Athlete, Football Player)
5022 Oak Farm Way
Flowery Branch, GA 30542-5273, USA

Smiley, Don (Baseball Player, President)
Florida Marlins
3233 Huntington
Weston, FL 33332-1820, USA

Smiley, Don (Baseball Player)
10539 NW Loth St
Fort Lauderdale, FL 33322, USA

Smiley, Jane (Writer)
c/o Lynn Pleshette *Lynn Pleshette Literary Agency*
2700 N Beachwood Dr
Los Angeles, CA 90068-1922, USA

Smiley, Jane (Writer)
235 El Caminito Rd
Carmel Valley, CA 93924-9636, USA

Smiley, John (Athlete, Baseball Player)
208 W 3rd Ave
Trappe, PA 19426-2212, USA

Smiley, Justin (Athlete, Football Player)
2771 Regatta Way
Tuscaloosa, AL 35406-4022, USA

Smiley, Rickey (Comedian)
c/o Staff Member *Breakwind Entertainment*
2633 McKinney Ave Ste 130
Dallas, TX 75204-8630, USA

Smiley, Tavis (Radio Personality, Television Host)
The Tavis Smiley Show
4401 Sunset Blvd
Los Angeles, CA 90027, USA

Smiley, Tommie B (Athlete, Football Player)
5340 Timberline Ln
Beaumont, TX 77706-7343, USA

S. Miller, Candice (Congressman, Politician)
1034 Longworth Hob
Washington, DC 20515-0510, USA

Smirnoff, Karina (Dancer, Reality Star)
2975 Hollyridge Dr
Los Angeles, CA 90068-1949, USA

Smirnoff, Yakov (Actor, Comedian)
c/o Staff Member *Richard De La Font Agency*
3808 W South Park Blvd
Broken Arrow, OK 74011-1261, USA

Smith, Adam (Congressman, Politician)
2402 Rayburn Hob
Washington, DC 20515-0548, USa

Smith, Adrian (Athlete, Basketball Player, Olympic Athlete)
2829 Saddleback Dr
Cincinnati, OH 45244-3914, USA

Smith, Adrian (Congressman, Politician)
503 Canoonhob
Washington, DC 20515-0001, USA

Smith, Adrian (Musician)
Chipster Entertainment
1976 E High St Ste 101
Pottstown, PA 19464-3277, USA

Smith, Akili (Athlete, Football Player)
PO Box 95
Jamul, CA 91935-0095, USA

Smith, Al (Athlete, Basketball Player)
308 S Sterling Ave
Peoria, IL 61604-6063, USA

Smith, Al (Athlete, Football Player)
49 Finnigan Ave Apt M19
Saddle Brook, NJ 07663-6091, USA

Smith, Al (Athlete, Football Player)
15 Pembroke St
Sugar Land, TX 77479-2929, USA

Smith, Aldon (Football Player)
c/o Tom Condon *CAA (St. Louis)*
222 S Central Ave Ste 1008
Saint Louis, MO 63105-3509, USA

Smith, Alex (Athlete, Football Player)
17662 Daves Ave
Monte Sereno, CA 95030-3216, USA

Smith, Alice (Musician)
c/o Staff Member *Paradigm (Monterey)*
404 W Franklin St
Monterey, CA 93940-2303, USA

Smith, Allison (Actor)
Innovative Artists
1505 10th St
Santa Monica, CA 90401-2805, USA

Smith, Amber (Actor, Model)
c/o Jerry Shandrew *Shandrew Public Relations*
1050 S Stanley Ave
Los Angeles, CA 90019-6634, USA

Smith, Andre (Athlete, Football Player)
c/o Ben Dogra *CAA (St. Louis)*
222 S Central Ave Ste 1008
Saint Louis, MO 63105-3509, USA

Smith, Ann (Athlete, Tennis Player)
3737 Cole Ave Apt 110
Dallas, TX 75204-1594, USA

Smith, Anna Deavere (Actor, Producer, Writer)
c/o Johnnie Planco *Parseghian Planco LLC*
388 2nd Ave
New York, NY 10010-5616, USA

Smith, Anthony (Athlete, Football Player)
PO Box 573
Fontana, CA 92334-0573, USA

Smith, Antowain (Athlete, Football Player)
2121 Hepburn St Apt 917
Houston, TX 77054-3221, USA

Smith, April (Writer)
427 7th St
Santa Monica, CA 90402-1907, USA

Smith, Art (Chef)
c/o Staff Member *Premier Management Group (PMG Sports)*
115 Crescent Commons Dr Ste 250
Cary, NC 27518-8134, USA

Smith, Arthur (Producer)
A. Smith and Company Properties
9911 W Pico Blvd Ste 250
Los Angeles, CA 90035-2737, USA

Smith, Artie (Athlete, Football Player)
3809 W 68th St
Stillwater, OK 74074-2428, USA

Smith, Barbara (Business Person)
B. Smith Enterprises
1120 Avenue of the Americas Fl 4
New York, NY 10036-6700, USA

Smith, Barry (Athlete, Football Player)
725 Richland Creek Dr
Blaine, TN 37709-5441, USA

Smith, Barty (Athlete, Football Player)
2290 Dabney Rd
Richmond, VA 23230-3344, USA

Smith, Beau (Cartoonist)
PO Box 706
Ceredo, WV 25507-0706, USA

Smith, Ben (Athlete, Football Player)
1127 Riverbend Club Dr SE
Atlanta, GA 30339-2817, USA

Smith, Ben (Athlete, Hockey Player, Olympic Athlete)
47 Norwood Hts
Gloucester, MA 01930-1212, USA

Smith, Ben (Cartoonist)
c/o Staff Member *King Features Syndication*
300 W 57th St Fl 15
New York, NY 10019-5238, USA

Smith, Bennett W (Religious Leader)
Progressive National Baptist Convention
601 50th St NE
Washington, DC 20019-5498, USA

Smith, Bernie (Athlete, Baseball Player)
PO Box 513
Lutcher, LA 70071-0513, USA

Smith, Bill (Athlete, Football Player)
19 Woodcrest Dr
Lexington, NC 27295-1661, USA

Smith, Bill (Athlete, Hockey Player)
New York Islanders
1255 Hempstead Tpke
Uniondale, NY 11553-1200

Smith, Billy (Athlete, Baseball Player)
5304 Vicksburg Dr
Arlington, TX 76017-4944, USA

Smith, Billy (Athlete, Baseball Player)
333 Rolling Hills Dr
Conroe, TX 77304-1280, USA

Smith, Billy (Athlete, Hockey Player)
8356 Quail Meadow Way
West Palm Beach, FL 33412-1505, USA

Smith, Billy Ray Jr (Athlete, Football Player)
XX Sports Radio
6160 Cornerstone Ct E Ste 100
San Diego, CA 92121-3724, USA

Smith, Bob (Athlete, Baseball Player)
102 Dean Rd
East Lyme, CT 06333-1509, USA

Smith, Bob (Golfer)
PO Box 6511
Ventura, CA 93006-6511, USA

Smith, Bobby (Athlete, Baseball Player)
2822 60th Ave
Oakland, CA 94605-1502, USA

Smith, Bobby (Athlete, Hockey Player)
10800 E Cactus Rd Unit 46
Scottsdale, AZ 85259-2505, USA

Smith, Bobby Gene (Athlete, Baseball Player)
1267 Tucker Rd Unit 15
Hood River, OR 97031-8601, USA

Smith, Brad (Athlete, Hockey Player)
Colorado Avalanche
1000 Chopper Cir
Denver, CO 80204-5805

Smith, Brad (Musician)
Shapiro Co
9229 W Sunset Blvd Ste 607
West Hollywood, CA 90069-3406, USA

Smith, Bradley (Brad) (Athlete, Football Player)
Brad Smith's True Foundation
1151 Mansell Dr
Youngstown, OH 44505-2242, USA

Smith, Brent (Athlete, Football Player)
258 Ridgewood Dr
Pontotoc, MS 38863-3532, USA

Smith, Brian (Athlete, Baseball Player)
203 Bo Howard Rd
Toney, AL 35773-9235, USA

Smith, Brick (Athlete, Baseball Player)
6706 Easton Pl
Charlotte, NC 28212-5649, USA

Smith, Brooke (Actor)
c/o Sue Leibman *Barking Dog Entertainment*
609 Greenwich St Fl 6
New York, NY 10014-3610, USA

Smith, Bruce W (Director)
c/o Staff Member *Jambalaya Studio*
111 N Maryland Ave # 300
Glendale, CA 91206-4238, USA

Smith, Bryn (Athlete, Baseball Player)
1239 Highway 1
Santa Maria, CA 93455-5909, USA

Smith, Calvin (Athlete, Track Athlete)
16703 Sheffield Park Dr
Lutz, FL 33549-6833, USA

Smith, Carolyn Renee
PO Box 813
North Hollywood, CA 91603-0813

Smith, Chad (Musician)
c/o Peter Mensch *Q Prime*
729 7th Ave Ste 1600
New York, NY 10019-6880, USA

Smith, Charles (Athlete, Basketball Player)
PO Box 190
Cedar Grove, NJ 07009-0190, USA

Smith, Charles Martin (Actor, Director)
c/o David Saunders *Agency for the Performing Arts (APA-LA)*
405 S Beverly Dr Ste 500
Beverly Hills, CA 90212-4425, USA

Smith, Charlie E (Athlete, Football Player)
1906 Crescent Dr
Monroe, LA 71202-3024, USA

Smith, Charlie H (Athlete, Football Player)
14074 Skyline Blvd
Oakland, CA 94619-3622, USA

Smith, Chelsi
335 E San Augustine St
Deer Park, TX 77536-4185

Smith, Chris (Athlete, Baseball Player)
4206 Dawn Ln
Oceanside, CA 92056-4716, USA

Smith, Chris (Golfer)
208 S Bellerive Dr
Peru, IN 46970-8060, USA

Smith, Chris M (Athlete, Football Player)
1424 Martway Cir Apt A
Olathe, KS 66061-5820, USA

Smith, Chuck (Athlete, Baseball Player)
1300 Saint Charles Pl Apt 810
Pembroke Pines, FL 33026-3340, USA

Smith, Chuck (Athlete, Football Player)
1155 Havenbrook Ct
Suwanee, GA 30024-2877, USA

Smith, Clifford (Method Man) (Musician, Television Host)
c/o Shauna Garr *Smart Girl Productions*
8335 W Sunset Blvd Ste 222
Los Angeles, CA 90069-1534, USA

Smith, Colleen (Actor)
c/o Mark Scroggs *David Shapira & Associates*
193 N Robertson Blvd
Beverly Hills, CA 90211-2103, USA

Smith, Connie (Music Group, Musician)
Gurley Co
1204B Cedar Ln
Nashville, TN 37212-5910, USA

Smith, Cotter (Actor)
15332 Antioch St # 800
Pacific Palisades, CA 90272-3628, USA

Smith, Dallas (Athlete, Hockey Player)
4390 SW 107th Ave Apt 4
Beaverton, OR 97005-3192

Smith, Dan (Athlete, Baseball Player)
715 N Carbon St
Girard, KS 66743-1025, USA

Smith, Daniel E. (Actor)
c/o Worthy Patterson *Evolution Entertainment (LA)*
901 N Highland Ave
Los Angeles, CA 90038-2412, USA

Smith, Danny (Actor)
c/o Lisa Harrison *William Morris Endeavor (LA)*
9601 Wilshire Blvd
Beverly Hills, CA 90210-5213, USA

Smith, Dante (Mos Def) (Actor, Musician)
c/o Linda Carbone *Press Here Publicity*
138 W 25th St Ste 900
New York, NY 10001-7470, USA

Smith, Darden (Music Group, Musician, Songwriter, Writer)
AGF Entertainment
30 W 21st St # 700
New York, NY 10010-6905, USA

Smith, Darrin (Athlete, Football Player)
7395 NW 19th Ct
Hollywood, FL 33024-1015, USA

Smith, Daryl (Athlete, Football Player)
2302 Winterwood Rd
Baltimore, MD 21209-3703, USA

Smith, Daryl (Athlete, Baseball Player)
3 Sunny Mills Ct
Randallstown, MD 21133-4449, USA

Smith, Dave (Athlete, Football Player)
214 W Kaler Dr
Phoenix, AZ 85021-7241, USA

Smith, Dave (Athlete, Baseball Player)
16330 Jersey Dr
Jersey Village, TX 77040-2020, USA

Smith, Dave (Athlete, Football Player)
650 S 13th St Apt 123-20
Indiana, PA 15701-3566, USA

Smith, Dean (Athlete, Basketball Player)
105 Fox Run
Chapel Hill, NC 27516-0608, USA

Smith, Dean E (Athlete, Basketball Player, Coach)
University of North Carolina
PO Box 2126
Chapel Hill, NC 27515-2126, USA

Smith, Dennis (Athlete, Football Player)
2450 Achilles Dr
Los Angeles, CA 90046-1626, USA

Smith, Derek (Athlete, Football Player)
4949 Centennial Blvd
Santa Clara, CA 95054-1229, USA

Smith, Derek (Athlete, Hockey Player)
201 Bramblewood Ln
East Amherst, NY 14051-2228

Smith, Dick (Athlete, Baseball Player)
2615 Gates Rd
Lincolnton, NC 28092-7968, USA

Smith, Dick (Athlete, Baseball Player)
6850 Downing Rd Spc 35
Central Point, OR 97502-3418, USA

Smith, Dick (Athlete, Baseball Player)
1926 Norwood Ln
State College, PA 16803-1326, USA

Smith, Dick (Athlete, Coach, Swimmer)
PO Box 1831
Dewey, AZ 86327-1831, USA

Smith, Dick (Athlete, Football Player)
5718 Chillum Pl NE
Washington, DC 20011-2528, USA

Smith, D.J. (Athlete, Football Player)
c/o Peter Schaffer *All Pro Sports and Entertainment*
36 Steele St Ste 100
Denver, CO 80206-5709, USA

Smith, Donald L (Athlete, Football Player)
3338 Pineview Dr
Holiday, FL 34691-9732, USA

Smith, Doug (Athlete, Basketball Player)
25482 Pennsylvania Ave
Novi, MI 48375-1785, USA

Smith, Doug (Athlete, Football Player)
25661 Pacific Crest Dr
Mission Viejo, CA 92692-5040, USA

Smith, Doug (Coach, Football Coach, Football Player)
University of Southern California
Heritage Hall
Los Angeles, CA 90089-0001, USA

Smith, Douglas (Doug) (Actor)
c/o Beverly Strong *Strong Management*
9350 Wilshire Blvd Ste 224
Beverly Hills, CA 90212-3204, USA

Smith, Dr Robin (Doctor, Writer)
226 W Rittenhouse Sq Apt 210
Philadelphia, PA 19103-5738, USA

Smith, Dwight (Athlete, Baseball Player)
PO Box 98
Varnville, SC 29944-0098, USA

Smith, Earl (Athlete, Baseball Player)
2764 N Leonard Ave
Fresno, CA 93737-9720, USA

Smith, Elliot (Athlete, Football Player)
1343 Cadillac Dr
Jackson, MS 39213-4811, USA

Smith, Elmore (Athlete, Basketball Player)
PO Box 24147S
Cleveland, OH 44124, USA

Smith, Emmitt (Athlete, Football Player)
Pat & Emmitt Smith Charities
16000 Dallas Pkwy # 550N
Tollway Plaza North
Dallas, TX 75248-6607, USA

Smith, Eric (Race Car Driver)
Southtown Motorsports
1701 W Washington St
Bloomington, IL 61701-3701, USA

Smith, Eugene (Baseball Player)
Cincinnati Buckeyes
8337 Flora Ave
Saint Louis, MO 63114-6203, USA

Smith, F Dean (Athlete, Track Athlete)
PO Box 71
Breckenridge, TX 76424-0071, USA

Smith, Floyd (Athlete, Hockey Player)
138 Stonehenge Dr
Orchard Park, NY 14127-2845

Smith, Forry
3500 W Olive Ave Ste 1400
Burbank, CA 91505-5512

Smith, Frankie (Athlete, Football Player)
620 N Grayson St
Groesbeck, TX 76642-1157, USA

Smith, Frederick W (Business Person)
FDX Corp
942 Shady Grove Rd S
Memphis, TN 38120-4117, USA

Smith, Garfield (Athlete, Basketball Player)
2006 Idylwild Ct
Richmond, KY 40475-3606, USA

Smith, G E
24 Thorndike St
Cambridge, MA 02141-1882, USA

Smith, G Elaine (Religious Leader)
American Baptist Churches USA
PO Box 851
Valley Forge, PA 19482-0851, USA

Smith, George (Cartoonist)
Universal Press Syndicate
4520 Main St Ste 340
Kansas City, MO 64111-7705, USA

Smith, Gerald C (Government Official)
2425 Tracy Pl NW
Washington, DC 20008-1628, USA

Smith, Gord (Athlete, Hockey Player)
6 Carriage Dr
West Haven, CT 06516-5514

Smith, Gordon (Politician)
8611 Country Club Dr
Bethesda, MD 20817-4579, USA

Smith, Greg (Athlete, Baseball Player)
1863 Gettysburg Village Dr Ste 995
Gettysburg, PA 17325-6707, USA

Smith, Greg (Athlete, Basketball Player)
9930 SW Lumbee Ln
Tualatin, OR 97062-7355, USA

Smith, Greg (Athlete, Hockey Player)
909 56th St W
Billings, MT 59106-2240

Smith, Gregory (Actor, Producer)
c/o JJ Harris *One Talent Management*
3680 1/2 Fredonia Dr
Los Angeles, CA 90068-1208, USA

Smith, Guy (Race Car Driver)
Tasman Motorsports
4192 Weaver Ct
Columbus, OH 43206, USA

Smith, Hal (Athlete, Baseball Player)
637 Houston St
Columbus, TX 78934-2618, USA

Smith, Hal (Athlete, Football Player)
PO Box 570517
Tarzana, CA 91357-0517, USA

Smith, Harry (Bowler)
580 E Cuyahoga Falls Ave
Akron, OH 44310-1540, USA

Smith, Harry (Correspondent)
c/o Staff Member *Early Show, The (NY)*
524 W 57th St
New York, NY 10019-2924, USA

Smith, Harry E (Black Jack) (Athlete,
Coach, Football Coach, Football Player)
805 Leawood Ter
Columbia, MO 65203-2729, USA

Smith, Hedrick L (Journalist)
4204 Rosemary St
Chevy Chase, MD 20815-5218, USA

Smith, Helen (Athlete, Baseball Player)
1600 Westbrook Ave Apt 436
Richmond, VA 23227-3318, USA

Smith, Hillary B
8730 W Sunset Blvd Ste 480
West Hollywood, CA 90069-2277, USA

Smith, Hunter (Athlete, Football Player)
320 W Cedar St
Zionsville, IN 46077-1301, USA

Smith, Huston (Writer)
c/o Staff Member *Red Wheel / Weiser
/Conari*
65 Parker St Ste 7
Newburyport, MA 01950-4600, USA

Smith, Ian (Doctor)
c/o Linda Shafran *Linda Shafran*
424 Wisconsin Ave Apt 1N
Oak Park, IL 60302-3678, USA

Smith, Jack (Athlete, Baseball Player)
250 Doubles Dr
Covington, GA 30016-1736, USA

Smith, Jackie L (Athlete, Football Player)
1566 Walpole Dr
Chesterfield, MO 63017-4615, USA

Smith, Jaclyn (Actor)
10398 W Sunset Blvd
Los Angeles, CA 90077-3613, USA

Smith, Jacob (Actor)
c/o Elaine Lively *LA Entertainment*
1375 S San Fernando Blvd
Suite 505
Burbank, CA 91504, USA

Smith, Jaden (Actor, Musician)
1401/1405/1409 Cold Canyon Rd
Calabasas, CA 91302, USA

Smith, James (Bonecrusher) (Boxer)
355 Keith Hills Rd
Lillington, NC 27546, USA

Smith, Jamie Renee (Actor)
c/o Pam Grimes *Hervey/Grimes Talent
Agency*
3002 Midvale Ave Ste 206
Los Angeles, CA 90034-3418, USA

Smith, Jason V (Athlete, Basketball Player)
c/o Mark Bartelstein *Priority Sports &
Entertainment - Chicago*
312 N La Salle
Suite 650
Chicago, IL 60610, USA

Smith, J D (Athlete, Football Player)
1615 County Road 204
Richland Springs, TX 76871, USA

Smith, J D Jr (Athlete, Football Player)
3332 Florida St
Oakland, CA 94602-3808, USA

Smith, Jean (Baseball Player)
5400 5 Mile Creek Rd
Harbor Springs, MI 49740-9783, USA

Smith, Jermaine (Athlete, Football Player)
1345 12th St
Augusta, GA 30901-3260, USA

Smith, Jim (Athlete, Baseball Player)
1730 S Arroyo Ln
Gilbert, AZ 85295-4815, USA

Smith, Jim (Athlete, Football Player)
2639 Round Table Blvd
Lewisville, TX 75056-5723, USA

Smith, Jim Field (Actor, Director)
c/o Trevor Engelson *Underground
Management*
447 S Highland Ave
Los Angeles, CA 90036-3530, USA

Smith, Jimmy (Athlete, Football Player)
c/o Drew Rosenhaus *Rosenhaus Sports
Representation*
6400 Allison Rd
Miami Beach, FL 33141-4540, USA

Smith, Jimmy Lee (Athlete, Football
Player)
1302 Charter Ct E
Jacksonville, FL 32225-2658, USA

Smith, Jim Ray (Athlete, Football Player)
7049 Cliffbrook Dr
Dallas, TX 75254-7909, USA

Smith, Joe (Basketball Player)
7639 Leafwood Dr
Norfolk, VA 23518-4536, USA

Smith, John (Actor)
c/o Alan Ellsweig *Shadow Entertainment*
655 N Central Ave Fl 17
Glendale, CA 91203-1439, USA

Smith, John (Race Car Driver)
5611 Highway 81 N
Williamston, SC 29697-9742, USA

Smith, John L (Coach, Football Coach)
Michigan State University
Daugherty Field House
East Lansing, MI 48824, USA

Smith, John M (Athlete, Football Player)
184 Centre St
Dover, MA 02030-2413, USA

Smith, John W (Wrestler)
5315 S Sangre Rd
Stillwater, OK 74074-2071, USA

Smith, Josh (Athlete, Basketball Player)
c/o Brian Dyke *Shibumi Sports*
4771 Sweetwater Blvd # 228
Sugar Land, TX 77479-3121, USA

Smith, J Robert (Athlete, Football Player)
6102 Timberlake Ct
Flower Mound, TX 75022-5627, USA

Smith, J T (Athlete, Football Player)
10110 Planters Row Dr
Frisco, TX 75033-0255, USA

Smith, Justin (Athlete, Football Player)
c/o Jim Steiner *CAA (St. Louis)*
222 S Central Ave Ste 1008
Saint Louis, MO 63105-3509, USA

Smith, Karin
2300 Palisades Ave
Los Osos, CA 93402-3910

Smith, Katie (Athlete, Basketball Player,
Olympic Athlete)
2494 Farleigh Rd
Columbus, OH 43221-2618, USA

Smith, Keith (Athlete, Baseball Player)
15711 Ada St
Canyon Country, CA 91387-1891, USA

Smith, Keith (Athlete, Baseball Player)
5823 13th St E
Bradenton, FL 34203-6819, USA

Smith, Kellita (Actor)
c/o Lynn Jeter *Lynn Jeter & Associates*
3699 Wilshire Blvd Ste 850
Los Angeles, CA 90010-2737, USA

Smith, Ken (Athlete, Baseball Player)
Bluff City Jaguar 6335 Wheel Cv Attn
Sales Dept
Memphis, TN 38119, USA

Smith, Kenneth L (Athlete, Baseball
Player, Football Player)
3802 Athens Dr
Pasadena, TX 77505-3349, USA

Smith, Kenny (Athlete, Basketball Player,
Sportscaster)
17414 Magnolia Blvd
Encino, CA 91316-2578, USA

Smith, Kerr (Actor, Director)
4828 Oak Park Ave
Encino, CA 91316-4115, USA

Smith, Kevin (Actor, Director, Producer,
Writer)
c/o Staff Member *View Askew
Productions Inc*
PO Box 400
Red Bank, NJ 07701-0400, USA

Smith, Kevin (Athlete, Football Player)
7001 Parkwood Blvd Apt 3204
Plano, TX 75024-7176, USA

Smith, Kim (Actor)
c/o Staff Member *Clipse Management*
279 W Main St
Dallas, TX 75208, USA

Smith, Kurtwood (Actor)
c/o Kelly Garner *Pop Art Management*
PO Box 55363
Sherman Oaks, CA 91413-0363, USA

Smith, Labradford (Athlete, Basketball
Player)
410 Thompson Dr
Bay City, TX 77414-7910, USA

Smith, Lamar (Congressman, Politician)
2409 Rayburn Hob
Washington, DC 20515-4317, USA

Smith, Lance (Athlete, Football Player)
14907 Rocky Top Dr
Huntersville, NC 28078-2648, USA

Smith, Larry (Athlete, Basketball Player)
1767 Lakeside Dr
Vicksburg, MS 39180-9369, USA

Smith, Larry (Athlete, Football Player)
3601 Bayshore Blvd
Tampa, FL 33629-8942, USA

Smith, Lauren Lee (Actor)
c/o Kim Callahan *Industry Entertainment*
955 Carrillo Dr Ste 300
Los Angeles, CA 90048-5400, USA

Smith, Laverne (Athlete, Football Player)
2122 N Homestead St
Wichita, KS 67208-1872, USA

Smith, Lawrence Leighton
Louisville Symphony
611 W Main St
Louisville, KY 40202-2963, USA

Smith, Lee (Athlete, Baseball Player)
PO Box 399
Castor, LA 71016-0399, USA

Smith, Lee A (Baseball Player)
Atlanta Braves
2124 Highway 507
Castor, LA 71016-4069, USA

Smith, Leonard P (Athlete, Football
Player)
18053 Creek Hollow Rd
Baton Rouge, LA 70817-3304, USA

Smith, Liz (Journalist)
160 E 38th St Apt 33C
New York, NY 10016-2615, USA

Smith, Liz (Writer)
160 E 38th St
New York, NY 10016-2651, USA

Smith, Lois (Actor)
c/o Steve Stone *Cornerstone Talent Agency*
37 W 20th St Ste 1007
New York, NY 10011-3714, USA

Smith, Lonnie (Athlete, Baseball Player)
145 Wesley Forest Dr
Fayetteville, GA 30214-1094, USA

Smith, Louise (Race Car Driver)
International Motorsports
PO Box 1018
Talladega, AL 35161-1018, USA

Smith, Lovie (Athlete, Coach, Football Coach, Football Player)
c/o Matthew Smith *IMG Coaches*
601 Carlson Pkwy Ste 610
Hopkins, MN 55305-5215, USA

Smith, Malcolm (Race Car Driver)
Motorsports HOF
PO Box 194
Novi, MI 48376-0194, USA

Smith, Margaret (Producer, Writer)
c/o Gail Stocker *Gail Stocker Presents*
1025 N Kings Rd Apt 113
West Hollywood, CA 90069-6007, USA

Smith, Margo (Musician, Songwriter, Writer)
Tristar Enterprises Inc
PO Box 3367
Brentwood, TN 37024-3367, USA

Smith, Marilynn (Golfer)
3784 N 162nd Ln
Goodyear, AZ 85395-8017, USA

Smith, Mark (Athlete, Baseball Player)
907 Forest Green Rd
Reedville, VA 22539-3577, USA

Smith, Mark (Athlete, Baseball Player)
1312 Elmhurst Ln
Flower Mound, TX 75028-3847, USA

Smith, Mark (Athlete, Hockey Player)
Ayla Boutique
381 E Campbell Ave
Campbell, CA 95008-2013

Smith, Marquis (Athlete, Football Player)
843 51st St
San Diego, CA 92114-1002, USA

Smith, Martha (Actor, Model)
9690 Heather Rd
Beverly Hills, CA 90210-1757, USA

Smith, Marvel (Athlete, Football Player)
30 Waterfront Dr
Pittsburgh, PA 15222-4748, USA

Smith, Marvin (Smitty) (Musician)
Joel Chriss
300 Mercer St Apt 3J
New York, NY 10003-6732, USA

Smith, Melanie (Actor)
Innovative Artists
1505 10th St
Santa Monica, CA 90401-2805, USA

Smith, Michael (Athlete, Basketball Player)
PO Box 91912
Washington, DC 20090-1912, USA

Smith, Michael Bailey (Actor)
c/o Alexandra Karrys *Divine Management*
117 N Orlando Ave
Los Angeles, CA 90048-3403, USA

Smith, Michael W (Musician, Songwriter, Writer)
c/o Staff Member *Creative Artists Agency (CAA-TN)*
401 Commerce St PH
Nashville, TN 37219-2516, USA

Smith, Mike (Athlete, Baseball Player)
101 Dover Rd
Millis, MA 02054-1338, USA

Smith, Mike (Athlete, Baseball Player)
3226 Livingston Rd
Jackson, MS 39213-6106, USA

Smith, Mike (Athlete, Baseball Player)
7605 Antique Oak St
Live Oak, TX 78233-3102, USA

Smith, Mike (Athlete, Football Player)
619 Feamster Dr
Houston, TX 77022-2505, USA

Smith, Mike (Cartoonist)
Las Vegas Sun
2275 Corporate Cir Ste 300
Editorial Dept
Henderson, NV 89074-7745, USA

Smith, Mike (Race Car Driver)
Paul Smith Racing
800 NE 3rd St Ste 2
Boynton Beach, FL 33435-3194, USA

Smith, Mike (Horse Racer)
3445 NE 210th St
Miami, FL 33180-3587, USA

Smith, Mindy (Musician, Songwriter, Writer)
Vanguard Records
11400 W Olympic Blvd Ste 1450
Los Angeles, CA 90064-1649, USA

Smith, Mitchell (Race Car Driver)
Mitchell Smith Racing
4570 W State Road 32
Anderson, IN 46011-1542, USA

Smith, Monika (Actor)
c/o David Gardner *Principato/Young Management (LA)*
9465 Wilshire Blvd Ste 900
Beverly Hills, CA 90212-2608, USA

Smith, Myron (Athlete, Football Player)
6604 Sandgate Dr
Arlington, TX 76002-5549, USA

Smith, Nate (Athlete, Baseball Player)
6365 Tahoe Dr
Atlanta, GA 30349-4052, USA

Smith, Neil (Athlete, Football Player)
5366 W 95th St
Prairie Village, KS 66207-3204, USA

Smith, Noland (Athlete, Football Player)
4338 Watkins Dr
Jackson, MS 39206-4450, USA

Smith, O C
1650 Broadway Ste 508
New York, NY 10019-6833, USA

Smith, O Guinn (Athlete, Track Athlete)
1 Hawthorne Pl Apt 3P
Boston, MA 02114-2333, USA

Smith, Orin R (Business Person)
Engelhard Corp
101 Wood Ave S
Iselin, NJ 08830-2749, USA

Smith, Orlando (Tubby) (Coach)
University of Kentucky
Athletic Dept
Lexington, KY 40536-0001, USA

Smith, Osborne E (Ozzie) (Athlete, Baseball Player)
PO Box 251
Saint Albans, MO 63073-0251, USA

Smith, Otis (Athlete, Basketball Player)
607 Applewood Ave
Altamonte Springs, FL 32714-7301, USA

Smith, Paul (Athlete, Baseball Player)
711 Trevino Ln
Conroe, TX 77302-3835, USA

Smith, Pete (Athlete, Baseball Player)
10030 Halstead Dr
Suwanee, GA 30024-5397, USA

Smith, Pete (Athlete, Baseball Player)
3512 Dixon Ln
The Villages, FL 32162-7150, USA

Smith, Putter (Actor)
1414 Lyndon St
South Pasadena, CA 91030-3812, USA

Smith, Quanterus (Athlete, Football Player)
c/o Jordan Woy *Willis and Woy Management*
3030 Olive St Ste 520
Dallas, TX 75219-7629, USA

Smith, Quincy (Baseball Player)
Cleveland Buckeyes
715 S 14th St
Terre Haute, IN 47807, USA

Smith, Quinn (Actor)
1738 Whitley Ave
Los Angeles, CA 90028-4809

Smith, Rachel (Beauty Pageant Winner)
c/o Margot Menzel *Evolution Entertainment (LA)*
901 N Highland Ave
Los Angeles, CA 90038-2412, USA

Smith, Ralph (Athlete, Football Player)
PO Box 1406
McComb, MS 39649-1406, USA

Smith, Ralph (Cartoonist)
c/o Staff Member *King Features Syndication*
300 W 57th St Fl 15
New York, NY 10019-5238, USA

Smith, Randy (Baseball Player)
7941 E Via De Luna Dr
Scottsdale, AZ 85255-4113, USA

Smith, Ray (Athlete, Baseball Player)
17183 Poblado Ct
San Diego, CA 92127-1431, USA

Smith, Ray E (Religious Leader)
Open Bible Standard Churches
2020 Bell Ave
Des Moines, IA 50315-1096, USA

Smith, RD (Race Car Driver)
Congdon Racing
4500 Turnberry Ct SW
Concord, NC 28027-0432, USA

Smith, Regan (Race Car Driver)
Furniture Row Racing
4000 Forest St
Denver, CO 80216-4537, USA

Smith, Reggie (Athlete, Basketball Player)
6975 Claywood Way
San Jose, CA 95120-2241, USA

Smith, Reggie (Athlete, Baseball Player)
Reggie Smith Baseball Center
16161Ventura Blvd Ste 775
Encino, CA 91436, USA

Smith, Remy (Remy Ma) (Musician)
c/o Staff Member *ReachGlobal Music Publishing*
4201 W Burbank Blvd
Burbank, CA 91505-2124, USA

Smith, Renee Felice (Actor)
c/o Hannah Roth *Don Buchwald & Associates (LA)*
6500 Wilshire Blvd Ste 2200
Los Angeles, CA 90048-4942, USA

Smith, Rex (Actor)
16986 Encino Hills Dr
Encino, CA 91436-4008, USA

Smith, Richard A (Publisher)
Harcourt general
275 Washington St
Newton, MA 02458-1611, USA

Smith, Rickie (Race Car Driver)
Rt 3 Box 19
Kirby Rd
King, NC 27021, USA

Smith, Rico (Athlete, Football Player)
8976 Foothill Blvd Unit B7-389
Rancho Cucamonga, CA 91730-3400, USA

Smith, Riley (Actor)
c/o Mark Armstrong *Sanders Armstrong Caserta*
2120 Colorado Ave Ste 120
Santa Monica, CA 90404-3561, USA

Smith, R Jackson (Swimmer)
122 Palmers Hill Rd Unit 3101
Stamford, CT 06902-2147, USA

Smith, Robert (Athlete, Baseball Player)
1274 Norman Rd
Colton, CA 92324-1713, USA

Smith, Robert (Musician)
c/o Staff Member *Geffen Records*
9126 Sunset Blvd
West Hollywood, CA 90069, USA

Smith, Robert B (Athlete, Football Player)
1012 S Royal St
Bogalusa, LA 70427-5457, USA

Smith, Robert C (Bob) (Senator)
9012 Rocky Lake Ct
Sarasota, FL 34238-4008, USA

Smith, Robert L (Athlete, Football Player)
426 Cape Lookout Ln
Corpus Christi, TX 78412-2636, USA

Smith, Robert S (Athlete, Football Player)
5668 Harrison Ave
Maple Heights, OH 44137-3331, USA

Smith, Robyn (Jockey)
1155 San Ysidro Dr
Beverly Hills, CA 90210-2102, USA

Smith, Rod (Athlete, Football Player)
821 W 4th St
Charlotte, NC 28202-1103, USA

Smith, Roger (Actor)
2707 Benedict Canyon Dr
Beverly Hills, CA 90210-1024, USA

Smith, Roger Guenveur (Actor, Writer)
Luna Ray Films
2018 Vine St
Los Angeles, CA 90068-3915, USA

Smith, Rogers
PO Box 2907
Mammoth Lakes, CA 93546-2907, USA

Smith, Rolland (Correspondent)
CBS-TV
524 W 57th St
News Dept
New York, NY 10019-2924, USA

Smith, Ron (Athlete, Football Player)
1804 Park Ave
Richmond, VA 23220-2821, USA

Smith, Ron (Athlete, Football Player)
266 York St
Trussville, AL 35173-3224, USA

Smith, Ron (Race Car Driver)
14933 175th Pl SE
Renton, WA 98059, USA

Smith, Roy (Athlete, Baseball Player)
908 Woodbridge Ct
Safety Harbor, FL 34695-2951, USA

Smith, Roy (Athlete, Baseball Player)
472 Gramatan Ave Apt G2
Mount Vernon, NY 10552-2940, USA

Smith, Russell (Musician)
LC Media
PO Box 965
Antioch, TN 37011-0965, USA

Smith, Sam (Athlete, Basketball Player)
5790 Cedar Bay Dr
Millington, TN 38053-8410, USA

Smith, Sam (Musician)
c/o Kirk Sommer *William Morris Endeavor (LA)*
9601 Wilshire Blvd
Beverly Hills, CA 90210-5213, USA

Smith, Sarah Christine (Actor)
c/o Staff Member *Hervey/Grimes Talent Agency*
3002 Midvale Ave Ste 206
Los Angeles, CA 90034-3418, USA

Smith, Sean (Athlete, Football Player)
c/o Roger Green *William Morris Endeavor (LA)*
9601 Wilshire Blvd
Beverly Hills, CA 90210-5213, USA

Smith, Seth (Athlete, Baseball Player)
117 Langdon Dr
Madison, MS 39110-7077, USA

Smith, Shawnee (Actor)
c/o Brian Wilkins *Kritzer Levine Wilkins Entertainment (KLWG)*
11872 La Grange Ave Fl 1
Los Angeles, CA 90025-5283, USA

Smith, Shelley (Actor)
4184 Colfax Ave
Studio City, CA 91604-2165, USA

Smith, Sherman (Athlete, Football Player)
1421 Primrose Ln
Franklin, TN 37064-9333, USA

Smith, Shevin (Athlete, Football Player)
10110 Farmingdale Pl
Tampa, FL 33624-5419, USA

Smith, Sid (Athlete, Football Player)
1939 Melody Ln
Richmond, TX 77406-2411, USA

Smith, Sinjin (Athlete, Volleyball Player)
Beach Volleyball Camps
PO Box 1714
Pacific Palisades, CA 90272-1714, USA

Smith, Skip (Race Car Driver)
2143C Statesville Blvd # 117
Salisbury, NC 28147-1411, USA

Smith, Sonny (Baseball Player)
Chicago American Giants
3549 N College Ave
Indianapolis, IN 46205-3733, USA

Smith, Stan
194 Bellevue Ave
Newport, RI 02840-3515

Smith, Stanley (Race Car Driver)
1740 Rd # 39
Chelsea, AL 35043, USA

Smith, Stanley R (Stan) (Tennis Player)
ProServe
1101 Woodrow Wilson Blvd
#1800
Arlington, VA 22209, USA

Smith, Stephen A (Correspondent, Radio Personality)
c/o Steven Arcieri *Arcieri & Associates Inc*
60 E 42nd St Ste 2315
New York, NY 10165-5015, USA

Smith, Steve (Athlete, Baseball Player, Olympic Athlete)
240 W Escalones
San Clemente, CA 92672-5109, USA

Smith, Steve (Athlete, Football Player)
c/o Tom Condon *CAA (St. Louis)*
222 S Central Ave Ste 1008
Saint Louis, MO 63105-3509, USA

Smith, Steve (Athlete, Football Player)
c/o Kevin Cahill *Encore Sports and Entertainment*
703 Palomar Airport Rd Ste 200
Carlsbad, CA 92011-1042, USA

Smith, Steve (Race Car Driver)
c/o Staff Member *RacingWest*
1772 Los Arboles
Suite #J-186
Thousand Oaks, CA 91362, USA

Smith, Steven L (Astronaut)
15728 Lake Lodge Dr
Houston, TX 77062, USA

Smith, Stevonne (Steve Sr) (Athlete, Football Player)
c/o Derrick Fox *Derrick Fox Management*
Prefers to be contacted by telephone
CA, USA

Smith, Susan
Leath Correctional Institution
2809 Airport Rd
Leath Correctional Institution
Greenwood, SC 29649-9245

Smith, Taran (Actor)
Full Circle Mgmt
12665 Kling St
Studio City, CA 91604-1143, USA

Smith, Tasha (Actor)
c/o CeCe Yorke *True Public Relations*
6725 W Sunset Blvd Ste 470
Los Angeles, CA 90028-7180, USA

Smith, Telvin (Athlete, Football Player)
c/o Adisa P. Bakari *Dow Lohnes PLLC*
1299 Pennsylvania Ave NW Ste 700
Washington, DC 20004-2431, USA

Smith, Terry (Sportscaster)
12 Cleome St
Ladera Ranch, CA 92694-0858, USA

Smith, Thomas (Athlete, Football Player)
RR 1 Box 198
Gates, NC 27937, USA

Smith, Tommie (Athlete, Olympic Athlete, Track Athlete)
1800 Lilburn Stone Mountain Rd
Stone Mountain, GA 30087-1720, USA

Smith, Tommy (Athlete, Baseball Player)
1299 E Cannon Ave
Albemarle, NC 28001-4360, USA

Smith, Tony (Athlete, Football Player)
4610 Hackberry Grove Cir Apt 2231
Charlotte, NC 28269-1595, USA

Smith, Tony (Athlete, Basketball Player)
2645 N 40th St
Milwaukee, WI 53210-2505, USA

Smith, Torrey (Athlete, Football Player)
c/o Deb Poquette *Prestige Lifestyle Management*
1300 Saint Michaels Rd
Mount Airy, MD 21771-3228, USA

Smith, Travian (Athlete, Football Player)
13941 County Road 2167D
Tatum, TX 75691-3214, USA

Smith, Travis (Athlete, Baseball Player)
1865 Cherry St
Clarkston, WA 99403-8717, USA

Smith, Troy (Athlete, Football Player, Heisman Trophy Winner)
c/o Staff Member *Baltimore Ravens*
1 Winning Dr
Owings Mills, MD 21117-4776, USA

Smith, Tyron (Football Player)
c/o Eric Metz *Lock Metz Milanovic LLC*
6900 E Camelback Rd Ste 600
Scottsdale, AZ 85251-8044, USA

Smith, Vern (Athlete, Hockey Player)
15 Meadowlark Dr
East Longmeadow, MA 01028-3173

Smith, Vernice (Athlete, Football Player)
4347 Arajo Ct
Belle Isle, FL 32812-2854, USA

Smith, Vince (Musician)
Process Talent Management
439 Wiley Ave
Franklin, PA 16323-2834, USA

Smith, Wallace B (Religious Leader)
Reorganized Church of Latter Day Saints
PO Box 1059
Independence, MO 64051-0559, USA

Smith, Walter S
11301 Cielo Pi
Santa Ana, CA 92705, USA

Smith, Wayne (Athlete, Football Player)
7730 S Bishop St
Chicago, IL 60620-4127, USA

Smith, Will (Actor, Musician, Producer)
1409 Cold Canyon Rd
Calabasas, CA 91302, USA

Smith, William (Actor)
3202 Anacapa St
Santa Barbara, CA 93105, USA

Smith, William A. (Athlete, Basketball Player)
4379 Tami Ln
Central Point, OR 97502-1040, USA

Smith, William Jay (Writer)
62 Luther Shaw Rd
RR 1 Box 151
Cummington, MA 01026, USA

Smith, Willie (Athlete, Baseball Player)
1330 E 68th St
Savannah, GA 31404-5718, USA

Smith, Willie (Football Player)
Baltimore Ravens
Ravens Stadium
11001 Russell St
Baltimore, MD 21230, USA

Smith, Willow (Actor)
c/o Miguel Melendez *Overbrook Entertainment*
10202 Washington Blvd
Culver City, CA 90232-3119, USA

Smith, W Lawrence (Athlete, Football Player)
3601 Bayshore Blvd
Tampa, FL 33629-8942, USA

Smith, Wyatt (Athlete, Hockey Player)
6154 Sugar Mill Ln
Mound, MN 55364-8624

Smith, Yeardley (Actor)
c/o Meredith O'Sullivan *42West (LA)*
1840 Century Park E Ste 700
Los Angeles, CA 90067-2122, USA

Smith, Zadie (Writer)
Random House
1745 Broadway Frnt 3 # B1
New York, NY 10019-4343, USA

Smith, Zane (Athlete, Baseball Player)
420 Windship Pl
Atlanta, GA 30327-4967, USA

Smithberg, Roger (Athlete, Baseball Player)
988 Glenmore Ln
Elgin, IL 60124-2303, USA

Smithereens, The (Music Group, Musician)
c/o Len Fico *Fuel Management Group*
Prefers to be contacted via telephone or email
CA, USA

Smitherman, Stephen (Athlete, Baseball Player)
HC 74 Box 240-10
Hartshorne, OK 74547, USA

Smithers, Jan (Actor)
c/o Staff Member *Innovative Artists (LA)*
1505 10th St
Santa Monica, CA 90401-2805, USA

Smithers, William (Actor)
2202 Anacapa St
Santa Barbara, CA 93105-3506, USA

Smith III, Earl (J.R.) (Athlete, Basketball Player)
c/o Shawn Zanotti *Exact Publicity Sports PR & Marketing*
1 S Dearborn St Ste 2100
Chicago, IL 60603-2307, USA

Smith Jr, John F (Jack) (Business Person)
General Motors Corp
100 Renaissance Ctr Fl 13
Detroit, MI 48243-1002, USA

Smith Jr, Lonnie Liston (Musician)
Associated Booking Corp
1995 Broadway # 501
New York, NY 10023-5882, USA

Smith-McPhee, Sianoa (Actor)
c/o Kenny Goodman *The Schiff Company*
9220 W Sunset Blvd Ste 106
West Hollywood, CA 90069-3500, USA

Smith Osborne, Madolyn (Actor)
United Talent Agency
9336 Civic Center Dr
Beverly Hills, CA 90210-3604, USA

Smithson, Mike (Athlete, Baseball Player)
2540 Swan Creek Rd
Centerville, TN 37033-4374, USA

Smithson, Ryan (Writer)
c/o Staff Member *HarperCollins Publishers*
195 Broadway Fl 2
Cellar 1
New York, NY 10007-3132, USA

Smit-McPhee, Kodi (Actor)
c/o Kenny Goodman *The Schiff Company*
9220 W Sunset Blvd Ste 106
West Hollywood, CA 90069-3500, USA

Smitrovich, Bill (Actor)
c/o Steven Siebert *Lighthouse Entertainment*
9220 W Sunset Blvd Ste 200
West Hollywood, CA 90069-3501, USA

Smits, Jimmy (Actor)
c/o Daniel (Danny) Sussman *Brillstein Entertainment Partners (LA)*
9150 Wilshire Blvd Ste 350
Beverly Hills, CA 90212-3453, USA

Smits, Rik (Athlete, Basketball Player)
8346 E 550 S
Zionsville, IN 46077-8610, USA

Smolan, Rick (Artist, Photographer)
Workman Publishers
225 Varick St Fl 9
New York, NY 10014-4381, USA

Smolinski, Bryan (Athlete, Hockey Player)
4869 Stoneleigh Rd
Bloomfield Hills, MI 48302-2171

Smolinski, Mark (Athlete, Football Player)
3300 Country Club Rd
Petoskey, MI 49770-8211, USA

Smolka, James W Ltcol
PO Box 2123
Lancaster, CA 93539-2123, USA

Smollett, Jurnee (Actor)
c/o Jon Leshay *Storefront Entertainment*
647 N Martel Ave Ste 102
Los Angeles, CA 90036-1930, USA

Smoltz, John A (Athlete, Baseball Player)
700 Foxhollow Run
Alpharetta, GA 30004-0962, USA

Smoot, Fred (Athlete, Football Player)
c/o Bus Cook *Bus Cook Sports, Inc*
1 Willow Bend Dr
Hattiesburg, MS 39402-8552, USA

Smoove, J.B. (Actor, Writer)
c/o Staff Member *Rain Management Group (RMG)*
1631 21st St
Santa Monica, CA 90404-3914, USA

Smothers, Dick (Actor, Comedian)
c/o Staff Member *William Morris Endeavor (LA)*
9601 Wilshire Blvd
Beverly Hills, CA 90210-5213, USA

Smothers, Tom (Actor, Comedian)
PO Box 759
Kenwood, CA 95452-0759, USA

Smothers Brothers, The (Comedian)
c/o Staff Member *William Morris Endeavor (LA)*
9601 Wilshire Blvd
Beverly Hills, CA 90210-5213, USA

Smrek, Peter (Athlete, Hockey Player)
J Mazura 14/52
Martin 1, 3 SLOVA

Smulders, Cobie (Actor)
c/o Staff Member *ROAR (LA)*
9701 Wilshire Blvd Fl 8
Beverly Hills, CA 90212-2008, USA

Smurfit, Victoria (Actor)
c/o Richard Cook *William Morris Endeavor (LA)*
9601 Wilshire Blvd
Beverly Hills, CA 90210-5213, USA

S. Murphy, Christopher (Congressman, Politician)
412 Cannon Hob
Washington, DC 20515-2509, USA

Smyth, Joe (Music Group, Musician)
Sawyer Brown Inc
5200 Old Harding Rd
Franklin, TN 37064-9406, USA

Smyth, Kevin (Athlete, Hockey Player)
4881 Key St
Blaine, WA 98230-7000

Smyth, Patty (Musician)
23712 Malibu Colony Rd
Malibu, CA 90265-6629, USA

Smyth, Ryan (Athlete, Hockey Player)
52314th St
Manhattan Beach, CA 90266

Smyth, Steve (Athlete, Baseball Player)
44005 Northgate Ave
Temecula, CA 92592-3000, USA

Smythe, Marcus (Actor)
c/o Bob Waters *Bob Waters Agency*
9301 Wilshire Blvd Ste 300
Beverly Hills, CA 90210-6119, USA

Snapp, Helen
800 SW 142nd Ave Apt 212
Pembroke Pines, FL 33027-1571, USA

Snare, Ryan (Athlete, Baseball Player)
5315 Wickershire Dr
Peachtree Corners, GA 30092-1693, USA

Snarr, Trevor (Actor)
c/o Elizabeth Knight *KnightStar Multimedia*
PO Box 893
Lehi, UT 84043-0893, USA

Snead, Esix (Athlete, Baseball Player)
1332 42nd St
Orlando, FL 32839-1276, USA

Snead, Jesse Caryle (J C) (Golfer)
PO Box 782170
Wichita, KS 67278-2170, USA

Snead, Norman B (Norm) (Athlete, Football Player)
508 Veranda Way Apt C204
Naples, FL 34104-6049, USA

Snead, W T Sr (Religious Leader)
Baptist Convention Missionary
1404 Firestone Blvd
Los Angeles, CA 90001-3827, USA

Sneaker Pimps (Music Group)
c/o Staff Member *Paradigm (Monterey)*
404 W Franklin St
Monterey, CA 93940-2303, USA

Snedden, Stephen (Actor)
c/o Don Carroll *Don Carroll Management*
14211 Hatteras St
Van Nuys, CA 91401-4207, USA

Sneddon, Bob (Athlete, Football Player)
9564 Brentford Dr
Highlands Ranch, CO 80130-3782, USA

Snedeker, Brandt (Athlete, Golfer)
2509 Iron Gate Ct
Franklin, TN 37069-7240, USA

Sneed, Ed (Golfer)
4155 Nottinghill Gate Rd
Columbus, OH 43220-3942, USA

Sneed, Floyd (Musician)
McKenzie Accountancy
5171 Caliente St Unit 134
Las Vegas, NV 89119-2198, USA

Snell, Ian (Athlete, Baseball Player)
90 Beechwood Ave
Dover, DE 19901-5236, USA

Snell, Matthews (Matt) (Athlete, Football Player)
S C I Limited Inc
175 Clendenny Ave
Jersey City, NJ 07304-1201, USA

Snell, Nate (Athlete, Baseball Player)
7299 Old State Rd
Holly Hill, SC 29059-8514, USA

Snell, Peter (Athlete, Olympic Athlete, Track Athlete)
6452 Dunstan Ln
Dallas, TX 75214-2239, USA

Snell, Ray (Athlete, Football Player)
10306 Councils Way
Temple Terrace, FL 33617-4058, USA

Snelling, Chris (Athlete, Baseball Player)
18122 Rhodes Lake Rd E
Bonney Lake, WA 98391-8143, USA

Snelling, Jason (Athlete, Football Player)
c/o Scott Smith *XAM Sports*
PO Box 1725
Madison, WI 53701-1725, USA

Sneva, Jerry (Race Car Driver)
2652 E 35th Ave
Spokane, WA 99223-4678, USA

Sneva, Tom (Race Car Driver)
3301 E Valley Vista Ln
Paradise Valley, AZ 85253-3739, USA

Sniadecki, Jim (Athlete, Football Player)
1220 Marina Cir
Discovery Bay, CA 94505-9481, USA

Snicket, Lemony (Writer)
Harper Collins Publishers
195 Broadway Fl 2
New York, NY 10007-3132, USA

Snider, Dee (Musician)
c/o Phil Carson *Phil Carson Management*
4931 Coldwater Canyon Ave Apt 1
Sherman Oaks, CA 91423-2229, USA

Snider, Edward M (Ed) (Athlete, Hockey Player)
PO Box 25088
Philadelphia, PA 19147-0288

Snider, George (Race Car Driver)
7404 Lucille Ave
Bakersfield, CA 93308-2725, USA

Snider, Mike (Musician)
PO Box 610
Gleason, TN 38229-0610, USA

Snider, Stacey (Business Person)
c/o Staff Member *Dreamworks Television*
100 Universal Plz Bldg 5125
Universal City, CA 91608, USA

Snider, Todd (Music Group, Musician, Songwriter, Writer)
Al Bunneta Mgmt
33 Music Sq W Ste 102B
Nashville, TN 37203-6607, USA

Snider, Travis (Athlete, Baseball Player)
18511 31st Ave SE
Bothell, WA 98012-8822, USA

Snider, Van (Athlete, Baseball Player)
1615 Windsor Dr
Cleveland, OH 44124-3616, USA

Snipes, Wesley (Actor)
1330 Shelter Rock Rd
Orlando, FL 32835-8032, USA

Snipscheer, Fred (Athlete, Hockey Player)
13404 Macaw Pl
Carmel, IN 46033-8964, USA

Snitker, Brian (Athlete, Baseball Player)
3148 Pine Needle Ct SW
Lilburn, GA 30047-1972, USA

Snitzier, Larry (Musician)
Lindy Martin Mgmt
5 Loblolly Ct
Pinehurst, NC 28374-9349, USA

Snodgrass, William (Writer)
3061 Hughes Rd
Erieville, NY 13061-4128, USA

Snodgrass, William D (Writer)
3061 Hughes Rd
Erieville, NY 13061-4128, USA

Snook, Frank (Athlete, Baseball Player)
2580 Elysium Ave
Eugene, OR 97401-7441, USA

Snopek, Chris (Athlete, Baseball Player)
103 Bradford Dr
Cynthiana, KY 41031, USA

Snow, Al (Race Car Driver)
1227 Leland Ave
Lima, OH 45805-1935, USA

Snow, Brittany (Actor)
c/o Marcel Pariseau *True Public Relations*
6725 W Sunset Blvd Ste 470
Los Angeles, CA 90028-7180, USA

Snow, DeShawn (Reality Star)
c/o Abbey Sibucao-MacDonald *New Wave Entertainment (LA)*
2660 W Olive Ave
Burbank, CA 91505-4525, USA

Snow, Eric (Athlete, Basketball Player)
2229 Edgartown Ln SE
Smyrna, GA 30080-6501, USA

Snow, Garth (Athlete, Hockey Player)
New York Islanders
1255 Hempstead Tpke
Uniondale, NY 11553-1200

Snow, Garth (Athlete, Hockey Player, Olympic Athlete)
4 Weeping Willow Ct
Glen Head, NY 11545-2420

Snow, Gene (Race Car Driver)
5719 Airport Fwy
Haltom City, TX 76117-6007, USA

Snow, John (Politician)
122 Tempsford Ln
Richmond, VA 23226-2319, USA

Snow, J T (Athlete, Baseball Player)
750 W California Way
Woodside, CA 94062-4057, USA

Snow, Justin (Athlete, Football Player)
1826 Milford St
Carmel, IN 46032-7207, USA

Snow, Kate (Television Host)
c/o Staff Member *Good Morning America*
(NY)
147 Columbus Ave Fl 6
Abc
New York, NY 10023-6503, USA

Snow, Percy L (Athlete, Football Player)
2010 48th St NE
Canton, OH 44705-3082, USA

Snowden, Alison (Director, Writer)
c/o Melissa Myers *William Morris*
Endeavor (LA)
9601 Wilshire Blvd
Beverly Hills, CA 90210-5213, USA

Snowdon, Lisa (Actor, Model)
c/o Marki Costello *Creative Management*
Entertainment Group (CMEG)
2050 S Bundy Dr Ste 280
Los Angeles, CA 90025-6128, USA

Snowe, Olympia (Politician)
337 Foreside Rd
Falmouth, ME 04105-1431, USA

Snow Patrol (Music Group)
c/o Staff Member *Paradigm (Monterey)*
404 W Franklin St
Monterey, CA 93940-2303, USA

Snuggerud, Dave (Athlete, Hockey Player,
Olympic Athlete)
968 Bavaria Hills Ter
Chaska, MN 55318-2722, USA

Snuka, Jimmy (Superfly) (Actor, Wrestler)
647 Pacific Ave
Atco, NJ 08004-2117

Snvder, Kyle (Athlete, Baseball Player)
1869 Upper Cove Ter
Sarasota, FL 34231-5437, USA

Snyder, Ben (Comedian)
c/o Staff Member *Gersh (LA)*
9465 Wilshire Blvd Ste 600
Beverly Hills, CA 90212-2605, USA

Snyder, Bill (Coach, Football Coach)
Kansas State University
Athletic Dept
Manhattan, KS 66506, USA

Snyder, Brian (Athlete, Baseball Player)
14834 Wood Home Rd
Centreville, VA 20120-1546, USA

Snyder, Chris (Athlete, Baseball Player)
4921 W Electra Ln
Glendale, AZ 85310-3838, USA

Snyder, Cory (Athlete, Baseball Player,
Olympic Athlete)
468 N Loafer Dr
Payson, UT 84651-4535, USA

Snyder, Daniel (Football Executive)
c/o Staff Member *Washington Redskins*
21300 Redskin Park Dr
Ashburn, VA 20147-6100, USA

Snyder, Dick (Athlete, Basketball Player)
4621 E Mockingbird Ln
Paradise Valley, AZ 85253-2420, USA

Snyder, Dylan Riley (Actor)
c/o Alexandra Heller *Persona PR (LA)*
8840 Wilshire Blvd Ste 212
Beverly Hills, CA 90211-2606, USA

Snyder, Earl (Athlete, Baseball Player)
58 Diamond Ave
Plainville, CT 06062-2904, USA

Snyder, Evan (Doctor)
Harvard Medical School
25 Shattuck St
Boston, MA 02115-6092, USA

Snyder, Fonda (Actor)
c/o Staff Member *William Morris*
Endeavor (LA)
9601 Wilshire Blvd
Beverly Hills, CA 90210-5213, USA

Snyder, Gary (Writer)
18442 MacNab Cypress Rd
Nevada City, CA 95959-8504, USA

Snyder, Gary S (Writer)
18442 MacNab Cypress Rd
Nevada City, CA 95959-8504, USA

Snyder, James (Actor)
c/o Brad Schenck *Paradigm (LA)*
360 N Crescent Dr
North Bldg
Beverly Hills, CA 90210-4874, USA

Snyder, Jerry (Athlete, Baseball Player)
29603 Imperial Creek Dr
Tomball, TX 77377-3975, USA

Snyder, Jim (Athlete, Baseball Player)
7516 Dunbridge Dr
Odessa, FL 33556-2270, USA

Snyder, John (Athlete, Baseball Player)
18241 W Cinnabar Ave
Waddell, AZ 85355-4351, USA

Snyder, Joshua (Actor)
c/o Staff Member *Main Title Entertainment*
8383 Wilshire Blvd Ste 408
Beverly Hills, CA 90211-2435, USA

Snyder, Kyle (Athlete, Baseball Player)
1869 Upper Cove Ter
Sarasota, FL 34231-5437, USA

Snyder, Liza (Actor)
c/o Susan Smith *Susan Smith Company,*
The
2001 Wilshire Blvd Ste 400
Santa Monica, CA 90403-5686, USA

Snyder, Loren (Athlete, Football Player)
12852 War Horse St
San Diego, CA 92129-2222, USA

Snyder, Rick (Governor, Politician)
Office of the Governor
PO Box 30013
Lansing, MI 48909-7513, USA

Snyder, Russ (Athlete, Baseball Player)
PO Box 264
Nelson, NE 68961-0264, USA

Snyder, Solomon H (Doctor)
3801 Canterbury Rd Unit 1001
Baltimore, MD 21218-2379, USA

Snyder, Suzanne (Actor)
Premiere Artists Agency
1875 Century Park E Ste 2250
Los Angeles, CA 90067-2563, USA

Snyder, Todd (Football Player)
Atlanta Falcons
850 S Valley Ln
Palatine, IL 60067-7185, USA

Snyder, Todd (Race Car Driver)
Brian Stewart Racing
PO Box 251
L.P.O.
Niagara Falls, NY 14304-0251, usa

Snyder, William (Journalist)
508 Young St
Dallas, TX 75202-4808, USA

Snyder, William D (Journalist,
Photographer)
Dallas Morning News
Communications Center
Editorial Dept
Dallas, TX 75265, USA

Snyder, Zack (Director, Writer)
c/o Staff Member *Believe Media*
1040 N Las Palmas Ave Bldg 10
Los Angeles, CA 90038-2409, USA

Snyderman, Nancy (Doctor, Television
Host)
c/o Staff Member *NBC News (NY)*
30 Rockefeller Plz
New York, NY 10112-0015, USA

So, Linda (Model)
6130 W Tropicana Ave # 280
Las Vegas, NV 89103-4604

Soares, Jr., John (Race Car Driver)
4004 Dyer Rd
Livermore, CA 94551-7489, USA

Sobchuk, Dennis (Athlete, Hockey Player)
37300 N Tom Darlington Dr N # N
Carefree, AZ 85377, USA

Sobel, Barry
9000 W Sunset Blvd Ste 1200
West Hollywood, CA 90069-5812

Sobers, Rickey (Athlete, Basketball Player)
6530 Annie Oakley Dr Apt 1414
Henderson, NV 89014-2171, USA

Sobers, Ricky
6S3E Annie Oakley Dr Apt 1414
Henderson, NV 89014, USA

Sobieski, Leelee (Actor)
c/o Shelley Browning *Magnolia*
Entertainment (LA)
9595 Wilshire Blvd Ste 601
Beverly Hills, CA 90212-2506, USA

Sobkowiak, Scott (Athlete, Baseball
Player)
1732 Borman Pl
Downers Grove, IL 60516-3743, USA

Sobule, Jill (Musician, Songwriter, Writer)
c/o Jonny (Jon) Podell *Podell Talent*
Agency LLC
22 W 21st St Fl 9
New York, NY 10010-7095, USA

Sochor, James (Jim) (Coach, Football
Coach)
1018 Kent Dr
Davis, CA 95616-0933, USA

Social Distortion (Music Group,
Musician)
c/o Jim Guerinot *Rebel Waltz Inc*
31652 2nd Ave
Laguna Beach, CA 92651-8244, USA

Society, Honor (Music Group, Musician)
c/o Staff Member *Walt Disney Music*
500 S Buena Vista St
Burbank, CA 91521-0007, USA

Soderbergh, Steven (Director, Producer)
c/o Michael Sugar *Anonymous Content*
(LA)
3532 Hayden Ave
Culver City, CA 90232-2413, USA

Soderholm, Eric (Athlete, Baseball Player)
10S360 Hampshire Ln
Willowbrook, IL 60527, USA

Soderstrom, Steve (Athlete, Baseball
Player)
301 N Faith Home Rd
Turlock, CA 95380-9458, USA

Sodowsky, Client (Athlete, Baseball
Player)
2801 Tropicana Ave
Norman, OK 73071-1711, USA

Soetaert, Doug (Athlete, Hockey Player)
8116 N Elmwood Ave
Kansas City, MO 64119-8602

Sofer, Rena (Actor)
c/o Nancy Iannios *Nancy Iannios PR*
PO Box 430
Signal Mountain, TN 37377-0430, USA

Soff, Ray (Athlete, Baseball Player)
146 Drew Ave
Deerfield, MI 49238-9787, USA

Soffer, Jesse Lee (Actor)
c/o Christina Gualazzi *Silver Lining*
Entertainment
421 S Beverly Dr Fl 7
Beverly Hills, CA 90212-4408, USA

Sofield, Rick (Athlete, Baseball Player)
18811 Big Cypress Dr
Jupiter, FL 33458-3728, USA

Sofie von Otter, Anne (Musician)
c/o Staff Member *ICM Partners (LA)*
10250 Constellation Blvd Fl 7
Los Angeles, CA 90067-6207, USA

Sogard, Eric (Athlete, Baseball Player)
15039 N 19th Way
Phoenix, AZ 85022-3904, USA

Sohmer, Steve
2625 Larmar Rd
Los Angeles, CA 90068-2631

Sohn, Sonja (Actor)
c/o James Suskin *James Suskin*
Management
2 Charlton St Apt 5K
New York, NY 10014-4970, USA

Sojo, Luis (Athlete, Baseball Player)
17647 SW 20th St
Miramar, FL 33029-5238, USA

Soklosky, Bing (Cinematographer)
4654 Cartwright Ave
North Hollywood, CA 91602-1451, USA

Sokol, Marilyn (Actor)
24 W 40th St # 1700
New York, NY 10018-3904, USA

Sokoloff, Marla (Actor)
The Firm
9100 Wilshire Blvd Ste 100W
Beverly Hills, CA 90212-3435, USA

Sokolosky, John (Football Player)
Detroit Lions
13240 Leech Dr
Sterling Heights, MI 48312-3253, USA

Sokolov, Grigory L (Musician)
Trawick Artists
1926 Broadway
New York, NY 10023-6915, USA

Solano, Jose (Actor)
c/o Staff Member *Stephany Hurkos*
Management
11935 Kling St
Valley Village, CA 91607-4072, USA

Solars, Stephen
241 Dover St
Brooklyn, NY 11235-3721

Solder, Nate (Football Player)
c/o David Dunn *Athletes First, LLC*
23091 Mill Creek Dr
Laguna Hills, CA 92653-1258, USA

Soleil, Stella (Music Group, Musician)
Kurfirst/Blackwell
350 W End Ave Apt 1A
New York, NY 10024-6818, USA

Soles, Pamela Jayne (PJ) (Actor)
c/o Bill Philputt *Re-Evolution*
Prefers to be contacted via telephone
West Hollywood, CA 90069, USA

Solich, Frank (Coach, Football Coach)
University of Nebraska
Athletic Dept
Lincoln, NE 68588, USA

Solis, Alex (Horse Racer)
411 N Cedros Ave
Solana Beach, CA 92075-4204, USA

Solis, Christina
9300 Wilshire Blvd Ste 555
Beverly Hills, CA 90212-3211

Solo, Hope (Athlete, Olympic Athlete, Soccer Player)
c/o Dan Levy *Wasserman Media Group (NC)*
4208 Six Forks Rd Ste 1020
Raleigh, NC 27609-5738, USA

Solo, Ksenia (Actor)
c/o Pamela Kohl *3 Arts Entertainment (LA)*
9460 Wilshire Blvd Fl 7
Beverly Hills, CA 90212-2713, USA

Soloman, Freddie (Athlete, Football Player)
18110 Palm Beach Dr
Tampa, FL 33647-4047, USA

Soloman, Richard
1550 M St NW Ste 700
Washington, DC 20005-1703, USA

Solomon, Ariel (Football Player)
Pittsburgh Steelers
3142 5th St
Boulder, CO 80304-2504, USA

Solomon, Bruce
3518 Cahuenga Blvd W # 316
Los Angeles, CA 90068-1304

Solomon, David (Director)
c/o Cori Wellins *William Morris Endeavor (LA)*
9601 Wilshire Blvd
Beverly Hills, CA 90210-5213, USA

Solomon, Ed (Writer)
c/o Todd Feldman *Creative Artists Agency (CAA-LA)*
2000 Avenue of the Stars Ste 100
Los Angeles, CA 90067-4705, USA

Solomon, Harold (Tennis Player)
Int'l Mgmt Group
1 Erieview Plz
1360 E 9th St #1300
Cleveland, OH 44114-1738, USA

Solomon, Jesse (Athlete, Football Player)
Minnesota Vikings
401 SW Bunker St
Madison, FL 32340-1902, USA

Solomon, Sophie (Musician)
c/o Staff Member *Paradigm (Monterey)*
404 W Franklin St
Monterey, CA 93940-2303, USA

Solondz, Todd (Director, Writer)
Industry Entertainment
955 Carrillo Dr Ste 300
Los Angeles, CA 90048-5400, USA

Solovey, Sam (Actor)
c/o Staff Member *Ruth Webb Enterprises*
10580 Des Moines Ave
Porter Ranch, CA 91326-2926, USA

Soloway, Jill (Producer)
c/o Staff Member *ICM Partners (LA)*
10250 Constellation Blvd Fl 7
Los Angeles, CA 90067-6207, USA

Solt, Ron (Athlete, Football Player)
1200 Thornhurst Rd
Bear Creek Township, PA 18702-8212, USA

Soltau, Gordie (Athlete, Football Player)
620 Sand Hill Rd Apt 105E
Palo Alto, CA 94304-2605, USA

Soltau, Gordon (Gordy) (Football Player)
620 Sand Hill Rd Apt 105E
Palo Alto, CA 94304-2605, USA

Soltau, Gordy
1111 Hamilton Ave
Palo Alto, CA 94301-2217

Soluna (Music Group)
c/o Staff Member *Creative Artists Agency (CAA-LA)*
2000 Avenue of the Stars Ste 100
Los Angeles, CA 90067-4705, USA

Solzhenitsyn, Ignat (Musician)
Columbia Artists Mgmt Inc
165 W 57th St
New York, NY 10019-2201, USA

Somerhalder, Ian (Actor)
c/o Alissa Vradenburg *Untitled Entertainment (LA)*
350 S Beverly Dr Ste 200
Beverly Hills, CA 90212-4819, USA

Somers, Gwen (Actor, Model)
Alice Fries Agency
1927 Vista Del Mar St
Los Angeles, CA 90068-4004, USA

Somers, Suzanne (Actor)
Port Carling Productions
23961 Craftsman Rd
Calabasas, CA 91302-1417, USA

Somerset, Willie (Athlete, Basketball Player)
6441 Oak View Dr
Harrisburg, PA 17112-1889, USA

Somerville, Bonnie (Actor)
c/o Staff Member *McKeon-Myones Management*
3500 W Olive Ave Ste 770
Burbank, CA 91505-5527, USA

Something Corporate (Music Group)
c/o Staff Member *Agency for the Performing Arts (APA-LA)*
405 S Beverly Dr Ste 500
Beverly Hills, CA 90212-4425, USA

Sommars, Julie (Actor)
7272 Outlook Cove Dr
Los Angeles, CA 90068, USA

Sommer, Rich (Actor)
c/o Staff Member *Davis Spylios Management*
244 W 54th St Ste 707
New York, NY 10019-5515

Sommer, Roy (Athlete, Hockey Player)
65 Roman Dr
Shrewsbury, MA 01545-5819

Sommer, Roy (Athlete, Hockey Player)
Worcester Sharks
50 Foster St
Worcester, MA 01608-1305

Sommerfeld, Kent (Sportscaster)
Milwaukee Brewers
13935 W Maria Dr
New Berlin, WI 53151-6891, USA

Sommers, Denny (Athlete, Baseball Player)
210 W Bath St Apt 133
Hortonville, WI 54944-9459, USA

Sommers, Gordon L (Religious Leader)
Moravian Church Northem Province
1021 Center St
Bethlehem, PA 18018-2838, USA

Sommers, Joanie (Musician)
Xentel
900 SE 3rd Ave Ste 201
Fort Lauderdale, FL 33316-1118, USA

Sommers, Stephen (Director, Producer, Writer)
c/o Stuart Rosenthal *Bloom Hergott Diemer Rosenthal Laviolette Feldman Schenkman & Goodman*
150 S Rodeo Dr Fl 3
Beverly Hills, CA 90212-2410, USA

Sommore (Comedian)
c/o Staff Member *ICM Partners (LA)*
10250 Constellation Blvd Fl 7
Los Angeles, CA 90067-6207, USA

Sondheim, Stephen (Musician)
246 E 49th St
New York, NY 10017-1502, USA

Sondrini, Joe (Athlete, Baseball Player)
16712 Stockland Ct
Huntersville, NC 28078-6438, USA

Sonenclar, Carly Rose (Musician)
c/o Terri Edelman *The Edelman Group*
750 3rd Ave Fl 32
New York, NY 10017-2725, USA

Song, Brenda (Actor)
27014 Slate Ct
Valencia, CA 91381-0656, USA

Songaila, Darius
141 S Longfellow Ln
Mooresville, NC 28117-7116, USA

Songin, Tom (Athlete, Hockey Player)
70 Cascade Ter
Walpole, MA 02081-3239, USA

Songz, Trey (Musician)
801 Brickell Key Blvd Apt 2408
Miami, FL 33131-3720, USA

Soni, Jimmy (Journalist, Writer)
c/o Staff Member *St Martins Press*
175 5th Ave Ste 400
Publicity Dept
New York, NY 10010-7848, USA

Soni, Rebecca (Athlete, Swimmer)
c/o Staff Member *USA Swimming Association*
1 Olympic Plz Bldg 2A
Colorado Springs, CO 80909-5770, USA

Sonmor, Glen (Athlete, Hockey Player)
2301 Vtllase Ln Apt 214
Minneapolis, MN 55431, USA

Sonnanstine, Andy (Athlete, Baseball Player)
5301 Gulf Blvd Apt D406
Saint Petersburg, FL 33706-2380, USA

Sonnenfeld, Barry (Director)
c/o Richard Lovett *Creative Artists Agency (CAA-LA)*
2000 Avenue of the Stars Ste 100
Los Angeles, CA 90067-4705, USA

Sonnenschein, Klaus (Actor)
Breisgauer Str. 15a
Berlin, GE D-141

Sonnier, Jo-El (Musician)
Entertainment Artists
2409 21st Ave S Ste 100
Nashville, TN 37212-5317, USA

Sons of the Desert (Music Group)
c/o Staff Member *William Morris Endeavor (Nashville)*
1600 Division St Ste 300
Nashville, TN 37203-2755, USA

Sons of the Pioneers
117 Berms Cir Apt 4
Branson, MO 65616-3875

Sonzero, Jim (Writer)
c/o Andrew Cannava *United Talent Agency (UTA-LA)*
9336 Civic Center Dr
Beverly Hills, CA 90210-3604, USA

Soo Hoo, Hayward (Actor)
1411 Solar Dr
Monterey Park, CA 91754-4548, USA

Soomekh, Bahar (Actor)
c/o Paul Kohner *Kohner Agency, The*
9300 Wilshire Blvd Ste 555
Beverly Hills, CA 90212-3211, USA

Soon-Shiong, Patrick (Doctor)
NantHealth
9920 Jefferson Blvd
Culver City, CA 90232-3506, USA

Sopel, Brent (Athlete, Hockey Player)
5506 S Park Ave
Hinsdale, IL 60521-5019, USA

Sopkovic, Kay (Athlete, Baseball Player)
6540 W Butler Dr Unit 62
Glendale, AZ 85302-4313, USA

Sorbo, Kevin (Actor)
c/o Sherry Marsh *Marsh Entertainment*
12444 Ventura Blvd Ste 203
Studio City, CA 91604-2409, USA

Sorel, Louise (Actor)
10808 Lindbrook Dr
Los Angeles, CA 90024-3007, USA

Sorel, Ted (Actor)
c/o Staff Member *Kerin-Goldberg Associates*
155 E 55th St Ste 5D
New York, NY 10022-4038, USA

Sorensen, Lary (Athlete, Baseball Player)
42515 Northville Place Dr Apt 406
Northville, MI 48167-3186, USA

Sorensen, Nick (Athlete, Football Player)
305 Grandview Dr
Blacksburg, VA 24060-6222, USA

Sorensen, Zach (Athlete, Baseball Player)
441 W Granite Dr
Washington, UT 84780-8331, USA

Sorenson, Heidi (Actor, Model)
Shelly & Pierce
13775A Mono Way # 220
Sonora, CA 95370-8813, USA

Sorenson, Reed (Race Car Driver)
Richard Petty Motorsports
320 Aviation Dr
Statesville, NC 28677-2509, USA

Sorenson, Theodore
1285 Avenue of the Americas Rm 200
New York, NY 10019-6028

Sorenson, Zach (Athlete, Baseball Player)
2690 E 1400 South Cir
Saint George, UT 84790-6198, USA

Sorenstam, Annika (Golfer)
c/o Staff Member *IMG (Cleveland)*
1360 E 9th St Ste 100
Cleveland, OH 44114-1730, USA

Sorenstam, Charlotta (Golfer)
c/o Patrick Bruce
1411 W Whitman Ct
Anthem, AZ 85086-3927, USA

Sorey, Revie (Athlete, Football Player)
485 Saint Moritz Dr
Glen Ellyn, IL 60137-4320, USA

Sorgi, Jim (Athlete, Football Player)
72 Hollaway Blvd
Brownsburg, IN 46112-8355, USA

Soria, Oscar (Sportscaster)
111 E Beth Dr
Phoenix, AZ 85042-7657, USA

Soriano, Alfonso G (Baseball Player)
Texas Rangers
1000 Ballpark Way Ste 400
Arlington, TX 76011-5170, USA

Soriano, Rafael (Athlete, Baseball Player)
7601 60th Dr NE # A
Marysville, WA 98270-3301, USA

Sorkin, Aaron (Producer, Writer)
c/o Rick Rosen *William Morris Endeavor (LA)*
9601 Wilshire Blvd
Beverly Hills, CA 90210-5213, USA

Sorkin, Andrew Ross (Commentator)
c/o Matthew Snyder *Creative Artists Agency (CAA-LA)*
2000 Avenue of the Stars Ste 100
Los Angeles, CA 90067-4705, USA

Sorkin, Arleen (Actor)
623 S Beverly Glen Blvd
Los Angeles, CA 90024-2531, USA

Sorrentino, Mike (The Situation) (Reality Star)
MPS Entertainment
138 Filbert Run
Freehold, NJ 07728-4116, USA

Sorrento, Paul (Athlete, Baseball Player)
5918 Mont Blanc Pl NW
Issaquah, WA 98027-7859, USA

Sorrento, Paul A (Baseball Player)
5918 Mont Blanc Pl NW
Issaquah, WA 98027-7859, USA

Sortun, Henrik (Athlete, Football Player)
6708 16th Ave NW
Seattle, WA 98117-5513, USA

Sorum, Matt (Musician)
c/o Todd Cameron *Abrams Artists Agency (LA)*
9200 W Sunset Blvd PH 11
West Hollywood, CA 90069-3601, USA

Sorvino, Mira (Actor)
25253 Malibu Rd
Malibu, CA 90265-4625, USA

Sorvino, Paul (Actor)
c/o Kieran Maguire *The Arlook Group*
205 S Beverly Dr Ste 209
Beverly Hills, CA 90212-3899, USA

Sosa, Elias (Athlete, Baseball Player)
333 Red Barn Trl
Matthews, NC 28104-5447, USA

Sosa, Sammy (Athlete, Baseball Player)
667 Ocean Blvd
Golden Beach, FL 33160-2217, USA

Sosenka, Don (Race Car Driver)
Mr Magoo
PO Box 679
Spring Branch, TX 78070-0679, USA

Sospiri, Vincenzo (Race Car Driver)
Dan Gurney's All American Racing
2334 S Broadway
Santa Ana, CA 92707-3250, USA

Sossamon, Lou (Athlete, Football Player)
6308 Exum Dr
West Columbia, SC 29169-7184, USA

Sossamon, Shannyn (Actor)
c/o Oren Segal *Radius Entertainment*
9229 W Sunset Blvd Ste 301
West Hollywood, CA 90069-3417, USA

Soter, Paul (Comedian)
c/o Staff Member *United Talent Agency (UTA-LA)*
9336 Civic Center Dr
Beverly Hills, CA 90210-3604, USA

Soto, Blanca (Actor)
c/o Bryan Brucks *Luber Roklin Management*
5815 W Sunset Blvd Ste 206
Los Angeles, CA 90028-6481, USA

Soto, Geovany (Athlete, Baseball Player)
6319 Perch Creek Dr
Houston, TX 77049-3447, USA

Soto, Mario M (Athlete, Baseball Player)
6319 Perch Creek Dr
Houston, TX 77049-3447, USA

Soto, Talisa (Actor)
c/o Peg Donegan *Framework Entertainment (LA)*
9057 Nemo St Ste C
West Hollywood, CA 90069-5511, USA

Sotomayor Sanabria, Javier (Athlete, Track Athlete)
Int'l Mgmt Group
1 Erieview Plz
1360 E 9th St #1300
Cleveland, OH 44114-1738, USA

Soucy, Christian (Athlete, Hockey Player)
274 Wildflower Cir
Williston, VT 05495-9391, USA

Souders, Cecil (Athlete, Football Player)
1803 Channingway Ct E
Reynoldsburg, OH 43068, USA

Soul Asylum (Music Group)
c/o Wesley Kidd *Red Light Management (VA)*
321 E Main St Ste 500
Charlottesville, VA 22902-3201, USA

Sound Tribe Sector 9 (Music Group)
c/o Staff Member *Paradigm (Monterey)*
404 W Franklin St
Monterey, CA 93940-2303, USA

Souray, Sheldon (Athlete, Hockey Player)
27927 Pacific Coast Hwy
Malibu, CA 90265-4326, USA

Soutar, Dave (Bowler)
6910 Chickasaw Falls Ave
Bradenton, FL 34203, USA

Soutar, Judy (Bowler)
3914 102nd Pl N
Clearwater, FL 33762-5404, USA

Soutendijk, Renee (Actor)
Marion Rosenberg
PO Box 69826
West Hollywood, CA 90069-0826, USA

Souter, David H (Attorney)
US Supreme Court
214 Hopkins Green Rd
Contoocook, NH 03229-2611, USA

South, Mike
PO Box 1288
Tucker, GA 30085-1288

Southam, James (Athlete, Olympic Athlete, Track Athlete)
18230 Norway Dr
Anchorage, AK 99516-6033, USA

Souther, J D (Musician, Songwriter, Writer)
8263 Hollywood Blvd
Los Angeles, CA 90069-1611, USA

Southerland, Ron (Race Car Driver)
7416 E Palo Verde Dr
Scottsdale, AZ 85250-6030, USA

Southerland II, Steve (Congressman, Politician)
1229 Longworth Hob
Washington, DC 20515-1315, USA

Southern, Silas (Eddie) (Athlete, Track Athlete)
2006 Custer Pkwy
Richardson, TX 75080-3403, USA

Southern Belles
11150 W Olympic Blvd Ste 1100
Los Angeles, CA 90064-1845

Southworth, Bill (Athlete, Baseball Player)
320 Dobbin Rd
Saint Louis, MO 63119-4515, USA

Southworth, Carrie (Actor)
c/o Van Johnson *Van Johnson Company*
350 S Beverly Dr Ste 200
Beverly Hills, CA 90212-4819, USA

Souza, Karla (Actor)
c/o Alejandro Asensi *Asensi Management*
1100 Glendon Ave Ste 1100
Los Angeles, CA 90024-3515, USA

Souza, Mark (Athlete, Baseball Player)
10001 Woodcreek Oaks Blvd Unit 817
Roseville, CA 95747-5105, USA

Sova, Peter M (Cinematographer)
1492 Roses Brook Rd
South Kortright, NY 13842-2514, USA

Sovereign, Lady (Musician)
c/o Staff Member *Paradigm (Monterey)*
404 W Franklin St
Monterey, CA 93940-2303, USA

Sovey, William P (Business Person)
Newell Co
20 E Milwaukee St Ste 212
Janesville, WI 53545-3061, USA

Sovran, Gino (Athlete, Basketball Player)
2669 Cheswick Dr
Troy, MI 48084-1069, USA

Soward, R J (Athlete, Football Player)
7660 Chipwood Ln
Jacksonville, FL 32256-2338, USA

Sowell, Arnold (Arnie) (Athlete, Track Athlete)
1647 Waterstone Ln # 1
Charlotte, NC 28262-3176, USA

Sowells, Rich (Athlete, Football Player)
3406 Ash Creek Dr
Missouri City, TX 77459-4953, USA

Sowers, Barbara (Athlete, Baseball Player)
30329 Cedar Rd
Punta Gorda, FL 33982-3307, USA

Sowers, Jeremy (Athlete, Baseball Player)
1005 Pueblo Ridge Pl
Cary, NC 27519-0832, USA

Soyer, David (Musician)
PO Box 307
Brattleboro, VT 05302-0307, USA

Spacek, Jaroslav (Athlete, Hockey Player)
6301 Osprey Ter
Coconut Creek, FL 33073-2624, USA

Spacek, Sissy (Actor)
Beau Val Farm
PO Box 22
Keswick, VA 22947-0022, USA

Spacey, Kevin (Actor, Producer)
c/o Joanne Horowitz *Joanne Horowitz Management*
9350 Wilshire Blvd Ste 224
Beverly Hills, CA 90212-3204, USA

Spade, David (Actor, Comedian)
c/o Marc Gurvitz *Brillstein Entertainment Partners (LA)*
9150 Wilshire Blvd Ste 350
Beverly Hills, CA 90212-3453, USA

Spade, Kate (Designer, Fashion Designer)
2 Park Ave Rm 8R
New York, NY 10016-5613, USA

Spader, James (Actor)
254 S Windsor Blvd
Los Angeles, CA 90004-3820, USA

Spagnardi, Darren (Athlete, Baseball Player)
2364 W Center Street Ext
Lexington, NC 27295-5943, USA

Spagnola, John S (Athlete, Football Player)
414 Hillbrook Rd
Bryn Mawr, PA 19010-3634, USA

Spahn, Ryan (Actor)
c/o Ann Kelly *Ann Kelly Management*
245 W 51st St Apt 411
New York, NY 10019-6281, USA

Spahr, Charles E (Business Person)
800 Beach Rd
Vero Beach, FL 32963-3392, USA

Spain, Douglas (Actor)
Innovative Artists
1505 10th St
Santa Monica, CA 90401-2805, USA

Spalding, Esperanza (Musician)
c/o Scott Southard *International Music Network (IMN)*
278 Main St
Gloucester, MA 01930-6022, USA

Spalding, Leslie (Athlete, Golfer)
1055 O Malley Dr
Billings, MT 59102-2524, USA

Spall, Timothy (Actor)
c/o Laura Berwick *Berwick & Kovacik*
9465 Wilshire Blvd Ste 420
Beverly Hills, CA 90212-2603, USA

Spanarkel, Jim (Athlete, Basketball Player)
436 Edgewood Pl
Rutherford, NJ 07070-2662, USA

Spanger, Amy (Actor)
c/o Maureen Taran *New Wave Entertainment (LA)*
2660 W Olive Ave
Burbank, CA 91505-4525, USA

Spangler, Al (Athlete, Baseball Player)
27202 Afton Way
Huffman, TX 77336-3601, USA

Spangler, Al (Athlete, Baseball Player)
27202 Afton Way
Huffman, TX 77336-3601, USA

Spang-McCook, Laurette (Actor)
4154 Colbath Ave
Sherman Oaks, CA 91423-4208, USA

Spanhel, Martin (Athlete, Hockey Player)
299 Lazelle Place Ln
Lewis Center, OH 43035-8830, USA

Spani, Gary (Athlete, Football Player)
3920 NE Sequoia St
Lees Summit, MO 64064-1574, USA

Spanjers, Martin (Actor)
c/o Sommer Smith *Innovative Artists (LA)*
1505 10th St
Santa Monica, CA 90401-2805, USA

Spano, Joe (Actor)
EC Assoc
10315 Woodley Ave Ste 110
Granada Hills, CA 91344-6900, USA

Spano, Nick (Actor)
c/o Justin Evans *The Independent Group*
6363 Wilshire Blvd Ste 115
Los Angeles, CA 90048-5734, USA

Spano, Robert (Musician)
c/o Staff Member *ICM Partners (LA)*
10250 Constellation Blvd Fl 7
Los Angeles, CA 90067-6207, USA

Spano, Vincent (Actor)
c/o Jo Kincaid *Gilbertson Management*
1334 3rd Street Promenade Ste 201
Santa Monica, CA 90401-1320, USA

Spanos, Alex (Football Executive)
1533 W Lincoln Rd
Stockton, CA 95207-2447, USA

Spanoulis, Vassilis (Athlete, Basketball Player)
c/o Jeff Schwartz *Excel Sports Management (NY)*
1700 Broadway Fl 29
New York, NY 10019-5905, USA

Spanswick, Bill (Athlete, Baseball Player)
1200 Commonwealth Cir Apt 202
Naples, FL 34116-6631, USA

Sparks
106 N Buffalo St Ste 200
Warsaw, IN 46580-2755

Sparks, Dana (Actor)
VOX
6420 Wilshire Blvd Ste 1080
Los Angeles, CA 90048-5539, USA

Sparks, Daniel (Athlete, Basketball Player)
2396 N Bruceville Rd
Vincennes, IN 47591-9698, USA

Sparks, Hal (Actor, Comedian, Musician, Producer)
c/o Sarah Klegman *Levity Entertainment Group (LEG)*
6701 Center Dr W Ste 1111
Los Angeles, CA 90045-1552, USA

Sparks, Hayley
5757 Wilshire Blvd # 512
Los Angeles, CA 90036-5810

Sparks, Jeff (Athlete, Baseball Player)
714 W 42nd St
Houston, TX 77018-4429, USA

Sparks, Joe (Athlete, Baseball Player)
3915 E Cholla St
Phoenix, AZ 85028-2116, USA

Sparks, Jordin (Musician)
3007 Lakeridge Dr
Los Angeles, CA 90068-1809, USA

Sparks, Kylie (Actor)
c/o Myrna Lieberman *Myrna Lieberman Management*
3001 Hollyridge Dr
Los Angeles, CA 90068-1951, USA

Sparks, Mike (Referee)
c/o Staff Member *World Wrestling Entertainment (WWE)*
1241 E Main St
Titan Towers
Stamford, CT 06902-3520, USA

Sparks, Nicholas (Writer)
c/o Theresa Park *Park Literary*
270 Lafayette St Ste 1504
New York, NY 10012-3327, USA

Sparks, Phillippi (Athlete, Football Player)
3315 W Walter Way
Phoenix, AZ 85027-1084, USA

Sparks, Stephanie (Golfer)
48 Redwood Ln
Wheeling, WV 26003-4854, USA

Sparks, Steve (Athlete, Baseball Player)
23378 Wilson Dr
Loxley, AL 36551-8559, USA

Sparks, Steve (Athlete, Baseball Player)
4019 Colony Oaks Dr
Sugar Land, TX 77479-2420, USA

Sparlis, Alexander (Al) (Athlete, Football Player)
HC 4 Box 243
Porterville, CA 93257-9706, USA

Sparrow, Guy (Athlete, Basketball Player)
8875 Highway 128
Savannah, TN 38372-5986, USA

Sparrow, Rory (Athlete, Basketball Player)
111 Valley Rd
Montclair, NJ 07042-2322, USA

Sparv, Camilla (Actor)
1500 Ocean Dr Apt 602
Miami Beach, FL 33139-3179, USA

Sparxxx, Bubba (Musician)
c/o Staff Member *Paradigm (Monterey)*
404 W Franklin St
Monterey, CA 93940-2303, USA

Speake, Bob (Athlete, Baseball Player)
4742 SW Urish Rd
Topeka, KS 66610-9758, USA

Speakman, Jeff (Actor)
11141 Woodview Dr
Rch Cucamonga, CA 91730-6728, USA

Speaks, Ruben L (Religious Leader)
African Methodist Episcopal Zion Church
PO Box 32843
Charlotte, NC 28232-2843, USA

Spearman, Alvin (Athlete, Baseball Player)
635 E 49th St Apt 3
Chicago, IL 60615-1556, USA

Spearritt, Hannah (Actor, Musician)
c/o Jeb Brandon *Kritzer Levine Wilkins Entertainment (KLWG)*
11872 La Grange Ave Fl 1
Los Angeles, CA 90025-5283, USA

Spears, Aries (Actor)
c/o Staff Member *AKA Talent Agency*
6310 San Vicente Blvd Ste 200
Los Angeles, CA 90048-5488, USA

Spears, Britney (Dancer, Musician)
398 W Stafford Rd
Thousand Oaks, CA 91361-5000, USA

Spears, Eddie (Actor)
c/o Jennie Saks *NASS Talent Management*
2212 Lea Ave
Bozeman, MT 59715-2264, USA

Spears, Ernest (Athlete, Football Player)
528 Clark Rd
Northfield, VT 05663-6182, USA

Spears, Jamie Lynn (Actor, Musician)
c/o Lou Taylor *Tri Star Sports & Entertainment Group (LA)*
1800 Century Park E Ste 1000
Los Angeles, CA 90067-1513, USA

Spears, Marcus (Athlete, Football Player)
10402 Reading Rd
Richmond, TX 77469-7330, USA

Spears, Peter (Actor)
c/o Jaclyn Travers *Creative Artists Agency (CAA-LA)*
2000 Avenue of the Stars Ste 100
Los Angeles, CA 90067-4705, USA

Spears, Randy (Adult Film Star)
c/o Staff Member *Wicked Pictures*
9040 Eton Ave
Canoga Park, CA 91304-1616, USA

Spears, William D (Football Player)
63 Waterbridge Pl
Ponte Vedra Beach, FL 32082-2323, USA

Specht, Greg (Athlete, Football Player)
8650 SW Woodside Dr
Portland, OR 97225-1742, USA

Speck, Cliff (Athlete, Baseball Player)
43773 Pettirosso St
Indio, CA 92203-2728, USA

Specter, Rachel (Actor)
c/o Adam Griffin *Kritzer Levine Wilkins Entertainment (KLWG)*
11872 La Grange Ave Fl 1
Los Angeles, CA 90025-5283, USA

Spector, Phil (Business Person, Songwriter)
1700 Grand View Dr
Alhambra, CA 91803-2639, USA

Speech (Artist, Musician)
William Morris Agency
1325 Avenue of the Americas Bsmt 2
New York, NY 10019-6047, USA

Speed, Horace (Athlete, Baseball Player)
6821 State Boulevard Ext
Meridian, MS 39305-8420, USA

Speed, Lake (Race Car Driver)
c/o Staff Member *NASCAR*
1801 W Speedway Blvd
Daytona Beach, FL 32114-1243, USA

Speed, Lizz (Producer)
c/o Staff Member *Jackoway Tyerman Wertheimer Austen Mandelbaum Morris & Klein*
1925 Century Park E Fl 22
Los Angeles, CA 90067-2701, USA

Speedman, Scott (Actor)
c/o Frank Frattaroli *Circle of Confusion (LA)*
8931 Ellis Ave
Los Angeles, CA 90034-3336, USA

Speedwagon, REO (Music Group, Musician)
c/o Keith Naisbitt *Agency Group Ltd, The (LA)*
1880 Century Park E Ste 711
Los Angeles, CA 90067-1618, USA

Speer, Del (Athlete, Football Player)
17620 NW 40th Ave
Miami Gardens, FL 33055-3864, USA

Speers, Ted (Athlete, Hockey Player)
61515 Brookway Dr
South Lyon, MI 48178-7056, USA

Spehr, Tim (Athlete, Baseball Player)
8524 Briargrove Dr
Woodway, TX 76712-2305, USA

Speier, Chris (Athlete, Baseball Player)
3102 N Manor Dr W
Phoenix, AZ 85014-5525, USA

Speier, Jackie (Congressman, Politician)
211 Cannon Hob
Washington, DC 20515-0549, USA

Speier, Justin (Athlete, Baseball Player)
9405 S 51st St
Phoenix, AZ 85044-5686, USA

Speier, Ryan (Athlete, Baseball Player)
5516 E 75th St
Tulsa, OK 74136-7119, USA

Speight, Derrick (Producer)
c/o Staff Member *Screen Door Entertainment*
15223 Burbank Blvd
Van Nuys, CA 91411-3505, USA

Speight, Lester (Rasta) (Actor)
c/o Staff Member *William Morris Endeavor (LA)*
9601 Wilshire Blvd
Beverly Hills, CA 90210-5213, USA

Speigner, Levale (Athlete, Baseball Player)
1041 Bond St
Thomasville, GA 31757-0221, USA

Speir, Chris
6114 E Montecito Ave
Scottsdale, AZ 85251-1936

Spektor, Regina (Actor, Musician)
c/o Marsha Vlasic *ICM Partners (LA)*
10250 Constellation Blvd Fl 7
Los Angeles, CA 90067-6207, USA

Spelke, Elizabeth S (Doctor)
Harvard University
Psychology Dept
Cambridge, MA 02138, USA

Spelling, Candy (Actor)
c/o Kevin Sasaki *Kevin Sasaki Public Relations & Media Counsel*
8491 W Sunset Blvd Ste 224
West Hollywood, CA 90069-1911, USA

Spelling, Randy (Actor)
c/o Staff Member *Innovative Artists (LA)*
1505 10th St
Santa Monica, CA 90401-2805, USA

Spelling, Tori (Actor)
c/o Meghan Prophet *PMK/BNC Public Relations (PMK-LA)*
8687 Melrose Ave Ste 8
West Hollywood, CA 90069-5746, USA

Spellman, Alonzo R (Athlete, Football Player)
1300 Marigold Way
Pflugerville, TX 78660-4137, USA

Spellman, John D (Ex-Governor)
Carney Stephenson Badley
701 5th Ave Ste 3600
Columbia Center
Seattle, WA 98104-7010, USA

Spelvin, Georgina (Actor)
3121 Ledgewood Dr
Los Angeles, CA 90068-1913

Spence, Blake (Athlete, Football Player)
300 NW 8th Ave Apt 802
Portland, OR 97209-3561, USA

Spence, Bob (Athlete, Baseball Player)
3081 Bonita Woods Dr
Bonita, CA 91902-2020, USA

Spence, Gerry (Attorney)
PO Box 548
Jackson, WY 83001-0548, USA

Spence, Sebastian (Actor)
c/o Lesa Kirk *Open Entertainment*
1051 Cole Ave Ste B
Los Angeles, CA 90038-2601, USA

Spencer, Abigail (Actor)
c/o Jon Rubinstein *Authentic Talent and Literary Management*
20 Jay St Ste M17
Brooklyn, NY 11201-8300, USA

Spencer, Andre (Athlete, Basketball Player)
1315 W Gage Ave
Los Angeles, CA 90044-2733, USA

Spencer, Anthony (Athlete, Football Player)
c/o Eugene Parker *Maximum Sports Management*
6435 W Jefferson Blvd # 197
Fort Wayne, IN 46804-6203, USA

Spencer, Chaske (Actor)
c/o Staff Member *Josselyne Herman & Associates*
345 E 56th St Apt 3B
New York, NY 10022-3745, USA

Spencer, Chris (Actor)
c/o Julia Buchwald *Don Buchwald & Associates (LA)*
6500 Wilshire Blvd Ste 2200
Los Angeles, CA 90048-4942, USA

Spencer, Darryl (Athlete, Football Player)
1473 Beechfern Dr
Melbourne, FL 32935-5989, USA

Spencer, Daryl (Athlete, Baseball Player)
2740 S Larkin Dr
Wichita, KS 67216-1258, USA

Spencer, Elizabeth (Writer)
402 Longleaf Dr
Chapel Hill, NC 27517-3042, USA

Spencer, Elmore (Athlete, Basketball Player)
2770 Foxlair Trl
Atlanta, GA 30349-4436, USA

Spencer, Felton (Athlete, Basketball Player)
4102 Nicholas Roy Ct
Prospect, KY 40059-8209, USA

Spencer, Freddie (Race Car Driver)
Freddie Specer's
7055 Speedway Blvd # E-106
Las Vegas, NV 89115-1807, USA

Spencer, GC (Race Car Driver)
698 Pickens Bridge Rd
Johnson City, TN 37615-4017, USA

Spencer, George (Athlete, Baseball Player)
8160 Hickory Ave
Galena, OH 43021-8508, USA

Spencer, Jesse (Actor)
c/o Jason Weinberg *Untitled Entertainment (LA)*
350 S Beverly Dr Ste 200
Beverly Hills, CA 90212-4819, USA

Spencer, Jimmy (Football Player)
5331 Talavero Pl
Parker, CO 80134-2799, USA

Spencer, Jimmy (Race Car Driver)
160 Gasoline Aly
Mooresville, NC 28117-6502, USA

Spencer, J Robert (Actor)
c/o Nyle Brenner *Brenner Management*
9171 Wilshire Blvd Ste 441
Beverly Hills, CA 90210-5516, USA

Spencer, Lara (Television Host)
c/o Jonathan Rosen *William Morris Endeavor (NY)*
1325 Avenue of the Americas
New York, NY 10019-6026, USA

Spencer, Marc (Radio Personality)
c/o Staff Member *WPKX*
1331 Main St Ste 4
Springfield, MA 01103-1621, USA

Spencer, Maurice (Athlete, Football Player)
61 W 62nd St
New York, NY 10023-7015, USA

Spencer, Octavia (Actor)
c/o Melissa Kates *Viewpoint Inc (LA)*
8820 Wilshire Blvd Ste 220
Beverly Hills, CA 90211-2622, USA

Spencer, Roderick
602 Bay St
Santa Monica, CA 90405-1215

Spencer, Sean (Athlete, Baseball Player)
3584 E Calistoga Ct
Port Orchard, WA 98366-4084, USA

Spencer, Shane (Athlete, Baseball Player)
2858 Manzanita View Rd
Alpine, CA 91901-3988, USA

Spencer, Stan (Athlete, Baseball Player)
502 Lexington Way
Vancouver, WA 98664-1218, USA

Spencer, Timothy (Tim) (Athlete, Football Player)
1435 Sherborne Ln
Powell, OH 43065-7604, USA

Spencer, Tom (Athlete, Baseball Player)
2021 E Conner Stra
Tucson, AZ 85719-3206, USA

Spencer, Tracie (Musician)
Rogers & Cowan
6340 Breckenridge Run
Rex, GA 30273-1841, USA

Spencer, Willie (Athlete, Football Player)
1109 Johnson St SE
Massillon, OH 44646-8266, USA

Spencer-Devlin, Muffin (Golfer)
1278 Glenneyre St Apt 155
Laguna Beach, CA 92651-3103, USA

Spenn, Fred (Athlete, Baseball Player)
5201 Desoto Rd
Sarasota, FL 34235-3607, USA

Sperber Carter, Paula (Bowler)
10331 SW 102nd Ave
Miami, FL 33176-3507, USA

Sperling, Gene (Government Official, Politician)
National Economic Council
1600 Pennsylvania Ave NW
Washington, DC 20506, USA

Spero, Nancy
530 Laguardia Pl Apt 2
New York, NY 10012-1427, USA

Sperring, Rob (Athlete, Baseball Player)
13302 Chriswood Dr
Cypress, TX 77429-2066, USA

Spevack, Jason (Actor)
c/o Dana Fletcher *Coast to Coast Talent Group*
3350 Barham Blvd
Los Angeles, CA 90068-1404, USA

Speyrer, Cotton (Athlete, Football Player)
7905 San Felipe Blvd Apt 117
Austin, TX 78729-7638, USA

Spezza, Jason (Athlete, Hockey Player)
The Orr Hockey Group
PO Box 290836
Charlestown, MA 02129-0215, USA

Spheeris, Penelope (Director)
PO Box 1128
Studio City, CA 91614-0128, USA

Spice 1 (Artist, Musician)
JL Entertainment
18653 Ventura Blvd # 340
Tarzana, CA 91356-4103, USA

Spice Girls (Music Group)
35 Parkgate Rd # 32
London, EN SW11

Spicer, Bob (Athlete, Baseball Player)
423 McPhee Dr
Fayetteville, NC 28305-5129, USA

SPider Loc (Musician)
c/o Staff Member *Interscope Records (NY)*
1755 Broadway
New York, NY 10019-3743, USA

Spiegelman, Art (Writer)
c/o Staff Member *Steven Barclay Agency*
12 Western Ave
Petaluma, CA 94952-2907, USA

Spieier, Patrick (Baseball Player)
6635 S 108th Ave
Omaha, NE 68137-4733, USA

Spielberg, David (Actor)
10537 Cushdon Ave
Los Angeles, CA 90064-3315, USA

Spielberg, Steven (Director, Producer)
1680 Old Oak Rd
Los Angeles, CA 90049-2506, USA

Spieler, Patrick (Athlete, Baseball Player)
6635 S 108th Ave
Omaha, NE 68137-4733, USA

Spielman, Chris (Athlete, Football Player, Sportscaster)
OSU 336 LLC
PO Box 20236
Attn: Carry Billy
Columbus, OH 43220-0236, USA

Spiers, Bill (Athlete, Baseball Player)
9233 Old State Rd
Cameron, SC 29030-8129, USA

Spiers, Judi (Actor)
1-3 Charlotte St
London, EN W1P 1

Spiezio, Ed (Athlete, Baseball Player)
2550 Gore Rd
Morris, IL 60450-8686, USA

Spiezio, Scott (Athlete, Baseball Player)
2550 Gore Rd
Morris, IL 60450-8686, USA

Spikes, Brandon (Athlete, Football Player)
c/o Gary Uberstine *Premier Sports Management*
16133 Ventura Blvd Ste 500
Encino, CA 91436-2402, USA

Spikes, Cameron (Athlete, Football Player)
3001 Fraternity Row # 132
College Station, TX 77845, USA

Spikes, Charlie (Athlete, Baseball Player)
531 N Border Dr
Bogalusa, LA 70427-3307, USA

Spikes, Jack E (Athlete, Football Player)
9537 Highland View Dr
Dallas, TX 75238-1025, USA

Spikes, Takeo (Athlete, Football Player)
5005 Heatherwood Ct
Roswell, GA 30075-2285, USA

Spilborghs, Ryan (Athlete, Baseball Player)
2220 Elise Way
Santa Barbara, CA 93109-1814, USA

Spilde, Jenna (Model, Reality Star)
c/o Staff Member *The Sports Illustrated Fresh Faces Competition*
Nbc Entertainment
3000 W Alameda Ave #5366
Burbank, CA 91523-0001, USA

Spilker, Angela
425 N Oakhurst Dr
Beverly Hills, CA 90210-3982

Spiller, Michael A (Cinematographer)
2418 Roscomare Rd
Los Angeles, CA 90077, USA

Spillner, Dan (Athlete, Baseball Player)
18505 SE Newport Way Unit C113
Issaquah, WA 98027-9032, USA

Spilman, Harry (Athlete, Baseball Player)
4423 Saint Phillips Rd S
Mount Vernon, IN 47620-9629, USA

Spin Doctors, The (Music Group)
c/o Staff Member *Paradigm (Monterey)*
404 W Franklin St
Monterey, CA 93940-2303, USA

Spinella, Stephen (Actor)
c/o Staff Member *Innovative Artists (LA)*
1505 10th St
Santa Monica, CA 90401-2805, USA

Spinelli, Jerry (Writer)
331 Melvin Rd
Phoenixville, PA 19460, USA

Spiner, Brent (Actor)
c/o Becca Kovacik *Berwick & Kovacik*
9465 Wilshire Blvd Ste 420
Beverly Hills, CA 90212-2603, USA

Spinks, Michael (Athlete, Boxer, Olympic Athlete)
Butch Lewis Productions
PO Box 77684
Seattle, WA 98177-0684, USA

Spinks, Scipio (Athlete, Baseball Player)
11422 Rock Bridge Ln
Sugar Land, TX 77498-0923, USA

Spinney, Caroll (Actor)
940 Brickyard Rd
Woodstock, CT 06281-1302, USA

Spinotti, Dante (Cinematographer)
Smith/Gosnell/Nicholson
PO Box 1156
Studio City, CA 91614-0156, USA

Spires, Greg (Athlete, Football Player)
175 Centre St # 520
Quincy, MA 02169-8600, USA

Spiridakos, Tracy (Actor)
c/o Melissa Raubvogel *Baker Winokur Ryder Public Relations (BWR-NY)*
292 Madison Ave Fl 12
New York, NY 10017-6415, USA

Spiro, Jordana (Actor)
c/o Larry Taube *Principal Entertainment (LA)*
9255 W Sunset Blvd Ste 500
West Hollywood, CA 90069-3301, USA

Spiro, Lev L (Director)
c/o Staff Member *William Morris Endeavor (LA)*
9601 Wilshire Blvd
Beverly Hills, CA 90210-5213, USA

Spitler, Austin (Athlete, Football Player)
c/o Joe Flanagan *BTI Sports Advisors*
170 N Scoville Ave
Oak Park, IL 60302-2647, USA

Spitz, Mark (Athlete, Olympic Athlete, Swimmer)
c/o Staff Member *Premier Management Group (PMG Sports)*
115 Crescent Commons Dr Ste 250
Cary, NC 27518-8134, USA

Spitzer, Eliot (Ex-Governor, Talk Show Host)
985 5th Ave
New York, NY 10075-0142, USA

Spivey, Junior (Athlete, Baseball Player)
4140 S Ambrosia Dr
Chandler, AZ 85248-4804, USA

Spivey, Sebron (Athlete, Football Player)
435 Capitol View Dr
Columbus, OH 43203-1037, USA

Splatt, Rachel (Race Car Driver)
12631 N Tatum Blvd
Phoenix, AZ 85032-7710, USA

Splatt, Rachelle (Race Car Driver)
12631 N Tatum Blvd
Phoenix, AZ 85032-7710, USA

Spoelstra, Erik (Basketball Coach)
3060 Matilda St
Miami, FL 33133-4546, USA

Spoiler, The
3615 W Waters Ave # 110
Tampa, FL 33614-2783

Spoliaric, Paul (Athlete, Baseball Player)
545 Gramiak Rd
Kelownabc V1x 1k4, BC CANAD, USA

Spoljario, Paul (Baseball Player)
Toronto Blue Jays
13261 N 73rd Ave
Peoria, AZ 85381-6054, USA

Sponable, Jess M (Astronaut)
1501 Quail St Spc 102
Newport Beach, CA 92660-2726, USA

Spong, John S (Religious Leader)
24 Puddingstone Rd
Morris Plains, NJ 07950-1114, USA

Spooneybarger, Tim (Athlete, Baseball Player)
4109 Bamboo Dr
Pensacola, FL 32526-8425, USA

Spork, Shirley (Golfer)
PO Box 637
Palm Desert, CA 92261-0637, USA

Sporkin, Stanley (Government Official, Judge)
US District Court
Courthouse
3rd & Constitution NW
Washington, DC 20001, USA

Sporleder, Gregory (Actor)
c/o Julia Buchwald *Don Buchwald & Associates (LA)*
6500 Wilshire Blvd Ste 2200
Los Angeles, CA 90048-4942, USA

Sposa, Mike (Golfer)
3 Pine Valley Ct
Spartanburg, SC 29306-6633, USA

Spottiswoode, Roger (Director)
c/o Staff Member *ICM Partners (LA)*
10250 Constellation Blvd Fl 7
Los Angeles, CA 90067-6207, USA

Spottsville, Ray (Baseball Player)
Houston Eagles
PO Box 591
Colfax, LA 71417-0591, USA

Spound, Michael (Actor)
James/Levy/Jacobson
3500 W Olive Ave Ste 1470
Burbank, CA 91505-5514, USA

Spradlin, Danny (Athlete, Football Player)
1011 Laurie St
Maryville, TN 37803-6731, USA

Spradlin, Jerry (Athlete, Baseball Player)
2824 E Diana Ave
Anaheim, CA 92806-4412, USA

Spradling, Charlie (Actor)
c/o Staff Member *Don Buchwald & Associates (NY)*
10 E 44th St Frnt 1
New York, NY 10017-3654, USA

Spragan, Donnie (Athlete, Football Player)
312 Riviera Dr
Union City, CA 94587-3722, USA

Sprague, Ed (Athlete, Baseball Player)
19015 N Davis Rd
Lodi, CA 95242-9203, USA

Sprague, Ed (Athlete, Olympic Athlete, Swimmer)
4677 Pine Valley Cir
Stockton, CA 95219-1881, USA

Sprague, Jack (Race Car Driver)
X-Press Motorsports
610 Performance Rd
Mooresville, NC 28115-9595, USA

Sprayberry, Dylan (Actor)
c/o Laura Pallas *Pallas Management*
5301 Bellaire Ave
Valley Village, CA 91607-2329, US

Spreitler, Taylor (Actor)
c/o Cameron Curtis *Curtis Talent Management*
9607 Arby Dr
Beverly Hills, CA 90210-1202, USA

Sprewell, Latrell (Athlete, Basketball Player)
1120 E Pleasant St
Milwaukee, WI 53202-2125, USA

Spriggs, George (Athlete, Baseball Player)
77A W Bay Front Rd # A
Lothian, MD 20711-9711, USA

Spriggs, Larry (Athlete, Basketball Player)
7870 Boeing Ave
Los Angeles, CA 90045-3142, USA

Spring, Jack (Athlete, Baseball Player)
PO Box 118
Colbert, WA 99005-0118, USA

Spring, Sherwood C (Astronaut)
2116 McDonough Ln
San Diego, CA 92106-6087, USA

Spring, Sherwood C Colonel (Astronaut)
2104 McDonough Ln
San Diego, CA 92106-6087, USA

Springer, Dennis (Athlete, Baseball Player)
537 Sherwood Ct
Hanford, CA 93230-6859, USA

Springer, Jerry (Talk Show Host, Television Host)
454 N Columbus Dr # 200
Chicago, IL 60611-5807, USA

Springer, Michael (Golfer)
1482 E Forest Oaks Dr
Fresno, CA 93730-3443, USA

Springer, Mike (Golfer)
1482 E Forest Oaks Dr
Fresno, CA 93730-3443, USA

Springer, Robert C (Astronaut)
202 Village Cir
Sheffield, AL 35660-5632, USA

Springer, Robert C Colonel (Astronaut)
202 Village Cir
Sheffield, AL 35660-5632, USA

Springer, Russ (Athlete, Baseball Player)
PO Box 185
4357 Highway 8
Pollock, LA 71467-0185, USA

Springer, Steve (Athlete, Baseball Player)
616 7th St
Huntington Beach, CA 92648-4613, USA

Springfield, Marty (Athlete, Baseball Player)
5164 Flicker Field Cir
Sarasota, FL 34231-3242, USA

Springfield, Rick (Actor, Musician)
30635 La Sonora Dr
Malibu, CA 90265-3125, USA

Springgs, Marcus (Athlete, Football Player)
830 Regal St
Houston, TX 77034-1231, USA

Springs, Kirk (Athlete, Football Player)
4925 Paddock Rd
Cincinnati, OH 45237-5548, USA

Springs, Shawn (Football Player)
Washington Redskins
21300 Redskin Park Dr
Ashburn, VA 20147-6100, USA

Springsteen, Bruce (Musician, Songwriter)
3561 Ambassador Dr
Wellington, FL 33414-6817, USA

Springsteen, Pamela (Actor, Photographer)
c/o Caryn Weiss *Weiss Artists*
6311 Romaine St # 7234
Los Angeles, CA 90038-2617, USA

Sprinkel, Beryl W (Government Official)
20140 Saint Andrews Dr
Olympia Fields, IL 60461-1169, USA

Sproles, Darren (Athlete, Football Player)
c/o Jimmy Sexton *CAA (Memphis)*
6060 Poplar Ave Ste 470
Memphis, TN 38119-0910, USA

Sprotte, Jimmy (Athlete, Football Player)
2163 E Palmcroft Dr
Tempe, AZ 85282-3062, USA

Sprouse, Cole (Actor)
c/o Megan Moss Pachon *ID Public Relations (LA)*
7060 Hollywood Blvd Fl 8th
Los Angeles, CA 90028-6021, USA

Sprouse, Dylan (Actor)
c/o Megan Moss Pachon *ID Public Relations (LA)*
7060 Hollywood Blvd Fl 8th
Los Angeles, CA 90028-6021, USA

Sprout, Bob (Athlete, Baseball Player)
227 County Road 740
Enterprise, AL 36330-6827, USA

Sprowl, Bobby (Athlete, Baseball Player)
4711 Leeward Ave
Northport, AL 35473-1934, USA

Spruill, Marquis (Athlete, Football Player)
c/o Joe Linta *JL Sports*
1204 Main St Ste 179
Branford, CT 06405-3787, USA

Spurgeon, Jay (Athlete, Baseball Player)
212 Hartsdale Rd
Rochester, NY 14622-2007, USA

Spurling, Chris (Athlete, Baseball Player)
27247 Copper Ridge Dr
Wesley Chapel, FL 33544-7331, USA

Spurlock, Morgan (Actor)
c/o Richard Arlook *The Arlook Group*
205 S Beverly Dr Ste 209
Beverly Hills, CA 90212-3899, USA

Spurrier, Steve (Athlete, Coach, Football Coach, Football Player, Heisman Trophy Winner)
126 Beaver Ridge Dr
Elgin, SC 29045-8210, USA

Spurrior, Stephen O (Steve) (Coach, Football Player)
17050 Silver Charm Pl
Leesburg, VA 20176-7152, USA

Spuzich, Sandra (Golfer)
Ladies Pro Golf Assn
100 International Golf Dr
Daytona Beach, FL 32124-1082, USA

Spyro Gyro
200 W Superior St Ste 202
Chicago, IL 60654-3554, USA

Square, Damion (Athlete, Football Player)
c/o Brian E. Overstreet *E.O. Sports Management*
2211 Norfolk St Ste 210
Houston, TX 77098-4055, USA

Squerciati, Marina (Actor)
c/o Myrna Jacoby *MJ Management*
130 W 57th St Apt 11A
New York, NY 10019-3311, USA

Squibb, June (Actor)
c/o Martin Gage *Gage Group, The (LA)*
5757 Wilshire Blvd Ste 659
Los Angeles, CA 90036-3682, USA

Squierek, Jack (Football Player)
4051 Vezber Dr
Seven Hills, OH 44131-6233, USA

Squirek, Jack (Athlete, Football Player)
4051 Vezber Dr
Seven Hills, OH 44131-6233, USA

Squires, Mike (Athlete, Baseball Player)
3646 Whicker Pointe
Kalamazoo, MI 49006-6413, USA

Squirrel Nut Zippers
2756 N Green Valley Pkwy # 449
Henderson, NV 89014-2120

Sri Chinmoy (Religious Leader)
85-45 Sri Chinmoy St
Jamaica, NY 11432, USA

St, Clair Carl
Pacific Symphony Orchestra
1231 E Dyer Rd
Santa Ana, CA 92705-5606, USA

Staab, Rebecca (Actor)
Don Buchwald
6500 Wilshire Blvd Ste 2200
Los Angeles, CA 90048-4942, USA

Staal, Eric (Athlete, Hockey Player)
The Orr Hockey Group
PO Box 290836
Charlestown, MA 02129-0215, USA

Staal, Jordan (Athlete, Hockey Player)
c/o Rick Curran *The Orr Hockey Group (PA)*
411 Timber Ln
Devon, PA 19333-1232, USA

Staats, Dewayne (Sportscaster)
1170 Gulf Blvd Apt 1601
Clearwater Beach, FL 33767-2785, USA

Staats, Dewayne (Baseball Player, Sportscaster)
Tampa Bay Devil Rays
1170 Gulf Blvd Apt 1601
Clearwater Beach, FL 33767-2785, USA

Stabenow, Deborah (Politician)
238 9th St SE
Washington, DC 20003-2111, USA

Stabile, Nick
c/o Staff Member *Diverse Talent Group*
9911 W Pico Blvd Ste 340W
Los Angeles, CA 90035-2703, USA

Stablein, George (Athlete, Baseball Player)
2903 Penman
Tustin, CA 92782-3314, USA

Stabler, Ken
260 N Joachim St
Mobile, AL 36603-6472

Stabler, Ken M (Kenny) (Football Player)
260 N Joachim St
Mobile, AL 36603-6472, USA

Stables, Kelly (Actor)
c/o Kurt Patino *Patino Management Company*
4370 Tujunga Ave Ste 120
Studio City, CA 91604-2763, USA

Stacey, Siran (Athlete, Football Player)
PO Box 131
Hartford, AL 36344-0131, USA

Stacey Q (Actor, Music Group, Musician)
641 S Palm St Ste D
La Habra, CA 90631-5758, USA

Stack, Brian (Writer)
c/o Staff Member *3 Arts Entertainment (LA)*
9460 Wilshire Blvd Fl 7
Beverly Hills, CA 90212-2713, USA

Stack, Rosemarie (Actor)
PO Box 49488
Los Angeles, CA 90049-0488, USA

Stack, Timothy
10635 Santa Monica Blvd Ste 130
Los Angeles, CA 90025-8306

Stackhouse, Charles (Athlete, Football Player)
240 Shady Grove St
Marion, AR 72364-9412, USA

Stackhouse, Jerry (Athlete, Basketball Player)
S266 Settles Bridge Rd
Suwanee, GA 30024, USA

Stacom, Kevin (Athlete, Basketball Player)
14 Florida Ave
Jamestown, RI 02835-1548, USA

Stacy, Billy (Athlete, Football Player)
400 Colonial Cir
Starkville, MS 39759-4214, USA

Stacy, Hollis (Golfer)
405 74th St
Holmes Beach, FL 34217-1111, USA

Stacy, James (Actor)
478 Severn Ave
Tampa, FL 33606-3842, USA

Stadlen, Lewis J. (Actor)
c/o Staff Member *Access Talent Voice Overs*
171 Madison Ave Ste 900
New York, NY 10016-5110

Stadler, Craig (Golfer)
113 Elk Xing
Evergreen, CO 80439-4114, USA

Staehle, Marv (Athlete, Baseball Player)
19421 Cromwell Ct Apt 208
Fort Myers, FL 33912-0386, USA

Staffieri, Joe (Athlete, Football Player)
6825 Polo Fields Pkwy
Cumming, GA 30040-5731, USA

Stafford, Ben (Horse Racer)
22 Glen Dr
Voorhees, NJ 08043-1404, USA

Stafford, Jerry (Baseball Player)
2316 Catalina Cir Apt 276
Oceanside, CA 92056-5395, USA

Stafford, Jim (Musician, Songwriter)
PO Box 509
Winter Haven, FL 33882-0509, USA

Stafford, Jimmy (Musician)
9562 Hampton Reserve Dr
Brentwood, TN 37027-8491, USA

Stafford, John R (Business Person)
American Home Products
1901 Doolittle Dr
Bridgewater, NJ 08807-7032, USA

Stafford, Matthew (Athlete, Football Player)
c/o Tom Condon *CAA (St. Louis)*
222 S Central Ave Ste 1008
Saint Louis, MO 63105-3509, USA

Stafford, Michelle (Actor)
c/o Marlan Willardson *MWPR*
10153 Riverside Dr # 157
Toluca Lake, CA 91602-2562, USA

Stafford, Nancy (Actor)
PO Box 3353
Westlake Village, CA 91359-0353, USA

Stafford, Steve (Actor)
Studio Wings, Inc.
855 Aviation Dr
Camarillo, CA 93010-8849, USA

Stageman-Roberts, Donna (Athlete, Baseball Player)
1831 Jerome Pl
Helena, MT 59601-4735, USA

Staggers, Jon (Athlete, Football Player)
3835 Oakes Dr
Hayward, CA 94542-1720, USA

Staggs, Jeff (Athlete, Football Player)
4641 Jeri Way
El Cajon, CA 92020-8329, USA

Staggs, Steve (Athlete, Baseball Player)
4001 Bentbrook Pl
Norman, OK 73072-4020, USA

Stagliano, John
14141 Covello St Ste 8C
Van Nuys, CA 91405-1400

Stagus, Gus (Coach, Swimmer)
University of Michigan
Athletic Dept
Ann Arbor, MI 48104, USA

Stahl, Jerry (Actor, Writer)
c/o Staff Member *United Talent Agency (UTA-LA)*
9336 Civic Center Dr
Beverly Hills, CA 90210-3604, USA

Stahl, Larry (Athlete, Baseball Player)
1506 E Main St # A
Belleville, IL 62221-5436, USA

Stahl, Lesley (Journalist)
c/o Staff Member *William Morris Endeavor (LA)*
9601 Wilshire Blvd
Beverly Hills, CA 90210-5213, USA

Stahl, Leslie (Actor)
c/o Staff Member *William Morris Endeavor (LA)*
9601 Wilshire Blvd
Beverly Hills, CA 90210-5213, USA

Stahl, Lisa (Actor)
Don Buchwald
6500 Wilshire Blvd Ste 2200
Los Angeles, CA 90048-4942, USA

Stahl, Nick (Actor)
c/o Sean Fay *Kritzer Levine Wilkins Entertainment (KLWG)*
11872 La Grange Ave Fl 1
Los Angeles, CA 90025-5283, USA

Stahley, Adele (Baseball Player)
3700 SE Jennings Rd Apt 214W
Port St Lucie, FL 34952-7701, USA

Stahoviak, Scott (Athlete, Baseball Player)
507 Balmoral Ct
Grayslake, IL 60030-9303, USA

Stai, Brendon (Athlete, Football Player)
1431 Teal Trce
Pittsburgh, PA 15237-3848, USA

Staib, David P (Astronaut)
6905 Vantage Dr
Alexandria, VA 22306-1245, USA

Staiger, Roy (Athlete, Baseball Player)
1233 Tyler Dr
Lebanon, MO 65536-4121, USA

Staind (Music Group)
c/o Staff Member *Mitch Schneider Organization (MSO)*
14724 Ventura Blvd Ste 410
Sherman Oaks, CA 91403-3537, USA

Staios, Steve (Athlete, Hockey Player)
1213 Newbridge Tree NE
Atlanta, GA 30319, USA

Stairs, Matt (Athlete, Baseball Player)
76 Skyline Rd
Bangor, ME 04401, USA

Staite, Jewel (Actor)
c/o Nils Larsen *Principato/Young Management (LA)*
9465 Wilshire Blvd Ste 900
Beverly Hills, CA 90212-2608, USA

Stalcup, Jerry (Athlete, Football Player)
1023 Westchester Dr
Rockford, IL 61107-3442, USA

Staley, Bill (Athlete, Football Player)
9210 Todd Rd
Potter Valley, CA 95469-9727, USA

Staley, Dawn (Athlete, Basketball Player, Olympic Athlete)
Dawn Staley Foundation
1224 Glenwood Rd
Columbia, SC 29204-3351, USA

Staley, Dawn M (Basketball Player, Coach)
1228 Callowhill St # 603
Philadelphia, PA 19123, USA

Staley, Joan (Actor)
24516 Windsor Dr Unit B
Valencia, CA 91355-4430, USA

Staley, Lex (Radio Personality)
c/o Staff Member *The Lex & Terry Morning Radio Network*
11700 Central Pkwy
Jacksonville, FL 32224-2600, USA

Staley, Matthew R (Actor, Musician)
PO Box 590
New York, NY 10108-0590, USA

Staley, Walter (Athlete, Hockey Player)
214 Teal Lake Rd
Mexico, MO 65265-3705, USA

Stallard, Tracy (Athlete, Baseball Player)
PO Box 905
Wise, VA 24293-0905, USA

Stallings, Gene (Athlete, Football Coach, Football Player)
6508 County Road 43200
Powderly, TX 75473-5320, USA

Stallings, Larry (Athlete, Football Player)
555 Town Hall Ct
Saint Louis, MO 63141-7228, USA

Stallings, Matthew Davey (Race Car Driver)
632 Wears Valley Rd
Pigeon Forge, TN 37863-7752, USA

Stallone, Jackie (Actor)
PO Box 491550
Los Angeles, CA 90049-9550, USA

Stallone, Sylvester (Actor, Director, Producer)
30 Beverly Park Ter
Beverly Hills, CA 90210-1563, USA

Stalls, David (Athlete, Football Player)
2100 Stout St
Denver, CO 80205-2827, USA

Stallworth, Bud (Athlete, Basketball Player)
14 Westwood Rd
Lawrence, KS 66044-4560, USA

Stallworth, Dave (Athlete, Basketball Player)
4400 N Rushwood St
Wichita, KS 67226-1475, USA

Stallworth, Donte (Athlete, Football Player)
6601 53rd St
Sacramento, CA 95823-1410, USA

Stallworth, Johnny L (John) (Athlete, Football Player)
302 Osman Dr
Madison, AL 35756-3499, USA

Stallworth, Ron (Athlete, Football Player)
1834 Parkview Dr S
Montgomery, AL 36117-7701, USA

Stalmaster, Lynn
12400 Wilshire Blvd Ste 920
Los Angeles, CA 90025-1040

Stam, Jessica (Model)
c/o Staff Member *IMG*
304 Park Ave S Fl 12
New York, NY 10010-4314, USA

Stam, Katie (Beauty Pageant Winner)
The Miss America Organization
222 New Rd Ste 700
Linwood, NJ 08221-1286, USA

Stamatopoulos, Dino (Writer)
c/o Greg Cavic *Creative Artists Agency (CAA-LA)*
2000 Avenue of the Stars Ste 100
Los Angeles, CA 90067-4705, USA

Stamberg, Josh (Actor)
c/o James Suskin *James Suskin Management*
2 Charlton St Apt 5K
New York, NY 10014-4970, USA

Stamler, Lorne (Athlete, Hockey Player)
1011 Orca Ct
Holiday, FL 34691-9817, USA

Stamm, Michael (Mike) (Athlete, Swimmer)
3929 Everett Ave
Oakland, CA 94602-1763, USA

Stammen, Craig (Athlete, Baseball Player)
13235 State Route 127
Rossburg, OH 45362-9505, USA

Stamos, John (Actor, Musician)
c/o Daniel (Danny) Sussman *Brillstein Entertainment Partners (LA)*
9150 Wilshire Blvd Ste 350
Beverly Hills, CA 90212-3453, USA

Stamp, Terence (Actor)
c/o Beth Holden-Garland *Untitled Entertainment (LA)*
350 S Beverly Dr Ste 200
Beverly Hills, CA 90212-4819, USA

Stamps, Sylvester (Athlete, Football Player)
Atlanta Falcons
951 Royal Oak Dr
Jackson, MS 39209-6736, USA

Stams, Frank (Athlete, Football Player)
2870 Marcia Blvd
Cuyahoga Falls, OH 44223-1146, USA

Stan, Sebastian (Actor)
c/o Emily Gerson Saines *Brookside Artists Management (NY)*
250 W 57th St Ste 2303
New York, NY 10107-2399, USA

Stanback, Haskel (Athlete, Football Player)
1530 Kingston Dr
Kannapolis, NC 28083-9280, USA

Stanchfield, Darby (Actor)
c/o Michael Smith *Principal Entertainment (LA)*
9255 W Sunset Blvd Ste 500
West Hollywood, CA 90069-3301, USA

Standen, Clive (Actor)
c/o Caryn Leeds *Sunshine Sachs (NY)*
136 Madison Ave Fl 17
New York, NY 10016-6734, USA

Standly, Mike (Golfer)
2306 Columbia Cir
League City, TX 77573-7622, USA

Standridge, Jason (Athlete, Baseball Player)
6228 Cardinal Dr
Pinson, AL 35126-3492, USA

Stanek, Al (Athlete, Baseball Player)
96 Allyn St
Holyoke, MA 01040-2549, USA

Stanfel, Richard (Dick) (Athlete, Coach, Football Player)
1104 Juniper Pkwy
Libertyville, IL 60048-3543, USA

Stanfield, Fred (Athlete, Hockey Player)
59 Cheshire Ln
East Amherst, NY 14051-2602, USA

Stanfield, Jack (Athlete, Hockey Player)
5715 Logan Ln
Houston, TX 77007-8005, United States

Stanfield, Kevin (Athlete, Baseball Player)
7565 Newcomb St
San Bernardino, CA 92410-4333, USA

Stanfill, Dennis
908 Oak Grove Ave
San Marino, CA 91108-1022

Stanfill, William T (Bill) (Athlete, Football Player)
3117 Wisteria Ct
Albany, GA 31721-2988, USA

Stanford, Aaron (Actor)
c/o Lainie Sorkin Becky *Management 360*
9111 Wilshire Blvd
Beverly Hills, CA 90210-5508, USA

Stanford, Angela (Golfer)
525 Buckstone Dr
Fort Worth, TX 76179-1245, USA

Stanford, Jason (Athlete, Baseball Player)
4505 W Mesquital Del Oro
Tucson, AZ 85742-9704, USA

Stange, Lee (Athlete, Baseball Player)
436 Dolphin St
Melbourne Beach, FL 32951-2916, USA

Stangel, Eric (Producer, Writer)
c/o Staff Member *3 Arts Entertainment (LA)*
9460 Wilshire Blvd Fl 7
Beverly Hills, CA 90212-2713, USA

Stangel, Justin (Producer, Writer)
c/o Staff Member *3 Arts Entertainment (LA)*
9460 Wilshire Blvd Fl 7
Beverly Hills, CA 90212-2713, USA

Stanger, Patti (Business Person, Reality Star)
c/o Lance Klein *William Morris Endeavor (LA)*
9601 Wilshire Blvd
Beverly Hills, CA 90210-5213, USA

Stanhouse, Don (Athlete, Baseball Player)
4 Creekmere Dr
Roanoke, TX 76262-9755, USA

Stanicek, Pete (Athlete, Baseball Player)
525 Wilson St
Downers Grove, IL 60515-3845, USA

Stanicek, Steve (Athlete, Baseball Player)
16354 Lanfear Dr
Lockport, IL 60441-4747, USA

Stanich, George (Athlete, Baseball Player, Beauty Pageant Winner, Olympic Athlete)
15816 Marigold Ave
Gardena, CA 90249-4837, USA

Stanifer, Rob (Athlete, Baseball Player)
10618 Park Place Dr
Largo, FL 33778-3402, USA

Stanis, Bernadette (Actor)
Sheba Media Group
11152 Westheimer Rd # 299
C/O Vanessa Morman
Houston, TX 77042-3208, USA

Stanka, Joe (Athlete, Baseball Player)
32718 Weymouth Ct
Fulshear, TX 77441-4164, USA

Stankavage, Scott (Athlete, Football Player)
3843 Somerset Dr
Durham, NC 27707-5016, USA

Stankiewicz, Andy (Athlete, Baseball Player)
9729 Wren Bluff Dr
San Diego, CA 92127-3462, USA

Stankowski, Paul (Athlete, Golfer)
4705 Saint Clair Ct
Flower Mound, TX 75022-1038, USA

Stanley, Bob (Athlete, Baseball Player)
30 Tansy Ave
Stratham, NH 03885-2288, USA

Stanley, Chad (Athlete, Football Player)
17496 US Highway 69 S
Tyler, TX 75703-8094, USA

Stanley, Christopher (Actor)
c/o Dan Baron *Agency for the Performing Arts (APA-LA)*
405 S Beverly Dr Ste 500
Beverly Hills, CA 90212-4425, USA

Stanley, Frank (Cinematographer)
PO Box 2230
Los Angeles, CA 90078-2230, USA

Stanley, Fred (Athlete, Baseball Player)
2109 Winthrop Hill Rd
Argyle, TX 76226-2103, USA

Stanley, Israel (Athlete, Football Player)
3850 S Miner St
Milwaukee, WI 53221-1250, USA

Stanley, James (Producer)
c/o Staff Member *United Talent Agency (UTA-LA)*
9336 Civic Center Dr
Beverly Hills, CA 90210-3604, USA

Stanley, Marianne Crawford (Coach)
New York Liberty
125 W End Ave # 6
Madison Square Garden
New York, NY 10023-6387, USA

Stanley, Marlanne Crawford (Basketball Player, Coach)
Washington Mystics
601 F St NW
Mci Center
Washington, DC 20004-1605, USA

Stanley, Mike (Athlete, Baseball Player)
1108 NE 10th Ave
Fort Lauderdale, FL 33304-2115, USA

Stanley, Paul (Musician)
c/o Doc McGhee *McGhee Entertainment*
8730 W Sunset Blvd Ste 175
West Hollywood, CA 90069-2246, USA

Stanley, Ralph (Music Group, Musician)
Press Office
2607 Westwood Dr
Nashville, TN 37204-2709, USA

Stanley, Richard (Athlete, Football Player)
4248 S FM 2869
Hawkins, TX 75765-5300, USA

Stanley, Scott M (Writer)
University of Denver
2199 S University Blvd
Denver, CO 80210-4700, USA

Stanley, Walter (Athlete, Football Player)
23977 E Alamo Pl
Aurora, CO 80016-4247, USA

Stansberry, Craig (Athlete, Baseball Player)
3433 Adirondack Ln
Frisco, TX 75033-1398, U S A

Stansbury, Terence
901 N Franklin St # 2
Wilmington, DE 19806-4529, USA

Stansbury, Terrace (Athlete, Basketball Player)
901 N Franklin St # 2
Wilmington, DE 19806-4529, USA

Stansfield, Claire
9300 Wilshire Blvd Ste 555
Beverly Hills, CA 90212-3211

Stanton, Andrew (Animator, Director, Writer)
c/o Staff Member *Pixar Animation Studios*
1200 Park Ave
Emeryville, CA 94608-3677, USA

Stanton, Drew (Athlete, Football Player)
c/o Mark Bartelstein *Priority Sports & Entertainment - Chicago*
312 N La Salle
Suite 650
Chicago, IL 60610, USA

Stanton, Giancarlo (Athlete, Baseball Player)
c/o Joel Wolfe *Wasserman Media Group (LA)*
12100 W Olympic Blvd Ste 200
Los Angeles, CA 90064-1075, USA

Stanton, Harry Dean (Actor)
14527 Mulholland Dr
Los Angeles, CA 90077-1713, USA

Stanton, Jeff (Race Car Driver)
1137 Athens Rd
Sherwood, MI 49089-9721, USA

Stanton, Leroy (Athlete, Baseball Player)
1751 N Norwood Ln
Florence, SC 29506-6901, U S A

Stanton, Mike (Athlete, Baseball Player)
3801 E Van Buren St
Camano Island, AZ 98282, USA

Stanton, Molly (Actor)
c/o Rick Kurtzman *Creative Artists Agency (CAA-LA)*
2000 Avenue of the Stars Ste 100
Los Angeles, CA 90067-4705, USA

Stanton, Paul (Athlete, Hockey Player)
2061 Snook Dr
Naples, FL 34102-1574, USA

Stapf, David (Business Person)
c/o Staff Member *CBS Paramount Network Television*
4024 Radford Ave
Cbs Studios
Studio City, CA 91604-2190, USA

Stapinski, Helene (Writer)
Saint Martin's Press
175 5th Ave Ste 400
New York, NY 10010-7848, USA

Staples, Mavis (Music Group, Musician)
PO Box 498360
Chicago, IL 60649-0159, USA

Staple Singers, The
PO Box 170429
San Francisco, CA 94117-0429

Stapleton, Dave (Athlete, Baseball Player)
418 S Galaxy Dr
Chandler, AZ 85226-4644

Stapleton, Dave (Athlete, Baseball Player)
51 N Bayview St
Fairhope, AL 36532-2537, USA

Stapleton, Jacinta (Actor)
c/o Stacey Testro *Stacey Testro International*
8265 W Sunset Blvd Ste 102
West Hollywood, CA 90046-2433, USA

Stapleton, Kevin (Actor)
Gersh Agency
232 N Canon Dr
Beverly Hills, CA 90210-5302, USA

Stapleton, Mike (Athlete, Hockey Player)
7719 Cottage Dr
Bellaire, MI 49615-9228, USA

Stapleton, Oliver (Cinematographer)
MacCorkindale & Holton
1640 5th St Ste 205
Santa Monica, CA 90401-3325, USA

Stapleton, Sullivan (Actor)
c/o Lindsay Galin *Rogers & Cowan PR (NY)*
919 3rd Ave Fl 18
New York, NY 10022-3902, USA

Stapp, Scott (Musician)
c/o Staff Member *Wind-up Records*
72 Madison Ave Fl 8
New York, NY 10016-8731, USA

Star, Darren (Doctor, Producer, Writer)
c/o Tracey Jacobs *United Talent Agency (UTA-LA)*
9336 Civic Center Dr
Beverly Hills, CA 90210-3604, USA

Star, Marilyn (Adult Film Star)
1521 Alton Rd # 369
Miami Beach, FL 33139-3301, USA

Star, Ryan (Musician)
c/o Mike Esterman *Esterman.Com, LLC*
Prefers to be contacted via email
Baltimore, MD XXXXX, USA

Starbird, Kate (Basketball Player)
Indiana Fever
125 S Pennsylvania St
Conseco Fieldhouse
Indianapolis, IN 46204-3610, USA

Starbuck, Jo Jo (Athlete, Figure Skater, Olympic Athlete)
33 Pomeroy Rd
Madison, NJ 07940-2638, USA

Starch, Ken (Athlete, Football Player)
603 E Hillcrest Dr
Verona, WI 53593-1517, USA

Starfield, Barbara H (Doctor)
Johns Hopkins University
624 N Broadway
Hygiene School
Baltimore, MD 21205-1900, USA

Stargell, Tony (Athlete, Football Player)
131 Jenny Rd
Grantville, GA 30220-2134, USA

Starikov, Sergei (Athlete, Hockey Player)
209 Greenbrook Rd
Green Brook, NJ 08812-2205, USA

Stark, Chad (Athlete, Football Player)
300 Broadway N Apt 401
Fargo, ND 58102-4726, USA

Stark, Collin (Actor)
c/o Peter Himberger *Impact Artists Group LLC*
42 Hamilton Ter
New York, NY 10031-6403, USA

Stark, Dennis (Athlete, Baseball Player)
213 N Elm St
Edgerton, OH 43517-9672, USA

Stark, Don (Actor)
c/o Tom Harrison *Diverse Talent Group*
9911 W Pico Blvd Ste 340W
Los Angeles, CA 90035-2703, USA

Stark, Matt (Athlete, Baseball Player)
721 Shirehampton Dr
Las Vegas, NV 89178-1233, USA

Stark, Melissa (Correspondent, Sportscaster)
NBC-TV
30 Rockefeller Plz
News Dept
New York, NY 10112-0015, USA

Stark, Rohn T (Athlete, Football Player)
PO Box 10067
Lahaina, HI 96761-0067, USA

Starke, Anthony (Actor)
c/o Staff Member *Paradigm (LA)*
360 N Crescent Dr
North Bldg
Beverly Hills, CA 90210-4874, USA

Starkey, Jason (Athlete, Football Player)
1525 Washington Ave # 1
Huntington, WV 25704-1520, USA

Starks, Duane (Athlete, Football Player)
811 NW 199th St
Miami, FL 33169, USA

Starks, James (Athlete, Football Player)
c/o Dave Butz *Sportstars Inc*
1350 Avenue of the Americas Fl 28
New York, NY 10019-4702, USA

Starks, John (Athlete, Basketball Player)
PO Box 8146
Stamford, CT 06905-8146, USA

Starks, Max (Athlete, Football Player)
c/o Ashley Smith Becker *Relativity Sports (LA)*
9242 Beverly Blvd Ste 300
Beverly Hills, CA 90210-3728, USA

Starks, Randy (Athlete, Football Player)
c/o Tony Paige *Perennial Sports and Entertainment*
1455 Pennsylvania Ave NW Ste 225
Washington, DC 20004-1026, USA

Starner, Shelby (Music Group, Musician)
Morebam Music
30 Hillcrest Ave
Morristown, NJ 07960-5090, USA

Starnes, John G (Athlete, Football Player)
8826 Shade Tree
San Antonio, TX 78254-6821, USA

Staroba, Paul (Athlete, Football Player)
9235 McWain Rd
Grand Blanc, MI 48439-8006, USA

Starr, Albert (Doctor)
1792 SW Montgomery Dr
Portland, OR 97201-2437, USA

Starr, Bart (Athlete, Football Coach, Football Player)
Healthcare Realty Services
2647 Rocky Ridge Ln
Birmingham, AL 35216-4809, USA

Starr, Beau (Actor)
c/o Geneva Bray *GVA Talent Agency Inc*
8981 W Sunset Blvd Ste 101
West Hollywood, CA 90069-1850, USA

Starr, Brenda K (Music Group, Musician)
Brothers Mgmt
141 Dunbar Ave
Fords, NJ 08863-1551, USA

Starr, David (Race Car Driver)
Boys Will Be Boys Racing
610 Performance Rd
Mooresville, NC 28115-9595, USA

Starr, Dick (Athlete, Baseball Player)
613 N Crescent Dr
Kittanning, PA 16201-2214, USA

Starr, Fredro (Actor, Artist, Musician)
c/o Keith Brown *KBiz Entertainment*
6938 Laurel Canyon Blvd Unit 214
North Hollywood, CA 91605-6850, USA

Starr, Garrison (Musician)
c/o Staff Member *MCT Management*
104 W 29th St Rm 1101
New York, NY 10001-5310, USA

Starr, Kay (Music Group, Musician)
Ira Okun Entertainment
708 Palisades Dr
Pacific Palisades, CA 90272-2800, USA

Starr, Keith (Athlete, Basketball Player)
1S83 Graystone Canyon Ave
Las Vegas, NV 89183, USA

Starr, Kenneth (Government Official, Judge)
Pepperdine Law School
24255 Pacific Coast Hwy
Malibu, CA 90263-3999, USA

Starr, Leonard (Cartoonist)
Tribune Media Services
319 Bayberry Ln
Westport, CT 06880-1314, USA

Starr, Martin (Actor)
c/o Ben Feigin *Anonymous Content (LA)*
3532 Hayden Ave
Culver City, CA 90232-2413, USA

Starr, Randy (Music Group, Musician, Songwriter, Writer)
DDS
230 Park Ave
New York, NY 10169-0005, USA

Starr, Ringo (Actor, Musician)
918 N Hillcrest Rd
Beverly Hills, CA 90210-2611, USA

Starr, Steve (Journalist, Photographer)
720 Arcadia Place
720 Arcadia Pl
Colorado Springs, CO 80903-2813, USA

Starrette, Herm (Athlete, Baseball Player)
103 Howard Pond Loop
Statesville, NC 28625-2280, USA

Starring, Stephen (Athlete, Football Player)
6120 W Tropicana Ave Ste A16
Las Vegas, NV 89103-4697, USA

Starsailor (Music Group)
c/o Staff Member *Paradigm (Monterey)*
404 W Franklin St
Monterey, CA 93940-2303, USA

Starship
9850 Sandalfoot Blvd # 458
Boca Raton, FL 33428-6645

Starting Line (Music Group)
c/o Staff Member *Virgin Records (NY)*
150 5th Ave Fl 7
New York, NY 10011-4372, USA

Stasey, Caitlin (Actor)
c/o Shelley Browning *Magnolia Entertainment (LA)*
9595 Wilshire Blvd Ste 601
Beverly Hills, CA 90212-2506, USA

Stashwick, Todd (Actor)
c/o Staff Member *Meghan Schumacher Management*
13351D Riverside Dr # 387
Sherman Oaks, CA 91423-2508, USA

Stassforth, Bowen (Athlete, Olympic Athlete, Swimmer)
26203 Birchfield Ave
Rancho Palos Verdes, CA 90275-1719, USA

Stastny, Paul (Athlete, Hockey Player)
465 S Mason Rd
Saint Louis, MO 63141-8519, USA

Stastny, Peter (Athlete, Hockey Player)
465 S Mason Rd
Saint Louis, MO 63141-8519, USA

Stastny, Yan (Athlete, Hockey Player)
465 S Mason Rd
Saint Louis, MO 63141-8519, USA

Staszak, Ray (Athlete, Hockey Player)
8273 96th Ct S
Boynton Beach, FL 33472-4405, USA

Stata, Raymond S (Business Person)
Analog Devices Inc
1 Technology Way
Norwood, MA 02062-2666, USA

Staten, Vince (Writer)
9323 Loch Lea Ln
Louisville, KY 40291-1477, USA

Statham, Jason (Actor)
2427 Castilian Dr
Los Angeles, CA 90068-2616, USA

Static, Wayne (Musician)
Andy Gould Mgmt
9100 Wilshire Blvd Ste 400W
Beverly Hills, CA 90212-3464, USA

Statler Brothers (Music Group)
The Statler Brothers, LLC
PO Box 2703
Staunton, VA 24402-2703, USA

Staton, Aaron (Actor)
4437 Farmdale Ave
North Hollywood, CA 91602-2001, USA

Staton, Candi (Music Group, Musician)
Capital Entertainment
1201 N St NW # A5
Washington, DC 20005-5115, USA

Staton, Dave (Athlete, Baseball Player)
2175 Arnold Dr
Rocklin, CA 95765-5901, USA

Staton, Joe (Athlete, Baseball Player)
2929 76th Ave SE Apt 201
Mercer Island, WA 98040-2715, USA

Staton, Leroy (Athlete, Baseball Player)
1751 N Norwood Ln
Florence, SC 29506-6901, USA

Staton, Mike (Athlete, Baseball Player)
19602 Indigo Lake Dr
Magnolia, TX 77355-3158, USA

Staub, Chelsea (Actor)
c/o Margot Menzel *Evolution Entertainment (LA)*
9111 Wilshire Blvd
Beverly Hills, CA 90210-5508, USA

Staub, Daniel J (Rusty) (Athlete, Baseball Player)
WWOR-Radio
9 Broadcast Plz
Secaucus, NJ 07094-2913, USA

Staub, Danielle (Reality Star)
c/o Jeffre Phillips *Ja-Tail Enterprises*
8306 Wilshire Blvd Ste 528
Beverly Hills, CA 90211-2304, USA

Staubach, Roger (Athlete, Football Player, Heisman Trophy Winner)
5242 Ravine Dr
Dallas, TX 75220-2260, USA

Staubach, Scott (Athlete, Football Player)
6701 Miwok Ct
Bakersfield, CA 93309-3436, USA

Stauber, Liz (Actor)
c/o Sally Ware *Gersh (NY)*
41 Madison Ave
New York, NY 10010-2202, USA

Stauber, Robb (Athlete, Hockey Player)
Stauber's Goal Crease
7401A Washington Aves
Minneapolis, MN 55439, USA

Stauffer, Tim (Athlete, Baseball Player)
2790 Bellezza Dr
San Diego, CA 92108-6745, USA

Stauffer, William A (Bill) (Athlete, Basketball Player)
913 Shoalcreek Pl
Wilmington, NC 28405-5211, USA

Staurovsky, Jason (Athlete, Football Player)
4822 E 87th Pl
Tulsa, OK 74137-2825, USA

Stause, Chrishell (Actor)
c/o Staff Member *Rooster Films*
5225 Wilshire Blvd Ste 701
Los Angeles, CA 90036-4351, USA

Stautberg, Gerald (Athlete, Football Player)
3200 Park Rd
Monkton, MD 21111, USA

Stavinoha, Nick (Athlete, Baseball Player)
19402 Indigo Lake Dr
Magnolia, TX 77355-3156, USA

Stavropoulos, William S (Business Person)
Dow Chemical
2030 Dow Ctr
Midland, MI 48674-2030, USA

Staysniak, Joseph A (Joe) (Athlete, Football Player)
4094 Forest Dr
Brownsburg, IN 46112-8672, USA

St. Clair, Jessica (Actor)
c/o Christie Smith *Mosaic Media Group*
9200 W Sunset Blvd Ste 10
West Hollywood, CA 90069-3608, USA

St Clair, Mike (Athlete, Football Player)
1606 Birchwood Ave
Cincinnati, OH 45224-2002, USA

St Clair, Robert B (Bob) (Athlete, Football Player)
3312 Parker Hill Rd
Saratoga, CA 95070, USA

St Claire, Randy (Athlete, Baseball Player)
7117 State Route 8
Brant Lake, NY 12815-2234, USA

StClaire, Randy (Athlete, Baseball Player)
7117 State Route 8
Brant Lake, NY 12815-2234, USA

Stead, Eugene A Jr (Doctor)
5113 Townsville Rd
Bullock, NC 27507-9438, USA

Steadman, J Richard (Doctor)
Steadman Hawkins Clinic
181 W Meadow Dr Ste 400
Vail, CO 81657-5058, USA

Steadman, Mark (Writer)
450 Pin Du Lac Dr
Central, SC 29630-9435, USA

Steadman, Robert L (Cinematographer)
15925 Temecula St
Pacific Palisades, CA 90272-4239, USA

Steall, Ben (Horse Racer)
1289 Brampton Cv
Wellington, FL 33414-8984, USA

Stearns, Cliff (Congressman, Politician)
2306 Rayburn Hob
Washington, DC 20515-3516, USA

Stearns, Jeff
9200 W Sunset Blvd Ste 1130
West Hollywood, CA 90069-3606

Stearns, John (Athlete, Baseball Player)
1155 W Mound St
Columbus, OH 43223-2211, USA

Stebbins, Richard (Athlete, Olympic Athlete, Track Athlete)
9305 Bahia Track Way
Ocala, FL 34472-2627, USA

Stechschulte, Gene (Athlete, Baseball Player)
206 Wellington Pl
Findlay, OH 45840-8303, USA

Steckel, David (Athlete, Hockey Player)
1516 Jefferson St
West Bend, WI 53090-1343, USA

Steckel, Les (Athlete, Football Coach, Football Player)
195 Blew Ct
E Brunswick, NJ 08816-1834, USA

Steckler, Ray Dennis (Director)
2375 E Tropicana Ave
Las Vegas, NV 89119-6564, USA

Steck-Weiss, Elma (Athlete, Baseball Player)
12543 W Skyview Dr
Sun City West, AZ 85375-5168, USA

Steding, Katy (Athlete, Basketball Player, Olympic Athlete)
21625 SW 100th Dr
Tualatin, OR 97062-8581, USA

Steed, Joel (Athlete, Football Player)
2639 Holly St
Denver, CO 80207-3229, USA

Steel, Amy (Actor)
Innovative Artists
1505 10th St
Santa Monica, CA 90401-2805, USA

Steel, Danielle (Writer)
2080 Washington St
San Francisco, CA 94109-2844, USA

Steel, John (Musician)
Lustig Talent
PO Box 770850
Orlando, FL 32877-0850, USA

Steele, Alex (Actor)
c/o Alvina Roman *Roman Empire Management*
Prefers to be contacted via telephone or email
Beverly Hills, CA 90210, USA

Steele, Allan (Actor)
c/o Staff Member *Baumgarten Management*
1447 Cloverfield Blvd Ste 101
Santa Monica, CA 90404-2979, USA

Steele, Barbara (Actor)
2460 Benedict Canyon Dr
Beverly Hills, CA 90210-1433, USA

Steele, Billy (DJ)
c/o Len Evans *Project Publicity*
312 W 53rd St Ste 202
New York, NY 10019-5743, USA

Steele, Brian (Actor)
c/o Joan Vento-Hall *Law Offices of Joan Vento-Hall, The*
10250 Constellation Blvd Fl 19
Los Angeles, CA 90067-6219, USA

Steele, Dave (Race Car Driver)
Team Sabco
114 Meadow Hill Cir
Mooresville, NC 28117-8089, USA

Steele, Glen (Athlete, Football Player)
303 E 5th St
Ligonier, IN 46767-2205, USA

Steele, Joshua (Flux Pavilion) (DJ, Producer)
c/o Staff Member *Atlantic Records (NY)*
1290 Avenue of the Americas Fl 28
New York, NY 10104-0106, USA

Steele, Joyce (Athlete, Baseball Player)
627 Sr 4010
Mehoopany, PA 18629-8841, USA

Steele, Larry (Athlete, Basketball Player)
PO Box 372
Slip 25
Vernonia, OR 97064-0372, USA

Steele, Michael (Musician)
Bangles Mall
1341 W Fullerton Ave # 180
Chicago, IL 60614-2362, USA

Steele, Michael (Politician)
Republican National Committee
310 1st St SE
Washington, DC 20003-1885, USA

Steele, Richard (Boxer, Referee)
2438 Antler Point Dr
Henderson, NV 89074-6269, USA

Steele, Riley (Actor, Adult Film Star, Model)
c/o Staff Member *Media Artists Group (LA)*
8222 Melrose Ave Ste 203
Los Angeles, CA 90046-6838, USA

Steele, Robert (Football Player)
3045 S Pioneer Way
Las Vegas, NV 89117-3244, USA

Steele, Shelby (Writer)
San Jose State University
English Dept
San Jose, CA 95192-0001, USA

Steele, Tim (Race Car Driver)
24th Ave
Marne, MI 49435, USA

Steel Magnolia (Music Group, Musician)
c/o Staff Member *Big Machine Records*
1219 16th Ave S
Nashville, TN 37212-2901, USA

Steels, Jim (Athlete, Baseball Player)
1654 Via Rico
Santa Maria, CA 93454-2609, USA

Steely Dan (Music Group)
c/o Irving Azoff *Azoff Music Management*
1100 Glendon Ave Ste 2000
Los Angeles, CA 90024-3524, USA

Steen, Jessica (Actor)
Innovative Artists
1505 10th St
Santa Monica, CA 90401-2805, USA

Steenburgen, Mary (Actor)
11 Latimer Rd
Santa Monica, CA 90402-1011, USA

Steenstra, Ken (Athlete, Baseball Player)
1228 Pheasant Ct
Liberty, MO 64068-8464, USA

Steenstra, Kennie (Athlete, Baseball Player)
1228 Pheasant Ct
Liberty, MO 64068-8464, USA

Steeples, Eddie (Actor)
c/o Staff Member *LRB Publicity*
2206 Rockefeller Ln Unit 1
Redondo Beach, CA 90278-3723, USA

Steere, Richard (Athlete, Football Player)
1810 Fox Bridge Ct
Fallbrook, CA 92028-8745, USA

Steers, Burr (Director)
c/o Shawn Simon *Anonymous Content*
(LA)
3532 Hayden Ave
Culver City, CA 90232-2413, USA

Steevens, Morrie (Athlete, Baseball
Player)
14465 Cadillac Dr
San Antonio, TX 78248-1001, USA

Stefan, Greg (Athlete, Hockey Player)
37648 Baywood Dr Unit 33
Farmington Hills, MI 48335-3604, USA

Stefan, Patrik (Athlete, Hockey Player)
1450 Bluebird Canyon Dr
Laguna Beach, CA 92651-3007, USA

Stefani, Gwen (Fashion Designer,
Musician, Songwriter)
c/o Irving Azoff *Azoff Music Management*
1100 Glendon Ave Ste 2000
Los Angeles, CA 90024-3524, USA

Stefanich, Jim (Bowler)
1444 Coral Bell Dr
Joliet, IL 60435-3979, USA

Stefanik, Mlke (Race Car Driver)
106 Pierremount Ave
New Britain, CT 06053-2345, USA

Stefanson, Leslie (Actor)
c/o Andy Cohen *Gersh (LA)*
9465 Wilshire Blvd Ste 600
Beverly Hills, CA 90212-2605, USA

Stefanyshyn-Piper, Heidemarie M
(Astronaut)
3722 W Pine Brook Way
Houston, TX 77059-3105, USA

Stefanyshyn-Piper, Heidemarie M Cdr
(Astronaut)
4 Saint Christophers Ln
Coronado, CA 92118-3275, USA

Stefero, John (Athlete, Baseball Player)
6239 Chestnut Oak Ln
Linthicum Heights, MD 21090-2148, USA

Steffen, Dave (Baseball Player)
30531 Maple View Ln
Flat Rock, MI 48134-2744, USA

Steffen, Jim (Athlete, Football Player)
1440 Westway
Arnold, MD 21012-2428, USA

Steffes, Kent (Athlete, Volleyball Player)
14675 Titus St
Panorama City, CA 91402-4922, USA

Stefy (Music Group)
Wind-up Records
72 Madison Ave Fl 8
New York, NY 10016-8731, USA

Stegall, Keith (Musician)
c/o Staff Member *Sony Music Nashville*
8 Music Sq W
Nashville, TN 37203-3204, USA

Stegall, Milt (Athlete, Football Player)
51 Springside Dr SE
Atlanta, GA 30354-2145, USA

Stegent, Larry (Athlete, Football Player)
1177 West Loop S Ste 525
Houston, TX 77027-9049, USA

Steger, Michael (Actor)
c/o Alex Spieller *IMPR*
357 S Robertson Blvd
Beverly Hills, CA 90211-3602, USA

Stegman, Dave (Athlete, Baseball Player)
3234 Simmons Dr
Grove City, OH 43123-1835, USA

Stehlin, Savannah (Actor)
c/o Sharon Lane *Lane Management Group*
13017 Woodbridge St
Studio City, CA 91604-1431, USA

Steiger, Ueli (Cinematographer)
2222 Kenilworth Ave
Los Angeles, CA 90039-3010, USA

Stein, Ben (Actor, Comedian, Producer,
Writer)
602 N Crescent Dr
Beverly Hills, CA 90210-3330, USA

Stein, Bill (Athlete, Baseball Player)
8117 Chamizal Dr
Fort Worth, TX 76137-5373, USA

Stein, Blake (Athlete, Baseball Player)
115 Formosa Dr
Brandon, MS 39047-7912, USA

Stein, Bob (Basketball Player, Misc)
Minnesota Timberwolves
600 1st Ave N
Target Center
Minneapolis, MN 55403-1400, USA

Stein, Chris (Musician)
Shore Fire Media
32 Court St Ste 1600
Brooklyn, NY 11201-4441, USA

Stein, Garth (Writer)
c/o Staff Member *HarperCollins Publishers*
10 E 53rd St Fl 8
Cellar 1
New York, NY 10022-5076, USA

Stein, Gilbert (Gil) (Athlete, Hockey
Player)
650 5th Ave Ste 3300
New York, NY 10019-6108, USA

Stein, Irving (Writer)
7000 N McCormick Blvd Apt 208
Lincolnwood, IL 60712-2734, USA

Stein, James (Business Person)
Fluor Corp
3353 Michelson Dr
Irvine, CA 92612-7622, USA

Stein, Joel (Writer)
c/o Roger Green *William Morris Endeavor*
(LA)
9601 Wilshire Blvd Fl 3
Beverly Hills, CA 90210-5219, USA

Stein, Mark (Music Group, Musician)
Future Vision
280 Riverside Dr Apt 12L
New York, NY 10025-9032, USA

Stein, Pamela Jean
2112 Broadway
Santa Monica, CA 90404-2912

Steinbach, Alice (Journalist)
Baltimore Sun
501 N Calvert St
Editorial Dept
Baltimore, MD 21278-1000, USA

Steinbach, Terry (Athlete, Baseball Player)
PO Box 181
Terry Steinbach Scholarship Fund
Hamel, MN 55340-0181, USA

Steinberg, K.J. (Actor)
c/o Ari Greenburg *William Morris*
Endeavor (LA)
9601 Wilshire Blvd
Beverly Hills, CA 90210-5213, USA

Steinberg, Paul (Cartoonist)
New Yorker Magazine
4 Times Sq Fl 22
Editorial Dept
New York, NY 10036-6592, USA

Steinbrenner, Hal (Baseball Player)
4926 Andros Dr
Tampa, FL 33629-4802, USA

Steinbrenner, Hank (Baseball Player)
402 Saint Andrews Dr
Belleair, FL 33756-1935, USA

Steindorff, Scott (Producer, Writer)
c/o Staff Member *Stone Village*
Entertainment
9200 W Sunset Blvd Ste 520
West Hollywood, CA 90069-3507, USA

Steinel, Laura (Actor)
c/o Staff Member *Principato/Young*
Management (LA)
9465 Wilshire Blvd Ste 900
Beverly Hills, CA 90212-2608, USA

Steinem, Gloria (Journalist, Writer)
118 E 73rd St
New York, NY 10021-4238, USA

Steiner, Charley (Sportscaster)
867 S Bundy Dr
Los Angeles, CA 90049-5216, USA

Steiner, Mel (Baseball Player)
11296 Linda Way
Los Alamitos, CA 90720-3918, USA

Steiner, Paul (Cartoonist)
Washington Times
3600 New York Ave NE
Washington, DC 20002-1996, USA

Steiner, Peter (Cartoonist)
New Yorker Magazine
4 Times Sq Fl 22
Editorial Dept
New York, NY 10036-6592, USA

Steiner, Rebel (Athlete, Football Player)
112 Aaronvale Cir
Birmingham, AL 35242-7353, USA

Steiner, Reed (Producer)
c/o Staff Member *William Morris*
Endeavor (LA)
9601 Wilshire Blvd
Beverly Hills, CA 90210-5213, USA

Steines, Mark (Television Host)
c/o Staff Member *Entertainment Tonight*
(ET)
4024 Radford Ave
Studio City, CA 91604-2101, USA

Steinfeld, Hailee (Actor)
c/o Doug Wald *Anonymous Content (LA)*
3532 Hayden Ave
Culver City, CA 90232-2413, USA

Steinfeld, Jake (Actor, Athlete, Fitness
Expert)
622 Toyopa Dr
Pacific Palisades, CA 90272-4471, USA

Steinfort, Fred (Athlete, Football Player)
PO Box 24981
Denver, CO 80224-0981, USA

Steinhardt, Arnold (Musician)
Herbert Barrett
266 W 37th St # 2000
New York, NY 10018-6609, USA

Steinhauer, Sherri (Golfer)
5010 Hammersley Rd
Madison, WI 53711-2616, USA

Steinkraus, William (Athlete, Olympic
Athlete)
PO B40 Great Is
Darien, CT 06820, USA

Steinkuhler, Dean (Athlete, Football
Player)
PO Box 247
Syracuse, NE 68446-0247, USA

Steinman, Jim (Songwriter, Writer)
DAS Communications
83 Riverside Dr
New York, NY 10024-5713, USA

Steinmetz, Richard (Actor)
c/o Staff Member *Personal Management*
Company
425 N Robertson Blvd
West Hollywood, CA 90048-1735, USA

Steinseifer Bates, Carrie (Swimmer)
9309 Benzon Dr
Pleasanton, CA 94588-4767, USA

Steirer, Ricky (Athlete, Baseball Player)
1015 Haverhill Rd
Baltimore, MD 21229-5115, USA

Stela, Annie (Musician)
c/o Staff Member *Paradigm (Monterey)*
404 W Franklin St
Monterey, CA 93940-2303, USA

Stelmaszek, Rick (Athlete, Baseball Player)
2734 E 97th St
Chicago, IL 60617-4928, USA

Stember, Jeff (Athlete, Baseball Player)
9517 E Altadena Ave
Scottsdale, AZ 85260-5865, USA

Stemie, Steve (Athlete, Baseball Player)
4011 Weatherby Way
New Albany, IN 47150-9676, USA

Stemkowski, Peter (Athlete, Hockey
Player)
146 Albany Blvd Apt 21C
Atlantic Beach, NY 11509-1207, USA

Stemle, Steve (Athlete, Baseball Player)
927 Saint Johns Church Rd NE
Lanesville, IN 47136-8567, USA

Stempniak, Lee (Athlete, Hockey Player)
4469 Clinton St
Buffalo, NY 14224-1700, USA

Stemrick, Greg (Athlete, Football Player)
1012 Matthews Dr
Cincinnati, OH 45215-1804, USA

Stenberg, Amandla (Actor)
c/o Mimi DiTrani *The Schiff Company*
9220 W Sunset Blvd Ste 106
West Hollywood, CA 90069-3500, USA

Stenberg, Brigitta
11484th St # 116
Santa Monica, CA 90403

Stenger, Brian (Athlete, Football Player)
7921 Kellogg Creek Dr
Mentor, OH 44060-7111, USA

Stenhouse, Dave (Athlete, Baseball Player)
20 Hayward St
Cranston, RI 02910-2701, USA

Stenhouse, Mike (Athlete, Baseball Player)
70 Woodbury Rd
Cranston, RI 02905-3317, USA

Stenko, Paul (Athlete, Football Player)
414 Martzville Rd
Berwick, PA 18603-5642, USA

Stennett, Rennie (Athlete, Baseball Player)
6519 Boticelli Dr
Lake Worth, FL 33467-7037, USA

Stensrud, Mike (Athlete, Football Player)
304 S Winnebago St
Lake Mills, IA 50450-1637, USA

Stenstrom, Steve (Athlete, Football Player)
3197 Lynwood Ave
Highlands Ranch, CO 80126-8046, USA

Stepanova, Maria (Basketball Player)
Phoenix Mercury
201 E Jefferson St
American West Arena
Phoenix, AZ 85004-2412, USA

Stephanopoulos, George (Politician)
20 Dunemere Ln
East Hampton, NY 11937-2706, USA

Stephen, Buzz (Athlete, Baseball Player)
15512 Sycamore St
Porterville, CA 93257-2594, USA

Stephen, Scott (Athlete, Football Player)
4132 Palm Tree Ct
La Mesa, CA 91941-7238, USA

Stephen, Shamar (Athlete, Football Player)
c/o Alan Herman *Sportstars Inc*
1350 Avenue of the Americas Fl 28
New York, NY 10019-4702, USA

Stephens, Everette (Athlete, Basketball Player)
2449 Hopkins Dr
West Lafayette, IN 47906-5171, USA

Stephens, Gene (Athlete, Baseball Player)
602 Erin Ave
Monroe, LA 71201-4710, USA

Stephens, Hal (Athlete, Football Player)
221 W Virginia St
Rocky Mount, NC 27804-4940, USA

Stephens, Jamain (Athlete, Football Player)
105 W 6th St
Tabor City, NC 28463-1633, USA

Stephens, James
8271 Melrose Ave Ste 110
Los Angeles, CA 90046-6800

Stephens, John (Athlete, Baseball Player)
1325 Oak Point Ct
Venice, FL 34292-1635, USA

Stephens, John (Athlete, Football Player)
PO Box 496
Shreveport, LA 71162-0496, USA

Stephens, Laraine
10800 Chalon Rd
Los Angeles, CA 90077-3220

Stephens, Ray (Athlete, Baseball Player)
1065 Council Rd NE
Charleston, TN 37310-6232, USA

Stephens, Robert (Business Person)
Adaptec Inc
691 S Milpitas Blvd Ste 100
Milpitas, CA 95035-5476, USA

Stephens, Santo (Athlete, Football Player)
1205 Winding Meadows Rd
Rockledge, FL 32955-8404, USA

Stephens, Stanley (Politician)
210 Columba Ln
Kalispell, MT 59901-2601, USA

Stephens, Toby (Actor)
c/o Simon Halls *Slate Public Relations*
9000 W Sunset Blvd Ste 915
West Hollywood, CA 90069-5809, USA

Stephens, Tom (Athlete, Football Player)
69 Orchard Rd
Swampscott, MA 01907-2349, USA

Stephenson, Dwight E (Athlete, Football Player)
4785 Tree Fern Dr
Delray Beach, FL 33445-7025, USA

Stephenson, Earl (Athlete, Baseball Player)
4043 Zacks Mill Rd
Angier, NC 27501-7185, USA

Stephenson, Garrett (Athlete, Baseball Player)
947 W State St
Eagle, ID 83616-4807, USA

Stephenson, John (Athlete, Baseball Player)
7 Mauroner Dr
Hammond, LA 70401-1728, USA

Stephenson, Kay (Athlete, Football Player)
310 Plantation Hill Rd
Gulf Breeze, FL 32561-4818, USA

Stephenson, Phil (Athlete, Baseball Player)
1307 Hancock St
Dodge City, KS 67801-3451, USA

Stepp, Craig
6310 San Vicente Blvd Ste 520
Los Angeles, CA 90048-5421

Steppe, Brook (Athlete, Basketball Player)
3486 Clare Cottage Trce SW
Marietta, GA 30008-6075, USA

Steppenwolf (John Kay)
108 E Matilija St
Ojai, CA 93023-2639

Steptoe, Jack (Athlete, Football Player)
77777 Country Club Dr Apt 109
Palm Desert, CA 92211-0460, USA

Steranko, Jim (Cartoonist)
PO Box 974
Reading, PA 19603-0974, USA

Sterban, Richard (Musician)
125 Bluegrass Cir
Hendersonville, TN 37075-2726, USA

Stereo Fuse (Music Group)
c/o Staff Member *Wind-up Records*
72 Madison Ave Fl 8
New York, NY 10016-8731, USA

Stereo MC's (Music Group)
c/o Staff Member *Paradigm (Monterey)*
404 W Franklin St
Monterey, CA 93940-2303, USA

Sterger, Jenn (Model, Television Host)
PO Box 2642
Lutz, FL 33548-2642, USA

Sterkel, Jill (Athlete, Olympic Athlete, Swimmer)
2206 Heritage Well Ln
Pflugerville, TX 78660-2968, USA

Sterling, Annette (Music Group, Musician)
Soundedge Personal Mgmt
332 Southdown Rd
Huntington, NY 11743-1053, USA

Sterling, Ashleigh (Actor)
10 Silkleaf
Irvine, CA 92614-5404, USA

Sterling, Donald (Business Person)
9441 Wilshire Blvd
Beverly Hills, CA 90212-2808, USA

Sterling, John (Sportscaster)
185 Spook Rock Rd
Suffern, NY 10901-3616, USA

Sterling, Mindy (Actor)
7307 Melrose Ave
Los Angeles, CA 90046-7512, USA

Sterling, Nici (Adult Film Star)
c/o Staff Member *Atlas Multimedia Inc*
9005 Eton Ave Ste C
Canoga Park, CA 91304-6533, USA

Sterling, Rachel (Actor)
c/o Leland LaBarre *Bleu, An Entertainment Company*
5225 Wilshire Blvd Ste 336
Los Angeles, CA 90036-4380, USA

Sterling, Randy (Athlete, Baseball Player)
2516 Linda Ave
Key West, FL 33040-5114, USA

Sterling, Tisha (Actor)
PO Box 788
Ketchum, ID 83340-0788, USA

Stern, Adam (Athlete, Baseball Player)
40 Summit Ave
London, ON N6H 4S3, USA

Stern, Daniel (Actor)
PO Box 6788
Malibu, CA 90264-6788, USA

Stern, David J (Basketball Player, Misc)
National Basketball Assn
122 E 55th St
Olympic Tower
New York, NY 10022-4535, USA

Stern, Dawn (Actor)
c/o Holly Shelton *Precision Entertainment*
465 N Croft Ave
Los Angeles, CA 90048-2508, USA

Stern, Gardner (Producer, Writer)
c/o Dave Brown *Echo Lake Management*
421 S Beverly Dr Fl 8
Beverly Hills, CA 90212-4408, USA

Stern, Howard (Radio Personality, Talk Show Host)
Howard Stern Production Company
10 E 44th St
New York, NY 10017-3601, USA

Stern, Joseph (Actor, Producer)
c/o Chris Simonian *Creative Artists Agency (CAA-LA)*
2000 Avenue of the Stars Ste 100
Los Angeles, CA 90067-4705, USA

Stern, Michael (Mike) (Musician)
Tropix International
163 3rd Ave # 206
New York, NY 10003-2523, USA

Stern, Shoshannah (Actor)
c/o David Ginsberg *Insight*
PO Box 36359
Los Angeles, CA 90036-0359, USA

Sternberg, Stuart (Baseball Player)
85 Bellevue Ave
Rye, NY 10580-1840, USA

Sternberg, Thomas (Business Person)
Staples Inc
PO Box 9265
Framingham, MA 01701-9265, USA

Sternecky, Neal (Cartoonist)
52 Bluebird Ln
Naperville, IL 60565-1347, USA

Sternhagen, Frances (Actor)
152 Sutton Manor Rd
New Rochelle, NY 10801-5756, USA

Stetter, Mitch (Athlete, Baseball Player)
4135 N Olcott Ave
Norridge, IL 60706-1112, USA

Steuert-Armstrong, Beverly (Athlete, Baseball Player)
211 Cathi Ln
Kernersville, NC 27284-9363, USA

Steussie, Todd E (Athlete, Football Player)
34535 Emigrant Trl
Shingletown, CA 96088-9342, USA

Steve, Rehage (Athlete, Football Player)
2632 Montana Ave
Metairie, LA 70003-5246, USA

Steve Miller Band (Music Group)
c/o Staff Member *Paradigm (Nashville)*
124 12th Ave S Ste 410
Nashville, TN 37203-3170, USA

Stevens, Amber (Actor)
c/o Robert Enriquez *Red Baron Management*
1600 Rosecrans Ave
Manhattan Beach, CA 90266-3708, USA

Stevens, Andrew (Actor)
Irv Schechter
9300 Wilshire Blvd Ste 410
Beverly Hills, CA 90212-3228, USA

Stevens, April (Music Group, Musician)
19530 Superior St
Northridge, CA 91324-1648, USA

Stevens, Bob (Producer)
c/o Staff Member *United Talent Agency (UTA-LA)*
9336 Civic Center Dr
Beverly Hills, CA 90210-3604, USA

Stevens, Brad (Basketball Coach)
c/o Sandy Montag *IMG Artists Worldwide (NY)*
825 7th Ave
New York, NY 10019-6014, USA

Stevens, Brinke (Actor, Athlete)
PO Box 7112
Van Nuys, CA 91409-7112, USA

Stevens, Chuck (Athlete, Baseball Player)
12591 George Reyburn Rd
Garden Grove, CA 92845-2404, USA

Stevens, Connie (Actor, Music Group, Musician)
243 Delfern Dr
Los Angeles, CA 90077-3544, USA

Stevens, Dave (Athlete, Baseball Player)
2630 Candlewood Way
La Habra, CA 90631-6203, USA

Stevens, Dirk (Race Car Driver)
PO Box 1197
Huntersville, NC 28070-1197, USA

Stevens, Dodie (Musician)
c/o Jim Wagner *American Management*
19948 Mayall St
Chatsworth, CA 91311-3522, USA

Stevens, Earl (E-40) (Musician)
c/o Staff Member *Warner Bros Records (LA)*
PO Box 6868
Burbank, CA 91510-6868, USA

Stevens, Eric Sheffer (Actor)
c/o Greg Weiss *Vanguard Management Group (NY)*
220 5th Ave PH West
New York, NY 10001-7745, USA

Stevens, Fisher (Actor)
329 N Orange Grove Ave
Los Angeles, CA 90036-2135, USA

Stevens, Gary (Horse Racer)
1308 Isleworth Dr
Louisville, KY 40245-5252, USA

Stevens, George Jr (Producer)
New Liberty Productions
John F Kennedy Center
Washington, DC 20566-0001, USA

Stevens, Howard (Athlete, Football Player)
846 Saint Catherines Dr
Wake Forest, NC 27587-6639, USA

Stevens, Jeremy (Actor, Producer, Writer)
c/o Staff Member *William Morris Endeavor (LA)*
9601 Wilshire Blvd
Beverly Hills, CA 90210-5213, USA

Stevens, Jerramy (Athlete, Football Player)
10047 Main St Apt 515
Bellevue, WA 98004-5319, USA

Stevens, John (Athlete, Hockey Player)
Los Angeles Kings
1111 S Figueroa St Ste 3100
Attn Coaching Staff
Los Angeles, CA 90015-1333, USA

Stevens, John Paul (Attorney)
US Supreme Court
United States Supreme Court 11th St NE
Washington, DC 20543-0001, USA

Stevens, Kevin (Athlete, Hockey Player, Olympic Athlete)
70 Onion Hill Rd
Duxbury, MA 02332-3808, USA

Stevens, Laraine
10800 Chalon Rd
Los Angeles, CA 90077-3220

Stevens, Lee (Athlete, Baseball Player)
940 Graland Pl
Highlands Ranch, CO 80126-5573, USA

Stevens, Mick
PO Box 344
West Tisbury, MA 02575-0344

Stevens, Ray (Musician, Songwriter)
1707 Grand Ave
Nashville, TN 37212-2205, USA

Stevens, Richard (Athlete, Football Player)
4100 Cimmaron Trl
Granbury, TX 76049-5252, USA

Stevens, Richie (Race Car Driver)
Richie Stevens Fan Club
9600 Chef Menteur Hwy
New Orleans, LA 70127-4234, USA

Stevens, Robert J (Business Person)
Lockheed Martin Corp
6801 Rockledge Dr
Bethesda, MD 20817-1877, USA

Stevens, Rogers (Musician)
Shapiro Co
9229 W Sunset Blvd Ste 607
West Hollywood, CA 90069-3406, USA

Stevens, Scott (Athlete, Hockey Player)
New Jersey Devils
165 Mulberry St
Attn Special Assignment Coach
Newark, NJ 07102-3607, USA

Stevens, Scott (Athlete, Hockey Player)
280 Spook Hollow Rd
Far Hills, NJ 07931-2707, USA

Stevens, Shadoe (Radio Personality)
2934 N Beverly Glen Cir # 399
Los Angeles, CA 90077-1724, USA

Stevens, Stella (Actor, Model)
2180 Coldwater Canyon Dr
Beverly Hills, CA 90210-1735, USA

Stevens, Steve (Musician)
c/o Staff Member *J H Cohn LLP*
720 E Palisade Ave
Englewood Cliffs, NJ 07632-3053, USA

Stevens, Steven (Actor)
Stevens Group
3518 Cahuenga Blvd W
Los Angeles, CA 90068-1304, USA

Stevens, Sufjan (Musician)
c/o Ali Hedrick *Billions Corporation, The*
833 W Chicago Ave Ste 101
Chicago, IL 60642-8408, USA

Stevens, Tony (Musician)
Lustig Talent
PO Box 770850
Orlando, FL 32877-0850, USA

Stevens, William S (Athlete, Football Player)
6176 Los Robles Dr
El Paso, TX 79912-1933, USA

Stevenson, Adlai
20 N Clark St Ste 750
Chicago, IL 60602-4116, USA

Stevenson, Cynthia (Actor)
c/o Elizabeth Much *Much and House Public Relations*
8075 W 3rd St Ste 500
Los Angeles, CA 90048-4325, USA

Stevenson, DeShawn (Basketball Player)
Utah Jazz
1348 Lake Whitney Dr
301 W South Temple
Windermere, FL 34786-6072, USA

Stevenson, James (Actor)
c/o Melissa Prophet *Melissa Prophet Management*
Prefers to be contacted by telephone
CA, USA

Stevenson, Jeremy (Athlete, Hockey Player)
7899 W 6 Mile Rd
Brimley, MI 49715-9281, USA

Stevenson, Parker (Actor)
c/o Laina Cohn *Cohn / Torgan Management*
Prefers to be contacted by telephone or email
Los Angeles, CA, USA

Stevenson, Rosemary (Athlete, Baseball Player)
19123 120th Ave
Nunica, MI 49448-9460, USA

Stevenson, Turner (Athlete, Hockey Player)
23924 NE 31st Way
Sammamish, WA 98074-5466, USA

Stevenson, Venetia (Actor)
1403 Keys Crossing Dr NE
Atlanta, GA 30319-4043, USA

Steverson, Todd (Athlete, Baseball Player)
109 W Glenhaven Dr
Phoenix, AZ 85045-0717, USA

Steward, Robert L
2864 S Circle Dr Ste 800
Colorado Springs, CO 80906-4163, USA

Stewart, Al (Music Group, Musician, Songwriter, Writer)
Chapman & Co
14011 Ventura Blvd Ste 405
Sherman Oaks, CA 91423-5230, USA

Stewart, Alana (Actor)
c/o Arnold Robinson *Rogers & Cowan PR (LA)*
8687 Melrose Ave Ste 7
West Hollywood, CA 90069-5721, USA

Stewart, Alexandra
37 Avenue De La Dame Blanche
San Francisco, CA 94120

Stewart, Amy (Actor)
c/o Lisa DiSante-Frank *DiSante Frank & Company*
10061 Riverside Dr # 377
Toluca Lake, CA 91602-2560, USA

Stewart, Andy (Athlete, Baseball Player)
641 Geddes St
Wilmington, DE 19805-3718, USA

Stewart, Bill (Athlete, Baseball Player)
44842 Aspen Ridge Dr
Northville, MI 48168-4435, USA

Stewart, Bill (Musician)
Blue Note Records
6920 W Sunset Blvd
Los Angeles, CA 90028-7010, USA

Stewart, Blair (Athlete, Hockey Player)
1604 Cottenham Ln
Virginia Beach, VA 23454-6406, USA

Stewart, Bob (Athlete, Hockey Player)
16756 Kehrs Mill Estates Dr
Chesterfield, MO 63005-6526, USA

Stewart, BooBoo (Actor)
c/o Siri Garber *Platform Public Relations*
2666 N Beachwood Dr
Los Angeles, CA 90068-2308, USA

Stewart, Boo Boo (Actor)
c/o Staff Member *Osbrink Talent Agency*
4343 Lankershim Blvd Ste 100
North Hollywood, CA 91602-2705, USA

Stewart, Cam (Athlete, Hockey Player)
2929 Buffalo Speedway Unit 218
Houston, TX 77098-1719, USA

Stewart, Cameron Deane (Actor)
c/o Pamela Fisher *Abrams Artists Agency (LA)*
9200 W Sunset Blvd PH 11
West Hollywood, CA 90069-3601, USA

Stewart, Catherine Mary (Actor)
c/o Philip Adelman *Gage Group, The (NY)*
1650 Broadway Ste 1410
New York, NY 10019-6957, USA

Stewart, Danica (Actor)
c/o Terrance Hines *Hines and Hunt Entertainment*
1213 W Magnolia Blvd
Burbank, CA 91506-1829, USA

Stewart, Darian (Athlete, Football Player)
c/o Dave Butz *Sportstars Inc*
1350 Avenue of the Americas Fl 28
New York, NY 10019-4702, USA

Stewart, Dave (Athlete, Baseball Player)
17762 Vineyard Ln
Poway, CA 92064-1061, USA

Stewart, David K (Dave) (Baseball Player)
Los Angeles Dodgers
17762 Vineyard Ln
Poway, CA 92064-1061, USA

Stewart, Fivel (Actor)
c/o Siri Garber *Platform Public Relations*
2666 N Beachwood Dr
Los Angeles, CA 90068-2308, USA

Stewart, Freddie
4862 Excelente Dr
Woodland Hills, CA 91364-4011

Stewart, French (Actor)
c/o JC Robbins *JC Robbins Management*
865 S Sherbourne Dr
Los Angeles, CA 90035-1809, USA

Stewart, James B (Journalist)
Wall Street Journal
200 Liberty St
Editorial Dept
New York, NY 10281-1003, USA

Stewart, Jermaine (Music Group, Musician)
Richard Walters
1800 Argyle Ave # 408
Los Angeles, CA 90028-5253, USA

Stewart, Jim (Athlete, Hockey Player)
57 Lincoln St
Spencer, MA 01562-1623, USA

Stewart, Jimmy (Athlete, Baseball Player)
1884 Talcott Ct
Auburn, AL 36830-0274, USA

Stewart, John (Athlete, Hockey Player)
1085 Southlake Cv
Hoover, AL 35244-3283, USA

Stewart, John A (Athlete, Hockey Player)
16424 Grenwich Ter
Eden Prairie, MN 55346-1421, USA

Stewart, Jon (Actor, Comedian, Television Host)
c/o Staff Member *The Daily Show with Jon Stewart*
733 11th Ave
New York, NY 10019-5051, USA

Stewart, Jonathan (Athlete, Football Player)
c/o Ben Dogra *CAA (St. Louis)*
222 S Central Ave Ste 1008
Saint Louis, MO 63105-3509, USA

Stewart, Josh (Actor)
c/o Marcel Pariseau *True Public Relations*
6725 W Sunset Blvd Ste 470
Los Angeles, CA 90028-7180, USA

Stewart, Josh (Athlete, Baseball Player)
182 Stewart Ln
Ledbetter, KY 42058-9549, USA

Stewart, Kimberly (Actor, Model)
c/o Kenya Knight *Nous Model Management*
117 N Robertson Blvd
Los Angeles, CA 90048-3101, USA

Stewart, Kordell (Athlete, Football Player)
PO Box 1043
Roswell, GA 30077-1043, USA

Stewart, Kristen (Actor)
1963 De Mille Dr
Los Angeles, CA 90027-1705, USA

Stewart, Ian (Athlete, Baseball Player)
12 Ocaso Dr
Asheville, NC 28806-8202, USA

Stewart, Lisa (Actor, Producer)
c/o Staff Member *Vinyl Films*
5555 Melrose Ave
Los Angeles, CA 90038-3989, USA

Stewart, Lisa (Musician)
1344 Lexington Ave
Friedman & Larosa
New York, NY 10128-1507, USA

Stewart, Martha (Business Person, Television Host)
Martha Stewart Living Omnimedia
601 W 26th St Rm 900
New York, NY 10001-1143, USA

Stewart, Maxine (Actor)
180 Comanche
Topanga, CA 90290-4426, USA

Stewart, Mel (Athlete, Olympic Athlete, Swimmer)
7308 Seneca Falls Loop
Austin, TX 78739-2216, USA

Stewart, Melvin Jr (Swimmer)
c/o Scott Karp *The Syndicate*
10203 Santa Monica Blvd Fl 5
Los Angeles, CA 90067-6416, USA

Stewart, Michael (Athlete, Football Player)
717 Palo Verde St
Bakersfield, CA 93309-1863, USA

Stewart, Michael
6234 Louise Cove Dr
Windermere, FL 34786-8941, USA

Stewart, Natalie (Musician, Songwriter, Writer)
DreamWorks Records
9268 W 3rd St
Beverly Hills, CA 90210-3713, USA

Stewart, Norman (Athlete, Basketball Player)
University of Missouri
3201 Westcrest Cir
Columbia, MO 65203, USA

Stewart, Patrick (Actor, Director, Producer)
288 7th St # 3
Brooklyn, NY 11215-3210, USA

Stewart, Paul (Athlete, Hockey Player)
16 Bridgeview Cir
Walpole, MA 02081-3766, USA

Stewart, Paul Anthony (Actor)
c/o Paul Reisman *Abrams Artists Agency (NY)*
275 7th Ave Fl 26
New York, NY 10001-6708, USA

Stewart, Peggy (Actor)
PO Box 2468
Toluca Lake, CA 91610, USA

Stewart, Porsha (Reality Star)
2045 Caladium Way
Roswell, GA 30075-2401, USA

Stewart, Robert L (Astronaut, General)
2303 Covemont Dr SE
Huntsville, AL 35801-2258, USA

Stewart, Robert L Brig Gen (Astronaut)
2303 Covemont Dr SE
Huntsville, AL 35801-2258, USA

Stewart, Rod (Musician, Songwriter)
1435 S Ocean Blvd
Palm Beach, FL 33480-5005, USA

Stewart, Ryan (Athlete, Football Player)
2715 Owens Ave SW
Marietta, GA 30064-4253, USA

Stewart, Sammy (Athlete, Baseball Player)
PO Box 399
Craggy Correctional Center
Asheville, NC 28802-0399, USA

Stewart, Scott (Actor)
c/o Jeff Okin *Anonymous Content (LA)*
3532 Hayden Ave
Culver City, CA 90232-2413, USA

Stewart, Scott (Athlete, Baseball Player)
5243 Hickory Knoll Ln
Mount Holly, NC 28120-9344, USA

Stewart, Shannon (Athlete, Baseball Player)
14348 SW 156th Ave
Miami, FL 33196-6072, USA

Stewart, Shannon H (Athlete, Baseball Player)
14348 SW 156th Ave
Miami, FL 33196-6072, USA

Stewart, Steve (Athlete, Football Player)
1161 Jeans Ln
Amery, WI 54001-5109, USA

Stewart, Tonea (Actor)
Alabama State University
Theater Arts Dept
Montgomery, AL 36101, USA

Stewart, Tony (Race Car Driver)
Tony Stewart Racing
6001 Haas Way
Kannapolis, NC 28081-7730, USA

Stewart, Tyler (Musician)
Nettwerk Mgmt
8730 Wilshire Blvd # 304
Beverly Hills, CA 90211-2716, USA

Stewart, Will Foster (Actor)
8730 Santa Monica Blvd # 1
West Hollywood, CA 90069-4547, USA

Stewart-Hardway, Donna (Actor)
PO Box 777
Pinch, WV 25156-0777, USA

Steyer, Tom (Business Person)
Farallon Capital Management LLC
1 Maritime Plz Ste 2100
San Francisco, CA 94111-3528, USA

Steyn, Mark (Writer)
Mark Steyn Enterprises Inc
PO Box 30
Woodsville, NH 03785-0030, USA

Sticht, J Paul (Business Person)
11732 Lake House Ct
North Palm Beach, FL 33408-3320, USA

Stickel, Fred A (Publisher)
Portland Oregonian
1320 SW Broadway
Portland, OR 97201-3411, USA

Stickles, Montford (Monty) (Athlete, Football Player)
1363 3rd Ave
San Francisco, CA 94122-2718, USA

Stickles, Ted (Swimmer)
1142 Sharynwood Dr
Baton Rouge, LA 70808-6069, USA

Stidham, Howard (Athlete, Football Player)
185 Bell Dr W
Winchester, TN 37398-5401, USA

Stidham, Phil (Athlete, Baseball Player)
5025 Malabar Blvd
Melbourne Beach, FL 32951-3268, USA

Stieb, David (Dave) A (Athlete, Baseball Player)
3375 Corey Dr
Reno, NV 89509-3991, USA

Stieber, Tamar (Journalist)
Albuquerque Journal
7777 Jefferson St NE
Editorial Dept
Albuquerque, NM 87109-4360, USA

Stiegler, Josef (Pepi) (Skier)
PO Box 290
Teton Village, WY 83025-0290, USA

Stiegler, Resi (Athlete, Olympic Athlete, Skier)
PO Box 1150
Wilson, WY 83014-1150, USA

Stienke, Jim (Athlete, Football Player)
4707 Interlachen Ln
Austin, TX 78747, USA

Stiers, David Ogden (Actor)
c/o Staff Member *Mitchell K Stubbs & Assoc (MKS)*
8675 Washington Blvd Ste 203
Culver City, CA 90232-7486, USA

Stieve, Terry (Athlete, Football Player)
1407 Vail Pl
Saint Louis, MO 63104-2570, USA

Stigers, Curtis (Actor, Musician)
Shore Fire Media
32 Court St Fl 16
Brooklyn, NY 11201-4441, USA

Stigman, Dick (Athlete, Baseball Player)
12914 5th Ave S
Burnsville, MN 55337-3504, USA

Stiles, Darron (Athlete, Golfer)
130 Wild Turkey Run
Pinehurst, NC 28374-9658, USA

Stiles, Jackie (Basketball Player)
Patrick J Stiles
115 E Hamilton St
Claflin, KS 67525-5200, USA

Stiles, Julia (Actor)
143 Avenue B Apt 9E
New York, NY 10009-5027, USA

Stiles, Ryan (Actor, Comedian)
c/o Kay Liberman *Liberman/Zerman Management*
252 N Larchmont Blvd Ste 200
Los Angeles, CA 90004-3754, USA

Still, Arthur B (Art) (Athlete, Football Player)
9813 Betsy Ross Ln
Liberty, MO 64068-8527, USA

Still, Bryan (Athlete, Football Player)
3812 Brennen Robert Pl
Glen Allen, VA 23060-2505, USA

Still, Devon (Athlete, Football Player)
c/o Drew Rosenhaus *Rosenhaus Sports Representation*
6400 Allison Rd
Miami Beach, FL 33141-4540, USA

Still, Ken (Golfer)
1210 Princeton St
Fircrest, WA 98466-6035, USA

Still, Susan L (Astronaut)
NASA
2101 Nasa Pkwy Spc Johnsoncenter
Houston, TX 77058-3696, USA

Stiller, Ben (Actor, Comedian, Director)
c/o Staff Member *Red Hour Films*
629 N La Brea Ave
Los Angeles, CA 90036-2013, USA

Stiller, Jerry (Actor, Comedian)
c/o Pearl Wexler *Kohner Agency, The*
9300 Wilshire Blvd Ste 555
Beverly Hills, CA 90212-3211, USA

Stiller, Stephen (Music Group, Musician)
17525 Ventura Blvd Ste 210
Encino, CA 91316-5111, USA

Stillman, Cory (Athlete, Hockey Player)
1 Panther Pkwy
Attn: Player Development Dept
Sunrise, FL 33323-5315, USA

Stillman, Royle (Athlete, Baseball Player)
580 Jb Ct
Glenwood Springs, CO 81601-8733, USA

Stillman, Whit (Director)
International Creative Mgmt
10250 Constellation Blvd Fl 1
Los Angeles, CA 90067-6241, USA

Stills, Chris (Musician)
Atlantic Records
9229 W Sunset Blvd Ste 900
West Hollywood, CA 90069-3410, USA

Stills, Ken (Athlete, Football Player)
PO Box 340732
Tampa, FL 33694-0732, USA

Stills, Stephen (Musician)
c/o Marsha Vlasic *ICM Partners (LA)*
10250 Constellation Blvd Fl 7
Los Angeles, CA 90067-6207, USA

Stills, The (Music Group)
c/o Staff Member *Paradigm (Monterey)*
404 W Franklin St
Monterey, CA 93940-2303, USA

Stillwagon, Jim (Athlete, Football Player)
890 Gatehouse Ln
Columbus, OH 43235-1734, United States

Stillwagon, Jim R (Athlete, Football Player)
3999 Parkway Ln
Hilliard, OH 43026-1252, USA

Stillwell, Kurt (Athlete, Baseball Player)
1105 Lassen View Dr
Westwood, CA 96137-9537, USA

Stillwell, Ron (Athlete, Baseball Player)
1105 Lassen View Dr
Westwood, CA 96137-9537, USA

Stilson, Jeff (Comedian, Producer)
c/o Bonnie Burns *Burns & Burns Management*
10523 Mars Ln
Los Angeles, CA 90077-3109, USA

Stilwell, Victoria (Television Host)
c/o Cristina Dennstedt *Sarah Hall Productions Inc*
670 Broadway Rm 504
New York, NY 10012-2318, USA

Stinchcomb, Matt (Athlete, Football Player)
3817 Sweet Bottom Dr
Duluth, GA 30096-3159, USA

Stincic, Thomas (Athlete, Football Player)
2121 E Oasis St
Mesa, AZ 85213-9743, USA

Stine, Richard (Cartoonist)
PO Box 348
Hansville, WA 98340-0348, USA

Stine, Robert L (R L) (Writer)
Scholastic Book Services
555 Broadway
New York, NY 10012-3919, USA

Stine, Robert (RL) (Writer)
225 W 71st St
New York, NY 10023-3726, USA

Sting (Musician)
c/o Kathy Schenker *KSM Inc.*
1776 Broadway Ste 2205
New York, NY 10019-2016, USA

Sting, Charlotte (Athlete, Basketball Player)
333 E Trade St
Charlotte, NC 28202-2331, USA

Stinnett, Kelly (Athlete, Baseball Player)
845 N Harris Dr
Mesa, AZ 85203-5720, USA

Stinson, Bob (Athlete, Baseball Player)
1309 Bando Ln
The Villages, FL 32162-0115, USA

Stinson, Ed (Athlete, Football Player)
c/o Drew Rosenhaus *Rosenhaus Sports Representation*
6400 Allison Rd
Miami Beach, FL 33141-4540, USA

Stipanovich, Steve (Athlete, Basketball Player)
840 Wenneker Dr
Saint Louis, MO 63124-2042, USA

Stipe, Michael (Musician)
255 Best Dr
Athens, GA 30606-2811, USA

Stiritz, William P (Business Person)
Ralston Purina Co
Checkerboard Square
Saint Louis, MO 63164-0001, USA

Stirling, Lindsey (Musician)
c/o April King *ICM Partners (LA)*
10250 Constellation Blvd Fl 7
Los Angeles, CA 90067-6207, USA

Stirling, Rachel (Actor)
c/o Staff Member *Management Inc*
2032 Pinehurst Rd
Los Angeles, CA 90068-3732

Stirling, Steve (Athlete, Coach, Hockey Player)
118 Sassamon Ave
Milton, MA 02186-5828, USA

Stirvins, Alex (Athlete, Basketball Player)
11330 N Sundown Dr
Scottsdale, AZ 85260-5538, USA

Stith, Bryant (Athlete, Basketball Player)
20697 Governor Harrison Pkwy
Freeman, VA 23856-2451, USA

Stith, Samuel (Athlete, Basketball Player)
36 Madison St NE
Washington, DC 20011-2352, USA

Stith, Thomas (Athlete, Basketball Player)
105 Overlook Dr
Farmingville, NY 11738-3107, USA

Stivers, Steve (Congressman, Politician)
1007 Longworth Hob
Washington, DC 20515-0539, USa

Stivrins, Alex
11330 N Sundown Dr
Scottsdale, AZ 85260-5538, USA

St James, James (Jimmy) (Actor, Radio Personality)
The Real Jimmy Hollywood
7510 W Sunset Blvd # 333
Los Angeles, CA 90046-3408, USA

St. James, Lyn (Race Car Driver)
57 Gasoline Aly Ste D
Indianapolis, IN 46222-5932, USA

St. James, Rebecca (Musician)
c/o Staff Member *Smallbone Management*
PO Box 1524
Franklin, TN 37065-1524, USA

St Jean, Garry (Basketball Player, Coach)
Golden State Warriors
1001 Broadway
Oakland, CA 94607-4019, USA

St Jean, Len (Athlete, Football Player)
32 Ledgebrook Ave
Stoughton, MA 02072-1054, USA

St John, Andrew (Actor)
c/o Loch Powell *Leverage Management*
3030 Pennsylvania Ave
Santa Monica, CA 90404-4112, USA

St John, Gina (Actor, Television Host)
Howard Talent West
17000 Ventura Blvd Ste 210
Encino, CA 91316-4153, USA

St John, Jill (Actor)
115 Johnson Dr
Aspen, CO 81611-9719, USA

St John, Kristoff (Actor)
c/o Steve Rohr *Lexicon Public Relations*
8430 Santa Monica Blvd Ste 203
West Hollywood, CA 90069-4253, USA

St John, Lara (Musician)
Columbia Artists Mgmt Inc
165 W 57th St
New York, NY 10019-2201, USA

St John, Mia (Boxer)
c/o Staff Member *Amsel, Eisenstadt & Frazier Talent Agency (AEF)*
5055 Wilshire Blvd Ste 860
Los Angeles, CA 90036-6108, USA

St Louis, Martin (Athlete, Hockey Player)
22 Pilot Rock Ln
Riverside, CT 06878-2621, USA

Stoa, Ryan (Athlete, Hockey Player)
9634 12th Avenue Cir
Minneapolis, MN 55425-2510, USA

Stock, Barbara (Actor)
7329 Capistrano Ave
West Hills, CA 91307-1715, USA

Stock, Mark (Athlete, Football Player)
9344 Crest Hill Rd
Marshall, VA 20115-3017, USA

Stock, Wes (Athlete, Baseball Player)
PO Box 1309
Allyn, WA 98524-1309, USA

Stockdale, Gretchen
520 Washington Blvd # 248
Marina Del Rey, CA 90292

Stockdale, James
Hoover Inst
Stanford, CA 94305, USA

Stockemer, Ralph (Athlete, Football Player)
3401 Seltzer Dr
Plano, TX 75023-5805, USA

Stocker, Kevin (Athlete, Baseball Player)
1204 N Murray Ln
Liberty Lake, WA 99019-7555, USA

Stocker-Bottazzi, Jeanette (Athlete, Baseball Player)
1440 W Walnut St Apt 811
Allentown, PA 18102-4444, USA

Stockham, Benjamin (Actor)
c/o Beverly Strong *Strong Management*
9350 Wilshire Blvd Ste 224
Beverly Hills, CA 90212-3204, USA

Stocklin, Erik (Actor)
c/o Gabrielle Krengel *Domain Talent*
9229 W Sunset Blvd Ste 710
West Hollywood, CA 90069-3407, USA

Stockman, David (Politician)
Blackstone Group
150 Greenfield Rd
Winter Haven, FL 33884-1306, USA

Stockman, Phil (Athlete, Baseball Player)
2013 Red Oak Rd
Norcross, GA 30071-3819, USA

Stockman, Shawn (Music Group, Musician)
c/o Steve C Smith *Creative Talent Management Group (CTMG)*
433 N Camden Dr Ste 600
Beverly Hills, CA 90210-4416, USA

Stockmayer, Walter H (Doctor, Misc)
Willey Hill
Norwich, VT 05055, USA

Stockton, Dave K (Golfer)
222 Escondido Dr
Redlands, CA 92373-7215, USA

Stockton, David (Golfer)
222 Escondido Dr
Redlands, CA 92373-7215, USA

Stockton, David Jr (Golfer)
10 Carrera Pl
Rancho Mirage, CA 92270-3227, USA

Stockton, Dick (Sportscaster)
2470 NW 63rd St
Boca Raton, FL 33496-3627, USA

Stockton, John (Athlete, Basketball Player)
The Warehouse
538 W Sumner Ave
Spokane, WA 99204-3738, USA

Stockton, Richard L (Dick) (Tennis Player)
715 Stadium Dr
San Antonio, TX 78212-7201, USA

Stockwell, Dean (Actor)
95723 Highway 99 W
Junction City, OR 97448-9395, USA

Stockwell, Jeff (Writer)
c/o Staff Member *United Talent Agency (UTA-LA)*
9336 Civic Center Dr
Beverly Hills, CA 90210-3604, USA

Stockwell, John (Actor)
United Talent Agency
9336 Civic Center Dr
Beverly Hills, CA 90210-3604, USA

Stoddard, Bob (Athlete, Baseball Player)
15760 Sunnyside Ave
Morgan Hill, CA 95037-5331, USA

Stoddard, Brandon
241 N Glenroy Ave
Los Angeles, CA 90049

Stoddard, Tim (Athlete, Baseball Player)
104 Hawthorne Dr
Twin Lakes, WI 53181-9564, USA

Stofa, John (Athlete, Football Player)
5893 Falling Brook Dr
Mason, OH 45040-2587, USA

Stoffer, Karen (Race Car Driver)
1408 Industrial Way Ste 16
Gardnerville, NV 89410-5719, USA

Stoitchkov, Hristo (Soccer Player)
DC United
14120 Newbrook Dr
Chantilly, VA 20151-2273, USA

Stojakovic, Peja
501 Gibson Dr Apt 424
Roseville, CA 95678-6501, USA

Stokes, Brian (Athlete, Baseball Player)
12140 66th Ave
Seminole, FL 33772-6122, USA

Stokes, Chris (Business Person, Director, Musician)
c/o Staff Member *Tobin & Associates PR*
4929 Wilshire Blvd Ste 245
Los Angeles, CA 90010-3859, USA

Stokes, Fred (Athlete, Football Player)
735 Mosleytown Rd
Tarrytown, GA 30470-4052, USA

Stokes, Greg (Athlete, Basketball Player)
2505 Plymouth St
Marion, IA 52302-5609, USA

Stokes, Jesse (Athlete, Football Player)
5810 Cayuga Dr
San Antonio, TX 78228-4325, USA

Stokes, Sims (Athlete, Football Player)
1011 Wind Ridge Cir
Duncanville, TX 75137-3741, USA

Stokkan, Bill (Race Car Driver)
Championship Auto Racing
5350 Lakeview Parkway South Dr
Indianapolis, IN 46268-5129, USA

Stokley, Brandon (Athlete, Football Player)
12479 Autumn Gate Way
Carmel, IN 46033-8284, USA

Stoklos, Randy (Athlete, Volleyball Player)
Beach Volleyball Camps
PO Box 1714
Pacific Palisades, CA 90272-1714, USA

Stole, Mink (Actor)
635 Colorado Ave Apt 3B
Baltimore, MD 21210-2135, USA

Stolhandske, Tom (Athlete, Football Player)
518 Mirepoix
San Antonio, TX 78232-1950, USA

Stolhanske, Erik (Comedian)
c/o Staff Member *United Talent Agency (UTA-LA)*
9336 Civic Center Dr
Beverly Hills, CA 90210-3604, USA

Stoll, Corey (Actor)
c/o James Suskin *James Suskin Management*
2 Charlton St Apt 5K
New York, NY 10014-4970, USA

Stoll, Jarret (Athlete, Hockey Player)
2021 Monterey Blvd
Hermosa Beach, CA 90254-2913, USA

Stolle, Frederick S (Tennis Player)
Turnberry Isle Yacht & Racquet Club
19735 Turnberry Way
Miami, FL 33180-2797, USA

Stollery, David (Actor)
3203 Bern Ct
Laguna Beach, CA 92651-2007, USA

Stolley, Paul D (Doctor)
10205 Wincopin Cir Apt 312
Columbia, MD 21044-3435, USA

Stolper, Pinchas (Religious Leader)
Orthodox Jewish Congregations Union
11 Broadway
New York, NY 10004-1303, USA

Stoltenberg, Bryan (Athlete, Football Player)
3207 W Farmington Ln
Sugar Land, TX 77479-1883, USA

Stoltz, Eric (Actor, Director, Producer)
c/o Helen Sugland *Landmark Artists*
4116 W Magnolia Blvd Ste 101
Burbank, CA 91505-2700, USA

Stoltzfus, Levi (Horse Racer)
234A N Harvest Rd
Ronks, PA 17572-9727, USA

Stomare, Peter
1129 N Poinsettia Pl
West Hollywood, CA 90046-5715

Stone, Albert L (Race Car Driver)
700 Central Ave
PO Box 8427
Louisville, KY 40208-1212, USA

Stone, Andrew L (Director)
2132 Century Park Ln Apt 212
Los Angeles, CA 90067-3320, USA

Stone, Angie (Musician)
c/o Jonathan Clardy *CN Publicity*
9107 Wilshire Blvd Ste 450
Beverly Hills, CA 90210-5535, USA

Stone, Benjamin (Actor)
c/o Mara Santino *Luber Roklin Management*
5815 W Sunset Blvd Ste 206
Los Angeles, CA 90028-6481, USA

Stone, Biz (Business Person)
Twitter Inc
1355 Market St Ste 900
San Francisco, CA 94103-1337, USA

Stone, Curtis (Chef, Television Host)
3220 Tahoe Pl
Los Angeles, CA 90068-1657, USA

Stone, Dean (Athlete, Baseball Player)
1451 20th Ave Apt 204
East Moline, IL 61244-2332, USA

Stone, Dee Wallace (Actor)
23035 Cumorah Crest Dr
Woodland Hills, CA 91364-3709, USA

Stone, Doug (Musician)
PO Box 943
Springfield, TN 37172-0943

Stone, Eddie (Adult Film Star)
c/o Staff Member *Diva Central Inc*
7510 W Sunset Blvd Ste 1445
Los Angeles, CA 90046-3408, USA

Stone, Emma (Actor)
1853 Noel Pl
Beverly Hills, CA 90210-1743, USA

Stone, Gene (Athlete, Baseball Player)
6897 Highway 262 SE
Othello, WA 99344-9761, USA

Stone, George H (Athlete, Baseball Player)
1304 Fairfield Dr
Ruston, LA 71270-3540, USA

Stone, Jack (Athlete, Football Player)
16125 Crestridge Ave
Sonora, CA 95370-8542, USA

Stone, Jack (Religious Leader)
Church of Nazarene
6401 Paseo Blvd
Kansas City, MO 64131-1213, USA

Stone, Jeff (Athlete, Baseball Player)
69 County Highway 244
Portageville, MO 63873-9587, USA

Stone, Jennifer (Actor)
c/o Laura Ackerman *Persona PR (LA)*
8840 Wilshire Blvd Ste 212
Beverly Hills, CA 90211-2606, USA

Stone, Joss (Musician, Songwriter)
c/o Rob Light *Creative Artists Agency (CAA-LA)*
2000 Avenue of the Stars Ste 100
Los Angeles, CA 90067-4705, USA

Stone, Ken (Athlete, Football Player)
1158 Jason Way
West Palm Beach, FL 33406-5255, USA

Stone, Lara (Model)
c/o Staff Member *IMG World (NY)*
200 5th Ave Bsmt 7
New York, NY 10010-3312, USA

Stone, Matt (Animator, Director, Producer, Writer)
2337 McKinley Ave
Venice, CA 90291-4623, USA

Stone, Michael (Athlete, Football Player)
c/o Eugene Parker *Maximum Sports Management*
6435 W Jefferson Blvd # 197
Fort Wayne, IN 46804-6203, USA

Stone, Moses (Musician)
c/o Lee Runchey *Chrome PR*
9107 Wilshire Blvd Ste 450
Beverly Hills, CA 90210-5535, USA

Stone, Nicole (Athlete, Olympic Athlete, Skier)
5272 Heather Ln
Park City, UT 84098-5967, USA

Stone, Nikki (Skier)
Podium Enterprises
PO Box 680-332
Park City, UT 84068, USA

Stone, Oliver (Actor, Director, Producer)
c/o Staff Member *Ixtlan Corporation*
12233 W Olympic Blvd Ste 322
Los Angeles, CA 90064-1085, USA

Stone, Richard (Politician)
4440 Willard Ave Apt 831
Chevy Chase, MD 20815-3762, USA

Stone, Ricky (Athlete, Baseball Player)
6494 Lakeview Ct
Hamilton, OH 45011-8139, USA

Stone, Rob
8033 W Sunset Blvd # 450
Los Angeles, CA 90046-2401

Stone, Robert (Director)
c/o Staff Member *Robert Stone Productions*
11 Morton Rd
Studio Building
Rhinebeck, NY 12572-2534, USA

Stone, Robert A (Writer)
Donadio & Ashworth
121 W 27th St Ste 704
New York, NY 10001-6262, USA

Stone, Roger D (Politician)
34 W 88th St
New York, NY 10024-2558, USA

Stone, Ron (Athlete, Baseball Player)
11720 NW Lovejoy St
Portland, OR 97229-5028, USA

Stone, Sammy
PO Box 2825
Port Arthur, TX 77643-2825

Stone, Sharon (Actor)
c/o Chuck Binder *Binder & Associates*
1465 Lindacrest Dr
Beverly Hills, CA 90210-2519, USA

Stone, Steve (Athlete, Baseball Player, Sportscaster)
9261 N 128th Way
Scottsdale, AZ 85259-6233, USA

Stone, William J (Athlete, Football Player)
618 Woodland Knolls Rd
Germantown Hills, IL 61548-9429, USA

Stonebreaker, Mike (Athlete, Football Player)
3300 Delaware Ave Apt A
Kenner, LA 70065-3689, USA

Stonecipher, Harry C (Business Person)
Boeing Co
PO Box 3707
Seattle, WA 98124-2207, USA

Stone Foxes, The (Music Group, Musician)
c/o Rob Weldon *Wingman Music*
Prefers to be contacted by email or telephone
CA, USA

Stone III, Charles (Actor, Director, Writer)
c/o Barbara Dreyfus *United Talent Agency (UTA-LA)*
9336 Civic Center Dr
Beverly Hills, CA 90210-3604, USA

Stoneman, Bill (Athlete, Baseball Player)
2519 N San Miguel Dr
Orange, CA 92867-8604, USA

Stoner, Alyson (Musician)
c/o Cindy Osbrink *Osbrink Talent Agency*
4343 Lankershim Blvd Ste 100
North Hollywood, CA 91602-2705, USA

Stoner, Bob (Race Car Driver)
Vapor Racing
10785 Oakland Dr
Portage, MI 49024-6758, USA

Stoner, Sherri (Actor, Producer, Writer)
c/o Tom Strickler *William Morris Endeavor (LA)*
9601 Wilshire Blvd
Beverly Hills, CA 90210-5213, USA

Stoner, Tobi (Athlete, Baseball Player)
2930 W Stuart St Apt 2
Fort Collins, CO 80526-6614, USA

Stone-Richards, Lucille (Athlete, Baseball Player)
17 Stonemeadow Dr
Bridgewater, MA 02324-1995, USA

Stones
4790 Irvine Blvd Ste 105
Irvine, CA 92620-1998

Stones, Dwight E (Athlete, Olympic Athlete)
27472 Portola Pkwy Ste 205
Foothill Ranch, CA 92610-2853, USA

Stonesipher, Don (Athlete, Football Player)
557 McHenry Rd Apt 218
Wheeling, IL 60090-9207, USA

Stone Sour (Music Group)
c/o Cory Brennan *Sanctuary Artist Management (NY)*
75 9th Ave
New York, NY 10011-7006, USA

Stonestreet, Eric (Actor)
12311 Cantura St
Studio City, CA 91604-2506, USA

Stookey, Paul (Music Group, Musician, Songwriter, Writer)
Newworld
RR 175
South Blue Hill Falls, ME 04615, USA

Stoops, Bob (Coach, Football Coach)
University of Oklahoma
Athletic Dept
108 Brooks St
Norman, OK 73069, USA

Stoops, Jim (Athlete, Baseball Player)
205 Foster Dr
Oswego, IL 60543-4053, USA

Stoops, Mike (Coach, Football Coach)
Arizona State University
Athletic Dept
Tempe, AZ 85287-0001, USA

Stopanovich, Steve (Athlete, Basketball Player)
14 Ridgecreek
Saint Louis, MO 63141-8042, USA

Stopel, Terry (Athlete, Football Player)
804 Saddlebrook Dr S
Bedford, TX 76021-5360, USA

Storch, Larry (Actor)
330 W End Ave # 17F
New York, NY 10023-8171, USA

Storch, Scott (Producer)
c/o Tracy Christian *TCA/Jed Root*
6500 Wilshire Blvd Ste 2200
Los Angeles, CA 90048-4942, USA

Storey, June
338 Morgan Pl
Vista, CA 92083-8018

Stork, Jeff (Athlete, Coach, Volleyball Player)
California State University Northridge
Athletic Dept
18111 Nordhoff St
Northridge, CA 91330-0001, USA

Stork, Travis (Doctor, Talk Show Host)
The Doctors
5555 Melrose Ave
Mae West Building, Second Floor
Los Angeles, CA 90038-3989, USA

Storke, Adam (Actor)
c/o Marc Epstein *Marc Epstein Entertainment*
108 Breeze Ave
Venice, CA 90291-3360, USA

Storm, Avery (Musician)
c/o Staff Member *Derrty Entertainment*
9648 Olive Blvd # 230
Saint Louis, MO 63132-3002, USA

Storm, Hannah (Correspondent, Sportscaster)
c/o Staff Member *ESPN (Main)*
935 Middle St
Espn Plaza
Bristol, CT 06010-1000, USA

Storm, Jim (Athlete, Hockey Player)
2609 Harvest Hill Dr
Brighton, MI 48114-8299, USA

Storm, Jim
13576 Cheltenham Dr
Sherman Oaks, CA 91423-4818

Storm, Lauren (Actor)
c/o Staff Member *Aquarius Public Relations*
5320 Sylmar Ave
Sherman Oaks, CA 91401-5612, USA

Storm, Tempest (Dancer)
3905 Cambridge St Unit 3
Las Vegas, NV 89119-7402, USA

Stormare, Peter (Actor)
c/o Jeff Golenberg *Silver Lining Entertainment*
421 S Beverly Dr Fl 7
Beverly Hills, CA 90212-4408, USA

Storms, Kirsten (Actor)
c/o Nils Larsen *Principato/Young Management (LA)*
9465 Wilshire Blvd Ste 900
Beverly Hills, CA 90212-2608, USA

Storr, Jamie (Athlete, Hockey Player)
Jamie Storr Goalie School
650 N Sepulveda Blvd
Los Angeles, CA 90049-2108, USA

Storraro, Vittorio (Cinematographer)
c/o Paul Hook *ICM Partners (LA)*
10250 Constellation Blvd Fl 7
Los Angeles, CA 90067-6207, USA

Story, Tim (Director)
c/o Michael Sheresky *United Talent Agency (UTA-LA)*
9336 Civic Center Dr
Beverly Hills, CA 90210-3604, USA

Story, Winston (Actor)
c/o Brian McCabe *Venture IAB*
3211 Cahuenga Blvd W Ste 104
Los Angeles, CA 90068-1372, USA

Storz, Erik (Athlete, Football Player)
114 Andrea Dr
Rockaway, NJ 07866-3702, USA

Stossel, John (Journalist)
211 Central Park W Apt 15-K
New York, NY 10024-6020, USA

Stott, Nicole P (Astronaut)
NASA
2007 Golden Bay Ln
League City, TX 77573-3968, USA

Stottlemyre, Melvin L (Mel) (Athlete, Baseball Player)
3314 Meadowlark Dr
Lewiston, ID 83501-8609, USA

Stottlemyre, Todd (Athlete, Baseball Player)
10839 E Gold Dust Ave
Scottsdale, AZ 85259-4842, USA

Stottlemyre Jr, Mel (Athlete, Baseball Player)
26004 SE 27th St
Sammamish, WA 98075-9140, USA

Stotts, Terry (Athlete, Basketball Coach, Basketball Player, Coach)
3109 Douglas Cir
Lake Oswego, OR 97035-3550, USA

Stoudamire, Damon (Athlete, Basketball Player)
c/o Lon Rosen *Magic Johnson Enterprises Inc*
5335 Wisconsin Ave NW Ste 850
Washington, DC 20015-2052, USA

Stoudemire, Amare (Athlete, Basketball Player)
16800 Berkshire Ct
Southwest Ranches, FL 33331-1332, USA

Stouder, Sharon M (Swimmer)
144 Loucks Ave
Los Altos, CA 94022-1045, USA

Stoudt, Bud (Bowler)
431 Lehman St
Lebanon, PA 17046-3639, USA

Stoudt, Cliff (Athlete, Football Player)
326 Doe Run Cir
Henderson, NV 89012-2701, USA

Stouffer, Kelly (Athlete, Football Player)
HC 81 Box 55
Rushville, NE 69360, USA

Stoughton, Blaine (Athlete, Hockey Player)
7526 Wakefield Ln Apt C
Maineville, OH 45039-8560, USA

Stovall, Da Rond (Athlete, Baseball Player)
1107 Goelz Dr
East Saint Louis, IL 62203-1917, USA

Stovall, Jerry L (Athlete, Football Player)
7948 Wrenwood Blvd Apt C
Baton Rouge, LA 70809-1787, USA

Stove, Betty (Tennis Player)
Advantage International
1025 Thomas Jefferson St NW # 450
Washington, DC 20007-5201, USA

Stover, George (Actor)
PO Box 10005
Towson, MD 21285-0005, USA

Stover, Irwin Russ Juno (Athlete, Swimmer)
512 Lanai Cir
Union City, CA 94587-4113, USA

Stover, Jeff (Athlete, Football Player)
260 Cohasset Rd Ste 190
Chico, CA 95926-2282, USA

Stover, Matt (Athlete, Football Player)
10024 Rustleleaf Dr
Dallas, TX 75238-2143, USA

Stover, Stewart (Athlete, Football Player)
9334 La Highway 82
Abbeville, LA 70510-2356, USA

Stowe, David H Jr (Business Person)
Deere Co
John Deere Road
Moline, IL 61265, USA

Stowe, Hal (Athlete, Baseball Player)
1361 Union New Hope Rd
Gastonia, NC 28056-8574, USA

Stowe, Madeleine
c/o Cynthia Pett-Dante *Brillstein Entertainment Partners (LA)*
9150 Wilshire Blvd Ste 350
Beverly Hills, CA 90212-3453, USA

Stowe, Medeleine (Actor)
United Talent Agency
9336 Civic Center Dr
Beverly Hills, CA 90210-3604, USA

Stowe, Otto (Athlete, Football Player)
546 Mills Way
Goleta, CA 93117-4021, USA

Stowers, Chris (Athlete, Baseball Player)
3773 Wakefield Hall Sq SE
Smyrna, GA 30080-4917, USA

Stowers, Tommie (Athlete, Football Player)
2435 NW Valley View Dr
Lees Summit, MO 64081-1977, USA

Stoya (Actor, Adult Film Star, Model)
c/o Drew Elliot *Artists International Management (NY)*
333 E 43rd St Apt 115
New York, NY 10017-4822, USA

Stoyanovich, Peter (Athlete, Football Player)
24383 Ravine Dr
South Lyon, MI 48178-8358, USA

St Patrick, Mathew (Actor)
c/o Steve Smith *Stagecoach Entertainment*
938 5th St Apt 4
Santa Monica, CA 90403-2653, USA

St. Pierre, Georges (Athlete)
c/o Staff Member *Creative Artists Agency (CAA-LA)*
2000 Avenue of the Stars Ste 100
Los Angeles, CA 90067-4705, USA

Strachan, Gordon (Politician)
PO Box 3747
Park City, UT 84060-3747, USA

Strachan, Mike (Athlete, Football Player)
PO Box 642007
Kenner, LA 70064-2007, USA

Strachan, Rod (Athlete, Olympic Athlete, Swimmer)
11632 Ranch Hl
Santa Ana, CA 92705-3130, USA

Strachan, Steve (Athlete, Football Player)
46 Crimson Rd
Billerica, MA 01821-5420, USA

Strachan, Tyaon (Athlete, Hockey Player)
5550 Flint Creek Ave
Dublin, OH 43016-9645, USA

Straczynski, J Michael (Actor)
c/o Chris Harbert *Creative Artists Agency (CAA-LA)*
2000 Avenue of the Stars Ste 100
Los Angeles, CA 90067-4705, USA

Strader, Cam (Athlete, Race Car Driver)
10974 Heritage Green Dr
Cornelius, NC 28031-7407, USA

Stradlin, Izzy (Musician)
605 McAndrew Rd
Ojai, CA 93023-9313, USA

Stradling, Harry A Jr (Cinematographer)
23388 Mulholland Dr # 55
Woodland Hills, CA 91364-2733, USA

Strahan, Michael (Athlete, Football Player)
491 N Tigertail Rd
Los Angeles, CA 90049-2807, USA

Strahler, Mike (Athlete, Baseball Player)
8 Canyon Draw
Alamogordo, NM 88310-3613, USA

Strahovski, Yvonne (Actor)
1603 Tower Grove Dr
Beverly Hills, CA 90210-2143, USA

Straight, Bering (Music Group)
c/o Staff Member *Creative Artists Agency (CAA-TN)*
401 Commerce St PH
Nashville, TN 37219-2516, USA

Strain, Joe (Athlete, Baseball Player)
8668 E Otero Cir
Centennial, CO 80112-3351, USA

Strain, Julie (Actor, Model)
Cooking with Mama
8491 W Sunset Blvd Ste 1850
West Hollywood, CA 90069-1911, USA

Strain, Sammy (Music Group, Musician)
Associated Booking Corp
1995 Broadway # 501
New York, NY 10023-5882, USA

Strait, Bob (Race Car Driver)
Carnes-Miller Motorsports
12515 Kenedo Cir
Elbert, CO 80106-8819, USA

Strait, George (Musician)
c/o Erv Woolsey *Erv Woolsey Agency*
1000 18th Ave S
Nashville, TN 37212-2184, USA

Strait, Steven (Actor)
c/o Chris Andrews *Creative Artists Agency (CAA-LA)*
2000 Avenue of the Stars Ste 100
Los Angeles, CA 90067-4705, USA

Straker, Lee (Athlete, Baseball Player)
Philadelphia Phillies
1 Citizens Bank Way Ofc
Attn: Venezulan Baseball Academy
Philadelphia, PA 19148-5249, USA

Strampe, Bob (Athlete, Baseball Player)
19210 W Lance Hill Rd
Cheney, WA 99004-7907, USA

Strampe, Bob (Bowler)
31029 Louise Ct
Warren, MI 48088-2005, USA

Strand, Mark (Writer)
5825 S Dorchester Ave Apt 9W
Chicago, IL 60637-1701, USA

Strand, Robin (Actor)
4083 Camellia Ave
Studio City, CA 91604-3007, USA

Strang, Deborah (Actor)
Henderson/Hogan
8285 W Sunset Blvd Ste 1
West Hollywood, CA 90046-2420, USA

Strange, Doug (Athlete, Baseball Player)
435 Heights Dr
Gibsonia, PA 15044-6032, USA

Strange, Pat (Athlete, Baseball Player)
156 Mill St
Springfield, MA 01108-1022, USA

Strange, Sarah (Actor)
c/o Ryan Martin *Agency for the Performing Arts (APA-LA)*
405 S Beverly Dr Ste 500
Beverly Hills, CA 90212-4425, USA

Strange Boys, The (Music Group)
c/o Staff Member *Paradigm (Monterey)*
404 W Franklin St
Monterey, CA 93940-2303, USA

Strange-Hansen, Martin (Actor)
c/o Staff Member *Gersh (LA)*
9465 Wilshire Blvd Ste 600
Beverly Hills, CA 90212-2605, USA

Stransky, Bob (Athlete, Football Player)
5970 W Colgate Pl
Denver, CO 80227-3814, USA

Strasburg, Stephen (Athlete, Baseball Player)
7511 Blue Lake Dr
San Diego, CA 92119-3010, USA

Strasser, Teresa (Comedian, Television Host)
c/o Anthony Mattero *Vigliano Associates*
405 Park Ave Ste 1700
New York, NY 10022-9402, USA

Strasser, Todd (Writer)
PO Box 859
Larchmont, NY 10538-0859, USA

Strassman, Marcia (Actor)
4024 Dixie Canyon Ave
Sherman Oaks, CA 91423-4832, USA

Strathairn, David (Actor)
Ryan Entertainment
4302 Agnes Ave
C/O Madeline Ryan
Studio City, CA 91604-1701, USA

Stratham, Jason (Actor)
International Creative Mgmt
10250 Constellation Blvd Fl 1
Los Angeles, CA 90067-6241, USA

Strathiam, David (Actor)
United Talent Agency
9336 Civic Center Dr
Beverly Hills, CA 90210-3604, USA

Stratton, Dan
65 Broadway Ste 504
New York, NY 10006-2541, USA

Stratton, Frederick P Jr (Business Person)
Briggs & Stratton
PO Box 702
Milwaukee, WI 53201-0702, USA

Stratton, Mike (Athlete, Football Player)
2611 Shore Line Rd
Knoxville, TN 37932-1724, USA

Stratus, Trish (Wrestler)
c/o Michael Braverman *Braverman Bloom Company*
6399 Wilshire Blvd
Los Angeles, CA 90048-5703, USA

Straub, Peter (Writer)
53 W 85th St
New York, NY 10024-4132, USA

Straub, Peter F (Writer)
53 W 85th St
New York, NY 10024-4132, USA

Strauss, Neil (Writer)
8491 W Sunset Blvd # 348
West Hollywood, CA 90069-1911, USA

Strauss, Peter (Actor)
Wolf/Kasteller
335 N Maple Dr Ste 351
Beverly Hills, CA 90210-5174, USA

Strauss-Schulson, Todd (Director)
c/o Christie Smith *Mosaic Media Group*
9200 W Sunset Blvd Ste 10
West Hollywood, CA 90069-3608, USA

Straw, Syd (Musician)
c/o Staff Member *The Agency Group (NYC)*
142 W 57th St Fl 6
New York, NY 10019-3300, USA

Strawberry, Darryl E (Athlete, Baseball Player)
Strawberry's Sports Grill
1802 Sterling Oaks Dr
Saint Peters, MO 63376-1187, USA

Strawberry, D J (Athlete, Basketball Player)
943 Bellevue St
Cape Girardeau, MO 63701-5401, USA

Stray Cats (Music Group, Musician)
c/o Dave Kaplan *Dave Kaplan Management*
1126 S Coast Hwy Ste 101
Encinitas, CA 92024-5003, USA

Strayed, Cheryl (Writer)
c/o Shari Smiley *Resolution (LA)*
1801 Century Park E Ste 2300
Los Angeles, CA 90067-2325, USA

Strayhorn, Les (Athlete, Football Player)
109 Sir Richard Ln
Chapel Hill, NC 27517-5531, USA

Streep, Meryl (Actor)
c/o Michelle Benson *42West (LA)*
1840 Century Park E Ste 700
Los Angeles, CA 90067-2122, USA

Street, Huston (Athlete, Baseball Player)
8300 Big View Dr
Austin, TX 78730-1520, USA

Street, John (Politician)
Mayor's Office
City Hall
23 N Juniper St
Philadelphia, PA 19107, USA

Street, Picabo (Athlete, Olympic Athlete, Skier)
PO Box 321
Hailey, ID 83333-0321, USA

Street, Rebecca (Actor)
19 W 69th St Apt 101
New York, NY 10023-4754, USA

Streeter, George (Athlete, Football Player)
117 Daniel Dr
North Prairie, WI 53153-9778, USA

Streiber, Whitley (Writer)
c/o Paul Canterna *Seven Summits Pictures & Management*
8906 W Olympic Blvd
Ground Floor
Beverly Hills, CA 90211-3550, USA

Streisand, Barbra (Actor, Director, Musician, Producer)
6838 Zumirez Dr
Malibu, CA 90265-4317, USA

Streit, Clarence K (Journalist)
2853 Ontario Rd NW Apt 509
Washington, DC 20009-2238, USA

Streit, Mark (Athlete, Hockey Player)
C A A Sports
2000 Avenue of the Stars Fl 3
Los Angeles, CA 90067-4704, USA

Stremme, David (Race Car Driver)
Penske Racing
200 Penske Way
Mooresville, NC 28115-8022, USA

Strenger, Rich (Athlete, Football Player)
1064 Arbroak Way
Lake Orion, MI 48362-2500, USA

Streuli, Wait (Athlete, Baseball Player)
1107 Westminster Dr
Greensboro, NC 27410-4545, USA

Streuli, Walt (Athlete, Baseball Player)
1107 Westminster Dr
Greensboro, NC 27410-4545, USA

Stricker, Bill (Athlete, Basketball Player)
2930 Driftwood Pl Apt 70
Stockton, CA 95219-8027, USA

Stricker, Steve (Athlete, Golfer)
5804 N Sherman Ave
Madison, WI 53704-2147, USA

Strickland, Donald (Athlete, Football Player)
1110 Gilman Ave
San Francisco, CA 94124-3623, USA

Strickland, Gail (Actor)
14732 Oracle Pl
Pacific Palisades, CA 90272-2642, USA

Strickland, Jim (Athlete, Baseball Player)
2139 Equestrian Rd
Paso Robles, CA 93446-4149, USA

Strickland, KaDee (Actor)
c/o Jason Trawick *William Morris Endeavor (LA)*
9601 Wilshire Blvd
Beverly Hills, CA 90210-5213, USA

Strickland, Rod (Athlete, Basketball Player)
14401 Darren Ct
Bowie, MD 20721-1213, USA

Strickland, Scott (Athlete, Baseball Player)
415 Enchanted River Dr
Spring, TX 77388-5981, USA

Stricklin, Hut (Race Car Driver)
9990 Caldwell Rd
Mount Ulla, NC 28125-8704, USA

Strieber, Whitley (Writer)
c/o Staff Member *Gersh (LA)*
9465 Wilshire Blvd Ste 600
Beverly Hills, CA 90212-2605, USA

Striker, Jake (Athlete, Baseball Player)
PO Box 5041
Salem, OR 97304-0041, USA

Stringer, Howard (Business Person)
Sony Corporation of America
Sony Drive
Park Ridge, NJ 07656, USA

Stringer, Rob (Business Person)
c/o Staff Member *Epic Records Group*
550 Madison Ave Fl 6
New York, NY 10022-3211, USA

Stringer, Vivian (Athlete, Basketball Coach)
6 Lavender Dr
Princeton, NJ 08540-9448, USA

Stringert, Hal (Athlete, Football Player)
1711 Dole St Apt 603
Honolulu, HI 96822-4946, USA

Stringfield, Sherry (Actor)
c/o Leanne Coronel *Coronel Group*
1100 Glendon Ave Fl 17
Los Angeles, CA 90024-3588, USA

Strittmatter, Mark (Athlete, Baseball Player)
8196 Keith Ct
Castle Rock, CO 80108-9257, USA

Strobel, Eric (Athlete, Hockey Player, Olympic Athlete)
6617 129th St W
Saint Paul, MN 55124-7967, USA

Stroble, Bobby (Golfer)
313 N Ingleside Dr
Albany, GA 31707-4130, USA

Strock, Donald J (Don) (Athlete, Coach, Football Coach, Football Player)
1512 Passion Vine Cir
Weston, FL 33326-3656, USA

Strode, Lester (Athlete, Baseball Player)
2523 Trenton Sta
Saint Charles, MO 63303-2913, USA

Strohmayer, John (Athlete, Baseball Player)
4379 Wild Flower Way
Redding, CA 96001-3776, USA

Strokes, The (Music Group)
c/o Juliet Casablancas *Wiz Kid Management*
123 E 7th St
New York, NY 10009-5747, USA

Strom, Brent (Athlete, Baseball Player)
2202 N Catalina Vista Loop
Tucson, AZ 85749-7908, USA

Strom, Brock T (Football Player)
4301 W 110th St
Leawood, KS 66211-1424, USA

Strom, Rick (Athlete, Football Player)
8905 Moor Park Run
Duluth, GA 30097-6622, USA

Stroma, Freddie (Actor)
c/o Danny Mancini *Inspire Entertainment*
425 N Robertson Blvd
West Hollywood, CA 90048-1735, USA

Stroman, Susan (Director)
c/o Leslee Dart *42West (NYC)*
220 W 42nd St Fl 12
New York, NY 10036-7200, USA

Stromberg, Mike (Athlete, Football Player)
PO Box 1510
Shelter Island, NY 11964-1510, USA

Stronach, Belinda (Business Person)
Magna International
600 Wilshire Dr
Troy, MI 48084-1625, USA

Strong, Brenda (Actor)
c/o Kay Liberman *Liberman/Zerman Management*
252 N Larchmont Blvd Ste 200
Los Angeles, CA 90004-3754, USA

Strong, Danny (Actor, Producer, Writer)
c/o Staff Member *The Gotham Group Inc*
9255 W Sunset Blvd Ste 515
West Hollywood, CA 90069-3308, USA

Strong, Derek (Athlete, Basketball Player)
5434 Hillcrest Dr
Los Angeles, CA 90043-2323, USA

Strong, Jamal (Athlete, Baseball Player)
12635 Versaille St
Victorville, CA 92394-9568, USA

Strong, Jeremy (Actor)
c/o Meredith Wechter *ICM Partners (LA)*
10250 Constellation Blvd Fl 7
Los Angeles, CA 90067-6207, USA

Strong, Jim (Athlete, Football Player)
9303 Oxted Ln
Spring, TX 77379-6621, USA

Strong, Joe (Athlete, Baseball Player)
1340 Corcoran Ave
Vallejo, CA 94589-1878, USA

Strong, Johnny (Actor)
c/o Beverly Strong *Strong Management*
9350 Wilshire Blvd Ste 224
Beverly Hills, CA 90212-3204, USA

Strong, Mack (Football Player)
c/o Staff Member *Maxx Sports &
Entertainment*
546 5th Ave Fl 6
New York, NY 10036-5000, USA

Strong, Rider (Actor)
c/o Ellen Meyer *Ellen Meyer Management*
8899 Beverly Blvd Ste 612
Los Angeles, CA 90048-2429, USA

Strong, Tara (Actor)
c/o Jeff Danis *Danis, Panaro, Nist (DPN)*
9201 W Olympic Blvd
Beverly Hills, CA 90212-4605, USA

Strossen, Nadine (Politician)
57 Worth St
New York, NY 10013-2926, USA

Stroud, Don (Actor)
500 Lunalilo Home Rd Apt 16A
Honolulu, HI 96825-1718, USA

Stroud, Morris (Athlete, Football Player)
11214 College Ave
Kansas City, MO 64137-2221, USA

Stroughter, Steve (Athlete, Baseball Player)
247 E Ashland Ave
Visalia, CA 93277-6702, USA

Stroup, Jessica (Actor)
c/o Erica Tarin *ID Public Relations (LA)*
7060 Hollywood Blvd Fl 8th
Los Angeles, CA 90028-6021, USA

Struber, Larry (Producer)
c/o Staff Member *William Morris
Endeavor (LA)*
9601 Wilshire Blvd
Beverly Hills, CA 90210-5213, USA

Strudwick, Suzanne (Golfer)
5500 Crestwood Dr
Knoxville, TN 37914-5108, USA

Strug, Kerri (Athlete, Gymnast, Olympic Athlete)
2611 N Santa Lucia Dr
Tucson, AZ 85715-3137, USA

Strus, Lusia (Actor)
c/o Staff Member *Steve Himber
Entertainment*
211 S Beverly Dr # 601
Beverly Hills, CA 90212-3807, USA

Struthers, Sally (Actor)
c/o Vincent Cirrincione *Vincent
Cirrincione Associates*
1516 N Fairfax Ave
Los Angeles, CA 90046-2608, USA

Struycken, Carel (Actor)
1665 E Mountain St
Pasadena, CA 91104-3936, USA

Stryker, Bradley (Actor)
c/o Staff Member *House of
Representatives, The*
1434 6th St Ste 1
Santa Monica, CA 90401-2527, USA

Stuart, Brad (Athlete, Hockey Player)
C A A Sports
2000 Avenue of the Stars Fl 3
Los Angeles, CA 90067-4704, USA

Stuart, Eric (Actor, Musician)
330 Carroll St
Brooklyn, NY 11231-5008, USA

Stuart, Jason (Actor, Comedian)
c/o Bonny Dore *Bonny Dore Management*
8530 Wilshire Blvd Ste 400
Beverly Hills, CA 90211-3131

Stuart, Lyle (Publisher)
1530 Palisade Ave Apt 6L
Fort Lee, NJ 07024-5402, USA

Stuart, Mark (Athlete, Hockey Player)
6320 Oak Meadow Ln NW
Rochester, MN 55901-8820, USA

Stuart, Marty (Musician, Songwriter)
c/o Staff Member *Paradigm (Monterey)*
404 W Franklin St
Monterey, CA 93940-2303, USA

Stuart, Roy (Athlete, Football Player)
PO Box 3339
Tulsa, OK 74101-3339, USA

Stubblefield, Dana W (Athlete, Football Player)
2464 Cottle Ave
San Jose, CA 95125-4010, USA

Stubblefield, Marga (Golfer)
PO Box 140
Kailua, HI 96734-0140, USA

Stubblefield, Mickey (Athlete, Baseball Player)
Kansas City Monarchs
4870 Seldon Way SE
Smyrna, GA 30080-9266, USA

Stubbs, Franklin (Athlete, Baseball Player)
13706 Mockingbird Dr
Prospect, KY 40059-9026, USA

Stubing, Larry (Moose) (Athlete, Baseball Player, Coach)
10821 Laconia Dr
Villa Park, CA 92861-6408, USA

Stuckey, Henry (Athlete, Football Player)
3615 Winchester Ave
Atlantic City, NJ 08401-3544, USA

Stuckey, James (Jim) (Football Player)
San Francisco 49ers
2044 Egret Ln
Charleston, SC 29414-5302, USA

Stuckey, Rodney (Athlete, Basketball Player)
c/o Steve Banks *Banks Sports Ventures*
1126 17th Ave
Seattle, WA 98122-4645, USA

Studaway, Mark (Athlete, Football Player)
4524 Saint Honore Dr
Memphis, TN 38116-2012, USA

Studdard, Ruben (Musician)
c/o Cara Lewis *Creative Artists Agency
(CAA-NY)*
162 5th Ave Fl 6
New York, NY 10010-6047, USA

Studdard, Vern (Athlete, Football Player)
11449 Tara Blvd
Lovejoy, GA 30250, USA

Studi, Wes (Actor)
c/o Nevin Dolcefino *Innovative Artists
(LA)*
1505 10th St
Santa Monica, CA 90401-2805, USA

Studnicka-Caden, Mary Lou (Athlete, Baseball Player)
29 Mazarron Dr
Hot Springs Village, AR 71909-5827, USA

Studnicki-Caden, Mary Lou (Baseball Player)
29 Mazarron Dr
Hot Springs Village, AR 71909-5827, USA

Studstill, Patrick L (Pat) (Athlete, Football Player)
2235 Linda Flora Dr
Los Angeles, CA 90077-1410, USA

Studwell, Scott (Athlete, Football Player)
10415 Brown Farm Cir
Eden Prairie, MN 55347-4926, USA

Stuffel, Paul (Athlete, Baseball Player)
62 Ridgewood Pkwy
Newport News, VA 23608-1924, USA

Stuhlbarg, Michael (Actor)
c/o Lisa Loosemore *Viking Entertainment*
445 W 23rd St Ste 1A
New York, NY 10011-1445, USA

Stuhr-Thompsen, Beverly (Athlete, Baseball Player)
6379 N Muscatel Ave
San Gabriel, CA 91775-1843, USA

Stuhr-Thompson, Beverly (Baseball Player)
6379 N Muscatel Ave
San Gabriel, CA 91775-1843, USA

Stukes, Charles (Athlete, Football Player)
2040 Bishop St
Petersburg, VA 23805-2220, USA

Stull, Everett (Athlete, Baseball Player)
1667 Fieldgreen Overlook
Stone Mountain, GA 30088-3112, USA

Stults, Eric (Athlete, Baseball Player)
13810 Ranier Dr
Middlebury, IN 46540-8786, USA

Stults, Geoff (Actor)
c/o Staff Member *Eleven Eleven Films*
8350 Wilshire Blvd Ste 200
Beverly Hills, CA 90211-2348, USA

Stults, George (Actor)
c/o Staff Member *Bleu, An Entertainment
Company*
5225 Wilshire Blvd Ste 336
Los Angeles, CA 90036-4380, USA

Stump, David (Cinematographer)
HFWD Creative Representation
394 E Glaucus St
Encinitas, CA 92024-1734, USA

Stump, Gene (Athlete, Basketball Player)
542 S Hampton Ave
Orlando, FL 32803-6514, USA

Stump, Jim (Athlete, Baseball Player)
7432 Creekside Dr
Lansing, MI 48917-9693, USA

Stump, Patrick (Musician)
c/o Staff Member *Fueled By Ramen*
PO Box 1803
Tampa, FL 33601-1803, USA

Stumpel, Jozef (Athlete, Hockey Player)
12057 NW 69th Ct
Parkland, FL 33076-3335, USA

Stumps, Kathy (Actor)
c/o Staff Member *Gersh (LA)*
9465 Wilshire Blvd Ste 600
Beverly Hills, CA 90212-2605, USA

Stunyo-Korpak, Jeanne (Athlete, Diver, Olympic Athlete)
1435 Almagre Peak Dr
Colorado Springs, CO 80921-3659, USA

Stuper, John (Athlete, Baseball Player)
38 Lake St
Hamden, CT 06517-2315, USA

Sturckow, Frederick W (Rick) (Astronaut)
RR 2 Box 14
Dickinson, TX 77539, USA

Sturckow, Frederick W "Rick" Lt Colonel
(Astronaut)
30410 Rollingoak Dr
Tehachapi, CA 93561-8569, USA

Sturgeon, Bob
3903 Lewis Ave
Long Beach, CA 90807-3617

Sturgess, Jim (Actor)
c/o Jodi Gottlieb *Independent Public
Relations*
7060 Hollywood Blvd Fl 8th
Los Angeles, CA 90028-6021, USA

Sturgess, Shannon (Actor)
1223 Wilshire Blvd # 577
Santa Monica, CA 90403-5406, USA

Sturm, Jerry (Athlete, Football Player)
1900 E Girard Pl Apt 1503
Englewood, CO 80113-3114, USA

Sturm, Marco (Athlete, Hockey Player)
500 Atlantic Ave Unit 14P
Boston, MA 02210-2245, USA

Sturr, Jimmy (Musician)
United Polka Artists
PO Box 1
Florida, NY 10921-0001, USA

Sturt, Fred (Athlete, Football Player)
120 N Berkey Southern Rd
Swanton, OH 43558-8907, USA

Sturtze, Tanyon (Athlete, Baseball Player)
7946 Monarch Ct
Delray Beach, FL 33446-3682, USA

Stutter, Jason (Director, Producer, Writer)
c/o Simon Millar *Rumble Media*
1620 Broadway Ste C
Santa Monica, CA 90404-2777, USA

Stuttering John (Radio Personality)
c/o Staff Member *Howard Stern Show*
1221 Avenue of the Americas
Sirius Satellite Radio
New York, NY 10020-1001, USA

Stutzman, Martin (Congressman, Politician)
1728 Longworth Hob
Washington, DC 20515-4307, USA

Styler, Kara (Actor)
PO Box 8002
Honolulu, HI 96830-0002

Styles, Harry (Musician)
9551 Oak Pass Rd
Beverly Hills, CA 90210-1229, USA

Stynes, Chris (Athlete, Baseball Player)
1980 NE 7th St Ste 106
Deerfield Beach, FL 33441-3778, USA

Styx (Music Group, Musician)
c/o Keith Naisbitt *Agency Group Ltd, The (LA)*
1880 Century Park E Ste 711
Los Angeles, CA 90067-1618, USA

Suarez, Ken (Athlete, Baseball Player)
6000 Forest Ln
Fort Worth, TX 76112-1060, USA

Suazo, Chloe (Actor)
c/o Cindy Osbrink *Osbrink Talent Agency*
4343 Lankershim Blvd Ste 100
North Hollywood, CA 91602-2705, USA

Sublime (Music Group, Musician)
c/o Jon Phillips *Silverback Professional Artist Management*
9469 Jefferson Blvd Ste 101
Culver City, CA 90232-2915, USA

Subways, The (Music Group)
c/o Staff Member *Paradigm (Monterey)*
404 W Franklin St
Monterey, CA 93940-2303, USA

Such, Alec John (Musician)
Bon Jovi Mgmt
248 W 17th St Apt 501
New York, NY 10011-5330, USA

Such, Dick (Athlete, Baseball Player)
7614 Divot Dr
Sanford, NC 27332-8804, USA

Sucherman, Todd (Musician)
c/o Sterling Bacon *TBA Artist Management (Atlanta)*
1111 Alderman Dr Ste 285
Alpharetta, GA 30005-5433, USA

Suchet, David (Actor, Producer)
c/o Sarah Jackson *Seven Summits Pictures & Management*
8906 W Olympic Blvd
Ground Floor
Beverly Hills, CA 90211-3550, USA

Suci, Robert (Athlete, Football Player)
2341 Morton Ave
Flint, MI 48507-4445, USA

Sucsy, Michael (Director)
c/o Michael Sugar *Anonymous Content (LA)*
3532 Hayden Ave
Culver City, CA 90232-2413, USA

Sudakis, Bill (Athlete, Baseball Player)
79834 Bethpage Ave
Indio, CA 92201-0922, USA

Sudano, Brooklyn (Actor)
c/o Staff Member *Resolution (LA)*
1801 Century Park E Ste 2300
Los Angeles, CA 90067-2325, USA

Sudduth, Jill (Athlete, Swimmer)
9917 Calabasas Ave
Las Vegas, NV 89117-7513, USA

Sudduth, Skipp (Actor)
c/o Heather Reynolds *One Entertainment (NY)*
12 W 57th St PH
New York, NY 10019-3900, USA

Sudduth-Smith, Jill (Athlete, Olympic Athlete, Swimmer)
7615 Kiva Dr
Austin, TX 78749-2915, USA

Sudeikis, Jason (Actor, Comedian)
c/o Geoff Cheddy *Brillstein Entertainment Partners (LA)*
9150 Wilshire Blvd Ste 350
Beverly Hills, CA 90212-3453, USA

Sudol, Alison (Actor, Musician)
c/o Julie Colbert *William Morris Endeavor (LA)*
9601 Wilshire Blvd
Beverly Hills, CA 90210-5213, USA

Sugar, Leo T (Athlete, Football Player)
7161 Golden Eagle Ct Apt 1012
Fort Myers, FL 33912-1708, USA

Sugarcult (Actor)
Kio Novina Management & Booking
545 N Rossmore Ave Apt 3
Los Angeles, CA 90004-2440

Sugarland (Music Group)
c/o Jason Owen *Sandbox Entertainment*
54 Music Sq E Ste 200
Nashville, TN 37203-4360, USA

Sugarman, Burt (Producer)
3688/3700 E Lakeshore Dr
Whitefish, MT 59937, USA

Sugarman, Joseph (Joe) (Business Person, Writer)
Blublocker Corp
3350 Palm Center Dr
Las Vegas, NV 89103-5668, USA

Sugg, Diana K (Journalist)
Baltimore Sun
501 N Calvert St
Editorial Dept
Baltimore, MD 21278-1000, USA

Suggs, M Louise (Golfer)
424 Royal Crescent Ct
Saint Augustine, FL 32092-2786, USA

Suggs, Shafer (Athlete, Football Player)
1232 Strieff Ln
Flossmoor, IL 60422-1657, USA

Suggs, Terrell (Athlete, Football Player)
c/o Denise White *EAG Sports Management*
909 N Sepulveda Blvd Ste 360
El Segundo, CA 90245-3864, USA

Suggs, Walt (Athlete, Football Player)
11105 Bradyville Pike
Readyville, TN 37149-4513, USA

Suh, Ndamukong (Athlete, Football Player)
c/o Roosevelt Barnes *Maximum Sports Management*
6435 W Jefferson Blvd # 197
Fort Wayne, IN 46804-6203, USA

Suh, Ndamunkong (Athlete, Football Player)
c/o Jimmy Sexton *CAA (Memphis)*
6060 Poplar Ave Ste 470
Memphis, TN 38119-0910, USA

Suhey, Matthew J (Matt) (Athlete, Football Player)
550 Carriage Way
Deerfield, IL 60015-4535, USA

Suhonen, Alpo (Coach)
Chicago Blackhawks
1901 W Madison St
United Center
Chicago, IL 60612-2459, USA

Suhor, Yvonne (Actor)
J Michael Bloom
233 Park Ave S # 1000
New York, NY 10003-1606, USA

Suhrstedt, Timothy (Cinematographer)
Gersh Agency
232 N Canon Dr
Beverly Hills, CA 90210-5302, USA

Suits, Julia (Cartoonist)
Creators Syndicate
737 3rd St
Hermosa Beach, CA 90254-4714, USA

Sukla, Ed (Athlete, Baseball Player)
16 Perch
Irvine, CA 92604-3688, USA

Sularz, Guy (Athlete, Baseball Player)
10818 N 83rd St
Scottsdale, AZ 85260-6550, USa

Suleman, Nadya (Octomom) (Reality Star)
2051 Madonna Ln
La Habra, CA 90631-3344, USA

Sulkin, Gregg (Actor)
c/o Danielle Allman-Del *D2 Management*
9255 W Sunset Blvd Ste 600
West Hollywood, CA 90069-3306, USA

Sulliman, Doug (Athlete, Hockey Player)
PO Box 28964
Scottsdale, AZ 85255-0166, USA

Sullivan, Brian (Athlete, Hockey Player)
392 E Beach Rd
Charlestown, RI 02813-1311, USA

Sullivan, Charlotte (Actor)
c/o Evan Hainey *Untitled Entertainment (LA)*
350 S Beverly Dr Ste 200
Beverly Hills, CA 90212-4819, USA

Sullivan, Chip (Golfer)
49 Homestead Cir
Troutville, VA 24175-6995, USA

Sullivan, CHris (Athlete, Football Player)
64 Wagon Wheel Rd
North Attleboro, MA 02760-3576, USA

Sullivan, Cory (Athlete, Baseball Player)
PO Box 6
Kittredge, CO 80457-0006, USA

Sullivan, Dan (Athlete, Football Player)
25 Algonquin Ave
Andover, MA 01810-5527, USA

Sullivan, Daniel (Producer, Writer)
c/o Alan Wertheimer *Jackoway Tyerman Wertheimer Austen Mandelbaum Morris & Klein*
1925 Century Park E Fl 22
Los Angeles, CA 90067-2701, USA

Sullivan, Erik Per (Actor)
c/o Jodi Peikoff *Peikoff Mahan Law Office*
173-175 E Broadway
Suite C1
New York, NY 10002, USA

Sullivan, Frank (Athlete, Baseball Player)
PO Box 1873
Lihue, HI 96766-5873, USA

Sullivan, Franklin L (Frank) (Athlete, Baseball Player)
PO Box 1873
Lihue, HI 96766-5873, USA

Sullivan, George (Athlete, Football Player)
41 Howard St
Norwood, MA 02062-2323, USA

Sullivan, Greg (Musician)
David Levin Mgmt
200 W 57th St Ste 308
New York, NY 10019-3211, USA

Sullivan, Jazmine (Musician)
c/o Daniel Kim *Creative Artists Agency (CAA-LA)*
2000 Avenue of the Stars Ste 100
Los Angeles, CA 90067-4705, USA

Sullivan, John (Athlete, Baseball Player)
24 Highland Ave
Dansville, NY 14437-1648, USA

Sullivan, John (Athlete, Football Player)
c/o David Dunn *Athletes First, LLC*
23091 Mill Creek Dr
Laguna Hills, CA 92653-1258, USA

Sullivan, John (Congressman, Politician)
434 Cannon Hob
Washington, DC 20515-2004, USA

Sullivan, Kathleen (Journalist)
1025 N Kings Rd Apt 202
West Hollywood, CA 90069-6008, USA

Sullivan, Kathryn D (Astronaut)
795 Old Oak Trce
Columbus, OH 43235-1761, USA

Sullivan, Kathryn D Dr (Astronaut)
795 Old Oak Tree
Columbus, OH 43235, USA

Sullivan, Kevin (Journalist)
Washington Post
Editorial Dept
1150 15th St NW
Washington, DC 20071-0001, USA

Sullivan, Kevin Rodney (Actor, Director, Producer, Writer)
c/o Arnold Robinson *Rogers & Cowan PR (LA)*
8687 Melrose Ave Ste 7
West Hollywood, CA 90069-5721, USA

Sullivan, Louis (Politician)
Morehouse College
PO Box 578
Oak Bluffs, MA 02557-0578, USA

Sullivan, Marc (Athlete, Baseball Player)
2038 W 1st St Ste 100
Fort Myers, FL 33901-3109, USA

Sullivan, Michael J (Mike) (Politician)
Rothgerber, Johnson, & Lyons
1124 S Durbin St
Casper, WY 82601-4328, USA

Sullivan, Mike (Athlete, Coach, Hockey Player)
275 Elm St
Duxbury, MA 02332-4820, USA

Sullivan, Mike (Athlete, Football Player)
Cleveland Brown
76 Lou Groza Blvd
Attn: Coaching Staff
Berea, OH 44017-1269, USA

Sullivan, Nicole (Actor)
c/o Jonathan Howard *Innovative Artists (LA)*
1505 10th St
Santa Monica, CA 90401-2805, USA

Sullivan, Pat (Coach, Football Coach, Football Player, Heisman Trophy Winner)
1717 Indian Creek Dr
Vestavia, AL 35243-1745, USA

Sullivan, Phil (Athlete, Football Player)
4113 Rollingwood Ct
Jacksonville, FL 32257-7665, USA

Sullivan, Russ (Athlete, Baseball Player)
1701 Hill N Dale St
Fredericksburg, VA 22405-2735, USA

Sullivan, Scott (Athlete, Baseball Player)
1649 Mayfair Ct
Auburn, AL 36830-2128, USA

Sullivan, Steve (Athlete, Hockey Player)
9820 E Thompson Peak Pkwy Unit 832
Scottsdale, AZ 85255-6663, USA

Sullivan, Susan (Actor)
15355 Mulholland Dr
Los Angeles, CA 90077-1622, USA

Sullivan, Tim (Director)
Agency for Performing Arts
9200 W Sunset Blvd Ste 900
West Hollywood, CA 90069-3604, USA

Sullivan, Tom (Actor, Writer)
c/o Chris Ridenhour *Evolution Entertainment (LA)*
901 N Highland Ave
Los Angeles, CA 90038-2412, USA

Sullivan Jr, Brendon V
725 12th St NW
Washington, DC 20005-3901, USA

Sultanov, Alexel (Musician)
Columbia Artists Mgmt Inc
165 W 57th St
New York, NY 10019-2201, USA

Sum 41 (Music Group)
c/o Ron Laffitte *Red Light Management (LA)*
8439 W Sunset Blvd Ste 2
West Hollywood, CA 90069-1925, USA

Sumerfelt, Josh
6550 Yucca St Apt 310
Los Angeles, CA 90028-4226

Sumika, Aya (Actor)
c/o Jill Littman *Impression Entertainment*
9229 W Sunset Blvd Ste 700
West Hollywood, CA 90069-3407, USA

Summer, Cree (Actor)
Monterey Peninsula Artists
509 Hartnell St
Monterey, CA 93940-2825, USA

Summer-Francks, Cree (Actor)
PO Box 5617
Beverly Hills, CA 90209-5617

Summerhays, Bob (Athlete, Football Player)
12345 SE 91st Ave
Summerfield, FL 34491-8251, USA

Summerhays, Boyd (Athlete, Golfer)
297 Frontier Rd
Farmington, UT 84025-2616, USA

Summerleigh, George A (Pat) (Athlete, Football Player)
710 S White Chapel Blvd
Southlake, TX 76092-7319, USA

Summers, Andy (Musician)
1111 San Vicente Blvd
Santa Monica, CA 90402-2007, USA

Summers, Champ (Athlete, Baseball Player)
13708 SW 111th Ave
Dunnellon, FL 34432-8797, USA

Summers, Dana (Cartoonist)
Orlando Sentinel
633 N Orange Ave Lbby
Editorial Dept
Orlando, FL 32801-1349, USA

Summers, Jerry (Musician)
American Promotions
2011 Ferry Ave Apt U19
Camden, NJ 08104-1900, USA

Summers, Lawrence (Politician)
Harvard University
207 Fisher Ave
Brookline, MA 02445-4223, USA

Summers, Marc (Actor, Chef, Director, Producer, Television Host)
c/o Staff Member *Marc Summers Productions*
23705 Vanowen St Ste 105
West Hills, CA 91307-3030, USA

Summers, Tara (Actor)
c/o Lena Roklin *Luber Roklin Management*
5815 W Sunset Blvd Ste 206
Los Angeles, CA 90028-6481, USA

Summers, Wilbur (Athlete, Football Player)
PO Box 72734
Louisville, KY 40272, USA

Summitt, Pat (Athlete, Basketball Player, Olympic Athlete)
3720 River Trace Ln
Knoxville, TN 37920-7118, USA

Sumner, Walt (Athlete, Football Player)
PO Box 112
Ocilla, GA 31774-0112, USA

Sumners, Rosalynn (Athlete, Figure Skater, Olympic Athlete)
7815 115th Pi NE
Kirkland, WA 98033, USA

Sumpter, Jeremy (Actor)
c/o Mark Robert *Mark Robert Management*
2208 Patricia Ave
Los Angeles, CA 90064-2318, USA

Sumpter, Tika (Actor)
c/o Emily Gerson Saines *Brookside Artists Management (NY)*
250 W 57th St Ste 2303
New York, NY 10107-2399, USA

Sumpter, Tony (Athlete, Football Player)
702 S Gray St
Stillwater, OK 74074-4331, USA

Sunday, Gabriel (Actor)
c/o Judy Savage *Savage Agency*
6212 Banner Ave
Los Angeles, CA 90038-2802, USA

Sundberg, Jim (Athlete, Baseball Player)
2308 Newforest Ct
Arlington, TX 76017-2638, USA

Sunde, Milt (Athlete, Football Player)
6008 W 104th St
Minneapolis, MN 55438-1826, USA

Sunderland, Zac (Athlete)
1710 N Moorpark Rd # 212
Thousand Oaks, CA 91360-5133, USA

Sundhage, Pia (Coach)
U.S. Soccer Federation
1801 S Prairie Ave
Women's National Team
Chicago, IL 60616-1356, USA

Sundin, Gordie (Athlete, Baseball Player)
28132 Goby Trl
Bonita Springs, FL 34135-8469, USA

Sundvold, Jon (Athlete, Basketball Player)
2700 Westbrook Way
Columbia, MO 65203-5221, USA

Sung, Elizabeth (Actor)
GVA Talent
9229 W Sunset Blvd Ste 320
West Hollywood, CA 90069-3403, USA

Sunjata, Daniel (Actor)
c/o Meg Mortimer *Principal Entertainment (NY)*
1133 Avenue Of The Americas Ste 1621
New York, NY 10036-6710, USA

Sunshine, Caroline (Actor)
c/o Reg Reg Askew *Fly Guy Management*
1 W 34th St Rm 201
New York, NY 10001-3011, USA

Sunshine Underground, The (Music Group)
c/o Staff Member *Paradigm (Monterey)*
404 W Franklin St
Monterey, CA 93940-2303, USA

Sununu, John E (Politician)
49 Linden Rd
Hampton Falls, NH 03844-2035, USA

Suomi, Al (Athlete, Hockey Player)
5847 Sunset Ave
La Grange Highlands, IL 60525-7118, USA

Superdrag (Music Group)
c/o Staff Member *Paradigm (Monterey)*
404 W Franklin St
Monterey, CA 93940-2303, USA

Supergrass (Music Group)
c/o Staff Member *Paradigm (Monterey)*
404 W Franklin St
Monterey, CA 93940-2303, USA

Supernaw, Kywin (Athlete, Football Player)
1123 Clairborne Ct
Indianapolis, IN 46280-1100, USA

Supertramp
16530 Ventura Blvd Ste 201
Encino, CA 91436-4586

Suplee, Ethan (Actor)
Don Buchwald
6500 Wilshire Blvd Ste 2200
Los Angeles, CA 90048-4942, USA

Suppan, Jeff (Athlete, Baseball Player)
25315 Prado De La Felicidad
Calabasas, CA 91302-3651, USA

Sura, Bob (Basketball Player)
Atlanta Hawks
190 Marietta St NW Ste 405
Atlanta, GA 30303-2717, USA

Sure, Al B (Musician)
c/o Staff Member *ICM Partners (LA)*
10250 Constellation Blvd Fl 7
Los Angeles, CA 90067-6207, USA

Surhoff, BJ (Athlete, Baseball Player, Olympic Athlete)
2205 Pine Hill Farms Ln
Cockeysville, MD 21030-1023, USA

Surhoff, Rick (Athlete, Baseball Player)
1839 White Oak Dr
Reading, PA 19608-9468, USA

Surkowski-Delmonico, Lee (Athlete, Baseball Player)
10 Via Las Colinas Apt 1
Rancho Mirage, CA 92270-6015, USA

Surma, Damian (Athlete, Hockey Player)
1057 Emmons Blvd
Lincoln Park, MI 48146-4240, USA

Surratt, Al (Baseball Player)
Kansas City Monarchs
3448 E 54th St
Kansas City, MO 64130-4027, USA

Sursok, Tammin (Actor)
c/o David Gardner *Principato/Young Management (LA)*
9465 Wilshire Blvd Ste 900
Beverly Hills, CA 90212-2608, USA

Surtain, Patrick (Athlete, Football Player)
14557 Sherwood Rd
Overland Park, KS 66224-9807, USA

Surtees, John (Race Car Driver)
Team Surtees
PO Box 1018
Talladega, AL 35161-1018, USA

Survivor
PO Box 1821
Ojai, CA 93024-1821

Susana, Marta (Actor)
c/o Staff Member *Univision*
605 3rd Ave Fl 12
New York, NY 10158-0034, USA

Susco, Stephen (Producer, Writer)
c/o Chris Ridenhour *Evolution Entertainment (LA)*
901 N Highland Ave
Los Angeles, CA 90038-2412, USA

Susi, Carol Ann (Actor)
846 N Sweetzer Ave Apt 2
West Hollywood, CA 90069-5942, USA

Susman, Todd (Actor)
Pakula/King
9229 W Sunset Blvd Ste 315
West Hollywood, CA 90069-3403, USA

Sussin, Christen (Actor)
c/o Elizabeth Much *Much and House Public Relations*
8075 W 3rd St Ste 500
Los Angeles, CA 90048-4325, USA

Sussman, Adam (Writer)
c/o Staff Member *McKuin Frankel Whitehead*
141 El Camino Dr Ste 100
Beverly Hills, CA 90212-2717, USA

Sussman, Kevin (Actor)
c/o Jill McGrath *The Group Entertainment*
115 W 29th St Rm 1102
New York, NY 10001-5106, USA

Sussman, Susan
927 Noyes St
Evanston, IL 60201-6206

Sutcliffe, David (Actor)
c/o Robert Stein *Robert Stein Management*
PO Box 3797
Beverly Hills, CA 90212-0797, USA

Sutcliffe, Richard L (Rick) (Athlete, Baseball Player)
616 NE Seabrook Ct
Lees Summit, MO 64064-1261, USA

Suter, Gary (Athlete, Hockey Player, Olympic Athlete)
2128 County Road D
Lac Du Flambeau, WI 54538-9726, USA

Suter, Ryan (Athlete, Hockey Player)
1554 Shining Ore Dr
Brentwood, TN 37027-2218, USA

Sutera, Paul
11365 Ventura Blvd Ste 100
Studio City, CA 91604-3148

Sutherin, Don (Athlete, Football Player)
1043 Cayuga Trl SW
Hartville, OH 44632-9488, USA

Sutherland, Angus (Actor)
6369 Ivarene Ave
Los Angeles, CA 90068-2821, USA

Sutherland, Bill (Actor)
c/o Staff Member *Select Artists Ltd (CA-Westside Office)*
1138 12th St Apt 1
Santa Monica, CA 90403-5459, USA

Sutherland, Darrell (Athlete, Baseball Player)
1011 NW Jeffrey Pl
Beaverton, OR 97006-6335, USA

Sutherland, David (Golfer)
5431 Tree Side Dr
Carmichael, CA 95608-5958, USA

Sutherland, Donald (Actor, Musician, Producer, Writer)
c/o Catherine Olim *PMK/BNC Public Relations (PMK-LA)*
8687 Melrose Ave Ste 8
West Hollywood, CA 90069-5746, USA

Sutherland, Doug (Athlete, Football Player)
511 Kenilworth Ave
Duluth, MN 55803-2113, USA

Sutherland, Gary (Athlete, Baseball Player)
338 Oakcliff Rd
Monrovia, CA 91016-1823, USA

Sutherland, Kevin (Golfer)
1230 Carter Rd
Sacramento, CA 95864-5328, USA

Sutherland, Kiefer (Actor, Director, Producer)
c/o Suzan Bymel *Management 360*
9111 Wilshire Blvd
Beverly Hills, CA 90210-5508, USA

Sutherland, Kristine (Actor)
c/o Staff Member *SMS Talent*
8383 Wilshire Blvd Ste 230
Beverly Hills, CA 90211-2436, USA

Sutherland, Leo (Athlete, Baseball Player)
12082 Nieta Dr
Garden Grove, CA 92840-3524, USA

Sutherland, Shirley (Athlete, Baseball Player)
9613 Ritter Dr
Machesney Park, IL 61115-1759, USA

Sutherland, Thomas
229 Columbine Ct
Fort Collins, CO 80521-1715

Sutko, Glenn (Athlete, Baseball Player)
4475 Settles Bridge Rd
Suwanee, GA 30024-1981, USA

Sutor, George (Athlete, Basketball Player)
29840 State Highway 27
Holcombe, WI 54745-8798, USA

Sutorius, James
14014 Milbank St Unit 1
Sherman Oaks, CA 91423-2983

Sutter, Bruce (Athlete, Baseball Player)
59 Waterside Dr SE
Cartersville, GA 30121-6615, USA

Sutter, Duane (Athlete, Hockey Player)
3703 High Pine Dr
Coral Springs, FL 33065-6014, USA

Sutter, Eddie (Athlete, Hockey Player)
5104 N Bevalon Pl
Peoria, IL 61614-4606, USA

Sutter, Kurt (Producer)
c/o Katherine Rowe *Slate Public Relations*
9000 W Sunset Blvd Ste 915
West Hollywood, CA 90069-5809, USA

Sutter, Ryan (Athlete, Football Player)
2405 Rollingwood Dr
Fort Collins, CO 80525-1943, USA

Sutter, Trista (Reality Star)
c/o Babette Perry *IMG (LA)*
2049 Century Park E Ste 2460
Los Angeles, CA 90067-3126, USA

Suttle, Dane (Athlete, Basketball Player)
138 W 69th St
Los Angeles, CA 90003-1824, USA

Sutton, Andy (Athlete, Hockey Player)
491 Peachtree Battle Ave NW
Atlanta, GA 30305-4062, USA

Sutton, Betty (Congressman, Politician)
1519 Longworth Hob
Washington, DC 20515-1601, USA

Sutton, Daron (Baseball Player)
8645 E Cheryl Dr
Scottsdale, AZ 85258-1435, USA

Sutton, Don (Athlete, Baseball Player)
611 Riverlawn Ct
Atlanta, GA 30339-2993, USA

Sutton, Drew (Athlete, Baseball Player)
5107 Hawks Nest
McKinney, TX 75070-5354, USA

Sutton, Greg (Athlete, Basketball Player)
PO Box 1801
Edmond, OK 73083-1801, USA

Sutton, Hal (Golfer)
40 Duck Haven Pt
Bossier City, LA 71111-8173, USA

Sutton, John (Athlete, Baseball Player)
536 Blueberry Blvd
Dallas, TX 75217-4201, USA

Sutton, Kelly (Race Car Driver)
8410 Streamview Dr Apt G
Huntersville, NC 28078-6117, USA

Sutton, Larry (Athlete, Baseball Player)
14209 Woodward St
Overland Park, KS 66223-2561, USA

Sutton, Michael (Actor)
Somers Teitelbaum David
8840 Wilshire Blvd # 200
Beverly Hills, CA 90211-2606, USA

Sutton, Percy E (Politician)
10 W 135th St
New York, NY 10037-2602, USA

Sutton, Ricky (Athlete, Football Player)
1112 To Lani Farm Rd
Stone Mountain, GA 30083-5364, USA

Sutton, Will (Athlete, Football Player)
c/o Bruce Tollner *REP 1 Sports Group*
2 Corporate Park Ste 106
Irvine, CA 92606-5103, USA

Suvadova, Silvia (Actor)
c/o Michael Henderson *Heresun Management*
4119 W Burbank Blvd
Burbank, CA 91505-2122, USA

Suvari, Mena (Actor)
c/o Jason Barrett *Alchemy Entertainment*
7024 Melrose Ave Ste 420
Los Angeles, CA 90038-3394, USA

Suwyn, Mark A (Business Person)
Louisiana-Pacific Corp
111 SW 5th Ave
Portland, OR 97204-3604, USA

Suzor, Mark (Athlete, Hockey Player)
1639 Hillcrest Dr
Sheridan, WY 82801-3242, USA

Suzuki, Ichiro (Athlete, Baseball Player)
4101 185th Pl SE
Issaquah, WA 98027-9765, USA

Suzuki, Kurt (Athlete, Baseball Player)
733 S Juanita Ave
Redondo Beach, CA 90277-4357, USA

Suzuki, Mac (Athlete, Baseball Player)
5122 E Shea Blvd Unit 1164
Scottsdale, AZ 85254-4677, USA

Suzuki, Pat
343 E 30th St
New York, NY 10016-6417

Suzy (Writer)
18 E 68th St # 1B
New York, NY 10065-5807, USA

Svatos, Marek (Athlete, Hockey Player)
10322 Bluffmont Dr
Lone Tree, CO 80124-5579, USA

Svejkovsky, Jaroslav (Yogi) (Athlete, Hockey Player)
PO Box 276
Point Roberts, WA 98281-0276, USA

Svendsen, George (Football Player)
163 Wayzata Blvd W Apt 315
Wayzata, MN 55391-1566, USA

Svenson, Bo (Actor)
312 Bellino Dr
Pacific Palisades, CA 90272-3103, USA

Sveum, Dale (Athlete, Baseball Player)
13483 E Estrella Ave
Scottsdale, AZ 85259-5417, USA

Svihus, Bob (Athlete, Football Player)
23000 Guidotti Dr
Salinas, CA 93908-1022, USA

Svitov, Alexander (Athlete, Hockey Player)
Puckagency LLC
1 Sunset Dr N
Attn Jay Grossman
Chappaqua, NY 10514-1613, USA

Svoboda, Petr (Athlete, Hockey Player)
2453 Chelsea Pl Apt 1
Santa Monica, CA 90404-2027, USA

Swaby, Don (Actor)
c/o Staff Member *Stone Manners Salners Agency (LA)*
6100 Wilshire Blvd Ste 1500
Los Angeles, CA 90048-5110, USA

Swagerty, Jane (Swimmer)
9128 N 70th St
Paradise Valley, AZ 85253-1960, USA

Swagerty, Keith (Athlete, Basketball Player)
22232 17th Ave SE Ste 205
Bothell, WA 98021-7411, USA

Swaggert, Jimmy
8912 World Ministry Ave
Baton Rouge, LA 70810

Swaggerty, Bill (Athlete, Baseball Player)
31 W Mayer Dr
Finksburg, MD 21048-1844, USA

Swail, Julie (Athlete, Coach)
University of California
Athletic Dept
Irvine, CA 92697-0001, USA

Swaim, Caskey
1605 N Cahuenga Blvd # 202
Los Angeles, CA 90028-6201

Swain, Brennan (Athlete)
c/o Jerry Shandrew *Shandrew Public Relations*
1050 S Stanley Ave
Los Angeles, CA 90019-6634, USA

Swain, Chelse (Actor)
c/o Staff Member *Identity Talent Agency (ID)*
9107 Wilshire Blvd Ste 500
Beverly Hills, CA 90210-5526, USA

Swain, Dominique (Actor)
c/o Michael Garnett *Leverage Management*
3030 Pennsylvania Ave
Santa Monica, CA 90404-4112, USA

Swain, Garry (Athlete, Hockey Player)
PO Box 33
Seeley Lake, MT 59868-0033, USA

Swain, John (Athlete, Football Player)
409 E 135th St
Burnsville, MN 55337-4019, USA

Swan, Charles W (Actor)
2043 Golf Course Rd
Halifax, VA 24558-3069, USA

Swan, Craig (Athlete, Baseball Player)
16704 Bobcat Dr
Fort Myers, FL 33908-4327, USA

Swan, Michael (Actor)
13576 Cheltenham Dr
Sherman Oaks, CA 91423-4818, USA

Swan, Serinda (Actor)
c/o Alex Cole *Elevate Entertainment*
5757 Wilshire Blvd Ste 460
Los Angeles, CA 90036-3658, USA

Swanagon, Mary Lou (Baseball Player)
2193 E Amarillo Way
Palm Springs, CA 92264-8637, USA

Swanepoel, Candice (Model)
c/o Liz Carpenter *IMG Models (NY)*
304 Park Ave S Fl 12
New York, NY 10010-4314, USA

Swank, Hilary (Actor)
400 W 12th St Apt 16A
New York, NY 10014-1861, USA

Swanke, Karl (Athlete, Football Player)
4 Butternut Ct
Essex Junction, VT 05452-3959, USA

Swann, Lynn C (Athlete, Football Player, Sportscaster)
506 Hegner Way # 2
Sewickley, PA 15143-1552, USA

Swann, Pedro (Athlete, Baseball Player)
9 Westbury Dr
New Castle, DE 19720-8812, USA

Swanson, Jackie (Actor)
154 San Vicente Blvd Apt 22
Santa Monica, CA 90402-1537, USA

Swanson, John (Race Car Driver)
235-237 Main St
Maynard, MA 01754, USA

Swanson, Judith (Actor)
Persona Mgmt
40 E 9th St
New York, NY 10003-6421, USA

Swanson, Kristy (Actor, Model)
c/o Leo Bozzuto *Inphenate*
9701 Wilshire Blvd Fl 10
Beverly Hills, CA 90212-2010, USA

Swanson, Red (Athlete, Baseball Player)
1139 Chippenham Dr
Baton Rouge, LA 70808-5694, USA

Swanson, Stan (Athlete, Baseball Player)
688 Bass Ln
Corvallis, MT 59828-9739, USA

Swanson, Steven R Dr (Astronaut)
1414 Blueberry Ln
Friendswood, TX 77546-5213, USA

Swanson, Travis (Athlete, Football Player)
c/o David Dunn *Athletes First, LLC*
23091 Mill Creek Dr
Laguna Hills, CA 92653-1258, USA

Swarbrick, George (Athlete, Hockey Player)
14918 Ridgeview Dr
Plattsmouth, NE 68048-8798, USA

Sward, Melinda (Actor)
c/o Sheila Wenzel *Innovative Artists (LA)*
1505 10th St
Santa Monica, CA 90401-2805, USA

Swardson, Nick (Actor, Musician)
c/o Tim Sarkes *Brillstein Entertainment Partners (LA)*
9150 Wilshire Blvd Ste 350
Beverly Hills, CA 90212-3453, USA

Swarn, George (Football Player)
442 Daisy St
Mansfield, OH 44903-1305, USA

Swartwoudt, Gregg (Athlete, Football Player)
202 Anderson Rd
Esko, MN 55733-9413, USA

Swartz, Steven R (Business Person)
Hearst
300 W 57th St Fl 34
New York, NY 10019-3741, USA

Swartzbaugh, Dave (Athlete, Baseball Player)
113 Orchard St
Middletown, OH 45044-4920, USA

Swatek, Barret (Actor)
c/o Tammy Rosen *Sanders Armstrong Caserta*
425 N Robertson Blvd
West Hollywood, CA 90048-1735, USA

Swatland, Richard (Athlete, Football Player)
178 Club Rd
Stamford, CT 06905-2120, USA

Sway (Television Host)
c/o Staff Member *MTV (NYC)*
1515 Broadway
New York, NY 10036-8901, USA

Swayne, Harry (Football Player)
Tampa Bay Buccaneers
956 Cheswick Dr
Gurnee, IL 60031-5600, USA

Swayze, Don
247 S Beverly Dr # 102
Beverly Hills, CA 90212-3830

Swearingen, John E Jr (Business Person)
1420 N Lake Shore Dr
Chicago, IL 60610-6657, USA

Swearinger, D.J. (Athlete, Football Player)
c/o Todd France *Five Star Athlete Management*
3500 Lenox Rd NE
Atlanta, GA 30326-4228, USA

Sweat, Keith (Musician, Songwriter)
c/o Michael Irving *Emancipated Talent*
215 Clinton St
Brooklyn, NY 11201, USA

Swedberg, Heidi (Actor)
c/o Staff Member *Marathon Entertainment*
8060 Melrose Ave Ste 400
Los Angeles, CA 90046-7038

Swedlin, Rosalie (Producer)
c/o Staff Member *Jackoway Tyerman Wertheimer Austen Mandelbaum Morris & Klein*
1925 Century Park E Fl 22
Los Angeles, CA 90067-2701, USA

Sweeney, Alison (Actor)
c/o Carrie Simons *Triple 7 PR (LA)*
11693 San Vicente Blvd # 333
Los Angeles, CA 90049-5105, USA

Sweeney, Bob (Athlete, Hockey Player)
110 Brookview Dr
North Andover, MA 01845-3253, USA

Sweeney, Brian (Athlete, Baseball Player)
111 Old Coach Rd
Clifton Park, NY 12065-7618, USA

Sweeney, Calvin (Athlete, Football Player)
4120 Olympiad Dr
View Park, CA 90043-1632, USA

Sweeney, D B (Actor)
c/o Staff Member *Lighthouse Entertainment*
9220 W Sunset Blvd Ste 200
West Hollywood, CA 90069-3501, USA

Sweeney, Don (Athlete, Hockey Player)
100 Legends Way Ste 250
Attn: Asst General Manager
Boston, MA 02114-1390, USA

Sweeney, Don (Athlete, Hockey Player)
10 Munroe Rd
Lexington, MA 02421-7812, USA

Sweeney, John J (Politician)
AFL-CIO
8000 Corporate Dr Ste 100
Hyattsville, MD 20785-7210, USA

Sweeney, Julia (Actor, Comedian)
c/o Staff Member *William Morris Endeavor (LA)*
9601 Wilshire Blvd
Beverly Hills, CA 90210-5213, USA

Sweeney, Kevin (Athlete, Football Player)
12401 N Via Tuscania Ave
Clovis, CA 93619-8382, USA

Sweeney, Mark (Athlete, Baseball Player)
1821 Horseman Ln
Rcho Santa Fe, CA 92091-4605, USA

Sweeney, Michael J (Mike) (Athlete, Baseball Player)
2802 E Tam O Shanter Ct
Ontario, CA 91761, USA

Sweeney, Pepper
1930 Century Park W # 403
Los Angeles, CA 90067-6802

Sweeney, Ryan (Athlete, Baseball Player)
1212 Millet St
Naperville, IL 60563-2754, USA

Sweeney, Sunny (Musician)
c/o Staff Member *William Morris Endeavor (Nashville)*
1600 Division St Ste 300
Nashville, TN 37203-2755, USA

Sweeney, Terry (Actor, Comedian, Writer)
c/o Staff Member *Creative Artists Agency (CAA-LA)*
2000 Avenue of the Stars Ste 100
Los Angeles, CA 90067-4705, USA

Sweeney, Tim (Athlete, Hockey Player)
47 Ledgewood Dr
Hanover, MA 02339-1329, USA

Sweet, Joe (Athlete, Football Player)
1503 NE 89th Ct
Vancouver, WA 98664-6413, USA

Sweet, Matthew (Musician, Songwriter, Writer)
Russell Carter Artists Mgmt
315 W Ponce De Leon Ave Ste 755
Decatur, GA 30030-2497, USA

Sweet, Rachel (Producer)
c/o Staff Member *William Morris Endeavor (LA)*
9601 Wilshire Blvd
Beverly Hills, CA 90210-5213, USA

Sweet, Rick (Athlete, Baseball Player)
1503 NE 89th Ct
Vancouver, WA 98664-6413, USA

Sweet, Shay (Adult Film Star)
c/o Staff Member *Atlas Multimedia Inc*
9005 Eton Ave Ste C
Canoga Park, CA 91304-6533, USA

Sweeten, Madylin (Actor)
c/o Dino May *Dino May Management*
6362 Hollywood Blvd # 422
Los Angeles, CA 90028-6323, USA

Sweethearts of the Rodeo
5101 Overton Rd
Nashville, TN 37220-1920

Sweetin, Jodie (Actor)
c/o Staff Member *Savage Agency*
6212 Banner Ave
Los Angeles, CA 90038-2802, USA

Sweetlin, Jodie
6212 Banner Ave
Los Angeles, CA 90038-2802

Sweetney, Mike (Basketball Player)
New York Knicks
125 W End Ave # 6
Madison Square Garden
New York, NY 10023-6387, USA

Swenson, August
1702 Azores Dr
Pflugerville, TX 78660

Swenson, Eliza (Actor, Musician)
Ad Astra Management
5118 Vineland Ave # 102
North Hollywood, CA 91601-3814, USA

Swenson, Inga (Actor, Musician)
3351 Halderman St
Los Angeles, CA 90066-1719, USA

Swenson, Robert C (Bob) (Athlete, Football Player)
910 Cypress Ln
Louisville, CO 80027-9428, USA

Swerling Jr, Jo
25745 Vista Verde Dr
Calabasas, CA 91302-2165, USA

Swick, Mike (Athlete)
c/o Staff Member *Zinkin Entertainment & Sports Management*
5 E River Park Pl W Ste 203
Fresno, CA 93720-1557, USA

Swider, Larry (Athlete, Football Player)
1903 W 93rd Ave
Crown Point, IN 46307-1809, USA

Swienton, Gregory T (Business Person)
Ryder System Inc
3600 NW 82nd Ave
Doral, FL 33166-6623, USA

Swierc, Carl (Athlete, Football Player)
Carl Swierc
Houston, TX 77018, USA

Swift, Billy (Athlete, Baseball Player)
5880 E Sapphire Ln
Paradise Valley, AZ 85253-2200, USA

Swift, Doug (Athlete, Football Player)
265 S 25th St
Philadelphia, PA 19103-5551, USA

Swift, Harley (Athlete, Basketball Player)
357 Cliffside Dr
Kingsport, TN 37660-7103, USA

Swift, Stephanie (Adult Film Star)
PO Box 9864
Canoga Park, CA 91309-0864, USA

Swift, Stromile (Athlete, Basketball Player)
1111 Lincoln Rd Fl 4
Miami Beach, FL 33139-2439, USA

Swift, Taylor (Musician)
2201 Harding Pl
Nashville, TN 37215-4105, USA

Swilley, Dennis (Athlete, Football Player)
1020 Gruene River Dr
New Braunfels, TX 78132-3298, USA

S. Wilson, Frederica (Congressman, Politician)
208 Cannon Hob
Washington, DC 20515-0107, USA

Swindell, Cole (Musician)
c/o Staff Member *William Morris Endeavor (Nashville)*
1600 Division St Ste 300
Nashville, TN 37203-2755, USA

Swindell, F Gregory (Greg) (Athlete, Baseball Player)
6213 Terwilliger Way
Houston, TX 77057-2803, USA

Swindell, Jeff (Race Car Driver)
TW Racing
1921 W 4th St
Marion, IN 46952-6200, USA

Swindell, Sammy (Race Car Driver)
7540 Bartlett Corporate Cv E
Memphis, TN 38133-3963, USA

Swindells, William Jr (Business Person)
Williamette Industries
1300 SW 5th Ave
Portland, OR 97201-5667, USA

Swindle, Orson
500 University Ave Apt 309
Honolulu, HI 96826-4903

Swindle, RJ (Athlete, Baseball Player)
9382 Ayscough Rd
Summerville, SC 29485-8677, USA

Swindoll, Luci (Writer)
Thomas Nelson, Inc
PO Box 141000
Nashville, TN 37214-1000, USA

Swinford, Wayne (Athlete, Football Player)
100 Beacham Dr
Athens, GA 30606-4004, USA

Swingle, Paul (Athlete, Baseball Player)
6844 S Whetstone Pl
Chandler, AZ 85249-9149, USA

Swink, James E (Jim) (Athlete, Football Player)
723 Euclid Ave
Rusk, TX 75785-1919, USA

Swinney, Clovis
963 N Patrick St
Jonesboro, AR 72401-8161, USA

Swinson, Aaron (Athlete, Basketball Player)
1004 Longley Cv
Lake Mary, FL 32746-1921, USA

Swisher, Nick (Athlete, Baseball Player)
c/o Team Member *New York Yankees*
Yankee Stadium
161st St & River Ave
Bronx, NY 10451, USA

Swisher, Steve (Athlete, Baseball Player)
432 60th St
Vienna, WV 26105-8091, USA

Swisshelm, Ann (Athlete, Olympic Athlete)
855 W Erie St Apt 106
Chicago, IL 60642-5948, USA

Swisten, Amanda (Actor)
c/o Staff Member *WNWN Media*
348 Hauser Blvd # PH414
Los Angeles, CA 90036-3276, USA

Swistowicz, Mike (Athlete, Football Player)
2519 S Drake Ave
Chicago, IL 60623-3919, USA

Swit, Loretta (Actor)
310 Tahiti Way Apt 103
Marina Del Rey, CA 90292-6741, USA

Switchfoot (Music Group)
c/o Staff Member *Red Light Management (LA)*
8439 W Sunset Blvd Ste 2
West Hollywood, CA 90069-1925, USA

Switzer, Barry (Athlete, Coach, Football Coach, Football Player)
700 W Timberdell Rd
Norman, OK 73072-6323, USA

Switzer, Barry (Basketball Player)
PO Box 43021
Lubbock, TX 79409-3021, USA

Switzer, Jon (Athlete, Baseball Player)
2110 Paramount Ave
Austin, TX 78704-3936, USA

Switzer, Veryl (Athlete, Football Player)
1412 Wreath Ave
Manhattan, KS 66503-2402, USA

Swoboda, Ron (Athlete, Baseball Player)
315 Alonzo St
New Orleans, LA 70115-2119, USA

Swoopes, Sheryl (Athlete, Basketball Player, Olympic Athlete)
14110 Scarborough Fair St
Houston, TX 77077-1820, USA

Swope, Tracy Brooks
8730 W Sunset Blvd Ste 480
West Hollywood, CA 90069-2277

Sword, Sam (Athlete, Football Player)
2781 San Leandro Blvd
San Leandro, CA 94578-2583, USA

SWV
6464 W Sunset Blvd Ste 610
Los Angeles, CA 90028-7527

Sydney, Harry (Athlete, Football Player)
2025 Argonne St
Green Bay, WI 54304-4007, USA

sydor, Darryl (Athlete, Hockey Player)
11374 Wagon Wheel Curv
Saint Paul, MN 55129-6726, USA

Sydor, Darryl
317 Washington St
Attn Coaching Staff
Saint Paul, MN 55102-1609, USA

Sykes, Bob (Athlete, Baseball Player)
1451 County Road 900 E
Carmi, IL 62821, USA

Sykes, Eugene (Gene) (Athlete, Football Player)
8155 Jefferson Hwy Apt 903
Baton Rouge, LA 70809-1616, USA

Sykes, Phil (Athlete, Hockey Player)
1486 Brooke Ct
Hastings, MN 55033-3266, USA

Sykes, Wanda (Actor, Comedian)
c/o Danica Smith *PMK/BNC Public Relations (PMK-LA)*
8687 Melrose Ave Ste 8
West Hollywood, CA 90069-5746, USA

Sylbert, Anthea (Designer)
13949 Ventura Blvd # 309
Sherman Oaks, CA 91423-3584, USA

Sylvester, Chuck (Horse Racer)
PO Box 1066
Williamstown, NJ 08094-5066, USA

Sylvester, Dean (Athlete, Hockey Player)
51 Upland Rd
Plympton, MA 02367-1602, USA

Sylvester, Harold (Actor)
International Creative Mgmt
10250 Constellation Blvd Fl 1
Los Angeles, CA 90067-6241, USA

Sylvester, Steven P (Athlete, Football Player)
10425 Londonderry Ct
Cincinnati, OH 45242-5029, USA

Sylvester, Stevenson (Athlete, Football Player)
c/o Peter Schaffer *All Pro Sports and Entertainment*
36 Steele St Ste 100
Denver, CO 80206-5709, USA

Sylvia (Musician)
So Much More Media
PO Box 120426
Nashville, TN 37212-0426, USA

Symington, Fife (Politician)
1700 W Washington St
Phoenix, AZ 85007-2812, USA

Symmonds, Nick (Athlete, Olympic Athlete, Track Athlete)
c/o Staff Member *Total Sports Management*
115 Beechnut St Apt D3
Johnson City, TN 37601-1540, USA

Symms, Steven (Politician)
43527 Butler Pl
Leesburg, VA 20176-7428, USA

Symon, Michael (Chef, Television Host)
c/o Jeff Googel *William Morris Endeavor (NY)*
1325 Avenue of the Americas
New York, NY 10019-6026, USA

Symone, Raven (Actor)
c/o Todd Diener *Untitled Entertainment (LA)*
350 S Beverly Dr Ste 200
Beverly Hills, CA 90212-4819, USA

Symonette, Josh (Athlete, Football Player)
4923 Forrest Run
Lithonia, GA 30038-2794, USA

Sypek, Ryan (Actor)
c/o Nils Larsen *Principato/Young Management (LA)*
9465 Wilshire Blvd Ste 900
Beverly Hills, CA 90212-2608, USA

Syreeta
6255 W Sunset Blvd Ste 1800
Los Angeles, CA 90028-7419

System of a Down (Music Group)
c/o David Benveniste *Velvet Hammer*
9014 Melrose Ave
West Hollywood, CA 90069-5610, USA

Sytsma, John F (Politician)
Locomotive Engineers Brotherhood
1370 Ontario St
Cleveland, OH 44113-1701, USA

Szajda, Pawel (Actor)
c/o Staff Member *Stone Manners Salners Agency (LA)*
6100 Wilshire Blvd Ste 1500
Los Angeles, CA 90048-5110, USA

Szarabajka, Keith (Actor)
c/o Staff Member *Bauman Redanty & Shaul Agency*
5757 Wilshire Blvd
Suite 473
Beverly Hills, CA 90212, USA

Szczerbiak, Wally (Athlete, Basketball Player, Sportscaster)
c/o Jim Ornstein *William Morris Endeavor (NY)*
1325 Avenue of the Americas
New York, NY 10019-6026, USA

Szczerbiak, Walt (Wally) (Athlete, Basketball Player)
20 Peabody Rd
Cold Spring Harbor, NY 11724-1709, USA

Szegedy, Todd (Race Car Driver)
13 Mallory Hill Rd
Ridgefield, CT 06877-6302, USA

Szep, Paul M (Cartoonist)
10610 Andrew Ln
Seminole, FL 33777-1223, USA

Szigmond, Vilmos (Cinematographer)
PO Box 2230
Los Angeles, CA 90078-2230, USA

Szmanda, Eric (Actor)
c/o Michael Gruber *After Dark Management Group*
Prefers to be contacted via telephone
West Hollywood, CA 90069, USA

Szohr, Jessica (Actor)
c/o Lena Roklin *Luber Roklin Management*
5815 W Sunset Blvd Ste 206
Los Angeles, CA 90028-6481, USA

Szotkiewicz, Ken (Athlete, Baseball Player)
849 Dusky Sap Ct
Griffin, GA 30223-5994, USA

Szott, David (Athlete, Football Player)
11 Manor Dr
Morristown, NJ 07960-2600, USA

Szuminski, Jason (Athlete, Baseball Player)
2 Townsend St Apt 1214
San Francisco, CA 94107-2035, USA

Szymanski, Jim (Athlete, Baseball Player)
541 Riverwalk Dr
Mason, MI 48854-9361, USA

Szymanski, Richard (Dick) (Athlete, Football Player)
5270 Forest Edge Ct
Sanford, FL 32771-7160, USA

Ta'amu, Alameda (Athlete, Football Player)
c/o Bruce Tollner *REP 1 Sports Group*
2 Corporate Park Ste 106
Irvine, CA 92606-5103, USA

Tabackin, Lewis B (Lew) (Musician)
38 W 94th St Apt 1
New York, NY 10025-7123, USA

Tabaka, Jeff (Athlete, Baseball Player)
1481 Norview Dr
New Franklin, OH 44216-8804, USA

Tabaracci, Rick (Athlete, Hockey Player)
PO Box 982001
Park City, UT 84098-2001, USA

Tabb, Jerry (Athlete, Baseball Player)
20711 Winston Lake Dr
Richmond, TX 77406-6403, USA

Taber, Catherine (Actor)
c/o Staff Member *Charles Riley*
7122 Beverly Blvd Ste F
Los Angeles, CA 90036-2572, USA

Tabor, Greg (Athlete, Baseball Player)
29317 Whalebone Way
Hayward, CA 94544-6427, USA

Tabor, Paul (Athlete, Football Player)
3308 Riverwalk Dr
Norman, OK 73072-4852, USA

Tabor, Phil (Athlete, Football Player)
PO Box 1523
Ardmore, OK 73402-1523, USA

Tabori, Laszlo (Athlete, Track Athlete)
2221 W Olive Ave
Burbank, CA 91506-2659, USA

Taccone, Jorma (Writer)
c/o Julie Darmody *Mosaic Media Group*
9200 W Sunset Blvd Ste 10
West Hollywood, CA 90069-3608, USA

Tackett, Jeffrey (Jeff) (Athlete, Baseball
Player)
1574 Frazier St
Camarillo, CA 93012-4431, USA

Taco (Musician)
8124 W 3rd St Ste 204
Los Angeles, CA 90048-4341, USA

Tada, Joni Eareckson (Writer)
Joni And Friends headquarters
PO Box 3333
Agoura Hills, CA 91376-3333, USA

Taeger, Ralph
5619 Mother Lode Dr
Placerville, CA 95667-8232

Taff, Russ
PO Box 570815
Tarzana, CA 91357-0815

Taffe, Jeff (Athlete, Hockey Player)
1455 Truax Cir
Hastings, MN 55033-2476, USA

Taffoni, Joe (Athlete, Football Player)
103 Pine Valley Dr
Medford, NJ 08055-9210, USA

Tafone, Phil (Horse Racer)
419 Star St
East Meadow, NY 11554-3308, USA

Tafoya, Michele (Sportscaster)
CBS-TV
51 W 52nd St
Sports Dept
New York, NY 10019-6119, USA

Tafoya, Michele (Sportscaster)
c/o Staff Member *ESPN (Main)*
935 Middle St
Espn Plaza
Bristol, CT 06010-1000, USA

Taft, John
5224 Oaklawn Ave
Minneapolis, MN 55424-1307, USA

Taft, Reed (Athlete, Football Player)
1101 Atlanta St
Hattiesburg, MS 39401-1454, USA

Taft, Robert (Politician)
2933 Lower Bellbrook Rd
Spring Valley, OH 45370-8761, USA

Taft, William H IV (Government Official)
1001 Pennsylvania Ave NW
Washington, DC 20004-2505, USA

Taft, William Howard (Politician)
PO Box 5703
Wakefield, RI 02880-5703, USA

Tagawa, Cary-Hiroyuki (Actor)
c/o Joseph (Joe) Rice *Abrams Artists
Agency (LA)*
9200 W Sunset Blvd PH 11
West Hollywood, CA 90069-3601, USA

Tagge, Jerry (Athlete, Football Player)
3127 S 169th Plz
Omaha, NE 68130-2101, USA

Taghmaoui, Said (Actor)
c/o Leonard Torgan *The Collective*
8383 Wilshire Blvd Ste 1050
Beverly Hills, CA 90211-2415, USA

Tagliabue, Paul (Business Person, Football
Executive)
4149 Parkglen Ct NW
Washington, DC 20007-2137, USA

Taglianetti, Peter (Athlete, Hockey Player)
PO Box 120
Lawrence, PA 15055-0120, USA

Tagliani, Alex (Race Car Driver)
Players//Forsythe Racing
7321 Georgetown Rd
Indianapolis, IN 46268, USA

Taguchi, So (Athlete, Baseball Player)
12931 Twin Meadows Ct
Saint Louis, MO 63146-1803, USA

Tai, Kobe (Adult Film Star)
c/o Staff Member *Atlas Multimedia Inc*
9005 Eton Ave Ste C
Canoga Park, CA 91304-6533, USA

Tailes, Devin Star (Dev) (Musician)
c/o Jenn Tolman *Paradigm (LA)*
360 N Crescent Dr
North Bldg
Beverly Hills, CA 90210-4874, USA

Tait, John (Athlete, Football Player)
11344 E Newcastle Ave
Mesa, AZ 85209-3001, USA

Tait, John E (Business Person)
Penn Mutual Life
Independence Square
Philadelphia, PA 19172-0001, USA

Tait, Tristan (Actor)
Paradigm Agency
10100 Santa Monica Blvd Ste 2500
Los Angeles, CA 90067-4116, USA

Taka, Miiko
14560 Round Valley Dr
Sherman Oaks, CA 91403-4631

Takac, Robby (Musician)
c/o Staff Member *Atlas/Third Rail
Entertainment*
9200 W Sunset Blvd Ste 10
West Hollywood, CA 90069-3608, USA

Take 6 (Music Group, Musician)
c/o Staff Member *Agency for the
Performing Arts (APA-LA)*
405 S Beverly Dr Ste 500
Beverly Hills, CA 90212-4425, USA

Takei, George (Actor)
c/o Michael Greenwald *Don Buchwald &
Associates (LA)*
6500 Wilshire Blvd Ste 2200
Los Angeles, CA 90048-4942, USA

Takezawa, Kyoko (Musician)
I C M Artists
40 W 57th St
New York, NY 10019-4001, USA

Takko, Kari (Athlete, Hockey Player)
2601 Avenue of the Stars Ste 100
Attn Dir European Scouting
Frisco, TX 75034-9016, USA

Takter, Jimmy (Horse Racer)
1079 Old York Rd
East Windsor, NJ 08520-4710, USA

Tal, Alona (Actor)
c/o Laura Myones *McKeon-Myones
Management*
3500 W Olive Ave Ste 770
Burbank, CA 91505-5527, USA

Talafous, Dean (Athlete, Hockey Player)
2418 Foxglove Cir
Hudson, WI 54016-8251, USA

Talalay, Rachel (Director)
1047 Grant St
Santa Monica, CA 90405-1411, USA

Talamini, Robert (Athlete, Football Player)
1312 Calle Lajas
Las Cruces, NM 88007-8809, USA

Talancon, Ana Claudia (Actor)
c/o Carlos Carreras *Agency for the
Performing Arts (APA-LA)*
405 S Beverly Dr Ste 500
Beverly Hills, CA 90212-4425, USA

Talavera, Tracee (Gymnast)
1761 Fisher Dr
Concord, CA 94520-4064, USA

Talbert, Billy (Athlete)
194 Bellevue Ave
Newport, RI 02840-3515, USA

Talbert, Diron (Athlete, Football Player)
PO Box 388
Rosenberg, TX 77471-0388, USA

Talbert, Don (Athlete, Football Player)
PO Box 261
3027 Highway 123
Richmond, TX 77406-0007, USA

Talbot, Bob (Athlete, Baseball Player)
608 W Kaweah Ave
Visalia, CA 93277-2510, USA

Talbot, Dale (Baseball Player)
Chicago Cubs
608 W Kaweah Ave
Visalia, CA 93277-2510, USA

Talbot, Diron V (Athlete, Football Player)
3803 B F Terry Blvd
Rosenberg, TX 77471-5657, USA

Talbot, Fred (Athlete, Baseball Player)
7701 Lunceford Ln
Falls Church, VA 22043-1207, USA

Talbot, Maxime (Athlete, Hockey Player)
111 Bellevue Ave
Pittsburgh, PA 15229-1705, USA

Talbot, Mitch (Athlete, Baseball Player)
1138 Brook St
Cedar City, UT 84721-6340, USA

Talbot, Nita (Actor)
3420 Merrimac Rd
Los Angeles, CA 90049-1034, USA

Talbot, Susan (Actor)
Media Artists Group
6300 Wilshire Blvd Ste 1470
Los Angeles, CA 90048-5200, USA

Talbott, Gloria (Actor)
2066 Montecito Dr
Glendale, CA 91208-1824, USA

Talbott, John H (Doctor)
Commodore Club
177 Ocean Lane Dr
Key Biscayne, FL 33149-1437, USA

Talbott, John R (Writer)
c/o Staff Member *St Martins Press*
175 5th Ave Ste 400
Publicity Dept
New York, NY 10010-7848, USA

Talbott, Michael (Actor)
231A Tano Rd
Santa Fe, NM 87506-7030, USA

Talbott, Strobe (Journalist)
State Department
2201 C St NW
Washington, DC 20520-0099, USA

Talent, James (Politician)
1470 Country Lake Estates Dr
Chesterfield, MO 63005-4347, USA

Talese, Gay (Writer)
154 E Atlantic Blvd
Ocean City, NJ 08226-4511, USA

Taliaferro, George (Athlete, Football
Player)
2708 S Olcott Blvd
Bloomington, IN 47401-4417, USA

Taliaferro, Lorenzo (Athlete, Football
Player)
c/o Joby Branion *Athletes First, LLC*
23091 Mill Creek Dr
Laguna Hills, CA 92653-1258, USA

Taliaferro, Mike (Athlete, Football Player)
7332 Oakbluff Dr
Dallas, TX 75254-2739, USA

Talib, Aqib (Athlete, Football Player)
c/o Todd France *Five Star Athlete
Management*
3500 Lenox Rd NE Ste 1400
Atlanta, GA 30326-4231, USA

Talla (DJ)
c/o Staff Member *Diva Central Inc*
7510 W Sunset Blvd Ste 1445
Los Angeles, CA 90046-3408, USA

Tallackson, Barry (Athlete, Hockey Player)
10011 Colorado Ave N
Minneapolis, MN 55445-2363, USA

Tallas, George (Race Car Driver)
21st Century Racing
5245 Crooked Mountain Ct
Las Vegas, NV 89149-6462, USA

Tallas, Rob
1 Panther Pkwy
Attn: Coaching Staff
Sunrise, FL 33323-5315, USA

Tallas, Rob (Athlete, Hockey Player)
1844 Classic Dr
Pompano Beach, FL 33071, USA

Tallet, Brian (Athlete, Baseball Player)
3167 McClendon Ct
Baton Rouge, LA 70810-8376, USA

Talley, Darryl V (Athlete, Football Player)
7517 Clementine Way
Orlando, FL 32819-4607, USA

Talley, Gary (Musician)
Horizon Mgmt
PO Box 8770
Endwell, NY 13762-8770, USA

Talley, Stan (Athlete, Football Player)
24241 Porto Cristo
Dana Point, CA 92629-4511, USA

Tallinder, Henrik (Athlete, Hockey Player)
40 Maple Ave
Madison, NJ 07940-2618, USA

Tallman, Patricia (Actor)
PMB 2161
1801 E Tropicana Ave Ste 9
Las Vegas, NV 89119-6559, USA

Tallon, Dale (Athlete, Hockey Player)
1480 Ocean Dr Apt 3H
Vero Beach, FL 32963-5345, USA

Tallon, Dale
1 Panther Pkwy
Attn: General Manager
Sunrise, FL 33323-5315, USA

Tall Paul (Musician)
111 Lakewood Dr
Madison, TN 37115-5343, USA

Talor, Vanessa
11271 Ventura Blvd # 396
Studio City, CA 91604-3136

Talore, Brandy (Adult Film Star)
524 Hull Ave
Findlay, OH 45840-5602, USA

Talton, Tim (Athlete, Baseball Player)
130 Hardy Talton Rd NW
Pikeville, NC 27863-8601, USA

Tam, Jeffrey (Jeff) (Athlete, Baseball
Player)
3350 Davis Macaulay Pl
Melbourne, FL 32934-8387, USA

Tamahori, Lee W (Director)
International Creative Mgmt
10250 Constellation Blvd Fl 1
Los Angeles, CA 90067-6241, USA

Tamargo, John (Athlete, Baseball Player)
19018 Fern Meadow Loop
Lutz, FL 33558-4000, USA

Tamaro, Janet (Journalist)
c/o Rob Kenneally Creative Artists Agency
(CAA-LA)
2000 Avenue of the Stars Ste 100
Los Angeles, CA 90067-4705, USA

Tambellini, Roger (Athlete, Golfer)
32531 N Scottsdale Rd Ste 105
Scottsdale, AZ 85266-1519, USA

Tamberino, Paul (Referee)
349 Homeland Southway
Baltimore, MD 21212-4153, USA

Tamblyn, Amber (Actor)
c/o Joan Hyler Hyler Management
20 Ocean Park Blvd Unit 25
Santa Monica, CA 90405-3590, USA

Tamblyn, Russ (Actor, Dancer)
2310 6th St Apt 2
Santa Monica, CA 90405-2443, USA

Tambor, Jeffrey (Actor)
c/o Leslie Siebert Gersh (LA)
9465 Wilshire Blvd Ste 600
Beverly Hills, CA 90212-2605, USA

Tamburello, Ben (Athlete, Football Player)
4385 Milner Rd W
Birmingham, AL 35242-7355, USA

Tamer, Chris (Athlete, Hockey Player)
4215 Cornwell Ln
Whitmore Lake, MI 48189-9771, USA

Tamke, George W (Business Person)
Emerson Electric Co
PO Box 4100
Saint Louis, MO 63136-8506, USA

Tamm, Ralph (Athlete, Football Player)
2670 Atlantic Ave
Bensalem, PA 19020-3507, USA

Tan, Amy (Writer)
c/o Staff Member Steven Barclay Agency
12 Western Ave
Petaluma, CA 94952-2907, USA

Tan, Phillip (Actor)
c/o Michael Henderson Heresun
Management
4119 W Burbank Blvd
Burbank, CA 91505-2122, USA

Tanabe, David (Athlete, Hockey Player)
2321 Fieldstone Curv
Saint Paul, MN 55129-6218, USA

Tanaka, Masahiro (Athlete, Baseball
Player)
c/o Casey Close Excel Sports Management
(LA)
9665 Wilshire Blvd Ste 500
Beverly Hills, CA 90212-2312, USA

Tanana, Frank (Athlete, Baseball Player)
28492 S Harwich Dr
Farmington Hills, MI 48334-4281, USA

Tancill, Chris (Athlete, Hockey Player)
14 Kingswood Cir
Verona, WI 53593-7921, USA

Tancredo, Tom (Politician)
15342 W Iliff Dr
Denver, CO 80228-6443, USA

Tandy, Meagan (Actor)
c/o Pamela Sharp Sharp & Associates
Public Relations
1516 N Fairfax Ave
Los Angeles, CA 90046-2608, USA

Tang, Felicia (Race Car Driver)
9461 Charleville Blvd # 352
Beverly Hills, CA 90212-3017, USA

Tango, Dave (Reality Star)
c/o Joe Rose Abrams Artists Agency (LA)
9200 W Sunset Blvd PH 11
West Hollywood, CA 90069-3601, USA

Tani, Daniel M (Astronaut)
PO Box 1453
Great Falls, VA 22066-8453, USA

Tanka, Aiko (Model)
PO Box 1025
Beverly Hills, CA 90213-1025, USA

Tankersley, Dennis (Athlete, Baseball
Player)
1032 Pearview Dr
Saint Peters, MO 63376-2269, USA

Tankersley, Taylor (Athlete, Baseball
Player)
853 Chartier Ct
Asheboro, NC 27205-0545, USA

Tankian, Serj (Musician)
c/o David Holmes 3D Management
520 S Westgate Ave
Los Angeles, CA 90049-4212, USA

Tannahill, Don (Athlete, Hockey Player)
10113 Lakeview Dr
Rancho Mirage, CA 92270-1474, USA

Tannehill, Ryan (Athlete, Football Player)
c/o Pat Dye Jr SportsTrust Advisors (GA)
3340 Peachtree Rd NE Fl 16
Atlanta, GA 30326-1000, USA

Tannen, Steve (Athlete, Football Player)
8301 SW 57th Pl
Gainesville, FL 32608-5563, USA

Tanner, Antwon (Actor)
c/o Jeff Golenberg Silver Lining
Entertainment
421 S Beverly Dr Fl 7
Beverly Hills, CA 90212-4408, USA

Tanner, Barron (Athlete, Football Player)
7556 W Oregon Ave
Glendale, AZ 85303-5685, USA

Tanner, Bruce (Athlete, Baseball Player)
324 Hearthstone Dr
New Castle, PA 16105-1374, USA

Tanner, Joseph R (Astronaut)
800 Nelson Park Ln
Longmont, CO 80503-7688, USA

Tannous, Afif I (Government Official)
6912 Oak Ct
Annandale, VA 22003-5929, USA

Taormina, Sheila (Athlete, Olympic
Athlete, Swimmer)
16087 Riverside St
Livonia, MI 48154-2460, USA

Tapani, Kevin (Athlete, Baseball Player)
781 Ferndale Rd N
Wayzata, MN 55391-1010, USA

Tapert, Robert (Director, Producer,
Writer)
c/o Staff Member Renaissance Pictures /
Ghost House Pictures
315 S Beverly Dr Ste 216
Beverly Hills, CA 90212-4310, USA

Tapes N Tapes (Music Group)
c/o Staff Member Paradigm (Monterey)
404 W Franklin St
Monterey, CA 93940-2303, USA

Tapia, Roberto (Musician)
c/o Staff Member Universal Music Group
(UMG - LA)
2220 Colorado Ave
Santa Monica, CA 90404-3506, USA

Tapp, Darryl (Athlete, Football Player)
c/o Fletcher Smith Blueprint Sports Group
221 W Jefferson Ave
Naperville, IL 60540-5355, USA

Tapper, Brad (Athlete, Hockey Player)
8132 Bibiana Way Apt 103
Fort Myers, FL 33912-9022, USA

Tapply, William G. (Writer)
c/o Staff Member St Martins Press
175 5th Ave Ste 400
Publicity Dept
New York, NY 10010-7848, USA

Tapscott, Mark
5663 Ruthwood Dr
Calabasas, CA 91302-1053

Tarabay, Nick (Actor)
c/o Jordyn Palos Persona PR (LA)
8840 Wilshire Blvd Ste 212
Beverly Hills, CA 90211-2606, USA

Tarango, Jeff (Athlete, Olympic Athlete,
Tennis Player)
1166 Longfellow Dr
Manhattan Beach, CA 90266-6848, USA

Tarantina, Brian (Actor)
c/o Staff Member Cunningham Escott
Slevin & Doherty (CESD-LA)
10635 Santa Monica Blvd Ste 130
Los Angeles, CA 90025-8306, USA

Tarantino, Quentin (Actor, Director,
Producer, Writer)
7471 Woodrow Wilson Dr
Los Angeles, CA 90046-1322, USA

Tarasco, Tony (Athlete, Baseball Player)
3528 Maplewood Ave
Los Angeles, CA 90066-3020, USA

Tarasova, Tatiana (Coach, Figure Skater)
Connecticut Skating Center
300 Alumni Rd
Newington, CT 06111-1868, USA

Tarasovic, George (Athlete, Football
Player)
1503 Michael Dr
Pittsburgh, PA 15227-3958, USA

Tardits, Richard (Athlete, Football Player)
3590 Round Bottom Rd
Cincinnati, OH 45244-3026, USA

Tarkanian, Jerry (Basketball Coach,
Coach)
4767 Ocean Blvd Unit 1005
San Diego, CA 92109-8903, USA

Tarkenton, Fran (Athlete, Business Person,
Football Player)
3340 Peachtree Rd NE Ste 2570
Atlanta, GA 30326-1088, USA

Tarle, Jim (Athlete, Football Player)
2125 Willesdon Dr E
Jacksonville, FL 32246-0549, USA

Tarnasky, Nick (Athlete, Hockey Player)
6010 Lnterba Blvd
Tampa, FL 33611, USA

Tarpey, Erin
77 W 66th St
New York, NY 10023-6201

Tarpley, Ron (Athlete, Basketball Player)
819 Foxridge Dr
Arlington, TX 76017-6451, USA

Tarpley, Roy (Athlete, Basketball Player)
819 Foxridge Dr
Arlington, TX 76017-6451, USA

Tarrant, Chris (Game Show Host)
c/o Staff Member Who Wants to Be a
Millionaire
30 W 67th St
New York, NY 10023-0038

Tarr Jr, Robert J (Publisher)
58 River Marsh Ln
Johns Island, SC 29455-5202, USA

Tarses, Matt (Producer)
c/o Staff Member William Morris
Endeavor (LA)
9601 Wilshire Blvd
Beverly Hills, CA 90210-5213, USA

Tartabull, Danilio (Dan) (Athlete, Baseball
Player)
8200 Redlands St Apt 112
Playa Del Rey, CA 90293-6101, USA

Tartabull, Danny (Athlete, Baseball
Player)
28990 Oak Creek Ln Apt 1611
Agoura Hills, CA 91301-6437, USA

Tartabull, Jose (Athlete, Baseball Player)
1658 W 72nd St
Hialeah, FL 33014-4443, USA

Tartaglia, John (Actor, Producer, Writer)
Shrek, The Musical
1681 Broadway
Broadway Theatre
New York, NY 10019-5827, USA

Tartakovsky, Genndy (Director, Producer,
Writer)
c/o Staff Member William Morris
Endeavor (LA)
9601 Wilshire Blvd
Beverly Hills, CA 90210-5213, USA

Tarver, Antonio (Athlete, Boxer, Olympic
Athlete)
3959 Van Dyke Rd
Lutz, FL 33558-8025, USA

Tarver, John (Athlete, Football Player)
12056 SE Mt Scott Blvd
Happy Valley, OR 97086-6939, USA

Tarver, Katelyn (Musician)
c/o Marta Michaud Cinematic
Management
249 1/2 E 13th St
New York, NY 10003-5602, USA

The Celebrity Black Book 2015

Tarver, Laschelle (Athlete, Baseball Player)
4410 N Emerson Ave
Fresno, CA 93705-1203, USA

Tasby, Willie (Athlete, Baseball Player)
1210 E Renfro St
Plant City, FL 33563-5850, USA

Taschner, Jack (Athlete, Baseball Player)
2170 Hidden Creek Rd
Neenah, WI 54956-8916, USA

Tasker, Steven J (Steve) (Athlete, Football Player, Sportscaster)
16 Gypsy Ln
East Aurora, NY 14052-2108, USA

Tata, Joe E (Actor)
c/o Jeffrey Leavitt *Leavitt Talent Group*
8222 Melrose Ave Ste 203
Los Angeles, CA 90046-6838, USA

Tata, Jordan (Athlete, Baseball Player)
709 Sunfish St
Lakeway, TX 78734-4409, USA

Tata, Terry (Athlete, Baseball Player)
23 Stonegate Cir
Cheshire, CT 06410-3461, USA

Tatar, Jerome F (Business Person)
Mead Corp
Courthouse Plaza N
Dayton, OH 45463, USA

Tatarek, Bob (Athlete, Football Player)
5829 Southhall Rd
Birmingham, AL 35213-1017, USA

Tataurangi, Phil (Golfer)
PO Box 15325
Irvine, CA 92623-5325, USA

Tate, Ben (Athlete, Football Player)
c/o David Dunn *Athletes First, LLC*
23091 Mill Creek Dr
Laguna Hills, CA 92653-1258, USA

Tate, Brandon (Athlete, Football Player)
c/o Joel Segal *Lagardere Unlimited (NYC)*
845 United Nations Plz
New York, NY 10017-3540, USA

Tate, Bruce (Musician)
David Harris Enterprises
24210 E East Fork Rd Spc 9
Azusa, CA 91702-6249, USA

Tate, David (Athlete, Football Player)
3481 S Blackhawk Way
Aurora, CO 80014-3984, USA

Tate, Frank (Boxer)
12731 Water Oak Dr
Missouri City, TX 77489-3903, USA

Tate, Golden (Athlete, Football Player)
c/o Todd France *Five Star Athlete Management*
3500 Lenox Rd NE
Atlanta, GA 30326-4228, USA

Tate, James (Writer)
PO Box 9668
North Amherst, MA 01059-9668, USA

Tate, Kevin
6834 Hollywood Blvd # 303
Los Angeles, CA 90028-6116

Tate, Lahmard (Actor)
c/o Rob D'Avola *Rob DAvola & Associates*
9107 Wilshire Blvd Ste 450
Beverly Hills, CA 90210-5535, USA

Tate, Larena
4116 W Magnolia Blvd Ste 101
Burbank, CA 91505-2700

Tate, Larenz (Actor)
c/o Thea Ellis *Fifteen Minutes (LA)*
8436 W 3rd St Ste 650
Los Angeles, CA 90048-4131, USA

Tate, Lee (Athlete, Baseball Player)
6905 Pratt St
Omaha, NE 68104-2528, USA

Tate, Randy (Athlete, Baseball Player)
670 Old Highway 20
Tuscumbia, AL 35674-6086, USA

Tate, Randy (Politician)
Chrsitian Coalition
100 Centerville Tumpike
Virginia Beach, VA 23463-0001, USA

Tate, Stu (Athlete, Baseball Player)
107 Conger Rd
Madison, AL 35758-8647, USA

TATU (Music Group)
c/o Robert Hayes *Sound Management*
1525 S Winchester Blvd
San Jose, CA 95128-4335, USA

Tatum, Bradford
1505 10th St
Santa Monica, CA 90401-2805

Tatum, Channing (Actor)
c/o William Choi *Management 360*
9111 Wilshire Blvd
Beverly Hills, CA 90210-5508, USA

Tatum, Craig (Athlete, Baseball Player)
1031 Old Highway 24
Sumrall, MS 39482-3808, USA

Tatum, Earl (Athlete, Basketball Player)
2300 W Skyline Rd
Milwaukee, WI 53209-2176, USA

Tatum, Jim (Athlete, Baseball Player)
7433 Indian Wells Cv
Lone Tree, CO 80124-4207, USA

Tatum, Ken (Athlete, Baseball Player)
19 Oakdale Dr
Montevallo, AL 35115-5435, USA

Tatum, Kinnon (Athlete, Football Player)
4109 Knollwood Dr
Fayetteville, NC 28304-5208, USA

Tatupu, Lofa (Athlete, Football Player)
5817 106th Ave NE
Kirkland, WA 98033-7410, USA

Taubensee, Ed (Athlete, Baseball Player)
7149 Broomshedge Trl
Winter Garden, FL 34787-6374, USA

Taubman, A Alfred (Business Person)
Taubman Co
200 E Long Lake Rd Ste 200
Bloomfield Hills, MI 48304-2336, USA

Ta'ufo'ou, Will (Athlete, Football Player)
c/o Ryan Tollner *REP 1 Sports Group*
2 Corporate Park Ste 106
Irvine, CA 92606-5103, USA

Taupin, Bernie (Musician, Songwriter, Writer)
2905 Roundup Rd
Santa Ynez, CA 93460-9558, USA

Taurasi, Diana (Basketball Player)
c/o Staff Member *Phoenix Mercury*
201 E Jefferson St
Phoenix, AZ 85004-2412, USA

Taurel, Sidney (Business Person)
Eli Lilly Co
Lilly Corporate Center
Indianapolis, IN 46285-0001, USA

Tausch, Terry (Athlete, Football Player)
2804 Ryder Ct
Plano, TX 75093-3426, USA

Tauscher, Mark (Athlete, Football Player)
2245 Red Tail Gin
De Pere, WI 54115, USA

Tauskey, Mary (Athlete, Horse Racer, Olympic Athlete)
6 Morris Rd
Ambler, PA 19002-5407, USA

Taussig, Don (Athlete, Baseball Player)
1111 Ocean Dunes Cir
Jupiter, FL 33477-9128, USA

Tautalatasi, Junior (Athlete, Football Player)
1032 Eagle Ave Apt A
Alameda, CA 94501-1111, USA

Tautolo, Terry (Athlete, Football Player)
5713 E Huntdale St
Long Beach, CA 90808-2717, USA

Tavare, Jay (Actor)
c/o Paul Greenstone *Paul Greenstone Entertainment*
3008 Sorrelwood Dr
San Ramon, CA 94582-5008, USA

Tavares, John (Athlete, Hockey Player)
c/o Pat Brisson *Creative Artists Agency (CAA-LA)*
2000 Avenue of the Stars Ste 100
Los Angeles, CA 90067-4705, USA

Tavarez, Christopher (Actor, Football Player)
c/o Staff Member *Ella Bee*
Prefers to be contacted by telephone or email
Atlanta, GA, USA

Tavarez, Julian (Athlete, Baseball Player)
1108 Fireside Trl
Broadview Heights, OH 44147-3625, USA

Taveras, Willy (Athlete, Baseball Player)
6014 Floyd St
Houston, TX 77007-5008, USA

Taxier, Arthur (Actor)
Pakula/King
9229 W Sunset Blvd Ste 315
West Hollywood, CA 90069-3403, USA

Taylor, Aaron (Athlete, Baseball Player, Sportscaster)
c/o Jim Ornstein *William Morris Endeavor (NY)*
1325 Avenue of the Americas
New York, NY 10019-6026, USA

Taylor, Alphonso (Athlete, Football Player)
254 W Trenton Ave Apt 314B
Morrisville, PA 19067-2077, USA

Taylor, Anthony (Athlete, Basketball Player)
5300 Parkview Dr Apt 1093
Lake Oswego, OR 97035-8728, USA

Taylor, Billy (Athlete, Football Player)
385 Seminary Ave # 1
Rahway, NJ 07065-3407, USA

Taylor, Billy (Athlete, Baseball Player)
201 Washington Pl
Thomasville, GA 31792-4785, USA

Taylor, Bob (Athlete, Baseball Player)
27 Sunnybrook Rd
Springfield, MA 01119-2209, USA

Taylor, Bobby ""The Chief" (Athlete, Hockey Player)
3912 Americana Dr
Tampa, FL 33634-7405, USA

Taylor, Bobby ""The Chief"" (Athlete,
401 Channelside Dr
Attn Broadcast Dept
Tampa, FL 33602-5400, USA

Taylor, Brian (Athlete, Basketball Player)
3622 Green Vista Dr
Encino, CA 91436-4038, USA

Taylor, Brien (Baseball Player)
147 Brien Taylor Ln
Beaufort, NC 28516-6664, USA

Taylor, Bruce (Athlete, Baseball Player)
8 Highland Park Rd
Rutland, MA 01543-1742, USA

Taylor, Bruce L. (Athlete, Football Player)
1652 Arabian Ln
Palm Harbor, FL 34685-3341, USA

Taylor, Buck (Actor)
1305 Clyde Dr
Marrero, LA 70072-3609, USA

Taylor, Carl (Athlete, Baseball Player)
2356 Riviera Dr
Sarasota, FL 34232-3522, USA

Taylor, Chad (Musician)
Freedman & Smith
1790 Broadway # 131
New York, NY 10019-1412, USA

Taylor, Charles R (Charley) (Athlete, Football Executive, Football Player)
12023 Canter Ln
Reston, VA 20191-2129, USA

Taylor, Chris (Athlete, Hockey Player)
24 W Ham Cir
North Chili, NY 14514-9762

Taylor, Chris (Athlete, Hockey Player)
Rochester Americans
1 War Memorial Sq Ste 228
Rochester, NY 14614-2192

Taylor, Christian (Actor)
c/o Staff Member *KST Productions*
5543 Edmondson Pike # 1
Nashville, TN 37211-5808, USA

Taylor, Christine (Actor)
71 Hog Hill Rd
Chappaqua, NY 10514, USA

Taylor, Christy (Actor)
10990 Massachusetts Ave Apt 3
Los Angeles, CA 90024-5530, USA

Taylor, Cindy (Actor)
c/o Allee Newhoff *Elite Model Management (Miami)*
119 Washington Ave Ste 501
Miami Beach, FL 33139-7228, USA

Taylor, Clarice (Actor)
380 Elkwood Ter
Englewood, NJ 07631-1935, USA

Taylor, Cordell (Athlete, Football Player)
1825 Chasewood Park Dr
Marietta, GA 30066-4298, USA

Taylor, Corey (Musician)
c/o Staff Member *Agency Group Ltd, The (LA)*
1880 Century Park E Ste 711
Los Angeles, CA 90067-1618, USA

Taylor, Dana (Actor)
100 S Sunrise Way # 468
Palm Springs, CA 92262-6779, USA

Taylor, Dave (Athlete, Hockey Player)
18920 Pasadero Dr
Tarzana, CA 91356-5122, USA

Taylor, David (Athlete, Football Player)
304 Paddington Rd
Baltimore, MD 21212-3812, USA

Taylor, David (Writer)
c/o Author Mail *Bantam-Dell Publishing
(NY)*
1745 Broadway Fl 18
New York, NY 10019-4642, USA

Taylor, Dennis (Race Car Driver)
1255 N Tustin Ave
Anaheim, CA 92807-1603, USA

Taylor, Dorn (Athlete, Baseball Player)
405 Avenue D
Horsham, PA 19044-2020, USA

Taylor, Doug (Race Car Driver)
6630 Denver Industrial Park Rd
Denver, NC 28037-9795, USA

Taylor, Dwight (Athlete, Baseball Player)
5163 Queen Mary Ln
Jackson, MS 39209-3141, USA

Taylor, Ed (Athlete, Football Player)
2901 Clarke Rd
Memphis, TN 38115-2402, USA

Taylor, Eunice (Baseball Player)
955 Carroll Ln
Mount Dora, FL 32757-3726, USA

Taylor, Fred (Athlete, Football Player)
7975 Monterey Bay Dr
Jacksonville, FL 32256-2927, USA

Taylor, Gary (Athlete, Baseball Player)
PO Box 459
Dimondale, MI 48821-0459, USA

Taylor, Glen (Basketball Player)
Minnesota Timberwolves
600 1st Ave N
Target Center
Minneapolis, MN 55403-1400, USA

taylor, Graham (Athlete, Baseball Player)
2705 Vera Cruz Dr
Villa Hills, KY 41017-1070, USA

Taylor, Harry (Athlete, Baseball Player)
2125 Cooks Ln
Fort Worth, TX 76120-5301, USA

Taylor, Henry S (Writer)
1120 Aqua Vista Dr NW
Gig Harbor, WA 98335-1536, USA

Taylor, Holland (Actor)
c/o Bob Gersh *Gersh (LA)*
9465 Wilshire Blvd Ste 600
Beverly Hills, CA 90212-2605, USA

Taylor, Hosea (Athlete, Football Player)
208 Bobby St
Longview, TX 75602-3804, USA

Taylor, Jack (Business Person)
Enterprise Rent-A-Car
600 Corporate Park Dr
Saint Louis, MO 63105-4204, USA

Taylor, James Arnold (Actor)
c/o Pat Brady *Cunningham Escott Slevin
& Doherty (CESD-LA)*
10635 Santa Monica Blvd Ste 130
Los Angeles, CA 90025-8306, USA

Taylor, James C (Jim) (Athlete, Football
Player)
7840 Walden Rd
Baton Rouge, LA 70808-5939, USA

Taylor, James (JT) (Musician)
c/o Carlos Keyes *Red Entertainment
Agency*
505 8th Ave Rm 1004
New York, NY 10018-6529, USA

Taylor, Jason (Athlete, Football Player)
2980 Paddock Rd
Weston, FL 33331-3604, USA

Taylor, Jeff (Race Car Driver)
2017 E 5th St
Lumberton, NC 28358-6111, USA

Taylor, Jennifer Bini (Actor)
c/o Brad Warshaw *Brad Warshaw*
PO Box 931332
Los Angeles, CA 90093-1332, USA

Taylor, Jim (Writer)
c/o Staff Member *William Morris
Endeavor (LA)*
9601 Wilshire Blvd
Beverly Hills, CA 90210-5213, USA

Taylor, Jonathan (Producer)
c/o Staff Member *United Talent Agency
(UTA-LA)*
9336 Civic Center Dr
Beverly Hills, CA 90210-3604, USA

Taylor, Josh (Actor)
4151 Vanalden Ave
Tarzana, CA 91356-5527, USA

Taylor, Kerry (Athlete, Baseball Player)
1705 33 1/2 St S
Moorhead, MN 56560-3945, USA

Taylor, Kim (Musician)
c/o Staff Member *Paradigm (Monterey)*
404 W Franklin St
Monterey, CA 93940-2303, USA

Taylor, Kitrick L (Athlete, Football Player)
18215 Foothill Blvd Apt 94
Fontana, CA 92335-8512, USA

Taylor, Lawrence (Athlete, Football
Player)
532 Enclave Cir E
Pembroke Pines, FL 33027-1214, USA

Taylor, Lili (Actor)
c/o Staff Member *Dontanville/Frattaroli
(D/F)*
270 Lafayette St Ste 402
New York, NY 10012-3327, USA

Taylor, Lionel (Athlete, Coach, Football
Coach, Football Player)
201 Pinnacle Dr SE Apt 3614
Rio Rancho, NM 87124-0458, USA

Taylor, Livingston (Musician)
Fat City Artists
830 Tannahill Dr SE
Huntsville, AL 35802-1956, USA

Taylor, Mams (Musician)
12427 Kling St
Studio City, CA 91604-1215, USA

Taylor, Marianne (Actor)
Jack Scagnatti
5118 Vineland Ave # 102
North Hollywood, CA 91601-3814, USA

Taylor, Mark L (Actor)
7919 Norton Ave
West Hollywood, CA 90046-5204, USA

Taylor, Maurice (Basketball Player)
Houston Rockets
2 Greenway Plz
Toyota Center
Houston, TX 77046-0297, USA

Taylor, Meldrick (Athlete, Boxer, Olympic
Athlete)
2736 W Lehigh Ave
Philadelphia, PA 19132-3128, USA

Taylor, Michael (Athlete, Football Player)
5014 Crane St
Detroit, MI 48213-2917, USA

Taylor, Mick (Musician)
Jacobson & Colin
347 5th Ave Rm 810
New York, NY 10016-5035, USA

Taylor, Mike (Athlete, Football Player)
19632 Quiet Bay Ln
Huntington Beach, CA 92648-2614, USA

Taylor, Natascha (Actor)
c/o Staff Member *ICM Partners (LA)*
10250 Constellation Blvd Fl 7
Los Angeles, CA 90067-6207, USA

Taylor, Niki (Actor, Model)
121 Stanton Hall Ln
Franklin, TN 37069-8432, USA

Taylor, Ollie (Athlete, Basketball Player)
6405 Hillock Ln
Pearland, TX 77584-9293, USA

Taylor, Otis (Athlete, Football Player)
6608 Woodson Rd
Raytown, MO 64133-5400, USA

Taylor, Penny (Basketball Player)
Cleveland Rockers
1 Center Ct
Gund Arena
Cleveland, OH 44115-4001, USA

Taylor, Phil (Football Player)
c/o Peter Schaffer *All Pro Sports and
Entertainment*
36 Steele St Ste 100
Denver, CO 80206-5709, USA

Taylor, Priscilla (Actor, Model)
c/o Staff Member *Crystal Sky Pictures*
10203 Santa Monica Blvd Fl 5
Los Angeles, CA 90067-6416, USA

Taylor, Rachael (Actor)
c/o Rebecca Sides Capellan *ID Public
Relations (NY)*
150 W 30th St Fl 19
New York, NY 10001-4119, USA

Taylor, Reggie (Athlete, Baseball Player)
828 Havird St
Newberry, SC 29108-3727, USA

Taylor, Regina (Actor)
8048 Dusenberg Ct
Sacramento, CA 95828-5834, USA

Taylor, Renee (Actor)
613 N Arden Dr # 309
Beverly Hills, CA 90210-3509, USA

Taylor, Rip (Actor, Comedian)
1133 N Clark St Apt 301
West Hollywood, CA 90069-2075, USA

Taylor, Rod (Actor)
2375 Bowmont Dr
Beverly Hills, CA 90210-1808, USA

Taylor, Roland (Athlete, Basketball Player)
3018 Carpenter Rd
Ashtabula, OH 44004-9789, USA

Taylor, Roosevelt (Athlete, Football
Player)
7331 Ebbtide Dr
New Orleans, LA 70126-2057, USA

Taylor, Ryan (Athlete, Football Player)
c/o Joby Branion *Athletes First, LLC*
23091 Mill Creek Dr
Laguna Hills, CA 92653-1258, USA

Taylor, Sam (Sammy) (Athlete, Baseball
Player)
248 N 74th St
East Saint Louis, IL 62203-2411, USA

Taylor, Sandra (Actor, Model)
c/o Craig Wyckoff *Epstein Wyckoff Corsa
Ross (LA)*
11350 Ventura Blvd Ste 100
Studio City, CA 91604-3140, USA

Taylor, Scott (Athlete, Baseball Player)
1349 N Forestview Ct
Wichita, KS 67235-7033, USA

Taylor, Stepfan (Athlete, Football Player)
c/o Doug Hendrickson *Octagon Football*
832 Sansome St Fl 1
San Francisco, CA 94111-1558, USA

Taylor, Stephen Monroe (Actor)
c/o Staff Member *Main Title Entertainment*
8383 Wilshire Blvd Ste 408
Beverly Hills, CA 90211-2435, USA

Taylor, Tamara (Actor)
3704 Sheridge Dr
Sherman Oaks, CA 91403-5005, USA

Taylor, Tate (Director)
c/o John Norris *Artists and Directors
Cooperative*
1041 N Formosa Ave
Writers Building Suite 8
West Hollywood, CA 90046-6703, USA

Taylor, Terry (Athlete, Baseball Player)
743 W Walnut Ave
Crestview, FL 32536-3919, USA

Taylor, Tommy (Athlete, Baseball Player)
Kansas City Monarchs
524 Whitehall St
Jackson, TN 38301-5535, USA

Taylor, Tony (Athlete, Baseball Player)
8415 NW 165th Ter
Miami Lakes, FL 33016-6137, USA

Taylor, TW (Race Car Driver)
22909 Airpark Dr
North Dinwiddie, VA 23803-6969, USA

Taylor, Tyrod (Athlete, Football Player)
c/o Adisa P. Bakari *Dow Lohnes PLLC*
1299 Pennsylvania Ave NW Ste 700
Washington, DC 20004-2431, USA

Taylor, Tyshawn (Athlete, Basketball
Player)
c/o Jeff Schwartz *Excel Sports
Management (NY)*
1700 Broadway Fl 29
New York, NY 10019-5905, USA

Taylor, Vaughn (Golfer)
2536 Queens Ct
Grovetown, GA 30813-4520, USA

Taylor, Wade (Athlete, Baseball Player)
6 Sleepy Hollow Cv
Longwood, FL 32750-3845, USA

Taylor, Wayne (Race Car Driver)
501 N Orlando Ave Ste 313-189
Winter Park, FL 32789-7310, USA

Taylor, Wilson H (Business Person)
CIGNA Corp
1 Liberty Pl
1650 Market St
Philadelphia, PA 19103-4201, USA

Taylor-Compton, Scout (Actor)
c/o Nicki Fioravante *PMK/BNC Public Relations (PMK-LA)*
8687 Melrose Ave Ste 8
West Hollywood, CA 90069-5746, USA

Taylor-Johnson, Aaron (Actor)
7475 Hillside Ave
Los Angeles, CA 90046-2228, USA

Taylor-Lukin, Norna (Baseball Player)
7934 W Maple Grove Rd
Andrews, IN 46702-9518, USA

Taylor-Taylor, Courtney (Musician)
Monqui Records
PO Box 5908
Portland, OR 97228-5908, USA

Taylor-Young, Leigh (Actor)
11300 W Olympic Blvd Ste 610
Los Angeles, CA 90064-1643, USA

Taymor, Julie (Director, Producer, Writer)
c/o Jeff Berg *Resolution (LA)*
1801 Century Park E Ste 2300
Los Angeles, CA 90067-2325, USA

Teaff, Grant (Coach, Football Coach)
8265 Forest Ridge Dr
Woodway, TX 76712-2405, USA

Teagarden, Taylor (Baseball Player)
2007 Bluestem Ln
Carrollton, TX 75007-5313

Teagle, Terry (Athlete, Basketball Player)
2111 Heatherwood Dr
Missouri City, TX 77489-3277, USA

Teague, George (Athlete, Football Player)
6561 Meadow Lark Dr
Montgomery, AL 36116-4227, USA

Teague, Jeff (Athlete, Basketball Player)
c/o Andy Miller *ASM Sports*
920 Undercliff Ave
Edgewater, NJ 07020-1558, USA

Teague, Kerry (Race Car Driver)
3110 Roberta Rd
Concord, NC 28027-9080, United States

Teague, Lewis
2190 N Beverly Glen Blvd
Los Angeles, CA 90077-2404

Teague, Marshall (Actor)
c/o Richard Lewis *Geddes Agency, The*
1203 Greenacre Ave
West Hollywood, CA 90046-5707, USA

Teahen, Mark (Athlete, Baseball Player)
8610 E Via Del Sol Dr
Scottsdale, AZ 85255-5253, USA

Teal, Jeff (Athlete, Hockey Player)
1840 Wood Duck Ln
Excelsior, MN 55331-6507

Teal, Jim F (Athlete, Football Player)
38444 Kingsway Ct
Farmington Hills, MI 48331-1651, USA

Teal, Jimmy D (Athlete, Football Player)
2636 Spring Branch Rd
Mesquite, TX 75181-2668, USA

Teal, Willie (Athlete, Football Player)
1322 Westchester Dr
Baton Rouge, LA 70810-5234, USA

Tea Leaf Green (Music Group)
c/o Staff Member *Paradigm (Monterey)*
404 W Franklin St
Monterey, CA 93940-2303, USA

Tearry, Larry (Athlete, Football Player)
1334 Kienast Dr
Fayetteville, NC 28314-5422, USA

Tears For Fears (Music Group)
c/o Staff Member *Creative Artists Agency (CAA-LA)*
2000 Avenue of the Stars Ste 100
Los Angeles, CA 90067-4705, USA

Teasdale, Kathryn (Race Car Driver)
PO Box 4950
Pinehurst, NC 28374-4950, USA

Teasley, Nikki (Basketball Player)
Los Angeles Sparks
1111 S Figueroa St
Staples Center
Los Angeles, CA 90015-1300, USA

Teasley, Ron (Athlete, Baseball Player)
New York Cubans
19317 Coyle St
Detroit, MI 48235-2039, USA

Tebow, Tim (Athlete, Football Player, Heisman Trophy Winner)
9200 Otis Rd
Jacksonville, FL 32220, USA

Tedder, Ryan (Musician)
60 Music Sq E Ste 390
Nashville, TN 37203-4412, USA

Tedeschi, Susan (Musician)
Blue Sky Artists
761 Washington Ave N
Minneapolis, MN 55401-1101, USA

Tedford, Travis (Actor)
c/o Staff Member *Acme Talent & Literary (LA)*
1400 Atlantic Ave Ste 274
Long Beach, CA 90813-2013, USA

Teed, Dick (Athlete, Baseball Player)
53 Church St
Windsor Locks, CT 06096-2332, USA

Teegarden, Aimee (Actor)
c/o Tara Friedlander *ID Public Relations (LA)*
7060 Hollywood Blvd Fl 8th
Los Angeles, CA 90028-6021, USA

Teerlinck, John (Athlete, Football Player)
9713 Bay Hill Dr
Lone Tree, CO 80124-3182, USA

Teeter, Mike (Athlete, Football Player)
4393 E Mount Garfield Rd
Fruitport, MI 49415-9782, USA

Teevens, Buddy (Coach, Football Coach)
Stanford University
Athletic Dept
Stanford, CA 94395, USA

Tefkin, Blair (Actor)
Lucie Gamelon
8022 Sunset Blvd # 4049
Los Angeles, CA 90046, USA

Teglianetti, Peter (Athlete, Hockey Player)
PO Box 120
Lawrence, PA 15055-0120, USA

Teichner, Helmut (Skier)
4250 N Marine Dr Apt 2101
Chicago, IL 60613-1733, USA

Teigen, Chrissy (Model)
c/o Britney Ross *42West (LA)*
8687 Melrose Ave Ste 7
West Hollywood, CA 90069-5721, USA

Teitel, Robert (Producer)
c/o Staff Member *Creative Artists Agency (CAA-LA)*
2000 Avenue of the Stars Ste 100
Los Angeles, CA 90067-4705, USA

Teitelbaum, Philip (Doctor)
University of Florida
Psychology Dept
Gainesville, FL 32611-0001, USA

Teitler, William (Producer)
c/o Staff Member *ICM Partners (LA)*
10250 Constellation Blvd Fl 7
Los Angeles, CA 90067-6207, USA

Teixeira, Mark (Athlete, Baseball Player)
c/o Scott Boras *Boras Corporation*
3 San Joaquin Plz Ste 100
Newport Beach, CA 92660-5944, USA

Tejada, Miguel O M (Athlete, Baseball Player)
3013 NE 20th Ct # C
Ft Lauderdale, FL 33305-1807, USA

Tejeda, Robinson (Baseball Player)
45 Appletree Ln Apt D
Old Bridge, NJ 08857-4586

Tejera, Michael (Athlete, Baseball Player)
15639 SW 16th St
Miami, FL 33185-5849, USA

Tekulve, Kenton C (Kent) (Athlete, Baseball Player)
350 Fruitwood Dr
Bethel Park, PA 15102-1008, USA

Telemaco, Amaury (Athlete, Baseball Player)
830 S Webster Ave
Scranton, PA 18505-4384, USA

Telford, Anthony (Athlete, Baseball Player)
9109 Cypress Keep Ln
Odessa, FL 33556-3150, USA

Telgheder, David (Athlete, Baseball Player)
50 Orchard Crest Dr
Westtown, NY 10998-3425, USA

Tellem, Nancy (Business Person)
c/o Staff Member *CBS Paramount International Television*
7800 Beverly Blvd
Los Angeles, CA 90036-2112, USA

Teller (Actor, Comedian, Magician)
7570 Gary Ave
Las Vegas, NV 89178-9236, USA

Teller, Edward (Doctor)
PO Box 808
Livermore, CA 94551-0808, USA

Telles, Rick (Director, Producer)
c/o Josh Levenbrown *Agency for the Performing Arts (APA-LA)*
405 S Beverly Dr Ste 500
Beverly Hills, CA 90212-4425, USA

Tellez, Steve (Actor)
c/o Staff Member *Innovative Artists (LA)*
1505 10th St
Santa Monica, CA 90401-2805, USA

Tellman, Tom (Athlete, Baseball Player)
1021 Yankee Bush Rd
Warren, PA 16365-8536, USA

Tellmann, Tom (Baseball Player)
1021 Yankee Bush Rd
Warren, PA 16365-8536, USA

Tellqvist, Mikael (Athlete, Hockey Player)
7932 E Feathersong Ln
Scottsdale, AZ 85255-6418

Telnaes, Ann (Cartoonist)
Tribune Media Services
435 N Michigan Ave Ste 1500
Chicago, IL 60611-4012, USA

Teltscher, Eliot (Coach, Tennis Player)
Pepperdine University
Athletic Dept
Malibu, CA 90265, USA

Teltschik, John (Athlete, Football Player)
9624 Nathan Way
Plano, TX 75025-5896, USA

Telushkin, Rabbi Joseph (Writer)
2316 Delaware Ave Ste 266
Ste 4-B
Buffalo, NY 14216-2638, USA

Telymonde, Louis (Horse Racer)
190 Biabou Dr
Toms River, NJ 08757-3731, USA

Temchen, Sybil (Actor)
c/o Staff Member *Untitled Entertainment (LA)*
350 S Beverly Dr Ste 200
Beverly Hills, CA 90212-4819, USA

Temesvari, Andrea (Tennis Player)
ProServe
1101 Woodrow Wilson Blvd
#1800
Arlington, VA 22209, USA

Temko, Allan B (Journalist)
San Francisco Chronicle
2440 Geary Blvd Apt C
Editorial Dept
San Francisco, CA 94115-3375, USA

Temp, Jim (Athlete, Football Player)
311 Roselawn Blvd
Green Bay, WI 54301-1305, USA

Tempero, Bill (Race Car Driver)
915 Turman Dr
Fort Collins, CO 80525-9312, USA

Temple, Collins (Athlete, Basketball Player)
2614 Dalrymple Dr
Baton Rouge, LA 70808-2038, USA

Temple, Collis (Athlete, Basketball Player)
1974 San Antonio Spurs
Baton Rouge, LA 70808

Temple, Josh (Television Host)
c/o Steven Neibert *Imperium 7 Talent Agency*
5455 Wilshire Blvd Ste 1706
Los Angeles, CA 90036-4217, USA

Temple, Juno (Actor)
c/o Jessica Kolstad *Relevant*
Prefers to be contacted by telephone or email
CA, USA

Templeman, Simon (Actor)
305 15th St
Santa Monica, CA 90402-2211, USA

Templeton, Ben (Cartoonist)
Tribune Media Services
435 N Michigan Ave Ste 1500
Chicago, IL 60611-4012, USA

Templeton, Garry L (Athlete, Baseball Player)
13552 Del Poniente Rd
Poway, CA 92064-2230, USA

Tempo, Nino (Actor)
9255 Doheny Rd Apt 2504
W Hollywood, CA 90069-3238

Temptations, The (Music Group)
c/o Steve Levine *ICM Partners (LA)*
10250 Constellation Blvd Fl 7
Los Angeles, CA 90067-6207, USA

Tenace, F Gene (Athlete, Baseball Player, Coach)
2650 Cliff Hawk Ct
Redmond, OR 97756-7301, USA

Tenenbaum, Stephen (Producer)
c/o Staff Member *Morra Brezner Steinberg & Tenenbaum (MBST) Entertainment*
345 N Maple Dr Ste 200
Beverly Hills, CA 90210-5174, USA

Tennant, Andy (Actor, Director, Writer)
c/o Eddie Michaels *Insignia Public Relations*
1507 20th St Ste B
Santa Monica, CA 90404-3474, USA

Tennant, David (Actor)
c/o Billy Lazarus *United Talent Agency (UTA-LA)*
9336 Civic Center Dr
Beverly Hills, CA 90210-3604, USA

Tennant, Victoria (Actor)
PO Box 929
Beverly Hills, CA 90213-0929, USA

Ten Napel, Garth (Athlete, Football Player)
PO Box 26
Carmen, ID 83462-0026, USA

Tenney, Jon (Actor)
c/o Brian Wilkins *Kritzer Levine Wilkins Entertainment (KLWG)*
11872 La Grange Ave Fl 1
Los Angeles, CA 90025-5283, USA

Tennille, Toni (Actor, Musician)
10787 N Saddle Pass Rd
Prescott, AZ 86305-4574, USA

Tennison, Chalee (Musician)
Tanasi Entertainment
1204 17th Ave S
Nashville, TN 37212-2802, USA

Tennon, Julius (Actor)
c/o Estelle Lasher *Lasher Group*
1133 Avenue Of The Americas Ste 1621
New York, NY 10036-6710, USA

Tennyson, Brian (Athlete, Golfer)
3014 Robert Oliver Ave
Fernandina Beach, FL 32034-4532, USA

Tenorio, Pedro P (Ex-Governor)
PO Box 567
Saipan, MP 96950, USA

Tensi, Steve (Athlete, Football Player)
300 Flannery Fork Rd
Blowing Rock, NC 28605-9333, USA

Tenth Avenue North (Musician)
c/o Staff Member *Reunion Records*
741 Cool Springs Blvd
Provident Music Group / Sony Bmg
Franklin, TN 37067-2750, USA

Tenuta, Judy (Actor, Comedian)
13504 Contour Dr
Sherman Oaks, CA 91423-4702, USA

Tepedino, Frank (Athlete, Baseball Player)
2 Pear Ct
Saint James, NY 11780-2143, USA

Tepper, David (Business Person)
Appaloosa Management
51 John F Kennedy Pkwy
Short Hills, NJ 07078-2704, USA

Tepper, Lou (Coach, Football Coach)
University of Illinois
Assembly Hall
Champaign, IL 61820, USA

Tepper, Stephen (Athlete, Hockey Player)
35 Brook St
Shrewsbury, MA 01545-4804

Tequila, Tila (Model, Reality Star)
c/o Gina Rodriguez *GR Media*
Prefers to be contacted via telephone or email
Reseda, CA 91335, USA

TerBlanche, Esta (Actor)
c/o Chris Schmidt *Paradigm (LA)*
360 N Crescent Dr
North Bldg
Beverly Hills, CA 90210-4874, USA

Tereshinski, Joe (Athlete, Football Player)
6508 Millwood Rd
Bethesda, MD 20817-6056, USA

Tergesen, Lee (Actor)
Gersh Agency
232 N Canon Dr
Beverly Hills, CA 90210-5302, USA

Ter Horst, Jerald F (Government Official, Journalist)
21 N Oak Forest Dr
Asheville, NC 28803-3333, USA

Terlecki, Bob (Athlete, Baseball Player)
113 Shady Brook Dr
Langhorne, PA 19047-8028, USA

Terlecky, Greg (Athlete, Baseball Player)
2130 Camino Laurel
San Clemente, CA 92673-5650, USA

Terlesky, John (Actor)
14229 Dickens St Apt 5
Sherman Oaks, CA 91423-4107, USA

Termeer, Henricus A (Business Person)
Genzyme Corp
1 Kendall Sq
Cambridge, MA 02139-1562, USA

Terminator X (Musician)
c/o Staff Member *William Morris Endeavor (LA)*
9601 Wilshire Blvd
Beverly Hills, CA 90210-5213, USA

Terpko, Jeff (Athlete, Baseball Player)
3546 Riverside Dr
Sayre, PA 18840-7864, USA

Terraciano, Andrew (Actor)
c/o Jaime Misher *Innovative Artists (NY)*
235 Park Ave S Fl 7
New York, NY 10003-1405, USA

Terraciano, Tony (Actor)
c/o Jaime Misher *Innovative Artists (NY)*
235 Park Ave S Fl 7
New York, NY 10003-1405, USA

Terranova, Joe (Musician)
Joe Taylor Mgmt
PO Box 279
Williamstown, NJ 08094-0279, USA

Terranova, Phil (Boxer)
30 Bogardus Pl
New York, NY 10040-2320, USA

terraro, Dave (Bowler)
672 E Chester St
Kingston, NY 12401-1742, USA

Terrasson, Jacky (Musician)
Joel Chriss
300 Mercer St Apt 3J
New York, NY 10003-6732, USA

Terrell, David (Athlete, Football Player)
43628 Cather Ct
Ashburn, VA 20147-4789, USA

Terrell, Ira (Athlete, Basketball Player)
1327 Fernwood Ave
Dallas, TX 75216-1265, USA

Terrell, Jerry (Athlete, Baseball Player)
1301 NE Sunny Creek Ln
Blue Springs, MO 64014-2041, USA

Terrell, Pat (Athlete, Football Player)
40 Hidden Lake Dr
Burr Ridge, IL 60527-8371, USA

Terrell, Walt (Athlete, Baseball Player)
1304 Oxley Ct
Union, KY 41091-7145, USA

Terreri, Chris (Athlete, Hockey Player, Olympic Athlete)
767 Riverside Dr
Hillsborough, NJ 08844-3325, USA

Terrero, Jessy (Director, Producer)
c/o Charles King *William Morris Endeavor (LA)*
9601 Wilshire Blvd
Beverly Hills, CA 90210-5213, USA

Terris, Malcolm (Actor)
14 England S Ln
London, EN NW3

Terry, Chuck (Athlete, Basketball Player)
11 Ravenna
Irvine, CA 92614-5329, USA

Terry, Clark (Musician)
4720 S Beech St
Pine Bluff, AR 71603-7327, USA

Terry, Claude (Athlete, Basketball Player)
3938 E Dubois Ave
Gilbert, AZ 85298-9153, USA

Terry, Hilda (Cartoonist)
8 Henderson Pl
New York, NY 10028-7557, USA

Terry, Jason (Basketball Player)
Atlanta Hawks
190 Marietta St NW Ste 405
Atlanta, GA 30303-2717, USA

Terry, Lee (Congressman, Politician)
2331 Rayburn Hob
Washington, DC 20515-3214, USA

Terry, Megan D (Writer)
2309 Hanscom Blvd
Omaha, NE 68105-3143, USA

Terry, Nat (Athlete, Football Player)
3003 W Palmetto St
Tampa, FL 33607-2936, USA

Terry, Ralph W (Athlete, Baseball Player)
801 Park St
Larned, KS 67550-2632, USA

Terry, Richard E (Business Person)
Peoples Energy Corp
130 E Randolph St Ste 300
Chicago, IL 60601-6203, USA

Terry, Rick (Athlete, Football Player)
109 Highgate Ln
Lexington, NC 27292-5372, USA

Terry, Ruth (Actor, Musician)
622 Hospitality Dr
Rancho Mirage, CA 92270-1312, USA

Terry, Scott (Athlete, Baseball Player)
4943 Montford Dr
Saint Louis, MO 63128-3134, USA

Terry, Tony (Musician)
Richard Walters
1800 Argyle Ave # 408
Los Angeles, CA 90028-5253, USA

Terwilliger, Wayne (Athlete, Baseball Player)
1909 Clear Creek Dr
Weatherford, TX 76087-3802, USA

Tesh, John (Musician)
TeshMedia Group
13245 Riverside Dr Ste 305
Sherman Oaks, CA 91423-5608, USA

Tesher, Howard (Horse Racer)
525 E 72nd St Apt 22B
New York, NY 10021-9607, USA

Teske, Rachel (Golfer)
c/o Staff Member *Pro Golfers Association (PGA) Tour*
112 Tpc Blvd
Ponte Vedra Beach, FL 32082, USA

Tesori, Kathleen (Fitness Expert, Model)
PO Box 853
Clearfield, UT 84089-0853, USA

Tess, John (Business Person)
Oregon Cultural Trust
775 Summer St NE
Suite 200
Portland, OR 97209, USA

Tessler-Lavigne, Marc (Doctor)
361 Ridgeway Rd
Woodside, CA 94062-2343, USA

Tessmer, Jay (Athlete, Baseball Player)
2359 Livingston Bridge Rd
Norman Park, GA 31771-4258, USA

Testa, Nick (Athlete, Baseball Player)
1 Consulate Dr Apt 2L
Tuckahoe, NY 10707-2432, USA

Testaverde, Vinny (Athlete, Football Player, Heisman Trophy Winner)
Jesuit High School of Tampa
4701 N Himes Ave
Attn: Boys Football Program Coach
Tampa, FL 33614-6694, USA

Tester, Hans
6310 San Vicente Blvd Ste 401
Los Angeles, CA 90048-5427

Testerman, Don (Athlete, Football Player)
3101 Bridges St
Morehead City, NC 28557-3365, USA

Testi, Fabio (Actor)
Via Francesco Siacci 38
Rome, IT I-001

Testone, Elise (Musician)
c/o Staff Member *19 Entertainment (LA)*
9000 W Sunset Blvd Ste 1574
West Hollywood, CA 90069-5817, USA

Tetarenko, Joey (Athlete, Hockey Player)
PO Box 1582
Iowa, LA 70647-1582

Teteak, Deral (Athlete, Football Player)
9458 S County Road G
Suring, WI 54174, USA

Teter, Hannah (Athlete, Olympic Athlete, Snowboarder)
1554 Plumas Cir
South Lake Tahoe, CA 96150-4822, USA

Tetrault, Roger E (Business Person)
McDermott International
1450 Poydras St
New Orleans, LA 70112-1227, USA

Tetro-Atkinson, Barbara (Athlete, Baseball Player)
7110 Cross Creek Blvd
Louisville, KY 40228-1305, USA

Tettleton, Mickey (Athlete, Baseball Player)
3500 Hollister Trl
Norman, OK 73071-5043, USA

Tetzlaff, Christian (Musician)
Shuman Assoc
120 W 58th St Apt 8D
New York, NY 10019-2156, USA

Teufel, Tim (Athlete, Baseball Player)
PO Box 3517
Jupiter, FL 33469-1009, USA

Teut, Nate (Athlete, Baseball Player)
2010 Sugar Creek Dr # D
Waukee, IA 50263-8093, USA

Teutul Jr, Paul (Business Person, Reality Star)
Orange County Choppers
14 Crossroads Ct
Newburgh, NY 12550-5064, USA

Teutul Sr, Paul (Reality Star, Television Host)
c/o Sean Perry *William Morris Endeavor (LA)*
9601 Wilshire Blvd
Beverly Hills, CA 90210-5213, USA

Tewell, Doug (Athlete, Golfer)
15216 Fairview Farm Rd
Edmond, OK 73013-1327, USA

Tewes, Lauren (Actor)
c/o Staff Member *The Actor's Group Talent and Literary Agency*
3400 Beacon Ave S
Seattle, WA 98144-6702, USA

Tewkesbury, Joan F (Director, Writer)
c/o Staff Member *Creative Artists Agency (CAA-LA)*
2000 Avenue of the Stars Ste 100
Los Angeles, CA 90067-4705, USA

Tewksbury, Bob (Athlete, Baseball Player)
63 Ridge Rd
Concord, NH 03301-3034, USA

Texada, Tia (Actor)
c/o Staff Member *Rogers & Cowan PR (LA)*
8687 Melrose Ave Ste 7
West Hollywood, CA 90069-5721, USA

Tezak-Papesh, Virginia (Athlete, Baseball Player)
1400 Clement St
Joliet, IL 60435-4209, USA

Thacker, Tom (Athlete, Basketball Player)
3655 Dogwood Ln
Cincinnati, OH 45213-2601, USA

Thackery, Jimmy (Musician)
Mongrel Music
743 Center Blvd
Fairfax, CA 94930-1764, USA

Thagard, Norman E (Astronaut, Physicist)
502 N Ride
Tallahassee, FL 32303-5127, USA

Thagard, Norman E Dr (Astronaut)
502 N Ride
Tallahassee, FL 32303-5127, USA

Thal, Eric (Actor)
c/o Phillip Carlson *Carlson Menashe Agency*
149 5th Ave Ste 1204
New York, NY 10010-6801

Thalia (Actor, Musician)
c/o Staff Member *William Morris Endeavor (LA)*
9601 Wilshire Blvd
Beverly Hills, CA 90210-5213, USA

Thames, Marcus (Athlete, Baseball Player)
5505 Rawls Rd
Tampa, FL 33625-1324, USA

Tharp, Twyla (Dancer)
Twyla Tharp Productions
336 Central Park W Apt 17B
New York, NY 10025-7127, USA

Tharpe, Larry (Athlete, Football Player)
3665 Greenbriar Rd E
Macon, GA 31204-4228, USA

Thatcher, Joe (Athlete, Baseball Player)
310 Ruddell Dr
Kokomo, IN 46901-4249, USA

Thatcher, Roland (Golfer)
18 Flowertuft Ct
Spring, TX 77380-1529, USA

Thaxton, Galand (Athlete, Football Player)
1571 N 22nd St
Laramie, WY 82072-2387, USA

Thaxton, James (Athlete, Football Player)
4319 Deergrove Rd
Memphis, TN 38141-7021, USA

Thayer, Brynn (Actor)
c/o Steven Neibert *Imperium 7 Talent Agency*
5455 Wilshire Blvd Ste 1706
Los Angeles, CA 90036-4217, USA

Thayer, Dale
9611 Woodlawn Dr
Huntington Beach, CA 92646-3635

Thayer, Greg (Athlete, Baseball Player)
1000 3rd St N
Sauk Rapids, MN 56379-2417, USA

Thayer, Helen (Skier)
PO Box 233
Snohomish, WA 98291-0233, USA

Thayer, Maria (Actor)
c/o Barry McPherson *Agency for the Performing Arts (APA-NY)*
135 W 50th St Fl 17
New York, NY 10020-1201, USA

Thayer, Tom (Athlete, Football Player)
330 W Diversey Pkwy Apt 2303
Chicago, IL 60657-6204, USA

Thayer, Tommy (Musician)
PO Box 7147
Westlake Village, CA 91359-7147, USA

Thayer, W Paul (Business Person, Government Official)
10200 Hollow Way Rd
Dallas, TX 75229-6635, USA

The Academy Is (Music Group)
c/o Bob McLynn *Crush Management*
60-62 E 11th St
7th Floor
New York, NY 10003, USA

The Band Perry (Music Group, Musician)
c/o Staff Member *Bob Doyle & Associates*
1111 17th Ave S
Nashville, TN 37212-2203, USA

The Beach Boys (Music Group)
c/o Elliott Lott *Boulder Creek Entertainment*
PO Box 91002
San Diego, CA 92169-3002, USA

The Bronx (Music Group)
c/o Jonathan Daniel *Crush Management*
60-62 E 11th St
7th Floor
New York, NY 10003, USA

The Color Fred (Music Group, Musician)
c/o Matt Galle *Paradigm (NY)*
360 Park Ave S Fl 16
New York, NY 10010-1716, USA

The Dear & Departed (Music Group, Musician)
c/o Stephen Looker *Knives Out Management*
PO Box 480519
Los Angeles, CA 90048-1519, USA

The Decemberists (Music Group)
c/o Ron Laffitte *Red Light Management (LA)*
8439 W Sunset Blvd Ste 2
West Hollywood, CA 90069-1925, USA

Thedford, Marcello (Actor)
c/o JC Robbins *JC Robbins Management*
865 S Sherbourne Dr
Los Angeles, CA 90035-1809, USA

The Expendables (Music Group, Musician)
c/o Jon Phillips *Silverback Professional Artist Management*
9469 Jefferson Blvd Ste 101
Culver City, CA 90232-2915, USA

The Fabulous Thunderbirds (Music Group)
c/o Patrick McAuliff *Monterey International (Chicago)*
200 W Superior St Ste 202
Chicago, IL 60654-6422, USA

The Fall of Troy (Music Group)
c/o David Benveniste *Velvet Hammer*
9014 Melrose Ave
West Hollywood, CA 90069-5610, USA

The Fray (Music Group)
c/o Jonathan Adelman *Paradigm (NY)*
360 Park Ave S Fl 16
New York, NY 10010-1716, USA

The Godfathers (Music Group, Musician)
c/o Matt Suhar *Tantrum Management*
3341 W Berteau Ave
Chicago, IL 60618-2305, USA

The Good The Bad & The Queen (Music Group)
c/o Staff Member *Paradigm (Monterey)*
404 W Franklin St
Monterey, CA 93940-2303, USA

The Great Khali (Writer)
c/o Kerry Rodgerson *World Wrestling Entertainment (WWE)*
1241 E Main St
Titan Towers
Stamford, CT 06902-3520, USA

The Imponderables (Music Group, Musician)
c/o Monique Moss *Integrated PR*
8060 Melrose Ave Fl 4
Los Angeles, CA 90046-7038, USA

The Insult Comic Dog, Triumph (Actor, Comedian)
c/o Staff Member *Creative Artists Agency (CAA-LA)*
2000 Avenue of the Stars Ste 100
Los Angeles, CA 90067-4705, USA

Theis, Dave (Athlete, Baseball Player)
7250 Lewis Ridge Pkwy Apt 206
Minneapolis, MN 55439-1938, USA

Theismann, Joe (Athlete, Football Player)
PO Box 186
Leesburg, VA 20178-0186, USA

Theiss, Duane (Athlete, Baseball Player)
66 Juniper Ave
Westerville, OH 43081-1700, USA

The Jets (Music Group)
c/o Staff Member *Lustig Talent Enterprises Inc*
PO Box 770850
Orlando, FL 32877-0850, USA

The Jonas Brothers (Music Group)
c/o Staff Member *Hollywood Records*
500 S Buena Vista St
Burbank, CA 91521-0002, USA

The Killers (Music Group)
c/o Staff Member *Island Records*
825 8th Ave Rm C2
New York, NY 10019-7472, USA

Thelan, Jodi (Actor)
8428 Melrose Pl Ste C
West Hollywood, CA 90069-5300

Theler, Derek (Actor)
c/o Daniel Spilo *Industry Entertainment*
955 Carrillo Dr Ste 300
Los Angeles, CA 90048-5400, USA

The Lonely Island (Music Group)
c/o Staff Member *Silva Artist Management (SAM)*
722 Seward St
Los Angeles, CA 90038-3504, USA

The Maine (Music Group)
c/o Tim Kirch *8123 Management*
Prefers to be contacted by telephone or email
New York, NY, USA

Themmen, Paris (Actor)
2109 S Wilbur Ave
Walla Walla, WA 99362-9048, USA

The National (Music Group)
c/o Dawn Berger *Post Hoc Management*
320 7th Ave # 145
Brooklyn, NY 11215-4194, USA

The Neptunes (Musician, Producer)
c/o Staff Member *Star Trak Entertainment*
1755 Broadway Frnt 3
New York, NY 10019-3743, USA

Theobald, Ron (Athlete, Baseball Player)
319 Jacaranda Pl
Fullerton, CA 92832-1434, USA

Theodore, Donna
10000 Santa Monica Blvd # 305
Los Angeles, CA 90067

Theodore, George (Athlete, Baseball Player)
1388 E Princeton Ave
Salt Lake City, UT 84105-1921, USA

Theodosakis, Jason (Doctor, Writer)
Saint Martin's Press
175 5th Ave Ste 400
New York, NY 10010-7848, USA

Theodosius, Primate Metropolitian (Religious Leader)
Orthodox Church in America
PO Box 675
Syosset, NY 11791-0675, USA

Theofiledes, Harry (Athlete, Football Player)
17806 Carrollwood Dr
Dallas, TX 75252-6357, USA

The Pointer Sisters (Music Group, Musician)
c/o Konrad Leh *Creative Talent Group*
1900 Avenue of the Stars Ste 2475
Los Angeles, CA 90067-4512, USA

The Pretenders (Music Group)
c/o Staff Member *William Morris Endeavor (LA)*
9601 Wilshire Blvd
Beverly Hills, CA 90210-5213, USA

The Prize Fighter Inferno (Music Group, Musician)
c/o Blaze James *Black Sheep Fellowship*
6255 W Sunset Blvd Ste 910
Los Angeles, CA 90028-7410, USA

Therefore I Am (Music Group, Musician)
c/o Cody DeLong *Kenmore Agency, The*
1032 W 18th St Ste A3
Costa Mesa, CA 92627-4553, USA

Therien, Chris (Athlete, Hockey Player)
15 Milford Dr
Marlton, NJ 08053-5408

Therien, Chris (Athlete, Hockey Player)
Philadelphia Flyers
3601 S Broad St Ste 2
Philadelphia, PA 19148-5297

Theriot, Ryan (Athlete, Baseball Player)
241 Granville Ct
Baton Rouge, LA 70810-4860, USA

The Rockers
PO Box 3859
Stamford, CT 06905

Theron, Charlize (Actor, Model)
2572 Outpost Dr
Los Angeles, CA 90068-2647, USA

Theroux, Justin (Actor)
c/o Nick Frenkel *3 Arts Entertainment (LA)*
9460 Wilshire Blvd Fl 7
Beverly Hills, CA 90212-2713, USA

Therrien, Michel (Athlete, Hockey Player)
3800 Hillcrest Dr Apt 1204
Hollywood, FL 33021-7940

The Script (Music Group, Musician)
c/o Cindi Berger *PMK/BNC Public Relations (PMK-NY)*
622 3rd Ave Fl 8
New York, NY 10017-6707, USA

These New Puritans (Music Group)
c/o Frank Riley *High Road Touring*
751 Bridgeway Fl 2
Sausalito, CA 94965-2174, USA

The Snake The Cross The Crown (Music Group, Musician)
c/o Staff Member *Equal Vision Records*
PO Box 38202
Albany, NY 12203-8202, USA

The The (Music Group)
c/o Staff Member *Paradigm (Monterey)*
404 W Franklin St
Monterey, CA 93940-2303, USA

Theus, Reggie (Athlete, Basketball Player)
2364 Tuscan Hills Ln
Las Cruces, NM 88011-4105, USA

The Vaccines (Music Group, Musician)
c/o Staff Member *Paradigm (NY)*
360 Park Ave S Fl 16
New York, NY 10010-1716, USA

The Veronicas (Music Group, Musician)
c/o Staff Member *Wilhelmina Dan Agency*
1503 Union Ave Ste 211
Kimbrough Office Tower
Memphis, TN 38104-3739, USA

The Weeknd (Music Group, Musician)
c/o Jenny Boddy *Press Here Publicity*
138 W 25th St Ste 900
New York, NY 10001-7470, USA

Thewlis, David (Actor)
c/o Staff Member *United Talent Agency (UTA-LA)*
9336 Civic Center Dr
Beverly Hills, CA 90210-3604, USA

Theys, Didier (Race Car Driver)
5773 N 78th Pl
Scottsdale, AZ 85250-6169, USA

Thibaud, Todd (Musician)
c/o Staff Member *Paradigm (Monterey)*
404 W Franklin St
Monterey, CA 93940-2303, USA

Thibaudet, Jean-Yves (Musician)
3601 Griffith Park Blvd
Los Angeles, CA 90027-1406, USA

Thibeaux, Peter (Athlete, Basketball Player)
2036 Paradise Dr Apt 2
Belvedere Tiburon, CA 94920-1985, USA

Thibert, Jim (Athlete, Football Player)
1365 County Road L
Swanton, OH 43558-9791, USA

Thibiant, Aida (Designer, Fashion Designer)
Institut de Beaute
449 N Canon Dr
Beverly Hills, CA 90210-4819, USA

Thibodeau, Tom (Basketball Coach)
c/o Terry Prince *CAA Sports (LA)*
2000 Avenue of the Stars Ste 100
Los Angeles, CA 90067-4705, USA

Thibodeaux, Keith (Actor)
5372 Jamaica Dr
Jackson, MS 39211-4057, USA

Thicke, Alan (Actor)
7110 Gobernador Canyon Rd
Carpinteria, CA 93013-3127, USA

Thicke, Robin (Musician)
1568 Blue Jay Way
Los Angeles, CA 90069-1215, USA

Thieben, Bill (Athlete, Basketball Player)
225 Jayne Ave
Patchogue, NY 11772-2628, USA

Thiel, Bert (Athlete, Baseball Player)
W11077 County Road D
Marion, WI 54950-9068, USA

Thiel, Peter (Business Person)
The Thiel Foundation
1 Letterman Dr Ste 400
San Francisco, CA 94129-1496, USA

Thielemann, Ray C (R C) (Athlete, Football Player)
210 Rose Meadow Ln
Alpharetta, GA 30005-8339, USA

Thielemans, Jean B (Toots) (Musician)
Peter Levinson Communications
2575 Palisade Ave Apt 11H
Bronx, NY 10463-6149, USA

Thieriot, Max (Actor)
c/o Ruth Bernstein *Viewpoint Inc (LA)*
8820 Wilshire Blvd Ste 220
Beverly Hills, CA 90211-2622, USA

Thierry, John F (Athlete, Football Player)
1431 Federal Rd
Opelousas, LA 70570-1172, USA

Thies, Dave (Baseball Player)
35737 Tympani Cir
Palm Desert, CA 92211-3067

Thies, Jake (Athlete, Baseball Player)
4 Cornflower Ct
Florissant, MO 63033-6530, USA

Thiessen, Tiffani (Actor)
c/o Jai Khanna *Brillstein Entertainment Partners (LA)*
9150 Wilshire Blvd Ste 350
Beverly Hills, CA 90212-3453, USA

Thievery Corporation (Music Group, Musician)
c/o Staff Member *William Morris Endeavor (LA)*
9601 Wilshire Blvd
Beverly Hills, CA 90210-5213, USA

Thigpen, Bobby (Athlete, Baseball Player)
926 Brookstown Ave
Winston Salem, NC 27101-3625, USA

Thigpen, Curtis (Athlete, Baseball Player)
345 Logan Ranch Rd
Georgetown, TX 78628-1208, USA

Thile, Chris (Actor, Musician)
c/o Staff Member *IMG Artists Worldwide (NY)*
825 7th Ave
New York, NY 10019-6014, USA

Thimmesch, Nicholas (Journalist)
6301 Broad Branch Rd
Chevy Chase, MD 20815-3343, USA

Thinnes, Roy (Actor)
952 Peekskill Hollow Rd
Putnam Valley, NY 10579-1705, USA

Third Day (Music Group)
c/o Staff Member *Red Light Management (LA)*
8439 W Sunset Blvd Ste 2
West Hollywood, CA 90069-1925, USA

Third Eye Blind (Music Group)
c/o Carla Parisi *Kid Logic*
156 Liberty St Apt 12
Little Ferry, NJ 07643-1768, USA

Third World (Music Group)
Lion Entertainment
PO Box 5231
Hollywood, FL 33083-5231, USA

Thirlby, Olivia (Actor)
c/o William Choi *Management 360*
9111 Wilshire Blvd
Beverly Hills, CA 90210-5508, USA

This Time Next Year (Music Group, Musician)
c/o Staff Member *Equal Vision Records*
PO Box 38202
Albany, NY 12203-8202, USA

Thobe, J J (Athlete, Baseball Player)
902 Grovemont St
Santa Ana, CA 92706-2046, USA

Thobe, Tom (Baseball Player)
19856 Berkshire Ln
Huntington Beach, CA 92646-4210

Thoenen, Dick (Athlete, Baseball Player)
862 Smith St
Harrisburg, OR 97446-9505, USA

Thom, Sandi (Musician)
c/o Staff Member *Paradigm (Monterey)*
404 W Franklin St
Monterey, CA 93940-2303, USA

Thoma, Tyrus
32 Wellesley Cir
Northbrook, IL 60062-1137, USA

Thomas, Aaron (Athlete, Football Player)
2906 NW Golf Course Dr
Bend, OR 97701-5504, USA

Thomas, Adalius (Athlete, Football Player)
1 Willow Bend Dr
Hattiesburg, MS 39402-8552, USA

Thomas, Alex (Actor)
c/o Staff Member *Identity Talent Agency (ID)*
11956 Gorham Ave Apt 3
Los Angeles, CA 90049-5396, USA

Thomas, Andrew S W (Andy) (Astronaut)
NASA
2101 Nasa Pkwy Spc Johnsoncenter
Houston, TX 77058-3696, USA

Thomas, AndrewS W Dr (Astronaut)
2421 Clopper St
Seabrook, TX 77586-3738, USA

Thomas, Aurelius (Athlete, Football Player)
PO Box 91157
Columbus, OH 43209-7157, USA

Thomas, Ben (Athlete, Football Player)
2572 Weston St
Auburn, AL 36832-3550, USA

Thomas, Betty (Actor, Director, Producer)
c/o Bryan Lourd *Creative Artists Agency (CAA-LA)*
2000 Avenue of the Stars Ste 100
Los Angeles, CA 90067-4705, USA

Thomas, BJ (Musician)
c/o Staff Member *Gloria Thomas Inc*
1424 Crownhill Dr
Arlington, TX 76012-2816, USA

Thomas, B J (Musician, Songwriter, Writer)
Gloria Thomas
1324 Crownhill Dr
Arlington, TX 76012, USA

Thomas, Blair (Athlete, Football Player)
401 Gulph Ridge Dr
King Of Prussia, PA 19406-3213, USA

Thomas, Bobbie (Television Host)
c/o Lauren Hale *Creative Artists Agency (CAA-LA)*
2000 Avenue of the Stars Ste 100
Los Angeles, CA 90067-4705, USA

Thomas, Broderick (Athlete, Football Player)
12004 Opal Creek Dr
Pearland, TX 77584-1647, USA

Thomas, Bruce (Actor)
c/o Jerry Shandrew *Shandrew Public Relations*
1050 S Stanley Ave
Los Angeles, CA 90019-6634, USA

Thomas, Calvin (Athlete, Football Player)
4931 NW 21st St
Gainesville, FL 32605-5473, USA

Thomas, Carl (Athlete, Baseball Player)
3212 N Miller Rd Apt 333
Scottsdale, AZ 85251-6988, USA

Thomas, Carl (Musician)
c/o Staff Member *Red Entertainment Agency*
505 8th Ave Rm 1004
New York, NY 10018-6529, USA

Thomas, Charles (Athlete, Baseball Player)
137 Black Oak Dr
Asheville, NC 28804-1835, USA

Thomas, Chris (Musician)
Associated Booking Corp
1995 Broadway # 501
New York, NY 10023-5882, USA

Thomas, Chuck (Athlete, Football Player)
2201 Purple Majesty Ct
Las Vegas, NV 89117-2747, USA

Thomas, Clarence (Attorney)
US Supreme Court
United States Supreme Court 11th St NE
Washington, DC 20543-0001, USA

Thomas, Clendon (Athlete, Football Player)
7508 Rumsey Rd
Oklahoma City, OK 73132-5335, USA

Thomas, Clete (Athlete, Baseball Player)
802 Wyoming Ave
Lynn Haven, FL 32444-1963

Thomas, Craig (Producer)
Bays Thomas Productions
10201 W Pico Blvd Bldg 88
Los Angeles, CA 90064-2606, USA

Thomas, Dallas (Athlete, Football Player)
c/o Bill Johnson *SportsTrust Advisors (GA)*
3340 Peachtree Rd NE Fl 16
Atlanta, GA 30326-1000, USA

Thomas, Daniel (Athlete, Football Player)
c/o Mitchell Frankel *Impact Sports - Boca Raton*
2799 NW 2nd Ave Ste 203
Boca Raton, FL 33431-6709, USA

Thomas, Dave (Comedian)
c/o David Boxerbaum *Paradigm (LA)*
405 S Beverly Dr Ste 500
Beverly Hills, CA 90212-4425, USA

Thomas, Dave G (Athlete, Football Player)
1504 Avalon Sq
Glen Cove, NY 11542-2849, USA

Thomas, David (Athlete, Football Player)
c/o Staff Member *New England Patriots*
1 Patriot Pl
Foxboro, MA 02035-1388, USA

Thomas, David (Business Person)
Thomson Corp
1 Station Pl Ste 5
Metro Center
Stamford, CT 06902-6893, USA

Thomas, De'Anthony (Athlete, Football Player)
c/o Joe Panos *Athletes First, LLC*
23091 Mill Creek Dr
Laguna Hills, CA 92653-1258, USA

Thomas, DeAnthony (Athlete, Football Player)
c/o David Dunn *Athletes First, LLC*
23091 Mill Creek Dr
Laguna Hills, CA 92653-1258, USA

Thomas, Debra J (Deb) (Figure Skater)
Mentor Mgmt
202 S Michigan St Ste 810
South Bend, IN 46601-2012, USA

Thomas, Demaryius (Athlete, Football Player)
c/o Todd France *Five Star Athlete Management*
3500 Lenox Rd NE
Atlanta, GA 30326-4228, USA

Thomas, Dennis (DT) (Musician)
c/o Staff Member *Pyramid Entertainment Group*
377 Rector Pl Apt 21A
New York, NY 10280-1439, USA

Thomas, Derrel (Athlete, Baseball Player)
c/o Staff Member *JD Legends Promotions*
10808 Foothill Blvd Ste 160-454
Rancho Cucamonga, CA 91730-3889, USA

Thomas, Dominic R (Religious Leader)
Church of Jesus Christ
6th & Lincoln Sts
Monongahela, PA 15063, USA

Thomas, Donald (Athlete, Football Player)
c/o Drew Rosenhaus *Rosenhaus Sports Representation*
6400 Allison Rd
Miami Beach, FL 33141-4540, USA

Thomas, Donald A (Astronaut)
1029 Hart Rd
Towson, MD 21286-1630, USA

Thomas, Donald A Dr (Astronaut)
1029 Hart Rd
Towson, MD 21286-1630, USA

Thomas, Doug (Athlete, Football Player)
11220 NE 53rd St
Kirkland, WA 98033-7505, USA

Thomas, Duane (Athlete, Football Player)
55 Sedona St
Sedona, AZ 86351-7753, USA

Thomas, Earl (Athlete, Football Player)
1000 Farrah Ln Apt 825
Stafford, TX 77477-6046, USA

Thomas, Earlie (Athlete, Football Player)
PO Box 1445
Laporte, CO 80535-1445, USA

Thomas, Eddie Kaye (Actor)
2516 Hargrave Dr
Los Angeles, CA 90068-2218, USA

Thomas, Elizabeth Marshall (Writer)
80 E Mountain Rd
Peterborough, NH 03458-2318, USA

Thomas, Emmitt (Athlete, Football Player)
5318 Harbury Cv
Suwanee, GA 30024-7544, USA

Thomas, Ernest (Actor)
Coast to Coast Talent
3350 Barham Blvd
Los Angeles, CA 90068-1404, USA

Thomas, Etan (Athlete, Basketball Player)
c/o Arn Tellem *Wasserman Media Group (LA)*
12100 W Olympic Blvd Ste 200
Los Angeles, CA 90064-1075, USA

Thomas, Evan (Writer)
c/o Staff Member *Public Affairs Books*
1094 Flex Dr
Jackson, TN 38301-5070, USA

Thomas, Frank J (Athlete, Baseball Player)
118 Doray Dr
Pittsburgh, PA 15237-3681, USA

Thomas, George (Athlete, Baseball Player)
5804 Ivrea Dr
Sarasota, FL 34238-4730

Thomas, Gorman (Athlete, Baseball Player)
W331S5179 Hood Pkwy
North Prairie, WI 53153-9719, USA

Thomas, Heather (Actor)
1433 San Vicente Blvd
Santa Monica, CA 90402-2203, USA

Thomas, Henry (Actor)
c/o Jennifer Craig *Gersh (LA)*
9465 Wilshire Blvd Ste 600
Beverly Hills, CA 90212-2605, USA

Thomas, Henry L Jr (Athlete, Football Player)
3040 Fm 1960 Rd Ste 125
Houston, TX 77073-2617, USA

Thomas, Henry W (Writer)
3214 Warder St NW
Washington, DC 20010-2521, USA

Thomas, Hollis (Athlete, Football Player)
920 Yeadon Ave
Lansdowne, PA 19050-3713, USA

Thomas, Irma (Musician)
c/o Staff Member *Concerted Efforts*
PO Box 440326
Somerville, MA 02144-0004, USA

Thomas, Irving (Athlete, Basketball Player)
5117 Lakosee Ct
Orlando, FL 32818-8330, USA

Thomas, Isaac (Athlete, Football Player)
510 Grady Ln
Cedar Hill, TX 75104-4212, USA

Thomas, Jabe (Race Car Driver)
850 Mountain View Dr
Christiansburg, VA 24073-4330, USA

Thomas, Jake (Actor)
c/o Connie Tavel *Forward Entertainment*
9255 W Sunset Blvd Ste 805
West Hollywood, CA 90069-3305, USA

Thomas, Jay (Actor)
c/o Christine Holder *Zero Gravity Management (II)*
9255 W Sunset Blvd Ste 1010
West Hollywood, CA 90069-3307, USA

Thomas, Joe L (Musician)
c/o Staff Member *Kedar Entertainment*
365 Bridge St Apt 20C
Brooklyn, NY 11201-3821, USA

Thomas, Joey (Athlete, Football Player)
c/o Eugene Parker *Maximum Sports Management*
6435 W Jefferson Blvd # 197
Fort Wayne, IN 46804-6203, USA

Thomas, John (Bud) (Athlete, Baseball Player)
2475 Woodland Dr
Sedalia, MO 65301-8915, USA

Thomas, Johnny (Athlete, Football Player)
1818 Darby Ln
Fresno, TX 77545-9233, USA

Thomas, Jonathan Taylor (Actor)
c/o Abby Bluestone *Innovative Artists (LA)*
1505 10th St
Santa Monica, CA 90401-2805, USA

Thomas, Josh (Athlete, Football Player)
c/o Alan Herman *Sportstars Inc*
1350 Avenue of the Americas Fl 28
New York, NY 10019-4702, USA

Thomas, J T (Athlete, Football Player)
408 Arden Dr
Monroeville, PA 15146-4855, USA

Thomas, Julius (Athlete, Football Player)
c/o Frank Bauer *Sun West Sports*
7883 N Pershing Ave
Stockton, CA 95207-1749, USA

Thomas, Khleo (Actor)
c/o Staff Member *Beverly Hecht Agency*
6320 Canoga Ave Fl 15
Woodland Hills, CA 91367-2563, USA

Thomas, Kurt (Athlete, Basketball Player)
1826 Brook Terrace Trl
Dallas, TX 75232-3708, USA

Thomas, Kurt (Athlete, Gymnast, Olympic Athlete)
4421 Hidden Hill Rd
Norman, OK 73072-2899, USA

Thomas, Lamar (Athlete, Football Player)
10524 NW 13th Ln
Gainesville, FL 32606-8091, USA

Thomas, Larry (Actor)
c/o Dora Whitaker *Whitaker Agency, The*
4924 Vineland Ave
N Hollywood, CA 91601-3847, USA

Thomas, Larry (Athlete, Baseball Player)
3825 Graham Ln
Eight Mile, AL 36613-2306, USA

Thomas, LaToya (Basketball Player)
San Antonio Silver Stars
1 at and T Center Pkwy
San Antonio, TX 78219-3604, USA

Thomas, Lavale (Athlete, Football Player)
712 Bradford Creek Trl # M
Duluth, GA 30096-1402, USA

Thomas, Lee (Athlete, Baseball Player)
14260 Manderleigh Woods Dr
Chesterfield, MO 63017-8051, USA

Thomas, Logan (Athlete, Football Player)
c/o David Dunn *Athletes First, LLC*
23091 Mill Creek Dr
Laguna Hills, CA 92653-1258, USA

Thomas, Mark A (Athlete, Football Player)
556 Hillsboro St
Monticello, GA 31064-1046, USA

Thomas, Marlo (Actor)
420 E 54th St
22F
New York, NY 10022-5179, USA

Thomas, Mary (Musician)
Superstars Unlimited
PO Box 371371
Las Vegas, NV 89137-1371, USA

Thomas, Mava Lee (Athlete, Baseball
Player)
9163 SE 48th Court Rd
Ocala, FL 34480-4203, USA

Thomas, Mike (Athlete, Baseball Player)
4808 Gregory Cv
Jonesboro, AR 72401-7943, USA

Thomas, Mike (Athlete, Football Player)
PO Box 446
Missouri City, TX 77459-0446, USA

Thomas, Norris (Athlete, Football Player)
4510 Chippewa Ave
Pascagoula, MS 39581-2501, USA

Thomas, Pamela (Business Person)
c/o Staff Member *CNBC (Main)*
900 Sylvan Ave
Englewood Cliffs, NJ 07632-3312, USA

Thomas, Pat (Athlete, Football Player)
5301 W Spring Creek Pkwy Apt 1132
Plano, TX 75024-4907, USA

Thomas, Philip Michael (Actor)
PO Box 23714
Brooklyn, NY 11202-3714, USA

Thomas, Pierre (Athlete, Football Player)
c/o Lamont Smith *All Pro Sports and
Entertainment*
36 Steele St Ste 100
Denver, CO 80206-5709, USA

Thomas, Ralph (Athlete, Football Player)
3270 Alum Creek Ct
Reno, NV 89509-7117, USA

Thomas, Randy (Athlete, Football Player)
2945 Jones St Apt 4
Atlanta, GA 30344-4130, USA

Thomas, Richard (Actor)
c/o Emily Gerson Saines *Brookside Artists
Management (NY)*
250 W 57th St Ste 2303
New York, NY 10107-2399, USA

Thomas, Ricky (Athlete, Football Player)
7890 Morgan Pointe Cir
Reno, NV 89523-4805, USA

Thomas, Rob (Director, Producer, Writer)
c/o Ari Greenburg *William Morris
Endeavor (LA)*
9601 Wilshire Blvd
Beverly Hills, CA 90210-5213, USA

Thomas, Rob (Musician, Songwriter)
c/o Michael Lippman *Lippman
Entertainment*
23586 Calabasas Rd Ste 208
Calabasas, CA 91302-1361, USA

Thomas, Robb (Athlete, Football Player)
179 NW Outlook Vista Dr
Bend, OR 97701-5472, USA

Thomas, Robert D (Publisher)
223 Mariomi Rd
New Canaan, CT 06840-3315, USA

Thomas, Robert L (Athlete, Football
Player)
2810 W Slauson Ave Apt 5
Los Angeles, CA 90043-2583, USA

Thomas, Robert R (Athlete, Football
Player)
970 Ridgewood Dr
West Chicago, IL 60185-5007, USA

Thomas, Robin (Actor)
c/o Staff Member *Marshak/Zachary
Company, The*
8840 Wilshire Blvd Fl 1
Beverly Hills, CA 90211-2606, USA

Thomas, Ross (Actor)
c/o Bryan Bukowski *Simmons & Scott
Entertainment*
7942 Mulholland Dr
Los Angeles, CA 90046-1225, USA

Thomas, Roy (Athlete, Baseball Player)
6881 SW 167th Pl
Beaverton, OR 97007-6312, USA

Thomas, Scott (Athlete, Hockey Player)
3621 Herba De Maria
Sierra Vista, AZ 85650-9552

Thomas, Sean Patrick (Actor)
c/o Karen Samfilippo *IMPR*
357 S Robertson Blvd
Beverly Hills, CA 90211-3602, USA

Thomas, Serena Scott (Actor)
S M S Talent
8383 Wilshire Blvd Ste 230
Beverly Hills, CA 90211-2436, USA

Thomas, Stan (Athlete, Baseball Player)
10827 159th Ct NE
Redmond, WA 98052-2691, USA

Thomas, Stayve (Slim Thug) (Musician)
c/o Wes Stevens *Vox*
6420 Wilshire Blvd Ste 1080
Los Angeles, CA 90048-5539, USA

Thomas, Ted (Business Person)
C/O Jones & Trevor Marketing
234 Willard St Ste C
Cocoa, FL 32922-7984, USA

Thomas, Thurman L (Athlete, Football
Player)
240 Pound Rd
Elma, NY 14059-9681, USA

Thomas, Tim (Athlete, Hockey Player)
PO Box 408
Green Mountain Falls, CO 80819-0408

Thomas, Tony (Actor, Producer)
Witt/Thomas/Harris Productions
11901 Santa Monica Blvd Ste 596
Los Angeles, CA 90025-5188, USA

Thomas, Tra (Athlete, Football Player)
1 Novacare Way
Philadelphia, PA 19145-5900, USA

Thomas, Wayne (Athlete, Hockey Player)
525 W Santa Clara St
San Jose, CA 95113-1520

Thomas, William H Jr (Athlete, Football
Player)
2401 Echo Dr
Amarillo, TX 79107-6405, USA

Thomas, William J (Athlete, Football
Player)
16 Russell St
Waltham, MA 02453-8505, USA

Thomas, Zach (Athlete, Football Player)
989 Hillsboro Mile
Hillsboro Beach, FL 33062-2301, USA

Thomaselli, Rich (Athlete, Football Player)
96A Seneca St
Weirton, WV 26062-2627, USA

Thomas III, Isiah L (Athlete, Basketball
Player)
1 Azalea Cir
Purchase, NY 10577-1131, USA

Thomas III, Leon (Actor)
c/o Bryan Leder *Management 101*
11271 Ventura Blvd # 102
Studio City, CA 91604-3136, USA

Thomas Jr, Frank E (Athlete, Baseball
Player)
1515 Sunnyview Rd
Libertyville, IL 60048-5328, USA

Thomas Jr, James (Athlete, Basketball
Player)
4499 Willow Hill Rd
Portal, GA 30450-5344, USA

Thomason, Bob (Athlete, Football Player)
2645 Bucknell Ave
Charlotte, NC 28207-2649, USA

Thomason, CJ (Actor)
c/o Staff Member *Robert Stein
Management*
PO Box 3797
Beverly Hills, CA 90212-0797, USA

Thomason, Erskine (Athlete, Baseball
Player)
932 Dial Pl
Laurens, SC 29360-8850, USA

Thomason, Harry (Producer)
c/o Staff Member *Mozark Productions*
4024 Radford Ave Bldg 5
Studio City, CA 91604-2101, USA

Thomason, Harry Z (Producer)
10732 Riverside Dr
North Hollywood, CA 91602-2313, USA

Thomason, Marsha (Actor)
c/o Kesha Williams *KW Entertainment*
425 N Robertson Blvd
West Hollywood, CA 90048-1735, USA

Thomasson, Gary (Athlete, Baseball
Player)
8300 N 53rd St
Paradise Valley, AZ 85253-2512, USA

Thome, Jim (Athlete, Baseball Player)
c/o Ashley Smith Becker *Relativity Sports
(LA)*
9242 Beverly Blvd Ste 300
Beverly Hills, CA 90210-3728, USA

Thomerson, Tim (Actor)
2635 28th St Apt 14
Santa Monica, CA 90405-2960, USA

Thomlinson, John (Baseball Player)
Negro Baseball Leagues
2351 Beach Way SW
Atlanta, GA 30310-1005, USA

Thomopoulos, Anthony (Business Person)
1280 Stone Canyon Rd
Los Angeles, CA 90077-2920, USA

Thompkins, Kenbrell (Athlete, Football
Player)
c/o Drew Rosenhaus *Rosenhaus Sports
Representation*
6400 Allison Rd
Miami Beach, FL 33141-4540, USA

Thompson, Ahmir-Khalib (Musician)
c/o Sara Ramaker *Paradigm (LA)*
360 N Crescent Dr
North Bldg
Beverly Hills, CA 90210-4874, USA

Thompson, Alana (Honey Boo Boo)
(Reality Star)
PO Box 72
Mc Intyre, GA 31054-0072, USA

Thompson, Andrea (Actor)
Dayton Milrad Cho Management
8306 Wilshire Blvd # 56
Beverly Hills, CA 90211-2304, USA

Thompson, Andy (Athlete, Baseball
Player)
1405 Bayshore Blvd
Tampa, FL 33606-3001, USA

Thompson, Anthony (Athlete, Coach,
Football Coach, Football Player)
Athletic Dept
Bloomington, IN 47405, USA

Thompson, Arland (Athlete, Football
Player)
6692 S Routt St
Littleton, CO 80127-4962, USA

Thompson, Aundra (Athlete, Football
Player)
12060 Galva Dr
Dallas, TX 75243-3702, USA

Thompson, Barbara (Athlete, Baseball
Player)
1721 Edgebrook Dr
Rockford, IL 61107-1320, USA

Thompson, Bennie (Athlete, Football
Player)
Baltimore Ravens
11001 Russell St
Baltimore, MD 21230, USA

Thompson, Billy (Athlete, Basketball
Player)
32 Lake Side Trl
Lake Placid, FL 33852-8413, USA

Thompson, Brent (Athlete, Hockey Player)
Bridgeport Sound Tigers
600 Main St Ste 1
Bridgeport, CT 06604-5106

Thompson, Brian
1010 Olive Ln
La Canada Flintridge, CA 91011-2367

Thompson, Brooks (Athlete, Basketball
Player)
29222 Oakview Rdg
Boerne, TX 78015-4457, USA

Thompson, Caroline W (Director,
Producer, Writer)
c/o Brian Sher *Category 5 Entertainment*
300 71st St Ste 620
Miami Beach, FL 33141-3089, USA

Thompson, Charissa (Actor, Sportscaster)
c/o Nick Khan *Creative Artists Agency
(CAA-LA)*
2000 Avenue of the Stars Ste 100
Los Angeles, CA 90067-4705, USA

Thompson, Cornelius (Athlete, Basketball
Player)
207 Lamentation Dr
Berlin, CT 06037-3727, USA

Thompson, Craig (Athlete, Football
Player)
913 C St
Hartsville, SC 29550-3166, USA

Thompson, Daley (Athlete)
1 Church Row Wandsworth Pln
London, EN SW18

Thompson, Darrell (Athlete, Football
Player)
4220 Oakview Ln N
Minneapolis, MN 55442-2773, USA

Thompson, Derek (Athlete, Baseball Player)
3212 Pine Shadow Dr
Land O Lakes, FL 34639-4516, USA

Thompson, Donnell (Athlete, Football Player)
1302 Village Crossing Dr
Chapel Hill, NC 27517-7572, USA

Thompson, Emma (Actor)
c/o Catherine Olim *PMK/BNC Public Relations (PMK-LA)*
8687 Melrose Ave Ste 8
West Hollywood, CA 90069-5746, USA

Thompson, Fred dalton (Politician)
10024 Colvin Manor Ct
Great Falls, VA 22066-1854, USA

Thompson, Gary (Basketball Player)
2531 Park Vista Cir
Ames, IA 50014-4568, USA

Thompson, Gary Scott (Producer, Writer)
c/o Rob Carlson *William Morris Endeavor (LA)*
9601 Wilshire Blvd
Beverly Hills, CA 90210-5213, USA

Thompson, Gina (Musician)
Richard Walters
1800 Argyle Ave # 408
Los Angeles, CA 90028-5253, USA

Thompson, Glenn (Congressman, Politician)
124 Cannon Hob
Washington, DC 20515-4401, USA

Thompson, G Ralph (Religious Leader)
Seventh-Day Adventists
12501 Old Columbia Pike
Silver Spring, MD 20904-6600, USA

Thompson, Jack (Athlete, Football Player)
2507 29th Ave W
Seattle, WA 98199-3323, USA

Thompson, Jack E (Business Person)
Homestake Mining Co
650 California St
San Francisco, CA 94108-2702, USA

Thompson, James R (Jim) Jr (Politician)
Winston & Strawn
35 W Wacker Dr Ste 4200
Chicago, IL 60601-1695, USA

Thompson, Jason (Athlete, Baseball Player)
10535 Oak Terrace Ave
Las Vegas, NV 89149-1504, USA

Thompson, Jason D (Athlete, Baseball Player)
4056 Summerfield Dr
Troy, MI 48085-7033, USA

Thompson, Jennifer (Jenny) (Swimmer)
USA Swimming
1 Olympic Plz Bldg 2A
Colorado Springs, CO 80909-5770, USA

Thompson, Jenny
1 Olympic Plz Bldg 2A
Colorado Springs, CO 80909-5746

Thompson, Jill (Cartoonist)
DC Comics
1700 Broadway Fl 6
New York, NY 10019-5905, USA

Thompson, J Lee
9595 Lime Orchard Rd
Beverly Hills, CA 90210-1315, USA

Thompson, John (Athlete, Basketball Player, Olympic Athlete)
Basketball Hall of Fame
1000 Hall of Fame Ave Ste 100
Springfield, MA 01105-2545, USA

Thompson, Justin (Athlete, Baseball Player)
32807 Clearwater Ct
Magnolia, TX 77354-3233, USA

Thompson, Kenan (Actor)
c/o Michael Goldman *Michael Goldman Management*
7471 Melrose Ave Ste 11
Los Angeles, CA 90046-7551, USA

Thompson, Kevin (Athlete, Basketball Player)
9808 Westpark Dr
Benbrook, TX 76126-3125, USA

Thompson, Lasalle (Athlete, Basketball Player)
111 W Main St Apt 2A
Carmel, IN 46032-2034, USA

Thompson, Lea (Actor)
c/o Gordon Gilbertson *Gilbertson Management*
1334 3rd Street Promenade Ste 201
Santa Monica, CA 90401-1320, USA

Thompson, Leonard (Athlete, Football Player)
5534 W Glenrosa Ave
Phoenix, AZ 85031-2220, USA

Thompson, Leonard (Golfer)
9010 Marsh View Ct
Ponte Vedra Beach, FL 32082-1928, USA

Thompson, Leroy (Athlete, Football Player)
5005 Princess Ann Ct
Knoxville, TN 37918-9274, USA

Thompson, Linda (Actor)
25254 Eldorado Meadow Rd
Hidden Hills, CA 91302-1242, USA

Thompson, Linda (Musician)
High Road
751 Bridgeway Fl 2
Sausalito, CA 94965-2174, USA

Thompson, Mark (Athlete, Baseball Player)
1122 Lord Murphy Way
Bowling Green, KY 42104-5539, USA

Thompson, Marty (Athlete, Football Player)
1290 Lone Star Ct
Calimesa, CA 92320-1501, USA

Thompson, Mike (Athlete, Baseball Player)
7565 Turner Dr
Denver, CO 80221-3432, USA

Thompson, Mike (Congressman, Politician)
231 Cannon Hob
Washington, DC 20515-3311, USA

Thompson, Milt (Athlete, Baseball Player)
PO Box 663
Williamstown, NJ 08094-0663, USA

Thompson, Morgan
c/o Jeff Morrone *Intellectual Artists Management*
9350 Wilshire Blvd Ste 224
Beverly Hills, CA 90212-3204, USA

Thompson, Mychal (Athlete, Basketball Player)
11 Paverstone Ln
Ladera Ranch, CA 92694-0454, USA

Thompson, Norm (Athlete, Football Player)
PO Box 4552
Hayward, CA 94540-4552, USA

Thompson, Paul (Athlete, Basketball Player)
3422 N 40th St
Milwaukee, WI 53216-3637, USA

Thompson, Ray (Athlete, Football Player)
1501 N Johnson St Apt A208
New Orleans, LA 70116-1720, USA

Thompson, Raynoch (Athlete, Football Player)
1739 2nd St
New Orleans, LA 70113-1657, USA

Thompson, Reyna (Athlete, Football Player)
1502 NW 183rd Ter
Pembroke Pines, FL 33029-3095, USA

Thompson, Rich (Athlete, Baseball Player)
7 Chambers Ct
Huntington Station, NY 11746-2620, USA

Thompson, Rich (Athlete, Baseball Player)
47 Murray St
Binghamton, NY 13905-4522, USA

Thompson, Richard (Musician, Songwriter, Writer)
Elizabeth Rush Agency
100 Park St Apt 4
Montclair, NJ 07042-2996, USA

Thompson, Richard K (Religious Leader)
African Methodist Episcopal Zion Church
PO Box 32843
Charlotte, NC 28232-2843, USA

Thompson, Ricky (Athlete, Football Player)
815 Woodland West Dr
Woodway, TX 76712-3415, USA

Thompson, Robert (Athlete, Football Player)
Deerfield Beach High School
910 SW 15th St
Deerfield Beach, FL 33441-6299, USA

Thompson, Robert L (Athlete, Football Player)
16924 White Pine Way
Canyon Country, CA 91387-3992, USA

Thompson, Robert R (Robby) (Athlete, Baseball Player)
PO Box 4100
Seattle, WA 98194-0100, USA

Thompson, Rocky (Athlete, Hockey Player)
Oklahoma City Barons
501 N Walker Ave Ste 140
Oklahoma City, OK 73102-1233

Thompson, Ryan (Athlete, Baseball Player)
2153 Fullerton Dr
Indianapolis, IN 46214-2130, USA

Thompson, Sarah (Actor)
c/o Gerry Harrington *Brillstein Entertainment Partners (LA)*
9150 Wilshire Blvd Ste 350
Beverly Hills, CA 90212-3453, USA

Thompson, Scot (Athlete, Baseball Player)
6142 Penn Dr
Butler, PA 16002-0406, USA

Thompson, Scottie (Actor)
c/o David Guillod *Intellectual Artists Management*
10585 Santa Monica Blvd Ste 135
Los Angeles, CA 90025-6392, USA

Thompson, Shaun (Dancer, Fitness Expert)
c/o Tom Estey *Tom Estey Publicity*
144 E 22nd St Apt 1B
New York, NY 10010-6333, USA

Thompson, Shawn
5319 Biloxi Ave
North Hollywood, CA 91601-3514

Thompson, Steve M (Athlete, Football Player)
11115 Vernon Rd
Lake Stevens, WA 98258-8541, USA

Thompson, Sue (Musician)
Curb Entertainment
3907 W Alameda Ave Ste 200
Burbank, CA 91505-4359, USA

Thompson, Susanna
PO Box 15717
Beverly Hills, CA 90209-1717

Thompson, Ted (Athlete, Football Player)
Green Bay Packers
PO Box 10628
Director of Player Personnel
Green Bay, WI 54307-0628, USA

Thompson, Tessa (Actor)
c/o Siri Garber *Platform Public Relations*
2666 N Beachwood Dr
Los Angeles, CA 90068-2308, USA

Thompson, Tim (Athlete, Baseball Player)
536 Summit Dr
Lewistown, PA 17044-1252, USA

Thompson, Tommy (Politician)
1313 Manassas Trl
Madison, WI 53718-8243, USA

Thompson, Weegie (Athlete, Football Player)
14501 Felbridge Way
Midlothian, VA 23113-6721, USA

Thompson, William A (Athlete, Football Player)
14616 E Hawaii Pl
Aurora, CO 80012-5747, USA

Thompson, William P (Religious Leader)
World Council of Churches
475 Riverside Dr Ste 727
New York, NY 10115-0070, USA

Thompson-Griffin, Viola (Athlete, Baseball Player)
232 Guthrie Rd
Belton, SC 29627-8900, USA

Thompson Square (Music Group, Musician)
c/o Staff Member *William Morris Endeavor (Nashville)*
1600 Division St Ste 300
Nashville, TN 37203-2755, USA

Thoms, Art (Athlete, Football Player)
90 Goodfellow Dr
Moraga, CA 94556-1584, USA

Thomsen, Cecilie (Actor)
c/o Staff Member *Special Artists Agency*
9200 W Sunset Blvd Ste 410
West Hollywood, CA 90069-3506, USA

Thomsen, Ulrich (Actor)
Paradigm Agency
10100 Santa Monica Blvd Ste 2500
Los Angeles, CA 90067-4116, USA

Thomson, Anna (Actor)
Innovative Artists
1505 10th St
Santa Monica, CA 90401-2805, USA

Thomson, Cyndi (Musician)
The Firm
9100 Wilshire Blvd Ste 100W
Beverly Hills, CA 90212-3435, USA

Thomson, David (Business Person)
The Thomson Corporation
1 Station Pl Ste 5
Metro Center
Stamford, CT 06902-6893, USA

Thomson, Dorrie
3349 Cahuenga Blvd W Ste 2
Los Angeles, CA 90068-1379

Thomson, Gordon (Actor)
3914 Fredonia Dr
Los Angeles, CA 90068-1214, USA

Thomson, John (Athlete, Baseball Player)
1414 E Kent Dr
Sulphur, LA 70663-5017, USA

Thomson, June (Correspondent)
KNBC-TV
News Dept
3000 W Alameda Ave
Burbank, CA 91523-0001, USA

Thomson, Rob (Athlete, Baseball Player)
17428 Equestrian Trl
Odessa, FL 33556-1846, USA

Thomson, Scott (DJ)
c/o Staff Member *Sharp Talent*
5538 Willowcrest Ave
North Hollywood, CA 91601-2830, USA

Thon, Dickie (Athlete, Baseball Player)
C17 Calle Lirio Del Mar
Urb Dorado Del Mar
Dorado, PR 00646-2126, USA

Thone, Charles (Ex-Governor)
Erickson & Sederstrom
301 S 13th St Ste 400
Lincoln, NE 68508-2532, USA

Thor, Brad (Writer)
c/o Staff Member *Sanford J Greenburger Associates Inc*
55 5th Ave
New York, NY 10003-4301, USA

Thora (Actor)
CunninghamEscottDipene
10635 Santa Monica Blvd Ste 130
Los Angeles, CA 90025-8306, USA

Thorburn, Christine (Athlete, Cycler, Olympic Athlete)
141 Mimosa Way
Portola Valley, CA 94028-7429, USA

Thorell, Clarke (Actor)
Bauman, Redanty & Shaul Agency
5757 Wilshire Blvd Ste 473
Los Angeles, CA 90036-3632

Thoren, Skip (Athlete, Basketball Player)
330 Buckland Trce
Louisville, KY 40245-4272, USA

Thorin, Christopher (Musician)
Shapiro Co
9229 W Sunset Blvd Ste 607
West Hollywood, CA 90069-3406, USA

Thormodsgard, Paul (Athlete, Baseball Player)
7752 E Rose Ln
Scottsdale, AZ 85250-4724, USA

Thorn, Paul (Musician)
c/o Staff Member *Paradigm (Monterey)*
404 W Franklin St
Monterey, CA 93940-2303, USA

Thorn, Rod (Athlete, Basketball Player)
20 Loewen Ct
Rye, NY 10580-2823, USA

Thornberry, Mac (Congressman, Politician)
2209 Rayburn Hob
Washington, DC 20515-3010, USA

Thornbladh, Robert (Athlete, Football Player)
3775 Bradford Square Dr
Ann Arbor, MI 48103-6317, USA

Thornburgh, Richard (Dick) (Politician)
2540 Massachusetts Ave NW Ste 405
Washington, DC 20008-2843, USA

Thornburgh, Richard L (Dick) (Ex-Governor)
1601 K St NW
Washington, DC 20006-1682, USA

Thorne, Bella (Actor)
c/o Adam Griffin *Kritzer Levine Wilkins Entertainment (KLWG)*
11872 La Grange Ave Fl 1
Los Angeles, CA 90025-5283, USA

Thorne, Callie (Actor)
c/o Lindsay Porter *Gersh (NY)*
41 Madison Ave Ste 4001
New York, NY 10010-2239, USA

Thorne, Dyanne (Actor)
5192 Placentia Pkwy
Las Vegas, NV 89118-1489, USA

Thorne, Frank (Cartoonist)
1967 Grenville Rd
Scotch Plains, NJ 07076-2907, USA

Thorne, Gary (Correspondent)
ABC-TV
77 W 66th St
Sports Dept
New York, NY 10023-6201, USA

Thorne, Remy (Actor)
c/o Adam Griffin *Kritzer Levine Wilkins Entertainment (KLWG)*
11872 La Grange Ave Fl 1
Los Angeles, CA 90025-5283, USA

Thorne-Smith, Courtney (Actor, Model)
c/o Staff Member *IMPR*
357 S Robertson Blvd
Beverly Hills, CA 90211-3602, USA

Thornhill, Arthur H Jr (Publisher)
50 S School St
Portsmouth, NH 03801-5258, USA

Thornhill, Josh (Athlete, Football Player)
1108 Willow Cir
Clarksville, TN 37043-6856, USA

Thornton, Andre (Athlete, Baseball Player)
PO Box 395
Chagrin Falls, OH 44022-0395, USA

Thornton, Billy Bob (Actor, Director)
3354 Mandeville Canyon Rd
Los Angeles, CA 90049-1018, USA

Thornton, Bob (Athlete, Basketball Player)
27865 Espinoza
Mission Viejo, CA 92692-2151, USA

Thornton, Bruce (Athlete, Football Player)
3117 Hazlewood Ct
Bedford, TX 76021-2953, USA

Thornton, George (Athlete, Football Player)
2830 Marti Ln
Montgomery, AL 36116-3139, USA

Thornton, James (Athlete, Football Player)
1010 Fuller Rd
Gurnee, IL 60031-1834, USA

Thornton, Joe (Athlete, Hockey Player)
c/o Staff Member *San Jose Sharks*
525 W Santa Clara St
San Jose, CA 95113-1500, USA

Thornton, John (Athlete, Football Player)
7340 Indian Hill Rd
Cincinnati, OH 45243-4022, USA

Thornton, John (Athlete, Football Player)
6192 Otoole Ln
Mount Morris, MI 48458-2628, USA

Thornton, Kalen (Athlete, Football Player)
c/o Eugene Parker *Maximum Sports Management*
6435 W Jefferson Blvd # 197
Fort Wayne, IN 46804-6203, USA

Thornton, Kathryn C (Astronaut)
100 Bedford Pl
Charlottesville, VA 22903-4622, USA

Thornton, Kathryn C Dr (Astronaut)
100 Bedford Pl
Charlottesville, VA 22903-4622, USA

Thornton, Lou (Athlete, Baseball Player)
725 Henderson Rd
Hope Hull, AL 36043-4429, USA

Thornton, Matt (Athlete, Baseball Player)
5203 N Monte Vista Dr
Paradise Valley, AZ 85253-7065, USA

Thornton, Melody (Musician)
c/o Page Jeter *Entertainment Fusion Group*
6363 Wilshire Blvd Ste 206
Los Angeles, CA 90048-5736, USA

Thornton, Otis (Athlete, Baseball Player)
4312 Avenue L
Birmingham, AL 35208-1812, USA

Thornton, Shawn (Athlete, Hockey Player)
1427 NW 126th Dr
Coral Springs, FL 33071-5436, USA

Thornton, Sidney (Athlete, Football Player)
748 Royal St
Natchitoches, LA 71457-5741, USA

Thornton, Terrence (Pusha T) (Musician)
c/o Mitch Blackman *ICM Partners (NY)*
730 5th Ave
New York, NY 10019-4105, USA

Thornton, Tiffany (Actor)
c/o Nikki Pederson *Nikki Pederson Talent*
Prefers to be contacted via telephone or email
The Woodlands, TX, USA

Thornton, William E (Astronaut)
7640 Pimlico Ln
Boerne, TX 78015-4820, USA

Thornton, William E Dr (Astronaut)
2501 Monterey St
Sarasota, FL 34231-5275, USA

Thornton, Zach (Soccer Player)
Chicago Fire
980 N Michigan Ave Ste 1998
Chicago, IL 60611-7504, USA

Thorogood, George (Musician)
c/o Staff Member *Monterey International*
PO Box 297
Carmel By The Sea, CA 93921-0297, USA

Thorpe, Alexis (Actor)
c/o Marv Dauer *Marv Dauer Management*
2236 The Terrace
Los Angeles, CA 90049-1171, USA

Thorpe, James (Director)
20 Loeffler Rd Apt T320
Bloomfield, CT 06002-2277, USA

Thorpe, Otis (Athlete, Basketball Player)
632 Casper Ave
West Palm Beach, FL 33413-1227, USA

Thorson, Celeste (Producer, Writer)
c/o Alex Fox *Nu Talent*
10635 Santa Monica Blvd Ste 130
Los Angeles, CA 90025-8306, USA

Thorson, Linda (Actor)
S M S Talent
8383 Wilshire Blvd Ste 230
Beverly Hills, CA 90211-2436, USA

Those, Tom (Athlete, Baseball Player)
740 E Mingus Ave Apt 1012
Cottonwood, AZ 86326-3780, USA

Thousand Foot Krutch (Music Group)
Tooth & Nail Records
PO Box 12698
Seattle, WA 98111-4698, USA

Thout, Pierre
6606 Patrick Ct
Centreville, VA 20120-3754

Thranhardt, Carlo (Actor)
Brauweilerstr. 14
Koln, GE D-508

Thrash, James (Athlete, Football Player)
16005 Hampton Rd
Hamilton, VA 20158-3311, USA

Threats, Jabbar (Athlete, Football Player)
2015 Miracle Mile
Springfield, OH 45503-2836, USA

Threatt, Sedale (Athlete, Basketball Player)
8400 E Dixileta Dr Unit 191
Scottsdale, AZ 85266-2270, USA

Three 6 Mafia (Music Group, Musician)
c/o Jennifer Wilson *Entertainment Fusion Group*
6363 Wilshire Blvd Ste 206
Los Angeles, CA 90048-5736, USA

Three Days Grace (Music Group, Musician)
c/o Cliff Burnstein *Q Prime Inc*
729 7th Ave Ste 1600
New York, NY 10019-6880, USA

Threets, Erick (Athlete, Baseball Player)
2080 Vintage Ln
Livermore, CA 94550-8202, USA

Threshie, R David Jr (Publisher)
Orange County Register
625 N Grand Ave
Santa Ana, CA 92701-4347, USA

Thrice (Music Group)
c/o Staff Member *Nick Ben-Meir CPA*
652 N Doheny Dr
West Hollywood, CA 90069-5526, USA

Thrift, Cliff (Athlete, Football Player)
705 Trisha Ln
Norman, OK 73072-3718, USA

Throop, George (Athlete, Baseball Player)
239 Windwood Ln
Sierra Madre, CA 91024-2677, USA

Thrower, Jim (Athlete, Football Player)
17421 Pontchartrain Blvd
Detroit, MI 48203-1720, USA

Thuot, Pierre
21700 Atlantic Blvd
Sterling, VA 20166-6860

Thuot, Pierre J (Astronaut)
6606 Patrick Ct
Centreville, VA 20120-3754, USA

Thuot, Pierre J Captain (Astronaut)
22897 Thornbury Dr
Hollywood, MD 20636-4228, USA

Thurlow, Steve (Athlete, Football Player)
198 Shore Rd
Old Greenwich, CT 06870-2421, USA

Thurman, Annie (Actor)
c/o Tina Treadwell *Treadwell
Entertainment*
1327 W Valleyheart Dr
Burbank, CA 91506-3035, USA

Thurman, Corey (Athlete, Baseball Player)
653 Sinking Springs Ln
York, PA 17404-8488, USA

Thurman, Dennis L (Athlete, Football
Player)
4501 Eli Dr Apt G
Owings Mills, MD 21117-3798, USA

Thurman, Gary (Athlete, Baseball Player)
225 W 32nd St
Indianapolis, IN 46208-4603, USA

Thurman, Mike (Athlete, Baseball Player)
1360 7th St
West Linn, OR 97068-4718, USA

Thurman, Uma (Actor, Producer)
502/522 Mink Hollow Rd
Bearsville, NY 12409, USA

Thurmond, Mark (Athlete, Baseball
Player)
1614 Kings Castle Dr
Katy, TX 77450-4300, USA

Thurmond, Nate (Athlete, Basketball
Player)
5094 Diamond Heights Blvd # B
San Francisco, CA 94131-1653, USA

Thursday (Music Group)
c/o Staff Member *Island Records*
825 8th Ave Rm C2
New York, NY 10019-7472, USA

Thurston, Frederick C (Fuzzy) (Athlete,
Football Player)
704 Oconto Pl
De Pere, WI 54115-3669, USA

Thurston, Joe (Athlete, Baseball Player)
2219 Fairfield Ave
Fairfield, CA 94533-2017, USA

Thwaites, Brenton (Actor)
c/o Daniel Spilo *Industry Entertainment*
955 Carrillo Dr Ste 300
Los Angeles, CA 90048-5400, USA

Thyer, Mario (Athlete, Hockey Player)
170 Silver Rd
Bangor, ME 04401-5829

Thyne, TJ (Actor)
4715 Camellia Ave
N Hollywood, CA 91602-1105, USA

Thyssen, Greta (Actor)
444 E 82nd St Apt 33F
New York, NY 10028-5944, USA

T.I. (Actor, Musician)
3309 Lost Valley Dr
Jonesboro, GA 30236-5479, USA

Tiant, Luis (Athlete, Baseball Player)
392 Clubhouse Rd
Wells, ME 04090-7375, USA

Tibbetts, Billy (Athlete, Hockey Player)
79 Jericho Rd
Scituate, MA 02066-4809

Tibbs, Jay (Athlete, Baseball Player)
1100 Stonebrook Ln
Oneonta, AL 35121-1601, USA

Tice, John (Athlete, Football Player)
1004 Bartlett Loop Apt B
West Point, NY 10996-1201, USA

Tice, Michael P (Mike) (Athlete, Football
Coach, Football Player)
2114 Gail Ave Apt A
Jacksonville Beach, FL 32250-6170, USA

Tichenor, Todd (Athlete, Baseball Player)
PO Box 434
Holcomb, KS 67851-0434, USA

Tichnor, Alan (Religious Leader)
*United Synagogues of Conservative
Judaism*
155 5th Ave
New York, NY 10010-6858, USA

Tichy, Milan (Athlete, Hockey Player)
2413 NW 7th St
Boynton Beach, FL 33426-8783

Tickner, Charles (Athlete, Figure Skater,
Olympic Athlete)
1826 Dolphin Ct
Discovery Bay, CA 94505-9362, USA

Ticotin, Rachel (Actor)
c/o Staff Member *Stone Manners Salners
Agency (LA)*
6100 Wilshire Blvd Ste 1500
Los Angeles, CA 90048-5110, USA

Tidrow, Dick (Athlete, Baseball Player)
324 NE Warrington Ct
Lees Summit, MO 64064-1605, USA

Tiefenbach, Dov (Actor)
c/o Staff Member *Bauman Redanty &
Shaul Agency*
5757 Wilshire Blvd
Suite 473
Beverly Hills, CA 90212, USA

Tiefenthaler, Verfe (Athlete, Baseball
Player)
1852 Quint Ave
Carroll, IA 51401-3567, USA

Tiefenthaler, Verle (Athlete, Baseball
Player)
1852 Quint Ave
Carroll, IA 51401-3567, USA

Tiegs, Cheryl (Model, Television Host)
9663 Santa Monica Blvd # 339
Beverly Hills, CA 90210-4303, USA

Tiernan, Andrew (Actor)
c/o Paula Rosenberg *ICA Talent*
818 12th St Apt 9
Santa Monica, CA 90403-1727, USA

Tierney, Maura (Actor)
211 Sherman Canal
Venice, CA 90291-4514, USA

Tiesto (DJ, Musician)
c/o Mike Liotta *True Public Relations*
6725 W Sunset Blvd Ste 470
Los Angeles, CA 90028-7180, USA

Tiffany (Musician)
c/o Stephen Ford *Diva Central Inc*
7510 W Sunset Blvd Ste 1445
Los Angeles, CA 90046-3408, USA

Tiffee, Terry (Athlete, Baseball Player)
4 Epernay Cir
Little Rock, AR 72223-5527, USA

Tiffin, Pamela (Actor)
15 W 67th St
New York, NY 10023-6226, USA

Tighe, Kevin (Actor)
c/o Joanna (Joanie) Burstein *Burstein
Company, The*
15304 W Sunset Blvd Ste 208
Pacific Palisades, CA 90272-3656, USA

Tilberg, Tasha (Model)
c/o Staff Member *Next (LA)*
8447 Wilshire Blvd Ste 301
Beverly Hills, CA 90211-3206, USA

Tilford, Terrell (Actor)
c/o Staff Member *SMS Talent*
8383 Wilshire Blvd Ste 230
Beverly Hills, CA 90211-2436, USA

Tilker, Ewald (Athlete)
2767 40th Ave
San Francisco, CA 94116-2707, USA

Till, Brian (Race Car Driver)
13701 S Lake Dr
Plainfield, IL 60544-8113, USA

Till, Lucas (Actor)
c/o Ellen Meyer *Ellen Meyer Management*
8899 Beverly Blvd Ste 612
Los Angeles, CA 90048-2429, USA

Tilleman, Mike (Athlete, Football Player)
180 County Road 800 NW
Havre, MT 59501-5714, USA

Tiller, Chris (Athlete, Baseball Player)
604 Morningside
Bullard, TX 75757-5181, USA

Tiller, Joe (Coach, Football Coach)
Purdue University
Athletic Dept
W Lafayette, IN 47907, USA

Tilley, Patrick L (Pat) (Athlete, Coach,
Football Coach, Football Player)
1906 Winter St
Houston, TX 77007-4419, USA

Tilley, Tom (Athlete, Hockey Player)
14724 Maple St
Overland Park, KS 66223-1216

Tillis, Mel (Musician, Songwriter, Writer)
PO Box 305
Silver Springs, FL 34489-0305, USA

Tillis, Pam (Musician, Songwriter)
Fitzgerald Hartley Co
1908 Wedgewood Ave
Nashville, TN 37212-3733, USA

Tillison, Ed (Athlete, Football Player)
38504 James Crosby Rd
Pearl River, LA 70452-3431, USA

Tillman, Andre (Athlete, Football Player)
PO Box 743204
Dallas, TX 75374-3204, USA

Tillman, Charles (Athlete, Football Player)
Charles Tillman Cornerstone Foundation
4 E Ogden Ave # 801
Westmont, IL 60559-3506, USA

Tillman, Kerry Rusty (Athlete, Baseball
Player)
35119th St
Atlantic Beach, FL 32233, USA

Tillman, Lewis (Athlete, Football Player)
PO Box 166
Madison, MS 39130-0166, USA

Tillman, Robert L (Business Person)
Lowe's Companies
1605 Curtis Bridge Rd
Wilkesboro, NC 28697-2263, USA

Tillman, Rusty (Athlete, Baseball Player)
8711 Newton Rd Apt 61
Jacksonville, FL 32216-4661, USA

Tillman Jr, George (Director, Producer,
Writer)
State Street Pictures
10201 W Pico Blvd Bldg 52
Los Angeles, CA 90064-2606, USA

Tillotson, Johnny (Musician)
American Mgmt
19948 Mayall St
Chatsworth, CA 91311-3522, USA

Tilly, Jennifer (Actor)
c/o Sue Leibman *Barking Dog
Entertainment*
609 Greenwich St Fl 6
New York, NY 10014-3610, USA

Tilton, Charlene (Actor)
c/o Staff Member *Bohemia Group (LA)*
1680 Vine St Ste 412
Los Angeles, CA 90028-8800, USA

Tilton, Charline (Actor)
c/o Staff Member *Bohemia Group (LA)*
1680 Vine St Ste 412
Los Angeles, CA 90028-8800, USA

Tilton, Glenn F (Business Person)
UAL Corp
1200 E Algonquin Rd
Arlington Heights, IL 60005-4712, USA

Timberlake, Gary (Athlete, Baseball
Player)
14016 Waters Edge Dr
Louisville, KY 40245-5250, USA

Timberlake, George (Athlete, Football
Player)
13880 Canoe Brook Dr Apt 4D
Seal Beach, CA 90740-3856, USA

Timberlake, Justin (Actor, Musician)
3100 Torreyson Pl
Los Angeles, CA 90046-1230, USA

Timberlake, Robert W (Bob) (Athlete,
Football Player)
2219 E Jarvis St
Milwaukee, WI 53211-2149, USA

Timchal, Cindy (Coach)
University of Maryland
Athletic Dept
College Park, MD 20742-0001, USA

Times, Ken (Athlete, Football Player)
2603 S Sanford Ave
Sanford, FL 32773-5298, USA

Timken, William R Jr (Business Person)
Timken Co
1835 Dueber Ave SW
Canton, OH 44706-2798, USA

Timlin, Mike (Athlete, Baseball Player)
355 High Ridge Way
Castle Pines, CO 80108-3422, USA

Timmerman, Adam (Athlete, Football Player)
1635 585th St
Cherokee, IA 51012-7295, USA

Timmermann, Tom (Athlete, Baseball Player)
197 Coyote Ct
Pinckney, MI 48169-8022, USA

Timmins, Call (Actor)
The Agency
1800 Avenue of the Stars Ste 400
Los Angeles, CA 90067-4206, USA

Timmons, Harold
PO Box 140571
Nashville, TN 37214-0571

Timmons, Jeff (Musician)
DAS Communications
83 Riverside Dr
New York, NY 10024-5713, USA

Timmons, Ozzie (Athlete, Baseball Player)
4901 S 83rd St
Tampa, FL 33619-7101, USA

Timmons, Tim (Athlete, Baseball Player)
PO Box 574
New Albany, OH 43054-0574, USA

Timmons, Tim (Athlete, Baseball Player)
5055 Johnstown Rd
New Albany, OH 43054-9578, USA

Timonen, Kimmo (Athlete, Hockey Player)
125 Upland Way
Haddonfield, NJ 08033-3603, USA

Timpner, Clay (Athlete, Baseball Player)
3847 Shaftburv Pi
Oviedo, FL 32765, USA

Timpson, Michael D (Athlete, Football Player)
1823 Derby Glen Dr
Orlando, FL 32837-8103, USA

Tingelhoff, Mick (Athlete, Football Player)
20517 Kalmeadow Ct
Lakeville, MN 55044-6705, USA

Tingle, Scott D Cmdr (Astronaut)
2106 Bayou Cove Ln
League City, TX 77573-3248, USA

Tinglehoff, H Michael (Mick) (Athlete, Football Player)
19288 Judicial Rd
Prior Lake, MN 55372, USA

Tingley, Leeann (Beauty Pageant Winner)
Miss Rhode Island Pageant
PO Box 3509
Cranston, RI 02910-0509, USA

Tingley, Ron (Athlete, Baseball Player)
349 Omni Dr
Sparks, NV 89441-7295, USA

Tinker, Grant (Business Person)
531 Barnaby Rd
Los Angeles, CA 90077-3213, USA

Tinoco, Joe
118 N Keeler St
Olathe, KS 66061-3716

Tinsley, George (Athlete, Basketball Player)
The Tinsley Group
PO Box 1442
Auburndale, FL 33823-1442, USA

Tinsley, Jamaal (Basketball Player)
Indiana Pacers
125 S Pennsylvania St
Conseco Fieldhouse
Indianapolis, IN 46204-3610, USA

Tinsley, Lee (Athlete, Baseball Player)
237 Tenor St
Shelbyville, KY 40065-9255, USA

Tinsley, Scott (Athlete, Football Player)
26852 Sommerset Ln
Lake Forest, CA 92630-5800, USA

Tin Tin, Rin
PO Box 27
Crockett, TX 75835-0027

Tippet, Andre B (Athlete, Football Player)
17 Knob Hill St
Sharon, MA 02067-3119, USA

Tippett, Dave (Athlete, Hockey Player)
Phoenix Coyotes
6751 N Sunset Blvd Ste E200
Glendale, AZ 85305-3158

Tippett, Dave (Athlete, Coach, Hockey Player)
19468 N Lolst St
Scottsdale, AZ 85255

Tippin, Aaron (Musician, Songwriter)
Tip Top Entertainment
PO Box 41689
Nashville, TN 37204-1689, USA

Tippins, Ken (Athlete, Football Player)
RR 2 Box 173
Adel, GA 31620, USA

Tipton, Analeigh (Actor)
c/o Paul Nelson *Mosaic Media Group*
9200 W Sunset Blvd Ste 10
West Hollywood, CA 90069-3608, USA

Tipton, Daniel (Religious Leader)
Churches of Christ in Christian Union
PO Box 30
Circleville, OH 43113-0030, USA

Tipton, Dave L (Athlete, Football Player)
915 Bonneville Way
Sunnyvale, CA 94087-3038, USA

Tirico, Mike (Sportscaster)
ABC-TV
77 W 66th St
Sports Dept
New York, NY 10023-6201, USA

Tisch, James S (Business Person)
Loews Corp
667 Madison Ave Fl 7
New York, NY 10065-8087, USA

Tisch, Preston R (Business Person, Government Official)
Loews Corp
667 Madison Ave Fl 7
New York, NY 10065-8087, USA

Tisch, Steve (Writer)
1162 Tower Rd
Beverly Hills, CA 90210-2131, USA

Tischinski, Tom (Athlete, Baseball Player)
9905 N Donnelly Ave
Kansas City, MO 64157-7861, USA

Tischiski, Tom (Athlete, Baseball Player)
9905 N Donnelly Ave
Kansas City, MO 64157-7861, USA

Tisdale, Ashley (Actor)
4314 Mariota Ave
Toluca Lake, CA 91602-2912, USA

Tisdale, Jennifer (Actor)
c/o Bill Perlman *Perlman Management Group*
PO Box 2939
Beverly Hills, CA 90213-2939, USA

Titanic, Morris (Athlete, Hockey Player)
120 Cambrook Row
Buffalo, NY 14221-5228

Titensor, Glen (Athlete, Football Player)
729 Montrose Ct
Flower Mound, TX 75022-8000, USA

Tito, Dennis (Astronaut)
1800 Alta Mura Rd
Pacific Palisades, CA 90272-2700, USA

Titone, Jackie (Actor)
c/o Staff Member *William Morris Endeavor (LA)*
9601 Wilshire Blvd
Beverly Hills, CA 90210-5213, USA

Titov, Vladimir
3 Hovanskaya St 8
Moscow, RU 12951

Tittle, Y A (Athlete, Football Player)
1890 N Shoreline Blvd Fl 2
Mountain View, CA 94043-1320, USA

Tittle, Yelberton A (Y A) (Athlete, Football Player)
2500 E Camino Real
Palo Alto, CA 94306, USA

Titus, Christopher (Comedian, Television Host)
c/o Jeff Abraham *Jonas Public Relations*
240 26th St Ste 3
Santa Monica, CA 90402-2542, USA

Tixby, Dexter (Musician)
David Harris Enterprises
24210 E East Fork Rd Spc 9
Azusa, CA 91702-6249, USA

Tiziani, Mario (Athlete, Golfer)
c/o Jim Lehrman *SFX Golf*
36855 W Main St Ste 200
Purcellville, VA 20132-3561, USA

Tizon, Albert (Journalist)
Seattle Times
1000 Denny Way # 5
Editorial Dept
Seattle, WA 98109-5340, USA

Tizzio, Thomas R Sr (Business Person)
American Int'l Group
70 Pine St
New York, NY 10270-0001, USA

Tkachuk, Keith (Athlete, Hockey Player, Olympic Athlete)
Pro-Athletes Management
2 Center Plz Ste 420
Boston, MA 02108-1929, USA

Tkaczuk, Ivan (Religious Leader)
Ukrainian Orthodox Church
3 Davenport Ave Apt 2A
New Rochelle, NY 10805-3438, USA

T. King, Peter (Congressman, Politician)
339 Cannon Hob
Washington, DC 20515-3003, USA

TLC (Music Group)
c/o Staff Member *Creative Artists Agency (CAA-LA)*
2000 Avenue of the Stars Ste 100
Los Angeles, CA 90067-4705, USA

T. McCaul, Michael (Congressman, Politician)
131 Cannon Hob
Washington, DC 20515-2501, USA

TNA Wrestling (Wrestler)
c/o Staff Member *Paradigm (Monterey)*
404 W Franklin St
Monterey, CA 93940-2303, USA

To, Tony (Director, Producer)
c/o Staff Member *Walt Disney Co, The (Buena Vista Motion Picture Group)*
500 S Buena Vista St
Burbank, CA 91521-0007

Toback, James (Director)
c/o Jeff Berg *Resolution (LA)*
1801 Century Park E Ste 2300
Los Angeles, CA 90067-2325, USA

Tobeck, Robbie (Athlete, Football Player)
2018 Newport Way NW
Issaquah, WA 98027-5392, USA

Tobey, James (Actor)
Paradigm Agency
10100 Santa Monica Blvd Ste 2500
Los Angeles, CA 90067-4116, USA

Tobias, Andrew (Business Person, Writer)
146 Central Park W
New York, NY 10023-6297, USA

Tobias, Randall L (Business Person)
Eli Lilly Co
Lilly Corporate Center
Indianapolis, IN 46285-0001, USA

Tobias, Stephen C (Business Person)
Norfolk Southern Corp
3 Commercial Pl Ste 1A
Norfolk, VA 23510-2108, USA

Tobik, Dave (Athlete, Baseball Player)
848 Chancellor Heights Dr
Ballwin, MO 63011-3580, USA

Tobin, Don (Cartoonist)
12312 Ranchwood Rd
Santa Ana, CA 92705-3349, USA

Tobin, Vince (Athlete, Coach, Football Coach, Football Player)
15997 W Monterey Way
Goodyear, AZ 85395-8054, USA

Tobolowsky, Stephen (Actor, Director, Writer)
c/o Steven Levy *Framework Entertainment (LA)*
9057 Nemo St Ste C
West Hollywood, CA 90069-5511, USA

Toburen, Nelson (Athlete, Football Player)
1007 Village Dr
Pittsburg, KS 66762-3552, USA

Tobymac (Musician)
c/o Staff Member *True Artist Management*
227 3rd Ave N
Franklin, TN 37064-2504, USa

Toca, Jorge (Athlete, Baseball Player)
7940 NW 167th Ter
Miami Lakes, FL 33016-3424, USA

Tocchet, Rick (Athlete, Hockey Player)
PO Box 13563
Pittsburgh, PA 15243-0563, USA

Todd, Anne E (Actor)
2419 Oregon St
Berkeley, CA 94705-1113, USA

Todd, Hallie (Actor)
Ann Morgan Guilbert
550 Erskine Dr
Pacific Palisades, CA 90272-4247, USA

Todd, Jackson (Athlete, Baseball Player)
8958 E 76th St
Tulsa, OK 74133-4406, USA

Todd, James R (Jim) (Athlete, Baseball Player)
21639 Hill Gail Way
Parker, CO 80138-7249, USA

Todd, Josh (Musician)
The Firm
9100 Wilshire Blvd Ste 100W
Beverly Hills, CA 90212-3435, USA

Todd, Kendra (Business Person, Reality Star)
C/O Eric Hanson
423 W 55th St Fl 2
New York, NY 10019-4460, USA

Todd, Kevin (Athlete, Hockey Player)
15 Narla Ln
Utica, NY 13501-5560

Todd, Rachel (Actor)
6310 San Vicente Blvd Ste 520
Los Angeles, CA 90048-5421, USA

Todd, Richard (Football Player)
New York Jets
PO Box 471
Sheffield, AL 35660-0471, USA

Todd, Tony (Actor)
c/o Jeff Goldberg *Jeff Goldberg Management*
817 Monte Leon Dr
Beverly Hills, CA 90210-2629, USA

Todd, Trisha (Actor)
c/o Staff Member *Henry Downey Talent Management*
4045 Vineland Ave PH 538
Studio City, CA 91604-4481, USA

Todd, Virgil H (Religious Leader)
Memphis Theological
168 E Parkway S
Memphis, TN 38104-4340, USA

Todman, Jordan (Athlete, Football Player)
c/o David Dunn *Athletes First, LLC*
23091 Mill Creek Dr
Laguna Hills, CA 92653-1258, USA

Toews, Jeffrey M (Jeff) (Athlete, Football Player)
11924 Silver Oak Dr
Davie, FL 33330-1911, USA

Toews, Jonathan (Athlete, Hockey Player)
c/o Pat Brisson *Creative Artists Agency (CAA-LA)*
2000 Avenue of the Stars Ste 100
Los Angeles, CA 90067-4705, USA

Toews, Loren (Athlete, Football Player)
165 Hawthorne Ave
Los Altos, CA 94022-3704, USA

Tofani, Loretta A (Journalist)
Philadelphia Inquirer
400 N Broad St
Editorial Dept
Philadelphia, PA 19130-4099, USA

Toffler, Alvin (Writer)
Randon House
1745 Broadway # B1
New York, NY 10019-4640, USA

Toft, Rod (Bowler)
1120 Oryan Trl N
Stillwater, MN 55082-1887, USA

Tognoni, Gina (Actor)
c/o Marnie Sparer *Innovative Artists (LA)*
1505 10th St
Santa Monica, CA 90401-2805, USA

Togo, Jonathan (Actor)
c/o Cynthia Shelton-Droke *Sweet Mud Group*
648 Broadway # 1002
New York, NY 10012-2348, USA

Togunde, Victor (Actor)
c/o Staff Member *GVA Talent Agency Inc*
8981 W Sunset Blvd Ste 101
West Hollywood, CA 90069-1850, USA

Toilolo, Levine (Athlete, Football Player)
c/o Frank Bauer *Sun West Sports*
7883 N Pershing Ave
Stockton, CA 95207-1749, USA

Tolan, Robert (Bobby) (Athlete, Baseball Player)
2213 Signal Hill Dr
Pearland, TX 77584-1672, USA

Tolar, Kevin (Athlete, Baseball Player)
6412 Lake Joanna Cir
Panama City, FL 32404-3401, USA

Tolbert, Berlinda (Actor)
c/o Staff Member *Pallas Management*
5301 Bellaire Ave
Valley Village, CA 91607-2329, US

Tolbert, Jim (Athlete, Football Player)
2435 Corinna Ct
San Diego, CA 92105-5303, USA

Tolbert, Ray (Athlete, Basketball Player)
12890 Freedom Dr
Fishers, IN 46037-5967, USA

Tolbert, Tom (Athlete, Basketball Player)
368 Creedon Cir
Alameda, CA 94502-7793, USA

Tolbert, Tony L (Athlete, Football Player)
475 S White Chapel Blvd
Southlake, TX 76092-7314, USA

Toldeo, Esteban (Golfer)
135 Spring Vly
Irvine, CA 92602-0919, USA

Tolentino, Jose (Athlete, Baseball Player)
26711 Caceres Cir
Mission Viejo, CA 92691-5503, USA

Toler, Greg (Athlete, Football Player)
c/o Hadley Engelhard *Enter-Sports Management*
5 Concourse Pkwy Ste 3000
Atlanta, GA 30328-7106, USA

Toler, Ken (Athlete, Football Player)
2064 Brecon Dr
Jackson, MS 39211-5838, USA

Toles, Alvin (Athlete, Football Player)
106 Todd Creek Pl
Forsyth, GA 31029, USA

Toles, Ted (Athlete, Baseball Player)
822 Braceville Robinson Rd SW
Newton Falls, OH 44444-9529, USA

Tolins, Jonathan (Writer)
c/o Cori Wellins *William Morris Endeavor (LA)*
9601 Wilshire Blvd
Beverly Hills, CA 90210-5213, USA

Toliver, Freddie (Athlete, Baseball Player)
674 Medical Center Dr
San Bernardino, CA 92411-2520, USA

Toliver, Jerry (Mad Man) (Race Car Driver)
7402 Mountjoy Dr Ste A
Huntington Beach, CA 92648-1238, USA

Tolkan, James (Actor)
Paradigm Agency
10100 Santa Monica Blvd Ste 2500
Los Angeles, CA 90067-4116, USA

Tollberg, Brian (Athlete, Baseball Player)
2104 39th St W
Bradenton, FL 34205-1334, USA

Tollefsen, Ole-Kristian (Athlete, Hockey Player)
250 Daniel Burnham Sq Unit 702
Columbus, OH 43215-2697, USA

Tolles, Tommy (Golfer)
c/o Staff Member *Pro Golfers Association (PGA) Tour*
112 Tpc Blvd
Ponte Vedra Beach, FL 32082, USA

Tolleson, Steve (Athlete, Baseball Player)
313 Mossycup Oak Ct
Spartanburg, SC 29306-6627, USA

Tolleson, Wayne (Athlete, Baseball Player)
313 Mossycup Oak Ct
Spartanburg, SC 29306-6627, USA

Tollin, Michael (Director, Producer, Writer)
c/o Staff Member *Tollin/Robbins Management*
4130 Cahuenga Blvd Ste 305
Toluca Lake, CA 91602-2847, USA

Tolliver, Billy Joe (Athlete, Football Player)
9837 Neesonwood Dr
Shreveport, LA 71106-7738, USA

Tolman, Allison (Actor)
c/o Naomi Odenkirk *Odenkirk Provissiero Entertainment*
1936 N Bronson Ave
Raleigh Studios
Los Angeles, CA 90068-5602, USA

Tolman, Tim (Athlete, Baseball Player)
11425 N Ingot Loop
Tucson, AZ 85737-9450, USA

Tolsky, Susan (Actor)
10815 Acama St
North Hollywood, CA 91602-3204, USA

Tolson, Billy
2710 N Stemmons Fwy Ste 700
Dallas, TX 75207-2208

Tolson, Byron (Athlete, Basketball Player)
4012 N Orchard St
Tacoma, WA 98407-4215, USA

Tolzien, Scott (Athlete, Football Player)
c/o Joe Panos *Athletes First, LLC*
23091 Mill Creek Dr
Laguna Hills, CA 92653-1258, USA

Tom, Braatz (Athlete, Football Player)
3131 NE 55th Ct
Fort Lauderdale, FL 33308-3428, USA

Tom, David
3033 Vista Crest Dr
Los Angeles, CA 90068-1824

Tom, Dimmick (Athlete, Football Player)
204 Broadmoor Blvd
Lafayette, LA 70503-5114, USA

Tom, Duniven (Athlete, Football Player)
503 Seis Lagos Trl
Wylie, TX 75098-8228, USA

Tom, Heather (Actor)
c/o Staff Member *Michael Einfeld Management*
10630 Moorpark St Unit 101
North Hollywood, CA 91602-2797, USA

Tom, Kiana (Actor, Fitness Expert)
KT Productions
555 N El Camino Real Ste A401
San Clemente, CA 92672-6740, USA

Tom, Lauren (Actor)
c/o Kelly Garner *Pop Art Management*
PO Box 55363
Sherman Oaks, CA 91413-0363, USA

Tom, Logan (Athlete, Olympic Athlete, Volleyball Player)
2001 E 21st St Unit 136
Signal Hill, CA 90755-5960, USA

Tom, Nicholle (Actor)
c/o Michael Einfeld *Michael Einfeld Management*
10630 Moorpark St Unit 101
North Hollywood, CA 91602-2797, USA

Tom, Nicolle
3033 Vista Crest Dr
Los Angeles, CA 90068-1824

Toma, David (Writer)
PO Box 854
Clark, NJ 07066-0854, USA

Tomaini, Amadeo (Athlete, Football Player)
3750 Oakhill Dr
Titusville, FL 32780-3521, USA

Tomaino, Jamie (The Jet) (Race Car Driver)
Impact Motorsports
6610 Hudspeth
Harrisburg, NC 28075, USA

Tomanek, Dick (Athlete, Baseball Player)
165 Duff Dr
Avon Lake, OH 44012-1234, USA

Tomanovich, Dara
8016 Willow Glen Rd
Los Angeles, CA 90046-1617

Tomas, Hildi Santo (Actor, Television Host)
2768 Broughton Ln SE
Atlanta, GA 30339-4196, USA

Tomasetti, Louis (Athlete, Football Player)
100 Powell St
Old Forge, PA 18518-1728, USA

Tomasik, Kathleen (Director)
c/o David Krintzman *Morris Yorn Barnes Levine Krintzman Rubenstein Kohner & Gellman*
2000 Avenue of the Stars Ste 300N
3rd Floor, North Tower
Los Angeles, CA 90067-4704, USA

Tomasina Keough, Jeana (Reality Star)
c/o Patrick Hughes *Intellectual Artists Management*
22817 Ventura Blvd # 471
Woodland Hills, CA 91364-1202, USA

Tomberlin, Andy (Athlete, Baseball Player)
7411 Crooked Creek Church Rd
Monroe, NC 28110-8283, USA

Tomberlin, Pat (Athlete, Football Player)
891 Arthur Moore Dr
Green Cove Springs, FL 32043-9510, USA

Tomblin, Earl Ray (Governor)
State Capitol Bldg
Charleston, WV 25305, USA

Tombs, Tina (Golfer)
1916 E Medlock Dr
Phoenix, AZ 85016-4127, USA

Tomczak, Mike (Athlete, Football Player)
400 Broad St Ste 106
Sewickley, PA 15143-1500, USA

Tomei, Concetta (Actor)
765 Linda Flora Dr
Los Angeles, CA 90049-1626, USA

Tomel, Marisa (Actor)
Three Arts Entertainment
9460 Wilshire Blvd Ste 700
Beverly Hills, CA 90212-2713, USA

Tomey, Dick (Coach, Football Coach)
San Francisco 49ers
4949 Centennial Blvd
Santa Clara, CA 95054-1254, USA

Tomfohrde, Heinn F (Business Person)
GAF Corp
1361 Alps Rd
Wayne, NJ 07470-3687, USA

Tomich, Jared (Athlete, Football Player)
2222 Red River Dr
Schererville, IN 46375-4492, USA

Tomita, Tamlyn (Actor)
c/o Nancy Moon-Broadstreet Geddes
Agency, The
1203 Greenacre Ave
West Hollywood, CA 90046-5707, USA

Tomjanovich, Rudolph (Rudy) (Athlete,
Basketball Player, Coach)
19 West Ln
Houston, TX 77019-1007, USA

Tom Jr, Layne (Actor)
3838 Humboldt Dr
Huntington Beach, CA 92649-2156, USA

Tomkins, Calvin (Writer)
c/o Staff Member Henry Holt & Company
175 5th Ave Ste 400
New York, NY 10010-7726, USA

Tomko, Brett (Athlete, Baseball Player)
14008 Lake Poway Rd
Poway, CA 92064-1421, USA

Tomlin, Chris (Musician)
c/o Shelley Giglio Six Steps Records
PO Box 14145
Atlanta, GA 30324-1145, USA

Tomlin, Dave (Athlete, Baseball Player)
2020 Clayton Pike
Manchester, OH 45144-9429, USA

Tomlin, Lily (Actor, Comedian)
c/o Jennifer Allen Viewpoint Inc (LA)
8820 Wilshire Blvd Ste 220
Beverly Hills, CA 90211-2622, USA

Tomlin, Mike (Athlete, Football Coach,
Football Player)
1224 Shady Ave
Pittsburgh, PA 15232-2812, USA

Tomlin, Randy (Athlete, Baseball Player)
153 Ridgeview Ln
Madison Heights, VA 24572-6037, USA

Tomlinson, LaDainian (Athlete, Football
Player)
c/o Tom Condon CAA (St. Louis)
222 S Central Ave Ste 1008
Saint Louis, MO 63105-3509, USA

Tommy Tutone (Music Group, Musician)
c/o Jake Hooker Hook Entertainment
26033 Mulholland Hwy
Calabasas, CA 91302-1946, USA

Tompkins, Allie (Baseball Player)
Pittsburgh Crawfords
931 1/2 Clarissa St
Pittsburgh, PA 15219-5770, USA

Tompkins, Angel (Actor)
Hurkos
11935 Kling St Apt 10
Valley Village, CA 91607-5406, USA

Tompkins, Barry (Sportscaster)
100 South St Apt 105
Sausalito, CA 94965-2502, USA

Tompkins, Dariene (Actor)
15413 Hall Rd # 230
Macomb, MI 48044-3840, USA

Tompkins, Paul F (Writer)
3018 Gracia St
Los Angeles, CA 90039-2306, USA

Tompkins, Ron (Athlete, Baseball Player)
25072 Leucadia St Unit G
Laguna Niguel, CA 92677-7598, USA

Tompkins, Susie (Designer, Fashion
Designer)
2500 Steiner St PH
San Francisco, CA 94115-1100, USA

Toms, David (Golfer)
6606 Gilbert Dr
Shreveport, LA 71106-2300, USA

Toms, Tommy (Athlete, Baseball Player)
126 Leadbetter Rd
Wayne, ME 04284-3144, USA

Tom Scholz (Music Group, Musician)
c/o Gail Parenteau Parenteau Guidance
132 E 35th St # 3J
New York, NY 10016-3892, USA

Tomsco, George (Musician)
Fireballs Entertainment
1224 Cottonwood St
Raton, NM 87740-3513, USA

Tomsic, Dubravka (Musician)
Trawick Artists
1926 Broadway
New York, NY 10023-6915, USA

Tomsic, Ronald (Athlete, Basketball
Player, Olympic Athlete)
22 Twilight Blf
Newport Coast, CA 92657-2126, USA

Toneff, Robert (Bob) (Athlete, Football
Player)
18 Dutch Valley Ln
San Anselmo, CA 94960-1016, USA

Tonelli, John (Athlete, Hockey Player)
4 Vincent Ln
Armonk, NY 10504-1245

Tone Loc (Musician)
c/o Bobby Bessone Entertainment Artists
2409 21st Ave S Ste 100
Nashville, TN 37212-5317, USA

Toner, Mike (Journalist)
Atlanta Journal-Constitution
72 Marietta St NW
Editorial Dept
Atlanta, GA 30303-2804, USA

Toner Jr, Ed (Athlete, Football Player)
12 Preston Ct
Swampscott, MA 01907-1650, USA

Toner Sr, Ed (Athlete, Football Player)
225 Ocean St
Lynn, MA 01902-3269, USA

Toney, Andrew (Athlete, Basketball
Player)
1044 Villa Rica Ct Apt A
Birmingham, AL 35215-6854, USA

Toney, Sedric (Athlete, Basketball Player)
3831 Sweetwater Dr
Brecksville, OH 44141-4102, USA

Tong, Jian (Figure Skater)
c/o Staff Member Champions on Ice
3500 American Blvd W Ste 190
Minneapolis, MN 55431-4431, USA

Tong, Pete (DJ, Musician)
c/o Joel Zimmerman William Morris
Endeavor (NY)
1325 Avenue of the Americas
New York, NY 10019-6026, USA

Tong, Stanley (Director)
c/o Ramses Ishak United Talent Agency
(UTA-LA)
9336 Civic Center Dr
Beverly Hills, CA 90210-3604, USA

Tongue, Marco (Athlete, Football Player)
8051 Winding Wood Rd
Glen Burnie, MD 21061-5020, USA

Tonic (Music Group)
Tonic Tonic
652 N Doheny Dr
West Hollywood, CA 90069-5526

Tonis, Mike (Athlete, Baseball Player)
9231 Bella Vista Pl
Elk Grove, CA 95624-2152, USA

Tonko, Paul (Congressman, Politician)
422 Cannon Hob
Washington, DC 20515-3303, USA

Tonkovich, Andy (Athlete, Basketball
Player)
2400 Forest Dr Apt 210
Inverness, FL 34453-3705, USA

Too, Slim (Musician)
New Frontier Mgmt
1921 Broadway
Nashville, TN 37203-2719, USA

Tookey, Tim (Athlete, Hockey Player)
21008 W Ridge Rd
Buckeye, AZ 85396-1590

Tool (Music Group)
Tool Dissectional
2311 W Empire Ave
Burbank, CA 91504-3318, USA

Toolson, Andy (Athlete, Basketball Player)
722 Ranch Cir
Alpine, UT 84004-1971, USA

Toomay, John (Athlete, Basketball Player)
7103 Primrose Way
Carlsbad, CA 92011-4834, USA

Toomay, Pat (Athlete, Football Player)
5603 Guadalupe Trl NW
Albuquerque, NM 87107-5423, USA

Toomer, Amani (Athlete, Football Player)
25 Regency Pl
Weehawken, NJ 07086-6600, USA

Toomey, Bill (Athlete, Decathlon Athlete,
Olympic Athlete)
240 Pelton Ln
Incline Village, NV 89451-9304, USA

Toomey, Sean (Athlete, Hockey Player)
1741 Saunders Ave
Saint Paul, MN 55116-2432

Toomey, Toomey (Cartoonist, Writer)
Andrews & McMeel
4520 Main St Ste 340
Kansas City, MO 64111-7705, USA

Toon, Al (Athlete, Football Player)
4915 Champions Run
Middleton, WI 53562-4078, USA

Toon, Nick (Athlete, Football Player)
c/o Jeff Sperbeck The Novo Agency
3201 Danville Blvd Ste 295
Alamo, CA 94507-1978, USA

Tootoo, Jardin (Athlete, Hockey Player)
2600 Hillsboro Pike Apt 359
Nashville, TN 37212-5666

Toots & The Maytals (Music Group)
c/o Staff Member William Morris
Endeavor (NY)
1325 Avenue of the Americas
New York, NY 10019-6026, USA

Top, Carrot (Actor, Comedian)
11 Isle of Sicily
Winter Park, FL 32789-1505, USA

Topor, Ted (Athlete, Football Player)
2840 Condit St
Highland, IN 46322-1605, USA

Toporowski, Shayne (Athlete, Hockey
Player)
26 Creston St
Worcester, MA 01604-2814

Topp, Robert (Athlete, Football Player)
2580 Lakeshore Dr
Fennville, MI 49408-9622, USA

Topper, John (Musician)
Monterey Peninsula Artists
509 Hartnell St
Monterey, CA 93940-2825, USA

Toppin, Rupe (Athlete, Baseball Player)
PO Box 25724
Miami, FL 33102-5724, USA

Topping, Marshall (Race Car Driver)
2950 Randolph Ave
Costa Mesa, CA 92626-4312, USA

Toradze, Alexander (Musician)
Columbia Artists Mgmt Inc
165 W 57th St
New York, NY 10019-2201, USA

Torborg, Jeff (Athlete, Baseball Player,
Coach)
47 Railroad Ave
Manahawkin, NJ 08050-3932, USA

Torcato, Tony (Athlete, Baseball Player)
798 SE Miller Ave
Dallas, OR 97338-2637, USA

Torchett, John (Athlete, Hockey Player)
14 Crows Nest Ln
Marshfield, MA 02050-3161

Torchetti, John (Athlete, Hockey Player)
Houston Aeros
317 Washington St
Saint Paul, MN 55102-1609

Torczon, Laverne J (Athlete, Football Player)
6472 Country Club Dr
Columbus, NE 68601-8338, USA

Toregas, Wyatt (Athlete, Baseball Player)
1461 Brown St
Akron, OH 44301-2302, USA

Torgeson, Lavern (Athlete, Football Player)
17672 Gainsford Ln
Huntington Beach, CA 92649-4723, USA

Tork, Peter (Musician)
614 Wormwood Hill Rd
Mansfield Center, CT 06250-1040, USA

Torkelson, Eric (Athlete, Football Player)
1196 Pleasant Valley Dr
Oneida, WI 54155-8634, USA

Torkildsen, Justin
7800 Beverly Blvd # 3371
Los Angeles, CA 90036-2112

Torme, Daisy (Actor)
c/o Steven Neibert *Imperium 7 Talent Agency*
5455 Wilshire Blvd Ste 1706
Los Angeles, CA 90036-4217, USA

Torme, Steve March (Actor, Musician)
c/o Mark Lourie *Skyline Music*
28 Union St
Whitefield, NH 03598-3503, USA

Tormohlen, Gene (Athlete, Basketball Player)
2248 Walker Dr
Lawrenceville, GA 30043-2472, USA

Torn, Rip (Actor)
c/o Alan Somers *Somers Mauldin The Rose Group*
1925 Century Park E Ste 2320
Los Angeles, CA 90067-2724, USA

Torok, Mitchell (Musician)
5100 Weaver Rd Apt 702
Lake Charles, LA 70605-6060, USA

Torre, Joe (Athlete, Baseball Player, Coach)
c/o Maury Gostfrand *Vision Sports Group*
675 Thrd Ave
Suite 2500
New York, NY 10017, USA

Torre, Steve (Horse Racer)
240 Court Pi Apt B
Brick, NJ 08723, USA

Torrealba, Yorvit (Athlete, Baseball Player)
3801 S Ocean Dr Apt 15F
Hollywood, FL 33019-2901, USA

Torrence, Gwendolyn (Gwen) (Athlete, Track Athlete)
Gold Medal Mgmt
1750 14th St
Boulder, CO 80302-6332, USA

Torres, Dara (Athlete, Olympic Athlete, Swimmer)
c/o Staff Member *Premier Management Group (PMG Sports)*
115 Crescent Commons Dr Ste 250
Cary, NC 27518-8134, USA

Torres, Dayanara (Actor, Model)
c/o Sheila Legette *Media Artists Group (LA)*
8222 Melrose Ave Ste 203
Los Angeles, CA 90046-6838, USA

Torres, Diego (Actor)
c/o Jon Simmons *Simmons & Scott Entertainment*
7942 Mulholland Dr
Los Angeles, CA 90046-1225, USA

Torres, Felix (Athlete, Baseball Player)
HC 1 Box 6424
Santa Isabel, PR 00757-9777, USA

Torres, Gina (Actor)
c/o Christopher Barrett *Metropolitan (MTA)*
4526 Wilshire Blvd
Los Angeles, CA 90010-3801, USA

Torres, Harold (Musician)
Brothers Mgmt
141 Dunbar Ave
Fords, NJ 08863-1551, USA

Torres, Hector (Athlete, Baseball Player)
662 Lexington St
Dunedin, FL 34698-8405, USA

Torres, Jacques (Chef, Television Host)
c/o Staff Member *Food Network, The*
1180 Avenue of the Americas Fl 11
New York, NY 10036-8401, USA

Torres, Jose (Boxer)
364B Greenwich St
#B
New York, NY 10013, USA

Torres, Oscar (Athlete, Basketball Player)
c/o Michael Esola *William Morris Endeavor (LA)*
9601 Wilshire Blvd
Beverly Hills, CA 90210-5213, USA

Torres, Rusty (Athlete, Baseball Player)
250 N Cedar St
Massapequa, NY 11758-2822, USA

Torres, Salomon (Athlete, Baseball Player)
101 Crimson Dr
Pittsburgh, PA 15237-1069, USA

Torres, Tia Maria (Reality Star)
Villalobos Rescue Center
PO Box 1544
Canyon Country, CA 91386-1544, USA

Torres, Tico (Musician)
Bon Jovi Mgmt
248 W 17th St Apt 501
New York, NY 10011-5330, USA

Torres, Tommy (Musician)
c/o Staff Member *Sony Music Miami*
605 Lincoln Rd Ste 700
Miami Beach, FL 33139-2901, USA

Torretta, Gino (Athlete, Football Player, Heisman Trophy Winner)
7830 SW 48th Ct
Miami, FL 33143-6131, USA

Torrey, Rich (Cartoonist)
c/o Staff Member *King Features Syndication*
300 W 57th St Fl 15
New York, NY 10019-5238, USA

Torrez, Mike (Athlete, Baseball Player)
1015 Frances Ct
Naperville, IL 60563-3370, USA

Torricelli, Robert (Politician)
PO Box 229
Rosemont, NJ 08556-0229, USA

Torriero, Talan (Actor)
c/o Scott Karp *The Syndicate*
10203 Santa Monica Blvd Fl 5
Los Angeles, CA 90067-6416, USA

Torrini, Emiliana (Musician)
c/o Staff Member *Paradigm (Monterey)*
404 W Franklin St
Monterey, CA 93940-2303, USA

Torry, Guy (Actor, Comedian)
c/o Janean Glover *Screen Partners*
9663 Santa Monica Blvd # 639
Beverly Hills, CA 90210-4303, USA

Torry, Joe (Comedian)
c/o Staff Member *William Morris Endeavor (LA)*
9601 Wilshire Blvd Ste 700
Beverly Hills, CA 90210-5211, USA

Torti, Robert (Actor)
388 Rushing Creek Ct
Henderson, NV 89014-4518, USA

Tortorella, John (Athlete, Coach, Hockey Player)
108 3rd Avenue St Pete
Saint Petersburg, FL 33706, USA

Tortorella, Nico (Actor)
c/o Brian Wilkins *Kritzer Levine Wilkins Entertainment (KLWG)*
11872 La Grange Ave Fl 1
Los Angeles, CA 90025-5283, USA

Torv, Anna
c/o Christine Tripicchio *Shelter PR*
9350 Wilshire Blvd Ste 450
Beverly Hills, CA 90212-3230, USA

Torvaids, Linus (Designer)
Transmeta Corp
3990 Freedom Cir
Santa Clara, CA 95054-1204, USA

Torve, Kelvin (Athlete, Baseball Player)
18701 Hammock Ln
Davidson, NC 28036-8836, USA

Tosca, Carlos (Athlete, Baseball Player, Coach)
PO Box 3623
Brandon, FL 33509-3623, USA

Toscano, Andrew (Horse Racer)
PO Box 34
Verbank, NY 12585-0034, USA

Toscano, Harry (Golfer)
3209 Mercer Rd
New Castle, PA 16105-5311, USA

Toscano, Linda (Horse Racer)
49 Euretta Ave
Freehold, NJ 07728-2631, USA

Toscano, Pia (Musician)
c/o Mark DiDia *Red Light Management (LA)*
8439 W Sunset Blvd Ste 2
West Hollywood, CA 90069-1925, USA

Tosh, Daniel (Actor, Comedian)
c/o Christie Smith *Mosaic Media Group*
9200 W Sunset Blvd Ste 10
West Hollywood, CA 90069-3608, USA

Toski, Bob (Golfer)
20914 Hamaca Ct
Boca Raton, FL 33433-2716, USA

Totenberg, Nina (Correspondent)
National Public Radio
News Dept
615 Main Ave NW
Washington, DC 20024, USA

Toth, Tom (Athlete, Football Player)
13723 Lindsay Dr
Orland Park, IL 60462-7011, USA

Toth, Zollie (Athlete, Football Player)
1612 Hideaway Ct
Baton Rouge, LA 70806-7674, USA

Totmianina, Tatyana (Figure Skater)
c/o Staff Member *Champions on Ice*
3500 American Blvd W Ste 190
Minneapolis, MN 55431-4431, USA

Totten, Robert (Director)
PO Box 7180
Big Bear Lake, CA 92315-7180, USA

Totter, Audrey (Actor)
Motion Picture Country Home
23388 Mulholland Dr
Woodland Hills, CA 91364-2792, USA

Toub, Shaun (Actor)
818 N Doheny Dr Apt 605
West Hollywood, CA 90069-4858, USA

Tountas, Pete (Bowler)
10100 N Calle Del Camero
Tucson, AZ 85737, USA

Toussaint, Beth (Actor)
c/o Staff Member *Don Buchwald & Associates (LA)*
6500 Wilshire Blvd Ste 2200
Los Angeles, CA 90048-4942, USA

Toussaint, Lorraine (Actor)
c/o Jonathan Howard *Innovative Artists (LA)*
1505 10th St
Santa Monica, CA 90401-2805, USA

Tovar, Lupita
1527 N Tigertail Rd
Los Angeles, CA 90049-1430

Tovar, Steven E (Steve) (Athlete, Football Player)
1026 Brower Rd
Lima, OH 45801-2316, USA

Tovoli, Luciano (Cinematographer)
United Talent Agency
9336 Civic Center Dr
Beverly Hills, CA 90210-3604, USA

Towe, Monte (Athlete, Basketball Player, Coach)
2125 Gold Valley Dr
Murfreesboro, TN 37130-8423, USA

Tower, Keith (Athlete, Basketball Player)
12530 Aldershot Ln
Windermere, FL 34786-6610, USA

Tower, Rob (Race Car Driver)
TBE Inc
33 Patton St
Fitchburg, MA 01420-7218, USA

Towers, Constance (Actor)
c/o Staff Member *Stone Manners Salners Agency (LA)*
6100 Wilshire Blvd Ste 1500
Los Angeles, CA 90048-5110, USA

Towers, Josh (Athlete, Baseball Player)
1033 Crescent Falls St
Henderson, NV 89011-2506, USA

Towers, Kevin (Baseball Player)
5580 La Jolla Blvd
La Jolla, CA 92037-7651, USA

Towery, Blackie (Athlete, Basketball Player)
943 Youth Camp Rd
Marion, KY 42064-6569, USA

Towle, Stephen R (Steve) (Athlete, Football Player)
609 NE Lake Pointe Dr
Lees Summit, MO 64064-1193, USA

Towles, J R (Athlete, Baseball Player)
13806 Lowell Ave
Tomball, TX 77377-7218, USA

Towles, Tom (Actor)
c/o Craig Dorfman *Frontline Management*
5670 Wilshire Blvd Ste 1370
Los Angeles, CA 90036-5679, USA

Towne, Katharine (Actor)
United Talent Agency
9336 Civic Center Dr
Beverly Hills, CA 90210-3604, USA

Towne, Robert (Writer)
1417 San Remo Dr
Pacific Palisades, CA 90272, USA

Towner, Ralph N (Musician)
Ted Kurtland
173 Brighton Ave
Allston, MA 02134-2003, USA

Townes, Linton (Athlete, Basketball Player)
PO Box 254
Luray, VA 22835-0254, USA

Townes, Willie (Athlete, Football Player)
5714 Logancraft Dr
Dallas, TX 75227-2847, USA

Towns, Bobby (Athlete, Football Player)
1351 Jennings Mill Rd Unit A
Watkinsville, GA 30677-7237, USA

Towns, Edolphus (Congressman, Politician)
2232 Rayburn Hob
Washington, DC 20515-3210, USA

Towns, Morris (Athlete, Football Player)
7102 Rustling Oaks Dr
Richmond, TX 77469-7338, USA

Townsell, Jo Jo (Athlete, Football Player)
PO Box 606
Gardnerville, NV 89410-0606, USA

Townsend, Andre (Athlete, Football Player)
6206 Providence Club Dr
Mableton, GA 30126-3697, USA

Townsend, Colleen (Actor)
645 E Champlain Dr Apt 150
Fresno, CA 93730-1295, USA

Townsend, Raymond (Athlete, Basketball Player)
5160 Caibari Knls
Anchorage, CA 99513, USA

Townsend, Robert (Actor, Director, Producer, Writer)
c/o Jeff Witjas *Agency for the Performing Arts (APA-LA)*
405 S Beverly Dr Ste 500
Beverly Hills, CA 90212-4425, USA

Townsend, Roscoe (Religious Leader)
Evangelical Friends
2018 W Maple St
Wichita, KS 67213-3314, USA

Townsend, Stuart (Actor)
c/o Vanessa Pereira *Artists Independent Management (LA)*
1522 2nd St
Santa Monica, CA 90401-2303, USA

Townsend, Tammy (Actor)
c/o Marni Goldman *Abrams Artists Agency (LA)*
9200 W Sunset Blvd PH 11
West Hollywood, CA 90069-3601, USA

Townsend, Wade (Athlete, Baseball Player)
Columbus Catfish
PO Box 2744
Columbus, GA 31902-2744, USA

Townshend, Graeme (Athlete, Hockey Player)
PO Box 1231
Saco, ME 04072-1231, USA

Tozzi, Tahyna (Actor)
c/o Elise Konialian *Untitled Entertainment (NY)*
435 Hudson St Fl 9
New York, NY 10014-3995, USA

T Pain (Musician)
c/o Staff Member *Jive Records*
550 Madison Ave Fl 6
New York, NY 10022-3211, USA

T-Pain (Musician)
c/o Michael Blumstein *Chase Entertainment*
7378 W Atlantic Blvd # 250
Margate, FL 33063-4214, USA

Traa (Musician)
East West America Records
75 Rockefeller Plz
New York, NY 10019-6908, USA

Traber, Billy (Athlete, Baseball Player)
836 Lomita St
El Segundo, CA 90245-2541, USA

Traber, Jim (Athlete, Baseball Player)
1917 Rosebrook
Norman, OK 73072-3104, USA

Trabert, Tony (Actor)
115 Knotty Pine Trl
Ponte Vedra, FL 32082-3024

Tracewski, Dick (Athlete, Baseball Player, Coach)
5 Flora Dr
Peckville, PA 18452-1004, USA

Trachsel, Stephen P (Steve) (Athlete, Baseball Player)
18750 Heritage Dr
Poway, CA 92064-6643, USA

Trachta, Jeff (Actor)
PO Box 124
Skyforest, CA 92385-0124, USA

Trachte, Don (Cartoonist)
c/o Staff Member *King Features Syndication*
300 W 57th St Fl 15
New York, NY 10019-5238, USA

Trachtenberg, Lyle
18619 Collins St Apt F7
Tarzana, CA 91356-2169

Trachtenberg, Michelle (Actor)
c/o Peg Donegan *Framework Entertainment (LA)*
9057 Nemo St Ste C
West Hollywood, CA 90069-5511, USA

Tracy, Andy (Athlete, Baseball Player)
2226 Park Cir
Lewis Center, OH 43035-6052, USA

Tracy, Brian (Business Person, Writer)
Brian Tracy International
462 Stevens Ave Ste 305
Solana Beach, CA 92075-2066, USA

Tracy, Chad (Athlete, Baseball Player)
9422 Sir Huon Ln
Waxhaw, NC 28173-0112, USA

Tracy, James E (Jim) (Athlete, Baseball Player, Coach)
6753 Ross Ln
Mason, OH 45040-4658, USA

Tracy, Jeanie (Musician)
c/o Staff Member *Diva Central Inc*
7510 W Sunset Blvd Ste 1445
Los Angeles, CA 90046-3408, USA

Tracy, Michael C (Dancer, Director)
Pilobolus Dance Theater
PO Box 388
Washington Depot, CT 06794-0388, USA

Tracy, Paul (Race Car Driver)
Hogan Penske Racing
9700 Highridge Dr
Las Vegas, NV 89134-6723, USA

Trafficant, James (Politician)
125 Market St
Youngstown, OH 44503-1780

Trafton, Stephanie Brown (Athlete, Track Athlete)
c/o Staff Member *USA Track & Field*
132 E Washington St Ste 800
Indianapolis, IN 46204-3674, USA

Trager, Milton (Doctor)
Trager Institute
3800 Park East Dr Ste 100
Beachwood, OH 44122-4322, USA

Traill, Phil (Director)
c/o Rosalie Swedlin *Anonymous Content (LA)*
3532 Hayden Ave
Culver City, CA 90232-2413, USA

Train (Music Group)
c/o Jon Lullo *Crush Management*
60-62 E 11th St
7th Floor
New York, NY 10003, USA

Trainor, Jerry (Actor)
c/o Staff Member *Burstein Company, The*
15304 W Sunset Blvd Ste 208
Pacific Palisades, CA 90272-3656, USA

Trainor, Mary Ellen (Actor)
c/o Stephanie Nese *Framework Entertainment (LA)*
9057 Nemo St Ste C
West Hollywood, CA 90069-5511, USA

Trainor, Meghan (Musician)
c/o Staff Member *Epic Records Group*
550 Madison Ave Fl 6
New York, NY 10022-3211, USA

Trammell, Alan (Athlete, Baseball Player, Coach)
5852 Box Canyon Rd
La Jolla, CA 92037-7405, USA

Trammell, Sam (Actor)
c/o Gene Parseghian *Parseghian Planco LLC*
388 2nd Ave
New York, NY 10010-5616, USA

Trammell, Terry (Doctor)
Orthopedics-Indianapolis
1801 Senate Blvd Ste 200
Indianapolis, IN 46202-1230, USA

Trammell, Thomas (Bubba) (Athlete, Baseball Player)
PO Box 643629
Vero Beach, FL 32964-3629, USA

Tramps, The
102 Ryders Ln
East Brunswick, NJ 08816-1328

Tranelli, Deborah (Actor, Musician)
c/o Staff Member *Image Entertainment*
6320 Canoga Ave Ste 790
Woodland Hills, CA 91367-2561, USA

Trang, Thuy
12651 Olaf Pl
Granada Hills, CA 91344-1052

Traore, Rokia (Actor, Composer)
c/o Staff Member *Concerted Efforts*
PO Box 440326
Somerville, MA 02144-0004, USA

Trapp, John (Athlete, Basketball Player)
1836 Remembrance Hill St
Las Vegas, NV 89144-5420, USA

Trask, Thomas E (Religious Leader)
Assemblies of God
1445 N Boonville Ave
Springfield, MO 65802-1894, USA

Traue, Antje (Actor)
c/o Staff Member *Anthem Entertainment*
9595 Wilshire Blvd Ste 900
Beverly Hills, CA 90212-2509, USA

Trauth, AJ (Actor)
c/o Felicia Sager *Sager Management*
260 S Beverly Dr Ste 205
Beverly Hills, CA 90212-3812, USA

Trautwein, John (Athlete, Baseball Player)
882 Beach Rd
Sanibel, FL 33957-6907, USA

Trautwig, Al (Sportscaster)
ABC-TV
77 W 66th St
Sports Dept
New York, NY 10023-6201, USA

Travanti, Daniel J (Actor)
10866 Wilshire Blvd Fl 10
Los Angeles, CA 90024-4350, USA

Travers, Bill (Athlete, Baseball Player)
10 Shoreline Dr
Foxboro, MA 02035-1115, USA

Travers, Pat (Musician)
ARM
1257 Arcade St
Saint Paul, MN 55106-2022, USA

Travis (Music Group)
c/o Staff Member *MCT Management*
104 W 29th St Rm 1101
New York, NY 10001-5310, USA

Travis, Kylie (Actor, Model)
1196 Summit Dr
Beverly Hills, CA 90210-2248, USA

Travis, Mack (Athlete, Football Player)
605 Holland Ave
Las Vegas, NV 89106-2651, USA

Travis, Nancy (Actor, Producer)
c/o Adena Chawke *Greenlight Management and Production*
9713 Santa Monica Blvd Ste 219
Beverly Hills, CA 90210-4215, USA

Travis, Randy (Musician, Songwriter)
12 Avenida De Rey
Santa Fe, NM 87506-8202, USA

Travis, Stacey (Actor)
c/o Brian Alexander *Essential Talent Management*
6399 Wilshire Blvd Ste 401
Los Angeles, CA 90048-5716, USA

Travolta, Ellen (Actor)
6470 E Sunnyside Rd
Coeur D Alene, ID 83814-9503, USA

Travolta, Joey (Actor)
c/o Staff Member *Stephany Hurkos Management*
11935 Kling St
Valley Village, CA 91607-4072, USA

Travolta, John (Actor)
735 N Bonhill Rd
Los Angeles, CA 90049-2303, USA

Traya, Misti (Actor)
c/o Andrew Edwards *Wishlab*
2225A Hyperion Ave
Los Angeles, CA 90027-4709, USA

Trayham, Jerry (Athlete, Football Player)
6606 S Tomaker Ln
Spokane, WA 99223-6202, USA

Traylor, B Keith (Athlete, Football Player)
1000 Football Dr
Lake Forest, IL 60045, USA

Traylor, Keith (Athlete, Football Player)
11043 S 4317
Chouteau, OK 74337-6063, USA

Traylor, Susan (Actor)
Propaganda Films Mgmt
1741 Ivar Ave
Los Angeles, CA 90028-5105, USA

Traynham, Wade (Athlete, Football Player)
PO Box 176
Wake, VA 23176-0176, USA

Traynor, Jay (Musician)
Jet Music
17 Pauline Ct
Rensselaer, NY 12144-9780, USA

Traynowicz, Mark (Athlete, Football Player)
1668 Sioux St
Lincoln, NE 68502-4737, USA

Treach (Musician)
International Creative Mgmt
10250 Constellation Blvd Fl 1
Los Angeles, CA 90067-6241, USA

Treadaway, John (Athlete, Football Player)
3140 N 83rd Ave
Phoenix, AZ 85033-4724, USA

Treadway, Edward A (Politician)
Elevator Constructors Union
5565 Sterrett Pl
Columbia, MD 21044-2665, USA

Treadway, James C Jr (Government Official)
Laurel Ledge Farm
Croton Lake Road
RR 4
Mount Kisco, NY 10549, USA

Treadway, Jeff (Athlete, Baseball Player)
8812 Estes Rd
Macon, GA 31220-5649, USA

Treadway, Nick (Athlete, Baseball Player)
50 Treasure Island Dr
Troy, MO 63379-2337, USA

Treadway, Ty (Actor)
c/o Frank Gonzales *The Agency (CA)*
3711 Ocean Front Walk # 1
Marina Del Rey, CA 90292-5705, USA

Treadwell, David (Athlete, Football Player)
5445 Dtc Pkey
Suite 800
Englewood, CO 80111, USA

Treanor, Matt (Athlete, Baseball Player)
1440 Coral Ridge Dr
Coral Springs, FL 33071-5433, USA

Treat, Dr Casey (Religious Leader)
Christian Faith Center
33645 20th Ave S
Federal Way, WA 98003-7743, USA

Trebek, Alex (Game Show Host)
10202 Washington Blvd
Culver City, CA 90232-3119, USA

Trebelhorn, Thomas L (Tom) (Athlete, Baseball Player, Coach)
7753 E Montebello Ave
Scottsdale, AZ 85250-6165, USA

Trebi, Dan (Athlete, Hockey Player)
8551 Big Woods Ln
Eden Prairie, MN 55347-5361

Trebunskaya, Anna (Dancer, Reality Star)
c/o Staff Member *ABC Television (LA)*
500 S Buena Vista St
Burbank, CA 91521-0001, USA

Tree, Michael (Musician)
45 E 89th St Apt 12F
New York, NY 10128-1228, USA

Trejo, Danny (Actor)
15226 Lassen St
Mission Hills, CA 91345-3042, USA

Tremblay, Yannick (Athlete, Hockey Player)
9911 Carrington Ln
Alpharetta, GA 30022-8527

Trembley, Dave (Athlete, Baseball Player, Coach)
Baltimore Orioles
3145 S Atlantic Ave Apt 601
Daytona Beach, FL 32118-6273, USA

Tremie, Chris (Athlete, Baseball Player)
484 Marion Ln
New Waverly, TX 77358-4504, USA

Tremko, Anne
10100 Santa Monica Blvd Ste 2500
Los Angeles, CA 90067-4116

Tremont, Ray C (Religious Leader)
Volunteers of America
3939 N Causeway Blvd Ste 400
Metairie, LA 70002-1777, USA

Trenary, Jill (Athlete, Figure Skater, Olympic Athlete)
4115 Stone Manor Hts
Colorado Springs, CO 80906-5799, USA

Trendy, Bobby (Designer)
c/o Darryl Marshak *Marshak/Zachary Company, The*
8840 Wilshire Blvd Fl 1
Beverly Hills, CA 90211-2606, USA

Treniers, The
520 N Camden Dr
Beverly Hills, CA 90210-3202

Trent, Buck (Musician)
Buck Trent Breakfast Theater
118 Hampshire Dr
Branson, MO 65616-3765, USA

Trent, Gary (Athlete, Basketball Player)
1150 Northwood Cir
New Albany, OH 43054-9056, USA

Trenyce (Reality Star)
c/o Staff Member *Diva Central Inc*
7510 W Sunset Blvd Ste 1445
Los Angeles, CA 90046-3408, USA

Trese, Adam (Actor)
c/o Staff Member *Robert Stein Management*
PO Box 3797
Beverly Hills, CA 90212-0797, USA

Tressel, Jim (Coach, Football Coach)
Ohio State University
Athletic Dept
Columbus, OH 43210, USA

Trestman, Marc (Football Player)
Minnesota Vikings
PO Box 888
Phoenix, AZ 85001-0888, USA

Tresvant, John (Athlete, Basketball Player)
14814 61st Dr SE
Snohomish, WA 98296-4221, USA

Tretiak, Vladislav (Athlete, Hockey Player)
1925 Birch Rd
Northbrook, IL 60062-5911

Treu, Adam (Athlete, Football Player)
556 Creedon Cir
Alameda, CA 94502-7794, USA

Treuel, Ralph (Athlete, Baseball Player)
15 Middleton Rd
Wolfeboro, NH 03894-4421, USA

Trevanian (Writer)
Jove Books
375 Hudson St Bsmt 3
Berkeley Publishing Group
New York, NY 10014-7465, USA

Trevathan, Danny (Athlete, Football Player)
c/o Bus Cook *Bus Cook Sports, Inc*
1 Willow Bend Dr
Hattiesburg, MS 39402-8552, USA

Trevelyan, Edward (Athlete, Olympic Athlete, Sailor)
25028 Maplewood Dr
Saint Michaels, MD 21663-2753, USA

Trevino, Alex (Athlete, Baseball Player)
PO Box 288
Houston, TX 77001-0288, USA

Trevino, Lee (Athlete, Golfer)
4906 Park Ln
Dallas, TX 75220-2031, USA

Trevino, Michael (Actor)
c/o Lena Roklin *Luber Roklin Management*
5815 W Sunset Blvd Ste 206
Los Angeles, CA 90028-6481, USA

Trevino, Rick (Musician)
William Morris Agency
2100 W End Ave Ste 1000
Nashville, TN 37203-5240, USA

Triandos, C Gus (Athlete, Baseball Player)
PO Box 5642
San Jose, CA 95150-5642, USA

Trias, Jasmine (Musician)
c/o Stephen Ford *Diva Central Inc*
7510 W Sunset Blvd Ste 1445
Los Angeles, CA 90046-3408, USA

Tribbett, Tye (Musician)
c/o Staff Member *Sony Music International*
550 Madison Ave Fl 6
New York, NY 10022-3211, USA

Trice, Obie (Musician)
BME Recordings
2144 Hills Ave NW
D2
Atlanta, GA 30318-2209, USA

Trichter, Judd
10264 Rochester Ave
Los Angeles, CA 90024-5331

Trick, Cheap (Music Group, Musician)
c/o Dave Frey *Red Light Management (VA)*
321 E Main St Ste 500
Charlottesville, VA 22902-3201, USA

Trick Daddy (Musician)
16573 SW 19th St
Miramar, FL 33027-4466, USA

Trickey, Paula
PO Box 261098
Encino, CA 91426-1098

Trickle, Dick (Race Car Driver)
Donlavey Racing
5415 Vesuvius Furnace Rd
Iron Station, NC 28080-7729, USA

Trickside (Music Group)
c/o Staff Member *Wind-up Records*
72 Madison Ave Fl 8
New York, NY 10016-8731, USA

Triffle, Carol (Director)
Imago Theater
PO Box 15182
Portland, OR 97293-5182, USA

Trigg, Alex (Baseball Player)
Detroit Stars
900 Turner Ln
Shreveport, LA 71106-4528, USA

Trigger, Sarah (Actor)
Paradigm Agency
10100 Santa Monica Blvd Ste 2500
Los Angeles, CA 90067-4116, USA

Triggs, Trini
3178 Allen Marthaville Rd
Robeline, LA 71469-4528

Trillin, Calvin M (Writer)
New Yorker Magazine
4 Times Sq Fl 22
Editorial Dept
New York, NY 10036-6592, USA

Trimble, Solomon (Actor)
c/o Kaili Canfield *Arthouse Talent and Literary*
107 SE Washington St Ste 156
Portland, OR 97214-2105, USA

Trimble, Vivian (Musician)
Metropolitan Entertainment
2 Penn Plz # 2600
New York, NY 10121-0101, USA

Trina (Musician)
c/o Staff Member *Pyramid Entertainment Group*
377 Rector Pl Apt 21A
New York, NY 10280-1439, USA

Trinh, Eugene (Astronaut)
NASA Headquarters
300 E St SW
Washington, DC 20546-0005, USA

Trinh, Eugene H Dr (Astronaut)
3549 Kelton Ave
Los Angeles, CA 90034-5505, USA

Trinidad, Felix (Tito) (Boxer)
RR 6 Box 11479
San Juan, PR 00926, USA

Trinneer, Connor (Actor)
c/o Gregg A Klein *AKA Talent Agency*
6310 San Vicente Blvd Ste 200
Los Angeles, CA 90048-5488, USA

Triola, Michelle
23215 Mariposa De Oro St
Malibu, CA 90265-4909

Triplet, Kirk (Golfer)
8141 E Overlook Dr
Scottsdale, AZ 85255-6481, USA

Triplett, Bill (Athlete, Football Player)
222 Beachwood Dr
Youngstown, OH 44505-4282, USA

Triplett, Kirk (Golfer)
8141 E Overlook Dr
Scottsdale, AZ 85255-6481, USA

Triplett, Wally (Athlete, Football Player)
4250 Fullerton St
Detroit, MI 48238-3235, USA

Tripp, Linda
27285 Boyce Mill Rd
Greensboro, MD 21639-1332

Tripp, Valerie (Writer)
Pleasant Company Publications
PO Box 620991
Middleton, WI 53562-0991, USA

Trippi, Charles L (Charlie) (Athlete, Football Player)
125 Riverhill Ct
Athens, GA 30606-4034, USA

Tripplehorn, Jeanne (Actor)
c/o Cynthia Pett-Dante *Brillstein Entertainment Partners (LA)*
9150 Wilshire Blvd Ste 350
Beverly Hills, CA 90212-3453, USA

Tripplett, Larry (Athlete, Football Player)
5324 Overdale Dr
Windsor Hills, CA 90043-2023, USA

Triptow, Dick (Athlete, Basketball Player)
1100 Pembridge Dr Apt 213
Lake Forest, IL 60045-4215, USA

Tripucka, Kelly (Athlete, Basketball Player)
14 Devon Rd
Boonton, NJ 07005-9305, USA

Tritt, Travis (Actor, Musician)
c/o Duke Cooper *Quantum Management*
5340 Forest Acres Dr
Nashville, TN 37220-2123, USA

Trivium (Music Group)
c/o Staff Member *Roadrunner Records Inc*
1290 Avenue Of The Americas Fl CONC4
New York, NY 10104-0106, USA

Trixter
210 Westfield Ave
Clark, NJ 07066-1539

Trlicek, Rick (Athlete, Baseball Player)
PO Box 1109
La Grange, TX 78945-1109, USA

Troche, Rose (Actor, Director, Producer, Writer)
c/o Staff Member *Gersh (NY)*
2701 Queens Plz N Ste 1
Long Island City, NY 11101-4021, USA

Troedson, Rich (Athlete, Baseball Player)
899 Bowen Ave
San Jose, CA 95123-5303, USA

Troegel, Butch (Athlete, Football Player)
230 Norcross St
Bossier City, LA 71111-6046, USA

Trohman, Joe (Musician)
4058 Woking Way
Los Angeles, CA 90027-1324, USA

Trombley, Mike (Athlete, Baseball Player)
2 Hilltop Park
Wilbraham, MA 01095-1753, USA

Trone, Roland (Don) (Musician)
Mars Talent
27 L Ambiance Ct
Bardonia, NY 10954-1421, USA

Tronnier, Ellen (Athlete, Baseball Player)
328 Anemone Ave
Palmyra, WI 53156-9326, USA

Trosch, Gene (Athlete, Football Player)
6393 Oak Tree Dr
Mc Calla, AL 35111-3926, USA

Trosky, Hal (Athlete, Baseball Player)
1414 Curtis Bridge Rd NE
Swisher, IA 52338-9588, USA

Trotter, Deedee (Athlete, Olympic Athlete, Track Athlete)
9900 Brannigan Cir
Knoxville, TN 37923-1965, USA

Trottier, Bryan J (Athlete, Coach, Hockey Player)
133 Highcroft Cir
Eighty Four, PA 15330-1003

Trottier, Guy (Athlete, Hockey Player)
1003 Hazel Ave
Englewood, OH 45322-2426

Trottier, Rocky (Athlete, Hockey Player)
13668 Blooming Orchard Dr
Fishers, IN 46038-4265

Trotz, Barry (Athlete, Hockey Player)
718 N Highland St
Arlington, VA 22201-2040

Trotz, Barry (Athlete, Hockey Player)
Nashville Predators
501 Broadway
Nashville, TN 37203-3980

Trouble, Valli (Musician)
Q Prime
729 7th Ave Ste 1600
New York, NY 10019-6880, USA

Troup, Guppy (Bowler)
60 Dwayne Dr
Taylorsville, NC 28681-8243, USA

Troup, Tom
8829 Ashcroft Ave
West Hollywood, CA 90048-2401

Troupe, Tom (Actor)
8829 Ashcroft Ave
West Hollywood, CA 90048-2401, USA

Trousdale, Chris (Actor, Musician)
c/o Staff Member *Adonis Productions*
175 Skillman St
Brooklyn, NY 11205-3901, USA

Trout, David (Athlete, Football Player)
408 Paddock Ct
Sewell, NJ 08080-2509, USA

Trout, Mike (Athlete, Baseball Player)
257 Cherry Ln
Millville, NJ 08332-4129, USA

Trout, Steve (Athlete, Baseball Player)
PO Box 1155
Tinley Park, IL 60477-7955, USA

Trower, Robin (Musician)
Stardust Enterprises
4600 Franklin Ave
Los Angeles, CA 90027-4202, USA

Troxel, Gary
11471 Earle Dr
Mount Vernon, WA 98273-7261, USA

Troxel, Melanie (Race Car Driver)
PO Box 637
Brownsburg, IN 46112-0637, USA

Troy, Cowboy (Musician)
919 Sam Johnson Rd
Columbia, TN 38401-7754, USA

Troy, Drake (Athlete, Football Player)
20103 Desert Forest Dr
Ashburn, VA 20147-3179, USA

Troy, Mike (Athlete, Olympic Athlete, Swimmer)
21187 E Alyssa Rd
Queen Creek, AZ 85142-6558, USA

Troyer, Maynard (Race Car Driver)
4555 Lyell Rd
Rochester, NY 14606-4316, United States

Troyer, Verne (Actor)
c/o Elaina Bertnolli *Fonolli Management*
11218 Osborne St
Sylmar, CA 91342-6604, USA

Truax, Billy (Athlete, Football Player)
735 Ruth Ave
Gulfport, MS 39501-1056, USA

Truax, Dalton (Athlete, Football Player)
77 Chateau Magdelaine Dr
Kenner, LA 70065-2026, USA

Truax, Mike (Athlete, Football Player)
5925 Cleveland Pl
Metairie, LA 70003-1047, USA

Truby, Chris (Athlete, Baseball Player)
2 Stadium Way
Attn: Managers Office
Lakewood, NJ 08701-4536

Truby, Chris (Athlete, Baseball Player)
12244 Silverado Dr
Fishers, IN 46037-8328, USA

Trucco, Michael (Actor)
McKeon-Myones
3500 W Olive Ave Ste 770
Burbank, CA 91505-5527, USA

Trudeau, Garry (Cartoonist)
14 Governors Is
Branford, CT 06405, USA

Trudeau, Jack F (Athlete, Football Player)
PO Box 375
Zionsville, IN 46077-0375, USA

Trudeau, Margaret (Writer)
c/o Staff Member *HarperCollins Publishers*
195 Broadway Fl 2
Cellar 1
New York, NY 10007-3132, USA

TRUE, Rachel (Actor)
c/o Ben Levine *LINK Entertainment*
11872 La Grange Ave Fl 1
Los Angeles, CA 90025-5283, USA

Truesdale, Yanic (Actor)
c/o Danielle Allman-Del *D2 Management*
9255 W Sunset Blvd Ste 600
West Hollywood, CA 90069-3306, USA

Truex Jr, Martin (Race Car Driver)
c/o Staff Member *Michael Waltrip Racing*
20310 Chartwell Center Dr
Cornelius, NC 28031-5253, USA

Trufant, Desmond (Athlete, Football Player)
c/o Doug Hendrickson *Octagon Football*
832 Sansome St Fl 1
San Francisco, CA 94111-1558, USA

Trufant, Isaiah (Athlete, Football Player)
c/o Doug Hendrickson *Octagon Football*
832 Sansome St Fl 1
San Francisco, CA 94111-1558, USA

Trufant, Marcus (Athlete, Football Player)
11220 NE 53rd St
Kirkland, WA 98033-7505, USA

Truhitte, Dan
4630 Sapp Rd
Concord, NC 28025-1567

Truhitte, Daniel (Actor)
4630 Sapp Rd
Concord, NC 28025-1567, USA

Truitt, Ansley (Athlete, Basketball Player)
18601 Cairo Ave
Carson, CA 90746-1715, USA

Truitt, Olanda (Athlete, Football Player)
1901 16th Way N
Bessemer, AL 35020-3930, USA

Trujillo, J J (Athlete, Baseball Player)
1329 York Ave
Corpus Christi, TX 78415-4337, USA

Trujillo, Mike (Athlete, Baseball Player)
16373 6475 Rd
Montrose, CO 81403-8578, USA

Trujillo, Solomon D (Business Person)
US West Inc
1801 California St Ste 3850
Denver, CO 80202-2601, USA

Trull, Don (Athlete, Football Player)
16435 Elmwood Point Ln
Sugar Land, TX 77498-7134, USA

Truman, Dan (Musician)
Dreamcatcher Artists Mgmt
2908 Poston Ave
Nashville, TN 37203-1312, USA

Trumbo, Karen (Actor)
c/o Staff Member *Creative Artists Management (OR)*
909 SW Saint Clair Ave
Portland, OR 97205-1300, USA

Trumbo, Mark (Athlete, Baseball Player)
1801 E Katella Ave Apt 4131
Anaheim, CA 92805-6672, USA

Trumka, Richard L (Politician)
AFL-CIO
8000 Corporate Dr Ste 100
Hyattsville, MD 20785-7210, USA

Trump, Blaine
166 Avenue of the Americas
New York, NY 10013-1207, USA

Trump, Donald (Business Person, Reality Star)
721 5th Ave Apt 39G
New York, NY 10022-2537, USA

Trump, Ivana (Business Person, Misc, Model)
10 E 64th St
New York, NY 10065-7212, USA

Trump, Ivanka (Business Person, Reality Star)
Ivanka Trump Flagship Boutique
109 Mercer St
New York, NY 10012-3964, USA

Trump, Melania (Model)
Trump Tower
725 5th Ave Bsmt A
New York, NY 10022-2516, USA

Trumpy, Robert T (Bob) Jr (Athlete, Football Player, Sportscaster)
75 Oak St
Cincinnati, OH 45246-4437, USA

Trundy, Natalie (Actor)
2109 S Wilbur Ave
Walla Walla, WA 99362-9048, USA

Truscott, Lucian K IV (Writer)
Avon/William Morrow
1350 Avenue of the Americas
New York, NY 10019-4702, USA

Truth, Hurts (Actor, Songwriter, Writer)
Aftermath/Interscope Records
2220 Colorado Ave
Santa Monica, CA 90404-3506, USA

Truvillion, Eric (Athlete, Football Player)
10436 Saint Tropez Pl
Tampa, FL 33615-4213, USA

Truvillion, Tobias (Actor)
c/o Kim Matuka Online Talent Group
Prefers to be contacted via email or telephone
West Hollywood, CA 90069, USA

Tryba, Ted (Athlete, Golfer)
6321 Cheryl St
Orlando, FL 32819-7511, USA

Tryon, Ty (Golfer)
8313 Citrus Chase Dr
Orlando, FL 32836-5432, USA

Tsai, Cheryl (Actor)
c/o Jason Solomon Full Circle Management
4932 Lankershim Blvd Ste 202
North Hollywood, CA 91601-4452, USA

Tsakalidis, Iakovos (Jake) (Basketball Player)
Memphis Grizzlies
175 Toyota Plz Ste 150
Memphis, TN 38103-6601, USA

Tsamis, George (Athlete, Baseball Player)
12 Sweetbriar Ct
Colchester, CT 06415-1887, USA

Tsamis, George (Athlete, Baseball Player)
St Paul Saints 1771 Energy Park Dr
Attn Managers Office
Saint Paul, MN 55108

Tsang, Bion (Musician)
Columbia Artists Mgmt Inc
165 W 57th St
New York, NY 10019-2201, USA

Tschida, Tim (Athlete, Baseball Player)
274 15 1/2 Ave
Turtle Lake, WI 54889-8825, USA

T. Schilling, Robert (Congressman, Politician)
507 Cannon Hob
Washington, DC 20515-2703, USA

Tschogl, John (Athlete, Basketball Player)
295 Shirley St
Chula Vista, CA 91910-1101, USA

Tseng, Yani (Athlete, Golfer)
9138 Sloane St
Orlando, FL 32827-7024, USA

Tsioropoulos, Lou (Athlete, Basketball Player)
2404 Chattesworth Ct
Louisville, KY 40242-2852, USA

Tsitouris, John (Athlete, Baseball Player)
5207 Austin Rd
Monroe, NC 28112-7948, USA

Tskitishvili, Nikoloz (Basketball Player)
Denver Nuggets
1000 Chopper Cir
Pepsi Center
Denver, CO 80204-5805, USA

Tsongas, Niki (Congressman, Politician)
1607 Longworth Hob
Washington, DC 20515-3009, USA

Tsu, Irene (Actor)
c/o Richard A. Castleberry Castleberry Talent
636 Acanto St Apt 205
Los Angeles, CA 90049-2128, USA

Tuaolo, Esera (Athlete, Football Player)
6520 Promontory Dr
Eden Prairie, MN 55346-1915, USA

Tubbs, Billy (Coach)
Lamar University
Athletic Dept
Beaumont, TX 77710, USA

Tubbs, Greg (Athlete, Baseball Player)
833 Clay Ave
Cookeville, TN 38501-2261, USA

Tubbs, Winfred (Athlete, Football Player)
RR 1 Box 800
Oakwood, TX 75855, USA

Tubert, Marcelo (Actor)
c/o Staff Member Richard Schwartz Management
2934 1/2 N Beverly Glen Cir # 107
Los Angeles, CA 90077-1724, USA

Tuberville, Tommy (Coach, Football Coach)
Aubum University
Athletic Dept
Auburn University, AL 36849-0001, USA

Tubiola, Nicole (Actor)
c/o Charlton Blackburne A Management Company
9107 Wilshire Blvd Ste 650
Beverly Hills, CA 90210-5544, USA

Tucci, Michael (Actor)
1425 Irving Ave
Glendale, CA 91201-1274, USA

Tucci, Stanley (Actor, Director)
c/o Jennifer Plante SLATE Public Relations - NY
307 7th Ave Rm 2401
New York, NY 10001-6019, USA

Tuck, Gary (Athlete, Baseball Player)
20819 79th Ave E
Bradenton, FL 34202-8216, USA

Tuck, Hillary (Actor)
c/o Justin Evans The Independent Group
6363 Wilshire Blvd Ste 115
Los Angeles, CA 90048-5734, USA

Tuck, Jessica (Actor)
Brett Adams
448 W 44th St
New York, NY 10036-5220, USA

Tucker, Barbara (Musician)
c/o Staff Member Diva Central Inc
7510 W Sunset Blvd Ste 1445
Los Angeles, CA 90046-3408, USA

Tucker, Bill (Bowler)
26126 Meadowcrest Blvd
Huntington Woods, MI 48070-1534, USA

Tucker, Bob (Athlete, Football Player)
8 Hunter Rd
Hazleton, PA 18201-6817, USA

Tucker, Brett (Actor)
c/o Tiffany Kuzon Evolution Entertainment (LA)
901 N Highland Ave
Los Angeles, CA 90038-2412, USA

Tucker, Chris (Actor, Comedian)
c/o Samantha Mast Rogers & Cowan PR (LA)
8687 Melrose Ave Ste 7
West Hollywood, CA 90069-5721, USA

Tucker, Corin (Musician)
Legends of 21st Century
7 Trinity Row
Florence, MA 01062-1931, USA

Tucker, Darcy (Athlete, Hockey Player)
Turning Point Sports Management
102 W Main St Ste 301
Auburn, WA 98001-4926, USA

Tucker, Eddie (Athlete, Baseball Player)
2216 Red Maple Ln
Dawsonville, GA 30534-8032, USA

Tucker, Elizabeth (Athlete, Baseball Player)
4037 N Fremont Ave
Tucson, AZ 85719-1065, USA

Tucker, Jason (Athlete, Football Player)
620 Remington Park
Robinson, TX 76706-7255, USA

Tucker, Jerry (Actor)
788 Saint Anns Ave
Copiague, NY 11726-4516, USA

Tucker, Jim
1654 Waters Edge Dr
Fleming Island, FL 32003-8674

Tucker, John (Athlete, Hockey Player)
19833 Michigan Ave
Odessa, FL 33556-4237

Tucker, Jonathan (Actor)
8265 W Sunset Blvd Ste 201
West Hollywood, CA 90046-2470, USA

Tucker, Marshall Band (Music Group)
c/o Ron Rainey Ron Rainey Management Inc.
315 S Beverly Dr Ste 300
Beverly Hills, CA 90212-4309, USa

Tucker, Michael (Actor, Producer)
PO Box 843
Santa Ynez, CA 93460-0843, USA

Tucker, Michael (Athlete, Baseball Player, Olympic Athlete)
407 Maple Ave N
Lehigh Acres, FL 33972-4001, USA

Tucker, Rex (Athlete, Football Player)
2300 Culpeper Dr
Midland, TX 79705-6314, USA

Tucker, Ryan (Athlete, Football Player)
c/o Team Member Cleveland Browns
76 Lou Groza Blvd
Berea, OH 44017-1269, USA

Tucker, Tanya (Musician)
c/o Staff Member Webster & Associates PR
3573 Couchville Pike
Hermitage, TN 37076-4012, USA

Tucker, T J (Athlete, Baseball Player)
6616 Ridge Top Dr
New Port Richey, FL 34655-5614, USA

Tucker, Tony (Boxer)
Club Prana
1619 E 7th Ave
Ybor City
Tampa, FL 33605-3705, USA

Tucker, Travis (Athlete, Football Player)
1568 Lee Terrace Dr
Wickliffe, OH 44092-1604, USA

Tucker, Trent (Athlete, Basketball Player)
433 River St
Minneapolis, MN 55401-2515, USA

Tucker, Wendell (Athlete, Football Player)
2042 E 171st Pl
South Holland, IL 60473-3718, USA

Tucker, Y Arnold (Athlete, Football Player)
PO Box 514
Hilbert, WI 54129, USA

Tuckwell, Barry E
13140 Fountain Head Rd
Hagerstown, MD 21742-2839, USA

Tudor, John (Athlete, Baseball Player)
5 Nathan Ln
Middleton, MA 01949-1531, USA

Tudyk, Alan (Actor)
c/o Nick Collins Gersh (LA)
9465 Wilshire Blvd Ste 600
Beverly Hills, CA 90212-2605, USA

Tueting, Sarah (Athlete, Hockey Player, Olympic Athlete)
PO Box 980608
Park City, UT 84098-0608, USA

Tufts, Bob (Athlete, Baseball Player)
6738 108th St Apt A27
Forest Hills, NY 11375-2358, USA

Tuggle, Anthony (Athlete, Football Player)
12345 Plymouth Dr
Baton Rouge, LA 70807-1961, USA

Tuggle, Jessie (Athlete, Football Player)
540 Avala Ct
Alpharetta, GA 30022-5576, USA

Tuiasosopo, Marques (Athlete, Football Player)
5569 Gold Creek Dr
Castro Valley, CA 94552-5442, USA

Tuinei, Tom (Athlete, Football Player)
714 Kihapai Pl Apt B2
Kailua, HI 96734-2677, USA

Tuipala, Joe (Athlete, Football Player)
43845 Thornberry Sq Unit 103
Leesburg, VA 20176-3403, USA

Tullis, Willie (Athlete, Football Player)
10018 Knoboak Dr Apt 4
Houston, TX 77080-6445, USA

Tulloch, Stephen (Athlete, Football Player)
c/o Drew Rosenhaus *Rosenhaus Sports Representation*
6400 Allison Rd
Miami Beach, FL 33141-4540, USA

Tully, Darrow (Publisher)
9862 Bridgeton Dr
Tampa, FL 33626-1802, USA

Tulowitzki, Troy (Athlete, Baseball Player)
2001 Blake St
Unit A
Denver, CO 80205-2060, USA

Tumpane, John (Athlete, Baseball Player)
9900 S 55th Ct Apt 3M
Oak Lawn, IL 60453, USA

Tumulty, Tom (Athlete, Football Player)
167 Woodside Ln
Verona, PA 15147-3425, USA

Tune, Tommy (Actor, Dancer)
222 Park Ave S Apt 12C
New York, NY 10003-1508, USA

Tunie, Tamara (Actor)
c/o Jean-Pierre (JP) Henraux *Henraux Management*
Prefers to be contacted by telephone
CA, USA

Tunnell, Lee (Athlete, Baseball Player)
6000 Kingsbridge Dr
Oklahoma City, OK 73162-3208, USA

Tunney, John V (Politician, Senator)
1819 Ocean Ave
Santa Monica, CA 90401-3215, USA

Tunney, Robin (Actor)
c/o Joan Hyler *Hyler Management*
20 Ocean Park Blvd Unit 25
Santa Monica, CA 90405-3590, USA

Tupa, Thomas J (Tom) (Athlete, Football Player)
5921 Fawn Ln
Brecksville, OH 44141-2849, USA

Tupman, Matt (Athlete, Baseball Player)
3 Lincoln St
Concord, NH 03301-2404, USA

Tupou, Christian (Athlete, Football Player)
c/o Jeff Sperbeck *The Novo Agency*
3201 Danville Blvd Ste 295
Alamo, CA 94507-1978, USA

Tupper, James (Actor)
c/o Alissa Vradenburg *Untitled Entertainment (LA)*
350 S Beverly Dr Ste 200
Beverly Hills, CA 90212-4819, USA

Tupper, Jeff (Athlete, Football Player)
3263 W 164th Ter
Stilwell, KS 66085-8822, USA

Turang, Brian (Athlete, Baseball Player)
3014 McNab Ave
Long Beach, CA 90808-4002, USA

Turco, Marty (Athlete, Hockey Player)
3616 Wolcott Dr
Flower Mound, TX 75028-8712

Turco, Paige (Actor)
c/o Rhonda Price *Gersh (NY)*
41 Madison Ave
New York, NY 10010-2202, USA

Turcotte, Alfie (Athlete, Hockey Player)
816 Hawk Dr
Wolverine Lake, MI 48390-3011

Turcotte, Mel (Horse Racer)
4260 NW 12th St
Coconut Creek, FL 33066-1506, USA

Turcotte, Ron (Horse Racer, Jockey)
PO Box 215
Van Buren, ME 04785-0215, USA

Tureaud, Laurence (Mr T) (Actor)
c/o Peter Young *Sovereign Talent Group*
8421 Wilshire Blvd Ste 200
Beverly Hills, CA 90211-3204, USA

Turgeon, Pierre (Athlete, Hockey Player)
2930 E Iliff Ave
Denver, CO 80210-5507

Turiaf, Ronny (Athlete, Basketball Player)
c/o Mark Bartelstein *Priority Sports & Entertainment - Chicago*
312 N La Salle
Suite 650
Chicago, IL 60610, USA

Turin Brakes (Music Group)
c/o Staff Member *Paradigm (Monterey)*
404 W Franklin St
Monterey, CA 93940-2303, USA

Turk, Brian (Actor)
c/o Staff Member *House of Representatives, The*
1434 6th St Ste 1
Santa Monica, CA 90401-2527, USA

Turk, Godwin (Athlete, Football Player)
1303 Magnolia Cir
Orange, TX 77632-8996, USA

Turk, Stephen (Cartoonist)
927 Westbourne Dr
West Hollywood, CA 90069-4113, USA

Turkel, Ann (Actor)
c/o Mark Baintree *Brian Baintree Agency*
4 W 58th St
New York, NY 10019-2515, USA

Turkoglu, Hidayet (Hedo) (Athlete, Basketball Player)
100 S Eola Dr Unit 1603
Orlando, FL 32801-6601, USA

Turley, Kyle (Football Player)
c/o Staff Member *St Louis Rams*
1 Rams Way
Earth City, MO 63045-1525, USA

Turlik, Gordon (Athlete, Hockey Player)
3618 E Garnet Ave
Spokane, WA 99217-6916

Turlington, Christy (Model)
c/o Lisa Jacobson *United Talent Agency (UTA-LA)*
9336 Civic Center Dr
Beverly Hills, CA 90210-3604, USA

Turman, Glynn (Actor, Director, Musician)
48421 3 Points Rd
Lake Hughes, CA 93532-1124, USA

Turnbow, Derrick (Athlete, Baseball Player)
25257 SE 192nd St
Maple Valley, WA 98038-7307, USA

Turnbow, Scot (Baseball Player)
Anaheim Angels
404 Newbary Ct
Franklin, TN 37069-1848, USA

Turnbull, Ian (Athlete, Hockey Player)
23930 Ocean Ave Apt 154
Torrance, CA 90505-5880

Turnbull, Perry (Athlete, Hockey Player)
2186 Cedar Forest Ct
Chesterfield, MO 63017-7201

Turnbull, Wendy (Tennis Player)
822 Boylston St Ste 203
Chestnut Hill, MA 02467-2504, USA

Turner, Aiden (Actor)
c/o Marnie Sparer *Innovative Artists (LA)*
1505 10th St
Santa Monica, CA 90401-2805, USA

Turner, Bake (Athlete, Football Player)
PO Box 277
Alpine, TX 79831-0277, USA

Turner, Bree (Actor)
c/o Jai Khanna *Brillstein Entertainment Partners (LA)*
9150 Wilshire Blvd Ste 350
Beverly Hills, CA 90212-3453, USA

Turner, Cathy (Speed Skater)
251 East Ave
Hilton, NY 14468-1333, USA

Turner, Cecil (Athlete, Football Player)
2717 Dog Leg Trl
McKinney, TX 75069-8043, USA

Turner, Chris (Athlete, Baseball Player)
28S53 N Quarry Dr
Elberta, AL 36530, USA

Turner, Dean (Athlete, Hockey Player)
26900 Captains Ln
Franklin, MI 48025-1717

Turner, Debbye (Doctor)
PO Box 12450
Saint Louis, MO 63132-0150, USA

Turner, Elston (Athlete, Basketball Player)
23 Commanders Cv
Missouri City, TX 77459-6517, USA

Turner, Evan (Athlete, Basketball Player)
c/o David Falk *F.A.M.E*
Prefers to be contacted via telephone
Washington, DC, USA

Turner, Floyd (Athlete, Football Player)
27822 Stonehurst Ln
Katy, TX 77494-4021, USA

Turner, Fred (Race Car Driver)
107 Brush Rd
Greensboro, NC 27409-9658, USA

Turner, Glenn (Business Person)
PO Box 952608
Lake Mary, FL 32795-2608, USA

Turner, Grant
PO Box 414
Brentwood, TN 37024-0414

Turner, Guinevere (Actor)
Gersh Agency
41 Madison Ave Ste 3301
New York, NY 10010-2210, USA

Turner, Hamp (Athlete, Football Player)
430172 Milledge Ter
Athens, GA 30605, USA

Turner, Herschel (Athlete, Football Player)
16622 Equestrian Ln
Chesterfield, MO 63005-4880, USA

Turner, Hersh (Athlete, Basketball Player)
1706 Lamberton Creek Ct NE
Grand Rapids, MI 49505-7702, USA

Turner, Jackie Lee (Athlete, Basketball Player)
2402 H St
Bedford, IN 47421-5122, USA

Turner, James A (Jim) (Athlete, Football Player)
14155 W 59th Pl
Arvada, CO 80004-3724, USA

Turner, James Jr (Business Person)
General Dynamics
3190 Fairview Park Dr
Falls Church, VA 22042-4530, USA

Turner, Janine (Actor, Model)
c/o Tiffany Smith *Binder & Associates*
1465 Lindacrest Dr
Beverly Hills, CA 90210-2519, USA

Turner, Jeff
1590 Woodland Ave
Winter Park, FL 32789-2773, USA

Turner, Jerry (Athlete, Baseball Player)
1935 18th St Apt B
Santa Monica, CA 90404-4732, USA

Turner, Jesse
1502 N 5th St
Boise, ID 83702-3703

Turner, Jim (Actor)
c/o Margrit Polak *Margrit Polak Management*
1920 Hillhurst Ave Ste 405
Los Angeles, CA 90027-2712, USA

Turner, John (Athlete, Football Player)
3217 Cedar Ave S
Minneapolis, MN 55407-3802, USA

Turner, Josh (Musician)
c/o Staff Member *Modern Management*
1625 Broadway Ste 600
Nashville, TN 37203-3141, USA

Turner, Karri (Actor)
Premiere Artists Agency
1875 Century Park E Ste 2250
Los Angeles, CA 90067-2563, USA

Turner, Kathleen (Actor)
200 Riverside Blvd Apt 39A
New York, NY 10069-0914, USA

Turner, Keena (Athlete, Coach, Football Coach, Football Player)
8200 W Erb Way
Tracy, CA 95304-8896, USA

Turner, Ken (Athlete, Baseball Player)
PO Box 252
San Marcos, CA 92079-0252, USA

Turner, Kenneth (Race Car Driver)
1081 S Trade St
Tryon, NC 28782-3790, USA

Turner, Kevin (Athlete, Football Player)
414 Shady Nook Dr
Deatsville, AL 36022-3496, USA

Turner, Kriss (Producer)
c/o Staff Member *William Morris Endeavor (LA)*
9601 Wilshire Blvd
Beverly Hills, CA 90210-5213, USA

Turner, Kristopher (Actor)
c/o Shelley Browning *Magnolia Entertainment (LA)*
9595 Wilshire Blvd Ste 601
Beverly Hills, CA 90212-2506, USA

Turner, Lane (Musician)
c/o Staff Member *Paradigm (Monterey)*
404 W Franklin St
Monterey, CA 93940-2303, USA

Turner, Marcus (Athlete, Football Player)
5032 Meadow Wood Ave
Lakewood, CA 90712-2855, USA

Turner, Matt (Athlete, Baseball Player)
829 Della Dr
Lexington, KY 40504-2319, USA

Turner, Maurice (Athlete, Football Player)
3558 Tiffany Ln
Saint Paul, MN 55126-3072, USA

Turner, Michael (Football Player)
c/o Staff Member *Atlanta Falcons*
4400 Falcon Pkwy
Flowery Branch, GA 30542-3176, USA

Turner, Norv (Athlete, Coach, Football
Coach, Football Player)
1256 Rose Ln
Lafayette, CA 94549-3032, USA

Turner, Odessa (Athlete, Football Player)
1416 Perry Ave
Bastrop, LA 71220, USA

Turner, Richard (Athlete, Football Player)
408 Piney Oak Dr
Norman, OK 73072-4603, USA

Turner, Ryan (Baseball Player)
1221 Shafter St
San Mateo, CA 94402-2901, USA

Turner, Shane (Athlete, Baseball Player)
3032 Van Reed Rd
Reading, PA 19608-1037, USA

Turner, Sherri (Athlete, Golfer)
PO Box 26
Yale, OK 74085-0026, USA

Turner, Sophie (Actor, Model)
c/o Noel Palm *Element Talent Agency*
120 S Vignes St Apt 202
Los Angeles, CA 90012-4336, USA

Turner, Stacie (Business Person, Reality
Star)
c/o Staff Member *Bravo (NY)*
30 Rockefeller Plz Fl 270E
New York, NY 10112-0299, USA

Turner, Stansfield
488 River Bend Rd
Great Falls, VA 22066-4016, USA

Turner, Ted (Business Person, Producer)
Turner Foundation
133 Luckie St NW Fl 2
Atlanta, GA 30303-2038, USA

Turner, Thomas (Athlete, Baseball Player)
4817 Delhi Arnheim Rd
Georgetown, OH 45121-8229, USA

Turner, Toby (Actor)
c/o Dan Weinstein *The Collective*
8383 Wilshire Blvd Ste 1050
Beverly Hills, CA 90211-2415, USA

Turner, Trai (Athlete, Football Player)
c/o Peter Schaffer *All Pro Sports and
Entertainment*
36 Steele St Ste 100
Denver, CO 80206-5709, USA

Turner, Tyrin (Actor)
c/o David Saunders *Agency for the
Performing Arts (APA-LA)*
405 S Beverly Dr Ste 500
Beverly Hills, CA 90212-4425, USA

Turner, Vernon (Athlete, Football Player)
86 Crosshill St
Staten Island, NY 10301-3308, USA

Turner, William (Athlete, Basketball
Player)
3271 Wisteria Tree St
Las Vegas, NV 89135-1787, USA

Turnesa, Jim (Golfer)
24 Poplar St
Elmsford, NY 10523-3726, USA

Turnesa, Mike (Golfer)
c/o Staff Member *Pro Golfers Association
(PGA) Tour*
112 Tpc Blvd
Ponte Vedra Beach, FL 32082, USA

Turnesa, Willie (Golfer)
41 Sheraton Dr
Poughkeepsie, NY 12601-5629, USA

Turney, Maura
PO Box 5617
Beverly Hills, CA 90209-5617

Turow, Scott (Writer)
c/o Robert (Bob) Bookman *Paradigm (LA)*
2000 Avenue of the Stars
Los Angeles, CA 90067-4700, USA

Turpin, Miles (Athlete, Football Player)
8444 Wildflower Pl
Lone Tree, CO 80124-3022, USA

Turris, Kyle (Athlete, Hockey Player)
19820 N 84th St
Scottsdale, AZ 85255-3964

Turteltaub, Jon (Director)
Junction Entertainment
500 S Buena Vista St
Animation Building Ste 1B
Burbank, CA 91521-0001, USA

Turtles, The
PO Box 1821
Ojai, CA 93024-1821

Turturro, Aida (Actor)
c/o Peg Donegan *Framework
Entertainment (LA)*
9057 Nemo St Ste C
West Hollywood, CA 90069-5511, USA

Turturro, John (Actor)
c/o Bart Walker *ICM Partners (LA)*
10250 Constellation Blvd Fl 7
Los Angeles, CA 90067-6207, USA

Turturro, Nicholas (Nick) (Actor)
PO Box 570824
Tarzana, CA 91357-0824, USA

Turturro, Nick (Actor)
c/o Adam Griffin *Kritzer Levine Wilkins
Entertainment (KLWG)*
11872 La Grange Ave Fl 1
Los Angeles, CA 90025-5283, USA

Tush, Bill
1 City Cnn Ctr Box 105366
Atlanta, GA 30348

Tushingham, Rita (Actor)
4 Kingly St
London, EN W1R 5

Tuten, Rick (Athlete, Football Player)
1146 SE 15th St
Ocala, FL 34471-4514, USA

Tutera, David (Reality Star)
c/o Eda Kalkay *EKPR*
470 Fashion Ave Fl 11
New York, NY 10018-7195, USA

Tutson, Tom (Athlete, Football Player)
6655 Poplar Grove Way
Stone Mountain, GA 30087-4791, USA

Tuttle, Perry (Athlete, Football Player)
14224 King Eider Dr
Charlotte, NC 28273-6714, USA

Tuttle, Steve (Athlete, Hockey Player)
928 Belfair Rd
Bellevue, WA 98004-4013

Tuzzolino, Tony (Athlete, Hockey Player)
31 Eagles Trce
Buffalo, NY 14221-1483

Tveit, Aaron (Actor)
c/o Elin McManus-Flack *Elin Flack
Management*
435 W 57th St Apt 3M
New York, NY 10019-1724, USA

Tverdovsky, Oleg (Athlete, Hockey
Player)
17832 Margate St # 6
Encino, CA 91316-2223

Tvrdon, Roman (Athlete, Hockey Player)
Mierova 1435/53
Galanta, 92 SLOVA

Twain, Shania (Actor, Musician)
c/o Jason Owen *Sandbox Entertainment*
54 Music Sq E Ste 200
Nashville, TN 37203-4360, USA

Twardzik, Dave (Athlete, Basketball
Player)
2139 Alaqua Lakes Blvd
Longwood, FL 32779-3206, USA

Tway, Bob (Golfer)
6405 Oak Tree Cir
Edmond, OK 73025-2512, USA

Tweed, Shannon (Actor, Model, Reality
Star)
2650 Benedict Canyon Dr
Beverly Hills, CA 90210-1023, USA

Tweeden, Leeann (Actor, Model,
Sportscaster)
c/o Jon Orlando *WNWN Media*
348 Hauser Blvd # PH414
Los Angeles, CA 90036-3276, USA

Tweet, Rodney (Athlete, Football Player)
2096 Placita De Vida
Santa Fe, NM 87505-5489, USA

Twigg, Rebecca (Athlete, Cycler, Olympic
Athlete)
7001 Old Redmond Rd Apt E318
Redmond, WA 98052-4293, USA

Twiggs, Greg (Golfer)
c/o Staff Member *Pro Golfers Association
(PGA) Tour*
112 Tpc Blvd
Ponte Vedra Beach, FL 32082, USA

Twilight Singers (Music Group)
c/o Staff Member *Paradigm (Monterey)*
404 W Franklin St
Monterey, CA 93940-2303, USA

Twilley, Howard J Jr (Athlete, Football
Player)
3109 S Columbia Cir
Tulsa, OK 74105-2329, USA

Twilly, Dwight
PO Box 1821
Ojai, CA 93024-1821

Twist, Tony (Athlete, Hockey Player)
63 Nordic Ln
Defiance, MO 63341-2332

Twista (Actor, Musician)
c/o Staff Member *Violator Management*
36 W 25th St Fl 2
New York, NY 10010-2768, USA

Twitty, Howard (Golfer)
8007 E Mercer Ln
Scottsdale, AZ 85260-6563, USA

Twitty, Jeff (Athlete, Baseball Player)
136 Parapet Trl
Chapin, SC 29036-7350, USA

Twohy, David (Actor)
c/o John Burnham *ICM Partners (LA)*
10250 Constellation Blvd Fl 7
Los Angeles, CA 90067-6207, USA

Twohy, Mike (Cartoonist)
605 Beloit Ave
Kensington, CA 94708-1117, USA

Twohy, Robert (Cartoonist)
New Yorker Magazine
4 Times Sq Fl 22
Editorial Dept
New York, NY 10036-6592, USA

Twyford, Dwan (Business Person)
Millionaire Mindset Collection
15 Gramercy Park S Fl 3
New York, NY 10003-1793, USA

Tydings, Joseph D (Politician, Senator)
2705 Pocock Rd
Monkton, MD 21111-2311, USA

Tyers, Kathy (Writer)
Martha Millard Agency
204 Park Ave
Madison, NJ 07940-1128, USA

Tyga (Musician)
25212 Prado Del Misterio
Calabasas, CA 91302-3600, USA

Tyler, Aisha (Actor, Comedian)
c/o Jordan Tilzer *ROAR (LA)*
9701 Wilshire Blvd Fl 8
Beverly Hills, CA 90212-2008, USA

Tyler, Anne (Writer)
c/o Staff Member *Random House
Publicity*
1745 Broadway Frnt 3
New York, NY 10019-4343, USA

Tyler, B J
1994 Philadelphia 76ERS
Port Arthur, TX 77640, USA

Tyler, Brian (Race Car Driver)
4410 W Alva St
Tampa, FL 33614-7639, USA

Tyler, Cory
9955 Balboa Blvd
Northridge, CA 91325-1610

Tyler, James Michael (Actor)
c/o Craig Mobbs *AKA Talent Agency*
6310 San Vicente Blvd Ste 200
Los Angeles, CA 90048-5488, USA

Tyler, Jess (Radio Personality)
c/o Staff Member *WPKX*
1331 Main St Ste 4
Springfield, MA 01103-1621, USA

Tyler, Karmyn (Actor, Musician)
c/o Staff Member *BMI (LA)*
8730 W Sunset Blvd Fl 3
West Hollywood, CA 90069-2210

Tyler, Liv (Actor)
255 W 11th St
New York, NY 10014-2412, USA

Tyler, Maurice (Athlete, Football Player)
7066 Whitfield Dr
Riverdale, GA 30296-2161, USA

Tyler, Mia (Actor)
c/o Staff Member *Core/Lapides Lear Entertainment*
14724 Ventura Blvd PH
Sherman Oaks, CA 91403-3513, USA

Tyler, Nikki
4F S Main St PMB 307
West Bridgewater, MA 02379-1766

Tyler, Richard (Designer, Fashion Designer)
c/o Staff Member *Richard Tyler*
525 Mission St
S Pasadena, CA 91030-3035, USA

Tyler, Robert (Actor)
Innovative Artists
1505 10th St
Santa Monica, CA 90401-2805, USA

Tyler, Steven (Musician, Songwriter)
8306 Grand View Dr
Los Angeles, CA 90046-1918, USA

Tyler, Terry (Athlete, Basketball Player)
6500 Tauton Rd NW
Albuquerque, NM 87120-2061, USA

Tyler, Wendell A (Athlete, Football Player)
4083 W Avenue L Apt 294
Lancaster, CA 93536-4202, USA

Tyler, Willie
1650 Broadway # 705
New York, NY 10019-6833

Tylo, Hunter (Actor)
11684 Ventura Blvd # 910
Studio City, CA 91604-2699

Tylo, Michael (Actor)
11684 Ventura Blvd # 910
Studio City, CA 91604-2699

Tylo, Noa (DJ)
c/o Len Evans *Project Publicity*
312 W 53rd St Ste 202
New York, NY 10019-5743, USA

Tylski, Richard (Athlete, Football Player)
5456 Tierra Verde Ln
Jacksonville, FL 32258-2281, USA

Tynan, Ronan (Musician)
c/o Lynnette Crouse *CMI Entertainment*
925 E 9th St
Port Angeles, WA 98362-8012, USA

Tyne, George
1449 Benedict Canyon Dr
Beverly Hills, CA 90210-2021

Tyner, Charles (Actor)
Dade/Schultz
6442 Coldwater Canyon Ave Ste 206
North Hollywood, CA 91606-1174, USA

Tyner, Jason (Athlete, Baseball Player)
5535 Sul Ross Ln
Beaumont, TX 77706-3435, USA

Tyner, Tray (Athlete, Golfer)
103 Ridges End Dr
Boerne, TX 78006-7833, USA

Tyree, David (Athlete, Football Player)
514 Boonton Ave
Boonton, NJ 07005-1510, USA

Tyrell, Steve (Musician)
c/o Staff Member *William Morris Endeavor (LA)*
9601 Wilshire Blvd
Beverly Hills, CA 90210-5213, USA

Tyrone, Jim (Athlete, Baseball Player)
1115 Park Vista Dr Apt 703
Arlington, TX 76012-2349, USA

Tyrone, Wayne (Athlete, Baseball Player)
505 Tish Cir Apt 404
Arlington, TX 76006-3549, USA

Tyronn, Lue
2926 Montessouri St
Las Vegas, NV 89117-3152

Tyrrell, Tim (Athlete, Football Player)
17 Fallstone Dr
Streamwood, IL 60107-1071, USA

Tysoe, Ronald W (Business Person)
Federated Department Stores
151 W 34th St
New York, NY 10001-2101, USA

Tyson, Deangelo (Athlete, Football Player)
c/o Anthony J. Agnone *Eastern Athletic Services*
11350 McCormick Rd
Suite 800 - Executive Plaza
Hunt Valley, MD 21031-1002, USA

Tyson, Dick (Athlete, Football Player)
PO Box 4307
Kansas City, KS 66104-0307, USA

Tyson, Laura D'Andrea (Politician)
1600 Pennsylvania Ave NW
Washington, DC 20500-0005, USA

Tyson, Mike (Athlete, Baseball Player)
479 Thunderhead Canyon Dr
Ballwin, MO 63011-1736, USA

Tyson, Mike (Athlete, Boxer)
1294 Imperia Dr
Henderson, NV 89052-4051, USA

Tyson, Neil deGrasse
Hayden Planetarium & Dept Of Astrophysics
American Museum Of Natural History
Central Park West At 79th St
New York, NY 10024, USA

Tyson, Richard (Actor)
c/o Staff Member *Cunningham Escott Slevin & Doherty (CESD-LA)*
10635 Santa Monica Blvd Ste 130
Los Angeles, CA 90025-8306, USA

Tyus, Wyomia (Athlete, Olympic Athlete, Track Athlete)
1102 Keniston Ave
Los Angeles, CA 90019-1709, USA

Tyutin, Fedor (Athlete, Hockey Player)
2434 Lane Rd
Columbus, OH 43220-2832

U2 (Musician)
c/o Guy Oseary *Untitled Entertainment (LA)*
350 S Beverly Dr Ste 200
Beverly Hills, CA 90212-4819, USA

Ubach, Alanna (Actor)
1544 12th St Apt 204
Santa Monica, CA 90401-3042, USA

Uberroth, Peter (Baseball Player)
Baseball Commissioner's Office
184 Emerald Bay
Laguna Beach, CA 92651-1209, USA

Ubriaco, Gene (Athlete, Coach, Hockey Player)
Chicago Wolves
621 Winston Dr
Melrose Park, IL 60160-2350

Ubriaco, Gene (Athlete, Hockey Player)
Chicago Wolves
2301 Ravine Way
Glenview, IL 60025-7627

Uchida, Mitsuko (Musician)
Arts Management Group
1133 Broadway Ste 1025
New York, NY 10010-7985, USA

Udenio, Fabiana (Actor)
Michael Slessinger
8730 W Sunset Blvd Ste 220W
West Hollywood, CA 90069-2275, USA

Udoka, Ime
PO Box 4E8E2
Portland, OR 97240, USA

Udrih, Beno (Athlete, Basketball Player)
825 N Prospect Ave Unit 23E2
Milwaukee, WI 53202-3979

Udvar-Hazy, Steven (Business Person)
67 Beverly Park Ct
Beverly Hills, CA 90210-1543, USA

Udy, Helene (Actor)
Sterling/Winters
10877 Wilshire Blvd # 15
Los Angeles, CA 90024-4341, USA

Ueberroth, John A (Business Person)
Preferred Hotel Group
311 S Wacker Dr Ste 1900
Chicago, IL 60606-6676, USA

Ueberroth, Peter (Baseball Player)
184 Emerald Bay
Laguna Beach, CA 92651-1209

Uecker, Bob (Athlete, Baseball Player, Sportscaster)
c/o Deborah Miller *Shelter Entertainment*
9255 W Sunset Blvd Ste 320
West Hollywood, CA 90069-3313, USA

Uecker, Keith (Athlete, Football Player)
1230 Sunset View Dr
Akron, OH 44313-7839, USA

Uehara, Koji (Athlete, Baseball Player)
c/o Staff Member *SFX Sports Management*
5335 Wisconsin Ave NW Ste 850
Washington, DC 20015-2052, USA

Uelses, John (Athlete, Track Athlete)
30660 Rolling Hills Dr
Valley Center, CA 92082-3351, USA

Ufland, Len (Actor, Director)
4400 Hillcrest Dr Apt 901
Hollywood, FL 33021-7979, USA

Uggams, Leslie (Actor, Musician)
c/o Philip Adelman *Gage Group, The (NY)*
1650 Broadway Ste 1410
New York, NY 10019-6957, USA

Uggla, Dan (Athlete, Baseball Player)
3325 Piedmont Rd NE Unit 3201
Atlanta, GA 30305-4821, USA

Ugueto, Luis (Athlete, Baseball Player)
21915 NE 85th St
Redmond, WA 98053-2204, USA

Uh Huh Her (Music Group)
c/o Staff Member *Paradigm (Monterey)*
404 W Franklin St
Monterey, CA 93940-2303, USA

Uhlenhake, Jeffrey (Athlete, Football Player)
635 Marburn Dr
Columbus, OH 43214-3417, USA

Uhlig, Anneliese (Actor)
1519 Escalona Dr
Santa Cruz, CA 95060-3311

Uhry, Alfred F (Writer)
Marshall Purdy
226 W 47th St Ste 900
New York, NY 10036-1413, USA

Ujdur, Jerry (Athlete, Baseball Player)
112 Riveness Rd
Duluth, MN 55811-2873, USA

Ulene, Art (Doctor)
6511 Moore Dr
Los Angeles, CA 90048-5325, USA

Ulevich, Neal (Journalist, Photographer)
11954 Glencoe Dr
Thornton, CO 80233-1895, USA

Ulion, Gretchen (Athlete, Hockey Player)
22181 Toro Hills Dr
Salinas, CA 93908-1132, USA

Ulion-Silverman, Gretchen (Athlete, Hockey Player, Olympic Athlete)
505 Westledge Dr
Torrington, CT 06790-4490, USA

Ullger, Scott (Athlete, Baseball Player)
1 Twins Way
Minneapolis, MN 55403-1418, USA

Ulliel, Gaspard (Actor)
c/o Brinda Bhatt *Innovative Artists (LA)*
9560 Wilshire Blvd Fl 5
Beverly Hills, CA 90212-2401, USA

Ullman, Ricky (Actor)
c/o Terry Saperstein *Nani/Saperstein Management*
481 8th Ave # 1575
New York, NY 10001-1809, USA

Ullman, Tracey (Actor, Comedian)
1200 N Tigertail Rd
Los Angeles, CA 90049-1425, USA

Ulloa, Christina (Actor)
c/o Michael Greenwald *Don Buchwald & Associates (LA)*
6500 Wilshire Blvd Ste 2200
Los Angeles, CA 90048-4942, USA

Ulmar, Bin Hassan (Musician)
Agency Group
1775 Broadway Ste 2300
New York, NY 10019-1907, USA

Ulmer, Arthur (Athlete, Football Player)
1133 Lloyd Dr
Forest Park, GA 30297-1516, USA

Ulmer, Kristen (Athlete)
3671 E Willow Canyon Dr
Salt Lake City, UT 84121-6184, USA

Ulrich, Kim Johnston (Actor)
S D B Partners
315 S Beverly Dr Ste 411
Beverly Hills, CA 90212-4301, USA

Ulrich, Lars (Musician)
Q Prime Inc
729 7th Ave Ste 1600
New York, NY 10019-6880, USA

Ulrich, Skeet (Actor)
3585 Woodhill Canyon Rd
Studio City, CA 91604-3657, USA

Ultra, Nate (Musician)
Peach Bisquit
451 Washington Ave Apt 5A
Brooklyn, NY 11238-1838, USA

Ultraista (Musician)
c/o Steve Martin *Nasty Little Man*
110 Greene St Ste 605
New York, NY 10012-3838, USA

Umansky, Mauricio (Business Person,
Reality Star)
The Agency
331 Foothill Rd Ste 100
Beverly Hills, CA 90210-3667, USA

Umbach, Arnie (Athlete, Baseball Player)
7828 Al Highway 147 N
Auburn, AL 36879-4208, USA

Umbarger, Jim (Athlete, Baseball Player)
10701 N 99th Ave Lot 161
Peoria, AZ 85345-5442, USA

Umberger, Andy (Actor)
c/o Claire Miller *Bauman Redanty &
Shaul Agency*
5757 Wilshire Blvd
Suite 473
Beverly Hills, CA 90212, USA

Umberger, RJ (Athlete, Hockey Player)
1616 Woodland Hall Dr
Delaware, OH 43015-7109, USA

Umbers, Mark (Actor)
c/o Nick Frenkel *3 Arts Entertainment (LA)*
9460 Wilshire Blvd Fl 7
Beverly Hills, CA 90212-2713, USA

Umenyiora, Osi (Athlete, Football Player)
c/o Tom Condon *CAA (St. Louis)*
222 S Central Ave Ste 1008
Saint Louis, MO 63105-3509, USA

Umphlett, Tommy (Athlete, Baseball
Player)
104 Berkley Rd
Ahoskie, NC 27910-9575, USA

Umphrey's McGee (Music Group)
c/o Staff Member *Paradigm (Monterey)*
404 W Franklin St
Monterey, CA 93940-2303, USA

Underhill, Matt (Athlete, Hockey Player)
22 Madison St
Medford, MA 02155-2231, USA

Underwood, Blair (Actor)
c/o Ron West *Thruline Entertainment*
9250 Wilshire Blvd Ste 100
Ground Floor
Beverly Hills, CA 90212-3343, USA

Underwood, Carrie (Musician)
8 Wentworth Pl
Brentwood, TN 37027-8934, USA

Underwood, Cecil (Politician)
1578 Kanawha Blvd E Apt 1C
Charleston, WV 25311-2459, USA

Underwood, Jacob (Musician)
Trans Continental Records
7380 W Sand Lake Rd # 350
Orlando, FL 32819-5248, USA

Underwood, Jay (Actor)
6100 Wilshire Blvd Ste 1170
Los Angeles, CA 90048-5116, USA

Underwood, Matthew (Sportscaster)
c/o Glenn Hughes III *Gem Entertainment
Group*
10920 Wilshire Blvd Ste 150
Los Angeles, CA 90024-3990, USA

Underwood, Olen (Athlete, Football
Player)
302 N Main St
Conroe, TX 77301-2810, USA

Underwood, Pat (Athlete, Baseball Player)
708 Riverview Dr
Kokomo, IN 46901-7024, USA

Underwood, Ron (Director)
United Talent Agency
9336 Civic Center Dr
Beverly Hills, CA 90210-3604, USA

Underwood, Sarah Jean (Actor)
c/o Matt Cohen *IAG Entertainment &
Sports*
5189 Argonne Ct
San Diego, CA 92117-1054, USA

Underwood, Scott (Musician)
Jon Landua
80 Mason St
Greenwich, CT 06830-5515, USA

Underwood, Sheryl (Actor)
c/o EJ Johnson *William Morris Endeavor
(LA)*
9601 Wilshire Blvd
Beverly Hills, CA 90210-5213, USA

Unger, Billy (Actor)
c/o Matt Luber *Luber Roklin Management*
5815 W Sunset Blvd Ste 206
Los Angeles, CA 90028-6481, USA

Unger, Brian (Television Host)
c/o Staff Member *Extra (LA)*
1840 Victory Blvd
Telepictures Productions
Glendale, CA 91201-2558, USA

Unger, Brian
5750 Wilshire Blvd
Los Angeles, CA 90036-3697

Unger, Deborah Kara (Actor)
c/o Sarah Jackson *Seven Summits Pictures
& Management*
8906 W Olympic Blvd
Ground Floor
Beverly Hills, CA 90211-3550, USA

Union, Gabrielle (Actor)
c/o Jeff Morrone *Intellectual Artists
Management*
10585 Santa Monica Blvd Ste 135
Los Angeles, CA 90025-6392, USA

Union, Sarah (Actor)
c/o Jason Barrett *Alchemy Entertainment*
7024 Melrose Ave Ste 420
Los Angeles, CA 90038-3394, USA

Unkefer, Ronald A (Business Person)
Good Guys Inc
1600 Harbor Bay Pkwy
Alameda, CA 94502-3085, USA

Unrein, Mitch (Athlete, Football Player)
c/o Frank Bauer *Sun West Sports*
7883 N Pershing Ave
Stockton, CA 95207-1749, USA

Unroe, Tim (Athlete, Baseball Player)
2719 S Joplin
Mesa, AZ 85209-2508, USA

Unruh, James A (Business Person)
5426 E Morrison Ln
Paradise Valley, AZ 85253-3017, USA

Unseld, Wes (Athlete, Basketball Player,
Coach)
2210 Cedar Circle Dr
Catonsville, MD 21228, USA

Unser, Al (Race Car Driver)
7625 Central Ave NW
Albuquerque, NM 87121-2115, USA

Unser, Bobby (Race Car Driver)
7700 Central Ave SW
Albuquerque, NM 87121-2113, USA

Unser, Del (Athlete, Baseball Player)
33516 N 79th Way
Scottsdale, AZ 85266-4244, USA

Unser, Johnny (Race Car Driver)
13701 S Lake Dr
Plainfield, IL 60544-8113, United States

Unser Jr, Al (Race Car Driver)
Galles Racing
130 Lomas Blvd
Albuquerque, NM 87102, USA

Unutoa, Morris (Athlete, Football Player)
821B Country Club Pkwy
Mount Laurel, NJ 08054-2714, USA

Upchurch, Rickie (Rick) (Athlete, Football
Player)
463 Hagens Aly
Mesquite, NV 89027-5815, USA

Upham, Misty (Actor)
c/o Richard Kerner *Kerner Management
Associates*
311 N Robertson Blvd Ste 288
Beverly Hills, CA 90211-1705, USA

Upshaw, Marv (Athlete, Football Player)
3851 Madrone Ave
Oakland, CA 94619-2731, USA

Upshaw, Regan (Athlete, Football Player)
21300 Redskin Park Dr
Ashburn, VA 20147-6100, USA

Upshaw, Willie (Athlete, Baseball Player)
500 Main St Attn Ofc
Bridgeport, CT 06604-5136, USA

Upton, Fred (Congressman, Politician)
2183 Rayburn Hob
Washington, DC 20515-1803, USA

Upton, Justin (Athlete, Baseball Player)
7755 N Foothill Dr S
Paradise Valley, AZ 85253-3067, USA

Upton, Kate (Model)
c/o Ilene Feldman *LBI Entertainment*
2000 Avenue of the Stars
Floor 3, North Tower
Los Angeles, CA 90067-4700, USA

Upton, Melvin (B J) (Athlete, Baseball
Player)
637 Riviera Dr
Tampa, FL 33606-3809, USA

Upton, Melvin ""B J"" (Athlete, Baseball
Player)
637 Riviera Dr
Tampa, FL 33606-3809, USA

Urb, Johann (Actor)
c/o Lena Roklin *Luber Roklin
Management*
5815 W Sunset Blvd Ste 206
Los Angeles, CA 90028-6481, USA

Urban, Brent (Athlete, Football Player)
c/o Todd France *Five Star Athlete
Management*
3500 Lenox Rd NE
Atlanta, GA 30326-4228, USA

Urban, Karl (Actor)
c/o Jennifer Rawlings *Principato/Young
Management (LA)*
9465 Wilshire Blvd Ste 900
Beverly Hills, CA 90212-2608, USA

Urban, Keith (Musician)
200 11th Ave # PH1
New York, NY 10011-1055, USA

Urban, Thomas N (Business Person)
Pioneer Hi-Bred Int'l
400 Locust St Ste 500
Capital Square
Des Moines, IA 50309-2355, USA

Urbanchek, Jon (Coach)
University of Michigan
Athletic Dept
Ann Arbor, MI 48109, USA

Urbani, Luca Dr (Astronaut)
18290 Upper Bay Rd
Houston, TX 77058-4122, USA

Urbani, Tom (Athlete, Baseball Player)
2999 Chen Way
Soquel, CA 95073-2849, USA

Urbano, Mike (Musician)
c/o Staff Member *Creative Artists Agency
(CAA-LA)*
2000 Avenue of the Stars Ste 100
Los Angeles, CA 90067-4705, USA

Urbanski, Douglas (Actor, Producer,
Writer)
Douglas Management Group (
9713 Little Santa Monica Blvd
Suite 218
Beverly Hills, CA 90210, USA

Urbik, Kraig (Athlete, Football Player)
c/o Joe Panos *Athletes First, LLC*
23091 Mill Creek Dr
Laguna Hills, CA 92653-1258, USA

Urch, Scott (Athlete, Football Player)
14 Elmo Dr
Macomb, IL 61455-9505, USA

Urenda, Herman (Athlete, Football Player)
225 Upton Pyne Dr
Brentwood, CA 94513-6425, USA

Uresti, Omar (Golfer)
7005 Mitra Dr
Austin, TX 78739-2037, USA

Uribe, Diane (Actor)
23874 Via Jacara
Valencia, CA 91355-2520, USA

Uribe, Juan (Athlete, Baseball Player)
1817 Micanopy Ave
Miami, FL 33133-3329, USA

Urich, Justin (Actor)
Talent Group
5670 Wilshire Blvd Ste 820
Los Angeles, CA 90036-5613, USA

Urie, Brendon (Musician)
c/o Staff Member *Fueled By Ramen*
PO Box 1803
Tampa, FL 33601-1803, USA

Urie, Michael (Actor)
7135 Hollywood Blvd Apt 1002
Los Angeles, CA 90046-3960, USA

Urlacher, Brian (Football Player)
15044 W Little Saint Marys Rd
Libertyville, IL 60048-9676, USA

Urmanov, Alexei
Luzhnetskaya nab. 8
Moscow, RU 11987

Urrea, John (Athlete, Baseball Player)
75 E 24th St
Upland, CA 91784-8353, USA

Urschel, John (Athlete, Football Player)
c/o Jim Ivler *Sportstars Inc*
1350 Avenue of the Americas Fl 28
New York, NY 10019-4702, USA

Urseth, Bonnie (Actor)
c/o Staff Member *Gage Group, The (LA)*
5757 Wilshire Blvd Ste 659
Los Angeles, CA 90036-3682, USA

Urshan, Nathaniel A (Religious Leader)
United Pentecostal Church International
8855 Dunn Rd
Hazelwood, MO 63042-2212, USA

Used, The (Music Group)
c/o John Reese *Freeze Management*
32941 Calle Perfecto # C
San Juan Capistrano, CA 92675-4705,
USA

Usery, William J Jr (Politician, Secretary)
1101 S Arlington Ridge Rd
Arlington, VA 22202-1951, USA

Usher, Bob (Athlete, Baseball Player)
1022 N 5th St
San Jose, CA 95112-4413, USA

Usher, Thomas J (Business Person)
USX Corp
600 Grant St Ste 153
Pittsburgh, PA 15219-2750, USA

Ushkowitz, Jenna (Actor)
c/o Jill Fritzo *PMK/BNC Public Relations
(PMK-NY)*
622 3rd Ave Fl 8
New York, NY 10017-6707, USA

Uslan, Michael (Producer, Writer)
Branded Entertainment
333 Crestmont Rd
Cedar Grove, NJ 07009-1907, USA

Usova, Maya (Figure Skater)
Connecticut Skating Center
300 Alumni Rd
Newington, CT 06111-1868, USA

Ustorf, Stefan (Athlete, Hockey Player)
8502 Waynesboro Way
Waynesville, OH 45068-7720

Utay, William (Actor)
c/o Staff Member *Days of Our Lives*
3000 W Alameda Ave
Burbank, CA 91523-0001, USA

Utley, Chase (Athlete, Baseball Player)
210 W Washington Sq Apt 12SW
Philadelphia, PA 19106-3579, USA

Utley, Mike (Athlete, Football Player)
PO Box 349
Orondo, WA 98843-0349, USA

Utley, Stan (Golfer)
20701 N Scottsdale Rd # 107-619
Scottsdale, AZ 85255-6413, USA

Utt, Ben (Athlete, Football Player)
3378 Habersham Rd NW
Atlanta, GA 30305-1171, USA

v, Avram
Technion 1 Efron Street PO Box 9697
Wrightsville, GA 31096, USA

Vaca, Joselito (Soccer Player)
Dallas Burn
14800 Quorum Dr Ste 300
Dallas, TX 75254-1442, USA

Vacanti, Charles A (Doctor)
Massachusetts University Med Center
Anesthesiology Dept
Cambridge, MA 02139, USA

Vacariu, Alina (Model)
c/o Staff Member *Elite Model
Management (LA)*
345 N Maple Dr Ste 176
Beverly Hills, CA 90210-5193, USA

Vaccaro, Brenda (Actor)
c/o Stephen (Steve) LaManna *Innovative
Artists (LA)*
1505 10th St
Santa Monica, CA 90401-2805, USA

Vacendak, Steve (Athlete, Basketball
Player)
608 Gaston St Ste 100
Raleigh, NC 27603-1258, USA

Vachon, Christine (Producer)
c/o Staff Member *Killer Films (US)*
526 W 26th St Rm 715
New York, NY 10001-5524, USA

Vachon, Nicholas (Athlete, Hockey
Player)
1926 Curtis Ave Apt B
Redondo Beach, CA 90278-2313

Vachon, Rogatien R (Rogie) (Athlete,
Coach, Hockey Player)
2228 Glyndon Ave
Venice, CA 90291-4043

Vachon, Rogie (Athlete, Hockey Player)
Los Angeles Kings
1111 S Figueroa St Ste 3100
Los Angeles, CA 90015-1333

Vack, Peter (Actor)
c/o Michael Greenwald *Don Buchwald &
Associates (LA)*
6500 Wilshire Blvd Ste 2200
Los Angeles, CA 90048-4942, USA

Vactor, Ted (Athlete, Football Player)
11504 Channing Dr
Silver Spring, MD 20902-2908, USA

Vaglica, Jim (Actor)
c/o Lisa Lobel *Boston Casting Inc*
129 Braintree St Ste 107
Allston, MA 02134-1613, USA

Vai, Steve (Musician)
c/o Ruta Seopetys *Sepetys Entertainment
Group*
5543 Edmondson Pike Ste 8A
Nashville, TN 37211-5808, USA

Vaidisova, Nicole (Tennis Player)
c/o Staff Member *IMG (Cleveland)*
1360 E 9th St Ste 100
Cleveland, OH 44114-1730, USA

Vaidya, Daya (Actor)
c/o Rob D'Avola *Rob DAvola &
Associates*
9107 Wilshire Blvd # 405
Beverly Hills, CA 90210-5531, USA

Vail, Eric (Athlete, Hockey Player)
10055 Piney Ridge Walk
Alpharetta, GA 30022-5065

Vail, Justina (Actor)
651 N Kilkea Dr
Los Angeles, CA 90048-2213, USA

Vail, Mike (Athlete, Baseball Player)
2348 Aztec Ruin Way
Henderson, NV 89044-4496, USA

Vails, Nelson (Athlete, Cycler, Olympic
Athlete)
7914 Tanager Ln
Indianapolis, IN 46256-1720, USA

Vajna, Andrew (Andy) (Producer)
c/o Staff Member *Cinergi Productions*
2308 Broadway
Santa Monica, CA 90404-2916, USA

Valabik, Boris (Athlete, Hockey Player)
13 South Ave SE
Atlanta, GA 30315, USA

Valance, Holly (Musician)
c/o Andrew Edwards *Wishlab*
2225A Hyperion Ave
Los Angeles, CA 90027-4709, USA

Valar, Paul (Skier)
34 Hubertus Ring
Franconia, NH 03580-5114, USA

Valastro, Buddy (Chef)
Carlos Bakery
95 Washington St Ste A
Hoboken, NJ 07030-4533, USA

Valbuena, Gary (Athlete, Football Player)
5040 Breckenridge Ave
Banning, CA 92220-7140, USA

Valderrama, Carlos (Soccer Player)
Colorado Rapids
555 17th St Ste 3350
Denver, CO 80202-3909, USA

Valderrama, Wilmer (Actor)
c/o Glenn Rigberg *Inphenate*
9701 Wilshire Blvd Fl 10
Beverly Hills, CA 90212-2010, USA

Valdes, Ismael (Athlete, Baseball Player)
13732 SW 285th St
Homestead, FL 33033-5708, USA

Valdes, Jesus (Chucho) (Musician)
IMN
278 Main St
Gloucester, MA 01930-6022, USA

Valdes, Marc (Athlete, Baseball Player)
PO Box 598
Binghamton, NY 13902-0598, USA

Valdes, Mark (Athlete, Baseball Player)
7519 Paula Dr
Tampa, FL 33615-4113, USA

Valdespino, Sandy (Athlete, Baseball
Player)
3831 NW 79th Way
Hollywood, FL 33024-8331, USA

Valdes-Rodriguez, Alisa (Writer)
c/o Staff Member *Greater Talent Network
Inc*
437 5th Ave Ste 8A
New York, NY 10016-2205, USA

Valdez, Erik (Actor)
c/o Ray Hughes *Ray Hughes Management*
12400 Ventura Blvd Ste 630
Studio City, CA 91604-2406, USA

Valdez, Ismael (Athlete, Baseball Player)
4001 26th St
Vero Beach, FL 32960-1930, USA

Valdez, Luis (Writer)
El Teatro Capesino
705 4th St
San Juan Bautista, CA 95045, USA

Valdivielso, Jose (Athlete, Baseball Player)
14 Rita Dr
Mount Sinai, NY 11766-2215, USA

Vale, Tina (Musician)
DreamWorks Records
9268 W 3rd St
Beverly Hills, CA 90210-3713, USA

Vale, Virginia
4039 Edenhurst Ave
Los Angeles, CA 90039-1469

Valen, Nancy (Actor)
c/o Michael Livingston *Artists Agency Inc
(LA)*
8255 W Sunset Blvd
West Hollywood, CA 90046-2417, USA

Valencia, Danny (Athlete, Baseball Player)
2289 NW 36th St
Boca Raton, FL 33431-5417, USA

Valensi, Nick (Musician)
615 Alta Vista Cir
South Pasadena, CA 91030-3605, USA

Valent, Eric (Athlete, Baseball Player)
1739 Colony Dr
Reading, PA 19610-1101, USA

Valenti, Carl M (Publisher)
Information Services
200 Liberty St
Dow Jones Telerate
New York, NY 10281-1003, USA

Valentin, Dave (Musician)
Turi's Music Enterprises
103 Westwood Dr
Miami, FL 33166, USA

Valentin, John (Athlete, Baseball Player)
1601 Avenida Cesar Chavez SE
Albuquerque, NM 87106-3930, USA

Valentin, Jose (Athlete, Baseball Player)
Fort Wayne Tincaps 1301 Ewing Street
Attn Managers Office
Fort Wayne, IN 46802, USA

Valentine, Bill (Athlete, Baseball Player)
15 Blue Ridge Cir
Little Rock, AR 72207-1901, USA

Valentine, Bobby (Athlete, Baseball
Player, Coach)
48 Chestnut Woods Rd
Redding, CT 06896-1819, USA

Valentine, Brooke (Musician)
c/o Staff Member *Virgin Records (NY)*
150 5th Ave Fl 7
New York, NY 10011-4372, USA

Valentine, Dan (Business Person)
C-Cube Microsystems
1551 McCarthy Blvd
Milpitas, CA 95035-7437, USA

Valentine, Darnell (Athlete, Basketball
Player, Olympic Athlete)
7546 SW Ashford St
Portland, OR 97224-7143, USA

Valentine, Donald T (Business Person)
Network Appliance Inc
495 E Java Dr
Sunnyvale, CA 94089-1125, USA

Valentine, Ellis (Athlete, Baseball Player)
2708 Bridgemarker Dr
Grand Prairie, TX 75054-7262, USA

Valentine, Fred (Athlete, Baseball Player)
4838 Blagden Ave NW
Washington, DC 20011-3716, USA

Valentine, Gary (Actor, Comedian)
c/o Shawn McDonald *William Morris Endeavor (LA)*
9601 Wilshire Blvd
Beverly Hills, CA 90210-5213, USA

Valentine, James (Musician)
c/o Staff Member *Creative Artists Agency (CAA-LA)*
2000 Avenue of the Stars Ste 100
Los Angeles, CA 90067-4705, USA

Valentine, Joe (Athlete, Baseball Player)
4168 Chiffon Ln
North Port, FL 34287-3236, USA

Valentine, Karen (Actor)
PO Box 1410
Washington, CT 06793-0410, USA

Valentine, Scott (Actor)
17465 Flanders St
Granada Hills, CA 91344-2211, USA

Valentine, Stacy (Adult Film Star)
200 W Houston St
New York, NY 10014-4828, USA

Valentine, Steve (Actor)
c/o Staff Member *Greater Vision Artists Talent Agency (GVA)*
8981 W Sunset Blvd Ste 101
West Hollywood, CA 90069-1850, USA

Valentine, William N (Doctor)
2009 Skylark Ln
San Luis Obispo, CA 93401-3001, USA

Valentine, Zack (Athlete, Football Player)
162 Harvest Rd
Swedesboro, NJ 08085-1427, USA

Valentinetti, Vito (Athlete, Baseball Player)
271 Summit Ave
Mount Vernon, NY 10552-3309, USA

Valentino, Bobby (Musician)
c/o Staff Member *Island Def Jam Group*
825 8th Ave Fl 28
New York, NY 10019-7416, USA

Valenzuela, Fernando (Athlete, Baseball Player)
2123 N Beachwood Dr
Los Angeles, CA 90068-3403, USA

Valera, Julio (Athlete, Baseball Player)
685 Urb Colinas
Verdes D4
San Sebastian, PR 00685, USA

Valeriani, Richard G (Correspondent)
23 Island View Dr
Sherman, CT 06784-2036, USA

Valetta, Amber (Model)
c/o Daniel Spilo *Industry Entertainment*
955 Carrillo Dr Ste 300
Los Angeles, CA 90048-5400, USA

Valicevic, Rob (Athlete, Hockey Player)
54666 Sassafras Dr
Shelby Township, MI 48315-6902

Valiee, Bert L (Doctor)
300 Boyksti St
#712
Boston, MA 02116, USA

Valladolid, Marcela (Chef)
c/o Staff Member *Fluent Media Group*
5230 Alton Rd
Miami Beach, FL 33140-2005, USA

Valle, Dave (Athlete, Baseball Player)
2260 95th Ave NE
Clyde Hill, WA 98004-2516, USA

Valle, Hector (Athlete, Baseball Player)
HC 2 Box 19813
Cabo Rojo, PR 00623, USA

Vallely, James (Jim) (Writer)
c/o Staff Member *Creative Artists Agency (CAA-LA)*
2000 Avenue of the Stars Ste 100
Los Angeles, CA 90067-4705, USA

Vallely, John (Athlete, Basketball Player)
PO Box 39
Newport Beach, CA 92662-0039, USA

Valletta, Amber (Actor, Model)
c/o Sarah Shyn *3 Arts Entertainment (LA)*
9460 Wilshire Blvd Fl 7
Beverly Hills, CA 90212-2713, USA

Valley, Mark (Actor)
c/o Christine Tripicchio *Shelter PR*
9350 Wilshire Blvd Ste 450
Beverly Hills, CA 90212-3230, USA

Vallez, Emilio (Football Player)
Chicago Bears
General Delivery
Polvadera, NM 87828-9999, USA

Valli, Frankie (Musician)
5603 Winton Ct
Calabasas, CA 91302-3164, USA

Valmon, Andrew (Athlete, Olympic Athlete, Track Athlete)
16403 Danforth Ct
Rockville, MD 20853-3278, USA

Valot, Daniel L (Business Person)
Total Petroleum
900 19th St
Denver, CO 80202, USA

Valverde, Jose (Athlete, Baseball Player)
773 W Raven Dr
Chandler, AZ 85286-4484, USA

Valverde, Rawley (Actor)
15207 Magnolia Blvd Unit 106
Sherman Oaks, CA 91403-1105, USA

Vampire Weekend (Music Group)
c/o Ian Montone *LBI Entertainment*
2000 Avenue of the Stars
Floor 3, North Tower
Los Angeles, CA 90067-4700, USA

Van, Allen (Athlete, Hockey Player)
4890 Ashley Ln Apt 206
Inver Grove Heights, MN 55077-1234, USA

Van, Joey
48607 Presidential Dr # 2
Macomb, MI 48044-1985

Van Allsburg, Chris (Writer)
222 Berkeley St Fl 8
C/O Houghton Mifflin Children's Books
Boston, MA 02116-3748, USA

VanAmerongen, Jerry (Cartoonist)
2533 Washburn Ave S
Minneapolis, MN 55416-4350, USA

Van Ark, Joan (Actor)
4556 Dundee Dr
Los Angeles, CA 90027-1214, USA

VanArsdale, Dick (Athlete, Basketball Player)
6028 E Calle Tuberia
Scottsdale, AZ 85251-4229, USA

VanArsdale, Tom (Athlete, Basketball Player)
5434 E Lincoln Dr
Paradise Valley, AZ 85253-4118, USA

Van Benschoten, John (Athlete, Baseball Player)
5918 Milburne Dr
Milford, OH 45150-4101, USA

VanBerg, John C (Jack) (Coach)
420 Fair Hill Dr # 1
Elkton, MD 21921-2573, USA

Vanbiesbrouck, John (Athlete, Hockey Player, Olympic Athlete)
15467 Oak Ridge Dr
Spring Lake, MI 49456-2195, USA

Van Boxmeer, John (Athlete, Hockey Player)
8033 E Santa Cruz Ave
Orange, CA 92869-5652

Van Brabant, Ozzie (Athlete, Baseball Player)
5389 William Dr
Lexington, MI 48450-8864, USA

Van Breda Kolff, Jan (Athlete, Basketball Player)
1102 French Town Ln
Franklin, TN 37067-4666, USA

Van Buren, Ebert (Athlete, Football Player)
2100 Highway 165 S
Monroe, LA 71202-8219, USA

Van Buren, Jermaine (Athlete, Baseball Player)
557 Acree Ln
Columbus, OH 43228-8907, USA

Van Burkleo, Ty (Athlete, Baseball Player)
19681 Rabon Valley Rd
Grass Valley, CA 95949-8166, USA

VanCamp, Emily (Actor)
c/o Marc Hamou *Thruline Entertainment*
9250 Wilshire Blvd Ste 100
Ground Floor
Beverly Hills, CA 90212-3343, USA

Vance, Cory (Athlete, Baseball Player)
1321 Surrey Rd
Vandalia, OH 45377-1646, USA

Vance, Courtney B (Actor, Producer)
4710 Hillard Ave
La Canada Flintridge, CA 91011-2006, USA

Vance, Cyrus
425 Lexington Ave Fl 15
New York, NY 10017-3903

Vance, Ellis (Athlete, Basketball Player)
6 Carriage Way
Champaign, IL 61821-5119, USA

Vance, Eric (Athlete, Football Player)
17613 Archland Pass Rd
Lutz, FL 33558-8034, USA

Vance, Kenny (Musician)
PO Box 116
Far Rockaway, NY 11695-0116, USA

Vance, Sandy (Athlete, Baseball Player)
5863 Chelton Dr
Oakland, CA 94611-2423, USA

VanClief, D G (Race Car Driver)
Breeders Cup Ltd
PO Box 8
Esmont, VA 22937-0008, USA

Van Dam, Rob (Actor)
c/o Staff Member *Coast to Coast Talent Group*
3350 Barham Blvd
Los Angeles, CA 90068-1404, USA

Van Damme, Jean-Claude (Actor)
4803 Roma Ct
Marina Del Rey, CA 90292-6793, USA

Vande Berg, Ed (Athlete, Baseball Player)
4903 S Meadows Pl
Chandler, AZ 85248-5460, USA

Vande Hei, Mark T Lt Colonel (Astronaut)
1831 Raintree Cir
El Lago, TX 77586-5930, USA

Vande Hei, Mark T Ltcolonel (Astronaut)
1831 Raintree Cir
El Lago, TX 77586-5930, USA

Vandeman, George
1600 Waverly Rd
San Marino, CA 91108-2038

VandenBerg, Lodewijk (Astronaut)
Constellation Technology Corp
7887 Bryan Dairy Rd Ste 100
Seminole, FL 33777-1498, USA

Van Den Berg, Lodewijk Dr (Astronaut)
9658 Leeward Ave
Largo, FL 33773-4423, USA

Vanden Bosch, Kyle (Athlete, Football Player)
5847 E Calle Tuberia
Phoenix, AZ 85018-4633, USA

Vander, Musetta (Actor)
c/o Jeff Goldberg *Jeff Goldberg Management*
817 Monte Leon Dr
Beverly Hills, CA 90210-2629, USA

Van Der Beek, James (Actor)
12147 Morrison St
Valley Village, CA 91607-3624, USA

Vanderbeek, Matt (Athlete, Football Player)
4 Monstad St
Aliso Viejo, CA 92656-6246, USA

Vanderbilt, Gloria (Writer)
c/o Staff Member *HarperCollins Publishers*
195 Broadway Fl 2
Cellar 1
New York, NY 10007-3132, USA

Vanderbundt, Skip (Athlete, Football Player)
4225 Los Coches Way
Sacramento, CA 95864-5241, USA

Van Derbur, Marilyn (Actor)
195 S Dahlia St
Denver, CO 80246-1046, USA

Vanderbush, Carin Cone (Athlete, Olympic Athlete, Swimmer)
47 Rose Dr
Highland Falls, NY 10928-4310, USA

Vandergriff Jr, Bob (Race Car Driver)
845 McFarland Pkwy
Alpharetta, GA 30004-3365, USA

Vanderkaay, Peter (Athlete, Olympic Athlete, Swimmer)
292 W Woodland St
Ferndale, MI 48220-2706, USA

Vanderkelen, Ron (Athlete, Football Player)
5300 Vernon Ave S Apt 102
Minneapolis, MN 55436-2328, USA

Vanderlip-Ozburn, Dolly (Athlete, Baseball Player)
W18878 US Highway 53 54 93
Galesville, WI 54630-2805, USA

Vanderloo, Mark (Model)
Wilhelmina Models
300 Park Ave S # 200
New York, NY 10010-5313, USA

Vandermeer, Jim (Athlete, Hockey Player)
17967 N 95th St
Scottsdale, AZ 85255-6086

Van Der Meer, Johnny
4005 W Leona St
Tampa, FL 33629-8506

Van der Pol, Anneliese (Actor, Musician)
c/o Victoria Morris *Kazarian, Measures, Ruskin & Associates (LA)*
11969 Ventura Blvd Fl 3
Studio City, CA 91604-2630, USA

Vanderpump, Lisa (Business Person, Reality Star)
Villa Blanca Restaurant
9601 Brighton Way
Beverly Hills, CA 90210-5109, USA

Vandersea, Phil (Athlete, Football Player)
34 Hunting Ave
Shrewsbury, MA 01545-3177, USA

VanDerveer, Tara (Athlete, Basketball Player, Olympic Athlete)
1036 Cascade Dr
Menlo Park, CA 94025-6629, USA

Vandervoort, Laura (Actor)
c/o Mona Loring *MLC PR*
7080 Hollywood Blvd Ste 903
Los Angeles, CA 90028-6936, USA

Vander Wal, John (Athlete, Baseball Player)
5474 Highbury Dr SE
Ada, MI 49301-7736, USA

VandeSande, Theo A (Cinematographer)
8180 Mannix Dr
Los Angeles, CA 90046-1936, USA

Van Devere, Trish (Actor)
7036 Grasswood Ave
Malibu, CA 90265-4247, USA

Vandeweghe, Ernie (Athlete, Basketball Player)
18025 Green Meadow Dr
Encino, CA 91316-4424, USA

Vandeweghe, Kiki (Athlete, Basketball Player)
c/o Staff Member *Denver Nuggets*
1000 Chopper Cir
Denver, CO 80204-5805, USA

Van Dien, Casper (Actor)
c/o Steven Siebert *Lighthouse Entertainment*
9220 W Sunset Blvd Ste 200
West Hollywood, CA 90069-3501, USA

Vandis, Titos
1930 Century Park W # 303
Los Angeles, CA 90067-6802

Van Doren, Mamie (Actor)
3419 Via Lido # 184
Newport Beach, CA 92663-3908, USA

Van Dusen, Fred (Athlete, Baseball Player)
319 N Rowan Ave
Los Angeles, CA 90063-2323, USA

Van Dusen, Granville
10974 Alta View Dr
Studio City, CA 91604-3903

VanDusen, Granville (Actor)
10974 Alta View Dr
Studio City, CA 91604-3903, USA

Van Dyk, Paul (DJ, Musician)
c/o Joel Zimmerman *William Morris Endeavor (NY)*
1325 Avenue of the Americas
New York, NY 10019-6026, USA

Van Dyke, Barry (Actor)
27800 Blythedale Rd
Agoura Hills, CA 91301-1824, USA

Van Dyke, Bruce (Athlete, Football Player)
143 Lakeview Dr
Canonsburg, PA 15317-2747, USA

Van Dyke, Dick (Actor)
23215 Mariposa De Oro St
Malibu, CA 90265-4909, USA

Van Dyke, Jerry (Actor)
503 Jonah Ln
Malvern, AR 72104-7409, USA

Van Dyke, Leroy
29000 Highway V
Smithton, MO 65350-3629

VanDyke, Philip (Actor)
1464 Madera Rd # 108N
Simi Valley, CA 93065-3077, USA

Van Eeghen, Mark (Athlete, Football Player)
2207 Station Cir
Dedham, MA 02026-4588, USA

Van Egmond, Tim (Athlete, Baseball Player)
8839 Callaway Rd
Gay, GA 30218-1817, USA

Vanek, Thomas (Athlete, Hockey Player)
2302 Nicolle Ave N
Stillwater, MN 55082-1782, USA

Van Eman, Charles
12304 Santa Monica Blvd Ste 104
Los Angeles, CA 90025-2586

Van Ert, Sondra (Athlete, Olympic Athlete, Snowboarder)
PO Box 5910
Hailey, ID 83333-5910, USA

Van Every, Jonathan (Athlete, Baseball Player)
555 Dixton Dr
Brandon, MS 39047-8125, USA

Van Exel, Nick (Athlete, Basketball Player)
3102 Noble Lakes Ln
Houston, TX 77082-6809, USA

Van Galder, Don (Athlete, Football Player)
1611 Giles St
Austin, TX 78722-1242, USA

Van Galder, Tim (Athlete, Football Player)
11851 Charlemagne Dr
Maryland Heights, MO 63043-1505, USA

Vangelis (Musician)
c/o Staff Member *Robert Urband & Associates*
8981 W Sunset Blvd Ste 311
W Hollywood, CA 90069-1881, USA

Vangen, Scott D (Astronaut)
2101 Nasa Pkwy Spc Centerbldg
Houston, TX 77058-3607, USA

Van Gorder, Dave (Athlete, Baseball Player)
7858 E Hawthorne St
Tucson, AZ 85710-1645, USA

Van Gorkum, Harry (Actor)
22933 Leonora Dr
Woodland Hills, CA 91367-6121, USA

Vangsness, Kirsten (Actor)
137 N Larchmont Blvd Ste 234
Los Angeles, CA 90004-3704, USA

Van Gundy, Jeff (Sportscaster)
c/o Staff Member *William Morris Endeavor (LA)*
9601 Wilshire Blvd
Beverly Hills, CA 90210-5213, USA

Van Gundy, Stan (Basketball Coach, Coach)
7500 Deer Park Trl
Clarkston, MI 48346-1221, USA

Van Halen (Music Group)
c/o Irving Azoff *Azoff Music Management*
1100 Glendon Ave Ste 2000
Los Angeles, CA 90024-3524, USA

Van Halen, Alex (Musician)
c/o Irving Azoff *Azoff Music Management*
1100 Glendon Ave Ste 2000
Los Angeles, CA 90024-3524, USA

Van Halen, Eddie (Musician)
10100 Santa Monica Blvd Ste 2460
Los Angeles, CA 90067-4146, USA

Van Hekken, Andy (Athlete, Baseball Player)
1064 Cobblestone Rd
Holland, MI 49423-8864, USA

Van Heusen, Billy (Athlete, Football Player)
835 Hudson St
Denver, CO 80220-4436, USA

Van Hoften, James D Dr (Astronaut)
131 Camelia Ln
Lafayette, CA 94549-2733, USA

Van Hollen, Chris (Congressman, Politician)
1707 Longworth Hob
Washington, DC 20515-0523, USA

Van Hollen, Chris (Congressman, Politician)
51 Monroe St Ste 507
Rockville, MD 20850-2406, USA

Van Holt, Brian (Actor)
c/o Carlos Carreras *Agency for the Performing Arts (APA-LA)*
405 S Beverly Dr Ste 500
Beverly Hills, CA 90212-4425, USA

VanHorn, Buddy (Director)
4409 Ponca Ave
Toluca Lake, CA 91602-2513, USA

Van Horn, Doug (Athlete, Football Player)
149 Feronia Way
Rutherford, NJ 07070-2437, USA

Van Horn, Kelly (Producer, Writer)
c/o Staff Member *Mirisch Agency*
8840 Wilshire Blvd Ste 100
Beverly Hills, CA 90211-2606, USA

Van Horn, Patrick
9200 W Sunset Blvd Ste 1130
West Hollywood, CA 90069-3606

Van Horne, Dave (Sportscaster)
202 Bent Tree Dr
Palm Beach Gardens, FL 33418-3401, USA

Van Horne, Keith (Football Player)
c/o Staff Member *Dallas Mavericks*
2909 Taylor St
Dallas, TX 75226-1909, USA

Van Houten, Leslie
#W13378 Bed #1B314U CA Inst. for Women16756 Chino Corona
Frontera, CA 91720

Vanilla Fudge
141 Dunbar Ave
Fords, NJ 08863-1551

Van Impe, Ed (Athlete, Hockey Player)
Philadelphia Flyers Alumni Association
137 W 5th Ave Apt B9
Conshohocken, PA 19428-1646, USA

van Johnson, Rodney (Actor)
c/o Staff Member *Passions*
4024 Radford Ave
Studio City, CA 91604-2101, USA

Van Kemp, Merete
10000 Santa Monica Blvd # 305
Los Angeles, CA 90067

Van Kempen, Simon (Reality Star)
c/o Staff Member *Bravo (NY)*
30 Rockefeller Plz
New York, NY 10112-0015, USA

Van Keulen, Isabelle (Musician)
c/o Staff Member *Columbia Artists Mgmt Inc*
1790 Broadway Fl 6
New York, NY 10019-1537, USA

Van Landingham, William (Athlete, Baseball Player)
3023 Old Hillsboro Rd
Franklin, TN 37064-9544, USA

van Munster, Bertram (Producer)
c/o Staff Member *Earthview Inc*
200 Continental Blvd Fl 2
El Segundo, CA 90245-4510, USA

Van Note, Jeff (Athlete, Football Player)
345 Hollyberry Dr
Roswell, GA 30076-1215, USA

Van Noy, Kyle (Athlete, Football Player)
c/o David Dunn *Athletes First, LLC*
23091 Mill Creek Dr
Laguna Hills, CA 92653-1258, USA

Van Ornum, John (Athlete, Baseball Player)
PO Box 26808
Fresno, CA 93729-6808, USA

Vanous, Lucky (Actor, Model)
28345 La Calenta Msn
Mission Viejo, CA 92692, USA

Vanover, Larry (Athlete, Baseball Player)
3037 Sterling Ct
Owensboro, KY 42303-6393, USA

Vanover, Larry (Baseball Player)
801 Glenn Ct
Owensboro, KY 42303-0520, USA

Vanover, Tamarick (Athlete, Football Player)
703 NW Wilson St
Lake City, FL 32055-1863, USA

Vanoy, Vern (Athlete, Football Player)
3710 E 51st St Apt 409
Kansas City, MO 64130-3061, USA

Van Patten, Dick (Actor)
c/o Daniel Bernstein *Bernstein Entertainment*
12581 Venice Blvd Ste 204
Los Angeles, CA 90066-3707, USA

Van Patten, James
14411 Riverside Dr Apt 15
Sherman Oaks, CA 91423-1739

Van Patten, Joyce
c/o Staff Member *SMS Talent*
8383 Wilshire Blvd Ste 230
Beverly Hills, CA 90211-2436, USA

Van Patten, Nels
14411 Riverside Dr Apt 18
Sherman Oaks, CA 91423-1740

Van Patten, Tim (Actor, Director, Producer, Writer)
c/o Chris Simonian *Creative Artists Agency (CAA-LA)*
2000 Avenue of the Stars Ste 100
Los Angeles, CA 90067-4705, USA

Van Patten, Timothy
13920 Magnolia Blvd
Sherman Oaks, CA 91423-1230

Van Patten, Vincent
13926 Magnolia Blvd
Sherman Oaks, CA 91423-1230

Van Peebles, Mario (Actor, Director, Producer)
4016 Kenway Ave
View Park, CA 90008-4808, USA

Van Peebles, Melvin (Writer)
353 W 56th St Apt 10F
New York, NY 10019-3777, USA

Van Pelt, Alex (Athlete, Football Player)
7209 Quaker Rd
Orchard Park, NY 14127-2008, USA

Van Pelt, Bo (Athlete, Golfer)
c/o Jim Lehrman *SFX Golf*
36855 W Main St Ste 200
Purcellville, VA 20132-3561, USA

Van Pelt, Erika (Musician)
c/o Staff Member *19 Entertainment (LA)*
9000 W Sunset Blvd Ste 1574
West Hollywood, CA 90069-5817, USA

Van Pier, Andre
PO Box 555
New York, NY 10156-0555, USA

Van Poppel, Todd (Athlete, Baseball Player)
340 Springfield Bnd
Argyle, TX 76226-6848, USA

Van Praagh, James (Actor, Producer, Writer)
Spiritual Horizons
PO Box 60517
Pasadena, CA 91116-6517, USA

Van Raaphorst, Dick (Athlete, Football Player)
720 Devon Ct
San Diego, CA 92109-8005, USA

Van Riemsdyk, James (Athlete, Hockey Player)
54 Foxwood Run
Middletown, NJ 07748-2428, USA

Van Ryn, Ben (Athlete, Baseball Player)
8911 Saddle Trl Unit 1
San Antonio, TX 78255-2372, USA

Van Ryn, Mike (Athlete, Hockey Player)
Houston Aeros
317 Washington St
Saint Paul, MN 55102-1609

Van Ryn, Mike (Athlete, Hockey Player)
17681 SW 54th St
Southwest Ranches, FL 33331-2308

Van Sant, Doug G (Director)
c/o Gabrielle (Gaby) Morgerman *William Morris Endeavor (LA)*
9601 Wilshire Blvd
Beverly Hills, CA 90210-5213, USA

Van Sant, Gus (Actor, Director, Producer, Writer)
c/o Gabrielle (Gaby) Morgerman *William Morris Endeavor (LA)*
9601 Wilshire Blvd
Beverly Hills, CA 90210-5213, USA

VanSanten, Shantel (Actor)
c/o Loch Powell *Leverage Management*
3030 Pennsylvania Ave
Santa Monica, CA 90404-4112, USA

Van Sant-Machado, Helene (Baseball Player)
1221 Marion Ave
San Bernardino, CA 92407-1217, USA

Vanska, Osmo
Minnesota Symphony
1111 Nicollet Mall
Orchestra Hall
Minneapolis, MN 55403-2406, USA

Van Slyke, Andy (Athlete, Baseball Player)
21 Frontenac Estates Dr
Saint Louis, MO 63131-2615, USA

Van Susteren, Greta (Television Host)
c/o Staff Member *Fox News (NY)*
1211 Avenue of the Americas Lowr C1
New York, NY 10036-8705, USA

Van Valkenberg, Pete (Athlete, Football Player)
3072 Ninebark Cir
Saint George, UT 84790-8226, USA

Van Valkenburgh, Deborah
2025 Stanley Hills Dr
Los Angeles, CA 90046-7752

VanValkenburgh, Deborah (Actor)
Gaye West
PO Box 1515
Studio City, CA 91614-0515, USA

Van Varenberg, Kristopher (Actor)
c/o Jack Gilardi *ICM Partners (LA)*
10250 Constellation Blvd Fl 7
Los Angeles, CA 90067-6207, USA

Vanvieren, Pete (Baseball Player, Sportscaster)
Atlanta Braves
12260 Magnolia Cir
Alpharetta, GA 30005-7234, USA

Van Vleet, Michael (Athlete, Baseball Player)
8462 Grapevine Cir
Mattawan, MI 49071-8433, USA

Van Vleet, Michael (Baseball Player)
118 Dreamfield Dr
Battle Creek, MI 49014-7846, USA

Van Vooren, Monique
165 E 66th St
New York, NY 10065-6132

Van Wageningen, Yorick (Actor)
c/o Staff Member *Nine Yards Entertainment*
5815 W Sunset Blvd Ste 206
Los Angeles, CA 90028-6481, USA

Van Wagner, James (Athlete, Football Player)
5246 N Royal Dr
Traverse City, MI 49684-6984, USA

Van Wieren, Pete (Athlete, Baseball Player)
12260 Magnolia Cir
Alpharetta, GA 30005-7234, USA

Van Winkle, Travis (Actor)
c/o Scott Fish *Velocity Entertainment Partners*
5455 Wilshire Blvd Ste 802
Los Angeles, CA 90036-4271, USA

Van Wormer, Steve (Actor)
c/o Staff Member *Innovative Artists (LA)*
1505 10th St
Santa Monica, CA 90401-2805, USA

Van Zandt, Caitlin (Actor)
Persona Management
40 E 9th St Apt 11J
New York, NY 10003-6426, USA

Van Zandt, Steven (Actor)
c/o Staff Member *Renegade Nation Holdings*
434 6th Ave Fl 6
New York, NY 10011-8411, USA

Van Zant, Donnie (Musician)
c/o Staff Member *Vector Management*
PO Box 120479
Nashville, TN 37212-0479, USA

Vanzant, Iyanla (Television Host, Writer)
Inner Visions Institute for Spiritual Development
PO Box 8517
Silver Spring, MD 20907-8517, USA

Van Zeeland, Kathy (Designer)
77 Beverly Park Ln
Beverly Hills, CA 90210-1571, USA

Varada, Vaclav (Athlete, Hockey Player)
9042 Stonebriar Dr
Clarence Center, NY 14032

Vardalos, Nia (Actor)
c/o Evan Hainey *Untitled Entertainment (LA)*
350 S Beverly Dr Ste 200
Beverly Hills, CA 90212-4819, USA

Vardell, Tommy (Athlete, Football Player)
PO Box 1261
Alamo, CA 94507-7261, USA

Varela, Leonor (Actor)
c/o Adam Griffin *Kritzer Levine Wilkins Entertainment (KLWG)*
11872 La Grange Ave Fl 1
Los Angeles, CA 90025-5283, USA

Vargas, Elizabeth (Television Host)
c/o Staff Member *ABC News*
77 W 66th St Fl 3
New York, NY 10023-6201, USA

Vargas, Jacob (Actor)
c/o Ben Feigin *Anonymous Content (LA)*
3532 Hayden Ave
Culver City, CA 90232-2413, USA

Vargas, Jason (Athlete, Baseball Player)
14775 Keota Ln
Apple Valley, CA 92307-5137, USA

Vargas, Roberto (Baseball Player)
Chicago American Giants
Urb Runoz Rivera 24 Calle Brizaida
Guaynabo, PR 00969, USA

Vargo, Ed (Athlete, Baseball Player)
101 Freedom Rd
Butler, PA 16001-1304, USA

Vargo, Larry (Athlete, Football Player)
23337 S Colonial Ct
Saint Clair Shores, MI 48080-2605, USA

Vargo, Tim (Business Person)
AutoZone Inc
123 S Front St
Memphis, TN 38103-3618, USA

Varitek, Jason (Athlete, Baseball Player)
c/o Scott Boras *Boras Corporation*
3 San Joaquin Plz Ste 100
Newport Beach, CA 92660-5944, USA

Varma, Indira (Actor)
c/o Tammy Rosen *Sanders Armstrong Caserta*
2120 Colorado Ave Ste 120
Santa Monica, CA 90404-3561, USA

Varnado, Victor (Actor, Comedian)
c/o Staff Member *The Luedtke Agency*
1674 Broadway Ste 7A
New York, NY 10019-5855, USA

Varney, Pete (Athlete, Baseball Player)
14 Juniper Ridge Rd
Acton, MA 01720-2213, USA

Varone, Phil (Musician)
c/o Barbara Papageorge *Barbara Papageorge Publicity*
790 Amsterdam Ave
New York, NY 10025-5738, USA

Varoni, Miguel (Actor)
c/o Oswaldo Pisfil *NCM Productions*
10770 NW 66th St Apt 512
Doral, FL 33178-3781, USA

Varrela, Leonor (Actor)
c/o Mimi DiTrani *The Schiff Company*
9220 W Sunset Blvd Ste 106
West Hollywood, CA 90069-3500, USA

Varrichione, Frank (Athlete, Football Player)
4118 Jefferson Pl
Bellingham, MA 02019-6305, USA

Varrichone, Frank (Athlete, Football Player)
RR 72 Box 319
Alton, NH 03809, USA

Varsho, Gary (Athlete, Baseball Player, Coach)
11921 Starr Rd
Chili, WI 54420-9502, USA

Vartan, Michael (Actor)
1811 Rising Glen Rd
Los Angeles, CA 90069-1246, USA

Vartan, Sylvie (Musician)
Scotti
706 N Beverly Dr
Beverly Hills, CA 90210-3322, USA

Varvatos, John (Designer, Fashion Designer)
John Varvatos
315 Bowery Frnt 2
New York, NY 10003-7151, USA

Vaske, Dennis (Athlete, Hockey Player)
9750 Crescent Park Cir Unit 389
Orland Park, IL 60462-7507

Vasquez, Junior (DJ, Musician)
Junior Vasquez Music
647 9th Ave Apt 3
New York, NY 10036-3661, USA

Vasquez, LaLa (Television Host)
c/o Stephanie Simon *Untitled Entertainment (LA)*
350 S Beverly Dr Ste 200
Beverly Hills, CA 90212-4819, USA

Vasquez, Randy
10600 Holman Ave Apt 1
Los Angeles, CA 90024-5931

Vasquez, Virgil (Athlete, Baseball Player)
32 Saint Francis Way
Santa Barbara, CA 93105-2552, USA

Vass, Zita (Actor)
c/o Kim Matuka *Online Talent Group*
Prefers to be contacted via email or telephone
West Hollywood, CA 90069, USA

Vasser, Jimmy (Race Car Driver)
8605 Robinson Ridge Dr
Las Vegas, NV 89117-5807, USA

Vassey, Liz (Actor)
c/o Nevin Dolcefino *Innovative Artists (LA)*
1505 10th St
Santa Monica, CA 90401-2805, USA

Vassilieva, Sofia (Actor)
c/o Jason Trawick *William Morris Endeavor (LA)*
9601 Wilshire Blvd
Beverly Hills, CA 90210-5213, USA

Vasys, Arunas (Athlete, Football Player)
2525 Hanford Ln
Aurora, IL 60502-6971, USA

Vataha, Randy (Athlete, Football Player)
183 Nobscot Rd
Sudbury, MA 01776-3339, USA

Vatcher, Jim (Athlete, Baseball Player)
16039 Northfield St
Pacific Palisades, CA 90272-4261, USA

Vatterott, Charles (Athlete, Football Player)
662 W Forest Dr
Houston, TX 77079-6916, USA

Vaughan, Charlie (Athlete, Baseball Player)
5717 Brazilwood Ct
Harlingen, TX 78552-2027, USA

Vaughan, Denis E (Musician)
c/o Staff Member *Schofer/Gold Agency*
51 Riverside Dr
New York, NY 10024, USA

Vaughan, Greg (Actor)
c/o Alex Cole *Elevate Entertainment*
5757 Wilshire Blvd Ste 460
Los Angeles, CA 90036-3658, USA

Vaughan, Jimmie (Musician)
c/o Cory L Moore *The Luther Wolf Agency*
PO Box 685318
Austin, TX 78768-5318, USA

Vaughan, Stoll (Musician)
c/o Staff Member *Paradigm (Monterey)*
404 W Franklin St
Monterey, CA 93940-2303, USA

Vaughn, Bruce (Golfer)
5615 N Monroe St
Hutchinson, KS 67502-3251, USA

Vaughn, Charles (Athlete, Basketball Player)
21358 State Highway 127
Tamms, IL 62988-3318, USA

Vaughn, Countess (Actor)
c/o Staff Member *Amsel, Eisenstadt & Frazier Talent Agency (AEF)*
5055 Wilshire Blvd Ste 860
Los Angeles, CA 90036-6108, USA

Vaughn, Damian (Athlete, Football Player)
423 Danvers Ct
Orrville, OH 44667-9579, USA

Vaughn, David (Basketball Player)
New Jersey Nets
390 Murray Hill Pkwy
East Rutherford, NJ 07073-2109, USA

Vaughn, Dewayne (Athlete, Baseball Player)
5501 NW 37th St
Warr Acres, OK 73122-2210, USA

Vaughn, Gregory L (Greg) (Athlete, Baseball Player)
10830 Sheldon Woods Way
Elk Grove, CA 95624-9630, USA

Vaughn, Jacque (Athlete, Basketball Player)
c/o Jeff Austin *Octagon Home Office*
1751 Pinnacle Dr Fl 15
Mc Lean, VA 22102-3833, USA

Vaughn, Jimmie (Musician)
Mark I Mgmt
PO Box 29480
Austin, TX 78755-6480, USA

Vaughn, John H (Johnny) (Athlete, Coach, Football Player)
Highway 6 W
Oxford, MS 38655, USA

Vaughn, Jonathan S (Jon) (Athlete, Football Player)
224 N Highway 67
Florissant, MO 63031-5904, USA

Vaughn, Linda (Race Car Driver)
PO Box 352
Newville, PA 17241-0352, USA

Vaughn, Matthew (Actor, Director)
c/o Naren Desai *Brillstein Entertainment Partners (LA)*
9150 Wilshire Blvd Ste 350
Beverly Hills, CA 90212-3453, USA

Vaughn, Maurice (Mo) (Athlete, Baseball Player)
Omni New York LLC 1 Dag Hammarskjold Plz Bsmt C
New York, NY 10017, USA

Vaughn, Ned (Actor)
James/Levy/Jacobson
3500 W Olive Ave Ste 920
Burbank, CA 91505-5514, USA

Vaughn, Robert (Actor)
PO Box 2071
Los Angeles, CA 90051-0071, USA

Vaughn, Terri J (Actor)
c/o Sandra Siegal *Siegal Company, The*
9025 Wilshire Blvd Ste 400
Beverly Hills, CA 90211-1828, USA

Vaughn, Thomas R (Athlete, Football Player)
860 E Linda Ln
Gilbert, AZ 85234-5969, USA

Vaughn, Vince (Actor)
106 Terraza Pl
Manhattan Beach, CA 90266-6831, USA

Vaught, Loy (Athlete, Basketball Player)
838 Andover Ct SE
Grand Rapids, MI 49508-4770, USA

Vaugier, Emmanuelle (Actor)
c/o David (Dave) Fleming *Mosaic Media Group*
9200 W Sunset Blvd Ste 10
West Hollywood, CA 90069-3608, USA

Vavra, Joe (Athlete, Baseball Player)
E4640 483rd Ave
Menomonie, WI 54751-5481, USA

Vayda, Brandon Michael (Actor)
c/o Omar Mayet *Gel Entertainment*
9255 W Sunset Blvd Ste 803
West Hollywood, CA 90069-3305, USA

Vaydik, Greg (Athlete, Hockey Player)
6041 Village Bend Dr Apt 1007
Dallas, TX 75206-3610

Vaynerchuk, Gary (Business Person, Writer)
c/o Staff Member *Vaynermedia*
586 Morris Ave
Springfield, NJ 07081-1017, USA

Vaziri, Khosrow (Wrestler)
c/o Eric Simms *ESS Promotions*
PO Box 52
Marlboro, NJ 07746-0052, USA

Vazquez, Armondo (Baseball Player)
Indianapolis Clowns
160 W 85th St Apt 1K
New York, NY 10024-4410, USA

Vazquez, Javier (Athlete, Baseball Player)
1441 S Prairie Ave
Chicago, IL 60605-2886, USA

Vazquez, LaLa (Actor)
c/o Shannon Barr *Rogers & Cowan PR (LA)*
8687 Melrose Ave Ste 7
West Hollywood, CA 90069-5721, USA

Vazquez, Yul (Actor)
c/o Sarah Fargo *Paradigm (NY)*
360 Park Ave S Fl 16
New York, NY 10010-1716, USA

Veal, Coot (Athlete, Baseball Player)
238 Stonegables Dr
Gray, GA 31032-5526, USA

Veal, Donnie (Athlete, Baseball Player)
2971 E Wildhorse Dr
Gilbert, AZ 85297-2162, USA

Veale, Robert A (Bob) (Athlete, Baseball Player)
2833 Bush Blvd
Birmingham, AL 35208-2227, USA

Veals, Elton (Athlete, Football Player)
2981 Joyce Dr
Baton Rouge, LA 70814-2568, USA

Vedder, Eddie (Musician)
8001 44th Ave SW
Seattle, WA 98136-2209, USA

Vega, Alexa (Actor, Musician)
c/o John Carrabino *John Carrabino Management*
5900 Wilshire Blvd Ste 406
Los Angeles, CA 90036-5015, USA

Vega, Makenzie (Actor)
c/o Ro Diamond *SDB Partners Inc*
315 S Beverly Dr Ste 411
Beverly Hills, CA 90212-4301, USA

Vega, Paz (Actor)
c/o Scott Henderson *Paradigm (LA)*
9601 Wilshire Blvd
Beverly Hills, CA 90210-5213, USA

Vega, Suzanne (Musician)
c/o Staff Member *William Morris Endeavor (NY)*
1325 Avenue of the Americas
New York, NY 10019-6026, USA

Vega 4 (Music Group)
c/o Staff Member *Paradigm (Monterey)*
404 W Franklin St
Monterey, CA 93940-2303, USA

Vegas, Dirty (Music Group)
c/o Staff Member *Creative Artists Agency (CAA-LA)*
2000 Avenue of the Stars Ste 100
Los Angeles, CA 90067-4705, USA

Veils, The (Music Group)
c/o Staff Member *Paradigm (Monterey)*
404 W Franklin St
Monterey, CA 93940-2303, USA

Veingrad, Alan (Athlete, Football Player)
614 SE 26th Ave
Fort Lauderdale, FL 33301-2708, USA

Veisor, Mike (Athlete, Hockey Player)
16091 W Lakepoint Ct
Prairieville, LA 70769-4980

Veitch, Darren (Athlete, Hockey Player)
3410 Maricopa Hwy
Ojai, CA 93023-9520

Vejar, Chico (Boxer)
56 Glenbrook Rd
#3214
Stamford, CT 06902, USA

Velaquez, Nydia M. (Congressman, Politician)
266 Broadway Ste 201
Brooklyn, NY 11211-6306, USA

Velarde, Randy (Athlete, Baseball Player)
4902 Thames Ct
Midland, TX 79705-1796, USA

Velasquez, Cain (Athlete)
c/o Bob Cook *Zinkin Entertainment & Sports Management*
5 E River Park Pl W Ste 203
Fresno, CA 93720-1557, USA

Velasquez, Guillermo (Athlete, Baseball Player)
13842 Clear Trail Ln
Houston, TX 77034-2158, USA

Velasquez, Jaci (Musician)
Jaci Inc
PO Box 158659
Nashville, TN 37215-8659, USA

Velasquez, Jorge
770 Allerton Ave
Bronx, NY 10467-8879, USA

Velasquez, Jorge L Jr (Jockey)
770 Allerton Ave
Bronx, NY 10467-8879, USA

Velasquez, Patricia (Actor, Model)
c/o Staff Member *Principal Entertainment (LA)*
9255 W Sunset Blvd Ste 500
West Hollywood, CA 90069-3301, USA

Velazquez, Gil (Athlete, Baseball Player)
5101 Evergreen Meadow Ave
Las Vegas, NV 89130-7021, USA

Velazquez, John (Horse Racer)
133 Avon Pl
West Hempstead, NY 11552, USA

Velazquez, Nadine (Actor, Model)
c/o Patricia Mora *Metro Public Relations*
8383 Wilshire Blvd Ste 208
Beverly Hills, CA 90211-2432, USA

Velez, Eddie (Actor)
c/o Staff Member *Stone Manners Salners Agency (LA)*
6100 Wilshire Blvd Ste 1500
Los Angeles, CA 90048-5110, USA

Velez, Fermin (Race Car Driver)
701 S Girls School Rd
Indianapolis, IN 46231-3132, USA

Velez, Gloria (Model)
c/o Mike Esterman *Esterman.Com, LLC*
Prefers to be contacted via email
Baltimore, MD XXXXX, USA

Velez, Lauren (Actor)
c/o Tina Thor *TMT Entertainment Group*
648 Broadway # 1002
New York, NY 10012-2348, USA

Velez, Lisa Lisa (Musician)
c/o Staff Member *William Morris Endeavor (LA)*
9601 Wilshire Blvd
Beverly Hills, CA 90210-5213, USA

Velez, Otto (Baseball Player)
33 Villas De Cambalache
Guaynabo, PR 00966, USA

Velez-Mitchell, Jane (Actor, Correspondent)
c/o Staff Member *CNN (NY)*
1 Time Warner Ctr
New York, NY 10019-6038, USA

Vel Johnson, Reginald (Actor)
DGRW
1501 Broadway Ste 703
New York, NY 10036-5501

Veljohnson, Reginald (Actor)
9637 Allenwood Dr
Los Angeles, CA 90046, USA

Vella, John (Athlete, Football Player)
1890 Saint George Rd
Danville, CA 94526-6253, USA

Vellucci, Mike (Athlete, Hockey Player)
6036 Valencia Ct
Raleigh, NC 27614-7666

Velvet, Jimmy
PO Box 808
Lititz, PA 17543-0538

Velvet Revolver (Music Group)
c/o Staff Member *RCA Records (LA)*
8750 Wilshire Blvd Fl 2
Beverly Hills, CA 90211-2715, USA

Vemtrone, Raymond (Athlete, Hockey Player)
c/o Staff Member *Boston Bruins*
100 Legends Way Ste 250
Td Banknorth Garden
Boston, MA 02114-1389, USA

Venable, Mac (Athlete, Baseball Player)
107 Clark St
San Rafael, CA 94901-3604, USA

Venable, Max (Athlete, Baseball Player, Coach)
107 Clark St
San Rafael, CA 94901-3604, USA

Venable, Will (Athlete, Baseball Player)
107 Clark St
San Rafael, CA 94901-3604, USA

Venafro, Mike (Athlete, Baseball Player)
15271 McGregor Blvd Ste 16
Fort Myers, FL 33908-1900, USA

Venasky, Vic (Athlete, Hockey Player)
4307 W 234th Pl # Pi
Torrance, CA 90505-4506

Vendt, Erik (Athlete, Olympic Athlete, Swimmer)
17 Amberwood Ct
Buzzards Bay, MA 02532-8324, USA

Veneziale, Mike (Baseball Player)
110 Cloverdale Ln
Williamstown, NJ 08094-2341, USA

Venita, Carla (Musician)
3087 James Rd
Memphis, TN 38128-2921, USA

Venora, Diane (Actor)
Innovative Artists
1505 10th St
Santa Monica, CA 90401-2805, USA

Ventimiglia, John (Actor)
c/o Stacy Abrams *Abrams Entertainment*
5225 Wilshire Blvd Ste 515
Los Angeles, CA 90036-4349, USA

Ventimiglia, John
9150 Wilshire Blvd Ste 350
Beverly Hills, CA 90212-3453

Ventimiglia, Milo (Actor)
c/o Jason Heyman *Creative Artists Agency (CAA-LA)*
3500 W Olive Ave Ste 1400
Burbank, CA 91505-5512, USA

Ventimilia, Jeffrey (Actor)
c/o Staff Member *ICM Partners (LA)*
10250 Constellation Blvd Fl 7
Los Angeles, CA 90067-6207, USA

Vento, Mike (Athlete, Baseball Player)
7142 Kendall Heath Way
Land O Lakes, FL 34637-7554, USA

Ventresca, Vincent (Actor)
Mindel/Donigan
9057 Nemo St # C
West Hollywood, CA 90069-5511, USA

Ventrone, Raymond (Athlete, Football Player)
c/o Staff Member *New England Patriots*
1 Patriot Pl
Foxboro, MA 02035-1388, USA

Ventura, Cassandra (Cassie) (Musician)
c/o Carrie Gordon *42West (NYC)*
220 W 42nd St Fl 12
New York, NY 10036-7200, USA

Ventura, Jesse (Politician, Talk Show Host)
c/o Barry Bloom *Braverman Bloom Company*
6399 Wilshire Blvd
Los Angeles, CA 90048-5703, USA

Ventura, Robin (Athlete, Baseball Player)
1088 Newsom Springs Rd
Arroyo Grande, CA 93420-3618, USA

Ventura, Robin M (Baseball Player)
106 Dingletown Rd
Greenwich, CT 06830-3540, USA

Ventura-Manina, Virginia (Athlete, Baseball Player)
205 Midwood Dr
E Stroudsburg, PA 18301-8947, USA

Venturella, Michelle (Athlete, Olympic Athlete, Softball Player)
219 Carver Hawkeye Arena
Iowa University Softball
Iowa City, IA 52242-1020, USA

Ventures, The (Music Group)
11761 E Speedway Blvd
Tucson, AZ 85748-2017, USA

Venturi, Rick (Athlete, Football Coach, Football Player)
910 Banbury Rd
Noblesville, IN 46062-9088, USA

Venturini, Bill (Race Car Driver)
7621 Texas Trl
Boca Raton, FL 33487-1423, USA

Venturini, Tisha (Athlete, Olympic Athlete, Soccer Player)
7101 Del Rio Dr
Modesto, CA 95356-9643, USA

Venus Hum (Music Group)
c/o Staff Member *Paradigm (Monterey)*
404 W Franklin St
Monterey, CA 93940-2303, USA

Veras, Quilvio (Athlete, Baseball Player)
4244 Vineyard Cir
Weston, FL 33332-2153, USA

Verastegui, Eduardo (Producer)
c/o Staff Member *Rain Management Group (RMG)*
1631 21st St
Santa Monica, CA 90404-3914, USA

Verba, Ross (Athlete, Football Player)
3066 Arden Pl
Saint Paul, MN 55129-5211, USA

Verbanic, Joe (Athlete, Baseball Player)
9722 Groffs Mill Dr Ste 107
Owings Mills, MD 21117-6341, USA

Verbeek, Lotte (Actor)
c/o Lindsay Galin *Rogers & Cowan PR (NY)*
Prefers to be contacted via telephone and email
New York, NY, USA

Verbeek, Pat (Athlete, Hockey Player)
Tampa Bay Lightning
401 Channelside Dr
Tampa, FL 33602-5400

Verbinski, Gore (Director, Producer)
c/o Dave Morrison *Anonymous Content (LA)*
3532 Hayden Ave
Culver City, CA 90232-2413, USA

Verble, Gene (Athlete, Baseball Player)
633 Camrose Cir NE
Concord, NC 28025-3280, USA

Verboom, Hanna (Actor)
c/o Greg Siegel *William Morris Endeavor (LA)*
9601 Wilshire Blvd
Beverly Hills, CA 90210-5213, USA

Verchota, Phil (Athlete, Hockey Player, Olympic Athlete)
PO Box 1181
Bemidji, MN 56619-1181, USA

Verdin, Clarence (Athlete, Football Player)
6221 Eastover Dr
New Orleans, LA 70128-3619, USA

Verdugo, Elena
PO Box 2048
Chula Vista, CA 91912-2048

Vereen, Ben (Actor, Dancer, Musician)
The Cooper Company
729 7th Ave
New York, NY 10019-6831, USA

Vereen, Carl (Athlete, Football Player)
300 River Glen Dr
Roswell, GA 30075-4873, USA

Vereen, Shane (Athlete, Football Player)
c/o David Dunn *Athletes First, LLC*
23091 Mill Creek Dr
Laguna Hills, CA 92653-1258, USA

Veres, Dave (Athlete, Baseball Player)
871 Diamond Ridge Cir
Castle Rock, CO 80108-7812, USA

Veres, Randy (Athlete, Baseball Player)
9213 W Frank Ave
Peoria, AZ 85382-5364, USA

Vergara, Sofia (Actor)
1156 San Ysidro Dr
Beverly Hills, CA 90210-2146, USA

Verhoeven, John (Athlete, Baseball Player)
20805 Paseo De La Rambla
Yorba Linda, CA 92887-2429, USA

Verhoeven, Paul (Director, Writer)
14980 Camarosa Dr
Pacific Palisades, CA 90272-4427, USA

Verhoeven, Peter (Athlete, Basketball Player)
12722 Fargo Ave
Hanford, CA 93230-9645, USA

Verica, Tom (Actor)
c/o Laura Fogelman *Independent Artists (LA)*
9601 Wilshire Blvd Ste 750
Beverly Hills, CA 90210-5228, USA

Veris, Garin (Athlete, Football Player)
23 Nichols Ave
Newmarket, NH 03857-1207, USA

Verlander, Justin (Athlete, Baseball Player)
1238 Hawkwell Dr
Maidens, VA 23102-2240, USA

Vermeil, Dick (Athlete, Coach, Football Coach, Football Player)
775 Fairview Rd
Coatesville, PA 19320-4453, USA

Vermette, Antoine (Athlete, Hockey Player)
8687 Melrose Ave Ste 7
West Hollywood, CA 90069-5721

Vermilyea, Jamie (Athlete, Baseball Player)
7051 E Calle Arandas
Tucson, AZ 85750-2563, USA

Vernarsky, Kris (Athlete, Hockey Player)
24323 Tallman Ave
Warren, MI 48089-1847, USA

Vernon, Conrad (Actor)
c/o Ilan Breil *Mosaic Media Group*
9200 W Sunset Blvd Ste 10
West Hollywood, CA 90069-3608, USA

Vernon, Kate (Actor)
c/o Staff Member *Shelter Entertainment*
9255 W Sunset Blvd Ste 320
West Hollywood, CA 90069-3313, USA

Vernon, Olivier (Athlete, Football Player)
c/o Drew Rosenhaus *Rosenhaus Sports Representation*
6400 Allison Rd
Miami Beach, FL 33141-4540, USA

Vernon Jr, Gary Wayne (Gary Levox) (Musician)
c/o Jake Basden *Big Machine Records*
1219 16th Ave S
Nashville, TN 37212-2901, USA

Verplank, Scott (Athlete, Golfer)
1850 W Waterloo Rd
Edmond, OK 73025-1801, USA

Verraros, Jim (Musician)
PO Box 99
Dundee, IL 60118-0099

Verreos, Nick (Fashion Designer)
NIKOLAKI DESIGN
3579 Tacoma Ave
Los Angeles, CA 90065-1725, USA

Verser, David (Athlete, Football Player)
2600 SW Arvonia Pl
Topeka, KS 66614-5294, USA

Vertical Horizon (Music Group)
c/o Staff Member *Paradigm (Monterey)*
404 W Franklin St
Monterey, CA 93940-2303, USA

Veruca Salt (Music Group)
Veruca Salt/Louise Post
PO Box 291105
Los Angeles, CA 90029-9105, USA

Verveen, Arie (Actor)
c/o Scott Karp *The Syndicate*
10203 Santa Monica Blvd Fl 5
Los Angeles, CA 90067-6416, USA

Verve Pipe, The (Music Group)
c/o Staff Member *Paradigm (Monterey)*
404 W Franklin St
Monterey, CA 93940-2303, USA

Verve, The (Music Group)
c/o Staff Member *Paradigm (Monterey)*
404 W Franklin St
Monterey, CA 93940-2303, USA

Verwey, Bob (Golfer)
I M G
1360 E 9th St Ste 100
Cleveland, OH 44114-1730, USA

Veryzer, Tom (Athlete, Baseball Player)
41 Union Ave
Islip, NY 11751-3919, USA

Vesey, Jim (Athlete, Hockey Player)
11 Ellwood St
Charlestown, MA 02129-3809

Vessey, Tricia (Actor)
c/o Staff Member *Brillstein Entertainment Partners (LA)*
9150 Wilshire Blvd Ste 350
Beverly Hills, CA 90212-3453, USA

Vest, Jake (Cartoonist)
PO Box 350757
Grand Island, FL 32735-0757, USA

Vest, R Lamar (Religious Leader)
Church of God
PO Box 2430
Cleveland, TN 37320-2430, USA

Veters, Michael (Race Car Driver)
Black Stallion Racing
17137 Black Stallion Ln
Hagerstown, MD 21740-1891, USA

Vetri, Victoria (Actor)
610 N Van Ness Ave
Los Angeles, CA 90004-1536, USA

Vetter, Jack (Athlete, Football Player)
312 N Grand St
McPherson, KS 67460-4428, USA

Vettrus, Richard J (Religious Leader)
Church of Lutheran Brethren
12229 W 80th Ave
Arvada, CO 80005-3351, USA

Vez, El
3322 Hamilton Way
Los Angeles, CA 90026-2112

V. Gutterrez, Luis (Congressman, Politician)
2266 Rayburn Hob
Washington, DC 20515-0308, USA

Viaene, David (Athlete, Football Player)
W9859 School Rd
Hortonville, WI 54944-9630, USA

Viardo, Vladimir V (Musician)
457 Piermont Rd
Cresskill, NJ 07626-1524, USA

Viciedo, Dayan (Athlete, Baseball Player)
1450 Brickell Ave Ste 1800
Miami, FL 33131-3452, USA

Vicius, Nicole (Actor)
c/o Mimi DiTrani *The Schiff Company*
9220 W Sunset Blvd Ste 106
West Hollywood, CA 90069-3500, USA

Vick, Michael (Athlete, Football Player)
12 Haywagon Trl
Hampton, VA 23669-1165, USA

Vick, Roger (Athlete, Football Player)
12919 Windfern Rd Apt 1902
Houston, TX 77064-3068, USA

Vickaryous, Scott (Actor)
c/o Staff Member *Artists Only Management*
10203 Santa Monica Blvd
Los Angeles, CA 90067-6405, USA

Vickers, Brian (Race Car Driver)
BLV Motorsports
42 High Tech Blvd
Thomasville, NC 27360-5560, USA

Vickers, Kipp (Athlete, Football Player)
PO Box 78365
Indianapolis, IN 46278-0365, USA

Vickers, Steve (Athlete, Hockey Player)
209 Washington Ave
Batavia, NY 14020-2211, USA

Vickerson, Kevin (Athlete, Football Player)
c/o Drew Rosenhaus *Rosenhaus Sports Representation*
6400 Allison Rd
Miami Beach, FL 33141-4540, USA

Victor, James
1944 Whitley Ave Apt 306
Los Angeles, CA 90068-4100

Victorino, Shane (Athlete, Baseball Player)
1997 Alcova Ridlle Dr
Las Vegas, NV 89135, USA

Victorin (Ursache), Archbishop (Religious Leader)
Romanian Orthodox Church
19959 Riopelle St
Highland Park, MI 48203-1249, USA

Vida Blue (Music Group)
c/o Staff Member *Paradigm (Monterey)*
404 W Franklin St
Monterey, CA 93940-2303, USA

Vidal, Christina (Actor)
c/o Bob McGowan *McGowan Management*
8733 W Sunset Blvd Ste 103
West Hollywood, CA 90069-2241, USA

Vidal, Deborah (Golfer)
2033 Paramount Dr
Los Angeles, CA 90068-3120, USA

Vidal, Lisa (Actor)
c/o Bob McGowan *McGowan Management*
8733 W Sunset Blvd Ste 103
West Hollywood, CA 90069-2241, USA

Vidali, Lynn (Swimmer)
14750 Mosegard Ln
Morgan Hill, CA 95037-9604, USA

Vidmar, Peter (Athlete, Gymnast, Olympic Athlete)
455 Camino Flora Vis
San Clemente, CA 92673-6901, USA

Vidrine, David M (Astronaut)
11847 N Potosi Point Dr
Tucson, AZ 85737-3734, USA

Vidro, Jose (Athlete, Baseball Player)
PO Box 385
Sabana Grande, PR 00637-0385, USA

Vie, Richard C (Business Person)
PO Box 191
Lake Forest, IL 60045-0191, USA

Vieira, Meredith (Game Show Host, Television Host)
Meredith Vieira Productions
888 7th Ave
New York, NY 10106-0001, USA

Vieluf, Vince (Actor)
c/o Tammy Rosen *Sanders Armstrong Caserta*
425 N Robertson Blvd
West Hollywood, CA 90048-1735, USA

Viener, John (Actor)
c/o Kevin Crotty *ICM Partners (LA)*
10250 Constellation Blvd Fl 7
Los Angeles, CA 90067-6207, USA

Viera, Joey
4253 Navajo Ave
Toluca Lake, CA 91602-2913

Viereck, Peter (Writer)
1346 Murrell Ave
Columbus, OH 43212-3558, USA

View, The (Music Group)
c/o Staff Member *Paradigm (Monterey)*
404 W Franklin St
Monterey, CA 93940-2303, USA

Vig, Butch (Musician)
c/o Staff Member *Borman Entertainment (TN)*
4322 Harding Pike Ste 429
Nashville, TN 37205-2661, USA

Vigman, Gillian (Actor)
c/o Jeanne Newman *Hansen, Jacobson, Teller, Hoberman, Newman, Warren & Richman*
450 N Roxbury Dr Fl 8
Beverly Hills, CA 90210-4222, USA

Vigneron, Thierry (Athlete, Track Athlete)
Adidas USA
5675 N Blackstock Rd
Spartanburg, SC 29303-6329, USA

Vigoda, Abe (Actor)
c/o Staff Member *Cunningham Escott Slevin & Doherty (CESD-LA)*
10635 Santa Monica Blvd Ste 130
Los Angeles, CA 90025-8306, USA

Vigorito, Tommy (Athlete, Football Player)
19 Garden Pl
Pompton Plains, NJ 07444-1409, USA

Viguerie, Richard
7777 Leesburg Pike
Falls Church, VA 22043-2411

Vila, Bob (Actor, Producer, Television Host)
Vila Ventures
162 5th Ave Ste 901
Attn: Agnieszka
New York, NY 10010-6047, USA

Vilanch, Bruce (Comedian, Writer)
c/o Joan Hyler *Hyler Management*
20 Ocean Park Blvd Unit 25
Santa Monica, CA 90405-3590, USA

Vilanich, Bruce (Comedian)
c/o Staff Member *William Morris Endeavor (LA)*
9601 Wilshire Blvd
Beverly Hills, CA 90210-5213, USA

Vilar, Tracy (Actor)
c/o Doug Wald *Anonymous Content (LA)*
3532 Hayden Ave
Culver City, CA 90232-2413, USA

Vilasuso, Jordie (Actor)
c/o Staff Member *Innovative Artists (LA)*
1505 10th St
Santa Monica, CA 90401-2805, USA

Vilella, Edward
905 Lincoln Blvd
Miami Beach, FL 33139

Villacis, Eduardo (Athlete, Baseball Player, Coach)
Casper Rockies
PO Box 1293
Attn: Coaching Staff
Casper, WY 82602-1293, USA

Villa-Cryan, Marge (Athlete, Baseball Player)
16305 Summershade Dr
La Mirada, CA 90638-2742, USA

Villafuerte, Brandon (Athlete, Baseball Player)
PO Box 188
North Bridgton, ME 04057-0188, USA

Villalon, Jade Valerie (Musician)
c/o Staff Member *Universal Records*
825 8th Ave
New York, NY 10019-7416, USA

Villano, Mike (Baseball Player)
Bowman
451 Village Green Blvd Apt 103
Ann Arbor, MI 48105-2700, USA

Villanueva, Carlos (Athlete)
c/o Staff Member *SFX Sports Management*
5335 Wisconsin Ave NW Ste 850
Washington, DC 20015-2052, USA

Villanueva, Charlie (Athlete, Basketball Player)
c/o Jeff Schwartz *Excel Sports Management (NY)*
1700 Broadway Fl 29
New York, NY 10019-5905, USA

Villanueva, Danny (Athlete, Football Player)
PO Box 258
Somis, CA 93066-0258, USA

Villapiano, Phillip J (Phil) (Athlete, Football Player)
21 Riverside Dr
Rumson, NJ 07760-1026, USA

Villaraigosa, Antonio (Politician)
City of Los Angeles
200 N Spring St Ste 303
Los Angeles, CA 90012-3239, USA

Villari, Guy (Musician)
293 Airport Rd
Liberty, NY 12754-2613, USA

Villarrial, Chris (Athlete, Football Player)
254 Hidden Meadow Ln
Ebensburg, PA 15931-7511, USA

Villegas, Camilo (Athlete, Golfer)
c/o Staff Member *IMG Miami*
1500 S Douglas Rd # 230
Coral Gables, FL 33134-4108, USA

Villemure, Gilles (Athlete, Hockey Player)
38 Grey Ln
Levittown, NY 11756-4498, USA

Villone, Ron (Athlete, Baseball Player)
800 W Willis Rd Apt 2019
Chandler, AZ 85286-6532, USA

Vilma, Jonathan (Athlete, Football Player)
c/o Mitchell Frankel *Impact Sports - LA*
11331 Ventura Blvd Ste 1A
Studio City, CA 91604-3147, USA

Vilsack, Thomas (Politician)
3501 30th St NW
Washington, DC 20008-3251, USA

Viltz, Theo (Athlete, Football Player)
2729 E De Soto St
Long Beach, CA 90814-2337, USA

Vina, Fernando (Athlete, Baseball Player)
11703 Colony Rd
Galt, CA 95632-8547, USA

Vinatieri, Adam (Athlete, Football Player)
11595 Ditch Rd
Carmel, IN 46032-8888, USA

Vince, Pruitt Taylor (Actor)
c/o Joanna (Joanie) Burstein *Burstein Company, The*
15304 W Sunset Blvd Ste 208
Pacific Palisades, CA 90272-3656, USA

Vincent, Cerina (Actor)
c/o Adam Seid *Bohemia Group (LA)*
1680 Vine St Ste 412
Los Angeles, CA 90028-8800, USA

Vincent, Fay (Athlete, Baseball Player)
290 Harbor Dr
Stamford, CT 06902-8700, USA

Vincent, Jay (Athlete, Basketball Player)
PO Box 27459
Lansing, MI 48909-0459, USA

Vincent, June
1541 Via Entrada Del Lago
San Marcos, CA 92078-5254

Vincent, Marjorie
1325 Boardwalk
Atlantic City, NJ 08401-7240

Vincent, Rhonda (Musician)
c/o Scott Clayton *Creative Artists Agency (CAA-TN)*
401 Commerce St PH
Nashville, TN 37219-2516, USA

Vincent, Rick (Musician, Songwriter, Writer)
Carter Career Mgmt
1028 18th Ave S # B
Nashville, TN 37212-2105, USA

Vincent, Sam (Athlete, Basketball Player)
6727 Fairway Cove Dr
Orlando, FL 32835-5747, USA

Vincent, Troy (Athlete, Football Player)
18900 Longhouse Pl
Leesburg, VA 20176-6464, USA

Vinci, Charles (Athlete, Olympic Athlete, Weightlifter)
10915 Burns Ave
Elyria, OH 44035-7515, USA

Vinci, Vince (Horse Racer)
9 Summit Dr
Denville, NJ 07834-2312, USA

Vincz, Melanie (Actor)
2212 Earle Ct
Redondo Beach, CA 90278-5003, USA

Vines, C Jerry (Religious Leader)
First Baptist Church
124 W Ashley St
Jacksonville, FL 32202-3189, USA

Vines, Ellsworth
4680 Irvine Blvd # 203
Irvine, CA 92620

Vines, The (Music Group)
c/o Rick Roskin *Creative Artists Agency (CAA-LA)*
2000 Avenue of the Stars Ste 100
Los Angeles, CA 90067-4705, USA

Vineyard, Dave (Athlete, Baseball Player)
1850 Tariff Rd
Left Hand, WV 25251-9542, USA

Vinge, Vernor (Writer)
Tom Doherty Associates, LLC
175 5th Ave
New York, NY 10010-7703, USA

Vining, David (Doctor, Scientist)
1955 Greenberry Rd
Baltimore, MD 21209-4555, USA

Vining, Ken (Athlete, Baseball Player)
341 Fischer Rd
Rd
Fort Mill, SC 29715-5921, USA

Vinnie (Artist, Music Group)
International Creative Mgmt
10250 Constellation Blvd Fl 1
Los Angeles, CA 90067-6241, USA

Vinson, Charlie (Athlete, Baseball Player)
3821 Walters Ln
District Heights, MD 20747-3943, USA

Vinson, Fernandus (Athlete, Football Player)
6572 Glenwood Ave Apt 221
Raleigh, NC 27612-7156, USA

Vinson, Fred (Athlete, Basketball Player)
925 1/2 E Fairview Blvd
Inglewood, CA 90302-1426, USA

Vinson, Fred (Athlete, Football Player)
11220 NE 53rd St
Kirkland, WA 98033-7505, USA

Vinson, Sharni (Actor)
c/o David (Dave) Fleming *Mosaic Media Group*
9200 W Sunset Blvd Ste 10
West Hollywood, CA 90069-3608, USA

Vint, Jesse
10637 Burbank Blvd
North Hollywood, CA 91601-2512

Vint, Jesse Lee III (Actor)
Film Artists
13563 1/2 Ventura Blvd # 200
Sherman Oaks, CA 91423, USA

Vinton, Bobby (Musician)
820 Manasota Key Rd
Englewood, FL 34223, USA

Vinton, Will (Animator, Cartoonist, Director, Producer)
c/o Rob Kenneally *Creative Artists Agency (CAA-LA)*
2000 Avenue of the Stars Ste 100
Los Angeles, CA 90067-4705, USA

Viola, Frank
844 Sweetwater Island Cir
Longwood, FL 32779-2345

Viola, Frank J Jr (Athlete, Baseball Player)
9868 Kilgore Rd
Orlando, FL 32836-5708, USA

Viola, Lisa (Dancer)
Paul Taylor Dance Co
552 Broadway
New York, NY 10012-3922, USA

Viola, Vincent (Business Person)
Virtu Financial
645 Madison Ave Fl 16
New York, NY 10022-1010, USA

Violent Femmes (Music Group)
15030 Ventura Blvd # 710
Sherman Oaks, CA 91403-5470, USA

Violetta-Kunkel, Karen (Athlete, Baseball Player)
904 Garfield Ave
Marquette, MI 49855-3214, USA

Violette, Chris (Actor)
c/o Staff Member *Power Rangers SPD*
500 S Buena Vista St
Burbank, CA 91521-0001, USA

Virden, Claude (Athlete, Basketball Player)
337 Fernwood Dr
Akron, OH 44320-2317, USA

Virdon, William C (Bill) (Athlete, Baseball Player, Coach)
1311 E River Rd
Springfield, MO 65804-7901, USA

Virgil Jr, Ozzie (Athlete, Baseball Player)
4316 W Mescal St
Glendale, AZ 85304-4132, USA

Virgins, The (Music Group)
c/o Staff Member *Paradigm (Monterey)*
404 W Franklin St
Monterey, CA 93940-2303, USA

Virts, Terry W Jr (Astronaut)
1904 Edgewater Dr
Friendswood, TX 77546-7845, USA

Virts, Terry W Major (Astronaut)
1904 Edgewater Dr
Friendswood, TX 77546-7845, USA

Virtue, Frank (Musician)
8309 Rising Sun Ave
Philadelphia, PA 19111, USA

Virtue, Thomas (Tom) (Actor)
c/o Staff Member *Gage Group, The (LA)*
5757 Wilshire Blvd Ste 659
Los Angeles, CA 90036-3682, USA

Vis, Anthony (Religious Leader)
Reformed Church in America
475 Riverside Dr Ste 1606
New York, NY 10115-0093, USA

Viscardi, Johnston Catherine (Publisher)
Mirabella Magazine
200 Madison Ave
New York, NY 10016-3903, USA

Visclosky, Pete (Congressman, Politician)
7895 Broadway Ste A
Merrillville, IN 46410-5529, USA

Visconti, Tony (Musician, Producer)
c/o Joe D'Ambrosio *Joe D'Ambrosio Management Inc*
1311 Mamaroneck Ave Ste 220
Star Mgmt. Group
White Plains, NY 10605-5222, USA

Visculo, Sal
6491 Ivarene Ave
Los Angeles, CA 90068-2823

Viscuso, Sal (Actor)
6491 Ivarene Ave
Los Angeles, CA 90068-2823, USA

Vise, David A (Journalist)
Washington Post
Editorial Dept
1150 15th St NW
Washington, DC 20071-0001, USA

Vishnevski, Vitali (Athlete, Hockey Player)
International Sports Advisors
878 Ridge View Way
Franklin Lakes, NJ 07417-1524, USA

Visitor, Nana (Actor)
c/o Staff Member *Diverse Talent Group*
9911 W Pico Blvd Ste 340W
Los Angeles, CA 90035-2703, USA

Visnjic, Goran (Actor)
c/o Elyse Scherz *William Morris Endeavor (LA)*
9601 Wilshire Blvd
Beverly Hills, CA 90210-5213, USA

Visnovsky, Lubomir (Athlete, Hockey Player)
15319th St
Manhattan Beach, CA 90266, USA

Visscher, Maurice B (Doctor)
120 Melbourne Ave SE
Minneapolis, MN 55414-3516, USA

Visser, Lesley (Sportscaster)
c/o Staff Member *CBS Television*
51 W 52nd St
New York, NY 10019-6119, USA

Viswanathan, Padma
213 N Summit Ave
Fayetteville, AR 72701-1312, USA

Vitale, Dick (Athlete, Basketball Player, Coach, Sportscaster)
7810 Mathern Ct
Lakewood Ranch, FL 34202-2592, USA

Vitale, Joe (Business Person, Writer)
The Vitale Estate
121 Canyon Gap Rd
Wimberley, TX 78676-6314, USA

Vitale, Tony (Actor, Director, Writer)
c/o Staff Member *Hansen, Jacobson, Teller, Hoberman, Newman, Warren & Richman*
450 N Roxbury Dr Fl 8
Beverly Hills, CA 90210-4222, USA

Vitamin-C (Actor, Musician)
c/o Carter Cohn *ICM Partners (LA)*
10250 Constellation Blvd Fl 7
Los Angeles, CA 90067-6207, USA

Vitez, Michael (Journalist)
Philadelphia Inquirer
400 N Broad St
Editorial Dept
Philadelphia, PA 19130-4099, USA

Vitiello, Joe (Athlete, Baseball Player)
13615 Old El Camino Real
San Diego, CA 92130-3088, USA

Vitiello, Sandro (Athlete, Football Player)
9 Dwight Cir
Commack, NY 11725-3313, USA

Vitko, Joe (Athlete, Baseball Player)
608 George St Rear
Turtle Creek, PA 15145-1524, USA

Vito, Don (Producer)
606 Treecrest Pkwy
Decatur, GA 30035-3564, USA

Vitolo, Dennis (Race Car Driver)
Payton-Coyne Racing
13400 S Budler Rd
Plainfield, IL 60544-9493, USA

Vitrano, Bob (Horse Racer)
16 Farnworth Close
Freehold, NJ 07728-3852, USA

Viviano, Joseph P (Business Person)
Hershey Foods Corp
100 Crystal A Dr Unit 8
Hershey, PA 17033-9702, USA

Vizcaino, Jose (Athlete, Baseball Player)
5976 Germaine Ln
La Jolla, CA 92037-7430, USA

Vizquel, Omar E (Athlete, Baseball Player)
2704 212th Ave SE
Sammamish, WA 98075-7167, USA

V. Johnson, Timothy (Congressman, Politician)
8426 Porter Ln
Alexandria, VA 22308-2139, USA

Vlardo, Vladimir V (Musician)
457 Piermont Rd
Cresskill, NJ 07626-1524, USA

Vlasic, Mark (Athlete, Football Player)
12809 Catalina St
Leawood, KS 66209-3327, USA

Vlassic, Robert
716 Ocean Dr
North Palm Beach, FL 33408-1911

Voce, Gary (Athlete, Basketball Player)
25912 147th Ave
Rosedale, NY 11422-3321, USA

Vodianova, Natalia (Model)
c/o Staff Member *DNA Model Management*
555 W 25th St Fl 6
New York, NY 10001-5542, USA

Vogel, Bob (Athlete, Football Player)
2065 N Galena Rd
Sunbury, OH 43074-9588, USA

Vogel, Dariene (Actor)
Michael Slessinger
8730 W Sunset Blvd Ste 220W
West Hollywood, CA 90069-2275, USA

Vogel, Frank (Basketball Coach)
c/o Lonnie Cooper *Career Sports and Entertainment*
150 Interstate North Pkwy SE Ste 100
Atlanta, GA 30339-2101, USA

Vogel, Matt (Athlete, Olympic Athlete, Swimmer)
204 Elm St Apt 6
South Portland, ME 04106-4366, USA

Vogel, Mike (Actor)
c/o Geordie Frey *GEF Entertainment*
611 N Cherokee Ave
Los Angeles, CA 90004-1008, USA

Vogel, Mitch (Actor)
3335 Honeysuckle Ave
Palmdale, CA 93550-1305, USA

Vogelsong, Ryan (Athlete, Baseball Player)
1231 E Judi St
Casa Grande, AZ 85122-6736, USA

Vogelstein, Bert (Doctor, Scientist)
Johns Hopkins University
Medical School
Oncology Center
Baltimore, MD 21218, USA

Vogler, Tim (Athlete, Football Player)
6710 Woodland Dr
Hamburg, NY 14075-6521, USA

Vogt, Lars (Musician)
c/o Staff Member *ICM Partners (NY)*
730 5th Ave
New York, NY 10019-4105, USA

Vogt, Paul (Actor)
c/o Judy Coppage *Coppage Company, The*
5411 Camellia Ave
North Hollywood, CA 91601-2615, USA

Vogtli, Jillian (Athlete, Olympic Athlete, Skier)
PO Box 683153
Park City, UT 84068-3153, USA

Voight, Jon (Actor, Producer, Writer)
9660 Oak Pass Rd
Beverly Hills, CA 90210-1232, USA

Voight, Karen (Fitness Expert)
Entertaining Fitness, Inc
827 Chautauqua Blvd
Pacific Palisades, CA 90272-3802, USA

Voight, Stu (Athlete, Football Player)
8832 Hunters Way
Saint Paul, MN 55124-9478, USA

Voigt, Cynthia (Writer)
866 3rd Ave
New York, NY 10022-6221, USA

Voigt, Jack (Athlete, Baseball Player)
1759 Bayshore Rd
Nokomis, FL 34275-1413, USA

Voinovich, George (Ex-Governor, Politician, Senator)
17820 Rosecliff Rd
Cleveland, OH 44119-1346, USA

Voisard, Mark (Baseball Player)
222 Meadowlane Dr
Sidney, OH 45365-7000, USA

Vokoun, Tomas (Athlete, Hockey Player)
6685 NW 122nd Ave
Parkland, FL 33076-3325, USA

Volchenkov, Anton (Athlete, Hockey Player)
Puckagency LLC
1 Sunset Dr N
Attn Jay Grossman
Chappaqua, NY 10514-1613, USA

Volcker, Paul (Politician)
151 E 79th St Fl 7
New York, NY 10075-0564, USA

Voldstad, John (Actor)
24812 Van Owen St
West Hills, CA 91300, USA

Volek, Billy (Athlete, Football Player)
13946 Sagewood Dr
Poway, CA 92064-1406, USA

Volek, David (Athlete, Hockey Player)
5 Blue Sky Ct
Huntington, NY 11743-2901, USA

Volibracht, Michaele (Artist, Designer, Fashion Designer)
General Delivery
Safety Harbor, FL 34695, USA

Volk, Patricia (Writer)
Gloria Loomis
133 E 35th St
New York, NY 10016-3886, USA

Volk, Phil (Musician)
Paradise Artists
108 E Matilija St
Ojai, CA 93023-2639, USA

Volk, Richard R (Rick) (Athlete, Football Player)
533 Wyngate Rd
Lutherville Timonium, MD 21093-2841, USA

Volkov, Alexander (Athlete, Basketball Player)
1413 Waterford Green Dr
Marietta, GA 30068-2910, USA

Vollebak, Knut (Government Official)
Royal Norwegian Embassy
2720 34th St NW
Washington, DC 20008-2705, USA

Vollmer, Dana (Athlete, Olympic Athlete, Swimmer)
260 Dahlia St
Nipomo, CA 93444-5022, USA

Vollmer, Sebastian (Athlete, Football Player)
c/o Ben Dogra *CAA (St. Louis)*
222 S Central Ave Ste 1008
Saint Louis, MO 63105-3509, USA

Volmar, Doug (Athlete, Hockey Player, Olympic Athlete)
19 Eliot St
Framingham, MA 01702-6403, USA

Volodos, Arcadl (Musician)
Columbia Artists Mgmt Inc
165 W 57th St
New York, NY 10019-2201, USA

Volstad, Chris (Athlete, Baseball Player)
11774 Hemlock St
Palm Beach Gardens, FL 33410-2637, USA

Volstad, John (Actor)
c/o Brandon Pender *Ithaca Entertainment Media Group*
PO Box 1880
Studio City, CA 91614-0880, USA

VOltaggio, Vic (Athlete, Baseball Player)
1049 Florian Way
Spring Hill, FL 34609-9021, USA

Volz, Wilbur (Athlete, Football Player)
35 Seminary Hl Apt C-31
West Lebanon, NH 03784-1728, USA

Von Bargen, Daniel (Actor)
c/o Mitchell Stubbs *Mitchell K Stubbs & Assoc (MKS)*
8675 Washington Blvd Ste 203
Culver City, CA 90232-7486, USA

Vonderau, Kathryn (Athlete, Baseball Player)
7224 Hawthorn Ave NE
Albuquerque, NM 87113-2084, USA

von Detten, Erik (Actor)
c/o Elissa Leeds-Fickman *Reel Talent Management*
PO Box 491035
Los Angeles, CA 90049-9035, USA

von Dohlen, Lenny (Actor)
c/o Martin Gage *Gage Group, The (LA)*
5757 Wilshire Blvd Ste 659
Los Angeles, CA 90036-3682, USA

Von Drachenberg, Katherine (Artist, Reality Star)
High Voltage Tattoo
1259 N La Brea Ave
West Hollywood, CA 90038-1023, USA

Von Erich, Jaret (Actor, Musician)
c/o Linda Kordek *Agency Group Ltd, The (LA)*
1880 Century Park E Ste 711
Los Angeles, CA 90067-1618, USA

VonEschenbach, Andrew (Doctor)
National Cancer Institute
9000 Rockville Pike # 12N226
Bethesda, MD 20892-0001, USA

Von Frankenstein, Clement (Actor)
c/o Staff Member *Matt Sherman Management*
7510 W Sunset Blvd Ste 1413
Los Angeles, CA 90046-3408, USA

Von Furstenberg, Betsy (Actor)
230 Central Park W
New York, NY 10024-6029, USA

VonFurstenberg, Betsy (Actor)
230 Central Park W Apt 2D
New York, NY 10024-6036, USA

Von Furstenberg, Diane (Fashion Designer)
DVF
874 Washington St
New York, NY 10014-1102, USA

VonFurstenberg, Egon (Designer, Fashion Designer)
50 E 72nd St
New York, NY 10021-4246, USA

VonGarnier, Katja (Director, Writer)
c/o John Campisi *Creative Artists Agency (CAA-LA)*
2000 Avenue of the Stars Ste 100
Los Angeles, CA 90067-4705, USA

Vongerichten, Jean-Georges (Chef)
Jean-Georges Enterprises, LLC
19 Greene St
New York, NY 10013-2535, USA

Von Hoff, Bruce (Athlete, Baseball Player)
11033 Lynn Lake Cir
Tampa, FL 33625-5642, USA

Vonn, Lindsey (Athlete, Skier)
c/o Mark Ervin *IMG (LA)*
2049 Century Park E Ste 2460
Los Angeles, CA 90067-3126, USA

Vonnegut Jr, Kurt (Writer)
Seven Stories Press
140 Watts St
New York, NY 10013-1738, USA

Von Nieda, Whitey (Athlete, Basketball Player)
1105 James Buchanan Dr
Elizabethtown, PA 17022-3169, USA

Vonoelhoffen, Kimo (Athlete, Football Player)
1503 Scarlet Oak Dr
Wexford, PA 15090-6931, USA

Von Ohlen, Dave (Athlete, Baseball Player)
653 Windmill Ave
West Babylon, NY 11704-4403, USA

Vonohlen, Dave (Baseball Player)
St Louis Cardinals
74 Elizabeth St
Floral Park, NY 11001-2129, USA

Vonoimoana, Eric
715 S Circle Dr
Colorado Springs, CO 80910-2324

Von Oy, Jenna (Actor)
c/o Kelly Garner *Pop Art Management*
PO Box 55363
Sherman Oaks, CA 91413-0363, USA

von Pfetten, Stefanie (Actor)
c/o Marina D'Amico *Precision Entertainment*
465 N Croft Ave
Los Angeles, CA 90048-2508, USA

Von Puttkamer, Jesco
Nassau MS Ml
Washington, DC 20546-0001, USA

VonRunkle, Theodora (Designer, Fashion Designer)
8805 Lookout Mountain Ave
Los Angeles, CA 90046-1819, USA

VonSaltza Olmstead, S Christine (Chris) (Swimmer)
7060 Fairway Pl
Carmel, CA 93923-9586, USA

Von Schamann, Uwe (Athlete, Football Player)
PO Box 5562
Norman, OK 73070-5562, USA

Von Scherler Mayer, Daisy (Director)
c/o Keith Addis *Industry Entertainment*
955 Carrillo Dr Ste 300
Los Angeles, CA 90048-5400, USA

Vonsonn, Andrew (Athlete, Football Player)
PO Box 791538
Paia, HI 96779-1538, USA

Von Sydow, Max (Actor)
c/o Staff Member *United Talent Agency (UTA-LA)*
9336 Civic Center Dr
Beverly Hills, CA 90210-3604, USA

Von Teese, Dita (Dancer, Model)
c/o Melissa Dishell *Dishell Multimedia Group*
8306 Wilshire Blvd PMB 833
Beverly Hills, CA 90211-2304, USA

Voog, Ana (Music Group, Musician, Songwriter, Writer)
MCA Records
1755 Broadway Fl 6
New York, NY 10019-3793, USA

Voorhees, John J (Doctor)
3965 Waldenwood Dr
Ann Arbor, MI 48105-3008, USA

Voorhies, Lark (Actor)
10635 Santa Monica Blvd Ste 130
Los Angeles, CA 90025-8306, USA

Vorgan, Gigi (Actor)
3637 Stone Cyn
Sherman Oaks, CA 91403, USA

Vorhies, Lark (Actor)
c/o Geoff Cheddy *Brillstein Entertainment Partners (LA)*
9150 Wilshire Blvd Ste 350
Beverly Hills, CA 90212-3453, USA

Voronina, Irina (Model)
7119 W Sunset Blvd # 293
Los Angeles, CA 90046-4411, USA

Vos, Rich (Actor, Comedian)
c/o Jason Steinberg *Steinberg Talent Management Group*
1560 Broadway # 405
New York, NY 10036-1537, US

Vosberg, Ed (Athlete, Baseball Player)
7839 E Marquise Dr
Tucson, AZ 85715-3774, USA

Voskuhl, Jake
20 White Birch Rdg
Weston, CT 06883-3015, USA

Vosloo, Arnold (Actor)
c/o James (Jim) Gosnell *Agency for the Performing Arts (APA-LA)*
405 S Beverly Dr Ste 500
Beverly Hills, CA 90212-4425, USA

Voss, Bill (Athlete, Baseball Player)
10625 E Oak Creek Trl
Cornville, AZ 86325-5824, USA

Voss, Brian (Bowler)
1635 Old 41 Hwy NW Ste 112
Kennesaw, GA 30152-4481, USA

Votaw, Ty (Golfer)
Ladies Pro Golf Assn
100 International Golf Dr
Daytona Beach, FL 32124-1082, USA

Voth, Julia (Actor)
c/o Alex Fox *Nu Talent*
10635 Santa Monica Blvd Ste 130
Los Angeles, CA 90025-8306, USA

Votto, Joey (Athlete, Baseball Player)
c/o Staff Member *Cincinnati Reds*
100 Main St
Great American Ball Park
Cincinnati, OH 45202-5108, USA

Vouyer, Vince (Adult Film Star)
Vouyer Media Inc
9020 Eton Ave Ste G
Canoga Park, CA 91304-6514, USA

Vowell, Sarah (Actor, Writer)
c/o Staff Member *Steven Barclay Agency*
12 Western Ave
Petaluma, CA 94952-2907, USA

Voyce, Inez (Athlete, Baseball Player)
PO Box 4284
Sunland, CA 91041-4284, USA

Voyles, Brad (Athlete, Baseball Player)
314 East Ave
Casco, WI 54205-9679, USA

Voytek, Edward (Athlete, Football Player)
2111 NW 13th St
Blue Springs, MO 64015-7734, USA

Vrabel, Mike (Athlete, Football Player)
74 Concerto Ct
North Easton, MA 02356-2762, USA

Vrabel, Mike (Athlete, Football Player)
8552 Misty Woods Cir
Powell, OH 43065-8356, USA

Vranes, Danny (Athlete, Basketball Player, Olympic Athlete)
3540 E Bengal Blvd
Salt Lake City, UT 84121-5902, USA

Vranes, Slavko (Basketball Player)
c/o Staff Member *Portland Trail Blazers*
1 N Center Court St Ste 200
Portland, OR 97227-2103, USA

Vuckovich, Peter D (Pete) (Athlete, Baseball Player)
86 Leonard St
Johnstown, PA 15902-1234, USA

Vukota, Mick (Athlete, Hockey Player)
PO Box 3213
7 Peases Point Rd
Edgartown, MA 02539-3213, USA

Vukovich, George (Athlete, Baseball Player)
305 W Calle Gota
Sahuarita, AZ 85629-7845, USA

Vulkovich, Frances (Athlete, Baseball Player)
258 W 28th St
Holland, MI 49423-4939, USA

Vullo, Maria T (Attorney)
1285 Avenue of the Americas
New York, NY 10019-6031, USA

Vyent, Louise (Model)
Pauline's Talent Corp
379 W Broadway # 502
New York, NY 10012-5121, USA

W

W, Kristine (Musician)
8585 La Cienega St
Las Vegas, NV 89123-1648, USA

Waalkes, Otto (Actor)
Papenhuder Str. 61
Hamburg, GE D-220

Wach, Caitlin (Actor)
c/o David Brownstein *Art Work Entertainment*
5900 Wilshire Blvd Ste 2150
Los Angeles, CA 90036-5021, USA

Wachowski, Andy (Director, Producer, Writer)
2213 Grand Canal
Venice, CA 90291-4571, USA

Wachowski, Larry (Director, Producer, Writer)
2309 Ocean Front Walk
Venice, CA 90291-4317, USA

Wachsberger, Patrick (Producer)
c/o Staff Member *Summit Entertainment*
2700 Colorado Ave Ste 200
Santa Monica, CA 90404-5502, USA

Waddell, Charles (Athlete, Football Player)
3600 Bon Rea Dr
Charlotte, NC 28226-3146, USA

Waddell, Don (Athlete, Hockey Player)
522 Harbor Dr N
Indian Rocks Beach, FL 33785-3117, USA

Waddell, Ernest (Actor)
c/o Bob McGowan *McGowan Management*
8733 W Sunset Blvd Ste 103
West Hollywood, CA 90069-2241, USA

Waddell, Jason (Athlete, Baseball Player)
12080 Pigeon Pass Rd Apt G262
Moreno Valley, CA 92557-6960, USA

Waddell, Justine (Actor)
International Creative Mgmt
10250 Constellation Blvd Fl 1
Los Angeles, CA 90067-6241, USA

Waddell, Tom (Athlete, Baseball Player)
77 S Shadow Creek Pl
Tucson, AZ 85748-3270, USA

Waddell-Wyatt, Helen (Athlete, Baseball Player)
7714 Deerfield Rd
Loves Park, IL 61111-3218, USA

Waddle, Tom (Athlete, Football Player)
8190 Tollbridge Ct
West Chester, OH 45069-1690, USA

Waddy, Billy (Athlete, Football Player)
2838 Highway 88
Minneapolis, MN 55418-3243, USA

Wade, Adam (Musician)
118 E 25th St # 600
New York, NY 10010-2915, USA

Wade, Charlie (Athlete, Football Player)
3109 E Raines Rd
Memphis, TN 38118-6756, USA

Wade, Cory (Athlete, Baseball Player)
c/o Staff Member *Los Angeles Dodgers (LA Dodgers)*
1000 Elysian Park Ave
Los Angeles, CA 90012-1112, USA

Wade, Dwyane (Athlete, Basketball Player)
5980 N Bay Rd
Miami Beach, FL 33140-2044, USA

Wade, Ed (Actor)
436 SW 50th Ave
Pratt, KS 67124-7731, USA

Wade, Ed (Athlete, Baseball Player)
169 Pitman Downer Rd
Sewell, NJ 08080-1878, USA

Wade, Edgar L (Religious Leader)
4466 Elvis Presley Blvd Ste 222
Memphis, TN 38116-7100, USA

Wade, Gale (Athlete, Baseball Player)
4809 Granada Blvd
Sebring, FL 33872-1531, USA

Wade, Jason (Musician)
3725 Medea Creek Rd
Agoura Hills, CA 91301-2743, USA

Wade, Jenny (Actor)
c/o Courtney Kivowitz *The Schiff Company*
9220 W Sunset Blvd Ste 106
West Hollywood, CA 90069-3500, USA

Wade, Kevin (Writer)
c/o David Lonner *Oasis Media Group*
8730 W Sunset Blvd Ste 700
West Hollywood, CA 90069-2249, USA

Wade, Mark (Athlete, Basketball Player)
405 S Centre St Apt 37
San Pedro, CA 90731-2732, USA

Wade, Russell
47287 W Eldorado Dr
Indian Wells, CA 92210-8654

Wade, Sonny (Athlete, Football Player)
943 Jones Ridge Rd
Axton, VA 24054-2888, USA

Wade, Terrell (Athlete, Baseball Player)
6380 Dinkins Mill Rd
Rembert, SC 29128-9789, USA

Wade, Todd (Athlete, Football Player)
217 Hendricks Isle Apt 302
Fort Lauderdale, FL 33301-5753, USA

Wade, Tom (Athlete, Football Player)
3309 Oak Knoll Dr
Tyler, TX 75707-1619, USA

Wade, William J (Bill) Jr (Athlete, Football Player)
7740 Buffalo Rd
Nashville, TN 37221-5501, USA

Wadhams, Wayne (Musician)
73 Hemenway St
Boston, MA 02115-2941, USA

Wadkins, Bobby (Golfer)
204 Kinloch Rd
Manakin Sabot, VA 23103-2911, USA

Wadkins, Lanny (Athlete, Golfer)
5200 Keller Springs Rd Apt 1217
Dallas, TX 75248-2751, USA

Wadsworth, Andre (Athlete, Football Player)
14003 N 99th Way
Scottsdale, AZ 85260-8851, USA

Wadsworth, Charles W (Musician)
PO Box 157
Charleston, SC 29402-0157, USA

Wadsworth, Fred (Golfer)
823 Bryon Rd
Columbia, SC 29205, USA

Waechter, Doug (Athlete, Baseball Player)
4590 13th Way NE
Saint Petersburg, FL 33703-5324, USA

Waelsch, Salome G (Doctor, Scientist)
90 Morningside Dr
New York, NY 10027-7124, USA

Wafer, Von (Athlete, Basketball Player)
2503 Dallas St
Houston, TX 77003-3605, USA

Wages, Harmon (Athlete, Football Player)
1846 Margaret St Apt 3C
Jacksonville, FL 32204-4423, USA

Wages, William (Cinematographer)
Innovative Artists
1505 10th St
Santa Monica, CA 90401-2805, USA

Waggoner, Lyle (Actor)
1124 Oak Mirage Pl
Westlake Village, CA 91362-5622, USA

Wagner, Alex (Journalist)
c/o Staff Member *MSNBC*
30 Rockefeller Plz Fl 2
New York, NY 10112-0043, USA

Wagner, Allison (Athlete, Olympic Athlete, Swimmer)
912 NW 45th Ter
Gainesville, FL 32605-4590

Wagner, Amanda
PO Box 1294
Los Alamos, NM 87544-1294

Wagner, Bret (Baseball Player)
US Olympic Team Bowman
489 Ridge Rd
Lewisberry, PA 17339-9308, USA

Wagner, Brett (Actor, Television Host)
1487 Queens Rd
Los Angeles, CA 90069-1914, USA

Wagner, Bruce (Writer)
United Talent Agency
9336 Civic Center Dr
Beverly Hills, CA 90210-3604, USA

Wagner, Bryan (Athlete, Football Player)
6020 Arlyne Ln
Medina, OH 44256-6852, USA

Wagner, Chuck (Actor, Musician)
1200 Maldonado Dr
Gulf Breeze, FL 32561-2244, USA

Wagner, Dajuan (Basketball Player)
Cleveland Cavaliers
1 Center Ct
Gund Arena
Cleveland, OH 44115-4001, USA

Wagner, Fred (Cartoonist)
c/o Staff Member *King Features Syndication*
300 W 57th St Fl 15
New York, NY 10019-5238, USA

Wagner, Gary (Athlete, Baseball Player)
1707 Northbrook Ct
Seymour, IN 47274-4801, USA

Wagner, Harold A (Business Person)
Air Products & Chemicals
7201 Hamilton Blvd
Allentown, PA 18195-9642, USA

Wagner, Jack (Actor, Musician)
314 Waverly Place Ct
Chesterfield, MO 63017-7819, USA

Wagner, Jane
PO Box 27700
Los Angeles, CA 90027-0700

Wagner, Jill (Actor)
c/o Staff Member *United Talent Agency (UTA-LA)*
9336 Civic Center Dr
Beverly Hills, CA 90210-3604, USA

Wagner, John (Cartoonist)
Hallmark Cards
101 McDonald Dr
Shoebox Division
Lawrence, KS 66044-1056, USA

Wagner, Katey (Actor)
1500 Old Oak Rd
Los Angeles, CA 90049-2504, USA

Wagner, Katie (Actor, Television Host)
c/o Staff Member *TV Guide Channel*
7140 S Lewis Ave
Tulsa, OK 74136-5437, USA

Wagner, Lindsay (Actor)
1106 Manhattan Ave Apt 3
Hermosa Beach, CA 90254-3727, USA

Wagner, Lou (Actor)
21224 Celtic St
Chatsworth, CA 91311-1468, USA

Wagner, Maggie (Actor)
Stephany Hurkos Management
11935 Kling St Apt 10
Valley Village, CA 91607-5406, USA

Wagner, Mark (Athlete, Baseball Player)
1838 Willow Arms Dr
Ashtabula, OH 44004-7810, USA

Wagner, Matt (Athlete, Baseball Player)
1112 Lilac Ln
Cedar Falls, IA 50613-5342, USA

Wagner, Matt (Cartoonist)
DC Comics
1700 Broadway Fl 6
New York, NY 10019-5905, USA

Wagner, Michael R (Mike) (Athlete, Football Player)
203 E Cherry Dr
Mars, PA 16046, USA

Wagner, Mike (Athlete, Football Player)
874 Bayou View Dr
Brandon, FL 33510-2018, USA

Wagner, Natasha Gregson (Actor)
1327 Vienna Way
Venice, CA 90291-4028, USA

Wagner, Paul (Athlete, Baseball Player)
N1960 State Road 67
Neosho, WI 53059-9723, USA

Wagner, Paula (Producer)
Chestnut Ridge Productions
3000 Olympic Blvd Bldg 2515
Santa Monica, CA 90404-5073, USA

Wagner, Philip M (Writer)
32 Montgomery St
Boston, MA 02116-6111, USA

Wagner, Phillip (Athlete, Basketball Player)
328 Glenloch Ln
Stockbridge, GA 30281-5920, USA

Wagner, Ricky (Athlete, Football Player)
c/o Joe Panos *Athletes First, LLC*
23091 Mill Creek Dr
Laguna Hills, CA 92653-1258, USA

Wagner, Robert (Actor)
115 Johnson Dr
Aspen, CO 81611-9719, USA

Wagner, Robin S A (Designer)
Robin Wagner Studio
890 Broadway
New York, NY 10003-1211, USA

Wagner, Roy H (Actor, Director)
c/o Lisa Helsing Lenhoff *Lenhoff & Lenhoff*
830 Palm Ave
West Hollywood, CA 90069-4009

Wagner, Ryan (Athlete, Baseball Player)
59 County Road 311
Yoakum, TX 77995-6014, USA

Wagner, William E (Billy) (Athlete, Baseball Player)
5066 Jones Mill Rd
Crozet, VA 22932-2610, USA

Wagoner, Dan (Athlete, Football Player)
PO Box 476
Lyman, SC 29365-0476, USA

Wagoner, David R (Writer)
5416 154th Pl SW
Edmonds, WA 98026-4348, USA

Wagoner, Richard (Rick) (Business Person)
General Motors Corp
100 Renaissance Ctr
Detroit, MI 48243-1114, USA

Wahl, Ken (Actor)
c/o Susan Balistocky *Law Offices of Sysan Balistocky*
1901 Avenue of the Stars Ste 1900
Los Angeles, CA 90067-6020, USA

Wahlberg, Donnie (Actor, Musician)
c/o Jonathan Baruch *Rain Management Group (RMG)*
1631 21st St
Santa Monica, CA 90404-3914, USA

Wahlberg, Mark (Actor, Model, Musician)
71 Beverly Park
Beverly Hills, CA 90210-1542, USA

Wahle, Mike (Athlete, Football Player)
26 Wood Haven Way
Fitchburg, WI 53711-5527, USA

Wahlquist, Heather (Actor)
c/o Troy Begnaud *Evolution Entertainment (LA)*
901 N Highland Ave
Los Angeles, CA 90038-2412, USA

Wahlstrom, Becky (Actor)
c/o Rob D'Avola *Rob DAvola & Associates*
9107 Wilshire Blvd Ste 450
Beverly Hills, CA 90210-5535, USA

Waihee, John D III (Politician)
4405 Kilauea Ave
Honolulu, HI 96816-5114, USA

Wain, Bea (Musician)
9955 Durant Dr Unit 305
Beverly Hills, CA 90212-1601, USA

Wainhouse, Dave (Athlete, Baseball Player)
160 Waverly Way
Kirkland, WA 98033-5307, USA

Wainscott, Loyd (Athlete, Football Player)
401 Tarpey Rd
Texas City, TX 77591-3159, USA

Wainwright, Adam (Athlete, Baseball Player)
2100 Brook Hill Ct
Chesterfield, MO 63017-7941, USA

Wainwright, James (Actor)
Lew Sherrell
937 N Sinova
Mesa, AZ 85205-5438, USA

Wainwright, Loudon (Actor)
c/o Harriet Sternberg *Harriet Sternberg Management*
4530 Gloria Ave
Encino, CA 91436-2718, USA

Wainwright, Loudon III (Musician, Songwriter, Writer)
Teddy Wainwright
521 SW Halpatiokee St
Stuart, FL 34994-2815, USA

Wainwright, Marcus (Designer)
Rag & Bone
425 W 13th St Ofc 2
New York, NY 10014-1123, USA

Wainwright, Rufus (Musician)
36 Jay Rd
Montauk, NY 11954-5035, USA

Wainwright, Rupert (Director)
1756 N Sierra Bonita Ave
Los Angeles, CA 90046, USA

Waite, John (Musician, Songwriter)
506 Walt Whitman Rd
Melville, NY 11747-2109, USA

Waite, Liam
c/o Staff Member *Gersh (LA)*
9465 Wilshire Blvd Ste 600
Beverly Hills, CA 90212-2605, USA

Waiters, Granville (Athlete, Basketball
Player)
481 Oakwood Ave
Columbus, OH 43205-1935, USA

Waiters, Van (Athlete, Football Player)
6021 NW 201st Ln
Hialeah, FL 33015-4865, USA

Waitley, Denis (Business Person)
The Waitley Institute
PO Box 197
Rancho Santa Fe, CA 92067-0197, USA

Waits, Cy (Business Person)
2020 Doral Ct
Henderson, NV 89074-1074, USA

Waits, Rick (Athlete, Baseball Player)
PO Box 1001
Patagonia, AZ 85624-1001, USA

Waits, Tom (Musician)
1020 Freestone Ranch Rd
Sebastopol, CA 95472, USA

Waitt, Theodore W (Ted) (Business
Person)
Gateway Inc
7565 Irvine Center Dr Ste 150
Irvine, CA 92618-4933, USA

Waitz, Richard H (Cinematographer)
405 Zenith Ave
Lafayette, CO 80026-3104, USA

Wajda, Andrezei
u1 Jezefa Hauke Boska 14
Warsaw, PO 19725

Wakamatsu, Don (Athlete, Baseball
Player)
8740 Ramblewood Ct
Keller, TX 76248-0361, USA

Wakata, Koichi (Astronaut)
NASA
2022 Converse St
Houston, TX 77006-1302, USA

Wakefield, Abbey-May (Actor)
c/o Simon Millar *Rumble Media*
1620 Broadway Ste C
Santa Monica, CA 90404-2777, USA

Wakefield, Andre (Athlete, Basketball
Player)
320 Wisconsin Ave Apt 519
Oak Park, IL 60302-3459, USA

Wakefield, Bill (Athlete, Baseball Player)
1 Baypoint Village Dr
San Rafael, CA 94901-8409, USA

Wakefield, Cameron (Actor)
c/o Simon Millar *Rumble Media*
1620 Broadway Ste C
Santa Monica, CA 90404-2777, USA

Wakefield, Rhys (Actor)
c/o Sandra Chang *Anonymous Content
(LA)*
3532 Hayden Ave
Culver City, CA 90232-2413, USA

Wakefield, Tim (Athlete, Baseball Player)
241 Lansing Island Dr
Indian Harbour Beach, FL 32937-5102,
USA

Wakeland, Chris (Athlete, Baseball Player)
60997 Luttrell Ln
Saint Helens, OR 97051-9126, USA

Wakely, Ernie (Athlete, Hockey Player)
11052 E Roundup Dr
Dewey, AZ 86327-5411, USA

Wakoski, Diane (Writer)
607 Division St
East Lansing, MI 48823-3428, USA

Walackas, Augie (Race Car Driver)
255 Plymouth St
Whitman, MA 02382-1626, USA

Walbeck, Matt (Athlete, Baseball Player)
8216 Olive Ave
Fair Oaks, CA 95628-7623, USA

Walberg, Mark L. (Actor, Television Host)
c/o Staff Member *William Morris
Endeavor (LA)*
9601 Wilshire Blvd
Beverly Hills, CA 90210-5213, USA

Walberg, Tim (Congressman, Politician)
418 Cannon Hob
Washington, DC 20515-0301, USA

Walcott, Gregory (Actor)
22246 Saticoy St
Canoga Park, CA 91303-1043, USA

Walcott, Jennifer (Model)
4400 N Scottsdale Rd Ste 9
Scottsdale, AZ 85251-3331, USA

Walcutt, John (Actor)
c/o Staff Member *MC Talent Management*
4821 Lankershim Blvd # F329
N Hollywood, CA 91601-4538, USA

Walczak, Mark (Athlete, Football Player)
PO Box 372
Scottsdale, AZ 85252-0372, USA

Wald, Jeff (Producer)
c/o Jeff Wald *Jeff Wald Entertainment*
3000 Olympic Blvd Bldg 1400
Santa Monica, CA 90404-5073, USA

Waldemore, Stan (Athlete, Football
Player)
PO Box 611
New Vernon, NJ 07976-0611, USA

Walden, Erik (Athlete, Football Player)
c/o Eugene Parker *Maximum Sports
Management*
6435 W Jefferson Blvd # 197
Fort Wayne, IN 46804-6203, USA

Walden, Greg (Congressman, Politician)
2182 Rayburn Hob
Washington, DC 20515-3310, USA

Walden, Robert (Actor)
1408 Mesa Ridge Ln
Austin, TX 78735-1635, USA

Walden, Robert E (Bobby) (Athlete,
Football Player)
1403 Douglas Dr
Bainbridge, GA 39819-5176, USA

Walden, Ronnie (Athlete, Baseball Player)
1007 Autumn Way
Blanchard, OK 73010-8961, USA

Walder, Katie
c/o Jeff Morrone *Intellectual Artists
Management*
9350 Wilshire Blvd Ste 224
Beverly Hills, CA 90212-3204, USA

Waldie, Marc (Athlete, Volleyball Player)
Murray Lampert Construction
3545 Camino Del Rio S Ste C
San Diego, CA 92108-4025, USA

Waldman, Suzyn (Sportscaster)
8 Foster Ct
Croton On Hudson, NY 10520-3303,
USA

Waldo, Janet
15735 Royal Oak Rd
Encino, CA 91436

Waldorf, Duffy (Golfer)
26850 Boulder Crest Dr
Valencia, CA 91381-0624, USA

Wales, Jimmy (Business Person)
Wikimedia Foundation
PO Box 78350
San Francisco, CA 94107-8350, USA

Wales, Ross (Swimmer)
2730 Walsh Rd
Cincinnati, OH 45208-3425, USA

Waletrs, David (Politician)
RR 2
Watts, OK 74964, USA

Walewander, Jim (Athlete, Baseball
Player)
5809 Seven Pines Ct
Haymarket, VA 20169-8102, USA

Walger, Sonya (Actor)
20860 Big Rock Dr
Malibu, CA 90265-5314, USA

Walheim, Rex J (Astronaut)
142 Hidden Lake Dr
League City, TX 77573-6976, USA

Walheim, Rex J Lt Colonel (Astronaut)
142 Hidden Lake Dr
League City, TX 77573-6976, USA

Walik, Billy (Athlete, Football Player)
PO Box 10712
Bainbridge Island, WA 98110-0712, USA

Walk, Bob (Athlete, Baseball Player)
2494 Shadowbrook Dr
Wexford, PA 15090-7982, USA

Walk, Neal (Athlete, Basketball Player)
6030 N 11th Ave
Phoenix, AZ 85013-1415, USA

Walken, Christopher (Actor)
142 Cedar Rd
Wilton, CT 06897-3631, USA

Walker, Adam (Athlete, Football Player)
915 Brookline Way
Alpharetta, GA 30022-3745, USA

Walker, Alice M (Writer)
PO Box 378
Philo, CA 95466, USA

Walker, Ally (Actor)
321 20th St
Santa Monica, CA 90402-2413, USA

Walker, Anetia
19551 Turtle Ridge Ln
Porter Ranch, CA 91326-3808

Walker, Ann (Actor)
c/o Pam Ellis *Ellis Talent Group*
4705 Laurel Canyon Blvd Ste 300
Valley Village, CA 91607-5901, USA

Walker, Antoine (Athlete, Basketball
Player)
3950 Wood Ave
Miami, FL 33133-6429, USA

Walker, Arnetia (Actor)
19551 Turtle Ridge Ln
Porter Ranch, CA 91326-3808, USA

Walker, Benjamin (Actor)
c/o Cara Tripicchio *Shelter PR*
9350 Wilshire Blvd Ste 450
Beverly Hills, CA 90212-3230, USA

Walker, Bree (Actor)
3347 Tareco Dr
Los Angeles, CA 90068-1527

Walker, Brian (Cartoonist)
c/o Staff Member *King Features
Syndication*
300 W 57th St Fl 15
New York, NY 10019-5238, USA

Walker, Bruce (Athlete, Football Player)
279 Eastlawn St
Detroit, MI 48215-3072, USA

Walker, Butch (Musician)
c/o Jonathan Daniel *Crush Management*
60-62 E 11th St
7th Floor
New York, NY 10003, USA

Walker, Caroline (Actor)
c/o Staff Member *Badgley-Connor-King*
9229 W Sunset Blvd Ste 311
West Hollywood, CA 90069-3403, USA

Walker, Charles D (Astronaut)
Boeing Co
12771 N Morgan Ranch Rd
Oro Valley, AZ 85755-6767, USA

Walker, Chet (Athlete, Basketball Player)
PO Box 9451
Marina Del Rey, CA 90295-1851, USA

Walker, Chico (Athlete, Baseball Player)
450 W Huron St
Chicago, IL 60654-3495, USA

Walker, Chuck (Athlete, Football Player)
9701 Armelise Dr
Myrtle Beach, SC 29579-5301, USA

Walker, Clarence "Foots (Athlete,
Basketball Player)
706 NE Hunters Rd
Blue Springs, MO 64014-6530, USA

Walker, Clay (Musician)
1040 Natchez Valley Ln
Franklin, TN 37064-4704, USA

Walker, Cleo (Athlete, Football Player)
512 Tecumseh Dr
Shepherdsville, KY 40165-7060, USA

Walker, Clint (Actor)
101 W McKnight Way Ste B
B-202
Grass Valley, CA 95949-9613, USA

Walker, Darnell (Athlete, Football Player)
501 N 44th St
Muskogee, OK 74401-2326, USA

Walker, Darrell (Athlete, Basketball
Player, Coach)
16122 Patriot Dr
Little Rock, AR 72212-2669, USA

Walker, David (Government Official)
General Accounting Office
441 G St NW
Washington, DC 20548-0002, USA

Walker, Denard (Athlete, Football Player)
1221 Mackey St
Garland, TX 75040-1215, USA

Walker, Dewayne (Athlete, Football Player)
605 W Surf Spray Ln
Ponte Vedra Beach, FL 32082-2785, USA

Walker, Django (Musician)
c/o Jon Folk *Red 11 Music (Nashville)*
Prefers to be contacted via telephone or email
Nashville, TN, USA

Walker, Dreama (Actor)
c/o Randi Goldstein *Gersh (NY)*
41 Madison Ave
New York, NY 10010-2202, USA

Walker, Duane (Athlete, Baseball Player)
2509 Georgia Ave
Deer Park, TX 77536-4732, USA

Walker, Dwight (Athlete, Football Player)
2616 Decatur St
Kenner, LA 70062-5024, USA

Walker, Eamonn (Actor)
c/o Scott Schachter *United Talent Agency (UTA-LA)*
9336 Civic Center Dr
Beverly Hills, CA 90210-3604, USA

Walker, Glen (Athlete, Football Player)
5592 Nelson St
Cypress, CA 90630-3147, USA

Walker, Greg (Athlete, Baseball Player)
630 Lazy Nine Rd
Pearson, GA 31642-5733, USA

Walker, Greg (Cartoonist)
c/o Staff Member *King Features Syndication*
300 W 57th St Fl 15
New York, NY 10019-5238, USA

Walker, Herschel (Athlete, Football Player, Heisman Trophy Winner)
2210 King Fisher Dr
Westlake, TX 76262-4815, USA

Walker, Hezekiah (Musician)
c/o Staff Member *The Alliance Agency*
1035 Bates Ct
Hendersonville, TN 37075-8864, USA

Walker, Hugh (Baseball Player)
Bowman
24 Georgeann Dr
Jacksonville, AR 72076-5352, USA

Walker, Jackie (Athlete, Football Player)
13014 N Dale Mabry Hwy # 120
Tampa, FL 33618-2808, USA

Walker, Jamie (Athlete, Baseball Player)
11450 W 187th St
Spring Hill, KS 66083-7593, USA

Walker, Jason (Musician)
c/o Len Evans *Project Publicity*
312 W 53rd St Ste 202
New York, NY 10019-5743, USA

Walker, Javon (Athlete, Football Player)
59 Wincrest Falls Dr
Cypress, TX 77429-5217, USA

Walker, Jeff (Athlete, Football Player)
3712 Ringgold Rd Apt 204
Chattanooga, TN 37412-1638, USA

Walker, Jerry (Athlete, Baseball Player)
2015 Collins Blvd
Ada, OK 74820-7015, USA

Walker, Jerry Jeff (Musician, Songwriter)
Tried & True Music
PO Box 39
Austin, TX 78767-0039, USA

Walker, Jimmie (Actor, Comedian)
8977 Rivers Edge Dr
Las Vegas, NV 89117-5425, USA

Walker, Joe Louis (Musician)
Rick Bates Mgmt
714 Brookside Ln
Sierra Madre, CA 91024-1426, USA

Walker, Johnny (Athlete, Baseball Player)
Raleigh Tigers
718 Franklin St SE
Grand Rapids, MI 49507-1307, USA

Walker, Junior
141 Dunbar Ave
Fords, NJ 08863-1551

Walker, Kenny (Athlete, Basketball Player)
7235 Darsena
Grand Prairie, TX 75054-6508, USA

Walker, Kenyatta (Athlete, Football Player)
14813 Tudor Chase Dr
Tampa, FL 33626-3353, USA

Walker, Kevin (Athlete, Baseball Player)
759 Chestnut Ave
Holtville, CA 92250-1410, USA

Walker, Kurt (Athlete, Hockey Player)
196 N Wesley Chapel Rd
Eatonton, GA 31024-6047, USA

Walker, Larry (Athlete, Baseball Player)
1667 Flagler Pkwy
West Palm Beach, FL 33411-1874, USA

Walker, Leslie David (Actor)
13952 Hartsook St
Sherman Oaks, CA 91423-1210, USA

Walker, Luke (Athlete, Baseball Player)
316 Loma Linda St
Wake Village, TX 75501-8638, USA

Walker, Malcolm (Athlete, Football Player)
7140 Winterwood Ln
Dallas, TX 75248-5246, USA

Walker, Marquis (Athlete, Football Player)
17576 Cherrylawn St
Detroit, MI 48221-2508, USA

Walker, Mickey (Athlete, Football Player)
22828 S Maple Point Rd
Pickford, MI 49774-9145, USA

Walker, Mike (Athlete, Baseball Player)
24616 Marks Rd
Splendora, TX 77372-3407, USA

Walker, Mike (Athlete, Baseball Player)
23195 Tankersley Rd
Brooksville, FL 34601-4818, USA

Walker, Mort (Cartoonist)
61 Studio Rd
Stamford, CT 06903-4724, USA

Walker, Nicholas
1900 Avenue of the Stars Ste 1640
Los Angeles, CA 90067-4407

Walker, Olene (Politician)
3135 Jacob Hamblin Dr
Saint George, UT 84790-7807, USA

Walker, Pete (Athlete, Baseball Player)
2 White Oak Ln
Quaker Hill, CT 06375-1045, USA

Walker, Phillip (Athlete, Basketball Player)
720 E Phil Ellena St
Philadelphia, PA 19119-1531, USA

Walker, Polly (Actor)
c/o Jon Rubinstein *Authentic Talent and Literary Management*
20 Jay St Ste M17
Brooklyn, NY 11201-8300, USA

Walker, Rick (Athlete, Football Player)
906 Winstead St
Great Falls, VA 22066-2546, USA

Walker, Ronald C (Publisher)
Smithsonian Magazine
900 Jefferson Dr SW
Washington, DC 20560-0005, USA

Walker, Sammy (Athlete, Football Player)
1031 Kings Row
McKinney, TX 75069-6207, USA

Walker, Scott (Director)
c/o BeBe Lerner *ID Public Relations (LA)*
7060 Hollywood Blvd Fl 8th
Los Angeles, CA 90028-6021, USA

Walker, Scott (Governor, Politician)
State Capitol
PO Box 7863
Madison, WI 53702-0001, USA

Walker, Shannon Dr (Astronaut)
2421 Clopper St
Seabrook, TX 77586-3738, USA

Walker, Todd (Athlete, Baseball Player)
212 Madonna Dr
Benton, LA 71006-4217, USA

Walker, Tom (Athlete, Baseball Player)
817 Whippoorwill Hill Rd
Gibsonia, PA 15044-8985, USA

Walker, Tony (Athlete, Baseball Player)
931 Gingerwood Ct
Vacaville, CA 95687-7701, USA

Walker, Tyler (Athlete, Baseball Player)
400 Sansome St
San Francisco, CA 94111-3353, USA

Walker, Tyler (Race Car Driver)
222 Raceway Dr
Mooresville, NC 28117-6510, United States

Walker, Val Joe (Athlete, Football Player)
3857 S Versailles Ave
Dallas, TX 75209-5927, USA

Walker, Wally (Athlete, Basketball Player)
154 Lombard St Apt 58
San Francisco, CA 94111-1125, USA

Walker, Wayne (Athlete, Football Player)
2033 S White Pine Ln
Boise, ID 83706-4048, USA

Walker, Wesley D (Athlete, Football Player)
PO Box 20438
Huntington Station, NY 11746-0857, USA

Walker, William D (Business Person)
Tektronix Inc
26600 Sourtwest Pkwy
Wilsonville, OR 97070, USA

Walker Jr, Robert (Actor)
TOPS
23410 Civic Center Way Ste C1
Malibu, CA 90265-5925, USA

Walkom, Stephen (Athlete, Hockey Player)
1709 Wheatland Dr
Coraopolis, PA 15108-9208, USA

Wall, Carolyn (Publisher)
Newsweek Magazine
251 W 57th St
New York, NY 10019-1802, USA

Wall, Donne (Athlete, Baseball Player)
116 River Breeze Way
Saint Louis, MO 63129-4855, USA

Wall, Frederick T (Athlete, Football Player)
2044 Kerwood Ave
Los Angeles, CA 90025-6007, USA

Wall, John (Athlete, Basketball Player)
c/o Dan Fegan *Relativity Sports (LA)*
9242 Beverly Blvd Ste 300
Beverly Hills, CA 90210-3728, USA

Wall, Lindsay (Hockey Player)
University of Minnesota
Athletic Dept
Minneapolis, MN 55455, USA

Wall, Paul (Musician)
c/o Drew Elliot *Artists International Management (NY)*
333 E 43rd St Apt 115
New York, NY 10017-4822, USA

Wall, Shana (Actor)
c/o Elizabeth Much *Much and House Public Relations*
8075 W 3rd St Ste 500
Los Angeles, CA 90048-4325, USA

Wall, Stan (Athlete, Baseball Player)
9907 E 80th St
Raytown, MO 64138-1929, USA

Wallace, Aaron (Athlete, Football Player)
612 Gardenia St
Desoto, TX 75115-1449, USA

Wallace, Aria (Actor)
c/o DebraLynn Findon *Discover Inc Management*
11425 Moorpark St
North Hollywood, CA 91602-2009, USA

Wallace, Barron Steven (Steve) (Athlete, Football Player)
705 Town Blvd NE Apt 417
Brookhaven, GA 30319-3075, USA

Wallace, Ben (Basketball Player)
c/o Staff Member *Chicago Bulls*
1901 W Madison St
Chicago, IL 60612-2459, USA

Wallace, B J (Athlete, Baseball Player, Olympic Athlete)
12775 River Creek Dr
Fairhope, AL 36532-6501, USA

Wallace, Bob (Athlete, Football Player)
44111 N 43rd Dr
New River, AZ 85087-5956, USA

Wallace, Bruce (Doctor, Scientist)
940 McBryde Ln
Blacksburg, VA 24060-3221, USA

Wallace, Chris (Correspondent)
2439 Wyoming Ave NW
Washington, DC 20008-1644, USA

Wallace, Cooper (Athlete, Football Player)
c/o Chad Speck *Allegiant Athletic Agency*
35 Market Sq Ste 201
Knoxville, TN 37902-1420, USA

Wallace, Craig K (Doctor)
National Institutes of Health
9000 Rockville Pike
Bethesda, MD 20892-0002, USA

Wallace, Dave (Athlete, Baseball Player)
82 Whipple Brook Rd
Wrentham, MA 02093-2512, USA

Wallace, Derek (Athlete, Baseball Player)
5951 SE Crooked Oak Ave
Hobe Sound, FL 33455-8311, USA

Wallace, Don (Actor)
c/o Staff Member *SMS Talent*
8383 Wilshire Blvd Ste 230
Beverly Hills, CA 90211-2436, USA

Wallace, Don (Athlete, Baseball Player)
23 Kris Ln
Manitou Springs, CO 80829-2709, USA

Wallace, George (Musician)
c/o Staff Member *Paradigm (Monterey)*
404 W Franklin St
Monterey, CA 93940-2303, USA

Wallace, Gerald (Athlete, Basketball Player)
8381 Providence Rd
Charlotte, NC 28277-9753, USA

Wallace, Jeff (Athlete, Baseball Player)
2417 Fairchild Cir NW
Uniontown, OH 44685-6630, USA

Wallace, Kenny (Race Car Driver)
8995 Harris Rd
Concord, NC 28027-8670, USA

Wallace, Laurie (Actor)
PO Box 3023
West New York, NJ 07093-6023

Wallace, Mike (Athlete, Baseball Player)
12483 Elk Run Rd
Midland, VA 22728-2316, USA

Wallace, Mike (Race Car Driver)
Morgan-McClure Racing
26502 Newbanks Rd
Abingdon, VA 24210-7500, USA

Wallace, Randall (Actor, Director, Producer, Writer)
c/o Staff Member *Wheelhouse, The*
15464 Ventura Blvd
Sherman Oaks, CA 91403-3002

Wallace, Rasheed (Athlete, Basketball Player)
1979 Arthurs Way
Rochester Hills, MI 48306-3363, USA

Wallace, Ray (Athlete, Football Player)
2480 Port Kembla Dr
Mount Juliet, TN 37122-7512, USA

Wallace, Rheagan (Actor)
c/o Linda McAlister *Linda McAlister Talent*
100 Oak Ln
Waxahachie, TX 75167-8412, USA

Wallace, Rick (Director, Producer)
29033 Grayfox St
Malibu, CA 90265-4256, USA

Wallace, Rodney (Athlete, Football Player)
20566 E Maplewood Pl
Centennial, CO 80016-1264, USA

Wallace, Roger (Athlete, Football Player)
408 N Oakland St
Urbana, OH 43078-1521, USA

Wallace, Rusty (Race Car Driver)
c/o Lou Oppenheim *Headline Media Management*
888 7th Ave Ste 503
New York, NY 10106-0501, USA

Wallace, Steve (Race Car Driver)
c/o Staff Member *Rusty Wallace Racing, LLC*
PO Box 5510
Mooresville, NC 28117-0510, USA

Wallace, Tommy Lee (Director)
Innovative Artists
1505 10th St
Santa Monica, CA 90401-2805, USA

Wallace, Will (Actor)
c/o Andrew Stawiarski *ADS Management*
269 S Beverly Dr # 441
Beverly Hills, CA 90212-3851, USA

Wallach, Tim (Athlete, Baseball Player)
21750 Deveron Cv
Yorba Linda, CA 92887-2662, USA

Wallechinsky, David (Writer)
c/o Staff Member *HarperCollins Publishers*
195 Broadway Fl 2
Cellar 1
New York, NY 10007-3132, USA

Wallem, Linda (Actor, Producer)
c/o Staff Member *Creative Artists Agency (CAA-LA)*
2000 Avenue of the Stars Ste 100
Los Angeles, CA 90067-4705, USA

Wallenberg, Raoul Committee
823 United Nations Plz Fl 8
New York, NY 10017-3510

Wallendas, The Great
138 Frog Hollow Rd
Southampton, PA 18966-1031

Waller, Dwight (Athlete, Basketball Player)
1038 S Brookside Dr
Gallatin, TN 37066-5612, USA

Waller, Jamie (Athlete, Basketball Player)
904 Owens Ave
South Boston, VA 24592-3728, USA

Waller, Robert (Writer)
12 Old Harper Rd
Harper, TX 78631-5255, USA

Waller, Ron (Athlete, Football Player)
900 Concord Rd
Seaford, DE 19973, USA

Waller, Ty (Athlete, Baseball Player)
16963 Silver Crest Dr
San Diego, CA 92127-2816, USA

Waller, Tye (Athlete, Baseball Player)
16963 Silver Crest Dr
San Diego, CA 92127-2816, USA

Wallflowers, The (Music Group)
c/o Rick Roskin *Creative Artists Agency (CAA-LA)*
2000 Avenue of the Stars Ste 100
Los Angeles, CA 90067-4705, USA

Walliams, David (Actor, Producer, Writer)
c/o Kevin McLaughlin *Baker Winokur Ryder Public Relations (BWR-LA)*
9100 Wilshire Blvd Ste 500
West Tower Suite 500
Beverly Hills, CA 90212-3426, USA

Wallin, Niclas (Athlete, Hockey Player)
244 Johnson Ave
Los Gatos, CA 95030-6218, USA

Walling, Camryn (Actor)
c/o Staff Member *Abrams Artists Agency (LA)*
9200 W Sunset Blvd PH 11
West Hollywood, CA 90069-3601, USA

Walling, Denny (Athlete, Baseball Player)
PO Box 1312
Waynesboro, VA 22980-0902, USA

Wallis, Annabelle (Actor)
c/o Craig Schneider *Pinnacle Public Relations*
8721 Santa Monica Blvd Ste 133
West Hollywood, CA 90069-4507, USA

Wallis, Joe (Athlete, Baseball Player)
PO Box 2284
Saint Louis, MO 63109-0284, USA

Wallis, Kevin (Horse Racer)
2874 NE 33rd St
Lighthouse Point, FL 33064-8551, USA

Wallis, Quvenzhane (Actor)
c/o Steven Kavovit *Thruline Entertainment*
9250 Wilshire Blvd Ste 100
Ground Floor
Beverly Hills, CA 90212-3343, USA

Wallis, Shani (Actor)
2119 Via Puerta Unit Q
Laguna Woods, CA 92637-2462, USA

Wallner, Hakan (Horse Racer)
PO Box 3153
Pompano Beach, FL 33072, USA

Walls, Denise (Nee-C) (Musician, Songwriter, Writer)
2113 South Ave
Youngstown, OH 44502-2255, USA

Walls, Everson C (Athlete, Football Player)
1925 Antwerp Ave
Plano, TX 75025-3320, USA

Walls, Herkie (Athlete, Football Player)
1002 Cherrywood Dr
Garland, TX 75040-7437, USA

Walls, Jeannette (Writer)
c/o Jennifer Rudolph Walsh *William Morris Endeavor (NY)*
1325 Avenue of the Americas
New York, NY 10019-6026, USA

Walls, Lenny (Athlete, Football Player)
2800 Bush St
San Francisco, CA 94115-2905, USA

Walls, Wesley (Athlete, Football Player)
8711 Lake Challis Ln
Charlotte, NC 28226-2666, USA

Walmsley, Jon (Actor)
217 Grand Ave Apt 5
Long Beach, CA 90803-6135, USA

Walrond, Les (Athlete, Baseball Player)
209 King Arthur Cir
Franklin, TN 37067-6468, USA

Walser, Don (Musician, Songwriter, Writer)
Nancy Fly Agency
6618 Wolfcreek Pass
Austin, TX 78749-1744, USA

Walsh, Addie (Writer)
c/o Staff Member *William Morris Endeavor (LA)*
9601 Wilshire Blvd
Beverly Hills, CA 90210-5213, USA

Walsh, Amanda (Actor)
c/o Laina Cohn *Cohn / Torgan Management*
Prefers to be contacted by telephone or email
Los Angeles, CA, USA

Walsh, Arthur
12360 Riverside Dr
Valley Village, CA 91607-3644

Walsh, Chris (Athlete, Football Player)
4834 N 74th St
Scottsdale, AZ 85251-1306, USA

Walsh, Dave (Athlete, Baseball Player)
500 Concord Ln
Edmond, OK 73003-6127, USA

Walsh, David M (Cinematographer)
15066 Sutton St
Sherman Oaks, CA 91403-4020, USA

Walsh, Don (Athlete, Swimmer)
International Maritime Inc
14758 Sitkum Ln
Myrtle Point, OR 97458-9692, USA

Walsh, Donnie (Basketball Coach, Coach)
5625 Audubon Ridge Ln
Indianapolis, IN 46250-2320, USA

Walsh, Dylan (Actor)
c/o Bob McGowan *McGowan Management*
8733 W Sunset Blvd Ste 103
West Hollywood, CA 90069-2241, USA

Walsh, JD (Actor)
6631 Saloma Ave
Van Nuys, CA 91405-4539, USA

Walsh, Joe (Congressman, Politician)
432 Cannon Hob
Washington, DC 20515-4004, USA

Walsh, Joe (Musician, Songwriter)
400 Porter St
Easton, PA 18042-1726, USA

Walsh, Kate (Actor)
15837 Royal Oak Rd
Encino, CA 91436-3909, USA

Walsh, Kerri (Athlete, Volleyball Player)
c/o Brandon Swibel *The Legacy Agency*
1500 Broadway Ste 2501
New York, NY 10036-4082, USA

Walsh, Maiara (Actor)
c/o Staff Member *Mattie Management*
1438 N Gower St Ste 57
Los Angeles, CA 90028-8358, USA

Walsh, Matt (Actor, Comedian)
c/o Antonio D'Alessandro *AntonioPaulPR*
PO Box 801651
Santa Clarita, CA 91380-1651, USA

Walsh, M Emmet (Actor)
4173 Motor Ave
Culver City, CA 90232-3414, USA

Walsh, Mike (Athlete, Hockey Player)
29 North St
Andover, NH 03216, USA

Walsh, Morgan (Actor)
c/o Glenn Salners *Stone Manners Salners Agency (LA)*
6100 Wilshire Blvd Ste 1500
Los Angeles, CA 90048-5110, USA

Walsh, Patrick C (Doctor)
Johns Hopkins University
Brady Urological Institute
Baltimore, MD 21205, USA

Walsh, Peter (Designer)
Peter Walsh Design
15030 Ventura Blvd # 19-881
Sherman Oaks, CA 91403-5470, USA

Walsh, Sheila (Musician, Writer)
PO Box 150783
Nashville, TN 37215-0783, USA

Walsh, Shelia (Musician, Writer)
PO Box 1516
Celina, TX 75009-1516, USA

Walsh, Stephen J (Steve) (Athlete,
Football Player)
339 Flamingo Dr
West Palm Beach, FL 33401-7721, USA

Walsh, Sydney (Actor)
Innovative Artists
1505 10th St
Santa Monica, CA 90401-2805, USA

Walsh, Ward (Athlete, Football Player)
1658 W Carson St Ste C
Torrance, CA 90501-2897, USA

Walske, Steven (Business Person)
Parametric Technology
140 Kendrick St
Needham Heights, MA 02494-2739, USA

Walsman, Leanna (Actor)
c/o Chris Andrews *Creative Artists Agency*
(CAA-LA)
2000 Avenue of the Stars Ste 100
Los Angeles, CA 90067-4705, USA

Walte, Grant (Golfer)
9380 S Magnolia Ave
Ocala, FL 34476-7535, USA

Walter, Gene (Athlete, Baseball Player)
1901 Fairway Dr
La Grange, KY 40031-9697, USA

Walter, Jessica (Actor)
22 Kinnicut Rd
Pound Ridge, NY 10576-1800, USA

Walter, Joe (Athlete, Football Player)
4136 Binley Dr
Richardson, TX 75082-3723, USA

Walter, Lisa Ann (Actor)
c/o Mel McKeon *McKeon-Myones*
Management
3500 W Olive Ave Ste 770
Burbank, CA 91505-5527, USA

Walter, Michael (Athlete, Football Player)
30460 SW Ruth St Unit 4802
Wilsonville, OR 97070-6680, USA

Walter, Mike (Athlete, Football Player)
30460 SW Ruth St Unit 4802
Wilsonville, OR 97070-6680, USA

Walter, Robert D (Business Person)
Cardinal Health
7000 Cardinal Pl
Dublin, OH 43017-1091, USA

Walter, Tracey (Actor)
257 N Rexford Dr
Beverly Hills, CA 90210-4907, USA

Walters, Barbara (Journalist, Talk Show
Host)
944 5th Ave
New York, NY 10021-2656, USA

Walters, Charles (Director)
23922 De Ville Way Apt A
Malibu, CA 90265-4844, USA

Walters, Charlie (Athlete, Baseball Player)
1717 Sutton Ln
Saint Paul, MN 55118-3717, USA

Walters, David (Politician)
RR 2
Watts, OK 74964, USA

Walters, Harry N (Government Official)
DHC Holdings Corp
125 Thomas Dl
Williamsburg, VA 23185-6576, USA

Walters, Hugh (Actor)
15 Christchurch Ave
London, EN NW6 7

Walters, Jamie (Actor, Musician)
4702 Ethel Ave
Sherman Oaks, CA 91423-3315, USA

Walters, Julie (Actor)
c/o Tom Burke *ICM Partners (LA)*
10250 Constellation Blvd Fl 7
Los Angeles, CA 90067-6207, USA

Walters, Lisa (Athlete, Golfer)
211 S Westland Ave Unit 2
Tampa, FL 33606-1721, USA

Walters, Melora (Actor)
2740 Lake Hollywood Dr
Los Angeles, CA 90068-1630, USA

Walters, Mike (Athlete, Baseball Player)
79070 Desert Stream Dr
La Quinta, CA 92253-4295, USA

Walters, Phil (Race Car Driver)
23 Sycamore
Homosassa, FL 32646, USA

Walters, PJ (Athlete, Baseball Player)
29476 Oakstone Dr E
Daphne, AL 36526-5602, USA

Walters, Rex (Athlete, Basketball Player)
21602 W 99th St
Lenexa, KS 66220-2678, USA

Walters, Scot (Race Car Driver)
Brewco Motorsports
PO Box 37
321 W. Reservoir
Central City, KY 42330-0037, USA

Walters, Stan (Athlete, Football Player)
10 Lcklingham Wood
Sewell, NJ 08080, USA

Walters, Susan (Actor)
c/o Gabrielle Krengel *Domain Talent*
9229 W Sunset Blvd Ste 710
West Hollywood, CA 90069-3407, USA

Walters, Tom (Athlete, Football Player)
8 Heritage Ln
Magnolia, TX 77354-1337, USA

Walterschield, Len (Athlete, Football
Player)
2312 I Rd
Grand Junction, CO 81505-9646, USA

Walther, Paul (Athlete, Basketball Player)
6555 Riverside Dr
Atlanta, GA 30328-2705, USA

Waltman, Sean (X-Pac) (Athlete, Wrestler)
c/o Staff Member *World Wrestling*
Entertainment (WWE)
1241 E Main St
Titan Towers
Stamford, CT 06902-3520, USA

Walton, Alice (Business Person)
Wal-Mart Stores
702 SW 8th St
Bentonville, AR 72716-6299, USA

Walton, Ann (Business Person)
1807 W Nifong Blvd
Columbia, MO 65203-5913, USA

Walton, Anthony J (Tony) (Designer)
International Creative Mgmt
40 W 57th St Fl 5
New York, NY 10019-4001, USA

Walton, Bennie (Baseball Player)
188 S Palm Villas Way
Palm Springs, FL 33461-1084, USA

Walton, Bill (Athlete, Basketball Player,
Sportscaster)
1010 Myrtle Way
San Diego, CA 92103-5123, USA

Walton, Bruce (Athlete, Baseball Player)
10704 Sunset Canyon Dr
Bakersfield, CA 93311-2746, USA

Walton, Christy (Business Person)
Wal-Mart Stores
702 SW 8th St
Bentonville, AR 72712-6209, USA

Walton, Danny (Athlete, Baseball Player)
PO Box 296
Huntsville, UT 84317-0296, USA

Walton, David (Actor)
c/o Nick Collins *Gersh (LA)*
9465 Wilshire Blvd Ste 600
Beverly Hills, CA 90212-2605, USA

Walton, Jerome (Athlete, Baseball Player)
4500 Shannon Blvd Apt 8C
Union City, GA 30291-1534, USA

Walton, Jess (Actor)
69372 Camp Polk Rd
Sisters, OR 97759-9705, USA

Walton, Jim (Business Person)
The Walton Family Foundation
PO Box 2030
Bentonville, AR 72712-2030, USA

Walton, John (Athlete, Football Player)
401 New York Ave
Elizabeth City, NC 27909-5939, USA

Walton, Joseph (Joe) (Athlete, Coach,
Football Coach, Football Player)
8 Windycrest Dr
Beaver Falls, PA 15010-3041, USA

Walton, Lawrence (Athlete, Football
Player)
8636 N 96th Ln
Peoria, AZ 85345-7759, USA

Walton, Luke (Athlete, Basketball Player)
332 Downham Ct
Walnut Creek, CA 94598-2320, USA

Walton, Reggie (Athlete, Baseball Player)
1142 S Curson Ave
Los Angeles, CA 90019-6611, USA

Walton, Robin (Golfer)
8404 SW 50th Ln
Gainesville, FL 32608-4307, USA

Walton, S Robson (Business Person)
Wal-Mart Stores
702 SW 8th St
Bentonville, AR 72716-6299, USA

Walton, Whip (Athlete, Football Player)
748 E Solana Cir
Solana Beach, CA 92075-2356, USA

Walton Laurie, Nancy (Business Person)
1186 MacDonald Ranch Dr
Henderson, NV 89012-7272, USA

Waltrip, Darrell (Race Car Driver)
110 Deerfield
Franklin, TN 37064, USA

Waltrip, Michael (Race Car Driver)
Michael Waltrip Racing
8566 Dog Leg Rd
Sherrills Ford, NC 28673, USA

Waltrip, Robert L (Business Person)
Service Corp International
1929 Allen Pkwy
Houston, TX 77019-2506, USA

Waltz, Christoph (Actor)
c/o Lisa Kasteler *WKT Public Relations*
(LA)
9350 Wilshire Blvd Ste 450
Beverly Hills, CA 90212-3230, USA

Waltz, Lisa (Actor)
c/o Donald Spradlin *Essential Talent*
Management
6399 Wilshire Blvd Ste 401
Los Angeles, CA 90048-5716, USA

Waltz, Rich (Sportscaster)
820 5th Ave NW
Issaquah, WA 98027-2816, USA

Walz, Carl E (Astronaut)
129 Lake Point Dr
League City, TX 77573-6973, USA

Walz, Carl E Col (Astronaut)
15506 Eagle Tavern Ln
Centreville, VA 20120-3701, USA

Walz, Wes (Athlete, Hockey Player)
2377 Fieldstone Curv
Saint Paul, MN 55129-6218, USA

Walz, Zach (Athlete, Football Player)
6270 E Wilshire Dr
Scottsdale, AZ 85257-1114, USA

Wambach, Abby (Athlete, Olympic
Athlete, Soccer Player)
446 Monterey Blvd Apt H2
Hermosa Beach, CA 90254-4575, USA

Wambaugh, Joseph (Writer)
30 Linda Isle
Newport Beach, CA 92660-7206, USA

Wambold, Richard L (Business Person)
Pactiv Corp
1900 W Field Ct
Lake Forest, IL 60045-4828, USA

Wamsley, Rick (Athlete, Hockey Player)
1171 Wildhorse Meadows Dr
Chesterfield, MO 63005-1349, USA

Wan, James (Director)
9332 Nightingale Dr
Los Angeles, CA 90069-1119, USA

Wang, Alexander (Fashion Designer)
Alexander Wang Inc
386 Broadway Fl 3
New York, NY 10013-6021, USA

Wang, Garrett (Actor)
501 E Del Mar Blvd Apt 310
Pasadena, CA 91101-3613, USA

Wang, Taylor G (Astronaut, Physicist)
4999 Tyne Ridge Ct
Nashville, TN 37220-1531, USA

Wang, Vera (Designer, Fashion Designer)
610 Cole Pl
Beverly Hills, CA 90210-1918, USA

Wang, Wayne (Director)
1888 Century Park E Ste 1888
Los Angeles, CA 90067-1722, USA

Wang Zhi Zhi (Basketball Player)
Miami Heat
601 Biscayne Blvd
American Airlines Arena
Miami, FL 33132-1801, USA

Wannsdedt, David R (Dave) (Coach, Football Coach)
12600 N Stonebrook Cir
Davie, FL 33330-1288, USA

Wannstedt, David R (Dave) (Athlete, Coach, Football Coach, Football Player)
1625 Gordon Dr
Naples, FL 34102-7417, USA

Wansel, Dexter (Musician)
Walt Reeder Productions
PO Box 27641
Philadelphia, PA 19118-0641, USA

Wanzer, Bobby (Athlete, Basketball Player)
28 Greenwood Park
Pittsford, NY 14534-2965, USA

Waples, Ron (Horse Racer)
7 Mill Run W
Hightstown, NJ 08520-3021, USA

Wapner, Joseph (Joe) (Attorney)
2388 Century Hl
Los Angeles, CA 90067-3514, USA

Wapnick, Steve (Athlete, Baseball Player)
7518 Plateau Rd
Greeley, CO 80634-9388, USA

War
250 W 57th St # 407
New York, NY 10107-0001

Warburton, Patrick (Actor)
2850 Los Fresnos Cir
Santa Rosa Valley, CA 93012-8810, USA

Ward, Aaron (Athlete, Hockey Player)
112 Ronsard Ln
Cary, NC 27511-6019, USA

Ward, Andre (Athlete, Boxer)
c/o Marylyn Aceves *Aceves Public Relations*
PO Box 32008
Los Angeles, CA 90032-0008, USA

Ward, Anita (Musician)
c/o Staff Member *Diva Central Inc*
7510 W Sunset Blvd Ste 1445
Los Angeles, CA 90046-3408, USA

Ward, Bert (Actor)
c/o Wes Stevens *Vox*
6420 Wilshire Blvd Ste 1080
Los Angeles, CA 90048-5539, USA

Ward, Bryan (Athlete, Baseball Player)
140 Bannock Ct
East Dundee, IL 60118-1626, USA

Ward, Charlie (Athlete, Basketball Player, Football Player, Heisman Trophy Winner)
2611 Dunsinane Rd
Pensacola, FL 32503-5812, USA

Ward, Chris (Athlete, Baseball Player)
12858 Williams Ranch Rd
Moorpark, CA 93021-2109, USA

Ward, Chris (Athlete, Football Player)
1920 Sylvan Ridge Dr SW
Atlanta, GA 30310-4945, USA

Ward, Christopher L (Chris) (Athlete, Football Player)
PO Box 1365
Inglewood, CA 90308-1365, USA

Ward, Colby (Athlete, Baseball Player)
1508 Hobble Creek Dr
Springville, UT 84663-2890, USA

Ward, Colin (Athlete, Baseball Player)
1220 E Commerce Ave
Gilbert, AZ 85234-4856, USA

Ward, Daryle (Athlete, Baseball Player)
18073 Granite Ave
Riverside, CA 92508-9777, USA

Ward, Dedric (Athlete, Football Player)
3435 N 45th St
Phoenix, AZ 85018-6028, USA

Ward, Ed (Athlete, Hockey Player)
9150 Weathervane Trl
Galesburg, MI 49053-9777, USA

Ward, Fred (Actor)
1214 Cabrillo Ave
Venice, CA 90291-3704, USA

Ward, Gary (Athlete, Baseball Player)
18073 Granite Ave
Riverside, CA 92508-9777, USA

Ward, Gemma (Actor, Model)
c/o Staff Member *Caliber Media Company*
5670 Wilshire Blvd Ste 1600
Los Angeles, CA 90036-5659, USA

Ward, Gerry (Athlete, Basketball Player)
14 Comstock Ct
Ridgefield, CT 06877-5826, USA

Ward, Hines (Athlete, Football Player)
6215 Riverside Dr
Atlanta, GA 30328-3623, USA

Ward, Jason (Athlete, Hockey Player)
133 Emerald Hill Way
Valrico, FL 33594

Ward, Jeff (Race Car Driver)
AJ Foyt Racing
64L5 Toledo St
Houston, TX 77008, USA

Ward, Joe (Athlete, Hockey Player)
2218 199th St SW
Lynnwood, WA 98036-7014, USA

Ward, Joel (Athlete, Hockey Player)
Cooney Management
220 Boylston St Apt 1202
Boston, MA 02116-3950, USA

Ward, John (Athlete, Football Player)
9501 Silver Lake Dr
Oklahoma City, OK 73162-7547, USA

Ward, John F (Business Person)
Russell Corp
1357 Lee St
Alexander City, AL 35010-2613, USA

Ward, Jon P (Business Person)
RR Donnelley & Sons
77 W Wacker Dr
Chicago, IL 60601-1604, USA

Ward, Kevin (Athlete, Baseball Player)
160 E Ave
Coronado, CA 92118-1321, USA

Ward, Mary B (Actor)
Innovative Artists
1505 10th St
Santa Monica, CA 90401-2805, USA

Ward, Mateus (Actor)
c/o Nicole Miller *Nicole Miller Agency*
Prefers to be contacted by telephone or email
CA, USA

Ward, Megan (Actor)
PO Box 481219
Los Angeles, CA 90036, USA

Ward, Micky (Athlete, Boxer)
c/o Nick Cordasco *Prince Marketing Group*
18 Carillon Cir
Livingston, NJ 07039-2600, USA

Ward, Pete (Athlete, Baseball Player)
575 G Ave
Lake Oswego, OR 97034-2272, USA

Ward, Preston (Athlete, Baseball Player)
4371 De Silva Pl
Las Vegas, NV 89121-5347, USA

Ward, R Duane (Athlete, Baseball Player)
PO Box 312
361 S Camino Del Rio
Durango, CO 81302-0312, USA

Ward, Robert R (Bob) (Athlete, Football Player)
PO Box 535
Riva, MD 21140-0535, USA

Ward, Ronald L (Ron) (Athlete, Hockey Player)
3178 W 140th St
Cleveland, OH 44111-1442, USA

Ward, Sela (Actor)
1492 Stone Canyon Rd
Los Angeles, CA 90077-1909, USA

Ward, Sterling (Religious Leader)
Brethren Church
524 College Ave
Ashland, OH 44805-3703, USA

Ward, Susan (Actor)
c/o Staff Member *Agency Group Ltd, The (LA)*
1880 Century Park E Ste 711
Los Angeles, CA 90067-1618, USA

Ward, Turner M (Athlete, Baseball Player)
232 Autumn Dr
Saraland, AL 36571-2619, USA

Ward, Wendy (Golfer)
12845 Sassin Station Rd N
Edwall, WA 99008-9564, USA

Ward, Zach (Actor)
Diverse Talent Group
1875 Century Park E Ste 2250
Los Angeles, CA 90067-2563, USA

Warden, Jon (Athlete, Baseball Player)
9573 Loveland Madeira Rd
Loveland, OH 45140-8947, USA

Wardle, Curt (Athlete, Baseball Player)
13900 Pheasant Knoll Ln
Moreno Valley, CA 92553-5330, USA

Ware, Andre (Athlete, Football Player, Heisman Trophy Winner)
3910 Wood Park
Sugar Land, TX 77479-2838, USA

Ware, Clyde (Director, Producer, Writer)
1942 Grace Ave Apt 222
Los Angeles, CA 90068-3871, USA

Ware, DeMarcus (Athlete, Football Player)
c/o Pat Dye Jr *SportsTrust Advisors (GA)*
3340 Peachtree Rd NE Fl 16
Atlanta, GA 30326-1000, USA

Ware, Derek (Athlete, Football Player)
2315 W Shannon St
Chandler, AZ 85224-3470, USA

Ware, Jeff (Athlete, Baseball Player)
2560 Mulberry Loop
Virginia Beach, VA 23456-7818, USA

Warfield, Eric (Athlete, Football Player)
718 Meadows Rd
Texarkana, AR 71854-8341, USA

Warfield, Paul D (Athlete, Football Player)
16 Normandy Way
Rancho Mirage, CA 92270-1635, USA

Warford, Larry (Athlete, Football Player)
c/o Neil Schwartz *Schwartz & Feinsod*
contact via telephone or email
White Plains, NY 10603

Wargo, Tom (Athlete, Golfer)
2801 Putter Dr
Centralia, IL 62801-6183, USA

Warhola, James (Writer)
56 Walkers Hl
Tivoli, NY 12583-5806, USA

Warhols, James (Writer)
PO Box 748
Rhinebeck, NY 12572-0748, USA

Warhop, George (Athlete, Football Coach, Football Player)
4767 Hill Top View Pl
San Jose, CA 95138-2708, USA

Wariner, Steve (Musician, Songwriter)
Steve Wariner Productions
PO Box 1647
Franklin, TN 37065-1647, USA

Waring, Todd (Actor)
Artists Agency
1180 S Beverly Dr Ste 301
Los Angeles, CA 90035-1154, USA

Warlick, Ernie (Athlete, Football Player)
10353 Tapestry Bnd
Lake Elmo, MN 55042-6006, USA

Warlock, Billy (Actor)
c/o Staff Member *Peter Strain & Associates Inc (LA)*
5455 Wilshire Blvd Ste 1812
Los Angeles, CA 90036-4268, USA

Warmenhoven, Daniel (Business Person)
Network Appliance Inc
495 E Java Dr
Sunnyvale, CA 94089-1125, USA

Warmerdam, Cornelius
3976 N 1st St
Fresno, CA 93726-4304

Warne, Jim (Athlete, Football Player)
5850 Hardy Ave
Apt 112
San Diego, CA 92115, USA

Warner, Amelia (Actor)
c/o Jon Rubinstein *Authentic Talent and Literary Management*
20 Jay St Ste M17
Brooklyn, NY 11201-8300, USA

Warner, Charley (Athlete, Football Player)
1890 Rena St
Beaumont, TX 77705-4729, USA

Warner, Chris (Cartoonist)
Dark House Publishing
10956 SE Main St
Milwaukie, OR 97222-7644, USA

Warner, Cornell (Athlete, Basketball Player)
2479 Glen Meadow Ln
Escondido, CA 92027-2810, USA

Warner, Dan (Actor)
c/o Staff Member *Players Talent Agency*
7700 W Sunset Blvd # 1
Los Angeles, CA 90046-3913, USA

Warner, Jack (Athlete, Baseball Player)
5938 W Calle Lejos
Glendale, AZ 85310-3505, USA

Warner, Jackie (Fitness Expert, Reality Star)
c/o Jean Kwolek *Artist & Brand Management (LA)*
132 N Laurel Ave
Los Angeles, CA 90048-3512, USA

Warner, Jackie (Athlete, Baseball Player)
19136 US Highway 18
Apple Valley, CA 92307-2507, USA

Warner, John (Politician)
2011 Fort Dr
Alexandria, VA 22307-1133, USA

Warner, Julie (Actor, Director, Producer)
333 S Roxbury Dr
Beverly Hills, CA 90212-3710, USA

Warner, Kirk (Athlete, Football Player)
110 S 5th St
Cochran, GA 31014-6632, USA

Warner, Kurt (Athlete, Football Player)
c/o Michael McCartney *Priority Sports & Entertainment - Chicago*
312 N La Salle
Suite 650
Chicago, IL 60610, USA

Warner, Malcolm-Jamal (Actor)
3671 Alta Mesa Dr
Studio City, CA 91604-4004, USA

Warner, Margaret (Correspondent)
News Hour Show
2700 S Quincy St Ste 250
Arlington, VA 22206-2222, USA

Warner, Mark (Politician)
1227 King St
Alexandria, VA 22314, USA

Warner, T C (Actor)
S D B Partners
315 S Beverly Dr Ste 411
Beverly Hills, CA 90212-4301, USA

Warner, Tom (Producer)
Carsey-Warner Productions
4024 Radford Ave Bldg 3
Studio City, CA 91604-2101, USA

Warner, Ty (Designer)
Ty Inc
PO Box 5377
Oak Brook, IL 60522-5377, USA

Warner, William W (Writer)
2243 47th St NW
Washington, DC 20007-1034, USA

Warnes, Jennifer (Musician, Songwriter, Writer)
Donald Miller
12746 Kling St
Studio City, CA 91604-1125, USA

Warnke, Paul
5037 Garfield St NW
Washington, DC 20016-3465

Warnock, John (Business Person)
Adobe Systems
345 Park Ave
San Jose, CA 95110-2704, USA

Warren, Cash (Producer)
1913 N Beverly Dr
Beverly Hills, CA 90210-1612, USA

Warren, Chris (Athlete, Football Player)
Seattle Seahawks
13707 Black Spruce Way
Chantilly, VA 20151-2346, USA

Warren, Cicero (Athlete, Baseball Player)
Homestead Grays
119 Brookwood St # 1
East Orange, NJ 07018-2317, USA

Warren, Diane (Musician, Songwriter)
Realsongs
6363 W Sunset Blvd # 810
Los Angeles, CA 90028-7317, USA

Warren, Don (Athlete, Football Player)
Centerville High School
6001 Union Mill Rd
Attn: Athletic Dept
Clifton, VA 20124-1131, USA

Warren, Estella (Actor, Model)
c/o Steven Jensen *Vincent Cirrincione Associates*
1516 N Fairfax Ave
Los Angeles, CA 90046-2608, USA

Warren, Gerard (Football Player)
c/o Staff Member *Denver Broncos*
13655 Broncos Pkwy
Englewood, CO 80112-4151, USA

Warren, Gloria (Actor, Musician)
16872 Bosque Dr
Encino, CA 91436-3531, USA

Warren, Jennifer (Actor)
1675 Old Oak Rd
Los Angeles, CA 90049-2505, USA

Warren, Karle (Actor)
c/o Justine Hunt *Hines and Hunt Entertainment*
1213 W Magnolia Blvd
Burbank, CA 91506-1829, USA

Warren, Kenneth S (Doctor, Scientist)
Picower Medical Research Institute
350 Community Dr
Manhasset, NY 11030-3816, USA

Warren, Kiersten (Actor)
2458 N Beachwood Dr
Los Angeles, CA 90068-3005, USA

Warren, Lesley Ann (Actor)
3619 Meadville Dr
Sherman Oaks, CA 91403-4311, USA

Warren, Martina (Adult Film Star)
Penthouse Pets
8675 Washington Blvd Ste 203
Culver City, CA 90232-7486, USA

Warren, Michael
11500 W Olympic Blvd Ste 510
Los Angeles, CA 90064-1527

Warren, Michael (Mike) (Actor, Basketball Player)
21216 Escondido St
Woodland Hills, CA 91364-5905, USA

Warren, Mike (Athlete, Baseball Player)
12281 Diane St
Garden Grove, CA 92840-3224, USA

Warren, Neil Clark
eHarmony
PO Box 3640
C/O Eharmony.Com
Santa Monica, CA 90408-3640, USA

Warren, Rick (Religious Leader, Writer)
Saddleback Church
1 Saddleback Pkwy
Lake Forest, CA 92630-8700, USA

Warren, Robert (Athlete, Basketball Player)
989 Hardin Wadesboro Rd
Hardin, KY 42048-9034, USA

Warren, Ron (Athlete, Baseball Player)
Detroit Stars
4025 Paddock Rd Apt 401
Cincinnati, OH 45229-1635, USA

Warren, Rosanna (Writer)
11 Robinwood Ave
Needham, MA 02492-2112, USA

Warren, Sahron (Actor)
c/o Kathryn Boole *Studio Talent Group*
1328 12th St Apt 1
Santa Monica, CA 90401-2051, United states

Warren, Tom (Athlete)
2393 La Marque St
San Diego, CA 92109-2342, USA

Warren, Ty (Athlete, Football Player)
c/o Staff Member *New England Patriots*
1 Patriot Pl
Foxboro, MA 02035-1388, USA

Warren Brothers
PO Box 120479
Nashville, TN 37212-0479, USA

Warren Brothers, The (Music Group)
c/o Staff Member *Creative Artists Agency (CAA-TN)*
401 Commerce St PH
Nashville, TN 37219-2516, USA

Warrener, Rhett (Athlete, Hockey Player)
761 W Ferry St
Buffalo, NY 14222-1618, USA

Warren G (Artist, Music Group, Musician)
Richard Walters
1800 Argyle Ave # 408
Los Angeles, CA 90028-5253, USA

Warren Jr, Christopher C (Chris) (Athlete, Football Player)
1020 W Casino Rd Apt C115
Everett, WA 98204-7915, USA

Warrenskjold, Dorothy
165 W 57th St
New York, NY 10019-2201

Warrick, Peter (Athlete, Football Player)
1508 11th Ave E
Palmetto, FL 34221-4195, USA

Warrington, Clint (Horse Racer)
69 Oakcrest Ln
Westampton, NJ 08060-5729, USA

Warrington, Steve (Horse Racer)
31926 Lambson Forest Rd
Galena, MD 21635-1523, USA

Warrington, Walter (Horse Racer)
31930 Lambson Forest Rd
Galena, MD 21635-1523, USA

Warthen, Dan (Athlete, Baseball Player)
3933 SW Wapato Ave
Portland, OR 97239-1412, USA

Warwick, Carl (Athlete, Baseball Player)
14102 Bonney Brier Dr
Houston, TX 77069-1324, USA

Warwick, Dionne (Musician)
3849 Crestway Dr
View Park, CA 90043-1738, USA

Warwick, Ken (Producer)
1149 Calle Vista Dr
Beverly Hills, CA 90210-2507, USA

Warwick, Lonnie (Athlete, Football Player)
828 Main St
Mount Hope, WV 25880-1321, USA

Warzeka, Ron (Athlete, Football Player)
9390 W Ustick Rd Unit 32
Boise, ID 83704-5501, USA

Wasdin, John (Athlete, Baseball Player)
2676 Riverport Dr S
Jacksonville, FL 32223-7115, USA

Wash, Martha (Musician)
c/o Stephen Ford *Diva Central Inc*
7510 W Sunset Blvd Ste 1445
Los Angeles, CA 90046-3408, USA

Washbrook, Johnny (Actor)
66 RR 1
Edgartown, MA 02539, USA

Washburn, Abigail (Musician)
c/o Staff Member *Paradigm (Monterey)*
404 W Franklin St
Monterey, CA 93940-2303, USA

Washburn, Beverly (Actor)
2339 Great Elk Dr
Henderson, NV 89052-7070, USA

Washburn, Greg (Athlete, Baseball Player)
1685 E Stellon St
Diamond, IL 60416-6028, USA

Washburn, Jarrod M (Athlete, Baseball Player)
10003 Olinger Rd
Webster, WI 54893-7435, USA

Washburn, Ray C (Athlete, Baseball Player)
1103 N 49th St
Seattle, WA 98103-6630, USA

Washington, Algernod Lanier (Plies) (Musician)
c/o Cara Donatto *Atlantic Records (LA)*
3400 W Olive Ave Fl 2
Burbank, CA 91505-5538, USA

Washington, Alonzo (Cartoonist)
Omega 7
PO Box 171046
Kansas City, KS 66117-0046, USA

Washington, Baby (Musician)
Headline Talent
1650 Broadway Ste 508
New York, NY 10019-6833, USA

Washington, Chris (Athlete, Football Player)
PO Box 17823
San Diego, CA 92177-7823, USA

Washington, Claudell (Athlete, Baseball Player)
4081 Clayton Rd Apt 227
Concord, CA 94521-2615, USA

Washington, Cornelius (Athlete, Football Player)
c/o Anthony J. Agnone *Eastern Athletic Services*
11350 McCormick Rd
Suite 800 - Executive Plaza
Hunt Valley, MD 21031-1002, USA

Washington, Daryl (Athlete, Football Player)
c/o Jordan Woy *Willis and Woy Management*
3030 Olive St Ste 520
Dallas, TX 75219-7629, USA

Washington, Denzel (Actor)
41 Beverly Park Cir
Beverly Hills, CA 90210-1567, USA

Washington, Dewayne (Athlete, Football Player)
6205 Rocky Creek Way
Wake Forest, NC 27587-6267, USA

Washington, Don
8 Thurston Dr
Upper Marlboro, MD 20774-1426, USA

Washington, Dwayne (Pearl) (Basketball Player)
206 Grenadier Dr # 206C
Liverpool, NY 13090-2744, USA

Washington, Eugene (Gene) (Athlete, Football Player)
2725 Jewel Ln N
Minneapolis, MN 55447-1737, USA

Washington, Evelyn Ashford (Athlete, Olympic Athlete, Track Athlete)
1804 12th St Apt 12
Riverside, CA 92507-5359, USA

Washington, Gene A (Athlete, Football Player)
10521 Bellagio Rd
Los Angeles, CA 90077-3820, USA

Washington, Hayma (Producer)
c/o Lindsay Williams *The Gotham Group Inc*
9255 W Sunset Blvd Ste 515
West Hollywood, CA 90069-3308, USA

Washington, Herb (Athlete, Baseball Player)
640 Saddlebrook Dr
Youngstown, OH 44512-4781, USA

Washington, Isaiah (Actor)
c/o Vincent Cirrincione *Vincent Cirrincione Associates*
1516 N Fairfax Ave
Los Angeles, CA 90046-2608, USA

Washington, Jascha (Actor)
c/o Staff Member *House of Representatives, The*
1434 6th St Ste 1
Santa Monica, CA 90401-2527, USA

Washington, Jim (Athlete, Basketball Player)
1108 Cardinal Way SW
Atlanta, GA 30311-2417, USA

Washington, Joe (Athlete, Football Player)
4 Treadwell Ct
Lutherville Timonium, MD 21093-3716, USA

Washington, Joe (Athlete, Football Player)
434 E 42nd Pl
Chicago, IL 60653-2916, USA

Washington, Joe D (Athlete, Football Player)
2350 W Joppa Rd
Lutherville Timonium, MD 21093-4616, USA

Washington, Keith (Athlete, Football Player)
548 Parkview Dr
Grand Prairie, TX 75052-3168, USA

Washington, Kelley (Athlete, Football Player)
c/o Chad Speck *Allegiant Athletic Agency*
35 Market Sq Ste 201
Knoxville, TN 37902-1420, USA

Washington, Kermit (Athlete, Basketball Player)
7208 NE Hazel Dell Ave
Vancouver, WA 98665-8341, USA

Washington, Kerry (Actor)
c/o Kathy Atkinson *Washington Square Arts (NY)*
310 Bowery Fl 2
New York, NY 10012-2861, USA

Washington, Larue (Athlete, Baseball Player)
3315 Sturbridge Ave
Easton, PA 18045-8139, USA

Washington, Lionel (Athlete, Football Player)
5 Gleneagles Dr
La Place, LA 70068-1612, USA

Washington, MaliVai (Tennis Player)
52 San Juan Dr
Ponte Vedra Beach, FL 32082-1320, USA

Washington, Marcus (Athlete, Football Player)
2196 Wedgewood Ct
Auburn, AL 36830-2581, USA

Washington, Mickey (Athlete, Football Player)
9420 Riggs St
Beaumont, TX 77707-1164, USA

Washington, Mike L (Athlete, Football Player)
3235 Hernon Rd
Montgomery, AL 36106, USA

Washington, Richard (Athlete, Basketball Player)
4606 SE Logus Rd
Portland, OR 97222-5150, USA

Washington, Rico (Athlete, Baseball Player)
2050 Old Clinton Rd
Macon, GA 31211-1064, USA

Washington, Ron (Athlete, Baseball Player, Coach)
2406 Copper Ridge Rd
Arlington, TX 76006-2726, USA

Washington, Ron (Athlete, Baseball Player)
7365 Perth St
New Orleans, LA 70126-1753, USA

Washington, Ronnie (Athlete, Football Player)
2204 Burg Jones Ln
Monroe, LA 71202-4411, USA

Washington, Russ (Athlete, Football Player)
9060 Gramercy Dr
San Diego, CA 92123-2395, USA

Washington, Sam (Athlete, Football Player)
7111 Cumberland Pl
Tampa, FL 33617-8423, USA

Washington, Ted (Athlete, Football Player)
PO Box 434
Waxhaw, NC 28173-1047, USA

Washington, Theodore (Ted) (Athlete, Football Player)
3522 E 26th Ave
Tampa, FL 33605-1602, USA

Washington, U L (Athlete, Baseball Player)
PO Box 164
Stringtown, OK 74569-0164, USA

Washington, Wilson (Athlete, Basketball Player)
2625 Mapleton Ave
Norfolk, VA 23504-3717, USA

Wasikowska, Mia (Actor)
c/o Christine Tripicchio *Shelter PR*
9350 Wilshire Blvd Ste 450
Beverly Hills, CA 90212-3230, USA

Wasinger, Mark (Athlete, Baseball Player)
303 S Seneca St
Wichita, KS 67213-5539, USA

Waskiewicz, Jim (Athlete, Football Player)
14365 Erin Ct
Broomfield, CO 80023-9579, USA

Waslewski, Gary (Athlete, Baseball Player)
1799 E Terrestrial Pl
Tucson, AZ 85737-3469, USA

Wass, Ted (Actor)
3825 Longridge Ave
Sherman Oaks, CA 91423-4921, USA

Wasserman, Allan (Actor)
c/o Judy Orbach *Judy O Productions*
6136 Glen Holly St
Los Angeles, CA 90068-2338, USA

Wasserman, Dale (Writer)
Casa Blanca Estates
#37
Victor, AZ 95253, USA

Wasserman, Kevin (Noodles) (Musician)
c/o Staff Member *Sugaroo! LLC*
3650 Helms Ave
Culver City, CA 90232-2417, USA

Wasserman, Rob (Musician)
Leslie Wiener Financial Services
PO Box 245
Sausalito, CA 94966-0245, USA

Wasserman, Robert H (Doctor)
Cornell University
Veterinary Medicine College
Ithaca, NY 14853, USA

Wasserman Schultz, Debbie (Congressman, Politician)
118 Cannon Hob
Washington, DC 20515-4403, USA

Wasserstein, Wendy (Writer)
c/o Robert (Bob) Bookman *Paradigm (LA)*
2000 Avenue of the Stars
Los Angeles, CA 90067-4700, USA

Wasson, Erin (Model)
I M G Models
304 Park Ave S # 1200
New York, NY 10010-4301, USA

Waszgis, B J (Athlete, Baseball Player)
2708 Dover Ln
Albany, GA 31721-1583, USA

Waszgis, BJ (Athlete, Baseball Player)
2708 Dover Ln
Albany, GA 31721-1583, USA

Watanabe, Gedde
1632 Westerly Ter
Los Angeles, CA 90026-1234

Watanabe, Ken (Actor)
c/o Will Ward *ROAR (LA)*
9701 Wilshire Blvd Fl 8
Beverly Hills, CA 90212-2008, USA

Watanabe, Sadao (Musician)
International Music Network
278 S Main St # 400
Gloucester, MA 01930, USA

Waterbury, Steve (Athlete, Baseball Player)
808 S Bentley St # A
Marion, IL 62959-2033, USA

Waterman, Felicity (Actor)
PO Box 234
Elk, CA 95432-0234, USA

Waters, Alice (Chef)
Chez Panisse
1517 Shattuck Ave
Berkeley, CA 94709-1598, USA

Waters, Brian (Athlete, Football Player)
1417 Wolf Dr
Desoto, TX 75115-1736, USA

Waters, Charles T (Charlie) (Athlete, Coach, Football Coach, Football Player)
9305 Moss Trl
Dallas, TX 75231-1409, USA

Waters, Crystal (Musician)
c/o Stephen Ford *Diva Central Inc*
7510 W Sunset Blvd Ste 1445
Los Angeles, CA 90046-3408, USA

Waters, Derek (Actor)
c/o Naomi Odenkirk *Odenkirk Provissiero Entertainment*
1936 N Bronson Ave
Raleigh Studios
Los Angeles, CA 90068-5602, USA

Waters, Drew (Actor, Producer)
Argentum Entertainment
21201 Kittridge St Apt 4412
Woodland Hills, CA 91303-5020, USA

Waters, Frank (Muddy) (Coach, Football Coach)
4850 Gratiot Rd
No. 2D
Saginaw, MI 48638-6202, USA

Waters, John (Director)
10 W Highfield Rd
Baltimore, MD 21218-1152, USA

Waters, John B (Government Official)
405 Burridge Waters Edge
Sevierville, TN 37862, USA

Waters, Lou (Correspondent)
Cable News Network
1050 Techwood Dr NW
News Dept
Atlanta, GA 30318-5695, USA

Waters, Mark (Director)
c/o Robert (Bob) Bookman *Paradigm (LA)*
2000 Avenue of the Stars
Los Angeles, CA 90067-4700, USA

Waters, Maxine (Congressman, Politician)
2344 Rayburn Hob
Washington, DC 20515-0535, USA

Waters, Richard (Publisher)
13919 Woods Run Ct
Centreville, VA 20121-3078, USA

Waters, Roger (Musician)
157 E 61st St # 5
New York, NY 10065-8112, USA

Waterston, James (Actor)
c/o Beth Colt *Gateway Management Company Inc*
860 Via De La Paz Ste F10
Pacific Palisades, CA 90272-3631, USA

Waterston, Katherine (Actor)
c/o Jason Shapiro *Silver Lining Entertainment*
421 S Beverly Dr Fl 7
Beverly Hills, CA 90212-4408, USA

Waterston, Sam (Actor)
92 Great Hollow Rd
West Cornwall, CT 06796-1806, USA

Watford, Earl (Athlete, Football Player)
c/o Anthony J. Agnone *Eastern Athletic Services*
11350 McCormick Rd
Suite 800 - Executive Plaza
Hunt Valley, MD 21031-1002, USA

Wathan, Dusty (Athlete, Baseball Player)
725 Amanda Dr
Matthews, NC 28104-9397, USA

Wathan, John D (Athlete, Baseball Player, Coach)
1354 NE Todd George Rd
Lees Summit, MO 64086-5337, USA

Watkins, Bob (Athlete, Baseball Player)
4417 W 58th Pl
Windsor Hills, CA 90043-3409, USA

Watkins, Bobby (Athlete, Football Player)
1112 Devonshire Dr
Desoto, TX 75115-3756, USA

Watkins, Carlene (Actor)
104 Fremont Pl
Los Angeles, CA 90005-3867, USA

Watkins, Danny (Football Player)
c/o Joe Panos *Athletes First, LLC*
6900 E Camelback Rd Ste 600
Scottsdale, AZ 85251-8044, USA

Watkins, Dave (Athlete, Baseball Player)
506 Ridgewood Rd
Louisville, KY 40207-1325, USA

Watkins, Marilyn
217 N San Marino Ave
San Gabriel, CA 91775-2909

Watkins, Michaela (Actor, Comedian)
c/o Amy Slomovits *Evolution Entertainment (LA)*
901 N Highland Ave
Los Angeles, CA 90038-2412, USA

Watkins, Michelle (Actor)
Capital Artists
6404 Wilshire Blvd Ste 950
Los Angeles, CA 90048-5529, USA

Watkins, Pat (Athlete, Baseball Player)
1205 Fowler Dr
Garner, NC 27529-4420, USA

Watkins, Robert A (Athlete, Football Player)
6 White Alder Way
South Dartmouth, MA 02748-1429, USA

Watkins, Sammy (Athlete, Football Player)
c/o Eugene Parker *Maximum Sports Management*
6435 W Jefferson Blvd # 197
Fort Wayne, IN 46804-6203, USA

Watkins, Scott (Athlete, Baseball Player)
14660 W 18th St S
Sand Springs, OK 74063-4405, USA

Watkins, Steve (Athlete, Baseball Player)
3408 Evanston Ave
Lubbock, TX 79407-4039, USA

Watkins, Tionne (T-Boz) (Artist, Musician)
c/o Randy Cabrera *Venture IAB*
3211 Cahuenga Blvd W Ste 104
Los Angeles, CA 90068-1372, USA

Watkins, Tommy (Athlete, Baseball Player)
Beloit Snappers
PO Box 855
Attn: Coaching Staff Beloit
Beloit, WI 53512, USA

Watkins, Tuc (Actor)
115 S Almont Dr
Los Angeles, CA 90048-2910, USA

Watkins, William D (Business Person)
Seagate Technology
215 El Pueblo Rd
Scotts Valley, CA 95066-4229, USA

Watley, Jody (Musician)
Baker Winokur Rider
9100 Wilshire Blvd Ste 600
Beverly Hills, CA 90212-3494, USA

Watling, Leonor (Actor)
c/o Staff Member *William Morris Endeavor (LA)*
9601 Wilshire Blvd
Beverly Hills, CA 90210-5213, USA

Watlington, Neal (Athlete, Baseball Player)
PO Box 418
Yanceyville, NC 27379-0418, USA

Watney, Heidi (Baseball Player)
2406 Daibes Ct
Edgewater, NJ 07020-1072, U S A

Watney, Nick (Athlete, Golfer)
c/o Staff Member *Gaylord Sports Management*
13845 N Northsight Blvd Ste 200
Scottsdale, AZ 85260-3609, USA

Watros, Cynthia (Actor)
c/o Marsha McManus *Principal Entertainment (LA)*
9255 W Sunset Blvd Ste 500
West Hollywood, CA 90069-3301, USA

Watrous, Cynthia (Actor)
c/o Staff Member *Innovative Artists (LA)*
1505 10th St
Santa Monica, CA 90401-2805, USA

Watson, Alberta (Actor)
c/o Staff Member *Cathy Atkinson*
2629 Main St PMB 129
Santa Monica, CA 90405-4001, USA

Watson, Allen (Athlete, Baseball Player)
6144 65th St
Middle Village, NY 11379-1027, USA

Watson, Angela (Actor)
c/o Tom Chasin *Chasin Agency, The*
8899 Beverly Blvd Ste 716
Los Angeles, CA 90048-2449, USA

Watson, Barry (Actor)
c/o Ruth Bernstein *Viewpoint Inc (LA)*
8820 Wilshire Blvd Ste 220
Beverly Hills, CA 90211-2622, USA

Watson, Benjamin (Athlete, Football Player)
c/o Staff Member *New England Patriots*
1 Patriot Pl
Foxboro, MA 02035-1388, USA

Watson, Bill (Athlete, Hockey Player)
1725 Vermilion Rd
Duluth, MN 55803-2508, USA

Watson, Bob (Athlete, Baseball Player)
9319 Montridge Dr
Houston, TX 77080-5429, USA

Watson, Brandon (Athlete, Baseball Player)
22273 Del Valle St
Woodland Hills, CA 91364-1516, USA

Watson, Bryan (Athlete, Hockey Player)
24663 Long Haul Rd
St Michaels, MD 21663, USA

Watson, Bubba (Athlete, Golfer)
178 Foxglove Ln
Lexington, NC 27292-0011, USA

Watson, Cecil J (Doctor)
Abbott Northwestern Hospital
2727 Chicago Ave
Minneapolis, MN 55407-3707, USA

Watson, Dale (Musician)
Crowley Artist Mgmt
602 Wayside Dr
Wimberley, TX 78676-5151, USA

Watson, Dave (Athlete, Hockey Player)
1431 Pinecroft Dr
Winston Salem, NC 27104-1351, USA

Watson, Dekoda (Athlete, Football Player)
c/o Peter Schaffer *All Pro Sports and Entertainment*
36 Steele St Ste 100
Denver, CO 80206-5709, USA

Watson, Denis (Athlete, Golfer)
14209 Evans Rd
Pacific Palisades, CA 90272, USA

Watson, Emily (Actor)
c/o George Freeman *William Morris Endeavor (LA)*
9601 Wilshire Blvd
Beverly Hills, CA 90210-5213, USA

Watson, Gene (Musician)
Bobby Roberts
909 Meadowlark Ln
Goodlettsville, TN 37072-2309, USA

Watson, Jamie (Athlete, Basketball Player)
PO Box 761
Elm City, NC 27822-0761, USA

Watson, Jim (Athlete, Hockey Player)
1702 Coventry Ln
Glen Mills, PA 19342-9426, USA

Watson, Jim (Athlete, Hockey Player)
8190 W Deer Valley Rd Ste 104
Peoria, AZ 85382-2126, USA

Watson, Joe (Athlete, Hockey Player)
220 Park Pi
Media, PA 19063, USA

Watson, Mark (Athlete, Baseball Player)
555 Spender Trce
Atlanta, GA 30350-5017, USA

Watson, Martha (Athlete, Olympic Athlete)
5509 Royal Vista Ln
Las Vegas, NV 89149-6644, USA

Watson, Matt (Athlete, Baseball Player)
636 Quail Crk
Manheim, PA 17545-8770, USA

Watson, Max P Jr (Business Person)
BMC Software
2101 Citywest Blvd
Houston, TX 77042-2828, USA

Watson, Mills (Actor)
PO Box 600
Talent, OR 97540-0600, USA

Watson, Robert (Athlete, Basketball Player)
1625 Sherwood Dr
Owensboro, KY 42301-3578, USA

Watson, Robert M (Bobby) Jr (Musician)
Split Second Timing
11 Ridge Rd
Chappaqua, NY 10514-2508, USA

Watson, Stephen E (Business Person)
Dayton Hudson
1000 Nicollet Mall
Minneapolis, MN 55403-2542, USA

Watson, Stephen R (Athlete, Football Player)
4675 S Vine Way
Englewood, CO 80113-6044, USA

Watson, Tim (Athlete, Football Player)
113 Crestwood Dr
RR 13
Fort Valley, GA 31030, USA

Watson, Tom (Athlete, Golfer)
Assured Management Company
1901 W 47th Pl Ste 200
Mission, KS 66205-1834, USA

Watson, Wayne (Musician)
TBA Artist Mgmt
300 10th Ave S
Nashville, TN 37203-4125, USA

Watson, Whit (Sportscaster)
1640 Walnut Ave
Winter Park, FL 32789-2036, USA

Watson-Johnson, Vernee (Actor)
Gage Group
5757 Wilshire Blvd Ste 659
Los Angeles, CA 90036-3682, USA

Watson Jr, Jack H (Government Official)
Long Aldridge Norman
1900 K St NW
Washington, DC 20006-1110, USA

Watson Richardson, Lillian (Pockey) (Swimmer)
4960 Maunalani Cir
Honolulu, HI 96816-4016, USA

Watt, Eddie (Athlete, Baseball Player)
940 Locust St
North Bend, NE 68649-4543, USA

Watt, James (Politician)
1558 Calle Encantado
Wickenburg, AZ 85390-3132, USA

Watt, Jim (Athlete, Hockey Player)
5249 1st Ave
Duluth, MN 55803-9469, USA

Watt, J.J. (Football Player)
c/o Tom Condon *CAA (St. Louis)*
222 S Central Ave Ste 1008
Saint Louis, MO 63105-3509, USA

Watt, Mike (Musician)
c/o Staff Member *The Agency Group (NYC)*
142 W 57th St Fl 6
New York, NY 10019-3300, USA

Watt, Mike (Athlete, Hockey Player)
N84W27677 Twin Pines Cir
Hartland, WI 53029-8572, USA

Wattelet, Frank (Athlete, Football Player)
4 Deer Run Dr
Joplin, MO 64804-5832, USA

Wattenberg, Ben J (Television Host)
Think Tank with Ben Wattenberg
4455 Connecticut Ave NW Ste C100
Washington, DC 20008-2372, USA

Watters, Richard J (Rickie) (Athlete,
Football Player)
11100 NE 8th St Ste 600
Bellevue, WA 98004-4402, USA

Watters, Ricky (Athlete, Football Player)
8815 Conroy Windermere Rd # 332
Orlando, FL 32835-3129, USA

Watters, Tim (Athlete, Hockey Player)
219 E Oregon Ave
Phoenix, AZ 85012-1435, USA

Watterson, John B (Brett) (Astronaut)
2508 Via Anacapa
Palos Verdes Estates, CA 90274-4333,
USA

Wattle, Dave (Athlete, Olympic Athlete,
Track Athlete)
9245 Forest Hill Ln
Germantown, TN 38139-7906, USA

Wattles, Stan (Race Car Driver)
2391 Old Dixie Hwy
Riviera Beach, FL 33404-5456, USA

Watts, Andre (Musician)
205 W 57th St
New York, NY 10019-2105, USA

Watts, Brandon (Athlete, Football Player)
c/o Joe Linta *JL Sports*
1204 Main St Ste 179
Branford, CT 06405-3787, USA

Watts, Brian (Athlete, Golfer)
55 Main St Ste 310
Colleyville, TX 76034-2957, USA

Watts, Brian (Athlete, Hockey Player)
1300 Via Coronel
Palos Verdes Estates, CA 90274-1938,
USA

Watts, D Henry (Business Person)
Norfolk Southern Corp
3 Commercial Pl Ste 1A
Norfolk, VA 23510-2108, USA

Watts, Donald (Athlete, Basketball Player)
51315 256th Ave NE
Redmond, WA 98135, USA

Watts, Ernest J (Ernie) (Musician)
DeLeon Artists
4031 Panama Ct
Oakland, CA 94611-4930, USA

Watts, Ernie (Designer, Director)
International Creative Mgmt
40 W 57th St Fl 5
New York, NY 10019-4001, USA

Watts, JC (Athlete, Football Player)
3512 Rose Crest Ln
Fairfax, VA 22033-1636, USA

Watts, J C (Politician)
600 13th St NW Ste 790
Washington, DC 20005-3021, USA

Watts, Kristi (Religious Leader, Television
Host)
c/o 700 Club *Christian Broadcasting
Network (CBN)*
977 Centerville Tpke
Virginia Beach, VA 23463-1001, USA

Watts, Naomi (Actor)
12307 7th Helena Dr
Los Angeles, CA 90049-3932, USA

Watts, Quincy (Athlete, Track Athlete)
First Team Marketing
PO Box 67581
Los Angeles, CA 90067-0581, USA

Watts, Robert (Athlete, Football Player)
99 Villa Dr
San Pablo, CA 94806-3736, USA

Watts, Rolonda (Actor, Musician)
6002/6010 Graciosa Dr
Los Angeles, CA 90068, USA

Watts, Ronald (Athlete, Basketball Player)
11800 Sunset Hills Rd Unit 908
Reston, VA 20190-4787, USA

Waugh, Seth (Athlete, Business Person,
Golfer)
11572 Turtle Beach Rd
North Palm Beach, FL 33408-3345, USA

Waxenberg, Alan M (Publisher)
Good Housekeeping Magazine
959 8th Ave
New York, NY 10019-3737, USA

Waxman, Henry (Congressman,
Politician)
2204 Rayburn Hob
Washington, DC 20515-0530, USA

Waxman, Keoni (Director, Writer)
c/o Jeff Okin *Anonymous Content (LA)*
3532 Hayden Ave
Culver City, CA 90232-2413, USA

Way, Gerard (Musician)
1621 Silverwood Ter
Los Angeles, CA 90026-1447, USA

Wayans, Damien Dante (Actor, Director,
Producer)
7317 Caverna Dr
Los Angeles, CA 90068-2021, USA

Wayans, Damon (Actor)
951 Ocean Ave Unit 402
Santa Monica, CA 90403-2461, USA

Wayans, Keenen Ivory (Actor, Director,
Producer)
4932 Avenida Oriente
Tarzana, CA 91356-4631, USA

Wayans, Kim (Actor)
c/o Staff Member *Wayans Brothers
Entertainment*
8730 W Sunset Blvd Ste 290
W Hollywood, CA 90069-2247, USA

Wayans, Marlon (Actor, Comedian)
4528 Cedros Ave
Sherman Oaks, CA 91403-2804, USA

Wayans, Shawn (Actor, Comedian, DJ,
Producer, Writer)
PO Box 48347
Los Angeles, CA 90048-0347, USA

Wayans Jr, Damon (Actor)
c/o Christie Smith *Mosaic Media Group*
9200 W Sunset Blvd Ste 10
West Hollywood, CA 90069-3608, USA

Wayne, Fredd
117 Strand St Apt 7
Santa Monica, CA 90405-2294

Wayne, Gary (Athlete, Baseball Player)
5762 W Asbury Pl
Lakewood, CO 80227-2550, USA

Wayne, Jimmy (Musician)
Big Machine Music
1219 16th Ave S
Nashville, TN 37212-2901, USA

Wayne, John (Bowler)
5018 S Barley Ct
Gilbert, AZ 85298-8633, USA

Wayne, Justin (Athlete, Baseball Player)
8294 Banpo Bridge Way
Delray Beach, FL 33446-0031, USA

Wayne, Nathaniel (Athlete, Football
Player)
128 Slate Dr
Buford, GA 30518-1662, USA

Wayne, Patrick (Actor)
10502 Whipple St
Toluca Lake, CA 91602-2838, USA

Wayne, Reggie (Athlete, Football Player)
16850 Stratford Ct
Southwest Ranches, FL 33331-1359, USA

Wayt, Russell (Athlete, Football Player)
PO Box 9
White Oak, TX 75693-0009, USA

W. Boustany Jr., Charles (Congressman,
Politician)
1431 Longworth Hob
Washington, DC 20515-4802, USA

W. Dent, Charles (Congressman,
Politician)
1009 Longworth Hob
Washington, DC 20515-3511, USA

Wearstler, Kelly (Writer)
c/o Staff Member *HarperCollins Publishers*
195 Broadway Fl 2
Cellar 1
New York, NY 10007-3132, USA

Weatherholtz, Walter (Trey) (Reality Star)
c/o Mike Esterman *Esterman.Com, LLC*
Prefers to be contacted via email
Baltimore, MD XXXXX, USA

Weatherly, Gerald (Athlete, Football
Player)
506 1/2 E Clayton St
Cuero, TX 77954-2820, USA

Weatherly, Jim (Athlete, Football Player)
23679 Calabasas Rd Apt 558
Calabasas, CA 91302-1502, USA

Weatherly, Michael (Actor)
2607 Nichols Canyon Rd
Los Angeles, CA 90046-1343, USA

Weatherly, Shwan (Actor, Beauty Pageant
Winner)
135 N Westgate Ave
Los Angeles, CA 90049-2916, USA

Weathers, Carl (Actor)
c/o Matt Luber *Luber Roklin Management*
5815 W Sunset Blvd Ste 206
Los Angeles, CA 90028-6481, USA

Weathers, Carl (Athlete, Football Player)
2228 Walnut Ave
Venice, CA 90291-4035, USA

Weathers, Dave (Athlete, Baseball Player)
979 Lexington Hwy
Loretto, TN 38469-2732, USA

Weatherspoon, Cephus (Athlete, Football
Player)
210 E Chapman Ave Apt 28
Placentia, CA 92870-4641, USA

Weatherspoon, Clarence (Athlete,
Basketball Player)
PO Box 117
Crawford, MS 39743-0117, USA

Weatherspoon, Sean (Athlete, Football
Player)
c/o David Dunn *Athletes First, LLC*
23091 Mill Creek Dr
Laguna Hills, CA 92653-1258, USA

Weatherspoon, Teresa G (Basketball
Player)
Los Angeles Sparks
1111 S Figueroa St
Staples Center
Los Angeles, CA 90015-1300, USA

Weatherwax, Bob
16133 Soledad Canyon Rd
Canyon Country, CA 91387-1821

Weaver, Delores (Business Person,
Football Executive)
6120 San Jose Blvd W
Jacksonville, FL 32217-2345, USA

Weaver, Dewitt (Athlete, Golfer)
5640 Golf Club Dr
Braselton, GA 30517-2426, USA

Weaver, Eric (Athlete, Baseball Player)
2641 Weaver Rd
Illiopolis, IL 62539-3640, USA

Weaver, Fritz (Actor)
161 W 75th St Apt 15A
New York, NY 10023-1809, USA

Weaver, Gary (Athlete, Football Player)
3496 Arden Rd
Hayward, CA 94545-3906, USA

Weaver, Herman (Athlete, Football
Player)
8105 Hamilton Mill Dr
Chattanooga, TN 37421-2766, USA

Weaver, Jacki (Actor)
c/o Alex Cole *Elevate Entertainment*
5757 Wilshire Blvd Ste 460
Los Angeles, CA 90036-3658, USA

Weaver, James (Race Car Driver)
165 Smith St
Poughkeepsie, NY 12601-2100, United
States

Weaver, Jed (Athlete, Football Player)
696 E 16th Ave
Eugene, OR 97401, USA

Weaver, Jeff (Athlete, Baseball Player,
Olympic Athlete)
1740 Classic Rose Ct
Westlake Village, CA 91362-5134, USA

Weaver, Jered (Athlete, Baseball Player)
c/o Staff Member *Los Angeles Dodgers
(LA Dodgers)*
1000 Elysian Park Ave
Los Angeles, CA 90012-1112, USA

Weaver, Jim (Athlete, Baseball Player)
3221 Stagecoach Trl
Wimauma, FL 33598-7526, USA

Weaver, Jim (Athlete, Baseball Player)
626 Prince George Dr
Lancaster, PA 17601-8802, USA

Weaver, John (Athlete, Football Player)
520 E Ward St
Versailles, OH 45380-1436, USA

Weaver, John (Race Car Driver)
Dream Weaver Family Racing
9246 Lacey Blvd
Hanford, CA 93230-4733, USA

Weaver, Michael (Actor)
960 16th St Apt 10
Santa Monica, CA 90403-3215, USA

Weaver, Patty (Actor)
PO Box 16458
Beverly Hills, CA 90209-2458, USA

Weaver, Roger (Athlete, Baseball Player)
65 Moyer St
Canajoharie, NY 13317-1430, USA

Weaver, Sigourney (Actor)
626 Langley Park Way
Long Lake, NY 12847, USA

Weaver, Wayne (Business Person, Football Executive)
6120 San Jose Blvd W
Jacksonville, FL 32217-2345, USA

Webb, Brandon (Athlete, Baseball Player)
8750 Tipton Ross Rd
Ashland, KY 41102-8920, USA

Webb, Chloe (Actor)
PO Box 2824
Venice, CA 90294-2824, USA

Webb, Hank (Athlete, Baseball Player)
1309 Lindenwood Dr
Tarpon Springs, FL 34688-7639, USA

Webb, James R (Jimmy) (Athlete, Football Player)
1319 S Prairie Flower Rd
Turlock, CA 95380-9367, USA

Webb, Jeff (Athlete, Basketball Player)
8011 FM 621
Martindale, TX 78655-2597, USA

Webb, Joe (Athlete, Football Player)
c/o Pat Dye Jr *SportsTrust Advisors (GA)*
3340 Peachtree Rd NE Fl 16
Atlanta, GA 30326-1000, USA

Webb, Karrie (Athlete, Golfer)
725 Presidential Dr
Boynton Beach, FL 33435-2431, USA

Webb, Katherine (Beauty Pageant Winner)
c/o Alexander Shekarchian *AS Management*
9440 Santa Monica Blvd Ste 700
Beverly Hills, CA 90210-4609, USA

Webb, Lee (Religious Leader, Television Host)
c/o 700 Club *Christian Broadcasting Network (CBN)*
977 Centerville Tpke
Virginia Beach, VA 23463-1001, USA

Webb, Lucy (Actor, Comedian)
1360 N Crescent Heights Blvd # 38
West Hollywood, CA 90046-4553, USA

Webb, Marc (Director)
c/o Michael Sugar *Anonymous Content (LA)*
3532 Hayden Ave
Culver City, CA 90232-2413, USA

Webb, Morgan (Actor)
c/o Andrea Ross *Creative Artists Agency (CAA-LA)*
2000 Avenue of the Stars Ste 100
Los Angeles, CA 90067-4705, USA

Webb, Richmond J (Athlete, Football Player)
4120 Humphrey Dr
Dallas, TX 75216-4908, USA

Webb, Russell (Athlete)
611 Knob Hill Ave
Redondo Beach, CA 90277-4255, USA

Webb, Sonny (Baseball Player)
Negro Baseball Leagues
3194 Jordan Rd
Pleasant Plain, OH 45162-9238, USA

Webb, Spud (Athlete, Basketball Player)
1453 Mosslake Dr
Desoto, TX 75115-7709, USA

Webb, Steve (Athlete, Hockey Player)
27 Barberry Ln
Center Moriches, NY 11934-1410, USA

Webb, Tamilee (Athlete)
1770 Haydn Dr
Cardiff By The Sea, CA 92007-2306, USA

Webb, Veronica (Actor, Model)
c/o Rae Ruff *Don Buchwald & Associates (NY)*
10 E 44th St Frnt 1
New York, NY 10017-3654, USA

Webb, Wayne (Bowler)
5850 Freeport Blvd
Sacramento, CA 95822-3505, USA

Webb, William H (Business Person)
Altria Group
120 Park Ave
New York, NY 10017-5577, USA

Webber, Chris (Sportscaster)
c/o Andy Elkin *Creative Artists Agency (CAA-LA)*
2000 Avenue of the Stars Ste 100
Los Angeles, CA 90067-4705, USA

Webber, Julian Lloyd (Musician)
Columbia Artists Mgmt Inc
165 W 57th St
New York, NY 10019-2201, USA

Webber, Mark (Actor, Producer)
3174 Deronda Dr
Los Angeles, CA 90068-1608, USA

Webber, Mayce (Athlete, Basketball Player)
21731 Ventura Blvd Ste 31313
Woodland Hills, CA 91364-1845, USA

Webby, Chris
c/o Jesse Kirschbaum *New Universal Entertainment Agency*
1115 Broadway Fl 12
New York, NY 10010-3452, USA

Weber, Amy (Actor, Model, Musician)
c/o Staff Member *Select Artists Ltd (CA-Westside Office)*
1138 12th St Apt 1
Santa Monica, CA 90403-5459, USA

Weber, Ben (Actor)
c/o Amy Guenther *Gateway Management Company Inc*
860 Via De La Paz Ste F10
Pacific Palisades, CA 90272-3631, USA

Weber, Ben (Athlete, Baseball Player)
5550 Baird St
Groves, TX 77619-3231, USA

Weber, Bruce (Coach)
University of Illinois
Athletic Dept
Assembly Hall
Champaign, IL 61820, USA

Weber, Charlie (Actor)
c/o Bernard Kira *Vanguard Management Group*
8060 Melrose Ave Fl 4
Los Angeles, CA 90046-7038, USA

Weber, Chuck (Athlete, Football Player)
12740 Cobblestone Creek Rd
Poway, CA 92064-5348, USA

Weber, Jack (Actor)
Gersh Agency
232 N Canon Dr
Beverly Hills, CA 90210-5302, USA

Weber, Jake (Actor)
c/o Brad Schenck *Paradigm (LA)*
360 N Crescent Dr
North Bldg
Beverly Hills, CA 90210-4874, USA

Weber, Leyna Juliet
c/o Staff Member *Atlas Talent Agency*
15 E 32nd St Fl 6
New York, NY 10016-5423, USA

Weber, Mary E (Astronaut)
14 Hawkview St
Portola Valley, CA 94028-8037, USA

Weber, Mary Ellen Dr (Astronaut)
14 Hawkview St
Portola Valley, CA 94028-8037, USA

Weber, Neil (Athlete, Baseball Player)
1 Morning Vw
Irvine, CA 92603-3716, USA

Weber, Peter D (Pete) (Bowler)
10500 Saint Xavier Ln
Saint Ann, MO 63074-2607, USA

Weber, Robert M (Bob) (Cartoonist)
New Yorker Magazine
4 Times Sq Fl 22
Editorial Dept
New York, NY 10036-6592, USA

Weber, Shea (Athlete, Hockey Player)
4527 Yancey Dr
Nashville, TN 37215-4115, USA

Weber, Steven (Actor)
727 Superba Ave
Venice, CA 90291-3868, USA

Weber Jr, Bob (Cartoonist)
c/o Staff Member *King Features Syndication*
300 W 57th St Fl 15
New York, NY 10019-5238, USA

Webster, Ben (Horse Racer)
452 Oak Haven Dr
Altamonte Springs, FL 32701-6318, USA

Webster, Corey (Athlete, Football Player)
c/o Jimmy Sexton *CAA (Memphis)*
6060 Poplar Ave Ste 470
Memphis, TN 38119-0910, USA

Webster, Cornell (Athlete, Football Player)
4575 Palm Ave Apt H
Riverside, CA 92501-3966, USA

Webster, Daniel (Congressman, Politician)
1039 Longworth Hob
Washington, DC 20515-0917, USA

Webster, Jason (Athlete, Football Player)
c/o Staff Member *New England Patriots*
1 Patriot Pl
Foxboro, MA 02035-1388, USA

Webster, Jeff (Athlete, Basketball Player)
10405 SE 15th St
Oklahoma City, OK 73130-5714, USA

Webster, Kayvon (Athlete, Football Player)
c/o Drew Rosenhaus *Rosenhaus Sports Representation*
6400 Allison Rd
Miami Beach, FL 33141-4540, USA

Webster, Larry (Athlete, Football Player)
12 Oakridge Ct
Elkton, MD 21921-3928, USA

Webster, Lenny (Athlete, Baseball Player)
6211 Bridgeport Dr
Charlotte, NC 28215-2319, USA

Webster, Mitch (Athlete, Baseball Player)
3120 NE 91st Ter
Kansas City, MO 64156-1071, USA

Webster, Ray (Athlete, Baseball Player)
311 5th St
Marysville, CA 95901-5714, USA

Webster, Robert D (Bob) (Athlete, Swimmer)
269 Hacienda Carmel
Carmel, CA 93923-7947, USA

Webster, Tom (Athlete, Coach, Hockey Player)
1750 Longfellow Dr
Canton, MI 48187-2995, USA

Webster, Victor (Actor)
744 N Curson Ave
Los Angeles, CA 90046-7416, USA

Webster, William H (Government Official, Politician)
4777 Dexter St NW
Washington, DC 20007-1060, USA

We Came As Romans (Music Group, Musician)
c/o Matthew Stewart *Outerloop Management*
2200 Clarendon Blvd Ste 1400
Arlington, VA 22201-3331, USA

Wechsler, Nick (Actor)
c/o Gordon Gilbertson *Gilbertson Management*
1334 3rd Street Promenade Ste 201
Santa Monica, CA 90401-1320, USA

Wecht, Cyril H
5420 Darlington Rd
Pittsburgh, PA 15217-1506, USA

Weddington, Mike (Athlete, Football Player)
237 Sycamore Grove St
Big Creek, CA 93605, USA

Weddington, Sarah R (Attorney)
709 W 14th St
Austin, TX 78701-1707, USA

Weddle-Hines, Mary (Athlete, Baseball Player)
329 Park Hills Rd
Corbin, KY 40701-2583, USA

Wedeen, Kelsey (Actor)
c/o Staff Member *Select Artists Ltd (CA-Westside Office)*
1138 12th St Apt 1
Santa Monica, CA 90403-5459, USA

Wedge, Chris (Actor, Director, Writer)
c/o Staff Member *Blue Sky Studios*
1 American Ln Ste 210
Greenwich, CT 06831-2563, USA

Wedge, Eric M (Athlete, Baseball Player, Coach)
25 Old Post Rd
Lancaster, NY 14086-3242, USA

Wedgeworth, Ann (Actor)
70 Riverside Dr
New York, NY 10024-5714, USA

Wedman, Scott (Athlete, Basketball Player)
7912 NW Scenic Dr
Kansas City, MO 64152-1645, USA

Weed, Kent (Director, Producer, Writer)
c/o Staff Member *Arthur Smith & Co*
1811 Centinela Ave
Santa Monica, CA 90404-4203, USA

Weeden, Brandon (Athlete, Football Player)
c/o Sean Howard *Octagon Football*
832 Sansome St Fl 1
San Francisco, CA 94111-1558, USA

Weege, Reinhold (Producer)
2035 Via Don Benito
La Jolla, CA 92037-6427, USA

Weekend Players (Music Group)
c/o Staff Member *Paradigm (Monterey)*
404 W Franklin St
Monterey, CA 93940-2303, USA

Weekley, Thomas (Boo) (Athlete, Golfer)
2555 New York St
Jay, FL 32565-2956, USA

Weeks, Claire
11048 Chimineas Ave
Porter Ranch, CA 91326-2820

Weeks, Michelle
c/o Staff Member *Diva Central Inc*
7510 W Sunset Blvd Ste 1445
Los Angeles, CA 90046-3408, USA

Weeks, Rickie (Athlete, Baseball Player)
353 Woldunn Cir
Lake Mary, FL 32746-3942, USA

Weeks, Rosey (Baseball Player)
1290 Menna St
Jacksonville, FL 32205-8330, USA

Weeks, Steve (Athlete, Hockey Player)
1178 Pine Acre Dr
Sugar Hill, GA 30518-6710, USA

Weezer (Music Group)
c/o Don Muller *William Morris Endeavor (LA)*
9601 Wilshire Blvd Ste 500
Beverly Hills, CA 90210-5207, USA

Wegener, Mike (Athlete, Baseball Player)
336 Britton Dr
Geneva, OH 44041-1248, USA

Weger, Mike (Athlete, Football Player)
2044 Earl Rd
Fort Myers, FL 33901-8000, USA

Wegman, Bill (Athlete, Baseball Player)
20521 Heather Ct
Lawrenceburg, IN 47025-9396, USA

Wegman, Marie (Baseball Player)
4158 Westwood Northern Blvd
Cincinnati, OH 45211-2444, USA

Wegman, William G (Artist, Photographer)
239 W 18th St
New York, NY 10011-4502, USA

Wegner, Mark (Baseball Player)
874 Bayou View Dr
Brandon, FL 33510-2018, USA

Wegner, Mark (Athlete, Baseball Player)
1722 Open Field Loop
Brandon, FL 33510-2094, USA

Wehner, John (Athlete, Baseball Player)
105 Averys Way
Cranberry Twp, PA 16066-3303, USA

Wehr, Dick (Athlete, Basketball Player)
4425 Thomas Dr Unit 813A
Panama City, FL 32408-8320, USA

Wehrli, Roger R (Athlete, Football Player)
46 Fox Meadows Ct
Saint Charles, MO 63303-1701, USA

Wehrmeister, Dave (Athlete, Baseball Player)
4216 Dubhe Ct
Concord, CA 94521-1820, USA

Wei, Dan-Wen (Musician)
Columbia Artists Mgmt Inc
165 W 57th St
New York, NY 10019-2201, USA

Weibel, Robert (Doctor)
University of Pennsylvania
Med School
Pediatrics Dept
Philadelphia, PA 19104, USA

Weibring, D A (Athlete, Golfer)
5865 Versailles Ave
Frisco, TX 75034-5957, USA

Weich, Gillian (Musician)
DS Mgmt
1017 16th Ave S Ste A
Nashville, TN 37212-2324, USA

Weicker, Lowell P Jr (Ex-Governor, Ex-Senator, Politician)
Trust for America's Health
PO Box 877
Old Lyme, CT 06371-0877, USA

Weickgenannt, Bob (Race Car Driver)
B&B Racing
8835 Columbia 100 Pkwy Ste M
Columbia, MD 21045-2147, USA

Weide, Bob (Director)
Wahyaduck Productions
4804 Laurel Canyon Blvd PMB 502
Valley Village, CA 91607-3717, USA

Weide, Robert B (Director, Producer)
c/o Jonathan Brandstein *Morra Brezner Steinberg & Tenenbaum (MBST) Entertainment*
345 N Maple Dr Ste 200
Beverly Hills, CA 90210-5174, USA

Weider, Betty (Actor)
131 S Hudson Ave
Los Angeles, CA 90004-1033, USA

Weidner, Bert (Athlete, Football Player)
517 NW 106th Ave
Plantation, FL 33324-1629, USA

Weidner, Brant (Athlete, Basketball Player)
1111 Colfax St
Evanston, IL 60201-2610, USA

Weigel, Teri (Actor, Adult Film Star, Model)
Web It Promotions
2551 SW Buena Vista Dr
Palm City, FL 34990-5499, USA

Weigert, Robin (Actor)
c/o Staff Member *Frontline Management*
5670 Wilshire Blvd Ste 1370
Los Angeles, CA 90036-5679, USA

Weight, Doug (Athlete, Hockey Player, Olympic Athlete)
72 Feeks Ln
Locust Valley, NY 11560-2022, USA

Weihenmayer, Erik (Mountaineer)
682 Partridge Cir
Golden, CO 80403-1548, USA

Weikel, M Keith (Business Person)
Manor Care Inc
333 N Summit St Ste 100
Toledo, OH 43604-2617, USA

Weil, Andrew (Doctor, Writer)
c/o Richard S. Pine *Inkwell Management*
521 5th Ave Fl 3
New York, NY 10175-0399, USA

Weil, Cynthia (Musician, Songwriter)
c/o Staff Member *Gorfaine/Schwartz Agency Inc*
4111 W Alameda Ave Ste 509
Burbank, CA 91505-4171, USA

Weil, Jeri (Actor)
11564 Kling St # N
North Hollywood, CA 91602-1054, USA

Weil, Liza (Actor)
c/o Kim Hodget *Creative Artists Agency (CAA-LA)*
2000 Avenue of the Stars Ste 100
Los Angeles, CA 90067-4705, USA

Weiland, Scott (Musician, Songwriter)
c/o Staff Member *Sanctuary Artist Management*
8750 Wilshire Blvd Ste 200
Beverly Hills, CA 90211-2707, USA

Weill, Claudia B (Director)
2800 Seattle Dr
Los Angeles, CA 90046-1209, USA

Weill, Dave (Athlete, Olympic Athlete)
120 Mountain Spring Ave
San Francisco, CA 94114-2120, USA

Weill, Sanford I (Sandy) (Business Person)
Citigroup Inc
399 Park Ave Bsmt
New York, NY 10022-4699, USA

Weinbach, Arthur F (Business Person)
Automatic Data Processing
1 Adp Blvd Ste 1
Roseland, NJ 07068-1728, USA

Weinbach, Lawrence A (Business Person)
Unisys Corp
Unisys Way
Blue Bell, PA 19424-0001, USA

Weinberg, Max (Musician)
2/36 Bayside Dr
Atlantic Highlands, NJ 07716, USA

Weinberg, Mike (Actor)
c/o Elissa Leeds-Fickman *Reel Talent Management*
PO Box 491035
Los Angeles, CA 90049-9035, USA

Weinberg, Robert A (Doctor, Scientist)
Whitehead Institute
9 Cambridge Ctr
Cambridge, MA 02142-1479, USA

Weinberger, Caspar (Publisher, Secretary)
Rogers & Wells
2001 K St NW
Washington, DC 20006-1037, USA

Weinbrecht, Donna (Athlete, Olympic Athlete, Skier)
177 High Crest Dr
West Milford, NJ 07480-3707, USA

Weiner, Eric (Producer, Writer)
c/o Staff Member *ICM Partners (LA)*
10250 Constellation Blvd Fl 7
Los Angeles, CA 90067-6207, USA

Weiner, Jennifer (Writer)
c/o Jake Weiner *Benderspink*
8447 Wilshire Blvd Ste 250
Studio E
Beverly Hills, CA 90211-3224, USA

Weiner, Marc (Comedian)
102 West Ln
Stamford, CT 06905-3955, USA

Weiner, Matthew (Producer)
1760 Courtney Ave
Los Angeles, CA 90046-2103, USA

Weiner, Timothy E (Tim) (Journalist, Writer)
c/o Staff Member *Creative Artists Agency (CAA-LA)*
2000 Avenue of the Stars
Los Angeles, CA 90067-4700, USA

Weiner-Davis, Michele (Writer)
c/o Staff Member *21st Century Speakers*
1352 Lake Ave
Gouldsboro, PA 18424, USA

Weinhandl, Mattias (Athlete, Hockey Player)
Puckagency LLC
1 Sunset Dr N
Attn Jay Grossman
Chappaqua, NY 10514-1613, USA

Weinke, Chris (Athlete, Football Player, Heisman Trophy Winner)
John Madden Football Academy
5500 34th St W
Attn: Directors Office
Bradenton, FL 34210-3506, USA

Weinman, Roz (Producer)
c/o Staff Member *Wolf Films Inc (LA)*
100 Universal City Plz
Universal City, CA 91608-1002, USA

Weinrich, Eric (Athlete, Hockey Player, Olympic Athlete)
337 Sea Meadows Ln
Yarmouth, ME 04096-5556, USA

Weinstein, Bob (Business Person, Producer)
c/o Staff Member *Weinstein Company, The*
99 Hudson St Fl 4
New York, NY 10013-2858, USA

Weinstein, Eric
c/o Staff Member *Home Box Office (HBO-LA)*
2500 Broadway Ste 400
Santa Monica, CA 90404-3176, USA

Weinstein, Harvey (Business Person, Producer)
c/o Staff Member *Weinstein Company, The*
99 Hudson St Fl 4
New York, NY 10013-2858, USA

Weintraub, Carl
10390 Santa Monica Blvd Ste 300
Los Angeles, CA 90025-5091

Weintraub, Jerry (Producer)
661 Doheny Rd
Beverly Hills, CA 90210-2939, USA

Weir, Amanda (Athlete, Olympic Athlete, Swimmer)
765 Barongate Dr
Lawrenceville, GA 30044-6079, USA

Weir, Bill (Correspondent)
c/o Staff Member *Good Morning America (NY)*
147 Columbus Ave Fl 6
Abc
New York, NY 10023-6503, USA

Weir, Bob (Musician)
PO Box 9357
San Rafael, CA 94912-9357, USA

Weir, Johnny (Athlete, Figure Skater, Olympic Athlete)
c/o Laina Cohn *Cohn / Torgan Management*
Prefers to be contacted by telephone or email
Los Angeles, CA, USA

Weir, Mike (Athlete, Golfer)
2960 E Oberland Rd
Sandy, UT 84092-7128, USA

Weir, Stephnie (Actor)
1406 W Riverside Dr
Burbank, CA 91506-3026, USA

Weirs, Peter (Director)
c/o Staff Member *Anonymous Content (LA)*
3532 Hayden Ave
Culver City, CA 90232-2413, USA

Weis, Al (Athlete, Baseball Player)
902 S Poplar Ave
Elmhurst, IL 60126-4547, USA

Weis, Charlie (Athlete, Coach, Football Coach, Football Player)
50905 Fox Trl
Rail # T-5
Granger, IN 46530-9042, USA

Weis, Scott (Race Car Driver)
Wiseguys/Weis Racing
5401 Lakeside Ave
Henrico, VA 23228-6009, USA

Weisacosky, Ed (Athlete, Football Player)
15321 Lawrence 2090
Mount Vernon, MO 65712-7281, USA

Weisberg, Tim (Musician)
c/o Staff Member *Pyramid Entertainment Group*
377 Rector Pl Apt 21A
New York, NY 10280-1439, USA

Weisburg, Alyssa (Producer)
c/o Staff Member *Casting Society of America*
606 N Larchmont Blvd Ste 4B
Los Angeles, CA 90004-1309, USA

Weishoff, Paula (Athlete, Olympic Athlete, Volleyball Player)
20021 Colgate Cir
Huntington Beach, CA 92646-4913, USA

Weishuhn, Clayton (Athlete, Football Player)
4521 Kropala Rd
San Angelo, TX 76905-7412, USA

Weisman, Annie (Comedian)
c/o Staff Member *Gersh (LA)*
9465 Wilshire Blvd Ste 600
Beverly Hills, CA 90212-2605, USA

Weisman, Kevin (Actor)
c/o Holly Lebed *Holly Lebed Personal Management*
10535 Wilshire Blvd Apt 808
Los Angeles, CA 90024-4556, USA

Weisman, Sam (Actor, Director)
United Talent Agency
9336 Civic Center Dr
Beverly Hills, CA 90210-3604, USA

Weiss, Barry (Reality Star)
Storage Wars
308 W Verdugo Ave
C/O Original Production
Burbank, CA 91502-2340, USA

Weiss, Brian L (Writer)
c/o Staff Member *William Morris Endeavor (LA)*
9601 Wilshire Blvd
Beverly Hills, CA 90210-5213, USA

Weiss, Daniel B (D.B.) (Producer, Writer)
c/o Guymon Casady *Management 360*
9111 Wilshire Blvd
Beverly Hills, CA 90210-5508, USA

Weiss, Frank (Athlete, Football Player)
729 Fairfax Dr
Salinas, CA 93901-1250, USA

Weiss, Gary (Athlete, Baseball Player)
1700 Weiss Ln
Brenham, TX 77833-7063, USA

Weiss, Janet (Musician)
Legends of 21st Century
7 Trinity Row
Florence, MA 01062-1931, USA

Weiss, Julie (Designer)
International Creative Mgmt
10250 Constellation Blvd Fl 1
Los Angeles, CA 90067-6241, USA

Weiss, Karen (Athlete, Golfer)
1135 Raymond Ave
Saint Paul, MN 55108-1922, USA

Weiss, Margaret (Writer)
TSR
PO Box 707
Renton, WA 98057-0707, USA

Weiss, Michael (Figure Skater)
PO Box 12311
Burke, VA 22009-2311, USA

Weiss, Michael T (Actor, Director)
2616 Strongs Dr
Venice, CA 90291-4434, USA

Weiss, Morry (Business Person)
American Greetings Corp
1 American Rd
Cleveland, OH 44144-2398, USA

Weiss, Roberta (Actor)
Sarnoff Co
3500 W Olive Ave Ste 300
Burbank, CA 91505-4647, USA

Weiss, Robert W (Bob) (Athlete, Basketball Player, Coach)
1600 Windermere Dr E
Seattle, WA 98112-3738, USA

Weiss, Shaun
c/o Jeff Morrone *Intellectual Artists Management*
9350 Wilshire Blvd Ste 224
Beverly Hills, CA 90212-3204, USA

Weiss, Stephen (Athlete, Hockey Player)
1346 Washington Blvd
Birmingham, MI 48009-4155, USA

Weiss, Walter W (Walt) (Athlete, Baseball Player)
1275 Castle Pointe Dr
Castle Rock, CO 80104-3258, USA

Weissenhofer, Ron (Athlete, Football Player)
16156 Seneca Lake Cir
Crest Hill, IL 60403-1500, USA

Weisser, Morgan (Actor)
1030 Superba Ave
Venice, CA 90291-3940, USA

Weisser, Norbert (Actor)
1030 Superba Ave
Venice, CA 90291-3940, USA

Weissman, Robert (Business Person)
IMS Health Inc
1499 Post Rd
Fairfield, CT 06824-5940, USA

Weisz, Martin (Director)
c/o Doreen Wilcox Little *Anonymous Content (LA)*
3532 Hayden Ave
Culver City, CA 90232-2413, USA

Weisz, Rachel (Actor)
200 Diamond Ln
Peconic, NY 11958-3000, USA

Weithorn, Michael (Director, Writer)
363 18th St
Santa Monica, CA 90402-2405, USA

Weitz, Bruce (Actor)
18826 Erwin St
Tarzana, CA 91335-6827, USA

Weitz, Chris (Actor, Director, Writer)
20000 Pacific Coast Hwy
Malibu, CA 90265-5422, USA

Weitz, Paul (Director, Writer)
Depth of Field
1424 2nd St Fl 3
Santa Monica, CA 90401-2379, USA

Weitz, Paul J (Astronaut)
3086 N Tam Oshanter Dr
Flagstaff, AZ 86004-7405, USA

Weitzenberg, Charles B (Athlete, Olympic Athlete, Water Polo Player)
1699 Happy Valley Rd
Santa Rosa, CA 95409-4000, USA

Weitzman, Rick (Athlete, Basketball Player)
76 Birch St
Peabody, MA 01960-2059, USA

Weixler, Jess (Actor)
c/o Rhonda Price *Gersh (NY)*
41 Madison Ave
New York, NY 10010-2202, USA

Wejbe, Jolean (Actor)
c/o Bob McGowan *McGowan Management*
8733 W Sunset Blvd Ste 103
West Hollywood, CA 90069-2241, USA

Wek, Alek (Model)
c/o Staff Member *IMG*
304 Park Ave S Fl 12
New York, NY 10010-4314, USA

Welbourn, John (Athlete, Football Player)
3301 Palos Verdes Dr N
Palos Verdes Estates, CA 90274-1030, USA

Welbring, D A (Golfer)
c/o Staff Member *Pro Golfers Association (PGA) Tour*
112 Tpc Blvd
Ponte Vedra Beach, FL 32082, USA

Welch, Brian (Head) (Musician)
4025 E Chandler Blvd Ste 70-B3
Phoenix, AZ 85048-8829, USA

Welch, Claxton (Athlete, Football Player)
9721 SE Ankeny St
Portland, OR 97216-2311, USA

Welch, Gillian (Musician)
PO Box 60007
Nashville, TN 37206-0007, USA

Welch, Herb (Athlete, Football Player)
999 La Senda
Santa Barbara, CA 93105-4512, USA

Welch, Jack (Business Person)
Jack Welch Management Institute
2303 Dulles Station Blvd # 6C
Strayer University Office of the General Counsel
Herndon, VA 20171-6353, USA

Welch, Lenny (Musician)
Brothers Mgmt
141 Dunbar Ave
Fords, NJ 08863-1551, USA

Welch, Michael (Actor)
c/o Susan Curtis *Curtis Talent Management*
9607 Arby Dr
Beverly Hills, CA 90210-1202, USA

Welch, Mike (Athlete, Baseball Player)
3 Inca Dr
Nashua, NH 03063-3544, USA

Welch, Milt (Athlete, Baseball Player)
818 Jannette Ct
Springfield, OR 97477-3694, USA

Welch, Peter
1404 Longworth Hob
Washington, DC 20515-3702, USA

Welch, Raquel (Actor)
3011 N Beverly Glen Cir
Los Angeles, CA 90077-1727, USA

Welch, Tahnee (Actor, Model)
PO Box 823
Beverly Hills, CA 90213-0823, USA

Welchel, Don (Athlete, Baseball Player)
21518 Patton Ave
Lago Vista, TX 78645-6770, USA

Welch Jr, John F (Business Person)
General Electric Co
3135 Easton Tpke
Fairfield, CT 06828-0001, USA

Weld, Tuesday (Actor)
c/o Alexa Pagonas *Michael Black Management*
9701 Wilshire Blvd Fl 10
Beverly Hills, CA 90212-2010, USA

Weld, William (Ex-Governor, Politician)
120 Zaccheus Mead Ln
Greenwich, CT 06831-3751, USA

Weldon, Ann (Actor)
c/o Staff Member *Sutton Barth & Vennari Inc*
5900 Wilshire Blvd Ste 700
Los Angeles, CA 90036-5009, USA

Weldon, Joan (Actor)
67 E 78th St
New York, NY 10075-0273, USA

Weldon, W Casey (Athlete, Football Player)
380 Castleton Cir
Tallahassee, FL 32312-1404, USA

Welk, Lawrence (Actor)
841 N Saint Elena St
Gilbert, AZ 85234-3586, USA

Welk, Tanya (Actor)
9633 La Tuna Canyon Rd
Sun Valley, CA 91352-2233, USA

Welke, Tim (Athlete, Baseball Player)
7790 Doubletree Ct
Kalamazoo, MI 49009-9771, USA

Welke, William (Bill) (Athlete, Baseball Player)
54 Country Hls
Marshall, MI 49068-9674, USA

Welker, Frank (Actor)
c/o Staff Member *Cunningham Escott Slevin & Doherty (CESD-LA)*
10635 Santa Monica Blvd Ste 130
Los Angeles, CA 90025-8306, USA

Welker, Wes (Athlete, Football Player)
251 SW 87th Ter
Plantation, FL 33324-2602, USA

Wellborn, Joe (Athlete, Football Player)
803 Paulus St
Schulenburg, TX 78956-1424, USA

Wellemeyer, Todd (Athlete, Baseball Player)
8402 Westover Dr
Prospect, KY 40059-9497, USA

Weller, Freddy (Musician)
c/o Case
3231 Hazel Pl
Westminster, CO 80031-2724, USA

Weller, Paul (Musician)
c/o Staff Member *Variety Artists International Inc*
1924 Spring St
Paso Robles, CA 93446-1620, USA

Weller, Peter (Actor)
37 Riverside Dr # Phb
New York, NY 10023-8027, USA

Weller, Robb (Television Host)
349 S Linden Dr Apt A
Beverly Hills, CA 90212-3741, USA

Welles, Tori (Actor, Adult Film Star, Model)
c/o Staff Member *Sirius/XM Satellite Radio*
1221 Avenue of the Americas Fl 19
New York, NY 10020-1011, USA

Welling, Tom (Actor)
Tom Welling Productions
16000 Ventura Blvd Ste 900
Encino, CA 91436-2760, USA

Wellman, Brad (Athlete, Baseball Player)
733 Graham Ct
Danville, CA 94526-4326, USA

Wellman, Gary (Athlete, Football Player)
1638 Wellington Pl
Westlake Village, CA 91361-1535, USA

Wellman Jr, William (Actor)
15935 Meadowcrest Rd
Sherman Oaks, CA 91403-4715, USA

Wells, Annie (Journalist, Photographer)
Press Democrat
427 Mendocino Ave
Editorial Dept
Santa Rosa, CA 95401-6385, USA

Wells, Audrey (Director, Writer)
c/o David Lonner *Oasis Media Group*
8730 W Sunset Blvd Ste 700
West Hollywood, CA 90069-2249, USA

Wells, Bob (Athlete, Baseball Player)
154 Wilcox Rd
Cowiche, WA 98923-9775, USA

Wells, Carole (Actor)
c/o Staff Member *Burton Moss*
10533 Strathmore Dr
Los Angeles, CA 90024-2540, USA

Wells, Casper (Athlete, Baseball Player)
252 Guy Park Ave
Amsterdam, NY 12010-2333, USA

Wells, Charles (Athlete, Baseball Player)
Philadelphia Stars
1035 Beaver Creek Dr
Duncanville, TX 75137-3731, USA

Wells, Chris (Athlete, Hockey Player)
PO Box 880883
Boca Raton, FL 33488-0883, USA

Wells, Claudia (Actor)
c/o Staff Member *Privilege Talent Agency*
PO Box 260860
Encino, CA 91426-0860, USA

Wells, Cory (Musician)
3853 Carbon Canyon Rd
Malibu, CA 90265-5004, USA

Wells, Dan (Actor)
c/o Jon Simmons *Simmons & Scott Entertainment*
7942 Mulholland Dr
Los Angeles, CA 90046-1225, USA

Wells, David (Dave) (Athlete, Baseball Player)
16956 Laurel Hill Ln Unit 197
San Diego, CA 92127-6869, USA

Wells, Dawn (Actor)
11684 Ventura Blvd # 965
Studio City, CA 91604-2699, USA

Wells, Dean (Athlete, Football Player)
1146 Copperfield Dr
Georgetown, IN 47122-9082, USA

Wells, Gawen D (Bonzi) (Basketball Player)
c/o Staff Member *Sacramento Kings*
1 Sports Pkwy
Sacramento, CA 95834-2301

Wells, Greg (Athlete, Baseball Player)
1 Sterling Ct
Cartersville, GA 30120-6469, USA

Wells, Harold (Athlete, Football Player)
2315 New Bern Ave
Raleigh, NC 27610-2434, USA

Wells, Jane (Correspondent)
c/o Staff Member *CNBC (Main)*
900 Sylvan Ave
Englewood Cliffs, NJ 07632-3312, USA

Wells, Joel (Athlete, Football Player)
11 Flicker Pt
Greenville, SC 29609-6646, USA

Wells, John (Producer)
356 S Hudson Ave
Los Angeles, CA 90020-4804, USA

Wells, Kip (Athlete, Baseball Player)
12891 Westbrook Dr
Tyler, TX 75704-2460, USA

Wells, LLewellyn (Producer)
c/o Wayne Fitterman *United Talent Agency (UTA-LA)*
9336 Civic Center Dr
Beverly Hills, CA 90210-3604, USA

Wells, Mark (Athlete, Hockey Player, Olympic Athlete)
25004 Portside Ct
Harrison Township, MI 48045-3265, USA

Wells, Norman (Athlete, Football Player)
600 Lakes Edge Dr
Oxford, MI 48371-5229, USA

Wells, Patricia (Journalist)
Harper Collins Publishers
195 Broadway Fl 2
New York, NY 10007-3132, USA

Wells, Scott (Athlete, Football Player)
291 Jones Pkwy
Brentwood, TN 37027-4458, USA

Wells, Terry (Athlete, Baseball Player)
110 Seymour Creek Dr
Cary, NC 27519-5870, USA

Wells, Terry (Athlete, Football Player)
25036 Polktown Rd
Lucedale, MS 39452, USA

Wells, Thelma (Writer)
1934 Lanark Ave
Dallas, TX 75203-4523, USA

Wells, Theodore V (Attorney)
Paul, Weiss, Rifkind, Warton & Garrison, LLC 1285 Avenue ofthe Americas
New York, NY 10019, USA

Wells, Vernon (Athlete, Baseball Player)
2251 King Fisher Dr
Westlake, TX 76262-4816, USA

Wells, Warren (Athlete, Football Player)
1399 Pipkin St
Beaumont, TX 77705-2056, USA

Wells, Wayne (Athlete, Olympic Athlete, Wrestler)
PO Box 69
Arcadia, OK 73007-0069, USA

Wells-Hawkes, Sharlene (Beauty Pageant Winner)
77 W Lund Ln
Centerville, UT 84014-2710, USA

Welp, Christian (Athlete, Basketball Player)
149 NW Tupelo Way
Poulsbo, WA 98370-8378, USA

Welsh, Chris (Athlete, Baseball Player)
12640 Huey Ln
Walton, KY 41094-9511, USA

Welsh, Dave (Musician)
2417 W 32nd Ave Unit 7
Denver, CO 80211-3374, USA

Welsh, Stephanie (Journalist, Photographer)
PO Box 277
Wayne, ME 04284-0277, USA

Welsom, Elleen (Journalist)
Albuquerque Tribune
7777 Jefferson St NE
Editorial Dept
Albuquerque, NM 87109-4360, USA

Welsome-Martin, Eileen (Journalist, Photographer)
2040 Locust St
Denver, CO 80207-3941, USA

Welteroth, Dick (Athlete, Baseball Player)
270 W 3rd St
Williamsport, PA 17701-6428, USA

Welti, Lisa (Actor)
c/o Staff Member *Select Artists Ltd (CA-Westside Office)*
1138 12th St Apt 1
Santa Monica, CA 90403-5459, USA

Wendeii-Pohl, Krissy (Athlete, Hockey Player, Olympic Athlete)
10812 Falling Water Ln Unit G
Saint Paul, MN 55129-5267, USA

Wendell, Krissy (Hockey Player)
University of Minnesota
Athletic Dept
Minneapolis, MN 55455, USA

Wendell, Ryan (Athlete, Football Player)
c/o Staff Member *New England Patriots*
1 Patriot Pl
Foxboro, MA 02035-1388, USA

Wendell, Steven "Turk" (Athlete, Baseball Player)
11245 E Palmer Divide Ave
Larkspur, CO 80118-5009, USA

Wendelstedt, Hunter (Athlete, Baseball Player)
101 Hawthorne Hollow Dr
Madisonville, LA 70447-9340, USA

Wendkos, Gina (Writer)
c/o Staff Member *Industry Entertainment*
955 Carrillo Dr Ste 300
Los Angeles, CA 90048-5400, USA

Wendt, George (Actor)
3856 Vantage Ave
Studio City, CA 91604-3636, USA

Wenge, Ralph (Correspondent)
Cable News Network
1050 Techwood Dr NW
News Dept
Atlanta, GA 30318-5695, USA

Wengert, Don (Athlete, Baseball Player)
13100 Cedarwood Ave
Clive, IA 50325-8568, USA

Wenglikowski, Alan (Athlete, Football Player)
422 Lake Ave
Franklin, OH 45005-3521, USA

Wengren, Mike (Musician)
c/o Staff Member *Mitch Schneider Organization (MSO)*
14724 Ventura Blvd Ste 410
Sherman Oaks, CA 91403-3537, USA

Wenham, David (Actor, Producer)
2326 Hollyridge Dr
Los Angeles, CA 90068-3518, USA

Wenner, Jann S (Publisher)
Wenner Media
1290 Avenue of the Americas Fl 2
New York, NY 10104-0295, USA

Wennington, Bill (Athlete, Basketball Player)
1085 Oak Grove Ln
Lake Forest, IL 60045-1629, USA

Wensink, John (Athlete, Hockey Player)
29311 Bidwell Creek Rd
Fredericktown, MO 63645-8900, USA

Wenstrom, Matt (Athlete, Basketball Player)
15714 Blanco Trails Ln
Cypress, TX 77429-4618, USA

Wente, Jean R (Business Person)
California State Automobile Assn
PO Box 422940
San Francisco, CA 94142-2940, USA

Wente, Jr., Bob (Race Car Driver)
59 Windam Place Dr
Saint Charles, MO 63304-7417, USA

Wentworth, Alexandra (Ali) (Actor, Comedian)
20 Dunemere Ln
East Hampton, NY 11937-2706, USA

Wentz, Pete (Musician)
3767 Reklaw Dr
Studio City, CA 91604-3830, USA

Wenz, Fred (Athlete, Baseball Player)
1 Circle Dr
Branchburg, NJ 08876-3905, USA

Wenzell, Margaret (Athlete, Baseball Player)
74835 Waring Ct
Palm Desert, CA 92260-3100, USA

Wenzell, Marge (Baseball Player)
78287 Brookhaven Ln
Palm Desert, CA 92211-2735, USA

Wepner, Chuck (Boxer)
153 Avenue E
Bayonne, NJ 07002-4434, USA

Werb, Mike (Director, Producer)
9270 Sierra Mar Dr
Los Angeles, CA 90069-1735, USA

Werbowy, Daria (Model)
c/o Staff Member *IMG*
304 Park Ave S Fl 12
New York, NY 10010-4314, USA

Werdann, Robert (Athlete, Basketball Player)
4739 40th St Apt 5F
Sunnyside, NY 11104-4035, USA

Werhas, Johnny (Athlete, Baseball Player)
22875 Savi Ranch Pkwy Ste A
Yorba Linda, CA 92887-4619, USA

Werkheiser, Devon (Actor)
3120 Hollyridge Dr
Los Angeles, CA 90068-1954, USA

Werner, Anna (Correspondent)
KHOU
1945 Allen Pkwy
News Department
Houston, TX 77019-2596, USA

Werner, Bjoern (Athlete, Football Player)
c/o Ben Dogra *CAA (St. Louis)*
222 S Central Ave Ste 1008
Saint Louis, MO 63105-3509, USA

Werner, Clyde (Athlete, Football Player)
3009 Islandview Ct
Gig Harbor, WA 98335-1258, USA

Werner, Don (Athlete, Baseball Player)
2204 Briarwood Blvd
Arlington, TX 76013-3316, USA

Werner, Roger L Jr (Television Host)
Prime Sports Ventures
10000 Santa Monica Blvd
Los Angeles, CA 90067, USA

Werner, Tom (Producer)
c/o Staff Member *Carsey-Werner-Mandabach*
16027 Ventura Blvd Ste 600
Encino, CA 91436-2798, USA

Wersching, Annie (Actor)
c/o Tara Friedlander *ID Public Relations (LA)*
7060 Hollywood Blvd Fl 8th
Los Angeles, CA 90028-6021, USA

Wersching, Raimund (Ray) (Athlete, Football Player)
18 Buttercup Ln
San Carlos, CA 94070-1528, USA

Wert, Don (Athlete, Baseball Player)
341 Smithville Rd
New Providence, PA 17560-9729, USA

Werth, Dennis (Athlete, Baseball Player)
2713 Tartan Way
Springfield, IL 62711-6717, USA

Werth, Jayson (Athlete, Baseball Player)
2713 Tartan Way
Springfield, IL 62711-6717, USA

Wertheimer, Linda (Correspondent)
National Public Radio
2025 M St NW
News Dept
Washington, DC 20036-3309, USA

Wertz, Bill (Athlete, Baseball Player)
26514 Mingo Dr
Perrysburg, OH 43551-5437, USA

Wescott, Scott (Athlete, Snowboarder)
c/o Ben Morrill *Octagon*
2 Union St Ste 300
Portland, ME 04101-4295, USA

Wesley, Dante (Athlete, Football Player)
104 Fawn Cv
White Hall, AR 71602-4774, USA

Wesley, David (Athlete, Basketball Player)
2S06 Baywater Canyon Dr
Pearland, TX 77S84, USA

Wesley, Glen (Athlete, Hockey Player)
5305 Newstead Manor Ln
Raleigh, NC 27606-9515, USA

Wesley, James (Musician)
c/o Staff Member *Broken Bow Records*
209 10th Ave S Ste 230
Cummins Station
Nashville, TN 37203-0722, USA

Wesley, Norman (Business Person)
Fortune Brands Inc
300 Tower Pkwy
Lincolnshire, IL 60069-3640, USA

Wesley, Paul (Actor)
2769 Westshire Dr
Los Angeles, CA 90068-1929, USA

Wesley, Rutina (Actor)
c/o Holly Shakoor Fleischer *42West (LA)*
1840 Century Park E Ste 700
Los Angeles, CA 90067-2122, USA

Wesley, Walt (Athlete, Basketball Player)
6417 Scott Ln
Fort Myers, FL 33966-4713, USA

Wessinger, Jim (Athlete, Baseball Player)
4275 Altair Crse
Liverpool, NY 13090-2230, USA

Wessling, John (Actor, Comedian)
c/o Nick Nuciforo *Creative Artists Agency (CAA-LA)*
2000 Avenue of the Stars Ste 100
Los Angeles, CA 90067-4705, USA

Wesson, Barry (Athlete, Baseball Player)
36 Shore Dr NE
Brookhaven, MS 39601-8756, USA

West, Adam (Actor)
PO Box 3477
Ketchum, ID 83340-3477, USA

West, Bob (Athlete, Football Player)
3915 Boston Ave
San Diego, CA 92113-3318, USA

West, Chandra
c/o Staff Member *Industry Entertainment*
955 Carrillo Dr Ste 300
Los Angeles, CA 90048-5400, USA

West, David (Athlete, Baseball Player)
1242 SW Seahawk Way
Palm City, FL 34990-4246, USA

West, David (Basketball Player)
New Orleans Homets
1501 Girod St
New Orleans Arena
New Orleans, LA 70113-3124, USA

West, Delonte (Athlete, Basketball Player)
c/o Aaron Goodwin *Goodwin Sports Management*
121 Lakeside Ave Ste 100B
Seattle, WA 98122-6587, USA

West, Doug (Athlete, Basketball Player)
Villanova University see E Lancaster Ave
Attn Basketball Coaching Staff
Nahant, PA 1908S, USA

West, Ed (Athlete, Football Player)
1930 Ma Lee Dr
Moody, AL 35004-2813, USA

West, Jeff (Athlete, Football Player)
12376 Adair Creek Way NE
Redmond, WA 98053-5686, USA

West, Jerry (Athlete, Basketball Player, Olympic Athlete)
Golden State Warriors
1011 Broadway
Attn: Executive Board
Oakland, CA 94607-4027, USA

West, Joe (Athlete, Baseball Player)
17531 Cobblestone Ln
Clermont, FL 34711-5906, USA

West, Joel (Model)
William Morris Agency
1325 Avenue of the Americas Bsmt 2
New York, NY 10019-6047, USA

West, Kanye (Musician)
113 16th St
Manhattan Beach, CA 90266-4616, USA

West, Leslie (Musician)
James Faith Entertainment
318 Wynn Ln Ste 14
Port Jefferson, NY 11777-1699, USA

West, Lizzie (Musician)
Warner Bors Records
3300 Warner Blvd
Burbank, CA 91505-4694, USA

West, Lori (Golfer)
2110 Augusta Dr SE
Marietta, GA 30067-8215, USA

West, Lyle (Athlete, Football Player)
719 1st St SE
Moultrie, GA 31768-5509, USA

West, Mario (Athlete, Basketball Player)
390 Vine Mountain Way
Mableton, GA 30126-7255, USA

West, Mark (Athlete, Basketball Player)
644 Old Wagner Rd
Petersburg, VA 23805-9319, USA

West, Matthew (Musician)
c/o Mandy Parsons *Savvy Media Solutions*
133 Holiday Ct
Franklin, TN 37067-1384, USA

West, Maura (Actor)
c/o Marnie Sparer *Innovative Artists (LA)*
1505 10th St
Santa Monica, CA 90401-2805, USA

West, Nathan (Actor)
c/o Jason Egenberg *United Talent Agency (UTA-LA)*
9336 Civic Center Dr
Beverly Hills, CA 90210-3604, USA

West, Paula (Musician)
PO Box 2142
San Francisco, CA 94126-2142, USA

West, Peter
4708 Largo Way
Las Vegas, NV 89121-2836

West, Price (Athlete, Baseball Player)
Raleigh Tigers
3540 Mill Point Dr SE
Grand Rapids, MI 49512-9337, USA

West, Red (Actor)
c/o Anne Geddes *Geddes Agency, The*
1203 Greenacre Ave
West Hollywood, CA 90046-5707, USA

West, Roland (Athlete, Basketball Player)
7464 Shaker Run Ln
West Chester, OH 45069-6301, USA

West, Ronnie (Athlete, Football Player)
PO Box 110
Pineview, GA 31071-0110, USA

West, Shane (Actor)
2820 Westshire Dr
Los Angeles, CA 90068-1932, USA

West, Simon (Director)
2158 La Mesa Dr
Santa Monica, CA 90402-2342, USA

West, Troy (Athlete, Football Player)
725 N Greenberry Ave
West Covina, CA 91790-1331, USA

West, Willie (Athlete, Football Player)
PO Box 50430
Eugene, OR 97405-0980, USA

Westbrook, Bryant (Athlete, Football Player)
28017 N 17th Dr
Phoenix, AZ 85085-5350, USA

Westbrook, Erinn (Actor)
c/o Tina Treadwell *Treadwell Entertainment*
1327 W Valleyheart Dr
Burbank, CA 91506-3035, USA

Westbrook, Jake (Athlete, Baseball Player)
PO Box 574
Danielsville, GA 30633-0574, USA

Westbrook, Jimi (Musician)
56 Annandale
Nashville, TN 37215-5819, USA

Westbrook, Michael (Athlete, Football Player)
1585 Oregon Trl
Elk Grove Village, IL 60007-2853, USA

Westbrook, Nicole (Musician)
c/o Siri Garber *Platform Public Relations*
2666 N Beachwood Dr
Los Angeles, CA 90068-2308, USA

Westbrook, Russell (Athlete, Basketball Player)
c/o Arn Tellem *Wasserman Media Group (LA)*
12100 W Olympic Blvd Ste 200
Los Angeles, CA 90064-1075, USA

Westbrooks, Greg (Athlete, Football Player)
3832 10th Avenue Pl
Moline, IL 61265-2429, USA

Westcott, Seth (Athlete, Snowboarder)
c/o Staff Member *US Ski And Snowboard Association*
Box 199
Park City, UT 84060, USA

Westenhoefer, Suzanne (Actor, Comedian)
100 S 4th St
Los Angeles, CA 90046

Wester, Travis (Actor)
c/o Abby Bluestone *Innovative Artists (LA)*
1505 10th St
Santa Monica, CA 90401-2805, USA

Westerberg, Paul (Musician, Songwriter)
4107 W 42nd St
Minneapolis, MN 55416-5005, USA

Westerfeld, Scott (Writer)
c/o Jill Grinberg *Jill Grinberg Literary Management*
392 Vanderbilt Ave
Brooklyn, NY 11238-1505, USA

Westerfield, Putney (Publisher)
501 Portola Rd Apt 8021
Portola Valley, CA 94028-7667, USA

Westerman-Austin, Helen (Baseball Player)
1837 Stonehenge Rd
Springfield, IL 62702-3244, USA

Western, Johnny (Musician)
19 E 16th Ave
Hutchinson, KS 67501-5533, USA

Western Underground (Music Group)
c/o Staff Member *Paradigm (Monterey)*
404 W Franklin St
Monterey, CA 93940-2303, USA

Westfall, Ed (Athlete, Hockey Player)
PO Box 39
Locust Valley, NY 11560-0039

Westfall, V Edward (Ed) (Athlete, Hockey Player)
699 Hillside Ave
New Hyde Park, NY 11040-2512, USA

Westfeldt, Jennifer (Actor)
2035 N Catalina St
Los Angeles, CA 90027-1825, USA

Westfield, Ernest (Athlete, Baseball Player)
PO Box 7091
Champaign, IL 61826-7091, USA

Westhead, Barb (Golfer)
9820 E Thompson Peak Pkwy
Pkwy Unit 707
Scottsdale, AZ 85255-6614, USA

Westhead, Paul (Athlete, Basketball Coach, Basketball Player, Coach)
2217 Via Alamitos
Palos Verdes Estates, CA 90274-1652, USA

Westheimer, Doctor Ruth (Doctor)
7 Wildwood Ln
Putnam Valley, NY 10579-2243, USA

Westheimer, Gerald (Doctor, Misc)
582 Santa Barbara Rd
Berkeley, CA 94707-1746, USA

Westlake, Wally (Athlete, Baseball Player)
3800 61st St
Sacramento, CA 95820-2421, USA

Westmore, McKenzie (Actor)
3904 Laurel Canyon Blvd
#766
Studio City, CA 91604, USA

Westmoreland, Dick (Athlete, Football Player)
5601 Sea Reef Pl
San Diego, CA 92154, USA

Westmoreland, James (Actor)
52940 Avenida Navarro
La Quinta, CA 92253-3333, USA

Westmoreland, Lynn (Congressman, Politician)
2433 Rayburn Hob
Washington, DC 20515-1602, USA

Weston, Celia (Actor)
c/o Staff Member *Innovative Artists (LA)*
1505 10th St
Santa Monica, CA 90401-2805, USA

Weston, Jeff (Athlete, Football Player)
7235 Alakoko St
Honolulu, HI 96825-2712, USA

Weston, Kim (Musician)
Powerplay
5434 W Sample Rd PMB 533
Margate, FL 33073-3453, USA

Weston, Mickey (Athlete, Baseball Player)
2702 Eisenhower Ave
Valparaiso, IN 46383-3273, USA

Weston, Randolph (Randy) (Musician)
PO Box 749
Maplewood, NJ 07040-0749, USA

Weston, Wesley (Lil' Flip) (Musician)
c/o Staff Member *Sony Music Entertainment*
555 Madison Ave
New York, NY 10022-3301, USA

Weston-Jones, Tom (Actor)
c/o Esther Chang *William Morris Endeavor (LA)*
9601 Wilshire Blvd
Beverly Hills, CA 90210-5213, USA

Westphal, Paul D (Athlete, Basketball Player, Coach)
1424 Granvia Altamira
Palos Verdes Estates, CA 90274-2131, USA

Westwick, Ed (Actor)
c/o Melanie Greene *Affirmative Entertainment*
425 N Robertson Blvd
West Hollywood, CA 90048-1735, USA

We The Kings (Musician)
c/o Staff Member *Ozone Entertainment*
60-62 E 11th St
7th Floor
New York, NY 10003, USA

Wetherbee, James D (Astronaut)
3818 Trailstone Ln
Katy, TX 77494-2472, USA

Wetherbee, James D Captain (Astronaut)
3818 Trailstone Ln
Katy, TX 77494-2472, USA

Wetherby, Jeff (Athlete, Baseball Player)
28410 Great Bend Pl
Wesley Chapel, FL 33543-5726, USA

Wetnight, Ryan S (Athlete, Football Player)
3156 Griffon Ct
Simi Valley, CA 93065-0500, USA

Wetoska, Robert (Athlete, Football Player)
1295 Forest Glen Dr S
Winnetka, IL 60093-1427, USA

Wetteland, John (Athlete, Baseball Player)
352 Old Justin Rd
Argyle, TX 76226-3508, USA

Wetterich, Brett (Athlete, Golfer)
147 Castle Island Pl
Jupiter, FL 33458-1616, USA

Wettig, Patricia (Actor)
21700 Oxnard St Ste 950
Woodland Hills, CA 91367-3607, USA

Wetton, John (Musician)
Entourage Talent
133 W 25th St # 500
New York, NY 10001-7206, USA

Wetzel, Carl (Athlete, Hockey Player)
609 4th St # 477
Gaylord, MN 55334-4465, USA

Wetzel, John (Athlete, Basketball Player, Coach)
13011 N Sunrise Canyon Ln
Marana, AZ 85658-4035, USA

Wetzel, Rosemarie
111 E 22nd St # 200
New York, NY 10010-5400

Wever, Stefan (Athlete, Baseball Player)
7 Corte Los Sombras
Greenbrae, CA 94904-1149, USA

Wexler, Anne (Government Official)
1317 F St NW Ste 600
Washington, DC 20004-1105, USA

Wexler, Haskell (Cinematographer)
201 Ocean Ave Unit 904B
Santa Monica, CA 90402-1465, USA

Wexner, Leslie H (Business Person)
Limited Inc
3 Limited Pkwy
PO Box 16000
Columbus, OH 43230-1467, USA

Weyerhaeuser, George (Business Person)
Weyerhaeuser Co
33663 32nd Ave S
Federal Way, WA 98023, USA

Whalen, Dorothy (Baseball Player)
8315 125th St
Kew Gardens, NY 11415-2705, USA

Whalen, Jim (Athlete, Football Player)
222 High Rd
Newbury, MA 01951-2215, USA

Whalen, Lindsay (Basketball Player)
Connecticut Sun
Mohegan Sun Arena
Uncasville, CT 06382, USA

Whalen, Sara (Athlete, Olympic Athlete, Soccer Player)
10 Francis Dr
Greenlawn, NY 11740-2504, USA

Whaley, Frank (Actor)
c/o Staff Member *Shelter Entertainment*
9255 W Sunset Blvd Ste 320
West Hollywood, CA 90069-3313, USA

Whaley, Joanne (Actor)
c/o Staff Member *Creative Artists Agency (CAA-LA)*
2000 Avenue of the Stars Ste 100
Los Angeles, CA 90067-4705, USA

Whalin, Justin (Actor)
c/o Deborah Miller *Shelter Entertainment*
9255 W Sunset Blvd Ste 320
West Hollywood, CA 90069-3313, USA

Whalley, Joanne (Actor)
1435 Lindacrest Dr
Beverly Hills, CA 90210-2519, USA

Whalum, Kirk (Musician)
Cole Classic Mgmt
PO Box 231
Canoga Park, CA 91305-0231, USA

Whang, Suzanne (Actor)
c/o Staff Member *Kragen & Company*
2103 Ridge Dr
Los Angeles, CA 90049-1153, USA

Whannell, Leigh (Actor, Writer)
c/o Stacey Testro *Stacey Testro International*
8265 W Sunset Blvd Ste 102
West Hollywood, CA 90046-2433, USA

W. Hanorable, Colleen (Congressman, Politician)
238 Cannon Hob
Washington, DC 20515-3502, USA

Whatley, Ennis (Athlete, Basketball Player)
42 Brinkwood Rd
Brookeville, MD 20833-2303, USA

Wheatley, Terrence (Athlete, Football Player)
c/o Staff Member *New England Patriots*
1 Patriot Pl
Foxboro, MA 02035-1388, USA

Wheatley, Tyrone (Athlete, Football Player)
20730 Westhampton St
Oak Park, MI 48237-2710, USA

Wheaton, David (Tennis Player)
20045 Cottagewood Ave
Excelsior, MN 55331-9239, USA

Wheaton, Kenny (Athlete, Football Player)
6427 S 21st Pl
Phoenix, AZ 85042-4652, USA

Wheaton, Wil (Actor)
460 S Lamer St
Burbank, CA 91506-2948, USA

Whedon, Joss (Director, Producer, Writer)
c/o Chris Harbert *Creative Artists Agency (CAA-LA)*
2000 Avenue of the Stars Ste 100
Los Angeles, CA 90067-4705, USA

Wheeler, Blake (Athlete, Hockey Player)
c/o Staff Member *Boston Bruins*
100 Legends Way Ste 250
Td Banknorth Garden
Boston, MA 02114-1389, USA

Wheeler, Charles F (Cinematographer)
79125 Jack Rabbit Trl
La Quinta, CA 92253-4514, USA

Wheeler, Cheryl (Musician, Songwriter, Writer)
Morningstar Mgmt
PO Box 1770
Hendersonville, TN 37077-1770, USA

Wheeler, Chris (Sportscaster)
302 Saint Andrews Pl
Blue Bell, PA 19422-1290, USA

Wheeler, Clinton (Athlete, Basketball Player)
199 Scenic View Ln
Stone Mountain, GA 30087-6222, USA

Wheeler, Daniel (Dan) (Athlete, Baseball Player)
215 Harrison Ave
Belleair Beach, FL 33786-3619, USA

Wheeler, Dwight (Athlete, Football Player)
2124 Blair Blvd
Nashville, TN 37212-4902, USA

Wheeler, Ellen (Actor)
13576 Cheltenham Dr
Sherman Oaks, CA 91423-4818

Wheeler, John (Actor)
Levin Agency
8484 Wilshire Blvd Ste 745
Beverly Hills, CA 90211-3235, USA

Wheeler, Maggie (Actor)
1960 Palmerston Pl
Los Angeles, CA 90027-1816, USA

Wheeler, Mark (Athlete, Football Player)
101 Meadowridge Cv
San Marcos, TX 78666-2251, USA

Wheelock, Douglas H Lt Colonel
(Astronaut)
PO Box 580408
Houston, TX 77258-0408, USA

Wheelock, Gary (Athlete, Baseball Player)
3354 N Park St
Buckeye, AZ 85396-8390, USA

Whelan, Jill (Actor)
c/o Staff Member Scott Stander &
Associates
13701 Riverside Dr Ste 201
Sherman Oaks, CA 91423-2447, USA

Whelan, Nicky (Actor)
c/o Lena Roklin Luber Roklin
Management
5815 W Sunset Blvd Ste 206
Los Angeles, CA 90028-6481, USA

Whelchel, Lisa (Actor)
1370 Meadows Ave
Lantana, TX 76226-6624, USA

Whelpley, John (Actor)
c/o Staff Member Lenhoff & Lenhoff
830 Palm Ave
West Hollywood, CA 90069-4009

Whibley, Deryck (Musician)
15445 Varden St
Sherman Oaks, CA 91403-3815, USA

Whigham, Larry (Athlete, Football Player)
6110 Midway Rd
Raymond, MS 39154-8357, USA

Whigham, Shea (Actor)
c/o Larry Taube Principal Entertainment
(LA)
9255 W Sunset Blvd Ste 500
West Hollywood, CA 90069-3301, USA

Whillock, Jack (Athlete, Baseball Player)
2118 River Ridge Rd
Arlington, TX 76017-2758, USA

Whinnery, Barbara (Actor)
Baier/Kleinman
3575 Cahuenga Blvd W Ste 500
Los Angeles, CA 90068-1344, USA

Whipple Jr, Allen (Race Car Driver)
GAS Motorsports
Route 11 & 103 Newport Rd.
Claremont, NH 03743, USA

Whirry, Shannon (Actor)
Shapiro-Lichtman
8827 Beverly Blvd
Los Angeles, CA 90048-2405, USA

Whisenant, Matt (Athlete, Baseball Player)
1035 Fairview Dr
La Canada Flintridge, CA 91011-2351,
USA

Whisenhunt, Ken (Athlete, Football Player)
1511 W Grand Canyon Dr
Chandler, AZ 85248-4816, USA

Whisenton, Larry (Athlete, Baseball Player)
524 Main St
Canton, MS 39046-3208, USA

Whiskey Myers (Music Group, Musician)
c/o Joey Lee William Morris Endeavor
(Nashville)
1600 Division St Ste 300
Nashville, TN 37203-2755, USA

Whisler, J Steven (Business Person)
Phelps Dodge Corp
1 N Central Ave Ste 100
Phoenix, AZ 85004-4464, USA

Whisler, Randy (Athlete, Baseball Player)
6920 Hilyard Ct
Klamath Falls, OR 97603-9620, USA

Whisler, Wes (Athlete, Baseball Player)
1094 Pebble Brook Dr
Noblesville, IN 46062-8442, USA

Whisman, Greg (Athlete, Golfer)
1908 129th Pl SE
Everett, WA 98208-7121, USA

Whiston, Don (Athlete, Hockey Player,
Olympic Athlete)
2 Jeffreys Neck Rd
Ipswich, MA 01938-1328, USA

Whitacre, Edward E Jr (Business Person)
SBC Communications
175 E Houston St
San Antonio, TX 78205-2255, USA

Whitaker, Alaina (Musician)
PO Box 703165
Tulsa, OK 74170-3165, USA

Whitaker, Denzel (Actor)
c/o Brad Slater William Morris Endeavor
(LA)
9601 Wilshire Blvd
Beverly Hills, CA 90210-5213, USA

Whitaker, Ed (Race Car Driver)
923 Wagner Rd
Bristol, VA 24201-2436, USA

Whitaker, Forest (Actor, Director,
Producer)
3036 Beckman Rd 3040 Munro Cir
Los Angeles, CA 90068, USA

Whitaker, Jack (Sportscaster)
225 Broadway Fl 20
New York, NY 10007-3001, USA

Whitaker, Johnny
4924 Vineland Ave
North Hollywood, CA 91601-3847

Whitaker, Louis R (Lou) Jr (Athlete,
Baseball Player)
17 Brownstone Ln
Greensboro, NC 27410-5145, USA

Whitaker, Pernell (Athlete, Boxer,
Olympic Athlete)
3808 Cranberry Ct
Virginia Beach, VA 23456-8109, USA

Whitaker, Roger
1730 Tree Blvd Ste 2
Saint Augustine, FL 32084-4193

Whitaker, Steve (Athlete, Baseball Player)
900 SE 6th Ct
Fort Lauderdale, FL 33301-3018, USA

Whitaker, William (Athlete, Football
Player)
Lake Road 135
Gravois Mills, MO 65037, USA

Whitbank, Ben (Baseball Player)
203 E Apollo Ln
Milton, DE 19968-9781, USA

Whitby, Bill (Athlete, Baseball Player)
13926 Huntersville Concord Rd
Huntersville, NC 28078-6262, USA

Whitcomb, Bob (Race Car Driver)
Whitcomb Racing
9201 Garrison Rd
Charlotte, NC 28278, USA

Whitcomb, Edgar D (Ex-Governor)
3905 Highwater Rd
Cannelton, IN 47520-5869, USA

Whitcomb, Ian (Musician, Songwriter,
Writer)
PO Box 451
Altadena, CA 91003-0451, USA

White, Adrian (Athlete, Football Player)
686 Allen Ln
Orange Park, FL 32073-3986, USA

White, Albert (Baseball Player)
St Louis Browns
32 Jessana Hts
Colorado Springs, CO 80906-7902, USA

White, Andre (Athlete, Football Player)
5122 Hunters Luck
Stone Mountain, GA 30088-3123, USA

White, Anna
9950 Durant Dr Unit 402
Beverly Hills, CA 90212-1610

White, Ben (Horse Racer)
452 Oak Haven Dr
Altamonte Springs, FL 32701-6318, USA

White, Betty (Actor, Comedian)
PO Box 491965
Los Angeles, CA 90049-8965, USA

White, Bob W (Athlete, Football Player)
763D Espada Dr
El Paso, TX 79912-1913, USA

White, Bradley
8730 W Sunset Blvd Ste 480
West Hollywood, CA 90069-2277

White, Brain (Athlete, Hockey Player)
3 Godlclc Rd
Burlington, MA 01803, USA

White, Brian (Actor)
c/o Lena Roklin Luber Roklin
Management
5815 W Sunset Blvd Ste 206
Los Angeles, CA 90028-6481, USA

White, Brooke (Musician)
c/o Rick Canny Sanctuary Artist
Management
8750 Wilshire Blvd Ste 200
Beverly Hills, CA 90211-2707, USA

White, Bryan (Musician, Songwriter)
910 Stuart Ln
Brentwood, TN 37027-5822, USA

White, Charles (Athlete, Football Player,
Heisman Trophy Winner)
31841 Via Faisan
Trabuco Canyon, CA 92679-4182, USA

White, Charlie (Figure Skater, Olympic
Athlete)
US Figure Skating
20 1st St
Colorado Springs, CO 80906-3697, USA

White, Cheryl (Musician)
Hallmark Direction
713 18th Ave S
Nashville, TN 37203-3214, USA

White, Chris (Athlete, Football Player)
c/o Bus Cook Bus Cook Sports, Inc
1 Willow Bend Dr
Hattiesburg, MS 39402-8552, USA

White, Chris (Musician)
Lustig Talent
PO Box 770850
Orlando, FL 32877-0850, USA

White, Cody (Athlete, Football Player)
c/o David Dunn Athletes First, LLC
23091 Mill Creek Dr
Laguna Hills, CA 92653-1258, USA

White, Colin (Athlete, Hockey Player)
1221 Crosstns Way
Wayne, NJ 07470, USA

White, Dana (Business Person)
Zuffa LLC
2960 W Sahara Ave Ste 200
Las Vegas, NV 89102-1709, USA

White, Danny (Athlete, Coach, Football
Player)
111 S Saint Joseph St
South Bend, IN 46601-1901, USA

White, Dean (Producer)
c/o Sean Freidin ICM Partners (LA)
10250 Constellation Blvd Fl 7
Los Angeles, CA 90067-6207, USA

White, Derrick (Athlete, Baseball Player)
4212 Frederick Ave
Baltimore, MD 21229-3513, USA

White, Devon M (Athlete, Baseball
Player)
6440 E Sierra Vista Dr
Paradise Valley, AZ 85253-4351, USA

White, DeVoreaux
4505 Santa Rosalia Dr Apt 2
Los Angeles, CA 90008-1512

White, Diz (Actor)
203 N Plymouth Blvd
Los Angeles, CA 90004-3833, USA

White, Donna (Athlete, Golfer)
200 Caribe Ct
Greenacres, FL 33413-2150, USA

White, Dwayne (Athlete, Football Player)
1916 Dickinson St
Philadelphia, PA 19146-4662, USA

White, Ed (Athlete, Football Player)
PO Box 1437
Julian, CA 92036-1437, USA

White, Ed
1225 Grand View Dr
Berkeley, CA 94705-1629

White, Edmund (Writer)
185 Nassau St Rm 224
Princeton, NJ 08544-2003, USA

White, Edward A (Ed) (Athlete, Football
Player)
PO Box 1437
Julian, CA 92036-1437, USA

White, Eric (Athlete, Basketball Player)
1945 Bush St Apt K
San Francisco, CA 94115-3226, USA

White, Eugene (Baseball Player)
Chicago American Giants
4166 Lockhart Dr N
Jacksonville, FL 32209-1928, USA

White, Frank (Athlete, Baseball Player)
PO Box 573
Blue Springs, MO 64013-0573, USA

White, Gabe (Athlete, Baseball Player)
1571 Lakeview Dr
Sebring, FL 33870-7940, USA

White, Gerald (Athlete, Football Player)
Halo Creative Concepts
1501 Halo Dr
Troy, MI 48084, USA

White, Glodean (Musician)
8000 Oceanus Dr
Los Angeles, CA 90046-2047, USA

White, Hubie (Athlete, Basketball Player)
101 E Gowen Ave
Philadelphia, PA 19119-1613, USA

White, Jack (Musician)
5055 Franklin Pike
Nashville, TN 37220-1523, USA

White, Jahidi (Athlete, Basketball Player)
c/o Staff Member *Washington Wizards*
601 F St NW
Washington, DC 20004-1605, USA

White, Jaleel (Actor)
1440 Via Anita
Pacific Palisades, CA 90272-2357, USA

White, James
7529 Franklin Ave
Los Angeles, CA 90046-2241

White, James C (Athlete, Football Player)
14430 Andrea Way Ln
Houston, TX 77083-7712, USA

White, Jamie (Radio Personality)
c/o Staff Member *Star 98.7 FM*
3400 W Olive Ave Ste 550
Burbank, CA 91505-5544, USA

White, Jan (Athlete, Football Player)
6507 Burkwood Dr
Clayton, OH 45315-9602, USA

White, Jason (Athlete, Football Player,
Heisman Trophy Winner)
3203 Stone Dr
Tuttle, OK 73089-7972, USA

White, Jeremy Allen (Actor)
c/o Jillian Roscoe *ID Public Relations (LA)*
7060 Hollywood Blvd Fl 8th
Los Angeles, CA 90028-6021, USA

White, Jeris (Athlete, Football Player)
PO Box 3031
Frederick, MD 21705-3031, USA

White, Jerry (Athlete, Baseball Player)
343 N Wildwood
Hercules, CA 94547-3523, USA

White, Jessica (Model)
c/o Staff Member *IMG*
304 Park Ave S Fl 12
New York, NY 10010-4314, USA

White, Jonah (Business Person)
Billy Bob Teeth, Inc.
PO Box 389
Hardin, IL 62047-0389, USA

White, Joseph (Jo Jo) (Athlete, Basketball
Player)
2 Mansfield Rd
Middleton, MA 01949-1515, USA

White, Joy Lynn (Musician)
Buddy Lee
38 Music Sq E Ste 300
Nashville, TN 37203-4304, USA

White, Julie (Actor)
c/o Alex Spieller *IMPR*
357 S Robertson Blvd
Beverly Hills, CA 90211-3602, USA

White, Karyn (Musician)
222 Monterey Rd Unit 905
Glendale, CA 91206-2035, USA

White, Lari (Actor)
c/o Staff Member *William Morris
Endeavor (LA)*
9601 Wilshire Blvd
Beverly Hills, CA 90210-5213, USA

White, Larri (Musician, Songwriter,
Writer)
Carter Career Mgmt
1028 18th Ave S # B
Nashville, TN 37212-2105, USA

White, Larry (Athlete, Baseball Player)
PO Box 54455
Phoenix, AZ 85078-4455, USA

White, Lee (Athlete, Football Player)
600 Langtry Dr
Las Vegas, NV 89107-2019, USA

White, Leon (Athlete, Football Player)
11033 Paseo Castanada
La Mesa, CA 91941-7330, USA

White, Lorenzo (Athlete, Football Player)
3450 NW 7th St
Fort Lauderdale, FL 33311-6505, USA

White, Marilyn (Athlete, Track Athlete)
9605 S 6th Ave
Inglewood, CA 90305-3207, USA

White, Mark (Musician)
DAS Communications
84 Riverside Dr
New York, NY 10024-5723, USA

White, Marsh (Athlete, Football Player)
7502 Bayhill Dr
Rowlett, TX 75088-5465, USA

White, Matt (Athlete, Baseball Player)
1853 Old Route 9
Windsor, MA 01270-9397, USA

White, Michael Jai (Actor)
c/o Craig Baumgarten *Baumgarten
Management*
1447 Cloverfield Blvd Ste 101
Santa Monica, CA 90404-2979, USA

White, Mike (Actor)
c/o Staff Member *Black and White
Productions*
100 Universal City Plz Bldg 4113
Universal City, CA 91608-1002, USA

White, Mike (Athlete, Baseball Player)
26438 S Jardin Dr
Sun Lakes, AZ 85248-7114, USA

White, Mike (Athlete, Coach, Football
Coach, Football Player)
115 Grand Canal
Newport Beach, CA 92662-1329, USA

White, Miles D (Business Person)
Abbott Laboratories
100 Abbott Park Rd
North Chicago, IL 60064-3500, USA

White, Myron (Athlete, Baseball Player)
3201 S Deegan Dr
Santa Ana, CA 92704-6614, USA

White, Nera (Athlete, Basketball Player)
RR 3 Box 165
Lafayette, TN 37083, USA

White, Paula (Religious Leader, Television
Host, Writer)
Paula White Ministries
PO Box 585217
Orlando, FL 32858-5217, USA

White, Persia (Actor)
3792 Berry Dr
Studio City, CA 91604-3856, USA

White, Peter (Actor)
S M S Talant
8383 Wilshire Blvd Ste 230
Beverly Hills, CA 90211-2436, USA

White, Randy L (Athlete, Football Player)
Randy White's HOF BBQ
9225 Preston Rd
Frisco, TX 75033-3916, USA

White, Raymond P Jr (Doctor)
205 Cedar Meadows Ln
Chapel Hill, NC 27517-7221, USA

White, Reggie (Athlete, Football Player)
3631 Washington Ave
Windsor Mill, MD 21244-3776, USA

White, Rex (Race Car Driver)
187 Rivers Rd Lot 222
Fayetteville, GA 30214-3250, USA

White, Rick (Athlete, Baseball Player)
2860 Windy Ridge Dr
Springfield, OH 45502-7230, USA

White, Robert M II (Journalist)
4871 Glenbrook Rd NW
Washington, DC 20016-3245, USA

White, Roddy (Athlete, Football Player)
c/o Neil Schwartz *Schwartz & Feinsod*
contact via telephone or email
White Plains, NY 10603

White, Rodney (Basketball Player)
Denver Nuggets
1000 Chopper Cir
Pepsi Center
Denver, CO 80204-5805, USA

White, Ron (Actor, Comedian)
c/o Drew Edwards *Electra Star
Management*
9229 W Sunset Blvd Ste 415
West Hollywood, CA 90069-3404, USA

White, Rondell (Athlete, Baseball Player)
11111 Pine Lodge Trl
Davie, FL 33328-7317, USA

White, Rory (Athlete, Basketball Player)
S303 32nd St S
Fargo, NO S8104, USA

White, Roy (Athlete, Baseball Player)
M D M Sports Marketing
218 Washington Ave Apt C14
Attn:David Ratner
Cedarhurst, NY 11516-1510, USA

White, Roy H (Baseball Player)
1001 2nd St
Sacramento, CA 95814-3201, USA

White, Russell (Athlete, Football Player)
17450 Vanowen St Unit 4
Van Nuys, CA 91406-4312, USA

White, Sammy (Athlete, Football Player)
102 Margaret Dr
Monroe, LA 71203-9588, USA

White, Santi (Santigold) (Musician)
c/o Staff Member *Girlie Action*
243 W 30th St Fl 12
New York, NY 10001-2812, USA

White, Sharon
380 Forest Retreat
Hendersonville, TN 37075

White, Shaun (Athlete, Snowboarder)
7157 Birdview Ave
Malibu, CA 90265-4108, USA

White, Sheldon (Athlete, Football Player)
PO Box 622
Novi, MI 48376-0622, USA

White, Sherman (Athlete, Football Player)
2710 Summerland Rd
Aromas, CA 95004-9117, USA

White, Shernan E (Sherm) (Athlete,
Football Player)
PO Box 1856
Pebble Beach, CA 93953-1856, USA

White, Stan (Athlete, Football Player)
10716 Pot Spring Rd
Cockeysville, MD 21030-3021, USA

White, Stephen (Writer)
Penguin Books
375 Hudson St Bsmt 3
New York, NY 10014-3672, USA

White, Steve (Athlete, Football Player)
11928 Middlebury Dr
Tampa, FL 33626-2520, USA

White, Tony (Athlete, Basketball Player)
1213 Holston Park Rd
Knoxville, TN 37914-5733, USA

White, Tony L (Business Person)
PE Corp
710 Bridgeport Ave
Shelton, CT 06484-4750, USA

White, Vanna (Model, Television Host)
75 Beverly Park Ln
Beverly Hills, CA 90210-1571, USA

White, Verdine (Musician)
c/o Staff Member *Atlas/Third Rail
Entertainment*
9200 W Sunset Blvd Ste 10
West Hollywood, CA 90069-3608, USA

White, Walter (Athlete, Football Player)
504 NW 44th Ter
Kansas City, MO 64116-1580, USA

White, Wilford (Athlete, Football Player)
30A S MacDonald Ste A
Mesa, AZ 85210-1322, USA

White, William (Athlete, Football Player)
4619 Sandwich Ct
Dublin, OH 43016-8292, USA

White, William B (Bill) (Athlete, Baseball Player)
PO Box 199
Upper Black Eddy, PA 18972-0199, USA

Whited, Ed (Athlete, Baseball Player)
PO Box 34
Carmel, IN 46082-0034, USA

Whitefield, A D (Athlete, Football Player)
807 Tangle Way Ct
Cedar Hill, TX 75104-7817, USA

Whitehead, Barb (Athlete, Golfer)
9820 E Thompson Peak Pkwy Unit 707
Scottsdale, AZ 85255-6656, USA

Whitehead, Bud (Athlete, Football Player)
5438 N Brooks Ave
Fresno, CA 93711-2913, USA

Whitehead, Geoffrey (Actor)
81 Shaftesbury Ave
London, EN W1

Whitehead, Jerome (Athlete, Basketball Player)
PO Box 5932
Playa Del Rey, CA 90296-5932, USA

Whitehead, Kimberly (Race Car Driver)
Miss Dirt Motorsports
PO Box 206
Sussex, NJ 07461-0206, USA

Whitehead, Paxton (Actor)
c/o Robert Attermann *Abrams Artists Agency (NY)*
9200 W Sunset Blvd PH 11
West Hollywood, CA 90069-3601, USA

Whitehead, Tahir (Athlete, Football Player)
c/o Chad Wiestling *Integrated Sports Management*
2120 Texas St Apt 2204
Houston, TX 77003-3054, USA

Whitehouse, Len (Athlete, Baseball Player)
300 Shore Rd
Burlington, VT 05408-2632, USA

Whitehurst, C David (Athlete, Football Player)
11010 Linbrook Ln
Duluth, GA 30097-1772, USA

White Jr, Josh (Musician)
23625 Ripple Crk
Novi, MI 48375-3546, USA

Whitemore, Hugh (Writer)
c/o Staff Member *Creative Artists Agency (CAA-LA)*
2000 Avenue of the Stars Ste 100
Los Angeles, CA 90067-4705, USA

Whitemore, Willet F Jr (Doctor, Scientist)
2 Hawthorne Ln
Manhasset, NY 11030-1505, USA

Whiten, Mark (Athlete, Baseball Player)
5810 Jefferson Park Dr
Tampa, FL 33625-3313, USA

Whiten, Richard (Actor)
247 S Beverly Dr # 102
Beverly Hills, CA 90212-3830, USA

White's
PO Box 2158
Hendersonville, TN 37077-2158

Whitesell, Emily (Producer, Writer)
c/o Staff Member *William Morris Endeavor (LA)*
9601 Wilshire Blvd
Beverly Hills, CA 90210-5213, USA

Whitesell, Josh (Athlete, Baseball Player)
1719 Deanna Way
Redlands, CA 92374-4716, USA

Whitesell, Sean (Actor, Producer)
c/o Staff Member *United Talent Agency (UTA-LA)*
9336 Civic Center Dr
Beverly Hills, CA 90210-3604, USA

Whiteside, Eli (Athlete, Baseball Player)
1018 County Road 373
New Albany, MS 38652-9690, USA

Whiteside, Matt (Athlete, Baseball Player)
255 Palisades Ridge Ct
Eureka, MO 63025-3706, USA

Whiteside, Sean (Athlete, Baseball Player)
3506 N Hills Dr
Haleyville, AL 35565-6746, USA

Whiteside, Sean (Athlete, Baseball Player)
654 W Olymoic Pi Apt 501
Seattle, WA 98119, USA

White Stripes, The (Music Group, Musician)
c/o Ian Montone *Monotone Inc.*
820 Seward St
Los Angeles, CA 90038-3602, USA

Whitfield, Dondre T (Actor)
c/o Jonathan Baruch *Rain Management Group (RMG)*
1631 21st St
Santa Monica, CA 90404-3914, USA

Whitfield, Ed (Congressman, Politician)
2368 Rayburn Hob
Washington, DC 20515-0105, USA

Whitfield, Fred (Athlete, Baseball Player)
119 Highway 480
Vandiver, AL 35176-7169, USA

Whitfield, Fredricka (Correspondent)
c/o Staff Member *CNN (Atlanta)*
1 Cnn Ctr NW
PO Box 105366
Atlanta, GA 30303-2762, USA

Whitfield, Lynn (Actor)
c/o Staff Member *Innovative Artists (LA)*
1505 10th St
Santa Monica, CA 90401-2805, USA

Whitfield, Mal (Athlete, Olympic Athlete, Track Athlete)
1322 28th St SE Apt 3
Washington, DC 20020-3647, USA

Whitfield, Sheree (Designer, Reality Star)
c/o Staff Member *Bravo (NY)*
30 Rockefeller Plz
New York, NY 10112-0015, USA

Whitfield, Terry (Athlete, Baseball Player)
849 Clearfield Dr
Millbrae, CA 94030-2148, USA

Whitfield, Trent (Athlete, Hockey Player)
5 Bryant Ln
Kennebunkport, ME 04046-7242, USA

Whitford, Brad (Musician)
12811 Ninebark Trl
Charlotte, NC 28278-6837, USA

Whitford, Bradley (Actor)
485 Maylin St
Pasadena, CA 91105-1629, USA

Whitley, Kim E (Actor, Producer)
c/o Judy Apperson *Morra Brezner Steinberg & Tenenbaum (MBST) Entertainment*
345 N Maple Dr Ste 200
Beverly Hills, CA 90210-5174, USA

Whitley, Kym (Actor, Producer)
5230 Babcock Ave
Valley Village, CA 91607-2302, USA

Whitlow, Bob (Athlete, Football Player)
315 W Gordon Pike
Bloomington, IN 47403-4570, USA

Whitman, Kari (Actor, Model)
1155 N La Cienega Blvd Apt 104
West Hollywood, CA 90069-2430, USA

Whitman, Mae (Actor)
c/o Daniel Spilo *Industry Entertainment*
955 Carrillo Dr Ste 300
Los Angeles, CA 90048-5400, USA

Whitman, Meg (Business Person)
HP
3000 Hanover St
Palo Alto, CA 94304-1112, USA

Whitman, Stuart (Actor)
749 San Ysidro Rd
Santa Barbara, CA 93108-1328, USA

Whitmer, Dan (Athlete, Baseball Player)
823 Robinhood Ln
Redlands, CA 92373-6665, USA

Whitmore, Darrell (Athlete, Baseball Player)
301 E 15th St
Front Royal, VA 22630-4112, USA

Whitmyer, Nat (Athlete, Football Player)
5305 W Goldenwood Dr
Inglewood, CA 90302-1037, USA

Whitney, Ashley (Athlete, Olympic Athlete, Swimmer)
124 Hearthstone Manor Cir
Brentwood, TN 37027-4344, USA

Whitney, CeCe (Actor)
16857 San Fernando Mission Blvd Unit 46
Granada Hills, CA 91344-4261, USA

Whitney, David (Athlete, Baseball Player)
Kansas City Monarchs
2178 Popps Ferry Rd
Biloxi, MS 39532-4233, USA

Whitney, Ray (Athlete, Hockey Player)
9820 E Thompson Peak Pkwy Unit 722
Scottsdale, AZ 85255-6657, USA

Whitney, Russ (Business Person, Misc)
Whitney Education Group Inc
1612 Cape Coral Pkwy E
Cape Coral, FL 33904-9618, USA

Whitney, Ryan (Athlete, Hockey Player)
179 Edward Foster Rd
Scituate, MA 02066-4342, USA

Whitney-Dearfield, Norma (Athlete, Baseball Player)
1803 Delaware Ave
White Oak, PA 15131-1660, USA

Whitney-Lee, Grace (Actor)
PO Box 79
Coarsegold, CA 93614, USA

Whitsett, Vivicca (Actor)
c/o Karin Olsen *Amazon PR*
269 S Beverly Dr # 750
Beverly Hills, CA 90212-3851, USA

Whitson, Ed (Athlete, Baseball Player)
10473 MacKenzie Way
Dublin, OH 43017-8775, USA

Whitson, Peggy A (Astronaut)
306 Lakeview Cir
El Lago, TX 77586-5846, USA

Whitson, Peggy A Dr (Astronaut)
306 Lakeview Cir
El Lago, TX 77586-5846, USA

Whitt, Ernie (Athlete, Baseball Player)
37370 Moravian Dr
Clinton Township, MI 48036-3604, USA

Whittaker, James (Jim) (Mountaineer)
2023 E Sims Way # 277
Port Townsend, WA 98368-6905, USA

Whittaker, Roger (Musician, Songwriter, Writer)
BML Mgmt
426 Marsh Point Cir
Saint Augustine, FL 32080-5863, USA

Whitted, Alvis (Athlete, Football Player)
2508 Bedford Ct
Fort Collins, CO 80526-5228, USA

Whittinghill, Dick
11310 Valley Spring Ln
North Hollywood, CA 91602-2613

Whittington, Art (Athlete, Football Player)
6709 La Tijera Blvd Apt 190
Los Angeles, CA 90045-2017, USA

Whittington, Bill (Race Car Driver)
1881 W State Road 84
Fort Lauderdale, FL 33315-2208, USA

Whittington, C L (Athlete, Football Player)
2332 Galilee Rd Apt 121
Hallsville, TX 75650-6189, USA

Whittington, Dale (Race Car Driver)
1881 W State Road 84
Fort Lauderdale, FL 33315-2208, USA

Whittington, Don (Race Car Driver)
1881 W State Road 84
Ft Lauderdale, FL 33315-2208, USA

Whittington, Michael S (Athlete, Football Player)
4246 Turtle Mound Rd
Melbourne, FL 32934-8505, USA

Whittle, Ricky (Athlete, Football Player)
c/o Naisha Arnold *Untitled Entertainment (LA)*
350 S Beverly Dr Ste 200
Beverly Hills, CA 90212-4819, USA

Whitwam, David R (Business Person)
Whirlpool Corp
2000 N State St
RR 63
Benton Harbor, MI 49022, USA

Whitwell, Mike (Athlete, Football Player)
PO Box 6
Cotulla, TX 78014-0006, USA

Whitworth, Andrew (Athlete, Football Player)
c/o Pat Dye Jr *SportsTrust Advisors (GA)*
3340 Peachtree Rd NE Fl 16
Atlanta, GA 30326-1000, USA

Whitworth, Johnny
c/o Lena Roklin *Luber Roklin Management*
5815 W Sunset Blvd Ste 206
Los Angeles, CA 90028-6481, USA

Whitworth, Kathy (Athlete, Golfer)
1735 Mistletoe Dr
Flower Mound, TX 75022-5316, USA

Whitworth, Kathy
5990 Lindenshire Ln Apt 101
Dallas, TX 75230-2726

Wholey, Dennis (Television Host)
Dennis Wholey Enterprises
1333 H St NW
Washington, DC 20005-4707, USA

Whoppers, Wendy (Actor)
c/o Staff Member *Wow Entertainment Inc*
8362 Pines Blvd # 296
Pembroke Pines, FL 33024-6600, USA

Whyte, Kenneth (Writer)
c/o Staff Member *Counterpoint*
2117 4th St Ste D
Berkeley, CA 94710-2205, USA

Whyte, Sandra (Athlete, Hockey Player,
Olympic Athlete)
81 Golden Hills Rd
Saugus, MA 01906-4010, USA

Whyte, Sean (Athlete, Hockey Player)
600 W Grove Pkwy # 1026
Mesa, AZ 85210, USA

WI, Charlie (Athlete, Golfer)
9400 Burnet Ave Unit 109
North Hills, CA 91343-7907, USA

Wick, Charles Z (Government Official)
US Information Agency
400 C St SW
Washington, DC 20024-2800, USA

Wick, Douglas (Producer)
c/o David O'Connor *Creative Artists
Agency (CAA-LA)*
2000 Avenue of the Stars Ste 100
Los Angeles, CA 90067-4705, USA

Wickander, Kevin (Athlete, Baseball
Player)
4319 W Banff Ln
Glendale, AZ 85306-3601, USA

Wicker, Floyd (Athlete, Baseball Player)
1758 W Greensboro Chapel Hill Rd
Snow Camp, NC 27349-9544, USA

Wicker, tom (Writer)
PO Box 361
Rochester, VT 05767-0361

Wickersham, Dave (Athlete, Baseball
Player)
25340 Quivira Rd
Louisburg, KS 66053-5204, USA

Wickert, Tom (Athlete, Football Player)
3717 Beach Dr SW
Seattle, WA 98116-3060, USA

Wickham, Daniel (Athlete, Baseball
Player)
3221 E Mountain Vista Dr
Phoenix, AZ 85048-5802, USA

Wickman, Robert J (Bob) (Athlete,
Baseball Player)
6568 Cheyenne Dr
Abrams, WI 54101-9434, USA

Wicks, Chuck (Musician)
c/o Staff Member *Webster & Associates
PR*
3573 Couchville Pike
Hermitage, TN 37076-4012, USA

Wicks, Sidney (Athlete, Basketball Player)
112 Great Oak Dr
Hampstead, NC 28443-2142, USA

Wicks, Sue (Basketball Player)
New York Liberty
125 W End Ave # 6
Madison Square Garden
New York, NY 10023-6387, USA

Wicoff, Erika (Athlete, Golfer)
7815 Four Leaf Dr
Greenville, IN 47124-9524, USA

Widby, G Ronald (Ron) (Athlete,
Basketball Player, Football Player)
1521 Lesli Dr
Royse City, TX 75189-3574, USA

Widdoes, Kathleen (Actor)
24 E 11th St
New York, NY 10003-4402, USA

Widdoes, Kathleen (Actor)
As the World Turns"" Show
524 W 57th St # 5330
Cbs-Tv
New York, NY 10019-2930, USA

Widell, Dave (Athlete, Football Player)
13050 Wexford Hollow Rd N
Jacksonville, FL 32224-9625, USA

Widell, Doug (Athlete, Football Player)
870 21st St
Vero Beach, FL 32960-5314, USA

Wideman, Dennis (Athlete, Hockey
Player)
26 Stillman St Apt 5-2
Boston, MA 02113-1695, USA

Wideman, John Edgar (Writer)
University of Massachusetts
Englesh Dept
Amherst, MA 01003, USA

Widenhouse, Bill (Race Car Driver)
PO Box 34
Highway 601
Midland, NC 28107-0034, USA

Widenhouse, Dink (Race Car Driver)
693 Warren St NE
Concord, NC 28025-3120, USA

Widger, Chris (Athlete, Baseball Player)
43 Goose Ln
Pennsville, NJ 08070-2638, USA

Widman, Herbert (Herb) (Athlete,
Swimmer)
844 Monarch Cir
San Jose, CA 95138-1343, USA

Widmer, Corey (Athlete, Football Player)
2640 Lake Shore Dr Unit 2508
Riviera Beach, FL 33404-4674, USA

Widmer, Jason (Athlete, Hockey Player)
PO Box 55289
Lexington, KY 40555-5289, USA

Wie, Michelle (Athlete, Golfer)
189 Bears Club Dr
Jupiter, FL 33477-4201, USA

Wieand, Ted (Athlete, Baseball Player)
216 S Walnut St
Slatington, PA 18080-2026, USA

Wiebe, Mark (Athlete, Golfer)
4123 S Elkhart St
Aurora, CO 80014-8100, USA

Wieber, Jordyn (Athlete, Gymnast,
Olympic Athlete)
Twistars Gymnastics
9410 Davis Hwy
Dimondale, MI 48821-9439, USA

Wiedenbauer, Tom (Athlete, Baseball
Player)
1460 Kilrush Dr
Ormond Beach, FL 32174-2882, USA

Wiedlin, Jane (Musician)
420 S San Pedro St Apt 612
Los Angeles, CA 90013-1887, USA

Wiegart, Zach (Athlete, Football Player)
3747 Saltmeadow Ct S
Jacksonville, FL 32224-9652, USA

Wiegert, Zach (Athlete, Football Player)
919 N 264th St
Waterloo, NE 68069-6207, USA

Wieghaus, Tom (Athlete, Baseball Player)
9724 E 8000N Rd
Grant Park, IL 60940-5364, USA

Wiegmann, Casey (Athlete, Football
Player)
30051 N Waukegan Rd
North Chicago, IL 60064, USA

Wiehl, Christopher (Actor)
2625 6th St Apt 3
Santa Monica, CA 90405-4431, USA

Wiemer, Jim
152 Country Ln
Rochester, NY 14626-3308, USA

Wier, Murray (Athlete, Basketball Player,
Coach)
118 Goodwater St
Georgetown, TX 78633-4505, USA

Wiesel, Elie (Nobel Prize Laureate, Writer)
Boston University
555 Madison Ave Fl 20
New York, NY 10022-3301, USA

Wiesenhahn, Robert (Athlete, Basketball
Player)
3315 Hickorycreek Dr
Cincinnati, OH 45244-2533, USA

Wiesler, Bob (Athlete, Baseball Player)
2325 Indiancup Dr
Florissant, MO 63033-1736, USA

Wiesner, Kenneth (Athlete, Olympic
Athlete)
996 Meta Lake Rd
Eagle River, WI 54521-9549, USA

Wiest, Dianne (Actor)
230 W 79th St
New York, NY 10024-6246, USA

Wieters, Matt (Athlete, Baseball Player)
1204 Suncast Ln Ste 2
El Dorado Hills, CA 95762-9665, USA

Wigger, Lones (Athlete, Olympic Athlete,
Shooter)
630 Wuthering Heights Dr
Colorado Springs, CO 80921-2533, USA

Wiggin, Paul (Athlete, Coach, Football
Coach, Football Player)
5013 Ridge Rd
Minneapolis, MN 55436-1013, USA

Wiggins, Al (Athlete, Olympic Athlete,
Swimmer)
167 Chancery Ln
Ligonier, PA 15658-1286, USA

Wiggins, Audrey (Musician)
William Morris Agency
2100 W End Ave Ste 1000
Nashville, TN 37203-5240, USA

Wiggins, Candice (Athlete, Basketball
Player)
BDA Sports Management
700 Ygnacio Valley Rd Ste 330
Walnut Creek, CA 94596-3838, USA

Wiggins, Jermaine (Athlete, Football
Player)
403 Overlook Dr
Beckley, WV 25801-9255, USA

Wiggins, John (Musician)
William Morris Agency
2100 W End Ave Ste 1000
Nashville, TN 37203-5240, USA

Wiggins, Mitchell (Athlete, Basketball
Player)
PO Box 5072
Kinston, NC 28503-5072, USA

Wiggins, Scott (Athlete, Baseball Player)
17 N Crescent Ave
Fort Thomas, KY 41075-2109, USA

Wigginton, Ty (Athlete, Baseball Player)
605 Kenway Loop
Mooresville, NC 28117-8414, USA

Wight, Paul (Big Show) (Athlete, Wrestler)
c/o Staff Member *World Wrestling
Entertainment (WWE)*
1241 E Main St
Titan Towers
Stamford, CT 06902-3520, USA

Wigiser, Margaret (Athlete, Baseball
Player)
7101 SE Quincy Ter
Hobe Sound, FL 33455-7357, USA

Wihtol, Sandy (Athlete, Baseball Player)
496 1st St Ste 200
Los Altos, CA 94022-3678, USA

Wiig, Kristen (Actor)
1430 Broadway Fl 17
New York, NY 10018-3355, USA

Wiik, Sven (Skier)
PO Box 774484
Steamboat Springs, CO 80477-4484, USA

Wilander, Mats (Athlete, Tennis Player)
104 Cove Creek Rd
Hailey, ID 83333-5100, USA

Wilber, Doreen V H (Athlete)
1401 W Lincoln Way
Jefferson, IA 50129-1675, USA

Wilber, Kyle (Athlete, Football Player)
c/o Andy Ross *Octagon Football*
832 Sansome St Fl 1
San Francisco, CA 94111-1558, USA

Wilborn, Ted (Athlete, Baseball Player)
6671 Pocket Rd
Sacramento, CA 95831-1904, USA

Wilbur, Richard P (Writer)
88 Dodwells Rd
Cummington, MA 01026-9705, USA

Wilbur, Richard S (Doctor)
985 Hawthome Pl
Lake Forest, IL 60045, USA

Wilburn, J R (Athlete, Football Player)
13908 Turnberry Ct
Midlothian, VA 23113-6488, USA

Wilburn, Ken (Athlete, Basketball Player)
17 E Meyran Ave
Somers Point, NJ 08244-2720, USA

Wilburn Brothers
PO Box 50
Goodlettsville, TN 37070-0050, USA

Wilcher, Mary (Actor)
c/o Staff Member *Levine Management*
9028 W Sunset Blvd PH 1
West Hollywood, CA 90069-1830, USA

Wilcox, Chris (Athlete, Basketball Player)
c/o Jeff Schwartz *Excel Sports Management (NY)*
1700 Broadway Fl 29
New York, NY 10019-5905, USA

Wilcox, Davie (Dave) (Athlete, Football Player)
94471 Willamette Dr
Junction City, OR 97448-9606, USA

Wilcox, J.J. (Athlete, Football Player)
c/o Anthony J. Agnone *Eastern Athletic Services*
11350 McCormick Rd
Suite 800 - Executive Plaza
Hunt Valley, MD 21031-1002, USA

Wilcox, John (Athlete, Football Player)
105 Sedgwick Ct
Walla Walla, WA 99362-9244, USA

Wilcox, Larry (Actor)
6763 Daryn Dr
West Hills, CA 91307-2709, USA

Wilcox, Lisa (Actor)
c/o Kate Ward *Ward Agency*
1617 N El Centro Ave Ste 15
Los Angeles, CA 90028-6429, USA

Wilcox, Milt (Athlete, Baseball Player)
10064 Vernon Ave
Huntington Woods, MI 48070-1522, USA

Wilcox, Shannon (Actor)
1753 Centinela Ave Apt A
Santa Monica, CA 90404-4204, USA

Wilcutt, Terence W (Terry) (Astronaut)
1216 Red Wing Dr
Friendswood, TX 77546-5888, USA

Wilcutt, Terrence W Colonel (Astronaut)
1216 Red Wing Dr
Friendswood, TX 77546-5888, USA

Wilde, Abby
c/o Ileane Rusch *Superior Talent Agency*
11712 Moorpark St Ste 209
Studio City, CA 91604-2164, USA

Wilde, Olivia (Actor)
66 9th Ave Apt 2W
New York, NY 10011-4956, USA

Wilder, Alan (Musician)
Reach Media
295 Greenwich St # 109
New York, NY 10007-1049, USA

Wilder, Bert (Athlete, Football Player)
501 Willow View Dr
Greensboro, NC 27455-1379, USA

Wilder, Don (Cartoonist)
North American Syndicate
235 E 45th St
New York, NY 10017-3305, USA

Wilder, Gene (Actor, Director, Writer)
476 Scofieldtown Rd
Stamford, CT 06903-3306, USA

Wilder, James (Actor)
Stone Manners
6500 Wilshire Blvd # 550
Los Angeles, CA 90048-4920, USA

Wilder, L Douglas (Politician)
2805 E Weyburn Rd
Richmond, VA 23235-3257, USA

Wilder, Sharon (Athlete, Golfer)
72730 Homestead Rd
Palm Desert, CA 92260-6581, USA

Wilder, Yvonne (Actor)
11836 Hesby St
Valley Village, CA 91607-3218

Wilding, Anna (Actor)
c/o Staff Member *Carpe Diem Films LLC*
9663 Santa Monica Blvd # 557
Beverly Hills, CA 90210-4303, USA

Wildman, George (Cartoonist)
262 Magee Dr
Hamden, CT 06514-1313, USA

Wildman, Valerie (Actor)
110 Hurricane St Apt 305
Marina Del Rey, CA 90292-5935, USA

Wild Orchid (Music Group)
c/o Staff Member *Diva Central Inc*
7510 W Sunset Blvd Ste 1445
Los Angeles, CA 90046-3408, USA

Wild Orchid
PO Box 90370
City Of Industry, CA 91715-0370

Wilds, Tristan (Actor)
c/o Elise Koseff *J Mitchell Management*
440 Park Ave S
New York, NY 10016-8012, USA

Wiles, Jason (Actor)
2381 Kimridge Rd
Beverly Hills, CA 90210-1830, USA

Wiles, Randy (Athlete, Baseball Player)
3716 Lake Catherine Dr
Harvey, LA 70058-5509, USA

Wiley, Enloe Steve (Baseball Player)
Negro Baseball Leagues
1222 Cedar St
Clarksville, TN 37040-3515, USA

Wiley, Lee (Musician)
Country Crossroads
7787 Monterey St
Gilroy, CA 95020-5217, USA

Wiley, Marcellus (Athlete, Football Player)
PO Box 83070
Los Angeles, CA 90083-0070, USA

Wiley, Marcus D. (Actor)
1614 Holman St
Houston, TX 77004-3839, USA

Wiley, Mark (Athlete, Baseball Player)
22273 Vista Lago Dr
Boca Raton, FL 33428-4765, USA

Wiley, Michael (Athlete, Basketball Player)
2461 Elm Ave Apt 2
Long Beach, CA 90806-3142, USA

Wiley, Michael E (Business Person)
Atlantic Richfield Co
333 S Hope St
Los Angeles, CA 90071-1406, USA

Wiley, Morlan (Athlete, Basketball Player)
2521 Fallview Ln
Carrollton, TX 75007, USA

Wiley, Morlon (Athlete, Basketball Player)
1967 Legacy Cove Dr
Maitland, FL 32751-7524, USA

Wiley-Sears, Janet (Baseball Player)
19629 Gilmer St
South Bend, IN 46614-5605, USA

Wilfong, Rob (Athlete, Baseball Player)
126 Maverick Dr
San Dimas, CA 91773-1127, USA

Wilford, John Noble Jr (Journalist)
232 W 10th St
New York, NY 10014-2976, USA

Wilfork, Vince (Athlete, Football Player)
c/o Staff Member *New England Patriots*
1 Patriot Pl
Foxboro, MA 02035-1388, USA

Wilheim, Jim (Athlete, Baseball Player)
348 Laurel Way
Mill Valley, CA 94941-4046, USA

Wilhelm, Erik (Athlete, Football Player)
6452 SE Division St
Portland, OR 97206-1278, USA

Wilhelm, Jim (Athlete, Baseball Player)
348 Laurel Way
Mill Valley, CA 94941-4046, USA

Wilhite, Jonathan (Athlete, Football Player)
c/o Staff Member *New England Patriots*
1 Patriot Pl
Foxboro, MA 02035-1388, USA

Wilhoite, Kathleen (Actor)
PO Box 5617
Beverly Hills, CA 90209-5617, USA

Wilk, Brad (Musician)
c/o Don Muller *William Morris Endeavor (LA)*
9601 Wilshire Blvd
Beverly Hills, CA 90210-5213, USA

Wilk, Vic (Athlete, Golfer)
1350 N Town Center Dr Unit 2082
Las Vegas, NV 89144-0587, USA

Wilkens, Lanny
2660 Peachtree Rd NW Apt 39F
Atlanta, GA 30305-3683

Wilkens, Lenny (Athlete, Basketball Coach, Basketball Player, Coach)
3429 Evergreen Point Rd
Medina, WA 98039-1022, USA

Wilkerson, Bob (Bobby) (Athlete, Basketball Player)
PO Box 7453
Upper Marlboro, MD 20792, USA

Wilkerson, Brad (Athlete, Baseball Player, Olympic Athlete)
8657 Man O War Rd
Palm Beach Gardens, FL 33418-7724, USA

Wilkerson, Bruce (Athlete, Football Player)
10822 Admiral Bend Way
Knoxville, TN 37934-3062, USA

Wilkerson, Curtis (Athlete, Baseball Player)
PO Box 182993
Arlington, TX 76096-2993, USA

Wilkerson, Doug (Athlete, Football Player)
PO Box 7090
Rancho Santa Fe, CA 92067-7090, USA

Wilkerson, Muhammad (Football Player)
c/o Chad Wiestling *Integrated Sports Management*
2120 Texas St Apt 2204
Houston, TX 77003-3054, USA

Wilkerson, Tim (Race Car Driver)
Demand Flow Racing
2901 Adlai Stevenson Dr
Springfield, IL 62703-4551, USA

Wilkes, Donna
16228 Maplegrove St
La Puente, CA 91744-1348

Wilkes, Glenn (Basketball Player, Coach)
Stetson University
Athletic Dept
Campus Box 8359
Deland, FL 32720, USA

Wilkes, Jamal (Athlete, Basketball Player)
1060 Colleen Way
Santa Barbara, CA 93111-1102, USA

Wilkes, Reggie (Athlete, Football Player)
6912 Wissahickon Ave
Philadelphia, PA 19119-3728, USA

Wilkie, Bob (Athlete, Hockey Player)
303 S Forge Rd
Palmyra, PA 17078-2613, USA

Wilkie, David (Athlete, Hockey Player)
8918 N 159th Ave
Bennington, NE 68007-5507, USA

Wilkin, Richard E (Religious Leader)
Winebrenner Theological Seminary
950 N Main St
Findlay, OH 45840-3652, USA

Wilkins, Damien
10490 Bent Tree Vw
Duluth, GA 30097-4423, USA

Wilkins, Dean (Athlete, Baseball Player)
10974 Tobago Rd
San Diego, CA 92126-2040, USA

Wilkins, Dominique (Athlete, Basketball Player)
4415 Felix Way SE
Smyrna, GA 30082-4700, USA

Wilkins, Donna (Athlete, Golfer)
1330 Southgate Dr
Villa Rica, GA 30180-7956, USA

Wilkins, Eddie Lee (Athlete, Basketball Player)
3045 Mockingbird Ln
Atlanta, GA 30344, USA

Wilkins, Eric (Athlete, Baseball Player)
1650 W Joshua St
Meridian, ID 83642-6194, USA

Wilkins, Mac (Athlete, Olympic Athlete, Track Athlete)
1915 NW Columbine Ln
Portland, OR 97229-9173, USA

Wilkins, Marc (Athlete, Baseball Player)
3473 Oakstone Dr
Ontario, OH 44903-8439, USA

Wilkins, Mardell (Athlete, Golfer)
26982 Durango Ln
Mission Viejo, CA 92691-4431, USA

Wilkins, Rick (Athlete, Baseball Player)
12766 Longview Dr W
Jacksonville, FL 32223-2620, USA

Wilkins, Roger (Journalist)
George Mason University
207 E Building
Fairfax, VA 22030, USA

Wilkins Myrick, Sue (Congressman, Politician)
230 Cannon Hob
Washington, DC 20515-3309, USA

Wilkinson, Adrienne (Actor)
c/o Ryan Hayden *Ideal Talent Agency (I.T.A.)*
10806 Ventura Blvd Ste 2
Studio City, CA 91604-3300, USA

Wilkinson, Amanda (Music Group, Musician)
Fitzgerald-Hartley
1908 Wedgewood Ave
Nashville, TN 37212-3733, USA

Wilkinson, Bill (Athlete, Baseball Player)
3738 Yuhas Ave
Helena, MT 59602-7404, USA

Wilkinson, Bruce (Writer)
Global Vision Resources
6400 Atlantic Blvd
Peachtree Corners, GA 30071-1291, USA

Wilkinson, Dale (Athlete, Basketball Player)
2168 E 3100 N
Layton, UT 84040-8479, USA

Wilkinson, Dan (Athlete, Football Player)
222 Republic Dr
Allen Park, MI 48101-3650, USA

Wilkinson, June (Actor, Model)
4060 E Grenora Way
Long Beach, CA 90815-2613, USA

Wilkinson, Kendra (Model, Reality Star)
c/o Liza Anderson *Anderson Group Public Relations*
8060 Melrose Ave Fl 4
Los Angeles, CA 90046-7038, USA

Wilkinson, Laura (Athlete, Diver, Olympic Athlete)
PO Box 131961
Spring, TX 77393-1961, USA

Wilkinson, Neil
PO Box 57
Sherwood, OR 97140-0057, USA

Wilkinson, Steve (Musician)
Fitzgerald Hartley
1908 Wedgewood Ave
Nashville, TN 37212-3733, USA

Wilkinson, Tom (Actor)
c/o Larry Taube *Principal Entertainment (LA)*
9255 W Sunset Blvd Ste 500
West Hollywood, CA 90069-3301, USA

Wilkinson, Tyler (Musician)
Fritzgerald Hartley
1908 Wedgewood Ave
Nashville, TN 37212-3733, USA

Wilkos, Steve (Television Host)
1122 N Dearborn St Apt 11B
Chicago, IL 60610-5065, USA

Wilks, Jim (Athlete, Football Player)
4314 Leaflock Ln
Katy, TX 77450-8251, USA

Will, George (Journalist)
9 Grafton St
Chevy Chase, MD 20815-3427, USA

Willard, Fred (Actor, Comedian)
5056 Woodley Ave
Encino, CA 91436-1411, USA

Willard, Jerry (Athlete, Baseball Player)
1421 Kumquat Pl
Oxnard, CA 93036-6219, USA

Willard, Kenneth H (Ken) (Athlete, Football Player)
3071 Viewpoint Rd
Midlothian, VA 23113, USA

Willard, Rod (Athlete, Hockey Player)
7736 Arboretum Dr Apt 108
Charlotte, NC 28270-0348

Willerth, Jeffrey
6615 W Tamarack Ave
Sun Valley, CA 91352

Willets, Kathy (Actor)
3251 Spanish River Dr
Pompano Beach, FL 33062-6809

Willett, Chad
PO Box 5617
Beverly Hills, CA 90209-5617

Willett, Malcolm (Cartoonist)
Universal Press Syndicate
4520 Main St Ste 340
Kansas City, MO 64111-7705, USA

Willett, Walter (Doctor, Scientist)
Harvard Medical School
25 Shattuck St
Boston, MA 02115-6092, USA

Willette, Jo Ann
9300 Wilshire Blvd Ste 400
Beverly Hills, CA 90212-3210

Willey, Cary (Athlete, Baseball Player)
PO Box 64
Cherryfield, ME 04622-0064, USA

Willey, Kathleen
2642 New Timber Way
Powhatan, VA 23139-5220

Will-Halpin, Maggie (Athlete, Golfer)
12423 Carnoustie Ln
North Chesterfield, VA 23236-4172, USA

Willhite, Gerald (Athlete, Football Player)
10464 Iliff Ct
Rancho Cordova, CA 95670-5409, USA

Willhite, Kevin (Athlete, Football Player)
9784 W Taron Dr
Elk Grove, CA 95757-8193, USA

Will.I.Am (Musician)
1965 De Mille Dr
Los Angeles, CA 90027-1705, USA

William, Edward (Religious Leader)
Bible Way Church
5118 Clarendon Rd
Brooklyn, NY 11203-5329, USA

Williams, Aaron (Athlete, Football Player)
c/o Tom Condon *CAA (St. Louis)*
222 S Central Ave Ste 1008
Saint Louis, MO 63105-3509, USA

Williams, Adrian (Basketball Player)
Phoenix Mercury
201 E Jefferson St
American West Arena
Phoenix, AZ 85004-2412, USA

Williams, Aeneas D (Athlete, Football Player)
PO Box 16291
Saint Louis, MO 63105-0991, USA

Williams, Al (Athlete, Baseball Player)
3428 E Shore Rd
Miramar, FL 33023-4978, USA

Williams, Al (Athlete, Basketball Player)
2809 S 36th St
Fort Smith, AR 72903-4501, USA

Williams, Alfred H (Athlete, Football Player)
Sportsradio 950 The Fan
7800 E Orchard Rd Ste 400
Greenwood Village, CO 80111-2599, USA

Williams, Allison (Actor, Musician)
c/o Lindsay Galin *Rogers & Cowan PR (NY)*
919 3rd Ave Fl 18
New York, NY 10022-3902, USA

Williams, Anson (Actor)
24612 Skyline View Dr
Malibu, CA 90265-4720, USA

Williams, Anthony A (Politician)
Mayor's Office
District Building
14th & E Sts NW
Washington, DC 20004, USA

Williams, Ashley (Actor)
c/o Lena Roklin *Luber Roklin Management*
5815 W Sunset Blvd Ste 206
Los Angeles, CA 90028-6481, USA

Williams, Barbara (Actor)
Innovative Artists
1505 10th St
Santa Monica, CA 90401-2805, USA

Williams, Barry (Actor, Musician)
c/o Anthony Anzaldo *Good Guy Entertainment*
3733 Oakfield Dr
Sherman Oaks, CA 91423-4430, USA

Williams, Bernabe (Bernie) (Athlete, Baseball Player)
180114th St Unit 210
Oakland, CA 94607, USA

Williams, Bernard (Athlete, Football Player)
1570 Waverly Ave
Memphis, TN 38106-2424, USA

Williams, Bernie (Athlete, Baseball Player)
77 Havemeyer Ln Unit 92
Stamford, CT 06902-2160, USA

Williams, Billy (Athlete, Baseball Player)
586 Prince Edward Rd
Glen Ellyn, IL 60137-6711, USA

Williams, Billy (Athlete, Baseball Player)
3227 Randolph Ave
Oakland, CA 94602-1539, USA

Williams, Billy Dee (Actor)
c/o Bradley Kramer *Kramer Management*
5699 Kanan Rd # 275
Agoura Hills, CA 91301-3358, USA

Williams, Bob A (Athlete, Football Player)
602 Stone Barn Rd
Towson, MD 21286, USA

Williams, Branden (Actor)
c/o Staff Member *Edward Horowitz*
1155 N La Cienega Blvd Apt 203
West Hollywood, CA 90069-2430, USA

Williams, Brandon (Athlete, Football Player)
c/o Pat Dye Jr *SportsTrust Advisors (GA)*
3340 Peachtree Rd NE Fl 16
Atlanta, GA 30326-1000, USA

Williams, Brian (Athlete, Football Player)
1226 Night Trl
Waconia, MN 55387-4558, USA

Williams, Brian (Athlete, Baseball Player)
2409 Colt Ln
Crowley, TX 76036-4703, USA

Williams, Brian (Athlete, Football Player)
5319 Lyoncrest Ct
Dallas, TX 75287-5500, USA

Williams, Brian (Correspondent, Television Host)
209 Sunset Hill Rd
New Canaan, CT 06840-4006, USA

Williams, Brooke (Actor)
c/o Staff Member *United Talent Agency (UTA-LA)*
9336 Civic Center Dr
Beverly Hills, CA 90210-3604, USA

Williams, Bryan (Baby) (Musician)
c/o Staff Member *Universal Music Group (UMG - LA)*
2220 Colorado Ave
Santa Monica, CA 90404-3506, USA

Williams, Bryan (Birdman) (Musician)
c/o Staff Member *Young Money Cash Money*
1755 Broadway Fl 7
New York, NY 10019-3743, USA

Williams, Buck (Athlete, Basketball Player)
9219 Fox Meadow Ln
Potomac, MD 20854-4619, USA

Williams, Calvin (Athlete, Football Player)
5032 Yellowwood Ave
Baltimore, MD 21209-4602, USA

Williams, Cara (Actor)
Dann
9903 Santa Monica Blvd # 606
Beverly Hills, CA 90212-1671, USA

Williams, Carlton (Athlete, Football Player)
5 Pinegate Ct
Peachtree City, GA 30269-1144, USA

Williams, Carnell (Cadillac) (Football Player)
c/o Jim Steiner *CAA (St. Louis)*
222 S Central Ave Ste 1008
Saint Louis, MO 63105-3509, USA

Williams, Charlie (Athlete, Baseball Player)
44 Frederick Ave
Port Orange, FL 32127-8628, USA

Williams, Charlie (Athlete, Basketball Player)
374 S Belvoir Blvd
Cleveland, OH 44121-2349, USA

Williams, Charlie (Athlete, Football Player)
2607 Encina
Irving, TX 75038-5559, USA

Williams, Chris (Actor)
c/o Carolyn Govers *Anonymous Content (LA)*
1119 Colorado Ave Ste 12
Santa Monica, CA 90401-3009, USA

Williams, Chris (Athlete, Football Player)
c/o Bill Johnson *SportsTrust Advisors (GA)*
3340 Peachtree Rd NE Fl 16
Atlanta, GA 30326-1000, USA

Williams, Chris A (Athlete, Football Player)
2800 Christopher Blvd
Hamburg, NY 14075-3456, USA

Williams, Christopher (Musician)
c/o Ken Maldonado *Zia Artists*
168 W 123rd St
New York, NY 10027-5510, USA

Williams, Cindy (Actor)
10470 Riverside Dr # 202
Westlake Village, CA 91361, USA

Williams, C K (Writer)
Princeton University
English Dept
Princeton, NJ 08544-0001, USA

Williams, Clarence (Journalist)
Los Angeles Times
145 S Spring St
Los Angeles, CA 90012-3601, USA

Williams, Cliff (Musician)
417 E Charlton St
Savannah, GA 31401-4609, USA

Williams, Clyde (Baseball Player)
Cleveland Buckeyes
17135 San Juan Dr
Detroit, MI 48221-2622, USA

Williams, Clyde (Athlete, Football Player)
9754 Highway 79
Bethany, LA 71007, USA

Williams, Colleen (Correspondent)
KNBC-TV
News Dept
3000 W Alameda Ave
Burbank, CA 91523-0001, USA

Williams, Cress (Actor)
c/o Marni Rosenzweig *Abrams Artists Agency (LA)*
9200 W Sunset Blvd PH 11
West Hollywood, CA 90069-3601, USA

Williams, Curtis (Actor)
c/o Sharyn Berg *Sharyn Talent Management*
PO Box 18033
Encino, CA 91416-8033, USA

Williams, Cynda (Actor)
Innovative Artists
1505 10th St
Santa Monica, CA 90401-2805, USA

Williams, Dallas (Athlete, Baseball Player)
7638 Allenwood Cir
Indianapolis, IN 46268-4738, USA

Williams, Dan (Athlete, Football Player)
c/o Joel Segal *Lagardere Unlimited (NYC)*
845 United Nations Plz Apt 40D
New York, NY 10017-3534, USA

Williams, Dana (Athlete, Baseball Player)
121 Arlene Dr
North Versailles, PA 15137-2432, USA

Williams, Dana (Musician)
Dreamcatcher Artists Mgmt
2908 Poston Ave
Nashville, TN 37203-1312, USA

Williams, Darnell (Actor)
Stone Manners
6500 Wilshire Blvd # 550
Los Angeles, CA 90048-4920, USA

Williams, Darryl (Athlete, Football Player)
2841 NW 82nd Way
Pembroke Pines, FL 33024-3177, USA

Williams, Dave (Athlete, Baseball Player)
157 Carter Ln
Camden, DE 19934-1212, USA

Williams, David (Athlete, Football Player)
31 Turn About Ct
Waynesville, NC 28785-7232, USA

Williams, David (Athlete, Football Player)
109 E Oxford St
Valley Stream, NY 11580-4622, USA

Williams, David (Athlete, Football Player)
30826 Tanoa Rd
Evergreen, CO 80439-7963, USA

Williams, David (Athlete, Hockey Player)
5 Barn Swallow Ln
Duxbury, MA 02332-3628, USA

Williams, Davida (Actor)
c/o Marvet Britto *Britto Agency PR*
90 Franklin St Apt 4N
New York, NY 10013-3489, USA

Williams, David W (Athlete, Football Player)
108 E Oxford St
Valley Stream, NY 11580, USA

Williams, DeAngelo (Athlete, Football Player)
c/o Jimmy Sexton *CAA (Memphis)*
6060 Poplar Ave Ste 470
Memphis, TN 38119-0910, USA

Williams, Delvin (Athlete, Football Player)
173 Sierra Vista Ave Apt 11
Mountain View, CA 94043-4468, USA

Williams, Deniece (Musician)
Green Light Talent Agency
PO Box 3172
Beverly Hills, CA 90212-0172, USA

Williams, Deren (Athlete, Basketball Player)
PO Box 270
Draper, UT 84020-0270, USA

Williams, Deron (Athlete, Basketball Player)
c/o Bob McClaren *McClaren Sports*
1401 McKinney St Ste 2222
Houston, TX 77010-4038, USA

Williams, Derwin (Athlete, Football Player)
12014 Windermere Crossing Cir
Winter Garden, FL 34787-5518, USA

Williams, D.J. (Athlete, Football Player)
c/o Mitchell Frankel *Impact Sports - Boca Raton*
2799 NW 2nd Ave Ste 203
Boca Raton, FL 33431-6709, USA

Williams, Don (Athlete, Baseball Player)
117 Greene Road 1250
Paragould, AR 72450-7377, USA

Williams, Don (Athlete, Basketball Player)
6109 Rosedale Dr
Hyattsville, MD 20782-2296, USA

Williams, Don (Musician, Songwriter)
2000 Neptune Rd
Ashland City, TN 37015-6172, USA

Williams, Donald E (Astronaut)
Science Applications Int'l
2450 Nasa Pkwy
Houston, TX 77058-3711, USA

Williams, Donald E Captain (Astronaut)
16430 Larkfield Dr
Houston, TX 77059-5415, USA

Williams, Donald "Spin" (Athlete, Baseball Player)
240 Shoute Division
El Dorado, AR 71730-8984, USA

Williams, Doug (Comedian)
c/o James Kellem *JKA Talent*
12725 Ventura Blvd Ste H
Studio City, CA 91604-2437, USA

Williams, Douglas L (Doug) (Athlete, Coach, Football Coach, Football Player)
10120 Lemon Rd
Zachary, LA 70791-6407, USA

Williams, Dudley (Dancer)
Alvin Alley American Dance Foundation
211 W 61st St # 300
New York, NY 10023-7832, USA

Williams, Duke (Athlete, Football Player)
c/o Adisa P. Bakari *Dow Lohnes PLLC*
1299 Pennsylvania Ave NW Ste 700
Washington, DC 20004-2431, USA

Williams, Easy (Actor)
Judy Schoen
606 N Larchmont Blvd Ste 309
Los Angeles, CA 90004-1309, USA

Williams, Ed (Athlete, Football Player)
3824 N Oak Grove Dr Apt 840
Oklahoma City, OK 73110-3534, USA

Williams, Eddie (Athlete, Baseball Player)
22809 Boxwood Ln
Santa Clarita, CA 91390-4155, USA

Williams, Edy (Actor, Model)
PO Box 6325
Woodland Hills, CA 91365-6325, USA

Williams, Eli (Baseball Player)
St Louis Stars
214 Thomas Ct NW
Fort Walton Beach, FL 32548-4139, USA

Williams, Ellery (Athlete, Football Player)
1987 Wimbledon Pl
Los Altos, CA 94024-7062, USA

Williams, Elmo (Director, Producer)
1249 Iris St
Brookings, OR 97415-9643, USA

Williams, Eric (Football Player)
c/o Staff Member *Saint Louis Cardinals (St Louis Cardinals)*
700 Clark Ave
Saint Louis, MO 63102-1727, USA

Williams, Eric (Football Player)
c/o Staff Member *Pittsburgh Steelers*
3400 S Water St
Pittsburgh, PA 15203-2358, USA

Williams, Eric M (Athlete, Football Player)
13330 Noel Rd Apt 825
Dallas, TX 75240-5092, USA

Williams, Erik (Athlete, Football Player)
1 Wortham Ct
Bear, DE 19701-2060, USA

Williams, Ernie (Athlete, Football Player)
45 Oakwood Dr
Chapel Hill, NC 27517-5650, USA

Williams, Erwin (Athlete, Football Player)
33 Manly St
Portsmouth, VA 23702-1019, USA

Williams, Frank (Basketball Player)
New York Knicks
125 W End Ave # 6
Madison Square Garden
New York, NY 10023-6387, USA

Williams, Freeman (Athlete, Basketball Player)
450 W 41st Pl
Los Angeles, CA 90037-2119, USA

Williams, Gary (Basketball Player, Coach)
University of Maryland
Athletic Dept
College Park, MD 20742-0001, USA

Williams, Gary Anthony (Actor)
4178 Dixie Canyon Ave
Sherman Oaks, CA 91423-4338, USA

Williams, George (Athlete, Baseball Player)
606 Paden Dr
Cedar Park, TX 78613-7023, USA

Williams, Gerald (Athlete, Baseball Player)
17011 Candeleda De Avila
Tampa, FL 33613-5213, USA

Williams, Gerald (Athlete, Football Player)
9613 Callis Ct
Harrisburg, NC 28075-9619, USA

Williams, Gluyas (Cartoonist)
New Yorker Magazine
4 Times Sq Fl 22
Editorial Dept
New York, NY 10036-6592, USA

Williams, Greg (Actor)
1680 Vine St Ste 604
Los Angeles, CA 90028-8833, USA

Williams, Gregg (Athlete, Coach, Football Coach, Football Player)
16897 Bold Venture Dr
Leesburg, VA 20176-7162, USA

Williams, Gregory Alan (Actor)
c/o Staff Member *Pakula/King & Associates*
9229 W Sunset Blvd Ste 315
West Hollywood, CA 90069-3403, USA

Williams, Gus (Athlete, Basketball Player)
PO Box 262
Mount Vernon, NY 10552-0262, USA

Williams, Hal (Actor)
Marter
PO Box 14227
Palm Desert, CA 92255-4227, USA

Williams, Harland (Actor)
8260 Grand View Dr
Los Angeles, CA 90046-1916, USA

Williams, Hayley (Musician)
1538 N Ogden Dr
Los Angeles, CA 90046-2616, USA

Williams, Herb (Athlete, Basketball Coach, Basketball Player, Coach)
67 Revonah Cir
Stamford, CT 06905-4026, USA

Williams, Howard E (Howie) (Basketball Player)
1940 Hamilton Ln
Carmel, IN 46032-3521, USA

Williams, Howard L (Howie) (Athlete, Football Player)
4731 Proctor Ave
Oakland, CA 94618-2540, USA

Williams, Hype (Actor, Director, Producer)
c/o Staff Member *Creative Artists Agency (CAA-LA)*
2000 Avenue of the Stars Ste 100
Los Angeles, CA 90067-4705, USA

Williams, Ivy (Writer)
Mediachase
834 N Harper Ave
Los Angeles, CA 90046-6804, USA

Williams, Jaimie (Actor)
1019 Kane Concourse Ste 202
Bay Harbor Islands, FL 33154-2138, USA

Williams, Jamal (Athlete, Football Player)
4020 Murphy Canyon Rd
San Diego, CA 92123-4407, USA

Williams, James A (Froggy) (Athlete,
Football Player)
296 Sugarberry Cir
Houston, TX 77024-7248, USA

Williams, James F (Jimy) (Athlete,
Baseball Player, Coach)
1506 S Evergreen Ave
Clearwater, FL 33756-2263, USA

Williams, James (Fly) (Athlete, Basketball
Player)
672 Ralph Ave Apt 4A
Brooklyn, NY 11212-3852, USA

Williams, James "Fly"
682 Ralph Ave Apt 2E
Brooklyn, NY 11212-3853, USA

Williams, James O (Athlete, Football
Player)
330 S Western Ave
Lake Forest, IL 60045-3245, USA

Williams, Jason (Athlete, Basketball
Player)
6103 Louise Cove Dr
Windermere, FL 34786-8939, USA

Williams, Jason (Athlete, Football Player)
c/o Dave Butz *Sportstars Inc*
1350 Avenue of the Americas Fl 28
New York, NY 10019-4702, USA

Williams, Jay (Athlete, Football Player)
1503 Alydar Ct
Waxhaw, NC 28173-6672, USA

Williams, Jay (Basketball Player)
Chicago Bulls
1901 W Madison St
United Center
Chicago, IL 60612-2459, USA

Williams, Jayson (Basketball Player,
Sportscaster)
NBC-TV
30 Rockefeller Plz
Sports Dept
New York, NY 10112-0015, USA

Williams, Jeff (Athlete, Football Player)
9710 15th Ave NW
Seattle, WA 98117-2314, USA

Williams, Jeffrey N (Astronaut)
4918 Cross Creek Ln
League City, TX 77573-6267, USA

Williams, Jeffrey N Colonel (Astronaut)
4918 Cross Creek Ln
League City, TX 77573-6267, USA

Williams, Jennifer (Fitness Expert, Reality
Star)
Flirty Girl Fitness
PO Box 8349
Van Nuys, CA 91409-8349, USA

Williams, Jerrol (Athlete, Football Player)
937 Lord Crewe St
Las Vegas, NV 89138-6036, USA

Williams, Jesse (Actor)
c/o Michael Guy *Atlas Talent Agency*
15 E 32nd St Fl 6
New York, NY 10016-5423, USA

Williams, Jessica (Musician)
c/o Staff Member *Diva Central Inc*
7510 W Sunset Blvd Ste 1445
Los Angeles, CA 90046-3408, USA

Williams, Jim (Athlete, Baseball Player)
16 Stone Pne
Aliso Viejo, CA 92656-2132, USA

Williams, Jimmy (Athlete, Baseball Player,
Coach)
4 Old Sound Rd
Joppa, MD 21085-4525, USA

Williams, JoBeth (Actor)
801 Tarcuto Way
Los Angeles, CA 90077-3216, USA

Williams, Joel (Athlete, Football Player)
1515 Penn Ave Apt 305
Wilkinsburg, PA 15221-2659, USA

Williams, John A (Writer)
693 Forest Ave
Teaneck, NJ 07666-2042, USA

Williams, John T (Actor, Composer)
c/o Staff Member *Gorfaine/Schwartz
Agency Inc*
4111 W Alameda Ave Ste 509
Burbank, CA 91505-4171, USA

Williams, Joseph R (Publisher)
Memphis Commercial Appeal
495 Union Ave
Memphis, TN 38103-3221, USA

Williams, Juan (Correspondent)
c/o 21st Century Speakers
Box 1422
Gouldsboro, PA 18424, USA

Williams, Justin (Athlete, Hockey Player)
7 Hart Ln
Ventnor City, NJ 08406-1215, USA

Williams, Kameelah (Musician)
c/o Staff Member *Creative Artists Agency
(CAA-LA)*
2000 Avenue of the Stars Ste 100
Los Angeles, CA 90067-4705, USA

Williams, Karen (Comedian)
HaHA Institute
27360 Beech Dr
Euclid, OH 44132-2139, USA

Williams, Karl (Athlete, Football Player)
6502 Falcon St
Rowlett, TX 75089-8260, USA

Williams, Katt (Actor, Comedian)
c/o Staff Member *Thicker Than Thieves*
1539 1/2 Westwood Blvd
Los Angeles, CA 90024-5601, USA

Williams, Keith (Athlete, Baseball Player)
1756 N Avignon Ln
Clovis, CA 93619-3799, USA

Williams, Kelli (Actor, Musician)
c/o John Carrabino *John Carrabino
Management*
5900 Wilshire Blvd Ste 406
Los Angeles, CA 90036-5015, USA

Williams, Ken (Athlete, Baseball Player)
409 E Benton Pl
Chicago, IL 60601-7288, USA

Williams, Kevin (Athlete, Basketball
Player)
1102 Blake Ave # 2
Brooklyn, NY 11208-3634, USA

Williams, Kevin (Athlete, Football Player)
9520 Viking Dr
Eden Prairie, MN 55344-3825, USA

Williams, Kevin (Athlete, Football Player)
2201 Wembley Downs Dr
Arlington, TX 76017-4548, USA

Williams, Kiely Alexis (Actor, Director,
Musician)
c/o Laurie Pozmantier *William Morris
Endeavor (LA)*
9601 Wilshire Blvd
Beverly Hills, CA 90210-5213, USA

Williams, Kim (Athlete, Golfer)
34350 Tuscany Ave
Sorrento, FL 32776-6921, USA

Williams, Kimberly Kevon (Actor)
c/o TJ Stein *Stein Entertainment Group*
1351 N Crescent Heights Blvd Apt 312
West Hollywood, CA 90046-4549, USA

Williams, Lauryn (Athlete, Track Athlete)
PO Box 8008
Johnson City, TN 37615-0008, USA

Williams, Lee E (Athlete, Football Player)
11651 NW 4th St
Plantation, FL 33325-2509, USA

Williams, Leona (Musician)
Leona Williams Enterprises
PO Box 777
Vienna, MO 65582-0777, USA

Williams, Lucinda (Musician, Songwriter)
11487 Laurelcrest Dr
Studio City, CA 91604-3873, USA

Williams, Madieu (Athlete, Football
Player)
5430 Beech Ave
Bethesda, MD 20814-1730, USA

Williams, Maiya (Producer)
c/o Staff Member *Principal Entertainment
(LA)*
9255 W Sunset Blvd Ste 500
West Hollywood, CA 90069-3301, USA

Williams, Malinda (Actor)
c/o Staff Member *Leverage Management*
3030 Pennsylvania Ave
Santa Monica, CA 90404-4112, USA

Williams, Mario (Athlete, Football Player)
c/o Jim Steiner *CAA (St. Louis)*
222 S Central Ave Ste 1008
Saint Louis, MO 63105-3509, USA

Williams, Mark (Bowler)
Professional Bowlers Assn
55 E Jackson Blvd Ste 401
Chicago, IL 60604-4307, USA

Williams, Mark (Athlete, Baseball Player)
1453 Trumansburg Rd
Ithaca, NY 14850-9530, USA

Williams, Mary Alice (Correspondent)
c/o Staff Member *CBS News (NY)*
524 W 57th St Fl 8
New York, NY 10019-2930, USA

Williams, Matt (Athlete, Baseball Player)
205 Tearose Ln
Lake Jackson, TX 77566-6043, USA

Williams, Matt (Athlete, Baseball Player)
4400 N Scottsdale Rd Ste 381
Scottsdale, AZ 85251-3331, USA

Williams, Matt (Writer)
Zeiderman
211 E 48th St
New York, NY 10017-1538, USA

Williams, Maurice (Musician)
Willis Blume Agency, The
PO Box 509
Orangeburg, SC 29116-0509, USA

Williams, Merriwether (Producer)
c/o Bruce Gellman *Felker, Toczek,
Gellman, Suddleson*
10880 Wilshire Blvd Ste 2070
Los Angeles, CA 90024-4118, USA

Williams, Michael (Athlete, Basketball
Player)
1005 Lakeridge Ct
Colleyville, TX 76034-2825, USA

Williams, Michael D (Mike) (Athlete,
Baseball Player)
302 Horseshoe Farm Rd
Pembroke, VA 24136-3478, USA

Williams, Michael K (Actor)
c/o Matt Goldman *Silver Lining
Entertainment*
421 S Beverly Dr Fl 7
Beverly Hills, CA 90212-4408, USA

Williams, Micheal (Basketball Player)
1415 Reynoldston Ln
Dallas, TX 75232-2411, USA

Williams, Michelle (Actor)
275 Conover St Apt 3A
Brooklyn, NY 11231-1036, USA

Williams, Michelle (Musician)
3035 London Dr
Olympia Fields, IL 60461-1858, USA

Williams, Mike (Athlete, Football Player)
c/o Hadley Engelhard *Enter-Sports
Management*
5 Concourse Pkwy Ste 3000
Atlanta, GA 30328-7106, USA

Williams, Mike (Athlete, Football Player)
c/o Mitchell Frankel *Impact Sports - Boca
Raton*
2799 NW 2nd Ave Ste 203
Boca Raton, FL 33431-6709, USA

Williams, Mikell (Athlete, Football Player)
222 W Edwards St
Covington, LA 70433-1626, USA

Williams, Mitch (Athlete, Baseball Player)
67 Highbridge Blvd
Medford, NJ 08055-3341, USA

Williams, Montel (Actor, Producer, Talk
Show Host)
c/o Staff Member *Montel Media Group*
331 W 57th St Ste 233
New York, NY 10019-3101, USA

Williams, Natalie (Basketball Player)
Indiana Fever
125 S Pennsylvania St
Conseco Fieldhouse
Indianapolis, IN 46204-3610, USA

Williams, Natashia (Actor)
c/o Teresa Valente *Beverly Hecht Agency*
6320 Canoga Ave Fl 15
Woodland Hills, CA 91367-2563, USA

Williams, Nate (Athlete, Basketball Player)
132 Stanmore Cir
Vallejo, CA 94591-6859, USA

Williams, Nicholas (Trinidad James)
(Musician)
c/o Joshua Dick *The Agency Group (NYC)*
142 W 57th St Fl 6
New York, NY 10019-3300, USA

Williams, Nick (Athlete, Football Player)
21760 Parklane St
Farmington Hills, MI 48335-4221, USA

Williams, O L (Religious Leader)
United Free Will Baptist Church
1101 University St
Kinston, NC 28501, USA

Williams, Oliver (Athlete, Football Player)
622 W 121st St
Los Angeles, CA 90044-3911, USA

Williams, Olivia (Actor)
c/o Risa Shapiro *The Schiff Company*
9220 W Sunset Blvd Ste 106
West Hollywood, CA 90069-3500, USA

Williams, Parker (Adult Film Star)
c/o Staff Member *Diva Central Inc*
7510 W Sunset Blvd Ste 1445
Los Angeles, CA 90046-3408, USA

Williams, Pat (Football Player)
DVA Brand Communications
1968 W Adams Blvd Ste 205
C/O Danielle Gibbs
Los Angeles, CA 90018-3515, USA

Williams, Patrick (Musician)
3156 Mandeville Canyon Rd
Los Angeles, CA 90049-1014, USA

Williams, Paul H (Actor)
c/o Chris Fenton *DMG Entertainment*
3431 Wesley St Ste E
Culver City, CA 90232-2365, USA

Williams, Perry (Athlete, Football Player)
273 Old Laurinburg Rd
Hamlet, NC 28345-8069, USA

Williams, Perry (Athlete, Football Player)
480 Canyon Oaks Dr Apt A
Oakland, CA 94605-3858, USA

Williams, Pete (Writer)
c/o Chris Fenton *DMG Entertainment*
3431 Wesley St Ste E
Culver City, CA 90232-2365, USA

Williams, Pharrell (Actor, Composer)
c/o Amanda Silverman *42West (NYC)*
220 W 42nd St Fl 12
New York, NY 10036-7200, USA

Williams, Phillip L (Publisher)
Los Angeles Times
202 W 1st St Ste 500
Editorial Dept
Los Angeles, CA 90012-4401, USA

Williams, Prince Charles (Boxer)
Boxing Ministry
3675 Polley Dr
Youngstown, OH 44515-3349, USA

Williams, Randy (Athlete, Baseball Player)
11410 Fm 586 S
Brookesmith, TX 76827-4010, USA

Williams, Randy (Athlete, Track Athlete)
5655 N Marty Ave Apt 204
Fresno, CA 93711-1575, USA

Williams, Reggie (Athlete, Baseball Player)
8855 Lake Edge Cv W
Cordova, TN 38016-4603, USA

Williams, Reggie (Athlete, Baseball Player)
920 E Estates Blvd Apt E
Charleston, SC 29414-5455, USA

Williams, Reggie (Athlete, Basketball Player)
2016 Callaway St
Temple Hills, MD 20748-4354, USA

Williams, Reginald (Reggie) (Athlete, Football Player)
503 Jennifer Ln
Windermere, FL 34786-8400, USA

Williams, Reuben (Baseball Player)
Chicago American Giants
PO Box 3982
Winter Haven, FL 33885-3982, USA

Williams, Rick (Athlete, Baseball Player, Coach)
1217 Wessmith Way
Madera, CA 93638-1854, USA

Williams, Ricky (Athlete, Football Player)
c/o Drew Rosenhaus *Rosenhaus Sports Representation*
6400 Allison Rd
Miami Beach, FL 33141-4540, USA

Williams, R J
1505 10th St
Santa Monica, CA 90401-2805, USA

Williams, Robbie (Musician)
3312 Clerendon Rd
Beverly Hills, CA 90210-1068, USA

Williams, Robert (Baseball Player)
Newark Eagles
6233 Delancey St
Philadelphia, PA 19143-1019, USA

Williams, Robert A (Athlete, Football Player)
602 Stone Barn Rd
Towson, MD 21286-1418, USA

Williams, Robert C (Athlete, Football Player)
347 Walnut Grove Ln
Coppell, TX 75019-5342, USA

Williams, Robert J (Ben) (Athlete, Football Player)
5961 Huntview Dr
Jackson, MS 39206-2128, USA

Williams, Robert (Meek Mill) (Musician)
c/o Staff Member *Warner Bros Records (LA)*
PO Box 6868
Burbank, CA 91510-6868, USA

Williams, Rodney (Athlete, Football Player)
44520 15th St E Unit 3
Lancaster, CA 93535-6321, USA

Williams, Roland (Athlete, Football Player)
6209 Mid Rivers Mall Dr
Saint Charles, MO 63304-1102, USA

Williams, Rosel (Athlete, Baseball Player)
Birmingham Black Barons
PO Box 442
Ninety Six, SC 29666-0442, USA

Williams, Roshumba (Model)
c/o Gail Parenteau *Parenteau Guidance*
132 E 35th St # 3J
New York, NY 10016-3892, USA

Williams, Roy (Athlete, Football Player)
1 Cowboys Pkwy
Irving, TX 75063-4924, USA

Williams, Sam (Athlete, Football Player)
33078 Hampshire Rd
Livonia, MI 48154-2953, USA

Williams, Sam (Athlete, Basketball Player)
9751 W Teresa Ln
Milwaukee, WI 53224-4651, USA

Williams, Samuel (Athlete, Basketball Player)
6116 S Verdun Ave
Los Angeles, CA 90043-3632, USA

Williams, Scott (Basketball Player)
Phoenix Suns
3405 N Valencia Ln
Phoenix, AZ 85018-6162, USA

Williams, Scott (Athlete, Football Player)
284 Heathrow Dr
Riverdale, GA 30274-2729, USA

Williams, Sean
4399 Whitmore Ln
Fairfield, OH 45014-8553, USA

Williams, Serena (Athlete, Olympic Athlete, Tennis Player)
1201 Stone Canyon Rd
Los Angeles, CA 90077-2919, USA

Williams, Shad (Athlete, Baseball Player)
4682 E Cornell Ave
Fresno, CA 93703-1607, USA

Williams, Shammond (Athlete, Basketball Player)
3809 Nashville Ave
New Orleans, LA 70125-4345, USA

Williams, Shaun (Athlete, Football Player)
11738 Gruen St
Sylmar, CA 91342-6117, USA

Williams, Shawn (Athlete, Football Player)
c/o Anthony J. Agnone *Eastern Athletic Services*
11350 McCormick Rd
Suite 800 - Executive Plaza
Hunt Valley, MD 21031-1002, USA

Williams, Shawne (Athlete, Basketball Player)
c/o Travis King *Relativity Sports (LA)*
9242 Beverly Blvd Ste 300
Beverly Hills, CA 90210-3728, USA

Williams, Sherman (Athlete, Football Player)
119 Patricia Ave
Mobile, AL 36610-2114, USA

Williams, Sidney (Athlete, Football Player)
1044 W 82nd St
Los Angeles, CA 90044-3518, USA

Williams, Stanley W (Stan) (Athlete, Baseball Player)
4702 Hayter Ave
Lakewood, CA 90712-3509, USA

Williams, Stepfret (Athlete, Football Player)
913 S Talton St
Minden, LA 71055-5448, USA

Williams, Stephanie E (Actor)
S M S Talent
8383 Wilshire Blvd Ste 230
Beverly Hills, CA 90211-2436, USA

Williams, Steven (Actor)
Geddes Agency
1203 Greenacre Ave
West Hollywood, CA 90046-5707, USA

Williams, Sun ita L Cdr (Astronaut)
1522 Festival Dr
Houston, TX 77062-4526, USA

Williams, Sylvester (Athlete, Football Player)
c/o Todd France *Five Star Athlete Management*
3500 Lenox Rd NE
Atlanta, GA 30326-4228, USA

Williams, Tamika (Basketball Player)
Minnesota Lunx
600 1st Ave N
Target Center
Minneapolis, MN 55403-1400, USA

Williams, Tank (Athlete, Football Player)
c/o Staff Member *New England Patriots*
1 Patriot Pl
Foxboro, MA 02035-1388, USA

Williams, Tavares (Monty) (Athlete, Basketball Coach, Basketball Player, Coach)
c/o Steve Kauffman *Kauffman Sports Management Group*
Prefers to be contacted by telephone
Malibu, CA, USA

Williams, Terrance (Athlete, Football Player)
c/o W Vann McElroy *Select Sports Group*
2700 Post Oak Blvd Ste 1450
Houston, TX 77056-5785, USA

Williams, Terry Tempest
Brandt & Brandt Literary Agency
1501 Broadway Ste 2310
New York, NY 10036-5689

Williams, Todd (Actor)
c/o Steve Caserta *Sanders Armstrong Caserta*
2120 Colorado Ave Ste 120
Santa Monica, CA 90404-3561, USA

Williams, Todd (Athlete, Baseball Player)
16707 Whispering Glen Dr
Lutz, FL 33558-4960, USA

Williams, Tony (Athlete, Football Player)
3966 Evans Ct
Yorkville, IL 60560-5102, USA

Williams, Tonya Lee (Actor)
Artists Agency
1180 S Beverly Dr Ste 301
Los Angeles, CA 90035-1154, USA

Williams, Treat (Actor)
589 North Rd
Manchester Center, VT 05255-9336, USA

Williams, Trent (Athlete, Football Player)
c/o Eugene Parker *Maximum Sports Management*
6435 W Jefferson Blvd # 197
Fort Wayne, IN 46804-6203, USA

Williams, Tyler James (Actor)
c/o Staff Member *Osbrink Talent Agency*
4343 Lankershim Blvd Ste 100
North Hollywood, CA 91602-2705, USA

Williams, Tyrone (Athlete, Football Player)
9516 Valley Ranch Pkwy E Apt 1024
Irving, TX 75063-7851, USA

Williams, Ulis (Athlete, Track Athlete)
2511 29th St
Santa Monica, CA 90405-2913, USA

Williams, Van (Athlete, Football Player)
1804 Parkwood Ln Apt 26
Johnson City, TN 37604-7784, USA

Williams, Van (Actor)
Pierce & Shelly
117/121 Aspen Lakes Dr
Hailey, ID 08333, USA

Williams, Vanessa (Actor, Musician)
150 Old Farm Rd N
Chappaqua, NY 10514-3706, USA

Williams, Venus (Athlete, Olympic Athlete, Tennis Player)
c/o Lisa Sorensen *LSPR*
116 W 23rd St Fl 5
New York, NY 10011-2599, USA

Williams, Victoria (Musician, Songwriter, Writer)
PO Box 342
Joshua Tree, CA 92252-0342, USA

Williams, Virginia (Actor)
c/o Lisa Blum *723 Productions*
8569 Holloway Dr Apt 1
West Hollywood, CA 90069-6918, USA

Williams, Wade (Actor)
5445 Buffalo Ave
Sherman Oaks, CA 91401-5224, USA

Williams, Walt (Athlete, Basketball Player)
3240 Beaumont St
Temple Hills, MD 20748-4541, USA

Williams, Walt (Athlete, Baseball Player)
2417 Monterey St
Brownwood, TX 76801, USA

Williams, Walter (Athlete, Baseball Player)
Newark Eagles
15700 Good Hope Rd
Silver Spring, MD 20905-4034, USA

Williams, Walter (Musician)
Associated Booking Corp
1995 Broadway # 501
New York, NY 10023-5882, USA

Williams, Warren Milton (Butch) (Athlete, Hockey Player)
518 N 15th Ave E
Duluth, MN 55812-1237, USA

Williams, W Clyde (Religious Leader)
Christian Methodist Episcopal Church
4466 Elvis Presley Blvd
Memphis, TN 38116-7180, USA

Williams, Wendy (Radio Personality, Talk Show Host)
The Wendy Williams Show
221 W 26th St
New York, NY 10001-6703, USA

Williams, Wendy Lian (Swimmer)
Advantage International
1025 Thomas Jefferson St NW # 450
Washington, DC 20007-5201, USA

Williams, William A (Astronaut)
Environmental Protection Agency
200 SW 35th St
Corvallis, OR 97333-4902, USA

Williams, Willie (Athlete, Football Player)
1402 Forest Edge Ct
Wexford, PA 15090-9598, USA

Williams, Willie (Athlete, Football Player)
4928 Country Club Dr
Mesquite, TX 75150-1169, USA

Williams, Willie (Baseball Player)
Newark Eagles
2729 20th St
Sarasota, FL 34234-7807, USA

Williams, Woody (Athlete, Baseball Player)
5110 Newpoint Dr
Fresno, TX 77545-9212, USA

Williams, Zelda (Actor)
2330 Bronson Hill Dr
Los Angeles, CA 90068-2410, USA

Williams & Ree
PO Box 163
Hendersonville, TN 37077-0163

Williams Brothers (Music Group, Musician)
c/o Staff Member *M.A.G./Universal Attractions*
15 W 36th St Fl 8
New York, NY 10018-7927, USA

Williams III, Clarance (Actor)
c/o Staff Member *Abrams Artists Agency (LA)*
9200 W Sunset Blvd PH 11
West Hollywood, CA 90069-3601, USA

Williams III, James (Fly) (Actor)
c/o Margaret Matuka *Schuller Talent Agency*
276 5th Ave Rm 206
New York, NY 10001-4509, USA

Williams III, Shelton Hank (Musician)
c/o Mitch Schneider *Mitch Schneider Organization (MSO)*
14724 Ventura Blvd Ste 410
Sherman Oaks, CA 91403-3537, USA

Williams Jr, Hank (Actor, Musician, Songwriter)
PO Box 40929
Nashville, TN 37204-0929, USA

Williams Jr, Walter Ray (Bowler)
303 SE 17th St # 309-171
Ocala, FL 34471-4421, USA

Williams Jr, Warren (Athlete, Football Player)
1935 Pauldo St
Fort Myers, FL 33916-4122, USA

Williamson, Antone (Athlete, Baseball Player)
6322 W Kent Dr
Chandler, AZ 85226-1172, USA

Williamson, Corliss (Basketball Player)
c/o Staff Member *Sacramento Kings*
1 Sports Pkwy
Sacramento, CA 95834-2301

Williamson, Cris (Musician)
Bird Ankles Music
PO Box 30067
Seattle, WA 98113-2067, USA

Williamson, Fred (Actor, Athlete, Football Player)
c/o Stephany Hurkos *Stephany Hurkos Management*
11935 Kling St
Valley Village, CA 91607-4072, USA

Williamson, Jay (Athlete, Golfer)
24 Clermont Ln
Saint Louis, MO 63124-1346, USA

Williamson, Joanne S (Writer)
c/o Staff Member *Bethlehem Books*
10194 Garfield St S
Bathgate, ND 58216-4031, USA

Williamson, Kerry (Writer)
c/o Staff Member *Gersh (LA)*
9465 Wilshire Blvd Ste 600
Beverly Hills, CA 90212-2605, USA

Williamson, Kevin (Director, Producer, Writer)
652 N Laurel Ave
Los Angeles, CA 90048-2321, USA

Williamson, Marianne (Radio Personality, Writer)
PO Box 2428
Nipomo, CA 93444-2428, USA

Williamson, Mark (Athlete, Baseball Player)
1260 Hidden Mountain Dr
El Cajon, CA 92019-3639, USA

Williamson, Michael (Journalist)
Washington Post
1945 Westchester Dr
Silver Spring, MD 20902-3564, USA

Williamson, Mykelti (Actor)
c/o Jim Hess *Silver Lining Entertainment*
421 S Beverly Dr Fl 7
Beverly Hills, CA 90212-4408, USA

Williamson, Richard (Athlete, Football Coach, Football Player)
5137 Morrowick Rd
Charlotte, NC 28226-7365, USA

Williamson, Scott (Athlete, Baseball Player)
2623 Foran Dr
Cincinnati, OH 45238-2164, USA

Williams-Paisley, Kimberly (Actor, Producer)
15309 Earlham St
Pacific Palisades, CA 90272-4344, USA

Willie, Reid
2690 Hunters Point Dr
Wexford, PA 15090-7991, USA

Williford, Duncan (Athlete, Basketball Player)
3703 Westfield St
High Point, NC 27265-2113, USA

Williford, Vann (Athlete, Basketball Player)
4455 Fair Oaks Ln
High Point, NC 27265-8705, USA

Willig, Matt (Athlete, Football Player)
22040 Saticoy St
Canoga Park, CA 91303-1132, USA

Willingham, Josh (Athlete, Baseball Player)
108 Cascade Dr
Florence, AL 35633-7621, USA

Willingham, Larry (Athlete, Football Player)
226 W 8th Ave
Gulf Shores, AL 36542-5902, USA

Willingham, Tyrone (Coach, Football Coach)
University of Washington
Athletic Dept
Seattle, WA 98195-0001, USA

Willis, Bruce (Actor)
PO Box 21084
New York, NY 10025-0017, USA

Willis, Carl (Athlete, Baseball Player)
6811 Lipscomb Dr
Durham, NC 27712-9292, USA

Willis, Connie (Writer)
c/o Staff Member *Random House Publicity*
1745 Broadway Frnt 3
New York, NY 10019-4343, USA

Willis, Dale (Athlete, Baseball Player)
3415 Hayes Bayou Dr
Ruskin, FL 33570-6157, USA

Willis, Dave (Writer)
c/o Staff Member *William Morris Endeavor (LA)*
9601 Wilshire Blvd
Beverly Hills, CA 90210-5213, USA

Willis, Dontrelle (Athlete, Baseball Player)
9820 E Thompson Peak Pkwy Unit 726
Scottsdale, AZ 85255, USA

Willis, Fred (Athlete, Football Player)
31 Blithewood Ave Apt 601
Worcester, MA 01604-3558, USA

Willis, Garrett (Athlete, Golfer)
628 Mountain Pass Ln
Knoxville, TN 37923-5725, USA

Willis, Jim (Athlete, Baseball Player)
PO Box 35
Boyce, LA 71409-0035, USA

Willis, Keith (Athlete, Football Player)
116 Coffeeberry Ct
Garner, NC 27529-5934, USA

Willis, Kelly (Musician)
c/o Staff Member *Davis McLarty Agency*
4609 Eagle Feather Dr
Austin, TX 78735-6474, USA

Willis, Kevin A (Athlete, Basketball Player)
1481 Jones Rd
Roswell, GA 30075-2723, USA

Willis, Mark (Musician)
c/o Staff Member *William Morris Endeavor (Nashville)*
1600 Division St Ste 300
Nashville, TN 37203-2755, USA

Willis, Mike (Athlete, Baseball Player)
6234 Taggart St
Houston, TX 77007-2051, USA

Willis, Mitch (Athlete, Football Player)
1398 Fairhaven Dr
Mansfield, TX 76063-3765, USA

Willis, Nadine (Model)
c/o Staff Member *New York Model Management*
596 Broadway # 701
New York, NY 10012-3396, USA

Willis, Patrick (Athlete, Football Player)
c/o Denise White *EAG Sports Management*
909 N Sepulveda Blvd Ste 360
El Segundo, CA 90245-3864, USA

Willis, Pete (Musician)
Q Prime Mgmt
729 7th Ave Ste 1400
New York, NY 10019-6889, USA

Willis, Peter Tom (Athlete, Football Player)
PO Box 237
Morris, AL 35116-0237, USA

Willis, Rumer (Actor)
8052 Woodrow Wilson Dr
Los Angeles, CA 90046-1117, USA

Willison, Mike (Musician)
Metropolitan Entertainment Group
2 Penn Plz # 2600
New York, NY 10121-0101, USA

Willman, David (Journalist)
Los Angeles Times
202 W 1st St Ste 500
Editorial Dept
Los Angeles, CA 90012-4401, USA

Willman, Justin (Actor, Magician)
c/o Nicole Chabot *Re: Group*
815 Broadway St Ste 2
Venice, CA 90291-3407, USA

Willmon, Trent (Musician)
Hallmark Direction Company
713 18th Ave S
C/O Shelia Shipley Biddy
Nashville, TN 37203-3214, USA

Willoughby, Bill (Basketball Player)
350 W Englewood Ave
Englewood, NJ 07631-3239, USA

Willoughby, Jim (Athlete, Baseball Player)
PO Box 707
Eufaula, OK 74432-0707, USA

Wills, Dave (Sportscaster)
PO Box 4057
Eatonton, GA 31024-4057, U S A

Wills, Elliott (Bump) (Athlete, Baseball Player)
1124 S Robinhood St
Spokane Valley, WA 99206-6951, USA

Wills, Maurice M (Maury) (Athlete, Baseball Player, Coach)
M & R Sports Marketing
5 Dalton Valley Dr
Saint Peters, MO 63376-7720, USA

Wills, Rick (Musician)
Hard to Handle Mgmt
16501 Ventura Blvd Ste 602
Encino, CA 91436-2072, USA

Wills, Ted (Athlete, Baseball Player)
5545 N El Adobe Dr
Fresno, CA 93711-2373, USA

Will to Power (Music Group)
c/o Staff Member *Diva Central Inc*
7510 W Sunset Blvd Ste 1445
Los Angeles, CA 90046-3408, USA

Wilmes, Gary (Actor)
c/o Ruthanne Secunda *ICM Partners (LA)*
10250 Constellation Blvd Fl 7
Los Angeles, CA 90067-6207, USA

Wilmet, Paul (Athlete, Baseball Player)
PO Box 330074
Nashville, TN 37203-7500, USA

Wilmore, Barry E (Astronaut)
3002 Bryant Ln
Webster, TX 77598-6011, USA

Wilmore, Barry E Cdr (Astronaut)
3002 Bryant Ln
Webster, TX 77598-6011, USA

Wilmore, Larry (Actor, Producer)
c/o David Miner *3 Arts Entertainment (LA)*
9460 Wilshire Blvd Fl 7
Beverly Hills, CA 90212-2713, USA

Wilmsmeyer, Klaus (Athlete, Football Player)
1509 Bellingham Ct
Louisville, KY 40245-4488, USA

Wilpon, Fred (Baseball Player)
New York Mets
100 Sheep Ln
Locust Valley, NY 11560-1115, USA

Wilson, Adrian (Athlete, Football Player)
c/o Eugene Parker *Maximum Sports Management*
6435 W Jefferson Blvd # 197
Fort Wayne, IN 46804-6203, USA

Wilson, Al (Athlete, Football Player)
3445 Stratford Rd NE Apt 3901
Atlanta, GA 30326-1728, USA

Wilson, Alexandra (Actor)
c/o Staff Member *GVA Talent Agency Inc*
8981 W Sunset Blvd Ste 101
West Hollywood, CA 90069-1850, USA

Wilson, Ann (Actor, Musician)
1915 Interlaken Dr E
Seattle, WA 98112-3431, USA

Wilson, Behn (Athlete, Hockey Player)
955 Bolender Dr
Delray Beach, FL 33483-4970, USA

Wilson, Ben (Athlete, Football Player)
3230 W Little York Rd Apt 3311
Houston, TX 77091-1566, USA

Wilson, Bill (Athlete, Baseball Player)
132 Wickenby Ct
Roseville, CA 95661-4044, USA

Wilson, Blaine (Athlete, Gymnast, Olympic Athlete)
7441 Murrayfield Dr
Columbus, OH 43085-1739, USA

Wilson, Bob (Athlete, Baseball Player)
111 W Monroe St Ste 1000
Chicago, IL 60603-4098, USA

Wilson, Brian (Athlete, Baseball Player)
741 S Banning Cir
Mesa, AZ 85206-4104, USA

Wilson, Brian (Athlete, Basketball Player)
1201 Hummingbird Hill Rd
Chapel Hill, NC 27517-7791, USA

Wilson, Brian (Musician, Songwriter)
3320 Clerendon Rd
Beverly Hills, CA 90210-1059, USA

Wilson, Brian Anthony (Actor)
Bernard Liebhaber
352 7th Ave Rm 301
New York, NY 10001-5012, USA

Wilson, Carnie (Musician)
c/o Terry Anzaldo *Good Guy Entertainment*
3733 Oakfield Dr
Sherman Oaks, CA 91423-4430, USA

Wilson, Casey (Actor)
c/o Staff Member *Odenkirk Provissiero Entertainment*
1936 N Bronson Ave
Raleigh Studios
Los Angeles, CA 90068-5602, USA

Wilson, Cassandra (Musician)
Dream Street Mgmt
4346 Redwood Ave Unit 307
Marina Del Rey, CA 90292-6495, USA

Wilson, Chandra (Actor)
1720 Rogers Pl Unit 16E
Burbank, CA 91504-3666, USA

Wilson, Charles (Athlete, Football Player)
5444 Calder Dr
Tallahassee, FL 32317-1429, USA

Wilson, Charlie (Uncle Charlie) (Musician)
c/o Carlos Keyes *Red Entertainment Agency*
505 8th Ave Rm 1004
New York, NY 10018-6529, USA

Wilson, Cherilyn (Actor)
c/o Jon Simmons *Simmons & Scott Entertainment*
7942 Mulholland Dr
Los Angeles, CA 90046-1225, USA

Wilson, Chris (Musician)
c/o Staff Member *Fein Music*
81 Pondfield Rd
Bronxville, NY 10708-3818, USA

Wilson, Cindy (Musician)
5343 Vernon Lake Dr
Atlanta, GA 30338-3526, USA

Wilson, Craig (Athlete, Baseball Player)
461 S Brent St
Ventura, CA 93003-4706, USA

Wilson, Dan (Musician, Songwriter, Writer)
Monterey Peninsula Artists
509 Hartnell St
Monterey, CA 93940-2825, USA

Wilson, Daniel A (Dan) (Athlete, Baseball Player)
2161 E Interlaken Blvd
Seattle, WA 98112-3432, USA

Wilson, Daniel H (Writer)
c/o Linda Chester *Linda Chester Literary Agency*
630 5th Ave # 2036
Rockefeller Center
New York, NY 10111-0100, USA

Wilson, Dave (Athlete, Football Player)
2120 Radnor Ave
Long Beach, CA 90815-3253, USA

Wilson, Dean (Athlete, Golfer)
12488 Carmel Cpe
San Diego, CA 92130-2252, USA

Wilson, De'Angelo (Actor)
c/o Staff Member *Overbrook Entertainment*
10202 Washington Blvd
Culver City, CA 90232-3119, USA

Wilson, Debra (Actor)
c/o Joan Rosenberg *Joan Rosenberg & Assoc Ltd*
3 Adams St
Floral Park, NY 11001-2809, USA

Wilson, Desi (Athlete, Baseball Player)
8 Janet Ln
Glen Cove, NY 11542-2809, USA

Wilson, Desire (Race Car Driver)
4197 Serenade Rd
Castle Rock, CO 80104-7716, USA

Wilson, Don The Dragon
178 S Victory Blvd Ste 205
Burbank, CA 91502-2881

Wilson, Dorien (Actor)
c/o Susie Tobin *Peter Strain & Associates Inc (LA)*
5455 Wilshire Blvd Ste 1812
Los Angeles, CA 90036-4268, USA

Wilson, Doug (Athlete, Hockey Player)
San Jose Sharks
525 W Santa Clara St
Attn: General Manager
San Jose, CA 95113-1500, USA

Wilson, Doug (Athlete, Hockey Player)
5620 Country Club Pkwy
San Jose, CA 95138-2220, USA

Wilson, Duane (Athlete, Baseball Player)
1945 N Porter Ave Apt A54
Wichita, KS 67203-2293, USA

Wilson, Earl (Athlete, Football Player)
122 W Reading Ave
Pleasantville, NJ 08232-1317, USA

Wilson, Earle L (Religious Leader)
Wesleyan Church
PO Box 50434
Indianapolis, IN 46250-0434, USA

Wilson, Edward O (Writer)
Harvard University
Department of Organismic and Evolutionary Biology
Cambridge, MA 02138, USA

Wilson, Elizabeth (Actor)
c/o Staff Member *Paradigm (NY)*
360 Park Ave S Fl 16
New York, NY 10010-1716, USA

Wilson, F Paul (Writer)
1933 State Route 35 Ste 337
Wall Township, NJ 07719-3502, USA

Wilson, Frank (Race Car Driver)
North Carlonia Motor Speedway
PO Box 500
Rockingham, NC 28380, USA

Wilson, Gahan (Cartoonist)
New Yorker Magazine
PO Box 1558
Sag Harbor, NY 11963-0057, USA

Wilson, Gale (Race Car Driver)
203 Nortbmont Dr
Statesville, NC 28625, USA

Wilson, Gary (Athlete, Baseball Player)
713 Ouachita 64
Camden, AR 71701-9616, USA

Wilson, Gary (Athlete, Baseball Player)
327 40th St
Sacramento, CA 95819-2027, USA

Wilson, George (Athlete, Basketball Player, Olympic Athlete)
151 Twin Lakes Dr
Fairfield, OH 45014-5257, USA

Wilson, Glenn (Athlete, Baseball Player)
300 Tara Park
Conroe, TX 77302-3756, USA

Wilson, Gretchen (Musician)
c/o Dale Morris *Morris Artists Management*
818 19th Ave S
Nashville, TN 37203-3202, USA

Wilson, Harry (Athlete, Football Player)
2600 N Lawrence St Apt 307
Philadelphia, PA 19133-3140, USA

Wilson, Harry C (Religious Leader)
Wesleyan Church Int'l Center
6060 Castleway West Dr
Indianapolis, IN 46250-1906, USA

Wilson, Hugh (Director, Producer, Writer)
c/o Staff Member *ICM Partners (LA)*
10250 Constellation Blvd Fl 7
Los Angeles, CA 90067-6207, USA

Wilson, Jack (Athlete, Baseball Player)
365 E Avenida De Los Arboles
Thousand Oaks, CA 91360-2975, USA

Wilson, James (Athlete, Football Player)
463 NW Baughn St
Lake City, FL 32055-5814, USA

Wilson, J C (Athlete, Football Player)
4785 Young Rd
Waldorf, MD 20601-4483, USA

Wilson, J C (Athlete, Football Player)
13410 Buchanan Dr
Fort Washington, MD 20744-2931, USA

Wilson, Jean D (Doctor)
Texas Southwestern Medical Center
5323 Harry Hines Blvd # Y8322
Dallas, TX 75390-7208, USA

Wilson, Jeannie (Actor)
General Delivery
Ketchum, ID 83340-9999, USA

Wilson, Jennifer
1947 Lake Shore Dr
Branson, MO 65616-9476

Wilson, Jerry (Athlete, Football Player)
4272 Ironwood Ct
Weston, FL 33331-3827, USA

Wilson, Jerry (Athlete, Football Player)
2117 Mountain View Dr
Vestavia, AL 35216-2023, USA

Wilson, Jim (Athlete, Baseball Player)
8112 NW Bacon Rd
Vancouver, WA 98665-6634, USA

Wilson, Jimmy (Athlete, Football Player)
c/o Drew Rosenhaus *Rosenhaus Sports Representation*
6400 Allison Rd
Miami Beach, FL 33141-4540, USA

Wilson, Joe (Athlete, Football Player)
135 Ridge Rd
Phoenixville, PA 19460-1531, USA

Wilson, Joe (Congressman, Politician)
2229 Rayburn Hob
Washington, DC 20515-2105, USA

Wilson, Josh (Athlete, Baseball Player)
2304 Cramden Rd
Pittsburgh, PA 15241-2438, USA

Wilson, J Tylee (Business Person)
PO Box 2057
Ponte Vedra Beach, FL 32004-2057, USA

Wilson, Julie (Actor, Musician)
415 W 55th St
New York, NY 10019-4435, USA

Wilson, Justin (Musician)
David Levin Mgmt
200 W 57th St Ste 308
New York, NY 10019-3211, USA

Wilson, Kim (Musician)
Ricci Assoc
15260 Ventura Blvd Ste 2100
Sherman Oaks, CA 91403-5360, USA

Wilson, Kris (Athlete, Baseball Player)
PO Box 15
Chillicothe, MO 64601-0015, USA

Wilson, Kristen (Actor)
c/o Norman Aladjem *Levity Entertainment Group (LEG)*
6701 Center Dr W Fl 11
Los Angeles, CA 90045-1535, USA

Wilson, Lambert (Actor)
c/o Estelle Lasher *Lasher Group*
1133 Avenue Of The Americas Ste 1621
New York, NY 10036-6710, USA

Wilson, Landon (Athlete, Hockey Player)
127 Tennyson Pl
Coppell, TX 75019-5364

Wilson, Lawrence F (Larry) (Athlete, Football Player)
11834 N Blackheath Rd
Scottsdale, AZ 85254-4809, USA

Wilson, Luke (Actor)
615 San Lorenzo St
Santa Monica, CA 90402-1321, USA

Wilson, Mara (Actor)
c/o Bonnie Liedtke *Principato/Young Management (LA)*
9465 Wilshire Blvd Ste 900
Beverly Hills, CA 90212-2608, USA

Wilson, Marc (Athlete, Football Player)
18020 157th Ave NE
Woodinville, WA 98072-9238, USA

Wilson, Marc D (Athlete, Football Player)
113113 Mount Wallace Ct
Rancho Cucamonga, CA 91737, USA

Wilson, Marie
6 Oakdale
Irvine, CA 92604-3221

Wilson, Mark (Athlete, Golfer)
N41W27751 Ishnala Trl
Pewaukee, WI 53072-2140, USA

Wilson, Mary (Musician)
21 Hassayampa Trl
Henderson, NV 89052-6668, USA

Wilson, Melanie (Actor)
Irv Schechter
9300 Wilshire Blvd Ste 410
Beverly Hills, CA 90212-3228, USA

Wilson, Michael G (Producer)
c/o Staff Member *Danjaq*
2400 Colorado Ave
Suite 310
Santa Monica, CA 90404, USA

Wilson, Michael (Tack) (Athlete, Baseball Player)
768 Forest St Aot 6
Roswell, GA 30075, USA

Wilson, Mike (Athlete, Hockey Player)
4647 Lake Charles Dr
Independence, OH 44131-6062, USA

Wilson, Mike D (Athlete, Football Player)
1967 Litchfield Ave
Dayton, OH 45406-3811, USA

Wilson, Mike R (Athlete, Football Player)
2908 N Poinsettia Ave
Manhattan Beach, CA 90266-2405, USA

wilson, Mitch (Athlete, Hockey Player)
PO Box 343
Brinnon, WA 98320-0343, USA

Wilson, Mookie (Athlete, Baseball Player)
1111 Heyward Wilson Rd
Eastover, SC 29044-9627, USA

Wilson, Nancy (Actor, Composer, Musician)
7618 238th St SE
Woodinville, WA 98072-9527, USA

Wilson, Neal C (Religious Leader)
Seventh-Day Adventists
12501 Old Columbia Pike
Silver Spring, MD 20904-6600, USA

Wilson, Neil (Athlete, Baseball Player)
4300 Highway 412 W
Lexington, TN 38351-5423, USA

Wilson, Nemiah (Athlete, Football Player)
11000 E Idaho Pl
Aurora, CO 80012-4118, USA

Wilson, Othell (Athlete, Basketball Player)
3413 Caledonia Cir
Woodbridge, VA 22192-1069, USA

Wilson, Otis (Athlete, Football Player)
7B W 15th St
Chicago, IL 60605-2723, USA

Wilson, Owen (Actor)
947 23rd St
Santa Monica, CA 90403-2103, USA

Wilson, Patrick (Actor, Musician)
23447 Continental Dr
Canyon Lake, CA 92587-7750, USA

Wilson, Paul (Athlete, Baseball Player)
949 Lenmore Ct
Orlando, FL 32812-1980, USA

Wilson, Peta (Actor)
c/o James Moore *Full Moon & High Tide Productions*
6201 Sunset Blvd # 149
Los Angeles, CA 90028

Wilson, Preston (Athlete, Baseball Player)
136 Paloma Dr
Coral Gables, FL 33143-6545, USA

Wilson, Rainn (Actor)
5683 Colodny Dr
Agoura Hills, CA 91301-2217, USA

Wilson, Rebel (Actor)
c/o Stephanie Ritz *William Morris Endeavor (LA)*
9601 Wilshire Blvd
Beverly Hills, CA 90210-5213, USA

Wilson, Red (Athlete, Baseball Player)
8301 Old Sauk Rd Apt 201
Middleton, WI 53562-4392, USA

Wilson, Reinard (Athlete, Football Player)
2595 NW 49th Ave Apt 108
Lauderdale Lakes, FL 33313-3354, USA

Wilson, Rick (Athlete, Basketball Player)
535 E Ormsby Ave
Louisville, KY 40203-2620, USA

Wilson, Rick (Athlete, Coach, Hockey Player)
1624 Reno Run
Lewisville, TX 75077-7522, USA

Wilson, Rick (Race Car Driver)
PO Box 304
Mulberry, FL 33860-0304, USA

Wilson, Ricky (Athlete, Basketball Player)
3014 NW Chapin Dr
Portland, OR 97229-8070, USA

Wilson, Rik (Athlete, Hockey Player)
345 Lakewood Dr
Ballwin, MO 63011-2410, USA

Wilson, Rita (Actor)
c/o Heidi Schaeffer *PMK/BNC Public Relations (PMK-LA)*
8687 Melrose Ave Ste 8
West Hollywood, CA 90069-5746, USA

Wilson, Robert Charles (Writer)
Tom Doherty Associates, LLC
175 5th Ave
New York, NY 10010-7703, USA

Wilson, Robert E (Bobby) (Athlete, Football Player)
1034 Liberty Park Dr Apt 408R
Austin, TX 78746-6854, USA

Wilson, Robert M (Actor)
RW Work
131 Varick St Ste 908
New York, NY 10013-1444, USA

Wilson, Robert N (Business Person)
Johnson & Johnson
1 Johnson and Johnson Plz
New Brunswick, NJ 08933-0002, USA

Wilson, Roger (Actor)
c/o Staff Member *Joel Stevens Entertainment*
5627 Allott Ave
Van Nuys, CA 91401-4502, USA

Wilson, Ron (Athlete, Coach, Hockey Player)
17 Middleton Gardens Pl # Pi
Bluffton, SC 29910-4954, USA

Wilson, Russell (Athlete, Football Player)
c/o Bus Cook *Bus Cook Sports, Inc*
1 Willow Bend Dr
Hattiesburg, MS 39402-8552, USA

Wilson, Ruth (Actor)
c/o Jason Weinberg *Untitled Entertainment (LA)*
350 S Beverly Dr Ste 200
Beverly Hills, CA 90212-4819, USA

Wilson, Ryan (Actor)
c/o Cindy Osbrink *Osbrink Talent Agency*
4343 Lankershim Blvd Ste 100
North Hollywood, CA 91602-2705, USA

Wilson, Scott
PO Box 5617
Beverly Hills, CA 90209-5617

Wilson, Sherlee (Actor)
c/o Staff Member *Cunningham Escott Slevin & Doherty (CESD-LA)*
10635 Santa Monica Blvd Ste 130
Los Angeles, CA 90025-8306, USA

Wilson, Stephanie D (Astronaut)
14910 Hollydale Dr
Houston, TX 77062-2907, USA

Wilson, Stephen (Athlete, Basketball Player)
71 S Jones Creek Ln
Pine, CO 80470-9675, USA

Wilson, Steve (Athlete, Football Player)
3503 Brymore Ct
Pearland, TX 77584, USA

Wilson, Steven (Musician)
c/o Kim Estlund *Baker Winokur Ryder Public Relations (BWR-LA)*
9100 Wilshire Blvd Ste 500
West Tower Suite 500
Beverly Hills, CA 90212-3426, USA

Wilson, Tavon (Athlete, Football Player)
c/o Chad Wiestling *Integrated Sports Management*
2120 Texas St Apt 2204
Houston, TX 77003-3054, USA

Wilson, Thomas L (Athlete, Football Player)
4342 Oakdale Pl
Pittsburg, CA 94565-6256, USA

Wilson, Thomas (Tom) F (Actor)
c/o Alex Murray *Brillstein Entertainment Partners (LA)*
9150 Wilshire Blvd Ste 350
Beverly Hills, CA 90212-3453, USA

Wilson, TJ (Tyson Kidd) (Athlete, Wrestler)
6617 Marina Pointe Village Ct
Tampa, FL 33635-9053, USA

Wilson, Tom (Athlete, Baseball Player)
2771 Holiday Dr
Lake Havasu City, AZ 86403-6079, USA

Wilson, Torrie (Model, Wrestler)
525 Woods Landing Trl
Oldsmar, FL 34677-4220, USA

Wilson, Trevor (Athlete, Baseball Player)
5173 Woodcrest Ln
Lake Oswego, OR 97035-1319, USA

Wilson, Trevor (Athlete, Basketball Player)
824 15th St
Hermosa Beach, CA 90254-3202, USA

Wilson, Troy (Athlete, Football Player)
14213 W 138th Pl
Olathe, KS 66062-5877, USA

Wilson, Vance (Athlete, Baseball Player)
6368 Elizabeth Ave
Springdale, AR 72762-4234, USA

Wilson, Wade (Athlete, Football Player)
6126 Mimosa Ln
Dallas, TX 75230-5042, USA

Wilson, Wayne (Athlete, Football Player)
5430 Lynx Ln Apt 152
Columbia, MD 21044-2319, USA

Wilson, Wendy (Musician)
4316 Bellaire Ave
Studio City, CA 91604-1526, USA

Wilson, William (Athlete, Basketball
Player)
130 Belmont St
Englewood, NJ 07631-1502, USA

Wilson, Willie (Athlete, Baseball Player)
PO Box 34665
Kansas City, MO 64116-1065, USA

Wilson, Woody (Cartoonist)
c/o Staff Member *King Features
Syndication*
300 W 57th St Fl 15
New York, NY 10019-5238, USA

Wilson Phillips (Music Group)
c/o Seth Shomes *Day After Day
Productions*
436 1st St Ste 102
Solvang, CA 93463-3710, USA

Wilson-Sampras, Bridgette (Actor)
c/o Andrea Pett-Joseph *Brillstein
Entertainment Partners (LA)*
9150 Wilshire Blvd Ste 350
Beverly Hills, CA 90212-3453, USA

Wiltsie, Brian (Athlete, Hockey Player)
45 Meadowbrook Rd
Randolph, NJ 07869-3862, USA

Wilzig, Ivan (Musician)
1874 Deerfield Rd
Water Mill, NY 11976-2109, USA

Wimmer, Brian (Actor)
c/o Jean-Pierre (JP) Henraux *Henraux
Management*
Prefers to be contacted by telephone
CA, USA

Wimmer, Chris (Athlete, Baseball Player,
Olympic Athlete)
4027 E Countryside Plz
Wichita, KS 67218-4103, USA

Wimmer, Kurt (Actor, Director, Producer,
Writer)
c/o Tom Strickler *William Morris
Endeavor (LA)*
9601 Wilshire Blvd
Beverly Hills, CA 90210-5213, USA

Wimmer, Scott (Race Car Driver)
Richard Childress Racing
425 Industrial Dr
Welcome, NC 27374, USA

Winans
1420 Coleman Rd
Franklin, TN 37064-7452

Winans, BeBe (Musician)
2409 Deerbourne Dr
Brentwood, TN 37027-3708, USA

Winans, CeCe (Musician)
47 Annandale
Nashville, TN 37215-5821, USA

Winans, Jeff (Athlete, Football Player)
175 21st Ave SE
Saint Petersburg, FL 33705-2826, USA

Winans, Mario (Musician)
c/o Staff Member *Bad Boy Worldwide
Entertainment*
1440 Broadway Fl 19
New York, NY 10018-2301, USA

Winans, Matthew (Matt) (Athlete,
Baseball Player)
17 Sanford St
Melrose, MA 02176-3611, USA

Winans, Tydus (Athlete, Football Player)
92 W Rall Ave
Clovis, CA 93612-4308, USA

Winans, Vickie (Musician)
c/o Staff Member *Covenant Agency, The*
123 California Ave Apt 116
Santa Monica, CA 90403-3560, USA

Winborne, Jamie (Athlete, Football Player)
195 Roscoe Lee Cir
Wetumpka, AL 36092-3681, USA

Winbush, Angela (Musician, Songwriter,
Writer)
Joyce Agency
370 Harrison Ave
Harrison, NY 10528-2714, USA

Winbush, Camille (Actor)
c/o Judy Landis *Judy Landis Management*
Prefers to be contacted by telephone or
email
Thousand Oaks, CA 91362, USA

Winbush, Troy (Actor)
c/o Staff Member *Paradigm (LA)*
360 N Crescent Dr
North Bldg
Beverly Hills, CA 90210-4874, USA

Winceniak, Ed (Athlete, Baseball Player)
10828 S Avenue O
Chicago, IL 60617-6543, USA

Wincer, Simon (Director, Producer)
c/o Adam Kanter *Paradigm (LA)*
2000 Avenue of the Stars
Los Angeles, CA 90067-4700, USA

Winchester, Brad (Athlete, Hockey
Player)
611 Boggan Pointe Ct
Ballwin, MO 63011-1759, USA

Winchester, Philip (Actor)
c/o Michael (Mike) Jelline *United Talent
Agency (UTA-LA)*
9336 Civic Center Dr
Beverly Hills, CA 90210-3604, USA

Winchester, Scott (Athlete, Baseball
Player)
4705 Oakridge Dr
Midland, MI 48640-7409, USA

Wincott, Jeff P (Actor)
Judy Shane & Associates
606 N Larchmont Blvd
Los Angeles, CA 90004-1321

Winder, Sammy (Athlete, Football Player)
Winder Construction
4823 Greens Crossing Rd
Ridgeland, MS 39157-5042, USA

Winders, Rich (Bowler)
720 Augusta St
Racine, WI 53402-4412, USA

Winders, Wim (Director)
Paul Kohner
9300 Wilshire Blvd Ste 555
Beverly Hills, CA 90212-3211, USA

Windhorn, Gordie (Athlete, Baseball
Player)
145 Bent Creek Rd
Danville, VA 24540-5213, USA

Windis, Tony (Athlete, Basketball Player)
404 1st St
Rawlins, WY 82301-5502, USA

Windsor, Jason Windsor (Athlete,
Baseball Player)
23972 Dublin St
Lake Forest, CA 92630-2927, USA

Windsor, Robert E (Athlete, Football
Player)
2625 Legends Way
Ellicott City, MD 21042-2257, USA

Wine, Bobby (Athlete, Baseball Player,
Coach)
2614 Woodland Ave
Norristown, PA 19403-1636, USA

Wine, David M (Religious Leader)
Church of Brethren
1451 Dundee Ave
Elgin, IL 60120-1694, USA

Wine, Robbie (Athlete, Baseball Player)
240 Bryce Jordan Ctr
University Park, PA 16802-7102, USA

Winegardner, Mark (Writer)
Random House
1745 Broadway Frnt 3
New York, NY 10019-4343, USA

Winer, Jason (Director)
c/o Michael Lasker *Mosaic Media Group*
9200 W Sunset Blvd Ste 10
West Hollywood, CA 90069-3608, USA

Winfield, Antoine (Athlete, Football
Player)
230 S Fazio Way
Spring, TX 77389-2711, USA

Winfield, David (Dave) (Athlete, Baseball
Player)
2235 Stratford Cir
Los Angeles, CA 90077-1316, USA

Winfield, Earl (Athlete, Football Player)
8817 Oxford Cir
Waynesboro, PA 17268-9225, USA

Winfield, Peter (Actor)
3725 Goodland Ave
Studio City, CA 91604-2313, USA

Winfrey, Oprah (Business Person,
Producer, Talk Show Host)
c/o Staff Member *OWN: The Oprah
Winfrey Network*
5700 Wilshire Blvd Ste 120
Los Angeles, CA 90036-3644, USA

Winfrey, Travis (Actor)
c/o Peter Kluge *Impact Artist Group LLC
(LA)*
244 N California St
1st Floor
Burbank, CA 91505-3505, USA

Wing, Ted (Horse Racer)
23 Wavey Willow Ln
Montgomery, NY 12549-1524, USA

Wingate, David (Athlete, Basketball
Player)
11404 Glaetzer Ln
Charlotte, NC 28270-1574, USA

Wingate, Elmer (Athlete, Football Player)
807 Wellington Rd
Baltimore, MD 21212-1931, USA

Wingate, J W (Athlete, Baseball Player)
Kansas City Monarchs
3215 Case St
Beaumont, TX 77703-3607, USA

Winger, Debra (Actor)
280 Riverside Dr Apt 13A
New York, NY 10025-9032, USA

Winger, Kip (Musician)
2001 Galbraith Dr
Nashville, TN 37215-3406, USA

Winget, Larry (Business Person,
Motivational Speaker, Writer)
6929 N Hayden Rd Ste C4-619
Scottsdale, AZ 85250-7282, USA

Wingfield, Dantonio (Athlete, Basketball
Player)
1602 Gadsden Dr
Albany, GA 31701-3566, USA

Wingfield, Dontonio (Athlete, Basketball
Player)
1602 Gadsden Dr
Albany, GA 31701-3566, USA

Wingle, Blake (Athlete, Football Player)
8200 Stockdale Hwy Apt 10
Bakersfield, CA 93311-1091, USA

Wing-Merrill, Toby
PO Box 889
Mathews, VA 23109-0889

Wingo, Harthorne (Athlete, Basketball
Player)
862 Macon St Apt 2B
Brooklyn, NY 11233-5405, USA

Wingreen, Jason
4224 Teesdale Ave
Studio City, CA 91604-1544

Winings, Meagan (Beauty Pageant
Winner)
PO Box 21
Atkinson, NE 68713-0021, USA

Winkelsas, Joe (Athlete, Baseball Player)
213 Virgil Ave
Buffalo, NY 14216-1836, USA

Winkleman, Sophie (Actor)
c/o Gabriel Cohen *Management 360*
9111 Wilshire Blvd
Beverly Hills, CA 90210-5508, USA

Winkler, David (Director)
Rigberg Roberts Rugoto
1180 S Beverly Dr Ste 604
Los Angeles, CA 90035-1158, USA

Winkler, Francis M (Athlete, Football
Player)
8223 Creekside Cir S
Cordova, TN 38016-5117, USA

Winkler, Henry (Actor, Producer)
334 S Cliffwood Ave
Los Angeles, CA 90049-3826, USA

Winkler, Irwin (Director, Producer)
Irwin Winkler Productions
211 S Beverly Dr # 220
Beverly Hills, CA 90212-3807, USA

Winkler, Marvin (Athlete, Basketball
Player)
PO Box 759
Zapata, TX 78076-0759, USA

Winkles, Bobby B (Athlete, Baseball
Player, Coach)
3470 Summersorin11S Dr
Las Vegas, NV 89129, USA

Winklevoss, Cameron (Business Person)
Winklevoss Capital
30 W 24th St Fl 4
New York, NY 10010-3558, USA

Winklevoss, Tyler (Business Person)
Winklevoss Capital
30 W 24th St Fl 4
New York, NY 10010-3558, USA

Winn, Billy (Athlete, Football Player)
c/o Jeff Sperbeck *The Novo Agency*
3201 Danville Blvd Ste 295
Alamo, CA 94507-1978, USA

Winn, Jim (Athlete, Baseball Player)
3440 S Delaware Ave Apt 123
Springfield, MO 65804-6447, USA

Winn, Randy (Athlete, Baseball Player)
12221 Broadwater Loop
Thonotosassa, FL 33592-3954, USA

Winner, Charley (Athlete, Football Coach,
Football Player)
14970 Lake Olive Dr
Fort Myers, FL 33919-8336, USA

Winnes, Chris (Athlete, Hockey Player)
9 Greenlawn Ave
Warren, RI 02885-2810, USA

Winnick, Katheryn (Actor)
c/o Jason Barrett *Alchemy Entertainment*
7024 Melrose Ave Ste 420
Los Angeles, CA 90038-3394, USA

Winningham, Herm (Athlete, Baseball
Player)
1542 Belleville Rd
Orangeburg, SC 29115-3702, USA

Winningham, Mare (Actor)
c/o Christy Hall *Paradigm (LA)*
8730 W Sunset Blvd Ste 490
West Hollywood, CA 90069-2248, USA

Winokur, Marissa Jaret (Actor)
c/o Michael Valeo *Valeo Entertainment*
8581 Santa Monica Blvd Ste 570
West Hollywood, CA 90069-4120, USA

Winslet, Kate (Actor)
c/o Heidi Lopata *42West (LA)*
1840 Century Park E Ste 700
Los Angeles, CA 90067-2122, USA

Winslow, Dan (Musician)
3807 114th Ln NE
Minneapolis, MN 55449-7031, USA

Winslow, Don (Writer)
The Story Factory
141 S Barrington Ave Ste E
Los Angeles, CA 90049-3314, USA

Winslow, George (Athlete, Football
Player)
14 Daisy Ln
Ambler, PA 19002-2326, USA

Winslow, Michael (Actor, Comedian)
c/o Damon Frank *Venture IAB*
3211 Cahuenga Blvd W Ste 104
Los Angeles, CA 90068-1372, USA

Winslow Jr, Kellen (Athlete, Football
Player)
c/o Staff Member *EAG Sports
Management*
909 N Sepulveda Blvd Ste 360
El Segundo, CA 90245-3864, USA

Winspear, Jacqueline (Writer)
c/o Amy Rennert *The Amy Rennert
Agency*
98 Main St Ste 302
Belvedere Tiburon, CA 94920-2517, USA

Winstead, Mary Elizabeth (Actor)
c/o Doug Wald *Anonymous Content (LA)*
3532 Hayden Ave
Culver City, CA 90232-2413, USA

Winston, Dennis (Athlete, Football Player)
150 Chesterfield Ln Apt 8
Maumee, OH 43537-3881, USA

Winston, Hattie (Actor)
13025 Jarvis Ave
Los Angeles, CA 90061-2247, USA

Winston, Roy C (Athlete, Football Player)
708 Highway 401
Napoleonville, LA 70390-3205, USA

Winter, Alex (Actor)
c/o Chris Ridenhour *Evolution
Entertainment (LA)*
901 N Highland Ave
Los Angeles, CA 90038-2412, USA

Winter, Ariel (Actor)
12954 Magnolia Blvd
Sherman Oaks, CA 91423-1619, USA

Winter, Blaise (Athlete, Football Player)
3520 Rose Mallow Loop
Oviedo, FL 32766-6647, USA

Winter, Edgar (Musician)
9233 Burton Way Unit 402
Beverly Hills, CA 90210-3718, USA

Winter, Eric (Actor)
c/o Colton Gramm *Brillstein
Entertainment Partners (LA)*
9150 Wilshire Blvd Ste 350
Beverly Hills, CA 90212-3453, USA

Winter, Fred (Tex) (Coach)
Los Angeles Lakers
1111 S Figueroa St
Staples Center
Los Angeles, CA 90015-1300, USA

Winter, Morice ""Tex"" (Athlete,
Basketball Player)
Brian Winter
1812 Todd Rd
Manhattan, KS 66502-3408, USA

Winter, Paul T (Musician)
Living Music Records
PO Box 72
Litchfield, CT 06759-0072, USA

Winter, Ralph (Producer)
c/o Staff Member *1019 Entertainment*
1680 Vine St Ste 600
Los Angeles, CA 90028-8800, USA

Winter, Terence (Producer)
c/o Staff Member *Creative Artists Agency
(CAA-LA)*
2000 Avenue of the Stars Ste 100
Los Angeles, CA 90067-4705, USA

Winter, Terrence (Producer, Writer)
c/o Staff Member *Jackoway Tyerman
Wertheimer Austen Mandelbaum Morris
& Klein*
1925 Century Park E Fl 22
Los Angeles, CA 90067-2701, USA

Winter, William F (Ex-Governor)
190 E Capitol St Ste 800
Jackson, MS 39201-2155, USA

Winters, Brian (Athlete, Basketball Player)
8652 E Kettle Cir
Centennial, CO 80112-2707, USA

Winters, Chris (Actor, Model)
933 Backspin Ct
Newport News, VA 23602-9428, USA

Winters, Dean (Actor)
c/o Bill Butler *Industry Entertainment*
955 Carrillo Dr Ste 300
Los Angeles, CA 90048-5400, USA

Winters, Frank (Football Player)
Cleveland Browns
820 17th St
Union City, NJ 07087-1928, USA

Winters, Matt (Athlete, Baseball Player)
1201 Foxfire Dr
Greensboro, NC 27410-3253, USA

Winters, Mike (Athlete, Baseball Player)
13644 Boquita Dr
Del Mar, CA 92014-3408, USA

Winters, Scott William (Actor)
c/o Staff Member *Levine Okwu Erickson
Management*
2126 N Commonwealth Ave
Los Angeles, CA 90027-2118, USA

Winters, Voise (Athlete, Basketball Player)
7305 S Rockwell St
Chicago, IL 60629-2037, USA

Winther, Richard (Athlete, Football
Player)
1620 6th Way NW
Center Point, AL 35215-5374, USA

Wintour, Anna (Business Person)
Vogue Magazine
4 Times Sq Fl 1200
New York, NY 10036-6518, USA

Winwood, Steve (Musician)
1865 Laurel Ridge Dr
Nashville, TN 37215-4808, USA

Wire II, William S (Business Person)
706 Overton Park
Nashville, TN 37215-2452, USA

Wirgowski, Dennis (Athlete, Football
Player)
1127 Brissette Beach Rd
Kawkawlin, MI 48631-9454, USA

Wirth, Alan (Athlete, Baseball Player)
2858 E Jasmine St
Mesa, AZ 85213-3123, USA

Wirth, Billy (Actor, Director)
c/o Molly Conners *Rogues Gallery*
20 Clinton St Apt C7
New York, NY 10002-1755, USA

Wirth, Timothy E (Politician, Senator)
United Nations Foundation
2201 Est NW
Washington, DC 20521-0001, USA

Wisdom, Robert (Actor)
Paradigm
10100 Santa Monica Blvd Fl 25
Los Angeles, CA 90067-4003

Wise, Dewayne (Athlete, Baseball Player)
709 Old Lexington Hwy
Chapin, SC 29036-7980, USA

Wise, Matt (Athlete, Baseball Player)
11627 E Twilight Ct
Chandler, AZ 85249-4546, USA

Wise, Ray (Actor)
c/o Brady McKay *Evolution Entertainment
(LA)*
9320 Wilshire Blvd Ste 202
Beverly Hills, CA 90212-3217, USA

wise, Richard C (Rick) (Athlete, Baseball
Player)
8235 SW 184th Ave
Beaverton, OR 97007-5764, USA

Wise, Robert (Ex-Governor, Politician)
Alliance for Excellent Education
1201 Connecticut Ave NW Ste 901
Washington, DC 20036-2615, USA

Wise, William A (Business Person)
El Paso Energy Corp
1001 Louisiana St
Houston, TX 77002-5083, USA

Wise, Willie (Athlete, Basketball Player)
1903 NE 19th Pl
Renton, WA 98056-2611, USA

Wiseman, Brian (Athlete, Hockey Player)
2960 Walnut Ridge Dr
Ann Arbor, MI 48103-2189, USA

Wiseman, Frederick (Producer)
Zipporah Films
1 Richdale Ave Unit 4
Cambridge, MA 02140-2610, USA

Wiseman, Gregory Reid Ltcmdr
(Astronaut)
2436 Mountain Falls Ct
Friendswood, TX 77546-5590, USA

Wiseman, Len (Director, Writer)
c/o Nick Reed *ICM Partners (LA)*
10250 Constellation Blvd Fl 7
Los Angeles, CA 90067-6207, USA

Wiseman, Mac (Musician)
PO Box 17028
Nashville, TN 37217-0028, USA

Wisener, Gary (Athlete, Football Player)
10 Encantado Way
Hot Springs Village, AR 71909-7405, USA

Wish Bone (Actor, Composer, Musician)
c/o Staff Member *Creative Artists Agency
(CAA-LA)*
2000 Avenue of the Stars Ste 100
Los Angeles, CA 90067-4705, USA

Wisin and Yandel (Musician)
c/o Staff Member *Universal Music
Publishing Group (Latin)*
420 Lincoln Rd Ste 200
Miami Beach, FL 33139-3014, USA

Wiska, Jeffrey R (Athlete, Football Player)
18579 Fox Hollow Ct
Northville, MI 48168-8848, USA

Wismann, Pete (Athlete, Football Player)
7923 Caledonia Dr
San Jose, CA 95135-2112, USA

Wisniewski, Andreas (Actor)
Gage Group
5757 Wilshire Blvd Ste 659
Los Angeles, CA 90036-3682, USA

Wisniewski, Leo (Athlete, Football Player)
1900 Village Rd
Pittsburgh, PA 15205-1578, USA

Wisniewski, Stephen A (Steve) (Athlete, Football Player)
36 El Alamo Ct
Danville, CA 94526-1455, USA

Wisoff, Jeff Dr (Astronaut)
4268 Brindisi Pl
Pleasanton, CA 94566-2238, USA

Wisoff, Peter J K (Jeff) (Astronaut)
4268 Brindisi Pl
Pleasanton, CA 94566-2238, USA

Wissel, Sharon (Figure Skater)
c/o Staff Member *Bobby Ball Talent Agency*
3500 W Olive Ave Ste 300
Burbank, CA 91505-4647, USA

Wissman, Dave (Athlete, Baseball Player)
PO Box 38
Derby, VT 05829-0038, USA

Wiste, Jim (Athlete, Hockey Player)
701 S University Blvd
Denver, CO 80209-4722, USA

Wistert, Albert A (Ox) (Athlete, Football Player)
256 Gunnell Rd
Grants Pass, OR 97526-9621, USA

Wistert, Alvin L (Moose) (Athlete, Football Player)
10250 7 Mile Rd
Northville, MI 48167-9107, USA

Wistrom, Grant (Athlete, Football Player)
5769 S Fox Hollow Ave
Springfield, MO 65810-2326, USA

Witasick, Jay (Athlete, Baseball Player)
200 Wellin11TON Ct
Bel Air, MD 21014, USA

Withem, Shannon (Athlete, Baseball Player)
39668 Dorchester Cir
Canton, MI 48188-5016, USA

Withers, Bill (Musician, Songwriter)
PO Box 16698
Beverly Hills, CA 90209-2698, USA

Withers, Jane (Actor)
c/o Staff Member *Keller & Vanderneth Inc*
1133 Broadway Ste 911
New York, NY 10010-8029, USA

Witherspoon, John (Actor, Comedian)
14957 Valley Vista Blvd
Sherman Oaks, CA 91403-4022, USA

Witherspoon, Reese (Actor, Producer)
1129 Amalfi Dr
Pacific Palisades, CA 90272-4031, USA

Withrow, Phil (Athlete, Football Player)
730 Oakland Hills Cir Apt 106
Lake Mary, FL 32746-5833, USA

Withrow, Ray (Athlete, Baseball Player)
3842 Bordeaux Loop S
Owensboro, KY 42303-2550, USA

with Spencer Davis, Strawberry Alarm Clock (Music Group)
c/o Geoffrey Blumenauer *Geoffrey Blumenauer Artists*
PO Box 343
Burbank, CA 91503-0343, USA

Witiuk, Doris (Baseball Player)
11821 N Hemlock St
Spokane, WA 99218-2718, USA

Witman, Jon (Athlete, Football Player)
568 Woodsview Ln
Hellam, PA 17406-9344, USA

Witmeyer, Ron (Athlete, Baseball Player)
PO Box 763
Rancho Santa Fe, CA 92067-0763, USA

Witt, Alexander (Director)
c/o Ann Murtha *Murtha Agency*
1025 Colorado Ave Ste B
Santa Monica, CA 90401-2847, USA

Witt, Alicia (Actor)
c/o Daniel (Danny) Sussman *Brillstein Entertainment Partners (LA)*
9150 Wilshire Blvd Ste 350
Beverly Hills, CA 90212-3453, USA

Witt, Bobby (Athlete, Baseball Player, Olympic Athlete)
4601 Winewood Ct
Colleyville, TX 76034-4887, USA

Witt, Brendan (Athlete, Hockey Player)
PO Box 907
Darby, MT 59829-0907, USA

Witt, George (Athlete, Baseball Player)
2209 Catalina
Laguna Beach, CA 92651-3607, USA

Witt, Katarina (Figure Skater)
c/o Gail Parenteau *Parenteau Guidance*
132 E 35th St # 3J
New York, NY 10016-3892, USA

Witt, Kevin (Athlete, Baseball Player)
6350 Concho Bay Dr
Houston, TX 77041-6171, USA

Witt, Michael A (Mike) (Athlete, Baseball Player)
37 Poppy Hills Rd
Laguna Niguel, CA 92677-1010, USA

Witte, Luke (Athlete, Basketball Player)
3223 Arbor Pointe Dr
Charlotte, NC 28210-7994, USA

Witten, Jason (Athlete, Football Player)
2001 Navasota Cv
Westlake, TX 76262-4801, USA

Wittma, Randy (Athlete, Basketball Coach, Basketball Player, Coach)
c/o Lonnie Cooper *Career Sports and Entertainment*
150 Interstate North Pkwy SE Ste 100
Atlanta, GA 30339-2101, USA

Wittrock, Finn (Actor)
c/o Jim Weissenbach *Weissenbach Management*
5951 Airdrome St
Los Angeles, CA 90035-4635, USA

Wittwer, Linda Jezek (Athlete, Olympic Athlete, Swimmer)
673 Oak Park Way
Emerald Hills, CA 94062-4041, USA

Witty, Chris (Athlete, Olympic Athlete, Speed Skater)
2644 E 2940 S
Salt Lake City, UT 84109-2527, USA

Witucki, Casimir (Athlete, Football Player)
3909 Spring Ter
Temple Hills, MD 20748-3439, USA

Witwer, Sam (Actor)
c/o Gordon Gilbertson *Gilbertson Management*
1334 3rd Street Promenade Ste 201
Santa Monica, CA 90401-1320, USA

Wizbicki, Alex (Athlete, Football Player)
10B Hayes Ct
Superior, WI 54880-2939, USA

Wlcek, James (Actor)
c/o Terrie Marroquin *Tlynn Talent Management*
10153 Riverside Dr Ste 566
Toluca Lake, CA 91602-2562, USA

W. Meeks, Gregory (Congressman, Politician)
2234 Rayburn Hob
Washington, DC 20515-2202, USA

Wockenfuss, John (Athlete, Baseball Player)
26 Wallamsey Ln
Chesapeake City, MD 21915-1821, USA

Woerner, Scott (Athlete, Football Player)
6570 Highway 356
Sautee Nacoochee, GA 30571-1814, USA

Wofford, Harris L (Politician, Senator)
260 Burch Dr
Coraopolis, PA 15108-3153, USA

Wofford, James (Athlete, Horse Racer, Olympic Athlete)
22145 Greengarden Rd
Upperville, VA 20184-3105, USA

Woggon, Bill (Cartoonist)
2724 Cabot Ct
Thousand Oaks, CA 91360-1640, USA

Wohl, Dave (Athlete, Basketball Player, Coach)
137 Morley Cir
Melville, NY 11747-4843, USA

Wohlers, Mark E (Athlete, Baseball Player)
135 Old Cedar Ln
Alpharetta, GA 30004-3795, USA

Wohlford, Jim (Athlete, Baseball Player)
3700 W Mineral King Ave
Visalia, CA 93291-5531, USA

Wohlhuter, Richard (Athlete, Olympic Athlete, Track Athlete)
13609 Danhurst Way
Jacksonville, FL 32224-1308, USA

Wohlwender-Fricker, Marian (Athlete, Baseball Player)
14006 Castle Hill Way
Fort Myers, FL 33919-7369, USA

Woiwode, Larry (Writer)
State University of New York
English Dept
Binghamton, NY 13901, USA

Wojciechowski, John (Athlete, Football Player)
13317 Clyde Rd
Holly, MI 48442-9010, USA

Wojciechowski, Steve (Athlete, Baseball Player)
4646 Thornberry Hill Ct NE
Grand Rapids, MI 49525-9489, USA

Wojcik, John (Athlete, Baseball Player)
8303 Salford Way
Louisville, KY 40222-5529, USA

Wojna, Ed (Athlete, Baseball Player)
225 Sussex Pl
Carson City, NV 89703-5372, USA

Wolaner, Robin P (Publisher)
Sunset Publishing Corp
80 Willow Rd
Menlo Park, CA 94025-3661, USA

Wolanin, Craig (Athlete, Hockey Player)
4891 Gallagher Rd
Rochester, MI 48306-1508, USA

Wolcott, Bob (Athlete, Baseball Player)
3323 Bryson Way
Medford, OR 97504-5811, USA

Wolf, David A (Astronaut)
1714 Neptune Ln
Houston, TX 77062-6108, USA

Wolf, David A Dr (Astronaut)
1714 Neptune Ln
Houston, TX 77062-6108, USA

Wolf, Dick (Producer)
c/o Staff Member *Wolf Films Inc (LA)*
100 Universal City Plz
Universal City, CA 91608-1002, USA

Wolf, Jim (Athlete, Baseball Player)
8054 Royer Ave
Canoga Park, CA 91304-3535, USA

Wolf, Joe (Athlete, Football Player)
2324 Lehigh Pkwy N
Allentown, PA 18103-3748, USA

Wolf, Naomi (Writer)
Random House
1745 Broadway Frnt 3 # B1
New York, NY 10019-4343, USA

Wolf, Randy (Athlete, Baseball Player)
18580 Corte Fresco
Rancho Santa Fe, CA 92091-0227, USA

Wolf, Ross (Athlete, Baseball Player)
15524 N 400th St
Wheeler, IL 62479-2300, USA

Wolf, Scott (Actor)
5250 Oak Park Ave
Encino, CA 91316-2624, USA

Wolf, Wally (Athlete, Baseball Player)
18580 Corte Fresco
Rancho Santa Fe, CA 92091-0227, USA

Wolfe, Bernie (Athlete, Hockey Player)
8012 Glenbrook Rd
Bethesda, MD 20814-2608, USA

Wolfe, Bob (Athlete, Football Player)
13165 Emiline Cir
Omaha, NE 68138, USA

Wolfe, Brian (Athlete, Baseball Player)
39398 Calle Anita
Temecula, CA 92592-8213, USA

Wolfe, David (Writer)
1259 N Crescent Heights Blvd Apt D
C/O Angela Hartman
West Hollywood, CA 90046-5018, USA

Wolfe, Derek (Athlete, Football Player)
c/o Joe Panos *Athletes First, LLC*
23091 Mill Creek Dr
Laguna Hills, CA 92653-1258, USA

Wolfe, George C (Director)
Shakespeare Festival
425 Lafayette St
New York, NY 10003-7087, USA

Wolfe, Jenna (Actor, Correspondent)
c/o Staff Member *IF Management, Inc.*
152 W 57th St Fl 14
New York, NY 10019-3993, USA

Wolfe, Kenneth L (Business Person)
Hershey Foods Corp
100 Crystal A Dr Unit 8
Hershey, PA 17033-9702, USA

Wolfe, Larry (Athlete, Baseball Player)
5200 Blossomwood Ct
Fair Oaks, CA 95628-3836, USA

Wolfe, Michael (Producer)
c/o Rosanna Bilow *Creative Artists
Agency (CAA-LA)*
2000 Avenue of the Stars Ste 100
Los Angeles, CA 90067-4705, USA

Wolfe, Mike (Reality Star)
Antique Archaeology
1300 Clinton St Ste 130
Nashville, TN 37203-7007, USA

Wolfe, Paul (Race Car Driver)
Baldwin Racing
182 Raceway Dr # B
Mooresville, NC 28117-6509, USA

Wolfe, Sterling (Actor)
2609 W Wyoming Ave Ste A
Burbank, CA 91505-1950, USA

Wolfe, Tom (Writer)
21 E 79th St Fl 14
New York, NY 10075-0182, USA

Wolfe, Traci (Actor)
c/o Staff Member *Cunningham Escott
Slevin & Doherty (CESD-LA)*
10635 Santa Monica Blvd Ste 130
Los Angeles, CA 90025-8306, USA

Wolff, Alex (Musician)
c/o Cindi Berger *PMK/BNC Public
Relations (PMK-NY)*
622 3rd Ave Fl 8
New York, NY 10017-6707, USA

Wolff, Bob (Sportscaster)
3 Salisbury Pt Apt 2E
Nyack, NY 10960-4726, USA

Wolff, Nat (Musician)
Naked Brothers Band
1909 3rd St N
C/O Yovia
Jacksonville Beach, FL 32250-7427, USA

Wolff, Tobias J A (Writer)
Stanford University
English Dept
Stanford, CA 94305, USA

Wolfley, Craig (Athlete, Football Player)
1767 Robson Dr
Pittsburgh, PA 15241-2617, USA

Wolford, Will (Athlete, Football Player)
205 Waterleaf Way
Louisville, KY 40207-5720, USA

Wolfson, Louis E (Business Person)
10205 Collins Ave
Bal Harbour, FL 33154-1403, USA

Wolk, James (Actor)
c/o Adena Chawke *Greenlight
Management and Production*
9713 Santa Monica Blvd Ste 219
Beverly Hills, CA 90210-4215, USA

Wolk, Jimmy (Actor)
c/o Adena Chawke *Greenlight
Management and Production*
9713 Santa Monica Blvd Ste 219
Beverly Hills, CA 90210-4215, USA

Wolken, Jonathan (Artist, Dancer,
Director)
Pilobolus Dance Theater
PO Box 388
Washington Depot, CT 06794-0388, USA

Woll, Deborah Ann (Actor)
923 Hauser Blvd
Los Angeles, CA 90036-4723, USA

Wollman, Harvey L (Ex-Governor)
40004 184th St
Frankfort, SD 57440-7311, USA

Wolman, M Gordon (Football Player,
Physicist)
1070 Stable Run Dr
Cordova, TN 38018-0109, USA

Wolov, Julia Lea (Actor, Writer)
c/o Jonathan Brandstein *Morra Brezner
Steinberg & Tenenbaum (MBST)
Entertainment*
345 N Maple Dr Ste 200
Beverly Hills, CA 90210-5174, USA

Wolpe, Lenny (Actor)
c/o Staff Member *Gage Group, The (LA)*
5757 Wilshire Blvd Ste 659
Los Angeles, CA 90036-3682, USA

Wolski, Dariusz (Director)
The Mack Agency
4705 Laurel Canyon Blvd Ste 204
Valley Village, CA 91607-3998, USA

Wolter, Sherilyn (Actor)
128 Old Topanga Canyon Rd
Topanga, CA 90290-3807

Wolters, Kara (Basketball Player)
137 Westfield Dr
Holliston, MA 01746-1256, USA

W. Olver, John (Congressman, Politician)
1111 Longworth Hob
Washington, DC 20515-3229, USA

Womack, Bruce L (Athlete, Football
Player)
2834 Triway Ln
Houston, TX 77043-1809, USA

Womack, Dooley (Athlete, Baseball
Player)
209 Weeping Cherry Ln
Columbia, SC 29212-8617, USA

Womack, Floyd (Athlete, Football Player)
c/o Eugene Parker *Maximum Sports
Management*
6435 W Jefferson Blvd # 197
Fort Wayne, IN 46804-6203, USA

Womack, Lee Ann (Actor, Musician)
133 Woodward Hills Pl
Brentwood, TN 37027-4236, USA

Womack, Steve (Congressman, Politician)
1508 Longworth Hob
Washington, DC 20515-3804, USA

Womack, Tony (Athlete, Baseball Player)
8301 Marcliffe Ct
Waxhaw, NC 28173-5500, USA

Wombats, The (Music Group)
c/o Staff Member *Paradigm (Monterey)*
404 W Franklin St
Monterey, CA 93940-2303, USA

Womble, Royce (Athlete, Football Player)
6350 Newt Patterson Rd
Mansfield, TX 76063-6157, USA

Wonder, Stevie (Musician, Songwriter)
Steveland Morris Music
4616 W Magnolia Blvd
Burbank, CA 91505-2731, USA

Wonders, Rich (Bowler)
720 Augusta St
Racine, WI 53402-4412, USA

Wong, B D (Actor)
c/o Richie Jackson *Jackson Group
Entertainment*
400 W 12th St Apt 5C
New York, NY 10014-1861, USA

Wong, Kailee (Athlete, Football Player)
1200 Paseo Redondo
Burbank, CA 91501-1624, USA

Wong, Mike (Athlete, Hockey Player)
16081 Hyland Ave
Lakeville, MN 55044-6221, USA

Wong, Russell (Actor)
International Creative Mgmt
10250 Constellation Blvd Fl 1
Los Angeles, CA 90067-6241, USA

Wonsley, George (Athlete, Football
Player)
6418 Amblewood Pl
Jackson, MS 39213-7803, USA

Woo, John (Director, Producer)
1655 Amalfi Dr
Pacific Palisades, CA 90272-2756, USA

Wood, Anna (Actor)
c/o Lenore Zerman *Liberman/Zerman
Management*
252 N Larchmont Blvd Ste 200
Los Angeles, CA 90004-3754, USA

Wood, Brandon (Athlete, Baseball Player)
5209 E Kathleen Rd
Scottsdale, AZ 85254-1738, USA

Wood, Brenton (Musician)
PO Box 4127
Inglewood, CA 90309-4127, USA

Wood, Carolyn (Swimmer)
4380 SW 86th Ave
Portland, OR 97225-2428, USA

Wood, Carri (Athlete, Golfer)
2001 Sabal Ridge Ct Apt H
Palm Beach Gardens, FL 33418-8922,
USA

Wood, Danny (Musician)
770 NE 69th St Apt 3B
Miami, FL 33138-5763, USA

Wood, Darin ""Dody"" (Athlete, Hockey
Player)
4941 S Woodside Ave
Independence, MO 64055-5738, USA

Wood, David (Athlete, Basketball Player)
15200 Chateau Ave
Reno, NV 89511-4524, USA

Wood, Dick (Athlete, Football Player)
1327 Briarvista Way NE
Atlanta, GA 30329-3632, USA

Wood, Duane (Athlete, Football Player)
PO Box 601
Wilburton, OK 74578-0601, USA

Wood, Eddie (Race Car Driver)
21 Performance Dr
Route 2 Box 77
Stuart, VA 24171-4000, USA

Wood, Eden (Beauty Pageant Winner,
Reality Star)
c/o Staff Member *VH1 Television*
1515 Broadway
New York, NY 10036-8901, USA

Wood, Elijah (Actor)
608 W Mary St
Austin, TX 78704-4136, USA

Wood, Eric (Athlete, Football Player)
c/o Joby Branion *Athletes First, LLC*
23091 Mill Creek Dr
Laguna Hills, CA 92653-1258, USA

Wood, Evan Rachel (Actor)
12 29th Ave Apt 2
Venice, CA 90291-4322, USA

Wood, Glen (Race Car Driver)
Wood Bros Racing
21 Performance Dr
Route 2 Box 77
Stuart, VA 24171-4000, USA

Wood, Jake (Athlete, Baseball Player)
9129 Daytona Dr
Pensacola, FL 32506-2904, USA

Wood, James (Business Person)
Great A & P Tea Co
2 Paragon Dr
Montvale, NJ 07645-1768, USA

Wood, James N (Director)
Art Institute of Chicago
111 S Michigan Ave
Chicago, IL 60603-6488, USA

Wood, Janet (Actor)
Acme Talent
4727 Wilshire Blvd Ste 333
Los Angeles, CA 90010-3874, USA

Wood, Jason (Athlete, Baseball Player)
9899 N Cascade Dr
Fresno, CA 93730-0864, USA

Wood, Jeff (Race Car Driver)
821 N Linden Ct
Wichita, KS 67206-4005, USA

Wood, Jon (Race Car Driver)
137 High Hills Dr
Mooresville, NC 28117-9000, USA

Wood, Kerry (Athlete, Baseball Player)
6838 E Cheney Dr
Paradise Valley, AZ 85253-3525, USA

Wood, Lana (Actor)
1131 Oriole Cir
Fillmore, CA 93015-1601, USA

Wood, Len (Race Car Driver)
21 Performance Dr
Route 2 Box 77
Stuart, VA 24171-4000, USA

Wood, Leon (Athlete, Basketball Player,
Olympic Athlete)
234 Turtle Crest Dr
Irvine, CA 92603-1001, USA

Wood, Martin "Al" (Athlete, Basketball
Player)
411 Belvedere Ln
Waxhaw, NC 28173-6581, USA

Wood, Maurice (Doctor)
RR 2 Box 543B
Hot Springs, VA 24445, USA

Wood, Mike (Athlete, Baseball Player)
1199 Cherlynn Ter
West Palm Beach, FL 33406-5272, USA

Wood, Mike (Athlete, Football Player)
630 N Geyer Rd
Saint Louis, MO 63122-2756, USA

Wood, Rachel Hurd (Actor)
c/o Michael Lazo *Untitled Entertainment (LA)*
350 S Beverly Dr Ste 200
Beverly Hills, CA 90212-4819, USA

Wood, Randy (Athlete, Hockey Player)
2 Bridge St
Manchester, MA 01944-1408, USA

Wood, Richard (Athlete, Football Player)
5413 Windbrush Dr
Tampa, FL 33625-4051, USA

Wood, Robert (Athlete, Basketball Player)
12930 Echo Dr
Rockton, IL 61072-2816, USA

Wood, Robert E (Publisher)
Peninsula Times Tribune
435 N Michigan Ave Ste 1609
Chicago, IL 60611-4008, USA

Wood, Robert J (Astronaut)
McDonnell Douglas Corp
PO Box 516
Saint Louis, MO 63166-0516, USA

Wood, Ronnie (Musician)
c/o Adam Nelson *Workhouse Publicity*
1 Little West 12th St
New York, NY 10014-1302, USA

Wood, Ted (Athlete, Baseball Player)
1810 Beckley Pl NW
Kennesaw, GA 30152-4265, USA

Wood, Ted (Athlete, Baseball Player)
1810 Becklev Pi NW
Kennesaw, GA 30152, USA

Wood, Tom
6310 San Vicente Blvd Ste 520
Los Angeles, CA 90048-5421

Wood, Wilbur F (Athlete, Baseball Player)
3 Elmbrook Rd
Bedford, MA 01730-1810, USA

Wood, William V (Athlete, Football Player)
7516 Piney Branch Rd
Silver Spring, MD 20910-5101, USA

Wood, William V (Willie) (Athlete, Football Player)
Willie Wood Mechanical Systems
7941 16th St NW
Washington, DC 20012-1230, USA

Wood, Willie (Athlete, Golfer)
6309 Oak Tree Dr
Edmond, OK 73025-2678, USA

Woodall, Al (Athlete, Football Player)
131 Field Crest Rd
New Canaan, CT 06840-6331, USA

Woodall, Brad (Athlete, Baseball Player)
4990 Borchers Beach Rd
Waunakee, WI 53597-9174, USA

Woodall, Rob (Congressman, Politician)
1725 Longworth Hob
Washington, DC 20515-0532, USA

Woodard, Alfre (Actor)
602 Bay St
Santa Monica, CA 90405-1215, USA

Woodard, Bob (Writer)
2907 Q St NW
Washington, DC 20007-3010, USA

Woodard, Charlayne (Actor, Writer)
c/o Alan Harris *Alan M Harris Management*
3278 Wilshire Blvd Apt 901
Los Angeles, CA 90010-1425, USA

Woodard, Darrell (Athlete, Baseball Player)
1227 E 69th St
Los Angeles, CA 90001-1657, USA

Woodard, Lynette (Athlete, Basketball Player, Olympic Athlete)
4807 Pin Oak Park Apt 3210
Houston, TX 77081-2229, USA

Woodard, Mike (Athlete, Baseball Player)
PO Box 35
Maywood, IL 60153-0035, USA

Woodard, Ray (Athlete, Football Player)
1917 FM 352
Corrigan, TX 75939-6822, USA

Woodard, Rickey (Musician)
JVC Music
3800 Barham Blvd Ste 409
Los Angeles, CA 90068-1042, USA

Woodard, Steven L (Steve) (Athlete, Baseball Player)
800 Frost Ct SW
Hartselle, AL 35640-2714, USA

Woodbine, Bokeem (Actor)
c/o Johnny Gallo *Artist Representation Group*
9701 Wilshire Blvd Fl 10
Beverly Hills, CA 90212-2010, USA

Wood Brothers, The (Music Group)
c/o Staff Member *Paradigm (Monterey)*
404 W Franklin St
Monterey, CA 93940-2303, USA

Woodburn, Danny (Actor)
12134 Viewcrest Rd
Studio City, CA 91604-3639, USA

Wooden, Shawn (Athlete, Football Player)
17741 SW 12th St
Pembroke Pines, FL 33029-4811, USA

Woodeshivk, Tom (Athlete, Football Player)
PO Box 716
Blakeslee, PA 18610-0716, USA

Woodforde, Mark (Athlete, Tennis Player)
c/o Staff Member *Octagon (VA)*
7231 Forest Ave Ste 103
Richmond, VA 23226-3785, USA

Woodhead, Cynthia (Swimmer)
PO Box 1193
Riverside, CA 92502-1193, USA

Wooding, Michelle (Athlete, Golfer)
3825 E Camelback Rd Unit 148
Phoenix, AZ 85018-2645, USA

Woodland, Lauren
c/o Jerry Shandrew *Shandrew Public Relations*
1050 S Stanley Ave
Los Angeles, CA 90019-6634, USA

Woodland, Rich (Race Car Driver)
Rich Woodland Racing
2000 Pitts School Rd
Concord, NC 28027, USA

Woodlawn, Holly (Actor)
PO Box 27766
Los Angeles, CA 90027-0766

Woodley, Dan
15852 Deer Ridge Dr
Morrison, CO 80465-9631, USA

Woodley, Shailene (Actor)
c/o Nils Larsen *Principato/Young Management (LA)*
9465 Wilshire Blvd Ste 900
Beverly Hills, CA 90212-2608, USA

Woodlief, Doug (Athlete, Football Player)
7928 Wilkinson Ave
N Hollywood, CA 91605-2209, USA

Woodruff, Billie (Actor)
c/o Joe Gatta *Gersh (NY)*
41 Madison Ave
New York, NY 10010-2202, USA

Woodruff, Blake (Actor)
c/o Justine Hunt *Hines and Hunt Entertainment*
1213 W Magnolia Blvd
Burbank, CA 91506-1829, USA

Woodruff, Bob (Journalist)
c/o Staff Member *ABC News*
77 W 66th St Fl 3
New York, NY 10023-6201, USA

Woodruff, Dwayne (Athlete, Football Player)
10382 Grubbs Rd
Wexford, PA 15090-9420, USA

Woodruff, Judy C (Correspondent, Television Host)
Cable News Network
820 1st St NE Ste 1000
News Dept
Washington, DC 20002-4363, USA

Woods, Al (Athlete, Baseball Player)
2600 San Leandro Blvd Apt 1004
Blvd Act 1004
San Leandro, CA 94578-5032, USA

Woods, Al (Athlete, Baseball Player)
2600 San Leandro Blvd Apt 1004
San Leandro, CA 94578-5032, USA

Woods, Barbara Alyn (Actor)
Honey Prod
22611 Federalist Rd
Calabasas, CA 91302-4807, USA

Woods, Chris (Athlete, Football Player)
202 Stone Ridge Trl
Irondale, AL 35210-1730, USA

Woods, Christine (Actor)
c/o David DeCamillo *Gersh (LA)*
9465 Wilshire Blvd Ste 600
Beverly Hills, CA 90212-2605, USA

Woods, Della (Race Car Driver)
302 Bellevue Ave
Lake Orion, MI 48362-2708, USA

Woods, Don (Athlete, Football Player)
10415 Johncock Ave SW
Albuquerque, NM 87121-9414, USA

Woods, Elbert (Ickey) (Athlete, Football Player)
505 E Sharon Rd # A
Cincinnati, OH 45246-4726, USA

Woods, Gary (Athlete, Baseball Player)
PO Box 151
Solvang, CA 93464-0151, USA

Woods, George (Athlete, Track Athlete)
7631 Green Hedge Rd
Edwardsville, IL 62025-6135, USA

Woods, Jake (Athlete, Baseball Player)
1405 Mehlert St
Kingsburg, CA 93631-2423, USA

Woods, James (Actor)
230 W Shore Dr
Exeter, RI 02822-1917, USA

Woods, Jerome (Athlete, Football Player)
1 Arrowhead Dr
Kansas City, MO 64129-1651, USA

Woods, Jerry L (Athlete, Football Player)
8976 Stratford Ct
Minneapolis, MN 55443-2976, USA

Woods, Jim (Athlete, Baseball Player)
4509 Gardenia Ave
Keyes, CA 95328-9701, USA

Woods, Michael (Actor)
c/o Staff Member *GVA Talent Agency Inc*
8981 W Sunset Blvd Ste 101
West Hollywood, CA 90069-1850, USA

Woods, Paul (Athlete, Hockey Player)
600 Civic Center Dr
Attn Broadcast Dept
Detroit, MI 48226-4408, USA

Woods, Paul (Athlete, Hockey Player)
4276 S Shore St
Waterford, MI 48328-1157, USA

Woods, Pierre (Athlete, Football Player)
c/o Staff Member *New England Patriots*
1 Patriot Pl
Foxboro, MA 02035-1388, USA

Woods, Qyntel (Basketball Player)
Portland Trail Blazers
1 N Center Court St Ste 200
Rose Garden
Portland, OR 97227-2103, USA

Woods, Rick (Athlete, Football Player)
713 Baldwin St
Meadville, PA 16335-1959, USA

Woods, Robert E (Athlete, Football Player)
c/o Andrew Kessler *Athletes First, LLC*
23091 Mill Creek Dr
Laguna Hills, CA 92653-1258, USA

Woods, Robert S (Actor)
ITA
PO Box 492
Kinderhook, NY 12106-0492, USA

Woods, Ron (Athlete, Baseball Player)
5209 Desert Star Dr
Las Vegas, NV 89130-0159, USA

Woods, Simon (Actor)
c/o Staff Member *ICM Partners (LA)*
10250 Constellation Blvd Fl 7
Los Angeles, CA 90067-6207, USA

Woods, Stuart (Writer)
Harper Collins Publishers
195 Broadway Fl 2
New York, NY 10007-3132, USA

Woods, Tiger (Athlete, Golfer)
Tiger Woods Foundation
1 Tiger Woods Way
Anaheim, CA 92801-5039, USA

Woods, Victoria (Musician)
c/o John Elias *Three Twins Entertainment, Inc*
PO Box 100210
Staten Island, NY 10310-0210, USA

Woodside, DB (Actor)
Paradigm Agency
10100 Santa Monica Blvd Ste 2500
Los Angeles, CA 90067-4116, USA

Woodson, Alli (Musician)
Superstars Unlimited
PO Box 371371
Las Vegas, NV 89137-1371, USA

Woodson, Charles (Athlete, Football Player, Heisman Trophy Winner)
10010 Tavistock Rd
Orlando, FL 32827-7053, USA

Woodson, Darren (Athlete, Football Player)
6821 Memorial Dr
Frisco, TX 75034-7295, USA

Woodson, Dick (Athlete, Baseball Player)
27879 Panorama Hills Dr
Menifee, CA 92584-7401, USA

Woodson, Kerry (Athlete, Baseball Player)
19392 La Serena Dr
Fort Myers, FL 33967-0525, USA

Woodson, Michael (Mike) (Athlete, Basketball Coach, Basketball Player)
525 New Haven Ct SW
Atlanta, GA 30331-9012, USA

Woodson, Rod (Athlete, Football Player)
c/o Eugene Parker Maximum Sports Management
6435 W Jefferson Blvd # 197
Fort Wayne, IN 46804-6203, USA

Woodson, Sean (Athlete, Football Player)
1135 Ellis Ave
Jackson, MS 39209-7325, USA

Woodson, Tracy (Athlete, Baseball Player)
9027 Fascine Ct
Mechanicsville, VA 23116-6570, USA

Woodson, Warren V (Coach, Football Coach)
12680 Hillcrest Rd Apt 1106
Dallas, TX 75230-2019, USA

Woodville, Kate (Actor)
PO Box 6613
Malibu, CA 90264-6613, USA

Woodward, Bob (Journalist)
3305 Old Point Rd
Edgewater, MD 21037-3110, USA

Woodward, Chris (Athlete, Baseball Player)
72 Bay Woods Dr
Safety Harbor, FL 34695-5401, USA

Woodward, Jim (Athlete, Golfer)
4205 NW 147th St
Oklahoma City, OK 73134-1812, USA

Woodward, Joanne (Actor)
270/274 North Ave
Westport, CT 06880, USA

Woodward, Morgan (Actor)
2051 N Highland Ave Apt 338
Los Angeles, CA 90068-3092, USA

Woodward, Neil W Cdr (Astronaut)
1935 Edgemont Pl W
Seattle, WA 98199-3914, USA

Woodward, Peter (Actor)
c/o Vincent Cirrincione Vincent Cirrincione Associates
1516 N Fairfax Ave
Los Angeles, CA 90046-2608, USA

Woodward, Rob (Athlete, Baseball Player)
58 Eastman Hill Rd
Lebanon, NH 03766-2103, USA

Woodward, Shannon (Actor)
6961 La Presa Dr
Los Angeles, CA 90068-3102, USA

Woodward, Woody (Athlete, Baseball Player)
10 San Marco Ct
Palm Coast, FL 32137-2104, USA

Woodward III, Neil W (Astronaut)
5701 Ridgefield Rd
Bethesda, MD 20816-1250, USA

Woody, Damien (Football Player)
New England Patriots
12170 Ashland Heights Rd
Ashland, VA 23005-7634, USA

Woody, Woody (Athlete, Football Player)
9122 Weymouth Dr
Houston, TX 77031-3034, USA

Woog, Doug (Athlete, Hockey Player)
433 Wentworth Ave
South St Paul, MN 55075-1602, USA

Woogon, Bill (Cartoonist)
2724 Cabot Ct
Thousand Oaks, CA 91360-1640, USA

Wooldridge, Dean E (Business Person)
355 S Grand Ave Ste 2600
Los Angeles, CA 90071-1505, USA

Woolery, Chuck (Actor, Television Host)
Chuck Woolery Signature Products
26135 Plymouth Rd
Redford, MI 48239-2173, USA

Woolfolk, Andre (Athlete, Football Player)
460 Great Circle Rd
Nashville, TN 37228-1404, USA

Woolfolk, Harold (Butch) (Football Player)
New York Giants
4519 Magnolia Ln
Sugar Land, TX 77478-5457, USA

Woolford, Donnell (Athlete, Football Player)
2925 Spur Ave
Fayetteville, NC 28306-8387, USA

Woolford, Gary (Athlete, Football Player)
6321 S Four Peaks Pl
Chandler, AZ 85249-3946, USA

Woollard, Bob (Athlete, Basketball Player)
166 Barnard Mill Rd
Hamptonville, NC 27020-7377, USA

Woolley, Catherine (Writer)
PO Box 67
Higgins Hollow Road
Orleans, MA 02653-0067, USA

Woolley, Jason (Athlete, Hockey Player)
4019 Quarton Rd
Bloomfield Hills, MI 48302-4061, USA

Woolley, Jordan (Actor)
c/o Suzanne Bennett-Harrison Diverse Talent Group
9911 W Pico Blvd Ste 340W
Los Angeles, CA 90035-2703, USA

Woolley, Sheb (Musician)
PO Box 2124
Hendersonville, TN 37077-2124

Woolsey, Elizabeth D (Skier)
Trail Creek Ranch
Wilson, WY 83014, USA

Woolsey, Ralph A (Cinematographer)
23388 Mulholland Dr # 109
Woodland Hills, CA 91364-2733, USA

Woolsey, Roland (Football Player)
Dallas Cowboys
24100 N Can Ada Rd
Star, ID 83669-5026, USA

Woolsey, William Tripp (Athlete, Olympic Athlete, Swimmer)
1032 Seascape Cir
Rodeo, CA 94572-1815, USA

Woolstenhume Jr, Rick (Musician)
23345 Hamlin St
West Hills, CA 91307-3316, USA

Woolwine, Chris (Race Car Driver)
Woolwine Motorsports
2705 6th St # 107
Galveston, TX 77551, USA

Woosnam, Ian H (Athlete, Golfer)
I M G
1360 E 9th St Ste 100
Cleveland, OH 44114-1730, USA

Wooten, Hubert (Daddy) (Athlete, Baseball Player)
120 Sandy Dr
Goldsboro, NC 27534-8803, USA

Wooten, Jim (Correspondent)
ABC-TV
5010 Creston St
News Dept
Hyattsville, MD 20781-1216, USA

Wooten, John (Athlete, Football Player)
505 Boronia Rd
Arlington, TX 76002-4515, USA

Wooten, Morgan (Coach)
De Matha High School
Athletic Dept
Hyattsville, MD 20781, USA

Wooten, Nicholas (Producer)
c/o Staff Member William Morris Endeavor (LA)
9601 Wilshire Blvd
Beverly Hills, CA 90210-5213, USA

Wooten, Ron (Football Player)
New England Patriots
2401 Lewis Grove Ln
Raleigh, NC 27608-1380, USA

Wooten, Shawn (Athlete, Baseball Player)
15724 50th Pl N
Minneapolis, MN 55446-3472, USA

Wooten, Victor (Musician)
1020 Yellow Hammer Dr
Kingston Springs, TN 37082-5233, USA

Wooton, John (Football Player)
Cleveland Browns
13520 Darley Ave
Cleveland, OH 44110-2122, USA

Wootten, Morgan (Athlete, Basketball Player)
6912 Wells Pkwy
University Park, MD 20782-1051, USA

Wootton, Corey (Athlete, Football Player)
c/o Michael McCartney Priority Sports & Entertainment - Chicago
312 N La Salle
Suite 650
Chicago, IL 60610, USA

Wopat, Tom (Actor, Musician)
2614 Woodlawn Dr
Nashville, TN 37212-5222, USA

Word, Barry (Athlete, Football Player)
5746 Janneys Mill Cir
Haymarket, VA 20169-6196, USA

Word, Roscoe (Football Player)
New York Jets
175 Richardson Rd
Ridgeland, MS 39157-9781, USA

Worden, Al Colonel (Astronaut)
5355 Corsica Pl
Vero Beach, FL 32967-7632, USA

Worden, Alfred M (Astronaut)
PO Box 8065
Vero Beach, FL 32963, USA

Worden, Neil (Football Player)
Philadelphia Eagles
5217 Country Club Dr
Brentwood, TN 37027-5175, USA

Working Title, The (Music Group)
c/o Staff Member Paradigm (Monterey)
404 W Franklin St
Monterey, CA 93940-2303, USA

Workman, Hank (Athlete, Baseball Player)
307 19th St
Santa Monica, CA 90402-2409, USA

Workman, Haywoode (Athlete, Basketball Player)
8350 Savannah Trace Cir Apt 208
Tampa, FL 33615-5513, USA

Workman, Shanelle (Actor)
12954 Magnolia Blvd
Sherman Oaks, CA 91423-1619, USA

Workman, Tom (Athlete, Basketball Player)
422 NE Roth St
Portland, OR 97211-1084, USA

Workman, Vincent (Vince) (Athlete, Football Player)
98 Southfield Ave Apt 605
Stamford, CT 06902-7654, USA

World Party (Music Group)
c/o Staff Member Paradigm (Monterey)
404 W Franklin St
Monterey, CA 93940-2303, USA

Worley, Darryl (Musician)
c/o Staff Member International Artist Management
311 Robinhood Rd
Brentwood, TN 37027-5137, USA

Worley, Jo Anne (Actor)
4714 Arcola Ave
Toluca Lake, CA 91602-1522, USA

Worley, Tim (Athlete, Football Player)
531 Sydnor Ave
Ridgecrest, CA 93555-3143, USA

Wormald, Kenny (Actor)
c/o Dallas Sonnier Caliber Media Company
5670 Wilshire Blvd Ste 1600
Los Angeles, CA 90036-5659, USA

Woronov, Mary (Actor)
4350 1/4 Beverly Blvd
Los Angeles, CA 90004, USA

Worrell, Mark (Athlete, Baseball Player)
3400 Harmon Ave Apt 364
Austin, TX 78705-2367, USA

Worrell, Peter (Athlete, Hockey Player)
3560 Aladdin Ave
Boynton Beach, FL 33436-2752, USA

Worrell, Tim (Athlete, Baseball Player)
4719 W El Cortez Pl
Phoenix, AZ 85083-2206, USA

Worrell, Todd (Athlete, Baseball Player)
810 Simmons Ave
Saint Louis, MO 63122-2754, USA

Worth, Jody (Actor, Producer)
c/o Jeff Jacobs *Creative Artists Agency (CAA-LA)*
2000 Avenue of the Stars Ste 100
Los Angeles, CA 90067-4705, USA

Wortham, Barron (Athlete, Football Player)
8608 Busch Gardens Dr
Fort Worth, TX 76123-1445, USA

Wortham, Rich (Athlete, Baseball Player)
1708 Mira Vis
Leander, TX 78641-8821, USA

Worthen, Sam (Athlete, Basketball Player)
Harlem Wizards
36 Harmon Cove Tower Ste 2
Secaucus, NJ 07094-1772, USA

Worthington, Al (Athlete, Baseball Player)
12070 Highwav 55
Sterrett, AL 35147, USA

Worthington, Al (Athlete, Baseball Player)
12070 Highway 55
Sterrett, AL 35147-9601, USA

Worthington, Cal
3815 Florin Rd
Sacramento, CA 95823-1801

Worthington, Craig (Athlete, Baseball Player)
10019 Mattock Ave
Downey, CA 90240-3528, USA

Worthington, Melvin L (Religious Leader)
Free Will Baptists
PO Box 5002
Antioch, TN 37011-5002, USA

Worthington, Sam (Actor)
c/o Sandra Chang *Anonymous Content (LA)*
3532 Hayden Ave
Culver City, CA 90232-2413, USA

Worthy, Calum (Actor)
c/o Paul Young *Principato/Young Management (LA)*
9465 Wilshire Blvd Ste 900
Beverly Hills, CA 90212-2608, USA

Worthy, James (Athlete, Basketball Player, Sportscaster)
5750 Corbett St
Los Angeles, CA 90016-4545, USA

Worthy, Rick (Actor)
c/o Charles Silver *SMS Talent*
8383 Wilshire Blvd Ste 230
Beverly Hills, CA 90211-2436, USA

Wortman, Keith (Football Player)
Green Bay Packers
421 Bordeaux Way
Saint Peters, MO 63376-2789, USA

Wortman, Kevin (Athlete, Hockey Player)
42 David Dr
Saugus, MA 01906-1214, USA

Wosniak, Stephen (Actor, Writer)
c/o Staff Member *Inevitable Film Group*
8484 Wilshire Blvd Ste 465
Beverly Hills, CA 90211-3233, USA

Wosniak, Steve (Business Person)
c/o Bob Thomas *Worldwide Speakers Group, LLC*
99 Canal Center Plz Ste 100
Alexandria, VA 22314-1588, USA

Wottie, David J (Dave) (Athlete, Track Athlete)
9245 Forest Hill Ln
Germantown, TN 38139-7906, USA

Wottle, Dave
9245 Forest Hill Ln
Germantown, TN 38139-7906, USA

Wotus, Ron (Athlete, Baseball Player)
6 Monteira Ln
Martinez, CA 94553-9768, USA

Wouk, Herman (Writer)
303 W Crestview Dr
Palm Springs, CA 92264-8920, USA

Wow, Bow (Actor, Musician)
2838 Grey Moss Pass
Duluth, GA 30097-5226, USA

Wozniacki, Caroline (Athlete, Tennis Player)
c/o Staff Member *Women's Tennis Association (WTA (US))*
1 Progress Plz Ste 1500
St Petersburg, FL 33701-4335, USA

Wozniak, Steve (Business Person)
16400 Blackberry Hill Rd
Los Gatos, CA 95030-7513, USA

Wozniewski, Andy (Athlete, Hockey Player)
322 Lakeview Dr
Buffalo Grove, IL 60089-1788, USA

Wregget, Ken (Athlete, Hockey Player)
1778 McMillan Rd
Pittsburgh, PA 15241-2654, USA

Wren, Darryl (Football Player)
New England Patriots
1418 Skipjack Dr
Fort Washington, MD 20744-4216, USA

Wren, Frank (Baseball Player)
500 Tuxedo Ln
Peachtree City, GA 30269-4070, USA

Wrenn, Peter (Horse Racer)
5215 Wren Ct
Carmel, IN 46033-9646, USA

Wrenn, Robert (Bob) (Athlete, Golfer)
8911 Alendale Rd
Henrico, VA 23229-7701, USA

Wright, Alexander (Athlete, Football Player)
501 S Mississippi St
Amarillo, TX 79106-8735, USA

Wright, Ben (Sportscaster)
CBS-TV
51 W 52nd St
Sports Dept
New York, NY 10019-6119, USA

Wright, Betty (Musician)
Rodgers Redding
1048 Tattnall St
Macon, GA 31201-1537, USA

Wright, Bracey (Basketball Player)
c/o Staff Member *Minnesota Timberwolves*
600 1st Ave N
Minneapolis, MN 55403-1400, USA

Wright, Brad (Athlete, Basketball Player)
1050 S Cloverdale Ave
Los Angeles, CA 90019-6732, USA

Wright, Charles (Football Player)
St Louis Cardinals
2698 Wakefield Ln
Westlake, OH 44145-3837, USA

Wright, Chase (Athlete, Baseball Player)
6703 Kit Carson Trl
Wichita Falls, TX 76310-2708, USA

Wright, Chely (Musician)
1904 Boscobel St
Nashville, TN 37206-2018, USA

Wright, Clyde (Athlete, Baseball Player)
528 S Jeanine St
Anaheim, CA 92806-4415, USA

Wright, Dan (Athlete, Baseball Player)
310 Vernon Dr
Batesville, AR 72501-4112, USA

Wright, David (Athlete, Baseball Player)
1105 Hillston Ct
Chesapeake, VA 23322-9534, USA

Wright, Dick (Cartoonist)
Columbus Dispatch
34 S 3rd St
Editorial Dept
Columbus, OH 43215-4241, USA

Wright, Donald C (Don) (Cartoonist)
PO Box 1176
Palm Beach, FL 33480-1176, USA

Wright, Dorell (Athlete, Basketball Player)
158 Twin Peaks Dr
Walnut Creek, CA 94595-1728, USA

Wright, Doug (Writer)
c/o Staff Member *ICM Partners (NY)*
730 5th Ave
New York, NY 10019-4105, USA

Wright, Elmo (Football Player)
Kansas City Chiefs
11419 Olympia Dr
Houston, TX 77077-6419, USA

Wright, Eric (Athlete, Football Player)
c/o Tony Fleming *Impact Sports - LA*
11331 Ventura Blvd Ste 1A
Studio City, CA 91604-3147, USA

Wright, Evan (Writer)
c/o Susan Solomon *Principato/Young Management (LA)*
9465 Wilshire Blvd Ste 900
Beverly Hills, CA 90212-2608, USA

Wright, Felix (Football Player)
Cleveland Browns
2698 Wakefield Ln
Westlake, OH 44145-3837, USA

Wright, Felix E (Business Person)
Leggett & Platt Inc
1 Leggett Rd
Carthage, MO 64836-9649, USA

Wright, Geoffrey (Actor)
Innovative Artists
1505 10th St
Santa Monica, CA 90401-2805, USA

Wright, George (Athlete, Baseball Player)
3306 Tranquility Dr
Arlington, TX 76016-2057, USA

Wright, George (Football Player)
Baltimore Colts
10627 Seaford Dr
Houston, TX 77089-1425, USA

Wright, Gerald (Director)
Guthrie Theatre
725 Vineland Pl
Minneapolis, MN 55403-1139, USA

Wright, Howard (Athlete, Basketball Player)
3019 Kingswood Way
Louisville, KY 40216-4914, USA

Wright, Hugh (Musician)
William Morris Agency
2100 W End Ave Ste 1000
Nashville, TN 37203-5240, USA

Wright, Irving S (Doctor)
25 E End Ave
New York, NY 10028-7052, USA

Wright, Jamey (Athlete, Baseball Player)
4325 Fairfax Ave
Dallas, TX 75205-3026, USA

Wright, Jaret (Athlete, Baseball Player)
3816 Vista Azul
San Clemente, CA 92672-4541, USA

Wright, Jarius (Athlete, Football Player)
c/o Ryan Morgan *MAG Sports Agency*
8222 Melrose Ave Fl 2
Los Angeles, CA 90046-6825, USA

Wright, Jay (Writer)
General Delivery
Piermont, NH 03779, USA

Wright, Jeff (Athlete, Football Player)
23426 N 21st Pl
Phoenix, AZ 85024-8631, USA

Wright, Jeff (Football Player)
Minnesota Vikings
6341 Rolf Ave
Minneapolis, MN 55439-1434, USA

Wright, Jeffrey (Actor)
c/o Jimmy Darmody *Creative Artists Agency (CAA-LA)*
2000 Avenue of the Stars Ste 100
Los Angeles, CA 90067-4705, USA

Wright, Jim (Athlete, Baseball Player)
549 E Randall St
Coopersville, MI 49404-9649, USA

Wright, Jim (Athlete, Baseball Player)
513 W Wyndermere Ct
Peoria, IL 61614-2919, USA

Wright, Joby (Athlete, Basketball Player)
University of Wyoming
PO Box 3434
Athletic Dept
Laramie, WY 82071, USA

Wright, Johnny (Producer)
Wright Entertainment Group
7680 Universal Blvd Ste 500
Orlando, FL 32819-8998, USA

Wright, Joseph "Joby" (Athlete, Basketball Player)
6010 Buck Trail Rd
Indianapolis, IN 46237-9773, USA

Wright, Julian (Athlete, Basketball Player)
50 Pinehurst Dr
New Orleans, LA 70131-3355, USA

Wright, Keith (Athlete, Football Player)
4419 Coldbrook Ln
Sachse, TX 75048-4595, USA

Wright, Ken (Athlete, Baseball Player)
1651 Ora Dr
Pensacola, FL 32506-8250, USA

Wright, Larry (Athlete, Basketball Player)
7610 Lakeside Manor Ln
Pearland, TX 77581-7528, USA

Wright, Louie (Football Player)
Denver Broncos
2263 S Quentin Way # 301
Aurora, CO 80014-7316, USA

Wright, Louis D (Athlete, Football Player)
3140 S Peoria St # K274
Seismic Corp
Aurora, CO 80014-3178, USA

Wright, Max (Actor)
241 Valley Dr
Hermosa Beach, CA 90254-4660, USA

Wright, Michael (Actor)
c/o Steven Arcieri *Arcieri & Associates Inc*
60 E 42nd St Ste 2315
New York, NY 10165-5015, USA

Wright, Michael W (Business Person)
Super Valu Inc
11840 Valley View Rd
Eden Prairie, MN 55344-3691, USA

Wright, Michelle (Musician)
Savannah Music
5114 Victoria Cv
Brentwood, TN 37027-6807, USA

Wright, Mickey (Athlete, Golfer)
2972 SE Treasure Island Rd
Port Saint Lucie, FL 34952-5773, USA

Wright, Mike (Athlete, Football Player)
c/o Staff Member *New England Patriots*
1 Patriot Pl
Foxboro, MA 02035-1388, USA

Wright, Nathaniel (Nate) (Football Player)
Atlanta Falcons
9256 Kornbrust Dr
Lone Tree, CO 80124-5550, USA

Wright, N'Bushe (Actor)
c/o Staff Member *Innovative Artists (LA)*
1505 10th St
Santa Monica, CA 90401-2805, USA

Wright, Pamela (Athlete, Golfer)
8031 N 73rd St
Scottsdale, AZ 85258-2713, USA

Wright, Pat (Musician)
Superstars Unlimited
PO Box 371371
Las Vegas, NV 89137-1371, USA

Wright, Petra (Actor)
c/o Bob Glennon *One Talent Management*
3680 1/2 Fredonia Dr
Los Angeles, CA 90068-1208, USA

Wright, Randy (Football Player)
Green Bay Packers
3591 Richie Rd
Verona, WI 53593-9649, USA

Wright, Ricky (Athlete, Baseball Player)
2502 Clark Ln
Paris, TX 75460-6220, USA

Wright, Robin (Actor, Producer)
265 Water St Apt 5
New York, NY 10038-1718, USA

Wright, Ron (Athlete, Baseball Player)
310 S 2100 E
Saint George, UT 84790-1465, USA

Wright, Ronald (Winkie) (Boxer)
c/o James Prince *Prince Boxing Enterprises*
3030 Jensen Dr
Houston, TX 77026-5511, USA

Wright, Roy (Athlete, Baseball Player)
331 Pinehurst Cir
Chickamauga, GA 30707-1459, USA

Wright, Samuel E (Actor)
c/o Marvin Josephson *Marvin A Josephson Management*
16 W 22nd St Fl 10
New York, NY 10010-5967, USA

Wright, Sarah (Actor)
c/o Ellen Meyer *Ellen Meyer Management*
8899 Beverly Blvd Ste 612
Los Angeles, CA 90048-2429, USA

Wright, Sharone (Athlete, Basketball Player)
6080 Lakeview Rd Apt 3504
Warner Robins, GA 31088-9157, USA

Wright, Stephen T (Athlete, Football Player)
14 Conifer Sq
Augusta, GA 30909-4505, USA

Wright, Steve (Athlete, Football Player)
15 Camel Point Dr
Laguna Beach, CA 92651-6988, USA

Wright, Steven (Actor, Comedian)
c/o Tim Sarkes *Brillstein Entertainment Partners (LA)*
9150 Wilshire Blvd Ste 350
Beverly Hills, CA 90212-3453, USA

Wright, Tim (Athlete, Football Player)
c/o Joe Flanagan *BTI Sports Advisors*
170 N Scoville Ave
Oak Park, IL 60302-2647, USA

Wright, Tom (Actor)
c/o Steven Siebert *Lighthouse Entertainment*
9220 W Sunset Blvd Ste 200
West Hollywood, CA 90069-3501, USA

Wright, Tom (Athlete, Baseball Player)
1116 Poplar Springs Church Rd
Shelby, NC 28152-8071, USA

Wright, Trevor (Actor)
c/o Tiffany Kuzon *Evolution Entertainment (LA)*
901 N Highland Ave
Los Angeles, CA 90038-2412, USA

Wright, Tyler (Athlete, Hockey Player)
200 W Nationwide Blvd Unit 1
Attn Coaching Staff
Columbus, OH 43215-2561, USA

Wright, Van Earl (Actor)
c/o Jill Smoller *William Morris Endeavor (LA)*
9601 Wilshire Blvd
Beverly Hills, CA 90210-5213, USA

Wright, Weldon (Athlete, Football Player)
701 E Bluff St Apt 6406
Fort Worth, TX 76102-2372, USA

Wright, Wesley (Athlete, Baseball Player)
9661 Colleton Pl
Montgomery, AL 36117-8458, USA

Wright, Willie (Athlete, Football Player)
13456 Dry Gulch Rd
Paonia, CO 81428-7119, USA

Wright, Winky (Athlete, Boxer)
c/o Staff Member *Violator Management*
36 W 25th St Fl 2
New York, NY 10010-2768, USA

Wright Jr, Charles P (Writer)
940 Locust Ave
Charlottesville, VA 22901-4030, USA

Wrightman, Tim (Football Player)
Chicago Bears
3505 S Denison Ave
San Pedro, CA 90731-6803, USA

Wrightson, Bernard (Bernie) (Swimmer)
924 Birch Ave
Escondido, CA 92027-3903, USA

Wrigley Jr, William (Business Person)
William Wrigley Jr Co
410 N Michigan Ave Ste 376
Chicago, IL 60611-4221, USA

Wrona, Rick (Athlete, Baseball Player)
2946 E 57th St
Tulsa, OK 74105-7404, USA

Wu, Alice (Writer)
c/o Staff Member *Creative Artists Agency (CAA-LA)*
2000 Avenue of the Stars Ste 100
Los Angeles, CA 90067-4705, USA

Wu, David (Congressman, Politician)
2338 Rayburn Hob
Washington, DC 20515-0546, USA

Wu, Jason (Designer)
Jason Wu
240 W 35th St Fl 11
New York, NY 10001-2506, USA

Wu, Kristy (Actor)
c/o Craig Dorfman *Frontline Management*
5670 Wilshire Blvd Ste 1370
Los Angeles, CA 90036-5679, USA

Wu, Lisa (Reality Star)
c/o Staff Member *Bravo (NY)*
30 Rockefeller Plz
New York, NY 10112-0015, USA

Wu, Vivian (Actor)
McKeon-Myones Management
9100 Wilshire Blvd Ste 350W
C/O Laura Myones
Beverly Hills, CA 90212-3437, USA

Wudunn, Sheryl (Journalist)
35 W 89th St
New York, NY 10024-2016, USA

Wuerffel, Danny (Athlete, Football Player, Heisman Trophy Winner)
424 Mimosa Dr
Decatur, GA 30030-3736, USA

Wuertz, Michael (Athlete, Baseball Player)
15029 N Thompson
Peak Pkwy Ste B111
Scottsdale, AZ 85260, USA

Wuhl, Robert (Actor)
10590 Holman Ave
Los Angeles, CA 90024-6042, USA

Wuhrer, Kari (Actor, Musician)
PO Box 69188
West Hollywood, CA 90069-0188, USA

Wunsch, Jerry (Football Player)
Tampa Bay Buccaneers
2601 Red Maple Rd
Wausau, WI 54401-9151, USA

Wunsch, Kelly (Athlete, Baseball Player)
13017 Zen Gardens Way
Austin, TX 78732-1656, USA

Wu-Tang Clan (Music Group)
PO Box 405
Asbury Park, NJ 07712-0405, USA

Wuycik, Dennis (Athlete, Basketball Player)
31 Rogerson Dr
Chapel Hill, NC 27517-4037, USA

Wyant, Fred (Football Player)
Washington Redskins
516 Westwood Ave
Morgantown, WV 26505-2125, USA

Wyatt, Alvin (Football Player)
Oakland Raiders
PO Box 244
Daytona Beach, FL 32115-0244, USA

Wyatt, Doug (Athlete, Football Player)
23 Andante Trail Pl
Shenandoah, TX 77381-2775, USA

Wyatt, Jennifer (Golfer)
Carolina Group
2321 Devine St Ste A
Columbia, SC 29205-2428, USA

Wyatt, Keke (Musician)
Universal Attractions
145 W 57th St # 1500
New York, NY 10019-2220, USA

Wyatt, Shannon (Actor)
8949 Falling Creek Ct
Annandale, VA 22003-4108, USA

Wyatt, Sharon (Actor)
23622 Calabasas Rd Ste 107
Calabasas, CA 91302-1584, USA

Wyatt, Summer (Beauty Pageant Winner)
2015 Unity Rd
Princeton, WV 24739-8587, USA

Wyatt Jr, Oscar S (Business Person)
Coastal Corp
6955 S Union Park Ctr Ste 540
Midvale, UT 84047-6520, USA

Wyche, Samuel D (Sam) (Athlete, Coach, Football Coach, Football Player, Sportscaster)
PO Box 1570
Pickens, SC 29671-1570, USA

Wycheck, Frank (Athlete, Football Player)
4674 Sunrise Ave
Bensalem, PA 19020-1112, USA

Wycinsky, Craig (Football Player)
Cleveland Browns
6890 E Sunrise Dr Ste 120
Tucson, AZ 85750-0739, USA

Wycoff, Brooks (Athlete)
1 Mohegan Sun Blvd
Uncasville, CT 06382-1355

Wyden, Ron (Politician)
312 A St NE
Washington, DC 20002-5938, USA

Wygal, Terry (Business Person)
Express Home Solutions Ltd
3005 Woodland Hills Dr
Kingwood, TX 77339-1403, USA

Wylde, Chris (Actor, Comedian)
3313 1/2 Barham Blvd
Los Angeles, CA 90068-1450, USA

Wylde, Peter (Athlete, Horse Racer, Olympic Athlete)
247 Wood Dale Dr
Wellington, FL 33414-4719, USA

Wylde, Zakk (Musician)
31329 Sloan Canyon Rd
Castaic, CA 91384-3415, USA

Wylde Bunch, The (Music Group)
c/o Staff Member *Paradigm (Monterey)*
404 W Franklin St
Monterey, CA 93940-2303, USA

Wyle, Noah (Actor, Director, Producer)
3065 Long Canyon Rd
Santa Ynez, CA 93460-9349, USA

Wylie, Adam (Actor)
14011 Ventura Blvd Ste 202
Sherman Oaks, CA 91423-3594, USA

Wylie, Joe (Athlete, Football Player)
8312 Bucknell Dr
Tyler, TX 75703-5103, USA

Wylie, Paul (Athlete, Figure Skater,
Olympic Athlete)
9819 Deer Brook Ln
Charlotte, NC 28210-8144, USA

Wyman, David (Football Player)
Seattle Seahawks
2114 204th Pl NE
Sammamish, WA 98074-4390, USA

Wyman, Joel (Producer, Writer)
c/o Staff Member *Creative Artists Agency
(CAA-LA)*
2000 Avenue of the Stars Ste 100
Los Angeles, CA 90067-4705, USA

Wynalda, Eric (Soccer Player)
2313 Stormcroft Ct
Westlake Village, CA 91361-2054, USA

Wynant, H M
300 S Raymond Ave Ste 11
Pasadena, CA 91105-2639, USA

Wynder, A J (Athlete, Basketball Player)
1 Cardenti Ct
Newark, DE 19702-6833, USA

Wynegar, Butch (Athlete, Baseball Player)
PO Box 915811
Longwood, FL 32791-5811, USA

Wyner, George (Actor)
3450 Laurie Pl
Studio City, CA 91604-3881, USA

Wynn, Bob (Athlete, Golfer)
78455 Calle Orense
La Quinta, CA 92253-2370, USA

Wynn, Jimmy (Athlete, Baseball Player)
5507 Sandy Field Ct
Rosharon, TX 77583-2040, USA

Wynn, Renaldo (Football Player)
Jacksonville Jaguars
19805 Rothschild Ct
Ashburn, VA 20147-4124, USA

Wynn, Spergon (Football Player)
Cleveland Browns
614 32nd St
Galveston, TX 77550, USA

Wynn, Stephen A (Business Person)
Wynn Las Vegas
3131 Las Vegas Blvd S
Las Vegas, NV 89109-1967, USA

Wynn, Steve (Business Person)
Wynn Las Vegas
3131 Las Vegas Blvd S
Las Vegas, NV 89109-1967, USA

Wynne, Billy (Athlete, Baseball Player)
7722 Greenwich Ct W
Jacksonville, FL 32277-0924, USA

Wynne, Marvell (Athlete, Baseball Player)
39640 Del Val Dr
Murrieta, CA 92562-4038, USA

Wynorski, Jim (Director, Producer)
5124 Sunnyslope Ave
Sherman Oaks, CA 91423-1420, USA

Wynter, Sarah (Actor)
2443 Solar Dr
Los Angeles, CA 90046-1740, USA

Wyrozub, Randy (Athlete, Hockey Player)
6717 Westminster Dr
East Amherst, NY 14051-2805, USA

Wysocki, Ben (Musician)
4500 W 30th Ave
Denver, CO 80212-3019, USA

Wyss, Amanda (Actor)
c/o Staff Member *Badgley-Connor-King*
9229 W Sunset Blvd Ste 311
West Hollywood, CA 90069-3403, USA

Xscape (Musician)
c/o Staff Member *So So Def Recordings
Inc*
1350 Spring St NW Ste 750
Atlanta, GA 30309-2870, USA

Xuereb, Emanuel (Actor)
c/o Staff Member *Pantheon Talent*
1801 Century Park E Ste 1910
Los Angeles, CA 90067-2321, USA

Xuereb, Salvator (Actor)
2418 St George St
Los Angeles, CA 90027-3206, USA

Xzibit (Musician)
5173 Baza Ave
Woodland Hills, CA 91364-1802, USA

Yabians, Frank (Producer)
88 Bull Path
East Hampton, NY 11937-4622, USA

Yablans, Frank (Producer)
100 Bull Path
East Hampton, NY 11937-4601, USA

Yablonski, Jeremy (Athlete, Hockey
Player)
11646 W Fenchurch St
Boise, ID 83709-4471, USA

Yabu, Keiichi (Athlete, Baseball Player)
c/o Team Member *San Francisco Giants*
24 Willie Mays Plz
Sbc Park
San Francisco, CA 94107-2199, USA

Yachmenev, Vitali (Athlete, Hockey
Player)
1485 Gulf of Mexico Dr Unit 104
Longboat Key, FL 34228-3472, USA

Yaeger, Andrea (Tennis Player)
1490 S Ute Ave
Aspen, CO 81611-2814, USA

Yager, Rick (Cartoonist)
North American Syndicate
235 E 45th St
New York, NY 10017-3305, USA

Yagher, Jeff (Actor)
15057 Sherview Pl
Sherman Oaks, CA 91403-5037, USA

Yago, Gideon (Journalist, Television Host)
c/o Staff Member *MTV (NYC)*
1515 Broadway
New York, NY 10036-8901, USA

Yaguda, Stan (Musician)
Joyce Agency
370 Harrison Ave
Harrison, NY 10528-2714, USA

Yagudin, Alexei (Figure Skater)
Connecticut Skating Center
300 Alumni Rd
Newington, CT 06111-1868, USA

Yahr, Betty (Athlete, Baseball Player)
10360 Timber Ridge Dr
Milan, MI 48160-8929, USA

Yakavonis, Ray (Athlete, Football Player)
8 Strand St
Hanover Township, PA 18706-4011, USA

Yake, Terry (Athlete, Hockey Player)
7827 Wind Hill Dr
O Fallon, MO 63368-4135, USA

Yale, Brian (Musician)
2616 Bayview Dr
Ft Lauderdale, FL 33306-1766, USA

Yaleborough, Cale (Race Car Driver)
2723 W Palmetto St Unit B
Florence, SC 29501-5929, USA

Yallop, Frank (Coach)
San Jose Earthquakes
3550 Stevens Creek Blvd Ste 200
San Jose, CA 95117-1031, USA

Yamagata, Rachel (Musician)
c/o Staff Member *Paradigm (Monterey)*
404 W Franklin St
Monterey, CA 93940-2303, USA

Yamaguchi, Kristi (Athlete, Figure Skater,
Olympic Athlete)
Always Dream Foundation
1203 Preservation Park Way Ste 102
Oakland, CA 94612-1246, USA

Yamaguchi, Roy (Business Person)
Roy's Restaurant
6600 Kalanianaole Hwy
Kai Corporate Plaza
Honolulu, HI 96825-1273, USA

Yamame, Marlene Mitsuko (Actor)
Herb Tannen
10801 National Blvd Ste 101
Los Angeles, CA 90064-4140, USA

Yamaoka, Seigen H (Religious Leader)
Buddhist Churches of America
1710 Octavia St
San Francisco, CA 94109-4341, USA

Yamasaki, Lindsey (Athlete, Basketball
Player)
767 Union St
San Francisco, CA 94133-2723, USA

Yamasaki, Taro M (Journalist)
People Magazine Editorial Dept
Time-Life Building
New York, NY 10020, USA

Yamazaki, Naoko (Astronaut)
500 Blue Dolphin Dr
Seabrook, TX 77586, USA

Yamin, Elliott (Actor, Musician)
c/o Mark Gorlick *The Collective*
8383 Wilshire Blvd Ste 1050
Beverly Hills, CA 90211-2415, USA

Yan, Esteban (Athlete, Baseball Player)
8842 Cameron Crest Dr
Tampa, FL 33626-4712, USA

Yanchar, William (Athlete, Football
Player)
PO Box 460141
Aurora, CO 80046-0141, USA

Yancy, Emily (Actor)
Henderson/Hogan
8285 W Sunset Blvd Ste 1
West Hollywood, CA 90046-2420, USA

Yancy, Hugh (Athlete, Baseball Player)
1708 Marilyn Ave
Bradenton, FL 34207-4633, USA

Yanda, Marshal (Athlete, Football Player)
c/o Neil Cornrich *NC Sports, LLC*
best to contact via email
Columbus, OH 43201, USA

Yandle, Keith (Athlete, Hockey Player)
646 Canton Ave
Milton, MA 02186-3133, USA

Yanez, Eduardo (Actor)
c/o Thomas Richards *Corsa Agency, The*
11704 Wilshire Blvd Ste 204
Los Angeles, CA 90025-1510, USA

Yang, Janet (Producer)
Manifest Film Company
PO Box 832
Santa Monica, CA 90406-0832, USA

Yang, Jerry (Business Person)
26535 Altamont Rd
Los Altos Hills, CA 94022-4334, USA

Yang, Young A (Athlete, Golfer)
5451 Millenia Lakes Blvd Apt 422
Orlando, FL 32839-6319, USA

Yankee, Daddy (Musician)
c/o Staff Member *Relentless Agency*
261 E 134th St Fl 2
Bronx, NY 10454-4405, USA

Yankey, David (Athlete, Football Player)
c/o Michael McCartney *Priority Sports &
Entertainment - Chicago*
312 N La Salle
Suite 650
Chicago, IL 60610, USA

Yankovic, Al (Weird Al) (Comedian,
Musician)
1631 Magnetic Ter
Los Angeles, CA 90069-1149, USA

Yankowski, George (Athlete, Baseball
Player)
3073 Saint Michael Ln
The Villages, FL 32162-7484, USA

Yankowski, Ron (Athlete, Football Player)
1318 Saint Paul Rd
Ballwin, MO 63021-8208, USA

Yanni (Musician, Songwriter)
PO Box 107
8983 Okeechobee Blvd #202
West Palm Beach, FL 33402-0107, USA

Yaralian, Zaven (Athlete, Football Player)
PO Box 1080
Summerland, CA 93067-1080, USA

Yarber, Eric (Athlete, Football Player)
Oregon State University
325 Valley Football Ctr
Attn: Football Program
Corvallis, OR 97331-8544, USA

Yarborough, Glenn (Musician)
PO Box 158
Malibu, CA 90265-0158, USA

Yarborough, W Caleb (Cale) (Race Car Driver)
Yarborough Racing
2723 W Palmetto St
Florence, SC 29501-5929, USA

Yarbrough, Cedric (Actor)
c/o Jenni Weinman *Patricola Lust PR*
9171 Wilshire Blvd Ste 441
Beverly Hills, CA 90210-5516, USA

Yarbrough, Curtis (Religious Leader)
General Baptists Assn
100 Stinson Dr
Poplar Bluff, MO 63901-8746, USA

Yarbrough, Glenn (Musician, Songwriter, Writer)
150 Avenida Presidio
San Clemente, CA 92672-3170, USA

Yarbrough, Jim (Athlete, Football Player)
720 N Phelps Ave
Winter Park, FL 32789-2757, USA

Yarbrough, Jim (Athlete, Football Player)
440 Capricorn St
Cedar Hill, TX 75104-8106, USA

Yardbirds, The (Music Group)
PO Box 1821
Ojai, CA 93024-1821, USA

Yarkin, Cori (Musician)
GreeneHouse Management
PO Box 151234
C/O Allan Greene
Altamonte Springs, FL 32715-1234, USA

Yarlett, Claire (Actor)
c/o Lorraine Berglund *Lorraine Berglund Management*
11537 Hesby St
North Hollywood, CA 91601-3618, USA

Yarmuth, John (Congressman, Politician)
435 Cannon Hob
Washington, DC 20515-4312, USA

Yarmuth, John A (Congressman, Politician)
600 Dr Martin Luther King Pl
Romano Mazzoli Federal Building
Louisville, KY 40202-2239, USA

Yarnall, Celeste (Actor)
2899 Agoura Rd # 315
Westlake Village, CA 91361-3218, USA

Yarnall, Ed (Athlete, Baseball Player)
9837 Vouvray Dr
Baton Rouge, LA 70817-7646, USA

Yarnell, Ed (Athlete, Baseball Player)
9837 Vouvray Dr
Baton Rouge, LA 70817-7646, USA

Yarno, George (Athlete, Football Player)
1529 18th St
Lewiston, ID 83501-3657, USA

Yarno, John (Athlete, Football Player)
10535 158th Ave NE
Redmond, WA 98052-2659, USA

Yarrow, Peter (Musician, Songwriter, Writer)
27 W 67th St # 5E
New York, NY 10023-6258, USA

Yary, A Ronald (Ron) (Athlete, Football Player)
38886 Calle De Companero
Murrieta, CA 92562-8877, USA

Yasbeck, Amy (Actor)
1205 Benedict Canyon Dr
Beverly Hills, CA 90210-2727, USA

Yashin, Alexei (Athlete, Hockey Player)
6 Polo Dr
Old Westbury, NY 11568-1043, USA

Yastrzemski, Carl (Athlete, Baseball Player)
22 Lakeshore Rd
Boxford, MA 01921-1115, USA

Yastrzemski, Carl
255 State St
Boston, MA 02109-2617, USA

Yasukawa, Roger (Race Car Driver)
2304 Nearcliff St
Torrance, CA 90505-7030, USA

Yasutake, Patti (Actor)
145 S Fairfax Ave Ste 310
Los Angeles, CA 90036-2176, USA

Yates, Bill (Cartoonist)
c/o Staff Member *King Features Syndication*
300 W 57th St Fl 15
New York, NY 10019-5238, USA

Yates, Billy (Athlete, Football Player)
c/o Staff Member *New England Patriots*
1 Patriot Pl
Foxboro, MA 02035-1388, USA

Yates, Bob (Athlete, Football Player)
125 Sunflower St
Georgetown, TX 78633-4556, USA

Yates, Doug (Race Car Driver)
Doug Yates Racing
112 Byers Creek Rd
Mooresville, NC 28117-4376, USA

Yates, Jim (Race Car Driver)
Commonwealth Service & Supply
4740 Eisenhower Ave
Alexandria, VA 22304-4806, USA

Yates, Robert (Race Car Driver)
18923 Coveside Ln
Cornelius, NC 28031-5252, USA

Yates, Tyler (Athlete, Baseball Player)
c/o Pat Rooney *SFX Baseball*
400 Skokie Blvd Ste 280
Northbrook, IL 60062-7939, USA

Yates, Wayne (Athlete, Basketball Player)
210 Yates Rd
Robeline, LA 71469, USA

Yates, Yvette (Producer)
c/o Staff Member *Payaso Entertainment*
5555 Melrose Ave Bldg 233
Los Angeles, CA 90038-3989, USA

Yavari, Leila (Actor)
c/o Staff Member *Cunningham Escott Slevin & Doherty (CESD-LA)*
10635 Santa Monica Blvd Ste 130
Los Angeles, CA 90025-8306, USA

Yavneh, Cyrus (Producer)
c/o Staff Member *ICM Partners (LA)*
10250 Constellation Blvd Fl 7
Los Angeles, CA 90067-6207, USA

Yawney, Trent (Athlete, Hockey Player)
7750 E Appaloosa Trl
Orange, CA 92869-2407, USA

Yayo, Tony (Musician)
c/o Staff Member *Interscope Records (NY)*
1755 Broadway
New York, NY 10019-3743, USA

Yazpik, Jose Maria (Actor)
c/o Carlos Carreras *Agency for the Performing Arts (APA-LA)*
405 S Beverly Dr Ste 500
Beverly Hills, CA 90212-4425, USA

Yeager, Steve (Athlete, Baseball Player)
JD Legends Promotions
PO Box 34184
Granada Hills, CA 91394-4184, USA

Yeagley, Jerry (Coach)
1418 S Sare Rd
Bloomington, IN 47401-4431, USA

Yeah Yeah Yeahs (Music Group)
c/o Tony Cuilla *Ciulla Management*
2015 Castilian Dr
Los Angeles, CA 90068-2608, USA

Yeakel, Scott (Astronaut)
30 Ticcoma Way
Nantucket, MA 02554-6078, USA

Yearley, Douglas C (Business Person)
Phelps Dodge Corp
1 N Central Ave Ste 100
Phoenix, AZ 85004-4464, USA

Yearwood, Trisha (Musician)
PO Box 120895
Nashville, TN 37212-0895, USA

Yeates, Jeff (Athlete, Football Player)
3793 Club Dr NE
Atlanta, GA 30319-1107, USA

Yeats, Matthew (Athlete, Hockey Player)
2947 W Riverwalk Cir Unit F
Littleton, CO 80123-7118, USA

Yelchin, Anton (Actor)
3866 Berry Dr
Studio City, CA 91604-3859, USA

Yelding, Eric (Athlete, Baseball Player)
PO Box 325
Montrose, AL 36559-0325, USA

Yeley, JJ (Race Car Driver)
Mayfield Motorsports
2220 Highway 49 N
Harrisburg, NC 28075, USA

Yelle, Stephane (Athlete, Hockey Player)
1423 Foothills Village Dr
Henderson, NV 89012-7265, USA

Yellen, Larry (Athlete, Baseball Player)
3886 Toccoa Falls Dr
Duluth, GA 30097-8105, USA

Yellen, Linda B (Director, Producer)
3 Sheridan Sq
New York, NY 10014-6828, USA

Yellowcard (Musician)
Capitol Records
1750 Vine St # T-06
Los Angeles, CA 90028-5274, USA

Yelvington, Richard J (Athlete, Football Player)
2105 Barbe St
Lake Charles, LA 70601-9017, USA

Yeo, Gwendoline (Actor)
c/o Anne Geddes *Geddes Agency, The*
1203 Greenacre Ave
West Hollywood, CA 90046-5707, USA

Yeo, Mike (Athlete, Hockey Player)
317 Washington St
Attn Coaching Staff
Saint Paul, MN 55102-1609, USA

Yeoh, Michelle (Actor)
c/o Lee Stollman *The Gotham Group Inc*
9255 W Sunset Blvd Ste 515
West Hollywood, CA 90069-3308, USA

Yeoman, Owain (Actor)
16255 Ventura Blvd Ste 625
Encino, CA 91436-2307, USA

Yeoman, William F (Bill) (Athlete, Coach, Football Coach, Football Player)
3030 Country Club Blvd
Sugar Land, TX 77478-3630, USA

Yepremian, Garabed S (Garo) (Athlete, Football Player)
613 Martin Dr
Avondale, PA 19311-1316, USA

Yerman, Jack (Athlete, Olympic Athlete, Track Athlete)
753 Camellia Dr
Paradise, CA 95969-3817, USA

Yes (Music Group)
c/o Staff Member *10th Street Entertainment (LA)*
700 N San Vicente Blvd Ste G410
West Hollywood, CA 90069-5060, USA

Yetnikoff, Walter
c/o Daniel Strone *Trident Media Group LLC*
41 Madison Ave Fl 36
New York, NY 10010-2257, USA

Yett, Rich (Athlete, Baseball Player)
5840 E Fairbrook Cir
Mesa, AZ 85205-5559, USA

Yeun, Steven (Actor)
c/o Peter McHugh *The Gotham Group Inc*
9255 W Sunset Blvd Ste 515
West Hollywood, CA 90069-3308, USA

Yeutter, Clayton (Politician)
10955 Martingale Ct
Potomac, MD 20854-1500, USA

Yewcic, Thomas (Tom) (Athlete, Baseball Player, Football Player)
15 Danby Rd
Stoneham, MA 02180-3003, USA

Yi, Charlyne (Actor, Producer, Writer)
c/o Christie Smith *Mosaic Media Group*
9200 W Sunset Blvd Ste 10
West Hollywood, CA 90069-3608, USA

Ying Yang Twins (Music Group)
TVT Records
23 E 4th St Fl 3
New York, NY 10003-7023, USA

Yip, Vern (Designer, Television Host)
24 Wakefield Dr NE
Atlanta, GA 30309-1515, USA

Yoakam, Dwight (Musician, Songwriter)
7615 Mulholland Dr
Los Angeles, CA 90046-1218, USA

Yoba, Malik (Actor)
c/o Matt Luber *Luber Roklin Management*
5815 W Sunset Blvd Ste 206
Los Angeles, CA 90028-6481, USA

Yochim, Len (Athlete, Baseball Player)
316 Nelson Dr
New Orleans, LA 70123-1958, USA

Yochum, Dan (Athlete, Football Player)
88 Doges Promenade
Lindenhurst, NY 11757-6408, USA

Yocum, Matt (Race Car Driver)
9910 Devonshire Dr
Huntersville, NC 28078-5965, USA

Yoder, Kevin (Congressman, Politician)
214 Cannon Hob
Washington, DC 20515-3007, USA

Yohn, John (Athlete, Football Player)
12 Riverview Dr
Middletown, PA 17057-3433, USA

Yoho, Mack (Athlete, Football Player)
2205 Sacramento St Apt 304
San Francisco, CA 94115-2394, USA

Yoken, Mel B (Writer)
261 Carroll St
New Bedford, MA 02740-1412, USA

Yonakor, Rich (Athlete, Basketball Player)
38140 Tamarac Blvd Apt 106
Willoughby, OH 44094-3448, USA

Yonder Mountain String Band (Music Group)
c/o Staff Member *Paradigm (Monterey)*
404 W Franklin St
Monterey, CA 93940-2303, USA

Yoo, Aaron (Actor)
c/o Tony Cloer *Blue Ridge Entertainment*
41 Union Sq W Ste 809
New York, NY 10003-3264, USA

Yoo, Paula (Writer)
c/o Nancy Etz *ICM Partners (LA)*
10250 Constellation Blvd Fl 7
Los Angeles, CA 90067-6207, USA

Yore, Jim (Athlete, Football Player)
1084 Westlake Woods Dr
Springfield, MI 49037-7665, USA

York, Francine (Actor)
6430 W Sunset Blvd Ste 1205
Los Angeles, CA 90028-8002, USA

York, Jim (Athlete, Baseball Player)
31262 Via Del Verde
San Juan Capistrano, CA 92675-6315, USA

York, John J (Actor)
4846 Agnes Ave
Valley Village, CA 91607-3703, USA

York, Kathleen (Bird) (Actor)
2235 Alcyona Dr
Los Angeles, CA 90068-2804, USA

York, Michael (Actor)
9100 Cordell Dr
Los Angeles, CA 90069-1718, USA

York, Michael M (Journalist)
Lexington Herald-Leader
Editorial Dept
Main & Midland
Lexington, KY 40507, USA

York, Mike (Athlete, Baseball Player)
8001 S 84th Ct
Justice, IL 60458-1420, USA

York, Mike (Athlete, Hockey Player, Olympic Athlete)
6105 W Longview Dr
East Lansing, MI 48823-9739, USA

York, Morgan (Actor)
c/o Meredith Fine *Coast to Coast Talent Group*
3350 Barham Blvd
Los Angeles, CA 90068-1404, USA

York, Ray (Jockey)
27918 Highway 119
Taft, CA 93268-9612, USA

York, Taylor (Musician)
813 Lealand Ct
Nashville, TN 37204-4006, USA

Yorke, Thom (Musician)
c/o Staff Member *Creative Artists Agency (CAA-LA)*
2000 Avenue of the Stars Ste 100
Los Angeles, CA 90067-4705, USA

Yorkin, Bud (Director, Producer)
Bud Yorkin Productions
250 Delfem Dr
Los Angeles, CA 90077, USA

Yorkin, Peg (Politician)
Fund for Feminist Majority
1600 Wilson Blvd Ste 704
Arlington, VA 22209-2505, USA

Yorn, Peter (Musician, Songwriter, Writer)
c/o Rick Yorn *LBI Entertainment*
2000 Avenue of the Stars Ste 300N
Floor 3, North Tower
Los Angeles, CA 90067-4704, USA

Yorzyk, William (Athlete, Olympic Athlete, Swimmer)
174 Lane 7
Sturbridge, MA 01566, USA

Yost, David (Actor)
8837 Cortina Cir
Roseville, CA 95678-2940, USA

Yost, Ned (Athlete, Baseball Player, Coach)
Milwaukee Brewers
2854 Piedmont Lake Rd
Pine Mountain, GA 31822-3595, USA

Yothers, Tina (Actor, Musician)
1834 S Helen Ave
Ontario, CA 91762-6023, USA

Youel, Jim (Athlete, Football Player)
1102 Avenue F
Fort Madison, IA 52627-2743, USA

Youkilis, Kevin (Athlete, Baseball Player)
19475 N Grayhawk Dr Unit 1083
Scottsdale, AZ 85255-7420, USA

Youmans, Floyd (Athlete, Baseball Player)
1915 E Noel St
Tampa, FL 33610-6157, USA

Youmans, Maury (Athlete, Football Player)
300 Beach Dr NE Apt 2104
Saint Petersburg, FL 33701-3461, USA

Young, Ace (Musician)
c/o Stephen Ford *Diva Central Inc*
7510 W Sunset Blvd Ste 1445
Los Angeles, CA 90046-3408, USA

Young, Adrian (Musician)
4220 Lakewood Dr
Lakewood, CA 90712-3839, USA

Young, Al (Athlete, Football Player)
1947 Green Forest Dr
North Augusta, SC 29841-2174, USA

Young, Alan (Actor)
24072 La Hermosa Ave
Laguna Niguel, CA 92677-2227, USA

Young, Almon (Athlete, Football Player)
PO Box 983
Mc Crory, AR 72101-0983, USA

Young, Angus (Musician, Songwriter, Writer)
c/o Christopher Dalston *Creative Artists Agency (CAA-LA)*
2000 Avenue of the Stars Ste 100
Los Angeles, CA 90067-4705, USA

Young, Anthony (Athlete, Baseball Player)
13107 Ellesmere Dr
Houston, TX 77015-2111, USA

Young, Anthony (Athlete, Football Player)
914 Colonial Ct
Coatesville, PA 19320-1685, USA

Young, Archie (Athlete, Baseball Player)
Birmingham Black Barons
1804 Ethel Ave SW
Birmingham, AL 35211-4914, USA

Young, Bellamy (Actor)
c/o Steven Levy *Framework Entertainment (LA)*
9057 Nemo St Ste C
West Hollywood, CA 90069-5511, USA

Young, Bob (Cartoonist)
c/o Staff Member *King Features Syndication*
300 W 57th St Fl 15
New York, NY 10019-5238, USA

Young, Brian (Musician)
MOB Agency
6404 Wilshire Blvd Ste 505
Los Angeles, CA 90048-5507, USA

Young, Bryant C (Athlete, Football Player)
2324 Vernon Dr
Charlotte, NC 28211-1842, USA

Young, Burt (Actor)
Higgins Harte International
11 W Pioneer Blvd Ste D
Mesquite, NV 89027-3510, USA

Young, Charle E (Athlete, Football Player)
16035 Mink Rd NE
Woodinville, WA 98077-9460, USA

Young, Charles E (Athlete, Football Player)
16035 Mink Rd NE
Woodinville, WA 98077-9460, USA

Young, Charles L (Athlete, Football Player)
3152 La Costa Way
Raleigh, NC 27610-8280, USA

Young, Chris (Athlete, Baseball Player)
c/o Staff Member *Arizona Diamondbacks*
PO Box 2095
Phoenix, AZ 85001-2095, USA

Young, Chris (Musician)
c/o Rob Beckham *William Morris Endeavor (Nashville)*
1600 Division St Ste 300
Nashville, TN 37203-2755, USA

Young, CJ (Athlete, Hockey Player, Olympic Athlete)
130 Hoover Rd
Needham Heights, MA 02494-1548, USA

Young, Curt (Athlete, Baseball Player)
10800 E Cactus Rd Unit 2
Scottsdale, AZ 85259-2503, USA

Young, Cy (Athlete, Olympic Athlete)
518 Grimes Ave
Modesto, CA 95358-8308, USA

Young, Danny (Athlete, Baseball Player)
1841 Lascassas Pike Apt J153
Murfreesboro, TN 37130-0609, USA

Young, Dean (Cartoonist)
c/o Staff Member *King Features Syndication*
300 W 57th St Fl 15
New York, NY 10019-5238, USA

Young, Delmon (Athlete, Baseball Player)
5904 Pelican Bay Plz S
Gulfport, FL 33707-3943, USA

young, Delwyn (Athlete, Baseball Player)
2212 Radcourt Dr
Hacienda Heights, CA 91745-5716, USA

Young, Dmitri (Athlete, Baseball Player)
26 SE Loth Ave
Fort Lauderdale, FL 33301, USA

Young, Don (Athlete, Baseball Player)
4911 E Hillery Dr
Scottsdale, AZ 85254-2210, USA

Young, Don (Congressman, Politician)
2314 Rayburn Hob
Washington, DC 20515-4907, USA

Young, Duane (Athlete, Football Player)
2255 River Run Dr
San Diego, CA 92108-5888, USA

Young, Earl (Athlete, Track Athlete)
4344 Livingston Ave
Dallas, TX 75205-2608, USA

Young, Eric O (Athlete, Baseball Player)
120 Brewster Ave
Piscataway, NJ 08854-2205, USA

Young, Ernie (Athlete, Baseball Player, Olympic Athlete)
8995 E Palm Ridge Dr
Scottsdale, AZ 85260-7533, USA

Young, Frank
5600 Fishers Ln
Rockville, MD 20852-1750, USA

Young, Frank E (Government Official, Scientist)
Food & Drug Administration
5600 Fishers Ln
Rockville, MD 20852-1750, USA

Young, Fred (Musician)
Mitchell Fox Mgmt
212 3rd Ave N Ste 301
Nashville, TN 37201-1632, USA

Young, Fredd (Athlete, Football Player)
4200 Real Del Sur
Las Cruces, NM 88011-7204, USA

Young, George (Athlete, Olympic Athlete)
8926 N Cox Rd
Casa Grande, AZ 85194-7230, USA

Young, Gerald (Athlete, Baseball Player)
10014 Rain Cloud Dr
Houston, TX 77095-2442, USA

Young, Guard (Athlete, Gymnast, Olympic Athlete)
4000 Worthington Dr
Norman, OK 73072-1777, USA

Young, H Edwin (Religious Leader)
Southern Baptist Convention
901 Commerce St Ste 400
Nashville, TN 37203-3628, USA

Young, Jacob (Actor)
c/o Alex D'Andrea *Edmonds Management*
1635 N Cahuenga Blvd Fl 5
Los Angeles, CA 90028-6201, USA

Young, James (Athlete, Football Player)
9630 Hillis St
Houston, TX 77078-2825, USA

Young, Jason (Athlete, Baseball Player)
1021 Washington St
San Francisco, CA 94108-1107, USA

Young, Jesse Colin (Musician, Songwriter, Writer)
Skyline Music
PO Box 31
Lancaster, NH 03584-0031, USA

Young, Jewell L (Basketball Player)
4480 Fairways Blvd Apt 203
Bradenton, FL 34209-8027, USA

Young, Jim (Coach, Football Coach)
US Military Academy
Athletic Dept
West Point, NY 10966, USA

Young, Joe (Athlete, Football Player)
33261 Windtree Ave
Wildomar, CA 92595-8235, USA

Young, John (Athlete, Baseball Player)
124 W 57th St
Los Angeles, CA 90037-4114, USA

Young, John A (Business Person)
Norvell Inc
122 E 1700 S
Provo, UT 84606-6194, USA

Young, John Lloyd (Actor)
c/o Staff Member *Dona R Miller*
8391 Beverly Blvd
3378
Los Angeles, CA 90048-2633, USA

Young, John W (Astronaut)
NASA
221 Lakeshore Dr
Seabrook, TX 77586-6128, USA

Young, Judith Knight (Actor)
Ann Steel
330 W 42nd St # 1800
New York, NY 10036-6902, USA

Young, J Warren (Publisher)
Boys Life Magazine
1325 W Walnut Hill Ln
Irving, TX 75038-3008, USA

Young, Kathryn (Athlete, Golfer)
323 Date Ave
Imperial Beach, CA 91932-1915, USA

Young, Kathy (Musician)
Cape Entertainment
1161 NW 76th Ave
Plantation, FL 33322-5120, USA

Young, Keone (Actor)
Gage Group
5757 Wilshire Blvd Ste 659
Los Angeles, CA 90036-3682, USA

Young, Kevin (Athlete, Baseball Player)
832 E Taurus Pl
Chandler, AZ 85249-3655, USA

Young, Kevin (Athlete, Track Athlete)
8860 Corbin Ave
Northridge, CA 91324-3309, USA

Young, Kip (Athlete, Baseball Player)
2570 US Highway 62
Winchester, OH 45697-9517, USA

Young, Larry (Athlete, Baseball Player)
PO Box 255
Roscoe, IL 61073-0255, USA

Young, Laurence Retman (Astronaut)
217 Thorndike St Apt 108
Cambridge, MA 02141-1504, USA

Young, Laurence R Prof (Astronaut)
217 Thorndike St Apt 108
Cambridge, MA 02141-1504, USA

Young, Lonnie (Athlete, Football Player)
Express Personnel Services
6437 S Cedar St
Lansing, MI 48911-5960, USA

Young, M Adrian (Athlete, Football Player)
10300 4th St Ste 100
Rancho Cucamonga, CA 91730-5808, USA

Young, Mark L. (Actor)
c/o Marty Berneman *Precision Entertainment*
465 N Croft Ave
Los Angeles, CA 90048-2508, USA

Young, Matt (Athlete, Baseball Player)
17 S Grand Ave
Pasadena, CA 91105-1602, USA

Young, Melissa (Actor)
Badgley Connor Talent
9229 W Sunset Blvd Ste 311
West Hollywood, CA 90069-3403, USA

Young, Michael (Athlete, Baseball Player)
3508 Bryn Mawr Dr
Dallas, TX 75225-7438, USA

Young, Michael (Athlete, Basketball Player)
6707 Broad Oaks Dr
Dr
Richmond, TX 77406-7629, USA

Young, Mighty Joe (Musician)
Jay Reil
3430 Bayberry Dr
Northbrook, IL 60062-2217, USA

Young, Mike (Athlete, Baseball Player)
1166 Rockspring Way
Antioch, CA 94531-8308, USA

Young, Mike (Athlete, Football Player)
20 Cherry Hills Farm Dr
Englewood, CO 80113-7165, USA

Young, Neil (Musician)
3240 Bear Gulch Rd
Redwood City, CA 94062, USA

Young, Nick (Athlete, Basketball Player)
c/o Mark Bartelstein *Priority Sports & Entertainment - Chicago*
312 N La Salle
Suite 650
Chicago, IL 60610, USA

Young, Parker (Actor)
c/o Mona Loring *MLC PR*
7080 Hollywood Blvd Ste 903
Los Angeles, CA 90028-6936, USA

Young, Paul (Musician)
What Mgmt
PO Box 1463
Culver City, CA 90232-1463, USA

Young, Pete (Athlete, Baseball Player)
PO Box 95
Summit, MS 39666-0095, USA

Young, Ric (Actor)
c/o Staff Member *Coast to Coast Talent Group*
3350 Barham Blvd
Los Angeles, CA 90068-1404, USA

Young, Richard (Actor)
1275 Westwood Blvd
Los Angeles, CA 90024-4811, USA

Young, Rickey (Athlete, Football Player)
13670 Valley View Rd Apt 116
Eden Prairie, MN 55344-1977, USA

Young, Robert (Athlete, Football Player)
RR 7 Box 306
Carthage, MS 39051, USA

Young, Roynell (Athlete, Football Player)
11823 Beinhorn Dr
Houston, TX 77065-1607, USA

Young, Sam (Athlete, Football Player)
c/o Drew Rosenhaus *Rosenhaus Sports Representation*
6400 Allison Rd
Miami Beach, FL 33141-4540, USA

Young, Scott (Athlete, Hockey Player, Olympic Athlete)
17 Sandy Ridge Rd
Sterling, MA 01564-2361, USA

Young, Sean (Actor)
105 W 55th St Apt 9B
6C
New York, NY 10019-5337, USA

Young, Shelby (Actor)
c/o Katie Mason *Luber Roklin Management*
5815 W Sunset Blvd Ste 206
Los Angeles, CA 90028-6481, USA

Young, Steve (Athlete, Football Player, Sportscaster)
245 Southwood Dr
Palo Alto, CA 94301-3137, USA

Young, Tim (Athlete, Baseball Player, Olympic Athlete)
20730 SE Sherry Ave
Blountstown, FL 32424-2265, USA

Young, Tim (Athlete, Hockey Player)
15808 Park Terrace Dr
Eden Prairie, MN 55346-2433, USA

Young, Tom (Coach)
Washington Wizards
601 F St NW
Mci Centre
Washington, DC 20004-1605, USA

Young, Ulysses (Athlete, Baseball Player)
7008 State Highway 215 N
Blair, SC 29015-9009, USA

Young, Vince (Athlete, Football Player)
c/o Denise White *EAG Sports Management*
909 N Sepulveda Blvd Ste 360
El Segundo, CA 90245-3864, USA

Young, Vincent (Actor)
Don Buchwald
6500 Wilshire Blvd Ste 2200
Los Angeles, CA 90048-4942, USA

Young, Walter (Athlete, Baseball Player)
134 Center St
Purvis, MS 39475-4540, USA

Young, Warren (Athlete, Hockey Player)
5960 Murray Ave
Bethel Park, PA 15102-3489, USA

Young, Wayne (Athlete, Gymnast, Olympic Athlete)
505 W 400 N
Orem, UT 84057-1950, USA

Young, Wendell (Athlete, Hockey Player)
1616 E Campbell St
Arlington Heights, IL 60004-6550, USA

Young, Wendell (Athlete, Hockey Player)
2301 Ravine Way
Attn: General Manager
Glenview, IL 60025-7627, USA

Young, Wilbur (Athlete, Football Player)
121 W Bannister Rd
Kansas City, MO 64114-4010, USA

Young, Wiliam Paul (Writer)
Wind Rumors Inc
PO Box 2107
Oregon City, OR 97045-0107, USA

Young, William Allen (Actor)
c/o Bruce Tufeld *Tufeld Entertainment Group*
19521 Rosita Stt
Tarzana, CA 91356, USA

Youngberg, Renae (Athlete, Baseball Player)
418 Stoney Ridge Loop
Maggie Valley, NC 28751-8653, USA

Youngblood, George (Athlete, Football Player)
16429 Lazare Ln
Huntington Beach, CA 92649-1862, USA

Youngblood, H Jackson (Jack) (Athlete, Football Player, Sportscaster)
4377 Steed Ter
Winter Park, FL 32792-7630, USA

Youngblood, Jimmy L (Jim) (Athlete, Football Player)
322 Allendale Rd
Oxford, AL 36203-9738, USA

Youngblood, Joel (Athlete, Baseball Player)
4446 E Camelback Rd Unit 113
Phoenix, AZ 85018-2837, USA

Youngblood, Rob (Actor)
1604 N Vista St
Los Angeles, CA 90046-2818, USA

Youngen, Lois (Athlete, Baseball Player)
45 Prall Ln
Eugene, OR 97405-3335, USA

Younger, Ben (Director, Writer)
c/o Joseph Cohen *Creative Artists Agency (CAA-LA)*
2000 Avenue of the Stars Ste 100
Los Angeles, CA 90067-4705, USA

Youngfellow, Barrie (Actor)
c/o Staff Member *Gage Group, The (LA)*
5757 Wilshire Blvd Ste 659
Los Angeles, CA 90036-3682, USA

Young Gunz (Musician)
c/o Staff Member *Roc-A-Fella Records*
825 8th Ave Fl 23
New York, NY 10019-7472, USA

Younghans, Tom (Athlete, Hockey Player)
6133 Sheridan Ave S
Minneapolis, MN 55410-2917, USA

Young Jeezy (Musician)
c/o Kevin Liles *KWL Management*
304 Park Ave S Fl 11
New York, NY 10010-4305, USA

Young Jr, Walter R (Business Person)
Champion Enterprises
2710 University Dr
Auburn Hills, MI 48326, USA

Young Knives, The (Music Group)
c/o Staff Member *Paradigm (Monterey)*
404 W Franklin St
Monterey, CA 93940-2303, USA

Young MC (Musician)
Universal Attractions
145 W 57th St # 1500
New York, NY 10019-2220, USA

Young Money (Music Group, Musician)
c/o Staff Member *Motown Records (NY)*
1755 Broadway Fl 7
New York, NY 10019-3743, USA

Yount, Larry (Athlete, Baseball Player)
5701 E Mockingbird Ln
Paradise Valley, AZ 85253-2221, USA

Yount, Robin (Athlete, Baseball Player)
5040 E Shea Blvd Ste 254
Scottsdale, AZ 85254-4687, USA

Yount, Robin R (Athlete, Baseball Player)
5040 E Shea Blvd Ste 254
Scottsdale, AZ 85254-4687, USA

Youso, Frank (Athlete, Football Player)
PO Box 1046
International Falls, MN 56649-1046, USA

Yowarsky, Walt (Athlete, Football Player)
395 Dogwood Pl NW
Cleveland, TN 37312-4414, USA

Yo-Yo (Musician)
William Morris Agency
1325 Avenue of the Americas Bsmt 2
New York, NY 10019-6047, USA

Y. Schwartz, Allyson (Congressman, Politician)
1227 Longworth Hob
Washington, DC 20515-1403, USA

Yu, Ronnie (Director, Producer, Writer)
c/o Richard Arlook *The Arlook Group*
205 S Beverly Dr Ste 209
Beverly Hills, CA 90212-3899, USA

Yuan, Ron (Actor)
c/o Laura Pallas *Pallas Management*
5301 Bellaire Ave
Valley Village, CA 91607-2329, US

Yuen, Biao (Actor)
c/o Staff Member *The Agency Group (NYC)*
142 W 57th St Fl 6
New York, NY 10019-3300, USA

Yuen, Corey (Actor, Director)
c/o Steve Chasman *Current Entertainment*
9200 W Sunset Blvd Ste 600
West Hollywood, CA 90069-3196, USA

Yulin, Harris (Actor)
40 W 86th St # 5C
New York, NY 10024-3605, USA

Yune, Johnny (Actor, Comedian)
1921 Scenic Sunrise Dr
Las Vegas, NV 89117-7237, USA

Yune, Rick (Actor)
c/o David Gardner *Principato/Young Management (LA)*
9465 Wilshire Blvd Ste 900
Beverly Hills, CA 90212-2608, USA

Yun-Fat, Chow (Actor)
c/o Lee Stollman *The Gotham Group Inc*
9255 W Sunset Blvd Ste 515
West Hollywood, CA 90069-3308, USA

Yun Lee, Will (Actor)
c/o Sam Maydew *The Collective*
8383 Wilshire Blvd Ste 1050
Beverly Hills, CA 90211-2415, USA

Yurak, Jeff (Athlete, Baseball Player)
PO Box 1931
Sumner, WA 98390-0420, USA

Yushkevich, Dmitri (Athlete, Hockey Player)
878 Ridge View Way
Franklin Lakes, NJ 07417-1524, USA

Ywecic, Tom (Athlete, Football Player)
15 Danby Rd
Stoneham, MA 02180-3003, USA

Yzerman, Steve (Athlete, Hockey Player)
401 Channelside Dr
Attn: General Manager
Tampa, FL 33602-5400, USA

Zaa, Charlie (Musician)
c/o Staff Member *Sony Music Miami*
605 Lincoln Rd Ste 700
Miami Beach, FL 33139-2901, USA

Zabel, Steven G (Steve) (Athlete, Football Player)
6000 Oak Tree Rd
Edmond, OK 73025-2625, USA

Zabiela, James (DJ, Musician)
c/o Joel Zimmerman *William Morris Endeavor (NY)*
1325 Avenue of the Americas
New York, NY 10019-6026, USA

Zaborowski, Robert R J M (Religious Leader)
Mariavite Old Catholic Church
2803 10th St
Wyandotte, MI 48192-4994, USA

Zabriski, Bruce (Athlete, Golfer)
6228 Winding Lake Dr
Jupiter, FL 33458-3787, USA

Zabriskie, Grace (Actor)
1536 Murray Dr
Los Angeles, CA 90026-1646, USA

Zac Brown Band (Music Group)
173 Arnold Rd
Fayetteville, GA 30215-5246, USA

Zachar, Jacob (Actor)
c/o Jamie Freed *Paris Hilton Entertainment*
2934 1/2 N Beverly Glen Cir # 383
Los Angeles, CA 90077-1724, USA

Zachary, Ken (Football Player)
San Diego Chargers
General Delivery
Newalla, OK 74857-9999, USA

Zacherle, John (Actor)
125 W 96th St Apt 4B
New York, NY 10025-6423, USA

Zachry, Pat (Athlete, Baseball Player)
7611 Bosque Blvd
Woodway, TX 76712-3766, USA

Zackham, Justin (Director, Producer)
8489 Crescent Dr
Los Angeles, CA 90046-1802, USA

Zadan, Craig (Director, Producer)
8452 Harold Way
Los Angeles, CA 90069-1903, USA

Zadel, C William (Business Person)
Millipore Corp
80 Ashby Rd
Bedford, MA 01730-2200, USA

Zadora, Pia (Actor)
69 Hawk Ridge Dr
Las Vegas, NV 89135-7864, USA

Zagurski, Mike (Athlete, Baseball Player)
2723 Via Capri Unit 819
Clearwater, FL 33764-3991, USA

Zahn, Geoffrey C (geof) (Athlete, Baseball Player)
6536 Walsh Rd
Dexter, MI 48130-9656, USA

Zahn, Paula (Journalist)
188 E 76th St Apt 26A
New York, NY 10021-2856, USA

Zahn, Steve (Actor)
133 Cane Run Rd
Georgetown, KY 40324, USA

Zahn, Timothy (Writer)
PO Box 1755
Coos Bay, OR 97420-0340, USA

Zahn, Wayne (Bowler)
2143 E Center Ln
Tempe, AZ 85281-7719, USA

Zahn, Wayne
5018 S Barley Ct
Gilbert, AZ 85298-8633, USA

Zaillian, Steve (Director, Producer)
30918 Broad Beach Rd
Malibu, CA 90265-2664, USA

Zajac, Travis (Athlete, Hockey Player)
10 Elsway Rd
Short Hills, NJ 07078-1617, USA

Zaks, Jerry (Director)
c/o Susan Weaving *William Morris Endeavor (NY)*
1325 Avenue of the Americas
New York, NY 10019-6026, USA

Zal, Roxana (Actor)
c/o Staff Member *Main Title Entertainment*
8383 Wilshire Blvd Ste 408
Beverly Hills, CA 90211-2435, USA

Zalapski, Zarley (Athlete, Hockey Player)
Eishockey Club
Olten AG Postfach 523
Olten, PA CH-46, USA

Zaloom, Paul (Actor, Writer)
c/o Staff Member *Washington Square Arts (LA)*
1041 N Formosa Ave
the Lot Writers Bldg, Room 305
West Hollywood, CA 90046-6703, USA

Zambrano, Carlos (Athlete, Baseball Player)
c/o Staff Member *Chicago Cubs Spring Training*
HoHoKam Stadium
1235 N St
Mesa, AZ 85201, USA

Zambri, Chris (Athlete, Golfer)
1329 La Culebra Cit
Camarillo, CA 93012, USA

Zamka, George D (Astronaut)
12101 Lyre Ct
Manassas, VA 20112-5900, USA

Zamka, George D Lt Colonel (Astronaut)
12101 Lyre Ct
Manassas, VA 20112-5900, USA

Zamora, Oscar (Athlete, Baseball Player)
5301 SW 98th Ct
Miami, FL 33165-7244, USA

Zamora, Tye (Musician)
77 Marathon St
Arlington, MA 02474-6936, USA

Zamprogna, Dominic (Actor)
c/o Margie Weiner *Margie Weiner Management*
8205 Santa Monica Blvd Ste 1450
West Hollywood, CA 90046-5967, USA

Zamuner, Rob (Athlete, Hockey Player)
4317 Beau Rivage Cir
Lutz, FL 33558-5353, USA

Zander, Carl (Athlete, Football Player)
2536 W Palomino Dr
Chandler, AZ 85224-1639, USA

Zander, Robin (Musician)
533 Harbor Grove Cir
Safety Harbor, FL 34695-4977, USA

Zanders, Emanuel (Athlete, Football Player)
11015 Goodwood Blvd
Baton Rouge, LA 70815-5222, USA

Zane, Billy (Actor)
c/o Chris Dennis *Underground Management*
447 S Highland Ave
Los Angeles, CA 90036-3530, USA

Zane, Frank (Fitness Expert)
PO Box 1090
La Mesa, CA 91944-1090, USA

Zane, Lisa (Actor)
505 N Lake Shore Dr Apt 5407
Chicago, IL 60611-6446, USA

Zanes, Dan (Musician, Songwriter, Writer)
c/o Harriet Sternberg *Harriet Sternberg Management*
4530 Gloria Ave
Encino, CA 91436-2718, USA

Zanetti, Eugenio (Actor, Director)
c/o Frank Wuliger *Gersh (LA)*
9465 Wilshire Blvd Ste 600
Beverly Hills, CA 90212-2605, USA

Zanni, Dom (Athlete, Baseball Player)
7 Sussex Ave
Massapequa, NY 11758-2434, USA

Zano, Nick (Actor)
4440 Sancola Ave
Toluca Lake, CA 91602-2520, USA

Zanon, Greg (Athlete, Hockey Player)
512 Marmik Cir
Hastings, MN 55033-4042, USA

Zanotto, Kendra (Athlete, Olympic Athlete, Swimmer)
18834 Lakeview Ct
Los Gatos, CA 95033-9593, USA

Zanuck, Lili Fini (Director, Producer)
Zanuck Co
1131 Miradero Rd
Beverly Hills, CA 90210-2531, USA

Zanuck, Ron (Athlete, Hockey Player)
1135 Trailwood N
Hopkins, MN 55343-7914, USA

Zanussi, Ron (Athlete, Hockey Player)
PO Box 11326
Saint Paul, MN 55111-0326, USA

Zapalac, Willie (Athlete, Football Player)
1400 Shannon Oaks Trl
Austin, TX 78746-7345, USA

Zapiec, Chuck (Athlete, Football Player)
PO Box 6055
Hilton Head Island, SC 29938-6055, USA

Zapp, Jim (Athlete, Baseball Player)
Baltimore Elite Giants
1409 Summer Glen Dr
Harker Heights, TX 76548-8807, USA

Zappa, Ahmet (Producer)
114 N McCadden Pl
Los Angeles, CA 90004-1022, USA

Zappa, Dweezil (Actor, Musician)
10508 Woodbridge St
Toluca Lake, CA 91602-2825, USA

Zappa, Moon (Musician)
PO Box 5265
N Hollywood, CA 91616-5265, USA

Zarate, Carlos (Boxer)
Gene Aguilera
PO Box 113
Montebello, CA 90640-0113, USA

Zardon, Jose (Athlete, Baseball Player)
7261 NW 1st Mnr
Plantation, FL 33317-2272, USA

Zarin, Jill (Reality Star)
c/o Robyn Bluestone *Robyn Bluestone Management*
11021 73rd Rd Apt 4G
Forest Hills, NY 11375-6316, USA

Zarley, Kermit (Athlete, Golfer)
16600 N Thompson Peak Pkwy Unit 2081
Scottsdale, AZ 85260-2185, USA

Zarnas, August C (Gust) (Athlete, Football Player)
850 Jennings St
Bethlehem, PA 18017-7010, USA

Zaske, Jeff (Athlete, Baseball Player)
2404 185th Pl SE
Bothell, WA 98012-6999, USA

Zaslavski, Anton (Zedd) (Producer)
c/o Clayton Blaha *Biz 3 Publicity*
1321 N Milwaukee Ave Ste 452
Chicago, IL 60622-9151, USA

Zastudil, Dave (Athlete, Football Player)
c/o Neil Cornrich *NC Sports, LLC*
best to contact via email
Columbus, OH 43201, USA

Zatkoff, Roger (Athlete, Football Player)
882 Hidden Ravines Ct
Birmingham, MI 48009-1681, USA

Zaun, Gregg (Athlete, Baseball Player)
1204 Rocky Top Cir
Macedonia, OH 44056-2364, USA

Zaunbrecher, Godfrey (Athlete, Football Player)
3126 N 205th St
Elkhorn, NE 68022-4708, USA

Zavada, Clay (Athlete, Baseball Player)
1794 E 12th Rd
Streator, IL 61364-9366, USA

Zavaleta, Cara (Actor, Model)
c/o Staff Member *Gersh (LA)*
9465 Wilshire Blvd Ste 600
Beverly Hills, CA 90212-2605, USA

Zavaras, Clint (Athlete, Baseball Player)
9675 S Thimbleberry Way
Parker, CO 80134-8860, USA

Zawadzkas, Gerald (Athlete, Football Player)
2712 Alcazar St NE
Albuquerque, NM 87110-3514, USA

zawadzki, lance (Athlete, Baseball Player)
259 Cordaville Rd
Southborough, MA 01772-2085, USA

Zayas, David (Actor)
c/o Andrew Tetenbaum *ATA Management*
12 Desbrosses St
New York, NY 10013-1704, USA

Z. Bordallo, Madeleine (Congressman, Politician)
2441 Rayburn Hob
Washington, DC 20515-1604, USA

Zdeb, Joe (Athlete, Baseball Player)
5717 Greenwood St
Shawnee, KS 66216-4676, USA

Zdrok, Victoria (Adult Film Star)
PO Box 332
Pompton Lakes, NJ 07442-0332, USA

Zduriencik, Jack (Baseball Player)
14800 SE 51st St
Bellevue, WA 98006-3516, USA

Zea, Natalie (Actor)
c/o Robert Semon *True Management*
8964 W 25th St
Los Angeles, CA 90034-2012, USA

Zeal, Meredith (Actor)
c/o Marv Dauer *Marv Dauer Management*
2236 The Terrace
Los Angeles, CA 90049-1171, USA

Zeber, George (Athlete, Baseball Player)
18826 Winnwood Ln
Santa Ana, CA 92705-1233, USA

Zecher, Rich (Athlete, Football Player)
PO Box 1859
Eureka, MT 59917-1859, USA

Zedlitz, Jean (Athlete, Golfer)
4587 Gatetree Cir
Pleasanton, CA 94566-6031, USA

Zednik, Richard (Athlete, Hockey Player)
4401 N Federal Hwy Ste 201
Boca Raton, FL 33431-5164, USA

Zee, Ona (Adult Film Star)
2523A Folsom St
San Francisco, CA 94110-2621, USA

Zegers, Kevin (Actor)
12841 Woodbridge St Unit 12
Studio City, CA 91604-1503, USA

Zehetner, Nora (Actor)
c/o Staff Member *Anonymous Content (LA)*
3532 Hayden Ave
Culver City, CA 90232-2413, USA

Zeidel, Larry (Athlete, Hockey Player)
6663 Erdrick St
Philadelphia, PA 19135-2601, USA

Zeier, Eric (Athlete, Football Player)
PO Box 327
Nashville, GA 31639-0327, USA

Zeigler, Alma (Athlete, Baseball Player)
403 Gold St
Auburn, CA 95603-5521, USA

Zeigler, Dusty (Athlete, Football Player)
440 Hodgeville Rd
Guyton, GA 31312-7103, USA

Zeigler, Heidi (Actor)
c/o Staff Member *Mary Grady Agency (MGA)*
4400 Coldwater Canyon Ave Ste 135
the Landmark Bldg
Studio City, CA 91604-5038, USA

Zeigler, Marie (Athlete, Baseball Player)
2502 N 22nd Ave
Phoenix, AZ 85009-1926, USA

Zeile, Todd E (Actor, Athlete, Baseball Player, Producer)
1670 Fairmount Rd
Westlake Village, CA 91362-4305, USA

Zeilic, Mauricio (Actor)
c/o Staff Member *Telemundo*
2470 W 8th Ave
Hialeah, FL 33010-2000, USA

Zeitler, Kevin (Athlete, Football Player)
c/o Joe Panos *Athletes First, LLC*
23091 Mill Creek Dr
Laguna Hills, CA 92653-1258, USA

Zell, Samuel (Business Person)
Itel Corp
2 N Riverside Plz
Chicago, IL 60606-2600, USA

Zellars, Ray (Athlete, Football Player)
1327 Island Ave
Pittsburgh, PA 15212-2845, USA

Zeller, Bart (Athlete, Baseball Player)
13885 E Lupine Ave
Scottsdale, AZ 85259-3719, USA

Zeller, David (Athlete, Basketball Player)
2260 Greenlawn Dr
Toledo, OH 43614-5122, USA

Zellner, Peppi (Athlete, Football Player)
31 Dew Pl
Forsyth, GA 31029-3302, USA

Zellweger, Renee (Actor, Musician, Producer)
c/o John Carrabino *John Carrabino Management*
5900 Wilshire Blvd Ste 406
Los Angeles, CA 90036-5015, USA

Zelman, Aaron (Writer)
c/o Staff Member *ICM Partners (LA)*
10250 Constellation Blvd Fl 7
Los Angeles, CA 90067-6207, USA

Zeman, Ed (Athlete, Football Player)
3002 Jeffrey Dr Apt C
Costa Mesa, CA 92626-2929, USA

Zeman, E Robert (Athlete, Football Player)
6333 La Jolla Blvd Unit 268
La Jolla, CA 92037-6619, USA

Zeman, Jacklyn (Actor)
STone Manners
6500 Wilshire Blvd # 550
Los Angeles, CA 90048-4920, USA

Zeman, Zoe (Adult Film Star)
PO Box 343
Walpole, MA 02081-0343, USA

Zembriski, Walter (Athlete, Golfer)
6507 Doubletrace Ln
Orlando, FL 32819-4653, USA

Zemeckis, Robert (Director, Producer, Writer)
c/o Staff Member *ImageMovers*
100 Universal City Plz Ste 484
Universal City, CA 91608-1002, USA

Zemlak, Richard (Athlete, Hockey Player)
17092 Adelmann St SE Apt 209
Prior Lake, MN 55372-3999, USA

Zendaya (Actor, Musician)
c/o Jessie Greene *Monster Talent Management*
6333 W 3rd St Ste 912
Los Angeles, CA 90036-3176, USA

Zendejas, Luis (Athlete, Football Player)
6609 S 47th Pl
Phoenix, AZ 85042-5352, USA

Zeno, Lance (Athlete, Football Player)
530 Landfair Ave
Los Angeles, CA 90024-2104, USA

Zeno, Tony (Athlete, Basketball Player)
4419 Fulton Ave Apt 30
Sherman Oaks, CA 91423-5116, USA

Zent, Jason (Athlete, Hockey Player)
271 Dartmouth St Apt 4G
Boston, MA 02116-2827, USA

Zepeda, David (Actor)
c/o Raul Xumalin *MAFAE Artist Management*
8491 NW 17th St
Doral, FL 33126-1025, USA

Zepp, Bill (Athlete, Baseball Player)
15000 Farmbrook Dr
Plymouth, MI 48170-2748, USA

Zeppelin, Dread (Musician)
The M.O.B Agency
6404 Wilshire Blvd Ste 700
Los Angeles, CA 90048-5509

Zeppelin, Led (Music Group, Musician)
c/o Seth Rappaport *The Agency Group (NYC)*
142 W 57th St Fl 6
New York, NY 10019-3300, USA

Zerbe, Anthony (Actor)
411 W 115th St Apt 51
New York, NY 10025-1730, USA

Zerbe, Chad (Athlete, Baseball Player)
7248 Palomino St
Highland, CA 92346-5032, USA

Zereoue, Amos (Athlete, Football Player)
116 Tanglewood Dr
Wexford, PA 15090-8692, USA

Zerhouni, Elias A (Doctor, Government Official)
National Institutes of Health
9000 Rockville Pike
Bethesda, MD 20892-0002, USA

Zero, Mark (Musician)
PO Box 656507
Fresh Meadows, NY 11365-6507, USA

Zervas, Nicholas T (Doctor)
100 Canton Ave
Milton, MA 02186-3507, USA

Zeta-Jones, Catherine (Actor)
541 Guard Hill Rd
Bedford, NY 10506-1046, USA

Zetterberg, Henrik (Athlete, Hockey Player)
1300 Division Rd Ste 202
Attn: Marc Levine
West Warwick, RI 02893-7558, USA

Zgonina, Jeff (Athlete, Football Player)
41 Hawthorne Ln
Barrington, IL 60010-5109, USA

Zhamnov, Alexei (Athlete, Hockey Player)
9601 Collins Ave Apt 509
Bal Harbour, FL 33154-2211, USA

Zhang, Ziyi (Actor)
c/o Gary Mantoosh *Baker Winokur Ryder Public Relations (BWR-LA)*
9100 Wilshire Blvd Ste 500
West Tower Suite 500
Beverly Hills, CA 90212-3426, USA

Zhang, Ziyl (Actor)
c/o Ling Lucas *Nine Muses and Apollo Inc*
525 Broadway Rm 201
New York, NY 10012-4482, USA

Zherdev, Nikolai (Athlete, Hockey Player)
251 Daniel Burnham Sq # 253
Columbus, OH 43215-2681, USA

Zhitnik, Alexei (Athlete, Hockey Player)
30 Shelter Rock Rd
Manhasset, NY 11030-3240

Zhitnik, Alexel (Athlete, Hockey Player)
1 Seymour St
Buffalo, NY 14210, USA

Zicherman, Stu (Director)
c/o Staff Member *William Morris Endeavor (LA)*
9601 Wilshire Blvd
Beverly Hills, CA 90210-5213, USA

Zick, Bob (Athlete, Baseball Player)
12028 S 45th St
Phoenix, AZ 85044-2436, USA

Zidek, George (Athlete, Basketball Player)
551 Landfair Ave
Los Angeles, CA 90024-2172, USA

Zidlicky, Marek (Athlete, Hockey Player)
2006 Sweetbriar Ave
Nashville, TN 37212-5412, USA

Ziegelmeyer, Nicole (Athlete, Olympic Athlete, Speed Skater)
5908 Mastodon Pines Dr
Imperial, MO 63052-2175, USA

Ziegler, Alicia (Actor)
c/o Peter Himberger *Impact Artists Group LLC*
42 Hamilton Ter
New York, NY 10031-6403, USA

Ziegler, Brad (Athlete, Baseball Player)
1908 W High Point St
Springfield, MO 65810-2265, USA

Ziegler, Jack (Cartoonist)
New Yorker Magazine
4 Times Sq Fl 22
Editorial Dept
New York, NY 10036-6592, USA

Ziegler, Larry (Athlete, Golfer)
10315 Luton Ct
Orlando, FL 32836-3733, USA

Ziegler Jr, John A (Athlete, Hockey Player)
Dickinson Wright
500 Woodward Ave Fl 40
Detroit, MI 48226-3425, USA

Ziem, Steve (Athlete, Baseball Player)
79885 Fiesta Dr
La Quinta, CA 92253-4308, USA

Zien, Chip (Actor)
c/o Staff Member *Gersh (LA)*
9465 Wilshire Blvd Ste 600
Beverly Hills, CA 90212-2605, USA

Zien, Sam (Chef, Producer, Television Host, Writer)
c/o Staff Member *Wiley John & Sons Incorporated*
111 River St Ste 3
Author's Mail (Publicity)
Hoboken, NJ 07030-5773, USA

Ziering, Ian (Actor)
2700 Jalmia Dr
Los Angeles, CA 90046-1720, USA

Ziering, Nikki (Actor)
c/o Jerry Shandrew *Shandrew Public Relations*
1050 S Stanley Ave
Los Angeles, CA 90019-6634, USA

Ziff, Sanford (Business Person, Philanthropist)
6931 SW 62nd Ct
South Miami, FL 33143-3340, USA

Zikarsky, Bjorn (Swimmer)
555 California St Ste 2600
San Francisco, CA 94104-1602, USA

Zikes, Les (Bowler)
424 S Stuart Ln
Palatine, IL 60067-6730, USA

Zilinskas, Annette (Actor, Musician)
c/o Staff Member *Creative Artists Agency (CAA-LA)*
2000 Avenue of the Stars Ste 100
Los Angeles, CA 90067-4705, USA

Zima, Madeline (Actor)
c/o Steven Levy *Framework Entertainment (LA)*
9057 Nemo St Ste C
West Hollywood, CA 90069-5511, USA

Zima, Yvonne (Actor)
c/o Danny Mancini *Inspire Entertainment*
425 N Robertson Blvd
West Hollywood, CA 90048-1735, USA

Zimbalist, Stephanie (Actor, Writer)
4536 Libbit Ave
Encino, CA 91436-2110, USA

Zimerman, Krystian (Musician)
Columbia Artists Mgmt Inc
165 W 57th St
New York, NY 10019-2201, USA

Zimmer, Constance (Actor)
4119 Elmer Ave
North Hollywood, CA 91602-3311, USA

Zimmer, Dawn (Politician)
59 Madison St # 1
Hoboken, NJ 07030-1805, USA

Zimmer, Norma (Actor)
31200 Santiago Rd
Temecula, CA 92592-3110

Zimmer, Tom (Athlete, Baseball Player)
7296 Marathon Dr Apt 602
Seminole, FL 33777-3837, USA

Zimmerlink, Geno (Athlete, Football Player)
318 Crestwood Dr
Milltown, NJ 08850-1849, USA

Zimmerman, Denny (Race Car Driver)
36 Gooseberry Dr
Suffield, CT 06078-2177, USA

Zimmerman, Don (Athlete, Football Player)
107 Coretta St
Monroe, LA 71202-6901, USA

Zimmerman, Gary W (Athlete, Football Player)
17450 Skyliners Rd
Bend, OR 97701-5203, USA

Zimmerman, H Leroy (Athlete, Football Player)
808 Willis Ace
Madera, CA 93637, USA

Zimmerman, James M (Business Person)
Federated Department Stores
151 W 34th St
New York, NY 10001-2101, USA

Zimmerman, Jordan (Athlete, Baseball Player)
15354 W Old Oak Ln
Surprise, AZ 85379-8153, USA

Zimmerman, Kent (Publisher)
Friendly Exchange Magazine
1999 Shepard Rd
Saint Paul, MN 55116-3210, USA

Zimmerman, Mary Beth (Athlete, Golfer)
2403 Bonshaw Ln
Marietta, GA 30064-5756, USA

Zimmerman, Philip (Phil) (Designer)
Network Assoc
4677 Old Ironsides Dr
Santa Clara, CA 95054-1809, USA

Zimmerman, Ryan (Athlete, Baseball Player)
c/o Staff Member *Washington Nationals*
1500 S Capitol St SE
Washington, DC 20003-3599, USA

Zim Zum (Musician)
c/o Staff Member *Mitch Schneider Organization (MSO)*
14724 Ventura Blvd Ste 410
Sherman Oaks, CA 91403-3537, USA

Zinczenko, David (Writer)
Rodale
33 E Minor St
Emmaus, PA 18098-0099, USA

Zink, Charlie (Athlete, Baseball Player)
893 Queen Victoria Ct
El Dorado Hills, CA 95762-4100, USA

Zinner, Nick (Musician)
Yeah Yeah Yeahs
249 Metropolitan Ave
Brooklyn, NY 11211-4009, USA

Zinter, Alan (Athlete, Baseball Player)
3064 E Trigger Way
Gilbert, AZ 85297-6038, USA

Zipadelli, Greg (Race Car Driver)
114 Whaling Ln
Mooresville, NC 28117-6034, USA

Zipfel, Bud (Athlete, Baseball Player)
57 Whiteside Dr
Belleville, IL 62221-2542, USA

Zippel, David (Musician)
Kraft-Benjamin-Engel
15233 Ventura Blvd Ste 200
Sherman Oaks, CA 91403-2244, USA

Zirinsky, Susan (Producer)
c/o Staff Member *CBS Television*
51 W 52nd St
New York, NY 10019-6119, USA

Zisk, Randall (Director, Producer)
1823 Old Ranch Rd
Los Angeles, CA 90049-2206, USA

Zisk, Richard W (Richie) (Athlete, Baseball Player)
7678 Doubleton Dr
Delray Beach, FL 33446-3631, USA

Zito, Barry (Athlete, Baseball Player)
9270 Kinglet Dr
Los Angeles, CA 90069-1114, USA

Zito, Chuck (Actor, Boxer)
c/o Darren Prince *Prince Marketing Group*
18 Carillon Cir
Livingston, NJ 07039-2600, USA

Zlotoff, Lee (Director)
c/o Wendi Niad *Niad Management*
15021 Ventura Blvd Ste 860
Sherman Oaks, CA 91403-2442, USA

Zmed, Adrian (Actor)
18344 Collins St Unit E
Tarzana, CA 91356-2402, USA

Zmeskal, Kim (Gymnast)
Cincinnati Gymnastics Academy
3635 Woodridge Blvd
Fairfield, OH 45014-8521, USA

Zmievskaya Petrenko, Galina (Nina) (Coach)
International Skating Center
1375 Hopmeadow St
Simsbury, CT 06070-1423, USA

Zmolek, Doug (Athlete, Hockey Player)
537 Frederichs Dr NW
Rochester, MN 55901-3840, USA

Zobrist, Ben (Athlete, Baseball Player)
4694 Peytonsville Rd
Franklin, TN 37064-7610, USA

Zoccolillo, Pete (Athlete, Baseball Player)
11 Triumph Ct
Flanders, NJ 07836-4404, USA

Zoch, Jacqueline (Athlete, Olympic Athlete, Rower)
3421 Charing Wood Ln
Birmingham, AL 35242-3927, USA

Zoe, Deborah (Actor)
c/o Kim Matuka *Online Talent Group*
Prefers to be contacted via email or telephone
West Hollywood, CA 90069, USA

Zoe, Rachel (Reality Star, Stylist)
c/o Holly Shakoor Fleischer *42West (LA)*
1840 Century Park E Ste 700
Los Angeles, CA 90067-2122, USA

ZoeGirl (Music Group)
EMI Christian Music Group
101 Winners Cir N
Brentwood, TN 37027-5352, USA

Zoeller, Fuzzy (Athlete, Golfer)
418 Deer Run Trce
Floyds Knobs, IN 47119-8505

Zofko, Mickey (Athlete, Football Player)
321 W Fern Ave
Foley, AL 36535-2128, USA

Zohn, Ethan (Motivational Speaker, Reality Star)
CAMPUSPEAK, Inc.
PO Box 440560
Aurora, CO 80044-0560, USA

Zolak, Scott (Athlete, Football Player)
40 Comstock Dr
Wrentham, MA 02093-1852, USA

Zolciak-Biermann, Kim (Reality Star)
c/o Staff Member *Bravo (NY)*
30 Rockefeller Plz
New York, NY 10112-0015, USA

Zolot, Natassia (Kreayshawn) (Musician)
c/o Matt Galle *Paradigm (NY)*
360 Park Ave S Fl 16
New York, NY 10010-1716, USA

Zomalt, Eric (Athlete, Football Player)
25387 Delphinium Ave
Moreno Valley, CA 92553-7153, USA

Zombie, Rob (Musician)
555 S Muirfield Rd
Los Angeles, CA 90020-4825, USA

Zombie, Sheri Moon (Actor)
8491 W Sunset Blvd # 215
West Hollywood, CA 90069-1911, USA

Zombo, Frank (Athlete, Football Player)
c/o Joe Flanagan *BTI Sports Advisors*
170 N Scoville Ave
Oak Park, IL 60302-2647, USA

Zombo, Rick (Athlete, Hockey Player)
2918 Ossenfort Rd
Glencoe, MO 63038-1718, USA

Zook, John E (Athlete, Football Player)
4302 N Spyglass Cir
Wichita, KS 67226-3355, USA

Zook, Ron (Coach, Football Coach)
University of Illinois
Athletic Dept
Champaign, IL 61820, USA

Zopf, Bill (Athlete, Basketball Player)
351 Wealdstone Rd
Cranberry Township, PA 16066-8310,
USA

Zophres, Mary (Designer)
c/o Staff Member *United Talent Agency
(UTA-LA)*
9336 Civic Center Dr
Beverly Hills, CA 90210-3604, USA

Zordich, Mike (Athlete, Football Player)
373 S Hazelwood Ave
Youngstown, OH 44509-2228, USA

Zorich, Christopher R (Chris) (Athlete,
Football Player)
47 W Polk St Ste 100
Chicago, IL 60605-2085, USA

Zorich, Louis (Actor)
c/o Staff Member *Susan Smith Company,
The*
2001 Wilshire Blvd Ste 400
Santa Monica, CA 90403-5686, USA

Zorn, James A (Jim) (Coach, Football
Coach)
c/o Staff Member *Washington Redskins*
21300 Redskin Park Dr
Ashburn, VA 20147-6100, USA

Zorn, Jim (Athlete, Football Player)
2006 W Mercer Way
Mercer Island, WA 98040-2020, USA

Zorrilla, Alberto (Swimmer)
580 Park Ave
New York, NY 10065-7313, USA

Zosky, Eddie (Athlete, Baseball Player)
233 W Everglade Ave
Clovis, CA 93619-3776, USA

Zsigmond, Vilmos (Cinematographer)
c/o Shari Shankewitz *Innovative Artists
(LA)*
1505 10th St
Santa Monica, CA 90401-2805, USA

Zuber, Jon (Athlete, Baseball Player)
197 Fernwood Dr
Moraga, CA 94556-2315, USA

Zubov, Sergei (Athlete, Hockey Player)
3 Carriage Hill Rd
White Plains, NY 10604-1525, USA

Zubrus, Dainius (Athlete, Hockey Player)
92 Union St
Montclair, NJ 07042-2613, USA

Zubrus, Dainus (Athlete, Hockey Player)
92 Union St
Montclair, NJ 07042-2613, USA

Zucco, Victor (Athlete, Football Player)
2276 Wulfert Rd
Sanibel, FL 33957-2209, USA

Zucker, Arianne (Actor, Model)
4226 Babcock Ave
Studio City, CA 91604-1509, USA

Zucker, Jeff (Business Person)
c/o Staff Member *NBC Universal (LA)*
100 Universal City Plz
Universal City, CA 91608-1002, USA

Zucker, Jerry (Director, Producer)
c/o Staff Member *Zucker Productions*
1250 6th St Ste 201
Santa Monica, CA 90401-1637, USA

Zuckerberg, Mark (Business Person,
Internet Star)
Facebook
156 University Ave Ste 200
Palo Alto, CA 94301-1688, USA

Zuckerberg, Randi (Business Person)
c/o Steven Grossman *Untitled
Entertainment (LA)*
8383 Wilshire Blvd Ste 1050
Beverly Hills, CA 90211-2415, USA

Zuckerman, Andrew (Director, Producer)
c/o Jon Rubinstein *Authentic Talent and
Literary Management*
20 Jay St Ste M17
Brooklyn, NY 11201-8300, USA

Zuckerman, Eugenia (Musician)
Brooklyn College of Music
Bedford & H Aves
Brooklyn, NY 11210, USA

Zuckerman, Josh (Actor)
c/o Anne Woodward *ROAR (LA)*
9701 Wilshire Blvd Fl 8
Beverly Hills, CA 90212-2008, USA

Zuckerman, Mortimer (Business Person,
Publisher)
Boston Properties
599 Lexington Ave Fl 18
New York, NY 10022-7661, USA

Zuckoff, Mitchell (Writer)
c/o Richard Abate *3 Arts Entertainment
(NY)*
16 W 22nd St Ste 201
New York, NY 10010-5842, USA

Zugsmith, Albert (Director)
23388 Mulholland Dr
Woodland Hills, CA 91364-2733, USA

Zuiker, Anthony (Producer)
27033 Sea Vista Dr
Malibu, CA 90265-4434, USA

Zukav, Gary (Writer)
Fireside/Simon & Schuster
1230 Avenue of the Americas Fl CONC1
New York, NY 10020-1586, USA

Zuke, Mike (Athlete, Hockey Player)
430 Norman Gate Dr
Ballwin, MO 63011-2440, USA

Zuker, Danny (Producer, Writer)
c/o Keith Addis *Industry Entertainment*
955 Carrillo Dr Ste 300
Los Angeles, CA 90048-5400, USA

Zukerman, Eugenia (Musician)
Brooklyn College of Music
Bedford & H Aves
Brooklyn, NY 11210, USA

Zuleta, Julio (Athlete, Baseball Player)
16381 Shenandoah Cir
Fort Myers, FL 33908-7818, USA

Zullo, Alan (Cartoonist)
Tribune Media Services
435 N Michigan Ave Ste 1500
Chicago, IL 60611-4012, USA

Zumaya, Joel (Athlete, Baseball Player)
12874 Holdenberry Ln
Windermere, FL 34786, USA

Zuniga, Daphne (Actor)
c/o Jonathan Baruch *Rain Management
Group (RMG)*
1631 21st St
Santa Monica, CA 90404-3914, USA

Zuniga, Jose (Actor)
c/o Laura Myones *McKeon-Myones
Management*
3500 W Olive Ave Ste 770
Burbank, CA 91505-5527, USA

Zuniga, Miles (Musician)
c/o Staff Member *Russell Carter Artists*
567 Ralph McGill Blvd NE
Atlanta, GA 30312-1110, USA

Zupcic, Bob (Athlete, Baseball Player)
1005 Baybrook Dr
Waxhaw, NC 28173-7061, USA

Zurer, Ayelet (Actor)
c/o Ilene Feldman *LBI Entertainment*
2000 Avenue of the Stars
Floor 3, North Tower
Los Angeles, CA 90067-4700, USA

Zusi, Graham (Athlete, Soccer Player)
Sporting Kansas City
1 Sporting Way
Kansas City, KS 66111-1702, USA

Zuvella, Paul (Athlete, Baseball Player)
2040 Canyon Crest Ave
San Ramon, CA 94582-4841, USA

Zuverink, George (Athlete, Baseball
Player)
1027 E McNair Dr
Tempe, AZ 85283-4733, USA

Zuvic, Daniella Monet (Actor)
c/o Staff Member *LA Entertainment*
1375 S San Fernando Blvd
Suite 505
Burbank, CA 91504, USA

Zvereva, Natasha (Athlete, Tennis Player)
c/o Staff Member *Women's Tennis
Association (WTA (US))*
1 Progress Plz Ste 1500
St Petersburg, FL 33701-4335, USA

Zvonareva, Vera (Athlete, Tennis Player)
c/o Staff Member *SFX Sports (Miami)*
846 Lincoln Rd # 500
Miami Beach, FL 33139-2878, USA

Zwart, Harald (Director)
c/o Spencer Baumgarten *Creative Artists
Agency (CAA-LA)*
2000 Avenue of the Stars Ste 100
Los Angeles, CA 90067-4705, USA

Zweibel, Alan (Writer)
c/o Lee Kernis *Brillstein Entertainment
Partners (LA)*
9150 Wilshire Blvd Ste 350
Beverly Hills, CA 90212-3453, USA

Zweig, Ivan (Athlete, Baseball Player)
6502 Duffield Dr
Dallas, TX 75248-1314, USA

Zwerling, Darrell (Actor)
c/o Staff Member *CLInc Talent*
843 N Sycamore Ave
Los Angeles, CA 90038-3316, USA

Zwick, Alyse (Actor, Model)
c/o Staff Member *OmniPop Talent Group
(LA)*
4605 Lankershim Blvd Ste 201
North Hollywood, CA 91602-1874, USA

Zwick, Edward (Actor, Director, Producer)
c/o Staff Member *Bedford Falls Company,
The*
409 Santa Monica Blvd PH
Santa Monica, CA 90401-2232, USA

Zwick, Joel (Director)
c/o Brian Wilkins *Kritzer Levine Wilkins
Entertainment (KLWG)*
11872 La Grange Ave Fl 1
Los Angeles, CA 90025-5283, USA

Zwigoff, Terry (Director)
c/o Tracey Jacobs *United Talent Agency
(UTA-LA)*
9336 Civic Center Dr
Beverly Hills, CA 90210-3604, USA

Zydeco, Buckwheat (Musician)
c/o Staff Member *Concerted Efforts*
PO Box 440326
Somerville, MA 02144-0004, USA

Zyglis, Adam (Artist, Cartoonist)
Buffalo News
PO Box 100
Editorial Dept
Buffalo, NY 14220-0100, USA

Zylka, Chris (Actor)
c/o Jon Simmons *Simmons & Scott
Entertainment*
7942 Mulholland Dr
Los Angeles, CA 90046-1225, USA

Zyman, Sergio (Business Person)
c/o Staff Member *BigSpeak*
23 S Hope Ave Ste E
Santa Barbara, CA 93105-5114, USA

Zyuzin, Andrei (Athlete, Hockey Player)
2426 Westgate Ave
San Jose, CA 95125-4039, USA

CPSIA information can be obtained at www.ICGtesting.com
Printed in the USA
LVOW09s2347020115

421315LV00013B/359/P

9 781604 870169